MW01093162

THE GEORGETOWN DICTIONARY OF IRAQI ARABIC

Arabic–English, English–Arabic

THE GEORGETOWN DICTIONARY OF IRAQI ARABIC

Arabic–English, English–Arabic

Editor

MOHAMED MAAMOURI

GEORGETOWN UNIVERSITY PRESS
WASHINGTON, DC

A previous edition of this book was cataloged as follows:

Library of Congress Cataloging-in-Publication Data

A dictionary of Iraqi Arabic.
p. cm. – (Georgetown classics in Arabic language and linguistics)
Consists of two previously published dictionaries.
Includes bibliographical references.
Contents: English-Arabic / Beverly E. Clarity, Karl Stowasser, and Ronald G. Wolfe, editors – Arabic-English / D.R. Woodhead and Wayne Beene, editors.
ISBN 0-87840-136-9 (pbk. : alk. paper)
1. English language—Dictionaries—Arabic. 2. Arabic language—Dialects—Iraq—Dictionaries. I. Series.

PJ6826.D53 2003
492.7321—dc21

2003045211

Paperback isbn: 978-1-58901-915-7

∞ This book is printed on acid-free paper meeting the requirements of the American National Standard for Permanence in Paper for Printed Library Materials.

15 14 13 9 8 7 6 5 4 3 2 First printing

CONTENTS

INTRODUCTION

The goal of *The Georgetown Dictionary of Iraqi Arabic: Arabic–English, English–Arabic* is to help speakers of English gain proficiency in colloquial Arabic. It is an updated, expanded, and enhanced edition of the seminal dictionaries originally published by Georgetown University Press in the 1960s.

The Georgetown Dictionary of Iraqi Arabic is the first of several dialectal Arabic dictionaries to be published by Iraqi Georgetown University Press (GUP) and the Linguistic Data Consortium (LDC) of the University of Pennsylvania. Its preparation has been long and challenging but also a very rewarding experience. We include in this revised edition much of what we think might be of interest. We hope that, beyond probable weaknesses and possible mistakes, this dictionary will inform and inspire future generations of Arabic scholars and learners.

Updates and Changes

This revised dictionary contains about 17,500 Iraqi Arabic entries under about 4,300 roots/skeletons and includes many examples of the words in use. Of these, some 30 percent are new to this edition. It also presents about 10,750 English-to-Iraqi entries. The dictionary emphasizes the language used by educated residents of Baghdad in everyday speech and assumes that conversation is the primary focus—hence, technical or specialized terminology is not included.

The Georgetown Dictionary of Iraqi Arabic adds several new and very significant features:

- Entries are listed in conventional Arabic script to provide etymological information.
- Pronunciation is included using a standardized version of the International Phonetic Alphabet (IPA).
- Relevant parts of speech for all entries in the Iraqi–English section are indicated.

We assume that readers are familiar with the Arabic alphabet, the standard organization of Arabic dictionaries along the triconsonantal-root system, and the formation of Arabic verb forms. As was done in the earlier editions, we use the American variety of English and provide extensive examples that illustrate how the Iraqi words are actually used.

Origins

Georgetown University Press (GUP) has, for many years, sustained the tradition of excellent research and publication in Arabic dialects led by the late Richard S. Harrell in the mid-twentieth century. The original publication of the Arabic dialect dictionaries, developed under his direction and guidance in the 1960s, represented enormous progress in the development of the body of resources available to those who wished and still wish to gain proficiency in colloquial Arabic.

The original dictionaries are:

- *A Dictionary of Syrian Arabic: English–Arabic*, Karl Stowasser and Moukhtar Ani, editors, published in 1964 and reissued in 2004;
- *A Dictionary of Iraqi Arabic, English–Arabic*, B. E. Clarity, Karl Stowasser, and Ronald G. Wolfe, editors, published in 1964 and reissued in 2003, and *A Dictionary of Iraqi Arabic, Arabic–English*, D. R. Woodhead and Wayne Beene, editors, published in 1964 and reissued in 2003; and
- *A Dictionary of Moroccan Arabic, Moroccan–English*, Richard S. Harrell, editor, published in 1966 and reissued in 2004, and *A Dictionary of Moroccan Arabic, English–Moroccan*, Harvey Sobelman and Richard S. Harrell, editors, published in 1966 and reissued in 2004.

These dictionaries have withstood the test of time and have remained essential resources throughout the current period of heightened national and global awareness of the Arab region. However, language in general, and, to an exaggerated extent, spoken/colloquial language changes over time. It soon became clear that these valuable but dated dictionaries needed to be updated and modernized. Moreover, Arabic language departments and instructors worldwide attest to the recent flood of interest in modern Arab culture, society, and political life. To pursue knowledge and scholarship in these areas requires up-to-date dialectal Arabic language resources that promote successful daily communication with native Arabic speakers.

The Linguistic Data Consortium (LDC) of the University of Pennsylvania and Georgetown University Press received a grant from the US Department of Education (DOE) International Research Studies (IRS) program in order to digitize, update, and enhance the three existing Arabic dialect dictionaries originally published by GUP under two funding contracts from the US Department of Health, Education, and Welfare: contract SAE-8706 for the English–Arabic portions and contract OE-2-14-029 for the Arabic–English portions. Funding for the required lexical research and software development work for the updated dictionaries was provided in 2008 by the DOE-IRS grant P017A050040.

The four-year grant received by the LDC and GUP resulted in the production of this new *Georgetown Dictionary of Iraqi Arabic*, which is a direct descendant of the two Iraqi dictionaries originally published in the 1960s. The updated versions of the original dictionaries within the scope of this project aim to provide English-speaking learners and teachers of Arabic with current and complete lexical information for specific dialects of Arabic in order to enable them to communicate orally with Arabic speakers. The newly developed print and digital tools may additionally help to integrate the instruction of dialectal Arabic and Modern Standard Arabic (MSA).

Key Features

This dictionary uses emerging standards in electronic dictionary development along with contemporary principles of computational linguistics and current pedagogical requirements to:

- Reflect current vocabulary and usage;
- provide attested conventional Arabic script for main entries, example phrases and idioms with needed diacritics to help with the reading and writing of Iraqi Arabic text;
- provide a standardized International Phonetic Alphabet (IPA), based system of transcription to aid pronunciation by providing the closest sound representation for all entries; and
- identify the part of speech (morphological category) of each entry with its corresponding English meaning(s).

Updated Vocabulary and Usage

Because this dictionary is corpus-based, we built the initial Iraqi Arabic database content by extracting and structuring the text from Word document files created via manual keyboarding from the original printed dictionaries. Additional content was added from existing LDC resources (available from LDC's catalog as LDC2006S45, LDC2006T16), mostly culled from a collection of recorded conversations with transcripts, as well as a larger collection of transcribed Iraqi–English dialogs collected for the DARPA TRANSTAC program. Based on lexicon development work that had been done specifically for TRANSTAC, we selected Iraqi words that were likely to be novel relative to the source GUP Iraqi content and created annotation tools to have native Iraqi speakers review each term, confirm whether it was already covered in the database, and add it, if appropriate, filling in an English gloss and all other features needed for completion of the dictionary entry.

Use of Arabic Script

The use of the Arabic script in the presentation of all dialectal Arabic—from entry words (citation forms or lemmas) to illustrative sentences—is one of the most essential additions to the new LDC–GUP dictionaries. This choice follows trends in research and practice of Arabic language pedagogy current at the time the project was conceived and developed. Most foreign language students still learn MSA first and later turn to a spoken dialect of Arabic. Learners of MSA are most likely to see Arabic written in the Arabic script. By presenting dialectal Arabic text in that same script, the presentation of MSA and dialectal Arabic becomes more uniform. Thus, we have narrowed the gap between the presentation of dialectal Arabic and MSA to learners. This is a vital step that may ease the movement between dialectal Arabic and MSA for learners. Moreover, this choice ensures the preservation of a word's Arabic/Semitic root and origin, and it increases the likelihood that learners will be able to recognize a word or connect it to its etymologically related forms. Because of the centrality of derivative words in the Arabic language, this is an especially critical consideration.

Readers who know MSA and spoken Arabic well understand that making this editorial decision required some additional decisions. We also decided to retain the original MSA spellings even when dialectal pronunciation might appear to warrant a deviation. For instance, the letter 'ذ' is pronounced /ð/ in the Iraqi dialect but /d/ in Moroccan and /z/ in Egyptian. Despite the capability of the Arabic script to clearly represent all three of these sounds by changing the spelling, we decided that the written entry of an Arabic word in any of the colloquial dictionaries would retain the letter 'ذ'. We also decided not to include Persian letters that represent sounds used in Iraqi Arabic because, although they reflect Iraqi pronunciation, they do not fit into the root structure.

Other important choices include (a) using the taa marbuta to indicate the feminine, although it is not pronounced in Iraqi Arabic, and (b) using hamzat-al-wasl (the alif with regular vocalic diacritics as in إ) in Iraqi nouns and verbs when that use corresponds to the standard use of initial hamzat-al-wasl for same or similar MSA words. So, in this dictionary, hamzat-al-wasl is used not only in the following verb forms إنفِعَل (ʔi)nfiʕal إفتِعَل (ʔi)ftiʕal, إفعَلّ (ʔi)fʕall, and إستَفعَل (ʔi)stafʕal, but also in many nouns and verbs such as in: إسم ʔism *name*, إستَأذَن ʔistaʔðan *to ask for permission*, or إلتَقى ʔiltaqa *to meet*. In general, we used diacritics to indicate consonantal length (e. g., shaddah) and short vowel structure. However, diacritics were mostly used sparingly and only to indicate unpredictable pronunciations.

Use of the International Phonetic Alphabet

Although we tried to follow standard spelling conventions, we did not ignore the Iraqi dialect's characteristic pronunciation. In addition to the importance of preserving etymological roots, it is also necessary to safeguard the phonetic specificity and integrity of the colloquial pronunciations. For this reason, this updated dictionary also contains IPA representation of all entries and example phrases to demonstrate the correct pronunciation.

We acknowledge that disparities may exist between some of the Arabic script forms and their corresponding IPA representations. Two or more Arabic letters may be represented by the same IPA symbol, and many IPA symbols may be represented by the same Arabic letter. While the disparities may cause some initial confusion for novice learners, this system is methodical and is amply compensated for by the advantages of improving cross-dialect word recognition and preserving the majority of the etymological relations. (See the section "Pronouncing Iraqi Arabic" for detailed information on the IPA used for this dictionary.)

Parts of Speech

This edition indicates parts of speech for each entry or subentry in the Iraqi–English section. More detailed information can be found in "How to Use This Dictionary."

HOW TO USE THIS DICTIONARY

The Iraqi Arabic-to-English Section

The Iraqi Arabic-to-English portion of the dictionary contains most of the introduced changes and innovations, such as the use of the Arabic script to write all headwords and phrases, adding a part of speech tag to identify the morphology of all word entries, and adding a usage tag to indicate whether the word is in current use or is an older, less frequently used word. The Iraqi-to-English database described in the introduction is the core of the dialectal Iraqi Arabic dictionary. The information below explains how each section of the Iraqi Arabic dictionary is structured.

Organization of the Iraqi–English Dictionary

Consonantal roots

The twenty-eight sections in the Iraqi–English dictionary are based on the Modern Standard Arabic (MSA) alphabet, and each section is organized according to the triconsonantal root. This root is the traditional Arabic lexicographic convention whereby words of Semitic origin tend to fall into various patterns of semantic relatedness in accordance with fairly regular patterns of syllabification, vowel qualities, and affixes on the root. Users will find this organizing principle similar to what they find in MSA dictionaries.

Skeletal roots of borrowed words

In the case of Iraqi Arabic, in which many commonly used words are borrowed from other languages, we extend this organizing principle to include the consonantal skeletons of borrowed words, even though these consonant sequences apply only to the specific borrowings and do not establish classes of semantically related terms. For example, in the Arabic letter ك (kaaf), a section labeled ك ت ب (/k t b/) contains the various words related to this Semitic root. Shortly after is a section labeled ك ت د ر ء (/k t d r ʔ/), which represents the consonantal skeleton of a borrowed word meaning *cathedral* and contains only that word. While this is slightly unusual, we think that users will use the logic of the language and of the root system and will be able to find these borrowed words.

We have used established lexicographical patterns for ordering numerous words that appear within a root/skeleton:

(a) When there are words with different parts of speech (POS), verbs are listed first, then nouns and adjectives, then any other categories (if available).

(b) When there are many verb entries, these are ordered according to their verb form number, such as the conventional Arabic verb forms I to X: فَعَل faʕal, فَعَّل faʕʕal, فَاعَل faaʕal, أَفعَل ʔafʕal, تفَعَّل tfaʕʕal, تفَاعَل tfaaʕal, إنفِعَل (ʔi)nfiʕal, إفتِعَل (ʔi)ftiʕal, إفعَلّ (ʔi) fʕall, إستَفعَل (ʔi)stafʕal. The numeric form designations themselves are not shown but can easily be found in all standard MSA dictionaries and grammar books.

(c) When there are numerous nouns, adjectives, and other parts of speech, the subentries within each entry are ordered according to the length of the word (counting letters only, not diacritic marks). Note that gerunds (*masdars*) are labeled as nouns and participles are labeled as adjectives.

This ordering may pose a challenge to beginning learners of Arabic because it requires an ability to discern the root and derivation of a word in order to know where to look for it. It also presents them with an opportunity to expand their knowledge of Arabic in general, as they learn how to use a dictionary and how to speak Iraqi Arabic.

Words with prefixes

There are many commonly used words that begin with "m," "n," or "t" by virtue of being formed with standard prefixes attached to Arabic verbal stems. To the three prefixes n-, t-, y- (used for person marking),we can add two initial clitics b-, l- (both prepositions), and the initial consonant m-, which marks all past participle forms. Readers will not find these words within the sections corresponding to these prefix letters but, instead, would need to locate each entry under the initial consonant of its respective root (unless the root happens to begin with the same letter as the prefix). To aid the novice learner, we have provided a separate index where we list each entry word whose initial consonant is different from the section that contains the word, and we give its root or skeleton where the entry can be found to direct the user to the appropriate section. All the words in the index are ordered strictly by Arabic alphabetic sequence.

Structure of entries in the English-Iraqi (top) and Iraqi-English (bottom)

English word
Arabic equivalent
Arabic term in IPA
Arabic example
Arabic example in IPA
English example

☞ the Arabic idiom is different from the English concept

Arabic root
Iraqi word in Arabic script
IPA pronunciation
Part of speech
English definition (sense)
Example in Arabic script
Example in IPA
English translation of example

Grammatical information

The morphological categories of all the citation forms of the Arabic-to-English dictionary are listed as follows: verb, auxiliary verb, pseudo verb, noun, proper noun, adjective, comparative adjective, pronoun, demonstrative, determiner, interjection, particle, interrogative particle, negative particle, conjunction, and subordinating conjunction. The key to the abbreviations used for parts of speech in the Arabic-to-English section is indicated at the bottom of each page.

We prefer not to use the term "participle" to represent the Arabic present and past participles – إسم الفاعل (ʔism fa:ʕil) for the active participle and إسم مفعول (ʔism mafʕu:l) for the passive participle and the "gerund" for مصدر *(maSdar)* because all three are, in fact, mainly used as either nouns or adjectives and rarely in a verbal function.

We use the term "preposition" to represent the closed class of words that have traditionally been identified as prepositions in Arabic and that seem to have lost their original nominal quality.

We reserve the use of the term "prepositional" for the open class of nouns whose function is that of prepositions but that have not lost their nominal status, such as تَحت *under*, بَعد *after*, and أمَامْ *in front of.*

The term "adverb" is used for the class of pure adverbs that is made of function words that are invariable and nonproductive. Adverbs do not always have etymologies linking them to nouns. Another term, "adverbial," represents the open class of nouns in the inflected dependent form that appears to correspond to English adverbs. Example: عِلمِيّاً *scientifically* from the noun عِلم *science.*

Usage

Usage is indicated for each headword as follows: common, archaic, obsolete, idiom, MSA, foreign, or unknown. This dictionary purports to describe the Iraqi Arabic dialect words and phrases as they are currently used at the time of publication.

The English–Iraqi Arabic Section

The major additions to the English–Iraqi Arabic section in this edition are the presentation of the Iraqi meanings in Arabic script and the provision of the pronunciation of the Iraqi words in IPA. In our enhancement of the Iraqi–English section, we added new Iraqi terms as look-up words and, to a lesser extent, added new English meanings for words that were present in the older edition. It was not possible to perform the same scope of work for the English–Iraqi section for this edition. In particular, English glosses for newly added IA terms have not been added as new English headwords. While some of the example phrases from the older edition have been updated to improve the Arabic or English wording, no new entries or example phrases have been added; in particular, none of the new Iraqi look-up terms have example phrases.

In the English–Iraqi portion of the dictionary, each English look-up term is given one or more Iraqi term(s) as its definition. This section provides the plural, feminine, and/or collective forms of nouns and adjectives. Verbs are quoted in the conventional third-person singular masculine of the Perfective. Whereas free prepositional complements are relegated to the illustrative sentences for demonstration, obligatory prepositional complements appear with the headword entry, e.g. 'to affect أثَّر عَلَى [ʔaθθar ʕala]' or 'to fall for, اِنخِدَع بِ- [ʔinxidaʕ b-]. Verb forms are followed by the 'masdar' or verbal noun (vn:), the stem vowel (sv) of the Imperfective with the appropriate vowel, and the passive form (p:) of the verb when it exists, indicated by the use of the proper prefix t- or ʔin-. The Iraqi Arabic dialect does not have an inflectional passive form. It uses derivational verbs (typically V تفَعَّل [tfaʕʕal], VII اِنفِعل [ʔinfiʕal] or VIII اِفتِعل [ʔiftiʕal]) to convey the passive or a passive-like (reflexive, resultative, or mediopassive) sense of the action involved in the verb. The meaning of these derived verbs is usually rendered in English by the passive.

PRONOUNCING IRAQI ARABIC

The Consonants

There are twenty-eight consonants in Iraqi Arabic. Twenty of them have a one-to-one fit with their IPA equivalents. One of these, the glottal stop or hamza, has six letter or graphemic representations in the Arabic script but is always represented by the same symbol /ʔ/ in IPA transcription. The six graphemic representations of the hamza (and its letter supports) are: ء أ إ آ ؤ ئ .

Arabic Name	Arabic Letter	IPA Symbol	Sun/Moon	Phonetic Description
alif/hamza	ا	ʔ	M	glottal stop/catch; similar to the pronunciation of Cockney English *bottle* where a catch replaces the *t* sound.
baa	ب	b (p)	M	voiced bilabial stop; similar to English *b* as in *boy*.
taa	ت	t	S	voiceless dental stop; similar to English *t* as in *toy*.
thaa	ث	θ (f, t)	S	voiceless interdental fricative; similar to English *th* as in *three*.
jiym	ج	ǰ (č)	S	voiceless palatal affricate, similar to English *j* as in *joy*.
haa	ح	ħ	M	voiceless pharyngeal fricative, no English equivalent.
xaa	خ	x	M	voiceless velar fricative; no English equivalent but similar to German *ch* as in *Bach*.
dal	د	d	S	voiced dental stop; similar to English *d* as in *day*.
dhal	ذ	ð (ð̣)	S	voiced interdental fricative; similar to English *th* as in *this*.
raa	ر	r	S	apico-alveolar trill, usually voiced. A single tap when short and a multiple trill when long (*rr*). Similar to Italian or Spanish *r*, as in *burro*.
zayn	ز	z	S	voiced dental fricative; similar to English *z* as in *zoo*.

Arabic Name	Arabic Letter	IPA Symbol	Sun/Moon	Phonetic Description
siin	س	s (ṣ)	S	voiceless dental fricative; similar to English *s* as in *say*.
shiin	ش	š, č (ǰ)	S	voiceless palatal fricative; similar to English *sh* as in *she*.
ṣaad	ص	ṣ (s)	S	velarized voiceless dental fricative; close to a velarized English *s* as in *sox* or sow.
dhaad	ض	ð̣	S	velarized voiced interdental fricative; close to a velarized English th.
ṭaa	ط	ṭ	S	voiceless dental stop. No equivalent in English.
dhaa	ظ	ð̣	S	velarized voiced interdental fricative; close to a velarized English th.
ayn	ع	ʕ	M	voiced pharyngeal fricative. No equivalent in English or other European languages.
ghayn	غ	ɣ	M	voiced velar fricative. A 'gurgle' sound produced in the back of the mouth similar to Parisian French r in Paris or the Spanish g in *lago* but more strongly articulated.
faa	ف	f	M	labio-dental fricative; similar to English *f* in *fun*.
qaaf	ق	q, g (k, ǰ)	M	voiceless pharyngeal stop. No English equivalent but close to a velarized (post velar) sound.
kaaf	ك	k, č (g)	M	voiceless velar stop; similar to English *k* in *cook*.
laam	ل	l	S	voiced alveo-dental lateral; similar to English l in love.
miim	م	m	M	voiced bilabial nasal; similar to English *m* in *man*.
nuun	ن	n	S	voiced dental nasal; similar to English *n* in *none*.
haa	ه	h	M	voiceless glottal fricative; similar to English *h* in *hat*.
waaw	و	w	M	voiced high back rounded semivowel, similar to English *w* in *war*.
yaa	ي	y	M	voiced high front unrounded semivowel ; similar to English *y* in *yes*.

Six of these twenty consonants have no English equivalents but are the same as they are in MSA. These are:

ح /ħ/, خ /x/ (similar to ch in German, as in Bach),
ط /ṭ/, ع /ʕ/, غ /ɣ/ (similar to some occurrences of French r), and
ق /q/ (similar to an English k sound that is pronounced way deep in the throat).

Note that some letters have multiple IPA sound representations. IPA symbols in parentheses in the above table indicate that the sounds they represent have a relatively low frequency of occurrence. Although they both have the same pronunciation of ð̣ in Iraqi Arabic, ض and ظ are listed separately in order to maintain consistency with written standard Arabic orthographic conventions.

The predominant issues of phonetic variation from MSA in Iraqi Arabic can be summarized as follows:

1. The letter ب normally represents /b/ but is also used for [p] in words that are of Persian, Turkish, or other foreign origin.

   Examples: بانسيَون / pa:nsyu:n *boarding house*, بيصوان / pi:ṣwa:n a *night guard*.

2. The letter ث generally stands for [θ] but in rare cases it can represent [t] as in ثلاثَة / tla:θa *three* and ثلاثِين / tlaθi:n *thirty* or [f] as in فالُولَة /falu:la *wart*.
3. The letter ج stands for [ǰ] but also occasionally represents the sound [č] as in بَرجَم for parčam *bangs, fringe of hair cut straight across the forehead.*
4. The letter ش stands for [š] and [č] but sometimes also represents [ǰ].

   Examples: شَرشَف / čarčaf *large cloth, tablecloth, bedsheet* or شِلَك / čilak *strawberry* and إنش / ʔinǰ *inch* or سَندَوِيش / sandawiyǰ *sandwich.*

5. The two Arabic letters ض and ظ have the same pronunciation in Iraqi Arabic and are both represented in IPA by the symbol [ð̣]. Because of our choice of strict adherence to the orthographic conventions of MSA and in order to keep the correct etymological structures separate, we made sure that each one of these two letters was correctly used according to strict MSA rules.

   Examples: مَضبَطَة / mað̣baṭa *petition* or مُضادّ / muð̣a:dd *opposed* versus عَظَمَة / ʕað̣ama *haughtiness, arrogance* and مَحفَظَة / maħfað̣a *file, folder, attaché case.*

6. The letter ق has the most varied sound renderings. It is pronounced [g] in Iraqi but its classical Arabic pronunciation [q] is also frequently used. The division between the two pronunciations is random.

   Example: قَنطَرَة is pronounced either qanṭara or ganṭara for *bridge*. However, قَهوَة *coffee* and قَمَرَة / قمَر *moon* are always pronounced gahwa and gamra /gumar in Baghdadi Arabic. The words for قُبلَة / qubla *kiss* and قَزان / qaza:n *kettle, cauldron* are always pronounced with [q]. Moreover, ق is sometimes pronounced [k] as in قِتَل kital *to kill, to beat up* or مَقتُول maktu:l *dead, beaten up*. ق is rarely used to represent the sound [ǰ] as in مُطبِق / muṭbiǰ *side-by-side*; قِدِر / ǰidir *pot, cooking vessel.*

7. The letter ك is usually pronounced [k] but is also very frequently pronounced [č]. This is a specific trait of the Iraqi Arabic dialect. There is a certain randomness about when a ك is used for [č] and when it is used for [k], as no rules seem to exist.

   Examples: كَلِب can be pronounced čalib or kalib *dog* but مَكلُوب *nasty, rabid* is only pronounced mačlu:b. أحكِيلِك *I tell you* is pronounced ʔaħči:lik when addressing a man and ʔaħči:lič when addressing a woman.

   Finally, the letter ك is sometimes used to represent the sound [g], which does not have a letter counterpart in the Arabic orthographic system.

   Example: كُمَز / gumaz *to jump*. This can result in some confusing phrases, such as يا كَلبِي, which is used for ya: galbi *my heart, my beloved* when it can also be ya: čalbi *my dog.*

8. A dot beneath a letter indicates that that letter represents an emphantic consonantal sound. Apart for the three main emphatics (ص /ṣ , ض – ظ / ð̣ , ط / ṭ), the following consonants seem to be affected by this variant phonetic spread of velarization: ṛ ḷ ṃ ḅ ṇ (and less frequently z and f). In our description of Iraqi sounds, we consider these secondary emphatic consonants to be only phonetic variants of their respective nonemphatic sounds and we therefore do not include them in our dialectal Iraqi Arabic dictionary IPA representation.
9. Arabic sun letters (marked with S in the table) assimilate when they are clustered with some other consonants across morpheme boundaries. For example, ʔal + šams becomes ʔaššams (*the* + *sun*) because ش is a sun letter. Moon letters (marked with M) do not assimilate. It is to be noted that ج [ǰ] assimilates in dialectal Arabic (but not in MSA ʔal-ǰamalu *the camel*). Most assimilation phenomena are not shown in the Arabic script. This is done in order to preserve the morphological integrity of Iraqi words. However, assimilation of root consonants to adjacent consonants is shown in the IPA structure.

   Examples: تزاحَم / dza:ħam *to compete* or تذَمَّر / dðammar *to complain, to grumble*, where ت is pronounced as [d] due to its assimilation with the letter that follows it.

The Vowels

Arabic dialects are characterized by their great vocalic diversity and considerable speaker-to-speaker vocalic inconsistency. Although we focus on the Baghdadi dialect of Iraqi Arabic exclusively in this book, it is sometimes difficult to have our native speaker informants agree on the exact vocalic nature of some words.

Iraqi Arabic has three short vowels /i, a, u/ and three long vowels /iː/, /aː/, and /uː/. The three short vowels are marked graphemically by three diacritics *kasra* for /i/, *fatha* for /a/, and *dhamma* for /u/. Short vowel diacritics are included in the Arabic transcription of all dictionary entries except in cases where these vowels become predictable and redundant as in the following environments: /a/ before an *alif*, /i/ before a *yaa*, and /u/ before a *waaw in* vocalic length marking.

Each of the Iraqi Arabic short vowel phonemes has many phonetic variants representing the range of different possible phonetic pronunciations. Some of these variants are as follows:

- /i/ short, unrounded, high vowel that represents the following allophonic variants: centralized [I] and [ə]
- /a/ short, low, central vowel that represents the following allophonic variants: [e], [æ], and back vowel [ɑ]
- /u/ short, high, back-rounded vowel that also represents the following allophonic variants: [o] and [U]

There are also two diphthongs, /aw/ and /ay/, in the Iraqi Arabic dialect. Our dictionary annotation shows that most words with possible diphthong pronunciations in the Arabic script may show long vowels in IPA (/ay/ is frequently represented by /iː/ or /iy/ and /aw/ by /uː/or a phonetic variant [oː]). For instance, زيت 'oil' is pronounced [zayt] or [zi:t] زور 'fraud' is pronounced [zu:r] and خير 'better' is pronounced xi:r or [xayr]. On the other hand, ذوق is pronounced [ð̣awq] for 'taste' in fashion and clothes and [ð̣ u:g]for 'taste' in food. We also have two attested pronunciations for شلونك *How are you?* namely šlawnik and šluːnik.

There are no given rules as to when an Iraqi Arabic diphthong should be pronounced /ay/ /or /i:/ and /aw/ or /u:/. Attested uses of diphthongized and nondiphthongized occurrences are indicated in our IPA annotation throughout the Iraqi Arabic dictionary. Our users will have to adapt their own pronunciation according to their Iraqi native speaker contacts.

ACKNOWLEDGMENTS

Tribute should be paid to all those who worked after founding editor Richard S. Harrell on the Iraqi Arabic dictionary, namely Wallace M. Erwin, Beverly E. Clarity, Karl Stowasser, Ronald G. Wolfe, D. R. Woodhead, Wayne Beene, and the numerous native Iraqi Arabic informants whose names are too numerous to mention. The contribution of these American and Arab scholars should in no way be underestimated. Without their effort there would have been no significant or important further progress.

Funding for the present collaboration between the Linguistic Data Consortium of the University of Pennsylvania and Georgetown University Press for the enhancement and development of electronic dialectal Arabic dictionaries and the significant research effort that ensued was provided by the Department of Education International Research and Studies Program (84.017A), Instructional Materials-03 Grant Award PO17A080044l. Their assistance is gratefully acknowledged here.

Georgetown University Press, in particular Hope LeGro and Gail Grella, are to be thanked for making their dictionaries available for the learning of Arabic dialects once again and in a new electronic format, especially at this time of critical national need. Without their trust and support the LDC's effort in the field of electronic dictionary development would not have been possible.

The LDC team led by Dr. Mohamed Maamouri bears final responsibility for the edited old and the newly added contents. David Graff, senior programmer at LDC, authored the IA database and created all annotation tools. He also took care of the annotation workflow. My debt to him is greater than can be expressed here. Alyaa Abboud helped with the supervision of all annotation phases. Her strong commitment to the project and her contribution to the annotation effort are greatly appreciated. Thanks and gratitude go to all our Iraqi annotators: Tamara Ali Janeb, Zainab Alsawaf, Safa Ismail, and all those who contributed in one way or another to this huge undertaking. Finally, thanks are also owed to Emily Goshey, who edited the English contents and helped with final editing tasks.

This has been a long but rewarding experience and it is hoped that these materials will benefit the teaching of Arabic in the United States and worldwide by bridging the gap between the Arabic dialects and the standard written language, and by helping users achieve a higher Arabic language proficiency and communicative competence.

My final thanks go to my wife Terry who has always given my work her full support and to my friend and dear colleague the late Dr. Fadhel Al Jammali, who first introduced me to Iraqi Arabic and to his beloved country Iraq.

PART – I

ARABIC–ENGLISH

ء

ء

ء ب

آب [ʔaːb] *n:* • **1.** August

ء ب ب ي

أبِّي [ʔabbi] *adj:* أبِّيات [ʔabbiyyaːt] *pl:* • **1.** main – أبِّي الماي [ʔabbi ʔilmaːy] water main • **2.** main line (elec.) • **3.** main switch, master switch (elec.)

ء ب د

أبَّد [ʔabbad] *v:* • **1.** to be eternal, perpetual, to last forever – خُو مُو راح تأبِّد؛ لازِم تمُوت فَدّ يوم [xuː muː raːħ tʔabbid; laːzim ʔitmuːt fadd yuːm] Well you're not going to last forever; you've got to die some day.

أبَد [ʔabad] *n:* • **1.** (limited to a few phrases), ever, never – أبَد ما [ʔabad maː] never. أبَد ما أقُولَه [ʔabad maː ʔaguːllah] I'll never tell him. إلَى الأبَد [ʔila ʔilʔabad] forever, to the end. هَذا مُخلِص إلَى الأبَد [haːða muxliṣ ʔila ʔilʔabad] He's faithful to the end. ما أنسَى فضلَك عَلَيّا إلَى الأبَد [maː ʔansaː faðlak ʕalayya ʔila ʔilʔabad] I won't ever forget the favor you did me.

أبَدِيَّة [ʔabadiyya] *n:* • **1.** eternity

أبَدِي [ʔabadi] *adj:* • **1.** eternal, everlasting – اِنحِكَم أبَدِي [ʔinħikam ʔabadi] He was sentenced to life imprisonment.

مُؤَبَّد [muʔabbad] *adj:* • **1.** for life – مَحكُوم مُؤَبَّد [maħkuːm muʔabbad] sentenced to life imprisonment. حُكُم مُؤَبَّد [ħukum muʔabbad] a life sentence. سِجِن مُؤَبَّد [siǰin muʔabbad] life imprisonment.

أبَداً [ʔabadan] *adverbial:* • **1.** /with neg./ never – أبَداً ما يِجِي هنا [ʔabadan maː yiǰi hna] He never comes here. • **2.** at all – ما عِندِي فلُوس أبَداً [maː ʕindi fluːs ʔabadan] I don't have any money at all. • **3.** /alone/ never, not at all – أبَداً! ما أقبَل ترُوح وِيّاه [ʔabadan! maː ʔaqbal truːħ wiyyaːh] Never! I won't have you go with him. أبَداً! وَلا فَكّ حَلقَه [ʔabadan! wala fakk ħalgah] Not at all! He didn't even open his mouth.

ء ب د س خ ن

أبدَسخانَة [ʔabdasxaːna] *n:* • **1.** toilet, especially that of a mosque

ء ب ر

أُبرَة [ʔubra] *n:* أُبَر [ʔubar] *pl:* • **1.** needle • **2.** by extension, hypodermic syringe, and loosely, a shot, an injection – ضَعفان. صايِر أُبرَة وخَيط [ðaʕfaːn. ṣaːyir ʔubra wxayṭ] You're skinny. You've gotten thin as a rail (lit. needle and thread).

ء ب ر ش

أبرَشِيَّة [ʔabrašiyya] *n:* • **1.** parish

ء ب ر ق

إبرِيق [ʔibriːg] *n:* أبارِيق [ʔabaːriːg] *pl:* • **1.** pitcher (for water)

ء ب ر و

آبرُو، وَرَق آبرُو [ʔaːbru, waraq ʔaːbru] *n:* • **1.** construction paper, glossy and colored on the face, plain white on the back

آبري [ʔaːbri] *n:* • **1.** construction paper, glossy and colored on the front face, plain white on the back

ء ب ط

أُبُط، أُباط [ʔubuṭ, ʔubaːṭ] *n:* أباطات، أباطات [ʔubaːṭaːt, ʔabaːṭaːt] *pl:* • **1.** armpit

جَوَّة أُبُط [jawwat ʔubuṭ] *n:* • **1.** underarm, armpit • **2.** under the arm – شايِل جَرِيدتَه جَوَّة أُبطَه [šaːyil ǰariːdtah ǰawwa ʔubṭah] He's carrying his newspaper under his arm. هَذا أطوَل مِنَّه هوايَة؛ يخَلِّيه جَوَّة أُبطَه [haːða ʔaṭwal minnah hwaːya; yxalliːh ǰawwa ʔubṭah] That guy's a lot taller than he; he can put him under his arm. المُعاوِن خَلَّى المُدِير جَوَّة أُبطَه [ʔalmuʕaːwin xalla: ʔilmudiːr ǰawwa ʔubṭah] The assistant's gotten the director under his control. هَذا شِمعَرّفَه يِلعَب شِطرَنج؟ أقدَر أخَلِّيه جَوَّة أُبطِي [haːða šimʕarrfah yilʕab šiṭranǰ? ʔagdar ʔaxalliːh ǰawwa ʔubṭi] What does he know about playing chess? I can put him in my pocket. أصدِقائَه خَشّوا جَوَّة أُبطَه وخَلّوه يبِيع كُلّ أملاكَه [ʔaṣdiqaːʔah xaššaw ǰawwa ʔubṭah wxalluːh yibiːʕ kull ʔamlaːkah] His friends got hold of him and had him sell all his property. خَشّ جَوَّة أُبطَه وَخَلّاه يِصرُف كُلّ فلُوسَه عالرّاقِصات [xašš ǰawwa ʔubṭah wxallaːh yiṣruf kull fluːsah ʕarraːqiṣaːt] He got hold of him and had him spend all his money on dancers.

ء ب ل س

إبلِيس [ʔibliːs] *n:* أبالِيسَة [ʔabaːlisa] *pl:* • **1.** the Devil – إبلِيس اِستَولَى عَلَى عَقلَه [ʔibliːs ʔistawla: ʕala ʕaqlah] The Devil has gotten control of him. • **2.** devil – هَذا إبلِيس؛ ما يِنغُلُب [haðaː ʔibliːs; maː yinɣulub] He's a devil; he can't be beaten.

ء ب ن

أبَّن [ʔabban] *v:* • **1.** to eulogize a deceased person, deliver a funeral sermon – أبَّنَه بقَصِيدَة مُمتازَة [ʔabbanah bqaṣiːda mumtaːza] He eulogized him with an excellent poem.

تَأبِين [taʔbiːn] *n:* • **1.** commemoration, eulogizing – حَفلَة تَأبِين [ħaflat taʔbiːn] commemorative celebration (in memory of a dead person).

تَأبِينِي [taːʔbiːni] *adj:* • **1.** commemorative – حَفلَة تَأبِينِيَّة [ħafla taʔbiːniyya] commemorative ceremony.

ء

ء ب ن س

أَبَنوس [ʔabanuːs] *n:* • **1.** ebony • **2.** various tropical Asian or African trees

ء ب و [1]

أَب [ʔab] *n:* آباء [ʔaːbaːʔ] *pl:* • **1.** father • **2.** Father (title of a Christian priest) – الأَب سَركِيس مُو بِالكَنِيسَة هَسَّة [ʔilʔab sarkiːs muː bilkaniːsa hassa] Father Sarkis isn't in the church now.

أَبُو [ʔabu] *n:* • **1.** owner of, possessor of, one distinguished by – أَبُو الجَّرايِد [ʔabu ʔiǰǰaraːyid] the newspaper boy, newspaper vendor. كُرسي أَبُو يَدّتَين [kursi ʔabu yaddtayn] arm chair. أَبُو بَيت [ʔabu bayt] household manager. هُوَّ أَبُو بَيت مُمتاز. يُعرُف شِيشتِري [huwwa ʔabu bayt mumtaːz. yuʕruf šyištiri] He's a fine manager of household affairs. He knows what to buy. أَبُو الجَّعَل [ʔabu ʔiǰǰaʕal] dung beetle. أَبُو الجِّنّيب [ʔabu ʔiǰǰinniːb] crab. أَبُو برَيص [ʔabu brayṣ] a type of small lizard. أَبُو فلَيس [ʔabu flays] miser, penny-pincher. • **2.** father (construct state of أَب); followed by name of oldest son: a friendly way of addressing or speaking of a man; followed by a conventional male name: a form of address among friends to a man who is not married and has no children

أُبُوَّة [ʔubuwwa] *n:* • **1.** fatherhood, paternity

يابَا، يَابَة [yaːba] *n:* • **1.** dad

الأَبَوَين [ʔilʔabawayn] *n:* • **1.** the parents – اِحتِرام الأَبَوَين واجِب [ʔiħtiraːm ʔilʔabawayn waːǰib] Respecting the parents is a duty.

أَبَوي [ʔabawi] *adj:* • **1.** paternal, fatherly – واجِب أَبَوي [waːǰib ʔabawi] paternal duty. حَنان أَبَوي [ħanaːn ʔabawi] fatherly affection.

أَباً، أَباً عَن جِدّ [ʔaban, ʔaban ʕan ǰidd] *adverbial:* • **1.** for generations – هَالبَيت مُلكنا أَباً عَن جِدّ [halbayt mulukna ʔaban ʕan ǰidd] This house has been our property for generations.

يابَة، ياب [yaːba, yaːb] *int:* • **1.** oh father, hey dad – يابَة العَشا حاضِر [yaːba ʔilʕašaː haːðir] Hey, dad! Supper's ready. • **2.** hey fella, say pal – يابَة، خَلّي نرُوح لِلسِّينَما [yaːba, xalliː nruːħ lissinama] Say, buddy, let's go to the movies. • **3.** (general exclamation of approval, astonishment, anguish) boy, wow, man – يا أَبّ [yaː ʔabb]) يابَة، شلُون جَمال هَذا [yaːba, šluːn ǰamaːl haːða] Boy, oh boy, what a beauty! هَلَو ياب! طَلَّع كُول اللّاخ [halaw yaːb! ṭallaʕ guːl ʔillaːx] Good, good! He scored another goal.

ء ب و [2]

بابَة [baːba] *n:* باباوات [baːbaːwaːt] *pl:* • **1.** The Pope • **2.** (a familiar form of address by a child to his father) daddy, papa • **3.** بابَة man, friend, pal, buddy (form of address)

بابا [baːba] *n:* باباوات [baːbaːwaːt] *pl:* • **1.** The Pope

البابَوِيَّة [ʔilbaːbawiyya] *n:* • **1.** Papacy

بابَوِي [baːbawi] *adj:* • **1.** papal – أَمُر بابَوِي [ʔamur baːbawi] a papal edict.

ء ب و ذ ي

أَبُوذِيَّة [ʔabuːðiyya] *n:* • **1.** type of poetry in which homonymous endings are used for three lines and -iyya for the fourth Usually used in song prologue, and popular in rural areas

ء ب ي

تأَبَّى [tʔabbaː] *v:* • **1.** to be careful, cautious, to proceed with caution – لازِم تِتأَبَّى مِن تِحكِي وِيّاه تَرَة يِتأَذَّى [laːzim titʔabbaː min tiħči wiyyaːh tara yitʔaððaː] You should be careful when you talk to him or he'll take offense. لازِم تِتأَبَّى فَدّ كَم يوم وَبَعدين أُكُل شما تريد [laːzim titʔabbaː fadd čam yuːm wbaʕdiːn ʔukul šma triːd] You should watch yourself for a few days and then eat whatever you want. لازِم تِتأَبَّى مِن البَرِد لِأَنَّك مَرِيض [laːzim titʔabbaː min ʔilbarid liʔannak mariːð̣] You should stay out of the cold because you are sick. إِنتَ ما تِتأَبَّه إِلّا واحِد يكَسِّر راسَك صُدُق [ʔinta maː titʔabbah ʔilla waːħid ykassir raːsak ṣudug] You won't learn prudence until someone really breaks your head.

أَبِي [ʔabi] *n:* • **1.** proud, prideful – هَذا ما يقبَل إِهانَة. نَفسَه أَبِيَّة [haːða maː yiqbal ʔihaːna. nafsah ʔabiyya] He won't take insults. He has a proud nature. وَلَد أَبِي [walad ʔabi] a proud boy.

ء ت ق

أَتَق [ʔatag] *n:* أَتَقات [ʔatagaːt] *pl:* • **1.** slip • **2.** petticoat, half-slip

ء ت م

مَأتَم [maʔtam] *n:* مَآتِم [maʔaːtim] *pl:* • **1.** funeral procession • **2.** wake, mourning ceremony

ء ت م ت ك

أُوتُوماتِيكِي [ʔutumatiːki] *adj:* • **1.** automatic

ء ث ث

أَثَّث [ʔaθθaθ] *v:* • **1.** to furnish (a house) – دَأَثَّث البَيت الجِّدِيد [daʔaθθiθ ʔilbayt ʔiǰǰidiːd] I'm furnishing the new house.

تأَثَّث [tʔaθθaθ] *v:* • **1.** to be furnished

أَثاث [ʔaθaːθ] *n:* • **1.** furniture, furnishings

مأَثَّث [mʔaθθaθ] *adj:* • **1.** furnished

ء ث ر

أَثَّر [ʔaθθar] *v:* • **1.** to affect, influence, have an effect upon – الضَّرُب ما دَيأَثِّر بِيه [ʔið̣ð̣arub maː dayʔaθθir biːh] Beating doesn't have any effect on him. هَالدُّوا ما دَيأَثِّر بِيك بَعَد [hadduwaː maː dayʔaθθir biːk baʕad] That medicine doesn't have any effect on you any more. كُثرَة الشُّرب مأثَره عَلى نَظَرَه [kuθrat ʔaššurub mʔaθθira ʕala naðarah] Too much drinking has affected his vision. المُعَلِّم أثَّر عَلى تَفكِير تَلامِيذَه [ʔilmuʕallim ʔaθθar ʕala tafkiːr talaːmiːðah] The teacher influenced the thinking of his students. • **2.** to move, touch emotionally – حكايتَه أثَّرَت بيّا [ħčaːytah ʔaθθirat biyya] His story moved me.

تأثَّر [tʔaθθar] *v:* • **1.** to be affected – اللَّكَّة بِهالثُّوب وَلا تأثَّرَت بِالغَسِل [ʔillakka bhaθθuːb wala tʔaθθrat bilɣasil] The stain in this shirt wasn't affected at all by the washing. عينِي تِتأثَّر بِالشَّمِس. لازِم أَلبَس مَناظِر شَمِس [ʕayni titʔaθθar biššamis. laːzim ʔalbas manaːðir šamis] My eyes are affected by the sun. I have to wear sunglasses. كان الفِلِم مُؤلِم، وَتأثَّر بِيه هوايَة [čaːn ʔilfilim muʔlim, wtʔaθθar biːh hwaːya] The film was sad, and he was touched very much by it. تأثَّر مِن حكايتَك هوايَة [tʔaθθar min ħčaːytak hwaːya] He got very mad at your remark.

أثَر [ʔaθar] *n:* آثار [ʔaːθaːr] *pl:* • **1.** track, print – آثار أقدام [ʔaːθaːr ʔaqdaːm] footprints. آثار أصابع [ʔaːθaːr ʔaṣaːbiʕ] fingerprints. • **2.** trace, vestige – اِنهِزمَوا وَما تِركَوا وَراهُم أثَر [ʔinhizmaw wma tirkaw waraːhum ʔaθar] They escaped without leaving a trace. لِقَوا أثَر زَرنِيخ بِمِعِدتَه [ligaw ʔaθar zarniːx bmiʕidtah] They found a trace of arsenic in his stomach. • **3.** (mostly pl.) ruin, historical monument, antiquity – عِلم الآثار [ʕilm ʔilʔaːθaːr] archaeology. • **4.** effect – أثَر المَرَض بَعدَه مبَيِّن عَلَيك [ʔaθar ʔilmarað baʕda mbayyin ʕaliːk] The effect of the disease is still showing on you. إلَه أثَر رَجعِي [ʔilah ʔaθar rajʕi] It has retroactive effect. • **5.** impression – خِطابَه تِرَك أثَر عَمِيق بِنفُوسنا [xiṭaːbah tirak ʔaθar ʕamiːq bnufuːsna] His speech left a deep impression on us.

تأثُّر [taʔaθθur] *n:* • **1.** emotion, agitation. effect – التَّأثُّر دَيبَيِّن عَلى وُجَّه [ʔittaʔaθθur daybayyin ʕala wuččah] Emotion is showing on his face.

تأثِير [taʔθiːr] *n:* • **1.** effect – هَالدُّوا ما إلَه أيّ تأثِير عَلى مَرَضَك [hadduwaː maː ʔilah ʔayy taʔθiːr ʕala maraðak] This medicine has no effect on your illness. زيارَة الرَّئِيس راح يكُون إلها تأثِير قَوِي عَلى عَلاقاتنا [ziyaːrat ʔirraʔiːs raːħ ykuːn ʔilha taʔθiːr qawi ʕala ʕalaːqaːtna] The president's visit will have a pronounced effect on our relations.

أثَري [ʔaθari] *adj:* • **1.** ancient, antique – قِطَع نُقود أثَرِيَّة [quṭaʕ nuquːd ʔaθariyya] antique coins.

مُؤثِّر [muʔaθθir] *adj:* • **1.** touching, moving – قُصَّة الفِلِم مُؤثِّرَة [quṣṣat ʔilfilim muʔaθθira] The story of the movie is touching. • **2.** effective – هَالبُندُقِيَّة مُؤثِّرَة مِن مَسافَة خَمِس مِيَّة مَتِر [halbunduqiyya muʔaθθira min masaːfat xamis miyyat matir] This rifle is effective at a distance of five hundred meters.

أثِير [ʔaθiːr] *adj:* • **1.** favored, preferred

مأثُور [maʔθuːr] *adj:* • **1.** handed down, traditional – قَول مأثُور [qawl maʔθuːr] a traditional saying.

متأثِّر [mitʔaθθir] *adj:* • **1.** under influence, influenced

آثاري [ʔaθaːri] *int:* • **1.** it seems, it turns out – آثارِي يرِيدُونِي أسكُن ويّاهُم حَتّى أصرُف عَلَيهُم [ʔaθaːri yriːduːni ʔaskun wiyyaːhum ħatta ʔaṣruf ʕalayhum] It seems they want me to live with them so I can spend my money on them. عَبالِي جارِي مُعَلِّم؛ آثارِي ضابُط [ʕabaːli ǰaːri muʕallim; ʔaθaːri ḍaːbuṭ] I thought my neighbor was a teacher; it turns out he's an officer. آثارِيهُم مِن ولايَتنا [ʔaθaːriːhum min wlaːyatna] It seems they're from our city. • **1.** for this reason

ء ث ل

أثَل [ʔaθal] *n:* • **1.** tamarisk

ء ث م

إثَم [ʔiθam] *v:* • **1.** to sin – إثَمِت عِند الله [ʔiθamit ʕind ʔallah] You sinned in the eyes of God.

إثِم [ʔiθim] *n:* آثام [ʔaːθaːm] *pl:* • **1.** sin

ء ث و ر

آثُوري [ʔaːθuːri] *adj:* • **1.** Assyrian, referring to a Christian people living NE of Mosul in Iraq • **2.** an Assyrian • **3.** Assyrian (language)

ء ث ي ر

أثِير [ʔaθiːr] *n:* • **1.** person's name • **1.** ether

ء ج ر

أجَّر [ʔaǰǰar] *v:* • **1.** to rent, let, lease – أجَّرلِي الدُّكّان مالَه [ʔaǰǰarli ʔiddukkaːn maːlah] He rented me his shop. أجَّرلِي بَيتِي بخوش سِعر [ʔaǰǰarli bayti bxuːš siʕir] He leased my house for me at a good price. • **2.** to rent, hire, lease – أجَّرنا بَلَم مُدَّة ساعتين [ʔaǰǰarna balam muddat saːʕtayn] We rented a boat for two hours.

تأجَّر [tʔaǰǰar] *v:* • **1.** pass. of – أجَّر [ʔaǰǰar] مَعَ الأسَف، البَيت تأجَّر البارحَة [maʕa ʔilʔasaf, ʔilbayt tʔaǰǰar ʔilbaːrħa] I'm sorry, the house was rented yesterday.

اِستأجَر [ʔistaʔǰar] *v:* • **1.** to hire, rent, charter – مِنُو اِستأجَر بَيتَك؟ [minu ʔistaʔǰar baytak?] Who rented your house?

أجِر [ʔaǰir] *n:* • **1.** reward, recompense – أجرَك عَظِيم عِند الله [ʔaǰrak ʕaðiːm ʕind ʔallah] Your reward will be great in Heaven.

آجر [ʔaːǰirr] *n:* • **1.** (coll.) hard, over-fired brick(s)

أجرَة [ʔuǰra] *n:* أجُور [ʔuǰuːr] *pl:* • **1.** rent, rental, hire • **2.** pay (rate), wage (rate) – شقَدّ أجُرتَك بِاليُوم؟ [šgadd ʔuǰurtak bilyuːm?] How much is your pay per day? الشَّرِكَة قَرَّرَت تزَيِّد أجُور العُمّال [ʔiššarika qarrarat dzayyid ʔuǰuːr ʔilʕummaːl] The company decided to increase the wages of the workers. • **3.** fee, rate, fare – أجرَة الباص [ʔuǰrat ʔilpaːṣ] bus fare. شقَدّ الأجرَة عَلى هَالمَكتُوب بِالطَّيّارَة؟ [šgadd ʔilʔuǰra ʕala halmaktuːb biṭṭiyyaːra?] How much

is the airmail rate on this letter? أُجُور الدِّراسَة [ʔuǰuːr ʔiddiraːsa] tuition.
مُؤَجِّر [muʔaǰǰir] *n:* مُؤَجِّرِين [muʔaǰǰiriːn] *pl:* • **1.** landlord, lessor
آجِرَّة [ʔaːǰirra] *n:* آجِرّات [ʔaːǰirraːt] *pl:* • **1.** a hard, overfired brick
إيجار [ʔiːǰaːr] *n:* • **1.** rent, rental – أَكُو يَمّكُم بَيت لِلإيجار؟ [ʔaku yammkum bayt lilʔiːǰaːr?] Is there a house for rent near you?
تَأجِير [taʔǰiːr] *n:* • **1.** letting, renting, leasing, hiring out
مِستَأجِر [mistaʔǰir] *n:* مِستَأجِرِين [mistaʔǰiriːn] *pl:* • **1.** tenant, renter, lessee
أَجِير [ʔaǰiːr] *adj:* • **1.** salaried, paid • **2.** as Noun: paid worker
مَأجُور [maʔǰuːr] *adj:* • **1.** hired, brided, bought – عَمِيل مَأجُور لِلإستِعمار [ʕamiːl maʔǰuːr lilʔistiʕmaːr] a hired agent of imperialism. هَذا واحِد مَأجُور [haːða waːħid maʔǰuːr] He's in the pay of someone.

ء ج غ

آجُغ [ʔaːčuɣ] *adj:* • **1.** light, light colored – ماوِي آجُغ [maːwi ʔaːčuɣ] light blue. • **2.** uncovered, unguarded (chiefly in backgammon) • **3.** unemployed, idle – كُلّ أَصدِقائي اِشتِغلَوا وَأنِي بقَيت آجُغ [kull ʔaṣdiquaːʔi ʔištiɣlaw waʔaːni bqiːt ʔaːčuɣ] All my friends went to work and I remained idle.

ء ج ل

أَجَّل [ʔaǰǰal] *v:* • **1.** to postpone, delay, defer, put off – أَجَّلت السَّفرَة مالتِي لِلإسبُوع الجّاي [ʔaǰǰalt ʔissafra maːlti lilʔisbuːʕ ʔiǰǰaːy] I postponed my trip till next week. ما عِندِي فلُوس. تِقدَر تأَجِّلِي هَالقِسِط؟ [maː ʕindi fluːs. tigdar tʔaǰǰilli halqisiṭ?] I haven't got any money. Can you defer this payment for me? أَجِّلَوا الجُّندِيَّة مالتِي إلَى السَّنَة الجّايَّة [ʔaǰǰilaw ʔiǰǰundiyya maːlti ʔila ʔissana ʔiǰǰaːyya] They deferred my military service till next year.
تأَجَّل [tʔaǰǰal] *v:* • **1.** to be postponed – الاجتِماع تأَجَّل إلَى يوم الخَمِيس [ʔilʔiǰtimaːʕ tʔaǰǰal ʔila yuːm ʔilxamiːs] The meeting's been postponed to Thursday.
أَجِل، لأَجِل، مِن أَجِل [ʔaǰil, lʔaǰil, min ʔaǰil] *n:* • **1.** for the sake of, because of – ضَحَّيت بوَظِيفتِي لأَجلَك [ðaħħiːt bwaðiːfti lʔaǰlak] I sacrificed my job for your sake. مِن أَجِل هَذا، ما نِقدَر نشَغّلَك [min ʔaǰil haːða, maː nigdar nšaɣɣlak] Because of this, we can't employ you.
أَجَل [ʔaǰal] *n:* آجال [ʔaːǰaːl] *pl:* • **1.** time, instant of death – أَجَلَه جاي [ʔaǰalah ǰaːy] His time is coming. الآجال بإيد الله [ʔilʔaːǰaːl bʔiːd ʔallah] Men's lives are in God's hands.
تأجِيل [taʔǰiːl] *n:* تأجِيلات [taʔǰiːlaːt] *pl:* • **1.** delay, postponement
مُؤَجَّل [muʔaǰǰal] *adj:* • **1.** postponed, delayed, deferred • **2.** sum of money arranged before marriage to be paid to the wife in the event of divorce
آجِلاً [ʔaːǰilan] *adverbial:* • **1.** later

ء ج ن

أُجُن [ʔuǰun] أُجُن، أُجُن أُجُن [ʔuǰun, ʔuǰun ʔuǰun] *adj:* • **1.** bit by bit, slowly, carefully, gently.

ء ح د [1]

أَحَّد [ʔaħħad] *n:* • **1.** someone, anyone – ماكُو أَحَّد هنا [maːku ʔaħħad hna] There isn't anyone here. مَحَّد، لا حَدّ [maħħad, laː ħadd] no one, nobody. مَحَّد خابَرَك [maħħad xaːbarak] No one called you. لا حَدّ يحكِي [laː ħadd yiħči] Don't anyone say anthing.
الأَحَّد، يوم الأَحَّد [ʔilʔaħħad, yuwm ilʔaħħad] *n:* • **1.** Sunday
الآحاد [ʔilʔaːħaːd] *n:* • **1.** (pl.) the units (math.)
أُحادِي [ʔuħaːdi] *adj:* • **1.** single, mono, solo

ء ح د [2]

لَحّد [laħħad] *v:* • **1.** nobody
مَحَّد [maħħad] *n:* • **1.** nobody

ء ح ن

إحنا [ʔiħna] *pronoun:* • **1.** we

ء خ

آخ [ʔaːx] *int:* • **1.** an exclamation, approx.: ow! ouch!, and a cry of distress, approx.: oh! – آخ، راسِي يَوجَعنِي [ʔaːx, raːsi yawǰaʕni] Oh, my head hurts!

ء خ ذ

أَخَذ مِن، أَخَذ عَلَى [ʔaxað min, ʔaxað ʕala] *v:* • **1.** to take (something) – أُخُذ شقَدّ ما ترِيد [ʔuxuð šgadd maː triːd] Take as much as you want. الخَيّاط أَخَذلِي أُولچِي [ʔilxayyaːṭ ʔaxaðli ʔuːlči] The tailor took my measurements. عِند يا رَسّام أَخَذِت هَالرَّسِم؟ [ʕind yaː rassaːm ʔaxaðit harrasim?] At which photographer's did you have this picture taken? خَلِّي ناخُذ هَالطَّرِيق. هَذا أَقصَر [xalliː naːxuð haṭṭriːq. haːða ʔaqṣar] Let's take this road. It's shorter. راح آخُذ هَالشُّغُل عَلَى عاتقِي [raːħ ʔaːxuð halšuɣul ʕala ʕaːtqi] I will take this job on myself. أَخَذلَه فال [ʔaxaðlah faːl] He told his fortune. اِنطِيه عَشِر فلُوس حَتَّى ياخُذلَك فال [ʔinṭiːh ʕašir fluːs ħatta yaːxuðlak faːl] Give him ten fils so he will tell your fortune. أُخُذ قِرفَة. صار لَو لا؟ [ʔuxuð girfa. ṣaːr law laː?] Face the facts. Did it happen or not? أُخُذ قِرفَة. أَوَّل ما خَلَّص الكُلِّيَّة، صار أُستاذ [ʔuxuð girfa. ʔawwal maː xallaṣ ʔilkulliyya, ṣaːr ʔustaːð] Face it. As soon as he finished college, he became a professor. • **2.** to take, take away – مِنُو أَخَذ قَلَمِي؟ [minu ʔaxað qalami?] Who took my pencil? اِلحَقلَه. الماي أَخَذَه [ʔilħaglah. ʔilmaːy ʔaxaðah] Go get him. The current's taken him. الله ياخُذ رُوحَك [ʔallah yaːxuð ruːħak] May God take your life! أَخَذ وِحدَة مِن بَناتهُم [ʔaxað wiħda min banaːthum] He married one of their daughters.

أخذُوه جُندِي [ʔaxðawh ǰundi] They took him into the army. أَخَذ بَكارَتها [ʔaxað baka:ratha] He took her virginity. خَلِّي نرُوح ناخُذ مِن خاطرَه [xalli: nru:ħ na:xuð min xa:ṭrah] Let's go ease his mind (of grief, anger). • **3.** to take along – راح آخذَك ويّايا [ra:ħ ʔa:xðak wiyya:ya] I'll take you with me. • **4.** to get, receive, obtain – أَخَذِت جَواب لَو بَعَد؟ [ʔaxaðit ǰawa:b law baʕad?] Did you get an answer yet? أَخَذِت خَبَر راح يِجِي [ʔaxaðit xabar ra:ħ yiǰi] I got word he's coming. شقَدّ تاخُذ بِالإسبُوع؟ [šgadd ta:xuð bilʔisbu:ʕ?] How much do you get per week? اليُوم ناخُذ مَعاشنا [ʔilyu:m na:xuð maʕa:šna] We get our pay today. شقَدّ أَخَذِت بِالحِساب؟ [šgadd ʔaxaðit bilħisa:b?] How much did you get in arithmetic? الرّاديُو مالِي ما دَياخُذ مَصِر [ʔirra:dyu ma:li ma: daya:xuð maṣir] My radio won't get Egypt. أَخَذِت حَيفَك مِنَّه؟ [ʔaxaðit ħayfak minnah?] Did you take your revenge on him? لازِم ترُوح لِدائرَة البَرِيد وَتاخُذ الرُّزمَة بنَفسَك [la:zim tru:ħ lida:ʔirat ʔilbari:d wta:xuð ʔirruzma bnafsak] You have to go to the Post Office and pick up the package yourself. • **5.** to accept, take – أخذَه عَلَى قَدّ عَقلَه [ʔuxðah ʕala gadd ʕaqlah] Accept him for what he is. لا تاخُذ كَلامَه راس [la: ta:xuð kala:mah ra:s] Don't take what he says seriously. مِن قِلِت الشُّغُل ما دَيمشِي، أَخَذ عَلَى نَفسَه وَزِعَل [min gilit ʔiššuɣul ma: dayimši, ʔaxað ʕala nafsah waziʕal] When I said the work's not moving, he took it personally and got mad. ما أَقدَر أتفاهَم وِيّاه. ما ياخُذ وَما ينطِي [ma: ʔagdar ʔatfa:ham wiyya:h. ma: ya:xuð wma yinṭi] I can't reach an understanding with him. He won't give and take. • **6.** to take, require – عَبالِي أَخَلِّص هَالشّغلَة بساعَة لَكِن أخذت نَهار كامِل [ʕaba:li ʔaxalliṣ haššaɣla bsa:ʕa la:kin ʔaxðat naha:r ka:mil] I thought I'd finish this job in an hour up, occupy, take. هَالميز ياخُذ مَكان هوايَة [halmi:z ya:xuð maka:n hwa:ya] This desk takes up a lot of room. راح آخُذ الصَّدِر وَحدِي وأرتاح [ra:ħ ʔa:xuð ʔiṣṣadir waħdi wʔarta:ħ] I'm going to take the front seat to myself and be comfortable. • **7.** to adopt, follow – أُخُذ بِرَأيَه لِأَنّ يفتِهِم [ʔuxuð braʔyah liʔann yiftihim] Follow his opinion because he knows what he is talking about. • **8** to take up, take on, acquire, absorb – الحايِط ماخِذ رُطُوبَة [ʔilħa:yiṭ ma:xið ruṭu:ba] The wall's taken up moisture. الأكِل بِالقُوطِيَّة جايِف لِأَنّ أَخَذ هَوا [ʔilʔakil bilqu:ṭiyya ǰa:yif liʔann ʔaxað hawa] The food in the can is rotten because it got some air in it. • **9** to take hold, catch hold, catch on – لُقاح الجِّدرِي مالِي ما أَخَذ [luqa:ħ ʔiǰǰidri ma:li ma: ʔaxað] My smallpox vaccination didn't take. عُودَة الشّخّاط ما دَتاخُذ. يمكِن مبَلِّلَة [ʕu:dat ʔiššixxa:ṭ ma: data:xuð. yimkin mballila] The match won't strike. Maybe it's wet. • **10.** to engage in, accomplish, make, take – أُخُذلَك فَرَّة بالسُّوق إلَى أن أَخَلِّص شُغلِي [ʔuxuðlak farra bissu:g ʔila ʔan ʔaxalliṣ šuɣli] Take a turn in the market till I finish my business. بَعَد ما يُقعُد مِن النُّوم، ياخُذ شناو [baʕad ma: yugʕud min ʔinnu:m, ya:xuð šna:w] After he gets out of bed, he does push-ups. • **11.** to take up, assume, strike (a pose, position) – أُخُذ وَضع إستِعداد مِن تِحكِي ويّا الضُّبّاط [ʔuxuð waḍiʕ ʔistiʕda:d min tiħči wiyya ʔiḍḍubba:ṭ] Assume a position of attention when you speak to officers. أُخُذ حَذَرَك مِنَّه [ʔuxuð ħaðarak minnah] Be on your guard against him. مِن يمُرّ الضّابُط، أُخُذلَه سَلام [min yumurr ʔiḍḍa:buṭ, ʔuxuðlah sala:m] When the officer passes by, give him a salute. • **12.** to take, catch, get the better of – أَخَذنِي فلاحَة ملاكَة. ظَلّ يحكِي نُصّ ساعَة وَلا خَلّانِي أجاوبَه [ʔaxaðni fla:ħa mla:ča. ḍall yiħči nuṣṣ sa:ʕa wala xalla:ni ʔaǰa:wbah] He took me by storm. He kept talking a half hour and didn't give me a chance to answer him. أَخَذنِي كراخَة؛ ما نطانِي مَجال أحكِي وَلا كِلمَة [ʔaxaðni kra:xa; ma: nṭa:ni maǰa:l ʔaħči wala čilma] He took me by storm; didn't give me a chance to say a word. أَخَذنِي عَلَى غَفلَة [ʔaxaðni ʕala ɣafla] He took me by surprise. أَخَذنِي النُّوم مِن كِنِت دَأقرا الجَّرِيدَة [ʔaxaðni ʔinnu:m min činit daʔaqra: ʔiǰǰari:da] Sleep overcame me while I was reading the newspaper. أَخذَتها العَبرَة [ʔaxðatha ʔilʕabra] She was overcome by sobbing. لا تآخذَه. بَعدَه جدِيد [la: tʔa:xðah. baʕdah ǰidi:d] Don't blame him. He's still inexperienced. • **13.** with ب (to begin) to take on, acquire – ظَلّ ناعِم إلَى أن صار عُمرَه أربَاطَعَش وَأَخَذ بالطُّول [ḍall na:ʕim ʔila ʔan ṣa:r ʕumrah ʔarba:ṭaʕaš waʔaxað bittu:l] He remained small until he was fourteen years old and then he took on some height. دَياخُذ بالعُرُض لِأَنّ مَرتَه تأكّلَه زين [daya:xuð bilʕuruḍ liʔann martah tʔakklah zi:n] He's getting fat because his wife feeds him well. • **14.** to catch, contract, get – ما أعتِقِد أخذَت؛ لازِم نوَدّيها لِلفَحَل مَرَّة اللُّخ [ma: ʔaʕtiqid ʔaxðat; la:zim nwaddi:ha lilfaħal marrat ʔillux] I don't think she took; we'll have to take her to the stud again.

واخذ [wa:xað] *v:* • **1.** to reproach • **2.** to excuse, pardon

تواخذ [twa:xað] *v:* • **1.** to be reproached

إنأخذ [ʔinʔixað] *v:* • **1.** to be taken

إتّخذ [ʔittixað] *v:* • **1.** to take – إتِّخَذنا كُلّ التَّدابِير الضُّرُورِيَّة [ʔittixaðna kull ʔittada:bi:r ʔiḍḍuru:riyya] We took all the necessary measures. • **2.** to take on, assume, adopt – إتَّخَذ مَوقِف مُعادِي لِلحُكُومَة [ʔittaxað mawqif muʕa:di lilħuku:ma] He took a position unfriendly to the government. الحُكُومَة إتّخذَت قَرار خَطِير [ʔilħuku:ma ʔittixðat qara:r xaṭi:r] The government adopted an important decision. • **3.** to take as, employ as, use as – إتَّخَذ مَرَضَه حِجَّة حَتَّى ما يرُوح لِلشُّغُل [ʔittaxað maraḍah ħiǰǰa ħatta ma: yru:ħ liššuɣul] He used his sickness as an excuse not to go to work. إتّخَذنِي آلَة لِتَحقِيق أغراضَه [ʔittixaðni ʔa:la litaħqi:q ʔaɣra:ḍah] He used me as a tool to achieve his ends.

أخذ [ʔaxið] *n:* • **1.** taking, receiving, acceptance • **2.** taking away, removal – أخِذ وَرَدّ [ʔaxið wradd]

ء

controversy, debate. هَذا ما بِيه أَخِذ وَرَدّ [haːða maː biːh ʔaxið wradd] There's no argument about that. القَضِيَّة بين أَخِذ وَرَدّ [ʔilqaðiyya bayn ʔaxið wradd] The matter is in dispute.

اِتِّخاذ [ʔittixaːð] *n:* • **1.** taking, receiving; acceptance

مُؤاخَذَة [muʔaːxaða] *n:* • **1.** censure, blame – بَلا مُؤاخَذَة، راح أَضطَرّ أَتْرُكَك [bala muʔaːxaða, raːħ ʔaðṭarr ʔaturkak] No offense, but I'm going to have to leave you.

مَأخُوذ [maʔxuːð] *adj:* • **1.** taken, possessed

ء خ ر

أَخَّر [ʔaxxar] *v:* • **1.** to delay, make late, hold up – ظَلّ يِحكِي وَأَخَّرنِي نُصّ ساعَة [ðall yiħči wʔaxxarni nuṣṣ saːʕa] He kept talking and delayed me a half hour. المُطَر أَخَّر تَقَدُّمنا [ʔilmuṭar ʔaxxar taqaddumna] The rain slowed our advance. أَرِيد الإِيجار واحِد بِالشَّهَر. لا يكُون تأَخّره [ʔariːd ʔilʔiːǰaːr waːħid biššahar. laː ykuːn tʔaxxrah] I want the rent the first of the month. You're not to hold it up. • **2.** to postpone, put off – أَخّرَوا الاِجتِماع عَلَى مُودِي [ʔaxxraw ʔilʔiǰtimaːʕ ʕala muːdi] They postponed the meeting on my account. دِزّ المَكتُوب اليُوم؛ لا تأَخّرَه إِلَى باكِر [dizz ʔilmaktuːb ʔilyuːm; laː tʔaxxrah ʔila baːčir] Send the letter today; don't put it off till tomorrow.

تأَخَّر [tʔaxxar] *v:* • **1.** to be delayed – وُصُول الطَّيّارَة تأَخَّر نُصّ ساعَة [wuṣuːl ʔiṭṭiyyaːra tʔaxxar nuṣṣ saːʕa] The plane's arrival was delayed a half hour. • **2.** to become late, get late, be late – الوَقت تأَخَّر. خَلِّي نرُوح [ʔilwakt tʔaxxar. xalliːnruːħ] It's gotten late. Let's go. المُطَر تأَخَّر هالسَّنَة [ʔilmuṭar tʔaxxar hassana] The rain is late this year. لِيش تأَخَّرت هَالقَدّ؟ الفِلم بِدا هَسَّة [liːš tʔaxxarit halgadd? ʔilfilim bidaː hassa] Why'd you take so long? The movie's begun now. • **3.** with عَن to fall behind – تأَخَّر عَن جَماعتَه لِأَنّ تمَرَّض السَّنَة اللِّي فاتَت [tʔaxxar ʕan ǰamaːʕtah liʔann tmarrað ʔissana ʔilli faːtat] He fell behind his group because he got sick last year.

لُخ [lux] *n:* • **1.** other (contraction of الأُخرَى) – راوِينِي إِيدَك اللُّخ [raːwiːni ʔiːdak ʔillux] Show me your other hand. شِفتَه مَرَّة لُخ [šiftah marra lux] I saw him another time.

آخِر [ʔaːxir] *n:* أَواخِر [ʔawaːxir] *pl:* • **1.** last, final – هاي آخِر مَرَّة راح أَقُلَّك [haːy ʔaːxir marra raːħ ʔagullak] This is the last time I'm going to tell you. آخِر كَلام، دِينارَين [ʔaːxir kalaːm, dinaːrayn] The final price is two dinars. • **2.** latest – سَيّارتَك آخِر مُودَيل [sayyaːrtak ʔaːxir muːdiːl] Your car's the latest model. • **3.** last, end, last portion – آخِر الشَّهَر [ʔaːxir ʔiššahar] the last (part) of month. هَالحَكِي ما إِلَه آخِر [halħači maː ʔilah ʔaːxir] There's no end to this talk.

لاخ [laːx] *n:* • **1.** other (contraction of الآخَر) – أَرجُوك، إِنطِينِي شاي لاخ [ʔarǰuːk, ʔinṭiːni čaːy laːx] Please give me another tea.

مُؤَخَّر [muʔaxxar] *n:* • **1.** delayed, postponed • **2.** sum of money agreed upon before marriage to be paid to the in the event of divorce

تأَخُّر [taʔaxxur] *n:* • **1.** delay, being late

تأخِير [taʔxiːr] *n:* تأخِيرات [taʔxiːraːt] *pl:* • **1.** delay, postponement

الآخرَة [ʔilʔaːxra] *n:* • **1.** the hereafter, the world to come

إِلَى آخِرِه [ʔila ʔaːxirihi] *n:* • **1.** etc., and so on – البارحَة باللَّيل سِكَرنا، وَلِعَبنا قمار، رِحنا لِلكَلَّجِيَّة، إِلَى آخِرِه [ʔilbaːrħa billayl sikarna, wliʕabna qmaːr, riħna lilkallačiyya, ʔila ʔaːxirih] Last night we got drunk, played cards, went to the red light district, and so on.

آخَر [ʔaːxar] *adj:* آخَرِين [ʔaːxariːn] *pl:* أُخرَى [ʔuxra] *feminine:* • **1.** another – هَذا مَوضُوع آخَر [haːða mawðuːʕ ʔaːxar] That's another matter. الرِّجّال الآخَر ما قال شِي [ʔirriǰǰaːl ʔilʔaːxar maː gaːl ši] The other man didn't say anything. مِن وَقِت لِآخَر، نرُوح لِلمَسبَح [min wakit lʔaːxar, nruːħ lilmasbaħ] From time to time, we go swimming.

أَخِير [ʔaxiːr] *adj:* • **1.** last – إِنتَ دائِماً أَخِير واحِد يُوصَل [ʔinta daːʔiman ʔaxiːr waːħid yuːṣal] You're always the last one to arrive. • **2.** latest • **3.** rearmost • **4.** rear, back, rear section – ماكُو مُكان هنا. أُقعُد بِالأَخِير [maːku mukaːn hna ʔugʕud bilʔaxiːr] There's no room here. Sit in the rear.

مِتأَخِّر [mitʔaxxir] *adj:* • **1.** late, delayed – لِيش هِيكِي مِتأَخِّر؟ [liːš hiːči mitʔaxxir?] Why are you so late? • **2.** backward, underdeveloped – أَهِل هَالمَنطِقَة كُلِّش مِتأَخّرِين [ʔahil halmanṭiqa kulliš mitʔaxxriːn] The people of this area are very backward.

أَخِيراً [ʔaxiːran] *adverbial:* • **1.** finally, eventually – أَخِيراً، اِشتِرَى السَّيّارَة التَّنتَة [ʔaxiːran, ʔištiraː ʔissayyaːra ʔittanta] Finally, he bought the convertible. • **2.** lately – الشَّهر اللِّي فات، الشُّغُل ما كان زين، لَكِن أَخِيراً تحَسَّن [ʔiššahr ʔilli faːt, ʔiššuɣul maː čaːn ziːn, laːkin ʔaxiːran tħassan] Last month, business wasn't good, but lately it's picked up.

ء خ ط ب و ط

أَخطَبُوط [ʔaxṭabuːṭ] *n:* أَخطَبُوطات [ʔaxṭabuːṭaːt] *pl:* • **1.** octopus

ء خ و

أَخ [ʔax] *n:* أُخوَة [ʔuxwa] *pl:* • **1.** brother (in a religious or ideological sense) – الإِخوان المُسلِمِين [ʔilʔixwaːn ʔalmuslimiːn] The Moslem Brotherhood. • **2.** brother الأَخ polite term for a stranger – مِنُو الأَخ وَمنَين؟ [minu ʔilʔax wminayn?] Who is the gentleman and where is he from? • **3.** (familiar form of address) friend, buddy, pal

أُخُت [ʔuxut] *n:* أَخوات، خوات [ʔaxwaːt, xwaːt] *pl:* • **1.** sister • **2.** /with feminine nouns/ mate, twin, the same as – هاي أُخُت سَيّارتِي [haːy ʔuxut sayyaːrti] This one is exactly like my car. اِشتِرَيتها أُخت البَلاش [ʔištiraytha ʔuxt ʔalbalaːš] I bought it for next to nothing. • **3.** Baghdad boil, a long-term skin eruption which leaves a large, round, flat depression on healing

أَخُو [ʔaxu] *n:* • **1.** brother

أخوه [ʔaxuːh] *n:* • **1.** his brother
خويَا [xuːya] *n:* • **1.** (familiar form of address) pal, buddy, friend
إخاء [ʔixaːʔ] *n:* • **1.** brotherhood, fraternity – جَمعيَّة الإخاء الوَطَنِي [ǰamʕiyyat ʔilʔixaːʔ ʔilwaṭani] Society of National Brotherhood.
أخُوَّة [ʔuxuwwa] *n:* • **1.** friendship, brotherhood – لا تسَوِّي هِيكِي أشياء إذا تريد أخُوَّتنا تِستَمِرّ [laː tsawwiː hiːči ʔašyaːʔ ʔiða triːd ʔuxuwwatna tistamirr] Don't do that sort of thing if you want our friendship to last.
تآخي [taʔaːxi] *n:* • **1.** friendship – التَّآخِي بَينكُم يعَجِّب [ʔittaʔaːxi baynkum yʕaǰǰib] The friendship between you is amazing.
أخُويَا [ʔaxuːya] *n:* • **1.** my brother • **2.** (by extension) pal, buddy, friend • **3.** /with masculine nouns/ mate, equal, like – شِفِت بَيت أخُو بَيتِي تَماماً [šifit bayt ʔaxuː bayti tamaːman] I saw a house exactly like my house! هَذا فَدّ خُوش وَلَد. ما يِنلِقِي أخُوه [haːða fadd xuːš walad. maː yinligi ʔaxuːh] He's a real nice guy. One like him can't be found. اِشتِرَينا هَالبَيت أخُو البَلاش [ʔištirayna halbiyt ʔaxuː ʔalbalaːš] We bought this house dirt cheap.
أخَوي [ʔaxawi] *adj:* أخَوِيَّة [ʔaxawiyya] *pl:* • **1.** brotherly love, deep friendship between two men • **2.** platonic friendship with a girl

ء د ب

أدَّب [ʔaddab] *v:* • **1.** to rear properly, bring up right, teach manners – يِظهَر أهلَك ما أدِّبوك [yiðhar ʔahlak maː ʔaddibuːk] Apparently your family didn't bring you up right. • **2.** (by extension) to teach a lesson – إذا ما تِسكُت، تَرَة أجِي أئَدِّبَك [ʔiða maː tiskut, tara ʔaji ʔaʔaddibak] If you don't shut up, I'll come and teach you a lesson. • **3.** to punish, discipline – مِن يِجِي أبُوك أقُلّه يأدّبَك [min yiji ʔabuːk ʔagullah yʔaddbak] When your father comes I'll tell him to punish you.
تأدَّب [tʔaːddab] *v:* • **1.** to be or become polite – تأدَّب، لَك! لا تِحكِي هِيكِي قِدّام النِّسوان [tʔaddab, lak! laː tiħči hiːči giddaːm ʔinniswaːn] Watch your manners, you! Don't talk like that in front of women.
أدَب [ʔadab] *n:* آداب [ʔaːdaːb] *pl:* • **1.** literature – كُلِّيَّة الآداب [kulliyyat ʔilʔaːdaːb] College of Arts. • **2.** manners, breeding, upbringing – قَلِيل الأدَب [qaliːl ʔilʔadab] lacking in manners. • **3.** toilet
أدِيب [ʔadiːb] *n:* أدَباء [ʔudabaːʔ] *pl:* • **1.** writer, author, literateur
تأدُّب [taʔaddub] *n:* • **1.** civility, politeness
تأدِيب [taʔdiːb] *n:* • **1.** discipline – مَجلِس تأدِيب [maǰlis taʔdiːb] disciplinary board.
أدَبِي [ʔadabi] *adj:* • **1.** literary – مَجَلَّة أدَبِيَّة [maǰalla ʔadabiyya] literary magazine.
مُؤدَّب [muʔaddab] *adj:* • **1.** well-mannered, well brought up – وَلَد كُلِّش مُؤدَّب [walad kulliš muʔaddab] a very well brought up boy.
أدَبسِزّ [ʔadabsizz] *adj:* أدَبسِزِّيَّة [ʔadabsizziyya] *pl:* • **1.** mannerless, crude, boorish, impolite
تأدِيبِي [taʔdiːbi] *adj:* • **1.** punitive
أدَبِيّاً [ʔadabiyyan] *adverbial:* • **1.** morally, socially – إنتَ أدَبِيّاً مَسؤُول عَن إبنَك [ʔinta ʔadabiyyan masʔuːl ʕan ʔibnak] You're morally responsible for your son. إذا ما تسَلِّم عَليها، أدَبِيّاً ما صَحِيح [ʔiða maː tsallim ʕaliːha, ʔadabiyyan maː ṣaħiːħ] If you don't say hello to her, it's not socially correct.

ء د ب خ ن

أدَبخانَة [ʔadabxaːna] *n:* أدَبخانات [ʔadabxaːnaːt] *pl:* • **1.** toilet, rest room, w.c

ء د م

آدَم [ʔaːdam] *n:* • **1.** Adam – بَنِي آدَم [bani ʔaːdam] (invar.) human being, man.
آدَمِي [ʔaːdami] *adj:* أوادِم [ʔawaːdim] *pl:* • **1.** human being, person – ما يصِير تعامِلنِي هِيكِي. آنِي آدَمِي، مُو كَلِب [maː yṣiːr tʕaːmilni hiːči. ʔaːni ʔaːdami, muː čalib] You can't treat me that way. I'm a human being, not a dog. جِيرانّا خُوش أوادِم [ǰiːraːnna xuːš ʔawaːdim] Our neighbors are nice people. • **2.** valet, man servant • **3.** a good man, nice guy – إبن أوادِم [ʔibin ʔawaːdim] man from a good family, well-bred man.
آدَمِيَّة [ʔaːdamiyya] *adj:* آدَمِيّات [ʔaːdamiyyaːt] *pl:* • **1.** person (fem.), woman, girl • **2.** a good girl – صِيرِي آدمِيَّة؛ لا تسَوِّين هِيكِي بَعَد [ṣiːri ʔaːdmiyya; laː tsawwiːn hiːči baʕad] Be a good girl; don't do that again.

ء د و

أداة [ʔadaːt] *n:* أدَوات [ʔadawaːt] *pl:* • **1.** tool, piece of equipment, and by extension, a person being used as a tool – أداة التَّعرِيف [ʔadaːt ʔittaʕriːf] the definite article (gram.). • **2.** piece, part (of a machine) – أدَوات اِحتِياطِيَّة [ʔadawaːt ʔiħtiyaːṭiyya] spare parts.

ء د ي

أدَّى [ʔaddaː] *v:* • **1.** to lead. (see also w-d-y.) – هَالطَّرِق وين يأدِّي؟ [hattarriq wiːn yʔaddi?] Where's this road lead? عَمَلَك هَذا يأدِّي إلَى نَتائِج خَطِيرَة [ʕamalak haːða yʔaddi ʔila nataːʔiǰ xaṭiːra] This action of yours will lead to serious consequences. • **2.** to carry out, discharge, do, fulfill – الشُّرطِي أدَّى واجبَه [ʔiššurṭi ʔaddaː waːǰbah] The policeman did his duty. هَالسَّيّارَة تأدِّي المَطلُوب [hassayyaːra tʔaddi ʔilmaṭluːb] This car will do what you require. • **3.** to perform, execute, render – الحَرَس أدَّى التَّحِيَّة لآمِر اللِّواء [ʔilħaras ʔaddaː ʔittaħiyya lʔaːmir ʔilliwaːʔ] The guard rendered a salute to the major general. أدَّى اليَمِين القانُونِي [ʔaddaː ʔilyamiːn ʔilqaːnuːni] He took the oath of office. • **4.** to pay, hand over – إذا ما تأدِّي الفلُوس، ما أخَلِّيك تِطلَع

[ʔiða maː tʔaddi ʔilflușs, maː ʔaxalliːk titlaʕ] If you don't pay the money, I won't let you leave.
أداء [ʔadaːʔ] *n:* • **1.** performance
تأدِيَة [taʔdiya] *n:* • **1.** performance, rendering • **2.** interpretation
مُؤدِّي [muʔaddi] *adj:* • (as **n**:) **1.** performer • **2.** actor

ء ذ

إذا [ʔiða] *subordinating conjunction:* • **1.** if – إذا سِأل عَنِّي، قُلَّه راح لِلسِّينَما [ʔiða siʔal ʕanni, gullah raːħ lissinama] If he asks about me, tell him I went to the movies. • **2.** whether, if – إذا يِشتِريها أو ما يِشتِريها، تِنباع ثاني يوم [ʔiða yištiriːha ʔaw maː yištiriːha, tinbaːʕ θaːni yuːm] Whether he buys it or doesn't buy it, it'll be sold some other day.
إلّا إذا [ʔilla ʔiða] *subordinating conjunction:* • **1.** except that, unless – راح أشتِكي عَليك إلّا إذا إنطَيتني فلوسي اليَوم [raːħ ʔaštiki ʕaliːk ʔilla ʔiða ʔințiːtni fluːsi ʔilyuːm] I'll take you to court unless you give me my money today.

ء ذ ر

آذار [ʔaːðaːr] *n:* • **1.** March

ء ذ ن

إذَن [ʔiðan] *v:* • **1.** to give permission – مِنُو إذَنلَك تخُشّ بهالغُرفَة؟ [minu ʔiðanlak txušš bhalɣurfa?] Who gave you permission to enter this room?
أذَّن، وَذَّن [ʔaððan, waððan] *v:* • **2.** to give the call to prayer
اِستَأذَن [ʔistaʔðan] *v:* • **1.** to ask permission – لازِم تِستَأذِن قَبُل ما تِطلَع [laːzim tistaʔðin gabul maː titlaʕ] You should ask permission before you leave.
إذِن [ʔiðin] *n:* • **1.** permission, authorization – بإذِن الله [bʔiðn ʔallah] God willing, with God's permission.
إذِن [ʔiðin] *n:* إذانات [ʔiðaːnaːt] *pl:* • **1.** ear – زِرفوا إذِنها [zirfaw ʔiðinha] They pierced her ears. اِنطِيه إذِن الطَّرشَة [ʔințiːh ʔiðin ʔițțarša] Pay no attention to him (lit., give him the deaf ear).
إذان [ʔiðaːn] *n:* إذان، إذانات [ʔiðaːn, ʔiðaːnaːt] *pl:* • **1.** ear
أذان، وَذان [ʔaðaːn, waðaːn] *n:* أذانات [ʔaðaːnaːt] *pl:* • **1.** a call to prayer
مَأذونِيَّة [maʔðuːniyya] *n:* مَأذونِيّات [maʔðuːniyyaːt] *pl:* • **1.** permission, authorization
مُوَذِّن، مُؤذِّن [muwaððin, muʔaððin] *n:* مُوَذِّنين [muwaððiniːn] *pl:* • **1.** muezzin, man who calls the people to prayer
إذَن [ʔiðan] *adv:* • **1.** therefore, then – إذَن ما راح تِجي؟ [ʔiðan maː raːħ tiji?] Then you're not going to come? إذَن، عَلَى هالحَكي، ما راح تِقدَر تِشتُغُل [ʔiðan, ʕala halħači, maː raːħ tigdar tištuɣul] Therefore, from what's been said, you won't be able to work.

ء ذ ي

آذَى [ʔaːðaː] *v:* • **1.** to hurt – جيراني دَيأذِيني هوايَة [jiːraːni dayʔaðiːni hwaːya] My neighbor is annoying me a lot.
أذَّى [ʔaððaː] *v:* • **1.** to hurt – هِدْني؛ دَتأذِّيني [hiddni; dataʔaððiːni] Let me go; you're hurting me. • **2.** to harm, do harm – إذا ما تِسمَع كَلامَه، يأذِّيك [ʔiða maː tismaʕ kalaːmah, yʔaððiːk] If you don't listen to what he says, he can do you harm. • **3.** to damage, do damage – المُطَر أذَّى الزَّرِع هالسَّنَة [ʔilmuțar ʔaððaː ʔizzariʕ hassana] Rain damaged the crops this year. • **4.** to molest, annoy, irritate, trouble, pester – إذا تظَلّ تأذِّيها، يجُوز تعَوِّرها [ʔiða dðall tʔaððiːha, yjuːz tʕawwirha] If you keep on pestering her, you might injure her.
تأذَّى [tʔaððaː] *v:* • **1.** to get hurt, hurt oneself – تأذَّيت هوايَة مِن هالشَّراكَة [tʔaððiːt hwaːya min haššaraːka] I've hurt myself a lot in this partnership. • **2.** to feel hurt, feel sorry – تأذَّيت هوايَة مِن سِمَعِت خَبَر فَصلَك [tʔaððayt hwaːya min simaʕit xabar fașlak] I was very sorry to hear about your getting fired. • **3.** to be hurt, suffer – تأذَّى هوايَة بِشَبابَه [tʔaððaː hwaːya bšabaːbah] He suffered a lot in his youth. شُغلي تأذَّى هوايَة طُول رَمَضان [šuɣli tʔaððaː hwaːya țuːl ramaḍaːn] My business has suffered a lot all Ramadan.
أذَى [ʔaða] *n:* • **1.** harm, damage, injury • **2.** trouble, grief, misfortune • **3.** annoyance, trouble, irritation
أذِيَّة [ʔaðiyya] *n:* أذِيّات [ʔaðiyyaːt] *pl:* • **1.** trouble, annoyance
مُؤذي [muʔði] *adj:* • **1.** harmful, damaging, injurious, noxious • **2.** hateful, spiteful, mean, offensive • **3.** annoying, irksome, irritating, troublesome
مِتأذِّي [mitʔaðði] *adj:* • **1.** suffering • **2.** In pain

ء ر ب ط ع ش

أرباطَعَش، أربَعطَعَش [ʔarbaːțaʕaš, ʔarbaʕțaʕaš] *n:* • **1.** fourteen

ء ر ت و ز

إرتوازي [ʔirtiwaːzi] *adj:* • **1.** artesian – بير إرتوازي [biːr ʔirtiwaːzi] artesian well.

ء ر خ

أرَّخ [ʔarrax] *v:* • **1.** to date, affix the date to – لا تِنسَى تأرِّخ المَكتُوب قَبُل ما تدِزَّه [laː tinsaː tʔarrix ʔilmaktuːb gabul maː ddizzah] Don't forget to date the letter before you send it.
مُؤرِّخ [muʔarrix] *n:* مُؤرِّخين [muʔarrixiːn] *pl:* • **1.** historian, chronicler
تاريخ [taːriːx] *n:* تَواريخ [tawaːriːx] *pl:* • **1.** date – تاريخ اليوم [taːriːx ʔilyuːm] today's date. إلَى هالتّاريخ [ʔila hattaːriːx] to date, to this date. • **2.** history – تاريخ حَياة [taːriːx ħayaːt] life story, biography.

تاريخي [taːriːxi] *adj:* • **1.** historical – مَوقع تاريخي [mawqiʕ taːriːxi] historical site.

ء ر د ن

الأُردُن [ʔilʔurdun] *n:* • **1.** Jordan – نَهر الأُردُن [nahr ʔilʔurdun] the Jordan River. شَرق الأُردُن [šarq ʔilʔurdun] Trans-Jordan.

أُردُني [ʔurduni] *adj:* • **1.** Jordanian • **2.** a Jordanian

ء ر ز

أرز، أرزَة [ʔarz, ʔarza] *n:* • **1.** cedar, cedar tree

ء ر ض

أرض [ʔarð̣] *n:* أراضي [ʔaraːð̣i] *pl:* • **1.** earth, ground • **2.** land, piece of land

أرضَة [ʔarð̣a] *n:* • **1.** (pl. only) termites

أرضِيَّة [ʔarð̣iyya] *n:* أرَضِيّات [ʔarð̣iyyaːt] *pl:* • **1.** floor • **2.** ground, background (of a fabric, painting) • **3.** charge for use of floor space, storage charge

أرضِي [ʔarð̣i] *adj:* أرضِيَّة [ʔarð̣iyya] *pl:* • **1.** ground – طابِق أرضِي [ṭaːbiq ʔarð̣i] ground floor. • **2.** electrical ground, ground wire

ء ر ق

إرَق [ʔiraq] *v:* • **1.** to have or get insomnia

تأرَّق [tʔarraq] *v:* • **1.** to suffer from insomnia

أرَق [ʔaraq] *n:* • **1.** insomnia

ء ر ك ل

أركِيلَة، نَركِيلَة [ʔargiːla, nargiːla] *n:* أركِيلات، أراكِيل، نَركِيلات، نَراكِيل [ʔargiːlaːt, ʔaraːgiːl, nargiːlaːt, naraːgiːl] *pl:* • **1.** narghile, hookah, water pipe

ء ر ك ن د ش ن

إيركُندِشِن [ʔiyrkundišin] *n:* • **1.** air conditioning

ء ر م ن

أرمَني [ʔarmani] *adj:* أرمَن [ʔarman] *pl:* • **1.** Armenian, • **2.** an Armenian

ء ر ن ب

أرنَب [ʔarnab] *n:* أرانِب [ʔaraːnib] *pl:* • **1.** rabbit

ء ر و ل

أروَل [ʔarwal] *n:* أراوِل [ʔaraːwil] *pl:* • **1.** monitor lizard

ء ر ي ل

أريَل [ʔaryal] *n:* أريَلات [ʔaryalaːt] *pl:* • **1.** aerial, antenna

ء ز ز

أزّاكي [ʔazzaːči] *n:* أزّاكِيَّة [ʔazzaːčiyya] *pl:* • **1.** pharmacist, druggist

أزّخانَة [ʔazzaxaːna] *n:* أزّخانات [ʔazzaxaːnaːt] *pl:* • **1.** pharmacy, drug store

ء ز ل

أزَل [ʔazal] *n:* • **1.** eternity, everlasting

أزَلي [ʔazali] *adj:* • **1.** eternal

ء ز م

أزَّم [ʔazzam] *v:* • **1.** to be or become critical, come to a head (situation, relation)

تأزَّم [tʔazzam] *v:* • **1.** to become critical – الحالَة تأزّمَت بَعَد سُقُوط الوزارَة [ʔilħaːla tʔazzmat baʕad suquːṭ ʔilwizaːra] The situation got critical after the fall of the cabinet.

أزمَة [ʔazma] *n:* أزمات [ʔazmaːt] *pl:* • **1.** crisis

مِتأزِّم [mitʔizzim] *adj:* • **1.** critical (situation)

ء ز ن ف

آزنِيف [ʔazniːf] *n:* • **1.** variant form of the game of dominoes

ء س

آس [ʔaːs] *n:* آسات [ʔaːsaːt] *pl:* • **1.** ace (playing cards)

ء س ب ن

إسبانيا [ʔisbaːnya] *n:* • **1.** Spain

إسباني [ʔisbaːni] *adj:* • **1.** Spanish • **2.** a Spaniard

ء س ت ذ

أُستاذ [ʔustaːð] *n:* أساتِذَة [ʔasaːtiða] *pl:* • **1.** professor • **2.** master – أُستاذ بِالشِّطرَنج [ʔustaːð biššiṭranǰ] a master at chess. أُستاذ بِالمَقام [ʔustaːð bilmaqaːm] a master in singing the Maqam • **3.** sir (a polite form of address to an educated man) – دَفتَر الأُستاذ [daftar ʔalʔustaːð] ledger. • **4.** supervisor, superintendent, boss

ء س ت ر ل

أُستراليا [ʔustraːliya] *n:* • **1.** Australia

أُسترالي [ʔustraːli] *adj:* • **1.** Australian • **2.** an Australian • **3.** draft horse • **4.** (as a contemptuous form of address) dumb ox

ء س ت ف ن ي ك

أستَفَنِيك [ʔastafaniːk] *n:* • **1.** creosote

ء س ت ك ن

إستِكان [ʔistikaːn] *n:* إستِكانات [ʔistikaːnaːt] *pl:* • **1.** a small glass used for drinking tea

ء س د

إستأسَد [ʔistaʔsad] *v:* • **1.** to become strong, rugged, tough – هَالوَلَد الكِبِير إستأسَد بِالمَحَلَّة [halwalad ʔiččibiːr ʔistaʔsad bilimħalla] This big kid has become the

ء

toughest in the neighborhood. • **2.** to achieve power, influence – هَذا اِستَأسَد مِن تزَوَّج بِتّ المُدِير [ha:ða ʔistaʔsad min dzawwaǰ bitt ʔilmudi:r] That guy's sitting pretty since he married the director's daughter.
أسَد [ʔasad] *n:* أُسُود [ʔusu:d] *pl:* • **1.** lion • **2.** (by extension) a brave man

ء س ر

إِسَر [ʔisar] *v:* • **1.** to capture – العَدُو إِسَر مِيَّة مِن جِنُودنا [ʔilʕadu ʔisar miyya min ǰinu:dna] The enemy captured one hundred of our soldiers. • **2.** (by extension) to captivate – إِسرَتَه بِجَمالها [ʔisratah bǰama:lha] She captivated him by her beauty.
أَسَّر [ʔassar] *v:* • **1.** to capture – أَسَّرنا فَصِيل مِن جِنُود العَدُو [ʔassarna faṣi:l min ǰinu:d ʔilʕadu] We captured a platoon of the enemy's soldiers.
تأَسَّر [tʔassar] *v:* • **1.** to be captured – واحِد مِن ضُبّاطنا تأَسَّر [wa:ħid min ðubba:ṭna tʔassar] One of our officers was captured.
أسِر [ʔasir] *n:* • **1.** captivity
أُسرَة [ʔusra] *n:* أُسَر [ʔusar] *pl:* • **1.** clan, dynasty, family
أسِير [ʔasi:r] *adj:* أسرَى [ʔasra:] *pl:* • **1.** captive, prisoner
أُسَّرِي [ʔussari] *adj:* • **1.** family, domestic • **2.** dynastic
أَسِير حَرُب [ʔasi:r ħarub] *adj:* • **1.** prisoner of war

ء س ر ء ل

إِسرائِيل [ʔisra:ʔi:l] *n:* • **1.** Israel
إِسرائِيلِي [ʔisra:ʔi:li] *adj:* • **1.** Israeli • **2.** an Israeli

ء س س

أَسَّس [ʔassas] *v:* • **1.** to lay a foundation – شوَقِت راح تأَسِّس وَتِبنِي؟ [šwakit ra:ħ tʔassis wtibni?] When are you going to lay the foundation and start building? • **2.** to found, establish, set up – أَسَّس جَمعِيَّة لِلأَساتِذَة [ʔassas ǰamʕiyya lilʔasa:tiða] He founded a society for professors.
تأَسَّس [tʔassas] *v:* • **1.** to be founded – النّادِي تأَسَّس السَّنَة اللّي فاتَت [ʔinna:di tʔassas ʔissana ʔilli fa:tat] The club was founded last year.
أُسّ [ʔuss] *n:* • **1.** exponent of a power (math.) – عَشرَة أُسّ خمُسطَعَش [ʕašra ʔuss xmusṭaʕaš] ten to the fifteenth power.
أُسُس [ʔusus] *n:* • **1.** principles
أساس [ʔasa:s] *n:* أساسات [ʔasa:sa:t] *pl:* • **1.** foundation, basis – عَلَى الأَساس [ʕala ʔalʔasa:s] on the basis of. مِن الأَساس [min ʔilʔasa:s] from the beginning, thoroughly. • **2.** foundation (of a building, etc)
تأسِيس [taʔsi:s] *n:* تأسِيسات [taʔsi:sa:t] *pl:* • **1.** facilities, utilities (plumbing and wiring)
مُؤَسَّسَة [muʔassasa] *n:* • **1.** establishment • **2.** foundation, establishment
مُؤَسِّس [muʔassis] *adj:* • **1.** (as n:) founder
أساسِي [ʔasa:si] *adj:* • **1.** basic, fundamental – السَّبَب الأَساسِي [ʔissabab ʔilʔasa:si] the basic reason. حَجَر أَساسِي [ħaǰar ʔasa:si] cornerstone.
تأسِيسِي [tʔasi:si] *adj:* تأسِيسِيّات [tʔasi:siyya:t] *pl:* • **1.** founding, foundational, fundamental • **2.** constituent (as in مَجلِس تأسِيسِي constituent assembly)
اساساً [ʔasa:sa:n] *adverbial:* • **1.** originally, basically, • **2.** mainly

ء س ط

أُسطَة [ʔusṭa] *n:* أُسطَوات [ʔusṭawa:t] *pl:* • **1.** master of a trade, also, form of address for such a man – أُسطَة بِالنِّجارَة [ʔusṭa binniǰa:ra] master carpenter. أُسطَة عُمران [ʔusṭa ʕumra:n] a variety of dates.

ء س ط ب ل

إِسطَبِل [ʔisṭabil] *n:* • **1.** stable • **1.** barn

ء س ط و ل

أُسطُول [ʔusṭu:l] *n:* أَساطِيل [ʔasa:ṭi:l] *pl:* • **1.** fleet

ء س ط و ن

أُسطُوانَة [ʔusṭuwa:na, ʔisṭuwa:na] *n:* أُسطُوانات [ʔusṭuwa:na:t, ʔisṭuwa:na:t] *pl:* • **1.** cylinder • **2.** phonograph record
إِسطِوانِي [ʔisṭiwa:ni] *adj:* • **1.** cylindrical

ء س ف

إِسَف [ʔisaf] *v:* • **1.** to feel sorry, be sad – إِسَفِت هوايَة مِن سِمَعِت بِمَرَضَك [ʔisafit hwa:ya min simaʕit bmaraðak] I was very sorry to hear of your sickness. طِرَدتَه وَبَعدين إِسَفِت عَلَى عَمَلِي [ṭiradtah wbaʕdi:n ʔisafit ʕala ʕamali] I fired him and then regretted my act.
تأَسَّف [tʔassaf] *v:* • **1.** to be sorry
أَسَف [ʔasaf] *n:* • **1.** regret – مَعَ الأَسَف، بِكُلّ أَسَف [maʕa ʔilʔasaf, bkull ʔasaf] unfortunately.
آسِف [ʔa:sif] *adj:* • **1.** sorry, regretful – آنِي آسِف لَكِن ما أَقدَر أَسَوِّي شِي [ʔa:ni ʔa:sif la:kin ma: ʔagdar ʔasawwi: ši] I'm sorry but I can't do anything.
مُؤسِف [muʔsif] *adj:* • **1.** regrettable – هَذا حادِث مُؤسِف [ha:ða ħa:diθ muʔsif] That's a regrettable accident.
متأَسِّف [mitʔassif] *adj:* • **1.** sorry, regretful – مِتأَسِّف، ما عِندِي خُردَة [mitʔassif, ma: ʕindi xurda] Sorry, I don't have any change.

ء س ف ل ت

إِسفَلت [ʔisfalt] *n:* • **1.** asphalt

ء س ف ن ج

إِسفَنجِي [ʔisfanǰi] *adj:* • **1.** spongy, porous

ء س ف ن ي ك

أَسفَنِيك [ʔasfani:k] *n:* • **1.** creosote

ع

ء س ق ف
أسقُف [ʔasqaf] *n:* أساقِفة [ʔasa:qifa] *pl:* • **1.** bishop

ء س ق ي
آسقِي [ʔa:sqi] *n:* آسقِيّات [ʔa:sqiyya:t] *pl:* • **1.** elastic, elastic fabric • **2.** suspenders • **3.** garters • **4.** coatrack, usually a board with hooks, attached to the wall of an entryway. Also occasionally a stand, with a mirror, for the same purpose

ء س ك ل
أسكَلّة [ʔaskalla] *n:* أسكَلّات [ʔaskalla:t] *pl:* • **1.** scaffold, scaffolding • **2.** pier, wharf • **3.** pumpkin – شِجَر أسكَلّة [šiǰar ʔaskala] pumpkin.

ء س ل
أسَل [ʔasal] *n:* • **1.** rush, a variety of marsh grass used in weaving

ء س م
See also: س م ي
إسِم [ʔisim] *n:* أسامِي، أسماء [ʔasa:mi, ʔasma:ʔ] *pl:* • **1.** name – هَذا رِجّال بالإسِم بَسّ [ha:ða riǰǰa:l bilʔisim bass] He's a man in name only. بِسِم الله [bisim ʔallah] in the name of God. قَبُل ما تاكُل، قُول بِسِم الله [gabul ma: ta:kul, gu:l bisim ʔallah] Before you eat, say 'In the name of God. ' إسم الله عَليه. شلُون خُوش وَلَد [ʔism ʔallah ʕali:h. šlu:n xu:š walad] God bless him. What a good boy he is! بَعَدنا بإسِم الله [baʕadna bʔism ʔallah] We have just begun. We are barely under way. الطّبِيخ ما بِيه حَتّى وَلا إسِم مِلِح [ʔiṭṭibi:x ma: bi:h ħatta wala ʔisim miliħ] There isn't even a trace of salt in the rice. • **2.** reputation, standing, prestige – إلَه إسِم كِبِير بالسُّوق [ʔilah ʔisim čibi:r bissu:g] He has a big reputation in the market. • **3.** (gram.) noun
إسمِي [ʔismi] *adj:* • **1.** in name only, nominal – المال الإسمِي لِلشَّرِكَة [ʔilma:l ʔilʔismi liššarika] the nominal capital of the company. • **2.** nominal (gram.)

ء س و
واسَى [wa:sa:] *v:* • **1.** to console, comfort – سمَعِت بَيت سَعِيد اِحتِرَق. خَلّي نرُوح نواسِيه [smaʕit bayt saʕi:d ʔiħtirag. xalli: nru:ħ nwa:si:h] I heard Said's house burned. Let's go comfort him. خَلّي نرُوح نواسِيه عَلَى وَفاة إبنَه [xalli: nru:ħ nwa:si:h ʕala wafa:t ʔibnah] Let's go offer condolences to him on the death of his son.
مَأساة [maʔsa:t] *n:* مَآسِي [maʔa:si] *pl:* • **1.** tragedy
مُواساة [muwa:sa:t] *n:* • **1.** consolation

ء س ي
آسيا [ʔa:sya] *n:* • **1.** Asia
آسيَوِي [ʔa:syawi] *adj:* • **1.** Asian • **2.** Asiatic

ء ش [1]
آش [ʔa:š] *n:* • **1.** a thick type of soup made from several kinds of grains and vegetables

ء ش [2]
آشكِي [ʔa:šči] *n:* آشكِيَّة [ʔa:ščiyya] *pl:* • **1.** cook

ء ش [3]
إش [ʔiš] *interrogative:* • **1.** (interrogative prefix)

ء ش ر
أشَّر [ʔaššar] *v:* • **1.** to check, indicate, mark – أشِّر عالمَوادّ اللّي تِستِلِمها [ʔaššir ʕalmawa:dd ʔilli tistilimha] Check the items you receive. قِيس بهَالمَسطَرَة وَأشِّر بقَلَم بَصمَة [qi:s bhalmasṭara waʔaššir bqalam baṣma] Measure with this ruler and make a mark with a lead pencil. جِبِتلَك مِسوَدَّة المَكتُوب حَتَّى تأشِّرها قَبُل ما نِطبَعَه [ǰibitlak miswaddat ʔilmaktu:b ħatta tʔašširha gabul ma: niṭbaʕah] I brought you the draft of the letter to O. K. before we type it. • **2.** to indicate, point to, point out – أشِّرلِي عَالرِّجّال اللّي شِفتَه دَيخُشّ بالبَيت البارحَة [ʔašširli ʕarriǰǰa:l ʔilli šiftah dayxušš bilbayt ʔilba:rħa] Point out the man you saw entering the house yesterday. أبرَة البَوصلَة دَتأشِّر عَالشِّمال [ʔubrat ʔilbu:ṣla daʔitʔaššir ʕaššima:l] The compass needle is pointing toward the north. • **3.** to signal, gesture – لمّا أئَشِّرلَك، إبدِي تسَجِّل الحَكِي [lamma ʔaʔašširlak, ʔibdi tsaǰǰil ʔilħači] When I signal you, start to record the talk. ما يِقدَر يحكِي بَلا ما يأشِّر [ma: yigdar yiħči bala ma: yiʔaššir] He can't talk without making gestures. • **4.** to note, make note of – أشِّر المُلاحَظات اللّي أقُلَّك إيّاها وَقَدِّملِي بِيها تَقرِير [ʔaššir ʔilmula:ħaða:t ʔilli ʔagullak ʔiyya:ha waqaddimli bi:ha taqri:r] Make a note of the comments I give you and submit a report about them to me.
مُؤَشِّر [muʔaššir] *n:* مُؤَشِّرِين [muʔašširi:n] *pl:* • **1.** pointer, indicator
إشارَة [ʔiša:ra] *n:* إشارات [ʔiša:ra:t] *pl:* • **1.** signal, sign, indication • **2.** gesture, motion, nod, wink, wave • **3.** mark, indicator
تَأشِيرَة [taʔši:ra] *n:* • **1.** visa

ء ش ر ب
إشارب [ʔiša:rb] *n:* إشاربات [ʔiša:rba:t] *pl:* • **1.** kerchief, (woman's) scarf

ء ش و
أشُو [ʔašu] *int:* • **1.** it seems, it looks as if, it appears – الكُتُب وَينها؟ أشُو ماكُو [ʔilkutub wi:nha? ʔašu: ma:ku] Where are the books? Looks like there aren't any. أشُو ما دَتبَيِّن هَالأيّام [ʔašu: ma: dathayyin halʔayya:m] It seems you're not coming around these days. أشُو مِثِل حِسّها [ʔašu: miθil ħissha] It seems just like her voice. • **2.** (interjection, approx.:) well then, okay then, well now – هَذا غَلَط؟ أشُو إنتَ جاوُب [ha:ða ɣalaṭ? ʔašu: ʔinta ǰa:wub] That's wrong? Okay then, you answer it. then, you answer it. أشُو تَعال وَخَلّي أفحَصَه [ʔašu: taʕa:l wxalli ʔafħaṣah] Now come here and

let me examine it. أَشُو أُقعُد هنا حَتَّى أَلَبّسَك قُندَرَة [ʔašuː ʔugʕud hna ħatta ʔalabbsak qundara] Well sit down here so I can put shoes on you.

ء ش و ر

آشُور [ʔaːšuːr] *n:* • **1.** Assyria

آشُورِي [ʔaːšuːri] *adj:* • **1.** Assyrian • **2.** an Assyrian

ء ص ل

تأَصَّل [tʔaṣṣal] *v:* • **1.** to become firmly rooted, deep-rooted, ingrained – العادَة تأَصِّلَت بِيه مِن كان صغَيِّر [ʔilʕaːda tʔaṣṣilat biːh min čaːn ṣɣayyir] The habit became ingrained in him when he was young.

أَصِل [ʔaṣil] *n:* أُصُول [ʔuṣuːl] *pl:* • **1.** origin, source, original form or state – أَصل الحكايَة [ʔaṣl ʔilħčaːya] the story in its original form. هَالسَّيّارَة بالأَصِل كانَت مالتِي [hassayyaːra bilʔaṣil čaːnat maːlti] This car was originally mine. البايسِكِل كان مَكسُور مِن الأَصِل. مُو آنِي كِسَرتَه [ʔilpaːysikil čaːn maksuːr min ʔilʔaṣil. muː ʔaːni kisartah] The bicycle was broken from the begining. I wasn't the one who broke it. • **2.** foundation, basis • **3.** one who counts, important one – لا تغار منهُم. إنتَ الأَصِل [laː tɣaːr minhum. ʔinta ʔilʔaṣil] Don't be jealous of them. You're the important one. • **4.** lineage, stock, descent, pedigree • **5.** (pl. only) customs, traditions, proprieties – حَسَب الأُصُول [ħasab ʔilʔuṣuːl] properly, according to the rules. • **6.** pl. أصال plant, seedling, set

أَصالَة [ʔaṣaːla] *n:* • **1.** originality

أَصلي [ʔaṣli] *adj:* • **1.** original – النُّسخَة الأَصليَّة [ʔannusxa ʔilʔaṣliyya] the original copy. التّايَرات الأَصليَّة مال سَيّارَة [ʔattaːyaraːt ʔilʔaṣliyya maːl sayyaːra] the original tires on a car. • **2.** genuine, authentic – غَراض أَصليَّة [ɣaraːð̣ ʔaṣliyya] genuine parts. • **3.** real – كَذّاب أَصلِي [čaððaːb ʔaṣli] a real liar. أَكِل عِراقِي أَصلِي [ʔakil ʕiraːqi ʔaṣli] real Iraqi food. • **4.** primary, initial – واحِد أَصلِي [waːħid ʔaṣli] low low, the lowest gear on a 4-speed truck transmission, and, by extension, 1st gear on a 4-speed auto transmission.

أَصِيل [ʔaṣiːl] *adj:* • **1.** of pure or noble origin – حصانٍ أَصِيل [ħṣaːn ʔaṣiːl] a purebred horse.

أُصُولِي [ʔuṣuːli] *adj:* • **1.** in accordance with traditions, rules, established practice – لا تِقلَق أَبَداً. عَمَلَك أُصُولِي كُلِّش [laː tiqlaq ʔabadan. ʕamalak ʔuṣuːli kulliš] Don't worry at all. Your action is quite proper.

مِتأَصِّل [mitʔaṣṣil] *adj:* • **1.** deep-rooted, deep-seated – العادَة مِتأَصّلَة بِيه [ʔilʕaːda mitʔaṣṣla biːh] The habit is deep rooted in him.

أَصلاً [ʔaṣlan] *adverbial:* • **1.** actually, as a matter of fact – أَصلاً ما كِنِت بِبَغداد البارحَة [ʔaṣlan maː činit bibaɣdaːd ʔilbaːrħa] Actually I wasn't in Baghdad yesterday. ما راح أَدفَع شِي. أَصلاً كُلّ التّلامِيذ قالوا نَفس الشِّي [maː raːħ ʔadfaʕ ši. ʔaṣlan kull ʔittalaːmiːð gaːlaw nafs ʔišši] I'm not going to pay anything. Actually, all the students said the same thing.

ء ط ر

إطار [ʔiṭaːr] *n:* إطارات [ʔiṭaːraːt] *pl:* • **1.** (picture) frame

ء ط ر ق

أَطرَقچِي [ʔaṭraqči] *n:* أَطرَقچِيَّة [ʔaṭraqčiyya.] *pl:* • **1.** rug merchant

ء ط ل س

أَطلَس [ʔaṭlas] *n:* أَطالِس [ʔaṭaːlis] *pl:* • **1.** collection of maps

أَطلَسِي [ʔaṭlasi] *adj:* • **1.** the Atlantic Ocean – المُحِيط الأَطلَسِي [ʔilmuħiːṭ ʔilʔaṭlasi] the Atlantic Ocean.

ء ط ل ن ط

أَطلَنطِي [ʔaṭlanṭi] *adj:* • **1.** the Atlantic Ocean – المُحِيط الأَطلَنطِي [ʔilmuħiːṭ ʔilʔaṭlanṭi] the Atlantic Ocean.

ء غ

أَغشَمكِي [ʔaɣšamči] *n:* أَغشَمكِيَّة [ʔaɣšamčiyya] *pl:* • **1.** night watchman (who guards until midnight)

ء غ ر ق

الإغرِيق [ʔalʔiɣriːq] *n:* • **1.** the Greeks – زَمَن الإغرِيق [zaman ʔiliɣriːq] the time of the Greeks, the Greek period.

إغرِيقِي [ʔiɣriːqi] *adj:* • **1.** Greek, Grecian – تِمثال إغرِيقِي [timθaːl ʔiɣriːqi] a Greek statue. فَلسَفَة إغرِيقِيَّة [falsafa ʔiɣriːqiyya] Greek philosophy.

ء غ و

آغا [ʔaɣa] *adj:* أَغوات [ʔaɣawaːt] *pl:* • **1.** rich landowner • **2.** lord, master (as form of address) • **3.** better, superior – هُوَّ أَغاتَك بِالشِّطرَنج [huwwa ʔaɣaːtak biššiṭranǰ] He's your superior at chess. لا تِحكِي عَلَيّا هِيكِي. آنِي أَغاتَك [laː tiħči ʕalayya hiːči. ʔaːni ʔaɣaːtak] Don't talk about me like that. I'm a better man than you.

ء ف ر ق

أَفرِيقيا [ʔafriːqya] *n:* • **1.** Africa

أَفرِيقِي [ʔafriːqi] *adj:* • **1.** African • **2.** an African

ء ف غ ن

أَفغانِي [ʔafɣaːni] *adj:* • **1.** Afghanistani, Afghan • **2.** an Afghanistani, an Afghan

الأَفغان [ʔilʔafɣaːn] *adj:* • **1.** the Afghans (coll.) • **2.** Afghanistan

ء ف غ ن س ت ن

أَفغانِستان [ʔafɣanistaːn] *n:* • **1.** Afghanistan

ء ف ف

تأفّف [tʔaffaf] *v:* • **1.** to moan, groan, complain – كُلّما أنطِيه شوَيَّة شُغُل، يِتأفّف [kullma ʔanṭiːh šwayya šuɣul, yitʔaffaf] Whenever I give him a little work, he moans and groans.

أفّ، أوفّ [ʔuff, ʔuːff] *int:* • **1.** (an exclamation of dismay or pain, approx.:) oh – أفّ، يا ربِّي! شلُون ويّا هالوَلَد؟ [ʔuff, yaː rabni! šluːn wiyya halwalad?] Oh, my God! What are we going to do with this boy? أوفّ، أوفّ، راسي دَيمَوِّتني [ʔuːff, ʔuːff, raːsi daymawwitni] Oh, oh, my head is killing me! أوفّ مِنّك! راح أهِجّ [ʔuːff minnak! raːħ ʔahijj] You're a pain in the neck! I'm leaving.

ء ف ق

أُفُق [ʔufuq] *n:* • **1.** horizon – أفقه واسِع [ʔufqah waːsiʕ] His horizon is wide, i.e.; He has imagination.

أُفُقِي [ʔufuqi] *adj:* • **1.** horizontal

ء ف ن د ي

أفَنْدي [ʔafandi] *n:* أفَنديَّة [ʔafandiyya] *pl:* • **1.** gentleman, a non-Westerner wearing Western clothes • **2.** a jocular or ironic form of address – أفَندِي، ما تِشتُغُل عاد [ʔafandi, maː tištuɣul ʕaːd] Get to work, Mac!

ء ف ي ن

أفْيُون [ʔafyuːn] *n:* • **1.** opium

ء ق ر

أقَر، أقَر... أقَر [ʔagar, ʔagar... ʔagar] *n:* • **1.** whether... or, either... or, – أقَر مِنّه أقَر مِنّك، آني أرِيد فلُوسِي [ʔagar minnah ʔagar minnak, ʔaːni ʔariːd fluːsi] Whether it's from him or from you, I want my money.

ء ق ل م

إقْلِيم [ʔiqliːm] *n:* أقالِيم [ʔaqaːliːm] *pl:* • **1.** territory, region • **2.** province, district, administrative subdivision

ء ك د

أكّد، وَكّد [ʔakkad, wakkad] *v:* • **1.** to confirm, make sure about, check on – أكّد عَليه يكتِب المَكتُوب [ʔakkid ʕaliːh yiktib ʔilmaktuːb] Make sure that he writes the letter. • **2.** to confirm – عَلِي أكّدلي الخَبَر [ʕali ʔakkadli ʔilxabar] Ali confirmed the story for me. • **3.** to give assurance – أكّدلي إنّو ما يعُرفَه [ʔakkadli ʔinnu maː yʕurfah] He assured me that he doesn't know him.

تأكّد، إتوَكّد [tʔakkad, ʔitwakkad] *v:* • **1.** to be assured – إتأكّد، آني مالِي عِلاقَة بِالمَوضُوع [ʔitʔakkad, ʔaːni maːli ʕilaːqa bilmawðuːʕ] Rest assured, I have no connection with the matter. • **2.** to be confirmed – هَسّة الخَبَر تأكّد [hassa ʔilxabar tʔakkad] The news has been confirmed now. • **3.** to be or become sure, certain, convinced, to reassure oneself, convince oneself – إتأكّد قَبُل ما تِحكِي [ʔitʔakkad gabul maː tiħči] Be sure of yourself before you speak out.

تأكِيد [taʔkiːd] *n:* تأكِيدات [taʔkiːdaːt] *pl:* • **1.** assurance, confirmation – كُلّ هَالتّأكِيدات وَما تصَدِّق؟ [kull hattaʔkiːdaːt wma tṣaddig?] All these assurances and you don't believe it? • **2.** follow-up, check (on a previous letter) – راح أجِي ساعَة خَمسَة بِالتّأكِيد [raːħ ʔaji saːʕa xamsa bittaʔkiːd] I'll come at five o'clock without fail. بِكُلّ تأكِيد! مَحَّد يِستِحِقّ تَرفِيع أكثَر مِنّه [bkull tʔakiːd! maħħad yistiħiqq tarfiːʕ ʔakθar minnah] Certainly! No one deserves promotion more than he does.

أكِيد [ʔakiːd] *adj:* • **1.** certainly, surely – أكِيد؛ هَذا ما يِنرادلَه حَكِي [ʔakiːd; haːða maː yinraːdlah ħači] Certainly; this needs no discussion. هَذا أكِيد راح يُغلُب [haːða ʔakiːd raːħ yuɣlub] That one's certainly going to win.

مُؤَكَّد [muʔakkad] *adj:* • **1.** certain, sure, confirmed – هَذا شِي مُؤَكَّد [haːða ši muʔakkad] That's a sure thing.

مِتأكِّد [mitʔakkid] *adj:* • **1.** positive, certain, sure – إنتَ مِتأكِّد هُوَّ اللّي ضِرَبَك جِيب؟ [ʔinta mitʔakkid huwwa ʔilli ðirabak jiːb?] Are you sure he's the one who picked your pocket?

ء ك د م

أكادِيمِيَّة [ʔakadimiyya] *n:* • **1.** academy

أكادِيمِي [ʔakadiːmi] *adj:* • **1.** academic

ء ك د ن ي

إجِّدِنيَة [ʔiggidinya] *n:* • **1.** loquat

ء ك س ب ر س

إكسِبرَس [ʔiksibras] *adj:* • **1.** express

ء ك س س و ر

إكسِسوار [ʔiksiswaːr] *n:* إكسِسوارات [ʔiksiswaːraːt] *pl:* • **1.** accessory

ء ك ل

أكَل [ʔakal] *v:* • **1.** to eat – ما أكَلت شِي طُول النّهار [maː ʔakalt ši ṭuːl ʔinnahaːr] I haven't eaten a thing all day long. مَأكُول العافيَة [maʔkuːl ʔalʕaːfya] May it be eaten in health. ساعتَك تاكُل شعِير [saːʕtak taːkul šʕiːr] Your watch is running slow (lit. eating barley). • **2.** to eat up, consume, take – القاط ياكُل ثلَث ياردات [ʔilqaːṭ yaːkul tlaθ yaːrdaːt] The suit will take three yards. لازِم تِدفَع الدَّين لأنّ الفايز راح ياكُل البَيت [laːzim tidfaʕ ʔiddayn liʔann ʔalfaːyiz raːħ yaːkul ʔilbayt] You should pay the debt because the interest will take the house. بِجَهَنَّم؛ عَسَى نارهُم تاكُل حَطَبهُم [bijahannam; ʕasaː naːrhum taːkul ħaṭabhum] To hell (with them); let them kill each other off (let their fire consume their firewood). • **3.** to gnaw, eat away, corrode, erode – الزِّنجار ماكِل البُورِي [ʔizzinjaːr maːkil ʔilbuːri] Rust

ء

has eaten away the pipe. الماي ماكِل الجُرُف هو مِن هنا [ʔilmaːy maːkil ʔijjuruf hwaːya min hna] The water has eaten away the bank extensively here. حكايتَك دَتاكُل بقَلبي [ħčaːytak dataːkul bigalbi] Your remark is gnawing at my heart. لازِم أنطِيه فلُوسَه؛ هَذا أكَل راسي [laːzim ʔanṭiːh fluːsah; haːða ʔakal raːsi] I've got to give him his money; he's insistent as hell (lit.: ate my head.) • **4.** to take, get (something unpleasant) – أكَل الإهانَة وَسِكَت [ʔakal ʔilʔihaːna wsikat] He took the insult and kept quiet. أخُويَا إلحَقلِي، تَرَة أكَلتها [ʔaxuːya ʔilħagli, tara ʔakaltha] Help me out, friend, or I've had it. راح تاكُلها غير أكلَة [raːħ taːkulha ɣiːr ʔakla] You're going to get a real comeuppance. • **5.** to capture, take – الجُندِي مالِي راح ياكُل الحِصان مالَك [ʔijjundi maːli raːħ yaːkul ʔilħiṣaːn maːlak] My pawn will capture your knight. مُو عِيب تاكُل حَرام؟ [muː ʕiːb taːkul ħaraːm?] Don't you think it's wrong to be so dishonest? أكَل حَقِّي. ما نطانِي كُلّ اللِّي أطلبَه إياه [ʔakal ħaqqi. maː nṭaːni kull ʔilli ʔaṭulbah ʔiyaːh] He cheated me out of what was mine. He didn't give me all that he owes me.

أكّل، وَكّل [ʔakkal, wakkal] *v:* • **1.** to feed – لا تِنسِين تأكّلين الجّاهِل [laː tinsiːn tʔakkliːn ʔijjaːhil] Don't forget to feed the baby.

تآكَّل [tʔakkal] *v:* • **1.** to be corroded, eaten away – الجّامُولُغ تآكّل مِن الزِّنجار [ʔaččaːmulluɣ tʔakkal min ʔizzinjaːr] The fender was eaten away by rust.

انِاكَل [ʔinʔikal] *v:* • **1.** pass. of أكَل to eat – The food's all been eaten • **2.** pass. of أكَل to eat, eat up, consume – الأكِل كُلّه انِاكَل [ʔilʔakil kullah ʔinʔikal] The food's all been eaten.

أكِل [ʔakil] *n:* • **1.** eating, dining – غُرفَة أكِل [ɣurfat ʔakil] dining room. خاشُوقَة أكِل [xaːšuːgat ʔakil] tablespoon. • **2.** food

أكلَة [ʔakla] *n:* أكلات [ʔaklaːt] *pl:* • **1.** meal, repast • **2.** dish, bit of food

مَأكُولات [maʔkuːlaːt] *n:* • **1.** (pl. only) foodstuffs, food

مَأكُولات مُعَلَّبَة [maʔkuːlaːt muʕallaba] *n:* • **1.** canned foods

آكِل [ʔaːkil] *adj:* • **1.** cannibal

أكّال [ʔakkaːl] *adj:* أكّالِين [ʔakkaːliːn] *pl:* • **1.** big eater, glutton

أكُول [ʔakuːl] *adj:* أكُولِين [ʔakuːliːn] *pl:* • **1.** hearty eater, gourmand

ماكِل [maːkil] *adj:* • **1.** eating

ء ك ل ي

إكِلّي [ʔikilli] *n:* • **1.** deuce (in native Iraqi card games).

ء ك و

أكُو [ʔaku] *v:* • **1.** there is, there are – أكُو خَمسِين دِينار بِجيبِي [ʔaku xamsiːn dinaːr bjiːbi] There's fifty dinars in my pocket. أكُو أحَّد بِالبَيت؟ [ʔaku ʔaħħad bilbayt?] Is there anyone at home? أكُو عِندَه [ʔaku ʕindah] he has. أكُو عِندَك قَلَم؟ [ʔaku ʕindak qalam?] Do you have a pencil?

ماكُو [maːku] *v:* • **1.** there isn't, there is no, there is nothing – اِستَعجِل، ماكُو وَقت [ʔistaʕjil, maːku wakit] Hurry, there's no time. ماكُو غير باكِر أرُوح عالشُّرطَة [maːku ɣiːr baːčir ʔaruːħ ʕaššurṭa] There's nothing else to do but to go to the police tomorrow. دَيقَتّلُون بِهَالنّاس وَماكُو [daykattiluːn bihannaːs wmaːku] They're slaughtering those people and there's no end to it.

شَكُو [šaku] *interrogative:* • **1.** what is there? what? – شَكُو بِ- شَكُو عِندَه؟ [šaku bi? šaku ʕindah?] what about? what is there about? what is wrong with? الطَّبِيب راد يُعرُف شَكُو بِيه [ʔiṭṭabiːb raːd yuʕruf šaku biːh] The doctor wanted to know what was ailing him. شَكُو عِندَك مِستَعجِل؟ [šaku ʕindak mistaʕjil?] Why are you hurrying? شَكُو ماكُو؟ [šaku maːku?] What's been going on lately? How have you been?

ء ل ب

إلبَة [ʔilba] *n:* • **1.** milk from a fresh cow or goat, boiled to a thick consistency

ء ل ب م

ألبُوم [ʔalbuːm] *n:* • **1.** album

ء ل ج غ

ألجَغ [ʔalčaɣ] *adj:* ألاجِغ [ʔalaːčiɣ] *pl:* • **1.** rotten, low-down, no-good

ء ل ف 1

ألِف [ʔalf] *n:* آلاف، ألُوف [ʔaːlaːf, ʔuluːf] *pl:* • **1.** thousand

ء ل ف 2

ألِف [ʔalif] *n:* • **1.** name of the first letter in the alphabet

ء ل ف 3

إلَف [ʔilaf] *v:* • **1.** to be or become tame – بَعَد خَمس سنِين، الأسَد إلَف [baʕad xams sniːn, ʔilʔasad ʔilaf] After five years, the lion grew tame. • **2.** to be or become accustomed to, habituated to, used to – مِن أوَّل نَهار، إلِفت حَياة الجِّبال [min ʔawwal nahaːr, ʔilafit ħayaːt ʔijjibaːl] From the first day, I got used to the life in the mountains. يوم، يومَين، وَيألَف عَلَيكُم [yuːm, yuːmayn, wyiʔlaf ʕaliːkum] A day or so and he'll get used to you.

ألَّف [ʔallaf] *v:* • **1.** to form, make up, put together – خَلّي نألّف لَجنَة تِدرُس المُشكِلَة [xalli nʔallif lajna tidrus ʔilmuškila] Let's form a committee to study the problem. • **2.** to compose, compile, write – ألَّفِت كتاب عَن العِراق [ʔallafit ktaːb ʕan ʔilʕiraːq] I wrote a book about Iraq.

تألَّف [tʔallaf] *v:* • **1.** to be formed, made up, compiled, to consist – اللُّجنَة مِتألّفَة مِن المُدِير وَمُعاونَه [ʔillujna mitʔallfa min ʔilmudiːr wamuʕaːwnah] The committee consists of the director and his assistant.

إئتِلَف [ʔiʔtilaf] *v:* • **1.** to harmonize, agree, go well, get along well – ما راح أسافِر لِأنّ ما أئتِلِف وِيّاهُم [maː raːħ ʔasaːfir liʔann maː ʔaʔtilif wiyyaːhum] I'm not going to go because I don't get along with them.
ألف [ʔulf] *n:* • **1.** intimacy
ألفَة [ʔulfa] *n:* • **1.** close association, intimate relationship
مُؤَلِّف [muʔallif] *n:* مُؤَلِّفِين [muʔallifiːn] *pl:* • **1.** author, writer
تَألِيف [taʔliːf] *n:* • **1.** composition
مُؤَلَّفَة [muʔallafa] *n:* مُؤَلَّفات [muʔallafaːt] *pl:* • **1.** literature
إئتِلاف [ʔiʔtilaːf] *n:* • **1.** harmony, concord, agreement • **2.** pl. political coalition
ألِيف [ʔaliːf] *adj:* • **1.** tame – أسَد ألِيف [ʔasad ʔaliːf] a tame lion. • **2.** domestic, domesticated – حَيوانات ألِيفَة [ħaywaːnaːt ʔaliːfa] domestic animals. • **3.** friendly – جاهِل ألِيف [jaːhil ʔaliːf] a friendly baby.
مألُوف [maʔluːf] *adj:* • **1.** familiar, accustomed, habituated • **2.** usual, customary, familiar (thing or action) – وُجُود الجِنُود والدَّبّابات بالشَّوارِع صار شِي مألُوف [wujuːd ʔijjinuːd widdabbaːbaːt biššawaːriʕ ṣaːr ši maʔluːf] The presence of soldiers and tanks in the streets has become a usual thing.
إئتِلافِي [ʔiʔtilaːfi] *adj:* • **1.** coalition – وِزارَة إئتِلافِيَّة [wizaːra ʔiʔtilaːfiyya] coalition government.

ء ل ق

تألَّق [tʔallaq] *v:* • **1.** to glow, glisten, shine • **2.** to be on top
تألُّق [taʔalluq] *n:* • **1.** glisten, shine, glow

ء ل ك ت ر ن

إلِكتِرُون [ʔilkitruːn] *n:* إلِكتِرُونِيّات [ʔilkitruniyyaːt] *pl:* • **1.** electron
ألِكتِرُونِي [ʔalkitruːni] *adj:* • **1.** electronic

ء ل ل

إلّا [ʔilla] *preposition:* • **1.** except – دَزَّيتهُم كُلّهُم إلّا آني [dazziːthum kullhum ʔilla ʔaːni] You sent them all except me. ما أشُوفَه إلّا مَرَّة بالإسبُوع [maː ʔašuːfah ʔilla marra bilʔisbuːʕ] I don't see him except once a week. • **2.** just, only – إلّا أرِيد البايسِكِل مالِي. بِيش ألعَب؟ [ʔilla ʔariːd ʔilpaːaysikil maːli. biːš ʔalʕab?] I just want my bicycle. What'll I play with? ما أقبَل. إلّا أرِيد قَلَمِي نَفسَه [maː ʔaqbal. ʔilla ʔariːd qalami nafsah] I don't want (this). I only want my own pen. إلّا أشتِري هَالنّوع. ما أشتِري غَيرَه [ʔilla ʔaštiri hannawʕ. maː ʔaštiri ɣayrah] I'll only buy this type. I won't buy other than it. لا. إلّا ألف دِينار [laː. ʔilla ʔalf diːnaːr] No. It's nothing but a thousand dinars. يَعنِي إلّا هَالقاط لَو ما يصِير؟ [yaʕni ʔilla halqaːṭ law maː yṣiːr?] In other words either this suit or nothing doing? • **3.** (denoting inevitability or necessity, approx.:) must – وَالله ما يصِير. إلّا تِجِي [wallah maː yṣiːr. ʔilla tiji] No, that can't be. You've got to come. شِفتَه بِالجّادَّة وَما حاكانِي. هَذا إلّا زَعلان [šiftah bijjaːdda wma ħaːčaːni. haːða ʔilla zaʕlaːn] I saw him on the way and he didn't speak to me. He must be mad. يَعنِي إلّا توَسِّخ القُبَّة مِن تِلعَب؟ [yaʕni ʔilla twassix ʔalgubba min tilʕab?] Do you have to dirty the room when you play? خَلِّي أشُوفَه، إلّا أمَوّتَه مِن البَسِط [xalliː ʔašuːfah, ʔilla ʔamawwtah min ʔalbasiṭ] Let me see him, and I'll beat him to death! بَسّ أشُوفَه إلّا أبُسطَه [bass ʔašuːfah ʔilla ʔabusṭah] As soon as I see him I'll sure beat him up good.
وَإلّا [waʔilla] *conjunction:* • **1.** or, or else, otherwise – تُسكُت وَإلّا أجِي أمَوّتَك [tuskut waʔilla ʔaji ʔamawwtak] You be quiet or I'll come kill you. ترِيد هَذا وَإلّا ذاك؟ [triːd haːða waʔilla ðaːk?] Do you want this one or that? ما عِندِي فلُوس، وَإلّا كان جِيت وِيّاكُم [maː ʕindi fluːs, waʔilla čaːn jiːt wiyyaːkum] I have got no money, or else I would have come with you. ما إستَعمَل الدُّوا مالَه، وَإلّا كان طاب [maː ʔistaʕmal ʔidduwaː maːlah, waʔilla čaːn ṭaːb] He didn't take his medicine, or otherwise he would have gotten well. غير أخُوه المُدِير؟ وَإلّا هَذا شيرَفّعَه؟ [ɣiːr ʔaxuːh ʔilmudiːr? waʔilla haːða šyraffʕah?] Isn't it that his brother is the director? How else would he get promoted?
إلّا إذا [ʔilla ʔiða] *conjunction:* • **1.** unless – راح أشتِكِي عَلِيه إلّا إذا إنطانِي الفلُوس اليُوم [raːħ ʔaštiki ʕaliːh ʔilla ʔiða ʔinṭaːni ʔilfluːs ʔilyuːm] I'm going to sue him unless he gives me the money today.

ء ل ي

اللِّي [ʔilli] *pronoun:* • **1.** who, which, that – مِنُو اللِّي قَلَّك؟ [minu ʔilli gallak?] Who's the one who told you? أُخُذ القَلَم اللِّي ترِيدَه [ʔuxuð ʔilqalam ʔilli triːdah] Take the pencil that you want. • **2.** whoever, whichever, whatever – اللِّي يوافُق، يِرفَع إيدَه [ʔilli ywaːfuq, yirfaʕ ʔiːdah] Whoever agrees, raise his hand.

ء ل م

ألَّم [ʔallam] *v:* • **1.** to cause pain to (someone), to pain, hurt, grieve – مَنظَر المَجرُوحِين ألَّمنِي كُلِّش [manðar ʔilmajruːħiːn ʔallamni kulliš] The sight of the wounded caused me great pain. حكايتَه ألَّمَتنِي هوايَة [ħčaːytah ʔallimatni hwaːya] His remark hurt me a lot. الجَّرِح دَيألِّمنِي [ʔijjariħ dayʔallimni] The wound is hurting me.
تألَّم [tʔallam] *v:* • **1.** to suffer pain – تألَّمِت مِن سِمَعتَه يِحكِي هِيكِي عَن اللاّجِئِين [tʔallamit min simaʕtah yiħči hiːči ʕan ʔallaːjiʔiːn] I was grieved to hear him talk like that about the refugees. تألَّمِت كُلِّش مِن سِمَعِت بخَبَر وَفاتَه [tʔallamit kulliš min simaʕit bxabar wafaːtah] I was deeply pained when I heard the news of his death.
ألَم [ʔalam] *n:* آلام [ʔaːlaːm] *pl:* • **1.** pain, suffering, agony

ع

أَلِيم [ʔali:m] *adj:* • **1.** painful, grievous, sad
مُؤلِم [muʔlim] *adj:* • **1.** painful, aching, sore • **2.** painful
مِتأَلِّم [mitʔallim] *adj:* • **1.** hurt, in pain

ع ل م س [1]

أَلماسَة [ʔalma:za] *n:* أَلماسات [ʔalma:za:t] *pl:* • **1.** diamond
أَلماس [ʔalma:z] *adj:* • **1.** (coll.) diamond(s)

ع ل م س [2]

أَلماسَة [ʔalma:za] *n:* • **1.** the root of a variety of the taro plant, resembling ginger root in appearance

ع ل م ن

أَلمان [ʔalma:n] *n:* • **1.** the German people, the Germans
أَلمانيا [ʔalma:nya] *proper noun:* • **1.** Germany
أَلماني [ʔalma:ni] *adj:* أَلمان [ʔalma:n] *pl:* • **1.** German • **2.** pl. أَلمانِيِّين [ʔalma:niyyi:n] a German

ع ل م ن ي و م

أَلَمنيَوم [ʔalaminyu:m] *n:* • **1.** aluminum

ع ل ه

الله [ʔallah] *n:* • **1.** بَيت الله [bayt ʔallah] the Kaaba • **2.** (by extension) Mecca – يا الله! شلُون وِيّاك؟ [ya: ʔallah! šlu:n wiyya:k?] My God! what am I going to do with you? لا تدِير بال. خَلِّيهَا يَمّ الله [la: ddi:r ba:l. xalli:ha yamm ʔallah] Don't worry. Leave it in God's hands. الله عَلِيك لا تقُلَّه [ʔallah ʕali:k la: tgullah] By God, don't you tell him. الله شاهِد، ما قِبَل ياخُذ فلُوس [ʔallah ša:hid, ma: qibal ya:xuð flu:s] As God is my witness, he wouldn't take any money. شلَونَك؟ شلُون صِحّتَك؟ [šlawnak? šlu:n ṣiħħtak?])
إِلاه [ʔila:h] *n:* آلِهَة [ʔa:liha] *pl:* • **1.** god, deity – يا إِلاهِي [ya: ʔila:hi] My God! إِله الحَرب [ʔila:h ʔilħarb] the god of war.
الله [ʔallah, ʔalla:h] *n:* • **1.** God, Allah – الله ينطِيك العافيَة [ʔallah yinṭi:k ʔalʕa:fya] God give you strength. (said to someone carrying a heavy load, or engaged in strenuous or difficult work.) أَعُوذ بِالله [ʔaʕu:ð billa:h] God forbid (lit. I take shelter with God). قَسَماً بِالله، ما أعرُف [qasaman billa:h, ma: ʔaʕruf] I swear by God I don't know. لِلّه دَرّه، شلُون شاعِر [lillahi darrah, šlu:n ša:ʕir] My God what a poet! (lit. his achievement is due to God). الحَمدُ لِله [ʔilħamdu lilla:h] thank God, praise God. الحمدُ لله، صِحّتِي زينَة [ʔilħamdu liʔallah, ṣiħħti zi:na] I'm in good health, thank you. سُبحان الله [subħa:n ʔallah] (lit., praise the Lord, an expression of surprise) my God, my goodness. سُبحان الله، العام كان مِفلِس وهَسَّة زَنكِين [subħa:n ʔallah, ʔilʕa:m ča:n miflis whassa zangi:n] My God, last year he was broke, and now he's rich. سُبحان الله عَلَى هَالجَمال [subħa:n ʔallah ʕala hajjama:l] My goodness what beauty! سُبحان الله عَلَى هَالكِذب [subħa:n ʔallah ʕala haččiðb] My God what a lie! سُبحان الله، اللّي ما عِندَه واسطَة، ما يِمشِي شُغلَه [subħa:n ʔallah, ʔilli ma: ʕindah wa:sṭa, ma: yimši šuɣlah] My God, anyone without pull won't get anywhere.
حَيّالله [ħayyallah] *n:* • **1.** (from حَيَّ الله) God present, grant anything at all, anyone at all
إلاهَة [ʔila:ha] *n:* إلاهات [ʔila:ha:t] *pl:* • **1.** goddess
إلاهِي [ʔila:hi] *adj:* • **1.** divine, of God – غَضَب إلاهِي [ɣaðab ʔila:hi] divine wrath.
بالله [ballah, billa:h] *int:* • **1.** please – بالله ما تجُوز مِنّي؟ آني تَعبان [ballah ma: dju:z minni? ʔa:ni taʕba:n] Won't you please leave me alone? I'm tired. بالله ما تناوُشني المِلِح؟ [ballah ma: tna:wušni ʔilmiliħ?] Would you please pass me the salt? • **2.** (an expression of surprise) really? my gosh! – بالله؟ وَشلُون لَعَد ما يقُلّي؟ [ballah? wšlu:n laʕad ma: ygulli?] Really? Then how come he didn't tell me? بالله عَلِيك [ballah ʕali:k] my gosh, my word. بالله عَلِيك! شِفتَه شسَوَّى بِيّا بَعَد تَعَبِي وِيّاه؟ [ballah ʕali:k! šiftah ššawwa: biyya baʕad taʕabi wiyya:h?] My gosh! Did you see what he did to me after all I did for him? بالله عَلِيك! شقَلَّك؟ [ballah ʕali:k! šgallak?] Oh come on! What did he tell you?
يَالله [yallah] *int:* • **1.** (exclamation) Oh God! – يَالله، يَالله! حَصَّلِت وَظِيفَة زِينَة وَأَهلِي يرِيدُونِي أَترُكها [yallah, yallah! ħaṣṣalit waðiːfa zi:na wʔahli yiri:du:ni ʔatrukha] Oh my God! I got a good job and my family wants me to leave it. • **2.** come on, go on, hurry up – يَالله، عَلِي، خَلّي نرُوح [yallah, ʕali, xalli:nru:ħ] Come on, Ali, let's go! دِيالله، خَلّي ناكُل [diyallah, xalli: na:kul] Oh let's eat. دِيالله، هَذا مُو كَتّال [diyallah, ha:ða mu: katta:l] Oh come now, he's not a killer! • **3.** then – نرِيدها تكَمِّل الكُلِّيَّة يَالله تِتزَوَّج [nri:dha tkammil ʔilkulliyya yallah tidzawwaj] We want her to finish college then get married. مِن عِرَف آني أخُوك يَالله حِكَى وِيّايا [min ʕiraf ʔa:ni ʔaxu:k yallah ħiča: wiyya:ya] When he learned I'm your brother, then he talked to me. إنطِيتَه دِينار يَالله قِبَل [ʔinṭi:tah dina:r yallah gibal] I gave him a dinar, then he accepted. • **4.** just, just barely, – الفلُوس اللّي عِندِي يَالله تكَفِّي [ʔilflu:s ʔilli ʕindi yallah tkaffi] The money I've got will just do. بَعَدنِي يَالله بدَيت. لا تِستَعجِل [baʕadni yallah bidi:t. la: tistaʕjil] I just started. Don't be in a hurry.
وَالله [wallah, wʔallah] *int:* • **1.** definitely, really – وَالله ما أَقبَل أَقَلّ مِن مِيَّة دِينار [wallah ma: ʔaqbal ʔaqall min miyyat dina:r] I really won't accept less than one hundred dinars. • **2.** (as a mere expletive) well, uh, umm – وَالله، أَبُويَا بَعدَه مَرِيض [wallah, ʔabu:ya baʕdah mari:ð] My father's still sick. • **3.** (an expression of surprise) really? my gosh! – وَالله؟ صُدُق اِنقِبَل بِالجّامعَة؟ [wallah? ṣudug ʔinqibal bijja:miʕa?] Really? Did he actually get accepted in the university?

وَالله [walla:hi] *int:* • **1.** by God) =
اللّهُمَّ [ʔalla:humma] *int:* • **1.** Oh God – اللّهُمَّ أُخذ رُوحَه [ʔallahumma ʔuxuð ru:ħah] Oh God kill him! اللّهُمَّ إلّا إذا [ʔallahumma ʔilla ʔiða] that is, unless. راح أقضِي الصَّيف كُلّه هنا؛ اللّهُمَّ إلّا إذا خِلصَت فلُوسِي [ra:ħ ʔagđi ʔiṣṣayf kullah hna: ʔallahumma ʔilla ʔiða xilṣat flu:si] I'm going to spend the whole summer here; that is unless my money runs out.
حَيَّ الله [ħayyallah] *int:* • **1.** literally: God present, God grant • **2.** anything at all, anyone at all
إسِم الله [ʔisim ʔallah, ʔismallah] *int:* • **1.** the name of God, a phrase to ward off potential evil, to express solicitousness and occasionally, admiration.) – إسِم الله! خُو ما تعَوَّرت؟ [ʔismallah! xu: ma: tʕawwarit?] God save you! You didn't get hurt, did you? إسِم الله! بِعِيد الشَّرّ عَنّه [ʔismallah! biʕi:d ʔiššarr ʕannah] Heaven forbid. I hope he'll be all right. إسِم الله عَليه، سَخَّن شوَيَّة [ʔismallah ʕali:h, saxxan šwayya] Poor thing, he's gotten a slight fever! إسِم الله يابَة، شلُون بنَيَّة حِلوَة [ʔismallah ya:ba, šlu:n bnayya ħilwa] God, man, what a pretty girl!
بِسم الله، بِأسِم الله [bismilla:h] *int:* • **1.** in the name of God – قَبِل ما تاكُل، قُول بِسِم الله [gabil ma: ta:kul, gu:l bʔisimillah] Before you eat, say 'In the name of God.'
ما شاء الله [ma:ša:llah, ma: ša:ʔ ʔalla:h] *int:* • **1.** good, thank goodness – ما شاء الله، صِحّتَك تحَسِّنَت [ma: ša:llah, ṣiħħtak tħassinat] Good, your health has improved. • **2.** (an exclamation of surprise) amazing! – ما شاء الله! ياهُو اللّي يِيجِي يصِير وَزِير [ma: ša:llah! ya:hu ʔalyiǰi yṣi:r wazi:r] Amazing! Anyone who comes along can become a minister.
إن شاءَ الله [ʔin ša:ʔa ʔalla:h, ʔinša:llah] *int:* • **1.** if God wills, God willing, if possible, it's to be hoped – إن شاء الله تصِير وَزِير [ʔinša:llah tṣi:r wazi:r] You'll become a minister, I hope. (Often a mere mechanical phrase when speaking of a plan or happening in the near or distant future.) إن شاء الله رَح أشترِي سَيّارَة اليُوم [ʔinša:llah raħ ʔaštiri sayya:ra ʔilyu:m] I'm planning to buy a car today. (Sometimes indicating an intentional vagueness of one's own plans.) تِجِي باكِر؟ إن شاء الله [tiǰi ba:čir? ʔinša:llah] Are you coming tomorrow? I might.

ء ل و

آلَة [ʔa:la] *n:* آلات [ʔa:la:t] *pl:* • **1.** instrument – آلَة مُوسِيقِيَّة [ʔa:la mu:si:qiyya] musical instrument. آلَة جِراحِيَّة [ʔa:la ǰira:ħiyya] surgical instrument. • **2.** mechanical device, gadget • **3.** small part (of a device) – آلات ساعَة [ʔa:la:t sa:ʕa] works of a watch, watch movement. آلات تَلَفِزيَون [ʔa:la:t talafizyu:n] parts of a television set. • **4.** spices (mainly dill, parsley, and fenugreek) used to season spinach
آلاتِي [ʔa:la:ti] *n:* آلاتِيَّة [ʔa:la:tiyya] *pl:* • **1.** musician
آلِي [ʔa:li] *adj:* • **1.** mechanical • **2.** mechanized, motorized – قُوَّة آلِيَّة [quwwa ʔa:liyya] mechanized force.

ء ل و ب ل و

آلُوبالُو [ʔa:luba:lu] *n:* • **1.** (coll.) variety of large cherries resembling plums
آلُوبالُوّة [ʔa:luba:luwwa] *n:* آلُوبالُوّات [ʔa:luba:luwwa:t] *pl:* • **1.** (coll) variety of large cherries resembling plums

ء ل و ج

آلُوجَة [ʔa:lu:ča] *n:* • **1.** (coll.) a variety of dried plums
آلُوجايَة [ʔa:lu:ča:ya] *n:* آلُوجايات [ʔa:lu:ča:ya:t] *pl:* • **1.** a variety of dried plums

ء ل ي

إلَى [ʔila] *preposition:* • **1.** to, toward – وَصَّلنِي إلَى هنا [waṣṣalni ʔila hna] He brought me here. • **2.** up to, as far as – لِحَقنِي إلَى الدّائِرَة [liħagni ʔila ʔidda:ʔira] He followed me as far as the office. • **3.** till, until, up to – إلَى هَسَّة، ما جا [ʔila hassa, ma: ǰa:] Up to now, he hasn't come. أجَّلنا الاجتِماع إلَى باكِر [ʔaǰǰalna ʔilʔiǰtima:ʕ ʔila ba:čir] We postponed the meeting till tomorrow. إلَى آخِره [ʔila ʔa:xirih] and so on, et cetera. إلَى أن [ʔila ʔan] until. اِنتَظرَه إلَى أن يرجَع [ʔintađrah ʔila ʔan yirǰaʕ] Wait for him until he comes back.

ء م

أمّا [ʔamma] *particle:* • **1.** as for, as to, as far as... is concerned – أمّا آنِي، راح أكُون مَشغُول باكِر [ʔamma ʔa:ni, ra:ħ ʔaku:n mašɣu:l ba:čir] As for me, I'll be busy tomorrow. • **2.** but – أمّا هَالمُختَبَر بَسّ للإستِعمال المُعَلِّمِين [ʔamma halmuxtabar bass lilʔistiʕma:l ʔilmuʕallimi:n] But this lab is just for the teachers' use. • **3.** (an exclamation of surprise or astonishment, approx.:) my! well now! – أمّا تَمام طِلَع مِثِل ما قِلت [ʔamma tama:m ṭilaʕ miθil ma: gilit] My! He sure did turn out like you said. أمّا هاي صُدُق خُوش نُكتَة [ʔamma ha:y ṣudug xu:š nukta] Well now that's really a good joke! أمّا تَمام! شلُون ما جَتِّي عَلَى بالِي؟ [ʔamma tama:m! šlu:n ma: ǰatti ʕala ba:li?] Well of course! How come I didn't think of it? • **4.** what, what a – أمّا جَمال [ʔamma ǰama:l] What beauty! أمّا عيُون [ʔamma ʕyu:n] What eyes!
إمّا [ʔimma] *conjunction:* • **1.** either – أرِيد إمّا هَذا لَو ذاك [ʔari:d ʔimma ha:ða law ða:k] I want either this or that.

ء م ب ر

أمبِير [ʔampi:r] *n:* أمبِيرات [ʔampi:ra:t] *pl:* • **1.** ampere

ء م ب ر ط و ر

إمبراطُور [ʔimbraṭu:r] *n:* إمبراطُورِيَّة [ʔimbraṭu:riyya] *pl:* • **1.** emperor

إمبراطورِيَّة [ʔimbraṭu:riyya] *n:* إمبراطُورِيّات [ʔimbraṭu:riyya:t] *pl:* • **1.** empire

إمبراطوري [ʔimbraṭu:ri] *adj:* • **1.** imperial

ء م ر

إئتُمَر [ʔiʔtumar] *v:* • **1.** to obey, take orders – ما يِأتُمُر بأمُر أحَّد [ma: yiʔtumur bʔamur ʔaħħad] He won't take orders from anyone. • **2.** to be ordered

أمَر [ʔumar] *v:* • **1.** to order, command, bid, direct – المُدِير أمَرنِي أطبَع هَالمَكتُوب [ʔilmudi:r ʔumarni ʔaṭbaʕ halmaktu:b] The director ordered me to type this letter. اللُّجنَة أُمرَت بطَردَه [ʔillujna ʔumrat bṭardah] The committee ordered his discharge. تُؤمُر. هَسَّة أطبَعَه [tuʔmur. hassa ʔaṭbaʕah] Yes sir. I'll type it now.

أمَّر [ʔammar] *v:* • **1.** to give authority – مِنُو أمَّرَك عَلينا؟ [minu ʔammarak ʕali:na?] Who set you over us?

تأمَّر [tʔammar] *v:* • **1.** to behave imperiously, be domineering, throw one's weight around – بَسّ ترَفَّع، قام يِتأمَّر عَلينا [bass traffaʕ, ga:m yitʔammar ʕali:na] As soon as he got promoted, he began to lord it over us.

تآمَر [tʔa:mar] *v:* • **1.** to plot, conspire – تآمرَوا عَلَى حَياة الوَزِير [tʔa:mraw ʕala ħaya:t ʔilwazi:r] They plotted against the life of the minister.

أمُر [ʔamur] *n:* أوامِر [ʔawa:mir] *pl:* • **1.** order, command, directive, instruction – سَوَّيتها حَسَب أمرَك [sawwi:tha ħasab ʔamrak] I did it according to your order. جَوَّة أمري [jawwa ʔamri] at my disposal. صِيغَة الأمُر [ṣi:ɣat ʔilʔamur] (gram.) imperative mood. • **2.** pl. أمُور affair, concern, business

أمُر [ʔamur] *n:* أمُور [ʔumu:r] *pl:* • **1.** matter, subject

آمِر [ʔa:mir] *n:* • **1.** commander, commandant

أمِير [ʔami:r] *n:* أمَراء [ʔumara:ʔ, ʔumara:] *pl:* • **1.** prince, emir • **2.** commander, one who gives orders, leader – أمِير لِواء [ʔami:r liwa:ʔ] military rank corresponding to American major general.

أمرَة [ʔumra] *n:* • **1.** authority, command

تآمُر [taʔa:mur] *n:* • **1.** conspiracy

إمارَة [ʔima:ra] *n:* إمارات [ʔima:ra:t] *pl:* • **1.** principality, emirate

أمِيرَة [ʔami:ra] *n:* أمِيرات [ʔami:ra:t] *pl:* • **1.** princess

مُؤامَرَة [muʔa:mara] *n:* مُؤامَرات [muʔa:mara:t] *pl:* • **1.** plot, conspiracy

مَأمُور [maʔmu:r] *n:* مأمُورِين [maʔmu:ri:n] *pl:* • **1.** subordinate, one who takes orders – إنتَ الآمِر وَأنِي المَأمُور بِهَالدّائرَة [ʔinta ʔilʔa:mir waʔa:ni ʔilmaʔmu:r bhadda:ʔira] You're the boss and I'm the one who takes orders in this office. • **2.** one delegated authority, official – مَأمُور الجُمرُك [maʔmu:r ʔilgumrug] customs official. مَأمُور المَركَز [maʔmu:r ʔalmarkaz] the chief of a police station. مَأمُور بَرِيد [maʔmu:r bari:d] postmaster.

مُؤتَمَر [muʔtamar] *n:* مُؤتَمَرات [muʔtamara:t] *pl:* • **1.** conference, convention, congress

مَأمُورِيَّة [maʔmu:riyya] *n:* مأمُوريّات [maʔmu:riyya:t] *pl:* • **1.** assignment, mission

إستِمارَة [ʔistima:ra] *n:* إستِمارات [ʔistima:ra:t] *pl:* • **1.** form, blank

أمِيري [ʔami:ri] *adj:* • **1.** state, government – أرض أمِيريَّة [ʔarð ʔami:riyya] state land.

مِتآمِر [mitʔa:mir] *adj:* مِتآمِرين [mitʔa:miri:n] *pl:* • **1.** conspirator

ء م ر ك

تأمرَك [tʔamrak] *v:* • **1.** to become Americanized – مِن رُوحتَه لِأمرِيكا، تأمرَك [min ru:ħtah liʔamri:ka, tʔamrak] Since his trip to America, he's become Americanized.

أمرِيكا [ʔamri:ka, ʔamiri:ka] *n:* • **1.** America

أمرِيكي [ʔamri:ki] *adj:* أمرِيكان [ʔamri:ka:n] *pl:* • **1.** American

أمرِيكانِي [ʔamri:ka:ni] *adj:* أمرِيكان [ʔamri:ka:n] *pl:* • **1.** American

ء م ر ل

أمِيرال [ʔamira:l] *n:* أمِيرالات، أمِيرالِيَّة [ʔamira:la:t, ʔamira:liyya] *pl:* • **1.** admiral

ء م ز ق

أمزُق [ʔumzug] *n:* أمزُقات [ʔumzuga:t] *pl:* • **1.** cigarette holder

ء م ل

أمَّل [ʔammal] *v:* • **1.** to raise hopes, give reason to hope – أمَّلنِي تُوصَل السَّيّارَة راس الشَّهَر [ʔammalni tu:ṣal ʔissayya:ra ra:s ʔiššahar] He gave me hope the car would come at the beginning of the month. • **2.** to put off, keep waiting, ask to wait – مِن طالَبتَه بِالفلُوس، أمَّلنِي إلَى أن ياخُذ مَعاشَه [min ṭa:labtah bilfilu:s, ʔammalni ʔila ʔan ya:xuð maʕa:šah] When I dunned him for the money, he asked me to wait until he gets his salary. رِحِت عَليه عَلَى شُغُل وَأمَّلنِي لباكِر [riħit ʕali:h ʕala šuɣul waʔammalni lba:čir] I went to him for work and he put me off until tomorrow. • **3.** to hope, expect – وَلَو ما قارِي زين، يأمِّل يِنجَح [walaw ma: qa:ri zi:n, yʔammil yinjaħ] Although he hasn't studied well, he expects to pass.

تأمَّل [tʔammal] *v:* • **1.** to hope – أتأمَّل البَيت يِعجبَك [ʔatʔammal ʔilbayt yiʕijbak] I hope you'll like the house. • **2.** to expect – أتأمَّل صَدِيقِي يُوصَل باكِر [ʔatʔammal ṣadi:qi yu:ṣal ba:čir] I expect my friend to arrive tomorrow. • **3.** to wait, be patient – تأمَّل شوَيَّة. لا تِستَعجِل [tʔammal šwayya. la: tistaʕjil] Wait a while. Don't be in a hurry.

أمَل [ʔamal] *n:* آمال [ʔa:ma:l] *pl:* • **1.** hope, expectation

مِتأمِّل [mitʔammil] *adj:* • **1.** hopeful

مَأمُول [maʔmu:l] *adj:* • **1.** prospective

ء

ء م ن [1]

إِمَن [ʔiman] *v:* • **1.** to be safe from, be secure from – الشُّرطَة لِزمَت هَالأشقِياء والنَّاس إمنَوا شَرّهُم [ʔiššurṭa lizmat halʔašqiyaːʔ winnaːs ʔimmnaw šarrahum] The police got those thugs and people are safe from their wickedness.

آمَن [ʔaːman] *v:* • **1.** to believe – هَذا ما يآمِن بالله [haːða maː yʔaːmin bʔallah] He doesn't believe in God. هَسَّة آمَنِت اللّي قِتلَك إيّاه صُدُق؟ [hassa ʔaːmanit ʔilli gitlak ʔiyyaːh ṣudug?] Now do you believe that what I told you is true?

أَمَّن [ʔamman] *v:* • **1.** to assure, ensure, guarantee, safeguard – حَصَّل عَلَى شَهادَة وَأَمَّن مُستَقبَلَه [ħaṣṣal ʕala šahaːda wʔamman mustaqbalah] He got a degree and ensured his future. • **2.** to place in safekeeping, to leave in trust – أَمَّن قَراضَه عِندِي [ʔamman garaːð̣ah ʕindi] He left his things in my keeping. خَلِّي نأَمِّن جِنَطنا بِالمَحَطَّة [xalliː nʔammin ǰinaṭna bilmaħaṭṭa] Let's check our bags in the station. • **3.** to assure, reassure, to set (someone's) mind at ease – أَمَّنِّي مِن طَرَف الوَظِيفَة [ʔammanni min ṭaraf ʔilwað̣iːfa] He reassured me about the position. أَمَّنِّي كُلّشِي يِخلَص باكِر [ʔammanni kullši yixlaṣ baːčir] He assured me everything would be done tomorrow. • **4.** to get insurance, take out insurance – أَمَّن عَلَى مَخزَنَه ضِدّ الحَرِيق [ʔamman ʕala maxzanah ð̣idd ʔilħariːq] He insured his warehouse against fire. • **5.** to believe, be assured, trust, have faith – مِن شافنِي، يَالله أَمَّن آنِي بِبَغداد [min šaːfni, yallah ʔamman ʔaːni bibaɣdaːd] When he saw me, then he believed I was in Baghdad. يِظهَر ما تأَمِّن بِحكايتِي [yið̣har maː tʔammin bičaːyti] It seems you don't believe my story. ما يأَمِّن بأَحَّد [maː yʔammin bʔaħħad] He doesn't trust anyone. ما دَيأَمِّن مِن عُمّالَه. ما يخَلِّي فلُوس عالمِيز أَبَداً [maː dayʔammin min ʕummaːlah. maː yxalli fluːs ʕalmiːz ʔabadan] He doesn't trust his workers. He doesn't ever leave money on the table. أَمِّن، ما راح أَحكِي لأَحَّد [ʔammin, maː raːħ ʔaħči lʔaħħad] Rest assured, I'm not going to talk to anyone. • **6.** to feel safe – ما دَيأَمِّن يرُوح وَحدَه بِاللَيل [maː dayʔammin yiruːħ waħdah billayl] He doesn't feel safe going out alone at night. • **7.** with عَلَى to confirm, corroborate, bear out – كُلّ المَوجُودِين أَمّنوا عَلَى حكايتَه [kull ʔilmawǰuːdiːn ʔammnaw ʕala ħčaːytah] All those present confirmed his statement.

تأَمَّن [tʔamman] *v:* • **1.** to be placed in safekeeping – جِنَطِي ما مُمكِن تِتأَمَّن بِالمَطار أكثَر مِن يوم واحِد [ǰinaṭi maːmumkin titʔamman bilmaṭaːr ʔakθar min yuːm waːħid] My suitcases can't be left in safekeeping at the airport more than one day. • **2.** to rest assured, have peace of mind – أَمِّن ما أَغُشَّك [ʔammin maː ʔaɣuššak] Rest assured that I won't cheat you. • **3.** to be trustworthy, reliable, honest – أَرِيد أَقُلَّه فَدّ سِرّ. تِعتِقِد يِتأَمَّن؟ [ʔariːd ʔagullah fadd sirr. tiʕtiqid yitʔamman?] I want to tell him a secret. Do you think he is trustworthy? لا تِشّارَك وِيّاه. هَذا ما يِتأَمَّن [laː tiššaːrak wiyyaːh. haːða maː yitʔamman] Don't go in partnership with him. He can't be trusted.

اِئتِمَن [ʔiʔtiman] *v:* • **1.** to be trusted (somebody)

اِستَئمَن [ʔistaʔman] *v:* • **1.** to trust, to guarantee, to assure

أَمِن [ʔamin] *n:* • **1.** safety • **2.** security, peace – الأَمن العامّ [ʔilʔamn ʔilʕaːmm] public safety. مَجلِس الأَمِن [majlis ʔilʔamin] the Security Council (of the United Nations). شُرطَة الأَمِن [šurṭat ʔilʔamin] security forces, investigative branch of the Iraqi police system.

أَمان [ʔamaːn] *n:* • **2.** security, safety – ماكُو حاجَة تُقفُل الباب؛ الدِّنيا أَمان [maːku ħaːǰa tuqful ʔilbaːb; ʔiddinya ʔamaːn] No need to lock the door; the area's safe. الدِّنيا أَمان [ʔiddinya ʔamaːn] All is well.

أَمنِي [ʔamni] *adj:* • **1.** secure, safe

مُؤمِن [muʔmin] *n:* • **1.** believer, religious

أَمانَة [ʔamaːna] *n:* • **1.** trustworthiness, reliability • **2.** honesty • **3.** confidence, trust, good faith • **4.** office or position of trust, trusteeship – أَمانَة الصَّندُوق [ʔamaːnat ʔiṣṣanduːq] office or position of treasurer or cashier.

تأمِين [taʔmiːn] *n:* • **1.** assurance • **2.** safeguarding • **3.** assurance, reassurance • **4.** insurance • **5.** (usually pl.)

إيمان [ʔiːmaːn] *n:* • **1.** faith, belief – بإيمانَك شقَلَّك؟ [biʔimaːnak šgallak?] By your faith, what did he tell you?

مَأمُون [maʔmuːn] *adj:* • **1.** trustworthy, reliable – ما نِقدَر نِترُك الجِّهال وِيّاه. هَذا واحِد ما مَأمُون [maː nigdar nitruk ʔiǰǰihaːl wiyyaːh. haːða waːħid maː maʔmuːn] We can't leave the children with him. He's not trustworthy. • **2.** safe, secure – نِقدَر نخَيِّم هنا؛ هَالمَنطَقَة مَأمُونَة [nigdar nxayyim hnaː; halmanṭaqa maʔmuːna] We can camp here; this area is safe.

اِئتِمان [ʔiʔtimaːn] *n:* • **1.** trust

اِستِئمان [ʔistiʔmaːn] *n:* • **1.** trust, confidence • **2.** credit

أَمِين [ʔamiːn] *adj:* • **1.** trustworthy, reliable, honest • **2.** one entrusted with something, trustee, custodian, guardian, keeper – أَمِين الصَّندُوق [ʔamiːn ʔiṣṣanduːq] treasurer, cashier أَمِين المَكتَبَة [ʔamiːn ʔilmaktaba] custodian of the library. أَمِين المَتحَف [ʔamiːn ʔalmatħaf] curator of the museum. أَمِين عامّ [ʔamiːn ʕaːmm] secretary general. أَمِين العاصِمَة [ʔamiːn ʔilʕaːṣima] an appointed officer in the Baghdad city government with limited administrative responsibility.

مأمِّن [mʔammin] *adj:* • **1.** feeling safe, safe

مُؤتَمَن [muʔtaman] *adj:* • **1.** entrusted, confidant

اِئتِمانِي [ʔiʔtimaːni] *adj:* • **1.** fiduciary, credit (in compounds), credit markets, credit facilitations

أَمنِياً [ʔamniyaːn] *adverbial:* • **1.** security-wise, regarding security

ء م ن [2]

أَمان [ʔamaːn] *int:* • **1.** (an expression of enthusiastic approval of a singer) great, wonderful – أَمان، أَمان، يا عينِي [ʔamaːn, ʔamaːn, yaː ʕiːni] Great, great!

ء

ء م و 1

أمّ [ʔamm] *v:* • **1.** to lead in prayer – مِنُو راح يِئِمّ الجَّماعَة اليُوم؟ [minu raːħ yʔimm ʔiǰǰamaːʕa ʔilyuːm?] Who's going to lead the congregation in prayer today?

أَمَّم [ʔammam] *v:* • **1.** to nationalize – الحُكُومَة أَمِّمَت صِناعَة السِّمَنت [ʔilħukuːma ʔammimat ṣinaːʕat ʔassimant] The government nationalized the cement industry.

تأمَّم [tʔammam] *v:* • **1.** to be nationalized – كُلّ البُنُوك تأَمِّمَت بهَالبَلَد [kull ʔilbunuːg tʔammimat bhalbalad] All the banks in this country were nationalized.

أمّ [ʔumm] *n:* أُمَّهات [ʔummahaːt] *pl:* • **1.** mother – الحاجَة أُمّ الاختِراع [ʔilħaːǰa ʔumm ʔilʔixtiraːʕ] Necessity is the mother of invention. • **2.** the woman with, the one with – أُمّ الخُبُز [ʔumm ʔilxubuz] the baker woman. أُمّ الثُّوب الأخضَر [ʔumm ʔiθθuːb ʔilʔaxðar] the one in the green dress. سِكِّينَة أُمّ الياي [siččiːna ʔumm ʔilyaːy] switchblade knife.

أُمَّة [ʔumma] *n:* أُمَم [ʔumam] *pl:* • **1.** The United Nations – الأُمَم المُتَّحِدَة [ʔilʔumam ʔilmuttaħida] The United Nations.

أُمِّيَّة [ʔummiyya] *n:* • **1.** illiteracy, analphabetism

أمام [ʔamaːm] *n:* • **1.** in front of, ahead of – الفِرقَة المُوسِيقِيَّة دَتِمشِي أمام الجَّيش [ʔilfirqa ʔalmuːsiːqiyya datimši ʔamaːm ʔiǰǰiayš] The band's marching ahead of the army. المُلازِم يِمشِي أمام جِنُودَه [ʔilmulaːzim yimši ʔamaːm ǰinuːdah] The lieutenant walks at the head of his troops. • **2.** in front of, in the presence of – ما أرِيدَك تِحكِي هِيكِي حَكِي أمام الجِّهال [maːʔariːdak tiħči hiːči ħači ʔamaːm ʔiǰǰihaːl] I don't want you to talk that way in front of the children. الحادِثَة صارَت أمام عيُونِي [ʔilħaːdiθa ṣaːr ʔamaːm ʕyuːni] The accident occurred right before my eyes. • **3.** front – باوِع لِلأمام [baːwiʕ lilʔamaːm] Look to the front. Face forward. خَلِّي نِقعُد بِالأمام [xalliːnigʕud bilʔamaːm] Let's sit down front. إلَى الأمام سِرّ [ʔila ʔilʔamaːm sirr] Forward- march!

إمام [ʔimaːm] *n:* • **1.** Imam (Islamic religious official) • **2.** prayer leader

أمّايَة [ʔummaːya] *n:* أمّايات [ʔummaːyaːt] *pl:* • **1.** matriarch, woman in charge • **2.** diminutive of mother

أُمُومَة [ʔumuːma] *n:* • **1.** motherhood • **2.** maternity

إمامَة [ʔimaːma] *n:* • **1.** leading in prayer

أُمِّي [ʔummi] *adj:* • **1.** illiterate • **2.** an illiterate

أُمَمِي [ʔumami] *adj:* • **1.** international

أمامِي [ʔamaːmi] *adj:* • **1.** front, forward – الخُطُوط الأمامِيَّة [ʔilxuṭuːṭ ʔilʔamaːmiyya] the front lines. غُرفَة أمامِيَّة [ɣurfa ʔamaːmiyya] front room.

ء م و 2

أمَوِي [ʔamawi] *adj:* • **1.** Ummayyad • **2.** an Ummayyad

ء م ي ب

أمِيبا [ʔamiːba] *n:* أمِيبات [ʔamiːbaːt] *pl:* • **1.** amoeba

ء ن 1

آنَة، أبُو إلآنَة [ʔaːna, ʔabuː ʔilʔaːna] *n:* • **1.** the one responsible, the one in charge

أنّ، إن، إنُّو [ʔan, ʔin, ʔinnu] *subordinating conjunction:* • **1.** that – ما دام إحنا بِالبَنك، مِن الأَحسَن أن نِصرُف الصِّكُوك [maː daːm ʔiħna bilbang, min ʔilʔaħsan ʔan niṣruf ʔiččikuːk] As long as we're in the bank, it's best that we cash the checks. اِتّفقوا أن يِرحُون لِلسِّينَما سُوَة [ʔittifqaw ʔan yirħuːn lissinama suwa] They agreed to go to the movies together. قال إنهُم ما يحِبُّون يدِرسُون [gaːl ʔinhum maː yħibbuːn ydirsuːn] He said that they don't like to study. قال إنُّو راجِع بَعَد نُصّ ساعَة [gaːl ʔinnu raːǰiʕ baʕad nuṣṣ saːʕa] He said that he's coming back after a half hour. قَلِّي إنُّو القَضِيَّة راح تِنتِهِي باكِر [galli ʔinnu ʔilqaðiyya raːħ tintihi baːčir] He told me that the matter would be settled tomorrow. إلَى أن [ʔila ʔan] until. اِنتِظِرنِي هنا إلَى أن أخَلِّص [ʔintiðirni hnaː ʔila ʔan ʔaxalliṣ] Wait for me here till I finish. طَيَّر إشاعَة بِأن الوَزِير راح يِستَقِيل [ṭayyar ʔišaːʕa bʔan ʔilwaziːr raːħ yistaqiːl] He spread a rumor to the effect that the minister was going to resign. راد يِقنِعهُم بِأن آنِي المُصوج [raːd yiqniʕhum bʔan ʔaːni ʔilmuṣwič] He wanted to convince him that I was to blame. عَلَى أن [ʕala ʔan] provided that, providing. وافق يِشتِرِيها عَلَى أن يِنطُوه تَخفِيض خَمسَة بِالمِيَّة [waːfaq yištiriːha ʕala ʔan yintuːh taxfiːð xamsa bilmiyya] He agreed to buy it providing they gave him a five percent discount. اِشتِرطَوا عَلِيه عَلَى أن يِدفَع نُصّ المَبلَغ [ʔištirṭaw ʕaliːh ʕala ʔan yidfaʕ nuṣṣ ʔilmablaɣ] They set a condition that he pay half the amount. ما إشتِرَيتَه لِأنّ غالِي [maː ʔištiraytah liʔann ɣaːli] The teacher isn't going to come because he's sick. وَلَو أن [walaw ʔan] even though. أخَذتها مِنَّه وَلَو أن كان يمانِع [ʔaxaðitha minnah walaw ʔan čaːn ymaːniʕ] I took it from him even though he objected. لازِم يِشتُغُل وَلَو إنُّو ما يرِيد [laːzim yištuɣul walaw ʔinnu maː yriːd] He has to work even though he doesn't want to.

ء ن 3

أنانِي [ʔanaːni] *adj:* • **1.** selfish – خَلِّي أستَعمِل القامُوس. لا تصِير أنانِي [xalliː ʔastaʕmil ʔilqaːmuːs. laː tṣiːr ʔanaːni] Let me use the dictionary. Don't be selfish.

أنانِيَّة [ʔanaːniyya] *n:* • **1.** selfishness

ء ن ب

أنَّب [ʔannab] *v:* • **1.** to rebuke, censure, upbraid, scold (someone) – أنَّبتَه مِيَّة مَرَّة لَكِن ما يجُوز [ʔannabtah miyyat marra laːkin maː yǰuːz] I rebuked him a hundred times but he won't stop. ضَمِيرِي دَيأَنِّبنِي لِأنّ ما نطَيتَه الفلُوس

[ðamiːri dayʔannibni liʔann maː nṭiːtah ʔilfluːs] My conscience is bothering me because I didn't give him the money.

ء ن ب ب

أنبُوب، أنبُوبَة [ʔunbuːb, ʔunbuːba] *n:* أنابِيب [ʔanaːbiːb] *pl:* • **1.** oil pipeline – أنبُوب اختِبار [ʔunbuːb ʔixtibaːr] test tube. خَطّ أنابِيب نَفُط [xaṭṭ ʔanaːbiːb nafuṭ] oil pipeline.

ء ن ب ق

إنبِيق [ʔinbiːq] *n:* أنابِيق [ʔanaːbiːq] *pl:* • **1.** retort (chem.)

ء ن ت

إنتَ [ʔinta] *pronoun:* إنتُم [ʔintum] *pl:* • **1.** fem إنتِي you – إنتَ شعلَيك؟ [ʔinta šaʕliːk?] What's it to you?

ء ن ت ر ن ت

إنتَرنَيت [ʔintarniːt] *n:* • **1.** Internet

ء ن ت ك

أنتِيك [ʔantiːk] *adj:* • **1.** antique

ء ن ث

أنَّث [ʔannaθ] *v:* • **1.** to make feminine (gram.) – شلُون تأنِّث هَالكِلمَة؟ [šluːn tʔanniθ haččilma?] How do you make this word feminine?

تأنَّث [tʔannaθ] *v:* • **1.** to become feminine – هَالإسِم ما يِتأنَّث [halʔisim maː yitʔannaθ] This noun doesn't become feminine.

أُنثَى [ʔunθa] *n:* إناث [ʔinaːθ] *pl:* • **1.** female • **2.** a female – الأُنثَى تاخُذ نُصّ الذَّكَر بالمِيراث [ʔilʔunθaː taːxuð nuṣṣ ʕiððakar bilmiːraːθ] The female gets half of what the male gets in the inheritance. أُنثَى العَنكَبُوت تُقتُل الفَحَل [ʔunθaː ʔalʕankabuːt tuktul ʔilfaħal] The female spider kills the male.

أُنوثَة [ʔunuːθa] *n:* • **1.** femininity

مُؤَنَّث [muʔannaθ] *adj:* • **1.** feminine – كِلمَة مُؤَنَّثَة [čilma muʔannaθa] feminine word.

ء ن ج

إنش [ʔinǰ] *n:* إنشات [ʔinǰaːt] *pl:* • **1.** inch

ء ن ج ل

إنجِيل [ʔinǰiːl] *n:* أناجِيل [ʔanaːǰiːl] *pl:* • **1.** gospel • **2.** Bible

ء ن د ن س ي

أندُونِيسيا [ʔanduniːsya] *n:* • **1.** Indonesia

ء ن د و ن ي س

أندَونِيسِي [ʔanduniːsi] *adj:* • **1.** Indonesian

ء ن س

وَنَّس [wannas] *v:* • **1.** to entertain, amuse, provide entertainment – هَالفِلِم يوَنِّس هوايَة [halfilim ywannis hwaːya] This movie is very entertaining. أُخُذ الجّاهِل وَوَنّسَه شوَيَّة [ʔuxuð ʔiǰǰaːhil wwannisah šwayya] Take the kid and amuse him for a while. إذا تِجِي لِبَغداد، أوَنّسَك [ʔiða tiǰi libaɣdaːd, ʔawannsak] If you come to Baghdad, I'll show you a good time.

توَنَّس [twannas] *v:* • **1.** to be entertained, to enjoy oneself – توَنَّستُوا البارحَة بِالحَفلَة وَإلّا لا؟ [twannastuː ʔilbaːrħa bilħafla waʔilla laː?] Did you enjoy yourselves yesterday at the party or not?

إستَأنَس، إستانَس [ʔistaʔnas, ʔistaːnas] *v:* • **1.** to enjoy oneself, have a good time – إستَأنَسِت وِيّاك هوايَة [ʔistaʔnasit wiyyaːk hwaːya] I enjoyed myself a lot with you. خَلِّي نبقَى بَعَد؛ آنِي مِستَأنِس [xalliː nibqaː baʕad; ʔaːni mistaʔanis] Let's stay a little longer; I'm having a good time. مِستَأنِس بِالبايسِكِل كُلِّش [mistaʔnis bilpaːysikil kulliš] He's having a good time with the bicycle.

إنس [ʔins] *n:* • **1.** (coll.) man, mankind, humanity – لا إنس وَلا جِنّ [laː ʔins wala ǰinn] neither man nor beast.

آنِسَة [ʔaːnisa] *n:* آنِسات، أوانِس [ʔaːnisaːt, ʔawaːnis] *pl:* • **1.** young lady, miss (also as a polite form of address)

وَنسَة [wansa] *n:* • **1.** pleasure, fun

إنسان [ʔinsaːn] *n:* • **1.** man, mankind, humankind, the human race • **2.** human being

إنسانِيَّة [ʔinsaːniyya] *n:* • **1.** humanity, humaneness, kindness • **2.** humanity, mankind • **3.** pl. ات humane act, humane deed, a kindness

إنسِي [ʔinsi] *adj:* إنسِيَّة [ʔinsiyya] *feminine:* • **1.** human • **2.** human being

مِتوَنِّس [mitwannis] *adj:* • **1.** cheerful

إنسانِي [ʔinsaːni] *adj:* • **1.** human • **2.** humane, humanitarian

ء ن ف

إنَف [ʔinaf] *v:* • **1.** to disdain, scorn – آنِي أنَف أشتُغُل. وِيّا هِيكِي ناس [ʔaːni ʔaːni ʔaʔnaf ʔaštugul. wiyya hiːči naːs] I am too proud to work with such people.

إستَأنَف [ʔistaʔnaf] *v:* • **1.** to appeal (a legal case) – راح أستأنِف الدَّعوَة [raːħ ʔastaʔnif ʔiddaʕwa] I'm going to appeal the case.

أنِف [ʔanif] *n:* أُنوف [ʔunuːf] *pl:* • **1.** **nose** • **2.** رَغُم أنف [raɣum ʔanf] in spite of, in defiance of. سَوَّيتها رَغُم أنفَك [sawwiːtha raɣum ʔanfak] I did it in spite of you.

أنَفَة [ʔanafa] *n:* • **1.** pride • **2.** haughtiness • **3.** scorn, disdain • **4.** rejection

أنُوف [ʔanuːf] *adj:* • **1.** proud, haughty, stuck-up, supercilious, disdainful

إستِئناف [ʔistiʔnaːf] *n:* • **1.** appeal (to the lower courts) – قَدَّم إستِئناف [qaddam ʔistiʔnaːf] He made an appeal. مَحكَمَة الاستِئناف [maħkamat ʔalʔistiʔnaːf] appeals court.

أَنفِي [ʔanfi] *adj:* • **1.** nasal – الجِّيُوب الأَنفِيَّة [ʔiǰǰiyu:b ʔalʔanfiyya] the nasal sinuses.

ء ن ف ل و ن ز

إنفلُوَنزَة [ʔinfluwanza] *n:* • **1.** influenza

ء ن ق

تأَنَّق [tʔannaq] *v:* • **1.** to be chic, elegant – يِتأَنَّق بِلِبسَه هوايَة [yitʔannaq blibsah hwa:ya] He's very elegant in his dress.

أَناقَة [ʔana:qa] *n:* • **1.** elegance

أَنِيق [ʔani:q] *adj:* • **1.** neat, chic, elegant

ء ن ك ل ت ر

إنكِلتَرا [ʔingiltara] *n:* • **1.** England

ء ن ك ل ي ز

إنكِلِيزي [ʔingili:zi] *n:* إنكِلِيز [ʔingili:z] *pl:* إنكِلِيزِيَّة [ʔingili:ziyya] *feminine:* • **1.** English • **2.** English

ء ن ن

أَنّ [ʔann] *v:* • **1.** to moan, groan – بُقَى يِئِنّ لِلصُّبُح [buqa: yʔinn liṣṣubuḥ] He kept moaning until morning.

أَنَّة [ʔanna] *n:* أَنّات [ʔanna:t] *pl:* • **1.** moan

أَنِين [ʔani:n] *n:* • **1.** moaning

ء ن ن س

أَناناس [ʔanana:s] *n:* • **1.** pineapple

ء ن ي

تأَنَّى [tʔanna:] *v:* • **1.** to act slowly, proceed deliberately and unhurriedly, take one's time – لَو تِتأَنَّى، ما تِغلَط [law titʔanna:, ma: tiɣlaṭ] If you take your time, you won't make a mistake. أُدرُس المَوضُوع قَبُل ما تِحتَجّ [ʔudrus ʔilmawḍu:ʕ gabul ma: tiḥtaǰǰ] Take your time. Study the matter before you protest.

تَأَنِّي [taʔanni] *n:* • **1.** deliberateness, unhurriedness

آني [ʔa:ni] *pronoun:* • **1.** I (for masc. and feminine)

ء ن ي م

أَنِيميا [ʔani:miya] *n:* • **1.** anemia

ء ه ب

تَأَهَّب [taʔahhab] *v:* • **1.** to be ready, get ready, to prepare oneself – تأَهَّبتُوا لِلسَّفرَة لَو بَعَد؟ [tʔahhabtu lissafra law baʕad?] Are you ready for the trip yet?

ء ه ل

أَهَّل [ʔahhal] *v:* • **1.** to qualify, fit, make suitable – نَظَره ما يأَهّلَه يصِير طَيّار [naḍarah ma: yʔahhlah yṣi:r ṭayya:r] His eyesight doesn't qualify him to be a pilot. ثَقافتَه ما تأَهّلَه لِهالوَظِيفَة [θaqa:ftah ma: tʔahhlah lihalwaḍi:fa] His education doesn't qualify him for this position.

تأَهَّل [tʔahhal] *v:* • **1.** to get married – سِمَعِت أَخُوك راح يِتأَهَّل [simaʕit ʔaxu:k ra:ḥ yitʔahhal] I heard your brother is going to get married. • **2.** to pass, to be qualified

اِستاهَل [ʔista:hal] *v:* • **1.** to deserve, merit, be worthy of – أستاهَل التَّرفِيع [ʔasta:hal ʔitttarfi:ʕ] He deserved the promotion. تِستاهِل. ما قِتلَك أقعُد راحَة؟ [tista:hil. ma: gitlak ʔugʕud ra:ḥa?] You deserve it. Didn't I tell you to be good? مِستاهِل، حيل بيه. لازم كان ينطِرِد مِن زَمان [mista:hil, ḥi:l bi:h. la:zim ča:n yinṭirid min zama:n] He deserved it, and more. He should have been fired long ago. لِيش ما يِستاهِلها؟ قابِل عائِلَتها أَحسَن مِن عائِلَته؟ [li:š ma: yista:hilha? qa:bil ʕa:ʔilatha ʔaḥsan min ʕa:ʔiltah?] Why isn't he worthy of her? Is her family better than his? مِستاهِلها وشايِف الخير، إن شاء الله [mista:hilha wša:yif ʔilxayr, ʔinša:llah] You deserve it. Good luck. (congratulatory phrase for use on occasions of new acquisitions).

أَهَل [ʔahal] *n:* أَهالِي [ʔaha:li] *pl:* • **1.** family, relatives • **2.** wife • **3.** people – أَهَل بَغداد [ʔahal baɣda:d] the people of Baghdad. أَهل السَّيّارات [ʔahl ʔissayya:ra:t] the people owning cars.

أَهلِي [ʔahli] *n:* • **1.** civil, civilian – مَلابِس أَهلِيَّة [mala:bis ʔahliyya] civilian clothes. • **2.** civil, national – حَرب أَهلِيَّة [ḥarib ʔahliyya] civil war. • **3.** private – بَنك أَهلِي [bang ʔahli] private bank. مَدرَسَة أَهلِيَّة [madrasa ʔahliyya] private school. • **4.** family, domestic – وَقُف أَهلِي [waquf ʔahli] family wakf -- inalienable religious endowment in Islamic law.

أَهالِي [ʔaha:li] *n:* • **1.** people, populace – أَهالِي المَنطَقَة [ʔaha:li ʔalmanṭaqa] the population of the area. • **2.** civilian populace (as distinct from government employees) • **3.** natives, native population

مُؤَهِّلات [muʔahhila:t] *n:* • **1.** (pl. only) qualifications, aptitudes

مُؤَهَّل [muʔahhal] *adj:* • **1.** qualified, eligible

أَهلِيَّة [ʔahliyya] *n:* • **1.** aptitude, suitability, fitness, competence • **2.** relatives, family

مَأهُول [maʔhu:l] *adj:* • **1.** inhabited, populated – مَنطِقَة ما مَأهُولَة [manṭiqa ma: maʔhu:la] an uninhabited area.

متأَهِّل [mitʔahhil] *adj:* • **1.** married

أَهلاً [ʔahlan] *adverbial:* • **1.** welcome – أَهلاً وَسَهلاً، أَهلاً بِيك [ʔahlan wasahlan, ʔahlan bi:k] welcome!

ء ه ي ن

آهِين [ʔa:hi:n] *n:* • **1.** cast iron

ء و

أَو [ʔaw] *conjunction:* • **1.** or – لَو تداينِّي الفلُوس أَو تقُلّي مِنَين أَتدايَنها [law dda:yinni ʔilflu:s ʔaw dgulli: mini:n ʔadda:yanha] Either lend me the money or tell me where I can borrow it from.

إمّا تِجي ويّايا أو تِبقَى بالبَيت [ʔimma tiǰi wiyyaːya ʔaw tibqaː bilbayt] Either come with me or stay at home. أو هَذا أو ذاك [ʔaw haːða ʔaw ðaːk] Either this or that.

ء و ب ر

أوبرا [ʔuːbra] *n:* • **1.** opera

ء و ت ج

أوتِجي [ʔuːtači] *n:* أوتَجِيَّة [ʔuːtačiyya] *pl:* • **1.** presser, ironer • **2.** presser's shop, cleaner's

ء و ت ل

أوتَيل، أتيل [ʔutiːl] *n:* أوتَيلات [ʔutiːlaːt] *pl:* • **1.** hotel

ء و ت ي

أوتي [ʔuːti] *n:* أوتيّات [ʔuːtiyyaːt] *pl:* • **1.** iron, flat iron – ضِرَب أوتي [ðirab ʔuːti] to iron, press. ضرَبتي الثّوب مالي أوتي؟ [ðrabti ʔiθθuːb maːli ʔuːti?] Did you iron my shirt?

ء و ج

أوج [ʔawǰ] *n:* • **1.** peak, top (e.g., of power or fame)

ء و د

أودَة [ʔuːda] *n:* أودات، أوَد [ʔuːdaːt, ʔuwad] *pl:* • **1.** room

ء و ر ب ب

أورُبّا [ʔuːruppa] *n:* • **1.** Europe

أورُبّي [ʔuːruppi] *adj:* • **1.** European, a European

ء و ر ت

أورطي [ʔuːrṭi] *n:* أورطيّات [ʔuːrṭiyyaːt] *pl:* • **1.** sheet, bed-sheet • **2.** a large rug covering more than one room

ء و ر ط

أورطَة [ʔuːrṭa] *n:* أورطات [ʔuːrṭaːt] *pl:* • **1.** a kind of very large Persian rug

ء و ف

آفَة [ʔaːfa] *n:* آفات، آفَوات، أوافي [ʔaːfaːt, ʔafawaːt, ʔawaːfi] *pl:* • **1.** tough person, tough guy, terror • **2.** rascal, sly guy • **3.** efficient person, one who gets things done, whiz

ء و ك س ج ي ن

أوكسِجين [ʔuksiǰiːn] *n:* • **1.** oxygen

ء و ل [1]

أوَّل [ʔawwal] *v:* • **1.** to interpret – أوّل حكايتي مِثلما تريد. ما يهِمّني [ʔawwil ḥčaːyti miθilmaː triːd. maː yhimmni] Interpret my remark any way you want. I don't care.

تَأويل [taʔwiːl] *n:* تَأويلات [taʔwiːlaːt] *pl:* • **1.** interpretation, explanation

أوَّل [ʔawwal] *adj:* أوائِل [ʔawaːʔil] *pl:* أولَى [ʔuwla] *feminine:* • **1.** beginning – أوَّل الشّارِع [ʔawwal ʔiššaːriʕ] the beginning of the street. أوَّل الإسبوع [ʔawwal ʔilʔisbuːʕ] the beginning of the week. كان مِن الأوَّل قُتلي حَتَّى ما أتَعّب نَفسِي [čaːn min ʔilʔawwal gutli ḥatta maː ʔataʕʕib nafsi] You should have told me in the first place so I wouldn't go to such effort. • **2.** earlier, previous – أحسَن مِن الأوَّل [ʔaḥsan min ʔilʔawwal] better than before. أوَّل البارحَة، أوَّلَة البارحَة [ʔawwal ʔilbaːrḥa, ʔawwalat ʔilbaːrḥa] the day before yesterday. • **3.** (pl. only) – كُتُب الأوَّلين وَالآخَرين [kutub ʔilʔawwaliːn wilʔaːxariːn] the books of early and contemporary (Islamic) writers. • **4.** first – الجّائِزَة الأولَى [ʔiǰǰaːʔiza ʔilʔuːla] the first prize.

أوَّلي [ʔawwali] *adj:* • **1.** first, initial – مِسوَدَّة أوَّلِيَّة [miswadda ʔawwaliyya] first draft. اِجتِماع أوَّلِي [ʔiǰtimaːʕ ʔawwali] preliminary meeting. اِنتِخابات أوَّلِيَّة [ʔintixaːbaːt ʔawwaliyya] primary elections (the popular choosing of electors). مَوادّ أوَّلِيَّة [mawaːdd ʔawwaliyya] raw materials.

أوَّلِيَّة [ʔawwaliyya] *n:* أوَّليّات [ʔawwaliyyaːt] *pl:* • **1.** precedence, priority • **2.** first place • **3.** (pl. only)

أوَّلاً [ʔawwalan] *adverbial:* • **1.** first, firstly, first of all – أوَّلاً خَلِّي نحَضِّر الغَراض [ʔawwalan xalli: nḥaððir ʔilɣaraːð] First let's get the things ready.

أوَّل ما [ʔawwal maː] *subordinating conjunction:* • **1.** as soon as

ء و ل [2]

آل [ʔaːl] *n:* • **1.** family, clan

ء و ل ج

أولجي [ʔuːlči] *n:* أولجِيَّة [ʔuːlčiyya] *pl:* • **1.** tape, tapeline, tape measure – أخَذ أولجِي [ʔaxað ʔuːlči] to take measurements. الخَيّاط أخَذلي أولجي [ʔilxayyaːṭ ʔaxaðli ʔuːlči] The tailor took my measurements.

ء و ن

الآن [ʔilʔaːn] *n:* • **1.** now – سَوِّي هَالمُعامَلَة الآن، رَجاءاً [sawwi: halmuʕaːmala ʔalʔaːn, raǰaːʔan] Do this job now, please. حَتَّى الآن ما صار شِي [ḥatta ʔalʔaːn maː ṣaːr ši] Until now, nothing's happened. بَعد الآن، ما أريدَك تسَوّي هيكِي شِي [baʕd ʔilʔaːn, maːʔariːdak tsawwi: hiːči ši] From now on, I don't want you to do such a thing. مِن الآن فَصاعِداً [min ʔilʔaːn faṣaːʕidan] ; مِن الآن وصاعِد [min ʔalʔaːn wṣaːʕid] from now on. مِن الآن فَصاعِداً، وَقِت الدَّوام راح يِتغَيَّر [min ʔalʔaːn faṣaːʕidan, waqit ʔiddawaːm raːḥ yidɣayyar] From now on, working hours will be changed.

أوان [ʔawaːn] *n:* آوِنَة [ʔaːwina] *pl:* • **1.** until the time was past – قَبُل أوانَه [gabul ʔawaːnah] prematurely.

ء

إلّا بَعَد فَوات الأَوان [ʔilla baʕad fawaːt ʔilʔawaːn] until the time was past.

ءونص

أونصَة [ʔuːnṣa] *n:* • **1.** ounce

ءوه

تأوّه [tʔawwah] *v:* • **1.** to moan, groan – بَعدَك تِتأوّه لِهَسّة؟ [baʕdak titʔawwah lhassa?] Are you still moaning?
آهَة [ʔaːha] *n:* آهات [ʔaːhaːt] *pl:* • **1.** moan, groan
تأوّه [taʔawwuh] *n:* • **1.** groan, groaning
آه [ʔaːh] *int:* • **1.** um, ah, eh, OK

ءوي

آوَى [ʔaːwaː] *v:* • **1.** to shelter, take in, put up – آواهُم إلَى أن لِقَوا بَيت جِدِيد [ʔaːwaːhum ʔila ʔan ligaw bayt ǰidiːd] He put them up until they found a new house. هَالشّيخ آوَى كُلّ اللّي اِنهِزمَوا مِن الشّمال [haššiːx ʔaːwaː kull ʔilli ʔinhizmaw min ʔiššimaːl] That ruler sheltered all who fled from the north.
آوَى، إبن آوَى [ʔawa, ʔibin ʔaːwa] *n:* • **1.** jackal
مَأوَى [maʔwa] *n:* مَآوِي [maʔaːwi] *pl:* • **1.** shelter, refuge
مُآوات [muʔaːwaːt] *n:* • **1.** sheltering

ءي [1]

إي [ʔiː] *int:* • **1.** yes • **2.** look, okay

ءي [2]

أيُّو [ʔayyu] *interrogative:* • **1.** which? which one? • **2.** whichever, whatever

ءي [3]

آيَة [ʔaːya] *n:* آيات [ʔaːyaːt] *pl:* • **1.** wonder, marvel – هِيَّ آيَة بِالجَّمال [hiyya ʔaːya bijǰamaːl] She's a marvel of beauty. • **2.** a verse of the Koran

ءيد

أيَّد [ʔayyad] *v:* • **1.** to support, back – كُلّ المُوَظّفِين أيّدَوا المُدِير بِمَوقفَه [kull ʔilmuwaððafiːn ʔayydaw ʔilmudiːr bimawqifah] All the employees supported the director's stand. • **2.** to confirm, corroborate – عَلِي أيَّد الخَبَر [ʕali ʔayyad ʔilxabar] Ali confirmed the news.
تأيَّد [tʔayyad] *v:* • **1.** to be backed • **2.** to be supported
تأيِيد [taʔyiːd] *n:* • **1.** support, backing • **2.** confirmation, corroboration
مُؤيِّد [muʔayyid] *adj:* • **1.** supporting, supporter

ءير

أيّار [ʔayyaːr] *n:* • **1.** May

ءيرن

إيران [ʔiraːn] *n:* • **1.** Iran
إيرانِي [ʔiraːni] *adj:* • **1.** Iranian • **2.** an Iranian

ءيس

أيَّس [ʔayyas] *v:* • **1.** to give up hope, to despair – أيَّس مِن التَّرفِيع [ʔayyas min ʔittarfiːʕ] He gave up hope of promotion. أيِّس! ما راح يِجِي اليُوم [ʔayyis! maː raːħ yiǰi ʔilyuːm] Forget it! He won't come today.

ءيش

أيش، إش [ʔayš, ʔiːš] *interrogative:* • **1.** what? /used only following prepositions/ – عَلَى ويش هَالصياح؟ [ʕala wiːš haṣṣyaːħ?] What's all the shouting about?
مِنيش، مِن أيش [miniːš, min ʔayš] *interrogative:* • **1.** from what? – مِنّ أيش مَعمُولَة؟ [min ʔiːš maʕmuːla?] What is it made of? • **2.** why? for what reason?
إبَيش، بَيش [ʔibayš, biːš] *interrogative:* • **1.** with what? how? • **2.** at what, how much – بيش كَلَّفتَك؟ [biːš kallifatak?] How much did it cost you? السّاعَة بيش؟ [ʔissaːʕa biyš?] What time is it?

ءيض

أيضاً [ʔayðan] *adverbial:* • **1.** also, too – المُعَلِّم أيضاً قَلّي [ʔilmuʕallim ʔayðan galli] The teacher also told me.

ءيلل

أيلُول [ʔayluːl, ʔiːluːl] *n:* • **1.** September

ءيي

أيّ، أي [ʔayy, ʔay] *interrogative:* • **1.** what? which? – أيّ نُوع؟ [ʔayy nuːʕ?] What kind? Which type? أيّ مُدِير وأيّ بَطّيخ؟ [ʔayy mudiːr wʔayy baṭṭiːx?] What sort of a director is that (lit., what director and what melon) ? • **2.** any – أيّ واحِد [ʔayy waːħid] anyone, whoever. أيّ شِي [ʔayy ši] anything, whatever.

ب

ب

ب [b] *preposition:* • **1.** in, at, into – هُوَّ مُو بالغُرفَة هَسَّة [huwwa mu: bilɣurfa hassa] He's not in the room now. أبُويَا بَعدَه بَالدّائِرَة [ʔabu:ya baʕdah bidda:ʔira] My father's still at the office. سِبَحِت بِالشَّطّ اليُوم [sibaħit biššaṭṭ ʔilyu:m] I swam in the river today. ماكُو مِثلَه بِالدِّنيا [ma:ku miθlah biddinya] There's no one like him in the world. قرَيتَه بِالجَّرِيدَة [qiraytah bijjari:da] I read it in the paper. دَوِّر بِبَين هَالأقلام، بَلكِي تشُوف اللّي تريدَه [dawwir bbayn halʔaqla:m, balki tšu:f ʔilli tri:dah] Look through these pencils; maybe you'll find the one you want. خَشّ بِالقُبَّة [xašš bilgubba] He went into the room. حَطّيت شَكَر بِالشّاي لَو بَعَد؟ [ħaṭṭi:t šakar bičča:y law baʕad?] Did you put sugar in the tea yet? حُطّ دِهِن بِشَعرَك حَتَّى يُقعُد [ħuṭṭ dihin bišaʕrak ħatta yugʕud] Put some oil on your hair so it'll stay down. خَشّ بِبَيناتهُم وفاكَكهُم [xašš bibayna:thum wfa:kakhum] He stepped in between them and separated them. هَالسَّلَّة أَعتِقِد بِيها كَيلُوَين عَلَى الأقَلّ [hassalla ʔaʕtiqid bi:ha kiluwayn ʕala ʔilʔaqall] I figure this basket weighs two kilos at least. شبِيها السَّيّارَة؟ ما تِمشِي بَعَد؟ [šbi:ha ʔissayya:ra? ma: timši baʕad?] what's wrong with the car? Won't it run anymore? شبِيه؟ ما دَيِشتُغُل أبَداً [šbi:h? ma: dayištuɣul ʔabadan] What's ailing him? He never works. بِيهُم تِيفُو. ما لازِم تخُشّ بِالقُبَّة [bi:hum ti:fu. ma: la:zim txušš bilgubba] They've got typhoid. You mustn't go in the room. هَسَّة بِيك. إنتَ أرْكُض [hassa bi:k. ʔinta ʔurkuð̣] Now you're 'it'. You run. • **2.** in, at (time) – بأوَّل الشَّهَر [bʔawwal ʔiššahar] the first of the month. بالوَقِت المُعَيَّن [bilwakt ʔalmuʕayyan] at the appointed time. سَوّاها بنُصّ ساعَة [sawwa:ha bnuṣṣ sa:ʕa] He did it in a half hour. صرَفِت هوايَة فلُوس بِهَالشَّهَر [ṣrafit hwa:ya flu:s bhaššahar] I spent a lot of money this month. بِحَياتِي ما شايِف هِيكِي [biħaya:ti ma: ša:yif hi:či] I've never seen such a thing in my life. السّاعَة بِالخَمسَة [ʔissa:ʕa bilxamsa] It's five o'clock. السّاعَة بيش، يا شَباب؟ [ʔissa:ʕa biyš, ya: šaba:b?] What time is it, fellows? بيش ساعتَك؟ [biyš sa:ʕtak?] What time have you got? السّاعَة بيش تِجِي؟ [ʔissa:ʕa biyš tiji?] At what time will you come? • **3.** in, at (signifying the pursuit of an action) – غلَبتَه بِالشِّطرَنج [ɣilabtah biššiṭranj] I beat him at chess. خِسَر فلُوسَه بِالقُمار [xiṣar flu:sah bilquma:r] He lost his money in gambling. غِلَب دِينار بِالرَّيسِز [gilab dina:r birraysiz] He won a dinar at the races. نِجَحِت بِالإمتِحان [nijaħit bilʔimtiħa:n] I passed the exam. يضَيِّع وَقتَه بِاللِّعِب [yiðayyiʕ waktah billaʕib] He wastes his time in play. مَخبُوص بِالشُّغُل [maxbu:ṣ biššuɣul] He's all wrapped up in the work. تعارکوا بِالحَكِي [tʕa:rkaw bilħači] They had an argument. • **4.** with, by means of – إغسِلَه بماي وَصابُون [ʔigislah bma:y wṣa:bu:n] Wash it with water and soap. يِكتِب بِقَلَم بَصمَة [yiktib bqalam baṣma] He writes with a pencil. راح ترُوح بِالقِطار؟ [ra:ħ tru:ħ bilqiṭa:r?] Are you going to go by train? زَعَّلنِي بِحَكيَه [zaʕʕalni bħačyah] He angered me with his talk. خابرَه بِالتَّلِفُون [xa:brah bittalifu:n] Call him on the phone. نِشرَوا الخَبَر بِالإذاعَة [nišraw ʔilxabar bilʔiða:ʕa] They broadcast the news on the radio. تزَحلَق بِقشِر مُوز [dzaħlag bigišir mu:z] He slipped on a banana peel. إختِنَق بِعَظم سِمَك [ʔixtinag bʕaðum simač] He choked on a fish bone. رُوح بَيش ما يِعجبَك [ru:ħ bi:š ma: yiʕijbak] Go any way you want. (by redundant use of • **5.** for (price) – أبِيعهُم الدَّرزَن بِعِشرِين فِلِس [ʔabi:ʕhum ʔaddarzan bʕiʃri:n filis] I sell them for twenty fils a dozen. شقَدّ دِفَعِتلَه بَالسَّيّارَة؟ [šgadd difaʕitlah bissayya:ra?] How much did you pay him for the car? أخَذِتها بِبَلاش [ʔaxaðitha bibala:š] I got it for free. هَالثُّوب بيش؟ [haθθu:b biyš?] How much is this shirt? راح أشترِيها بَيش ما يقُول [ra:ħ ʔaštri:ha bi:š ma: yigu:l] I'll buy it for whatever he says. • **6.** by – فِرقَتنا غِلبَتهُم بِخَمِس نُقاط أزيَد [firqatna ɣilbathum bxamis nuqa:ṭ ʔazyad] Our team beat them by five points. آنِي أكبَر مِن أخُويَا بِخَمس سنِين [ʔa:ni ʔakbar min ʔaxu:ya bxams sni:n] I'm five years older than my brother. أضرُب خَمسَة بِستَّة [ʔuðrub xamsa bsitta] Multiply five by six. مَساحَة هَالغُرفَة سِتّ أمتار بِخَمسَة [masa:ħat halɣurfa sitt ʔamta:r bixamsa] The area of this room is six meters by five. • **7.** per – شقَدّ تاخُذ بِاليُوم؟ [šgadd ta:xuð bilyu:m?] How much do you get a day? أصرُف مِيَّة دِينار بِالشَّهَر [ʔaṣruf miyyat dina:r biššahar] I spend a hundred dinars a month. أشُوفهُم مَرَّة بِالسَّنَة [ʔašu:fhum marra bissana] I see them once a year. إبلَع ثلَث حَبّات بِاليُوم [ʔiblaʕ tlaθ ħabba:t bilyu:m] Take three pills a day. • **8.** in the condition or state of (frequently paraphrases an English adverb) – يَالله بِالعَجَل [yallah bilʕajal] Come on, make it snappy! جا بسُرعَة [ja: bsurʕa] He came in a hurry. إلبِسَه بِالعافيَة [ʔilibsah bilʕa:fya] Wear it in health. بِالخير، إن شاء الله [bilxi:r, ʔinša:llah] Hope you have good luck. شِفتَه بِالصِّدفَة [šiftah biṣṣidfa] I saw him by accident. ماكُو أحَّد بِقُوتَه [ma:ku ʔaħħad biquwwtah] There's no one with his strength. • **9.** (as a particle of oath, approx.:) by – بدِينَك، آنِي قِتلَك هِيكِي؟ [bdi:nak, ʔa:ni gitlak hi:či?] By your religion, did I tell you that? بِشَرَفِي، آنِي ما أعُرفَه [bišarafi, ʔa:ni ma: ʔaʕurfah] On my honor, I don't know him.

بِلا ما [bila maː] *subordinating conjunction:* • **1.** (conj.) without, unless – راح أَقُلَّك بَلا ما تِسأَل [raːħ ʔagullak bala maː tisʔal] I'll tell you without your asking. مَرَّت أَيّام بَلا ما نِسمَع مِنَّه [marrat ʔayyaːm bala maː nismaʕ minnah] Days passed without our hearing from him. ما تِقدَر تسُوق بَلا ما تِتعَلَّم سِياقَة [maː tigdar tsuːq bala maː titʕallam siyaːqa] You can't drive unless you take driving lessons.

ب ء

باء [baːʔ] *n:* • **1.** name of the letter

ب ء ب ء

بُؤبُؤ [buʔbuʔ] *n:* • **1.** pupil (of the eye)

ب ء ر

بُؤرَة [buʔra] *n:* بُؤَر [buʔar] *pl:* • **1.** focal point

بُؤرِي [buʔri] *adj:* • **1.** focal – طُول بُؤرِي [ṭuːl buʔri] focal length.

ب ء س

بَأس، لا بَأس [baʔs, laː baʔs] *n:* • **1.** no objection – لا بَأس. خُذها [laː baʔs. xuðha] No objections. Take it. • **2.** not bad – صِحّتَه لا بَأس بِيها [ṣiħħtah laː baʔs biːha] His health is pretty good. لا بَأس بِيه، لَكِن ما يِسوَى رُبُع دِينار [laː baʔs biːh, laːkin maː yiswaː rubuʕ dinaːr] It's all right, but it's not worth a quarter dinar.

بُؤس [buʔs] *n:* • **1.** misery, wretchedness

بائِس [baːʔis] *adj:* • **1.** wretched, miserable

ب ب ت و ت ي

بِبِتُوتِي [bibituːti] *n:* بِبِتُوتِيّات [bibituːtiyyaːt] *pl:* • **1.** parrot

ب ب س

بِيبسِي [biːbsi] *n:* • **1.** pepsi

ب ب غ ء

بَبَغاء [babaɣaːʔ] *n:* بَبَغاءات [babaɣaːʔaːt] *pl:* • **1.** parrot

ب ب ل

بابِل [baːbil] *n:* • **1.** Babylon

بابِلِي [baːbili] *adj:* • **1.** Babylonian • **2.** a Babylonian

ب ب م ت و

بِبِمَتُّو [bibimattu] *n:* بِبِمَتُّوات [bibimattuwaːt] *pl:* • **1.** parrot

ب ب ن ج

بابُونَّج [baːbuːnnag] *n:* • **1.** camomile (bot.)

ب ب و ج

بابُوج [baːbuːǰ] *n:* بوابِيج [bwaːbiːǰ] *pl:* • **1.** slipper, a sandal-like slipper worn mostly by women

ب ب و ر

بابُور [baːbuːr] *n:* بابُورات، بوابِير [baːbuːraːt, bwaːbiːr] *pl:* • **1.** a long cigarette holder, consisting of two types; one in which the cigarette fits upright, and one in which it fits lengthwise. Often decorated with engraving, it is peculiar to the rural North • **2.** opium pipe – أَبُو بابُور، شَرّاب بابُور [ʔabu baːpuːr, šarraːb baːpuːr] dope addict.

ب ت ت [1]

بَتّ [batt] *v:* • **1.** to decide – المُدِير بَعَد ما بَتّ بِقَضِيتَك [ʔilmudiːr baʕad maː batt biqaðiːtak] The director hasn't yet decided on your case. المَوضُوع بَعَد ما مَبتُوت بِيه [ʔilmawðuːʕ baʕad maː mabtuːt biːh] The matter still hasn't been decided upon.

بُتَّة [putta] *n:* • **1.** an expensive sort of iridescent, silk fabric

باتّ [baːtt] *adj:* • **1.** definite, decided, absolute – جَواب باتّ [ǰawaːb baːtt] definite answer. مَنِع باتّ [maniʕ baːtt] categorical prohibition.

بَتاتاً [bataːtan] *adverbial:* • **1.** positively, absolutely, definitely, decidedly, categorically – التَّدخِين مَمنُوع بَتاتاً [ʔattadxiːn mamnuːʕ bataːtan] Smoking is absolutely forbidden.

ب ت ت [2]

بَتّ [batt] *n:* • **1.** luck, break – جاب خُوش بَتّ وَغِلَبهُم كُلّهُم [ǰaːb xuːš batt wɣilabhum kullhum] He had good luck and beat them all.

ب ت ت [3]

بَتّ [batt] *n:* بتُوت [btuːt] *pl:* • **1.** thin bracelet, usually worn several at a time

ب ت ر

بِتَر [bitar] *v:* • **1.** to cut off, sever – بِتَر قُمع الخيارَة بِالسِّكِّينَة [bitar gumʕ ʔilxyaːra bissičči:na] He chopped off the cucumber stem with the knife. جرُوخ القِطار بِترَت رِجلَيه [čruːx ʔilqiṭaːr bitrat rijlayh] The train wheels severed his legs. لا تِبتِر الحكايَة؛ قُلّ إلنا شصار [laː tibtir ʔilħčaːya; gull ʔilna ššaːr] Don't cut the story short; tell us what happened. • **2.** to amputate – الطَّبِيب بِتَر إيدَه [ʔiṭṭabiːb bitar ʔiːdah] The doctor amputated his arm.

بَتَّر [battar] *v:* • **1.** to chop off – بَتَّر ذيُول خَيلهُم حَتَّى يِنتِقِم مِنهُم [battar ðyuːl xiːlhum ħatta yintiqim minhum] He cut off their horses' tails to get revenge on them. • **2.** to flow steadily – اِنجِرحَت إيدَه بِالسِّكِّين وَالدَّم ظَلّ يبَتِّر [ʔinǰirħat ʔiːdah bissičči:n widdamm ðall ybattir] His hand got cut on the knife and the blood kept flowing.

اِنبِتَر [ʔinbitar] *v:* • **1.** to be cut off, be severed – إيدَه اِنبِترَت بِالحادِث [ʔiːdah ʔinbitrat bilħaːdiθ] His arm was severed in the accident.

بَتِر [batir] *n:* • **1.** cutting off, severance
أبتَر [ʔabtar] *adj:* • **1.** having a bobbed, docked, or clipped tail – كَلِب أبتَر [čalib ʔabtar] dog with a bobbed tail.
بَتّار [batta:r] *adj:* • **1.** sharp – هَالسَّيف صارلَه بِعائِلتِي مِيَّة سَنَة وَبَعدَه لهَسَّة بَتّار [hassayf ṣa:rlah bʕa:ʔilti miyyat sana wbaʕdah lhassa batta:r] This sword has been in my family a hundred years and it's still sharp as a razor. لسانَه بَتّار [lsa:nah batta:r] His tongue is sharp.
مبتَّر [mbattar] *adj:* • **1.** cut off, severed • **2.** cut off, removed, severed, amputated
مَبتُور [mabtu:r] *adj:* • **1.** amputated, cut off • **2.** pruned, lopped off, removed

ب ت ر ي
باترِي [pa:tri] *n:* باترِيّات [pa:triyya:t] *pl:* • **1.** battery

ب ت ن
بَيتُونَة [baytu:na] *n:* • **1.** attic (a small room)

ب ت و
بَتُو [patu] *n:* بَتُووات [patuwa:t] *pl:* • **1.** blanket

ب ت ي ت
بُتَيتَة [putayta] *n:* • **1.** (coll.) potato(es)
بُتَيتايَة [putayta:ya] *n:* بُتَيتايات [putaytaya:t] *pl:* • **1.** potato

ب ث ث
بَثّ [baθθ] *v:* • **1.** to spread, tell (a secret) – لا تِحكِيلَه القُصَّة، تَرَة يبِثها بين النّاس [la: tiħči:lah ʔilquṣṣa, tara ybiθθha bi:n ʔinna:s] Don't tell him the story or he'll spread it around. • **2.** to broadcast, transmit – مَحَطَّة بَغداد تبِثّ عَلَى مَوجتَين [maħaṭṭat baɣda:d tbiθθ ʕala mawijtayn] The Baghdad station transmits on two wave lengths.
بَثّ [baθθ] *n:* • **1.** broadcast

ب ث ل
بِثِل [biθil] *n:* • **1.** (tea) leaves • **2.** (coffee) grounds

ب ج
باجَة [pa:ča] *n:* باجات [pa:ča:t] *pl:* • **1.** leg, calf of the leg • **2.** a stew made of meat from the head, feet, stomach, and neck of an animal
باجَجِي [pa:čači] *n:* باجَجِيَّة [pa:čačiyya] *pl:* • **1.** a man who cooks and serves the heads of sheep

ب ج ح
تبَجَّح [tbajjaħ] *v:* • **1.** to boast • **2.** to boast, brag, vaunt
تَبَجُّح [tabajjuħ] *n:* • **1.** bragging, boasting
مِتبَجِّح [mitbajjiħ] *adj:* • **1.** bragger, braggart

ب ج غ
بَجَغ [bajaɣ] *n:* بَجَغات [bajaɣa:t] *pl:* • **1.** good-looking young man, pretty boy. • **2.** jack, knave (in cards).

ب ج ل
بِجَامَة [bajal] *n:* بِجَامَات [bija:ma:t] *pl:* • **1.** a mild form of syphilis causing sores on the belly

ب ج م
بِجَامَة [bija:ma] *n:* بِجَامَات [bija:ma:t] *pl:* • **1.** pajamas

ب ج ي
باجِي [ba:ji] *n:* باجِيّات [ba:jiyya:t] *pl:* • **1.** fem. a close friend (among women), also a polite term of address among women not related by blood
باجِيَّة [ba:jiyya] *n:* • **1.** whore • **2.** elder sister, aunt (used generally for adult women)

ب ح ب ح
بَحبَح [baħbaħ] *v:* • **1.** to prosper, be prosperous – هَذا بَحبَح أثناء الحَرب [ha:ða baħbaħ ʔaθna:ʔ ʔilħarb] He prospered during the war. مبَحبِح لأنّ يِشتُغل ويّا عَشِر بَنات [mbaħbiħ liʔann yištuɣul wiyya ʕašir bana:t] He's in clover since he's working with ten girls. • **2.** to enjoy oneself, have a good time – بَحبِح، الله رَبَّك [baħbiħ, ʔallah rabbak] Enjoy yourself, God's taking care of you. تبَحبَح بِهالشُّغُل السَّهل [tbaħbaħ bhaššuɣul ʔissahil] He enjoyed himself with that easy job.
بَحبُوح [baħbu:ħ] *adj:* • **1.** merry
مبَحبَح [mbaħbaħ] *adj:* • **1.** prosperous, well-to-do – مَلعُون مبَحبِح، دَيحَصِّل عَشِر دَنانِير بِاليُوم [malʕu:n mbaħbiħ, dayħaṣṣil ʕašir dana:ni:r bilyu:m] The prosperous son of a gun, he's making ten dinars a day.

ب ح ت
بَحت [baħt] *adj:* • **1.** pure, unadulterated, sheer – هَذا كِذِب بَحت [ha:ða čiðib baħt] That's pure lies. هاي لِمَنفَعتَك الشَّخصِيَّة البَحتَة [ha:y limanfaʕtak ʔiššaxṣiyya ʔalbaħta] That's for your own personal benefit. الحَقِيقَة البَحتَة [ʔilħaqi:qa ʔalbaħta] the unadulterated truth.

ب ح ث
بِحَث [biħaθ] *v:* • **1.** to look, search – الشُّرطَة دَتِبحَث عَنَّك [ʔiššurṭa datibħaθ ʕannak] The police are looking for you. بِحَث بالغُرفَة وَما لِقَى شِي [biħaθ bilɣurfa wama: liga: ši] He searched the room and didn't find anything. • **2.** to study, examine, investigate – الوِزارَة دَتِبحَث مَوقِفنا بِهالمُشكِلَة [ʔilwiza:ra datibħaθ mawqifna bihalmuškila] The cabinet's studying our stand on this problem. • **3.** to discuss – بِحَثناها ويّا المُدِير [biħaθna:ha wiyya ʔilmudi:r] We discussed it with the

director. • **4.** to scratch, dig – الدِّجاج دَيبحَث بِالحَدِيقَة [ʔiddiǰa:ǰ dayibħaθ bilħadi:qa] The chickens are scratching in the garden.
باحَث [ba:ħaθ] *v:* • **1.** to talk to, consult with, confer with – مُمَثِّلنا باحَث مُمَثِّل الشَّرِكَة حَول زِيادَة الأُجُور [mumaθθilna ba:ħaθ mumaθθil ʔiššarika ħawil ziya:dat ʔilʔuǰu:r] Our representative talked to the company representative about the pay raise.
تباحَث [tba:ħaθ] *v:* • **1.** to confer, discuss together – راح نِتباحَث بِالقَضِيَّة [ra:ħ nitba:ħaθ bilqaðiyya] We're going to confer on the matter.
بَحِث [baħiθ] *n:* بُحُوث، أبحاث [buħu:θ, ʔabħa:θ] *pl:* • **1.** research – بَحِث عِلمِي [baħiθ ʕilmi] scientific research. • **2.** report, paper – قَدَّم بَحِث بالمُؤتَمَر [qaddam baħiθ bilmuʔtamar] He presented a paper at the conference.
تَباحُث [taba:ħuθ] *n:* • **1.** conferring, discussing
مُباحَثَة [muba:ħaθa] *n:* مُباحَثات [muba:ħaθa:t] *pl:* • **1.** talk, conference, negotiation
باحِث [ba:ħiθ] *n:* • **1.** researching

ب ح ح

بَحّ [baħħ] *v:* • **1.** to be or become hoarse, husky, harsh – حِسِّي بَحّ مِن العِياط [ħissi baħħ min ʔilʕiya:ṭ] My voice got hoarse from shouting.
اِنبَحّ [ʔinbaħħ] *v:* • **1.** to be hoarse
بَحَّة [baħħa] *n:* • **1.** hoarseness
مَبحُوح [mabħu:ħ] *adj:* • **1.** hoarse – شبِيك؟ حِسَّك مَبحُوح [šbi:k? ħissak mabħu:ħ] What's the matter? your voice's hoarse!

ب ح ر

بَحَّر [baħħar] *v:* • **1.** to look closely, look carefully – بَحِّر بِهالرَّسِم وقُلِّي مِنُو هَالمَرَة [baħħir bharrasim wgulli minu halmara] Examine this picture closely and tell me who this woman is.
أبحَر [ʔabħar] *v:* • **1.** to sail, put to sea – الباخِرَة تِبحِر يوم الإثنين الصُّبُح [ʔilba:xira tibħir yu:m ʔilʔiθni:n ʔiṣṣubuħ] The ship sails Monday morning.
تبَحَّر [tbaħħar] *v:* same as بَحَّر • **1.** to examine – ماكُو حاجَة تِتبَحَّر بيه هالقَدّ أَنَكِّدلَك أصله [ma:ku ħa:ǰa titbaxxar bi:h halgadd. ʔaʔakkidlak ʔaṣlu] No need to examine it so closely. I assure you it is genuine.
بَحَر [baħar] *n:* أبحُر، بِحار، بُحُور [ʔabħur, bħa:r, bħu:r] *pl:* • **1.** sea – الكِيمِياء بَحَر؛ مَحَّد يِقدَر يِختِمها [ʔilki:miya baħar; maħħad yigdar yixtimha] Chemistry is like a sea; no one can know it all.
بَحّار [baħħa:r] *n:* بَحّارَة [baħħa:ra] *pl:* • **1.** sailor
بَحرِيَّة [baħriyya] *n:* بَحريّات [baħriyya:t] *pl:* • **1.** navy
بُحَيرَة [buħayra] *n:* بُحَيرات [buħayra:t] *pl:* • **1.** lake
البَحرَين [ʔilbaħri:n, ʔilbaħrayn] *n:* • **1.** Bahrain
بَحرِي [baħri] *adj:* • **1.** sea, marine – حَيوان بَحرِي [ħaywa:n baħri] marine animal. • **2.** naval – ضابُط بَحرِي [ða:buṭ baħri] naval officer.
متبَحِّر [mitbaħħir] *adj:* • **1.** experienced, familiar – مِتبَحِّر بِفَرعَه [mitbaħħir bifarʕah] He's thoroughly familiar with his specialty.
بَحراني [baħra:ni] *adj:* بحارنَة [bħa:rna] *pl:* • **1.** Bahraini, from Bahrain • **2.** a Bahraini

ب ح ل ق

بَحلَق [baħlaq] *v:* • **1.** to stare – لِيش دَتبَحلِق بوِجهِي؟ [li:š datbaħliq bwičči?] Why are you staring at me? مِن شاف أَبُو المِيَّة، عَينَه بَحلقَت [min ša:f ʔabu ʔilmiyya, ʕaynah baħliqat] When he saw the hundred dinar bill, his eyes opened wide.
بَحلَقَة [baħlaqa] *n:* • **1.** gaze
مبَحلِق [mbaħliq] *adj:* • **1.** staring

ب خ ت

بَخَت [baxat] *n:* • **1.** luck – شلُون بَخَت عِندَه! كُلّما يلعَب، يِربَح [šlu:n baxat ʕindah! kullma: yilʕab, yirbaħ] What luck he has! Every time he plays, he wins. آني بِبَختَك؛ لا تُضرُبنِي [ʔa:ni bbaxtak; la: tuðrubni] I'm at your mercy; don't hit me! ببَختَك! توَنَّس [bbaxtak! twannas] You lucky guy! Have a good time! ببَختَك! آني قِلِت فَدّ شِي ما زَين؟ [bbaxtak! ʔa:ni gilit fadd ši ma: zayn?] Now I ask you! Did I say anything wrong? بِبَخت الله، فُكّني. عِندِي عَشِر جهال [bbaxt ʔallah, fukkni. ʕindi ʕašir ǰha:l] For the love of God, let me go! I have ten kids. عَلَى بَختَك؛ آني أَقُول هِيكِي شِي؟ [ʕala baxtak; ʔa:ni ʔagu:l hi:či ši?] By your conscience; would I say such a thing? عَلَى بَختَك؛ النَّهار كُلَّه ما أَكَلت [ʕala baxtak; ʔinnaha:r kullah ma: ʔakalt] Have a heart, I haven't eaten all day. عَلَى بَختَك! شلُون راح أَطَعِّم الجِّهال؟ [ʕala baxtak! šlu:n ra:ħ ʔaṭaʕʕum ʔiǰǰiha:l?] My God! How am I going to feed the kids? عَلَى بَختَك! المَسكِين! شوَقِت مات؟ [ʕala baxtak! ʔilmaski:n! šwakit ma:t?] For God's sake! The poor guy! When did he die? عَلَى بَختَك؛ البانزِين خِلَص [ʕala baxtak;ʔilbanzi:n xilaṣ] Now what do we do? We're out of gas.
بُختَة [puxta] *n:* • **1.** (invar.) mush – شدَعوَة طُبَختِي الأَكِل هَالقَدّ؟ صايِر بُختَة [šdaʕwa ṭubaxti ʔilʔakil halgadd? ṣa:yir puxta] Why'd you cook the food so much? It's gotten mushy. صار بُختَة مِن التَّعَب [ṣa:r puxta min ʔittaʕab] He got dead tired.
مَبخُوت [mabxu:t] *adj:* • **1.** fortunate, lucky • **2.** (as *n:*) a lucky person

ب خ ت ر

تبَختَر [tbaxtar] *v:* • **1.** to strut – يِتبَختَر بمَشِيتَه [yitbaxtar bmaši:tah] He struts when he walks.
بَختَرَة [baxtara] *n:* • **1.** strutting

ب خ خ

بَخّ [baxx] *v:* • **1.** to spray, sprinkle – شوَيَّة ماي عالثُّوب قَبُل ما تضرُبَه أُوتِي [šwayya ma:y ʕaθθu:b gabul ma: ðurbah ʔu:ti] Sprinkle a little water on the shirt before you iron it. بُخّ الثَّمَن بِشوَيَّة مَيّ

[buxx ʔittimman bšwayyat mayy] Sprinkle the rice with a little water.
بَخّ [baxx] *n:* • **1.** spraying

ب خ ر

بَخَّر [baxxar] *v:* • **1.** to vaporize, evaporate – الشَّمِس بِالصَّيف تبَخِّر هوايَة ماي مِن البُحَيرَة [ʔiššamis bişṣayf tbaxxir hwa:ya ma:y min ʔilbuħayra] The sun evaporates a lot of water from the lake in the summer. • **2.** to disinfect, fumigate – بَخِّرَوا التَّمُر حَتَّى يصَدِّرُوه [baxxiraw ʔittamur ħatta yṣaddru:h] They fumigated the dates in order to export them. • **3.** to expose to burning incense – بَخِّرَوا الغُرفَة لِأَنّ الشَّيخ عِندَه خُطّار [baxxiraw ʔilɣurfa liʔann ʔašši:x ʕindah xuṭṭa:r] They burned incense in the room because the chief is having guests. بَخِّرَوا لِلمَرِيض حَتَّى يطُردُون الشِّيطان [baxxiraw lilmari:ḍ ħatta yṭurdu:n ʔišši:ṭa:n] They burned incense for the sick man in order to chase away the Evil One.
تبَخَّر [tbaxxar] *v:* • **1.** to evaporate – المَيّ يِتبَخَّر بالحَرارَة [ʔilmayy yitbaxxar bilħara:ra] Water evaporates with the heat. • **2.** to disappear, evaporate – قَبُل ما أَخُشّ لِلإمتِحان، مَعلُوماتِي كُلّها تبَخّرَت [gabul ma: ʔaxušš lilʔimtiħa:n, maʕlu:ma:ti kullha tbaxxrat] Before I went in for the exam, my knowledge all disappeared. هَسَّة كان هنا؛ عَبالَك تبَخَّر [hassa ča:n hna; ʕaba:lak tbaxxar] He was just here; looks as if he vanished into thin air.
بُخار [buxa:r] *n:* • **1.** steam • **2.** fumes, vapor
بُخُور [buxu:r] *n:* • **1.** incense
تَبَخُّر [tabaxxur] *n:* • **1.** evaporation
بخارَة [bxa:ra] *n:* • **1.** a variety of small preserved plum, mostly imported from Afghanistan or Iran
مَبخَرَة [mabxara] *n:* مَباخِر [maba:xir] *pl:* • **1.** censer
باخِرَة [ba:xira] *n:* بَواخِر [bawa:xir] *pl:* • **1.** He went by steamer • **2.** steamer, steamship – راح بِالباخِرَة [ra:ħ bilba:xira] He went by steamer.
تَبخِير [tabxi:r] *n:* • **1.** steaming
بُخارِي [buxa:ri] *adj:* • **1.** steam, steam-driven – مَكِينَة بُخارِيَّة [maki:na buxa:riyya] steam engine.

ب خ ش ش

بَخشَش [baxšaš] *v:* • **1.** to give a tip
بَخشِيش [baxši:š] *n:* • **1.** tip, gratuity

ب خ ل

بِخَل [bixal] *v:* • **1.** to be stingy, niggardly, miserly – إِنتَ شلُون صَدِيق! تِبخَل عَلَيّا بِهَالكامِيرا اللّي ما تِسوَى [ʔinta šlu:n ṣadi:q! tibxal ʕalayya bhalkamira ʔilli ma: tiswa:] Some friend you are! You're being stingy with me about this worthless camera. لا تِبخَل عَلَى نَفسَك بالأَشياء الضَّرُورِيَّة [la: tibxal ʕala nafsak bilʔašya:ʔ ʔiððaru:riyya] Don't stint yourself on the necessities. لا تِبخَل علينا بِزيارتَك [la: tibxal ʕali:na bziya:rtak] Don't be stingy with your visits to us.
بُخُل [buxul] *n:* • **1.** stinginess
بَخِيل [baxi:l] *adj:* بُخَلاء [buxala:ʔ] *pl:* • **1.** stingy, miserly, niggardly • **2.** (as *n:*) a stingy person
أَبخَل [ʔabxal] *comparative adjective:* • **1.** more or most stingy, miserly

ب د ء

بِدا، بِدَء [bida:, bidaʔ] *v:* • **1.** to begin, start – الفِلِم بِدا قَبُل خَمِس دَقايِق [ʔilfilim bida: gabul xamis daqa:yiq] The film started five minutes ago.
بَدَّى [badda:] *v:* • **1.** to give precedence or priority to – يبَدِّي الخُطّار عَلَى نَفسَه [ybaddi ʔilxuṭṭa:r ʕala nafsah] He puts the guests before himself. يبَدِّي صَدِيقَه عَلَى أَخُوه [ybaddi ṣadi:qah ʕala ʔaxu:h] He prefers his friend over his brother.
انبِدا [ʔinbida:] *v:* • **1.** to begin • **2.** to get started
ابتِدا [ʔibtida:] *v:* • **1.** to begin, start – شوَقِت راح نِبتِدِي نِشتُغُل؟ [šwakit ra:ħ nibtidi ništuɣul?] When are we going to start working?
بَدوَة [badwa] *n:* بَدوات [badwa:t] *pl:* • **1.** beginning, start
مَبدَأ [mabdaʔ] *n:* مَبادِئ [maba:diʔ] *pl:* • **1.** principle • **2.** doctrine, ideology • **3.** fundamentals, guiding principles – مَبادِئ القِراءَة [maba:diʔ ʔilqira:ʔa] fundamentals of reading. • **4.** ideology – المَبادِئ الهَدّامَة [ʔilmaba:diʔ ʔilhadda:ma] the subversive ideology.
بِدايَة [bida:ya] *n:* بِدايات [bida:ya:t] *pl:* • **1.** beginning, start – at first, in the beginning – مَحكَمَة البِدايَة [maħkamat ʔilbida:ya] court of first instance, ranking above مَحكَمَة الصُّلُح [maħkamat ʔaṣṣuluħ] and handling suits and crimes involving money.
بَداءَة [bada:ʔa] *n:* • **1.** formal variant of بِدايَة
مُبتَدَى [mubtada:] *n:* • **1.** subject of an equational sentence. (gram.)
اِبتِدائِيَّة [ʔibtida:ʔiyya] *n:* • **1.** primary school
اِبتِداءً مِن [ʔibtida:ʔan min] *n:* • **1.** starting with, beginning from, as of – اِبتِداءً مِن باكِر، الدَّوام راح يِبدِي ساعَة ثمانيَة [ʔibtida:ʔan min ba:čir, ʔiddawa:m ra:ħ yibdi sa:ʕa θma:nya] As of tomorrow, office hours will commence at eight o'clock. مَدرَسَة اِبتِدائِيَّة [madrasa ʔibtida:ʔiyya] elementary school.
بادِئ [ba:diʔ] *adj:* • **1.** beginning – ببادِئ الأَمُر، ما قِبَل [bba:diʔ ʔilʔamur, ma: qibal] At first, he wouldn't agree.
مَبدَئِي [mabdaʔi] *adj:* • **1.** initial, preliminary – حَلّ مَبدَئِي [ħall mabdaʔi] initial solution, temporary solution. دِراسَة مَبدَئِيَّة [dira:sa mabdaʔiyya] preliminary study. بِصُورَة مَبدَئِيَّة [bṣu:ra mabdaʔiyya] provisionally, tentatively. وافَق بِصُورَة مَبدَئِيَّة، لَكِن بَعدين غَيَّر رَأيَه [wa:faq bṣu:ra mabdaʔiyya, la:kin baʕdi:n ɣayyar raʔyah] He agreed tentatively, but then he changed his mind. بِصُورَة مَبدَئِيَّة، ما عِندِي مانِع، لَكِن يِمكِن تِطلَع مَشاكِل

[bṣu:ra mabdaʔiyya, ma: ʕindi ma:niʕ, la:kin yimkin titlaʕ maša:kil] Offhand, I have no objections, but problems may arise.
بدائي [bida:ʔi] *adj:* • **1.** primitive – عِيشَة بِدائِيَّة [ʕi:ša bida:ʔiyya] a primitive way of life.
مُبتَدِئ [mubtadiʔ] *adj:* مُبتَدِئين [mubtadiʔi:n] *pl:* • **1.** beginner, novice
اِبتِدائي [ʔibtidiʔi] *adj:* • **1.** primary, initial
مَبدَئِيّاً [mabdaʔiyyan] *adverbial:* • **1.** initially, originally, as a beginning, to start with – صِرَفنا مِيَّة أَلِف دِينار مَبدَئِيّاً عَلَى بِناء أُتِيلات بِالشِّمال [ṣirafna miyyat ʔalif dina:r mabdaʔiyyan ʕala bina:ʔ ʔuti:la:t biššima:l] We spent one hundred thousand dinars initially for building hotels in the North. • **2.** provisionally, tentatively – وافَق مَبدَئِيّاً لَكِن بَعدين غَيَّر رأيَه [wa:faq mabdaʔiyyan la:kin baʕdi:n ɣayyar raʔyah] He agreed provisionally but then changed his mind. الحُكُومَة خَصِّصَت مِليون دِينار مَبدَئِيّاً، إِلَى أَن يِجتِمِع المَجلِس [ʔilħuku:ma xaṣṣiṣat milyu:n dina:r mabdaʔiyyan, ʔila ʔan yijtimiʕ ʔilmajlis] The government appropriated a million dinars provisionally till parliament convenes.

ب د د

بَدَّد [baddad] *v:* • **1.** to waste, squander – بَدِّدَوا كُلّ جُهُودهُم [baddidaw kull juhu:dhum] They wasted all their efforts. بَدَّد فلُوسَه [baddad flu:sah] He squandered his money.
بَدَّى [badda:] *v:* • **1.** to spill – بَدَّى المَيّ عالزُّولِيَّة [badda: ʔilmayy ʕazzu:liyya] He spilled the water on the carpet.
تبَدَّى [tbadda:] *v:* • **1.** to be spilled – شلُون تبَدَّى الشَّكَر؟ [šlu:n tbadda: ʔiššakar?] How did the sugar get spilled?
اِستَبَدّ [ʔistabadd] *v:* • **1.** to act arbitrarily, high-handedly – المُدِير اِستِبَدّ بِالمُوَظَّفِين [ʔilmudi:r ʔistibadd bilmuwaððafi:n] The director acted arbitrarily with the employees. اِستِبَدّ بِرَأيَه وَما توَصَّلنا إِلَى نَتِيجَة [ʔistibadd braʔyah wma twaṣṣalna ʔila nati:ja] He was obstinate and we didn't reach any conclusion. • **2.** to act despotically, tyrannically – الدِّكتاتُور اِستِبَدّ بِحُكمَه [ʔiddiktatu:r ʔistibadd biħukmah] The dictator was a tyrant in his rule.
تَبدِيد [tabdi:d] *n:* • **1.** waste
اِستِبداد [ʔistibda:d] *n:* • **1.** arbitrariness • **2.** despotism
مِستِبِدّ [mistibidd] *adj:* • **1.** arbitrary, high-handed, tyrannical, despotic – المُدِير السّابِق كان مِستِبِدّ [ʔilmudi:r ʔissa:biq ča:n mistibidd] The former director was highhanded. مَلِك مِستِبِدّ [malik mistibidd] a tyrannical king. هُوَّ مِستِبِدّ بِرَأيَه [huwwa mistibidd braʔyah] He's opinionated. • **2.** (as *n:*) a despot, a tyrant
اِستِبدادي [ʔistibda:di] *adj:* • **1.** despotic – حُكُم اِستِبدادي [ħukum ʔistibda:di] despotic rule.
بُدّ [budd] *n:* • **1.** way out, escape (usually in set phrases as:) – لا بُدّ نقُلَّه [la: budd ngullah] We have no choice but to tell him. لازِم تِجُون مِن كُلّ وَلا بُدّ [la:zim tiju:n min kull wala: budd] You absolutely must come without fail. مِن كُلّ بُدّ [min kull budd] in any case, under any circumstances, without fail. أَرِيدَك تِحكِي وِيّا المُدِير اليُوم مِن كُلّ بُدّ [ʔari:dak tiħči wiyya ʔilmudi:r ʔilyu:m min kull budd] I want you to talk to the director today definitely.

ب د ر

تبادَر [tba:dar] *v:* • **1.** to initiate
بادِرَة [ba:dira] *n:* بَوادِر [bawa:dir] *pl:* • **1.** sign, omen – هاي بادرَة خير [ha:y ba:drat xi:r] That's a good sign. مُو خُوش بادرَة؛ ما دَيطِيعُون الأَوامِر [mu: xu:š ba:dra; ma: dayti:ʕu:n ʔilʔawa:mir] That's a bad sign; they're not obeying orders.
تَبادُر [taba:dur] *n:* • **1.** initiating
مُبادَرَة [muba:dara] *n:* مُبادَرات [muba:dara:t] *pl:* • **1.** initiative, unexpected action, idea
بَدِر [badir] *n:* • **1.** full moon – القُمَر بَدِر اللَّيلَة [ʔilgumar badir ʔillayla] The moon is full tonight. تزَوَّج وِحدَة مِثل البَدِر [dzawwaj wiħda miθl ʔalbadir] He married a girl pretty as the full moon.

ب د ع

بَدَّع [baddaʕ] *v:* • **1.** to achieve excellence, to excel, be outstanding – بَدَّعِت بِالإمتِحان [baddaʕit bilʔimtiħa:n] I did very well in the examination. الكُولچِي بَدَّع [ʔilgu:lči baddaʕ] The goalkeeper did an excellent job. هَذا صُدُق بَدَّع إبداع بهالصُّورَة [ha:ða ṣudug baddaʕ ʔibda:ʕ bhaṣṣu:ra] He really came up with something fine in this picture.
بِدعَة [bidʕa, budʕa] *n:* بِدَع [bidaʕ] *pl:* • **1.** (heretical) innovation
بَداعَة [bada:ʕa] *n:* • **1.** (invar.) an outstanding, amazing thing, a marvel, a wonder – كانَت طالعَة بَداعَة [ča:nat ṭa:lʕa bada:ʕa] She looked wonderful. بَداعَة! وَالله، يِستاهِل يصِير وَزِير [bada:ʕa! wallah, yista:hil yṣi:r wazi:r] Wonderful! He really deserves to be a minister. هَذا خَبَر بَداعَة [ha:ða xabar bada:ʕa] That's great news.
إِبداع [ʔibda:ʕ] *n:* • **1.** unique, wonderful achievement
بَدِيع [badi:ʕ] *adj:* • **1.** excellent, outstanding, wonderful, marvelous – شلُون مَنظَر بَدِيع [šlu:n manðar badi:ʕ] What a marvelous view!
مُبدِع [mubdiʕ] *adj:* • **1.** outstanding, exceptional, unique • **2.** outstanding person
أَبدَع [ʔabdaʕ] *comparative adjective:* • **1.** more or most outstanding, excellent, wonderful, amazing

ب د ق

بِدَق [bidag] *v:* • **1.** to be aware, to note – إِنتَ دَتِبدِق عالقَصِد مالَه؟ [ʔinta datibdig ʕalqaṣid ma:lah?] Are you aware of his intention? بادِق عَلَى هَالكِذِب؟ [ba:dig ʕala haččiðib?] Did you catch those lies? • **2.** to pay attention – إبدِق عَليه وشُوف شدَيِحكِي [ʔibdig ʕali:h wšu:f šdayiħči] Pay attention to him and see what he is saying. إذا ما تِبدقِلي، شلُون تِفتِهِم؟ [ʔiða ma: tibdigli, šlu:n tiftihim?] If you don't pay attention to me, how will you comprehend?

بِدَق [bidag] *v:* • **1.** to look at, eye (someone), pay special attention to

ب د ق ر

بادقِير [ba:dgi:r] *n:* بادقِيرات [ba:dgi:ra:t] *pl:* • **1.** air vent, air duct • **2.** chimney

ب د ل

بَدَّل [baddal] *v:* • **1.** to exchange, replace – أقدَر أبَدِّل هَالثُّوب؟ طِلَع صغَيِّر عَليّا [ʔagdar ʔabaddil haθθu:b? ṭilaʕ ṣɣayyir ʕalayya] Can I exchange this shirt? It's too small for me. أقدَر أبَدِّل هَالقَلَم بهَذا؟ [ʔagdar ʔabaddil halqalam bha:ða?] Can I exchange this pen for that one? الفِيتَر جِي بَدَّل بلَكَّين بسَيَّارتِي [ʔalfitarči baddal plakkayn bsayya:rti] The mechanic changed two spark plugs in my car. مِنُو بَدَّل القَبُّوط مالِي؟ [minu baddal ʔilqappu:ṭ ma:li?] Who switched overcoats with me? لازِم نبَدِّل هَالفَصِيل لِأنّ صارلَه بِالجَّبهَة مُدَّة طُوِيلَة [la:zim nbaddil halfaṣi:l liʔann ṣa:rlah bijjabha mudda ṭuwi:la] We've got to replace that platoon because they've been in the front lines a long time. • **2.** to change, alter – بَدِّلَوا مَوقع الجِّسِر [baddilaw mawqiʕ ʔijjisir] They changed the site of the bridge. هَالكَلِمَة تبَدِّل كُلّ مَعنى الجُّملَة [halkalima tbaddil kull maʕna: ʔijjumla] That word alters the whole meaning of the sentence. ما أدرِي شبَدَّلَه [ma: ʔadri šbaddalah] I don't know what changed him. • **3.** to change, change clothes, to get dressed – إذا ما طالِع بَعَد، لِيش ما تبَدِّل؟ [ʔiða ma: ṭa:liʕ baʕad, li:š ma: tbaddil?] If you're not going out again, why don't you change clothes? اِنتِظِرنِي حَتَّى أبَدِّل [ʔintiðirni ħatta ʔabaddil] Wait for me while I change. قُوم، بَدِّل. صار وَقِت المَدرَسَة [gu:m, baddil. ṣa:r wakit ʔilmadrasa] Get up; get dressed. It's time for school. يَالله، بَدِّل هدُومَك [yallah, baddil hdu:mak] Come on, get dressed. أبُويَا بَعدَه ما مبَدِّل. يِقُول "خَلِّي يِنتَظرُونِي" [ʔabu:ya baʕdah ma: mbaddil. yigu:l "xalli yintaðru:ni"] My father's not dressed yet. He says, 'Have them wait for me.' شُوف عَلِي شلُون مبَدِّل! طالِع فَلَّة [šu:f ʕali šlu:n mbaddil! ṭa:liʕ falla] Look at Ali, all dressed up! He looks sharp. شلُون حِلو مبَدِّل [šlu:n ħilw mbaddil] How nicely dressed he is! • **4.** to shift, switch, change – ما تِقدَر تِصعَد الجِّبَل إذا ما تبَدِّل عَالثّنَين [ma: tigdar tiṣʕad ʔijjibal ʔiða ma: tbaddil ʕaθθinayn] You won't be able to get up the mountain unless you shift into second. ما إفتِهَمت وَلا كِلمَة لِأنّ كُلّ ساع يبَدِّل مِن العَرَبِي لِلإنكِلِيزِي [ma: ʔiftihamit wala čilma liʔann kull sa:ʕ ybaddil min ʔilʕarabi lilʔingili:zi] I didn't understand a word because every moment he switches from Arabic to English.

بادَل [ba:dal] *v:* • **1.** to exchange, trade – لِيش أبادِل حصانِي بِحصانَك اللّي ما غِلَب أبَداً؟ [li:š ʔaba:dil ħṣa:ni biħṣa:nak ʔilli ma: ɣilab ʔabadan?] Why should I trade my horse for your horse which has never won? • **2.** to reciprocate – بادَلها الحُبّ [ba:dalha ʔalħubb] He returned her love.

تبَدَّل [tbaddal] *v:* • **1.** to be changed – رَقَم تَلَفونِي تبَدَّل [raqam talifu:ni tbaddal] My telephone number was changed.

تبادَل [tba:dal] *v:* • **1.** to exchange – الوَزِيرَين تبادلَوا الآراء حَول المَوضُوع [ʔilwazi:rayn tba:dlaw ʔalʔa:ra:ʔ ħawl ʔilmawðu:ʕ] The two ministers exchanged opinions on the case. تبادلَوا بِساعاتهُم [tba:dlaw bsa:ʕa:thum] They exchanged watches.

إستَبدَل [ʔistabdal] *v:* • **1.** to replace

بَدَل [badal] *n:* • **1.** substitute, alternate, replacement – ضَيَّع القَلَم مالِي وَإنطانِي هَذا بِبَدَلَه [ðayyaʕ ʔilqalam ma:li wʔinṭa:ni ha:ða bbadalah] He lost my pencil and gave me this in place of it. أنطِيك بَدَل القَلَم اللّي ضَيَّعِت لَك إيّاه [ʔanṭi:k badal ʔilqalam ʔilli ðayyaʕit lak ʔiyya:h] I'll give you a replacement for the pencil I lost. • **2.** compensation, reimbursement, recompense, allowance – بَدَل لَيالِي [badal laya:li] overnight travel allowance. • **3.** fee, rate, price – بَدَل الاشتِراك [badal ʔalʔištira:k] subscription rate. • **4.** in place of, instead of – هاك دِينارَين بَدَل كتابَك لِأنّ ضَيَّعتَه [ha:k dina:rayn badal kta:bak liʔann ðayyaʕtah] Here's two dinars in place of your book since I lost it.

بَدلَة [badla] *n:* بَدلات [badla:t] *pl:* • **1.** suit – بَدلَة رَسمِيَّة [badla rasmiyya] uniform. بَدلَة عَسكَرِيَّة [badla ʕaskariyya] military uniform.

بِدال، بَدَل [bida:l, badal] *n:* • **1.** in lieu of, in place of, in exchange for – أرِيد دِينار بِدال القَلَم اللّي كسَرتلِي إيّاه [ʔari:d dina:r bida:l ʔilqalam ʔilli ksaritli: ʔiyya:h] I want a dinar in exchange for the pen you broke. ماكُو طَماطَة بالسُّوق. شتِرِيد بِبدالهَا؟ [ma:ku ṭama:ṭa bissu:g. šitri:d bibda:lha?] There aren't any tomatoes in the market. What do you want in place of them? مالِي خُلُق. رُوح بِدالِي [ma:li xulug. ru:ħ bida:li] I don't feel well. Go in my place. ترِيد قَلَمِي؟ زِين، شتِنطِينِي بداله؟ [tri:d qalami? zi:n, štinṭi:ni bda:lah?] You want my pen? Okay, what'll you give me in exchange for it? الله بدالَك [ʔallah bda:lak] I wouldn't cheat you (lit., God is in your place).

بَدِيل [badi:l] *n:* • **1.** city, village • **2.** substitute

بَدّالَة [badda:la] *n:* بَدّالات [badda:la:t] *pl:* • **1.** telephone exchange • **2.** switchboard

تَبادُل [taba:dul] *n:* • **1.** exchange – تَبادُل الآراء [taba:dul ʔalʔa:ra:ʔ] exchange of opinions. تَبادُل إطلاق النّار [taba:dul ʔiṭla:q ʔinna:r] exchange of gunfire.

ب

تبديل [tabdi:l] *n:* • **1.** replacement • **2.** change, exchange
بَدَلاً مِن، بَدَلاً عَن [badalan min, badalan ʕan] *n:* • **1.** instead of – اِستَعمِل هَالدُّوا بَدَلاً مِن الدُّوا العَتيق [ʔistaʕmil hadduwa: badalan min ʔidduwa: ʔilʕati:g] Use this medicine instead of the old kind. هُوَّ راح بَدَلاً عَنِّي [huwwa ra:ħ badalan ʕanni] He went instead of me.
اِستِبدال [ʔistibda:l] *n:* • **1.** exchange, replacement • **2.** exchange • **3.** replacement
مبَدَّل [mbaddal] *adj:* • **1.** replaced, altered
بَدَلچي [badalči] *adj:* بَدَلچِيَّة [badalčiyya] *pl:* • **1.** man who has paid the fee to shorten his military service
مُتَبادَل [mutaba:dal] *adj:* • **1.** mutual
بَدَلما [badalma] *subordinating conjunction:* • **1.** instead of – بَدَل ما يساعِدني، عافني وَراح [badalma: ysa:ʕidni, ʕa:fni wra:ħ] Instead of helping me, he left me and went off.
بِدَل ما [bidal ma:] *subordinating conjunction:* • **1.** in exchange for (the fact that) – بِدال ما ساعَدتِني راح أَشتُغُل بِمُكانَك [bida:l ma: sa:ʕadtni ra:ħ ʔaštuɣul bmuka:nak] In exchange for your helping me, I'm going to work in your place. • **2.** instead of – بِدال ما تِلعَب، تَعال إدرُس [bida:l ma: tilʕab, taʕa:l ʔidrus] Instead of playing, come and study.

ب د م

بادَم [ba:dam] *n:* • **1.** (coll.) a variety of hard glazed cookie

ب د ن

بَدَن [badan] *n:* أَبدان [ʔabda:n] *pl:* • **1.** body, trunk, torso • **2.** physique – فَحِص بَدَن [fahiṣ badan] physical examination. طَبيب أَبدان [ṭabi:b ʔabda:n] general practitioner (commonly excluding eye, ear, nose, and throat).
بَدَني [badani] *adj:* • **1.** physical – رِياضَة بَدَنِيَّة [riya:ḍa badaniyya] physical exercise.

ب د ه

بَدِيهَة [badi:ha] *n:* • **1.** intuition
بَداهَة [bada:ha] *n:* • **1.** intuition
بَديهِيَّة [badi:hiyya] *n:* بَدِيهِيّات [badi:hiyya:t] *pl:* • **1.** axiom, self-evident fact • **2.** truism, platitude
بَديهي [badi:hi] *adj:* • **1.** self-evident, obvious – مَسأَلَة بَدِيهِيَّة [masʔala badi:hiyya] a self-evident matter. • **2.** naturally, obviously – بَديهي يعُرفَه لِأَنّ هاي شَغِلتَه [badi:hi yʕurfah liʔann ha:y šaɣiltah] Of course he knows it because that's his business.

ب د و [1]

أَبدَى [ʔabda:] *v:* • **1.** to express, utter, voice – تحِبّ تِبدِي رَأيَك بِالمَوضُوع؟ [tħibb tibdi raʔayak bilmawḍu:ʕ?] Do you want to express your opinion on the subject? أَبدَى رَغُبتَه بِشِراء البَيت [ʔabda: raɣubtah bšira:ʔ ʔilbayt] He expressed his desire to buy the house. • **2.** to offer – السُّلطات أَبدَت لِهُم كُلّ المُساعَدات المُمكِنَة [ʔissulṭa:t ʔabdat lihum kull ʔalmusa:ʕada:t ʔilmumkina] The authorities offered them all possible assistance.
بَداوَة [bada:wa] *n:* • **1.** Bedouinism, nomadism. People who live in the desert – حَياة البَداوَة تقَوِّي الأَجسام [ħaya:t ʔilbada:wa tqawwi ʔilʔajsa:m] The Bedouin life strengthens the body.
بادِيَة [ba:diyya] *n:* بَوادِي [bawa:di] *pl:* • **1.** desert
بَدوي [bidwi, bdi:wi, badawi] *adj:* • **1.** Bedouin, nomad, nomadic – خَيل بِدوِي [xayl bidwi] Bedouin horses. • **2.** a nomad, a Bedouin
بادي [ba:di] *adj:* • **1.** evident, apparent
بَدَوِيَّة [badawiyya] *n:* بَدَوِيّات [badawiyya:t] *pl:* • **1.** Bedouin woman or girl

ب د و [2]

بَدو [badw] *n:* • **1.** coll. Bedouins

ب د و س

بايدَوس [pa:ydu:s] *n:* • **1.** quitting time, closing time, time to stop work – ما تِقدَر تِشتِري طابِع. هَسَّة بايدُوس [ma: tigdar tištiri ṭa:biʕ. hassa pa:ydu:s] You can't buy any stamps. It's closing time.

ب ذ ء

بَذِيئ [baði:ʔ] *adj:* • **1.** foul, obscene, dirty – حَكِي بَذِيئ [ħači baði:ʔ] dirty talk. بَذِيئ اللِّسان [baði:ʔ ʔillisa:n] foul-mouthed.

ب ذ خ

بِذَخ [biðax] *v:* • **1.** to spend lavishly – يِبذِخ عَلَى وِلدَه هوايَة [yibðix ʕala wildah hwa:ya] He spends a lot on his sons. بِذَخ هوايَة بِالحَفلَة اللِّي سَوّاها لِلوَزير [biðax hwa:ya bilħafla ʔilli sawwa:ha lilwazi:r] He really put on the dog in the party he gave for the minister.
بَذِخ [baðix] *n:* • **1.** extravagance • **2.** splendor, high style
بَذّاخ [baðða:x] *adj:* بَذّاخِين [baðða:xi:n] *pl:* • **1.** spendthrift, wastrel

ب ذ ر

بِذَر [biðar] *v:* • **1.** to seed
بَذَّر [baððar] *v:* • **1.** to waste, squander – بَذَّر كُلّ فلُوسَه عالونسَة [baððar kull flu:sah ʕalwinsa] He squandered all his money on pleasure. • **2.** to go to seed – لازِم أَخَلِّي طَماطَة وِحدَة تبَذِّر لِلسَّنَة الجّايَة [la:zim ʔaxalli ṭama:ṭa wiħda tbaððir lissana ʔijja:yya] I have to let one tomato go to seed for next year.
تبَذَّر [tbaððar] *v:* • **1.** to be wasted – كُلّ جُهُودِي تبَذِّرَت [kull juhu:di tbaððirat] All my efforts were wasted.

اِنبِذَر [ʔinbiðar] *v:* • **1.** to be seeded • **2.** to be wasted
بَذِر [baðir] *n:* • **1.** (coll.) pl • **2.** coll. seed(s)
بَذرَة [baðra] *n:* بَذرات، بِذُور [baðra:t, biðu:r] *pl:* • **1.** seed
مُبَذِّر [mubaððir] *adj:* مُبَذِّرِين [mubaððiri:n] *pl:* • **1.** spend-thrift

ب ذ ل

بِذَل [biðal] *v:* • **1.** to give or spend freely – عِندَه اِستِعداد يِبذِل عَلَى أَصدِقائَه [ʕindah ʔistiʕda:d yibðil ʕala ʔaṣdiqa:ʔah] He's ready to spend freely on his friends. بِذَلِت كُلّ جُهدِي حَتَّى أَساعدَه [biðalit kull ǰuhdi ħatta ʔasa:ʕdah] I made every effort to help him. بِذَلت الغالِي وَالرِّخِيص بِسَبِيلَك [biðalt ʔilɣa:li wʔirrixi:ṣ bsabi:lak] I sacrificed everything for your sake.
تبَذَّل [tbaððal] *v:* • **1.** to debase, cheapen oneself, to display crude, vulgar traits – تبَذَّل بِأَواخِر أَيّامَه [tbaððal biʔawa:xir ʔayya:mah] He got vulgar in his old age. المُدِير مِتبَذِّل. تشُوفَه بالمايخانات ويّا القحاب [ʔilmudi:r mitbaððil. tšu:fah bilmayxa:na:t wiyya ʔilgħa:b] The director's degraded himself. You see him in the bars with prostitutes.
اِنبِذَل [ʔinbiðal] *v:* • **1.** to be exerted • **2.** to sacrifice one's self
بَذِل [baðil] *n:* • **1.** exerting, spending, extending
مِتبَذِّل [mitbaððil] *adj:* • **1.** vulgar, crude, cheap, debased
مَبذُول [mabðu:l] *adj:* • **1.** spent, given, sacrificed freely • **2.** plentiful, abundant, rife – هَالنَّوع مِن القُماش مَبذُول بالسُّوق [hannu:ʕ min ʔalquma:š mabðu:l bissu:g] This type of cloth is very plentiful in the market

ب ر [1]

بار [ba:r] *n:* بارات [ba:ra:t] *pl:* • **1.** bar, counter • **2.** bar, tavern

ب ر [2]

بارَة [pa:ra] *n:* بارات [pa:ra:t] *pl:* • **1.** the smallest unit of turkish money, hence, an insignificant, almost worthless thing – ما يِسوَى وَلا بارَة [ma: yiswa: wala pa:ra] It's not worth a red cent.

ب ر ء [1]

البارِي [ʔilba:ri] *adj:* • **1.** the Creator

ب ر ء [2]

بَرَّأ [barraʔ] *v:* • **1.** to clear, acquit, absolve – بَرِّتَه المَحكَمَة مِن الدَّعوتَين [barratah ʔilmaħkama min ʔiddaʕwtayn] The court cleared him of the two charges.
تبَرَّى [tbarra:] *v:* • **1.** to disassociate oneself – تبَرَّى مِن إبنَه بِالمَحكَمَة [tbarra: min ʔibnah bilmaħkama] He disowned his son in court. • **2.** to be acquitted, be cleared – عَلِي تبَرَّى لَكِن شَرِيكَه اِنحِكَم سَنتَين [ʕali tbarra: la:kin šari:kah ʔinħikam santayn] Ali was acquitted but his partner got two years.
بَراءَة [bara:ʔa] *n:* • **1.** innocence, guiltlessness – حُكم البَراءَة [ħukm ʔalbara:ʔa] acquittal decision. • **2.** guilelessness, naiveté • **3.** patent (on an invention)
تَبرِئَة [tabriya, tabriʔa] *n:* • **1.** acquittal – حِضَر المَحكَمَة وَطِلَع تَبرِيَة [ħiðar ʔilmaħkama wṭilaʕ tabriya] He went to court and came out a free man.
بَرِيء [bari:ʔ, bari:] *adj:* بَرِيئِين، أَبرِياء [bari:ʔi:n, ʔabriya:ʔ] *pl:* • **1.** guiltless, innocent – طِلَع بَرِيء [ṭilaʕ bari:ʔ] He turned out to be innocent. حكايَة بَرِيئَة [hča:ya bari:ʔa] an innocent remark.

ب ر ب خ

بُربُخ [burbux] *n:* بَرابِخ [bara:bix] *pl:* • **1.** drain, drainpipe • **2.** section of drainpipe

ب ر ب ر

بَربَر [barbar] *v:* • **1.** to jabber, prattle, chatter – صارلَه ساعَة يبَربِر [ṣa:rlah sa:ʕa ybarbir] He's been jabbering away for an hour.
بَربَرِي [barbari] *n:* بَرابِرَة [bara:bira] *pl:* • **1.** Berber • **2.** barbarian – جُيُوش بَربَرِيَّة [ǰuyu:š barbariyya] barbarian armies.
البَربَر [ʔilbarbar] *n:* • **1.** the Berbers
بَربَرِيَّة [barbariyya] *n:* • **1.** barbarianism, barbarism

ب ر ب ع

بَربَع [barbaʕ] *v:* • **1.** to thrive, prosper – الغَنَم راح تبَربِع بِهَالخَضار [ʔilɣanam ra:ħ tbarbiʕ bhalxaða:r] The sheep will thrive in this pasturage. بَربَع بِهالشُّغُل [barbaʕ bhaššuɣul] He prospered in that business. بَربِع! الله رَبَّك [barbiʕ! ʔallah rabbak] Enjoy yourself! God's taking care of you. • **2.** to soak, sop, dip, dunk – بَربِع الخُبزَة بالحَلِيب وَإنطِيها لِلطِّفِل [barbiʕ ʔilxubza bilħali:b waʔinṭi:ha liṭṭifil] Soak the piece of bread in milk and give it to the baby.
تبَربَع [tbarbaʕ] *v:* • **1.** to be soaked, sopped, dipped, dunked – الخُبزَة تبَربِعَت بِالشُّوربَة [ʔilxubza tbarbiʕat biššu:rba] The bread was soaked in the soup.
مبَربِع [mbarbiʕ] *adj:* • **1.** soaked, dipped (in) • **2.** (idiomatic:) having a lot of (something)

ب ر ب ن

بَربِين [barbi:n] *n:* • **1.** an edible wild green plant

ب ر ت غ ل

بُرتُغال [purtuɣa:l] *n:* • **1.** Portugal
بُرتُغالِي [purtuɣa:li] *adj:* • **1.** Portuguese

ب ر ت ق ل

بُرتُقال [burtuqa:l, buritqa:l] *n:* • **1.** (coll.) orange(s)

ب

بُرتُقالَة [burtuqaːla] *n:* بُرتُقالات [burtuqaːlaːt] *pl:* • **1.** orange
بُرتُقالِي [burtuqaːli] *adj:* • **1.** orange, orange-colored

ب ر ج

بُرِج [burij] *n:* بُرُوج، أَبراج [buruːǰ, ʔabraːǰ] *pl:* • **1.** tower – بُرج المُراقَبَة [burǰ ʔilmuraːqaba] watch tower, control tower. • **2.** dovecote, pigeon house • **3.** sign of the zodiac – بُرج الجِّدِي [burǰ ʔiǰǰidi] Capricorn
بارِجَة [baːriǰa] *n:* بَوارِج [bawaːriǰ] *pl:* • **1.** battleship

ب ر ج ز

بِرجِز [birǰiz] *n:* بَراجِز [baraːǰiz] *pl:* • **1.** riding breeches

ب ر ج ك ت ر

برُوجَكتَر [pruːǰaktar] *n:* • **1.** projector

ب ر ج م 1

بَرجَم [parčam] *n:* بَراجِم [paraːčim] *pl:* • **1.** bang

ب ر ج م 2

بَرجَم [parčam] *v:* • **1.** to rivet – بَرجِمَوا شَيلمان البِنايَة [parčimaw šiːlmaːn ʔilbnaːya] They riveted the girders of the building. بَرجَمها لِلقَضِيَّة [parčamha lilqaðiyya] He took care of the matter once and for all. He settled the matter finally.
تبَرجَم [tparčam] *v:* • **1.** to be riveted – هَالحَدِيدَة لازِم تِتبَرجَم وِيّا اللّي يَمّها [halħadiːda laːzim titparčam wiyya ʔilli yammha] This piece of metal has to be riveted to the one next to it.

ب ر ح

البارحَة [ʔilbaːrħa] *n:* • **1.** yesterday – أَوَّل البارحَة [ʔawwal ʔilbaːrħa] or أَوَّلَة البارحَة [ʔawwalat ʔilbaːrħa] day before yesterday.

ب ر د 1

بُرَد [burad] *v:* • **1.** to cool, cool off (also figuratively) – المَيّ بُرَد هَسَّة؛ تِقدَر تِشرَب مِنَّه [ʔilmayy burad hassa; tigdar tišrab minnah] The water's cooled off now; you can drink some of it. بُردَت الدِّنيا هوايَة [burdat ʔiddinya hwaːya] The weather got very cold. راح يسافِر أَخُوك؟ لا، يِظهَر بُرَد عَن القَضِيَّة [raːħ ysaːfir ʔaxuːk? laː, yiðhar burad ʕan ʔilqaðiyya] Is your brother going to go? No, it looks like he's cooled toward the idea. تِقدَر تحاكِيه. بُرَد هَسَّة [tigdar tħaːčiːh. burad hassa] You can talk to him now. He's cooled off.
بَرَّد [barrad] *v:* • **1.** to cool, chill – بَرَّد المَيّ بِالثَّلّاجَة [barrad ʔilmayy biθθallaːǰa] He cooled the water in the refrigerator. المُطَر بَرَّد الجَّوّ [ʔilmuṭar barrad ʔiǰǰaww] The rain cooled the air. بَرَّدها لمَرتَه بِحَكيَه اللَّطِيف [barradha lmartah bħačyah ʔillaṭiːf] He cooled his wife's anger with his gentle words. لَمّا حِكالِي عَن حَرّ وُلايتَه بَرَّدنِي عَن الرَّواح لِيها [lamma ħičaːli ʕan ħarr wulaːytah barradni ʕan ʔirrawaːħ liːha] When he told me about his city's hot weather, he dampened my enthusiasm for going there.
تبَرَّد [tbarrad] *v:* • **1.** to be cooled – الماي ما يِتبَرَّد أَكثَر مِن هَذا؛ يِجمَد [ʔilmaːy maː yitbarrad ʔakθar min haːða; yiǰmad] The water can't be cooled any more than that; it'll freeze. • **2.** to cool off, cool oneself – فَكّيت ياختِي حَتَّى أَتبَرَّد شوَيَّة [fakkiːt yaːxti ħatta ʔatbarrad šwayya] I opened my collar so I could cool off a bit.
اِستَبرَد [ʔistabrad] *v:* • **1.** to catch a cold – لازِم اِستَبرَد البارحَة باللَّيل [laːzim ʔistabrad ʔilbaːrħa billayl] He must have caught a cold last night.
بَرِد [barid] *n:* • **1.** cold, coldness, coolness, chill – قَرصَة بَرِد [garṣat barid] a touch of cold. • **2.** cold, catarrh – أَخَذ بَرِد [ʔaxað barid] He caught cold.
بَردَة [barda] *n:* بَردات [bardaːt] *pl:* • **1.** cold spell, cold snap, frost
بَردِي [bardi] *n:* • **1.** (coll.) papyrus
بَردَة [parda] *n:* بَردات [pardaːt] *pl:* • **1.** curtain, drapery
بُرُودَة [buruːda] *n:* • **1.** coldness, coolness, (also of emotions)
بَرّادَة [barraːda] *n:* بَرّادات [barraːdaːt] *pl:* • **1.** water cooler
مُبَرِّدَة [mubarrida] *n:* مُبَرِّدات [mubarridaːt] *pl:* • **1.** cooling device • **2.** air conditioner
بَردِيَّة [bardiyya] *n:* بَردِيّات [bardiyyaːt] *pl:* • **1.** papyrus branch – يطُوف عَلَى بَردِيَّة [yṭuːf ʕala bardiyya] He's happy-go-lucky (lit., he'd float on a papyrus twig).
بُرُود [buruːd] *adj:* • **1.** coldness, coolness – صار بَيناتهُم بُرُود [ṣaːr biːnaːthum buruːd] They've gotten cool to each other. قابَلنِي بِبُرُود [qaːbalni biburuːd] He received me halfheartedly. • **2.** emotional coldness – بُرُود طَبعَه يعَجِّب [buruːd ṭabʕah yʕaǰǰib] His coolness of disposition is amazing.
بارِد [baːrid] *adj:* • **1.** cold, cool, chilly – فَدّ واحِد بارِد كُلِّش [fadd waːħid baːrid kulliš] a real slowpoke. تِتِن بارِد [titin baːrid] mild tobacco. نُكتَة باردَة [nukta baːrda] a dull joke. طَبُع بارِد [ṭabuʕ baːrid] a phlegmatic disposition. دَمَّه بارِد [dammah baːrid] He's cool headed. راسَه بارِد [raːsah baːrid] He has no problems. He is carefree.
بَردان [bardaːn] *adj:* • **1.** cold – لِبَسِت قَبُّوط وبَعَدنِي بَردان [libasit qappuːṭ wbaʕadni bardaːn] I put on an overcoat and I'm still cold.
أَبرَد [ʔabrad] *comparative adjective:* • **1.** colder, coldest

ب ر د 2

بُرَد [burad] *v:* • **1.** to file – بُرَد المِحبَس حَتَّى قِدَر يلِبسَه [burad ʔilmiħbas ħatta gidar yilbsah] He filed out the ring until he could slip it on.

بَرّاد [barra:d] *n:* • **1.** fitter, mechanic (esp. in the military)
مُبرَد [mubrad, mabrad] *n:* مَبارِد [maba:rid] *pl:* • **1.** file, rasp
بِرادَة [bira:da] *n:* • **1.** fitter's trade or work
بُرادَة [bra:da] *n:* • **1.** iron filings

ب ر د 3
بَرِيد [bari:d] *n:* • **1.** post, mail
بَرِيدِي [bari:di] *adj:* • **1.** postal – حَوّالَة بَرِيدِيَّة [ħawwa:la bari:diyya] postal money order.

ب ر د س و ن
بَردَسُون [pardasu:n] *n:* بَردَسُونات [pardasu:na:t] *pl:* • **1.** overcoat, topcoat

ب ر د غ
بَردَغ [pardaɣ] *v:* • **1.** to get a close shave – الحَلّاق بَردَغ وِجهِي كُلِّش زين [ʔilħalla:q pardaɣ wičči kulliš zi:n] The barber gave me a very close, smooth shave.
پردَغ [pirdaɣ] *n:* بَرادِيغ [para:di:ɣ] *pl:* • **1.** carpet
بَرداغ [barda:ɣ] *n:* بَرادِيغ [bara:di:ɣ] *pl:* • **1.** drinking glass

ب ر ر 1
بَرّ [barr] *v:* • **1.** to fulfill, keep. After two years, he kept his promise – بَعَد سَنتَين، بَرّ بِوَعدَه [baʕad santayn, barr bwaʕdah] After two years, he kept his promise.
بَرَّر [barrar] *v:* • **1.** to warrant, justify, vindicate – شلُون تبَرِّر مَوقِفَك؟ [šlu:n tbarrir mawqifak?] How do you justify your stand?
مُبَرِّر [mubarrir] *n:* مُبَرِّرات [mubarrira:t] *pl:* • **1.** justification, excuse
تَبرِير [tabri:r] *n:* • **1.** justification
بارّ [ba:rr] *adj:* • **1.** dutiful, devoted – وَلَد بارّ [walad ba:rr] a dutiful son. زَوج بارّ [zawǰ ba:rr] a devoted husband.
مَبرُور [mabru:r] *adj:* • **1.** blessed – عَمَل مَبرُور [ʕamal mabru:r] a blessed act.

ب ر ر 2
بَرّ [barr] *n:* • **1.** dry land, terra firma – بِالبَرّ وَالبَحَر [bilbarr wilbaħar] on land and sea. • **2.** desert wilderness
بَرَّة [barra] *prepositional:* • **1.** (prep.) outside – خَلِّي الكَلِب بَرَّة البَيت [xalli: ʔiččalib barra ʔilbayt] Leave the dog outside the house. • **2.** (adverbial:) out, outside الجِّهال دَيِلعَبُون بَرَّة [ʔiǰǰiha:l dayilʕabu:n barra] The children are playing outside. لا، بَعدَه بَرَّة. راح يِرجَع لِبَغداد باكِر [la:, baʕdah barra. ra:ħ yirǰaʕ lbayda:d ba:čir] No he's still away. He'll return to Baghdad tomorrow. طِلَع بَرَّة [ṭilaʕ barra] He went out.
بَرِّي [barri] *adj:* • **1.** land, terrestrial – قُوّات بَرِّيَّة [quwwa:t barriyya] land forces. • **2.** wild – حَيوانات بَرِّيَّة [ħaywa:na:t barriyya] wild animals.
بَرّانِي [barra:ni] *adj:* • **1.** outside, outer, exterior – الصَّفحَة البَرّانِيَّة [ʔaṣṣafħa ʔalbarra:niyya] the outer side. الطَّبقَة البَرّانِيَّة [ʔiṭṭabaqa ʔalbarra:niyya] the exterior layer. • **2.** external, extrinsic – هَذا شِي بَرّانِي مالَه عِلاقَة بِالمَسألَة [ha:ða ši barra:ni ma:lah ʕila:qa bilmasʔala] That's an external thing that has no connection with the problem. هُوَّ رَجُل بَرّانِي مالَه دَخَل بِالمَوضُوع [huwwa raǰul barra:ni ma:lah daxal bilmawðu:ʕ] He's an outsider who has no concern with the matter. نسَوِّي رَهان بَرّانِي بَينِي وبينَك [nsawwi: raha:n barra:ni bayni wbi:nak] Let's make a side bet between us.

ب ر ز
بِرَز [biraz] *v:* • **1.** to appear, show up, emerge – بُرَز ذَكائَه مِن خَلَّص الدِّراسَة الابتِدائِيَّة [buraz ðaka:ʔah min xallaṣ ʔiddira:sa ʔilʔibtida:ʔiyya] His intelligence showed up when he finished elementary education. • **2.** to stand out, attain prominence – بِرَز بين المُوَظَّفِين بمُدَّة قَصِيرَة [biraz bi:n ʔilmuwaððafi:n bmudda qaṣi:ra] He stood out among the employees in a short time. بِرَز بالحِزِب [biraz bilħizib] He became prominent in the party. • **3.** to display, show – إبرِز هَوِيتَك لِلمُوَظَّف قَبُل ما تخُشّ [ʔubruz hawiyytak lilmwaððaf gabul ma: txušš] Show your identification to the official before you go in.
بارَز [ba:raz] *v:* • **1.** to duel, engage in a sword fight with – البَطَل هِجَم عَلَيه وَبارَزَه [ʔalbaṭal hiǰam ʕali:h wba:razah] The hero charged him and engaged him in swordplay. • **2.** to compete in a contest – آنِي حاضِر أَبارزَك بِالشِّطرَنج [ʔa:ni ħa:ðir ʔaba:rzak biššiṭranǰ] I'm ready to take you on in chess.
أبرَز [ʔabraz] *v:* • **1.** to present, show, display – أَبرَز كُلّ ما عِندَه مِن وَثايِق حَتَّى يِكسِب الدَّعوَة [ʔabraz kull ma: ʕindah min waθa:yiq ħatta yiksib ʔiddaʕwa] He presented all he had in the way of documents to win the case. أَبرَز هَوِيتَه بِالباب قَبُل ما يخُشّ [ʔabraz hawi:tah bilba:b gabul ma: yxušš] He showed his identification at the gate before entering.
تبارَز [tba:raz] *v:* • **1.** to duel
بُرُوز [buru:z] *n:* • **1.** prominence, eminence
إبراز [ʔibra:z] *n:* • **1.** presentation, showing
مُبارَزَة [muba:raza] *n:* مُبارَزات [muba:raza:t] *pl:* • **1.** swordfight, duel • **2.** competition, contest
أبرَز [ʔabraz] *comparative adj:* • **1.** more or most prominent, outstanding, etc
بارِز [ba:riz] *adj:* • **1.** prominent – عُضُو بارِز بِالحِزِب [ʕuðw ba:riz bilħizib] a prominent member of the party. • **2.** raised, embossed, in relief – حُرُوف بارِزَة [ħuru:f ba:riza] embossed letters.

ب

ب ر ز ن

بَرَزان [baraza:n] *n:* بَرَزانات [baraza:na:t] *pl:* • **1.** horn, trumpet, bugle

ب ر س م

بريسَم [bri:sam] *n:* • **1.** silk

ب ر ش ت

بَرَشُوت [parašu:t] *n:* • **1.** parachute

ب ر ص [1]

بَرَص [baraṣ] *n:* • **1.** a birth defect resulting in unpigmented patches of skin • **2.** (by extension) albinism

بريص، أبو برَيص [brayṣ, ʔabu brayṣ] *n:* أبُوبرَيصات [ʔabu brayṣa:t] *pl:* • **1.** lizard, wall gecko

برَيعصِي [brayʕṣi, bri:ʕṣi] *n:* • **1.** lizard

أبرَص [ʔabraṣ] *adj:* بُرُص، بَرصِين [buruṣ, barṣi:n] *pl:* بَرصَة [barṣa] *feminine:* • **1.** having light patches of skin • **2.** person with light patches of skin • **3.** albino • **4.** an albino

ب ر ص [2]

بُرصَة، بُورصَة [burṣa, bu:rṣa] *n:* بُورصات [bu:rṣa:t] *pl:* • **1.** bourse, stock exchange

ب ر ط

بُرَط [puraṭ, paruṭ] *v:* • **1.** to disclose inadvertently (a secret) – دِير بالَك لا تُبرُط السِّرّ [di:r ba:lak la: tupruṭ ʔissirr] Watch out you don't give away the secret. بُرَطها لِلحكايَة [puraṭha lilħča:ya] He let the cat out of the bag.

بَرِط [pariṭ] *n:* • **1.** disclosing inadvertently (a secret)

ب ر ط ل

بَرطَل [barṭal] *v:* • **1.** to bribe – بَرطَلَه بخَمسِين دِينار [barṭalah bxamsi:n dina:r] He bribed him with fifty dinars.

تبَرطَل [tbarṭal] *v:* • **1.** to be bribed – هَذا يِتبَرطَل بِالعَجَل [ha:ða yitbarṭal bilʕaǰal] He's easily bribed.

بَرطِيل [barṭi:l, burṭi:l] *n:* بَراطِيل [bara:ṭi:l] *pl:* • **1.** bribe

ب ر ط م [1]

بَرطَم [barṭam] *v:* • **1.** to pout – لمّا ما نطَيتَه البايسِكِل، بَرطَم وَبَعد شوَيَّة راح يِبكِي [lamma ma: nṭi:tah ʔilpa:ysikil, barṭam wbaʕd šwayya ra:ħ yibči] When I didn't give him the bicycle, he pouted and a bit later started to cry.

بَراطِم [bara:ṭim] *n:* • **1.** swollen lips

مبَرطَم [mbarṭum] *adj:* • **1.** pout, pouting • **2.** having pursed lips (esp. out of anger)

ب ر ط م [2]

بَرطَمان [barṭama:n] *n:* • **1.** glass jar, jelly jar

ب ر ط ن

بريطانيا [briṭa:nya] *n:* • **1.** Great Britain • **2.** Britain

ب ر ع

بِرَع [biraʕ] *v:* • **1.** to be skillful, proficient – بِرَع بتَقلِيد المُمَثِّلِين [biraʕ btaqli:d ʔilmumaθθili:n] He was skillful at impersonating actors.

تبَرَّع [tbarraʕ] *v:* • **1.** to donate, contribute, give freely – يِتبَرَّع هوايَة لِلجَمعِيّات الخَيرِيَّة [yitbarraʕ hwa:ya lijǰamʕiyya:t ʔalxayriyya] He contributes a lot to charitable organizations. تبَرَّع بألِف دِينار [tbarraʕ bʔalif dina:r] He donated a thousand dinars. • **2.** to volunteer – تبَرَّع يِبنِي غُرفَة جِدِيدَة لِلجّامِع [tbarraʕ yibni ɣurfa ǰidi:da lijǰa:miʕ] He volunteered to build a new room for the mosque.

تبَرُّع [tabarruʕ] *n:* تبَرُّعات [tabarruʕa:t] *pl:* • **1.** donation, contribution

بَراعَة [bara:ʕa] *n:* • **1.** skill, proficiency

بارِع [ba:riʕ] *adj:* • **1.** skilled, skillful, proficient – بارِع بِالرَّسِم [ba:riʕ birrasim] skillful at drawing. خَطِيب بارِع [xaṭi:b ba:riʕ] a skillful speaker.

أبرَع [ʔabraʕ] *comparative adjective:* • **1.** more or most skillful, proficient

ب ر ع م

بَرعَم [barʕam] *v:* • **1.** to bud, blossom

بُرعُم [burʕum] *n:* بَراعِم [bara:ʕim] *pl:* • **1.** bud (bot.)

ب ر غ ث

بَرغُوث [barɣu:θ] *n:* • **1.** (coll.) flea(s)

بَرغُوثَة [barɣu:θa] *n:* بَراغِيث [bara:ɣi:θ] *pl:* • **1.** flea

ب ر غ ش

بَرغَش [barɣaš] *n:* • **1.** (coll.) small, non-biting, swarming insect(s), midge(s)

بَرغَشَة [barɣaša] *n:* بَرغَشات، بَراغِيش [barɣaša:t, bara:ɣi:š] *pl:* • **1.** small, nonbiting, swarming insect(s), midge(s)

ب ر غ ل

بُرغُل [burɣul] *n:* • **1.** bulgur, boiled dried and crushed wheat

ب ر غ ي

بُرغِي [burɣi] *n:* بَراغِي [bara:gi] *pl:* • **1.** screw, bolt • **2.** winding stem (of a watch)

ب ر ق

بِرَق [biraq] *v:* • **1.** to flash (of lightning) – السِّما برِقَت وَرِعدَت [ʔissima birqat wriʕdat] There was thunder and lightning. • **2.** to wire, telegraph, cable – بِرَقلِي بَرقِيَّة يطالبنِي بِالفلُوس [biraqli barqiyya yṭa:libni bilfilu:s] He wired me asking for the money.

بَرق [barq] *n:* بُرُوق [buru:q] *pl:* • **1.** lightning, flash of lightning • **2.** telegraph – دائِرَة البَرق [da:ʔirat ʔilbarq] telegraph office.
بَرقِي [barqi] *n:* • **1.** telegraph, telegraphic – المُواصَلات البَرقِيَّة [ʔalmuwa:ṣala:t ʔilbarqiyya] telegraph connections. خَطّ بَرقِي [xaṭṭ barqi] telegraph line.
بَرِيق [bari:q] *n:* • **1.** glitter
بَرّاق [barra:q] *n:* • **1.** shining, flashing
بَرقِيَّة [barqiyya] *n:* بَرقِيّات [barqiyya:t] *pl:* • **1.** telegram, wire, cable
بارِق [ba:riq] *adj:* • **1.** shiny, brilliant
بَرقِيّاً [barqiyyan] *adverbial:* • **1.** by telegraph

ب ر ك [1]

بُرَك [burak] *v:* • **1.** to kneel – بُرَك عَلَى رُكُبتَه وَنَيشَن عالهَدَف [burak ʕala rukubtah wanayšan ʕalhadaf] He knelt on one knee and aimed at the target.
بارَك [ba:rak] *v:* • **1.** to bestow a blessing (said of God) – الله يبارِك. يوم عَلَى يوم دَيصِير أزكَن [ʔallah yba:rik. yu:m ʕala yu:m dayṣi:r ʔazgan] Bless his heart. Day by day he gets richer. • **2.** to offer congratulations, felicitations – بارَكلَه عالنَّجاح [ba:raklah ʕannaja:ħ] He congratulated him on his success. سمَعِت جالَه وَلَد. خَلّي نرُوح نبارِكلَه [smaʕit ja:lah walad. xalli nru:ħ nba:riklah] I heard he has a son. Let's go congratulate him. أشكُرَك، الله يبارِكلَك [ʔaškurak, ʔallah yba:riklak] Thank you, the same to you (an answer to
تبَرَّك [tbarrak] *v:* • **1.** to be blessed, get a blessing – خَلّي أتبَرَّك بِالحايِط مال الجّامِع [xalli ʔatbarrak bilħa:yiṭ ma:l ʔijja:miʕ] Let me get a blessing from touching the wall of the mosque.
بُركَة، بِركَة [burka, birka] *n:* بِرَك [birak] *pl:* • **1.** puddle, pool, pond
بَرَكَة [baraka] *n:* • **1.** blessing, boon – هالسَّنَة بَرَكَة. المَحصُول كُلِّش زين [hassana baraka. ʔilmaħṣu:l kulliš zi:n] This year is a lucky one. The harvest is very good. هالفلُوس ما بيها بَرَكَة [halfilu:s ma: bi:ha baraka] This money doesn't do any good. ما شاء الله بَرَكَة؛ يوم عَلَى يوم يزيد [ma: ša:llah baraka; yu:m ʕala yu:m yzi:d] God's been bounteous; there's more every day. عالبَرَكَة نَجاحَك [ʕalbaraka naja:ħak] Congratulations on your success. مِن بَرَكَة الله، شُغلي زين [min barakat ʔallah, šuɣli zi:n] Thank God, my business is good.
بُرُوك [buru:k] *n:* • **1.** kneeling down
مبارَك [mba:rak] *adj:* • **1.** blessed, fortunate, also congratulations – مبارَك، سِمَعِت نِجَحت [mba:rak, simaʕit nijaħit] Congratulations, I heard you passed. مبارَك عَلَى قاطَك الجِّدِيد [mba:rak ʕala qa:ṭak ʔijjidi:d] Congratulations on your new suit. مبارَك عِيدَك [mba:rak ʕi:dak] Blessings on your feast day.
مَبرُوك [mabru:k] *n:* • **1.** congratulations

ب ر ك [2]

بَرَّك [barrak] *v:* • **1.** to park

ب ر ك [3]

برَيك [brayk] *n:* • **1.** brake

ب ر ك ن

بُركان [burka:n] *n:* بَراكِين [bara:ki:n] *pl:* • **1.** volcano
بُركانِي [burka:ni] *adj:* • **1.** volcanic – حَجَر بُركانِي [ħajar burka:ni] volcanic rock. مَنطِقَة بُركانِيَّة [manṭiqa burka:niyya] a volcanic region.

ب ر ك ن د

بَرَكَندَة [parakanda] *n:* بَرَكَندِيَّة [parakandiyya] *pl:* • **1.** disorderly, untidy, disorganized – لا تصِير بَرَكَندَة. رَتِّب غَراضَك [la: tṣi:r parakanda. rattib ɣara:ḍ̣ak] Don't be disorderly. Straighten up your things. • **2.** untidy person

ب ر ل م ن

بَرلَمان [barlama:n] *n:* بَرلَمانات [barlama:na:t] *pl:* • **1.** parliament
بَرلَمانِي [barlama:ni] *adj:* • **1.** parliamentary

ب ر م

بُرَم [buram] *v:* • **1.** to twist – أبرُم الخيط وشَمِّعَه حَتَّى يُقوَى [ʔubrum ʔilxi:ṭ wšammiʕah ħatta yuqwa:] Twist the string and wax it so it'll be strong. بُرَم إيدِي وَأذّانِي [buram ʔi:di wʔaððа:ni] He twisted my arm and hurt me. • **2.** to brag, talk big, show off – شدَعوَة تُبرُم هَالقَدّ؟ [šdaʕwa tubrum halgadd?] Why do you brag so much?
بارَم [ba:ram] *v:* • **1.** to brag, talk big – هَذا يبارُم هوايَة [ha:ða yba:rum hwa:ya] He brags a lot.
تبارَم [tba:ram] *v:* • **1.** to brag to each other – كُلَما يشُوف بَنات، يقُوم يِتبارَم [kullma: yšu:f bana:t, ygu:m yitba:ram] Wherever he sees girls, he starts talking big. إبنِي وَإبنَك كانَوا يِتبارمُون [ʔibni waʔibnak ča:naw yitba:rmu:n] My son and your son were bragging to each other.
انبُرَم [ʔinburam] *v:* • **1.** to be twisted, to be entwined • **2.** to be settled, established
بَرُم [barum] *n:* • **1.** twisting • **2.** bragging, showing off
بُرمَة [burma] *n:* • **1.** (coll.) bourma, a Mid-Eastern pastry
بَرمَة [barma] *n:* • **1.** twist
إبرام [ʔibra:m] *n:* • **1.** settlement, establishment
بُرمايَة [burma:ya] *n:* بُرمايات [burma:ya:t] *pl:* • **1.** a Mid-Eastern pastry
ابرام [ʔibra:m] *n:* • **1.** bragging, showing off

ب

بَرّام [barraːm] *adj:* بَرّامَة [barraːma] *pl:* • **1.** braggart, bragger

مُبرَم [mubram] *adj:* • **1.** real, veritable – هَالطِّفِل غَضَب مُبرَم [haṭṭifil ɣaðab mubram] That kid's a real pest. المُدِير الجِّدِيد بَلاء مُبرَم [ʔilmudiːr ʔiǰǰidiːd balaːʔ mubram] The new director is a real ball of fire.

ب ر م ء

بَرمائي [barmaːʔi] *adj:* • **1.** amphibious – الحَيوانات البَرمائِيَّة [ʔalħaywaːnaːt ʔilbarmaːʔiyya] the amphibious animals.

ب ر م ج

بَرمَج [barmaǰ] *v:* • **1.** to program

بَرمَجَة [barmaǰa] *n:* • **1.** programming

بَرنامِج [barnaːmiǰ] *n:* بَرامِج [baraːmiǰ] *pl:* • **1.** broadcasting schedule, list of programs – بَرنامِج إذاعَة [barnaːmiǰ ʔiðaːʕa] broadcasting schedule, list of programs.

بَرنامَج [barnaːmaǰ] *n:* • **1.** program

مبَرمِج [mbarmiǰ] *adj:* • **1.** programmer

مُبَرمَج [mubarmaǰ] *adj:* • **1.** programmed

ب ر م ز

بريمِز [braymiz, briːmiz] *n:* بريمِزات [braymizaːt] *pl:* • **1.** Primus stove

ب ر م ك

بَرمَكي [barmaki] *adj:* بَرمَكِيَّة [barmakiyya] *pl:* • **1.** sweetened, dark-colored vinegar – خَلّ بَرمَكِي [xall barmaki] sweetened, dark-colored vinegar. • **2.** generous

ب ر م ل

بَرمِيل [barmiːl] *n:* بَرامِيل [baraːmiːl] *pl:* • **1.** barrel, drum

ب ر ن

بَرنَو [barnaw] *n:* • **1.** kind of rifle

ب ر ن ج

برنج [prinǰ] *n:* • **1.** brass • **2.** bronze

ب ر ن ز

برُونز [brunz] *n:* • **1.** bronze

برُنزِي [brunzi] *adj:* • **1.** bronze – تِمثال برُونزي [timθaːl bruwnzi] a bronze statue. • **2.** bronze-like, bronze-colored

ب ر ن ص

بُرنُص [burnuṣ] *n:* بَرانِص [baraːniṣ] *pl:* • **1.** burnoose, hooded robe

ب ر ن ط

بَرنُوطِي [barnuːṭi] *n:* • **1.** snuff

بُرنيطَة [burniːṭa] *n:* بُرنيطات، بَرانيط [burniːṭaːt, baraːniːṭ] *pl:* • **1.** (Western style) hat

ب ر ه ن

بَرهَن [barhan] *v:* • **1.** to prove, demonstrate – بَرهَن إنُّو واحِد مِنهُم [barhan ʔinnu waːħid minhum] He proved that he's one of us. تِقدَر تبَرهِن عَلَى حَقِيقَة قَولَك؟ [tigdar tbarhin ʕala ħaqiːqat qawlak?] Can you prove the truth of what you say?

بُرهان [burhaːn] *n:* بَراهِين [baraːhiːn] *pl:* • **1.** proof

ب ر و

براوَة [praːwa] *n:* براوات [praːwaːt] *pl:* • **1.** fitting at the tailor's – الخَيّاط سَوّالِي براوتَين [ʔilxayyaːṭ sawwaːli praːwtayn] The tailor gave me two fittings. • **2.** tailor's fitting

ب ر و ت س

برُوتِستانِيَّة [prutistaːniyya] *n:* • **1.** Protestantism

برُوتِستانِي [prutistaːni] *adj:* • **1.** Protestant

ب ر و ت ك ل

برُوتوكول [prutukuːl] *n:* • **1.** protocol

ب ر و ت ن

برُوتُون [prutuːn] *n:* • **1.** proton

ب ر و د

بارُود [baːruːd] *n:* • **1.** gunpowder – صار مِثل البارُود [ṣaːr miθl ʔalbaːruːd] He became apoplectic.

ب ر و ف س ر

برُوفِيسُور [prufisuːr] *n:* • **1.** professor

ب ر و ن

بَرَوانَة [parawaːna] *n:* بَرَوانات [parawaːnaːt] *pl:* • **1.** propeller, fan

ب ر ي 1

بِرَى [biraː] *v:* • **1.** to sharpen (a pencil) – هَالمُقطاطَة تِبرِي القَلَم مُمتاز [halmuqṭaːṭa tibri ʔilqalam mumtaːz] This sharpener sharpens the pencil very well.

بارَى [baːraː] *v:* • **1.** to vie with, compete with – بَعَدما غِلَب كُلّ المِتنافِسِين، راح يباري البَطَل نَفسَه [baʕadmaː ɣilab kull ʔilmitnaːfsiːn, raːħ ybaːri ʔalbaṭal nafsah] Now that he has beaten all contenders, he is going to compete with the champion himself.

تبارَى [tbaːraː] *v:* • **1.** to vie, compete with each other – وِيّا أيّ فَرِيق راح تِتبارُون الإسبُوع الجّاي؟ [wiyya ʔayy fariːq raːħ titbaːruːn ʔilʔisbuːʕ ʔiǰǰaːy?] Which team are you going to compete with next week?

بَرِي [bary] *n:* • **1.** sharpening of (a pencil)
بارِيَة [baːrya] *n:* بوارِي [bwaːri] *pl:* • **1.** large, heavy, woven bamboo mat
مُباراة [mubaːraːt] *n:* مُبارَيات [mubaːrayaːt] *pl:* • **1.** match, tournament, contest – مُباراة كُرَة القَدَم [mubaːraːt kurat ʔilqadam] football game.

ب ر ي 2
بارِيَة [baːrya] *n:* بوارِي [bwaːri] *pl:* • **1.** large woven bamboo mat

ب ر ي ن
بَرِينَة [bariːna] *n:* بَرايِن [baraːyin] *pl:* • **1.** drill
بِريانِي [biryaːni] *n:* • **1.** a dish made of rice, meat, and hot spices, originally from India

ب ز 1
بازَة [baːza] *n:* • **1.** cotton flannel

ب ز 2
باز [baːz] *n:* بازات [baːzaːt] *pl:* • **1.** falcon

ب ز ب ز
بَزبَز [bazbaz] *v:* • **1.** to dart, shift (of the eyes) – عيُونَه تبَزبِز عَلَى طُول [ʕyuːnah tbazbiz ʕala ṭuːl] His eyes dart about all the time.
بِزبِز [bizbiz] *n:* بِزابِز [bizaːbiz] *pl:* • **1.** rat, a nocturnal animal resembling the mink

ب ز ب ن د
بازبَند [baːzband] *n:* بازبَندات [baːzbandaːt] *pl:* • **1.** a talisman in the form of a leather bracelet worn on the upper arm (also called زَنّادِي [zannaːdi])

ب ز ر 1
بِزَر [bizar] *v:* • **1.** to beget – يِسأَل عَن النَغَل وَمِنُو اللّي بزَرَه [yisʔal ʕan ʔinnaɣal waminu ʔilli bazrah] He's a nosy old busybody (lit., he asks about the bastard and who begat him).
بَزَّر [bazzar] *v:* • **1.** to go to seed – الوَرِد بَزَّر [ʔilwarid bazzar] The flower's gone to seed. البَيتِنجان بَزَّر [ʔlbaytinǰaːn bazzar] The eggplant has gotten old and seedy.
بَزِر [bazir] *n:* • **1.** seed(s) • **2.** semen • **3.** offspring, kid(s), brat(s)
بَزرَة [bazra] *n:* بَزرات، بزُور [bazraːt, bzuːr] *pl:* • **1.** seed • **2.** offspring, kids, brats
بِزار [bizaːr] *n:* • **1.** a person who meddles or gossips • **2.** losing track – تخَربَط عَليه البِزار [txarbaṭ ʕaliːh ʔilibzaːr] He got confused.
بزارَة [bzaːra] *n:* بزارات [bzaːraːt] *pl:* • **1.** date molasses factory

ب ز ر 2
بزار [bzaːr] *n:* بزارات [bzaːraːt] *pl:* • **1.** scaffold.

ب ز ز 1
بَزّ [bazz] *v:* • **1.** to defeat, beat, outstrip, excel – بَزّ كُل التَّلامِيذ بِالرِّياضِيّات [bazz kull ʔittalaːmiːð birriyaːḍiyyaːt] He outdid all the students in sports. • **2.** to spit or spray – الجّاهِل بَزّ المَيّ عالبَزّونَة [ʔiǰǰaːhil bazz ʔilmayy ʕalbazzuːna] The child spat the water on the cat.
اِبتَزّ [ʔibtazz] *v:* • **1.** to take away (unlawfully) – اِبتَزّ أَموال الأَغنِياء بِمَحَلّتَه بِالتَّهدِيد [ʔibtazz ʔamwaːl ʔilʔaɣniyaːʔ bimħalltah bittahdiːd] He extracted money from the rich in his neighborhood by threats. اِبتَزّ أَموالهُم بِدُون أَن يشِعرُون [ʔibtazz ʔamwaːlhum biduːn ʔan yšiʕruːn] He got their money without them catching on.
بَزّ [bazz] *n:* • **1.** defeating, spitting, spraying
اِبتِزاز [ʔibtizaːz] *n:* • **1.** extortion, robbery, fleecing

ب ز ز 2
بِزّ [bizz] *n:* • **1.** a large Iraqi food fish
بَزّاز [bazzaːz] *n:* بَزّازَة، بَزّازِين [bazzaːza, bazzaːziːn] *pl:* • **1.** cloth merchant, yard goods dealer
بزازَة [bzaːza] *n:* • **1.** cloth trade

ب ز و ن
بَزّون [bazzuːn] *n:* بِزازِين [bizaːziːn] *pl:* • **1.** cat, tom cat
بَزّونَة [bazzuːna] *n:* بَزّونات، بزازِين [bazzuːnaːt, bzaːziːn] *pl:* • **1.** cat, female cat • **2.** hoist, chain hoist, chain falls, and by extension, derrick, crane

ب ز ع
بِزَع [bizaʕ] *v:* • **1.** to be or become exasperated, disgusted, fed up – بزَعِت مِن أَعمالَك [bzaʕit min ʔaʕmaːlak] I've gotten fed up with your actions.
بَزَّع [bazzaʕ] *v:* • **1.** to exasperate, irritate – بَزَّعتنِي. بَسّ عاد [bazzaʕtni. bass ʕaːd] You've exasperated me. That's enough, now!

ب ز غ
بِزَغ [bizaɣ] *v:* • **1.** to emerge
بزُوغ [bizuːɣ] *n:* • **1.** rise, appearance, dawn

ب ز ق
بُزُق [buzuq] *n:* بُزُوقات [buzuːqaːt] *pl:* • **1.** a mandolin-like musical instrument

ب ز ل
بِزَل [bizal] *v:* • **1.** to drain – وِزارَة الزِّراعَة قَرَّرَت تِبزِل هالمَنطِقَة [wizaːrat ʔizziraːʕa

qarrarat tibzil halmanṭiqa] The Ministry of Agriculture has decided to drain this area. إبزِلي التِّمَّن زين حَتَّى لا يِنلَكّ [ʔibizli ʔittimman ziːn ħatta laː yinlakk] Drain the rice well so it won't stick together.
بَزِل [bazil] *n:* • **1.** drain, draining
مَبزَل [mabzal] *n:* مَبازِل [mabaːzil] *pl:* • **1.** drainage ditch

ب ز ل ي
بَزاليا [bazaːlya] *n:* • **1.** green peas

ب ز م
بُزمَة [buzma] *n:* بُزمات، بُزَم [buzmaːt, buzam] *pl:* • **1.** cuff (of a shirt sleeve)

ب ز ي م
بزيم [bziːm] *n:* بزيمات، بزايِم [bziːmaːt, bzaːyim] *pl:* • **1.** buckle

ب س ت
بَستَة [pasta] *n:* بَستات [pastaːt] *pl:* • **1.** a kind of Iraqi folk song or verse • **2.** tale, story – طَلَّعلي غير بَستَة حَتَّى يبَرِّر غِيابَه [ṭallaʕli ɣiːr pasta ħatta ybarrir ɣiyaːbah] He told me quite a tale to justify his absence.

ب س ت ج
بَستَج [bastaǰ] *n:* • **1.** frankincense, used primarily for chewing gum – عِلِك بَستَج [ʕilič bastaǰ] frankincense gum.

ب س ت ر
بَستَر [bastar] *v:* • **1.** to pasteurize – المَعمَل يبَستِر الحَليب قبُل ما يعَبّي بِالبطالَة [ʔilmaʕmal ypastir ʔilħaliːb gabul maː yʕabbi bilbṭaːla] The plant pasteurizes the milk before they fill the bottles with it.
مبَستَر [mpastar] *adj:* • **1.** pasteurized – حَليب مبَستَر [ħaliːb mpastar] pasteurized milk.

ب س ت ك
بَستُوكَة [bastuːga] *n:* بَستُوكات [bastuːgaːt] *pl:* • **1.** glazed pottery jar

ب س ت ن
بستان [bistaːn] *n:* بساتِين [bsaːtiːn] *pl:* • **1.** orchard, grove
بَستَنَة [bastana] *n:* • **1.** horticulture

ب س ر
باسُور [baːsuːr] *n:* بواسِير [bwaːsiːr] *pl:* • **1.** hemorrhoid

ب س س
بَسّ [bass] *adv:* • **1.** enough – بَسّ؛ لا تخَلّي بَعَد [bass; laː txalliː baʕad] That's enough; don't put in any more. بُسَطتَه حَتَّى قال بَسّ [busaṭtah ħatta gaːl bass] I beat him till he said uncle. بَسَّك عاد! شقَدّ تِحكي [bassak ʕaːd! šgadd tiħči] That's enough out of you now! You talk too much! • **2.** only, just – بَسّ صار عُمرَه عَشِر سنين، قام يريد بايسِكِل [bass ṣaːr ʕumrah ʕašir sniːn, gaːm yriːd paːysikil] He just turned ten, and here he wants a bicycle. بَسّ جَرّ نَفَس واحِد مِن السِجارَة وَذَبّها [bass ǰarr nafas waːħid min ʔaǰǰigaːra waðabbha] He just took one puff of the cigarette, and threw it away. عِندي بَسّ ثلَث أيّام عُطلَة [ʕindi bass tlaθ ʔayyaːm ʕuṭla] I've only got three days' vacation. بَسّ يقُحّ اللّيل كُلَّه [bass yguħħ ʔillayl kullah] He simply coughs all night. بَسّ لَو عِندي خَمس دَنانير [bass law ʕindi xams danaːniːr] If I only had five dinars! • **3.** but, however, on the other hand – هَذا طِبيخ مُمتاز، بَسّ أعتِقِد يصير أحسَن إذا تحُطّ بيه شوَيَّة فِلفِل [haːða ṭibiːx mumtaːz, bass ʔaʕtiqid yṣiːr ʔaħsan ʔiða tħuṭṭ biːh šwayya filfil] This is excellent food, but I think it'll be better if you put in some pepper. بَسّ المُصيبَة ويّا إبن خالِك [bass ʔilmuṣiːba wiyya ʔibin xaːlič] But the problem is with your cousin. تكُون هنا ساعَة خَمسَة وَبَسّ [tkuːn hna saːʕa xamsa wbass] Be here at five and no arguments.

ب س ط
بُسَط [busaṭ] *v:* • **1.** to beat, thrash – الشُرطَة إجَوا وَبِدَوا يبُسطُون الطُّلاب [ʔiššurṭa ʔiǰaw wabidaw ybusṭuːn ʔiṭṭullaːb] The police arrived and began to beat the students. إبن الجِّيران بُسَطني [ʔibin ʔiǰǰiːraːn busaṭni] The neighbor's son beat me up.
بَسَّط [bassaṭ] *v:* • **1.** to spread out, display (i.e. wares, merchandise) – راح أبَسِّط قِدّام هَالبِنايَة. يبَيِّن أكُو هوايَة ناس هنا [raːħ ʔabassiṭ giddaːm halbinaːya. yibayyin ʔaku hwaːya naːs hna] I'm going to spread out my wares in front of this building. It seems there's a lot of people here. • **2.** (by extension) to open, open up, open for business – ما لازِم تبَسِّط يوم الجُّمعَة [maː laːzim tbassiṭ yuːm ʔiǰǰimʕa] You shouldn't open for business on Friday. • **3.** to simplify – تِقدَر تبَسِّطلي هَالقَضِيَّة؟ ما دَأفهَمها [tigdar tbassiṭli halqaðiyya? maː daʔafhamha] Can you simplify this thing for me? I don't understand it. بَسَّطِتها لِلقَضِيَّة هوايَة [baṣṣaṭitha lilqaðiyya hwaːya] You've over-simplified the matter.
تباسَط [tbaːsaṭ] *v:* • **1.** to fight, beat each other – تباسَط ويّا صاحِب المَحَلّ [tbaːṣaṭ wiyya ṣaːħib ʔilmaħall] He got in a fight with the owner of the shop.
انبُسَط [ʔinbusaṭ] *v:* • **1.** to be beaten, be punished
بَسِط [basiṭ] *n:* • **1.** beating, thrashing
بَسطَة [basṭa] *n:* بَسطات [basṭaːt] *pl:* • **1.** display of wares, merchandise • **2.** a beating, thrashing, flogging
بساط [bṣaːṭ] *n:* بُسُط [buṣuṭ] *pl:* • **1.** rug, thin and simple in pattern

بَساطَة [basa:ṭa] *n:* • **1.** simplicity, uncomplicatedness, plainness • **2.** naivete, ingenuousness
تَبسِيط [tabsi:ṭ] *n:* • **1.** simplicity • **2.** simplification
مباسَط [mba:saṭ] *n:* • **1.** fight
البَسِيطَة [ʔilbasi:ṭa] *n:* • **1.** the earth, the world – عَلَى وَجه البَسِيطَة [ʕala wajh ʔilbasi:ṭa] on the face of the earth.
بَسِيط [baṣi:ṭ] *adj:* بَسِيطِين [baṣi:ṭi:n] *pl:* • **1.** simple, uncomplicated – مُشكِلَة بَسِيطَة [muškila basi:ṭa] a simple problem. عَقلِيتَه بَسِيطَة [ʕaqli:tah basi:ṭa] He has a simple mind. بَسِيطَة. خَلِّيهَا عَلَيّا. إنتَ إدفَع مَرَّة اللُّخ [basi:ṭa. xalli:ha ʕalayya. ʔinta ʔidfaʕ marra ʔillux] It's nothing. Leave it to me. You pay next time. بَسِيطَة. دَربِي مِن هِنا [basi:ṭa. darbi min hina] No trouble. It's on my way. بَسِيطَة. ماكُو حاجَة تِشكُرنِي [basi:ṭa. ma:ku ħa:ja tiškurni] Don't mention it. There's no need to thank me. بَسِيطَة. آنِي أَدَبُّر لَك إيّاه باكِر [basi:ṭa. ʔa:ni ʔadabbur lak ʔiyya:h ba:čir] No problem. I'll arrange it for you tomorrow. مَحَّد تعَوَّر؛ لا تخابُر الشُّرطَة. بَسِيطَة، بَسِيطَة [maħħad tʕawwar; la: txa:bur ʔiššurṭa. basi:ṭa, basi:ṭa] No one's injured; don't call the police. It's nothing. • **2.** small, modest, trivial, trifling – مَبلَغ بَسِيط [mablaɣ basi:ṭ] a small sum. شِي بَسِيط [ši basi:ṭ] a trivial thing, nothing. نَشلَة بَسِيطَة [našla basi:ṭa] an ordinary cold, a little cold.
مِنبَسِط [minbasaṭ] *adj:* • **1.** beaten
مَبسُوط [mabsu:ṭ] *adj:* • **1.** flat
أبسَط [ʔabsaṭ] *comparative adjective:* • **1.** more or most uncomplicated, etc • **2.** more or most insignificant, etc • **3.** more or most naive, ingenuous, etc

ب س ط ر م

باسطِرمَة [ba:sṭirma] *n:* • **1.** (coll.) a type of large flat sausage stuffed with highly seasoned meat

ب س ط ل

بُسطال [busṭa:l] *n:* بَساطِيل [basa:ṭi:l] *pl:* • **1.** military boots

ب س ط ن

باسطُون [ba:sṭu:n] *n:* باسطُونات [pa:sṭu:na:t] *pl:* • **1.** walking stick, cane

ب س ف ر

البُسفُور [ʔilbusfu:r] *n:* • **1.** The Bosporus

ب س ك ت

بِسكِت [biskit] *n:* • **1.** (coll.) cookie(s), biscuit(s)
بِسكِيتَة [biski:ta, biskita:ya] *n:* بِسكِيتَة، بِسكِيتايات [biski:ta, biskita:ya:t] *pl:* • **1.** cookie, biscuit

ب س ك ل

بايسِكِل [pa:ysikil, ba:ysikil] *n:* بايسِكِلات [pa:ysikila:t, ba:ysikila:t] *pl:* • **1.** bicycle
بَسكُولَة [pasku:la] *n:* بَسكُولات [pasku:la:t] *pl:* • **1.** tassel (on a fez)

ب س ك و ي ت

بَسكَوِيت [baskawi:t] *n:* • **1.** (coll.) cookie(s), biscuit(s)
بِسكوِيتَة [biskwi:ta] *n:* بِسكوِيتات [biskwi:ta:t] *pl:* • **1.** cookie, biscuit

ب س ل 1

اِستَبسَل [ʔistabsal] *v:* • **1.** to be fearless, defy death – هَالجُندِي اِستَبسَل بِالمَعرَكَة [halǰundi ʔistabsal bilmaʕraka] This soldier defied death in battle. الجَّيش العِراقِي اِستَبسَل بِالدِّفاع عَن العِراق [ʔiǰǰayš ʔilʕira:qi ʔistabsal biddifa:ʕ ʕan ʔilʕira:q] The Iraqi Army was intrepid in its defense of Iraq.
بَسالَة [basa:la] *n:* • **1.** courage, bravery
اِستِبسال [ʔistibsa:l] *n:* • **1.** heroism • **2.** death defiance, bravery, courage, intrepidity
باسِل [ba:sil] *adj:* • **1.** brave, fearless, intrepid – الجَّيش الباسِل [ʔiǰǰayš ʔilba:sil] the fearless army.

ب س ل 2

بِسَل [bisal, bizal] *v:* • **1.** to cull – ما أَقدَر أَبِيعلَك طَماطَة قَبُل ما أبزِلها [ma: ʔagdar ʔabi:ʕlak ṭama:ṭa gabul ma: ʔabzilha] I can't sell you any tomatoes before I cull them.
بَسِل [basil] *n:* • **1.** culling, sorting the bad from the good • **2.** culls, throw-aways, things culled out – الخيار الزِّين اِنباع وَمابُقَى غير البَزِل [ʔilxya:r ʔizzi:n ʔinba:ʕ wma buqa: ɣi:r ʔilbazil] The good cucumbers are sold out and nothing is left but the culls.

ب س م

بَسَّم [bassam] *v:* • **1.** to smile – ما ضِحَك، لَكِن بَسَّم [ma: ðiħak, la:kin bassam] He didn't laugh, but he smiled.
تبَسَّم [tbassam] *v:* • **1.** to smile – مِن يِحكِي، يِتبَسَّم [min yiħči, yitbassam] He smiles when he talks. مِن يبتِسِم، تِقدَر تشُوف سِنَّه الذَّهَب [min yibtisim, tigdar tšu:f sinnah ʔiððahab] When he smiles, you can see his gold tooth. عَلَى طُول تشُوفَه مِبتِسِم [ʕala ṭu:l tšu:fah mibtisim] You always see him smiling.
بَسمَة [basma] *n:* بَسمات [basma:t] *pl:* • **1.** smile
اِبتِسام [ʔibtisa:m] *n:* • **1.** smiling, smile
اِبتِسامَة [ʔibtisa:ma] *n:* اِبتِسامات [ʔibtisa:ma:t] *pl:* • **1.** a smile
مِبتَسِم [mibtasim] *adj:* • **1.** smiling – وِجه مُبتِسِم [wiǰh mibtisim] a smiley face

ب س م ر

بَسمَر [basmar] *v:* • **1.** to nail, fasten with nails

ب

تبَسمَر [tbasmar] *v:* • **1.** to be nailed – هَاللَّوحَة ما تِتبَسمَر بِسُهُولَة [hallawħa maː titbasmar bsuhuːla] That board can't be nailed easily. مِن شافنِي، تبَسمَر بمُكانَه [min šaːfni, tbasmar bmukaːnah] When he saw me, he was riveted to the spot.

بِسمار [bismaːr] *n:* بسامِير [bsaːmiːr] *pl:* • **1.** nail • **2.** corn (on the foot)

ب س و ر ق

باسَورَق [basawrag, basuːrag] *n:* • **1.** (coll.) an edible nut, similar to the almond but smaller, with a smooth, dark shell

باسَورقَة [basawrga] *n:* باسَورقات [basawrgaːt] *pl:* • **1.** (coll) an edible nut, similar to the almond but smaller, with a smooth dark shell

ب ش

باش [baːš] *n:* • **1.** /in compounds/ head, chief – باش حَمّال [baːš ħammaːl] head porter. باش كاتِب [baːš kaːtib] chief clerk.

باشَة [baːša, paːša] *n:* باشاوات [bašawaːt, pašawaːt] *pl:* • **1.** pasha • **2.** a well-liked, popular fellow – هَذا خُوش وَلَد باشا [haːða xuːš walad paːša] He's a good guy - a prince.

ب ش ب ز غ

باشبُزُغ، باشبُزُق [baːšbuzuɣ, baːšbuzuq] *n:* • **1.** native or eastern dress – ما يصِير تِجِي لِلدّائِرَة لابِس باشبُزُغ [maː yṣiːr tiji liddaːʔira laːbis baːšbuzuɣ] You can't come to the office in native clothes. هَذا الباشبُزُغ، شماعَرّفَه؟ [haːða ʔilbaːšbuzuɣ, šmaʕarrfah?] That guy in native dress, what does he know?

ب ش ت

بِشِت [bišit] *n:* بشُوت، بشاتِي [bšuːt, bšaːti] *pl:* • **1.** a thin aba worn in summer

بُشت [pušt] *n:* بُشتِيَّة [puštiyya] *pl:* • **1.** a bad character, degenerate

ب ش ت م ل

بَشتَمال [paštamaːl] *n:* بَشتَمالات [paštamaːlaːt] *pl:* • **1.** sarong-like, tight-fitting garment, usually worn in public baths, etc

ب ش ت و

بِشتاوَة [bištaːwa] *n:* بِشتاوات [bištaːwaːt] *pl:* • **1.** flintlock pistol, old-fashioned handgun

ب ش ر [1]

بِشَر [bišar] *v:* • **1.** to rejoice – إبشِر! عَمَّك صار مُدِيرنا [ʔibšir! ʕammak ṣaːr mudiːrna] Rejoice! Your uncle has been made our director. نَظِّف الغُرفَة زين . . . إبشِر [naððuf ʔilɣurfa ziːn. . . ʔibšir] Clean the room well . . . Yes sir! • **2.** to be cordial – المُدِير بِشَر بِيه هوايَة [ʔilmudiːr bišar biːh hwaːya] The manager was very cordial to him.

بَشَّر [baššar] *v:* • **1.** to bear glad tidings, to tell (someone) good news – عَمَّك، مَرتَه جابَت وَلَد. رُوح بَشّرَه [ʕammak, martah ǰaːbat walad. ruːħ bašširah] Your uncle's wife had a boy. Go give him the good news. بَشَّرَك الله بِالخير [baššarak ʔallah bilxiːr] (polite reply to someone bringing good news, approx.:) May God gladden you also with good tidings. • **2.** (with ب) to spread, propagate, preach – دَيبَشّرُون بالإسلام بأفرِيقِيَا [daybaššruːn bilʔislaːm bʔafriːqiya] They're spreading Islam in Africa.

إستَبشَر [ʔistabšar] *v:* • **1.** to rejoice, be delighted, be happy – إستَبشَر هوايَة بهَالخَبَر [ʔistabšar hwaːya bhalxabar] He became very happy with this news.

بَشِر [bašir] *n:* • **1.** annunciation, joy, good news

بَشِير [bašiːr] *n:* بَشِيرِين [baširiːn] *pl:* • **1.** bearer of good news

بشارَة [bšaːra] *n:* بِشايِر [bšaːyir] *pl:* • **1.** good news, glad tidings

تَبشِير [tabšiːr] *n:* • **1.** missionary activity

مُبَشِّر [mubaššir] *adj:* مُبَشّرِين [mubašširiːn] *pl:* • **1.** bearer of glad tidings • **2.** missionary, evangelist

ب ش ر [2]

باشَر [baːšar] *v:* • **1.** to treat, attend, give medical treatment to • **2.** (with ب-) to begin, start, commence – راح أباشِر بالبِناء باكِر [raːħ ʔabaːšir bilbinaːʔ baːčir] I'm going to start building tomorrow. باشَرت بشُغلي الجِّدِيد البارحَة [baːšarit bšuɣli ʔiǰǰidiːd ʔilbaːrħa] I began work in my new job yesterday. طَبِيبنا باشَرَه [ṭabiːbna baːšarah] Our doctor treated him.

بَشَر [bašar] *n: (coll.)* • **1.** human being, man • **2.** mankind, men – ما تِلقِي مِثلَه بِالبَشَر [maː tilgi miθlah bilbašar] You won't find anyone like him in the world.

بَشَرَة [bašara] *n:* • **1.** complexion – بَشَرَة سَمرَة [bašara samra] dark complexion.

بَشَرِيَّة [bašariyya] *n:* • **1.** mankind, human race

مُباشَرَة [mubaːšara] *n:* • **1.** start, commencement, beginning • **2.** medical treatment

بَشَري [bašari] *adj:* • **1.** human – الجِّنس البَشَرِي [ʔiǰǰins ʔalbašari] the human race.

مُباشِر [mubaːšir] *adj:* • **1.** direct, immediate – السَّبَب المُباشِر لِمَرَضَه [ʔissabab ʔilmubaːšir limaraðah] the direct reason for his illness.

مُباشَرَةً [mubaːšaratan] *adverbial:* • **1.** immediately, directly – راح أرُوح عَليه مُباشَرَةً وأقُلَّه [raːħ ʔaruːħ ʕaliːh mubaːšaratan wagullah] I'm going to go straight to him and tell him.

ب

ب ش ش 1

بَشّ [bašš] *v:* • **1.** to smile – بَشّ بوُجهنا وَرَحَّب بِينا [bašš bwuččna wraħħab biːna] He smiled at us and welcomed us. • **2.** to be friendly, cheerful – مِن زرِته، بَشّ بِيّا [min zirtah, bašš biyya] When I visited him, he was very friendly to me.

بَشاشَة [bašaːša] *n:* بَشاشات [bašaːšaːt] *pl:* • **1.** happy face – اِستَقبَلنِي بِبَشاشَة [ʔistaqbalni bibašaːša] He received me with a big smile.

بَشُوش [bašuːš] *adj:* • **1.** smiling, cheerful, friendly – وِجِه بَشُوش [wiǰih bašuːš] cheerful face.

ب ش ش 2

بَشّ [bašš] *n:* • **1.** blot

ب ش ش 3

بَشّ [bašš] *n:* • **1.** (coll.) a variety of large, light-colored domesticated duck

بَشَّة [bašša] *n:* بَشّات، بشُوش [baššaːt, bšuːš] *pl:* • **1.** goose

ب ش ع

بَشاعَة [bašaːʕa] *n:* • **1.** ugliness

بَشِع [bašiʕ] *adj:* • **1.** ugly – وِجِه بَشِع [wiǰih bašiʕ] ugly face. • **2.** disgusting, repulsive • **3.** ugly

أَبشَع [ʔabšaʕ] *adj:* • **1.** uglier, ugliest • **2.** more or most disgusting, revolting, loathsome

ب ش ق 1

بَشقَة [bašqa] *adj:* • **1.** (invar.) different – لا، هَذا مَوضُوع بَشقَة [laː, haːða mawðuːʕ bašqa] No, that's another matter.

ب ش ق 2

باشَق [baːšaq, baːšak] *n:* بواشِق [bwaːšiq, bwaːšik] *pl:* • **1.** sparrow hawk

ب ش ك ر

بَشكِير [baškiːr] *n:* بَشاكِير [bašaːkiːr] *pl:* • **1.** hand towel

ب ص

باص [paːṣ, baːṣ] *n:* باصات [paːṣaːt, baːṣaːt] *pl:* • **1.** pass, authorization paper • **2.** bus

ب ص ب ص

بَصبَص [baṣbaṣ] *v:* • **1.** to cast sly, stealthy glances – مِن يشُوف بنَيَّة، يظَلّ يبَصبُص عَلَيها [min yšuːf bnayya, yðall ybaṣbuṣ ʕaliːha] When he sees a girl, he keeps making eyes at her. لا تِكتِب قِدّامَه تَرَة يبَصبُص [laː tiktib giddaːmah tara ybaṣbuṣ] Don't write in front of him or he'll look on. • **2.** with prep ب to wag – الكَلِب بَصبَصلِي بذَيلَه [ʔiččalib baṣbaṣli biðiːlah] The dog wagged his tail at me.

تبَصبَص [tbaṣbaṣ] *v:* • **1.** to fawn, apple-polish, curry favor – دائماً يِتبَصبَص لِلمُدِير [daːʔiman yitbaṣbaṣ lilmudiːr] He's always fawning on the director.

بَصِيص [baṣiːṣ] *n:* • **1.** glow, shine, glimpse, ray

ب ص ر 1

تبَصَّر [tbaṣṣar] *v:* • **1.** to reflect, ponder – لازم تِتبَصَّر بالأُمُور [laːzim titbaṣṣar bilʔumuːr] You have to think things through.

تباصَر [tbaːṣar] *v:* • **1.** to confer – خَلِّي نِتباصَر بِالقَضِيَّة وَنشُوف فَدّ حَلّ [xalliː nitbaːṣar bilqaðiyya winšuːf fadd ħall] Let's confer on the matter and find a solution.

بَصَر [baṣar] *n:* • **1.** vision, eyesight – بَصَرَه ضَعِيف [baṣarah ðaʕiːf] His eyesight is weak. قَصِير البَصَر [qaṣiːr ʔilbaṣar] nearsighted. اِختِفَى بِلَمح البَصَر [ʔixtifaː blamħ ʔilbaṣar] He disappeared in the blink of an eye. بِالصَّحراء تشُوف رَمُل عَلَى مَدّ البَصَر [biṣṣaħraːʔ tšuːf ramul ʕala madd baṣar] In the desert the sand stretches as far as the eye can see.

بَصِير [baṣiːr] *adj:* • **1.** seeing, endowed with vision – العين بَصِيرَة وَاليَدّ قَصِيرَة [ʔilʕayn baṣiːra wʔilyadd qaṣiːra] I see your problem but I can't help (lit., the eye sees but the arm is short). • **2.** (as a euphemism) blind – المِسكِين بَصِير بِالعَينتَين [ʔilmiskiːn baṣiːr bilʕayntayn] The poor man is blind in both eyes.

ب ص ر 2

البَصرَة [ʔilbaṣra] *n:* • **1.** Basra (port in Southern Iraq) – نُومِي بَصرَة [nuːmi baṣra] a condiment made of dried lemons imported through/from Basra.

بَصرِي [baṣri] *adj:* • **1.** Basra-, of, from, or pertaining to Basra • **2.** native of Basra

بَصراوِي [baṣraːwi] *adj:* • **1.** from, of, or pertaining to Basra

ب ص ل

بُصَل [buṣal] *n:* • **1.** onion(s) • **2.** bulb(s) – راح يِزرَع بُصَل [raːħ yizraʕ buṣal] He's pushing up daisies.

بُصلَة [buṣla] *n:* بُصلات [buṣlaːt] *pl:* • **1.** onion

بَصَلِي [baṣali] *adj:* • **1.** light orange (onion skin color)

ب ص م

بُصَم [buṣam] *v:* • **1.** to stamp, print – بِالنَّجَف أَكُو مَحَلّات تُبصُم بَردات، شَراشِف، وَبُقَچ [binnaǰaf ʔaku maħallaːt tubṣum pardaːt, čaraːčif, wbuqač] In Nejef there are places that hand print curtains, handkerchiefs and cloths for bundling up articles. • **2.** to trace – بُصَم نُسخَة عَلَى هَالخَرِيطَة [buṣam nusxa ʕala halxariːṭa] He made a tracing of this map.

بَصُم [baṣum] *n:* • **1.** stamping, printing

ب

بَصمَة [başma] *n:* بَصمات [başma:t] *pl:* • **1.** imprint, impression – بَصمَة أصابِع [başmat ʔaşa:biʕ] fingerprint. قَلَم بَصمَة [qalam başma] pencil.
بَصمَجي [başmači] *n:* بَصمَجِيَّة [başmačiyya] *pl:* • **1.** an artisan who hand prints material
بَصّام [başşa:m] *adj:* بَصّامَة [başşa:ma] *pl:* • **1.** an artisan who hand prints material

ب ص و ن

بَصوان، بَصونجي [paşwa:n, paşwanči] *n:* بَصونجِيَّة [paşwančiyya] *pl:* • **1.** night watchman
بيصوان [pi:şwa:n] *n:* بيصوانِيَّة [pi:şwa:niyya] *pl:* • **1.** night watchman

ب ض ع

بِضاعَة [biḍa:ʕa] *n:* بَضايِع [baḍa:yiʕ] *pl:* • **1.** goods, merchandise, wares, commodities

ب ط

باطَة [pa:ṭa] *adj:* • **1.** even – لِعَبِت وَرَق ساعَة وَطلَعِت باطَة [liʕabit waraq sa:ʕa wṭlaʕit pa:ṭa] I played cards an hour and broke even.

ب ط ء

بُطَى [buṭa:] *v:* • **1.** to be slow, take a long time – لِيش تُبطِي هَالقَدّ بِاللِّبِس؟ [li:š tubṭi halgadd billibis?] Why are you so slow getting dressed? • **2.** to tarry, linger – رُوح، بَسّ لا تُبطِي [ru:ħ, bass la: tubṭi] Go, but don't be long. بُطَى هواية بالسُّوق؛ ما أدري شصار بِيه [buṭa: hwa:ya bissu:g; ma: ʔadri šṣa:r bi:h] He's stayed a long time at the market; I don't know what happened to him.
بَطّى [baṭṭa:] *v:* • **1.** to slow up, delay, make late – لا تبَطِّي الشُّغُل عِندَك [la: tbaṭṭi ʔiššuɣul ʕindak] Don't hold the work up at your end. أُخذَه ويّاك بَسّ لا تبَطّي [ʔuxðah wiyya:k bass la: tbaṭṭi] Take him with you but don't make him late.
اِستَبطَى [ʔistabṭa:] *v:* • **1.** to consider (someone or something) late, slow, to get impatient about, wait anxiously for – اِستَبطَيت النَّجّار وَقُمِت أشتُغُل بالمَكتَبَة بنَفسِي [ʔistabṭi:t ʔinnajja:r wagumit ʔaštuɣul bilmaktaba bnafsi] I got tired of waiting for the carpenter and started to work on the bookcase myself. اِستَبطَيناك وَخابَرنا الشُّرطَة [ʔistabṭi:na:k wxa:barna ʔiššurṭa] We got worried about you and called the police. لا تِستَبطُونِي. يجُوز أتأَخَّر [la: tistabṭu:ni. yǰu:z ʔatʔaxxar] Don't be expecting me. I might be late.
بُطء [buṭuʔ] *n:* • **1.** slowness, tardiness
بطيء [buṭʔi, baṭi:ʔ] *adj:* • **1.** slow – بَطِيء بِالتَّفكِير [baṭi:ʔ bilttafki:r] slow thinking. • **2.** late – الدِّنيا بُطئِيَّة، الوَقِت بَطِيء [ʔiddinya buṭʔiyya, ʔilwakit baṭi:ʔ] It's late. صار بَطِيء [şa:r baṭi:ʔ] It's gotten late.
بَطِيء [baṭi:ʔ] *adj:* • **1.** slow – مُوَظَّف بَطِيء [muwaððaf baṭi:ʔ] a slow worker. يِشتُغُل بَطِيء [yištuɣul baṭi:ʔ] He works slowly.
أبطأ [ʔabṭaʔ, ʔabṭa] *comparative adjective:* • **1.** slower, slowest • **2.** later, latest

ب ط ب ط

بَطبَط [baṭbaṭ] *v:* • **1.** to blister, become blistered – إيدي بَطبُطَت مِن شِلت الجِّدر الحارّ [ʔi:di baṭbuṭat min šilt ʔijǰidr ʔilħa:rr] My hand got blistered when I lifted the hot pot.
بُطباطَة [buṭba:ṭa] *n:* بُطباطات، بَطابِيط [buṭba:ṭa:t, baṭa:bi:ṭ] *pl:* • **1.** blister
مبَطبُط [mbaṭbuṭ] *adj:* • **1.** blistered • **2.** chubby

ب ط ح

بُطَح [buṭaħ] *v:* • **1.** to throw down, fall, prostrate
باطَح [ba:ṭaħ] *v:* • **1.** to wrestle with (someone) – رَح أباطحَه لعَلِي باكِر [raħ ʔaba:ṭħah lʕali ba:čir] I'm wrestling with Ali tomorrow.
تباطَح [tba:ṭaħ] *v:* • **1.** to wrestle each other, wrestle with each other – ويّامَن راح تِتباطَح باكِر؟ [wiyya:h man ra:ħ titba:ṭaħ ba:čir?] Who are you wrestling with tomorrow?
اِنبُطَح [ʔinbuṭaħ] *v:* • **1.** to prostrate oneself, lie down, sprawl flat – بَسّ دِفَعتَه، اِنبُطَح [bass difaʕtah, ʔinbuṭaħ] I just pushed him and he fell down. • **2.** to be prostrated
بَطِح [baṭiħ] *n:* • **1.** throwing, prostrating
بَطحَة [baṭħa] *n:* بَطحات [baṭħa:t] *pl:* • **1.** fall, pin (wrestling)
اِنبِطاح [ʔinbiṭa:ħ] *n:* • **1.** lying
مَبطُوح [mabṭu:ħ] *adj:* • **1.** stretched out, prone – شِفتَه مَبطُوح عَلَى بَطنَه، جَوَّة القَنفَة [šiftah mabṭu:ħ ʕala baṭnah, ǰawwa ʔalqanafa] I found him lying on his stomach, under the couch. • **2.** the loser, one who got pinned (wrestling)
أبطَح [ʔabṭaħ] *comparative adjective:* • **1.** flatter, smoother

ب ط خ

بَطِّيخ [baṭṭi:x] *n:* • **1.** (coll.) melon, cantaloupe
بَطِّيخَة [baṭṭi:xa] *n:* بَطِّيخات [baṭṭi:xa:t] *pl:* • **1.** melon • **2.** canteloupe

ب ط ر

بَطَّر [baṭṭar] *v:* • **1.** to make reckless, dissatisfied – الوَظِيفَة بَطَّرَته [lwaði:fa baṭṭratah] The job went to his head.
تبَطَّر [tbaṭṭar] *v:* • **1.** to have big ideas, to be dissatisfied with one's lot – قام يِتبَطَّر مِن صار مُدِير [ga:m yitbaṭṭar min şa:r mudi:r] He got delusions of grandeur when he became a director. لا تِتبَطَّر. مُو عِندَك سَيّارَة [la: titbaṭṭar. mu: ʕindak

sayya:ra] Don't be dissatisfied. You already have a car! لا تِتبَطَّر، تَرَة هاي خُوش وَظِيفَة [la: titbaṭṭar, tara ha:y xu:š waḏi:fa] Don't hold out, because that's a good position. دَيتبَطَّر عَلينا. أيّ وَظِيفَة نِنطِيه، ما يِرضَى [dayitbaṭṭar ʕali:na. ʔayy waḏi:fa ninṭi:h, ma: yirḏa:] He's being high hat with us. Any position we give him, he's not satisfied.

بُطَر [buṭar] *n:* • **1.** desire for something better, dissatisfaction

بَطران [baṭra:n] *adj:* • **1.** discontent, dissatisfied with one's lot • **2.** malcontent, person who is dissatisfied with his lot

مِتبَطِّر [mitbaṭṭir] *adj:* • **1.** dissatisfied • **2.** dissatisfied (with)

ب ط ر س

بُطرُس [buṭrus] *n:* • **1.** Peter

ب ط ر ق

بَطرِيق [baṭri:q] *n:* • **1.** Patriarchate. Penguin like

ب ط ر ي

بَطارِيَّة [baṭa:riyya] *n:* بَطاريّات [baṭa:riyya:t] *pl:* • **1.** battery (mil.)

ب ط ر ي ق

بَطرِيقِيَّة [baṭri:qiyya] *n:* • **1.** Patriarchate. Penguin like

ب ط ش 1

بُطَش [buṭaš] *v:* • **1.** to throw down, knock down – شالَه وَبُطَشَه بِالقاع [ša:lah wbuṭašah bilga:ʕ] He lifted him and threw him on the ground.

اِنبُطَش [ʔinbuṭaš] *v:* • **1.** to throw oneself down – بَسّ جا لِلبَيت، خَشّ لِلقُبَّة وَاِنبُطَش عَالقاع [bass ǰa: lilbayt, xašš lilgubba wʔinbuṭaš ʕalga:ʕ] As soon as he reached the house, he went in the room, and threw himself on the floor.

بَطِش [baṭiš] *n:* • **1.** violence, tyranny

ب ط ش 2

بَطُّوش [baṭṭu:š] *n:* • **1.** a variety of small melon

ب ط ط 1

بَطّ [baṭṭ] *v:* • **1.** to poke, prick (the eye) – أخُويَا بَطّ عينِي بإصبعَه [ʔaxu:ya baṭṭ ʕayni bʔiṣibʕah] My brother poked me in the eye with his finger.

اِنبَطّ [ʔinbaṭṭ] *v:* • **1.** to be poked – دِير بالَك؛ لا تِنبَطّ عينَك [di:r ba:lak; la: tinbaṭṭ ʕaynak] Watch out; don't get poked in the eye. عينِي اِنبَطَّت بِالعَركَة [ʕi:ni ʔinbaṭṭat bilʕarka] My eye was poked during the fight.

بَطّ [baṭṭ] *n:* بَطّات [baṭṭa:t] *pl:* • **1.** (coll.) ducks – تِمشِي مِثل البَطَّة [timši miθl ʔilbaṭṭa] She wiggles her hips nicely when she walks.

ب ط ط 2

بَطاطَة [baṭa:ṭa] *n:* • **1.** (coll.) potato(es)

بَطاطايَة [baṭa:ṭa:ya] *n:* بَطاطايات [baṭa:ṭa:ya:t] *pl:* • **1.** potato

ب ط ق

بِطاقَة [biṭa:qa] *n:* بِطاقات، بِطايِق [biṭa:qa:t, biṭa:yiq] *pl:* • **1.** ticket • **2.** card – بِطاقَة تَعزِيَة [biṭa:qat taʕziya] card of condolence. بِطاقَة مُعايَدَة [biṭa:qat muʕa:yada] greeting card.

ب ط ل 1

بُطَل [buṭal] *v:* • **1.** to be or become null, void, invalid, to expire, become obsolete – الباسبُورت مالَك بُطَل؛ لازِم تاخُذ غَيرَه [ʔilpa:spu:rt ma:lak buṭal; la:zim ta:xuð ɣayrah] Your passport has expired; you'll have to get another one. النَّفنُوف القَصِير بُطلَت المُودَة مالتَه [ʔannafnu:f ʔilqaṣi:r buṭlat ʔilmu:da ma:ltah] The short dress has gone out of style.

بَطَّل [baṭṭal] *v:* • **1.** to stop, cease, leave off, quit – المُطَر بَطَّل [ʔilmuṭar baṭṭal] The rain stopped. ما تبَطِّل، هَذا وَلا يُغلُب [ma: tbaṭṭil, ha:ða wala yuɣlub] Aw! quit it! He'll never win. صارلَه إسبُوع مبَطِّل التَّدخِين [ṣa:rlah ʔisbu:ʕ mbaṭṭil ʔittadxi:n] He's been off smoking for a week. لِيش بَطَّلِت مِن شُغلَك؟ [li:š baṭṭalit min šuɣlak?] Why'd you quit your job? • **2.** to make (someone) stop, cease, quit – ظَلّ يلِحّ عَلَيّا إلَى أن بَطَّلنِي مِن العادَة [ðall yliħħ ʕalayya ʔila ʔan baṭṭalni min ʔilʕa:da] He kept after me until he made me quit the habit. • **3.** to fire, lay off – بَطَّلُونِي مِن الشُّغُل [baṭṭilu:ni min ʔiššuɣul] They laid me off the job.

تبَطَّل [tbaṭṭal] *v:* • **1.** to quit

بُطُل [buṭul] *n:* • **1.** falseness, untruth. Also, bottle – شِهادتَه بُطُل [šiha:dtah buṭul] His testimony is false. هَالحَكِي كُلَّه بُطُل [halħači kullah buṭul] That talk is all false.

تبُطُّل [tbuṭṭul] *n:* • **1.** cancelation, stopping; laying off (employment)

بَطالَة [baṭa:la] *n:* • **1.** idleness, inactivity • **2.** unemployment

تَبطِيل [tabṭi:l] *n:* • **1.** cancelation, stopping • **2.** laying off • **3.** stopping

بَطّال [baṭṭa:l] *adj:* • **1.** unemployed, out of work – صارلِي شَهرَين بَطّال [ṣa:rli šahrayn baṭṭa:l] I've been unemployed for two months.

باطِل [ba:ṭil] *adj:* • **1.** groundless, baseless, unfounded, false – لا تِتهِم العالَم بِالباطِل [la: tithim

ʔilʕa:lam bilba:ṭil] Don't accuse people without evidence. • **2.** null, void, invalid – كُمبيالَة باطلَة [kumpya:la ba:ṭla] a voided promissory note.

ب

ب ط ل 2

بُطُولَة [buṭu:la] *n:* • **1.** heroism, bravery, valor • **2.** lead, leading role – دُور البُطُولَة [duwr ʔilbuṭu:la] the leading role, the starring role. • **3.** championship

بَطَل [baṭal] *adj:* أبطال [ʔabṭa:l] *pl:* • **1.** hero – دُور البَطَل [duwr ʔalbaṭal] the role of the hero. • **2.** champion – بَطَل المُلاكَمَة بِالوَزن الثَّقِيل [baṭal ʔalmula:kama bilwazn ʔiθθaqi:l] heavy-weight boxing champion.

بُطُولِي [buṭu:li] *adj:* • **1.** heroic

ب ط ل 3

بُطِل [buṭil] *n:* بطُولَة [bṭu:la] *pl:* • **1.** bottle

ب ط م

بُطُم [buṭum] *n:* • **1.** (coll.) terebinth nut(s)

بُطمَة [buṭma] *n:* بُطمات [buṭma:t] *pl:* • **1.** terebinth nut

بُطمايَة [buṭma:ya] *n:* بُطمايات [buṭma:ya:t] *pl:* • **1.** terebinth nut

ب ط ن

بَطَّن [baṭṭan] *v:* • **1.** to line (a garment) – الخَيّاط بَطَّن سِترِتي بِحَرِير [ʔilxayya:ṭ baṭṭan sitirti bħari:r] The tailor lined my jacket with silk. القماش مال القَنَفَة مبَطَّن بِقُونِيَّة [ʔilqma:š ma:l ʔilqanafa mbaṭṭan bgu:niyya] The cloth on the sofa is lined with burlap.

بَطِن [baṭin] *n:* بطُون [bṭu:n] *pl:* • **1.** belly, stomach, abdomen • **2.** pregnancy, delivery – أوَّل بَطِن جابَت وَلَد [ʔawwal baṭin ǰa:bat walad] On her first pregnancy she had a boy. جابَت ثلاث بطُون [ǰa:bat tlaθ bṭu:n] She's had three babies. • **3.** interior, inside – شَكُو بِبَطن الصَّندُوق؟ [šaku bibaṭn ʔiṣṣandu:g?] What's inside the trunk? حَطّ دِينار بِبَطن الكِتاب [ħaṭṭ dina:r bibaṭn ʔilkita:b] He put a dinar in the book. الوَلَد مات بِبَطنها [ʔilwalad ma:t bibaṭnha] The child died inside her. شَقُّوا بَطِنها وَطَلَّعوا الجّاهِل [šaggaw baṭinha wṭallʕaw ʔiǰǰa:hil] They opened her womb to remove the baby.

بطانَة [bṭa:na] *n:* إبطانات [ʔibṭa:na:t] *pl:* • **1.** lining (of a garment)

بَطّانِيَّة [baṭṭa:niyya] *n:* بَطّانِيّات [baṭṭa:niyya:t] *pl:* • **1.** blanket

باطِني [ba:ṭini] *adj:* • **1.** internal – مَرَض باطِنِي [marað ba:ṭini] internal disease.

ب ط ن ش

بَطَناش، ضِرَب بَطَناش [baṭana:š, ðirab baṭana:š] *n:* • **1.** to spin, slip, lose traction (esp. of a wheel) – لا تدُوس عَالبّانزِين هوايَة تَرَة تُضرُب بَطَناش [la: ddu:s ʕalbanzi:n hwa:ya tara tuðrub baṭana:š] Don't give it too much gas or you'll spin the wheels. الوِيل دَيِضرُب بَطَناش [ʔilwi:l dayiðrub baṭana:š] The wheel's spinning.

ب ع ب ص

بَعبَص [baʕbaṣ] *v:* • **1.** to poke, or pretend to poke, lewdly with a finger – مِن كانَت تِمشِي قِدّامَه، بَعبَصها وشِرَد [min ča:nat timši gidda:mah, baʕbaṣha wširad] As she was walking in front of him, he poked her and ran away. • **2.** to make a lewd gesture with the middle finger, suggesting poking

بَعبُوص، بَعبُوصَة [baʕbu:ṣ, baʕbu:ṣa] *n:* بَعابِيص [baʕa:bi:ṣ] *pl:* • **1.** act of lewd poking • **2.** (by extension) the middle finger – هُوَّ بقَدّ البَعبُوص ويحكِي كبار [huwwa bgadd ʔilbaʕbu:ṣ wyiħči kba:r] He's a runty little shrimp and still he talks big.

ب ع ث

بِعَث [biʕaθ] *v:* • **1.** to send, send out, dispatch – لِيش ما تبعَثلَه مَكتُوب؟ [li:š ma: tibʕaθlah maktu:b?] Why don't you send him a letter? البَعث، حِزب البَعث [ʔilbaʕθ, ħizb ʔilbaʕθ] The Ba'ath Party, Renaissance Party.

بَعِث [baʕiθ] *n:* • **1.** sending out, dispatching

بِعثَة [biʕθa] *n:* بِعثات [biʕθa:t] *pl:* • **1.** delegation, mission – بِعثَة عَسكَرِيَّة [biʕθa ʕaskariyya] military mission. • **2.** student exchange (for studying abroad at Government expense) – طالِب بِعثَة [ṭa:lib biʕθa] bursary student.

باعِث [ba:ʕiθ] *n:* • **1.** reason, cause, motive – الباعِث عالجَّرِيمَة [ʔilba:ʕiθ ʕaǰǰari:ma] the motive for the crime.

بَعثِي [baʕθi] *adj:* • **1.** of or pertaining to the Ba'ath Party • **2.** member of the Ba'ath Party

مَبعُوث [mabʕu:θ] *adj:* • **1.** dispatched, delegated

ب ع ث ر

بَعثَر [baʕθar] *v:* • **1.** to scatter, strew – لا تبَعثِر غَراضَك هنا وَهناك [la: tbaʕθir ɣara:ðak hna whna:k] Don't scatter your things all around. • **2.** to squander – بَعثَر كُلّ فلُوسَه عالقحاب [baʕθar kull flu:sah ʕalgħa:b] He squandered all his money on whores.

تبَعثَر [tbaʕθar] *v:* • **1.** to become scattered – غَراضِي تبَعثَرت مِن وُقعَت الجُنطَة [ɣara:ði tbaʕθart min wugʕat ʔiǰǰunṭa] My things got scattered when the suitcase fell.

بَعثَرَة [baʕθara] *n:* • **1.** scattering, dispersing

مبَعثَر [mbaʕθar] *adj:* • **1.** scattered, dispersed

ب ع د

بِعَد [biʕad] *v:* • **1.** to go far away, become distant – المَوكِب بِعَد مِنّا هوايَة [ʔilmawkib biʕad minna hwa:ya] The parade has gotten a long way from us. الطَّيارَة بِعدَت هوايَة. ما أقدَر أشُوفها بَعَد [ʔiṭṭiyya:ra biʕdat hwa:ya. ma: ʔagdar ʔašu:fha baʕad] The plane has gotten very distant. I can't see it anymore. بِعَدنا عَن الوِلايَة؛ تَرَة البَنزين يخلَص [biʕadna ʕan ʔilwila:ya; tara ʔilbanzi:n yixlaṣ] We've gotten far from the city; the gas may run out.

بَعَّد [baʕʕad] *v:* • **1.** to remove, move away – بَعِّد المَنقَل مِن يَمِّي [baʕʕid ʔilmanqal min yammi] Move the brazier away from me. • **2.** to deport – الحُكُومَة بَعّدَته إلَى إيران لأنّ دِخَل العِراق بَلا باسبُورت [ʔilħuku:ma baʕʕdatah ʔila ʔira:n liʔann dixal ʔilʕira:q bala pa:spu:rt] The government deported him to Iran because he entered Iraq without a passport. • **3.** to go far away, become distant – بَعَّدنا عَن الجُرُف. خَلِّي نِرجَع [baʕʕadna ʕan ʔijjuruf. xalli: nirjaʕ] We've gotten far from the shore. Let's go back. مِن يشَوِّت، يبَعِّد هوايَة [min yšawwit, ybaʕʕid hwa:ya] When he shoots for a goal, he overshoots it by quite a lot.

باعَد [ba:ʕad] *v:* • **1.** to separate

أبعَد [ʔabʕad] *v:* • **1.** to banish, exile – مَجلِس الوُزَراء أبعَدَه [majlis ʔilwuzara:ʔ ʔabʕadah] The council of ministers exiled him. • **2.** to remove, send away, deport – الشُّرطَة أبعدُوه عَن العِراق [ʔiššurṭa ʔabʕidu:h ʕan ʔilʕira:q] The police threw him out of Iraq.

تبَعَّد [tbaʕʕad] *v:* • **1.** to be banished, to be exiled – تبَعَّد مِنَّه، تَرَة يعَضَّك [tbaʕʕad minnah, tara yʕaðððak] Get away from him, or he'll bite you.

اِبتَعَد [ʔibtiʕad] *v:* • **1.** to move or go far away, to get distant – اِبتِعَد عَن الجُرُف وَغِرَق [ʔibtiʕad ʕan ʔijjuruf waɣirag] He got far away from the shore and sank. الماطُور اِبتِعَد هوايَة؛ ما دَنِقدَر نشُوفَه بَعَد [ʔilma:ṭu:r ʔibtiʕad hwa:ya; ma: danigdar nšu:fah baʕad] The launch has gotten very far away; we can't see it any more. • **2.** to withdraw, pull away, avoid – اِبتِعَد عَن جَماعتَه لأنّ قامَوا يسِكرُون وَيِلعَبُون قمار [ʔibtiʕad ʕan jama:ʕtah liʔann ga:maw ysikru:n wyilʕabu:n qma:r] He's moved away from his group because they began to drink and gamble. مِن تشُوفَه، اِبتِعِد عَنَّه؛ دائِماً يشِيل مُسَدَّس [min tšu:fah, ʔibtiʕid ʕannah; da:ʔiman yši:l musaddas] When you see him, keep away from him; he always carries a pistol. حاوِل تِبتِعِد عَن هِيكِي مَشاكِل [ħa:wil tibtiʕid ʕan hi:či maša:kil] Try to avoid problems like this.

اِستَبعَد [ʔistabʕad] *v:* • **1.** to consider unlikely, to doubt – أستَبعِد يِجِي باكِر [ʔastabʕid yiji ba:čir] I doubt he'll come tomorrow. أستَبعِد قُصّتَه عَن الحادِث [ʔastabʕid quṣṣtah ʕan ʔilħa:diθ] I doubt his account of the accident. أستَبعِد هالعَمَل مِنَّك [ʔastabʕid halʕamal minnak] I wouldn't have expected that of you. ما أستَبعِد هَذا مِنَّه أبَداً [ma: ʔastabʕid ha:ða minnah ʔabadan] I wouldn't ever put that past him.

بُعُد، بِعِد [buʕud, biʕid] *n:* • **1.** remoteness • **2.** farsightedness, hyperopia • **3.** foresightedness, foresight

بَعَد [baʕad] *n:* • **1.** still, yet – بَعدَه دَياكُل [baʕdah daya:kul] He's still eating. بَعَدها مَرِيضَة [baʕadha mari:ða] She's still sick. وَصَّى السَّيّارَة قَبُل شَهَر لَكِن بَعَد ما إستِلَمها [waṣṣa: ʔissayya:ra gabul šahar la:kin baʕad ma: ʔistilamha] He ordered the car a month ago but he still hasn't received it. خَلَّصِت لَو بَعَد؟ [xallaṣit law baʕad?] Have you finished yet? لَكِن بَعَد ما شافَه الطَّبِيب [la:kin baʕad ma: ša:fah ʔiṭṭabi:b] But he hasn't seen the doctor yet. • **2.** after – راح أرجَع بَعد شوَيَّة [ra:ħ ʔarjaʕ baʕd šwayya] I'll return after a while. راح يوصَل لِهنا بَعَد شَهَر [ra:ħ yu:ṣal lihna baʕad šahar] He'll arrive here a month from now. سبَحنا شوَيَّة بَعد الظُّهُر [sbaħna šwayya baʕd ʔiðððuhur] We swam a bit in the afternoon. • **3.** more – ترِيد بَعَد فلُوس؟ [tri:d baʕad flu:s?] Do you want more money? بَعَد شتِرِيد؟ [baʕad šitri:d?] What else do you want? خِلَص! آني شِعلَيَّا بَعَد؟ [xilaṣ! ʔa:ni ʔiš ʕlayya baʕad?] That settles it! What does it matter to me anymore? بَعَدلِي ثلَث دَنانِير وَيصِير عِندِي ألف [baʕadli tlaθ dana:ni:r wyṣi:r ʕindi ʔalf] Just three more dinars and I'll have a thousand. شقَدّ بَعَدلَك وَتخَلِّص؟ [šgadd baʕadlak wtxalliṣ?] How much longer until you finish?

إبعاد [ʔibʕa:d] *n:* • **1.** banishment, deportation, expulsion

مِتباعِد [mitba:ʕid] *adj:* • **1.** separate, infrequent

اِبتِعاد [ʔibtiʕa:d] *n:* • **1.** separation

بِعِيد، بَعِيد [biʕi:d, baʕi:d] *adj:* • **1.** far, distant, remote – بَيتنا بِعِيد [baytna biʕi:d] Our house is far away. بَعِيد النَّظَر [baʕi:d ʔinnaðar] farsighted, foresighted. بَعِيد الاحتِمال [baʕi:d ʔalʔiħtima:l] unlikely, improbable. مُو بَعِيد يِجِي بِنَفِس الوَقِت اللّي نِطلَع بِيه [mu: baʕi:d yiji bnafis ʔilwaqit ʔilli nitlaʕ bi:h] It isn't unlikely that he'll come at the same time we're leaving. بِعِيد عَنَّك [biʕi:d ʕannak] (a polite expression used when speaking of an unpleasant occurrence, approx.:) May it never happen to you. بِعِيد عَنَّك، إنطاك عُمرَه البارحَة [biʕi:d ʕannak, ʔinṭa:k ʕumrah ʔilba:rħa] God forbid. He died yesterday. مِن بِعِيد [min biʕi:d] distantly. يِقرَبلِي مِن بِعِيد [yigrabli min biʕi:d] He's distantly related to me. مالِي بِيه عِلاقَة، لا مِن قَرِيب وَلا مِن بِعِيد [ma:li bi:h ʕila:qa, la: min qari:b wala min biʕi:d] I've no connection with him, neither close nor distant.

مُبعَد [mubʕad] *n:* • **1.** deportee, exile

مُستَبعَد [mustabʕad] *adj:* • **1.** unlikely, improbable – قُصَّة مُستَبعَدَة [quṣṣa mustabʕada] an unlikely story.

بَعدِين [baʕdi:n] *adv:* • **1.** then, after that – وَبَعدِين شصار؟ [wbaʕdi:n šṣa:r?] And then what

ب

happened? • **2.** afterwards, later – أَحكي وِيّاك بَعدين [ʔahči wiyyaːk baʕdiːn] I'll talk to you later. وَبَعدين مِن إيدَك؟ شراح نسَوّي؟ [wbaʕdiːn min ʔiːdak? šraːħ nsawwiː?] What's next from you? What are we going to do? وَبَعدين وِيّاك؟ ما تِسكُت عاد [wbaʕdiyn wiyyaːk? maː tiskut ʕaːd] What's next? Why don't you shut up!

بَعَد ما [baʕad maː] *subordinating conjunction:* • **1.** (conj.) after – بَعَد ما تعَشّينا، رِحنا لِلسِّينَما [baʕad maː tʕaššiːna, riħna lissinama] After we had supper, we went to the movies.

ب ع ر

بَعرَر [baʕrar] *v:* • **1.** to defecate (of sheep, goats, and camels) – الخَرُوف دَيِمشِي وَيبَعرِر [ʔilxaruːf dayimši wybaʕrir] The sheep's walking along and dropping dung. هَذا يبَعرِر بحَكيَه. لا تديرلَه بال [haːða ybaʕrir bħačyah. laː ddiːrlah baːl] He's talking nonsense. Don't pay any attention to him.

بعير [biʕiːr] *n:* بعران، أباعِر [biʕraːn, ʔabaːʕir] *pl:* • **1.** camel

بَعرَة [baʕra] *n:* بَعرُور [baʕruːr] *pl:* • **1.** camel dung

بَعرُور [baʕruːr] *n:* • **1.** (coll.) dung, manure (sheep, goat, or camel)

بَعرُورَة [baʕruːra] *n:* بَعرُورات، بَعرُور [baʕruːraːt, baʕruːr] *pl:* • **1.** dung, manure (sheep, goat, or camel)

ب ع ص

بُعَص [buʕaṣ] *v:* • **1.** to poke lewdly with the finger – بِعَصتَه مِن شِفتَه لابِس قاط جِدِيد [biʕaṣtah min šiftah laːbis qaːṭ ǰidiːd] I poked him when I saw him wearing a new suit. • **2.** to non-plus, confound, deflate – بُعصَه بِهَالحكايَة [buʕṣah bhalħčaːya] He took the wind out of his sails with that remark. • **3.** to mess up, foul up, ruin, wreck – بُعَصها لِقَضِيَّة السَّفرَة. ما راح يجِيب سَيّارتَه [buʕaṣha lqaðiyyat ʔissafra. maː raːħ yǰiːb sayyaːrtah] He messed up the business of the trip. He's not going to bring his car. بُعصَه بِهَالمُعامَلَة [buʕṣah bhalmuʕaːmala] He messed him up on that deal.

بَعَص [baʕaṣ] *n:* • **1.** poking lewdly with the finger • **2.** ruining, wrecking • **3.** nonplussing, confounding, deflating

ب ع ض

بَعَض، بَعض [baʕað, baʕð] *n:* • **1.** some, a few – بَعض التَّلامِيذ [baʕð ʔittalaːmiːð] some of the students. بَعض الشّي [baʕð ʔišši] something, a little bit. إسأل عَلي؛ يِفتِهِم بَعض الشّي بِهَالمَوضُوع [ʔisʔal ʕali; yiftihim baʕð ʔišši bhalmawðuːʕ] Ask Ali; he knows a little about this subject. عَلَى بَعض [ʕala baʕð] /plus pronominal ending/ up to sorts, one's usual self. شبِيك اليُوم؟ مُو عَلَى بَعضَك [šbiːk ʔilyuːm? muː ʕala baʕðak] What's ailing you today? You aren't your usual self. بَعض مَعَ بَعض [baʕað maʕa baʕað] each other, among themselves. خَلِّيهُم يِتباسطُون بَعَضهُم مَعَ بَعَض [xalliːhum yitbaːsṭuːn baʕaðhum maʕa baʕað] Let them fight it out among themselves.

بَعضاً [baʕðan] *adverbial:* • **1.** sometimes, at times, occasionally – بَعضاً وَلا يِعجِبنِي أشتُغُل [baʕðan wala yiʕǰibni ʔaštuɣul] Sometimes I don't like to work at all.

ب غ

باغَة [baːɣa] *n:* • **1.** plastic • **2.** celluloid

ب غ ت

باغَت [baːɣat] *v:* • **1.** to surprise, come unexpectedly upon – الشُّرطَة باغتُوه مِن كان دَيِكسِر القاصَة [ʔiššurṭa baːɣtuːh min čaːn dayiksir ʔilqaːṣa] The police surprised him while he was cracking the safe.

ب غ د د

بَغداد [baɣdaːd] *n:* • **1.** Baghdad

بَغدادِي [baɣdaːdi] *adj:* بَغادَّة، بَغدادِيِّين [baɣdaːdiyyiːn, bɣaːdda] *pl:* • **1.** from Baghdad, Baghdadi • **2.** native of Baghdad, Baghdadi

ب غ ض

بُغَض [buɣað] *v:* • **1.** to loathe, detest, hate – لِيش تُبغُضنِي؟ [liːš tubɣuðni?] Why do you hate me?

انبُغَض [ʔinbuɣað] *v:* • **1.** pass. of بُغَض to hate – انبُغَض مِن كُلّ التَّلامِيذ [ʔinbuɣað min kull ʔittalaːmiːð] He's hated by all the students.

بُغُض [buɣuð] *n:* • **1.** hatred, hate

مَبغُوض [mabɣuːð] *adj:* • **1.** hated, loathed, detested

أبغَض [ʔabɣað] *comparative adjective:* • **1.** more or most hated, loathed, detested

ب غ ل

بَغَل [baɣal] *n:* بغال، بغُولَة [bɣaːl, bɣuːla] *pl:* • **1.** mule

بَغلَة [baɣla] *n:* بَغلات [baɣlaːt] *pl:* • **1.** female mule

ب غ ي

انبِغَى [ʔinbiɣaː] *v:* • **1.** /in pres. tense/ to be necessary, desirable – كان يِنبِغي تقُلَّه [čaːn yinbiɣi dgullah] You should have told him. ما تظُنّ يِنبِغِي تِفتَح دَفتَر جِدِيد؟ [maː dðunn yinbiɣi tiftaħ daftar ǰidiːd?] Don't you think you ought to start a new ledger?

بَغاء [baɣaːʔ] *n:* • **1.** prostitution

مَبغَة [mabɣa] *n:* مَباغِي [mabaːɣi] *pl:* • **1.** brothel

بُغيَة [buɣya, baɣya] *n:* بُغيات [buɣyaːt] *pl:* • **1.** desired object, goal – تِرَكها بَعَد ما نال بُغيتَه [tirakha baʕad maː naːl buɣiːtah] He left her after he got what he wanted.

ب ق ب ق

بَقبَق [baqbaq] *v:* • **1.** to bubble, gurgle – التِّمَّن دَيبَقبُق. خَلّي عَليه شوَيَّة ماي [ʔittimman daybaqbuq. xalliː ʕaliːh šwayya maːy] The rice is bubbling. Put

some water in it. • **2.** to cluck – الدِّجاجَة دَتبَقبُق [ʔiddiǰa:ǰa datbaqbuq] The hen is clucking.
بَقبَقَة [baqbaqa] *n:* • **1.** bubbling
بُقباقَة [buqba:qa] *n:* بُقباقات، بُقابِيق [buqba:qa:t, buqa:bi:q] *pl:* • **1.** bubble

ب ق ج

بَقَّج [baqqač] *v:* • **1.** to bundle, gather up in a bundle – بَقَّج الهدُوم واخَذها لِلمَكوِي [baqqač ʔilhdu:m wʔaxaðha lilmakwi] He bundled up the clothes and took them to the cleaner's.
بُقجَة [buqča] *n:* بُقَج [buqač] *pl:* • **1.** cotton cloth used to tie up things in a bundle
بَقجَة [baqča] *n:* بَقجات [baqča:t] *pl:* • **1.** small flower garden.

ب ق ر

بَقَر [baqar] *n:* • **1.** (coll.) cow(s), cattle – لَحم البَقَر [laħm ʔilbaqar] beef.
بَقَرَة [baqara] *n:* بَقَرات [baqara:t] *pl:* • **1.** cow
بَقَرِي [baqari] *adj:* • **1.** bovine, cow-like

ب ق ص م

بَقصَم [baqṣam] *n:* • **1.** (coll.) rusk(s), zwieback
بَقصَمَة [baqṣama] *n:* بَقصَمات [baqṣama:t] *pl:* • **1.** rusk, zwieback (a type of crisp, sweetened bread)

ب ق ع

بَقَّع [baggaʕ] *v:* • **1.** to get stained, spotted – شُوف ثُوبِي بَقَّع مِن العَرَق [šu:f θu:bi baggaʕ min ʔalʕarag] Look how my shirt got stained from the sweat.
بُقعَة [buqʕa] *n:* • **1.** spot
أَبقَع [ʔabgaʕ] *adj:* بُقُع [buguʕ] *pl:* بَقعَة [bagʕa] *feminine:* • **1.** spotted, speckled (of animals) – حصان أَبقَع [ħṣa:n ʔabgaʕ] piebald horse.
مبَقَّع [mbaggaʕ] *adj:* • **1.** spotted, speckled (of animals)

ب ق ق

بَقّ [bagg] *n:* • **1.** mosquito(es) • **2.** gnat(s)
بَقَّة [bagga] *n:* بَقّات [bagga:t] *pl:* • **1.** mosquito(es), gnat(s)

ب ق ل

بَقّال [bagga:l] *n:* بَقّالِين، بقاقِيل [bagga:li:n, bga:gi:l] *pl:* • **1.** grocer
بقالَة [bga:la] *n:* • **1.** grocery business

ب ق ل و

بَقلاوَة [baqla:wa] *n:* • **1.** (coll.) baklava, a Near Eastern confection
بَقلاوايَة [baqla:wa:ya] *n:* بَقلاوايات [baqla:wa:ya:t] *pl:* • **1.** a piece of baklava

ب ق ي

بُقَى [buqa:] *v:* • **1.** to remain, stay – بُقِيت بِبَغداد إِسبُوع [buqi:t bibaɣda:d ʔisbu:ʕ] I stayed in Baghdad a week. إِنتَ جاي ويّانا لَو باقِي؟ [ʔinta ǰa:y wiyya:na law ba:qi?] Are you coming with us or staying? ما أَدرِي وِين بُقَى؛ هُوَّ السُّوق هِيّاتَه [ma: ʔadri wi:n buqa:; huwwa ʔissu:g hiyya:tah] I don't know where he's keeping himself; the market is close-by here. بُقَى عِندِي بَسّ دِينارَين [buqa: ʕindi bass dina:rayn] I've only got two dinars left. إِذا جُوعان، أَكُو أَكِل باقِي [ʔiða ǰu:ʕa:n, ʔaku ʔakil ba:qi] If you're hungry, there's some food left. باقِيلَه سَنتَين عالتَّخَرُّج [ba:qi:lah santayn ʕattaxarruǰ] He's got two years left to graduation. شقَدّ باقِي عالعِيد؟ [šgadd ba:qi ʕalʕi:d?] How much longer till the holiday? اللَّحَم يُبقَى بِالثَّلّاجَة إِسبُوع وَما يِتلَف [ʔillaħam yubqa: biθθalla:ǰa ʔisbu:ʕ wma yitlaf] Meat will last in the refrigerator a week and not spoil. • **2.** to continue, go on, keep on – بُقَينا نِلعَب ساعَة [buqayna nilʕab sa:ʕa] We kept on playing for an hour. ما بُقَى غير تِضرُبنِي [ma: buqa: ɣi:r tiðrubni] There's nothing left now except for you to hit me.
بَقَّى [baqqa:] *v:* • **1.** to cause or allow (something or someone) to remain, stay, or be left – بَقَّيت شِي مِن الأَكِل، لَو أَكَلتَه كُلَّه؟ [baqqayt ši min ʔilʔakil, law ʔakaltah kullah?] Did you leave any of the food, or did you eat it all? بَقِّيه عَالنّار شوَيَّة اللُّخ [baqqi:h ʕanna:r šwayya ʔillux] Leave it on the fire a little longer. المُدِير بَقّانِي أَشتُغُل إِلَى هَسَّة [ʔilmudi:r baqqa:ni ʔaštuɣul ʔila hassa] The director kept me working till now.
أَبقَى [ʔabqa:] *v:* • **1.** to preserve
تبَقَّى [tbaqqa:] *v:* • **1.** pass. of بَقَّى remain – شقَدّ راح يِتبَقَّى مِن الدَّين؟ [šgadd ra:ħ yitbaqqa: min ʔiddayn?] How much of the debt will be left?
اِنبُقَى [ʔinbuqa:] *v:* • **1.** pass. of بُقَى stay – هَالمَحَلّ ما يِنبُقِي بِيه أَكثَر مِن ساعَة لِأَنّ حارّ [halmaħall ma: yinbuqi bi:h ʔakθar min sa:ʕa liʔann ħa:rr] You can't stay in this place more than an hour, it's so hot.
بَقاء [baqa:ʔ] *n:* • **1.** remaining, staying
باقِي [ba:qi] *adj:* • **1.** rest, remainder • **2.** remainder (arith.) • **3.** everlasting, eternal – الحَيّ الباقِي [ʔilħayy ʔilba:qi] the Eternal Being.
إِبقاء [ʔibqa:ʔ] *n:* • **1.** preservation, continuation, retention, maintenance
بَقِيَّة [baqiyya] *adj:* • **1.** remainder, rest – بَقِيَّة الفلُوس [baqiyyat ʔilflu:s] the rest of the money. البَقِيَّة بحَياتَك [ʔilbaqiyya bħaya:tak] polite formula for expressing condolences to the bereaved. • **2.** well, so – بَقِيَّة لا تِفاتِحنِي بِهالمَوضُوع بَعَد [baqiyya la: tifa:tiħni bhalmawðu:ʕ baʕad] So-don't bring up the matter with me again.

ب ك ب ك

تبَكبَك [tbačbač] *v:* • **1.** to whine, wheedle, pout tearfully – ظَلَّت تِتبَكبَك حَتَّى إِشتِرالها البَدلَة [ðallat titbačbač ħatta ʔištira:lha ʔalbadla] She kept whining around until he brought the suit for her.

ب

ب ك ت

بَكَتا [bakata:] *n:* • **1.** heavy machine gun
باكِيت [ba:ki:t] *n:* • **1.** packet

ب ك ت ي ر ي

بَكتِيريا [bakti:rya] *n:* • **1.** bacteria

ب ك ر 1

بِكِر [bičir] *n:* • **1.** /masc. and fem./ first child, first-born
باكِر [ba:čir] *n:* • **1.** tomorrow – عُقُب باكِر [ʕugub ba:čir] the day after tomorrow. أَبُو باكِر [ʔabu ba:čir] (lit. the father of tomorrow, i.e.:) the master of his own fate. مِنُو أَبُو باكِر؟ [minu ʔabu ba:čir?] Who knows what the future will bring?
بُكرَة [bukra] *n:* • **1.** = • **2.** tomorrow
مُبَكِّر [mubaččir] *adj:* • **1.** early

ب ك ر 2

اِبتِكَر [ʔibtikar] *v:* • **1.** to invent – اِبتِكَر مَكِينَة جِدِيدَة [ʔibtikar maki:na ǰidi:da] He invented a new machine. • **2.** to originate, create, start – بارِيس تِبتِكِر أَحدَث أَزياء النِّسوان [pa:ri:s tibtikir ʔaħdaθ ʔazya:ʔ ʔinniswa:n] Paris creates the latest women's fashions.
اِبتِكار [ʔibtika:r] *n:* اِبتِكارات [ʔibtika:ra:t] *pl:* • **1.** creation, fashion design • **2.** creative idea
مُبتَكِر [mubtakir] *adj:* • **1.** original

ب ك ر 3

بَكرَة [bakra] *n:* بَكرات، بَكَر [bakra:t, bakar.] *pl:* • **1.** spool, reel • **2.** pulley • **3.** winch

ب ك ر 4

بَكارَة [baka:ra] *n:* • **1.** virginity
باكِر، باكرَة [ba:kir, ba:kra] *adj:* بَواكِر [bawa:kir] *pl:* • **1.** virgin

ب ك ل

بُكلَة [bukla] *n:* بُكلات [bukla:t] *pl:* • **1.** lock of hair on the fore part of the head

ب ك ل ت

باكلايت [ba:kla:yt] *n:* • **1.** back light (automotive)

ب ك ل و ر ي

بَكَلُوريا [bakalu:rya] *n:* • **1.** baccalaureate – اِمتِحان بَكالُوريا [ʔimtiħa:n bakalu:rya] baccalaureate examination. شَهادَة بَكالُوريا [šaha:da bakalu:rya] high school degree, baccalaureate.

ب ك ل و ر ي س

بَكالُورِيُوس [bakalu:riyus] *n:* • **1.** bachelor's degree – شَهادَة بَكالُورِيُوس [šaha:da bakalu:ryus]. بَكالُورِيُوس بِالعُلُوم [bakalu:ryus bilʕulu:m] bachelor of science degree. • **2.** bachelor's degree

ب ك ي

بِكَى [biča:] *v:* • **1.** to cry, weep – رُوح شُوف لِيش الجّاهِل دَيِبكِي [ru:ħ šu:f li:š ʔiǰǰa:hil dayibči] Go see why the baby's crying. مِن مات أَبُوها، بِكَت هوايَة [min ma:t ʔabu:ha, bičat hwa:ya] When her father died, she cried very much.
بَكَّى [bačča:] *v:* • **1.** to make cry – أَخَذ الطُّوبَة مِن الجّاهِل وَبَكّاه [ʔaxað ʔiṭṭu:ba min ʔiǰǰa:hil wbačča:h] He took the ball away from the child and made him cry.
تبَكِّي [tbačči] *v:* • **1.** to be made to cry – يِتبَكَّى بأَقَلّ شِي [yitbačča: biʔaqall ši] He bawls at any little thing.
تباكَى [tba:ča:] *v:* • **1.** to implore tearfully, plead – راح لِلمُدِير وتباكالَه حَتَّى ما يِنُقلَه [ra:ħ lilmudi:r witba:ča:lah ħatta ma: ynuqqlah] He went to the director and cried on his shoulder so that he wouldn't transfer him.
اِنبِكَى [ʔinbiča:] *v:* • **1.** to cry, weep – الماضِي ما يِنبِكِي عَليه [ʔalma:ḍi ma: yinbiči ʕali:h] The past isn't worth crying over.
بَكيَة [bačya] *n:* • **1.** a cry, a crying moment

ب ل ب ل 1

بِلبِل [bilbil] *n:* بَلابِل [bala:bil] *pl:* • **1.** nightingale

ب ل ب ل 2

بَلبَل [balbal] *v:* • **1.** to disquiet, make uneasy or restive, stir up, rouse, trouble, confuse
بَلبُولَة [balbu:la] *n:* بَلبُولات [balbu:la:t] *pl:* • **1.** spout (of a pitcher, teapot)

ب ل ب ل 3

تبَلبَل [tbalbal] *v:* • **1.** to become confused, uneasy
تَبَلبُل [tabalbul] *n:* • **1.** confusion, muddle
مبَلبَل [mbalbal] *n:* • **1.** chaotic, anarchic
بَلبَلَة [balbala] *n:* • **1.** anxiety, uneasiness, concern, confusion

ب ل ت

بلَيتَة [pli:ta] *n:* • **1.** plate

ب ل ت ن

بلاتِين [pla:ti:n] *n:* • **1.** platinum

ب ل ج

بِلاج [bila:ǰ] *n:* • **1.** beach

ب ل د

بَلَد، بِلاد [balad, bila:d] *n:* بُلدان، بِلاد [bulda:n, bila:d] *pl:* • **1.** country

بَلدَة [balda] *n:* بَلدات [balda:t] *pl:* • **1.** city, town, community

بَلَدِي [baladi] *n:* • **1.** municipal – المَجلِس البَلَدِي [ʔilmajlis ʔilbaladi] the municipal council.

بَلَدِيَّة [baladiyya] *n:* • **1.** municipal administration, city government

بَلادَة [bala:da] *n:* • **1.** stupidity

بَلِيد [bali:d] *adj:* بَلِيدِين، بُلَداء [bali:di:n, bulada:ʔ] *pl:* • **1.** a stupid student – تِلمِيذ بَلِيد [tilmi:ð bali:d] a stupid student.

بلادِي [bla:di] *adj:* • **1.** foreign – بِضاعَة بلادِيَّة [biða:ʕa bla:diyya] foreign goods. • **1.** domestic, not imported (of goods)

أبلَد [ʔablad] *comparative adjective:* • **1.** more or most stupid

ب ل د ي

بالدِي [ba:ldi] *n:* بالدِيّات [ba:ldiyya:t] *pl:* • **1.** drum, metal barrel

ب ل س ت ك

بلاستِك [blasti:k] *n:* • **1.** plastic

بلاستِيكِي [blasti:ki] *adj:* • **1.** plastic

ب ل س م

بَلسَم [balsam] *n:* • **1.** balsam, balm

ب ل س ي

بلِسَي [plisi:] *adj:* بلِسات [plisa:t] *pl:* • **1.** pleated (in clothing), with pleats • **2.** (as *n:*) pleat

ب ل ش

بِلَش [bilaš] *v:* • **1.** to become involved, get entangled, get mixed up – ما أرِيد أبلَش وِيّا هِيكِي ناس [ma: ʔari:d ʔablaš wiyya hi:či na:s] I don't want to get mixed up with that kind of people. شلُون تِبلَش بهِيكِي شَغلَة؟ [šlu:n tiblaš bhi:či šaɣla?] How did you ever get messed up in such a deal? • **2.** to get stuck, get a bad deal, get the dirty end of the stick – وَالله بِلَشِت بِهَالسَّيّارَة البَلَشقَة [wallah bilašit bhassayya:ra ʔilpalašqa] I really got stuck with this junky car. تزَوَّجها وَبِلَش بِيها [dzawwajha wbilaš bi:ha] He married her and got stuck with her.

بَلَّش [ballaš] *v:* • **1.** to stick, give (someone) the dirty end of the stick – شبَلَّشَك بِهَالسَّيّارَة؟ [šballašak bhassayya:ra?] How did you get stuck with this car? وَالله، بَلَّشنِي بِهَالشَّروَة [wallah, ballašni bihaššarwa] Gosh, he stuck me on that deal. وَالله، ما رِدِت أشترِيها بَسّ هُوَّ بَلَّشنِي [wʔallah, ma: ridit ʔaštiri:ha bass huwwa ballašni] By golly, I didn't want to buy it but he stuck me with it. • **2.** to commence, start, go ahead – شوَقِت راح تبَلِّش بالبِناء؟ [šwakit ra:ħ tballiš bilbina:ʔ?] When are you going to start building?

تبالَش [tba:laš] *v:* • **1.** to pick fights, get into fights – لا تِتبالَش وِيّا العالَم [la: titba:laš wiyya ʔilʕa:lam] Don't fight with people.

بَلشَة [balša, bilša] *n:* بَلشات [balša:t] *pl:* • **1.** mess, muddle • **2.** bother, pain in the neck

بَلُّوشِي [ballu:ši] *n:* • **1.** free, no cost

تَبلِيش [tabli:š] *n:* • **1.** begining, starting

بَلاش [bala:š] *adj:* • **1.** (invar.) free, gratis – اِنطانِي قَلَم بَصمَة بَلاش [ʔinṭa:ni qalam başma bala:š] He gave me a pencil free. اِشتِرَيتها بَلاش [ʔištiraytha bala:š] I bought it cheap. يا بَلاش! وَالله بَلاش [ya: bala:š! wallah bala:š] My, that's cheap, that's a steal! البَلاش ما يِنحاش [ʔalbala:š ma: yinħa:š] You don't get something for nothing.

ب ل ش ق

بَلَشقَة [palašqa] *adj:* بَلَشقات [palašqa:t] *pl:* • **1.** crude, simple wagon or cart • **2.** dilapidated car, jalopy – ما تبِيع هَالسَّيّارَة؟ صارَت بَلَشقَة [ma: tbi:ʕ hassayya:ra? ṣa:rat palašqa] Why don't you sell that car? It's gotten to be a jalopy.

ب ل ط [1]

بَلَّط [ballaṭ] *v:* • **1.** to pave – راح يبَلّطُون الشّارِع وَنِخلَص مِن التَّراب [ra:ħ yballṭu:n ʔišša:riʕ wʔinixlaṣ min ʔittira:b] They're going to pave the street and we'll be rid of the dust. خَلّي سَيّارتَك هنا. شارِعهُم ما مبَلَّط [xalli: sayya:rtak hna. ša:riʕhum ma: mballaṭ] Leave your car here. Their street isn't paved.

تَبلِيط [tabli:ṭ] *n:* • **1.** paving, pavement, surface (of a road or sidewalk)

مبَلَّط [mballaṭ] *adj:* • **1.** paved – شَوارِع مبَلَّطَة [šawa:riʕ mballaṭa] paved street.

ب ل ط [2]

بَلُّوط [ballu:ṭ] *n:* • **1.** oak(s) • **2.** acorn(s)

بَلُّوطَة [ballu:ṭa] *n: (coll)* بَلُّوط [ballu:ṭ] بَلُّوطات، [ballu:ṭa:t] *pl:* • **1.** oak • **2.** acorn

بَلُّوطِي [ballu:ṭi] *adj:* • **1.** made of oak, oaken

ب ل ط [3]

بَلطَة [balṭa] *n:* بَلطات [balṭa:t] *pl:* • **1.** axe, hatchet

ب ل ع

بِلَع [bilaʕ] *v:* • **1.** to swallow, put up with, stomach – لِسانِي مِلتِهِب؛ ما أقدَر أبلَع رِيقِي [lisa:ni miltihib; ma: ʔagdar ʔablaʕ ri:gi] My tongue's swollen; I can't swallow. ما يِقدَر يِبلَع الحَبّايَة بِلا مَيّ [ma: yigdar yiblaʕ ʔilħabba:ya bila mayy] He can't swallow the pill

without water. ما أقدَر أبلَع هَالإهانات [maː ʔagdar ʔablaʕ halʔihaːnaːt] I can't put up with these insults.
بَلَّع [ballaʕ] *v:* • **1.** to make swallow – الأُمّ بَلَّعت إبنها الحَبّايَة [ʔilʔumm balliʕat ʔibinha ʔilħabbaːya] The mother forced her son to swallow the pill.
بَلِع [baliʕ] *n:* • **1.** swallowing
بَلّوع، بَلّوعَة [balluːʕ, balluːʕa] *n:* بَلّوعات، بلاليع [balluːʕaːt, blaːliːʕ] *pl:* • **1.** drain, cesspool

ب ل ع م

بَلعَم [balʕam] *v:* • **1.** to astound, dumbfound – حكايتَه بَلعِمَتني [ħčaːytah balʕimatni] His remark floored me.
تبَلعَم [tbalʕam] *v:* • **1.** to be unable to speak, to stammer – كُلّما المُعَلّم يِسألَه سُؤال، يِتبَلعَم [kullmaː ʔilmuʕallim yisʔalah suʔaːl, yitbalʕam] Whenever the teacher asks him a question, he gets tongue-tied. • **2.** to be hesitant to speak, to hem and haw, beat around the bush – لَمّا طلَبت مِنَّه ينطِيني النَّتيجَة، قام يِتبَلعَم [lamma ṭlabit minnah yinṭiːni ʔinnatiːǰa, gaːm yitbalʕam] When I asked him to give me the result, he started hemming and hawing.
بَلعُوم [balʕuːm] *n:* بلاعيم [blaːʕiːm] *pl:* • **1.** throat • **2.** (pl. only) tonsils – إدهَن بَلعُومَه حَتّى يمَشّي قَضِيتَك [ʔidhan balʕuːmah ħatta ymašši qaðiːtak] Bribe him so he'll put your case through.

ب ل غ

بِلَغ [bilaɣ] *v:* • **1.** to reach, get to, arrive at, come to – التَّعَدّي بِلَغ حَدَّه؛ بَعَد ما أتحَمَّل [ʔittaʕaddi bilaɣ ħaddah; baʕad maː ʔatħammal] The aggression has reached its limit; I can't take it anymore. يخَلّوا يتصَرَّف بفلوسَه مِن يبلَغ سِنّ الرُّشد [yxalluːh yitṣarraf bfluːsah min yibluɣ sinn ʔirrušid] They will let him manage his money when he comes of age. • **2.** to reach puberty, become sexually mature – راح يزَوّجُوا بَسّ يبلَغ [raːħ yzawwǰuːh bass yiblaɣ] They're going to get him married as soon as he reaches puberty.
بَلَّغ [ballaɣ] *v:* • **1.** to convey, transmit, impart, communicate, report – بَلَّغ تَحِيّاتنا لِلأهَل وَالأصدِقاء [ballaɣ taħiyyaːtna lilʔahal wilʔaṣdiqaːʔ] He conveyed our greetings to the family and friends. • **2.** to notify officially – بَلَّغتَه بالدَّعوَى البارحَة [ballaɣtah biddaʕwaː ʔilbaːrħa] I served him with a summons yesterday. بَلَّغتَه الشُّرطَة بِلُزُوم حُضُورَه لِلمَحكَمَة [ballɣatah ʔiššurṭa bluzuːm ħuðuːrah lilmaħkama] The police notified him he had to appear in court.
بالَغ [baːlaɣ] *v:* • **1.** to exaggerate – يبالِغ هوايَة بوَصفَه لأي شِي [ybaːliɣ hwaːya bwaṣfah lʔay ši] He exaggerates a lot in describing anything.
تبَلَّغ [tballaɣ] *v:* • **1.** pass. of بَلَّغ to notify – تبَلَّغ وَراح يِحضَر المُحاكَمَة [tballaɣ wraːħ yiħðar ʔilmuħaːkama] He was officially notified and he's going to attend the trial.

بَلاغ [balaːɣ] *n:* بَلاغات [balaːɣaːt] *pl:* • **1.** communication, report, communiqué, bulletin
بُلُوغ [buluːɣ, biluːɣ] *n:* • **1.** attainment, reaching, arrival at • **2.** puberty, sexual maturity – سِنّ البلُوغ [sinn ʔilbiluːɣ] the age of puberty.
مَبلَغ [mablaɣ] *n:* مَبالِغ [mabaːliɣ] *pl:* • **1.** amount, sum of money • **2.** (by extension) price, cost
مُبَلِّغ [muballiɣ] *n:* مُبَلِّغِين [muballiɣiːn] *pl:* • **1.** process server (of a court)
تَبلِيغ [tabliːɣ] *n:* تَبلِيغات [tabliːɣaːt] *pl:* • **1.** subpoena, summons
بَلاغَة [balaːɣa] *n:* • **1.** eloquence
بالِغ [baːliɣ] *n:* • **1.** adolescent, having reached puberty • **2.** an adolescent • **3.** adult, mature • **4.** an adult
بَلِيغ [baliːɣ] *adj:* • **1.** eloquent
مُبالَغَة [mubaːlaɣa] *n:* مُبالَغات [mubaːlaɣaːt] *pl:* • **1.** exaggeration

ب ل غ م

بَلغَم [balɣam] *n:* • **1.** phlegm

ب ل ف

بِلَف [bilaf] *v:* • **1.** to bluff, deceive, trick – بِلَفها وَأخَذ فلُوسها مِنها [bilafha wʔaxað fluːsha minha] He tricked her and took her money. بِلَفَه وَخَلّاه يدايِنَه فلُوس [bilafah wxallaːh ydaːynah fluːs] He bluffed him and made him loan him money.
بَلِف [balif] *n:* • **1.** bluffing, deceiving, tricking
بَلفَة [balfa] *n:* بَلفات [balfaːt] *pl:* • **1.** bluff, trick
بَلّاف [ballaːf] *adj:* بَلّافَة، ـِين [ballaːfa, -iːn] *pl:* • **1.** trickster, deceiver, bluffer

ب ل ك

بُلكَة [pulka] *n:* بُلكات، بُلَك [pulkaːt, pulak] *pl:* • **1.** spangle • **2.** fringe
بَلكِي، بَلكَت، بَلكَن [balki, balkat, balkan] *conjunction:* • **1.** perhaps, maybe – بَلكِي مات باكِر؛ خَلّي نِسألَه هَسَّة [balki maːt baːčir; xalliː nisʔalah hassa] Maybe he'll die tomorrow; let's ask him now. اِنتِظِر فَدّ عَشِر دَقايِق؛ بَلكَت يِجي [ʔintiðir fadd ʕašir daqaːyiq; balkat yiǰi] Wait about ten minutes; perhaps he'll come. سمَعِت صار جَنَرال. . . بَلكَت [smaʕit ṣaːr ǰanaraːl. . . balkat] I heard he became a general. . . It could be.

ب ل ك ك

بلَك [plakk] *n:* بلَكّات [plakkaːt] *pl:* • **1.** (electrical) plug • **2.** spark plug • **3.** electrical outlet

ب ل ك ن

بَلكُون، بالكُون [balkuːn, baːlkuːn] *n:* بالكُونات [baːlkuːnaːt] *pl:* • **1.** balcony

ب ل ل

بَلّ [ballal] *v:* • **1.** to wet, soak, moisten – بَلِّل إيدَك قَبُل ما تِعجِن العَجِين [ballil ʔiːdak gabul maː tiʕǰin ʔilʕaǰiːn] Wet your hands before you knead the dough. المُطَر بَلَّل هدُومِي [ʔilmuṭar ballal hduːmi] The rain soaked my clothes. بَلَّل الطّابِع بلِسانَه وَلِزَقَه [ballal ʔiṭṭaːbiʕ bilsaːnah wlizagah] He moistened the stamp with his tongue and stuck it on. المِبَلَّل ما يخاف مِن المُطَر [ʔilimballal maː yxaːf min ʔilmuṭar] What more is there to lose? (lit., whoever's gotten soaked isn't afraid of the rain).

تبَلّ [tballal] *v:* • **1.** to get wet, be soaked – تبَلِّلت بالمُطَر [tballalit bilmuṭar] I got wet in the rain.

بَلَّة، زاد الطِّين بَلَّة [balla, zaːd ʔiṭṭiːn balla] *n:* • **1.** That made things worse

مبَلَّل [mballal] *adj:* • **1.** wet, moist

ب ل ل ي

بِلّي [billi] *n:* بِلّيّات [billiyyaːt] *pl:* • **1.** ace (in cards)

ب ل م

بَلَم [balam] *n:* بلام [blaːm] *pl:* • **1.** small rowboat, skiff • **2.** lateen rigged sailing barge, dhow • **3.** large porcelain serving platter

بَلّام [ballaːm] *n:* بَلّامَة [ballaːma] *pl:* • **1.** man who operates a rowboat

ب ل م ن

بُلمَن، سَيّارَة بُلمَن [pulman, sayyaːra pulman] *n:* • **1.** "'Pullman'" bus, an air conditioned passenger trailer and tractor

ب ل ه

بَلاهَة [balaːha] *n:* • **1.** stupidity • **2.** idiocy

أبلَه [ʔablah] *adj:* • **1.** idiot, stupid person

ب ل ه ر س

بِلهارِسيا [bilhaːrisya, bilhaːriːzya] *n:* • **1.** bilharziasis, schistosomiasis

ب ل و

بالُو، حَفلَة بالُو [baːlu, ħafla baːlu] *n:* • **1.** ball, formal dance

ب ل و ر

بَلُّور [balluːr] *n:* • **1.** crystal • **2.** crystal glass

بَلُّورَة [balluːra] *n:* بَلُّورات [balluːraːt] *pl:* • **1.** piece of crystal

بَلُّورِي [balluːri] *n:* • **1.** crystal, crystalline

ب ل و ز

بلُوز [bluːz] *n:* بلُوزات [bluːzaːt] *pl:* • **1.** blouse • **2.** sweater, pullover

ب ل و ك

بلُوك [bluːk] *n:* • **1.** block

ب ل و ن

بالُون [baːluːn] *n:* بالُونات [baːluːnaːt] *pl:* • **1.** balloon • **2.** dirigible, blimp

بِليُون [bilyuːn] *n:* بَلايِين [balaːyiːn] *pl:* • **1.** billion

ب ل ي 1

بلَى [bilaː] *v:* • **1.** to accuse – الجِّيران بِلُوه بالبوقَة [ʔiǰǰiːraːn biluːh bilbuːga] The neighbors accused him of the theft. • **2.** to afflict, try, torment – المُعَلِّم بِلانا بالإمتِحانات [ʔilmuʕallim bilaːna bilʔimtiħaːnaːt] The teacher bothered us continually with examinations. بِلانِي بابِنَه [bilaːni bʔibnah] He pestered me continually about his son. مِن قِتلَه مَرتَه ماتَت، وَلا بالَى [min gitlah martah maːtat, wala baːla] When I told him his wife died, he wasn't concerned at all. يِحكِي شما يرِيد وَما يبالِي [yiħči šma yriːd wma ybaːli] He says what he wants and doesn't worry about the consequences. ما سِمَعِت الأخبار؟ أشُو وَلا مبالِي [maː simaʕit ʔilʔaxbaːr? ʔašu wala mbaːli] Didn't you hear the news? It seems you're not concerned at all.

اِنبِلَى [ʔimbilaː] *v:* • **1.** to be accused, to be afflicted, to be tormented – خَطِيَّة، اِنبِلَى بالبوقَة [xaṭiyya, ʔinbilaː bilbawga] Poor guy, he was accused of the theft.

اِبتِلَى [ʔibtilaː] *v:* • **1.** to be afflicted, get stuck – أخُويَا مات وَخَلّانِي أبتِلِي بوِلدَه [ʔaxuːya maːt wxallaːni ʔabtili bwildah] My brother died and left me saddled with his kids. يَعنِي اِبتِلَيت بِيك؟ ما تِشتُغُل [yaʕni ʔibtilayt biːk? maː tištuɣul] How did I get stuck with you? Get to work! اِبتِلَيت بسَيّارتِي؛ كُلّ يوم يِطلَع بِيها عِيب جِدِيد [ʔibtilayt bsayyaːrti; kull yuːm yiṭlaʕ biːha ʕiːb ǰidiːd] I got stuck on my car; every day a new defect turns up in it. خَطِيَّة، مِبتِلِي بابِنَه [xaṭiyya, mibtili bʔibnah] Poor guy, he's got his hands full with his son. • **2.** to get involved, get in trouble – لا تِمشِي ويّاه، تَرَة تِبتِلِي [laː timši wiyyaːh, tara tibtili] Don't associate with him, or you'll find yourself in trouble. خَلِّي نرُوح قَبُل ما تِجِي الشُّرطَة تَرَة نِبتِلِي [xalliː nruːħ gabul maː tiǰi ʔiššurṭa tara nibtili] Let's go before the police come or we may get ourselves in trouble. وَالله اِبتِلَيت! ما أدرِي إلمَن أخدِم [wallah ʔibtilayt! maː ʔadri ʔilman ʔaxdim] God, I'm in a mess! I don't know who to take orders from. بِمَن اِبتِلَيت! هَذا يُعرُف نُصّ الدِّنيا [biman ʔibtilayt! haːða yuʕruf nuṣṣ ʔiddinya] Look who you've tangled with! He knows everybody. فُوت مِن قِدّامِي قَبُل ما أبتِلِي بِيك [fuːt min giddaːmi gabul maː ʔabtili biːk] Get out of my sight before I get your blood on my hands.

بَلِي [baly] *n:* • **1.** accusation

بَلاء، بَلَة [balaːʔ, bala] *n:* • **1.** affliction, visitation – هَذا بَلاء مِن الله [haːða balaːʔ min ʔallah] This is an affliction from God. هَذا بَلاء مال الله. يَومِيّاً يسَوِّيلَه عَركَة [haːða balaːʔ maːl ʔallah. yawmiyyan ysawwiːlah ʕarka] He's a holy terror. Every day he starts a fight. هَذا كَلِب لَو بَلا أَسوَد؟ [haːða čalib law bala ʔaswad?] Is that a dog or a black terror?

بَلوَة [balwa] *n:* بَلاوِي [balaːwiː] *pl:* • **1.** Don't interfere because there's only misfortune to come of it – هَذا غير بَلوَة؛ يَومِيّاً جايِب السَّيّارَة لِلكَراج [haːða ɣiːr balwa; yawmiyyan ǰaːyib ʔissayyaːra lilgaraːǰ] He's a real affliction; he brings the car to the garage every day. هَذا غير بَلوَة؛ كُلّ النّاس يخافُون مِنَّه [haːða ɣiːr balwa; kull ʔinnaːs yxaːfuːn minnah] He's a real terror; everyone's scared of him. لا تِتداخَل تَرَة وَراها بَلوَة [laː tiddaːxal tara waraːha balwa] Don't interfere because there's only misfortune to come of it.

بالِية [baːlya] *n:* • **1.** ballet

مُبالاة [mubaːlaːt] *n:* • **1.** attention, heed – بَلا مُبالاة [bala mubaːlaːt] without paying attention, unconcernedly.

اِبتِلاء [ʔibtilaːʔ] *n:* • **1.** affliction, tribulation – اِبتِلائَه بِالقمار حَطَّمَه [ʔibtilaːʔah bilqmaːr ħaṭṭamah] His affliction with gambling destroyed him. هَذا شلُون اِبتِلاء مِن الله! و لا يِشتُغُل؛ يذِبّ كُلّ الشُّغُل عَلَيّا [haːða šluːn ʔibtilaːʔ min ʔallah! w laː yištuɣul; yðibb kull ʔiššuɣul ʕalayya] What an affliction he is! He won't work; he lets me do it all.

لا أُبالِي [laː ʔubaːli] *adj:* • **1.** indifferent, unconcerned, careless, heedless, inattentive • **2.** indifferent, unconcerned person

ب ل ي 2

بَلِي [bali] *int:* • **1.** yes, of course, certainly – بَلِي، تَمام [bali, tamaːm] Yes, that's right. بَلِي، أَتصَوَّر يِقدَر يِنجَح [bali, ʔatṣawwar yigdar yinǰaħ] Yes, I think he can succeed. بَلِي، أَغاتِي! لِيش لا؟ [bali, ʔaɣaːti! liːš laː?] Sure, man! Why not? بَلِي، أَغاتِي! لِيش ما يركَب كَدِيلاك إِذا تزَوَّج وِحدَة زَنكِينَة؟ [bali, ʔaɣaːti! liːš maː yirkab kadiːlaːk ʔiða dzawwaǰ wiħda zangiːna?] Sure, man! Why shoudn't he ride in a Cadillac if he's married a rich girl? أَبُو بَلِي [ʔabu bali] yes man, sycophant. • **2.** (as a question) pardon? eh? – بَلِي؟ شقِلِت؟ ما سِمَعِت [bali? šgilit? maː simaʕit] Pardon? What'd you say? I didn't hear.

ب ل ي 3

بِلا، بلَيّا [balaː, bila, blayya]: • **1.** (prep.) without – دِخَل السِّينَما بِلا بِطاقَة [dixal ʔissiːnama bila biṭaːqa] He went in the movie without a ticket. بِلا لَغوَة. ما يعِجبَك، لا تِجِي [bila laɣwa. maː yʕiǰbak, laː tiǰi] No nonsense. If you don't want to, don't come. بِلا زَعَل. ماكُو مُكان بِالسَّيّارَة [bila zaʕal. maːku mukaːn bissayyaːra] Don't get mad. There isn't any room in the car.

ب ل ي ر د

بِليارد [bilyaːrd] *n:* • **1.** billiards

ب ل ي س

بلايِس [plaːyis] *n:* بلايِسات [plaːyisaːt] *pl:* • **1.** pliers, pincers

ب م ي

بامية [baːmya, baːnya] *n:* • **1.** (coll.) okra

بامياية [baːmyaːya, baːnyaːya] *n:* بامِيايات [baːmyayaːt] *pl:* • **1.** pod of okra

ب ن ت ر

بَنتَر، قَندَرَة شِكِل بَنتَر [pantar, qandara šikil pantar] *adj:* • **1.** shoes with decorative stitched welts on the toes and sides

ب ن ج

بَنَّج [bannaǰ] *v:* • **1.** to anesthetize – الدُّكتُور ما بَنَّجنِي قَبِل العَمَلِيَّة [ʔidduktuːr maː bannaǰni gabil ʔilʕamaliyya] The doctor didn't anesthetize me before the operation.

بَنج [banǰ] *n:* • **1.** anesthetic

مبَنَّج [mbannaǰ] *adj:* • **1.** anesthetized

ب ن ج ر

بَنجَر [pančar] *v:* • **1.** to break down, fail mechanically – بَنجِرَت السَّيّارَة بنُصّ الدَّرُب [pančirat ʔissayyaːra bnuṣṣ ʔaddarub] The car broke down halfway down the road. وُصَل الصَّفّ الرّابِع وبَنجَر [wuṣal ʔiṣṣaff ʔirraːbiʕ wpančar] He got to the fourth grade and couldn't get any further. دَأقُلَّك صِحّتِي مبَنجرَة. كَلِّف غيرِي يسَوِّيها [daʔagullak ṣiħħti mpančira. kallif ɣayri ysawwiːha] I tell you my health is run down. Have someone else do it.

بَنجَر [pančar] *n:* بَناجِر [panaːčir] *pl:* • **1.** puncture, leak, hole • **2.** flat

بَنجَرجِي [pančarči] *n:* بَنجَرجِيَّة [pančarčiyya] *pl:* • **1.** tire repairman

ب ن د 1

بَنَّد [bannad] *v:* • **1.** to stop working, be idle (with a commercial vehicle) – راح أَبَنِّد السَّيّارَة السّاعَة خَمسَة [raːħ ʔabannid ʔissayyaːra ʔissaːʕa xamsa] I'm going to put the car away at five. راح نبَنِّد باكِر [raːħ nbannid baːčir] We're not going to drive tomorrow. شُغل التَّكسِيّات مُو زين. صارلِي إِسبُوع مبَنِّد [šuɣl ʔittaksiyyaːt muː ziːn. ṣaːrli ʔisbuːʕ mbannid] The taxi business is bad. I haven't been driving for a week. • **2.** to suspend – بَنّدَوا هَالجّاكِي إِسبُوعَين [bannidaw hajǰaːki ʔisbuːʕayn] They suspended that jockey for two weeks.

ب ن د [2]

بَند [band] *n:* بُنُود [bunu:d] *pl:* • **1.** a bundle of 100 large sheets of paper • **2.** clause, article, paragraph (of a contract)

بَنِد [banid] *n:* • **1.** var. of wrapping string, parcel string

ب ن د [3]

بَنِد، بَنِيد [banid, bani:d] *n:* بنُود [bnu:d] *pl:* • **1.** bonnet, hood (of a car)

ب ن د ق [1]

بُنْدُق [bunduq] *n:* • **1.** (coll.) hazelnut, filbert • **2.** hazel, hazel tree(s)

بُنْدُقَة [bunduqa] *n:* بُنْدُقات، بَنادِق [bunduqa:t, bana:diq] *pl:* • **1.** hazelnut • **2.** filber nut • **3.** hazel, hazel tree

بُنْدُقِي [bunduqi] *n:* بُنْدُقِيَّة [bunduqiyya] *pl:* • **1.** (military) gunsmith, armorer

ب ن د ق [2]

بُنْدُقِيَّة [bunduqiyya] *n:* بَنادِق [bana:diq] *pl:* • **1.** rifle, gun • **2.** shotgun

ب ن د ق [3]

البُنْدُقِيَّة [ʔilbunduqiyya] *n:* • **1.** Venice

ب ن د ل

بَنْدُول [pandu:l] *n:* بَنْدُولات [pandu:la:t] *pl:* • **1.** pendulum

ب ن د ن

باندان [pa:nda:n] *n:* باندانات [ba:nda:na:t] *pl:* • **1.** fountain pen, ink pen

قَلَم بَنْدَان [qalam pa:nda:n] *n:* • **1.** fountain pen

ب ن ز ن

بانزين [banzi:n] *n:* • **1.** gasoline

بَانْزِينخانَة [banzi:nxa:na] *n:* بانزينخانات [banzi:nxa:na:t] *pl:* • **1.** gas station

ب ن س ي و ن

بانسيَون [pansyu:n] *n:* بانسيَونات [pansyu:na:t] *pl:* • **1.** boarding house • **2.** apartment house

ب ن ص ر

بُنْصُر [bunṣur] *n:* • **1.** ring finger

ب ن ط ر و ن

بَنطَرُون [panṭaru:n, panṭaru:n] *n:* بَنطَرُونات، بَناطِير [panṭaru:na:t, pana:ṭi:r] *pl:* • **1.** pants, trousers

ب ن ف س ج

بَنَفسَجِي [banafsaǰi] *n:* • **1.** violet (adj) – أَشِعَّة فَوق البَنَفسَجِيَّة [ʔašiʕʕa fu:q ʔilbanafsaǰiyya] ultra-violet rays. • **1.** purple

ب ن ف ش

بَنَفشَة [banafša] *n:* • **1.** a purplish carbonated drink • **2.** date drink

ب ن ك [1]

بَنك [bang] *n:* بِنُوك [binu:g] *pl:* • **1.** bank, banking house

ب ن ك [2]

بَنكَة [panka] *n:* بَنكات [panka:t] *pl:* • **1.** electric fan

ب ن ن

إبِن [ʔibin] *n:* أبناء [ʔabna:ʔ] *pl:* • **1.** son – إبِن العَمّ [ʔibin ʔilʕamm] (uncle's son) = cousin on the father's side. إبِن الخال [ʔibin ʔalxa:l] (uncle's son) = cousin on mother's side. إبِن الأخ [ʔibin ʔalʔax] (brother's son) = nephew. إبِن حَرام [ʔibin ħara:m] illegitimate son, bastard, son of a bitch, stinker. إبِن قَحبَة [ʔibin gaħba] son of a whore, son of a bitch, stinker. إبِن أَبُوه [ʔibin ʔabu:h] (his father's son) brave, clever man. • **2.** one of, one from, member of – إبِن صَفِّي [ʔibin ṣaffi] a member of my class. إبِن طَرَف [ʔibin ṭaraf] and إبِن المَحَلَّة [ʔibin ʔilmaħalla] man from the neighborhood. إبِن ولايتِي [ʔibin wla:yti] man from my home town. إبِن ثلاثِين [ʔibin θla:θi:n] a man of thirty. إبِن السَّبِت [ʔibin ʔissabit] Jew. إبِن عَرَب [ʔibin ʕarab] an Arab. إبِن أَوادِم [ʔibin ʔawa:dim] and إبِن حَمُولَة [ʔibin ħamu:la] honorable, respected, dignified man. إبِن نُصّ الدِّنيا [ʔibin nuṣṣ ʔiddinya] man of great influence from an important family.

بِنت، بِتّ [bint, bitt] *n:* بَنات [bana:t] *pl:* • **1.** daughter – بِنت العَمّ [bint ʔilʕamm] (uncle's daughter) = cousin on father's side. بِنت الخال [bint ʔalxa:l] (uncle's daughter) = cousin on mother's side. بِنت الأخ [bint ʔalʔax] (brother's daughter) = niece. بِنت أَبُوها [bint ʔabu:ha] (her father's daughter) a girl displaying commendable traits. بِنت حَرام [bint ħara:m] illegitimate daughter, and by extension, bitch, brat. بِنت قَحبَة [bint gaħba] daughter of a whore, and by extension, bitch. • **2.** one of, one from, a member of – بِنت المَحَلَّة [bint ʔilmaħalla] a woman from the neighborhood. بِنت الثّلاثِين [bint ʔiθθila:θi:n] a woman of thirty. بِنت عَرَب [bint ʕarab] an Arab woman. بِنت وُردان، بِتّ مُردان [bint wurda:n, bitt murda:n] cockroach. بِنت الشَّقَّة [bint ʔiššaqqa] ladybug, ladybird beetle. • **3.** queen (in cards)

بنَيَّة [bnayya] *n:* بنَيّات [bnayya:t] *pl:* • **1.** daughter • **2.** girl • **3.** virgin, maiden

ب

بَنِي آدَم، بَنيادَم [bani: ʔa:dam, banya:dam] *n:* • **1.** human being, man – بَنِي آدَم! ما يِتأمَّن [bany ʔa:dam! ma: yitʔamman] He's only human. You can't trust him. البَني آدَم طَمّاع [ʔilbany ʔa:dam ṭamma:ʕ] Man is greedy. (see also ء - ب - ن)

بُنِّي [bunni] *adj:* • **1.** brown, coffee colored – قاط بُنِّي [qa:ṭ bunni] a brown suit.

ب ن ن ي

بُنِّي [bunni] *n:* • **1.** (coll.) a common variety of edible fish similar to the carp

بِنِّيَّة [binniyya] *n:* بِنِّيات [bunniyya:t] *pl:* • **1.** a common variety of edible fish similar to the carp

ب ن ي 1

بِنَى [bnai:] *v:* • **1.** to build, construct, erect – بِناله بَيت جِدِيد [bina:lah bayt ǰidi:d] He built him a new house. اِشتِرَيت قِطعَة رُكُن. راح أبنِيها بَيت [ʔištirayt qiṭʕa rukun. ra:ħ ʔabni:ha bayt] I bought a corner lot. I'm going to build a house on it.

اِنبِنَى [ʔinbina:] *v:* • **1.** to be built

بَنَّا [banna] *n:* بَنّايَة [banna:ya] *pl:* • **1.** mason, master bricklayer

بِناء [bina:ʔ] *n:* • **1.** building, construction

بُنيَة [bunya] *n:* • **1.** build, frame, physique, constitution

مَبنَى [mabna:] *n:* مَبانِي [maba:ni] *pl:* • **1.** building, construction, foundation

بِنايَة [bina:ya] *n:* • **1.** building, construction

بُنيان [bunya:n] *n:* • **1.** construction, structure, building

بِناءاً عَلَى [bina:ʔan ʕala] *n:* • **1.** based on, due to, on the basis of – بِناءاً عَلَى مَرَضَه، إنطُوه إجازَة شَهَر [bina:ʔan ʕala maraðah, ʔinṭu:h ʔiǰa:zat šahar] Due to his illness, they gave him a month's leave. بِناءاً عَلَى هَذا، كُلّ التَّرفِيعات توَقّفَت [bina:ʔan ʕala ha:ða, kull ʔattarfi:ʕa:t twaqqfat] Because of this, all promotions have been stopped.

مَبنِي [mabni] *adj:* • **1.** built, made, constructed – مَبنِي مِن صَخَر [mabni min ṣaxar] built of stone.

بانِي [ba:ni] *adj:* • **1.** built

ب ن ي 2

تبَنَّى [tbanna:] *v:* • **1.** to adopt – تبَنَّينا يَتِيم مِن المَيتَم الإسلامِي [tbanni:na yati:m min ʔilmaytam ʔilʔisla:mi] We adopted an orphan from the Islamic Orphanage. • **2.** to adopt, take an interest in, take up the cause of – وَزِير الدّاخِلِيَّة نَفسَه تبَنَّى هَالمَشرُوع [wazi:r ʔidda:xiliyya nafsah tbanna: halmašru:ʕ] The Minister of the Interior himself has embraced this project.

تَبَنِّي [tabanni] *n:* • **1.** adoption

مِتبَنِّي [mitbanni] *adj:* • **1.** adopting, sponsor

ب ن ي ن

بانيانِ [ba:nya:ni] *n:* بانيان [ba:nya:n] *pl:* • **1.** Hindu, or any non-Moslem Indian • **2.** an ignorant person

ب ن ي و

بانيُو [ba:nyu] *n:* بانيُوات [ba:nyuwa:t] *pl:* • **1.** bathtub

ب ه ت

بِهَت [bihat] *v:* • **1.** to be or become astonished, amazed, surprised, flabbergasted – بِهَتِت مِن خَشّ عَلَيّا وَراوانِي ألف دِينار [bihatit min xašš ʕalayya wra:wa:ni ʔalf dina:r] I was amazed when he came up and showed me a thousand dinars. • **2.** to astonish, amaze, surprise – خَبَر نَقلَه بِهَتنِي. وَلا كِنت أتصَوَّر يِنِّقِل [xabar naqlah bihatni. wala čint ʔatṣawwar yinniqil] The news of his transfer amazed me. I'd never have imagined he'd be transferred.

اِنبِهَت [ʔinbihat] *v:* • **1.** to be amazed, astonished – اِنبِهَتِت مِن سِمَعِت اللِّي تطَلّقَت [ʔinbihatit min simaʕit ʔilli ṭṭalligat] I was amazed when I heard that she was divorced.

بَهِت [bahit] *n:* • **1.** astonishment, surprise

بُهتان [buhta:n] *n:* • **1.** slander, lies

باهِت [ba:hit] *adj:* • **1.** pale, faded – لُون باهِت [lu:n ba:hit] a pale color.

مَبهُوت [mabhu:t] *adj:* • **1.** amazed, astonished, surprised, startled – شبِيك مَبهُوت؟ ما تِحكِي [šbi:k mabhu:t? ma: tiħči] What're you, flabbergasted? Talk, why don't you!

ب ه ج

اِبتِهَج [ʔibtihaǰ] *v:* • **1.** to be glad, happy, delighted – اِبتِهَج هوايَة بِخَبَر نَجاح إبنَه [ʔibtihaǰ hwa:ya bxabar naǰa:ħ ʔibnah] He was very joyful at the news of his son's success.

بَهجَة [bahǰa] *n:* بَهجات [bahǰa:t] *pl:* • **1.** joy, delight

مُبهِج [mubhiǰ] *adj:* • **1.** festive

مِبتِهِج [mibtihiǰ] *adj:* • **1.** gay • **2.** happy, glad

ب ه د ل

بَهدَل، بَهذَل [bahðal] *v:* • **1.** to ridicule, embarrass – عَلَى دِينارَين، بَهدَلنِي قِدّام النّاس [ʕala dina:rayn, bahdalni gidda:m ʔinna:s] For two dinars, he ridiculed me in front of people. • **2.** to make a mess of, disrupt, ruin – المُطَر بَهذَلنا وَإضطَرَّينا نبَدِّل [ʔilmuṭar bahðalna waʔiðṭarayna nbaddil] The rain made a mess of us and we had to change clothes. لِيش مبَهذِل نَفسَك هِيكِي؟ ما تِلبَس هِدُوم زينَة [li:š mbahðil nafsak hiːči? maː tilbas hiduːm ziːna] Why're you letting yourself go? Wear some good clothes! إذا أشُوفَه، أبَهذِل أحوالَه [ʔiða ʔašuːfah, ʔabahðil ʔaħwaːlah] If I see him, I'll mess him up. • **3.** to waste, squander – أبُوه خَلَّفلَه ثَروَة، لَكِن بَهذَلها بِالعَجَل [ʔabuːh xallaflah θarwa, laːkin bahðalha bilʕaǰal] His father left him a fortune, but he squandered it right away.

تبَهدَل [tbahðal] *v:* • **1.** to be or become mixed up, get in bad shape, go to ruin – مِن تزَوَّجِت، تبَهذَلِت؛ عَلَى طُول مِفلِس [min dzawwaǰit, tbahðalit; ʕala ṭuːl miflis] When I got married, I got all messed up; I'm always broke.

بَهذَلَة [bahðala] *n:* بَهذَلات [bahðalaːt] *pl:* • **1.** abuse, insult – البَهدَلَة ما تِنفَع وِيّاه [ʔilbahdala maː tinfaʕ wiyyaːh] Abuse won't do any good with him. • **2.** humiliation, degradation – الشَّغُل بِهَالدّائِرَة بَهذَلَة. مَحَّد يِحتُرُم الواحِد [ʔiššɣul bhaddaːʔira bahðala. maħħad yiħturum ʔilwaːħid] Working in this office is a trauma. No one respects you. • **3.** mess, disorder, sloppiness – شِنُو هَالبَهذَلَة؟ ما تصَفُّط غَراضَك [šinu halbahðala? maː tṣaffuṭ ɣaraːđak] What's this mess? Arrange your things, will you!

مبَهدَل [mbahðal] *adj:* • **1.** sloppy, unkempt – شُوفَه شلُون مبَهذَل، لا ممَشَّط وَلا مزَيِّن [šuːfah šluːn mbahðal, laː mmaššiṭ wala mzayyin] Look how sloppy he is, uncombed and unshaven.

ب ه ر 1

بُهَر [buhar] *v:* • **1.** to dazzle, overwhelm – ضُوَا الشَّمِس بُهَر عينِي [đuwa ʔiššamis buhar ʕiːni] The sunlight dazzled me. جَمالها يبهُر [ǰamaːlha yibhur] Her beauty is dazzling.

اِنبُهَر [ʔinbuhar] *v:* • **1.** to be dazzled

بَهَر [bahar] *n:* • **1.** dazzlement

بَهار [bahaːr] *n:* بَهارات [bahaːraːt] *pl:* • **1.** spice, seasoning

باهِر [baːhir] *adj:* • **1.** splendid, brilliant, dazzling – نَجاح باهِر [naǰaːħ baːhir] a brilliant success.

ب ه ر 2

بَهار [bahaːr] *adj:* • **1.** the beginning of Spring

بَهارِي [bahaːri] *adj:* • **1.** spring, vernal – قاط بَهارِي [qaːṭ bahaːri] spring suit.

ب ه ر 3

بُهرَة [buhra] *n:* • **1.** a Moslem sect concentrated in India and Pakistan

ب ه ر ز

بَهرِيز [pahriːz] *n:* • **1.** diet, prescribed regimen

ب ه ض

باهِض [baːhiđ] *adj:* • **1.** excessive, exorbitant, enormous

ب ه ل

بُهُل [buhul] *n:* • **1.** (invar.) stupid, backward – نِسوان بُهُل [niswaːn buhul] stupid women.

بَهلُول [bahluːl] *n:* بَهالِيل [bahaːliːl] *pl:* • **1.** clown, buffoon, jester • **2.** dunce, simpleton, fool

ب ه ل و ن

بَهلَوان [pahlawaːn] *n:* • **1.** circus performer • **2.** acrobat • **3.** strong-man

بَهلَوانِي [pahlawaːni] *adj:* • **1.** acrobatic

ب ه م

بَهِيمَة [bahiːma] *n:* • **1.** beast of burden • **2.** a stupid animal

إبهام [ʔibhaːm, bhaːm] *n:* إبهامات [ʔibhaːmaːt] *pl:* • **1.** thumb • **2.** big toe

مُبهَم [mubham] *adj:* • **1.** vague, ambiguous – حَكِي مُبهَم [ħači mubham] vague talk.

ب ه و

بَهُو [bahw] *n:* • **1.** large hall, auditorium, recreation hall

ب ه ي 1

باهَى [baːhaː] *v:* • **1.** to pride oneself, be proud, boast – عَلَى طُول يباهِي بِسَيّارتَه [ʕala ṭuːl ybaːhi bsayyaːrtah] He's always bragging about his car.

تباهَى [tbaːhaː] *v:* • **1.** to pride oneself, be proud, boast – شدَعوَة تِتباهَى بنَفسَك [šdaʕwa titbaːhaː bnafsak] You sure are proud of yourself!

ب ه ي 2

بَهائِي [bahaːʔi] *adj:* بَهائِيَّة [bahaːʔiyya] *pl:* • **1.** Bahai • **2.** a Bahai, adherent of the Bahai sect

البَهائِيَّة [ʔilbahaːʔiyya] *adj:* • **1.** Bahai, the Bahai religion

ب و ء

بِيئَة [biːʔa] *n:* • **1.** environment

ب و ب

بَوَّب [bawwab] *v:* • **1.** to divide into parts or sections – الكِتاب مبَوَّب إلَى ثلَاث أبواب [ʔilkitaːb mbawwab ʔila tlaθ ʔabwaːb] The book's divided into three parts. • **2.** to classify, arrange in groups – أرِيدَك تبَوُّبلِي هالمَعلُومات [ʔariːdak tbawwubli halmaʕluːmaːt] I want you to classify this information for me.

باب [ba:b] *n:* أبواب، بيبان [ʔabwa:b, bi:ba:n] *pl:* • **1.** door, doorway • **2.** gate, gateway – باب الشَّرجي [ba:b ʔaššarji] (the South Gate) a quarter of Baghdad. • **3.** sluice gate • **4.** part, section (of a book) • **5.** class, type, category
بَوّاب [bawwa:b] *n:* بَوّابين [bawwa:bi:n] *pl:* • **1.** doorman
بَوّابَة [bawwa:ba] *n:* بَوّابات [bawwa:ba:t] *pl:* • **1.** gate, sluice gate
تَبويب [tabwi:b] *n:* • **1.** arrangement, grouping
مُبَوَّب [mubawwab] *adj:* • **1.** classified, classed, arranged in groups

ب و ت س

بُوتاسَة [pu:ta:sa] *n:* بُوتاسات [pu:ta:sa:t] *pl:* • **1.** torpedo, a home-made, impact-detonating firecracker

ب و ت ن

بَوتِين [pu:ti:n] *n:* بُوتينات [pu:ti:na:t] *pl:* • **1.** (pair of) leather boots

ب و ح

باح [ba:ħ] *v:* • **1.** (with بـ-) to disclose, divulge, reveal – لَو تقُتلَه ما يبُوح بِالسِّرّ [law tkutlah ma: ybu:ħ bissirr] Even if you kill him he won't reveal the secret. • **2.** to permit, allow, sanction
بُوح [bu:ħ, bawħ] *n:* • **1.** disclosing
إباحَة [ʔiba:ħa] *n:* • **1.** openness, looseness, licentiousness, unrestrictedness (esp. sexual) (negative connotation)
إباحِي [ʔiba:ħi] *adj:* • **1.** licentious, amoral – فِكرَة إباحِيَّة [fikra ʔiba:ħiyya] an amoral idea. حُكُومَة إباحِيَّة [ħuku:ma ʔiba:ħiyya] an amoral government. • **2.** libertine, free-thinker
إباحِيَّة [ʔiba:ħiyya] *n:* • **1.** freethinking, libertinism

ب و خ

بَوَّخ [bawwax] *v:* • **1.** to steam, give off steam – الحَمّام دَيبَوِّخ. رُوح إغسِل [ʔilħamma:m daybawwix. ru:ħ ʔiɣsil] The Turkish bath is steaming. Go take a bath. بَوَّخ التِّمَّن. نَزِّل نارَه شوَيَّة [bawwax ʔittimman. nazzil na:rah šwayya] The rice has boiled. Turn down the fire under it a little.
بُوخَة، بواخ [bu:xa, bwa:x] *n:* • **1.** steam
بايِخ [ba:yix] *adj:* • **1.** stale, insipid, flat – نُكتَة بايخَة [nukta ba:yxa] a bad joke. حكايَة بايخَة [ča:ya ba:yxa] an insipid remark.

ب و د ر

بودَر [pu:dar, pawdar] *v:* • **1.** to powder, apply powder – بُودرَت المُكانات المِلتَهبَة بِجِسم الجّاهِل [pu:drat ʔalmuka:na:t ʔilmiltahba bjism ʔijja:hil] She powdered the inflamed areas on the baby's body.
تبودَر [tpu:dar] *v:* • **1.** to powder oneself – دَتِتبُودَر قِدّام المرايا [datitpu:dar gidda:m ʔilmra:ya] She's powdering herself in front of the mirror.
بودرَة [pu:dra] *n:* • **1.** powder

ب و ر

بار [ba:r] *v:* • **1.** to go to waste, to be left over – دَياكلُون كُلَّشي؛ ما كُو شِي راح يبُور [daya:klu:n kullši; ma: ku: ši ra:ħ ybu:r] They're eating everything; nothing's going to be left over. • **2.** to be unsaleable, stay on the shelf – هالبِضاعَة بارَت، مَحَّد يِشتِريها [halbiða:ʕa ba:rat, maħħad yištiri:ha] These goods didn't move; no one will buy them. • **3.** to fail to get a husband, become an old maid – بِنتِي ما راح تِبُور لِأنَّ زَنكِينَة [binti ma: ra:ħ tbu:r liʔann zangi:na] My daughter won't be left on the shelf because she's rich.
بُور، أراضِي بُور [bu:r, ʔara:ði bu:r] *adj:* • **1.** wasteland
بايِر [ba:yir] *adj:* • **1.** waste, uncultivated, unused, unwanted – أراضِي بايرَة [ʔara:ði ba:yra] wasteland. • **2.** unsold, left over, unwanted – بَضايِع بايرَة [baða:yiʕ ba:yra] goods left on the shelves.
بايرَة [ba:yra] *adj:* بايرات [ba:yra:t] *pl:* • **1.** an old maid • **2.** a woman whose husband has married a second wife

ب و ر ق

بُورَق [bu:rag] *n:* • **1.** borax • **2.** a type of stuffed pastry

ب و ر ن

بَورانِي [bu:ra:ni] *n:* • **1.** fried slices of eggplant, usually mixed with yogurt and garlic

ب و ر ي

بُورِي [bu:ri] *n:* بُورِيّات، بُوارِي [bu:riyya:t, bwa:ri] *pl:* • **1.** bugle • **2.** pipe, tube

ب و ز

بَوَّز [bawwaz] *v:* • **1.** to pout, look glum – مِن أخَذِت اللُّعّابَة مِنها، بَوّزَت [min ʔaxaðit ʔillaʕʕa:ba minha, bawwzat] When I took the doll from her, she pouted. شبِيك مبَوِّز؟ أكُو شِي؟ [šbi:k mbawwiz? ʔaku ši?] Why are you so glum? Is something wrong? • **1.** to shuffle
بُوز [bu:z] *n:* بُوزات [bu:za:t] *pl:* • **1.** snout, muzzle (of an animal), and by extension, a derogatory term for chin – شِفتَه شلُون بُوز عَليه؟ [šiftah šlu:n bu:z ʕali:h?] Did you see what a chin he's got?

مِشّ بُوزَك! ما راح تحَصِّل شِي [mišš bu:zak! ma: ra:ħ tħaṣṣil ši] Wipe your chin! You won't get anything.
مبَوَّز [mbawwaz] *adj:* • **1.** glum, bleak

ب و س

باس [ba:s] *v:* • **1.** to kiss – باس إبنَه بِقُصتَه [ba:s ʔibnah bguṣtah] He kissed his son on the forehead.
بَوَّس [bawwas] *v:* • **2.** with بـ- to kiss repeatedly, cover with kisses – ظَلّ يبَوِّس بِيها نُصّ ساعَة [ðall ybawwis bi:ha nuṣṣ sa:ʕa] He kept on kissing her for a half hour.
تباوَس [tba:was] *v:* • **1.** to kiss one another – بَعَد ما تلاقَوا، تباوَسَوا [baʕad ma: tla:gaw, tba:wasaw] After they met, they kissed each other.
بَوس [baws, bu:s] *n:* • **1.** kissing, (coll.) kisses
بَوسَة [bawsa] *n:* بَوسات [bawsa:t] *pl:* • **1.** kiss

ب و س ط

بُوسطَة [bu:sṭa] *n:* بُوسطات [bu:sṭa:t] *pl:* • **1.** mail, post – دِزّلِي الأَوراق بِالبُوسطَة [dizzli ʔilʔawra:q bilbu:sṭa] Send me the papers by mail. • **2.** post office – راح لِلبَوسطَة حَتَّى يِشتِرِي طَوابِع [ra:ħ lilbu:sṭa ħatta yištiri ṭawa:biʕ] He went to the post office to buy some stamps. • **3.** group of travelers – راح ترُوح وِيّا هَالبَوسطَة لِأَنّ كُلّهُم تُعرُفهُم [ra:ħ tru:ħ wiyya halbu:sṭa liʔann kullhum tuʕrufhum] You will go with this group because you know all of them.
بُوسطَجِي [bu:sṭači] *n:* بُوسطَجِيَّة [bu:sṭačiyya] *pl:* • **1.** postman

ب و ش

بَوَّش [bawwaš] *v:* • **1.** to put in neutral – بَوِّش الكير [bawwiš ʔilgi:r] Put the gears in neutral. • **1.** to set a car to neutral • **2.** to cause to wear a veil, to veil
تبَوَّش [tbawwaš] *v:* • **1.** to put on the veil, to veil oneself – لازِم تِتبَوّشِين قَبُل ما تطِلعِين [la:zim titpawwši:n gabul ma: ṭṭilʕi:n] You should put on your veil before you go out. • **2.** to wear a veil, go veiled – هِيَّ تِتبَوَّش حَتَّى مَحَّد يعرُفها [hiyya titpawwaš ħatta maħħad yuʕrufha] She wears a veil so no one will know her.
بُوشِي [pu:ši] *n:* بُوشِيّات، بوش [pu:ši:yya:t, pu:š] *pl:* • **1.** veil
بُوشِيَّة [pu:šiyya] *n:* بُوشِيّات [pu:šiyya:t] *pl:* • **1.** veil
بَوش [bawš, bu:š] *adj:* • **1.** empty – الِكوابَة البُوش [ʔilkwa:ba ʔilbu:š] the empty cups. • **2.** vain, useless – تَعَبِي كُلَّه راح بُوش [taʕabi kullah ra:ħ bu:š] All my efforts went to waste. • **3.** neutral (automotive) – المَكِينَة قاعِد تِشتُغُل بِالبُوش [ʔilmaki:na ga:ʕid tištuɣul bilbu:š] The motor's running in neutral. ذِبّ الكير عالبُوش [ðibb ʔilgi:r ʕalbu:š] Put the gearshift in neutral. • **4.** looseness, play – بُوش الإستَيرِن دَيزِيد يوم عَلَى يوم [bu:š ʔilʔisti:rin dayzi:d yu:m ʕala yu:m] The play in the steering is increasing all the time.

ب و ص ل

بَوصلَة [bawṣala, bu:ṣla] *n:* بُوصَلات [bawṣala:t, bu:ṣla:t] *pl:* • **1.** compass

ب و ط

بَوَّط [bawwaṭ] *v:* • **1.** to wrinkle and lose its shape – مِن تِغسِل السِّترَة، تبَوُّط [min tiɣsil ʔissitra, tbawwuṭ] As soon as you wash the jacket, it will wrinkle out of shape.
بَوط [pu:ṭ] *n:* بَوطات [pu:ṭa:t] *pl:* • **1.** faux pas, social error, slip – صاحِبنا كِسَر غير بُوط البارحَة عِند الوَزِير [ṣa:ħibna kisar ɣi:r pu:ṭ ʔilba:rħa ʕind ʔilwazi:r] Our friend pulled a big faux pas yesterday with the minister.
مبَوُّط [mbawwuṭ] *adj:* • **1.** out of shape (curved), crooked, hunched

ب و ع

باوَع [ba:waʕ] *v:* • **1.** to observe, watch – باوِع شدَأسَوِّي حَتَّى تسَوِّي مِثلِي [ba:wiʕ šdaʔasawwi: ħatta tsawwi: miθli] Observe what I do so you can do it the same way. • **2.** to look – باوِع مِن الشِّبّاك وشُوف شصار جَوَّة [ba:wiʕ min ʔiššibba:č wšu:f šṣa:r ǰawwa] Look out the window and see what happened down below. باوِع جَوَّة القَنَفَة [ba:wiʕ ǰawwa ʔalqanafa] Look under the couch. باوِع دَأَقُلَّك! آنِي ما أَخاف مِن التَّهدِيد [ba:wiʕ daʔagullak! ʔa:ni ma: ʔaxa:f min ʔittahdi:d] Now you look here! I'm not afraid of threats.

ب و ف ي

بُوفيَة [bu:fya] *n:* بُوفيَهات [bu:fyaha:t] *pl:* • **1.** buffet, sideboard

ب و ق 1

بُوق [bu:q] *n:* بواق [bwa:q] *pl:* • **1.** bugle – بُوق النَّوم [bu:q ʔinnu:m] taps. • **2.** spokesman, mouthpiece – بُوق لِلمُستَعمِرِين [bu:q lilmustaʕmiri:n] a mouthpiece for the colonialists.
بُوقِي [bu:qi] *n:* بُوقِيَّة [bu:qi:yya] *pl:* • **1.** (mil.) bugler

ب و ق 2

باق [ba:g] *v:* • **1.** to rob, burglarize – الحَرامِيَّة باقَوا البَيت [ʔilħara:miyya ba:gaw ʔilbayt] The thieves robbed the house. • **2.** to steal – باق نُصّ دِينار مِنِّي [ba:g nuṣṣ dina:r minni] He stole half a dinar from me. باق ألف دِينار بِالحِساب [ba:g ʔalf dina:r biliħsa:b] He embezzled a thousand dinars. أَبُوق نَفسِي مِن الشُّغُل نُصّ ساعَة [ʔabu:g nafsi min ʔiššuɣul nuṣṣ sa:ʕa] I'll drag myself away from work

ب

for a half hour. لَهِّي إبنِي حَتَّى أَبُوق نَفسِي [lahhi ʔibni ħatta ʔabuːg nafsi] Keep my son busy so I can sneak away.
بَوَّق [bawwag] *v:* • **1.** to steal (habitually) – بِأي شُغُل تخَلِّيه، يقُوم يبَوُّق [bʔay šuɣul txalliːh, yguːm ybawwug] Any job you put him in, he starts to steal. دَيبَوُّق فلُوس الشَّرِكَة [daybawwug fluːs ʔiššarika] He's stealing the company's money.
بَوق [bawg, buːg] *n:* • **1.** thievery, robbery, larceny, stealing
بُوقَة [buːga] *n:* بَوقات [bawgaːt, buːgaːt] *pl:* • **1.** a theft, a robbery • **2.** loot, swag, take, stolen goods
مَبيُوق [mabyuːg] *adj:* • **1.** stolen

ب و ق 3
باقَة [baːqa, baːga] *n:* باقات [baːgaːt] *pl:* • **1.** bunch, bouquet

ب و ك
باوَك [paːwak] *v:* • **1.** to pay back, pay off, settle (a debt) – باوَكِت كُلّ ديُونَك [paːwakit kull dyuːnak] You paid back all your debts.
تباوَك [tpaːwak] *v:* • **1.** to settle with each other, settle up – اِنطانِي الفلُوس وَتباوَكنا [ʔinṭaːni ʔilfluːs wtpaːwakna] He gave me the money and we were even.

ب و ك س
بُوكس [buːks] *n:* • **1.** punch

ب و ل 1
بال [baːl] *v:* • **1.** to urinate, make water – لا تبُول بِالدَّرُب [laː tbuːl biddarub] Don't urinate in the street.
بَوَّل [bawwal] *v:* • **1.** to make (someone) urinate – بَوِّلِي الجّاهِل [bawwli ʔijjaːhil] Take the kid to the potty.
بَول [bawl, buːl] *n:* • **1.** urine – مَرَض البُول السُّكَّرِي [marað ʔilbuːl ʔissukkari] sugar diabetes.
بُول [puːl] *n:* بوالَة [pwaːla] *pl:* • **1.** piece, man (backgammon, dominoes) • **2.** (archaic) postage stamp • **3.** small Persian coin
بُولَة [buːla] *n:* بُولات [buːlaːt] *pl:* • **1.** an act of urination
تَبَوُّل [tabawwul] *n:* • **1.** urination, peeing
مِبوَلَة [mibwala, mabwala] *n:* مَبوَلات، مَباوِل [mabwalaːt, mabaːwil] *pl:* • **1.** urinal • **2.** public urinal

ب و ل 2
بال [baːl] *n:* • **1.** mind – بالَه مَشغُول هوايَة [baːla mašɣuːl hwaːya] He's very preoccupied. خَلِّي بالَك يَمّ التِّلفُون [xalli: baːlak yamm ʔittilifuːn] Keep your mind on the telephone. إسمَه راح مِن بالِي [ʔismah raːħ min baːli] His name slipped my mind. خَلِّيها عَلَى بالَك. مُو تِنسَى [xalliːha ʕala baːlak. muː tinsaː] Keep it in mind. Don't you forget. إسمَه مُو عَلَى بالِي [ʔismah muː ʕala baːli] His name doesn't come to mind. إسمَه هَسَّة جا عَلَى بالِي [ʔismah hassa ǰaː ʕala baːli] His name just came to me. ببالَك مِن نزَل الثَّلج هنا قَبل إسبُوع؟ [bbaːlak min nizal ʔiθθaliǰ hna qabl ʔisbuːʕ?] Do you recall when the snow fell here a week ago? هِيكِي مُشكِلَة ما كانَت لا بِالبال وَلا بِالخاطِر [hiːči muškila maː čaːnat laː bilbaːl wala bilxaːṭir] Such a problem could never have been expected. بالَك وِيّاك [baːlak wiyyaːk] Take care not to. . . ! Mind that you don't. . . بالَك وِيّاك ترُوح مِن أَطلَع ! [baːlak wiyyaːk truːħ min ʔaṭlaʕ] Make sure you don't leave while I'm out. بالَك وِيّاك تِمشِي وِيّا هِيكِي ناس [baːlak wiyyaːk timši wiyya hiːči naːs] Watch yourself that you don't associate with such people. • **2.** attention – بالَك عَنِّي! هَسَّة أَفتَح الباب بِفَدّ دَفعَة [baːlak ʕanni! hassa ʔaftaħ ʔilbaːb bfadd dafʕa] Watch me! I'm going to open the door with one push. دار بال [daːr baːl] to pay attention, give heed. خَوُّفُوه بَسّ ما دار بال وَخَشّ بالمَقبَرَة [xawwufuːh bass maː daːr baːl wxašš bilmaqbara] They tried to frighten him but he paid no attention and went into the graveyard. لا تدِيرلَه بال شما يِحكِي [laː ddiːrlah baːl šmaː yiħči] Don't pay any attention to him whatever he says. دِير بالَك عَلَى شُغلَك [diːr baːlak ʕala šuɣlak] Pay attention to your work. دِير بالَك عَلَى غراضِي [diːr baːlak ʕala ɣaraːði] Watch my things. دِير بالَك مِن السَّيّارَة [diːr baːlak min ʔissayyaːra] Watch out for that car! ظَلّ بالَه [ðall baːla] He was worried, apprehensive. لا يضَلّ بالكُم. راح أَتأَخَّر اللَّيلَة [laː yðall baːlkum. raːħ ʔatʔaxxar ʔillayla] Don't worry. I'm going to be late tonight. وَبالَك وَبالَك [wbaːlak wbaːlak] a derisive expression of exaggerated emphasis. أَشُو تقُول راح أَساعدَك وَبالَك وَبالَك وَما بَيَّن شِي مِنَّك [ʔašuː dguːl raːħ ʔasaːʕdak wbaːlak wbaːlak wma bayyan ši minnak] It seems you say "I'll help you" and blah blah blah and nothing has appeared from you. بالَك وَبالَك؛ وُعَد يِنطِينا فلُوس وَمَقبَضنا شِي [baːlak wbaːlak; wuʕad yintiːna fluːs wmaqbaðna ši] He made a big fuss; he promised to give us some money and we didn't get a thing.
عَبال [ʕabaːl] *n:* • **1.** it seemed, it would have seemed – مِن دَقّ التِّلفُون، عَبالِي إنتَ [min dagg ʔittilifuːn, ʕabaːli ʔinta] When the phone rang, I thought it was you. توَهَّمِت. عَبالِي أَخُويَا [twahhamit. ʕabaːli ʔaxuːya] I got confused. I thought it was my brother. عَبالكُم أَجُوز مِن الطَّلَب؟ راح أَشتِكِي عَلَيكُم [ʕabaːlkum ʔaǰuːz min ʔiṭṭalab? raːħ ʔaštiki ʕaliːkum] Did you think I would abandon the debt? I'll sue you. لَعَد شعبالَك؟ بَسّ إنتَ تُعرُف؟ [laʕad šʕbaːlak? bass ʔinta tuʕruf?] So what did you think? You're the only one

who knows? قام يصَيِّح عَلَيّا عَبالَه يخَوُّفني [ga:m yṣayyiħ Ƹalayya Ƹaba:lah yxawwufni] He began to shout at me like he thought he'd scare me. وُقَع بالأكِل دَقّ عَبالَك ما ماكِل مُدَّة شَهَر [wugaƸ bilʔakil dagg Ƹaba:lak ma: ma:kil muddat šahar] He dug into the food as though he hadn't eaten for a month. • **2.** it seemed to (plus personal pronoun)

ب و ل 3
بالَة [ba:la] *n:* بالات [ba:la:t] *pl:* • **1.** bale

ب و ل س
بُولِيس [bu:li:s] *n:* • **1.** police, policeman
بُولِيسِي [bu:li:si] *adj:* • **1.** detective, police (in compounds)

ب و م
بُوم [bu:m] *n:* • **1.** (coll.) owl(s)
بُومَة [bu:ma] *n:* بُومات، بُوَم [bu:ma:t, buwam] *pl:* • **1.** owl – لا تصِير بُومَة. إذا يُضُربَك، إنتَ هَمّ أُضُربَه [la: tṣi:r bu:ma. ʔiða yuðurbak, ʔinta hamm ʔuðurbah] Don't be a chicken. If he hits you hit him back. هَذا بُومَة. الكُلّ يكَرِّبُون عَليه [ha:ða bu:ma. ʔilkull ykarribu:n Ƹali:h] He's a sheep. Everyone loads him with work.

ب و ن
باوَن [pa:wan] *n:* • **1.** pound (weight)

ب و ي
بُوي [bu:y] *n:* • **1.** waiter
بَويَة [bu:ya] *n:* بَويات [bu:ya:t] *pl:* • **1.** paint

ب و ي ن ب غ
بَوينباغ [bu:yinba:ɣ] *n:* بَوينباغات [bu:yinba:ɣa:t] *pl:* • **1.** neck tie

ب ي
بايَة [pa:ya] *n:* بايات [pa:ya:t] *pl:* • **1.** leg – بايات القَنَفَة مطَعطِعَة [pa:ya:t ʔilqanafa mṭaƸṭiƸa] The sofa legs are wobbly. • **2.** step, stair – السِّرداب ينزِل عِشرين بايَة [ʔassirda:b yinzil Ƹišri:n pa:ya] The cellar is twenty steps deep. • **3.** step, notch, degree – صَعّدَوا بايَة لُخ؛ سَوّاوَه مُدِير [ṣaƸƸdaw pa:ya lux; sawwa:wah mudi:r] They raised him another step; made him a supervisor. نَزَّلِت خَشمَه بايَة [nazzalit xašmah pa:ya] I took him down a peg.

ب ي ب
بِيب [pi:p] *n:* بياب [pya:p] *pl:* • **1.** barrel, keg, drum

ب ي ب م ت ت و
بِيمَتُّو [bibimattu] *n:* بِيمَتُّوّات [bibimattuwwa:t] *pl:* • **1.** neck tie

ب ي ب ي
بِيبِي [bi:bi] *n:* بِيبِيّات [bi:biyya:t] *pl:* • **1.** grandmother, granny
بِيبِيَّة [bi:biyya] *n:* بِيبِيّات [bi:biyya:t] *pl:* • **1.** grandmother from both sides

ب ي ت
بات [ba:t] *v:* • **1.** to spend the night, stay overnight – الخُطّار راح يبات عِدنا اليُوم [ʔilxuṭṭa:r ra:ħ yba:t Ƹidna ʔilyu:m] The guest is going to stay overnight with us tonight. • **2.** to sit overnight – إذا الأكِل يبات، ما يصِير طَيِّب [ʔiða ʔilʔakil yba:t, ma: yṣi:r ṭayyib] If the food sits overnight, it won't be tasty.
بَيَّت [bayyat] *v:* • **1.** to put up for the night – بَيِّتي بِنتي وَباكِر أجي آخُذها [bayyiti binti wba:čir ʔaǰi ʔa:xuðha] Keep my daughter overnight and tomorrow I'll come and get her. • **2.** to keep overnight, let stand overnight – تريدني أذِبّ الأكِل الباقي، لَو أبَيِّتَه لباكِر [tri:dni ʔaðibb ʔilʔakil ʔilba:qi, law ʔabayyitah liba:čir] Do you want me to throw out the remaining food, or keep it till tomorrow. بَيِّت الماي عالتِّيغَة، يبرَد للصُّبُح [bayyit ʔilma:y Ƹatti:ɣa, yibrad liṣṣubuħ] Let the water stand overnight on the wall of the roof to get cold for the morning. • **3.** to put, place – بَيِّت الكير عالواحِد [bayyit ʔilgi:r Ƹalwa:ħid] Put the gearshift in first. بَيِّت الرَّهَن عِند أخُوك [bayyit ʔirrahan Ƹind ʔaxu:k] Put the money for the bet in your brother's care. تُسكُت لَو أجي أبَيِّت رصاصَة براسَك [tuskut law ʔaǰi ʔabayyit rṣa:ṣa bra:sak] Shut up or I'll put a bullet in your head.
بَيت [bayt] *n:* بيُوت [biyu:t] *pl:* • **1.** house, home – آني رايح لِلبَيت [ʔa:ni ra:yiħ lilbayt] I'm going home. مال بَيت [ma:l bayt] home-made, home. خُبُز مال بَيت [xubuz ma:l bayt] home-made bread. طَبُخ مال بَيت [ṭabux ma:l bayt] home cooking. • **2.** family – بَيت الچَلَبي [bayt ʔiččalabi] the Chalabi family. بَيت عَمّي [bayt Ƹammi] my uncle's family. • **3.** case, covering, sheath, box – بَيت مُسَدَّس [bayt musaddas] pistol holster.
بَيتَة، بَيتُوتَة [bayta, baytu:ta] *n:* بَيتُوتات [baytu:ta:t] *pl:* • **1.** overnight stop, stay
مَبِيت [mabi:t] *n:* مَبِيتات [mabi:ta:t] *pl:* • **1.** overnight stop, stay • **2.** shelter for the night
بَيتُونَة [baytu:na] *n:* • **1.** attic
بَيتِي [bayti] *adj:* • **1.** home-, domestic, house- – أشغال بَيتِيَّة [ʔašɣa:l baytiyya] household chores.
بايِت [ba:yit] *adj:* • **1.** left overnight, stale, old

ب

ب ي ت ن ج ن

بَيتِنجان [baytinǰa:n] *n:* • **1.** (coll.) eggplant
بَيتِنجانَة [baytinǰa:na] *n:* بَيتِنجانات [baytinǰa:na:t] *pl:* • **1.** eggplant
بَيتِنجانايَة [baytinǰana:ya] *n:* بَيتِنجانايات [baytinǰanaya:t] *pl:* • **1.** eggplant
بِيتِنجانِي [baytinǰa:ni] *adj:* • **1.** dark-purple (eggplant color)

ب ي ج م

بيجامَة [bi:ǰa:ma] *n:* بيجامات [bi:ǰa:ma:t] *pl:* • **1.** pajamas

ب ي د 1

باد [ba:d] *v:* • **1.** to destroy, exterminate – الفلِتّ باد كُلّ الحَشَرات [ʔilflitt ba:d kull ʔilħašara:t] The flyspray killed all the insects.
إبادَة [ʔiba:da] *n:* • **1.** extermination
بائِد، بايِد [ba:ʔid, ba:yid] *adj:* • **1.** past, bygone – العَهد البايِد [ʔilʕahd ʔilba:yid] the bygone era, the former regime.

ب ي د 2

بيادَة [pya:da] *n:* • **1.** on foot, walking – سَيّارتِي خَربانَة؛ جَينا بيادَة [sayya:rti xarba:na; ǰi:na pya:da] My car's out of commission; we came on foot.

ب ي د ر

بَيدَر [baydar] *n:* بَيدَرات، بَيادِر [baydara:t, baya:dir] *pl:* • **1.** threshing floor, threshing area • **2.** pile, heap – بَيدَر تِبِن [baydar tibin] pile of straw. بَيدَر دُخُن [baydar duxun] pile of millet.
بايدار [pa:yda:r] *n:* بايدارات [pa:ydara:t] *pl:* • **1.** a pedal (bicycle) Pedal hard – أُضرُب بايدار حيل [ʔuð̣rub pa:ydar ħi:l] Pedal hard.

ب ي د ق

بَيدَق [baydaq] *n:* بَيادِق [baya:diq] *pl:* • **1.** pawn (in chess)

ب ي ر 1

بِير [bi:r] *n:* بيارَة، آبار [bya:r, ʔa:ba:r] *pl:* • **1.** well wells – آبار النَّفُط [ʔa:ba:r ʔinnafuṭ] oil wells.

ب ي ر 2

بِيرَة [bi:ra] *n:* بِيرات [bi:ra:t] *pl:* • **1.** beer • **2.** a beer, a bottle of beer

ب ي ر غ

بِيرَغ [bi:raɣ] *n:* بيارِغ [bya:riɣ] *pl:* • **1.** banner, flag

ب ي ر ق

بَيرَق [bayraq] *n:* بَيارِق [baya:riq] *pl:* • **1.** flag, banner, standard

ب ي ر و ت

بَيرُوت [bayru:t, bi:ru:t] *n:* • **1.** Beirut
بَيرُوتِي [bayru:ti, bi:ru:ti] *n:* بَيرُوتِيَّة، بَيارِتَة [bayru:tiyya, baya:rita] *pl:* • **1.** Beiruti, from Beirut • **2.** a Beiruti, a native of Beirut

ب ي ز

بَيزَة [bi:za] *n:* • **1.** penny

ب ي ز ن ط

بِيزَنطِي [bi:zanṭi] *adj:* • **1.** Byzantine – الحَضارَة البِيزَنطِيَّة [ʔilħað̣a:ra ʔilbi:zanṭiyya] Byzantine civilization. • **2.** a Byzantine

ب ي ض

باض [ba:ð̣] *v:* • **1.** to lay (an egg) – الدِّجاجَة باضَت اليُوم [ʔiddiǰa:ǰa ba:ð̣at ʔilyu:m] The hen laid eggs today. باضَت الدِّجاجَة خَمِس بَيضات بِهَالإسبُوع [ba:ð̣at ʔiddiǰa:ǰa xamis bayð̣a:t bhalʔisbu:ʕ] The hen laid five eggs this week. ما تبِيضها لِلحكايَة عاد [ma: tbi:ð̣ha lilħča:ya ʕa:d] Come on, out with it!
بَيَّض [bayyað̣] *v:* • **1.** to make white, whiten – الحَرُب بَيِّضَت شَعرِي [ʔilħarub bayyið̣at šaʕri] The war turned my hair white. بَيَّض الله وِجهَك [bayyað̣ ʔallah wiččak] A phrase said to the bearer of good news, lit., May God lighten your face. • **2.** whitewash – اليُوم راح نبَيِّض الحِيطان [ʔilyu:m ra:ħ nbayyið̣ ʔalħi:ṭa:n] Today we're going to whitewash the walls. • **3.** to make a fair copy, to copy neatly – دَأكتِب الدَّرِس بِهَالأوراق وَبَعدين أبَيِّضَه بِالدَّفتَر [daʔaktib ʔiddaris bihalʔawra:q wbaʕdi:n ʔabayyið̣ah biddaftar] I'm writing the lesson on these slips of paper and later I'll enter them neatly in the notebook. • **4.** to lay eggs – هَالدِّجاجَة ما تبَيِّض أبَداً [haddiǰa:ǰa ma: tbayyið̣ ʔabadan] This chicken doesn't ever lay eggs. • **5.** to tinplate, cover with tin – لازِم تبَيِّض الجِّدُورَة قَبُل ما تُطبُخ بِيها [la:zim tbayyið̣ ʔiǰǰdu:ra gabul ma: tuṭbux bi:ha] You should coat the inside of the pots with tin before you cook with them.
اِبيَضّ [ʔibyað̣ð̣] *v:* • **1.** to turn white – شَعرَه كُلَّه اِبيَضّ [šaʕrah kullah ʔibyað̣ð̣] His hair all turned white.
بَيض [bayð̣] *n:* • **1.** (coll.) egg(s) – بَيض اللَّقلَق [bayð̣ ʔillaglag] a frothy, colored confection.
بَيضَة [bayð̣a] *n:* بَيضات [bayð̣a:t] *pl:* • **1.** egg
بَياض [baya:ð̣] *n:* • **1.** white, whiteness – عَليها غير بَياض [ʕali:ha ɣayr baya:ð̣] She has a very light complexion. طِلَع بِبَياض الوُجِه. ما ثِبَت ضِدَّه شِي [ṭilaʕ bbaya:ð̣ ʔalwuǰih. ma: θibat ð̣iddah ši] He came out smelling like a rose. Nothing was proven against him. • **2.** white, white part – بَياض البَيض [baya:ð̣ ʔilbi:ð̣] egg white, albumen. بَياض العَين [baya:ð̣ ʔilʕayn] white of the eye. • **3.** whitewash

بَيّاض [bayya:ð̣] *n:* بَيّاضَ، بيايِيض [bayya:ð̣a, bya:yi:ð̣] *pl:* • **1.** tinner, man who plates copper pots
مَبِيض [mabi:ð̣] *n:* مَبايِض [maba:yið̣] *pl:* • **1.** ovary
مبَيِّض [mbayyið̣] *n:* • **1.** tinner, tinplater
أبيَض [ʔabyað̣] *adj:* بِيض [bi:ð̣] *pl:* بَيضَة [bi:ð̣a] *feminine:* • **1.** white – ثُوب أبيَض [θu:b ʔabyað̣] white shirt. هٰذا صَحِيفتَه بيضَة [ha:ða ṣaħi:ftah bi:ð̣a] His record's clean. سِلاح أبيَض [sila:ħ ʔabyað̣] bayonet, sword, cold steel.
بَيضَوي [bayð̣awi] *adj:* • **1.** egg-shaped, oval
بَيّاضَة [bayya:ð̣a] *adj:* بَيّاضات [bayya:ð̣a:t] *pl:* • **1.** good layer, productive hen
مبيَضَّة [mibyað̣ð̣a] *adj:* مِبيَضّات [mibyað̣ð̣a:t] *pl:* • **1.** (as *n:*) fair copy, a final copy
أبيَضاني [ʔabyað̣a:ni] *adj:* • **1.** white

ب ي ط ر

بَيطَر [bayṭar] *v:* • **1.** to beat severely – بَيطرُوه البارحَة [bayṭru:h ʔilba:rħa] They beat the devil out of him yesterday.
بَيطَري [bayṭari] *adj:* بَيطَرِيَّة [bayṭari:yya] *pl:* • **1.** veterinarian
بَيطار [bayṭa:r] *n:* بَياطرَة [baya:ṭra] *pl:* • **1.** veterinarian
بَيطَرَة [bayṭara] *n:* • **1.** veterinary science
بَيطَري [bi:ṭari] *n:* • **1.** veterinary – الطِّبّ البَيطَري [ʔiṭṭibb ʔilbi:ṭari] veterinary medicine.

ب ي ع

باع [ba:ʕ] *v:* • **1.** to sell – سِمَعِت بِعت البَيت مالَك [simaʕit biʕt ʔilbayt ma:lak] I heard you sold your house. باعلِي سَيّارتَه [ba:ʕli sayya:rtah] He sold me his car. دَيبِيع رَزانَة بِراسِي [daybi:ʕ raza:na bra:si] He's trying to show off his dignity to me. لا تبيع شَقاوَة بِراسِي [la: tbi:ʕ šaqa:wa bra:si] Don't get tough with me.
بَيَّع [bayyaʕ] *v:* • **1.** to make sell, cause to sell – وِلد الجِّيران راح يبَيِّعُونا البَيت [wild ʔijji:ra:n ra:ħ ybayyiʕu:na ʔilbayt] The neighbors' kids are going to force us to sell the house.
بِيع [bayʕ, bi:ʕ] *n:* بُيُوع، بِيعات [buyu:ʕ] *pl:* • **1.** sale
بَيع [bayʕ] *n:* • **1.** selling
بَيعَة [bayʕa] *n:* بَيعات [bayʕa:t] *pl:* • **1.** sale
بَيّاع [bayya:ʕ] *n:* بَيّاعِين، بَيّاعَة [bayya:ʕa, bayya:ʕi:n] *pl:* • **1.** salesman, sales clerk
بايِع [ba:yiʕ] *n:* • **1.** seller
بَيّاعَة [bayya:ʕa] *adj:* بَيّاعات [bayya:ʕa:t] *pl:* • **1.** salesgirl

ب ي ك

بَيك [bayk] *n:* • **1.** (formerly a title of respect, now used sarcastically:) – هٰذا بَيك؛ ما يِشتُغُل [ha:ða bayk; ma: yištuɣul] He's a privileged character; he doesn't work. شِنُو، يا بَيك، قابِل نِسَيتنِي؟ [šinu:, ya: bi:g, qa:bil nisi:tni?] Hey, stuck up, have you forgotten me?
بَيك [pi:k] *n:* بَيكات [pi:ka:t] *pl:* • **1.** shot, dram (of liquor) • **2.** shot glass, jigger

ب ي ل ج

البايُولُوجِيَة [bayulu:ǰiya] *n:* • **1.** biology
بَيُولُوجِي [bayulu:ǰi] *adj:* • **1.** biological

ب ي ن

بَيَّن [bayyan] *v:* • **1.** to explain, expound – بَيَّنلِي القَضِيَّة بِالتَّفصِيل [bayyanli ʔilqað̣iyya bittafṣi:l] He explained the matter to me in detail. • **2.** to appear, show up, become evident – الطَّيّارَة بَيّنَت مِن بِعِيد [ʔilṭayya:ra bayynat min biʕi:d] The plane appeared in the distance. بَيَّن شِي مِن قَضِيَّة تَعيِينَك؟ [bayyan ši min qað̣iyyat taʕyi:nak?] Has anything come up on the business of your appointment? عَلِي بَعدَه دَيبَيِّن بِالقَهوَة كُلّ لَيلَة؟ [ʕali baʕdah daybayyin bilgahwa kull layla?] Does Ali still show up in the café every evening? هَسَّة مَوقِفَه بِالقَضِيَّة بَيَّن [hassa mawqifah bilqað̣iyya bayyan] Now his stand on the matter has come out. المَرَض بَيَّن عَلِيك. أحسَنلَك ترُوح لِلبَيت [ʔilmarað̣ bayyan ʕali:k. ʔaħsanlak tru:ħ lilbayt] The illness has begun to show on you. You'd better go home. • **3.** to be visible, to show – الطَّيّارَة بَعدها تبَيِّن [ʔiṭṭayya:ra baʕadha tbayyin] The plane is still visible. مِن يِضحَك، سنُونَه كُلّها تبَيِّن [min yið̣ħak, snu:nah kullha tbayyin] When he grins, his teeth all show. إكتِب بهالقَلَم حَتَّى الكِتابَة تبَيِّن [ʔiktib bhalqalam ħatta ʔilkita:ba tbayyin] Write with this pen so the writing will show up. • **4.** to seem, appear to be – يبَيِّن ضِجِت. تحِبّ نِرجَع؟ [yibayyin ð̣ijit. tħibb nirjaʕ?] It looks like you're bored. Would you rather we go back? يبَيِّن عَلِيك تَعبان [yibayyin ʕali:k taʕba:n] It seems that you're tired, you look tired.
تبَيَّن [tbayyan] *v:* • **1.** to turn out, prove to be, appear – تبَيَّنلِي إنُّو مُو صَدِيق [tbayyanli ʔinnu mu: ṣadi:q] It became evident to me that he's not a friend. تبَيَّن بِالأخِير الحُكُومَة ما راح تسَوِّيها [tbayyan bilʔaxi:r ʔilħuku:ma ma: ra:ħ tsawwi:ha] It turned out finally that the government isn't going to do it. يِتبَيَّنلِي ما لهُم ثِقَة بأي واحِد [yitbayyanli ma: lhum θiqa bʔay wa:ħid] It looks to me like they have no confidence in anyone.
بَين [bi:n] *n:* • **1.** between – بين الدِّنَقتَين [bayn ʔiddinagtayn] between the two columns. بينهُم، بَيناتهُم [baynhum, bayna:thum] between them. دِخَل بَيناتهُم وفاكَكهُم [dixal bi:na:thum wfa:kakhum] He stepped in between them and separated them. هٰذا قَضِيَّة بَينِي وبينَك بَسّ [ha:ða qað̣iyya bayni wbaynak bass] This is a matter just between me and you. بين يوم ويُوم [bayn yu:m wyu:m] from day to day, occasionally. بين مُدَّة وَمُدَّة [bayn mudda wmudda] from time to

ب

time, now and then. • **2.** among, amidst – بين الكُتُب [biːn ʔilkutub] among the books. بَين هَالأَقلام [bayn halʔaqlaːm] among these pencils. بين الجَّماعَة [bayn ʔiǰǰamaːʕa] in the midst of the group. • **3.** bad luck, misfortune – لاحقَه البَين [laːħgah ʔalbayn] Wherever he goes bad luck is after him. • **4.** death – إن شاء الله ياخذَك [ʔinšaːllah yaːxðak] Plague take you! (lit. God grant that death take you). شالَه البَين [šaːlah ʔalbayn] Death claimed him, he died.

بَيان [bayaːn] *n:* بَيانات [bayaːnaːt] *pl:* • **1.** statement, official report • **2.** announcement, proclamation

بَيّنَة [bayyna] *n:* • **1.** evidence

بِينات [biːnaːt, baynaːt] *adv:* • **1.** between

تَبايُن [tabaːyun] *n:* • **1.** contrast

مبَيِّن [mbayyin] *adj:* • **1.** obvious

مِتبايِن [mitbaːyin] *adj:* • **1.** unclear, non-specific, ambiguous

بايِن عَلَى [baːyin ʕala] *adj:* • **1.** /plus pronominal endings/ it seems that, it appears that – بايِن عَليه يرِيد يِشتِرِيلها هَدِيَّة [baːyin ʕaliːh yriːd yištiriːlha hadiyya] He seems to want to buy her a gift. بايِن عَلِيك تَعبان [baːyin ʕaliːk taʕbaːn] You seem to be tired.

ب ي ن و

بيانُو [pyaːnu, byaːnu] *n:* • **1.** piano

ت

ت ء

تاء [ta:ʔ] *n:* • **1.** name of the letter

ت ب ب

تَبَّة [tabba] *n:* تَبّات [tabba:t] *pl:* • **1.** hilltop

ت ب د ر

تَبْدُور [tabbadu:r] *n:* **1.** (coll.) cork

تَبْدُورَة [tabbadu:ra] *n:* تَبّدُورات [tabbadu:ra:t] *pl:* • **1.** piece of cork, cork

ت ب س ي

تبسي [tabsi] *n:* تبسِيّات، تَباسِي [tabsi:yya:t, taba:si] *pl:* • **1.** tray • **2.** large, flat pan

ت ب ع

تِبَع [tibaʕ] *v:* • **1.** to follow, pursue, to trail, track – اِتبَعَه وشُوف وِين يرُوح [ʔitbaʕah wšu:f wi:n yiru:ħ] Follow him and see where he goes. • **2.** to come after, succeed, follow – هَالبَرد والمُطَر راح يِتبَعهُم صَحو [halbarid wilmuṭar ra:ħ yitbaʕhum ṣaħw] Clear weather will follow this rain and cold. • **3.** to use as a guide, adhere to, follow – لَو تِتبَع هَالتَّعلِيمات، تِلقِي المُكان بسُهُولَة [law titbaʕ hattaʕli:ma:t, tilgi ʔalmuka:n bsuhu:la] If you adhere to these directions, you'll find the place easily. المُدِير الجِّدِيد دَيِتبَع سِياسَة تَقلِيل المَصرُوفات [ʔilmudi:r ʔijjidi:d dayitbaʕ siya:sat taqli:l ʔilmaṣru:fa:t] The new director is following a policy of cutting expenditures. • **4.** to be attached to, be fastened to – عِندَه بَيت يِتبَعَه مُشتَمَل وَكَراج [ʕindah bayt yitbaʕah muštamal wgara:j] He has a house with a cottage and a garage attached to it. • **5.** to be attached to, under the authority of – هَالفَرع يِتبَع الفَرع الرَّئِيسِي اللِّي بِبَغداد [halfariʕ yitbaʕ ʔilfariʕ ʔirraʔi:si ʔilli bibaɣda:d] This branch office is subsidiary to the main branch which is in Baghdad.

تَبَّع [tabbaʕ] *v:* • **1.** to follow, follow along – آنِي أقرا وَإنتَ تَبِّع وَقُلِّي إذا أغلَط [ʔa:ni ʔaqra: wʔinta tabbiʕ wgulli ʔiða ʔaɣlaṭ] I'll read and you follow along and tell me if I make a mistake. ما يِقدَر يِقرا إذا ما يتَبِّع [ma: yigdar yiqra: ʔiða ma: ytabbiʕ] He can't read if he doesn't follow the line with his finger.

تابَع [ta:baʕ] *v:* • **1.** to keep under surveillance, watch, keep an eye on, follow the progress of – ظَلّ يتابِع القَضِيَّة بنَفسَه [ðall yta:biʕ ʔilqaðiyya bnafsah] He kept an eye on the case personally. • **2.** to continue, go on with, pursue – تابَع الخِطاب مالَه بَعَد ما صَلّحَوا المايكرُفُون [ta:baʕ ʔilxiṭa:b ma:lah baʕad ma: ṣallħaw ʔilma:krufu:n] He continued his speech after they fixed the microphone.

اِتَّبَع [ʔittibaʕ] *v:* • **1.** to adhere to, follow, go along with, pursue – لَو مِتِّبع تَعلِيماتِي، هَالغَلَطات ما كان صارَت [law mittibiʕ taʕli:ma:ti, halɣalṭa:t ma: ča:n ṣa:rat] If you'd followed my instructions, these mistakes wouldn't have happened. الوِزارَة الجِّدِيدَة دَتِتَّبِع سِياسَة الحِياد [ʔilwiza:ra ʔijjidi:da datittibiʕ siya:sat ʔilħiya:d] The new cabinet is pursuing a policy of neutrality.

اِتَّبَّع [ʔittabbaʕ] *v:* • **1.** to track down, trail, follow, pursue – الشُّرطَة تِتَبّعَته إلَى البَصرَة [ʔiššurṭa ʔittabbʕatah ʔila ʔilbaṣra] The police traced him to Basra. الكِلاب تَبّعَت أثَر الحَرامِيَّة [ʔiččila:b tabbiʕat ʔaθar ʔilħara:miyya] The dogs followed the criminals' tracks.

تِبّاعَة [tibba:ʕa] *n:* تِبّاعات [tibba:ʕa:t] *pl:* • **1.** pointer (used to follow the line in reading)

تابعَة [ta:biʕa] *n:* تَوابِع [tawa:biʕ] *pl:* • **1.** female servant • **2.** female demon who accompanies a woman, appurtenance, appendage

تَبَعِيَّة [tabaʕiyya] *n:* • **1.** subordination, dependency, state of being subject, of pertaining or belonging to (a group, class, country)

تَتابُع [tata:buʕ] *n:* • **1.** succession, relay

تَتَبُّع [tatabbuʕ] *n:* • **1.** following (esp. of an argument, of a development), pursuit, succession, course

مُتابَعَة [muta:baʕa] *n:* • **1.** pursuit, continuation

تابِع [ta:biʕ] *adj:* أتباع [ʔatba:ʕ] *pl:* • **1.** following, succeeding – هَالمَقال تابِع لِمَقالِي مال الإسبُوع اللِّي فات [halmaqa:l ta:biʕ limaqa:li ma:l ʔilʔisbu:ʕ ʔilli fa:t] This article is a continuation of my article of last week. • **2.** subordinate – هَالشَّرِكَة تابعَة لشَرِكَتنا [haššarika ta:bʕa lšarikatna] That company is subordinate to our company. هَالدُّوَل كانَت تابعَة لِلحُكم الإنكلِيزِي [hadduwal ča:nat ta:bʕa lilħukm ʔilʔingli:zi] Those countries were under British rule. • **3.** follower, disciple – أتباعَه كُلّهُم تِركَوا [ʔatba:ʕah kullhum tirkawh] His followers all left him.

تَبِيع [tabi:ʕ] *adj:* تِباع [tiba:ʕ] *pl:* • **1.** following attached, attending, adjunct

مَتبُوع [matbu:ʕ] *adj:* مَتبُوعِين [matbu:ʕi:n] *pl:* • **1.** followed, succeeded

مُتَتابِع [mutata:biʕ] *adj:* • **1.** successive, consecutive

تِباعاً [tiba:ʕan] *adverbial:* • **1.** in succession, successively, consecutively, one after the other, one by one

ت ب غ

تِبِغ [tibiɣ] *n:* • **1.** tobacco

ت ب ل[1]

تِبَل، تَبَل [tibal, tabal] *n:* تِبَل، تَبَلات [tibal, tabala:t] *pl:* • **1.** burden, hardship **2.** burdensome or troublesome person

تَبُولَة [tabbu:la] *n:* • **1.** a type of salad made with bulgur

ت ب ل 2

توابل [tawa:bil] *n:* • **1.** pl. only spices

ت ب ل ي

تِبلِيَة [tibilya] *n:* تِبلِيات [tibilya:t] *pl:* • **1.** thick strap used for climbing palm trees, safety strap

ت ب ن

تِبَن [tiban] *v:* • **1.** to founder – لا تأكِّل الحِصان هوايَة، تَرَة تِبَنَّه [la: tʔakkil ʔilħiṣa:n hwa:ya, tara tibannah] Don't feed the horse too much or you'll founder him. البارحَة تِبَنِتها زين بالعَزِيمَة [ʔilba:rħa tibanitha zi:n bilʕazi:ma] Yesterday I really stuffed myself at the dinner party.

اِنتِبَن [ʔintiban] *v:* • **1.** to be or become foundered – لا تِنطِي لِلحصان شِعِير هوايَة تَرَة يِنتِبِن [la: tinṭi lilħṣa:n šiʕi:r hwa:ya tara yintibin] Don't give the horse too much barley or he'll get foundered.

تِبِن [tibin] *n:* • **1.** straw, hay

تِبِن [tibin] *n:* • **1.** stuffing

تِبنِي [tibni] *adj:* • **1.** straw colored

ت ب و ت

تابُوت [ta:bu:t] *n:* تَوابِيت [tawa:bi:t] *pl:* • **1.** coffin, casket

ت ت ن

تِتِن [titin] *n:* • **1.** tobacco

تِتِنجِي [titinči, tatanči] *n:* تَتَنجِيَّة [tatančiyya] *pl:* • **1.** tobacconist, tobacco vendor, cigarette maker

ت ج ر

تاجَر [ta:ǰar] *v:* • **1.** to do business, deal, buy and sell, trade – يتاجِر بِالحَرِير [yta:ǰir bilħari:r] He deals in silk. هُوَّ يتاجِر بِأعراض النّاس [huwwa yta:ǰir bʔaʕra:ḍ ʔinna:s] He buys and sells people's honor.

تاجِر [ta:ǰir] *n:* تُجّار [tuǰǰa:r] *pl:* • **1.** retailer – تاجِر جُملَة [ta:ǰir ǰumla] wholesaler. تاجِر مُفرَد [ta:ǰir mufrad] retailer.

تِجارَة [tiǰa:ra] *n:* • **1.** commerce, trade, business – وِزارَة التِّجارَة [wiza:rat ʔittiǰa:ra] Ministry of Commerce.

تِجارِي [tiǰa:ri] *adj:* • **1.** commercial, trading, business – شَرِكَة تِجارِيَّة [šarika tiǰa:riyya] trading company.

ت ح ت

تَحت [taħit, taħat] *n:* • **1.** (prep.) under – الشُّرطَة حَطَّت هَالبَيت تَحت المُراقَبَة [ʔiššurṭa ħaṭṭat halbayt taħt ʔilmura:qaba] The police put that house under surveillance. خَلّى سَيّارتَه تَحت تَصَرُّفِي [xalla: sayya:rtah taħat taṣarrufi] He put his car at my disposal. • **2.** (adv.) down below, downstairs – نَزِّل هَالأغراض تَحَت [nazzil halʔaɣra:ḍ taħat] Take these things downstairs. اِنتِظِرنِي تَحَت [ʔintiḍirni taħat] Wait for me downstairs. دَوَّرنا البِنايَة مِن فُوق إلَى تَحَت [dawwarna ʔilbina:ya min fu:g ʔila taħat] We searched the building from top to bottom.

تَحتانِي [taħta:ni] *n:* • **1.** lower, underneath – القاط التَّحتانِي [ʔilqa:ṭ ʔittaħta:ni] the lower floor. مَلابِس تَحتانِيَّة [mala:bis taħta:niyya] underclothes.

تَحتِيَّة [taħtiyya] *adj:* • **1.** lower, infra

ت ح ف

تِحَف [tiħaf] *v:* • **1.** to present – تِحَفنِي بهَدِيَّة فاخرَة [tiħafni bhadiyya fa:xra] He presented me with an exquisite present. إتِحفِنا بكَم نُكتَة [ʔitħifna bčam nukta] Favor us with some jokes.

تُحفَة [tuħfa] *n:* تُحَف، تُحَفِيات [tuħaf, tuħafiya:t] *pl:* • **1.** unique object, curiosity, rarity – هَالتِّمثال تُحفَة؛ ماكُو مِثلَه [hattimθa:l tuħfa; ma:ku miθlah] This statute is a rarity; there's no other like it. • **2.** work of art – المَتحَف مَليان تُحَف فَنِّيَّة [ʔilmatħaf malya:n tuħaf fanniyya] The museum's full of unique works of art. • **3.** something exceptionally good, something special, really something – هَالنَّوع مِن التِّفّاح تُحفَة [hannu:ʕ min ʔattiffa:ħ tuħfa] This kind of apple is something special. هَالمَقال تُحفَة؛ لازِم تِقراه [halmaqa:l tuħfa; la:zim tiqra:h] This article is a great one; you must read it. بانِيلَه بَيت تُحفَة [ba:ni:lah bayt tuħfa] He's built himself a marvelous house.

مَتحَف [matħaf] *n:* مَتاحِف [mata:ħif] *pl:* • **1.** museum • **2.** (art) gallery

ت خ ت

تَخَت [taxat] *n:* تخُوت [txu:t] *pl:* • **1.** unupholstered couch, bench with back and arms – يُضرُب بِالتَّخَت [yuḍrub bittaxat] He tells fortunes. He predicts the future. هُوَّ تَختَه ناقِص [huwwa taxtah na:giṣ] He's slightly crazy. His mind has slipped a notch.

تَختَة [taxta] *n:* تَختات [taxta:t] *pl:* • **1.** small box-like stool • **2.** chopping board, bread board • **3.** card for winding yarn on

ت خ ت خ

تَختَخ [taxtax] *v:* • **1.** to be stunned, stupefied, overwhelmed – مِن شاف جَمالها، تَختَخ [min ša:f ǰama:lha, taxtax] When he saw her beauty, he was stupefied. • **2.** to seduce, overcome the resistance of – إذا ترِيد تِتَختِخها، إنطِيها مَشرُوب [ʔiða tri:d ʔittaxtixha, ʔinṭi:ha mašru:b] If you want to weaken her resistance, give her a drink.

تَختَخَة [taxtaxa] *n:* • **1.** satisfaction, relaxing

مَتخَتِخ [mtaxtix] *adj:* • **1.** relaxed

ت خ م

تِخَم [tixam] *v:* • **1.** to satiate, fill up – ما أقدَر آكُل وَلا شِي، لِأنَّ الأكلَة تِخمَتنِي [ma: ʔagdar ʔa:kul wala ši, liʔann ʔilʔakla tixmatni] I can't eat a thing -- the meal filled me up. • **2.** to give indigestion, make sick – هَالأكلَة الدِّهِينَة تِخمَتنِي [halʔakla ʔiddihi:na tixmatni] That greasy food gave me indigestion.

تَخَّم [taxxam] *v:* • **1.** to loaf, hang around, dawdle, kill time – ما عِندَه شُغُل. بَسّ يتَخِّم بِالدَّرابِين [maː ʕindah šuɣul. bass ytaxxim biddaraːbiːn] He has no job. He just loafs around in the streets.
اِنتِخَم [ʔintixam] *v:* • **1.** to be satiated, filled up – مِن يشُوف أَكِل، يوقَع بِيه دَقّ، إِلَى أَن يِنتِخُم [min yšuːf ʔakil, yawgaʕ biːh dagg, ʔila ʔan yintixum] When he sees food, he digs in until he's stuffed. • **2.** to get indigestion, get sick – اِنتِخَمِت. لازِم آخُذ فَدّ شِي يصَرُّف الأَكِل [ʔintixamit. laːzim ʔaːxuð fadd ši yṣarruf ʔilʔakil] I've got indigestion. I should take something to digest the food.
تُخُم [tuxum] *n:* تخامَة [txaːma] *pl:* • **1.** cigarette holder
تَخِم [taxim] *n:* • **1.** satiating, filling up
تُخمَة [tuxma] *n:* • **1.** indigestion, dyspepsia

ت ر ب
تَرَّب [tarrab] *v:* • **1.** to make dusty, get dirty, cover with dust – وُقَع وَتَرَّب هدُومَه [wugaʕ wtarrab hduːmah] He fell and got his clothes dusty.
تَّرَّب [ttarrab] *v:* • **1.** to become dusty or dirty – لا تخُشّ بمَعمَل الشّبِنتُو تَرَة تِتَّرَّب [laː txušš ʔibmaʕmal ʔiččbintu tara tittarrab] Don't go in the cement factory or you'll get dusty.
تُرَب [turab] *n:* • **1.** turban
تُربَة [turba] *n:* تراب [trrab] *pl:* • **1.** soil, earth • **2.** ground • **3.** clean piece of clay, usually taken from the river at the holy city of Karbala, used by the Shiite sect of Islam in their prayer rites
تراب [traːb] *n:* تُربان [turbaːn] *pl:* • **1.** dirt, dust, soil, earth
متَرَّب [mtarrab] *adj:* • **1.** dusty
تُرابِي [turaːbi] *adj:* • **1.** dusty • **2.** powdery, dust-like

ت ر ب س
تِرباس [tirbaːs] *n:* تَرابِيس [taraːbiːs] *pl:* • **1.** bolt, latch – بُندُقِيَّة أُمّ التِّرباس [bunduqiyya ʔumm ʔittirbaːs] bolt-action rifle.

ت ر ب ن
تُربِين [turbiːn] *n:* • **1.** turbine

ت ر ج م
تَرجَم [tarǰam] *v:* • **1.** to translate, interpret – تَرجُملِي هالمَقالَة لِلعَرَبِي [tarǰumli halmaqaːla lilʕarabi] Translate this article into Arabic for me. آني ما أعرُف عَرَبِي، لَكِن راح أَجِيب واحِد وِيّايا يتَرجُملِي [ʔaːni maː ʔaʕruf ʕarabi, laːkin raːħ ʔaǰiːb waːħid wiyyaːya ytarǰumli] I don't know Arabic, but I'll bring someone along to interpret for me.
تَرجَمَة [tarǰama, tarǰuma] *n:* تَراجِم [taraːǰim] *pl:* • **1.** translation, interpretation
مُتَرجِم [mutarǰim] *n:* مُتَرجِمِين [mutarǰimiːn] *pl:* • **1.** translator, interpreter
مُتَرجَم [mutarǰam] *adj:* • **1.** translated
تُرجُمان [turǰumaːn] *n:* تُرجُمانِيَّة [turǰumaːniyya] *pl:* • **1.** translator, interpreter

ت ر ج ي
تِرچِيَّة [tirčiyya] *n:* تراچي [taraːči] *pl:* • **1.** earring

ت ر خ
تارِيخِي [taːriːxi] *adj:* • **1.** historic

ت ر س
تِرَس [tiras] *v:* • **1.** to fill, fill up – الجّاهِل تِرَس جيبَه بِالچُكلَيت [ʔiǰǰaːhil tiras ǰiːbah biččukliːt] The child filled his pocket with candy chocolate.
تَرَّس [tarras] *v:* • **1.** to fill, fill up – آنِي أَناوشَك البِيب وَإِنتَ تَرِّس البُطالَة [ʔaːni ʔanaːwšak ʔilpiːp wʔinta tarris ʔilbṭaːla] I'll hand you the barrel and you fill the bottles.
اِنتِرَس [ʔintiras] *v:* • **1.** to be or become filled, get full – اِنتِرَس السِّرداب ماي [ʔintiras ʔissirdaːb maːy] The cellar got filled with water.
تَرِس [taris] *n:* • **1.** filling
تَرَس [taras] *n:* تَرَسِيَّة [tarasiyya] *pl:* • **1.** person of low morals, person with bad character • **2.** clever person, sly fox, sneak
مَترُوس [matruːs] *adj:* • **1.** filled

ت ر ف
تَرَف [taraf] *n:* • **1.** luxury, opulence, affluence
تَرِف [tarif] *adj:* • **1.** neat, clean, tidy – هدُوم تَرفَة [hduːm tarfa] neat clothes.
تَرافَة [taraːfa] *adj:* • **1.** neatness, cleanness, tidiness

ت ر ق و
تَرقوَة، عَظم التَّرقُوَة [tarquwa, ʕaðum ʔiltarquwa] *n:* • **1.** clavicle, collarbone

ت ر ك [1]
تِرَك [tirak] *v:* • **1.** to give up, forswear, swear off – لازِم تِترُك هَالعادَة [laːzim titruk halʕaːda] You've got to stop this habit. كان يِلعَب قمار بَسّ بَعدين تِرَك [čaːn yilʕab qmaːr bass baʕdiːn tirak] He used to gamble but later gave it up. صارلَه مُدَّة تارِك التَّدخِين [ṣaːrlah mudda taːrik ʔittadxiːn] He's been off smoking for some time. • **2.** to leave – إِذا ما لِقِيتَه، إِترُكلَه خَبَر [ʔiða maː ligiːtah, ʔitruklah xabar] If you don't find him, leave him a message. ما تِرَكلِي مَجال لِلتَّفاهُم [maː tirakli maǰaːl littafaːhum] He didn't give me a chance to explain. • **3.** to leave, abandon, forsake, give up, leave behind – ما يصِير تِترُك سَيّارتَك بنُصّ الشّارِع [maː yṣiːr titruk sayyaːrtak bnuṣṣ ʔiššaːriʕ] You can't just leave your car in the middle of the street. • **4.** to leave alone, stay away from – تُركَه! الإِلحاح ما يفِيد

[turkah! ʔilʔilħa:ħ ma: yfi:d] Leave him alone! Insisting won't help. تُركَه لهالمَوضُوع [turkah lhalmawđu:ʕ] Drop the subject.
تَرَّك [tarrak] *v:* • **1.** to cause to give up – لازِم أتَرِّكَك العادَة [la:zim ʔatarrikak ʔilʕa:da] I've got to cure you of the habit.
اِنتِرَك [ʔintirak] *v:* • **1.** to be abandoned
تَرِك [tarik] *n:* • **1.** leaving, omission
تَركَة [tarka] *n:* تَركات [tarka:t] *pl:* • **1.** pinch of salt – تَركَة مِلح [tarkat miliħ] pinch of salt.
تَرِكَة [tarika] *n:* تَرِكات [tarika:t] *pl:* • **1.** heritage, legacy, bequest
تارِك [ta:rik] *adj:* • **1.** reluctant, projecting, disinclined
مَترُوك [matru:k] *adj:* • **1.** abandoned

ت ر ك ²

تُركِيا [turkya] *n:* • **1.** Turkey
تُركِي [turki] *adj:* تُرُك، أتراك [turuk, ʔatra:k] *pl:* • **1.** Turk, person from Turkey • **2.** Turkish

ت ر ك ت ر

تَرَكتَر [traktar] *n:* تَرَكتَرات [traktara:t] *pl:* • **1.** tractor

ت ر ك م ن

تُركماني [turkma:ni] *adj:* تُركمان [turkma:n] *pl:* • **1.** Turkoman (a Turkic people in North Iraq, who speak a dialect of Turkish)

ت ر م

ترام [tra:m] *n:* ترامات [tra:ma:t] *pl:* • **1.** streetcar, tram

ت ر و ك

تِرواكَة [tirwa:ka] *n:* تِرواكات [tirwa:ka:t] *pl:* • **1.** three-quarter length jacket, worn by women

ت ر ي ش

تِرِيشَة [tiri:ša] *n:* ترايِش [tra:yiš] *pl:* • **1.** slat, lath, long, thin piece (of wood, metal, etc.)

ت ر ي ع

تتَريَع [ttaryaʕ, ʔitdaryaʕ] *v:* • **1.** to belch, burp – مِن ياكُل فِجِل يِتَّريَع هوايَة [min ya:kul fij̄il yittaryaʕ hwa:ya] When he eats radishes he belches a lot.
تَريُوعَة [taryu:ʕa] *n:* تَريُوعات [taryu:ʕa:t] *pl:* • **1.** belch, burp

ت ر ي ك

تِرياك [tirya:k] *n:* • **1.** opium
تِريَكجِي [tiryakči] *n:* تِريَكجِيَّة [tiryakčiyya] *pl:* • **1.** addicted to opium, dope or strong tea • **2.** person fond of strong tea
تِرياكِي [tirya:ki] *adj:* تِرياكِيَّة [tirya:kiyya] *pl:* • **1.** person addicted to opium, dope addict • **2.** person fond of strong tea

ت ر ي ل

تَرَيلَة [trayla, tri:la] *n:* تَرَيلات [trayla:t] *pl:* • **1.** heavy vehicle

ت ز

تازَة [ta:za] *adj:* • **1.** fresh – فَواكِه تازَة [fawa:kih ta:za] fresh fruit. • **2.** recent, new – خَبَر تازَة [xabar ta:za] recent news.

ت س ع

تُسُع [tusuʕ] *n:* أتساع [ʔatsa:ʕ] *pl:* • **1.** one ninth
تِسعَة [tisʕa] *n:* تِسعات [tisʕa:t] *pl:* • **1.** nine
تِسعِين [tisʕi:n] *n:* • **1.** ninetieth
تِسعمِئَة [tisʕmiʔa] *n:* • **1.** nine hundred
تاسِع [ta:siʕ] *adj:* • **1.** ninth (ordinal)

ت س ع ط ع ش

تساطَعَش [tsa:ṭaʕaš] *n:* • **1.** nineteen

ت س ق

تِسقا [tisga] *n:* تِسقايات [tisga:ya:t] *pl:* • **1.** carpenter's workbench

ت ش ر ت

تِيشُرت [ti:šurt] *n:* تِيشُرتات [ti:šurta:t] *pl:* • **1.** T-shirt

ت ش ر ن ¹

تَشرَن [tašran] *v:* • **1.** to become inflamed – الجَرِح مال إيدَك مِتشَرِن [ʔij̄jariħ ma:l ʔi:dak mtašrin] The wound on your hand is blue and swollen.

ت ش ر ن ²

تَشرِين [tašri:n, tišri:n] *n:* • **1.** October – تَشرِين أوَّل، تَشرِين ثانِي [tašri:n ʔawwal, tašri:n θa:ni] November.

ت ش ق ل

تَشقَل [tašqal] *v:* • **1.** with عَلَى to cheat, swindle, dupe – دِير بالَك مِنَّه؛ هَذا يتَشقِل عالنّاس [di:r ba:lak minnah; ha:ða ytašqil ʕanna:s] Watch out for him; he cheats people. ما يِقدَر يبِيعلَك الباص. تَشقَل عَلِيك [ma: yigdar ybi:ʕlak ʔilpa:ṣ. tašqal ʕali:k] He can't sell you the bus. He swindled you.

ت ع ب

تِعَب [tiʕab] *v:* • **1.** to work hard, toil, slave – تِعَبِت عَلَى هَالبَيت هوايَة [tiʕabit ʕala halbayt hwa:ya] I put a lot of effort into this house. نِسِيت شقَد تِعَبِت عَلِيك مِن كِنت صغَيِّر؟ [nisi:t šgad tiʕabit ʕali:k min čint ṣγayyir?] Have you forgotten how much trouble I went to for you when you were young? • **2.** to be or become tired, weary – تِعَبِت؛ خَلِّي أستِرِيح شوَيَّة [tiʕabit; xalli: ʔastiri:ħ šwayya] I've gotten tired; let me sit down a bit.

تَعَّب [taʕʕab] *v:* • **1.** to make tired, to tire, to weary – الرِّكِض تَعَّبني هوايَة [ʔirrikiđ taʕʕabni hwaːya] The running tired me a lot. • **2.** to trouble, inconvenience, bother – تَعَّبتَك هوايَة بهَالقَضِيَّة [taʕʕabtak hwaːya bhalqađiyya] I've caused you a lot of trouble with this matter.
تَعَب [taʕab] *n:* • **1.** fatigue, weariness, tiredness • **2.** pl. أتعاب trouble, effort, exertion, inconvenience
مَتاعِب [mataːʕib] *n:* • **1.** problems
مُتعِب [mutʕib] *adj:* • **1.** tiring, difficult, wearisome • **2.** dull, boring, tedious
تَعبان [taʕbaːn] *adj:* • **1.** tired, weary, exhausted
مَتعُوب [matʕuːb] *adj:* • **1.** tired, out of shape
أتعَب [ʔatʕab] *comparative adjective:* • **1.** more or most tired • **2.** more or most tiring

ت ع س

تَعاسَة [taʕaːsa] *n:* • **1.** misery, wretchedness
تَعِس، تَعِيس [taʕis, taʕiːs] *adj:* تَعِس، تَعِيسِين، تُعَساء [taʕis, taʕiːsiːn, tuʕasaːʔ] *pl:* • **1.** miserable, wretched, unfortunate, poor • **2.** miserable person, wretch
أتعَس [ʔatʕas] *comparative adjective:* • **1.** more or most miserable

ت ع ل

تَعال، تَعالِي، تَعالُوا [taʕaːl, taʕaːli, taʕaːlu] *v:* • **1.** come on, let's go – تَعال فَهمَه لِلأُستاذ [taʕaːl fahhmah lilʔustaːđ] Come on, explain to the gentleman. دَتَعال عاد! مُو صارلِي ساعَة أنتَظرَك؟ [ditaʕaːl ʕaːd! muː ṣaːrli saːʕa ʔantađrak?] Come on there! Haven't I been waiting for you an hour already? تَعال دَأقُلَّك، هَالشَّغلَة ما تِنراد [taʕaːl daʔagullak, haššaγla maː tinraːd] Let me tell you, that work isn't desirable. • **2.** (imperative direct address) come, come here – تَعال يَمِّي. دَأحكِيلَك شِي [taʕaːl yammi. daʔaħčiːlak ši] Come here. I'll tell you something. رُوح وَتَعال بِالعَجَل [ruːħ wataʕaːl bilʕajal] Go and come back quickly. تَعال، شُوف بِمَن اِبتِلِيت [taʕaːl, šuːf biman ʔibtiliːt] Come here and look who I got stuck with!

ت ف ح

تَفَّح [taffaħ] *v:* • **1.** to glow with good health, to have rosy cheeks – تَفَّح وِجه الجّاهِل عَلَى هالهوا والأكِل [taffaħ wijħ ʔijjaːhil ʕala halhawa wilʔakil] The child's face glowed with good health from this climate and food. شُوف وِجهه شلُون مَتَفِّح [šuːf wiččah šluːn mtaffiħ] Look how pink-cheeked and healthy he is!
تِفّاح [tiffaːħ, tuffaːħ] *n:* • **1.** apple(s) • **2.** apple tree(s)
تِفّاحَة [tiffaːħa, tuffaːħa] *n:* تِفّاحات [tiffaːħaːt, tuffaːħaːt] *pl:* • **1.** apple
مَتَفِّح [mtaffiħ] *adj:* • **1.** pink-cheeked, healthy

ت ف خ

تُفَخ [tufax, tuffaːxa] *v:* • **1.** var. of نُفَخ see under نفخ

ت ف ر

تَفَر [tafar] *n:* تَفَرات [tafaraːt] *pl:* • **1.** crupper, breeching strap (of donkey's harness).

ت ف س

تَفِس [tafis] *adj:* • **1.** filthy, dirty

ت ف ق

اِتَّفَق [ʔittaffag] *v:* • **1.** to arm oneself with a rifle, to take up arms – اِتَّفُقوا قَبُل ما يهجمُون [ʔittaffugaw gabul maː yhijmuːn] They armed themselves with rifles before they attacked.
تُفَقَة [tufga] *n:* تُفَق، تُفقات [tufag, tufgat] *pl:* • **1.** BB gun, air rifle – تُفقَة صَيد [tufgat ṣiːd] shotgun. تُفقَة صَچِم [tufgat ṣačim] BB gun, air rifle.
تَفّاق [taffaːg] *adj:* تَفّاقَة [taffaːga] *pl:* • **1.** rifleman
متَفَّق [mtaffag] *adj:* • **1.** carrying a rifle, armed

ت ف ل

تِفَل [tifal] *v:* • **1.** to spit, expectorate – تِفلَت بوجهَه لان فَشَّر عَليها [tiflat bwiččah laːn faššar ʕaliːha] She spit in his face because he talked dirty to her. واحِدهُم تافِل بِحَلق الثّانِي [waːħidhum taːfil bħalg ʔiθθaːni] They both say exactly the same thing.
تَفَّل [taffal] *v:* • **1.** to spit, expectorate – لا تتَفِّل بلقاع. اِستَعمِل كَفِّيَّة [laː ttaffil bilgaːʕ. ʔistaʕmil čaffiyya] Don't spit on the floor. Use a handkerchief.
تِفِل [tifil] *n:* • **1.** var. of • **2.** var. of تِلِف see under ت ل ف pulp (of fruit, etc)
تَفِل [tafil] *n:* • **1.** expectoration, spitting
تفال [tfaːl] *n:* تفالات، مَتافِل [tfaːlaːt, mataːfil] *pl:* • **1.** spit, spittle, saliva • **2.** (coll) spit, spittle, saliva
تَفلَة [tafla] *n:* • **1.** spit
مَتفَلَة [matfala] *n:* مَتفَلات، مَتافِل [matfalaːt, mataːfil] *pl:* • **1.** cuspidor, spittoon

ت ف ه

تَفاهَة [tafaːha] *n:* • **1.** triviality, paltriness, insignificance
تافِه [taːfih] *adj:* • **1.** trivial, paltry, unimportant, trifling, insignificant
أتفَه [ʔatfah] *comparative adjective:* • **1.** more trivial, unimportant, most trivial, unimportant

ت ف و س

تِيفُوس [tiːfuːs] *n:* • **1.** typhus

ت ق ن

تِقَن [tiqan] *v:* • **1.** to master, know thoroughly – بُقَى بأمريكا سَنتَين وَتِقَن الإنكليزي [buqaː bʔamriːka santayn wtiqan ʔalʔingiliːzi] He stayed in America two years and mastered English.
مُتقَن [mutqan] *n:* • **1.** perfect
إتقان، إتِّقان [ʔitqaːn, ʔittiqaːn] *n:* • **1.** perfection • **2.** proficiency, skill • **3.** mastery, command

تَقنِيَّة [taqniyya] *n:* تَقنِيّات [taqniyya:t] *pl:* • **1.** technique
تِقَنِي [tiqani] *adj:* • **1.** technical • **2.** (as n:) technician

ت ق ي

See also: و ق ي

ت ك ت

تِكِت [tikit] *n:* تِكِتات [tikita:t] *pl:* • **1.** ticket

ت ك ت ك

تَكتَك [taktak] *v:* • **1.** to plan, arrange something • **2.** to tick (clock)
تَكتِيك [takti:k] *n:* • **1.** tactic
تَكتَكَة [taktaka] *n:* • **1.** ticking, ticktock (of a clock), ticking noise • **2.** tactic
تَكتِيكِي [takti:ki] *adj:* • **1.** tactical

ت ك س ي

تَكسِي [taksi] *n:* تَكسِيّات [taksiyya:t] *pl:* • **1.** taxi, taxicab

ت ك ك

تَكّ [takk] *n:* • **1.** one of a pair, mate, match – وِين تَكّ هَالجَوراب؟ [wi:n takk hajǰu:ra:b?] Where's the mate to this sock? ضاع تَكّ مِن قُندَرتِي [ða:ʕ takk min qundarti] One of my shoes got lost. وِين تَكَّك؟ مُو إنتُو كُلّ يوم سُوَة؟ [wi:n takkak? mu: ʔintu kull yuwm suwa?] Where is your bosom buddy? Aren't you always together? • **2.** one, a single – أَقدَر أمَوّتَك بِتَكّ عِجِل [ʔagdar ʔamawwtak btakk ʕiǰil] I could kill you with a single slap. • **3.** alone, only – لا، آني بتَكّ نَفسِي [la:, ʔa:ni btakk nafsi] No, I'm all by myself. سَوّاها بتَكّ نفسَه [sawwa:ha btakk nafsah] He did it all by himself.
تِكَّة [tiča] *n:* تِكَك [tičač] *pl:* • **1.** drawstring (in the waist-band)
تِكَّة [tikka] *n:* • **1.** kabob, shish kebab, meat cooked on a skewer • **2.** draw-string (in the waist-band)

ت ك ك ي

تُكِّي [tukki] *n:* • **1.** mulberry(ies) • **2.** mulberry tree(s)
تُكِّيَّة [tukkiyya] *n:* تُكِّيّات [tukkiyya:t] *pl:* • **1.** mulberry tree (see also under ت - و - ث)

ت ك م

تُكمَة [tukma] *n:* تُكمات، تُكَم [tukama:t, tukam] *pl:* • **1.** pillar, column • **2.** brace, support • **3.** (invar.) well-built, solid, stout – بَيت تُكمَة [bayt tukma] a sturdy house.
تُكمَاجِي [tukma:či] *n:* تُكمَاجِيَّة [tukma:čiyya] *pl:* • **1.** antique dealer

ت ك ن ل ج

تَكنُولُوجِي [taknu:lu:ǰi] *adj:* • **1.** technological

ت ك ن ل و ج

تَكنلُوجيا [taknulu:ǰya] *n:* • **1.** technology

ت ك ي

تَكيَّة [takiyya] *n:* تَكيّات [takiyya:t] *pl:* • **1.** monastery of a Moslem order • **2.** school for the study of a branch of Moslem theology

ت ل

تال [ta:l] *n:* • **1.** (coll.) palm seedling(s), palm shoot(s), slip(s)
تالَة [ta:la] *n:* تالات [ta:la:t] *pl:* • **1.** palm seedling, palm shoot, palm

ت ل س ك و ب

تَلِسكُوب [talisku:b] *n:* • **1.** telescope

ت ل غ ر ف

تِلَغراف [talaɣra:f] *n:* تَلَغرافات [talaɣra:fa:t] *pl:* • **1.** telegraph • **2.** telegram, wire, cable
تِلَغرافِي [talaɣra:fi] *adj:* • **1.** telegraphic – مُواصَلات تَلَغرافِيَّة [muwa:ṣala:t talaɣra:fiyya] telegraph communications.

ت ل ف

تِلَف [tilaf] *v:* • **1.** to be or become damaged, spoiled, ruined – خَلِّي اللَّحَم بِالثَّلّاجَة قَبُل ما يِتلَف [xalli: ʔillaħam biθθalla:ǰa gabul ma: yitlaf] Put the meat in the refrigerator before it spoils. تلفِت مِن الدِّراسَة [tlafit min ʔiddira:sa] I got worn out from studying. تلفِت عَليها، لَكِن ما دارتلي بال [tlafit ʕali:ha, la:kin ma: da:ratli ba:l] I went to pieces over her, but she didn't pay me any attention. • **2.** to destroy – إتلِف كُلّ الأوراق اللّي عِندَك قَبُل ما يكبسُون البَيت [ʔitlif kull ʔilʔawra:q ʔilli ʕindak gabul ma: ykibsu:n ʔilbayt] Destroy all the papers you have before they raid the house. • **3.** to ruin, spoil – تِلَف صِحّتَه بشِرب العَرَق [tilaf ṣiħħtah bširb ʔilʕarag] He ruined his health drinking liquor. • **4.** to waste, squander – تِلَف فلُوسَه بالقمار [tilaf flu:sah bilqma:r] He frittered away his money gambling.
إنتِلَف [ʔintilaf] *v:* • **1.** to get ruined, damage
تَلَف [talaf] *n:* • **1.** damage, destruction • **2.** waste, spoilage
تِلِف [tilif, tifil] *n:* • **1.** pulp (of fruit) • **2.** grounds (of coffee) • **3.** leaves (of tea)
إتلاف [ʔitla:f] *n:* • **1.** destruction, annihilation
تالِف [ta:lif] *adj:* • **1.** damaged
تَلفان [talfa:n] *adj:* • **1.** damaged, ruined, destroyed – مَدِينَة تَلفانَة [madi:na talfa:na] a ruined city. • **2.** spoiled, rotten – لَحَم تَلفان [laħam talfa:n] spoiled meat. فَواكِه تَلفانَة [fawa:kih talfa:na] rotten fruit. • **3.** worn-out. sayya:ra talfa:na a worn-out car

ت ل ف ز

تِلِفِزيُون [tilifizyu:n] *n:* تَلَفِزيُونات [talifizyuwna:t] *pl:* • **1.** television

ت ل ف ن

تَلفَن [talfan] *v:* • **1.** to call some one
تَلِيفُون [talifu:n, tilifu:n] *n:* • **1.** phone

ت ل ل

تَلّ [tall] *n:* تلال، تلُول [tla:l, tlu:l] *pl:* • **1.** hill, mound, elevation, rise
تَلّكِي [tallači] *n:* تَلّكِيَّة [tallačiyya] *pl:* • **1.** gambler, gambling house owner
تَلّخانَ [tallaxa:na] *n:* تَلّخانات، تَلّخاين [tallaxa:na:t, tallaxa:yin.] *pl:* • **1.** gambling den, casino

ت ل م ذ

تتَلمَذ [ttalmað] *v:* • **1.** to be or become a student or apprentice – هُوَّ تِتَلمَذ عَلَى إيد هَالأُستاذ [huwwa ʔittalmað ʕala ʔi:d halʔusta:ð] He became a student under that professor.
تَلمَذَة [talmaða] *n:* • **1.** student status, student life – أيّام التَّلمَذَة [ʔayya:m ʔattalmaða] student days.
تلمِيذ [tilmi:ð] *n:* تَلامِيذ [tala:mi:ð] *pl:* • **1.** pupil, student

ت ل و

تِلَى [tila:] *v:* • **1.** to read aloud, recite – تِلَى عَلينا التَّعلِيمات [tila: ʕali:na ʔittaʕli:ma:t] He read the instructions aloud to us. • **2.** to follow after, succeed, come behind – هالهَدِيَّة راح تِتلِيها هَدايا [halhadiyya ra:ħ titli:ha hada:ya] Gifts will follow this gift.
تِلاوَة [tila:wa] *n:* • **1.** oral reading, recitation, recital
تالِي [ta:li] *n:* تُوالِي [tuwa:li] *pl:* • **1.** final portion, last part, end – بتالِي عُمرَه، صار مِتدَيِّن [bta:li ʕumrah, ṣa:r middayyin] Toward the end of his life, he became religious. تالِيها طِلَع ما يُعرُف شِي [ta:li:ha ṭilaʕ ma: yuʕruf ši] In the end he turned out not to know a thing. العِنَب الزّين ينزِل بتُوالِي المَوسِم [ʔilʕinab ʔizzi:n yinzil btuwa:li ʔilmu:sim] The good grapes appear toward the last days of the season. هاي التُّوالِي. إسبُوع الجّاي ما تِلقِي طَماطَة بالسُّوق [ha:y ʔittuwa:li. ʔisbu:ʕ ʔiǰǰa:y ma: tilgi ṭama:ṭa bissu:g] These are the last ones. Next week you won't find tomatoes in the market. إنتَ رُوح. آني أجِي تالِي [ʔinta ru:ħ. ʔa:ni ʔaǰi ta:li] You go ahead. I'll come later. أخذُوا كِفايَتكُم. آني أبقَى بالتّالِي [ʔuxðu: kifa:yatkum. ʔa:ni ʔabqa: bitta:li] Take what you need. I'll wait until last. عِدنا خُوش قُمصان. إلحَقُوا عَلَى تالِيها [ʕidna xu:š qumṣa:n. ʔilħagu: ʕala ta:li:ha] We have fine quality shirts. Get them while they last. هَذا مالَه تالِي. ما شِفتَه شسَوَّى بِيّا؟ [ha:ða ma:lah ta:li. ma: šiftah ššawwa: biyya?] You just can't tell about him. Did you see what he did to me? • **2.** outcome, result, conclusion, final issue – هاي تالِيها؟ مُو آني صَدِيقَك؟ [ha:y ta:li:ha? mu: ʔa:ni ṣadi:qak?] Is that the end result? Aren't I your friend? التّالِي راح تِشتِكِي بالفلُوس عَلَى جِيرانها [ʔitta:li ra:ħ tištiki bilfilu:s ʕala ǰi:ra:nha] The upshot is that she's going to sue her neighbor for the money. إذا ما تِدرُس، ما تقُلّي شِنُو تالِيَك؟ [ʔiða ma: tidrus, ma: tgulli šinu ta:liyyak?] If you don't study, would you tell me just what'll become of you? صارلِي مِيَّة مَرَّة أداعِيك بالفلُوس وَما تِنطِينِي. تالِيها ويّاك؟ [ṣa:rli miyyat marra ʔada:ʕi:k bilfilu:s wma tinṭi:ni. ta:li:ha wiyya:k?] I've asked you a hundred times for the money and you don't give it to me. What am I going to do with you? تالِيها ويّا إبنَك؟ بَعدَه دَيشلَع وَردِي [ta:li:ha wiyya ʔibnak? baʕdah dayišlaʕ wardi] What's going to become of your son? He's still pulling up my flowers. التّالِي شصار؟ [ʔitta:li šṣa:r?] Then what happened? تالِي ما تالِي [ta:li ma: ta:li] finally, after all that, in the end. تالِي ما تالِي، ما يرِيد يساعِدنِي [ta:li: ma: ta:li, ma: yri:d ysa:ʕidni] After all that, he doesn't want to help me.
تالانِي [ta:la:ni] *adj:* • **1.** toward the end, at the last, end, final, concluding, terminal – ناوِشنِي الكِتاب التّالانِي [na:wišni ʔilkita:b ʔitta:la:ni] Hand me the book on the end.

ت ل ي ت

تُواليت [tuwali:t] *n:* • **1.** coiffure, hairdo (also, long hair style for men) • **2.** bathroom

ت م ب ك

تمباك [timba:k] *n:* • **1.** a kind of tobacco, used mostly in the narghile and water-pipe smoking

ت م ت م

تَمتَم [tamtam] *v:* • **1.** to mutter, mumble – دَتتَمتِم وَما دَأفهَم [dattamtim wma daʔafham] You're muttering and I can't understand.
تَمتَمَة [tamtama] *n:* • **1.** mumbling

ت م ر

تَمُر [tamur] *n:* • **1.** (coll.) date(s) (particularly dried dates) – تَمُر هِندِي [tamur hindi] tamarind.
تَمرَة [tamra] *n:* تَمرات [tamra:t] *pl:* • **1.** a date • **2.** clump, chunk, piece of packed dates
تَمرايَة [tamra:ya] *n:* تَمرايات [tamra:ya:t] *pl:* • **1.** date

ت م س ح

تِمساح [timsa:ħ] *n:* تَماسِيح [tama:si:ħ] *pl:* • **1.** crocodile • **2.** alligator

ت م م

تَمّ [tamm] *v:* • **1.** to stay, remain, abide – لِيش ما تِتَمّ عِدنا هاللَّيلَة؟ [li:š ma: titAmm ʕidna hallayla?] Why don't you stay with us tonight? وين تَمِّيت لِهَسَّة؟

[wi:n tammi:t lhassa?] Where've you been till now? ما تَمّ أَحّد ما سِمَع [ma: tamm ʔaħħad ma: simaʕ] No one remained who hadn't heard. • **2.** to continue to completion, to be complete – فَرحَتنا ما تِتَّم إذا ما تِجي [farħatna ma: titamm ʔiða ma: tiǰi] Our joy won't be complete if you don't come.
تَمَّم [tammam] *v:* • **1.** to complete, finish, wind up, conclude – تَمِّم شُغلَك وَتعال [tammim šuɣlak wataʕa:l] Finish your work and come on.
تمام [tama:m] *n:* • **1.** completeness, entirety, wholeness – إستِلَمت فلُوسي بِالتَّمام [ʔistilamt flu:si bittama:m] I received my money in full. • **2.** exact, real, true, complete – هُوَّ صَدِيق تَمام [huwwa ṣadi:q tama:m] He's a real friend. • **3.** true, correct, right – هَذا تَمام، لَكِن [ha:ða tama:m, la:kin] That's true, but. . . وَالله، تَمام! هَذا خُوش وَلَد [wallah, tama:m! ha:ða xu:š walad] You can say that again! He's a nice guy. تَمام، بَسّ هَذا مُو عُذُر [tama:m, bass ha:ða mu: ʕuður] All right, but that's not an excuse. هَذا تَمام! هَذا بِالضَبُط اللُّون اللّي أَرِيدَه [ha:ða tama:m! ha:ða biððabuṭ ʔillu:n ʔilli ʔari:dah] That's it! That's the color I want exactly. أَمّا تَمام طِلَع مِثِلما قِلت [ʔamma tama:m ṭilaʕ miθilma gilit] He sure did turn out like you said.
تَتِمَّة [tatimma] *n:* تَتِمّات [tatimma:t] *pl:* • **1.** supplement • **2.** completion
تامّ [ta:mm] *adj:* • **1.** complete, perfect • **2.** genuine, real
تَماماً [tama:man] *adverbial:* • **1.** precisely, exactly • **2.** completely, entirely

ت م ن

تِمَّن [timman] *n:* • **1.** rice

ت م و ز

تَمُّوز [tammu:z] *n:* • **1.** July

ت ن ب ل

تَنبَلخانَة [tanbalxa:na] *n:* تَنبَلخانات [tanbalxa:na:t] *pl:* • **1.** place to relax – مِن تِجي لِلشُّغُل لازِم تِشتُغُل؛ هَذِي مُو تَنبَلخانَة [min tiǰi liššuɣul la:zim tištuɣul; ha:ði mu: tanbalxa:na] When you come to work, you better work; this isn't any place to goof off!
تَنبَل [tanbal] *adj:* تَنبَلِيَّة، تَنابِل [tanbaliyya, tana:bil] *pl:* • **1.** lazy, slothful, indolent • **2.** lazy person – تَنبَل بالنُّوم [tanbal binnu:m] heavy sleeper, deep sleeper.

ت ن ت

تَنتَة [tanta] *adj:* تَنتات [tanta:t] *pl:* • **1.** convertible car – سَيّارَة تَنتَة [sayya:ra tanta] convertible car.

ت ن ت ر ي و ك

تَنتَرِيُوك [tantaryu:k] *n:* • **1.** tincture of iodine

ت ن ح

تَنَّح [tannaħ] *v:* • **1.** to bend over
مَتَنِّح [mtannaħ] *adj:* • **1.** stooping, bending

ت ن س

تِنِس [tannis] *n:* • **1.** tennis

ت ن ق

تَتَنَّق [ttannag, ʔittannag] *v:* • **1.** to be made taut or tight, to be strained – الحَبِل تتَنَّق [ʔilħabil ʔittannag] The rope was tightened.
تَنَّق [tannag] *v:* • **1.** to draw tight, make taut, stretch, strain – تَنِّق الحَبِل قَبُل ما تخَلّي الهِدُوم عَليه [tannig ʔilħabil gabul ma: txalli: ʔilhdu:m ʕali:h] Stretch the rope tight before you put the clothes on it. الخَيّاط تَنَّق سِترِتي كُلِّش [ʔilxayya:ṭ tannag sitirti kulliš] The tailor made my coat very tight. عَبّي القُونِيَّة تِمَّن بَسّ لا تتَنِّقها [ʕabbi ʔilgu:niyya timman bass la: ʔittannigha] Fill the gunny sack with rice but don't strain it. الوَضع السِّياسِي متَنِّق [ʔalwaðʕ ʔissiya:si mtannig] The political situation is tense. العَلاقات بَيناتهُم متَنِّقَة [ʔilʕala:qa:t bayna:thum mtanniga] Relations between them are strained.
تُنقَة [tunga] *n:* تِنَق [tinag] *pl:* • **1.** clay water jug
تَنقَة نَفَس [tanga nafas] *n:* • **1.** asthma
تَنق، تَنَق [tang, tanag (tanig)] *adj:* • **1.** tight, strained – هدُوم تَنقَة [hdu:m tanga] tight clothes. • **2.** tense, nervous – رِجّال تَنق [riǰǰa:l tang] a nervous man.

ت ن ك

تَنَك [tanak] *n:* • **1.** tin
تَنَكَة [tanaka] *n:* تَنَكات [tanaka:t] *pl:* • **1.** piece of tin • **2.** jerry can, five-gallon can
تَنَكچِي [tanakči] *adj:* تَنَكچِيَّة [tanakčiyya] *pl:* • **1.** tinsmith • **2.** automobile body and fender repairman

ت ن ك ر

تانكر [tankar] *n:* تَناكِر، تانكرات [tana:ki:r, tankara:t] *pl:* • **1.** tank

ت ن ك ي

تانكِي [ta:nki] *n:* تانكِيّات [ta:nkiya:t] *pl:* • **1.** tank, metal container

ت ن ن

تِنِّين [tinni:n] *n:* تَنانِين [tanani:n] *pl:* • **1.** dragon

ت ن و ر

تَنُّور [tannu:r] *n:* تنانِير [tna:ni:r] *pl:* • **1.** large, mud outdoor oven for baking bread
تَنُّورَة [tannu:ra] *n:* تَنُّورات [tannu:ra:t] *pl:* • **1.** woman's skirt

ت ن ي

تِنَى [tina:] *v:* • **1.** to wait, to await, wait for – تناه فَدّ شوَيَّة. هَسَّة يِجي [tnah: fadd šwayya. hassa yiǰi]

Wait for him a little while. He's coming now. راح نتانيك وَما ناكُل إلَى أن تِجي [ra:ħ nta:ni:k wma na:kul ʔila ʔan tiǰi] We will wait for you and not eat until you come. إنتَ إلمَن تاني؟ [ʔinta ʔilman ta:ni?] Who are you waiting for?
متاني [mta:ni] *adj:* • **1.** waiting

ت و ب

تاب [ta:b] *v:* • **1.** to forswear, renounce, turn from – القُمارجي تاب مِن لِعِب القُمار [ʔilqumarči ta:b min liʕib ʔalquma:r] The gambler swore off gambling. راح البَيت الله وَتاب مِن أكِل الحَرام [ra:ħ ʔilbayt ʔallah wta:b min ʔakil ʔalħara:m] He went to Mecca and swore off cheating. • **2.** to learn one's lesson, to go straight, reform – مِن ذِيك البَسطَة، تاب. بَعَد ما يذِبّ حجار عالنّاس [min ðiːč ʔalbaṣṭa, ta:b. baʕad ma: yðibb ħǰa:r ʕanna:s] Since that beating, he's reformed. He doesn't throw rocks at people any more. راح أبُسطَك إلَى أن تِقُول "تِبِت" [ra:ħ ʔabusṭak ʔila ʔan tigu:l "tibit"] I'm going to beat you till you say 'I've learned my lesson!'.
تَوَّب [tawwab] *v:* • **1.** to cause to go straight, reform, teach a lesson to – الخَسارَة تَوَّبَته مِن هَالشَّغلَة [ʔilxaṣa:ra tawwubatah min haššaɣla] The losses made him give up this business. تَوَّبتَه. بَعَد وَلا يبُوق [tawwabtah. baʕad wala ybu:g] I straightened him out. He won't steal again.
تُوبَة [tu:ba] *n:* • **1.** repentance, contrition – الأمّ بُسطَت إبِنها حَتَّى قال "التَّوبَة!" [ʔilʔumm busṭat ʔibinha ħatta ga:l "ʔittu:ba!"] The mother beat her son until he said 'I'll never do it again!'. التَّوبَة إذا أكفَل واحِد مِن هِيكِي ناس [ʔittu:ba ʔiða ʔakfal wa:ħid min hi:či na:s] That's the last time I'll ever co-sign with one of those people!
تايِب [ta:yib] *adj:* • **1.** contrite, penitent, sorry, remorseful, repentant, regretful, repenting

ت و ث

تُوث [tu:θ] *n:* • **1.** (coll.) mulberry wood, mulberry trees
تُوثَة [tu:θa] *n:* تُوثات [tu:θa:t] *pl:* • **1.** mulberry tree
تُوثِيَّة [tu:θiyya] *n:* تواثِي [twa:θi] *pl:* • **1.** billy club, night-stick

ت و ج

تَوَّج [tawwaǰ] *v:* • **1.** to crown – تَوّجُوه مَلِك عالعِراق [tawwiǰu:h malik ʕalʕira:q] They crowned him king of Iraq.
تاج [ta:ǰ] *n:* تِيجان [ti:ǰa:n] *pl:* • **1.** crown, miter
تَتوِيج [tatwi:ǰ] *n:* • **1.** coronation, crowning
متَوَّج [mtawwaǰ] *adj:* • **1.** crowned, coronated

ت و ر

تُورَة [tu:ra] *n:* تُورات [tu:ra:t] *pl:* • **1.** Torah • **2.** synagogue

ت و ر ج

تُورِج [tu:rič] *n:* • **1.** flashlight

ت و ر ن

تُورنَة [tu:rna] *n:* تُورنات [tu:rna:t] *pl:* • **1.** lathe
تَورنَجِي [tu:rnači] *adj:* تَورنَجِيَّة [tu:rnačiyya] *pl:* • **1.** machinist, lathe operator

ت و ك ي

تُوكِي [tu:ki] *n:* • **1.** a children's game similar to hopscotch

ت و م

تَوم [tawm] *n:* تَوامَة [twa:ma] *pl:* • **1.** twin – مَرتَه جابَت تَوم [martah ǰa:bat tawm] His wife had twins. أخُوه التَّوم [ʔaxu:h ʔattawm] his twin brother. • **2.** one of any multiple birth – مَرتَه جابَت تلَث تَوامَة [martah ǰa:bat tlaθ twa:ma] His wife had triplets.
تَوأم [tawʔam] *n:* • **1.** twin

ت و ن س

تُونِس [tu:nis] *n:* • **1.** Tunis • **2.** Tunisia
تُونِسِي [tu:nisi] *adj:* • **1.** Tunisian, a Tunisian

ت و و

تَوّ [taww] *adv:* • **1.** /with pronominal suffix/ just now, just this minute, just a second ago – تَوّنِي وُصَلِت. خَلّي أرتاح [tawwni wuṣalit. xalli: ʔarta:ħ] I just arrived. Let me rest. تَوَّة كان هنا [tawwa ča:n hna] He was just here. هَسَّة تَوَّك [hassa tawwak] Now you're on the right track! You've hit the nail on the head!

ت ي ت ي

تِيتِي [ti:ti] *n:* تِيتِيَّات [ti:tiyya:t] *pl:* • **1.** ticket taker, conductor

ت ي خ

تاخ [ta:x] *v:* • **1.** to wear out, to become dilapidated, old, run-down – سِكَنّا بِالبَيت إلَى أن تاخ [sikanna: bilbayt ʔila ʔan ta:x] We lived in the house till it wore out. لا تِمشِي عالسَّطِح تَرَة تايِخ [la: timši ʕaṣṣaṭiħ tara ta:yix] Don't walk on the roof because it's dilapidated.
تِيخَة [ti:xa] *n:* تِيَخ [tiyax] *pl:* • **1.** date stalk (after the dates are removed)
تايِخ [ta:yix] *adj:* • **1.** worn out

ت ي ر[1]

تَيّار [tayya:r] *n:* تَيّارات [tayya:ra:t] *pl:* • **1.** current, flow, stream, movement – تَيّار كَهرَبائِي [tayya:r kahraba:ʔi] electric current. • **2.** draft (of air)

ت ي ر[2]

تايَر [ta:yar] *n:* • **1.** tire

ت

ت ي ز ب

تِيزاب [tiːzaːb] *n:* • **1.** aqua regia (chem.)

ت ي س

تَيس [tays] *n:* تيُوس [tyuːs] *pl:* • **1.** billy goat

ت ي غ

تِيغَة [tiːɣa] *n:* تِيَغ [tiyaɣ] *pl:* • **1.** wall around the roof of a house

ت ي ف و

تِيفُو [tiːfu] *n:* • **1.** typhoid

ت ي ل

تيل [tiːl] *n:* تيُولَة [tyuːla] *pl:* • **1.** wire • **2.** metallic thread • **3.** wire screen, window screen • **4.** power line, high-tension line – لا تِندَقّ بتِيلَه [laː tindagg btiːlah] Don't get mixed up with him.

ت ي ن

تين [tiːn] *n:* • **1.** fig(s) • **2.** fig tree(s)

تِينَة [tiːna] *n:* • **1.** unit noun of تين fig • **2.** fig tree

ت ي ه

تاه [taːh] *v:* • **1.** to get lost, go astray, lose one's way, wander, stray – طِلَع لِلصّيد وتاه بالجّول [ṭilaʕ liṣṣiːd wtaːh bičču:l] He went out hunting and got lost in the wilderness. فِكري تايِه؛ ما دَأقدَر أشتُغُل [fikri taːyih; maː daʔagdar ʔaštuɣul] My mind is wandering; I can't work.

تَيَّه [tayyah] *v:* • **1.** to lose, mislead, lead astray, confuse, confound – الشُّرطِي راد يِلزَمني لَكِن رِكَضِت وَتَيَّهتَه [ʔiššurṭi raːd yilzamni laːkin rikaðit wtayyahtah] The policeman tried to catch me but I ran and lost him. مِن وُصَلِت يَمّ السِّينَما، تَيَّهت الطَّرِيق [min wuṣalit yamm ʔissiːnama, tayyaht ʔiṭṭariːq] When I got near the movie, I lost the way. لا تتَيِّه عَلَيّا الحساب [laːttayyih ʕalayya ʔilħsaːb] Don't make me lose count. هَالشّوارِع تتَيِّه [haššawaːriʕ ttayyih] These streets are confusing.

تياه [tyaːh] *n:* • **1.** anarchy, confusion

مَتاهَة [mataːha] *n:* مَتاهات [mataːhaːt] *pl:* • **1.** maze

تايِه [taːyih] *adj:* • **1.** lost, stray, errant, wandering – رصاصَة تايِهَة [rṣaːṣa taːyha] a stray bullet. • **2.** confused, perplexed

ت ي و ب

تيُوب [tyuːb] *n:* • **1.** tube

ث

ث

ثاء [θaːʔ] *n:* • **1.** name of the letter

ث ء ر

ثأر [θiʔar] *v:* • **1.** to take blood revenge – راح نِثأر مِن كُل أعدائنا [raːħ niθʔar min kull ʔaʕdaːʔna] We're going to take revenge on all our enemies. عائِلتَه ثِأرَتلَه [ʕaːʔiltah θiʔaratlah] His family avenged him.

ثار [θaːr] *n:* ثارات [θaːraːt] *pl:* • **1.** revenge, blood revenge, vengeance

ث ب ت

ثِبَت [θibat] *v:* • **1.** to be steady, firm, unshakable, stable – هَل قَدّ ما شارُب، ما دَيقدَر يِثبِت عَلَى رِجلَيه [hal gadd maː šaːrub, maː dayigdar yiθbit ʕala rijlayh] He's so drunk, he can't stay on his feet. • **2.** to hold on, to abide, stick – ثِبَت عَلَى رأيَه [θibat ʕala raʔyah] He held to his opinion. هَذا ما يِثبِت عَلَى كَلامَه [haːða maː yiθbit ʕala kalaːmah] He doesn't stick to his word. • **3.** to withstand, resist, hold out – جَيشنا ثِبَت بِالمَعرَكَة إِلَى النِّهايَة [jayšna θibat bilmaʕraka ʔila ʔinnihaːya] Our army held out in the battle till the end. • **4.** to be or become established, proven, definite – الجَّرِيمَة ثِبتَت عَليه [ʔajjariːma θibtat ʕaliːh] The crime was proven against him. ثِبَت إنُّو هُوَّ البايِق [θibat ʔinnu huwwa ʔilbaːyig] It was established that he's the thief. ثِبَتلِي مالَه عِلاقَة بِالمَوضُوع [θibatli maːlah ʕilaːqa bilmawðuːʕ] It's clear to me that he has no connection with the matter.

ثَبَّت [θabbat] *v:* • **1.** to set firmly, stabilize – ثَبِّتها بمُكانها زين، لا تُوقَع [θabbitha bmukaːnha ziːn, laː tuːgaʕ] Set it in place well, so it doesn't fall. • **2.** to appoint permanently, confirm – ثَبِّتُوه بوَظِيفتَه بَعَد اِنتِهاء مُدَّة التَّجرُبَة [θabbituːh bwaðiːftah baʕad ʔintihaːʔ muddat ʔittajruba] They appointed him to his position permanently at the end of the probationary period.

أثبَت [ʔaθbat] *v:* • **1.** to prove, establish, validate – خَلِّي أثبِتلَك الحكايَة [xalliː ʔaθbitlak ʔilħčaːya] Let me prove the story to you. أثبَت شَجاعتَه قِدّام النّاس [ʔaθbat šajaːʕtah giddaːm ʔinnaːs] He established his bravery before the people.

تثَبَّت [tθabbat] *v:* • **1.** to make sure of, become certain of, verify, establish

ثُبُوت [θubuːt] *n:* • **1.** permanence, stability • **2.** certainty, sureness – ثُبُوت رَمَضان [θubuːt ramaðaːn] official determination of the beginning of Ramadan (by two witnesses who have seen the moon).

ثبات [θbaːt] *n:* ثباتات [θbaːtaːt] *pl:* • **1.** proof, corroboration • **2.** stake, peg, pin

إثبات [ʔiθbaːt] *n:* إثباتات [ʔiθbaːtaːt] *pl:* • **1.** establishment

ثابتَة [θaːbta] *n:* ثَوابِت [θawaːbit] *pl:* • **1.** point of reference (e.g. star), landmark

مَثبُوت [maθbuːt] *adj:* • **1.** established, comfirmed, certain, sure, positive, assured, proven

ثُبُوتِيَّة [θubuːtiyya] *n:* • **1.** identity

ثِبِت [θabit] *adj:* • **1.** steady

ثابِت [θaːbit] *adj:* • **1.** steady, invariable, constant, stable – النِّسبَة الثّابِتَة [ʔinnisba ʔaθθaːbita] pi (math.). • **2.** permanent, lasting, durable, enduring – صُبُغ ثابِت [ṣubuɣ θaːbit] color-fast dye. حِبر ثابِت [ħibir θaːbit] indelible ink. • **3.** confirmed, proven, established

مُثَبَّت [muθabbat] *adj:* • **1.** fixed, affirmative, probative; (as n:) stabilizer, fastener

مُثَبِّت [muθabbit] *adj:* • **1.** (as n:) fixative, fixing fluid

إثباتِي [ʔiθbaːti] *adj:* • **1.** affirmative, cofirmatory, corroborative, positive

أثبَت [ʔaθbat] *comparative adjective:* • **1.** more or most stable, certain, reliable, etc

ث ب ر 1

ثُبَر [θubar] *v:* • **1.** to pester, keep after, bother continually – البارحَة ظَلّ يِحكِيلنا عَلَى مُغامَراته وَثُبَرنا أربَع ساعات [ʔilbaːrħa ðall yiħčiːlna ʕala muɣaːmaraːtah wθubarna ʔarbaʕ saːʕaːt] Yesterdy he kept talking to us about his adventures and pestered us for four hours. ثُبَرنِي عَالفلُوس [θubarni ʕalfluːs] He pestered me for the money. الجّاهِل ثُبَرنِي، النَّهار كُلَّه يِبكِي [ʔijjaːhil θubarni, ʔinnahaːr kullah yibči] The baby gave me a pain, he has been crying all day. • **2.** to puzzle, perplex, stump, stymie – الأستاذ ثُبَرنا بالإمتِحان بِسُوال صَعُب [ʔilʔustaːð θubarna bilʔimtiħaːn bsuʔaːl ṣaʕub] The professor stymied us on the exam with a hard question.

اِنثُبَر [ʔinθubar] *v:* • **1.** to be or become puzzled, perplexed, stumped, stymied – اِنثُبَرت بِالإمتِحان وَما جاوَبِت زين [ʔinθubarit bilʔimtiħaːn wma jaːwabit zayn] I got muddled on the exam and didn't answer well. • **2.** to be or become caught, stuck – اِنثُبَرت بِيه وَما تخَلَّصِت مِنَّه إلّا بِصُعُوبَة [ʔinθubarit biːh wma txallaṣit minnah ʔilla bṣuʕuːba] I got stuck with him and only got away from him with difficulty.

ثَبُر [θabur] *n:* • **1.** ruin, destruction

ث ب ر 2

ثابَر [θaːbar] *v:* • **1.** with عَلَى to persist

ثُبُور [θubuːr] *n:* • **1.** ruin, destruction, doom, jeopardy, perdition

مُثابَرَة [muθaːbara] *n:* • **1.** persistence, perseverence, endurance • **2.** diligence, assiduity, painstaking

ث

مُثابِر [muθaːbir] *adj:* • **1.** persistent

ث ب ط

ثَبَّط [θabbaṭ] *v:* • **1.** demoralize, daunt, dishearten, dissuade, dispirit

تثبِيط [taθbiːṭ] *n:* • **1.** discouragement

ث خ ن

ثِخَن [θixan] *v:* • **1.** to thicken, to be or become thick – بَقِّي المرَبَّى عَالنّار حَتَّى تِثخَن [baqqi ʔalmrabba ʕannaːr ħatta tiθxan] Leave the jam on the fire so that it'll thicken. مِن إستعمَل هَالدُّوا، بدا شَعرَه يِثخَن [min ʔistaʕmal hadduwa bidaː šaʕrah yiθxan] When he used that medicine his hair began to get thicker. • **2.** to be or become thick, fat, heavy – هَذا الفايِل ثِخَن هوايَة؛ إفتَحلَه مُلحَق [haːða ʔilfaːyil θixan hwaːya; ʔiftaħlah mulħaq] That file's gotten awfully fat; start an appendix to it. راح يِثخَن عَلَى هَالأَكِل [raːħ yiθxan ʕala halʔakil] He's going to get fat on this food. • **3.** to become serious, complicated, more involved, more serious – ثِخنَت القَضِيَّة بَيناتهُم ووُصلَت لِلمباسَط [θixnat ʔilqaḍiyya baynaːthum wwuṣlat lilmbaːsaṭ] The matter got serious between them and it came to blows.

ثَخَّن [θaxxan] *v:* • **1.** to make thick, thicken – النّار راح تثَخِّن المِربَّى إذا ما تطَفِّيها [ʔinnaːr raːħ tθaxxin ʔilimrabbaː ʔiða maː ʔiṭṭaffiːha] The fire will make the jam thick if you don't turn it off. • **2.** to exaggerate • **3.** to over-do, go too far – مُو ثَخَّنِتها؟ ما أعتِقِد هَالقَدّ بَخِيل [muː θaxxanitha? maː ʔaʕtiqid halgadd baxiːl] Aren't you exaggerating? I don't think he's that stingy. طلَعِت مِن الدّائرَة عِشرِين مَرَّة هَاليُوم. مُو ثَخَّنِتها؟ [ṭlaʕit min ʔiddaːʔira ʕišriːn marra halyuːm. muː axxanitha?] You've left the office twenty times today. Aren't you overdoing it? – يَزّي عاد؛ مُو ثَخَّنِتها [yazzi ʕaːd; muː θaxxanitha] Hold on now; you've gone too far!

ثُخُن، ثخُونَة [θuxun, θxuːna] *n:* • **1.** thickness, density • **2.** seriousness, severity, complexity

تَثخِين [taθxiːn] *n:* • **1.** thickening

ثِخِين [θixiːn] *adj:* ثخان [θxaːn] *pl:* • **1.** thick, dense • **2.** thick, fat, heavy • **3.** serious, complicated, deep, weighty

أثخَن [ʔaθxan] *comparative adjective:* • **1.** thicker, thickest • **2.** more or most serious, complicated

ث د ي

ثِدَى، ثَدي [θida, θady] *n:* ثِداية [θidaːya] *pl:* • **1.** breast, udder

ث ر ب

ثِرب [θirib] *n:* • **1.** (coll.) pl. ثُرُوب [θuruːb] *pl:* fish eggs, roe

ثِربَة [θirba] *n:* ثِربات [θirbaːt] *pl:* • **1.** fish eggs, roe

ث ر ث ر

ثَرثَر [θarθar] *v:* • **1.** to chatter, prattle – صارلَك ساعَة تثَرثِر. ما تِسكُت عاد [ṣaːrlak saːʕa tθarθir. maː tiskut ʕaːd] You've been chattering an hour. Why don't you shut up!

ثَرثَرَة [θarθara] *n:* • **1.** chatter, idle talk

ثَرثار [θarθaːr] *adj:* ثَرثارين [θarθaːriːn] *pl:* • **1.** chatterbox, prattler

ث ر د

ثِرَد [θirad] *v:* • **1.** to crumble, break (bread) – إثرِد الخُبُز بالماعُون [ʔiθrid ʔilxubuz bilmaːʕuːn] Crumble the bread in the plate.

ثرِيد [θiriːd] *n:* • **1.** crumbled bread with stew or broth poured over it

مَثرُودَة [maθruːda] *n:* • **1.** a dish made of pieces of dried bread and spices boiled in water

ث ر م also ف - ر - م

ثِرَم، فِرَم [θiram, firam] *v:* • **1.** to chop, cut up – إثرُم اللَّحَم ناعِم [ʔiθrum ʔillaħam naːʕim] Chop the meat fine.

ثَرَّم، فَرَّم [θarram, farram] *v:* • **1.** to chop up, cut up – ثَرَّم البُصَل وَخَلّاه عالزَّلاطَة [θarram ʔilbuṣal wxallaːh ʕazzalaːṭa] He chopped up the onions and put them on the salad.

تفرَّم [tθarram] *v:* • **1.** to be chopped, to get cut up – اللَّحَم ما يِتثَرَّم بهَالسِّكِّينَة [ʔillaħam maː yitθarram bhassiččiːna] The meat can't be chopped with this knife.

انفِرَم [ʔinθiram] *v:* • **1.** to be chopped, to get cut up – اللَّحَم لازِم يِنثِرِم أَوَّل [ʔillaħam laːzim yinθirim ʔawwal] The meat has to be cut up first.

فَرُم [θarum] *n:* • **2.** chopping

فُرمَة [θurma] *n:* فُرَم [θuram] *pl:* • **1.** shred, small piece

مَفرُوم [maθruːm] *adj:* • **1.** chopped up, hashed, chopped, minced

ث ر م و م ت ر

ثَرمُومَتِر [θarmuːmatir] *n:* • **1.** thermometer

ث ر ي

ثِرا [θira] *v:* • **1.** to become wealthy, rich, to prosper – إذا تُدخُل بهَالشَّغلَة، تِثرِي [ʔiða tudxul bhaššaɣla, tinθiri] If you get into this business, you'll get rich.

ثُرَيَّة [θurayya] *n:* ثُرَيّات [θurayyaːt] *pl:* • **1.** chandelier

ثَروَة [θarwa] *n:* • **1.** fortune

ثَري [θari] *adj:* أثرياء [ʔaθriyaːʔ] *pl:* • **1.** wealthy, rich • **2.** (as n:) a rich person

مُثري [muθri] *adj:* مُثرِيِّين [muθriyyiːn] *pl:* • **1.** wealthy, rich • **2.** (as n:) a rich person

ث ع ل ب

ثَعلَب [θaʕlab] *n:* ثَعالِب [θaʕaːlib] *pl:* • **1.** fox

ثَعلَبِيَّة [θaʕlabiyya] *n:* • **1.** tapioca pudding

ث غ ر

ثَغرَة [θaɣra] *n:* ثَغرات [θaɣraːt] *pl:* • **1.** breach, crack, rift, opening

ث ق ب

ثُقُب [θugub] *n:* • **1.** puncture

ث ق ف

ثَقَّف [θaqqaf] *v:* • **1.** to impart education or culture, to educate – هَالكُتُب راح تثَقِّفَك [halkutub raːħ tθaqqifak] These books will give you an education.

تثَقَّف [tθaqqaf] *v:* • **1.** to acquire education or culture, to become educated – إذا تريد تِتثَقَّف، أُدخُل كُلِّيَّة [ʔiða triːd titθaqqaf, ʔudxul kulliyya] If you want to get educated, enter a college.

ثَقافَة [θaqaːfa] *n:* • **1.** education, culture

مُثَقَّف [muθaqqaf] *adj:* • **1.** educated, cultured, refined

ثَقافِي [θaqaːfi] *adj:* • **1.** educational, cultural, intellectual – مُلحَق ثَقافِي [mulħaq θaqaːfi] cultural attache.

أثقَف [ʔaθqaf] *comparative adjective:* • **1.** more or most cultured, refined, educated

ث ق ل

ثِقَل [θigal] *v:* • **1.** to be or become heavy, burdensome – الصَّندُوق ثِقَل. ما أقدَر أشِيلَه بَعَد [ʔiṣṣanduːg θigal. maː ʔagdar ʔašiːlah baʕad] The trunk's gotten heavy. I can't lift it anymore. إذا يِثقَل حِمل الزُّمال، ما يِمشِي سَرِيع [ʔiða yiθgal ħiml ʔizzumaːl, maː yimši sariːʕ] If the donkey's load is heavy, he won't go fast. • **2.** to be or become serious, somber – مِن تزَوَّج، ثِقَل هوايَة [min dzawwaǰ, θigal hwaːya] Since he got married, he's gotten awfully serious.

ثَقَّل [θaggal, θaqqal] *v:* • **1.** to make heavy, add weight down – ثَقِّل الأوراق بشِي حَتَّى لا يطَيِّرها الهَوا [θaggil ʔilʔawraːq bši ħatta laː yṭayyirha ʔilhawa] Put weight on the papers so the wind won't blow them around. • **2.** to make too heavy – لا تحُطّ بَعَد تَرَة تثَقِّل الحِمِل عالحصان [laː tħuṭṭ baʕad tara tθaggil ʔilħimil ʕalħṣaːn] Don't put any more or you'll make the load too heavy for the horse. • **3.** to make difficult, troublesome, or onerous – الأُستاذ ثَقَّل الأسئِلَة بهالإمتِحان [ʔilʔustaːð θaggal ʔilʔasʔila bhalimtiħaːn] The teacher made the questions on this exam difficult. • **4.** to overload – سَيّارَة الحِمِل مالتَك ما راح تِمشِي، لِأنّ ثَقَّلتها [sayyaːrat ʔilħimil maːltak maː raːħ timši, liʔann θaggalitha] Your truck won't go because you overloaded it. • **5.** to make indifferent, make cool – شِنُو المثَقِّلَك عَلَيّا؟ [šinu mθagglak ʕalayya?] What's made you so cool to me? • **6.** with عَلَى to be a burden to, to inconvenience – خَلِّي نرُوح، عاد. ثَقَّلنا عالجَّماعَة هوايَة [xalliː nruːħ, ʕaːd. θaggalna ʕaǰǰamaːʕa hwaːya] Let's go, then. We've inconvenienced them too much.

تثاقَل [tθaːqal] *v:* • **1.** to feel imposed upon, to be recalcitrant, reluctant – مِن سِمَع أرِيد أرُوح وِيّاه، تثاقَل [min simaʕ ʔariːd ʔaruːħ wiyyaːh, tθaːqal] When he heard that I want to go with him, he felt imposed upon. لا تِتثاقَل. هَذا صَدِيقَك؛ لازِم تساعدَه [laː titθaːqal. haːða ṣadiːqak; laːzim tsaːʕdah] Don't feel burdened. He's your friend; you must help him. مِن تكَلّفَه بشِي، يِتثاقَل [min tkallfah bši, yitθaːqal] When you ask him to do something, he moans and groans.

اِستَثقَل [ʔistaθqal] *v:* • **1.** to find annoying or unpleasant, to dislike – يِستَثقِل أيّ شُغُل تِنطِيه [yistaθqil ʔayy šuɣul tintiːh] He considers any work you give him as an imposition. أستَثقِلَه لِهذا. ما أقدَر أقعُد وِيّاه [ʔastaθqilah lhaːða. maː ʔagdar ʔagʕud wiyyaːh] I find him boring. I can't sit with him. أستَثقِل هوايَة الرَّوحَة لِلمَطار [ʔastaθqil hwaːya ʔirrawħa lilmaṭaːr] I dislike going to the airport very much.

ثُقُل [θuqul] *n:* أثقال [ʔaθqaːl] *pl:* • **1.** weight-lifting (athlet.) – رَمي الثُّقُل [ramy ʔiθθuqul] the shot put (athlet. event) – رَفع الأثقال [rafiʕ ʔilʔaθqaːl] weight-lifting (athlet.).

ثُقُل [θugul] *n:* ثقال [θgaːl] *pl:* • **1.** weight, burden, load • **2.** seriousness, gravity, importance – دَيبِيع ثُقُل بِراسِي [daybiːʕ θugul braːsi] He's being pompous toward me. • **3.** inconvenience, bother, trouble

مِثقال [miθqaːl] *n:* مَثاقِيل [maθaːqiːl] *pl:* • **1.** a unit of jeweler's weight – يِحكِي بالمثاقِيل [yiħči bilmθaːqiːl] He's a man of few words.

ثِقّالَة [θiggaːla] *n:* ثِقّالات [θiggaːlaːt] *pl:* • **1.** paperweight

ثِقِيل [θigiːl] *adj:* • **1.** heavy • **2.** burdensome, weighty, cumbersome, oppressive, unpleasant, onerous • **3.** serious, grave, somber – دَمَّه ثِقِيل [dammah θigiːl] He's a dull bore. He's too serious. سَمعَه ثِقِيل [samʕah θigiːl] He's hard hearing.

أثقَل [ʔaθqal] *comparative adjective:* • **1.** heavier, heaviest • **2.** more or most burdensome, oppressive, unpleasant, etc

ث ك ل

ثِكَل [θikal] *v:* • **1.** to lose (in death), to be bereaved of a loved one – ثِكلَتَك أُمَّك، إن شاء الله! ما ترُوح مِن هنا [θiklatak ʔummak, ʔinšaːllah! maː truːħ min hna] May your mother lose you, God willing! Get out of here! أثكِل إبنِي إذا أعرُف شِي عَن هَذا [ʔaθkil ʔibni ʔiða ʔaʕruf ši ʕan haːða] May I lose my son if I know anything about that.

ث ك ن

ثَكَنَة [θakana,θakna] *n:* ثَكَنات [θakanaːt] *pl:* • **1.** barracks (mil)

ث

ث ل ث

ثِلِث [θiliθ, θuluθ] *n:* أثلاث [ʔaθla:θ] *pl:* • **1.** one third, a third part
ثلَث [tlaθ] *n:* • **1.** three
مُثَلَّث [muθallaθ] *n:* • **1.** tripled, triple, triangular • **2.** (pl. only) trigonometry
ثلاثَة [tla:θa] *n:* • **1.** three
ثالُوث [θa:lu:θ] *n:* • **1.** Trinity – الثّالُوث المُقَدَّس [ʔiθθa:lu:θ ʔalmuqaddas] the Holy Trinity.
ثُلثَين [θulθayn] *n:* • **1.** two thirds
ثلاثِين الثّلاثِين [tla:θi:n, ʔittla:θi:n] *n:* • **1.** thirty, thirtieth
الثِلاثاء، يُوم الثِلاثاء [ʔiθθila:θa, yu:m ʔiθθila:θa] *n:* • **1.** Tuesday
ثالِث [θa:liθ] *adj:* • **1.** third (ordinal)
ثُلاثِي [θula:θi] *adj:* • **1.** tri-partite, tri-, triliteral – فِعِل ثُلاثِي [fiʕil θula:θi] triliteral verb, verb with three radicals.
ثالِثاً [θa:liθan] *adverbial:* • **1.** thirdly

ث ل ج

ثِلَج [θilaǰ] *v:* • **1.** to snow, sleet – شُوف! الدِّنيا دَتِثلِج [šu:f! ʔiddinya datiθliǰ] Look! It's snowing! بمَنطِقَة الجِّبال، ثِلجَت هوايَة هَالإسبُوع [bmanṭiqat ʔiǰǰiba:l, θilǰat hwa:ya halʔisbu:ʕ] In the mountain area, it snowed a lot this week.
ثَلَّج [θallaǰ] *v:* • **1.** to be or become frozen (fig.), to get cold – ثَلَّجِت. إنطِينِي بَطّانِيَّة لُخ [θallaǰit. ʔinṭi:ni baṭṭa:niyya lux] I'm half frozen. Give me another blanket. ثَلِّجَت رِجلَيّا مِن البَرِد [θalliǰat riǰlayya min ʔilbarid] My legs froze from the cold. الدِّنيا ثَلَّجَت. خَلِّي نسَوِّي مَنقَلَة [ʔiddinya θallǰat. xalli: nsawwi: manqala] The weather's gotten cold. Let's start the brazier.
ثَلِج [θaliǰ] *n:* ثلُوج [θulu:ǰ] *pl:* • **1.** snow • **2.** sleet • **3.** ice
ثَلّاجَة [θalla:ǰa] *n:* ثَلّاجات [θalla:ǰa:t] *pl:* • **1.** refrigerator, icebox • **2.** iceberg
ثَلجِي [θalǰi] *adj:* • **1.** snowy • **2.** ice, ice-, glacial – العَصر الثَّلجِي [ʔilʕaṣr ʔiθθalǰi] the Ice Age. مَناطِق ثَلجِيَّة [mana:ṭiq θalǰiyya] arctic regions.
مثَلَّج [mθallaǰ] *adj:* • **1.** iced, icy, ice-cold – شاي مثَلَّج [ča:y mθallaǰ] iced tea.

ث ل ط ع ش

ثلَطَّعَش [tlaṭṭaʕaš, θlaṭṭaʕaš] *n:* • **1.** thirteen

ث ل م

ثِلَم [θilam] *v:* • **1.** to chip, nick, break the edge of, make jagged – ثِلَم الماعُون مِن كان يِغسلَه [θilam ʔilma:ʕu:n min ča:n yγislah] He chipped the edge of the dish when he was washing it. مِنُو ثِلَم هَالسِّكِّينَة؟ [minu θilam hassičči:na?] Who nicked this knife?
ثَلَّم [θallam] *v:* • **1.** to chip, nick – ثَلَّم الكاسَة بعِدَّة مُكانات [θallam ʔalka:sa bʕiddat muka:na:t] He chipped the edge of the bowl in several places. هَالسِّكِّينَة كُلّها مثَلَّمَة [hassičči:na kullha mθallma] This knife is all nicked.
ثَلِم [θalim] *n:* • **1.** chipping, breaking the edge of
ثِلمَة [θilma] *n:* ثِلمات، ثِلَم [θilma:t, θilam] *pl:* • **1.** chip, nick, notch
متثَلِّم [mitθallim] *adj:* • **1.** blunted, blunt, cracking
مَثلُوم [maθlu:m] *adj:* • **1.** chipped

ث ل و ل also ف - ل - ل

ثالُول [fa:lu:l] *n:* • **1.** (coll.) wart(s)
ثالُولَّة [fa:lu:lla] *n:* ثالُولات [fa:lu:la:t] *pl:* • **1.** wart

ث م ر

ثُمَر [θumar] *v:* • **1.** to bear, bear fruit – هَالشَّجَرَة ما تِثمُر [haššaǰara ma: tiθmur] This tree doesn't bear. • **2.** to bear fruit, to show results – تَعَبنا بِدا يُثمُر أَخِيراً [taʕabna bida: yuθmur ʔaxi:ran] our work has finally begun to show results.
أَثمَر [ʔaθmar] *v:* • **1.** to bear
اِستَثمَر [ʔistaθmar] *v:* • **1.** to invest profitably, to exploit, utilize, derive benefit from – اِستَثمَر فلُوسَه بشَرِكَة السِّمَنت [ʔistaθmar flu:sah bšarikat ʔassimant] He invested his money in the cement company.
ثَمَر [θamar] *n:* • **1.** (coll.) pl. fruit
ثَمَرَة [θamara] *n:* ثَمَرات، أَثمار [θamara:t, ʔaθma:r] *pl:* • **1.** fruit • **2.** benefit, gain, profit – تَعَبَك ما بِيه ثَمَرَة [taʕabak ma: bi:h θamara] You're wasting your effort.
إثمار [ʔiθma:r] *n:* • **1.** fruition
اِستِثمار [ʔistiθma:r] *n:* • **1.** investment, utilization, exploitation • **2.** exploitation, selfish or unfair utilization
مُثمِر [muθmir] *adj:* • **1.** fructuous, productive, profitable, fruitful, juicy, yielding
مُستَثمِر [mustaθmir] *adj:* مُستَثمِرِين [mustaθmiri:n] *pl:* • **1.** investor • **2.** exploiter

ث م ن 1

ثَمَّن [θamman] *v:* • **1.** to appraise, assess, to set a value on – اللُّجنَة راح تِجِي باكِر تثَمِّن البَيت [ʔilluǰna ra:ћ tiǰi ba:čir tθammin ʔilbayt] The committee will come tomorrow to appraise the house.
تثَمَّن [tθamman] *v:* • **1.** to be appraised, assessed – ساعتِي تثَمَّنَت بِقِيمَة عَشِر دَنانِير [sa:ʕti tθammanat bqi:mat ʕašir dana:ni:r] My watch was appraised at ten dinars.
ثَمَن [θaman] *n:* أثمان [ʔaθma:n] *pl:* • **1.** price, cost • **2.** value
تَثمِين [taθmi:n] *n:* • **1.** appraisal
ثَمِين [θami:n] *adj:* • **1.** costly, precious, valuable
أَثمَن [ʔaθman] *comparative adjective:* • **1.** more or most valuable, precious, costly

ث م ن 2

ثُمُن [θumun] *n:* أثمان [ʔaθma:n] *pl:* • **1.** eight, one eighth, an eighth part
ثمانيَة [θma:nya] *n:* • **1.** eight
ثمانِين [θma:ni:n] *n:* • **1.** eighty
ثامِن [θa:min] *adj:* • **1.** eighth (ordinal)
مُثَمَّن [muθamman] *adj:* • **1.** eight-fold • **2.** eight-sided, octagonal

ث م ن ط ع ش

ثمُنطَعَش [θmunṭaʕaš] *n:* • **1.** eighteen

ث ن ع ش

ثنَعَش [θnaʕaš] *n:* • **1.** twelve

ث ن ي

ثِنَى [θina:] *v:* • **1.** to double, double up, fold – البَهلَوان ثِنَى الشِّيش [ʔalpahlawa:n θina: ʔišši:š] The strongman bent the bar. إثنِي حاشيَة الشَرشَف وخَيِّطها [ʔiθni ħa:šyat ʔaččarčaf wxayyiṭha] Fold the edge of the sheet and sew it up. • **2.** to bend, bend over – إثنِي نَفسَك عاليَمِين [ʔiθni nafsak ʕalyami:n] Bend over to the right.
ثَنَّى [θanna:] *v:* • **1.** to do twice, repeat
أثنَى [ʔaθna:] *v:* • **1.** to praise, laud, commend – الوَزِير أثنَى عَلَى خِطابَه [ʔilwazi:r ʔaθna: ʕala xiṭa:bah] The minister praised his speech.
تثَنَّى [tθanna:] *v:* • **1.** to walk with a graceful gait – شُوفها شلُون تِتثَنَّى بِمَشيِها [šu:fha šlu:n titθanna: bmašyiha] Look how she undulates when she walks!
إنثِنَى [ʔinθina:] *v:* • **1.** to be or become doubled, folded – هَالزُّولِيَّة ما تِنثِنِي [hazzu:liyya ma: tinθini] This carpet won't fold up. • **2.** to bend, bend over, lean, incline – لا تحُطّ هَالقَدّ ثُقُل عالتِّيل تَرَة يِنثِنِي [la: tħuṭṭ halgadd θugul ʕatti:l tara yinθini] Don't put so much weight on the wire or it'll get bent. اِنثِنِي لِجِهَة اليِسار [ʔinθini ljihat ʔalyisa:r] Lean to the left side.
اِستَثنَى [ʔistaθna:] *v:* • **1.** to exclude, except, exempt – عاقِبهُم كُلّهُم وَلا تِستَثنِي أحَّد [ʕa:qibhum kullhum wla: tistaθni ʔaħħad] Punish them all and don't make an exception for anyone. القانُون يِستَثنِي الوُزَراء مِن الخِدمَة العَسكَرِيَّة [ʔilqa:nu:n yistaθni lwuzara:ʔ min ʔilxidma ʔilʕaskariyya] The law exempts cabinet ministers from military service.
ثَني [θany] *n:* • **1.** doubling up, folding up
ثَنيَة [θanya] *n:* ثَنيَات [θanya:t] *pl:* • **1.** fold • **2.** cuff
ثنَين [θnayn] *n:* ثنَينات [θnayna:t] *pl:* • **1.** two • **2.** pair • **3.** deuce, two (cards) • **4.** /plus pronominal suffix/ both, both of, the two of – عَلِي وأخُوه ثنَينهُم إجَوا [ʕali wʔaxu:h θnaynhum ʔ ijaw] Ali and his brother both came.
ثَناء [θana:ʔ] *n:* • **1.** appreciation, praise
مُثَنَّى [muθanna] *adj:* • **1.** dual • **1.** doubled, twofold
أثناء [ʔaθna:ʔ] *n:* • **1.** during, in the course of – لا تخَلِّي أحَّد يخُشّ لِلغُرفَة أثناء الاِجتِماع [la: txalli: ʔaħħad yxušš lilɣurfa ʔaθna:ʔ ʔilʔijtima:ʕ] Don't let anybody come in the room during the meeting. • **2.** time, moment, instant – بهالأثناء، بَيَّن رَجِلها [bhalʔaθna:ʔ, bayyan rajilha] At that moment, her husband appeared. بَعَض أثناء شقَدّ خُوش وَلَد [baʕað ʔaθna:ʔ šgadd xu:š walad] Sometimes he's such a nice guy!
ثانيَة [θa:niya] *n:* ثَوانِي [θawa:ni] *pl:* • **1.** second (unit of time)
ثنَينات [θnayna:t] *n:* • **1.** /plus pronominal suffix/ both
ثانَوِيَّة [θanawiyya] *n:* • **1.** secondary school, high school – خِرِّيج ثانَوِيَّة [xirri:j θanawiyya] high school graduate.
الاِثنَين، يَوم الاِثنَين [ʔilʔiθni:n, yawm ʔilʔiθnayn] *n:* • **1.** Monday
اِستِثناء [ʔistiθna:ʔ] *n:* اِستِثناءات [ʔistiθna:ʔa:t] *pl:* • **1.** with the exception of, except, excluding
ثانِي [θa:ni] *adj:* • **1.** second (ordinal) • **2.** next, following
ثانَوِي [θanawi] *adj:* • **1.** secondary – مَدرَسَة ثانَوِيَّة [madrasa θanawiyya] secondary school, high school. • **2.** minor – مَسألَة ثانَوِيَّة [masʔala θanawiyya] a minor matter.
ثُنائِي [θuna:ʔi] *adj:* • **1.** bilateral, dual
اِستِثنائِي [ʔistiθna:ʔi] *adj:* • **1.** exceptional, special – جَلسَة اِستِثنائِيَّة [jalsa ʔistiθna:ʔiyya] emergency session.
ثانِياً [θa:niyan] *adverbial:* • **1.** secondly, in the second place, furthermore – أوَّلاً ما شِفتَه. وَثانِياً شَعلَيَّا؟ [ʔawwalan ma: šiftah. wθa:niyan šaʕlayya?] First of all I didn't see him. And secondly, what's it to me?
أثناء ما [ʔaθna:ʔ ma:] *subordinating conjunction:* • **1.** while, when – لا تِزعِجنِي أثناء ما دَأشتُغُل [la: tizʕijni ʔaθna:ʔ ma: daʔaštuɣul] Don't bother me while I'm working.

ث و ب

تثاوَب [tθa:wab] *v:* • **1.** to yawn – أشُو دَتِتثاوَب. إنتَ نَعسان؟ [ʔašu datitθa:wab. ʔinta naʕsa:n?] I see you're yawning. Are you sleepy?
ثُوب [θu:b, θawb] *n:* ثِياب [θya:b] *pl:* • **1.** shirt • **2.** blouse
ثَواب [θawa:b] *n:* ثَوابات [θawa:ba:t] *pl:* • **1.** reward from God for good deeds • **2.** merit, credit (in the eyes of God)
أثوَب [ʔaθwab] *comparative adjective:* • **1.** more or most meritorious, deserving reward (in the eyes of God)

ث و ر

ثار [θa:r (u)] *v:* • **1.** to revolt, rebel, make a revolution – بَعض القَبائِل ثارَت عَالحُكُومَة [baʕð ʔilqaba:ʔil θa:rat ʕalħuku:ma] Some of the tribes revolted against the government. • **2.** to erupt, explode, flare up – هَالبُركان ثار مَرّتَين هالسَّنَة [halburka:n θa:r marrtayn hassana] This volcano erupted twice this year.

يثور بالعَجَل، مِن أقَلّ كِلمَة [yθuːr bilʕaǰal, min ʔaqall čilma] He flares up easily, at the slightest thing. ثار العَجاج مِن فاتَت الخَيل [θaːr ʔalʕaǰaːǰ min faːtat ʔilxayl] The dust swirled up when the horses passed. • **3.** to fire, go off – ثار المُسَدَّس بايد الوَلَد [θaːr ʔilmusaddas bʔiːd ʔilwalad] The revolver went off in the boy's hand. هَالطَّلْقَة فاسدَة. ما تثور [haṭṭalqa faːsda. maː tθuːr] This bullet is defective. It won't go off.

ثَوَّر [θawwar] *v:* • **1.** to incite to revolution, to stir up, arouse – ثَوَّر كُلّ القَبائِل عَالحُكُومَة [θawwar kull ʔilqabaːʔil ʕalħukuːma] He stirred up all the tribes against the government. • **2.** to have an erection

أثار [ʔaθaːr] *v:* • **1.** to stir up, arouse, kindle, provoke – لا تثير إلنا مُشكِلَة [laː tθiːr ʔilna muškila] Don't stir up trouble for us. • **2.** to raise, pose, bring up, interject – باكِر راح أثير المَوضُوع وأشُوف شيقُولُون [baːčir raːħ ʔaθiːr ʔilmawðuːʕ wʔašuːf šyguːluːn] Tomorrow I'll bring up the subject and see what they say.

انثار [ʔinθaːr] *v:* • **1.** to get excited, to get sexually excited

استثار [ʔistaθaːr] *v:* • **1.** to provoke, inflame, arouse, infuriate – إنتَ راح تِستثِيرَه بهالحكايَة [ʔinta raːħ tistiθiːrah bhalħčaːya] You'll infuriate him with that remark.

ثور [θuːr] *n:* ثيران [θiːraːn] *pl:* • **1.** bull, steer • **2.** ox • **3.** (by extension) a stubborn, bull-headed person

ثَورَة [θawra] *n:* ثَورات [θawraːt] *pl:* • **1.** revolution, rebellion, revolt • **2.** commotion, turmoil

إثارَة [ʔiθaːra] *n:* • **1.** provocation, agitation

ثَورِي [θawri] *adj:* • **1.** revolutionary

ثايِر، ثائِر [θaːyir, θaːʔir] *adj:* • **1.** rebellious, agitated, stirred up • **2.** exciting • **3.** provocative, stimulating

مُثير [muθiːr] *adj:* • **1.** provocative • **2.** sexy

ثَورَوِي [θawrawi] *adj:* • **1.** revolutionary

ث و ل

ثَوَل [θawall] *v:* • **1.** to be or become confused, disturbed, mixed-up – مِن واحِد يراقبَه بالشُّغُل، يِثوَل [min waːħid yraːqbah biššuɣul, yiθwall] When someone watches him at work, he gets all confused.

ثُوَل [θuwal] *v:* • **1.** to confuse, muddle, mix up – قِعَد يَمِّي وظَلّ يضحَك إلَى أن ثُوَلني [giʕad yammi wðall yiðħak ʔila ʔan θuwalni] He sat near me and kept laughing until he mixed me up. شثُوَلَك؟ مُو تُعرُف المَوضُوع زين [šθuwalak? muː tuʕruf ʔilmawðuːʕ ziːn] What came over you? You know the subject well!

ثَوَّل [θawwal] *v:* • **1.** to confuse, unnerve, upset – ثَوَّلتني بطَلَباتَك [θawwaltni bṭalabaːtak] You've driven me crazy with your demands!

انثوَل [ʔinθuwal] *v:* • **1.** to become confused, mixed up – انثوَلت؛ ما قدَرت أجاوُب أسئلَة المُدير [ʔinθiwalit; maː gidarit ʔaǰaːwub ʔasʔilat ʔalmudiːr] I got confused; I couldn't answer the director's questions.

ثَوِل [θawil] *n:* • **1.** confusion

أثوَل [ʔaθwal] *adj:* ثُول، ثَولين [θuːl, θuːliːn.] *pl:* ثُولَة [θuːla] *feminine:* • **1.** confused, absent-minded • **2.** scatter-brained

ث و م

ثُوم [θuːm,θawm] *n:* • **1.** garlic راس ثُوم [raːs θuːm] a clove of garlic.

ثُومَة [θuːma, θawma] *n:* • **1.** clove of garlic

ث ي ل

ثَيِّل [θayyil] *n:* • **1.** grass • **2.** lawn

ج

ج

جا [ča:, ǰa:] *conjunction:* • **1.** then, so, in that case

ج ب ب

جُبَّة [ǰubba] *n:* جُبَب [ǰubab] *pl:* • **1.** a long, plain outer garment, collarless, with wide sleeves, usually worn by religious men

ج ب ج ب

تَجَبجَب [dǰabǰab] *v:* • **1.** to be unsure, hesitant, timid, shy – دِفُوت قُلّه! لا تِتجَبجَب [difu:t gullah! la: tidǰabǰab] Go on in and tell him! Don't be hesitant! هُوَّ دَيتجَبجَب مِن هَالوَظِيفَة [huwwa dayidǰabǰab min halwaðˤi:fa] He's not too sure about this position. آنِي دَإتجَبجَب مِنّه هواية [ʔa:ni daʔidǰabǰab minnah hwa:ya] I am very unsure about him.

متجَبجِب [mitǰabǰib] *adj:* • **1.** hesitant

ج ب ر

جُبَر [ǰubar] *v:* • **1.** to force, compel, coerce – جُبرَونِي أتزَوَّجها [ǰubrawni ʔadzawwaǰha] They forced me to marry her.

جَبَّر [ǰabbar] *v:* • **1.** to set (a broken bone) – المجَبُّر جَبَّر إيدِي المَكسُورَة [ʔilmǰabbur ǰabbar ʔi:di ʔalmaksu:ra] The bonesetter set my broken arm.

اِنجُبَر [ʔinǰubar] *v:* • **1.** to be forced, compelled – اِنجُبَرت أترُك شُغلِي و أرُوح وِيّاهُم [ʔinǰubarit ʔatruk šuɣli wʔaru:ħ wiyya:hum] I had to leave my work and go with them. • **2.** to fall in love – اِنجُبَر بيها وتزَوَّجها [ʔinǰubar bi:ha wdzawwaǰha] He fell in love with her and married her.

جَبِر [ǰabir] *n:* • **1.** algebra

مجَبِّر [mǰabbir] *n:* مجَبِّرين [mǰabbiri:n] *pl:* • **1.** bonesetter

جبِيرَة [ǰibi:ra] *n:* • **1.** cast (as for a broken bone)

تَجبِير [taǰbi:r] *n:* • **1.** casting

إجبارِي [ʔiǰba:ri] *n:* • **1.** compulsory, obligatory, forced – جُندِي إجبارِي [ǰundi ʔiǰba:ri] draftee. أخذُوه إجبارِي [ʔaxðuwh ʔiǰba:ri] They drafted him.

جَبُر [ǰabur] *n:* • **1.** force, coercion, compulsion, duress

جَبرِي [ǰabri] *adj:* • **1.** compulsory, obligatory, forced

جَبّار [ǰabba:r] *adj:* • **1.** almighty, omnipotent • **2.** thick, large (in circumference) • **3.** pl. جَبابِرَة mighty, powerful, strong

مَجبُور [maǰbu:r] *adj:* • **1.** forced, compelled • **2.** in love, enamored – هُوَّ مَجبُور بِيها [huwwa maǰbu:r bi:ha] He's in love with her.

مجَبِّرجِي [mǰabbirči] *adj:* مجَبِّرجِيَّة [mǰabbirči:yya] *pl:* • **1.** bonesetter

أجبَر [ʔaǰbar] *comparative adjective:* • **1.** stronger, strongest • **2.** thicker, thickest

جَبراً [ǰabran] *adverbial:* • **1.** forcibly, by force – ما قِبَل يرُوح لكِن الشُّرطَة وَدّوه جَبراً [ma: qibal yiru:ħ la:kin ʔiššurṭa waddawh ǰabran] He wouldn't go but the police took him forcibly. إبنِي ما يِدرُس إلّا جَبراً [ʔibni ma: yidrus ʔilla ǰabran] My son won't study unless forced to. شبِيدِي؟ سَوَّيتها جَبراً [šbi:di? sawwi:tha ǰabran] What could I do? I did it because I had to. جَبراً عَن [ǰabran ʕan] in spite of, despite. اِضطَرَّيت أقبَل الشَّغلَة جَبراً عَنِّي [ʔiðˤṭarri:t ʔaqbal ʔiššaɣla ǰabran ʕanni] I had to accept the job in spite of myself. عَيّنَوا هالمُوَظَّف جَبراً عَن رَئِيسَه [ʕayynaw halmuwaðˤðˤaf ǰabran ʕan raʔi:sah] They appointed that employee against the wishes of his boss.

ج ب ر ل

جبرائِيل [ǰibri:l, ǰibra:ʔi:l] *n:* • **1.** Gabriel

ج ب س

جِبس [ǰibs] *n:* • **1.** gypsum • **2.** plaster of paris

جَبَّس [ǰabbas] *n:* • **1.** to set (a broken bone) with a cast

ج ب ل

جِبَل [ǰibal] *n:* جبال [ǰiba:l] *pl:* • **1.** mountain

جَبَلِي [ǰabali] *adj:* • **1.** mountainous, hilly, mountain- • **2.** (as a n:) a mountain dweller, mountaineer

ج ب ن

جِبَن [ǰiban] *v:* • **1.** to be cowardly, fearful, scared, afraid – مِن شاف الأسَد قِدّامَه، جِبَن [min ša:f ʔilʔasad gidda:mah, ǰiban] When he saw the lion before him, he was scared. • **2.** to mix (mortar, cement) – إجبِن هَالجُصّ حَتَّى نبنِي بِيه الطّابُوق [ʔiǰbin halǰuṣṣ ħatta nibni bi:h ʔiṭṭa:bu:g] Mix this mortar so that we can use it to lay the bricks.

جَبَّن [ǰabban] *v:* • **1.** to curdle, become curdled – الحَلِيب جَبَّن. صار مِثل القالَب [ʔilħali:b ǰabban. ṣa:r miθl ʔalqa:lab] The milk's curdled. It's gotten solid.

جِبِن [ǰibin] *n:* • **1.** cheese

جُبُن [ǰubun] *n:* • **1.** cowardice

جَبنَة [ǰabna] *n:* جَبنات [ǰabna:t] *pl:* • **1.** mixing, batch (of mortar, cement)

جبِين [ǰibi:n] *n:* • **1.** forehead

جبان [ǰaba:n] *adj:* جُبَناء [ǰubana:ʔ] *pl:* • **1.** coward

مَجبنَة [maǰibna, maǰbna] *n:* • **1.** part of the stomach of the baby lamb, used as a fermenting agent in making cheese

ج ب ه

جابَه [ǰa:bah] *v:* • **1.** to confront, face, encounter – لازِم نجابهَه بِالحَقِيقَة [la:zim nǰa:bhah bilħaqi:qa] We'll have to face him with the truth. راح تجابِه صُعُوبات هوايَة بهالسَّفرَة [ra:ħ dǰa:bih ṣuʕu:ba:t hwa:ya bhassafra] You will encounter many hardships on this journey.

جَبهَة [ǰabha] *n:* جَبَهات [ǰabaha:t] *pl:* • **1.** front, front part, facade • **2.** forehead, brow • **3.** front lines, front (mil.)

ج ب ي

جِبَى [ǰiba:] *v:* • **1.** to collect, levy (taxes) – الحُكُومَة تِجبِي الضَّرايِب مِن الفُقَراء وَتجُوز مِن الزَّناكِين [ʔilħuku:ma tiǰbi ʔiððara:yib min ʔilfuqara:ʔ wdǰu:z min ʔizzana:gi:n] The government collects taxes from the poor and leaves the rich alone.

جَبَّى [ǰabba:] *v:* • **1.** to sit or lie down (with the buttocks prominently displayed) – شايفَه مِن يُقعُد شلُون يجَبِّي؟ [ša:yfah min yugʕud šlu:n yǰabbi?] Have you seen how he sticks his butt out when he sits down? لِيش مجَبِّي عَالقاع؟ ما تقُوم [li:š mǰabbi ʕalga:ʕ? ma: tgu:m] Why are you prostrated on the ground? Get up!

جابِي [ǰa:bi] *n:* جُباة [ǰuba:t] *pl:* • **1.** collector, collection agent • **2.** bus conductor

جِبايَة [ǰiba:ya] *n:* • **1.** collecting, levying

ج ت ت

جَتّ [ǰatt] *n:* • **1.** clover • **2.** hay

ج ث ث

جِثَّة [ǰiθθa] *n:* جِثَث [ǰiθaθ] *pl:* • **1.** corpse, cadaver, body

جِثِيث [ǰiθi:θ] *adj:* جِثِيثِين، جثاث [ǰiθi:θi:n, ǰθa:θ.] *pl:* • **1.** fat, obese, corpulent • **2.** obese person

ج ث م

جِثمان [ǰiθma:n] *n:* جِثمانات [ǰiθma:na:t] *pl:* • **1.** body, remains, corpse

جَيثُوم [ǰayθu:m] *n:* جَيثُومات [ǰayθu:ma:t] *pl:* • **1.** incubus • **2.** nightmare

ج ح د

جِحَد [ǰiħad] *v:* • **1.** to disclaim, disavow, deny – هَذا جِحَد النِّعمَة [ha:ða ǰiħad ʔinniʕma] He proved ungrateful.

جُحُود [ǰuħu:d] *n:* • **1.** denial, rejection

جاحِد [ǰa:ħid] *adj:* جاحِدِين [ǰa:ħidi:n] *pl:* • **1.** denier, ungrateful

ج ح ر

جُحُر [ǰuħur] *n:* جحار، جحُور [ǰħa:r, ǰħu:r] *pl:* • **1.** anus • **2.** buttocks

ج ح ش

جَحَّش [ǰaħħaš] *v:* • **1.** to marry a woman, consummate the marriage, and then divorce her (in order to make her eligible to re-marry her former husband) – جَحَّشها حَتَّى يِقدَر يتزَوَّجها رَجِلها السّابِق [ǰaħħašha ħatta yigdar yidzawwaǰha raǰilha ʔassa:biq] He married her, slept with her, and divorced her so that her former husband could marry her.

جَحَش [ǰaħaš] *n:* جحاش، جحُوش [ǰħa:š, ǰħu:š] *pl:* • **1.** young donkey

ج ح ف ل

جَحفَل [ǰaħfal] *n:* جَحافِل [ǰaħa:fil] *pl:* • **1.** group, battle group (mil.) – آمِر الجَّحفَل [ʔa:mir ʔiǰǰaħfal] battle group commander.

ج ح ي م

جَحِيم [ǰaħi:m] *n:* • **1.** hell, hellfire

ج د ح also ق - د - ح

جِدَح [ǰidaħ] *v:* • **1.** to spark, make sparks – هَالنَّوع مِن الحَجَر ما يِجدَح زين [hannawʕ min ʔalħaǰar ma: yiǰdaħ zi:n] This kind of flint doesn't spark well.

جَدِح [ǰadiħ] *n:* • **1.** sparking

جِدّاحَة [ǰidda:ħa] *n:* جِدّاحات [ǰidda:ħa:t] *pl:* • **1.** cigarette lighter

ج د د 1

جِدّ [ǰidd] *n:* جدُود، أجداد [ǰdu:d, ʔaǰda:d] *pl:* • **1.** grandfather

جِدَّة [ǰidda] *n:* جِدّات [ǰidda:t] *pl:* • **1.** grandmother • **2.** midwife

جَدَّة [ǰadda] *n:* • **1.** grandmother

ج د د 2

جَدَّد [ǰaddad] *v:* • **1.** to renew, revive – خَلِّي نجَدِّد عَلاقَتنا [xalli nǰaddid ʕala:qatna] Let's renew our relationship. ما تِقدَر تسافِر إذا ما تجَدِّد الباسبَورت [ma: tigdar tsa:fir ʔiða ma: dǰaddid ʔilpa:spu:rt] You can't travel if you don't renew your passport. • **2.** to remodel, restore, renovate, modernize – لازِم نجَدِّد البَيت قَبُل ما نأَجّرَه [la:zim nǰaddid ʔilbayt gabul ma: nʔaǰǰrah] We've got to renovate the house before we rent it. • **3.** to begin anew, start, try again – فلُوسَك خِلصَت. راح تبَطِّل لَو تجَدِّد؟ [flu:sak xilṣat. ra:ħ tbaṭṭil law dǰaddid?] Your money's gone. Are you going to quit or play again? ما مَعقُولَة شبَعِت. جَدِّد [ma: maʕqu:la šbaʕit. ǰaddid] You can't possibly be full. Have some more!

تجَدَّد [dǰaddad] *v:* • **1.** to be started anew, be revived – المَشاكِل تجَدِّدَت بِالشِّمال [ʔilmaša:kil dǰaddidat biššima:l] The troubles have cropped up again in the North. • **2.** to be modern, keep up to date – يِتجَدَّد بكُلّ أعمالَه [yidǰaddad bkull ʔaʕma:lah] He keeps up to date in everything he does.

جِدّ [ǰidd] *n:* • **1.** seriousness, earnestness – دَقُلَّك إياه بِكُل جِدّ [dagullak ʔiyya:h bkull ǰidd] I'm telling you this in all seriousness. دَتِتشَاقَى لَو جِدّ؟ [datitša:qa: law ǰidd?] Are you kidding or serious?
جادَّة [ja:dda] *n:* جادّات [ja:dda:t] *pl:* • **1.** boulevard, main street, large street
تَجدِيد [tajdi:d] *n:* • **1.** renovation, renewal
جِدِّي [ǰiddi] *adj:* • **1.** serious, earnest, sincere
جادّ [ja:dd] *adj:* • **1.** serious, in earnest – كان جادّ مِن حِكاها [ča:n ja:dd min ħiča:ha] He was serious when he said it.
جِدِّيَّة [ǰiddiyya] *adj:* جِدِّيّات [ǰiddiyya:t] *pl:* • **1.** seriously. I'm not joking – جِدِّيّات ما دَأتشَاقَى [ǰiddiyya:t. ma: daʔatša:qa:] Seriously. I'm not joking. • **2.** with earnestness, seriousness, gravity بجِدِّيَّة [bǰiddiyya]
جِدِيد [ǰidi:d] *adj:* • **1.** new, recent – مِن جِدِيد [min ǰidi:d] anew, again, from the start.
مِتجَدِّد [mitǰaddid] *adj:* • **1.** modern, progressive, up-to-date
مِستَجِدّ [mistaǰidd] *adj:* • **1.** new, recent – جُندِي مِستَجِدّ [ǰundi mistaǰidd] (military) recruit.
أجدَد [ʔaǰdad] *comparative adjective:* • **1.** newer, newest, more or most recent
جِدّاً [ǰiddan] *adverbial:* • **1.** very much – أحتُرُم أبُويَا جِدّاً [ʔaħturum ʔabu:ya ǰiddan] I respect my father very much.
جِدِّياً [ǰiddiyan] *adverbial:* • **1.** seriously, earnestly, in earnest

ج د ر [1]

جَدَّر [ǰaddar] *v:* • **1.** to be or become infected with smallpox – جَدَّر مِن كان عُمرَه خَمس سنِين [ǰaddar min ča:n ʕumrah xams sni:n] He had smallpox when he was five years old. آنِي مجَدِّر قَبُل [ʔa:ni mǰaddir gabul] I've had smallpox before.
جِدرِي [ǰidri] *n:* • **1.** smallpox • **2.** smallpox vaccination – ضَرُب جِدرِي [ḍarub ǰidri] smallpox vaccination.

ج د ر [2]

جَدارَة [ǰada:ra] *n:* • **1.** worthiness • **2.** fitness, suitability, aptitude, qualification • **3.** appropriateness
جَدِير [ǰadi:r] *adj:* • **1.** worthy, deserving • **2.** proper, suited, suitable, fit, appropriate – هَذا مُو جَدِير بهَالوَظِيفَة [ha:ða mu: ǰadi:r bhalwaḍi:fa] That man's not qualified for this position.
أجدَر [ʔaǰdar] *adj:* • **1.** more or most worthy, deserving

ج د ر [3]

جِدرِيَّة [ǰidriyya] *n:* جِدرِيّات [ǰidriyya:t] *pl:* • **1.** small pot

ج د ر [4]

جِدارِي [ǰida:ri] *n:* • **1.** mural, wall

ج د ف

See also: ج ذ ف

ج د ل [1]

جادَل [ǰa:dal] *v:* • **1.** to debate, argue with, bicker with – جادَلنِي بِمَوضُوع ما يُعرُف عَنَّه شِي [ǰa:dalni bmawḍu:ʕ ma: yuʕruf ʕannah ši] He argued with me on a subject he knew nothing about.
تجادَل [dǰa:dal] *v:* • **1.** to engage in argument, to argue with each other – تجادلَوا ساعَة وَما تفاهمَوا [dǰa:dlaw sa:ʕa wma tfa:hmaw] They argued an hour and didn't reach an understanding. تجادَل ويّانا عَلَى شِي تافِه [dǰa:dal wiyya:na ʕala ši ta:fih] He argued with us about a trivial thing.
جَدَل [ǰadal] *n:* • **1.** debate, dispute, argument, controversy
جِدال [ǰida:l] *n:* جِدالات [ǰida:la:t] *pl:* • **1.** quarrel, argument, debate
مُجادَلَة [muǰa:dala] *n:* مُجادَلات [muǰa:dala:t] *pl:* • **1.** argument, discussion, debate, quarrel
جَدَلِي [ǰadali] *adj:* جَدَلِيِّين [ǰadaliyyi:n] *pl:* • **1.** disputant • **2.** argumentative (person)

ج د ل [2]

جَدوَل [ǰadwal] *n:* جَداوِل [ǰada:wil] *pl:* • **1.** canal • **2.** small stream, brook • **3.** table, schedule, chart – جَدوَل مَواعِيد القِطار [ǰadwal mawa:ʕi:d ʔilqiṭa:r] train schedule. جَدوَل الضَّرُب [ǰadwal ʔiḍḍarub] multiplication table.

ج د و

جَدوَى، جِدوَى [ǰadwa ǰidwa] *n:* • **1.** benefit, advantage, gain, avail – بَلا جَدوَى [bala ǰadwa] or مِن غير جَدوَى [min ɣayr ǰadwa] to no avail, with no benefit. مِن جَدوَى [min ǰadwa] concerning, about. مِن جَدوَى الفلُوس اللّي أطلبَك إيّاها؛ تَرَة أرِيدها [min ǰadwa ʔilflu:s ʔilli ʔaṭulbak ʔiyya:ha; tara ʔari:dha] About the money you owe me; well, I want it.

ج د ي

جَدَّى [ǰadda:, gadda:] *v:* • **1.** to beg – كُلّ يوم يُقعُد هنا وَيجَدِّي [kull yu:m yugʕud hna: waygaddi] He sits here every day and begs. لا يِغنِيك وَلا يخَلِّيك تجَدِّي [la: yiɣni:k wala yxalli:k tǰaddi] He won't let you do anything (lit., he won't make you rich and he won't let you beg).
جِديَة [ǰidya, gidya] *n:* • **1.** begging
تجِدِّي [dgiddi] *n:* • **1.** begging
جدايَة [ǰda:ya, gda:ya] *n:* • **1.** begging
مجَدِّي [mǰaddi, mgaddi] *adj:* مجادِي [mǰa:di, mga:di] *pl:* • **1.** begger

ج ذ ب

جِذَب [ǰiðab] *v:* • **1.** to attract, draw in, pull in – المِغنَطِيس يِجذِب الحَدِيد [ʔilmiɣnaṭi:s yiǰðib ʔilħadi:d]

A magnet attracts iron. بِهَالمَنهَج، نِقدَر نِجذِب كُلّ الشَّباب [bhalmanhaǰ, nigdar niǰðib kull ʔaššaba:b] With this program, we can attract all the young people. بخِطابَه، جِذَبهُم كُلّهُم لِلحِزِب [bxiṭa:bah, ǰiðabhum kullhum lilħizib] With his speech, he drew them all into the political party.

اِنجِذَب [ʔinǰiðab] *v:* • **1.** to attract • **2.** with إِلَّى to be attracted to • **3.** with ب to be fascinated by, charmed by, captivated by, infatuated with, attracted by

جَذِب [ǰaðib] *n:* • **1.** attraction

تَجاذُب [taǰa:ðub] *n:* • **1.** attracting one another

جاذِبِيَّة [ǰa:ðibiyya] *n:* • **1.** attraction, lure, enticement • **2.** attractiveness, charm • **3.** magnetic force • **4.** gravitational force, gravity

اِنجِذاب [ʔinǰiða:b] *n:* • **1.** attraction

جَذّاب [ǰaðða:b] *adj:* • **1.** attractive, appealing, enticing – مَنظَر جَذّاب [manðar ǰaðða:b] an attractive sight.

مِنجَذِب [minǰaðib] *adj:* • **1.** attracted

ج ذ ر

جَذِر [ǰaðir] *n:* جذُور [ǰðu:r] *pl:* • **1.** square root (math.) جَذِر تَربِيعِي [ǰaðir tarbi:ʕi] square root (math.). • **2.** lower end

جَذرِي [ǰaðri] *adj:* • **1.** radical, basic, substantial

ج ذ ع

جِذِع [ǰiðiʕ] *n:* جِذُوع [ǰiðu:ʕ] *pl:* • **1.** tree trunk • **2.** stump

ج ذ ف also ج - د - ف ج - د - ف

جِذَف [ǰidaf, ǰiðaf] *v:* • **1.** to row, paddle – البَلَم كان بِيه فَدّ واحِد يِجذِف [ʔilbalam ča:n bi:h fadd wa:ħid yiǰðif] There was one person in the boat rowing.

جَذِف [ǰadif, ǰaðif] *n:* • **1.** paddling

مِجذاف [miǰda:f, miǰða:f] *n:* مَجاذِيف [maǰa:ði:f] *pl:* • **1.** paddle • **2.** oar

تَجدِيف [taǰdi:f, taǰði:f] *n:* • **1.** rowing (sport), oaring

ج ر [1]

جارَة [ǰa:ra] *n:* جارات [ǰa:ra:t] *pl:* • **1.** afterbirth, placenta

ج ر [2]

جارَة [ča:ra] *n:* جارات [ča:ra:t] *pl:* • **1.** cure, remedy – هَالمَرَض ما إلَه جارَة [halmarað ma: ʔilah ča:ra] There's no cure for this disease. ما يصِيرلَه جارَة. راح يمُوت [ma: yṣi:rlah ča:ra. ra:ħ ymu:t] There's no curing him. He's going to die شِنُو جارتَه لِهذا؟ كُلّ سَنَة يِسقُط بالمَدرَسَة [šinu: ča:rtah lha:ða? kull sana yisquṭ bilmadrasa] What is to be done with him? He fails in school every year. • **2.** escape, way out – ماكُو جارَة. لازم يسَوِّي عَمَلِيَّة [ma:ku ča:ra. la:zim ysawwi: ʕamaliyya] There's no way out. He has to have an operation. هاي ما إلها غير جارَة [ha:y ma: ʔilha ɣi:r ča:ra] There's no other solution for it. تِقدَر تسَوِّي فَدّ جارَة وَتشُوفلَه شُغُل؟ [tigdar tsawwi: fadd ča:ra wtšu:flah šuɣul?] Could you manage somehow to find work for him?

ج ر ء

جِرَأ [ǰira?] *v:* • **1.** to dare, have the courage – ما يِجرأ يِحكِي ويّاه [ma: yiǰra? yiħči wiyya:h] He doesn't dare talk with him.

تجَرَّأ [dǰarra?] *v:* • **1.** to dare, to have the nerve – شلُون تِتجَرَّأ تِحكِي ويّا المُدِير هِيكِي؟ [šlu:n tidǰarra? tiħči wiyya ʔilmudi:r hi:či?] How do you dare talk with the director like that? • **2.** to be insolent, disrespectful, to take liberties – أرِيد هَالمُوظَّف ينفُصِل لِأَنّ تجَرَّأ عَلَيّا [ʔari:d hallmuwaððaf yinfuṣil liʔann dǰarra? ʕalayya] I want that employee to be fired because he was insolent toward me.

جُرأة [ǰurʔa] *n:* • **1.** courage, daring, nerve –

جَرِئ، جَرِيئ [ǰari?, ǰari:?] *adj:* • **1.** courageous, bold, daring • **2.** insolent, immodest, forward

أجرَأ [ʔaǰra?] *comparative adjective:* • **1.** more or most bold, courageous, daring • **2.** more or most insolent, forward

ج ر ب

جَرَبّ [ǰrabb] *v:* • **1.** to get the mange – كَلبِي جرَبّ [čalbi ǰrabb] My dog got mange. • **2.** to fade, lose color – قاطِي جرَبّ مِن الشَّمِس [qa:ṭi ǰrabb min ʔiššamis] My suit faded from the sun.

جَرَّب [ǰarrab] *v:* • **1.** to test, try out – جَرُّب هالمِفتاح. بَلكِي تِقدَر تفُكّ الباب [ǰarrub halmifta:ħ. balki tigdar tfukk ʔilba:b] Try this key. May be you can open the door.

جَرَب [ǰarab] *n:* • **1.** mange • **2.** scabies, itch

جراب [ǰra:b] *n:* جُربان [ǰurba:n] *pl:* • **1.** fraud, blow hard, incompetent

تَجرُبَة [taǰruba] *n:* تَجارُب [taǰa:rub] *pl:* • **1.** experiment, test – التَّجرُبَة ما نِجحَت [ʔittaǰruba ma: niǰħat] The experiment didn't succeed. • **2.** trial, test – بَعدَه تَحت التَّجرُبَة، وَما يِستِحِق إجازَة براتِب [baʕdah taħt ʔittaǰruba, wma yistiħiqq ʔiǰa:za bra:tib] He's still on probation and isn't entitled to vacation with pay. • **3.** experience, practice – تِتعَلَّم بالتَّجرُبَة [titʕallam bittaǰruba] You learn by experience. هَذا شايِف تَجارُب هوايَة؛ اِشتِغَل ويّا أنواع النّاس [ha:ða ša:yif taǰa:rub hwa:ya; ʔištiɣal wiyya ʔanwa:ʕ ʔinna:s] He's had a lot of experiences; he's worked with different types of people.

أجرَب [ʔaǰrab] *adj:* جربِين [ǰirbi:n] *pl:* • **1.** mangy

جَربَة [ǰarba] *adj:* جَربات [ǰarba:t] *pl:* • **1.** (fem.) mangy

مجَرَّب [mǰarrab] *adj:* • **1.** experienced, seasoned عامِل مجَرِّب [ʕa:mil mǰarrib] an experienced workman. • **2.** (as n:) experimenter, tester, examiner

تَجرِيبِي [taǰri:bi] *adj:* • **1.** experimental

ج ر ب ز

جَربَزَة [ǰarbaza] *n:* جَربَزات [ǰarbaza:t] *pl:* • **1.** irascible person, crank, crab, grouch

ج ر ب ع

جَربُوع [ǰarbu:ʕ] *n:* جَرابِيع [ǰara:bi:ʕ] *pl:* • **1.** jerboa, kangaroo rat • **2.** a kind of desert lizard or rat

ج ر ب ي

جُربايَة [čurpa:ya] *n:* جُربايات، جَرابِي [čurpa:ya:t, čara:pi] *pl:* • **1.** bed, bedstead

جُربايَة أَمّ نَفَرَين [čurpa:ya ʔumm nafarayn] *n:* • **1.** double bed

ج ر ث م

جَرثُوم [ǰarθu:m] *n:* جَراثِيم [ǰara:θi:m] *pl:* • **1.** microbe, germ

ج ر ج ت

جِرجَيت [ǰirǰayt] *n:* • **1.** a kind of thin, translucent cloth

ج ر ج ر

جَرجَر [ǰarǰar] *v:* • **1.** to jerk, tug, pull – ما يرِيد يرُوح. لا تجَرجِر بِيه [ma: yri:d yiru:ħ. la: dǰarǰir bi:h] He doesn't want to go. Don't tug at him. • **2.** to stall, procrastinate, hedge, delay – ظَلّ يجَرجِر سَنَة وَبَعدين دِفَع الفلُوس [ðall yǰarǰir sana wbaʕdi:n difaʕ ʔilflu:s] He kept stalling for a year and then paid the money.

جِرجِير [ǰirǰi:r] *n:* جِرجِيرين [ǰirǰi:ri:n] *pl:* • **1.** procrastinator, staller • **2.** sing watercress

مجَرجَر [mǰarǰar] *adj:* • **1.** procrastinated, stalled

ج ر ح

جِرَح [ǰiraħ] *v:* • **1.** to wound, injure, cut – جِرَحَه بصَدرَه، وَودُّوه لِلمُستَشفَى [ǰiraħah bṣadrah, wawaddu:h lilmustašfa] He wounded him in the chest, and they took him to the hospital. لا تِلعَب بِالمُوس، تَرَة تِجرَح نَفسَك [la: tilʕab bilmu:s, tara tiǰraħ nafsak] Don't play with the razor blade, or you'll cut yourself. لا تِجرَح عَواطفه بهِيكِي كَلِمات [la: tiǰraħ ʕawa:ṭfah bhi:či kalima:t] Don't hurt his feelings with such remarks.

جَرَّح [ǰarraħ] *v:* • **1.** to wound, cut to pieces, cut up – شلُون مزَيِّن! جَرَّحنِي [šlu:n mzayyin! ǰarraħni] What a barber! He cut me all up.

تجَرَّح [dǰarraħ] *v:* • **1.** to be wounded

اِنجِرَح [ʔinǰiraħ] *v:* • **1.** to be injured

جَرِح [ǰariħ] *n:* جرُوح [ǰru:ħ] *pl:* • **1.** wound, cut, injury

جَرّاح [ǰarra:ħ] *n:* جَرّاحِين [ǰarra:ħi:n] *pl:* • **1.** surgeon

جَرِيح [ǰari:ħ] *adj:* • **1.** wounded

جِراحَة [ǰira:ħa] *n:* • **1.** surgery

جارِح [ǰa:riħ] *adj:* • **1.** dangerous, injurious – آلات جارِحَة [ʔa:la:t ǰa:riħa] dangerous instruments. • **2.** rapacious, predatory – طيُور جارِحَة [ṭyu:r ǰa:riħa] predatory birds.

مجَرَّح [mǰarraħ] *adj:* • **1.** wounded

جِراحِي [ǰira:ħi] *adj:* • **1.** surgical

مَجرُوح [maǰru:ħ] *adj:* مَجارِيح [maǰariyħ] *pl:* • **1.** wounded

ج ر خ [1]

جِرَخ [čirax] *v:* • **1.** to turn on a lathe – يِجرَخ الخِشبَة ويسَوِّي مِنها مُصرَع [yičrax ʔilxišba wysawwi: minha muṣraʕ] He turns the wood and makes a top out of it.

جَرِخ [čarix] *n:* جرُوخ [čru:x] *pl:* • **1.** wheelchair – كُرسِي أَبُو جرُوخ [kursi ʔabu čru:x] wheelchair.

جَرِخ [čarix] *n:* • **1.** turning on a lathe

جَرّاخ [čarra:x] *n:* جَرّاخِين [čarra:xi:n] *pl:* • **1.** lathe operator • **2.** man who sharpens knives, scissors on a grinding wheel, scissors grinder

ج ر خ [2]

جَرخَجِي [čarxači] *n:* جَرخَجِيَّة [čarxačiyya] *pl:* • **1.** night watchman, patrolman

ج ر د

جِرَد [ǰirad] *v:* • **1.** to take stock, make an inventory – راح تِجِي لَجنَة تِجرِد المَخزَن باكِر [ra:ħ tiǰi lajna tiǰrid ʔilmaxzan ba:čir] A committee's coming to inventory the stores tomorrow.

جَرَّد [ǰarrad] *v:* • **1.** to divest, strip, dispossess, deprive – جَرِّدَوه مِن رُتُبتَه وَمَدالياتَه [ǰarridawh min rutubtah wmadalya:tah] They stripped him of his rank and medals.

اِنجِرَد [ʔinǰirad] *v:* • **2.** pass. of جِرَد to be inventoried – المَخزَن لازِم ينجِرِد مَرَّة بِالسَّنَة [ʔilmaxzan la:zim yinǰirid marra bissana] The store should be inventoried once a year.

جَرِد [ǰarid] *n:* • **1.** stocktaking, inventory

جَراد [ǰara:d] *n:* • **1.** (coll.) locust(s)

جرِيد [ǰiri:d] *n:* • **1.** palm branch(es) stripped of leaves, palm-leaf stalk(s)

جَرادَة [ǰara:da] *n:* جَرادات [ǰara:da:t] *pl:* • **1.** locust

جَرِيدَة [ǰarri:da] *n:* جَرايِد [ǰara:yid] *pl:* • **1.** newspaper

مُجَرَّد [muǰarrad] *adj:* • **1.** stripped, divested, bare – أَكثَر النُّجُوم ما تِنشاف بِالعَين المُجَرَّدَة [ʔakθar ʔinnuǰu:m ma: tinša:f bilʕayn ʔilmuǰarrada] Most of the stars can't be seen with the naked eye. • **2.** pure, mere, nothing more than هَذا مُجَرَّد سُؤال، لا غير [ha:ða muǰarrad suʔa:l, la: ɣi:r] This is merely a question, nothing else. بمُجَرَّد ما تِضحَك، يِزعَل [bmuǰarrad ma: tiðħak, yizʕal] If you barely laugh, he gets mad.

جوَيرِد، أبُو جوَيرِد [ǰwayrid, ʔabu ǰwayrid] *n:* • **1.** the first cold wind of fall, the harbinger of autumn
مَجرُود [majru:d] *adj:* • **1.** stocked, packed

ج ر د م

جَردَم [ǰardam] *v:* • **1.** to infect with leprosy, or loosely, any skin blemish – لا ترُوح يَمَّه تَرَة يجَردِمَك [la: tru:ħ yammah tara yǰardimak] Don't go near him or he'll infect you with leprosy.
تجَردَم [dǰardam] *v:* • **1.** to be or become infected with leprosy or, loosely, any skin blemish – وِجهه تجَردَم مِن البَقّ [wiččah dǰardam min ʔilbagg] His face was blotched by mosquito bites.
جِردام [ǰirda:m] *n:* • **1.** leprosy
مجَردَم [mǰardam] *adj:* • **1.** leprous • **2.** leper

ج ر ر

جَرّ [ǰarr] *v:* • **1.** to pull, tug, jerk – المُعَلِّم جَرّ إذن التِّلمِيذ لَمّا ضِرَب اللِّي يَمَّه [ʔilmuʕallim ǰarr ʔiðn ʔittilmi:ð lamma ḍirab ʔilli yammah] The teacher pulled the student's ear when he hit the one beside him. جَرّ حَصرَة وَرا حَصرَة [ǰarr ħaṣra wara ħaṣra] He heaved sigh after sigh. جَرّلَه نَفَس مِن جِيكارتِي [ǰarrlah nafas min ǰiga:rti] He took a puff from my cigarette. • **2.** to tow, pull, drag along, draw – كان الجّاهِل يجُرّ عَرَبانتَه بحَبِل [ča:n ʔiǰǰa:hil yǰurr ʕaraba:ntah bħabil] The child was pulling his wagon with a rope. جَرّ سَيّارتِي بسَيّارتَه لِلكَراج [ǰarr sayya:rti bsayya:rtah lilgara:ǰ] He towed my car with his car to the garage. • **3.** to extract, draw out, pull out – جَرّ عَلَيّا خَنجَر [ǰarr ʕalayya xanǰar] He pulled a knife on me. جَرّت الرَّقُم مالِي باليانَصِيب [ǰarrat ʔirraqum ma:li bilya:naṣi:b] She drew my number in the lottery. جُرّ إيدَك تَرَة أمَوّتَك [ǰurr ʔi:dak tara ʔamawwtak] Take your hand off or I'll kill you. جُرّ نَفسَك مِن هَالقَضِيَّة [ǰurr nafsak min halqaḍiyya] Get out of that affair. ترِيد ناخُذ راحَة شوَيَّة مِن الشُّغُل لَو نجُرها فَدّ جَرَّة؟ [tri:d na:xuð ra:ħa šwayya min ʔiššuɣul law nǰurrha fadd ǰarra?] Shall we take a short rest from working or get right on with it? جَرّيناها فَدّ جَرَّة لِبَغداد [ǰarri:na:ha fadd ǰarra libaɣda:d] We hurried straight through to Baghdad.
اِنجَرّ [ʔinǰarr] *v:* • **1.** with مِن to shun, avoid, stay away from – كُلّ المُوَظَّفِين ينجَرُّون مِنَّه [kull ʔilmuwaððafi:n yinǰarru:n minnah] All the employees shy away from him. إذا تِنجَرّ مِن عِدهُم، أحسَنلَك [ʔiða tinǰarr min ʕidhum, ʔaħsanlak] If you avoid them, it'll be better for you.
اِجتَرّ [ʔiǰtarr] *v:* • **1.** to ruminate – باوِع! الهايشَة دَتِجتَرّ [ba:wiʕ! ʔilha:yša datiǰtarr] Look! The cow is chewing its cud.
جَرّ [ǰarr] *n:* • **1.** pulling, towing, tugging, drawing, dragging – سِباق جَرّ الحَبِل [siba:q ǰarr ʔilħabil] tug-of-war contest. حَرُف جَرّ [ħaruf ǰarr] preposition (gram.).
جَرَّة [ǰarra] *n:* جَرّات [ǰarra:t] *pl:* • **1.** a pull, a tug, a jerk – يِقدَر يبَدِّل الوَضِع بجَرَّة قَلَم [yigdar ybaddil ʔilwaḍiʕ bǰarrat qalam] He can alter the situation with a stroke of the pen. • **2.** large earthenware jug
مجَرّ [mǰarr] *n:* مَجَرّات [majarra:t] *pl:* • **1.** drawer (of a desk, table, etc.)
جَرّار [ǰarra:r] *n:* جَرّارات [ǰarra:ra:t] *pl:* • **1.** drawer (of desk, etc.) • **1.** tractor
جَرّاء [ǰarra:ʔ] *n:* • **1.** by, because, the cause of/to
مَجَرَّة [majarra] *n:* • **1.** galaxy
جَرّارَة [ǰarra:ra] *n:* جَرّارات [ǰarra:ra:t] *pl:* • **1.** trailer
مُجتَرّ [muǰtarr] *adj:* • **1.** ruminant • **2.** a ruminant

ج ر ي

جِرّي [ǰirri] *n:* • **1.** (coll.) a type of catfish
جِرِّيَّة [ǰirriyya] *n:* جِرِّيّات [ǰirriyya:t] *pl:* • **1.** a type of catfish

ج ر س

جَرَس [ǰaras] *n:* أجراس [ʔaǰra:s] *pl:* • **1.** bell

ج ر ش

جِرَش [ǰiraš] *v:* • **1.** to grind, crush, crack (grain, etc.) – اِجرُش شوَيَّة عَدَس لِلشُّوربَة [ʔiǰruš šwayyat ʕadas liššu:rba] Grind up a few lentils for the soup.
جَرِش [ǰariš] *n:* • **1.** grinding, crushing, cracking (grain)
جرِيش [ǰiri:š] *n:* • **1.** ground grain
مِجرَشَة، مِجراشَة [miǰraša, miǰra:ša] *n:* مِجارِش [miǰa:riš] *pl:* • **1.** grinder, cracking machine
جارُوشَة [ǰa:ru:ša] *n:* جارُوشات [ǰa:ru:ša:t] *pl:* • **1.** grinder, cracking machine

ج ر ع

جِرَع [ǰiraʕ] *v:* • **1.** to gulp, swallow, drink down hurriedly – جِرَع نُصّ كلاص عَرَق بشُربَة وِحدَة [ǰiraʕ nuṣṣ gla:ṣ ʕarag bšurba wiħda] He downed half a glass of arrack in one draught. • **2.** to endure, bear, stand, take – ظَلّ عِدنا يومَين بَسّ ما قِدَرت أجِرعَه [ðall ʕidna yu:mayn bass ma: gidart ʔaǰirʕah] He was with us for two days but I couldn't stand him. جِرَعت المُرّ مِن إيد هَالوَلَد [ǰiraʕt ʔilmurr min ʔi:d halwalad] I've had nothing but trouble from this boy.
جَرَّع [ǰarraʕ] *v:* • **1.** to endure, bear, stand, take • **2.** to gulp, swallow, drink hurriedly
جِرَّع [ǰirraʕ] *v:* • **1.** to drink like an animal, to drink sloppily, gulp down, guzzle – لا تجَرِّع بالحَلِيب؛ مُو خَلَّصتَه [la: tčarriʕ bilħali:b; mu: xallaṣtah] Don't gulp the milk down; you've almost finished it! لا تكَرِّع مِن تِشرَب! حُطّ بالكلاص وإشرَب [la: tčarriʕ min tišrab! ħuṭṭ bilgla:ṣ wʔišrab] Don't put your nose in it when you drink! Put it in the glass and drink properly.
اِنجِرَع [ʔinǰiraʕ] *v:* • **1.** to be bearable, sufferable – دِهن الخِروِع ما ينجِرِع [dihn ʔilxirwiʕ ma: yinǰiriʕ] Castor oil is unbearable.
جَرِع [ǰariʕ] *n:* • **1.** gulp, swallow

جُرعَة [ǰurʕa] *n:* جُرعات، جُرَع [ǰurʕa:t, ǰuraʕ] *pl:* • **1.** mouthful, gulp, swallow • **2.** dose (of medicine) Editor's Note: The above entries could use an itinitial ك for

ج ر غ د

جَرغَد [čarɣad] *n:* جَراغِد [čara:ɣid] *pl:* • **1.** woman's head-cloth

ج ر ف

جِرَف [ǰiraf] *v:* • **1.** to sweep away, carry downstream – الماي جِرَف البَلَم مِن ضَيَّعِت المِجداف [ʔilma:y ǰiraf ʔilbalam min ðayyaʕit ʔilmiǰda:f] The water took the boat when I lost the oar. • **2.** to wash away – الماي جِرَف كُلّ الغَراض اللّي خَلّيناها عالشَّط [ʔilma:y ǰiraf kull ʔilɣara:ð ʔilli xallayna:ha ʕaššaṭ] The water washed away all the things we left on the bank.
اِنجِرَف [ʔinǰiraf] *v:* • **1.** to be swept
جَرُف [ǰaruf] *n:* • **1.** clearance, shoveling away
جُرُف [ǰuruf] *n:* جُرُوف [ǰuru:f] *pl:* • **1.** bank, shore, cliff
مِجرَفَة [miǰrafa] *n:* مَجارِف [maǰa:rif] *pl:* • **1.** kind of shovel shaped like a hoe with a curved blade
جَرّافَة [ǰarra:fa] *n:* • **1.** harrow, rake

ج ر ق ع

تجَرقَع [tčarqaʕ] *v:* • **1.** to be or become worn out, run down – بُقَت السَّيّارَة عِندَه سَنتَين وَبَعدين تجَرقعَت [buqat ʔissayya:ra ʕindah santayn wbaʕdi:n tčarqiʕat] He had the car for two years and then it went to pieces.
مجَرقَع [mčarqaʕ] *adj:* • **1.** worn out, run down, dilapidated

ج ر م

جِرَم [ǰiram] *v:* • **1.** to commit a crime or offense, to do wrong – إذا يِجرِم مَرَّة ثانيَة، ما يِعفِي عَنَّه الحاكِم [ʔiða yiǰrim marra θa:nya, ma: yiʕfi ʕannah ʔilħa:kim] If he commits another crime, the judge won't pardon him. جِرَم عَلَى وِلدَه؛ ما دَخَّلهُم مَدارِس [ǰiram ʕala wildah; ma: daxxalhum mada:ris] He wronged his children; he didn't put them in school.
اِنجِرَم [ʔinǰiram] *v:* • **1.** to be wronged, mistreated, cheated – اِنجِرَمِت بِهالشَّروَة [ʔinǰiramit bhaššarwa] I got cheated on that deal.
جُرُم [ǰurum] *n:* أجرام [ʔaǰra:m] *pl:* • **1.** crime, offense
إجرام [ʔiǰra:m] *n:* • **1.** crime – مُكافَحَة الإجرام [muka:fahat ʔilʔiǰra:m] crime prevention. عِلم الإجرام [ʕilm ʔilʔiǰra:m] criminology.
جَرِيمَة [ǰari:ma] *n:* جَرايِم [ǰara:yim] *pl:* • **1.** crime
مُجرِم [muǰrim] *adj:* مُجرِمِين [muǰrimi:n] *pl:* • **1.** criminal
إجرامِي [ʔiǰra:mi] *adj:* • **1.** criminal

ج ر و

جِرو [ǰirw] *n:* جراوَة [ǰra:wa] *pl:* • **1.** puppy, whelp, cub

ج ر و ي

جَرّاوِيَّة [čarra:wiyya] *n:* جَرّاوِيّات [čarra:wiyya:t] *pl:* • **1.** cloth wound around the head • **2.** small, simple turban

ج ر ي

جِرَى [ǰira:] *v:* • **1.** to flow, stream, run – المَيّ دَيجري بِالسّاقيَة صارلَه ساعتين [ʔilmayy dayiǰri bissa:gya ṣa:rlah sa:ʕtayn] The water has been running in the ditch for two hours. • **2.** to take place, come to pass, happen, occur – حَوادِث الرُّوايَة تِجري بِالجِبال [ħawa:diθ ʔirruwa:ya tiǰri biǰǰiba:l] The action of the story takes place in the mountains. لَو تِدري شجِرَى بِيّا [law tidri šǰira: biyya] If you only knew what happened to me! كُلّشِي جِرَى بلَحظَة وِحدَة [kullši ǰira: blaħða wiħda] Everything happened at once. شجارِيلَك تِشتِري سَيّارَة مُستَعمَلَه وَتِتوَرَّط بِيها؟ [šǰa:ri:lak tištiri sayya:ra mustaʕmalah watitwarraṭ bi:ha?] What ever impelled you to buy a used car and get stuck with it?
جارَى [ǰa:ra:] *v:* • **1.** to co-operate with, go along with, to adapt to, adjust to – جارِيه بَعدلَه إسبُوعَين يِنِّقِل [ǰa:ri:h. baʕadlah ʔisbu:ʕayn yinniqil] Go along with him. He's got two more weeks before he's transferred.
أجرَى [ʔaǰra:] *v:* • **1.** to carry out, perform – أجرَى تَجارُب هوايَة عَلَى هَالدُّوا [ʔaǰra: taǰa:rub hwa:ya ʕala hadduwa] He conducted many experiments on that medicine.
جَرِي [ǰari] *adj:* • **1.** flowing, streaming, running
مَجرَى [maǰra] *n:* مَجارِي [maǰa:ri] *pl:* • **1.** watercourse, stream • **2.** channel, stream-bed • **3.** flow, stream – لازِم أكُو شِي سادّ مَجرَى الماي. النَّهَر دَيصعَد [la:zim ʔaku ši sa:dd maǰra: ʔilma:y. ʔinnahar dayiṣʕad] There must be something blocking the flow of water. The river's rising. قِطعَوا عَن الثُّوّار مَجرَى الماي [giṭʕaw ʕan ʔiθθuwwa:r maǰra: ʔilma:y] They cut off the supply of water to the rebels. • **4.** course, progress, passage (of events) – صارلِي مُدَّة مَدا أتّبِع مَجرَى الحَوادِث بأمرِيكا [ṣa:rli mudda madaʔattibiʕ maǰra ʔilħawa:diθ bʔamri:ka] For some time I haven't been following the course of events in America.
جَرَيان [ǰaraya:n] *n:* • **1.** flow, movement • **2.** current
إجراء [ʔiǰra:ʔ] *n:* إجراءات [ʔiǰra:ʔat] *pl:* • **1.** performance, execution, act of carrying out • **2.** measure, step, proceeding – الحُكُومَة راح تاخُذ إجراءات شَدِيدَة ضِدّ المِتضاهِرِين [ʔilħuku:ma ra:ħ ta:xuð ʔiǰra:ʔa:t šadi:da ðidd ʔilmidða:hiri:n] The government's going to take stern measures against the demonstrators. راح آخُذ إجراءات قانُونِيَّة بحَقَّك [ra:ħ ʔa:xuð ʔiǰra:ʔa:t qa:nu:niyya bħaqqak] I'm going to take legal steps against you.
مَجارِي [maǰa:ri] *n:* • **1.** sewage
مُجاراةً لِ [muǰa:ra:tan li] *n:* • **1.** out of regard for in accordance with, in conformity with

بقيت ساكِت مُجاراتاً لِشعُورَه [biqi:t sa:kit mujara:tan lišuʕu:rah] I kept still out of regard for his feelings.
جاري [ǰa:ri] *adj:* • **1.** flowing, running, circulating – الماي الجّاري نَظِيف [ʔilma:y ʔiǰǰa:ri naði:f] Flowing water is clean.

ج ر ي د

جريدي [ǰraydi] *n:* جرَيديَّة [ǰraydiyya] *pl:* • **1.** large tree-climbing rodent – جريدي نَخَل [ǰri:di naxal] a large tree-climbing rodent.

ج ز ء

جَزَّأ [ǰazzaʔ] *v:* • **1.** to divide, break up, separate, partition, cut up – إذا تجَزَّأ السُّؤال، يِنفِهِم بسُهُولَة [ʔiða dǰazziʔ ʔissuʔa:l, yinfihim bsuhu:la] If you break up the question, it will be easily understood.
جُزُء [ǰuzuʔ] *n:* أجزاء [ʔaǰza:ʔ] *pl:* • **1.** part, portion – قريت جُزُء مِن الكِتاب وَما عِجَبني [qrayt ǰuzuʔ min ʔilkta:b wma ʕiǰabni] I read a part of the book and I didn't like it. • **2.** fraction – البَيت ما كَلَّفه إلّا جُزُء بَسِيط مِن ثَرُوته [ʔilbayt ma: kallafah ʔilla ǰuzuʔ basi:ṭ min θarwwtah] The house didn't cost him more than a small fraction of his fortune. • **3.** one of the thirty sections of the Koran • **4.** volume, section, part – اِشترَيت الجُزء الأوَّل مِن الكِتاب [ʔištirayt ʔiǰǰuzʔ ʔilʔawwal min ʔilkta:b] I bought the first volume of the book.
جُزَيئة [ǰuzayʔa] *n:* • **1.** molecule
جُزئي [ǰuzʔi] *adj:* • **1.** partial • **2.** minor, trivial, insignificant, petty
جُزئيّاً [ǰuzʔiyyan] *adverbial:* • **1.** partially

ج ز ج ز

جَزجَز [ǰazǰaz] *v:* • **1.** to squeak – هاليَمَني يِجَزجُز. لازِم خُوش شُغُل [halyamani yiǰazǰuz. la:zim xu:š šuɣul] These slippers squeak. They must be well made.

ج ز د ن

جِزدان [ǰizda:n] *n:* جِزدانات، جزادين [ǰizda:na:t, ǰaza:di:n] *pl:* • **1.** wallet • **2.** change purse

ج ز ر

جَزَّر [ǰazzar] *v:* • **1.** to be or become dried out – لا تفُكّ الجِّدِر، حَتَّى لا يجَزِّر الشّوَندَر [la: tfukk ʔiǰǰidir, ħatta la: yǰazzir ʔiššuwanðar] Don't open up the pot, so the beets won't dry out.
جِزَر [ǰizar] *n:* • **1.** (coll.) carrot(s) – راس جِزَر [ra:s ǰizar] a carrot, one carrot.
جَزِر [ǰazir] *n:* • **1.** ebb (of the tide) • **2.** low tide • **3.** shortage, deficiency – أكُو جَزِر بِالحساب [ʔaku ǰazir bilħsa:b] There is a shortage in the accounts.
جِزرَة [ǰizra] *n:* جِزرات [ǰizra:t] *pl:* • **1.** carrot
جَزرَة [ǰazra] *n:* جَزرات [ǰazra:t] *pl:* • **1.** island • **2.** sandbar شُبُه جَزِيرَة [šubuh ǰazi:ra] peninsula.
جَزّار [ǰazza:r] *n:* جَزّارين [ǰazza:ri:n] *pl:* • **1.** butcher
مَجزَرَة [majzara] *n:* مَجازِر [maǰa:zir] *pl:* • **1.** slaughterhouse • **2.** massacre, slaughter, carnage
جَزيرَة [ǰazi:ra] *n:* جَزائِر، جُزُر [ǰaza:ʔir, ǰuzur] *pl:* • **1.** island
الجَزائِر [ʔiǰǰaza:ʔir] *n:* • **1.** Algeria
جَزائري [ǰaza:ʔiri] *adj:* • **1.** Algerian, from Algeria • **2.** an Algerian

ج ز ز

جَزّ [ǰazz] *v:* • **1.** to shear, clip off – دَيجُزُّون صُوف الخَرُوف [dayǰuzzu:n ṣu:f ʔilxaru:f] They're shearing the sheep. • **2.** to squeak – قُندَرتِي الجِّدِيدَة دَتجَزّ [qundarti ʔiǰǰidi:da dadǰuzz] My new shoes are squeaking.
جَزّ [ǰazz] *n:* • **1.** shearing, clipping
جِزَّة [ǰizza] *n:* جِزَز [ǰizaz] *pl:* • **1.** the wool from one sheep – جِزَّة صُوف [ǰizza ṣu:f] the wool from one sheep, a clip of wool. • **2.** fleece, a clip of wool

ج ز ع

جِزَع [ǰizaʕ] *v:* • **1.** to be or become bored, to tire – الجّاهِل ما يِجزَع مِن اللِّعِب [ʔiǰǰa:hil ma: yiǰzaʕ min ʔilliʕib] The child doesn't get tired of playing. • **2.** to be or become disgusted, fed up, impatient, dissatisfied – طالَبتَه بِالفِلُوس مُدَّة وَبَعدين جِزَعِت [ṭa:labtah bilfilu:s mudda wbaʕdi:n ǰizaʕit] I asked him for the money a few times and then got disgusted.
جَزَّع [ǰazzaʕ] *v:* • **1.** to make restless, impatient, disgusted, to upset, make nervous – أظَلّ أدُقّ بِراسَه حَتَّى أجَزِّعَه [ʔaðall ʔadugg bira:sah ħatta ʔaǰazziʕah] I keep pestering him until I get his goat.
جَزَع [ǰazaʕ] *n:* • **1.** anxiety, worry

ج ز ف

جازَف [ǰa:zaf] *v:* • **1.** to act recklessly, heedlessly, to take chances – لا تجازِف هَالقَدّ؛ سُوق عَلَى كَيفَك [la: dǰa:zif halgadd; su:q ʕala kayfak] Don't take chances so much; drive slowly. • **2.** with ب to risk, hazard, stake – جازَف بِحَياتَه حَتَّى يِنقُذ المَرَة [ǰa:zaf bħaya:tah ħatta yinquð ʔilmara] He risked his life to save the woman.
مُجازَفَة [muǰa:zafa] *n:* مُجازَفات [muǰa:zafa:t] *pl:* • **1.** risk, hazard • **2.** recklessness • **3.** dangerous adventure
مُجازِف [muǰa:zif] *adj:* • **1.** reckless, foolhardy • **2.** adventurous

ج ز ل

جَزِيل [ǰazi:l] *n:* • **1.** abundant, opulent, overabundant, numerous

ج ز م [1]

جِزَم [ǰizam] *v:* • **1.** to be certain, positive, sure – ما تِقدَر تِجزِم بِأن الصُّوچ مِنَّه [ma: tigdar tiǰzim bʔan ʔiṣṣu:č minnah] You can't be positive that the blame is his.

جَزِم [ǰazim] *n:* • **1.** assertiveness
جازِم [ǰaːzim] *n:* • **1.** decisive • **2.** final, definite • **3.** absolutely certain, firmly convinced

ج ز م 2

جُزمَة [ǰuzma, čazma] *n:* جُزَم [ǰuzam, čuzam] *pl:* • **1.** rubber boots

ج ز و

جَزوَة [ǰazwa] *n:* جَزوات [ǰazwaːt] *pl:* • **1.** coffee pot (for Turkish coffee) • **2.** reward

ج ز ي

جَزَّى [ǰazzaː] *v:* • **1.** to fine – الحاكِم جَزّانِي دِينارَين [ʔilħaːkim ǰazzaːni dinaːrayn] The judge fined me two dinars. • **2.** to reward – جَزّاك الله خير [ǰazzaːk ʔallah xiːr] May God reward you.
جازَى [tǰaːzaː] *v:* • **1.** to repay, recompense – يِجِي يوم أَجازِيك عَلَى فَضلَك [yiǰi yuːm ʔaǰaːziːk ʕala fađlak] The day will come when I'll repay you for your favor. • **2.** to reward – الله يجازِيك عَلَى عَمَلَك [ʔallah yǰaːziːk ʕala ʕamalak] May God reward you for your act. • **3.** to punish – إذا ما تحَضِّر وَظِيفتَك، المُعَلِّم يجازِيك [ʔiða maː tħađđir wađiːftak, ʔilmuʕallim yǰaːziːk] If you don't prepare your lessons, the teacher will punish you.
تجازَى [dǰaːzaː] *v:* • **1.** to be recompensed, rewarded • **2.** to be reward
جَزاء [ǰazaːʔ] *n:* جَزاءات [ǰazaːʔaːt] *pl:* • **1.** reward – اللّي يِتصَدَّق عالفُقَراء، جَزائَه عِند الله عَظِيم [ʔilli yitṣaddaq ʕalfuqaraːʔ, ǰazaːʔah ʕind ʔallah ʕađiːm] The man who gives to the poor will have a great reward in heaven. • **2.** punishment, penalty – مَرَّة اللُّخ جَزاءَك يكُون حَبِس [marrat ʔillux ǰazaːʔak ykuːn ħabis] Next time your punishment will be jail. مَحكَمَة الجَّزاء [maħkamat ʔaǰǰazaːʔ] Penal Court (the second from the bottom of criminal court hierarchy, above ṣuluħ and below kubra • **3.** fine, judgment – إذا ما تِدفَع الجَّزاء، يحِبسُوك إسبُوعَين [ʔiða maː tidfaʕ ʔaǰǰazaːʔ, yħibsuːk ʔisbuːʕayn] If you don't pay the fine, they'll jail you for two weeks.
جِزيَة [ǰizya] *n:* • **1.** tribute • **2.** tax on free (non-slave) non-Muslims under Muslim rulers
مجازاة [mǰaːza(ːt)] *n:* • **1.** repayment, remuneration, bounty, bonus, recompense, fine, reward, fee • **2.** revenge, comeuppance, castigation, chastening, chastisement, penalization, retribution, retaliation
مُجزِي [muǰzi] *adj:* • **1.** profitable
جَزائِي [ǰazaːʔi] *adj:* • **1.** penal, punitive

ج س ب

جَسِب [ǰasib] *n:* • **1.** (coll.) dried date(s)
جَسبَة [ǰasba] *n:* جَسبات [ǰasbaːt] *pl:* • **1.** dried date
مجَسِّب [mgassib] *adj:* • **1.** crisp

ج س ر

جِسَر [ǰisar] *v:* • **1.** to venture, dare – شلُون جِسَرت وقِتلَه لِلمُعَلِّم هِيكِي؟ [šluːn ʔitǰisarit wgitlah lilmuʕallim hiːči?] How could you be so bold as to tell the teacher such a thing? إذا تِجسُر بكِلمَة وِحدَة، أَشُقَّه لِحَلقَك [ʔiða tiǰsur bčilma wiħda, ʔašuggah lħalgak] If you dare say one word, I'll smack you. • **2.** to have the courage, have the nerve – ما يِجسُر يُطلُب مِنَّه الفلُوس [maː yiǰsur yuṭlub minnah ʔilfluːs] He doesn't have the nerve to ask him for the money. • **3.** to be disrespectful, impudent, insolent – هَالوَلَد يِجسُر عَلَى أَبُوه [halwalad yiǰsur ʕala ʔabuːh] This boy is disrespectful toward his father.
جَسَّر [ǰassar] *v:* • **1.** to embolden, encourage, to make disrespectful, impudent – شِنُو اللّي جَسَّرَك هِيكِي؟ [šinuː ʔilli ǰassarak hiːči?] What was it that made you so impudent?
تجاسَر [dǰaːsar] *v:* • **1.** to be bold, forward, insolent, impudent – عِيب تِتجاسَر عَلَى أَبُوك [ʕiːb tidǰaːsar ʕala ʔabuːk] Shame on you, being insolent to your father! الطّالِب تجاسَر عالمُدَرِّس [ʔiṭṭaːlib dǰaːsar ʕalmudarris] The student was impudent toward the instructor.
جِسِر [ǰisir] *n:* جسُور، جسُورَة [ǰsuːr, ǰsuːra] *pl:* • **1.** bridge, span, overpass, viaduct • **2.** dental bridge • **3.** beam, girder, rafter
جَسرَة [ǰasra] *n:* • **1.** spunk, valor, nerve, heart, guts, stoutheartedness, nerviness, undauntedness, boldness, fearlessness, audacity, pluck, intrepidity, dauntlessness, courage, daring, bravery
جَسارَة [ǰasaːra] *n:* • **1.** boldness, courage • **2.** insolence, impudence, forwardness, nerve
تَجاسُر [taǰaːsur] *n:* • **1.** dare, venture, adventure, • **2.** heart, daring, valor, valiance, undauntedness, nerve, guts, stoutheartedness, nerviness, bravery, boldness, spunk, audacity, intrepidity, courage, fearlessness, dauntlessness
جَسِر [ǰasir] *adj:* • **1.** bold, courageous • **2.** impudent, insolent, forward
جَسُور [ǰasuːr] *adj:* • **1.** aggressive • **1.** bold, courageous, impudent, insolent, forward
متجاسِر [mitǰaːsir] *adj:* • **1.** forward • **1.** bold, impudent, insolent, impertinent
أَجسَر [ʔaǰsar] *comparative adjective:* • **1.** more or most insolent, impudent

ج س س 1

تجَسَّس [dǰassas] *v:* • **1.** to spy, engage in espionage – دَزُّوه يِتجَسَّس إلهُم [dazzawh yidǰassas ʔilhum] They sent him to spy for them.
جاسُوس [ǰaːsuːs] *n:* جواسِيس [ǰwaːsiːs] *pl:* • **1.** spy
جاسُوسِيَّة [ǰaːsuːsiyya] *adj:* • **1.** spying, espionage

ج س س 2

جَسّ [ǰass] *v:* • **1.** to feel, probe, examine by touch – الطَّبِيب جَسّ النَّبُض مالَه [ʔiṭṭabiːb ǰass ʔannabuđ maːlah]

The doctor felt his pulse. خَلِّي نجُسّ نَبضَه قَبُل ما نِسألَه [xalli: nǰuss nabðah gabul ma: nisʔalah] Let's feel him out before we ask him. • **2.** to try to find out, try to gain information – جِسِّلِي الخَبَر حَتَّى أعرُف شأسَوِّي [ǰissli ʔilxabar ħatta ʔaʕruf šʔasawwi:] Find out for me what's happening so I'll know what to do.
جاس [ga:s] *v:* • **1.** to touch – بَسّ تِجيسَه يقُوم يِبكِي [bass dgi:sah yguːm yibči] The minute you touch him he starts crying. البارحَة جاسنِي الشَّيطان [ʔilba:rħa ga:sni ʔišši:ṭa:n] I had an emission last night. • **2.** to blister – القُندَرَة جاسَت رِجلِي [ʔilqundara ga:sat riǰli] The shoe blistered my foot.
اِنجاس [ʔinga:s] *v:* • **1.** to be touched – بُقَى الأكِل مِثِلما هُوَّ. وَلا اِنجاس [buqa: ʔilʔakil miθilma huwwa. wala ʔinga:s] The food remained the way it was. It wasn't touched. • **2.** to be blistered – رِجلِي اِنجاسَت بِالقُندَرَة [riǰli ʔinga:sat bʔilqundara] My foot was blistered by the shoe.
جَسّ [ǰass] *n:* • **1.** feeling, palpate • **2.** contact with finger, feel, sense, touch

ج س م

جَسَّم [ǰassam] *v:* • **1.** to play up, magnify, enlarge, exaggerate – ماكُو شي. هَذا صاحبَك يجَسِّم الأُمُور [ma:ku ši. ha:ða ṣa:ħbak yǰassim ʔilʔumu:r] It's nothing. Your friend here just builds things up out of proportion.
تجَسَّم [dǰassam] *v:* • **1.** to become corporeal, materialize, assume form, take shape – تجَسِّمَت أمامَه حادِثَة مُوتَة عَمَّه وَبِكَى [tǰassimat ʔama:mah ħa:diθat mu:tat ʕammah wbiča:] A vision of the death of his uncle materialized before him and he cried.
جِسِم [ǰisim] *n:* أجسام [ʔaǰsa:m] *pl:* • **1.** body, • **2.** figure, form, shape • **3.** bulk, mass
جَسامَة [ǰasa:ma] *n:* • **1.** size, volume • **2.** immensity
جَسِيم [ǰasi:m] *adj:* • **1.** huge, immense
مُجَسَّم [muǰassam] *adj:* • **1.** bodily, corporeal • **2.** material, tangible • **3.** three-dimensional – خَرِيطَة مُجَسَّمَة [xari:ṭa muǰassama] three-dimensional relief map. هَندَسَة مُجَسَّمَة [handasa muǰassama] Solid geometry.
جِسماني [ǰisma:ni] *adj:* • **1.** physical

ج ش ع

جَشَع [ǰašaʕ] *n:* • **1.** greediness, covetousness
جَشِع [ǰašiʕ] *adj:* • **1.** greedy, covetous
أجشَع [ʔaǰšaʕ] *comparative adjective:* • **1.** more or most covetous

ج ص ص

جُصّ [ǰuṣṣ] *n:* • **1.** lime • **2.** mortar, plaster

ج ط ل

جِطَل [ǰiṭal] *v:* • **1.** to lay, place horizontal – إجطُل الجّاهِل عالميز وَلَفلِفَه [ʔiǰṭul ʔiǰǰa:hil ʕalmi:z wlaflifah] Lay the child on the table and wrap him up.
جَطَّل [ǰaṭṭal] *v:* • **1.** to lay out, flatten – ضُرَبهُم بُوكسات وَجَطَّلهُم عَالقاع [ðurabhum bu:ksa:t wǰaṭṭalhum ʕalga:ʕ] He hit them several times and laid them on the ground.
اِنجِطَل [ʔinǰiṭal] *v:* • **1.** to lie down, recline – تَعبان؛ راح أنجِطِل عالفراش [taʕba:n; ra:ħ ʔanǰiṭil ʕalifra:š] I'm tired; I'm going to lie down on the bed.
جَطلَة ,جَطَل [čaṭal, čaṭla] *n:* جَطَلات [čaṭala:t] *pl:* • **1.** fork (utensil) • **2.** shuttle, shuttle train • **3.** jumper cable (elec.) – جِيب سَيّارتَك يَمّ سَيّارتِي وَنسَوِّي جَطَل عالباتري مالَك [ǰi:b sayya:rtak yamm sayya:rti wnsawwi: čaṭal ʕa:lpa:tri ma:lak] Bring your car up to mine and we'll run a jumper to your battery.
جَطَل [čaṭal] *n:* • **1.** jump start

ج ع ب

جِعِب [ǰiʕib] *n:* جعُوبَة [ǰʕu:ba] *pl:* • **1.** hips, buttocks
جُعبَة [ǰuʕba] *n:* جُعبات [ǰuʕaba:t] *pl:* • **1.** lump of flesh on a bird's tail

ج ع د

جَعَّد [ǰaʕʕad] *v:* • **1.** to curl, make curly – شَعرك حِلو. ماكُو حاجَة تجَعّدِيه [šaʕrič ħilw. ma:ku ħa:ǰa tǰaʕʕdi:h] Your hair's nice. There's no need to curl it. • **2.** to wave – وين جَعَّدتِي شَعرِك؟ [wi:n ǰaʕʕadti šaʕrič?] Where'd you get your hair waved?
تجَعَّد [tǰaʕʕad] *v:* • **1.** to become wrinkled – مِن الوَجعَة ضِعَف وَجِلِد وُجَّه تجَعَّد [min ʔilwaǰʕa ðiʕaf wǰilid wuččah tǰaʕʕad] He got thin from the illness and the skin of his face became wrinkled. • **2.** to become curly or wavy • **3.** to become wavy
تَجعِيد [taǰʕi:d] *n:* • **1.** curl
تَجاعِيد [taǰa:ʕi:d] *n:* • **1.** (pl. only) wrinkles, lines (in the face)
مجَعَّد [mǰaʕʕad] *adj:* • **1.** curly, kinky – شَعَرها مجَعَّد مِن طَبِيعتَه [šaʕarha mǰaʕʕad min ṭabi:ʕtah] Her hair is naturally curly. • **2.** wrinkled, creased, furrowed – بَعدَه جاهِل لَكِن وِجهه مجَعَّد [baʕdah ǰa:hil la:kin wiččah mǰaʕʕad] He's still young but his face is wrinkled.

ج ع ر

جِعَر [ǰiʕar] *v:* • **1.** to bray – شُوفَه شلُون دَيِجعَر مِثل الزُّمال. ما يقدَر يحكِي يَواش [šu:fah šlu:n dayiǰʕar miθl ʔizzuma:l. ma: yigdar yiħči yawa:š] Look at him braying like a donkey. He can't talk softly.
جَعِر [ǰaʕir] *n:* • **1.** braying

ج ع ص

جِعَص [ǰiʕaṣ] *v:* • **1.** to crush, mash, squash. عَلَى كَيفَك! لا تِجعَص الطَّماطَة [ʕala kayfak! la: tiǰʕaṣ ʔiṭṭama:ṭa] Watch it! Don't mash the tomatoes. لا تُقعُد يَمّ هَذا السِّمين تَرَة يِجعَصك [la: tugʕud yamm ha:ða

ʔissimiːn tara yiǰʕṣak] Don't sit next to that fat guy or he'll squeeze you. راح تِتصارَع ويّا هالسِّمين؟ هَذا يِقدَر يجعَصَك [raːħ titṣaːraʕ wiyya hassimiːn? haːða yigdar yiǰʕaṣak] Are you going to wrestle with that fat guy? He could squash you.
جَعِص [ǰaʕiṣ] *n:* • **1.** crushing, mashing, squashing
تَجعِيص [taǰʕiːṣ] *n:* • **1.** crushing, mashing
مجَعَّص [mǰaʕʕaṣ] *adj:* • **1.** mashed, crushed
مَجعُوص [maǰʕuːṣ] *adj:* • **1.** mashed, crushed

ج ع ل

جِعَل [ǰiʕal] *v:* • **1.** to consider, regard, assume – إنطِيها كَم فِلِس وَاجعَلها صَدَقَة [ʔinṭiːha čam filis wʔiǰʕalha ṣadaqa] Give her a little money and consider it charity. إجعَل نَفسَك ما تِدري وَإسأله [ʔiǰʕal nafsak maː tidri wʔisʔalah] Pretend you don't know and ask him.
جَعَل، أَبُو جَعَل [ǰaʕal, ʔabu ǰaʕal] *n:* • **1.** dung roller, dung beetle

ج ع م ر

مجَعمَر [mǰaʕmar] *adj:* • **1.** lop-sided, misshapen

ج ع م ص

جَعمَص [ǰaʕmaṣ] *v:* • **1.** (vulgar) to talk nonsense – لا تِنتِبِهلَه. دَيجَعمُص [laː tintibihlah. dayǰaʕmuṣ] Don't pay any attention to him. He's just talking nonsense.
جَعمُوص [ǰaʕmuːṣ] *n:* جَعامِيص [ǰaʕaːmiːṣ] *pl:* • **1.** (vulgar) the product of an act of defecating, a piece of feces

ج غ ر ف

جُغرافِيَة [ǰuɣraːfya] *n:* • **1.** geography
جُغرافِي [ǰuɣraːfi] *adj:* • **1.** geographic, (as n:) geographer

ج ف ت

جَفَّت [ǰaffat] *v:* • **1.** to overhaul, rebuild (a motor) – شوَقِت راح تجَفِّت مَكِينَة السَّيّارَة؟ [šwakit raːħ dǰaffit makiːnat ʔissayyaːra?] When are you going to overhaul the car motor?
جِفت [ǰift] *n:* • **1.** an even number, multiple of two – إذا تجِيب جِفت، تُغلُب [ʔiða dǰiːb ǰift, tuɣlub] If you get an even number, you win. • **2.** double بُندُقِيَّة جِفت [bunduqiyya ǰift] double-barreled shotgun.
جُفتَة [ǰufta] *n:* جُفَت [ǰufat] *pl:* • **1.** in dominoes, a piece with the same number on both ends

ج ف ج ر

جَفجِير [čafčiːr] *n:* جَفاجِير [čafaːčiːr] *pl:* • **1.** a slightly concave metal spatula with holes in it

ج ف ر

جُفرَة [ǰufra] *n:* جُفَر [ǰufar] *pl:* • **1.** pit, hole in the ground • **2.** dug-out arena or ring for wrestling and athletic contests

ج ف ف

جَفّ [ǰaff] *v:* • **1.** to dry, become dry – خَلّاها بِالشَّمِس حَتَّى تجِفّ [xallaːha biššamis ħatta dǰiff] He put it in the sun to dry.
جَفَّف [ǰaffaf] *v:* • **1.** to dry out, make dry – يجَفِّفُون الفَواكِه حَتَّى ياكلُوها بِالشِّتا [yǰaffifuːn ʔalfawaːkih ħatta yaːkluːha biššita] They dry fruits in order to eat them in the winter.
جَفاف [ǰafaːf] *n:* • **1.** dryness
جافّ [ǰaːff] *adj:* • **1.** dry – بَغداد جَوّها جافّ بِالصَّيف [baɣdaːd ǰawwha ǰaːff bissayf] Baghdad's climate is dry in the summer. قَلَم حِبِر جافّ [qalam ħibir ǰaːff] ball-point pen. • **2.** stale, uninteresting, dry – يِسأَل أَسئِلَة جافَّة [yisʔal ʔasʔila ǰaːffa] He asks uninteresting questions.

ج ف ل

جِفَل [ǰifal] *v:* • **1.** to start, startle, jump with fright – جِفَلِت مِن طِلَعلي مِن وَرا الباب [ǰifalit min ṭilaʕli min wara ʔilbaːb] I got a start when he came out from behind the door. • **2.** to shy – الحصان جِفَل مِن سِمَع الطَّلقَة [ʔilħṣaːn ǰifal min simaʕ ʔiṭṭalqa] The horse shyed when he heard the shot.
جَفَّل [ǰaffal] *v:* • **1.** to startle, frighten – خَلِّي نِختِل وَرا الباب وَنجَفّلَه [xalliː nixtil wara ʔilbaːb wnǰafflah] Let's hide behind the door and startle him.
جَفِل [ǰafil] *n:* • **1.** jumping with fright • **2.** fear, fright
جافِل [ǰaːfil] *adj:* • **1.** frightened, alarmed

ج ف ن

جِفِن [ǰifin] *n:* جفُون [ǰfuːn] *pl:* • **1.** eyelid

ج ق ل

أَجقَل [ʔačqal] *adj:* جُقُل، جَقلِين [čuqul, čaqliːn] *pl:* جَقلَة [čaqla] *feminine:* • **1.** cross-eyed or walleyed – عيُونَه جُقُل [ʕyuːnah čuqul] His eyes are crossed. • **2.** cross-eyed or walleyed person

ج ك ت

جاكِيت [ǰakiːt] *n:* • **1.** jacket

ج ك ك

جَكّ [ǰagg] *n:* • **1.** jack

ج ك ل ت

جُكلِيت [čukliːt] *n:* • **1.** chocolate • **2.** various types of wrapped candies, such as caramels, toffee, etc – بَزِر جُكلَيت [bazir čukliːt] person who has lived a wealthy, soft life.

ج ك ل ي ت

جُكلَيتَة [čuklayta, čukliːta] *n:* • **1.** one piece of chocolate

ج ك م ج

جَكمَجَة [čakmača] *n:* جَكمَجات [čakmača:t] *pl:* • **1.** drawer • **2.** glove compartment (of a car)

ج ك ن م

جَكنَمَة [čaknama] *n:* • **1.** coziness

مجَكنَم [mčaknam] *adj:* • **1.** cozy, comfortable, snug – غُرفَة مجَكنَمَة [ɣurfa mčaknama] a cozy room.

ج

ج ك و ج

جاكُوج [ča:ku:č] *n:* جواكِيج [čwa:ki:č] *pl:* • **1.** hammer

ج ك ي

جاكِي [ǰa:ki] *n:* • **1.** jockey

ج ل ب

جِلَب [ǰilab] *v:* • **1.** to attract, draw – هدُوم هَالرِّجّال تِجلِب النَّظَر [hdu:m harriǰǰa:l tiǰlib ʔinnaðar] This man's clothes attract attention. • **2.** to bring, bring about, cause – إنتَ راح تِجلِب إلنا مَشاكِل [ʔinta ra:ħ tiǰlib ʔilna maša:kil] You will bring us problems.

جَلِب [ǰalib] *n:* • **1.** bringing, fetching, arraignment (of the accused before the court), procurement, bringing on, bringing about, attracting

جَلّابِيَة [ǰalla:biya, galla:biya] *n:* جَلّابِيات [ǰalla:biya:t, galla:biya:t] *pl:* • **1.** galabia (long, handmade traditional dress for women)

جَلَب [ǰalab] *adj:* • **1.** of poor quality, shoddy, cheap • **2.** imitation, copied

جَلّاب [ǰalla:b] *adj:* • **1.** cold and refreshing, invigorating

ج ل ت ن

جَلاتِين [ǰala:ti:n] *n:* • **1.** gelatin

ج ل خ

جِلَخ [ǰilax] *v:* • **1.** to scratch, scrape open, wound – البَزُّونَة خَرمُشَتنِي وَجِلخَت إيدِي [ʔilbazzu:na xarmušatni wǰilxat ʔi:di] The cat clawed me and scratched my hand.

جَلَّخ [ǰallax] *v:* • **1.** to scratch up – الجِّهال تعاركَوا وواحِد جَلَّخ وُجِه اللّاخ [ʔiǰǰiha:l tʕa:rkaw wwa:ħid ǰallax wučč ʔilla:x] The children had a fight and one scratched the other's face all up.

تجَلَّخ [tǰallax] *v:* • **1.** to get all scratched – لِيش تجَلّخَت إيدَك هِيكِي؟ [li:š dǰallxat ʔi:dak hi:či?] How'd your hand get all scratched up like that?

إنجِلَخ [ʔinǰilax] *v:* • **1.** to be scratched, scraped – إنجِلخَت رُكُبتَه مِن كان يِحبِي [ʔinǰilxat rukubtah min ča:n yiħbi] His knee got scraped when he was crawling.

جَلخ [ǰalix] *n:* جلُوخ [ǰlu:x] *pl:* • **1.** scratch, scrape

تَجلِيخ [taǰli:x] *n:* • **2.** scratching

مجَلَّخ [mǰallax] *adj:* • **1.** scratched

مَجلُوخ [maǰlu:x] *adj:* • **1.** scratched

ج ل د

جِلَد [ǰilad] *v:* • **1.** to whip, flog, lash – قَبِل ما يجِلدُوه، الطَّبِيب فُحَصَه [gabil ma: yǰildu:h, ʔiṭṭabi:b fuħaṣah] Before they flogged him, the doctor examined him.

جَلَّد [ǰallad] *v:* • **1.** to bind (a book) – بيش جَلَّدِت الكِتاب؟ [biyš ǰalladit ʔilkita:b?] How much did it cost you to bind the book?

تجَلَّد [tǰallad] *v:* • **1.** to take heart, buck up, compose oneself – تجَلَّد؛ لا تبَيِّن ضُعفَك قِدّام النّاس [dǰallad; la: tbayyin ðuʕfak gidda:m ʔinna:s] Pull yourself together; don't show your weakness in front of people.

جِلِد [ǰilid] *n:* جُلُود [ǰulu:d] *pl:* • **1.** skin, hide, pelt • **2.** leather

جَلِد [ǰalid] *n:* • **1.** lashing, whipping

جَلدَة [ǰalda] *n:* جَلدات [ǰalda:t] *pl:* • **1.** lash, stroke with a whip

جَلّاد [ǰalla:d] *n:* جَلّادِين [ǰalla:di:n] *pl:* • **1.** executioner, hangman

مُجَلِّد [muǰallid] *n:* مُجَلِّدِين [muǰallidi:n] *pl:* • **1.** book-binder

مُجَلَّد [muǰallad] *n:* • **1.** bound (book) • **3.** pl. مُجَلَّدات volume (of a book)

تَجلِيد [taǰli:d] *n:* • **1.** the binding of a book

جَلِد، طَير جَلِد [ǰalid, ṭi:r ǰalid] *adj:* • **1.** tame pigeon, homing pigeon

جَلِد [ǰalid] *adj:* • **1.** strong

جِلدِي [ǰildi] *adj:* • **1.** dermal, pertaining to the skin أمراض جِلدِيَّة [ʔamra:ð ǰildiyya] skin diseases.

ج ل س

جَلسَة [ǰalsa] *n:* جَلسات [ǰalsa:t] *pl:* • **1.** session, meeting, gathering

مَجلِس [maǰlis] *n:* مَجالِس [maǰa:lis] *pl:* • **1.** conference, council, congress – مَجلِس الأُمَّة [maǰlis ʔalʔumma] parliament. مَجلِس الأعيان [maǰlis ʔalʔaʕya:n] the senate. مَجلِس النُّوّاب [maǰlis ʔinnuwwa:b] the lower house, chamber of deputies. مَجلِس الأمِن [maǰlis ʔilʔamin] the Security Council. مَجلِس الإدارَة [maǰlis ʔilʔida:ra] board of directors.

جِلُوس [ǰilu:s] *n:* • **1.** sitting

جَلِيس [ǰali:s] *adj:* • **1.** participant, companion, (baby) sitter

ج ل ط

جِلَط [ǰilaṭ] *v:* • **1.** to shave • **2.** to disturb, irritate

إنجِلَط [ʔinǰilaṭ] *v:* • **1.** to have a heart attack, blood clot, stroke

جَلطَة [ǰalṭa] *n:* • **1.** stroke, blood clot, heart attack

مَجلُوط [maǰlu:ṭ] *adj:* • **1.** bothered • **2.** shaved, waxed • **3.** having a heart attack or stroke

ج ل ف

جِلَف [ǰilaf] *v:* • **1.** to scrub, scour – جِلفِي رِجلِك زين؛ بَعَدها وَسخَة [ǰilfi rijlič zi:n; baʕadha

wasxa] Scrub your feet well; they're still dirty. دَتجلِف قُفَا الجِّدِر بِمَسحُوق خاصّ [datiǰlif gufa ʔiǰǰidir bmasħuːq xaːṣṣ] She's scouring the outside of the pot with a special powder.
جَلِف [ǰalif] *n:* • **1.** scrubbing
جَلّافَة [ǰallaːfa] *n:* جَلّافات [ǰallaːfaːt] *pl:* • **1.** scouring pad
جَلافَة [ǰalaːfa] *n:* • **1.** rudeness
جِلِف [ǰilif] *adj:* أجلاف [ʔaǰlaːf] *pl:* • **1.** boorish, rude, ill-mannered • **2.** rude person
جِلفِي [ǰilfi] *adj:* • **1.** uncivilized, crude, common • **2.** colloquial, informal – عِراقِي جِلفِي [ʕiraːqi ǰilfi] colloquial Iraqi. ما يصِير تِحكِي جِلفِي بِالصَّفّ [maː yṣiːr tiħči ǰilfi biṣṣaff] You shouldn't use colloquial speech in class.

ج ل ف ط

جَلفُوطَة [ǰalfuːṭa] *n:* جلافِيط [ǰlaːfiːṭ] *pl:* • **1.** gristle, fat, waste (of meat)
مجَلفُط [mǰalfuṭ] *adj:* • **1.** fatty, fattening

ج ل ق

جَلَق [ǰlagg] *v:* • **1.** to sag, droop (of the eyelid) – عَينَه جلَقَّت مِن كان جاهِل [ʕaynah ǰlaggat min čaːn ǰaːhil] His eyelid drooped when he was a child.
جِلِق [ǰiliq] *v:* • **1.** to masturbate
جَلَّق [čallaq] *v:* • **1.** to boot
تجَلَّق [tčallaq] *v:* • **1.** to be kicked
جُلُق، ضَرُب الجُّلُق [ǰuluq, ðarub ʔiǰǰuluq] *n:* • **1.** masturbation
جِلاق [čillaːq] *n:* • **1.** kick
تَجلِيق [tačliːq] *n:* • **1.** kicking
أجلَق [ʔaǰlag] *adj:* جُلُق، جَلقِين [ǰulug, ǰalgiːn] *pl:* جَلقَة [ǰalqa] *feminine:* • **1.** having a drooping eyelid

ج ل ك ن

جِيلكان [ǰiːlikaːn] *n:* • **1.** container, jerrycan

ج ل ل 1

جَلّ [ǰall] *v:* • **1.** to be great, exalted, sublime – الله عَزَّ وَجَلّ [ʔallah ʕazz wǰall] God is powerful and exalted. • **2.** with عَن to be above, too good for – هَذا يجِلّ عَن هِيكِي عَمَل [haːða yǰill ʕan hiːči ʕamal] He's above such an act.
أجَلّ [ʔaǰall] *v:* • **1.** to revere, venerate, esteem highly, exalt – هالعالِم الدِّينِي كُلّهُم يجِلُّوه [halʕaːlim ʔiddiːni kullhum yiǰilluːh] They all revere this religious advisor. أجَلَّك الله [ʔaǰallak ʔallah] (an expression of apology for mentioning a distasteful topic, approx.:) Pardon the expression, but. . ., excuse me for saying so, but. . . . أجَلَّك الله، هَذا كَذّاب حَقِير [ʔaǰallak ʔallah, haːða čaððaːb ħaqiːr] You should pardon the expression, he's a low-down liar.
جِلَّة [ǰilla] *n:* جِلَل [ǰilal] *pl:* • **1.** basket made of palm leaves
جلال [ǰlaːl] *n:* جلالات [ǰlaːlaːt] *pl:* • **1.** canvas pack-saddle (for a donkey)
جَلال [ǰalaːl] *n:* • **1.** loftiness, sublimity, augustness
جَلِيل [ǰaliːl] *adj:* • **1.** revered, respected • **2.** exalted, lofty, sublime
جَلالَة [ǰalaːla] *adj:* • **1.** majesty صاحِب الجَّلالَة المَلِك [ṣaːħib ʔiǰǰalaːla ʔilmalik] His Majesty the King.

ج ل ل 2

مَجَلَّة [maǰalla] *n:* مَجَلّات [maǰallaːt] *pl:* • **1.** periodical • **2.** magazine • **3.** bulletin, journal

ج ل ي 1

جِلَى [ǰilaː] *v:* • **1.** to polish, shine, clean – أقدَر أجلِي الصِّينِيَّة وأخَلِّيها تِلمَع [ʔagdar ʔaǰli ʔiṣṣiːniyya wʔaxalliːha tilmaʕ] I can polish the tray and make it shine. • **2.** to evacuate, pull out, depart
جَلِي [ǰaly] *n:* • **1.** polishing
جالِي [ǰaːli] *n:* • **1.** heartburn, indigestion – أكَلت هوايَة وصار عِندِي جالِي [ʔakalt hwaːya wṣaːr ʕindi ǰaːli] I ate a lot and got indigestion.
جالِيَة [ǰaːliya] *n:* جالِيّات [ǰaːliyaːt] *pl:* • **1.** colony (of foreigners)

ج ل ي 2

جَلَّة [ǰalla] *n:* • **1.** (coll.) animal droppings, dung (specifically, of a donkey, horse, or camel)
جِلّايَة [ǰillaːya] *n:* جِلّايات [ǰillaːyaːt] *pl:* • **1.** sponge • **2.** scrubber (for washing dishes)

ج م

جام [ǰaːm] *n:* • **1.** (coll.) glass, plate glass, sheet glass
جامَة [ǰaːma] *n:* جامات [ǰaːmaːt] *pl:* • **1.** pane of glass • **2.** photographic plate or negative
جامخانَة [ǰaːmxaːna] *n:* جامخانات [ǰaːmxaːnaːt] *pl:* • **1.** glassed cabinet • **2.** showcase • **3.** store show window

ج م ب د

جُمبُدَة [ǰumbuda] *n:* • **1.** bud

ج م ب ر

جُمبارَة [čumpaːra] *n:* جُمبارات [čumpaːraːt] *pl:* • **1.** finger cymbal • **2.** castanet

ج م ب ز

جُمباز [ǰumbaːz] *n:* • **1.** gymnastics
جُمبازِي [ǰumbaːzi] *adj:* جُمبازِيّات [ǰumbaːziyyaːt] *pl:* • **1.** gymnast • **2.** dishonest shopkeeper

ج م ج

جَمجَة [čamča] *n:* جَمجات [čamča:t] *pl:* • **1.** ladle, dipper

ج م ج م

جُمجُمَة [ǰumǰuma] *n:* جماجُم [ǰma:ǰum] *pl:* • **1.** skull

ج م د [1]

جِمَد [ǰimad] *v:* • **1.** to freeze – المَيّ جِمَد بسُرعَة [ʔilmayy ǰimad bsurʕa] The water froze quickly. • **2.** to congeal, harden, set, become solid – الشّوربَة جِمدَت بِالهَوا البارِد [ʔiššu:rba ǰimdat bilhawa ʔilba:rid] The soup congealed in the cool air. الكَنكَرِيت يرِيدلَه ساعَة حَتّى يِجمَد [lkankari:t yri:dlah sa:ʕa ħatta yiǰmad] The concrete needs an hour to set. • **3.** to stop dead, stand stock still, freeze – الصَّيّاد، مِن شاف السَّبِع، جِمَد [ʔiṣṣayya:d, min ša:f ʔissabiʕ, ǰimad] The hunter froze when he saw the lion.

جَمَّد [ǰammad] *v:* • **1.** to freeze – ثَلّاجَتنا تجَمِّد المَيّ بِالعَجَل [θalla:ǰatna dǰammid ʔilmayy bilʕaǰal] Our refrigerator freezes water quickly. صاح بِيه صَيحَة جَمَّدَه بمُكانَه بِيها [ṣa:ħ bi:h ṣi:ħa ǰammadah bmuka:nah bi:ha] He gave him a shout that froze him in his place. • **2.** to freeze (assets) – الحُكومَة جَمِّدَت أموال هَالشَّرِكتَين [ʔilħuku:ma ǰammidat ʔamwa:l haššariktayn] The government froze the assets of these two companies.

تجَمَّد [tǰammad] *v:* • **1.** to be or become frozen – بِهَالجَوّ، المَيّ يِتجَمَّد بِسُرعَة [bhaǰǰaww, ʔilmayy yidǰammad bsurʕa] In this weather, water becomes frozen quickly.

جَماد [ǰama:d] *n:* جَمادات [ǰama:da:t] *pl:* • **1.** a solid • **2.** inorganic body • **3.** inanimate body, inanimate being

جُمُود [ǰumu:d] *n:* • **1.** inactivity, inaction • **2.** lethargy, apathy

جامِد[ǰa:mid]*adj:* • **1.** frozen • **2.** hard,solid • **3.** stiff • **4.** inanimate • **5.** dry, dull, boring • **6.** impervious to progress or innovation, ultraconservative

ج م د [2]

جَمادِي، جَمادِي الأوَّل [ǰama:di, ǰama:di ʔilʔawwal] *n:* • **1.** Jumada I, the fifth month of the Moslem year جَمادِي الثّانِي [ǰama:di θθa:ni] Jumada II, the sixth month of the Moslem year.

ج م ر

جَمَّر [ǰammar] *v:* • **1.** to cut the core from a young palm tree – جَمَّر الطّالِع بِالفاس [ǰammar ʔiṭṭa:laʕ bilfa:s] He cored the young palm tree with the adze. • **2.** to place fresh coals upon – بالله جَمُّرلِي النَّرقِيلَة [ballah ǰammurli ʔinnargi:la] Put fresh coals on the narghile for me, please.

جَمُر [ǰamur] *n:* جَمرات [ǰamra:t] *pl:* • **1.** (coll.) ember(s), live coal(s) – الجَمرَة الخَبِيثَة [ʔiǰǰamra ʔilxabi:θa] anthrax.

جُمّار [ǰumma:r] *n:* • **1.** edible heart of the young palm tree

جَمرَة [ǰamra] *n:* • **1.** live coal

ج م ر ك

جَمرَك [gamrag] *v:* • **1.** to impose a duty or customs tax on – مَأمُور الجُمرُك فَتَّش غراضِي وَجَمرَك بَسّ الجِّكايِر [maʔmu:r ʔilgumrug fattaš ɣara:ḍi wgamrag bass ʔiǰǰiga:yir] The customs inspector inspected my things and imposed duty only on the cigarettes. اللُّجنَة راح تجَمرُك هَالبَضايِع حَسَب قانُون الكَمارِك [ʔilluǰna ra:ħ tgamrug halbaḍa:yiʕ ħasab qa:nu:n ʔilgama:rig] The committee is going to impose a duty on these goods in accordance with the customs law. • **2.** to take a portion – لا تراوِي الرِّسُوم لعَلِي تَرَة يجَمرُكها [la: tra:wi ʔirrisu:m lʕali tara ygamrugha] Don't show the pictures to Ali or he'll take some of them. • **3.** to process through customs, put through customs – ما تِقدَر تاخُذها قَبُل ما يجَمرُكُوها [ma: tigdar ta:xuðha gabul ma: ygamrugu:ha] You can't take it before they process it through customs.

جُمرُك [gumrug] *n:* جَمارِك [gama:rig] *pl:* • **1.** customs duty or tax • **2.** customs inspection house

جُمرُكِي [gumrugi] *adj:* • **1.** related to customs

ج م ع

جِمَع [ǰimaʕ] *v:* • **1.** to collect – الطُّلّاب دَيجمَعُون فلُوس لِلهِلال الأحمَر [ʔiṭṭulla:b dayiǰmaʕu:n flu:s lilhila:l ʔilʔaħmar] The students are collecting money for the Red Crescent. • **2.** to gather, collect (specimens) – أخُويَا يِجمَع طَوابِع [ʔaxu:ya yiǰmaʕ ṭawa:biʕ] My brother collects stamps. • **3.** to assemble – المُدِير جِمَع كُلّ التَّلامِيذ [ʔilmudi:r ǰimaʕ kull ʔittala:mi:ð] The principal called all the students together. سُبحان اللِّي جِمَعهُم [subħa:n ʔilli ǰimaʕhum] Only the Sublime could have brought them together. • **4.** to add, add up, total – إجمَع هَالأعداد [ʔiǰmaʕ halʔaʕda:d] Add up these figures. • **5.** to make plural, pluralize – شلُون تِجمَع هَالإسِم؟ [šlu:n tiǰmaʕ halʔisim?] How do you make this noun plural?

جَمَّع [ǰammaʕ] *v:* • **1.** to save, pile up, amass, accumulate – صارلِي سَنتَين أجَمِّع فلُوس حَتّى أشتِري رادِيُو [ṣa:rli santayn ʔaǰammiʕ flu:s ħatta ʔaštiri ra:dyu] I've been saving money for two years to buy a radio.

جامَع [ǰa:maʕ] *v:* • **1.** to have sexual intercourse – ما لازِم تجامِع هوايَة وَإنتَ مَرِيض [ma: la:zim dǰa:miʕ hwa:ya wʔinta mari:ḍ] You shouldn't have intercourse often when you're sick.

تجَمَّع [tǰammaʕ] *v:* • **1.** to assemble, congregate, gather – الطُّلّاب تجَمّعوا بِساحَة المَدرَسَة [ʔiṭṭulla:b dǰammiʕaw bsa:ħat ʔilmadrasa] The students gathered in the school yard. قُوّات العَدُو تجَمّعَت خارِج المَدِينَة [quwwa:t ʔilʕadu dǰammiʕat xa:riǰ ʔilmadi:na] The enemy forces assembled outside the city. • **2.** to accumulate, collect – الماي تجَمَّع بِالسِّرداب [ʔilma:y dǰammaʕ bissirda:b] The water collected in the basement.

تجامَع [tǰa:maʕ] *v:* • **1.** reciprocal of • **1.** reciprocal of جامَع to have sexual intercourse

انجمع [ʔinǰimaʕ] *v:* • **1.** to be collected
اجتمع [ʔiǰtimaʕ] *v:* • **1.** to assemble, meet, convene – اللُّجنَة راح تِجتِمِع باكِر [ʔilluǰna raːħ tiǰtimiʕ baːčir] The committee will meet tomorrow. • **2.** to meet, confer, get together – المُدير اجتِمَع ويّا الوَزير مَرّتَين هَالإسبوع [ʔilmudiːr ʔiǰtimaʕ wiyya ʔilwaziːr marrtayn halʔisbuːʕ] The director has conferred with the minister twice this week.
استجمع [ʔistaǰmaʕ] *v:* • **1.** to gather
جمع [ǰamiʕ] *n:* **1.** gathering **2.** collection • **3.** accumulation • **4.** addition
جمع [ǰimiʕ] *n:* جموع [ǰmuːʕ] *pl:* • **1.** fist, clenched hand • **2.** a blow with the fist
جُمعَة، الجُمعَة، يَوم الجُمعَة [ǰumʕa, ʔiǰǰumʕa, yuːm ʔiǰǰumʕa] *n:* • **1.** Friday
جَميع [ǰamiːʕ] *n:* • **1.** all, entirety – خبَّرِت جَميع التَّلاميذ [xabbarit ǰamiːʕ ʔittalaːmiːð] I told all the students. الجَّميع وافقوا [ʔiǰǰamiːʕ waːfqaw] Everyone agreed.
أجمَع، أجمَعين [ʔaǰmaʕ, ʔaǰmaʕiːn] *n:* • **1.** (reply to a wish for good health, fortune, approx.:) May it be the same for all
مَجمَع [maǰmaʕ] *n:* مَجامِع [maǰaːmiʕ] *pl:* • **1.** meeting place, assembly point • **2.** convention, assembly, gathering • **3.** academy – مَجمَع عِلمي [maǰmaʕ ʕilmi] academy of sciences.
جماع [ǰimaːʕ] *n:* • **1.** sexual intercourse
مُجَمَّع [muǰammaʕ] *n:* • **1.** compound, accumulator, totality collected
تَجَمُّع [taǰammuʕ] *n:* تَجَمُّعات [taǰammuʕaːt] *pl:* • **1.** gathering • **2.** congregation, assembly
جَمعِيَّة [ǰamʕiyya] *n:* جَمعِيّات [ǰamʕiyyaːt] *pl:* • **1.** organization, association, club, society – جَمعِيَّة الرِّفق بِالحَيوان [ǰamʕiyyat ʔirrifq bilħaywaːn] Society for the Prevention of Cruelty to Animals (SPCA)
جَماعَة [ǰamaːʕa] *n:* جَماعات [ǰamaːʕaːt] *pl:* • **1.** group, bunch – شِفتَه يِحكي ويّا جَماعَة مِن الفَلّاحين [šiftah yiħči wiyya ǰamaːʕa min ʔilfallaːħiːn] I saw him talking with a group of peasants. هاي جَماعتي. كُلّ يوم نُقعُد بِالقَهوَة سُوَة [haːy ǰamaːʕti. kull yuːm nugʕud bilgahwa suwa] This is my gang. We sit at the café together every day. جَماعات جَماعات [ǰamaːʕaːt ǰamaːʕaːt] by groups / in groups – المُصَلّين دَيطِلعُون مِن الجّامِع جَماعات جَماعات [ʔilmuṣalliːn dayṭilʕuːn min ʔiǰǰaːmiʕ ǰamaːʕaːt ǰamaːʕaːt] The worshippers are coming out of the mosque in groups.
إجماع [ʔiǰmaːʕ] *n:* • **1.** unanimity وافقوا عَالإقتِراح بِالإجماع [waːfqaw ʕalʔiqtiraːħ bilʔiǰmaːʕ] They agreed on the proposal unanimously.
جامِعَة [ǰaːmiʕa] *n:* جامِعات [ǰaːmiʕaːt] *pl:* • **1.** league, union, association – الجّامِعَة العَرَبِيَّة [ʔiǰǰaːmiʕa ʔilʕarabiyya] the Arab League. • **2.** university
مَجمُوع [maǰmuːʕ] *n:* • **1.** collected, gathered • **2.** totality, whole • **3.** pl. مَجاميع sum, total
مُجتَمَع [muǰtamaʕ] *n:* مُجتَمَعات [muǰtamaʕaːt] *pl:* • **1.** society, community, human society
اجتِماع [ʔiǰtimaːʕ] *n:* اِجتِماعات [ʔiǰtimaːʕaːt] *pl:* • **1.** meeting • **2.** get-together, gathering, assembly • **3.** community life, social life – عِلم الاِجتِماع [ʕilm ʔilʔiǰtimaːʕ] sociology.
مَجمُوعَة [maǰmuːʕa] *n:* مَجمُوعات [maǰmuːʕaːt] *pl:* • **1.** collection (of objects) • **2.** group • **3.** aggregate • **4.** complex
اِستِجماع [ʔistiǰmaːʕ] *n:* • **1.** gathering
اِجتِماعِيّات [ʔiǰtimaːʕiyyaːt] *n:* • **1.** pl. only humanities
جامِع [ǰaːmiʕ] *adj:* • **1.** comprehensive, extensive, broad, general, (as n:) • **2.** (book) compiler • **3.** collector • **4.** mosque • **5.** collector (of) • **6.** pl. جَوامِع mosque
جَماعي [ǰamaːʕi] *adj:* • **1.** communal, mass
مِتجَمِّع [mitǰammiʕ] *adj:* • **1.** gathered, collected
مِجتِمِع [miǰtimiʕ] *adj:* • **1.** meeting (with), associating, gathering
جامِعي [ǰaːmiʕi] *adj:* • **1.** academic, collegiate
اِجتِماعي [ʔiǰtimaːʕi] *adj:* • **1.** social – الحالَة الاجتِماعِيَّة بِالعِراق زينَة [ʔilħaːla ʔiliǰtimaːʕiyya bilʕiraːq ziːna] Social conditions are good in Iraq. وِزارَة الشّؤون الاجتِماعِيَّة [wizaːrat ʔiššʔuːn ʔilʔiǰtimaːʕiyya] ministry of social affairs. • **2.** sociological – عالِم اِجتِماعي [ʕaːlim ʔiǰtimaːʕi] sociologist. • **3.** sociable, friendly – لِيش ما تصير اِجتِماعي وَتروح تِحكي ويّا الخُطّار؟ [liːš maː tṣiːr ʔiǰtimaːʕi wtruːħ tiħči wiyya ʔilxuṭṭaːr?] Why don't you be sociable and go talk with the guests?

ج م ل [1]

جَمَّل [ǰammal] *v:* • **1.** to beautify, make beautiful – دَيجَمِّلُون الشَّوارِع بِسَعَف وَضُوايات [dayǰammiluːn ʔiššawaːriʕ bsaʕaf waḍuwaːyaːt] They're beautifying the streets with palm branches and lights. الحَديقَة تجَمِّل البَيت [ʔilħadiːqa dǰammil ʔilbayt] The garden makes the house beautiful.
جامَل [ǰaːmal] *v:* • **1.** to be polite, courteous – جامَلني بِشُرب القَهوَة، وَلَو الطَّبيب مانعَه [ǰaːmalni bšurb ʔilgahwa, walaw ʔiṭṭabiːb maːnʕah] He was polite to me, drinking the coffee even though the doctor had told him not to. الأُستاذ يجامِل طُلّابَه هوايَة [ʔilʔustaːð yǰaːmil ṭullaːbah hwaːya] The professor treats his students very politely. ماكُو حاجَة تجامِلني. آني مُو غَريب [maːku ħaːǰa dǰaːmilni. ʔaːni muː ɣariːb] No need to treat me special. I'm not a stranger.
تجَمَّل [tǰammal] *v:* • **1.** to beautify oneself, make oneself pretty – عُمُرها سِتّين سَنَة ويعجبها تِتجَمَّل [ʕumurha sittiːn sana wyiʕǰibha tidǰammal] She's sixty years old and still likes to make herself pretty.
تجامَل [tǰaːmal] *v:* • **1.** to be polite with one another, treat each other with courtesy – بَينهُم عَداوَة بَسّ دَيتجامَلُون قِدّامنا [baynhum ʕadaːwa bass dayidǰaːmluːn giddaːmna] There is animosity between them but they're being polite to each other in our presence.

جُملَة [ǰumla] *n:* جُمَل [ǰumal] *pl:* • **1.** totality, sum, total – مِن جُملَة الأشياء اللّي قالها عَنَّك، إنَّك كَذّاب [min ǰumlat ʔilʔašyaːʔ ʔilli gaːlha ʕannak, ʔinnak kaððab] Among the things he said about you was that you're a liar. • **2.** group, body – الحُكُومَة دَتُفصُل مُوَظَفِين بِالجُملَة [ʔilħukuːma datufṣul muwaḍafiːn biǰǰumla] The government is firing employees in whole groups. • **3.** wholesale – بَيّاع جُملَة [bayyaːʕ ǰumla] wholesale dealer. هالمَخزَن يِبِيع بِالجُملَة [halmaxzan yibiːʕ biǰǰumla] This store sells wholesale. • **4.** (gram.) sentence, clause – إنطِينِي جُملَة بِيها هَالكِلمَة [ʔinṭiːni ǰumla biːha haččilma] Give me a sentence with this word in it.

جَمال [ǰamaːl] *n:* • **1.** beauty

تَجمِيل، جِراحَة تَجمِيل [tajmiːl, ǰiraːħat tajmiːl] *n:* • **1.** plastic surgery

مُجامَلَة [muǰaːmala] *n:* مُجامَلات [muǰaːmalaːt] *pl:* • **1.** courtesy • **2.** amiability, civility • **3.** flattery

جَمِيل [ǰamiːl] *adj:* • **1.** beautiful, pretty, comely, handsome • **2.** favor, service, good turn

مُجامِل [muǰaːmil] *adj:* • **1.** courteous • **2.** complimentary

أجمَل [ʔaǰmal] *comparative adjective:* • **1.** more or most beautiful, handsome, etc

ج م ل ²

جَمَل [ǰamal] *n:* جِمال [ǰimaːl] *pl:* • **1.** camel, male camel

جَمّال [ǰammaːl] *n:* جَمّالَة [ǰammaːla] *pl:* • **1.** camel driver • **2.** camel herder

ج م ل ⁵

جَمّالِي، سَقُف جَمّالِي [ǰammaːli, saguf ǰammaːli] *adj:* • **1.** pitched roof

ج م ل غ

جامُلُّغ، جامُرلُغ [čaːmulluɣ, čaːmurluɣ] *n:* جامُرلُغات [čaːmurluɣaːt] *pl:* • **1.** fender (of a car)

ج م ل و ن

جَملَون، سَقُف جَملَون [ǰamaluːn, saguf ǰamaluːn] *n:* • **1.** pitched roof

ج م ه ر

تجمهَر [dǰamhar] *v:* • **1.** to gather, flock together – لِيش هَالنّاس مِتجَمهرِين هنا؟ [liːš hannaːs mitǰamhiriːn hna?] Why are these people gathered here?

جَمهُور [ǰamhuːr] *n:* جَماهِير [ǰamaːhiːr] *pl:* • **1.** crowd, throng, group, mass (of people) – الشُّرطَة فَرِّقَت الجَّماهِير [ʔiššurṭa farriqat ʔiǰǰamaːhiːr] The police broke up the crowds. • **2.** the public, the people, the masses – الجَّمهُور ما يأيِّد الحُكُومَة بِسِياسَتها [ʔiǰǰamhuːr maː yʔayyid ʔilħukuːma bsiyaːsatha] The public doesn't support the government in its policy.

جَمهَرَة [ǰamhara] *n:* • **1.** gathering, throng

جَمهُورِيَّة [ǰamhuːriyya] *n:* جَمهُورِيّات [ǰamhuːriyyaːt] *pl:* • **1.** republic

جَمهُورِي [ǰamhuːri] *adj:* • **1.** republican – نِظام جِمهُورِي [niḍaːm ǰimhuːri] republican system (of government).

ج م و س

جامُوس [ǰaːmuːs] *n:* جوامِيس، جِمَس [ǰwaːmiːs, ǰimas] *pl:* • **1.** buffalo, water buffalo

جامُوسَة [ǰaːmuːsa] *n:* جامُوسات، جوامِيس [ǰaːmuːsaːt, ǰwaːmiːs] *pl:* • **1.** buffalo cow

ج ن ب ¹

جَنَّب [ǰannab] *v:* • **1.** to avert from, ward away from – هَذا يجَنِّبَك هوايَة مَشاكِل [haːða yǰannibak hwaːya mašaːkil] That'll spare you a lot of problems.

تجَنَّب [tǰannab] *v:* • **1.** to avoid, keep away from – لازِم تِتجَنَّب هَالوَلَد [laːzim tiǰannab halwalad] You've got to avoid that boy.

اِجتِنَب [ʔiǰtinab] *v:* • **1.** to avoid

جَنِب [ǰanib, ǰamb] *n:* • **1.** side – مَرَض ذات الجَّنب [marað ðaːt ʔiǰǰamb] pleurisy.

جَناب [ǰanaːb] *n:* • **1.** a title of respect (also used facetiously) – يا جَناب الحاكِم [yaː ǰanaːb ʔilħaːkim] Your Honor. . . . جَنابَك، لِيش زِعَلِت؟ [ǰanaːbak, liːš ziʕalit?] Why did Your Lordship get angry?

جِنُوب [ǰinuːb, ǰanuːb] *n:* • **1.** south

جِنِّيب، أبُو جِنِّيب [ǰinniːb, ʔabu ǰinniːb] *n:* • **1.** crab

جانِب [ǰaːnib] *n:* جَوانِب [ǰawaːnib] *pl:* • **1.** side – الجّانبَين ما اِتِّفقوا عَلَى شِي [ʔiǰǰaːnbayn maː ʔittifqaw ʕala ši] The two sides didn't agree on anything. آنِي مِن جانبَك [ʔaːni min ǰaːnbak] I'm on your side.

تَجَنُّب [taǰannub] *n:* • **1.** avoidance, avoiding

جَنَبات [ǰanabaːt] *n:* • **1.** (invar.) in a state of ritual impurity from sexual intercourse (of men only) ما أقدَر أخُشّ بِالجامِع؛ آنِي جَنَبات [maː ʔagdar ʔaxušš biǰǰaːmiʕ; ʔaːni ǰanabaːt] I can't go in the mosque; I am unclean.

مُجنِب، مِجنِب [muǰnib, miǰnib] *adj:* • **1.** in a state of religious impurity from sexual intercourse ما أقدَر أصَلِّي؛ آنِي مِجنِب [maː ʔagdar ʔaṣalli; ʔaːni miǰnib] I can't pray; I'm unclean.

جِنُوبِي [ǰinuːbi] *adj:* • **1.** southern لَهجَة جِنُوبِيَّة [lahǰa ǰinuːbiyya] southern accent.

جانِبِي [ǰanibi] *adj:* • **1.** lateral, side – أخَذنا مَنظَر جانِبِي لِلبِنايَة [ʔaxaðna manḍar ǰaːnibi lilbinaːya] We took a side view of the building.

أجنَبِي [ʔaǰnabi] *adj:* • **1.** foreign, alien

ج ن ب ²

جِنَّب [ǰinnab] *n:* • **1.** hemp

ج ن ج ل

جنجِل [ǰinǰil] *n:* جِنجِلات [ǰinǰilaːt] *pl:* • **1.** sty, growth on the eye

جناجِل [ǰanaːǰiːl] *n:* • **1.** gold or silver anklets with bells attached, worn by small children learning to walk

ج ن ح

جَنَّح [ǰannaħ] *v:* • **1.** to fledge – فرُوخ الطَّير جَنِّحَت وَراح تطِير [fruːx ʔiṭṭiːr ǰanniħat wraːħ ṭṭiːr] The squabs have fledged and are about to fly. • **2.** to strut, walk with the chest stuck out – شُوفَه شلُون مجَنِّح. عَبالَك هُوَّ بَطَل [šuːfah šluːn mǰanniħ. ʕabaːlak huwwa baṭal] Look at him all puffed up. You would think he is a champion.

جِنِح [ǰiniħ] *n:* • **1.** wing

جُنحَة [ǰunħa] *n:* جُنَح [ǰunaħ] *pl:* • **1.** misdemeanor (jur.)

جناح [ǰinaːħ] *n:* جِناحات، أَجنِحَة [ǰinaːħaːt, ʔaǰniħa] *pl:* • **1.** wing (of a bird, airplane, building, or air force)

مجَنَّح [mǰannaħ] *adj:* • **1.** winged, flanked

ج ن د 1

جَنَّد [ǰannad] *v:* • **1.** to draft, conscript, induct, recruit -- الحُكُومَة راح تجَنِّد كُلّ شابّ اللّي يِقدَر يشِيل سلاح [ʔilħukuːma raːħ dǰannid kull šaːbb ʔilli yigdar yšiːl slaːħ] The government's going to induct every young man who can bear arms.

تجَنَّد [tǰannad] *v:* • **1.** to be drafted, recruited – كُلّ وِلدِي تجَنّدَوا [kull wildi dǰannidaw] All my sons were drafted.

جُندِي [ǰundi] *n:* جنُود [ǰinuːd] *pl:* • **1.** soldier – جُندِي نَفَر [ǰundi nafar] private. جُندِي أَوَّل [ǰundi ʔawwal] private first class. • **2.** pawn (in chess)

مُجَنَّد [muǰannad] *n:* • **1.** recruit, conscript, draftee

تَجنِيد [taǰniːd] *n:* • **1.** recruitment, enlistment, mobilization

جُندِيَّة [ǰundiyya] *adj:* • **1.** the army, the military • **2.** military service

ج ن د 2

جِندَة [ǰinda] *n:* جِندات، جِنَد [ǰindaːt, ǰinad] *pl:* • **1.** porter's back pad

ج ن د ر م

جَندِرمَة [ǰandirma] *n:* جَندِرمات [ǰandirmaːt] *pl:* • **1.** dullard, dim-wit, lout

ج ن د ل

جَندَلَة [ǰandala] *n:* جَندَلات، جَنادِل [ǰandalaːt, ǰanːdil] *pl:* • **1.** giant • **2.** big person

ج ن ز

جَنَّز [ǰannaz] *v:* • **1.** to kill, murder – جَنَّزَه مِن البَسُط [ǰannazah min ʔilbasuṭ] He beat him within an inch of his life.

تجَنَّز [tǰannaz] *v:* • **1.** to act dead, be lazy – لا تِتجَنَّز. خُفّ إيدَك [laː tidǰannaz. xuff ʔiːdak] Don't goof off. Get a move on.

جَنّاز [ǰannaːz] *n:* جَنّازَة [ǰannaːza] *pl:* • **1.** person who accompanies the deceased from where he died to the city where he is to be buried

جَنازَة [ǰanaːza] *n:* جَنازات، جَنايِز [ǰanaːzaːt, ǰanaːyiz] *pl:* • **1.** coffin (with corpse), bier آنِي صايِر جَنازَة [ʔaːni ṣaːyir ǰanaːza] I'm dead tired.

ج ن س

تجَنَّس [dǰannas] *v:* • **1.** to become a naturalized citizen – راح أتجَنَّس بِالجِّنسِيَّة العِراقِيَّة [raːħ ʔadǰannas biǰǰinsiyya ʔilʕiraːqiyya] I'm going to get naturalized with Iraqi citizenship.

جِنِس [ǰinis] *n:* أجناس [ʔaǰnaːs] *pl:* • **1.** kind, sort, variety – عِندِي طيُور مِن كُلّ جِنِس [ʕindi ṭyuːr min kull ǰinis] I have all varieties of pigeons. عِندَه عَشِر قُوط؛ كُلّ واحِد جِنِس [ʕindah ʕašir quːṭ; kull waːħid ǰinis] He has ten suits, each one a different kind. لا تِمشِي وِيّاه. هَذا مُو مِن جِنسَك [laː timši wiyyaːh. haːða muː min ǰinsak] Don't hang around with him. He's not your sort of person. • **2.** sex, gender – الجِّنس اللَّطِيف [ʔiǰǰins ʔillaṭiːf] the fair sex. • **3.** race – الجِّنس البَشَرِي [ʔiǰǰins ʔalbašari] the human race. الجِّنس الزَّنجِي [ʔiǰǰins ʔizzinǰi] the black race.

جِنسِيَّة [ǰinsiyya] *n:* جِنسِيّات، جَناسِي [ǰinsiyyaːt, ǰanaːsi] *pl:* • **1.** nationality, citizenship

جِنسِي [ǰinsi] *adj:* • **1.** generic • **2.** sexual • **3.** racial

ج ن ط

جُنطَة [ǰunṭa] *n:* جُنَط، جَنطات [ǰunaṭ, ǰanṭaːt] *pl:* • **1.** suitcase, valise, satchel • **2.** briefcase • **3.** (woman's) purse, handbag

ج ن ف ص

جِنفاص [ǰinfaːṣ, činfaːṣ] *n:* • **1.** canvas • **2.** sackcloth

ج ن ك ل

جَنكَل [čangal] *v:* • **2.** see also شَنكَل

ج ن ك و

جِينكُو [čiːnku] *n:* • **1.** (coll.) galvanized sheet metal

جِينكُوَّة [čiːnkuwwa] *n:* جِينكُوّات [čiːnkuwwaːt] *pl:* • **1.** piece of galvanized sheet metal

ج ن ن

جَنّ [ǰann] *v:* • **1.** to be or become insane – صار عِندَه مَرَض عَصَبِي وَبَعدين جَنّ [ṣaːr ʕindah maraḏ ʕaṣabi wbaʕdiyn ǰann] He got a nervous disease and later went insane. مِن شاف جَمالها، جَنّ [min šaːf ǰamaːlha, ǰann] When he saw her beauty, he went out of his mind.

جَنَّن [ǰannan] *v:* • **1.** to make insane, to craze, madden إبنَك جَنَّنِّي اليُوم [ʔibnak ǰannanni ʔilyuːm] Your son

drove me nuts today. جَمالها يجَنِّن [ǰamaːlha yǰannin] Her beauty is maddening.
اِنجَنّ [ʔinǰann] *v:* • **1.** to become insane – إذا يشُوف إبنَه مَرِيض، يِنجَنّ [ʔiða yšuːf ʔibnah mariːð̣, yinǰann] If he finds out his son is sick, he'll go out of his mind.
جِنّ [ǰinn] *n:* • **1.** (coll.) genie(s), jinn
جِنّي [ǰinni] *n:* جِن [ǰinn] *pl:* • **1.** genie
جَنَّة [ǰanna] *n:* • **1.** heaven, paradise
جَنِين [ǰaniːn] *n:* أجِنَّة [ʔaǰinna] *pl:* • **1.** embryo, fetus
جُنُون [ǰunuːn] *n:* • **1.** insanity, madness, mania • **2.** delusion – جُنُون العَظَمَة [ǰunuːn ʔilʕað̣ama] delusions of grandeur, superiority complex.
جُنُونِي [ǰunuːni] *adj:* • **1.** crazy, insane, mad
مَجنُون [majnuːn] *adj:* • **1.** crazed, crazy, insane, mad • **2.** madman, maniac, lunatic • **3.** fool

ج ن ي

جِنَى [ǰinaː] *v:* • **1.** with عَلَى to wrong, injure, harm
جَنِي [ǰany] *n:* • **1.** with عَلَى hurting, abusing (someone)
جانِي [ǰaːni] *n:* جُناة [ǰunaːt] *pl:* • **1.** perpetrator (of a crime) • **2.** culprit, criminal
جِنايَة [ǰinaːya] *n:* جِنايات [ǰinaːyaːt] *pl:* • **1.** felony, crime
جِنائِي [ǰinaːʔi] *adj:* • **1.** criminal – عَمَل جِنائِي [ʕamal ǰinaːʔi] a criminal act.

ج ه

جاه [ǰaːh] *n:* • **1.** standing, dignity, position

ج ه د

جاهَد [ǰaːhad] *v:* • **1.** to strive, endeavor, to put forth one's best effort – جاهِد تقَنّعَه يِجِي وِيّانا [ǰaːhid tqannʕah yiji wiyyaːna] Do your best to persuade him to come with us. شقَدّ ما جاهَدت أبَدِّل فِكرَه، ما فاد [šgadd maː ǰaːhadit ʔabaddil fikrah, maː faːd] As much as I tried to change his mind, it still didn't work. • **2.** to fight, to do battle – كُلّنا مُستَعِدِّين نجاهِد فِي سَبِيل الوَطَن [kullna mustaʕiddiːn nǰaːhid fi sabiːl ʔilwaṭan] We're all ready to fight in our country's behalf.
أجهَد [ʔaǰhad] *v:* • **1.** to strain, overtax, overwork – لا تِجهِد نَفسَك بِالشُّغُل. مُو زين [laː tiǰhid nafsak biššuɣul. muː ziːn] Don't strain yourself with work. It's not good.
اِجتِهَد [ʔiǰtihad] *v:* • **1.** to work hard, put forth one's best effort إذا تِجتِهِد، تِنجَح [ʔiða tiǰtihid, tinǰaħ] If you work hard, you'll succeed. اِجتِهَدِتلَك هوايَة لٰكِن اِنطَوا الوَظِيفَة لغَيرَك [ʔiǰtihaditlak hwaːya laːkin ʔinṭaw ʔilwað̣iːfa lɣayrak] I did all I could for you but they gave the job to someone else.
جُهُد [ǰuhud] *n:* • **1.** effort, attempt, endeavor – كُلّ جُهُد [kull ǰuhud] every possible effort. بِذَلِت كُلّ جُهدِي حَتَّى أصالِحهُم [biðalit kull ǰuhdi ħatta ʔaṣaːliħhum] I did all I could to reconcile them. جُهُد الإمكان [ǰuhud ʔilʔimkaːn] as far as possible, as much as possible. حاوَلِت جُهد إمكانِي، لَكِن ما راد [ħaːwalit ǰuhd ʔimkaːni, laːkin maː raːd] I tried as hard as I could, but he wasn't willing.
جِهاد [ǰihaːd] *n:* • **1.** jihad, holy war
إجهاد [ʔiǰhaːd] *n:* • **1.** overwork, over-exertion, strain – إجهاد عَصَبِي [ʔiǰhaːd ʕaṣabi] nervous strain.
مَجهُود [majhuːd] *n:* مَجهُودات [majhuːdaːt] *pl:* • **1.** effort, endeavor, exertion, work, trouble
اِجتِهاد [ʔiǰtihaːd] *n:* اِجتِهادات [ʔiǰtihaːdaːt] *pl:* • **1.** effort, exertion, pains, trouble • **2.** interpretation, individual opinion • **3.** pl. إجتِهادات individual interpretation of a religious matter based on The Koran
جَهِيد [ǰahiːd] *adj:* • **1.** extreme
مُجهَد [muǰhad] *adj:* • **1.** tired, exhausted
مُجهِد [muǰhid] *adj:* • **1.** strenuous, grueling
مُجاهِد [muǰaːhid] *n:* مُجاهِدِين [muǰaːhidiːn] *pl:* • **1.** warrior, religious warrior • **2.** fanatic crusader
مُجتَهِد [muǰtahid] *adj:* مُجتَهِدِين [muǰtahidiːn] *pl:* • **1.** diligent, industrious • **2.** pl. مُجتَهِدِين one who interprets Koranic law through precedents

ج ه ر [1]

جاهَر [ǰaːhar] *v:* • **1.** to declare openly, publicly – يجاهِر بآرائَه. ما يخاف مِن أحَّد [yǰaːhir baːraːʔah. maː yxaːf min ʔaħħad] He expresses his opinions openly. He's not afraid of anyone.
مِجهَر [miǰhar] *n:* مِجهَرات، مَجاهِر [miǰharaːt, maǰaːhir] *pl:* • **1.** microscope
مِجهَرِي [miǰhari] *adj:* • **1.** microscopic
جَهراً [ǰahran] *adverbial:* • **1.** publicly, openly, in public ما خاف. قالها جَهراً [maː xaːf. gaːlha ǰahran] He wasn't afraid. He said it openly.

ج ه ر [2]

چِهرَة [čihra] *n:* چِهَر، چهرات [čihraːt, čihar] *pl:* • **1.** unsightly face, (insulting term for face, approx:) mug, puss, ugly face – لا تراوِينِي چِهرتَك بَعَد [laː traːwiːni čihirtak baʕad] Don't let me see your ugly mug again. عَليها چِهرَة ما تِتباوَع [ʕaliːha čihra maː titbaːwaʕ] She has an unsightly face.
چِهرَسِزّ [čihrasizz] *adj:* • **1.** (invar.) ugly, homely هِيَّ چَهرَسِزّ [hiyya čahrasizz] She's ugly.

ج ه ز

جَهَّز [ǰahhaz] *v:* • **1.** to supply, provide, furnish, equip جَهَّزنا الجَّيش بأحدَث الأسلِحَة [ǰahhazna ʔiǰǰayš bʔaħdaθ ʔilʔasliħa] We supplied the army with the most modern arms.
تجَهَّز [dǰahhaz] *v:* • **2.** pass. of – هُمَّ دائماً يجَهَّزُون بِدَفاتِر وَأقلام جَهَّز [humma daːʔiman yiǰahhazuːn bdafaːtir wʔaqlaːm] They are always provided with notebooks and pencils.
جِهاز [ǰihaːz] *n:* أجهِزَة [ʔaǰhiza] *pl:* • **1.** apparatus, instrument, appliance, gadget, utensil • **2.** things

bought with the trousseau • **3.** system – الجِّهاز العَصَبِي [ʔijjiha:z ʔilʕaṣabi] the nervous system.
مُجَهِّز [mujahhiz] *n:* • **1.** supplier, provider • **1.** provider
تَجهِيز [tajhi:z] *n:* • **1.** equipping, equipment • **2.** coll. equipment, gear, material
جاهِز [ja:hiz] *adj:* • **1.** ready-made – مَلابِس جاهزَة [mala:bis ja:hza] ready-made clothes.
مُجَهَّز [mujahhaz] *adj:* • **1.** equipped, supplied

ج ه ض

إجهاض [ʔijha:ð̣] *n:* • **1.** miscarriage, abortion – صار عِندها إجهاض بَعَد ما وُقعَت مِن الدَّرَج [ṣa:r ʕindha ʔijha:ð̣ baʕad ma: wugʕat min ʔiddaraj] She had a miscarriage after she fell down the stairs.

ج ه ل

تجاهَل [tja:hal, dja:hal] *v:* • **1.** to ignore, disregard – تجاهَلَه. سَوِّي نَفسَك ما شِفتَه [dja:halah. sawwi: nafsak ma: šiftah] Ignore him. Make as if you didn't see him. • **2.** to pretend ignorance, feign a lack of knowledge – لا تِتجاهَل. تِدري عَلَى مَن دَنِحكِي [la: tidja:hal. tidri ʕala man daniħči] don't pretend ignorance. You know who we're talking about.
جَهَل [jahal] *n:* • **1.** ignorance • **2.** illiteracy
جُهُل [juhul] *n:* • **1.** childhood
جاهِل [ja:hil] *n:* جَهال، جِهال [jaha:l, jiha:l] *pl:* • **1.** baby, child, youngster, kid
جاهِل [ja:hil] *adj:* جَهَلَة [jahala] *pl:* • **1.** ignorant, uneducated, illiterate • **2.** uneducated person
مَجهُول [majhu:l] *adj:* • **1.** unknown
أجهَل [ʔajhal] *comparative adjective:* • **1.** more or most ignorant, uneducated • **2.** more or most youthful

ج ه م

جهامَة [jha:ma] *n:* جَهامات، جهايِم [jaha:ma:t, jha:yim] *pl:* • **1.** mug, puss, ugly face

ج ه ن م

جِهَنَّم [jihannam] *n:* • **1.** hell, hellfire – بِجهَنَّم! يِستاهِل [bijihannam! yista:hil] To hell with him! He deserves it.

ج و

جاوَة [ja:wa] *n:* • **1.** Java
جاوِي [ja:wi] *n:* • **1.** Javanese, a Javanese

ج و ب [1]

جاوَب [ja:wab] *v:* • **1.** to answer, reply to, respond to – حَتَّى لَو يسِبَّك، لا تجاوبَه [ħatta law ysibbak, la: dja:wbah] Even if he insults you, don't answer him. جاوُب عَلَى سُؤالَين بَسّ [ja:wab ʕala suʔa:layn bass] He answered two questions only.
تجاوَب [tja:wab, dja:wab] *v:* • **1.** to respond, to react
اِستَجوَب [ʔistajwab] *v:* • **1.** to interrogate, examine, question – الشُّرطَة اِستَجوُبَتَه ساعَة [ʔiššurṭa ʔistajwubatah sa:ʕa] The police questioned him an hour.
اِستَجاب [ʔistaja:b] *v:* • **1.** to respond, reply
جَواب [jawa:b] *n:* أَجوِبَة [ʔajwiba] *pl:* • **1.** answer, reply
إجابَة [ʔija:ba] *n:* • **1.** answer
تَجاوُب [taja:wub] *n:* • **1.** response, consent
مِتجاوِب [mitja:wib] *n:* • **1.** harmonious
اِستِجواب [ʔistijwa:b] *n:* اِستِجوابات [ʔistijwa:ba:t] *pl:* • **1.** interrogation, questioning
اِستِجابَة [ʔistija:ba] *n:* • **1.** compliance, response

ج و ب [2]

جُوب [ču:b] *n:* جُوبات، جواب، جوابَة [ču:ba:t, čwa:b, čwa:ba] *pl:* • **1.** tube, inner tube • **2.** bladder (of a ball)

ج و ت [1]

جُوت [ju:t] *n:* • **1.** jute
جوِيت [čwi:t] *n:* • **1.** a blueing agent used in washing clothes

ج و ت [2]

جويتِي [čwi:ti] *adj:* • **1.** bluish purple

ج و خ

جَوخ [čawx, *n:* جوَاخ [čwa:x] *pl:* • **1.** heavy broadcloth • **2.** felt

ج و د

جاد [ja:d] *v:* • **1.** with ب to grant or bestow generously – جاد عَلينا بألِف دِينار [ja:d ʕali:na bʔalif dina:r] He generously granted us a thousand dinars. لِيش ما تجُود عَلينا بسُكُوتَك [li:š ma: dju:d ʕali:na bsuku:tak] Why don't you favor us with your silence!
جَوَّد [jawwad] *v:* • **1.** to recite the Koran – فِتَح القُرآن وقام يجَوِّد [fitaħ ʔilqurʔa:n wga:m yjawwid] He opened the Koran and began to recite.
أجاد [ʔaja:d] *v:* • **1.** to excel at, be a master of, to do (something) well, know (something) well – هُوَّ يجِيد العَزف عالكَمَنجَة [huwwa yji:d ʔilʕazif ʕalkamanja] He excels at playing the violin. يجِيد ثلاث لُغات [yiji:d tlaθ luɣa:t] He knows three languages well.
جُود [ju:d] *n:* • **1.** generosity, liberality, open-handedness • **2.** pl. جواد small bag made from animal skin
جَودَة [jawda] *n:* • **1.** quality
جَيِّد [jayyid] *adj:* • **1.** good, perfect • **2.** excellent, outstanding
أجاوِيد [ʔaja:wi:d] *adj:* • **1.** (pl. only) generous people
أجوَد [ʔajwad] *comparative adjective:* • **1.** better, best

ج و د ر

جَودَر [čawdar] *v:* • **1.** to pitch a tent, to make camp – خَلِّي نجُودِر هنا هاللَّيلَة [xalli: nčawdir hna hallayla] Let's

camp here tonight. أَشُو صارلَك مجُوبِر هنا ساعتين. شَكُو عِندَك؟ [ʔašuː ṣaːrlak mčuːdir hnaː saːʕtayn. šaku ʕindak?] You've been hanging around here two hours. What are you after?
جادِر [čaːdir] *n:* جُوادِر [čwaːdir] *pl:* • **1.** tent

ج و ر 1

جار [ǰaːr] *v:* • **1.** with عَلى to wrong, persecute, oppress, commit an outrage against – جُور عَالوَلَد إذا تدزَّه لِلسُّوق بِهَالمُطَر [ǰuːr ʕalwalad ʔiða ddizzah lissuːg bhalmuṭar] You're being unfair to the boy if you send him to the market in this rain.
جاوَر [ǰaːwar] *v:* • **1.** to be the neighbor of, to live next door to – جاوَرنا سَنتَين وَبَعدين تحَوَّل [ǰaːwarna santayn wbaʕdiːn tħawwal] He was our neighbor for two years and then he moved. • **2.** to border, border on – إيران تجاوِر العِراق [ʔiraːn dǰaːwir ʔilʕiraːq] Iran borders on Iraq.
تجاوَر [dǰaːwar] *v:* • **1.** to neighbor, to be neighbors with
اِستَجار [ʔistaǰaːr] *v:* • **1.** to seek refuge, protection, help, aid – راح نِستَجِير بأي واحِد يقدَر ينقُذنا [raːħ nistaǰiːr bʔay waːħid yigdar yinquðna] We will appeal for aid from anyone who can save us.
جور [ǰuːr] *n:* • **1.** injustice • **2.** oppression, tyranny
جار [ǰaːr] *n:* جِيران، جِيارِين، جُوارِين [ǰiːraːn, ǰiyaːriːn, ǰuwaːriːn] *pl:* • **1.** neighbor
جيران [ǰiːraːn] *n:* جِيارِين، جُوارِين [ǰiyaːriːn, ǰuwaːriːn] *pl:* • **1.** neighbor(s)
مُجاوَرَة [muǰaːwara] *n:* • **1.** neighborhood, proximity
مُجاوِر [muǰaːwir] *adj:* • **1.** neighboring, adjacent, close, touching

ج و ر 2

جُورِي، وَرِد جُورِي [ǰuːri, warid ǰuːri] *adj:* • **1.** damask rose

ج و ر ب

جوراب [ǰuːraːb] *n:* جواريب [ǰwaːriːb] *pl:* • **1.** one sock, a stocking تَكّ جُوراب [takk ǰuːraːb] one sock, a stocking.

ج و ز 1

جاز [ǰaːz] *v:* • **1.** to be possible, conceivable – كُلّ شِي يجُوز [kull ši yǰuːz] Anything's possible. يجُوز. لَكِن ما أتصَوَّر هِيكِي [yǰuːz. laːkin maː ʔatṣawwar hiːči] It's possible. But I don't think so. خابرَه هَسَّة. يجُوز بِالبَيت [xaːbrah hassa. yǰuːz bilbayt] Call him now. He may be home. شلُون يجُوزلَك تطَلّعَه مِن الشُّغُل؟ [šluːn yiǰuːzlak ttallʕah min ʔiššuɣul?] What gives you the right to fire him? • **2.** to let go of, let alone – جُوز مِن هَالجّاهِل [ǰuːz min haǰǰaːhil] Leave that child alone! الشُّرطِي جاز مِنِّي بَعَد ما راوِيتَه هَوِيتِي [ʔiššurṭi ǰaːz minni baʕad maː raːwiːtah hawiːti] The cop let me go after I showed him my identification. • **3.** with مِن to stop, quit, give up – جُوز مِن أكِل الخيار؛ ما زَين إلَك [ǰuːz min ʔakil ʔilxyaːr; maː ziːn ʔilak] Stop eating cucumbers; it's not good for you. قابِل آني جايِز مِن حَياتِي، أركَب طَيّارَة وِيّاه؟ [qaːbil ʔaːni ǰaːyiz min ħayaːti, ʔarkab ṭiyyaːra wiyyaːh?] You think I've given up my life, to ride an airplane with him?
جَوَّز [ǰawwaz] *v:* • **1.** to break
جاوَز [ǰaːwaz] *v:* • **1.** to over-step, go beyond – جاوَز كُلّ الحُدُود بِالحَكِي مالَه [ǰaːwaz kull ʔilħuduːd bilħači maːlah] He overstepped all the bounds with his talk. • **2.** to exceed, surpass – مِيزانِيَّتنا جاوزَت المَليُون دِينار هالسَّنَة [miːzaːniyyatna ǰaːwazat ʔilmalyuːn dinaːr hassana] Our budget exceeded a million dinars this year.
أجاز [ʔaǰaːz] *v:* • **1.** to license
تجاوَز [tǰaːwaz, dǰaːwaz] *v:* • **1.** to over-step, exceed, go beyond – تجاوَز الحُدُود بِحَكيَه [dǰaːwaz ʔilħuduːd bħačyah] He stepped out of bounds in what he said.
اِجتاز [ʔiǰtaːz] *v:* • **1.** to pass through, go through, traverse – اِجتاز الغابَة وَحدَه [ʔiǰtaːz ʔilɣaːba waħdah] He passed through the woods by himself. • **2.** to cross, go across – جيش العَدُو اِجتاز حُدُودنا البارحَة [ǰayš ʔilʕadu ʔiǰtaːz ħuduːdna ʔilbaːrħa] The enemy army crossed our borders yesterday. خَلِّي نِجتاز الشّارِع من هنا [xalliː niǰtaːz ʔiššaːriʕ min hna] Let's cut across the street here. • **3.** to get through, come through – اِجتاز الامتِحان بتَفَوُّق [ʔiǰtaːz ʔilʔimtiħaːn btafawwuq] He passed the exam with flying colors.
جَواز [ǰawaːz] *n:* • **1.** possibility, conceivability • **2.** quitting, giving up • **3.** relinquishing • **4.** passport, travel document
مُوجَز [muːǰaz] *n:* • **1.** summary, brief
مَجاز [maǰaːz] *n:* • **1.** corridor
إجازَة [ʔiǰaːza] *n:* إجازات [ʔiǰaːzaːt] *pl:* • **1.** authorization • **2.** license, permit • **3.** leave, vacation – إجازَة دِراسِيَّة [ʔiǰaːza diraːsiyya] leave of absence for study.
تَجاوُز [taǰaːwuz] *n:* تَجاوُزات [taǰaːwuzaːt] *pl:* • **1.** encroachment, unwarranted act • **2.** overdraft, overdrawing (of an account)
جائِزَة [ǰaːʔiza] *n:* جَوائِز [ǰawaːʔiz] *pl:* • **1.** prize, award, premium • **2.** reward
تَجوِيز [taǰwiːz] *n:* • **1.** training or forcing someone to quit a bad habit
جائِز [ǰaːʔiz] *adj:* • **1.** possible, conceivable
مُجاز [muǰaːz] *adj:* • **1.** on vacation, on leave • **2.** licensed, authorized
متجاوِز [mitǰaːwiz] *adj:* • **1.** passing, trespassing • **2.** outstripping, outdistancing, overreaching, transcending, overstepping, exceeding, overtaking

ج و ز 2

جوز [ǰawz, ǰuːz] *n:* • **1.** (coll.) walnut(s) – جُوز هِند، جُوز هِندِي [ǰuːz hind, ǰuːz hindi] coconut (s).
جَوزَة [ǰawza] *n:* جَوزات [ǰawzaːt] *pl:* • **1.** Adam's apple • **2.** walnut

جُوزبَوَّة [ǰu:zbawwa] *n:* • **1.** nutmeg
جَوزِي [ǰawzi] *adj:* • **1.** walnut-colored, nut brown

ج و ع

جاع [ja:ʕ] *v:* • **1.** to be or become hungry – شِبساع جِعِت! هَسَّة أكَلنا [šibsa:ʕ jiʕit! hassa ʔakalna] You sure got hungry fast! We just ate.
جَوَّع [ǰawwaʕ] *v:* • **1.** to starve, cause to starve – لِيش دَتجَوِّع الحِصان مالَك؟ [li:š dadǰawwiʕ ʔilhiṣa:n ma:lak?] Why are you starving your horse? • **2.** to make hungry – هَوا الجِّبال يجَوِّع [hawa ʔiǰǰiba:l yǰawwiʕ] Mountain air makes one hungry.
جُوع [ǰu:ʕ] *n:* • **1.** hunger, starvation
مَجاعَة [maǰa:ʕa] *n:* مَجاعات [maǰa:ʕa:t] *pl:* • **1.** famine
جُوعِيّات [ǰu:ʕiyya:t] *n:* • **1.** sponging, free-loading ما تجُوز مِن الجُّوعِيّات [ma: dǰu:z min ʔiǰǰu:ʕiyya:t] Why don't you quit sponging!
جُوعِي [ǰu:ʕi] *adj:* جُوعِيِّين [ǰu:ʕiyyi:n] *pl:* • **1.** cadger, free-loader, sponger, cheapskate
جُوعان [ǰu:ʕa:n] *adj:* جُوعانِين، جواعَة [ǰu:ʕa:ni:n, ǰwa:ʕa] *pl:* • **1.** hungry, starved, famished

ج و ع ر

جَوعَر [ǰawʕar] *v:* • **1.** to bray – وَخِّر هَالزُّمال من هنا. دَيجَوعِر عَلَى طُول [waxxir hazzuma:l min hna. dayǰawʕir ʕala ṭu:l] Get this donkey away from here. He brays continuously.

ج و ف

تَجوِيف [taǰwi:f] *n:* تَجاوِيف [taǰa:wi:f] *pl:* • **1.** hollow space
مجَوَّف [mǰawwaf] *adj:* • **1.** hollow • **2.** hollowed out, hollow
أجوَف، جَوفاء [ʔaǰwaf, ǰawfa:ʔ] *adj:* • **1.** hollow, empty, vain

ج و ق

جَوق [ǰawq] *n:* أجواق [ʔaǰwa:q] *pl:* • **1.** band, orchestra
جَوقَة [ǰawga] *n:* • **1.** a group of people, band

ج و ل

جال [ǰa:l] *v:* • **1.** to get around • **1.** to wander around
تجَوَّل [tǰawwal] *v:* • **2.** to patrol, make the rounds – يعجِبنِي أتجَوَّل ببارِيس [yiʕǰibni ʔadǰawwal bpa:ri:s] I like to go wandering around in Paris. الشُّرطَة تِتجَوَّل بالمَناطِق الحَسّاسَة بالبَلدَة [ʔiššurṭa tidǰawwal bilmana:ṭiq ʔilħassa:sa bilbalda] The police patrol the sensitive areas in the city.
جَول [čawl , ču:l] *n:* • **1.** wilderness, wasteland, desert – إذا ترُوح لِلمَدرَسَة باللَّيل، تِلقِيها جَول [ʔiða tru:ħ lilmadrasa billayl, tilgi:ha čawl] If you go to the school at night you'll find it deserted.
جَولَة [ǰawla] *n:* جَولات [ǰawla:t] *pl:* • **1.** tour, excursion, outing • **2.** circuit, round, patrol • **3.** round (in sports)
جَوّال [ǰawwa:l] *n:* جَوّالَة [ǰawwa:la] *pl:* • **1.** a senior Boy Scout • **2.** cell phone
مَجال [maǰa:l] *n:* مَجالات [maǰa:la:t] *pl:* • **1.** room, space – أكُو مَجال كافِي لِلسَّيّارَة تفُوت جَوَّة الطّاق [ʔaku maǰa:l ka:fi lissayya:ra tfu:t ǰawwa ʔiṭṭa:g] There's clearance enough for the car to go under the arch. • **2.** place, opening – ماكُو مَجال بالمِلاك نعَيِّنَه [ma:ku maǰa:l bilmila:k nʕayynah] There's no opening we can appoint him to in the organization. • **3.** field, domain, sphere – هُوَّ مَعرُوف بِالمَجال السِّياسِي [huwwa maʕru:f bilmaǰa:l ʔissiya:si] He is well-known in the political field. • **4.** free scope, freedom, opportunity, chance – بِهَالوَظِيفَة، عِندِي مَجال واسِع أستَعمِل ذَكائِي [bhalwaḏi:fa, ʕindi maǰa:l wa:siʕ ʔastaʕmil ðaka:ʔi] In this job, I have great opportunity for using my intelligence. راح أخابرَك إذا صارلِي مَجال [ra:ħ ʔaxa:brak ʔiða ṣa:rli maǰa:l] I'll call you if I get a chance.
تَجَوُّل [taǰawwul] *n:* • **1.** going about, moving around مَنع التَّجَوُّل [maniʕ ʔattaǰawwul] curfew.
تَجوال [taǰwa:l] *n:* • **1.** going about, moving around, wandering, travelling
مُتَجَوِّل [mutaǰawwil] *adj:* • **1.** moving, wandering, itinerant, traveling, roving

ج و م

جُومَة [ǰu:ma] *n:* جُوَم [ǰuwam] *pl:* • **1.** hole in the ground or floor for mounting a loom • **2.** a loom

ج و ن

جاوَن [ǰa:wan] *n:* • **1.** large mortar, hollowed log used as a mortar, large bowl • **2.** hollowed log used as a mortar • **3.** whirlpool

ج و ه ر

جَوهَر [ǰawhar] *n:* جَواهِر [ǰawa:hir] *pl:* • **1.** essence, quintessence, essential nature • **2.** tint, dye, coloring
جَوهَرَة [ǰawhara] *n:* جَواهِر [ǰawa:hir] *pl:* • **1.** gem, jewel, precious stone
جَوهَرجِي [ǰawharči] *n:* جَوهَرجِيَّة [ǰawharčiyya] *pl:* • **1.** jeweler • **2.** merchant who charges high prices, profiteer
مُجَوهَرات [muǰawhara:t] *n:* • **1.** jewelry • **2.** jewels, gems
جَوهَرِي [ǰawhari, ǰu:hari] *adj:* • **1.** basic • **1.** essential

ج و و

جَوّ [ǰaww] *n:* أجواء [ʔaǰwa:ʔ] *pl:* • **1.** air – الجَّوّ بارِد هنا باللَّيل [ʔiǰǰaww ba:rid hna: billayl] The air's cold here at night. • **2.** atmosphere – الجَّوّ بِهَالدّائِرَة مُو مُرِيح [ʔiǰǰaww bhadda:ʔira mu: muri:ħ]

ج

The atmosphere in this office is not relaxed. • **3.** weather, climate جَوّ مُمطِر [ǰaww mumṭir] rainy weather.
جَوَّة [ǰawwa] *n:* • **1.** in, inside – خَشّ جَوَّة [xašš ǰawwa] He went inside. فُوت بِالباص وَاُقعُد جَوَّة كُلِّش [fu:t bilpa:ṣ wugʕud ǰawwa kulliš] Get on the bus and sit all the way in the back. جَوَّة العَبا [ǰawwa ʔilʕaba] behind the scenes, unseen, covert. • **2.** down, downstairs – خَلّي ننزل جوَّة [xalli: ninzil ǰawwa] Let's go downstairs. • **3.** under, beneath, underneath – الكَلِب نايِم جَوَّة السَّيّارَة [ʔiččalib na:yim ǰawwa ʔissayya:ra] The dog is sleeping under the car. جَوَّة الإيد [ǰawwa ʔilʔi:d] at hand, handy, available.
جُوَّة [ǰuwwa] *n:* جُوّات، جُوَو [ǰuwwa:t, ǰuwaw] *pl:* • **1.** patch, plot, bed (in a garden)
جَوِّي [ǰawwi] *adj:* • **1.** air, aerial, aero- بَرِيد جَوِّي [bari:d ǰawwi] air mail.
جَوّانِي [ǰawwa:ni] *adj:* • **1.** inner, inside, interior • **2.** lower, bottommost

ج ي ء

إِجَى [ʔiǰa:] *v:* • **1.** to come
جا [ǰa:] *v:* **1.** to come, come to – جا لِلدّائِرَة مِتأَخِّر [ǰa: lidda:ʔira mitʔaxxir] He came to the office late. إِجَونا خُطّار البارحَة [ʔiǰawna xuṭṭa:r ʔilba:rħa] We had guests yesterday. صَدِيقَك جا عَلِيك البارحَة [ṣadi:qak ǰa: ʕali:k ʔilba:rħa] Your friend came to see you yesterday. جانِي مِن وَرا وِضِرَبنِي [ǰa:ni min wara wđirabni] He approached me from behind and hit me. إِلّلي ما يِجِي وِيّاك، تَعال وِيّاه [ʔilli ma: yiǰi wiyya:k, taʕa:l wiyya:h] If he doesn't go along with you, compromise (lit. whoever won't come with you, go with him). إِذا تِجِي وِيّاه بِاللِّين، يِقبَل [ʔiđa tiǰi wiyya:h billi:n, yiqbal] If you approach him gently, he will agree. إِذا تِجِيه بلسان طَيِّب، يوافُق [ʔiđa tiǰi:h bilsa:n ṭayyib, ywa:fuq] If you approach him in a nice manner, he'll agree. إِسمَه ما دَ يِجِي عَلَى بالِي [ʔismah ma: da yiǰi ʕala ba:li] His name doesn't occur to me. ظَلّ يِرُوح ويِجِي بالقُبَّة [đall yiru:ħ wyiǰi bilgubba] He kept pacing back and forth in the room. جَتنِي خُوش فِكرَة [ǰatni xu:š fikra] A good idea occurred to me. جاك خَبَر مِن أَخُوك؟ [ǰa:k xabar min ʔaxu:k?] Have you gotten any news from your brother? جَتِّي براسِي وَضِرَبتَه [ǰatti bra:si wđirabtah] I got mad and hit him. • **2.** to arrive – شوَقِت تِجِي الطَّيّارَة؟ [šwakit tiǰi ʔiṭṭiyya:ra?] What time does the plane arrive? أَجَلَه جا وَمات [ʔaǰalah ǰa: wma:t] His time came and he died. جا المُطَر وَدُمَر كُلّ الوَرِد [ǰa: ʔilmuṭar wdumar kull ʔilwarid] The rain came and damaged all the flowers. مِن يِجِي الخير، يِجِي فَدّ مَرَّة [min yiǰi ʔilxi:r, yiǰi fadd marra] When properity comes, it comes all at one time. مِن تِجِي العُطلَة، راح أَتعَلَّم سِبِح [min tiǰi ʔilʕuṭla, ra:ħ ʔatʕallam sibiħ] When vacation comes around, I'll learn swimming. هَمّ جا الصَّيف [hamm ǰa: ʔiṣṣayf] Summer has come again. جا وَقِت الرَّقِّي [ǰa: wakit ʔirraggi] Watermelons are in season. إِجا ظَهرَه [ʔiǰa đahrah] He had an orgasm. هَالقُماش يِجِي بِخَمس أَلوان [halquma:š yiǰi bxams ʔalwa:n] This cloth comes in five colors. • **3.** to reach, get to – الماي جانِي لِصَدرِي [ʔilma:y ǰa:ni lṣadri] The water came to my chest. مَيّ الجَّدوَل يِجِي لِلحزام [mayy ʔiǰǰadwal yiǰi lilħza:m] The water in the channel comes up to the waist. • **4.** to come to, accrue to, come one's way – دَيِجِي خُوش مَورِد مِن البِستان [dayiǰi xu:š mawrid min ʔilbista:n] He's getting a good income from the orchard. مِن مات أَبُوه، جَتَّه فلُوس هوايَة [min ma:t ʔabu:h, ǰattah flu:s hwa:ya] When his father died, he came into a lot of money. جَتَّك زِيادَة وِيّا بَقِيَة العُمّال؟ [ǰattak ziya:da wiyya baqiyat ʔilʕumma:l?] Did you get a raise with the rest of the workers? جانِي الأَس [ǰa:ni ʔilʔa:s] I got the ace. جاه وَلَد [ǰa:h walad] He had a son. شدَيجِيك مِن وَرا أَذِيَة النّاس؟ [šdayǰi:k min wara ʔađiyyat ʔinna:s?] What are you gaining from hurting people? تقَرَّب عَالبَنكَة. ما دَيجِيك هَوا [tqarrab ʕalpanka. ma: dayǰi:k hawa] Move closer to the fan. You aren't getting any air. • **5.** to descend upon, befall – شجاك؟ مُو تُعرُف الأَجوِبَة [šǰa:k? mu: tuʕruf ʔilʔaǰwiba] What came over you? You know the answers! إِذا تغَمُّض عينَك، يِجِيك النَّوم [ʔiđa tɣammuđ ʕaynak, yiǰi:k ʔinnawm] If you close your eyes, sleep will come to you. جانِي النُّوم. خَلّي نِرجَع لِلبَيت [ǰa:ni ʔinnawm. xalli: nirǰaʕ lilbayt] I've gotten sleepy. Let's go home. جَتنِي الدَّوخَة وَأَنِي دَأَكتِب [ǰatni ʔiddawxa waʔa:ni daʔaktib] I was overcome by dizziness as I was writing. أَهلِي ما جَتها العادَة شَهرَين [ʔahli ma: ǰatha ʔilʕa:da šahrayn] My wife hasn't gotten her period for two months. جاك المُوت إِن شاء الله [ǰa:k ʔilmu:t ʔinša:llah] I hope death takes you. • **6.** (as a set phrase) approximately – عِندِي يِجِي خَمس دَنانِير [ʕindi yiǰi xams dana:ni:r] I have almost five dinars. • **7.** with عَلَى to fit, be big enough – هَالشَّفقَة ما تِجِي عَلِيك [haššafqa ma: tiǰi ʕali:k] This hat is too small for you.
جَيَّة [ǰayya] *n:* جَيّات [ǰayya:t] *pl:* • **1.** coming, arrival – جَيِّتَه كانَت بمَحَلّها [ǰayytah ča:nat bmaħallha] His arrival was timely. جَيِّتَك منِين؟ [ǰayytak mni:n?] Where did you arrive from? إِجا البَرِد فَدّ جَيَّة [ʔiǰa ʔilbarid fadd ǰayya] The cold weather came all at once. • **2.** visit, call – بقَيت دَقِيقتَين. هَذِي مُو جَيَّة [bqayt daqi:qtayn. ha:đi mu: ǰayya] You stayed two minutes. That's no visit!

ج ي ب 1

جاب [ǰa:b] *v:* • **1.** to bring, fetch – جابلِي ساعَة مِن سويسرا [ǰa:bli sa:ʕa min swi:sra] He brought me a watch from Switzerland. إِذا تبِيعها هَسَّة، دَتجِيبلَك خُوش فلُوس [ʔiđa ʔitbi:ʕha hassa, datǰi:blak xu:š flu:s] If you sell it now, it will bring you a good price. • **2.** to come up with, get hold of – ما تجِيب الفلُوس عاد! مُو صار شَهرَين أَطالبَك؟ [ma: dǰi:b ʔilflu:s ʕa:d! mu: ṣa:r šahrayn ʔaṭa:lbak?] Why don't you come up with the money, then! Haven't I been after you for two months? • **3.** to bring out, come out with, pull off – جاب الحكايَة بمُكانها [ǰaːb ʔilħčaːya bmukaːnha] He made a pertinent remark. جاب خُوش نَقِش وَقِدَر ياخُذها مِنها [ǰaːb xuːš naqiš wgidar yaːxuðha minha] He pulled a slick trick and was able to get it from her. • **4.** to receive, get, have – جاب خُوش شانص. غِلَب مِيَّة دِينار [ǰaːb xuːš čaːnṣ. ɣilab miyyat dinaːr] He had good luck. He won a hundred dinars. جِبِت دُوشَيش [ǰibit duːšiːš] I drew a double six. • **5.** to give birth to, have (a child) – زَوجتِي جابَت وَلَد [zawiǰti ǰaːbat walad] My wife had a boy.

جَيَّب [ǰayyab] *v:* • **1.** to attend (a woman) in childbirth – أَيّ طَبِيب جَيَّب مَرتَك؟ [ʔayy ṭabiːb ǰayyab martak?] Which doctor attended your wife in childbirth? جِيرانَتنا دَتِطلَق وَماكُو وِحدَة تجَيِّبها [ǰiːraːnatna datiṭlag wmaːku wiħda dǰayyibha] Our neighbor is in labor and there's no one to act as midwife for her.

جَيبُوبَة [ǰaybuːba] *n:* جَيبُوبات [ǰaybuːbaːt] *pl:* • **1.** delivery, birth (of a baby)

ج ي ب 2

جيب [ǰiːb] *n:* • **1.** pocket – دِير بالَك مِنَّه، تَرَة يُضرُب جيب [diːr baːlak minnah, tara yuðrub ǰiːb] Be careful of him, because he picks pockets.

ج ي ر

جَيَّر [ǰayyar] *v:* • **1.** to endorse (a check) – جَيَّرتَه لِلشِّيك؟ [ǰayyartah liččiːk?] Did you endorse the check?

جِير [ǰiːr] *n:* • **1.** asphalt – وَإذا سِقَط، بِالجِّير [wʔiðaː siqaṭ, biǰǰiːr] And if he fails, the hell with him! خِسَر هوايَة بِالقمار. . . بِالجِّير [xisar hwaːya bilqmaːr. . . biǰǰiːr] He lost a lot gambling. . . That's good enough for him!

ج ي ش

جَيش [ǰayš, ǰiːš] *n:* جِيُوش [ǰiyuːš] *pl:* • **1.** army, armed forces

ج ي ف

جاف [ǰaːf] *v:* • **1.** to be or become putrid, to stink – الجُثَّة بُقَت مَذبُوبَة هنا إِلَى أَن جافَت [ʔiǰǰuθθa buqat maðbuːba hnaː ʔila ʔan ǰaːfat] The body was left here till it began to stink. اللَّحَم جاف. لازِم تذِبَّه [ʔillaħam ǰaːf. laːzim dðibbah] The meat's spoiled. You'd better throw it out. المَيّ إِذا يِبقَى بمُكان واحِد، يجِيف [ʔilmayy ʔiða yibqaː bmukaːn waːħid, yǰiːf] If water stays in one place, it becomes foul.

جَيَّف [ǰayyaf] *v:* • **1.** to go too far, carry something too far – هَذا جَيَّفها. كُلّ يوم يِطلَع قَبِل الدَّوام [haːða ǰayyafha. kull yuːm yiṭlaʕ gabil ʔiddawaːm] He's carried it too far. Every day he leaves early.

جَيف [ǰayf, ǰiːf] *n:* • **1.** stink, putrid smell

جِيفَة [ǰiːfa] *n:* جِيَف [ǰiyaf] *pl:* • **1.** rotting carcass, carrion • **2.** bad odor, stink, putrid smell

جايِف [ǰaːyif] *adj:* • **1.** stinking, putrid • **2.** rotten, spoiled

ج ي ك

جَيَّك [čayyak] *v:* • **1.** to check

تَجِييك [tačyiːk] *n:* تَجِييكات [tačyiːkaːt] *pl:* • **1.** check, check up

مجَيَّك [mčayyak] *adj:* • **1.** checked

ج ي ل

جِيل [ǰiːl] *n:* أَجيال [ʔaǰyaːl] *pl:* • **1.** generation

ج ي م 1

جِيم [ǰiːm] *n:* • **1.** name of the letter

ج ي م 2

جَيَّم [ǰayyam] *v:* • **1.** to jam, to get stuck (in traffic)

تجَيَّم [tǰayyam, dǰayyam] *v:* • **1.** to jam

تَجِييم [taǰyiːm] *n:* • **1.** jamming

مجَيِّم [mǰayyim] *adj:* • **1.** jammed

ج ي م 3

جيم [ǰaym, ǰiːm] *n:* • **1.** game

ج ي ن ز

جِينز [ǰiːnz] *n:* • **1.** jeans

ح

ح

حاء -حَ [ħa, ħa:] n: • **1.** name of the letter

ح ب ب [1]

حَبّ [ħabb] *v:* • **1.** to love, like – أَحِبّ مَرتِي هوايَة [ʔaħibb marti hwa:ya] I love my wife a lot. ما أَحِبّ هَاللَّون [ma: ʔaħibb hallawn] I don't like this color. تحِبّ تِجي وِيّانا؟ [tħibb tiǰi wiyya:na?] Would you like to come with us? • **2.** to kiss – حَبّها بِشفاها [ħabbha bišfa:ha] He kissed her on her lips.

حَبَّب [ħabbab] *v:* • **1.** to endear, to cause to be loved or liked – يُعرُف شلُون يحَبِّب نَفسَه لِلنّاس [yuʕruf šlu:n yħabbib nafsah linna:s] He knows how to endear himself to people.

حابَى [ħa:ba:] *v:* • **1.** to show favoritism, take sides – المُلاحِظ يحابِي لِأَهل ولايتَه [ʔilmula:ħið yiħa:bi lʔahl wla:ytah] The supervisor favors the people from his home town. يحابِي بين الجِّهال [yiħa:bi bi:n ʔiǰǰiha:l] He plays favorites among the children.

تحَبَّب [tħabbab] *v:* • **1.** to show love, reveal affection – دائماً يتحَبَّب لها وهِيَّ ما تدِيرلَه بال [da:ʔiman yitħabbab ʔilha whiyya ma: ddi:rlah ba:l] He's always demonstrating his affection for her and she doesn't pay him any attention.

تحابَب [tħa:bab] *v:* • **1.** to love each other – تحابِبَوا مِن هُمَّ صغار [tħa:bibaw min humma ṣɣa:r] They've loved each other since they were kids.

حُبّ [ħubb] *n:* • **1.** love, affection – حُبّ الاستِطلاع [ħubb ʔilʔistiṭla:ʕ] curiosity. حُبّ الظُّهُور [ħubb ʔiððuhu:r] love of display, love of being known. حُبّ الذّات [ħubb ʔiðða:t] love of self, egotism. وُقَع بالحُبّ [wugaʕ bilħubb] He fell in love. واقِع بحُبّ بنَيَّة مُو حِلوَة [wa:giʕ bħubb bnayya ma: ħilwa] He's in love with an unattractive girl.

حَبِيب [ħabi:b] *n:* أَحِبَّة، أَحباب [ʔaħibba, ʔaħba:b] *pl:* • **1.** beloved, lover, sweetheart • **2.** dear friend – أَصدِقائِي وأَحبابِي [ʔaṣdiqa:ʔi wʔaħba:bi] my closest friends.

مَحَبَّة [maħabba] *n:* • **1.** affection, love

حَبِيبَة [ħabi:ba] *n:* حَبايِب [ħaba:yib] *pl:* • **1.** beloved (fem.), sweetheart, darling

مُحاباة، مُحابات [muħa:ba:t] *n:* • **1.** favoritism

مُحِبّ [muħibb] *adj:* • **1.** lover

حَبُّوب [ħabbu:b] *adj:* • **1.** likeable, lovable, friendly, pleasant – مُوَظَّفنا الجِّدِيد كُلِّش حَبُّوب [muwaððafna ʔiǰǰidi:d kulliš ħabbu:b] Our new employee is very likeable.

حَبّاب [ħabba:b] *adj:* • **1.** polite, nice

مَحبُوب [maħbu:b] *adj:* • **1.** beloved, dear • **2.** lovable, likeable • **3.** popular

مُستَحَبّ [mustaħabb] *adj:* • **1.** recommended, desirable (said of acts which are not required by religion but which are commendable)

مَحَبَّتاً [maħabbatan] *adverbial:* • **1.** through love, from affection – سَوَّيتَه مَحَبَّتاً إِلَك [sawwi:tah maħabbatan ʔilak] I did it out of affection for you.

ح ب ب [2]

حَبّ [ħabb] *n:* • **1.** Coll. seed, grain, kernel • **2.** Coll. pimple, pustule, acne • **3.** Coll. pill, capsule, tablet, pellet

حَبَّة [ħabba] *n:* حَبّات [ħabba:t] *pl:* • **1.** a seed, a grain, a kernel; pimple, pustule, acne; a pill, a capsule, a tablet, a pellet

حَبّايَة [ħabba:ya] *n:* حَبّايات [ħabba:ya:t] *pl:* • **1.** There isn't a single bit left • **2.** a capsule, a tablet, a pellet

محَبِّب [mħabbib] adj: • **1.** someone with an acne, pimpled

ح ب ب [3]

حِبّ [ħibb] *n:* حباب، حبُوب [ħba:b, ħbu:b] *pl:* • **1.** large, porous, pottery vessel for storing drinking water

ح ب ذ

حَبَّذ [ħabbað] *v:* • **1.** to approve of, think well of – آنِي أَحَبِّذ هَالفِكرَة [ʔa:ni ʔaħabbið halfikra] I approve of this idea.

مُحَبَّذ [muħabbað] *adj:* • **1.** desirable, preferable

ح ب ر

حِبِر [ħibir] *n:* • **1.** ink

مَحبَرَة [maħbara] *n:* مَحابِر [maħa:bir] *pl:* • **1.** inkpot, inkwell

حَبارِي، طِير حَبارِي [ħaba:ri, ṭi:r ħaba:ri] *n:* • **1.** bustard

ح ب س

حِبَس [ħibas] *v:* • **1.** to confine, restrict, block – بالله تَعال بِالعَجَل؛ لا تِحبِسنِي [ballah taʕa:l bilʕaǰal; la: tiħbisni] Please come quickly; don't leave me stranded. آنِي مَحبُوس ومااَقدَر أَطلَع لِأَنّ أَخُويَا راح يِجِي [ʔa:ni maħbu:s wma ʔagdar ʔaṭlaʕ liʔann ʔaxu:ya ra:ħ yiji] I'm tied down, and can't go out because my brother's coming. حِبَسِت البُول مالَك؛ ما تِقدَر تحَرِّكَه [ħibasit ʔilpu:l ma:lak; ma: tigdar tħarrikah] I've blocked your piece; you can't move it. • **2.** to jail, imprison – حِبسوه سَنَة وَطَلّعوه [ħibsawh sana wṭalliʕawh] They locked him up for a year and turned him loose. • **3.** to pen up – إِحبِس الدِّجاج قَبُل ما تظَلِّم [ʔiħbis ʔiddiǰa:ǰ gabul ma: dðallum] Pen the chickens up before it gets dark. • **4.** to jail, lock up

اِنحِبَس [ʔinħibas] *v:* • **1.** pass. of – حِبَس

حَبِس [ħabis] *n:* • **1.** imprisonment, confinement, detention, jailing

مِحبَس [miħbas] *n:* محابِس [mħa:bis] *pl:* • **1.** ring (jewelry)

مَحَيبِس [mħaybis] *n:* • **1.** a game, usually played during the nights of Ramadan, in which one team hides an object in a member's closed fist and the other team must find it

مَحبُوس [maħbu:s] *adj:* • **1.** blocked, restricted – طاولي مَحبُوس [ṭa:wli maħbu:s] a variant of backgammon in which the opponent's pieces are blocked by landing one's pieces on the same file after them. • **2.** مَحابِيس [mħa:bi:s] prisoner, convict

ح ب ش

الحَبَشَة [ʔilħabaša] *n:* • **1.** Abyssinia, Ethiopia

حَبَشِي [ħabaši] *adj:* • **1.** Ethiopian, an Ethiopian

ح ب ل 1

حَبِل [ħabil] *n:* • **1.** rope, line, cord – سِباق جَرّ الحَبِل [siba:q ǰarr ʔilħabil] tug-o-war. شَرَّه عَالحَبِل [šarrah ʕalħabil] He hung him up for all to see (lit., he hung him on the line). الجَّرِيدَة شَرَّت الوَزِير عَالحَبِل. تقُول ياخُذ رَشاوِي [ʔiǰǰari:da šarrat ʔilwazi:r ʕalħabil. dgu:l ya:xuð raša:wi] The newspaper exposed the minister. They say he takes bribes. يِلعَب عَلى حَبلَين [yilʕab ʕala ħablayn] He plays both ends against the middle. حَبل السُّرَّة [ħabl ʔissurra] umbilical cord. • **2.** pl. حِبال [ħiba:l] rope, line, cord

ح ب ل 2

حِبَل [ħibal] *v:* • **1.** to be or become pregnant – حِبلَت بَعَد شَهرَين مِن الزَّواج [ħiblat baʕad šahrayn min ʔizzawa:ǰ] She got pregnant after two months of marriage. طَلَّق مَرتَه لِأَنّ ما تِحبَل [ṭallag martah liʔann ma: tiħbal] He divorced his wife because she can't have kids.

حَبَّل [ħabbal] *v:* • **1.** to make pregnant – بَعَد ما حَبَّلها، اِضطَرّ يِتزَوَّجها [baʕad ma: ħabbalha, ʔiðṭarr yidzawwaǰha] Once he'd made her pregnant, he had to marry her.

حَبَل [ħabal] *n:* • **1.** pregnancy

حبالَة [ħba:la] *n:* • **1.** pregnancy

حِبلَة [ħibla] *adj:* حِبلات [ħibla:t] *pl:* • **1.** pregnant women – نِسوان حِبلات [niswa:n ħibla:t] pregnant women.

حَبلانَة [ħabla:na] *adj:* حَبلانات [ħabla:na:t] *pl:* • **1.** pregnant • **2.** pregnant (woman)

ح ب ن

حُبّانَة [ħubba:na] *n:* حُبّانات [ħubba:na:t] *pl:* • **1.** pottery drinking cup.

ح ب ي

حِبَى [ħiba:] *v:* • **1.** to crawl, creep – الجّاهِل قام يِحبِي [ʔiǰǰa:hil ga:m yiħbi] The baby's started to crawl.

حَبِي [ħaby] *n:* • **1.** crawling

ح ت م

حَتَّم [ħattam] *v:* • **1.** to make necessary, make a duty – مِنُو حَتَّم عَلِيك الرَّوحَة؟ [minu ħattam ʕali:k ʔirrawħa?] Who made it your duty to go? • **2.** to impose – حَتَّم عَلَى أَبُوه يِشتِرِيلَه ساعَة [ħattam ʕala ʔabu:h yištiri:lah sa:ʕa] He insisted that his father buy him a watch.

حَتمِي [ħatmi] *adj:* • **1.** inevitable, irrevocable, unalterable, definite, final, conclusive – الامتِحان النِّهائِي فَدّ شِي حَتمِي [ʔilʔimtiħa:n ʔinniha:ʔi fadd ši ħatmi] The final exam is something unavoidable.

حَتماً [ħatman] *adverbial:* • **1.** decidedly, definitely, certainly, inevitably – حَتماً راح أَرُوح [ħatman ra:ħ ʔaru:ħ] I'm definitely going to go. راح تُمطُر الدِّنيا حَتماً [ra:ħ tumṭur ʔiddinya ħatman] It will certainly rain.

ح ت ي

حَتَّى [ħatta] *conjunction:* • **1.** until, till, up to, as far as – بقَينا نِسبَح حَتَّى السّاعَة خَمسَة [bqayna nisbaħ ħatta ʔissa:ʕa xamsa] We kept swimming until five o'clock. بُقَى بِالباص حَتَّى آخِر مَوقِف [buqa: bilpa:ṣ ħatta ʔa:xir mawqif] He stayed on the bus until the last stop. ما طِلَع حَتَّى شافهُم كُلّهُم [ma: ṭilaʕ ħatta ša:fhum kullhum] He didn't leave until he saw them all. • **2.** (conj.) in order to, so that – لازِم نرُوح عالوَقِت حَتَّى نَلحِّق بِالقِطار [la:zim nru:ħ ʕalwakit ħatta nlaħħig bilqiṭa:r] We've got to go early in order to catch the train. إحكِيلَه كُلّ القُصَّة حَتَّى يِفهَم شدَ يصِير بِالدّائِرَة [ʔiħči:lah kull ʔilquṣṣa ħatta yifham šdayṣi:r bidda:ʔira] Tell him the whole story so that he'll know what's going on in the office. بَعَد ما شِفتَه الطَّبِيب حَتَّى أَقُلَّه عَليها [baʕad ma: šiftah ʔiṭṭabi:b ħatta ʔagullah ʕali:ha] I still haven't seen the doctor to tell him about it. لازِم تِنطِينِي فلُوس كافيَة حَتَّى أَقدَر أَسافِر [la:zim tiṭi:ni flu:s ka:fya ħatta ʔagdar ʔasa:fir] You'll have to give me enough money so I'll be able to travel. • **3.** even – بِالبَيت عِدنا كُلّشِي، حَتَّى تَلَفزيَون [bilbayt ʕidna kullši, ħatta talafizyu:n] We've got everything in the house, even a television. ما يِفشِي بأي سِرّ حَتَّى لَو تبُسطَه [ma: yifši bʔay sirr ħatta law tbusṭah] He won't reveal any secret even if you beat him. حَتَّى وَلا [ħatta wala] not even, never even. حَتَّى وَلا حِكَى وِيّايا [ħatta wala ħiča: wiyya:ya] He didn't even talk to me. حَتَّى وَلا يِسأَل سُؤال [ħatta wala yisʔal suʔa:l] He never even asks a single question.

ح ث ث

حَثّ [ħaθθ] *v:* • **1.** to urge, encourage, prod – حِثّ أَخُوك عَالدِّراسَة تَرَة يِسقُط [ħiθθ ʔaxu:k ʕaddira:sa tara yisquṭ] Urge your brother on to study or he's going to fail.

حَثّ [ħaθθ] *n:* • **1.** encouragement

ح ج ب

حِجَب [ħijab] *v:* • **1.** to veil, cover, screen, shelter, seclude – لازِم نعَلِّي الحايِط حَتَّى يِحجِب الحَدِيقَة عَن الشّارِع [la:zim nʕalli ʔilħa:yiṭ ħatta yiħǰib ʔilħadi:qa ʕan ʔiššа:riʕ] We've got to raise the wall so it'll screen the garden from the street. • **2.** to hide, obscure, conceal, block off – هَالشِّجرَة دَتِحجِب عَنّا المَنظَر [haššiǰra datiħǰib ʕannah ʔilmanðar] This tree is obscuring the view for us. لا تِبنِي الحايِط عالِي تَرَة يِحجِب الشَّمِس عَن الحَدِيقَة [la: tibni ʔilħa:yiṭ ʕa:li tara yiħǰib ʔiššamis ʕan ʔilħadi:qa] Don't build the wall too high or it'll block the sun from the garden.

تحَجَّب [tħaǰǰab] *v:* • **1.** to put on a veil, to wear a veil – بِنتَه سافِرَة بَسّ مَرتَه تِتحَجَّب [bintah sa:fira bass martah titħaǰǰab] His daughter is unveiled but his wife wears a veil.

حَجِب [ħaǰib] *n:* • **1.** withholding, veiling, screening off

حِجاب [ħiǰa:b] *n:* • **1.** (woman's) veil • **2.** diaphragm – الحِجاب الحاجِز [ʔilħiǰa:b ʔilħa:ǰiz] the diaphragm (anat.).

حاجِب [ħa:ǰib] *n:* حَواجِب [ħawa:ǰib] *pl:* • **1.** eyebrow

مُحَجَّب [muħaǰǰab] *adj:* • **1.** veiled, obscured, screened – مَرَة مُحَجَّبَة [mara muħaǰǰaba] a woman who goes veiled.

ح ج ج

حَجّ [ħaǰǰ] *v:* • **1.** to make the pilgrimage (to Mecca) – حَجّ بَيت الله [ħaǰǰ bayt ʔallah] He made a pilgrimage to Mecca.

حاجَج [ħa:ǰaǰ] *v:* • **1.** to dispute with, argue with – سَوِّيها مِثلما قِتلَك؛ لا تحاجِجنِي [sawwi:ha miθilma gitlak; la: tħa:ǰiǰni] Do it the way I told you; don't give me an argument.

تحَجَّج [tħaǰǰaǰ] *v:* • **1.** to make excuses, to find an excuse – بَسّ تِطلُب مِنَّه شِي، يقُوم يِتحَجَّج [bass titlub minnah ši, ygu:m yitħaǰǰaǰ] Just ask him for something, and he begins to make excuses. لا تِتحَجَّج بتَعبَك [la: titħaǰǰaǰ btaʕbak] Don't use your tiredness as an excuse.

تحاجَج [tħa:ǰaǰ] *v:* • **1.** to debate, carry on an argument – يِتحاجَج ويّا المُعَلِّم [yitħa:ǰaǰ wiyya ʔilmuʕallim] He argues with the teacher.

اِحتَجّ [ʔiħtaǰǰ] *v:* • **1.** to protest, object – كُلّ ما نسَوِّي، يِحتَجّ [kull ma: nsawwi:, yiħtaǰǰ] Whatever we do, he objects. راح أرُوح لسَفارَتنا أحتَجّ [ra:ħ ʔaru:ħ lsafa:ratna ʔaħtaǰǰ] I'm going to our embassy to protest. اِحتَجّ عِند المُدِير [ʔiħtaǰǰ ʕind ʔilmudi:r] He protested to the director. اِحتَجّ عَلَى مُعامَلَة الشُّرطَة إلَه [ʔiħtaǰǰ ʕala muʕa:malat ʔiššurṭa ʔilah] He protested about the treatment he got from the police.

حَجّ [ħaǰǰ] *n:* • **1.** pilgrimage

حِجَّة، ذُو الحِجَّة [ħiǰǰa, ðu ʔilħiǰǰa] *n:* • **1.** the twelfth month of the Moslem calendar

حِجَّة [ħiǰǰa] *n:* حِجَات، حِجَج [ħiǰǰa:t, ħiǰaǰ] *pl:* • **1.** excuse, pretext – بِحِجَّة مَرِيض ما جا لِلشُّغُل تلَث إيام [bħiǰǰat mari:ð ma: ǰa: liššuɣul tlaθʔiya:m] On the pretense of being sick, he didn't come to work for three days. طَلَّع حِجَّة حَتَّى ما يرُوح [ṭallaʕ ħiǰǰa ħatta ma: yiru:ħ] He made up an excuse not to go. • **2.** a pilgrimage to Mecca • **3.** deed, title (to real property)

حُجَّة [ħuǰǰa] *n:* حُجَج [ħuǰaǰ] *pl:* • **1.** authoritative source, competent authority

حَجِّي [ħaǰǰi] *n:* حِجاج [ħiǰǰa:ǰ] *pl:* • **1.** person who has made the pilgrimage, pilgrim

حاجّ [ħa:ǰǰ] *n:* • **1.** pilgrim

تَحاجُج [taħa:ǰuǰ] *n:* • **1.** arguing with some one, argumentation

اِحتِجاج [ʔiħtiǰa:ǰ] *n:* • **1.** protest, objection, exception

مُحاجَجَة [muħa:ǰaǰa] *n:* • **1.** argumentation

مُحتَجّ [muħtaǰǰ] *n:* • **1.** protester, demonstrator, objector

ح ج ر 1

حِجَر [ħiǰar] *v:* • **1.** to quarantine

اِنحِجَر [ʔinħiǰar] *v:* • **1.** to deny access, detain, lock into a room

حَجِر، حَجِر صِحِّي [ħaǰir, ħaǰir ṣiħħi] *n:* • **1.** quarantine

حِجِر [ħiǰir] *n:* • **1.** lap

حُجرَة [ħuǰra] *n:* حُجَر [ħuǰar] *pl:* • **1.** room • **2.** an office stall in an old building • **3.** stall in an automobile repair shop rented by a specialist such as a body and fender man

مَحجَر صِحِّي [maħǰar ṣiħħi] *n:* مَحاجِر صِحِّيَّة [maħa:ǰir ṣiħħiyya] *pl:* • **1.** quarantine station • **2.** sanatorium for communicable diseases

ح ج ر 2

حَجَّر [ħaǰǰar] *v:* • **1.** to turn to stone, petrify, harden (fig.) قَلبَه حَجَّر مِن كُثرَة ما شاف قَتِل بِالحَرُب [galbah ħaǰǰar min kuθrat ma: ša:f qatil bilħarub] He became hard-hearted from seeing so much killing in the war. • **2.** to scrub with pumice – حَجِّر رِجلَك قَبُل ما تِغسِلها بِالصّابُون [ħaǰǰir riǰlak gabul ma: tiɣsilha bişşa:bu:n] Scrub your feet with pumice before you wash them with soap.

تحَجَّر [tħaǰǰar] *v:* • **1.** to be hardened

حَجَرَة [ħaǰara] *n:* حَجَر، حَجَرات [ħaǰar, ħaǰara:t] *pl:* • **1.** stone, rock – الحَجَر الأَساسِي [ʔilħaǰar ʔilʔasa:si] the cornerstone. • **2.** jewel (watchmaking) • **3.** flint (in a lighter) • **4.** pl. حَجَرات pumice stone

حجار [ħiǰa:r] *n:* • **1.** (coll.) rock(s), stone(s)

مَحجَر [maħǰar] *n:* مَحاجِر [maħa:ǰir] *pl:* • **1.** (stone) quarry

حجارَة [ħǰa:ra] *n:* حجارات، حِجار [ħǰa:ra:t, ħiǰa:r] *pl:* • **1.** rock, stone

حجَيرَة [ħǰayra] *n:* • **1.** cell • **1.** small room

حَجَرِي [ħaǰari] *adj:* • **1.** stony, stone – العَصر الحَجَرِي [ʔilʕaṣr ʔilħaǰari] the Stone Age.

متحَجِّر [mitħaǰǰir] *adj:* • **1.** petrified, hardened (fig.) – قَلبَه متحَجِّر. مَنظَر القَتِل ما يأَثِّر عَليه [galbah mitħaǰǰir. manðar ʔilqatil ma: yaʔaθθir ʕali:h] He's hard-hearted.

The sight of killing doesn't affect him. هَذا دَماغَه مِتحَجِّر [haːða damaːɣah mitħajjir] That guy's thickheaded.

ح ج ز

حَجَز [ħijaz] *v:* • **1.** to separate – ماكُو شِي يِحجِز حَدِيقَتنا مِن حَدِيقَتهُم [maːku ši yiħjiz ħadiːqatna min ħadiːqathum] There's nothing separating our garden from their garden. • **2.** to seize, confiscate – الحُكُومَة حِجزَت عَلَى كُلّ أَموالَه [ʔilħukuːma ħijzat ʕala kull ʔamwaːlah] The government seized all his property. الحُكُومَة حِجزَت البَيت مالَه [ʔilħukuːma ħijzat ʔilbayt maːlah] The government seized his house. • **3.** to reserve – إحجِزلِي غُرفَة بِنَفس أُوتيلَك [ʔiħjizli ɣurfa bnafis ʔutiːlak] Reserve me a room in the same hotel you're in. • **4.** to make a reservation – حِجَزِت اليُوم بِالطَّيّارَة [ħijazit ʔilyuːm biṭṭiyyaːra] I made a reservation today on the plane.

حاجَز [ħaːjaz] *v:* • **1.** to separate, come between – شُوف واحِد دَيمَوِّت اللّاخ! حاجِزهُم [šuːf waːħid daymawwit ʔillaːx! ħaːjizhum] Look, one of them's killing the other! Separate them. خَلِّيهُم يِتعارِكُون. لا تحاجِز بينهُم [xalliːhum yitʕaːrkuːn. laː tħaːjiz biːnhum] Let them fight. Don't separate them.

اِنحِجَز [ʔinħijaz] *v:* • **1.** to be detained, seized, confiscated

حَجِز [ħajiz] *n:* • **1.** separation • **2.** seizure, confiscation • **3.** reservation • **4.** detaining, booking

حِجاز [ħijaːz] *n:* • **1.** Hijaz, or, by extension, Saudi Arabia

حاجِز [ħaːjiz] *n:* حَواجِز [ħawaːjiz] *pl:* • **1.** divider • **2.** partition, dividing wall, screen – الحِجاب الحاجِز [ʔilħijaːb ʔilħaːjiz] the diaphragm. • **3.** pl. حَواجِز dividers

اِحتِجاز [ʔiħtijaːz] *n:* • **1.** detention

حِجازِي [ħijaːzi] *adj:* • **1.** from Hijaz, or, by extension, from Saudi Arabia • **2.** person from Hijaz or from Saudi Arabia

مَحجُوز [maħjuːz] *adj:* • **1.** held under arrest, detained

مُحتَجَز [muħtajaz] *adj:* • **1.** held under arrest, (as n:) hostage, detainee

ح ج ل

حِجِل [ħijil] *n:* حجُول [ħjuːl] *pl:* • **1.** (pair of) anklets

حَجلَة [ħajla] *n:* حَجلات [ħajlaːt] *pl:* • **1.** a small stand with wheels for teaching children to walk

مَحَجَّل [mħajjal] *adj:* • **1.** wearing anklets – مَرَة مَحَجَّلَة [mara mħajjala] ankleted woman. طَير محَجَّل [ṭiːr mħajjal] pigeon with feathers covering its feet. • **2.** white-footed, white-ankled – حصان محَجَّل [ħṣaːn mħajjal] white-ankled horse.

ح ج م

حَجَم [ħijam] *v:* • **1.** to cup, subject to blood-letting – اليُوم حِجمُوه واخذُوا دَمّ هوايَة مِنَّه [ʔilyuːm ħijmawh wʔaxðaw damm hwaːya minnah] Today they cupped him and took a lot of blood. هُوَّ حِجَم مَرّتَين هَالشَّهَر [huwwa ħijam marrtayn haššahar] He was bled twice this month.

حَجِم [ħajim] *n:* حُجُوم، أَحجام [ħujuːm, ʔaħjaːm] *pl:* • **1.** volume of a tank – حَجِم الرّاديُو كِبِير [ħajim ʔirraːdyu čibiːr] The radio's too large a size. حَجِم تانكِي [ħajim taːnki] volume of a tank.

حَجّام [ħajjaːm] *n:* حَجّامَة [ħajjaːma] *pl:* • **1.** blood-letter, cupper

حِجامَة [ħijaːma] *n:* • **1.** cupping, blood-letting

ح خ م

حاخام [ħaːxaːm] *n:* حاخامِيَّة [ħaːxaːmiyya] *pl:* • **1.** rabbi

ح د ب

حَدَّب [ħaddab] *v:* • **1.** to stoop, hunch the back – هَالشّايِب يحَدِّب مِن يِمشِي [haššaːyib yħaddib min yimši] That old man hunches his back when he walks.

تحَدَّب [tħaddab] *v:* • **1.** to become hunched – ظَهرَه تحَدَّب مِن صار عُمرَه سِتِّين [ðahrah tħaddab min ṣaːr ʕumrah sittiːn] His back became hunched by the time he was sixty.

حِدبَة [ħidba] *adj:* حِدبات، حِدَب [ħidbaːt, ħidab] *pl:* • **1.** hump on the back

أَحدَب [ʔaħdab] *adj:* حِدِب، حَدبِين [ħidib, ħadbiːn] *pl:* حَدبَة [ħadba] *feminine:* • **1.** hunch-backed • **2.** (as n:) a hunch-back

محَدِّب [mħaddib] *adj:* • **1.** hunched up • **2.** convex, arched

محَودِب [mħawdib] *adj:* • **1.** hunched up • **2.** convex, arched

ح د ث

حِدَث [ħidaθ] *v:* • **1.** to happen, occur, take place – الحادِثَة وِين حِدثَت؟ [ʔilħaːdiθa wiːn ħidθat?] Where did the accident occur?

أَحدَث [ʔaħdaθ] *v:* • **1.** to found, establish – أَحدِثَوا شُعبَة جِدِيدَة بِالدّائِرَة [ʔaħdiθaw šuʕba jidiːda biddaːʔira] They set up a new section in the office.

تحَدَّث [tħaddaθ] *v:* • **1.** to speak, talk – راح يِتحَدَّث عَن الأُمَم المُتَّحِدَة [raːħ yitħaddaθ ʕan ʔilʔumam ʔilmuttaħida] He'll speak about the U. N.

حَدَث [ħadaθ] *n:* أَحداث [ʔaħdaːθ] *pl:* • **1.** event

حادِث، حادِثَة [ħaːdiθ, ħaːdiθa] *n:* حَوادِث [ħawaːdiθ] *pl:* • **1.** occurrence, event, incident, happening – حادِث وَفاة [ħaːdiθ wafaːt] a death. حادِث قَتِل [ħaːdiθ qatil] a killing. حادِث دَعِس [ħaːdiθ daʕis] pedestrian accident. • **2.** accident, mishap

حُدُوث [ħuduːθ] *n:* • **1.** occurrence, happening

حَداثَة [ħadaːθa] *n:* • **1.** newness, recency, novelty

تَحدِيث [taħdiːθ] *n:* • **1.** updating, renewing

مُحادَثَة [muħaːdaθa] *n:* مُحادَثات [muħaːdaθaːt] *pl:* • **1.** conversation, discussion, talk, parley – دَرِس مُحادَثَة [daris muħaːdaθa] conversation class.

إحداثِيَّة [ʔiħda:θiyya] *n:* إحداثِيّات [ʔiħda:θiyya:t] *pl:* • **1.** coordinates
إستِحداث [ʔistiħda:θ] *n:* • **1.** invention, creation
حَدِيث [ħadi:θ] *adj:* • **1.** modern, up to date – أجهزَة حَدِيثَة [ʔajhiza ħadi:θa] modern equipment. مَكاين حَدِيثَة [maka:yin ħadi:θa] modern machinery. • **2.** pl. أحادِيث [ʔaħa:di:θ] talk, address, speech • **3.** prophetic tradition, Hadith, the deeds and sayings of the Prophet
مُتَحَدِّث [mutaħaddiθ] *adj:* • **1.** speaking (باِسم on behalf of)
مُستَحدَث [mustaħadθ] *adj:* • **1.** newly made, recent
أحدَث [ʔaħdaθ] *comparative adjective:* • **1.** more or most modern, up-to-date

ح د ج

حَدِيجَة [ħadi:ja] *n:* حَدايِج [ħada:yij] *pl:* • **1.** camel saddle

ح د د

حَدّ [ħadd] *v:* • **1.** to sharpen, hone – السِّكِّينَة عَميَة. لازِم تحِدّها [ʔissičči:na ʕamya. la:zim tħiddha] The knife's dull. You'd better sharpen it. البَزّونَة نايمَة جَوَّة القَفَص. يبَيِّن حادَّة سنُونها عَالطِّير [ʔilbazzu:na na:yma ǰawwa ʔilqafaṣ. yibayyin ħa:dda snu:nha ʕaṭṭi:r] The cat's lying under the cage. Looks like she's after the bird. حِشدَوا جِيُوشهُم عالحُدُود. يبَيِّن حادِّين سنُون عَلينا [ħišdaw ǰiyu:šhum ʕalħudu:d. yibayyin ħa:ddi:n snu:n ʕali:na] They've massed their troops on the border. They seem to be ready to pounce on us. المُدِير حادّ سنُونَه عَليك [ʔilmudi:r ħa:dd snu:nah ʕali:k] The director's got it in for you. يِظهَر صَدِيقَك حَدّ سنُونَه عَلَى هَالوَظِيفَة [yiðhar ṣadi:qak ħadd snu:nah ʕala halwaði:fa] It looks like your friend has really worked up an appetite for this job. حِدّ سنُونَك؛ تَرَة هالفُرصَة ما تِحصَل بَعَد [ħidd snu:nak; tara halfurṣa ma: tiħṣal baʕad] Get ready; maybe the chance won't come again. • **2.** to impede, hinder, check, curb – المُطَر راح يحِدّ مِن شِدَّة الحَرّ [ʔilmuṭar ra:ħ yħidd min šiddat ʔilħarr] The rain will reduce the intensity of the heat. • **3.** to border upon, be adjoining – إيران تحِدّ العِراق مِن الشَّرق [ʔira:n tħidd ʔilʕira:q min ʔiššarq] Iran borders Iraq on the east.
حَدَّد [ħaddad] *v:* • **1.** to delimit, demarcate – لَجنَة راح تحَدِّد الحُدُود بين العِراق وَإيران [lajna ra:ħ tħaddid ʔilħudu:d bi:n ʔilʕira:q wʔira:n] A committee's going to demarcate the border between Iraq and Iran. راح يِجِي مُهَندِس يحَدِّد القاع مالتِي [ra:ħ yiǰi muhandis yħaddid ʔilga:ʕ ma:lti] A surveyor's coming to set the boundaries of my land. • **2.** to limit, restrict, confine – الحُكُومَة حَدِّدَت مَساحَة القاع اللِّي لازِم تِنزرِع تِتِن ʔilħuku:ma ħaddidat masa:ħat ʔilga:ʕ ʔilli la:zim tinziriʕ titin] The government limited the amount of land which can be planted in tobacco. شما أسَوِّي بكَيفِي. قابِل ترِيد تحَدِّدنِي؟ [šma: ʔasawwi: bkayfi. qa:bil tri:d tħaddidni?] Whatever I do is my business. Do you mean you want to restrict me? • **3.** to hobble, chain – حَدِّدَوا المَسجُون بزِناجِيل غِلاظ [ħaddidaw ʔilmasǰu:n bizna:ǰi:l ɣla:ð] They hobbled the prisoner with thick chains. • **4.** to set a limit, fix a deadline – حَدَّدلِي إلَى يوم الجُمعَة أرَجِّعلَه الفلُوس [ħaddadli ʔila yu:m ʔiǰǰumʕa ʔaraǰǰiʕlah ʔilflu:s] He gave me until Friday to return the money. حَدَّدلِي الوَقِت اللِّي أخَلِّص الشُّغُل بيه [ħaddadli ʔilwaqit ʔilli ʔaxalliṣ ʔiššuɣul bi:h] He set a deadline for me to finish the work. • **5.** to determine, appoint, assign, schedule, establish, set down – حَدَّدلِي السّاعَة اللِّي أشُوفَه بيها [ħaddadli ʔissa:ʕa ʔilli ʔašu:fah bi:ha] He set the time for me to see him. • **6.** to fix – راتِب المُوَظَّف محَدَّد بالقانُون [ra:ṭib ʔilmuwaððaf mħaddad bilqa:nu:n] The employee's salary is fixed by law.
حادَد [ħa:dad] *v:* • **1.** to border, adjoin – العِراق يحادِد تُركيا مِن الشِّمال [ʔilʕira:q yħa:did turkiya min ʔiššima:l] Iraq borders Turkey in the north.
إحتَدّ [ʔiħtadd] *v:* • **1.** to be or become angry – شدَعوَة تِحتَدّ بالعَجَل؟ [šdaʕwa tiħtadd bilʕaǰal?] Why do you get mad so fast? اِحتَدّ عَلَيّا عَلَى شِي ما يِسوَى [ʔiħtadd ʕalayya ʕala ši ma: yiswa:] He got mad at me over a trifle.
اِنحَدّ [ʔinħadd] *v:* • **1.** to be sharpened, honed • **2.** to be bordered
حَدّ [ħadd] *n:* حُدُود [ħudu:d] *pl:* • **1.** border, boundary, borderline – حُدُود البَلَد طُولها ميتَين مِيل [ħidu:d ʔilbalad ṭu:lha mitayn mi:l] The borders of the country are two hundred miles long. • **2.** limit, end – طَمَعَه ما إلَه حَدّ [ṭamaʕah ma: ʔilah ħadd] His greed has no limit. هَذا حَدَّك. إذا تقُول كِلمَة لُخ، أدُمرَك [ha:ða ħaddak. ʔiða dgu:l čilma lux, ʔadumrak] That's enough from you. If you say one more word, I'll beat you up. وَقَّفتَه عِند حَدَّه، لأنّ ثَخّنها [waggaftah ʕind ħaddah, liʔann θaxxanha] I stopped him right there, because he went too far. شحَدِّي أعترِض! يفَصُلنِي بالعَجَل [šħaddi ʔaʕtirið! yufṣulni bilʕaǰal] I don't dare object! He would fire me right away. شحَدَّه يطُبّ! الكَلِب يعَضَّه [šħaddah yṭubb! ʔiččalib yʕaððah] He wouldn't dare go in! The dog would bite him. • **3.** extent, degree, point – هُوَّ بَخِيل إلَى حَدّ عَجِيب [huwwa baxi:l ʔila ħadd ʕaǰi:b] He's stingy to an extraordinary degree. كان يعتِمِد عَلَيّا إلَى حَدّ كبِير [ča:n yiʕtimid ʕalayya ʔila ħadd čabi:r] He used to depend on me to a large extent. إلَى حَدّ [ʔila ħadd] until, till, up to, to the extent of, to the point of. رِكَض إلَى حَدّ الجِّسِر، وَتِعَب [rikað ʔila ħadd ʔiǰǰisir, waṭaʕab] He ran as far as the bridge and got tired. عراكهُم وُصَل لِحَدّ الضَّرُب [ʕra:khum wuṣal liħadd ʔiððarub] Their fight reached the point of blows. وُصلَت إلَى حَدّ ما ينحِمِل بَعَد [wuṣlat ʔila ħadd ma: yinħimil baʕad] It's reached the point where it's not bearable any more. بِذَل جُهدَه إلَى أقصى حَدّ لمُساعَدتِي [biðal ǰuhdah ʔila ʔaqṣa: ħadd lmusa:ʕadti] He exerted his efforts to the utmost extent in helping me. إلَى حَدّ الآن

[ʔila ħadd ʔilʔaːn] till now, up to now. لِحَدّ الآن، ما جا [liħadd ʔilʔaːn, maː ǰaː] Up to now, he hasn't come. إلَى حَدّ ما [ʔila ħadd maː] to the point that. لَحّ عَلَيّا إلَى حَدّ ما ضَوَّجني [laħħ ʕalayya ʔila ħadd maː ðawwaǰni] He kept insisting, to the point where he irritated me. بحَدّ ذاتَه [bħadd ðaːtah] by itself, in itself, as such. الرَّقِّي بحَدّ ذاتَه مُدَرِّر [ʔirraggi bħadd ðaːtah mudarrir] Watermelon by itself is a diuretic. • **4.** sharpening, whetting

حِدَّة [ħidda] *n:* • **1.** sharpness, intensity, severity • **2.** rage, fury, anger

حِداد [ħidaːd] *n:* • **1.** mourning – عِلنَوا حِداد عَلَى رَئِيس الوُزَراء [ʕilnaw ħidaːd ʕala raʔiːs ʔilwuzaraːʔ] They declared (a period of) mourning for the prime minister. لابِس أسوَد حِداداً عَلَى مَرتَه [laːbis ʔaswad ħidaːdan ʕala martah] He's wearing black in mourning for his wife.

حَدِيد [ħadiːd] *n:* • **1.** iron – حَدِيد الخام [ħadiːd ʔilxaːm] crude iron, pig iron. • **2.** (loosely) steel, or any metal – أعصاب مِن حَدِيد [ʔaʕṣaːb min ħadiːd] nerves of steel. سِكَّة حَدِيد [siččat ħadiːd] railroad, railroad tracks.

حَدِيدَة [ħadiːda] *n:* حَدايِد [ħadaːyid] *pl:* • **1.** piece of iron

حِدادَة [ħdaːda] *n:* • **1.** blacksmithing, trade of smithing

تَحدِيد [taħdiːd] *n:* • **1.** demarcation – تَحدِيد الحُدُود [taħdiːd ʔilħuduːd] demarcation of the border. • **2.** restriction – تَحدِيد الأسعار [taħdiːd ʔilʔasʕaːr] price restriction. • **3.** specifically – بِالتَّحدِيد [bittaħdiːd] المُدِير عَيَّن إسمَك بِالتَّحدِيد [ʔilmudiːr ʕayyan ʔismak bittaħdiːd] The director selected your name specifically. ما أعرُف مِنُو هُمَّ بِالتَّحدِيد [maː ʔaʕruf minu humma bittaħdiːd] I don't know who they are specifically.

مِستَحَدّ [mistaħadd] *n:* مِستَحَدّات [mistaħaddaːt] *pl:* • **1.** whetstone, sharpening stone

حادّ [ħaːdd] *adj:* • **1.** sharpened, sharp, keen – سِچِّينَة حادَّة [siččiːna ħaːdda] a sharp knife. زاوِيَة حادَّة [zaːwiya ħaːdda] acute angle. • **2.** acute, severe, intense – اِلتِهاب حادّ [ʔiltihaːb ħaːdd] acute inflammation. • **3.** fiery, vehement, impetuous – طَبعَه حادّ. يِزعَل بِالعَجَل [ṭabʕah ħaːdd. yizʕal bilʕaǰal] He has a fiery nature. he gets mad easily.

حَدّاد [ħaddaːd] *adj:* حَدّادِين [ħaddaːdiːn] *pl:* • **1.** blacksmith

مُحَدَّد [muħaddad] *adj:* • **1.** set, determined, defined

مِحتَدّ [miħtadd] *adj:* • **1.** angry, furious, exasperated

حَدِيدِي [ħadiːdi] *adj:* • **1.** iron, made of iron or, loosely, of any metal – عَضَلات حَدِيدِيَّة [ʕaðalaːt ħadiːdiyya] iron muscles.

مَحدُود [maħduːd] *adj:* • **1.** limited, delimited, restricted, fixed – كَمِّيَّة مَحدُودَة [kammiyya maħduːda] a limited number, a small number. لازِم تشُوف المُدِير. آنِي سُلُطتِي مَحدُودَة [laːzim tšuːf ʔilmudiːr. ʔaːni suluṭti maħduːda] You'll have to see the director. My powers are limited. شَرِكَة مَحدُودَة [šarika maħduːda] a limited company, a corporation.

حِدُودِي [ħiduːdi] *adj:* • **1.** relating to frontiers or borders

أحَدّ [ʔaħadd] *comparative adjective:* • **1.** sharper, sharpest • **2.** more or most intense, severe • **3.** more or most vehement, impetuous

ح د ر

حِدَر [ħidar] *v:* • **1.** to wash away, sweep away, carry downstream – المَيّ حِدَر البَلَم [ʔilmayy ħidar ʔilbalam] The current carried the boat downstream.

اِنحِدَر [ʔinħidar] *v:* • **1.** to be washed away, be swept away, carried downstream – البَلَم اِنقِطَع وَانحِدَر وِيّا المَيّ [ʔilbalam ʔingiṭaʕ wʔinħidar wiyya ʔilmayy] The boat got free and was washed away with the current.

حَدِر [ħadir] *n:* • **1.** descent, slant, slope, inclination

حَدرَة [ħadra] *n:* • **1.** slide

حِدرِيَّة [ħidriyya] *n:* حَدارِي [ħadaːri] *pl:* • **1.** skull cap

مُنحَدَر [munħadar] *n:* • **1.** sloping ground, incline, descent, declivity

اِنحِدار [ʔinħidaːr] *n:* • **1.** slant, dip, pitch, descent, slope اِنحِدار قَوِي [ʔinħidaːr qawi] steep slope, steep incline, steep pitch. • **2.** fall – اِنهِدار النَّهَر [ʔinhidaːr ʔinnahar] the fall of the river.

حَدّار [ħaddaːr] *adj:* • **1.** fast, swirling – لا تِسبَح هنا؛ المَيّ حَدّار [laː tisbaħ hna; ʔilmayy ħaddaːr] Don't swim here; the current's fast.

مِنحِدِر [minħadir, minħidir] *adj:* • **1.** slanting, sloping – قاع مِنحَدرَة [gaːʕ minħadra] sloping land.

ح د ق 1

حَدَقَة [ħadaqa] *n:* حَدَقات، أحداق [ħadaqaːt, ʔaħdaːq] *pl:* • **1.** pupil (of the eye)

ح د ق 2

حَدِيقَة [ħadiːqa] *n:* حَدايِق [ħadaːyiq] *pl:* • **1.** garden • **2.** public park – حَدِيقَة حَيوانات [ħadiːqat ħaywaːnaːt] zoo.

ح د ق د ق

حِدِقدِقَة [ħidigdiga] *n:* حِدِقدِقات [ħidigdigaːt] *pl:* • **1.** sty (med.)

ح د و 1

حِدَى [ħidaː] *v:* • **1.** to sing or chant to camels, to urge them on – حِدَى لِلجِمال مِن بِدَت تِتعَب [ħidaː liǰǰimaːl min bidat titʕab] He sang at the camels when they began to tire.

تحَدَّى [tħaddaː] *v:* • **1.** to challenge – أتحَدّاك أن تِلعَب شِطرَنج [ʔatħaddaːk ʔan tilʕab šiṭranǰ] I challenge you to play chess with me. • **2.** to defy, oppose, resist لا تِتحَدَّى سُلطَة المُدِير [laː tithaddaː sulṭat ʔilmudiːr] Don't defy the director's authority.

حَادِي [ħaːdi] *n:* • **1.** camel driver, cameleer
حَدِي [ħady] *n:* singing to urge on camels.
تَحَدِّي [taħaddi] *n:* • **1.** challenge
مُتَحَدِّي [mutaħaddi] *n:* • **1.** challenger, provoker

ح د و 2

حدَيَّة [ħdayya] *n:* حدَيّات [ħdayyaːt] *pl:* • **1.** kite (zool.)

ح ذ ر

حِذَر [ħiðar] *v:* • **1.** to be cautious, beware, be on guard – إحذَر مِن هَالشَّخِص [ʔiħðar min haššaxiṣ] Watch out for that guy.
حَذَّر [ħaððar] *v:* • **1.** to warn, caution, put on guard – ما حَذَّرتِك مِن الطَّلعَة باللَّيل؟ [maː ħaððartič min ʔiṭṭalʕa billayl?] Didn't I warn you about going out at night?
تحَذَّر [tħaððar] *v:* • **1.** to take care, be careful, be wary – تحَذَّر مِن السَّيّارات [tħaððar min ʔissayyaːraːt] Watch out for the cars.
اِحتِذَر [ʔiħtiðar] *v:* • **1.** to be on guard, take care, be cautious – اِحتِذَر مِن المُدِير لِأَنّ سِمَع عَنَّه حَكِي قَبُل [ʔiħtiðar min ʔilmudiːr liʔann simaʕ ʕannah ħači gabul] He was on his guard against the director, since he'd heard talk about him before.
حَذَر [ħaðar] *n:* • **1.** caution, wariness, watchfulness – الجُنُود خَشّوا لِلبَيت بحَذَر [ʔijjunuːd xaššaw lilbayt bħaðar] The soldiers entered the house cautiously.
عَلَى حَذَر [ʕala ħaðar] on guard, alert, watchful.
كُونُوا عَلَى حَذَر. مُمكِن يهجمُون عَلينا هاللَّيلَة [kuːnuː ʕala ħaðar. mumkin yhijmuːn ʕaliːna hallayla] Be on your guard. They may attack us tonight.
تَحذِير [taħðiːr] *n:* • **1.** warning, cautioning
حَذِر [ħaðir] *adj:* • **1.** cautious, wary, careful
مَحذُور [maħðuːr] *adj:* مَحاذِير [maħaːðiːr] *pl:* • **1.** something to beware, something to be careful about • **2.** danger, peril – الله يدِفَع عَنَّك كُلّ مَحذُور [ʔallah yidfaʕ ʕannak kull maʕðuːr] God protect you from any peril.
مِتحَذِّر [mitħaððir] *adj:* • **1.** careful

ح ذ ف

حِذَف [ħiðaf] *v:* • **1.** to delete, cancel, drop, omit, leave out, take away – حِذفَوا إسمَه مِن القائِمَة [ħiðfaw ʔismah min ʔilqaːʔima] They removed his name from the list.
حِذفَوا ألف دِينار مِن مِيزانِيَّة شُعُبتي [ħiðfaw ʔalf dinaːr min miːzaːniyyat šuʕubti] They cut out a thousand dinars from my section's budget.
اِنحِذَف [ʔinħiðaf] *v:* • **1.** to be canceled, deleted, dropped
حَذِف [ħaðif] *n:* • **1.** removal, dropping
حِذّاف [ħiððaːf] *n:* • **1.** a variety of wild bird
مَحذُوف [maħðuːf] *adj:* • **1.** dropped, canceled, crossed

ح ذ ف ر

حَذافِير، بِحَذافِيرَه [ħaðaːfiːr, biħaðaːfiːrah] *n:* • **1.** in its entirety – حِكالِي الحَقِيقَة بِحَذافِيرها [ħičaːli ʔilħaqiːqa bħaðaːfiːrha] He told me the truth in its entirety.

ح ذ و

حاذَى [ħaːðaː] *v:* • **1.** to parallel, run parallel to – الطَّرِيق يحاذِي النَّهَر لِمَسافَة مِيل [ʔiṭṭariːq yħaːði ʔinnahar limasaːfat miːl] The road parallels the river for a mile.
حِذاء [ħiðaːʔ] *n:* أَحذِيَة [ʔaħðiya] *pl:* • **1.** shoe – مَعمَل أَحذِيَة [maʕmal ʔaħðiya] shoe factory.
بِمُحاذاة [bmuħaːðaːt] *n:* • **1.** along, alongside of, parallel to – خَلِّي نِمشِي بمُحاذاة الشَّطّ [xalliː nimši bmuħaːðaːt ʔiššaṭṭ] Let's walk along the river.
مُحاذِي [muħaːði] *adj:* • **1.** next to, along – النَّهَر مُحاذِي لِلسِّكَّة [ʔinnahar muħaːði lissičča] The river's next to the tracks.

ح ر ب

حارَب [ħaːrab] *v:* • **1.** to fight, combat, battle – جَيشنا دَيحارُب بِجَبهتَين [jayšna dayħaːrub bjabihtayn] Our army's fighting on two fronts – راح نحارُب الأعداء لِلمُوت [raːħ nħaːrub ʔilʔaʕdaːʔ lilmuːt] We'll battle the enemy to the death.
جَمعِيَّتنا تحارُب القُمار [jamʕiyyatna tħaːrub ʔalqumaːr] Our association is combatting gambling.
كُلّ المُوَظَّفِين دَيحاربُونِي لِأَنّ آنِي الوَحِيد عِندِي شَهادَة عالِيَة [kull ʔilmuwaððafiːn dayħaːrbuːni liʔann ʔaːni ʔilwaħiːd ʕindi šahaːda ʕaːlya] All the other employees are giving me a hard time because I'm the only one with an advanced degree.
تحارَب [tħaːrab] *v:* • **1.** to fight (each other), be engaged in war – تحارَبنا ويّا هَالدَّولَة لِمُدَّة سِتّ أَشهُر [tħaːrabna wiyya haddawla limuddat sitt ʔašhur] We fought with that nation for a period of six months.
حَرُب [ħarub] *n:* حُرُوب [ħuruːb] *pl:* • **1.** war, warfare • **2.** fight, battle, combat
حَربَة [ħarba] *n:* حِراب [ħiraːb] *pl:* • **1.** bayonet
حراب [ħraːb] *n:* حرابات [ħraːbaːt] *pl:* • **1.** rock fight, a fight with slings • **2.** knife (used as a weapon)
حَرباء [ħarbaːʔ] *n:* حَرابِي [ħaraːbi] *pl:* • **1.** chameleon
مِحراب [miħraːb] *n:* مَحارِيب [maħaːriːb] *pl:* • **1.** recess in a mosque indicating the direction of prayer • **1.** mihrab, prayer niche
مُحارِب [muħaːrib] *n:* مُحارِبِين [muħaːribiːn] *pl:* • **1.** fighter • **2.** belligerent
حَربِي [ħarbi] *adj:* • **1.** war, military, martial – الكُلِّيَّة الحَربِيَّة [ʔilkulliyya ʔilħarbiyya] the military academy.
مِتحارُب [mitħaːrub] *adj:* • **1.** belligerent

ح ر ث

حِرَث [ħiraθ] *v:* • **1.** to plow, plow up – راح يحِرثُون القاع ويزرَعُوها حُنطَة [raːħ yħirθuːn ʔilgaːʕ wyizraʕuːha ħunṭa] They'll plow up the land and plant it in wheat.

حَرِث [ħariθ] *n:* • **1.** cultivation
مِحراث [miħraːθ] *n:* مَحارِيث [maħaːriːθ] *pl:* • **1.** plow
حِراثَة [ħiraːθa] *n:* • **1.** tillage

ح ر ج

حِرَج [ħiraǰ] *v:* • **1.** to embarrass, to put (someone) on the spot, to put in a tight spot – لِيش حِرَجِتنِي قِدّام مَرتِي؟ [liːš ħiraǰitni giddaːm marti?] Why did you put me on the spot in front of my wife?
حَرَّج [ħarraǰ] *v:* • **1.** to be persistent – حَرَّج عَلَى أَبُوه يِشتِرِيلَه بايسِكِل [ħarraǰ ʕala ʔabuːh yištiriːlah paːysikil] He insisted that his father buy him a bicycle.
أحرَج [ʔaħraǰ] *v:* • **1.** to embarrass
اِنحِرَج [ʔinħiraǰ] *v:* • **1.** pass. of حِرَج to be embarrassed – مِن سِألنِي السُّؤال، اِنحِرَجِت وَما عِرَفِت شأجاوُب [min siʔalni ʔissuʔaːl, ʔinħiraǰit wama ʕirafit šʔaǰaːwub] When he asked me the question, I was embarrassed and didn't know what to answer. اِنحِرَج وَاِضطَرّ يِدفَع المَبلَغ [ʔinħiraǰ wʔiðṭarr yidfaʕ ʔilmablaɣ] He got put on the spot and was forced to pay the sum.
إحراج [ʔiħraːǰ] *n:* • **1.** embarassment
حَرِج [ħariǰ] *adj:* • **1.** difficult, embarrassing – خَلّانِي بوَضِع حَرِج [xallaːni bwaðiʕ ħariǰ] He put me in a bind. • **2.** critical – الحالَة بالبَلدَة حَرجَة [ʔilħaːla bilbalda ħarǰa] The situation in the city is critical.
مُحرِج [muħriǰ] *adj:* • **1.** embarrassing

ح ر ح ر

حِرحارَة [ħirħaːra] *n:* حِرحارات [ħirħaːraːt] *pl:* • **1.** palm of the hand

ح ر ر

حَرَّر [ħarrar] *v:* • **1.** to liberate, free – راح أحَرِّر الوَطَن [raːħ ʔaħarrir ʔilwaṭan] I'm going to free the country. • **2.** to edit – مِنُو يحَرِّر هَالجَّرِيدَة؟ [minu yħarrir hajǰariːda?] Who edits this newspaper?
تحَرَّر [tħarrar] *v:* • **1.** to be freed – العَبِيد تحَرِّرَوا مِن زَمان [ʔilʕabiːd tħarriraw min zamaːn] The slaves were freed long ago.
اِحتَرّ [ʔiħtarr] *v:* • **1.** to be or become heated, hot – اِحتَرَّيت. بالله ما تفُكّ الشِّبّاك؟ [ʔiħtarrayt. ballah maː tfukk ʔiššibbaːč?] I'm hot. Would you please open the window?
حُرِّيَّة [ħurriyya] *n:* حُرِّيّات [ħurriyyaːt] *pl:* • **1.** freedom, liberty • **2.** independence
حَرِير [ħariːr] *n:* • **1.** silk
مُحَرِّر [muħarrir] *n:* مُحَرِّرِين [muħarririːn] *pl:* • **1.** liberator, emancipator • **2.** editor
حَرِيرَة [ħariːra] *n:* • **1.** a pudding of starch and sugar, served hot
حَرارَة [ħaraːra] *n:* • **1.** heat • **2.** warmth (also of emotions) • **3.** temperature دَرَجَة الحَرارَة [daraǰat ʔilħaraːra] What is the temperature. • **4.** fever blister, cold sore
مِحرار [miħraːr] *n:* مَحارِير [maħaːriːr] *pl:* • **1.** thermometer
تَحرِير [taħriːr] *n:* • **1.** liberation, emancipation • **2.** editing مُدِير التَّحرِير [mudiːr ʔittaħriːr] editor-in-chief.
حرُورَة [ħruːra] *n:* • **1.** heat, fever
حُرّ [ħurr] *adj:* أحرار [ʔaħraːr] *pl:* • **1.** pure, unadulterated دِهِن حُرّ [dihin ħurr] clarified butter. • **2.** free صَحافَة حُرَّة [ṣaħaːfa ħurra] free press. • **3.** liberal (pol.) تَفكِير حُرّ [tafkiːr ħurr] liberal thinking. • **4.** a liberal حِزب الأحرار [ħizb ʔilʔaħraːr] the Liberal Party (lit. party of the free)
حُرِّي، طِين حُرِّي [ħurri, ṭiːn ħurri] *adj:* • **1.** a type of red alluvial clay
حارّ [ħaːrr] *adj:* • **1.** hot نَهار حارّ [nahaːr ħaːrr] a hot day. راسَه حارّ [raːsah ħaːrr] He's hot-tempered. • **2.** strong, hot, biting تِتِن حارّ [titin ħaːrr] strong tobacco.
محتَرّ [miħtarr] *adj:* • **1.** hot, feeling too warm
متحَرِّر [mitħarrir] *adj:* • **1.** emancipated هَذِي مِتحَرِّرَة بآرائها [haːði mitħarrira bʔaːraːʔha] She's emancipated in her opinions. • **2.** liberal-minded, liberal المَلِك الجِّدِيد مِتحَرِّر [ʔilmalik ʔiǰǰidiːd mitħarrir] The new king is liberal-minded.
حَرارِي [ħaraːri] *adj:* • **1.** thermal
حَرِيرِي [ħariːri] *adj:* • **1.** silky
تَحرِيرِي [taħriːri] *adj:* • **1.** recorded in writing, written, in writing اِمتِحان تَحرِيرِي [ʔimtiħaːn taħriːri] written examination. بِصُورَة تَحرِيرِيَّة [bṣuːra taħriːriyya] in written form.
أحَرّ [ʔaħarr] *comparative adjective:* • **1.** hotter, hottest

ح ر ز

حِرَز [ħiraz] *v:* • **1.** to stockpile, store up البُصَل هوايَة بالسُّوق. خَلِّي نِحرِز كَم كِيلُو مِنَّه [ʔilbuṣal hwaːya bissuːg. xalliː niħriz čam kiːlu minnah] Onions are plentiful at the market. Let's stock up with a few kilos of them.
أحرَز [ʔaħraz] *v:* • **1.** with عَلَى to achieve, obtain, attain
حِرِز [ħiriz] *n:* • **1.** custody, protection بِحِرِز الرَّحمن [bħirz ʔirraħman] (under the protection of the Merciful) God be with you (said to anyone starting on a journey.) • **2.** pl. حرُوز amulet
حَرِز [ħariz] *n:* • **1.** storing, stockpiling

ح ر س

حِرَس [ħiras] *v:* • **1.** to guard, watch – خمس جنُود يِحرسُون المُخَيَّم كُلّ لَيلَة [xams ǰnuːd yħirsuːn ʔilmuxayyam kull layla] Five soldiers guard the camp each night. المَعمَل ما كان مَحرُوس مِن اِحتِرَق [ʔilmaʕmal maː čaːn maħruːs min ʔiħtirag] The factory wasn't guarded when it caught fire. • **2.** to secure, protect, safeguard, preserve, keep الله يِحرسَك [ʔallah yħirsak]

ح

God preserve you. دِزّ وِيّاهُم سَيّارَة مصَفَّحَة تِحرِسهُم [dizz wiyya:hum sayya:ra mṣaffaħa tiħrishum] Send an armored car along to protect them.
تحَرَّس [tħarras] *v:* • **1.** to beware, be wary, be on guard – تحَرَّس مِنَّه. تَرَة هَذا فَتّان [tħarras minnah. tara ha:ða fatta:n] Be wary of him. He's a talebearer.
اِحترِس [ʔiħtiras] *v:* • **1.** to beware, be wary, be on guard – اِحتِرِس هوايَة تَرَة تاخُذ بَرِد [ʔiħtiris hwa:ya tara ta:xuð barid] Be very careful or you'll catch cold.
حَرَس [ħaras] *n:* • **1.** watch, guard – واقُف حَرَس [wa:guf ħaras] standing guard. عَلِي واقُف حَرَس اللَّيلَة [ʕali wa:guf ħaras ʔillayla] Ali's standing guard tonight. • **2.** guard detachment, guard, escort • **3.** sentry, guard
حارِس [ħa:ris] *n:* حُرّاس [ħurra:s] *pl:* • **1.** watchman • **2.** guard, sentry
حِراسَة [ħira:sa] *n:* • **1.** guarding, watching • **2.** watch, guard duty – ضَرِيبَة الحِراسَة [ḍari:bat ʔilħira:sa] night watch tax.
اِحتِراس [ʔiħtira:s] *n:* • **1.** caution, wariness • **2.** precaution, taking precautions
مَحرُوس [maħru:s] *adj:* • **1.** guarded, safeguarded – المُعَسكَر مَحرُوس زين [ʔilmuʕaskar maħru:s zi:n] The post is well guarded. • **2.** protected (by God) – رُوح، مَحرُوس بِالله [ru:ħ, maħru:s bʔallah] God go with you. • **4.** pl. مَحرُوسِين, protected (by god), a polite term for a man's son – طاب المَحرُوس مِن مَرِضتَه وَإلّا بَعَد؟ [ṭa:b ʔilmaħru:s min mariḍtah waʔilla baʕad?] Has your boy recovered from his sickness yet?
مِحتِرِس [miħtiris] *adj:* • **1.** cautious

ح ر ش

حارَش [ħa:raš] *v:* • **1.** to provoke, incite, stir up trouble with – لِيش حارَشتَه؟ ما قِتلَك جُوز مِنَّه؟ [li:š ħa:raštah? ma: gitlak ǰu:z minnah?] Why'd you provoke him? Didn't I tell you to leave him alone?
تحَرَّش [tħarraš] *v:* • **1.** to start trouble, pick a fight – دائِماً يِتحَرَّش بِولد الجِّيران [da:ʔiman yitħarraš bwild ʔiǰǰi:ra:n] He's always provoking the neighbor's kids. • **2.** to be forward, be rude, be fresh – لا تِتحَرَّش بِالبَنات [la: titħarraš bilbana:t] Don't get fresh with the girls.
تحارَش [tħa:raš] *v:* • **1.** to pick a quarrel, to provoke or start trouble – إذا ما تِتحارَش بِيه، ما يأذِّيك [ʔiða ma: titħa:raš bi:h, ma: yʔaððiːk] If you don't provoke him, he won't hurt you. لِيش تِتحارَش بِالصِّغار؟ رُوح عَلِّبقَلبِك [li:š titħa:raš biṣṣiɣa:r? ru:ħ ʕallibgaddak] Why pick on the little kids? Go find someone your own size. • **2.** to be forward, rude, fresh – لا تِتحارَش بِيها. هَذِي بِنِت مَستُورَة [la: titħa:raš bi:ha. ha:ði binit mastu:ra] Don't get fresh with her. She's a chaste girl.
حَرِش [ħariš] *n:* • **1.** (coll.) a variety of small fish
حَرشَة [ħarša] *n:* حَرشات [ħarša:t] *pl:* • **1.** variety of small fish
حِرشَة [ħirša] *n:* حِرشات [ħirša:t] *pl:* • **1.** provocation, act of provocation
أحراش [ʔaħra:š] *n:* • **1.** forest

ح ر ص

حِرَص [ħiraṣ] *v:* • **1.** with عَلَى to be concerned with, be intent upon – يِحرِص عَلَى مَصلَحَة بَلَدَه [yiħriṣ ʕala maṣlaħat baladah] He is very concerned with the welfare of his country. يِحرُص عَلَى كُلّ دَقِيقَة مِن وَقتَه [yiħruṣ ʕala kull daqi:qa min waktah] He husbands every minute of his time.
حِرص [ħiriṣ] *n:* • **1.** dedication, intentness, concern – حِرص عَالدِّراسَة [ħiriṣ ʕaddira:sa] dedication to studying.
حَرِيص [ħari:ṣ] *adj:* • **1.** concerned, dedicated, intent – حَرِيص عَلَى سُمُعتَه [ħari:ṣ ʕala sumuʕtah] concerned about his reputation. شدَعوَة هَالقَدّ حَرِيص؟ أُخُذ راحَة [šdaʕwa halgadd ħari:ṣ? ʔuxuð ra:ħa] Why so eager? Take a rest.
أحرَص [ʔaħraṣ] *comparative adjective:* • **1.** more or most dedicated or concerned

ح ر ض

حَرَّض [ħarraḍ] *v:* • **1.** to incite, provoke, rouse, stir up
حَرَّض التَّلامِذ عالإضراب [ħarraḍ ʔittala:mi:ð ʕalʔiḍra:b] • **1.** He incited the students to strike
تحَرَّض [tħarraḍ] *v:* • **1.** to be provoked
مُحَرِّض [muħarriḍ] *n:* مُحَرِّضِين [muħarriḍi:n] *pl:* • **1.** instigator, inciter, provoker • **2.** rabble-rouser, demagogue
تَحرِيض [taħri:ḍ] *n:* • **1.** provocation, incitement

ح ر ف

حِرَف [ħiraf] *v:* • **1.** to tilt to one side – إحرُف البِسمار لِليَمِين، تَرَة مُو عَدِل [ʔiħruf ʔilbisma:r lilyami:n, tara mu: ʕadil] Tilt the nail to the right; it's not straight. لَو ما أحرُف راسِي، كان الحجارَة صابَتنِي [lu: ma: ʔaħruf ra:si, ča:n ʔilħǰa:ra ṣa:batni] If I hadn't ducked my head, the stone would have struck me. • **2.** to turn (someone) aside – هُوَّ اللِّي حِرَفها عَن الطَّرِيق العَدِل [huwwa ʔilli ħirafha ʕan ʔiṭṭari:q ʔilʕadil] He's the one who turned her aside from the straight and narrow.
حَرَّف [ħarraf] *v:* • **1.** to distort, twist, pervert, corrupt, misconstrue – إنتَ لِيش تحَرُّف الحَكِي؟ آني ما قِلت هِيكِي [ʔinta li:š tħarruf ʔilħači? ʔa:ni ma: gilit hi:či] Why do you twist what's said? I didn't say that.
اِنحِرَف [ʔinħiraf] *v:* • **1.** to deviate, digress, turn away, depart – اِنحِرَف عَن المَبدَأ اللِّي كان مِتمَسِّك بِيه [ʔinħiraf ʕan ʔilmabdaʔ ʔilli ča:n mitmassik bi:h] He deviated from the principle that he had adhered to.
اِحتِرَف [ʔiħtiraf] *v:* • **1.** to take as a profession, to do professionally اِحتِرَف المُلاكَمَة [ʔiħtiraf ʔalmula:kama] He made boxing his profession.

حَرف [ħaruf] *n:* حُرُوف [ħuru:f] *pl:* • **1.** letter (of the alphabet) – حَرُف بحَرُف [ħaruf bħaruf] word by word, exactly. حِكالِي القُصَّة حَرُف بحَرُف [ħiča:li ʔilquṣṣa ħaruf bħaruf] He told me the story word for word. • **2.** consonant • **3.** particle – حَرُف جَرّ [ħaruf ǰarr] preposition (gram.).

حِرفَة [ħirfa] *n:* • **1.** profession, craft, occupation, career, metier, trade, vocation

مِنحِرف [minħirif] *n:* • **1.** pervert

اِحتِراف [ʔiħtira:f] *n:* • **1.** professionalism (as opposed to amateurism)

اِنحِراف [ʔinħira:f] *n:* • **1.** perversion

حَرفِي [ħarfi] *adj:* • **1.** literal, word-for-word, direct – تَرجُمَة حَرفِيَّة [tarǰuma ħarfiyya] a literal translation. نَقِل حَرفِي [naqil ħarfi] a word-for-word copy. بِصُورَة حَرفِيَّة [bṣu:ra ħarfiyya] literally, word for word. أرِيدَك تِتَرجُملِي هَالمَكتُوب بِصُورَة حَرفِيَّة [ʔari:dak ʔittarǰumli halmaktu:b bṣu:ra ħarfiyya] I want you to translate this letter for me literally.

مُحتَرِف [muħtarif] *adj:* • **1.** professional – لاعِب كُرَة القَدَم مُحتَرِف [la:ʕib kurat ʔilqadam muħtarif] a professional soccer player.

مُنحَرِف [munħarif] *adj:* • **1.** diagonal • **2.** aberrant, perverse • **3.** slanted, sidelong, slantwise • **4.** crooked • **5.** different from what you expected to find

حَرفِيّاً [ħarfiyyan] *adverbial:* • **1.** literally, directly – تَرجُملِي هَالمَكتُوب حَرفِيّاً [tarǰumli halmaktu:b ħarfiyyan] Translate this letter for me literally. • **2.** word for word, word by word – عاد كَلامِي حَرفِيّاً [ʕa:d kala:mi ħarfiyyan] He repeated my remark word for word. قَلِّي كُلّ شِي حَرفِيّاً [galli kull ši ħarfiyyan] He told me the whole thing word by word.

ح ر ق

حِرَق [ħirag] *v:* • **1.** to burn – جِكارتَك حِرقَت إيدِي [ǰiga:rtak ħirgat ʔi:di] Your cigarette burned my hand. المُتَظاهِرِين حِرقَوا السَّفارَة [ʔilmutaðа:hiri:n ħirgaw ʔissafa:ra] The demonstrators set fire to the embassy. البانيان يِحرِقُون المَيِّت [ʔilba:niya:n yħirgu:n ʔilmayyit] The Hindus cremate the dead. حِرَقَة لِقَلبِي. ظَلّ ساعَة يِحكِي عَلَى شِي ما يِفهَم بِيه [ħiraga lgalbi. ðall sa:ʕa yiħči ʕala ši ma: yifham bi:h] He exasperated me. Kept talking for an hour about something he doesn't understand. زَعَّل خَطِيبتِي عَلَيّا وَحِرَق قَلبِي [zaʕʕal xaṭi:bti ʕalayya wħirag galbi] He got my fiancée mad at me and burned me up. • **2.** to burn, sting, smart – الصّابُون خَشّ بعَينِي وَقام يِحرِقها [ʔiṣṣa:bu:n xašš bʕayni wga:m yiħrigha] The soap got in my eyes and started to sting. عينِي قامَت تِحرِقنِي مِن الصّابُون [ʕi:ni ga:mat tiħrigni min ʔiṣṣa:bu:n] My eyes began to sting from the soap.

تحَرَّق [tħarrag] *v:* • **1.** to be consumed (by an emotion), be pained, eat one's heart out – بَعدَك تِتحَرَّق عَالوَظِيفَة؟ [baʕdak titħarrag ʕalwaði:fa?] Are you still eating your heart out over the position?

اِحترَق [ʔiħtirag] *v:* • **1.** to catch fire, burn, burn up – اِحترقَت سَيّارتِي وَما كانَت عِندِي مِطفاَة حَرِيق [ʔiħtirgat sayya:rti wma ča:nat ʕindi miṭfaʔat ħari:q] My car caught fire and I had no fire extinguisher. الأكِل اِحترَق [ʔilʔakil ʔiħtirag] The food got burned. اِحترَق قَلبِي عَلَى هالفَقِير الجَّوعان [ʔiħtirag galbi ʕala halfaqi:r ʔiǰǰawʕa:n] My heart bled for that poor, hungry man. اِحترَق الأخضَر بِسِعِر اليابِس [ʔiħtirag ʔilʔaxðar bsiʕir ʔilya:bis] The innocent got hung with the guilty (lit., the green things got burned up with the dry). • **2.** to burn out – الكلُوب اِحترَق [ʔilglu:b ʔiħtirag] The light bulb burned out. • **3.** to be consumed (with emotion) – اِحترَق مِن سِمَع ترَفَّعِت [ʔiħtirag min simaʕ traffaʕit] He was consumed with jealousy when he heard I got promoted.

حَرِق [ħarig] *n:* • **1.** burning • **2.** pl. حرُوق, burn, burn mark

حَرقَة، حُرقَة [ħarga, ħurga] *n:* • **1.** stinging, burning sensation (of heartburn)

حَرِيق [ħari:q] *n:* حَرايِق [ħara:yiq] *pl:* • **1.** fire, conflagration

مِحرَقَة [miħraqa] *n:* مَحارِق [maħa:riq] *pl:* • **1.** incinerator

مَحرَقَة [maħraqa] *n:* • **1.** burning chamber, crematory

اِحتِراق [ʔiħtira:q] *n:* • **1.** burn, burning

حارِق [ħa:riq] *adj:* • **1.** burning

حَرّاق [ħarra:g] *adj:* حَرّاقَة [ħarra:ga] *pl:* • **1.** envious

مَحرُوق [maħru:g] *adj:* • **1.** burned, scorched, charred, burned up – مَحرُوق إصِبعَه [maħru:g ʔiṣibʕah] a dish made of dried bread and spices boiled in water. شدَعوَة قَلبَك مَحرُوق عَليه! يِستاهِل [šdaʕwa galbak maħru:g ʕali:h! yista:hil] My you're awfully agitated about him! He deserves it. • **2.** irritated, burned up – إنتَ شبِيك مَحرُوق؟ آنِي اللِّي خِسَرت ألف دِينار [ʔinta šbi:k maħru:g? ʔa:ni ʔilli xṣarit ʔalf dina:r] What are you burned up about? I'm the one who lost the thousand dinars. • **3.** burned out – كلُوب مَحرُوق [glu:b maħru:g] a burned out light bulb.

ح ر ك

حَرَّك [ħarrak] *v:* • **1.** to move, to set in motion, make move, propel – حَرِّك المِيز شوَيَّة. خَلِّي أشُوف شَكُو جَوّاه [ħarrik ʔilmi:z šwayya. xalli: ʔašu:f šaku ǰawwa:h] Move the desk a little. Let me see what's under it. إذا تحَرِّك المِيز، ما أقدَر أكتِب [ʔiða tħarrik ʔilmi:z, ma: ʔagdar ʔaktib] If you jiggle the table, I can't write. ما يُعرُف يحَرِّك هَالمَكِينَة [ma: yuʕruf yħarrik halmaki:na] He doesn't know how to make this machine operate. لا تحَرِّك ساكِن [la: tħarrik sa:kin] Let sleeping dogs lie! Don't stir things up! ظَلّ قاعِد يِتفَرَّج وَلا حَرَّك ساكِن [ðall ga:ʕid yitfarraǰ wala ħarrak sa:kin] He just sat watching and never lifted a finger. • **2.** to start, get started, get under way – خَلّي نحَرِّك الصُّبُح ساعَة خَمسَة [xalli: nħarrik ʔiṣṣubuħ sa:ʕa xamsa] Let's get started at five in the morning. صِعدُوا. راح يحَرِّك الباص [ṣiʕdu:. ra:ħ yħarrik ʔilpa:ṣ] Get on. The bus is about to leave. • **3.** to incite, instigate, provoke, stir up – حَرَّك العَشايِر حَتَّى يثُورُون [ħarrak ʔilʕaša:yir ħatta yθu:ru:n] He incited the tribes to revolt. حَرَّك العُمّال عَالشَّرِكَة وخَلّاهُم يضِربُون [ħarrak ʔilʕumma:l ʕaššarika wxalla:hum yḍirbu:n] He stirred up the workers against the company and got them to go on strike. حَرَّكِت مَرتَه عَليه [ħarrakit martah ʕali:h] I stirred up his wife against him. • **4.** to vowel, put in vowel markings (gram.) – إكتِب الكِلمات وَحَرِّكها [ʔiktib ʔiččilma:t wħarrikha] Write the words and put the vowel markings on them.

تحَرَّك [tħarrak] *v:* • **1.** to move, stir, budge – لا تِتحَرَّك. أرُوح أجِرحَك بالمُوس [la: titħarrak. ʔaru:ħ ʔajirħak bilmu:s] Don't move. I might cut you with the razor. بَسّ يُقعُد، بَعَد ما يِتحَرَّك مِن مُكانَه [bass yugʕud, baʕad ma: yitħarrak min muka:nah] Once he sits down, then he won't move out of his place. • **2.** to start moving, get moving – تحَرَّك عاد! ما بُقَى وَقِت [tħarrak ʕa:d! ma: buqa: wakit] Get a move on! There's no time left. • **3.** to start out, get under way – شوَقِت تحَرَّكتُوا مِن البَصرَة؟ [šwakit tħarraktu: min ʔilbaṣra?] When did you start out from Basra? الجَّيش تحَرَّك لِلحُدُود [ʔijjayš tħarrak lilħudu:d] The army moved out toward the border. • **4.** to leave, depart – الباص تحَرَّك قَبُل خَمِس دَقِيقَة [ʔilba:ṣ tħarrak gabul xamis daqi:qa] The bus left five minutes ago. • **5.** to be agitated, be excited, to act up – تحَرَّك عَليه سِنَّه وَما قِدَر ينام [tħarrak ʕali:h sinnah wma gidar yna:m] His tooth acted up on him and he couldn't sleep.

حَرَكَة [ħaraka] *n:* • **1.** movement, motion • **2.** activity – سُوق التِّمَّن ما بيه حَرَكَة اليُوم [su:g ʔittimman ma: bi:h ħaraka ʔilyu:m] There's no activity in the rice market today. • **3.** traffic • **4.** disturbance, trouble • **5.** social movement, cause • **6.** vowel, vowel marking (gram.) • **7.** (taboo) erection

مُحَرِّك [muħarrik] *n:* مُحَرِّكات [muħarrika:t] *pl:* • **1.** pl. مُحَرِّكِين trouble-maker, instigator, agitator • **2.** pl مُحَرِّكات motor, engine

تَحَرُّك [taħarruk] *n:* تَحَرُّكات [taħarruka:t] *pl:* • **1.** movement

تَحرِيك [taħri:k] *n:* • **1.** motivation, shake

حَرِك [ħarik] *adj:* • **1.** lively, brisk, agile, nimble • **2.** mischievous

مِتحَرِّك [mitħarrik] *adj:* • **1.** active, lively • **2.** mischievous

ح ر م

حِرَم [ħiram] *v:* • **1.** to deprive, dispossess, withhold, deny, refuse – لا تِحرُمنا مِن شَوفتَك [la: tiħrumna min šu:ftak] Don't deprive us of the pleasure of seeing you. مَنع التَّجَوُّل حِرَمني مِن شُوفَة أصدِقائي [maniʕ ʔittajawwul ħiramni min šu:fat ʔaṣdiqa:ʔi] The curfew prevented me from seeing my friends. لا تِحرُم الوَلَد مِن اللِّعب ويّا أصدِقائه [la: tiħrum ʔilwalad min ʔilliʕib wiyya ʔaṣdiqa:ʔah] Don't keep the boy from playing with his friends. حَطّ إيدَه الوَسخَة بِالأكِل وحِرَمنا مِنَّه [ħaṭṭ ʔi:dah ʔilwasxa bilʔakil wħiramna minnah] He put his dirty hand in the food and spoiled it for us. خَطِيَّة، مَحرُومَة مِن كُلّ شِي [xaṭiyya, maħru:ma min kull ši] Poor thing, she's been deprived of everything. • **2.** to exclude, cut off – حِرَم إبنَه الكِبير مِن المِيراث [ħiram ʔibnah ʔiččibi:r min ʔilmi:ra:θ] He excluded his oldest son from the inheritance. الكُلّ ترَفّعَوا. بَسّ آني المَحرُوم [ʔilkull traffʕaw. bass ʔa:ni ʔilmaħru:m] Everyone got promoted. I'm the only one who was excluded.

حَرَّم [ħarram] *v:* • **1.** to declare unlawful, forbidden, to forbid – الدِّين يحَرِّم شُرُب العَرَق [ʔiddi:n yħarrum šurub ʔilʕarag] Religion forbids drinking arrack. أبُويا حَرَّم عَلَيّا الطَّلعَة باللَّيل [ʔabu:ya ħarram ʕalayya ʔiṭṭalʕa billayl] My father told me not to go out at night. حَرَّم عَلَى نَفسَه أيّ وِنسَة [ħarram ʕala nafsah ʔayy winsa] He denies himself all pleasure. • **2.** to waste, squander sinfully – لا تحَرُّم الوَرَق. إذا ترِيد تشَخبُط، إستَعمِل وَرَق رخِيص [la: tħarrum ʔilwaraq. ʔiða tri:d tšaxbuṭ, ʔistaʕmil waraq rixi:ṣ] Don't waste the paper. If you want to scribble, use cheap paper.

تحَرَّم [tħarram] *v:* • **1.** to be wasted, go to waste – القَصّاب باع نُصّ اللَّحَم وَالنُّصّ اللاخ تحَرَّم عَليه [ʔilgaṣṣa:b ba:ʕ nuṣṣ ʔillaħam winnuṣ ʔilla:x tħarram ʕali:h] The butcher sold half the meat and the other half went to waste. مَواهبَه تحَرَّمَت بِالجَيش [mawa:hbah tħarrmat bijjayš] His talents were wasted in the army.

إنحِرَم [ʔinħiram] *v:* • **1.** to be deprived – الجّاهِل إنحِرَم مِن كُلشي [ʔijja:hil ʔinħiram min kullši] The kid was deprived of everything. مِن صِرِت بهَالوَظِيفَة، إنحِرَمِت مِن شُوفَة ولدِي [min ṣirit bhalwaḍi:fa, ʔinħiramit min šu:fat wildi] Since I got this position, I've been prevented from seeing my kids.

إحتِرَم [ʔiħtiram] *v:* • **1.** to respect, esteem, revere – لازِم تِحتِرُم أبُوك [la:zim tiħtirum ʔabu:k] You have to respect your father. يِحتُرُم نَفسَه هوايَة. ما يِتدَاخَل بِقَضايات الجِّهال [yiħturum nafsah hwa:ya. ma: yidda:xal bqaḍa:ya:t ʔijjiha:l] He's very self-respecting. He doesn't meddle in the children's affairs.

إستَحرَم [ʔistaħram] *v:* • **1.** to consider sinful, unlawful, forbidden – يِستَحرِم مِن شُرُب المَشرُوبات الرُّوحِيَّة [yistaħrum min šurub ʔilmašru:ba:t ʔirru:ħiyya] He considers drinking alcoholic beverages sinful. ما ياخُذ فائِدَة عَلَى فلُوسَه لِأنَّه يِستَحرِم [ma: ya:xuð fa:ʔida ʕala flu:sah liʔannah yistaħrim] He doesn't take interest on his money because he considers it a sin.

حَرَم [ħaram] *n:* أحرام [ʔaħra:m] *pl:* • **1.** holy, sacred, sacrosanct • **2.** forbidden place, esp. the family quarters of a house, where guests are not allowed • **3.** sacred place, consecrated part (of a mosque or shrine) – الحَرَم الشَّريف [ʔilħaram ʔiššariːf] the Kaaba and Mecca.

حُرمَة [ħurma] *n:* • **1.** sanctity, sacredness, inviolability – كُلّ بَيت لَه حُرمَة [kull biːtʔ lah ħurma] Every house is private. • **2.** woman, lady • **3.** wife

حَرام [ħaraːm] *adj:* • **1.** forbidden, prohibited – شُرُب العَرَق حَرام [šurub ʔilʕarag ħaraːm] Drinking arrack is forbidden. إبِن حَرام [ʔibin ħaraːm] illegitimate son, bastard. حَرام عَلِيك [ħaraːm ʕaliːk] Shame on you! You shouldn't do that! هَذا ياكُل مال حَرام [haːða yaːkul maːl ħaraːm] He's dishonest. He cheats. حَرام، بالحَرام [ħaraːm, bilħaraːm] I swear. بالحَرام، ما تِنطِي [bilħaraːm, maː tinṭi] By God, I won't let you pay. حَرام، ما أعرُف [ħaraːm, maː ʔaʕruf] Cross my heart, I don't know.

حَرِيم [ħariːm] *n:* • **1.** harem • **2.** women of a family • **3.** family

إحرام [ʔiħraːm] *n:* • **1.** state of ritual consecration of a Mecca pilgrim

حَرامِي [ħaraːmi] *n:* حَرامِيَّة [ħaraːmiyya] *pl:* • **1.** thief, bandit

حِرمان [ħirmaːn] *n:* • **1.** privation

حَرامات [ħaraːmaːt] *n:* • **1.** regrettable waste – تَعَبِي كُلّه راح حَرامات [taʕabi kullah raːħ ħaraːmaːt] My effort all went to waste.

إحتِرام [ʔiħtiraːm] *n:* إحتِرامات [ʔiħtiraːmaːt] *pl:* • **1.** deference, respect, regard, esteem قَدِّم إحتِراماتِي لِلأَهِل [qaddim ʔiħtiraːmaːti lilʔahil] Give my regards to the family. عامَلنِي بإحتِرام [ʕaːmalni bʔiħtiraːm] He treated me with respect.

حرام [ħraːm] *adj:* حرامات [ħraːmaːt] *pl:* • **1.** white sheet worn by pilgrims in Mecca • **2.** thin, coarse-textured blanket

مُحَرَّم [muħarram] *adj:* • **1.** forbidden, prohibited شُرُب العَرَق فَدّ شِي مُحَرَّم [šurub ʔilʕarag fadd ši muħarram] Drinking arrack is a forbidden thing. • **2.** forbidden act • **3.** Muharram, first month of the Moslem calendar

مُحرِم [muħrim] *adj:* مُحرِمِين [muħrimiːn.] *pl:* • **1.** Mecca pilgrim in a state of ritual consecration

مُحتَرَم [muħtaram] *adj:* • **1.** honored, esteemed, respected هَذا كُلِّش مُحتَرَم بين النّاس [haːða kulliš muħtaram biːn ʔinnaːs] He's very much respected among the people.

مَحرُوم [maħruːm] *adj:* • **1.** disadvantaged, destitute, poverty-stricken, poor, necessitous, needy

إحتِراماً [ʔiħtiraːman] *adverbial:* • **1.** out of respect وُقفَوا إحتِراماً لِلحاكِم [wugfaw ʔiħtiraːman lilħaːkim] They stood out of respect for the judge.

ح ر م س

حِرمِس [ħirmis] *n:* • **1.** very small biting insects

ح ر م ل

حَرمَل [ħarmal] *n:* • **1.** African rue (used against evil eye)

ح ر ن

حِرَن [ħiran] *v:* • **1.** to be or become obstinate, stubborn, head-strong – مِن تكَلّفَه بشِي، يِحرِن [min tkallfah bši, yiħrin] When you ask him for anything, he gets stubborn. الحصان حِرَن وَما يِقبَل يِمشِي بَعَد [ʔilħṣaːn ħiran wma yiqbal yimši baʕad] The horse balked and refused to go on.

حَرِن [ħarin] *n:* • **1.** stubbornness

حارِن [ħaːrin] *adj:* • **1.** stubborn

ح ر ي

تحَرَّى [tħarraː] *v:* • **1.** to investigate – ما نِقدَر نعَيّنَك قَبُل ما الشُّرطَة تِتحَرَّى عَنَّك [maː nigdar nʕayynak gabul maː ʔiššurṭa titħarraː ʕannak] We can't appoint you before the police investigate you. • **2.** to inquire, make inquiries – الشُّرطَة دَتِتحَرَّى عَنَّك [ʔiššurṭa datitħarraː ʕannak] The police are looking for you.

تَحَرِّي [taħarri] *n:* تَحَرِّيات [taħarriːyyaːt] *pl:* • **1.** investigation – شُرطَة التَّحَرِّي [šurṭat ʔittaħarri] detective force. شُرطِي تَحَرِّي [šurṭi taħarri] detective. • **2.** inquiry, check

ح ز ب

تحَزَّب [tħazzab] *v:* • **1.** to band together, stick together, join forces – تحَزّبوا ضِدَّه لِأَنّ يخافُون مِنَّه [tħazzbaw ḍiddah liʔann yxaːfuːn minnah] They banded together against him because they're afraid of him. – أَهِل هَالولايَة يِتحَزّبُون. الغَرِيب ما يِقدَر يعِيش ويّاهُم [ʔahil halwlaːya yitħazzibuːn. ʔilɣariːb maː yigdar yiʕiːš wiyyaːhum] The people of that town stick together. A stranger can't live with them. • **2.** to show favoritism, bias, to take sides – يِتحَزَّب لِقَرايبَه [yitħazzab ligaraːybah] He shows favoritism toward his relatives. المُدِير يِتحَزَّب هوايَة. ما يعَيِّن أَحَّد إلّا مِن وُلايتَه [ʔilmudiːr yitħazzab hwaːya. maː yʕayyin ʔaħħad ʔilla min wulaːytah] The director plays favorites. He only appoints people from his home town.

حِزِب [ħizib] *n:* أحزاب [ʔaħzaːb] *pl:* • **1.** political party • **2.** faction, clique, group, band

تَحَزُّب [taħazzub] *n:* • **1.** group loyalty • **2.** favoritism, bias • **3.** factionalism

حِزبِي [ħizbi] *adj:* • **1.** party, factional – جَرِيدَة حِزبِيَّة [ǰariːda ħizbiyya] party newspaper. غَرَض حِزبِي [ɣarað ħizbi] party goals.

حِزبِيَّة [ħizbiyya] *adj:* حِزبِيّات [ħizbiyyaːt] *pl:* • **1.** party activity, political campaigning • **2.** partisanship, partiality • **3.** factionalism • **4.** patronage, favoritism

مِتحَزِّب [mitħazzib] *adj:* • **1.** partial, biased • **2.** partisan

ح ز ر

حِزَر [ħizar] *v:* • **1.** to guess, make a guess – تِقدَر تِحزِر شَكُو بِيدِي؟ [tigdar tiħzir šaku biːdi?] Can you guess what's in my hand?

حَزَّر [ħazzar] *v:* • **1.** to quiz, make guess – حَزَّرتَه شقَدّ كَلّفتنِي السَّيّارَة [ħazzartah šgadd kallfatni ʔissayyaːra] I made him guess how much the car cost me. خَلّي أحَزّرَك شِي. شجِبتلَك؟ [xalliː ʔaħazzrak ši. šjibitlak?] Let me quiz you on something. What did I bring you? كان يحَزّرنا بأشياء ما تِجِي عَالبال [čaːn yħazzirna bʔašyaːʔ maː tiji ʕalbaːl] He was giving us riddles about things you'd never think of.

حَزِر [ħazir] *n:* • **1.** guessing

حَزُّورَة [ħazzuːra] *n:* حَزُّورات [ħazzuːraːt] *pl:* • **1.** riddle, puzzle

ح ز ر ن

حُزَيران [ħuzayraːn] *n:* • **1.** June

ح ز ز

حَزّ [ħazz] *v:* • **1.** to notch, nick – حَزّ الخِشبَة بالسِّكّينَة [ħazz ʔilxišba bissiččiːna] He notched the piece of wood with the knife. • **2.** to split – ضِرَبَه بالفاس وَحَزّه لِراسَه [ðirabah bilfaːs wħazzah liraːsah] He hit him with an ax and split his head.

اِنحَزّ [ʔinħazz] *v:* • **1.** to be or become notched, nicked – الأثاث كُلّه اِنحَزّ بِالنَّقِل [ʔilʔaθaːθ kullah ʔinħazz binnaqil] The furniture all got nicked in moving. • **2.** to be split – راسَه اِنحَزّ مِن الضَّربَة [raːsah ʔinħazz min ʔiððarba] His head was split by the blow.

حَزّ [ħazz] *n:* حزُوز [ħzuːz] *pl:* • **1.** nick, notch

حَزازَة [ħazaːza] *n:* حَزازات، حَزازيات [ħazaːzaːt] *pl:* • **1.** enmity, hostility, rancor, hatred, hate

ح ز م

حِزَم [ħizam] *v:* • **1.** to tie up, bundle, wrap up, pack – إحزِم هالفايلات سُوَة، وَدِزّهُم لِلوِزارَة [ʔiħzim halfaːylaːt suwa, wdizzhum lilwizaːra] Tie up these files and send them to the ministry.

حَزَّم [ħazzam] *v:* • **1.** to strap, strap up – هَالصَّندُوق مُو قَوِي. حَزّمَه بِقَيد [haṣṣanduːg muː qawi. ħazzmah bqayd] This trunk isn't very strong. Strap it up with steel bands. حَزّمتَه بزِيق [ħazzamtah bziːg] I gave him a Bronx cheer. مِن قال راح يصِير المُدِير، حَزّمتَه بزِيق [min gaːl raːħ yṣiːr ʔilmudiːr, ħazzamtah bziːg] When he said he's going to be the director, I gave him a Bronx cheer.

تحَزَّم [tħazzam] *v:* • **1.** to put on a belt – لِبَس البَنطَرُون بَسّ ما تحَزَّم [libas ʔilpanṭaruːn bass maː tħazzam] He put on the pants but didn't put on a belt. • **2.** to gird oneself, get ready, prepare oneself – تحَزَّمِتلَه لِلإمتِحان [tħazzamitlah lilʔimtiħaːn] I got ready for the exam. • **3.** to pitch in, throw oneself wholeheartedly into – ما كان خَلَّصنا الشُّغُل كُلّه لَو ما نِتحَزَّملَه [maː čaːn xallaṣna ʔiššuɣul kullah law maː nitħazzamlah] We wouldn't have finished all the work if we hadn't pitched right into it. تحَزَّملِي بقَضِيَّة تَرفِيعِي [tħazzamli bqaðiyyat tarfiːʕi] He got right down to work on the matter of my promotion. قُوم تحَزَّم وَنَظُّف البَيت [guːm tħazzam wnaððuf ʔilbayt] Get to work and clean the house.

حَزِم [ħazim] *n:* • **1.** packaging, wrapping • **2.** resoluteness, firmness, determination – لا تصِير ضَعِيف. عامِل المُوَظَّفِين بِحَزِم [laː tṣiːr ðaʕiːf. ʕaːmil ʔilmuwaððafiːn bħazim] Don't be weak. Handle the employees with firmness.

حزام [ħzaːm] *n:* حِزِم [ħizim] *pl:* • **1.** belt • **2.** girdle • **3.** truss, supporter

مَحزَم [maħzam] *n:* مَحازِم [maħaːzim] *pl:* • **1.** waist

حازِم [ħaːzim] *adj:* • **1.** resolute, decisive, energetic, forceful – هَالوَظِيفَة يِراد إلها فَدّ رَجُل حازِم؛ يقَرِّر شِي وَينَفّذَه [halwaðiːfa yiraːd ʔilha fadd rajul ħaːzim; yqarrir ši wynaffðah] This position needs a decisive man; one who'll decide a thing and carry it out.

متحَزِّم [mitħazzim] *adj:* • **1.** having a belt on, strengthened • **2.** resolute, decided

ح ز ن

حِزَن [ħizan] *v:* • **1.** to mourn, be in mourning – حِزنَت عَلَى رَجِلها سنِين [ħiznat ʕala rajilha sniːn] She mourned her husband for years. حِزنَت سَنَة عَلَى إبنها المَيِّت [ħiznat sana ʕala ʔibinha ʔilmayyit] She mourned her dead son for a year.

أحزَن [ʔaħzan] *v:* • **1.** to grieve, sadden, make sad – وَفاتَه أحزِنَتنِي هوايَة [wafaːtah ʔaħzinatni hwaːya] His death grieved me greatly.

حِزِن [ħizin, ħuzun] *n:* • **1.** grief, sorrow, sadness • **2.** mourning – بَعَدهُم ما فَكّوا الحِزِن مالهُم [baʕadhum maː fakkaw ʔilħizin maːlhum] They still haven't come out of mourning.

حَزِين [ħaziːn] *adj:* • **1.** sorrowing, mournful, grieved – مالِك الحَزِين [maːlik ʔilħaziːn] heron.

مُحزِن [muħzin] *adj:* • **1.** sad – هَالفِلِم كُلّش مُحزِن [halfilim kulliš muħzin] This movie's very sad.

حَزنان [ħaznaːn] *adj:* • **1.** in mourning – ما يِحلِق وِجهه لأنّ بَعدَه حَزنان [maː yiħliq wiččah liʔann baʕdah ħaznaːn] He doesn't shave his face because he's still in mourning.

حَزايِني [ħazaːyni] *adj:* • **1.** (invar.) funereal, mourning – مُوسِيقَى حَزايِني [muːsiːqaː ħazaːyni] mourning music.

ح س ب

حِسَب [ħisab] *v:* • **1.** to compute, reckon, calculate – خَلّي نِحسِب مَصرَفنا هَالشَّهَر [xalliː niħsib maṣrafna haššahar] Let's figure out our expenses for this month. • **2.** to count – حِسَب الفلُوس وشاف أكُو زِيادَة [ħisab ʔilfluːs wšaːf ʔaku ziyaːda] He counted the

انحسب [ʔinħisab] *v:* • **1.** to be counted • **2.** to be considered • **3.** to be on someone's expense

حَسَب [ħasab] *n:* • **1.** esteem, high regard • **2.** noble descent – إبن حَسَب ونَسَب [ʔibin ħasab wnasab] man from an esteemed, noble family.

حَسبَة [ħasba] *n:* حَسبات [ħasba:t] *pl:* • **1.** arithmetical problem • **2.** matter, business, question, affair, problem – حَسبَة البَيت، شصار مِنها؟ اِشترَيته لَو بَعَد؟ [ħasbat ʔilbayt, šṣa:r minha? ʔištiraytah law baʕad?] What happened about the matter of the house? Have you bought it yet? أعتِقد هِيَّ حَسبَة عِشرين دينار، مُو أكثَر [ʔaʕtiqid hiyya ħasbat ʕišri:n dina:r, mu: ʔakθar] I think it's a matter of twenty dinars, no more.

حساب [ħsa:b] *n:* • **1.** arithmetic, calculus – بِنتِك ضَعِيفَة بِالحِساب [bintič ðaʕi:fa biliħsa:b] Your daughter is weak in arithmetic. • **2.** count, score – آني أصَفُّط الكِياس وإنتَ إلزَم حِساب [ʔa:ni ʔaṣaffuṭ ʔiččya:s wʔinta ʔilzam ħisa:b] I'll stack the bags and you keep count. حِسَبِت مِيَّة واحِد وتاه الحساب عَلَيّا [ħisabit miyyat wa:ħid wta:h ʔilħsa:b ʕalayya] I counted one hundred people and then lost count. خَلّي نِلعَب طاولي وعَلي يِلزَم الحساب [xalli: nilʕab ṭa:wli wʕali yilzam ʔilħsa:b] Let's play backgammon and Ali'll keep score. ما إلَه حساب [ma: ʔilah ħsa:b] countless, innumerable. حاطّين كَراسِي ما إلها حساب بِالحَدِيقَة [ħa:ṭṭi:n kara:si ma: ʔilha ħsa:b bilħadi:qa] They've put innumerable chairs in the garden. بِلا حساب، بلَيّا حساب [bila ħsa:b, blayya ħsa:b] without limits, recklessly, heedlessly. دَيِصرُف فلُوسَه بلَيّا حساب [dayiṣruf flu:sah blayya ħsa:b] He's spending his money heedlessly. • **3.** bill, check • **4.** account, reckoning – حساب بِالبَنك [ħsa:b bilbang] bank account. اِنطِيه حسابَه وَخَلّيه يوَلّي [ʔinṭi ħsa:bah wxalli:h ywalli:] Give him what you owe him and make him scram. • **5.** at the expense of – شايَك عَلَى حسابِي [ča:yak ʕala ħsa:bi] Your tea's on me. ما قِبَل ياخُذ فلُوس. صَلَّحها عَلَى حسابَه [ma: qibal ya:xuð flu:s. ṣallaħha ʕala ħsa:bah] He wouldn't take any money. He fixed it at his own expense. • **6.** on the account of, by oneself – أخِذت السَّيّارَة عَلَى حسابِي لِأنّ مستَعجِل [ʔaxiðt ʔissayya:ra ʕala ħsa:bi liʔann mistaʕjil] I took the taxi all to myself because I was in a hurry. أخَذِت سَيّارَة عَلَى حسابَك لَو رِحت عِبري؟ [ʔaxaðit sayya:ra ʕala ħsa:bak law riħit ʕibri?] Did you hire a car by yourself or come by jitney? • **7.** on the account of, for the sake of عَلَى حسابَك، راح أطرُدَه [ʕala ħsa:bak, ra:ħ ʔaṭurdah] I'll fire him for your sake. عَلَى أيّ حِساب فِصلوه؟ [ʕala ʔayy ħisa:b fiṣlawh?] On what grounds did they fire him? سَوّى دَعوَة عَلَى حساب زَواج أخُوه [sawwa: daʕwa ʕala ħsa:b zawa:ǰ ʔaxu:h] He gave a party on the occasion of his brother's marriage. • **8.** (pl. only) شُعبَة الحِسابات [šuʕbat ʔilħisa:ba:t] finance section, accounting section.

money and saw that there was a surplus. • **3.** to enumerate – تِقدَر تِحسِبلِي كَم إبن عَمّ عِندَك؟ [tigdar tiħsibli čam ʔibin ʕamm ʕindak?] Can you tell me how many cousins you have? – إحسِبلِي القارّات الخمسَة [ʔiħsibli ʔilqa:rra:t ʔilxamsa] Enumerate the five continents for me. • **4.** to consider, deem, think – دَيِحسِب نَفسَه رِجّال [dayiħsib nafsah rijja:l] He considers himself a man. رَفّعُوه لِأنّ حِسبُوه عالوَزِير [raffʕu:h liʔann ħisbu:h ʕalwazi:r] They promoted him because they figured he was a protege of the minister. • **5.** to consider, regard, count – إحسِبَه وِيّا الجّايين [ʔiħsibah wiyya ʔiǰǰa:yi:n] Count him with those that are coming. مِن تكَلّفَه بشِي، إحسِبَه صار [min tkallfah bši, ʔiħisbah ṣa:r] When you ask him for something, you can consider it done. حِسَبنِي واحِد مِن إخوانَه [ħisabni wa:ħid min ʔixwa:nah] He considered me one of his brothers. إحسِبها عَلَيّا؛ هَذا جاهِل [ʔiħsibha ʕalayya; ha:ða ǰa:hil] Do it for my sake; he's just a kid. • **6.** to price – إذا تِشتِرِي الكِتاب، أحسِبلَك القَلَم بِخَمسِين فِلِس [ʔiða tištiri ʔilkita:b, ʔaħsiblak ʔilqalam bxamsi:n filis] If you buy the book, I'll sell you the pencil for fifty fils. بيش حِسبُولَك هَالثُّوب؟ [biyš ħisbu:lak haθθu:b?] How much did they charge you for this shirt? حِسَب حِساب [ħisab ħisa:b] He took account of everything. He took everything into consideration. لازِم تِحسِب حِسابَك قَبُل ما تِشتِرِيها [la:zim tiħsib ħisa:bak gabul ma: tištiri:ha] You must take all things into account before you buy it. لازِم تِحسِبلَه ألِف حِساب [la:zim tiħsiblah ʔalif ħisa:b] You should take every little thing about him into consideration. إحسِب حِساب المُستَقبَل [ʔiħsib ħisa:b ʔilmustaqbal] Consider the future.

حَسَّب [ħassab] *v:* • **1.** to consider, think – ما حَسَّبِت يِترُكنِي [ma: ħassabit yitrukni] I never thought he would leave me. • **2.** to ponder, meditate – شبِيك تحَسِّب؟ عِندَك مُشكِلَة؟ [šbi:k tħassib? ʕindak muškila?] Why are you pondering? Have you got a problem? • **3.** to be or become apprehensive, anxious, concerned – لَمّا تأخّر إبنها، ظَلَّت تحَسِّب هوايَة [lamma tʔaxxar ʔibinha, ðallat tħassib hwa:ya] When her son was late, she became very apprehensive.

حاسَب [ħa:sab] *v:* • **1.** to call to account, ask for an accounting – يسَوّون شما يِردُون لِأنّ ماكُو واحِد يحاسِبهُم [ysawwu:n šma yirdu:n liʔann ma:ku wa:ħid yħa:sibhum] They do whatever they want because there's no one to call them to account. • **2.** to hold responsible, make answerable – يحاسِبنِي عَلَى كُلّ فِلِس [yħa:sibni ʕala kull filis] He holds me responsible for every penny.

تحاسَب [tħa:sab] *v:* • **1.** to settle a mutual account – خَلّي نُقعُد نِتحاسَب [xalli: nugʕud nitħa:sab] Let's sit down and settle accounts. صُدُق حِكَى عَلَيّا؟ بَسّ أشُوفَه أتحاسَب ويّاه [ṣudug ħiča: ʕalayya? bass ʔašu:fah ʔatħa:sab wiyya:h] Did he really talk about me? Just let me see him and I'll settle with him.

حاسِبَة [ħa:siba] *n:* حاسِبات [ħa:siba:t] *pl:* • **1.** adding machine – آلَة حاسِبَة [ʔa:la ħa:siba] adding machine.
مُحاسِب [muħa:sib] *n:* مُحاسِبين [muħa:sibi:n] *pl:* • **1.** accountant, bookkeeper • **2.** paymaster
حاسُوب [ħa:su:b] *n:* • **1.** computer
حُسبان [ħusba:n] *n:* • **1.** calculation • **2.** assumption, view, thinking
مُحاسَبَة [muħa:saba] *n:* مُحاسَبات [muħa:saba:t] *pl:* • **1.** accounting • **2.** bookkeeping – دائِرَة المُحاسَبات [da:ʔirat ʔilmuħa:saba:t] accounting office.
مَحسُوبِيَّة [maħsu:biyya] *n:* • **1.** favoritism, patronage
مِحَسِّب [mħassib] *adj:* • **1.** considered, taken into account
حِسابِي [ħisa:bi] *adj:* • **1.** arithmetical, mathematical – عَمَلِيَّة حِسابِيَّة [ʕamaliyya ħisa:biyya] a mathematical calculation.
مَحسُوب [maħsu:b] *adj:* • **1.** reckoned, figured, calculated, counted – الضَرِيبَة مَحسُوبَة وِيّا الكُلفَة [ðari:ba maħsu:ba wiyya ʔilkulfa] tax included in the cost. • **2.** considered, deemed – إِنتَ مَحسُوب واحِد مِنّا [ʔinta maħsu:b wa:ħid minna] You're considered one of us. • **3.** pl. مَحسُوبِين protege, pet, favorite
حَسَب [ħasab] *adv:* • **1.** (prep.) according to, in accordance with, commensurate with, depending on – أُصبُغ البَيت حَسَب ذَوقَك [ʔuṣbuɣ ʔilbayt ħasab ðawqak] Paint the house according to your own taste. سَوَّيتها حَسَب طَلَب المُدِير [sawwi:tha ħasab ṭalab ʔilmudi:r] I did it in accordance with the director's request. القُندَرجِي يسَوِّي قَنادِر حَسَب الطَّلَب [ʔilqundarči ysawwi: qana:dir ħasab ʔiṭṭalab] The shoemaker makes shoes according to demand. حَسَب أَمرَك؛ هَسَّة راح أَجِيب لَك إِيّاه [ħasab ʔamrak; hassa ra:ħ ʔaǰi:b lak ʔiyya:h] At your orders; I'll bring it to you now.
حَسب بال [ħasb ba:l] *adv:* • **1.** /with pronominal suffix/ in the opinion of.. إِنطَيتَه فلُوس. حَسبالِي آدَمِي [ʔinṭi:tah flu:s. ħasab liy ʔa:dami] I gave him money. I thought he was an honorable man. • **2.** according to
حَسَبما [ħasabma] *subordinating conjunction:* • **1.** (conj.) according to what, as, as far as – سَوِّيت لَه إِيّاه حَسَب ما يرِيد [sawwi:t lah ʔiyya:h ħasab ma: yri:d] I made it for him just the way he wanted. حَسَب ما أَعرُف، مالَه عِلاقَة بِالقَضِيَّة [ħasab ma: ʔaʕruf, ma:lah ʕila:qa bilqaðiyya] As far as I know, he's got nothing to do with the affair.

ح س ب ل

حَسبال [ħasba:l-] *adv:* • **1.** see **2** • ح س ب

ح س د

حِسَد [ħisad] *v:* • **1.** to be envious, to envy – حِسَدنِي عَلَى وَظِيفتِي الجِّدِيدَة [ħisadni ʕala waði:fti ʔiǰǰidi:da] He envied me my new job.
اِنحِسَد [ʔinħisad] *v:* • **1.** to be envied – اِنحِسَدِت مِن اِشتِرَيت سَيّارَة جِدِيدَة [ʔinħisadit min ʔištirayt sayya:ra ǰidi:da] I've been envied since I bought a new car.
حَسَد [ħasad] *n:* • **1.** envy
حَسُود [ħasu:d] *adj:* • **1.** envious
مَحسُود [maħsu:d] *adj:* • **1.** envied

ح س ر

تحَسَّر [tħassar] *v:* • **1.** to sigh – مِن يِسمَع إِسِمها، يِتحَصَّر [min yismaʕ ʔisimha, yitħaṣṣar] When he hears her name, he sighs. • **2.** to long – دَيِتحَصَّر عَلَى شُوفَة خَطِيبتَه [dayitħaṣṣar ʕala šu:fat xaṭi:btah] He's longing for the sight of his fiancée. قام يِتحَصَّر عَلَى أَيّام شَبابَه [ga:m yitħaṣṣar ʕala ʔayya:m šaba:bah] He became nostalgic over the days of his youth. • **3.** to grieve, be grieved, be upset – صُرَف فلُوسَه كُلّها وَبَعدين قام يِتحَصَّر عَلَى فِلِس [ṣuraf flu:sah kullha wbaʕdi:n ga:m yitħaṣṣar ʕala filis] He spent all his money and then began to grieve for one fils.
حَسرَة [ħasra] *n:* حَسرات [ħasra:t] *pl:* • **1.** sigh – قِعَد قبالِي وَقام يجُرّ حَصرَة وَرا حَصرَة [giʕad gba:li wga:m yǰurr ħaṣra wara ħaṣra] He sat down across from me and began heaving sigh after sigh. • **2.** longing, nostalgia – مات بِحَصرَتها [ma:t bħaṣratha] He almost died of longing for her. حَصرَة عَلَى الأَيّام اللِّي فاتَت [ħaṣra ʕala ʔilʔayya:m ʔilli fa:tat] Ah, those were the days!

ح س س

حَسّ [ħass] *v:* • **1.** to feel, sense – خَشّ لِلقُبَّة، ووُقَف يَمِّي وَما حَسَّيت بِيه إِلَى أَن حِكَى وِيّايا [xašš lilgubba, wwugaf yammi wma: ħassi:t bi:h ʔila ʔan ħiča: wiyya:ya] He came in the room and stood beside me and I didn't sense it till he spoke to me. ما ترِيد تِحكِي وِيّاك. ما دَتحِسّ؟ [ma: tri:d tiħči wiyya:k. ma: datħiss?] She doesn't want to talk to you. Can't you sense it? • **2.** to notice – شلُون ما حَسَّيت؟ صارَت لَغوَة كِبِيرَة [šlu:n ma: ħassi:t? ṣa:rat laɣwa čibi:ra] How come you didn't notice? There was a big commotion. • **3.** to discover, find out – الشُّرطَة حَسَّت بِيه دَيبُوق وَوَقّفُوه [ʔiššurṭa ħassat bi:h daybu:g wwaqqfu:h] The police found out that he was stealing and arrested him. • **4.** to wake, wake up – ما حَسَّيت مِن النُّوم إِلَى الظُّهُر [ma: ħassi:t min ʔinnu:m ʔila ʔiððuhur] I didn't wake up till noon.
حَسَّس [ħassas] *v:* • **1.** to make aware, make conscious – حَسَّستَه بِتصَرُّفات المُوَظَّفِين ضِدَّه [ħassastah btaṣarrufa:t ʔilmuwaððafi:n ðiddah] I made him aware of the employees' actions against him. • **2.** to wake, wake up, cause to wake – رُوح، حَسِّس أَبُوك مِن النُّوم [ru:ħ, ħassis ʔabu:k min ʔinnu:m] Go wake your father up.
تحَسَّس [tħassas] *v:* • **1.** to feel around, grope, probe – اِنطِفَى الضُوا، وَتحَسَّسِت طَرِيقِي لِبَرَّة [ʔinṭifa: ʔiððuwa, wtħassasit ṭari:qi libarra] The light went out and I groped my way outside.

حِسّ [ħiss] *n:* • **1.** feeling, sensation, sensory perception • **2.** voice • **3.** sound • **4.** noise
حاسَّة [ħaːssa] *n:* حَواسّ [ħawaːss] *pl:* • **1.** sensation • **2.** sense – الحَواسّ الخمسَة [ʔilħawaːss ʔilxamsa] the five senses. حاسَّة الشَّمّ [ħaːssat ʔiššamm] the sense of smell.
إحساس [ʔiħsaːs] *n:* • **1.** sensitivity, perception – قِلَّة إحساس [qillat ʔiħsaːs] insensitivity, obtuseness.
حَسّاسِيَّة [ħassaːsiyya] *n:* • **1.** sensitivity, allergy
حاسّ [ħaːss] *adj:* • **1.** aware
حَسّاس [ħassaːs] *adj:* • **1.** sensitive, readily affected – فَدّ شَخِص كُلِّش حَسّاس [fadd šaxiṣ kulliš ħassaːs] a very sensitive person. • **2.** delicate, sensitive – آلَة حَسّاسَة [ʔaːla ħassaːsa] a delicate instrument. • **3.** delicate, touchy – مَسأَلَة حَسّاسَة [masʔala ħassaːsa] a delicate matter.
حاسِس [ħaːsis] *adj:* • **1.** conscious
مَحسُوس [maħsuːs] *adj:* • **1.** perceptible, noticeable, tangible – تَحَسُّن مَحسُوس [taħassun maħsuːs] a noticeable improvement.

ح س ف

حَسافَة [ħasaːfa] *n:* • **1.** pity

ح س م [1]

حِسَم [ħisam] *v:* • **1.** to finish, complete, terminate, conclude – صارلَك تِتعامَل ساعَة. ما تِحسِم القَضِيَّة، عاد [ṣaːrlak titʕaːmal saːʕa. maː tiħsim ʔilqaḍiyya, ʕaːd] You've been bargaining for an hour. For goodness' sake, conclude the matter! • **2.** to decide – المُدِير هُوَّ الوَحِيد اللِّي يِقدَر يِحسِم هالمَسأَلَة [ʔilmudiːr huwwa ʔilwaħiːd ʔilli yigdar yiħsim halmasʔala] The director is the only one who can decide this question. • **3.** to settle – لِيش ما تِحسِم قَضِيَّة القاع ويّاهُم؟ [liːš maː tiħsim qaḍiyyat ʔilgaːʕ wiyyaːhum?] Why don't you settle the matter of the land with them?
حَسِم [ħasim] *n:* • **1.** termination
حاسِم [ħaːsim] *adj:* • **1.** decisive – مَعرَكَة حاسمَة [maʕraka ħaːsma] a decisive battle. • **2.** final, definite – جَواب حاسِم [ǰawaːb ħaːsim] a definite answer.

ح س م [2]

حُوسَم [ħuːsam] *v:* • **1.** to loot, steal

ح س ن

حَسَّن [ħassan] *v:* • **1.** to improve, make better – هالمَطعَم حَسَّن الأكِل [halmaṭʕam ħassan ʔilʔakil] This restaurant has improved its food.
أَحسَن [ʔaħsan] *v:* • **1.** to master, have command of, be proficient in – هُوَّ يِحسِن اللُّغَة الإنكِلِيزِيَّة [huwwa yiħsin ʔilluɣa ʔilʔingiliːziyya] He has a good knowledge of English. • **2.** to give alms – يِحسِن عَالفُقَراء [yiħsin ʕalfuqaraːʔ] He gives alms to the poor.
تحَسَّن [tħassan] *v:* • **1.** to be or become improved, get better – صِحّتَه تحَسّنَت [ṣiħħtah tħassnat] His health has improved.
إستَحسَن [ʔistaħsan] *v:* • **1.** to regard as best, appropriate, or advisable – أَستَحسِن نرُوح هَسَّة [ʔastaħsin nruːħ hassa] I think we'd better go now. أَستَحسِن نَقلَه مِن هَالشُّعبَة لِأَنّ هُوَّ والمُلاحِظ ما يتفاهمُون [ʔastaħsin naqlah min haššuʕba liʔann huwwa wilmulaːħiḍ maː yitfaːhmuːn] I approve of his transfer from this section since he and the supervisor don't get along.
حِسِن [ħisin] *n:* • **1.** beauty, loveliness, comeliness
حُسنَى، بالحُسنَى [ħusna, bilħusna] *n:* • **1.** amicably, in a friendly way – عامِلَه بِالحُسنَى [ʕaːmlah bilħusna] Treat him nicely.
حَسَنَة [ħasana] *n:* حَسَنات [ħasanaːt] *pl:* • **1.** good deed, charitable deed, benefaction – سَوِّيها حَسَنَة لِالله [sawwiːha ħasana lʔallah] Do it as a good deed for God's sake. • **2.** merit, advantage, attraction – هَالطَّرِيقَة إِلها حَسَناتها [haṭṭariːqa ʔilha ħasanaːtha] This way has its advantages.
تَحَسُّن [taħassun] *n:* تَحَسُّنات [taħassunaːt] *pl:* • **1.** improvement
تَحسِين [taħsiːn] *n:* تَحسِينات [taħsiːnaːt] *pl:* • **1.** improvement, improving, betterment.)
إحسان [ʔiħsaːn] *n:* • **1.** performance of good deeds, charity, alms-giving • **3.** pl. إحسانات good deed, good turn, favor
مَحاسِن [maħaːsin] *n:* • **1.** pros, good qualities
حُسَينِيَّة [ħusayniyya] *n:* حُسَينِيّات [ħusayniyaːt] *pl:* • **1.** shiite mosque
إستِحسان [ʔistiħsaːn] *n:* • **1.** approval, consent
حُسِن [ħusin] *n:* • **1.** goodness, excellence (in certain expressions:) – حُسُن السُّلُوك [ħusun ʔissuluːk] good conduct, good behavior. حُسُن التَّصَرُّف [ħusun ʔittaṣarruf] good judgment, discretion. حُسِن النِّيَّة [ħusin ʔinniyya] good faith, good intentions. سَوّاها بِحُسِن نِيَّة [sawwaːha bħusin niyya] He did it in good faith. حُسُن الظَّنّ [ħusun ʔiððann] good opinion. هَذا حُسِن ظَنَّك بِيّا [haːða ħusin ðannak biyya] You have a good opinion of me. أَشكُرَك عَلَى حُسِن ظَنَّك [ʔaškurak ʕala ħusin ðannak] I thank you for your good opinion. مِن حُسُن الحَظ [min ħusun ʔilħaðð] fortunately لِحُسُن الحَظ [liħusun ʔilħaðð] as goodluck would have it, fortunately. لِحُسُن الحَظّ، وُصَلنا عالوَقِت [liħusun ʔilħaðð, wuṣalna ʕalwakit] Fortunately, we arrived on time.
حَسِن [ħasin] *adj:* • **1.** beautiful, handsome, good-looking, comely, lovely – بِنتهُم حَسنَة [binithum ħasna] Their daughter is pretty. واحِد حَسِن [waːħid ħasin] a good-looking man. حَسِن الصُّورَة [ħasin ʔiṣṣuːra] good-looking, having good features. إبنَك حَسِن الصُّورَة [ʔibnak ħasin ʔiṣṣuːra] Your son has nice features.
حَسِين [ħasiːn] *adj:* • **1.** pretty, good-looking – بنَيَّة حَسِينَة [bnayya ħasiːna] a pretty girl.

مُحسِن [muħsin] *adj:* • **1.** charitable, beneficent, philanthropic أعمال مُحسِنَة [ʔaʕmaːl muħsina] charitable works. • **2.** pl. مُحسِنِين philanthropist, charitable person

مُحَسَّن [muħassan] *adj:* • **1.** improved, advanced

أحسَن [ʔaħsan] *comparative adjective:* • **1.** better, best – سَيّارتِي أحسَن مِن هاي [sayyaːrti ʔaħsan min haːy] My car's better than this one. لَو تِسألَه أوَّل أحسَن [law tisʔalah ʔawwal ʔaħsan] If you ask him first, it would be better. أحسَنلَك ترُوح قَبُل ما يزعَل [ʔaħsanlak truːħ gabul maː yizʕal] You'd better go before he gets mad. هَذا أحسَن طَبِيب بِبَغداد [haːða ʔaħsan ṭabiːb bibaɣdaːd] He's the best doctor in Baghdad. آنِي أحسَنهُم بِالشِّطرَنج [ʔaːni ʔaħsanhum biššiṭranǰ] I'm the best of them in chess. الأحسَن تقُلَّه قَبُل ما تسَوِّي شِي [ʔilʔaħsan dgullah gabul maː tsawwiː ši] The best thing would be to tell him before you do anything.

أحسَن ما [ʔaħsan maː] *subordinating conjunction:* • **1.** in preference to, rather than – أحسَن ما نخابرَه، خَلِّي نرُوحلَه لِلبَيت [ʔaħsan maː nxaːbrah, xalliː nruːħlah lilbayt] Better than calling him, let's go see him at home. بَطِّل أحسَن ما تِخسَر كُلّ فلُوسَك [baṭṭil ʔaħsan maː tixsar kull fluːsak] Quit rather than lose all your money.

ح س و

حَساوِي [ħasaːwi] *adj:* حَساوِيَّة [ħasaːwiyya] *pl:* • **1.** a kind of large, white donkey

ح ش د

حِشَد [ħišad] *v:* • **1.** to gather, mass, concentrate – حِشدَوا جُيُوشهُم عالحُدُود [ħišdaw ǰuyuːšhum ʕalħuduːd] They massed their troops on the border.

حَشَّد [ħaššad] *v:* • **1.** to mass, build up, concentrate – دَيحَشّدُون قُوّاتهُم قُرب العاصِمَة [dayħaššduːn guwwaːthum qurb ʔilʕaːṣima] They're concentrating their forces around the capital.

تحَشَّد [tħaššad] *v:* • **1.** to be massed, concentrate – الجُيُوش مِتحَشّدَة بِهالمَنطَقَة [ʔiǰǰuyuːš mitħaššda bhalmanṭaqa] The troops are concentrated in this area.

اِحتِشَد [ʔiħtišad] *v:* • **1.** to come together, assemble, congregate – عَشرَة آلاف جُندِي اِحتِشدَوا [ʕašrat ʔaːlaːf ǰundi ʔiħtišdaw] Ten thousand troops have assembled on the border.

حَشِد [ħašid] *n:* • **1.** crowd

مِحتِشِد [miħtišid] *adj:* • **1.** overcrowded, massed

ح ش ر

حِشَر [ħišar] *v:* • **1.** to stuff, pack, jam, squeeze, force – إحشِر هَالكِتاب بين بَقِيَّة الكُتُب [ʔiħšir halkitaːb biːn baqiyyat ʔilkutub] Stick this book in among the rest. إحشِر قَمِيصي وِيّا قُمصانَك بِالجَّنطَة [ʔiħšir qamiːṣi wiyya qumṣaːnak biǰǰanṭa] Stick my shirt in with your shirts in the bag. هَذا وَلَد صغَيِّر. إحشِرَه بِالصَّدِر [haːða walad ṣɣayyir. ʔiħšrah biṣṣadir] He's a small boy. Squeeze him into the front seat. السّايِق حِشَر النّاس بِالباص بَلا حساب [ʔissaːyiq ħišar ʔinnaːs bilpaːṣ bala ħsaːb] The driver jammed a whole crowd of people into the bus. شلُون حِشرَوا ألف شَخِص بهَالقاعَة الصّغَيّرَة؟ [šluːn ħišraw ʔalf šaxiṣ bhalqaːʕa ʔiṣṣiɣayyra?] How did they crowd a thousand people into that small hall? عَلَى طُول يحشر نَفسَه ويّانا بِالمُناقَشَة [ʕala ṭuːl yiħšir nafsah wiyyaːna bilmunaːqaša] He always intrudes himself into our discussion. لا تِحشِر إسمِي بهَالمَوضُوع [laː tiħšir ʔismi bhalmawḍuːʕ] Don't bring my name into this affair. المُدِير حِشَرنِي بهاللُّجنَة [ʔilmudiːr ħišarni bhalluǰna] The director stuck me on this committee. • **2.** to jam, stick, get stuck – الكَير حِشَر. خابُر الفِيتَرجِي [ʔilgiːr ħišar. xaːbur ʔilfiːtarči] The gearshift jammed. Call the mechanic.

حَشَّر [ħaššar] *v:* • **1.** to stuff, pack, squeeze

اِنحِشَر [ʔinħišar] *v:* • **1.** to crowd oneself, push oneself – كُلّما نُقعُد بِالقَهوَة، يِنحِشِر بَيناتنا [kullma nugʕud bilgahwa, yinħišir baynaːtna] Whenever we sit in the coffeeshop, he crowds in among us.

حَشِر، يَوم الحَشِر [ħašir, yuːm ʔilħašir] *n:* • **1.** Resurrection Day

حَشِر [ħašir] *n:* • **1.** stuffing, squeezing

حَشَرَة [ħašara] *n:* حَشَرات [ħašaraːt] *pl:* • **1.** insect, bug – عِلم الحَشَرات [ʕilm ʔilħašaraːt] entomology.

حِشَرِي [ħišari] *adj:* حِشَرِيَّة [ħišariyya] *pl:* حِشَرِيَّة [ħišariyya] *feminine:* • **1.** a person who meddles or gossips

حاشِر [haːšir] *adj:* • **1.** jammed, stuffed, packed

ح ش ش

حَشَّش [ħaššaš] *v:* • **1.** to smoke hashish – أهَل هَالمَنطِقَة كُلّهُم يحَشّشُون [ʔahal halmanṭiqa kullhum yħaššišuːn] The people of this area all smoke hashis. • **2.** to daydream, let one's mind wander – شبِيك محَشّش؟ ما تدِير بالَك عَالشّغُل [šbiːk mħaššiš? maː ddiːr baːlak ʕaššɣul] What's the matter with you, daydreaming? Pay attention to your work!

حَشِيش [ħašiːš] *n:* • **1.** wild grass, hay • **2.** hemp, hashish, cannabis, or loosely, any narcotic

حَشِيشَة [ħašiːša] *n:* • **1.** hemp, hashish, cannabis, or loosely, any narcotic

حَشّاش [ħaššaːš] *adj:* حَشّاشِين، حَشّاشَة [ħaššaːšiːn, ħaššaːša] *pl:* • **1.** narcotics addict • **2.** idiot, dope, dunce, ninny

محَشّش [mħaššiš] *adj:* • **1.** under the influence of hashish, or other narcotic – لِقوه محَشّش وَوَقّفُوه [ligawh mħaššiš wwaqqufuːh] They found him hopped up, and arrested him. • **2.** absent-minded – هَذا محَشّش. ما يِتذَكَّر وين خَلَّى الغَراض [haːða mħaššiš. maː yiðđakkar wiːn xallaː ʔilɣaraːð] He's absent-minded. He doesn't remember where he put the things. • **3.** (loosely) crazy, out of one's mind – هَذا مَحَشِّش. ماكُو اِجتِماع اليُوم [ha:ða mħaššiš. ma:ku ʔijtima:ʕ ʔilyu:m] He's out of his mind! There's no meeting today.

ح ش ف

حَشَف [ħašaf] *n:* • **1.** (coll.) under-developed, dried up, poor quality dates
حَشفَة [ħašfa] *n:* حَشَفات [ħašfa:t] *pl:* • **1.** (vulgar) glans penis • **2.** under-developed, dried up, poor quality dates

ح ش ك

حِشَك [ħišag] *v:* • **1.** to crowd, cram, stuff, jam, squeeze – إحشِك هَالكِتاب بين بَقِيَّة الكُتُب [ʔiħšig halkita:b bi:n baqiyyat ʔilkutub] Squeeze this book in with the rest of them.
تحَشَّك [tħaššag] *v:* • **1.** to crowd, jostle, brush – عِيب تِتحَشَّك بالبَنات [ʕi:b titħaššag bilbana:t] It's wrong to go brushing against the girls. • **2.** to interfere, meddle – هَذا يِتحَشَّك بالرّايح والجاي [ha:ða yitħaššag birra:yiħ wajja:y] He interferes in everyone's affairs.
تحاشَك [tħa:šag] *v:* • **1.** to crowd, jostle, push each other – لا تِتحاشكُون. أكُو مُكان واسِع [la: titħa:šku:n. ʔaku muka:n wa:siʕ] Don't jostle. There's a wide enough space.
اِنحِشَك [ʔinħišag] *v:* • **1.** to crowd, force oneself – قِعَد بِالباص يَمِّي وظَلّ يِنحِشِك بيّا [giʕad bilpa:ṣ yammi wđall yinħišig biyya] He sat next to me on the bus, and kept crowding me. إبني دائِماً يِنحِشِك بَيني وبَين مَرتي عالقَنَفَة [ʔibni da:ʔiman yinħišig bayni wbayn marti ʕalqanafa] My son always squeezes in between me and my wife on the sofa.
حَشِك [ħašig] *n:* • **1.** crowd, mob, jam
حَشكَة [ħašga] *n:* حَشكات [ħašga:t] *pl:* • **1.** crowd, mob, jam
مَحشُوك [maħšu:g] *adj:* • **1.** compact

ح ش م

اِحتِشَم [ʔiħtišam] *v:* • **1.** to be modest, proper, conservative, timid – تِحتِشِم هوايَة بلِبِسها [tiħtišim hwa:ya blibisha] She is very conservative in her dress.
حَشَم [ħašam] *n:* • **1.** compensation for an insult to one's reputation – هَالحكايَة عَليها حَشَم [halħča:ya ʕali:ha ħašam] That remark calls for recompense.
حِشمَة [ħišma] *n:* • **1.** modesty • **2.** decorum, decency
مَحشُوم [maħšu:m] *adj:* • **1.** blameless, undeserving of shame or guilt, proper, decorous – إنتَ مَحشُوم مِن الكِذب [ʔinta maħšu:m min ʔiččiðib] You're above lying. مَحشُوم! إنتَ ما إلَك عِلاقَة بالقُمار [maħšu:m! ʔinta ma: ʔilak ʕila:qa bilquma:r] You have nothing to be ashamed of! You have no connection with gambling. مَحشُوم؛ مُو بِالحَيف! إنتَ شجابَك عَالكِذب؟ [maħšu:m; mu: bilħayf! ʔinta šja:bak ʕaččiðib?] You're not to blame; far from it! What could you have to do with lying?
مُحتَشِم [muħtašim] *adj:* • **1.** modest

ح ش و [1]

حِشَى [ħiša:] *v:* • **1.** to stuff, full
حَشَّى [ħašša:] *v:* • **1.** to stuff, fill – حَشَّى الدِّجاجَة بلُوز وكِشمِش [ħašša: ʔiddija:ja blu:z wkišmiš] He stuffed the chicken with almonds and raisins. • **2.** to fill (teeth) – طَبِيب الأسنان حَشَّى كَم سِنّ [ṭabi:b ʔilʔasna:n ħašša: čam sinn] The dentist filled some teeth. • **3.** to stick, stuff, pack – شدَعوَة مَحَشِّي هَالقَدّ قُطِن بإذنَك؟ [šdaʕwa mħašši halgadd guṭin bʔiðnak?] Why have you stuffed so much cotton in your ear? • **4.** to insert, stick in – شِمحَشِّي بين الأوراق؟ [šimħašši bi:n ʔilʔawra:q?] What's stuck in among the papers? حَشَّى الثَّمانيَة ويّا الأس حَتَّى يِبلِفني [ħašša: ʔiθθma:nya wiyya ʔilʔa:s ħatta yiblifni] He stuck the eight with the ace so as to bluff me.
تحَشَّى [tħašša:] *v:* • **1.** to be filled – هَالسِّنّ ما يِتحَشَّى. لازِم نِشلَعَه [hassinn ma: yitħašša:. la:zim nišlaʕah] This tooth can't be filled. We'll have to pull it.
تحاشَى [tħa:ša:] *v:* • **1.** to avoid, shun – آني دائماً أتحاشاه لأنَّه مُو خُوش رِجّال [ʔa:ni da:ʔiman ʔatħa:ša:h liʔannah mu: xu:š rijja:l] I'm always avoiding him because he's a nasty old man. تحاشَى تِذكُرلَه أيّ شِي عَن المَوضُوع [tħa:ša: tiðkurlah ʔayy ši ʕan ʔilmawđu:ʕ] Avoid mentioning anything about the subject to him. • **2.** to ignore – دَاحاوِل أتحاشاه. شما يِحكي، ما أدِيرلَه بال [daʔaħa:wil ʔatħa:ša:h. šma yiħči, ma: ʔadi:rlah ba:l] I'm trying to ignore him. Whatever he says, I don't pay him any attention.
اِنحِشَى [ʔinħiša:] *v:* • **1.** to be filled, stuffed
حَشو [ħašw] *n:* • **1.** stuffing, filling, that with which something is filled – حَشو مال قَنَفَة [ħašw ma:l qanafa] stuffing, or padding of a sofa. الحَشو مال الفلفِل [ʔilħašw ma:l ʔilfilfil] the stuffing in the pepper. • **2.** filling (of teeth) – حَشو مال سِنّ [ħašw ma:l sinn] filling of a tooth. • **3.** verbiage – القَصِيدَة مالتَه كُلها حَشو [ʔilqaṣi:da ma:ltah kullha ħašw] His poem is nothing but verbiage.
حَشوَة [ħašwa] *n:* حَشوات [ħašwa:t] *pl:* • **1.** (dent.) a filling
حاشِيَة [ħa:šiya] *n:* حَواشِي [ħawa:ši] *pl:* • **1.** edge – حاشيَة البِرداغ [ħa:šyat ʔilpirda:ɣ] the edge of the glass. حاشيَة الزُّولِيَّة [ħa:ṣyat ʔizzu:liyya] the edge of the carpet. هَالقَضِيَّة إلها حَواشِي هوايَة بَعَد [halqađiyya ʔilha ħawa:ši hwa:ya baʕad] There are many more facets to this affair. • **2.** retinue, entourage, followers
مَحشِي [maħši] *adj:* • **1.** stuffed, filled – طَماطَة مَحشِيَّة [ṭama:ṭa maħšiyya] stuffed tomatoes. هَالبَقلاوَة مَحشِيَّة بلُوز لَو جُوز؟ [halbaqla:wa maħšiyya blu:z law ju:z?] Is this baklava filled with almonds or walnuts?

محَشّا [mħaššaː] *adj:* • **1.** stuffed, filled – دِجاجَة محَشّايَة تِمَّن وكِشمِش وَلُوز [dijaːja mħaššaːya timman wkišmiš wluːz] chicken stuffed with rice, raisins, and almonds.

ح ش و [2]

حَشَى [ħašaː] *particle:* • **1.** except, with the exception of, excluding – كُلّ البَنات ملَعِّبات، حَشَى بَناتَك [kull ʔilbanaːt mlaʕʕibaːt, ħašaː banaːtak] All girls are fast, excepting your girls. عَساهُم بالعَمَى مِن حَشَى إبني [ʕasaːhum bilʕama min ħašaː ʔibni] I hope they all go blind, except for my son! هَالأكِل طُرَّهات، حَشَى النِّعمَة [halʔakil ṭurrahaːt, ħašaː ʔinniʕma] This food is lousy, save what is God's bounty. حَشاك، أستاذ، هَذا زمال [ħašaːk, ʔustaːð, haːða zmaːl] Saving your presence, sir, that guy is an ass. إنتَ حَشاك مِن الكِذِب [ʔinta ħašaːk min ʔiččiðib] You're above lying. • **1.** God forbid

ح ص ب

حَصَّب [ħaṣṣab] *v:* • **1.** to catch or have the measles – حَصَّب إبنها وَما راح لِلمَدرَسَة [ħaṣṣab ʔibinha wama raːħ lilmadrasa] Her son had measles and didn't go to school.

حَصبَة [ħaṣba, ħuṣba] *n:* • **1.** measles

محَصَّب [mħaṣṣub] *adj:* • **1.** having the measels

ح ص د

حِصَد [ħiṣad] *v:* • **1.** to reap, harvest – الفَلّاحِين دَيحِصدُون الحُنطَة [ʔilfallaːħiːn dayħiṣduːn ʔilħunṭa] The peasants are harvesting the wheat.

اِنحِصَد [ʔinħiṣad] *v:* • **1.** to be harvested – الشِّعِير بَعَد ما نحِصَد [ʔiššiʕiːr baʕad maː nħiṣad] The barley still hasn't been harvested.

حَصِد [ħaṣid] *n:* • **1.** reaping, harvesting

حَصاد [ħaṣaːd] *n:* حَصادات [ħaṣaːdaːt] *pl:* • **1.** harvesting, harvest • **2.** harvest time

مَحصُود [maħṣuːd] *n:* • **1.** harvest

حاصُودَة [ħaːṣuːda] *n:* • **1.** machine for harvesting

ح ص ر

حِصَر [ħiṣar] *v:* • **1.** to enclose – إحصِر هَالكِلمَة بين قَوسَين [ʔiħṣir haččilma biːn qawsayn] Enclose this word between parentheses. • **2.** to trap, corner, hem in, encircle – حِصرَوا الكَلِب بِالزُّوِيَّة وَكُمشَوه [ħiṣraw ʔiččalib bizzuwiyya wkumšuːh] They trapped the dog in the corner and caught him. حِصَر المَلِك مالِي بِهَالخانَة وماأقدَر أحَرّكَه بَعَد [ħiṣar ʔilmalik maːli bhalxaːna wma ʔagdar ʔaħarrkah baʕad] He trapped my king on that square and I can't move it. لِيش تِحصِر الوَزِير مالَك هِيكِي؟ مُو تِحتاجَه بَرَّة [liːš tiħṣir ʔilwaziːr maːlak hiːči? muː tiħtaːǰah barra] Why do you hem in your queen like that? You need it outside. ما يعجِبنِي هَالبَيت لِأَنّ مَحصُور بين بنايات عالية [maː yiʕǰibni halbayt liʔann maħṣuːr biːn binaːyaːt ʕaːlya] I don't like this house because it's sandwiched in between tall buildings. إجانِي لِلدّائرَة وَحِصَرنِي وَما طِلَع إلّا بَعَد ما أخَذ فلُوسَه [ʔijaːni liddaːʔira wħiṣarni wamaː ṭilaʕ ʔilla baʕad maː ʔaxað fluːsah] He came to me at the office, cornered me and wouldn't leave till he got his money. حِصَرنِي عالطَّلَب مالَه بوَقِت ما كان عِندِي فلُوس [ħiṣarni ʕaṭṭalab maːlah bwaqit maː čaːn ʕindi fluːs] He pressed me for what I owed him when I didn't have any money. • **3.** to narrow down, confine – حِصرَوا الشُّبهَه بِالخَدّامَة [ħiṣraw ʔiššubhah bilxaddaːma] They narrowed down the suspicion to the maid. إحصِر فِكرَك بِشُغلَك [ʔiħṣir fikrak bišuɣlak] Keep your mind on your work. إحصِر فِكرَك وحاوِل تِتذَكَّر [ʔiħṣir fikrak wħaːwil tiððakkar] Put your mind to it and try to remember. هَالولايَة تِحصِر الرُّوح [halwlaːya tiħṣir ʔirruːħ] This city's depressing (lit., restricts the spirit).

حاصَر [ħaːṣar] *v:* • **1.** to surround, encircle – الشُّرطَة حاصرَت الكُلِّيَّة مِن بِدَت المُظاهَرات [ʔiššurṭa ħaːṣrat ʔilkulliyya min bidat ʔilmuðaːharaːt] The police surrounded the college when the demonstrations started. • **2.** to besiege – العَدُو حاصَر المَدِينَة سَبعَة أيّام قَبُل ما اِتسَلّمِت [ʔilʕadu ħaːṣar ʔilmadiːna sabʕa ʔayyaːm gabul maː tsallamit] The enemy besieged the city for seven days before it surrendered.

اِنحِصَر [ʔinħiṣar] *v:* • **1.** to get caught, get trapped – اِنحِصَرنا بِباب الدّائرَة إلَى أن وُقَف المُطَر [ʔinħiṣarna bibaːb ʔiddaːʔira ʔila ʔan wugaf ʔilmuṭar] We got caught in the doorway of the office until the rain stopped. إيدِي اِنحِصرَت بِالباب وَإصبِعِي تعَوَّر [ʔiːdi ʔinħiṣrat bilbaːb wʔiṣibʕi tʕawwar] My hand got caught in the door and my finger got hurt. • **2.** to be crowded, be jammed – اِنحِصرَوا بِالباص وَما قِدَر الواحِد يِتحَرَّك [ʔinħiṣraw bilpaːṣ wma gidar ʔilwaːħid yitħarrak] They were crowded in the bus so that no one could move. إذا اِنحِصَرت وَما عِندَك وَلا فِلِس، إكتِبلِي [ʔiða ʔinħiṣarit wma ʕindak wala filis, ʔiktibli] If you get in a tight spot and don't have a bit of money, write me. • **3.** to have a full bladder, to have to go – الجّاهِل اِنحِصَر بُولَة. أكُو مِرحاض هنا؟ [ʔiǰǰaːhil ʔinħiṣar buːla. ʔaku mirħaːḍ hna?] The child has to go to the bathroom. Is there a toilet here? إذا اِنحِصَرت، المَراحِيض فوق [ʔiða ʔinħiṣarit, ʕilmaraːħiːḍ fuːg] If you feel the need, the toilets are upstairs.

اِحتِصَر [ʔiħtiṣar] *v:* • **1.** to be or become depressed, feel confined, restless, closed in – إذا يِبقَى وَحدَه بِالبَيت، يِحتِصِر [ʔiða yibqaː waħdah bilbayt, yiħtiṣir] If he stays alone in the house, he will get depressed. اِحتِصَرت بِبَعقُوبَة، لِأَنّ ماكُو شِي واحِد يِلتِهِي بِيه [ʔiħtiṣarit bbaʕguːba, liʔann maːku ši waːħid yiltihi biːh] I got depressed in Ba'kuba, because there's nothing to occupy oneself with.

حَصِر [ħaṣir] *n:* • **1.** enclosing

حَصِير [ħaṣiːr] *n:* • **1.** oven matting, woven mat

حِصار [ħiṣa:r] *n:* حِصارات [ħiṣa:ra:t] *pl:* • **1.** siege • **2.** blockade – حِصار اِقتِصادِي [ħiṣa:r ʔiqtiṣa:di] economic blockade.

حَصِيرَة [ħaṣi:ra] *n:* حَصِيرات [ħaṣi:ra:t] *pl:* • **1.** a woven mat

مُحاصَرَة [muħa:ṣara] *n:* مُحاصَرات [muħa:ṣara:t] *pl:* • **1.** blockade • **2.** siege

اِنحِصار [ʔinħiṣa:r] *n:* • **1.** restrictedness, limitation, confinement • **2.** (tobacco) monopoly – مُدِيرِيَّة اِنحِصار التَّبُغ العامَّة [mudi:riyyat ʔinħiṣa:r ʔittabuɣ ʔilʕa:mma] Directorate General of the Tobacco Monopoly.

حَصرِي [ħaṣri] *adj:* • **1.** exclusive

مَحصُور [maħṣu:r] *adj:* • **1.** limited, restricted, confined – تِجارَة الشّاي مَحصُورَة بين خَمِس تُجّار [tiǰa:rat ʔiččaːy maħṣu:ra bi:n xamis tuǰǰa:r] The tea trade is restricted to five merchants. • **2.** depressed, bored – كِنِت مَحصُور بهالولايَة الصَّغَيِّرَة [činit maħṣu:r bha:luwla:ya ʔilzɣayyra] I was bored in that small town. • **3.** feeling the need to urinate – آنِي مَحصُور. أَكُو خَلاء هنا؟ [ʔa:ni maħṣu:r. ʔaku xala:ʔ hna?] I've got to go. Is there a toilet here?

مُحاصَر [muħa:ṣar] *adj:* • **1.** under siege, in sanctions

ح ص ر م

حِصرِم، حُصرُم [ħiṣrim, ħuṣrum] *n:* • **1.** sour, unripe grapes

مَحصرُم [mħaṣrum] *adj:* • **1.** sour

ح ص ص

حُصَّة [ħuṣṣa, ħiṣṣa] *n:* حُصَص [ħuṣaṣ] *pl:* • **1.** share, part

مُحاصَصَة [muħa:ṣaṣa] *n:* • **1.** allotment, apportion

ح ص ف

حَصَف [ħaṣaf] *n:* • **1.** skin rash

ح ص ل

حِصَل [ħiṣal] *v:* • **1.** to happen, occur, take place, come to pass – حِصَل شِي بِغِيابِي؟ [ħiṣal ši biɣya:bi?] Did anything happen during my absence? هَذا شِي يِحصَل مَرَّة بِالسَّنَة [ha:ða ši yiħṣal marra bissana] This is a thing that happens only once a year. لازم حِصَل عِندَه مانِع أَخَّرَه [la:zim ħiṣal ʕindah ma:niʕ ʔaxxarah] Something must have come up to delay him. حِصلَت المُوافَقَة عَلَى نَقلَك اليُوم [ħiṣlat ʔilmuwa:faqa ʕala naqlak ʔilyu:m] The approval of your transfer went through today. • **2.** to be extant, available, obtainable – دَوَّرتلَك عالقماش لَكِن ما حِصَل [dawwartlak ʕalqma:š la:kin ma: ħiṣal] I looked for the cloth for you but it wasn't available. هَالثُّوب ما يِحصَل مِنَّه بالسُّوق [haθθu:b ma: yiħṣal minnah bissu:g] A shirt like this isn't to be found in the market. • **3.** with – عَلَى to obtain, attain, get, receive – شوَقِت حِصَلِت عَلَى شَهادتَك؟ [šwakit ħiṣalit ʕala šaha:dtak?] When did you get your diploma?

حَصَّل [ħaṣṣal] *v:* • **1.** to obtain, attain, get, receive – حَصَّل الوَظِيفَة اللِّي يرِيدها [ħaṣṣal ʔilwaðiːfa ʔilli yri:dha] He got the job he wanted. حَصَّلِتلَك المَعلُومات اللِّي ترِيدها [ħaṣṣalitlak ʔilmaʕlu:ma:t ʔilli tri:dha] I got you the information that you want. تِقدَر تحَصِّلِّي هَالكتاب مِن المَكتَبَة؟ [tigdar tħaṣṣilli halkta:b min ʔilmaktaba?] Can you get this book for me from the library? حَصِّلِي مُدِير الذّاتِيَّة [ħaṣṣilli mudi:r ʔiððaːtiyya] Get me the personnel supervisor (on the phone). دَيحَصِّل عَشِر دَنانِير بِاليُوم [dayħaṣṣil ʕašir dana:ni:r bilyu:m] He makes ten dinars a day. شتحَصِّل مِن أَذِيَّة النّاس؟ [šitħaṣṣil min ʔaðiyyat ʔinna:s?] What do you get from hurting people? • **2.** to collect, recover (a debt) – أَطلُب عَلِي خَمس دَنانِير وَ ما دَأَقدَر أَحَصِّلها مِنَّه [ʔaṭlub ʕali xams dana:ni:r wma daʔagdar ʔaħaṣṣilha minnah] Ali owes me five dinars and I can't collect it from him. • **3.** to profit, make a profit – بِعت سَيّارتِي بِأَلف دِينار وحَصَّلِت بِيها مِيَّة دِينار [biʕit sayya:rti bʔalif dina:r wħaṣṣalit bi:ha miyyat dina:r] I sold my car for a thousand dinars and made a hundred dinars profit on it. إذا تبِيع سَيّارتَك هَسَّة، ما راح تحَصِّل [ʔiða tbi:ʕ sayya:rtak hassa, ma: ra:ħ tħaṣṣil] If you sell your car now, you won't make any profit. • **4.** to yield a profit, be profitable – إذا أَبِيعها بهِيكِي قِيمَة، ما تحَصِّل [ʔiða ʔabi:ʕha bhi:či qi:ma, ma: tħaṣṣil] If I sell it for this price it won't yield any profit.

تحَصَّل [tħaṣṣal] *v:* • **1.** to be obtained – هِيكِي سَيّارَة ما تِتحَصَّل بأَقَلّ مِن أَلف دِينار [hi:či sayya:ra ma: titħaṣṣal bʔaqall min ʔalf dina:r] That sort of car can't be obtained for less than a thousand dinars. • **2.** to be collected – هَالدَّين ما يِتحَصَّل [haddi:n ma: yitħaṣṣal] This debt can't be collected.

حُصُول [ħuṣu:l] *n:* • **1.** obtainment, attainment حُصُول عالشَّهادَة [ħuṣu:l ʕaššaha:da] attainment of a degree.

حاصِل [ħa:ṣil] *n:* حاصِلات [ħa:ṣila:t] *pl:* • **1.** product – أَهَمّ حاصِلات العِراق النَّفُط وَالتَّمُر [ʔahamm ħa:ṣila:t ʔilʕira:q ʔinnafuṭ wittamur] The most important of the products of Iraq are oil and dates. • **2.** crop, harvest – المُطَر دَمَّر حاصِلاتنا مِن التَّمُر هالسَّنَة [ʔilmuṭar dammar ħa:ṣila:tna min ʔittamur hassana] The rain damaged our date production this year. • **3.** gist, essence, main content – الحاصِل، كُلّ تَعَبنا راح حَرَمات [ʔilħa:ṣil, kull taʕabna ra:ħ ħarama:t] To make a long story short, all our effort went for nothing. الحاصِل، اِشتِرَيت سَيّارَة لَو لا؟ [ʔilħa:ṣil, ʔištirayt sayya:ra law la:?] In point of fact, did you buy a car or not? الحاصِل، ما لِقَينا سَيّارَة تِعجِبنا [ʔilħa:ṣil, ma: ligi:na sayya:ra tiʕǰibna] In the end, we didn't find a car we liked.

تَحصِيل [taħṣi:l] *n:* تَحصِيلات [taħṣi:la:t] *pl:* • **1.** educational level – تَحصِيل عِلمِي [taħṣi:l ʕilmi] educational level.

مَحصُول [maħşu:l] *n:* مَحاصِيل [maħa:şi:l] *pl:* • **1.** produce, product • **2.** crop, harvest • **3.** yield, gain, profit
حَصّالَة [ħaşşa:la] *n:* • **1.** small safe, collection box
مُحَصَّل [muħaşşal] *adj:* • **1.** outcome, result

ح ص ن

حَصَّن [ħaşşan] *v:* • **1.** to fortify, entrench – الجَّيش حَصَّن هَالمَنطِقَة بِالحَرُب الأُولَى [ʔiǰǰayš ħaşşan halmanṭiqa bilħarub ʔilʔu:la] The army fortified this area in the first World War.
تحَصَّن [tħaşşan] *v:* • **1.** to take shelter, seek shelter – لَو ما تِتحَصَّن العَشايِر بِالجِبال، كان الجَّيش دَمَّرهُم [lu: ma: titħaşşan ʔilʕaša:yir biǰǰiba:l, ča:n ʔiǰǰi:š dammarhum] If the tribes hadn't taken shelter in the mountains, the army'd have destroyed them. الجِّنُود تحَصَّنَوا بِالسُّوبِيرات مِن صار الهُجُوم [ʔiǰǰinu:d tħaşşnaw bissu:pi:ra:t min şa:r ʔilhuǰu:m] The soldiers took cover in the trenches when the attack occurred.
حُصِن [ħuşin, ħişin] *n:* حُصُون [ħuşu:n] *pl:* • **1.** fort
حصان [ħşa:n] *n:* حُصُن [ħuşun] *pl:* • **1.** horse, specifically, a stallion – حصان إبلِيس [ħşa:n bli:s] mantis, praying mantis. • **1.** حصان البَحَر – sea horse, hippopotamus • **2.** horsepower – هَالمَكِينَة قُوَّتها مِيَّة حصان [halmaki:na quwwatha miyyat ħşa:n] This motor is one hundred horsepower. • **3.** knight (chess)
حصِينِي [ħşi:ni] *n:* حصَينِيَّة [ħşi:niyya] *pl:* • **1.** fox • **2.** jackal
حَصانَة [ħaşa:na] *n:* • **1.** immunity – حَصانَة دِبلُوماسِيَّة [ħaşa:na diblu:ma:siyya] diplomatic immunity. حَصانَة بَرلَمانِيَّة [ħaşa:na barlama:niyya] parliamentary immunity.
تَحصِين [taħşi:n] *n:* تَحصِينات [taħşi:na:t] *pl:* • **1.** fortification, entrenchment
مَحَصَّن [mħaşşan] *adj:* • **1.** fortified

ح ص و

حِصَى [ħişa:] *v:* • **1.** to count, enumerate – هَالنّاس اللّي بِالسِينَما شيِحصِيهُم؟ [hanna:s ʔilli bissinama šyiħşi:hum?] How could you ever count all these people in the movie theater? عِندَه فلُوس شيِحصِيها [ʕindah flu:s šyiħşi:ha] He has more money than he could count!
حَصو [ħaşw] *n:* • **1.** (coll.) pebble(s), gravel
حَصوَة [ħaşwa] *n:* حَصوات [ħaşwa:t] *pl:* • **1.** pebble, small stone • **2.** stone, calculus (med.)
إحصاء [ʔiħşa:ʔ] *n:* • **1.** count, counting – إحصاء النُّفُوس [ʔiħşa:ʔ ʔinnufu:s] census. • **2.** statistics • **3.** (pl. إحصَاءات [ʔiħşa:ʔa:t]) statistics, statistical datum
إحصائِيَّة [ʔiħşa:ʔiyya] *n:* إحصائِيّات [ʔiħşa:ʔiyya:t] *pl:* • **1.** count • **2.** statistics

ح ض ر

حِضَر [ħiðar] *v:* • **1.** to attend مِيَّة شَخِص حِضرَوا الإجتِماع [miyyat šaxiş ħiðraw ʔilʔiǰtima:ʕ] A hundred people attended the meeting. ما حِضَر الحَفلَة البارحَة [ma: ħiðar ʔilħafla ʔilba:rħa] He didn't attend the party yesterday. • **2.** to arrive – الطَّرَفَين حِضرَوا. ترِيد تشُوفهُم هَسَّة؟ [ʔiṭṭarafayn ħiðraw. tri:d tšu:fhum hassa?] The two parties have arrived. do you want to see them now? • **3.** to appear at, show up at – إذا ما تِحضَر المُحاكَمَة، تِخسَر الدَّعوَة [ʔiða ma: tiħðar ʔilmuħa:kama, tixsar ʔiddaʕwa] If you don't appear at the trial, you'll lose the case. • **4.** to be or become ready – شُوف الأكِل حِضَر لَو بَعَد [šu:f ʔilʔakil ħiðar law baʕad] See if the food's ready yet.
حَضَّر [ħaððar] *v:* • **1.** to prepare, make ready, ready – حَضِّر كُلّ غَراضَك لِلسَّفرَة [ħaððir kull ɣara:ðak lissafra] Get all your things ready for the trip. إذا تِنتِظِر خَمِس دَقايِق، راح أحَضِّرلَك الدُّوا [ʔiða tintiðir xamis daqa:yiq, ra:ħ ʔaħaððirlak ʔidduwa] If you wait five minutes, I'll prepare the medicine for you. • **2.** to produce, make, manufacture – شلُون تحَضِّر غاز الهَيدرُوجِين؟ [šlu:n tħaððir ɣa:z ʔilhidruǰi:n?] How do you produce hydrogen gas? • **3.** to fetch, get, bring – تِقدَر تحَضِّرلِي مِيَّة دِينار اليُوم العَصِر؟ [tigdar tħaððirli miyyat dina:r ʔilyu:m ʔilʕaşir?] Can you get me a hundred dinars by this afternoon? • **4.** to summon forth, make appear – هَالسّاحِر يِقدَر يحَضِّر أرواح [hassa:ħir yigdar yħaððir ʔarwa:ħ] This magician is able to summon spirits.
حاضَر [ha:ðar] *v:* • **1.** to lecture, give lectures – حاضَر بِهالكُلِّيَّة سَنتَين [ha:ðar bhalkulliyya santayn] He lectured in this college two years.
تحَضَّر [tħaððar] *v:* • **1.** to prepare oneself, get ready – تحَضَّرِت لِلإمتِحان زين [tħaððarit lilʔimtiħa:n zi:n] I prepared well for the exam. تحَضَّرنا مِن زَمان [tħaððarna min zama:n] We got ready some time ago. • **2.** to become civilized, settle down – طُول عُمرَك ما راح تِتحَضَّر [ṭu:l ʕumrak ma: ra:ħ titħaððar] You'll never in your life become civilized.
إنحِضَر [ʔinħiðar] *v:* • **1.** to be attended
إحتِضَر [ʔiħtiðar] *v:* • **1.** to die – دَيِحتِضِر وَما حَدّ يَمَّه [dayiħtiðir wma ħadd yammah] He is dying and there's no one by his side.
حَضَر [ħaðar] *n:* • **1.** settled population, town dwellers (as opposed to nomads)
حَضرَة [ħaðra] *n:* • **1.** presence – ما لازم تِقُول هِيكِي أشياء بِحَضرَة ناس أكبَر مِنَّك [ma: la:zim tigu:l hi:či ʔašya:ʔ bħaðrat na:s ʔakbar minnak] You shouldn't say such things in the presence of older people. • **2.** /in construct/ a polite form of address, sometimes used sarcastically – حَضرَة الأُستاذ [ħaðrat ʔilʔusta:ð] approx., the good professor, the honorable professor. حَضرَة الأُستاذ، لَو قارِي جَرِيدَة اليُوم، كان شِفِت مَعلُوماتَك غَلَط [ħaðrat ʔilʔusta:ð, law qa:ri ǰari:dat ʔilyu:m, ča:n šifit maʕlu:ma:tak ɣalaṭ] My dear sir, if you'd read today's

paper you'd have seen that your information is wrong. حَضرَتكُم لِيش زِعَلتُوا؟ [ħaḍratkum liːš ziʕaltuː?] Why did your Grace get mad? • **4.** most sacred chamber of a religious shrine, where the deceased is entombed
حُضُور [ħuḍuːr] *n:* • **1.** presence – حُضُورَك بِالمَحكَمَة مُو ضَرُورِي [ħuḍuːrak bilmaħkama muː ḍaruːri] Your presence in court isn't necessary. إنطاه الفلُوس بِحضُورِي [ʔinṭaːh ʔilfluːs biħḍuːri] He gave him the money in my presence. • **2.** attendance – الحُضُور بِلإجتِماع جَبري [ʔilħuḍuːr bilʔiǰtimaːʕ ǰabri] Attendance at the meeting is compulsory. • **3.** those present, the ones attending – مَحَّد مِن الحُضُور وافَق [maħħad min ʔilħuḍuːr waːfaq] None of those present would agree.
مَحضَر [maħḍar] *n:* مَحاضِر [maħaːðir] *pl:* • **1.** minutes (of a meeting, police deposition)
تَحَضُّر [taħaḍḍur] *n:* • **2.** civilization, urbanization, urbanism
حَضارَة [ħaḍaːra] *n:* حَضارات [ħaḍaːraːt] *pl:* • **1.** civilization • **2.** culture
حَضِيرَة [ħaḍiːra] *n:* حَضايِر [ħaḍaːyir] *pl:* • **1.** patrol (boy scouts) • **2.** squad (mil.)
مُحاضِر [muħaːḍir] *n:* مُحاضِرِين [muħaːḍiriːn] *pl:* • **1.** lecturer, speaker – دَولَة مِتحَضّرَة [dawla mitħaḍḍra] a civilized country.
تَحضِير [taħḍiːr] *n:* • **1.** preparation
مُحاضَرَة [muħaːḍara] *n:* مُحاضَرات [muħaːḍaraːt] *pl:* • **1.** lecture
حَضَرِي [ħaḍari] *adj:* • **1.** settled, sedentary, non-nomadic • **2.** settled person, town dweller
حاضِر [ħaːḍir] *adj:* • **1.** ready – الأكِل حاضِر [ʔilʔakil ħaːḍir] The food's ready. • **2.** dower paid by a man to his bride before their final marriage vows • **3.** present (physically, at a place), attending • **4.** present (time) – بالحاضِر، بالوَقت الحاضِر [bilħaːḍir, bilwakt ʔilħaḍir] at present, now, at the present time. بالوَقت الحاضِر ما عِدنا وَظِيفَة شاغرَة [bilwakt ʔilħaːḍir maː ʕiddna waḍiːfa šaːɣra] At the present time, we don't have a position vacant.
مِحَضَّر [mħaḍḍar] *adj:* • **1.** prepared, ready
حَضارِي [ħaḍaːri] *adj:* • **1.** civilized, cultured
مِتحَضِّر [mitħaḍḍir] *adj:* • **1.** prepared • **2.** civilized
تَحضِيرِي [taħḍiːri] *adj:* • **1.** preparatory • **2.** preparative

ح ض ر م و ت

حَضرَمَوت [ħaḍramawt] *n:* • **1.** Hadhramaut
حَضرَمَوتِي [ħaḍramawti] *adj:* • **1.** Hadhramautian, from Hadhramaut • **2.** Hadhramauti, man from Hadhramaut

ح ض ن

حِضَن [ħiḍan] *v:* • **1.** to embrace, hug حِضَن صَدِيقَه وَباسَه [ħiḍan ṣadiːqah wbaːsah] He embraced his friend and kissed him.
تحاضَن [tħaːḍan] *v:* • **1.** to embrace one another – مِن تلاقوا، تحاضَنوا [min tlaːgaw, tħaːḍnaw] When they met, they embraced.
حُضُن [ħuḍun] *n:* أحضان [ʔaħḍaːn] *pl:* • **1.** lap • **2.** bosom – حُضنَة حَطَب [ħuḍnat ħaṭab] an armload or apronload of firewood.
حَضِن [ħaḍin] *n:* • **1.** embracing
حَضنَة [ħaḍna] *n:* حَضنات [ħaḍnaːt] *pl:* • **1.** embrace, hug
حَضانَة، دار حَضانَة [ħaḍaːna, daːr ħaḍaːna] *n:* • **1.** day nursery, children's home
حَضِينَة [ħaḍiːna] *n:* حَضايِن [ħaḍaːyin] *pl:* • **1.** diaper • **2.** (baby's) diaper

ح ط ب

حَطَّب [ħaṭṭab] *v:* • **1.** to gather firewood – مَرَة الفَلّاح تحَطِّب وَرَجِلها يبِيع الحَطَب [marat ʔilfallaːħ tħaṭṭub wraǰilha yibiːʕ ʔilħaṭab] The peasant's wife gathers firewood and her husband sells it.
حَطَب [ħaṭab] *n:* • **1.** (coll.) firewood
حَطبَة [ħaṭba] *n:* حَطبات [ħaṭbaːt] *pl:* • **1.** stick, piece of firewood
حَطّاب [ħaṭṭaːb] *n:* حَطّابَة [ħaṭṭaːba] *pl:* • **1.** man who gathers and sells firewood, lumberjack

ح ط ط

حَطّ [ħaṭṭ] *v:* • **1.** to put, place, put down, set down – حُطّ بُوينباغِي بِجنُطتَك، رَجاءاً [ħuṭṭ buːyinbaːɣi bǰinuṭṭak, raǰaːʔan] Put my necktie in your suitcase, please. لا تحُطّ نَفسَك بهالقَضِيَّة [laː tħuṭṭ nafsak bhalqaḍiyya] Don't get yourself into that affair. كِنِت حاطّ عينِي عَلَى أُختها، لَكِن تزَوجَت [činit ħaːṭṭ ʕiːni ʕala ʔuxutha, laːkin dzawǰat] I had my eye on her sister, but she got married. • **2.** to alight, settle, land – ظَلّ الطِّير يحُوم نُصّ ساعَة قَبُل ما يحُطّ [ḍall ʔiṭṭiːr yħuːm nuṣṣ saːʕa gabul maː yħuṭṭ] The bird kept hovering for a half hour before he lit. • **3.** with – مِن, to lower, diminish, reduce, decrease, detract from هالعَمَل حَطّ مِن قِيمتَه [halʕamal ħaṭṭ min qiːmtah] That deed lowered his prestige.
اِنحَطّ [ʔinħaṭṭ] *v:* • **1.** to be put, placed, put down – هالرِّجّال ما ينحَطّ بالجِّيب [harriǰǰaːl maː yinħaṭṭ biǰǰiːb] That man can't be pushed around (lit., can't be put in one's pocket). • **2.** to deteriorate, decline, go down, decay – اِنحَطّت صِحّتَه هوايَة بالأشهُر الأخِيرَة [ʔinħaṭṭat ṣiħħtah hwaːya bilʔašhur ʔilʔaxiːra] His health has deteriorated a lot the last few months. الوَضِع اِنحَطّ مِن جَتّي هالوزارَة لِلحُكُم [ʔilwaḍiʕ ʔinħaṭṭ min ǰatti halwizaːra lilħukum] The situation has deteriorated since this government came to power. اِنحَطّت أخلاقَه هوايَة مِن قام يِمشِي ويّا هالجَماعَة [ʔinħaṭṭat ʔaxlaːqah hwaːya min gaːm yimši wiyya haǰǰamaːʕa] His morals have declined a lot since he started to go with that crowd. اِنحَطّ هوايَة. قام يبُوق وَيغِشّ

[ʔinħatt hwa:ya. ga:m ybu:g wyɣišš] He's become awfully debased. He has started to steal and cheat.
حَطّ [ħatt] *n:* • **1.** putting, placing • **2.** declining
مَحَطّ [maħatt] *n:* • **1.** center
مَحَطَّة [maħatta] *n:* • **1.** stop, stopping place – مَحَطَّة الباص [maħattat ʔilpa:ṣ] bus stop. • **2.** station – مَحَطَّة القِطار [maħattat ʔilqita:r] railroad station. محطَّة الإذاعَة [maħattat ʔilʔiða:ʕa] broadcasting station, radio station.
اِنحِطاط [ʔinħita:t] *n:* • **1.** decline – اِنحِطاط بِالأخلاق [ʔinħita:t bilʔaxla:q] a decline in morals.
مُنحَطّ [munħatt, minħatt] *adj:* • **1.** degraded, low, base, vile – هَذا مُنحَطّ. ما عِندَه لا ضَمِير وَلا أخلاق [ha:ða munħatt. ma: ʕindah la: ðami:r wala ʔaxla:q] He's degraded. he has neither conscience nor morals. مَرَة مُنحَطَّة [mara munħatta] a fallen woman.
مَحطُوط [maħtu:t] *adj:* مَحطُوطِين، مَحطُوطات [maħtuwta:t, maħtuwti:n] *pl:* • **1.** placed
أحَطّ [ʔaħatt] *comparative adjective:* • **1.** more or most deteriorated, etc • **2.** more or most debased.

ح ط م

حَطَّم [ħattam] *v:* • **1.** to wreck, destroy, ruin – اللُّوري دِعَم السَّيّارَة وَحَطَّمها [ʔillu:ri diʕam ʔissayya:ra wħattamha] The truck hit the car and demolished it. العَرَق حَطَّم صِحَّتَه [ʔilʕarag ħattam ṣiħħtah] Arrack destroyed his health. إذا أشُوفَه، أحَطّمَه [ʔiða ʔašu:fah, ʔaħattmah] If I see him, I'll bust him up! شَرِيكي حَطَّمنِي. ما يُعرُف يِشتُغُل [šari:ki ħattamni. ma: yuʕruf yištuɣul] My partner ruined me. He doesn't know how to do business.
تحَطَّم [tħattam] *v:* • **2.** to be wrecked, destroyed, ruined – الطَّيّارَة وُقعَت وَتحَطَّمَت [ʔittayya:ra wugʕat wtħattmat] The plane crashed and was wrecked. تحَطَّم مِن شُرُب العَرَق وَالقِمار [tħattam min šurub ʔilʕarag wiliqma:r] He was destroyed by drinking arrack and gambling. المِسكِين تحَطَّم. المَخزَن مالَه اِحتِرَق وَخِسَر كُلّ أموالَه [ʔilmiski:n tħattam. ʔilmaxzan ma:lah ʔiħtirag wxisar kull ʔamwa:lah] The poor guy was ruined. His store burned and he lost all his money.
حُطام [ħuta:m] *n:* • **1.** wreckage, wreck
مُحَطَّم [muħattam] *adj:* • **1.** crashed, destroyed

ح ظ ر

حِظَر [ħiðar] *v:* • **1.** to forbid, prohibit
حَظِيرَة [ħaði:ra] *n:* • **1.** stable, barn
مَحظُور [maħðu:r] *adj:* • **1.** banned, prohibited, forbidden

ح ظ ظ

حَظّ [ħaðð] *n:* حظُوظ [ħðu:ð] *pl:* • **1.** lot, fate, destiny • **2.** luck, fortune لِسُوء الحَظّ [lisu:ʔ ʔilħaðð] unfortunately. حُسُن الحَظّ [ħusun ʔilħaðð] good luck. مِن حُسُن الحَظّ [min ħusun ʔilħaðð] luckily, fortunately. لِحُسُن الحَظّ [liħusun ʔilħaðð] luckily, fortunately. لِحُسُن الحَظّ، ما يعَضّ [liħusun ʔilħaðð, ma: yʕaðð] Fortunately it doesn't bite. لِحُسُن حَظَّه، لِقَوا الأوراق الضايعَة [liħusun ħaððah, ligaw ʔilʔawra:q ʔiðða:yʕa] Fortunately for him, they found the lost papers.
حَظِيظ [ħaði:ð] *adj:* • **1.** fortunate, lucky هَذا. حَظِيظ. كُلّما يِلعَب وَرَق يِغلُب [ha:ða. ħaði:ð. kullma yilʕab waraq yiɣlub] He's lucky. Whenever he plays cards he wins.
مَحظُوظ [maħðu:ð] *adj:* • **1.** fortunate

ح ف ر

حُفَر [ħufar] *v:* • **1.** to dig – حُفَر نُقرَة غمِيقَة بِالحَدِيقَة [ħufar nugra ɣami:ja bilħadi:qa] He dug a deep hole in the garden. الجِّنُود دَيحُفرُون خَنادِق [ʔijjinu:d dayħufru:n xana:diq] The soldiers are digging trenches. • **2.** to drill – الشَّركَة دَتحُفُر آبار نَفُط جِدِيدَة [ʔiššarika datuħfur ʔa:ba:r nafuṭ jidi:da] The company's drilling new oil wells. طَبِيب الأسنان حُفَر سِنّي وَحَشّاه [ṭabi:b ʔilʔasna:n ħufar sinni wħašša:h] The dentist drilled out my tooth and filled it. • **3.** to carve – حُفَر إسمَه وَإسِمها بِالشِّجرَة [ħufar ʔismah wʔisimha biššijra] He carved his name and her name on the tree.
حَفَّر [ħaffar] *v:* • **1.** to dig up, tear up – العُمّال حَفَّرَوا الشّارِع كُلَّه وَما لِقَوا البُورِي المَكسُور [ʔilʕumma:l ħaffuraw ʔišša:riʕ kullah wama: ligaw ʔilbu:ri ʔilmaksu:r] The laborers dug up the whole street and didn't find the broken pipe. اللُّورِيّات حَفَّرَت الشّارِع مالنا [ʔillu:riyya:t ħaffrat ʔišša:riʕ ma:lna] The trucks have torn our street all up. الشّارِع تحَفَّر مِن اللُّورِييات [ʔišša:riʕ tħaffar min ʔillu:riyya:t] The street got all dug up by the trucks.
اِنحُفَر [ʔinħufar] *v:* • **1.** to be dug out
حَفُر [ħafur] *n:* • **1.** digging
حُفرَة [ħufra] *n:* حُفَر، حُفرِيّات [ħufar, ħufriyya:t] *pl:* • **1.** pl. حُفرِيّات excavation (archeol) • **2.** hole
حَفّار [ħaffa:r] *n:* حَفّارَة، حَفّارِين [ħaffa:ra, ħaffa:ri:n] *pl:* • **1.** digger حَفّار القبُور [ħaffa:r ʔilgbu:r] gravedigger. • **2.** driller
حافِر [ħa:fir] *n:* حَوافِر [ħawa:fir] *pl:* • **1.** hoof
مَحَفَّر [mħaffar] *adj:* • **1.** perforated
مَحفُور [maħfu:r] *adj:* • **1.** inscribed, engraved – مَحفُور عالمَرمَرَة مال القَبُر [maħfu:r ʕalmarmara ma:l ʔilgabur] Inscribed on the marble tombstone.

ح ف ز

حَفَّز [ħaffaz] *v:* • **1.** stab, urge, prompt
تحَفَّز [tħaffaz] *v:* • **1.** to prompt • **2.** to be prompted, urged
حافِز [ħa:fiz] *n:* حَوافِز [ħawa:fiz] *pl:* • **1.** spur, incentive
تَحَفُّز [taħaffuz] *n:* • **1.** preparedness, readiness
مِتحَفِّز [mitħaffiz] *adj:* • **1.** ready, prepared

ح ف ظ

حفَظ [ħifað] *v:* • **1.** to preserve – الثَّلِج حُفَظ الجِثَّة مُدَّة طويلَة [ʔiθθalij ħufað ʔijjiθθa mudda ṭwiːla] The snow preserved the corpse a long time. • **2.** to protect, guard, watch over – الله يحُفظَك [ʔallah yħufðak] God protect you. • **3.** to put away, store, file – خَلَّصنا شُغُلنا بِهَالإضبارات. أريدَك تُحفُظها كُلّها [xallaṣna šuɣulna bhalʔiðbaːraːt. ʔariːdak tuħfuðha kullha] We've finished with these files. I want you to put them all away. لازِم تِحفُظ كُلّ الأوراق [laːzim tiħfuð kull ʔilʔawraːq] You've got to file all the papers. المَكتُوب مَحفُوظ إلي بِشِبّاك البَريد [ʔilmaktuːb maħfuːð ʔili bšibbaːk ʔilbariːd] The letter is being held for me in care of general delivery. • **4.** to set aside, pigeonhole – المُدِير حُفَظ عَرِيضتِي. لازِم أقَدِّم طَلَب لاخ [ʔilmudiːr ħufað ʕariːðti. laːzim ʔaqaddim ṭalab laːx] The director pigeonholed my application. I'll have to submit another request. • **5.** to memorize, commit to memory – حِفَظِت القَصِيدَة كُلّها؟ [ħifaðit ʔilqaṣiːda kullha?] Did you memorize the whole poem? • **6.** to know by heart – خَمسَة مِن دُولَة التَّلامِيذ يحُفظُون القُرآن [xamsa min ðuːla ʔittalaːmiːð yħufðuːn ʔilqurʔaːn] Five of those students know the Koran by heart.

حَفَّظ [ħaffað] *v:* • **1.** to cause to memorize – ماكُو حاجَة تحَفُّظ الطُّلّاب هَالقَدّ قَصايِد [maːku ħaːja tħaffuð ʔiṭṭullaːb halgadd qaṣaːyid] There's no need to make the students learn so many poems. أَبُويَا حَفَّظنِي الشِّعِر [ʔabuːya ħaffaðni ʔiššiʕir] My father helped me memorize the poetry.

حافَظ [ħaːfað] *v:* • **1.** to guard, protect, defend – الجَيش دَيحافُظ عَلَى بَغداد مِن الثُّوّار [ʔijjayš dayħaːfuð ʕala baɣdaːd min ʔiθθuwwaːr] The army is guarding Baghdad from the rebels. الشُّرطَة حافظَتنا طُول الطَّرِيق [ʔiššurṭa ħaːfðatna ṭuːl ʔiṭṭariːq] The police protected us all the way. • **2.** with – عَلَى to maintain, sustain, keep up, preserve, uphold الماي حافَظ عَلَى مُستَواه [ʔilmaːy ħaːfað ʕala mustawaːh] The water maintained its level. بَعدَه محافُظ عَلَى صِحّتَه [baʕdah mħaːfuð ʕala ṣiħħtah] He is still keeping up his health. الشُّرطَة تحافُظ عالأمِن [ʔiššurṭa tħaːfuð ʕalʔamin] The police maintain the peace. حافَظ عَلَى وَعدَه وَإنطانِي الفلُوس مِثلما قال [ħaːfað ʕala waʕdah wʔinṭaːni ʔilfluːs miθilmaː gaːl] He kept his promise and gave me the money like he said.

تحَفَّظ [tħaffað] *v:* • **1.** to protect oneself – تحَفَّظ مِن البَرد. إلبَس قَبُّوطَك [tħaffað min ʔilbarid. ʔilbas qappuːṭak] Protect yourself from the cold. Put on your overcoat. • **2.** to be cautious, careful, wary, be on guard – تحَفَّظ بِحَكيَك. لا يكُون تقُول شِي غَلَط [tħaffað bħačyak. laː ykuːn dguːl ši ɣalaṭ] Be careful with what you say. Don't say anything wrong. هَذا مُجرِم خَطِر؛ تحَفَّظ مِنَّه [haːða mujrim xaṭir; tħaffað minnah] He's a dangerous criminal; be careful of him.

انحُفَظ [ʔinħufað] *v:* • **1.** to be memorized, kept, preserved

احتفَظ [ʔiħtifað] *v:* • **2.** to keep up, maintain, retain – اِحتِفَظ بصِحّتَه إلَى آخِر أيّامَه [ʔiħtifað bṣiħħtah ʔila ʔaːxir ʔayyaːmah] He kept his health up to the end of his life. • **3.** to hold, possess – اِحتِفَظ بالأوَّلِيَّة مِن أوَّل السِّباق لآخِرَه [ʔiħtifað bilʔawwaliyya min ʔawwal ʔissibaːq lʔaːxirah] He held first place from the beginning of the race to the end. اِحتِفَظ بالأوَّلِيَّة ثلاث سنِين [ʔiħtifað bilʔawwaliyya tlaθ sniːn] He retained first place for three years. • **4.** to keep, retain – اِحتِفَظ بِالباقِي لِنَفسَه [ʔiħtifað bilbaːqi linafsah] He kept the rest for himself. رَئِيس الوُزَراء اِحتِفَظ بِوِزارَة الدِّفاع لِنَفسَه [raʔiːs ʔilwuzaraːʔ ʔiħtifað bwizaːrat ʔiddifaːʕ linafsah] The prime minister retained the ministry of defense for himself. • **5.** with ب to maintain, uphold, reserve – أحتِفِظ بحَقِّي ألغِي العَقد شوَكِت ما أريد [ʔaħtifið bħaqqi ʔalɣi ʔilʕaqid šwakit maː ʔariːd] I reserve the right to break the contract whenever I want.

حُفُظ [ħufuð] *n:* • **1.** preserving

تحَفُّظ [taħaffuð] *n:* • **1.** caution, reticence, reserve • **2.** preventive custody

مَحفَظَة [maħfaða] *n:* مَحفَظات، مَحافِظ [maħfaðaːt, maħaːfið] *pl:* • **1.** folder, (and by extension) file, dossier • **2.** dispatch case, attache case, brief case, portfolio

مُحافِظ [muħaːfið] *n:* • **1.** conservative – نائِب مُحافِظ [naːʔib muħaːfið] a conservative deputy. • **2.** director, director general – مُحافِظ البَنك المَركَزِي [muħaːfið ʔilbang ʔilmarkazi] Director of the Central Bank. • **3.** conservative – حِزب المُحافِظِين [ħizb ʔilmuħaːfiðiːn] the conservative party.

حافِظَة [ħaːfiða] *n:* • **1.** wallet, container

تَحفِيظ [taħfiːð] *n:* • **1.** memorization

مُحافَظَة [muħaːfaða] *n:* • **1.** safeguarding • **2.** protection, defense • **3.** preservation, maintenance – المُحافَظَة عالأمِن [ʔilmuħaːfaða ʕalʔamin] preservation of the peace. مُحافَظَة عَالهدُوء [muħaːfaða ʕalhiduːʔ] maintenance of order.

احتفاظ [ʔiħtifaːð] *n:* • **1.** maintenance, preservation – لَو ما اِحتِفاظَه بِهدُوئَه، كان تصِير عَرَكَة [law maː ʔiħtifaːðah bhiduːʔah, čaːn tṣiːr ʕarka] But for his maintenance of his calm, there would've been a fight.

مَحفُوظَة [maħfuːða] *n:* مَحفُوظات [maħfuːðaːt] *pl:* • **1.** poetry memorization class – دَرس المَحفُوظات [dars ʔilmaħfuːðaːt] poetry memorization class.

حافِظ [ħaːfið] *adj:* حُفّاظ [ħuffaːð] *pl:* • **1.** man who knows the Koran by heart.

محتِفِظ [miħtifuð] *adj:* • **1.** keeping, preserving

ح ف ف

حَفّ [ħaff] *v:* • **1.** to depilate, remove hair, to pluck

حَفّ [ħaff] *n:* حَفّ، حفافات [ħaff, ħfaːfaːt] *pl:* • **1.** removing hair with thread – اليُوم راح يحِفُّون لِلعَرُوس [ʔilyuːm raːħ yħiffuːn lilʕaruːs] Today they're going to depilate the bride. هِيَّ تحِفّ لَو تزَيِّن شَعَر رِجلَيها؟ [hiyya

tħiff law dzayyin šaʕar rijli:ha?] Does she pluck or shave the hair on her legs? حَصَّل دَرَجَة عالحافَّة بالإمتِحان [ħaṣṣal daraja ʕalħa:ffa bilʔimtiħa:n] He got a marginal grade on the exam.
حَفَّة [ħaffa] *n:* • **1.** plucking
حَفّاف، حَفّافَة [ħaffa:f, ħaffa:fa] *n:* • **1.** plucker, one who plucks or tweezes facial hair
مَحفُوف [maħfu:f] *adj:* • **1.** charged (with)

ح ف ل

اِحتِفَل [ʔiħtifal] *v:* • **1.** with ب to celebrate, have a celebration – اِحتِفلَوا بفُوزهُم بالسِّباق [ʔiħtiflaw bfu:zhum bissiba:q] They celebrated their victory in the game.
حَفلَة [ħafla] *n:* حَفلات [ħafla:t] *pl:* • **1.** party • **2.** ceremony – حَفَلات تَعبين [ħafala:t taʔni:n] commemorative ceremony for a deceased person • **3.** show, presentation, performance – حَفلَة تَمثِيلِيَّة [ħafla tamθi:liyya] dramatic presentation, play. شوَقِت تِبتِدِي الحَفلَة لِهَالفِلِم؟ [šwakit tibtidi ʔilħafla lihalfilim?] What time does the showing of that movie start? • **4.** concert – حَفلَة مَوسِيقِيَّة [ħafla mu:si:qiyya] concert. حَفلَة غِنائِيَّة [ħafla ɣina:ʔiyya] a concert of vocal music.
مَحفَل [maħfal] *n:* • **1.** gathering, assembly
اِحتِفال [ʔiħtifa:l] *n:* اِحتِفالات [ʔiħtifa:la:t] *pl:* • **1.** celebration, festival
مِحتَفِل [miħtafil] *adj:* • **1.** participating in a festive event
اِحتِفالاً [ʔiħtifa:lan] *adverbial:* • **1.** in celebration – سَوَّى حَفلَة اِحتِفالاً بنَجاح إبنهُم [sawwa: ħafla ʔiħtifa:lan bnaja:ħ ʔibinhum] He gave a party in celebration of their son's graduation.

ح ف ن

حَفنَة [ħafna] *n:* حَفنات [ħafna:t] *pl:* • **1.** a double handful

ح ف و [1]

اِحتِفَى [ʔiħtifa:] *v:* • **1.** to behave with affection, be affectionate – مِن رِحنا نزُورهُم، اِحتِفَوا بينا هوايَة [min riħna nzu:rhum, ʔiħtifaw bi:na hwa:ya] When we went to visit them, they were very nice to us.
حَفاوَة [ħafa:wa] *n:* • **1.** friendly reception, welcome, hospitality – قابلُونا بحَفاوَة [qa:blu:na bħafa:wa] They received us with open arms.

ح ف و [2]

تحَفَّى [tħaffa:] *v:* • **1.** to be or become barefooted – لازِم تِتحَفَّى قَبُل ما تطُبّ بالجامِع [la:zim titħaffa: gabul ma: ṭṭubb bilja:miʕ] You must be barefooted before you enter the mosque. تحَفَّى. خَلِّي أفحَص رِجلَك [tħaffa:. xalli ʔafħaṣ rijlak] Take off your shoes and socks. Let me examine your feet.
حافّ [ħa:ff] *adj:* • **1.** plain, barefoot
حافِي [ħa:fi] *adj:* حِفّاي [ħiffa:y] *pl:* • **1.** barefooted طَير حافِي [ṭi:r ħa:fi] a bare-shanked pigeon. • **2.** barefoot person • **3.** ignorant, uneducated – حافِي بالكِيمياء [ħa:fi bilki:mya] ignorant of chemistry. • **4.** ignorant person, ignoramus

ح ف ي د

حَفِيد [ħafi:d] *n:* أحفاد [ʔaħfa:d] *pl:* • **1.** grandson • **2.** descendant

ح ق ب

حَقِيبَة [ħaqi:ba] *n:* • **1.** knapsack

ح ق د

حِقِد [ħiqid] *n:* أحقاد [ʔaħqa:d] *pl:* • **1.** grudge • **2.** hatred, malice
حَقُود [ħaqu:d] *adj:* • **1.** malicious • **2.** full of hatred, spiteful

ح ق ر

حَقَّر [ħaqqar] *v:* • **1.** to disparage, decry, deprecate – حَقَّرتَه عَلَى عَمَلَه الدَّنِيئ [ħaqqartah ʕala ʕamalah ʔiddani:ʔ] I gave him hell for his filthy trick. • **2.** to humiliate, humble, debase, degrade – شلُون حَقَّرُوه! لا نطوا مُكان يقعُد وَلا أَحَّد حِكَى ويّاه [šlu:n ħaqqiru:h! la: niṭawh muka:n yigʕud wala ʔaħħad ħiča: wiyya:h] They really humiliated him! They didn't give him a place to sit and no one talked to him. لِيش تحَقِّر نَفسَك وترُوح لِلعَزايِم بَلا دَعوَة؟ [li:š tħaqqir nafsak wtru:ħ lilʕaza:yim bala daʕwa?] Why do you degrade yourself and go to parties without invitation? حَقَّر نَفسَه بنَظَر المُوَظَّفِين [ħaqqar nafsah bnaðar ʔilmuwaððafi:n] He's lowered himself in the eyes of the employees. لا تحَقِّر نَفسَك وَترُوحلَه. خَلِّي هُوَّ يجِيك [la: tħaqqir nafsak wtru:ħlah. xalli: huwwa yiji:k] Don't lower yourself and go to him. Let him come to you.
اِحتِقَر [ʔiħtiqar] *v:* • **1.** to despise, scorn, disdain, look down on – آنِي أحتِقِر اللّي ياخُذ رَشوَة [ʔa:ni ʔaħtiqir ʔilli ya:xuð rašwa] I despise anyone who take a bribe.
حَقارَة [ħaqa:ra] *n:* • **1.** meanness, baseness • **2.** pettiness • **3.** contemptibility
تَحقِير [taħqi:r] *n:* • **1.** contempt, disdain, scorn – ماكُو حاجَة لِلتَّحقِير. إذا ما ترِيدنِي أشتُغُل هنا، قُلّي [ma:ku ħa:ja littaħqi:r. ʔiða ma: tri:dni ʔaštuɣul hna, gulli] There's no need for contempt. If you don't want me to work here, tell me.
اِحتِقار [ʔiħtiqa:r] *n:* • **1.** contempt, disdain, scorn – عامَلنِي بإحتِقار [ʕa:malni bʔiħtiqa:r] He treated me with contempt.
حَقِير [ħaqi:r] *adj:* حَقِيرِين، حُقَراء [ħaqi:ri:n, ħuqara:ʔ] *pl:* • **1.** low, base, vulgar – مِن عائِلَة حَقِيرَة [min ʕa:ʔila ħaqi:ra] from a low family. • **2.** mean, cheap, petty – عَمَل حَقِير [ʕamal ħaqi:r] a mean

action. • **3.** despicable, contemptible – شَخِص حَقِير [šaxiṣ ħaqiːr] a contemptible person.

أحقَر [ʔaħqar] *comparative adjective:* • **1.** more or most vulgar, despicable

ح ق ق

حَقّ [ħaqq, ħagg] *v:* • **1.** to be true, turn out to be true, be confirmed – هَسَّة حَقَّت الحَقِيقَة [hassa ħaqqat ʔilħaqiːqa] Now the truth has come out. • **2.** to be right, correct, proper, fitting – ما يحِقّلَك تعامِلني هِيكِي [maː yħiqqlak tʕaːmilni hiːči] You have no right to treat me that way. • **3.** to have a claim, be entitled – لا يَزال يحُقَّك بدِينارَين [laː yazaːl yħuqqak bdiːnaːrayn] He is still entitled to two dinars from you.

حَقَّق [ħaqqaq] *v:* • **1.** to realize – حَقَّقِت كُلّ آمالِي [ħaqqaqit kull ʔaːmaːli] I've realized all my hopes. • **2.** to inquire, check – اللُّجنَة دَتحَقِّق عَن مَصِير الأَوراق الضّايعَة [ʔillujna datħaqqiq ʕan maṣiːr ʔilʔawraːq ʔiððaːyʕa] The committee is inquiring into the where abouts of the lost papers. لِيش ما تحَقِّق عَن مَصدَر الحكايَة؟ [liːš maː tħaqqiq ʕan maṣdar ʔilħčaːya?] Why don't you check on the source of the story? رُوح حَقِّقلِي شُوف صُدُق راح يِتحَوّلُون [ruːħ ħaqqiqli šuːf ṣudug raːħ yitħawwluːn] Go find out for me if it's true they're going to move. • **3.** with – ب to investigate – الشُّرطة حَقَّقت بحادِث القَتِل، لَكِن ما لِقت أيّ دَلِيل [ʔiššurṭa ħaqqiqat bħaːdiθ ʔilqatil, laːkin maː ligat ʔayy daliːl] The police investigated the killing, but didn't find any clues. • **4.** with وِيّا to interrogate – الشُّرطَة حَقّقَت وِيّاه أكثَر مِن ساعَة [ʔiššurṭa ħaqqiqat wiyyaːh ʔakθar min saːʕa] The police interrogated him for more than an hour.

تحَقَّق [tħaqqaq] *v:* • **1.** to prove true, turn out to be true, be confirmed – الخَبَر تحَقَّق مِثلما قِتلَك [ʔilxabar tħaqqaq miθilma gitlak] The news turned out to be true, just like I told you. إشاعَة نَقلَه تحَقّقَت [ʔišaːʕat naqlah tħaqqiqat] The rumor of his transfer has been confirmed. • **2.** to be realized, be effected, come into effect, come to pass – أَمَلَه بِالحَياة تحَقَّق [ʔamalah bilħayaːt tħaqqaq] His goal in life has been realized. • **3.** to make sure, reassure oneself – تحَقَّق أكُو أَحَّد هناك قَبُل ما ترُوح [tħaqqaq ʔaku ʔaħħad hnaːk gabul maː truːħ] Make sure there's someone there before you go. تحَقَّق مِن الوَقِت اللّي يرِدُونا بيه [tħaqqaq min ʔilwakit ʔilli yriduːna biːh] Make sure of the time they want us. • **4.** with مِن to check, verify – أرِيدَك ترُوح تِتحَقَّق مِن الخَبَر [ʔariːdak truːħ titħaqqaq min ʔilxabar] I want you to go check out the news. تحَقَّق مِن هَويتَه قَبُل ما تِنطِيه الفلُوس [tħaqqaq min hawiːtah gabul maː tintiːh ʔilfluːs] Check his identity before you give him the money.

اِستَحَقّ [ʔistaħaqq] *v:* • **1.** to be entitled, have a claim – مَحَّد يِستِحِقّها لِلفلُوس غير إبنَه [maħħad yistiħiqqha lilifluːs ɣiːr ʔibnah] No one is entitled to the money but his son. ما دام كِسَرِت البايسِكِل مالَه، اِستَحَقَّك بعَشر دَنانِير [maː daːm kisarit ʔilpaːysikil maːlah, ʔistaħaqqak bʕašr danaːniːr] In as much as you broke his bicycle, he has a claim on you for ten dinars. إذا اِشتِكَى عَلِيك، يِستَحِقَّك بِالمَبلَغ كُلَّه [ʔiða ʔištikaː ʕaliːk, yistaħiqqak bilmablag kullah] If he sues you, he'll get you for the whole amount. • **2.** to deserve, merit – لِيش تعامله هِيكِي؟ ما يِستِحِق [liːš tʕaːmlah hiːči? maː yistiħiqq] Why do you treat him like that? He doesn't deserve it. هَذا ما يِستِحِقّ الواحِد يساعدَه [haːða maː yistiħiqq ʔilwaːħid ysaːʕdah] He doesn't deserve to have anyone help him. • **3.** to become payable, fall due – الكُمبِيالَة اِستَحَقَّت اليُوم [ʔilkumpiyaːla ʔistaħaqqat ʔilyuːm] The note became due today. إذا ما تشِيل غَراضَك، تِستِحِقّ عَليها أرضِيَّة يَومِيّاً دِينار [ʔiða maː tšiːl ɣaraːðak, tistiħiqq ʕaliːha ʔarðiyya yawmiyyan dinaːr] If you don't move your things, a daily charge of a dinar will be due on them. إذا ما تخَلِّص الشُّغُل خِلال شَهَر، تِستِحِق غَرامَة [ʔiða maː txalliṣ ʔiššuɣul xilaːl šahar, tistiħiqq ɣaraːma] If ou don't finish the job within a month, there'll be a penalty due against you.

حَقّ [ħaqq, ħagg] *n:* حُقُوق [ħuquːq, ħuguːg] *pl:* • **1.** truth – هَسَّة طِلَع الحَقّ، وَثِبتَت بَرائتِي [hassa ṭilaʕ ʔilħaqq, wθibtat baraːʔti] Now the truth has come out, and my innocence is established. الحَقّ وِيّاك [ʔilħaqq wiyyaːk] You're right. وَحَقّ الله، ما أعرُف [wħaqq ʔallah, maː ʔaʕruf] It's God's truth, I don't know. • **2.** one's due – حَقَّك. مِنُو يِتحَمَّل هذا؟ [ħaqqak. minu yitħammal haːða?] You're entirely justified. Who'd stand for that? حَقَّك. ما كان لازم يسِبَّك [ħaqqak. maː čaːn laːzim ysibbak] You're right. He shouldn't have insulted you. آنِي ما دَأطالِب غير بحَقّي [ʔaːni maː daʔaṭaːlib ɣiːr bħaqqi] I'm not asking for anything but what's due me. صُدُق حِكَى عَلَيّا؟ بَسّ أشُوفَه، آخُذ حَقّي مِنَّه [ṣudug ħičaː ʕalayya? bass ʔašuːfah, ʔaːxuð ħaqqi minnah] Did he really talk about me? Just let me see him and I'll get my revenge on him. أُخُذ حَقَّك وَخَلِّي حَقِّي [ʔuxuð ħaqqak wxalliː ħaqqi] Take what's yours and leave what's mine. كَمَّلِت شُغلِي. إنطِينِي حَقِّي وَخَلِّي أرُوح [kammalit šuɣli. ʔintiːni ħaqqi wxalliː ʔaruːħ] I've finished my work. Give me what's due me and let me go. حَقّ هَالعامِل رُبُع دِينار بِاليُوم [ħaqq halʕaːmil rubuʕ dinaːr bilyuːm] This worker's wage is a quarter of a dinar a day. خَلِّي نقَسِّمها قِسمَة حَقّ [xalliː nqassimha qismat ħaqq] Let's make a fair division of it. الحَقّ ضايع بِهالدِّنيا [ʔilħaqq ðaːyiʕ bhaddinya] There's no justice in this world. هَالحكايَة مُو زينَة بحَقَّه [halħčaːya muː ziːna bħaqqah] That story's not so good as regards him. قال هوايَة أشياء زينَة بحَقَّك [gaːl hwaːya ʔašyaːʔ ziːna bħaqqak] He said many nice things about you. قَسَّم الفلُوس عَلَى وِلدَه بِالحَقّ [qassam ʔilfluːs ʕala wildah bilħaqq] He divided the money justly among his sons. يِطلَع مِن حَقَّه [yiṭlaʕ min ħaqqah] He can handle it. He's capable of it. مَحَّد يِطلَع مِن حَقَّه غيرَك إنتَ إحكِي وِيّاه.

[ʔinta ʔiħči wiyyaːh. maħħad yitlaʕ min ħaqqah ɣiːrak] You speak to him. Nobody can handle him except you. • **3.** right, title, claim, legal claim – حَقّ التَّصويت [ħaqq ʔittaṣwiːt] the right to vote. ما إِلَك كُلّ حَقّ بيها [maː ʔilak kull ħaqq biːha] You have no right at all to it. حَقّها تداعِي بِالفِلُوس [ħaqqhah tdaːʕi bilfiluːs] She has the right to ask for the money. مِن حَقَّك تُطلُب تَعوِيض [min ħaqqak tuṭlub taʕwiːð] You have the right to ask for damages. ما إِلَك حَقّ عَلَيه. ما تداين مِنَّك [maː ʔilak ħaqq ʕaliːh. maː tdaːyan minnak] You have no claim against him. He didn't borrow from you. • **4.** (pl. only) law, jurisprudence, legal science – كُلِّيَّة الحُقُوق [kulliyyat ʔilħuquːq] law school.

حُقَّة [ħugga] *n:* حُقَق [ħugag] *pl:* • **1.** oka, a unit of weight equal to four kilograms – حُقَّة إِسطَنبُول [ħuggat ʔisṭanbuːl] the small Iraqi oka, 1. 28 kilos.

مُحَقِّق [muħaqqiq] *n:* مُحَقِّقِين [muħaqqiqiːn] *pl:* • **1.** investigator • **2.** interrogator

حَقِيقَة [ħaqiːqa] *n:* حَقايِق، حَقائِق [ħaqaːyiq, ħaqaːʔiq] *pl:* • **1.** truth, reality – بِالحَقِيقَة، غُرُفتَك أَلطَف [bilħaqiːqa, ɣuruftak ʔalṭaf] Actually, your room is nicer. • **2.** fact • **3.** true nature, essence – هَسَّة عِرَفِتها عَلَى حَقِيقَتها [hassa ʕirafitha ʕala ħaqiːqatha] Now I know her true colors.

أَحَقِّيَة [ʔaħaqqiyya] *n:* أَحَقِّيات [ʔaħaqqiyyaːt] *pl:* • **1.** legal claim, title, right

تَحقِيق [taħqiːq] *n:* تَحقِيقات [taħqiːqaːt] *pl:* • **1.** investigation • **2.** check, verification, realization, actualization, implementation

اِستِحقاق [ʔistiħqaːq] *n:* • **1.** claiming, worth, merit

مُحِقّ [muħiqq] *adj:* • **1.** correct, right – طلَعِت مُحِقّ برأيَك عَنها، لِأَنّ هَسَّة اِنكِشفَت حَقِيقَتها [tlaʕit muħiqq braʔyak ʕanha, liʔann hassa ʔinkišfat ħaqiːqatha] You turned out to be right in your opinion of her, because now her true nature has come out.

مُحَقَّق [muħaqqaq] *adj:* • **1.** sure, certain, indubitable, unquestionable – مُحَقَّق راح يِجِي [muħaqqaq raːħ yiǰi] It's certain he'll come. مُحَقَّق، شلُون ما يفزَعلِي؟ هَذا أَخُويَا [muħaqqaq, šluːn maː yifzaʕli? haːða ʔaxuːya] Sure, why shouldn't he back me up? He's my brother. • **2.** confirmed, established – جَيتَه صارَت مُحَقَّقَة [ǰaytah ṣaːrat muħaqqaqa] His arrival has been confirmed.

حَقِيقِي [ħaqiːqi] *adj:* • **1.** real, true, actual – قُصَّة حَقِيقِيَّة [quṣṣa ħaqiːqiyya] a true story. السَّبَب الحَقِيقِي [ʔissabab ʔilħaqiːqi] the real reason. غايتَه الحَقِيقِيَّة [ɣaːytah ʔilħaqiːqiyya] his real goal. • **2.** intrinsic, essential – الفَرق الحَقِيقِي بين الثّنَين [ʔilfarq ʔilħaqiːqi biːn ʔiθθnayn] the essential difference between the two.

حُقُوقِي [ħuquːqi] *adj:* • **1.** juristic, law, legal – دَعوَة حُقُوقِيَّة [daʕwa ħuquːqiyya] law suit, court case. مَعلُومات حُقُوقِيَّة [maʕluːmaːt ħuquːqiyya] legal knowledge. • **2.** graduate of a law school, lawyer, jurist

حَقّانِي [ħaqqaːni] *adj:* حَقّانِيَّة، حَقّانِيِّين [ħaqqaːniyya, ħaqqaːniyyiːn] *pl:* • **1.** just, honest, fair • **2.** an honest person

مُستَحِقّ [mustaħiqq, mistaħiqq] *adj:* • **1.** deserving, worthy – مُستَحِقّ كُلّ مُساعَدَة [mustaħiqq kull musaːʕada] deserving of help. • **2.** due, payable – الكُمبِيالَة مُستَحِقَّة [ʔilkumpiyaːla mustaħiqqa] The note is due. الدَّين مالَك مُستَحِقّ عَلَيه فايز [ʔiddayn maːlak mustaħiqq ʕaliːh faːyiz] Your debt has interest due on it. • **3.** worth of, deserving of – صارلِي شَهَر مُستَحِقّ تَرفِيع [ṣaːrli šahar mustaħiqq tarfiːʕ] I've been entitled to promotion for a month.

مُستَحَقّ [mustaħaqq] *adj:* • **1.** deserved – مُستَحَقّ! لَو دارِس، ما كان سِقَطِت [mustaħaqq! law daːris, maː čaːn siqaṭit] It was deserved! If you'd studied you wouldn't have failed. مُستَحَقّ بِيك! ما قِتلَك لا تِلعَب وِيّاه، تَرَة يُضُربَك؟ [mustaħaqq biːk! maː gitlak laː tilʕab wiyyaːh, tara yuðurbak?] You deserved it! Didn't I tell you not to play with him or he'd beat you up?

أَحَقّ [ʔaħaqq] *comparative adjective:* • **1.** more or most worthy, entitled, deserving

حَقِيقَةً [ħaqiːqatan] *adverbial:* • **1.** really, actually, truly, in fact, indeed

ح ق ل

حَقِل [ħaqil] *n:* حُقُول [ħuquːl] *pl:* • **1.** field • **2.** (fig.) realm, domain, field

ح ق ن

حِقَن [ħiqan] *v:* • **1.** to give an enema – حِقَن المَرِيض مَيّ ومِلِح حَتَّى تِمشِي بَطنَه [ħiqan ʔilmariːð mayy wmiliħ ħatta timši baṭnah] He gave the sick man an enema of salt water so he'd have a bowel movement.

اِحتِقَن [ʔiħtiqan] *v:* • **1.** to become congested – اِحتِقنَت عيُونَه بِسَبَب الحَسّاسِيَّة [ʔiħtiqnat ʕyuːnah bsabab ʔilħassaːsiyya] His eyes became congested because of the allergy.

حَقِن [ħaqin] *n:* • **1.** injection, retention, withholding

حُقنَة [ħuqna] *n:* حُقنات، حُقَن [ħuqnaːt, ħuqan] *pl:* • **1.** enema • **2.** apparatus for giving an enema, syringe • **3.** pain in the neck, dull person, clod, stick in the mud

مِحقان [miħgaːn] *n:* مَحاقِن [maħaːgin] *pl:* • **1.** funnel

اِحتِقان [ʔiħtiqaːn] *n:* • **1.** congestion – اِحتِقان الرِّئَة [ʔiħtiqaːn ʔirriʔa] lung congestion.

ح ك ر

اِحتِكار [ʔiħtikaːr] *n:* • **1.** monopoly

مُحتَكِر [muħtakir] *adj:* • **1.** monopolist

ح ك ك

حَكّ [ħakk] *v:* • **1.** to scratch لا تحُكّ الحَبّايَة تَرَة تِلتِهِب [laː tħukk ʔilħabbaːya tara tiltihib] Don't scratch the pimple or it'll get infected. ظَهري يُحُكِّني وما أَقدَر أَحُكَّه [ðahri yuħukkni wma ʔagdar ʔaħukkah] My back itches and I can't scratch it. • **2.** to itch – راسي يُحُكّني. أَعتِقِد وَسِخ [ra:si yuħukkni. ʔaʕtiqid waṣix] My head itches. I think it's dirty. أَشُو إيدي دَتحُكّني اليُوم. لازم راح أَحَصِّل شِي [ʔašu ʔi:di datħukkni ʔilyu:m. la:zim ra:ħ ʔaħaṣṣil ši] My hand is itching me today. I must be going to get something. جِلدَه دَيحُكَّه [ǰildah dayħukkah] He's itching for something (lit. his skin is itching him). ما قِتلَك أُقعُد راحَة؟ يبَيِّن جِلدَك دَيحُكَّك [ma: gitlak ʔugʕud ra:ħa? yibayyin ǰildak dayħukkak] Didn't I tell you to quit? Looks like you're itching for it. جِلدَه يحُكَّه. يريدلَه بَسطَة زينَة [ǰildah yħukkah. yri:dlah basṭa zi:na] He's itching for a good beating.

تحَكَّك [tħakkak] *v:* • **1.** to rub, brush – قِعَد يَمّي بِالباص وَقام يِتحَكَّك بِيّا [giʕad yammi bilpa:ṣ wga:m yitħakkak biyya] He sat next to me in the bus and began to brush against me.

تحاكَك [tħa:kak] *v:* • **1.** to engage in tribadism, and hence, to be a lesbian – ما تريد تِتزَوَّج لِأَنّ تِتحاكَك [ma: tri:d tidzawwaǰ liʔann titħa:kak] She doesn't want to get married because she's a lesbian.

اِنحَكّ [ʔinħakk] *v:* • **1.** to become frayed, worn – ياخَة الثُّوب اِنحَكَّت مِن الغَسِل [ya:xat ʔiθθu:b ʔinħakkat min ʔilɣasil] The shirt collar got worn from washing. اِنحَكّ البَنطَرُون مِن قَدّ ما يِزحَف [ʔinħakk ʔilpanṭaru:n min gadd ma: yizħaf] The pants got worn from his crawling so much.

اِحتَكّ [ʔiħtakk] *v:* • **1.** to come in contact, be in contact, be in touch – لا تِحتَكّ بِيه. تَرَة هَذا عَصَبي [la: tiħtakk bi:h. tara ha:ða ʕaṣabi] Don't get near him. He's irritable. آني ما رِدِت أَحاكِيه، بَسّ هُوَّ اِحتَكّ بِيّا [ʔa:ni ma: ridit ʔaħa:či:h, bass huwwa ʔiħtakk biyya] I didn't want to talk with him but he buttonholed me. • **2.** to bother, pick at, pick on, cause trouble – كُلّما اِنفُوت مِن هنا، يِحتَكّ بِينا [kullma: ʔinfu:t min hna, yiħtakk bi:na] Whenever we come by here, he starts trouble with us.

حَكّ [ħakk] *n:* • **1.** scratching, itching

حَكَّة [ħakka] *n:* حَكّات [ħakka:t] *pl:* • **1.** scratching • **2.** itching, itch • **3.** itch, scabies • **4.** rash

حِكاكَة [ħikka:ka] *n:* • **1.** the darkened rice at the bottom of a cooking pot

اِحتِكاك [ʔiħtika:k] *n:* • **1.** friction • **2.** close contact or touch • **3.** friction, dissention, dischord

حَكّاك [ħakka:k] *adj:* حَكّاكَة [ħakka:ka] *pl:* • **1.** lapidary

حَكّاكَة [ħakka:ka] *adj:* حَكّاكات [ħakka:ka:t] *pl:* • **1.** lesbian also **حَكّاكِيَّة** [ħakka:kiyya] حَكّاكِيّات [ħakka:kiyya:t]

مَحكُوك [maħku:k] *adj:* • **1.** frayed, worn – لِيش ما تخَيِّط ردانَك المَحكُوكَة؟ [li:š ma: txayyiṭ rda:nak ʔilmaħku:ka?] Why don't you have your frayed cuff repaired?

ح ك م

حِكَم [ħikam] *v:* • **1.** to pass judgment, express an opinion, judge – الحاكِم لازِم يُحكُم بِالعَدِل [ʔilħa:kim la:zim yuħkum bilʕadil] The judge must judge fairly. • **2.** to sentence – حِكموه لِلجّاسُوس بِالرَّمي بِالرِّصاص [ħikmawh liǰǰa:su:s birramy birriṣa:ṣ] They sentenced the spy to death by firing squad. حُكمَوه بالإعدام [ħukmawh bilʔiʕda:m] They sentenced him to death by hanging. حِكمَه الحاكِم عَشِر سنِين [ħikamah ʔilħa:kim ʕašir sni:n] The judge sentenced him to ten years. • **3.** to deliver a judgment, rule – الحَكَم حِكَم الضَّربَة كانَت آوت [ʔilħakam ħikam ʔiððarba ča:nat ʔa:wt] The referee ruled the ball was out-of-bounds. الحَكَم ما دَيحكُم زين. ما يُعرُف القَوانين [ʔilħakam ma: dayiħkum zi:n. ma: yuʕruf ʔilqawa:ni:n] The referee isn't doing a good job. He doesn't know the rules. • **4.** to govern, rule, control, dominate – حِكَم البَلَد عِشرين سَنَة [ħikam ʔilbalad ʕišri:n sana] He ruled the country for twenty years. حِكَمتني بِهَاللِّعبَة. لازِم أَحَرِّك المَلِك [ħikamtni bhalliʕba. la:zim ʔaħarrik ʔilmalik] You got the upper hand with that move. I'll have to move the king. • **5.** to come due, be due, arrive (of prayer time) شوَقِت تُحكُم صَلاة الظُّهُر؟ [šwakit tuħkum ṣala:t ʔiððuhur?] How soon is the noon prayer due? حُكمَت عَلينا الصَّلاة أَثناء السَّفرَة [ħukmat ʕali:na ʔiṣṣala ʔaθna:ʔ ʔissafra] Prayer time came on us during the trip. • **6.** with عَلَى to insist, demand, order – مِنُو حِكَم عَلِيك ترُوح؟ إنتَ اللّي كان عاجبَك [minu ħikam ʕali:k tru:ħ? ʔinta ʔilli ča:n ʕa:ǰbak] Who forced you to go? You're the one who was anxious. حِكَم عليّا لازِم أَشترِيلَه بايسِكِل [ħikam ʕalayya la:zim ʔaštiri:lah pa:ysikil] He insisted that I should buy him a bicycle.

حَكَّم [ħakkam] *v:* • **1.** to choose as judge or arbitrator, make the judge – حَكِّم عَقلَك بهَالقَضِيَّة وشُوف صُوج مَن [ħakkim ʕaqlak bhalqaðiyya wšu:f ṣu:č man] Let your reason be the judge of this matter and see who's at fault. • **2.** to adjust, regulate – حَكِّم الحَنَفِيَّة عالحُوض [ħakkim ʔilħanafiyya ʕalħu:ð] Adjust the faucet so it's over the basin. حَكَّم وَقِت وُصُولَه بوَقِت وُصُولي [ħakkam waqit wuṣu:lah bwaqit wuṣu:li] He adjusted his time of arrival to coincide with my time of arrival.

حاكَم [ħa:kam] *v:* • **1.** to arraign, bring to trial, try – ما يصِير نحاكِم الواحِد مَرّتَين بنَفس الجَّرِيمَة [ma: yṣi:r nħa:kim ʔilwa:ħid marrtayn bnafs ʔiǰǰari:ma] We can't try a person twice for the same crime. حاكمُوه بَعَد ما ثِبتَت عَليه التُّهمَة [ħa:kmu:h baʕad ma: θibtat ʕali:h ʔittuhma] They tried him once his guilt was established.

تحَكَّم [tħakkam] *v:* • **1.** to have one's own way, deal arbitrarily – مَحَّد يريد يِشتُغُل بهَالشُّعبَة لِأَنّ المُلاحِظ يِتحَكَّم بِالمُوَظَّفِين [maħħad yri:d yištuɣul bhaššuʕba liʔann ʔilmula:ħið yitħakkam bilmuwaððafi:n] No one wants to work in this section because the supervisor handles the employees arbitrarily. يتحَكَّم بيهُم مِثِلما يريد [yitħakkam biːhum miθilma yriːd] He can do anything he wants with them.

تحاكَم [tħaːkam] *v:* • **1.** to be arraigned, bring to trial

اِنحِكَم [ʔinħikam] *v:* • **1.** to be sentenced اِنحِكَم مُؤَبَّد [ʔinħikam muʔabbad] He was sentenced to life imprisonment.

اِحتِكَم [ʔiħtikam] *v:* • **1.** to seek judgment, appeal for a decision – اِحتِكموا عِند رَئِيس القَبِيلَة [ʔiħtikmaw ʕind raʔiːs ʔilqabiːla] They sought judgment from the head of the tribe.

حُكُم [ħukum] *n:* أَحكام [ʔaħkaːm] *pl:* • **1.** judgment, verdict, sentence – حُكُم خَفِيف [ħukum xafiːf] a light sentence. حُكُم غِيابِي [ħukum ɣiyaːbi] sentence in absentia. حُكُم بالإعدام [ħukum bilʔiʕdaːm] death sentence. حُكم البَراءَة [ħukm ʔalbaraːʔa] acquittal. • **2.** decision, ruling – حُكم الحَكَم [ħukm ʔilħakam] the decision of the referee. • **3.** rule, regulation, provision, ordinance, decree – أحكام القانُون [ʔaħkaːm ʔilqaːnuːn] provisions of the law. أَحكام عُرفِيَّة [ʔaħkaːm ʕurfiyya] martial law. الضَّرُورَة إلها أَحكام [ʔiððaruːra ʔilha ʔaħkaːm] Necessity knows no law (lit. necessity has its own rules). • **1.** by force of – سَوّاها بحُكم العادَة [sawwaːha bħukm ʔilʕaːda] He did it from force of habit. • **2.** almost, as good as, virtually – بحُكم المُستَحِيل [bħukm ʔilmustaħiːl] virtually impossible. • **3.** government, regime, rule – الحُكم الجُّمهُوري [ʔilħukm ʔijjamhuːri] the republican form of government. الحُكم التُّركي [ʔilħukm ʔitturki] The Turkish rule. الحُكم الذّاتي [ʔilħukm ʔiððaːti] self-rule, autonomy. • **5.** (invar.) inescapable, inevitable, certain, sure – راس شَهَر وَماخِذ مَعاشَه. هَذا حُكُم راح يِسكَر هاللَّيلَة [raːs šahar wmaːxið maʕaːšah. haːða ħukum raːħ yiskar hallayla] The first of the month and he is got his pay. He's certainly going to go out drinking tonight. حُكُم. لازِم يِجُون مِن هنَا [ħukum. laːzim yijuːn min hna] It's inevitable. They've got to come by here. هَذا حُكُم. لازِم تحَرِّك المَلِك مالَك [haːða ħukum. laːzim tħarrik ʔilmalik maːlak] It's obligatory. You've got to move your king.

حَكَم [ħakam] *n:* حُكّام، حَكَمِيَّة [ħukkaːm, ħakamiyya] *pl:* • **1.** umpire, referee

حِكمَة [ħikma] *n:* حِكَم [ħikam] *pl:* • **1.** wisdom • **2.** maxim • **3.** rationale, underlying reason

حاكِم [ħaːkim] *n:* حُكّام [ħukkaːm] *pl:* • **1.** governor – حاكِم عَسكَري [ħaːkim ʕaskari] military governor. • **2.** judge

تَحَكُّم [taħakkum] *n:* • **1.** control

حُكُومَة [ħukuːma] *n:* حُكُومات [ħukuːmaːt] *pl:* • **1.** government • **2.** administration, cabinet

مَحكَمَة [maħkama] *n:* مَحاكِم [maħaːkim] *pl:* • **1.** court, tribunal

تَحكِيم [taħkiːm] *n:* تَحكِيمات [taħkiːmaːt] *pl:* • **1.** arbitration

مُحاكَمَة [muħaːkama] *n:* مُحاكَمات [muħaːkamaːt] *pl:* • **1.** trial, court hearing

مَحكُومِيَّة [maħkuːmiyya] *n:* • **1.** sentence (legal)

حَكِيم [ħakiːm] *adj:* حُكَماء [ħukumaːʔ] *pl:* • **1.** wise, judicious • **2.** (as n:) wise man, sage • **3.** herb doctor

مُحكَم [muħkam] *adj:* • **1.** perfect

حُكُومي [ħukuːmi] *adj:* • **1.** government, official – سَيّارَة حُكُومِيَّة [sayyaːra ħukuːmiyya] an official car. • **2.** public, state, state-owned – قاع حُكُومِيَّة [gaːʕ ħukuːmiyya] public land. • **3.** administration, government – لمَنهَج الحُكُومي [ʔilmanhaǰ ʔilħukuːmi] the administration's program. • **4.** pro-administration, pro-government – النُّوّاب الحُكُومِيِّين [ʔinnuwwaːb ʔilħukuːmiyyiːn] the pro-government deputies.

حاكمِيَّة [ħaːkimiyya] *n:* • **1.** judgeship, position as judge

مَحكُوم عَلَيه [maħkuːm ʕaliːh] *adj:* • **1.** sentenced – هُوَّ مَحكُوم عَلَيه بالإعدام [huwwa maħkuːm ʕaliːh bilʔiʕdaːm] He's been condemned to death. • **2.** person who has been sentenced رَجّعوا المَحكُوم عَلَيه لِلسِّجِن [rajjʕaw ʔilmaħkuːm ʕaliːh lissijin] They returned the sentenced man to prison.

ح ك ي

حِكَى [ħičaː] *v:* • **1.** to tell, relate, report – إحكِيلِي، شصار؟ [ʔiħčiːli, šṣaːr?] Tell me, what happened? حِكالِي حكايَة طُوِيلَة [ħičaːli ħčaːya ṭuwiːla] He told me a long story. • **2.** to say, utter – حِكَى هوايَة أَشياء ما عِجبَتني [ħičaː hwaːya ʔašyaːʔ maː ʕijbatni] He said many things I didn't like. ما حِكَى وَلا كِلمَة [maː ħičaː wala čilma] He never said a word. ما سِمَعِت شحكَيت [maː simaʕit šħčiːt] I didn't hear what you said. • **3.** to speak, talk – حِكَيت وِيّاه بالتَّلِفُون [ħičiːt wiyyaːh bittalifuːn] I talked with him on the telephone. حِكَى هوايَة بالحَفلَة [ħičaː hwaːya bilħafla] He talked a lot at the party. إذا ما تزُورني ما أحكِي وِيّاك بَعَد [ʔiða maː dzuːrni maː ʔaħči wiyyaːk baʕad] If you don't visit me, I won't talk to you any more. صار مُدَّة ما يحكِي وِيّا أَبُوه [ṣaːr mudda maː yiħči wiyya ʔabuːh] He hasn't been speaking to his father for some time. يحكِي عالنّاس [yiħči ʕannaːs] He runs people down. حِكَى مِن يَمَّك مِن اِنتِقدُوك [ħičaː min yammak min ʔintiqduːk] He spoke in your behalf when they criticized you. أَرِيدَك تِحكِيلي وِيّا المُدِير [ʔariːdak tiħčiːli wiyya ʔilmudiːr] I want you to put in a word for me with the director. المُدِير صاحَه لغُرفتَه وحِكَى عَلَيه [ʔilmudiːr ṣaːħah lɣuruftah wħičaː ʕaliːh] The director called him into his office and dressed him down.

حَكَّى [ħaččaː] *v:* • **1.** to force to speak, make talk – راح أحَكِّيه بالقُوَّة [raːħ ʔaħaččiːh bilguwwa] I'm going to make him talk by force. لا تحَكِّيني. خَلِّي القَضِيَّة مستَّرَة [laː tħaččiːni. xalliː ʔilqaðiyya msattira] Don't make me talk. Let the matter rest.

حاكَى [ħaːča] *v:* • **1.** to talk to, speak to, converse with – أَرِيدَك تحكِيلي إيّاه لِلمُدِير [ʔariːdak taħčiːliː ʔiyyaːh lilmudiːr] I'd like you to speak to the director for me. شِفتَه اليُوم لَكِن ما حاكَيتَه [šiftah ʔilyuːm laːkin maː ħaːčiːtah] I saw him today but I didn't speak to him. حاكَيت المُدِير عَلَى تَرفِيعِي؟ [ħaːčiːt ʔilmudiːr ʕala tarfiːʕi?] Did you talk to the director about my promotion? صارلِي مُدَّة ما حاكِيه [ṣaːrli mudda maː ħaːčiːh] I haven't been speaking to him for some time.

تحَكَّى [tħaččaː] *v:* • **1.** to be willing to talk – هالمُوَظَّف ما يتحَكَّى. لا تراجِعَه بقَضِيتَك [halmuwaðððaf maː yitħakkaː. laː traːjiʕah bqaðiːtak] That official won't talk. Don't go to him with your case. لَو بَسّ يِتحَكَّى، كان أتفاهَم وِيّاه [law bass yitħaččaː, čaːn ʔatfaːham wiyyaːh] If he had only been willing to talk, I would have reached an understanding with him. مِن صار مُدِير، ما قام يتحَكَّى [min ṣaːr mudiːr, maː gaːm yitħaččaː] Since he's become a director, he doesn't speak. هَذا ما يِتحَكَّى. عَبالَه بَسّ هُوَّ عِندَه سَيّارَة [haːða maː yitħakkaː. ʕabaːlah bass huwwa ʕindah sayyaːra] He won't even talk terms. He thinks he's the only one with a car for sale.

تحاكَى [tħaːčaː] *v:* • **1.** to talk to one another, to converse – صارلهُم ساعَة دَيتحاكُون [ṣaːrilhum saːʕa dayitħaːčuːn] They've been talking together for an hour. صارلهُم سَنَة ما يتحاكُون [ṣaːrilhum sana maː yitħaːčuːn] They haven't been speaking to each other for a year.

انحكَى [ʔinħičaː] *v:* • **1.** to be said, uttered – هِيكِي شِي ما ينحِكِي قِدّام النِّسوان [hiːči ši maː yinħiči giddaːm ʔinniswaːn] This sort of thing isn't said in front of women.

حَكِي [ħači, ħačy] *n:* • **1.** talking, speaking • **2.** speech, talk – خُوش حَكِي [xuːš ħači] Good idea! That's the spirit! Now you're talking!

حكايَة [ħčaːya] *n:* حكايات [ħčaːyaːt] *pl:* • **1.** story, narrative, tale • **2.** remark, utterance speech

حَكّاي [ħaččaːy] *adj:* حَكّايَة [ħaččaːya], *pl:* • **1.** orator, convincing or persuasive speaker • **2.** glib person, fast talker • **3.** talkative person, articulate person

ح ل ب

حِلَب [ħilab] *v:* • **1.** to milk – تِحلِب الهايشَة السّاعَة أربَعَة الصُّبُح كُلّ يوم [tiħlib ʔilhaːyša ʔissaːʕa ʔarbaʕa ʔiṣṣubuħ kull yuːm] She milks the cow at four a. m. every day. الرّاقِصَة حِلبَتَه كُلّ فلُوسَه [ʔirraːqiṣa ħilbatah kull fluːsah] The dancer milked him of all his money.

انحِلَب [ʔinħilab] *v:* • **1.** to be milked – الصَّخلَة انحِلبَت حَلِبتَين [ʔiṣṣaxla ʔinħilbat ħalibtayn] The goat was milked twice.

حَلِب [ħalib] *n:* • **1.** milking

حَلَب [ħalab] *n:* • **1.** Aleppo (important town in Syria)

حَلبَة [ħalba] *n:* حَلبات [ħalbaːt] *pl:* • **1.** a milking

حِلبَة [ħilba] *n:* • **1.** fenugreek (herb with aromatic seeds)

حَلِيب [ħaliːb] *n:* • **1.** milk – ظَلَّت تِعتِنِي بِيه حَتَّى طِلَع حَلِيب أُمَّها مِن خَشِمها [ðallat tiʕtini biːh ħatta ṭilaʕ ħaliːb ʔummaha min xašimha] She kept worrying with him until she couldn't take it any more. حَلِيب سباع [ħaliːb sbaːʕ] arrack (lit., lions' milk). • **2.** (by extension) breeding, honor – حَلِيبَه ما يخَلِّيه يسَوِّي هِيكِي شِي [ħaliːbah maː yxalliːh ysawwiː hiːči ši] His breeding won't let him do such a thing. حَلِيبَه مُو زين [ħaliːbah muː ziːn] He's not honorable (i.e. his womenfolks' milk isn't good). حَلِيبَه نَظِيف وَما يخُون أيّ واحِد [ħaliːbah naðiːf wma yxuːn ʔayy waːhid] He is an honorable fellow and wouldn't betray anyone. إنتَ وحَلِيبَك. إذا أستاهِل فلُوس، إنطِينِي [ʔinta wħaliːbak. ʔiða ʔastaːhil fluːs, ʔinṭiːni] I leave it to your honor. If I deserve money, give it to me. راح تُقبُض مِن دَبَش. هُوَّ وَحَلِيبَه [raːħ tuqbuð min dabaš. huwwa wħaliːbah] You'll wind up holding the short end. That's how honorable he is. إنتَ وحَلِيبَك يا لِبَن [ʔinta wħaliːbak yaː liban] (an insult implying that one's mother's milk was soured because her character was questionable, approx.:) Your family honor is in question.

حالِب [ħaːlib] *n:* حَوالِب [ħawaːlib] *pl:* • **1.** ureter

حالُوب [ħaːluːb] *n:* • **1.** (coll.) hail, hailstones

حالُوبَة [ħaːluːba] *n:* حالُوبات، حالُوب [ħaːluːbaːt] *pl:* • **1.** a hailstone

محَلَّبِي [mħallabi] *n:* • **1.** a pudding made from milk, sugar, and rice flour or starch

حَلِيبِي [ħaliːbi] *adj:* • **1.** milky, milk-like – گلُوب حَلِيبِي [gluːb ħaliːbi] frosted light bulb.

حَلّابَة [ħallaːba] *adj:* حَلّابات، حَلّابِين [ħallaːbaːt] *pl:* • **1.** milkmaid, dairy-maid • **2.** good milker, cow which gives a lot of milk

ح ل ج

حِلَج [ħilaǰ] *v:* • **1.** to gin (cotton) – يحلِجُون القُطِن وَيصَدِّرُوه [yiħliǰuːn ʔilguṭin wyṣaddiruːh] They gin the cotton and export it.

حَلِج [ħaliǰ] *n:* • **1.** ginning cotton

مَحلَج [maħlaǰ] *n:* مَحالِج [maħaːliǰ] *pl:* • **1.** cotton ginning plant

ح ل ح ل

حَلحَل [ħalħal] *v:* • **1.** to wiggle, jiggle, work back and forth – حَلحِل سِنَّك حَتَّى ينشِلِع [ħalħil sinnak ħatta yinšiliʕ] Work your tooth back and forth so it can be pulled. تِقدَر تحَلحِل عَمُود الكَهرَباء؟ [tigdar tħalħil ʕamuːd ʔilkahrabaːʔ ?] Can you jiggle the power pole? • **2.** to move, budge – هَذا ثِقِيل؛ ما أقدَر أحَلحِلَه [haːða θigiːl; maː ʔagdar ʔaħalħilah] That's heavy; I can't move it. • **3.** to loosen (one's) clothes, make (oneself) comfortable – لِيش مَحَلحِل نَفسَك؟ مُو عِدنا خُطّار [liːš mħalħil nafsak? muː ʕidna xuṭṭaːr] Why've you loosened your clothes? We have guests!

تحَلحَل [tħalħal] *v:* • **1.** to wiggle, wobble, shake, move – سِنّي دَيتحَلحَل. راح أشلَعه [sinni dayitħalħal. ra:ħ ʔašlaʕah] My tooth is loose. I'm going to pull it. • **2.** to move oneself, move over – تحَلحَل شوَيَّة خاطِر أقعُد يَمَّك [tħalħal šwayya xa:ṭir ʔagʕud yammak] Move a little so I can sit down next to you. • **3.** to loosen one's clothes, make oneself comfortable آني تَعبان وَمحترّ. راح أتحَلحَل وآخُذ راحَة [ʔa:ni taʕba:n wmiħtarr. ra:ħ ʔatħalħal wa:xuð ra:ħa] I'm tired and hot. I'm going to loosen up my clothes and take a rest.

ح

ح ل ز ن

حَلَزُون [ħalazu:n] *n:* حَلَزُونات [ħalazu:na:t] *pl:* • **1.** snail

حَلَزُوني [ħalazu:ni] *adj:* • **1.** spiral – دَرَج حَلَزُوني [daraǰ ħalazu:ni] a spiral staircase.

ح ل ف

حِلَف [ħilaf] *v:* • **1.** to swear, vow – حِلَف بَعَد ما يلعَب قمار أبَداً [ħilaf baʕad ma: yilʕab qma:r ʔabadan] He swore that he'd never gamble again. حِلَف بِالله ما سَوّاه [ħilaf bʔallah ma: sawwa:h] He swore by God he didn't do it. حِلَف يَمِين مالَه عِلاقَة بِيهُم [ħilaf yami:n ma:lah ʕila:qa bi:hum] He took an oath that he has no connection with them.

حَلَّف [ħallaf] *v:* • **1.** to make swear, force to swear – حَلّفَه ما يرُوح [ħallfah ma: yru:ħ] Make him take an oath that he won't go. حَلَّفني إذا إلي عِلاقَة بالبوقَة [ħallafni ʔiða ʔili ʕila:qa bilbu:ga] He made me swear as to whether I had any connection with the theft. • **2.** to put under oath, swear in – حَلّفَوه قبِل ما ينطي شَهادتَه [ħallifawh gabil ma: yinṭi šaha:dtah] They swore him in before he gave his testimony.

حالَف [ħa:laf] *v:* • **1.** to form an alliance with, become an ally of – حالَفناهُم حَتَّى نِقدَر ننتِصِر عَلَى أعدائنا [ħa:lafna:hum ħatta nigdar nintiṣir ʕala ʔaʕda:ʔna] We formed an alliance with them so we could conquer our enemies. بَعَد ما نِكَت بيّا، تحَلَّفتلَه [baʕad ma: nikat biyya, tħallafitlah] After he made a fool of me, I swore I'd even the score with him. تَرَة المُدير مِتحَلِّفلَك. أقَلّ غَلطَة يفُصلَك [tara ʔilmudi:r mitħalliflak. ʔaqall ɣalṭa yfuṣlak] I'm telling you the director has got it in for you. The least mistake and he'll fire you. لا ترُوح للبَيت، تَرَة أبُوك مِتحَلِّفلَك [la: tru:ħ lilbayt, tara ʔabu:k mitħalliflak] Don't go home, because your father is laying for you.

تحالَف [tħa:laf] *v:* • **1.** to join together in an alliance, to ally oneself – الدَّولِتَين تحالفوا أثناء الحَرب [ʔiddawiltayn tħa:lfaw ʔaθna:ʔ ʔilħarb] The two countries allied themselves during the war. تحالَفنا ويّاهُم [tħa:lafna wiyyahum] We allied ourselves with them.

حِلِف [ħilif] *n:* أحلاف [ʔaħla:f] *pl:* • **1.** swearing, oath-taking, oath • **2.** pact, alliance

حَلفَة [ħalfa] *n:* • **1.** alfa, esparto, a long marsh grass commonly dried and used for packing material

حَلّاف [ħalla:f] *n:* حَلّافِين، حَلّافَة [ħalla:fi:n, ħalla:fa] *pl:* • **1.** (chronic) oath-taker, vow-maker

مُحَلّفِين [muħallifi:n] *n:* • **1.** jury (under oath persons)

حَلِيف [ħali:f] *adj:* • **1.** allied – الدُّوَل الحَليفَة [ʔidduwal ʔilħali:fa] the allied nations. • **2.** pl. حُلَفاء [ħulafa:ʔ] allies

ح ل ق

حِلَق [ħilaq] *v:* • **1.** to shave – يِحلِق وِجهه مَرّتَين يَومِيّاً [yiħliq wiččah marrtayn yawmiyyan] He shaves his face twice a day. هَذا يِحلِق راسَه بالمُوس [ha:ða yiħliq ra:sah bilmu:s] He shaves his head. • **2.** to shave off – رَبّالَه لِحيَة شَهرَين وَبَعدين حِلَقها [rabba:lah liħya šahrayn wbaʕdi:n ħilaqha] He grew a beard for two months and then shaved it off. • **3.** to barber, cut hair – الحَلاق غِسَل وَحِلَق راسي [ʔilħalla:q ɣisal wħilaq ra:si] The barber washed and cut my hair.

حَلِق [ħaliq] *v:* • **1.** to shave, to get a haircut

حَلِق [ħalig] *n:* حلُوق [ħlu:g] *pl:* • **1.** mouth – إذا تريد كُلّ النّاس يِسمَعُون هَالحكايَة حُطّها بِحَلِق عَلي [ʔiða tri:d kull ʔinna:s yismaʕu:n halħča:ya ħuṭṭha bħalig ʕali] If you want everyone to hear that story, let Ali know. لازِم أشتُغُل كُلّ يوم عَشِر ساعات لِأنَّ أطَعِّم عَشِر حلُوق [la:zim ʔaštuɣul kull yu:m ʕašir sa:ʕa:t liʔann ʔaṭaʕʕim ʕašir ħlu:g] I have to work ten hours every day since I have ten mouths to feed. حَلقَه وَسِخ [ħalgah waṣix] He's foul mouthed. • **2.** throat

حَلقَة [ħalqa, ħalaqa] *n:* حَلَقات [ħalaqa:t] *pl:* • **1.** ring (also nose-ring, earring) • **2.** wedding band • **3.** link (of a chain) • **4.** circle (also of people) • **5.** (vulgar) anus

حَلّاق [ħalla:q] *n:* حَلّاقِين [ħalla:qi:n] *pl:* • **1.** barber

حِلاقَة [ħila:qa] *n:* حِلاقات [ħila:qa:t] *pl:* • **1.** shaving, shave – مَكِينَة حِلاقَة [maki:nat ħila:qa] safety razor. • **2.** barber's trade, barbering

حالِق [ħa:lig] *adj:* • **1.** shaving

ح ل ق م

حَلقُوم [ħalqu:m] *n:* • **1.** Turkish delight

حَلقُومَة [ħalqu:ma] *n:* حَلقُومات، حَلقُوم [ħalqu:ma:t, ħalqu:m] *pl:* • **1.** piece of Turkish delight

ح ل ل

حَلّ [ħall] *v:* • **1.** to untie, unfasten, unravel, undo – إظافِرَك طوال. تِقدَر تحِلّ العُقدَة [ʔiða:firak ṭwa:l. tigdar tħill ʔilʕugda] Your fingernails are long. You can untie the knot. لا تضَيِّع وَقتَك. هَذا لا يحِلّ وَلا يربُط [la: dðayyiʕ waktak. ha:ða la: yħill wala yirbuṭ] Don't waste your time. He has no power (lit., he neither unties nor knots). • **2.** to solve, figure out – تِقدَر تحِلّ هَاللُّغز؟ [tigdar tħill halluɣuz?] Can you solve this riddle? الخَبِير ما يِقدَر يحِلّ رمُوز الشَّفرَة [ʔilxabi:r ma: yigdar yħill rumu:z ʔiššafra] The expert can't solve the key to the code. • **3.** to dissolve – هَاللَّكَّة عَلَى سِترَتَك ما يحِلّها إلّا الكُحُول [hallakka ʕala sitirtak ma: yħillha ʔilla ʔilkuħu:l] That spot on your suit can only be dissolved by alcohol. • **4.** to disband, break up, dissolve – الحُكُومَة حَلَّت المَجلِس [ʔilħuku:ma ħallat lmajlis] The government dissolved parliament. • **5.** to release, set free, let go – حَلّ نَفسَه وَانهِزَم [ħall nafsah wʔinhizam] He freed himself and escaped. حِلّنِي ما راح أنهِزِم [ħillni ma: ra:ħ ʔanhizim] Turn me loose! I'm not going to run away. حِلّ عَنّي! ما دَتشُوفنِي مَشغُول؟ [ħill ʕanni! ma: datšu:fni mašɣu:l?] Leave me alone! Don't you see I'm busy? • **6.** to be let off, be let go – العُمّال راح يحِلُّون السّاعَة أربَعَة [ʔilʕumma:l ra:ħ yħillu:n ʔissa:ʕa ʔarbaʕa] The workers will get off at four o'clock. لا تفَتّح قَبُل ما أصِيح حَلَّت [la: tfattiħ gabul ma: ʔaṣi:ħ ħallat] Don't open your eyes before I call okay. • **7.** to befall, occur, happen – شُوفَه شحَلّ بِيه! قِتلَه لا يِشتُغُل ويّا هَالجَماعَة [šu:fah šħall bi:h! gitlah la: yištuɣul wiyya haljama:ʕa] Look what happened to him! I told him not to go into business with that crowd. • **8.** to be or become due, payable – حَلَّت الوَعدَة. ما قِتلِي توَدِّينِي لِلسِّينَما يوم الجُمعَة؟ [ħallat ʔilwaʕda. ma: gitli twaddi:ni lissinama yu:m ʔijjumʕa?] The promise has come due. Didn't you tell me you'd take me to the movies Friday? • **9.** to be or become worthwhile, appropriate, timely – هَسَّة حَلَّت الرَّوحَة لِبَغداد. كُلّ قَرايبِي هناك [hassa ħallat ʔirrawħa libayda:d. kull gara:ybi hna:k] Now it's worthwhile going to Baghdad. All my relatives are there. • **10.** to be allowed, permitted, lawful, legitimate

حَلَّل [ħallal] *v:* • **1.** to analyze – حَلَّل المَوقِف بمَقال طِلَع بِالجَّرِيدَة اليُوم [ħallal ʔilmawqif bmaqa:l ṭilaʕ bijjari:da ʔilyu:m] He analyzed the situation in an article which came out in the paper today. • **2.** to make a chemical analysis – حَلِّل هالمَحلُول [ħallil halmaħlu:l] Analyze this solution. • **3.** to make permissible or lawful, sanction, justify, warrant – الله حَلَّل الزَّواج بأربَع نِسوان [ʔallah ħallal ʔizzawa:j bʔarbaʕ niswa:n] God sanctioned marriage to four women. قُوم اِشتُغُل، حَلِّل مَعاشَك [gu:m ʔištuɣul, ħallil maʕa:šak] Get to work and justify your salary. • **4.** to declare permissible, permit, allow – الدِّين يحَلِّل أكِل أنواع اللُّحُوم عَدا الخَنزِير [ʔiddi:n yħallil ʔakil ʔanwa:ʕ ʔilluħu:m ʕada: ʔilxanzi:r] The religion permits the eating of meats other than pork.

تحَلَّل [tħallal] *v:* • **1.** to be analyzed, broken down

اِنحَلّ [ʔinħall] *v:* • **1.** to be untied – العُقدَة اِنحَلَّت [ʔilʕugda ʔinħallat] The knot came loose. • **2.** to be solved – المُشكِلَة اِنحَلَّت [ʔilmuškila ʔinħallat] The problem was solved.

اِحتَلّ [ʔiħtall] *v:* • **1.** to occupy, take over – الجَّيش اِحتَلّ المَدِينَة [ʔijjayš ʔiħtall ʔilmadi:na] The army occupied the city. إبنِي اِحتَلّ السِّرداب كُلَّه لنَفسَه [ʔibni ʔiħtall ʔissirda:b kullah lnafsah] My son has taken over the whole basement for himself.

اِستَحَلّ [ʔistaħall] *v:* • **1.** to occupy, to regard as fair game, as easy prey, to seize unlawfully

حَلّ [ħall] *n:* حُلُول [ħulu:l] *pl:* • **1.** untying, unfastening, undoing – المُعاوِن هُوَّ اللّي بِيدَه الحَلّ وَالرَّبُط بهَالدّائِرَة [ʔalmuʕa:win huwwa ʔilli bi:dah ʔilħall wʔirrabuṭ bhadda:ʔira] The assistant is the one who has the power in this office (lit., in whose hands is the untying and the knotting). • **2.** solution • **3.** chemical solution • **4.** dissolution, disbandment, breaking up • **5.** release, liberation, freeing

حَلَّة [ħalla] *n:* حَلّات، حلال [ħalla:t, ħla:l] *pl:* • **1.** large, basket-like nest for pigeons

مَحَلّ [maħall] *n:* مَحَلّات [maħalla:t] *pl:* • **1.** place, location, site, spot – لَو بمَحَلَّك، ما كِنِت أقبَل بأقَلّ مِن مِيَّة دِينار [law bmaħallak, ma: činit ʔaqbal bʔaqall min miyyat dina:r] If I'd been in your place, I wouldn't have accepted for less than one hundred dinars. مِن أستَقِيل، مِنُو راح ياخُذ مَحَلِّي؟ [min ʔastaqi:l, minu ra:ħ ya:xuð maħalli?] When I resign, who's going to take my place? • **1.** appropriate – جاب حكايَة كُلَّش بمَحَلّها [ja:b ħča:ya kulliš bmaħallha] He came out with a very appropriate remark. • **2.** justified, warranted – حكايتَك مُو بمَحَلّها [ħča:ytak mu: bmaħallha] Your remark was out of place. • **3.** room, space • **4.** seat • **5.** desk, work area • **6.** shop, place • **7.** place, opening • **8.** grammatical function – هَالكِلمَة ما إلها مَحَلّ مِن الإعراب بهَالجُّملَة [haččilma ma: ʔilha maħall min ʔilʔiʕra:b bihajjumla] This word has no function grammatically in this sentence. • **9.** (hence, by extension) bearing, relevance – حكايتَك ما إلها مَحَلّ مِن الإعراب [ħča:ytak ma: ʔilha maħall min ʔilʔiʕra:b] Your remark has no relevance.

حَلال [ħala:l] *n:* • **1.** allowed, permitted, permissible, allowable, lawful, legal – هَذا حَلال بالإسلام [ha:ða ħala:l bilʔisla:m] That's permissible in Islam. • **2.** nice guy, good fellow, good man • **3.** due, owed, coming – حَلال عَلِيك. أُخذَه. مِن كُلّ قَلبِي [ħala:l ʕali:k. ʔuxðah. min kull galbi] It's rightfully yours. Take it. I really mean it. حَلال عَليه الوَظِيفَة. يِستاهِل [ħala:l ʕali:h lwaḍi:fa. yista:hil] The position is rightly his. He deserves it. الإجازَة حَلال عَليه لأنّ صارلَه سَنتَين ما ماخِذ إجازَة [ʔilʔija:za ħala:l ʕali:h liʔann ṣa:rlah santayn ma: ma:xið ʔija:za] The leave is due him since he's gone two years without one. • **4.** lawful possession – هَذا مُلكِي وَحَلالِي. أقدَر أسَوِّي بِيه شما أرِيد [ha:ða mulki wħala:li. ʔagdar ʔasawwi: bi:h šma ʔari:d] This is my legal property. I can do what I want with it. • **5.** literally a man with good values or morals; used sarcastically to mean bastard – إبن حَرام [ʔibin ħara:m] approx.:) son of a gun.

مَحَلَّة [maħalla] *n:* مَحَلّات، محالِيل [maħalla:t, mħa:li:l] *pl:* • **1.** section, part, quarter of a city, neighborhood

حَلّان، حِلّان [ħalla:n, ħilla:n] *n:* • **1.** bale(s) of pressed dates – تَمر الحِلّان [tamr ʔilħilla:n] dates in the bale. • **2.** the basket-like wrapping of the bale, woven of palm leaves • **3.** a kind of stone

مُحَلِّل [muħallil] *n:* مُحَلِّلِين [muħallili:n] *pl:* • **1.** analyzer, analyst

مُحتَلّ [muħtall] *n:* مُحتَلِّين [muħtalliyyn] *pl:* • **1.** invader, occupier

تَحَلُّل [tħallul] *n:* • **1.** moldiness, disintegration

حَلّانَة، حِلّانَة [ħalla:na, ħilla:na] *n:* حِلّانات [ħilla:na:t] *pl:* • **1.** unit noun of حَلّان • **2.** (by extension, jokingly) derriere (vulgar)

تَحلِيل [taħli:l] *n:* تَحلِيلات، تَحالِيل [taħli:la:t, taħa:li:l] *pl:* • **1.** analysis – تَحلِيل نَفسِي [taħli:l nafsi] psychoanalysis. سَوَّولَه تَحلِيل نَفسِي [sawwawlah taħli:l nafsi] They psychoanalyzed him. تَحلِيل دَمّ [taħli:l damm] blood test. تَحلِيل مَرَضِي [taħli:l maraði] a medical analysis. مُختَبَر التَّحلِيلات المَرَضِيَّة [muxtabar ʔittaħli:la:t ʔilmaraðiyya] medical analysis laboratory.

مَحلُول [maħlu:l] *n:* • **1.** loose, loosened – بُرغِي مَحلُول [burɣi maħlu:l] a loose screw. • **2.** united, unfastened, free, at large, loose – قِيطان قُندَرتَك مَحلُول [qi:ṭa:n qundartak maħlu:l] Your shoelace is untied. لا تخُشّ بِالحَدِيقَة، تَرَة الكَلِب مَحلُول [la: txušš bilħadi:qa, tara ʔiččalib maħlu:l] Don't go in the garden, because the dog is loose. • **3.** weakened, exhausted, languid – آنِي مَحلُول اليُوم؛ ما بِيَّا حيل أشتُغُل [ʔa:ni maħlu:l ʔilyu:m; ma: biyya ħi:l ʔaštuɣul] I'm tired today; I've got no energy to work. • **4.** pl. مَحالِيل liquid, solution (chem) – مَحلُول حامضِي [maħlu:l ħa:mði] an acidic solution.

اِنحِلال [ʔinħila:l] *n:* • **1.** slackening, loosening, relaxing – اِنحِلال الأخلاق [ʔinħila:l ʔilʔaxla:q] the decline in morals.

اِحتِلال [ʔiħtila:l] *n:* • **1.** occupation (mil.)

مَحَلِّي [maħalli] *adj:* • **1.** local – الإدارَة المَحَلِّيَّة [ʔilʔida:ra ʔilmaħalliyya] the local administration. • **2.** native, indigenous, local – صِناعات مَحَلِّيَّة [ṣina:ʕa:t maħalliyya] local industries. • **3.** (pl. only) – تِقدَر تلقِي المَحَلِّيّات بِالصَّفحَة الثّانيَة [tigdar tilgi ʔilmaħalliyya:t biṣṣafħa ʔiθθa:nya] You can find the local news on the second page. قرَيت خَبَر الزِّلزال بالمَحَلِّيّات؟ [qrayt xabar ʔizzilza:l bilmaħalliyya:t?] Did you read the earthquake story in the local news?

مِنحَلّ [minħall] *adj:* • **1.** loosened, relaxed – الأخلاق مِنحَلَّة بهالبَلَد [ʔilʔaxla:q minħalla bha:lbalad] Morals are loose in this country.

ح ل م

حِلَم [ħilam] *v:* • **1.** to dream – حِلمِت البارحَة راح أصِير مَلِك [ħilamit ʔilba:rħa ra:ħ ʔaṣi:r malik] I dreamed yesterday that I was going to become a king. حِلمِت بِيك البارحَة [ħilamit bi:k ʔilba:rħa] I dreamed about you yesterday. • **2.** to daydream – ما اِشتِغَل كُلّشِي هَاليُوم؛ دَيِحلَم بزَواجَه [ma: ʔištiɣal kullši halyu:m; dayiħlam bzawa:ǰah] He didn't do a thing today; he's dreaming about his marriage. دَتِحلَم. بَعَد عِشرِين سَنَة ما تصِير طَبِيب [datiħlam. baʕad ʕišri:n sana ma: tṣi:r ṭabi:b] You're dreaming. In twenty years you won't become a doctor.

تحَلَّم [tħallam] *v:* • **1.** to muse, reflect, daydream – دَيِتحَلَّم بسَفِرتَه لباريس [dayitħallam bsafirtah lpa:ri:s] He's daydreaming about his trip to Paris.

اِستَحلَم [ʔistaħlam] *v:* • **1.** to have a nocturnal emission

حِلِم [ħilim] *n:* أحلام [ʔaħla:m] *pl:* • **1.** dream – يعِيش بدِنيا الأحلام [yiʕi:š bdinya: ʔilʔaħla:m] He lives in a dream world.

حِلمَة [ħilma] *n:* حِلمات، حِلَم [ħilma:t, ħilam] *pl:* • **1.** nipple, teat, mammillary bodies (of a female)

حَلمان [ħalma:n] *adj:* • **1.** dreaming, in a state of dreaming – إنتَ حَلمان. ماكُو هِيكِي شِي [ʔinta ħalma:n. ma:ku hi:či ši] You're dreaming. There's no such thing.

مِحتِلِم [miħtilim] *adj:* • **1.** sexually mature • **2.** pubescent

ح ل و

حِلَى [ħila:] *v:* • **1.** to become sweet – كُلما تخَلِّي الرَّقِّي يبقَى بهِرشَه أزيَد، يِحلَى [kullma txalli: ʔirraggi yibqa: bhiršah ʔazyad, yiħla:] The longer you leave the watermelon on the vine, the sweeter it gets. • **2.** to become pleasant, nice, enjoyable – مِن جا مَجِيد، حِلَت القَعدَة [min ǰa: maǰi:d, ħilat ʔilgaʕda] When Majid came, the session became pleasant. القَعدَة عَالشَّطّ تِحلَى وَقِت المِغرب [ʔilgaʕda ʕaššaṭṭ tiħla: wakit ʔilmiɣrib] Sitting by the river gets pleasant at sunset. بَغداد تِحلَى بالرَّبِيع [baɣda:d tiħla: birrabi:ʕ] Baghdad gets pleasant in the spring. • **3.** to become pretty – دَتِحلَى يوم عَلَى يوم [datiħla: yu:m ʕala yu:m] She's getting prettier day by day.

حَلَّى [ħalla:] *v:* • **1.** to make sweet, sweeten – لا تحَلِّي الشاي مالِي زايِد [la: tħalli ʔičča:y ma:li za:yid] Don't sweeten my tea too much. • **2.** to make pleasant, nice, enjoyable – الغِنَى يحَلِّي الحَياة [ʔilɣina yħalli: ʔilħaya:t] Wealth makes life more enjoyable. • **3.** to make pretty, beautify – نَفنُوفِك الأسوَد يحَلِّيك أزيَد مِن اللاخ [nafnu:fič ʔilʔaswad yħalli:č ʔazyad min ʔilla:x] Your black dress becomes you more than the other. اللّايتات عَالسَّيّارَة مَحَلّيَتها [ʔilla:yta:t ʕassayya:ra mħallyatha] The lights on the car have improved its appearance.

حَلا، حَلَة [ħala:, ħala] *n:* • **1.** sweetness • **2.** pleasantness, niceness • **3.** beauty, prettiness

حَلاوَة [ħala:wa] *n:* • **1.** halvah, a flaky confection of crushed sesame seeds in a base of honey or other syrup • **2.** peace offering – ما دام تصالَحنا، خَلِّي أغَدِّيك حَلاوَة صُلُح [ma: da:m tṣa:laħna, xalli: ʔaɣaddi:k ħala:wat ṣuluħ] Since we've made up, let me take you to lunch as a peace offering. • **2.** present to a mediator – عَلِيَّة إنطَتها هَدِيَّة لِأُمّها حَلاوَة صُلُح لِأَنّ صالحَتها ويّا رَجِلها [ʕaliyya ʔinṭatha hadiyya lʔummha ħalaːwat ṣuluħ liʔann ṣaːlħatha wiyya rajilha] Aliya gave her mother a present as a token for mediation because she reconciled her and her husband. • **3.** an easy thing, a snap – الشُّغُل بِأَوَّل هَالإِسبُوع كان حَلاوَة، لَكِن صار صَعُب بَعدين [ʔiššuɣul bʔawwal halʔisbuːʕ čaːn ħalaːwa, laːkin ṣaːr ṣaʕub baʕdiːn] The work at the beginning of this week was a piece of cake, but it got hard later.

تَحلِيَة [taħliya] *n:* • **1.** desalinization, removing salt (from) • **2.** decoration

حَلوِيّات [ħalawiyyaːt] *n:* • **1.** (pl. only) sweet pastries

حِلو [ħilw] *adj:* • **1.** sweet, sweetened – شاي حِلو [čaːy ħilw] sweetened tea. ماي حِلو [maːy ħilw] fresh water, free of brackish qualities. • **2.** pleasant, nice, enjoyable – حَكِي حِلو [ħači ħilw] pleasant talk. دَيصرُف بِهَالفلُوس الحِلوَة [dayiṣruf bhalfluːs ʔilħilwa] He's spending all that nice money. • **3.** handsome, good-looking, pretty – بنَيَّة حِلوَة [bnayya ħilwa] a pretty girl. • **4.** (an exclamation of approval, also used sarcastically, approx.:) great! wonderful! – حِلو! لَعَد راح أَتوَنَّس هَالصَّيف [ħilw! laʕad raːħ ʔatwannas haṣṣayf] Wonderful! Then I'm going to have a good time this summer. حِلو! حِلو! لِيش حَرَّكت المَلِك؟ مُو راح تِخسَر [ħilw! ħilw! liːš ħarrakt ʔilmalik? muː raːħ tixsar] Great, great! Why did you move the king? You're going to lose now! • **5.** nicely – شُوفها شلُون تِمشِي حِلو [šuːfha šluːn timši ħilw] Look how nicely she walks. كان دَيِدرُس حِلو حِلو إِلَى أَن جا صَدِيقَه [čaːn dayidrus ħilw ħilw ʔila ʔan jaː ṣadiːqah] He was studying quite nicely till his friend came. • **6.** pl. حِلوِين buddy, pal

حِلوَة [ħilwa] *adj:* حِلوات [ħilwaːt] *pl:* • **1.** pretty girl – تَعالِي يا حِلوَة؛ إِنطِي بُوسَة لأَبُوك [taʕaːli yaː ħilwa; ʔinṭi buːsa lʔabuːč] Come on, pretty girl; give your father a kiss! حِلوَة المَحَلَّة [ħilwat ʔilmaħalla] the belle of the neighborhood.

أَحلَى [ʔaħla] *comparative adjective:* • **1.** sweeter, sweetest • **2.** more or most pleasant • **3.** more or most handsome.

ح م د

حِمَد [ħimad] *v:* • **1.** to praise, laud, extol – مُدِيرَك يحِبَّك وَيحِمدَك [mudiːrak yħibbak wyħimdak] Your boss likes you and praises you. المُعَلِّم يِحمِد بِيك هوايَة [ʔilmuʕallim yiħmid biːk hwaːya] The teacher praises you a lot. إحمِد الله وَأُشكُرَه! شِترِيد بَعَد؟ [ʔiħmid ʔallah wšukrah! šitriːd baʕad?] Praise God and thank Him! What else do you want?

حَمِد [ħamid] *n:* • **1.** praise, commendation – الحَمدُ لله، الحَمدُ لله [ʔilħamdu lillaːh, ʔilħamdu lillaːh] Praise be to God! Thank God! الحَمدُ لله، رِجَع سالِم [ʔilħamdu lillaːh, rijaʕ saːlim] Thank God, he returned safely!

حَمِيد [ħamiːd] *adj:* • **1.** praiseworthy, laudable, commendable – صِفَة حَمِيدَة [ṣifa ħamiːda] a laudable quality, a virtue. رَبَّك حَمِيد، ما سَوَّى إلنا شِي [rabbak ħamiːd, maː sawwaː ʔilna ši] Thank goodness, he didn't do anything to us. وَالله الحَمِيد، مالِي عِلاقَة بِيه [wʔallah ʔilħamiːd, maːli ʕilaːqa biːh] My goodness, I had nothing to do with it!

مُحَمَّدِي [muħammadi] *adj:* مُحَمَّدِيِّين [muħammadiyyin] *pl:* • **1.** (as n:) a follower of Mohammed, a Moslem

ح م ر

حَمَّر [ħammar] *v:* • **1.** to make red, redden, color red – العَرُوس حَمُّرَت خدُودها زايِد [ʔilʕaruːs ħammurat xduːdha zaːyid] The bride put too much rouge on her cheeks. • **2.** to roast – بِدال ما تفَوِّرها لِلدِّجاجَة، حَمُّرها عالنّار [bidaːl maː tfawwirha liddijaːja, ħammurha ʕannaːr] Instead of boiling the chicken, roast it on the fire. • **3.** to brown – الدِّجاجَة مِستَوِيَة لَكِن رَجِّعها عالنّار وَحَمُّرها [ʔiddijaːja mistawiya laːkin rajjiʕha ʕannaːr wħammurha] The chicken's done, but put it back on the fire and brown it.

إحمَرّ [ʔiħmarr] *v:* • **1.** to turn red, become red, redden – إحمَرَّت عَينَه مِن قَدّ ما يفرُكها [ʔiħmarrat ʕaynah min gadd maː yifrukha] His eyes turned red from his rubbing them so much. إحمَرّ وِجهه مِن الخَجَل [ʔiħmarr wiččah min ʔilxajal] He blushed from embarrassment.

حِمرِي [ħimri] *n:* • **1.** a kind of reddish-colored fish

حُمرَة [ħumra] *n:* • **1.** redness, red color, red coloration • **2.** rouge, lipstick – حُمرَة شفاف [ħumrat šfaːf] lipstick.

حمار [ħamaːr] *n:* • **1.** reddening, blushing • **2.** redness, red coloration

حمار [ħmaːr] *n:* حَمِير، حماير [ħamiːr, ħmaːyir] *pl:* • **1.** donkey, ass (also a derogatory term for a person) – هَذا شِنُو، هَالحِمار؟ [haːða šinu, haliħmaːr?] What does he matter, that jackass?

حِمرِين، جبال حِمرِين [ħimriːn, jibaːl ħimriːn] *n:* • **1.** a group of mountains in northern Iraq

أَحمَر [ʔaħmar] *adj:* حُمُر [ħumur] *pl:* حَمرَة [ħamra] *feminine:* • **1.** red – موت أَحمَر [muːt ʔaħmar] violent death. هاي شلُون وَظِيفَة! موت أَحمَر [haːy šluːn waðiːfa! muːt ʔaħmar] What a job! It's killing!

محَمَّر [mħammar] *adj:* • **1.** roasted – دِجاجَة محَمَّرَة [dijaːja mħammara] a roasted chicken.

ح م س 1

حِمَس [ħimas] *v:* • **1.** to excite, stir up – حِمَستَه مِن قُمِت أَحكِي وِيّا صَدِيقتَه [ħimastah min gumit ʔaħči wiyya ṣadiːqtah] I got him all worked up when I started talking with his girl friend.

حَمَّس [ħammas] *v:* • **1.** to excite, arouse, stir, make enthusiastic, work up – المُوسِيقَى العَسكَرِيَّة حَمّسَتنِي [ʔilmuːsiːqa ʔilʕaskariyya ħammsatni] The military music stirred me. حَمَّسنِي عَلَى الدُّخُول بِالسِّبَاق [ħammasni ʕala ʔidduxuːl bissibaːq] He made me enthusiastic about entering the race. خِطابَه حَمَّس الجَّماهِير، وقامَوا يهَوّسُون [xiṭaːbah ħammas ʔijǰamaːhiːr, wgaːmaw yhawwsuːn] His speech stirred up the crowd, and they began to go wild.

تحَمَّس [tħammas] *v:* • **1.** to be excited, aroused, stirred – تحَمَّسِت مِن سِمَعت الخِطاب [tħammasit min simaʕt ʔilxiṭaːb] I was stirred when I heard the speech. • **2.** to become enthusiastic, eager, zealous – تحَمَّس هوايَة لِلمَشرُوع وَكان عِندَه اِستِعداد يُصرُف فلُوس [tħammas hwaːya lilmašruːʕ wčaːn ʕindah ʔistiʕdaːd yuṣruf fluːs] He grew very enthusiastic toward the project and was ready to spend money.

حَماس، حَماسَة [ħamaːs, ħamaːsa] *n:* • **1.** enthusiasm, ardor, fervor, zeal, fanaticism

تَحَمُّس [taħammus] *n:* • **1.** enthusiasm

حَماسِي [ħamaːsi] *adj:* • **1.** stirring, rousing, thrilling – أناشِيد مَدرَسِيَّة حَماسِيَّة [ʔanaːšiːd madrasiyya ħamaːsiyya] stirring school songs.

مِتحَمِّس [mitħammis] *adj:* • **1.** enthusiastic, ardent, fiery, zealous – قَومِي مِتحَمِّس [qawmi mitħammis] an ardent nationalist.

ح م س 2

حِمَس [ħimas] *v:* • **1.** to fry (meat) in its own juices (without oil or grease) – حِمسَت اللَّحَم وَبَعدين خَلَّت عَليه مَيّ [ħimsat ʔillaħam wbaʕdiːn xallat ʕaliːh mayy] She fried the meat and then put water in it. راح أنزَع اليَلَك. الشَّمِس حِمسَتنِي [raːħ ʔanzaʕ ʔilyalag. ʔiššamis ħimsatni] I'm going to take off the vest. The sun has broiled me.

حَمِس [ħamis] *n:* • **1.** frying

حَمسَة [ħamsa] *n:* حَمسات [ħamsaːt] *pl:* • **1.** frying

حَمِيس [ħamiːs] *n:* • **1.** chunks of meat fried in their own juice with onion • **2.** pieces of liver broiled on a skewer

مَحمُوس [maħmuːs] *adj:* • **1.** boiled heart, lungs, and liver • **3.** chunks of meat fried in their own juices with onion

ح م س 3

حَمِيسَة، دُبَّة حَمِيسَة [ħamiːsa, dubba ħamiːsa] *adj:* • **1.** fat, obese

ح م ص

حَمَّص [ħammaṣ] *v:* • **1.** to roast – حَمُّص القَهوَة زين قَبُل ما تِطحَنها [ħammuṣ ʔilgahwa ziːn gabul maː tiṭħanha] Roast the coffee well before you grind it.

تحَمَّص [tħammaṣ] *v:* • **1.** to be roasted – خَلّي الدِّجاجَة تِتحَمَّص زين بِالفِرِن [xalliː ʔiddijaːja titħammaṣ ziːn bilfirin] Let the chicken get well roasted in the oven.

حُمُّص [ħummuṣ] *n:* • **1.** chick-peas – حُمُّص بِطحِينَة [ħummuṣ biṭħiːna] a dish made of ground chickpeas and sesame oil.

ح م ض

حُمَض [ħumað] *v:* • **1.** to sour, become sour or unpleasant – مِن صار وَزير أخلاقَه حُمضَت [min ṣaːr waziːr ʔaxlaːqah ħumðat] When he became a minister his manners went bad. تجادلَوا شوَيَّة وَبَعدين حُمضَت القَضِيَّة [dǰaːdlaw šwayya wbaʕdiːn ħumðat ʔilqaðiyya] They argued a little and then the matter really turned sour. حُمضَت عاد! صارلَك إسبُوع تواعِدنِي بِالفلُوس [ħumðat ʕaːd! ṣaːrlak ʔisbuːʕ twaːʕidni bilfiluːs] It's gone too far! You've been promising me the money for a week.

حَمَّض [ħammað] *v:* • **1.** to sour, become sour – خَلّي الحَلِيب بِالثَّلّاجَة قَبُل ما يحَمُّض [xalliː ʔilħaliːb biθθallaːǰa gabul maː yħammuð] Put the milk in the refrigerator before it sours. • **2.** to make (matters) unpleasant – يَزّي عاد! مُو حَمَّضِتها [yazzi ʕaːd! muː ħammaðitha] Enough now! You've gone too far!

حَمُض [ħamuð] *n:* • **1.** sourness • **2.** acidity

حُمُوضَة [ħumuːða] *n:* • **1.** sourness • **2.** acidity

حامُض [ħaːmuð] *adj:* • **1.** sour, acid – الحُصرُم حامُض كُلِّش [ʔilħuṣrum ħaːmuð kulliš] Green grapes are very sour. نُومِي حامُض [nuːmi ħaːmuð] lemon. شاي حامُض [čaːy ħaːmuð] lemon tea, a hot drink made by boiling crushed dried lemons. • **2.** sour, crabby – نَفسَه حامضَة؛ لا تِطلُب مِنَّه شِي [nafsah ħaːmða; laː titlub minnah ši] He's crabby; don't ask him for anything. ما تِقدَر تِحكِي وِيّاه؛ أخلاقَه حامضَة [maː tigdar tiħči wiyyaːh; ʔaxlaːqah ħaːmða] You can't talk to him; he's a sourpuss. • **3.** acid – حَوامِض [ħawaːmið] *Pl: n:*

محَمَّض [mħammuð] *adj:* • **1.** soured

ح م ق

حُمَق [ħumaq] *v:* • **1.** to be or become angry, mad, furious – حُمَق بِالعَجَل وَطِلَع مِن الغُرفَة [ħumaq bilʕaǰal wṭilaʕ min ʔilɣurfa] He got mad right away and left the room. • **2.** to anger, make mad, furious – حُمَقنِي بِالحَكِي مالَه [ħumaqni bilħači maːlah] He angered me with his talk.

اِنحُمَق [ʔinħumaq] *v:* • **1.** to get angry, mad, furious – اِنحُمَق عَلَيّا لِأنّ ما كَمَّلت الشُّغُل مالِي [ʔinħumaq ʕalayya liʔann maː kammalt ʔiššuɣul maːli] He got mad at me because I hadn't finished my work.

حُمُق [ħamuq] *n:* • **1.** stupidity • **2.** anger • **3.** foolishness

حَماقَة [ħamaːqa] *n:* حَماقات [ħamaːqaːt] *pl:* • **1.** stupidity, foolishness • **2.** hot-tempered person • **3.** pl. حَماقات stupid, foolish act or deed

ح

أحمَق [ʔaħmaq] *adj:* حُمُق، حَمقِين [ħumuq, ħamqiːn] *pl:* حَمقاء [ħamqaːʔ] *feminine:* • **1.** dumb, stupid, foolish, silly • **2.** fool, simpleton, idiot, jerk

حَمقان [ħamqaːn] *adj:* • **1.** angry, upset, mad – إسمَع حِسَّه؛ دَيصَيِّح. يبَيِّن هَمّ حَمقان [ʔismaʕ ħissah; dayṣayyiħ. yibayyin hamm ħamqaːn] Listen to his voice; he's shouting. Looks like he's mad again.

مَحمُوق [maħmuːq] *adj:* • **1.** angry, mad, furious – لِيش مَحمُوق؟ ما قِصَدها [liːš maħmuːq? maː qiṣadha] Why are you angry? He didn't mean it.

أحمَق [ʔaħmaq] *comparative adjective:* • **1.** more or most foolish

ح م ل

حِمَل [ħimal] *v:* • **1.** to bear, hold, support – هَالكُرسِي ما يِحِملَك [halkursi maː yħimlak] This chair won't bear your weight. • **2.** to bear, stand, endure, tolerate – دُكتُور، ما أقدَر أحمِل بَعَد. بَنِّجنِي [duktuːr, maː ʔagdar ʔaħmil baʕad. bannijni] Doctor, I can't take it any more. Anesthetize me. ما أقدَر أحمِلَه لِهذا. يِلغِي عَلَى طُول [maː ʔagdar ʔaħimlah lhaːða. yilɣi ʕala ṭuːl] I can't take him. He chatters constantly. لا تشاقِيه تَرَة ما يِحمِل [laː tšaːqiːh tara maː yiħmil] Don't tease him because he can't take it. حِمَلها لِلحكايَة لِأنّ ما راد يسَوِّي لَغوَة [ħimalha lilħčaːya liʔann maː raːd ysawwiː laɣwa] He took the remark because he didn't want to make a commotion. • **3.** to accept, entertain, harbor – يِحمِل أفكار شِيُوعِيَّة [yiħmil ʔafkaːr šiyuːʕiyya] He harbors communist ideas. عَقلِي ما يِحمِلها. مُستَحِيل [ʕaqli maː yiħmilha. mustaħiːl] My mind won't accept it. It's unbelievable. • **4.** to become pregnant – حِملَت مِنَّه [ħimlat minnah] She got pregnant by him. • **5.** to bear, bear fruit – شِجرَة البُرتُقال حِملَت هالسَّنَة [šijrat ʔilpurtuqaːl ħimlat hassana] The orange tree bore fruit this year. • **6.** to take, take hold – الجِّدرِي مالَك ما حِمَل. لازِم تُضرُب مَرَّة اللُّخ [ʔijjidri maːlak maː ħimal. laːzim tuðrub marrat ʔillux] Your vaccination didn't take. You'll have to be vaccinated again. • **7.** with عَلَى to attack, launch, make an attack against – مِن سِمَع راح أنافسَه عَالوَظِيفَة، حِمَل عَلَيّا قِدّام النّاس [min simaʕ raːħ ʔanaːfsah ʕalwaðiːfa, ħimal ʕalayya giddaːm ʔinnaːs] When he heard I'm going to compete with him for the position, he attacked me in front of everyone.

حَمَّل [ħammal] *v:* • **1.** to load – حَمّلَوا اللَّورِي رَقِّي [ħammilaw ʔilluːri raggi] They loaded the truck with watermelons. • **2.** to load, burden, impose on – المُدِير حَمَّل المُعاوِن مالَه مَسؤُولِيَّة كُلّ الأغلاط بالحِسابات [ʔilmudiːr ħammal ʔilmuʕaːwin maːlah masʔuːliyyat kull ʔilʔaɣlaːṭ bilħisaːbaːt] The director saddled his assistant with responsibility for all the mistakes in the accounts. عاوَنِّي بالشُّغُل وحَمَّلنِي مِنِّيَّة. هَسَّة يَومِيّاً يرِيدنِي أعاوِنَه [ʕaːwanni biššuɣul wħammalni minniyya. hassa yuːmiyyan yriːdni ʔaʕaːwnah] He helped me with the job and imposed an obligation. Now he wants me to help him everyday. حَمَّل الفلُوس دِينار فايز [ħammal ʔilfluːs dinaːr faːyiz] He added a dinar interest to the money. • **3.** to ship, transport – حَمَّل عِشرِين ماطَور حُنطَة لِلبَصرَة [ħammal ʕišriːn maːṭuːr ħunṭa lilbaṣra] He shipped twenty motor barges of wheat to Basra. راح أدِزّلَك حَمّالَين حَتَّى تحَمِّل كُلّ الغَراض [raːħ ʔadizzlak ħammaːlayn ħatta tħammil kull ʔilɣaraːð] I will send you two porters so you can transport all the things. • **4.** to become infected – الحَبّايَة راح إتحَمِّل إذا ما تداوِيها بسُرعَة [ʔilħabbaːya raːħ tħammil ʔiða maː ddaːwiːha bsurʕa] The pimple will get infected if you don't treat it quickly. • **5.** to take hold, take – الجِّدرِي مالَك مَحَمَّل [ʔijjidri maːlak maħammal] Your smallpox vaccination didn't take.

تحَمَّل [tħammal] *v:* • **1.** to be loaded – أرِيد اللَّورِي يِتحَمَّل قَبِل المَغرِب [ʔariːd ʔilluːri yitħammal gabil ʔilmaɣrib] I want the truck to be loaded before sundown. • **2.** to bear, hold, support, take – هَالجِسِر ما يِتحَمَّل لَورِيّات [haljisir maː yitħammal luːriyyaːt] This bridge won't take trucks. • **3.** to bear, stand, sustain, endure, tolerate, stomach – ما يِتحَمَّل ألَم [maː yitħammal ʔalam] He can't stand pain. مِنُو يِتحَمَّل هِيكِي مَرَة؟ [minu yitħammal hiːči mara?] Who can stand such a woman? تحَمَّل الرَّزالَة وسِكَت [tħammal ʔirrazaːla wsikat] He took the insult and kept quiet. الوَضِع ما يِتحَمَّل هِيكِي إجراءات [ʔilwaðiʕ maː yitħammal hiːči ʔijraːʔaːt] The situation won't allow such measures. • **4.** to undergo, suffer – تحَمَّلَت هوايَة بمَرَض إبنها [tħammilat hwaːya bmarað ʔibinha] She suffered a lot during her son's illness. • **5.** to accept, receive, admit, entertain – عَقلِي ما يِتحَمَّل راح يبَطِّل [ʕaqli maː yitħammal raːħ ybaṭṭil] My mind won't accept that he's going to quit. عَقلِي ما يِتحَمَّل الرِّياضِيات [ʕaqli maː yitħammal ʔirriyaːðiyyaːt] My mind has no capacity for mathematics.

تحامَل [tħaːmal] *v:* • **1.** with عَلَى to attack, criticize unjustly, pick on – ماكُو حاجَة تِتحامَل عَلِيه بغِيابَه [maːku ħaːja titħaːmal ʕaliːh bɣiyaːbah] There's no need for you to attack him in his absence. المُدِير عَلَى طُول يِتحامَل عَلَيّا [ʔilmudiːr ʕala ṭuːl yitħaːmal ʕalayya] The principal always picks on me.

إنحِمَل [ʔinħimal] *v:* • **1.** to be borne, stood, endured, tolerated, stomached – الوُجَع ما يِنحِمِل [ʔilwujaʕ maː yinħimil] The pain is unbearable. حكايتَك ما تِنحِمِل. إذا تقُولها مَرَّة اللُّخ، كَيفَك [ħčaːytak maː tinħimil. ʔiða tguːlha marrat ʔillux, kayfak] Your remark was unbearable. If you say it again, you're asking for it. دَمَّه ثقِيل؛ ما يِنحِمِل [dammah θigiːl; maː yinħimil] He's a stick in the mud; he's unbearable.

احتِمَل [ʔiħtimal] *v:* • **1.** to bear, stand, endure, take – مِنُو يِحتِمِل هَالعَذاب؟ [minu yiħtimil halʕaðaːb?] Who could stand this suffering? شلُون تحَمَّلِت كُلّ هَالمُدَّة بِلا مَرَة؟

[šlu:n tħammalit kull halmudda bila mara?] How'd you stand it all this time without a wife? ما أقدَر أحتِملَه. حَكيَه يسَوِّيني عَصَبي [ma: ʔagdar ʔaħtimlah. ħačyah ysawwi:ni ʕaṣabi] I can't stand him. His talk makes me mad. لِيش اِحتِمَلِت الإهانَة؟ كان لازِم تضرُبَه [li:š ʔiħtimalit ʔilʔiha:na? ča:n la:zim dd̦urbah] Why did you take the insult? You should have hit him. • **2.** to accept, receive, encompass – العَقِل ما يحتِمِل قُصّتَه [ʔilʕaqil ma: yiħtimil quṣṣtah] The mind boggles at his story. • **3.** to feel that something is possible, conceivable, or likely – يُحتَمَل يِجي باكِر [yuħtamal yiǰi ba:čir] It's possible he'll come tomorrow.

حَمِل [ħamil] *n:* • **1.** pregnancy

حِمِل [ħimil] *n:* حمُول [ħmu:l] *pl:* • **1.** cargo, load, burden

حَملَة [ħamla] *n:* حَملات [ħamla:t] *pl:* • **1.** attack, criticism • **2.** campaign – حَملَة اِنتِخابِيَّة [ħamla ʔintixa:biyya] election campaign. حَملَة عَسكَرِيَّة [ħamla ʕaskariyya] military campaign. • **3.** the ceremony of carrying the bride's belongings from her parents' house to the groom's house

حَمّال [ħamma:l] *n:* حَمّالين، حمامِيل [ħamma:li:n, ħma:mi:l] *pl:* • **1.** porter, carrier

تَحَمُّل [taħammul] *n:* • **1.** endurance, tolerance, resistance – تَحَمُّل لِلبَرِد [taħammul lilbarid] resistance to cold. • **2.** capacity, carrying capacity, strength – تَحَمُّل الفيُوز [taħammul ʔilfyu:z] the load capacity of the fuse. تَحَمُّل الأساسات أكثَر شِي أربَع قُوط [taħammul ʔilʔasa:sa:t ʔakθar ši ʔarbaʕ qu:ṭ] The bearing capacity of the foundations is at the most four floors.

حامِل [ħa:mil, ħa:mla] *n:* حَوامِل [ħawa:mil] *pl:* • **1.** fem. only pl. حَوامِل pregnant • **2.** as Adjective: masc. حامِل fem. حامْلَة holding, carrying

حمالَة [ħma:la] *n:* • **1.** porter's trade, occupation of being a porter • **2.** porterage, fee for carrying

حُمُولَة [ħumu:la] *n:* حُمُولات [ħumu:la:t] *pl:* • **1.** load capacity, load limit, capacity • **2.** tonnage (of a vessel)

تَحمِيل [taħmi:l] *n:* • **1.** loading

اِحتِمال [ʔiħtima:l] *n:* • **1.** tolerance, toleration, endurance, resistance – اِحتِمال لِلحَرّ [ʔiħtima:l lilħarr] tolerance for heat. • **2.** probability, likelihood, potentiality – أكُو اِحتِمال تُمطُر باكِر [ʔaku ʔiħtima:l tumṭur ba:čir] There's a good chance it will rain tomorrow.

تَحمِيلَة [taħmi:la] *n:* تَحامِيل [taħa:mi:l] *pl:* • **1.** suppository

مَحَمَّل [mħammal] *adj:* • **1.** loaded – اللُّوري مَحَمَّل أكثَر مِن اللّازِم [ʔillu:ri mħammal ʔakθar min ʔilla:zim] The truck's overloaded.

مَحَمِّل [mħammil] *adj:* • **1.** holder

حَمُولَة [ħamu:la] *adj:* حَمائِل [ħama:ʔil] *pl:* • **1.** a man from good stock – إبِن حَمُولَة [ʔibin ħamu:la] a man from good stock.

مُحتَمَل [muħtamal] *adj:* • **1.** probable, likely – لازِم كان يُوصَل قَبُل ساعتين. سَيّارتهُم عَتِيقَة؛ مُحتَمَل خُربَت [la:zim ča:n yu:ṣal gabul sa:ʕtayn. sayya:rathum ʕati:ga; muħtamal xurbat] They should've arrived two hours ago. Their car is old; it is likely it broke down. مُحتَمَل يرُوح بالطَّيّارَة لِبَغداد [muħtamal yiru:ħ biṭṭayya:ra libaɣda:d] He'll likely take the plane to Baghdad. • **2.** possible, conceivable – مُحتَمَل تُمطُر باكِر [muħtamal tumṭur ba:čir] It's possible it'll rain tomorrow. مُحتَمَل، لَكِن هَذا ما يركَب طَيّارَة أبَداً [muħtamal, la:kin ha:ða ma: yirkab ṭiyya:ra ʔabadan] It's possible, but he never goes by plane.

حامِلَة [ħa:mila] *adj:* حامِلات [ħa:mila:t] *pl:* • **2.** device for carrying or holding – حامِلَة طائِرات [ħa:milat ṭa:ʔira:t] aircraft carrier.

حامْلَة [ħa:mla] *adj:* حَمَلَة [ħamala] *pl:* • **1.** holder, carrier

مَحمُول [maħmu:l] *adj:* • **1.** carried • **2.** mobile (as n:) a mobile, cell phone

ح م م

تحَمَّم [tħammam] *v:* • **1.** to bathe, take a bath

حُمَّة [ħumma] *n:* حُمّايات [ħumma:ya:t] *pl:* • **1.** fever

حمام [ħama:m] *n:* • **1.** (coll.) pigeon(s), dove(s)

حَمّام [ħamma:m] *n:* حَمّامات [ħamma:ma:t] *pl:* • **1.** bath, Turkish bath – حَمّام عامّ [ħamma:m ʕa:mm] public bath. • **2.** bathroom, room for bathing

حَمامَة [ħama:ma] *n:* حَمامات [ħama:ma:t] *pl:* • **1.** pigeon, dove

حَمِيم [ħami:m] *adj:* • **1.** close

مَحمُوم [maħmu:m] *adj:* • **1.** feverish – الوَلَد صارلَه يومَين مَحمُوم [ʔilwalad ṣa:rlah yu:mayn maħmu:m] The boy has been feverish for two days.

ح م ن

حِمِّنِين [ħimmini:n] *n:* • **1.** chicken lice, small parasites found on chickens

ح م و 1

حِمَى [ħima:] *v:* • **1.** (by extension) to become heated – المُناقَشَة حِمَت وقامَوا يصَيِّحُون [ʔilmuna:qaša ħimat wga:maw yṣayyħu:n] The discussion became heated and they began to shout. • **2.** to heat, heat up, make warm – شُوف المَيّ حِمَى لَو بَعَد [šu:f ʔilmayy ħima: law baʕad] See if the water has gotten hot yet. إنتِي لِيش حِمَى حَمّامِك؟ مَحَّد جاب إسمِك [ʔinti li:š ħima: ħamma:mič? maħħad ǰa:b ʔismič] Don't get your water hot! No one mentioned your name. رُوحِي حَمِّيلي الحَمّام [ru:ħi ħammi:ly ʔilħamma:m] Go heat the bath for me!

حَمَّى [ħamma:] *v:* • **1.** to heat, make warm – حَمِّيلي شوَيَّة ماي [ħammi:li šwayya ma:y] Heat me some water.

تحَمَّى [tħamma:] *v:* • **1.** to warm oneself – تَعال تحَمَّى يَمّ النّار [taʕa:l tħamma: yamm ʔinna:r] Come get warm by the fire.

حَمِيَّة [ħamiyya] *n:* • **1.** zeal, ardor, fervor – حَمِيَّة قَومِيَّة [ħamiyya qawmiyya] nationalistic zeal. • **2.** enthusiasm – صاحِب حَمِيَّة [ṣa:ħib ħamiyya] a man with enthusiasm, dedicated man. • **3.** passion, rage, fury
حَماوَة [ħama:wa] *n:* • **1.** heat, warmth
حامِي [ħa:mi] *adj:* • **1.** warm, heated, violent, fierce – مُناقَشَة حامیَة [muna:qaša ħa:mya] a heated argument. لِعِب حامِي [liʕib ħa:mi] a fierce game.
حَميانَة [ħamya:na] *adj:* • **1.** overheating

ح م و 2

حِمَى [ħima:] *v:* • **1.** to protect, defend, shelter, shield – اللَّبوَة تِحمِي أشبالها [ʔillabwa tiħmi ʔašba:lha] The lioness protects her cubs. الجَّيش يِحمِي الوَطَن مِن الأعداء [ʔiǰǰayš yiħmi ʔilwaṭan min ʔalʔaʕda:ʔ] The army defends the country from her enemies.
حامَى [ħa:ma:] *v:* • **1.** to defend, protect – لا تخاف؛ أخُوك الكِبِير يحامِيك [la: txa:f; ʔaxu:k ʔiččibi:r yħa:mi:k] Don't worry; your older brother will protect you. • **2.** with ل to stand up for
اِحتِمَى [ʔiħtima:] *v:* • **1.** to seek protection, take shelter or refuge – الجّاهِل اِحتِمَى بِيّا مِن الكَلِب [ʔiǰǰa:hil ʔiħtima: biyya min ʔiččalib] The child took shelter behind me from the dog. خَلِّي نِحتِمِي بِالحايِط مِن الهَوَا [xalli: niħtimi bilħa:yiṭ min ʔillhawa] Let's take shelter from the wind behind the wall.
حَمِي [ħamy] *n:* • **1.** warming
حِمايَة [ħima:ya] *n:* • **1.** protecting, protection • **2.** pl. حِمايات protectorate
حامِيَة [ħa:miya] *n:* حامِيات [ħa:miya:t] *pl:* • **1.** protectress • **2.** garrison (mil.)
مَحمِيَّة [maħmiyya] *n:* مَحمِيّات [maħmiyya:t] *pl:* • **1.** protectorate (pol.)
مُحامِي [muħa:mi] *n:* مُحامِين [muħa:mi:n] *pl:* • **1.** lawyer, attorney
مُحاماة [muħa:ma:t] *n:* • **1.** legal profession, practice of law
مُحامِيَة [muħa:miya] *n:* مُحامِيات [muħa:miya:t] *pl:* • **1.** woman lawyer
حامِي [ħa:mi] *adj:* حامِين، حُماة [ħa:mi:n, ħuma:t] *pl:* • **1.** The protector turned out a thief – حامِيها حَرامِيها [ħa:mi:ha ħara:mi:ha] The protector turned out a thief. • **1.** protecting, defending, guarding
مَحمِي [maħmi] *adj:* • **1.** protected – المَلِف مالِي مَحمِي زين بِالفِيل [ʔilmalif ma:li maħmi zi:n bilfi:l] My king is well protected by the bishop.

ح م و 3

حَمَة [ħama] *n:* حِميان، حُمُوين [ħimya:n, ħumuwi:n] *pl:* • **1.** father-in-law – حَماه [ħama:h] his father-in-law
حَمَى، حَماة [ħama, ħama:t] *n:* حَمَوات [ħamawa:t] *pl:* • **1.** mother-in-law – حَماتِي [ħama:ti] my mother-in-law

ح م و ر ب ي

حَمُورابِي [ħamu:ra:bi] *n:* • **1.** code of Hammurabi

ح ن ء

حَنَّى [ħanna:] *v:* • **1.** to dye red (with henna), to apply henna to – حَنَّوا إيدَين العَرُوس وَرِجلَيها [ħannaw ʔi:dayn ʔilʕaru:s wrijli:ha] They dyed the bride's hands and feet with henna.
تحَنَّى [tħanna:] *v:* • **1.** to apply henna to oneself, to use henna as a cosmetic – بَنات المَدارِس ما يِتحَنُّون قَبُل زَواجهُم [bana:t ʔilmada:ris ma: yitħannu:n gabul zawa:ǰhum] Educated girls don't put on henna before their marriage.
حِنَّة [ħinna] *n:* • **1.** henna

ح ن ج ر

حَنجَرَة [ħinǰara] *n:* حَناجِر [ħana:ǰir] *pl:* • **1.** larynx, throat

ح ن ط

حَنَّط [ħannaṭ] *v:* • **1.** to mummify, embalm – المَصرِيِّين القُدَماء كانَوا يحَنِّطُون مَوتاهُم [ʔilmaṣriyyi:n ʔilqudama:ʔ ča:naw yħanniṭu:n mawta:hum] The ancient Egyptians used to mummify their dead. • **2.** to stuff, preserve – مِن يمُوت هالطَير راح أحَنِّطَه وَأحُطَّه بغُرفَة الخُطّار [min ymu:t hattTi:r ra:ħ ʔaħanniṭah waħuṭṭah bɣurfat ʔilxuṭṭa:r] When this bird dies I'm going to have it stuffed and put it in the parlor. بالمُختَبَر، يحَنِّطُون الحِيايَة بِسائِل كِيمياوِي [bilmuxtabar, yħanniṭu:n ʔilħiya:ya bsa:ʔil kimya:wi] In the lab, they preserve snakes in a chemical solution.
حُنطَة [ħunṭa] *n:* • **1.** wheat
حُنطايَة [ħunṭa:ya] *n:* حُنطايات [ħunṭa:ya:t] *pl:* • **1.** grain of wheat
حُنطِي [ħunṭi] *adj:* • **1.** wheat-colored, golden brown, tan
حِنطاوِي [ħinṭa:wi] *adj:* • **1.** brown-skinned, tan

ح ن ظ ل

حَنظَل [ħanðal] *adj:* • **1.** colocynth, a kind of very bitter wild gourd – مُرّ حَنظَل [murr ħanðal] as bitter as colocynth.

ح ن ف

حَنَفِيَّة [ħanafiyya] *n:* حَنَفِيّات [ħanafiyya:t] *pl:* • **1.** faucet, spigot
حَنَفِي [ħanafi] *adj:* • **1.** Hanafitic, pertaining to the theological school founded by Abu Hanifah • **3.** Hanafite, belonging to the Hanafi school of Islam

ح ن ق ب ز

حَنقَباز [ħanqaba:z] *n:* حَنقَبازِيَّة [ħanqaba:ziyya] *pl:* • **1.** juggler

ح ن ق ر ي ص
حِنقَرِيصَة [ħingariːṣa] *n:* حِنقَرِيصات [ħingariːṣaːt] *pl:* • **1.** orgasm, climax

ح ن ك
حِنِك [ħinič] *n:* حنُوك [ħnuːč] *pl:* • **1.** chin
مُحَنَّك [muħannak] *adj:* • **1.** experienced

ح ن ن
حَنّ [ħann] *v:* • **1.** to long, yearn, be anxious – دَأحِنّ لأيّام التَّلمَذَة [daʔaħinn lʔayyaːm ʔattalmaða] I'm longing for my student days. دَأحِنّ لِشُوفَتها مَرَّة اللُّخ [daʔaħinn lišuːfatha marrat ʔillux] I'm anxious to see her again. • **2.** to feel compassion, sympathy, to have mercy, take pity
حَنَّن [ħannan] *v:* • **1.** to fill with compassion, sympathy, or tenderness, to soften – الله يحَنِّن قَلب المُعَلِّم عَلِيك [ʔallah yħannin galb ʔilmuʕallim ʕaliːk] May God soften the teacher's heart toward you.
حَنان [ħanaːn] *n:* • **1.** sympathy, love, affection, tenderness • **2.** compassion, pity
مَحَنَّة [maħanna] *n:* • **1.** sympathy, tenderness • **2.** compassion, pity
حَنّونَة [ħannuːna] *n:* حَنّونات [ħannuːnaːt] *pl:* • **1.** small loaf of bread, usually made from the last bit of dough
حِنِّنين [ħinniniːn] *n:* • **1.** chicken lice, small parasites found on chickens
حَنُون [ħanuːn] *adj:* • **1.** tenderhearted, loving, softhearted
حَنِين [ħaniːn] *adj:* • **1.** softhearted, tenderhearted, compassionate, moving, touching, tender
أحَنّ [ʔaħann] *comparative adjective:* • **1.** more or most compassionate • **2.** more or most moving, touching

ح ن و also ح - ن - ي
حِنَى [ħinaː] *v:* • **1.** to bow, bend forward, tilt forward – إحنِي راسَك حَتّى أزَيِّن رُقُبتَك [ʔiħni raːsak ħatta ʔazayyin rugubtak] Bend your head forward so I can shave your neck. • **2.** to bend, bow, curve – الكُبُر حِنَى ظَهرَه [ʔilkubur ħinaː ðahrah] Age bent his back.
اِنحِنَى [ʔinħinaː] *v:* • **1.** to bend, curve, twist, turn – الطَّرِيق يِنحِني لِليَسار مِن هنا [ʔiṭṭariːq yinħini lilyasaːr min hna] The road curves to the left here. • **2.** to bow – اليابانِيِّين، مِن يسَلِّمُون عَلَى واحِد، يِنحِنُوالَه [ʔilyabaniyyiːn, min ysallimuːn ʕala waːħid, yinħinuːlah] The Japanese bow to a person when they greet him. • **3.** to bend forward – اِنحِنَى وشال القَلَم مِن القاع [ʔinħinaː wšaːl ʔilqalam min ʔilgaːʕ] He bent forward and picked up the pencil from the ground. راسَه اِنحِنَى مِن النَّعاس [raːsah ʔinħinaː min ʔinnaʕaːs] His head bent forward from fatigue.
حُنُو [ħunuw] *n:* • **1.** sympathy, compassion, tenderness, affection – حُنُوَّه عَلَى وِلدَه [ħunuwwah ʕala wildah] his affection for his children.
حَنيَة [ħanya] *n:* • **1.** bend • **2.** hunchback
مِنحِنِي [minħini] *adj:* • **1.** bent, bowed – ظَهرَه مِنحِني مِن الكُبُر [ðahrah minħini min ʔilkubur] His back is bent with age. • **2.** leaning, inclined – هَالشَّجَرَة مِنحَنيَة وَ راح تَوقَع. لازِم الهَوا كان كُلِّش قَوِي البارحَة [haššajara minħanya w raːħ tuːgaʕ. laːzim ʔilhawa čaːn kulliš qawi ʔilbaːrħa] That tree is leaning over and it's about to fall. The wind must have been real strong yesterday.

ح ن و ت
حانُوت [ħaːnuːt] *n:* حَوانِيت [ħawaːniːt] *pl:* • **1.** canteen, snack bar
حَنُوتي [ħaːnuːti] *adj:* حانُوتِيَّ [ħaːnuːtiyya] *pl:* • **1.** canteen operator

ح و ب
حَوبَة [ħawba, ħuːba] *n:* حُوبات [ħuːbaːt] *pl:* • **1.** divine retribution, punishment by God – هالعالِم الدِّينِي إلَه حَوبَتَه [halʕaːlim ʔiddiːni ʔilah ħuːbtah] That religious man can summon the wrath of God. قَتِل الكَلِب إلَه حَوبَة. تِتلَقّاها بِأَهلَك [qatil ʔiččalib ʔilah ħuːba. titlaggaːha bʔahlak] Killing the dog will bring retribution. You'll catch it through your family. شُوفَه شلُون عِمَت عَينَه؟ هاي حَوبَة الأيتام الأكَل فلُوسهُم [šuːfah šluːn ʕimat ʕaynah? haːy ħuːbat ʔilʔaytaːm ʔilʔakal fluːshum] See how he went blind? That's retribution for the orphans whose money he took. • **2.** revenge, satisfaction – أخَذِت حَوبتِي مِنَّه. بُسَطتَه بَسطَة زينَة لِأنّ فِتَن عَلَيّا عِند المُدِير [ʔaxaðit ħawbti minnah. busaṭṭah basṭa ziːna liʔann fitan ʕalayya ʕind ʔilmudiːr] I got my revenge on him. I beat him up because he told the principal on me.

ح و ت
حُوت [ħuːt] *n:* حِيتان [ħiːtaːn] *pl:* • **1.** whale

ح و ج
حَوَج [ħawaǰ] *v:* • **1.** to be necessary – ما يحوِج توَصِّلني لِلمَطار، لِأنّ الشَّركَة راح تدِزّلي سَيّارَة [maː yiħwiǰ twaṣṣilni lilmaṭaːr, liʔann ʔiššarika raːħ ddizzli sayyaːra] It isn't necessary for you to take me to the airport, because the company is going to send a car for me. ما يِحتاج تقُلَّه لأبُوك؛ أقدَر أنطِيك الفلُوس [maː yiħtaːǰ dgullah lʔabuːk; ʔagdar ʔanṭiːk ʔilfluːs] There's no need to tell your father; I can give you the money.
اِحتاج [ʔiħtaːǰ] *v:* • **1.** to need, want, require, be in want of – إذا تِحتاج شِي، قُلّي [ʔiða tiħtaːǰ ši, gulli] If you need anything, tell me. آني ما مِحتاج إلَى أيّ شِي هَسَّة [ʔaːni maː miħtaːǰ ʔila ʔayy ši hassa] I don't need anything right now. قَضِيَّة تَعيِينَك يِحتاجِلها دَفعَة

[qaðiyyat taʕyiːnak yiħtaːǰilha dafʕa] The matter of your appointment requires a push.
حاجَة [ħaːǰa] *n:* حاجات، حَوايِج [ħaːǰaːt, ħawaːyiǰ] *pl:* • **1.** need, necessity – أَكُو حاجَة تسَوِّي هِيكِي؟ [ʔaku ħaːǰa tsawwi: hiːči?] Is there any need to do this? لا تاخُذ البَرِينَة؛ إلِي حاجَة بِيها [laː taːxuð ʔilbariːna; ʔili ħaːǰa biːha] Don't take the drill; I need it. ماكُو حاجَة تِزعَل. سِأَلتَك سُؤال بَسِيط [maːku ħaːǰa tizʕal. siʔaltak suʔaːl basiːṭ] There's no need to get mad. I asked you a simple question. عِند الحاجَة [ʕind ʔilħaːǰa] in time of need, when necessary. ماكُو مانِع تِستَعمِل سَيّارتِي عِند الحاجَة [maːku maːniʕ tistaʕmil sayyaːrti ʕind ʔilħaːǰa] There's no objection to your using my car if necessary. بِحاجَة إِلَى [bħaːǰa ʔila] in need of, lacking. المُختَبَر بحاجَة إِلَى أَدوات جِدِيدَة [ʔilmuxtabar bħaːǰa ʔila ʔadawaːt ǰidiːda] The laboratory's in need of new equipment. • **2.** pressing need, neediness, poverty, destitution – لَو ما الحاجَة، ما أَقبَل هِيكِي شُغُل [law maː ʔilħaːǰa, maː ʔaqbal hiːči šuɣul] Were it not for pressing need, I wouldn't accept such a job. • **3.** need, necessary article, requisite – أُخُذ حاجتَك وَخَلِّي الباقِي [ʔuxuð ħaːǰtak wxalliː ʔilbaːqi] Take what you need and leave the rest. • **4.** matter, concern, business, job – رِحِت عالشَّخِص اللِّي دَزِّيتنِي عَليه وقِضَى حاجتِي [riħit ʕaššaxiṣ ʔilli dazziːtni ʕaliːh wgiðaː ħaːǰti] I went to the person you sent me to and he took care of my business. • **5.** concern, interest, responsibility – آنِي مالِي حاجَة بالغَير. إذا يِردُون يِتبارَعُون، كَيفهُم [ʔaːni maːli ħaːǰa bilɣayr. ʔiða yirduːn yitbaːraʕuːn, kayfhum] I've got no concern with the others. If they want to donate, let them. شما ترِيد سَوِّي. آنِي مالِي حاجَة [šma triːd sawwiː. ʔaːni maːli ħaːǰa] Do whatever you want. I'm not responsible. لا تخاف تفُوت مِن يَمّ الشُّرطِي. مالَه حاجَة بِيك [laː txaːf tfuːt min yamm ʔiššurṭi. maːlah ħaːǰa biːk] Don't be afraid of going by the policeman. He has no concern with you. • **6.** (pl. only) wares, merchandise – يبِيع حاجات أَجنَبِيَّة [yibiːʕ ħaːǰaːt ʔaǰnabiyya] He sells foreign goods.
حاجِيّات [ħaːǰiyyaːt] *n:* • **1.** (pl. only) goods, wares, merchandise
اِحتياج [ʔiħtiyaːǰ] *n:* • **1.** need
محتاج [miħtaːǰ] *adj:* مِحتاجِين [miħtaːǰiːn] *pl:* • **1.** in need, needy, poor, destitute • **2.** needy person, poor person

ح و د

حاد [ħaːd] *v:* • **1.** to turn aside, drive away, drive off – حُودَه لِلحصان لِلطُّولَة حَتَّى نسَرِّجَه [ħuːdah lilħṣaːn liṭṭuːla ħatta nsarrǰah] Drive the horse to the stable so we can saddle him. حُود الهوايِش لباب البُستان [ħuːd ʔilhwaːyiš lbaːb ʔilbustaːn] Drive the cows to the orchard gate. الشُّرطَة حادَت الطُّلّاب مِن السّاحَة إِلَى المَركَز [ʔiššurṭa ħaːdat ʔiṭṭullaːb min ʔissaːħa lilmarkaz] The police herded the students from the square to the station. كُلّ مَن يحُود النّار لِقُرصتَه [kull man yħuːd ʔinnaːr liguruṣtah] Everyone looks out for his own interests (lit., everyone pushes the fire toward his own loaf). حُود زمايلَك. دَياكلُون الوَرِد [ħuːd zmaːylak. dayaːkluːn ʔilwarid] Drive your donkeys away. They're eating the flowers. • **2.** to drive, herd, urge on
حَود [ħawd, ħuːd] *n:* • **1.** driving or herding

ح و ر

حَوَّر [ħawwar] *v:* • **1.** to change, alter, amend, modify, remodel, transform, reorganize – رُوح قُلَّه اللِّي قِلتلَك إيّاه بِالضَبُط. لا تحَوِّر شِي [ruːħ gullah ʔilli giltlak ʔiyyaːh biððabuṭ. laː tħawwir ši] Go tell him what I told you exactly. Don't change anything. إحكِي عَدِل. لا تحَوِّر الكَلام [ʔiħči ʕadil. laː tħawwir ʔilkalaːm] Talk straight. Don't alter the words.
تحَوَّر [tħawwar] *v:* • **1.** to be changed, to be modified
حارَة [ħaːra] *n:* حارات [ħaːraːt] *pl:* • **1.** neighborhood, area, section (of a city)
مِحوَر [miħwar] *n:* مَحاوِر [maħaːwir] *pl:* • **1.** pivot, core, heart, center – هُوَّ كان مِحوَر الحَدِيث [huwwa čaːn miħwar ʔilħadiːθ] He was the central figure of the discussion.
حَوارِي [ħawaːri] *n:* • **1.** disciple, follower
حُورِيَّة [ħuːriyya] *n:* حُورِيّات [ħuːriyyaːt] *pl:* • **1.** houri – حِلوَة مِثل الحُورِيَّة [ħilwa miθl ʔilħuːriyya] very pretty. • **2.** nymph – حُورِيَّة البَحَر [ħuːriyyat ʔilbaħar] mermaid, sea nymph.
مُحاوَرَة [muħaːwara] *n:* مُحاوَرات [muħaːwaraːt] *pl:* • **1.** dialogue, conversation, talk
مِحوَرِي [miħwari] *adj:* • **1.** axial

ح و ز

حاز [ħaːz] *v:* • **1.** with عَلَى to achieve, attain, obtain, get, receive – اِقتِراحَه حاز عَلَى تَأيِيد الكُلّ [ʔiqtiraːħah ħaːz ʕala taʔyiːd ʔilkull] His suggestion received the support of everyone. حاز عَلَى دَرَجَة شَرَف [ħaːz ʕala daraǰat šaraf] He got honors. He passed with honors.
تحَيَّز [tħayyaz] *v:* • **1.** to side, take sides, to be biased, be partial – هَالحَكَم يِتحَيَّز لِفِرقتكُم [halħakam yitħayyaz lfirqatkum] This referee is partial to your team.
اِنحاز [ʔinħaːz] *v:* • **1.** to side, take sides, to be biased, be partial
حِيز [ħiːz] *n:* حِيزِيَّة، حيُوزَة [ħiːziyya, ħyuːza] *pl:* • **1.** epithet for a man who submits to sodomy for profit or advancement, and by extension, a loose term of contempt
تَحَيُّز [taħayyuz] *n:* • **1.** prejudice, bias
حَوزَة [ħawza] *n:* • **1.** territory • **2.** possession
حِيازَة [ħiyaːza] *n:* • **1.** acquisition, obtainment, attainment • **2.** possession, holding – لِقَوا بحِيازتَه بَنادِق وَمُسَدَّسات [ligaw bħiyaːztah banaːdiq wmusaddasaːt] They found rifles and pistols in his possession.

منحاز [minħaːz] *adj:* • **1.** retired • **2.** biased
متحَيِّز [mitħayyiz] *adj:* • **1.** biased • **2.** unjust, aligned

ح و ش

حاش [ħaːš] *v:* • **1.** to gather, collect, amass, accumulate – رُوح حُوش شوَيَّة حَشِيش لِلخَرُوف [ruːħ ħuːš šwayya ħašiːš lilxaruːf] Go gather some grass for the sheep.
حُوش [ħuːš, ħawš] *n:* حَواش [ħwaːš] *pl:* • **1.** court, courtyard, patio • **2.** house

ح

ح و ص

حاص [ħaːṣ] *v:* • **1.** to fidget, be restless, nervous – شبِيك دِتخُوص أَشُو كُلّ دَقِيقَة راكِض لِلدَّرُب [šbiːk datħuːṣ ʔašu kull daqiːqa raːkiđ liddarub] Why are you fidgeting? Every minute you run to the street. شَكُو عِندَك دِتخُوص هَسَّة نرُوح [šaku ʕindak datħuːṣ? hassa nruːħ] Why are you so restless? We're going right away. دَيحُوص عَلَى هَالوَظِيفَة [dayħuːṣ ʕala halwađiːfa] He's really itching for that job.
حَوص [ħawṣ, ħuːṣ] *n:* • **1.** fidgeting

ح و ص ل

حُوصلَة [ħuːṣla] *n:* حَوصلات، حَواصِل [ħuːṣlaːt, ħawaːṣil] *pl:* • **1.** craw, corp, gizzard (of a bird) • **2.** patience, endurance – هَذا ما عِندَه حُوصلَة. يزهَق بِالعَجَل [haːđa maː ʕindah ħuːṣla. yizhag bilʕajal] He doesn't have any patience. He gets disgusted quickly.

ح و ض

حَوض [ħawđ, ħuːđ] *n:* أَحواض [ʔaħwaːđ] *pl:* • **1.** basin, trough, tank • **2.** pool, pond • **3.** seat of a car – الحَوض الوَرّاني [ʔilħawđ ʔilwarraːni] the back seat. أَخَذنِي حَوض. ما نطانِي مَجال أَحكِي [ʔaxađni ħuːđ. maː nṭaːni majaːl ʔaħči] He talked incessantly. He didn't give me a chance to speak.

ح و ط

حَوَّط [ħawwaṭ] *v:* • **1.** to wall in, build a wall around, to encircle, surround – لِيش ما تحَوُّط بَيتَك بِسِياج حَدِيدِي؟ [liːš maː tħawwuṭ baytak bsiyaːj ħadiːdi?] Why don't you surround your house with an iron fence?
أَحاط [ʔaħaːṭ] *v:* • **1.** to surround, encircle, encompass – حاطَوه غير حَوطَة وَما قدَرِت أَشُوفَه [ħaːṭawh ɣayr ħawṭa wma gdarit ʔašuːfah] They clustered around him and I couldn't see him.
اِحتاط [ʔiħtaːṭ] *v:* • **1.** to take precautions, to prepare oneself, make provision – إِذا ما تِحتاط لِلمُشكِلَة، تِتدَمَّر [ʔiđa maː tiħtaːṭ lilmuškila, tiddammar] If you aren't prepared for the problem, you'll be ruined. لازِم تِحتاط لِلمَوضُوع قَبُل ما تشُوفَه [laːzim tiħtaːṭ lilmawđuːʕ gabul maː tšuːfah] You should bone up on the subject before you see him.
حَوط [ħuːṭ] *n:* • **1.** surrounding
حُوطَة [ħuːṭa] *n:* حَوطات [ħuːṭaːt] *pl:* • **1.** circle, cluster
حايِط [ħaːyiṭ] *n:* حِيطان، حياطِين [ħiːṭaːn, ħyaːṭiːn] *pl:* • **1.** wall – آنِي مُو حايِط نصَيِّص [ʔaːni muː ħaːyiṭ nṣayyiṣ] I'm nobody to fool around with (lit., I'm not a low wall).
مُحِيط [muħiːṭ] *n:* مُحِيطات [muħiːṭaːt] *pl:* • **1.** circumference, periphery • **2.** ocean • **3.** milieu, environment, surroundings
اِحتِياط [ʔiħtiyaːṭ] *n:* • **1.** caution, cautiousness, prudence, carefulness • **2.** provision, precaution, care, prevention – أُخُذ وِيّاك قَبُّوط لِلإِحتِياط [ʔuxuđ wiyyaːk qappuːṭ lilʔiħtiyaːṭ] Take an overcoat with you just in case. • **3.** reserve – عِدنا فِرقَتَين اِحتِياط [ʕidna firiqtayn ʔiħtiyaːṭ] We have two divisions in reserve. • **4.** spare, replacement – أَدَوات اِحتِياطِيَّة [ʔadawaːt ʔiħtiyaːṭiyya] spare parts. • **5.** pl. اِحتِياطات precaution, precautionary measure or step – الشُّرطَة وَالجَيش أَخذَوا كُلّ الاحتِياطات اللّازمَة لِمَنع المُظاهَرات [ʔiššurṭa wijjayš ʔaxđaw kull ʔilʔiħtiyaːṭaːt ʔillaːzma limanʕ ʔilmuđaːharaːt] The police and army took all precautions necessary to prevent demonstrations. • **6.** pl. اِحتِياطِيِّن substitute
محَوَّط [mħawwaṭ] *adj:* • **1.** surrounded
مُحاط [muħaːṭ] *adj:* • **1.** surrounded
محاوُط [mħaːwuṭ] *adj:* • **1.** surrounding

ح و ف

حافَّة [ħaːffa] *n:* حافّات [ħaːffaːt] *pl:* • **1.** edge • **3.** border

ح و ك

حاك [ħaːk, ħaːč] *v:* • **1.** to weave – حاكلِي عَبايَة صُوف [ħaːkli ʕabaːya ṣuːf] He wove a woolen robe for me. • **2.** to knit – بِتّ عَمِّي حاكَتلِي بلُوز [bitt ʕammi ħaːkatli bluːz] My uncle's daughter knitted me a sweater. • **3.** to hit, strike – حاكَه بِبُوكس وَوَقَّعَه [ħaːkah bibuːks wwaggaʕah] He hit him with his fist and knocked him down.
حايِك [ħaːyik] *n:* • **1.** woven cloth
حَوك [ħawk] *n:* • **1.** striking, hitting – أَخَذنا حُوك بِالحَكِي مالَه [ʔaxađna ħuːk bilħači maːlah] He wouldn't let us get a word in edgewise.
حايِك [ħaːyik] *n:* حِيّاك [ħiyyaːk] *pl:* • **1.** weaver
حِياكَة [ħiyaːka] *n:* • **1.** weaving • **2.** knitting

ح و ل

حوَلّ [ħwall] *v:* • **1.** to be cross-eyed – حوَلّ مِن طِفُولتَه [ħwall min ṭifuːltah] He's been cross-eyed since childhood.
حال [ħaːl] *v:* • **1.** to be perennial (of plants) – هَالنَّوع مِن الوَرِد يِحُول [hannuːʕ min ʔilwarid yiħuːl]

This type of flower comes up each year. • **2.** to intervene, interfere, interpose – ماكُو شِي يِحُول بَينَه وَبَين السَّفرَة [maːku ši yiħuːl baynah wbayn ʔissafra] Nothing's going to come between him and his trip.

حال [ħaːl] *v:* • **1.** to transfer – حال دَينَه عَلَيّا [ħaːl daynah ʕalayya] He transferred his debt to me. حال نَفسَه عالتَّقاعُد [ħaːl nafsah ʕattaqaːʕud] He got himself on pension. • **2.** to refer – لا تحِيلنِي عَلَى دائرَة أُخرَى. إنتَ خَلِّص شُغلِي [laː tħiːlni ʕala daːʔira ʔuxra. ʔinta xalliṣ šuɣli] Don't refer me to another office. You take care of my business.

حَوَّل [ħawwal] *v:* • **1.** to change – حَوَّلِت مِيَّة دِينار إلَى دُولارات [ħawwalit miyyat dinaːr ʔila dularaːt] I changed a hundred dinars into dollars. • **2.** to convert (mathematically) – حَوِّل هَالكُسُور الاعتِيادِيَّة إلَى كُسُور عُشرِيَّة [ħawwil halkusuːr ʔilʔiʕtiyaːdiyya ʔila kusuːr ʕušriyya] Convert these common fractions to decimal fractions. • **3.** to transfer – المُدِير حَوَّلَه إلَى غير وَظِيفَة [ʔilmudiːr ħawwalah ʔila ɣiːr waḍiːfa] The director transferred him to another job. • **4.** to remit, send, transmit – حَوِّللِي مِيَّة دِينار بِالبَرِيد اليُوم [ħawwilli miyyat dinaːr bilbariːd ʔilyuːm] Send me a hundred dinars through the post office today. • **5.** to refer, pass on, hand on – راح أَحَوِّل مُعامَلتَك لِلمُدِير وأَشُوف شَيقُول [raːħ ʔaħawwil muʕaːmaltak lilmudiːr wʔašuːf šayguːl] I'm going to refer your affair to the director and find out what he says. راح أَحَوِّلَه عَلِيك. إنتَ إنطِيه إيّاه [raːħ ʔaħawwilah ʕaliːk. ʔinta ʔinṭiːh ʔiyyaːh] I'll unload him onto you. You give it to him. • **6.** to endorse, sign over – حَوَّل الشِّيك عَلَيّا وَأَنِي إنطَيتَه الفلُوس [ħawwal ʔiččiːk ʕalayya waʔaːni ʔinṭaytah ʔilfluːs] He signed the check over to me and I gave him the money. • **7.** to direct, turn, divert – حَوِّل المَيّ عَلَى هَاللُّوح [ħawwil ʔilmayy ʕala halluːħ] Divert the water into this plot. • **8.** to turn aside, avert – ما حَوَّل عَينَه عَن وُجهِي [maː ħawwal ʕaynah ʕan wuǰhi] He didn't move his eyes from my face.

حاوَل [ħaːwal] *v:* • **1.** to try, attempt, endeavor, make an attempt – حاوَل يِنهِزِم مِن السِّجِن [ħaːwal yinhizim min ʔissiǰin] He tried to escape from prison.

تحَوَّل [tħawwal] *v:* • **1.** to be changed, be converted – كُلّ الماي تحَوَّل إلَى بُخار [kull ʔilmaːy tħawwal ʔila buxaːr] All the water turned to steam. • **2.** to be transferred, reassigned – إذا ما أَتحَوَّل مِن هَالوَظِيفَة، أَبَطِّل [ʔiða maː ʔatħawwal min halwaḍiːfa, ʔabaṭṭil] If I don't get transferred from this position, I'll quit. • **3.** to move – تحَوَّلنا مِن بَيتنا [tħawwalna min baytna] We moved out of our house.

إحتال [ʔiħtaːl] *v:* • **1.** to cheat, dupe, deceive, beguile – إحتال عَلَيه وَأَخَذ مِنَّه نُصّ دِينار [ʔiħtaːl ʕaliːh wʔaxað minnah nuṣṣ dinaːr] He cheated him and took a half dinar from him. • **2.** with عَلَى to cheat, dupe, deceive, beguile

إستَحال [ʔistaħaːl] *v:* • **1.** to be impossible, to be or become unimaginable

حال [ħaːl] *n:* أَحوال [ʔaħwaːl] *pl:* • **1.** condition, state – شلُون حالَك؟ [šluːn ħaːlak?] How're you doing? • **2.** situation • **3.** circumstance – عَلَى كُلّ حال [ʕala kull ħaːl] at any rate, in any case, anyhow. عَلَى كُلّ حال، لا تدِيرلَه بال [ʕala kull ħaːl, laː ddiːrlah baːl] At any rate, don't pay attention to him. ما بَقَّى عَلَى حالِي حال [maː baqqaː ʕala ħaːli ħaːl] He didn't leave me a thing. • **4.** (pl. only) أَحوال matters, affairs, concerns – شلُون الأَحوال؟ [šluːn ʔilʔaħwaːl?] How are things?

حَول [ħawl] *n:* • **1.** power, might – لا حَول وَلا قُوَّة إلّا بِالله [laː ħawl wala quwwa ʔilla billaːh] There's no power and no strength save in God. • **2.** (prep.) around, about, in the area of – أَكُو دَكاكِين هوايَة حَول البِنايَة [ʔaku dakaːkiːn hwaːya ħawl ʔilbinaːya] There are many shops around the building. • **3.** about, concerning, re – حِكَى وِيّاك حَول المَوضُوع لَو لاء؟ [ħičaː wiyyaːk ħawl ʔilmawḍuːʕ law laːʔ?] Did he speak with you about the situation or not?

حَوَل [ħawal] *n:* • **1.** crossing (of the eyes) – حَوَل حِسِن [ħawal ħisin] a slight crossing of the eyes, regarded as a mark of beauty. عَينها حَولَة حَوَل حِسِن [ʕaynha ħawla ħawal ħisin] Her eyes are crossed in a charming way.

حول [ħuːl] *n:* • **1.** perennial (of plants)

حالَة [ħaːla] *n:* حالات [ħaːlaːt] *pl:* • **1.** condition, state – حالَة الطَّوارِئ [ħaːlat ʔiṭṭawaːriʔ] state of emergency. • **2.** situation • **3.** case – بِهالحالَة، إنتَ كُون المَسؤُول [bhalħaːla, ʔinta kuːn ʔilmasʔuːl] In this case, you be in charge.

حَولي [ħawli] *n:* حَولِيَّة [ħawliyya] *pl:* • **1.** a male calf • **2.** a hanger-on, one who fawns on another for ulterior motives

حِيلَة [ħiːla] *n:* حِيَل [ħiyal] *pl:* • **1.** trick, ruse, strategem, subterfuge – سَوَّى بِيّا حِيلَة وَأَخَذ فلُوسِي [sawwaː biyya ħiːla wʔaxað fluːsi] He played a trick on me and took my money.

تَحَوُّل [taħawwul] *n:* • **1.** turning

حَولِيَّة [ħawliyya] *n:* حَولِيّات [ħawliyyaːt] *pl:* • **1.** calf, heifer

حَوالَة [ħawaːla] *n:* حَوالات [ħawaːlaːt] *pl:* • **1.** (postal) money order

حَوالِي [ħawaːli] *n:* • **1.** around, about, in the area of – بُقَينا طايرِين حَوالِي بَغداد [buqayna ṭaːyriːn ħawaːli baɣdaːd] We kept flying around in the area of Baghdad. • **2.** approximately, about, roughly – عِندِي حَوالِي مِيتَين كتاب [ʕindi ħawaːli mitayn ktaːb] I have about two hundred books.

مُحَوِّلَة [muħawwila] *n:* مُحَوِّلات [muħawwilaːt] *pl:* • **1.** transformer (el.)

تحوِيل [taħwiːl] *n:* • **1.** transformation

تَحايُل [taħaːyul] *n:* • **1.** trickery, craft, deception

إحالَة [ʔiħaːla] *n:* • **1.** transformation • **2.** referral

ح

مُحاوَلَة [muħa:wala] *n:* مُحاوَلات [muħa:wala:t] *pl:* • **1.** attempt, endeavor, try

اِحتِيال [ʔiħtiya:l] *n:* • **2.** trickery, craft, deception

حَيلُولَة [ħaylu:la] *n:* • **1.** prevention

حَيل [ħayl, ħi:l] *adj:* • **1.** strength, force, power, vigor – سمَعِت عَلي اِنطِرَد مِن شُغلَه؟ حيل بِيه، يِستاهِل [smaʕit ʕali ʔinṭirad min šuɣlah? ħi:l bi:h, yista:hil] Did you hear that Ali was fired? Good, he deserves it. • **2.** (adv.) with force, with vigor – إدفَع حيل [ʔidfaʕ ħi:l] Push hard. إلزَم الحَبِل حيل [ʔilzam ʔilħabil ħi:l] Hold the rope tight. لا تِمشِي حيل [la: timši ħi:l] Don't walk fast. إحكِي حيل [ʔiħči ħi:l] speak up loudly!

حالِي [ħa:li] *adj:* • **1.** present, current, existing – الوَضِع الحالِي [ʔilwaðiʕ ʔilħa:li] the present situation.

حَيّال [ħayya:l] *adj:* حَيّالِين [ħayya:li:n] *pl:* • **1.** cunning, crafty, wily, or sly person – أيا حَيّال! شلُون دَبَّرتها؟ [ʔaya ħayya:l! šlu:n dabbartha?] You sly fox! How'd you manage it?

أحوَل [ʔaħwal] *adj:* حُول، حَولِين [ħu:l, ħu:li:n] *pl:* حُولَة [ħu:la] *feminine:* • **1.** cross-eyed • **2.** crossed-eyed person

مُحَوِّل [muħawwil] *adj:* • **1.** exchanger, converter

حايِل [ħa:yil] *adj:* • **1.** perennial

مُحتال [muħta:l] *adj:* مُحتالِين [muħta:li:n] *pl:* • **1.** swindler, cheat, impostor, fraud • **2.** crook, scoundrel

حالاً [ħa:lan] *adverbial:* • **1.** immediately, at once, right away – خابرَه حالاً [xa:brah ħa:lan] Call him immediately.

حالما [ħa:lama] *subordinating conjunction:* • **1.** as soon as, the moment that – قُلّي حالما تشُوفَه [gulli ħa:lama tšu:fah] Tell me as soon as you see him.

ح و م

حام [ħa:m] *v:* • **1.** to circle, hover, fly around – ظَلّ الطَّير يحُوم نُصّ ساعَة قَبُل ما يحُطّ [ðall ʔiṭṭi:r yħu:m nuṣṣ sa:ʕa gabul ma: yħuṭṭ] The bird kept circling for half an hour before he lit. حامَت الشُّبهَه عَليه [ħa:mat ʔiššubha ʕali:h] The suspicion centered on him. صارلَه مُدَّة يحُوم عَلَى هَالشُّغُل [ṣa:rlah mudda yħu:m ʕala haššuɣul] He's been after this job for quite a while.

حَوم [ħawm, ħu:m] *n:* • **1.** circling, hovering

ح و و

حَوّا [ħawwa:] *n:* • **1.** Eve – آدَم وَحَوّا [ʔa:dam wħawwa] Adam and Eve.

ح و ي

حُوَى [ħuwa:] *v:* • **1.** to gather, collect, amass – يِحوِي بِبَيتَه أنواع الطيُور [yiħwi bbaytah ʔanwa:ʕ ʔiṭṭyu:r] He collects different types of birds at his house. شوَقِت راح تِحوِي العِنجاص؟ [šwakit ra:ħ tiħwi ʔilʕinja:ṣ?] When are you going to pick the plums? • **2.** to contain, hold, comprise, include – بِستانَه يِحوِي أنواع الفَواكِه [bista:nah yiħwi ʔanwa:ʕ ʔalfawa:kih] His garden contains all kinds of fruits. المَحَلّ يِحوِي أشياء مُمتازَة [ʔilmaħall yiħwi ʔašya:ʔ mumta:za] The store has fine things.

اِحتوَى [ʔiħtiwa:] *v:* • **1.** with عَلَى to contain, hold,comprise, include – تَقرِيرِي يِحتِوِي عَلَى كُلّ التَّفاصِيل [taqri:ri yiħtiwi ʕala kull ʔittafa:ṣi:l] My report contains all the details. البَيت يِحتِوِي عَلَى ثلَث غُرَف ومَطبَخ وَحَمّام [ʔilbayt yiħtiwi ʕala tlaθ ɣuraf wmaṭbax wħamma:m] The house consists of three rooms and kitchen and bath.

حَوي [ħawy] *n:* • **1.** collecting

حاوِيَّة [ħa:wiyya] *n:* • **1.** bin, container

مُحتَوَى [muħtawa] *n:* • **1.** pl. مُحتَوَيات content

مُحتَوَيات [muħtawaya:t] *n:* • **1.** (pl. only) contents, ingredients

مِحتوِي [miħtawi, miħtiwi] *adj:* • **1.** containing

ح ي ث

حَيث، حِيث [ħayθ, ħi:θ] *n:* • **1.** with إلَى: to hell with, good riddance إلَى حَيث [ʔila ħiyθ] the hell with him, he deserves it, good riddance. صُدُق عَلِي اِنِّقَل؟ إلَى حَيث [ṣudug ʕali ʔinniqal? ʔila ħayθ] Was Ali really transferred? Good riddance. جِيرانَك ما راضِي عَنَّك. إلَى حَيث [ǰi:ra:nak ma: ra:ði ʕannak. ʔila ħi:θ] Your neighbor is not pleased with you. – The hell with him. • 2. with – ب in such a manner that, so that, in order that -- دِخَلِت لِلبَيت صَنتَة بحَيث ماحَد حَسّ بِيّا [dixalit lilbayt ṣanta bħayθ ma:ħad ħass biyya] I entered the house quietly so that no one would hear me.

حَيثِيَّة [ħayθiyya] *n:* حَيثِيّات [ħayθiyya:t] *pl:* • **1.** dignity, social distinction, high social standing – خِرَيت بحَيثِيتَه [xirayt bħayθi:tah] I really told him off.

ح ي د

حاد [ħa:d] *v:* • **1.** to deviate, stray, swerve – ما يحِيد عَن طَرِيق الحَقّ وَلَو ضِدّ مَصلَحتَه [ma: yħi:d ʕan ṭari:q ʔilħaqq walaw ðidd maṣlaħtah] He doesn't deviate from the way of truth even though it's against his own good.

حَيد [ħayd] *n:* • **1.** deviation, swerving

حِياد [ħiya:d] *n:* • **1.** neutrality – آنِي عَلَى الحِياد، وَما أتدَخَّل [ʔa:ni ʕala ʔilħiya:d, wma: ʔaddaxxal] I'm neutral, and I won't interfere. • **1.** with عَلَى neutral

مُحايِد [muħa:yid] *adj:* • **1.** neutral

حِيادِي [ħiya:di] *adj:* • **1.** neutral

ح ي ر

حار [ħa:r] *v:* • **1.** to become confused – لِيش حِرِت؟ يا كِتاب ترِيدَه أُخذَه [li:š ħirit? ya: kita:b tri:dah, ʔuxðah] Why are you confused? Whichever book you want, take it. مِن كُثرَة الصُّوَر، الواحِد يحِير عَلَى يا صُورَة

يباوِع [min kuθrat ʔiṣṣuwar, ʔilwaːħid yħiːr ʕala yaː ṣuːra ybaːwiʕ] Because there are so many pictures, one is perplexed as to which picture to look at. مِن تخُشّ لِغُرفَتها تحِير مِن كُثرَة الذَّهَب وَالمُجوهَرات [min txušš liɣurfatha tħiːr min kuθrat ʔiððahab wilmuǰawharaːt] When you enter her room, you'll be astonished at the amount of gold and jewelry. اِشتِرَيتها وَحِرت بِيها [ʔištiraytha wħirit biːha] I bought it and then didn't know what to do with it.

حَيَّر [ħayyar] *v:* • **1.** to perplex, confuse, baffle, puzzle – قُلّي شِتريد. مُو حَيَّرتني [gulli šitriːd. muː ħayyaritni] Tell me what you want. You've played games with me enough! أريد أرُوح. لا تحَيِّرني [ʔariːd ʔaruːħ. laː tħayyirni] I want to go. Don't waste my time. لا تحَيِّرني. تريدها لَو لا؟ [laː tħayyirni. triːdha law laː?] Make up your mind. Do you want it or not? هَالوَلَد حَيَّرني. مَرَّة يريد سَيّارَة ومَرَّة يريد ماطور [halwalad ħayyarni. marra yriːd sayyaːra wmarra yriːd maːṭuːr] This boy's given me a hard time. One time he wants a car and next he wants a motorboat. جَمالها يحَيِّر العَقِل [ǰamaːlha yħayyir ʔilʕaqil] Her beauty makes the mind reel.

تحَيَّر [tħayyar] *v:* • **1.** to become puzzled, perplexed, confused – تحَيَّرت وَما أدري شأسَوّي [tħayyarit wma ʔadri šʔasawwiː] I'm perplexed and don't know what to do. تحَيَّرت، ما أدري آخُذ هَالسَّيّارَة لَو ذيك [tħayyarit, maː ʔadri ʔaːxuð hassayyaːra law ðiːč] I am undecided whether to take this car or that.

اِحتار [ʔiħtaːr] *v:* • **1.** to become puzzled, perplexed, confused

حِيرَة [ħiːra] *n:* • **1.** confusion, perplexity, puzzlement, bewilderment – سافَر زَوجها وَخَلّاها بِحِيرَة [saːfar zawiǰha wxallha bħiːra] Her husband went away and left her helpless.

مِحَيَّر [mħayyar] *adj:* • **1.** confused

مِحتار [miħtaːr] *adj:* مِحتارين [miħtaːriːn] *pl:* • **1.** confused

ح ي ص

حِياصَة [ħiyaːṣa] *n:* حِياصات [ħiyaːṣaːt] *pl:* • **1.** cummerbund • **2.** wide woven belt

ح ي ض

حاض [ħaːð̣] *v:* • **1.** to menstruate – بأي سِنّ تِبتدِي البِنَيَّة تحِيض؟ [bʔay sinn tibtidi ʔilbnayya tħiːð̣?] At what age does a girl begin to menstruate?

حَيض [ħayð̣] *n:* • **1.** menstruation

ح ي ف

اِستَحيَف [ʔistaħyaf] *v:* • **1.** to consider (something) wrong, shameful – دَأستَحيِف أذِبّ هَالثّوب لِأنّ بَعدَه يِنلِبِس [daʔastaħyif ʔaðibb haθθuːb liʔann baʕdah yinlibis] I feel it's a shame to throw this shirt out because it still can be worn. • **2.** to regret – اِستَحيَفت ما اِشتِرَيت هَالبَدلَة المُمتازَة [ʔistaħyafit maː ʔištiriːt halbadla ʔilmumtaːza] I was sorry I didn't buy that fine suit of clothes.

حَيف [ħayf] *n:* • **1.** wrong, injustice, • **2.** pity, shame, waste – حَيف عَليه [ħayf ʕaliːh] What a pity! Too bad! حَيف عَليه، الدّائرَة خِسرَتَه [ħayf ʕaliːh, ʔiddaːʔira xisratah] It's a shame the office lost him! مُو بِالحَيف [muː bilħayf] Not a chance! It'll never happen! Not on your life! هَذا يغُلُبنِي؟ مُو بِالحَيف [haːða yuɣlubni? muː bilħayf] Him beat me? Not on your life! مُو بِالحَيف! لَو كُلّ أصدِقائك يِترُكوك آني ما أترُكَك [muː bilħiːf! law kull ʔaṣdiqaːʔak yiturkuːk ʔaːni maː ʔaturkak] Not a chance! Even if all of your friends leave you, I won't. • **3.** revenge – رُوح أخُذ حَيفَك مِن اللّي بُسَطَك [ruːħ ʔuxuð ħayfak min ʔilli buṣaṭak] Go get your revenge on the one who beat you up.

اِستِحياف [ʔistiħyaːf] *n:* • **1.** regret, remorse

مِستَحيِف [mistaħyif] *adj:* • **1.** regretful

ح ي ن

حِين [ħiːn] n: moment, time – فِي حِين [fiː ħiːn] while, at the time

أحيان، بَعض الأحيان [ʔaħyaːn, baʕð̣ ʔilʔaħyaːn] *n:* • **1.** sometimes, occasionally, once in a while, at times – بَعض الأحيان ما يِنحِمِل [baʕð̣ ʔilʔaħyaːn maː yinħimil] Sometimes he is insufferable.

أحياناً [ʔaħyaːnan] *adverbial:* • **1.** sometimes, occasionally, from time to time – أحياناً ما أفهَم عَليه [ʔaħyaːnan maː ʔafham ʕaliːh] Sometimes I don't understand him.

ح ي و

حَيوَة [ħaywa] *n:* • **1.** (coll.) quince(s)

حَيوايَة [ħaywaːya] *n:* حَيوايات [ħaywaːyaːt] *pl:* • **1.** quince

ح ي ي

حَيَّ، حَيَّ عَلَى الصَّلاة [ħayya, ħayya ʕala ʔiṣṣalaːt] *v:* • **1.** Come to prayer! – ماكُو حاجَة تِسأل؛ المَسألَة مبَيّنَة حَيَّ عَلَى الصَّلاة [maːku ħaːǰa tisʔal; ʔilmasʔala mbayyna ħayya ʕala ʔiṣṣala] There is no need to ask; the matter's as clear as daylight.

حِيا [ħiyaː] *v:* • **1.** to revive, give new life, rejuvenate – المُطَر يحِيِيها لِلقاع [ʔilmuṭar yiħyiːha lilgaːʕ] The rain adds new life to the land. بِهَالتَّصليح، حِيَيتها لِلسَّيّارَة [bhattaṣliːħ, ħiyiːtha lissayyaːra] By repairing it like that, you gave the car a new lease on life. • **3.** to stay awake – حِيا لِلصُّبُح، أبَد ما نام [ħiyaː liṣṣubuħ, ʔabad maː naːm] He stayed up until morning and never slept.

حَيّا [ħayyaː] *v:* • **1.** to hail, to greet (formally) – الجَّماهِير دَيحَيُّون المَلِك [ʔiǰǰamaːhiːr dayħayyuːn ʔilmalik] The crowds are cheering the king. • **2.** to salute – الجُّنُود دَيحَيُّون العَلَم [ʔiǰǰunuːd dayħayyuːn ʔilʕalam] The soldiers are saluting the flag. حَيّاك الله [ħayyaːk ʔallah] Bravo! Good for you!

أحيا [ʔaħya:] *v:* • **1.** to celebrate – أحيَوا ذِكِر المَرحُوم بِقَصائِد رَنّانَة [ʔaħyaw ðikir ʔilmarħu:m bqaṣa:ʔid ranna:na] They commemorated the memory of the deceased with fine poems. • **2.** to live, to revive, give new life, to stay awake

اِحتِيا [ʔiħtiya:] *v:* • **1.** to revive, come back to life – مات بَعد العَمَلِيَّة، بَسّ مِن سَوَّولَه تَنَفُّس اِصطِناعِي، اِحتِيا [ma:t baʕd ʔilʕamaliyya, bass min sawwawlah tanaffus ʔiṣṭina:ʕi, ʔiħtiya:] He died after the operation, but when they gave him artificial respiration, he revived.

اِستِحَى [ʔistiħa:] *v:* • **1.** to feel ashamed, be ashamed – ما تِستِحِي؟ لا تصَيِّح عَلَى أَبُوك [ma: tistiħi? la: tṣayyiħ ʕala ʔabu:k] Aren't you ashamed? Don't shout at your father! هُوَّ فَدّ واحِد ما يِستِحِي. يِكذِب عَلَى أيّ شَخِص [huwwa fadd wa:ħid ma: yistiħi. yičðib ʕala ʔayy šaxiṣ] He's a guy who doesn't know shame. He lies about anybody. • **2.** to be or become embarrassed, feel embarrassed – أستِحِي أطلُب مِنَّه فلُوس بَعَد [ʔastiħi ʔaṭlub minnah flu:s baʕad] I'm embarrased to ask him for more money. ما أقدَر أكَلِّفَه بِيها. أستِحِي [ma: ʔagdar ʔakallifah bi:ha. ʔastiħi] I can't bother him with it. I'd be embarrassed. • **3.** to be bashful, shy, diffident – ما قِبَل يحاكِيها. يِستِحِي هوايَة [ma: qibal yħa:či:ha. yistiħi hwa:ya] He wouldn't talk to her. He's very bashful.

حَيّ [ħayy] *n:* • **1.** neighborhood

حَيَّة [ħayya] *n:* حَيّات، حَيايَة [ħayya:t, ħaya:ya] *pl:* • **1.** snake in the grass, dirty rat – حَيَّة صَفرَة [ħayya ṣafra] snake in the grass, dirty rat. • **1.** snake, serpent, viper • **2.** yellow viper

حَيا، حَياء [ħaya:, ħaya:ʔ] *n:* • **1.** shame, diffidence, timidity, bashfulness

حَياة [ħaya:t] *n:* • **1.** life – بِحَياتِي ما شِفت هِيكِي شِي [biħaya:ti ma: šifit hi:či ši] I never saw such a thing in my life.

تَحِيَّة [taħiyya] *n:* تَحِيّات [taħiyya:t] *pl:* • **1.** greeting • **2.** salute

حَيوان [ħaywa:n] *n:* حَيوانات [ħaywa:na:t] *pl:* • **1.** animal, beast – لا تصِير حَيوان [la: tṣi:r ħaywa:n] Don't be an animal!

حَيَوِيَّة [ħayawiyya] *n:* • **1.** energy

مِستَحاة [mistaħa: (t)] *n:* • **1.** shyness, shame

حَيّ [ħayy] *adj:* أحياء [ʔaħya:ʔ] *pl:* • **1.** living, live, alive – ما أدرِي حَيّ لَو مَيِّت [ma: ʔadri ħayy law mayyit] I don't know if he's alive or dead. يَزِّي عاد! مُو وُصلَت اللَّحم الحَيّ [yazzi ʕa:d! mu: wuṣlat ʔillaħm ʔilħayy] Enough now! You've gotten to the quick! • **2.** pl. أحيَاء living beings, living things, living organisms – عِلم الأحياء [ʕilm ʔilʔaħya:ʔ] biology. دَرس أحياء [daris ʔaħya:ʔ] general science class.

حَيَوِي [ħayawi] *adj:* • **1.** vital, essential to life – مَسألَة حَيَوِيَّة [masʔala ħayawiyya] a vital matter.

حَياسِز [ħaya:sizz] *adj:* حَياسِزِّيَّة [ħaya:sizziyya] *pl:* • **1.** shameless, bold, brazen • **2.** brazen person

مِستِحِي [mistiħi] *adj:* • **1.** bashful, shy

خ

خ

خا, خاء [xaː] *n:* • **1.** name of the letter

خ ب ء

خَبّى [xabbaː] *v:* • **1.** to hide, conceal – قُلّي. لا تخَبّي عَلَيّا شِي [gulli. laː txabbi ʕalayya ši] Tell me. Don't hide anything from me.
تخَبّى [txabbaː] *v:* • **1.** to hide oneself – إجا الشُّرطِي. تخَبّى [ʔija ʔiššurṭi. txabbaː] The policeman's coming. Hide yourself!
اِختِبَى [ʔixtibaː] *v:* • **1.** to hide, conceal oneself – شُوفلَك فَدّ مُكان تِختِبي بِيه [šuːflak fadd mukaːn tixitibi biːh] Look for some place to hide.
مَخبَأ [maxbaʔ] *n:* • **1.** hiding place, shelter, refuge
مخَبّى [mxabba] *adj:* • **1.** hidden, concealed

خ ب ث

خَبَّث [xabbaθ] *v:* • **1.** to work malicious mischief – ما اِشتِغَل بمُكان إذا ما خَبَّث بِيه [maː ʔištiɣal bmukaːn ʔiða maː xabbaθ biːh] He's never worked anywhere that he didn't stir up trouble.
خُبُث [xubuθ] *n:* • **1.** trouble-making, viciousness
خَبِيث [xabiːθ] *adj:* خُبَثاء [xubaθaːʔ] *pl:* • **1.** troublesome, vicious, malicious – واحِد خَبِيث [waːħid xabiːθ] an instigator, troublemaker. • **2.** dangerous, serious, deadly, pernicious – مَرَض خَبِيث [marað̣ xabiːθ] a serious disease.
أخبَث [ʔaxbaθ] *comparative adjective:* • **1.** more or most troublesome, vicious

خ ب ر

خَبَّر [xabbar] *v:* • **1.** to tell, inform, advise – خَبَّرتَه باكِر ما راح نِشتُغُل [xabbartah baːčir maː raːħ ništuɣul] I told him we're not going to work tomorrow.
خابَر [xaːbar] *v:* • **1.** to telephone, phone – خابرَتني مَرّتَين البارحَة [xaːbratni marrtayn ʔilbaːrħa] She phoned me twice yesterday.
تخابَر [txaːbar] *v:* • **1.** to telephone, get in touch – تخابَرت وِيّاه [txaːbarit wiyyaːh] I got in touch with him.
اِختِبَر [ʔixtibar, ʔixtubar] *v:* • **1.** to test, examine, give an examination – اِختِبَرتَه وطِلَع صادِق [ʔixtibartah wṭilaʕ ṣaːdiq] I tested him and he was telling the truth. البارحَة المُدَرِّس اِختِبَرنا [ʔilbaːrħa ʔilmudarris ʔixtibarna] Yesterday the teacher gave us an examination.
اِستَخبَر [ʔistaxbar] *v:* • **1.** to ask, inquire – لازِم نِستَخبُر عَنّه [laːzim nistaxbur ʕannah] We have to inquire about it. • **2.** to learn, discover, find out – اِستَخبَرنا إنُّو هَذا المُجرِم بَعدَه بِالوِلايَة [ʔistaxbarna ʔinnu haːða ʔilmujrim baʕdah bilwilaːya] We've learned that the criminal is still in town.
خَبَر [xabar] *n:* أخبار [ʔaxbaːr] *pl:* • **1.** news item • **2.** news, word, information, report
خِبرَة [xibra] *n:* خِبرات، خِبَر [xibraːt, xibar] *pl:* • **1.** experience
خَبِير [xabiːr] *n:* خُبَراء [xubaraːʔ] *pl:* • **1.** expert
مُخَبِّر [muxabbir] *n:* • **1.** informant
إخبار [ʔixbaːr] *n:* إخبارات [ʔixbaːraːt] *pl:* • **1.** summons, subpoena – جانِي إخبار مِن المَحكَمَة [jaːni ʔixbaːr min ʔilmaħkama] I got a summons from the court.
مُختَبَر [muxtabar] *n:* مُختَبَرات [muxtabaraːt] *pl:* • **1.** laboratory
مُخابَرَة [muxaːbara] *n:* مُخابَرات [muxaːbaraːt] *pl:* • **1.** correspondence • **2.** communication, contact • **3.** telephone call • **4.** pl. مُخابَرات calls, intelligence
اِختِبار [ʔixtibaːr] *n:* • **1.** test
الخابُور [ʔilxaːbuːr] *n:* • **1.** a tributary of the Upper Euphrates
إخبارِيَّة [ʔixbaːriyya] *n:* • **1.** information, tip (about illegal act) • **2.** tip, information
اِستِخبار [ʔistixbaːr] *n:* اِستِخبارات [ʔistixbaːraːt] *pl:* • **1.** inquiry
مُخبِر [muxbir] *adj:* • **1.** reporter
مخابُر [mxaːbur] *adj:* • **1.** calling

خ ب ز

خُبَز [xubaz] *v:* • **1.** to bake bread – أُمَّه خُبزَت عِشرِين قُرصَة خُبُز [ʔummah xubzat ʕišriːn gurṣat xubuz] His mother baked twenty flat, round loaves of bread. صارلِي خَمس سنِين أشتُغُل وِيّاه. عِجَنتَه وَخُبَزتَه [ṣaːrli xams sniːn ʔaštuɣul wiyyaːh. ʕijantah wxubaztah] I have worked with him for five years. I know him thoroughly (lit., kneaded and baked him.) آنِي عاجنَه وخابزَه [ʔaːni ʕaːjnah wxaːbzah] I know all about it.
اِنخُبَز [ʔinxubaz] *v:* • **1.** to be baked • **2.** to be struck, hit
خُبُز [xubuz] *n:* • **1.** (coll.) bread
خَبُز [xabuz] *n:* • **1.** baking
خُبزَة [xubza] *n:* خُبزات [xubzaːt] *pl:* • **1.** piece of bread
خَبزَة [xabza] *n:* خَبزات [xabzaːt] *pl:* • **1.** batch, mixture (of bread dough)
خَبّاز [xabbaːz] *n:* خَبّازِين، خبابِيز [xabbaːziːn, xbaːbiːz] *pl:* • **1.** baker, bread maker
خُبّاز، خُبَّيز [xubbaːz, xubbiːz] *n:* • **1.** mallow
مَخبَز [maxbaz] *n:* مَخابِز [maxaːbiz] *pl:* • **1.** bakery, bread shop

خ ب ص

خُبَص [xubaṣ] *v:* • **1.** to mix up, distract, confuse, bother, rush – لا تُخبُصنِي. خَلِّينِي أشُوف دَربِي [laː tuxbuṣni. xalliːni ʔašuːf darbi] Don't bother me. Let me concentrate

on what I'm doing. شَكُو خابُص نَفسَك؟ عَلَى كَيفَك [šaku xaːbuṣ nafsak? ʕala kayfak] Why are you so worked up? Take it easy.
اِنخُبَص [ʔinxubaṣ] *v:* • **1.** to be or become rushed, busy, preoccupied – كان عِدنا عِرِس وَانخُبَصنا [čaːn ʕidna ʕiris wʔinxubaṣna] We had a wedding and we got all tied up with it. مِن يجُوه خُطّار يِنخُبُص بِيهُم [min yǰuːh xuṭṭaːr yinxubuṣ biːhum] When he has guests he gets completely occupied with them.
خَبُص [xabuṣ] *n:* • **1.** mess, confusion
خَبصَة [xabṣa] *n:* خَبصات [xabṣaːt] *pl:* • **1.** commotion, hustle and bustle, melee, madhouse • **2.** mess, hodgepodge, rat's nest
خِبِيصَة [xibiːṣa, xabiːṣa] *n:* خِبِيصات [xibiːṣaːt] *pl:* • **1.** commotion, hustle and bustle, melee, madhouse
مَخبُوص [maxbuːṣ] *adj:* • **1.** busy, occupied, tied up – مَخبُوص بشُغلَه [maxbuːṣ bšuɣlah] busy with his work.

خ ب ط

خُبَط [xubaṭ] *v:* • **1.** to mix – يُخبُط جَتّ وَتِبِن وَيِنطِيه لِلحصان [yuxbuṭ ǰatt wtibin wyinṭiːh lilḥṣaːn] He mixes alfalfa and straw and gives it to the horse. • **2.** to roil, stir up, muddy – فاتَت السَّيّارَة بِالجَدوَل وَخُبطَت المَيّ [faːtat ʔissayyaːra bilǰadwal wxubṭat ʔilmayy] The car went through the creek and muddied the water. • **3.** to become murky, muddy, roiled – مِن تضِيف هالمَسحُوق، لُون السّائِل يُخبُط [min dðiːf halmasḥuːq, luːn ʔissaːʔil yuxbuṭ] When you add this powder, the color of the liquid becomes murky. النَّهَر خابُط مِن كُثرَة المُطَر [ʔinnahar xaːbuṭ min kuθrat ʔilmuṭar] The river's muddy from all the rain.
خَبَّط [xabbaṭ] *v:* • **1.** to grope, stumble around – ظَلّ يخَبُّط مُدَّة بِالظَلمَة حَتَّى لِقَى السُّوِيج [ðall yxabbuṭ mudda biððalma ħatta ligaː ʔissuwiːč] He kept groping around for a while in the dark until he found the switch.
اِنخُبَط [ʔinxubaṭ] *v:* • **1.** to be mixed
خَبُط [xabuṭ] *n:* • **1.** mixing
خَبطَة [xabṭa] *n:* خَبطات [xabṭaːt] *pl:* • **1.** a mixing, an instance of mixing • **2.** mixture, batch
خَبّاطَة [xabbaːṭa] *n:* خَبّاطات [xabbaːṭaːt] *pl:* • **1.** mixer, cement mixer
خابُط [xaːbuṭ] *adj:* • **1.** muddy, murky, roiled – ماي خابُط [maːy xaːbuṭ] muddy water.
خَباطَة [xabaːṭa] *adj:* • **1.** (invar.) mentally unbalanced, touched in the head, odd, off
مَخبُوط [maxbuːṭ] *adj:* • **1.** mixed

خ ب ل

خَبَّل [xabbal] *v:* • **1.** to drive insane, rob of his senses – ما تاخذَه لإبنَك! مُو خَبَّلنِي [maː taːxðah lʔibnak! muː xabbalni] Look, take your son! He's driven me out of my mind! جَمالها يخَبُّل [ǰamaːlha yxabbul] Her beauty stuns you.
تخَبَّل [txabbal] *v:* • **1.** to go crazy, go wild – تخَبَّلَت مِن مات إبِنها [txabblat min maːt ʔibinha] She went crazy when her son died. مِن شاف السَّيّارَة، تخَبَّل عَليها [min šaːf ʔissayyaːra, txabbal ʕaliːha] When he saw the car, he was crazy about it.
خبال [xbaːl] *n:* • **1.** madness, insanity
تخُبُّل [txubbul] *n:* • **1.** madness, insanity
مخَبَّل [mxabbal] *adj:* مخابِيل [mxaːbiːl] *pl:* • **1.** insane person, madman
متخَبُّل [mitxabbul] *adj:* • **1.** angry, infuriated, furious – المُدِير متِخَبُّل لِأَنّ نُص المُوَظَّفِين ما إجَوا لِلشُّغُل [ʔilmudiːr mitxabbul liʔann nuṣṣ ʔilmuwaððafiːn maː ʔiǰaw liššuɣul] The director's furious because half of the employees didn't show up for work.

خ ت ل

خِتَل [xital] *v:* • **1.** to hide, conceal oneself – الحَرامِي خِتَل بِالسِّرداب [ʔilħaraːmi xital bissirdaːb] The thief hid in the cellar.
تخَتَّل [txattal] *v:* • **1.** intens. of hide – خِتَل [xital] دَتِتخَتَّل؟ هَذا عَمَّك، مُو غَرِيب [datitxattal? haːða ʕammak, muː ɣariːb] Why do you keep hiding? This is your uncle, not a stranger. • **2.** to be concealed
خَتِل [xatil] *n:* • **1.** deceitfulness, hiding
خَتلَة [xatla] *n:* خَتلات [xatlaːt] *pl:* • **1.** an isolated or concealed spot, a hiding place – مَكان خَتلَة [makaːn xatla] an isolated spot. وِين هَالخَتلَة؟ ما نشُوفَك [wiːn halxatla? maː nšuːfak] Where've you been hiding? We don't see you anymore.
مخَتِّل [mxattil] *adj:* • **1.** hiding
خِتّيلَة [xittayla, xittiːla] *n:* • **1.** the game of hide and seek
خاتِل [xaːtil] *adj:* • **1.** hiding
مخَتَّل [mxattal] *adj:* • **1.** hidden

خ ت م

خِتَم [xitam] *v:* • **1.** to seal – خِتَم الظَرُف بَعَد ما خَلَّى المَكتُوب بِيه [xitam ʔiððaruf baʕad maː xallaː ʔilmaktuːb biːh] He sealed the envelope after he placed the letter in it. • **2.** to stamp – إختِم العَرِيضَة وَدِّيها لِلمُدِير [ʔixtim ʔilʕariːḍa wwaddiːha lilmudiːr] Stamp the application and take it to the director. إختِم الطَّوابع بخَتَم اليُوم [ʔixtim ʔiṭṭawaːbiʕ bxatam ʔilyuːm] Cancel the postage stamps with the date stamp. • **3.** to conclude, terminate – خِتَم الكَلِمَة مالتَه بِالتَّرحِيب بِالضُيُوف [xitam ʔilkalima maːltah bittarhiːb biððuyuːf] He concluded his speech by welcoming the guests. • **4.** to finish, complete, wind up – خِتَم المَصلَحَة [xitam ʔilmaṣlaħa] He has finished his apprenticeship. • **5.** to read through, read from cover to cover (of the Koran) – إبِنها خِتَم القُرآن [ʔibinha xitam ʔilqurʔaːn] Her son has read the Koran from cover to cover.
خَتَّم [xattam] *v:* • **1.** to have someone read through – خَتِّمَوه القُرآن قَبُل ما يدَخِّلُوه المَدرَسَة [xattimawh ʔilqurʔaːn gabul maː ydaxxiluːh ʔilmadrasa] They made him read the Koran before they entered him in school.

اِختِتَم [ʔixtitam] *v:* • **1.** to conclude, finish,terminate – خِتمَوا الحَفلَة بِالسَّلام الجُمهُوري [xitmaw ʔilħafla bissala:m ʔiǰǰumhu:ri] They concluded the ceremony with the national anthem.
خَتِم، خَتَم [xatim, xatam] *n:* أختام [ʔaxta:m] *pl:* • **1.** seal, stamp
خَتمَة، وَرد الخَتمَة [xatma, warid ʔilxatma] *n:* • **1.** hollyhock • **2.** the end of a cyle of reading the Quran from cover to cover
خاتَم [xa:tam] *n:* خَواتِم [xawa:tim] *pl:* • **1.** ring
خِتام [xita:m] *n:* • **1.** closure, sealing • **2.** sealing
مَختُوم [maxtu:m] *adj:* • **1.** sealed
خِتامِي [xita:mi] *adj:* • **1.** final

خ ت و ن

خاتُون [xa:tu:n, xa:tu:na] *n:* خواتِين [xwa:ti:n] *pl:* • **1.** lady • **2.** polite form of address to a lady • **3.** good girl, little lady

خ ث ر

خِثَر [xiθar] *v:* • **1.** to curdle – خِثَر الحَلِيب وَإلّا بَعَد؟ [xiθar ʔilħali:b waʔilla baʕad?] Has the milk curdled yet?
خَثَّر [xaθθar] *v:* • **1.** to curdle – شَرُّب الجّاهِل حَلِيب والباقِي، خَثَّرَه [šarrub ʔiǰǰa:hil ħali:b wilba:qi, xaθθirah] Give the baby a drink of milk and curdle the rest. • **2.** to clot, make clot – هَالدُّوا يخَثِّر الدَّم [hadduwa yxaθθir ʔiddamm] This medicine makes blood clot.
تخَثَّر [txaθθar] *v:* • **1.** to be curdled • **2.** to be solid • **3.** to be thick
خَثِر [xaθir] *n:* • **1.** curd
خُثرَة [xuθra] *n:* خُثرات [xuθra:t] *pl:* • **1.** curdling agent
خاثِر [xa:θir] *n:* • **1.** A variety of yoghurt,

خ ج ل

خِجَل [xiǰal] *v:* • **1.** to be or become embarrassed – خِجَل لِأنّ جوابَه طِلَع غَلَط [xiǰal liʔann ǰawa:bah ṭilaʕ ɣalaṭ] He got embarrassed because his answer turned out to be wrong. هُوَّ يِخجَل مِن أَبُوه [huwwa yixǰal min ʔabu:h] He's embarrassed in front of his father. خِجَل مِن ما عِرَف يجاوُب [xiǰal min ma: ʕiraf yǰa:wub] He was embarrassed when he couldn't answer. • **2.** to be ashamed, feel shame – هُوَّ فَدّ شَخِص ما يِخجَل [huwwa fadd šaxiṣ ma: yixǰal] He's a person who feels no shame. خِجَل مِن أعمالَه [xiǰal min ʔaʕma:lah] He was ashamed of his action.
خَجَّل [xaǰǰal] *v:* • **1.** to embarrass, put to shame – لا تدِزَّه لِهذا، تَرَة يخَجِّلنا لِأنّ ما يُعرُف إنكِلِيزِي [la: ddizzah lha:ða, tara yxaǰǰilna liʔann ma: yuʕruf ʔingili:zi] Don't send him --- he'll embarrass us because he doesn't know English. خَجَّلنا بكَلامَه الخَشِن [xaǰǰalna bkala:mah ʔilxašin] He embarrassed us with his rough talk. خَجَّلتِني. ما أعرُف شلُون أجازِيك [xaǰǰaltini. ma: ʔaʕruf šlu:n ʔaǰa:zi:k] You've embarrassed me (with favors). I don't know how to repay you.
خَجَل [xaǰal] *n:* • **1.** embarrassment
خَجُول [xaǰu:l] *adj:* • **1.** shy, bashful, timid – وَلَد خَجُول هوايَة [walad xaǰu:l hwa:ya] a very timid boy.
مُخجِل [muxǰil] *adj:* • **1.** shameful, shocking – عَمَل مُخجِل [ʕamal muxǰil] a shameful act.
خَجلان [xaǰla:n] *adj:* • **1.** embarrassed – تِرَك القاعَة خَجلان [tirak ʔilqa:ʕa xaǰla:n] He left the hall in embarrassment.
أخجَل [ʔaxǰal] *comparative adjective:* • **1.** more or most shy

خ خ م

خاخام [xa:xa:m, ħa:xa:m] *n:* خاخامِيَّة [xa:xa:miyya] *pl:* • **1.** rabbi

خ د د 1

خَدّ [xadd] *n:* خدُود [xdu:d] *pl:* • **1.** cheek – تُفّاح أَبُو خَدّ وَخَدّ [tuffa:ħ ʔabu xadd wxadd] apples that are not all red.

خ د د 2

مُخَدَّة [muxadda] *n:* مَخادِيد، مُخَدّات [maxa:di:d, muxadda:t] *pl:* • **1.** pillow, cushion

خ د ر 1

خِدَر [xidar] *v:* • **1.** to become numb, tingle – قِعَدِت عَلَى رِجلِي، وَخِدرَت [giʕadit ʕala riǰli, wxidrat] I sat on my leg, and it went to sleep.
خَدَّر [xaddar] *v:* • **1.** to numb, deaden – ضِرَبَه أُبرَة جَوَّة السِّنّ حَتَّى يخَدِّر المُكان [ð̣irabah ʔubra ǰawwa ʔissinn ħatta yxaddir ʔilmuka:n] He gave him a shot next to the tooth to deaden the area. • **2.** to anesthetize – خَدِّر الأرنَب حَتَّى نشَرّحَه [xaddir ʔilʔarnab ħatta nšarrħah] Anesthetize the rabbit so we can dissect it.
تخَدَّر [txaddar] *v:* • **1.** to be numbed
خَدَر [xadar] *n:* • **1.** numbness, insensibility
مُخَدِّر [muxaddir] *n:* مُخَدِّرات [muxaddira:t] *pl:* • **1.** anesthetic, pain-killing, tranquilizing – مادَّة مُخَدِّرَة [ma:dda muxaddira] painkilling agent, material. pl. • **2.** when pl. مُخَدِّرات Noun: narcotics, drugs, dope
تَخدِير [taxdi:r] *n:* • **1.** anesthesia, narcotization, numbness
خَدران [xadra:n] *adj:* • **1.** numb, asleep – إيدِي خَدرانَة لِأنّ نِمت عَليها [ʔi:di xadra:na liʔann nimit ʕali:ha] My arm is asleep because I slept on it.
مُخَدَّرَة [muxaddara] *adj:* مُخَدَّرات [muxaddara:t] *pl:* • **1.** veiled women – نِسوان مُخَدَّرات [niswa:n muxaddara:t] veiled women.
مِتخَدِّر [mitxaddir] *adj:* • **1.** numb

خ د ر 2

خِدَر [xidar] *v:* • **1.** to brew, steep – خِدَر الشاي. صُبّ إلنا [xidar ʔičča:y. ṣubb ʔilna] The tea has brewed. Pour for us.

تَخَدَّر [txaddar] *v:* • **1.** to be brewed • **2.** to feel tingly, to feel numb
خَدِر [xadir] *n:* • **1.** brewing
تَخدِير [taxdiːr] *n:* • **1.** brewing
مِتخَدِّر [mitxaddir] *adj:* • **1.** brewing, steeping

خ د ش

خِدَش [xidaš] *v:* • **1.** to scratch
خَدَّش [xaddaš] *v:* • **1.** to scratch
تخَدَّش [txaddaš] *v:* • **1.** to be scratched
اِنخِدَش [ʔinxidaš] *v:* • **1.** to be scratched
خَدِش [xadiš] *n:* خِدُوش [xiduwš] *pl:* • **1.** scratch
خَدشَة [xadša] *n:* • **1.** scratch
تَخدِيش [taxdiːš] *n:* • **1.** scratching

خ د ع

خِدَع [xidaʕ] *v:* • **1.** to deceive, mislead, dupe, gull – لا تخَلِّي مَظهَرَه يِخدَعَك [laː txalliː maðharah yixdaʕak] Don't let his appearance fool you. بَعدَك لهَسَّة مَخدُوع بِيه؟ [baʕdak lihassa maxduːʕ biːh?] Are you still taken in by him?
اِنخِدَع [ʔinxidaʕ] *v:* • **1.** to be deceived – هَذا يِنخِدِع بِالعَجَل [haːða yinxidiʕ bilʕajal] He's easily taken in.
خَدِع [xadiʕ] *n:* • **1.** cheating, deception
خُدعَة [xudʕa] *n:* خُدَع [xudaʕ] *pl:* • **1.** trick
خِداع [xidaːʕ] *n:* • **1.** deceit
خَدّاع [xaddaːʕ] *adj:* • **1.** deceptive, deceiving – مَظهَرَه خَدّاع [maðharah xaddaːʕ] His appearance is deceiving.
مُخادِع [muxaːdiʕ] *adj:* • **1.** deceitful
خِداعِي [xidaːʕi] *adj:* • **1.** deceiving

خ د ق

خُدُق [xudug] *n:* • **1.** tickle, involuntary twitching movement, tickling sensation

خ د م

خِدَم [xidam] *v:* • **1.** to serve, be of service, work for – الرَّئِيس خِدَم الوَطَن مُدَّة طُوِيلَة [ʔirraʔiːs xidam ʔilwaṭan mudda ṭuwiːla] The president served his country a long time. خِدَم مَصالِح عَمَّه [xidam maṣaːliħ ʕammah] He served the interests of his uncle. • **2.** to serve, be a servant – خِدَم بِبَيتهُم شَهرَين [xidam bibaythum šahrayn] He served in their household for two months.
اِستَخدَم [ʔistaxdam] *v:* • **1.** to employ, hire – اِستَخدِمَتَه الحُكُومَة شَهرَين وَنُص [ʔistaxdimatah ʔilħukuːma šahrayn wnuṣṣ] The government employed him for two and a half months. • **2.** to employ, use, make use of – نِستَخدِم أَحدَث الأَجهِزَة بِهَالمُختَبَر [nistaxdim ʔaħdaθ ʔilʔajhiza bhalmuxtabar] We use the most modern equipment in this lab.
خِدمَة [xidma] *n:* خِدمات، خِدَم، خَدَمات [xidmaːt, xidam, xadamaːt] *pl:* • **1.** a service • **2.** hospitality, duties of a host • **3.** service, attendance – الخِدمَة العَسكَرِيَّة [ʔilxidma ʔilʕaskariyya] military service. آنِي بِخِدمَتكُم [ʔaːni bxidmatkum] I'm at your service.
مُستَخدَم [mustaxdam] *n:* • **1.** employee, official
مُستَخدِم [mustaxdim] *n:* • **1.** employer
استخدام [ʔistixdaːm] *n:* • **1.** use, utilization
خَدُوم [xaduːm] *adj:* • **1.** obliging – هَذا كُلِّش خَدُوم. أَيّ شِي تكَلّفَه بِيه، يسَوِّيه [haːða kulliš xaduːm. ʔayy ši tkallfah biːh, ysawwiːh] He's very obliging. Anything you ask, he'll do.
خادِم [xaːdim] *n:* خَدَم، خُدّام [xadam, xuddaːm] *pl:* خادِمَة [xaːdima] *feminine:* • **1.** servant, manservant
خَدَمِي [xadami] *adj:* • **1.** useful, subservient, serviceable
خَدّامَة [xaddaːma] *n:* خَدّامات [xaddaːmaːt] *pl:* • **1.** maid
خادمَة [xaːdma] *n:* خادمات [xaːdmaːt] *pl:* • **1.** maid

خ ر ب

خِرَب [xirab] *v:* • **1.** to be ruined, destroyed, spoiled – خُربَت المَدِينَة مِن مَرّ الجَّيش [xurbat ʔilmadiːna min marr ʔijjayš] The city was destroyed when the army came through. البَلَد خِرَب مِن أَعمال الدِّكتاتورِيَّة [ʔilbalad xirab min ʔaʕmaːl ʔiddiktaːtuːriyya] The country was ruined by the dictatorship's actions. • **2.** to go bad, spoil (of food) – خِرَب الأَكِل [xirab ʔilʔakil] The food got spoiled. • **3.** to break down, get out of order, broken – المَكِينَة خُربَت [ʔilmakiːna xurbat] The machine broke down. هَالسّاعَة كُلِّش دَقِيقَة؛ تِخرَب بِالعَجَل [hassaːʕa kulliš daqiːqa; tixrab bilʕajal] This watch is very delicate; it'll get out of order easily. • **4.** to go bad, be spoiled, change for the worse – كان خُوش وَلَد لَكِن خِرَب مِن قام يِمشِي وِيّا هَالجَماعَة [čaːn xuːš walad laːkin xirab min gaːm yimši wiyya hajjamaːʕa] He used to be a good boy, but he was ruined by going with this group. صَدِيقتِي خُربت عَلَيّا. لازم أَحَّد قالِلها شِي عَنِّي [ṣadiːqti xurbat ʕalayya. laːzim ʔaħħad gaːlilha ši ʕanni] My girlfriend turned against me. Someone must have told her something about me. • **5.** to collapse, to pass out – خِرَب الشّايِب مِن شِدَّة الحَرّ [xirab ʔiššaːyib min šiddat ʔilħarr] The old man collapsed from the intense heat. الجّاهِل وُقَع عَلَى وُجّه وَخِرَب [ʔijjaːhil wugaʕ ʕala wuččah wxirab] The child fell on his face and passed out.
خَرَّب [xarrab] *v:* • **1.** to destroy, ruin, spoil – الله يخَرُّب بَيتَك [ʔallah yxarrub baytak] I hope God will destroy your life. المُطَر غَرَّق الوِلايَة وَخَرَّب كُلّشِي [ʔilmuṭar ɣarrag ʔilwilaːya wxarrab kullši] The rain flooded the city and destroyed everything. • **2.** to put out of order, damage – لُويش خَرَّبت السّاعَة؟ [luwiːš xarrabt ʔissaːʕa?] Why did you mess up the watch? • **3.** to lead astray, influence for the worse – لا تِمشِي وِيّاه تَرَة يخَرُّبَك [laː timši wiyyaːh tara yxarrubak] Don't run around with him or he'll ruin you. لا تقُلّها هَالحِكايَة، تَرَة تخَرُّبها عَلَيّا [laː tgullha halħčaːya,

tara txarrubha ʕalayya] Don't tell her that story or you'll turn her against me. خَرَّب بَينِي وَبَين مَرتِي [xarrab bayni wbayn marti] He caused trouble between me and my wife.

خارَب [xa:rab] *v:* • **1.** to make mad at each other, stir up trouble between – راح تدَخَّل وَخارَبهُم [ra:ħ ddaxxal wxa:rabhum] He went and interfered and made them mad at each other.

تخارَب [txa:rab] *v:* • **1.** to get mad at each other, to quarrel, fall out – كُلّ يوم يِتخاربُون وَيِتصالحُون [kull yu:m yitxa:rbu:n wyitṣa:lħu:n] Every day they quarrel and make up. الإبن وأَبُوه تخاربَوا [ʔilʔibn wʔabu:h txa:rbaw] The son and his father had a falling out. تخارَبِت وِيّا صَدِيقِي وَما دَنِتحاكَى [txa:rabit wiyya ṣadi:qi wama: danitħa:ča:] I quarreled with my friend and we're not speaking.

خَراب [xara:b] *n:* • **1.** ruin, ruins • **2.** quarrel, split, falling out

خَرابَة [xara:ba] *n:* خَرابات، خَرايِب [xara:ba:t, xara:yib] *pl:* • **1.** ruin, ruins, dilapidated building

تَخرِيب [taxri:b] *n:* تَخرِيبات [taxri:ba:t] *pl:* • **1.** destruction, sabotage

مُخَرِّب [muxarrib] *n:* • **1.** saboteur

خَربان [xarba:n] *adj:* • **1.** broken, out of order – سَيّارتِي خَربانَة [sayya:rti xarba:na] My car is broken down. • **2.** knocked out, out cold – بُقَى خَربان ساعتِين [buqa: xarba:n sa:ʕtayn] He was unconscious for two hours.

تَخرِيبِي [taxri:bi] *adj:* تَخرِيبِيَّة [taxri:biyya] *pl:* • **1.** act of sabotage

خ ر ب ط

خَربَط [xarbaṭ] *v:* • **1.** to throw into disorder, mess up, confuse – الهَوا خَربَط شَعرِي [ʔilhawa xarbaṭ šaʕri] The wind messed up my hair. خَربَط الغَراض ولازِم أَعَدِّلها [xarbaṭ ʔilɣara:ð wla:zim ʔaʕaddilha] He mixed up the things and I have to straighten them out. خَربَطنِي بِحَكيَه وَما قدَرت أَجاوُب [xarbaṭni bħačyah wma: gdarit ʔaja:wub] He confused me with what he said and I couldn't answer. راح أَرُوح عَليه وَأَخَربُط أَحوالَه [ra:ħ ʔaru:ħ ʕali:h wʔaxarbuṭ ʔaħwa:lah] I'll go see him and tell him off. • **2.** to get mixed up, to foul up, malfunction – كُلّ الجِّنُود دَيمشُون عَدِل، بَسّ هُوَّ يخَربُط [kull ʔijjinu:d dayimšu:n ʕadil, bass huwwa yxarbuṭ] All the soldiers are marching properly; he's the only one who's messing it up. مَكِينَة سَيّارتِي دَتخَربُط. لازم أَضبُطها [maki:nat sayya:rti datxarbuṭ. la:zim ʔaðbuṭha] The motor in my car is running badly. I've got to tune it. مِعدتِي دَتخَربُط عَليّا [miʕidti datxarbuṭ ʕalayya] My stomach's bothering me. شِرَب بِيك وَخَربَط، صِعَد عالميز، وَقام يِرقُص [širab pi:k wxarbaṭ, ṣiʕad ʕalmi:z, wga:m yirguṣ] He had a shot and went wild; got up on the table and started to dance. دَيخَربُط بِحَكيَه [dayxarbuṭ bħačyah] He gets mixed up in talking. دَيخَربُط وَما دَيُعرُف شيحكِي [dayxarbuṭ wma: dayuʕruf šyiħči] He talks disjointedly and doesn't know what he is saying. رِجَع عَليه الوُجَع لِأَنّ خَربَط بِالأَكِل [rijaʕ ʕali:h ʔilwujaʕ liʔann xarbaṭ bilʔakil] The pain returned to him because he didn't eat right.

تخَربَط [txarbaṭ] *v:* • **1.** pass. of خَربَط to be thrown into disorder, be messed up, be confused – أَحوالَه تخَربُطَت مِن تزَوَّج [ʔaħwa:lah txarbuṭat min tzawwaj] Since he got married he's gone to pot. لا تِحكِي مِن أَكتِب تَرَة أَتخَربَط [la: tiħči min ʔaktib tara ʔatxarbaṭ] Don't talk when I'm writing or I'll get mixed up. أَبُوه تخَربَط بِاللَّيل وجابولَه الطَّبِيب [ʔabu:h txarbaṭ billayl wja:bu:lah ʔiṭṭabi:b] His father got sick at night and they brought the doctor for him. مِن بِلَع الحَبّايَة تخَربَط [min bilaʕ ʔilħabba:ya txarbaṭ] When he took the pill, he got worse.

خَربَطَة [xarbaṭa] *n:* خَرابِيط، خَربَطات [xara:bi:ṭ, xarbaṭa:t] *pl:* • **1.** mess, disorder, muddle, confusion

تخُربُط [txurbuṭ] *n:* • **1.** mess, disorder, muddle, confusion

مخَربَط [mxarbaṭ] *adj:* • **1.** mixed up, confused – وَضِع مخَربَط [waðiʕ mxarbaṭ] an unsettled situation. • **2.** disorderly, disarranged, messed up

مِتخَربُط [mitxarbuṭ] *adj:* • **1.** disarranged

خ ر ب ن د

خَربَندَة [xarbanda] *adj:* خَربَندِيَّة [xarbandiyya] *pl:* • **1.** an incompetent, incapacitated, or senile person • **2.** something useless or worn out, junk

خ ر ج

خِرَج [xiraj] *v:* • **1.** to spend – خِرَج كُلّ فلُوسَه بساعَة وِحدَة [xiraj kull flu:sah bsa:ʕa wiħda] He spent all his money in one hour.

خَرَّج [xarraj] *v:* • **1.** to graduate – الجّامِعَة خَرِّجَت أَلفَين طالِب هالسَّنَة [ʔijja:miʕa xarrijat ʔalfayn ṭa:lib hassana] The university graduated two thousand students this year. • **2.** to deduct, subtract – خَرِّج دِينارَين مِن الحساب [xarrij dina:rayn min ʔilħsa:b] Deduct two dinars from the account.

أَخرَج [ʔaxraj] *v:* • **1.** to throw out, eject, bounce – أَخرِجُوه مِن الحَفلَة مِن قام يصَيِّح [ʔaxriju:h min ʔilħafla min ga:m yṣayyiħ] They ejected him from the ceremony when he began to shout. • **2.** to direct – مِنُو أَخرَج هَالفِلِم؟ [minu ʔaxraj halfilim?] Who directed this movie?

تخَرَّج [txarraj] *v:* • **1.** to graduate, be graduated – تخَرَّج هالسَّنَة مِن الجّامِعَة [txarraj hassana min ʔijja:miʕa] He graduated this year from the university. • **2.** to manage, to take care of oneself – لا تدِزَّه وَحدَه. ما يُعرُف يِتصَرَّف [la: ddizzah waħdah. ma: yuʕruf yitṣarraf] Don't send him alone. He doesn't know how to get around.

اِستَخرَج [ʔistaxraj] *v:* • **1.** to extract, mine, recover – يِستَخرجُون العُطُور مِن الأَوراد [yistaxriju:n ʔilʕuṭu:r min

ʔilʔawra:d] They extract scents from flowers. هَالفَحَم ما يِستَخرِج بسُهُولَة [halfaħam ma: yistaxriǰ bsuhu:la] This coal can't be mined easily. الألماس يِستَخرِجُوه مِن الفَحَم [ʔilʔalma:s yistaxriǰu:h min ʔilfaħam] Diamonds are obtained from coal. البانزِين يِستَخرِجُوه مِن النَّفُط [ʔilbanzi:n yistaxriǰu:h min ʔinnafuṭ] Gasoline is extracted from petroleum.

خُرُج، خُرِج [xuruǰ, xuriǰ] *n:* خُرُوج [xuru:ǰ] *pl:* • **1.** saddlebags

خَرِج [xariǰ] *n:* • **1.** spending

خُرُوج [xuru:ǰ] *n:* • **1.** stool, feces

خارِج [xa:riǰ] *n:* • **1.** outside, exterior • **2.** foreign countries, the outside • **3.** (prep.) outside, out of – خارِج المَدِينَة [xa:riǰ ʔilmadi:na] outside the city.

مَخرَج [maxraǰ] *n:* مَخارِج [maxa:riǰ] *pl:* • **1.** exit, way out

مُخرِج [muxriǰ] *n:* • **1.** (stage or screen) director

خُرّاج [xurra:ǰ, xarra:ǰ] *n:* • **1.** abscess

خَرجِيَّة [xarǰiyya] *n:* • **1.** spending money

إخراج [ʔixra:ǰ] *n:* • **1.** direction • **2.** taking out • **3.** removal

اِستِخراج [ʔistixra:ǰ] *n:* • **1.** extraction, removal

خِرِّيج [xirri:ǰ] *adj:* • **1.** graduate

خارِجي [xa:riǰi] *adj:* • **1.** outer, outside, external – للإستِعمال الخارِجي [lilʔistiʕma:l ʔilxa:riǰi] external use. • **2.** nonresident – طُلّاب خارِجِيِّين [ṭulla:b xa:riǰiyyi:n] day students. عِيادَة خارِجِيَّة [ʕiya:da xa:riǰiyya] outpatient clinic.

مِتخَرِّج [mitxarriǰ] *adj:* • **1.** graduated

خارِجِيَّة [xa:riǰiyya] *adj:* • **1.** foreign office, foreign ministry – الشُّؤُون الخارِجِيَّة [ʔiššuʔu:n ʔilxa:riǰiyya] foreign affairs. وِزارَة الخارِجِيَّة [wiza:rat ʔilxa:riǰiyya] ministry of foreign affairs.

خ ر خ ر

خَرخَر [xarxar] *v:* • **1.** to drip, to leak – القِربَة مالتَك مَنقُوبَة وَدَتخَرخِر [ʔilgirba ma:ltak mangu:ba wadatxarxir] Your water bag has a hole in it and is dripping.

خ ر خ ش

خَرخَش [xarxaš] *v:* • **1.** to rattle – الجّاهِل دَيخَرخِش بقُوطِيَّة بِيها حَصو [ʔiǰǰa:hil dayxarxiš bqu:ṭiyya bi:ha ħaṣw] The kid is rattling a tin can with gravel in it.

خَرخَشَة [xarxaša] *n:* • **1.** stir

خِرخاشَة [xirxa:ša] *n:* خِرخاشات [xirxa:ša:t] *pl:* • **1.** rattle, baby's rattle

خ ر د

خُردَة [xurda] *n:* • **1.** change, small change

خُردَوات [xurdawa:t] *n:* • **1.** (pl.) notions, miscellaneous small articles

خ ر د ف ر و ش

خُردَفُرُوش [xurdafuru:š] *n:* خُردَفُرُوشِيَّة [xurdafuru:šiyya] *pl:* • **1.** dealer in notions, or miscellaneous small articles

خ ر د ل

خَردَل [xardal] *n:* • **1.** mustard

خ ر ر

خَرّ [xarr] *v:* • **1.** to drip, leak – مِن مَطرَت الدِّنيا، خِتَلِت جَوَّة الشِّجرَة، بَسّ المَيّ بُقَى يخُرّ عَلَى راسِي [min maṭrat ʔiddinya, xitalit ǰawwa ʔiššiǰra, bass ʔilmayy buqa: yxurr ʕala ra:si] When it rained, I sought shelter under the tree, but the rain kept dripping on my head. مِن تُمطُر الدِّنيا سَقُف الغُرفَة يخُرّ [min tumṭur ʔiddinya saguf ʔilɣurfa yxurr] When it rains, the ceiling of the room drips. ما بُقَى بِالكِتلِي مَيّ. أَعتِقِد يخُرّ مِنَّه [ma: buqa: bilkitli mayy. ʔaʕtiqid yxurr minnah] There's no water left in the kettle. I think it leaks out of it. • **2.** to fall, fall down, drop, dive, swoop down – شُوف، شُوف، نَجمَة خَرَّت [šu:f, šu:f, najma xarrat] Look, look, a star fell! طَيّارَة الجّاهِل خَرَّت وكَلِّبَت بِشِّجرَة [ṭayya:rat ʔiǰǰa:hil xarrat wčallibat bišiǰra] The kid's kite nose-dived and got hung up in a tree. الطَّيّارَة خَرَّت عَلَى ساحَة الألعاب [ʔiṭṭayya:ra xarrat ʕala sa:ħat ʔilʔalʕa:b] The airplane buzzed the playing field.

خَرّ [xarr] *n:* • **1.** leak

خ ر ز

خِرزَة [xirza] *n:* خِرزات، خِرَز [xirza:t, xiraz] *pl:* • **1.** bead

خرَيزَة [xri:za] *n:* • **1.** a small bead – طَمّ خرَيزَة [ṭamm xri:za] a children's game in which a small bead is hidden in one of two piles of earth. أَبُو خرَيزَة [ʔabu xri:za] a type of small, round-shaped river fish.

خ ر س

خرَس [xras] *v:* • **1.** to become mute, dumb – اِخرَسّ وَإطرَشّ مِن حادِث السَّيّارَة [ʔixrass wʔiṭrašš min ħadiθ ʔissayya:ra] He became mute and deaf from the car accident. شبِيك ما تِحكِي؟ خرَسِّيت؟ [šbi:k ma: tiħči? xrassi:t?] Why don't you talk? Have you lost your tongue?

خَرَّس [xarras] *v:* • **1.** to silence, make dumb – صاح بِيه صَيحَة خَرَّسَه بِيها [ṣa:ħ bi:h ṣi:ħa xarrasah bi:ha] He shut him up with a mighty shout.

خَرَس [xaras] *n:* • **1.** dumbness, muteness

أخرَس [ʔaxras] *adj:* خُرُس، خِرسان [xurus, xirsa:n] *pl:* خَرسَة [xarsa] *feminine:* • **1.** mute, dumb • **2.** mute, dumb person

خ ر س ن

خَرَسانَة [xarasa:na] *n:* خَرَسانات [xarasa:nat] *pl:* • **1.** cement

خ ر ش

خِرَش [xiraš] *v:* • **1.** to startle – خِرَشهُم بصَيحتَه [xirašhum bṣiːħtah] He startled them with his shout. • **2.** to astound, amaze – المُعَلِّم خِرَشنا بِحَكيَه عَن القُنبُلَة الذَّرِّيَّة [ʔilmuʕallim xirašna bħačyah ʕan ʔilqumbula ʔiððarriyya] The teacher astounded us with his talk on the atomic bomb. • **3.** to annoy, irritate, disturb, bother – حِسّ الرّاديُو عالِي يِخرِش الإذِن [ħiss ʔirraːdyu ʕaːli yixriš ʔilʔiðin] The volume of the radio is so high it is irritating. المَزيقَة هَالقَدّ عاليَة خِرشَتها لِلمحَلَّة [ʔilmaziːqa halgadd ʕaːlya xiršatha lilimħalla] The music was so loud that it shook the neighborhood.

خَرَّش [xarraš] *v:* • **1.** to startle, dumbfound – صَيحَة الزُّمال تخَرِّش [ṣiːħat ʔizzumaːl txarriš] The donkey's braying startles.

خَرِش [xariš] *n:* • **1.** startling

خِريش [xiriːš] *adj:* • **1.** eccentric, odd, touched in the head

خ ر ص ن

خارصِين [xaːrṣiːn] *n:* • **1.** zinc

خ ر ط

خِرَط [xiraṭ] *v:* • **1.** to talk nonsense, talk through one's hat – النَّهار كُلَّه يُخرُط بِراسِي عَن الأشياء اللّي سَوّاها بأمريكا [ʔinnahaːr kullah yuxruṭ braːsi ʕan ʔilʔašyaːʔ ʔilli sawwaːha bʔamriːka] All day long he gave me all this talk about the things he did in America. ظَلّ ساعَة يُخرُط وَسِكَت بَعدين [ðall saːʕa yuxruṭ wsikat baʕdiːn] He spent an hour talking nonsense and finally shut up. • **2.** to wipe out – أُخرُط اللِّبَن الباقِي بإصبعَك [ʔuxruṭ ʔilliban ʔilbaːqi bʔiṣibʕak] Wipe out the rest of the yoghurt with your finger.

خرط [xariṭ, xaruṭ] *n:* • **1.** rubbish, trash, baloney, nonsense – حَكيَه كُلَّه خَرِط [ħačyah kullah xariṭ] Everything he says is nonsense. • **2.** worthless thing, junk – لا تِشتِري هَالسَّيّارَة، تَرَة هِيَّ خَرِط [laː tištiri hassayyaːra, tara hiyya xariṭ] Don't buy that car --- it's a piece of junk. • **3.** worthless person, incompetent, jerk – شلَونَه مُعَلِّمكُم الجِّدِيد؟ خَرُط [šluːnah muʕallimkum ʔiǰǰidiːd? xaruṭ] How's your new teacher? Not worth a damn.

خريط [xriːṭ] *n:* • **1.** rubbish, junk, worthless thing • **2.** worthless person, incompetent

خَريطَة [xariːṭa] *n:* خَرايِط [xaraːyiṭ] *pl:* • **1.** map, chart, blueprint

مَخرُوط [maxruːṭ] *n:* مَخارِيط [maxaːriːṭ] *pl:* • **1.** cone (geom.)

خِراطَة [xirraːṭa] *n:* • **1.** turnery

مِخرَطَة [mixraṭa] *n:* • **1.** lathe

خَرّاط [xarraːṭ] *adj:* خَرّاطَة، خَرّاطِين [xarraːṭa, xarraːṭiːn] *pl:* • **1.** braggart, storyteller

خريطِي [xriːṭi] *adj:* • **1.** mess, of bad quality

مَخرُوطِي [maxruːṭi] *adj:* • **1.** cone-shaped – جِبَل مَخرُوطِي [ǰibal maxruːṭi] cone-shaped mountain.

أَخرَط [ʔaxraṭ] *comparative adjective:* • **1.** more or most useless

خ ر ط م [1]

خَرطُوم [xarṭuːm] *n:* خَراطِيم [xaraːṭiːm] *pl:* • **1.** hose

خَرطُومِي [xarṭuːmi] *adj:* • **1.** tubular

خ ر ط م [2]

خَرطُوم [xarṭuːm] *n:* خَراطِيم [xaraːṭiːm] *pl:* • **1.** Khartoum (capital of the Sudan)

خ ر ع

خَرَّع [xarraʕ] *v:* • **1.** to scare, frighten – جانِي مِن وَرا وَخَرَّعنِي [ǰaːni min wara wxarraʕni] He came from behind and scared me.

تخَرَّع [txarraʕ] *v:* • **1.** to be scared, alarmed – هَذا ما يِتخَرَّع بِالعَجَل [haːða maː yitxarraʕ bilʕaǰal] He doesn't get scared easily.

اِختِرَع [ʔixtiraʕ] *v:* • **1.** to become scared, alarmed – اِختِرَع بِالظَّلمَة [ʔixtiraʕ biððalma] He got scared in the dark. • **2.** to invent, devise – مِنُو اِختِرَع الرّاديُو؟ [minu ʔixtiraʕ ʔirraːdyu?] Who invented the radio?

خَرعَة [xarʕa] *n:* خَرعات [xarʕaːt] *pl:* • **1.** a scare, a fright

مُختَرِع [muxtariʕ] *n:* مُختَرِعِين [muxtariʕiːn] *pl:* • **1.** inventor

تَخريع [taxriːʕ] *n:* • **1.** frightening, scaring

اِختِراع [ʔixtiraːʕ] *n:* اِختِراعات [ʔixtiraːʕaːt] *pl:* • **1.** invention

خَرّاع، خُرّاعَة، خَرُّوعَة [xarraːʕ, xurraːʕa, xarruːʕa] *adj:* خَرّاع، خُرّاعَ، خَرُّوعات [xarraːʕ, xurraːʕa, xarruːʕaːt] *pl:* • **1.** frightening, also used as n: to mean: a frightening thing, something to frighten people – هَالكَلِب ما يعَضّ. خالِّيه خَرُّوعَة [haččalib maː yʕaðð. xalliːh xarruːʕa] That dog doesn't bite. He's just put there to scare people. خَرّاع خُضرَة [xarraːʕ xuðra] scarecrow. إنتَ شِنُو هنا، خَرّاع خُضرَة؟ [ʔinta šinuː hna, xarraːʕ xuðra?] What are you here for, a scare crow?

مِختِرِع [mixtiriʕ] *adj:* • **1.** scared – شبِيك مِختِرِع؟ ماكُو شِي [šbiːk mixtiriʕ? maːku ši] Why are you scared? There's nothing wrong.

خ ر ف

اِخرَفّ [ʔixraff] *v:* • **1.** to become senile, feeble minded – دَيِخرَفّ يوم عَن يوم [dayixraff yuːm ʕan yuːm] He's getting more senile every day.

خَرِيف [xariːf] *n:* • **1.** autumn, fall – فَصل الخَرِيف [faṣl ʔilxariːf] the autumn season.

خَرُوف [xaruːf] *n:* خِرفان [xirfaːn] *pl:* • **1.** sheep, and by extension, a stupid person

خُرافَة [xuraːfa] *n:* خُرافات [xuraːfaːt] *pl:* • **1.** fable, fairy tale

مِخرَفّ [mixraff] *adj:* • **1.** senile, feeble minded, and by extension, crazy

خُرافِي [xura:fi] *adj:* • **1.** fictitious, legendary – شَخِص خُرافِي [šaxiṣ xura:fi] legendary character. قُصَّة خُرافيَّة [quṣṣa xura:fiyya] fable.
خَرفان [xarfa:n] *adj:* • **1.** senile, feeble minded • **2.** crazy

خ ر ق

خِرَق [xiraq] *v:* • **1.** to violate, break (the law)
اِختِرَق [ʔixtiraq] *v:* • **1.** to pierce – الرَّصاصَة اِختِرقَت الباب [ʔirraṣa:ṣa ʔixtirqat ʔilba:b] The bullet went through the door. • **2.** to penetrate, pass through – دَبّاباتنا اِختِرقَت خُطُوط العَدُو [dabba:ba:tna ʔixtirqat xuṭu:ṭ ʔilʕadu] Our tanks penetrated the enemy lines.
خَرِق [xariq] *n:* • **1.** penetration, violation
خِرقَة [xirga] *n:* خِرَق [xirag] *pl:* • **1.** rag, scrap of cloth
اِختِراق [ʔixtira:q] *n:* • **1.** penetration, piercing, disruption
خارِق [xa:riq] *adj:* • **1.** unusual, extraordinary

خ ر ك

خُرَّكِي [xurraki] *adj:* خُرَّكِيَّة [xurrakiyya] *pl:* • **1.** coward, panty-waist, creampuff

خ ر م

خَرَّم [xarram] *v:* • **1.** to pierce, make holes in, perforate – أَرِيدَك تخَرُّملِي هَاللَّوحَة [ʔari:dak txarrumli hallawħa] I want you to make holes in this piece of wood for me. • **2.** to embroider – صَدر البلُوز مالها مخَرَّم [ṣadr ʔilblu:z ma:lha mxarram] The front of her blouse is embroidered.
تخَرَّم [txarram] *v:* • **1.** to be pierced
خُرُم [xurum] *n:* خرُوم [xru:m] *pl:* • **1.** needle's eye – خُرم الأُبرَة [xurm ʔilʔubra] needle's eye.
مخَرَّم [mxarram] *adj:* • **1.** perforated • **2.** embroidered

خ ر م ش

خَرمَش [xarmaš] *v:* • **1.** to scratch – دِير بالَك، لا تخَرمُشَك البَزُّونَة [di:r ba:lak, la: txarmušak ʔilbazzu:na] Be careful that the cat doesn't scratch you.
تخَرمَش [txarmaš] *v:* • **1.** to be scratched
خَرمُوش [xarmu:š] *n:* خرامِيش [xra:mi:š] *pl:* • **1.** stalk or bunch of dates
تخِرمُش [txirmuš] *n:* • **1.** scratch

خ ر و ع

خِروِع [xirwiʕ] *n:* • **1.** castor oil plant – دِهِن خِروِع [dihin xirwiʕ] castor oil.

خ ر ي

خِرَى [xira:] *v:* • **1.** to excrete, defecate, go to the toilet – الجّاهِل خِرَى عَالزُّولِيَّة [ʔiǰǰa:hil xira: ʕazzu:liyya] The baby messed on the carpet. لا تخَلِّي إبنَك يخرِي بِالشّارِع [la: txalli ʔibnak yixriy bišša:riʕ] Don't let your son go in the street. الكَلِب خِرَى قِدّام الباب [ʔiččalib xira: gidda:m ʔilba:b] The dog made a mess in front of the door. لا تِتجادَل وِيّاه، يِخرَى مِن حَلقَه [la: tiiǰǰa:dal wiyya:h, yixra: min ħalgah] Don't argue with him; he talks dirty. إجا وَخِرَى بِالوَسطَة [ʔiǰa wxira: bilwaṣṭa] He came and messed up the works. ماكُو زَمبُور يخرَى عَسَل [ma:ku zambu:r yixra: ʕasal] It sounds like baloney to me (lit., there's no wasp which excretes honey).
خَرَّى [xarra:] *v:* • **1.** to allow or cause to defecate – بَوِّلِي وَخَرِّي الجّاهِل قَبُل ما نِطلَع [bawwli wxarri ʔiǰǰa:hil gabul ma: niṭlaʕ] Make the child urinate and defecate before we go out. • **2.** to excrete, defecate, go to the toilet – البَزُّونَة دَاتِخَرِّي بِالحَدِيقَة [ʔilbazzu:na datxarri bilħadi:qa] The cat is messing in the garden.
خَرَة [xara] *n:* • **1.** feces, excrement – خِريان، خَريان [xirya:n, xarya:n] feces, excrement. هَذا أَثقَل مِن خَرَا الحَدّاد [ha:ða ʔaθgal min xara ʔilħadda:d] He's a real bore (lit., he's heavier than the blacksmith's rubbish).
خَرِي [xari] *n:* • **1.** feces, excrement
خَريَة [xarya] *n:* خَريات [xarya:t] *pl:* • **1.** feces, excrement
خَرائِي [xara:ʔi] *adj:* خَرائِيات [xara:ʔiya:t] *pl:* • **1.** fecal
أخرَى [ʔaxra:] *comparative adjective:* • **1.** worse or worst

خ ز ر

خِزَر [xizar] *v:* • **1.** to stare at – بين مُدَّة وَمُدَّة يِخزِر البنَيّات [bi:n mudda wmudda yixzir ʔilbnayya:t] From time to time he stares at the girls. • **2.** to glare at – الأَب خِزَر إبنَه مِن مَدّ إيدَه عَالأَكِل [ʔilʔab xizar ʔibnah min madd ʔi:dah ʕalʔakil] The father glared at his son when he stretched out his hand toward the food.
خَزَر، بَحَر الخَزَر [xazar, baħar ʔilxazar] *n:* • **1.** The Caspian Sea
خَزِر [xazir] *n:* • **1.** stare
خَزرَة [xazra] *n:* خَزرات [xazra:t] *pl:* • **1.** stare • **2.** scathing look

خ ز ف

خَزَف [xazaf] *n:* • **1.** (ancient) glazed pottery, earthenware
خَزَفِي [xazafi] *adj:* • **1.** pottery, earthenware – أَوانِي خَزَفِيَّة [ʔawa:ni xazafiyya] earthenware dishes.

خ ز ق

خَوزَق [xawzaq] *v:* • **1.** to stick, cheat, take in – لا تِشتِرِي مِنَّه تَرَة يخَوزِقَك [la: tištiri minnah tara yxawziqak] Don't buy from him or he'll stick you.
تخَوزَق [txawzaq] *v:* • **1.** to get stuck, to be taken in – آنِي تخَوزَقِت بهالشَّروَة [ʔa:ni txawzaqit bhaššarwa] I got stuck on this deal.
خازُوق [xa:zu:q] *n:* خَوازِيق [xawa:zi:q] *pl:* • **1.** (originally post or stake, now in expressions, approx:) shaft – أَكَل الخازُوق [ʔakal ʔilxa:zu:q] He got the shaft, he got taken. • **2.** pole, pipe

خ ز ل

اِختِزال [ʔixtizaːl] *n:* • **1.** shorthand, stenography

خ ز م

خِزّامَة [xizzaːma] *n:* خِزّامات [xizzaːmaːt] *pl:* • **1.** nose ring (for bulls, male camels or women) – طَوب أَبُو خِزّامَة [ṭuːb ʔabu xizzaːma] an old-fashioned type of cannon (with a ring on it for hitching to a horse)

خ ز ن

خِزَن [xizan] *v:* • **1.** to store – الحُكُومَة خِزنَت التِّتِن بِالشِّمال [ʔilħukuːma xiznat ʔittitin biššimaːl] The government stored the tobacco in the north.

خَزَّن [xazzan] *v:* • **1.** to become infected – الجَّرِح خَزَّن [ʔijǰariħ xazzan] The wound became infected.

خَزِن [xazin] *n:* • **1.** storing

خَزنَة [xazna] *n:* خَزنات [xaznaːt] *pl:* • **1.** treasure

خَزّان [xazzaːn] *n:* خَزّانات [xazzaːnaːt] *pl:* • **1.** reservoir

مَخزَن [maxzan] *n:* مَخازِن [maxaːzin] *pl:* • **1.** storeroom, storehouse • **2.** stockroom, supply room • **3.** store, shop

خَزِين [xaziːn] *n:* • **1.** stock, supply, inventory

خزانَة [xzaːna] *n:* خزانات، خزايِن [xzaːnaːt, xzaːyin] *pl:* • **1.** The hot water reservoir in a public bath house

خَزِينَة [xaziːna] *n:* خَزِينات [xaziːnaːt] *pl:* • **1.** treasury, public treasury

خازِن [xaːzin] *n:* • **1.** a storer, treasurer

مخَزَّن [mxazzan] *adj:* • **1.** stored

مَخزُون [maxzuːn] *adj:* • **1.** stored

خ ز ي

خَزَّى [xazzaː] *v:* • **1.** to disgrace, put to shame – خَزَّيتنا بِبُخلَك [xazzaytna bibuxlak] You've shamed us with your stinginess. راح أَرُوحلَه وَأَخَزِّيه عَالطَّلَب مالِي [raːħ ʔaruːħ lah wʔaxazziːh ʕaṭṭalab maːli] I'm going to him and take him to task about my money.

تخَزَّى [txazzaː] *v:* • **1.** to be disgraced, to be put to shame – إذا ما ندفَع الطَّلَب، تَرَة نِتخَزَّى [ʔiða maː nidfaʕ ʔiṭṭalab, tara nitxazzaː] If we don't pay the debt, we'll be disgraced.

اِختِزَى [ʔixtizaː] *v:* • **1.** to be ashamed – ما تِختِزِي عاد! مُو عِيب؟ [maː tixtizi ʕaːd! muː ʕiːb?] Aren't you ashamed of yourself? Isn't that something to be ashamed of?

خِزِي [xizi] *n:* • **1.** shame, disgrace

مُخزِي [muxzi] *adj:* • **1.** shameful, disgraceful

أَخزَى [ʔaxzaː] *comparative adjective:* • **1.** more or most disgraceful

خ س ء

خَسَى، تخَسَى [xasaː, txasaː] *n:* • **1.** (invar.) approx., aw, go on! come off it – تخَسَى! عاد وَالله اللِّي يُضرُبنِي أَمَوِّتَه [txasaː! ʕaːd wallah ʔilli yuðrubni ʔamawwtah] Baloney! Boy, anyone hits me, I'll kill him. تخَسَى، آنِي ما أَخاف مِن أَحَّد [txasaː, ʔaːni maː ʔaxaːf min ʔaħħad] Not me. I'm not afraid of anyone. فِرقَتنا راح تُغلُب فِرقَتكُم. تخَسَى [firqatna raːħ tuɣlub firqatkum. txasaː] Our team is going to beat your team. How could that be?

خ س ت خ ن

خَستَخانَة [xastaxaːna] *n:* خَستَخايِن، خَستَخانات [xastaxaːyin, xastaxaːnaːt] *pl:* • **1.** hospital

خ س ر

خِسَر [xisar] *v:* • **1.** to lose – خِسَرت دِينار بِالقُمار [xisarit dinaːr bilqumaːr] I lost a dinar gambling. خِسَر الدَّعوَة لَكِن راح يِستَأنِف [xiṣar ʔiddaʕwa laːkin raːħ yistaʔnif] He lost the case but he is going to appeal. دائِرتَه خِسرَتَه. ما يلقُون أَحسَن مِنَّه [daːʔirtah xisratah. maː yilguːn ʔaħsan minnah] His office lost him. They can't find anyone better than he was. فِرقَتنا خِسرَت اليُوم [firqatna xisrat ʔilyuːm] Our team lost today.

خَسَّر [xassar] *v:* • **1.** to make lose – لا تصِير شَرِيكَه، تَرَة يخَسّرَك كُلّ فلُوسَك [laː tṣiːr šariːkah, tara yxassrak kull fluːsak] Don't become his partner, or he'll make you lose all your money. عَلِي ما لِعَب زين، هُوَّ اللِّي خَسّرنا [ʕali maː liʕab ziːn, huwwa ʔilli xassarna] Ali didn't play well. He caused us to lose.

خَسارَة [xasaːra] *n:* خَسارات، خَسايِر [xasaːraː t, xasaːyir] *pl:* • **1.** loss, losses • **2.** waste, loss – يِرُوح عُمرَك خَسارَة [yiruːħ ʕumrak xasaːra] Your life will go to waste. • **3.** defeat, loss

خاسِر [xaːsir] *adj:* • **1.** loser

خَسران [xasraːn] *adj:* • **1.** loser

خ س س

خَسّ [xass] *n:* • **1.** lettuce – راس خَسّ [raːs xass] a head of lettuce.

خِسَّة [xissa] *n:* • **1.** meanness, baseness

خَسِيس [xasiːs] *adj:* • **1.** stingy, cheap, mean – رِجّال خَسِيس [rijǰaːl xasiːs] a stingy man.

خ س ف

خِسَف [xisaf] *v:* • **1.** to give way, cave in – السَّقُف خِسَف بِيهُم وَماتَوا [ʔissaguf xisaf biːhum wmaːtaw] The roof caved in under them and they died. كانَوا قاعدِين بِالقَهوَة وأَشُو فَدّ مَرَّة خِسفَت القاع بِيهُم [čaːnaw gaːʕdiːn bilgahwa wʔašuː fadd marra xisfat ʔilgaːʕ biːhum] They were sitting in the café and all of a sudden the floor sank under them. • **2.** to be eclipsed (moon only) – راح يِخسِف القُمَر باكِر [raːħ yixsif ʔilgumar baːčir] The moon will be eclipsed tomorrow.

خَسَّف [xassaf] *v:* • **1.** to dent, make dents in – الجّاهِل دَقدَق بِماعُون الفافَون وَخَسَّفَه [ʔijǰaːhil dagdag

خ

bma:ʕu:n ʔilfa:fu:n wxassafah] The child beat on the aluminum dish and made dents in it.
اِنخِسَف [ʔinxisaf] *v:* • **1.** to be dented or curved, to be sunk down • **2.** to be sinked down
خَسِف [xasif] *n:* • **1.** dent, curve
خَسفَة [xasfa] *n:* خَسفات [xasfa:t] *pl:* • **1.** dent • **2.** dimple
خُسُوف [xusu:f, xisu:f] *n:* • **1.** lunar eclipse
اِنخِساف [ʔinxisa:f] *n:* • **1.** occultation, eclipse

خ ش ب

خَشَّب [xaššab] *v:* • **1.** to become like wood, to stiffen, to become rigid – وُقَع عَلَى وُچَّه وَخَشَّب مِثِل المَيِّت [wugaʕ ʕala wuččah wxaššab miθl ʔilmayyit] He fell on his face and became rigid like a dead person. صَدرَه خَشَّب مِن هَالنَّشلَة القَوِيَّة [ṣadrah xaššab min hannašla ʔilqawiyya] His chest dried out and became painful from this strong cold.
خِشَب [xišab] *n:* • **1.** wood, lumber, timber – صَندُوق خِشَب [ṣandu:g xišab] a wooden box. خِشَب معاكَس [xišab mʕa:kas] plywood. خِشَب جام [xišab ča:m] crate wood. خِشَب جاوِي [xišab ǰa:wi] ironwood (lit. Java wood). خِشَب جُوز [xišab ǰu:z] walnut.
خِشبَة [xišba] *n:* خِشبات، خِشَب [xišba:t, xišab] *pl:* • **1.** piece of wood
خَشّاب [xašša:b] *n:* خَشّابَة [xašša:ba] *pl:* • **2.** a man who drums at Iraqi parties
خَشَبِي [xašabi] *adj:* • **1.** wooden – صَندُوق خَشَبِي [ṣandu:g xašabi] a wooden box.

خ ش خ ش

خَشخَش [xašxaš] *v:* • **1.** to rattle, to jingle – لازِم أَكُو شِي بِيه؛ مِن تخُضَّه يخَشخِش [la:zim ʔaku ši bi:h; min txuḍḍah yxašxiš] There must be something in it; when you shake it, it rattles. دَيخَشخِش الفلُوس بجِيبَه [dayxašxiš ʔilflu:s bǰi:bah] He's jingling the money in his pocket.
تخَشخَش [txašxaš] *v:* • **1.** to get around, socialize – يُعرُف كُلّ الوُزَراء لِأَنَّه يِتخَشخَش هوايَة [yuʕruf kull ʔilwuzara:ʔ liʔannah yitxašxaš hwa:ya] He knows all the ministers because he gets around a lot.
خَشخَشَة [xašxaša] *n:* خَشخَشات [xašxaša:t] *pl:* • **1.** (coll.) poppy, poppies
خِشخاشَة [xišxa:ša] *n:* خِشخاشات [xišxa:ša:t] *pl:* • **2.** rattle (toy)

خ ش ش

خَشّ [xašš] *v:* • **1.** to enter – آنِي ما أَخُشّ بِبَيتهُم أَبَداً [ʔa:ni ma: ʔaxušš bibaythum ʔabadan] I have never entered their house. هَالكِتاب كِبِير؛ ما يخُشّ بجِيبِي [halkita:b čibi:r; ma: yxušš bǰi:bi] This book is too big; it won't go into my pocket. شَوكَة خَشَّت بِيدِي [šawka xaššat bi:di] A thorn pricked my hand. خُشّ عالمُدِير وَقُولَّه [xušš ʕalmudi:r wgu:llah] Go on in to the director and tell him. مِن خَشّ لِلبَيت نِزَع سِترتَه [min xašš lilbayt nizaʕ sitirtah] When he entered the house he took off his jacket. هاي ما دَتخُشّ بعَقلِي [ha:y ma: datxušš bʕaqli] I can't believe that (lit., this cannot enter my mind). خَشّ بالخَمسِين [xašš bilxamsi:n] He just turned fifty. خَشّ ويّاها مَرّتَين [xašš wiyya:ha marrtayn] He slept with her twice. • **2.** to shrink – هَالقماش يخُشّ بالغَسِل [halqma:š yxušš bilɣasil] This material shrinks with washing.
خَشّش [xaššaš] *v:* • **1.** to put in, insert – خَشِّش الغَراض جَوَّة [xaššiš ʔilɣara:ḍ ǰawwa] Take the things inside. تِقدَر تخَشِّش إيدَك بالتُّنقَة؟ [tigdar txaššiš ʔi:dak bittunga?] Can you stick your hand in the jar? • **2.** to let in, get in – خَشَّشنِي بالحَفلَة بِلا بِطاقَة [xaššašni bilħafla bila biṭa:qa] He got me into the party without a ticket. كُلّما أَرُوح لهَالسِّينَما يخَشّشنِي بَلاش [kullma: ʔaru:ħ lhassinama yxaššišni bala:š] Everytime I go to this movie theater he lets me in for nothing.
خَشّ [xašš] *n:* • **1.** entrance
خَشَّة [xašša] *n:* خَشّات [xašša:t] *pl:* • **1.** entry, entrance • **2.** instance of fornication
خُشَّة [xušša] *n:* خُشّات [xušša:t] *pl:* • **1.** fat, pug nose

خ ش ع

خِشَع [xišaʕ] *v:* • **1.** to humble oneself – يصَلِّي وَيخشَع لرَبَّه [yṣalli wyixšaʕ ʔirrabbah] He prays and humbles himself to God. • **2.** to make someone feel humble – صَوتَه يخَشّع مِن يِقرا القُرآن [ṣu:tah yxaššiʕ min yiqra: ʔilqurʔa:n] His voice makes one feel humble when he reads the Koran.
خُشُوع [xušu:ʕ] *n:* • **1.** humbleness, humility

خ ش ف 1

خِشِف [xišif] *n:* خشُوف [xšu:f] *pl:* • **1.** fawn (of a gazelle).

خ ش ف 2

خِشّاف [xišša:f] *n:* • **1.** coll. bats (zool.)
خِشّافَة [xišša:fa] *n:* خِشّافات [xišša:fa:t] *pl:* • **2.** bat (zool.)

خ ش ل

خَشِل [xašil] *n:* • **1.** jewelry.
مُخَشَّلات [muxaššala:t] *n:* • **1.** (pl.) jewelry, valuables

خ ش م

خَشِم [xašim] *n:* خشُوم [xšu:m] *pl:* • **1.** nose – شايِل خَشمَه عَلينا [ša:yil xašmah ʕali:na] He stuck up his nose at us. المُدِير الجِّدِيد كِسَر خَشمَه، رَجَّعَه كاتِب [ʔilmudi:r ʔiǰǰidi:d kisar xašmah, raǰǰaʕah ka:tib] The new director put him in his place, and demoted him back to clerk. طِلعَت السَّفرَة مِن خَشمَه [ṭilʕat ʔissafra min xašmah] The trip turned out to be a pain. أَكسِر خَشمَه وَآخُذ فلُوسِي مِنَّه [ʔaksir xašmah wʔa:xuð flu:si minnah] I'll force him to give me my money. • **2.** breast (of lamb, a cut of meat).

خشيم، أبو خشيم [xšiːm, ʔabuː xšiːm] *n:* • **1.** variety of pigeons with a large protuberance above the beak • **2.** man with a large nose

خ ش ن

خُشُونَة [xušuːna] *n:* • **1.** coarseness, crudeness • **2.** rudeness • **3.** with ب - means coarsely, rudely • **4.** toughness

خَشِن [xašin] *adj:* • **1.** coarse, rough – قماش خَشِن [qmaːš xašin] coarse cloth. جِلِد خَشِن [jilid xašin] rough skin. • **2.** rough, crude, uncouth, rude – وَلَد خَشِن [walad xašin] an uncouth boy. أخلاق خَشنَة [ʔaxlaːq xašna] crude manners. • **3.** rough, hoarse, low-pitched – صُوت خَشِن [ṣuːt xašin] low voice, low note. • **4.** large, coarse – مِشمِش خَشِن [mišmiš xašin] large apricots. الجِّنس الخَشِن [ʔiǰǰins ʔilxašin] men, the stronger sex.

أخشَن [ʔaxšan] *comparative adjective:* • **1.** coarser • **2.** cruder, more uncouth • **3.** rougher, deeper, hoarser • **4.** larger

خ ش ي

خِشَى [xišaː] *v:* • **1.** to fear, dread – إذا تِخشَى رَبَّك، ما تبُوق [ʔiða tixšaː rabbak, maː tbuːg] If you fear your God, you won't steal.

اِختِشَى [ʔixtišaː] *v:* • **1.** to feel afraid, to be afraid – لا يِستِحِي وَلا يِختِشِي [laː yistiħi wlaː yixtiši] He feels no shame at all. اِختِشِي! شلُون تِحكِي هِيكِي قِدّام أبُوك؟ [ʔixtiši! šluːn tiħči hiːči giddaːm ʔabuːk?] For shame! How can you talk like that in front of your father?

خَشِي [xaši] *n:* • **1.** fear

خِشيَة [xišya] *n:* • **1.** fear

خ ص ب

خِصَب [xiṣab] *v:* • **1.** to make fertile, to fructify, fertilize

خَصَّب [xaṣṣab] *v:* • **1.** to make (something) fertile, fertilize

تخَصَّب [txaṣṣab] *v:* • **1.** to become fertile

خُصُوب [xuṣuːb] *n:* • **1.** fertility

مُخَصِّب [muxaṣṣib] *n:* • **1.** fertilizer

إخصاب [ʔixṣaːb] *n:* • **1.** fertility, fertilization

خُصُوبَة [xuṣuːba] *n:* • **1.** fertility

تَخصِيب [taxṣiyb] *n:* • **1.** fructification, fertilization

خَصِب [xaṣib] *adj:* • **1.** fertile – أَراضِي خَصبَة [ʔaraːḍ̣i xaṣba] fertile land.

خَصِيب [xaṣiːb] *adj:* • **1.** fertile – الهِلال الخَصِيب [ʔilhilaːl ʔilxaṣiːb] The Fertile Crescent.

أخصَب [ʔaxṣab] *comparative adjective:* • **1.** more fertile

خ ص ر

تخَصَّر [txaṣṣar] *v:* • **1.** to put one's hands on hips – تخَصَّر ووُقَف قِدّامِي [txaṣṣar wwugaf giddaːmi] He put his hands on his hips and stood in front of me.

اِختِصَر [ʔixtiṣar] *v:* • **1.** to condense, shorten – إذا ما تِختِصِر المَقال مالَك، ما نِقدَر نِنشِرَه [ʔiða maː tixtiṣir ʔilmaqaːl maːlak, maː nigdar ninišrah] If you don't condense your article, we can't publish it. • **2.** to summarize – اِختِصِر مَقال الوَزِير بصَفحَة وِحدَة [ʔixtiṣir maqaːl ʔilwaziːr bṣafħa wiħda] Summarize the minister's article in one page.

خِصِر [xiṣir] *n:* خُصُور [xuṣuːr] *pl:* • **1.** waist

مُختَصَر [muxtaṣar] *adj:* • **1.** brief, short – مَكتُوب مُختَصَر [maktuːb muxtaṣar] a short letter. زِيارَة مُختَصَرَة [ziyaːra muxtaṣara] a brief visit. حَفلَة مُختَصَرَة [ħafla muxtaṣara] small, informal party or get-together. مُختَصَر مُفِيد [muxtaṣar mufiːd] in short, in brief, to make a long story short.

خاصرَة [xaːṣra] *n:* خَواصِر [xawaːṣir] *pl:* • **1.** side (between the hip bone and false rib) • **2.** loin – لَحَم خاصرَة [laħam xaːṣra] loin meat.

اِختِصار [ʔixtiṣaːr] *n:* • **1.** shortening, condensation, summarization

خ ص ص

خَصّ [xaṣṣ] *v:* • **1.** to concern, pertain to – هَالشّي ما يخُصّنِي [hašši maː yxuṣṣni] That doesn't concern me. آنِي ما يخُصّنِي. إسأَل غَيرِي [ʔaːni maː yxuṣṣni. ʔisʔal ɣayri] That's not my business. Ask someone else. • **2.** to be related to – عَلِي يخُصّنِي [ʕali yxuṣṣni] Ali is related to me. شيخُصَّك هَذا؟ [šyxuṣṣak haːða?] How's he related to you? • **3.** to single out, bestow upon – صَدِيقَك عَلِي يخُصَّك بِالسَّلام [ṣadiːqak ʕali yxuṣṣak bissalaːm] Your friend Ali sends his greetings to you.

خَصَّص [xaṣṣaṣ] *v:* • **1.** to designate, set aside – خَصَّصِت ساعَة مِن وَقتِي كُلّ يوم لِلفرَنسِي [xaṣṣaṣit saːʕa min wakti kull yuːm lilfransi] I have set aside one hour of my time every day to study French. • **2.** to assign, reserve – خَصَّصنا هاي الغُرفَة لِلنِّسوان [xaṣṣaṣna haːy ʔilɣurfa linniswaːn] We've reserved this room for women. هَالغُرفَة مُخَصَّصَة لِلإجتِماعات [halɣurfa muxaṣṣaṣa lilʔiǰtimaːʕaːt] This room is reserved for meetings. • **3.** to allocate, allot, appropriate – الحُكُومَة خَصَّصَت مِليَون دِينار لِلجِّسِر الجِّدِيد [ʔilħukuːma xaṣṣiṣat milyuːn dinaːr liǰǰisir ʔiǰǰidiːd] The government appropriated a million dinars for the new bridge.

تخَصَّص [txaṣṣaṣ] *v:* • **1.** to specialize, become a specialist – تخَصَّص بِالأمراض الجِّلدِيَّة [txaṣṣaṣ bilʔamraːḍ̣ ʔiǰǰildiyya] He specialized in skin diseases.

اِختَصّ [ʔixtaṣṣ] *v:* • **1.** to specialize, become a specialist – اِختَصّ بِالقانُون الجِّنائِي [ʔixtaṣṣ bilqaːnuːn ʔiǰǰinaːʔi] He specialized in criminal law.

خَصّ [xaṣṣ] *n:* • **1.** specification

خُصُوص [xuṣuːṣ] *n:* • **1.** with مِن and ب in regard to, concerning • **2.** with عَلَى especially • **3.** in this respect

تَخَصُّص [taxaṣṣuṣ] *n:* • **1.** specialization

خ

خاصَّة [xaːṣṣa] *n:* خَواصّ، خاصِّيَّة [xawaːṣṣ, xaːṣṣiyya] *pl:* • **1.** property, characteristic, attribute

تَخصِيص [taxṣiːṣ] *n:* تَخصِيصات [taxṣiːṣaːt] *pl:* • **1.** allocation

خاصِّيَة [xaːṣṣiyya] *n:* خَصائِص [xaṣaːʔiṣ] *pl:* • **1.** characteristic

اِختِصاص [ʔixtiṣaːṣ] *n:* • **1.** jurisdiction, bailiwick • **2.** specialty, field, area of competence

مُخَصَّصات [muxaṣṣaṣaːt] *n:* • **1.** allocation, appropriation • **2.** allowances – راتِب وَمُخَصَّصات [raːtib wmuxaṣṣaṣaːt] salary and allowances.

خُصُوصِيَة [xuṣuːṣiyya] *n:* • **1.** privacy

أَخَصّ [ʔaxaṣṣ] *adj:* • **1.** in the phrases: عَلأَخَصّ, عَلَى الأَخَصّ, بِالأَخَصّ especially • **2.** more important

خاصّ [xaːṣṣ] *adj:* • **1.** special – حِسَبلِي إِيّاها بِسِعِر خاصّ [ħisabliː ʔiyyaːha bsiʕir xaːṣṣ] He gave it to me at a special price. ظُرُوف خاصَّة [ðuruːf xaːṣṣa] special circumstances. بِصُورَة خاصَّة [bṣuːra xaːṣṣa] especially, particularly. • **2.** reserved, limited, restricted – هَالقاعَة خاصَّة لِلأَعضاء [halqaːʕa xaːṣṣa lilʔaʕðaːʔ] This hall is reserved for members. باص خاصّ لِلطُّلّاب [paːṣ xaːṣṣ liṭṭullaːb] a bus reserved for students. • **3.** personal – حَرَس خاصّ [ħaras xaːṣṣ] personal guard. طَبِيب خاصّ [ṭabiːb xaːṣṣ] personal physician. • **4.** set aside, designated – دُكتُور خاصّ لِلمُوَظَّفِين [duktuːr xaːṣṣ lilmwaððafiːn] a doctor especially for the employees. مَبلَغ خاصّ لِلفُقَراء [mablaɣ xaːṣṣ lilfuqaraːʔ] an amount earmarked for the poor. • **5.** private – قَضِيَّة خاصَّة [qaðiyya xaːṣṣa] a private matter.

خاصَّة [xaːṣṣa] *n:* • **1.** (invar.) relatives

مخَصَّص [mxaṣṣaṣ] *adj:* • **1.** specified, dedicated

مِختَصّ [mixtaṣṣ] *adj:* • **1.** specialized, professional

خُصُوصِي [xuṣuːṣi] *adj:* • **1.** special – باسبُورت خُصُوصِي [paːspuːrt xuṣuːṣi] special passport. • **2.** personal, private – مَكاتِيب خُصُوصِيَّة [makaːtiːb xuṣuːṣiyya] personal letters. سَيّارَة خُصُوصِيَة [sayyaːra xuṣuːṣiya] private car.

مَخصُوص [maxṣuːṣ] *adj:* • **1.** special, particular, specific – رِحِتلَه مَخصُوص لِهَالقَضِيَّة [riħit lah maxṣuːṣ lihalqaðiyya] I went to see him specifically about that matter.

مِتخَصِّص [mitxaṣṣiṣ] *adj:* • **1.** specialized

أَخِصّائِي [ʔaxiṣṣaːʔi] *n:* • **1.** specialist

اِختِصاصِي [ʔixtiṣaːṣi] *n:* • **1.** specialist

خاصَّةً [xaːṣṣatan] *adverbial:* • **1.** especially, particularly

خُصُوصاً [xuṣuːṣan] *adverbial:* • **1.** especially – أَحِبّ الفاكِهَة، خُصُوصاً العِنَب [ʔaħibb ʔilfaːkiha, xuṣuːṣan ʔilʕinab] I like fruit, especially grapes.

خ ص ف

خِصّاف [xiṣṣaːf] *n:* • **1.** (coll.) a basket-like container for dates, woven of palm leaves

خِصّافَة [xiṣṣaːfa] *n:* خِصّافات [xiṣṣaːfaːt] *pl:* • **1.** a basket-like container for dates woven with palm leaves

خ ص ل

خِصلَة [xiṣla] *n:* خِصلات، خِصال، خُصَل، خِصَل [xiṣlaːt, xiṣaːl, xuṣal, xiṣal] *pl:* • **1.** good quality, good characteristic • **2.** character, good character • **3.** lock of hair

خ ص م

خِصَم [xiṣam] *v:* • **1.** to deduct, subtract – إِذا أَشتِرِي مِيَّة وِحدَة، يُخصُملِي كَم فِلِس مِن السِّعِر [ʔiða ʔaštiri miyyat wiħda, yuxṣumli čam filis min ʔissiʕir] If I buy a hundred, he deducts a few fils from the price. • **2.** to finish, be complete – قَضِيَّة نَقلِي خُصمَت [qaðiyyat naqli xuṣmat] the matter of my transfer was completed. صارلِي ساعَة واقُف. ما تُخصُمها عاد [ṣaːrli saːʕa waːguf. maː tuxṣumha ʕaːd] I've been standing here for an hour. Come on and finish with it. اِنطِيه عَشِر دَنانِير وَأُخصُمها وِيّاه [ʔinṭiːh ʕašir danaːniːr wʔuxṣumha wiyyaːh] Give him ten dinars and be done with him. أَقدَر أَخصُمها وِيّاه بخَمسَة وَثلاثِين دِينار [ʔagdar ʔaxṣumha wiyyaːh bxamsa wtlaːθiːn dinaːr] I can settle it with him for thirty-five dinars. إِذا ذُولَة تعَيّنَوا وُزَراء، لَعَد خُصمَت القَضِيَّة [ʔiða ðuːla tʕayynaw wuzaraːʔ, laʕad xuṣmat ʔilqaðiyya] If those guys have been appointed ministers, then it's all over. لا خُصمَت [laː xuṣmat] how could that be? it's not possible! شلُون خَلَّصِت شُغُل مال شَهَر بنُصّ ساعَة؟ لا خُصمَت! لَعَد قُول "سَوِّيتَه شَلّالِي" [šluːn xallaṣit šuɣul maːl šahar bnuṣṣ saːʕa? laː xuṣmat! laʕad guːl "sawwiːtah šallaːli"] How'd you finish a month's work in a half hour? It's impossible! Then say 'I did a sloppy job'! لا خُصمَت، هَذا يصِير مُدِير [laː xuṣmat, haːða yṣiːr mudiːr] I don't see how he can be a supervisor.

تخاصَم [txaːṣam] *v:* • **1.** to quarrel

خَصُم [xaṣum] *n:* خُصُوم [xuṣuːm] *pl:* • **1.** (sg or pl) opponent, opposing team • **2.** discount (sg only) – سِعِر الخَصُم [siʕir ʔilxaṣum] discount price.

خِصام [xiṣaːm] *n:* • **1.** quarrel

خُصُومَة [xuṣuːma] *n:* • **1.** discount, quarrel

تَخاصُم [taxaːṣum] *n:* • **1.** quarrel

مِتخاصُم [mitxaːṣum] *adj:* • **1.** belligerent

خ ص ي

خِصَى [xiṣaː] *v:* • **1.** to castrate, emasculate – إِذا تِخصِي الدِّيك، يِسمَن [ʔiða tixṣi ʔiddiːč, yisman] If you castrate a rooster, it becomes fat. إِذا يِجِي المُدِير الجِّدِيد، يِخصِيهُم كُلّهُم [ʔiða yiji ʔilmudiːr ʔijjidiːd, yixṣiːhum kullhum] If the new director comes, they'll be done for.

خَصَّى [xaṣṣaː] *v:* • **1.** to castrate, emasculate

خَصِي [xaṣy] *n:* • **1.** castration

خُصوَة [xuṣwa] *n:* خَصاوِي، خِصيان [xaṣaːwi, xiṣyaːn] *pl:* • **1.** testicle, testis

خِصِي [xiṣi] *adj:* خَصايَة [xaṣaːya] *pl:* • **1.** timid, coward, funky

مَخصِي [maxṣi] *adj:* مخاصِي [mxaːṣi] *pl:* • **1.** castrated male, eunuch, gelding, capon

خ ض خ ض

خَضخَض [xaðxað] *v:* • **1.** to shake – لا تخُضخِض البطالة [laː txaðxið ʔilbṭaːla] Don't shake the bottles.
مخَضخَض [mxaðxað] *adj:* • **1.** shaken

خ ض ر

خَضّر [xaððar] *v:* • **1.** to turn green – هَل قَدّ ما مُطرَت، القاع كُلّها خَضرَت [hal gadd maː muṭrat, ʔilgaːʕ kullha xaððrat] Because it rained so much, the whole land became green. • **2.** to sprout, send up shoots – البَزر اللّي زِرَعتَه كُلّه ما خَضّر [ʔilbazr ʔilli ziraʕtah kullah maː xaððar] None of the seeds I planted came up. • **3.** to bud, leaf – الشَّجَرَة اللّي بحَدِيقتِي خضّرَت [ʔiššajara ʔilli bħadiːqti xaððirat] The tree in my garden leafed. • **4.** to become infected – الحَبّايَة اللّي بِيدِي خَضّرَت [ʔilħabbaːya ʔilli biːdi xaððirat] The sore on my hand got infected.
اِخضَرّ [ʔixðarr] *v:* • **1.** to turn green – الماي بِالحوض اِخضَرّ [ʔilmaːy bilħuːð ʔixðarr] The water in the pool turned green. القِيعان راح تِخضَرّ مِن هَالمُطَر [ʔilgiːʕaːn raːħ tixðarr min halmuṭar] The landscape will turn green from this rain.
خُضرَة [xuðra] *n:* • **1.** greens, salad greens • **2.** خُضَر [xuðar] *pl*: vegetable garden • **3.** vegetables خُضرَوات [xuðrawaːt] *pl.*
خَضار [xaðaːr] *n:* • **1.** green, green color • **2.** vegetation, herbage, greenery
مخَضّر [mxaððar] *n:* مخضّرات، مخَاضِير [mxaððaraːt, mxaðiːr] *pl:* • **1.** vegetable(s)
الخِضِر [ʔilxiðir] *n:* • **1.** a legendary invisible religious man
خضِيري [xðiːri] *n:* خضَيريَّة [xðiːriyya] *pl:* • **1.** (coll.) a kind of wild duck, resembling the mallard
خِضّيري، أَبُو الخِضّير [xiððiːri, ʔabu ʔilxiððiːr] *n:* • **1.** a kind of wild green bird
خَضراوي [xaðraːwi] *n:* • **1.** A common variety of dates
مخَضّرجِي [mxaððarči] *n:* مخضّرجيَّة [mxaððarčiyya] *pl:* • **1.** vegetable merchant, greengrocer
أَخضَر [ʔaxðar] *adj:* خُضُر [xuður] *pl:* خَضرَة [xaðra] *feminine:* • **1.** green – عيُونها خُضُر [ʕyuːnha xuður] Her eyes are green.
مخَضّر [mxaððir] *adj:* • **1.** greenish, virescent
مخُوضِر [mxuːðir] *adj:* • **1.** greenish; green

خ ض ض

خَضّ [xaðð] *v:* • **1.** to shake – خُضّ البُوطِل قَبُل ما تِشرَب الدُّوا [xuðð ʔilbuːṭil gabul maː tišrab ʔidduwa] Shake the bottle before you take the medicine. خُضّ الماعُون بِشوَيَّة مَيّ [xuðð ʔilmaːʕuːn bšwayyat mayy] Rinse the plate in some water. • **2.** to threaten, shake up – راح أَخُضّلَك إيّاه خَضّة زينَة وأَخَوّفَه بِيها [raːħ ʔaxuððlak ʔiyyaːh xaðða ziːna wʔaxawwfah biːha] I will shake him up good for you and make him worry about it.
اِنخَضّ [ʔinxaðð] *v:* • **1.** to be shaken • **2.** to be afraid
خَضّ [xaðð] *n:* • **1.** shaking
خَضَّة [xaðða] *n:* • **1.** rinse • **2.** fear
خضاضَة [xðaːða] *n:* • **1.** rinse water • **2.** (by extension) a worthless person • **3.** buttermilk
مَخضُوض [maxðuːð] *adj:* • **1.** shaken • **2.** afraid

خ ض ع

خِضَع [xiðaʕ] *v:* • **1.** to bow, defer, yield, submit – العَشايِر كُلّها خِضعَت لِلحُكُومَة [ʔilʕašaːyir kullha xiðʕat lilħukuːma] All the tribes yielded to the government. هِيَّ ما تِخضَع لِرَّجِلها [hiyya maː tixðaʕ ʔirrajilha] She doesn't obey her husband.
خَضّع [xaððaʕ] *v:* • **1.** to subdue, subjugate – الحُكُومَة خَضّعَت القَبائِل بالقُوَّة [ʔilħukuːma xaððiʕat ʔilqabaːʔil bilquwwa] The government subdued the tribes by force.
أَخضَع [ʔaxðaʕ] *v:* • **1.** to subdue, subjugate
تخَضّع [txaððaʕ] *v:* • **1.** to abase oneself, grovel – مِن فِصلوه، راح يِتخَضّع لِلوَزِير [min fiṣlawh, raːħ yitxaððaʕ lilwaziːr] When they fired him, he went to grovel at the minister's feet.
خُضُوع [xuðuːʕ] *n:* • **1.** submission

خ ط ء

خِطَأ [xiṭaʔ] *v:* • **1.** to make a mistake – خِطَئ بِالحِساب [xiṭaʔ biliħsaːb] He made a mistake in arithmetic.
خِطَى [xiṭaː] *v:* • **1.** to miss – ضِرَبِت ثلَث رصاصات وَخِطِيتَه [ðirabit tlaθ rṣaːṣaːt wxiṭiːtah] I fired three shots, but I missed him.
خَطّأ [xaṭṭaʔ] *v:* • **1.** to cause to make a mistake – بَسّ تِحكِي، تخَطّأني [bass tiħči, txaṭṭiʔni] The minute you speak, you cause me to make a mistake.
اِستَخطَى [ʔistaxṭaː] *v:* • **1.** to deem sinful, consider sinful – أَستَخطِي أَصرُف فلُوس اليَتِيم [ʔastaxṭi ʔaṣruf fluːs ʔilyatiːm] I feel it's a sin to spend the orphan's money.
خَطَأ [xaṭaʔ] *n:* أَخطاء [ʔaxṭaːʔ] *pl:* • **1.** mistake
خَطأة [xaṭʔa] *n:* خَطآت [xaṭʔaːt] *pl:* • **1.** mistake
خَطِيئَة [xaṭiːʔa] *n:* • **1.** sin, crime, fault
خَطِيَّة [xaṭiyya] *adj:* • **1.** (in certain expressions:) – لا تشِيل خَطِيَّتها. إنت ما متأَكِّد [laː tšiːl xaṭiyyatha. ʔinta maː mitʔakkid] Don't accuse her wrongly. You're not really sure. لا تشِيل خَطِيتَه لِلرَّجّال. يجُوز مُو صُوجَه [laː tšiːl xaṭiːtah lirrajjaːl. yjuːz muː ṣuːčah] Don't accuse the man. Maybe it wasn't his fault. • **2.** (invar.) poor unfortunate, poor wretch – جُوز مِنّه، خَطِيَّة [juːz minnah, xaṭiyya] Let the poor guy alone.
مُخطِئ [muxṭiʔ] *adj:* • **1.** mistaken, wrong, at fault
خاطِئ [xaːṭiʔ] *adj:* • **1.** mistaken

خ ط ب

خِطَب [xiṭab] *v:* • **1.** to speak, give an address – الوَزِير خِطَب بِالتَّلامِيذ [ʔilwazi:r xiṭab bittala:mi:ð] The minister addressed the students. • **2.** to propose to, get engaged to – خِطَبلَه بنَيَّة حِلوَة [xiṭablah bnayya ħilwa] He got engaged to a pretty girl. خِطَبِت بِنِت جارنَا وَراح نِتزَوَّج شَهَر اللَّاخ [xiṭabit binit ǰa:rna wra:ħ nidzawwaǰ šahar ʔilla:x] I became engaged to the neighbor's daughter and we will be married next month. • **3.** to betroth, engage – دَزّ أُمَّه تُخطُبلَه بنَيَّة مِنهُم [dazz ʔummah tuxṭublah bnayya minhum] He sent his mother to propose to one of their girls for him.

خاطَب [xa:ṭab] *v:* • **1.** to speak to, talk to, address – آني دَأخاطبَك إلَك [ʔa:ni daʔaxa:ṭbak ʔilak] I'm talking to you.

اِنخِطَب [ʔinxiṭab] *v:* • **1.** to be betrothed, become engaged – اِنخِطبَت الشَّهر اللِّي فات [ʔinxiṭbat ʔiššahr ʔilli fa:t] She got engaged last month.

خَطَب [xaṭab] *n:* • **1.** giving a speech

خُطبَة [xuṭba] *n:* خُطَب [xuṭab] *pl:* • **1.** speech, address • **2.** sermon • **3.** engagement ceremoney, betrothal

خِطاب [xiṭa:b] *n:* خِطابات [xiṭa:ba:t] *pl:* • **1.** speech, address

خَطِيب [xaṭi:b] *n:* خُطَباء [xuṭaba:] *pl:* • **1.** preacher, speaker in a mosque • **2.** good speaker, orator • **3.** pl. خطبان fiance, betrothed

خَطِيب، خَطِيبَة [xaṭi:b, xaṭi:ba] *n:* خُطبان، خَطِيبات [xuṭba:n, xaṭi:ba:t] *pl:* • **1.** fiancé, fiancée, betrothed

خَطّابَة [xaṭṭa:ba] *n:* • **1.** betrothal delegation, matchmaking delegation

مُخاطَبَة [muxa:ṭaba] *n:* • **1.** address

مَخطُوب [maxṭu:b] *adj:* • **1.** engaged

خ ط ر

خِطَر [xiṭar] *v:* • **1.** to pass, go by – هَسَّة خِطَر مِن هِنا [hassa xiṭar min hina] He just passed by here. • **2.** to occur – إِسمَه ما دَيخطُر عَلَى بالِي [ʔismah ma: dayixṭur ʕala ba:li] His name doesn't come to mind. شِنُو؟ صار وَزِير؟ هَذا شِي ما يِخطُر عالبال [šinu? ṣa:r wazi:r? ha:ða ši ma: yixṭur ʕalba:l] What? He became a minister? I can't imagine that.

خاطَر [xa:ṭar] *v:* • **1.** to endanger, risk – ماكُو حاجَة تخاطِر بِحَياتَك [ma:ku ħa:ja txa:ṭir bħaya:tak] There's no need for you to risk your life.

أخطَر [ʔaxṭar] *v:* • **1.** to notify, serve notice – أخطِرتَه المَحكَمَة يِطلَع مِن البَيت [ʔaxṭirtah ʔilmaħkama yiṭlaʕ min ʔilbayt] The court notified him to vacate the house.

تخَطَّر [txaṭṭar] *v:* • **1.** to recall, recollect, remember – ما دَاتخَطَّر وين شايفَه [ma: daʔitxaṭṭar wi:n ša:yfah] I don't remember where I saw him.

اِنخِطَر [ʔinxiṭar] *v:* • **1.** to be endangered – بَغداد اِنخِطرَت بِالفَيَضان [baɣda:d ʔinxiṭrat bilfayaða:n] Baghdad was endangered by the flood.

خَطَر [xaṭar] *n:* أخطار [ʔaxṭa:r] *pl:* • **1.** danger, risk • **2.** menace, danger – خَطَر عَالمُجتَمَع [xaṭar ʕalmuǰtamaʕ] a menace to society.

خاطِر [xa:ṭir] *n:* • **1.** so, so as to, so that – خَلِّي اِنفُوت مِنَّا خاطِر ما يشُوفنا [xalli: ʔinfu:t minna xa:ṭir ma: yšuwfna] Let's go this way so as he won't see us. • **2.** (in certain expressions) for the sake of – لِخاطرَك، بدِينارَين [lxa:ṭrak, bdina:rayn] For your sake, two dinars. لخاطِر الله، بَسّ عاد [lxa:ṭir ʔallah, bass ʕa:d] For God's sake, quit it! ما عِندِي خاطِر عِندَك؟ [ma: ʕindi xa:ṭir ʕindak?] Don't I have any influence with you? خَلِّي نرُوح ناخُذ مِن خاطرَه. أَبُوه مات البارحَة [xalli: nru:ħ na:xuð min xa:ṭrah. ʔabu:h ma:t ʔilba:rħa] Let's go offer our condolences. His father died yesterday. رُوح أُخُذ مِن خاطِر أَبُوك وَلا تخَلِّيه زَعلان عَلِيك [ru:ħ ʔuxuð min xa:ṭir ʔabu:k wla: txalli:h zaʕla:n ʕali:k] Go make up with your father and don't leave him mad at you. لا يُبقَى بِخاطرَك؛ ما قصَدِت شِي [la: yubqa: bxa:ṭrak; ma: qṣadit ši] Don't be offended; I didn't mean anything.

خُطّار [xuṭṭa:r] *n:* خِطاطِير [xiṭa:ṭi:r] *pl:* • **1.** guest(s), company – راح خُطّار [ra:ħ xuṭṭa:r] He went visiting.

مُخاطَرَة [muxa:ṭara] *n:* مُخاطَرات [muxa:ṭara:t] *pl:* • **1.** adventure • **2.** hazard

خاطرانَة [xa:ṭra:na] *n:* • **1.** pull, influence • **2.** favoritism • **3.** pl. خاطرانات patron, sponsor

خَطِر [xaṭir] *adj:* • **1.** dangerous, hazardous, risky, serious – مُجرِم خَطِر [muǰrim xaṭir] a dangerous criminal. سابِقَة خَطرَة [sa:biqa xaṭra] a dangerous precedent. عَمَلِيَّة خَطرَة [ʕamaliyya xaṭra] a serious operation.

خَطِير [xaṭi:r] *adj:* • **1.** serious, grave – وَضع خَطِير [waðiʕ xaṭi:r] a serious situation. خَبَر خَطِير [xabar xaṭi:r] grave news. • **2.** important, weighty – نَبأ خَطِير [nabaʔ xaṭi:r] an important announcement.

مُخطِر [muxṭir] *adj:* • **1.** endangered, threatened – صِحّتَه مُخطِرَة [ṣiħħtah muxṭira] His health is endangered.

أَخطَر [ʔaxṭar] *comparative adjective:* • **1.** more or most dangerous

خ ط ط

خَطّ [xaṭṭ] *v:* • **1.** to draw (a line) – خُطّ خَطّ جَوَّة هَالكِلمَة [xuṭṭ xaṭṭ ǰawwa haččilma] Draw a line under this word. • **2.** to print, write, paint (calligraphy) – الخَطّاط خَطّها لِلقُطعَة بدِينارَين [ʔilxaṭṭa:ṭ xaṭṭha lilquṭʕa bdina:na:rayn] The calligrapher printed the sign for two dinars.

خَطَّط [xaṭṭaṭ] *v:* • **1.** to draw lines. rule – خَطِّط هالصَّفحَة بِالمَسطَرَة [xaṭṭiṭ ha:lṣafħa bilmasṭara] Draw lines on this page with the ruler. • **2.** mark off, line – خَلِّي نخَطِّط ساحَة التَّنِس [xalli nxaṭṭiṭ sa:ħat ʔittanis] Let's mark off the tennis court.

تخَطَّط [txaṭṭaṭ] *v:* • **1.** to apply eyebrow make-up – العَرُوس دَتِتخَطَّط قِدّام المرايا [ʔilʕaru:s datitxaṭṭaṭ gidda:m ʔilmra:ya] The bride is putting on eyebrow make-up in front of the mirror.

خَطّ [xaṭṭ] *n:* خُطُوط [xuṭu:ṭ] *pl:* • **1.** line • **2.** line of communication, route – خَطّ حَدِيدي [xaṭṭ ħadi:di] railroad line. الخُطُوط الجَوِّيَّة العِراقِيَّة [ʔilxuṭu:ṭ ʔijjawwiyya ʔilʕira:qiyya] Iraqi Airlines. خَطّ الباص [xaṭṭ ʔilpa:ṣ] the bus line. • **3.** telephone line – الخَطّ مَشغُول [ʔilxaṭṭ mašɣu:l] The line's busy. • **4.** line (mil.) – الخُطُوط الأَمامِيَّة [ʔilxuṭu:ṭ ʔilʔama:miyya] the front lines. • **5.** handwriting – خَطّ إيد [xaṭṭ ʔi:d] handwriting, penmanship. • **6.** calligraphy – خَطّ الرُّقعَة [xaṭṭ ʔirruqʕa] Ruq`a style calligraphy. • **7.** letter, note – خَطّ الاستِواء [xaṭṭ ʔilʔistiwa:ʔ] the equator. خَطّ العَرض [xaṭṭ ʔilʕarð] parallel (of latitude). خَطّ الطُّول [xaṭṭ ʔiṭṭu:l] meridian, circle of longitude.

خَطّي [xaṭṭi] *n:* • **1.** written, handwritten – جَواب خَطّي [ǰawa:b xaṭṭi] a written answer.

خُطَّة [xuṭṭa] *n:* خُطّات [xuṭṭa:t] *pl:* • **1.** a diagram drawn on pavement for children's games

خُطَّة [xuṭṭa] *n:* خُطَط [xuṭaṭ] *pl:* • **1.** plan, project, design • **2.** policy, line of action, aim, purpose, principle

خَطّاط [xaṭṭa:ṭ] *n:* • **1.** calligrapher • **2.** sign painter

خطاط [xṭa:ṭ] *n:* • **1.** eyebrow make-up, eyebrow pencil

مُخَطِّط [muxaṭṭiṭ] *n:* • **1.** planner

مُخَطَّط [muxaṭṭaṭ] *n:* • **1.** plan • **2.** design

تَخطِيط [taxṭi:ṭ] *n:* • **1.** planning

مَخطُوطَة [maxṭu:ṭa] *n:* مَخطُوطات [maxṭu:ṭa:t] *pl:* • **1.** (old) manuscript

مخَطَّط [mxaṭṭaṭ] *adj:* • **1.** striped

مَخطُوط [maxṭu:ṭ] *adj:* • **1.** handwritten • **2.** handwritten

تَخطِيطي [taxṭi:ṭi] *adj:* • **1.** graphic

خ ط ف

خِطَف [xiṭaf] *v:* • **1.** to pass, go by – خِطَف مِن هنا مِثل البَرق [xiṭaf min hna miθl ʔilbarq] He went by here like lightning. السَّيّارَة خِطفَت بسُرعَة [ʔissayya:ra xiṭfat bsurʕa] The car went by fast. لا تُخطُف مِن هنا القاع مبَلَّلَة [la: tuxṭuf min hna. ʔilga:ʕ mballila] Don't step across here. The ground is wet. • **2.** to duck – أُخطُف راسَك. الباب مُو عالي [ʔuxṭuf ra:sak. ʔilba:b mu: ʕa:li] Duck your head. The doorway's not very high. لَو ما خِطفِت، كان ضِرَبني حجارَة [lu: ma: xiṭafit, ča:n ðirabni ħja:ra] If I hadn't ducked, he'd have hit me with a rock. • **3.** to kidnap

انخِطَف [ʔinxiṭaf] *v:* • **1.** to be drained away (of color) – اِنخِطَف لَونها مِن قِلتلها الخَبَر [ʔinxiṭaf lu:nha min giltlha ʔilxabar] She turned pale when I told her the news. • **2.** to be dumbfounded, petrified – اِنخِطفِت مِن شِفت الكَلب جاي عَلَيّا [ʔinxiṭafit min šifit ʔiččalib ǰa:y ʕalayya] I was petrified when I saw the dog coming at me. • **3.** to be kidnapped

اختِطَف [ʔixtiṭaf] *v:* • **1.** to kidnap, abduct – اِختِطفَوا إبن الوَزِير [ʔixtiṭfaw ʔibin ʔilwazi:r] They kidnapped the minister's son.

خَطُف [xaṭuf] *n:* • **1.** grabbing, kidnapping • **2.** quick passing

خَطفَة [xaṭfa] *n:* خَطفات [xaṭfa:t] *pl:* • **1.** a short distance, a dash, a hop, skip, and a jump

خاطِف [xa:ṭif] *n:* • **1.** kidnapper

اختِطاف [ʔixtiṭa:f] *n:* اِختِطافات [ʔixtiṭa:fa:t] *pl:* • **1.** kidnapping

خاطِف [xa:ṭif] *adj:* • **1.** fast, rapid • **2.** kidnapping

مَخطُوف [maxṭu:f] *adj:* • **1.** kidnapped

خ ط و

خِطَى [xiṭa:] *v:* • **1.** to step – اللّي يِخطِي مِن هنا أَمَوّتَه [ʔilli: yixṭi min hna, ʔamawwtah] I'll kill anyone who moves from there. إخطِي خَطوَة لِقِدّام [ʔixṭi xaṭwa ligidda:m] Step forward one pace.

خَطّى [xaṭṭa:] *v:* • **1.** to pace, walk around – صار ساعَة دَيخَطّي بالقُبَّة [ṣa:r sa:ʕa dayxaṭṭi bilgubba] He has been pacing the room for one hour.

تخَطّى [txaṭṭa:] *v:* • **1.** to over-step, transgress – لا تِتخَطّى الحُدُود بحَكيَك ويّاها [la: titxaṭṭa: ʔilħudu:d bħačyak wiyya:ha] Don't overstep the bounds in talking with her. تخَطّى الأُصُول بتَصَرُّفاتَه [txaṭṭa: ʔilʔuṣu:l btaṣarrufa:tah] He violated the customs with his behavior. • **2.** to cross, go beyond – لا تِتخَطّى هَالحَدّ. قاعنا تِنتِهي هنا [la: titxaṭṭa: halħadd. ga:ʕna tintihi hna] Don't cross this boundary. Our land ends here. • **3.** to disregard, by-pass, go around – لا تِتخَطّى مَرجِعَك [la: titxaṭṭa: marǰiʕak] Don't by-pass your superior. • **4.** to take a stroll – خَلّي نِطلَع نِتخَطّى بالحَدِيقَة [xalli: niṭlaʕ nitxaṭṭa: bilħadi:qa] Let's go out and take a stroll in the garden.

خَطي [xaṭy] *n:* • **1.** stepping

خَطوَة [xaṭwa] *n:* خَطوات [xaṭwa:t] *pl:* • **1.** step – خَطوَة حاسمَة [xaṭwa ħa:sma] a decisive step.

خ ف ت

خِفَت [xifat] *v:* • **1.** to die away, fade – كُلّما يِبتِعِد، يِخفِت صَوتَه [kullma: yibtiʕid, yixfit ṣawtah] As he goes farther away, his voice fades. • **2.** to become silent, quiet down – بِكَى مُدَّة وَبَعدين خِفَت [biča: mudda wbaʕdi:n xifat] He cried a while and then quieted down. • **3.** to die down, subside – النّار راح تِخفِت [ʔinna:r ra:ħ tixfit] The fire will die down.

خَفت [xafit] *n:* • **1.** fading, dimming

خافِت [xa:fit] *adj:* • **1.** dim, soft, subdued – ضُوَا خافِت [ðuwa xa:fit] dim light.

أخفَت [ʔaxfat] *comparative adjective:* • **1.** weaker, softer

خ ف ر

خَفَر [xafar] *n:* • **1.** watching, watch, guard – الطَّبِيب الخَفَر [ʔiṭṭabi:b ʔilxafar] doctor on duty. مُمَرِّضَة خَفَر [mumarriða xafar] nurse on duty. جُندي خَفَر [ǰundi xafar] soldier on guard duty. صَيدَلِيَّة خَفَر [ṣaydaliyya xafar] pharmacy designated to stay open all night. الرَّئِيس أحمَد خَفَر باكِر [ʔirraʔi:s ʔaħmad xafar ba:čir] Captain Ahmed will be on guard duty tomorrow. • **2.** guard, guard detachment – ضابُط الخَفَر [ða:buṭ ʔilxafar] officer on duty.

خ

مَخفَر [maxfar] *n:* مَخافِر [maxa:fir] *pl:* • **1.** guard post, control post – مَخفَر شُرطَة [maxfar šurṭa] police station. مَخفَر حُدُود [maxfar ħidu:d] guard duty.
خَفارَة [xafa:ra] *n:* خَفارات [xafa:ra:t] *pl:* • **1.** guard duty – لِزَم خَفارَة [lizam xafa:ra] He was on guard duty.
مَخفُور [maxfu:r] *adj:* • **1.** under escort, under guard – جابَوه لِلمَركَز مَخفُور [ǰa:bawh lilmarkaz maxfu:r] They brought him to the police station under guard.

خ ف ش

خَفّاش [xaffa:š, xuffa:š] *n:* • **1.** bat

خ ف ض

خَفَّض [xaffað̣] *v:* • **1.** to lower, decrease, reduce, drop – إذا تخَفُّض السِّعِر، أشتِريها [ʔiða txaffuð̣ ʔissiʕir, ʔaštiri:ha] If you lower the price, I'll buy it. خَفُّض صَوتَك. أكُو جَماعَة يِتصَنَّطُون [xaffuð̣ ṣawtak. ʔaku ǰama:ʕa yitṣannaṭu:n] Lower your voice. There are people listening.
اِنخُفَض [ʔinxufað̣] *v:* • **1.** to sink, drop, decrease – أسعار الشَّكَر اِنخُفضَت هَالأَيّام [ʔasʕa:r ʔiššakar ʔinxufð̣at halʔayya:m] The price of sugar has dropped these days. اليُوم اِنخُفضَت دَرَجَة الحَرارَة هوايَة [ʔilyu:m ʔinxufð̣at darajat ʔilħara:ra hwa:ya] The temperature went down a lot today.
تَخفِيض [taxfi:ð̣] *n:* • **1.** reduction, discount
اِنخِفاض [ʔinxifa:ð̣] *n:* • **1.** reduction, decrease • **2.** dropping, low level (of water)
مُنخَفِض [munxafið̣] *adj:* • **1.** low – اِرتِفاع مُنخَفِض [ʔirtifa:ʕ munxafið̣] low altitude. أسعار مُنخَفضَة [ʔasʕa:r munxafð̣a] low prices.
أخفَض [ʔaxfað̣] *comparative adjective:* • **1.** more or most subdued

خ ف ف

خَفّ [xaff] *v:* • **1.** to become lighter, lose weight, decrease in weight – مِن تِنزِل بِالمَيّ، وَزنَك يخُفّ [min tinzil bilmayy, waznak yxuff] When you get in the water, your weight decreases. الحِمِل خَفّ عَلَيه مِن أخَذِت قِسِم مِنَّه [ʔilħimil xaff ʕali:h min ʔaxaðit qisim minnah] The load was lighter for him after I took some of it. تاه بالغابَة مُدَّة شَهَر وَعَقلَه خَفّ [ta:h bilγa:ba muddat šahar wʕaqlah xaff] He was lost in the jungle for a month and he went half crazy. • **2.** to decrease – الوُجَع خَفّ [ʔilwuǰaʕ xaff] The pain has let up. السُّرعَة مالته ما خَفَّت، تَرَة ما راح يُوقَف [ʔissurʕa ma:ltah ma: xaffat, tara ma: ra:ħ yu:gaf] His speed hasn't decreased; looks like he's not going to stop. • **3.** to become lighter in color – لا تحُطّ بِيه مَيّ بَعَد تَرَة لونَه يخُفّ [la: tħuṭṭ bi:h mayy baʕad tara lu:nah yxuff] Don't add anymore water or its color will become lighter. • **4.** to become easier, lighter – لَو أعرُف إنكِلِيزِي كان الامتِحان يخُفّ عَلَيّا [law ʔaʕruf ʔingili:zi ča:n ʔilʔimtiħa:n yxuff ʕalayya] If I knew English, the exam would be easier for me. مِن إجا المُوَظَّف الثّانِي، الشُّغُل مالِي خَفّ [min ʔiǰa ʔilmuwað̣ð̣af ʔiθθa:ni, ʔiššuγul ma:li xaff] When the new employee came, my work got lighter. • **5.** to thin, become thin, sparse – خَلّي نِبقَى بالبَيت إلَى أن يخُفّ الازدِحام [xalli: nibqa: bilbayt ʔila ʔan yxuff ʔilʔizdiħa:m] Let's stay at home until the crowd thins out. شَعرِي دَيخُفّ [šaʕri dayxuff] My hair is getting thinner. • **6.** to speed up, hurry, quicken – خُفّ رِجلَك، تأخَّرنا عالحَفلَة [xuff riǰlak, tʔaxxarna ʕalħafla] Speed up. We are late for the party. خُفّ إيدَك، المُدِير دَيرِيد المَكتُوب [xuff ʔi:dak, ʔilmudi:r dayri:d ʔilmaktu:b] Hurry up. The director wants the letter.
خَفَّف [xaffaf] *v:* • **1.** to lighten, make lighter – لازِم نخَفِّف الحِمِل حَتَّى نصَلِّح البَنجَر [la:zim nxaffif ʔilħimil ħatta nṣalliħ ʔilpančar] We've got to lighten the load in order to fix the flat. • **2.** to decrease, lessen – مِن تُوصَل قَرِيب مِن الجِّسِر خَفِّف السُّرعَة [min tu:ṣal qari:b min ʔiǰǰisir xaffif ʔissurʕa] When you get near the bridge, let up on the speed. • **3.** to ease, lighten, relieve – راح أضُربَك أبرَة تخَفُّف الوُجَع عَنَّك [ra:ħ ʔaðurbak ʔubra txaffuf ʔilwuǰaʕ ʕannak] I am going to give you a shot to ease your pain. خَلَّوا وِيّاه واحِد حَتَّى يخَفُّف عَلَيه الشُّغُل [xallaw wiyya:h wa:ħid ħatta yxaffuf ʕali:h ʔiššuγul] They put a man with him to make the work lighter on him. المَكتُوب اللّي دَزّلها إيّاه خَفَّف عَنها شوَيَّة [ʔilmaktu:b ʔilli dazzilha ʔiyya: xaffaf ʕanha šwayya] The letter which he sent her lifted her spirits a little. المُعَلِّم راح يخَفُّف الأسئِلَة هالمَرَّة [ʔilmuʕallim ra:ħ yxaffuf ʔilʔasʔila halmarra] The teacher is going to simplify the questions this time. • **4.** to dilute, thin, lighten – خَفِّف البُويَة، لِأنَّها ثخِينَة كُلِّش [xaffif ʔilbu:ya, liʔanh θxi:na kulliš] Thin the paint; it's too thick. خَفِّف الحامُض حَتَّى ما يِحرِق المَلابِس [xaffif ʔilħa:muð̣ ħatta ma: yiħrig ʔilmala:bis] Dilute the acid so it won't burn the clothes. الشاي طُوخ، خَفِّفلِي إيّاه [ʔičča:y ṭu:x, xaffifli: ʔiyya:h] The tea is dark. Lighten it for me. الحَلّاق خَفَّف شَعرِي بالمُقَصّ والمِشِط [ʔilħalla:q xaffaf šaʕri bilmugaṣṣ wilmišiṭ] The barber thinned my hair with the scissors and comb.
اِستَخَفّ [ʔistaxaff] *v:* • **1.** to ridicule, despise, disdain, scorn – اِستَخَفّ بفِكِرتِي [ʔistaxaff bfikirti] He ridiculed my idea. • **2.** to value lightly, take lightly – لا تِستِخِفّ بِهالشُّغُل. أصبُر وشُوف شلُون صَعُب [la: tistixiff bhaššuγul. ʔuṣbur wšu:f šlu:n ṣaʕub] Don't take this work too lightly. Wait and see how hard it gets.
خُفّ [xuff] *n:* أخفاف [ʔaxfa:f] *pl:* • **1.** hoof (especially of a camel)
خِفَّة [xiffa] *n:* • **1.** agility, nimbleness – خِفَّة الدَّم [xiffat ʔiddamm] amiability, charm, wittiness. • **2.** looseness, availability (of women)
اِستِخفاف [ʔistixfa:f] *n:* • **1.** contempt
خَفِيف [xafi:f] *adj:* خفاف [xfa:f] *pl:* • **1.** light, lightweight – جُنطَة خَفِيفَة [ǰunṭa xafi:fa] a light suitcase.

قماش خَفِيف [qmaːš xafiːf] lightweight cloth. وَرَق خَفِيف [waraq xafiːf] thin paper, onionskin. طَبَقَة خَفِيفَة [ṭabaqa xafiːfa] light, thin layer. أَكِل خَفِيف [ʔakil xafiːf] and أَكِل خَفِيف عالمعدَة [ʔakil xafiːf ʕalmiʕda] light, easily digestible food. مَطرَة خَفِيفَة [maṭra xafiːfa] a light shower. مُطَر خَفِيف [muṭar xafiːf] light rain. حُكُم خَفِيف [ħukum xafiːf] a light sentence. • **2.** slight, little, trivial, inconsequential – وُجَع خَفِيف [wujaʕ xafiːf] a slight pain. حمُوضَة خَفِيفَة [ħmuːða xafiːfa] a little sourness. حُمرَة خَفِيفَة [ħumra xafiːfa] a little lipstick. سُؤال خَفِيف [suʔaːl xafiːf] an easy question. شُغُل خَفِيف [šuɣul xafiːf] easy work. بُوكَر خَفِيف [puːkar xafiːf] low-stake poker. قمار خَفِيف [qmaːr xafiːf] gambling for low stakes. • **3.** thin, sparse, scanty – شَعرَه خَفِيف [šaʕrah xafiːf] His hair is thin. • **4.** thin, diluted – لِبَن خَفِيف [liban xafiːf] light yoghurt صُبُغ خَفِيف، بُويَة خَفِيفَة [ṣubuɣ xafiːf, buːya xafiːfa] thin paint. شاي خَفِيف [čaːy xafiːf] light tea. • **5.** agile, nimble, quick – صِير خَفِيف، تحَرَّك [ṣiːr xafiːf, tħarrak] Be quick about it; get a move on. خادمَة خَفِيفَة بالشُّغُل [xaːdma xafiːfa biššuɣul] a maid who is quick and efficient at her work إيدَه خَفِيفَة [ʔiːdah xafiːfa] He's a fast worker. خَفِيف الدَّم [xafiːf ʔiddamm] charming, amiable, witty. وَلَد خَفِيف عالمعدَة [walad xafiːf ʕalmiʕda] sociable, pleasant man. خَفِيف العَقِل [xafiːf ʔilʕaqil] simple-minded, feeble-minded. بنَيَّة خَفِيفَة [bnayya xafiːfa] loose, easily available girl.

خفايِف [xafaːyif] *adj:* • **1.** light, small

خفايِفي [xafaːyfi] *adj:* • **1.** (invar.) light, digestible – أَكلَة خفايِفي [ʔakla xafaːyfi] a little light food, a light meal, a snack.

أَخَفّ [ʔaxaff] *comparative adjective:* • **1.** more or most lightweight • **2.** more or most trivial • **3.** more or most sparse • **4.** more or most diluted • **5.** more or most agile

خ ف ق

خُفَق [xufag] *v:* • **1.** to palpitate, beat, throb – قَلبِي دَيُخفُق [galbi dayuxfug] My heart is palpitating. • **2.** to flap, beat, flutter – الطَّير خُفَق جناحَه مَرَّة وَمات [ʔiṭṭiːr xufag ǰnaːħah marra wmaːt] The pigeon flapped its wings once and died. • **3.** to beat, whip – أُخفُقلِي بَيضتَين لِلكَيكَة [ʔuxfugli bayðtayn lilkayka] Beat me two eggs for the cake. خُشّ جَوَّة لا يخُفقَك الهَوا البارِد [xušš ǰawwa laː yxufgak ʔilhawa ʔilbaːrid] Go inside so the cold wind won't hit you. • **4.** to stucco – البَنّة دَيُخفُق الحايِط بشِبِنتُو خَفِيف [ʔilbanna dayuxfug ʔilħaːyiṭ bčbintu xafiːf] The mason is stuccoing the wall with light grout.

خَفَّق [xaffag] *v:* • **1.** to flap, flutter, beat – شُوف الطَّير دَيخَفُّق بِجنحانَه [šuːf ʔiṭṭayr dayxaffug bǰinħaːnah] Look at the bird flapping its wings.

خَفُق [xafug] *n:* • **1.** palpitation, beating, throbbing • **2.** whipping, flapping, fluttering

خَفَقان [xafaqaːn] *n:* • **1.** palpitation

خ ف ي

خِفَى [xifaː] *v:* • **1.** to hide, conceal – إخفِيها بِفَدّ مُكان قَبُل ما يشُوفها [ʔixfiːha bfadd mukaːn gabul maː yšuːfha] Hide it somewhere before he sees it. • **2.** to conceal, keep secret – أَقُلَّك لَو أَدري. ما أَخفِي عَلِيك شِي [ʔagullak law ʔadri. maː ʔaxfi ʕaliːk ši] I'd tell you if I knew. I don't hide anything from you.

خَفَّى [xaffaː] *v:* • **1.** to hide

تخَفَّى [txaffaː] *v:* • **1.** to be hidden, keep out of sight – دَيتخَفَّى وَما حَدّ يدرِي وِين [dayitxaffaː wamaː ħadd yidri wiːn] He is in hiding and nobody knows where. • **2.** to disguise oneself – كان مِتخَفِّي بِهدُوم نِسوان [čaːn mitxaffi bihduːm niswaːn] He was disguised in women's clothing.

اِختِفَى [ʔixtifaː] *v:* • **1.** to hide, conceal oneself, keep out of sight – الصَّيّاد اِختِفَى حَتَّى ما يشُوفَه الطَّير [ʔiṣṣayyaːd ʔixtifaː ħatta maː yšuːfah ʔiṭṭiːr] The hunter concealed himself so the bird wouldn't see him. • **2.** to disappear, vanish – شلُون اِختِفَى! هَسَّة كان مَوجُود [šluːn ʔixtifaː! hassa čaːn mawǰuːd] He simply disappeared! He was just here. الشَّكَر اِختِفَى مِن السُّوق [ʔiššakar ʔixtifaː min ʔissuːg] Sugar has vanished from the market.

خَفِي [xafy] *n:* • **1.** hidding, keeping out

خِفيَة [xifya] *n:* • **1.** secretly, covertly – سَوّاها خِفيَة بَلا حِسّ أَحَّد [sawwaːha xifya bala ħiss ʔaħħad] He did it secretly without anyone's knowing it.

مَخفِي [maxfi] *adj:* • **1.** hidden, concealed

مِتخَفِّي [mitxafi] *adj:* • **1.** hiding, concealing

خ ك

خاكَة [xaːka] *n:* • **1.** dust. – خاكَت فَحَم [xaːkat faħam] charcoal dust. خاكَت قَند [xaːkat qand] the particles left from breaking up a block of sugar. • **2.** a rag with which a woman covers the lower part of her face

خ ك ي

خاكِي [xaːki] *n:* • **1.** khaki

خ ل ب

مَخلَب [maxlab] *n:* مَخالِب [maxaːlib] *pl:* • **1.** claw, talon

خ ل ج

خَلِيج [xaliːǰ] *n:* خِلجان [xilǰaːn] *pl:* • **1.** gulf, bay

خَلِيجِي [xaliːǰi] *adj:* • **1.** from the Arabian Gulf region

خ ل خ ل

خَلخَل [xalxal] *v:* • **1.** to shake, jiggle – مِن دَيشلَع البِسمار، خَلخَلَه لِلمَيز كُلَّه [min dayišlaʕ ʔilbismaːr, xalxalah lilmayz kullah] When he was pulling the nail, he shook the whole table.

خِلخال [xilxaːl] *n:* خَلاخِيل [xalaːxiːl] *pl:* • **1.** anklet, ankle bracelet (usually heavy and tinkling)

خ

خ ل د

خَلَّد [xallad] *v:* • **1.** to perpetuate, immortalize – سَوّولَه تَماثِيل حَتَّى يخَلّدُون ذِكراه [sawwawlah tama:θi:l ħatta yxallidu:n ðikra:h] They built statues of him to perpetuate his memory.

تخَلَّد [txallad] *v:* • **1.** to be perpetuated, immortalized – بِهَالتَّضحِيَة راح يِتخَلَّد ذِكرَه [bhattaðaħiya ra:ħ yitxallad ðikrah] By that sacrifice his memory will be immortalized.

خالِد [xa:lid] *adj:* • **1.** eternal

خ ل س

اِختِلَس [ʔixtilas] *v:* • **1.** to embezzle, misappropriate – اِختِلَس أَلف دِينار مِن فلُوس الشَّرِكَة [ʔixtilas ʔalf dina:r min flu:s ʔiššarika] He embezzled a thousand dinars from company funds.

اِختِلاس [ʔixtila:s] *n:* • **1.** embezzlement

خِلسَة [xilsa] *adj:* • **1.** secretly – طِلَع مِن البَيت خِلسَة وَما حَدّ دِرى بِيه [ṭilaʕ min ʔilbayt xilsa wama: ħadd dira: bi:h] He left the house secretly and no one knew about it.

مُختَلِس [muxtalis] *adj:* • **1.** fleeting, furtive

خ ل ص

خِلَص [xilaṣ] *v:* • **1.** to be freed, get rid of – باكر راح أَنَّقِل وأخلَص مِن هالشُّغُل [ba:čir ra:ħ ʔanniqil wʔaxlaṣ min haššuɣul] Tomorrow I am being transferred and will be relieved of this work. راح أَشتِرِي بَيت وَأخلَص [ra:ħ ʔaštiri bayt wʔaxlaṣ] I'm going to buy a house and be done with it. • **2.** to be saved, rescued, to escape – خِلَص مِن الحَبِس بِإعجُوبَة [xilaṣ min ʔilħabis bʔiʕǰu:ba] He avoided being imprisoned by a miracle. خِلَص مِن المَوت بإعجُوبَة [xilaṣ min ʔilmawt bʔiʕǰu:ba] He escaped from death by a miracle. قِضَينا الصَّيف بلُبنان وَخلَصنا مِن حَرّ بَغداد [giðiːna ʔiṣṣayf blabna:n wxlaṣna min ħarr baɣda:d] We spent the summer in Lebanon and escaped from Baghdad's heat. • **3.** to be finished, done, all through, over – سَيّارتَك خِلصَت. تَعال أخُذها [sayya:rtak xilṣat. taʕa:l ʔuxuðha] Your car is ready. Come and get it. القاط مالَك خِلَص [ʔilqa:ṭ ma:lak xilaṣ] Your suit is finished. قَضِيَّة تَعيينَك خِلصَت [qaðiyyat taʕyi:nak xilṣat] The matter of your appointment is all done. • **4.** to become finished, used up – مِتأَسِّف. ماكُو أكِل؛ كُلَّه خِلَص [mitʔassif. ma:ku ʔakil; kullah xilaṣ] I'm sorry. There's no food; it's all gone. الوَقِت خِلَص [ʔilwakit xilaṣ] The time is up. خِلصَت رُوحِي [xilṣat ru:ħi] I'm plumb fed up! خِلَص! آنِي شَعلَيَّا بَعَد؟ [xilaṣ! ʔa:ni šaʕlayya baʕad?] That does it! (That settles it! that's it!) What concern of mine is it then?

خَلَّص [xallaṣ] *v:* • **1.** to save, rescue, free, rid – المُحامِي خَلّصَه مِن السِّجِن [ʔilmuħa:mi xallaṣah min ʔissiǰin] The lawyer saved him from prison. راح يخَلِّص البَيت مِن الدِّبِيب [ra:ħ yxalliṣ ʔilbayt min ʔiddibi:b] He's going to rid the house of crawling insects. مَحَّد يِقدَر يخَلّصَك مِنِّي [maħħad yigdar yxallṣak minni] No one can save you from me. • **2.** to finish, complete, get through – الخَيّاط ما خَلَّص القاط مالِي [ʔilxayya:ṭ ma: xallaṣ ʔilqa:ṭ ma:li] The tailor hasn't finished my suit. خَلَّص سَنتَين وَبَعدلَه سَنَة [xallaṣ santayn wbaʕadlah sana] He completed two years and still has a year to go. أَرِيدَك تِحكِي وِيّاه وَتخَلِّصلِي القَضِيَّة [ʔari:dak tiħči wiyya:h watxalliṣli ʔilqaðiyya] I want you to talk with him and bring this matter to a close. شوَقِت تخَلِّص مِن الشُّغُل؟ [šwakit txalliṣ min ʔiššuɣul?] What time do you get off work? أَقدَر أَخَلِّصلَك السَّيّارَة بِألِف دِينار [ʔagdar ʔaxalliṣlak ʔissayya:ra bʔalif dina:r] I can get you the car for a thousand dinars. بُسَطتَه بَسطَة خَلّصتَه بِيها [busaṭṭah basṭa xallaṣtah bi:ha] I beat the tar out of him, I gave him a beating he'll never forget. • **3.** to use up, finish – لا تخَلِّص كُلّ الوَرَق [la: txalliṣ kull ʔilwaraq] Don't use up all the paper. لا تخَلِّص كُلّ الأكِل؛ بَعَد أُخوتَك ما أَكلَوا [la: txalliṣ kull ʔilʔakil; baʕad ʔuxwtak ma: ʔaklaw] Don't eat up all the food; your brothers haven't eaten yet. خَلَّص البُوطِل وَحدَه [xallaṣ ʔilbu:ṭil waħdah] He finished the bottle alone. • **4.** to clear, make it – مِن هَالصَّفحَة تخَلِّص، لَكِن يِمكِن تطُخّ بِالحايِط مِن صَفحَة اللُّخ [min haṣṣafħa txalliṣ, la:kin yimkin ṭṭuxx bilħa:yiṭ min ṣafħat ʔillux] You're clear on this side, but you might hit the wall on the other side. سُوق عَلَى كَيفَك. تِقدَر تخَلِّص [su:q ʕala kayfak. tigdar txalliṣ] Drive slowly --- you can make it. بِالكاد الطِّيّارَة خَلّصَت مِن الأشجار [bilka:d ʔiṭiyya:ra xallaṣat min ʔilʔašǰa:r] The airplane just barely cleared the trees.

أخلَص [ʔaxlaṣ] *v:* • **1.** to be devoted, faithful – أَخلَصِلها إِلَى آخِر يوم مِن حَياتَه [ʔaxlaṣilha ʔila ʔa:xir yu:m min ħaya:tah] He was faithful to her till his death.

تخَلَّص [txallaṣ] *v:* • **1.** to rid oneself – بِالقُوَّة يَالله تخَلَّصِت مِنَّه [bilguwwa yallah txallaṣit minnah] I got rid of him only after a lot of trouble. تخَلَّصِت مِن الدَّعوَة لِلحَفلَة [txallaṣit min ʔiddaʕwa lilħafla] I got out of going to the party. تخَلَّص مِن السُّؤال مالِي [txallaṣ min ʔissuʔa:l ma:li] He avoided my question.

اِستَخلَص [ʔistaxlaṣ] *v:* • **1.** to extract – نِستَخلِص عِدَّة مَوادّ مِن النَّفط الخام [nistaxliṣ ʕiddat mawa:dd min ʔinnafṭ ʔilxa:m] We extract several products from crude oil.

خَلاص [xala:ṣ] *n:* • **1.** way out, way around – هاي ما مِنها خَلاص [ha:y ma: minha xala:ṣ] There's no way out of it.

مَخلَص [maxlaṣ] *n:* • **1.** final offer, firm price – هَالسِّترَة مَخلَصها بدِينارَين [hassitra maxlaṣha bdina:rayn] The bottom price on this jacket is two dinars. ماكُو حاجَة لِلمُعامَلَة. مَخلَص بدِينارَين [ma:ku ħa:ǰa lilmuʕa:mala. maxlaṣ bdina:rayn] There's no use in bargaining. The final price is two dinars.

خُلاصَة [xula:ṣa] *n:* خُلاصات [xula:ṣa:t] *pl:* • **1.** essence, extract • **2.** substance, gist • **3.** summary, resume –

الخُلاصَة، هَذا مُو صَدِيق [ʔilxula:ṣa, ha:ða mu: ṣadi:q] In short, he's no friend.
إخلاص [ʔixla:ṣ] *n:* • **1.** loyalty
تَخلِيص [taxli:ṣ] *n:* • **1.** rescue
اِستِخلاص [ʔistixla:ṣ] *n:* • **1.** derivation
خالِص [xa:liṣ] *adj:* • **1.** pure, unadulterated – ذَهَب خالِص [ðahab xa:liṣ] pure gold.
مُخلِص [muxliṣ] *adj:* • **1.** loyal, faithful – صَدِيق مُخلِص [ṣadi:q muxliṣ] a loyal friend.
مخَلِّص [mxalliṣ] *adj:* • **1.** finished
خَلصان [xalṣa:n] *adj:* • **1.** free, rid of – إحنا خَلصانِين مِن شَرَّه الحَمد لله [ʔiħna xalṣa:ni:n min šarrah ʔilħamd lilla:h] We're rid of his annoying, thank God. آنِي خَلصان مِن هالمَشاكِل؛ بَعَدنِي ما مِتزَوِّج [ʔa:ni xalṣa:n min halmaša:kil; baʕadni ma: midzawwij] I'm free of those problems; I'm not married yet. • **2.** safe, saved, out of danger – المَدِينَة خَلصانَة مِن الغَرق هَسَّة [ʔilmadi:na xalṣa:na min ʔilɣarig hassa] The city is safe from the flood now. • **3.** finished, done, over – قاطَك خَلصان. تَعال أخذَه [qa:ṭak xalṣa:n. taʕa:l ʔuxðah] Your suit is ready. Come get it. الحَفلَة خَلصانَة [ʔilħafla xalṣa:na] The party is over. كُلّشِي خَلصان. راح يِتزَوَّج باكِر [kullši xalṣa:n. ra:ħ yidzawwaǰ ba:čir] Everything is done. He's going to get married tomorrow. • **4.** gone, finished, used up, worn out – ماكُو خُبُز. كُلَّه خَلصان [ma:ku xubuz. kullah xalṣa:n] There's no bread. It's all gone. هَالسَّيّارَة خَلصانَة. ما تِسوَى [hassayya:ra xalṣa:na. ma: tiswa:] This car's done for. It's not worth anything. المُدَّة خَلصانَة. لازِم تِدفَع اليُوم [ʔilmudda xalṣa:na. la:zim tidfaʕ ʔilyu:m] The time's up. You've got to pay today. قَلبِي خَلصان مِن القَهَر [galbi xalṣa:n min ʔilqahar] I'm sick from this misery.
أخلَص [ʔaxlaṣ] *comparative adjective:* • **1.** more or most faithful, loyal

خ ل ط

خَلَط [xilaṭ] *v:* • **1.** to mix, mingle, blend – هَالعَصِير قَوِي. لازِم تُخَلطَه بمَيّ [halʕaṣi:r qawi. la:zim tuxulṭah bmayy] This juice is too thick. You better mix it with water. لا تُخلُط هَالأوراق، خَلِّيها مَعزُولَة [la: tuxluṭ halʔawra:q, xalli:ha maʕzu:la] Don't mix these papers. Leave them separated. • **2.** to be or become confused, mixed up – دائِماً أخلُط بَينَه وَبَين أخُوه [da:ʔiman ʔaxluṭ baynah wbayn ʔaxu:h] I always confuse him with his brother. دَتُخلُط بين الكِلمتَين [datuxluṭ bayn ʔiččilimtayn] You're confusing the two words. هَذا يُخلُط بِحَكيَه [ha:ða yuxluṭ bħačyah] He gets all mixed up in his speech.
خالَط [xa:laṭ] *v:* • **1.** to mix, associate with – إبنَك دَيخالِط جَماعَة مُو زينَة [ʔibnak dayxa:liṭ ǰama:ʕa mu: zi:na] Your son is mixing with a bad group
تخالَط [txa:laṭ] *v:* • **1.** to integrate
اِنخلَط [ʔinxilaṭ] *v:* • **1.** to be mixed
اِختَلَط [ʔixtilaṭ] *v:* • **1.** to associate, mix – صَدِيقي ما يعجبَه يِختِلِط ويّا الغير [ṣadi:qi ma: yʕiǰbah yixtiliṭ wiyya ʔilɣayr] My friend doesn't like to associate with others. • **2.** to get all mixed up – اِختِلَط الحابِل بِالنّابِل [ʔixtilaṭ ʔilħa:bil binna:bil] Everything got all mixed up.
خَلط [xaliṭ] *n:* • **1.** mixing
خَلطَة [xalṭa] *n:* خَلطات [xalṭa:t] *pl:* • **1.** mixture, blend, mix
خَلّاطَة [xalla:ṭa] *n:* • **1.** mixer, blender
تَخالُط [taxa:luṭ] *n:* • **1.** company
اِختِلاط [ʔixtila:ṭ] *n:* اِختِلاطات [ʔixtila:ṭa:t] *pl:* • **1.** complication (med.)
مُخالَطَة [muxa:laṭa] *n:* • **1.** company, intercourse, association
مخَلَّط [mxallaṭ] *adj:* • **1.** a mixture of candies, nuts, cookies, or fruits – مخَلَّط يا لوز [mxallaṭ ya: lu:z] the cry of the nut vendor. موَظَّفِين هَالدّائِرَة مخَلَّط يا لوز [mwaðððafi:n hadda:ʔira mxallaṭ ya: lu:z] The employees in this office are a motley crew.
مُختَلَط [muxtalaṭ] *adj:* • **1.** mixed
مَخلُوط [maxlu:ṭ] *adj:* مَخلُوطِين [maxluwṭi:n] *pl:* • **1.** mixed

خ ل ع

خِلَع [xilaʕ] *v:* • **1.** to dislocate, wrench – جَرّنِي مِن إيدِي وَخِلَع كِتفِي [ǰarrni min ʔi:di wxilaʕ čitfi] He pulled me by my hand and dislocated my shoulder. • **2.** to depose, remove, dismiss – خِلعَوا المَلِك وخَلّوا إبنَه بمُكانَه [xilʕaw ʔilmalik wxallaw ʔibnah bmuka:nah] They dethroned the King and put his son in his place.
اِختِلَع [ʔixtilaʕ] *v:* • **1.** to tear out, pull out – اِختِلَع الشِّجرَة مِن جُذُورها [ʔixtilaʕ ʔiššiǰra min ǰuðu:rha] He pulled up the tree by its roots.
خَلِع [xaliʕ] *n:* • **1.** dislocation
خَلِيع [xali:ʕ] *adj:* • **1.** wanton, dissolute, dissipated, depraved – هُوَّ فَدّ واحِد خَلِيع ما يِستِحِي [huwwa fadd wa:ħid xali:ʕ ma: yistiħi] He's a depraved fellow who knows no shame.
خِلاعِي [xila:ʕi] *adj:* • **1.** lewd, bawdy – صُوَر خِلاعِيَّة [ṣuwar xila:ʕiyya] lewd pictures, pornography.
مَخلُوع [maxlu:ʕ] *adj:* • **1.** exiled, expelled

خ ل ف 1

خِلَف [xilaf] *v:* • **1.** to break, fail to keep – خِلَف المَوعِد مالِي [xilaf ʔilmawʕid ma:li] He broke the date with me. مُو صَحِيح تِخلِف الوَعَد [mu: ṣaħi:ħ tixlif ʔilwaʕad] It isn't right to break the promise.
خَلَّف [xallaf] *v:* • **1.** to have offspring – خَلَّف أربَع أطفال [xallaf ʔarbaʕ ʔaṭfa:l] He had four children. أنعَل أبُوك لابُو اللِّي خَلَّفَك [ʔanʕal ʔabu:k wʔabu ʔilli xallafak] Damn your father and your father's father! • **2.** to leave behind, leave – مِن مات خَلَّف ثَروَة لِولدَه [min ma:t xallaf θarwa lwildah] When he died he left a fortune to his kids.

خالَف [xaːlaf] *v:* • **1.** to contradict – أوّل مَرَّة قالِلها هِيكِي وَبَعدين خالَف نَفسَه [ʔawwal marra gaːlilha hiːči wbaʕdiyn xaːlaf nafsah] The first time he said it this way, and later contradicted himself. • **2.** to be different, to differ, to diverge, to be inconsistent, incompatible, not in keeping – رَأيَك يخالِف رَأيِي [raʔayak yxaːlif raʔyi] Your opinion differs from my opinion. آني أخالفَك بهالمَوضُوع [ʔaːni ʔaxaːlfak bhalmawðuːʕ] I differ with you on this subject. يِمشِي دائماً عَلَى قاعِدَة خالِف تُعرَف [yimši dayman ʕala qaːʕidat xaːlif tuʕraf] He always follows the principle: Be different and you'll be known. تَصَرُّفاتَه تخالِف الأُصُول [taṣarrufaːtah txaːlif ʔilʔuṣuːl] His conduct is at variance with good manners. شُرُب العَرَق يخالِف الدِّين [šurub ʔilʕarag yxaːlif ʔiddiːn] Drinking arrack is not in keeping with religion. • **3.** to matter, to make a difference – يخالِف شِي إذا أرُوح؟ [yxaːlif ši ʔiða ʔaruːħ?] Would there be any objection to my leaving? شيخالِف إذا قِلت هِيكِي؟ [šyxaːlif ʔiða gilit hiːči?] What difference does it make if I said that? ما يخالِف. ما عِندِي مانِع [maː yxaːlif. maː ʕindi maːniʕ] It doesn't make any difference. I've got no objections. • **4.** to break, violate, disobey – السّايِق خالَف القانُون [ʔissaːyiq xaːlaf ʔilqaːnuːn] The driver violated the law. ما يِصير تخالِف رَغبَة أبُوك [maː yṣiːr txaːlif raɣbat ʔabuːk] You mustn't go against your father's wishes.

تخَلَّف [txallaf] *v:* • **1.** to fail to appear, to stay away – سِقَط بِالصَّفّ الخامِس وَتخَلَّف عَن جَماعتَه [siqaṭ biṣṣaff ʔilxaːmis witxallaf ʕan ǰamaːʕtah] He failed in the fifth class and fell behind his group. تخَلَّف عَن الخِدمَة العَسكَرِيَّة وَحِبسَوه [txallaf ʕan ʔilxidma ʔilʕaskariyya wħibsuːh] He failed to appear for his military service and they jailed him.

اِختِلَف [ʔixtilaf] *v:* • **1.** to differ, be different, vary – هالقُماش يِختِلِف، مُو مِثل اللّي أرِيدَه [halqumaːš yixtilif, muː miθl ʔilli ʔariːdah] This cloth is different, not like the one I want. آراء الخُبَراء اِختِلفَت بِهالمَوضُوع [ʔaːraːʔ ʔilxubaraːʔ ʔixtilfat bhalmawðuːʕ] The opinions of the experts varied on this matter. • **2.** to disagree, argue, quarrel – وِلدَه اِختِلفَوا عَلَى تَقسِيم القاع [wildah ʔixtilfaw ʕala taqsiːm ʔilgaːʕ] His sons quarrelled over division of the land. الشُّهُود اِختِلفَوا. كُلّ واحِد حِكَى شِكِل [ʔiššuhuːd ʔixtilfaw. kull waːħid ħičaː šikil] The witnesses disagreed. Each one said something different.

خُلفَة [xulfa] *n:* خُلَف [xulaf] *pl:* • **1.** offspring, issue • **2.** ugly face, mug, puss

خِلاف [xilaːf] *n:* خِلافات [xilaːfaːt] *pl:* • **1.** difference, disparity, dissimilarity – خِلاف بِالرَّأي [xilaːf birraʔy] a difference of opinion. • **2.** disagreement, difference of opinion • **3.** dispute, controversy

خَلِيفَة [xaliːfa] *n:* خُلَفاء [xulafaːʔ] *pl:* • **1.** caliph

خِلافَة [xilaːfa] *n:* خِلافات [xilaːfaːt] *pl:* • **1.** caliphate

مُخالَفَة [muxaːlafa] *n:* مُخالَفات [muxaːlafaːt] *pl:* • **1.** violation, infringement • **2.** misdemeanor

اِختِلاف [ʔixtilaːf] *n:* اِختِلافات [ʔixtilaːfaːt] *pl:* • **1.** difference, disparity

خَلفَة [xalfa] *adj:* خَلفات [xalfaːt] *pl:* • **1.** apprentice, assistant

خَلفِي [xalfi] *adj:* • **1.** rear

مُخالِف [muxaːlif] *adj:* • **1.** dissenter, dissenting

مِختِلِف [mixtilif] *adj:* • **1.** different

مُخَلَّف [muxallaf] *adj:* مُخَلَّفات [muxallafaːt] *pl:* • **1.** residual, left behind, left over

مِتخالِف [mitxaːlif] *adj:* • **1.** contradictory

خَلف [xalf] *prepositional:* • **1.** behind

خَلفِيَّة [xalfiyya] *n:* • **1.** background

خ ل ف 2

خَلفَة [xalfa] *n:* • **1.** foreman

خ ل ف 3

مِخلِف [mixlif] *adj:* مَخالِف [maxaːlif] *pl:* • **1.** (adj. and n.) young male, immature male (bird)

خ ل ق

خِلَق [xilaq] *v:* • **1.** to create – الله خِلَق الأرض وَالسَّماوات [ʔallah xilaq ʔilʔarð wissamaːwaːt] God created the earth and the skies. الله يِخلِق وَمُحَمَّد يِبتِلِي [ʔallah yixliq wmuħammad yibtili] Man proposes and God disposes (lit., God creates and Mohammed suffers). Used to express exasperation at a nuisance that must be endured. لا تقُلِّي "ما أدرِي وينَه"! اِخلِقَه [laː tgulli "maː ʔadri wiːnah"! ʔixilqah] Don't tell me 'I don't know where he is. ' Pull him out of thin air!

اِختِلَق [ʔixtilaq] *v:* • **1.** to think up, concoct, fabricate – اِختِلَق قُصَّة خَيالِيَّة، وَالنّاس صَدّقَوا بِيه [ʔixtilaq quṣṣa xayaːliyya, winnaːs ṣaddgaw biːh] He made up a fanciful story, and people believed him. الحادِثَة مُو حَقِيقِيَّة. هُوَّ اختِلَقها [ʔilħaːdiθa muː ħaqiːqiyya. huwwa ʔixtilaqha] The incident is not true. He made it up.

خُلُق [xuluq] *n:* أخلاق [ʔaxlaːq] *pl:* • **1.** character, behavior • **2.** morals

خُلُق [xulug] *n:* • **1.** mood, temper, disposition – خُلقَه ضَيِّق [xulgah ðayyig] He's short-tempered. ضاق خُلقِي بِالبَيت؛ خَلِّي نِطلَع نِتمَشّى [ðaːg xulgi bilbayt; xalliː niṭlaʕ nitmaššaː] I feel confined in the house; let's go for a walk. لا تِحكِي وِيّاه. ما إلَه خُلُق [laː tiħči wiyyaːh. maː ʔilah xulug] Don't talk to him. He's in a bad mood. أخُذ إبنَك. آني مالِي خُلقَه [ʔuxuð ʔibnak. ʔaːni maːli xulgah] Take your son. I'm not in the mood to put up with him. مالِي خُلُق الدِّراسَة وَالإمتِحانات [maːli xulug ʔiddiraːsa wilʔimtiħaːnaːt] I don't have the get-up-and-go for study and examinations • **2.** patience, even temper – خُلقَه طَوِيل [xulgah ṭuwiːl] His patience is great. تَربِيَة الأطفال يرِيدِلها خُلُق [tarbiːt ʔilʔaṭfaːl yriːdilha xulug] Raising children requires patience.

خَلَق [xalag] *n:* • **1.** lowly, mere – خَلَق كاتِب [xalag ka:tib] a mere clerk. • **2.** worn out, useless, worn out, useless
خَلِق [xaliq] *n:* • **1.** creation
خِلقَة [xilqa] *n:* خِلَق [xilaq] *pl:* • **1.** face, countenance, looks – خِلقَة حِلوَة [xilqa ħilwa] an attractive face. خِلقَتَه اِنقِلبَت مِن سِمَع بالخَبَر [xilqatah ʔingilbat min simaʕ bilxabar] His face fell when he heard the news. خِلقَتها مَقلُوبَة لِأَنّ بَعَد ما مخَلِّيَّة مَساحِيق [xilqatha maglu:ba liʔann baʕad ma: mxalliyya masa:ħi:q] Her face is a mess because she hasn't put on her make-up yet.
خالِق [xa:liq] *n:* • **1.** creator
مَخلُوق [maxlu:q] *n:* مَخلُوقات [maxlu:qa:t] *pl:* • **1.** creature
أَخلاق [ʔaxla:q] *n:* • **1.** ethics
الخَلّاق [ʔilxalla:q] *n:* • **1.** The Creator
خَلُوق [xalu:q] *adj:* • **1.** polite, well-mannered – إبِن جِيرانّا شلُون خَلُوق [ʔibin ǰi:ra:nna šlu:n xalu:q] Our neighbors' son is awfully polite.
مخَلقَن [mxalgan] *adj:* • **1.** run-down, worn-out, shabby – مُوَظَّف مخَلقَن [mwaðððaf mxalgan] a seedy official. سَيّارَة مخَلقَنَة [sayya:ra mxalgana] a run-down car.
أَخلاقِي [ʔaxla:qi] *adj:* • **1.** moral – فِصلوه لأسباب أَخلاقِيَّة [fiṣlawh lʔasba:b ʔaxla:qiyya] They fired him for moral reasons.

خ ل ل

تخَلَّل [txallal] *v:* • **1.** to come between, be located between – التَّمثِيلِيّات كان تِتخَلَّلها قُطَع مُوسِيقِيَّة [ʔittamθi:liyya:t ča:n titxallalha quṭaʕ musi:qiyya] Musical selections were interspersed between the dramas.
اِختَلّ [ʔixtall] *v:* • **1.** to become disrupted, disturbed – كان دَيمشِي عالحَبِل لَكِن اِختَلّ تَوازنَه وَوُقَع [ča:n dayimši ʕalħabil la:kin ʔixtall tawa:znah wwugaʕ] He was walking on the rope, but he lost his balance and fell. اِختَلَّت المُواصَلات بين الثَّورَة [ʔixtallat ʔilmuwa:ṣala:t bi:n ʔiθθawra] Communications were disrupted during the revolution. إذا تخَلِّي إيدَك هنا، يِختَلّ التَّوازُن [ʔiða txalli: ʔi:dak hna, yixtall ʔittawa:zun] If you put your hand here, the balance will be disturbed. اِختَلّ عَقلَه وَوَدُّوه لمُستَشفى المَجانِين [ʔixtall ʕaqlah wawaddu:h lmustašfa ʔilmaǰa:ni:n] His mind became disturbed and they took him to the mental hospital.
خَلّ [xall] *n:* • **1.** vinegar
خَلَل [xalal] *n:* • **1.** a mechanical defect – خَلَل مِيكانِيكِي [xalal mikani:ki] a mechanical defect.
خِلَّة [xilla] *n:* خِلّات [xilla:t] *pl:* • **1.** defect, deficiency, flaw, fault, shortcoming
خِلال [xila:l] *n:* • **1.** (prep.) during – خِلال هَالمُدَّة [xila:l halmudda] during this time. • **2.** interval, space, period
خَلال [xala:l, xla:l] *n:* • **1.** (coll.) dates, crisp and not yet ripe
إخلال [ʔixla:l] *n:* إخلالات [ʔixla:la:t] *pl:* • **1.** breach, infraction, violation • **2.** disturbance – إخلال بالأَمِن [ʔixla:l bilʔamin] disturbance of the peace.
خَلالَة [xala:la] *n:* خَلالات [xala:la:t] *pl:* • **1.** (vulgar) glans penis
مُخِلّ، مُخِلّ بِالأَدَب [muxill, muxill bilʔadab] *adj:* • **1.** immoral, indecent, improper
مُختَلّ [muxtall] *adj:* • **1.** insane, unstable
مخَلَّل [mxallal] *adj:* • **1.** pickled

خ ل و

خَلَّى [xalla:] *v:* • **1.** to leave, allow or cause to remain – تعَشُّوا وَخَلُّولِي شوَيَّة [tʕaššu: wxallu:li šwayya] Eat your supper and leave me a little bit. خَلّيتَه بِالسِّينَما؛ راد يشُوف الفِلِم مَرَّة اللُّخ [xalli:tah bissinama; ra:d yšu:f ʔilfi lim marrat ʔillux] I left him behind at the movie; he wanted to see the film another time. مِن تِطلَع، لا تخَلِّي الباب مَفكُوك [min tiṭlaʕ, la: txalli: ʔilba:b mafku:k] When you go out, don't leave the door open. حِكَوا عَليها حَكِي وَما خَلُّوا شِي ما قالَوا [ħičaw ʕali:ha ħači wma xallaw šma ga:law] They talked about her and didn't leave anything unsaid. ما خَلَّى أَحَّد ما قَلَّه [ma: xalla: ʔaħħad ma: gallah] There was no one he didn't tell. • **2.** to keep, retain, hold – خَلِّي الفلُوس عِندَك إلَى أَن أحتاجها [xalli: ʔilflu:s ʕindak ʔila ʔan ʔaħta:ǰha] Keep the money with you until I need it. خَلِّي عينَك عَالجّاهِل [xalli: ʕaynak ʕaǰǰa:hil] Keep your eye on the child. بالله خَلِّي هَالقَضِيَّة عَلَى بالَك [ballah xalli: halqaðiyya ʕala ba:lak] Please keep this matter in mind. خَلُّولِي مُكان يَمّكُم [xallu:li muka:n yammkum] Save me a place next to you. • **3.** to put, place – خَلِّي خَمِس قَلَنات بانزِين بِالسَّيّارَة [xalli: xamis galana:t banzi:n bissayya:ra] Put five gallons of gas in the car. خَلِّي الكلاص عالميز [xalli: ʔilgla:ṣ ʕalmi:z] Put the glass on the table. خَلَّى واهسَه بِالقمار. لا دَيشتُغُل وَلا دَيدرُس [xalla: wahsah bilqma:r. la: dayištuɣul wala dayidrus] He has put all his energy into gambling. He's neither working nor studying. وين تخَلِّي المِفتاح؟ [wi:n txalli: ʔilmifta:ħ?] Where do you keep the key? بِنتِك خالَّة حُمرَة شفاف [bintič xa:lla ħumrat šfa:f] Your daughter is wearing lipstick. خالّ عَينَه عَلَى هَالسَّيّارَة؛ يرِيد يِشترِيها [xa:ll ʕaynah ʕala hassayya:ra; yri:d yištiri:ha] He's set on this car; he wants to buy it. لِيش خَلّيت نَفسَك؟ [li:š xallayt nafsak?] Why did you interfere? • **4.** to let, allow – هَالمَسجُون ما يخَلُّون واحِد يشُوفَه [halmasǰu:n ma: yxallu:n wa:ħid yšu:fah] They don't allow anyone to see this prisoner. خَلِّيه يِلبَس هدُومَه [xalli:h yilbas hdu:mah] Let him get dressed. خَلِّينِي أَفَكِّر [xalli:ni ʔafakkir] Let me think. • **5.** to cause, make, have – خَلِّيه يرُوح لِلبَنك [xalli:h yiru:ħ lilbang] Have him go to the bank. خَلَّى كُلّ النّاس يضِحكُون [xalla: kull ʔinna:s yðiħku:n] He made all the people laugh. هَالأَريَل يخَلِّي الرّاديُو يِشتُغُل أَحسَن [halʔaryal yxalli: ʔirra:dyu yištuɣul ʔaħsan] This aerial makes the radio operate better. • **6.** /in imperative/ (showing inclination, desire, command) let – خَلِّي نِلعَب وَرَق [xalli: nilʕab waraq] Let's play cards. يَالله، عاد، خَلِّي نرُوح [yallah, ʕa:d, xalli: nru:ħ] C'mon man, let's go! إذا ما تداوُم، يفصلُوك. خَلِّيهُم [ʔiða ma: dda:wum, yfuṣlu:k. xalli:hum] If you don't show up, they'll fire you. Let them.

أخلَى [ʔaxla:] *v:* • **1.** to vacate – الحُكُومَة قالَت لازِم نِخلِي البَيت مالنَا [ʔilħuku:ma ga:lat la:zim nixli ʔilbayt ma:lna] The government announced we have to vacate our house. • **2.** to evacuate – الفَصِيل الثّانِي أخلَى مَركَزَه [ʔilfaṣi:l ʔiθθa:ni ʔaxla: markazah] The second platoon evacuated its position. الجَّيش أخلَى المَدِينَة مِن السُّكّان [ʔijǰayš ʔaxla: ʔilmadi:na min ʔissukka:n] The army evacuated the populace from the city.

تخَلَّى [txalla:] *v:* • **1.** to give up, relinquish, abandon – ما خَلُّوه يِتزَوَّجها إلّا لَمّا تخَلَّى عَن نُصّ أملاكَه [ma: xallawh yidzawwaǰha ʔilla lamma txalla: ʕan nuṣṣ ʔamla:kah] They wouldn't let him marry her until he gave up half of his property. ما يِتخَلَّى عَن الصَّدِيق عِند الشِّدَّة [ma: yitxalla: ʕan ʔiṣṣadi:q ʕind ʔiššidda] He doesn't abandon a friend during a crisis. • **2.** to be left – الفلُوس ما تِتخَلَّى بهِيكِي مُكان [ʔilflu:s ma: titxalla: bhi:či muka:n] Money mustn't be left in this sort of place. هَذا ما يِتخَلَّى بِالعِبّ [ha:ða ma: yitxalla: bilʕibb] He's a tough nut to crack (lit. he can't be put in the pocket).

تخَلَّى [txalla:] *v:* • **1.** to visit the toilet – راح يِتخَلَّى وَهَسَّة يِجِي [ra:ħ yitxalla: whassa yiǰi] He went to visit the rest room and he'll be right back.

إختِلَى [ʔixtila:] *v:* • **1.** to go off, retire, be alone, withdraw – إختِلَى بِيه وَقالَّه بِالسِّرّ [ʔixtila: bi:h wga:llah bissirr] He stepped aside with him and told him about the secret.

خَلاء، بيت إلخَلاء [xala:ʔ, bi:t ʔilxala:ʔ] *n:* • **1.** toilet, water closet, restroom

خُلوَة [xalwa] *n:* خلوات [xalwa:t] *pl:* • **1.** secluded, isolated place

خَلوَة [xalwa] *n:* خَلاوِي [xala:wi] *pl:* • **1.** toilet, water closet

خَلِيَّة [xaliyya] *n:* خَلايا [xala:ya] *pl:* • **1.** cell (biol.) • **2.** beehive – خَلِيَّة عَسَل [xaliyyat ʕasal] beehive.

تَخَلِّي [taxilli] *n:* • **1.** giving up

إخلاء [ʔixla:ʔ] *n:* • **1.** emptying, vacating

خالِي [xa:li] *adj:* • **1.** empty, void – صَندُوق خالِي [ṣandu:g xa:li] an empty chest. • **2.** vacant – بَيت خالِي [bayt xa:li] a vacant house. • **3.** free, clear, devoid – مَيزِي خالِي مِن الأوراق [mayzi xa:li min ʔilʔawra:q] My desk is free of papers. بالَه خالِي [ba:la xa:li] His mind is clear. خُبُز خالِي [xubuz xa:li] plain bread.

مخَلِّي [mxalli] *adj:* • **1.** putting, leaving, keeping

خ م

خام [xa:m] *n:* • **1.** raw, unworked, unprocessed – مَوادّ خام [mawa:dd xa:m] raw materials. نَفُط خام [nafuṭ xa:m] crude oil. حَدِيد خام [ħadi:d xa:m] crude iron, pig iron, iron ore. جِلِد خام [ǰilid xa:m] untanned hide, raw leather. • **2.** inexperienced, green, wet behind the ears, naive, artless – هَالعامِل الجِّدِيد خام؛ ما يُعرُف كُلّ شِي [halʕa:mil ʔiǰǰidi:d xa:m; ma: yuʕruf kull ši] That new worker's green; he doesn't know anything. دَماغَه بَعدَه خام [dama:ɣah baʕdah xa:m] His mind is still undeveloped. • **3.** a type of cheap cotton cloth – خام أسمَر [xa:m ʔasmar] and خام سَواحِل [xa:m sawa:ħil] unbleached cotton cloth. خام أبيَض [xa:m ʔabyað] bleached cotton cloth.

خ م خ م

خمخَم [xamxam] *v:* • **1.** to become spoiled, tainted • **2.** to loaf, lounge – ما عِندَه شُغُل غير يخَمخُم بِالشَّوارِع [ma: ʕindah šuɣul ɣi:r yxamxum biššawa:riʕ] He has nothing to do but loaf around the streets. • **3.** to rummage, fumble about – لِيش دَتخَمخُم بالغَراض؟ [li:š datxamxum bilɣara:ð̣?] Why are you rummaging in the things?

خ م د

خِمَد [ximad] *v:* • **1.** to go out, die – لا تِترُك النّار قَبُل ما تُخمُد [la: titruk ʔinna:r gabul ma: tuxmud] Don't leave the fire until it goes out. • **2.** to calm down, die down, abate – البُركان خُمَد [ʔilburka:n xumad] The volcano became quiet. • **3.** to quiet down, shut up, be still – شقَدّ تِبكِي! ما راح تُخمُد؟ [šgadd tibči! ma: ra:ħ tuxmud?] You cry so much! Aren't you going to shut up?

خَمَّد [xammad] *v:* • **1.** to quench, put out – ذَبّ مَيّ عَالنّار وَخَمَّدها [ðabb mayy ʕanna:r wxammadha] He threw water on the fire and extinguished it.

أخمَد [ʔaxmad] *v:* • **1.** to quell, put down – الجَّيش أخمَد الثَّورَة بِسُرعَة [ʔiǰǰayš ʔaxmad ʔiθθawra bsurʕa] The army quelled the revolt quickly.

خَمُد [xamud] *n:* خُمُود [xumu:d] *pl:* • **1.** extinction

خُمُود [xumu:d] *n:* • **1.** extinction

خامِد [xa:mid] *adj:* • **1.** inactive – بُركان خامِد [burka:n xa:mid] an inactive volcano. • **2.** quiet, still, silent – الجّاهِل خامِد هَسَّة [ʔiǰǰa:hil xa:mid hassa] The kid is quiet now.

خ م ر

خَمَّر [xammar] *v:* • **1.** to leaven, raise, let rise – ما يصِير تُخبُز العَجِين بَلا ما تخَمُّرَه [ma: yṣi:r tuxbuz ʔilʕaǰi:n bala ma: txammurah] You shouldn't bake the dough without letting it rise. الخُمرَة هاي ما تخَمُّر العَجِين كُلَّه [ʔilxumra ha:y ma: txammur ʔilʕaǰi:n kullah] That leaven won't raise all the dough. • **2.** to rise – خَلِّي العَجِين يخَمُّر زين [xalli: ʔilʕaǰi:n yxammur zi:n] Let the dough rise well. • **3.** to let ferment, cause to ferment – بِالشِّمال، يخَمُّرُون عَصِير العِنَب، وَيسَوُّوه شَراب [biššima:l, yxammuru:n ʕaṣi:r ʔilʕinab, wysawwu:h šara:b] In the North, they ferment grape juice and make it into

wine. • **4.** to ferment – عَصِير العِنَب تخَمَّر؛ بَعَد ما يِنشُرُب [ʕaṣiːr ʔilʕinab txammar; baʕad maː yinšurub] The grape juice fermented; it's not drinkable any more.
تخَمَّر [txammar] *v:* • **1.** to veil oneself, wear a veil – البَدو بِالصَّحراء يِتخَمَّرُون، لَكِن تِقدَر تشُوف عيُونهُم [ʔilbadw biṣṣaḥraːʔ yitxammaruːn, laːkin tigdar tšuːf ʕyuːnhum] The Bedouins in the desert veil themselves but you can see their eyes. أُمَّه ما تِطلَع إذا ما تِتخَمَّر [ʔummah maː tiṭlaʕ ʔiða maː titxammar] His mother doesn't go out without putting on a veil. • **2.** to rise – خَلّي العَجِين يِتخَمَّر زين قَبُل ما تُخُبزَه [xalli: ʔilʕajiːn yitxammar ziːn gabul maː tuxubzah] Let the dough rise well before you bake it. • **3.** to ferment – عَصِير العِنَب تخَمَّر [ʕaṣiːr ʔilʕinab txammar] The grape juice has fermented.
اِختِمَر [ʔixtimar] *v:* • **1.** to rise – اِختِمَر العَجِين. خُبزِيه [ʔixtimar ʔilʕajiːn. xubziːh] The dough has risen. Bake it.
خَمُر [xamur] *n:* خُمُور [xumuːr] *pl:* • **1.** wine • **2.** liquor, alcoholic beverage
خُمرَة [xumra] *n:* خُمرات [xumraːt] *pl:* • **1.** fermenting agent, starter (in making yoghurt, bread), yeast
خَمّار [xammaːr] *n:* خَمّارَة [xammaːra] *pl:* • **1.** Alcoholic, drunkard • **2.** experienced drinker
خِمار [ximaːr] *n:* خِمارات [ximaːraːt] *pl:* • **1.** veil covering the head and face worn by women
خَمِيرَة [xamiːra] *n:* • **1.** yeast
خَمري [xamri] *adj:* • **1.** reddish brown, rosy – لُون خَمرِي [luːn xamri] wine color. خدُود خَمرِيَّة [xduːd xamriyya] rosy cheeks.
خمارِيَّة [xmaːriyya] *adj:* خمارِيّات [xmaːriyyaːt] *pl:* • **1.** hangover

خ م س

خَمَّس [xammas] *v:* • **1.** to divide (property) into fifths – خَمِّسَوا فلُوسَه مِن مات [xammisaw fluːsah min maːt] They divided his money into fifths when he died.
خُمُس [xumus] *n:* أخماس [ʔaxmaːs] *pl:* • **1.** one fifth
خَمسَة [xamsa] *n:* خَمسات [xamsaːt] *pl:* • **1.** five – خَمِس كَيلُوات [xamis kiluwaːt] five kilos. البارحَة بالعَزِيمَة ضِرَبنا بِالخَمسَة [ʔilbaːrḥa bilʕaziːma ðirabna bilxamsa] Yesterday at the dinner party we really dug in (lit. used all five fingers).
خمَيِّس، أبو خمَيِّس [xmayyis, ʔabu xmayyis] *n:* • **1.** a figurative term for a lion
خَمسِين [xamsiːn] *n:* خَمسِينات [xamsiːnaːt] *pl:* • **1.** fifty
الخَمِيس، يُوم الخَمِيس [ʔilxamiːs, yuːm ʔilxamiːs] *n:* • **1.** Thursday
خَمسِينات [xamsiːnaːt] *n:* • **1.** fifties
خامِس [xaːmis] *adj:* • **1.** fifth
مُخَمَّسَة [muxammasa] *adj:* • **1.** pentagon

خ م س ط ع ش

خُمُسطَعَش [xumusṭaʕaš] *n:* • **1.** fifteen

خ م ش

خُمَش [xumaš] *v:* • **1.** to snatch, to grab – لَمّا ما نطاه إيّاه، خُمَشها مِن إيدَه وشِرَد [lamma maː nṭaːh ʔiyyaːh, xumašha min ʔiːdah wširad] When he wouldn't give it to him, he snatched it from his hand and ran away.
خَمَّش [xammaš] *v:* • **1.** intens. of to snatch, grab – لُويش دَتخَمُّش؟ راح نِنطِيك إيّاهُم [luwiːš datxammuš? raːḥ ninṭiːk ʔiyyaːhum] Why are you grabbing so much? We will give them to you.
خَمُش [xamuš] *n:* • **1.** grabbing, snatching
خَمشَة [xamša] *n:* خَمشات [xamšaːt] *pl:* • **1.** a grab, a snatch

خ م ص

أخمَص [ʔaxmaṣ] *n:* • **1.** butt (of a rifle)

خ م ط

خُمَط [xumaṭ] *v:* • **1.** (vulgar) to mate with, to have intercourse with – الدِّيك خُمَط الدِّجاجَة [ʔiddiːč xumaṭ ʔiddijaːja] The rooster mated with the hen.
اِنخُمَط [ʔinxumaṭ] *v:* • **1.** to be snatched, to be grabbed, to be taken by force • **2.** to be stolen
خَمُط [xamuṭ] *n:* • **1.** grabbing, snatching
مَخمُوط [maxmuːṭ] *adj:* • **1.** snatched, grabbed, stolen

خ م ل

خِمَل [ximal] *v:* • **1.** to relax
خَملَة [xamla] *n:* • **1.** nap, pile, hairy surface (of a fabric)
مَخمَل [maxmal] *n:* • **1.** velvet
خُمُول [xumuːl] *n:* • **1.** weakness, drowsiness
خامِل [xaːmil] *adj:* • **1.** lazy, sluggish – فَدّ واحِد خامِل [fadd waːḥid xaːmil] a lazy guy.
مَخمَلِي [maxmali] *adj:* • **1.** velvety, plush • **2.** plush, amaranth, velvet

خ م م

خَمّ [xamm] *v:* • **1.** to check, try – خُمّ الأكِل، شُوفَه اِستِوَى [xumm ʔilʔakil, šuːfah ʔistiwaː] Check the food and see if it's done. خُمّ جيُوبَه؛ شُوفَه شايِل سِچِّينَة [xumm jyuːbah; šuːfah šaːyil siččiːna] Check his pockets; see if he's carrying a knife. خُمّ الجّاهِل، شُوفَه نايِم لَو لا [xumm ʔijjaːhil, šuːfah naːyim law laː] Check the baby and see if he's sleeping or not. خُمّلِي فِكرَة. راح يبِيع الحُوش لَو لا؟ [xummli fikra. raːḥ ybiːʕ ʔilḥuːš law laː?] Check out this idea for me. Is he going to sell his house or not? خَمِّيت بِكُلّ المَخازِن وَما لِقِيت هِيكِي قَلَم [xammiːt bkull ʔilmaxaːzin wma ligiːt hiːči qalam] I've tried in all the stores and couldn't find that sort of pencil. • **2.** to test, try – راد يخُمَّك أوَّل، يشُوفَك تِصلَح لِهالوَظِيفَة [raːd yxummak ʔawwal, yšuːfak tiṣlaḥ lhalwaðiːfa] He wanted to test you first, to see if you're suitable for that job. كان دَيخُمّني. راد يشُوف أبُوق شِي [čaːn dayxummni. raːd yšuːf ʔabuːg ši] He was testing me. He wanted to see if I'd steal something. • **3.** to search, explore, rummage – شَكُو عِندَك دَإِتخُمّ بالغَراض؟ [šaku ʕindak daʔitxumm bilɣara:ð̣?] How come you're rummaging through the things? خُمّ الجّاهِل وشُوف إذا أَكُو شِي بِجَيبَه [xumm ʔijǰa:hil wšu:f ʔiða ʔaku ši bǰaybah] Search the child and see if there's anything in his pocket. خَمَّيت السُّوق كُلَّه وَما شِفِت مِثِل هالكلاص [xammi:t ʔissu:g kullah wama: šifit miθil halgla:ṣ] I searched all through the market and didn't see a glass like this. آنِي خامّ أُورُبّا كُلّها [ʔa:ni xa:mm ʔu:ruppa kullha] I've travelled all over Europe.

خَمّ [xamm] *n:* • **1.** checking, trying

خ م ن

خَمَّن [xamman] *v:* • **1.** to assess, appraise, estimate – شقَدّ تخَمِّن إيجار هَالبَيت؟ [šgadd txammin ʔi:ǰa:r halbayt?] How much would you guess the rent of this house to be? راح يِجِي مُوَظَّف يخَمِّن البَيت اليوم [ra:ħ yiǰi muwað̣ð̣af yixammin ʔilbayt ʔilyu:m] An official is coming to appraise the house today. تِقدَر تخَمِّن سِعِر هَالبَيت؟ [tigdar txammin siʕir halbayt?] Can you estimate the price of this house?

تَخمِين [taxmi:n] *n:* تَخمِينات [taxmi:na:t] *pl:* • **1.** estimation

مُخَمَّن [muxamman] *adj:* • **1.** estimated, evaluated

مُخَمِّن [muxammin] *n:* • **1.** assessor, appraiser

خ ن

خان [xa:n] *n:* خانات [xa:na:t] *pl:* • **1.** old fashioned inn, hostelry • **2.** stable (usually boarding beasts of burden) • **3.** warehouse, storehouse

خانَة [xa:na] *n:* خانات [xa:na:t] *pl:* • **1.** space, row (chess, backgammon, etc.) • **2.** space, shelf, cubbyhole

خانَة [xa:na] *n:* • **1.** (usually used as the second constituent in a number of compound words of Turkish and Persian origin) place for ---, house for ---, etc., for instance: خستَخانَة sick house ie hospital

خانچِي [xa:nči] *n:* خانچِيَّة [xa:nči:yya] *pl:* • **1.** warehouseman

خ ن ث

خَنَّث [xannaθ] *v:* • **1.** to scare, terrify, cow – خَنَّثلَك إيّاه بصَيحَة وِحدَة [xannaθlak ʔiyya:h bṣi:ħa wiħda] He really terrified him with one roar. خَنَّثتَه بالشِّطرَنج البارحَة. غِلَبتَه خَمِس مَرّات وَبَعَد ما يِلعَب ويّايا [xannaθtah biššiṭranǰ ʔilba:rħa. ɣilabtah xamis marra:t wabaʕad ma: yilʕab wiyya:ya] I cowed him in chess yesterday. I beat him five times and now he won't play with me. • **2.** to get scared – مِن يشِيل عَليه السِّكّينَة، يخَنِّث [min yši:l ʕali:h ʔissičči:na, yxanniθ] When he pulls a knife on him, he turns chicken.

تخَنَّث [txannaθ] *v:* • **1.** to be effeminate – لا تِتخَنَّث بلِبسَك [la: titxannaθ blibsak] Don't be effeminate in your dress. • **2.** to turn coward, chicken out – مِن شافنِي جاي، تخَنَّث وَسِكَت [min ša:fni ǰa:y, txannaθ wsikat] When he saw me coming, he chickened out and shut up. فُوت عَليه! لا تِتخَنَّث [fu:t ʕali:h! la: titxannaθ] Go get him! Don't be chicken!

خناث، خَناث [xna:θ, xana:θ] *n:* خَناثات [xana:θa:t] *pl:* • **1.** vulva, female genitalia • **2.** effeminate or homosexual male

خُنثَى [xunθa] *adj:* • **1.** (no pl.) hermaphrodite

خَنِيث [xani:θ] *adj:* • **1.** coward, timid person, chicken – خَنِيث خَبِيث [xani:θ xabi:θ] trouble-making coward.

مخَنَّث [mxannaθ] *adj:* مَخانِيث، مخانثَة [maxa:ni:θ, mxa:nθa] *pl:* • **1.** effeminate man • **2.** coward, sissy • **3.** powerless, weak, ineffectual person

أخنَث [ʔaxnaθ] *comparative adjective:* • **1.** more or most cowardly – أخنَث مِن الدِّجاجَة [ʔaxnaθ min ʔiddiǰa:ǰa] More cowardly than the chicken.

خ ن ج ر

خَنجَر [xanǰar] *n:* خَناجِر [xana:ǰir] *pl:* • **1.** dagger, usually with a curved blade

خَنجَرلِيَّة [xanǰarliyya] *n:* خَنجَرلِيّات [xanǰarliyya:t] *pl:* • **1.** small dagger

خ ن خ ن

خَنخَن [xanxan] *v:* • **1.** to talk nasally, talk through one's nose – يخَنخِن بحَكيَه هوايَة [yxanxin bħačyah hwa:ya] He nasalizes his speech a lot.

خَنخَنَة [xanxana] *n:* • **1.** nasalization, nasal twang

خ ن د ق

خَندَق [xandaq] *n:* خَنادِق [xana:diq] *pl:* • **1.** moat • **2.** trench

خ ن ز ر

خَنزَر [xanzar] *v:* • **1.** to glare, stare angrily – لُويش دَتخنزر عَليّا؟ شسَوِّيت؟ [luwi:š datxanzir ʕalayya? šsawwi:t?] Why are you glaring at me? What did I do?

تخَنزَر [txanzar] *v:* • **1.** to be or become a swine, a bastard – مِن توَظَّف، تخَنزَر [min twað̣ð̣af, txanzar] When he got the job, he became a swine.

خَنزِير [xanzi:r, xinzi:r] *n:* خَنازِير [xana:zi:r] *pl:* • **1.** pig, hog, swine

خَنزِيرَة [xanzi:ra, xinzi:ra] *n:* خَنزِيرات [xinzi:ra:t] *pl:* • **1.** female pig, sow • **2.** water pump, hand pump

خ ن س

خِنَس [xinas] *v:* • **1.** to cower, withdraw, shrink back – خِنَس جَوَّة المِيز [xinas ǰawwa ʔilmi:z] He cowered under the table. صِيح بِيه، هَسَّة يخِنِس [ṣi:ħ bi:h, hassa yixnis] Shout at him and he'll shrink back. • **2.** to subside, quiet down, shut up – مِن صاح بإبنَه، خِنَس [min ṣa:ħ bʔibnah, xinas] When he shouted at his son, he shut up. هُوَّ خانِس وَقاعِد [huwwa xa:nis wga:ʕid] He's sitting subdued.

خَنَّس [xannas] *v:* • **1.** to cow, make cower – خَنَّسَه بصَيحَة وِحدَة [xannasah bṣiːħa wiħda] He made him cower with one shout.
خَنِس [xanis] *n:* • **1.** silence
الخَنّاس [ʔilxannaːs] *n:* • **1.** name for the Devil – لابِس كلاو الخَنّاس [laːbis klaːw ʔilxannaːs] He's invisible (lit., he's wearing the Devil's cap).

خ ن ص ر

خُنصُر [xunṣur] *n:* خَناصِر [xanaːṣir] *pl:* • **1.** little finger

خ ن ف س

خَنفَس [xanfas] *v:* • **1.** to die down, go down, subside, dim – النّار خَنفِسَت. حُطِّلها بَعَد فَحَم [ʔinnaːr xanfisat. ħuṭṭilha baʕad faħam] The fire's died down. Put some more coal on it. الفانُوس خَنفَس. يِمكِن خِلَص النَّفُط [ʔilfaːnuːs xanfas. yimkin xilaṣ ʔinnafuṭ] The lantern has dimmed. Maybe the oil is all gone. مِن شِعَلت الطَّبّاخ، الكلُوب خَنفَس [min šiʕalt ʔiṭṭabbaːx, ʔilgluːb xanfas] When I turned on the stove, the light dimmed. أَشُو الماي خَنفَس. يبَيِّن جيرانّا هَمّ قام يِسقُون حَدِيقَتهُم [ʔašu ʔilmaːy xanfas. yibayyin ǰiːraːnna hamm gaːm yisguːn ħadiːqathum] I notice the water pressure's gone down. Looks like the neighbors have started to water their garden again. • **2.** to quiet down, calm down – خَنفَس مِن شاف الرِّجّال شلُون قَوِي [xanfas min šaːf ʔirriǰǰaːl šluːn qawi] He quieted down when he saw how strong the man was.

خ ن ف س ن

خُنفِسان [xunfisaːn] *n:* • **1.** (coll.) beetle(s)
خُنفِسانَة [xunfisaːna] *n:* خُنفِسانات [xunfisaːnaːt] *pl:* • **1.** beetle

خ ن ق

خِنَق [xinag] *v:* • **1.** to choke – عَظُم سِمَك خِنَقنِي [ʕaðum simač xinagni] A fishbone choked me. الدُّخّان بهَالمَحَلّ يُخنُق [ʔidduxxaːn bhalmaħall yuxnug] The smoke in this place is choking. • **2.** to choke (a motor, usually by putting one's hand over the carburetor mouth) – إخنُق الكَبرِيتَر [ʔixnug ʔilkabriːtar] Choke the carburetor. • **3.** to choke to death, strangle, suffocate, smother – الجّاهِل خِنَق البَزّونَة [ʔiǰǰaːhil xinag ʔilbazzuːna] The kid strangled the cat. لِقوه بَالسَّيّارَة بِالكَراج مَيِّت. دُخّان السَّيّارَة خِنَقَه [ligawh bissayyaːra bilgaraːǰ mayyit. duxxaːn ʔissayyaːra xinagah] They found him in the car in the garage. The smoke from the car overcame him. وُقَع بِالشَّطّ والماي خِنَقَه [wugaʕ biššaṭṭ wilmaːy xinagah] He fell in the river and drowned.
خَنَّق [xinnag] *v:* • **1.** to choke, to choke to death • **2.** to choke to death
تخانَق [txaːnag] *v:* • **1.** to choke one another – فاكِك الجُّهّال. دَيِتخانقُون [faːkik ʔiǰǰahhaːl. dayitxaːnguːn] Separate the kids. They're choking each other. • **2.** to quarrel, dispute, pick a fight – ماكُو حاجَة تِتخانَق وِيّا النّاس [maːku ħaːǰa titxaːnag wiyya ʔinnaːs] There is no reason for you to jump down people's throats.
اِختِنَق [ʔixtinag] *v:* • **1.** to choke – ماكُو شِي. اِختِنَقِت بِالأَكِل [maːku ši. ʔixtinagit bilʔakil] It's nothing. I choked on the food. اِختِنَقِت مِن الدُّخّان [ʔixtinagit min ʔidduxxaːn] I choked from the smoke. • **2.** to choke to death, suffocate – وُقَف الأَكِل بزَردُومَه وَاِختِنَق [wugaf ʔilʔakil bzarduːmah wʔixtinag] The food caught in his throat and he choked to death. صار حَرِيق بِالغُرفَة مالتَه وَاِختِنَق [ṣaːr ħariːq bilɣurfa maːltah wʔixtinag] There was a fire in his room and he suffocated. اِختِنَق جَوَّة التُّراب [ʔixtinag ǰawwa ʔittiraːb] He suffocated under the dirt. وُقَع بِالماي وَاِختِنَق [wugaʕ bilmaːy wʔixtinag] He fell into the water and drowned.
خَنِق [xanig] *n:* • **1.** strangulation, suffocation
خَنقَة [xanga] *n:* خَنقات [xangaːt] *pl:* • **1.** congestion, crowding, jam • **2.** madhouse, mess, crowded place – السُّوق كان خَنقَة اليُوم [ʔissuːg čaːn xanga ʔilyuːm] The market was a madhouse today.
اِختِناق [ʔixtinaːq] *n:* • **1.** suffocation, asphyxia
مِختِنِق [mixtinig] *adj:* • **1.** suffocated
خَنّاق الدجاج [xannaːg ʔiddiǰaːǰ] *n:* • **1.** a type of plant poisonous to chickens

خ ن م

خانِم، خانُم [xaːnim, xaːnum] *n:* خَوانِم [xawaːnim] *pl:* • **1.** (a term of respectful address to a lady, approx.:) madam, ma'am • **2.** (a casual way of referring to a man's wife, approx.:) the little woman, the missus – إجا هُوَّ وِالخانُم مالتَه [ʔiǰa huwwa wilxaːnum maːltah] He and his wife came. الخانِم مالتَه راكُبتَه [lxaːnim maːltah raːkubtah] His missus wears the pants in the family.

خ ن ن

خَنّ [xann] *v:* • **1.** to speak nasally, nasalize – مِن يِحكِي يخِنّ [min yiħči yxinn] or يخِنّ بحَكيَه [yxinn bħačyah] He speaks nasally. يخِنّ بخَشمَه [yxinn bxašmah] He talks through his nose.
خَنّ [xann] *n:* • **1.** nasal twang
خَنَّة [xanna] *n:* • **1.** nasal twang – أَبُو خَنَّة [ʔabu xanna] man with a nasal twang.

خ ن و

خَناوَة [xanaːwa] *adj:* • **1.** (invar.) sissified, unmanly – لا تصِير خَناوَة [laː tṣiːr xanaːwa] Don't be a sissy.

خ و ب

خُو، خُوب [xuː, xuːb] *particle:* • **1.** an interjection implying apprehension or hope – خُو ما سِمَع؟ [xuː maː simaʕ?] He hasn't heard, has he? خُو ما زِعَل؟ [xuː maː ziʕal?] He didn't get mad, did he? خُو ما الماي بُرَد؟ [xuː maː ʔilmaːy burad?] The water hasn't cooled off, has it? خُو ما ترِيد ترُوح هَسَّة [xuː maː triːd truːħ hassa] You don't want to go now, I hope. • **2.** thus, therefore, so – خُو ما بِقَى عَلَيّا دَين [xuː maː biqaː ʕalayya dayn] So I don't owe anything anymore. خُو ما عِندَك حِجَّة بَعَد [xuː maː ʕindak ħijja baʕad] So you've got no more excuse. • **3.** (as an intensifier, approx.:) oh, why, heck – خُو الكُلّ يِعرفُون شقَدّ أَحِبَّك. ما مَعقُول أَسَوِّي بِيك هِيكِي [xuː ʔilkull yiʕrifuːn šgadd ʔaħibbak. maː maʕquːl ʔasawwiː biːk hiːči] Oh everyone knows how much I like you. I couldn't do anything like that to you. خُو أَيّ واحِد يِقدَر يسَوِّي هَذا [xuː ʔayy waːħid yigdar ysawwiː haːða] Heck, anyone can do that!

خ و خ

خُوخ [xawx, xuːx] *n:* • **1.** (coll.) peach(es)
خُوخَة [xuːxa] *n:* خُوخات [xuːxaːt] *pl:* • **1.** peach

خ و ذ

خُوذَة [xuːða] *n:* خُوَذ [xuwað] *pl:* • **1.** helmet

خ و ر

خار [xaːr] *v:* • **1.** to tour, wander around – خِرِت أُورُبّا كُلّها [xirit ʔuːruppa kullha] I went all over Europe.
خَوَّر [xawwar] *v:* • **1.** to run around, wander, roam – إبِنها ما عِندَه شُغُل؛ بَسّ يخَوُّر بِالدَّرابِين [ʔibinha maː ʕindah šuɣul; bass yxawwur biddaraːbiːn] Her son has no job and just bums around the streets.
خَور [xuːr] *n:* • **1.** wandering, strolling
خَورَة [xawra] *n:* خورات [xawraːt] *pl:* • **1.** tour, trip, spin, turn, round • **2.** whirlpool
خَوّار [xawwaːr] *adj:* خَوّارَة [xawwaːra] *pl:* • **1.** well traveled, having gotten around a lot – يُعرُف كُلّ مُكان بِالوِلايَة لِأَنَّه خَوّار هوايَة [yuʕruf kull mukaːn bilwilaːya liʔannah xawwaːr hwaːya] He knows every corner of the city because he's gotten around a lot.

خ و ر د

تخُورَد [txuːrad] *v:* • **1.** to treat – راح أَتخَورَد عَلِيك بدونَدِرمَة [raːħ ʔatxawrad ʕaliːk bduːndirma] I'll treat you to an ice cream. دَيِتخَورَد عالبنَيَّة بِفلُوس غَيرَه [dayitxawrad ʕalbnayya bifluːs ɣayrah] He's treating the girl with money that isn't his. يِتخَورَد عالرّايِح والجاي [yitxawrad ʕarraːyiħ wijjaːy] He pays for everyone whether he knows them or not.
خوارِدَة [xwaːrda] *adj:* • **1.** (invar.) generous – وَلَد خوارِدَة [walad xwaːrda] a generous fellow.

خ و ش

خُوش [xuːš] *n:* • **1.** good, fine, excellent – خُوش سَيّارَة [xuːš sayyaːra] a good car. خُوش وَلَد [xuːš walad] a nice guy. خُوش. أَشُوفَك السّاعَة سِتَّة [xuːš. ʔašuːfak ʔissaːʕa sitta] Good. I'll see you at six. خُوش حَكِي [xuːš ħači] Good idea! Now you're talking!
خُوشِي [xuːši] *adj:* • **1.** tart, bittersweet – رُمّانَة خُوشِيَّة [rummaːna xuːšiyya] a tart pomegranate.

خ و ش ق

خَوشَق [xawšag] *v:* • **1.** to eat with a spoon – شِفِتهُم يخُوشقُون بِالشُّوربَة [šifithum yxuːšguːn biššuːrba] I saw them eating soup with spoons. • **2.** to stir with a spoon – خَوشَقت الشّاي زين؟ [xawšagt ʔiččaːy zayn?] Did you stir up the tea well enough? • **3.** (by extension) to drink tea – طَبَّيت عَلَيهُم وَلقَيتهُم يخُوشقُون [ṭabbayt ʕaliːhum wilgaythum yxuːšguːn] I dropped in on them and found them drinking tea.
خاشُوقَة [xaːšuːga] *n:* خَواشِيق [xawaːšiːg] *pl:* • **1.** teaspoon – خاشُوقَة أَكِل [xaːšuːgat ʔakil] table spoon. خاشُوقَة شاي [xaːšuːgat čaːy] demi-tasse spoon. خاشُوقَة كُوب [xaːšuːgat kuːb] teaspoon.

خ و ص

خُوص [xuːṣ] *n:* • **1.** (coll.) palm leaf, palm leaves
خُوصَة [xuːṣa] *n:* خُوصات، خُوَص [xuːṣaːt, xuwaṣ] *pl:* • **1.** palm leaf • **2.** a type of bracelet in the form of a coil

خ و ض

خاض [xaːð̣] *v:* • **1.** to wade – شال دِشداشتَه وطَبّ يخُوض بِالمَيّ [šaːl dišdaːštah wṭabb yxuːð̣ bilmayy] He lifted his robe and went wading in the water.
خَوض [xawð̣] *n:* • **1.** wading

خ و ط

خاط [xaːṭ] *v:* • **1.** to stir
خَوط [xawṭ] *n:* • **1.** stir, (act of) stirring

خ و ف

خاف [xaːf] *v:* • **1.** to be scared, afraid, worried, concerned, apprehensive – خِفِت بِالعَركَة؛ وَلا طَلَّعِت راسِي [xifit bilʕarka; wala ṭallaʕit raːsi] I was scared during the fight; I never even stuck my head out. لا تخاف؛ الكَلِب ما يعَضّ [laː txaːf; ʔiččalib maː yʕað̣ð̣] Don't be afraid; the dog doesn't bite. أَخاف أَحكِي وِيّاه هَسَّة لِأَنّ مَشغُول [ʔaxaːf ʔaħči wiyyaːh hassa liʔann mašɣuːl] I'm afraid to talk to him now, because he's busy. يخاف مِن مَرتَه [yxaːf min martah] He is afraid of his wife. خاف الله وَلا تِحكِي عالنّاس [xaːf ʔallah wla tiħči ʕannaːs] Fear God and don't talk about people. أَخُوك خاف عَلِيك هُوايَة [ʔaxuːk xaːf ʕaliːk huwaːya] Your brother was worried about you a lot. لا تخاف عَليه. هُوَّ كُلِّش شاطِر [laː txaːf ʕaliːh. huwwa kulliš šaːṭir] Don't worry about him. He's very clever. خاف يِجِي لِلبَيت وَما يِلقانِي [xaːf yiji lilbayt wma yilgaːni] It's possible he'll come to the house and not find me. أَخاف ما عِندَه فلُوس وَلِهَالسَّبَب ما جا [ʔaxaːf maː ʕindah fluːs wilhassabab maː ǰaː] I'm afraid he didn't have money and that's the reason he didn't come. أخاف مِن طَرَف الفلوس [ʔaxaːf min ṭaraf ʔilfluːs] Maybe it's about money. أخاف عَن التَّرفِيع مالِي [ʔaxaːf ʕan ʔitttarfiːʕ maːli] Hey, maybe it's about my promotion! خاف يِسأل عَنِّي قُلّه هَسَّة يِجِي [xaːf yisʔal ʕanni gullah hassa yiǰi] Just in case he asks about me, tell him I'm coming right away. أُخُذ وِيّاك أَكِل خاف تِجُوع [ʔuxuð wiyyaːk ʔakil xaːf dǰuːʕ] Take some food with you in case you get hungry.

خَوَّف [xawwaf] *v:* • **1.** to scare, frighten, alarm, worry – طِلَعلِي مِن وَرا الباب وَخَوَّفنِي [ṭilaʕli min wara ʔilbaːb wxawwafni] He jumped at me from behind the door and scared me. خَوَّفنِي كُلّش مِن وُگَع مِن الدَّرَج [xawwafni kulliš min wugaʕ min ʔiddaraǰ] He scared me to death when he fell down the stairs. الحالَة دَتخَوُّف [ʔilħaːla datxawwuf] The situation is alarming. هَالكَلِب يخَوُّف [haččalib yxawwuf] This dog is frightening.

تخَوَّف [txawwaf] *v:* • **1.** to be scared, to be alarmed, to be worried, to be frightened – دَأتخَوَّف مِن الوَضِع [daʔatxawwaf min ʔilwaðiʕ] I am alarmed at the situation. لا تُطلُب مِنَّه يسَوِّيها. يِتخَوَّف هوايَة [laː tuṭlub minnah ysawwiːha. yitxawwaf hwaːya] Don't ask him to do it. He's very fearful.

خَوف [xawf, xuːf] *n:* • **1.** fear, fright

مَخاوُف [maxaːwuf] *n:* • **1.** fears

خَوّاف [xawwaːf] *adj:* • **1.** fearful, timid, faint-hearted – إبنَك خَوّاف هوايَة [ʔibnak xawwaːf hwaːya] Your son's very timid. • **2.** coward

مُخِيف [muxiːf] *adj:* • **1.** scary • **2.** scary, frightful, fear-inspiring

خايِف [xaːyif] *adj:* • **1.** fearful

متخَوُّف [mitxawwuf] *adj:* • **1.** scared, hesitant

أخوَف [ʔaxwaf] *comparative adjective:* • **1.** more or most cowardly – أخوَف مِن الدِّجاجَة [ʔaxwaf min ʔiddiǰaːǰa] more cowardly than the chicken.

خَوفاً [xawfan] *adverbial:* • **1.** for fear

خ و ل

خَوَّل [xawwal] *v:* • **1.** to authorize – خَوَّلنِي أوَقِّع الصُّكُوك مالتَه [xawwalni ʔawaqqiʕ ʔiṣṣukuːk maːltah] He authorized me to sign his checks.

تخَوَّل [txawwal] *v:* • **1.** to be authorized

خال [xaːl] *n:* خوال [xawaːl] *pl:* • **1.** maternal uncle

خالَة [xaːla] *n:* خالات [xaːlaːt] *pl:* • **1.** maternal aunt • **2.** (from of address to a much older woman approx.:) madam – خالَة، تِدرِين وِين دائِرَة البَرِيد؟ [xaːla, tidriːn wiːn daːʔirat ʔilbariːd?] Ma'am, do you know where the post office is?

خالُو [xaːlu] *n:* • **1.** (as a form of address) uncle – رُوح، يا صغَيِّر؛ جِيب خالُو [ruːħ, yaː ṣɣayyir; ǰiːb xaːlu] Go on, Junior; get Uncle.

تخوِيل [taxwiːl] *n:* • **1.** authorization

مُخَوَّل [muxawwal] *adj:* • **1.** authorized

خ و ل ي

خاولِي [xaːwli] *n:* خاولِيّات [xaːwliːyyaːt] *pl:* • **1.** towel, hand towel

خ و ن [1]

خان [xaːn] *v:* • **1.** to betray – رِموه بِالرِّصاص لِأنّ خان وَطَنَه [rimuːh birriṣaːṣ liʔann xaːn waṭanah] They shot him because he betrayed his country. لا تقُلَّه بِالسِّرّ تَرَة يخُونَك [laː tgullah bissirr tara yxuːnak] Don't tell him the secret or he will give you away. 2. to cheat, deceive. زَوجتَه تخُونَه عَلَى طُول [zawiǰtah txuːnah ʕala ṭuːl] His wife's cheating on him all the time. • **2.** to cheat, deceive

خَوَّن [xawwan] *v:* • **1.** to distrust, be suspicious of – إنتَ دَتخَوِّنِّي بشِي ما تُعرُف عَنَّه [ʔinta datxawwinni bši maː tuʕruf ʕannah] You're making me out to be dishonest in something you don't know about. ماكُو حاجَة تصِير شَكّاك وَتخَوِّن النّاس اللِّي يِشتَغلُون عِندَك [maːku ħaːǰa tṣiːr šakkaːk wtxawwin ʔinnaːs ʔilli yištaɣluːn ʕindak] There is no need to be suspicious and to mistrust the people who work for you.

خِيانَة [xiyaːna] *n:* • **1.** faithlessness, betrayal, perfidy

خائِن [xaːʔin, xaːyin] *adj:* خَونَة [xawana] *pl:* • **1.** traitor

خ و ن [2]

خان، خانَة [xaːn, xaːna] *n:* • **1.** old fashion inn, warehouse

خ و ي

خُوَى [xuwaː] *v:* • **1.** to extort money from – كُلَّما أشُوفَه يِخوِينِي سِجارَة [kullma ʔašuːfah yixwiːni sigaːra] Whenever I see him he bums a cigarette.

خَوِي [xawy] *n:* • **1.** extortion

خاوَة [xaːwa] *n:* • **1.** protection, protection money, protection fee – طِين خاوَة [ṭiːn xaːwa] a white clay used by women as beauty cream.

خ ي ب

خاب [xaːb] *v:* • **1.** to be dashed, let down, disappointed – خاب ظَنِّي بِيك [xaːb ðanni biːk] My opinion of you has been lowered. خاب أمَلِي بِالمُدِير الجِّدِيد [xaːb ʔamali bilmudiːr ʔiǰǰidiːd] My hopes in the new director were dashed.

خَيَّب [xayyab] *v:* • **1.** to dash, disappoint, let down – لا تخَيِّب أمَلِي بِيك [laː txayyib ʔamali biːk] Don't disappoint my hopes for you.

خَيب [xayb] *n:* • **1.** failure • **2.** disappointment

خَيبَة [xayba] *n:* • **1.** disappointment

خايِب، إبن الخايبَة [xaːyib, ʔibn ʔilxaːyba] *n:* • **1.** a failure in life (lit., son of a disappointed woman)

خ ي ر

خَيَّر [xayyar] *v:* • **1.** to let choose, to give a choice – خَيَّرتَه بين الثُّوب وَالبلُوز [xayyartah bi:n ʔiθθu:b wiliblu:z] I gave him the choice between the shirt and the sweater.
تخَيَّر [txayyar] *v:* • **1.** to choose, take one's choice – لَو تروُح تجِيبها، لَو تدِزّ واحِد يجِيبها؛ تخَيَّر [law tru:ħ dji:bha, law ddizz wa:ħid yji:bha; txayyar] Either you go get it or you send someone to get it; you make your choice.
اِختار [ʔixta:r] *v:* • **1.** to choose, select, pick – مِنُو اِختار هَاللُّون؟ [minu ʔixta:r hallu:n?] Who chose this color?
اِستَخار [ʔistaxa:r] *v:* • **1.** to ask (God) for guidance – اِستِخِير الله قَبُل ما تسافِر [ʔistixi:r ʔallah gabul ma: tsa:fir] Ask God for proper guidance before you go travelling.
اِستَخيَر [ʔistaxyar] *v:* • **1.** to choose, pick
خَير [xayr, xi:r] *n:* • **1.** good, excellent, outstanding, superior – هالسَّنَة خير. مُطرَت هوايَة وَالحُنطَة كُلِّش زينَة [hassana xi:r. muṭrat hwa:ya wilħunṭa kulliš zi:na] This year is prosperous. It rained a lot and the wheat is very good. • **2.** best – الخير فِي ما اِختارَه الله [ʔilxi:r fi: ma: ʔixta:rah ʔallah] Whatever God willed is best. سِمَعِت تزَوَّجِت. بيها الخير، إن شاء الله [simaʕit dzawwaǰit. bi:ha ʔilxi:r, ʔinša:llah] I heard you got married. I wish you the best. • **3.** good thing, blessing • **4.** good, benefit, advantage – هَذا ما بِيه خير [ha:ða ma: bi:h xi:r] He's not worth anything. إذا بِيك خير، تصارَع ويّا واحِد بقَدَّك [ʔiða bi:k xi:r, tṣa:raʕ wiyya wa:ħid bgaddak] If you're the man you think you are, fight with someone your own size. • **5.** charity – عَمَل الخير [ʕamal ʔilxi:r] charitable work.
خيار [xya:r] *n:* • **1.** (coll.) cucumber(s)
خِيرَة [xi:ra] *n:* خِيرات [xi:ra:t] *pl:* • **1.** best, choice, pick, elite, cream • **2.** fortune, lot – خَلّي آخُذلَك خِيرَة [xalli: ʔa:xuðlak xi:ra] Let me tell your fortune.
خِيار [xiya:r] *n:* • **1.** alternative
خيارَة [xya:ra] *n:* خيارات، خيار [xya:ra:t, xya:r] *pl:* • **1.** a cucumber
مُختار [muxta:r] *n:* مخاتِير [mxa:ti:r] *pl:* • **1.** mukhtar, the elected village or neighborhood leader
اِختِيار [ʔixtiya:r] *n:* اِختِيارات [ʔixtiya:ra:t] *pl:* • **1.** choice, selection, option – تزَوَّجها باِختِيارَه [dzawwaǰha bʔixtiya:rah] He married her of his own accord.
خَيِّر [xayyir] *adj:* • **1.** generous man • **2.** charitable, benevolent man
خَيري [xayri] *adj:* • **1.** charitable – جَمعِيَّة خَيرِيَّة [ǰamʕiyya xayriyya] a charitable organization.
اِختِياري [ʔixtiya:ri] *adj:* • **1.** voluntary – قَرار اِختِياري [qara:r ʔixtiya:ri] a voluntary decision. جُندِي اِختِياري [ǰundi ʔixtiya:ri] an enlistee. • **2.** optional – الحُضُور اِختِياري [ʔilħuḏu:r ʔixtiya:ri] Attendance is optional. مَوقِف اِختِياري [mawqif ʔixtiya:ri] optional (bus) stop, where the bus need not stop if there are no passengers. • **3.** elective – دُرُوس اِختِيارِيَّة [duru:s ʔixtiya:riyya] elective courses.
أَخيَر [ʔaxyar] *comparative adjective:* • **1.** more or most honorable, upstanding, etc

خ ي ز ر ن

خَيزَران [xayzara:n] *n:* • **1.** cane, rattan • **2.** cane plant
خَيزَرانَة [xayzara:na] *n:* خَيزَرانات [xay:zara:na:t] *pl:* • **1.** cane, rattan • **2.** cane plant

خ ي س

خاس [xa:s] *v:* • **1.** to spoil, rot, go bad – الطَّماطَة خاسَت [ʔiṭṭama:ṭa xa:sat] The tomatoes spoiled. الماي بِالحوض خاس [ʔilma:y bilħawð xa:s] The water in the pond got stagnant.
خَيَّس [xayyas] *v:* • **1.** to cause to rot, spoil • **2.** to steal
خَيس [xays, xi:s] *n:* • **1.** decomposition, decay
خِيسَة [xi:sa] *n:* • **1.** dirt, filth – إذا إجَوا مُفَتِّشِين تِطلَع الخِيسَة [ʔiða ʔiǰaw mufattiši:n tiṭlaʕ ʔilxi:sa] If any inspectors came the dirt would come out.
خايِس [xa:yis] *adj:* • **1.** rotten, spoiled – بُصَل خايِس [buṣal xa:yis] rotten onions. هَذا دَماغَه خايِس! أَكُو واحِد يِقبَل بهِيكِي مَشرُوع؟ [ha:ða dama:ɣah xa:yis! ʔaku wa:ħid yiqbal bhi:či mašru:ʕ?] He's out of his mind! Is there anyone who'd accept such a plan?

خ ي ط

خَيَّط [xayyaṭ] *v:* • **1.** to sew – بِنتَه تخَيِّط كُلِّش زين [bintah txayyiṭ kulliš zi:n] His daughter sews very well. ما تِحكِي. شبِيك، حَلقَك مخَيَّط؟ [ma: tiħči. šbi:k, ħalgak mxayyaṭ?] You aren't talking. What's wrong, is your mouth sewed up? ضِرَبَه سِتّ رصاصات، خَيَّطَه بمُكانَه [ḏirabah sitt rṣa:ṣa:t, xayyaṭah bmuka:nah] He hit him with six bullets and stitched him to the spot. • **2.** to tailor – مِنُو خَيَّطلَك هَالقاط؟ [minu xayyaṭlak halqa:ṭ?] Who made this suit for you?
خيط [xayṭ, xi:ṭ] *n:* خيُوط [xyu:ṭ] *pl:* • **1.** thread – خيط أَمَل [xayṭ ʔamal] a thread of hope. • **2.** string, twine, cord • **3.** chevron, stripe • **4.** trace, touch, bit
خياط [xya:ṭ] *n:* • **1.** seam, seams, sewing
خَيّاط [xayya:ṭ] *n:* خَيّاطِين [xayya:ṭi:n] *pl:* • **1.** tailor – خَيّاط فَرفُوري [xayya:ṭ farfu:ri] porcelain mender.
مُخيَط [muxyaṭ, mixyaṭ] *n:* مَخايِط [maxa:yiṭ] *pl:* • **1.** a large needle
خياطَة [xya:ṭa] *n:* • **1.** sewing – مَكِينَة خياطَة [maki:nat xya:ṭa] sewing machine.
خَيّاطَة [xayya:ṭa] *n:* خَيّاطات [xayya:ṭa:t] *pl:* • **1.** seamstress
مخَيَّط [mxayyaṭ] *adj:* • **1.** threaded, sewn

خ ي ل 1

خَيَّل [xayyal] *v:* • **1.** to be or become entranced – خَيَّل عَلَى جَمالها [xayyal ʕala ǰama:lha] He was entranced by her beauty. كُلَّما يشُوف بنَيَّة حِلوَة يخَيِّل

[kullma yšuːf bnayya ħilwa yxayyil] Every time he sees a pretty girl, he becomes entranced. • **2.** to become tipsy, intoxicated – شِرَبلَه بيك واحِد وَخَيَّل [širablah piːk waːħid wxayyal] He had one drink and became tipsy. • **3.** to daydream, woolgather – شُوف، دَيخَيِّل عَليها [šuːf, dayxayyil ʕaliːha] Look, he's dreaming about her. تخَيَّل نَفسَك مَلِك [txayyal nafsak malik] Imagine being a king!
تخَيَّل [txayyal] *v:* • **1.** to imagine
خَيال [xayaːl] *n:* • **1.** imagination • **2.** shadow • **3.** pl. خَيالات fantasy, vision
تَخَيُّل [taxayyul] *n:* • **1.** imagination
خَيالِي [xayaːli] *adj:* • **1.** fantastic

خ ي ل 2

خَيل [xayl, xiːl] *n:* • **1.** horse(s) • **2.** knights (chess)
خَيّال [xayyaːl] *n:* خَيّالَة [xayyaːla] *pl:* • **1.** rider, horseman
خَيّالَة [xayyaːla] *n:* • **1.** cavalry – شُرطَة خَيّالَة [šurṭa xayyaːla] mounted police.

خ ي م

خَيَّم [xayyam] *v:* • **1.** to set up camp, pitch a tent – خَيَّمنا المُغرُب [xayyamna ʔilmuɣrub] We set up camp at sunset. • **2.** to settle (of the night) – اللَّيل خَيَّم عالبَلدَة وَكُلّ النّاس نامَوا [ʔillayl xayyam ʕalbalda wkull ʔinnaːs naːmaw] Night settled over the city and everybody slept.
خَيمَة [xayma, xiːma] *n:* خِيَم، خيام [xiyam, xyaːm] *pl:* • **1.** Allah, God – أَبُو الخَيمَة الزَّرقَة [ʔabu ʔilxayma ʔizzarga] Allah, God.
مُخَيَّم [muxayyam] *n:* • **1.** camp ground, camp, encampment

د

د

دَ [da] *particle:* • **1.** progressive prefix, indicating continued, repeated, or habitual action – دَيبنُون جِسر جِدِيد هنا [dayibnu:n ǰisr ǰidi:d hna] They're building a new bridge here. دَيسَوِّيها هَسَّة [daysawwi:ha hassa] He's doing it now. ما دَأدري وين راح [ma: daʔadri wi:n ra:ħ] I don't know where he went. ما دَتِفتِهم اللّي قِتلَك؟ [ma: datiftihim ʔilli gitlak?] Don't you understand what I told you? إي، دَأشُوفها هَسَّة [ʔi, daʔašu:fha hassa] Yes, I see her now.

د ء ب

دَئِب [daʔib] *n:* • **1.** (invar.) habit

د ب ب

دِبَى [diba:] *v:* • **1.** to crawl

دَبَّب، دَبَب [dabbab] *v:* • **1.** to sharpen, point, taper – دَبِّب راس القَلَم بِهالمُوس [dabbib ra:s ʔilqalam bhalmu:s] Sharpen the pencil point with this razor blade.

دُبّ [dubb] *n:* دِبَبَة، دباب [dibaba, dba:b] *pl:* • **1.** bear – الدُّبّ الأصغَر [ʔiddubb ʔilʔaṣɣar] the Little Bear, Ursa Minor. الدُّبّ الأكبَر [ʔiddubb ʔilʔakbar] the Big Bear, Ursa Major.

دَبَّة [dabba] *n:* دَبّات [dabba:t] *pl:* • **1.** heavy jug or jar, made of porcelain or sheet metal, used for clarified butter.

ضِرَب دَبَّة [ðirab dabba] *v:* • **1.** to balk, be obstinate – ضِرَب دَبَّة؛ بَعَد ما يِمشِي [ðirab dabba; baʕad ma: yimši] He balked and won't go any further. ضِرَب دَبَّة إلّا يرُوح لِلسِّينَما [ðirab dabba ʔilla yiru:ħ lissinama] He's dead set on going to the movies. • **2.** to change one's mind, go back on one's word, back down – ضِرَب دَبَّة وَما قِبَل يبِيعها بدِينارَين [ðirab dabba wma: qibal ybi:ʕha bdina:rayn] He went back on his word and refused to sell it for two dinars. • **3.** to trick, fool – ضِرَبنِي دَبَّة وَأخَذ فلُوسِي [ðirabni dabba waʔaxað flu:si] He tricked me and took my money.

دَبِي [daby] *n:* • **1.** crawling, creeping

دبيب [dbi:b, dibi:b] *n:* • **1.** (coll.) crawling insect(s)

دابَّة [da:bba] *n:* دَوابّ [dawa:bb] *pl:* • **1.** a riding animal or beast of burden esp. a donkey • **2.** pl. water buffalo

دبيبَة [dbi:ba, dibi:ba] *n:* دبيبات [dbi:ba:t] *pl:* • **1.** crawling insect

دَبّابَة [dabba:ba] *n:* دَبّابات [dabba:ba:t] *pl:* • **1.** tank (mil)

دُبَّة [dubba,] *adj:* • **1.** (invar.) fat, obese – مَرَة دُبَّة (دُبَّة حَمِيسَة) [mara dubba (dubba ħami:sa)] a fat woman.

د ب ر

دُبَر [dubar] *v:* • **1.** to be arranged, managed – دُبرَت القَضِيَّة بِسُهُولَة [dubrat ʔilqaðiyya bsuhu:la] The matter was taken care of easily. الفلُوس دُبرَت؛ حَضِّر نَفسَك لِلسَّفَر باكِر [ʔilflu:s dubrat; ħaððir nafsak lissafar ba:čir] The money is arranged for; get yourself ready for travelling tomorrow.

دَبَّر [dabbar] *v:* • **1.** to arrange, manage, handle – تِقدَر تدَبُّرلِي عَشِر دَنانِير؟ [tigdar ddabburli ʕašir dana:ni:r?] Can you manage to get ten dinars for me? ما أعتِقِد يدَبُّرها [ma: ʔaʕtiqid ydabburha] I don't think he can handle it. هُوَّ دَبَّرلِي شُغُل بِهالشَّرِكَة [huwwa dabbarli šuɣul bhaššarika] He arranged a job for me with this company. • **2.** to contrive, devise, work out – الحَرامِيَّة دَبِّرَوا خِطَّة يبُوقُون بِيها البَيت [ʔilħara:miyya dabbiraw xiṭṭa yibu:gu:n bi:ha ʔilbayt] The thieves worked out a plan for robbing the house.

تدَبَّر [tdabbar] *v:* • **1.** to be arranged, managed

دِبِر، دُبُر [dibir, dubur] *n:* أدبار [ʔadba:r] *pl:* • **1.** anus

تَدبِير [tadbi:r] *n:* تَدابِير [tada:bi:r] *pl:* • **1.** organization, planning, preparation – تَدبِير مَنزِلِي [tadbi:r manzili] home economics. • **2.** pl. measure, step, move – سَوِّيلِي تَدبِير؛ القِسُط اِستَحَقّ وماعِندِي فلُوس [sawwi:li tadbi:r; ʔilqusuṭ ʔistaħaqq wma:ʕindi flu:s] Show me a way out; the payment is due and I don't have any money.

مدَبَّر [mdabbar] *adj:* • **1.** well-organized – مَرتَه مدَبَّرَة [martah mdabbara] His wife is a good manager.

د ب س

دِبِس [dibis] *n:* • **1.** date molasses

دَبّاس [dabba:s] *n:* دَبّاسَة [dabba:sa] *pl:* • **1.** a maker of date molasses

د ب ش

دَبَش [dabaš] *n:* • **1.** (only in the expression: قُبَض مِن دَبَش [qubað min dabaš] he never got it back) – إنطَيتَه عَشِر دَنانِير وراح أقبُض مِن دَبَش [ʔinṭaytah ʕašir dana:ni:r wra:ħ ʔaqbuð min dabaš] I gave him ten dinars and don't expect to get it back. • **2.** rubbish, junk, trash, goods

د ب غ

دُبَغ [dubaɣ] *v:* • **1.** to tan – نِشتِرِي جِلُود وَنِدبُغها [ništiri ǰilu:d wnidbuɣha] We buy hides and tan them.

دَبَّغ [dabbaɣ] *v:* • **1.** intens. of to tan دُبَغ [dubaɣ] – دُبَغ راح يدَبُّغُون الجِّلُود بِمَدبَغَتنا [dubaɣ ra:ħ ydabbuɣu:n ʔiǰǰilu:d bmadbaɣatna] They'll have the hides tanned at

our tannery. جلدَه مدَبَّغ مِن البَسِط؛ بَعَد ما يمُضّ بيه [ǰildah mdabbaɣ min ʔilbasiṭ; baʕad maː ymuđđ biːh] His hide is tanned from beating, so that it doesn't hurt him anymore. كُلّما تضُربَه ما يحِسّ. عَبالَك جِلدَه مدَبَّغ [kullmaː dđurbah maː yħiss. ʕabaːlak ǰildah mdabbaɣ] No matter how much you hit him he doesn't feel it. He must be tough as leather.
تدَبَّغ [tdabbaɣ] *v:* • **1.** to be tanned – الجُلُود ينرَاد إلها تَنظِيف قَبِل ما تِتدَبَّغ [ʔiǰǰuluːd yinraːd ʔilha tanđiːf gabil maː tiddabbaɣ] The skins need cleaning before they are tanned.
اِندُبَغ [ʔindubaɣ] *v:* • **1.** to be tanned – الجِّلُود تِندُبُغ هنا وَبَعدين يصَدِّرُوها [ʔiǰǰiluːd tindubuɣ hnaː wbaʕdiːn yṣaddiruːha] The hides are tanned here and then they export them.
دَبُغ [dabuɣ] *n:* • **1.** tanning
دباغ [dbaːɣ] *n:* • **1.** pomegranate peels used for tanning
دَبّاغ [dabbaːɣ] *n:* دَبّاغَة [dabbaːɣa] *pl:* • **1.** tanner – باكِر يوَدُّون جِلدَه لِلدَّبّاغ [baːčir ywadduːn ǰildah liddabbaːɣ] Tomorrow they're going to tan his hide.
دِباغَة، دباغة [dibaːɣa, dbaːɣa] *n:* • **1.** tanning, tanner's trade
مَدبَغَة [madbaɣa] *n:* مَدابُغ [madaːbuɣ] *pl:* • **1.** tannery
مَدبُوغ [madbuːɣ] *adj:* • **1.** tanned – جِلُود مَدبُوغة [ǰiluːd madbuːɣa] tanned hides.

د ب ق

دَبَّق [dabbag] *v:* • **1.** to make sticky – اِستَعمِل خاشُوقَة حَتَّى لا تدَبُّق إيدَك [ʔistaʕmil xaːšuːga ħatta laː ddabbug ʔiːdak] Use a spoon so you won't get your hands sticky.
تدَبَّق [ddabbag] *v:* • **1.** to get sticky – إيدِي تدَبقَت مِن التَّمُر [ʔiːdi ddabgat min ʔittamur] My hand got sticky from the dates.
دُبَق [dubag] *n:* • **1.** sticky place, stickiness – سِتِرتَك بِيها دُبَق [sitirtak biːha dubag] Your jacket has a stickylooking spot on it. كُلّ المُوَظَّفِين دَيِردُون هَالشُّعبَة، لازِم بِيها دُبَق [kull ʔilmuwađđafiːn dayirduːn haššuʕba, laːzim biːha dubag] All the employees want to work in this section. There must be something attractive there.
دُبَق [dubag] *adj:* • **1.** sticky – إيدَه دُبَق مِن الجُكلَيت [ʔiːdah dubag min ʔiččukliːt] His hand's sticky from the candy.
مدَبُّق [mdabbug] *adj:* • **1.** sticky

د ب ك

دَبَّك [dabbač] *v:* • **1.** to stamp one's feet – لا تدَبِّكُون. الطِّفِل نايِم [laː ddabbičuːn. ʔiṭṭifil naːyim] Don't stamp your feet. The baby's sleeping.
دَبكَة [dabča, dabka] *n:* • **1.** stamping of feet • **2.** a folk dance in which a group of dancers lined up with locked arms, stamp out the rhythm and sing

د ب ل [1]

دِبلَة [dibla] *n:* دِبلات، دِبَل [diblaːt, dibal] *pl:* • **1.** a plain ring

د ب ل [2]

دَبَل [dabal] *n:* • **1.** double

د ب ل [3]

دَبَل [dabal] *adj:* • **1.** double, extra, larger

د ب ل ج

دُوبلاج [dublaːǰ] *n:* • **1.** dubbing (in motion pictures)

د ب ل م

دِبلُوم [dibluːm] *n:* دِبلُومات [dibluːmaːt] *pl:* • **1.** diploma or associate degree awarded on successful completion of first two years of college

د ب ل و م س

دِبلُوماسِي [diblumaːsi] *adj:* • **1.** diplomatic • **2.** (as *n:*) a diplomat

د ب ن ق

دَبَنق [dabang] *adj:* دَبَنقِيَّة [dabangiyya] *pl:* • **1.** stupid, addle-brained, witless

د ث ر

دَثَّر [daθθar] *v:* • **1.** to cover, cover up – دَثِّر الجّاهِل حَتَّى لا يبرَد [daθθir ʔiǰǰaːhil ħatta laː yibrad] Cover up the kid so he won't get cold.
تدَثَّر [tdaθθar] *v:* • **1.** to wrap oneself up – تدَثَّر زين؛ الدِّنيا بارِدَة [ddaθθar ziːn; ʔiddinya baːrda] Cover up well; the weather's cold. تدَثَّر بالبَطّانِيَّة ونام [ddaθθar bilbaṭṭaːniyya wnaːm] He wrapped himself in the blanket and went to sleep. • **2.** to be covered – إذا تدَثَّر الجِّدِر زين، ينطُبُخ الأَكِل بِالعَجَل [ʔiđa ddaθθar ʔiǰǰidir ziːn, yinṭubux ʔilʔakil bilʕaǰal] If the pot is well covered, the food will cook quickly.
اِندِثَر [ʔindiθar] *v:* • **1.** to be wiped out, be obliterated – حَضارَتهُم اِندِثرَت مِن هاجمُوهُم المَغُول [ħađaːrathum ʔindiθrat min haːǰmuːhum ʔilmaɣuːl] Their civilization was wiped out when the Mongols attacked them. المَدِينَة اِندِثرَت بِالزِّلزال [ʔilmadiːna ʔindiθrat bizzilzaːl] The city was obliterated by the earthquake • **2.** to die out, disappear – أَهلَه اِندِثرَوا، ما بُقالَهُم أَثَر [ʔahlah ʔindiθraw, maː buqaːlahum ʔaθar] His family died out, and no trace of them remains.
دثار [dθaːr] *n:* دثارات [dθaːraːt] *pl:* • **1.** covers
مدَثَّر [mdaθθar] *adj:* • **1.** covered
مندِثِر [mindiθir] *adj:* • **1.** evanescent, temporary, hidden

د ث و

دِثو [diθw] *adj:* دِثاوَة [diθaːwa] *pl:* • **1.** (a contemptuous term) sloth, sluggard, slob, clod, idiot

د ج ت ل

دِجتال [diǰitaːl] *adj:* • **1.** digital

د ج ج

دِجاج [diǰaːǰ] *n:* • **1.** (coll.) chicken(s)
دِجاجَة [diǰaːǰa] *n:* دِجاجات [diǰaːǰaːt] *pl:* • **1.** chicken

د ج ل [1]

دَجَّل [dajǰal] *v:* • **1.** to swindle, cheat – لا تِشتِري مِن هَالتّاجِر. يدَجِّل عَلَى كُلّ واحِد [la: tištiri min hattaːǰir. ydaǰǰil ʕala kull waːħid] Don't buy from that merchant. He cheats everyone.
دَجَل [daǰal] *n:* • **1.** trickery, humbug, deceit
دَجّال [daǰǰaːl] *n:* • **1.** an imposter

د ج ل [2]

دِجلَة [diǰla] *n:* • **1.** the Tigris River

د ج ن

داجِن [daːǰin] *adj:* دَواجِن [dawaːǰin] *pl:* • **1.** tamed, domesticated – حَيوانات داجِنَة [ħaywaːnaːt daːǰina] domesticated animals. • **2.** domestic animal (usually chickens, ducks, and rabbits)

د ح د ح

تدَحدَح [tdaħdaħ] *v:* • **1.** to waddle – شُوفَه شلُون يِتدَحدَح بمَشيَه [šuːfah šluːn yiddaħdaħ bmašyah] Look at how he waddles when he walks.
مدَحدَح [mdaħdaħ] *adj:* • **1.** dumpy, squat, stocky

د ح ر

دِحَر [diħar] *v:* • **1.** to defeat, vanquish – دِحَرنا جيش العَدُو بسُهُولَة [diħarna ǰayš ʔilʕadu bsuhuːla] We defeated the enemy army easily.
دَحِر [daħir] *n:* • **1.** defeating

د ح ر ج

دَحرَج [daħraǰ] *v:* • **1.** to roll
تدَحرَج [tdaħraǰ] *v:* • **1.** to roll
دَحرَجَة [daħraǰa] *n:* • **1.** rolling

د ح س

دِحَس [diħas] *v:* • **1.** to stuff in, stick in, push in, shove in, crowd in – دِحَس ساعتَه بين البَطّانِيّات [diħas saːʕtah bayn ʔilbattaːniyyaːt] He shoved his watch in between the blankets. إدحَس هَالكِتاب بين كُتُبَك [ʔidħas halkitaːb bayn kutubak] Stick this book in among your books. كُلّما نُقعُد نِحكِي يِدحَس نَفسَه بَيناتنا [kullmaː nugʕud niħči yidħas nafsah baynaːtna] Every time we sit down to talk, he butts in among us.
دَحَّس [daħħas] *v:* • **1.** to stuff in, stick in
اِندِحَس [ʔindiħas] *v:* • **1.** to crowd oneself in – الجّاهِل اِندِحَس بين أَبُوه وأُمَّه [ʔiǰǰaːhil ʔindiħas bayn ʔabuːh wʔummah] The child crowded in between his father and mother.
دَحِس [daħis] *n:* • **1.** stuffing, filling

د ح ق

دَحَّق [daħħag] *v:* • **1.** to look – إذا تدَحِّق زين، تِقدَر تِقراها [ʔiða ddaħħig ziːn, tigdar tiqraːha] If you look carefully, you can read it. دَحِّق بِالصَّندُوق [daħħig biṣṣanduːg] Look in the trunk. دَحِّق زين وَإحزِر هَذا تَصوير مَن [daħħig ziːn wʔiħzir haːða taṣwiːr man] Look very closely and guess whose picture this is.

د خ ل

دِخَل [dixal] *v:* • **1.** to consummate the marriage, cohabit, sleep with one's wife – دِخَل عالعَرُوس إسبُوعَين بَعَد العَقِد [dixal ʕalʕaruːs ʔisbuːʕayn baʕad ʔilʕaqid] He slept with his bride two weeks after the signing of the contract. سمَعِت عَلِي دِخَل البارحَة؟ [smaʕit ʕali dixal ʔilbaːrħa?] Did you hear Ali consummated his marriage yesterday? • **2.** to be included – شُوف التَّلامِيذ دِخلَوا الصَّفّ لَو بَعَد [šuːf ʔittalaːmiːð dixlaw ʔiṣṣaff law baʕad] See if the students have gone into the classroom yet. إدخُل، الباب مَفتُوحَة [ʔidxul, ʔilbaːb maftuːħa] Come in, the door is open. قُوّاتنا دِخلَت أَراضِي العَدُو [quwwaːtna dixlat ʔaraːḍi ʔilʕadu] Our troops entered enemy territory. دِخَل بالغُرفَة لَكِن ما شافنِي [dixal bilɣurfa laːkin maː šaːfni] He entered the room but he didn't see me. لا تخَلِّي أَحَّد يِدخُل عَالمُدير [laː txalliː ʔaħħad yidxul ʕalmudiːr] Don't let anyone go in to the director. اللّي يِكذِب يِدخُل جَهَنَّم [ʔilli yikðib yidxul ǰahannam] He who lies goes to hell. إبنِي راح يِدخُل كُلِّيَة الطِّبّ [ʔibni raːħ yidxul kulliyyat ʔiṭṭibb] My son is going to enter the medical school. راح أَدخُل سِباق المِيَة مَتِر [raːħ ʔadxul sibaːq ʔilmiyat matir] I am going to enter the 100-meter dash. إسمَك دِخَل بِقائِمَة التَّرفِيعات [ʔismak dixal bqaːʔimat ʔattarfiːʕaːt] Your name has been put on the promotion list. خَلِّي نِدخُل بِالمَوضُوع. شِتريد؟ [xalliː nidxul bilmawḍuːʕ. šitriːd?] Let's get to the subject. What do you want? هَالسَّنَة الدِّنيا راح تِدخُل عَلَى جريدِي [hassana ʔiddinya raːħ tidxul ʕala ǰriːdi] The world is entering the year of the rat. العُمُولَة ما تِدخُل بِالسِّعِر [ʔilʕumuːla maː tidxul bissiʕir] The commission is not included in the price. الضَّريبَة داخلَة بضِمِن السِّعِر [ʔiððariːba daːxla bðimin ʔissiʕir] The tax is included in the price.
دَخَّل [daxxal] *v:* • **1.** to put in, stick in, place in, enter – دَخِّل الوايَر بِهَالزُّرُف [daxxil ʔilwaːyar bhazzuruf] Insert the wire in this hole. دَخِّل الكَلِب بالبَيت [daxxil ʔiččalib bilbayt] Bring the dog in the house.

دَخَّل إصبِعَه بعَينِي [daxxal ʔiṣibʕah bʕayni] He stuck his finger in my eye. البارحَة صِحّتَه تخربِطَت وَدَخلَوه لِلمُستَشفى [ʔilba:rha ṣiħħtah txarbiṭat wdaxxlawh lilmustašfa] Yesterday his condition worsened and they placed him in the hospital. ما يقبَل يدَخِّل أَحَّد عالوَزير [ma: yiqbal ydaxxil ʔaħħad ʕalwazi:r] He refuses to let anyone go in to see the minister. يدَخِّل نفسَه بكُلشِي [ydaxxil nafsah bikullši] He meddles in everything. لا تدَخِّلني بهَالمُشكِلَة [la: ddaxxilni bhalmuškila] Don't drag me into the problem. دَخِّل هَالكَلِمَة بجُملَة [daxxil halkalima bǰumla] Put this word in a sentence. ما دَخلَوا إسمَك بالقائِمَة [ma: daxxlaw ʔismak bilqa:ʔima] They didn't enter your name on the list. دَخِّل هَالدِّينار بحسابِي [daxxil haddina:r biħsa:bi] Put this dinar on my account.

أدخَل [ʔadxal] *v:* • **1.** formal equivalent of دَخَّل – المَجلِس أدخَل بَعض التَّعديلات بهالقانُون [ʔilmaǰlis ʔadxal baʕð̣ ʔittaʕdi:la:t bhalqa:nu:n] The parliament inserted some amendments in this law.

تدَخَّل [tdaxxal] *v:* • **1.** to be put in, entered – هَالوايَر لازِم يِتدَخَّل مِن هنا [halwa:yar la:zim yiddaxxal min hna] This wire has to go through here. • **2.** to involve oneself, take part, interfere – لا تِتدَخَّل بالسِّياسَة [la: tiddaxxal bissaya:sa] Don't involve yourself in politics. لِيش تِتدَخَّل بكُلّ مُناقَشَة؟ [li:š tiddaxxal bkull muna:qaša?] Why do you always take part in arguments? ما أقبَل تِتدَخَّل بشُغلِي [ma: ʔaqbal tiddaxxal bšuɣli] I won't have you interfering in my affairs. الشُّرطَة تدَخَّلَت بالإنتِخابات [ʔiššurṭa ddaxxalat bilʔintixa:ba:t] The police meddled in the elections.

تداخَل [tda:xal] *v:* • **1.** to get acquainted, make friends – شبالعَجَل يِتداخَل! ماكُو أحَّد ما يعُرفَه [šbilʕaǰal yidda:xal! ma:ku ʔaħħad ma: yʕurfah] How fast he makes friends! There's no one that doesn't know him. • **2.** to be put in – قِلتِلَك مِيَّة مَرَّة، لا تِتداخَل بشُغلِي [gilitlak miyyat marra, la: tidda:xal bšuɣli] I've told you a hundred times, don't interfere in my business.

دَخَل [daxal] *n:* دُخُول [duxu:l] *pl:* • **1.** income – ضَرِيبَة الدَّخَل [ð̣ari:bat ʔiddaxal] the income tax. • **2.** receipts, revenues, returns, take • **3.** till, cash drawer • **4.** bank for saving coins • **5.** (in certain expressions:) affair, business – مالَه دَخَل [ma:lah daxal] he has no business, he has nothing to do with, it's none of his business. آنِي مالِي دَخَل بهَالمَوضُوع [ʔa:ni ma:li daxal bhalmawð̣u:ʕ] I've got nothing to do with that affair. إنتَ شِنُو دَخَلَك؟ هاي بَينِي وَبَين أَخُويا [ʔinta šinu: daxalak? ha:y bayni wbayn ʔaxu:ya] What's this got to do with you? This is between me and my brother.

دَخلَة [daxla] *n:* دَخلات [daxla:t] *pl:* • **1.** the wedding night – يوم الدَّخلَة، لَيلَة الدَّخلَة [yu:m ʔiddaxla, laylat ʔiddaxlap] the wedding night.

دُخُول [duxu:l] *n:* • **1.** entry, entrance, admittance, admission – سِعِر الدُّخُول [siʕir ʔidduxu:l] the price of admission. عِيد الدُّخُول [ʕi:d ʔidduxu:l] Celebration of the Persian New Year, held in springtime, when the world comes under the sign of a different animal.

مدخَل [madxal] *n:* مَداخِل [mada:xil] *pl:* • **1.** entrance

تدَخُّل [tadaxxul] *n:* • **1.** intervention

تدخِيل [tadxi:l] *n:* • **1.** entering

دُخُولِيَّة [duxu:liyya] *n:* • **1.** admission, admission price

دخِيل [daxi:l] *adj:* • **1.** inward, internal, foreign, extraneous – دَخِيل الله، ما تقُلّي منِين جِبت الفلُوس؟ [daxi:l ʔallah, ma: tgulli mni:n ǰibit ʔilflu:s?] For the love of God, won't you tell me where you got the money? دَخِيلَك، لا تُضرُبنِي [daxi:lak, la: tuð̣rubni] Please don't hit me. ذَبّ نَفسَه دَخِيل عَلَيّا [ðabb nafsah daxi:l ʕalayya] He threw himself on my mercy. • **2.** as Noun: intermediary, go-between

داخِل [da:xil] *adj:* • **1.** interior, inside

داخِلِي [da:xili] *adj:* • **1.** internal, interior, inside – اِضطِرابات داخِلِيَّة [ʔið̣ṭira:ba:t da:xiliyya] internal disorders. قِسِم داخِلِي [qisim da:xili] (of a school) boarding department, boarding section. مَلابِس داخِلِيَّة [mala:bis da:xiliyya] underwear, underclothes.

داخِلِيَّة [da:xiliyya] *adj:* • **1.** interior – وِزارَة الدّاخِلِيَّة [wiza:rat ʔidda:xiliyya] ministry of the interior.

د خ ن

دَخَّن [daxxan] *v:* • **1.** to fumigate – دَخِّن الغُرفَة حَتَّى يرُوح البَقّ [daxxin ʔilɣurfa ħatta yiru:ħ ʔilbagg] Fumigate the room so that the mosquitoes will go away. • **2.** to smoke (cigarette, pipe, etc.) – أيّ نُوع جِكايِر تدَخِّن؟ [ʔayy nu:ʕ ǰiga:yir ddaxxin?] What kind of cigarettes do you smoke? • **3.** to smoke, give off smoke – الخِشَب دَيدَخِّن؛ يمكِن راح يِشتِعِل [ʔilxišab daydaxxin; yimkin ra:ħ yištiʕil] The wood is smoking; maybe it'll catch fire. الفتِيلَة مُو زينَة؛ تدَخِّن هوايَة [ʔilfiti:la mu: zi:na; ddaxxin hwa:ya] The lantern's no good; it smokes a lot.

دُخُن [duxun] *n:* • **1.** millet

مُدَخِّن [mudaxxin] *n:* • **1.** smoker

دُخّان [duxxa:n] *n:* • **1.** smoke, fumes • **2.** fumes, tobacco

مَدخَنَة [madxana] *n:* مداخِن [mda:xin] *pl:* • **1.** chimney, smokestack, funnel

تدخِين [tadxi:n] *n:* • **1.** (tobacco) smoking

مدَخِّن [mdaxxin] *adj:* • **1.** irritated, upset – طَبّ عَلينا مدَخِّن؛ مَحَّد يدرِي شبِيه [ṭabb ʕali:na mdaxxin; maħħad yidri šbi:h] He came in all upset; no one knows what was ailing him. • **2.** smoky, burning

دُخّانِي [duxxa:ni] *adj:* • **1.** smoky

د ر ب

دَرَّب [darrab] *v:* • **1.** to train, coach, drill – دَرَّب الفِرقَة هوايَة قَبُل السِّباق [darrab ʔilfirqa hwa:ya gabul ʔissiba:q] He coached the team a lot before the game. المُصارِع يِجِي لِلمَدرَسَة كُلّ يوم يدَرِّب التَّلامِيذ عالمُصارَعَة [ʔilmuṣa:riʕ yiǰi lilmadrasa kull yu:m ydarrub

ʔittala:mi:ð ʕalmuṣa:raʕa] The wrestler comes to school every day to train the students in wrestling. دَرَّب الكَلِب مالَه عالقَفُز [darrab ʔiččalib ma:lah ʕalqafuz] He trained his dog to jump. • **2.** to send (someone) on his way, send packing

تدَرَّب [ddarrab] *v:* • **1.** to get accustomed to, get used to – تدَرَّبت عَلَى هِيكِي حَياة مِن كِنِت جُندِي [ddarrabit ʕala hi:či ħaya:t min činit ǰundi] I got used to such a life when I was in the army. • **2.** to train, drill, practice – سَوَّى نَفسَه مَرِيض حَتَّى ما يِتدَرَّب وِيّا الجِّنُود [sawwa: nafsah mari:ð̣ ħatta ma: yiddarrab wiyya ʔiǰǰinu:d] He pretended to be sick so as not to drill with the soldiers. رُوح تدَرَّب كَم شَهَر وَبَعدين تَعال إلعَب شِطرَنج وِيّايا [ru:ħ ddarrab čam šahar wbaʕdi:n taʕa:l ʔilʕab šiṭranǰ wiyya:ya] Go practice for a few months and then come play chess with me. • **3.** to train (athletics) – دَأتدَرَّب لِلسِّباق [daʔaddarrab lissiba:q] I'm training for the race. دَأتدَرَّب عَلَى رَفع الأثقال كُلّ يوم [daʔaddarrab ʕala rafʕ ʔilʔaθqa:l kull yu:m] I'm training in weight lifting every day.

دَرُب [darub] *n:* دروب [dru:b] *pl:* • **1.** street, road • **2.** way, route – إذا دَربَك عالسُوق ما تِشتِرِيلِي كِيلُو شَكَر [ʔiða darbak ʕassu:g ma: tištiri:li ki:lu šakar] If you happen to go by the market would you buy me a kilo of sugar. تِقدَر تجِيبلِي طَوابِع بدَربَك؟ [tigdar dǰi:bli ṭawa:biʕ bdarbak?] Could you bring me some stamps on your way? ما عليه بكُلّ أحَّد. يرُوح بدَربَه ويجِي بدَربَه [ma: ʕli:h bkull ʔaħħad. yiru:ħ bdarbah wyiǰi bdarbah] He doesn't bother anyone. He goes his own way. دَرب الكَلِب عالقَصّاب [darb ʔiččalib ʕalgaṣṣa:b] He'll be around one of these days (lit., the dog's route goes to the butcher's). لا تلحّ عَلَيّا. خَلِّينِي أشُوف دَربِي [la: tliħħ ʕalayya. xalli:ni ʔašu:f darbi] Don't pester me. Let me concentrate on what I'm doing. إنطِينِي دَرُب حَتَّى أسَوِّيها [ʔinṭi:ni darub ħatta ʔasawwi:ha] Give me a chance to do it. ما نطَيتَه دَرُب يِحكِي [ma: nṭaytah darub yiħči] You didn't give him a chance to speak. شِفتلَه خُوش دَرُب. أقدَر أخابِر المُدِير وَهُوَّ يدَبُّرها [šiftlah xu:š darub. ʔagdar ʔaxa:bir ʔalmudi:r wahuwwa ydabburha] I've found a good way out. I can call the director and he'll take care of it. • **3.** trip, run – هَذا آخِر دَرُب لِلباص لِهَاللَيلَة [ha:ða ʔa:xir darub lilpa:ṣ lhallayla] This is the last bus run tonight. شِلت كُلّ الغَراض بدَربَين؟ [šilt kull ʔilgara:ð̣ bdarbayn?] Did you bring all the things in two trips? راح وِيّاها دَربَين [ra:ħ wiyya:ha darbayn] He went with her twice (euphemism for the act of sexual intercourse). جِيبلِي دَرُب رَمُل [ǰi:bli darub ramul] Bring me a load of sand.

مُدَرِّب [mudarrib] *n:* • **1.** trainer, coach

تَدَرُّب [tadarrub] *n:* • **1.** training

تَدرِيب [tadri:b] *n:* • **1.** practice, drill, training

مدَرَّب [mdarrab] *adj:* • **1.** veteran • **2.** trained

مُتَدَرِّب [mutadarrib] *adj:* • **1.** trained, accustomed (person)

تَدرِيبِي [tadri:bi] *adj:* • **1.** training – دَورَة تَدرِيبِيَّة [dawra tadri:biyya] a training course.

د ر ب ن

دَربِين [darbi:n] *n:* دَربِينات [darbi:na:t] *pl:* • **1.** binoculars

دَربُونَة [darbu:na] *n:* درابِين [dra:bi:n] *pl:* • **1.** alley, narrow street

د ر ج

دِرَج [diraǰ] *v:* • **1.** to be common, prevalent, popular

تدَرَّج [ddarraǰ] *v:* • **1.** to advance gradually – تدَرَّج بِالوَظايِف إلَى أن صار مُدِير [ddarraǰ bilwað̣a:yif ʔila ʔan ṣa:r mudi:r] He rose in grade till he became a director.

إستَدرَج [ʔistadraǰ] *v:* • **1.** to lure, coax, lead gradually – إستَدرِجَوه إلَى أن اِعتِرَف بِالجَّرِيمَة [ʔistadriǰawh ʔila ʔan ʔiʕtiraf biǰǰari:ma] They coaxed him until he confessed to the crime.

دَرَج [daraǰ] *n:* دَرَجات [daraǰa:t] *pl:* • **1.** stairs, steps, flight of stairs, staircase • **2.** ladder

دُرُج [duruǰ] *n:* • **1.** drawer

دَرجَة [darǰa] *n:* دَرجات [darǰa:t] *pl:* • **1.** step, stair

دَرَجَة [daraǰa] *n:* دَرَجات [daraǰa:t] *pl:* • **1.** degree – دَرَجَة غَلَيان الماي [daraǰat ɣalaya:an ʔilma:y] the boiling point of water. دَرَجَة الحَرارَة [daraǰat ʔilħara:ra] the temperature. • **2.** thermometer • **3.** degree, extent – بَخِيل إلَى دَرَجَة فَظِيعَة [baxi:l ʔila daraǰa fað̣i:ʕa] stingy to an extreme degree. سَوّانِي عَصَبِي إلَى دَرَجَة بَعد شوَيَّة أضُربَه [sawwa:ni ʕaṣabi ʔila daraǰa baʕd šwayya ʔað̣urbah] He made me so mad I was about to hit him. • **4.** class – دَرَجَة أُولَى [daraǰa ʔu:la:] first class. كَذّاب مِن الدَّرَجَة الأُولَى [čaððа:b min ʔiddaraǰa ʔilʔu:la] a first-class liar. • **5.** grade, mark (in school)

دَراج [dara:ǰ] *n:* • **1.** stairs, steps, flight of stairs, staircase

دَرّاج [darra:ǰ] *n:* • **1.** (coll.) a game bird resembling the pheasant

مُدَرَّج [mudarraǰ] *n:* مُدَرَّجات [mudarraǰa:t] *pl:* • **1.** stand, grandstand, bleachers

دَرّاجَة [darra:ǰa] *n:* دَرّاجات [darra:ǰa:t] *pl:* • **1.** bicycle –

تَدرِيج، بِالتَدرِيج [tadri:ǰ, bittadri:ǰ] *n:* • **1.** gradually, by degrees, by steps, step-by-step • **2.** by degrees, step by step الأمُور دَتِتحَسَّن بِالتَّدرِيج [ʔilʔumu:r datitħassan bittadri:ǰ] Things are getting better gradually.

متدَرِّج [mitdarriǰ] *adj:* • **1.** gradual

دارِج [da:riǰ] *adj:* • **1.** current, prevalent, common, popular – مَثَل دارِج [maθal da:riǰ] a wide-spread saying.

تَدرِيج [tadri:ǰ] *n:* • **1.** gradual, step by step

تَدرِيجِي [tadri:ǰi] *adj:* • **1.** gradual

تَدرِيجِيّاً [tadri:ǰiyyan] *adverbial:* • **1.** gradually, step by step

د ر د [1]

أدرَد [ʔadrad] *adj:* • **1.** toothless • **2.** toothless person

د ر د [2]

دَرِد [darid] *n:* • **1.** suffering, torment, affliction, misfortune, trouble, bad luck, problem – كُلّ مَن مِبتِلِي بِدَردَه [kull man mibtili bdardah] Everyone's got his own problems. ما دَأعرُف شِنُو دَردَه [maː daʔaʕruf šinu dardah] I can't figure out what's eating him. هَذا دَردِي. إبنِي سَيبَندِي [haːða dardi. ʔibni siːbandi] That's my luck. My son is a rotter. لِيش النَّهار كُلَّه ما يِحكِي؟ بَسّ لَو أعرُف شِنُو دَردَه [liːš ʔinnahaːr kullah maː yiħči? bass law ʔaʕruf šinu dardah] Why hasn't he said anything all day? If only I knew what his trouble was.

د ر د م

دَردَم [dardam] *v:* • **1.** to mumble, muttter – طِلَع زَعلان وَقام يدَردِم [ṭilaʕ zaʕlaːn wgaːm ydardim] He went out mad and began to mutter to himself.

د ر ر

دَرّ [darr] *v:* • **1.** to shower, heap – مِن صار أبُوهُم وَزِير، ظَلّ يدُرّ عَلَيهُم بِالفلُوس [min ṣaːr ʔabuːhum waziːr, ḏ̣all ydurr ʕaliːhum bilfiluːs] When their father became minister, he kept them in money. هَالشَّغلَة دَرّت عَلَيهُم فلُوس هوايَة [haššaɣla darrat ʕaliːhum fluːs hwaːya] That job showered a lot of money on them. • **2.** to be productive, give milk abundantly – قَبُل ما يِحلِبُون الهايشَة يخَلُّون إبنها يرضَع مِنها حَتَّى تدُرّ [gabul maː yiħlibuːn ʔilhaːyša yxalluːn ʔibinha yirḏ̣aʕ minha ħatta ddurr] Before they milk the cow they let her calf suck so that she will give plenty of milk.

دَرَّر [darrar] *v:* • **1.** to act as a diuretic, stimulate the kidneys – البِيرَة تدَرِّر [ʔilbiːra ddarrir] Beer makes you urinate.

دُرّ [durr] *n:* • **1.** pearl(s) • **2.** gem(s) • **3.** gemstone(s) – دُرّ نَجَف [durr najaf] crystalline quartz. حَكيَه دُرّ [ħačyah durr] His words are precious gems. يطَلِّع دُرّ مِن طِيز الكُرّ [yṭalliʕ durr min ṭiːz ʔilkurr] He's talking through his hat (lit., he gets gems from the young donkey's anus).

دُرَّة [durra] *n:* دُرّات، دُرَر [durraːt, durar] *pl:* • **1.** pearl • **2.** gem, gemstone • **3.** gemstone

مُدَرِّر [mudarrir] *n:* مُدَرِّرات، مُدَرِّرَة [mudarriraːt, mudarrira] *pl:* • **1.** (adj. and n.) diuretic

إدرار [ʔidraːr] *n:* • **1.** urine (as medical specimen)

د ر ز ن

دَرزَن [darzan] *n:* دَرازِن [daraːzin] *pl:* • **1.** dozen

د ر س

دِرَس [diras] *v:* • **1.** to study – مِن أكبَر راح أدرُس هَندَسَة [min ʔakbar raːħ ʔadrus handasa] When I grow up I'm going to study engineering. إدرُسها لِهَالقَضِيَّة زين وَقَدِّملِي تَقرِير [ʔidrusha lhalqaḏ̣iyya ziːn waqaddimli taqriːr] Study this case well and forward me a report. ما دِرَسِت بِهَالمَدرَسَة [maː dirasit bhalmadrasa] I didn't study at that school. دِرَس هوايَة لِلإمتِحان [diras hwaːya lilʔimtiħaːn] He studied a lot for the exam.

دَرَّس [darras] *v:* • **1.** to teach – يدَرِّس الاقتِصاد [ydarris ʔilʔiqtiṣaːd] He teaches economics.

دَرِس [daris] *n:* درُوس [druːs] *pl:* • **1.** class, class period • **2.** course, course of study • **3.** lesson, chapter (of a textbook) • **4.** lesson (from experience)

مُدَرِّس [mudarris] *n:* • **1.** teacher, instructor

دِراسَة [diraːsa] *n:* • **1.** study, studying – دِراسَة عالِيَة [diraːsa ʕaːliya] graduate study. أُجُور الدِّراسَة [ʔujuːr ʔiddiraːsa] tuition. • **2.** pl. دِراسات a study, an investigation

مَدرَسَة [madrasa] *n:* مَدارِس [madaːris] *pl:* • **1.** school

تَدرِيس [tadriːs] *n:* • **1.** teaching

دارِس [daːris] *adj:* • **1.** studying

دِراسِي [diraːsi] *adj:* • **1.** academic, scholastic – سَنَة دِراسِيَّة [sana diraːsiyya] an academic year.

مَدرَسِي [madrasi] *adj:* • **1.** scholastic, school – كِتاب مَدرَسِي [kitaːb madrasi] school book, text book.

مَدرُوس [madruːs] *adj:* • **1.** studied

تَدرِيسِي [tadriːsi] *adj:* • **1.** teaching, school

د ر س ن

دارسِين [daːrsiːn] *n:* • **1.** cinnamon

د ر ع

دِرِع [diriʕ] *n:* درُوع [druːʕ] *pl:* • **1.** shield • **2.** armor, suit of armor • **3.** mail, suit of mail

دريع [driːʕ] *adj:* • **1.** dull person, clod, jerk

مُدَرَّع [mudarraʕ] *adj:* • **1.** armored – سَيّارَة مُدَرَّعَة [sayyaːra mudarraʕa] armored car. قُوّات مُدَرَّعَة [quwwaːt mudarraʕa] armored forces. فِرقَة مُدَرَّعَة [firqa mudarraʕa] armored division.

د ر ف ع

دَرفَع [darfaʕ] *v:* • **1.** to push, shove – دَرفَعنِي ووَقَّعنِي [darfaʕni wwaggaʕni] He pushed me and knocked me down. عَلَى كَيفَك. لا تدَرفُع [ʕala kayfak. laː ddarfuʕ] Take it easy. Don't push. إذا إجا عَلِيك، دَرفُعَه [ʔiða ʔija ʕaliːk, darfuʕah] If he comes to you, send him away.

د ر ق

دَرَقِي [daraqi] *n:* • **1.** thyroid – الغُدَّة الدَّرَقِيَّة [ʔilɣudda ʔildaraqiyya] the thyroid gland.

درقَة [dirga] *n:* دِرقات [dirgaːt] *pl:* • **1.** shield • **2.** disc • **3.** steering wheel

د ر ك

دِرَك [dirak] *v:* • **1.** to attain puberty – زَوّجُوه قَبُل ما يِدرُك [zawwǰu:h gabul ma: yidruk] They married him off before he became sexually mature. • **2.** to understand, grasp, comprehend, realize – هُوَّ ما يِدرُك هِيكِي حَقايِق [huwwa ma: yidruk hi:či ħaqa:yiq] He doesn't understand such facts. ما دِرَك قَصِدهُم، وَأَكَلها [ma: dirak qaṣidhum, wʔakalha] He didn't realize what they were up to, and he got taken.

تدارَك [dda:rak] *v:* • **1.** to face, meet, check, take care of, take charge of – تدارَك القَضِيَّة قَبُل ما تِثخَن [dda:rak ʔilqaḍiyya gabul ma: tiθxan] Take charge of the matter before it gets any worse. إذا الطَّبِيب ما يِدّارَك المَجرُوح بسُرعَة، تَرَة يمُوت [ʔiða ʔiṭṭabi:b ma: yidda:rak ʔilmaǰru:ħ bsurʕa, tara ymu:t] If the doctor doesn't see to the patient quickly, he's going to die.

إدراك [ʔidra:k] *n:* • **1.** understanding, comprehension, grasp

مُدرِك [mudrik] *adj:* • **1.** intelligent • **2.** aware

مَدرُوك [madru:k] *adj:* • **1.** endangered – صِحّتَه مَدرُوكَة [ṣiħħtah madru:ka] His health is endangered.

دَرَكِيَّة [darakiyya] *adj:* • **1.** danger • **2.** regiment

د ر م

دُرّامَة، دِرّامَة [durra:ma, dirra:ma] *n:* دُرّامات، دِرّامات [durra:ma:t, dirra:ma:t] *pl:* • **1.** (vulgar) glans penis

د ر م ك

دَرمَك [darmak] *v:* • **1.** to stain, spot – الحِبِر اِنكَبّ عَلَيّا وَدَرمَك ثَوبِي [ʔilħibir ʔinčabb ʕalayya wdarmak θawbi] The ink got spilled on me and stained my shirt.

تدَرمَك [ddarmak] *v:* • **1.** to become spotted, stained – صُبَغ الثَّوب مالَه وَتدَرمَك [ṣubaɣ ʔiθθu:b ma:lah widdarmak] He dyed his shirt and it became spotty.

د ر ن ف ي س

دَرنَفِيس [darnafi:s] *n:* دَرنَفِيسات [darnafi:sa:t] *pl:* • **1.** screwdriver

د ر ن ق

درِنقَة [dringa] *n:* درِنقات [dringa:t] *pl:* • **1.** drunk as a skunk, dead drunk

د ر ه م

دِرهِم [dirhim] *n:* دَراهِم [dara:him] *pl:* • **1.** coin of fifty fils • **2.** a weight equalling 1/100 وقِيَّة [wgiyya] (10 grams) in the reformed weight system, and 1/96 وقِيَّة in the old.

درَيهِم [dri:him] *n:* درَيهمات [dri:hma:t] *pl:* • **1.** coin worth fifty fils (diminutive form)

د ر و ش

دَروِيش [darwi:š] *n:* دَراوِيش [dara:wi:š] *pl:* • **1.** dervish, a member of any of the various Moslem sects which take vows of poverty and self-denial

د ر ي

دِرَى [dira:] *v:* • **1.** to know – تِدرِي؟ هَالوَظِيفَة ما تِعجِبنِي [tidri? halwaḍi:fa ma: tiʕǰibni] You know what? I don't like this job. ما دَندرِي شراح يصِير باكِر [ma: danidri šra:ħ yṣi:r ba:čir] We don't know what's going to happen tomorrow. بَسّ أَدرِي وينَه، أَرُوح عَلِيه [bass ʔadri wi:nah, ʔaru:ħ ʕali:h] If I only knew where he was, I'd go to him. ما أَدرِي أَرُوح بِالسَّيّارَة لَو بِالطَّيّارَة [ma: ʔadri ʔaru:ħ bissayya:ra law biṭṭayya:ra] I don't know if I'll go by car or by plane. ما أَدرِي مِنُو قَلَّه [ma: ʔadri minu gallah] I wonder who told him. هَذا شمَدرِيه؟ بَعدَه جِدِيد هنا [ha:ða šmadri:h? baʕdah ǰidi:d hna] What does he know? He's still new here. الشَّبعان شمَدرِيه بِالجّوعان؟ [ʔiššabʕa:n šmadri:h biǰǰu:ʕa:n?] What does the well-fed man know about the hungry? آنِي شمَدرِينِي؟ إسأَل غَيرِي [ʔa:ni šmadri:ni? ʔisʔal ɣayri] What do I know? Ask someone else. • **2.** to find out – دِرَى بنَقلَه، لَو بَعَد؟ [dira: bnaqlah, law baʕad?] Has he learned of his transfer yet?

دارَى [da:ra:] *v:* • **1.** to take care of, care for – عَمّتِي دارَتنِي كُلِّش زين [ʕammti da:ratni kulliš zi:n] My aunt took good care of me. لِيش قاعِد؟ قُوم دارِي المِشتِريَّة [li:š ga:ʕid? gu:m da:ri ʔilmištiriyya] Why are you sitting? Get up and wait on the customers. لَو تدارِي هرُوش الوَرِد بِالمَيّ وَالسَّماد، ما يمُوتُون [law dda:ri hru:š ʔilwarid bilmayy wissama:d, ma: ymu:tu:n] If you'd provide the rose bushes with water and manure, they won't die. ما أَدرِي لِيش بَطَّل. كُلّ المُوَظَّفِين يحِبُّوه وَيدارُوه [ma: ʔadri li:š baṭṭal. kull ʔilmuwaððafi:n yħibbu:h wyda:ru:h] I don't know why he quit. All of the employees like him and do things for him.

اِندِرَى [ʔindira:] *v:* • **1.** to be known – ما يِندِرِي راح يِستِقِيل لَو يِبقَى [ma: yindiri ra:ħ yistiqi:l law yibqa:] It's not known if he's going to resign or stay.

مدارَة [mda:ra] *n:* • **1.** service, care, attention

دِرايَة [dira:ya] *n:* • **1.** knowledge

مدارِي [mda:ri] *adj:* • **1.** taking care of, paying attention to

أَدرَى [ʔadra:] *comparative adjective:* • **1.** more or most informed, knowledgeable

د ر ي و ل

دَرَيوِل [draywil] *n:* دَرَيوِلِيَّة [draywliyya] *pl:* • **1.** driver (of a taxi or car), chauffeur

د ز ز

دَزّ [dazz] *v:* • **1.** to send – دَزَّيت المَكتُوب لَو بَعَد؟ [dazzi:t ʔilmaktu:b law baʕad?] Did you send the

letter yet? دَزَّيت إبِنِي بِشُغُل [dazzi:t ʔibni bšuɣul] I sent my son on an errand. دَزَّيتلَه خَبَر وَراح يِجِي [dazzi:tlah xabar wra:ħ yiǰi] I sent him word and he will come.
اِندَزّ [ʔindazz] *v:* • **1.** to be sent
دَزّ [dazz] *n:* • **1.** sending
دَزَّة [dazza] *n:* دَزّات [dazza:t] *pl:* • **1.** trip, errand

د س ت
دَستَة [dasta] *n:* دَستات [dasta:t] *pl:* • **1.** deck (of cards) – دَستَة وَرَق [dasta waraq] a deck of cards. • **2.** dozen, set of twelve • **3.** mourning or funeral procession for a dignitary by the Shiites

د س ت ر
دَستَر [dastar] *v:* • **1.** to manage secretly
تدَستَر [ddastar] *v:* • **1.** to be managed secretly
دَستُور [dastu:r] *n:* دَساتِير [dasa:ti:r] *pl:* • **1.** constitution
دَستَرَة [dastara] *n:* • **1.** secrecy
دَستُورِي [dastu:ri] *adj:* • **1.** constitutional – الحُكُم الدَّستُورِي [ʔilħukum ʔiddastu:ri] constitutional rule.

د س س
دَسّ [dass] *v:* • **1.** to administer surreptitiously – دَسَّتلَه السَّمّ بِالشُّوربَة حَتَّى تمَوِّتَه [dassatlah ʔissamm biššu:rba ħatta tmawwtah] She slipped him the poison in the soup to kill him. • **2.** to inject double meanings, insinuate – دِير بالَك مِنَّه تَرَة يدِسّ بِالحَكِي مالَه [di:r ba:lak minnah tara ydiss bilħači ma:lah] Watch your step with him; he's insincere in his speech.
اِندَسّ [ʔindass] *v:* • **1.** to be infiltrated, to be inserted
دَسّ [dass] *n:* • **1.** subterfuge • **2.** insinuation
دَسِيسَة [dasi:sa] *n:* دَسائِس [dasa:ʔis] *pl:* • **1.** scheme, plot
دَسّاس [dassa:s] *adj:* دَسّاسِين [dassa:si:n] *pl:* • **1.** plotter, schemer

د س م
تدَسَّم [ddassam] *v:* • **1.** to become greasy, oily (from food) – ما أَقدَر آكُل بِيدِي لِأَنّ تِتدَسَّم [ma: ʔagdar ʔa:kul bi:di liʔann tiddassam] I can't eat with my hand because it'll get greasy.
دَسَم [dasam] *adj:* دُسُومات [dusu:ma:t] *pl:* • **1.** fat, grease, oil
دَسِم [dasim] *adj:* • **1.** fatty, greasy, oily – أَكِل دَسِم [ʔakil dasim] greasy food. لَحَم دَسِم [laħam dasim] fatty meat. • **2.** rich – حَلِيب دَسِم [ħali:b dasim] rich milk. راتِب دَسِم [ra:tib dasim] a fat salary.
أدسَم [ʔadsam] *comparative adjective:* • **1.** more or most fatty • **2.** richer or richest

د ش ب ل
دَشبُول [dašbu:l] *n:* دَشبُولات [dašbu:la:t] *pl:* • **1.** dashboard (of a car)

د ش د ش
دِشداشَة [dišda:ša] *n:* دِشادِيش [diša:di:š] *pl:* • **1.** an ankle-length robe, with a buttoned opening halfway down the front, the standard dress for children, and adults not wearing western clothing

د ش ش
دَشّ [dašš] *v:* • **1.** to jingle, make a jingling noise – مِن تِمشِي تدِشّ بِحجِلها [min timši ddišš bħiǰilha] When she walks, she makes a noise with her anklets.
دَشّ [dašš] *n:* • **1.** jingling

د ش ل م
دَشلَمَة، دِشلَمَة شاي [dašlama, dišlama ča:y] *n:* • **1.** tea strained through a lump of sugar held in the mouth

د ش ل ي
دِشلِي [dišli] *n:* دِشلِيّات، دِشالِي [dišliyya:t, diša:li] *pl:* • **1.** gear, cog wheel

د ش ن
دَشَّن [daššan] *v:* • **1.** (by extension) to use for the first time – الوَزِير دَشَّن السِّينَما الجِّدِيدَة [ʔilwazi:r daššan ʔissinama ʔiǰǰidi:da] The minister dedicated the new movie house. باكِر راح أَدَشِّن قاطِي [ba:čir ra:ħ ʔadaššin qa:ṭi] Tomorrow I'm going to wear my suit for the first time. جِدِيدَة؛ بَعدَها ما مدَشِّنَة [ǰidi:da; baʕdah ma: mdaššina] It's brand new; never been used. • **2.** to dedicate, inaugurate

د ط ل ي
داطلِي [da:ṭli] *n:* • **1.** (coll.) a type of pastry similar to doughnuts
داطلِيَّة [da:ṭliyya] *n:* داطلِيّات [da:ṭliyya:t] *pl:* • **1.** a piece of doughnut-like pastry

د ع ب ل
دَعبَل [daʕbal] *v:* • **1.** to roll into a ball, to round – هالطِّينَة تِقدَر تدَعبِلها بسُهُولَة [haṭṭi:na tigdar ddaʕbilha bsuhu:la] You can round this piece of clay easily. • **2.** to roll – دَعبِلِي الطُّوبَة [daʕbilli ʔiṭṭu:ba] Roll me the ball. دَعبَلِتلَه حكايات كبار لَكِن وَلا زِعَل [daʕbalitlah ħča:ya:t kba:r la:kin wala ziʕal] I threw some rough phrases his way, but he didn't get mad. حكَيت وِيّاه شوَيَّة وَدَعبَلتَه [ħči:t wiyya:h šwayya wdaʕbaltah] I talked to him a bit and sent him on his way.
تدَعبَل [ddaʕbal] *v:* • **1.** to roll – الصَّخرَة تدَعبِلَت مِن فُوق الجِّبَل [ʔiṣṣaxra ddaʕbilat min fu:g ʔiǰǰibal] The rock rolled from the top of the mountain. مِن يِمشِي يِتدَعبَل، هَل قَدّ ما سِمِين [min yimši yiddaʕbal, hal gadd ma: simi:n] When he walks he rolls, because he's so fat.

دُعبُل [duʕbul] *n:* • **1.** (coll.) marble(s)
دُعبُلَّة [duʕbulla] *n:* دُعبُلات، دَعابُل [duʕbullaːt, daʕaːbul] *pl:* • **1.** a marble
مدَعبَل [mdaʕbal] *adj:* • **1.** rounded, round, spherical – الدُّعبُلَّة مُو مدَعبَلَة [ʔidduʕbulla muː mdaʕbala] The marble's out of round. لَمّا كان طِفِل كان مدَعبَل [lamma čaːn ṭifil čaːn mdaʕbal] When he was a child, he was roly-poly. مُو كُلّ مدَعبَل جُوز [muː kull mdaʕbal ǰuːz] All that glitters is not gold. You can't judge a book by its cover (lit. not everything round is a walnut).

د ع ر

دَعارَة [daʕaːra] *n:* • **1.** prostitution

د ع س

دِعَس [diʕas] *v:* • **1.** to run over, knock down – دِعسَتَه السَّيّارَة وَمات [diʕsatah ʔissayyaːra wmaːt] The car ran over him and he died.
اِندِعَس [ʔindiʕas] *v:* • **1.** to be run over – اِندِعَس بلُوري وَرِجلَه اِنفُسخَت [ʔindiʕas bluːri wrijlah ʔinfusxat] He was run over by a truck and his leg was broken.
دَعِس [daʕis] *n:* • **1.** running over pedestrians – حَوادِث الدَّعِس [ħawaːdiθ ʔiddaʕis] pedestrian accidents.

د ع ش

دَعَش [daʕaš] *n:* • **1.** eleven

د ع ف س

دَعفَس [daʕfas] *v:* • **1.** to look, search, inquire, look into, explore
تدِعفِس [tidiʕfis] *n:* • **1.** exploration, research

د ع ك

دِعَك [diʕač] *v:* • **1.** to jostle, bump, shove, push, squeeze – لا تِدعَكني. بيدي شاي [laː tidʕačni. biːdi čaːy] Don't jostle me. I'm holding some tea. الكَلِب دِعَك نَفسَه بَيناتنا [ʔiččalib diʕač nafsah baynaːtna] The dog pushed himself between us. • **2.** to hurt (feelings), make someone feel bad
دَعَّك [daʕʕač] *v:* • **1.** to jostle, bump, shove, push, squeeze • **2.** to wrinkle
تدَعَّك [tdaʕʕač] *v:* • **1.** to become wrinkled – هدُومَك تدَعّكَت. بَدِّلها [hduːmak ddaʕʕčat. baddilha] your clothes are wrinkled. Better change them.
تداعَك [ddaːʕač] *v:* • **1.** to jostle
اِندَعَك [ʔindaʕač] *v:* • **1.** pass. of دِعَك – اِندِعَكِت بالإزدِحام وَكِتفِي تعَوَّر [ʔindiʕačit bilʔizdiħaːm wčitfi tʕawwar] I got shoved in the crowd and my shoulder was hurt. مِن قَلّي إطلَع بَرَّة، اِندِعَكِت مِن حكايتَه [min galli ʔiṭlaʕ barra, ʔindiʕačit min ħčaːytah] When he told me to get out, I was hurt by his remark. لا تقُلّه سِقَط بالإمتِحان؛ يِندِعِك [laː tgullah siqaṭ bilʔimtiħaːn; yindiʕič] Don't tell him he failed the exam; he'll feel bad. • **2.** reflex of دِعَج – الجّاهِل اِندِعَك بين أَبُوه وأُمَّه [ʔiǰǰaːhil ʔindiʕač biːn ʔabuːh wʔummah] The child pushed himself in between his father and mother. أَقدَر أَندِعِك بالحوض الوَرّاني [ʔagdar ʔandiʕič bilħuːð ʔilwarraːni] I can squeeze in the back seat.
دَعِك [daʕič] *n:* • **1.** shoving, pushing
مدَعَّك [mdaʕʕač] *adj:* • **1.** rubbed, massaged

د ع م

دِعَم [diʕam] *v:* • **1.** to run into, collide – كِنت أَباوِع لوَرا وَدِعَمت العمُود [čint ʔabaːwiʕ lwara wdiʕamt ʔilʕamuːd] I was looking back, and ran into the pole. دِعَمت اللُّوري بسَيّارتي [diʕamit ʔilluːri bsayyaːrti] I ran into the truck with my car. السّايِق مالي دِعَم السَّيّارَة وَتلَفها [ʔissaːyiq maːli diʕam ʔissayyaːra wtilafha] My chauffeur had an accident with the car and ruined it سَيّارتي اِندِعمَت بالحايِط [sayyaːrti diʕmat bilħaːyiṭ] My car collided with the wall. • **2.** to support, hold up • **3.** to support, back up – آني راح أَدعِم كُلّ اللّي تقُلّه [ʔaːni raːħ ʔadʕim kull ʔilli dgullah] I will back up everything you tell him.
تداعَم [ddaːʕam] *v:* • **1.** to collide, run into each other – السّايِق مالي وَسايقَك تداعمَوا [ʔissaːyiq maːli wsaːyiqak ddaːʕmaw] My chauffeur and yours collided.
اِندِعَم [ʔindiʕam] *v:* • **1.** to be run into, to be hit – هالسَّيّارَة اِندِعمَت أَربَع مَرّات [hassayyaːra ʔindiʕmat ʔarbaʕ marraːt] This car has been in four collisions.
دَعِم [daʕim] *n:* • **1.** support, holding, assistance
دَعمَة [daʕma] *n:* دَعمات [daʕmaːt] *pl:* • **1.** accident, collision
دَعّامِيَّة [daʕʕaːmiyya] *n:* دَعّامِيّات [daʕʕaːmiyyaːt] *pl:* • **1.** bumper (auto.)
داعِم [daːʕim] *adj:* • **1.** supporting • **2.** supporter
مُدَعَّم [mudaʕʕam] *adj:* • **1.** supported
مدعُوم [madʕuːm] *adj:* • **1.** supported • **2.** crashed

د ع و

دِعَى [diʕaː] *v:* • **1.** to summon, call for someone, send for someone – وِزارَة الدِّفاع دِعَت مَواليد سَنتي لِلخِدمَة [wizaːrat ʔiddifaːʕ diʕat mawaːliːd santi lilxidma] The defense ministry called my year group to service. • **2.** to invite – دِعَى كُلّ أَصدِقائَه لِلعَشا [diʕaː kull ʔaṣdiqaːʔah lilʕaša] He invited all his friends to supper. • **3.** to curse – لِيش دَتِدعِي عَلَيّا؟ [liːš datidʕi ʕalayya?] Why are you cursing me? • **4.** to pray
داعَى [daːʕaː] *v:* • **1.** to dun, ask for repayment – داعيتَه بفلُوسي عِدَّة مَرّات [daːʕiːtah bifluːsi ʕiddat marraːt] I dunned him for my money several times.
تداعَى [ddaːʕaː] *v:* • **1.** to argue, bicker, fight – ماكُو حاجَة تِتداعَى وِيّاه [maːku ħaːǰa tiddaːʕaː wiyyaːh] There is no need for your to argue with him. عَلي وَمَرتَه دائِماً يِدّاعُون [ʕali wmartah daːʔiman yiddaːʕuːn] Ali and his wife are always fighting.

إنتَ شقَدّ تِتداعَى وَتِتطالَب ويّا الجِّيران [ʔinta šgadd tiddaːʕaː wtiṭṭaːlab wiyya ʔijjiːraːn] My, how you argue with and make demands of the neighbors.
اِندعَى [ʔindiʕaː] *v:* • **1.** to pray
اِدَّعَى [ʔiddiʕaː] *v:* • **1.** to claim, allege, maintain – اِدَّعَى إنُّو يُعرُف السِّرّ [ʔiddʕaː ʔinnu yuʕruf ʔissirr] He claimed he knows the secret.
اِستَدعَى [ʔistadʕaː] *v:* • **1.** to summon, call in – وَزير الخارِجيَّة اِستَدعَى سَفيرنا لِدائرتَه [waziːr ʔilxaːrijiyya ʔistadʕaː safiːrna lidaːʔirtah] The foreign minister summoned our ambassador to his office. • **2.** to recall – اِستَدعَينا وَفِدنا قَبُل نِهايَة الاِجتِماع [ʔistadʕayna wafiðna gabul nihaːyat ʔilʔijtimaːʕ] We recalled our delegation before the end of the conference. • **3.** to call for, require, demand – الوَضِع اِستَدعَى هَالإجراءات [ʔilwaðiʕ ʔistadʕaː halʔijraːʔaːt] The situation called for these measures. • **4.** to apply, submit an application – لِيش ما ترُوح تِستَدعِي؟ يِمكِن تحَصِّل شِي [liːš maː truːħ tistadʕi? yimkin tħaṣṣil ši] Why don't you go apply? Maybe you'll get something. اِستَدعِيت عَلَى وَظِيفَة بدائرَة البَرِيد [ʔistadʕiːt ʕala waðiːfa bdaːʔirat ʔilbariːd] I applied for a position in the post office. اِستَدعَت بِالمَحكَمَة عَلَى حَقّها مِن الفلُوس [ʔistadʕat bilmaħkama ʕala ħaqqha min ʔilifluːs] She applied to the court for her share of the money.
دَعوَة [daʕwa] *n:* دَعوات، دَعاوِي [daʕwaːt, daʕaːwi] *pl:* • **1.** invitation • **2.** reception, party, fete • **3.** matter, case, affair – دَعوَة شَرَف [daʕwat šaraf] a matter of honor. دَعوَة دِينارَين [daʕwat dinaːrayn] a matter of two dinars. ما لِي دَعوَة بِيه؛ لازِم يِدرُس بنَفسَه [maːli daʕwa biːh; laːzim yidrus bnafsah] He's no concern of mine; he'll have to do his own studying. هاي دَعوَة المِجدّي؛ تِنطِيه فِلِس، يرِيد عَشرَة [haːy daʕwat ʔilimjaddi; tintiːh filis, yriːd ʕašra] That's the story with the beggar; give him a fils and he wants ten. شدَعوَة هَالقَدّ؟ ما يِسوَى أزيَد مِن دِينار [šdaʕwa halgadd? maː yiswaː ʔazyad min dinaːr] How come so much? It's not worth more than a dinar. شدَعوَة دَتُركُض؟ أكُو شِي؟ [šdaʕwa daturkuð? ʔaku ši?] Why are you running? Anything wrong? شدَعوَة هَالبِكا؟ [šdaʕwa halbiča?] Why all this crying? شدَعوَة شايِل خَشمَك عَلينا؟ [šdaʕwa šaːyil xašmak ʕaliːna?] Why are you looking down on us? شدَعوَة، يابَة؟ مَحَّد يشُوفَك [šdaʕwa, yaːba? maħħad yšuːfak] What's up, pal? We don't see you any more. • **4.** pl. دَعاوِي law suit, case, legal proceeding • **5.** prayer
دُعاء [duʕaːʔ] *n:* أدعِيَة [ʔadʕiya] *pl:* • **1.** prayer, supplication • **2.** curse, imprecation • **3.** a small scroll or paper carried as an amulet on which is written a religious phrase
داعَة، وداعَة [daːʕa, wdaːʕa] *n:* • **1.** For the sake, honor – وَداعَة أبُويَا، راح أسَوِّيها [wdaːʕat ʔabuːya, raːħ ʔasawwiːha] By my father's honor, I'll do it. وَداعَة الله ما شايفَه [wdaːʕat ʔallah maː šaːyfah] By God, I haven't seen him. وَداعتَك ما تِنطِي؛ خَلِّيهَا عَلَى حسابِي [wdaːʕtak maː tinṭi; xalliːha ʕala ħsaːbi] Not on your life; this is on me.
داعِي [daːʕi] *n:* دُعاة، دَواعِي [duʕaːt, dawaːʕiː] *pl:* • **1.** proponent, propagandist • **2.** host, person who has invited someone – آنِي اللِّي سَوَّيتَه، داعِيك [ʔaːni ʔilli sawwiːtah, daːʕiːk] I am the one who did it, yours truly.
دِعايَة [diʕaːya] *n:* • **1.** propaganda • **2.** advertising, promotion
اِدِّعاء [ʔiddiʕaːʔ] *n:* • **1.** claim
مُداعاة [mudaːʕaːt] *n:* • **1.** dunning, asking for repayment
اِستِدعاء [ʔistidʕaːʔ] *n:* • **1.** summons, invitation
مُدَّعِي [muddaʕi] *adj:* • **1.** phony
مُستَدعِي [mustadʕi] *adj:* • **1.** summoning, requiring attendence (e.g. summoning to court)
متداعِي [mitdaːʕi] *adj:* • **1.** tottering

د ع ي

See also: د ع و

د غ د غ

دَغدَغ [daɣdaɣ] *v:* • **1.** to tickle – دَغدِغ الجّاهِل حَتَّى يِضحَك [daɣdiɣ ʔijjaːhil ħatta yiðħak] Tickle the kid so he'll laugh.

د غ ش

دِغَش [diɣaš] *v:* • **1.** to cheat – دِغَشنِي. قَلِّي هَالقُماش إنكِلِيزِي، طِلَع وَطَنِي [diɣašni. galli halqumaːš ʔingiliːzi, ṭilaʕ waṭani] He cheated me. He said this material was English and it turned out to be a local product. هالبَقّال يِدغُش بكُلّشِي يبِيعَه [halbaggaːl yidɣuš bkullši ybiːʕah] This grocer cheats on everything he sells. يِدغُش بِالقمار [yidɣuš bilqmaːr] He cheats at gambling. • **2.** to insinuate, imply – وَلَو كَلِماتَه بَرِيئَة، لَكِن يِدغُش بحَكيَه [walaw kalimaːtah bariːʔa, laːkin yidɣuš bħačyah] Even though his words are innocuous, he makes insinuations.
دَغَش [daɣaš] *n:* • **1.** insinuation, innuendo

د غ ل

دَغَّل [daɣɣal] *v:* • **1.** to poke – لا تدَغِّل تَرَة أبُسطَك [laː ddaɣɣal tara ʔabusṭak] Don't poke or I'll sock you one.
دَغَل [daɣal] *n:* • **1.** clump(s) of grass or brush • **2.** thorn bush(es)
دَغلَة [daɣla] *n:* دَغلات [daɣlaːt] *pl:* • **1.** poke, jab

د غ ل ي

داغلِي [daːɣli] *n:* داغليّات [daːɣliyyaːt] *pl:* • **1.** king (in non-western card games).

د غ م

دِغَم [diɣam] *v:* • **1.** to dull, blunt, to bend or break the tip of – دِغَم الأبرَة وَبَعَد ما تخَيِّط [diɣam ʔilʔubra wabaʕad

maː txayyiṭ] He dulled the needle and it won't sew any more.
أدغَم [ʔadɣam] *adj:* دُغُم، دَغمِين [duɣum, daɣmiːn] *pl:* دَغمَة [daɣma] *feminine:* • **1.** gloomy-looking, sad-looking • **2.** gloomy-looking person – ألوان دَغمَة [ʔalwaːn daɣma] dark colors. الدِّنيا دَغمَة اليُوم [ʔiddinya daɣma ʔilyuːm] It's dark today. لُون رِصاصِي أدغَم [luːn riṣaːṣi ʔadɣam] dull grey color. لُون سِترتِي رِصاصِي أدغَم [luːn sitirti riṣaːṣi ʔadɣam] The color of my jacket is dull gray. • **3.** dark, dull, gloomy

د ف ء

دِفَى [difaː] *v:* • **1.** to get warm, warm up – لَفِّيت نَفسِي بالبَطّانِيَّة وَدِفِيت [laffiːt nafsi bilbaṭṭaːniyya wdifiːt] I wrapped myself in the blanket and got warm. المَيّ دِفَى. تِقدَر تِغسِل إذا ترِيد [ʔilmayy difaː. tigdar tiɣsil ʔiða triːd] The water has gotten warm. You can take a bath if you want. أكُو اِحتِمال الدِّنيا تِدفَى اليُوم [ʔaku ʔiħtimaːl ʔiddinya tidfaː ʔilyuːm] There's a possibility it will warm up today.
دَفَّى [daffaː] *v:* • **1.** to warm – خَلَّى الجّاهِل تَحت قَبُّوطَه حَتَّى يدَفِّيه [xallaː ʔijjaːhil taħat qappuːṭah ħatta ydaffiːh] He put the kid under his overcoat to warm him up. هَالصُّوبَة تدَفِّي الغُرفَة بنُصّ ساعَة [haṣṣuːpa ddaffi ʔilɣurfa bnuṣṣ saːʕa] This heater heats the room in a half hour.
تدَفَّى [tdaffaː] *v:* • **1.** to warm oneself, get warm – تَعال أقعُد يَمّ النّار، اِتدَفَّى [taʕaːl ʔugʕud yamm ʔinnaːr, ʔiddaffaː] Come sit near the fire, and get warm.
دَفُو [dafw, difw] *n:* • **1.** warmth
مَدفَأة [madfaʔa] *n:* • **1.** heater
دافِي [daːfi] *adj:* • **1.** warm – مَيّ دافِي [mayy daːfi] warm water. الدِّنيا دافيَة [ʔiddinya daːfya] The weather's warm.
دَفيان [dafyaːn] *adj:* • **1.** warm
أدفَى [ʔadfaː] *comparative adjective:* • **1.** warmer

د ف ت ر

دَفتَر [daftar] *n:* دَفاتِر [dafaːtir] *pl:* • **1.** He keeps a record of his expenses – دَفتَر خِدمَة [daftar xidma] service certificate --- a small booklet showing record of military service. مَسك الدَّفاتِر [mask ʔiddafaːtir] bookkeeping. يِلزَم دَفتَر بمَصرُوفاتَه [yilzam daftar bmaṣruːfaːtah] He keeps a record of his expenses. • **2.** note book

د ف ت ي ر ي

دَفتِيريَة [daftiːrya] *n:* • **1.** diphtheria • **2.** Notary Office

د ف ر

دُفَر [dufar] *v:* • **1.** to kick – الحصان دُفَرَه برِجلَه وَوَقَّعَه [ʔilħṣaːn dufarah brijlah wwaggaʕah] The horse kicked him and knocked him down.
دَفَّر [daffar] *v:* • **1.** to kick repeatedly – لا تدَفُّرَه؛ تِقدَر تقُولَّه إطلَع [laː ddaffurah; tigdar dguːllah ʔiṭlaʕ] Don't keep kicking him; you can tell him to get out.
تدافَر [tdaːfar] *v:* • **1.** to kick one another – شُوف الوِلِد دَيتدافرُون [šuːf ʔilwilid dayiddaːfruːn] Look at the boys kicking each other.
دَفُر [dafur] *n:* • **1.** kicking
دَفرَة [dafra] *n:* دَفرات [dafraːt] *pl:* • **1.** kick (like that of a horse)

د ف ع

دِفَع [difaʕ] *v:* • **1.** to push – الباب ما يِنفَكّ إذا ما تِدفَعها حيل [ʔilbaːb maː tinfakk ʔiða maː tidfaʕha ħiːl] The door won't open if you don't push it hard. دِفعَوا سَيّارتِي لِلبانزِين خانَة [difʕaw sayyaːrti lilbanziːn xaːna] They pushed my car to the gas station. جانِي مِن وَرا وَدِفَعنِي بِالمَيّ [jaːni min wara wdifaʕni bilmayy] He ran up behind me and shoved me into the water. وُقَفِت بِالباب حَتَّى ما يخُشّ لَكِن دِفَعنِي وَخَشّ [wugafit bilbaːb ħatta maː yxušš laːkin difaʕni wxašš] I stood in the door so he wouldn't come in, but he pushed me aside and entered. • **2.** to get rid of, send away – إنطِيه دِينار وَإدِفعَه [ʔinṭiːh dinaːr wʔidifʕah] Give him a dinar and get rid of him. الله يِدفَع عَنَّك كُلّ بَلا [ʔallah yidfaʕ ʕannak kull bala] God save you from all misfortune. دَفَع الله ما كان أعظَم لَو مَيِّت [dafaʕ ʔallah maː kaːn ʔaʕðam law mayyit] God spared him the worst or he'd have died. • **3.** to pay – ما دَأقدَر أبِيعها؛ مَحَّد دَيِدفَع بِيها شِي [maː daʔagdar ʔabiːʕha; maħħad dayidfaʕ biːha ši] I can't sell it; nobody will pay anything for it. شقَدّ تِدفَع بِهَالتَّلَفزِيُون؟ [šgadd tidfaʕ bhattalafizyuːn?] How much would you pay for this TV? دِفَع ديُونَه قَبُل ما سافَر [difaʕ dyuːnah gabul maː saːfar] He paid his debts before he left. • **4.** to offer – ما بِعت السَّيّارَة لأَنّ دِفعُولِي بِيها مِيَّة دِينار [maː biʕt ʔissayyaːra liʔann difʕuːli biːha miyyat dinaːr] I didn't sell the car because they offered me (only) a hundred dinars for it.
دَفَّع [daffaʕ] *v:* • **1.** intens. of push, shove – لا تدَفِّع، عاد! كُلّنا نخُشّ [laː ddaffiʕ, ʕaːd! kullna nxušš] Don't shove, Mac! We'll all get in. لا تدَفِّع بِيّا. خَلِّينِي أمشِي عَلَى كَيفِي [laː ddafiʕ biyya. xalliːni ʔamši ʕala kayfi] Don't push me. Let me walk slowly. • **2.** to make someone pay
دافَع [daːfaʕ] *v:* • **1.** to defend – دافعَوا عَن المُعَسكَر حَتَّى خِلصَت مَؤُونَتهُم [daːfʕaw ʕan ʔilmuʕaskar ħatta xilṣat maʔuːnathum] They held the barracks until their ammunition ran out. دافعَوا عَن بَلَدتهُم حَتَّى النَّفَس الأخِير [daːfʕaw ʕan baldathum ħatta ʔinnafas ʔilʔaxiːr] They defended their city unto the last breath.
تدافَع [tdaːfaʕ] *v:* • **1.** to push each other – النّاس تدافعَوا مِن فَتَّح المَخزَن [ʔinnaːs ddaːfʕaw min

fattaħ ʔilmaxzan] The people pushed each other when the store opened. ماكو حاجَة تِتدافَع ويّاه. خابِر الشُّرطَة [maːku ħaːja tiddaːfaʕ wiyyaːh. xaːbir ʔiššurṭa] There's no reason for you to struggle with him. Call the police.
اندفَع [ʔindifaʕ] *v:* • **1.** to be pushed – هَالسَّيّارَة ما تِندِفِع؛ ثِقِيلَة [hassayyaːra maː tindifiʕ; θigiːla] This car can't be pushed; it's too heavy. • **2.** to be gotten rid of, be sent away – ما اِندِفَع قَبُل ما ياخُذ دِينار مِنِّي [maː ʔindifaʕ gabul maː yaːxuð dinaːr minni] He wouldn't go away until he got a dinar from me. اِندِفِع، لَك. بَسّ تِلغِي [ʔindifiʕ, lak. bass tilɣi] Beat it, bud! You're talking nonsense. • **3.** to be carried away, to get worked up – مِن يِحكِي عَن الدِّين يِندِفِع هوايَة [min yiħči ʕan ʔiddiːn yindifiʕ hwaːya] When he talks about religion, he gets all worked up.
دَفع [dafiʕ] *n:* • **1.** pushing • **2.** payment
دَفعَة [dafʕa] *n:* دَفعات [dafʕaːt] *pl:* • **1.** push, shove, thrust – خَلِّي يِرُوح، دَفعَة مَردِي وَعَصا كُردِي [xalli: yiruːħ, dafʕa mardi wʕaṣaːt kurdi] Let him go, to hell with him. هاي تبَيِّن دَفعَة؛ لَو يريد يشَغّلَك كان دَزَّك لِلفَحِص [haːy tbayyin dafʕa; law yriːd yšaɣɣlak čaːn dazzak lilfaħiṣ] It looks like he wanted to get rid of you; if he wanted to give you a job, he would have given you a physical exam. • **2.** that which comes at any one time, a burst, a spurt, a gush, a rush • **3.** group, bunch – دَفعَة جِنُود [dafʕat ǰinuːd] a shipment of troops. دَفعَة فلُوس [dafʕat fluːs] a payment of money. دَفعَة وِحدَة [dafʕa wiħda] all at once, at one time. لَبِّسُونا جِنُود كُلّنا دَفعَة وِحدَة [labbisuːna ǰunuːd kullna dafʕa wiħda] They took all of us into the army at one time.
مَدفَع [madfaʕ] *n:* مَدافِع [madaːfiʕ] *pl:* • **1.** gun, cannon
دِفاع [difaːʕ] *n:* • **1.** defense (also jur. and sports) – وِزارَة الدِّفاع [wizaːrat ʔiddifaːʕ] Ministry of Defense. مُحامِي الدِّفاع [muħaːmi ʔiddifaːʕ] the lawyer for the defense. • **2.** pl. دِفاعِيَّة back (soccer)
دُفعَة [dufʕa] *n:* • **1.** batch
دافِع [daːfiʕ] *n:* • **1.** motivation, motive
مَدفَعِي [madfaʕi] *n:* • **1.** artillery, gun, cannon – ضابُط مَدفَعِي [ðaːbuṭ madfaʕi] artillery officer. بَطارِيَّة مَدفَعِيَّة [baṭaːriyya madfaʕiyya] artillery battery. وُكُر مَدفَعِي [wukur madfaʕi] gun emplacement. • **2.** artillery, gunner, cannon
مُدافِع [mudaːfiʕ] *n:* • **1.** back (in soccer)
مَدفَعِيَّة [madfaʕiyya] *n:* • **1.** artillery
اِندِفاع [ʔindifaːʕ] *n:* • **1.** impulse, enthusiasm
دِفاعِي [difaːʕi] *adj:* • **1.** defensive – خِطَّة دِفاعِيَّة [xiṭṭa difaːʕiyya] a defensive strategy.
مَدفُوع [madfuːʕ] *adj:* • **1.** paid
مُندَفِع [mundafiʕ] *adj:* • **1.** impulsive

د ف ف

دَفّ [daff] *n:* دفُوف [dfuːf] *pl:* • **1.** tambourine
دَفَّة [daffa] *n:* دَفّات [daffaːt] *pl:* • **1.** rudder (of a boat or plane) – دَفَّة الحُكُم [daffat ʔilħukum] the helm of government. • **2.** a shallow, conical clay brazier set by one's feet for warmth

د ف ق

تدَفَّق [ddaffaq] *v:* • **1.** to pour out, gush out – صارَت كَسرَة بِالسَّدّ وَقام يِدَّفَّق المَيّ مِنهَا [ṣaːrat kasra bissadd wgaːm yiddaffaq ʔilmayy minha] There was a break in the dam and the water began rushing out of it.

د ف ل

دِفلَة [difla] *n:* • **1.** oleander

د ف ن

دِفَن [difan] *v:* • **1.** to bury, inter – دِفنَوا المَيِّت بالمَقبَرَة [difnaw ʔilmayyit bilmaqbara] They buried the dead man in the cemetery. الزِّلزال دِفَنها لِلوِلايَة [ʔizzilzaːl difanha lilwilaːya] The earthquake buried the city. الكَلِب دِفَن العَظُم بِالحَدِيقَة [ʔiččalib difan ʔilʕaðum bilħadiːqa] The dog buried the bone in the yard. • **2.** to conceal, keep secret – إدفِن هالفايِل بين الفايلات حَتَّى لَا حَدّ يِلقِيه [ʔidfin halfaːyil biːn ʔilfaːylaːt ħatta laː ħadd yilgiːh] Conceal the file among the others so no one will find it. دِفنَوا الحِكايَة وَما خَلُّوها تِطلَع [difnaw ʔilħičaːya wma xalluːha tiṭlaʕ] They kept the story secret and didn't let it leak out.
اندِفَن [ʔindifan] *v:* • **1.** to be buried – المَرحُوم اِندِفَن بِمَقبَرَة العائِلَة [ʔilmarħuːm ʔindifan bmagbarat ʔilʕaːʔila] The deceased was buried in the family cemetery.
دَفِن [dafin] *n:* • **1.** burying, burial – فلُوس الدَّفِن [fluːs ʔiddafin] burial money. إجازَة الدَّفِن [ʔiǰaːzt ʔiddafin] burial permit. • **2.** innuendo, insinuation, implication – جِيب دَفِن [ǰiːb dafin] ash pocket (tailoring). قُندَرَة دَفِن [qundara dafin] shoe(s) with thin, inconspicuous soles.
دَفّان [daffaːn] *n:* • **1.** undertaker, mortician • **2.** mortician
دَفنَة [dafna] *n:* • **1.** burial
مَدفُونَة [madfuːna] *n:* • **1.** stuffed vegetable
مَدفُون [madfuːn] *adj:* مَدفُونات [madfuwnaːt] *pl:* • **1.** buried

د ق د ق [1]

دَقدَق [daqdaq] *v:* • **1.** to be fussy, particular – إكتِب العَرِيضَة كُلِّش زين، تَرَة هَالمُوَظَّف يدَقدِق هوايَة [ʔiktib ʔilʕariːða kulliš ziːn, tara halmuwaððaf ydaqdiq hwaːya] Write the petition very well, because that official's awfully fussy.
دِقداقِي [diqdaːqi] *adj:* دِقداقِيَّة [diqdaːqiyya] *pl:* • **1.** particular, fussy • **2.** fussy person

د ق د ق 2

دَقدَق [dagdag] *v:* • **1.** to bang, pound – شدَتِدَقدِق؟ أَرِيد أنام [šdatidagdig? ʔariːd ʔanaːm] What are you banging? I want to sleep. • **2.** to tattoo – الدَّقّاقَة تدَقدِق العَرُوس وَتحَفحِفها قَبُل ما تِتزَوَّج [ʔiddaggaːga ddagdig ʔilʕaruːs wtħafħifha gabul maː tidzawwaǰ] The tattooing woman will tattoo the bride and depilate her before she gets married.

دِقدِقَة [digdiga] *n:* دِقدِقات [digdigaːt] *pl:* • **1.** sty (med.) • **2.** a lump on the eyelid

مدَقدَق [mdagdag] *adj:* • **1.** tattooed – إِيد مدَقدِقَة [ʔiːd mdagdiga] a tattooed hand.

د ق ر

دِقَر [digar] *v:* • **1.** to bump, jostle, jiggle • **2.** to disturb, upset, bother, irritate – دِقَرنِي هوايَة بِهَالكِلمَة [digarni hwaːya bhaččilma] He upset me terribly with that remark.

اِندِقَر [ʔindigar] *v:* • **1.** to be bumped, be jostled, be jiggled – الكلاص اِندِقَر بِيدِي وَكَبّ المَيّ [ʔilglaːṣ ʔindigar biːdi wčabb ʔilmayy] The glass got bumped by my hand and spilled the water. أَشُو اِندِقَرت بِهَالكِلمَة [ʔašuː ʔindigarit bhaččilma] Seems you were upset by that remark.

دَقِر [dagir] *n:* • **1.** jiggling

د ق ق

دَقّ [daqq] *v:* • **1.** to sicken, make ill (with anxiety, impatience, irritation, etc.) – حَكيَه يدُقّ المُطِي [ħačyah yduqq ʔilmuṭi] His talk would make even a donkey sick. دَقنِي؛ قِرا المَكتُوب عَشِر مَرّات قَبُل ما يِفهَم المَسأَلَة [daqqni; qiraː ʔilmaktuːb ʕašir marraːt gabul maː yifham ʔilmasʔala] He made me sick; he read the letter ten times before he understood the problem. راح أَشَوّفه البايسِكِل مالِي وَأَدُقّه [raːħ ʔašawwfah ʔilpaːysikil maːli waʔaduqqah] I am going to show him my bicycle and make him green with envy.

دَقّ [dagg] *v:* • **1.** to grind, crush, pulverize – لازِم ندُقّ القَهوَة [laːzim ndugg ʔilgahwa] We've got to grind the coffee. • **2.** to strike – ساعَة الصَّراي هَسَّة دَقَّت بِالخَمسَة [saːʕat ʔiṣṣaraːy hassa daggat bilxamsa] The clock on the Serai just struck five. • **3.** to beat, throb – رِكَضِت شوَيَّة وَقَلبِي قام يدُقّ حيل [rikaðit šwayya wgalbi gaːm ydugg ħiːl] I ran a little, and my heart began to beat heavily. • **4.** to knock, rap, bang, pound, hammer – دُقّ الباب قَبُل ما تخُشّ [dugg ʔilbaːb gabul maː txušš] Knock on the door before you go in. دَقّ رِجلَه بِالقاع وقال إِلّا يِشتِري سَيّارَة [dagg riǰlah bilgaːʕ wgaːl ʔilla yištiri sayyaːra] He stamped his foot on the ground and said he's bound he'll buy a car. رُوح دُقّ راسَك بِالحايِط [ruːħ dugg raːsak bilħaːyiṭ] Go jump in the lake (lit., go bang your head against the wall). إِبنَك دَقّوه حيل [ʔibnak daggawh ħiːl] They beat up your son badly. راح أَدُقلَه بَرقِيَّة باكِر [raːħ ʔadugglah barqiyya baːčir] I will send him a telegram tomorrow. آني موافِق؛ دُقّها [ʔaːni mwaːfuq; duggha] I'm agreed; put her there! يعجِبها تدُقّ إِصبِعتَين مِن تُرقُص [yiʕǰibha ddugg ʔiṣbiʕtayn min turguṣ] She likes to snap her fingers when she dances. كِنّا ساكتِين أَشُو فُجأَةً دَقّها [činna saːktiːn ʔašu fuǰʔatan daggha] We were all quiet and suddenly he broke wind. • **5.** to pound in, drive – دُقّ هالبِسمار بِالحايِط [dugg halbismaːr bilħaːyiṭ] Hammer this nail into the wall. دُقّ هَالصُّورَة بِالحايِط [dugg haṣṣuːra bilħaːyiṭ] Nail up this picture on the wall. • **6.** to bump, touch – هَل قَدّ ما طوِيل، راسَه يدُقّ بِالسَّقُف [hal gadd maː ṭuwiːl, raːsah ydugg bissaguf] He is so tall, his head bumps the ceiling. حاشيَة شَرشَف الدَّوشَك مدَندِلَة وَقَرِيب تدُقّ بِالقاع [ħaːšyat čarčaf ʔiddawšag mdandila wqariːb ddugg bilgaːʕ] The edge of the bed sheet is dangling down and almost touching the floor. • **7.** to beat, strum, play – يدُقّ عُود زين [ydugg ʕuːd ziːn] He plays the lute well. دَقلِي طَبُل؛ ما ظَلّ أَحَّد ما سِمَع [daggli ṭabul; maː ðall ʔaħħad maː simaʕ] He noised it all over town. There isn't anyone left who hasn't heard. • **8.** to ring – الجّهال دَقّوا الجَّرَس وَانهِزمَوا [ʔiǰǰihaːl daggaw ʔiǰǰaras wʔinhizmaw] The children rang the bell and ran away. دَقّيتلَه تِلِفون، لَكِن ما كان بِبَيتَه [daggiːtlah tilifuːn, laːkin maː čaːn ʔibbaytah] I gave him a ring, but he wasn't home. • **9.** to ring, resound – التَّلِفون دَيدُقّ [ʔittalifuːn daydugg] The phone is ringing. لِيش الجَّرَس دَيدُقّ؟ [liːš ʔiǰǰaras daydugg?] Why's the bell ringing? • **10.** to tattoo – العَرُوس دَيدُقُّولها دَقَّة بحِنكها [ʔilʕaruːs dayduggu: lha dagga bħiničha] They are putting a tattoo on the bride's chin.

دَقَّق [daqqaq] *v:* • **1.** to scrutinize, look closely – راح يجِي مُفَتِّش، يدَقِّق حساباتنا [raːħ yiǰi mufattiš, ydaqqiq ħsaːbaːtna] An inspector's coming to check our accounts. لِيش ما دَقَّقت النَّظَر، قَبُل ما تِشتِري؟ [liːš maː daqqaqt ʔinnaðar, gabul maː tištiri?] Why didn't you look close before you bought it?

اِندَقّ [ʔindaqq] *v:* • **1.** pass. of – دَقّ to be crushed دَقّ اِندَقّ مِن شافنِي راكُب البايسِكِل الجِّدِيد [ʔindaqq min šaːfni raːkub ʔilpaːysikil ʔiǰǰidiːd] He became green with envy when he saw me riding the new bicycle. مَرتَه اِندَقَّت مِن تزَوَّج عَليها مَرَة [wugaʕ biːh dagg] [martah ʔindaqqat min tzawwaǰ ʕaliːha mara] His wife was crushed when he married a second wife.

اِندَقّ [ʔindagg] *v:* • **1.** to get involved – لا تِندَقّ بِيه، تَرَة مُو خُوش آدَمِي [laː tindagg biːh, tara muː xuːš ʔaːdami] Don't get involved with him because he's no good.

دَقّ [dagg] *n:* • **1.** (in the expression وُقَع بِيه دَقّ [wugaʕ biːh dagg]) لِزَم إِبنَه وَوُقَع بِيه دَقّ [lizam ʔibnah wwugaʕ biːh dagg] He grabbed his son and beat the tar out of him. وُقَع بِالشُّغُل دَقّ؛ وَلا تغَدَّى [wugaʕ biššuɣul dagg; wala tɣaddaː] He really tore into the work; didn't even have lunch. مِن ياكُل سِمَك، يَوقَع بِيه دَقّ [min yaːkul

simač, yu:gaʕ bi:h dagg] When he eats fish, he really digs into it.
دَقّ [dagg] *n:* • **1.** grinding, crushing, pulverizing
دِقَّة [diqqa] *n:* • **1.** accuracy, exactness, precision • **2.** with - ب means precisely, accurately
دَقَّة [dagga] *n:* دَقّات [dagga:t] *pl:* • **1.** knock, bang, rap • **2.** beat, throb • **3.** stroke, striking • **4.** ring, ringing, • **5.** tattoo, tattooed mark • **6.** dirty trick
دُقَّة [dugga] *n:* • **1.** cracked rice
دَقّاق [dagga:g] *n:* • **1.** a (male) nurse who gives shots – دَقّاق جِدرِي [dagga:g ǰidri] a man who gives smallpox vaccinations.
مَدَقَّة [madaqqa] *n:* • **1.** teasing
دَقِيقَة [daqi:qa] *n:* دَقايِق [daqa:yiq] *pl:* • **1.** minute
دَقّاقَة [dagga:ga] *n:* دَقّاقات [dagga:ga:t] *pl:* • **1.** door knocker • **2.** a woman who does tattooing
تَدقِيق [tadqi:q] *n:* • **1.** accuracy, precision, verification, checking
مَدقُوقَة [madgu:ga] *n:* • **1.** a confection made of crushed dates and sesame seeds
دَقِيق [daqi:q] *adj:* • **1.** small, minute, tiny – تَفاصِيل دَقِيقَة [tafa:ṣi:l daqi:qa] minute details. الأمعاء الدَّقِيقَة [ʔilʔamʕa:ʔ ʔiddaqi:qa] the small intestine. • **2.** precise, exact, accurate – ساعَة دَقِيقَة [sa:ʕa daqi:qa] an accurate watch. حساب دَقِيق [ħsa:b daqi:q] a precise account. • **3.** delicate, precarious, serious – قَضِيَّة دَقِيقَة [qaðiyya daqi:qa] a delicate matter. وَضِع دَقِيق [waðiʕ daqi:q] a precarious situation.
مُدَقِّق [mudaqqiq] *n:* • **1.** a civil servant ranking between the clerk and supervisor
مُدَقَّق [mudaqqaq] *adj:* • **1.** precise, accurate
مَدقُوق [madqu:q] *adj:* • **1.** teased
أَدَقّ [ʔadaqq] *comparative adjective:* • **1.** more or most exact, precise

د ق ل

دِقَل [digal] *n:* • **1.** (coll.) a variety of dates • **2.** mast (naut.)
دِقلَة [digla] *n:* دِقلات [digla:t] *pl:* • **1.** a variety of dates

د ق م

دَقَّم [daggam] *v:* • **1.** to button – دَقُّم قَبُوطَك. الدِّنيا بارِدَة [daggum qappu:ṭak. ʔiddinya ba:rda] Button up your overcoat. It's cold outside. تدَقَّم قَبُل ما تخُشّ عَالمُدِير [ddaggam gabul ma: txušš ʕalmudi:r] Button up before you go in to see the director.
تدَقَّم [ddaggam] *v:* • **1.** to button oneself up
دَقُم [dagum] *n:* • **1.** bending or breaking the tip of something
دُقمَة [dugma] *n:* دُقَم، دِقَم [dugam, digam] *pl:* • **1.** button • **2.** button, pushbutton – دُقمَة الضُّوَة [dugmat ʔiððuwa] the light switch.

د ق ن

دِقَن [digan] *n:* • **1.** rheum (eye gunk) sleep, the mucous substance in the eyes

د ق و ر

داقُور [da:gu:r] *n:* دواقِير [dwa:gi:r] *pl:* • **1.** a removable center door post used to hold shop doors together when the shop is closed.

د ك ت ر 1

دِكتاتُور [diktatu:tu:r] *n:* • **1.** dictator
دِكتاتُورِيَّة [diktatu:tu:riyya] *n:* • **1.** dictatorship
دِكتاتُورِي [diktatu:tu:ri] *adj:* • **1.** dictatorial

د ك ت ر 2

دَكتُور [daktu:r, duktu:r] *n:* دَكاتِرَة [daka:tra] *pl:* • **1.** doctor (physician), and Ph.D. holder
دِكتُوراه [diktu:ra:h] *n:* • **1.** Ph.D – شِهادَة الدِّكتُورا [šiha:dat ʔiddiktura] Ph.D. degree. • **2.** doctorate degree

د ك ك 1

دَكّ [dačč] *v:* • **1.** to tamp, pack – دَيدِكُّون الشّارِع بِالرَّولَة [daydičču:n ʔiššaːriʕ birrawla] They're packing the street down with the roller. إذا ما أَدِّكّ القاع زين، يقُبّ الكاشِي [ʔiða ma: ʔaddičč ʔilga:ʕ zi:n, ygubb ʔilka:ši] If you don't tamp the ground well, the tile will bulge. • **2.** to stuff, pack, jam – دِكّ هَالوُصلَة بِالزُّرُف حَتَّى لا يِجِي هَوا بارِد [dičč halwuṣla bizzuruf ħatta la: yiǰi hawa ba:rid] Stuff this piece of cloth in the hole so cold air won't come in. دِكّها زين، تَرَة ما راح ناكُل بَعَد لِلمِغرِب [diččha zi:n, tara ma: ra:ħ na:kul baʕad lilmiɣrib] Eat your fill --- we aren't going to eat again until evening.
دَكّ [dačč] *n:* • **1.** tamping, packing
دَكَّة [dačča] *n:* دَكّات، دِكَك [dačča:t, dičač] *pl:* • **1.** a low ledge or platform built against a wall and used as a seat, esp. in Turkish baths • **2.** door step, front step • **3.** brick grave cover • **4.** dunce, blockhead

د ك ك 2

دُكّان [dukka:n] *n:* دِكاكِين [dika:ki:n] *pl:* • **1.** shop, small store
دُكّانچِي [dukka:nči] *n:* دُكّانچِيَّة [dukka:nčiyya] *pl:* • **1.** shopkeeper

د ل

دال [da:l] *n:* • **1.** name of the letter

د ل ع

دَلَّع [dallaʕ] *v:* • **1.** to spoil, to fondle, to attribute
اِندِلَع [ʔindilaʕ] *v:* • **1.** to get started
دَلَع [dalaʕ] *n:* • **1.** coddling, spoiling; coquetry, coyness
دَلعَة [dalʕa] *n:* • **1.** open-necked shirt

دَلاعَة [dala:ʕa] *n:* • **1.** coyness, coddling, spoiling, coquetry
دِلّاعَة [dilla:ʕa] *n:* • **1.** charm
اِندِلاع [ʔindila:ʕ] *n:* • **1.** outbreak
دَلِع [daliʕ] *adj:* • **1.** open neck (for shirt or dress)
مدَلَّع [mdallaʕ] *adj:* • **1.** spoiled, open-necked shirt
مِندِلِع [mindiliʕ] *adj:* • **1.** flaring up

د ل غ

دِلَغ [dilaɣ] *v:* • **1.** to daydream, dream, woolgather – باوَع عَلَى رَسِمها وَدِلَغ [ba:waʕ ʕala rasimha wdilaɣ] He looked at her picture and daydreamed.
دَلَّغ [dallaɣ] *v:* • **1.** to daydream, dream, woolgather
دَلُغ [daluɣ] *n:* • **1.** daydreaming
دالغَة [da:lɣa] *n:* دالغات [da:lɣa:t] *pl:* • **1.** an unexpected thing, something sprung at the last minute, a surprise • **2.** question, problem, matter, affair • **3.** a strange or inconceivable thing, an unbelievable event or exploit, a wild tale • **4.** opium dream, pipe dream, day-dream • **5.** an odd statement or action, an eccentricity • **6.** a strange person, eccentric, nut – يِضرُب دالغَة [yiðrub da:lɣa] he day-dreams, contemplates, meditates.
دالغَجي [dalɣa:či] *adj:* دالغَجِيَّة [dalɣa:čiyya] *pl:* • **1.** woolgatherer, day-dreamer, contemplative person, absentminded person

د ل غ م

دَلغَم [dalɣam] *v:* • **1.** to look unhappy, glum – مِن قِتلَه ما يِصِير يرُوح، دَلغَم [min gitlah ma: yṣi:r yiru:ħ, dalɣam] When I told him he couldn't go, he looked glum.

د ل ف ن

دَولفِين [du:lfi:n] *n:* دَلافِين [dala:fi:n] *pl:* • **1.** dolphin

د ل ق

دَلَق [dalag] *n:* دَلَقات، دَلقات [dalaga:t, dalga:ṭ] *pl:* • **1.** column, vertical beam, support

د ل ك

دِلَك [dilak] *v:* • **1.** to rub – دِلَك صَدرَه وَخَلَّى عَليه دِهِن [dilak ṣadrah wxalla: ʕali:h dihin] He rubbed his chest and put oil on it.
دَلَّك [dallak] *v:* • **1.** to massage – مِن دَلِّكَت ظَهري راح الألَم مِنَّه [min dallikat ḍahri ra:ħ ʔilʔalam minnah] When she massaged my back, the pain left it.
دَلِك [dalik, dalk] *n:* • **1.** massaging, massage
دَلّاك [dalla:k] *n:* • **1.** masseur (in a Turkish bath, massages and washes the body)
مدَلِّكجي [mdallikči] *n:* مدَلِّكجِيَّة [mdallikčiyya] *pl:* • **1.** masseur
مدَلَّك [mdallak] *adj:* • **1.** massaged

د ل ك و

دِيلكُو [di:lku] *n:* دِيلكُوّات [di:lkuwwa:t] *pl:* • **1.** distributor (automotive)

د ل ل 1

دَلّ [dall] *v:* • **1.** to show, indicate, demonstrate – اِختِيارَك لِهالقاط يدُلّ عَلَى حُسُن ذَوقَك [ʔixtiya:rak lhalqa:ṭ ydull ʕala ħusun ðawqak] Your choosing this suit shows your good taste. جَوابَك ما يدُلّ عَلَى أيّ شِي [ǰawa:bak ma: ydull ʕala ʔayy ši] Your answer doesn't show anything. عَمَلَك يدُلّ عَلَى حُسُن نِيّتَك [ʕamalak ydull ʕala ħusun niyytak] Your action demonstrates your good will. • **2.** to prove – حَكيَك هَذا ما يدُلّ عَلَى إنُّو كَذّاب [ħačyak ha:ða ma: ydull ʕala ʔinnu kaðða:b] This remark of yours doesn't prove that he's a liar.
دَلّ، دَلَّى [dalla:] *v:* • **1.** to direct, give directions – تِقدَر تدَلِّينِي عَلَى مَحَطَّة القِطار؟ [tigdar ddalli:ni ʕala maħaṭṭat ʔilqiṭa:r?] Could you direct me to the train station? دَلَّى إبنِي عَلَى كُلّ الدِّرُوب اللّي مُو زينَة [dalla: ʔibni ʕala kull ʔiddiru:b ʔilli mu: zi:na] He steered my son on all the wrong paths. • **2.** to show the way, point out – إذا تاخُذنِي بِالسَّيّارَة، أقدَر أدَلّيك [ʔiða ta:xuðni bissayya:ra, ʔagdar ʔadalli:k] If you take me in the car, I can show you the way. باوِع من هنا حَتَّى أدَلّيك وينَه [ba:wiʕ min hna ħatta ʔadalli:k wi:nah] Look out from here and I'll show you where it is.
اِندَلّ [ʔindall] *v:* • **1.** to find – اِندَلّيت البَيت لَو لا؟ [ʔindalli:t ʔilbayt law la:?] Did you find the house or not? الجّاهِل ضَمّ القَلَم مالَه بمُكان ما نِندَلَّه [ʔiǰǰa:hil ḍamm ʔilqalam ma:lah bmuka:n ma: nindallah] The child hid his pencil in a place where we wouldn't find it. • **2.** to know, know where – تِندَلّ بَيتنا؟ [tindall baytna?] Do you know where our house is? مَحَّد يِندَلّ بَيتهُم وين صايِر [maħħad yindall baythum wi:n ṣa:yir] Nobody knows where they're living now. أندَلّ، بَسّ لهَسَّة ما قَلّي شِيرِيد [ʔandall, bass lhassa ma: galli šiyri:d] I know, but he still hasn't told me what he wants.
اِستَدَلّ [ʔistadall] *v:* • **1.** to gather, infer, conclude, draw conclusions – شتِستِدِلّ مِن هَالكَلام مالَه؟ [štistidill min halkala:m ma:lah?] What do you conclude from what he said?
دَلِيل [dali:l] *n:* أدِلَّة [ʔadilla] *pl:* • **1.** proof, evidence, clue • **2.** guide • **3.** guidebook, handbook – دَلِيل الجّامِعَة [dali:l ʔiǰǰa:miʕa] the college catalog. • **4.** directory, telephone book
مِندَل [mindal] *n:* • **1.** know the way
أدِلّاء [ʔadilla:ʔ] *n:* • **1.** testimony, utterance, statement

د ل ل 2

دَلَّل [dallal] *v:* • **1.** to auction off – مِن وُصَلِت لِلمَزاد، الدَّلّال كان دَيدَلِّل بِالكَمَنجَة [min wuṣalit lilmaza:d, ʔiddalla:l ča:n daydallil bilkamanǰa] When I got to the auction, the auctioneer was auctioning off the violin. • **2.** to peddle, hawk, sell – جيب دَلّال، خَلّي يدَلِّل بِالقَبُّوط مالَك بالسُّوق [ǰi:b dalla:l, xalli: ydallil bilqappu:ṭ ma:lak bissu:g] Get a peddler, let him sell your overcoat. يَالله، إطلَع، دَلِّل بِاللِّبَن، عاد [yallah, ʔiṭlaʕ, dallil billiban, ʕa:d] Go on, get out and peddle the yoghurt, why don't you! دَيدَلِّل بِبَناتَه وَما حَدّ دَيزَوَّجهُم [daydallil bibana:tah wma: ħadd dayizzawwaǰhum] He's trying to get rid of his daughters and no one wants to marry them. • **3.** to pamper, spoil – دَتدَلِّل إبنَك هوايَة [daddallil ʔibnak hwa:ya] You're pampering your son too much.

دَلّال [dalla:l] *n:* • **1.** auctioneer • **2.** hawker, peddler • **3.** agent, broker – دَلّال سَيّارات [dalla:l sayya:ra:t] car dealer.

دلالَة [dla:la] *n:* دلالات [dla:la:t] *pl:* • **1.** commission taken by a auctioneer

دَلالَة [dala:la] *n:* • **1.** auctioning

دَلالِيَّة [dala:liyya] *n:* • **1.** real estate agency

د ل ل 3

تدَلَّل [ddallal] *v:* • **1.** to make demands, ask for favors, take advantage • **2.** to be coy, to play hard to get – كَسِّحها لِهاي. بَسّ يِعجِبها تِدَّلَّل عَلَى كُلّ النّاس [kassiħha lha:y. bass yiʕǰibha tiddallal ʕala kull ʔinna:s] Forget about her. She just likes to be playing hard to get with everyone. هاي قابلَة تِتزَوَّجَه لَكِن دَتِتدَلَّل [ha:y qa:bla tidzawwaǰah la:kin datiddallal] She's willing to marry him but she's acting coy. لا تِتدَلَّل؛ دِفعَوا لَك خُوش فلُوس [la: tiddallal; difʕu:lak xu:š flu:s] Don't play hard to get; they offered you a good salary. راح أدَلَّل عَلَيهُم لِأَنّ يِحتاجُونِي [ra:ħ ʔadallal ʕali:hum liʔann yiħta:ǰu:ni] I'm going to hold them up for more because they need me. المَرَة تِتدَلَّل عَلَى رَجِلها لِأَنّ يحِبّها [ʔilmara tiddallal ʕala raǰilha liʔann yħibbha] The woman makes demands of her husband because he loves her. دَيِتدَلَّل عَلَيّا عَبالَك آني أبُوه [dayiddallal ʕalayya ʕaba:lak ʔa:ni ʔabu:h] He's asking favors of me as if I were his father.

دَلال [dala:l] *n:* • **1.** coyness, coquettishness • **2.** spoiling, coddling, pampering – وِلِد نِعمَة وَدَلال [wilid niʕma wdala:l] بَزر دَلال [bazir dala:l] / the pampered rich, somebody born with a silver spoon in his/her mouths.

تَدليل [tadli:l] *n:* • **1.** coyness

مدَلَّل [mdallal] *adj:* • **1.** spoiled (as of children, not of food)

د ل ل 4

دَلَّة [dalla] *n:* دَلّات، دلال [dla:l, dalla:t] *pl:* • **1.** coffee pot

د ل ه م

دَلهَم [dalham] *v:* • **1.** to become dark, cloudy – الدِّنيا دَلهِمَت ويمكِن تُمطُر [ʔiddinya dalhimat wyimkin tumṭur] The sky has turned dark and it might rain. عَلَوَيش مدَلهِم؟ أحَّد أذّاك؟ [ʕalawi:š mdalhim? ʔaħħad ʔaðða:k?] Why are you so gloomy? Did somebody treat you bad?

مدَلهِم [mdalhim] *adj:* • **1.** gloomy

د ل و

دَلو [dalw] *n:* دلاوَة [dla:wa] *pl:* • **1.** bucket, pail

دِلو [dilw] *adj:* دلاوَة [dla:wa] *pl:* • **1.** simpleton, dope, idiot.

د ل ي

دالِيَة [da:lya] *n:* • **1.** dahlia(s) (bot.)

د م

دامَة [da:ma] *n:* • **1.** checkers • **2.** a game played by moving counters through a series of depressions around a board

د م ج

دِمَج [dimaǰ] *v:* • **1.** to merge, combine, join – دِمجَوا شَرِكَتهُم ويّا شَرِكَة ثانيَة [dimǰaw šarikathum wiyya šarika θa:nya] They merged their company with another one. القائِدَين دِمجَوا قُوّاتهُم وهِجمَوا سُوَة [ʔilqa:ʔidayn dimǰaw quwwa:thum whiǰmaw suwa] The two commanders merged their forces and attacked together. المُعَلِّم دِمَج الصَّفَّين وَدَرَّسهُم [ʔilmuʕallim dimaǰ ʔiṣṣaffayn wdarrashum] The teacher combined the two classes and taught them that way.

دَمِج [damiǰ] *n:* • **1.** merging, combining

د م د م

دَمدَم [damdam] *v:* • **1.** to grumble

تدِمدِم [tdimdim] *n:* • **1.** grumble

د م ر 1

دُمَر [dumar] *v:* • **1.** to ruin, damage, wreck – المُطَر دُمَرها لحَديقتِي [ʔilmuṭar dumarha lħadi:qti] The rain ruined my garden. الأُوتَجِي دَمَر قاطِي [ʔilʔu:tači damar qa:ṭi] The presser made a mess of my suit. إبنِي مُو دمَرتنِي؛ ما يصِير تُصرُف هَالقَدّ فلُوس [ʔibni mu: dmaritni; ma: yṣi:r tuṣruf halgadd flu:s] You've ruined me, son; you can't go around spending so much money. بُسَطَه خُوش بَسطَة؛ دُمَرَه [busaṭah xu:š basṭa; dumarah] He gave him a good beating; messed him up good. شَغّلنا لِلمِغرب. دُمَرنِي [šaɣɣalna lilmiɣrib. dumarni] He worked us till evening. Knocked me out.

دَمَّر [dammar] *v:* • **1.** to destroy, ruin, wreck, demolish – القَنابُل دَمُّرَت البَلدَة [ʔilqana:bul dammurat ʔilbalda] The bombs destroyed the city. العَدُو دَمَّر جَيشنا [ʔilʕadu dammar ǰayšna] The enemy wiped out our army. دَمَّرها لِلسَّيّارَة لِأَنّ عَلَّم كُلّ أصدِقائَه السِّياقَة بِيها [dammarha lissayya:ra liʔann ʕallam kull ʔaṣdiqa:ʔah

ʔissiya:qa bi:ha] He ruined the car by teaching all of his friends to drive in it. الخَلّ يدَمُّر المَرَق [ʔilxall ydammur ʔilmarag] Vinegar ruins stew. كُلّما ألعَب شِطرَنج ويّاه يدَمُّرنِي [kullma: ʔalʕab šiṭranǰ wiyya:h ydammurni] Everytime I play chess with him he slaughters me. الأستاذ دَمَّرنا بالإمتِحان [ʔilʔusta:ð dammarna bilʔimtiħa:n] The professor ruined us with the test.
تدَمَّر [ddammar] *v:* • **1.** to be destroyed, ruined, demolished – هُوَّ ما صار بيه شِي لَكِن سَيّارتَه تدَمّرَت [huwwa ma: ṣa:r bi:h ši la:kin sayya:rtah ddammrat] Nothing happened to him, but his car was wrecked. المِسكِين تدَمَّر؛ طِردوه مِن الوَظِيفَة وَما حَدّ دَيشَغّلَه [ʔilmiski:n ddammar; ṭirdawh min ʔilwaði:fa wma: ħadd dayšaɣɣlah] The poor guy is ruined; they fired him from his job and no one will hire him. تدَمَّرِت هوايَة بهالسَّفرَة [ddammarit hwa:ya bhassafra] I had a lot of troubles on that trip.
اِندُمَر [ʔindumar] *v:* • **1.** to be destroyed, ruined, demolished – السَّيّارَة اِندُمرَت بهالدَّعمَة [ʔissayya:ra ʔindumrat bhaddaʕma] The car was wrecked in this accident. حَدِيقتَه اِندُمرَت مِن البزازِين [ħadi:qtah ʔindumrat min ʔilbza:zi:n] His garden was ruined by the cats. القاط مالَك اِندُمَر؛ صارلَك شَهَر لابسَه [ʔilqa:ṭ ma:lak ʔindumar; ṣa:rlak šahar la:bsah] Your suit is a mess; you've been wearing it a month.
دَمُر [damur] *n:* • **1.** ruin, damage
دَمار [dama:r] *n:* • **1.** ruin, destruction
مُدَمَّر [mudammar] *adj:* • **1.** destroyed
مَدمُور [madmu:r] *adj:* • **1.** in bad shape, messed up, ruined
مُدَمِّرَة [mudammira] *n:* مُدَمِّرات [mudammira:t] *pl:* • **1.** destroyer

د م ر 2

دَمار [dama:r] *n:* دَمارات [dama:ra:t] *pl:* • **1.** vein – لِزَمَه دَمار وَما قِدَر يِسبَح بَعَد [lizamah dama:r wma gidar yisbaħ baʕad] He got a cramp and couldn't swim any farther. آنِي أعرُف كُلّ دَماراتَه [ʔa:ni ʔaʕruf kull dama:ra:tah] I can read him like a book. I know what makes him tick.

د م س

دامِس [da:mis] *adj:* • **1.** pitch

د م ش ق

دِمَشق [dimašq] *n:* • **1.** Damascus
دِمِشقِي [dimišqi] *adj:* • **1.** Damascene

د م ع

دِمَع [dimaʕ] *v:* • **1.** to tear, shed tears, water (of the eyes) – لَمّا يِبكِي ما تِدمَع عَينَه أبَداً [lamma yibči ma: tidmaʕ ʕaynah ʔabadan] When he cries his eyes never shed tears. مِن تقَشِّر بُصَل عيُونها تِدمَع [min tgaššir buṣal ʕyu:nha tidmaʕ] When she peels onions her eyes water.
دَمَّع [dammaʕ] *v:* • **1.** intens. of to tear, cry, shed tears – مِن يباوِع بِالشَّمِس عيُونَه تقُوم تدَمِّع [min yba:wiʕ biššamis ʕyu:nah tgu:m ddammiʕ] When he looks at the sun his eyes begin to water.
دَمِع [damiʕ] *n:* • **1.** (coll.) tear(s) • **2.** pl. دمُوع tears
دَمعَة [damʕa] *n:* دَمعات [damʕa:t] *pl:* • **1.** tear

د م غ

دُمَغ [dumaɣ] *v:* • **1.** to hit someone on the head, to crown, to brain – دُمَغَه حيل وَوَقَّعَه عَالقاع [dumaɣah ħi:l wwaggaʕah ʕalga:ʕ] He brained him and knocked him down.
دَمَّغ [dammaɣ] *v:* • **1.** intens. of دُمَغ to hit someone on the head, to crown, to brain
دَمُغ [damuɣ] *n:* • **1.** hitting someone on the head
دَمغَة [damɣa] *n:* دَمغات [damɣa:t] *pl:* • **1.** blow on the top of the head (with the flat of the hand) • **2.** a light blow with the knuckles, generally to the ribs
دَماغ [dama:ɣ] *n:* أدمِغَة [ʔadmiɣa] *pl:* • **1.** brain • **2.** mind, brains, intelligence
دامُغ [da:muɣ] *n:* • **1.** tormentor – الكَلِب يحِبّ دامغَه [ʔiččalib yħibb da:mɣah] A dog loves its tormentor (said of anyone who submits to abuse).
مَدمَغَة [madmaɣa] *adj:* • **1.** (invar.) person who is easily abused or pushed around
دَماغسِز [dama:ɣsizz] *adj:* دَماغسِزِّيَّة [dama:ɣsizziyya] *pl:* • **1.** brainless

د م ق ر ط

دِمُقراطِيَّة، دِيمُقراطِيَّة [dimuqra:ṭiyya] *n:* • **1.** democracy
دِمُقراطِي، دِيمُقراطِي [dimuqra:ṭi] *adj:* • **1.** democratic • **2.** democrat

د م م

دَمّام [damma:m] *n:* دَمّامات [damma:ma:t] *pl:* • **1.** a flat, circular drum used to wake people in Ramadan, and in religious processions

د م ن

دامَن [da:man] *v:* • **1.** to become accustomed, get used – البَزُّونَة دامنَت عَالبَيت، وَتِجِي وَحَّدها [ʔilbazzu:na da:mnat ʕalbayt, wtiǰi waħħadha] The cat has gotten used to the house, and comes by itself. • **2.** to make a habit, to do regularly – إذا تدامِن عَلَى هَالدُّوا، صِحّتَك تِتحَسَّن [ʔiða dda:min ʕala hadduwa, ṣiħħtak titħassan] If you take this medicine regularly, your health will improve. دِمَن عالكِذِب وَما يِقدَر يبَطِّل بَعَد [diman ʕalčiðib wma yigdar ybaṭṭil baʕad] He made a habit of lying and he can't stop now. • **3.** to get a habit, become addicted – دِمَن عَلَى شُرُب السِّجايِر مِن كان صغَيِّر [diman ʕala šurub

ʔijjiga:yir min ča:n şɣayyir] He became addicted to smoking cigarettes when he was small.
أدمَن [ʔadman] *v:* • **1.** to become addicted – أدمَن عَلَى الحَشِيش [ʔadman ʕala ʔilhaši:š] He became addicted to hasheesh. إذا تِدمِن عَلَى شُرُب العَرَق، تِتدَهوَر صِحّتَك [ʔiða tidmin ʕala šurub ʔilʕarag, tiddahwar şiħħtak] If you addict yourself to drinking arrack, your health will be ruined.
دِمِن [dimin] *n:* • **1.** manure
إدمان [ʔidma:n] *n:* • **1.** addiction
مُدمِن [mudmin] *adj:* • **1.** addict, addicted • **2.** habitual drunkard • **3.** person who has the habit of smoking

د م ي

دَمَّى [damma:] *v:* • **1.** to bloody, cover with blood – دَمّاه بِالبَسُط [damma:h bilbasuṭ] he bloodied him with the beating. ظَلّ يضُربَه إلَى أن دَمّاه [ðall yðurbah ʔila ʔan damma:h] He kept hitting him until he'd covered him with blood.
تدَمَّى [ddamma:] *v:* • **1.** to be bloodied, be covered with blood – ظَلّوا يِتباسطُون حَتَّى تدَمّوا ثنَينهُم [ðallaw yitba:sṭu:n ħatta ddammaw θnaynhum] They continued to fight until they were covered with blood.
دَمّ [damm] *n:* دِماء [dima:ʔ] *pl:* • **1.** blood – أحمَر دَمّ [ʔaħmar damm] blood red. وُجَّه أحمَر دَمّ [wuččah ʔaħmar damm] His face is blood red. دَمَّه بِراحَة إيدَه [dammah bra:ħat ʔi:dah] He doesn't fear danger (lit., his blood is on the palm of his hand). • **2.** pl. – دمُوم, دَمّات a killing, a death, a life
دَمَوِي [damawi] *adj:* • **1.** blood – أوعِيَة دَمَوِيَّة [ʔawʕiya damawiyya] blood vessels. • **2.** bloody, sanguinary – حَرُب دَمَوِيَّة [ħarub damawiyya] a bloody war. • **3.** blood-red, bright red – نَفنُوف دَمَوِي [nafnu:f damawi] a bright red dress.
مدَمَّى [mdamma] *adj:* • **1.** bloody

د م ي ر

دَمِيرِي [dami:ri] *n:* • **1.** a kind of brocaded cloth

د ن ء

دَناءَة [dana:ʔa] *n:* • **1.** lowness, vileness, meanness
دَنِيء [dani:ʔ] *adj:* أدنِياء [ʔadniya:ʔ] *pl:* • **1.** lowness, vileness, meanness, depravity – عَمَل دَنِيء [ʕamal dani:ʔ] a foul deed, a dirty trick.

د ن ب س

دَنبَس [danbas, dambas] *v:* • **1.** to pin – دَمبِس البطانَة كُلّها [dambis ʔilbṭa:na kullha] Pin the whole lining in. • **2.** to clip – دَمبِس هَالوَرَقتَين بِالكِلبِس [dambis halwaraqti:n biliklips] Clip these two papers together with the paper clip.
دَنبُوس [danbu:s, dambu:s] *n:* دَنابِيس [dana:bi:s] *pl:* • **1.** pin, straight pin • **2.** pin, brooch • **3.** mace (weapon)

د ن ب ك

دُنبُك [dunbug, dumbug] *n:* دَنابُك [dana:bug] *pl:* • **1.** a tapering clay or brass drum with skin head
دُنبَكجِي [dunbakči, dumbakči] *n:* دُنبَكجِيَّة [dunbakčiyya, dumbakčiyya] *pl:* • **1.** a man who drums at Iraqi parties

د ن ب ل

دِنبِلَة [dinbila, dimbila] *n:* دَنابِل [dana:bil] *pl:* • **1.** boil, furuncle, infection of the hair follicle

د ن ت ل

دانتِيل [da:nti:l] *n:* دانتَيلات [da:nti:la:t] *pl:* • **1.** lace

د ن د ل

دَندَل [dandal] *v:* • **1.** to lower, let down, dangle – دَندِل الحَبِل بالبِير حَتَّى نشُوف شغُمقَه [dandil ʔilħabil bilbi:r ħatta nšu:f šɣumjah] Lower the rope into the well so we can see how deep it is. راح أنزِل جَوَّة وَإنتَ دَندِلِلي المِيز [ra:ħ ʔanzil jawwa wʔinta dandilli ʔilmi:z] I'll get down below and you let the table down to me. حاشيَة شَرشَف الدُوشَك مدَندِلَة وَقَرِيب تدُقّ بِالقاع [ħa:šyat čarčaf ʔiddu:šag mdandila wgari:b ddugg bilga:ʕ] The edge of the bed sheet is hanging down and almost touching the floor.
تدَندَل [ddandal] *v:* • **1.** to hang down, hang, dangle – البَهلَوان دَيِدَّندَل مِن الحَبِل [ʔalpahlawa:n dayiddandal min ʔilħabil] The acrobat is hanging on the rope. خَلِّي الجَّرَس يِدَّندَل من هنا [xalli: ʔijjaras yiddandal min hna] Hang the bell from here.
دَندُولَة [dandu:la] *n:* دَندُولات [dandu:la:t] *pl:* • **1.** something dangling, pendant

د ن ر

دِينار [dina:r] *n:* • **1.** diamonds (suit in cards). • **2.** currency

د ن س

دَنَّس [dannas] *v:* • **1.** to dirty, soil, sully (fig.) – دَنَّس سُمعَة العائِلَة مِن تزَوَّجها لِهاي [dannas sumʕat ʔilʕa:ʔila min dzawwajha lha:y] He dirtied the family's reputation when he married that woman. لا تِمشِي وِيّاه؛ تَرَة يدَنِّسَك بِأخلاقَه [la: timši wiyya:h; tara ydannisak bʔaxla:qah] Don't hang around with him; he'll contaminate you with his behavior.
مدَنَّس [mdannas] *adj:* • **1.** profane, defiled, sacrilegious

د ن ش

دانَش [da:naš] *v:* • **1.** to consult, seek advice from – رُوح دانِش أبُوك قَبُل ما تِشتِري السَّيّارَة [ru:ħ da:niš ʔabu:k gabul ma: tištiri ʔissayya:ra] Go consult your father before you buy the car.
تدانَش [dda:naš] *v:* • **1.** to confer, talk over something – تدانَش وِيّا أبُوك قَبُل ما تقَرِّر [dda:naš wiyya ʔabu:k gabul

maː tqarrir] Talk it over with your father before you decide.

د ن ق

دَنَّق [dannag, dannaǰ] *v:* • **1.** to bend, bow, lean – دَنَّق عَالطِّفِل وَشالَه [dannag ʕaṭṭifil wšaːlah] He bent over the baby and picked it up. دَنَّق راسَه حَتَّى أَشُوف شبيها عِلباتَه [dannag raːsah ħatta ʔašuːf šbiːha ʕilbaːtah] He bowed his head so I could see what was on the back of his neck. لا تدَنِّق هوايَة مِن الشِّبّاك، تَرَة تُوقَع [laː ddannig hwaːya min ʔiššibbaːč, tara tuːgaʕ] Don't lean too far out the window or you'll fall.

د ن ك

دِنكَة [dinga] *n:* دِنكات، دِنَك [dingaːt, dinag] *pl:* • **1.** concrete pole/column • **2.** (as adj:) stupid, thick-headed, dim

د ن ن

دنان [dnaːn] *n:* • **1.** (coll.) seeds of a variety of grass or weeds sometimes found in rice

دنانَة [dnaːna] *n:* دنانات [dnaːnaːt] *pl:* • **1.** coll. seeds of a variety of grass or weeds sometimes found in rice

د ن ي

دِنَى [dinaː] *v:* • **1.** to stoop to, lower oneself for – تِدني نَفسَه عالفِلِس [tidni nafsah ʕalfilis] He'd do anything for a buck. نَفسَه دِنَت عالخَدّامَة، لَكِن خاف مِن مَرتَه [nafsah dinat ʕalxaddaːma, laːkin xaːf min martah] He felt lust for the maid, but he was afraid of his wife.

دَنَّى [dannaː] *v:* • **1.** to bring close, move near – دَنِّي الكِتاب؛ ما دَأَقدَر أَشُوف من هنا [danni ʔilkitaːb; maː daʔagdar ʔašuːf min hna] Move the book closer; I can't see from here. دَنِّي الماعُون يَمِّي حَتَّى آكُل [danni ʔilmaːʕuːn yammi ħatta ʔaːkul] Move the dish near me so I can eat.

تدَنَّى [ddannaː] *v:* • **1.** to move close, go near – تدَنَّى! لِيش واقُف بِعِيد؟ [ddannaː! liːš waːguf biʕiːd?] Move closer. Why are you standing so far off? لا تِتدَنَّى يَمّ الكَلِب، تَرَة يعَضَّك [laː tiddannaː yamm ʔiččalib, tara yʕaðǒak] Don't go near the dog or he'll bite you. • **2.** to move over, shift one's position – تدَنَّى شوَيَّة وَسَوِّيلي مُكان [ddannaː šwayya wsawwiːli mukaːn] Move over a little and make a place for me.

دِنيا [dinya] *n:* • **1.** world – جا لِلدِّنيا أَوَّل رَمَضان [ǰaː liddinya ʔawwal ramaðaːn] He was born the first of Ramadan. • **2.** this world, this life (as opposed to • **3.** life, existence – هاي الدِّنيا [haːy ʔiddinya] and هاي دِنيا [haːy dinya] That's life. الدِّنيا جَتِّي وِيّاه فَدّ جَيَّة. صار صاحِب أَراضِي وَمَزارِع [ʔiddinya ǰatti wiyyaːh fadd ǰayya. ṣaːr ṣaːħib ʔaraːði wmazaːriʕ] Things are going his way. He's become the owner of land and farms. قِلَبها لِلدِّنيا مِن أَخِذت البايسِكِل مِنَّه [gilabha liddinya min ʔaxiðt ʔilpaːysikil minnah] He threw a fit when I took the bicycle from him. • **4.** weather – الدِّنيا طَيِّبَة اليُوم [ʔiddinya ṭayyba ʔilyuːm] The weather is nice today. الدِّنيا دَتُمطُر [ʔiddinya datumṭur] It is raining. • **5.** people, humanity – السُّوق مَترُوس دِنيا [ʔissuːg matruːs dinya] The market is full of people.

دِنِي [dini] *adj:* • **1.** greedy, self indulgent – نَفسَه دِنِيَّة [nafsah diniyya] greedy, selfindulgent, lacking self control. نَفسَه دِنِيَّة. كُلّ ما يشُوفَه، يرِيد [nafsah diniyya. kull maː yšuːfah, yriːd] He's greedy. He wants everything he sees.

دُنياوِي [dunyaːwi] *adj:* • **1.** practical, material, of the world

أَدنَى [ʔadna] *comparative adjective:* • **1.** more or most vile – أَدنَى مِن الآخَر [ʔadnaː min ʔilʔaːxar] more vile than the other. • **2.** more or most slight, small, etc – الحَدّ الأَدنَى [ʔilħadd ʔilʔadna] the lower limit. السِّعِر الأَدنَى [ʔissiʕir ʔilʔadna] the lowest price. إِذا تِحكِي أَدنَى كِلمَة أَزعَل [ʔiða tiħči ʔadnaː čilma ʔazʕal] If you say a single word, I'll get mad. يِزعَل عَلَى أَدنَى شِي [yizʕal ʕala ʔadnaː ši] He gets mad over the least thing. الشَّرق الأَدنَى [ʔiššarq ʔilʔadna] The Near East.

د ه د ر

دَهدَر [dahdar] *v:* • **1.** to send – دَهدِرَه لعَلِي عَليه، تَرَة صَدِيقَه [dahdirah lʕali ʕaliːh, tara ṣadiːqah] Send Ali to him, since he's his friend. • **2.** to let out (a remark) – دَهدِر البِيب مِن يَمَّك [dahdir ʔilpiːb min yammak] Roll the barrel away from you. دَهدِر القَلَم عالمَيز، وَوُقَع [dahdir ʔilqalam ʕalmayz, wwugaʕ] He started the pencil rolling on the table, and it fell off. دَهدَرها لِلحكايَة قِدّام النّاس [dahdarha lilħčaːya giddaːm ʔinnaːs] He let the remark slip in front of the people.

تدَهدَر [ddahdar] *v:* • **1.** to roll – وَخِّر! الصَّخرَة دتِتدَهدر [waxxir! ʔiṣṣaxra datiddahdar] Get out of the way! The rock is rolling. لَمّا تدَهدَر اللُّورِي بِلا ستُوب، قُمَز السّايِق مِنَه [lamma ddahdar ʔilluːri bila stuːb, gumaz ʔissaːyiq minah] When the truck rolled forward without any brakes, the driver jumped out. تدَهدَر مِن الجِبَل بسُرعَة [ddahdar min ʔiǰǰibal bsurʕa] He coasted down the mountain at high speed. أَكُو سَدّ عَالجِّبَل طَقّ وَتدَهدَر المَيّ كُلَّه [ʔaku sadd ʕaǰǰibal ṭagg widdahdar ʔilmayy kullah] There's a dam on the mountain which broke and all the water ran down.

د ه د و

دَهدَى [dahdaː] *v:* • **1.** var. of roll slowly

دِهدِيوَة [dihdiːwa] *n:* دِهدِيوات [dihdiːwaːt] *pl:* • **1.** downgrade, slope, incline

دِهدوانَة [dihidwaːna] *n:* دِهدِوانات [dihidwaːnaːt] *pl:* • **1.** downgrade, slope, incline

د ه ر

داهَر [da:har] *v:* • **1.** to tease – لا تزعَل؛ دَيداهرَك [la: tizʕal; dayda:hrak] Don't get mad; he's teasing you. لا تداهرني؛ تُعرُف وين كتابي لَو لا؟ [la: dda:hirni; tuʕruf wi:n kta:bi law la:?] Don't stall me; do you know where my book is or don't you?

تَداهَر [tda:har] *v:* • **1.** to tease one another – هذُولَة ما دَيتعاركُون؛ دَيتداهرُون بَسّ [hðu:la ma: dayitʕa:rku:n; dayidda:hru:n bass] They're not fighting; they're just stirring each other up. هذا دَيتداهَر ويّاك، الكِتاب عِندَه [ha:ða: dayidda:har wiyya:k, ʔilkita:b ʕindah] He is teasing you; he has the book. • **2.** to drag things out, to hold up matters – رُبع دينار. ما أتداهَر ويّاك [rubuʕ dina:r. ma: ʔadda:har wiyya:k] A quarter dinar. I won't haggle with you. لا تِدّاهَر. رُوح عاد. سَوّي اللّي قِلتلَك إيّاه [la: tidda:har. ru:ħ ʕa:d. sawwi: ʔilli giltlak ʔiyya:h] Don't keep arguing. Go on now. Do what I told you to. إنتَ شقَدّ تِتداهَر! فُضّني [ʔinta šgadd tidda:har! fuððni] You sure do prolong things! Let me be on my way.

دَهَر [dahar] *n:* دُهُور [duhu:r] *pl:* • **1.** long time, age • **2.** fate, destiny

دُهُر [duhur] *n:* • **1.** teasing • **2.** delaying, arguing, haggling

مداهَرَة [mda:hara] *n:* • **1.** teasing

دُهري [duhri] *adj:* • **1.** slowpoke

د ه ر ب

تدَهرب [ddahrab] *v:* • **1.** to roll oneself, roll – الجُّهال يعجِبهُم يتدَهربُون مِن راس التَّل [ʔijjaha:l yiʕjibhum yiddahrbu:n min ra:s ʔittall] The kids like to roll down from the top of the hill.

د ه س / د ع س

دِهَس - دِعَس [dihas - diʕas] *v:* • **1.** to run over, knock down

دَهِس, دَعِس [dahis, daʕis] n: running over, being knocked down

د ه ش

دِهَش [dihaš] *v:* • **1.** to astonish, surprise, amaze, impress – عَمَلَه دِهَشني [ʕamalah dihašni] His action astonished me. شِكلَه دِهَشني. عَبالي وَزير [šiklah dihašni. ʕaba:li wazi:r] His appearance impressed me. I thought he was a cabinet member.

اِندِهَش [ʔindihaš] *v:* • **1.** to be astonished, amazed, surprised – اِندِهَشت مِن جوابَه الخَشِن [ʔindihašit min ǰawa:bah ʔilxašin] I was taken aback by his rude answer. اِندِهَشت مِن جَمالها [ʔindihašit min ǰama:lha] I was overwhelmed by her beauty. اِندِهَشت مِن هَالمَنظَر الفَظيع [ʔindihašit min halmanðar ʔilfaði:ʕ] I was stunned by the gruesome sight.

دَهِش [dahiš] *n:* • **1.** surprise, amazement

دَهشَة [dahša] *n:* • **1.** astonishment, amazement, wonder, surprise • **2.** a magnificent, wondrous thing – إنتَ طالِع دَهشَة بِهَالقاط الجِّدِيد [ʔinta ṭa:liʕ dahša bhalqa:ṭ ʔiǰǰidi:d] You look great in that new suit.

اِندِهاش [ʔindiha:š] *n:* • **1.** surprise, amazement

مُدهِش [mudhiš] *adj:* • **1.** amazing, astonishing, surprising

مَدهُوش [madhu:š] *adj:* • **1.** amazed, astonished – شبيك مَدهُوش؟ ما شايف بنَيَّة؟ [šbi:k madhu:š? ma: ša:yif bnayya?] Why are you astonished? Haven't you ever seen a girl?

مِندِهِش [mindihiš] *adj:* • **1.** amazed, astonished

أدهَش [ʔadhaš] *comparative adjective:* • **1.** more or most surprising, astonishing, amazing

د ه ل

دِهلَة [dihla] *n:* • **1.** dense, stupid • **2.** dunce • **3.** roiled, turbid – مَيّ دِهلَة [mayy dihla] muddy water.

د ه ل ز

دِهليز [dihli:z] *n:* دَهاليز [daha:li:z] *pl:* • **1.** a narrow passage or corridor • **2.** a tunnel between buildings

د ه م

دِهَم [diham] *v:* • **1.** to break in, to raid

دَهِم [dahim] *n:* • **1.** breaking in, raiding, raid

مُداهَمَة [muda:hama] *n:* • **1.** breaking in, raid

د ه ن

دِهَن [dihan] *v:* • **1.** to oil, grease – دِهَن إيدَه حَتّى تخُشّ بسُهُولَة بالبَستُوكَة [dihan ʔi:dah ħatta txušš bsuhu:la bilbastu:ga] He greased his hand so it would go into the jar. المَكينَة بيها صَوت؛ لازم تِدهَنها [ʔilmaki:na bi:ha ṣawt; la:zim tidhanha] The machine's noisy; better oil it. دِهَن السَّير حَتّى ينطُوه إجازَة [dihan ʔissayr ħatta yinṭu:h ʔiǰa:za] He greased some palms so they'd give him a license. لازم دِهنَوا فَدّ كَم إيد يَالله قِدرَوا يحَصّلُون بطاقات [la:zim dihnaw fadd čam ʔi:d yallah gidraw yħaṣṣlu:n biṭa:qa:t] They must have greased some palms to be able to get tickets. • **2.** to rub, massage – دِهَن رِجلَه بزَيت الزَّيتُون [dihan riǰlah bzayt ʔizzaytu:n] He massaged his leg with olive oil. دِهنَت ظَهرَه بالكُحُول [dihnat ðahrah bilkuħu:l] She rubbed his back with alcohol. • **3.** to salve, apply, smear on, paint on (medicine, ointment) – دِهَنِت خَشمَك بالدُّوا؟ [dihanit xašmak bidduwa?] Did you apply the ointment to your nose? الطَّبيب دِهَن بَلعُومي بدُوَا مُرّ [ʔiṭṭabi:b dihan balʕu:mi bduwa murr] The doctor painted my throat with a bitter medicine. • **4.** to bribe, grease palms

دَهَّن [dahhan] *v:* • **1.** to oil – بَعَد ما تِغسِل الطّاوَة، دَهّنها حَتّى ما تزَنجِر [baʕad ma: tiɣsil ʔiṭṭa:wa, dahhinha ħatta ma: dzanǰir] After you wash the frying pan, oil it so it won't rust. • **2.** to cover with grease, get greasy – ما إشتِغَل بالمَكينَة إلّا ما دَهَّن إيدَه [ma: ʔištiɣal bilmaki:na ʔilla ma: dahhan ʔi:dah] He's never worked on an engine without getting his hands greasy.

دِهِن [dihin] *n:* • **1.** oil (lubricating, edible, or for the skin) • **2.** fat, butterfat – دِهِن حُرّ [dihin ħurr] clarified butter, ghee. • **3.** ointment – عَلِي وأحمَد صايرِين دِهِن وَدِبِس [ʕali wʔaħmad ṣa:yri:n dihin wdibis] Ali and Ahmed have become very good friends. هَالسَّيّارَة تِمشِي مِثل الدِّهِن [hassayya:ra timši miθl ʔiddihin] This car runs like a top. إيدَه بِالدِّهِن [ʔi:dah biddihin] He's fatcatting it. He's got it made. He's really living.

دَهِن [dahin] *n:* • **1.** oiling, greasing • **2.** painting

دَهِين [dahi:n] *n:* • **1.** a type of very rich, greasy pastry

دِهنِي [dihni] *adj:* • **1.** fatty – مادَّة دِهنِيَّة [ma:dda dihniyya] a fatty substance.

دِهِين [dihi:n] *adj:* • **1.** oily, greasy – التِّمَّن دِهِين [ʔittimman dihi:n] The rice is too oily. أكِل دِهِين [ʔakil dihi:n] greasy food. • **2.** rich (in butterfat) – حَلِيب دِهِين [ħali:b dihi:n] rich milk. ياخُذ راتِب دِهِين [ya:xuð ra:tib dihi:n] He gets a fat salary.

مدَهَّن [mdahhan] *adj:* • **1.** greasy

د ه و ر

دَهوَر [dahwar] *v:* • **1.** to damage, ruin, destroy – العَرَق دَهوَر صِحّتَه [ʔilʕarag dahwar ṣiħħtah] Arrack destroyed his health.

تدَهوَر [tdahwar] *v:* • **1.** to deteriorate – الوَضِع تدَهوَر بهَالبَلَد [ʔilwaðiʕ ddahwar bhalbalad] The situation has deteriorated in this country. البَيت تدَهوَر مِن المُطَر [ʔilbayt ddahwar min ʔilmuṭar] The house deteriorated from the rain.

تَدَهوِر [tadahwir] *n:* • **1.** deterioration

مِتدَهوِر [mitdahwir] *adj:* مِتدَهوُرِين [mitdahwuri:n] *pl:* • **1.** deteriorating

د ه ي [1]

دَهّى [dahha:] *v:* • **1.** to close (a door) – لا تِنسَى تدَهّي الباب مِن تِطلَع [la: tinsa: ddahhi ʔilba:b min tiṭlaʕ] Don't forget to close the door when you go out.

د ه ي [2]

داهِيَة [da:hiya] *n:* دَواهِي [dawa:hi] *pl:* • **1.** disaster, catastrophe, calamity – وُقَع بداهِيَة [wugaʕ bda:hiya] A disaster befell him.

د ه ي [3]

داهِيَة [da:hiya] *n:* دُهاة [duha:t] *pl:* • **1.** genius, clever, resourceful person

د و ء

داء [da:ʔ] *n:* • **1.** disease

د و ب

دُوبَة [du:ba] *n:* • **1.** barge • **2.** flat-car or gondola (R.R.) • **3.** sidecar (of a motorcycle)

دُوب [du:b] *adv:* • **1.** barely, hardly, scarcely – دُوب وُصَلنا عالوَقِت [du:b wuṣalna ʕalwakit] We just barely got there in time. دُوبها الفلُوس تكَفِّي [du:bha ʔilflu:s tkaffi] The money is barely sufficient. يا دُوب لَحّقنا مِن طِلَع القِطار [ya: du:b laħħagna min ṭilaʕ ʔilqiṭa:r] We had only just arrived when the train left.

د و ب ر

دُوبارَة [du:ba:ra] *n:* • **1.** two deuces (in rolling dice)

د و ح س

دَوحَس [dawħas] *v:* • **1.** to become seriously infected – اِنجِرَح إصبِعَه وَدَوحَس [ʔinjirah ʔiṣibʕah wdawħas] His finger was injured and became badly infected.

دَوحاس [dawħa:s] *n:* • **1.** infection

د و خ

داخ [da:x] *v:* • **1.** to get dizzy, feel dizzy – آنِي أدُوخ إذا أفتَرّ كَم مَرَّة [ʔa:ni ʔadu:x ʔiða ʔaftarr čam marra] I get dizzy if I spin around a few times. راسِي يدُوخ مِن أوَّل بِيك [ra:si ydu:x min ʔawwal pi:k] My head starts spinning on the first drink. • **2.** to get a headache, be bothered – دِخِت مِن عياط الجِّهال [dixit min ʕya:ṭ ʔijjiha:l] The kids' shouting gave me a headache. داخ راسِي مِن حِسّ المَكاين [da:x ra:si min ħiss ʔilmaka:yin] I got a headache from the noise of the machines. دِخِت. ما تسِكتُون، عاد [dixit. ma: tsiktu:n, ʕa:d] I'm fed up. Why don't you keep quiet now. • **3.** to be put to a lot of bother, have a lot of trouble – دِخِت بقَضِيّتَك. صارلِي إسبُوع ما دَأسَوِّي شِي؛ بَسّ أركُضلَك [dixit bqaðiyytak. ṣa:rli ʔisbu:ʕ ma: daʔasawwi ši; bass ʔarkuðlak] I've had a lot of trouble with your case. For a week I've been doing nothing but running around for you. عَلِي وَمَرتَه كانَوا بِبَغداد وَدِخنا بِيهُم [ʕali wmartah ča:naw bibaydа:d wdixna bi:hum] Ali and his wife were in Baghdad and we ran ourselves ragged for them. إذا تِشتِرِي هَالسَّيّارَة المِجرَقعَة راح تدُوخ بِيها [ʔiða tištiri hassayya:ra ʔilimčarqiʕa ra:ħ ddu:x bi:ha] If you buy this broken down old car you will be constantly having trouble with it. • **4.** to get sick, feel nauseous – ما يسافِر بِالطَّيّارَة لأنّ يدُوخ بِيها [ma: ysa:fir biṭṭayya:ra liʔann ydu:x bi:ha] He doesn't travel by plane because he gets sick on them.

دَوَّخ [dawwax] *v:* • **1.** to make dizzy – القِرايَة بِالسَّيّارَة تدَوِّخنِي [ʔilqra:ya bissayya:ra ddawwixni] Reading in a car makes me dizzy. • **2.** to give someone a headache, bother – دَوَّختنِي. ما تِسكُت [dawwaxtni. ma: tiskut] You give me a headache. Why don't you shut up! دَوّخنِي بِطَلَباتَه [dawwxni bṭalaba:tah] He bothered me with his requests. راح أظَلّ أطالبَه بِالفلُوس حَتَّى أدَوّخَه وَينطِينِي إياها [ra:ħ ʔaðall ʔaṭa:lbah bilfilu:s ħatta ʔadawwxah wyinṭi:ni ʔiyy:ha] I will keep asking him for the money until I drive him to distraction and he gives it to me.

دَوخَة [du:xa] *n:* • **1.** dizziness, vertigo • **2.** headache, trouble, bother, nuisance • **3.** nausea, motion sickness

مدَوِّخ [mdawwix] *adj:* • **1.** giddying, dizzying, vertiginous
دايخ [da:yix] *adj:* • **1.** dazed

د و خ ن

ديوَخانَة، ديوان خانَة [di:waxa:na, di:wa:n xa:na] *n:* دِيوَخانات، دِيوان خانات [di:waxa:na:t, di:wa:n xa:na:t] *pl:* • **1.** parlor, sitting room (where guests are entertained in traditional households)

د و د

دَوَّد [dawwad] *v:* • **1.** to become wormy, worm-eaten – التَّمُر دَوَّد، وما يِنّكِل [?ittamur dawwad, wama: yinnikil] The dates have gotten wormy and can't be eaten.
دُود [du:d] *n:* • **1.** worms • **2.** worm-like larvae, e.g. maggots, grubs – مِثل الدُود، ما يِنعَدُّون [miθl ?iddu:d, ma: yinʕaddu:n] There are so many of them, they can't be counted.
دُودَة [du:da] *n:* دُودات [du:da:t] *pl:* • **1.** unit noun of دُود. دُودَة الأَرض – دُود [du:d. du:dat ?il?arḍ] earthworm. دُودَة القَزّ [du:dat ?ilqazz] silkworm. الدُودَة الوَحِيدَة [?iddu:da ?ilwaħi:da] tapeworm.
مدَوِّد [mdawwid] *adj:* • **1.** wormy
دُودَكي [du:daki] *adj:* دُودَكِيَّة [du:dakiyya] *pl:* • **1.** homosexual who takes the female role

د و ر

ديوَر [daywar, di:war] *v:* • **1.** to turn, turn around – يَالله، ديوِر؛ خَلِّي نِرجَع [yallah, di:wir; xalli: nirǰaʕ] Come on, turn around; let's go back. خَفِّف السُّرعَة قَبِل ما تديوَر [xaffif ?issurʕa gabil ma: ddi:war] Slow up before you turn.
تدَيوَر [tdaywar, tdi:war] *v:* • **1.** pass. of دَيوَر to be turned around – السَّيّارَة ما تِدّيوَر بِهالدَّربُونَة [?issayya:ra ma: tiddi:war bhaddarbu:na] The car can't be turned around in this alley.
دار [da:r] *v:* • **1.** to turn, revolve, rotate, circle – مِن سِمَعنِي وَراه، اِندار [min simaʕni wara:h, da:r] When he heard me behind him, he turned. مَرَّة بِاليُوم، الأَرض تدُور عَلَى نَفِسها [marra bilyu:m, ?il?arḍ ddu:r ʕala nafisha] Once a day, the earth revolves on its axis. رُوح لِراس الشّارِع **وديور** لِلِيسرَة [ru:ħ lira:s ?išša:riʕ wdu:r lilyisra] Go to the end of the street and turn left. الأَرض تدُور حَول الشَّمِس [?il?arḍ ddu:r ħawl ?iššamis] The earth revolves around the sun. السَّنَة دارَت عَلَى ثَور [?issana da:rat ʕala θu:r] The year has come under the sign of the bull. الزَّمَن دار غير دورَة؛ العَوائِل العَتِيقَة اِنقِرضَت [?izzaman da:r ɣi:r du:ra; ?ilʕawa:?il ?ilʕati:ga ?inqirḍat] Times have changed; all the old families have died out. راسِي دار وَما دَأندَلّ [ra:si da:r wma: da?andall] I'm all turned around and can't find my way. • **2.** to turn something, turn something around – مِن قِعَدِت يَمَّه، دارلِي ظَهرَه [min giʕadit yammah, da:rli ḍahrah] When I sat near him, he turned his back on me. دَوِّر السَّيّارَة؛ خَلِّي نِرجَع [dawwir ?issayya:ra; xalli: nirǰa] Turn the car around; let's go back. ياخَة قَمِيصَك قايمَة. دُورها عَدِّلها [ya:xat qami:ṣak ga:yma. du:rha ʕaddilha] Your shirt collar's frayed. Have it turned. هالجِّهَة مِن المَيز وَسخَة. راح أَدُورها [hajǰiha min ?ilmi:z wasxa. ra:ħ ?adu:rha] This side of the table is dirty. I'm going to turn it around. • **3.** to move, transfer, change • **4.** to tour, travel, go around, wander around – كُلّ سَنَة يدُور أُورُبّا كُلّها [kull sana ydu:r ?u:ruppa kullha] Every year he travels all over Europe. دِرنا بَغداد كُلّها بِتلَث أَيّام [dirna bayda:d kullha bitlaθ ?ayya:m] We toured the whole of Baghdad in three days. دَيدُور عالمُوَظَّفِين يِجمَع مِنهُم فلُوس [daydu:r ʕa:lmuwaððafi:n yiǰmaʕ minhum flu:s] He's going around to the employees collecting money from them. شَكُو عِندَك تدُور هنا باللَّيل؟ [šaku ʕindak ddu:r hna: billayl?] What reason do you have for walking around here at night? هَذا دايِر عَكَّة وَمَكَّة [ha:ða da:yir ʕakka wmakka] He's been all over. He's widely traveled (lit. he's toured Acre and Mecca.). • **5.** to circulate, spread, be current, go around – الإشاعَة دارَت بِبَغداد [?il?iša:ʕa da:rat bibayda:d] The rumor has gone around Baghdad. هَالمُودَة دايرَة هَالسَّنَة [halmu:da da:yra hassana] This style is in fashion this year. • **6.** with عَلَى to turn against – اِندار عَلَيّا وَسَبّنِي [?inda:r ʕalayya wsabbni] He turned on me and cursed me. دارَوا عَليه كُلّهُم وَبُسطَوه [da:raw ʕali:h kullhum wbuṣṭu:h] They all turned against him and beat him up.
دار [da:r] *v:* • **1.** to turn, direct – دِير وِجهَك عَلَيّا [di:r wiččak ʕalayya] Turn your face to me. دِير التَّلِفِزيُون عَلينا، ما دَنشُوف [di:r ?ittalifizyu:n ʕali:na, ma: danšu:f] Turn the television towards us; we can't see. دار بالَه [da:r ba:lah] to pay attention, look out, be careful. لا تديرلَه بال؛ هَذا جاهِل [la: ddi:rlah ba:l; ha:ða ǰa:hil] Don't pay any attention to him; he's a child. دِير بالَك عَالجّاهِل إِلَى أَن أَرجَع مِن السُّوق [di:r ba:lak ʕaǰǰa:hil ?ila ?an ?arǰaʕ min ?issu:g] Look after the kid until I get back from the market. لا تدِير بال. مِنُو أَبُو باكِر؟ [la: ddi:r ba:l. minu ?abu ba:čir?] Don't worry about it. Who knows about tomorrow? دِير بالَك مِنَّه، تَرَة يكَذِّب [di:r ba:lak minnah, tara yčaððib] Be careful with him, or he'll lie to you. دِير بالَك! لا تِتعَوَّر [di:r ba:lak! la: titʕawwar] Watch out! Don't get hurt. • **2.** to pour – أَرجُوك، دِيرلِي فِنجان قَهوَة [?arǰu:k, di:rli finǰa:n gahwa] Please pour me a cup of coffee. دِير المَيّ الباقِي بالكلاص [di:r ?ilmayy ?ilba:qi bilgla:ṣ] Pour the rest of the water in the glass. • **3.** to manage, run, direct – ما أَعتَقِد يِقدَر يدِير هَالدّائِرَة [ma: ?aʕtiqid yigdar ydi:r hadda:?ira] I don't think he can manage this office. نِقدَر ندِير بَلَدنا بلَيّا نفُوذ أَجنَبي [nigdar ndi:r baladna blayya nufu:ð ?aǰnabi] We can run our country without foreign influence.

دَوَّر [dawwar] *v:* • **1.** to show around, take on a tour – دَوَّرنا كُلّ بَغداد بسَيّارتَه [dawwarna kull baɣdaːd bsayyaːrtah] He showed us around Baghdad in his car. • **2.** to look, search – دَوَّرت كُلّ جيُوبَه وَما لقَيت شِي [dawwarit kull ǰyuːbah wma lgayt ši] I searched all his pockets and didn't find anything. إذا تدَوُّر زين تِلقاها [ʔiða ddawwur ziːn tilgaːha] If you search carefully you'll find it. دَوَّرت بالسُّوق لَكِن ما لقَيت مِثِل هَالقَلَم [dawwarit bissuːg laːkin maː lgiːt miθil halqalam] I looked all over the market and didn't find another pen like this. هَذا دَيدَوِّر طلايِب. يريد يِتعارَك ويّا الرّايح وَالجاي [haːða daydawwir tlaːyib. yriːd yitʕaːrak wiyya ʔirraːyiħ wijǰaːy] He is looking for trouble. He wants to fight with everybody. يِكرَهُوه لِأنّ يِسكَر وَيدَوِّر قحاب [yikrahuːh liʔann yiskar wydawwir ɣhaːb] They despise him because he drinks and chases after whores. أبُوك دَيدَوُّر عَلِيك [ʔabuːk daydawwur ʕaliːk] Your father is looking for you. لا تدَوِّر دَفاتِر عِتّق [laː ddawwir dafaːtir ʕittag] Don't bring up old matters.

داوَر [daːwar] *v:* • **1.** to alternate, vary, change, exchange – لِيش تِلبَس هَالقاط كُلّ يوم وَتارك اللّاخ؟ داوِرهُم [liːš tilbas halqaːṭ kull yuːm wtaːrik ʔillaːx? daːwirhum] Why do you wear this suit every day and leave the other one? Alternate them. داوِر السِبَير وَالتّايَرات [daːwir ʔilispayr wittaːyaraːt] Rotate the spare and the tires. داوِر الخَلّ بِهَالبطالَة [daːwir ʔilxall bhalbṭaːla] Transfer the vinegar into these bottles.

اِندار [ʔindaːr] *v:* • **1.** to turn – مِن سِمَع حِسّي اِندار حَتّى يشُوفني [min simaʕ ħissi ʔindaːr ħatta yšuːfni] When he heard my voice he turned so he could see me. • **2.** to sneak in, slip in – اِندار عَلينا حَرامِي البارحَة باللّيل [ʔindaːr ʕaliːna ħaraːmi ʔilbaːrħa billayl] A thief broke into our place last night. ضَيَّعنا المِفتاح وَندارَينا مِن بَيت الجِّيران [ðayyaʕna ʔilmiftaːħ windaːrayna min bayt ʔijǰiːraːn] We lost the key and slipped in from the neighbor's house. • **3.** with عَلَى to turn against, on – الحَكِي كان عَلَيّا، لَكِن هَسَّة اِندار عَلِيك [ʔilħači čaːn ʕalayya, laːkin hassa ʔindaːr ʕaliːk] The talk was against me, but now it's turned against you. واحِد مِنهُم اِندار عَلَيّا؛ ضِرَبنِي مِيَّة جِلّاق [waːħid minhum ʔindaːr ʕalayya; ðirabni miyyat čillaːq] One of them turned on me; he kept kicking me.

دار [daːr] *n:* دُور [duːr] *pl:* • **1.** nursery (in hospital, etc.) – دار الأيتام [daːr ʔilʔaytaːm] orphanage. دار العَجَزَة [daːr ʔilʕaǰaza] old folks' home. دار المُعَلِّمين العالِيَة [daːr ʔilmuʕallimiːn ʔilʕaːliya] teachers college. دار الحَضانَة [daːr ʔilħaðaːna] nursery (in hospital, etc.). • **2.** House, home. **دَور** [dawr, duːr] *n:* أدوار [ʔadwaːr] *pl:* • **1.** round (in sports) • **2.** role, part (also of stage and screen) – لِعَب دَور مُهِمّ بِالتَّحقِيق [liʕab dawr muhimm bittaħqiːq] He played an important role in the investigation. • **3.** stage, phase, step • **4.** turn – الدُّور عَلِيك [ʔidduːr ʕaliːk] It's your turn. راح يُوصِلَك الدَّور [raːħ yuːṣlak ʔiddawr] Your turn will come.

دِير [diːr] *n:* • **1.** turning, directing

دارَة [daːra] *n:* دارات [daːraːt] *pl:* • **1.** circle • **2.** hand, round (cards)

دُورَة [duːra, dawra] *n:* دُورات [duːraːt] *pl:* • **1.** once, one time, time – دورَة يِضحَك وَدورَة يِبكِي [dawra yiðħak wdawraː yibči] Sometimes he laughs and sometimes he cries. فتَرّ دايِر البَيت دَورتَين [ftarr daːyir ʔilbayt duːrtayn] He went around the house twice. آنِي تَعبان. اِنتَ رُوح هَالدَّورَة [ʔaːni taʕbaːn. ʔinta ruːħ haddawra] I'm tired. You go this time. فَدّ دورَة قُول "آني ما أشتِرِك" [fadd duːra guːl "ʔaːni maː ʔaštirik"] You might as well say 'I don't participate.' آنِي تَعبان فَدّ دورَة؛ ما أقدَر أركُض [ʔaːni taʕbaːn fadd duːra; maː ʔagdar ʔarkuð] I'm completely exhausted; I can't run. الزَّمَن دار غير دورَة؛ العَوائِل العَتِيقَة اِنقِرضَت [ʔizzaman daːr ɣiːr duːra; ʔilʕawaːʔil ʔilʕatiːga ʔinqirðat] Times have changed; all the old families have died out.

دَورَة [dawra] *n:* دَورات [dawraːt] *pl:* • **1.** rotation, turn • **2.** orbit, circuit, lap • **3.** course, training course • **4.** session (of Parliament) – الدَّورَة الدَّمَوِيَّة [ʔiddawra ʔiddamawiyya] blood circulation.

دَوّار [dawwaːr] *n:* دَوّارِين، دَوّارَة [dawwaːriːn, dawwaːra] *pl:* • **1.** peddler, hawker, roving vendor

دِيرِي [diːri] *n:* • **1.** (coll.) variety of dried red dates, common in southern Iraq

دِيرَة [diːra] *n:* دِيرات [diːraːt] *pl:* • **1.** district, area, region

مُدِير [mudiːr] *n:* مُدَراء [mudaraːʔ] *pl:* • **1.** director, head, chief, manager • **2.** principal (of a school)

دَوار [dawaːr] *n:* • **1.** seasickness • **2.** dizziness, vertigo

مَدار [madaːr] *n:* • **1.** Tropic of Cancer • **2.** orbit

دَورِيَّة [dawriyya] *n:* دَورِيّات [dawriyyaːt] *pl:* • **1.** patrol

دوارَة [dwaːra] *n:* • **1.** showing around, taking on a tour, looking, searching

دَوَران [dawaraːn] *n:* • **1.** rotation, revolving • **2.** revolution, circuiting, orbiting

دائِرَة [daːʔira] *n:* دَوائِر [dawaːʔir] *pl:* • **1.** circle • **2.** agency, bureau, department • **3.** office, office building – دائِرَة المَعارِف [daːʔirat ʔilmaʕaːrif] encyclopedia.

دَيرِيَّة [dayriyya] *n:* دَيرِيّات [dayriyyaːt] *pl:* • **1.** (coll) a variety of dried, red dates, common in southern Iraq

إدارَة [ʔidaːra] *n:* • **1.** administration, management, managing • **2.** administrative section, administrative office • **3.** managerial ability, administrative ability – سَوَّى إدارَة [sawwaː ʔidaːra] to manage, make do.

مَرتِي ما تِقدَر تسَوِّي إدارَة عَلَى مِيَّة دِينار بِالشَّهَر [marti maː tigdar tsawwiː ʔidaːra ʕala miyyat dinaːr biššahar] My wife can't manage on a hundred dinars a month. • **4.** pl. إدارات administration, management, directorate

تَدوِير [tadwiːr] *n:* • **1.** turning

مُدِيرِيَّة [mudiːriyya] *n:* مُدِيريّات [mudiːriyyaːt] *pl:* • **1.** bureau, directorate, department, office

دارَة، فِلفِل دارَة [daːra, filfil daːra] *adj:* • **1.** hot pepper(s)

دَورِي [dawri] *adj:* • **1.** round robin, rotating – سِباق دَورِي [sibaːq dawri] round robin tournament.

دايِر [daːyir] *adj:* • **1.** around, surrounding – دايِر الوَسِط [daːyir ʔilwasiṭ] around the center.

مدَوَّر [mdawwar] *adj:* • **1.** round, circular – وِجِه مدَوَّر [wiǰih mdawwar] a round face.

إدارِي [ʔidaːri] *adj:* • **1.** administrative – أَمُر إدارِي [ʔamur ʔidaːri] an administrative order. • **2.** administrator

دائِرِي [daːʔiri] *adj:* • **1.** circular

مَديُور [madyuːr] *adj:* • **1.** turned

د و ر ب ي ن

دَورِبِين [duːrbiːn] *n:* دَورِبِينات [duːrbiːnaːt] *pl:* • **1.** binoculars

د و ز ي

دُوزِي، لَيمُون دُوزِي [duːzi, liːmuːn duːzi] *adj:* • **1.** crystalline citric acid, sour salt

د و س

داس [daːs] *v:* • **1.** to step, tread – لا تدُوس بقُندَرتَك عَالزُّولِيَّة [laː dduːs bqundartak ʕazzuːliyya] Don't step on the carpet with your shoes. رِجلِي اليِسرَى تُوجَعنِي. ما أَقدَر أدُوس عَليها [rijli ʔilyisra tuːǰaʕni. maː ʔagdar ʔaduːs ʕaliːha] My left foot is hurting me. I can't stand on it. سَبَّتَه لِأَنّ داس وِيّاها زايِد [sabbatah liʔann daːs wiyyaːha zaːyid] She cussed him out because he went too far with her. دُوس بانزِين! ما ظَلّ وَقِت [duːs baːnziːn! maː ðall wakit] Step on the gas! There's no time left. خَلِّي نسَوِّي نَفِسنا ما نشُوفَه. دُوس [xalliː nsawwiː nafisna maː nšuːfah. duːs] Let's pretend we don't see him. Step on it! • **2.** to press, push – لا تدُوس عَالجَّرِح؛ يَوجَعنِي [laː tduːs ʕaǰǰarih; yawǰaʕni] Don't press on the wound; it hurts me. داس الزِّرّ وَانهِزَم [daːs ʔizzirr wʔinhizam] He pushed the doorbell and ran. دُوس العُودَة حيل حَتَّى تخُشّ بِالزُّرُف [duːs ʔilʕuːda ħiːl ħatta txušš bizzuruf] Push the stick hard so it'll go into the hole. كُلّما يِحكِي يدُوس عَلَى قَلبِي [kullmaː yiħči yduːs ʕala galbi] Everything he says burns me up. دِسِت بِيدَه دِينار يَالله خَلّانِي أَخُشّ [disit biːdah dinaːr yallah xallaːni ʔaxušš] I slipped him a dinar and only then he let me enter. شقَدّ خُوش آدَمِي! لَو تدُوس عَلَى راسَه ما يِحكِي [šgadd xuːš ʔaːdami! law dduːs ʕala raːsah maː yiħči] What a nice guy! Even if you hurt him he won't say anything. • **3.** to roll over, flatten – الرَّولَة داسَت القاع [ʔirrawla daːsat ʔilgaːʕ] The steam roller packed the ground. السَّيّارَة داسَت وَلَد [ʔissayyaːra daːsat walad] The car ran over a boy. • **4.** to raid – الشُّرطَة داسَوا بَيتنا [ʔiššurṭa daːsaw baytna] The police raided our house.

دَوَّس [dawwas] *v:* • **1.** to trample – خَلُّوه جَوَّة رِجلَيهُم وقامَوا يدَوِّسُون عَليه [xalluːh ǰawwa riǰlayhum wgaːmaw ydawwisuːn ʕaliːh] They put it under their feet and started stamping on it.

اِنداس [ʔindaːs] *v:* • **1.** pass. of داس to be trampled – الكاشِي مُو يابِس؛ ما يِنداس عَليه [ʔilkaːši muː yaːbis; maː yindaːs ʕaliːh] The tile is not dry; it can't be walked on. القاع ما تِنداس بَعَد [ʔilgaːʕ maː tindaːs baʕad] The ground can't be packed down anymore. لَو ما يِركُض، كان اِنداس [law maː yirkuð, čaːn ʔindaːs] If he hadn't run, he'd have been run over. هَالدُّقمَة اِنداسَت بالغَلَط [haddugma ʔindaːsat bilɣalaṭ] This button was pushed by accident. اِنهَزمُوا تَرَةاِنداسَينا [ʔinhazmuː tara ʔindaːsiːna] Run --- we've been raided!

داس [daːs] *n:* دُوس [duːs] *pl:* • **1.** round, game, hand

دوس [duːs] *n:* • **1.** stepping, treading

دَوسَة [dawsa, duːsa] *n:* دَوسات [dawsaːt] *pl:* • **1.** plank, walkway, gang plank • **2.** running board

مداس [mdaːs] *n:* مداسات، مِدِس [mdaːsaːt, midis] *pl:* • **1.** slipper with the quarter folded in • **2.** slipper with a low heel and no quarter, mule – وِجهه مِثِل مداس [wiččah miθil mdaːs] His face is wrinkled up like the top of a soft shoe.

د و ش [1]

دَوش [dawš] *n:* • **1.** breast of lamb – لَحَم دَوش [laħam duːš] breast of lamb. • **1.** fatty meat

دَوشَة [duːša] *n:* • **1.** noise, racket, uproar

د و ش [2]

دُوش [duːš] *n:* • **1.** shower, shower bath

د و ش ك [1]

دَوشَك [dawšag, duːšag] *n:* دواشِك [dwaːšig] *pl:* • **1.** mattress

د و ش ك [2]

دُوشكا [duːška] *n:* • **1.** heavy machine gun

د و ش م

دَوشَمَة [dawšama] *n:* • **1.** upholstering, upholstery • **2.** upholstering, the upholsterer's trade

دَوشَمجِي [dawšamči] *n:* دَوشَمجِيَّة [dawšamčiyya] *pl:* • **1.** upholsterer

د و غ [1]

دُوغ، لِبَن دُوغ [duːɣ, liban duːɣ] *adj:* • **1.** thin, diluted yogurt

د و غ ²

دواغ [dwaːɣ] *n:* دواغات [dwaːɣaːt] *pl:* • **1.** bridal veil, often including the train

د و غ ر also د - غ - ر

دُغرِي, [duɣri] *adj:* • **1.** straight, direct – حَكِي دغرِي [ħači duːɣri] straight talk. رَجُل دغرِي [rajul duːɣri] an honest man, an upright man. • **2.** truth, straight story – حِكَى الدُّغرِي اللِّي قالَه كُلَّه صُدُق [ħičaː duːɣri. ʔilli gaːlah kullah ṣudug] He told the truth. Everything he said is right.

د و ق

دَوق [dawq, duːq] *n:* • **1.** duck, white duck, duck cloth

د و ل

تداوَل [ddaːwal] *v:* • **1.** to discuss – دَيدّاوَلُون بِالمُشكِلَة [dayiddaːwaluːn bilmuškila] They're discussing the problem. تداوَلِت وِيّا أَبُوك عَن قَضِيَّة دِراستَك؟ [ddaːwalit wiyya ʔabuːk ʕan qaḏiyyat diraːstak?] Did you discuss the matter of your studies with your father?
دَولَة [dawla] *n:* دَولات، دُوَل [dawlaːt, duwal] *pl:* • **1.** country, state – هَذا شكُبرَه! دَولَة مِن غير عَساكِر [haːða škubrah! dawla min ɣiːr ʕasaːkir] What a great man! He's a state by himself (lit. a state without soldiers). • **2.** dynasty
تَداوُل [tadaːwul] *n:* • **1.** circulation (of money) • **2.** negotiation • **3.** rotating (on tasks)
مُداوَلَة [mudaːwala] *n:* مُداوَلات [mudaːwalaːt] *pl:* • **1.** negotiation • **2.** discussion
دُولِي [dawli] *adj:* • **1.** international – القانُون الدَّولِي [ʔilqaːnuːn ʔiddawli] international law.
مُتَداوَل [mutadaːwal] *adj:* • **1.** circulating, current, common, in common use

د و ل ب

دِيلاب، دُولاب [diːlaːb, duːlaːb] *n:* دَوالِيب، دوالِيب [dawaːliːb, dwaːliːb] *pl:* • **1.** Ferris wheel – دِيلاب هَوا [diːlaːb hawa] Ferris wheel.

د و ل ر

دُولار [dulaːr] *n:* دُولارات [dularaːt] *pl:* • **1.** dollars

د و ل ك

دُولكَة [duːlka, duːlča] *n:* دُولكات [duːlkaːt, duːlčaːt] *pl:* • **1.** pitcher • **2.** dipper resembling a pitcher

د و ل م

دُولمَة [duːlma] *n:* • **1.** an all inclusive term for stuffed vegetables (and grape leaves)

د و م

دام [daːm] *v:* • **1.** to last, continue – الحَرُب دامَت سِتّ سنِين [ʔilħarub daːmat sitt sniːn] The war lasted six years. الفَرحَة ما دامَتلَه هوايَة [ʔilfarħa maː daːmatlah hwaːya] The enjoyment didn't last long for him. الدِّنيا ما تدُوم لِأَحَّد [ʔiddinya maː dduːm lʔaħħad] The world doesn't stand still for anyone. • **2.** to perpetuate, make permanent, cause to last – الله يدِيم هَالنِعمَة عَلَيك [ʔallah ydiːm hanniʕma ʕaliːk] God perpetuate this prosperity for you. أَشكُرَك، الله يدِيمَك [ʔaškurak, ʔallah ydiːmak] Thank you. God keep you.
دام [daːm] *v:* • **1.** to perpetuate, make permanent, cause to last
داوَم [daːwam] *v:* • **1.** to continue – راح أَداوُم بِالوَظِيفَة مِن باكِر [raːħ ʔadaːwum bilwaḏiːfa min baːčir] I'm going to start going to work tomorrow. راح يداوُم بِالمَدرَسَة هالسَّنَة [raːħ ydaːwum bilmadrasa hassana] He's going to start attending school this year. بَعدَه دَيداوُم بِالمَدرَسَة [baʕdah daydaːwum bilmadrasa] He is still going to school. راح أَداوُم عَلَى هَالدُّوا [raːħ ʔadaːwum ʕala hadduwa] I'm going to stay on this medicine.
أَدام [ʔadaːm] *v:* • **1.** to perpetuate, cause to last – يا رَبِّي، دِيمها لِهَالنِعمَة [yaː rabni, diːmha lhanniʕma] Oh, God, let this blessing continue.
دَوم [dawm, duːm] *n:* • **1.** always, perpetually, continually – دُوم يِجِي مِتأَخِّر [duːm yiji mitʔaxxir] He always arrives late. دُوم يِحكُون عالنّاس [duːm yiħčuːn ʕannaːs] They're always talking people down. دومَه يِجِي مِتأَخِّر [duːmah yiji mitʔaxxir] He always comes late. دومِي مِفلِس [duːmi miflis] I'm always broke. بُقَى وِيّايا دُوم الوَقِت [buqaː wiyyaːya duːm ʔilwakit] He stayed with me all the time.
دَوام [dawaːm] *n:* • **1.** working day – ساعات الدَّوام [saːʕaːt ʔiddawaːm] working hours, hours of business. الدَّوام بِالمَدرَسَة [ʔiddawaːm bilmadrasa] school hours. عِدنا نُصّ دَوام [ʕidna nuṣṣ dawaːm] We have a half day. دَوامَه مُنتَظَم [dawaːmah muntaḏam] His attendance is regular. الأَحوال مالها دَوام؛ كُلّشِي يِتبَدَّل [ʔilʔaħwaːl maːlha dawaːm; kullši yitbaddal] Things don't remain the same; everything changes. عَلَى الدَّوام [ʕala ʔiddawaːm] perpetually, at all times, always. يِتشَكَّى عَلَى الدَّوام [yitšakkaː ʕala ʔiddawaːm] He complains all the time.
إِدامَة [ʔidaːma] *n:* • **1.** maintenance
مُداوَمَة [mudaːwama] *n:* • **1.** perseverance, endurance
دائِم [daːʔim] *adj:* • **1.** continuous, continual, unceasing, constant – بخَطَر دائِم [bxaṭar daːʔim] in constant danger.
دائِمِي [daːʔimi] *adj:* • **1.** permanent – وَضِع دائِمِي [waḏiʕ daːʔimi] a permanent arrangement. بِصُورَة دائِمِيَّة [bṣuːra daːʔimiyya] permanently.
مداوُم [mdaːwum] *adj:* • **1.** continuous

أدوَم [ʔadwam] *comparative adjective:* • **1.** more or most lasting, enduring – الصُّوف أدوَم مِن القُطِن [ʔiṣṣuːf ʔadwam min ʔilguṭin] Wool is longer wearing than cotton.
دائِماً [daːʔiman] *adverbial:* • **1.** always – يزُورنا دائِماً مِن هُوَّ بِبَغداد [yzuːrna daːʔiman min huwwa bibaɣdaːd] He always visits us when he's in Baghdad. دائِماً يِتشَكّى [daːʔiman yitšakkaː] He always complains.
ما دام [maː daːm] *conjunction:* • **1.** as long as, while – تمَتَّع بحَياتَك ما دامَك شَباب [tmattaʕ bħayaːtak maː daːmak šabaːb] Enjoy your life while you're still young. • **2.** as long as, inasmuch as, since, because – ما دام ما عِندَك فلُوس، ما نِقدَر نوَدّيك ويّانا [maː daːm maː ʕindak fluːs, maː nigdar nwaddiːk wiyyaːna] As long as you don't have money, we can't take you with us. ما دام ما جا، لا تِدفَعلَه فلُوس [maː daːm maː ǰaː, laː tidfaʕlah fluːs] Since he didn't come, don't pay him any money.

د و م ن

دومنَة [duːmna] *n:* دومنات [duːmnaːt] *pl:* • **1.** dominoes

د و ن

دُون [duːn] *n:* • **1.** less than, under, below – اللّي دُون الثمُنطَعَش ما يصِير يصِير مُوَظَّف [ʔilli duːn ʔiliθmunṭaʕaš maː yṣiːr yṣiːr muwaðððaf] Anyone under eighteen cannot become a government employee.
ديوان [diːwaːn] *n:* دَواوين [dawaːwiːn] *pl:* • **1.** guest house of a village • **2.** collection of poems by one author • **3.** central office, central building (of a ministry)
دُوني [duːni] *adj:* • **1.** inferior, poor, bad – قماش دُوني [qmaːš duːni] poor quality cloth. • **2.** bad, spoiled, rotten – طَماطَة دُونيَّة [ṭamaːṭa duːniyya] spoiled tomatoes. • **3.** low, lowly, mean, base, despicable, depraved, degenerate – رياجيل دُونيِّين [riyaːǰiːl duːniyyiːn] contemptible men. مَرَة دُونيَّة [mara duːniyya] a bad woman, a slut. • **4.** pl. دُونيين, دُونيَّة bum, degenerate, debased or unscrupulous man
أدوَن [ʔadwan] *comparative adjective:* • **1.** worse or worst • **2.** more or most spoiled • **3.** more or most despicable, debased
بدُون [biduːn, bduːn] *conjunction:* • **1.** without – طِلَع بِدُون شَمسيَّة بهالمُطَر [ṭilaʕ biduːn šamsiyya bhalmuṭar] He went out without an umbrella in this rain. بِدُونَه القَعدَة ما تِسوَى [bduːnah ʔilgaʕda maː tiswaː] Without him a gathering isn't worthwhile.
بدُون ما، بِدُون ما [bduːn maː, biduːn maː] *subordinating conjunction:* • **1.** (conj.) without – لا ترُوح بِدُون ما تقُلّي [laː truːħ bduːn maː dgulli] Don't go without telling me.

د و ن د ر م

دوندرمَة [duːndirma] *n:* دوندِرمات [duːndirmaːt] *pl:* • **1.** an ice cream cone – كلاص بِسكِت دوندِرمَة [glaːṣ biskit duːndirma] an ice cream cone.

د و ن ك ي

دَونكِي [duːnki] *n:* دَونكِيّات [duːnkiyyaːt] *pl:* • **1.** billy club, nightstick

د و ن م

دَونَم [dawnam] *n:* دَونَمات، دوانِم [dawnamaːt, dwaːnim] *pl:* • **1.** a land measure of about 2500 square meters

د و و

دَوَّة [dawwa] *n:* دَوّات [dawwaːt] *pl:* • **1.** a shallow, conical clay brazier set by one's feet for warmth

د و ي 1

دُوَى [duwaː] *v:* • **1.** to resound, boom, make a dull, booming sound – سِمَعِت حِسّ المَدفَع يِدوِي؟ [simaʕit ħiss ʔilmadfaʕ yidwi?] Did you hear the cannon boom? المَكِينَة ظَلَّت تِدوِي اللَّيل كُلَّه [ʔilmakiːna ðallat tidwi ʔillayl kullah] The machine kept thudding all night. • **2.** to drone – الطَّيّارَة صارِلها ساعَة تِدوِي فُوق رُوسنا [ʔiṭṭayyaːra ṣaːrilha saːʕa tidwi fuːg ruːsna] The plane kept droning over our heads.
دَوِيّ [dawiyy] *n:* • **1.** making a dull, booming sound
دَويَة [dawya] *n:* دَويات [dawyaːt] *pl:* • **1.** boom, rumbling – دَويَة المَدفَع [dawyat ʔilmadfaʕ] the cannon's roar.
دوايَة [dwaːya] *n:* دوايات [dwaːyaːt] *pl:* • **1.** inkwell • **2.** candle or lantern holder

د و ي 2

داوَى [daːwaː] *v:* • **1.** to treat – ظَلّ الطَّبِيب يداويه شَهَر [ðall ʔiṭṭabiːb ydaːwih šahar] The doctor continued to treat him for a month. داوَيت السِّفلِس مالَك لَو لا؟ [daːwiːt ʔissiflis maːlak law laː?] Have you had your syphilis treated or not?
تداوَى [ddaːwaː] *v:* • **1.** to get treated, be treated – عِند يا طَبِيب دَتِدّاوَى؟ [ʕind yaː ṭabiːb datiddaːwaː?] What doctor are you being treated by?
دُوا [duwa] *n:* دُويات، أدوِيَة [duwayaːt, ʔadwiya] *pl:* • **2.** medicine, medication, remedy – إبنَك دُواه العَصَا [ʔibnak duwaːh ʔilʕaṣa] The best medicine for your son is a stick. العَقرَب دُواه النَّعال [ʔilʕagrab duwaːh ʔinnaʕaːl] The only way you'd be any good is dead (lit., the remedy for a scorpion is a sandal). دُوا حَمّام [duwaː ħammaːm] a depilatory made from quicklime and arsenic, used to remove pubic hairs. دَيُضرُب دُوا حَمّام [dayuðrub duwaː ħammaːm] He's putting on a depilatory. Also called شِيرَة [šiːra]
تَداوِي [tadaːwi] *n:* • **1.** treatment

د ي [1]

د، دِ [di, d] *particle:* • **1.** emphatic particle used with imperative – دَتعال نِتشارَك [ditaʕa:l nitša:rak] Come on; let's become partners! دِيالله! فات الوَقت [diyallah! fa:t ʔilwakit] Come on! It's late. دَقُوم! خَلِّي نرُوح لِلسِّينَما [dagu:m! xalli: nru:ħ lissinama] Get up! Let's go to the movies. لَك دَقُوم! شِمقَدّرَك تِلعَب وِيّايا؟ [lak dagu:m! šimgaddrak tilʕab wiyya:ya?] Oh go on! How could you play against me? درُوح! هَذا شمفَهّمَه؟ [dru:ħ! ha:ða šmafahhmah?] Oh go on! What does he understand? دَأكُل خاطِر نقُوم نرُوح [daʔukul xa:ṭir ngu:m nru:ħ] Eat up so we can get going. دَاِحكِي! مُو قِتلِي عِندَك أخبار؟ [diħči! mu: gitli ʕindak ʔaxba:r?] Speak up! Didn't you tell me you had some news?

دِي [di] *particle:* • **1.** come on, let's go – دِي! إدفَع حيل [di! ʔidfaʕ ħi:l] Come on! Push hard! دِي! ما تِنزِل عاد! فات الوَقِت [di! ma: tinzil ʕa:d! fa:t ʔilwakit] Let's go! Get down here! It's late. • **2.** (an emphatic expression of disagreement, approx.:) aw, come on, good God – دِي! هَذا شلُون شُغُل يضَوِّج [di! ha:ða šlu:n šuɣul yðawwij] My God! This is such irritating work! دِي! هاي هَمّ قَهوَة؟ [di! ha:y hamm gahwa?] Come on! Do you call this coffee?

د ي [2]

دايَة [da:ya] *n:* دايات [da:ya:t] *pl:* • **1.** wet nurse • **2.** seedling

د ي د

داد [da:d] *n:* • **1.** (in certain expressions:) – بَسّ عاد. مُو راح أصِيح الدّاد [bass ʕa:d. mu: ra:ħ ʔaṣi:ħ ʔidda:d] Quit it! I'm about to holler uncle, dammit! وُلد المَحَلّة صاحَوا الدّاد مِنَّه [wuld ʔilmaħalla ṣa:ħaw ʔidda:d minnah] The neighborhood kids have gotten sick of him. هَمّ سَكران وَجاي مِتأخِّر، الدّاد مِنَّك [hamm sakra:n wja:y mitʔaxxir, ʔidda:d minnak] Drunk again and coming in late, to hell with you! • **2.** (in certain expressions:) hell, dammit

داد [da:d] *int:* • **1.** brother (form of address used mostly in supplication) – داد، ما تساعِدنِي؟ [da:d, ma: tsa:ʕidni?] Say, old buddy, won't you give me a hand?

دادَة [da:da] *int:* • **1.** brother, (form of address infrequently, by a girl) sister

د ي ز

دِيزِي [di:zi] *n:* دِيزِيّات [di:ziyya:t] *pl:* • **1.** small round cooking pot, usually with handles at the side

د ي س

دِيس [di:s] *n:* دِيُوس [dyu:s] *pl:* • **1.** breast • **2.** udder

دِيس العَنز [di:s ʔilʕanz] *n:* • **1.** a variety of large, '''white''' grapes

د ي ك

دِيك [di:č] *n:* دِيُوكَة [dyu:ča] *pl:* • **1.** rooster, cock

دِيك هِندِي [di:č hindi] *n:* • **1.** turkey

دِيكِي، سُعال دِيكِي [di:ki, suʕa:l di:ki] *adj:* • **1.** whooping cough

د ي ن [1]

دايَن [da:yan] *v:* • **1.** to lend, loan – دايِنِّي خَمسِين فِلِس رَجاءاً [da:yinni xamsi:n filis raja:ʔan] Please lend me fifty fils. ما تدايِنِّي سَيّارتَك؟ [ma: dda:yinni sayya:rtak?] Would you lend me your car? ما يداين أحَّد [ma: yda:yin ʔaħħad] He doesn't lend to anyone. • **2.** to lend, to loan

أدان [ʔada:n] *v:* • **1.** to find guilty, convict – المَحكَمَة أدانَتَه [ʔilmaħkama ʔada:natah] The court found him guilty.

تدَيَّن [tdayyan] *v:* • **1.** to loan • **2.** to borrow

تدايَن [dda:yan] *v:* • **1.** to borrow – تدايَن مِنِّي خَمس دَنانِير [dda:yan minni xams dana:ni:r] He borrowed five dinars from me. كان مُضطَرّ يِتدايَن المَبلَغ [ča:n muḍṭarr yidda:yan ʔilmablaɣ] He was obliged to borrow the amount.

اِستَدان [ʔistada:n] *v:* • **1.** to borrow

دان [da:n] *n:* • **1.** cannonball(s) • **2.** bomb(s)

دَين [dayn] *n:* دِيُون [dyu:n] *pl:* • **1.** debt • **2.** a loan outstanding, money owed one • **3.** an obligation, a favor (owed, or due one) – بِالدَّين [biddayn] credit.

دانَة [da:na] *n:* دانات [da:na:t] *pl:* • **1.** checkers, a game played by moving counters through a series of depressions in a board

اِستِدانَة [ʔistida:na] *n:* • **1.** incurrence of debts

دَيّان [dayya:n] *adj:* دَيّانَة [dayya:na] *pl:* • **1.** creditor

مُدان [muda:n] *adj:* • **1.** convicted

مَديُون [madyu:n] *adj:* • **1.** indebted, in debt • **2.** obligated, under obligation

مدايِن [mda:yin] *adj:* • **1.** lender,creditor

مِتدايِن [midda:yin] *adj:* • **1.** indebeted, in debt, under obligation

د ي ن [2]

دِين [di:n] *n:* أديان [ʔadya:n] *pl:* • **1.** religion

دِيانَة [diya:na] *n:* ديانات [dya:na:t] *pl:* • **1.** religious • **2.** confession, denomination, sect

دَيِّن [dayyin] *adj:* • **1.** religious, pious, godly, devout

دِينِي [di:ni] *adj:* • **1.** religious, spiritual – اِجتِماع دِينِي [ʔijtima:ʕ di:ni] religious gathering. رَجُل دِينِي [rajul di:ni] religious functionary.

دِينسِز [di:nsizz] *adj:* دِينسِزِّيَّة [di:nsizziyya] *pl:* • **1.** faithless, lacking religion, person who violates religious laws • **2.** cruel, heartless, savage, barbarous • **3.** a mild term of jocular condemnation

مِتدَيِّن [middayyin] *adj:* • **1.** religious, pious, devout, godly

مِتدَيِّن [middayyin] *adj:* • **1.** indebted, in debt

د ي ن م ي ت

دِيناميت [dinami:t] *n:* • **1.** dynamite – إصبع دِينامِيت [ʔiṣbiʕ dinami:t] a stick of dynamite.

د ي و ث

دَيُّوث [dayyu:θ] *adj:* دَيُّوثِين [dayyu:θi:n] *pl:* • **1.** cuckold • **2.** procurer, pimp

د ي ن ر

دِينار [di:na:r] *n:* دَنانِير [dana:ni:r] *pl:* • **1.** the basic unit of Iraqi money, equal to the pound sterling

د ي ن م

دَينَمُو [di:namu] *n:* دِينَمَوات [di:namu:wa:ṭ] *pl:* • **1.** generator, dynamo

ذ

ذ

ذاك [ða:k] *demonstrative:* ذوك، ذولاك [ðu:k, ðu:la:k] *pl:* ذيك [ði:č] *feminine:* • **1.** that, those • **2.** that one, that person, that guy – كُلّشِي ما تبَدّل؛ ذاك الطّاس وذاك الحَمّام [kullši ma: tbaddal; ða:k ʔiṭṭa:s wðа:k ʔilħamma:m] Everything is unchanged; it's the same old song and dance. ذاك اليُوم [ða:k ʔilyu:m] the other day.

ذاكُوَّ، ذاك هُوَّ [ðakuwwa, ða:k huwwa] *demonstrative:* • **1.** That's him • **2.** There he is

ذ ب ب

ذَبّ [ðabb] *v:* • **1.** to toss, throw – ذَبّلِي الطَّوبَة [ðabbli ʔiṭṭawba] He threw me the ball. ذَبّ شوَيَّة شعِير لِلدِّجاج [ðabb šwayya šʕi:r liddiǰa:ǰ] He threw a little barley to the chickens. ذَبّها لِلحكايَة بوُجهَه [ðabbha liliħča:ya bwuččah] He threw the remark in his face. ذَبَّيتلَه حَكِي، لَكِن ما أفتِهَم [ðabbi:tlah ħači, la:kin ma: ʔaftiham] I threw out a hint to him, but he didn't understand. الجّاهِل ذَبّ نَفسَه عَلَى أُمَّه وَحِضَنها [ʔiǰǰa:hil ðabb nafsah ʕala ʔummah wħiðanha] The child threw himself on his mother and hugged her. ذَبّ نَفسَه مِن السَّطِح [ðabb nafsah min ʔissaṭiħ] He jumped from the roof. لَو تذِبّ نفسَك عالشُّغُل تخَلّصَه بساعَة [law dðibb nafsak ʕaššuɣul txallṣah bsa:ʕa] If you throw yourself into the work, you'll finish in an hour. ذَبّ نَفسَه تِبَل عَلَيّا إلَى أن إنطِيتَه الفلُوس [ðabb nafsah tibal ʕalayya ʔila ʔan ʔinṭi:tah ʔilflu:s] He pressured me until I gave him the money. ذَبّ نَفسَه عالمَوت، وَأنقَذ حَياة إبنَه [ðabb nafsah ʕalmawt, wʔanqað ħaya:t ʔibnah] He endangered himself and saved his son's life. بيا فَصِيل ذَبّوك؟ [bya: faṣi:l ðabbu:k?] In which platoon did they put you? ذَبّوني بِفَدّ ولايَة صغَيّرَة [ðabbawni bfadd wla:ya ṣɣayyra] They sent me to a small town. بالله ذِبّنِي يَمّ مَوقِف الباص [ballah ðibbni yamm mawqif ʔilpa:ṣ] Please drop me off near the bus stop. ذَبّ كُلّ شُغلَه عَلَيّا [ðabb kull šuɣlah ʕalayya] He pushed all of his work off on me. ذِبّلَه طُعُم. قُلّه إذا يِجِي نِنطِيه مِيَّة دِينار [ðibblah ṭuʕum. gullah ʔiða yiǰi ninṭi:h miyyat dina:r] Put out some bait for him. Tell him if he comes we'll give him a hundred dinars. ذَبّلَه نُكتَة ما تضَحِّك [ðabblah nukta ma: dðaħħik] He cracked a joke that wasn't funny. مِثل المَيِّت. ما دَيذِبّ لا إيد وَلا رجِل [miθl ʔilmayyit. ma: dayðibb la: ʔi:d wala riǰil] He's like a dead man. He isn't moving a hand or a leg. أُوقف بمُكانَك؛ لا تذِبّ وَلا خَطوَة [ʔu:gaf bmuka:nak; la: dðibb wala xaṭwa] Stop where you are; don't take another step. التّاكسِي مالِي ذَبّلِي دِينارَين اليُوم [ʔitta:ksi ma:li ðabbli dina:rayn ʔilyu:m] My taxi brought in two dinars today. راح أذِبّ الآس [ra:ħ ʔaðibb ʔilʔa:s] I am going to play the ace. ذَبَّيت دِينارَين عَلَى هَالحِصان وخِسَرت [ðabbi:t dina:rayn ʕala halħiṣa:n wxisarit] I put two dinars on this horse and he lost. ذِبّ الكير عالواحِد [ðibb ʔilgi:r ʕalwa:ħid] Put the gear into first. ذَبَّيت هوايَة عَرايِض [ðabbi:t hwa:ya ʕara:yið] I put in many applications. • **2.** to throw away, discard – رَجاءاً ذِبّ الزِّبِل بَرَّة [raǰa:ʔan ðibb ʔizzibil barra] Please throw the garbage outside. راح ألبَس الثُّوب فَدّ مَرَّة واذِبَّه [ra:ħ ʔalbas ʔiθθawb fadd marra waʔaðibbah] I'm going to wear the shirt one time and throw it away. الجّاهِل ذَبّ الثَّلِج مِن إيدَه [ʔiǰǰa:hil ðabb ʔiθθaliǰ min ʔi:dah] The child threw the ice away. إذا تِشتِرِي هَالسَّيّارَة تذِبّ فلُوسَك بِالشَّطّ [ʔiða tištiri hassayya:ra dðibb flu:sak biššaṭṭ] If you buy this car, you'll be throwing your money away. ذَبَّت الحِجاب مِن دِخلَت الكُلِّيَة [ðabbat ʔilħiǰa:b min dixlat ʔilkulliya] She discarded the veil when she entered college. ذِبّ كُلّشِي وَإطبَع هَالمَكتُوب [ðibb kullši wʔiṭbaʕ halmaktu:b] Drop everything and type the letter. ذَبّ مَرتَه وَجهالَه وَمِلتِهِي بِالونسَة [ðabb martah wǰha:lah wmiltihi bilwinsa] He dropped his wife and children and is busy having a good time. الطَّيّارَة دَتذِبّ مَناشِير [ʔiṭṭiyya:ra dadðibb mana:ši:r] The plane is dropping pamphlets. دَيذِبّ مِن راسَه [dayðibb min ra:sah] He is throwing up. صَلّحَوا البُورِي، لَو بَعدَه يذِبّ مَيّ؟ [ṣallħaw ʔilbu:ri, law baʕdah yðibb mayy?] Did they fix the pipe, or is it still leaking water?

انذَبّ [ʔinðabb] *v:* • **1.** to be thrown

ذَبّ [ðabb] *n:* • **1.** throwing

ذَبَّة [ðabba] *n:* ذَبّات [ðabba:t] *pl:* • **1.** habit, custom, quirk

مَذبُوب [maðbu:b] *adj:* • **1.** thrown away

ذ ب ح

ذِبَح [ðibaħ] *v:* • **1.** to slaughter, butcher – القَصّاب ذِبَح ثلَث هوايِش [ʔilgaṣṣa:b ðibaħ tlaθ hwa:yiš] The butcher slaughtered three cows. • **2.** to cut someone's throat – الحَرامِي شافَه نايِم بِالفراش وَذِبَحَه [ʔilħara:mi ša:fah na:yim bilfra:š wðibaħah] The thief found him lying in bed and cut his throat. أذبَحَك إذا ترُوح [ʔaðbaħak ʔiða tru:ħ] I'll kill you if you go. هَالحَرّ يِذبَح [halħarr yiðbaħ] This heat is murder. ذِبَحتنِي، لا تِشتُغُل وَلا تخَلِّي غيرَك يِشتُغُل [ðibaħitni, la: tištuɣul wala txalli: ɣi:rak yištuɣul] You kill me. You don't work and you don't let anyone else work. ذِبحَوه مِن البَسِط [ðibħawh min ʔalbasiṭ] They just about beat him to death. ذِبَح نَفسَه حَتَّى حَصَّل عَالوَظِيفَة [ðibaħ nafsah ħatta ħaṣṣal ʕalwaðii:fa] He almost killed himself until he got the job. • **3.** to massacre – الجَّيش ذِبَح أهل الوِلايَة [ʔiǰǰayš ðibaħ ʔahl ʔilwila:ya] The army massacred the people of the city.

ذَبَّح [ðabbaħ] *v:* • **1.** to slaughter (large numbers) – صارلَه ساعَة يذَبِّح صُخُول [ṣaːrlah saːʕa yðabbiħ ṣuxuːl] He's been slaughtering goats for an hour. • **2.** to massacre – الأشقِيائِيَّة ذَبّحَوا رُكّاب الباص [ʔilʔašqiyaːʔiyya ðabbħaw rukkaːb ʔilpaːṣ] The gangsters massacred the bus passengers.
انذِبَح [ʔinðibaħ] *v:* • **1.** to be slaughtered – اِنذِبَحِت مِن هالشُّغُل [ʔinðibaħit min haššuɣul] I'm dead tired from this work.
ذَبِح [ðabiħ] *n:* • **1.** slaughtering
ذَبّاح [ðabbaːħ] *n:* • **1.** slaughterer
ذَبحَة [ðabħa] *n:* • **1.** angina pectoris, angina
مَذبَح [maðbaħ] *n:* • **1.** abattoir, slaughterhouse, butchery
ذِبيحَة [ðibiːħa] *n:* ذِبايِح [ðibaːyiħ] *pl:* • **1.** animal for slaughter, slaughtered animal • **2.** sacrificial animal (given away, to the poor, after sacrifice)
مَذبَحَة [maðbaħa] *n:* مَذابِح [maðaːbiħ] *pl:* • **1.** massacre, carnage, slaughter
ذابِح [ðaːbiħ] *adj:* • **1.** slaughterer, also means: bothering, annoying
مَذبُوح [maðbuːħ] *adj:* • **1.** slaughtered

ذ ب ذ ب

ذَبذَب [ðabðab] *v:* • **1.** to strew, throw around – لُويش دَتذَبذِب كُتُبَك هنا وَهنا؟ [luwiːš dadðabðib kutubak hna whna?] Why do you throw your books here and there?
تذَبذَب [dðabðab] *v:* • **1.** to tailor one's opinions or statements to what is expected – هالمُوَظَّف يِتذَبذَب لِلمُدِير أكثَر مِن اللّازِم [hallmuwaððaf yidðabðab lilmudiːr ʔakθar min ʔillaːzim] That employee defers to the director unnecessarily. أحتقرَه لِأَنّ مِتذَبذِب [ʔaħtaqrah liʔann midðabðib] I despise him because he goes with the prevailing wind. • **2.** to be strewed, thrown around – ما يصِير أغراضَك تِذّبذَب هنا [maː yṣiːr ʔaɣraːðak tiððabðab hna] Your things shouldn't be strewn around here.
تَذَبذُب [taðabðub] *n:* • **1.** vibration
ذَبذَبَة [ðabðaba] *n:* • **1.** vibration
مِتذَبذِب [mitðabðib] *adj:* • **1.** hesitant

ذ ب ل

ذِبَل [ðibal] *v:* • **1.** to wilt, wither, shrivel – الخيار ذِبَل بِالحَرّ [ʔilxyaːr ðibal bilħarr] The cucumbers wilted in the heat. • **2.** to waste away, get run down – ذِبلَت مِن المَرَض [ðiblat min ʔilmarað̣] She wasted away with the illness.
ذَبِل [ðabil] *n:* • **1.** wilting, withering, shriveling
ذَبلان [ðablaːn] *adj:* • **1.** wilted, withered, dried up – وَرِد ذَبلان [warid ðablaːn] a wilted flower. • **2.** wasted away, run down – إبنَك يبَيِّن ذَبلان [ʔibnak yibayyin ðablaːn] Your son seems run down.

ذ ب ن

ذَبَّن [ðabban] *v:* • **1.** to become fly-infested – أعتقِد الباقِلَّة راح تذَبِّن [ʔaʕtiqid ʔilbaːgilla raːħ ððabbin] I think the horse beans are going to get flies in them.
ذِبّان [ðibbaːn] *n:* • **1.** (coll.) flies
ذِبّانَة [ðibbaːna] *n:* ذِبّانات [ðibbaːnaːt] *pl:* • **1.** a fly

ذ خ ر

ادِّخَر [ʔiddixar] *v:* • **1.** to save, lay away, be thrifty – إذا تِسرِف وَما تِدِّخِر، تَرَة تاكُلها [ʔiða tisrif wma tiddixir, tara taːkulha] If you spend everything and don't save, you'll be sorry. يِدِّخِر فلُوسَه بِصُندُوق البَرِيد [yiddixir fluːsah bṣunduːg ʔilbariːd] He saves his money in the postal savings bank.
ذُخُر [ðuxur] *n:* • **1.** mainstay (person) – إنتَ ذُخُر إلنا [ʔinta ðuxur ʔilna] You're our mainstay.
مَذخَر [maðxar] *n:* مَذاخِر [maðaːxir] *pl:* • **1.** warehouse, storehouse, especially for pharmaceuticals and drugs
ذَخِيرَة [ðaxiːra] *n:* ذَخايِر [ðaxaːyir] *pl:* • **1.** supplies, stores • **2.** ammunition (mil.)
إدِّخار [ʔiddixaːr] *n:* • **1.** storage, gathering, saving
مُدَّخِر [muddaxir] *adj:* مُدَّخَرات [muddaxaraːt] *pl:* • **1.** one who saves up or stocks (e.g. food, money)

ذ ر ر

ذَرَّة [ðarra] *n:* ذَرّات [ðarraːt] *pl:* • **1.** atom • **2.** tiny particle • **3.** speck, mote – ما عِندَه وَلا ذَرَّة عَقِل [maː ʕindah wala ðarrat ʕaqil] He doesn't have a bit of sense.
ذُرِّيَّة [ðurriyya] *n:* ذُرِّيّات [ðurriyyaːt] *pl:* • **1.** offspring, descendants, children
ذَرِّي [ðarri] *adj:* • **1.** atomic – قُنبُلَة ذَرِّيَّة [qunbula ðarriyya] atomic bomb.

ذ ر ع

ذِرَع [ðiraʕ] *v:* • **1.** to measure – إذرَع الغُرفَة وَقُلّي شقَدّ طُولها وَعُرُضها [ʔiðraʕ ʔilɣurfa wgulli šgadd ṭuːlha wʕuruðha] Measure the room and tell me its length and width.
تذَرَّع [dðarraʕ] *v:* • **1.** to resort, have recourse – يِتذَرَّع بأعذار سَخِيفَة [yidðarraʕ bʔaʕðaːr saxiːfa] He resorts to stupid excuses.
ذَرِع [ðariʕ] *n:* • **1.** measurement
ذراع [ðraːʕ] *n:* ذراعات، ذِرعان، أذرُع [ðraːʕaːt, ðirʕaːn, ʔaðruʕ] *pl:* • **1.** arm, forearm – حَصَّل الوَظِيفَة بِذراعَه [ħaṣṣal ʔilwaðiːfa biðraːʕah] He got the job by his own effort. • **2.** pl. أذرُع a unit of measure from the finger tips to the shoulder ذراع بَغداد [ðraːʕ baɣdaːd] approx. 0.8 meter
ذَرِيعَة [ðariːʕa] *n:* ذرائع [ðaraːyiʕ] *pl:* • **1.** excuse, reason
ذَرِيع [ðariːʕ] *adj:* • **1.** devastating, awful • **1.** awful

ذ ر ف

ذِرَف [ðiraf] *v:* • **1.** to shed

اِنذِرَف [ʔinðiraf] *v:* • **1.** to shed
ذَرِف [ðarif] *n:* • **1.** flowing, shedding

ذ ر و

ذَرَّى [ðarraː] *v:* • **1.** to winnow (grains)
دَيذَرُّون الحُنطَة بِالهَوَا [dayðarruːn ʔilħunṭa filhawa] They are winnowing the wheat in the wind.
ذِرَة، إذرَة [ðira, ʔiðra] *n:* • **1.** corn – إذرَة صَفرَة [ʔiðra ṣafra] corn, maize. إذرَة بيضَة [ʔiðra biːḍa] durra, grain sorghum.
ذَروَة [ðarwa] *n:* • **1.** peak, apex, top (of power or success)

ذ ر ي

See also: ذ ر و

ذ ع ر

ذُعُر [ðuʕur] *v:* • **1.** panic

ذ ع ن

أذعَن [ʔaðʕan] *n:* • **1.** to yield, submit, give in, obey. – إذا ما يِذعِن، نِستَعمِل قُوَّة وِيّاه [ʔiða maː yiðʕin, nistaʕmil quwwa wiyyaːh] If he doesn't obey, we'll use force on him. إذا تهَدِّدَه يِذعِنلَك [ʔiða thaddidah yiðʕinlak] If you threaten him, he'll give in to you.

ذ ق ن

ذِقِن [ðiqin] *n:* ذِقُون [ðiquːn] *pl:* • **1.** beard, whiskers (on the chin)

ذ ك ر

ذِكَر [ðikar] *v:* • **1.** to recall, remember – ما تِذكُر الزَّينِيّات اللّي سَوَّيتلَك إيّاها؟ [maː tiðkur ʔizzayniyyaːt ʔilli sawwiːtlak ʔiyyaːha?] Don't you recall all the favors I did for you? هَسَّة ذِكَرت أخُوك أخَذ قَلَمي [hassa ðikarit. ʔaxuːk ʔaxað qalami] Now I remember. Your brother took my pen. إذا تاكُل أكلَة طَيِّبَة، أُذكُرني [ʔiða taːkul ʔakla ṭayyba, ʔuðkurni] If you eat a good meal, think of me. • **2.** to speak of, talk about – إحنا دائِماً نِذُكرَك بِالخير [ʔiħna daːʔiman niðukrak bilxiːr] We always speak well of you. • **3.** to mention – أشُو ما دَ يِذكُر شي بِهالمَكتُوب عَن مَجِيئَه [ʔašuː maː da yiðkur ši bhalmaktuːb ʕan majiːʔah] I notice he mentions nothing about his coming in this letter.
ذَكَّر [ðakkar] *v:* • **1.** to remind, call to mind – بالله ذَكِّرني اليُوم أشتِري شَمسيَّة [ballah ðakkirni ʔilyuːm ʔaštiri šamsiyya] Please remind me today to buy an umbrella. شُوف هَالوَلَد. وُجَّه ما يذَكّرَك بِعَلي؟ [šuːf halwalad. wuččah maː yðakkrak bʕali?] Look at that boy. Doesn't his face remind you of Ali? • **2.** to make a word masculine – هالأسماء مُؤَنَّثَة. ذَكِّرها [halʔasmaːʔ muʔannaθa. ðakkirha] These nouns are feminine. Make them masculine.
تذَكَّر [dðakkar] *v:* • **1.** to remember, recollect – ما دَ أتذَكَّر شوَقِت قلّي أشُوفه [maː da ʔadðakkar šwakit galli ʔašuːfah] I don't remember what time he told me to see him.
تذاكَر [dðaːkar] *v:* • **1.** to confer, have a talk – مَرّ عَلَيّا لِلبَيت حَتَّى نِتذاكَر بِالقَضِيَّة [marr ʕalayya lilbayt ħatta niððaːkar bilqaḍiyya] He dropped by my house so we could confer about the matter.
ذِكِر [ðikir] *n:* • **1.** mentioning, mention – جاب ذِكِر القَضِيَّة [ǰaːb ðikir ʔilqaḍiyya] He brought up the matter. هَسَّة كِنّا بِذِكرَك [hassa činna bðikrak] We were just talking about you. عَلَى ذِكِر أخُوك، قُلّي هَسَّة شدَيسَوِّي [ʕala ðikir ʔaxuːk, gulli hassa šdaysawwiː] Speaking of your brother, tell me what he's doing now. • **2.** a religious ceremony in which the attributes of God are recited
ذَكَر [ðakar] *n:* ذُكُور [ðukuːr] *pl:* • **1.** male • **3.** penis – ذُكُور، ذكُورَة [ðukuːr, ðkuːra]) penis.
ذِكرَى [ðikra] *n:* ذِكرَيات [ðikrayaːt] *pl:* • **1.** anniversary – يوم ذِكرَى [yuːm ðikra] anniversary.
تِذكار [tiðkaːr] *n:* تِذكارات [tiðkaːraːt] *pl:* • **1.** souvenir, memento
ذاكِرَة [ðaːkira] *n:* • **1.** memory – قُوَّة الذّاكِرَة [quwwat ʔiððaːkira] power of recollection.
مُذَكَّرَة [muðakkara] *n:* مُذَكَّرات [muðakkaraːt] *pl:* • **1.** memorandum • **2.** appointment book
تذكِير [taðkiːr] *n:* • **1.** reminding • **2.** reminder
مُذَكَّر [muðakkar] *adj:* • **1.** masculine (gram.) – إسِم مُذَكَّر [ʔisim muðakkar] a masculine noun.
تِذكارِي [tiðkaːri] *adj:* تِذكارِيَّة [tiðkaːriyya] *pl:* • **1.** memorial, commemorative – نَصُب تِذكارِي [naṣub tiðkaːri] monument.

ذ ك و

ذَكاء [ðakaːʔ] *n:* • **1.** intelligence, mental acuteness, brightness
ذَكِي [ðaki] *adj:* أذكِياء [ʔaðkiyaːʔ] *pl:* • **1.** intelligent, clever, bright, smart, sharp-witted
أذكَى [ʔaðkaː] *comparative adjective:* • **1.** smarter, more intelligent

ذ ك ي

See also: ذ ك و

ذ ل

ذال, ذَل [ðal, ðaːl] *n:* • **1.** name of the letter

ذ ل ل

ذَلّ [ðall] *v:* • **1.** to go down – سِعِر الشِّعِير تذَلّ بواسطَة الاستيراد [siʕir ʔiššiʕiːr dðall bwaːsṭat ʔilʔistiːraːd] The price of barley went down as a result of imports. • **2.** to humble, humiliate – ماكُو حاجَة تذِلّ نَفسَك عَلَى دِينار [maːku ħaːǰa dðill nafsak ʕala dinaːr] There's no need to humiliate yourself for a dinar.
ذَلَّل [ðallal] *v:* • **1.** to humble, humiliate – لا تذَلِّل نَفسَك قِدّامه. قابِل هُوَّ رَبَّك؟ [laː dðallil nafsak

gidda:mah. qa:bil huwwa rabbak?] Don't humble yourself in front of him. Do you think he's your God? • **2.** to conquer, overcome – مُساعَدتَك راح تذَلِّل كُلّ الصُّعُوبات [musa:ʕadtak ra:ħ dðallil kull ʔiṣṣuʕu:ba:t] Your help will overcome all the difficulties.

تذَلَّل [dðallal] *v:* • **1.** to lower, humble oneself, be humble, cringe – شُوفَه شلُون يِتذَلَّل مِن يِحتاجَك [šu:fah šlu:n yidðallal min yiħta:ǰak] Look at how he humbles himself when he needs you. • **2.** to be overcome, be conquered – راح تِتذَلَّل كُلّ الصُّعُوبات أَمامِي [ra:ħ tidðallal kull ʔiṣṣuʕu:ba:t ʔama:mi] All the difficulties facing me will be overcome.

ذِلّ، ذُلّ [ðill, ðull] *n:* • **1.** subjugation, subjection, submission, humiliation – عِيشَة الذِّلّ ما تِنراد [ʕi:šat ʔiððill ma: tinra:d] A life of subjugation is unacceptable.

ذِلَّة [ðilla] *n:* • **1.** Lack of freedom is a humiliation عَدَم الإستِقلال ذِلَّة [ʕadam ʔilʔistiqla:l ðilla]

مَذَلَّة [maðalla] *n:* • **1.** humiliation

تَذلِيل [taðli:l] *n:* • **1.** getting over, ironing out, surmounting difficulties – تَذلِيل المَصاعِب [taðli:l ʔalmaṣa:ʕib]

ذَلِيل [ðali:l] *adj:* • **1.** low, down, depressed – سُوق الشَّعِير ذَلِيل [su:g ʔiššiʕi:r ðali:l] The barley market is depressed. • **2.** humble, submissive, servile, abject – شَعَب ذَلِيل [šaʕab ðali:l] a subservient people.

ذ م ر

تذَمَّر [dðammar] *v:* • **1.** to complain, grumble – دَيِتذَمَّر هوايَة مِن هالشُّغُل [dayidðammar hwa:ya min haššuɣul] He's grumbling a lot about this work.

تَذَمُّر [taðammur] *n:* • **1.** complaining, grumbling, griping

مِتذَمِّر [mitðammir] *adj:* • **1.** complainer

ذ م م

ذَمّ [ðamm] *v:* • **1.** to criticize, find fault with, damn – ياكُل عِدهُم وَيذِمّهُم [ya:kul ʕidhum wyðimmhum] He eats at their house and then finds fault with them. يذِمّ الأَكِل الأَورُبِّي [yðimm ʔilʔakil ʔilʔu:ruppi] He's always talking down European food.

ذَمّ [ðamm] *n:* • **1.** criticizing

ذِمَّة [ðimma] *n:* ذِمَم [ðimam] *pl:* • **1.** conscience – أَخَلِّيها يَمّ ذِمّتَك [ʔaxalli:ha yamm ðimmtak] I'll leave it to your discretion.

مَذَمَّة [maðamma] *n:* • **1.** censure, blame

مَذمُوم [maðmu:m] *adj:* • **1.** objectionable, reprehensible – آنِي مِثل السِّمَك، مَأكُول ومَذمُوم [ʔa:ni miθl ʔissimač, maʔku:l wmaðmu:m] I'm like the fish, eaten and then despised.

ذَمّاً [ðamman] *adverbial:* • **1.** derogatorily, disparagingly

ذ ن ب

أَذنَب [ʔaðnab] *v:* • **1.** to sin – إذا تِذنِب بِالدِّنيا تِتعَذَّب بِالآخِرَة [ʔiða tiðnib biddinya titʕaððab bilʔa:xira] If you sin in this life you will be tortured in the next life.

ذَنِب [ðanib] *n:* ذنُوب [ðnu:b] *pl:* • **1.** offense, sin, crime, misdeed • **2.** fault, error, mistake

ذِنبَة [ðinba] *n:* ذِنبات [ðinba:t] *pl:* • **1.** stinger (of an insect)

مُذَنَّب [muðannab] *n:* • **1.** comet

ذِنبايَة [ðinba:ya] *n:* • **1.** stinger of an insect

مُذنِب [muðnib] *adj:* • **1.** guilty • **2.** sinner

ذ ه ب

ذَهَّب [ðahhab] *v:* • **1.** to gild – إنطَيتَه صِينِيَّة الشّاي حَتَّى يذَهِّبها [ʔinṭi:tah ṣi:niyyat ʔičča:y ħatta yðahhibha] I gave him the tea tray to gild.

ذَهَب [ðahab] *n:* • **1.** gold – شدَعوَة الكِيلُو بدِينار! قابِل ذَهَب [šdaʕwa ʔilki:lu bdina:r! qa:bil ðahab] Imagine, a dinar a kilo! You'd think it was gold. شلُون خُوش وَلَد! ذَهَب [šlu:n xu:š walad! ðahab] What a good boy! He's a gem.

مَذهَب [maðhab] *n:* مَذاهِب [maða:hib] *pl:* • **1.** faith, denomination, religious creed • **2.** school of canonical law – بِمَذهَبَك، آنِي قِلِت شِي؟ [bmaðhabak, ʔa:ni gilit ši?] Honestly, did I say anything?

مذَهَّب، مذَهِّب [mðahhab, mðahhib] *adj:* • **1.** gilded – بَردَة مذَهِّبَة [parda mðahhiba] a gilded curtain.

ذَهَبِي [ðahabi] *adj:* • **1.** golden

مَذهَبِي [maðhabi] *adj:* • **1.** sectarian – تَعَصُّب مَذهَبِي [taʕaṣṣub maðhabi] sectarian bigotry.

ذ ه ل

ذِهَل [ðihal] *v:* • **1.** to amaze, astonish, astound, dumbfound – هَالصُّورَة تِذهِل اللِّي يشُوفها [haṣṣu:ra tiðhil ʔilli yšu:fha] This picture will astonish anyone who sees it. الفِلِم بِيه حَوادِث تِذهِل العَقِل [ʔilfilim bi:h ħawa:diθ tiðhil ʔilʕaqil] The film has events in it which stagger the imagination. • **2.** to frighten, scare – شِكِل هالحَيوان يِذهِل [šikil halħaywa:n yiðhil] This animal's looks are frightening.

أذهَل [ʔaðhal] *v:* • **1.** to astonish, dumbfound, amaze, astound – أذهَل المَحَلَّة كُلّها بجَرائِمَه [ʔaðhal ʔilmaħalla kullha bǰara:ʔimah] He terrorized the whole neighborhood with his crimes.

انذِهَل [ʔinðihal] *v:* • **1.** to be astonished – اِنذِهَلِت مِنَّه مِن طَبّ فُجأة [ʔinðihalit minnah min ṭabb fuǰʔa] I was frightened when he burst in. مِن سِمَع الخَبَر اِنذِهَل [min simaʕ ʔilxabar ʔinðihal] When he heard the news he was astonished.

مُذهِل [muðhil] *adj:* • **1.** staggering • **2.** astonishing

مَذهُول [maðhu:l] *adj:* • **1.** dumbfounded • **1.** astonished, stunned, amazed

مِنذِهِل [minðihil] *adj:* • **1.** startled

ذ ه ن

ذِهِن [ðihin] *n:* أذهان [ʔaðha:n] *pl:* • **1.** mind

ذ

ذِهني [ðihni] *adj:* • **1.** mental, intellectual – مَسأَلة رِياضِيَّة ذِهنِيَّة [masʔala riyaːd̩iyya ðihniyya] a perplexing mathematical problem. أَسئِلَة ذِهنِيَّة [ʔasʔila ðihniyya] questions requiring thought.

ذ و

ذات، بِالذّات [ðaːt, biððaːt] *n:* • **1.** self, ego – حُبّ الذّات [ħubb ʔiððaːt] egoism, self-love, selfishness. • **2.** -self – هُمَّ إِجَوا بِذاتهُم [humma ʔiǰaw bðaːthum] They came themselves. هُوَّ بِذاتَه. ماكُو أَحَّد يِشبَهَه [huwwa bðaːtah. maːku ʔaħħad yišbahah] It was he himself. There is no one that looks like him. بحَدّ ذات [bħadd ðaːt] by itself, in itself. السَّفَر بحَدّ ذاتَه مُفيد بَسّ مُتعِب [ʔissafar bħadd ðaːtah mufiːd bass mutʕib] Travelling in itself is beneficial but tiring. • **3.** conscience • **4.** with بـ- by itself, in itself

ذَوات، إِبن ذَوات [ðawaːt, ʔibin ðawaːt] *n:* • **1.** person from a prominent family

ذاتِي، حُكُم ذاتِي [ðaːti, ħukum ðaːti] *adj:* • **1.** autonomy, self-rule

ذاتِيَّة [ðaːtiyya] *adj:* • **1.** personnel – قِسِم الذّاتِيَّة [qisim ʔiððaːtiyya] personnel section.

ذاتاً [ðaːtan] *adverbial:* • **1.** anyway, anyhow

ذ و ب

ذاب [ðaːb] *v:* • **1.** to dissolve – كُلّ الشَّكَر ذاب بِالشّاي [kull ʔiššakar ðaːb biččaːy] All the sugar dissolved in the tea. • **2.** to melt – الثَّلِج كُلَّه ذاب [ʔiθθaliǰ kullah ðaːb] All the ice melted. ذابَت رُوحِي مِن الشَّمِس [ðaːbat ruːħi min ʔiššamis] I wilted from the sun. ذابَت رُوحِي مِن الجُوع [ðaːbat ruːħi min ʔiǰǰuːʕ] I became weak from hunger.

ذَوَّب [ðawwab] *v:* • **1.** to dissolve – ذَوِّب المِلِح بِهالكُوب [ðawwib ʔilmiliħ bhalkuːb] Dissolve the salt in this cup. • **2.** to melt – ذَوِّب الرَّصاص بِهالخاشُوقَة [ðawwib ʔirras̩aːs̩ bhalxaːšuːga] Melt the lead in this spoon. يذَوِّب القَلب هالجّاهِل [yðawwub ʔilgalub haǰǰaːhil] That kid's a pain in the neck.

ذَوَبان [ðawabaːn] *n:* • **1.** melting

ذ و ت

بَذّات [baððaːt] *adj:* • **1.** inconsiderate

ذ و ق [1]

ذاق [d̩aːg] *v:* • **1.** to taste, sample – ضاق المَرَق وَما قِبَل ياكُل [d̩aːg ʔilmarag wma qibal yaːkul] He tasted the stew and refused to eat. • **2.** to taste, experience, undergo, suffer, go through – ضاق الحِلو وَالمُرّ بحَياتَه [d̩aːg ʔilħilw wilmurr bħayaːtah] He tasted the sweet and the bitter in his lifetime. ضاقَت المُرّ بتَربِيتَه [d̩aːgat ʔilmurr btarbiːtah] She went through hell in raising him.

ذَوَّق [d̩awwag] *v:* • **1.** to give a taste of, let taste – راح أَطبُخ وَأذَوّقَك الطَّبُخ مالِي [raːħ ʔat̩bux waʔd̩awwgak ʔit̩t̩abux maːli] I'm going to cook and I'll give you a taste of my cooking.

ذوق [d̩uːg] *n:* • **1.** taste (in food)

ذوقَة [d̩uːga] *n:* ذوقات [d̩uːgaːt] *pl:* • **1.** tasting, experiencing (food)

ذ و ق [2]

اِستَذوَق [ʔistaðwaq] *v:* • **1.** to like, appreciate – ما يِستَذوِق الأَكِل بالمَطاعِم [maː yistaðwiq ʔilʔakil bilmat̩aːʕim] He doesn't like the food in restaurants. ما تِستَذوِق الفَصال الأَمرِيكِيَّة [maː tistaðwiq ʔilfas̩aːl ʔilʔamriːkiyya] She doesn't like American styles. اِستَذوَقِت الطَّبُخ مالها [ʔistaðwaqit ʔit̩t̩abux maːlha] I appreciated her cooking.

ذَوق [ðawq] *n:* • **1.** taste, manners, sense of propriety • **2.** taste, flavor • **3.** taste (clothing)

ذ ي ب

ذِيب [ðiːb] *n:* ذِياب [ðiyaːb] *pl:* • **1.** wolf

ذ ي ع

ذاع [ðaːʕ] *v:* • **1.** to spread, circulate – الخَبَر شِبساع ذاع! ما ظَلّ أَحَّد ما سِمعَه [ʔilxabar šibsaːʕ ðaːʕ! maː d̩all ʔaħħad maː simʕah] How fast the news spread! There's no one who hasn't heard it. • **2.** to broadcast, transmit – راح يذِيعُون الأَخبار ساعَة سِتَّة [raːħ yðiːʕuːn ʔilʔaxbaːr saːʕa sitta] They're going to broadcast the news at six o'clock.

اِنذاع [ʔinðaːʕ] *v:* • **1.** to be broadcast, transmitted – الأَخبار اِنذاعَت قَبُل ساعَة [ʔilʔaxbaːr ʔinðaːʕat gabul saːʕa] The news was broadcast an hour ago.

مُذِيع [muðiːʕ] *n:* • **1.** radio or television announcer

إِذاعَة [ʔiðaːʕa] *n:* • **1.** announcement, disclosure • **2.** broadcasting, radio – مَحَطَّة الإِذاعَة [maħat̩t̩at ʔilʔiðaːʕa] broadcasting station, transmitter station (radio and television). • **3.** pl. إذاعات broadcasting station

إِذاعِي [ʔiðaːʕi] *adj:* • **1.** radio (in compounds)

ذ ي ل

ذَيَّل [ðayyal] *v:* • **1.** to add on the end, add an appendage – دائِرَتنا ذَيِّلَت الكِتاب بطَلَب مُساعَدَة [daːʔiratna ðayyilat ʔilkitaːb bt̩alab musaːʕada] Our office attached an appendage to the letter with a request for assistance. ذَيِّل المَكتُوب بعِبارَة غَيِّرَت كُلّ المَعنَى [ðayyal ʔilmaktuːb bʕibaːra ɣayyirat kull ʔilmaʕna] He tacked on the end of the letter a clause changing the whole meaning. • **2.** (jocular) to fire, throw out of a job – صَدِيقِي ذَيِّلُوه البارحَة [s̩adiːqi ðayyiluːh ʔilbaːrħa] They fired my friend yesterday.

ذَيل [ðayl] *n:* ذيُول، ذيُولَة [ðyu:l, ðyu:la] *pl:* • **1.** tail (of an animal or bird, also of an airplane or kite) • **2.** hem, border (of a dress, skirt, or robe) • **3.** appendix (of a book) • **4.** (pl. only) ذيُول – ذيُول الثَّورَة [ðyu:l ʔiθθawra] the consequences of the revolution. أَشُو وَين ما أَرُوح تِلحَقنِي. شِنُو إِنتَ، قابِل ذَيلِي؟ [ʔašu: wayn ma: ʔaru:ħ tilħagni. šinu: ʔinta, qa:bil ðayli?] It seems wherever I go you follow me. What are you, my shadow?

ذِيال [ðiya:l] *n:* ذيالات [ðya:la:t] *pl:* • **1.** hem, border (of a dress, skirt, or robe) – شايلَة الطَّماطَة بِذيال عَبايَتها [ša:yla ʔiṭṭama:ṭa biðya:l ʕaba:yatha] She is carrying the tomatoes in the hem of her aba. الجَّهال مكَلِّبِين بِذيالات أُمَّهاتهُم حَتَّى لا يضِيعُون [ʔijjaha:l mčallibi:n biðya:la:t ʔummaha:thum ħatta la: yḏi:ʕu:n] The children are holding onto their mothers' coattails so they won't get lost.

ذوَيل [ðwayl] *n:* • **1.** tail (of an animal or bird, also of an airplane or kite) • **2.** hem, border of a dress, skirt, or robe. (diminutive form of ذَيل [ðwayl])

ر

ر

ر ء س

رِأَس [ri?as] *v:* • **1.** to lead, head, be in charge of – مِنو راح يِرأَس الجَمعِيَّة؟ [minu ra:ħ yir?as ?iǰǰamʕiyya?] Who's going to head the association?

رَأَّس [ra??as] *v:* • **1.** to appoint as leader, place in charge. heads – ما تقُلّي مِنو رَأَّسَك هنا؟ [ma: tgulli minu ra??asak hna?] Would you just tell me, who made you the boss around here?

ترَأَّس [tra??as] *v:* • **1.** to lead, head, be in charge of – مِنو ترَأَّس الوَفِد؟ [minu tra??as ?ilwafid?] Who headed the delegation?

راس [ra:s] *n:* رُؤُوس [ru?u:s, ru:s] *pl:* • **1.** head – يَعني قابِل يريد يِلعَب براسِي؟ [yaʕni qa:bil yri:d yilʕab bra:si?] You mean he thinks he's going to make a fool out of me? هَالقَضِيَّة مخَربُطَة؛ ما أعرُف راسها مِن كَعَبها [halqaðiyya mxarbuṭa; ma: ?aʕruf ra:sha min čaʕabha] This matter is confusing; I can't make heads or tails of it. بِنتَه إجَت عَلَى راس إبنَه [bintah ?iǰat ʕala ra:s ?ibnah] His daughter was born immediately after his son. عَلَى عِيني وراسِي [ʕala ʕi:ni wra:si] Very gladly, sir! At your service! Just as you say! عَلَى عِينِي وَراسِي. راح أسَوِّي مِثلما ترِيد [ʕala ʕi:ni wra:si. ra:ħ ?asawwi: miθilma tri:d] Certainly! I'll do as you wish. وراسَك العَزِيز [wra:sak ?ilʕazi:z] Honest! You can be sure! وراسَك العَزِيز، ما أعرُف [wra:sak ?ilʕazi:z, ma: ?aʕruf] Honestly, I don't know. لا تاخُذ كَلامَه راس [la: ta:xuð kala:mah ra:s] Don't take what he says seriously. • **2.** head (as a numerative of livestock) – كَم راس غَنَم عِندَك؟ [čam ra:s ɣanam ʕindak?] How many head of sheep do you have? • **3.** one, a single – راس خَسّ [ra:s xass] a head of lettuce. راس شَلغَم [ra:s šalɣam] one turnip. راس جِزَر [ra:s ǰizar] one carrot. راس باجَة [ra:s pa:ča] head, feet, and tripe from one animal. ما عِندِي جَهال؛ راسِي وَراس مَرتِي [ma: ʕindi ǰaha:l; ra:si wra:s marti] I have no children; there's only me and my wife. • **4.** tip, end – راس الخَشِم [ra:s ?ilxašim] the tip of the nose. راس السِّلّايَة [ra:s ?issilla:ya] the tip of the pen point. راس قَلَم [ra:s qalam] point of a pencil. رُؤُوس أقلام [ru?u:s ?aqla:m] notes. أخَذِت رُؤُوس أقلام بِالمُحاضَرَة [?axaðit ru?u:s ?aqla:m bilmuħa:ðara] I took notes in the lecture. رُؤُوس الإصابِع [ru?u:s ?il?iṣa:biʕ] tiptoes. لِيش دَتمِشِي عَلَى رُؤُوس أصابعَك؟ [li:š datimši ʕala ru?u:s ?aṣa:bʕak?] Why are you walking on tiptoe? • **5.** top, summit, peak – راس النَّخلَة [ra:s ?innaxla] the top of the palm tree. راس القائِمَة [ra:s ?ilqa:?ima] the top of the list. إترِس البُطِل لِلرّاس [?itris ?ilbuṭil lirra:s] Fill the bottle to the brim. إنطِينِي كِيلو طَماطَة مِن راس السَّلَّة [?inṭi:ni ki:lu ṭama:ṭa min ra:s ?issalla] Give me a kilo of tomatoes from the top of the basket. • **6.** end, extremity – راس الخيط [ra:s ?ilxi:ṭ] the end of the string. راس العَقِد [ra:s ?ilʕagid] the end of the alley, end of the lane. راس الشّارِع [ra:s ?išša:riʕ] end of the block, i.e., corner, intersection. • **7.** beginning – راس الشَّهَر [ra:s ?iššahar] the first of the month. راس السَّنَة [ra:s ?issana] the beginning of the year. إحكِيلِي كُلّشِي مِن الرّاس [?iħči:li kullši min ?irra:s] Tell me everything from the beginning.

رَأس [ra?s, ra:s] *n:* رُؤُوس [ru?u:s] *pl:* • **1.** cape, promontory, headland

رَئِيس [ra?i:s] *n:* رُؤَساء [ru?asa:, ru?asa:?] *pl:* • **1.** head, leader, chief, boss – رَئِيس العِصابَة [ra?i:s ?ilʕiṣa:ba] the leader of the gang. رَئِيس عُرَفاء [ra?i:s ʕurafa:?] master sergeant. رَئِيس تَحرِير الجَّرِيدَة [ra?i:s taħri:r ?iǰǰari:da] the editor in chief of the newspaper. • **2.** captain (mil.) – رَئِيس أوَّل [ra?i:s ?awwal] major. رَئِيس فِرقَة كُرَة القَدَم [ra?i:s firqat kurat ?ilqadam] captain of the football team. • **3.** president – رَئِيس الجَّمهُورِيَّة [ra?i:s ?iǰǰamhu:riyya] president of the republic. رَئِيس الوُزَراء، رَئِيس الوِزارَة [ra?i:s ?ilwuzara:?, ra?i:s ?ilwiza:ra] prime minister. رَئِيس البَلَدِيَّة [ra?i:s ?ilbaladiyya] chief of a municipality, mayor. رَئِيس أركان الجَّيش [ra?i:s ?arka:n ?iǰǰayš] army chief of staff.

رئاسَة، رياسَة [ri?a:sa, riya:sa] *n:* رِئاسات، رِياسات [ri?a:sa:t, riya:sa:t] *pl:* • **1.** premiership, prime ministry – رِئاسَة الوِزارَة [ri?a:sit ?ilwiza:ra] premiership, prime ministry.

رَأسمال [ra?sma:l, ra:sma:l] *n:* • **1.** capital, financial assets

رَأسمالِيَّة [ra?sma:liyya] *n:* • **1.** capitalism

رَئِيسِي [ra?i:si] *adj:* • **1.** leading, main, chief, principal – شارِع رَئِيسِي [ša:riʕ ra?i:si] a main street. دَور رَئِيسِي [dawr ra?i:si] a leading role.

مَرؤُوس [mar?u:s] *adj:* مَرؤُوسِين [mar?u:si:n] *pl:* • **1.** subordinate, underling

رَأسمالِي [ra?sma:li] *adj:* • **1.** capitalistic, capitalist • **2.** a capitalist

رَأساً [ra?san] *adverbial:* • **1.** directly, straight, straightaway – هَالطَّيّارَة ترُوح رَأساً لِبَغداد [haṭṭayya:ra tru:ħ ra?san lbayda:d] This plane goes directly to Baghdad. راح أوَدِّي السَّيّارَة لِلكَراج رَأساً [ra:ħ ?awaddi ?issayya:ra lilgara:ǰ ra?san] I'm going to take the car straight to the garage.

ر ء ف

رِأَف [ri?af] *v:* • **1.** to show pity, have mercy, be merciful – رِأَف بِيه وَما عاقبَه عالمُخالَفَة [ri?af bi:h wma ʕa:qabah ʕalmuxa:lafa] He took pity on him and didn't punish him for the violation.

رَأفَة [raʔfa] *n:* • **1.** mercy
رَؤُوف [raʔu:f] *adj:* • **1.** merciful, compassionate
أرأف [ʔarʔaf] *comparative adjective:* • **1.** more or most merciful, compassionate

ر ء و

رِئة، رِيَّة [riʔa, riyya] *n:* رِئات، رِيّات [riʔa:t, riyya:t] *pl:* • **1.** pneumonia – مَرَض ذات الرِّئة [marað ða:t ʔirriʔa] • **2.** lung
رِئوي [riʔawi] *adj:* • **1.** of the lung, pulmonary

ر ء ي

رَأي [raʔy] *n:* آراء [ʔa:ra:ʔ] *pl:* • **1.** opinion, view
رايَة [ra:ya] *n:* رايات [ra:ya:t] *pl:* • **1.** banner, flag
مرايَة [mra:ya] *n:* مِري، مرايات [miri, mra:ya:t] *pl:* • **1.** the behind – مرايَة الظَّهَر [mra:yat ʔiððahar] • **2.** mirror
مُرائي [mura:ʔi] *adj:* مُرائِين [mura:ʔi:n] *pl:* • **1.** hypocrite
تَرَة [tara] *int:* • **1.** or, or else, otherwise – أُوقَف، تَرَة أرميك [ʔu:gaf, tara ʔarmi:k] Stop or I'll shoot! لا تِتقَرَّب يَمّ الكَلِب، تَرَة يعَضَّك [la: titgarrab yamm ʔiččalib, tara yʕaððak] Don't go near the dog or else he'll bite you. لا تِشتِري هَالسَّيّارَة، تَرَة تِتوَرَّط بِيها [la: tištiri hassayya:ra, tara titwarraṭ bi:ha] Don't buy this car, or you'll have trouble with it. • **2.** since, because – لا تشُوف هَالفِلِم، تَرَة ما يِسوَى [la: tšu:f halfilim, tara ma: yiswa:] Don't see that film, because it is not worth it. • **3.** I tell you, I warn you, mind you – إذا ما تِنطِيني الفلُوس تَرَة أشتِكِي عَلِيك [ʔiða ma: tinṭi:ni ʔilflu:s tara ʔaštiki ʕali:k] If you don't give me the money, I warn you I'm going to sue. تَرَة ما أرِيدَك تِحكِي وِيّاه [tara ma: ʔari:dak tiħči wiyya:h] Mind you, I don't want you to talk with him. • **4.** well, well then, well now, so – تَرَة اليُوم جُمعَة. إنطِينِي الفلُوس مِثلما وُعَدِت [tara ʔilyu:m ǰumʕa. ʔinṭi:ni ʔilflu:s miθilma wuʕadit] Well, today's Friday. Give me the money like you promised. • **5.** actually, after all – تَرَة صُدُق هَذا خُوش وَلَد [tara ṣudug ha:ða xu:š walad] You know, he really is a good fellow.
ريت، يا ريت [ri:t, ya: ri:t] *pseudo-verb:* • **1.** I wish.. ! How nice it would be if.! Would that ! – رَيت ذِيك الأيّام تِرجَع [rayt ði:č ʔilʔayya:m tirǰaʕ] I wish those days would return. رَيتَك هنا [raytak hna] I wish you were here.

ر ب ب

رَبّ [rabb] *n:* أرباب، ربُوب [ʔarba:b, rbu:b] *pl:* • **1.** refined gentleman, well-liked, respected man – رَبّ العائِلَة [rabb ʔilʕa:ʔila] the head of the family. يا رَبِّي، هاي شلُون بَلوَة [ya: rabbi, ha:y šlu:n balwa] My God, what a calamity! الله رَبَّك؛ المُدِير أخُوك [ʔallah rabbak; ʔilmudi:r ʔaxu:k] God looks after you; the director's your brother. وَلَد أرباب [walad ʔarba:b] refined gentleman, well-liked, respected man. • **1.** the Lord, God
مرَبَّى [mrabba] *n:* مرَبّات، مرَبّايات [mrabba:t, mrabba:ya:t] *pl:* • **1.** jam, preserves, jelly
رُبّان [rubba:n] *n:* • **1.** captain (of ships), pilot
ربابَة [rba:ba, rubba:ba] *n:* ربابات، ربايِب [rba:ba:t, rba:yib] *pl:* • **1.** rebec, a stringed musical instrument resembling the fiddle • **2.** headache, bother – هاي شلُون ربابَة! ما أرِيد أرُوح لِلسِّينَما [ha:y šlu:n rba:ba! ma: ʔari:d ʔaru:ħ lissinama] What a pain in the neck! I don't want to go to the movies. لازِم أرُوح لِلمَكتَبَة، وادَوُّر عالكتاب. هاي ربابَة؛ أسهَلِّي أشترِيه [la:zim ʔaru:ħ lilmaktaba, wadawwur ʕalkta:b. ha:y rba:ba; ʔashalli ʔaštiri:h] I'll have to go to the library and look for the book. That's a bother; it's easier for me to buy it. • **3.** pl. ربايِب long, drawn-out affair
رَبّاني [rabba:ni] *adj:* • **1.** divine – عَمَل رَبّانِي [ʕamal rabba:ni] act of God.
رُبَّما [rubbama] *adv:* • **1.** perhaps, maybe, possibly – رُبَّما تأَخّرَوا بِالطَّرِيق [rubbama tʔaxxraw biṭṭari:q] Perhaps they got delayed on the way.

ر ب ح

رُبَح [rubaħ] *v:* • **1.** to gain, profit – أفرُض يمُوت. إنتَ شتِربَح؟ [ʔufruð ymu:t. ʔinta štirbaħ?] Assume he dies. What would you gain? رُبَح بِهالصَّفقَة عِشرِين دِينار [rubaħ bhaṣṣafqa ʕišri:n dina:r] He made twenty dinars on that deal. • **2.** to win – البِطاقَة رَقَم عِشرِين رُبحَت دِينار واحِد [ʔilbiṭa:qa raqam ʕišri:n rubħat dina:r wa:ħid] Ticket number twenty won one dinar. رُبَح ألف دِينار بِالقمار البارحَة [rubaħ ʔalf dina:r bilqma:r ʔilba:rħa] He won a thousand dinars gambling yesterday.
رَبَّح [rabbaħ] *v:* • **1.** to grant a profit, to allow to profit – الله يرَبّحَك بِهالبِيعَة [ʔallah yrabbħak bhalbi:ʕa] God grant that you profit from this sale.
رِبِح [ribiħ] *n:* أرباح [ʔarba:ħ] *pl:* • **1.** profit, gain • **2.** interest (on money) • **3.** winnings
رابِح [ra:biħ] *n:* • **1.** profitable, lucrative, gainful • **2.** pl. رابِحِين gainer, winner, profiter
مُربِح [murbiħ] *adj:* • **1.** profitable
رَبحان [rabħa:n] *adj:* رَبحانِين [rabħa:ni:n] *pl:* • **1.** gainer, winner, profiter
أربَح [ʔarbaħ] *comparative adjective:* • **1.** more or most profitable, lucrative

ر ب د

رَبُد [rabud] *n:* ربُود [rbu:d] *pl:* • **1.** pointed stick, stake • **1.** piece
رَبدَة، حِسّ رَبدَة [rabda, ħiss rabda] *n:* • **1.** clattering, banging, rattling noise

ر ب ر ب

رَبرَب [rabrab] *v:* • **1.** to complain vociferously, make a fuss – مِن ما لِقَى عَشا، قام يرَبرُب [min ma: liga: ʕaša, ga:m yrabrub] When he didn't find any supper, he started raising hell.

ر ب ط

رُبَط [rubaṭ] *v:* • **1.** to bind, tie up – أربُط الكُتُب بهَالخيط [ʔurbuṭ ʔilkutub bhalxi:ṭ] Tie up the books with this string. • **2.** to tie, fasten, attach, hitch – وين تريدِني أربُط الحصان؟ [wi:n tri:dni ʔarbuṭ ʔilħṣa:n?] Where do you want me to hitch the horse? أُربُط الخَرُوف بِالشَّجرَة [ʔurbuṭ ʔilxaru:f biššijra] Tie the sheep to the tree. • **3.** to connect – بِنَوا جِسِر بِبَغداد يربُط قِطار كَركُوك بقِطار البَصرَة [binaw ǰisir bibayda:d yirbuṭ qiṭa:r karku:k bqiṭa:r ʔilbaṣra] They built a bridge in Baghdad to connect the Kirkuk railroad with the Basra railroad. • **4.** to attach, annex – راح يِفُصلُون دائِرَتنا مِن وزارَة الزِّراعَة وَيِربُطوها بوزارَة التِّجارَة [ra:ħ yifuṣlu:n da:ʔiratna min wiza:rat ʔizzira:ʕa wyirubṭu:ha bwiza:rat ʔittiǰa:ra] They're going to detach our office from the Ministry of Agriculture and attach it to the Ministry of Commerce.

رابَط [ra:baṭ] *v:* • **1.** to hang around

انرُبَط [ʔinrubaṭ] *v:* • **1.** to be tied

اِرتُبَط [ʔirtubaṭ] *v:* • **1.** to bind oneself, commit oneself – اِرتُبَط بمَوعِد قَبِل ما يقُلِّي [ʔirtubaṭ bmawʕid gabil ma: ygulli] He got tied up with an appointment before he spoke to me.

رَبُط [rabuṭ] *n:* • **1.** binding, tying – بِيدَه الحَلّ وَالرَّبُط [bi:dah ʔilħall wʔirrabuṭ] He has absolute power (lit., in his hands is the untying and the tying). ما يفيد تِحكِي وِيّاه؛ الحَلّ وَالرَّبُط بايد مَرتَه [ma: yfi:d tiħči wiyya:h; ʔilħall wʔirrabuṭ bʔi:d martah] It won't do you any good to talk to him. She's the one who makes the decisions. • **2.** connecting, connection – حَكيَه ما بيه رَبُط [ħačyah ma: bi:h rabuṭ] His words don't make sense. تَعلِيقَك ما كان إلَه رَبُط [taʕli:qak ma: ča:n ʔilah rabuṭ] Your comment was irrelevant.

رَبطَة [rabṭa] *n:* رَبطات [rabṭa:t] *pl:* • **1.** bunch, bale, bundle • **2.** necktie

ربيط [rbi:ṭ] *n:* رِبَيطِيَّة [rbayṭiyya] *pl:* • **1.** an animal penned up for fattening

رباط [riba:ṭ] *n:* أربِطَة [ʔarbiṭa] *pl:* • **1.** necktie

رَبّاط [rabba:ṭ] *n:* • **1.** truss (supportive device)

رابِطَة [ra:biṭa] *n:* رَوابِط [rawa:biṭ] *pl:* • **1.** bond, tie – رَوابِط صَداقَة [rawa:biṭ ṣada:qa] bonds of friendship. • **2.** league, union, association – رابِطَة الطُّلّاب العَرَب [ra:biṭat ʔiṭṭulla:b ʔilʕarab] Arab Students League.

اِرتِباط [ʔirtiba:ṭ] *n:* اِرتِباطات [ʔirtiba:ṭa:t] *pl:* • **1.** connection, engagement • **2.** bond, binding

مُرابَطَة [mura:baṭa] *n:* • **1.** hanging around

مرَبَّط [mrabbaṭ] *adj:* • **1.** tied, connected

مِرتبُط [mirtibuṭ] *adj:* • **1.** committed, tied up, tied down – مِرتبُط بمَوعِد [mirtibuṭ bmawʕid] tied up with an appointment.

مَربُوط [marbu:ṭ] *adj:* • **1.** tied, connected

مرابُط [mra:buṭ] *adj:* • **1.** persistent

ر ب ع

رَبَّع [rabbaʕ] *v:* • **1.** to square – رَبُّع هَالعَدَد [rabbuʕ halʕadad] Square this number.

تربَّع [trabbaʕ] *v:* • **1.** to sit cross-legged – مِن يُقعُد عَالزُّولِيَّة، يِترَبَّع [min yugʕud ʕazzu:liyya, yitrabbaʕ] When he sits on the rug, he crosses his legs.

رَبُع [rabuʕ] *n:* • **1.** (group of) friends – عِندَه رَبُع هوايَة [ʕindah rabuʕ hwa:ya] He has a lot of friends. تصالَحنا وَصِرنا رَبُع [tṣa:laħna wṣirna rabuʕ] We made up and became buddies. جِيب رَبعَك وَأني أجِيب رَبعِي وخَلِّي نِلعَب [ǰi:b rabʕak waʔani ʔaǰi:b rabʕi wxalli: nilʕab] You bring your gang and I'll bring my gang and let's play.

رُبُع [rubuʕ] *n:* أرباع [ʔarba:ʕ] *pl:* • **1.** quarter, one-fourth, fourth part – ثلاث أرباع السّاعَة [tlatt ʔarba:ʕ ʔissa:ʕa] three quarter of an hour. رُبُع فِستِق [rubuʕ fistiq] a quarter kilo of pistachios. رُبُع عَرَق [rubuʕ ʕarag] a quarter liter bottle of arrack.

رَبيع [rabi:ʕ] *n:* • **1.** spring, springtime – رَبِيع الأوَّل [rabi:ʕ ʔilʔawwal] Rabia I, third month of the Moslem calendar. رَبِيع الثّانِي [rabi:ʕ ʔiθθa:ni] Rabia II, fourth month of the Moslem calendar.

ربيع [ribi:ʕ] *n:* • **1.** plenitude, abundance, sufficiency – واقِع بِربِيع [wa:giʕ bribi:ʕ] He's got it made. He's in high cotton.

أربَعَة [ʔarbaʕa] *n:* أربَعات [ʔarbaʕa:t] *pl:* • **1.** four

تَربيع [tarbi:ʕ] *n:* • **1.** squaring (a number) • **2.** floor tiling, flooring

أربَعِين [ʔarbaʕi:n] *n:* • **1.** forty

أربِعاء، يوم الأربِعاء [ʔarbiʕa:ʔ, yu:m ʔilʔarbaʕa:ʔ] *n:* • **1.** Wednesday

رابِع [ra:biʕ] *adj:* • **1.** fourth (ordinal)

مُرَبَّع [murabbaʕ] *adj:* • **1.** squared, square – عِشرِين مَتِر مُرَبَّع [ʕišri:n matir murabbaʕ] twenty square meters. • **2.** square (math.) • **3.** pl. مُرَبَّعات square (geom.)

رَبِيعِي [rabi:ʕi] *adj:* • **1.** spring – العُطلَة الرَّبِيعِيَّة [ʔilʕuṭla ʔirrabi:ʕiyya] spring vacation.

رُباعِي [ruba:ʕi] *adj:* • **1.** quadri-partite, consisting of four • **2.** (gram.) consisting of four radical letters, quadriliteral

مَربُوع [marbu:ʕ] *adj:* مَربُوعِين [marbu:ʕi:n] *pl:* • **1.** medium sized with broad shoulders

تَربِيعِي [tarbi:ʕi] *adj:* • **1.** square, quadratic – جَذِر تَربِيعِي [ǰaðir tarbi:ʕi] square root (math.).

ر ب ك

رِبَك [ribak] *v:* • **1.** to confuse – لا تِربِكنِي؛ خَلِّينِي أَحسِب [la: tirbikni; xalli:ni ʔaħsib] Don't confuse me; let me count.

أَربَك [ʔarbak] *v:* • **1.** to confuse

اِرتِبَك [ʔirtibak] *v:* • **1.** to become confused – اِرتِبَكِت بالإِمتِحان وَما قدَرت أَجاوُب زين [ʔirtibakit bilʔimtiħa:n wma gdarit ʔaǰa:wub zi:n] I got confused on the examination and couldn't answer properly.

رَبِك [rabik] *n:* • **1.** confusion, disconcertion

اِرتِباك [ʔirtiba:k] *n:* • **1.** confusion

مُربِك [murbik] *adj:* • **1.** confusing

مِرتبِك [mirtibik] *adj:* • **1.** confused

ر ب و

رُبَى [ruba:] *v:* • **1.** to grow, grow up – رُبَى ويّا العُربان وَتعَلَّم عاداتهُم [ruba: wiyya ʔilʕurba:n wtʕallam ʕa:da:thum] He grew up with the tribes and learned their customs.

رَبَّى [rabba:] *v:* • **1.** to cause to grow, let grow – دَيرَبِّيلَه شوارُب حَتَّى يكَوِّنلَه شَخصِيَّة [dayrabbi:lah šwa:rub ħatta ykawwinlah šaxṣiyya] He's growing himself a mustache to give himself a personality. • **2.** to raise, rear, bring up – رَبَّى جهالَه زين [rabba: ǰha:lah zi:n] He raised his children well. • **3.** to raise, breed – هَالدِّجاج مرَبَّى عَلَى حُنطَة وَشعِير [haddiǰa:ǰ mrabba ʕala ħunṭa wšʕi:r] These chickens have been raised on wheat and barley. • **4.** to strengthen, give added vigor – هَالدُّوا يرَبِّي القَلب [hadduwa yrabbi ʔilgalub] This medicine will strengthen the heart.

تَرَبَّى [trabba:] *v:* • **1.** to be raised, reared, brought up – عَلِي ترَبَّى وِيّانا [ʕali trabba: wiyya:na] Ali was raised with us.

رَبُو [rabw] *n:* • **1.** asthma

رِبَة [riba] *n:* • **1.** upbringing, raising, • **2.** breeding

رِبا [riba:] *n:* • **1.** interest, usury

تَربِيَة [tarbiya] *n:* • **1.** raising, rearing, bringing up • **2.** manners, breeding, civility • **3.** education, teaching, pedagogy • **4.** breeding, raising (of animals)

مُرَبِّيَة [murabbiya] *n:* مُرَبِّيات [murabbiya:t] *pl:* • **1.** nurse-maid • **2.** governess

مُرابِي [mura:bi] *n:* • **1.** loan shark • **1.** usurer

مرَبَّى [mrabba:] *adj:* • **1.** raised, brought up

تَربَوِي [tarbawi] *adj:* • **1.** educational

مِترَبِّي [mitrabbi] *adj:* • **1.** polite, well raised

ر ت ب

رَتَّب [rattab] *v:* • **1.** to arrange, put in order, organize – رَتِّب هالبِطاقات حَسَب الحُرُوف الهَجائِيَّة [rattib halbiṭa:qa:t ħasab ʔilħuru:f ʔilhaǰa:ʔiyya] Arrange these cards alphabetically. رَتِّب غُرفَة الخُطّار [rattib ɣurfat ʔilxuṭṭa:r] Straighten up the guest room. تِلبَس هِدُوم رِخِيصَة لَكِن تُعرُف ترَتِّب نَفِسها وَتِطلَع حِلوَة [tilbas hidu:m rixi:ṣa la:kin tuʕruf trattib nafisha wtiṭlaʕ ħilwa] She wears cheap clothes but she knows how to fix herself up and look nice. • **2.** to arrange, prepare – رَتَّبِت كُلّشِي. إحنا نِبقى هنا وهُمَّة يجُون ساعَة خَمسَة [rattabit kullši. ʔiħna nibqa: hna: whumma yiǰu:n sa:ʕa xamsa] I arranged everything. We stay here and they will come at five o'clock. رَتِّبلَك عُذُر زين تَرَة زَعلان [rattiblak ʕuður zayn tara zaʕla:n] Make up a good excuse for yourself because he's mad.

تَرَتَّب [trattab] *v:* • **1.** to be arranged, put in order – هَالأوراق أَبَد ما تِترَتَّب [halʔawra:q ʔabad ma: titrattab] These papers can't be arranged at all. • **2.** to be the result or consequence – تُعرُف شراح يِترَتَّب عَلَى عَمَلَك هَذا؟ [tuʕruf šra:ħ yitrattab ʕala ʕamalak ha:ða?] Do you know what's going to result from this action of yours?

رُتبَة [rutba] *n:* رُتَب [rutab] *pl:* • **1.** rank (mil.)

راتِب [ra:tib] *n:* رَواتِب [rawa:tib] *pl:* • **1.** salary, pay

تَرتِيب [tarti:b] *n:* • **1.** order, arrangement – حِلّ هالمَسائِل بِالتَّرتِيب [ħill halmasa:ʔil bittarti:b] Solve the problems in order. • **2.** pl. تَرتِيبات layout

مَرتَبَة [martaba] *n:* • **1.** level • **1.** grade, rank

مرَتَّب [mrattab] *adj:* • **1.** orderly, neat

ر ت ل

رَتَّل [rattal] *v:* • **1.** to recite the Koran

تَرَتَّل [trattal] *v:* • **1.** to be recited

رَتِل [ratil] *n:* أَرتال [ʔarta:l] *pl:* • **1.** column (of soldiers, etc), convoy – الرَّتل الخامِس [ʔirratl ʔilxa:mis] the fifth column.

رَتلَة [ratla] *n:* • **1.** mispronouncing the letter 'R' (speech impediment)

مُرَتِّل [murattil] *n:* • **1.** reciter of the Koran • **2.** chanter

رتيلَة [rti:la] *n:* رتِيلات [rti:la:t] *pl:* • **1.** harvestman (type of arachnid), daddy long-legs spider

تَرتِيل [tarti:l] *n:* تراتِيل [tra:ti:l] *pl:* • **1.** chanting, chanting manner of Koranic recitation

ر ت و ش

رِتُوش [ritu:š] *n:* • **1.** retouching (phot.)

ر ث ي

رِثَى [riθa:] *v:* • **1.** to elegize, lament, bewail – رِثَى الوَزِير المَرحُوم بِقَصِيدَة فَخمَة [riθa: ʔilwazi:r ʔilmarħu:m bqaṣi:da faxma] He elegized the deceased minister with a magnificent poem. • **2.** to pity, feel sorry – آنِي أَرثِي لِحال هالفَقِير [ʔa:ni ʔarθi lilħa:l halfaqi:r] I'm sorry about this poor man's situation.

رِثاء [riθa:ʔ] *n:* • **1.** lamentation

مُرثِي [murθi] *adj:* • **1.** pitiable

ر ج ب

رَجَب [raǰab] *n:* • **1.** Rajab, seventh month of the Moslem calendar

ر ج ج

رَجّ [rajj] *v:* • **1.** to convulse, shake, rock – الطُّلّاب رَجّوا الوِلايَة بِالمُظاهَرات [ʔiṭṭullaːb rajjaw ʔilwilaːya bilmuðaːharaːt] The students shook the city with their demonstrations.

اِرتَجّ [ʔirtajj] *v:* • **1.** to be convulsed, shake, tremble, quake – اِرتَجَّت الوِلايَة مِن أصوات المَدافِع [ʔirtajjat ʔilwilaːya min ʔaṣwaːt ʔilmadaːfiʕ] The city shook from the noise of the cannons.

رَجّ [rajj] *n:* • **1.** shaking

ر ج ح

See also: م ر ج ح

رَجَّح [rajjaħ] *v:* • **1.** to prefer, favor, consider preferable – آني أرَجِّح تخَلِّص شُغلَك قَبُل ما تِطلَع [ʔaːni ʔarajjiħ txalliṣ šuɣulak gabul maː tiṭlaʕ] I prefer that you finish your work before you leave.

راجِح [raːjiħ] *adj:* • **1.** preferable • **2.** probable, likely • **3.** heavy, generous, more than fair (of a merchant's weight) – إنطاك وَزِن راجِح [ʔinṭaːk wazin raːjiħ] He gave you more than a fair amount.

مُرَجَّح [murajjaħ] *adj:* • **1.** favored, preferred, probable

أرجَح [ʔarjaħ] *comparative adjective:* • **1.** more or most probable – عالأرجَح، يُوصَل اليُوم بالليل [ʕalʔarjaħ, yuːṣal ʔilyuːm billayl] Most probably, he will arrive tonight.

ر ج ع

رِجَع [rijaʕ] *v:* • **1.** to return, come back, come again – راح أرجَع بَعد شوَيَّة [raːħ ʔarjaʕ baʕd šwayya] I'll return after a while. لا تِجي ويّانا. إرجَع [laː tiji wiyyaːna. ʔirjaʕ] Don't come with us. Go back! إرجَع لوَرا [ʔirjaʕ lwara] Move back! رِجَع لِعَقلَه وَجاز مِن القمار [rijaʕ lʕaqlah wjaːz min ʔilqmaːr] He came to his senses and quit gambling. وُقَع بأوَّل ضَربَة، لَكِن قام ورجَعلَه ببُوكس [wugaʕ bʔawwal ðarba, laːkin gaːm wrijaʕlah bibuːks] He fell from the first blow but then he got up and retaliated with a punch. • **2.** to recur, come back, return – المَرَض رِجَع عَلَيّا [ʔilmarað rijaʕ ʕalayya] My sickness recurred. هَمّ رِجَع البَرِد [hamm rijaʕ ʔilbarid] Cold weather is back again. بِالصَّيف يِتلَف، لَكِن بِالشِّتا تِرجَع صِحّتَه [biṣṣayf yitlaf, laːkin biššita tirjaʕ ṣiħħtah] In the summer he gets run down but in the winter his health returns. رِجَع واهسَه بِالشِّطرَنج [rijaʕ waːhsah biššiṭranj] His interest in chess returned. • **3.** to begin again, resume, recommence – رِجَع عَلَى سوالفَه العَتيقَة [rijaʕ ʕala swaːlfah ʔilʕatiːga] He resumed his old stories. • **4.** to return to, revert to, go back to, become again – مِن تزَوَّج، رِجَع شَباب [min tzawwaj, rijaʕ šabaːb] When he got married, he became young again. إذا تغِسلَه بِهالصّابُون، يِرجَع أبيَض [ʔiða tɣislah bhaṣṣaːbuːn, yirjaʕ ʔabyað] If you wash it with this soap, it'll turn white again. كُلّما يِكبَر، يِرجَع لوَرا [kullma yikbar, yirjaʕ lwara] The older he gets, the more he regresses. • **5.** to be traceable, go back – أصلَه يِرجَع لِهارُون الرَّشيد [ʔaṣlah yirjaʕ lhaːruːn ʔirrašiːd] His ancestry goes back to Harun al Rashid. • **6.** to derive power from, rely on, depend on – شما يريد، سَوّي! هَذا يِرجَع لِلوَزير [šma yriːd, sawwiː! haːða yirjaʕ lilwaziːr] Whatever he wants, do! He's backed up by the minister. • **7.** with عَن to go back on, revoke, countermand – آني وافقِت وَما راح أرجَع عَن رَأيي [ʔaːni waːfaqit wma raːħ ʔarjaʕ ʕan raʔyi] I agreed and I'm not going to change my opinion. رِجَع عَن كَلامَه [rijaʕ ʕan kalaːmah] He went back on his word.

رَجَّع [rajjaʕ] *v:* • **1.** to return, give back – أرجُوك رَجِّعلي كتابي [ʔarjuːk rajjiʕli ktaːbi] Please return my book to me. هَالقاط ما دَيعجِبني؛ راح أرَجّعَه [halqaːṭ maː dayiʕjibni; raːħ ʔarajjʕah] I don't like this suit; I'm going to take it back. رَجّعَولِنا التِّلِفُون بَعَد ما دِفَعنا الفلُوس [rajjʕawlna ʔittilifuːn baʕad maː difaʕna ʔilfluːs] They reinstalled the telephone after we paid the money. الأكِل الزّين رَجَّعلي قُوتي [ʔilʔakil ʔizziːn rajjaʕli quːti] The good food gave me back my strength. رَجَّعلَه ضَربَة بِضَربَة [rajjaʕlah ðarba bðarba] He returned him punch for punch. • **2.** to bring back, take back, return – إذا أرُوح وِيّاك، لازِم ترَجِّعني بِسَيّارتَك [ʔiða ʔaruːħ wiyyaːk, laːzim trajjiʕni bsayyaːrtak] If I go with you, you'll have to bring me back in your car. صاح عَليه ورَجَّع عَقلَه بِراسَه [ṣaːħ ʕaliːh wrajjaʕ ʕaqlah braːsah] He shouted at him and brought him to his senses. اِستَعمِل هَالدُّوا؛ يرَجّعَك جاهِل [ʔistaʕmil hadduwa; yrajjʕak jaːhil] Take this medicine; it will make a young man of you. • **3.** to put back, return – رَجّعُوني لِوَظيفتي السّابقَة [rajjʕuːni lwaðiːfti ʔissaːbqa] They returned me to my previous position. رَجّعُوه إلَى رُتبَة رَئيس [rajjʕuːh ʔila rutbat raʔiːs] They reinstated him in the rank of captain. مِن يِلعَب شِطرَنج يرَجّع [min yilʕab šiṭranj yrajjiʕ] When he plays chess, he takes his moves back. • **4.** to take back – مِن نبيع شِي، بَعَد ما نرَجّعَه [min nbiːʕ ši, baʕad maː nrajjʕah] Once we sell something, we don't take it back. • **5.** to move back, set back – رَجِّع الكُرسي مالَك لوَرا شوَيَّة [rajjiʕ ʔilkursi maːlak lwara šwayya] Move your chair back a little. رَجَّع السّاعَة مالتَه عَشِر دَقايِق [rajjaʕ ʔissaːʕa maːltah ʕašir daqaːyiq] He set his watch back ten minutes.

راجَع [raːjaʕ] *v:* • **1.** to consult, ask, check with – ما أريدَك تِنطِي أيّ جَواب لأحَّد قَبُل ما تراجِعني [maː ʔariːdak tinṭi ʔayy jawaːb lʔaħħad gabul maː traːjiʕni] I don't want you to give an answer to anybody without consulting me. راجَعِت عِدَّة أطِبّاء لَكِن مَحَّد عِرَف شِنُو مَرَضي [raːjaʕit ʕiddat ʔaṭibbaːʔ laːkin maħħad ʕiraf šinu marað̣i] I consulted several doctors but no one found out what my disease was. راجِع شُعبَة الذّاتيَّة [raːjiʕ šuʕbat ʔiððaːtiyya] Check with personnel section.

راجِعني باكِر بالدّائِرَة [raːǰiʕni baːčir biddaːʔira] Check with me tomorrow in the office. راجِع عَقلَك قَبُل ما تقرِّر [raːǰiʕ ʕaqlak gabul maː tqarrir] Think it over before you decide. راجَعِت الكِتاب مَرّتَين قَبِل الامتِحان [raːǰaʕit ʔilkitaːb marrtayn gabil ʔilʔimtiħaːn] I went over the book twice before the exam. • **2.** to check, verify, examine critically – المُؤَلِّف ما طَبَع الكِتاب إلّا بَعَد ما راجَعَه مُؤَلِّف آخَر [ʔilmuʔallif maː ṭubaʕ ʔilkitaːb ʔilla baʕad maː raːǰaʕah muʔallif ʔaːxar] The author didn't print the book until after another author had reviewed it. راجَعت الحساب وَما لِقَيت أَيّ غَلَط [raːǰaʕt ʔilħsaːb wma ligiːt ʔayy ɣalaṭ] I checked the accounts and didn't find any error.

تَرَجَّع [traǰǰaʕ] *v:* • **1.** to be returned, to be moved back

تراجَع [traːǰaʕ] *v:* • **1.** to consult, confer – يِتراجَع ويّا المُدير بكُلّ قَضِيَّة مُهِمَّة [yitraːǰaʕ wiyya ʔilmudiːr bkull qaðiyya muhimma] He confers with the director on every important matter. • **2.** to withdraw, retreat, fall back, back off – جيش العَدُو تراجَع مِيَّة مِيل [ǰayš ʔilʕadu traːǰaʕ miyyat miːl] The enemy army retreated a hundred miles. • **3.** with – عَن to go back on, rescind, countermand, revoke – ما دَيِقبَل يِتراجَع عَن قَرارَه [maː dayiqbal yitraːǰaʕ ʕan qaraːrah] He won't agree to go back on his decision.

اِستَرجَع [ʔistarǰaʕ] *v:* • **1.** to get back, recover, regain – اِستَرجِعَوا مِنَّه جَميع المَبالِغ [ʔistarǰiʕaw minnah ǰamiːʕ ʔilmabaːliɣ] They recovered all the money from him.

رَجعَة [rajʕa] *n:* رَجعات [rajʕaːt] *pl:* • **1.** return, return trip

مَرجِع [marǰiʕ] *n:* مَراجِع [maraːǰiʕ] *pl:* • **1.** source, source material, authoritative reference work • **2.** immediate superior in a chain of command, authority one turns to

رُجوع [rujuːʕ] *n:* • **1.** returning

تَرجيع [tarǰiːʕ] *n:* • **1.** return

تَراجُع [taraːǰuʕ] *n:* • **1.** retreat • **2.** change of mind

إرجاع [ʔirǰaːʕ] *n:* • **1.** refundment, return

مُراجَعَة [muraːǰaʕa] *n:* مُراجَعات [muraːǰaʕaːt] *pl:* • **1.** review, reiteration, going over

اِسترجاع [ʔistirǰaːʕ] *n:* • **1.** retraction, retrieval

رَجعي [rajʕi] *adj:* • **1.** reactionary

مُرَجَّع [muraǰǰaʕ] *adj:* • **1.** (adj.) round-trip – تِكِت مُرَجَّع [tikit muraǰǰaʕ] a round-trip ticket.

رَجعِيَّة [rajʕiyya] *n:* • **1.** reactionism, reaction

مُراجِع [muraːǰiʕ] *adj:* مُراجِعين [muraːǰiʕiːn] *pl:* • **1.** petitioner, consulter, person who has business with an official • **2.** (doctor's) patient • **3.** petitioner, person who has business with an official

مَرجُوع [marǰuːʕ] *adj:* • **1.** returned, given back

ر ج ف

رِجَف [riǰaf] *v:* • **1.** to tremble, shiver, shudder, shake – الجّاهِل دَيِرجِف مِن البَرد [ʔiǰǰaːhil dayirǰif min ʔilbarid] The child is shivering from the cold. مِن يصير عَصَبي يِرجِف [min yṣiːr ʕaṣabi yirǰif] When he becomes angry he trembles.

اِنرِجَف [ʔinriǰaf] *v:* • **1.** to be made to shiver, to be shaken

رَجِف [rajif] *n:* • **1.** quaver

رَجفَة [rajfa] *n:* • **1.** quaver • **2.** shiver

رِجَّيفَة [riǰǰayfa] *n:* • **1.** trembling, shaking, shivering – لِزمَتَه الرِّجَّيفَة [lizmatah ʔirriǰǰayfa] He was seized with shivering.

ر ج ل

تَرَجَّل [traǰǰal] *v:* • **1.** to dismount – تَرَجَّل الفارِس مِن حصانَه [traǰǰal ʔilfaːris min ħṣaːnah] The horseman got down off his horse.

اِرتِجَل [ʔirtiǰal] *v:* • **1.** to improvise, extemporize, deliver off-hand – الشّاعِر اِرتِجَل قَصيدَة مُمتازَة [ʔiššaːʕir ʔirtiǰal qaṣiːda mumtaːza] The poet made up a wonderful poem on the spot.

اِستَرجَل [ʔistarǰal] *v:* • **1.** to act like a man, display masculine manners or qualities – اِستَرجِلَت وَلِبسَت هِدُوم رياجيل [ʔistarǰilat wlibsat hiduːm riyaːǰiːl] She looked like a man and wore men's clothing. • **2.** to be self-important, overbearing – مِن صار عَمَّه وَزير اِستَرجَل براسنا [min ṣaːr ʕammah waziːr ʔistarǰal braːsna] When his uncle became minister, he lorded it over us.

رِجِل [riǰil] *n:* رِجلَين، رِجلينات [riǰlayn, riǰliːnaːt] *pl:* • **1.** foot • **2.** leg (also of a table, etc.) – مَكِينَة أُمّ رِجِل [makiːna ʔumm riǰil] treadle-operated machine, foot-powered machine. خُفّ رِجلَك؛ تأَخَّرنا [xuff riǰlak; tʔaxxarna] Get a move on; we're late.

رَجِل [rajil] *n:* رجُولَة، رياجيل [rǰuːla, riyaːǰiːl] *pl:* • **1.** husband

رِجّال [riǰǰaːl] *n:* رِياجيل [riyaːǰiːl] *pl:* • **1.** man

مِرجَل [mirǰal] *n:* مَراجِل [maraːǰil] *pl:* • **1.** boiler (of a steam engine)

رُجُولَة [rujuːla] *n:* • **1.** manhood, masculinity, virility

مَراجِل [maraːǰil] *n:* • **1.** (pl. only) feats, deeds, exploits – دَيبيع مَراجِل براسي [daybiːʕ maraːǰil braːsi] He's trying to impress me with his exploits. لِيش تبيع مَراجِل براس البَنات؟ إذا بيك خير رُوح عالوُلِد [liːš tbiːʕ maraːǰil braːs ʔilbanaːt? ʔiða biːk xiːr ruːħ ʕalwulid] Why do you bully the girls? If you think you're somebody, go pick on the boys.

اِرتِجال [ʔirtiǰaːl] *n:* اِرتِجالات [ʔirtiǰaːlaːt] *pl:* • **1.** improvisation, extemporaneous creation

رِجالي [riǰaːli] *adj:* • **1.** men's, for men, male, masculine – أَلبِسَة رِجالِيَّة [ʔalbisa riǰaːliyya] men's clothing.

مُرتَجَل [murtaǰal] *adj:* • **1.** extemporaneous

اِرتِجالي [ʔirtiǰaːli] *adj:* • **1.** improvised, impromptu, offhand, extemporary, unprepared – خِطاب اِرتِجالي [xiṭaːb ʔirtiǰaːli] an extemporaneous speech. أعمالَه كُلّها اِرتِجالِيَّة [ʔaʕmaːlah kullha ʔirtiǰaːliyya] Everything he does is on the spur of the moment.

ر ج م

رِجَم [rijam] *v:* • **1.** to stone

رَجِم [rajim] *n:* • **1.** stoning

راجِمَة [ra:jima] *n:* راجمات [ra:jima:t] *pl:* • **1.** multiple rocket launcher

ر ج و

رِجَى [rija:] *v:* • **1.** to request, ask – رِجانِي أَتَرجُمله المَكتُوب [rija:ni ʔatarjumlah ʔilmaktu:b] He asked me to translate the letter for him. أَرجُوك ما تصرُّفلِي الدِّينار؟ [ʔarju:k ma: tsarrufli ʔiddina:r?] Would you please change the dinar for me? أَرجُوك لا تجِيب إِسمِي [ʔarju:k la: dji:b ʔismi] Please don't mention my name. أَرجُوك! آنِي شَعلَيَّا؟ [ʔarju:k! ʔa:ni šaʕlayya?] Now I ask you! What do I have to do with it?

رَجَّى [rajja:] *v:* • **1.** to hear a request, listen to – ما يفِيد، هَذا ما يرَجِّي أَحَّد [ma: yfi:d, ha:ða ma: yrajji ʔaħħad] It's no good. He won't listen to anyone.

تَرَجَّى [trajja:] *v:* • **1.** to request, ask, beg – جِيت أَترَجَّى مِنَّك تسَوِّيلِي زَينِيَّة [ji:t ʔatrajja: minnak tsawwi:li zi:niyya] I came to ask you to do me a favor. أَترَجّاك تساعِد إِبنِي [ʔatrajja:k tsa:ʕid ʔibni] I beg of you to help my son. أَترَجّاك، ما تقُلِّي وِين المَكتَبَة؟ [ʔatrajja:k, ma: tgulli wi:n ʔilmaktaba?] Would you please tell me where the library is?

اِرتِجَى [ʔirtija:] *v:* • **1.** to hope for, expect, anticipate – شتِرتِجِي مِنَّه؟ [štirtiji: minnah?] What can you expect from him?

رِجَا [rija] *n:* رِجايات [rija:ya:t] *pl:* • **1.** request, plea – الرِّجَا ما يِنفَع وِيّاه [ʔirrija ma: yinfaʕ wiyya:h] Begging won't help with him.

رَجاء [raja:ʔ] *n:* رَجاءات [raja:ʔa:t] *pl:* • **1.** hope – رَأس الرَّجاء الصّالِح [raʔs ʔirraja:ʔ ʔiṣṣa:liħ] Cape of Good Hope. • **2.** request, plea

مَرجُوّ [marjuw] *adj:* • **1.** hoped for, anticipated, expected – هَذا مَرجُوا مِنَّه [ha:ða marjuw minnah] That's expected of him.

رَجاءاً [raja:ʔan] *adverbial:* • **1.** please – رَجاءاً، لا تسَوِّي هَالقَدّ حِسّ [raja:ʔan, la: tsawwi: halgadd ħiss] Please don't make so much noise.

ر ج ي م

رِجِيم [riji:m] *n:* رَجِيمات [raji:ma:t] *pl:* • **1.** diet – سَوَّى رَجِيم [sawwa: raji:m] He went on a diet.

رِيجِيم [ri:ji:m] *n:* • **1.** diet, regimen – راح أَسَوِّي رِيجِيم [ra:ħ ʔasawwi: ri:ji:m] I'm going to go on a diet.

ر ح ب

رَحَّب [raħħab] *v:* • **1.** with – ب to welcome, make welcome – مِن شافنِي، رَحَّب بِيّا هوايَة [min ša:fni, raħħab biyya hwa:ya] When he saw me, he welcomed me heartily.

رَحابَة، رَحابَة صَدِر [raħa:ba, raħa:bat ṣadir] *n:* • **1.** magnanimity, generosity

تِرحاب [tirħa:b] *n:* تِرحابات [tirħa:ba:t] *pl:* • **1.** welcome, greeting – قابَلنِي بِالتِّرحاب [qa:balni bittirħa:b] He received me with open arms.

تَرحِيب [tarħi:b] *n:* • **1.** welcoming, welcome, greeting – حَفلَة تَرحِيب [ħaflat tarħi:b] a welcoming party, reception.

رَحِب [raħib] *adj:* • **1.** generous, roomy, unconfined

تَرحِيبِي [tarħi:bi] *adj:* • **1.** welcoming – حَفلَة تَرحِيبِيَّة [ħafla tarħi:biyya] reception, welcoming ceremony. • **2.** welcoming speech, word of welcome

مَرحَبا [marħaba] *int:* مَراحُب [mara:ħub] *pl:* • **1.** welcome! greetings! hello! – مَرحَبا بِيك [marħaba bi:k] an answer to "welcome" or "hello" مَرحَبا. أَهلاً وَمَرحَباً [marħaba. ʔahlan wmarħaban] Hello! ماكُو بَيناتنا غير المَرحَبا [ma:ku bayna:tna ɣi:r ʔilmarħaba] We don't do anything more than say hello to each other.

ر ح ت

رحاتِي، رَحّاتِي [rħa:ti:, raħħa:ti] *n:* رَحّاتِيّات، رَحاتِيّات [raħħa:ti:ya:t, raħa:ti:ya:t] *pl:* • **1.** funnel

ر ح ض

مِرحاض [mirħa:ð̣] *n:* مَراحِيض [mara:ħi:ð̣] *pl:* • **1.** toilet, lavatory, rest room, latrine

ر ح ل

رِحَل [riħal] *v:* • **1.** to migrate, move away – هَالقَبِيلَة راح ترِحَل مِن هَالمَنطِقَة لِأَنّ ماكُو عِشِب كافِي [halqabi:la ra:ħ tirħal min halmanṭiqa liʔann ma:ku ʕišib ka:fi] This tribe's going to move away from this area because there isn't enough grazing.

رَحَّل [raħħal] *v:* • **1.** to cause to migrate, to relocate, resettle – الحُكُومَة رَحِّلَت كُلّ القَبائِل بِهَالمَنطِقَة [ʔilħuku:ma raħħilat kull ʔilqaba:ʔil bhalmanṭiqa] The government relocated all the tribes in this area.

رَحلَة [raħla] *n:* رَحلات [raħla:t] *pl:* • **1.** desk, seat (in school)

رِحلَة [riħla] *n:* رِحلات [riħla:t] *pl:* • **1.** trip, tour, outing

رَحِيل [raħi:l] *n:* • **1.** emigration • **2.** departure

مَرحَلَة [marħala] *n:* مَراحِل [mara:ħil] *pl:* • **1.** phase, stage

رَحّال [raħħa:l] *adj:* رَحّالَة، رُحَّل [raħħa:la, ruħħal] *pl:* • **1.** migratory, wandering, nomadic • **2.** great traveler, explorer • **3.** قَبائِل رُحَّل nomadic tribes

ر ح م

رِحَم [riħam] *v:* • **1.** to have mercy upon, have comparison for – الله يِرحَمَه. كان خُوش آدَمِي [ʔallah yirħamah. ča:n xu:š ʔa:dami] God have mercy on him. He was a good man. تُعرُف الحاكِم رِحَمَك بِهَالحُكُم؟ [tuʕruf ʔilħa:kim riħamak bhalħukum?] Do you realize that

the judge was merciful to you in that verdict?
يرحَم أبُوك، ما تعاونِّي [yirħam ʔabu:k, ma: tʕa:winni] For goodness sake, will you please give me a hand!
رَحَّم [raħħam] *v:* • **1.** to seek the mercy of God, to ask God to have mercy – رَحَّم لأَبُوه [raħħam lʔabu:h] He asked God to have mercy upon his dead father.
ترَحَّم [traħħam] *v:* • **1.** to be merciful, be kind, show mercy – ترَحَّم عَليه بِبَدلَة عَتِيقَة [traħħam ʕali:h bbadla ʕati:ga] He showed mercy to him by giving him an old suit.
اِستَرحَم [ʔistarħam] *v:* • **1.** to plead for mercy – المَسجُون قَدَّم عَرِيضَة لِرَئِيس الجُمهُورِيَّة يِستَرحِم بِيها [ʔilmasǰu:n qaddam ʕari:ða liraʔi:s ʔiǰǰumhu:riyya yistarħim bi:ha] The prisoner presented a petition to the president in which he pleaded for mercy. اِستَرحَم مِن الحُكُومَة يفُكُّون إبنَه مِن الحَبِس لأَنّ صِحّتَه مُو زينَة [ʔistarħam min ʔilħuku:ma yfukku:n ʔibnah min ʔilħabis liʔann ṣiħħtah mu: zi:na] He pleaded with the government to relase his son from prison because his health was bad.
رَحَم [raħam] *n:* أرحام [ʔarħa:m] *pl:* • **1.** womb, uterus • **2.** kinship, family tie, relationship – هُوَّ مِن أرحامنا [huwwa min ʔarħa:mna] He's one of our kinfolk. • **3.** pity, compassion – وين أهل الرَّحَم؟ فلُوس عَشا ما عِندِي [wi:n ʔahl ʔirraħam? flu:s ʕaša ma: ʕindi] Where are the compassionate people? I don't have money for dinner.
رَحمَة [raħma] *n:* • **1.** compassion, pity • **2.** mercy – رَحمَة عَلى مَوتاك [raħma ʕala mu:ta:k] a polite formula for requesting aid. رَحمَة عَلى مَوتاك ما تفُكّلِي هالباب [raħma ʕala mu:ta:k ma: tfukk li halba:b] Would you please open that door for me. • **3.** pl. رَحمات an act of mercy from God, a blessing
مَرحَمَة [marħama] *n:* مَراحِم [mara:ħim] *pl:* • **1.** During the feast the prisoners receive a lightening of their sentences – بالعِيد المَساجِين يحَصّلُون عَلَى مَراحِم [bilʕi:d ʔilmasa:ǰi:n yħaṣṣlu:n ʕala mara:ħim] During the feast the prisoners receive a lightening of their sentences. • **2.** pity, sympathy, mercy, compassion
الرحمَن [ʔirraħma:n] *n:* • **1.** the Merciful (i.e. God) – بِسِم الله الرَّحمَن الرَّحِيم [bisim ʔallah ʔirraħma:n ʔirraħi:m] In the name of God, the Merciful, the Compassionate. وَالرَّحمَن، ما أدرِي [wirraħma:n, ma: ʔadri] I swear I don't know.
اِسترحام [ʔistirħa:m] *n:* اِسترحامات [ʔistirħa:ma:t] *pl:* • **1.** petition, plea for clemency
رَحِيم [raħi:m] *adj:* • **1.** merciful, compassionate – قَلبَه رَحِيم [galbah raħi:m] He's kind-hearted.
مَرحُوم [marħu:m] *adj:* • **1.** deceased, departed, late • **2.** (as *n:*) deceased person
أرحَم [ʔarħam] *comparative adjective:* • **1.** more or most merciful, compassionate

ر ح ي

رَحَّة [raħħa] *n:* رَحّات، رَحّيّات [raħħa:t, raħħayya:t] *pl:* • **1.** quern (stones used in pairs), hand mill
رَحّايَة، رَحيَّة [raħħa:ya, rħayya] *n:* رَحّايَة، رحَيّات، رِحِي [raħħa:ya, rħayya:t, riħi] *pl:* • **1.** grinder, molar tooth

ر خ خ

رُخّ [ruxx] *n:* • **1.** rook, castle (chess)

ر خ ص

رِخَص [rixaṣ] *v:* • **1.** to become inexpensive, cheap – الخيار رِخَص هوايَة [ʔilxya:r rixaṣ hwa:ya] The cucumbers got very cheap. سِعِر الشَّكَر يِرخَص بِالصَّيف [siʕir ʔiššakar yirxaṣ biṣṣayf] The price of sugar decreases in the summer.
رَخَّص [raxxaṣ] *v:* • **1.** to make cheap, inexpensive – إذا ترَخِّصها شوَيَّة، تبِيع مِنها هوايَة [ʔiða traxxiṣha šwayya, tbi:ʕ minha hwa:ya] If you lower the price a little, you'll sell a lot of it. • **2.** to permit, allow, give permission – بَعَد ما رَخَّصنِي، سافَرت [baʕad ma: raxxaṣni, sa:farit] Once he'd given me permission, I took the trip. • **3.** to authorize, license – مِنُو رَخَّصلَك تبِيع جِكايِر هنا؟ [minu raxxaṣlak tbi:ʕ ǰiga:yir hna?] Who authorized you to sell cigarettes here?
ترَخَّص [traxxaṣ] *v:* • **1.** to get permission
اِسترخَص [ʔistarxaṣ] *v:* • **1.** to find cheap, regard as inexpensive – اِستَرخَصَه لِلقماش وإشتِرَى مِنَّه هوايَة [ʔistarxaṣah liluqma:š wʔištira: minnah hwa:ya] He decided the cloth was cheap and bought a lot of it. • **2.** to ask permission – اِستَرخَص مِن أبُوه قَبُل ما يرُوح لِلسِّينَما [ʔistarxaṣ min ʔabu:h gabul ma: yru:ħ lissinama] He asked permission from his father before he went to the movies. آنِي أسترخِص [ʔa:ni ʔastarxiṣ] Excuse me (said when leaving a room or group).
رُخُص [ruxuṣ] *n:* • **1.** cheapness, inexpensiveness – الرُّخُص عَجِيب بهالُولايَة [ʔirruxuṣ ʕaǰi:b bhalwla:ya] Life is amazingly cheap in this city.
رُخصَة [ruxṣa] *n:* • **1.** permission, authorization – مِن رُخُصتَك [min ruxuṣtak] if you please, with your permission. مِن رُخُصتَك، أقدَر مِن هنا [min ruxuṣtak, ʔagdar ʔamurr min hna?] May I please get through here? مِن رُخُصتَك، ناوشنِي السَّلَّة [min ruxuṣtak, na:wišni ʔissalla] Please hand mc thc basket.
ترخِيص [tarxi:ṣ] *n:* تَرخِيصات، تَراخِيص [tarxi:ṣa:t, tara:xi:ṣ] *pl:* • **1.** permission • **2.** authorization • **3.** price cut, price reduction
رخِيص [rixi:ṣ] *adj:* • **1.** inexpensive, cheap – ما تِلقِي شِي رخِيص هنا [ma: tilgi ši rxi:ṣ hna] You won't find anything cheap here.
مُرَخَّص [muraxxaṣ] *adj:* • **1.** authorized, permitted • **2.** permissive, licensed

مَرخُوص [marxuːṣ] *adj:* • **1.** authorized, permitted – إنتَ ما مَرخُوص تاخُذ الفلُوس [ʔinta maː marxuːṣ taːxuð ʔilfluːs] you are not permitted to take the money.
أرخَص [ʔarxaṣ] *comparative adjective:* • **1.** more or most inexpensive

ر خ م
رُخام [ruxaːm] *n:* • **1.** marble

ر خ و
رِخَى [rixaː] *v:* • **1.** to become loose, slack – لِيش ما شَدَّيت الحَبِل زين؟ بَسّ عَلَّقت الهِدُوم بِيه، رِخَى [liːš maː šaddiːt ʔilħabil zayn? bass ʕallagit ʔilhduːm biːh, rixaː] Why didn't you tighten the rope well? The minute I hung the clothes on it, it sagged. مِن تِحكِي ويّاه بنَيَّة حِلوَة، يِرخَى [min tiħči wiyyaːh bnayya ħilwa, yirxaː] Whenever a pretty girl talks with him, he's helpless. • **2.** to accede, give in, be persuaded – حاكاها بلُطُف حَتَّى رِخَت [ħaːčaːha biluṭuf ħatta rixat] He talked to her gently until she gave in.
رَخَّى [raxxaː] *v:* • **1.** to slacken, loosen – رَخِّي الحَبِل حَتَّى أشِدَّه بالعَمُود [raxxi ʔilħabil ħatta ʔašiddah bilʕamuːd] Slacken the rope so I can tie it to the pole. • **2.** to persuade, win over, cause to give in – ظَلّ يِحكِي وياها عَالزَّواج إلَى أن رَخّاها [ðall yiħči wiyyaːha ʕazzawaːǰ ʔila ʔan raxxaːha] He kept on talking to her about marriage until he won her over.
تَرَخَّى [traxxaː] *v:* • **1.** to be loosened, slackened – هَالبُرغِي مزَنجِر. ما يِترَخَّى [halburɣi mzanǰir. maː yitraxxaː] This screw is rusted. It can't be loosened.
اِرتِخَى [ʔirtixaː] *v:* • **1.** to relax – اِرتِخِي شوَيَّة حَتَّى يُضُربَك أبرَة [ʔirtixi šwayya ħatta yuðurbak ʔubra] Relax a little so he can give you a shot. دِير بالَك. لا تِرتِخِي مِن يِحكُون وِيّاك [diːr baːlak. laː tirtixi min yiħčuːn wiyyaːk] Be careful. Don't let down your guard when they're talking to you.
رَخاء [raxaːʔ] *n:* • **1.** welfare
رَخاوَة [raxaːwa] *n:* • **1.** looseness, slackness • **2.** softness
تَراخِي [taraːxi] *n:* • **1.** limpness, looseness, semi-paralysis
رَخُو [raxw] *adj:* • **1.** soft
رِخِي [rixi] *adj:* • **1.** loose, slack – شِدّ الحزام رِخِي حَتَّى تاكُل أكثَر [šidd ʔilħzaːm rixi ħatta taːkul ʔakθar] Fasten your belt loosely so you can eat more.
راخِي [raːxi] *adj:* • **1.** loose, slack – القايِش مال المَكِينَة راخِي [ʔilqaːyis maːl ʔilmakiːna raːxi] The fan belt is loose. الوتَر مال الكَمَنجَة راخِي. ضُبَّه [ʔilwatar maːl ʔilkamanǰa raːxi. ðubbah] The violin string is loose. Tighten it. البُرغِي راخِي؛ ضُبَّه [ʔilburɣi raːxi; ðubbah] The screw is loose; tighten it.

ر د ء
تَرَدَّى [traddaː] *v:* • **1.** to become bad – صِحّتَه تردَّت هوايَة [ṣiħħtah traddat hwaːya] His health got very poor.
رَداءَة [radaːʔa] *n:* • **1.** badness, bad condition or state – رَداءَة الجَوّ [radaːʔat ʔiǰǰaww] the inclemency of the weather.
رَدِيء [radiːʔ] *adj:* • **1.** bad – هُوَّ سُمُعتَه رَدِيئَة [huwwa sumuʕtah radiːʔa] His reputation is bad. • **2.** of poor quality – هَالقماش مِن النَّوع الرَّدِيء [halqmaːš min ʔinnuːʕ ʔirradiːʔ] This is a shoddy sort of cloth. • **3.** in poor condition – صِحتَه رَدِيئَة [ṣiħtah radiːʔa] His health is poor.
أردَأ [ʔardaʔ] *comparative adjective:* • **1.** worse, worst

ر د د
رَدّ [radd] *v:* • **1.** to bring back, take back – إذا تِشتِرِي هَالسّاعَة بَعَد ما تِقدَر ترُدّها [ʔiða tištiri hassaːʕa baʕad maː tigdar truddha] If you buy this watch you won't be able to return it later. • **2.** to return, put back – أُخُذ الكِتاب وبَعَدما تقراه، رِدَّه بمُكانَه [ʔuxuð ʔilkitaːb wbaʕadma tiqraːh, riddah bmukaːnah] Take the book and after you read it, put it back where it belongs. بالله مِن تِطلَع، رُدّ الباب [ballah min tiṭlaʕ, rudd ʔilbaːb] When you go out, please close the door. • **3.** to throw back, repel, drive back, drive away – المُتَظاهِرِين رادوا يهجمُون عالبِنايَة لَكِن الشُّرطَة رَدَّتهُم [ʔilmutaðaːhiriːn raːdaw yhiǰmuːn ʕalbinaːya laːkin ʔiššurṭa raddathum] The demonstrators were going to attack the building but the police drove them off. • **4.** to refuse, reject, turn down, decline – ما رَدّلِي طَلَب لهَسَّة [maː raddli ṭalab lhassa] He hasn't refused me a request yet. ما يرِدّ أحَّد؛ بابَه عَلَى طُول مَفتُوح [maː yridd ʔaħħad; baːbah ʕala ṭuːl maftuːħ] He doesn't turn anyone away; his door is always open. • **5.** to hand back, give back, return, restore – مِن تِنطِيه دِينار، راح يرِدّلك الباقِي [min tintiːh dinaːr, raːħ yriddlak ʔilbaːqi] When you give him a dinar, he'll give you back the change. • **6.** to return – سَلَّمِت عَليه وَما رَدّ السَّلام [sallamit ʕaliːh wma radd ʔissalaːm] I greeted him and he didn't return the greeting. زارنا ولازم نرُدّ الزِّيارَة [zaːrna wlaːzim nrudd ʔizziyaːra] He visited us and we must return the visit. • **7.** to echo, sing a refrain – المُغَنِّيَة تغَنِّي وَالجُوق يرِدّ لها [ʔilmuɣanniya tɣanni wiǰǰuːq yriddilha] The singer sings and the band sings the refrain. مِن نخَلِّص رَدَّتنا، إنتُو رِدُّوا [min nxalliṣ raddatna, ʔintu ridduː] When we finish our chorus, you repeat it. • **8.** to dictate – إنتَ رِدّلِي وَآنِي أكتِب [ʔinta riddli wʔaːni ʔaktib] You dictate to me and I'll write. المُدِير رَدّ المَكتُوب لِسِكرِتِيرتَه وَكِتبَتَه [ʔilmudiːr radd ʔilmaktuːb lisikirtiːrtah wkitbatah] The director dictated the letter to his secretary and she wrote it down. قِعَد يَمِّي بِالإمتِحان وَرَدّلِي [giʕad yammi bilʔimtiħaːn wraddli] He sat next to me in the

examination and gave me the answers. • **9.** to return, come back, go back – دروح هسَّة؛ عُود مِن ترُدّ أنطيك إيّاها [duru:ħ hassa; ʕu:d min trudd ʔanṭi:k ʔiyya:ha] Go ahead now and then when you come back I'll give it to you. شَكُو عِندَه هَذا؟ أشُو دَيرُوح وَيرِدّ [šaku ʕindah ha:ða? ʔašu dayru:ħ wyridd] What's the matter with that guy? I notice he's pacing back and forth. رَدَّت صِحّتَه مِن تزَوَّج [raddat ṣiħħtah min tzawwaǰ] His health returned when he got married. هَمّ رَدِّينا عالعِراك وَالمَشاكِل [hamm raddayna ʕalʕra:k wilmaša:kil] We are back to fights and problems again. • **10.** with عَلَى to reply to, answer – لِيش ما ترِدّ عَالتَّلَفون؟ [li:š ma: tridd ʕattalifu:n?] Why didn't you answer the telephone? راح أرُدّ عَلَى مَقالتَه بِالجَّرِيدَة [ra:ħ ʔarudd ʕala maqa:ltah bijǰari:da] I'll reply to his article in the newspaper.

ردّد [raddad] *v:* • **1.** to repeat – يرَدِّد شما أقُول [yraddid šma ʔagu:l] He repeats whatever I say.

تردّد [traddad] *v:* • **1.** to come and go, appear frequently – دَيتِرَدَّد عالدّائِرَة. شَكُو عِندَه؟ [dayitraddad ʕadda:ʔira. šaku ʕindah?] He's always coming into the office. What's he up to? • **2.** to return, recur – إسمَه دَيتِرَدَّد عالألسِنَة [ʔismah dayitraddad ʕalʔalsina] His name is frequently mentioned. • **3.** to hesitate, waver, be uncertain, doubtful, reluctant – لا تِترَدَّد. رُوح اِشتِرِيها [la: titraddad. ru:ħ ʔištiri:ha] Don't hesitate. Go and buy it.

انرَدّ [ʔinradd] *v:* • **1.** to be answered, to be returned

اِسترَدّ [ʔistaradd] *v:* • **1.** to get back – اِستَرَدّ مِنَّه كُلّ المَبلَغ [ʔistaradd minnah kull ʔilmablaɣ] He got the whole amount back from him.

رَدّ [radd] *n:* رُدُود [rudu:d] *pl:* • **1.** reaction • **2.** reversal, turnabout, change of heart – صار عِندَه رَدّ فِعِل وَفُسَخ الخُطبَة [ṣa:r ʕindah radd fiʕil wfusax ʔilxuṭba] He had a change of heart and broke the engagement. بين أخِذ وَرَدّ [bi:n ʔaxið wradd] under discussion, under debate, in dispute. القَضِيَّة بين أخِذ وَرَدّ [ʔilqaðiyya bi:n ʔaxið wradd] The matter is in dispute. • **3.** pl. – رُدُود response, reply, answer

رَدَّة [radda] *n:* رَدّات [radda:t] *pl:* • **1.** return, returning • **2.** chorus, refrain (of a song or chant)

ردّاد [radda:d] *n:* رَدّادَة [radda:da] *pl:* • **1.** member of a chorus which repeats a refrain after a singer

ترَدُّد [taraddud] *n:* • **1.** hesitation

رادُود [ra:du:d] *n:* روادِيد [rwa:di:d] *pl:* • **1.** leader of a chorus or chant

مِترَدِّد [mitraddid] *adj:* • **1.** hesitating

ر د ف

مُرادِف [mura:dif] *n:* مُرادِفات [mura:difa:t] *pl:* • **1.** synonym (gram.)

ر د م

ردَم [ridam] *v:* • **1.** to fill in with dirt – الحُكُومَة دَترِدِم المُستَنقَعات [ʔilħuku:ma datirdim ʔilmustanqaʕa:t] The government is filling in the swamps. • **2.** to hit, crash into – السَّيّارَة رِدمَت العمُود [ʔissayya:ra ridmat ʔilʕamu:d] The car crashed into the pole.

ترادَم [tra:dam] *v:* • **1.** to collide, crash together, crash into each other – ترادمَت سَيّارَة وِيّا باص [tra:dmat sayya:ra wiyya pa:ṣ] A car collided with a bus.

رَدِم [radim] *n:* • **1.** filling in with dirt, hitting

ر د ن

رِدِن [ridin] *n:* ردانات [rda:na:t] *pl:* • **1.** sleeve

ردان [rda:n] *n:* • **1.** sleeve

ر د ه

رَدهَة [radha] *n:* رَدهات [radha:t] *pl:* • **1.** large room • **2.** ward (in a hospital, etc.)

ر د ي ت

رادِيتَة [radi:ta] *n:* رادِيتات [radi:ta:t] *pl:* • **1.** What's he doing all that shouting for? He must be boiling mad about something – شَكُو عِندَه يصَيِّح؟ لازِم الرّادِيتَة عِندَه حامِيَة [šaku ʕindah yṣayyiħ? la:zim ʔirradi:ta ʕindah ħa:mya] What's he doing all that shouting for? He must be boiling mad about something. • **2.** radiator

ر د ي و

رادِيُو [ra:dyu, ra:dyu:n] *n:* رادِيُوات [ra:dyuwa:t] *pl:* • **1.** radio

ر ذ ل

رَذِيلَة [raði:la] *n:* • **1.** vice

رَذِيل [raði:l] *adj:* • **1.** mean, base, vile

ر ر ي

رارَى [ra:ra:] *v:* • **1.** to be transparent, sheet – لابسَة أتَك لِأنّ نَفنُوفها يراري [la:bsah ʔatag liʔann nafnu:fha yra:ri] She's wearing a slip because her dress is transparent. • **2.** to show through, be visible behind sheer cloth – وِجهَها دَيراري مِن وَرا البُوشِيَّة [wiččha dayra:ri min wara ʔilpu:šiyya] Her face shows through from behind the veil.

ر ز ب

مِرزاب [mirza:b] *n:* مَرازِيب [mara:zi:b] *pl:* • **1.** spout

ر ز ز

رَزَّة [razza] *n:* رَزّات [razza:t] *pl:* • **1.** hasp • **2.** hook latch

ر ز ق

رِزَق [rizaq] *v:* • **1.** to provide (with a means of subsistence) – الله يرِزقَك [ʔallah yrizqak] May God provide you with a livelihood.

شُوف شقَدّ أَكُو بَيّاعَة هنا، لَكِن الله يِرزِقهُم كُلّهُم [šuːf šgadd ʔaku bayyaːʕa hna, laːkin ʔallah yirziqhum kullhum] Look how many vendors there are here, but God enables them all to make a living. • **2.** to bless with (esp. a child) – الله رِزَقَه وَلَد [ʔallah rizaqah walad] God blessed him with a son.
اِرتِزَق [ʔirtizaq] *v:* • **1.** to make a living, seek one's livelihood – دَيِرتِزِق مِن بَيع الخيار [dayirtiziq min bayʕ ʔilxyaːr] He's making a living selling cucumbers.
رِزِق [riziq] *n:* أَرزاق [ʔarzaːq] *pl:* • **1.** livelihood, subsistence, means of living • **2.** provision, ration
مُرتَزَقَة [murtazaqa] *n:* • **1.** hangers-on, freeloaders

ر ز ل

رَزَّل [razzal] *v:* • **1.** to give trouble, cause trouble, mess up, ruin – الزَّواج رَزَّلَه وَما خَلّى عِندَه فِلِس [ʔizzawaːǰ razzalah wama xallaːʕindah filis] Marriage ruined him and left him penniless. • **2.** to rebuke, upbraid, scold, berate – إذا أذّاك، أَرَزِّلَه [ʔiða ʔaððaːk, ʔarazzilah] If he hurt you, I'll tell him off.
تَرَزَّل [trazzal] *v:* • **1.** to have trouble, get in trouble – شُوفَه شلُون ترَزَّل. خِسَر كُلّ فلُوسَه بالقُمار وَطِردَوه مِن شُغلَه [šuːfah šluːn trazzal. xisar kull fluːsah bilqumaːr wṭirdawh min šuɣlah] Look what a mess he's in. He lost all his money gambling and they fired him from his job. بَسّ يغِشّ، يِترَزَّل [bass yɣišš, yitrazzal] As soon as he cheats, he'll be in trouble. إذا تُسقُط بِهَالإمتِحان، تِترَزَّل، لِأَنّ يفُصلُوك مِن المَدرَسَة [ʔiða tusquṭ bhalʔimtiħaːn, titrazzal, liʔann yfuṣluːk min ʔilmadrasa] If you fail this exam, you've had it, because they will kick you out of school. ما كانَت عِندي شَمسِيَّة وَترَزَّلِت بِالمُطَر [maː čaːnat ʕindi šamsiyya wtrazzalit bilmuṭar] I had no umbrella, and I really caught it in the rain.
رَزالَة [razaːla] *n:* رَزالات [razaːlaːt] *pl:* • **1.** trouble, mess, pain, pain in the neck – ماكُو غير الرَّزالَة مِن وَرا الزَّواج؛ مَصرَفَك يِزِيد وَمَرتَك تِتعارَك [maːku ɣiːr ʔirrazaːla min wara ʔizzawaːǰ; maṣrafak yiziːd wmartak titʕaːrak] There's nothing but trouble to be had from marriage; your expenses increase and your wife nags. تَصلِيح السَّيّارات رَزالَة. كُلّ يوم هدُومي تِتدَهَّن [taṣliːħ ʔissayyaːraːt razaːla. kull yuːm hduːmi tiddahhan] Repairing cars is for the birds. Every day my clothes get oil all over them. • **2.** rebuke, upbraiding, scolding, berating • **3.** humiliation
تَرزِيل [tarziːl] *n:* • **1.** chiding, censure, castigation, reproof, reprehension, scolding, reprimand, reproach, talking-to, upbraiding
رَزِيل [raziːl] *adj:* • **1.** base, mean, vile, contemptible, despicable • **2.** miserly, cheap, tight, pennypinching • **3.** a despicable character • **4.** tightwad, miser, skinflint

ر ز م

رِزَم [rizam] *v:* • **1.** to pack • **2.** to wrap up
رُزمَة [ruzma] *n:* رُزَم [ruzam] *pl:* • **1.** parcel, package
رَزّام [razzaːm] *n:* رَزّامِين [razzaːmiːn] *pl:* • **1.** junior clerical worker • **2.** file clerk

ر ز ن

رَزانَة [razaːna] *n:* • **1.** gravity, sedateness, staidness, dignity – دَيبِيع رَزانَة بِراسِي [daybiːʕ razaːna braːsi] He's trying to stand on his dignity with me.
رازُونَة [raːzuːna] *n:* روازِين [rwaːziːn] *pl:* • **1.** shelf • **2.** ledge • **3.** mantle • **4.** pigeonhole, niche
رَزِين، رَزِينَة [raziːn. raziːna] *adj:* • **1.** grave, serious, sedate, staid, dignified – لا تِشّاقَى وِيّاه. هُوَّ فَدّ واحِد رَزِين [laː tiššaːqaː wiyyaːh. huwwa fadd waːħid raziːn] Don't joke with him. He's a serious person.
أَرزَن [ʔarzan] *comparative adjective:* • **1.** more or most serious, staid

ر ز ن م

رُزنامَة [ruznaːma] *n:* رُزنامات [ruznaːmaːt] *pl:* • **1.** calendar

ر س ب

رِسَب [risab] *v:* • **1.** to sink to the bottom, settle – المَسحُوق كُلَّه رِسَب بِالقَعَر [ʔilmasħuːq kullah risab bilqaʕar] All the powder settled to the bottom. • **2.** to fail, flunk – رِسَب بدَرسَين بالإمتِحان النِّهائِي [risab bdarsayn bilʔimtiħaːn ʔinnihaːʔi] He failed two courses on the final exam.
رَسَّب [rassab] *v:* • **1.** to cause to settle – الشَّبّ يرَسِّب الطِّين [ʔiššabb yrassib ʔiṭṭiːn] Alum causes mud to settle. • **2.** to cause to fail, fail, give a failing grade – رَسَّبَه المُعَلِّم لِأَنّ غَشّ [rassabah ʔilmuʕallim liʔann ɣašš] The theacher flunked him because he cheated.
تَرَسَّب [trassab] *v:* • **1.** to settle to the bottom – إذا ترَكِّد الكلاص، الأملاح راح تِترَسَّب بِالكَعَب [ʔiða trakkid ʔilglaːṣ, ʔilʔamlaːħ raːħ titrassab biččaʕab] If you let the glass sit still, the grains of salt will settle to the bottom.
رُسُوب [rusuːb] *n:* • **1.** sediment, deposit • **2.** failure (in an examination)
راسِب [raːsib] *n:* رَواسِب [rawaːsib] *pl:* • **1.** sediment, remains
تَرَسُّبات [tarassubaːt] *n:* • **1.** pl. only deposits
راسِب [raːsib] *adj:* • **1.** failing, flunking
رِسُوبِي، صخُور رِسُوبِيَّة [risuːbi, ṣixuːr risuːbiyya] *adj:* • **1.** sedimentary

ر س ح

مَرسَح [marsaħ] *n:* • **1.** var. of مَسرَح theater

ر س خ

رِسَخ [risax] *v:* • **1.** to be or become firmly established, deeply rooted, to sink in, stick (in the mind) – قرَيت المَوضُوع عِدَّة مَرّات حَتَّى يِرسَخ بذِهنِي [qrayt ʔilmawðuːʕ ʕiddat marraːt ħatta yirsax bðihni] I read up on the subject several times so it would stick in my mind.

رَسَّخ [rassax] *v:* • **1.** to establish, impress, make take root – المُعَلِّم يرِيد يرَسِّخ هَالمَعلُومات بأذهانّا [ʔilmuʕallim yriːd yrassix halmaʕluːmaːt bʔaðhaːnna] The teacher wants to impress these instructions on our minds.

رُسُوخ [rusuːx] *n:* • **1.** firmness, stability

تَرسِيخ [tarsiːx] *n:* • **1.** establishment • **2.** rooting

راسِخ [raːsix] *adj:* • **1.** firm

ر س س

رِسّ [riss] *n:* • **1.** family background, breeding

ر س غ

رُسُغ [rusuɣ] *n:* أرساغ [ʔarsaːɣ] *pl:* • **1.** wrist

ر س ل

راسَل [raːsal] *v:* • **1.** to correspond with, carry on a correspondence with – ظَلّيت أراسلَه مُدَّة سَنَة [ðalliːt ʔaraːslah muddat sana] I kept corresponding with him for a year.

أرسَل [ʔarsal] *v:* • **1.** to send, forward, ship – راح أرسِلَّك القُمصان ويّا أخُوك [raːħ ʔarsillak ʔilqumṣaːn wiyya ʔaxuːk] I'll send you the shirts through your brother.

تراسَل [traːsal] *v:* • **1.** to exchange correspondence, correspond with each other – دَتِتراسلُون لَو بَطِّلتُوا؟ [datitraːsluːn law baṭṭaltuː?] Are you all corresponding with each other or did you stop?

رَسِل، عَلَى رَسلَه [rasil, ʕala raslah] *n:* • **1.** according to his own desire, however he wishes – مِن نُوصَل لرَاس الشّارِع، كُلّ واحِد راح يرُوح عَلَى رَسلَه [min nuːṣal lraːs ʔiššaːriʕ, kull waːħid raːħ yruːħ ʕala raslah] When we get to the corner, everyone will go his own way. كِنِت ماشِي عَلَى رَسلِي أشُو فَدّ مَرَّة واحِد هِجَم عَلَيّا [činit maːši ʕala rasli ʔašu fadd marra waːħid hijam ʕalayya] I was walking along minding my business when suddenly someone attacked me. إنتَ رُوح عَلَى رَسلَك [ʔinta ruːħ ʕala raslak] Go ahead with what you were doing.

رِسالَة [risaːla] *n:* رَسائِل [rasaːʔil] *pl:* • **1.** letter, note

مُراسِل [muraːsil] *n:* مُراسِلِين [muraːsiliːn] *pl:* • **1.** correspondent, reporter • **2.** orderly, houseboy (military)

مُرسِلَة [mursila] *n:* مُرسِلات [mursilaːt] *pl:* • **1.** (radio) transmitter

إرسال [ʔirsaːl] *n:* • **1.** sending

الرَّسُول [ʔirrasuːl] *n:* • **1.** the Messenger of God, Mohammed

مُراسَلَة [muraːsala] *n:* مُراسَلات [muraːsalaːt] *pl:* • **1.** correspondence, exchange of letters

إرسالِيَّة [ʔirsaːliyya] *n:* إرسالِيّات [ʔirsaːliyyaːt] *pl:* • **1.** consignment • **2.** shipment

رَسُولِي [rasuːli] *adj:* • **1.** apostolic

ر س م

رِسَم [risam] *v:* • **1.** to draw, sketch – تِقدَر ترِسِم فِيل؟ [tigdar tirsim fiːl?] Can you draw an elephant? • **2.** to paint – الفَنّان رِسَملِي خُوش لَوحَة [ʔilfannaːn risamli xuːš lawħa] The artist painted a good picture for me. • **3.** to sketch, outline (fig.) – رِسَملِي خِطَّة وَراح أمشِي عَليها [risamli xiṭṭa wraːħ ʔamši ʕaliːha] He outlined a plan for me and I'm going to follow it.

رَسَّم [rassam] *v:* • **1.** to set, fix, or establish a tax or duty on – ما تِطلَع مِن الجُمرُك قَبِل ما يرَسِّمُوها [maː tiṭlaʕ min ʔilgumrug gabil maː yrassimuːha] It won't come out of the customs office until they fix a tax on it.

ترَسَّم [trassam] *v:* • **1.** pass. of رَسَّم to be set, fixed, or established; set a tax or duty on – بِضاعتَك خَلّي تِترَسَّم وَبَعدين أخُذها [biðaːʕtak xalliː titrassam wbaʕdiːn ʔuxuðha] Let your goods have a tax set on them and then take them.

اِنرِسَم [ʔinrisam] *v:* • **1.** pass. of رِسَم to be drawn, sketched

رَسِم [rasim] *n:* • **1.** drawing, sketching, art (as a subject in school) • **2.** (rarely) photograph • **3.** duty, tax, tariff • **4.** pl. رُسُوم picture, sketch, drawing

رَسّام [rassaːm] *n:* رَسّامِين [rassaːmiːn] *pl:* • **1.** draftsman • **2.** painter, artist • **3.** (rarely) photographer

رَسمِي [rasmi] *adj:* • **1.** official, formal – لِباس رَسمِي [libaːs rasmi] formal dress. مَلابِس رَسمِيَّة [malaːbis rasmiyya] official dress, uniforms. بِصُورَة رَسمِيَّة [bṣuːra rasmiyya] officially. راح أواجهَه بِصُورَة رَسمِيَّة [raːħ ʔawaːǰhah bṣuːra rasmiyya] I'll see him officially.

مَرسُوم [marsuːm] *adj:* • **1.** drawn, sketched, traced • **2.** painted • **3.** (as *n:*) regulation, ordinance – مَراسِيم الحَفلَة [maraːsiːm ʔilħafla] rules of the ceremony, protocol, ceremonial procedures, rituals. • **4.** pl. مَراسِيم decree, edict

رَسمِيّاً [rasmiyyan] *adverbial:* • **1.** officially, formally

ر س ن

رِسَن [risan] *n:* أرسان [ʔarsaːn] *pl:* • **1.** halter

ر س و

رِسَى [risaː] *v:* • **1.** to anchor

رَسُو [rasw] *n:* • **1.** anchoring

مَرسَى [marsa] *n:* • **1.** anchorage, anchoring

مَرساة [marsaːt] *n:* • **1.** anchor

ر ش ح

رَشَّح [raššaħ] *v:* • **1.** to filter – النِّشّاف يرَشِّح كُلِّش زين [ʔinniššaːf yraššiħ kulliš ziːn] Blotter paper filters very well. • **2.** to nominate, put up as a candidate – رَشِّحوه لِرِئاسَة الوَفِد [raššiħuːh liriʔaːsat ʔilwafid] They nominated him for the chairmanship of the delegation.

تَرَشَّح [traššaħ] *v:* • **1.** to be nominated – مِنُو تَرَشَّح عَن هَالمَنطَقَة؟ [minu traššaħ ʕan halmanṭaqa?] Who was nominated from this district?

رَشَح [rašaħ] *n:* • **1.** cold • **2.** leak, leakage

تَرشِيح [taršiːħ] *n:* • **1.** candidacy

مُرَشَّح [muraššaħ] *n:* مُرَشَّحِين [muraššaħiːn] *pl:* • **1.** candidate, nominee

ر ش د

أرشَد [ʔaršad] *v:* • **1.** to lead, guide, direct, show the way – ماكُو واحِد يرشِدَه عَالطَّرِيق الصَّحِيح [maːku waːħid yrišdah ʕaṭṭariːq ʔiṣṣaħiːħ] There is no one who can show him the right way.

اِستَرشَد [ʔistaršad] *v:* • **1.** to be guided – آنِي دائِماً أستَرشِد بآراء أساتِذتِي [ʔaːni daːʔiman ʔastaršid bʔaːraːʔ ʔasaːtiðti] I'm always guided by the opinions of my professors.

رُشد، سِنّ الرُّشد [rušd, sinn ʔirrušd] *n:* • **1.** full legal age, majority (18 years or older)

رِشّاد [ršaːd, riššaːd] *n:* • **1.** pepper grass (eaten as a condiment with food)

مُرشِد [muršid] *n:* مُرشِدِين [muršidiːn] *pl:* • **1.** adviser, leader, conductor, counselor, instructor

إرشاد [ʔiršaːd] *n:* إرشادات [ʔiršaːdaːt] *pl:* • **1.** guidance • **2.** pl. only – إرشادات instructions, directions, directives

راشدِي [raːšdi] *n:* راشدِيّات [raːšdiyyaːt] *pl:* • **1.** a slap on the cheek

راشِد [raːšid] *adj:* راشِدِين [raːšidiːn] *pl:* • **1.** adult

ر ش ر ش

رَشرَش [rašraš] *v:* • **1.** to sprinkle, spray – الجّاهِل لازِم الصّوندَة وِيرَشرِش بِيها [ʔijjaːhil laːzim ʔiṣṣuːnda wyrašriš biːha] The kid's holding the hose and spraying water around with it.

ر ش ش

رَشّ [rašš] *v:* • **1.** to sprinkle – الأكِل فاهِي. رِشّ عَلِيه شوَيَّة مِلِح [ʔilʔakil faːhi. rišš ʕaliːh šwayya miliħ] The food is flat. Sprinkle a little salt on it. رُشّ القاع بِشوَيَّة مَيّ حَتَّى يِجِي هَوا بارِد [rušš ʔilgaːʕ bšwayyat mayy ħatta yiji hawa baːrid] Sprinkle the ground with a little water so we'll get some cool air. • **2.** to water – رَشَّيت الثَّيِّل وإلّا بَعَد؟ [raššayt ʔiθθayyil waʔilla baʕad?] Have you watered the lawn yet?

رَشّ [rašš] *n:* • **1.** sprinkling, spraying, showering, splashing – سَيّارَة الرَّشّ [sayyaːrat ʔirrašš] sprinkling truck.

رَشَّة [rašša] *n:* • **1.** sprinkling, drizzle • **2.** light drizzle, dash

رَشّاش [raššaːš] *n:* رَشّاشات [raššaːšaːt] *pl:* • **1.** sprinkling can, watering can

رَشّاشَة [raššaːša] *n:* رَشّاشات [raššaːšaːt] *pl:* • **1.** machine gun

ر ش ف

رِشَف [rišaf] *v:* • **1.** to sip, to sup (in small mouthfuls)

اِنرِشَف [ʔinrišaf] *v:* • **1.** to be sipped

رَشِف، رَشفَة [rašif, rašfa] *n:* رَشفات [rašfaːt] *pl:* • **1.** sip

ر ش ق

رَشاقَة [rašaːqa] *n:* • **1.** shapeliness, slenderness, graceful, slender build

رَشِيق [rašiːq] *adj:* • **1.** svelte, slender, slim, nimble, elegant – هَالرّاقِصَة رَشِيقَة [harraːqiṣa rašiːqa] This dancer is shapely.

ر ش م

رَشمَة [rašma] *n:* رَشمات [rašmaːt] *pl:* • **1.** halter • **1.** curb

ر ش و

رِشَى [rišaː] *v:* • **1.** to bribe – حاوَل يرشِي الشُّرطِي بَسّ ما قِدَر [ħaːwal yirši ʔiššurṭi bass maː gidar] He attempted to bribe the policeman but he couldn't.

اِرتِشَى [ʔirtišaː] *v:* • **1.** to accept bribery, to be corrupt – هَالمُوَظَّف ما يرتِشِي أبَداً [halmuwaððaf maː yirtiši ʔabadan] This employee won't ever take a bribe.

رَشو [rašw] *n:* • **1.** bribery

رَشوَة [rašwa] *n:* رَشوات، رَشاوِي [rašwaːt, rašaːwi] *pl:* • **1.** bribe

راشِي [raːši] *n:* • **1.** sesame oil • **2.** briber, palm greaser

ر ش ي ت

رَشِيتَة [rašiːta, račiːta] *n:* رَشِيتات [rašiːtaːt, račiːtaːt] *pl:* • **1.** prescription (med.)

ر ص د

رِصَد [riṣad] *v:* • **1.** to observe, watch – دَيرصِد نِجُوم مِن فُوق الجِّبَل [dayirṣid nijuːm min fuːg ʔijjibal] He is observing stars from the top of the hill. • **2.** to appropriate, set aside, earmark – الحُكُومَة رِصدَت مَليُون دِينار لِهَالمَشرُوع [ʔilħukuːma riṣdat malyuːn dinaːr lihalmašruːʕ] The government appropriated a million dinars for this project.

تَرَصَّد [traṣṣad] *v:* • **1.** keep eye on • **2.** to observe, watch

رَصِد [raṣid] *n:* • **1.** observation

رَصِيد [raṣi:d] *n:* أَرصِدَة [ʔarṣida] *pl:* • **1.** assets, capital • **2.** reserves • **3.** available funds – شَكّ بِلا رَصِيد [čakk bila raṣi:d] rubber check, check without funds to cover it. • **4.** backing, support – ما إِلَه رَصِيد بدائِرتَه [ma: ʔilah raṣi:d bda:ʔirtah] He gets no backing in his office.
مَرصَد [marṣad] *n:* مَراصِد [mara:ṣid] *pl:* • **1.** observatory
مِرصاد [mirṣa:d] *n:* • **1.** ambush – واقُف بالمِرصاد [wa:guf bilmirṣa:d] He's lying in wait. واقُفلِي بِالمِرصاد. شما أَسَوِّي، يِحتَجّ [wa:gufli bilmirṣa:d. šma ʔasawwi:, yiħtajj] He's keeping a sharp eye on me. Whatever I do, he protests. الشُّرطَة واقفَتلَه بالمِرصاد [ʔiššurṭa wa:gfatlah bilmirṣa:d] The police are watching him closely.
راصِد [ra:ṣid] *adj:* • **1.** observing, observer
مِترَصِّد [mitraṣṣid] *adj:* • **1.** lurker, observer

ر ص ر ص

رَصرَص [raṣraṣ] *v:* • **1.** to fill with melted lead, to weight – مَوِّع شوَيَّة رصاص وَرَصرِص الكَعَب [mawwiʕ šwayya rṣa:ṣ wraṣriṣ ʔiččaʕab] Melt a little lead and weight the bone.
مرَصرَص [mraṣraṣ] *adj:* • **1.** thickset • **2.** compacted, compact, compressed

ر ص ص

رَصّ [raṣṣ] *v:* • **1.** to fit tightly together, press together, compress, pack, tamp – عَبِّي هَالقُوطِيَّة بِتَمُر بَسّ رُصّها زين [ʕabbi halqu:ṭiyya btamur bass ruṣṣha zi:n] Fill this container with dates and pack them down well.
انرَصّ [ʔinraṣṣ] *v:* • **1.** to be pressed, to be compressed
رَصّ [raṣṣ] *n:* • **1.** compaction, pressing, compressing
رصاص [rṣa:ṣ] *n:* • **1.** lead – قَلَم رصاص [qalam rṣa:ṣ] pencil. • **2.** (coll.) bullets
رصاصَة [rṣa:ṣa] *n:* رصاصات [rṣa:ṣa:t] *pl:* • **1.** bullet
رِصاصِي [riṣa:ṣi] *adj:* • **1.** leaden, lead-colored, dull gray
مَرصُوص [marṣu:ṣ] *adj:* • **1.** compressed, pressed

ر ص ع

رَصَّع [raṣṣaʕ] *v:* • **1.** to set, stud, inlay – تاج المَلِكَة مرَصَّع بِياقُوت وَأَلماس [ta:j ʔilmalika mraṣṣaʕ bya:qu:t wʔalma:s] The queen's crown is set with rubies and diamonds.
رَصعَة [raṣʕa] *n:* رَصعات [raṣʕa:t] *pl:* • **1.** dent • **2.** dimple

ر ص ف

رِصَف [riṣaf] *v:* • **1.** to pave – راح يرُصفُون الشّارِع بطابُوق [ra:ħ yruṣfu:n ʔišša:riʕ bṭa:bu:g] They're going to pave the street with bricks.
تراصَف [tra:ṣaf] *v:* • **1.** to move together, draw closer to each other, close ranks – العَرِيف قال لِلجُنُود يِتراصفُون [ʔilʕari:f ga:l lijjunu:d yitra:ṣfu:n] The sergeant told the soldiers to close ranks.
رَصِف [raṣif] *n:* • **1.** paving
رَصِيف [raṣi:f] *n:* أَرصِفَة [ʔarṣifa] *pl:* • **1.** pavement • **2.** sidewalk • **3.** wharf, dock, pier • **4.** platform (of a railway station) • **5.** wharfage, fee for using a wharf
الرِصافَة، جانِب الرِصافَة [ʔirriṣa:fa, ja:nib ʔirriṣa:fa] *n:* • **1.** name of the section of Baghdad on the east side of the Tigris
مَرصُوف [marṣu:f] *adj:* • **1.** paved

ر ض خ

رِضَخ [riðax] *v:* • **1.** to submit
رِضُوخ [riðu:x] *n:* • **1.** submission

ر ض ر ض

رَضرَض [raðrað] *v:* • **1.** to break, smash, crush – إِذا ما تِسكُت، أَرَضرِض عظامَك [ʔiða ma: tiskut, ʔaraðrið ʕða:mak] If you don't shut up, I'll break your bones into pieces. آني أَرَضرِض الجُوز وَإِنتَ طَلِّع اللُبّ [ʔa:ni ʔaraðrið ʔijju:z wʔinta ṭalliʕ ʔillibb] I'll crack the walnuts and you take out the meat.

ر ض ض

رَضّ [raðð] *v:* • **1.** to bruise – وُقعَت الحَدِيدَة عَلَى زَندِي وَرَضَّتَه [wugʕat ʔilħadi:da ʕala zandi wraððatah] The piece of iron fell on my arm and bruised it.
انرَضّ [ʔinraðð] *v:* • **1.** to become bruised – فُخذَه انرَضّ مِن وُقَع عَليه الكُرسِي [fuxðah ʔinraðð min wugaʕ ʕali:h ʔilkursi] His thigh got bruised when the chair fell on him.
رَضّ [raðð] *n:* رضُوض [rðu:ð] *pl:* • **1.** bruise, bruising
رَضَّة [raðða] *n:* رَضّات [raðða:t] *pl:* • **1.** bruise, bruising

ر ض ع

رِضَع [riðaʕ] *v:* • **1.** to nurse, suck at the breast – الجّاهِل رِضَع إِلَى أَن صار عُمره سَنتَين [ʔijja:hil riðaʕ ʔila ʔan ṣa:r ʕumrah santayn] The baby nursed until he was two years old. البِزازِين رِضعَوا كُلّ حَلِيب أُمّهُم [ʔilbiza:zi:n riðʕaw kull ħali:b ʔummhum] The kittens sucked out all their mother's milk. • **2.** to nurse, suckle, feed at the breast – جابَوا دايَة حَتَّى ترَضِّع طِفِلهُم [ja:baw da:ya ħatta traððiʕ ṭifilhum] They brought a wet nurse to nurse their baby.
رَضَّع [raððaʕ] *v:* • **1.** to nurse, suckle, feed at the breast – قُومِي رَضِّعِي الجّاهِل [gu:mi raððiʕi ʔijja:hil] Go nurse the baby!
رَضِع [raðiʕ] *n:* • **1.** suckling

رَضِيع [raðiːʕ] *n:* رُضَعاء، رُضَّع [ruðaʕaːʔ, ruððaʕ] *pl:* • **1.** suckling, infant, baby
رِضاعَة [riðaːʕa] *n:* • **1.** breastfeeding • **2.** suckling
مُرضِع [murðiʕ] *adj:* • **1.** nursing, having a nursing child – هَالمَرَة مُرضِعَة [halmara murðiʕa] That woman's nursing a baby.
مُرضِعَة [murðiʕa] *adj:* مُرضِعات [murðiʕaːt] *pl:* • **1.** wet nurse

ر ض ي

رِضَى [riðaː] *v:* • **1.** to be satisfied, be content – شما تِنطِيه، ما يِرضَى [šma tinṭiːh, maː yirðaː] Whatever you give him, he isn't satisfied. • **2.** to agree, consent – ما دَيِرضَى يِشتِرِك بالوِزارَة [maː dayirðaː yištirik bilwizaːra] He won't consent to take a position in the cabinet. ما يِرضَى يِبيع بِهَالسِّعِر [maː yirðaː yibiːʕ bhassiʕir] He won't agree to sell at that price. ما دَيِرضَى يرُوح ويّانا [maː dayirðaː yiruːħ wiyyaːna] He isn't willing to go with us. • **3.** to be pleased – مَحَّد يِرضى عَلَى هِيكِي وَضِع [maħħad yirðaː ʕala hiːči waðiʕ] No one is pleased with these conditions. الله يِرضى عَنَّك [ʔallah yirðaː ʕannak] May God be pleased with you.
رَضَّى [raððaː] *v:* • **1.** to satisfy, please, gratify – هَذا شيرَضِّيه؟ كُلّ ما تِنطِيه، يريد بَعَد [haːða šyraððiːh? kull maː tinṭiːh, yriːd baʕad] What can satisfy him? The more you give him, the more he wants. ما مرَضّي أَحَّد مِن الموَظَّفِين [maː mraððì ʔaħħad min ʔilmuwaððafiːn] He hasn't made any of the employees happy. رَضَّى الجّاهِل بالجُّكلَيت [raðða ʔiǰǰaːhil biččukliːt] He placated the child with the candy. • **2.** to mollify, appease, placate, conciliate – أَبُوك زَعلان عَلِيك. رُوح رَضِّيه [ʔabuːk zaʕlaːn ʕaliːk. ruːħ raððiːh] Your father is mad at you. Go make up with him.
راضَى [raːðaː] *v:* • **1.** to conciliate, propitiate, make up with – زِعل عَلِيك. رُوح راضِيه [ziʕal ʕaliːk. ruːħ raːðih] He's mad at you. Go make up with him. • **2.** to reconcile – صارِلهُم شَهَر زِعالَة. خَلّي نرُوح نراضِيهُم [ṣaːrilhum šahar zʕaːla. xalliː nruːħ nraːðiːhum] They've been mad at each other for a month. Let's go reconcile them.
تَراضَى [traːðaː] *v:* • **1.** to come to terms, settle differences with each other – إِترُكهُم هُمَّ يِتراضُون وَحَدهُم [ʔitrukhum humma yitraːðuːn waħadhum] Leave them to settle their differences by themselves.
رِضا [riðaː] *n:* • **1.** agreement, consent, assent, acceptance, approval
تَراضِي [taraːði] *n:* • **1.** compromise • **2.** mutual consent
إِرضاء [ʔirðaːʔ] *n:* • **1.** satisfaction
مراضاة، بِلمراضاة [mraːða, bilmraːða] *n:* • **1.** amicably, with mutual satisfaction – اِنحَلَّت المُشكِلَة بِالمراضاة [ʔinħallat ʔilmuškila bilmraːða] The problem was solved amicably.
راضِي [raːði] *adj:* • **1.** satisfied, content – المُعَلِّم راضِي عَنَّك [ʔilmuʕallim raːði ʕannak] The teacher is satisfied with you. • **2.** willing, ready – هُوَّ راضِي يسَوِّيها [huwwa raːði ysawwiːha] He's willing to do it.
مُرضِي [murði] *adj:* • **1.** gratifying • **2.** satisfactory

ر ط ب

رَطَّب [raṭṭab] *v:* • **1.** to moisten, dampen – المُبَرِّدَة تَرَطِّب الهَوا حَتَّى يُبرَد [ʔilmubarrida traṭṭub ʔilhawa ħatta yubrad] The air cooler moistens the air so it gets cool. • **2.** to become succulent, mellow, ripen – الخلال بَعدَه ما رَطَّب [ʔilxlaːl baʕdah maː raṭṭab] The dates still haven't gotten ripe.
تَرَطَّب [traṭṭab] *v:* • **1.** to be dampened
اِستَرطَب [ʔistarṭab] *v:* • **1.** to become excited, become sexually aroused
رُطَب [ruṭab] *n:* • **1.** (coll.) ripe, fresh, succulent date(s)
رُطبَة [ruṭba] *n:* رُطبات، رُطَب [ruṭbaːt, ruṭab] *pl:* • **1.** ripe, fresh, succulent date
رُطُوبَة، مُرَطِّب [ruṭuːba, muraṭṭib] *n:* • **1.** moisturizer
رُطُوبَة [ruṭuːba] *n:* • **1.** moistness, dampness, humidity
تَرطِيب [tarṭiːb] *n:* • **1.** hydrating, moistening
مُرَطِّبات [muraṭṭibaːt] *n:* • **1.** (pl. only) refreshments, soft drinks
رَطِب [raṭib] *adj:* • **1.** moist, damp, humid – الهَوا رَطِب اليُوم [ʔilhawa raṭib ʔilyuːm] The air is humid today. القاع رَطبَة. لا تُقعُد عَلَيها [ʔilgaːʕ raṭba. laː tugʕud ʕaliːha] The ground is damp. Don't sit on it.
مَرطُوب [marṭuːb] *adj:* • **1.** damp, moist, wet – لا تِمشِي حافِي؛ القاع مَرطُوبَة [laː timši ħaːfi; ʔilgaːʕ marṭuːba] Don't walk barefooted; the ground is damp.

ر ط ن

رِطَن [riṭan] *v:* • **1.** to speak unintelligible language, talk gibberish, jabber
رَطِن [raṭin] *n:* • **1.** gibberish

ر ع ب

رِعَب [riʕab] *v:* • **1.** to horrify • **2.** to terrifiy
اِرتِعَب [ʔirtiʕab] *v:* • **1.** to be terrified
رُعُب [ruʕub] *n:* • **1.** fright, alarm, dismay
إِرعاب [ʔirʕaːb] *n:* • **1.** frightening, intimidation
مُرعِب [murʕib] *adj:* • **1.** terrifying, frightening • **2.** horrible
مَرعُوب [marʕuːb] *adj:* • **1.** horrified

ر ع د

رِعَد [riʕad] *v:* • **1.** to thunder – أَشُو دَتِرعِد وَما دَتُمطُر [ʔašuː datirʕid wma datumṭur] It seems to be thundering but it isn't raining.
رَعَد [raʕad] *n:* رُعُود [ruʕuːd] *pl:* • **1.** thunder, clap of thunder

ر

ر ع ر ع

تَرعَرَع [traʕraʕ] *v:* • **1.** to thrive
تَرَعرُع [taraʕruʕ] *n:* • **1.** flourishing, developing, thriving

ر ع ش

رِعَش [riʕaš] *v:* • **1.** to shake, tremble – أَبُوها يِرعِش مِن الكُبُر [ʔabu:ha yirʕiš min ʔilkubur] Her father trembles from old age.
اِرتِعَش [ʔirtiʕaš] *v:* • **1.** to shake, tremble – اِرتِعَش بَدَنَه مِن الخَوف [ʔirtiʕaš badanah min ʔilxawf] His body trembled from fear.
رَعِش [raʕiš] *n:* • **1.** shaking • **2.** trembling, tremor
رَعشَة [raʕša] *n:* رَعشات [raʕša:t] *pl:* • **1.** tremor, trembling, shaking • **1.** feverish shiver
اِرتِعاش [ʔirtiʕa:š] *n:* • **1.** tremor
مِرتِعِش [mirtiʕiš] *adj:* • **1.** shaky

ر ع ي

رِعَى [riʕa:] *v:* • **1.** to graze – الغَنَم دَتِرعَى بِهَالمَنطَقَة [ʔilɣanam datirʕa: bhalmanṭaqa] The sheep are grazing in this area.
راعَى [ra:ʕa:] *v:* • **1.** to observe, heed, respect, comply with – لازِم تراعُون القانُون [la:zim tra:ʕu:n ʔilqa:nu:n] You must observe the law. • **2.** to make allowance for, be lenient with – المُعَلِّم راعانا بِالإِمتِحان [ʔilmuʕallim ra:ʕa:na bilʔimtiħa:n] The teacher was lenient with us on the exam. • **3.** to treat well – إذا تراعِينِي، أَشتِرِي مِنَّك عَلَى طُول [ʔiða tra:ʕi:ni, ʔaštiri minnak ʕala ṭu:l] If you treat me well, I'll always buy from you. راعانِي بِالسِّعِر وَإِنطانِي الثُّوب بدِينار [ra:ʕa:ni bissiʕir wʔinṭa:ni ʔiθθu:b bdina:r] He did well by me on the price and gave me the shirt for a dinar.
رَعِي [raʕy] *n:* • **1.** grazing
مَرعَى [marʕa:] *n:* مَراعِي [mara:ʕi] *pl:* • **1.** meadow, grazing land, pasture
راعِي [ra:ʕi] *n:* رِعيان، رُعاة [riʕya:n, ruʕa:t] *pl:* • **1.** American cowboys – رُعاة البَقَرة الأَمرِيكِيِّين [ruʕa:t ʔilbaqar ʔilʔamri:kiyyi:n] American cowboys. • **1.** shepherd, herdsman
رِعايَة [riʕa:ya] *n:* • **1.** care, attention, consideration, regard • **2.** sponsorship, patronage, auspices – السِّباق تَحت رِعايَة الوَزِير [ʔissiba:q taħt riʕa:yat ʔilwazi:r] The game is sponsored by the minister.
مُراعاة [mura:ʕa:t] *n:* • **1.** consideration, regard, respect

ر غ ب

رِغَب [riɣab] *v:* • **1.** to desire, wish, want – تِرغَب تِجِي وِيّايا لِلسِّينَما؟ [tirɣab tiǰi wiyya:ya lissinama?] Would you like to come to the movies with me? هالسَّيّارَة، صارلها شَهرَين مَعرُوضَة لِلبَيع وَما حَدّ دَيِرغَب بِيها [hassayya:ra, ṣa:rilha šahrayn maʕru:ða lilbayʕ wma ħadd dayirɣab bi:ha] This car has been up for sale for two months and nobody wants it.
رَغَّب [raɣɣab] *v:* • **1.** to interest, excite interest – رَغَّبتَه بِبَيتَك يَالله إِشتِراه [raɣɣabtah bbi:tak yallah ʔištira:h] I got him interested in your house and he bought it. ما كانَت عِندِي نِيَّة أَشتِرِيها، بَسّ إِنتَ رَغَّبتِنِي عَلَيها [ma: ča:nat ʕindi niyya ʔaštiri:ha, bass ʔinta raɣɣabtini ʕali:ha] I had no intention of buying it, but you got me enthusiastic about it.
رَغبَة [raɣba] *n:* رَغبات [raɣba:t] *pl:* • **1.** wish, desire, craving – رَغبَة بِالدِّراسَة [raɣba biddira:sa] desire to study. رَغبَة بِالسَّفَر [raɣba bissafar] desire to travel.
تَرغِيب [tarɣi:b] *n:* • **1.** attraction, invitation
مَرغُوب [marɣu:b] *adj:* • **1.** coveted, sought after, in demand – هَالسَّيّارات مَرغُوبَة بِبَغداد [hassayya:ra:t marɣu:ba bibaɣda:d] These cars are in demand in Baghdad.

ر غ م

رِغَم [riɣam] *v:* • **1.** to force, compel, coerce – رِغمَوه يِستِقِيل [riɣmawh yistiqi:l] They forced him to resign.
أَرغَم [ʔarɣam] *v:* • **1.** to force, compel, coerce – أَرغُمُوه يِدفَع كُلّ المَبلَغ [ʔarɣumu:h yidfaʕ kull ʔilmablaɣ] They forced him to pay the whole amount.
رَغُم، بِالرَّغُم مِن [raɣum, birraɣum min] *n:* • **1.** in spite of, despite – نِجَح رَغم الصُّعُوبات اللِّي شافها [niǰaħ raɣm ʔiṣṣuʕu:ba:t ʔilli ša:fha] He succeeded despite the hardships that he experienced. سافَر بِالرَّغُم مِن مُعارَضَة أَبُوه [sa:far birraɣum min muʕa:raðat ʔabu:h] He went on a trip in spite of the objection of his father. راح أَرُوح رَغُم أَنفَك [ra:ħ ʔaru:ħ raɣum ʔanfak] I will go no matter what you do. رَغماً عَن [raɣman ʕan] in spite of, despite. راح أَدخُل رَغماً عَنَّك [ra:ħ ʔadxul raɣman ʕannak] I'm going in in spite of you.
رَغُم [raɣum] *n:* • **1.** forcing, compulsion, coercion
إِرغام [ʔirɣa:m] *n:* • **1.** compulsion
مَرغُوم [marɣu:m] *adj:* • **1.** reluctant, unwilling • **2.** reluctantly, unwillingly – سَوّاها مَرغُوم [sawwa:ha marɣu:m] He did it unwillingly.

ر غ ن

رُوغان [ru:ɣa:n] *adj:* • **1.** patent leather

ر غ و

رِغَى [riɣa:] *v:* • **1.** to lather
رَغوَة [raɣwa] *n:* • **1.** lather

ر ف ء

مَرفَأ [marfaʔ] *n:* مَرافِئ [mara:fiʔ] *pl:* • **1.** harbor

ر ف ت

رَفَّت [raffat] *v:* • **1.** to dismiss, discharge – بُقَى شَهَر بِالوَظِيفَة وَبَعدِين رَفِّتُوه [buqa: šahar bilwaði:fa wbaʕdi:n raffi ṭu:h] He stayed a month in the position and then they dismissed him.

ر

رَفتِيَّة [raftiyya] *n:* رَفتِيّات [raftiyya:t] *pl:* • **1.** clearance paper showing that commodity tax has been collected on a shipment of goods, also used as an invoice

ر ف ج

رِفِيج [rifi:ǰ] *n:* رِفجَان [rifǰa:n, rufǰa:n] *pl:* • **1.** friend, buddy, pal

ر ف د

رافِد [ra:fid] *n:* • **1.** tributary

ر ف ر ف

رَفرَف [rafraf] *v:* • **1.** to flutter, flap – الحَمامَة ظَلَّت تَرَفرِف قَبُل ما تحُطّ [ʔilħama:ma ð̣allat trafrif gabul ma: tħuṭṭ] The pigeon flapped its wings before it lit. العَلَم دَيرَفرِف عَلَى سَطح المَدرَسَة [ʔilʕalam dayrafrif ʕala saṭħ ʔilmadrasa] The flag is fluttering on the roof of the school. • **3.** to flap the wings

ر ف س

رُفَس [rufas] *v:* • **1.** to kick – لا ترُوح يَمّ الحِصان، تَرَة يُرفُس [la: tru:ħ yamm ʔilħiṣa:n, tara yurfus] Don't go near the horse, because he kicks. رُفَسَه بِبَطنَه وَخَلّاه يِبكِي [rufasah bbaṭnah wxalla:h yibči] He kicked him in his stomach and made him cry.

رَفَّس [raffas] *v:* • **1.** to keep kicking – الكَلِب المَضرُوب ظَلّ يرَفِّس مُدَّة قَبُل ما يمُوت [ʔiččalib ʔilmað̣ru:b ð̣all yraffus mudda gabul ma: ymu:t] The dog that got hit kicked for a while before he died.

اِنرِفَس [ʔinrifas] *v:* • **1.** to be kicked

رَفُس [rafus] *n:* • **1.** kicking

رَفسَة [rafsa] *n:* رَفسات [rafsa:t] *pl:* • **1.** kick

ر ف ش

رَفِش [rafiš] *n:* رُفُوش [rufu:š] *pl:* • **1.** variety of large turtle

ر ف ض

رُفَض [rufað̣] *v:* • **1.** to reject, turn down, decline, refuse to accept – بَعَد ما شاف النَّمُونَة، رُفَض كُلّ الإرسالِيَّة [baʕad ma: ša:f ʔinnamu:na, rufað̣ kull ʔilʔirsa:liyya] After he saw the sample, he rejected the whole shipment. اِتِّفقَوا يرُفضُون أيّ اِقتِراح يقَدِّمَه [ʔittifqaw yirufð̣u:n ʔayy ʔiqtira:ħ yqaddimah] They agreed to turn down any suggestion he submitted. أيّ مَدرَسَة يرُوحِلها ترُفضَه [ʔayy madrasa yiru:ħilha trufð̣ah] Any school he goes to rejects him. الحاكِم رُفَض شَكواه [ʔilħa:kim rufað̣ šakwa:h] The judge dismissed his complaint.

اِنرُفَض [ʔinrufað̣] *v:* • **1.** to be declined

رَفُض [rafuð̣] *n:* • **1.** refusal, rejection – كان جَوابَه بِالرَّفُض [ča:n ǰawa:bah birrafuð̣] His answer was a refusal.

رافِض [ra:fið̣] *adj:* • **1.** dismissive

مَرفُوض [marfu:ð̣] *adj:* • **1.** rejected, denied

ر ف ع

رُفَع [rufaʕ] *v:* • **1.** to lift, lift up, raise a loft, heave up, hoist up – رُفَع مِيَّة كِيلُو بِفَدّ إيد [rufaʕ miyyat ki:lu bfadd ʔi:d] He lifted one hundred kilos with one hand. • **2.** to raise – رُفَع العَلَم [rufaʕ ʔilʕalam] He raised the flag. • **3.** to raise, increase, make higher – الشَّرِكَة رُفعَت السِّعِر لَمّا زاد الطَّلَب [ʔiššarika rufʕat ʔissiʕir lamma za:d ʔiṭṭalab] The company raised the price when the demand increased. رُفَع صَوتَه [rufaʕ ṣawtah] He raised his voice. • **4.** to remove, take away – رُفَع جَمِيع العَراقِيل بِطَرِيق دِراستَه [rufaʕ ǰami:ʕ ʔilʕara:qi:l bṭari:q dira:stah] He removed the obstacles in the way of his studies. رُفعَوا عَنَّه التَّوبِيخ [rufʕaw ʕannah ʔittawbi:x] They removed the reprimand from his record. رُفَع زَحمَة [rufaʕ zaħma] to remove an inconvenience, get out of someone's way. إحنا راح نِرفَع الزَّحمَة. صار إلنا مُدَّة قاعدِين [ʔiħna ra:ħ nirfaʕ ʔizzaħma. ṣa:r ʔilna mudda ga:ʕdi:n] We'll get out of your way. We've been sitting around for some time. • **5.** to abolish, eliminate, lift, put an end to – شوَقت راح يِرفَعُون مَنع التَّجَوُّل؟ [šwakit ra:ħ yirfaʕu:n maniʕ ʔittaǰawwul?] When are they going to lift the curfew? • **6.** to submit, present, forward – رُفَع تَقرِير بِالقَضِيَّة [rufaʕ taqri:r bilqað̣iyya] He submitted a report on the matter. المُلاحِظ شِرَح عَالعَرِيضَة وَرُفَعها لرَئِيس المُلاحِظِين [ʔilmula:hið̣ širaħ ʕalʕari:ð̣a wrufaʕha ʔirraʔi:s ʔilmula:ħið̣i:n] The superintendent endorsed the request and forwarded it to the chief superintendent. رُفَع قَضِيتَه لمَجلِس الوُزَراء [rufaʕ qað̣i:tah ʔilmaǰlis ʔilwuzara:ʔ] He took his case to the Cabinet. رُفَع دَعوَة عَلَى [rufaʕ daʕwa ʕala] to instigate legal action against, to sue. رُفَع دَعوَة عَالشَّرِكَة [rufaʕ daʕwa ʕaššarika] He sued the company.

رَفَّع [raffaʕ] *v:* • **1.** to promote, raise in salary or rank – بَسّ يرَفِّعُونِي، أعزمكُم عَلَى عَشا بِأفخَر مَطعَم [bass yraffʕu:ni, ʔaʕzimkum ʕala ʕaša: bʔafxar maṭʕam] As soon as they promote me, I'll treat you to dinner at the best restaurant. • **2.** to thin, make thinner (in diameter) – تِقدَر ترَفِّع العُودَة بِالمُبرَد [tigdar traffuʕ ʔilʕu:da bilmubrad] You can make the stick thinner with the file.

ترَفَّع [traffaʕ] *v:* • **1.** to be promoted – صارلَه عَشِر سنِين بهالوَظِيفَة وَما ترَفَّع إلّا مَرَّة وِحدَة [ṣa:rlah ʕašir sni:n bhalwað̣i:fa wma traffaʕ ʔilla marra wiħda] He's been in this position for ten years and only been promoted once. • **2.** to become thinner, be made thinner (in diameter) – مِن تُبرُد الشِّيش، يِترَفَّع [min tubrud ʔišši:š, yitraffaʕ] When you file the rod, it becomes thinner. • **3.** to be or deem oneself above, to be too good, look down – أترَفَّع أتزَوَّج بنَيَّة مِنهُم

[ʔatraffaʕ ʔadzawwaǰ bnayya minhum] I'm above marrying one of their girls. ما أعتقِد يقبَل هالشُغُل. هُوَّ يترَفَّع عَن هيكي أشغال [maː ʔaʕtiqid yiqbal haššuɣul. huwwa yitraffaʕ ʕan hiːči ʔašɣaːl] I don't think he'll accept this job. He looks down on such tasks.

ترافَع [traːfaʕ] *v:* • **1.** with ب to plead, present (a case in court) – المُحامي ترافع بدَعوتَين هَاليوم [ʔilmuħaːmi traːfaʕ bdaʕwtayn halyuːm] The lawyer pleaded two cases today.

انرُفَع [ʔinrufaʕ] *v:* • **1.** to be raised, to be submitted

ارتِفَع [ʔirtifaʕ] *v:* • **1.** to rise, ascend, go up, become higher – مُستوَى الماي ارتِفَع بَعَد المُطَر [mustawaː ʔilmaːy ʔirtifaʕ baʕad ʔilmuṭar] The water level increased after the rain. بِدا يحكِي يَواش إلَى أن صار عَصَبي وحِسّه ارتِفَع [bidaː yiħči yawaːš ʔila ʔan ṣaːr ʕaṣabi wħissah ʔirtifaʕ] He started talking softly until he got mad and his voice rose. بِالشَّهَر الجّاي، راح يرتِفِع سِعِر اللَّحَم [biššahar ʔiǰǰaːy, raːħ yirtifiʕ siʕir ʔillaħam] In the next month, the price of meat will go up.

رَفع [rafiʕ] *n:* • **1.** lifting, hoisting – رَفع الأثقال [rafʕ ʔilʔaθqaːl] weight lifting.

رُفُع [rufuʕ] *n:* • **1.** thinness, slenderness – جيبلِي عُودَة بِهالرُّفُع [ǰiːbli ʕuːda bharrufuʕ] Bring me a stick this thin.

رَفُع [rafuʕ] *n:* • **1.** lifting

مَرفَع [marfaʕ] *n:* مَرافِع [maraːfiʕ] *pl:* • **1.** stand supporting a clay water urn

تَرفيع [tarfiːʕ] *n:* تَرفيعات [tarfiːʕaːt] *pl:* • **1.** promotion • **2.** raise in salary

رافِعَة [raːfiʕa] *n:* رافِعات [raːfiʕaːt] *pl:* • **1.** crane

مُرتَفَع [murtafaʕ] *n:* مُرتَفَعات [murtafaʕaːt] *pl:* • **1.** hills

مُرافَعَة [muraːfaʕa] *n:* مُرافَعات [muraːfaʕaːt] *pl:* • **1.** court proceeding, hearing, trial

ارتِفاع [ʔirtifaːʕ] *n:* ارتِفاعات [ʔirtifaːʕaːt] *pl:* • **1.** rise • **2.** increase • **3.** altitude, elevation, height

رفيع [rifiːʕ] *adj:* • **1.** thin in diameter, slender, fine, of small gauge – خيط رِفيع [xiːṭ rifiːʕ] thin string. • **2.** thin, high-pitched – صَوت رِفيع [ṣawt rifiːʕ] a highpitched voice.

مِرتَفِع [mirtafiʕ] *adj:* • **1.** rising, high

مَرفوع [marfuːʕ] *adj:* • **1.** nominative (gram.) • **2.** raised, uplifted, pointed

أرفَع [ʔarfaʕ] *comparative adjective:* • **1.** thinner, thinnest • **2.** more or most high-pitched • **3.** above, too good for – آني أرفَع مِن أن أسَوّي هيكي شِي [ʔaːni ʔarfaʕ min ʔan ʔasawwiː hiːči ši] I'm above doing such a thing.

ر ف ف

رَفّ [raff] *v:* • **1.** to twitch, quiver – عيني دَترُفّ [ʕiːni datruff] My eye is twitching. أحياناً يرُفّ مَتني بِلا سَبَب [ʔaħyaːnan yruff matni bila sabab] Sometimes my shoulder twitches without any reason.

رَفّ [raff] *n:* رفوف [rfuːf] *pl:* • **1.** shelf • **2.** ledge • **3.** flight, covey (of birds)

ر ف ق [1]

رُفَق [rufaq] *v:* • **1.** to be kind, friendly, nice, to show kindness – رُفَق بيه الحاكِم وعِفَى عَنّه [rufaq biːh ʔilħaːkim wʕifaː ʕannah] The judge took pity on him and let him go.

رافَق [raːfaq] *v:* • **1.** to accompany, escort – ثلاث صُحُفِيّين رافقوا الوَفِد [tlaθ ṣuħufiyyiːn raːfqaw ʔilwafid] Three newspapermen accompanied the delegation.

أرفَق [ʔarfaq] *v:* • **1.** to enclose, attach, append, add – لازِم ترفُق صُورتَك ويّا الاستِمارَة وَتدِزّها [laːzim tirfuq ṣuːrtak wiyya ʔilʔistimaːra widdizzha] You must enclose your picture with the application and send it in.

انرُفَق [ʔinrufaq] *v:* • **1.** to be enclosed, to be attached

رِفِق [rifiq] *n:* • **1.** kindness

رَفيق [rafiːq] *n:* رُفَقاء [rufaqaːʔ] *pl:* • **1.** friend, companion • **2.** comrade (in Marxist terminology) • **3.** pl. رفاق [rifaːq] buddy, pal

مُرفَق [murfaq] *n:* • **1.** attached, enclosed • **2.** *pl.* مُرفقات [murfaqaːt] enclosure (s)

مُرافِق [muraːfiq] *n:* مُرافِقين [muraːfiqiːn] *pl:* • **1.** companion, attendant • **2.** escort • **3.** aide, aide-de-camp, adjutant

مَرافُق [maraːfuq] *n:* • **1.** bathroom

إرفاق [ʔirfaːq] *n:* • **1.** attach

مُرافَقَة [muraːfaqa] *n:* • **1.** association, company, friendly relationship • **1.** escorting

ر ف ق [2]

رافَق [raːfaǰ] *v:* • **1.** to become on intimate terms with, become friends with, associate closely with – إذا ترافقه، تِتعَلَّم مِنّه هوايَة [ʔiða traːfǰah, titʕallam minnah hwaːya] If you become his close friend, you'll learn a lot from him. • **2.** to go with, be the lover of, keep as a mistress – رافَقها مُدَّة سَنتَين [raːfaǰha muddat santayn] He was her lover for two years.

ترافَق [traːfaǰ] *v:* • **1.** to become friendly, be intimate with one another – ترافَق ويّا أخُوها حَتّى يتزَوَّجها [traːfaǰ wiyya ʔaxuːha ħatta yidzawwaǰha] He became friendly with her brother, so that he could marry her.

رِفقَة [rifǰa] *n:* رِفقات [rifǰaːt] *pl:* • **1.** close friendship, comradeship

رِفيقَة [rifiːǰa] *n:* رِفيقات [rifiːǰaːt] *pl:* • **1.** girl friend • **2.** mistress, paramour

ر ف ه

رَفَّه [raffah] *v:* • **1.** to make life pleasant and comfortable – هالوِزارَة دَترَفِّه عَن المُوَظَّفين هوايَة [halwizaːra datraffih ʕan ʔilmuwaððafiːn hwaːya]

ر

This administration is making conditions a lot better for the employees. المُغَنِّيَة تبَرَّعَت ترُوح ترَفِّه عَن الجِّنُود [ʔilmuɣanniya tbarraʕat truːħ traffih ʕan ʔijjinuːd] The singer volunteered to go bring comfort to the soldiers.
ترَفَّه [traffah] *v:* • **1.** to live in comfort and ease – إذا يصِير راتبَك مِيتَين دِينار بِالشَّهَر، تِترَفَّه [ʔiða yṣiːr raːtbak mitayn dinaːr biššahar, titraffah] If your salary gets to two hundred dinars per month, you'll live well.
رَفاهِيَّة [rafaːhiyya] *n:* • **1.** luxury • **2.** easy living • **3.** personal comfort

ر ف و

راف [raːf] *v:* • **1.** to reweave, darn, mend – راف مُكان الحَرِق بِالسِّترَة كُلِّش زين [raːf mukaːn ʔilħarig bissitra kulliš ziːn] He rewove the burned place in the jacket very well. رُوف المُكانات القايمَة بِالجُّواريب [ruːf ʔalmukaːnaːt ʔilgaːyma bijjuwaːriːb] Darn the worn places in the socks.
رَوف [rawf, ruːf] *n:* • **1.** reweaving, mending
رَوّاف [rawwaːf] *n:* رَوّافَة [rawwaːfa] *pl:* • **1.** reweaver, mender (of woven material)
رِيافَة [riyaːfa] *n:* • **1.** reweaving, darning, mending

ر ق ب

راقَب [raːqab] *v:* • **1.** to watch, observe, regard closely, keep an eye on – مِنُو راقَب الصَّفّ اليوم؟ [minu raːqab ʔiṣṣaff ʔilyuːm?] Who watched over the class today? الشُّرطَة دَتراقبَه [ʔiššurṭa datraːqbah] The police have him under surveillance.
ترَقَّب [traqqab] *v:* • **1.** to expect, anticipate, await – كِنّا نِترَقَّب وُصُولَه بِأي لَحظَة [činna nitraqqab wuṣuːlah bʔay laħða] We were expecting his arrival at any moment.
رَقِيب [raqiːb] *n:* رُقَباء [ruqabaːʔ] *pl:* • **1.** censor
رُقبَة [rugba] *n:* رُقَب، رقاب [rugab, rgaːb] *pl:* • **1.** neck - رِسّجلا ،َبقُر [rugbat ʔijjisir] end of the bridge. • **2.** responsibility – رُقبَة الجِّسر [rugbat ʔijjisir] end of the bridge. برُقُبتَه خَمِس جَهّال بِالإضافَة إلَى مَرتَه [brugubtah xamis jihaːl bilʔiðaːfa ʔila martah] He's got the responsibility for five children in addition to his wife on his shoulders.
ترَقُّب [taraqqub] *n:* • **1.** expectation, anticipation
رَقابَة [raqaːba] *n:* • **1.** censorship
مُراقِب [muraːqib] *n:* مُراقِبِين [muraːqibiːn] *pl:* • **1.** prefect, monitor. • **2.** observer, inspector, supervisor
رقَيبَة، شِجَر أَبُو رقَيبَة [rgayba, šijar ʔabu rgayba] *n:* • **1.** long-necked squash
مُراقَبَة [muraːqaba] *n:* • **1.** observation, surveillance • **2.** monitoring, overseeing

ر ق د

مَرقَد [marqad] *n:* مَراقِد [maraːqid] *pl:* • **1.** mausoleum, tomb

ر ق ش

رَقِش [ragiš] *n:* رقاش [rgaːš] *pl:* • **1.** pockmark
أرقَش [ʔargaš] *adj:* رُقُش، رَقشِين [ruguš, ragšiːn.] *pl:* رَقشَة [ragša] *feminine:* • **1.** pockmarked • **2.** person with a pockmarked face

ر ق ص

See also: م ر ق ص
رِقَص [rigaṣ] *v:* • **1.** to dance – هِيَّ ما تُعرُف تُرقُص زين [hiyya maː tuʕruf turguṣ ziːn] She doesn't know how to dance well. قام يُرقُص مِن الفَرَح [gaːm yurguṣ min ʔilfaraħ] He jumped for joy.
رَقَّص [raggaṣ] *v:* • **1.** to make dance – جِيب الشّادِي مالَك وَرَقِّصَه [jiːb ʔiššaːdi maːlak wraggiṣah] Bring your monkey and make him dance. رَقِّصنِي. مَرَّة يرِيد هَذا ومَرَّة يرِيد ذاك [raggaṣni. marra yriːd haːða wmarra yriːd ðaːk] He kept me jumping. One time he wants this and next he wants that.
ترَقَّص [traggaṣ] *v:* • **1.** to dance – يِترَقَّص بمَشيَه [yitraggaṣ bmašyah] He prances when he walks.
رَقُص، رِقِص [raguṣ, rigiṣ] *n:* • **1.** dancing, dance
رَقّاص [raggaṣ, raqqaːṣ] *n:* رَقّاصَة [raqqaːṣa, raggaːṣa] *pl:* • **1.** dancer • **2.** pl. رَقّاصَة dancer • **3.** pl. رَقّاصات pendulum
رِقصَة [rigṣa] *n:* رِقصات [rigṣaːt] *pl:* • **1.** a dance
راقِصَة [raːqiṣa] *n:* راقِصات [raːqiṣaːt] *pl:* • **1.** woman dancer, belly or oriental dancer
راقُوص [raːguːṣ] *n:* رواقِيص [rwaːgiːṣ] *pl:* • **1.** dancer
رَقّاصَة [raqqaːṣa, raggaːṣa] *n:* رَقّاصات [raqqaːṣaːt, raggaːṣaːt] *pl:* • **1.** female dancer
راقِص [raːqiṣ] *adj:* • **1.** dancing – حَفلَة راقِصَة [ħafla raːqiṣa] dancing party. • **2.** pl. راقِيصِين dancer

ر ق ط

رَقَّط [raggaṭ] *v:* • **1.** to speckle, spot – رَقَّط وُصلَة القماش بِأخضَر وأحمَر [raggaṭ wuṣlat ʔilqmaːš bʔaxðar wʔaħmar] He speckled the piece of cloth with green and red.
أرقَط [ʔargaṭ] *adj:* • **1.** speckled, spotted – دِيك أرقَط [diːč ʔargaṭ] a speckled rooster.
مرَقَّط [mraqqaṭ, mraggaṭ] *adj:* • **1.** speckled, spotted

ر ق ع

رِقَع [rigaʕ] *v:* • **1.** to patch – رِقَع الدِّشداشَة بِوُصلَة مِن غير لُون [rigaʕ ʔiddišdaːša bwuṣla min ɣiːr luːn] He patched the robe with a piece of another color. • **2.** to slam, slap – مِن تِطلَع، لا ترِقَع الباب حيل [min tiṭlaʕ, laː tirgaʕ ʔilbaːb ħiːl] When you go out, don't slam the door hard. شال الكَلِب وَرِقعَه بِالقاع [šaːl ʔiččalib wrigaʕah bilgaːʕ] He picked up the dog and slammed him down on the ground. رِقعَه عِجِل دَوَّخَه [rigaʕah ʕijil dawwaxah] He slapped him and made him dizzy. ما أدرِي شَكُو. صار ساعَة الرِّصاص يرقع [maː ʔadri

šaku. ṣa:r sa:ʕa ʔirriṣa:ṣ yirgaʕ] I don't know what's happening. For an hour bullets have been flying around.
رَقَّع [raggaʕ] *v:* • **1.** to patch, mend – صار خَمِس مَرّات رَقَّعِت هَالقُندَرَة [ṣa:r xamis marra:t raggaʕit halqundara] I've mended this shoe for the fifth time now. دَترَقِّع البَنطَرُون [datraggiʕ ʔilpanṭaru:n] She's patching the pants. هِيَّ تشُق وَأُمّها ترَقِّعلها [hiyya tšugg wʔummha traggʕilha] She misbehaves and her mother patches things up for her.
رَقِع [ragiʕ] *n:* • **1.** slapping, patching
رُقعَة [rugʕa] *n:* رُقَع [rugaʕ] *pl:* • **1.** patch (of clothes or shoes) – هَالرُّقعَة لهَالبابُوج [harrugʕa lhalba:bu:ǰ] They're birds of a feather (lit., this patch for this slipper).
رَقّاع [ragga:ʕ] *n:* رقاقِيع [raga:gi:ʕ] *pl:* • **1.** shoe repairman, cobbler
مرَقَّع [mraggaʕ] *adj:* • **1.** patched
مَرقُوع [margu:ʕ] *adj:* • **2.** stitched

ر ق ق

رَق [raqq, račč] *v:* • **1.** to soften, relent, have pity – رَق قَلبِي عَليه وَإنطَيتَه أَكِل [raqq galbi ʕali:h wʔinṭaytah ʔakil] I took pity on him and gave him food. • **2.** to become weak, be weakened
رَق [ragg] *n:* • **1.** (coll.) turtle
رِقَّة [riqqa] *n:* • **1.** gentleness, mildness
رَقَّة [ragga] *n:* رَقّات [ragga:t] *pl:* • **1.** turtle • **2.** Volkswagen "beetle" car
رَقِّي [raggi] *n:* • **1.** (coll.) watermelon
رَقِّيَّة [raggiyya] *n:* رَقِّيّات [raggiyya:t] *pl:* • **1.** a watermelon
رَقِيق [raqi:q, riči:č] *adj:* • **1.** soft, tender, gentle – قَلبَه رَقِيق [galbah raqi:q] He has a kind heart. He's soft-hearted.
رقاق، خُبُز رقاق [rga:g, xubuz rga:g] *n:* • **1.** bread baked in thin loaves
أَرَق [ʔaraqq] *comparative adjective:* • **1.** more or most compassionate, tender-hearted

ر ق ل

رِقَل [rigal] *v:* • **1.** to wobble – الجَرخ القِدّامِي دَيُرقُل [ʔiččarix ʔilgidda:mi dayurgul] The front wheel is wobbling.
رَقلَة [ragla] *n:* • **1.** rough, bumpy, uneven ground

ر ق م

رِقَم [rigam] *v:* • **1.** to cover over, close off, seal off – رِقَم الصَّندُوق بخِشَب معاكَس [rigam ʔiṣṣandu:g bxišab mʕa:kas] He sealed up the box with plywood. رِقَم حَلق البِير بچِينكُو [rigam ħalg ʔilbi:r bči:nku] He closed up the mouth of the well with sheet metal.
رَقَّم [raqqam] *v:* • **1.** to affix numbers to, to number – رَقُّم صَفحات التَّقرِير [raqqum ṣafħa:t ʔittaqri:r] Number the pages of the report.
رَقَّم [raggam] *v:* • **1.** to close up, seal up – أَخَذ البسامِير والخِشَب وَرَقَّم الصَّنادِيق [ʔaxað ʔilbsa:mi:r wilxišab wraggam ʔiṣṣana:di:g] He took the nails and wood and sealed up the boxes.
رَقَم [raqam] *n:* أرقام [ʔarqa:m] *pl:* • **1.** record, official record (athlet.) • **2.** number, numeral – رَقَم قِياسِي [raqam qiya:si] record, official record (athlet.).
رَقُم [ragum] *n:* • **1.** closing off, sealing off

ر ق ي

رَقَّى [raqqa:] *v:* • **1.** to promote – أَخُوك، رَقُّوه وَإلّا بَعَد؟ [ʔaxu:k, raqqawh waʔilla baʕad?] Did they promote your brother yet? • **2.** to raise, further, promote, advance – يبَيِّن وَظِيفتَه رَقّاتَه عَلينا [yibayyin waðiːftah raqqa:tah ʕali:na] It seems his job has set him above us. شرَقّاك عَلَى أَصدِقائَك؟ [šraqqa:k ʕala ʔaṣdiqa:ʔak?] What made you feel you are better than your friends?
ترَقَّى [traqqa:] *v:* • **1.** to rise, ascend, go up – الأَسعار كُلّها ترَقّات [ʔilʔasʕa:r kullha traqqa:t] All the prices went up. • **2.** to advance, progress – الطِّب ترَقَّى هوايَة بالسِّنِين الأَخِيرَة [ʔiṭṭibb traqqa: hwa:ya bissini:n ʔilʔaxi:ra] Medicine has advanced a lot in the last few years.
ترَقِّي [taraqqi] *n:* • **1.** advance
ترقِيَة [tarqiya] *n:* • **1.** promotion
اِرتِقاء [ʔirtiqa:ʔ] *n:* • **1.** evolution • **2.** progress
راقِي [ra:qi] *adj:* • **1.** advanced, modern • **2.** superior, high-grade • **3.** educated, refined

ر ك ب

رِكَب [rikab] *v:* • **1.** to ride – ما يِقدَر يِركَب حصان [ma: yigdar yirkab ħṣa:n] He can't ride a horse. • **2.** to ride in, ride on, go in, on, or on board, travel in, on, or on board – الجّاهِل راكُب عَلَى مَتِن أُمَّه [ʔiǰǰa:hil ra:kub ʕala matin ʔummah] The child is riding on his mother's shoulder. رِكَب يَمِّي بِالقِطار [rikab yammi bilqiṭa:r] He rode beside me on the train. أَبَداً ما راكُب طَيّارَة [ʔabadan ma: ra:kub ṭiyya:ra] I've never ridden in an airplane. • **3.** to get in, get on, board, climb aboard – رِكَب سَيّارتَه وَراح عَليه [rikab sayya:rtah wra:ħ ʕali:h] He got in his car and went to see him. • **4.** to mount, breed with, mate with – خَرُوفنا رِكَب نَعجَتهُم [xaru:fna rikab naʕǰathum] Our ram mated with their ewe. • **5.** to bully, browbeat, intimidate, dominate – اللّي يصِير ضَعِيف، النّاس يِركَبُوه [ʔilli yṣi:r ðaʕi:f, ʔinna:s yirkabu:h] People bully anyone who is weak. مَرتَه شافتَه ضَعِيف وَرِكبَتَه [martah ša:fatah ðaʕi:f wrikbatah] His wife saw that he was weak and dominated him.
رَكَّب [rakkab] *v:* • **1.** to cause to ride, give a ride to – تِقدَر ترَكُّبنِي وِيّاك؟ [tigdar trakkubni wiyya:k?] Can you give me a ride with you? • **2.** to put on, put aboard – أُخُذ الجّاهِل وَرَكُّبَه بالباص [ʔuxuð ʔiǰǰa:hil wrakkubah

bilpa:ṣ] Take the child and put him on the bus. • **3.** to mount, fasten, insert, set, place, install – رَكَّب الجّامَة بِالشِّبّاك [rakkab ʔijja:ma biššibba:č] He installed the pane of glass in the window. • **4.** to put together, assemble, fit together – رَكَّب المَكِينَة بساعَة [rakkab ʔilmaki:na bsa:ʕa] He assembled the machine in one hour. • **5.** to cook, fix, or put together a meal – راح ترَكُّب بَعَد ما تِجِي مِن السُّوق [ra:ħ trakkub baʕad ma: tiji min ʔissu:g] She's going to fix a meal as soon as she comes from the market. • **6.** to graft – رَكَّبِت بُرتُقال عَلَى سِندِي [rakkabit purtuqa:l ʕala sindi] He grafted an orange onto a grapefruit.

ترَكَّب [trakkab] *v:* • **1.** to be set in, inserted, mounted, fitted – باب السَّيّارَة ما تِترَكَّب لِأَنّ مَعوُوجَة [ba:b ʔissayya:ra ma: titrakkab liʔann maʕwu:ja] The car door won't fit because it's bent. • **2.** to be composed, made up, consist – هالمادَّة تِترَكَّب مِن ثلَث عَناصِر [halma:dda titrakkab min tlaθ ʕana:ṣir] This substance is composed of three elements. • **3.** to be grafted – البُرتَقال ما يِترَكَّب عَلَى رُمّان [ʔilpurtaqa:l ma: yitrakkab ʕala rumma:n] An orange can't be grafted onto a pomegranate.

اِرتِكَب [ʔirtikab] *v:* • **1.** to commit, perpetrate – اِرتِكَب جَرائِم هوايَة [ʔirtikab jara:ʔim hwa:ya] He committed many crimes.

رُكبَة [rukba] *n:* رُكَب [rukab, rikab] *pl:* • **1.** knee

رَكبَة [rakba] *n:* رِكبات [rikba:t] *pl:* • **1.** ride

رِكاب [rka:b, rča:b] *n:* رُكاب، رِكابات [ruka:b, rča:ba:t] *pl:* • **1.** stirrup

مَركَب [markab] *n:* مَراكِب [mara:kib] *pl:* • **1.** ship, vessel, boat

راكِب [ra:kib] *n:* رُكّاب [rukka:b] *pl:* • **1.** passenger, rider

مُرَكِّب [murakkib] *n:* مُرَكِّبِين [murakkibi:n] *pl:* • **1.** installer, fitter – مُرَكِّب الأسنان [murakkib ʔilʔasna:n] prosthodontist. • **2.** assembler

مُرَكَّب [murakkab] *adj:* • **1.** mounted, fastened, fixed, fitted, inserted, installed • **2.** assembled, composed, put together, made up • **3.** compound, composite, complex – رِبح مُرَكَّب [ribiħ murakkab] compound interest. • **4.** grafted – تُكِّي مرَكَّب [tukki mrakkab] grafted mulberries. • **5.** complex (psych.) – مُرَكَّب نَقِص [murakkab naqiṣ] inferiority complex. • **6.** pl. مُرَكَّبات is used as Noun as in: composite, composition, compound

رُكُوب [ruku:b] *n:* • **1.** ride, travel • **2.** riding

مَركُوب [marku:b] *adj:* • **1.** ridden • **2.** boarded • **3.** mounted, mated, bred • **4.** pl. مراكِيب (as *n:*) (pair of) sandals

تَركِيب [tarki:b] *n:* • **1.** installation

اِرتِكاب [ʔirtika:b] *n:* • **1.** perpetration (of sin or crime) • **2.** commission

ر ك د

رِكَد [rikad] *v:* • **1.** to be still, motionless – بَسّ يِركُد المَيّ، كُلّ الطِّين يِنزِل لِلكَعَب [bass yirkud ʔilmayy, kull ʔiṭṭi:n yinzil liččaʕab] As soon as the water becomes still, all the mud settles to the bottom. شلُون أَضُربَك أُبرَة إذا ما تِركُد؟ [šlu:n ʔaðurbak ʔubra ʔiða ma: tirkud?] How can I give you a shot if you don't be still? • **2.** to abate, subside – رِكَد الوَجَع وَإلّا بَعَد؟ [rikad ʔilwajaʕ waʔilla baʕad?] Has the pain eased yet?

رَكَّد [rakkad] *v:* • **1.** to still, make quiet, motionless – رَكِّدِي الجّاهِل. دَوَّخني بصياحَه [rakkdi ʔijja:hil. dawwaxni bṣya:ħah] Calm that kid down. He's driving me nuts with his yelling. • **2.** to set firmly in place, to place solidly – رَكِّد الكاسَة حَتَّى لا تُوقَع [rakkid ʔalka:sa ħatta la: tu:gaʕ] Set the bowl firmly in place so it won't fall.

رَكدَة [rakda] *n:* رَكدات [rakda:t] *pl:* • **1.** base, foundation, level place

رُكُود [ruku:d] *n:* • **1.** motionlessness, stagnation

راكِد [ra:kid] *adj:* • **1.** still, motionless, stagnant – ماي راكِد [ma:y ra:kid] stagnant water. • **2.** sluggish – سُوق الحُنطَة راكِد اليُوم [su:g ʔilħunṭa ra:kid ʔilyu:m] The wheat market is sluggish today.

ر ك ز

رَكَّز [rakkaz] *v:* • **1.** to plant in the ground, set up – رَكِّز العَمُود بهَالنُّقرَة [rakkiz ʔilʕamu:d bhannugra] Set up the pole in this hole. • **2.** to fix, implant – إقراها عِدَّة مَرّات حَتَّى ترَكِّز المَعلُومات بِذِهنَك [ʔiqra:ha ʕiddat marra:t ħatta trakkiz ʔilmaʕlu:ma:t bðihnak] Read it several times so as to fix the information in your mind. • **3.** to concentrate – رَكَّز كُلّ جهُودَه عَلَى هَالقَضِيَّة [rakkaz kull jhu:dah ʕala halqaðiyya] He concentrated all his efforts on this matter. ما دَأقدَر أَرَكِّز مِن هَالصَّوت العالِي [ma: daʔagdar ʔarakkiz min haṣṣawt ʔilʕa:li] I can't concentrate because of this loud noise. • **4.** to focus – رَكِّز الكامِيرَة عَلَى بُعُد عَشِر أَقدام [rakkiz ʔilkamira ʕala buʕud ʕašir ʔaqda:m] Focus the camera at ten feet.

ترَكَّز [trakkaz] *v:* • **1.** pass. of – رَكَّز. • **2.** to be fixed, focused, concentrated

اِرتِكَز [ʔirtikaz] *v:* • **1.** to lean, support one's weight – رِجل المِيز مَكسُورَة. يِنرادلَه شِي يِرتِكِز عَلِيه [rijl ʔilmi:z maksu:ra. yinra:dlah ši yirtikiz ʕali:h] The table leg is broken. It needs something to support its weight on. • **2.** to rest, be based – خَلِّي حجارَة مِن هَالجِّهَة حَتَّى يِرتِكِز عَليها البِيب [xalli: ħja:ra min hajjiha ħatta yirtikiz ʕali:ha ʔilpi:p] Put a stone under this side so the barrel will rest on it.

مَركَز [markaz] *n:* مَراكِز [mara:kiz] *pl:* • **1.** station, police station • **2.** position (mil.) • **3.** center (of a circle and fig.) • **4.** position, situation, office, post • **5.** status, standing, position

رُكزَة [rukza] *n:* • **1.** comma

رَكِيزَة [raki:za] *n:* • **1.** base

مُرَكَّز [murakkaz] *adj:* • **1.** centralized, concentrated • **2.** condensed, concentrated – حامُض مُرَكَّز [ħa:muð murakkaz] concentrated acid.

مَرکَزِي [markazi] *adj:* • **1.** central – الحُكُومَة المَركَزِيَّة [ʔilħukuːma ʔilmarkaziyya] the central government.

ر ك س

رِكَس [rikas] *v:* • **1.** to sink, go down, become submerged – الحَدِيد يِركُس بِالمَيّ [ʔilħadiːd yirkus bilmayy] Iron sinks in water. • **2.** to plunge, fall, drop – رِكَس بِالنُّقرَة وتعَوَّر [rikas binnugra wtʕawwar] He fell in the hole and got hurt.

رَكَّس [rakkas] *v:* • **1.** to push down, submerge, immerse, dunk – رَكِّس الثُّوب زين بِالصُّبُغ [rakkis ʔiθθuːb ziːn bişşubuɣ] Immerse the shirt well in the dye.

رَكِس [rakis] *n:* • **1.** falling, plunging, dropping, sinking

ر ك ض

رِكَض [rikaḍ] *v:* • **1.** to race, rush, run – حصانِي راح يِركُض بثانِي هَدَّة [ħşaːni raːħ yirkuḍ bθaːni hadda] My horse will run in the second race. أُركُض حَتَّى تلَحِّق بِيه [ʔurkuḍ ħatta tlaħħig biːh] Run so you can catch up to him. كُلّما يِحتاج فلُوس، يُركُض عَلَى أَبُوه [kullmaː yiħtaːǰ fl uːs, yurkuḍ ʕala ʔabuːh] Whenever he needs money, he runs to his father. رِكَضلِي بقَضِيَّة الباسبَورت مالِي [rikaḍli bqaḍiyyat ʔilpaːspuːrt maːli] He did the running around for me on the matter of my passport. ساعتِي دَترُكُض [saːʕti daturkuḍ] My watch is too fast. المَكِينَة دَترُكُض؛ نَقِّصها [ʔilmakiːna daturkuḍ; naqqişha] The engine is racing; slow it down. يِركُض وَالعَشا خُبّاز [yirkuḍ wilʕašaː xubbaːz] He works hard and gets nowhere (lit., he runs and gets only greens for dinner).

رَكَّض [rakkaḍ] *v:* • **1.** to make race, rush, run – لازِم ترَكِّض الحِصان شوَيَّة قَبُل ما تدَخّلَه السِّباق [laːzim trakkiḍ ʔilħişaːn šwayya gabul maː ddaxxlah ʔissibaːq] You should make the horse run a little before you enter him in the race.

رِكِض [rikiḍ] *n:* • **1.** running • **2.** run, dash – سِباق رِكض الضّاحِيَة [sibaːq rikḍ ʔiḍḍaːħiya] cross-country race.

رَكُض [rakuḍ] *n:* • **1.** running, dash

رِكضَة [rikḍa] *n:* رِكضات [rikḍaːt] *pl:* • **1.** running, dash, run

راكِض [raːkiḍ] *adj:* • **1.** running, galloping • **2.** pl. راكِضِين racer, runner

راكُوض [raːkuːḍ] *adj:* • **1.** swift, fleet-footed • **2.** pl. راكُوضِين [rakuːḍiːn] racer, runner

ر ك ع

رِكَع [rikaʕ] *v:* • **1.** to bend the body (in prayer) – مِن يِركَع بِالصَّلاة، ظَهَرَه يقُوم يُوجعَه [min yirkaʕ bişşalaː, ḍaharah yguːm yuːǰʕah] When he bends over in prayer, his back begins go hurt.

رُكعَة [rukʕa] *n:* رُكَعات [rukʕaːt, rukaʕ] *pl:* • **1.** in Moslem prayer, a bending of the torso from a standing position, followed by putting the forehead to the floor

رُكُوع [rukuːʕ] *n:* • **1.** kneeling down, bowing

راكِع [raːkiʕ] *adj:* • **1.** kneeling

ر ك ك

رَكّ [račč] *v:* • **1.** to become weak, be weakened – لا تِغسِل ثوبَك هوايَة تَرَة يِركّ بِالغَسِل [laː tiɣsil θuːbak hwaːya tara yričč bilɣasil] Don't wash your shirt too much or it'll be weakened by the washing. رَكِّيت وَبَعَد ما أَقدَر أَشتُغُل [raččiːt wabaʕad maː ʔagdar ʔaštuɣul] I've gotten weak and can't work any more.

رَكّ [račč] *n:* • **1.** weakness

رِكِيك [ričiːč, rikiːk] *adj:* • **1.** weak, feeble – قماش رِكِيك [qmaːš ričiːč] weak cloth, shoddy cloth. عِبارَة رِكِيكَة [ʕibaːra ričiːča] a weak phrase. صِحّتَه رِكِيكَة [şiħħtah ričiːča] His health is poor. • **2.** loose, slack – الحَبِل ما مَشدُود زين عالجُنطَة. رِكِيك [ʔilħabil maː mašduːd ziːn ʕaǰǰunṭa. ričiːč]. The rope is not well tied on the suitase. It is loose.

ر ك م

تراكَم [traːkam] *v:* • **1.** to pile up

تَراكُم [taraːkum] *n:* • **1.** accumulation

مِتراكُم [mitraːkum] *adj:* • **1.** accumulated, piled up, amassed, heaped up

ر ك ن

رِكَن [rikan] *v:* • **1.** to park, put aside

رُكُن [rukun] *n:* أَركان [ʔarkaːn] *pl:* • **1.** corner – كُلّ واحِد قاعِد بِرُكُن. يبَيِّن زعالَة [kull waːħid gaːʕid brukun. yibayyin zʕaːla] Everyone is sitting in a corner. It seems they're mad. اِشتِرَيت قِطعَة رُكُن. راح أَبنِيها بَيت [ʔištirayt qiṭʕa rukun. raːħ ʔabniːha bayt] I bought a corner lot. I'm going to build a house on it. • **2.** (military) staff – ضابُط رُكُن [ḍaːbuṭ rukun] staff officer. رَئِيس أَركان الجَّيش [raʔiːs ʔarkaːn ʔiǰǰayš] military chief of staff.

مَركُون [markuːn] *adj:* • **1.** parked • **2.** antiquated

ر م ح

رُمُح [rumuħ] *n:* رماح [rmaːħ] *pl:* • **1.** lance, spear, javelin

ر م د

رُمَد [rumad] *v:* • **1.** to become inflamed (eye) – رُمدَت عَين الجّاهِل مِن قَدّ ما يِلعَب بِيها [rumdat ʕiːn ʔiǰǰaːhil min gadd maː yilʕab biːha] The child's eye became inflamed from his playing with it so much.

رَمَّد [rammad] *v:* • **1.** to inflame, make inflamed – الطُّوز يرَمِّد العَين [ʔiṭṭuːz yrammid ʔilʕayn] Dust inflames the eyes.

رَمَد [ramad] *n:* • **1.** inflammation of the eyes, ophthalmia, conjunctivitis

رماد [rmaːd, ramaːd] *n:* • **1.** ashes

ر

أرمَد [ʔarmad] *adj:* رُمُد، رَمدِين [rumud, ramdiːn] *pl:* رَمدَة [ramda] *feminine:* • **1.** sore-eyed, having inflamed, sore eyes • **2.** person with inflamed eyes
رمادِي [rmaːdi, ramaːdi] *adj:* • **1.** ashen, ash-colored, ash-gray – قاط رمادِي [qaːṭ rmaːdi] a light gray suit.

ر م ز
رِمَز [rimaz] *v:* • **1.** to symbolize, represent, stand for – هالحَرُف يِرمِز إِلَى الهَدرُوجِين [halħaruf yirmiz ʔila ʔilhadruːǰiːn] This letter stands for hydrogen. اللّون الماوي بالخَرِيطَة يِرمِز إِلَى المَيّ [ʔilluːn ʔilmaːwi bilxariːṭa yirmiz ʔila ʔilmayy] The light blue color on the map stands for water. • **2.** to use a symbol for, represent with a symbol – بالكِيمياء يِرمِزُون لكُلّ مَعدَن بِرَمِز [bilkiːmya yirmizuːn lkull maʕdan bramiz] In chemistry they represent each metal with a symbol. خَلِّي نِرمِز إلها حَرُف لاتِينِي [xalliː nirmiz ʔilha ħaruf laːtiːni] Let's use a Latin character to symbolize it.
رَمِز [ramiz] *n:* رُمُوز [rumuːz] *pl:* • **1.** symbol, symbolic figure, emblem, character • **2.** secret sign, code sign
رَمزِي [ramzi] *adj:* • **1.** symbolic – هَدِيَّة رَمزِيَّة [hadiyya ramziyya] a symbolic gift.

ر م ش
رِمَش [rimaš] *v:* • **1.** to twitch, flutter, to blink – جِفِن عينِي دَيرمِش هوايَة [ǰifin ʕiːni dayirmiš hwaːya] My eyelid is twitching a lot.
رِمِش [rimiš] *n:* رمُوش [rmuːš] *pl:* • **1.** eyelash
رَمِش [ramiš] *n:* • **1.** blinking
رَمّاش [rammaːš] *adj:* رَمّاشات [rammaːšaːt] *pl:* • **1.** blinking (light)

ر م ض
رَمَضان [ramaðaːn] *n.* • **1.** Ramadan, the ninth month of the Moslem calendar

ر م ل [1]
تَرَمَّل [trammal] *v:* • **1.** to become a widow – إذا تِرَمّلَت، شلُون راح تعَيِّش وِلِدها؟ [ʔiða trammulat, šluːn raːħ tʕayyiš wilidha?] If she became a widow, how would she provide for her children?
أرمَل [ʔarmal] *n:* أرامِل [ʔaraːmil] *pl:* • **1.** widower
أرمَلَة [ʔarmala] *n:* أرامِل [ʔaraːmil] *pl:* • **1.** widow

ر م ل [2]
رَمُل [ramul] *n:* • **1.** sand – يُضرُب بالتَّخَت رَمُل [yuðrub bittaxat ramul] He tells fortunes in sand.
رَملِي [ramli] *adj:* • **1.** sandy

ر م م
رَمَّم [rammam] *v:* • **1.** to repair, to restore, to overhaul
تَرَمَّم [trammam] *v:* • **1.** to be repaired, to be overhauled
تَرمِيم [tarmiːm] *n:* تَرمِيمات [tarmiːmaːt] *pl:* • **1.** repair, restoration, overhaul

ر م ن
رُمّان [rummaːn] *n:* • **1.** (coll.) pomegranate(s)
رُمّانَة [rummaːna] *n:* رُمّانات [rummaːnaːt] *pl:* • **1.** pomegranate • **2.** knob, ball • **3.** grenade
رُمّانِي [rummaːni] *adj:* • **1.** dark red, maroon

ر م ي
رِمَى [rimaː] *v:* • **1.** to throw, hurl, cast – رِمَى الرُّمُح إِلَى مَسافَة مِيَّة مَتِر [rimaː ʔirrumuħ ʔila masaːfat miyyat matir] He threw the javelin one-hundred meters. • **2.** to fire (a gun) – ظَلَّت المَدافع تِرمِي لِلصُّبُح [ðallat ʔilmadaːfiʕ tirmi lissubuħ] The artillery continued firing till morning. أُخُذ نِيشان زين قَبُل ما تِرمِي [ʔuxuð niːšaːn ziːn gabul maː tirmi] Take good aim before you fire. • **3.** to shoot (someone) – رِمُوه بِطلِقتَين بصَدرَه [rimuːh bṭliqtayn bṣadrah] They shot him twice in the chest. عيُونَه تِرمِي نار مِن الغَضَب [ʕyuːnah tirmi naːr min ʔilɣaðab] His eyes are flashing with anger.
اِنرِمَى [ʔinrimaː] *v:* • **1.** to be shot • **2.** to be thrown
رَمِي [ramy] *n:* • **1.** throwing, hurling – رَمِي القُرُص [ramy ʔilquruṣ] discus throwing. • **2.** firing, shooting – رَمِي حَقِيقِي [ramy ħaqiːqi] live firing, firing with live ammunition. رَمِي بِالرِّصاص [ramy birriṣaːṣ] death by firing squad.
رامِي [raːmi] *n:* • **1.** rummy (cards)
مَرمَى [marma] *n:* • **1.** range • **2.** goal • **3.** purpose

ر ن ح
تَرَنَّح [trannaħ] *v:* • **1.** to stagger, reel, totter, sway – يِترَنَّح بمَشيَه مِن السُّكُر [yitrannaħ bmašyah min ʔissukur] He's staggering from drunkenness.

ر ن د
رَندَة [randa] *n:* رَندات [randaːt] *pl:* • **1.** (carpenter's) plane – أُضرُبَه رَندَة إِلَى أَن يِتساوَى [ʔuðurbah randa ʔila ʔan yitsaːwaː] Use a plane on it till it is smooth. • **2.** food grater

ر ن د ج
رَندَج [randaǰ] *v:* • **1.** to plane – النَّجّار رَندَج اللّوحَة وصارَت ناعمَة [ʔinnaǰǰaːr randaǰ ʔilluːħa wṣaːrat naːʕma] The carpenter planed the board and it became smooth.
رَندَج [randaǰ] *n:* رَنادِج [ranaːdiǰ] *pl:* • **1.** (carpenter's) plane

ر ن ق [1]
رَونَق [rawnaq] *n:* • **1.** splendor, beauty, glamour, elegance

ر ن ق [2]

رنق [ring] *n:* رنقات [ringa:t] *pl:* • **1.** ring (esp. piston ring) – رنق مُلاكَمَة [ring mula:kama] boxing ring. • **2.** rim (of an automobile wheel) – آني قاعِد عالرِّنقات [ʔa:ni ga:ʕid ʕarringa:t] I'm flat broke.

ر ن ن

رَنّ [rann] *v:* • **1.** to ring, resound – الدِّرهِم، إذا ما يرِنّ، مُزَيَّف [ʔiddirhim, ʔiða ma: yrinn, muzayyaf] If the dirham doesn't ring, it's counterfeit.
رَنّ، رَنَّة [rann, ranna] *n:* رَنّات [ranna:t] *pl:* • **1.** sound, ringing, tone
رَنِين [rani:n] *n:* • **1.** ring(ing), toll(ing), peal, resonance
رَنّان [ranna:n] *adj:* • **1.** ringing, resounding, sonorous, resonant – خِطاب رَنّان [xiṭa:b ranna:n] a resounding speech. شَوكَة رَنّانَة [šawka ranna:na] tuning fork.

ر ه ب

أرهَب [ʔarhab] *v:* • **1.** to terrorize, to frighten
اِرتِهَب [ʔirtihab] *v:* • **1.** to become afraid, be frightened – اِرتِهَبِت مِن الظِّلمَة [ʔirtihabit min ʔiððalma] I got scared of the dark.
رَهبَة [rahba] *n:* • **1.** fear, fright, terror, awe
راهِب [ra:hib] *n:* رُهبان [ruhba:n] *pl:* • **1.** (Christian) monk
إرهاب [ʔirha:b] *n:* • **1.** terror, terrorism
راهِبَة [ra:hiba] *n:* راهِبات [ra:hiba:t] *pl:* • **1.** nun
رَهِيب [rahi:b] *adj:* • **1.** awful, terrible
إرهابِي [ʔirha:bi] *adj:* • **1.** terroristic • **2.** *pl.* إرهابِيِّين (as *n:*) terrorist

ر ه د ن

رَهدَن [rahdan] *v:* • **1.** to set or put in place, place – التُّنقَة وُقعَت لِأَنّ ما رَهدَنِتها زين [ʔittunga wugʕat liʔann ma: rahdanitha zi:n] The jug fell because you didn't place it carefully. • **2.** to situate, get settled, settle – رَهدِن مَرتَك وَولدَك بالأَوَّل، وبَعدين سافِر [rahdin martak wwildak bilʔawwal, wbaʕdi:n sa:fir] Get your wife and children settled first, and then take the trip.
تَرَهدَن [trahdan] *v:* • **1.** to become settled, situated – بَعَد ما أترَهدِن بِبَغداد، أدَوِّر عَلَى شُغُل [baʕad ma: ʔatrahdin bibaɣda:d, ʔadawwir ʕala šuɣul] After I get settled in Baghdad, I'll look for work.

ر ه ق

رِهَق [rihaq] *v:* • **1.** to make excessive demands
إرهاق [ʔirha:q] *n:* • **1.** pressure, oppression, heavy load
مُراهَقَة [mura:haqa] *n:* • **1.** adolescence
مُرهَق [murhaq] *adj:* مُرهَقِين [murhaqi:n] *pl:* • **1.** exhausted, overstrained
مُرهِق [murhiq] *adj:* • **1.** overworked, overtired, lean, languorous, languid
مُراهِق [mura:hiq] *n:* مُراهِقِين [mura:hiqi:n] *pl:* • **1.** adolescent

ر ه م

رِهَم [riham] *v:* • **1.** to harmonize – هَالبَوينباغ ما يِرهَم ويّا هَالقاط [halbuyinba:ɣ ma: yirham wiyya halqa:t] This tie doesn't go with this suit. • **2.** to come to agreement – إنطِيه فَدّ سِعِر زين وَبَلكِي تِرهَم ويّاه [ʔinṭi:h fadd siʕir zi:n wbalki tirham wiyya:h] Give him a good price and maybe you'll come to an agreement with him. • **3.** with عَلَى to fit – هالمِفتاح ما يِرهَم عالقُفُل [halmifta:ħ ma: yirham ʕalquful] This key doesn't fit the lock. سِترتَك تِرهَم عَلَيّا تَمام [sitirtak tirham ʕalayya tama:m] Your coat fits me fine. مِن أوَّل يوم، إيدَه رُهمَت عَالشُّغُل [min ʔawwal yu:m, ʔi:dah ruhmat ʕaššuɣul] From the first day, he took to the work. شلُون رِهمَت جَيّتَك اليُوم [šlu:n rihmat ǰayytak ʔilyu:m] Your arrival today was very appropriate!
رَهَّم [rahham] *v:* • **1.** to make fit, to fit – رَهَّم مِفتاح عَلَى قُفل الصَّندُوق وَفتَحَه [rahham mifta:ħ ʕala qufl ʔiṣṣandu:q wfitaħah] He fitted a key into the trunk's lock and opened it. الخَيّاط رَهَّم قاط أبُويا عَلَيّا [ʔilxayya:ṭ rahham qa:ṭ ʔabu:ya ʕalayya] The tailor fitted my father's suit to me.
تراهَم [tra:ham] *v:* • **1.** to fit with each other, be harmonious with each other – هَالثَّوب وَهَالقاط ما يِتراهمُون [haθθu:b whalqa:ṭ ma: yitra:hmu:n] This shirt and this suit don't go together. ما رِدِت أسافِر وِيّاه لِأَنّ ما نِتراهَم [ma: ridit ʔasa:fir wiyya:h liʔann ma: nitra:ham] I didn't want to travel with him because we don't get along together.
مَرهَم [marham] *n:* مَراهِم [mara:him] *pl:* • **1.** ointment, salve
تَرهِيم [tarhi:m] *n:* • **1.** fitting, harmonization
راهُم، راهِم [ra:hum, ra:him] *adj:* • **1.** fitting, proper – هَالحكايَة ما راهمَة مِنَّك [halhča:ya ma: ra:hma minnak] That statement isn't proper from you.

ر ه ن

رِهَن [rihan] *v:* • **1.** to pawn, deposit as security – رِهنَت كُلّ ذَهَبها [rihnat kull ðahabha] She pawned all of her jewelry. ما دايَنَه فلُوس إلّا لَمّا رِهَن ساعتَه [ma: da:yanah flu:s ʔilla lamma rihan sa:ʕtah] He wouldn't lend him any money until he left his watch as security. رِهَنِت بَيتِي بِألِف دِينار [rihanit bayti bʔalif dina:r] I mortgaged my house for a thousand dinars.
راهَن [ra:han] *v:* • **1.** to make a bet with (someone), to bet, wager – راهَنَه عَلَى فَدّ مَسألَة عَوِيصَة [ra:hanah ʕala fadd masʔala ʕawi:ṣa] He made a bet with him on a complex issue. أراهنَك راح يِتزَوَّج [ʔara:hnak ra:ħ yidzawwaǰ] I'll bet you he is going to get married.

راهَن بمِيَة دِينار عَلَى هَالحِصان [ra:han bmiyat dina:r ʕala halħiṣa:n] He wagered a hundred dinars on that horse.
تراهَن [tra:han] *v:* • **1.** to bet with each other – تراهنوا عَلَى مِيَّة دِينار [tra:hnaw ʕala miyyat dina:r] They bet each other a hundred dinars.
رَهَن [rahan] *n:* رُهُون [ruhu:n] *pl:* • **1.** pawn, pledge, security – مَصرَف الرُّهُون [maṣraf ʔirruhu:n] pledge bank, government bank which lends money upon deposit of collateral. • **2.** mortgage • **3.** bet, wager • **4.** money deposited on a bet
رَهِن [rahin] *n:* • **1.** pawning, deposit as security
رِهان [riha:n] *n:* • **1.** bet, wager
رَهِينَة [rahi:na] *n:* رَهاين [raha:yin, raha:ʔin] *pl:* • **1.** hostage
راهِن [ra:hin] *adj:* • **1.** present (time), present, actual, present-day, existing

ر ه و

ترَهَّى [trahha:] *v:* • **1.** to be or become skilled, proficient, thoroughly competent – هُوَّ راح يِترَهَّى عالشُّغُل بَعَد فَدّ سَنَة [huwwa ra:ħ yitrahha: ʕaššuɣul baʕad fadd sana] He will become proficient at the job after one year. إنطُوه شُغُل بَسِيط يترَهَّى عَليه [ʔinṭu:h šaɣla basi:ṭa yitrahha: ʕali:h] They gave him a simple job he could do easily. لازِم مِترَهِّي عَليه. دَيضُربَه شلُون ما يرِيد [la:zim mitrahhi ʕali:h. dayðurbah šlu:n ma: yri:d] He knows he's got him. He's hitting him any way he wants. • **2.** to be in control of the situation, be in good shape, to have an easy time of it – أقدَر أخَلِّص شُغلِي قَبِل الظُّهُر وَأني مِترَهِّي [ʔagdar ʔaxalliṣ šuɣli gabil ʔiððuhur waʔa:ni mitrahhi] I can finish my work before noon and have time to spare. هَذا حَكِي واحِد مِترَهِّي [ha:ða ħači wa:ħid mitrahhi] This is the talk of a man who's comfortably well off.
رَهاوَة [raha:wa] *n:* • **1.** surplus, extra amount – أرِيد تخَيِّطلِي قَمِيص بِيه رَهاوَة [ʔari:d txayyitli qami:ṣ bi:h raha:wa] I want you to sew me a shirt that will be a bit large. هَالبَنطَرُون بِيه رَهاوَة زايدَة [halpanṭaru:n bi:h raha:wa za:yda] These pants are a little too big. • **2.** confidence, assurance, authority – يِحكِي بِرَهاوَة لِأنّ يُعرُف كُلّشِي عَن المَوضُوع [yiħči braha:wa liʔann yuʕruf kullši ʕan ʔilmawðu:ʕ] He speaks with confidence because he knows all about the subject.
راهِي [ra:hi] *adj:* • **1.** ample, more than enough – ثلاث ياردات قماش راهيَة عَلَيّا. يصِير مِنها قاط وَيزِيد شوَيَّة [tlaθ ya:rda:t qma:š ra:hya ʕalayya. yṣi:r minha qa:ṭ wyzi:d šwayya] Three yards of cloth is ample for me. It will make a suit with a little left over. هَالسِّترَة راهيَة عَلَيّا [hassitra ra:hya ʕalayya] This jacket is too big for me.
مِترَهِّي [mitrahhi] *adj:* • **1.** skilled, proficient • **2.** relaxed, at ease, completely in control

ر و ب [1]

راب [ra:b] *v:* • **1.** to curdle – الحَلِيب راب [ʔilħali:b ra:b] The milk curdled.
رَوَّب [rawwab] *v:* • **1.** to curdle, make curdle – رَوُّب الحَلِيب بِهَالكاسَة [rawwub ʔilħali:b bhalka:sa] Curdle the milk in this bowl.
رُوبَة [ru:ba] *n:* • **1.** curdled milk, curds • **2.** thick yogurt
رايِب [ra:yib] *adj:* • **1.** curdled milk

ر و ب [2]

رُوب [ru:b] *n:* إرواب، روابَة [rwa:b, rwa:ba] *pl:* • **1.** robe, dressing gown, bathrobe

ر و ب ن

رُوبيان [rubya:n] *n:* • **1.** a kind of shrimp

ر و ت ن

رُوتِين [ru:ti:n] *n:* • **1.** routine
رُوتِينِي [ru:ti:ni] *adj:* • **1.** routine

ر و ث

رَوَّث [rawwaθ] *v:* • **1.** to defecate, drop dung (of an animal) – وَخِّر الحِصان مِنّا قَبِل ما يرَوِّث [waxxir ʔilħiṣa:n minna gabil ma: yrawwiθ] Get the horse away from us before he drops his dung.
رَوث [rawθ] *n:* • **1.** dung, manure (horse, donkey, or cow)

ر و ح

See also: ر ي ح
راح [ra:ħ] *v:* • **1.** to go, go away, leave, depart – لا ترُوح. أبقى هنا [la: tru:ħ. ʔubqa: hna] Don't go. Stay here. هَاللَّكَّة ما ترُوح [hallakka ma: tru:ħ] This spot won't go away. ظَلّ يِرُوح ويِجِي بالقُبَّة [ðall yiru:ħ wyiji bilgubba] He kept pacing back and forth in the room. تَعَبِي راح بَلاش [taʕabi ra:ħ bala:š] My efforts went for nought. هَالقاط راح؛ بَعَد ما يِنلِبِس [halqa:ṭ ra:ħ; baʕad ma: yinlibis] This suit's gone; it can't be worn anymore. القاط راحلَه أربَع ياردات قماش [ʔilqa:ṭ ra:ħlah ʔarbaʕ ya:rda:t qma:š] Four yards of material went into the suit. هَالبَيت شقَدّ راحلَه فلُوس؟ [halbayt šgadd ra:ħlah flu:s?] How much money did this house cost? • **2.** a pre-verb denoting likelihood of some alternate or future action – لا تسَوِّي هِيكِي أشياء قِدّام الجّاهِل. يِرُوح يِتعَلَّم مِنَّك [la: tsawwi:hi:či ʔašya:ʔ gidda:m ʔijja:hil. yiru:ħ yitʕallam minnak] Don't do such things in front of the child. He might learn from you. إذا تِنطِيه لِلجّاهِل فَدّ شِي ياكلَه، يِرُوح يِسكُت [ʔiða tinṭi:h lijja:hil fadd ši ya:klah, yiru:ħ yiskut] If you give the kid something to eat, he'll be quiet. لا تبَيِّنلَه شِي. يِرُوح يِشنَعنا [la: tbayyinlah ši. yiru:ħ yišnaʕna] Don't let him in on anything. He's likely

to give us away. أُخُذ شَمسِيَّة وِيّاك لا ترُوح تِتبَلّل [ʔuxuð šamsiyya wiyyaːk laː truːħ titballal] Take an umbrella with you or you'll get wet. لا تِلعَب قمار لا ترُوح تِخسَر [laː tilʕab qmaːr laː truːħ tixsar] Don't gamble or you might lose. جاوبَه عَلَى مَكتُوبَه لا يرُوح يزعَل [ǰaːwbah ʕala maktuːbah laː yruːħ yizʕal] Answer his letter or he might get mad. أنصُب السّاعَة لا ترُوح تُوقَف [ʔunṣub ʔissaːʕa laː truːħ tuːgaf] Wind the watch or it'll stop.
رَوَّح [rawwaħ] *v:* • **1.** to cause or allow to go away, – البانزين يِرَوِّح اللّكّات [ʔilbanziːn yirawwiħ ʔillakkaːt] Gasoline removes spots. لا ترَوِّح هَالسَّيّارَة مِن إيدَك [laː trawwiħ hassayyaːra min ʔiːdak] Don't let this car get through your hands. كانَت خُوش صَفقَة بَسّ إنتَ رَوَّحتها مِن إيدِي بِحَكيَك [čaːnat xuːš ṣafqa bass ʔinta rawwaħitha min ʔiːdi bħačyak] It was a good deal but you made it slip through my hands with your remark.
راوَح [raːwaħ] *v:* • **1.** to mark time, walk in place – الجِّنُود دَيراوحُون [ʔiǰǰinuːd dayraːwħuːn] The soldiers are marking time. صارلَه ثلاث سنين دَيراوِح بِالصَّفّ الرّابع [ṣaːrlah tlaθ sniːn dayraːwiħ bişṣaff ʔirraːbiʕ] He's been marking time for three years in the fourth grade.
تراوَح [traːwaħ] *v:* • **1.** to fluctuate, alternate, vary, vacillate – أسعار البَدلات تِتراوَح بين عَشرَة وَعِشرِين دِينار [ʔasʕaːr ʔilbadlaːt titraːwaħ biːn ʕašra wʕišriːn dinaːr] The prices of the suits range between ten and twenty dinars. • **2.** to take turns, alternate – إذا نِتراوَح بِالشُّغُل، ما نِتعَب [ʔiða nitraːwaħ biššuɣul, maː nitʕab] If we alternate doing the work, we won't get tired.
رُوح [ruːħ] *n:* أرواح [ʔarwaːħ] *pl:* • **1.** soul, breath of life – الرُّوح بإيد الله [ʔirruːħ bʔiːd ʔallah] A person's life is in God's hands. لا، مُو مَيِّت. بَعَد بِيه رُوح [laː, muː mayyit. baʕad biːh ruːħ] No, he's not dead. There's still life in him. البَزُّونَة بِيها تِسع أرواح [ʔilbazzuːna biːha tisʕ ʔarwaːħ] The cat has nine lives. ما قِدَرت أساعِد أحَّد. يَاالله خَلَّصِت رُوحِي [maː gidarit ʔasaːʕid ʔaħħad. yallah xallaṣit ruːħi] I couldn't help anyone. I barely saved myself. لا تدَخِّل رُوحَك بِهَالعَركَة [laː ddaxxil ruːħak bhalʕarka] Don't get yourself involved in this fight. ظَلّ يُضرُب الكَلِب إلَى أن طِلعَت رُوحَه [ðall yuðrub ʔiččalib ʔila ʔan ṭilʕat ruːħah] He continued beating the dog until it died. إذا تُبسُط إبنِي، أطَلِّع رُوحَك [ʔiða tubsuṭ ʔibni, ʔaṭalliʕ ruːħak] If you whip my son, I'll kill you. لُويش ما ساعَدتُوه؟ كُلّ مَن يقُول يا رُوحِي [luwiːš maː saːʕadtuːh? kull man yiguːl yaː ruːħi] Why didn't you all help him? Everyone's looking out for himself. شبيك دَتِبكِي، يا رُوحِي [šbiːk datibči, yaː ruːħi] Why are you crying, dear? ما عِندَه أحَّد. هَذا بطَرق رُوحَه [maː ʕindah ʔaħħad. haːða bṭarig ruːħah] He doesn't have anyone. He's all by himself. • **2.** spirit – وِلايَتكُم تُقبُض الرُّوح [wilaːyatkum tuqbuð ʔirruːħ] Your town is depressing (lit., constricts the spirit). رُوحَه طوِيلَة [ruːħah ṭwiːla] He has great patience. مِن شاف الدَّمّ، ماعَت رُوحَه [min šaːf ʔiddamm, maːʕat ruːħah] When he saw the blood, he passed out. • **3.** essence, spirit – رُوح الشَّكَر [ruːħ ʔiššakar] saccharine. رُوح الحَياة [ruːħ ʔilħayaːt] a type of cloth, similar to rayon.
رُوحَة [ruːħa, rawħa] *n:* رُوحات [ruːħaːt] *pl:* • **1.** act of going, departing
رَواح [rawaːħ] *n:* • **1.** departing, going
رُوحِي [ruːħi] *adj:* • **1.** spiritual – زَعِيم رُوحِي مَشهُور [zaʕiːm ruːħi mašhuːr] a famous spiritual leader. • **2.** spiritous, alcoholic – مَشرُوبات رُوحِيَّة [mašruːbaːt ruːħiyya] alcoholic beverages, spirits.
راح، رَح [raːħ, raħ] *particle:* • **1.** /followed by imperfect verb/ prefix indicating future tense – مُؤَكَّد راح تُمطُر اليُوم [muʔakkad raːħ tumṭur ʔilyuːm] It's definitely going to rain today. راح تِجِي لِلحَفلَة لَو لا؟ [raːħ tiǰi lilħafla law laː?] Are you going to come to the party or not? ما راح أشرَب جِكايِر إذا يِرفَعُون الأسعار [maː raːħ ʔašrab ǰigaːyir ʔiða yirfaʕuːn ʔilʔasʕaːr] I'm not going to smoke cigarettes if they raise the prices. يَعنِي شلُون وِيّاك؟ ما راح تبَطِّل مِن الشَّقَى؟ [yaʕni šluːn wiyyaːk? maː raːħ tbaṭṭil min ʔiššaqa?] Just what's to be done with you? Aren't you ever going to stop teasing?

ر و د

راد [raːd] *v:* • **1.** to want, wish, desire – شراد مِنَّك؟ [šraːd minnak?] What did he want from you? ترِيد تِجِي وِيّايا؟ [triːd tiǰi wiyyaːya?] Do you want to come with me? خالَة، إبنِي يرِيد بِنتِك [xaːla, ʔibni yriːd bintič] Ma'am, my son would like the hand of your daughter in marriage. أرِيد مِن الله ينطِينِي وَلَد [ʔariːd min ʔallah yintiːni walad] I'd like God to give me a son. ما رادلَك إلّا الخير [maː raːdlak ʔilla ʔilxiːr] He wished you nothing but the best. أرِيدَك بالعَمَى [ʔariːdak bilʕama] I wish you were blind. • **2.** to be desirable, important, necessary – البَيت يرِيدلَه صُبُغ [ʔilbayt yriːdlah ṣubuɣ] The house needs paint. ينرادلِي ألبَس قاط شِتوِي اليُوم [yinraːdli ʔalbas qaːṭ šitwi ʔilyuːm] I should have worn a winter suit today.
انراد [ʔinraːd] *v:* • **1.** to be wanted, desired, needed, necessary – ينرادلِي قَلَم باندان [yinraːdli qalam paːndaːn] I need a fountain pen.
رائِد [raːʔid] *n:* رُوّاد [ruwwaːd] *pl:* • **1.** explorer
إرادَة [ʔiraːda] *n:* • **1.** will, volition • **2.** wish, desire – هَذا ضِدّ إرادتِي [haːða ðidd ʔiraːdti] That's against my wishes. كُلّشِي صار حَسَب الإرادَة [kullši ṣaːr ħasab ʔilʔiraːda] Everything went as was desired. • **3.** will power – هَذا إرادتَه ضَعِيفَة [haːða ʔiraːdtah ðaʕiːfa] His will is weak. • **4.** pl. إرادات decree
مُراد [muraːd] adj.:/*n:* • **1.** wanted, desired • **2.** design, purpose, intention – تِرَكها بَعَد ما نال مُرادَه مِنها [tirakha baʕad maː naːl muraːdah minha] He left her after he got what he wanted from her.

ر

ر و ز

راز [ra:z] *v:* • **1.** to weigh, size up, examine – أقدَر أرُوز سَلّة الخُوخ وأقُلَّك شقَدّ بِيها [ʔagdar ʔaru:z sallat ʔilxu:x wʔagullak šgadd bi:ha] I can examine the basket of peaches and tell you how many are in it. رزتَه وشِفتَه ما يريد يِنطِي [riztah wšiftah ma: yri:d yinṭi] I sized him up and saw he didn't want to give.

روز [ru:z] *n:* • **1.** weight, examination

ر و س [1]

راوَس [ra:was] *v:* • **1.** to apportion equally, evenly, or fairly – لا تِنطِينِي مِشمِش صغار بَسّ. لازم تراوِس [la: tinṭi:ni mišmiš ṣɣa:r bass. la:zim tra:wis] Don't give me only small apricots. You should be fair. قَسِّم التِّفّاح عَلينا بَسّ راوسَه [qassim ʔittiffa:ħ ʕali:na bass ra:wsah] Divide the apples among us but be sure to divide them equally. • **2.** to settle, resolve, decide – القَضِيَّة كانَت مُعَلَّقَة وَهُوَّ اللّي راوَسلِي إيّاها [ʔilqaðiyya ča:nat muʕallaqa wahuwwa ʔilli ra:wasli ʔiyya:ha] The matter was undecided and he is the one who settled it for me. ما دَيقدَر يراوِس المَوضُوع لِأَنّ كُلّ مَن دَيرِيد غير شِي [ma: dayigdar yra:wis ʔilmawðu:ʕ liʔann kull man dayri:d ɣi:r ši] He isn't able to settle the matter because everybody wants something different.

تراوَس [tra:was] *v:* • **1.** to be crowded in – بَسّ عِدنا جُربايَة وِحدَة. لازم الجِّهال يِتراوسُون [bass ʕidna čurpa:ya wiħda. la:zim ʔiǰǰiha:l yitra:wsu:n] We only have one bed. The children will have to crowd in together.

ر و س [2]

رُوسيا [ru:sya] *n:* • **1.** Russia

رُوسِي [ru:si] *adj:* • **1.** Russian • **2.** pl. رُوسِيين [ru:siyyi:n] a Russian

ر و ض

رَيَّض [rayyað] *v:* • **1.** to exercise

رَوَّض [rawwað] *v:* • **1.** to tame

تريَّض [trayyað] *v:* • **1.** to be exercised

تروَّض [trawwað] *v:* • **1.** to be tamed

رَوضَة [rawða] *n:* رَوضات [rawða:t] *pl:* • **1.** kindergarten, nursery school

تَرَيُّض [tarayyuð] *n:* • **1.** exercise

رِياضَة [riya:ða] *n:* • **1.** physical exercise • **2.** athletics, sports

ترويض [tarwi:ð] *n:* • **1.** taming, training • **2.** training

رِياضِيّات [riya:ðiyya:t] *n:* • **1.** mathematics

رِياضِي [riya:ði] *adj:* • **1.** athletic, sporting – ألعاب رياضِيَّة [ʔalʕa:b riya:ðiyya] sports, sporting events. • **2.** mathematic, mathematical – مَسألَة رياضِيَّة [masʔala riya:ðiyya] a mathematical problem. • **3.** pl. رياضِيِّن [riya:ðiyyi:n] athlete, sportsman

ر و ع

رَوَّع [rawwaʕ] *v:* • **1.** to frighten, scare, alarm – هَالخَبَر رَوَّع كُلّ الوِلايَة [halxabar rawwaʕ kull ʔilwila:ya] This news alarmed the whole city.

اِرتاع [ʔirta:ʕ] *v:* • **1.** to be or become frightened, scared, alarmed – الجِّهال اِرتاعَوا مِن شَبَّت النّار [ʔiǰǰaha:l ʔirta:ʕaw min šabbat ʔinna:r] The children were terrified when the fire broke out.

رَوعَة [rawʕa] *n:* • **1.** beauty, splendor, magnificence • **2.** pl. رَوائع [rawa:ʔiʕ] a beautiful, splendid, or magnificent thing

رائع [ra:ʔiʕ] *adj:* • **1.** splendid, wonderful, marvelous, glorious, magnificent – صُورَة رائِعَة [ṣu:ra ra:ʔiʕa] a splendid picture.

مُرِيع [muri:ʕ] *adj:* • **1.** dreadful, terrible, horrible – أخبار مُرِيعَة [ʔaxba:r muri:ʕa] dreadful news.

مُروِّع [murawwiʕ] *adj:* • **1.** disastrous • **2.** dreadful

أروَع [ʔarwaʕ] *comparative adjective:* • **1.** more or most splendid, marvelous

ر و غ

راوَغ [ra:waɣ] *v:* • **1.** to dodge, to engage in low trickery

مُراوِغ [mura:wiɣ] *adj:* • **1.** cunning • **2.** devious

ر و ل

رولَة [ru:la] *n:* رولات [ru:la:t] *pl:* • **1.** roller • **2.** road roller, steam roller • **3.** hair roller, hair curler

ر و م [1]

رُوما [ru:ma] *n:* • **1.** Rome

رَوماني [ruma:ni] *adj:* • **1.** Roman

ر و م [2]

مَرام [mara:m] *n:* مَرامات [mara:ma:t] *pl:* • **1.** wish, desire • **2.** aspiration

ر و م ت ز م

رُوماتِيزم [ru:ma:ti:zm] *n:* • **1.** rheumatism

ر و ي

رُوَى [ruwa:] *v:* • **1.** to quench the thirst – ماكُو شِي يِروِي مِثل المَيّ البارِد [ma:ku ši yirwi miθl ʔilmayy ʔilba:rid] Nothing quenches thirst like cold water. • **2.** to water, irrigate – هَالجَدوَل يِروِي قِيعان واسِعَة [haǰ ǰadwal yirwi gi:ʕa:n wa:sʕa] This creek provides water for a vast area of land.

راوَى [ra:wa:] *v:* • **1.** to show, demonstrate, display – بَعَد ما راوانِي النَّمُونَة، اِشتِرَيت [baʕad ma: ra:wa:ni ʔinnamu:na, ʔištiri:t] After he showed me the sample, I made a purchase. راوانِي كُلّ كُتبَه [ra:wa:ni kull kutbah] He showed me all his books. إنتَ هَسَّة إحكِي عَلَيّا. آني بَعدين أراوِيك [ʔinta hassa ʔiħči

ʕalayya. ʔa:ni baʕdi:n ʔara:wi:k] Go ahead and talk about me now. I'll show you later.
ترَوَّى [trawwa:] *v:* • **1.** to ponder, reflect, think over – اِترَوَّى وَلا تِستَعجِل بِحُكمَك عَليه [ʔitrawwa: wla: tistaʕǰil bħukmak ʕali:h] Think it over and don't be hasty in your judgment of him.
تراوَى [tra:wa:] *v:* • **1.** to appear (in a vision or dream), materialize – المَيِّت لهَسَّة بَعدَه دَيِتراوالِي [ʔilmayyit lhassa baʕdah dayitra:wa:li] The vision of the corpse is still real to me now. بَسّ دَتِتراوالَك أَشباح [bass datitra:wa:lak ʔašba:ħ] You're just seeing things.
اِرتِوَى [ʔirtiwa:] *v:* • **1.** to quench one's thirst – ظَلّ يِشرَب مَيّ حَتَّى اِرتِوَى تَمام [ðall yišrab mayy ħatta ʔirtiwa: tama:m] He kept drinking water until he'd quenched his thirst completely. • **2.** to be watered, irrigated – خَلِّي القاع تِرتِوي زين [xalli:ʔilga:ʕ tirtiwi zi:n] Let the ground get plenty of water.
رَيّ [rayy] *n:* • **1.** watering, irrigation, supplying of water – مُدِيرِيَّة الرَّيّ العامَّة [mudi:riyyat ʔirrayy ʔilʕa:mma] general directorate of irrigation.
روا [riwa:] *n:* • **1.** watering, irrigation
رَوِي، رَيّ [rawy, rayy] *n:* • **1.** irrigation, watering, quenching
رُوايَة [ruwa:ya, riwa:ya] *n:* رُوايات [ruwa:ya:t] *pl:* • **1.** tale, story • **2.** novel • **3.** play, drama – رُوايَة هَزَلِيَّة [ruwa:ya hazaliyya] a comedy. • **4.** كَاتِب رُوَايَات playwright, dramatist
مراوَى [mra:wa] *n:* • **1.** viewing, examination, being shown – أَشتِريها عالمراواة [ʔaštiri:ha ʕalʔimra:wa] I'll buy it once I see it.
رَيّان [rayya:n] *adj:* • **1.** provided with a good supply of water • **2.** juicy, succulent, fresh – بُرتَقالَة رَيّانَة [purtaqa:la rayya:na] a juicy orange. بنَيَّة رَيّانَة [bnayya rayya:na] healthy, well-formed girl.

ر ي ب

اِرتاب [ʔirta:b] *v:* • **1.** to feel doubt, suspicion, or misgivings, to be suspicious – آني أَرتاب مِنَّه [ʔa:ni ʔarta:b minnah] I'm suspicious of him.
رِيبَة [ri:ba] *n:* رِيَب [riyab] *pl:* • **1.** suspicion, doubt, misgiving
اِرتِياب [ʔirtiya:b] *n:* • **1.** doubt, suspicion
مُرِيب [muri:b] *adj:* • **1.** suspicious, doubtful, dubious, questionable, fishy, equivocal
مِرتاب [mirta:b] *adj:* • **1.** doubtful

ر ي ت

رِيتَة [ri:ta] *n:* • **1.** the seeds of a certain plant, ground and used as soap in washing wool and delicate fabrics

ر ي ث

ترَيَّث [trayyaθ] *v:* • **1.** to stay, linger, tarry – ما أَقدَر أَترَيَّث لِأَنّ ماكُو طَيّارَة بَعد إِسبُوع [ma: ʔagdar ʔatrayyaθ liʔann ma:ku ṭayya:ra baʕd ʔisbu:ʕ] I can't stay because there isn't another plane for a week. • **2.** to be patient, bide one's time, wait – لا تسافِر هَسَّة. ترَيَّث شوَيَّة [la: tsa:fir hassa. trayyaθ šwayya] Don't go on a trip now. Wait a while.

ر ي ح

See also: ر و ح
راح [ra:ħ] *v:* • **1.** to give a rest to, rest, let rest – صارلَك ساعَة تِقرا. لِيش ما ترِيِّح عينَك؟ [ṣa:rlak sa:ʕa tiqra:. li:š ma: trayyiħ ʕaynak?] You've been reading for an hour. Why don't you rest your eyes? راح أَستِقِيل وَأَرَيِّح مُخِّي [ra:ħ ʔastiqi:l waʔarayyiħ muxxi] I'm going to resign and get some peace of mind. هَالنَّومَة رَيَّحَتنِي [hannu:ma rayyaħatni] That nap refreshed me. • **2.** to relieve, free, ease – المُوَظَّف الجِّدِيد رَيَّحنِي هوايَة. يُعرُف كُلشِي [ʔilmuwaððaf ʔiǰǰidi:d rayyaħni hwa:ya. yuʕruf kullši] The new employee took a lot off of me. He's very capable. إذا تاخُذ هَالشَّغلَة وَحدَك، ترِيِّحني هوايَة [ʔiða ta:xuð haššaɣla waħdak, trayyiħni hwa:ya] If you take over this job by yourself, you'll relieve me a lot. المُوَظَّف الجِّدِيد طِلَع شاغُول. رَيَّحنِي مِن كُثرَة الشُّغُل [ʔilmuwaððaf ʔiǰǰidi:d ṭilaʕ ša:ɣu:l. rayyaħni min kuθrat ʔiššuɣul] The new employee turned out to be a hard worker. He relieved me of a large part of the work.
رَيَّح، رَوَّح [rayyaħ, rawwaħ] *v:* • **1.** to rest, give a rest to, let rest – رَيِّح الحِصان مالَك [rayyiħ ʔilħiṣa:n ma:lak] Rest your horse.
أَراح [ʔara:ħ] *v:* • **1.** to give rest to, rest, let rest
ترَيَّح [trayyaħ] *v:* • **1.** to put perfume
اِرتاح [ʔirta:ħ] *v:* • **1.** to rest, relax – خَلِّي نرتاح شوَيَّة [xalli: nirta:ħ šwayya] Let's rest awhile. إذا تَعبان، اِرتاح [ʔiða taʕba:n, ʔirta:ħ] If you're tired, take a break. أُقعُد شوَيَّة وَإِرتاح [ʔugʕud šwayya wʔirta:ħ] Sit down for a while and relax. وُصلَوا بِالسَّلامَة. هَسَّة أَقدَر أَرتاح [wuṣlaw bissala:ma. hassa ʔagdar ʔarta:ħ] They arrived safely. Now I can relax. • **2.** to be relieved, be at ease – راح أَرَجِّعله إِيّاه حَتَّى ضَمِيرِي يِرتاح [ra:ħ ʔaraǰǰiʕlah ʔiyya:h ħatta ḍami:ri yirta:ħ] I'm going to return it to him so my mind will be at ease. مِن بِلَعت الحَبّايَة، اِرتاحِت [min bilaʕt ʔilħabba:ya, ʔirtaħit] When I took the pill, I felt relieved. • **3.** to be satisfied, be pleased – آني مِرتاح مِن سَيّارتِي [ʔa:ni mirta:ħ min sayya:rti] I'm well satisfied with my car.
اِستَراح [ʔistara:ħ] *v:* • **1.** to rest, take a break – كُلّ نُصّ ساعَة يِسترِيح عَشِر دَقايِق [kull nuṣṣ sa:ʕa yistiri:ħ ʕašir daqa:yiq] Every half hour he rests ten minutes. تعَبنا. خَلِّي نِستَراح شوَيَّة [tʕabna. xalli: nistara:ħ šwayya] We got tired. Let's rest a little. • **2.** to relax, make oneself comfortable – تفَضَّل اِسترِيح. هَسَّة يِجِي المُدِير [tfaððal ʔistiri:ħ. hassa yiǰi ʔilmudi:r] Please make yourself comfortable. The director will be with you in a moment. • **3.** to be saved, delivered, relieved – زَوِّجَه حَتَّى نِستَراح مِنَّه [zawwiǰah ħatta nistara:ħ minnah] Marry him off so we'll be rid of him.

ر

ريح [riːħ] *n:* • **1.** gas (on the stomach) – الصُّودا زينَة لِلرِّيح [ʔiṣṣuːda ziːna lirriːħ] Soda is good for gas on the stomach. فَتِق ريح [fatig riːħ] hernia.
رِيحَة [riːħa] *n:* رَوائِح، رَوايِح، رِيَّح [rawaːʔiħ, rawaːyiħ, riyyaħ] *pl:* • **1.** scent, odor, fragrance, smell • **2.** perfume, cologne
راحَة [raːħa] *n:* • **1.** rest, repose – المَريض يِحتاج إِلَى راحَة [ʔilmariːð yiħtaːǰ ʔila raːħa] The patient needs rest. خَلِّي ناخُذ راحَة [xalliː naːxuð (xannaːxuð) raːħa] Let's take a rest. أُخُذ راحتَك. آنِي أَقعُد هنا [ʔuxuð raːħtak. ʔaːni ʔagʕud hna] You take it easy. I'll sit over here. • **2.** ease, leisure – بِراحتَك. شوَقِت ما عِندَك مَجال، سَوِّيها [braːħtak. šwakit maː ʕindak maǰaːl, sawwiːha] At your convenience. Whenever you get a chance, do it. • **3.** comfort – وَسائِل الرّاحَة [wasaːʔil ʔirraːħa] conveniences. كُرسِي راحَة [kursi raːħa] deck chair, cloth garden chair.
ريحان [riːħaːn] *n:* • **1.** sweet basil
رُوَيحَة [rwayħa] *n:* • **1.** scent, odor, fragrance, smell
مَروَحَة [marwaħa] *n:* • **1.** fan
أَريَحِيَّة [ʔaryaħiyya] *n:* • **1.** generosity, open-handedness
تَراويح، صَلاة التَّراويح [taraːwiːħ, ṣalaːt ʔittaraːwiːħ] *n:* • **1.** a prayer performed during the evening in Ramadan
مِروَحِيَّة [mirwaħiyya] *n:* • **1.** helicopter
اِرتِياح [ʔirtiyaːħ] *n:* • **1.** satisfaction • **2.** relief
اِستِراحَة [ʔistiraːħa] *n:* • **1.** rest, repose, relaxation
مُريح [muriːħ] *adj:* • **1.** restful, reposeful • **2.** comfortable – كُرسِي كُلِّش مُرِيح [kursi kulliš muriːħ] a very comfortable chair.
أَريَحِي [ʔaryaħi] *adj:* أَريَحِيَّة [ʔaryaħiyya] *pl:* • **1.** generous, liberal, open-handed • **2.** having a relaxed, congenial personality
مِرتاح [mirtaːħ] *adj:* • **1.** comfortable, rested
أَروَح، أَريَح [ʔarwaħ, ʔaryaħ] *comparative adjective:* • **1.** more or most relaxed

ر ي ز

رِيزَة [riːza] *n:* • **1.** a kind of thin cotton cloth

ر ي ش

رَيَّش [rayyaš] *v:* • **1.** to become wealthy, feather one's nest – مَعلُوم يرَيِّش إذا راتبَه صار مِيَّة دِينار بالشَّهَر [maʕluːm yrayyiš ʔiða raːtbah ṣaːr miyyat dinaːr biššahar] Of course he's getting rich if his salary is a hundred dinars a month. آنِي راح أَرَيِّش بِهالرّاتِب [ʔaːni raːħ ʔarayyiš bharraːtib] I'll live in luxury on this salary. مِن يِحكُون عَن البَنات، يرَيِّش هواية [min yiħčuːn ʕan ʔilbanaːt, yrayyiš hwaːya] When they talk about girls, he gets a big charge out of it.
رِيش [riːš] *n:* • **1.** (coll.) feather(s)
رِيشَة [riːša] *n:* رِيشات، رِيَش [riːšaːt, riyaš] *pl:* • **1.** feather • **2.** blade of a fan or propeller • **3.** windshield wiper blade • **4.** nib of a pen
مرَيِّش [mrayyiš] *adj:* • **1.** feathered • **2.** rich

ر ي ع

رَيَّع [rayyaʕ] *v:* • **1.** to thrive, flourish, grow – الغَنَم ترَيِّع بِهَالعِشِب [ʔilɣanam trayyiʕ bhalʕišib] The sheep are thriving in this good pasture. أَكَلِت رَقِّيَّة وترَيَّعِت بِيها [ʔakalit raggiyya wtrayyaʕit biːha] I ate my fill of watermelon.
رَيعان، رَيعان الشَّباب [rayʕaːn, rayʕaːn ʔiššabaːb] *n:* • **1.** prime, in the prime of youth
مرَيِّع [mrayyiʕ] *adj:* • **1.** productive

ر ي ف

رِيف [riːf] *n:* أَرياف [ʔaryaːf] *pl:* • **1.** countryside, country (as opposed to city), rural area
رِيفِي [riːfi] *adj:* • **1.** rural, rustic, country – الحَياة الرِّيفِيَّة [ʔilħayaːt ʔirriːfiyya] the rural life.

ر ي ق

رَيَّق [rayyag] *v:* • **1.** to feed breakfast to, to provide with breakfast – رَيِّقِيه لِلوَلَد قَبُل ما تدزِّيه لِلمَدرَسَة [rayygiːh lilwalad gabul maː ddizziːh lilmadrasa] Give the boy some breakfast before you send him to school. راح أَرَيِّقَك بِهَالمَطعَم [raːħ ʔarayyagak bihaːlmaṭʕam] I'll treat you to breakfast in this restaurant.
ترَيَّق [trayyag] *v:* • **1.** to eat breakfast – شترَيَّقِت اليُوم؟ [štrayyagit ʔilyuːm?] What did you have for breakfast today?
رِيق [riːg] *n:* • **1.** saliva, spittle – رِيقِي ناشِف [riːgi naːšif] My mouth is dry. مِن أَبلَع رِيقِي، بَلعُومِي يُوجَعنِي [min ʔablaʕ riːgi, balʕuːmi yuːǰaʕni] When I swallow, my throat hurts me. عَلَى الرِّيق [ʕala ʔirriːg] before breakfast, on an empty stomach. لهَسَّة، بَعَدنِي عَلَى رِيقِي [lhassa, baʕadni ʕala riːgi] I haven't eaten a thing all day. فُكّ رِيقَك بِفَدّ شِي قَبُل ما تِشرَب سِجارَة [fukk riːgak bfadd ši gabul maː tišrab sigaːra] Get something in your stomach before you smoke a cigarette.
رَيُوق، رِيُوق [rayyuːg, riyuːg] *n:* رِيُوقات [ryuːgaːt] *pl:* • **1.** breakfast

ر ي ل

رِيال [ryaːl] *n:* رِيالات [ryaːlaːt] *pl:* • **1.** rial, two hundred fils coin

ر ي و ن

رايُون [raːyuːn] *n:* • **1.** rayon

ز

ز ء ب ق

زَيبَق، زئبَق [ziːbag, ziʔbaq] *n:* • **1.** quicksilver, mercury

ز ء ر

زأر [ziʔar] *v:* • **1.** to roar

زئير [zaʔiːr] *n:* • **1.** roar

ز ب ب

زِبّ [zibb] *n:* زبُوبَة، زباب [zbuːba, zbaːb] *pl:* • **1.** penis

ز ب د

زَبَّد [zabbad] *v:* • **1.** to foam

تزَبَّد [dzabbad] *v:* • **1.** to foam

زِبِد [zibid] *n:* • **1.** butter

زَبَد [zabad] *n:* • **1.** foam

زُبدَة [zubda] *n:* زُبدات، زُبَد [zubdaːt, zubad] *pl:* • **1.** What's the essence of the matter? – شِنُو زُبدَة المَوضُوع؟ [šinu zubdat ʔilmawḏuːʕ?] What's the essence of the matter? • **2.** essence, substance, gist, main point

ز ب ر ج د

زَبَرجَد [zabarǰad] *n:* • **1.** chrysolite, a dark green semi-precious gem

ز ب ع

زَوبَعَة [zawbaʕa] *n:* زَوابِع [zawaːbiʕ] *pl:* • **1.** storm, hurricane

زَوبَعِي [zawbaʕi] *adj:* • **1.** stormy

ز ب ق

زُبَق [zubag] *v:* • **1.** to slip out, slip away – زُبقَت السِّمكَة مِن إيدي [zubgat ʔissimča min ʔiːdi] The fish slipped out of my hand. الجّاهِل كان ويّانا وبَعدين زُبَق [ʔiǰǰaːhil čaːn wiyyaːna wbaʕdiːn zubag] The kid was with us and then slipped away. أزبُق قَبُل ما يشُوفَك [ʔuzbug gabul maː yšuːfak] Slip away before he sees you.

تزَبَّق [dzabbag] *v:* • **1.** to slip, dart, jump – شُوف هَالجّاهِل دَيتزَبَّق بين السَّيّارات [šuːf haǰǰaːhil dayidzabbag biːn ʔissayyaːraːt] Look at that kid zigzagging through the cars. • **2.** to slip, dart, jump

زَبُق [zabug] *n:* • **1.** slipping (as of mercury), darting

ز ب ل [1]

زَبَّل [zabbal] *v:* • **1.** to throw trash around, cause untidiness – لا تزَبِّل. هَسَّة كنَسنا البَيت [laː dzabbil. hassa knasna ʔilbayt] Now don't make a mess. We just swept the house.

زِبِل [zibil] *n:* • **1.** garbage, trash, rubbish, refuse

زَبّال [zabbaːl] *n:* زَبّالَة، زَبّالِين [zabbaːla, zabbaːliːn] *pl:* • **1.** garbage collector, trash man

زبالَة [zbaːla] *n:* • **1.** trash, garbage, rubbish, refuse

مَزبَلَة [mazbala] *n:* مَزابِل [mazaːbil] *pl:* • **1.** dump, trash heap – الدِّجاجَة تمُوت وَعِينها عالمَزبَلَة [ʔiddijaːǰa tmuːt wʕiːnha ʕalmazbala] He doesn't know when he's well off (lit., the chicken dies with its eye on the trash pile).

ز ب ل [2]

زبِيل [zbiːl] *n:* زِبلان [ziblaːn] *pl:* • **1.** flexible basket or satchel made of palm leaves

ز ب ن

زِبُون [zibuːn] *n:* زِبنات [zibnaːt] *pl:* • **1.** long, belted robe made of heavy material

زَبُون [zabuːn] *n:* زَبايِن، زَبائِن [zabaːyin, zabaːʔin] *pl:* • **1.** customer

زَبانَة [zabaːna] *n:* زَبايِن [zabaːyin] *pl:* • **1.** casing of heavy paper for custom-made cigarettes • **2.** brass casing of a cartridge

مزَبُّن، سِجايِر مزَبُّنَة [mzabbun, ǰigaːyir mzabbuna] *n:* • **1.** custom-made cigarettes in which the tobacco is packed in a pre-formed casing of heavy paper with one end closed

ز ب ي ب

زبِيب [zibiːb] *n:* • **1.** (coll.) large, dried grape(s), raisin(s)

زِبِيبَة [zibiːba] *n:* زِبِيبات [zibiːbaːt] *pl:* • **1.** pl. زِبِيبات unit noun of زِبِيب • **2.** raisins

ز ت ت

زَتّ [zatt] *v:* • **1.** to move quickly, rush (trans.) – زِتَّه بَالسَّيّارَة لبَيتَه وَتعال [zittah bissayyaːra lbiːtah wataʕaːl] Rush him home in the car and come back. لا تخاف. مِن تِخلَص الحَفلَة، آني راح أزِتّها لِبَيتها [laː txaːf. min tixlaṣ ʔilħafla, ʔaːni raːħ ʔazittha lbiːtha] Don't worry. When the party is over, I'll get her home quickly. أُخُذ مِنَّه المَكتُوب وَزِتَّه [ʔuxuð minnah ʔilmaktuːb wzittah] Take the letter from him and send him back. بالله زِتّ ماعُون الزِّبِد مِن يَمَّك [ballah zitt maːʕuːn ʔizzibid min yammak] Please slide the butter dish over here from where you are.

زَتّ [zatt] *n:* • **1.** rushing, moving quickly

ز ج ج

زُجاج [zuǰa:ǰ] *n:* • **1.** glass (as substance)
زُجاجَة [zuǰa:ǰa] *n:* • **1.** glass, bottle
زُجاجِي [zuǰa:ǰi] *adj:* • **1.** glass, of glass – عَين زُجاجِيَّة [ʕayn zuǰa:ǰiyya] a glass eye.

ز ج ر

زِجَر [ziǰar] *v:* • **1.** to reproach • **2.** to blame
اِنزِجَر [ʔinziǰar] *v:* • **1.** to be blamed
زَجِر [zaǰir] *n:* • **1.** reproach, blame

ز ح ر

زُحار [zuħa:r] *n:* • **1.** dysentery

ز ح ز ح

زَحزَح [zaħzaħ] *v:* • **1.** to move, shift, displace – زَحزِح المِيز شوَيَّة حَتَّى يصِير مُكان [zaħziħ ʔilmi:z šwayya ħatta yṣi:r muka:n] Move the table a little so there will be room. يبَيِّن مَسنُود بوَظِيفتَه. مَحَّد يقدَر يزَحزِحَه [yibayyin masnu:d bwaði:ftah. maħħad yiqdar yzaħziħah] It seems that he's protected in his job. No one can move him out.
تزَحزَح [dzaħzaħ] *v:* • **1.** to be moved, to be budged – هَالبِيب ثِقِيل هوايَة وَما يِتزَحزَح [halpi:p θigi:l hwa:ya wma yidzaħzaħ] This barrel is very heavy and won't budge. تزَحزَح شوَيَّة حَتَّى يصِيرلِي مُكان أَقعُد [dzaħzaħ šwayya ħatta yṣi:rli muka:n ʔagʕud] Move over a little so there'll be room for me to sit down.

ز ح ف

زِحَف [ziħaf] *v:* • **1.** to crawl, creep – شُوف الكَلِب؛ رِجلَيه مَكسُورَة وَدَيزحَف عَلَى بَطنَه [šu:f ʔiččalib; riǰlayh maksu:ra wadayizħaf ʕala baṭnah] Look at the dog; his legs are broken and he's crawling on his stomach. هَالجّاهِل عُمرَه سَنَة وَنُصّ وَبَعدَه يزحَف [haǰǰa:hil ʕumrah sana wnuṣṣ wbaʕdah yizħaf] This baby is one and a half years old and still crawling. • **2.** to march – الجَّيش راح يِزحَف عالحُدُود الفَجِر [ʔiǰǰayš ra:ħ yizħaf ʕalħudu:d ʔilfaǰir] The army will march toward the border at dawn.
زَحِف [zaħif] *n:* • **1.** crawling, creeping • **2.** marching, march, advance • **3.** a blanket wage increase for all civil servants, decreed periodically to cover cost-of-living increases
زاحِف [za:ħif] *adj:* • **1.** creeping, crawling • **2.** marching • **3.** زَواحِف [zawa:ħif] *pl:* reptile

ز ح ل ق

زَحلَق [zaħlag] *v:* • **1.** to cause to slide, slip – دِفَعَه وَزَحلَقَه عالطِّين [difaʕah wzaħlagah ʕaṭṭi:n] He pushed him and made him slide into the mud. • **2.** to be slippery – الثَّلِج يزَحلِق [ʔiθθaliǰ yzaħlig] The ice is slippery.
تزَحلَق [dzaħlag] *v:* • **1.** to glide, slide, slip, skid – تزَحلَق بِقشِر مُوز وَوُقَع [dzaħlag bigišir mu:z wwugaʕ] He slipped on a banana peel and fell. إمشِي عَلَى كَيفَك حَتَّى لا تِتزَحلَق [ʔimši ʕala kayfak ħatta la: tidzaħlag] Walk slowly so you won't slip. • **2.** to ski – راح نِتزَحلَق هَالشِّتوِيَّة بِجبال لُبنان [ra:ħ nidzaħlag haššitwiyya bǰiba:l lubna:n] We're going to ski this winter in the mountains of Lebanon.
تزِحلِق [dziħlig] *n:* • **1.** skating
زِحلَيقَة [ziħlayga] *n:* زِحلَيقات [ziħlayga:t] *pl:* • **1.** slide, place to slide • **2.** slippery spot

ز ح م

زَحَّم [zaħħam] *v:* • **1.** to inconvenience, trouble, bother – زَحَّمناك هوايَة بِمُشكِلَتنا [zaħħamna:k hwa:ya bmuškilatna] We've bothered you too much with our problem.
زاحَم [za:ħam] *v:* • **1.** to compete (for s.th.) – يبِيع رخِيص وَما حَدّ يقدَر يزاحمَه [yibi:ʕ rixi:ṣ wma ħadd yigdar yza:ħmah] He sells cheaply and nobody can compete with him.
تزاحَم [dza:ħam] *v:* • **1.** to compete with, vie with
اِزدِحَم [ʔizdiħam] *v:* • **1.** to crowd, crush, jam – اِزدِحَم الشّارِع بالنّاس [ʔizdiħam ʔišša:riʕ binna:s] The street was crowded with people.
اِستَزحَم [ʔistazħam] *v:* • **1.** to regard as an inconvenience – اِستَزحَم تَوصِيلَة أَخُويَا بَالسَّيّارَة [ʔistazħam tawṣi:lat ʔaxu:ya bissayya:ra] He thought it was too much trouble delivering my brother in the car.
زَحمَة [zaħma] *n:* زَحمات [zaħma:t] *pl:* • **1.** inconvenience, bother, trouble – بَلا زَحمَة، ما تفُكّ الباب؟ [bala zaħma, ma: tfukk ʔilba:b?] If it's not too much trouble, would you open the door? • **2.** jam, crowd, crush, throng
مُزاحِم [muza:ħim] *n:* مُزاحمِين [muza:ħmi:n] *pl:* • **1.** competitor
تزاحُم [taza:ħum] *n:* • **1.** huddling • **2.** competition
مُزاحَمَة [muza:ħama] *n:* مُزاحَمات [muza:ħama:t] *pl:* • **1.** competition • **2.** rivalry
زَحِم [zaħim] *adj:* • **1.** inconvenient, bothersome, difficult – عُبُور الشّارِع بهَالدَّقِيقَة زَحِم كُلِّش [ʕubu:r ʔišša:riʕ bhaddaqi:qa zaħim kulliš] Crossing the street right now is very difficult. هالشُّغُل كُلِّش زَحِم [haššuɣul kulliš zaħim] This work is a lot of trouble.
مِزدَحِم [mizdaħim] *adj:* • **1.** crowded

ز خ خ

زَخّ [zaxx] *v:* • **1.** to rain heavily, pour down rain, pour – المُطَر ظَلّ يزُخّ طُول اللَّيل [ʔilmuṭar ðall yzuxx ṭu:l ʔillayl] The rain kept pouring down all night long.

ز خ

زَخّ [zaxx] *n:* • **1.** heavy rain • **2.** downpour
زَخَّة [zaxxa] *n:* زَخّات [zaxxa:t] *pl:* • **1.** shower, heavy shower, downpour – زَخَّة خَفِيفَة [zaxxa xafi:fa] a light shower.

ز خ ر ف

زَخرَف [zaxraf] *v:* • **1.** to engrave, carve – أُخُذ هَاللَّوحَة وَزَخرُف عَليها فَدّ شِي لَطِيف [ʔuxuð hallawħa wzaxruf ʕali:ha fadd ši laṭi:f] Take this board and carve some nice design on it.
زُخرُف [zuxruf] *n:* زَخارِف [zaxa:rif] *pl:* • **1.** engraved decoration, embellishment • **2.** arabesque
زَخرَفَة [zaxrafa] *n:* زَخارُف [zaxa:ruf] *pl:* • **1.** adornment, decoration
مزَخرَف [mzaxraf] *adj:* • **1.** ornamental
زُخرُفِي [zuxrufi] *adj:* • **1.** arabesque • **2.** ornamental, decorative

ز خ م

زَخَم [zaxam] *n:* • **1.** momentum, impetus (phys.)
زخمَة [zaxma, zixma] *n:* زَخمات، زِخَم [zaxma:t, zixam] *pl:* • **1.** brassiere

ز ر

زار [za:r] *n:* زارات [za:ra:t] *pl:* • **1.** die • **2.** (pair of) dice • **3.** a large skin-covered earthen drum played at traditional oriental athletic events • **4.** dice

ز ر ب

زِرَب [zirab] *v:* • **1.** to have a bowel movement, defecate – الجَاهِل زِرَب بِلباسَه [ʔiǰǰa:hil zirab bilba:sah] The baby messed in his pants.
زَرَّب [zarrab] *v:* • **1.** to have a bowel movement, defecate
زَرُب [zarub] *n:* • **1.** defecation
زَربَة [zarba] *n:* زَربات [zarba:t] *pl:* • **1.** feces, stool
زراب [zra:b] *n:* • **1.** feces
زِرِيبَة [ziri:ba] *n:* زَرايِب [zara:yib] *pl:* • **1.** pen, corral, stockade, fold
مَزرِيب [mazri:b, mizri:b] *n:* مَزارِيب [maza:ri:b] *pl:* • **1.** drain spout

ز ر د [1]

زَرَد [zarad] *n:* • **1.** chain mail
زَردَة [zarda] *n:* • **1.** a thick pudding made of rice, milk, and sugar

ز ر د [2]

زَردُوم [zardu:m] *n:* زَرادِيم [zara:di:m] *pl:* • **1.** pharynx, throat • **2.** larynx, Adam's apple

ز ر ر

زِرّ [zirr] *n:* زرار، زرُور [zra:r, zru:r] *pl:* • **1.** button, push button • **3.** pl. زرُور thigh, leg

ز ر ز ر

زَرزُور [zarzu:r] *n:* زَرازِير [zara:zi:r] *pl:* • **1.** starling (type of birds)

ز ر ش ك

زرِشك [zrišk] *n:* • **1.** (coll.) currants
زرِشكَة [zriška] *n:* زرِشكات [zriška:t] *pl:* • **1.** currant

ز ر ع

زِرَع [ziraʕ] *v:* • **1.** to plant, grow, raise – إِزرَع هَالشَّجرَة بهالمُكان [ʔizraʕ haššiǰra bhalmuka:n] Plant that tree right here. راح يحِرثُون القاع ويزرَعُوها حُنطَة [ra:ħ yħirθu:n ʔilga:ʕ wyizraʕu:ha ħunṭa] They'll plow the land and plant wheat on it. راح نِزرَع حُنطَة وَشِعِير هالسَّنَة [ra:ħ nizraʕ ħunṭa wšiʕi:r hassana] We're going to grow wheat and barley this year. بالله تَعال بِسُرعَة. لا تِزرَعنِي [ballah taʕa:l bsurʕa. la: tizraʕni] Please come quickly. Don't leave me waiting.
اِنزِرَع [ʔinziraʕ] *v:* • **1.** to be grown
زَرِع [zariʕ] *n:* • **1.** planting, growing, cultivation (of crops) • **2.** pl. زرُوع crop, growing crop
زَرّاع [zarra:ʕ] *n:* زَرّاعَة [zarra:ʕa] *pl:* • **1.** farm-owner, farmer
زَرعَة [zarʕa] *n:* • **1.** plant
زِراعَة [zira:ʕa] *n:* • **1.** agriculture, farming – وِزارَة الزِّراعَة [wiza:rat ʔizzira:ʕa] ministry of agriculture.
مَزرَعَة [mazraʕa] *n:* مَزارِع [maza:riʕ] *pl:* • **1.** farm, plantation
مُزارِع [muza:riʕ] *n:* مُزارِعِين [muza:riʕi:n] *pl:* • **1.** farm-owner, farmer
زِراعِي [zira:ʕi] *adj:* • **1.** agricultural, agrarian, farm – وِزارَة الإصلاح الزِّراعِي [wiza:rat ʔilʔiṣla:ħ ʔizzira:ʕi] ministry of agrarian reform. مَكايِن زِراعِيَّة [maka:yin zira:ʕiyya] farm machinery. أَراضِي زِراعِيَّة [ʔara:ði zira:ʕiyya] arable lands. • **2.** agricultural, agrarian, farm- (in compound words)
مَزرُوع [mazru:ʕ] *adj:* مَزرُوعات [mazru:ʕa:t] *pl:* • **1.** planted

ز ر ف

زِرَف [ziraf] *v:* • **1.** to pierce, puncture, make a hole in – القَلَم زِرَفَه لِجَيبِي [ʔilqalam zirafah lǰi:bi] The pencil punched a hole in my pocket. راح نِزرُف إِذان البنَيَّة [ra:ħ nizruf ʔiða:n ʔilbnayya] We're going to pierce the girl's ears.
زَرَّف [zarraf] *v:* • **1.** to punch full of holes – بِيدَه المُخيَط وَيزَرُّف بِالمقَوّايَة [bi:dah ʔilmuxyaṭ wyzarruf bilmqawwa:ya] He has the big needle in his hand and he's punching holes in the cardboard.
اِنزِرَف [ʔinziraf] *v:* • **1.** pass. of زِرَف to be pierced – الكِيس اِنزِرَف [ʔiči:s ʔinziraf] The bag got a hole in it.

زُرُف [zuruf] *n:* زرُوف [zru:f] *pl:* • **1.** eye of the needle – زُرف الأبرَة [zurf ʔilʔubra] eye of the needle. • **2.** hole

زَرافَة [zara:fa] *n:* زَرافات [zara:fa:t] *pl:* • **1.** giraffe

مزرَف [mazraf, mizraf] *adj:* مزارُف [maza:ruf] *pl:* • **1.** awl • **2.** drill

مزَرَّف [mzarraf] *adj:* • **1.** pierced

مَزرُوف [mazru:f] *adj:* • **1.** pierced

ز ر ق

زِرَق [zirag] *v:* • **1.** to dash, hurry, go quickly – هَسَّة أَزرُق لِلسُّوق وَأَشتِرِيلَك إيّاها [hassa ʔazrug lissu:g wʔaštiri:lak ʔiyya:ha] I'll dash to the market right now and buy it for you. كُلّما أَلزَم السِّمكَة، تِزرُق مِن إيدِي [kullma ʔalzam ʔissimča, tizrug min ʔi:di] Every time I try to catch the fish, it slips from my hand.

اِزرَقّ [ʔizragg] *v:* • **1.** to become blue, turn blue – اِزرَقّ جِلدَه مِن البَرِد [ʔizragg ǰildah min ʔilbarid] His skin turned blue from the cold.

زَراق [zara:g] *n:* • **1.** blueness, blue coloration

زَرَق، زَرَق وَرَق [zaraq, zaraq waraq] *adj:* • **1.** colored or decorated paper for gift wrapping, etc – لابِس بُوينباغ زَرَق وَرَق [la:bis buyinba:ɣ zaraq waraq] He's wearing a loud, multicolored tie. • **2.** multicolored

أَزرَق [ʔazrag] *adj:* زُرُق، زَرقِين [zurug, zargi:n] *pl:* زَرقَة [zarga, zarqa] *feminine:* • **3.** blue

ز ر ك ش

زَركَش [zarkaš] *v:* • **1.** to embroider, decorate with brocade embroidery – زَركِشَت شَرشَف المِيز [zarkišat čarčaf ʔilmi:z] She embroidered the tablecloth.

مزَركَش [mzarkaš] *adj:* • **1.** decorated, embroidered

ز ر ن

زَرنَة [zarna] *n:* زَرنات [zarna:t] *pl:* • **1.** protruding corner, point where three converging lines meet – تعَوَّر راسَه بِزَرنَة المِيز [tʕawwar ra:sah bzarnat ʔilmi:z] He hurt his head on the corner of the table. • **2.** promontory, peak

ز ر ن خ

زَرنِيخ [zarni:x] *n:* • **1.** arsenic

ز ر و ق

زَروَق [zarwaq] *v:* • **1.** to decorate, adorn, embellish – زَروِق الهَدِيَّة قَبُل ما تدِزّلَه إيّاها [zarwiq ʔilhadiyya gabul ma: ddizzlah ʔiyya:ha] Decorate the present before you send it to him. زَروُقَت السِّمكَة بِنُومِي حامُض وَبصَل [zarwuqat ʔissimča bnu:mi ħa:muđ wbuṣal] She garnished the fish with lemon and onions.

تزَروَق [dzarwaq] *v:* • **1.** to garnish

تزِروِق [dzirwiq] *n:* • **1.** garnishing • **2.** decoration

ز ر ي

زَرِي، قماش زَرِي [zari, qma:š zari] *n:* • **1.** a type of cloth brocaded with gold or silver, imported from India (a sari or saree)

ز ع ت ر

زَعتَر [zaʕtar] *n:* • **1.** wild thyme

ز ع ج

زِعَج [ziʕaǰ] *v:* • **1.** to annoy, bother, upset – زِعَجنِي بِإلحاحَه [ziʕaǰni bʔilħa:ħah] He annoyed me with his insistence. زِعَجنِي هوايَة مِن رَدّ طَلَبِي [ziʕaǰni hwa:ya min radd ṭalabi] He upset me a lot when he turned down my request. • **2.** to disturb, alarm, make uneasy – جَوابَه زِعَجنِي [ǰawa:bah ziʕaǰni] His answer bothered me. لا تِزعِج نَفسَك وَتظَلّ تفَكِّر، راح يِدرُس وَيِنجَح [la: tizʕiǰ nafasak wdđall tfakkir, ra:ħ yidrus wyinǰaħ] Don't upset yourself and keep thinking about it. He's going to study and pass.

أَزعَج [ʔazʕaǰ] *v:* • **1.** to annoy, bother, upset, to disturb, alarm, make uneasy

اِنزِعَج [ʔinziʕaǰ] *v:* • **1.** pass. of زِعَج to be bothered, to be annoyed – يِنزِعِج مِن أَيّ كِلمَة تقُولها [yinziʕiǰ min ʔayy čilma tgu:lha] He gets upset at anything you say.

إزعاج [ʔizʕa:ǰ] *n:* • **1.** annoyance • **2.** disturbance

اِنزِعاج [ʔinziʕa:ǰ] *n:* • **1.** inconvenience, annoyance

مُزعِج [muzʕiǰ] *adj:* • **1.** bothersome, annoying

مَزعُوج [mazʕu:ǰ] *adj:* • **1.** annoyed

ز ع ز ع

زَعزَع [zaʕzaʕ] *v:* • **1.** to shake violently, rock – الهَوا زَعزَع كُلّ الأَشجار [ʔilhawa zaʕzaʕ kull ʔilʔašǰa:r] The wind shook all the trees. • **2.** to disturb, unsettle, disrupt – لا تزَعزِع الجّاهِل. خَلِّيه نايِم [la: dzaʕziʕ ʔiǰǰa:hil. xalli:h na:yim] Don't disturb the baby. Let him sleep. إنتَ زَعزَعتِنِي هوايَة. كُلّ مَرَّة تقَعِّدنِي بمُكان [ʔinta zaʕzaʕitni hwa:ya. kull marra tgaʕʕidni bmuka:n] You've upset me very much. You're always seating me in a different place. • **3.** to move, displace, dislodge – هَذا شِيزَعزِعَه مِن مَنصَبَه؟ الجَّيش وِيّاه [ha:đa šiyzaʕziʕah min manṣabah? ʔiǰǰayš wiyya:h] What could dislodge him from his position? The army is behind him.

تزَعزَع [dzaʕzaʕ] *v:* • **1.** pass. of زَعزَع • **2.** to be worked loose, to be shaken, to be wobbled

ز ع ط

مَزعَطَة [mazʕaṭa] *n:* • **1.** something for children (used in derisive phrases) – وِزارَتهُم مَزعَطَة [wiza:rathum mazʕaṭa] Their ministry is full of young punks. هَذا شُغُل حُكُومَة لَو مَزعَطَة؟ [ha:đa šuɣul ħuku:ma law mazʕaṭa?] Is this government work or child's play?

تزعطِط [tziʕṭiṭ] *n:* • **1.** immature behavior, acting childish
زَعطُوط [zaʕṭuːṭ] *adj:* زعاطِيط [zʕaːṭiːṭ] *pl:* • **1.** child, young person

ز ع ف ر ن

زَعفَران [zaʕfaraːn, zuʕufraːn] *n:* • **1.** saffron

ز ع ل

زِعَل [ziʕal] *v:* • **1.** to become annoyed, angry – يِزعَل بِالعَجَل [yizʕal bilʕaǰal] He gets mad quickly. زِعَلِت عَليه مِن ما دايَنّي الفلُوس [ziʕalit ʕaliːh min maː daːyanni ʔilfluːs] I got mad at him when he didn't lend me the money.
زَعَّل [zaʕʕal] *v:* • **1.** to vex, annoy, anger – زَعَّلنِي بِهالكِلمَة [zaʕʕalni bhaččilma] He made me mad with this remark.
تزَعَّل [dzaʕʕal] *v:* • **1.** to be angry, to be annoyed
تزاعَل [dzaːʕal] *v:* • **1.** to be angry at each other – تزاعلَوا عَلَى شِي سَخِيف [dzaːʕlaw ʕala ši saxiːf] They stopped speaking to each other over a silly thing.
انزِعَل [ʔinziʕal] *v:* • **1.** to be angered, made angry – هَذا ما ينزِعِل مِنَّه؛ بَعدَه جاهِل [haːða maː yinziʕil minnah; baʕdah ǰaːhil] One can't get mad at him; he's still a child.
زَعَل [zaʕal] *n:* • **1.** irritation, annoyance, vexation, anger – تَرَة ماكُو زَعَل [tara maːku zaʕal] Now don't get mad! ماكُو حاجَة لِلزَّعَل، سِألتَك سُؤال بَسِيط [maːku ħaːǰa lizzaʕal, siʔaltak suʔaːl basiːṭ] There's no need to get mad. I asked you a simple question. زَعَلهُم داوَم شَهرَين [zaʕalhum daːwam šahrayn] They didn't talk to each other for two months. بزَعَل [bzaʕal] in anger, angrily. حِكاها بزَعَل [ħičaːha bzaʕal] He said it angrily.
زَعلَة [zaʕla] *n:* زَعلات [zaʕlaːt] *pl:* • **1.** irritation, annoyance, vexation, anger
تزَعِيل [tazʕiːl] *n:* • **1.** annoyance, anger
زَعلان [zaʕlaːn] *adj:* زَعلانِين، زعالَة [zaʕlaːniːn, zʕaːla] *pl:* • **1.** peeved, vexed, angry, annoyed – مَرتَه بَعَدها زَعلانَة [martah baʕadha zaʕlaːna] His wife is still mad at him.

ز ع م

زِعَم [ziʕam] *v:* • **1.** to pretend
زَعَّم [zaʕʕam] *v:* • **1.** to make leader, appoint as leader – مِنُو اللّي زَعَّمَك عَلينا؟ [minu ʔilli zaʕʕamak ʕaliːna?] Who put you in charge of us?
تزَعَّم [dzaʕʕam] *v:* • **1.** to be the leader, to command, lead – مِنُو تزَعَّم هالحَرَكَة؟ [minu dzaʕʕam halħaraka?] Who was leader of this movement?
زَعَم [zaʕam] *n:* • **1.** supposing..., let's suppose..., just suppose..., let's assume..., let's pretend... – زَعَم آني أبُوه ولازِم أرشِدَه [zaʕam ʔaːni ʔabuːh wlaːzim ʔarišdah] Suppose I were his father and had to advise him. زَعَم آنِي العِصابَجِي وَإنتَ الشُّرطِي [zaʕam ʔaːni ʔilʕiṣaːbači wʔinta ʔiššurṭi] Pretend I'm the gangster and you're the policeman.
زَعِم [zaʕim] *n:* • **1.** pretending, allegation, claim
زَعِيم [zaʕiːm] *n:* زُعَماء [zuʕamaːʔ] *pl:* • **1.** leader • **2.** brigadier general
زَعامَة [zaʕaːma] *n:* • **1.** leadership, controlling position

ز غ

زاغ [zaːɣ] *n:* زاغات، زِيغان [zaːɣaːt, ziːɣaːn] *pl:* • **1.** crow

ز غ ب

زَغَب [zaɣab] *n:* • **1.** down • **2.** fluff, fuzz

ز غ ل

زاغَل [zaːɣal] *v:* • **1.** to cheat, break the rules, play unfairly – ما إلعَب وِيّاه بَعَد لِأنّ يزاغُل هوايَة [maː ʔalʕab wiyyaːh baʕad liʔann yzaːɣul hwaːya] I won't play with him any more because he cheats too much. زاغَل عَليَّا بِالحِساب [zaːɣal ʕalayya biliħsaːb] He cheated me on the bill. هَذا مِتزَوَّج ويزاغِل. عَلَى طُول أَشُوفَه وِيّا بَنات [haːða midzawwaǰ wyzaːɣil. ʕala ṭuːl ʔašuwfah wiyya banaːt] He's married and he cheats. I see him all the time with girls. إحكِي عَدِل. لا تزاغُل [ʔiħči ʕadil. laː dzaːɣul] Talk straight. Don't try to beat around the bush.
زُغُل [zuɣul] *n:* • **1.** cheating, deception, duplicity – كِسَب بِالزُّغُل [kisab bizzuɣul] He won by cheating.

ز غ ل ط

زَغلَط [zaɣlaṭ] *v:* • **1.** to cheat, break the rules – هِيَّ دَتزَغلُط وَما حَدّ يِدرِي بِيها [hiyya dadzaɣluṭ wma ħadd yidri biːha] She is slipping around and nobody knows about her.

ز ف ت

زَفَّت [zaffat] *v:* • **1.** to coat with tar or asphalt – زَفِّتَوا الشِّيلمان حَتَّى ما يزَنجِر [zaffitaw ʔiššiːlmaːn ħatta maː yzanǰir] They coated the girders with tar so they wouldn't rust.
زِفِت [zifit] *n:* • **1.** tar, asphalt

ز ف ر

زَفَّر [zaffar] *v:* • **1.** to make stink, to impart a stench to, to soil, dirty – إنتَ نَظِّف السِّمكَة. آني ما أَرِيد أزَفُّر إيدِي [ʔinta naððuf ʔissimča. ʔaːni maː ʔariːd ʔazaffur ʔiːdi] You clean the fish. I don't want to stink up my hands.
تزَفَّر [dzaffar] *v:* • **1.** pass. of زَفَّر to be stinky, to be dirty – تزَفَّرِت مِن شِلِت السِّمَك [dzaffarit min šilit ʔissimač] I got smelly when I carried the fish.

ز

زُفَر [zufar] *n:* • **1.** the slippery secretion of fish • **2.** fishy smell • **3.** grease, animal fat
زُفرَة [zufra] *n:* • **1.** smell, stench, stink
زَفِير [zafi:r] *n:* • **1.** exhaling
زَفِر [zafir] *adj:* • **1.** rancid, rank, stinking • **2.** dirty, filthy, unclean – حَلقَه زَفِر. يفَشِّر هوايَة [ħalgah zafir. yfaššir hwa:ya] He's got a dirty mouth. He's always using bad language.

ز ف ف
زَفّ [zaff] *v:* • **1.** to escort the bride or bridegroom to the new home – راح يزِفُّون العَرُوس اليُوم باللَّيل [ra:ħ yziffu:n ʔilʕaru:s ʔilyu:m billayl] They're going to escort the bride to her new home tonight. • **2.** to scold, upbraid – إذا عِثرِت بيه، أَزِفَّه [ʔiða ʕiθarit bi:h, ʔaziffah] If I run into him, I'll really read him the riot act!
زَفَّة [zaffa] *n:* زَفّات [zaffa:t] *pl:* • **1.** procession which ceremonially escorts the bride or bridegroom on the wedding night • **2.** scolding, tirade
زَفاف [zafa:f] *n:* • **1.** wedding, wedding ceremony

ز ق ز ق
زَقزَق [zaqzaq] *v:* • **1.** to chirp, peep, cheep – العَصفُور دَيزَقزِق [ʔilʕaṣfu:r dayzaqziq] The bird is cheeping.

ز ق ط
زِقَط [zigaṭ] *v:* • **1.** to kick (of an animal) – الزُّمال زِقَطَه [ʔizzuma:l zigaṭah] The donkey kicked him.
زَقَّط [zaggaṭ] *v:* • **1.** to have a tendency to kick
زاقَط [za:gaṭ] *v:* • **1.** to have a tendency to kick, to be in the habit of kicking – هَالزُّمال يزاقُط. دِير بالَك مِنَّه [hazzuma:l yza:guṭ. di:r ba:lak minnah] This donkey kicks. Be careful of him.
زَقُط [zaguṭ] *n:* • **1.** kicking
زَقطَة [zagṭa] *n:* زَقطات [zagṭa:t] *pl:* • **1.** a kick (of an animal)

ز ق ق [1]
زَقّ [zaqq] *v:* • **1.** to feed (of a bird) – العَصفُور دَيزُقّ فراخَه [ʔilʕaṣfu:r dayzuqq fra:xah] The sparrow is feeding its young. يَزّي تزُقّ الزَّعطُوط مَيّ [yazzi dzuqq ʔizzaʕṭu:ṭ mayy] You've fed the baby enough water now!
زَقّ [zaqq] *n:* • **1.** feeding

ز ق ق [2]
زُقاق [zuqa:q] *n:* زُقاقات، أَزِقَّة [zuqa:qa:t, ʔaziqqa] *pl:* • **1.** alley
زقاقِي [sqa:qi, zqa:qi] *adj:* زقاقِيَّة [sqa:qiyya, zqa:qiyya] *pl:* • **1.** street urchin • **2.** homosexual
زقاقِيَّة [sqa:qiyya] *adj:* زقاقِيّات [sqa:qiyya:t] *pl:* • **1.** street-walker, slut

ز ق م
زَقُّوم [zaqqu:m] *n:* • **1.** an infernal tree mentioned in the Koran, and also its fruit, used figuratively to mean poison – عَسَى تكُون هَالأَكلَة زَقُّوم [ʕasa: tku:n halʔakla zaqqu:m] I hope this meal is poison. صار عَلَيّا زَقُّوم [ṣa:r ʕalayya zaqqu:m] It was like poison to me.

ز ق ن ب
زَقنَب [zaqnab] *v:* • **1.** to feed (someone) something unpleasant, to cram down the throat, stuff into the mouth – زَقنِبِي الجّاهِل حَتَّى يِسكُت [zaqnibi ʔiǰǰa:hil ħatta yiskut] Feed the kid so he'll shut up.
تزَقنَب [dzaqnab] *v:* • **1.** to eat something unpleasant, to stuff in, shovel in – صارلَك ساعَة تِتزَقنَب ما تخَلِّص عاد [ṣa:rlak sa:ʕa titzaqnab; ma: txalliṣ ʕa:d] You've been stuffing yourself for an hour; why don't you finish! لِيش ما تِتزَقنَب قَبُل مَا تِجِي؟ [li:š ma: titzaqnab gabul ma: tiǰi?] Why don't you feed your face before you come?

ز ق ن ب و ت
زَقنَبُوت [zaqnabu:t] *n:* • **1.** an unpleasant meal, (figuratively) poison – ما إلتَذَّيت بِالعَشا مِن خَبصَتكُم. صار عَلَيّا زَقنَبُوت [ma: ʔiltaðði:t bilʕaša: min xabṣatkum. ṣa:r ʕalayya zaqnabu:t] I didn't enjoy dinner because of your commotion. It was like poison to me. زَقنَبُوت [zaqnabu:t] May you choke to death! Go eat worms!
زُكام [zuka:m] *n:* • **1.** common cold, head cold
ز - ك - م [zaka:] *n:* • **1.** alms-giving, alms, charity • **2.** alms tax (Islamic law)

ز ك و
زَكَّى [zakka:] *v:* • **1.** to vouch for, support, testify in favor of – آنِي أَزَكِّيك إذا تريد تِشتِرِك بِالنّادِي [ʔa:ni ʔazakki:k ʔiða tri:d tištirik binna:di] I'll vouch for you if you want to join the club. كُلّهُم زَكُّوه عِند المُدِير [kullhum zakku:h ʕind ʔilmudi:r] They all vouched for his integrity to the director. • **2.** to recommend – كُلّهُم زَكُّوه للرِّياسَة [kullhum zakku:h lirriya:sa] They all recommended him for the presidency.
زَكاة [zaka:] *n:* • **1.** alms-giving, alms, charity • **2.** alms tax (Islamic law)
تَزكِيَة [tazkiya] *n:* • **1.** pronouncement of support, favorable testimony • **2.** with بـ by acclamation

ز ك ي
See also: ز ك و

ز ل ب ي
زلابيَة [zla:bya] *n:* • **1.** a coil-shaped donut-like pastry, fried in oil or butter and covered with syrup

ز ل ج

تزَلَّج [dzallaǰ] *v:* • **1.** to skate
تزَلُّج [tazalluǰ] *n:* • **1.** skiing, skating
مِزلاج [mizla:ǰ] *n:* مَزالِج [maza:liǰ] *pl:* • **1.** (sliding) bolt (on a door)
زِلّاجَة [zilla:ǰa] *n:* • **1.** skate, roller-skate, skateboard
مُتَزَلِّج [mutazalliǰ] *n:* • **1.** skier

ز ل ز ل

زِلزال [zilza:l] *n:* زَلازِل [zala:zil] *pl:* • **1.** earthquake

ز ل ط

زلَط [zilaṭ] *v:* • **1.** to swallow whole, to gulp down – إعلِس الخُبُز زين. لا تزُلطَه [ʔiʕlis ʔilxubuz zi:n. la: dzulṭah] Chew the bread well. Don't swallow it whole.
انزِلَط [ʔinzilaṭ] *v:* • **1.** to be swallowed, to be gulped – المَوز يِنزِلُط بسُهُولَة [ʔilmu:z yinziluṭ bsuhu:la] Bananas go down easily.

ز ل ف [1]

تزَلَّف [dzallaf] *v:* • **1.** to fawn, curry favor, behave in a fawning, obsequious manner, fawn on – يِتزَلَّف هوايَة. ما عِندَه مانِع يكَذِّب [yidzallaf hwa:ya. ma: ʕindah ma:niʕ yčaððib] He curries favor all the time. He has no compunction about telling lies. يِزَّلَّف لرَئِيس الدّائِرَة [yizzallaf lraʔi:s ʔidda:ʔira] He fawns on the chief of the office.
مزَلِّف [mzallaf] *adj:* مزَلِّفِين [mzallafi:n] *pl:* • **1.** greedy. • **2.** miserly, stingy.

ز ل ف [2]

زِلِف [zilif] *n:* زلُوف [zlu:f] *pl:* • **1.** sideburns

ز ل ق

زِلَق [zilag] *v:* • **1.** to slip, slide – زِلَق بِطِّين وتوَسَّخَت هدُومَه [zilag biṭṭi:n wtwassaxat hdu:mah] He slipped in the mud and his clothes got dirty. • **2.** to make a mistake, commit an error, make a slip – إحكِي عَلَى كَيفَك وَلا تِزلَق [ʔiħči ʕala kayfak wla: tizlag] Talk slowly and don't make a slip.
زَلَّق [zallag] *v:* • **1.** to cause to make a mistake, to trip up – يِسألنِي هِيكِي أسئِلَة حَتَّى يزَلِّقنِي [yisʔalni hi:či ʔasʔila ħatta yzalligni] He asks me these questions to trip me up.
زَلقَة [zalga] *n:* • **1.** slip (of the tongue). See also زَلَّة
انزِلاق [ʔinzila:q] *n:* • **1.** slipping, sliding
زَلَق، زَلِق [zalag, zalig] *adj:* • **1.** slippery

ز ل ق ط

زَلقَط [zalgaṭ] *v:* • **1.** to bolt – أُقفُل الباب وَزَلقِطها [ʔuqful ʔilba:b wzalgiṭha] Lock the door and bolt it.
زِلقاطَة [zilga:ṭa] *n:* زِلقاطات [zilga:ṭa:t] *pl:* • **1.** (door) bolt, lock

ز ل ل

زَلّ [zall] *v:* • **1.** to slip, slip up, make a mistake – مِتأَسِّف. زَلّ لِسانِي [mitʔassif. zall lisa:ni] I'm sorry. My tongue slipped.
زَلَّة [zalla] *n:* زَلّات [zalla:t] *pl:* • **1.** mistake, error • **2.** زَلَّة لِسان [zallat lisa:n] a slip of the tongue

ز ل م

زِلمَة [zilma, zlima] *n:* زِلِم [zilim] *pl:* • **1.** man

ز ل ن ط ح

زَلَنطَح [zalanṭaħ] *n:* زَلَنطَحات [zalanṭaħa:t] *pl:* • **1.** snail – زَلَنطَح، زَلَنطَح، طَلِّع قرُونَك وَإنطَح [zalanṭaħ, zalanṭaħ, ṭalliʕ gru:nak wʔinṭaħ] Snail, snail, put out your horns and butt.

ز م ب ل

مزَمبِلَة [mzambila] *n:* مزَمبِلات [mzambila:t] *pl:* • **1.** faucet, spigot

ز م ب ل ك

زُمبَلَك [zumbalak] *n:* زُمبَلَكات [zumbalaka:t] *pl:* • **1.** mainspring of a watch – مَرَة زُمبَلَك [mara zumbalak] harridan, shrewish woman.

ز م ر

زَمَّر [zammar] *v:* • **1.** to toot. to play the horn – ظَلّ يزَمُّر إلَى أن دَوَّخنا [ðall yzammur ʔila ʔan dawwaxna] He kept on tooting the horn until he made us dizzy.
زُمرَة [zumra] *n:* زُمَر [zumar] *pl:* • **1.** gang, group (of people)
زِمِير [zimi:r] *n:* • **1.** flute, sound of flute
زُمّارَة [zumma:ra] *n:* زُمّارات [zumma:ra:t] *pl:* • **1.** zummara, a small flute-like wind instrument with a bell-shaped end • **2.** horn

ز م ر د

زُمَرَّد [zumarrad, zumrud] *n:* • **1.** (coll.) emerald(s)
زُمُرُّدَة [zumurruda] *n:* زُمُرُّدات [zumurruda:t] *pl:* • **1.** emerald

ز م ز م

زَمزَمِيَّة [zamzamiyya] *n:* زَمزَمِيّات [zamzamiyya:t] *pl:* • **1.** canteen, flask

ز م ط

زُمَط [zumaṭ] *v:* • **1.** to boast, brag, talk big – أشُو تِزمُط وَماكُو قَبُض [ʔašu tizmuṭ wma:ku qabuð] It seems you're always bragging but there's no results. • **2.** to kick
زَمُط [zamuṭ] *n:* • **1.** boasting, bragging, talking big

ز م ل

زامَل [za:mal] *v:* • **1.** to be a friend, colleague, associate of, to maintain a friendship with – زاملهُم مُدَّة سَنَة وَبَعدين تِرَكهُم [za:malhum muddat sana wbaʕdi:n tirakhum] He ran around with them for a year and then abandoned them.

تزَمَّل [dzammal] *v:* • **1.** to behave like an ass – لا تِزَّمَّل عاد [la: tizzammal ʕa:d] Stop acting like a jackass!

زَميل [zami:l] *n:* زُمَلاء [zumala:ʔ] *pl:* • **1.** friend, companion, associate, comrade • **2.** colleague

زمال [zma:l] *n:* زمايِل [zma:yil] *pl:* • **1.** jackass, donkey

زَمالَة [zama:la] *n:* زَمالات [zama:la:t] *pl:* • **1.** comradeship • **2.** colleagueship • **3.** friendship • **4.** fellowship, grant, stipend

مزَمِّلَة [mzammila] *n:* مزَمِّلات [mzammila:t] *pl:* • **1.** faucet, spigot

ز م ن

أزمَن [ʔazman] *v:* • **1.** to be or become chronic – الكَحَّة مالتَه أزمِنَت [ʔilgaħħa ma:ltah ʔazminat] His cough has become chronic.

تزامَن [dza:man] *v:* • **1.** to occur at the same time • **2.** to be (or live) simultaneously as • **3.** be a contemporary of

زَمَن [zaman] *n:* أزمِنَة [ʔazmina] *pl:* • **1.** During the Turkish period, all officials learned Turkish – بزَمَن الأتراك، كُلّ المُوَظَّفين تعَلّمَوا تُركي [bzaman ʔilʔatra:k, kull ʔilmuwaððafi:n tʕallmaw turki] During the Turkish period, all officials learned Turkish. • **2.** time, period, era

زَمان [zama:n, zima:n] *n:* أزمِنَة [ʔazmina] *pl:* • **1.** time, age, era, epoch – بزَماني هيكي شي ما كان يصير [bzama:ni hi:či ši ma: ča:n yṣi:r] In my day this sort of thing wouldn't have happened. هَذا شلون زَمان اللّي هَذا يصير نائِب؟ [ha:ða šlu:n zama:n ʔilli ha:ða yṣi:r na:ʔib?] What sort of times are these when that guy becomes a representative? هَالزَّمان، ما بيه صَديق مِن صُدُق [hazzama:n, ma: bi:h ṣadi:q min ṣudug] These days there are no real friends. صار زَمان ما شِفتَك [ṣa:r zama:n ma: šiftak] I haven't seen you in quite a while. صاحِب الزَّمان [ṣa:ħib ʔizzama:n] (Shiite) the Mahdi, the last imam who will come to purify Islam.

تَزامُن [taza:mun] *n:* • **1.** simultaneity

مُزمِن [muzmin] *adj:* • **1.** chronic, lasting, enduring, long-lived, deep-seated – دِزانتَري مُزمِن [diza:ntari muzmin] chronic dysentery.

زَمَني [zamani] *adj:* • **1.** temporal, time-oriented

متزامِن [mitza:min] *adj:* • **1.** simultaneous

ز م ه ر

زَمهَرير [zamhari:r] *adj:* • **1.** severe frost, bitter cold

ز م ي ج

زِميج [zimi:ǰ] *n:* • **1.** alluvial mud (used as fertilizer)

ز ن ب ر

زَنبور [zanbu:r] *n:* زنابير [zna:bi:r] *pl:* • **1.** wasp, hornet

ز ن ب ر ك

زُنبُرُك [zunburuk] *n:* • **1.** var. of [zumbalak] زُمبَلَك • **2.** mainspring of a watch

ز ن ب ق

زَنبَقَة، زَنبَق [zanbaqa, zanbaq] *n:* زَنابِق [zana:biq] *pl:* • **1.** lily • **2.** iris

ز ن ب ل

زَنبيل [zanbi:l, zambi:l] *n:* زَنابيل [zana:bi:l] *pl:* • **1.** large basket woven from palm leaves

ز ن ج

زَنجي [zanǰi] *n:* زُنُوج [zunu:ǰ] *pl:* • **1.** a black, a Negro

ز ن ج ر

زَنجَر [zanǰar] *v:* • **1.** to rust, be or become rusted – القُفُل زَنجَر وَما ينفِتِح [ʔilquful zanǰar wma yinfitiħ] The lock has rusted and won't open.

زنجار [zinǰa:r] *n:* • **1.** rust • **2.** verdigris

مزَنجِر [mzanǰir] *adj:* • **1.** rusty

زِنجاري، دَفّ زِنجاري [zinǰa:ri, daff zinǰa:ri] *n:* • **1.** tambourine

ز ن ج ل

زَنجَل [zanǰal] *v:* • **1.** to chain

تزَنجَل [dzanǰal] *v:* • **1.** to be chained

زَنجيل [zanǰi:l] *n:* زناجيل [zna:ǰi:l] *pl:* • **1.** chain, chain bracelet • **2.** zipper

زَنجَلَة [zanǰala] *n:* • **1.** chaining

مزَنجَل [mzanǰal] *adj:* • **1.** chained

ز ن د

زَند [zanid] *n:* زنود [znu:d] *pl:* • **1.** upper arm, between the shoulder and the elbow

زناد [zna:d] *n:* زنادات [zna:da:t] *pl:* • **1.** trigger (of a gun) • **2.** cigarette lighter

ز ن د ق

زَنديق [zandi:q] *adj:/n:* زَنادِق، زَنادِقَة [zana:diq, zana:diqa] *pl:* • **1.** atheist, unbeliever, free-thinker

ز ن ز ن

زِنزانَة [zinza:na] *n:* زنزانات [zinza:na:t] *pl:* • **1.** prison cell

ز ن ك ط

زُنكُطَة، زُنُكطة [zunguṭa, zunugṭa] *n:* زُنكُطات، زناكِط [zunguṭa:t, zunugṭa:t, zna:giṭ] *pl:* • **1.** pimple, skin blemish

ز ن ك ن

زَنكَن [zangan] *v:* • **1.** to bestow wealth, make wealthy – الوَظِيفَة ما تزَنكِن أَحَّد [lwaðiːfa maː dzangin ʔaħħad] Government work won't make anyone wealthy. إذا تدَبُّر القَضِيَّة، أزَنقِنَك بمِية دِينار [ʔiða ddabbur ʔilqaðiyya, ʔazanginak bmiyaːt dinaːr] If you take care of the matter, I'll give you a hundred dinars.

تزَنكَن [dzangan] *v:* • **1.** to be or become wealthy, to get rich – بوَقِت الحَرُب، تزَنكَنَوا ناس هوايَة [bwakit ʔilħarub, dzanganaw naːs hwaːya] During the war, many people got rich.

زَنكَنَة [zangana] *n:* • **1.** wealth, riches

زَنكِين [zangiːn] *adj:* زَناكِين [zanaːgiːn] *pl:* • **1.** wealthy, rich • **2.** a rich man

ز ن م

زَنِيم [zaniːm] *adj:* • **1.** low, despicable, mean, ignoble • **2.** pl. زَنِيمين despicable person

ز ن ن

زَنانَة، مال زَنانَة [zanaːna, maːl zanaːna] *adj:* • **1.** having to do with women, for women, feminine – شلُون تِلبَس هِيكِي قَنادِر؟ هَذِي مال زَنانَة [šluːn tilbas hiːči qanaːdir? haːði maːl zanaːna] How can you wear such shoes? These are for women! شلُون تسَوِّي هِيكِي بِيّا؟ هَذا عَمَل زَنانَة [šluːn tsawwiː hiːči biyya? haːða ʕamal zanaːna] How could you do that to me? That's something a woman would do. • **2.** effeminate – هَذا زَنانَة. ما يُقعُد وِيّا الرّياجِيل، يحِبّ حَكِي النِّسوان [haːða zanaːna. maː yugʕud wiyya ʔirriyaːǰiːl, yħibb ħači ʔinniswaːn] He's effeminate. He doesn't sit with the men; he likes women's talk. واحِد مِن وِلدَه رِجّال تَمام، وَاللّاخ زَنانَة [waːħid min wildah rijjaːl tamaːm, willaːx zanaːna] One of his boys is a real man, but the other is effeminate.

ز ن ي

زِنَى [zinaː] *v:* • **1.** to fornicate • **2.** to commit adultery – إذا تِزنِي، الله يعاقبَك [ʔiða tizni, ʔallah yʕaːqbak] If you commit adultery, God will punish you.

زِنا [zina] *n:* • **1.** fornication • **2.** adultery – إبِن زِنَا [ʔibin zina] bastard.

زانِي [zaːni] *adj:* زانِيِّين، زُناة [zaːniyyiːn, zunaːt] *pl:* • **1.** fornicator, adulterer

ز ه د

زَهدِي [zahdi] *adj:* • **1.** a cheap variety of dates

زاهِد [zaːhid] *adj:* • **1.** self-denying, detached (from worldly pleasures)

مِتزَهِّد [mitzahhid] *adj:* • **1.** ascetic

ز ه ر

اِزدِهَر [ʔizdihar] *v:* • **1.** to flourish, thrive, prosper – بَغداد اِزدِهرَت بزَمَن العَبّاسِيِّين [baɣdaːd ʔizdiharat bzaman ʔilʕabbaːsiyyiːn] Baghdad flourished during the Abbasid period.

زَهَر [zahar] *n:* • **1.** a kind of poison primarily used in poisoning fish

زُهَرَة [zuhara] *n:* • **1.** the planet Venus

زَهرَة [zahra] *n:* أزهار [ʔazhaːr] *pl:* • **1.** flower

مَزهَرِيَّة [mazhariyya] *n:* مَزهَرِيّات [mazhariyyaːt] *pl:* • **1.** flower vase

اِزدِهار [ʔizdihaːr] *n:* • **1.** prosperity, flourishing

زُهرِي، مَرَض زُهرِي [zuhri, marað zuhri] *n:* • **1.** venereal disease

زَهرِي [zahri] *adj:* • **1.** pink

مُزدَهِر [muzdahir] *adj:* • **1.** prosperous

ز ه ف

زِهَف [zihaf] *v:* • **1.** to make a mistake, err – دِير بالَك لا تِزهَف تَرَة ما يسامحَك [diːr baːlak laː tizhaf tara maː ysaːmħak] Be careful not to make a mistake or he won't forgive you.

زَهَّف [zahhaf] *v:* • **1.** to cause to make a mistake, to cause to err – لا تِحكِي. تَرَة تزَهِّفنِي [laː tiħči. tara dzahhifni] Don't talk. You'll make me make a mistake.

زَهِف [zahif] *n:* • **1.** mistake, error

زَهفَة [zahfa] *n:* زَهفات [zahfaːt] *pl:* • **1.** mistake, error

ز ه ق

زِهَق [zihag] *v:* • **1.** to be or become disgusted, fed up, tired – الرِّجّال زِهَق مِن مَرتَه [ʔirrijjaːl zihag min martah] The man got fed up with his wife.

زَهَّق [zahhag] *v:* • **1.** to make disgusted, fed up, tired, to antagonize, irritate, exasperate – يزَهِّقنِي. ساعَة يرِيد السَّيّارَة وساعَة ما يرِيدها [yzahhigni. saːʕa yriːd ʔissayyaːra wsaːʕa maː yriːdha] He disgusts me. One time he wants the car and one time he doesn't. لا تزَهِّقه لِلوَلَد تَرَة يبَطِّل [laː dzahhigah lilwalad tara ybaṭṭil] Don't antagonize the boy or he will quit.

تزَهَّق [tzahhag] *v:* • **1.** to be disgusted, fed up, tired

زَهِق [zahig] *n:* • **1.** boredom • **2.** tiredness

تزِهِّق [tzihhig] *n:* • **1.** boredom

زَهقان [zahgaːn] *adj:* • **1.** disgusted, fed up, tired, annoyed – آنِي زَهقان مِن هالعِيشَة [ʔaːni zahgaːn min halʕiːša] I'm disgusted with this life.

ز ه و

زِهَى [zihaː] *v:* • **1.** to be radiant, glow, gleam, shine brightly – الشّارِع اليُوم يِزهِي بِهالضُوايات

[ʔiššaːriʕ ʔilyuːm yizhi bhaðð̣uwaːyaːt] The street's radiant today with these lights.
زَهو [zahw] *n:* • **1.** overconfidence, pride
زاهِي [zaːhi] *adj:* • **1.** bright

ز و ج

زَوَّج [zawwaǰ] *v:* • **1.** to marry off, to give in marriage – إذا تِشتِرِك وِيّايا، أزَوِّجَك بِنتِي [ʔiða tištirik wiyyaːya, ʔazawwiǰak binti] If you'll go into partnership with me, I'll marry my daughter to you. مِن يِتخَرَّج إبنِي مِن الكُلِّيَّة، أزَوِّجَه [min yitxarraǰ ʔibni min ʔilkulliyya, ʔazawwiǰah] When my son graduates from college, I'll get him married.
زاوَج [zaːwaǰ] *v:* • **1.** to mate – زاوَج دِجاج أَمِيرِكِي وِيّا دِجاج عِراقِي [zaːwaǰ diǰaːǰ ʔamiːrki wiyya diǰaːǰ ʕiraːqi] He mated an American chicken with an Iraqi chicken.
تزَوَّج [dzawwaǰ] *v:* • **1.** to get married – تزَوّجوا قَبُل سَنَة وَهَسَّة عِدهُم بِنت [dzawwiǰaw gabul sana whassa ʕidhum bint] They got married a year ago and now they have a daughter.
زَوج [zuːǰ, zawǰ] *n:* زواج، أزواج [zwaːj, ʔazwaːǰ] *pl:* • **1.** husband • **2.** couple, pair – زوج قَنادِر [zuːǰ qanaːdir] a pair of shoes. الزّمال ضِرَبَه زوج [ʔizzumaːl ðirabah zuːǰ] The donkey kicked him with his two hind feet. سَوّوَه زوج وأخذوا فلوسَه [sawwawh zuːǰ wʔaxðaw fluːsah] They fooled him and took his money. • **3.** fool
زَوجَة [zawǰa] *n:* زَوجات [zawǰaːt] *pl:* • **1.** wife
زَواج [zawaːǰ] *n:* • **1.** marriage – تزَنگَن بزَواجَه مِنها [dzangan bzawaːjah minha] He got rich from his marriage with her. • **2.** wedding • **3.** matrimony
زَوجِيَة [zawǰiya] *n:* • **1.** marriage, matrimony, wedlock
تَزاوُج [tazaːwuǰ] *n:* • **1.** intermarriage
اِزدِواج [ʔizdiwaːj] *n:* • **1.** duality
زَوجِي [zawǰi] *adj:* • **1.** matrimonial, marital, conjugal • **2.** paired, in pairs • **3.** even – رَقَم زَوجِي [raqam zawǰi] an even number.
مِزواج [mizwaːǰ] *adj:* • **1.** frequently married • **2.** frequently marriying
مُزدَوِج [muzdawiǰ] *adj:* • **1.** double
مِتزَوِّج [mitzawwiǰ] *adj:* • **1.** married

ز و د

زَوَّد [zawwad] *v:* • **1.** to provide, supply, furnish – هَالدّائِرَة راح تزَوّدَك بِكُلّ المَعلُومات [haddaːʔira raːħ tzawwdak bkull ʔilmaʕluːmaːt] That office will furnish you with all the information.
تزَوَّد [dzawwad] *v:* • **1.** to be supplied
زاد [zaːd] *n:* • **1.** provisions, supplies, stores • **2.** food
مُزَوِّد [muzawwid] *n:* • **1.** supplier
تَزوِيد [tazwiːd] *n:* • **1.** supplying
مُزَوَّد [muzawwad] *adj:* • **1.** supplied

ز و ر

زار [zaːr] *v:* • **1.** to visit, call on, pay a visit to – زِرنا لُبنان زِيارَة قصَيِّرَة الصَّيف اللّي فات [zirna lubnaːn ziyaːra gṣayyra ʔiṣṣayf ʔilli faːt] We paid a short visit to Lebanon last summer. راح أزُور المُدِير بِبَيتَه [raːħ ʔazuːr ʔilmudiːr bibaytah] I will call on the director at his home. زِرنا العَتَبات المُقَدَّسَة [zirna ʔilʕatabaːt ʔilmuqaddasa] We visited the holy places. راح تزُور هالسَّنَة؟ [raːħ dzuːr hassana?] Are you going to the holy places this year?
زَوَّر [zawwar] *v:* • **1.** to guide, show around, conduct on a tour (particularly of a shrine) – شُوفلَك فَدّ واحِد يزَوّرَك المَقام [šuːflak fadd waːħid yzawwrak ʔilmaqaːm] Find yourself someone to guide you around the shrine. • **2.** to forge, falsify – يِقدَر يزَوِّر أيّ تَوقِيع [yigdar yzawwir ʔayy tawqiːʕ] He can forge any signature. ألغوا الانتِخابات لِأَنّ كانَت مُزَوَّرَة [ʔalɣaw ʔilintixaːbaːt liʔann čaːnat muzawwara] They voided the elections because they were rigged.
تزاوَر [dzaːwar] *v:* • **1.** to exchange visits, visit each other – إذا تظَلّون تِتزاوِرُون عَلَى طُول، يِمكِن تِتزَوَّجها [ʔiða tð̣alluːn tidzaːwruːn ʕala ṭuːl, yimkin tidzawwaǰha] If you keep on visiting with each other a long time, perhaps you will marry her.
زُور، شَهادَة زُور [zuːr, šahaːdat zuːr] *n:* • **1.** untruth, falsehood
زور [zuːr] *n:* • **1.** force – ما يسَوِّي شِي إلّا بِالزّور [maː ysawwiː ši ʔilla bizzuːr] He doesn't do anything unless he's forced to. خُو مُو بِالزُّور؛ ما يِعجِبنِي أرُوح لِلسِّينَما هاللَّيلَة [xuː muː bizzuːr; maː yiʕǰibni ʔaruːħ lissinama hallayla] Even force won't help; I don't want to go to the movies tonight. • **2.** undergrowth, thicket in a marshy area – أكُو خَنزِير بِالزُّور [ʔaku xanziːr bizzuːr] There's something that doesn't meet the eye (lit., there's a boar in the marsh growth).
زايِر [zaːyir, zaːʔir] *n:* زُوّار [zuwwaːr] *pl:* • **1.** visitor, caller, guest • **2.** visitor, pilgrim (to a shrine or holy place other than Mecca)
مُزَوِّر [muzawwir] *n:* • **1.** forger
مَزار [mazaːr] *n:* • **1.** shrine
زِيارَة [ziyaːra] *n:* • **1.** pl. زِيارات visit; call (social, business, etc.)
تَزوِير [tazwiːr] *n:* • **1.** forgery, falsification
مزَوُّرچِي [mzawwurči] *n:* مزَوِّرچِيَّة [mzawwirčiyya] *pl:* • **1.** guide at a shrine who leads people in prayers appropriate to the place
زورخانَة [zuːrxaːna] *n:* زورخانات [zuːrxaːnaːt] *pl:* • **1.** a kind of oriental gymnasium, devoted to body-building and physical culture
مزَوَّر [mzawwar] *adj:* • **1.** counterfeit
زُورخَنچِي [zuːrxanči] *adj:* • **1.** athlete who exercizes

in a gymnasium زورخانة devoted to body-building and physical culture

ز و ر ق

زَورَق [zawraq] *n:* زَوارِق [zawa:riq] *pl:* • **1.** boat

ز و ع

زاع [za:ʕ] *v:* • **1.** to vomit, retch, throw up – السَّكران زاع بالباص [ʔissakra:n za:ʕ bilpa:ṣ] The drunk vomited in the bus. مِن هَدَّدتَه، زاع كُلّ الفلُوس [min haddadtah, za:ʕ kull ʔilflu:s] When I threatened him, he coughed up all the money.

زَوَّع [zawwaʕ] *v:* • **1.** to vomit, retch, throw up – داخ وزَوَّع [da:x wzawwaʕ] He got dizzy and vomited. • **2.** to cause to vomit – أُمَّه اِنطَاتَه دُوا حَتَّى تزَوِّعَه [ʔummah ʔinṭa:tah duwa ħatta dzawwiʕah] His mother gave him some medicine to make him vomit. زَوَّعتَه كُلّ الفلُوس [zawwaʕtah kull ʔilflu:s] I squeezed all the money out of him.

زوع [zu:ʕ] *n:* • **1.** vomit

زواع [zwa:ʕ] *n:* • **1.** vomit

زوعَة، مَرَض أَبُو زوعَة [zu:ʕa, marað ʔabu zu:ʕa] *n:* • **1.** cholera

ز و ق

زَوَّق [zawwag] *v:* • **1.** to trim

تزَوَّق [dzawwag] *v:* • **1.** to trim

زواقَة [zwa:ga] *n:* • **1.** make-up

ز و ل

زال [za:l] *v:* • **1.** (a) /with negative only/ to cease (often equivalent to English "still, yet") – هُمَّ لا يَزالُون يِرحُون مَشِي لِلمَدرَسَة [humma la: yaza:lu:n yirħu:n mašy lilmadrasa] They haven't stopped walking to school. They still go to school on foot. هُوَّ لا يَزال مَوجُود بِبَغداد [huwwa la: yaza:l mawǰu:d bibaɣda:d] He's still in Baghdad. • **2.** to go away, leave, withdraw – الخَطَر زال عَنَّه [ʔilxaṭar za:l ʕannah] He's out of danger (lit., the danger went away from him). • **3.** to remove, eliminate, to make disappear or vanish – هالمَحلُول يزِيل اللَّكَّة [halmaħlu:l yzi:l ʔillakka] This solution will remove the spot.

زُولِيَّة [zu:liyya] *n:* زُولِيّات، زوالِي [zu:liyya:t, zwa:li] *pl:* • **1.** carpet, rug

مِزوَلَة [mizwala] *n:* مَزاوِل [maza:wil] *pl:* • **1.** sundial

زائِل [za:ʔil] *adj:* • **1.** mortal • **2.** transitory, passing, fleeting, short-lived

ز و ن [1]

زوان [zwa:n] *n:* • **1.** (coll.) freckle(s) • **2.** (coll.) blackhead(s), boil(s), pimple(s)

زوانَة [zwa:na] *n:* زوانات [zwa:na:t] *pl:* • **1.** freckle

ز و ن [2]

زان [za:n] *n:* • **1.** beech tree

زانَة [za:na] *n:* زانات [za:na:t] *pl:* • **1.** pole vaulting – طَفر الزّانَة [ṭafr ʔizza:na] pole vaulting. • **2.** pole

ز و ي

اِنزَوَى [ʔinzuwa:] *v:* • **1.** to hide oneself, go into seclusion – البَزُّونَة تِنزُوِي مِن تشُوف الكَلِب [ʔilbazzu:na tinzuwi min tšu:f ʔiččalib] The cat hides itself when it sees the dog. مِن فِشَل بِالإنتِخابات، اِنزُوَى [min fišal bilʔintixa:ba:t, ʔinzuwa:] When he lost in the election, he went into seclusion.

زُوِيَّة [zuwiyya] *n:* زوايا [zwa:ya] *pl:* • **1.** corner, nook

زاوِيَة [za:wiya] *n:* زَوايا [zawa:ya:] *pl:* • **1.** angle (math.)

ز ي ت

زَيَّت [zayyat] *v:* • **1.** to oil, grease

زَيت [zayt, zi:t] *n:* زيُوت [zyu:t] *pl:* • **1.** olive oil – زَيت الزَّيتُون [zayt ʔizzi:tu:n] olive oil. • **2.** pl. زيُوت oil (edible, fuel, etc)

زَيتِي [zayti, zayti] *adj:* • **1.** oily, oil – أَصباغ زَيتِيَّة [ʔaṣba:ɣ zaytiyya] (artist's) oil paints.

مزَيَّت [mzayyat] *adj:* • **1.** oiled • **2.** lubricated

ز ي ت ن

زَيتُون [zaytu:n, zi:tu:n] *n:* • **1.** olive(s) • **2.** olive tree(s)

زَيتُونَة [zaytu:na, zi:tu:na] *n:* زَيتُونات [zaytu:na:t, zi:tu:na:t] *pl:* • **1.** olive • **2.** olive tree

ز ي ت و ن

زَيتُونِي [zaytu:ni, zi:tu:ni] *adj:* • **1.** olivaceous, olive-colored, olive-green – نَفنُوف زَيتُونِي [nafnu:f zi:tu:ni] an olive-colored dress.

ز ي ح

زاح [za:ħ] *v:* • **1.** to take away, drive away, remove, banish – ما تزِيح هَالكُتُب مِن يَمِّي حَتَّى أَقدَر أَكتِب؟ [ma: dzi:ħ halkutub min yammi ħatta ʔagdar ʔaktib?] Would you move these books away from me so I can write? الوَزِير الجِّدِيد زاح المُدِير مِن ذاك المَنصِب [ʔilwazi:r ʔiǰǰidi:d za:ħ ʔilmudi:r min ða:k ʔilmanṣib] The new minister ousted the director from that position. أُخُذ هَالكَم دَرِس المَطلُوبَة حَتَّى تزِيحها عَنَّك [ʔuxuð halčam daris ʔilmaṭlu:ba ħatta dzi:ħha ʕannak] Take these few required courses so you can get them out of your way.

زَيح [zayħ, zi:ħ] *n:* • **1.** removing

ز ي د

زاد [za:d] *v:* • **1.** to become greater, become more, grow, increase, multiply – عَدَد الطُّلّاب زاد [ʕadad

ز

ʔiṭṭulla:b za:d] The number of students increased. وجَع راسِي دَيزِيد [wijaʕ ra:si dayzi:d] My headache is getting more severe. الشَّطّ يزِيد بِالرَّبِيع [ʔiššaṭṭ yzi:d birrabi:ʕ] The river rises in the spring. • **2.** to augment, increase, compound. add to, enlarge – زِيد الشّاي مالِي ماي [zi:d ʔiččа:y ma:li ma:y] Add some water to my tea. • **3.** to be in excess, be left over – كُلّ طالِب أَخَذ كِتاب وَزادَت خَمِس كُتُب [kull ṭa:lib ʔaxað kita:b wza:dat xamis kutub] Every student took a book and five books were left over. إذا يزُود شِي مِن القماش، أنطِيك إيّاه [ʔiða yzu:d ši min ʔilqma:š, ʔanṭi:k ʔiyya:] If there's anything left of the cloth, I'll give it to you. • **4.** with عَلَى or عَن to exceed, be greater than, be more than – المَصرَف زاد عَلَى الدَّخَل [ʔilmaṣraf za:d ʕala ʔiddaxal] The expense exceeded the income.

زَيَّد [zayyad] *v:* • **1.** to augment, increase, make greater or more – البَقّال راح يزَيِّد سِعِر الجِّزَر [ʔilbagga:l ra:ḥ yzayyid siʕir ʔijjizar] grocer is going to increase the price of carrots. زَيّدَوايُومِيّتِي [zayydaw yawmiyyti] They raised my daily allowance. • **2.** with عَلَى to outbid, to make a higher bid than – زَيَّد عَلَيّا بدِينارَين وَباعولَه إيّاه [zayyad ʕalayya bdina:rayn wba:ʕu:lah ʔiyya:h] He raised me two dinars and they sold it to him.

زايَد [za:yad] *v:* • **1.** to bid, offer a bid (at an auction) – الدَّلّال عِرَض الرّادِيُو بَسّ مَحَّد زايَد [ʔiddalla:l ʕirað ʔirra:dyu bass maḥḥad za:yad] The auctioneer showed the radio but no one bid.

تزَيَّد [dzayyad] *v:* • **1.** to be increased, to be aggravated

اِزداد [ʔizda:d] *v:* • **1.** to grow, increase, become more or greater – لا تِتجادَل وِيّاه تَرَة يزداد غَضَبَه [la: tidja:dal wiyya:h tara yizda:d ɣaðabah] Don't argue with him or he'll get madder (lit., his anger will increase).

مَزاد [maza:d] *n:* مَزادات [maza:da:t] *pl:* • **1.** auction, public sale

زِيادَة [ziya:da] *n:* • **1.** increase, growth – صارَت زِيادَة كِبِيرَة بِالشَّطّ هالسَّنَة [ṣa:rat ziya:da čibi:ra biššaṭṭ hassana] there was a big rise in the river this year. • **2.** excess, surplus, overage, over-plus – طِلعَت عِدنا زِيادَة بِالحِساب [ṭilʕat ʕidna ziya:da biliḥsa:b] We had an excess in our accounts. هالسَّنَة راح تصِير زِيادَة بالمِيزانِيَّة [hassana ra:ḥ tṣi:r ziya:da bilmi:za:niyya] This year there is going to be a surplus in the budget. غلَط بِالحِساب وَإنطانِي خَمسِين فِلِس زيادَة [ɣilaṭ biliḥsa:b wʔinṭa:ni xamsi:n filis zya:da] He made a mistake in figuring and gave me 50 fils too much. عِندِي فلُوس التِّكِت وَلا فِلِس زِيادَة [ʕindi flu:s ʔittikit wala filis ziya:da] I have money for the ticket, but not one fils more. هاي كُلّها زِيادَة مالها حاجَة [ha:y kullha zya:da ma:lha ḥa:ja] All of these things are unnecessary additions. الزِّيادَة بِكُلشِي مُو زِينَة [ʔizziya:da bikullši mu: zi:na] Excess in everything isn't good. • **3.** increase, augmentation, raising, stepping up – إنطَونِي زِيادَة نُصّ دِينار بِاليُوم [ʔinṭu:ni ziya:da nuṣṣ dina:r bilyu:m] They gave me a half dinar a day raise. باعلِي الأثاث بسِعر التَّكلِيف بَلا زِيادَة [ba:ʕli ʔilʔaθa:θ bsiʕr ʔittakli:f bala ziya:da] He sold me the furniture at cost without a mark-up. نِقلَه وَزِيادَة عَلَى ذلِك غَرَّمَه راتِب يومَين [niqalah wziya:da ʕala ða:lik ɣarramah ra:tib yu:mayn] He transferred him and, in addition to that, docked him two days pay.

زائِدَة، الزائِدَة الدُودِيَّة [za:ʔida, ʔizza:ʔida ʔiddu:diyya] *n:* • **1.** appendix, vermiform appendix (anat.)

مُزايَدَة [muza:yada] *n:* • **1.** bidding, offering of bids (at an auction)

اِزدِياد [ʔizdiya:d] *n:* • **1.** increase

زايِد، زائِد [za:yid, za:ʔid] *adj:* • **1.** increasing, growing, becoming more or greater • **2.** excessive, immoderate – هَذِي كانَت زايدَة مِنَّك. ما كان لازِم تقُول هِيكِي شِي [ha:ði ča:nat za:yda minnak. ma: ča:n la:zim dgu:l hi:či ši] That was uncalled for. You shouldn't have said such a thing. • **3.** additional, extra – عِندَك قَلَم زايِد؟ [ʕindak qalam za:yid?] Do you have an extra pencil? • **4.** excess, more than necessary – الشاي مالِي، شَكَرَه زايِد [ʔiččа:y ma:li, šakarah za:yid] My tea has too much sugar. العَشِر دَنانِير زايدَة عَلَيّا [ʔilʕašir dana:ni:r za:yda ʕalayya] The ten dinars is more than enough for me.

مزايِد [mza:yid, muza:yid] *n:* • **1.** bidder, outbidder (at an auction)

مِتزايِد [mitza:yid] *adj:* • **1.** increasing

أزيَد [ʔazyad] *comparative adjective:* • **1.** more or most excessive, high, great

ز ي ز ف و ن

زِيزَفُون [zi:zafu:n] *n:* • **1.** linden tree

ز ي ط

زِيطَة [zi:ṭa] *n:* زِيطات [zi:ṭa:t] *pl:* • **1.** wagtail, water thrush (common Iraqi birds)

ز ي ف

زَيَّف [zayyaf] *v:* • **1.** to counterfeit (money) – أكُو كَم واحِد دَيزَيِّفُون دَنانِير [ʔaku čam wa:ḥid dayzayyifu:n dana:ni:r] There are several people counterfeiting dinars.

تزَيَّف [dzayyaf] *v:* • **1.** to be counterfeited

تَزيِيف [tazyi:f] *n:* • **1.** forgery

مُزَيَّف [muzayyaf] *adj:* • **1.** counterfeit, false, spurious – حُبَّه إلها كان مُزَيَّف [ḥubbah ʔilha ča:n muzayyaf] His love for her was phony.

ز ي ق 1

زَيَّق [zayyag] *v:* • **1.** to give a Bronx cheer, raspberry – كُلّما أحكِي، يزَيِّق [kullma ʔaḥči, yzayyig] Everytime I say something, he gives a Bronx cheer.

زيق [zi:g, zi:ǰ] *n:* زياقة [zya:ga, zya:ǰa] *pl:* • **1.** a loud, derisive noise made by putting the tongue between the lips and blowing, Bronx cheer, raspberry – لَمّا هَدَّدني جِبتَه بزيق [lamma haddadni ǰibtah bzi:g] When he threatened me, I gave him the raspberry.

ز ي ق 2

زيق [zi:ǰ, zi:g] *n:* زياق [zya:ǰ, zya:g] *pl:* • **1.** shirt-front opening

ز ي ن

زَيَّن [zayyan] *v:* • **1.** to adorn, decorate, embellish, ornament, beautify – زَيِّنَوا الغُرفَة بورُود [zayyinaw ʔilɣurfa bwru:d] They decorated the room with flowers. • **2.** to shave, give a shave to – مِنُو زَيَّنَك الصُّبُح، أَبُو سامِي؟ [minu zayyanak ʔiṣṣubuḥ, ʔabu sa:mi?] Who shaved you this morning, Abu Sami? • **3.** to shave, get a shave – لِحيتَك طُويلَة. لِيش ما تزَيِّن؟ [liḥi:tak ṭuwi:la. li:š ma: dzayyin?] Your whiskers're pretty long. Why don't you shave? • **4.** to cut hair, give a haircut to – هُوَّ يزَيِّن إبنَه بِيدَه [huwwa yzayyin ʔibnah bi:dah] He gives his son haircuts himself. • **5.** to cut one's hair, get a haircut – لازِم تزَيِّن راسَك [la:zim dzayyin ra:sak] You have to have a haircut.

تزَيَّن [dzayyan] *v:* • **1.** to be decorated, be adorned, be beautified – الشَّوارِع تزَيِّنَت بهَالأَشجار [ʔiššawa:riʕ dzayyinat bhalʔašǰa:r] The streets have been improved by these trees. • **2.** to shave, get a shave – آني أَزَيِّن السّاعَة سَبعَة الصُّبُح كُلّ يوم [ʔa:ni ʔazayyin ʔissa:ʕa sabʕa ʔiṣṣubuḥ kull yu:m] I shave at seven o'clock every morning. • **3.** to get a haircut – آني رايِح لِلحَلّاق أَزَيِّن [ʔa:ni ra:yiḥ lilḥalla:q ʔazayyin] I'm going to the barber to get a haircut.

زِينَة [zi:na] *n:* زينات [zi:na:t] *pl:* • **1.** decoration, embellishment, ornament

زيان [zya:n] *n:* زيانات [zya:na:t] *pl:* • **1.** shave • **2.** haircut

مزَيِّن [mzayyin] *n:* مزَيِّنين [mzayyni:n] *pl:* • **1.** barber

زينِيَّة [zi:niyya] *n:* زينِيّات [zi:niyya:t] *pl:* • **1.** favor, kindness, good deed

تزيين [tazyi:n] *n:* • **1.** decoration, ornamentation

زين [zi:n, zayn] *adj:* • **1.** fine, good, nice – عِندَه شُغُل زين [ʕindah šuɣul zi:n] He has a good job. هَمّ زين ما قِلتلَه [hamm zi:n ma: giltlah] It's a good thing you didn't tell him. يَعني، مُو زين مِنَّه إنطاك سَيّارتَه تِستَعمِلها؟ [yaʕni, mu: zi:n minnah ʔinṭa:k sayya:rtah tistaʕmilha?] Now, wasn't that nice of him to give you his car to use? صِرِت زين لَو بَعدَك مَريض؟ [ṣirit zi:n law baʕdak mari:ð?] Did you get well or are you still sick? • **2.** (adv.) well, excellently – مَرتِي تُطبُخ زين [marti tuṭbux zi:n] My wife cooks well. • **3.** (interjection of compliance or approbation) fine, good, all right, O.K – زين، أَسَوِّيها بأَقرَب فُرصَة [zi:n, ʔasawwi:ha bʔaqrab furṣa] All right, I'll do it the first chance I get. زين، آني أَعَلِّمَك [zi:n, ʔa:ni ʔaʕallamak] O.K., I'll teach you.

مزَيِّن [mzayyin] *adj:* • **1.** shaved

مزَيَّن [mzayyan] *adj:* • **1.** decorated

ز ي ي

زَيّ [zayy] *n:* أَزياء [ʔazya:ʔ] *pl:* • **1.** costume • **2.** style of dress – مَعرَض أَزياء [maʕrað ʔazya:ʔ] fashion show.

ز

س

س ء ل

سِأَل [siʔal] *v:* • **1.** to ask, inquire – ما نِدري شرَاح يِسأَلنا بِالإمتِحان [maː nidri šrah yisʔalna bilʔimtiħaːn] We have no idea what he will ask us on the exam. إسأَل مِنَّه. بَلكِي يُعرُف [ʔisʔal minnah. balki yuʕruf] Ask him. Perhaps he knows. الشُّرطَة دَتِسأَل عَنَّك [ʔiššurṭa datisʔal ʕannak] The police are inquiring about you.
تسَأّل [tsaʔʔal] *v:* • **1.** to be inquisitive, ask questions – إذا تِتسَأّل هوايَة، يعُرفُوك غَرِيب [ʔiða titsaʔʔal hwaːya, yʕurfuːk ɣariːb] If you ask a lot of questions, they will know you're a stranger.
تسائَل [tsaːʔal] *v:* • **1.** to ask, to inquire
سُؤال [suʔaːl] *n:* أَسئِلَة [ʔasʔila] *pl:* • **1.** question, query, inquiry
مَسأَلَة [masʔala] *n:* مَسائِل [masaːʔil] *pl:* • **1.** problem, question • **2.** controversy, issue, thing in dispute • **3.** matter, affair, case – شصار مِن مَسأَلَة الزَّواج؟ [šṣaːr min masʔalat ʔizzawaːǰ?] What came of the wedding matter? شلُون مَسائِل دَتصِير بالدّائِرَة! المُوَظَّفِين يِتعارِكُون، وَالغَراض دَتِنباق [šluːn masaːʔil datṣiːr biddaːʔira! ʔilmuwaððafiːn yitʕaːrkuːn, wilɣaraːð datinbaːg] What goings-on are taking place in the office! The employees are fighting with each other and things are being stolen. ما تجُوز مِن هالمَسائِل! مُو عِيب تِحكِي عالنّاس [maː djuːz min halmasaːʔil! muː ʕiːb tiħči ʕannaːs] Why don't you quit this business! It's wrong to talk against people! عِندَه غير مَسائِل [ʕindah ɣiːr masaːʔil] or شلُون مَسائِل عِندَه [šluːn masaːʔil ʕindah] He's a real nut! What a character he is!
مَسؤُول [masʔuːl] *n:* • **1.** accountable, responsible, in charge – مِنُو المَسؤُول عَن اللّي صار؟ [minu ʔilmasʔuːl ʕann ʔilli ṣaːr?] Who's responsible for what happened? مِنُو المَسؤُول بِهالدّائِرَة؟ [minu ʔilmasʔuːl bhaddaːʔira?] Who's in charge of this office?
مِتسَوِّل [mitsawwil] *n:* مِتسَوِّلِين [mitsawwiliːn] *pl:* • **1.** beggar
مَسؤُولِيَّة [masʔuːliyya] *n:* مَسؤُولِيّات [masʔuːliyyaːt] *pl:* • **1.** responsibility
سَئّال [saʔʔaːl] *adj:* • **1.** inquisitive, curious, given to asking questions
سائِل [saːʔil] *adj:* سائِلِين [saːʔiliːn] *pl:* • **1.** questioner, asker • **2.** beggar

س ب ب

سَبّ [sabb] *v:* • **1.** to insult, abuse, call names, revile, curse – سَبّ البَزّاز اللّي غَشّه بِالقماش [sabb ʔilbazzaːz ʔilli ɣaššah bilqmaːš] He reviled the cloth dealer who cheated him on the material.
سَبَّب [sabbab] *v:* • **1.** to cause, bring about, provoke, produce – ما دَنُعرُف شِنُو اللّي دَيسَبِّب هَالمَرَض [maː danuʕruf šinu ʔilli daysabbib halmarað] We don't know what is causing this disease.
تسَبَّب [tsabbab] *v:* • **1.** to make a living, carry on a business – خَلّي الرِّجّال يِتسَبَّب ورُوح عَنَّه [xalliː ʔirrijjaːl yitsabbab wruːħ ʕannah] Let the man carry on his business; get away from him! • **2.** with مِن، عَن to be caused by, be the result or consequence of, to result from, spring from – هَالرُّطُوبَة دَتِتسَبَّب مِن البَلُّوعَة [harruṭuːba datitsabbab min ʔilballuːʕa] This dampness comes from the drain. • **3.** with ب to be the cause of, be to blame for – خَلّى إبنَه يصِير طَيّار وَتسَبَّب بمُوته [xallaː ʔibnah yṣiːr ṭayyaːr wtsabbab bmuːtah] He let his son become a pilot and caused his death.
تسَبَّب [tsabbab] *v:* • **1.** to cause
تسابَب [tsaːbab] *v:* • **1.** to exchange insults, insult each other – تسابَّوا مَرَّة ثانيَة بمَركَز الشُّرطَة [tsaːbbaw marra θaːnya bmarkaz ʔiššurṭa] They exchanged insults again in the police station.
سَبّ [sabb] *n:* • **1.** abuse, insult
سَبَب [sabab] *n:* أسباب [ʔasbaːb] *pl:* • **1.** reason, cause – شِنُو سَبَب اِستِقالتَه؟ [šinu sabab ʔistiqaːltah?] What's the reason for his resignation? إنتَ كِنِت سَبَب كُلّ هالمَشاكِل [ʔinta činit sabab kull halmašaːkil] You were the cause of all these difficulties. ما قِدَر يِجِي بِسَبَب المُطَر [maː gidar yiǰi bsabab ʔilmuṭar] He couldn't come because of the rain.
مَسَبَّة [masabba] *n:* مَسَبّات [masabbaːt] *pl:* • **1.** abuse, insult, vilification – اني ما مِستِعِدّ اكُل مَسَبّة [ʔaːni maː mistiʕidd ʔaːkul masabba] I'm not about to take insults.
سَبّابَة [sabbaːba] *n:* • **1.** index finger
مُسَبِّب [musabbib] *adj:* • **1.** causer, instigator
مِتسَبِّب [mitsabbib] *adj:* • **1.** with فِي causing, instigating

س ب ت

سَبِت، يَوم السَّبِت [sabit, yuːm ʔissabit] *n:* • **1.** Saturday

س ب ت ت ن ك

سَبتَتَنك [sabtatang] *n:* • **1.** septic tank

س ب ح

سِبَح [sibaħ] *v:* • **1.** to swim, go swimming – يِعجبَك نرُوح نِسبَح اليُوم؟ [yiʕiǰbak nruːħ nisbaħ ʔilyuːm?]

Would you like to go swimming today? • **2.** to bathe, take a bath – آنِي مُجنِب؛ لازِم أسبَح قَبُل ما أصَلِّي [ʔa:ni mujnib; la:zim ʔasbaħ gabul ma: ʔaṣalli] I'm ritually unclean; I've got to take a bath before I pray.
سَبَّح [sabbaħ] *v:* • **1.** to cause to swim, let swim – وَدِّي أخُوك الصّغَيِّر وَسَبّحَه بِالشَّطّ [waddi ʔaxu:k ʔiṣṣɣayyir wsabbħah biššaṭṭ] Take your little brother and let him swim in the river. • **2.** to finger one's beads toy with a string of prayer beads – صارلَك ساعَة دَتسَبِّح. إيدَك ما تِعبَت؟ [ṣa:rlak sa:ʕa datsabbiħ. ʔi:dak ma: tiʕbat?] You've been playing with your worry beads for an hour. Hasn't your hand gotten tired?
انسِبَح [ʔinsibaħ] *v:* • **1.** pass. of سِبَح to be swum (in)
سِبِح [sibiħ] *n:* • **1.** swimming
سِبحَة [sibħa] *n:* سِبَح [sibaħ] *pl:* • **1.** prayer beads, a string of beads resembling a rosary
سَبّاح [sabba:ħ] *n:* سَبّاحِين [sabba:ħi:n] *pl:* • **1.** swimmer
مَسبَح [masbaħ] *n:* مَسابِح [masa:biħ] *pl:* • **1.** swimming place, swimming pool
سِباحَة [siba:ħa] *n:* سِباحات [siba:ħa:t] *pl:* • **1.** float
سابُوح [sa:bu:ħ] *adj:* سابُوحِين، سوابِيح [sa:bu:ħi:n, swa:bi:ħ] *pl:* • **1.** expert swimmer, good swimmer

س ب خ

سَبِخ [sabix] *adj:* • **1.** alkaline – قاع سَبخَة [ga:ʕ ṣabxa] alkaline soil. • **2.** briny, alkaline

س ب د ج

سَبدَج [sabdaj] *v:* • **1.** to scrub with ceruse, apply ceruse – دَتسَبدِج وِجهَها [datsabdij wiččha] She's scrubbing her face with ceruse.
سِبداج [sibda:j] *n:* • **1.** white lead, ceruse, a cosmetic containing white lead

س ب ر ن ك

سِبرنك [sipring] *n:* سِبرنكات [sipringa:t] *pl:* • **1.** spring (as an elastic body) – سِبرِنقات لَوِي [sipringa:t lawy] coil springs

س ب ز

سَبزِي [sabzi] *n:* • **1.** spinach

س ب ط

سُبَط [subaṭ] *v:* • **1.** to stay in place, lie down (of hair) – إذا تحُطّ شوَيَّة مَيّ عَلَى شَعرَك، يُسبُط [ʔiða tħuṭṭ šwayya mayy ʕala šaʕrak, yusbuṭ] If you put a little water on your hair, it'll stay down.
سَبَّط [sabbaṭ] *v:* • **1.** to be still, remain motionless, stay calmly in place – إذا ما تسَبُّط، ما أقدَر أزَيِّنَك [ʔiða ma: tsabbuṭ, ma: ʔagdar ʔazayyinak] If you don't be still, I can't shave you.
سَبُط [sabuṭ] *n:* • **1.** staying in place • **2.** pl. أصباط descendents, future lineage
سُبّاطَة [subba:ṭa] *n:* سُبّاطات [subba:ṭa:t] *pl:* • **1.** hair-net

س ب ط ن

سَبَطانَة [sabaṭa:na] *n:* سَبَطانات [sabaṭa:na:t] *pl:* • **1.** barrel • **2.** bore (inside of a gun's barrel)

س ب ع

سَبَّع [sabbaʕ] *v:* • **1.** to make brave, courageous – هَذا مخَنَّث! شسَبَّعَه؟ [ha:ða mxannaθ! ššabbaʕah?] He's a coward! What made him brave?
تسَبَّع [tsabbaʕ] *v:* • **1.** to be made brave, to get up one's courage – تسَبَّع وَراح حِكَى وِيّاه [tsabbaʕ wra:ħ ħiča: wiyya:h] He got up his courage and went to talk with him.
اِستَسبَع [ʔistasbaʕ] *v:* • **1.** to become brave, work up courage, find courage – مِن إجا أبُوه، اِستَسبَع وَقام يسِبّنِي [min ʔija ʔabu:h, ʔistasbaʕ wga:m ysibbni] When his father came, he got brave and began to insult me. كان يخاف مِن خَيالَه. أشُو هَسَّة اِستَسبَع [ča:n yxa:f min xaya:lah. ʔašu hassa ʔistasbaʕ] He was afraid of his shadow. Now it seems he's gotten some courage. • **2.** with عَلَى to overpower, overcome – شافَه وَحدَه وَاِستَسبَع عَلِيه [ša:fah waħdah wʔistasbaʕ ʕali:h] He saw him alone and overpowered him.
سُبُع [subuʕ] *n:* أسباع [ʔasba:ʕ] *pl:* • **1.** one-seventh, seventh part
سَبِع [sabiʕ] *n:* سباع [sba:ʕ] *pl:* • **1.** lion
سَبعَة [sabʕa] *n:* سَبعات، سِبَع [sabʕa:t, sibaʕ] *pl:* • **1.** centipede, millipede • **2.** seven – سَبع مِيَّة [sabiʕ miyya] seven hundred. سَبع أقلام [sabiʕ ʔaqla:m] seven pencils. السَّبعَة بِيدِي [ʔissabʕa bi:di] I've the seven in my hand. أبُو سَبعَة وَسَبعِين [ʔabu sabʕa wsabʕi:n] centipede, millipede.
سَبعِين [sabʕi:n] *n:* • **1.** seventy
إسبُوع [ʔisbu:ʕ] *n:* أسابِيع [ʔasa:bi:ʕ] *pl:* • **1.** week
إسبُوعِيَّة [ʔisbuwʕiyya] *n:* • **1.** weekly wage
سَبِع [sabiʕ] *adj:* • **1.** brave • **2.** cunning • **3.** clever
سابِع [sa:biʕ] *adj:* • **1.** seventh (ordinal)
إسبُوعِي [ʔisbu:ʕi] *adj:* • **1.** weekly – مَعاش إسبُوعِي [maʕa:š ʔisbu:ʕi] a weekly salary.
أسبُوعِيّاً [ʔusbu:ʕiyyan] *adverbial:* • **1.** weekly, by the week

س ب ع ط ع ش

سباطَعَش [sba:ṭaʕaš] *n:* • **1.** seventeen

س ب ق

سِبَق [sibaq] *v:* • **1.** to be, come, go, get, act, or happen before or ahead of, to precede, antecede –

س

الفحص الطِّبّي يِسبِق التّعيين [ʔilfaḥṣ ʔiṭṭibbi yisbiq ʔittaʕyiːn] The medical examination precedes the appointment. أخُوك يِسبِقنِي بِالتَّرفِيع [ʔaxuːk yisbiqni bittarfiːʕ] Your brother is ahead of me in line for promotion. هُوَّ سابِقنِي بِصَفّين بِالثّانَوِيَّة [huwwa saːbiqni bṣaffayn biθθanawiyya] He is two grades ahead of me in high school. سِبَق وقِتلَه عَنَّك [sibaq wgitlah ʕannak] I already told him about you. ما سِبَق وَشِفتَه يصِير هِيكِي عَصَبِي [maː sibaq wšiftah yṣiːr hiːči ʕaṣabi] I haven't ever seen him so mad before. • 2. to surpass, beat, do better than – مَدرَستهُم سِبقَتنا بكُرَة السَّلَّة [madrasathum sibqatna bkurat ʔissalla] Their school beat us in basketball.

تسابَق [tsaːbaq] *v:* • **1.** to race, compete – لا تِتسابَق وِيّاه. سَيّارتَه كِبِيرَة [laː titsaːbaq wiyyaːh. sayyaːrtah čibiːra] Don't race him. His car is big. ترِيد تِتسابَق وِيّايا بِالرِّكِض؟ [triːd titsaːbaq wiyyaːya birrikið?] Do you want to see if you can outrun me?

سَبِق [sabiq, sibiq] *n:* • **1.** antecedence • **2.** precedence, priority – سَبِق لِسان [sabiq lisaːn] a slip of the tongue, impulsive utterance.

سِباق [sibaːq] *n:* سِباقات [sibaːqaːt] *pl:* • **1.** race • **2.** game, meet, match, contest

سابِقَة [saːbiqa] *n:* سَوابِق [sawaːbiq] *pl:* • **1.** previously convicted, having a criminal record *n:* مَعرُوف عَنَّه مِن أصحاب السَّوابِق [maʕruːf ʕannah min ʔaṣḥaːb ʔissawaːbiq] He is known to have been previously convicted • **2.** precedent, previous case

أسبَقِيَّة [ʔasbaqiyya] *n:* • **1.** precedence, priority • **2.** seniority – إنتُو إلكُم الأسبَقِيَّة بِالتَّرفِيع [ʔintu ʔilkum ʔilʔasbaqiyya bittarfiːʕ] You have the seniority for promotion.

مُسابَقَة [musaːbaqa] *n:* مُسابَقات [musaːbaqaːt] *pl:* • **1.** race • **2.** contest – مُسابَقَة أجمَل طِفِل [musaːbaqat ʔajmal ṭifil] most-beautiful child contest.

مِتسابِق [mitsaːbiq] *n:* • **1.** competitor

سابِق [saːbiq] *adj:* • **1.** prior, previous, preceding – الرَّوحَة السّابقَة [ʔirrawḥa ʔissaːbqa] the previous trip. • **2.** former, ex- بِالسّابِق [bissaːbiq] in the past, formerly, at one time. – بِالسّابِق، كانَوا يسافرُون بعَرَبايِن [bissaːbiq, čaːnaw ysaːfruːn bʕarabaːyin] In The past, they travelled by carriage. رِجعَت الأُمُور كَالسّابِق [rijʕat ʔilʔumuːr kassaːbiq] Everything returned to the way it was before.

مُسبَق [musbaq] *adj:* • **1.** previous, preceding, in advance • **2.** previous • **3.** in advance

أسبَق [ʔasbaq] *comparative adjective:* • **1.** earlier, or earliest, antecedent – إنتَ الأسبَق بِالتَّرفِيع [ʔinta ʔilʔasbaq bittarfiːʕ] You are the first in line for promotion.

سابِقاً [saːbiqan] *adverbial:* • **1.** formerly • **2.** previously

س ب ك

سِبَك [sibač] *v:* • **1.** to thicken, become thick – فَوُّرها نُصّ ساعَة حَتَّى تِسبِك [fawwurha nuṣṣ saːʕa ħatta tisbič] Boil it for half an hour so that it'll thicken.

سَبِك [sabič] *n:* • **1.** thickness

سِبّاك [sibbaːč] *n:* سِبّاكَة [sibbaːča] *pl:* • **1.** a maker of date molasses

مَسبَك [masbač] *n:* مَسابِك [masaːbič] *pl:* • **1.** a place where date molasses is made

سَبِيكَة [sabiːka] *n:* سَبائِك [sabaːʔik] *pl:* • **1.** ingot – سَبائِك ذَهَبِيَّة [sabaːʔik ðahabiyya] gold bullion.

سابِك [saːbič] *adj:* • **1.** viscous, syrupy, thick – شُوربَة سابكَة [šuːrba saːbča] thick soup.

أسبَك [ʔasbač] *comparative adjective:* • **1.** more or most syrupy, viscous, thick

س ب ل [1]

سَبَّل [sabbal] *v:* • **1.** to donate for charitable use – راح أسَبِّل تُنقَة مَيّ لِثَواب أبُويَا [raːħ ʔasabbil ṭungat mayy liðawaːb ʔabuːya] I will donate a jar of water (to people passing by) for the sake of my deceased father.

سَبِيل، سُبُل [sabiːl, subul] سَبِيل [sabiːl] donated for public use (especially at a religious shrine) – سَبِيل؛ مُو بِفلُوس هَالمَيّ [halmayy sabiːl; muː bifluːs] This water has been donated; it isn't to be paid for. إبِن السَّبِيل [ʔibin ʔissabiːl] • **1.** vagabond, tramp, hobo • **2.** wayfarer, traveler فِي سَبِيل [fi sabiːl] for the sake of, in behalf of. سَوَّيتها فِي سَبِيل الله [sawwiːtha fi sabiːl ʔallah] I did it for the sake of God. عَلَى سَبِيل [ʕala sabiːl] for the purpose of, by way of, as. عَلَى سَبِيل التَّجرُبَة [ʕala sabiːl ʔittajruba] for the purpose of trial, on a trial basis. عَلَى سَبِيل المِثال [ʕala sabiːl ʔilmiθaːl] as an example, for the purpose of an example. • **3.** path, way

سبِيل [sbiːl] *n:* سبِيلات، سبايِل [sbiːlaːt, sbaːyil] *pl:* • **1.** clay pipe

س ب ل [2]

سَبَّل [sabbal] *v:* • **1.** to wink

تَسبِيل [tasbiːl] *n:* • **1.** wink

س ب ل ت

سِبلِت [siblit] *n:* سَبالِت [sabaːlit] *pl:* • **1.** air conditioner

س ب ن

سبانَة [spaːna] *n:* سبانات، سبايِن [spaːnaːt, spaːyin] *pl:* • **1.** wrench, spanner

س ب ن د

سِيبَندِي [siːbandi] *adj:* سِيبَندِيَّة [siːbandiːyya] *pl:* • **1.** an unscrupulous person, slippery character, double-dealer

س ب ن غ

سبِيناغ [sbiːnaːɣ] *n:* • **1.** spinach

س ب و ر

سَبُّورَة [sabbuːra] *n:* سَبُّورات [sabbuːraːt] *pl:* • **1.** blackboard • **2.** slate

س ب و ر ت ر

سَبورتَر [sabu:rtar] *n:* • **1.** athletic supporter

س ب و س

سبُوس [sbu:s] *n:* • **1.** (coll.) rice hulls, rice husks
سبُوسَة [sbu:sa] *n:* سبُوسات [sbu:sa:t] *pl:* • **1.** rice hull, rice husk

س ب ي

سِبَى [siba:] *v:* • **1.** to capture, take prisoner – كِتلَوا زلِمهُم وَسِبَوا نِسوانهُم [kitlaw zilimhum wsibaw niswa:nhum] They killed their men and captured their women. • **2.** to exasperate, vex, bother greatly – سِباني. كُلّ عَشِر دَقايِق يخابُرنِي يِسأَل عَلَى نَتِيجَة اِمتِحانَه [siba:ni. kull ʕašir daqa:yiq yxa:burni yisʔal ʕala nati:ǰat ʔimtiħa:nah] He has thoroughly exasperated me. Every ten minutes he calls me to ask about the results of his exam. إصبِر شوَيَّة. مُو سِبَيتنِي [ʔiṣbir šwayya. mu: sibi:tni] Be patient a minute. You've bothered the hell out of me.
سَبِي [saby] *n:* • **1.** capture, captivity
سِبايَة [siba:ya] *n:* سِبايات [siba:ya:t] *pl:* • **1.** Shiite mourning ceremony

س ب ي ر

سبَير [spayr] *n:* سبَيرات [spayra:t] *pl:* • **1.** spare, spare tire, spare part

س ت ت [1]

سِتّ [sitt] *n:* • **1.** a polite term of address used by students when speaking or referring to a female teacher, approx.: Lady, Madame, Miss – مُعَلِّمَة الحِساب سِتّ هِندِي [muʕallimat ʔilħisa:b sitt hindi] The mathematics teacher is Miss Hindi.

س ت ت [2]

سِتَّة، سِتّ [sitta, sitt] *n:* • **1.** six
سِتِّين [sitti:n] *n:* • **1.** sixty

س ت ر

سِتَر [sitar] *v:* • **1.** to watch over, protect, guard – الله يِستُر عَليها. خُوش مَرَة [ʔallah yistur ʕali:ha. xu:š mara] God watch over her. She's a fine woman. الله يِستُر مِن هَالحَرب. يجُوز تدَمُّر العالَم [ʔallah yistur min halħarb. yǰu:z ddammur ʔilʕa:lam] God protect us from this war. It might destroy the world. جا يُوقَع بِالشَّط، لَكِن الله سِتَر [ǰa: yu:gaʕ biššaṭṭ, la:kin ʔallah sitar] He was about to fall into the river, but God prevented it. لا، ما تُسقُط. الله يِستُر [la:, ma: tusquṭ. ʔallah yistur] No, you won't fail. God forbid! • **2.** to hide, conceal, cover up – ما تمَكَّن يِستُر غَضَبَه [ma: tmakkan yistur ɣaðabah] He wasn't able to conceal his anger.

سَتَّر [sattar] *v:* • **1.** to watch over, protect, guard, hide, conceal, cover up
تسَتَّر [tsattar] *v:* • **1.** to cover, hide, conceal oneself – دَتِتسَتَّر وَتِعتِقِد النّاس ما يعُرفُون عَنها [datitsattar wtiʕtiqid ʔinna:s ma: yʕurfu:n ʕanha] She's covering up and she thinks people don't know about her.
سِتِر [sitir] *n:* • **1.** covering, protection
سِترَة [sitra] *n:* سِتَر [sitar] *pl:* • **1.** jacket, light coat • **2.** sport coat, suit jacket
سِتار [sita:r] *n:* سَتائِر [sata:ʔir] *pl:* • **1.** curtain (of theater) – السِّتار الحَدِيدِي [ʔissita:r ʔilħadi:di] the Iron Curtain.
سَتّار [satta:r] *n:* • **1.** the Veiler, the Coverer (attribute of God) • **2.** protector, guardian
ساتِر [sa:tir] *n:* سَواتِر [sawa:tir] *pl:* • **1.** fence, screen, curtain • **2.** protective fence around a building or shelter (esp. during war)
سِتارَة [sita:ra] *n:* • **1.** curtain • **2.** screen
مَستُور [mastu:r] *adj:* • **1.** hidden, concealed, covered up • **2.** chaste, proper, honorable
أستَر [ʔastar] *comparative adjective:* • **1.** more or most proper, honorable, respectable – أحسَن شِي وأستَر شِي الواحِد يُصرُف عَلَى قَدّ فلُوسَه [ʔaħsan ši wʔastar ši ʔilwa:ħid yuṣruf ʕala gadd flu:sah] The best and most proper thing is for one to spend according to how much money he has.

س ت ر ن

ستَيرِن [sti:rin] *n:* ستَيرِنات [sti:rina:t] *pl:* • **1.** steering wheel • **2.** steering mechanism, steering gear, steering

س ت ل ت

سَتَلايت [satala:yt] *n:* • **1.** satellite

و ت س

سَتَّى [satta:] *v:* • 1. to cook well, make well-done – سَتُّو اللَّحَم زين قَبل مَا تجِيبَه [sattu: ʔillaħam zi:n gabul ma: dǰi:bah] Cook the meat well-done before you bring it. سَتَّوت اللَّحَم [sattawt ʔillaħam] I cooked the meat well done.

س ت و و

سَتَوّ، -سَتَوّ- [staww, ʔistaww] *adv:* • **1.** variant of • **2.** var. of and هَستَوّ [hastaww-] (with pronoun suffix) now, right this moment

س ت ي ر ي و

ستَيريُو [sti:ryu] *n:* • **1.** stereo, operating device

س ت ي ل

ستِيل [sti:l] *n:* • **1.** steel

س ت ي ن

سِتيان [sitya:n] *n:* سِتيانات [sitya:na:t] *pl:* • **1.** bra

س

س ج د

سِجَد [sijad] *v:* • **1.** to bow down, prostrate oneself (in prayer) – ما دام ظَهرَك يُوجعَك، لا تِسجِد مِن تصَلّي [maː daːm ðahrak yuːjʕak, laː tisjid min tṣalli] Since your back hurts you, don't bow down when you pray. ما يِسجِد غير لِالله [maː yisjid ɣiːr lʔallah] He doesn't bow down to anyone except God.
سَجدَة [sajda] *n:* سَجدات [sajdaːt] *pl:* • **1.** prostration in prayer
سِجّاد [sijjaːd] *n:* • **1.** prayer rug(s) • **2.** rug(s), carpet(s)
مَسجِد [masjid] *n:* مساجِد [msaːjid] *pl:* • **1.** mosque
سُجُود [sujuːd] *n:* • **1.** prostration
سِجّادَة [sijjaːda] *n:* سِجّادات، سجاجِيد [sijjaːdaːt, sjaːjiːd] *pl:* • **1.** prayer rug, rug, carpet

س ج ر

سِجار [sigaːr] *n:* • **1.** cigar
سِجارَة [jigaːra] *n:* سِجايِر [jigaːyir] *pl:* • **1.** cigarette

س ج ع

سَجِع [sajiʕ] *n:* • **1.** rhymed prose

س ج ق

سُجُق [sujuq] *n:* • **1.** link sausage

س ج ل

سَجَّل [sajjal] *v:* • **1.** to register, record, put on record, enter in a register – سَجِّل إسمَك وعِنوانَك هنا [sajjil ʔismak wʕinwaːnak hna] Enter your name and address here. سَجِّلنِي؛ أرِيد أرُوح لِلسَّفرَة [sajjilni; ʔariːd ʔaruːħ lissafra] Put me down; I want to go on the trip. سَجِّل دِينار بحسابَه [sajjil dinaːr bħsaːbah] Enter a dinar on his account. لا تُوقف هنا تَرَة الشُّرطِي يسَجِّل عَلِيك مُخالَفَة [laː tuːgaf hnaː tara ʔiššurṭi ysajjil ʕaliːk muxaːlafa] Don't stop here or the cop will give you a ticket. • **2.** to enter, enroll (in a school, etc.) – أرِيد أسَجِّل إبنِي بِالمَدرَسَة [ʔariːd ʔasjjil ʔibni bilmadrasa] I want to enroll my boy in the school. • **3.** to record, make a recording of, cut a record of – أرِيد أسَجِّل أغانِيها الجِّدِيدَة [ʔariːd ʔasajjil ʔaɣaːniːha ʔijjidiːda] I want to record her new songs.
تسَجَّل [tsajjal] *v:* • **1.** to get registered
سِجِل [sijil] *n:* سِجِلّات [sijillaːt] *pl:* • **1.** register, list, record – سِجِلّات الشَّرِكَة [sijillaːt ʔiššarika] the company's records. سِجِل الزِّيارات [sijil ʔizziyaːraːt] guest register, visitors' book.
مُسَجِّل [musajjil] *n:* مُسَجِّلِين [musajjiliːn] *pl:* • **1.** recorder, registrar • **2.** tape recorder, recording device
تَسجِيل [tasjiːl] *n:* • **1.** recording
مُسَجَّل [musajjal] *adj:* • **1.** registered, recorded, listed – بَرِيد مُسَجَّل [bariːd musajjal] registered mail. عَلامَة مُسَجَّلَة، مارکَة مُسَجَّلَة [ʕalaːma musajjala, maːrka musajjala] registered trade mark.

س ج م

اِنسِجَم [ʔinsijam] *v:* • **1.** to harmonize, blend in, be in harmony – اللَّون الأحمَر ما ينسِجِم ويّا هِيكِي ألوان [ʔilluːn ʔilʔaħmar maː yinsijim wiyya hiːči ʔalwaːn] Red doesn't go with such colors. ما دَينسِجِم ويّا تَلامِيذ صَفَّه [maː dayinsijim wiyya talaːmiːð ṣaffah] He's not getting along with the students in his class. هُوَّ ما مِنسِجِم ويّا أصدِقائَه [huwwa maː minsijim wiyya ʔaṣdiqaːʔah] He doesn't get along with his friends.
اِنسِجام [ʔinsijaːm] *n:* • **1.** harmony

س ج ن

سِجَن [sijan] *v:* • **1.** to jail, imprison, confine – سِجنوه بَعَد ما صِدَر الحُکُم ضِدَّه [sijnuːh baʕad maː ṣidar ʔilħukum ðiddah] They put him in prison after the sentence was pronounced against him. البارحَة سجَنتِني بِالحَرّ ساعتِين [ʔilbaːrħa sjanitni bilħarr saːʕtayn] Yesterday you stranded me in the heat for two hours.
اِنسِجَن [ʔinsijan] *v:* • **1.** to be jailed, imprisoned – قِتَلَه وَانسِجَن عِشرِين سَنَة [kitalah wnsijan ʕišriːn sana] He killed him and was imprisoned for twenty years.
سِجِن [sijin] *n:* سِجُون [sijuːn] *pl:* • **1.** prison, jail, penitentiary • **2.** imprisonment, confinement – سِجِن اِنفِرادِي [sijin ʔinfiraːdi] solitary confinement. سِجِن شَدِيد [sijin šadiːd] confinement at hard labor.
سَجّان [sajjaːn] *n:* • **1.** jailer, prison guard, warden
سَجِين [sajiːn] *adj:* • **1.** prisoner
مَسجُون [masjuːn] *adj:* • **1.** imprisoned, jailed, confined – غِرقَت الباخِرَة وبُقَوا مَسجُونِين بالجَّزِيرَة سَنتَين [ɣirgat ʔilbaːxira wbuqaw masjuːniːn bijjaziːra santayn] The ship sank and they stayed stranded on the island for two years. • **2.** (as *n:*) pl. مَساجِين prisoner, prison inmate, convict

س ح ب

سِحَب [siħab] *v:* • **1.** to pull, draw, drag – سَيّارتِي ما دَتِشتُغُل. دِزِّلِي لورِي يِسحَبها [sayyaːrti maː datištuɣul. dizzli luːri yisħabha] My car isn't running. Send me a truck to tow it. سَيّارَة الجِّيب تِسحَب كُلِّش زين [sayyaːrat ʔijjiːb tisħab kulliš ziːn] A jeep pulls very well. خَلَّوا بَنكَة بِشِبّاك المَطبَخ حَتَّى تِسحَب الهَوا [xallaw panka bšibbaːč ʔilmaṭbax ħatta tisħab ʔilhawa] They put a fan in the kitchen window to draw the air out. • **2.** to withdraw, call back, pull back, pull out – سِحبَوا سَفِيرهُم [siħbaw safiːrhum] They recalled their ambassador. راح نِسحَب جَيشنا مِن الحِدُود [raːħ nisħab jayšna min ʔilħiduːd] We are going to pull our army back from the borders. • **3.** to take back, withdraw – إسحَب كَلامَك تَرَة أمَوّتَك [ʔisħab kalaːmak tara ʔamawwtak] Take back what you said or I'll kill you. إذا تسَوِّي مُخالَفَة، يِسحَبُون إجازتَك [ʔiða tsawwi muxaːlafa, yisħabuːn ʔijaːztak] If you break the law, they'll take away your license. سِحبَوا إيدَه مِن الوَظِيفَة إلَى أن يدَقِّقُون حساباتَه [siħbaw ʔiːdah min ʔilwaðiːfa ʔila ʔan ydaqqiquːn ħsaːbaːtah] They suspended him from the position until they check his books. • **4.** to take out, withdraw – سِحَبِت مِيَّة دِينار مِن البَنك [siħabit miyyat dinaːr min ʔilbank] I withdrew a hundred dinars from the bank. جابَوا بنَيَّة صغَيِّرَة تِسحَب أرقام الفائِزِين [ǰaːbaw bnayya zɣayyra tisħab ʔarqaːm ʔilfaːʔiziːn] They brought a little girl to draw the winners' numbers. • **5.** to draw (a check, bill of exchange, etc.) – دِزّلِي شَكّ مَسحُوب عَلَى بَنك الرّافِدَين [dizzli čakk masħuːb ʕala bang ʔirraːfidiːn] Send me a check drawn on the Rafidayn Bank. سِحَب عَلَيّا كُمبِيالَة بمِيَة دِينار [siħab ʕalayya kumpiyaːla bmiyat dinaːr] He made out a promissory note to me for a hundred dinars. • **6.** to pull, draw (a weapon) – سِحَب عَليه المُسَدَّس وراد يقُتلَه [siħab ʕaliːh ʔilmusaddas wraːd ykutlah] He drew the gun on him and wanted to kill him.

انسِحَب [ʔinsiħab] *v:* • **1.** to withdraw, retreat, pull back – جَيشنا انسِحَب مِن هَالمَنطِقَة [ǰayšna ʔinsiħab min halmanṭiqa] Our army retreated from the area. إذا ما تِقدَر تِتجادَل وِيّاهُم، انسِحِب [ʔiða maː tigdar tidǰaːdal wiyyaːhum, ʔinsiħib] If you can't argue with them, back off. ما أعتِقِد يِنتَخبُونِي. راح أنسِحِب [maː ʔaʕtiqid yintaxbuːni. raːħ ʔansiħib] I don't think they will elect me. I'm going to withdraw.

سَحِب [saħib] *n:* • **1.** drawing (in a lottery)

سَحبَة [saħba] *n:* سَحبات [saħbaːt] *pl:* • **1.** a withdrawal • **2.** a drawing (in a lottery)

ساحِبَة [saːħiba] *n:* ساحِبات [saːħibaːt] *pl:* • **1.** tow truck, wrecker • **2.** tractor (for hauling a semi-trailer)

سَحابَة [saħaːba] *n:* سَحاب [saħaːb] *pl:* • **1.** cloud

انسِحاب [ʔinsiħaːb] *n:* • **1.** pull back

ساحِب [saːħib] *adj:* • **1.** drawn

س ح ر

سِحَر [siħar] *v:* • **1.** to enchant, bewitch, charm, infatuate, fascinate – مَرتَه ترِيد تِسحَرَه حَتَّى بَلكِي يحِبها [martah triːd tisħarah ħatta balki yħibbha] His wife wants to cast a spell on him so he'll love her. عيُونك سِحرَتنِي [ʕyuːnič siħratni] Your eyes have bewitched me!

سَحَّر [saħħar] *v:* • **1.** to serve the Suhuur – بِتنا عِدهُم وَكَلَّب إلّا يسَحِّرنا [bitna ʕidhum wčallab ʔilla ysaħħirna] We spent the night with them and he insisted on serving us the Suhuur.

تسَحَّر [tsaħħar] *v:* • **1.** to eat the Suhuur – ما راح أتسَحَّر هاللَيلَة [maː raːħ ʔatsaħħar hallayla] I'm not going to eat the Suhuur tonight.

سِحِر [siħir] *n:* • **1.** bewitchment, enchantment, beguilement • **2.** magic, sorcery, witchcraft

سُحُور [suħuːr] *n:* سُحُورات [suhuːraːt] *pl:* • **1.** Suhuur, the meal before dawn during Ramadan

سَحّار [saħħaːr] *n:* سَحّارَة، سَحّارِين [saħħaːra, saħħaːriːn] *pl:* • **1.** sorcerer, magician, wizard

ساحِر [saːħir] *n:* ساحِرِين [saːħiriːn] *pl:* ساحِرَة [saːħira] *feminine:* • **1.** magician

سَحّارَة [saħħaːra] *n:* سَحّارات [saħħaːraːt] *pl:* • **1.** sorceress, witch

سِحرِي [siħri] *adj:* • **1.** magic, magical – ألعاب سِحرِيَّة [ʔalʕaːb siħriyya] magic tricks. فانُوس سِحرِي [faːnuːs siħri] magic lanter, slide projector.

مَسحُور [masħuːr] *adj:* • **1.** enchanted, under magical influence • **2.** under magical influence

س ح س ل

سَحسَل [saħsal] *v:* • **1.** to drag or scrape on the ground, to brush the ground – عَباتَه دَتسَحسِل بِالطِّين [ʕabaːtah datsaħsil biṭṭiːn] His robe is dragging in the mud. دَيِمشِي وَيسَحسِل بقُندَرتَه [dayimši wysaħsil bqundartah] He's walking along and shuffling his shoes. • **2.** to slide, drag, pull – إذا ما تِقدَر تشِيل الكِيس، سَحسِلَه [ʔiða maː tigdar tšiːl ʔiččiːs, saħsilah] If you can't carry the bag, drag it.

مسَحسَل [msaħsal] *adj:* • **1.** dragged • **2.** minimal, barely sufficient – غُلبَة مسَحسَلَة [ɣulba msaħsala] a close victory. نِجَح نَجاح مسَحسَل [nijaħ najaːħ msaħsal] He barely succeeded. يِحكِي إنكلِيزِي مسَحسَل [yiħči ʔingiliːzi msaħsal] He barely speaks English. هُوَّ فَدّ واحِد مسَحسَل [huwwa fadd waːħid msaħsal] He's a good-for-nothing loafer.

س ح ق

سِحَق [siħag] *v:* • **1.** to crush, mash, flatten – إسحَق عالجِّكارَة حَتَّى تِنطِفِي زين [ʔisħag ʕaǰǰigaːra ħatta tinṭifi ziːn] Crush the cigarette so it'll be really out. يِنرادِلنا رُولَة تِسحَق القاع [yinraːdilna ruːla tisħag ʔilgaːʕ] We need a steam-roller to pack down the ground. • **2.** to run over, run down, trample – كان يِمشِي بِنُصّ الشّارِع وَسِحقَتَه سَيّارَة [čaːn yimši bnuṣṣ ʔiššaːriʕ wsiħgatah sayyaːra] He was walking in the middle of the street and a car ran over him. وَخِّر، لا يِسحقَك الزُّمال [waxxir, laː ysiħgak ʔizzumaːl] Move out of the way so the donkey won't trample you. اللّي يُوقَف بطَرِيقَك، إسحقَه [ʔilli yuːgaf bṭariːqak, ʔisiħgah] Whoever stands in your way, run over him. بَس ما صار مُدِير، سِحَق المُوَظَّف اللّي كان ينافسَه [bas maː ṣaːr mudiːr, siħag ʔilmuwaððaf ʔilli čaːn ynaːfsah] As soon as he became director, he rode roughshod over the employee who was competing with him. • **3.** to annihilate, wipe out, destroy – جَيشنا سِحَق جيش العَدُو [ǰayšna siħag ǰayš ʔilʕadu] Our army crushed the enemy army. • **4.** to wear in, break in – القُندَرَة إذا تِسحَقها مُدَّة يومَين، بَعَد ما تُوجعَك [ʔilqundara ʔiða tisħagha muddat yawmayn, baʕad maː tuːǰʕak] If you break in the shoes for a couple of days, they won't hurt you anymore.

لازم تِسحَق مَكِينَة السَّيّارَة قَبُل ما تِمشِي بِسُرعَة زايدَة [la:zim tisħag maki:nat ʔissayya:ra gabul ma: timši bsurʕa za:yda] You should break in the car's motor before you go at high speed.
سَحَّق [saħħag] *v:* • **1.** intens. of سِحَق to crush, mash, flatten – خَلّاه جَوَّة رِجلَه وَقام يسَحِّق بِيه [xalla:h ǰawwa riǰlah wga:m ysaħħig bi:h] He put it underneath his foot and started stomping on it.
سَحِق [saħig] *n:* • **1.** crushing, mashing
سِحاق [siħa:q] *n:* • **1.** Lesbianism, tribady
سَحقَة [saħga] *n:* • **1.** humiliation
مَسحُوق [masħu:q] *n:* مَساحِيق [masa:ħi:q] *pl:* • **1.** powder • **2.** (pl.) make-up, cosmetics
سِحِق [siħig] *adj:* • **1.** worthless, no good – هَالسِّينَما تجِيب أفلام سِحِق [hassi:nama: dǰi:b ʔafla:m siħig] That theatre brings in no-good movies. هُوَّ زين بِاللُّغات بَسّ سِحِق بِالرِّياضِيّات [huwwa zi:n billuɣa:t bass siħig birriya:ðiyya:t] He's good in languages but not worth a damn at mathematics.
ساحِق [sa:ħiq] *adj:* • **1.** overwhelming, crushing – فاز فُوز ساحِق بِالإنتِخابات [fa:z fu:z sa:ħiq bilʔintixa:ba:t] He won an overwhelming victory in the election.
مسَحَّق [msaħħag] *adj:* • **1.** crushed, mashed, flattened, trampled – قِعَدِت الصُّبُح مسَحَّق [giʕadit ʔiṣṣubuħ msaħħag] I got up this morning feeling like I'd taken a beating.
سُحاقِيَّة [suħaqiyya] *adj:* سُحاقِيّات [suħa:qiyya:t] *pl:* • **1.** Lesbian

س ح ل

سِحَل [siħal] *v:* • **1.** to draw, drag, trail – شُوف الجُهّال دَيسِحلُون البَزُّونَة المَيتَة [šu:f ʔiǰǰaha:l daysiħlu:n ʔilbazzu:na ʔilmayyta] Look at the kids dragging the dead cat around.
سَحِل [saħil] *n:* • **1.** dragging
سَحلَة [saħla] *n:* • **1.** instance noun of سَحِل
ساحِل [sa:ħil] *n:* سَواحِل [sawa:ħil] *pl:* • **1.** rough, unbleached cotton cloth – خام سَواحِل [xa:m sawa:ħil] rough, unbleached cotton cloth. • **2.** seashore, coastline
سحالَة [sħa:la] *n:* • **1.** fine rice dust left over after polishing – • **2.** scum شِنُو هَالسحالات تِمشِي ويّاهُم؟ [šinu: halsħa:la:t timši wayya:hum?] What's this scum you are running around with? **مِسحال، مِسحال الكَبِش** [misħa:l, misħa:l ʔilkabiš] *n:* • **1.** the Milky Way

س ح ن

سِحَن [siħan] *v:* • **1.** to pulverize, grind, crush – دُقِّي المِلِح وَسِحنِيه زين [duggi ʔilmiliħ wsiħni:h zi:n] Pound the salt and pulverize it well.
سَحِن [saħin] *n:* • **1.** grinding, crushing • **2.** crushing

س ح ي

سَحايَة، مَرَض السَحايَة [saħa:ya, marað ʔissaħa:ya] *n:* • **1.** meningitis

مِسحَة [misħa] *n:* مَساحِي [masa:ħi] *pl:* • **1.** spade, shovel

س خ ت

سَختَة [saxta] *n:* سَختات [saxta:t] *pl:* • **1.** swindle, fraud – سَوَّى بِيّا سَختَة. قَلِّي القماش إنكِلِيزِي وَطِلَع وَطَنِي [sawwa: biyya saxta. galli ʔilqma:š ʔingili:zi wṭilaʕ waṭani] He pulled a fast one on me. He told me the cloth was British and it turned out to be locally made. لا تصَدِّق بِيه. هَذِي سَختَة مِن عِندَه [la: tṣaddig bi:h. ha:ði saxta min ʕindah] Don't believe him. That's a lot of baloney.
سَختَچِي [saxtači] *adj:* سَختَچِيَّة [saxtači:yya] *pl:* • **1.** swindler, fraud, con artist, smooth talker

س خ ت ن

سُختِيان [suxtiya:n] *n:* • **1.** a kind of fine, thin leather

س خ ر

سِخَر [sixar] *v:* • **1.** with مِن or بـ to laugh at, ridicule, mock – لا تِسخَر مِن الأَقدار [la: tisxar min ʔilʔaqda:r] Don't laugh at fate.
سَخَّر [ṣaxxar] *v:* • **1.** to ask (someone) to do something onerous, to trouble, impose upon – يسَخِّر المُوَظَّفِين يِقضُولَه أشغال خُصُوصِيَّة [ysaxxir ʔilmuwaððafi:n yigðu:lah ʔašɣa:l xuṣu:ṣiyya] He imposes on the employees to do personal jobs for him. لا تقُلَّه وَلا تِتعَب. سَخَّرتَه وَما قِبَل [la: tgullah wala titʕab. saxxartah wma qibal] Don't bother to tell him. I've asked him and he wouldn't agree. • **2.** to employ, utilize, make use of
تسَخَّر [tṣaxxar] *v:* • **1.** to do a charitable deed, put oneself out to help others – شلُون وَلَد! أبَد ما يِتسَخَّر [šlu:n walad! ʔabad ma: yitsaxxar] What kind of boy is he! He never does anything for others.
سُخرَة [ṣuxra] *n:* سُخرات [ṣuxra:t] *pl:* • **1.** imposition, burden, bother, trouble – أقدَر أسَخَّرَك سُخرَة؟ [ʔagdar ʔasaxxrak suxra?] Could I trouble you to do a favor? • **2.** corvee, work exacted by the authorities – مِن يصِير فَيَضان، قِسِم مِن العُمّال يِشتَغلُون بِالسُّخرَة [min yṣi:r fayaða:n, qisim min ʔilʕumma:l yištaɣlu:n bissuxra] When there's a flood, some of the workers work at forced labor.
مَسخَرَة [masxara] *n:* مَساخِر [masa:xir] *pl:* • **1.** object of ridicule, butt of jokes, laughingstock – هَذِي مُو إنتِخابات. هَذِي مَسخَرَة [ha:ði mu: ʔintixa:ba:t. ha:ði masxara] This is no election. This is joke.

س خ ط

ساخِط [sa:xiṭ] *adj:* • **1.** indignant

س خ ف

سَخَّف [saxxaf] *v:* • **1.** to be stupid, foolish
تسَخَّف [tsaxxaf] *v:* • **1.** to be stupid, foolish

سَخافَة [saxa:fa] *n:* سَخافات [saxa:fa:t] *pl:* • **1.** foolishness, folly, a foolish thing to do

سَخِيف [saxi:f] *adj:* • **1.** foolish, stupid, simple-minded • **2.** silly, ridiculous, absurd • **3.** pl. سُخَفاء fool, idiot

أَسْخَف [ʔasxaf] *comparative adjective:* • **1.** more or most foolish

س خ م

سَخَّم [saxxam] *v:* • **1.** to blacken, begrime, besmudge (with soot) – شال الجِّدِر وَسَخَّم إيدَه [ša:l ʔijjidir wsaxxam ʔi:dah] He lifted the pot and got his hands black. سَخَّم الله وِجهَك [ṣaxxam ʔallah wiččak] May God blacken your face! Shame on you! • **2.** to upbraid, berate, tell off – مِن سِمَعِت دَتِحكِي ويّا رَجلِي. سَخَّمِتها وَلَطَّمِتها [min simaʕit datiħči wiyya rajli. saxxamitha wlaṭṭamitha] When I heard she was talking with my husband, I gave her hell and slapped her around. • **3.** to ruin, disgrace, bring shame upon (and by extension, to rape) – سَخّمُوها وَبَعدين كِتلَوها [saxxumu:ha wbaʕdi:n kitlawha] They raped her and then killed her.

تسَخَّم [tsaxxam] *v:* • **1.** to be blackened – شِيل الجِّدِر بوُصلَة حَتَّى ما تِتسَخَّم إيدَك [ši:l ʔijjidir bwuṣla ħatta ma: titsaxxam ʔi:dak] Lift the pot with a piece of cloth so your hands won't get dirty. تسَخَّم وُجّه؛ عِرفوه كَذّاب [tsaxxam wuččah; ʕirfu:h čaððа:b] He's disgraced; they know he's a liar.

سخام [sxa:m] *n:* • **1.** soot

مسَخَّم [msaxxam] *adj:* • **1.** sooty, dirty

س خ ن

سَخَّن [saxxan] *v:* • **1.** to be or become feverish, get a fever – سَخَّنِت البارحَة وَما قدَرِت أرُوح لِلمَدرَسَة [saxxanit ʔilba:rħa wma: gdarit ʔaru:ħ lilmadrasa] I got a fever yesterday and wasn't able to go to school.

تسَخَّن [tsaxxan] *v:* • **1.** to be heated

سَخَّان [saxxa:n] *n:* • **1.** heater

سُخُونَة [suxu:na] *n:* • **1.** fever, temperature

مَسخَنَة، مَسِخنَة [masxana, masixna] *n:* مساخِن [msa:xin] *pl:* • **1.** large, long-necked copper water container

ساخِن [sa:xin] *adj:* • **1.** hot, warm

س خ و

سِخَى [sixa:] *v:* • **1.** to be or become generous, liberal – شلُون سِخَى يِنطِيك خَمس دَنانِير؟ [šlu:n sixa: yinṭi:k xams dana:ni:r?] How'd he get so generous as to give you five dinars? ما سِخَى يِنطِينِي السَّيّارَة [ma: sixa: yinṭi:ni ʔissayya:ra] He wasn't generous enough to give me the car.

سَخَّى [saxxa:] *v:* • **1.** to make generous, liberal – الله سَخّاه وَإنطانِي الفلُوس [ʔallah saxxa:h wʔinṭa:ni ʔiflu:s] God made him generous and he gave me the money. الله يسَخِّي قَلبَك عَلينا [ʔallah ysaxxi galbak ʕali:na] May God soften your heart toward us.

سَخاء [saxa:ʔ] *n:* • **1.** freely • **2.** liberality, munificence

سَخِي، سِخِي [saxi, sixi] *adj:* • **1.** generous, liberal – هَذا شقَدّ سَخِي [ha:ða šgadd saxi] My how generous he is!

س د د

سَدّ [sadd] *v:* • **1.** to plug, close up, stop up – بِثل القَهوَة سَدّ المَغسَل [biθl ʔilgahwa sadd ʔilmaɣsal] The coffee grounds stopped up the sink. سَدَّوا مَجرَى المَيّ لِأَنّ الزَّرِع كُلّه غِرَق [saddaw majra: ʔilmayy liʔann ʔizzariʕ kullah ɣirag] They dammed the water channel because all the crops had flooded. سِدّ زرُوف الحايِط بشِبِنتُو [sidd zru:f ʔilħa:yiṭ bčbintu] Fill in the cracks in the wall with cement. • **2.** to block, obstruct, close off – البَلَدِيَّة سَدَّت الشّارِع لِأَنّ دَيبَلّطُوه [ʔilbaladiyya saddat ʔišša:riʕ liʔann dayballṭu:h] The city closed off the street because they're paving it. سَدّ عَلَيّا الطَّرِيق [sadd ʕalayya ʔiṭṭari:q] He blocked my way. البَيت الجِّدِيد قبالنا سَدّ مَنظَر الحَدِيقَة عَلينا [ʔilbayt ʔijjidi:d gba:lna sadd manðar ʔilħadi:qa ʕali:na] The new house across from us obstructed our view of the park. • **3.** to cover, close up, stopper – إذا تسِدّ الجِّدِر، يفُور المَيّ بِساع [ʔiða tsidd ʔijjidir, yfu:r ʔilmayy bsa:ʕ] If you cover the pot, the water will boil quickly. • **4.** to close, shut – سِدّ المجَرّ [sidd ʔilmjarr] Close the drawer. سِدّ الباب مِن تِطلَع [sidd ʔilba:b min tiṭlaʕ] Close the door when you go out. سَدَّيت حسابِي بالبَنك [saddayt ħsa:bi bilbang] I closed out my account at the bank. سِدّ المَوضُوع! عَلِي جا [sidd ʔilmawḍu:ʕ! ʕali ja:] Drop the subject! Ali is coming. سِدّها عاد [siddha ʕa:d] All right, knock it off! • **5.** to turn off, shut off, cut off – سَدَّيت الماي مِن طِلَعِت؟ [saddayt ʔilma:y min ṭilaʕit?] Did you turn off the water when you left? سِدّ الضُّوَة [sidd ʔiḍḍuwa] Turn off the light. سَدّ التِّلفُون بوُجّهي [sadd ʔittalifu:n bwuččhi] He hung up the telephone on me. • **6.** to cover, satisfy, meet – الحُكُومَة اِقتِرضَت مِليون دِينار حَتَّى تسِدّ العَجَز بالمِيزانِيَّة [ʔilħuku:ma ʔiqtirḍat milyu:n dina:r ħatta tsidd ʔilʕajaz bilmi:za:niyya] The government borrowed a million dinars to meet the deficit in the budget. هَالفلُوس اللّي عِدنا تسِدّ حاجاتنا [halfilu:s ʔilli ʕidna tsidd ħa:ja:tna] The money we've got satisfies our needs. • **7.** to fill, close – سَدَّينا كُلّ الشَّواغِر [saddayna kull ʔiššawa:ɣir] We filled all the vacancies. مَحَّد يسِدّ الفَراغ اللّي حِصَل بَعَد وَفاتَه [maħħad ysidd ʔilfara:ɣ ʔilli ħiṣal baʕad wafa:tah] No one can fill the gap that was created by his death.

سَدَّد [saddad] *v:* • **1.** to settle, pay up, cover – سَدَّد كُلّ ديُونَه [saddad kull dyu:nah] He paid up all his debts.

اِنسَدّ [ʔinsadd] *v:* • **1.** to be closed

س

سَدّ [sadd] *n:* سُدُود [sudu:d] *pl:* • **1.** obstacle, obstruction • **2.** block • **3.** dike • **4.** dam
سَدَّة [sadda] *n:* سَدّات [sadda:t] *pl:* • **1.** dam
سَدّادَة [sadda:da] *n:* سَدّادات [sadda:da:t] *pl:* • **1.** plug, stopper, cork
تَسدِيد [tasdi:d] *n:* • **1.** payment, settlement, discharge
اِنسِداد [ʔinsida:d] *n:* • **1.** blockage
مسَدِّد [msaddid] *adj:* • **1.** paying, settling
مَسدُود [masdu:d] *adj:* • **1.** closed, blocked, jammed

س د ر

سِدِر [sidir] *n:* • **1.** a type of thorny bush or tree • **2.** the leaves of this tree, crushed and used as soap in rural areas
سِدارَة [sida:ra] *n:* سِدايِر [sida:yir] *pl:* • **1.** a common Iraqi headgear, usually of black velvet • **2.** overseas cap (mil.)

س د س

سُدُس [sudus] *n:* أسداس [ʔasda:s] *pl:* • **1.** a sixth part, one-sixth
مُسَدَّس [musaddas] *n:* مُسَدَّسات [musaddasa:t] *pl:* • **1.** hexagon • **2.** pistol, revolver
سادِس [sa:dis] *adj:* • **1.** sixth (ordinal)
سُداسِي [suda:si] *adj:* • **1.** hexagonal • **2.** sixfold

س د س د

سَدسَد [sadsad] *v:* • **1.** to clog, close
تسَدسَد [tsadsad] *v:* • **1.** to be clogged, to be closed
تسِدسِد [tsidsid] *n:* • **1.** plugging, closing
مسَدسَد [msadsad] *adj:* • **1.** plugged, closed

س د ن

سِدانَة [sida:na] *n:* سِدايِن [sida:yin] *pl:* • **1.** a clay container used for storing grain, and the like

س د و

سَدَّى [sadda:] *v:* • **1.** to weave, make a web – العَنكَبُوت دَيسَدِّي بِالزُّويَّة [ʔalʕankabu:t daysaddi bizzuwiyya] The spider is making a web in the corner. هِرش العِنَب سَدَّى عَالشِّبّاك [hirš ʔilʕinab sadda: ʕaššibba:č] The grape vine has covered the window.
سِدَة [sida] *n:* سدايَة [sda:ya] *pl:* • **1.** warp (of a fabric)
سَديَة [sadya] *n:* سَديات [sadya:t] *pl:* • **1.** stretcher, litter

س ذ ج

سَذاجَة [saða:ǰa] *n:* • **1.** innocence, ingenuousness, guilelessness
ساذِج [sa:ðij] *adj:* سُذَّج [suððaǰ] *pl:* • **1.** simple, naive, innocent, guileless • **2.** (as *n:*) naive person

س ر ب 1

سَرَّب [sarrab] *v:* • **1.** to leak, seep out
تسَرَّب [tsarrab] *v:* • **1.** to leak, seep out – المَيّ دَيتسَرَّب مِن جَوَّة الباب [ʔilmayy dayitsarrab min ǰawwa ʔilba:b] Water is leaking out from under the door. • **2.** to leak out, get out, spread – ما دَنُعرُف شلُون تسَرُّبَت هالمَعلُومات [ma: danuʕruf šlu:n tsarrubat halmaʕlu:ma:t] We don't know how this information leaked out.
سِرِب [sirib] *n:* أسراب [ʔasra:b] *pl:* • **1.** flock, covey, flight (of birds) • **2.** squadron, group, formation, flight (of aircraft) • **3.** swarm (of bees)
سَراب [sara:b] *n:* • **1.** mirage
تَسَرُّب [tasarrub] *n:* • **1.** leak, sneak
تَسرِيب [tasri:b] *n:* • **1.** leakage, infiltration

س ر ب 2

سَربَت [sarbat] *v:* • **1.** to let go free, to turn loose – سَربَت كلابَه بِالشَّوارِع [sarbat čla:bah biššawa:riʕ] He let his dogs run loose in the streets. اِنطِيه خَمسِين فِلِس وَسَربتَه [ʔinṭi:h xamsi:n filis wsarbtah] Give him fifty fils and let him go.
تسَربَت [tsarbat] *v:* • **1.** to wander away – لِغَى نُصّ ساعَة وَبَعدين تسَربَت [liɣa: nuṣṣ sa:ʕa wbaʕdi:n tsarbat] He prattled on for a half hour and then wandered away.
سَربُوت [sarbu:t] *adj:* • **1.** loafer, lazy bum

س ر ب س

سَربَس [sarbas] *n:* سَرابِس [sara:bis] *pl:* • **1.** reel

س ر ج 1

سِرَج [siraǰ] *v:* • **1.** to saddle – إسرِجَه لِلحصان [ʔisirǰah lilḥṣa:n] Saddle the horse.
سَرَّج [sarraǰ] *v:* • **1.** to harness • **2.** to saddle
تسَرَّج [tsarraǰ] *v:* • **1.** to be saddled
سَرِج [sariǰ] *n:* سرُوج [sru:ǰ] *pl:* • **1.** saddle –
سَرّاج [sarra:ǰ] *n:* سَرّاجِين، سَرّاجَة [sarra:ǰi:n, sarra:ǰa] *pl:* • **1.** saddler • **2.** leather craftsman
سِراجَة [sira:ǰa] *n:* • **1.** saddlery, saddler's trade
سِرُوجِيَّة [siru:ǰiyya] *n:* • **1.** saddlery, saddler's trade

س ر ج 2

سَرِج [sariǰ] *n:* • **1.** serge, serge pants – بَنطَرُون سَرِج [panṭaru:n sariǰ] serge pants.

س ر ج 3

سِراج [siraːǰ] *n:* • **1.** light, lamp, lantern – لَو بِالظَّلمَة لَو بِالسِّراجَين س ر ج ن [law biððalma law bissiraːǰayn] It is either a feast or a famine (lit., either in the dark or with two lamps)
سِرجِين [sirǰiːn] *n:* • **1.** dung, manure (especially of cattle)

س ر ح 1

سِرَح [siraħ] *v:* • **1.** to roam freely, graze freely – صَخلَتنا دَتِسرَح وِيّا الغَنَم [ṣaxlatna datisraħ wiyya ʔilɣanam] Our goat is grazing with the sheep. • **2.** to be distracted, let one's mind wander – يِنتِبِه شوَيَّة لِلمُحاضَرَة وَبَعدين يِسرَح [yintibih šwayya lilmuħaːðara wbaʕdiːn yisraħ] He pays attention to the lecture for a while and then his mind wanders. • **3.** to forget – إذا ما تأَكِّد عَلِيه، تَرَة يِسرَحها لِلقَضِيَّة [ʔiða maː tʔakkid ʕaliːh, tara yisraħha lilqaðiyya] If you don't remind him, he's going to forget about the matter.
سَرَّح [sarraħ] *v:* • **1.** to dismiss, discharge, release, set free – وِزارَة الدِّفاع راح تسَرِّح أَلف جُندِي هَالشَّهَر [wizaːrat ʔiddifaːʕ raːħ tsarriħ ʔalf ǰundi haššahar] The Ministry of Defense is going to dismiss a thousand soldiers this month. • **2.** to arrange, do up, fix (the hair) – صارِلها ساعَة تسَرِّح شَعَرها [ṣaːrilha saːʕa tsarriħ šaʕarha] She took an hour doing her hair.
تسَرَّح [tsarraħ] *v:* • **1.** to be layed off, to be combed
سَرِح [sariħ] *adj:* • **1.** straight, roaming freely
سِراح [siraːħ] *n:* • **1.** release – أَطلِقَوا سِراحَه بَعَد ما عُرفَوا مُو هُوَّ المُذنِب [ʔaṭliqaw siraːħah baʕad maː ʕurfaw muː huwwa ʔilmuðnib] They set him free after they learned he wasn't the guilty one.
مَسرَح [masraħ] *n:* مَسارِح [masaːriħ] *pl:* • **1.** stage (of a theater), theater
تَسرِيح [tasriːħ] *n:* • **1.** dismissal, straightness
تَسرِيحَة [tasriːħa] *n:* تَسرِيحات [tasriːħaːt] *pl:* • **1.** hairdo – تَسرِيحَة الشَّعَر [tasriːħat ʔiššaʕar] hairdo. • **2.** hairdo, coiffure
مَسرَحِيَّة [masraħiyya] *n:* مَسرَحِيّات [masraħiyyaːt] *pl:* • **1.** play
سَرحِي [sarħi] *adj:* سَرحِيِّن [sarħiyyin] *pl:* • **1.** forgetful, absent-minded
سارِح [saːriħ] *adj:* • **1.** smooth • **2.** absent-minded
مسَرَّح [msarraħ] *adj:* • **1.** straight, sleek • **2.** permitted, authorized
مَسرَحِي [masraħi] *adj:* • **1.** theatrical

س ر ح 2

سَراحِيَّة [saraːħiyya] *n:* سَراحِيّات [saraːħiyyaːt] *pl:* • **1.** water jar, carafe

س ر د

سِرَد [sirad] *v:* • **1.** to tell, present in detail, give a detailed account – إجانِي غَضبان وَسِرَد كُلّ اللّي عِندَه [ʔiǰaːni ɣaðbaːn wsirad kull ʔilli ʕindah] He came to me angrily and told me everything that was bothering him.
سَرِد [sarid] *n:* • **1.** presentation

س ر د ب

سِرداب [sirdaːb] *n:* سَرادِيب [saraːdiːb] *pl:* • **1.** cellar • **2.** basement

س ر د ن

سَردِينَة [sardiːna] *n:* • **1.** sardine

س ر ر

سَرّ [sarr] *v:* • **1.** to make happy, gladden, delight – يسُرِّنِي هوايَة أَن تِتقَدَّم بحَياتَك [ysurrni hwaːya ʔan titqaddam bħayaːtak] It makes me very happy that you're getting ahead in life. • **2.** to tell a secret, to confide in – أَقدَر أَسُرَّك بشِي وَما تقُول؟ [ʔagdar ʔasurrak bši wma tguːl?] Can I let you in on a secret without your telling?
إستَرّ [ʔistarr] *v:* • **1.** to become happy, be delighted – مِن سِمَع بالخَبَر، اِستَرّ هوايَة [min simaʕ bilxabar, ʔistarr hwaːya] When he heard the news, he became very happy.
اِنسَرّ [ʔinsarr] *v:* • **1.** to be pleased
سِرّ [sirr] *n:* أَسرار [ʔasraːr] *pl:* • **1.** secret – كَلِمَة السِّرّ [kalimat ʔissirr] password. ما يِكتِم سِرّ [maː yiktim sirr] He can't keep a secret.
سُرُور [suruːr] *n:* • **1.** joy, happiness, delight, pleasure – بِكُلّ سُرُور [bkull suruːr] gladly! with pleasure!
سَرِير [sariːr] *n:* سرايِر [sraːyir] *pl:* • **1.** bed • **2.** a mat of woven palm stalks
سِرِّي [sirri] *adj:* • **1.** secret – اِجتِماع سِرِّي [ʔiǰtimaːʕ sirri] a secret meeting. العادَة السِّرِّيَّة [ʔilʕaːda ʔissirriyya] masturbation. • **2.** confidential, classified – إضبارتَه مَحفُوظَة بالقَلَم السِّرِّي [ʔiðbaːrtah maħfuːða bilqalam ʔissirri] His file is kept in the classified section. • **3.** secret agent, undercover agent
سارّ [saːrr] *adj:* • **1.** joyful
مَسرُور [masruːr] *adj:* • **1.** glad, happy, delighted, pleased – آني مَسرُور بنَجاحَك [ʔaːni masruːr bnaǰaːħak] I am happy about your success.
سَرِيرِي [sariːri] *adj:* • **1.** clinical
سِرّانِي [sirraːni] *adj:* • **1.** discreet
سِرّاً [sirran] *adverbial:* • **1.** secretly

س ر س ر

سَرسَرِي [sarsari] *n:* سَرسَرِيَّة [sarsariːyya] *pl:* • **1.** tramp, vagabond, bum

س ر ط ن

سَرَطان [saraṭaːn] *n:* سَرَطانات [saraṭaːnaːt] *pl:* • **1.** lobster • **2.** cancer (med.) • **3.** Cancer (astron.) – مَدار السَّرَطان [madaːr ʔissaraṭaːn] Tropic of Cancer.

س ر ع

سَرَّع [sarraʕ] *v:* • **1.** to speed up, expedite – بَلْكِي تِقدَر تسَرِّعلِي المَسألَة [balki tigdar tsarriʕli ʔilmasʔala] Perhaps you can expedite this matter for me.

أَسرَع [ʔasraʕ] *v:* • **1.** to hurry, hasten, rush, run, dash – إذا تِسرِع، تلَحَّق بِيه [ʔiða tisriʕ, tlaħħag biːh] If you hurry, you'll catch up with him.

تسَرَّع [tsarraʕ] *v:* • **1.** to be rash, hasty, be in too much of a hurry – لا تِتسَرَّع وَتِستِقِيل. يِمكِن باكِر يبَدِّل رأيَه [laː titsarraʕ wtistiqiːl. yimkin baːčir ybaddil raʔyah] Don't be rash and resign. Maybe tomorrow he'll change his mind. أشُوف لَو ما تِتسَرَّع أحسَن [ʔašuːf law maː titsarraʕ ʔaħsan] I think it would be better not to be in a rush.

سُرعَة [surʕa] *n:* • **1.** speed, velocity – يسُوق بسُرعَة [ysuːq bsurʕa] He drives fast. • **2.** rapidity, quickness, promptness – شما تقُلَّه يصَدِّق بسُرعَة [šmaː dgullah yṣaddig bsurʕa] Whatever you tell him, he believes right away.

تَسَرُّع [tasarruʕ] *n:* • **1.** rashness, haste • **2.** haste

إسراع [ʔisraːʕ] *n:* • **1.** acceleration • **2.** haste

سَرِيع [sariːʕ] *adj:* • **1.** fast, quick, rapid, speedy, swift – حصان سَرِيع كُلِّش [ħṣaːn sariːʕ kulliš] a very fast horse. قِطار سَرِيع [qiṭaːr sariːʕ] express train. سَرِيع الالتِهاب [sariːʕ ʔilʔiltihaːb] highly inflammable. سَرِيع التَّأثُّر [sariːʕ ʔittaʔaθθur] easily affected, highly sensitive.

أَسرَع [ʔasraʕ] *comparative adjective:* • **1.** faster or fastest • **2.** quicker or quickest

سَرِيعاً [sariːʕan] *adverbial:* • **1.** at once • **2.** quickly

س ر ف

أسرَف [ʔasraf] *v:* • **1.** to waste, squander, spend lavishly, to be extravagant – إذا تِسرِف وَما تِدَّخِر، تَرَة تاكُلها [ʔiða tisrif wamaː tiddixir, tara taːkulha] If you waste and don't save, you'll be in trouble.

إسراف [ʔisraːf] *n:* • **1.** waste, squandering, extravagance

مُسرِف [musrif] *adj:* • **1.** extravagant, wasteful • **2.** spend-thrift

س ر ق

سِرَق [siraq] *v:* • **1.** to steal

انسِرَق [ʔinsiraq] *v:* • **1.** to be stolen

سَرِق [sariq] *n:* • **1.** stealing, filching, pilfering

سَرِقَة [sariqa] *n:* سَرِقات [sariqaːt] *pl:* • **1.** robbery, theft, larceny

مَسرُوقات [masruːqaːt] *adj:* • **1.** (invar. pl.) stolen goods, loot

س ر ك

سُركِي [surgi] *n:* سُركِيّات، سُراكِي [surgiːyyaːt, suraːgi] *pl:* • **1.** bolt, lock

س ر ن ج

سرِنجَة [srinǰa] *n:* • **1.** needle

س ر و

سَرُو [sarw] *n:* • **1.** (evergreen) cypress

س ر و ل

سِروال [sirwaːl] *n:* سِروالات [sirwaːlaːt] *pl:* • **1.** a sort of loose trousers

س ر ي

سِرَى [siraː] *v:* • **1.** to spread – السَّرَطان دَيِسرِي بجِسمَه [ʔissaraṭaːn dayisri bǰismah] Cancer's spreading through his body. • **2.** to take effect, be effective – الدُّوا راح يِسرِي مَفعُولَه بظَرُف خَمِس دَقايِق [ʔidduwaː raːħ yisri mafʕuːlah bðaruf xamis daqaːyiq] The medicine will take effect within five minutes. • **3.** to apply, be applicable – القانُون يِسرِي عالكُلّ [ʔilqaːnuːn yisri ʕalkull] The law applies to everyone.

سِرَة [sira] *n:* سِرَاوات [sirawaːt] *pl:* • **1.** line, row, column – خَلِّي نُقعُد بِالسِّرَة الوَرّانِي [xalli nugʕud bissira ʔilwarraːni] Let's sit in the last row. صُفّ السَّيّارات سِرايين [ṣuff ʔissayyaːraːt sirayayn] Line up the cars in two columns. • **2.** row of buttons (on a jacket) – سِترَة سِرَة واحِد [sitra sira waːħid] single-breasted jacket. قُوط سِراوَين [quːṭ siraːwayn] double-breasted suit. • **3.** place in line, turn – ما تِقدَر تقُصّ بِطاقَة إذا ما تاخُذ سِرَة [maː tigdar dguṣṣ biṭaːqa ʔiða maː taːxuð sira] You can't buy a ticket if you don't take a place in line. هَسَّة سِراك [hassa siraːk] Now it's your turn.

سَراي [saraːy] *n:* • **1.** see under ص-ر-ي

سَرِيَّة [sariyya] *n:* سَرايا [saraːya] *pl:* • **1.** company (mil.)

سارِيَة [saːriya] *n:* سارِيات [saːriyaːt] *pl:* • **1.** column, pole – سارِيَة عَلَم [saːriyat ʕalam] flagpole. • **2.** mast

سَرَيان [sarayaːn] *n:* • **1.** spreading

سارِي [saːri] *adj:* • **1.** contagious – أمراض سارِيَة [ʔamraːð saːrya] contagious diseases.

سِريانِي [siryaːni] *adj:* • **1.** Assyrian

س ز ز

-سِزّ [-sizz] *particle:* • **1.** fem. and pl. سِزِّيَّة a suffix of negation roughly comparable to English -less أدَبسِزّ ill-mannered, mannerless, مُخّسِزّ stupid, brainless

س س ي

سِسِّي [sissi] *n:* سِسِّيّات [sissiyyaːt] *pl.* سِسِّيَّة [sissiyya] *feminine:* • **1.** (coll.) a kind of edible nut with a fibrous, grayish-white shell, grown in Northern Iraq

س ط ح

سَطِح [saṭiħ] *n:* سطُوح [sṭuːħ] *pl:* • **1.** (flat) roof • **2.** surface سَطِح البَحَر [saṭiħ ʔilbaħar] sea level.

سَطحِي [satḥi] *adj:* • **1.** external • **2.** superficial – مَعلُومات سَطحِيَّة [maʕlu:ma:t satḥiyya] superficial knowledge.
مُسَطَّح [musattaḥ] *adj:* • **1.** flat, even
سَطحِيّاً [satḥiyyan] *adverbial:* • **1.** Superficial

س ط ر

سِطَر [siṭar] *v:* • **1.** to chop, hack, cleave, split (esp. with a cleaver) – راح أَقَصِّلَك لَحَم بَعَد ما أَسطُر اللَّشَّة [ra:ḥ ʔaguṣṣlak laḥam baʕad ma: ʔasṭur ʔillašša] I'll cut you some meat after I chop up the carcass. • **2.** to stun, daze, stupefy – جَمالها يِسطُر [ǰama:lha yisṭur] Her beauty dazzles you. بِيك واحِد سِطَرَه [pi:k wa:ḥid siṭarah] One drink addled him.
سَطَّر [saṭṭar] *v:* • **1.** to line up, arrange in a straight line – سَطِّر الكلاصات عالميز حَتَّى أَترُسها [saṭṭir ʔilgla:ṣa:t ʕalmi:z ħatta ʔatrusha] Line up the glasses on the table so I can fill them.
تسَطَّر [tsaṭṭar] *v:* • **1.** to be lined up, arranged in a straight line – شَكُو تسَطَّرتُوا قِدّامِي؟ ما تُرحُون؟ [šaku tsaṭṭartu: gidda:mi? ma: truḥu:n?] Why are you lined up in front of me? Why don't you leave?
اِنسِطَر [ʔinsiṭar] *v:* • **1.** to be or become stunned, dazed, stupefied – مِن سِمَع بالخَبَر، اِنسِطَر [min simaʕ bilxabar, ʔinṣiṭar] When he heard the news he was stupefied.
سَطِر [saṭir] *n:* سطُور [sṭu:r] *pl:* • **1.** line • **2.** column, row
سَطرَة [saṭra] *n:* سَطرات [saṭra:t] *pl:* • **1.** a slap on the face
ساطُور [sa:ṭu:r] *n:* سواطِير [swa:ṭi:r] *pl:* • **1.** (meat) cleaver – ذَبّها عالسّاطُور [ðabbha ʕassa:ṭu:r] He didn't care about the consequences.
مَسطَرَة [masṭara] *n:* مَساطِر [masa:ṭir] *pl:* • **1.** ruler, straight edge • **2.** clipping, sample (of cloth)
أُسطُورَة [ʔusṭu:ra] *n:* أَساطِير [ʔasa:ṭi:r] *pl:* • **1.** legend, fable, myth
مَسطَر [masṭar] *adj:* • **1.** in line, lined up in a row – أُوقفُوا مَسطَر حَتَّى أَحسِبكُم [ʔu:gfu: masṭar ħatta ʔaḥsibkum] Stand in a line until I count you.
مسَطَّر [msaṭṭar] *adj:* • **1.** lined up in a row
سُوطَرِي [su:ṭari] *adj:* • **1.** in a daze, oblivious, unaware, inattentive, unheeding, woolgathering, absent-minded – قاعِد بِالصَّفّ سُوطَرِي وَما يِدرِي شَكُو ماكُو [ga:ʕid biṣṣaff su:ṭari wma yidri šaku ma:ku] He's sitting in the class not paying attention and doesn't know what's what. سُوطَرِي! لِيش دَتدَوِّر هنا؟ ما قِتلَك الكِتاب هناك؟ [su:ṭari! li:š daddawwir hna? ma: gitlak ʔilkita:b hna:k?] Numbskull! Why are you looking here? Didn't I tell you the book was there? هَذا سُوطَرِي. لا تِعتِمِد عَليه [ha:ða su:ṭari. la: tiʕtimid ʕali:h] He's absent-minded. Don't depend on him.
مَسطُور [masṭu:r] *adj:* • **1.** dazed • **2.** suffering from severe pain

س ط ع

سِطَع [siṭaʕ] *v:* • **1.** to shine, gleam, be radiant – وِجهَها يِسطَع نُور [wiččha yisṭaʕ nu:r] Her face gleams.
سَطِع [saṭiʕ] *n:* • **1.** shine, gleam
ساطِع [sa:ṭiʕ] *adj:* • **1.** shining, gleaming, glowing, radiant, brilliant – نُور الشَّمِس ساطِع [nu:r ʔiššamis sa:ṭiʕ] The sunlight is bright.
أَسطَع [ʔasṭaʕ] *comparative adjective:* • **1.** more or most shining, gleaming, radiant

س ط ع ش

سِطَّعَش [siṭṭaʕaš] *n:* • **1.** sixteen

س ط ل

سَطِل [saṭil] *n:* سَطَلات، سطُولَة [saṭala:t, sṭu:la] *pl:* • **1.** bucket, pail
سَطِل [saṭil] *adj:* سطُول [sṭu:l] *pl:* • **1.** stupid, unintelligent, slow-witted
مَسطُول [masṭu:l] *adj:* • **1.** stupid, unintelligent, slow-witted, addicted • **2.** drugged

س ط م ب

سطَمبَة [sṭamba] *n:* • **1.** stamp

س ط و

سِطَى [siṭa:] *v:* • **1.** with عَلَى to break into, burglarize – الحَرامِيَّة سِطَوا عَلَى بَيتَه وَباقَوا زُولِيَّة [ʔilħara:miyya siṭaw ʕala baytah wba:gaw zu:liyya] The thieves broke into his house and stole a rug.
اِنسِطَى [ʔinsiṭa:] *v:* • **1.** to be broken into (of a place), to be attacked
سَطو [saṭw] *n:* • **1.** robbery
سَطوَة [saṭwa] *n:* سَطوات [saṭwa:t] *pl:* • **1.** a burglary • **2.** influence, authority, power

س ع د

سِعَد [siʕad] *v:* • **1.** to please, make happy – الله يِسعِدَك بزَواجَك [ʔallah ysiʕdak bzawa:ǰak] God make you happy in your marriage. مَرتَه سِعدَتَه [martah siʕdatah] His wife made him happy. يِسعِدنِي أَن تِتوَفَّق بِحَياتَك [yisʕidni ʔan titwaffaq bħaya:tak] It pleases me that you're getting ahead in your life.
ساعَد [sa:ʕad] *v:* • **1.** to help, aid, assist – ساعَدنِي بشُغلِي [sa:ʕadni bšuɣli] He helped me in my work. كَونَه مُسلِم ساعَدَه بِالإنتِخابات [kawnah muslim sa:ʕadah bilʔintixa:ba:t] His being a Moslem helped him in the elections. الحَرارَة تساعِد عَلَى ذَوَبان الأَملاح [ʔilħara:ra tsa:ʕid ʕala ðawaba:n ʔilʔamla:ħ] Heat is helpful in dissolving salts.
أَسعَد [ʔasʕad] *v:* • **1.** (also سِعَد) to please, make happy
تساعَد [tsa:ʕad] *v:* • **1.** to help each other – إذا ما نِتساعَد، ما يِطلَع شُغُل [ʔiða ma: nitsa:ʕad, ma:

yitlaʕ šuɣul] If we don't help each other, no work will get done.
ساعِد [sa:ʕid] *n:* سَواعِد [sawa:ʕid] *pl:* • **1.** forearm – هُوَّ السّاعِد الأيمَن لِلوَزِير [huwwa ʔissa:ʕid ʔilʔayman lilwazi:r] He's the minister's right-hand man.
سَعادَة [saʕa:da] *n:* • **1.** happiness • **2.** good fortune • **3.** a formal title roughly equiv. to His Excellency, His Grace – سَعادَة المُدِير [saʕa:dat ʔilmudi:r] His Excellency the Director.
مُساعِد [musa:ʕid] *n:* مُساعِدِين [musa:ʕidi:n] *pl:* • **1.** helper, aide, assistant – عامِل مُساعِد [ʕa:mil musa:ʕid] (chem.) catalyst.
مُساعَدَة [musa:ʕada] *n:* مُساعَدات [musa:ʕada:t] *pl:* • **1.** assistance, help, support, backing – مُساعَدَة مالِيَّة [musa:ʕada ma:liyya] financial assistance. مُساعَدات اِقتِصادِيَّة [musa:ʕada:t ʔiqtiṣa:diyya] economic aid. آني حاضِر لِأيّ مُساعَدَة تِرِيدُوها [ʔa:ni ħa:ðir liʔayy musa:ʕada tiri:du:ha] I'm ready to help in any way you want.
سَعِيد [saʕi:d] *adj:* سَعِيدِين، سُعَداء [saʕi:di:n, suʕada:ʔ] *pl:* • **1.** happy – أعتِقِد راح يكُون سَعِيد بزَواجَه مِنها [ʔaʕtiqid ra:ħ yiku:n saʕi:d bzawa:jah minha] I think he'll be happy in his marriage with her. أيّامكُم سَعِيدَة [ʔayya:mkum saʕi:da] Happy holiday! (a greeting used during two Moslem feast days). • **2.** fortunate, lucky – السَّعِيد اللّي ما يِحتاج وَظِيفَة [ʔissaʕi:d ʔilli ma: yiħta:ǰ waði:fa] The lucky one is the guy who doesn't need a government job.
سُعُودِي [suʕu:di] *adj:* • **1.** Saudi – المَملَكَة العَرَبِيَّة السُّعُودِيَّة [ʔilmamlaka ʔilʕarabiyya ʔissuʕu:diyya] The Kingdom of Saudi Arabia. • **2.** a Saudi Arab
أسعَد [ʔasʕad] *comparative adjective:* • **1.** happier or happiest • **2.** more or most fortunate

س ع ر

سَعَّر [saʕʕar] *v:* • **1.** to price, set a price on, fix the price of – الحُكُومَة سَعِّرَت أكثَر البَضائِع المُستَورَدَة [ʔilħuku:ma saʕʕirat ʔakθar ʔilbaða:ʔiʕ ʔilmustawrada] The government has fixed the price on most imported goods.
سِعِر [siʕir] *n:* أسعار [ʔasʕa:r] *pl:* • **1.** price
سِعرَة، سُعرَة [siʕra, suʕra] *n:* سُعرات [suʕra:t] *pl:* • **1.** calorie
تَسعِيرَة [tasʕi:ra] *n:* • **1.** pricing, price-fixing, price tag

س ع ف

أسعَف [ʔasʕaf] *v:* • **1.** to help, aid, assist • **2.** to render medical assistance – أسعَفوه بالأوكسِجِين حَتَّى صِحَى [ʔasʕafawh bilʔuksiǰi:n ħatta ṣiħa:] They treated him with oxygen until he regained consciousness.
سَعَف [saʕaf] *n:* سَعفات [saʕfa:t] *pl:* • **1.** (coll.) palm frond(s)
سَعفَة [saʕfa] *n:* سَعفات [saʕfa:t] *pl:* • **1.** palm frond
إسعاف [ʔisʕa:f] *n:* إسعافات [ʔisʕa:fa:t] *pl:* • **1.** aid, relief, help • **2.** medical assistance – إسعافات أوَّلِيَّة [ʔisʕa:fa:t ʔawwaliyya] first aid. سَيّارَة الإسعاف [sayya:rat ʔilʔisʕa:f] ambulance.
مُسعِف [musʕif] *adj:* • **1.** rescuer, life-saver • **2.** (as n.) a paramedic

س ع ل

سَعَّل [saʕʕal] *v:* • **1.** to catch whooping cough – إبنِي سَعَّل مِن كان عُمرَه سَبع سنِين [ʔibni saʕʕal min ča:n ʕumrah sabʕ sni:n] My son caught whooping cough when he was seven years old.
سُعال، سُعال دِيكِي [suʕa:l, suʕa:l di:ki] *n:* • **1.** whooping cough

س ع ل و

سِعلُوَّة [siʕluwwa] *n:* سِعلُوّات [siʕluwwa:t] *pl:* • **1.** large (female) monster, witch, goblin

س ع ي

سِعَى [siʕa:] *v:* • **1.** to work, endeavor, try – سِعالِي هوايَة لَكِن ما حَصَّلت الوَظِيفَة [siʕa:li hwa:ya la:kin ma: ħaṣṣalt ʔilwaði:fa] He did his best for me but I didn't get the position. إذا تِسعِي زين، تِنجَح [ʔiða tisʕi zi:n, tinǰaħ] If you work real hard, you'll succeed. ما سِعَى وَسِقَط بِالإمتِحان [ma: siʕa: wsiqaṭ bilʔimtiħa:n] He didn't study and he failed the exam. دَيسعِيلَك بِكِسران الرُّقبَة. دَيشَيِّع عَنَّك إنتَ شِيُوعِي [dayisʕi:lak bkisra:n ʔirrugba. dayšayyiʕ ʕannak ʔinta šiyu:ʕi] He's trying to hurt you. He's spreading it around that you're a communist.
سَعِي [saʕy] *n:* • **1.** walking, effort
ساعِي [sa:ʕi] *n:* سُعاة [suʕa:t] *pl:* • **1.** messenger, delivery boy – ساعِي البَرِيد [sa:ʕi ʔilbari:d] rural mail carrier.
مَسعَى [masʕa] *n:* مَساعِي [masa:ʕi] *pl:* • **1.** effort

س ف ح

سِفاح [sifa:ħ] *n:* • **1.** fornication
سَفّاح [saffa:ħ] *adj:* سَفّاحِين [saffa:ħi:n] *pl:* • **1.** shedder of blood, killer, murderer

س ف ر

سِفَر [sifar] *v:* • **1.** to unveil the face – مِن مات، بَناتَه سِفرَوا [min ma:t, bana:tah sifraw] When he died, his daughters took off their veils. بَنات بَغداد كُلّهُم سِفرَوا [bana:t bayda:d kullhum sifraw] Baghdad girls have all removed the veil.
سَفَّر [saffar] *v:* • **1.** to send on a journey, send off – سَفَّرنا ألف حَجِّي هَالإسبُوع [saffarna ʔalf ħaǰǰi halʔisbu:ʕ] We got a thousand pilgrims on their way this week. • **2.** to compel to leave, expel, deport – الشُّرطَة سَفِّرَت ثلاث أجانِب دِخلَوا بَلا باسبُورت [ʔiššurṭa

saffirat tlaθ ʔaǰa:nib dixlaw bala pa:spu:rt] The police deported three foreigners who entered without passports.
سافَر [sa:far] *v:* • **1.** to travel, take a trip – راح أسافِر لِأورُبّا هالصَّيف [ra:ħ ʔasa:fir liʔu:ruppa: haṣṣayf] I'm going to travel to Europe this summer. • **2.** to leave, depart – الوَفِد راح يسافِر باكِر [ʔilwafid ra:ħ ysa:fir ba:čir] The delegation will leave tomorrow. أريد أشوفَك قبِل ما تسافِر [ʔari:d ʔašu:fak gabil ma: tsa:fir] I want to see you before you leave town.
سَفَر [safar] *n:* • **1.** traveling, travel
سَفرَة [safra] *n:* سَفرات [safra:t] *pl:* • **1.** trip, journey • **2.** tour, outing
سُفرَة [sufra] *n:* سُفَر [sufar] *pl:* • **1.** a woven mat placed on the floor on which food is set at meal time – حَضّري السُّفرَة. راح ناكُل [ħaððri ʔissufra. ra:ħ na:kul] Set the table. We're going to eat.
سَفِير [safi:r] *n:* سُفَراء [sufara:ʔ] *pl:* • **1.** ambassador
سُفُور [sufu:r] *n:* • **1.** unveiling, uncovering the face • **2.** without a veil, with the face uncovered – بَغداد بِيها نِسوان هوايَة يِمشُون سُفُور [baɣda:d bi:ha niswa:n hwa:ya yimšu:n sufu:r] In Bagdad are many women who go around unveiled.
سَفارَة [safa:ra] *n:* سَفارات [safa:ra:t] *pl:* • **1.** embassy
مُسافِر [musa:fir] *n:* مُسافِرين [musa:firi:n] *pl:* • **1.** traveler • **2.** passenger
تَسفِير [tasfi:r] *n:* • **1.** transport • **2.** deporting
مُسافِرخانَة [musa:firxa:na] *n:* • **1.** old-fashioned hotel (esp. an old, dirty one)
سَفَري [safari] *adj:* • **1.** portable, movable, mobile
سافِر، سافرَة [sa:fir, sa:fra] *adj:* • **1.** unveiled, wearing no veil – بِنتَه سافِرَة بَسّ مَرتَه تِتحَجَّب [bintah sa:fira bass martah titħaǰǰab] His daughter goes unveiled but his wife wears a veil.
مسَفَّر [msaffar] *adj:* مسَفَّرِين [msaffari:n] *pl:* • **1.** deported

س ف ر ج ل

سفَرجَل [sfarǰal] *n:* • **1.** (coll.) quince(s)
سفَرجَلَة [sfarǰala] *n:* سفَرجَلات [sfarǰala:t] *pl:* • **1.** quince

س ف ر ط س

سَفَرطاس [safarṭa:s] *n:* سَفَرطاسات [safarṭa:sa:t] *pl:* • **1.** a set of separate pans fitted together to carry a hot meal, lunchbox

س ف ط

سُفَط [sufaṭ] *v:* • **1.** to stack, line up – أُسفُط هالكتابَين ويّا ذِيك الكُتُب [ʔuṣfuṭ halkta:bayn wiyya ði:č ʔilkutub] Stack these two books with those books. • **2.** to move close together – أُسفُط وِيّا أَخُوك حَتَّى يصِير مُكان لِأُختَك [ʔuṣfuṭ wiyya ʔaxu:k ħatta yṣi:r muka:n liʔuxtak] Sit close to your brother so there will be room for your sister.
سَفَّط [saffaṭ] *v:* • **1.** to line up, stack, stack up – سَفَّط الكُتُب بِهالرّازُونَة [saffaṭ ʔilkutub bharra:zu:na] Stack the books on this shelf. سَفُّط الكلاصات عالميز [ṣaffuṭ ʔilgla:ṣa:t ʕalmi:z] Arrange the glasses on the table. سَفُّط هدُومَك زين حَتَّى لا تِتعَقَّج [ṣaffuṭ hdu:mak zi:n ħatta la: titʕaqqač] Pack your clothes well so they won't wrinkle. صارلَه ساعَة يسَفُّط كِذِب براسِي [ṣa:rlah sa:ʕa yṣaffuṭ čiðib bra:si] He's been telling me lies on top of lies for an hour.
تسَفَّط [tsaffaṭ] *v:* • **1.** organized, to be tightened • **2.** to be stacked, lined up
سُفَط [sufaṭ] *n:* سفاطَة [sfa:ṭa] *pl:* • **1.** small women basket, usually used by women to hold sewing materials
سَفُط [safuṭ] *n:* • **1.** stacking, lining up
سَفطَة [safṭa] *n:* سَفطات [safṭa:t] *pl:* • **1.** stack, pile
تَسفِيط [tasfi:ṭ] *n:* • **1.** organizing, folding, arranging
مسَفَّط [msaffaṭ] *adj:* • **1.** organized, ordered – حَكيَه مسَفَّط، بَسّ نُصَّه كِذِب [ħačyah mṣaffaṭ, bass nuṣṣah čiðib] His talk is well organized, but half of it is lies.

س ف ف

سفُوف [sfu:f] *n:* • **1.** a medicinal mixture of ground herbs
سفِيفَة [sfi:fa] *n:* سفايِف [sfa:yif] *pl:* • **1.** protective bordering • **2.** piping, edging • **3.** molding

س ف ل

سَفالَة [safa:la] *n:* • **1.** lowness
سُفلي [sufli] *adj:* سُفليَّة [sufliyya] *pl:* • **1.** worthless person, derelict, bum • **2.** ruffian, hooligan, hoodlum
سافِل [sa:fil] *adj:* سَفلَة [safala] *pl:* • **1.** low, lowly, base, mean, despicable • **2.** despicable person

س ف ن

سَفّان [saffa:n] *n:* • **1.** sailor, man who works on a sailing ship
سَفِينَة [safi:na] *n:* سُفُن [sufun] *pl:* • **1.** ship, vessel, boat – سَفِينَة نُوح [safi:nat nu:ħ] Noah's ark.

س ف ن ج

إسفَنج [ʔisfanǰ] *n:* • **1.** (coll.) sponge(s)
إسفَنجَة [ʔisfanǰa] *n:* إسفَنجات [ʔisfanǰa:t] *pl:* • **1.** a sponge

س ف ه

تسَفَّه [tsaffah] *v:* • **1.** to behave unrestrainedly, enjoy oneself, have a good time – راح لِبَغداد حَتَّى يِتسَفَّه [ra:ħ lbayda:d ħatta yitsaffah] He went to Baghdad to relax and have a good time.
سَفاهَة [safa:ha] *n:* • **1.** silliness, foolishness, stupidity,

unrestrained conduct, intemperance, shamelessness, immodesty

سَفِيه [safi:h] *adj:* سُفَهاء [sufaha:ʔ] *pl:* • **1.** foolish, silly, stupid • **2.** intemperate, unrestrained • **3.** shameless

س ق ر

سَقَر [saqar] *n:* • **1.** hell, hell-fire – إلَه سَقَر [ʔilah saqar] to hell with him! يِقبَل ما يِقبَل، إلَه سَقَر [yiqbal ma: yiqbal, ʔilah saqar] Whether he agrees or doesn't agree, to hell with him.

س ق ط

سقّط [sgaṭṭ] *v:* • **1.** to be or become ruined, spoiled, wrecked – لا تقصِّر السِّترَة بَعَد. راح تِسقّط [la: tgaṣṣir ʔissitra baʕad. ra:ħ tisgaṭṭ] Don't shorten the coat any more. It's going to be ruined. لا تِلعَب بِالمَكِينَة تَرَة تِسقَط [la: tilʕab bilmaki:na tara tisgaṭṭ] Don't play with the engine or it'll get broken.

سِقَط [siqaṭ] *v:* • **1.** to fall, topple, collapse – أكُو اِحتِمال الوِزارَة تُسقُط [ʔaku ʔiħtima:l ʔilwiza:ra tusquṭ] There's a probability that the cabinet will fall. يِسقُط الخائِن [yisquṭ ʔilxa:ʔin] Down with the traitor! • **2.** to fall, drop, sink down, decline – سِقَط بِنَظَري مِن عِرَفِت يِكذِب [siqaṭ bnaðari min ʕirafit yičðib] He dropped in my estimation when I discovered he lies. • **3.** to fail, flunk – سِقَط بِالإمتِحان مَرّتَين [siqaṭ bilʔimtiħa:n marrtayn] He failed the examination twice.

سَقَّط [saqqaṭ] *v:* • **1.** to cause to fall, topple, collapse – إذا ثلاث وُزَراء اِستَقالَوا، يسَقِّطُون الوُزارَة [ʔiða tlaθ wuzara:ʔ ʔistaqa:law, ysaqqiṭu:n ʔilwuza:ra] If three ministers resign, they will force the cabinet to fall. سَقَّط الجِّنسِيَّة عَن [saqqaṭ ʔijǰinsiyya ʕan] to deprive of citizenship. سَقِّطَوا عَنَّه الجِّنسِيَّة لَمّا عُرفَوا عَنَّه يِتجَسَّس [saqqiṭaw ʕannah ʔiǰǰinsiyya lamma ʕurfaw ʕannah yidǰassas] They took away his citizenship when they learned he was spying. • **2.** to fail, flunk – المُعَلِّم سَقَّطَه لأَنّ نِقَل مِن اللّي يَمَّه [ʔilmuʕallim saqqaṭah liʔann niqal min ʔilli yammah] The teacher flunked him because he copied from the one next to him. • **3.** to renounce, give up one's citizenship – سَقَّط وَتِرَك البَلَد [saqqaṭ wtirak ʔilbalad] He gave up his citizenship and left the country. • **4.** to bolt (the door)

سَقَّط [saggaṭ] *v:* • **1.** to cripple, disable – الخَيّاط سَقَّط السِّترَة مالتِي [ʔilxayya:ṭ saggaṭ ʔissitra ma:lti] The tailor ruined my coat. الوَقعَة مِن السَّطِح سَقَّطَتَه [ʔilwagʕa min ʔissaṭiħ ṣaggiṭatah] The fall from the roof disabled him.

مَسقَط [masqaṭ] *n:* مَساقِط [masa:qiṭ] *pl:* • **1.** the place where something falls (is born) – مَسقَط الرّاس [masqaṭ ʔirra:s] birth-place.

سُقُوط [suqu:ṭ] *n:* • **1.** fall, collapse

سِقّاطَة [siqqa:ṭa, saqqa:ṭa] *n:* سِقّاطات [siqqa:ṭa:t, saqqa:ṭa:t] *pl:* • **1.** (door) bolt

سَقَط، سَقَط عَدِيم [saqaṭ, saqaṭ ʕadi:m] *n:* • **1.** worthless junk

سِقَط [sigaṭ] *adj:* • **1.** broken down, wrecked, ruined, no good, junk – الرّاديُو مالَك سِقَط. رَجِّعَه [ʔirra:dyu ma:lak sigaṭ. raǰǰiʕah] Your radio's junk. Return it. شلَونَه بِالدِّراسَة؟ سِقَط [šlu:nah biddira:sa? sigaṭ] How is he at studying? No damm good! • **2.** crippled, disabled – ما يِقدَر يِشتُغل. هُوَّ سِقَط [ma: yigdar yištuɣul. huwwa sigaṭ] He can't work. He is disabled.

ساقِط [sa:qiṭ] *adj:* سُقّاط [suqqa:ṭ] *pl:* • **1.** fallen • **2.** disreputable, notorious – شَخِص ساقِط [šaxiṣ sa:qiṭ] a disreputable person.

ساقطَة [sa:qṭa, ṣa:qṭa] *adj:* ساقطات [sa:qṭa:t] *pl:* • **1.** disreputable, notorious (woman)

س ق ف

سِقَف [sigaf] *v:* • **1.** to roast (fish) over an open fire – راح نِسقُف سِمَك اليُوم [ra:ħ nisguf simač ʔilyu:m] We're going to roast some fish over an open fire today. • **2.** to roof, provide with a roof or ceiling – سَقَّف الغُرفَة بطابُوق وَبشِيلمان [saggaf ʔilɣurfa bṭa:bu:g wbši:lma:n] He built a roof over the room with bricks and girders.

سَقَّف [saggaf] *v:* • **1.** to roof, provide with a roof or ceiling – باكِر راح نِبدِي نسَقِّف البَيت [ba:čir ra:ħ nibdi nsagguf ʔilbayt] Tomorrow we are going to begin to roof the house.

سَقُف [saguf] *n:* سقُوف [sgu:f] *pl:* • **1.** ceiling

سَقُف [saguf] *n:* • **1.** roasting (fish) over an open fire

سَقّاف [sagga:f] *n:* سَقّافَة، سَقّافِين [sagga:fa, sagga:fi:n] *pl:* • **1.** a man who is skilled at cooking fish over an open fire

سَقفِيَّة [sagfiyya] *n:* • **1.** roofing material

سِقِيفَة، زقِيفَة [sigi:fa, zigi:fa] *n:* سِقِيفات، زقِيفات، سِقايِف [sigi:fa:t, zigifa:t, siga:yif] *pl:* • **1.** a small hut made of tree branches • **2.** storeroom built on top of a house

مسَقَّف [msaggaf] *adj:* • **1.** roofed

مَسقُوف [masgu:f] *adj:* • **1.** broiled in front of an open fire – سِمَك مَسقُوف [simač masgu:f] broiled fish.

س ق م

سِقَم [sigam] *v:* • **1.** to bother, pester, keep after – لا تِسقُم أمَّك. خَلِّيهَا تِشتُغُل [la: tisgum ʔummak. xalli:ha tištuɣul] Don't pester your mother. Let her work.

سَقَّم [saggam] *v:* • **1.** to buy (something, after shopping around for it) – أُخُذ هَالمِيَة دِينار وَسَقُّملَك فَدّ دُكّان صغَيِّر [ʔuxuð halmiyat dina:r wsaggumlak fadd dukka:n zɣayyir] Take this hundred dinars and buy yourself a small shop.

تسَقَّم [tsaggam] *v:* • **1.** to cost, require in exchange – بيش تسَقَّم عَلِيك هَالقاط؟ [biyš tsaggam ʕali:k halqa:ṭ?] How much did that suit cost you?

سُقُم [sugum] *n:* • **1.** disturbance
سُقمان [sugma:n] *n:* • **1.** soot

س ق ي

سِقَى [siga:] *v:* • **1.** to water, provide water for – وَدِّي الخيل لِلشَّطّ وَإِسقِيها [waddi ʔilxi:l liššaṭṭ wʔisgi:ha] Take the horses to the river and water them. الحَدِيقَة يابسَة. لازِم تِسقِيها [ʔilħadi:qa ya:bsa. la:zim tizgi:ha] The garden's dry. You've got to water it. صَدِيقِي سِقانِي قَهوتَين اليُوم [ṣadi:qi siga:ni gahwti:n ʔilyu:m] My friend treated me to two coffees today. • **2.** to irrigate – هَالنَّهَر يِسقِي كُلّ هَالمَنطَقَة [hannahar yisgi kull halmanṭaqa] This river irrigates all this area. • **3.** to temper – يِستَورِد فُولَاذ ويِسقِيه ويسَوِّي مِنَّه سبرنقات [yistari:d fu:la:ð wyizgi:h wysawwi: minnah springa:t] He imports steel and tempers it and makes springs from it.
ساقَى [sa:qa:] *v:* • **1.** to put water in, to add water to – القَهوَة ثِخِينَة. ساقِيها [ʔilgahwa θixi:na. sa:qi:ha] The coffee is thick. Add water to it.
اِستَقَى [ʔistiqa:] *v:* • **1.** to draw, derive, obtain – يِستَقِي الأَخبار مِن مَصادِرها [yistiqi ʔilʔaxba:r min maṣa:dirha] He obtains the news from its sources.
سَقَّة [saqqa] *n:* سَقّايَة [saqqa:ya] *pl:* • **1.** water carrier, man who brings water from a river or village well to the houses – بِنت السَّقَّة [bint ʔissaqqa] ladybug, lady beetle, ladybird.
سِقَة [siga] *n:* سِقيات [sigya:t] *pl:* • **1.** milk-skin, hide bag for milk, yogurt, etc
سَقِي [sagy] *n:* • **1.** watering, irrigation
ساقيَة [sa:gya, sa:ǰya] *n:* سواقِي [swa:gi, swa:ǰi] *pl:* • **1.** irrigation channel, irrigation ditch • **2.** water carrier, woman who brings water from a river or village well to the houses
اِستِسقاء، صَلاة الاِستِسقاء [ʔistisqa:ʔ, ṣala:t ʔalʔistisqa:ʔ] *n:* • **1.** edema, dropsy, prayer for rain
ساقِي [sa:qi] *adj:* سُقات [suqa:t] *pl:* • **1.** waiter in a café

س ك ت

سِكَت [sikat] *v:* • **1.** to become silent, lapse into silence, shut up – أُسكُت! إِنتَ شتِفهَم بِالسَّيّارات؟ [ʔuskut! ʔinta štifham bissayya:ra:t?] Quiet! What do you know about cars? أُسكُت لَك، تَرَة أَمَوّتَك [ʔuskut lak, tara ʔamawwtak] Shut up, you, or I'll kill you. • **2.** to become quiet, quiet down, calm down, subside – الجّاهِل سِكَت بَعَدما بِكَى أَكثَر مِن رُبع ساعَة [ʔiǰǰa:hil sikat baʕadma: biča: ʔakθar min rubuʕ sa:ʕa] The child quieted down after crying more than a quarter of an hour. لَمّا المُعَلِّم دِخَل الصَّف، كُلنا سكَتنا [lamma ʔilmuʕallim dixal ʔiṣṣaff, kullna skatna] When the teacher entered the class, we all quieted down. لا تِسكُتلَه. إذا ضِرَبَك، أُضرُبَه [la: tiskutlah. ʔiða ḍirabak, ʔuḍurbah] Don't take it from him. If he hits you, hit him back. آنِي ما أَسكُتلَه عَلَى هَالدَّقَّة [ʔa:ni ma: ʔaskutlah ʕala haldagga] I won't forgive him for that dirty trick.
سَكَّت [sakkat] *v:* • **1.** to silence, quiet, calm – إِنطِيه دِينار وَسَكّتَه [ʔinṭi:h dina:r wsakkitah] Give him a dinar and silence him. سَكَّت الجّاهِل بِشوَيَّة جُكلَيت [sakkat ʔiǰǰa:hil bšwayyat čukli:t] He quieted the child with a little bit of chocolate.
سَكتَة [sakta] *n:* • **1.** silence, quiet – سَكتَة قَلبِيَّة [sakta qalbiyya] heart failure.
سُكُوت [suku:t] *n:* • **1.** quiet, silence • **2.** with -ب بسُكوت quietly
ساكِت [sa:kit] *adj:* • **1.** quiet, silent
سكُوتِي [sku:ti] *adj:* سكُوتِيِّن، سكُوتِيَّة [sku:tiyyi:n, sku:tiyya] *pl:* • **1.** taciturn, reticent person • **2.** secretive person

س ك ر [1]

سِكَر [sikar] *v:* • **1.** to get drunk, become intoxicated – سِكَر وَقام يخَربُط بحَكيَه [sikar wga:m yxarbuṭ bħačyah] He got drunk and his speech became muddled. • **2.** to drink (liquor) – ما تزَوِّجَته لِأَنّ يِسكَر [ma:dzawwiǰatah liʔann yiskar] She didn't marry him because he drinks. يَومِيّاً يِسكرُون بِهَالبار [yawmiyyan ysikru:n bhalba:r] They drink every day in this bar.
سَكَّر [sakkar] *v:* • **1.** to intoxicate, make drunk – البِيرَة ما تسَكِّر مِثل الوِسكِي [ʔilbi:ra ma: tsakkir miθl ʔilwiski] Beer doesn't make you drunk the way whiskey does. سَكّروه وأَخذوا فلُوسَه [sakkirawh wʔaxðaw flu:sah] They got him drunk and took his money.
سُكُر [sukur] *n:* • **1.** drunkenness
سَكرَة [sakra] *n:* سَكرات [sakra:t] *pl:* • **1.** drinking spree, instance of drunkenness
سِكِّير [sikki:r] *adj:* سِكِّيرين [sikki:ri:n] *pl:* • **1.** drunkard, habitual drinker
مُسَكِّر [musakkir] *adj:* مُسَكِّرات [musakkira:t] *pl:* • **1.** intoxicant • **2.** (as *n:*) intoxicants
سَكران [sakra:n] *adj:* سكارَة [ska:ra] *pl:* • **1.** drunk, intoxicated – سَكران طِينَة [sakra:n ṭi:na] dead drunk. • **2.** (as *n:*) a drunkard, an inebriated person

س ك ر [2]

سُكَّرِي [sukkari] *n:* • **1.** sugar, sugary – مَرَض البُول السُّكَّرِي [marað ʔilbu:l ʔissukkari] diabetes.

س ك ر [3]

سُكرِي [sukri] *n:* • **1.** small grains of baked clay used as an abrasive for cleaning

س ك ر ب

سِكراب [sikra:b] *n:* • **1.** scrap metal
مسَكرَب [msakrab] *adj:* • **1.** junk, old, broken

س

س ك ر ب ي ن

سكاربين [skarpi:n] *n:* سكاربيّات [skarpiyya:t] *pl:* • **1.** women's high-heeled shoes, and also, a pair of high-heeled shoes

س ك ر ت ي ر

سِكِرتير [sikirti:r] *n:* سِكِرتَيريَّة [sikirti:riyya] *pl:* • **1.** male secretary
سِكِرتيرَة [sikirti:ra] *n:* سِكِرتيرات [sikirti:ra:t] *pl:* • **1.** female secretary

س ك س

سَكس [saks] *n:* • **1.** sex, porn
سَكسِي [saksi] *adj:* • **1.** sexy, erotic, hot

س ك س ك

سَكسُوكَة [saksu:ka] *n:* • **1.** goatee

س ك ك

سَكّ [sačč] *v:* • **1.** to wander around
سَكّ [sakk] *v:* • **1.** to mint, coin – وين يسِكُّون فلُوسنا؟ [wi:n ysikku:n flu:sna?] Where do they mint our money? • **2.** to wander around
سَكّ [sakk] *n:* • **1.** minting, coining • **2.** wandering around
سِكَّة [sikka, sičča] *n:* سِكَك [sičač] *pl:* • **1.** die, mold – إنتَ غير سِكَّة سِكّتَك [ʔinta ɣi:r sičča siččtak] I can't figure you out (lit., you're different from your mold). • **2.** coined money, coin – السِّكَّة مالْتهُم ما تسَوِّي سِكّتنا [ʔissičča ma:lathum ma: tsawwi. siččatna] Their coins aren't equal to our coins. • **3.** railroad, railroad track – كان نايِم عالسِّكَّة وسِحَقَه القِطار [ča:n na:yim ʕassičča wsiħagah ʔilqiṭa:r] He was sleeping on the tracks and the train ran over him. المُطَر غَرَّق سِكَّة بَغداد البَصرَة [ʔilmuṭar ɣarrag siččat baɣda:d ʔilbaṣra] The rain flooded the Baghdad-Basra railroad line.

س ك ل س ب ن

سكُولسبانَة [sku:lspa:na] *n:* • **1.** wrench, spanner (all purposes)

س ك ل ل

سِكَلَّة [sikalla] *n:* سِكَلات [sikalla:t] *pl:* • **1.** scaffold
سكَلَّة [skalla] *n:* سكَلات [skalla:t] *pl:* • **1.** lumber yard, open storage and marketing area

س ك م ل

سِكَملِي [sikamli, skamli] *n:* سِكَمليّات [skamli:yya:t] *pl:* • **1.** chair

س ك ن 1

سِكَن [sikan] *v:* • **1.** to become still, tranquil, calm, to abate, subside – بَعَد نُصّ ساعَة، سِكَن الوُجَع [baʕad nuṣṣ sa:ʕa, sikan ʔilwuǰaʕ] After half an hour, the pain subsided. • **2.** to reside, dwell, live – صارلِي أسكُن بهالبَيت سَنتَين [ṣa:rli ʔaskun bihalbayt santayn] I've been living in this house two years. أبُوه يِسكُن ببَغداد [ʔabu:h yiskun bibaɣda:d] His father resides in Baghdad.
سَكَّن [sakkan] *v:* • **1.** to calm, soothe, alleviate – هَالدُّوا يسَكِّن الوُجَع [hadduwa: ysakkin ʔilwuǰaʕ] This medicine will alleviate the pain. • **2.** to settle, lodge, provide living quarters for – الشَّرِكَة سَكّنَت عُمّالها ببيُوت قَريبَة منها [ʔiššarika sakkinat ʕumma:lha bibyu:t qari:ba minha] The company settled its workers in houses close to it.
انسِكَن [ʔinsikan] *v:* • **1.** to be inhabited – هَالبَيت ما ينسِكِن بيه [halbayt ma: yinsikin bi:h] This house can't be lived in.
سَكَن [sakan] *n:* • **1.** house, place to stay, residency
سِكّين، سِكّينَة [sičči:n, sičči:na] *n:* سكاكِين [sča:či:n] *pl:* • **1.** knife
مَسكَن [maskan] *n:* مَساكِن [masa:kin] *pl:* • **1.** residence, home
سُكّان [sukka:n] *n:* • **1.** steering mechanism, steering • **2.** steering wheel • **3.** handle bars
سُكُون [suku:n] *n:* • **1.** tranquillity, calm, peace, silence, quiet
إسكان [ʔiska:n] *n:* • **1.** settling, settlement – مَشرُوع إسكان العَشايِر [mašru:ʕ ʔiska:n ʔilʕaša:yir] the project for settling the tribes. • **2.** housing, allocation of living quarters – وِزارَة الإسكان [wiza:rat ʔilʔiska:n] Ministry of Housing.
ساكِن [sa:kin] *adj:* • **1.** tranquil, calm, motionless, still – البَحَر اليُوم ساكِن [ʔilbaħar ʔilyu:m sa:kin] The sea is calm today. لا تحَرِّك ساكِن [la: tħarrik sa:kin] Let sleeping dogs lie. • **2.** quiet, phlegmatic – أخُوك فَدّ واحِد ساكِن. يحِكي كُلِّش قَليل [ʔaxu:k fadd wa:ħid sa:kin. yiħči kulliš qali:l] Your brother is a quiet one. He talks very little. • **3.** unvowelled (of a medial consonant) – حَرُف ساكِن [ħaruf sa:kin] an unvowelled medial consonant. • **4.** living, dwelling, residing – وين ساكِن هَسَّة؟ [wi:n sa:kin hassa?] Where're you living now? • **5.** (as *n:*) dweller, resident, inhabitant (pl. سُكّان which also means 'population')
مُسَكِّن [musakkin] *adj:* • **1.** pl. مُسَكِّنين pacifier, calmer, soother • **2.** **مُسَكِّنات** [musakkina:t] pl. ات sedative, tranquilizer
سَكَني [sakani] *adj:* • **1.** residential
مَسكُون [masku:n] *adj:* • **1.** inhabited, populated • **2.** haunted – هَالبَيت مَسكُون؛ بيه أشباح [halbayt masku:n; bi:h ʔašba:ħ] This house is haunted; there are ghosts in it.

س ك ن 3

سَكِن، سِكِن [sakin, sikin] *n:* سِكِنيَّة [sikiniyya] *pl:* • **1.** second, helper, assistant –

لَمّا السّايِق تِعَب السِكِن ساق الباس [lamma ʔissa:yiq tiʕab ʔissikin sa:q ʔilpa:s] When the driver got tired the relief driver drove the bus.
سِكنات [sikna:t] *n:* • **1.** back lights

س ك ن ج ب ي ل

سكَنجَبِيل، شَرَبَت سكَنجَبِيل [skanǰabi:l, šarbat skanǰabi:l] *n:* • **1.** ginger • **2.** a non-carbonated soft drink of ginger, sugar and water, sometimes sold as a concentrated syrup

س ك ن د ر

إسكَندَر [ʔiskandar] *n:* • **1.** Alexander
الإسكَندَرِيَّة [ʔilʔiskandariyya] *n:* • **1.** Alexandria (Egypt)

س ك و

ساكُو [sa:ku] *n:* ساكُوّات [sa:kuwwa:t] *pl:* • **1.** coat, jacket

س ك ي ت

سكَيت [skayt] *n:* • **1.** skate

س ل ب

سِلَب [silab] *v:* • **1.** to rob, steal, plunder, loot – ياهُو اللّي يمُرّ، يِسلِبُوه [ya:hu ʔilli ymurr, ysilbu:h] Whoever passes by, they rob him. سِلبَوا كُلّ ما عِندَه بِالطَّرِيق [silbaw kull ma: ʕindah biṭṭari:q] They stole everything he had along the way. • **2.** to bone, cut out the bone – أَرِيد شوَيَّة لَحَم وَيكُون تِسلِبلِي إياها شقَدّ ما تِقدَر [ʔari:d šwayyat laħam wyku:n tislibli ʔiyya:ha šgadd ma: tigdar] I want a little meat and bone it out for me as much as you can.
سَلَّب [sallab] *v:* • **1.** to rob, steal, plunder, loot – لا تسافِر باللّيل تَرَة الحَرامِيَّة يسَلّبُوك [la: tsa:fir billayl tara ʔilħara:miyya ysallibu:k] Don't travel by night or the thieves will rob you.
سَلِب [salib] *n:* • **1.** robbing, looting, plundering, pillage • **2.** negation – عَلامَة السّالِب [ʕala:mat ʔissa:lib] minus sign (math.).
سَلّاب [salla:b] *n:* سَلّابَة [salla:ba] *pl:* • **1.** bandit, robber, thief
سالِب [sa:lib] *adj:* سوالِب [sawa:lib] *pl:* • **1.** negative, minus
أُسلُوب [ʔuslu:b] *n:* أَسالِيب [ʔasa:li:b] *pl:* • **1.** way, method, procedure • **2.** manner, mode, fashion • **3.** style (esp. of text or author)
سِلبِيَّة [silbiyya] *n:* • **1.** negative attitude • **2.** negativism
تَسلِيب [tasli:b] *n:* • **1.** holdup • **2.** robbing
سَلبِي [salbi] *adj:* • **1.** negative, minus – إشارَة سَلبِيَّة [ʔiša:ra salbiyya] minus sign. • **2.** passive – مُقاوَمَة سَلبِيَّة [muqa:wama salbiyya] passive resistance.
سلاب [sla:b] *adj:* سلابات [sla:ba:t] *pl:* • **1.** clothing on a body at the time of death, and also, a derogatory term for any clothing • **2.** useless, worthless thing – جابَوا إلنا مُعَلّمِين كُلّهُم سلابات [ǰa:baw ʔilna muʕallimi:n kullhum sla:ba:t] They brought some teachers for us that were all worthless.
مَسلُوبَة [maslu:ba] *adj:* • **1.** boned, boneless – لَحمَة مَسلُوبَة [laħma maslu:ba] a boneless piece of meat.

س ل ب ح

سَلبُوح [salbu:ħ] *n:* سلابِيح [sla:bi:ħ] *pl:* • **1.** worm

س ل ب و

سِلِبُويَة [silibu:ya] *n:* • **1.** (coll.) watercolor
سِلِبُويايَة [silibuya:ya] *n:* سِلِبُويايات [silibuyaya:t] *pl:* • **1.** (coll.) watercolor(s)

س ل ت

سِلَت [silat] *v:* • **1.** to extract, pull out – سِلَت خيط مِن حاشيَة الوُصلَة وَراف بِيه بَنطَرُونَه [silat xi:ṭ min ħa:šyat ʔilwuṣla wra:f bi:h panṭaru:nah] He pulled a thread out of the edge of the cloth and darned his pants with it.
سَلَّت [sallat] *v:* • **1.** intens. of سِلَت to extract, pull out – لا تسَلِّت الخيُوط مال البُويِنباغ [la: tsallit ʔilixyu:ṭ ma:l ʔilbuyinba:ɣ] Don't pull the threads out of the tie.
سَلِت [salit] *n:* • **1.** extracting, pulling out
مسَلَّت [msallit] *adj:* • **1.** frayed – حاشيَة هَالكَفِّيَّة مسَلّتَة [ħa:šyat haččaffiyya msallita] The edge of this handkerchief is frayed.

س ل ح

سِلَح [silaħ] *v:* • **1.** to drop, put aside – يِظهَر سِلَحها لِلقَضِيَّة [yiðhar silaħha lilqaðiyya] It seems that he has put the matter aside.
سَلَّح [sallaħ] *v:* • **1.** to arm, provide with weapons – سَلّحهُم وَدَزّهُم لِلمَعرَكَة [sallaħhum wdazzhum lilmaʕraka] He armed them and sent them to the battlefield. • **2.** to reinforce, strengthen – لازِم نسَلِّح الأَساسات [la:zim nsalliħ ʔilʔasa:sa:t] We've got to reinforce the foundation.
تسَلَّح [tsallaħ] *v:* • **1.** to arm oneself – تسَلَّح بمُسَدَّس وَخَنجَر وَراح عَلَيهُم [tsallaħ bmusaddas wxanǰar wra:ħ ʕali:hum] He armed himself with a pistol and a dagger and went to see them.
إنسِلَح [ʔinsilaħ] *v:* • **1.** to be dropped, be put aside – يبَيِّن مَسألَة تَرفِيعِي إنسِلحَت [yibayyin masʔalat tarfi:ʕi ʔinsilħat] It seems that the question of my promotion was laid aside.
سَلِح [saliħ] *n:* • **1.** putting aside, dropping
سلاح [sla:ħ] *n:* أَسلِحَة [ʔasliħa] *pl:* • **1.** weapon
تَسَلُّح [tasalluħ] *n:* • **1.** armament
تَسلِيح [tasli:ħ] *n:* • **1.** arming, equipping, armament, rearmament, reinforcement (in ferroconcrete construction)

مُسَلَّح [musallaћ] *adj:* • **1.** armored – سَيّارَة مُسَلَّحَة [sayya:ra musallaћa] armored car. • **2.** reinforced – كُنكَرِيت مُسَلَّح [kunkari:t musallaћ] reinforced concrete.

س ل ح ف

سُلحَفاة [sulћafa:t] *n:* • **1.** tortoise, turtle

س ل خ

سِلَخ [silax] *v:* • **1.** to skin – القَصّاب دَيسلَخ الذَّبيحَة [ʔilgaṣṣa:b dayislax ʔiððibi:ћa] The butcher's skinning the slaughtered animal. • **2.** to strike, hit hard – سِلخَتَه براشدِي وَتفلَت بوِجهَه [silxatah bra:šdi wtiflat bwiččah] She slapped him hard and spit in his face. • **3.** to have sexual intercourse with • **4.** سُلَخ to lie, tell lies, – يُسلُخ بِحَكيَه هوايَة [yuṣlux bћačyah hwa:ya] He lies a lot in what he says.

سَلَّخ [sallax] *v:* • **1.** to strip, disrobe (someone) – الطَّبِيب سَلَّخَه وَأخَذ وَزنَه [ʔiṭṭabi:b ṣallaxah wʔaxað waznah] The doctor disrobed him and took his weight.

تسَلَّخ [tsallax] *v:* • **1.** to strip, disrobe, take off one's clothes – تسَلَّخ وَنزَل بالمَيّ [tsallax wnizal bilmayy] He stripped and went in the water.

سَلِخ [salix] *n:* • **1.** skinning, flaying • **2.** striking, hitting hard • **3.** having sexual intercourse with

مَسلَخ [maslax] *n:* مَسالِخ [masa:lix] *pl:* • **1.** slaughterhouse

مُسلَخ [muslux] *n:* مَسالِخ [masa:lix] *pl:* • **1.** drain

سُلُوخ [sulux] *adj:* • **1.** prevarication, lies

سلُوخ [slu:x] *adj:* • **1.** (invar.) stripped, naked, bare, unclothed – شُوف اللّي دَيسِبحُون؛ كُلّهُم سلُوخ [šu:f ʔilli daysibћu:n; kullhum slu:x] Look at the swimmers; they're all naked.

مسَلَّخ [msallax] *adj:* مسَلَّخِين، مسالِيخ [msallaxi:n, msa:li:x] *pl:* • **1.** naked

س ل س

سَلاسَة [sala:sa] *n:* • **1.** smoothness, fluency

سَلِس [salis] *adj:* • **1.** smooth, fluent, easy to read (of a style of writing) – التَّقرِير مالَه سَلِس [ʔittaqri:r ma:lah salis] His report is written in a smooth style.

أسلَس [ʔaslas] *comparative adjective:* • **1.** more or most fluent, smooth

س ل س ل

تسَلسَل [tsalsal] *v:* • **1.** to be connected, to be interlinked

سِلسِلَة [silsila] *n:* سَلاسِل [sala:sil] *pl:* • **1.** chain (also fig.) – سِلسِلَة جبال [silsilat ǰba:l] mountain chain. • **2.** series

تَسَلسُل [tasalsul] *n:* • **1.** sequence, succession – رَتِّب الكُتُب حَسَب تَسَلسُل أرقامها [rattib ʔilkutub ћasab tasalsul ʔarqa:mha] Stack the books in numerical order. • **2.** بِالتَّسَلسُل successively, consecutively

مُسَلسَلَة [musalsala] *n:* • **1** series, sequence (TV, radio)

مُتَسَلسِل [mutasalsil] *adj:* • **1.** continuous (numbering)

س ل ط

سَلَّط [sallaṭ] *v:* • **1.** to give power over, set up as overlord – الله سَلَّط عَلَيهُم واحِد يُعرُف شلُون يعامِلهُم [ʔallah sallaṭ ʕali:hum wa:ћid yuʕruf šlu:n yʕa:milhum] God put someone in control of them who knows how to treat them. مِنُو اللّي سَلَّطَك عَلينا؟ [minu ʔilli sallaṭak ʕali:na?] Who set you over us? • **2.** with عَلَى to set up, put over or above – سَلِّط المِزَمِّلَة عالحُوض [salliṭ ʔilimzammila ʕalћu:ð̣] Set the faucet over the pool. سَلَّط عَليه السَّيف إلَى أن قَرّ [sallaṭ ʕali:h ʔissayf ʔila ʔan qarr] He held the sword over him until he confessed.

تسَلَّط [tsallaṭ] *v:* • **1.** pass. of سَلَّط to be set up, to be put over or above • **2.** to be given power over, be set up

سُلطَة [sulṭa] *n:* سُلطات [sulṭa:t] *pl:* • **1.** power, authority, dominion, influence, jurisdiction • **2.** pl. سُلطات authority, official agency

سَلاطَة [zala:ṭa] *n:* سَلاطات، سَلَطات [zala:ṭa:t, zalaṭa:t] *pl:* • **1.** salad • **2.** a sure or easy thing, a snap, a cinch – هَالمَوضُوع زَلاطَة. ما يِنرادلَه قرايَة [halmawð̣u:ʕ zala:ṭa. ma: yinra:dlah qra:ya] This course is a cinch. There's no reading required for it.

سَلطَن، تسَلطَن [salṭa:n, tsalṭan] *v:* • **1.** سَلطَن to establish as ruler, تسَلطَن to become sultan or ruler

مسَلِّط [msalliṭ] *adj:* • **1.** authoritarian

سَلِيط [sali:ṭ] *adj:* • **1.** sharp

مِتسَلِّط [mitsalliṭ] *adj:* • **1** dominating

س ل ط ن

سُلطان، سَلاطِين [sulṭa:n] *n:* • **1.** sultan • **2.** ruler, holder of power

سَلطَنَة [salṭana] *n:* • **1.** sultanate • **2.** power of an authoritarian ruler

س ل ع

سِلعَة [silʕa] *n:* سِلَع [silaʕ] *pl:* • **1.** commodity, commercial article

س ل ف

سَلَّف [sallaf] *v:* • **1.** to lend, loan, advance – البَنك الصِّناعِي يسَلِّف أصحاب المَعامِل فلُوس [ʔilbank ʔiṣṣina:ʕi ysallif ʔaṣћa:b ʔilmaʕa:mil flu:s] The Industrial Bank lends money to factory owners. هَالبَنك يسَلِّف مُوَظَّفِينَه لِحَدّ الألف دِينار [halbang ysallif muwað̣ð̣ afi:nah liћadd ʔilʔalf dina:r] This bank advances its employees up to one thousand dinars.

اِستَلَف [ʔistilaf] *v:* • **1.** to borrow, get a loan, get an advance – اِستِلَفِت ألف دِينار مِن البَنك العَقارِي حَتَّى أبنِي بَيت [ʔistilafit ʔalf dina:r min ʔilbank ʔilʕaqa:ri ћatta ʔabni bayt] I borrowed a thousand dinars from the Real Estate

Bank to build a house. تِقدَر تِستِلِف وَتِشتِري الثَّلّاجَة [tigdar tistilif wtištiri ʔiθθallaːja] You can get an advance on your salary and buy the refrigerator.
سَلَف [salaf] *n:* • **1.** ancestors, forefathers – نَعلَة عَلَى سَلَف سَلفاك. ما قِتلَك لا تسَوِّي هِيكِي؟ [naʕla ʕala salaf salfaːk. maː gitlak laː tsawwiː hiːči?] Damn you. Didn't I tell you not to do that? إذا ما يرَجِّعلَك الفلُوس، أنعَل سَلفَة سَلفاه [ʔiða maː yrajjiʕlak ʔilfluːs, ʔanʕal salfat salfaːh] If he doesn't return the money to you, I'll raise hell with him.
سِلفَة، سُلفَة [silfa, sulfa] *n:* سِلَف [silaf] *pl:* • **1.** loan, advance (of money)
تَسلِيف [tasliːf] *n:* • **1.** credit, loan

س ل ق

سِلَق [silag] *v:* • **1.** to boil, scald, to cook in boiling water – سِلقَت بَيضتَين وَخَلّتهُم بجَيب إبنها [silgat bayḍtayn wxallathum bjiːb ʔibinha] She boiled two eggs and put them in her son's pocket. مِن رِحت لِلإمتِحان الشَّفَوِي المُعَلِّم سِلَقني بالأسئِلَة [min riħit lilʔimtiħaːn ʔiššafawi ʔilmuʕallim silagni bilʔasʔila] When I went for the oral examination, the teacher gave me a real hard time.
تسَلَّق [tsallaq] *v:* • **1.** to scale • **2.** to climb
سَلِق [salig] *n:* • **1.** boiling
سِلِق [silig] *n:* • **1.** a kind of chard
سَلقَة [salga] *n:* سَلقات [salgaːt] *pl:* • **1.** boiling
تَسَلُّق [tasalluq] *n:* • **1.** scaling • **2.** climbing
سلُوقِي [sluːgi, saluki] *adj:* سلُوقِيَّة [sluːgiyya] *pl:* • **1.** saluki, a breed of dog similar to the greyhound
مِتسَلِّق [mitsalliq] *adj:* • **1.** ascending • **2.** climbing

س ل ك

سِلَك [silak] *v:* • **1.** to behave, comport oneself – إذا تُسلُك سُلُوك زين، تِنجَح [ʔiða tusluk suluːk ziːn, tinjaħ] If you follow the rules of good behavior, you'll succeed. • **2.** to get along well, be on good terms – ما دَيِسلُك ويّا أبُوه [maː dayisluk wiyya ʔabuːh] He's not getting along with his father.
سَلَّك [sallak] *v:* • **1.** same as سِلَك: to get along well, be on good terms
سِلك [silk] *n:* أسلاك [ʔaslaːk] *pl:* • **1.** wire • **2.** filament (of a light bulb) • **3.** rayon • **4.** corps – السِّلك الدِّبلُوماسِي [ʔissilk ʔiddipluːmaːsi] the diplomatic corps.
سِلكَة [silka] *n:* سِلكات [silkaːt] *pl:* • **1.** a lightweight woolen fabric worn in summer
سُلُوك [suluːk, siluːk] *n:* • **1.** behavior, deportment, conduct, manners
مَسلَك [maslak] *n:* • **1.** career • **2.** path • **3.** method
سالِك [saːlik] *adj:* • **1.** paved • **2.** passable, clear
سِلُوكِي [siluːki, suluːki] *adj:* • **1.** behavioral
مَسلُوك [masluːk] *adj:* • **1.** passable

س ل ل

سَلّ [sall] *v:* • **1.** to draw, unsheath – سَلّ سَيفَه وَحَيّا الزَّعِيم [sall sayfah wħayyaː ʔizzaʕiːm] He drew his sword and saluted the brigadier. • **2.** to infect with tuberculosis, cause tuberculosis in – هِيكِي مَناخ يسِلّ الشَّخُص [hiːči manaːx ysill ʔiššaxuṣ] This climate gives people tuberculosis. • **3.** to bother, bug, annoy, give a pain – إبنَك يسِلّنِي. لا يرُوح لِلمَدرَسَة وَلا يِشتُغُل [ʔibnak ysillni. laː yiruːħ lilmadrasa wala yištuɣul] Your son gives me a pain. He doesn't go to school and he doesn't work.
اِنسَلّ [ʔinsall] *v:* • **1.** to catch tuberculosis, become consumptive – اِنسَلّ بشَبابَه [ʔinsall bšabaːbah] He got tuberculosis in his youth. • **2.** to be bothered by someone, annoyed
اِستَلّ [ʔistall] *v:* • **1.** to draw, unsheath – اِستَلّ سَيفَه وبدا يُضرُب بِيهُم [ʔistall sayfah wbidaː yuḍrub biːhum] He drew his sword and began to strike them.
سِلّ [sill] *n:* • **1.** tuberculosis, consumption
سَلَّة [salla] *n:* سلال، سَلّات [slaːl, sallaːt] *pl:* • **1.** basket – سَلَّة المُهمَلات [sallat ʔilmuhmalaːt] waste basket. كُرَة السَّلَّة [kurat ʔissalla] basketball.
سِلّي، سِلَّة [silli, silla] *n:* • **1.** (coll.) thorn(s)
سِلِّيَّة [silliyya] *n:* سِلِّيّات [silliyyaːt] *pl:* • **1.** a thorn
مَسَلَّة [masalla] *n:* مَسَلّات [masallaːt] *pl:* • **1.** obelisk
سَلِيل [saliːl] *n:* • **1.** descendent
سِلّايَة [sillaːya] *n:* سِلّايات [sillaːyaːt] *pl:* • **1.** thorn • **2.** point, nib (of a pen)
سُلالَة [sulaːla] *n:* سُلالات [sulaːlaːt] *pl:* • **1.** descendant, progeny, offspring, family, race, strain, stock
مَسلُول [masluːl] *adj:* • **1.** drawn, unsheathed – سَيف مَسلُول [sayf masluːl] a drawn sword. • **2.** tubercular, infected with tuberculosis • **3.** a person having tuberculosis

س ل م

سِلَم [silam] *v:* • **1.** to be safe, unharmed, intact, secure – بَسّ نُعبُر الحِدُود، نِسلَم [bass nuʕbur ʔilħiduːd, nislam] Once we cross the border, we're safe. إذا ترِيد تِسلَم عَلَى رُوحَك، لا تِمشِي ويّا هَالأشقِياء [ʔiða triːd tislam ʕala ruːħak, laː timši wiyya halʔašqiyaːʔ] If you want to be safe, don't run around with this gangster. • **2.** to escape, get away – سِلَم مِن الخَطَر [silam min ʔilxaṭar] He escaped from the danger. • **3.** to pass, get by – لَو بَسّ أسلَم بِالإنكِلِيزِي باقِي الدِّرُوس سَهلَة [law bass ʔaslam bilʔingiliːzi baːqi ʔiddiruːs sahla] If I only pass in English the rest of the courses are easy. مَحَّد سِلَم. كُلنا سِقَطنا بِالإمتِحان [maħħad silam. kullna siqaṭna bilʔimtiħaːn] No one made it. All of us failed the exam.
سَلَّم [sallam] *v:* • **1.** to protect from harm, keep safe, save, preserve – الله يسَلّمَك [ʔallah ysallmak] God preserve you! (a reply to شلُونَك؟) الله يسَلّمَك، وَإنتَ شلُونَك؟

[ʔallah ysallmak, wʔinta šlu:nak?] God keep you and how are you? شيسَلّمَه مِن ذُولَة؟ كُلّهُم شَقاوات [šysallmah min ðu:la? kullhum šaqa:wa:t] What will save him from them? They're all gangsters. الله سَلّمَه؛ كان بَعَد شوَيَّة يِغرَق [ʔallah sallamah; ča:n baʕad šwayya yiɣrag] God saved him; he was about to drown. الله يسَلّمَه؛ كُلّش خُوش وَلَد [ʔallah ysallimah; kulliš xu:š walad] God bless him; he's a real good boy. • **2.** to turn over, hand over, surrender – سَلّمِت جَمِيع الغَراض لِلمُوَظَّف الجِّدِيد [sallamit ǰami:ʕ ʔilɣara:ð lilmuwaððaf ʔiǰǰidi:d] I turned all the things over to the new employee. سَلَّم أمرَه لِالله [sallam ʔamrah lʔallah] He surrendered his fate to God. سَلَّم نَفسَه لِلشُّرطَة [sallam nafsah liššurṭa] He surrendered himself to the police. • **3.** to deliver to, hand over to, give to – سَلَّمَه المَكتُوب بِيدَه [sallamah ʔilmaktu:b bi:dah] He delivered the letter to him personally. سَلّمنِي مِفتاح البَيت [sallimli mifta:ћ ʔilbayt] Give the house key to me. البارحَة سَلَّمنِي خَمسِين دِينار [ʔilba:rћa sallamni xamsi:n dina:r] Yesterday he gave me fifty dinars. • **4.** to surrender, lay down one's arms – جيُوش العَدُو كُلّها سَلَّمَت [ǰiyu:š ʔilʕadu kullha sallimat] All of the enemy forces surrendered. • **5.** with عَلَى to greet, salute – مَرّ وَما سَلَّم عَلَيّا [marr wma sallam ʕalayya] he passed by and didn't say hello to me. مِن تشُوفَه، سَلّملِي عَليه [min tšu:fah, sallimli ʕali:h] When you see him, give him my regards. نسَلِّم عَلَيكُم. لا تِنسُون تِجُون عِدنا إسبُوع الجّاي [nsallim ʕali:kum. la: tinsu:n tiǰu:n ʕidna ʔisbu:ʕ ʔiǰǰa:y] Goodbye. Don't forget to come visit us next week.

أسلَم [ʔaslam] *v:* • **1.** to become a Moslem, embrace Islam – أسلَم وَحَجّ مَكَّة [ʔaslam wћaǰǰ makka] He became a Moslem and made a pilgrimage to Mecca.

تسَلَّم [tsallam] *v:* • **1.** to receive • **2.** to be delivered, to be submitted

تسالَم [tsa:lam] *v:* • **1.** to greet each other, exchange greetings – تسالَمِت وِيّاه البارحَة بالحَفلَة [tsa:lamit wiyya:h ʔilba:rћa bilћafla] I exchanged greetings with him yesterday at the party.

إستِلَم [ʔistilam] *v:* • **1.** to take delivery of, to receive, obtain, get – إستِلَمِت مَكتُوب اليُوم؟ [ʔistilamit maktu:b ʔilyu:m?] Did you receive a letter today? راح أستِلِم السَّيّارَة باكِر [ra:ћ ʔastilim ʔissayya:ra ba:čir] I will take delivery on the car tomorrow. • **2.** to take over, take possession of – إستِلَم إدارَة المَعمَل [ʔistilam ʔida:rat ʔilmaʕmal] He took over management of the factory. المُلاحِظ الجِّدِيد إستِلَم مِنِّي [ʔilmula:ћiḍ ʔiǰǰidi:d ʔistilam minni] The new supervisor took over from me.

إستَسلَم [ʔistaslam] *v:* • **1.** to submit, yield, give oneself over, succumb – ظَلّ يِحكِي وِيّاها مُدَّة إلَى أن إستَسلِمَتلَه [ðall yiћči wiyya:ha mudda ʔila ʔan ʔistaslimatlah] He kept talking to her for some time, until she gave in to him. • **2.** to convert to Islam, become a Moslem – ثنَين يَهُود إستَسلِمَوا [θnayn yahu:d ʔistaslimaw] Two Jews became Moslems.

سِلم [silim] *n:* • **1.** peace

سُلَّم [sullam] *n:* سَلالِم [sala:lim] *pl:* • **1.** scale (mus.)

سَلام [sala:m] *n:* • **1.** soundness, well-being – بِسَلامَة راسَك، ما نِحتاج شِي [bsala:mat ra:sak, ma: niћta:ǰ ši] As long as you're living, we don't need a thing. • **2.** peace, peacefulness – هَالشّعَب مُحِبّ لِلسَّلام [haššʕab muћibb lissala:m] These are peace-loving people. سَلام الله عَليه؛ شلُون سَبِع [sala:m ʔallah ʕali:h; šlu:n sabiʕ] God's peace on him; how brave he is! • **3.** security, safety – السَّلام عَلَيكُم [ʔissala:m ʕali:kum] Peace be with you (a standard greeting). • **4.** national anthem – السَّلام الجُّمهُورِي [ʔissala:m ʔiǰǰamhu:ri] the national anthem of the republic. • **5.** pl. سَلامات salute • **6.** with يا standard exclamation of amazement, surprise, dismay, grief, pity, etc • **7.** with وـ as in والسَّلام: that's all, that's final – ما أقبَل ترُوح والسَّلام [ma: ʔaqbal tru:ћ wassala:m] I don't want you to go and that's final.

سَلامَة [sala:ma] *n:* • **1.** unimpaired state, flawlessness – لازِم نِتأكَّد مِن سَلامَة الغَنَم مِن الأمراض قَبُل ما نِستَوردها [la:zim nitʔakkad min sala:mat ʔilɣanam min ʔilʔamra:ð gabul ma: nistawridha] We must make sure the sheep are free of disease before we import them. سَلامَة الذُّوق [sala:mat ʔiððuwq] good taste. سَلامَة النِّيَّة [sala:mat ʔinniyya] good faith, sincerity, guilelessness. قالها بِسَلامَة نِيَّة [ga:lha bsala:mat niyya] He said it in good faith. • **2.** well-being, welfare – سَلامتَك. ماكُو شِي [sala:mtak. ma:ku ši] Thank you, I'm all right. • **3.** safety, security – سَلامَة العِراق تِتوَقَّف عَلَى قُوَّة جَيشَه [sala:mat ʔilʕira:q titwaqqaf ʕala quwwat ǰayšah] The safety of the Iraq depends on the strength of its army. الحَمدُ لله عالسَّلامَة [ʔilћamdu lilla:h ʕassala:ma] Thank goodness you're all right! (said to a returning traveler). مَعَ السَّلامَة [maʕa ʔissala:ma] Goodbye (a standard farewell).

إسلام [ʔisla:m] *n:* • **1.** the religion of Islam, the Moslem religion • **2.** followers of Islam, Moslems

تَسلِيم [tasli:m] *n:* • **1.** handing over, delivery, submission

سَلامات [sala:ma:t] *n:* • **1.** Greetings! – سَلامات، سَلامات! بُقَى فِكِرنا عِندَك [sala:ma:t, sala:ma:t! buqa: fikirna ʕindak] Hello there! We've been thinking about you. إلَى هَسَّة سَلامات، لَكِن بَعَد عِندِي إمتِحانَين [ʔila hassa sala:ma:t, la:kin baʕad ʕindi ʔimtiћa:nayn] I'm okay till now, but I've still got two exams.

إستِلام [ʔistila:m] *n:* • **1.** reception

إستِسلام [ʔistisla:m] *n:* • **1.** resignation • **2.** surrender

سِلمِي [silmi] *adj:* • **1.** peaceful – مُظاهَرَة سِلمِيَّة [muḍa:hara silmiyya] a peaceful demonstration. • **2.** pacifist

سَلِيم [sali:m] *adj:* • **1.** safe, secure • **2.** unimpaired, undamaged, unhurt, sound, intact – صاغ سَلِيم

[ṣaːɣ saliːm] safe and sound, in perfect condition. طِلَع مِن المَركَب صاغ سَلِيم [ṭilaʕ min ʔilmarkab ṣaːɣ saliːm] He got off the boat safe and sound. إستِلَمت الرّاديُو صاغ سَلِيم [ʔistilamt ʔirraːdyu ṣaːɣ saliːm] I received the radio in perfect condition. • **3.** faultless, flawless – ذَوقَه سَلِيم [ðawqah saliːm] He has good taste. قَلبَه سَلِيم [galbah saliːm] He is good-natured. صَدِيقِي سَلِيم النِّيَّة [ṣadiːqi saliːm ʔinniyya] My friend is sincere.

سالِم [saːlim] *adj:* • **1.** safe, secure • **2.** free – سالِم مِن الأمراض المُعدِيَة [saːlim min ʔilʔamraːð̣ ʔilmuʕdiya] He's free from contagious diseases. • **3.** unblemished, flawless, undamaged, intact

مُسلِم [muslim] *adj:* مُسلِمِين [muslimiːn] *pl:* • **1.** Moslem

مُسالِم [musaːlim] *adj:* • **1.** peaceable, peaceful, peace-loving – شَعَب مُسالِم [šaʕab musaːlim] a peace-loving people.

مُستَلِم [mustalim] *adj:* • **1.** receiver

إسلامِي [ʔislaːmi] *adj:* • **1.** Islamic, Moslem – الدِّين الإسلامِي [ʔiddiːn ʔilʔislaːmi] The Moslem Religion. المَركَز الإسلامِي [ʔilmarkaz ʔilʔislaːmi] The Islamic Center.

أسلَم [ʔaslam] *comparative adjective:* • **1.** more or most safe, sound, intact

سِلمِياً [silmiyyan] *adverbial:* • **1.** peacefully

س ل ن د ر

سِلِندَر [silindar] *n:* سِلِندَرات [silindaraːt] *pl:* • **1.** cylinder (of a motor)

س ل ن ق

سلِنق [sling] *n:* سلِنقات [slingaːt] *pl:* • **1.** crane • **2.** sling hoist • **3.** block-and-tackle

س ل و

سَلَّى [sallaː] *v:* • **1.** to distract, divert, amuse, entertain – ما يُعرُف أحَّد هنا. هَمّ زين عِندَه تَلَفِزيَون يسَلِّيه [maː yuʕruf ʔaħħad hna. hamm zayn ʕindah talafizyuːn ysalliːh] He doesn't know anyone here. It's good that he has a television to amuse him.

تسَلَّى [tsallaː] *v:* • **1.** to derive amusement, entertainment, to amuse oneself – ما دام ما عِندَك شُغُل، ليش ما تِتعَلَّم فَدّ لِعبَة تِتسَلَّى بيها؟ [maː daːm maː ʕindak šuɣul, liːš maː titʕallam fadd liʕba titsallaː biːha?] Since you don't have work, why don't you learn some game to keep you amused?

سَلوَى [salwa] *n:* • **1.** consolation

تَسلِيَة [tasliya] *n:* تَسلِيات [tasliyaːt] *pl:* • **1.** amusement, distraction, diversion, entertainment, pastime

سَلوان [salwaːn] *n:* • **1.** consolation

مُسَلِّي [musalli] *adj:* • **1.** amusing

س م ب

سُمبَة [sumba] *n:* سُمبات [sumbaːt] *pl:* • **1.** chisel

س م ب د

سُمبادَة، وَرَق سُمبادَة، كاغَد سُمبادَة [sumbaːda, waraq sumbaːda, kaːɣad sumbaːda] *n:* • **1.** sandpaper

س م ب ل

سُمبَيلَة [sumbayla, sumbiːla] *n:* • **1.** leap frog

س م ح

سِمَح [simaħ] *v:* • **1.** to permit, allow, grant permission – إذا ما عِندَك بِطاقَة، ما يِسمَحُولَك تُدخُل [ʔiða maː ʕindak biṭaːqa, maː yismaħuːlak tudxul] If you don't have a ticket, they won't allow you to enter. مِنُو سِمَحلَك تِطلَع؟ [minu simaħlak titlaʕ?] Who let you go out? لا سَمَح الله [laː samaħ ʔallah] God forbid! إسمَحلِي دَقِيقَة. هَسَّة أقُلَّك [ʔismaħli daqiːqa. hassa ʔagullak] Excuse me a minute. I'll tell you right away. إسمَحلِي أشرَحلَك المَوضُوع [ʔismaħli ʔašraħlak ʔilmawð̣uːʕ] Permit me to explain the matter to you.

سامَح [saːmaħ] *v:* • **1.** to forgive – إشتِرِي مِن هَالبَقّال. يسامحَك بِالسِّعِر هوايَة [ʔištiri min halbaggaːl. ysaːmħak bissiʕir hwaːya] Buy from that grocer. He gives you very good prices. سامَحنِي دِينار بِالسِّعِر [saːmaħni dinaːr bissiʕir] He went down a dinar for me on the price. راح أسامحَك هَالمَرَّة [raːħ ʔasaːmħak halmarra] I'll forgive you this time. • **2.** to be indulgent, tolerant, generous

تسامَح [tsaːmaħ] *v:* • **1.** to be tolerant, forbearing, to show gentleness – تسامَح وِيّاه. هاي أوَّل مَرَّة يِغلَط [tsaːmaħ wiyyaːh. haːy ʔawwal marra yiɣlaṭ] Be tolerant with him. This is the first time he has done wrong. يِتسامَح هوايَة بمُعامَلتَه لِلمُوَظَّفِين [yitsaːmaħ hwaːya bmuʕaːmaltah lilmuwað̣ð̣afiːn] He is very tolerant in his dealings with the employees.

إنسِمَح [ʔinsimaħ] *v:* • **1.** to be allowed

سَماح [samaːħ] *n:* • **1.** permission, forbearance, tolerance, forgiveness

تَسامُح [tasaːmuħ] *n:* • **1.** tolerance, leniency, indulgence, forbearance

سَماحَة: سَماحَة ال- [samaːħa, samaːħat ʔil-] *n:* • **1.** His Eminence, the... (title usually used for religious dignitaries) • **2.** title usually used for religious dignitaries

سَمِح [samiħ] *adj:* • **1.** generous, magnanimous, liberal, kind – قَصّابنا سَمِح بِالسِّعِر [gaṣṣaːbna samiħ bissiʕir] Our butcher is generous about prices.

مَسمُوح [masmuːħ] *adj:* • **1.** permitted, permissible – ما مَسمُوح تِسبَحُون هنا [maː masmuːħ tisbaħuːn hna] You are not permitted to swim here.

متسامِح [mitsaːmiħ] *adj:* • **1.** tolerant, indulgent

س م د

سَمَّد [sammad] *v:* • **1.** to fertilize, spread manure on – راح أسَمِّد الحَدِيقَة بِالرَّبِيع [raːħ ʔasammid ʔilħadiːqa birrabiːʕ] I'm going to fertilize the garden in the spring.

س

سَماد [sama:d] *n:* أسمِدَة [ʔasmida] *pl:* • **1.** dung, manure • **2.** fertilizer as in سَماد كِيمياوِي [sama:d kimya:wi] chemical fertilizer

تَسمِيد [tasmi:d] *n:* • **1.** fertilizing, manuring

س م ر

سامَر [sa:mar] *v:* • **1.** to spend the night in a pleasent conversation, to chat

تسامَر [tsa:mar] *v:* • **1.** to spend the night in a pleasent conversation, to chat

اِسمَرّ [ʔismarr] *v:* • **1.** to turn brown, to tan – قِعدَت بِالشَّمِس حَتَّى يِسمَرّ جِلِدها [giʕdat biššamis ħatta yismarr ǰilidha] She sat in the sun so her skin would tan.

سَمَر [samar] *n:* • **1.** to chat, talk (generally) • **2.** to talk, chat in the evening or at night

سَمار [sama:r] *n:* • **1.** brownness, brown or tan coloration

مُسامَرَة [musa:mara] *n:* مُسامَرات [musa:mara:t] *pl:* • **1.** program of social entertainment, show • **2.** nightly or evening chat • **3.** conversation, chat, talk • **4.** conversation, chat, talk

أسمَر [ʔasmar] *adj:* سُمُر [sumur] *pl:* سَمرَة [samra] *feminine:* • **1.** brown, brown-skinned – مَرتَه شَقرَة لَكِن بِنتَه سَمرَة [martah šagra la:kin bintah samra] His wife is blonde but his daughter is brunette.

س م س م

سِمسِم [simsim] *n:* • **1.** sesame

س م ط

سُمَط [sumaṭ] *v:* • **1.** to scald – إذا ما تُسمُط المواعِين بمَيّ حارّ، ما يرُوح الدِّهِن [ʔiða ma: tusmuṭ ʔilmwa:ʕi:n bmayy ħa:rr, ma: yru:ħ ʔiddihin] If you don't scald the dishes in hot water, the grease won't come off. الشاي حارّ يِسمُط [ʔičča:y ħa:rr yiṣmuṭ] The tea is scalding hot.

سَمُط [samuṭ] *n:* • **1.** scalding, burning

سِمِيط [simi:ṭ] *n:* • **1.** (coll.) a type of hard bread, similar to bagels

سُماط [suma:ṭ] *n:* سُماطات [suma:ṭa:t] *pl:* • **1.** cloth on which food is served • **2.** spread, display of food – السُّماط كان من هنا لِكَعب الغُرفَة [ʔissuma:ṭ ča:n min hina: lčaʕb ʔilɣurfa] Food was set out from here to the end of the room.

سِمِيطَة [simi:ṭa] *n:* سِمِيطات [simi:ṭa:t] *pl:* • **1.** a type of hard bread similar to bagels

سُمّاطَة [summa:ṭa] *n:* سُمّاطات [summa:ṭa:t] *pl:* • **1.** pot holder, hot pad

س م ع

سِمَع [simaʕ] *v:* • **1.** to hear – سِمَعنِي أَحكِي بالنَّوم [simaʕni ʔaħči binnawm] He heard me talking in my sleep. سِمَعت الأَخبار؟ [simaʕt ʔilʔaxba:r?] Did you hear the news? ما سِمَعِت مِنهُم إلَى هَسَّة؟ [ma: simaʕit minhum ʔila hassa?] Didn't you hear from them yet? • **2.** to listen, pay attention, take heed – ما يِسمَع كَلام أَحَّد [ma: yismaʕ kala:m ʔaħħad] He won't listen to anybody. إبنَك يِسمَع كَلام [ʔibnak yismaʕ kala:m] Your son minds what he's told. ظَلَّت تِنقُر براس رَجِلها حَتَّى سِمَع كَلامها [ðallat tingur bra:s rajilha ħatta simaʕ kala:mha] She kept nagging her husband until he did what she wanted. إسمَع! ما أَرِيدَك تِجِي هنا [ʔismaʕ! ma: ʔari:dak tiǰi hna] Listen! I don't want you to come here!

سَمَّع [sammaʕ] *v:* • **1.** to make hear, cause to hear – حِكاها بصَوت عالِي حَتَّى يِسَمِّعنِي [ħiča:ha bṣawt ʕa:li ħatta yisammiʕni] He said it in a loud voice in order to make me hear him. دَيسَمِّعنِي حَكِي عالسَّيّارَة. يِبَيِّن ما راضِي عَنها [daysammiʕni ħači ʕassayya:ra. yibayyin ma: ra:ði ʕanha] He's hinting about the car. It seems he's dissatisfied with it.

تسَمَّع [tsammaʕ] *v:* • **1.** to listen in, eavesdrop – يِفتَرّ عَلَى كُلّ الشُّعَب يِتسَمَّع أَخبار [yiftarr ʕala kull ʔiššuʕab yitsammaʕ ʔaxba:r] He goes around to all the sections listening in on what is new.

اِنسِمَع [ʔinsimaʕ] *v:* • **1.** to be heard – إحكِي حيل. حِسَّك ما دَينسِمِع [ʔiħči ħi:l. ħissak ma: dayinsimiʕ] Speak louder. Your voice can't be heard.

اِستِمَع [ʔistimaʕ] *v:* • **1.** to listen closely, lend one's ear, give ear – راح نِستِمِع الخِطابَه وَنُعرُف شدَيصِير [ra:ħ nistimiʕ lxiṭa:bah wnuʕruf šdayṣi:r] We're going to listen closely to his speech and find out what is going on. سَمعَه ثِقِيل [samʕah θigi:l] He's hard of hearing.

سَمِع [samiʕ] *n:* • **1.** hearing

سُمعَة [sumʕa] *n:* • **1.** reputation, standing, name – سُمُعتَه رَدِيئَة [sumuʕtah radi:ʔa] His reputation is bad.

سَماع [sama:ʕ] *n:* • **1.** hearing, listening

سامِع [sa:miʕ] *n:* • **1.** hearer, listener • **2.** audient, auditor

مَسمَع [masmaʕ] *n:* • **1.** hearing distance, earshot

سِمّاعَة [simma:ʕa] *n:* سِمّاعات [simma:ʕa:t] *pl:* • **1.** earphone, earphones, headset • **2.** hearing aid • **3.** (telephone) receiver • **4.** stethoscope

مُستَمِع [mustamiʕ] *n:* مُستَمِعِين [mustamiʕi:n] *pl:* • **1.** hearer, listener • **2.** auditor (in a class)

اِستِماع [ʔistima:ʕ] *n:* • **1.** listening

سَماعِيّات [sama:ʕiyya:t] *n:* • **1.** acoustics

سَمعِي [samʕi] *adj:* • **1.** auditory, auditive, acoustic, acoustical

مَسمُوع [masmu:ʕ] *adj:* • **1.** audible, perceptible – كِلِمتَه مَسمُوعَة. شما يرِيد يِصِير [čilimtah masmu:ʕa. šma yri:d yiṣi:r] His word is law. Whatever he wants is done.

سَمعان [samʕa:n] *adj:* • **1.** heard

س م ق

سُمّاق [summa:g] *n:* • **1.** sumac (used as seasoning for food)

س م ك

سِمَك [simač] *n:* • **1.** (coll.) fish – دَيِحكِي عَن السِّمَك بِالمَيّ [dayihči ʕan ʔissimač bilmayy] He's counting his chickens before they hatch.
سِمكَة [simča] *n:* سِمكات [simča:t] *pl:* • **1.** a fish
سَمّاك [samma:č] *n:* سَمّاكَة [samma:ča] *pl:* • **1.** fishmonger
سمِيك [smi:k] *adj:* • **1.** thick

س م ك ر

سَمكَر [samkar] *v:* • **1.** to repair
سَمكَري [samkari] *n:* • **1.** plumber
سَمكَرَة [samkara] *n:* • **1.** plumbing

س م م

سَمّ [samm] *v:* • **1.** to poison – سَمّوه بِالسِّجِن وَمات [sammuawh bissijin wma:t] They poisoned him in prison and he died.
سَمَّم [sammam] *v:* • **1.** to poison, put poison in – خَلّي نسَمِّم الخُبُز حَتَّى الجِّريدِيَّة ياكلُوه وَيمُوتُون [xalli: nsammim ʔilxubuz ħatta ʔijjiri:diyya ya:klu:h wymu:tu:n] Let's poison the bread so the mice will eat it and die.
تسَمَّم [tsammam] *v:* • **1.** to be poisoned – أكَل شوَيَّة جِبِن وَتسَمَّم [ʔakal šwayya jibin wtsammam] He ate a little cheese and was poisoned.
سِمّ، سَمّ [simm, samm] *n:* سمُوم [sumu:m] *pl:* • **1.** poison, toxin • **2.** venom
تَسَمُّم [tasammum] *n:* • **1.** poisoning
مَسامَة [masa:ma] *n:* مَسامات، مَسام [masa:ma:t, masa:m] *pl:* • **1.** pore (of the skin)
سامّ [sa:mm] *adj:* • **1.** poisonous, toxic • **2.** venomous
مُسِمّ [musimm] *adj:* • **1.** poisonous
سمُوم، هَوا سمُوم [sumu:m, hawa: sumu:m] *adj:* • **1.** a hot, dry wind off the desert
مَسمُوم [masmu:m] *adj:* • **1.** poisoned, containing poison, poisonous – دِير بالَك مِنَّه. هُوَّ فَدّ واحِد مَسمُوم [di:r ba:lak minnah. huwwa fadd wa:ħid masmu:m] Watch out for him. He's poison.
مِتسَمِّم [mitsammim] *adj:* • **1.** poisoned

س م ن

سِمَن [siman] *v:* • **1.** to become fat, plump, stout, corpulent, obese, to gain weight – شقَدّ ما آكُل، ما دَأسمَن [šgadd ma: ʔa:kul, ma: daʔasman] No matter how much I eat, I don't gain weight.
سَمَّن [samman] *v:* • **1.** to fatten, make fat – دَينطِي الدِّجاج مالَه فَدّ نُوع مِن الأكِل يسَمِّنَه [dayinṭi ʔiddija:j ma:lah fadd nu:ʕ min ʔilʔakil ysamminah] He's giving his chickens some kind of food to make them fat.
سِمِن [simin] *n:* • **1.** fatness, corpulence, fleshiness • **2.** obesity • **3.** tallow, fat
سِمنَة [simna] *n:* • **1.** fatness, corpulence, fleshiness • **2.** obesity
سمِين [simi:n] *adj:* • **1.** fat, stout, corpulent, plump – إجا عَلَيك فَدّ واحِد سمِين وقصَيِّر [ʔija ʕali:k fadd wa:ħid simi:n wiqṣayyir] A short, fat guy came to see you. • **2.** obese • **3.** fatty, rich – أكِل سمِين [ʔakil simi:n] rich food.
سَمنان [samna:n] *adj:* • **1.** sleek, healthy – يبيِن عَلِيك سَمنان مِن هَوا لُبنان [ybayyin ʕali:k samna:n min hawa lubna:n] You look sleek from the Lebanese climate. سَمنان مِن كُثرَة الأكِل وَالرّاحَة [samna:n min kuθrat ʔilʔakil wirra:ħa] You've gained weight from eating a lot and doing nothing.
أسمَن [ʔasman] *comparative adjective:* • **1.** more or most corpulent

س م ن ت

سمِنت، شمِنتُو، شبِنتُو [smint, šmintu, šbintu] *n:* • **1.** cement

س م و [1]

سِما [sima] *n:* سَماوات [sama:wa:t] *pl:* • **1.** sky – لخاطِر السَّماوات، جُوز [lxa:ṭir ʔissama:wa:t, ju:z] For Heavens' sakes, cut it out!
سُمُو، صاحِب السُمُو [sumu, ṣa:ħib ʔissumu] *n:* • **1.** His Royal Highness (title of a prince)
سِمايَة [sima:ya] *n:* سِمايات [sima:ya:t] *pl:* • **1.** skylight, roof window
سامِي [sa:mi] *adj:* • **1.** lofty, exalted, eminent, sublime, august – أشكُر عَواطفَك السّامِيَة [ʔaškur ʕawa:ṭfak ʔissa:miya] I thank you for your noble sentiments.
سَماوِي [sama:wi] *adj:* • **1.** heavenly, celestial • **2.** sky-blue, azure – نَفنُوف سَماوِي [nafnu:f sama:wi] a sky-blue dress.
سَمائِي [sama:ʔi, sma:ʔi] *adj:* • **1.** baby blue

س م و [2]

سامِي [sa:mi] *adj:* • **1.** Semitic – العُنصُر السّامِي [ʔilʕunṣur ʔissa:mi] the Semitic race, Semitic stock. • **2.** a Semite

س م و ر

سَماوَر [sama:war] *n:* سَماوَرات [sama:wara:t] *pl:* • **1.** samovar (A metal urn with a spigot to boil water)

س م ي

See also: ء س م
سَمَّى [samma:] *v:* • **1.** to name, designate, call – شِتسَمِّي هَالشّي؟ [šitsammi hašši?] What do you call this thing? • **2.** to call, name, give a name to – سَمَّى إبنَه بإسِم أبُوه [samma: ʔibnah bʔisim ʔabu:h] He gave his son his father's name. • **3.** to say – "بِسِم الله الرَّحمَن الرَّحِيم". سَمِّي قَبُل ما تِنزِل لِلسِّرداب

["b?isimillah ?irrahma:n ?irrahi:m". sammi gabul ma: tinzil lissirda:b] Mention God's name before you go down into the basement. سَمِّي قَبُل ما تاكُل [sammi gabul ma: ta:kul] Say grace before you eat.

تسَمَّى [tsamma:] *v:* • **1.** to be named, called – تسَمَّى بإسِم جِدَّه [tsamma: b?isim ǰiddah] He is named after his grandfather. شتِعتقِد هَذا لازم يِتسَمَّى؟ [štiʕtiqid ha:ða la:zim yitsamma:?] What do you think this should be called?

تَسمِيَة [tasmiya] *n:* • **1.** naming, designation, appellation

مُسَمَّى [musamma:] *adj:* مُسَمَّيات [musammaya:t] *pl:* • **1.** named, called, by name of • **2.** pl. مُسَمَّيات name, designation, appellation

س ن ب ل

سُنبُلَة [sunbula, sumbula] *n:* سَنابِل [sana:bil] *pl:* • **1.** spike, ear (of grain)

س ن ت

سَنت [sant] *n:* • **1.** cent

س ن ت م

سَنتِيم [santi:m] *n:* سَنتِيمات [santi:ma:t] *pl:* • **1.** centime, one cent

س ن ت م ت ر

سَنتِمتِر [santimitir] *n:* سَنتِمِترات [santimitira:t] *pl:* • **1.** centimeter

س ن ج ب

سِنجاب [sinǰa:b] *n:* سناجِيب، سَناجِب [sna:ǰi:b, sana:ǰib] *pl:* • **1.** squirrel

س ن ح

سِنَح [sinah] *v:* • **1.** to present itself, offer itself – إذا تِسنَحلِي الفُرصَة، أزُورَك [?iða tisnahli ?ilfurṣa, ?azu:rak] If the opportunity presents itself to me. I'll visit you. • **2.** to afford

س ن د 1

سِنَد [sinad] *v:* • **1.** to prop up, support, provide support for – إسنِد السَّبُّورَة بِهَالعَمُود [?isnid ?issabbu:ra bhalʕamu:d] Prop up the blackboard with this pole. دَيحكِي بنِفس لِأَنّ أكُو واحِد يسِندَه [dayihči bnifas li?ann ?aku wa:hid ysindah] He speaks boldly because there's somebody backing him up.

سانَد [sa:nad] *v:* • **1.** to support, back, assist, help – سانَدهُم بِحَملَتهُم الانتِخابِيَّة [sa:nadhum bhamlathum ?il?intixa:biyya] He supported them in their election campaign.

أسنَد [?asnad] *v:* • **1.** to incriminate, charge to – أسنِدَوا التُّهمَة إلَه [?asnidaw ?ittuhma ?ilah] They charged the guilt to him. • **2.** with لـ to entrust to, vest in – أسنِدَوه إلَى مَنصِب نائِب وَزِير [?asnidawh ?ila manṣib na:?ib wazi:r] They entrusted him with the position of deputy minister.

انسِنَد [?insinad] *v:* • **1.** to be braced • **2.** to be supported

اِستِنَد [?istinad] *v:* • **1.** to rest one's weight, support one's weight – ما أقدَر أكتِب إذا ما أستِنِد عَلَى فَدّ شِي ما يِتحَرَّك [ma: ?agdar ?aktib ?iða ma: ?astinid ʕala fadd ši ma: yitharrak] I can't write if I don't support myself on something that won't move. • **2.** to be supported, based, founded – هَالمَقال يِستِنِد عَلَى إحصاءات مَوثُوق بيها [halmaqa:l yistinid ʕala ?ihṣa:?a:t mawθu:q bi:ha] This article is based on trustworthy statistics. • **3.** with عَلَى to use as a basis, rest one's case on, have as evidence – لازِم تِستِنِد عَلَى فَدّ شِي قَبُل ما تِتهِمَه [la:zim tistinid ʕala fadd ši gabul ma: tithmah] You must have something for a basis before you accuse him.

سَنَد [sanad] *n:* سَنَدات [sanada:t] *pl:* • **1.** something which can be relied upon, support, backing • **2.** document, deed, legal instrument • **3.** debenture, promissory note – سَنَدات القَرض [sanada:t ?ilqarð̣] government bonds.

مَسنَد [masnad] *n:* مَسانِد [masa:nid] *pl:* • **1.** support, prop, stay • **2.** back, arm-rest (of a chair)

إسناد [?isna:d] *n:* • **1.** support

مُستَنَد [mustanad] *n:* • **1.** credentials • **2.** record

اِستِناد [?istina:d] *n:* • **1.** dependence,depending, leaning, on the basis (of), on the strength (of)

مُسانَدَة [musa:nada] *n:* • **1.** support

مَسنُود [masnu:d] *adj:* • **1.** propped (up) • **2.** supported

س ن د 2

سِندِي [sindi] *n:* • **1.** (coll.) grapefruit(s)

السِند [?issind] *n:* • **1.** Sind, a province of West Pakistan – بَنات السِّند وَالهِند [bana:t ?issind w?ilhind] swallows (?).

سِندِيَّة [sindiyya] *n:* سِندِيّات [sindiyya:t] *pl:* • **1.** grapefruit

س ن د 3

سِندان [sinda:n] *n:* سِنادِين [sina:di:n] *pl:* • **1.** anvil

سِندانَة [sinda:na] *n:* سِندانات، سِنادِين [sinda:na:t, sina:di:n] *pl:* • 1. flower pot

س ن د و ي ج

سَندَوِيش [sandawi:ǰ] *n:* سَندَوِيشات [sandawiyǰa:t] *pl:* • **1.** sandwich

س ن ط ر

سَنطُور [santu:r] *n:* سَناطِير [sana:ṭi:r] *pl:* • **1.** dulcimer – طَيّارَة أمّ السَّناطِير [ṭiyya:ra ?umm ?issana:ṭi:r] kite equipped with a whistling noise maker.

س ن ك

سِنَك [sinak] *n:* • **1.** club (suit in cards)

س ن ك ن

سَنكِين [sanki:n, sangi:n] *adj:* • **1.** strong, dark – سَوِّي الشاي مالِي سَنقِين [sawwi: ʔičča:y ma:li sangi:n] Make my tea strong.

س ن م

سَنام [sana:m] *n:* سَنامات [sana:ma:t] *pl:* • **1.** hump (of a camel)

س ن ن

سَنّ [sann] *v:* • **1.** to sharpen, whet, hone – دَيسِنّ الخَنجَر [daysinn ʔilxanǰar] He is sharpening the dagger. • **2.** to enact, establish, pass – أكُو اِحتِمال يسِنُّون قانُون يمنَعُون بِيه القمار [ʔaku ʔiħtima:l ysinnu:n qa:nu:n yimnaʕu:n bi:h ʔilqma:r] They probably will pass a law prohibiting gambling.

سِنّ [sinn] *n:* أسنان [ʔasna:n] *pl:* • **1.** tooth – طَبِيب الأسنان [ṭabi:b ʔilʔasna:n] dentist. • **2.** cog, tooth (of a gear wheel) • **3.** bedrock • **4.** age – ما قِبلَوه بِالجُّندِيَّة لِصُغُر سِنَّه [ma: qiblawh biǰǰundiyya liṣuɣur sinnah] They didn't accept him in the army because he was underage.

سَنّ [sann] *n:* • **1.** sharpening, honing, whetting • **2.** enacting, establishment, passing

سُنَّة [sunna] *n:* • **1.** customary practice, usage – سُنَّة النَّبِي [sunnat ʔinnabi] the actions and sayings of Mohammed, later established as legally binding.

سُنّي [sunni] *adj:* سُنَّة، سُنِّيِّين [sunna, sunniyyi:n] *pl:* • **1.** Sunni, Sunnite, belonging to the orthodox sect of Islam • **2.** a Sunni, a Sunnite

مَسَنّ [masann] *adj:* مَسَنّات [masanna:t] *pl:* • **1.** whetstone, grindstone

مُسِنّ [musinn] *adj:* • **1.** old, aged, advanced in years – أبُوها رِجّال مُسِنّ وَما أدرِي أيّ ساعَة يمُوت [ʔabu:ha rijja:l musinn wama: ʔadri ʔayy sa:ʕa ymu:t] Her father is an old man and he's likely to die at any time.

مسَنَّن [msannan] *adj:* • **1.** toothed, notched, jagged

س ن و

سَنَة [sana] *n:* سَنَوات، سِنِين [sanawa:t, sini:n] *pl:* • **1.** year – سَنَة هِجرِيَّة [sana hiǰriyya] year of the Moslem calendar, A. H. سَنَة مِيلادِيَّة [sana mi:la:diyya] year of the Christian calendar, A. D.

سَنَوِيَّة [sanawiyya] *n:* • **1.** licence

سَنَوِي [sanawi] *adj:* • **1.** yearly, annual – وارِد سَنَوِي [wa:rid sanawi] yearly income.

سَنَوِيّاً [sanawiyyan] *adverbial:* • **1.** annually, each year, per year

س ه ر

سِهَر [sihar] *v:* • **1.** to stay awake, go without sleep, stay up at night – راح أنام هَسَّة حَتَّى أقدَر أسهَر بالليل [ra:ħ ʔana:m hassa ħatta ʔagdar ʔashar billayl] I'm going to sleep now so I can stay awake tonight. سِهَرنا البارحَة لِسّاعَة ثلاثَة [siharna ʔilba:rħa lissa:ʕa tla:θa] We stayed up last night until three o'clock. عيُونَه تِلفَت مِن قَدّ ما يِسهَر [ʕyu:nah tilfat min gadd ma: yishar] His eyes were ruined from his staying awake so much.

ساهَر [sa:har] *v:* • **1.** same as سِهَر: to stay awake, go without sleep, stay up at night – أيّام الامتِحان أكثَر الطُّلّاب يسَاهرُون [ʔayya:m ʔilʔimtiħa:n ʔakθar ʔiṭṭulla:b ysa:hru:n] Most of the students stay up late during exam time.

سَهَر [sahar] *n:* • **1.** staying up at night • **2.** wakefulness

سَهرَة [sahra] *n:* سَهرات [sahra:t] *pl:* • **1.** soiree, evening gathering • **2.** entertainment

سَهران [sahra:n] *adj:* • **1.** sleepless

س ه ل

سِهَل [sihal] *v:* • **1.** to become easy, facile, convenient – مِن اِشتِغَل وِيّانا، سِهلَت المَسألَة [min ʔištiɣal wiyya:na, sihlat ʔilmasʔala] When he worked with us, the problem became easier. • **2.** to purge, relieve of constipation – اِشتِرَيت دُوا مِن الصَيدَلِيَّة يِسهِل البَطِن [ʔištirayt duwa: min ʔiṣṣaydaliyya yishil ʔilbaṭin] I bought some medicine from the pharmacy which purges the bowels. • **3.** to move, be relieved, become loose – سِهلَت بَطنَه مَرّتَين اليُوم [sihlat baṭnah marrtayn ʔilyu:m] He had two bowel movements today.

سَهَّل [sahhal] *v:* • **1.** to make easier, to ease, facilitate – المُعَلِّم سَهَّل الأسئِلَة هالمَرَّة [ʔilmuʕallim sahhal ʔilʔasʔila halmarra] The teacher made the questions easy this time. هَالمَكِينَة تسَهِّل الشُّغُل هوايَة [halmaki:na tsahhil ʔiššuɣul hwa:ya] This machine makes the work a great deal easier. • **2.** to give a laxative – صار يومَين بَطن الوَلَد ما طِلعَت. لازِم نسَهِّلَه [ṣa:r yu:mayn baṭn ʔilwalad ma: ṭilʕat. la:zim nsahhlah] The boy has been constipated two days. We must give him a laxative.

تسَهَّل [tsahhal] *v:* • **1.** to be or become easy

تساهَل [tsa:hal] *v:* • **1.** to be indulgent, forbearing, lenient, tolerant, obliging – المُعَلِّم دَيتساهَل وِيّانا [ʔilmuʕallim dayitsa:hal wiyya:na] The teacher is being lenient with us. تساهَلُوا وِيّايا وَباعولِي السَّيّارَة بِالدَّين [tsa:hlaw wiyya:ya wba:ʕu:li ʔissayya:ra biddayn] They were obliging to me and sold me the car on credit.

اِستَسهَل [ʔistashal] *v:* • **1.** to consider easy, to deem easy – لا تِستَسهِل القَضِيَّة. راح تِطلَع بِيها تَعقِيدات [la: tistashil ʔilqaðiyya. ra:ħ titlaʕ bi:ha taʕqi:da:t] Don't consider the matter easy. There will be some complications to it.

س

سَهَل [sahal] *n:* سُهُول [suhu:l] *pl:* • **1.** plain, level ground
مُسهِل، مُسَهِّل [mushil, musahhil] *n:* مُسهِلات، مُسَهِّلات [mushila:t, musahhila:t] *pl:* • **1.** purgative, laxative
سُهُولَة [suhu:la] *n:* • **1.** easiness, facility, convenience – ماكو شِي بِسُهُولَة هالشُّغُل [ma:ku ši bsuhu:lat haššuɣul] There is nothing as easy as this work. تعَلَّم السِّياقَة بِسُهُولَة [tʕallam ʔissiya:qa bsuhu:la] He learned to drive easily.
إسهال [ʔisha:l] *n:* • **1.** diarrhea
تَساهِيل [tasa:hi:l] *n:* • **1.** pl. only facilities
تَسهِيلات [tashi:la:t] *n:* • **1.** pl. only facilitations
سَهِل [sahil] *adj:* • **1.** easy, facile, convenient – سَهلَة! أَيّ نُوع مِن الجِكايِر ترِيدُون؟ [sahla! ʔayy nu:ʕ min ʔijjiga:yir tri:du:n?] Sure, that's easy! What kind of cigarettes do you want?
مِتساهِل [mitsa:hil] *adj:* • **1.** easy-going • **2.** indulgent, tolerant, lenient, forbearing
أَسهَل [ʔashal] *comparative adjective:* • **1.** more or most facile, convenient

س ه م

ساهَم [sa:ham] *v:* • **1.** to have a share, to participate, share, take part (في in) – لازِم الكُلّ يساهمُون بِجَمع التَّبَرُّعات [la:zim ʔilkull ysa:hmu:n bǰamʕ ʔittabarruʕa:t] All must participate in collecting donations. هُوَّ ساهَم بِنُصّ راسمال الشَّرِكَة [huwwa sa:ham bnuṣṣ ra:sma:l ʔiššarika] He contributed half the capital of the company.
سَهَم [saham] *n:* أَسهُم [ʔashum] *pl:* • **1.** share, portion, lot • **2.** share (of stock) • **3.** dart • **4.** pl. سِهام arrow
مُساهِم [musa:him] *n:* مُساهِمِين [musa:himi:n] *pl:* • **1.** shareholder, stockholder
مُساهَمَة [musa:hama] *n:* • **1.** participation, taking part

س ه و

سِهَى [siha:] *v:* • **1.** to be forgetful, neglectful, inattentive – ما أَدرِي شلُون سِهَيت وَما خابَرتَه [ma: ʔadri šlu:n sihi:t wma xa:bartah] I don't know how I forgot and didn't call him. • **2.** with عَن to forget, neglect, overlook – الجّاهِل دَيلعَب. لا تِسهَى عَنَّه [ʔijja:hil dayilʕab. la: tisha: ʕannah] The kid is playing. Don't forget about him. ما يِسهَى عَن أَيّ شِي بشُغلَه [ma: yisha: ʕan ʔayy ši bšuɣlah] He doesn't neglect anything about his work.
سَهَّى [sahha:] *v:* • **1.** to cause to forget – ظَلّ يِحكِي وَسَهّانِي عَن الأَكِل اللِّي عَالنّار [ðall yiħči wsahha:ni ʕan ʔilʔakil ʔilli ʕanna:r] He kept talking and made me forget the food that was on the fire.
سَهُو [sahw] *n:* • **1.** inattentiveness, inattention, absent-mindedness • **2.** negligence, neglectfulness, forgetfulness • **3.** mistake, oversight
سَهواً [sahwan] *adverbial:* • **1.** inattentively, absent-mindedly, negligently • **2.** inadvertently, by mistake – طُبَعت المَكتُوب عَلَى وَرَق خَفِيف سَهواً [ṭubaʕt ʔilmaktu:b ʕala waraq xafi:f sahwan] I typed the letter on thin paper by mistake.

س ه و ن

ساهُون [sa:hu:n] *n:* • **1.** peanut brittle

س و ء

ساء، أَساء [sa:ʔ, ʔ asa:ʔa] *v:* • **1.** to do evil, do harm شما تسَوِّيلَه زين، لازِم يسِيئلَك [šma: tsawwi:lah zi:n, la:zim ysi:ʔlak] Whatever good you do for him, he always has to do you dirty. أساء فَهمِي [ʔasa:ʔ fahmi] He misunderstood me. أساء الظَّن بِيّا [ʔasa:ʔ ʔiððann biyya] He thought badly of me. لا تسِيِئ الظَّنّ بكُلّ واحِد ما يِتّفِق وِيّاك [la: tsi:ʔ ʔiððann bkull wa:ħid ma: yittifiq wiyya:k] Don't have a low opinion of everyone who doesn't agree with you. الشُّرطَة أَساءَت مُعامَلتَه بِالسِّجِن [ʔiššurṭa ʔasa:ʔat muʕa:maltah bissiǰin] The police mistreated him in prison.
إستاء [ʔista:ʔ] *v:* • **1.** to be or become offended, annoyed, disgusted, indignant, displeased – هُوَّ إستاء مِن هالوَضِع [huwwa ʔista:ʔ min halwaḍiʕ] He got disgusted with that situation.
إنساء [ʔinsa:ʔ] *v:* • **1.** to be abused, to be mistreated, to be treated poorly • **2.** to be ill-treated
سُوء [su:ʔ] *n:* • **1.** evil, ill – سُوء الحَظّ [su:ʔ ʔilħaḍḍ] bad luck, misfortune. لِسُوء الحَظّ [lisu:ʔ ʔilħaḍḍ] unfortunately. سُوء نِيَّة [su:ʔ niyya] evil intent, malice. بِسُوء النِّيَّة [bsu:ʔ ʔinniyya] with evil intent, maliciously. سُوء الفَهم [su:ʔ ʔilfahim] misunderstanding. سُوء هَضُم [su:ʔ haḍum] indigestion.
سَيِّئَة [sayyiʔa] *n:* سَيِّئات [sayyiʔa:t] *pl:* • **1.** misdeed, bad deed
مَساوِئ [masa:wiʔ] *n:* • **1.** pl. only disadvantages
إساءَة [ʔisa:ʔa] *n:* • **1.** offense, misdeed, affront, insult, sin
سَيِّئ [sayyiʔ] *adj:* • **1.** bad, evil, ill, poor • **2.** ill-mannered, ill-tempered – سَيِّئ الحَظّ [sayyiʔ ʔilħaḍḍ] unlucky, unfortunate. سَيِّئ السُّمعَة [sayyiʔ ʔissumʕa] of bad reputation. تَغذِيَة سَيِّئَة [taɣðiya sayyiʔa] malnutrition, poor nourishment.
مُسِيئ [musi:ʔ] *adj:* • **1.** offensive, inappropriate
أَسوَء [ʔaswaʔ] *comparative adjective:* • **1.** worse, worst

س و ت ي ن

سُوتيان [su:tya:n] *n:* سُوتيانات [su:tya:na:t] *pl:* • **1.** brassiere

س و ح

ساحَة [sa:ħa] *n:* ساحات [sa:ħa:t] *pl:* • **1.** open square, courtyard • **2.** open space, park, field – ساحَة رَمِي [sa:ħat ramy] firing range. ساحَة تَنِس [sa:ħat tanis]

tennis court. ساحَة مَدرَسَة [sa:ħat madrasa] school yard. ألعاب السّاحَة [ʔalʕa:b ʔissa:ħa] track and field sports.

س و د

سَوَّد [sawwad] *v:* • **1.** to blacken, make black, darken – الدُّخان سَوَّد كَعب الجِّدِر [ʔidduxxa:n sawwad čaʕb ʔiǰǰidir] The smoke blackened the bottom of the pot. سَوَّد وِجِه [sawwad wiǰih] to show up, expose, make a fool of, shame, discredit, disgrace, dishonor. سَوَّد وِجهي بِهالحكايَة [sawwad wičči bhalħča:ya] He made a fool of me with that remark. سَوَّد الله وِجهَك عَلَى هَالدَقَّة [sawwad ʔallah wiččak ʕala haldagga] May God shame you for this deed.
اِسوَدّ [ʔiswadd] *v:* • **1.** to be or become black, dark – الفُضَّة تِسوَدّ بِالعَجَل [lfuðða tiswadd bilʕaǰal] Silver turns dark quickly. اِسوَدّ وِجهه [ʔiswadd wiččah] He was disgraced. اِسوَدّ وِجهه؛ كُلّهُم عِرفُوه كَذّاب [ʔiswadd wiččah; kullhum ʕirfu:h čaðða:b] He's discredited; everyone knows he is a liar.
سَيِّد [sayyid] *n:* سادَة [sa:da] *pl:* • **1.** lord, master • **2.** (a title used in formal speech, approx.:) Mister – السَّيِّد عَلي [ʔassayyid ʕali] Mr. Ali. • **3.** (a formal title of address) Sir – سَيِّدي، المُلازِم أحمَد يرِيد يشُوفَك [sayyidi, ʔilmula:zim ʔaħmad yiri:d yišu:fak] Sir, Lt. Ahmad wants to see you. • **4.** a descendant of the Prophet, and also, the title used in addressing a sayyid
سَواد [sawa:d] *n:* • **1.** blackness, darkness • **2.** black clothing, mourning, crepe
سَيِّدَة [sayyida] *n:* سَيِّدات [sayyida:t] *pl:* • **1.** lady • **2.** Mrs
سُودان [su:da:n] *n:* • **1.** the Sudan
سَيِّدِيَّة [sayyidiyya] *n:* سَيِّدِيّات [sayyidiyya:t] *pl:* • **1.** (bestowal of the) title of sayyid • **2.** fez with a green band worn by descendants of Mohammed
سِيادَة [siya:da] *n:* • **1.** mastery, rule, dominion, sovereignty – سِيادَة الرَّئِيس [siya:dat ʔirraʔi:s] His Excellency the President.
مِسوَدَّة [miswadda] *n:* مِسوَدّات [miswadda:t] *pl:* • **1.** draft • **2.** rough draft (of a document), galley proof (printing) • **3.** (as *adj:*) blackened
سادَة [sa:da] *adj:* • **1.** (invar.) plain, unicolored, uniform – لُون سادَة [lu:n sa:da] a solid color. أحمَر سادَة [ʔaħmar sa:da] solid red. • **2.** (invar.) plain, unadulterated, straight – قَهوَة سادَة [gahwa sa:da] unsweetened coffee. شاي سادَة [ča:y sa:da] unsweetened tea. عَرَق سادَة [ʕarag sa:da] straight arrack.
أسوَد [ʔaswad] *adj:* سُود [su:d] *pl:* سُودَة [su:da] *feminine:* • **1.** black, dark – عَمَى أسوَد [ʕama: ʔaswad] total blindness. عَمَى أسوَد! مُو كِسَرِت رِجلي [ʕama: ʔaswad! mu: kisarit riǰli] May you be struck blind! You've just about broken my leg!
سَوداء [sawda:ʔ] *adj:* • **1.** black as in السُوق السَوداء black market

سُوداني [su:da:ni] *adj:* • **1.** Sudanese • **2.** (as *n:*) a Sudanese

س و د ن

سَودَن [sawdan] *v:* • **1.** to make crazy, drive insane – سُودَنِّي عَالطَّلَب [su:danni ʕaṭṭalab] He drove me crazy about the request.
تسَودَن [tsawdan] *v:* • **1.** to be made crazy, insane, to go mad – اِنصاب بِمَرَض عَصَبِي وَفُجأَةً تسَودَن [ʔinṣa:b bmarað ʕaṣabi wfuǰʔatan tsawdan] He got a nervous disease and suddenly went crazy.
سوادِين [swa:di:n] *n:* • **1.** frenzied madness, insanity • **2.** insane behavior

س و ر

سَوَّر [sawwar] *v:* • **1.** to enclose, fence in, build a wall or fence around – لازِم تسَوِّر الحَدِيقَة حَتَّى ما تخُشّلها الكِلاب [la:zim tsawwir ʔilħadi:qa ħatta ma: txuššlha ʔiččila:b] You should fence in the garden so the dogs won't get into it.
سُور [su:r] *n:* أسوار [ʔaswa:r] *pl:* • **1.** wall • **2.** fence – الجَّيش سُور الوَطَن [ʔiǰǰayš su:r ʔilwaṭan] The army is the bastion of the nation.
سوار [swa:r] *n:* سوارات [swa:ra:t] *pl:* • **1.** bracelet
سُورَة [su:ra] *n:* سُوَر [suwar] *pl:* • **2.** chapter of the Koran, surate, sura

س و ر ب

سَورَب [sawrab] *v:* • **1.** to see things – عينَك دَتسَورِب [ʕaynak datsawrib] Your eyes are deceiving you. You're seeing things.

س و ر ي [1]

سوارِي [swa:ri] *n:* سواريهات [swa:riyha:t] *pl:* • **1.** horseman, mounted patrolman

س و ر ي [2]

سُوريا [su:rya] *n:* • **1.** Syria
سُورِي [su:ri] *adj:* • **1.** Syrian • **2.** a Syrian

س و س

سَوَّس [sawwas] *v:* • **1.** to rot, decay, cause to decay (esp. the teeth) – الجُكلَيت يسَوِّس السِّنُون [ʔiččukli:t ysawwis ʔissnu:n] Chocolate decays teeth. سِنَّك مسَوِّس؛ لازِم أشلَعَه [sinnak msawwis; la:zim ʔašlaʕah] Your tooth is decayed; I'll have to extract it.
تسَوَّس [tsawwas] *v:* • **1.** pass. of سَوَّس to be decayed, rotten – إذا تاكُل حِلو هوايَة، سنُونَك تِتسَوَّس [ʔiða ta:kul ħilw hwa:ya, snu:nak titsawwas] If you eat sweets a lot, your teeth will decay.
سُوس، عِرق السُّوس [su:s, ʕirg ʔissu:s] *n:* • **1.** licorice
تَسَوُّس [tasawwus] *n:* • **1.** (dental) caries, rottenness
مسَوِّس [msawwis] *adj:* • **1.** decayed

س

مِتسَوِّس [mitsawwis] *adj:* • **1.** decayed

س و س ن

سَوسَن [sawsan] *n:* • **1.** lily of the valley (bot.)
سَوسَنَة [sawsana] *n:* سَوسَن [sawsan] *pl:* • **1.** lily-of-the-valley

س و ع

سوَيعَتي [swayʕati, swiːʕati] *adj:* • **1.** capricious

س و ف

ساف [saːf] *v:* • **1.** to become worn, worn down, worn out – البُرغي ساف. لازم نِستَعمِل غَيرَه [ʔilburɣi saːf. laːzim nistaʕmil ɣayrah] The screw is worn. We should use another one. عِيُونَك سافَت مِن القرايَة [ʕiyuːnak saːfat min ʔiliqraːya] Your eyes are worn out from reading.
سَوَّف [sawwaf] *v:* • **1.** to wear, wear down, wear out – سَوَّفت الكلَج مِن قَدّ ما تبَدِّل [sawwaft ʔilklač min gadd maː tbaddil] You wore out the clutch from shifting so much.
ساف [saːf] *n:* سُوف [suːf] *pl:* • **1.** row, file, rank • **2.** row, course, layer (as of bricks)
مَسافَة [masaːfa] *n:* مَسافات [masaːfaːt] *pl:* • **1.** distance, stretch, interval • **2.** interval, period (of time)

س و ف ت

سُوفياتِي [suːfyaːti] *adj:* • **1.** Soviet

س و ق

ساق [saːq] *v:* • **1.** to drive, operate (a vehicle) – تُعرُف تسُوق لوري؟ [tuʕruf tsuːq luːri?] Can you drive a truck? • **2.** to draft, conscript – ساقوه لِلجُندِيَّة [saːgawh lijjundiyya] They drafted him into the army. • **3.** to force to go – ساقوه لِلمُحاكَمَة [saːgawh lilmuħaːkama] They brought him to trial.
ساق [saːg] *v:* • **1.** to drive, herd (animals) – سُوق الزُّمال لِلبِستان [suːg ʔizzumaːl lilbistaːn] Drive the donkey out to the orchard. ساقها بتِبِنها [saːgha btibinha] He said it without thinking. • **2.** to hit, strike – ساقَه بِجلّاق [saːgah bčillaːq] He gave him a kick. ساقَه ببُوكس وَقَّعَه [saːgah bibuːks waggaʕah] He hit him and knocked him down. ساقه بِتَفلَة بُوجهَه [saːgah btafla bwuččah] He spit in his face.
تسَوَّق [tsawwag] *v:* • **1.** to go shopping – مَرتِي تِتسَوَّق يَومِيّاً [marti titsawwag yawmiyyan] My wife goes shopping every day.
ساق [saːq] *n:* سِيقان [siːqaːn] *pl:* • **1.** shank • **2.** leg
سُوق [suːg] *n:* أسواق [ʔaswaːq] *pl:* • **1.** marketplace, bazaar • **2.** market – هالبِضاعَة ما إلها سُوق [halbiðaːʕa maː ʔilha suːg] There's no market for these goods.
سُوق [suːg] *n:* • **1.** driving, herding (animals)
سايِق [saːyiq] *n:* سُوّاق [suwwaːq] *pl:* • **1.** driver • **2.** chauffeur
تِسواق [tiswaːg] *n:* • **1.** shopping, going to the market – عَلَى مَن التِّسواق اليُوم؟ [ʕala man ʔittiswaːg ʔilyuːm?] Whose turn is it to go to the market today?
مِسواق [miswaːg] *n:* • **1.** shopping, buying things from the market – المِسواق عَلَيّا اليُوم. شتِردُون أشتِري؟ [ʔilmiswaːg ʕalayya ʔilyuːm. štirduːn ʔaštiri?] I do the shopping today. What do you want me to buy? • **2.** things gotten in the market, supplies, groceries – راح نُطبُخ مِن يِجِيب أبُوك المِسواق [raːħ nuṭbux min yiǰiːb ʔabuːk ʔilmiswaːg] We'll start cooking when your father brings the groceries.
سواقَة [swaːga] *n:* • **1.** shopping
تَسوِيق [taswiːq] *n:* • **1.** marketing
سِياقَة [siyaːqa] *n:* • **1.** driving

س و ك

سَوَّك [sawwak] *v:* • **1.** to brush, scrub (the teeth) with a chewed twig – يسَوِّك سنُونَه بَعد الصَّلاة [ysawwik snuːnah baʕd ʔiṣṣalaːt] He brushes his teeth after prayer.
مِسواك [miswaːk] *n:* مساوِيك [msaːwiːk] *pl:* • **1.** frayed twig used for cleaning the teeth

س و ل ف

سُولَف [suːlaf] *v:* • **1.** to reminisce, to chat, carry on idle conversation, talk – ظَلّينا نسُولِف لنُصّ اللّيل [ðallayna nsuːlif lnuṣṣ ʔillayl] We kept on chatting until midnight. إي، سَولِف [ʔi, suːlif] Yes, go ahead and tell me.
سالفَة [saːlfa] *n:* سوالِف [swaːlif] *pl:* • **1.** tale, story, narrative
سالُوفَة [saːluːfa] *n:* سالُوفات، سُوالِيف [saːluːfaːt, suwaːliːf] *pl:* • **1.** tale, story, narrative

س و م

سام [saːm] *v:* • **1.** to quote a price on, to set a price for – هَالبَدلَة بيش سامها عَلِيك الخَيّاط؟ [halbadla biyš saːmha ʕaliːk ʔilxayyaːṭ?] What price did the tailor quote you on this suit? هَالبَزّاز يسُوم غالِي [halbazzaːz ysuːm ɣaːli] That yard-goods dealer sets his prices high.
ساوَم [saːwam] *v:* • **1.** to bargain, haggle with – ماكُو داعِي تساومَه. السِّعِر مَحدُود [maːku daːʕi tsaːwmah. ʔissiʕir maħduːd] There's no need to haggle with him. The price is fixed.
سَوم [sawm] *n:* • **1.** quoting a price on, setting a price for
مُساوَمَة [musaːwama] *n:* • **1.** bargaining

س و م ر

سُومَر [suːmar] *n:* • **1.** Sumeria
سُومَرِي [suːmari] *adj:* • **1.** Sumerian

س و ي

يِسوَى [yiswa:] *v:* • **1.** to be worth, equivalent to, equal to – هَالكِتاب شقَدّ يِسوَى؟ [halkita:b šgadd yiswa:?] How much is this book worth? القَضِيَّة ما كانَت تِسوَى العراك [ʔilqaðiyya ma: ča:nat tiswa: ʔiliʕra:k] The matter wasn't worth fighting about.

سَوّى[sawwa] *v:* • **1.** to do, to perform, execute, discharge, commit – شراح تسَوِّي هَاللَّيلَة؟ [šra:ħ tsawwi hallayla?] What are you going to do tonight? قُلّي شِتسَوِّي بيها حَتَّى أنطِيك إيّاها [gulli šitsawwi bi:ha ħatta ʔanṭi:k ʔiyya:ha] Tell me what you'll do with it and I'll give it to you. سَوّولَه عَمَلِيَّة [sawwawlah ʕamaliyya] They performed an operation on him. إذا تسَوِّي مُخالَفَة، يِسحَبُون إجازتَك [ʔiða tsawwi: muxa:lafa, yisħabu:n ʔiǰa:ztak] If you commit a violation, they'll withdraw your license. الطُّلّاب مسَوِّين مُظاهَرَة [ʔiṭṭulla:b msawwi:n muða:hara] The students have staged a demonstration. سَوّى بِيّا نُكتَة. قُلّي ماكو مَدرَسَة اليُوم [sawwa: biyya nukta. galli ma:ku madrasa ʔilyu:m] He played a trick on me. He told me there wasn't any school today. سَوّاها بِيّا. أخَذ فلُوسِي وَانهِزَم [sawwa:ha biyya. ʔaxað flu:si wʔinhizam] He tricked me. He took my money and fled. • **2.** to make, to produce, manufacture, fabricate – سَوِّي مِن هَالمقَوّايَة صَندُوق [sawwi: min halmqawwa:ya ṣandu:g] Make a box out of this cardboard. هَالمَعمَل يسَوِّي قنادِر [hallmaʕmal ysawwi: qana:dir] This factory manufactures shoes. يَاللّه عاد! سَوَّيتها طلابَة [yallah ʕa:d! sawwi:tha ṭla:ba] Come on now! You've made it a complicated thing. سَوّى فِتنَة وخَلّاهُم يِتعارکُون [sawwa: fitna wxalla:hum yitʕa:rku:n] He stirred up trouble and made them fight. راح يسَوُّون حَفلَة بِمُناسَبَة نَجاحَه [ra:ħ ysawwu:n ħafla bimuna:sabat naǰa:ħah] They will have a party to celebrate his success. المُدِير سَوّانِي مُراقِب عالصَّفّ [ʔilmudi:r sawwa:ni mura:qib ʕaṣṣaff] The principal made me monitor over the class. لا تسَوِّي نَفسَك كُلِّش ما تُعرُف [la: tsawwi: nafsak kulliš ma: tuʕruf] Don't act as though you don't know at all.

ساوَى [sa:wa:] *v:* • **1.** to equal, to be equal to, be equivalent to – ثنَين وإثنَين يساوِي أربَعَة [θnayn wʔiθnayn ysa:wi ʔarbaʕa] Two plus two equals four. • **2.** to level, make level, to smooth, smooth out – أرِيد أساوِي هالوُصلَة القاع [ʔari:d ʔasa:wi halwuṣlat ʔilga:ʕ] I want to level this piece of land. • **3.** to settle, smooth over, put in order, make up (a dispute, etc.) – سَوّوها لِلقَضِيَّة بساع وَما حَدّ عِرَف [sawwawha lilqaðiyya bsa:ʕ wma ħadd ʕiraf] They settled the matter quickly and no one found out. • **4.** with بَين to treat alike, be impartial toward – لازِم تساوِي بين المُوَظَّفِين [la:zim tsa:wi bi:n ʔilmuwaððafi:n] You've got to treat the employees all alike.

تساوَى [tsa:wa:] *v:* • **1.** to be equal, equivalent to each other, to come out equal – الرِّجّال وَالمَرَة يِتساوَوا بنَظَر القانُون [ʔirriǰǰa:l wilmara yitsa:waw bnaðar ʔilqa:nu:n] Man and woman are equal in the eyes of the law. المَجمُوعَين تساوَوا [ʔilmaǰmu:ʕayn tsa:waw] The two sums came out equal. • **2.** to be leveled – القاع بَعَدها ما تساوَت [ʔilga:ʕ baʕadha ma: tsa:wat] The ground is still not leveled.

اِستَوَى [ʔistuwa:] *v:* • **1.** to ripen, mature, be or become ripe – خَلّي الخَوخ عالشَّجَر حَتَّى يِستُوِي [xalli: ʔilxu:x ʕaššiǰar ħatta yistuwi] Leave the peaches on the trees until they ripen. • **2.** to become well-cooked, done – الأكِل اِستَوَى. تَعال أُكُل [ʔilʔakil ʔistuwa:. taʕa:l ʔukul] The food is done. Come and eat. لَحَم الهُوش ما يِستُوِي بالعَجَل [laħam ʔilhu:š ma: yistuwi bilʕaǰal] Beef doesn't cook quickly.

سُوَة، سُوا [suwa] *n:* • **1.** equal, the same, alike – كُلّهُم سُوَة عِندِي [kullhum suwa ʕindi] They're all the same to me. • **2.** together, in a body – خَلّي نرُوح سُوَة [xalli: nru:ħ suwa] Let's go together.

تَسوِيَة [taswiya] *n:* • **1.** leveling, smoothing • **2.** settlement, adjustment (of a dispute) – دائِرَة التَّسوِيَة [da:ʔirat ʔittaswiya] Office of Land Dispute Settlement.

مُساواة، مُساواء [musa:wa:t, musa:wa:ʔ] *n:* • **1.** equality, equal rights

تَساوِي [tasa:wi] *n:* • **1.** equality, equivalence, sameness – قَسَّم الشُّغُل عَلينا بالتَّساوِي [qassam ʔiššuɣul ʕali:na bittasa:wi] He divided the work for us equally.

مُستَوَى [mustawa] *n:* • **1.** level, standard – مُستَوَى البَحَر [mustawa: ʔilbaħar] sea level. مُستَوَى اِقتِصادِي [mustawa: ʔqtiṣa:di] economic level, standard of living.

اِستِواء، خَطّ الاِستِواء [ʔistiwa:ʔ, xaṭṭ ʔilʔistiwa:ʔ] *n:* • **1.** the equator

سَواسِي، سَواسِيَة [sawa:si, sawa:siya] *n:* • **1.** equal, alike (both forms used as both masc. and fem.)

مسَاوِي [msa:wi] *adj:* • **1.** done, finished

مِستُوِي [mistuwi] *adj:* • **1.** ripe, mature • **2.** done, cooked

مُساوِي [musa:wi] *adj:* • **1.** equivalent

مُستَوِي [mustawi] *adj:* • **1.** flat

متساوِي [mitsa:wi] *adj:* • **1.** equal

اِستِوائِي [ʔistiwa:ʔi] *adj:* • **1.** equatorial, tropical – مَنطَقَة اِستِوائِيَّة [manṭaqa ʔistiwa:ʔiyya] a tropical region.

س و ي ج

سوِيج [swi:č] *n:* • **1.** (car) key, electronic key • **2.** a crazy person

س ي ب

سَيَّب [sayyab] *v:* • **1.** to turn loose to wander, to abandon, neglect, forsake – ترُوح لِلقَبُولات وَتسَيِّب ولِدها بالشَّوارِع [tru:ħ lilqabu:la:t wtsayyib wilidha biššawa:riʕ] She goes to hen

س

parties and leaves her children to run loose in the streets. سافَر لِلُبنان وَسَيَّب أهلَه [sa:far lilubna:n wsayyab ʔahlah] He took off for Lebanon and abandoned his family.
تسَيَّب [tsayyab] *v:* • **1.** to be left to stray, to wander aimlessly, be without a leader – تسَيَّبَوا بَعَد مُوتَة أَبُوهُم [tsayyibaw baʕad mu:tat ʔabu:hum] They split up after their father's death.
سايِب [sa:yib] *adj:* • **1.** stray, abandoned, forsaken, neglected – كلاب سايبَة [čla:b sa:yba] stray dogs.

س ي ب ي

سِيبايَة [si:pa:ya] *n:* سَيبايات [si:pa:ya:t] *pl:* • **1.** luggage rack (on a car or bicycle) • **2.** rack used to hold pots over a cooking fire • **3.** tripod

س ي ج

سَيَّج [sayyaǰ] *v:* • **1.** to fence in, surround with a fence – راح نسَيِّج الحَدِيقَة بِشَرَك [ra:ħ nsayyiǰ ʔilħadi:qa bšarak] We're going to fence in the garden with barbed wire.
تسَيَّج [tsayyaǰ] *v:* • **1.** to be fenced in, surrounded with a fence
سِياج [siya:ǰ] *n:* سِياجات [siya:ǰa:t] *pl:* • **1.** fencing, fence
تَسيِيج [tasyi:ǰ] *n:* • **1.** fencing
مسَيَّج [msayyaǰ] *adj:* • **1.** fenced

س ي ح

ساح [sa:ħ] *v:* • **1.** to flow, run – المَيّ ساح وَغَطَّى الشّارِع [ʔilmayy sa:ħ wɣaṭṭa: ʔišša:riʕ] The water flowed along and covered the street. • **2.** to travel, make a tour
سيح [sayħ, si:ħ] *n:* • **1.** flow
سِياحَة [siya:ħa] *n:* • **1.** traveling, touring, tourism • **2.** pl. سِياحات tour, trip
سايِح [sa:yiħ] *n:* سِيّاح، سُوّاح [siyya:ħ, suwwa:ħ] *pl:* • **1.** traveler • **2.** tourist

س ي خ

سِيخ [si:x] *n:* سياخ [sya:x] *pl:* • **1.** skewer • **2.** rapier

س ي ر

سار [sa:r] *v:* • **1.** to march, to go forward – إلَى الأمام، سِرّ [ʔila ʔilʔama:m, sirr] Forward, march! • **2.** with عَلَى to follow, pursue, maintain – ما دَيسِير عَلَى خِطَّة مُعَيَّنَة [ma: daysi:r ʕala xiṭṭa muʕayyana] He's not following any specific plan of action.
سَيَّر [sayyar] *v:* • **1.** to order around, to make do one's bidding – مَرتَه تسَيِّرَه حَسَب ما ترِيد [martah tsayyirah ħasab ma: tri:d] His wife orders him around however she wants. • **2.** with عَلَى to call on, drop in on – راح نسَيِّر عَلَى جِيرانّا باكِر [ra:ħ nsayyir ʕala ǰi:ra:nna ba:čir] We're going to drop in on our neighbors tomorrow.
ساير [sa:yar] *v:* • **1.** to put up with, go along with, show patience or tolerance toward – لازم تسايرَه. ما تعُرفَه عَصَبِي؟ [la:zim tsa:yrah. ma: tʕurfah ʕaṣabi?] You should put up with him. Don't you know he's nervous?
سَير، سِيَر [sayr, siyar] *n:* سيُور، سيُورَة [syu:r, syu:ra] *pl:* • **1.** leather strap, band • **2.** strop • **3.** piece of harness. [ʔiða ma: tidhin ʔissayr ma: tħaṣṣal ʕala ši] If you don't bribe someone (lit. oil the harness) you won't get anything
سَير [sayr] *n:* • **1.** following, pursuing, maintaining
سِيرَة [si:ra] *n:* سِيَر [siyar] *pl:* • **1.** behavior, conduct, deportment
سَيّار [sayya:r] *adj:* • **1.** moving about, roving – القُوَّة السَّيّارَة [ʔilquwwa ʔissayya:ra] the roving patrol, the mobile force. • **2.** (as a *n:*) *pl.* سَيارات hose extentsion
مَسار [masa:r] *n:* • **1.** path
سَيّارَة [sayya:ra] *n:* سَيّارات [sayya:ra:t] *pl:* • **1.** automobile, car • **2.** vehicle – سَيّارَة إسعاف [sayya:rat ʔisʕa:f] ambulance.
مَسِيرَة [masi:ra] *n:* مَسِيرات [masi:ra:t] *pl:* • **1.** parade • **2.** march
تِسيارَة [tisya:ra] *n:* تِسيارات [tisya:ra:t] *pl:* • **1.** visit
مُسايَرَة [musa:yara] *n:* • **1.** adaptation, adjustment

س ي س [1]

سَيَّس [sayyas] *v:* • **1.** to float along, move on water – الرَّقِّيَّة سَيِّسَت بِالشَّطّ [ʔirraggiyya sayyisat biššaṭṭ] The watermelon floated away in the river.
سايَس [sa:yas] *v:* • **1.** to use extreme tact in handling, to curry favor with – إذا تسايِس أبُوها، تِقدَر تِتزَوَّجها [ʔiða tsa:yis ʔabu:ha, tigdar tidzawwaǰha] If you suck up to her father, you can marry her.
سايِس [sa:yis] *n:* سِيّاس [siyya:s] *pl:* • **1.** stableman, groom
سِياسَة [siya:sa] *n:* سِياسات [siya:sa:t] *pl:* • **1.** policy • **2.** politics • **3.** diplomacy
سِياسِي [siya:si] *adj:* • **1.** political • **2.** diplomaticas *n:* (as *n:*) • **3.** politician • **4.** diplomat, statesman
سِياسِيّاً [siya:siyyan] *adverbial:* • **1.** politically

س ي س [2]

ساس [sa:s] *n:* • **1.** a fencing game played with sticks and shields, often to the accompaniment of drum and pipe • **2.** same as أساس [ʔasa:s] foundation (of a building)

س ي س ي

سِيسِي [si:si] *n:* سِيسِيّات [si:siyya:t] *pl:* • **1.** pony, small horse

س ي ط ر

سَيطَر [sayṭar] *v:* • **1.** to master, acquire a command of – إذا ما تِقرا هالكتابَين، ما تِقدَر تسَيطِر عَالمَوضُوع [ʔiða ma:

tiqra: halkta:bayn, ma: tigdar tsayṭir ʕalmawḍu:ʕ] If you don't read these two books, you can't master the subject. • **2.** with عَلى to dominate, control, command – الشُّرطَة سيطِرَت عَالوَضِع [ʔiššurṭa ṣayṭirat ʕalwaḍiʕ] The police took control of the situation. ما دَيِقدَر يسَيطِر عَلَيهُم [ma: dayigdar ysi:ṭir ʕali:hum] He can't control them.

سَيطَرَة [sayṭara] *n:* • **1.** control, command, rule, domination – إلَه سَيطَرَة عَلَيهُم [ʔilah sayṭara ʕalayhum] He has control over them. • **2.** mastery, command – السَّيطَرَة عَاللُّغَة الفَرَنسِيَّة تِحتاج وَقِت [ʔissayṭara ʕalluɣa ʔilfaransiyya tiħta:ǰ wakit] Mastery of the French language takes time.

مسَيطِر [msayṭir] *adj:* • **1.** controlling • **2.** controlled

س ي ع

ساع، بساع [sa:ʕ, bsa:ʕ] *n:* • **1.** quickly, speedily, fast, in a hurry, right away – إذا تسِدّ الجِّدِر، يفُور المَيّ بِساع [ʔiða tsidd ʔiǰǰidir, yfu:r ʔilmayy bsa:ʕ] If you cover the pot, the water will boil quickly. شِبساع رجَعِت [šibsa:ʕ rǰaʕit] You sure got back fast! وَدّي إبنِي لِلمَدرَسَة وَتَعال بِساع [waddi ʔibni lilmadrasa wataʕa:l bsa:ʕ] Take my son to school and hurry back.

ساعَة [sa:ʕa] *n:* ساعات [sa:ʕa:t] *pl:* • **1.** time, moment – بيش السّاعَة رَجاءاً؟ [bi:š ʔissa:ʕa raǰa:ʔan?] What time is it, please? ساعَة الّي يوصَل، أَقُلَّه [sa:ʕat ʔilli: yu:ṣal, ʔagullah] The minute he comes, I'll tell him. • **2.** hour – الدَّرِس طَوَّل ساعَة وَنُصّ [ʔiddaris ṭawwal sa:ʕa wnuṣṣ] The lesson lasted an hour and a half. • **3.** pl. ساعات, سُوع watch, clock

ساعَجِي [sa:ʕači] *n:* ساعَجِيَّة [sa:ʕačiyya] *pl:* • **1.** watchmaker, watch and clock repairman or dealer

ساعاتِي [sa:ʕa:ti] *n:* ساعاتِيَّة [sa:ʕa:tiyya] *pl:* • **1.** watchmaker, watch and clock repairman or dealer • **2.** watch and clock repairman or dealer

س ي ف

سَيف [sayf] *n:* سِيُوف [syu:f] *pl:* • **1.** sword, saber, epee

سِيف [si:f] *n:* أسياف [ʔasya:f] *pl:* • **1.** grain or date warehouse

س ي ف ن

سِيفُون [si:fu:n] *n:* سِيفُونات [si:fu:na:t] *pl:* • **1.** siphon • **2.** chain-operated toilet flush tank • **3.** a kind of sweet, carbonated beverage

س ي ل

سال [sa:l] *v:* • **1.** to flow, run, stream – الدِّبِس دَيسِيل مِن التَّنَكَة [ʔiddibis daysi:l min ʔittanaka] The molasses is flowing out of the can.

سَيل [sayl, si:l] *n:* سيُول [syu:l] *pl:* • **1.** flood, inundation • **2.** torrent – مِن يِحكِي، يِنزِل مِثِل السَّيل [min yiħči, yinzil miθl ʔissi:l] When he talks, he comes out like a torrent.

سَيَلان [sayala:n] *n:* • **1.** gonorrhea

سِيلان [si:la:n] *n:* • **1.** date molasses

سيُولَة [syu:la] *n:* • **1.** liquidity • **2.** currency

إسالَة [ʔisa:la] *n:* • **1.** liquefaction

سَيّال [sayya:l] *adj:* • **1.** liquid, flowing, fluid – قِير سَيّال [gi:r sayya:l] liquid asphalt.

سايِل، سائِل [sa:yil, sa:ʔil] *adj:* • **1.** liquid, flowing, fluid • **2.** (as *n:*) *pl.* سَوائِل [sawa:ʔil] liquid, fluid • **3.** (as *n:*) (*pl.* سائِلِين) [sa:ʔili:n] beggar

مُسِيل [musi:l] *adj:* • **2.** liquefacient, solvent

س ي ل ن

سِيلان [si:la:n] *n:* • **1.** Ceylon

س ي م

سِيم [si:m] *n:* سيامَة [sya:ma] *pl:* • **1.** wire • **2.** stitches (surgical) • **3.** spoke of a wheel • **4.** thin metal rod

س ي ن [1]

سِين [si:n] *n:* • **1.** name of the letter 's'

س ي ن [2]

سَيَّن [sayyan] *v:* • **1.** to make muddy, dirty – الجَاهِل سَيَّن هدُومَه بِالشّارِع [ʔiǰǰa:hil sayyan hdu:mah biššaːriʕ] The kid got his clothes muddy in the street.

تسَيَّن [tsayyan] *v:* • **1.** to become muddy – لا تفُوت بهَالشّارِع تَرَة تِتسَيَّن [la: tfu:t bhašša:riʕ tara titsayyan] Don't go on that street or you'll get muddy.

سيان [sya:n] *n:* • **1.** muck, mire, mud

س ي ن ر ي و

سِينارِيُو [sina:ryu] *n:* • **1.** scenario

س ي ن م

سِينَما [sinama] *n:* سِينَمات [sinama:t] *pl:* • **1.** cinema, movie theater – البارحَة سَوّوا صَدِيقَك سِينَما [ʔilba:rħa sawwaw ṣadi:qak si:nama] Yesterday they made a laughingstock of your friend.

سِينَمائِي [si:nama:ʔi] *adj:* • **1.** cinematic, movie (*adj.*) – نَجِم سِينَمائِي [najim sinama:ʔi] movie star. رُوايَة سِينَمائِيَة [ruwa:ya sinama:ʔiyya] movie, film story.

س ي ه

سِياهَة [siya:ha] *n:* سِياهات [siya:ha:t] *pl:* • **1.** list, manifest, invoice

ش

ش

-ش [š-] *interrogative:* • **1.** (interrogatory prefix) what, who, which – شصار [šṣaːr] what happened? شِتسَوِّي [šitsawwiː] what are you doing? شاسمَك [šʔismak] What's your name? شبيك [šbiːk] What's (wrong) with you? شقَدّ [šgadd] How much?

شما [šmaː] *interrogative:* • **1.** whatever, whichever, what, which – سَوِّي شما يعجبَك [sawwi šma yiʕijbak] Do whatever you like. هَذا شمعَلّمه باِسمي ؟ [haːða šmʕallmah biʔismi?] How does he know my name?

ش ء م 1

تشائَم [tšaːʔam] *v:* • **1.** to be pessimistic, have a pessimistic attitude – لا تِتشائَم. الله يفرِجها [laː titšaːʔam. ʔallah yifrijha] Don't be pessimistic. God will take care of it. آني دَأتشائَم مِن هَالوَضِع [ʔaːni daʔatšaːʔam min halwaḏiʕ] I'm pessimistic about this situation. • **2.** to be superstitious – يِتشائم مِن شُوف البزازين السُّود [yitšaːʔam min šuːf ʔilbzaːziːn ʔissuːd] He is superstitious about seeing black cats.

شُؤُم، شُوم [šuʔum, šuːm] *n:* • **1.** bad luck, misfortune

تَشاؤُم [tašaːʔum] *n:* • **1.** pessimism

مَشؤُوم [mašʔuːm] *adj:* • **1.** unlucky, jinxed – عَدَد مَشؤُوم [ʕadad mašʔuːm] an unlucky number.

مِتشائِم [mitšaːʔim] *adj:* • **1.** pessimistic • **2.** (as n:) a pessimist

ش ء م 2

الشام [ʔiššaːm] *n:* • **1.** Damascus or, loosely, Syria

خام الشام [xaːm ʔiššaːm] *n:* • **1.** coarse, unbleached cotton fabric

شامي [šaːmi] *adj:* شامِيِّين [šaːmiːyyiːn] *pl:* • **1.** Damascene, Syrian • **3.** pl. شوام [šwaːm], شامِيِّين a Damascene, a Syrian

ش ء م 3

شامِيَّة [šaːmiyya] *n:* • **1.** popcorn

ش ء ن

شَأن [šaʔn] *n:* شُؤُون [šuʔuːn] *pl:* • **1.** matter, affair, concern, business – وِزارَة الشُّؤُون الاجتِماعِيَّة [wizaːrat ʔiššuʔuːn ʔilʔijtimaːʕiyya] Ministry of Social Affairs. حِكَيت وِيّاه بِشَأن المَوضُوع [ħičiːt wiyyaːh bšaʔn ʔilmawḏuːʕ] I talked to him concerning the subject.

ش ب ب

شَبّ [šabb] *v:* • **1.** to become a young man, to adolesce, grow up – مِن صار عُمرَه عَشِر سنِين، شَبّ فَدّ مَرَّة [min ṣaːr ʕumrah ʕašir sniːn, šabb fadd marra] When he became ten, he grew up fast. ما شاء الله شَبّ بِالعَجَل [maː šaːllah šabb bilʕajal] By golly, he's sprouted up quickly. • **2.** to break out, blaze up, start up (of fire, war, etc.) – النّار شَبَّت بالمَخزَن [ʔinnaːr šabbat bilmaxzan] A fire broke out in the warehouse. • **3.** with عَلَى to jump up on, to climb on top of, mount – الكَلِب شَبّ عَلَيّا [ʔiččalib šabb ʕalayya] The dog jumped up on me. الحصان شَبّ عالفَرَس [ʔilħṣaːn šabb ʕalfaras] The stallion mounted the mare. • **4.** with مِن to jump over – الكَلِب يِقدَر يِشِب مِن هَالسِّياج بسُهُولَة [ʔiččalib yigdar yšibb min hassiyaːǰ bsuhuːla] The dog can jump over this fence easily.

شَبَّب [šabbab] *v:* • **1.** to breed, cause to mate – تشَبِّب الفَرَس إلّا مِن حصان أبيَض [tšabbib ʔilfaras ʔilla min ħṣaːn ʔabyaḏ] Don't breed the mare with anything but a white stallion. جِيب حصانَك حَتَّى نشَبِّبَه عَلَى فَرَسنا [ǰiːb ħṣaːnak ħatta nšabbibah ʕala farasna] Bring your horse so we can mate it to our mare.

شَبّ [šabb] *n:* • **1.** alum

شَبَّة [šabba] *n:* شَبّات [šabbaːt] *pl:* • **1.** a platform on top of a pole for keeping food out of reach of prowling animals

شابّ [šaːbb] *n:* • **1.** youthful, young, juvenile • **2.** pl. شُبّان young man, youth

شَباب [šabaːb] *n:* • **1.** youthfulness, youth • **2.** (invar. sing. and pl.) juvenile, adolescent, youth, young person, young people

ش ب ث

تشَبَّث [tšabbaθ] *v:* • **1.** to be persistent, tenacious, to seek tenaciously – ظَلّ مُدَّة يِتشَبَّث حَتَّى توَظَّف [ðall mudda yitšabbaθ ħatta twaðððaf] He kept on trying for some time until he got a job. ما عِدنا وَظِيفَة؛ رُوح تشَبَّث بغَير دائِرَة [maː ʕidna waḏiːfa; ruːħ tšabbaθ bɣiːr daːʔira] We don't have a job; go try in another office. تشَبَّث عَلَى الوَظِيفَة لَكِن ما حَصَّلها [tšabbaθ ʕala lwaḏiːfa laːkin maː ħaṣṣalha] He tried hard for the job but he didn't get it. دَيِتشَبَّث عَلَى إجازَة فَتح مَلهَى [dayitšabbaθ ʕala ʔiǰaːzat fatiħ malha] He's trying hard to get a license to open a night club.

ش ب ح

شَبَح [šabaħ] *n:* أشباح [ʔašbaːħ] *pl:* • **1.** apparition • **2.** specter, spirit, ghost

ش ب خ

شِبَخ [šibax] *v:* • **1.** to take a large step – إشبُخ حَتَّى ما تِتبَلّل رجلَك بِالمَيّ [ʔišbux ħatta maː titballal rijlak bilmayy] Take a big step so your foot won't get wet in the water.

شَبَّخ [šabbax] *v:* • **1.** to spread the legs far apart – شَبُّخ زين حَتَّى تمُرّ الصَّخلَة مِن جَوّاك [šabbux ziːn ħatta tmurr ʔiṣṣaxla min ǰawwaːk] Spread your legs so the goat can go under you.
شَبُخ [šabux] *n:* • **1.** taking a large step
شَبخَة [šabxa] *n:* شَبخات [šabxaːt] *pl:* • **1.** giant step, stride

ش ب ر

شِبَر [šibar] *v:* • **1.** to measure with the span of the hand – إشبُر هالحَصِير وَقُلِّي إشقَدّ طُولَه [ʔišbur halħaṣiːr wgulli šgadd ṭuːlah] Measure this mat (with the span of your hand) and tell me how long it is.
شِبِر [šibir] *n:* شبار [šbaːr] *pl:* • **1.** a unit of measurement equal to the span of an outstretched hand – دافعَوا عَن كُلّ شِبِر مِن القاع [daːfʕaw ʕan kull šibir min ʔilgaːʕ] They defended every inch of ground.
شَبُر [šabur] *n:* • **1.** measuring with the span of the hand

ش ب ط

شباط [šbaːṭ] *n:* • **1.** February
شَبُّوط [šabbuːṭ] *n:* • **1.** a kind of large fish found in the Tigris and Euphrates rivers

ش ب ع

شِبَع [šibaʕ] *v:* • **1.** to satisfy one's appetite, eat one's fill, to become sated, full – ما راح أقُوم مِن الأكِل قَبُل ما أشبَع [maː raːħ ʔaguːm min ʔilʔakil gabul maː ʔašbaʕ] I'm not going to get up from the table before I get full. • **2.** to have enough, have one's fill, become sick and tired – بَعَد ما شِبَع مِنها، طِرَدها [baʕad maː šibaʕ minha, ṭiradha] After he satisfied himself with her, he threw her out. • **3.** to sate, satisfy, fill – التَّمُر يِشبِع الواحِد [ʔittamur yišbiʕ ʔilwaːħid] Dates fill you up.
شَبَّع [šabbaʕ] *v:* • **1.** to satisfy, fill, sate – أكِل هَالمَطعَم ما يشَبِّع [ʔakil halmaṭʕam maː yšabbiʕ] This restaurant's food doesn't fill one up.
هَذا طَمّاع؛ كُلّ فلُوس الدِّنيا ما تشَبِّع عَينَه [haːða ṭammaːʕ; kull fluːs ʔiddinya maː tšabbiʕ ʕaynah] He's greedy; all the money of the world wouldn't satisfy him.
دارَوا عَليه ثلاثتهُم وَشَبِّعوه بَسُط [daːraw ʕaliːh tlaːθathum wšabbiʕuːh basuṭ] The three of them converged on him and beat him thoroughly. • **2.** to satisfy, gratify
اِنشِبَع [ʔinšibaʕ] *v:* • **1.** to have enough, have one's fill – هَالأكِل كُلِّش طَيِّب. ما يِنشِبِع مِنَّه [halʔakil kulliš ṭayyib. maː yinšibiʕ minnah] This food is very good. You can never get enough of it.
شِبِع [šibiʕ] *n:* • **1.** satiation, saturation, surfeit • **2.** satiety
إشباع [ʔišbaːʕ] *n:* • **1.** satiation, saturation, surfeit
مُشبَع [mušbaʕ] *adj:* • **1.** satiated, filled • **2.** with ب full of, filled with
شَبعان [šabʕaːn] *adj:* • **1.** sated, satisfied, full • **2.** satiated, fed up, sick and tired – آني شَبعان مِن السِّينَمات [ʔaːni šabʕaːn min ʔissinamaːt] I'm fed up with movies.
هَذا عَينَه شَبعانَة. نَفسَه ما تِدني عَلَى هِيكِي شِي [haːða ʕaynah šabʕaːna. nafsah maː tidni ʕala hiːči ši] He's got everything. He wouldn't care to get such a thing.

ش ب ك 1

شِبَك [šibač, šibak] *v:* • **1.** to intertwine, interweave, lace together – شِبَك أصابعَه وَطَقطَقها [šibač ʔaṣaːbʕah wṭagṭagha] He laced his fingers together and cracked his knuckles.
تشابَك [tšaːbač] *v:* • **1.** to finger wrestle – لا تِتشابَك ويّاه تَرَة هُوَّ أقوَى مِنَّك [laː titšaːbač wiyyaːh tara huwwa ʔaqwa minnak] Don't finger wrestle with him because he's stronger than you.
اِشتِبَك [ʔištibak] *v:* • **1.** to become entangled, involved, engaged, embroiled – جَيشنا اِشتِبَك بمَعرَكَة وِيّا العَدُو [ǰayšna ʔištibak bmaʕraka wiyya ʔilʕadu] Our forces engaged in battle with the enemy.
شِبَك [šibač] *n:* • **1.** netting, net
شَبِك [šabič] *n:* • **1.** intertwining, interweaving
شِبكَة [šibča] *n:* شِبكات [šibčaːt] *pl:* • **1.** net, piece of netting
شِبّاك [šibbaːč, šibbaːk] *n:* شبابِيك [šbaːbiːč, šbaːbiːk] *pl:* • **1.** window • **2.** grill, grid, lattice-work • **3.** wicket • **4.** ventilator grill • **5.** a piece of زلابيَة [zlaːbya] (a popular confection made in a lattice shape)
مشَبَّك [mšabbač] *n:* • **1.** latticed, having a latticed or plaited design • **2.** pl. مشَبَّكات grill, latticework • **3.** زلابيَة a popular confection
شَبَكِيَّة [šabakiyya] *n:* شَبَكِيّات [šabakiyyaːt] *pl:* • **1.** retina (of the eye)
اِشتِباك [ʔištibaːk] *n:* • **1.** fight, scuffle, melee • **2.** involvement, entanglement
شابكَة [šaːbča] *adj:* • **1.** tangled up, complicated

ش ب ك 2

شُبَك [šubag] *v:* • **1.** to embrace, hug – بَسّ نِزَل مِن الطَّيّارَة، شُبَك إبنَه [bass nizal min ʔiṭṭiyyaːra, šubag ʔibnah] As soon as he got off of the plane, he embraced his son.
مِن شِفِت عَلِي، شُبَكتَه. صارلِي ثلاث سنين ما شايفَه [min šifit ʕali, šubaktah. ṣaːrli tlaθ sniːn maː šaːyfah] When I saw Ali, I embraced him. I hadn't seen him for three years.
شَبَّك [šabbag] *v:* • **1.** to keep hugging, keep embracing – ظَلّ يشَبُّك وَيبَوِّس بِيها مُدَّة [ðall yšabbug wybawwis biːha mudda] He hugged and kissed her for quite a while.
تشابَك [tšaːbag] *v:* • **1.** to embrace each other – بَسّ تلاقَوا، تشابكَوا [bass tlaːgaw, tšaːbgaw] The moment they met, they embraced.
شَبُك [šabug] *n:* • **1.** hug, hugging, embrace, embracing
شَبكَة [šabga] *n:* شَبكات [šabgaːt] *pl:* • **1.** an embrace, a hug

ش ب ل

شِبِل [šibil] *n:* أشبال [ʔašbaːl] *pl:* • **1.** lion cub

ش ب ن ت

شبِنت [šbint] *n:* • **1.** dill

ش ب ه

شِبَه [šibah] *v:* • **1.** to resemble, look like, be similar to – إبنَك يِشبَهَك كُلِّش [ʔibnak yišbahak kulliš] Your son resembles you a lot. • **2.** to cast suspicion upon, bring suspicion to, make suspect – شِبَهنِي مِن جاب إسمِي بالمَحكَمَة [šibahni min ǰaːb ʔismi bilmaħkama] He cast suspicion on me when he mentioned my name in court.

شَبَّه [šabbah] *v:* • **1.** to compare, liken – يشَبِّه حَبِيبتَه بِالغَزال [yšabbih ħabiːbtah bilɣazaːl] He compares his darling to a gazelle. • **2.** to consider similar or identical, to find a resemblance in – بيش تشَبِّه هَالنّوع مِن الفاكِهَة؟ [biyš tšabbih hannuːʕ min ʔilfaːkiha?] What does this variety of fruit remind you of? شُوف ذاك الرِّجّال. شَبَّهتَه بأخُوك [šuːf ðaːk ʔirrijjaːl. šabbahtah bʔaxuːk] Look at that man. I thought he was your brother.

شابَه [šaːbah] *v:* • **1.** to resemble, look like, be similar to – قماش سِترتي يشابِه السَّرج [qmaːš sitirti yšaːbih ʔissarij] The material of my jacket resembles serge. كُلّ أعضاء هَالنّادِي مُحامِين، وَأطِباء، وَما شابَه [kull ʔaʕðaːʔ hannaːdi muħaːmiːn, wʔaṭṭibaːʔ, wma šaːbah] All the members of this club are lawyers, physicians, and the like.

تشَبَّه [tšabbah] *v:* • **1.** with ب to imitate, copy, try to be like – هَالبنَيَّة تِتشَبَّه بِالنِّسوان [halbnayya titšabbah binniswaːn] That girl copies grown women.

تشابَه [tšaːbah] *v:* • **1.** to resemble each other, look alike, be similar to each other – هُوَّ وَأخُوه هوايَة يِتشابهُون [huwwa wʔaxuːh hwaːya yitšaːbhuːn] He and his brother look a lot alike.

انشِبَه [ʔinšibah] *v:* • **1.** to be or become under suspicion, be suspected – اِنشِبَه لِأنّ دائماً يمشِي ويّا المُجرِم [ʔinšibah liʔann daːʔiman yimši wiyya ʔilmujrim] He's suspected because he's always hanging around with the criminal.

اشتِبَه [ʔištibah] *v:* • **1.** to be mistaken, make a mistake – لازم اِشتِبَهت. التّفاح مُو هَالقَدّ غالِي [laːzim ʔištibahit. ʔittiffaːħ muː halgadd ɣaːli] You must be mistaken. Apples aren't that expensive. اِشتِبَهت بِالحِساب لِأنّ كِنِت تِحكِي [ʔištibahit biliħsaːb liʔann činit tiħči] I made a mistake on the accounts because you were talking. العَفو! اِشتِبَهت بِيك [ʔilʕafw! ʔištibahit biːk] Sorry! I mistook you for someone else. اِشتِبَه بِيّا وَاِعتِقَد آنِي نَجِم سِينَمائِي [ʔištibah biyya wʔiʕtiqad ʔaːni najim sinamaːʔi] He took me for someone else and thought I was a movie star. • **2.** with ب to suspect, be suspicious about – الشُّرطَة، أيّ واحِد تِشتِبِه بِيه، تاخذَه لِلمَرَكَز [ʔiššurṭa, ʔayy waːħid tištibih biːh, taːxðah lilmarkaz] Any one the police suspect, they take to the station.

شُبُه [šubuh, šabah] *n:* أشباه [ʔašbaːh] *pl:* • **1.** resemblance, similarity, likeness • **2.** image • **3.** -like, quasi, semi-, half- – شُبُه دِفاع [šubuh difaːʕ] halfback (soccer). شِبِه رَسمِي [šibih rasmi] semi-formal, semi-official. شُبُه مُنحَرِف [šubuh munħarif] trapezoid (geom.). شِبِه مُعَيَّن [šibih muʕayyan] rhomboid (geom.).

شَبَه، شَبِه [šabah, šabih] *n:* أشباه [ʔašbaːh] *pl:* • **1.** resemblance, similarity, likeness • **2.** image

شُبهَة [šubha] *n:* شُبهات [šubhaːt] *pl:* • **1.** suspicion – إنتَ ما عَلَيك شُبهَة [ʔinta maː ʕaliːk šubha] You're not under suspicion.

شَبِيه [šabiːh] *n:* أشباه [ʔašbaːh] *pl:* • **1.** like, counterpart – ما إلَه شَبِيه بِالدِّنيا [maː ʔilah šabiːh biddinya] There's no one like him in the world.

تَشابُه [tašaːbuh] *n:* • **1.** resemblance, similarity – أكُو تَشابُه بينهُم [ʔaku tašaːbuh biːnhum] There's a resemblance between them.

مُشابِه [mušaːbih] *adj:* • **1.** similar

اِشتِباه [ʔištibaːh] *n:* • **1.** resemblance, similarity, suspicion, dubiousness, doubtfulness, doubt,

مَشبُوه [mašbuːh] *adj:* • **1.** under suspicion, suspect, suspicious, doubtful, notorious – بَيت مَشبُوه [bayt mašbuːh] house of ill repute. • **2.** (as n:) pl. مَشبُوهِين [mašbuːhiːn] suspect

مِتشابِه [mitšaːbih] *adj:* • **1.** identical • **2.** corresponding, alike

أشبَه [ʔašbah] *comparative adjective:* • **1.** with ب more or most similar to – هاي أشبَه شِي بِالخَوخ [haːy ʔašbah ši bilxuːx] This is the closest thing to a peach.

ش ب و [1]

شِبَة [šiba] *adj:* • **1.** imitation gold, brass – خِزّامَة شِبَة [xizzaːma šiba] a brass nose ring.

ش ب و [2]

شَبَّى [šabbaː] *v:* • **1.** to breed, cause to mate – راح أشَبِّي الفَرَص مالتِي مِن أحسَن حصان مَوجُود [raːħ ʔašabbi ʔilfaraṣ maːlti min ʔaħsan ħṣaːn mawjuːd] I'm going to breed my mare to the best stallion available.

شبُوَّة، فَحَل شبُوَّة، حصان شبُوَّة [šbuwwa, faħal šbuwwa, ħṣaːn šbuwwa] *n:* • **1.** stud horse – يَعنِي جايبِيك لأمرِيكا تِدرُس لَو تصِير فَحَل شبُوَّة [yaʕni ǰaːybiːk lamriːka tidrus law tṣiːr faħal šbuwwa] You think they sent you to America to study or to be a stud?

ش ت ت

شَتَّت [šattat] *v:* • **1.** to scatter, disperse, break up, rout – العَدُو شَتَّت شَملهُم [ʔilʕadu šattat šamilhum] The enemy routed them.

تشَتَّت [tšattat] *v:* • **1.** to be scattered, to disperse – مِن إجَت الشُّرطَة، تشَتّتَوا [min ʔijat ʔiššurṭa, tšattitaw]

When the police came, they dispersed. جيش نابُليون تشَتَّت بِرُوسيا [ǰayš naːpulyuːn tšattat bruːsya] Napoleon's army fell apart in Russia.

ش ت ل

شِتَل [šital] *v:* • **1.** to plant, transplant – جِبِت كَم هِرِش وَرِد وَشِتَلِتهُم بِالحَدِيقَة [ǰibit čam hiriš warid wšitalithum bilħadiːqa] I got a few flower seedlings and transplanted them in the garden. • **2.** to constrain, stay, deter, hobble, confine – اِشتِل الطَّير حَتَّى ما يطِير [ʔištil ʔiṭṭiːr ħatta maː yṭiːr] Fasten the bird's wings so he won't fly. باالله تَعال بساع. لا تِشتِلنِي [ballah taʕaːl bsaːʕ. laː tištilni] Please come right away. Don't leave me here.

شِتِل [šitil] *n:* شتُول، شَتلات [štuːl, šatlaːt] *pl:* • **1.** young plant, seedling

شَتِل [šatil] *n:* • **1.** transplanting • **2.** waiting for a long time

مَشتَل [maštal] *n:* مَشاتِل [mašaːtil] *pl:* • **1.** nursery, arboretum

شَتلَة [šatla] *n:* شَتلات [šatlaːt] *pl:* • **1.** seedling, set, transplant

ش ت م

شِتَم [šitam] *v:* • **1.** to curse, revile, vilify, abuse – شِتَمتَه لِأَنّ فَشَّر عَلَيّا [šitamtah liʔann faššar ʕalayya] I cussed him out because he talked dirty to me.

شَتَّم [šattam] *v:* • **1.** intens. of شِتَم to curse, revile, vilify, abuse – تِقدَر تِحكِي بَلا ما تشَتِّم [tigdar tiħči bala maː tšattim] You can talk without cursing continually.

تشاتَم [tšaːtam] *v:* • **1.** to curse one another, vilify one another – تشاتموا وَبَعدين تباسطوا [tšaːtmaw wbaʕdiːn tbaːṣṭaw] They threw insults at each other and then got into a fight.

شَتِم [šatim] *n:* • **1.** curse, cursing • **2.** abuse, vilification

شَتمَة [šatma] *n:* شَتمات، شَتايِم [šatmaːt, šataːyim] *pl:* • **1.** insult, vilification

شَتُّومَة [šattuːma] *n:* شَتُّومات، شتايِم [šattuːmaːt, štaːyim] *pl:* • **1.** insult, vilification

ش ت و [1]

شَتَّى [šattaː] *v:* • **1.** to winter, spend the winter – يصَيِّف بِالشِّمال وَيشَتِّي بِالبَصرَة [yṣayyif biššimaːl wyšatti bilbaṣra] He spend his summers in the North and his winters in Basra. • **2.** to put on or wear winter clothing – أَشُو شَتَّيت بِالعَجَل. الدِّنيا بَعَدها حارَّة [ʔašu šattayt bilʕajal. ʔiddinya baʕadha ħaːrra] It looks like you put on winter clothes too soon. The weather is still hot.

شِتا [šitaː] *n:* شِتَايَات [šitaːyaːt] *pl:* • **1.** winter

مَشتَى [maštaː] *n:* مَشاتِي [mašaːti] *pl:* • **1.** winter resort

شِتوِيَّة [šitwiyya] *n:* شِتوِيّات [šitwiyyaːt] *pl:* • **1.** winter, winter time

شِتوِي [šitwi] *adj:* • **1.** winter, wintry – بَدلَة شِتوِيَّة [badla šitwiyya] a winter suit.

ش ت و [2]

شِتَى [šitaː] *v:* • **1.** to incite, turn loose, sick (a dog) – شِتَى الكَلِب عَلَى صَدِيقَه [šitaː ʔiččalib ʕala ṣadiːqah] He sicked the dog on his friend.

ش ج ب

مِشجَب [mišǰab] *n:* مَشاجِب [mašaːǰib] *pl:* • **1.** gun rack

ش ج ر

شِجَر [šiǰar] *v:* • **1.** to prepare the baking oven for baking flat bread – جِيبِلِي حَطَب حَتَّى أَشجَر التَّنُّور [ǰiːbli ħaṭab ħatta ʔašǰar ʔittannuːr] Bring me some kindling so I can heat up the outdoor oven.

شَجَّر [šaǰǰar] *v:* • **1.** to plant trees or bushes, to landscape – شَجّرَوا الشّارِع الجِّدِيد بكالِبتُوز [šaǰǰiraw ʔiššaːriʕ ʔiǰǰidiːd bkalibtuːz] They planted eucalyptus trees along the new street.

شِجَر [šiǰar, šiǰar] *n:* • **1.** (coll.) tree(s) • **2.** bush(es) • **3.** squash • **4.** pumpkin(s) – شِجَر أَسكَلَة، شِجَر أَحمَر [šiǰar ʔaskala, šiǰar ʔaħmar] pumpkin. • **5.** dope, dunce, fool, jerk – لا تِزعَل مِن حَكيَه. هُوَّ فَدّ واحِد شِجَر [laː tizʕal min ħačyah. huwwa fadd waːħid šiǰar] Don't get mad at what he says. He's a simple-minded fellow.

شِجرَة [šiǰra, šaǰra] *n:* شِجرات، أَشجار، شَجَرات [šiǰraːt, ʔašǰaːr, šaǰaraːt] *pl:* • **1.** squash • **2.** pumpkin • **4.** bush, shrub • **5.** pl. شِجرات, أَشجار tree

شَجَرَة [šaǰara] *n:* شَجَرات، أَشجار [šaǰaraːt, ʔašǰaːr] *pl:* • **1.** tree • **2.** bush, shrub

شاجُور [šaːǰuːr] *n:* • **1.** magazine

شُجَيرَة [šuǰayra] *n:* • **1.** shrub • **2.** small tree

شِجرايَة [šiǰraːya] *n:* شِجرايات [šiǰraːyaːt] *pl:* • **1.** squash • **2.** pumpkin

مشَجَّر [mšaǰǰar] *adj:* • **1.** embellished with trees or bushes, landscaped • **2.** having a floral design – لابسَة فِستان مشَجَّر [laːbsah fistaːn mšaǰǰar] She's wearing a floral print dress.

ش ج ع

شَجَّع [šaǰǰaʕ] *v:* • **1.** to encourage, embolden – شَجَّعَه عَلَى الدِّراسَة بأُورُبّا [šaǰǰaʕah ʕala ʔiddiraːsa bʔuːruppa] He encouraged him to study in Europe. كُلّ التَّلامِيذ إِجَوا لِلسّاحَة حَتَّى يشَجِّعُون الفِرقَة [kull ʔittalaːmiːð ʔiǰaw lissaːħa ħatta yšaǰǰiʕuːn ʔilfirqa] All the students came to the field to cheer the team. • **2.** to support, back, promote – لازِم نشَجِّع مَصنُوعاتنا الوَطَنِيَّة [laːzim nšaǰǰiʕ maṣnuːʕaːtna ʔilwaṭaniyya] We should support our domestic products.

تشَجَّع [tšaǰǰaʕ] *v:* • **1.** to take heart, pluck up courage, be encouraged – مِن حِكَينا وِيّاه، تشَجَّع [min ħičiːna wiyyaːh, tšaǰǰaʕ] When we talked to him, he was encouraged.

ش

شَجاعَة [šaja:ʕa] *n:* • **1.** courage, bravery, valor, boldness, audacity
تَشْجِيع [tašji:ʕ] *n:* • **1.** encouragement, support
شُجاع [šuja:ʕ] *adj:* شُجعان [šujʕa:n] *pl:* • **1.** brave, courageous, bold, audacious • **2.** courageous man
مُشَجِّع [mušajjiʕ] *adj:* مُشَجِّعِين [šijʕa:ni:n] *pl:* • **1.** encourager, supporter, advocate, proponent
أَشْجَع [ʔašjaʕ] *comparative adjective:* • **1.** more or most courageous

ش ح ب

شِحَب [šiħab] *v:* • **1.** to turn pale
شُحُوب [šuħu:b] *n:* • **1.** sallowness, paleness, wanness, emaciation
شاحِب [ša:ħib] *adj:* • **1.** pale, wan, emaciated, lean, haggard • **2.** sickly, ill looking, dull

ش ح ح

شَحّ [šaħħ] *v:* • **1.** to become scarce, run short, dwindle – اِشتِرِي هوايَة مِن هَالصّابُون. يِظهَر دَيشِحّ يوم عَن يوم [ʔištiri hwa:ya min haṣṣa:bu:n. yiðhar dayšiħħ yu:m ʕan yu:m] Buy a lot of this soap. It appears to be getting scarcer day after day.
شِحَّة [šiħħa] *n:* • **1.** scarcity, paucity, shortage, deficiency
شاحّ [ša:ħħ] *adj:* • **1.** scarce, tight
شَحِيح [šaħi:ħ] *adj:* • **1.** miser • **2.** stingy

ش ح ش ط

شَحشَط [šaħšaṭ] *v:* • **1.** to scrape, scuff, drag along – دَيمشِي وَيشَحشِط بنعالَه [dayimši wyšaħšiṭ bnʕa:lah] He's walking along and scuffing his sandals. إذا ما تِقدَر تشِيل القُونِيَّة، شَحشِطها [ʔiða ma: tiqdar tši:l ʔilgu:niyya, šaħšiṭha] If you can't carry the gunny sack, drag it. نِجَح نَجاح مشَحشَط [nijaħ naja:ħ mšaħšaṭ] He just barely passed.

ش ح ط

شِحَط [šiħaṭ] *v:* • **1.** to scrape, scuff, drag along – دَيمشِي وَيشحَط بنعالَه [dayimši wyišħaṭ bnʕa:lah] He's walking along and scuffing his sandals. • **2.** to irritate, cause a lump in (the throat) – النُّومِي الحامُض يِشحَط البَلعُوم [ʔinnu:mi ʔilħa:muð yišħaṭ ʔilbalʕu:m] Lemon puckers the throat.
شَحَّط [šaħħaṭ] *v:* • **1.** to make deficient, make too short – لا تشَحِّطها. إنطِينِي عَالأَقَلّ ثلَث ياردات [la: tšaħħiṭha. ʔinṭi:ni ʕalʔaqall tlaθ ya:rda:t] Don't make it too short. Give me at least three yards. هالوُصلَة القُماش مشَحَّطَة. ما تصِيرلَك قاط [halwuṣlat ʔilqma:š mšaħħiṭa. ma: tṣi:rlak qa:ṭ] This piece of material is too short. It won't make you a suit. هَالطَّماطَة تسَوِّي نُصّ كِيلُو مشَحَّط [haṭṭama:ṭa tsawwi: nuṣṣ ki:lu mšaħħaṭ] These tomatoes make barely half a kilo.
شَحُط [šaħuṭ] *n:* • **1.** scraping, dragging along
شَحطَة [šaħṭa] *n:* • **1.** irritation, lump (in the throat)
شَحّاطَة [šaħħa:ṭa] *n:* شَحّاطات [šaħħa:ṭa:t] *pl:* • **1.** sandal, flip-flop
مشَحَّط [mšaħħaṭ] *adj:* • **1.** measly

ش ح ف

مَشحُوف [mašħu:f] *n:* مَشاحِيف [maša:ħi:f] *pl:* • **1.** a kind of long boat, made of wood, or asphalt-covered straw, and propelled by a pole

ش ح م

شَحَّم [šaħħam] *v:* • **1.** to lubricate, grease – بَعَد ما شَحَّمت السَّيّارَة، قامَت تِمشِي زين [baʕad ma: šaħħamt ʔissayya:ra, ga:mat timši zi:n] After I lubricated the car, it began to run well.
تشَحَّم [tšaħħam] *v:* • **1.** pass. of شَحَّم to be lubricated, greased
شَحَم [šaħam] *n:* شُحُوم [šuħu:m] *pl:* • **1.** fat, suet, grease • **2.** tallow – صابُون شَحَم [ṣa:bu:n šaħam] tallow soap.
شَحمَة [šaħma] *n:* شَحمات [šaħama:t] *pl:* • **1.** piece of fat, suet, tallow, or lard – شَحمَة الإذِن [šaħmat ʔilʔiðin] earlobe.
تَشحِيم [tašħi:m] *n:* • **1.** lubrication
شَحمِي [šaħmi] *adj:* • **1.** fatty, greasy

ش ح ن

شِحَن [šiħan] *v:* • **1.** to ship, freight, consign – راح نِشحَن طَنَّين بُصَل لِلبَصرَة [ra:ħ nišħan ṭannayn buṣal lilbaṣra] We're going to ship two tons of onions to Basra. راح تِشحَن الرَّقِّي بِالقِطار لَو بِاللُّورِيّات؟ [ra:ħ tišħan ʔirraggi bilqiṭa:r law billu:riyya:t?] Are you going to ship the watermelons by train or by truck? • **2.** to charge, load with electricity – هَالمَكِينَة تِشحَن الباترِيّات [halmaki:na tišħan ʔilpa:triyya:t] This machine charges batteries.
اِنشِحَن [ʔinšiħan] *v:* • **1.** to be charged, to be loaded, to be shipped
شَحِن [šaħin] *n:* • **1.** shipping, freighting • **2.** charging, loading with electricity
شُحنَة [šuħna] *n:* شُحنات [šuħna:t] *pl:* • **1.** load, shipment, cargo • **1.** charge, freight
شاحِنَة [ša:ħina] *n:* شاحِنات [ša:ħina:t] *pl:* • **1.** charger, battery charger
مُشاحَنَة [muša:ħana] *n:* • **1.** quarrel, feud, grudge, hatred, enmity, controversy
مَشحُون [mašħu:n] *adj:* • **1.** loaded. laden, freighted, – لورِي مَشحُون طَماطَة [lu:ri mašħu:n ṭama:ṭa] a truck loaded with tomatoes. • **1.** charged (esp. ship)

ش

ش خ

شاخَة [šaːxa] *n:* شاخات [šaːxaːt] *pl:* • **1.** child's top with holes in the side to make noise

ش خ ب ط

شَخبَط [šaxbaṭ] *v:* • **1.** to scribble, scrawl – اِنطِيه القَلَم وَخَلّي يشَخبُط عَلَى هالوَرَقَة [ʔinṭi ʔilqalam wxalli: yšaxbuṭ ʕala halwaraqa] Give him the pen and let him scribble on this piece of paper.

ش خ خ

شَخ [šaxx] *v:* • **1.** to urinate, to piss, to make water – البَزُّونَة شَخَّت عالبَطّانِيَّة [ʔilbazzuːna šaxxat ʕalbattaːniyya] The cat wet on the blanket.
شَخَّخ [šaxxax] *v:* • **1.** to cause to urinate – شَخِّخَت الجّاهِل قَبِل ما تبَدِّلَه [šaxxixat ʔijjaːhil gabil maː tbaddillah] She made the child urinate before she'd change him.
شَخ [šaxx] *n:* • **1.** urine, piss
شَخَّة [šaxxa] *n:* شَخّات [šaxxaːt] *pl:* • **1.** urine, piss
شخاخ [šxaːx] *n:* • **1.** urine, piss

ش خ ر

شُوخَر [šuːxar] *v:* • **1.** to snore, to snort – شبِيك دَتشوخِر؟ خَشمَك مَسدُود؟ [šbiːk datšuːxir? xašmak masduːd?] Why are you snoring? Is your nose stopped up?
شِخَر [šixar] *v:* • **1.** to snore – بَس ما خَلَّى راسَه عالمخَدَّة، شِخَر [bas maː xallaː raːsah ʕalumxadda, šixar] As soon as he put his head on the pillow, he started to snore.
شَخُر [šaxur] *n:* • **1.** snoring
شَخِير، شخِير [šaxiːr, šxiːr] *n:* • **1.** snoring

ش خ ص

شَخَّص [šaxxaṣ] *v:* • **1.** to diagnose – الطَّبِيب ما قِدَر يشَخِّص المَرَض [ʔiṭṭabiːb maː gidar yšaxxiṣ ʔilmarað] The doctor couldn't diagnose the disease. • **2.** to identify, recognize – عِندَه قُصُر نَظَر وَما يِقدَر يشَخِّص الواحِد مِن بِعِيد [ʕindah quṣur naðar wma yigdar yšaxxiṣ ʔilwaːħid min biʕiːd] He's shortsighted and can't recognize anyone from a distance.
شَخِص [šaxiṣ] *n:* أشخاص [ʔašxaːṣ] *pl:* • **1.** person, individual – بِشَخصَه [bšaxṣah] himself, personally, in person. راح عَلِيه بِشَخصَه وحِكَى وِيّاه [raːħ ʕaliːh bšaxṣah wħičaː wiyyaːh] He went to see him personally and talked to him.
شَخصِيَّة [šaxṣiyya] *n:* شَخصِيّات [šaxṣiyyaːt] *pl:* • **1.** identity – ما نُعرُف شَخصِيَّة المَقتُول [maː nuʕruf šaxṣiyyat ʔilmaqtuːl] We don't know the murdered man's identity. • **2.** personality – حِكَى عَلِيه حَكِي حَطَّم شَخصِيتَه بِيه [ħičaː ʕaliːh ħači ħaṭṭam šaxṣiːtah biːh] He gave him a talking to that damaged his ego. • **3.** personage, big shot
تَشخِيص [tašxiːṣ] *n:* • **1.** identification • **2.** diagnosis
شَخصِي [šaxṣi] *adj:* • **1.** personal, private – مَسأَلَة شَخصِيَّة [masʔala šaxṣiyya] a private matter.
شَخصِياً [šaxṣiyyan] *adverbial:* • **1.** personally, from a personal viewpoint – آنِي شَخصِياً أفَضِّل العَرَق [ʔaːni šaxṣiyyan ʔafaððil ʔilʕarag] I personally prefer arrack.

ش خ ط

شِخَط [šixaṭ] *v:* • **1.** to scratch, mar, make a mark – شِخَط شُخطَين بالحايِط [šixaṭ šuxṭayn bilħaːyiṭ] He scratched two marks on the wall. • **2.** to cross out, scratch out, strike out – كِتَب الكِلمَة وَبَعدين شِخَطها [kitab ʔiččilma wbaʕdiːn šixaṭha] He wrote the word and then crossed it out. • **3.** to strike (a match) – شِخَطِت عُودتَين شِخّاط وَماكُو نار [šixaṭit ʕuːdtayn šixxaːṭ wmaːku naːr] I struck two matches and got no fire.
شَخَّط [šaxxaṭ] *v:* • **1.** intens. of شِخَط to scratch, mar, make a mark – بِيدَه البِسمار وَدَيشَخُّط بالباب [biːdah ʔilbismaːr wadayšaxxuṭ bilbaːb] He's got the nail in his hand and he's scratching up the door.
شَخُط [šaxuṭ, šuxuṭ] *n:* • **1.** scratching • **2.** crossing out • **3.** striking (a match) • **4.** pl. شخُوط scratch, mark
شَخطَة [šaxṭa] *n:* شَخطات [šaxṭaːt] *pl:* • **1.** scratch
شِخّاط [šixxaːṭ] *n:* • **1.** (coll.) match(es), lucifer(s) – عُودَة شِخّاط [ʕuːdat šixxaːṭ] a match.
شخُوط [šxuːṭ] *n:* • **1.** scratchings
شِخّاطَة [šixxaːṭa] *n:* شِخّاطات [šixxaːṭaːt] *pl:* • **1.** a match • **2.** a box of matches
مشَخَّط [mšaxxaṭ] *adj:* • **1.** scratched, marred, marked, scarred
مَشخُوط [mašxuːṭ] *adj:* • **1.** scratched, marred, marked, scarred • **2.** slightly crazy, touched in the head

ش د د

شَدّ [šadd] *v:* • **1.** to tie, fasten, bind – شَدّ خيط بِرِجل العَصفُور وَكُمَشَه حَتَّى ما يطِير [šadd xiːṭ brijl ʔilʕaṣfuːr wkumašah ħatta maː yṭiːr] He tied a string to the sparrow's leg and held it so it wouldn't fly. لا تشِدّ الشَّداد قَوِي [laː tšidd ʔiššadaːd qawi] Don't tie the bandage tight. لَجِّم الحصان قَبُل ما تشِدَّه بالعَرَبانَة [lajjim ʔilħṣaːn gabul maː tšiddah bilʕarabaːna] Bridle up the horse before you hitch him up to the cart. • **2.** to tie up, tie together, bind together – خَلّي الثِّياب بِالبُقجَة وَشِدها [xalliː ʔiθθiyaːb bilbuqča wšiddha] Put the shirts in the sheet and tie it up. • **3.** to mount, fasten on, assemble, put together – شِدّ الوِيلات القِدّامِيَّة أوَّل [šidd ʔilwiːlaːt ʔilgiddaːmiyya ʔawwal] Mount the front wheels first. يِقدَر يفُكّ البَنكَة وُصلَة وُصلَة وَبَعدين يشِدّها [yigdar yfukk ʔilpanka wuṣla wuṣla wbaʕdiːn yšiddha] He can take apart the fan piece by piece and then put it back

ش

together. شَدّلَه البايسِكِل بنُصّ ساعَة [šaddlah ʔilpaːysikil bnuṣṣ saːʕa] He put the bicycle together for him in half an hour. شِدّ حَيلَك وحاوِل تخَلِّص الشُّغُل [šidd ħiːlak wħaːwil txalliṣ ʔiššuɣul] Gather your strength and try to finish the work. • **4.** to stir up, cause trouble between – بَسّ يعجبَه يشِدّهُم وَيخَلّيهُم يتباسطُون [bass yʕiǰbah yšiddhum wyxalliːhum yitbaːṣṭuːn] He just likes to cause trouble between them and make them fight.

شَدَّد [šaddad] *v:* • **1.** to strengthen, intensify, make strong, harsh – ما دام كِذَبِت بالمَحكَمَة، الحاكِم راح يشَدِّد العُقُوبَة عَليك [maː daːm čiðabit bilmaħkama, ʔilħaːkim raːħ yšaddid ʔilʕuquːba ʕaliːk] Since you lied in court, the judge is going to make your sentence heavier. • **2.** to exert pressure, press – إذا تشَدِّد عَليه، ينطِيك الفلُوس [ʔiða tšaddid ʕaliːh, yinṭiːk ʔilfluːs] If you're firm with him, he'll give you the money.

شَدِّد [šaddid] *v:* • **1.** to emphasize, to insist

تشَدَّد [tšaddad] *v:* • **1.** to be harsh, strict, severe, stern – المُدِير الجِّدِيد دَيتشَدَّد هوايَة [ʔilmudiːr ʔiǰǰidiːd dayitšaddad hwaːya] The new principal is getting a lot more strict.

انشَدّ [ʔinšadd] *v:* • **1.** pass. of شَدّ to be tied, fastened – وُصلَت المَكاين كُلّها مفَكّكَة. لازِم تِنشَدّ بالمَحَلّ [wuṣlat ʔilmakaːyin kullha mfakkika. laːzim tinšadd bilmaħall] The machines arrived completely disassembled. They'll have to be put together in the shop.

اشتَدّ [ʔištadd] *v:* • **1.** to become hard, harsh, severe, intense – مِن وُقَع ثَلج بالشِّمال، اِشتَدّ البَرِد [min wugaʕ θalij biššimaːl, ʔištadd ʔilbarid] When the snow fell in the north, the cold became intense. • **2.** to become harder, harsher, more intense, severer – مِن يفُكّه البَنج، راح يِشتَدّ الوُجَع [min yfukkah ʔilbanǰ, raːħ yištadd ʔilwuǰaʕ] When the anesthetic wears off, the pain will become more severe. • **3.** to become aggravated, more critical – عِلنَوا الأحكام العِرفِيَّة. يبَيِّن اِشتَدَّت الأمُور [ʕilnaw ʔilʔaħkaːm ʔilʕirfiyya. yibayyin ʔištaddat ʔilʔumuːr] They proclaimed martial law. It seems matters have become more critical.

شَدّ [šadd] *n:* • **1.** tying, binding, fastening • **2.** tying up, fastening together • **3.** assembling

شَدَّة [šadda] *n:* شَدّات [šaddaːt] *pl:* • **1.** bundle, bunch, pack – شَدَّة أقلام [šaddat ʔaqlaːm] a bundle of pencils. شَدَّة جِزَر [šaddat ǰizar] a bunch of carrots. شَدَّة وَرد [šaddat warid] a bouquet of flowers. • **2.** tying, binding, fastening

شِدَّة [šidda] *n:* • **1.** intensity, severity, forcefulness, vehemence, violence • **2.** distress, hardship, adversity

مَشَدّ [mašadd] *n:* مَشَدّات [mašaddaːt] *pl:* • **1.** corset

شَدّاد، شداد [šaddaːd, šdaːd] *n:* شَدّادات، شدادات [šaddaːdaːt, šdaːdaːt] *pl:* • **1.** bandage

تَشدِيد [tašdiːd] *n:* • **1.** accent • **2.** strenghtening, intensification, emphasis

شَدِيد [šadiːd] *adj:* • **1.** strong, powerful, forceful, severe, hard, harsh, violent, vehement, intense – هالعُمّال إذا ما يكُون الواحِد شَدِيد ويّاهُم، ما يطلَع شُغُل [halʕummaːl ʔiða maː ykuːn ʔilwaːħid šadiːd wayyaːhum, maː yiṭlaʕ šuɣul] If one isn't severe with these workers, no work will get done.

مُشَدَّد [mušaddad] *adj:* • **1.** aggravating • **2.** intensive

مَشدُود [mašduːd] *adj:* • **1.** tied

متشَدِّد [mitšaddid] *adj:* • **1.** strict

أشَدّ [ʔašadd] *comparative adjective:* • **1.** more or most forceful, rigorous, intense

ش د ه

شِدَه [šidah] *v:* • **1.** to surprise, astonish, astound, amaze – لُون الجَّوهَرَة وكُبُرها شِدَهني [luːn ʔiǰǰawhara wkuburha šidahni] The color of the diamond and its size amazed me. جَمالها يشدَه [ǰamaːlha yišdah] Her beauty is dazzling. • **2.** to distract, preoccupy – شِدَهتنِي وَما قِدَرت أطبُخ زين [šidahtni wma gidarit ʔaṭbux ziːn] You distracted me and I couldn't cook well. مَشدُوه بشُغلَه وَما دَيقدَر يسافِر [mašduːh bšuɣlah wma dayigdar ysaːfir] He's preoccupied with his work and not able to take a trip.

اِنشِدَه [ʔinšidah] *v:* • **1.** to be surprised, astonished, amazed – مِن شاف المُجوهَرات، اِنشِدَه [min šaːf ʔilmuǰawharaːt, ʔinšidah] When he saw the jewelry, he was amazed. • **2.** to be distracted, preoccupied – البارحَة اِنشِدَهِت النَّهار كُلّه وَما صارلِي مَجال أخابرَك [ʔilbaːrħa ʔinšidahit ʔinnahaːr kullah wma ṣaːrli maǰaːl ʔaxaːbrak] Yesterday, I was preoccupied all day and had no chance to call you.

شَدِه [šadih] *n:* • **1.** astonishment, surprise • **2.** distraction

مَشدُوه [mašduːh] *adj:* • **1.** surprised, astonished, amazed • **2.** distracted, preoccupied – شبِيك مَشدُوه؟ ما دَتِسمَعني؟ [šbiːk mašduːh? maː datismaʕni?] Why are you so distracted? Aren't you listening to me?

ش د ي

شادي [šaːdi] *n:* شوادِي [šwaːdi] *pl:* • **1.** monkey

ش ذ ذ

شَذّ [šaðð] *v:* • **1.** to wander afield, become separated, isolated – دَتشِذّ عَن المَوضُوع وَما دَنِفهَم شِي [datšiðð ʕan ʔilmawḍuːʕ wma danifham ši] You're getting off the subject and we can't understand a thing. • **2.** to be exceptional, stand out – يشِذّ عَن بَقِيَة الطُّلّاب بِعِدَّة صِفات [yšiðð ʕan baqiyat ʔiṭṭullaːb biʕiddat ṣifaːt] He stands out from the rest of the students in several characteristics.

شُذُوذ، شِذُوذ [šuðuːð, šiðuːð] *n:* • **1.** irregularity, deviation, anomaly – شِذُوذ جِنسِي [šiðuːð ǰinsi] sexual deviation. • **2.** oddness, eccentricity

شاذ [ša:ðð] *adj:* شَواذ [šawa:ðð] *pl:* • **1.** irregular, anomalous, unusual, queer, odd, peculiar, extraordinary, strange, eccentric – حالَة شاذَّة [ħa:la ša:ðða] an exceptional situation. مِن الصَّعُب تِنسِجِم ويّاه. هُوَّ فَدّ واحِد شاذ [min ʔiṣṣaʕub tinsijim wiyya:h. huwwa fadd wa:ħid ša:ðð] It's difficult to get along with him. He's an eccentric character. • **2.** pl. شَواذ exception

ش ذ ر

شَذِر [šaðir] *n:* • **1.** (coll.) turquoise
شَذرَة [šaðra] *n:* شَذرات [šaðra:t] *pl:* • **1.** a turquoise, piece of turquoise
شَذرِي [šaðri] *adj:* • **1.** turquoise, turquoise blue – لُون شَذرِي [lu:n šaðri] turquoise colored.

ش ذ ر و ن

شَذِروان [šaðirwa:n, šadirwa:n] *n:* شَذِروانات [šaðirwa:na:t, šadirwa:na:t] *pl:* • **1.** fountain

ش ذ ي

شاذِي [ša:ði] *n:* شواذِي [šwa:ði] *pl:* • **1.** monkey

ش ر ب [1]

شِرَب [širab] *v:* • **1.** to drink – يِشرَب شاي هوايَة [yišrab ča:y hwa:ya] He drinks a lot of tea. لا تقَدِّملَه بيرَة؛ تَرَة ما يِشرَب [la: tqaddimlah bi:ra; tara ma: yišrab] Don't offer him beer; he doesn't drink. • **2.** to smoke – عُمرَه عَشِر سنِين وِيشرَب جِكايِر [ʕumrah ʕašir sni:n wyišrab ǰiga:yir] He's ten years old and smokes cigarettes.
شَرَّب [šarrab] *v:* • **1.** to make or let drink – الوَلَد ما دَيِشرَب الدُّوا مالَه. تَعال شَرّبَه [ʔilwalad ma: dayišrab ʔidduwa: ma:lah. taʕa:l šarrbah] The boy isn't drinking his medicine. Come make him drink. وَدِّي الخيل لِلشَّطّ، شَرُّبها مَيّ [waddi ʔilxi:l liššaṭṭ, šarrubha mayy] Take the horses to the river and water them. • **2.** to soak, saturate – شَرُّب الخُبُز بالمَرَق [šarrub ʔilxubuz bilmarag] Soak the bread in the gravy.
تشَرَّب [tšarrab] *v:* • **1.** to be saturated – خَلّي الخُبُز بِالشُّوربَة إِلَى أَن يِتشَرَّب زين [xalli: ʔilxubuz bilšu:rba ʔila ʔan yitšarrab zi:n] Leave the bread in the soup until it's well soaked.
اِنشِرَب [ʔinširab] *v:* • **1.** to be drunk – هَالمَيّ حارّ. ما يِنشُرُب [halmayy ħa:rr. ma: yinšurub] This water is hot. It can't be drunk.
شُرُب [šurub] *n:* • **1.** drinking
شَربَة [šarba] *n:* شَربات [šarba:t] *pl:* • **1.** large clay water jug
شُربَة، شِربَة [šurba, širba] *n:* شُربات، شِربات [šurba:t, širba:t] *pl:* • **1.** drink, draught, sip
شَراب [šara:b] *n:* • **1.** wine • **2.** syrup
مَشرَب [mašrab] *n:* مَشارُب [maša:rub] *pl:* • **1.** cigarette holder
شارِب [ša:rib] *n:* شوارُب [šwa:rub] *pl:* • **1.** moustache
تَشرِيب [tašri:b] *n:* • **1.** bread soaked in boiled meat juices, with meat on top (usually eaten for breakfast)
مَشرُوب [mašru:b] *n:* مَشارِيب [maša:ri:b] *pl:* • **1.** drink, (alcoholic) beverage
شُوربَة [šu:rba] *n:* شُوربات [šu:rba:t] *pl:* • **1.** soup
تَشرِيبايَة [tašri:ba:ya] *n:* • **1.** a dish made of dried bread and spices boiled in water (usually eaten for breakfast)
شَرّاب [šarra:b] *adj:* شَرّابِين [šarra:bi:n] *pl:* • **1.** heavy drinker, drunkard – شَرّاب جِكايِر [šarra:b ǰiga:yir] chain smoker.
شارُب [ša:rub] *adj:* شارِبِين [ša:rbi:n] *pl:* • **1.** drinker
شَرابِي [šara:bi] *adj:* • **1.** purple, wine-colored

ش ر ب [2]

شَربَت [šarbat] *n:* شَرابِت [šara:bit] *pl:* • **1.** sherbet, punch, non-carbonated soft drink • **2.** weak coffee

ش ر ب ت

شَربَت [šarbat] *v:* • **1.** to do hurriedly, carelessly, sloppily – شلُون خَلَّصت الشُّغُل بعَشِر دَقايِق؟ لازِم شَربَتَّه [šlu:n xallaṣt ʔiššuɣul bʕašir daqa:yiq? la:zim šarbattah] How did you finish the work in ten minutes? You must have done a sloppy job of it.

ش ر ب ك

شَربَك [šarbak] *v:* • **1.** to entangle, snarl – لا تشَربُكنِي بِهالمُشكِلَة [la: tšarbukni bihalmuškila] Don't get me into this problem.
تشَربَك [tšarbak] *v:* • **1.** to become entangled – رِجلِي تشَربِكَت بالحَبِل [riǰli tšarbikat bilħabil] My leg got tangled up in the rope.
شَربَكَة [šarbaka] *n:* • **1.** tangle

ش ر ح

شَرَح [šraħħ] *v:* • **1.** to be or become inflamed (in the eye) – بَسّ عاد تِبكِي! عينَك شرحَّت [bass ʕa:d tibči! ʕaynak šraħħat] Stop crying! Your eyes are all red.
شِرَح [širaħ] *v:* • **1.** to rip, cut down the middle, cut lengthwise – أُخُذ المِنشار وَإِشرَح هَاللَّوحَة [ʔuxuð ʔilminša:r wʔišraħ hallawħa] Take the saw and cut this board lengthwise. • **2.** to explain, elucidate, make clear or plain – الأُستاذ ما شِرَح الدَّرِس زين [ʔilʔusta:ð ma: širaħ ʔiddaris zi:n] The professor didn't explain the lesson well.
شَرَّح [šarraħ] *v:* • **1.** to cut up, cut in strips – شَرِّحها لِهَاللَّوحَة [šarriħha lhallawħa] Cut this board into strips. • **2.** to dissect, dismember – اليُوم راح نشَرِّح أَرنَب [ʔilyu:m ra:ħ nšarriħ ʔarnab] Today we're going to dissect a rabbit.

شَرِّحَوا المَيِّت حَتَّى يشُوفُون سَبَب مُوتَه [šarriħaw ʔilmayyit ħatta yšuːfuːn sabab muːtah] They performed an autopsy on the corpse to find out the cause of his death.
اِنشِرَح [ʔinširaħ] *v:* • **1.** to be explained, to be opened • **2.** to be happy, relaxed, to rejoice, to become glad
شَرِح [šariħ] *n:* • **1.** explanation, elucidation • **2.** ripping, cutting lengthwise
شِرحَة [širħa] *n:* شِرحات [širħaːt] *pl:* • **1.** slice, piece – شِرحَة لَحَم [širħat laħam] a piece of meat.
شريحَة [šriːħa] *n:* شَرايِح [šraːyiħ] *pl:* • **1.** strip, thin slice
تَشريح [tašriːħ] *n:* • **1.** dissecting, dissection – عِلم التَّشريح [ʕilm ʔittašriːħ] anatomy.
مَشرَحَة [mašraħa] *n:* • **1.** operating room, autopsy room
اِنشِراح [ʔinširaːħ] *n:* • **1.** joy, relaxation, delight, glee, gaiety
شِرِح [širiħ] *adj:* • **1.** lean – لَحَم شِرِح [laħam širiħ] lean meat.
أَشرَح [ʔašraħ] *adj:* شرحين، شُرُح [šrħiːn, šuruħ] *pl:* شَرحَة [šaraħa] *feminine:* • **1.** inflamed, infected (of the eye) • **2.** having an eye infection
مَشرُوح [mašruːħ] *adj:* • **1.** explained
تَشرِيحي [tašriːħi] *adj:* • **1.** anatomical

ش

ش ر خ

شَرَخ [šarix] *n:* • **1.** crack, splinter, fracture, break

ش ر د

شِرَد [širad] *v:* • **1.** to run away, flee – بَسّ شاف الشُّرطَة، شِرَد [bass šaːf ʔiššurṭa, širad] The moment he saw the police, he ran away. شارِد مِن السِّجِن وَدَيدَوّرُون عَليه [šaːrid min ʔissijin wadaydawwruːn ʕaliːh] He's escaped from prison and they're looking for him. قاعِد بِالصَّفّ وَفِكرَه شارِد [gaːʕid biṣṣaff wfikrah šaːrid] He is sitting in class but his mind is far away.
شَرَّد [šarrad] *v:* • **1.** to cause to flee, run away – شَرَّد الحَرامِيَّة بصياحَه [šarrad ʔilħaraːmiyya bṣyaːħah] He made the thieves run away with his shouting. الحَرُب شَرِّدَت هوايَة ناس مِن بيُوتهُم [ʔilħarub šarridat hwaːya naːs min byuːthum] The war drove a lot of people from their homes. شَرَّد اِبنَه قَبُل ما تِجِي الشُّرطَة تاخذَه [šarrad ʔibnah gabul maː tiji ʔiššurṭa taːxðah] He sent his son fleeing before the police came to take him.
تشَرَّد [tšarrad] *v:* • **1.** same as شِرَد to become homeless, vagabond – يِتشَرَّد مِن المَدرَسَة [yitšarrad min ʔilmadrasa] He runs away from school.
شَرِد [šarid] *n:* • **1.** running away, fleeing
شَردَة [šarda] *n:* شَردات [šardaːt] *pl:* • **1.** running away, fleeing
شراد [šraːd] *n:* • **1.** running away, fleeing; fugitive • **2.** fugitive, expatriated, vagabond, loafer, tramp
شارِد [šaːrid] *adj:* • **1.** running, fleeing, on the lam • **2.** pl. شارِدين fugitive, runaway, escapee, deserter, loafer, vagrant, vagabond
مِتشَرِّد [mitšarrid] *adj:* • **1.** tramp, loafer, • **2.** vagrant, homeless, vagabond

ش ر ر [1]

شَرّ [šarr] *v:* • **1.** to hang (on a line) – شُرّ هالهدُوم المبَلّلَة عَالحَبَل [šurr halhduːm ʔilimballila ʕalħabil] Hang these wet clothes on the line. شَرُّوه عَالحَبِل بِحَكِيهُم هَذا [šarruːh ʕalħabil bħačyhum haːða] They exposed him by talking like that.
اِنشَرّ [ʔinšarr] *v:* • **1.** to be hung (on a line), • **2.** revealed, exposed

ش ر ر [2]

شَرّ [šarr] *n:* • **1.** evil, wickedness, malice – اِنطِيه عَشِر دَنانِير وَتكَفَّى شَرَّه [ʔinṭi ʕašir danaːniːr wtčaffaː šarrah] Give him ten dinars and be done with him. لا تِحكِي وِيّاه، تَرَة دَيدَوِّر شَرّ [laː tiħči wiyyaːh, tara daydawwir šarr] Don't speak to him, because he's looking for trouble. • **2.** hanging (on a line)
شَرارَة [šaraːra] *n:* شَرارات [šaraːraːt] *pl:* • **1.** spark
شِرِّير [širriːr] *adj:* أشرار [ʔašraːr] *pl:* • **1.** very bad, very evil
شَرّانِي [šarraːni] *adj:* • **1.** evil

ش ر س [1]

شَراسَة [šaraːsa] *n:* • **1.** fierceness, ferociousness, • **1.** gnarl, querulousness
شَرِس [šaris] *adj:* • **1.** vicious, malicious, ill-tempered – هَالشُّرطِي شَرِس كُلِّش [haššurṭi šaris külliš] That cop is real mean. • **2.** wild, ferocious, fierce – السَّبِع حَيوان شَرِس [ʔissabiʕ ħaywaːn šaris] The lion is a ferocious animal.

ش ر س [2]

شريس [šriːs, šriːṣ] *n:* • **1.** glue, paste • **2.** a powder which becomes glue or paste when mixed with water

ش ر ش ف

شَرشَف [čarčaf] *n:* شَراشِف [čaraːčif] *pl:* • **1.** large cloth • **2.** tablecloth • **3.** bed-sheet – شَرشَف مخَدَّة [čarčaf mxadda] pillowcase.

ش ر ط

شِرَط [širaṭ] *v:* • **1.** to stipulate, to impose as a condition – شِرَط لازِم تكُون حُصَّتَه أكثَرهُم [širaṭ laːzim tkuːn ħuṣṣtah ʔakθarhum] He stipulated that his share must be biggest.
شَرَّط [šarraṭ] *v:* • **1.** to make an incision, cut into, lance – أَخَذ المُوس وَشَرَّط بِيه الحَبّايَة [ʔaxað ʔilmuːs

wšarraṭ bi:h ʔilħabba:ya] He took the razor and lanced the boil with it.
شارَط [ša:raṭ] *v:* • **1.** to bet, wager – أشارطَك راح يصِير وَزير بالوُزارَة الجِّديدَة [ʔaša:rṭak ra:ħ yiṣi:r wazi:r bilwuza:ra ʔijjidi:da] I bet you he'll be a minister in the new cabinet.
تشارَط [tša:raṭ] *v:* • **1.** to fix mutual conditions, to conclude an agreement – تشارَط ويّاهُم ياخُذ خُمُس الرِّبح [tša:raṭ wiyya:hum ya:xuð xumus ʔirribiħ] He made an agreement with them to take one-fifth of the profits. تشارَطنا إذا وُصَل قَبلي، أوَدِّيه لِلسِّينَما [tša:raṭna ʔiða wuṣal gabli, ʔawaddi:h lissinama] We made an agreement that if he got there before me, I would take him to the movies.
اِشتِرَط [ʔištiraṭ] *v:* • **1.** to stipulate, impose a condition – اِشتِرَط عَليهُم يدِزُّون البِضاعَة بالطَّيّارَة [ʔištiraṭ ʕali:hum ydizzu:n ʔilbiða:ʕa biṭṭayya:ra] He imposed on them the condition that they send the goods by plane.
شَرِط [šariṭ] *n:* شُرُوط [šuru:ṭ] *pl:* • **1.** condition, precondition, provision, stipulation – أرُوح لِلسِّينَما بِشَرِط تِجِي ويّايا [ʔaru:ħ lissinama bšarṭ tiji wiyya:ya] I'll go to the movies on condition that you come with me. يبِيع الرَّقِّي شَرط السِّكِّين [yibi:ʕ ʔirraggi šarṭ ʔissičči:n] He sells the watermelons on the condition that they are good.
شُرطَة [šurṭa] *n:* • **1.** (coll.) police, policemen, police force
شُرطِي [šurṭi] *n:* شُرطِيِّين، شُرطَة [šurṭi:yyi:n, šurṭa] *pl:* • **1.** policeman
شَرِيط [šari:ṭ] *n:* أشرِطَة، شَرائِط [ʔašriṭa, šara:yiṭ] *pl:* • **1.** ribbon, band, tape, strip – شَرِيط مُسَجِّل [šari:ṭ musajjil] recording tape. • **2.** ribbon, medal, decoration
مِشرَط [mišraṭ] *n:* مَشارِط [maša:riṭ] *pl:* • **1.** scalpel, lancet

ش ر ع

شراع [šra:ʕ] *n:* شراعات، أشرِعَة [šra:ʕa:t, ʔašriʕa] *pl:* • **1.** sail
شارِع [ša:riʕ] *n:* شَوارِع [šawa:riʕ] *pl:* • **1.** street – راس الشّارِع [ra:s ʔišša:riʕ] end of the block, intersection, corner.
مُشَرِّع [mušarriʕ] *n:* • **1.** legislator • **2.** law-giver
الشَّرِع [ʔiššariʕ] *n:* • **1.** the canonical law of Islam – خِلاف الشَّرِع [xila:f ʔiššariʕ] violation of religious law.
شَرعِيَّة [šarʕiyya] *n:* • **1.** lawfulness, legality, legitimacy
شِرِيعَة [širi:ʕa] *n:* شِرِيعات [širi:ʕa:t] *pl:* • **1.** an approach to a water hole, a level, flat place beside a body of water
تَشرِيع [tašri:ʕ] *n:* • **1.** legislation
مَشرُوع [mašru:ʕ] *adj:* • **1.** legal, lawful, legitimate – عَمَلَك مُو مَشرُوع [ʕamalak mu: mašru:ʕ] Your action isn't legal. • **2.** acceptable, allowable – هَذا عُذُر غير مَشرُوع [ha:ða ʕuður ɣi:r mašru:ʕ] That's not an acceptable excuse. • **3.** (as n:) project, undertaking, enterprise
الشَّرِيعَة [ʔiššari:ʕa] *n:* • **1.** the Sharia, the canonical law of Islam
شَرعِي [šarʕi] *adj:* • **1.** legal, lawful, legitimate – فَصلَه مِن الوَظِيفَة مُو شَرعِي [faṣlah min ʔilwaḍi:fa mu: šarʕi] Discharging him from his position was illegal. • **2.** dealing with religious law – مَحكَمَة شَرعِيَّة [maħkama šarʕiyya] religious court.
مُشَرَّع [mušarraʕ] *adj:* • **1.** legislated • **2.** widely opened
شراعِي [šra:ʕi] *adj:* • **1.** sail, sailing, rigged with sails – مَركَب شراعِي [markab šra:ʕi] sailboat.
تَشرِيعِي [tašri:ʕi] *adj:* • **1.** legislative – السُّلطَة التَّشرِيعِيَّة [ʔissulṭa ʔittašri:ʕiyya] the legislative branch.
شَرعاً [šarʕan] *adverbial:* • **1.** legally, in a legal sense – هَذا شِي شَرعاً ما مَقبُول [ha:ða ši šarʕan ma: maqbu:l] This sort of thing is legally unacceptable.

ش ر ف

شَرَّف [šarraf] *v:* • **1.** to honor – شَرِّفُونا دائِماً [šarrfu:na da:yman] Visit us often (lit., honor us always). • **2.** to be more noble, eminent, distinguished, honorable than – آني أشَرِّفَك وَأشَرُّف عائِلتَك [ʔa:ni ʔašarrfak wʔašarruf ʕa:ʔiltak] I'm worth more than you and your family.
أشرَف [ʔašraf] *v:* • **1.** with عَلَى to watch, supervise, oversee – إنتَ إشرِف عالشُّعبَة إلَى أن يرجَع المُلاحِظ مالكُم [ʔinta ʔišrif ʕaššuʕba ʔila ʔan yirjaʕ ʔilmula:ħiḍ ma:lkum] You watch over the section until your superintendent comes back. يا مُعاوِن يشرِف عَلَى شُعبَة المُحاسَبَة؟ [ya: muʕa:win yišrif ʕala šuʕbat ʔilmuħa:saba?] Which assistant supervises the personnel section? • **2.** to overlook, be above, command a view of – غُرُفتِي تِشرِف عَالشّارِع [ɣurufti tišrif ʕašša:riʕ] My room overlooks the street.
تشَرَّف [tšarraf] *v:* • **1.** to be honored, feel honored – تشَرَّفنا بمَعرفتَك [tšarrafna bmaʕriftak] I'm honored to make your acquaintance.
شَرَف [šaraf] *n:* • **1.** eminence, dignity, nobility, high standing • **2.** honor – راح نسَوِّي حَفلَة عَلَى شَرَفَه [ra:ħ nsawwi: ħafla ʕala šarafah] We're going to have a party in his honor. بِطاقَة شَرَف [biṭa:qat šaraf] invitation for an honored guest.
شُرفَة [šurfa] *n:* • **1.** balcony
مُشرِف [mušrif] *n:* • **1.** supervisor
إشراف [ʔišra:f] *n:* • **1.** supervision, superintendence, control, patronage, auspices
تَشرِيفاتِي [tašri:fa:ti] *n:* تَشرِيفاتِيَّة [tašri:fa:tiyya] *pl:* • **1.** usher, master of ceremonies, chief of protocol

ش

شَرِيف [šari:f] *adj:* أَشراف، شُرَفاء [ʔašra:f, šurafa:ʔ] *pl:* • **1.** distinguished, eminent, illustrious, noble • **2.** honorable, respectable, honest • **3.** (pl. شُرفَة) 'sherif', a descendant of Mohammed
مُشَرِّف [mušarrif] *adj:* • **1.** honorable
أَشرَف [ʔašraf] *comparative adjective:* • **1.** more or most distinguished, eminent • **2.** more or most honorable, respectable

ش ر ق

شِرَق [širag] *v:* • **1.** to split, crack – تِقدَر تِشرُق الخِشبَة بِالفاس [tigdar tišrug ʔilxišba bilfa:s] You can split the log with the axe. • **2.** to choke, swallow the wrong way – شِرَق لِأَنّ كان يِشرَب المَيّ بِسُرعَة [širag liʔann ča:n yišrab ʔilmayy bsurʕa] He choked because he was drinking the water fast.
شَرَّق [šarrag] *v:* • **1.** to split, crack repeatedly – شَرِّق السَّعفَة وطَلِّع مِنها عُوَد رفاع [šarrig ʔissaʕfa wṭalliʕ minha ʕuwad rfa:ʕ] Split up the palm leaf and get some thin sticks from it.
اِستَشرَق [ʔistašraq] *v:* • **1.** to become an Orientalist – اِستَشرَق وقِضَى عُمرَه يِدرُس عَرَبِي [ʔistašraq wgiða: ʕumrah yidrus ʕarabi] He adopted the Eastern culture and spent his life studying Arabic. • **2.** to adopt oriental manners
شَرق [šarq] *n:* • **1.** east – إيران تحِدّ العِراق مِن الشَّرق [ʔira:n tħidd ʔilʕira:q min ʔiššarq] Iran borders Iraq on the east. • **2.** the East, the Orient – الشَّرق الأَوسَط [ʔiššarq ʔilʔawṣaṭ] The Middle East.
شَرِق [šarig] *n:* شرُوق [šru:g] *pl:* • **1.** split, crack, fissure
شُرُوق [šuru:q] *n:* • **1.** sunrise
مَشرِق [mašriq] *n:* مَشارِق [maša:riq] *pl:* • **1.** east, place of sunrise, the east, the orient
إِشراق [ʔišra:q] *n:* • **1.** sunrise, brillance (of the morning), radiant brightness
اِستِشراق [ʔistišra:q] *n:* • **1.** oriental studies
شَرقِي [šarqi] *adj:* • **1.** eastern, easterly – المَنطَقَة الشَّرقِيَّة [ʔalmanṭaqa ʔiššarqiyya] the eastern region. • **2.** oriental, eastern – هدُوم شَرقِيَّة [hdu:m šarqiyya] oriental clothes. بَيت شَرقِي [bayt šarqi] a house built around a central patio. حَمّام شَرقِي [ħamma:m šarqi] eastern style bathroom, Turkish bath.
مُشرِق [mušriq] *adj:* • **1.** radiant, resplendent, • **2.** shiny, brilliant
شرُوقِي [šru:gi] *adj:* شرُوقِيَّة، شرُوق [šru:gi:yya, šru:g] *pl:* • **1.** person from the rural areas of southern Iraq
مُستَشرِق [mustašriq] *adj:* مُستَشرِقِين [mustašriqi:n] *pl:* • **1.** a person who studies the Orient • **2.** (as n:) Orientalist
شَرقاوِي [šarga:wi] *adj:* شراقوَة [šra:gwa] *pl:* • **1.** person from the rural areas of southern Iraq

ش ر ق ط

شِرقِيط [širgi:ṭ, širgi:l] *n:* • **1.** cramp, muscle spasm

ش ر ق ل

شِرقال [širga:l] *n:* • **1.** cramp, muscle spasm

ش ر ك

شِرَك [širak] *v:* • **1.** to make a partner, participant, associate, to give a share, include – لا تشِركُونِي بهَالقَضِيَّة العَوِيصَة [la: tširku:ni bhalqaðiyya ʔalʕawi:ṣa] Don't include me in this complicated matter.
شارَك [ša:rak] *v:* • **1.** to enter into partnership, association, participation with, to join, combine, be or become a partner with – شارَكتهُم وخسَرت [ša:rakthum wixsarit] I went into partnership with them and I lost money.
أَشرَك [ʔašrak] *v:* • **1.** as in شِرَك in شِرَك بِاللّه **2.** to make a partner, participant, associate, to give a share, include • **3.** to be a polytheist, hold others equal with God – اللِّي يِشرِك بالله يرُوح لِلنّار [ʔilli yišrik bʔallah yiru:ħ linna:r] He who holds others equal to God goes to hell.
تشارَك [tša:rak] *v:* • **1.** to form a partnership, enter into partnership – سِمَعِت راح تِتشارَك ويّا صاحِب هالمَخزَن [simaʕit ra:ħ titša:rak wiyya ṣa:ħib halmaxzan] I heard that you're going into partnership with the owner of this store.
اِشتِرَك [ʔištirak] *v:* • **1.** to involve oneself, to participate, take part, join in, collaborate – اِشتِرَكِت بِجَمعِيَّة المُعَلِّمِين [ʔištirakit bjamʕiyyat ʔilmuʕallimi:n] I became a member of the teachers' association. أَشُو ما دَتِشتِرِك وِيّانا. المَوضُوع ما يِعجبَك؟ [ʔašu ma: datištirik wiyya:na. ʔilmawðu:ʕ ma: yʕijbak?] I notice you're not joining in with us. The subject doesn't please you? طِيّاراتنا اِشتِركَت بِالمَعرَكَة [ṭiyya:ra:tna ʔištirkat bilmaʕraka] Our airplanes took part in the battle. • **2.** to subscribe – جُبَرنِي أَشتِرِك بهالمَجَلَّة السَّخِيفَة [ǰubarni ʔaštirik bhalmaǰalla ʔissaxi:fa] He forced me to subscribe to this silly magazine.
شَرَك [šarak] *n:* • **1.** barbed wire
شِرك [širk] *n:* • **1.** polytheism
شُركَة [šurka] *n:* • **1.** partnership, association
شَرِكَة [šarika] *n:* شَرِكات [šarika:t] *pl:* • **1.** company, firm, corporation
شَرِيك [šari:k] *n:* شُرَكاء، شُركان [šuraka:ʔ, šurka:n] *pl:* • **1.** partner • **2.** ally, associate • **3.** accomplice
شَراكَة [šara:ka] *n:* • **1.** partnership, association
مُشتَرِك [muštarik] *n:* مُشتَرِكِين [muštariki:n] *pl:* • **1.** subscriber, participant
تَشارُك [taša:ruk] *n:* • **1.** partnership, participation
مُشارِك [muša:rik] *n:* • **1.** partner, associate, participant
إِشراك [ʔišra:k] *n:* • **1.** involvment, polytheism

اِشتِراك [ʔištira:k] *n:* • **1.** participation, collaboration, sharing, joining • **2.** partnership • **3.** subscription fee, rate • **4.** dues, participation fee • **5.** pl. اِشتِراكات subscription
مُشارَكَة [muša:raka] *n:* • **1.** participation, partnership, cooperation, collaboration • **2.** complicity, accessoriness (jur.)
اِشتِراكِيَّة [ʔištira:kiyya] *n:* • **1.** socialism
مُشرِك [mušrik] *adj:* مُشرِكِين [mušriki:n] *pl:* • **1.** (as n:) a polytheist
مُشتَرَك [muštarak] *adj:* • **1.** joint, combined, collective, common, co-, communal – بَالَغ مُشتَرَك [ba:laɣ muštarak] joint communique. حَمّام مُشتَرَك [ħamma:m muštarak] communal bath house. قاسِم مُشتَرَك [qa:sim muštarak] common denominator (math.). السُّوق المُشتَرَكَة [ʔissu:q ʔilmuštaraka] The Common Market.
اِشتِراكِي [ʔištira:ki] *adj:* • **1.** socialist, socialistic • **2.** as a Noun: a socialist

ش ر م

شِرَم [širam] *v:* • **1.** to split, cleave, slit – التِّرچِيَّة شِرمَت إِذِنها [ʔittirčiyya širmat ʔiðinha] The earring split her ear.
شَرَّم [šarram] *v:* • **1.** to do a good job of, do thoroughly, do properly, do up brown – آنِي هَذا اللّي أعُرفَه. إنتَ عُود راح تشَرُّمها؟ [ʔa:ni ha:ða ʔilli ʔaʕurfah. ʔinta ʕu:d ra:ħ tšarrumha?] That's it as I know it. Now you think you're going to do it up right? عَبالِي يعُرف إنكلِيزِي. شَرَّمها! تَرجَم المَكتُوب غَلَط [ʕaba:li yuʕruf ʔingili:zi. šarramha! tarǰam ʔilmaktu:b ɣalaṭ] I thought he knew English. He really did it up brown! He translated the letter wrong. عَبالِي يِطلَع أحسَن مِن أخُوه. جا شَرَّمها [ʕaba:li yiṭlaʕ ʔaħsan min ʔaxu:h. ǰa: šarramha] I thought he'd turn out better than his brother. He sure did, by far!
شَرُم [šarum] *n:* • **1.** splitting, cleaving, slitting
شاوُرمَة [ša:wurma] *n:* • **1.** sliced beef sandwich, sliced chicken sandwich
أشرَم [ʔašram] *adj:* شُرُم، شَرمِين [šurum, šarmi:n] *pl:* شَرمَة [šarma] *feminine:* • **1.** having a harelip

ش ر م خ

شَرمَخ [šarmax] *v:* • **1.** to scratch

ش ر ن ق

شَرنَقَة [šarnaqa] *n:* شَرانِق [šara:niq] *pl:* • **1.** cocoon, especially of the silkworm

ش ر ه

شَراهَة [šara:ha] *n:* • **1.** gluttony, greediness for food – ياكُل بشَراهَة [ya:kul bšara:ha] He eats greedily.
شَرِه [šarih] *adj:* • **1.** greedy (for food), gluttonous – شقَدّ ما تخَلِّيلَه أكِل، ما يِكتِفِي. هُوَّ فَدّ واحِد شَرِه [šgadd ma: txalli:lah ʔakil, ma: yiktifi. huwwa fadd wa:ħid šarih] No matter how much food you give him, he isn't satisfied. He's greedy.

ش ر و ل

شِروال [širwa:l] *n:* شِروالات، شِراوِيل [širwa:la:t, šira:wi:l] *pl:* • **1.** a sort of loose-fitting trousers – الأكراد يِلبَسُون شِروال [ʔilʔakra:d yilbasu:n širwa:l] The Kurds wear (baggy) pants.

ش ر ي

شِرَى [šira:] *v:* • **1.** to purchase, buy – مِن يا قَصّاب اِشتَرَيت اللَّحَم؟ [min ya: gaṣṣa:b ʔištri:t ʔillaħam?] From which butcher did you buy the meat? بيش اِشرَيتها؟ [biyš ʔišraytha?] How much did you buy it for?
اِنشِرَى [ʔinšira:] *v:* • **1.** to be sold
اِشتِرَى [ʔištira:] *v:* • **1.** to purchase, buy – اِشتِرَى سَيّارَة جِدِيدَة [ʔištira: sayya:ra ǰidi:da] He bought a new car. يِشتِري العَركَة بفلُوس [yištiri ʔilʕarka bflu:s] He looks for trouble. هَذا شَيطان؛ يِشتِرِيك وَيبِيعَك [ha:ða ši:ṭa:n; yištiri:k wybi:ʕak] He's a tricky character; he'll take the shirt off your back.
شَروَة [šarwa] *n:* شَروات [šarwa:t] *pl:* • **1.** purchase, buy
شَرّاي [šarra:y] *n:* شَرّايَة [šarra:ya] *pl:* • **1.** purchaser, buyer – بَيّاع شَرّاي [bayya:ʕ šarra:y] dealer, merchant.
شِريان [širya:n] *n:* شَرايِين [šara:yi:n] *pl:* • **1.** artery
مُشتَري، مِشتَري [muštari, mištiri] *n:* مُشتَرِيَّة، مِشتِرِيَّة [muštariyya, mištiriyya] *pl:* • **1.** buyer, purchaser, customer
مِشتَرَى [mištara] *n:* مِشتَرَيات [mištaraya:t] *pl:* • **1.** buying, purchasing, acquisition • **2.** things purchased, purchased goods
شرايَة [šra:ya] *n:* • **1.** purchasing, buying
المُشتَري [ʔilmuštari] *n:* • **1.** the planet Jupiter
شِرائِي [šira:ʔi] *adj:* • **1.** purchasing (as in قُدرَة شِرائِيَّة) purchasing power
شِريانِي [širya:ni] *adj:* • **1.** relating to the arteries, arterial

ش ص ص

شُصّ [šuṣṣ] *n:* شصُوص [šṣu:ṣ] *pl:* • **1.** fishhook

ش ص ي

شاصِي [ša:ṣi] *n:* شاصِيّات [ša:ṣi:yya:t] *pl:* • **1.** chassis (automotive)

ش ط ب

شِطَب [šiṭab] *v:* • **1.** to cross out, mark out, strike out – شِطَب أكثَر الأشياء المَوجُودَة بالقائِمَة [šiṭab ʔakθar ʔilʔašya:ʔ ʔilmawǰu:da bilqa:ʔima] He crossed out most of the things on the list.

ش

شَطَّب [šaṭṭab] *v:* • **1.** intens. of شِطَب to cross out, mark out, strike out – لِزَم القَلَم وَقام يشَطُّب [lizam ʔilqalam wgaːm yšaṭṭub] He grabbed the pen and started crossing things out.
شَطُب [šaṭub] *n:* • **1.** crossing out, striking out, scratching out
شَطبَة [šaṭba] *n:* شَطبات [šaṭbaːt] *pl:* • **1.** crossing out

ش ط ح

شَطِح [šaṭiħ] *n:* • **1.** flat, shallow – ماعُون شَطِح [maːʕuːn šaṭiħ] a shallow dish.

ش ط ح ل

شطَحلي [šṭaħli] *n:* • **1.** a kind of card game

ش ط ر

شِطَر [šiṭar] *v:* • **1.** to cut into two equal parts – شِطَر اللَّحمَة بِالنُّصّ [šiṭar ʔillaħma binnuṣṣ] He cut the piece of meat right down the middle.
تشاطَر [tšaːṭar] *v:* • **1.** to exchange clever or flippant remarks, engage in repartee – لا تِتشاطَر ويّاه. ثنينكُم نفس الشّي [laː titšaːṭar wiyyaːh. θaynkum nafs ʔišši] Don't be smart with him. The two of you are just alike.
شَطِر [šaṭir] *n:* • **1.** cutting into two equal parts, a half
شَطارَة [šaṭaːra] *n:* • **1.** cleverness, shrewdness, cunning, adroitness, skill • **2.** industriousness
شاطِر [šaːṭir] *adj:* شُطَّر، شُطّار [šuṭṭar, šuṭṭaːr] *pl:* • **1.** clever, smart, bright, adroit, skillful – لا تخاف عَليه. هُوَّ كُلِّش شاطِر [laː txaːf ʕaliːh. huwwa kulliš šaːṭir] Don't worry about him. He's very clever. • **2.** industrious, diligent, hardworking – صِير شاطِر وَخَلِّص شُغلَك بالعَجَل [ṣiːr šaːṭir wxalliṣ šuɣlak bilʕajal] Be industrious and finish your work quickly. كُلّ التَّلاميذ كَسلانين. بَسّ إبنَك شاطِر [kull ʔittalaːmiːð kaslaːniːn. bass ʔibnak šaːṭir] All of the students are lazy. Your son's the only hard worker.
أشطَر [ʔašṭar] *comparative adjective:* • **1.** more or most clever, shrewd, adroit, skillful

ش ط ر ن ج

شِطرَنج [šiṭranǰ] *n:* • **1.** chess • **2.** pl. شِطرَنجات [šiṭranǰaːt] chess set

ش ط ط

شَطّ [šaṭṭ] *n:* شطُوط [šṭuːṭ] *pl:* • **1.** river
شاطِي [šaːṭi] *n:* شواطِي [šwaːṭi] *pl:* • **1.** flood plain, fields inundated at flood time – شاطِي شَباطِي، شاطِي باطِي [šaːṭi šabaːṭi, šaːṭi baːṭi] easily, effortlessly. لِعَب بيه شاطِي باطِي [liʕab biːh šaːṭi baːṭi] He made a fool of him. He beat him without any effort. لِعبَت بيه شاطِي شَباطِي [liʕbat biːh šaːṭi šabaːṭi] She made a mess out of him.

ش ط ف

شِطَف [šiṭaf] *v:* • **1.** to infatuate, enamor, fill with ardent passion – شِطفَتَه. ما دَيفكِّر بأحَّد غيرها [šiṭfatah. maː dayfakkir bʔaħħad ɣiːrha] She completely captivated him. He can't think about anyone but her. • **2.** to rinse in clean water, rinse off – آني أصُوبِن المواعِين وَإنتَ إشطُفها [ʔaːni ʔaṣuːbin ʔilmwaːʕiːn wʔinta ʔišṭufha] I'll soap the dishes and you rinse them. • **3.** to make ritually clean by dipping three times in water – إغسِل الماعُون وأشطفَه الكَلِب أكَل بيه [ʔiɣsil ʔilmaːʕuːn wʔušṭfah. ʔiččalib ʔakal biːh] Wash the plate and make it ritually clean. The dog ate off it. • **4.** to rebuke, belittle, scold, berate – شِطفَتَه غير شَطفَة [šiṭfatah ɣiːr šaṭfa] She gave him a good scolding.
شَطَّف [šaṭṭaf] *v:* • **1.** to wash the private parts – الخَدّامَة شَطُّفَت الجّاهِل وَبَدِّلَتلَه [ʔilxaddaːma šaṭṭufat ʔijǰaːhil wbaddilatlah] The maid washed the child's bottom and changed him.
تشَطَّف [tšaṭṭaf] *v:* • **1.** to wash one's private parts – لا تِطلَع مِن الخَلوَة قَبُل ما تِتشَطَّف [laː titlaʕ min ʔilxalwa gabul maː titšaṭṭaf] Don't leave the toilet before you wash yourself.
شَطُف [šaṭuf] *n:* • **1.** rinsing, cleansing, rebuking, scolding
مَشطُوف [mašṭuːf] *adj:* • **1.** madly in love, infatuated, enamored • **2.** rinsed, washed ritually clean

ش ع ب

تشَعَّب [tšaʕʕab] *v:* • **1.** to separate, split, diverge, branch out – هَالطَّرِيق بَعدين راح يتشَعَّب [haṭṭariːq baʕdiːn raːħ yitšaʕʕab] Later on this road will branch out.
شَعَب [šaʕab] *n:* شُعُوب [šuʕuːb] *pl:* • **1.** people, folk • **2.** ethnic group • **3.** nation
شُعبَة [šuʕba] *n:* شُعَب [šuʕab] *pl:* • **1.** section, portion, part, division • **2.** department, branch, section
تَشَعُّب [tašaʕʕub] *n:* • **1.** ramification, branching, branching off, spliting
شَعبِيَّة [šaʕbiyya] *n:* • **1.** popularity
شَعبان [šaʕbaːn] *n:* • **1.** Shaban, the eighth month of the Moslem calendar
شَعبِي [šaʕbi] *adj:* • **1.** popular, folk- – أغاني شَعبِيَّة [ʔaɣaːni šaʕbiyya] folk songs, popular songs. رَئِيس شَعبِي [raʔiːs šaʕbi] a popular leader.
متشَعِّب [mitšaʕʕib] *adj:* • **1.** ramified, manifold, branching • **2.** versatile, diverse. ramified, many-sided

ش ع ب ث

شَعبَث [šaʕbaθ] *v:* • **1.** to mess up, make a mess of – شَكُو عِندَك دَتشَعبِث الأغراض؟ [šaku ʕindak datšaʕbiθ ʔilʔaɣraːð?] Why are you messing up the things? لا تِحكِي قِدّامَه شي. هُوَّ فَدّ واحِد يشَعبِث [laː tiħči giddaːmah ši. huwwa fadd waːħid yšaʕbiθ] Don't say anything in front of him. He's the sort who makes a mess of everything.

ش ع ر

شِعَر [šiʕar] *v:* • **1.** to know, be cognizant – دَيِشعُر أن الكُلّ يحِبُّوه [dayišʕur ʔan ʔilkull yħibbuːh] He knows that everyone likes him. • **2.** to realize, notice – ظَلّوا يقَشمُرُون عَليه وَلا شِعَر [ðallaw yiqašmuruːn ʕaliːh walaː šiʕar] They kept pulling his leg and he never realized. • **3.** to feel, sense – الطَّبيب نِغَزَه بأبرَة وَلا شِعَر بيها [ʔiṭṭabiːb niɣazah bʔubra wala šiʕar biːha] The doctor poked him with a needle and he never felt it.

شَعَّر [šaʕʕar] *v:* • **1.** to make aware, conscious – شَعَّرتَه بالخَطَر وعِرَف شِيسَوِّي [šaʕʕartah bilxaṭar wʕiraf šiːsawwi] I awakened him to the danger and he knew what to do.

شَعَر [šaʕar] *n:* • **1.** (coll.) hair(s) – شَعَر بَنات [šaʕar banaːt] cotton candy. • **2.** fur

شِعِر [šiʕir] *n:* أشعار [ʔašʕaːr] *pl:* • **1.** poetry

شَعرَة [šaʕra] *n:* شَعرات [šaʕraːt] *pl:* • **1.** a hair – زين حَصَّلِت دِينار مِنَّه. شَعرَه مِن جِلِد خِنزِير [ziːn ħaṣṣalit dinaːr minnah. šaʕrah min jilid xinziːr] It's good you got a dinar from him. Getting anything from him is like trying to pluck a hog. البَلَم اِنقِلَب إلّا شَعرَه [ʔilbalam ʔingilab ʔilla šaʕrah] The boat missed turning over by a hair. قماش شَعري [qmaːš šaʕri] raw silk.

شِعرَة [šiʕra] *n:* • **1.** pubes, pubic area

شِعار [šiʕaːr] *n:* شِعارات [šiʕaːraːt] *pl:* • **1.** motto, slogan, watchword • **2.** emblem, badge, distinguishing mark, coat-of-arms • **3.** banner

شِعِير [šiʕiːr] *n:* • **1.** barley

شُعُور [šuʕuːr] *n:* • **1.** awareness, consciousness – غاب عَن الشُّعُور [ɣaːb ʕan ʔiššuʕuːr] He lost consciousness. شُعُور بالنَّقِص [šuʕuːr binnaqiṣ] feeling of inferiority. فُقَد شُعُورَه وَضُرَب إبنَه سِكّينَة [fuqad šuʕuːrah wðurab ʔibnah siččiːna] He lost his senses and stabbed his son. • **2.** sensitivity, sensibility, perceptiveness – ما عِندَك شُعُور [maː ʕindak šuʕuːr] You have no sensitivity.

مَشعَر [mašʕar] *n:* • **1.** pubes, pubic area

شاعِر [šaːʕir] *n:* شُعَراء [šuʕaraːʔ] *pl:* • **1.** poet

شَعرِيَّة [šaʕriyya] *n:* • **1.** vermicelli (pasta)

شُعَيرَة [šuʕayra] *n:* • **1.** gun pointer • **1.** a short strand of hair

مَشاعِر [mašaːʕir] *n:* • **1.** feelings

إشعار [ʔišʕaːr] *n:* • **1.** notice, notification, information

شَعّار [šaʕʕaːr] *adj:* شَعّارَة، شَعّارِين [šaʕʕaːriːn, šaʕʕaːra] *pl:* • **1.** a male dancer who does female impersonations • **2.** homosexual, fairy, pansy • **3.** procurer, pander, pimp

مُشعِر [mušʕir] *adj:* • **1.** hirsute, hairy, shaggy – بَعض البَنات يحِبُّون الرِّجّال المِشعِر [baʕð ʔilbanaːt yiħibbuːn ʔirrijjaːl ʔilmišʕir] Some girls like hairy men.

ش ع ع

شَعّ [šaʕʕ] *v:* • **1.** to radiate, beam, emit rays or beams – وِجهَها يشِعّ بالجَّمال [wiččha yšiʕʕ bijjamaːl] Her face is radiant with beauty.

شُعاع، شعاع [šuʕaːʕ, šʕaːʕ] *n:* أشِعَّة [ʔašiʕʕa] *pl:* • **1.** ray, beam • **2.** X-ray – خَلِّي ناخُذ أشِعَّة لِصَدرَك [xalliː naːxuð ʔašiʕʕa liṣadrak] Let's take an X-ray of your chest.

إشعاع [ʔišʕaːʕ] *n:* • **1.** radiation, irradiation

مُشِعّ [mušiʕʕ] *adj:* • **1.** radiative, radiant, emitting rays, radioactive • **2.** shiny

شُعاعِي [šuʕaːʕi] *adj:* • **1.** radiative, radiant

إشعاعِي [ʔišʕaːʕi] *adj:* • **1.** radiative

ش ع ل

شِعَل [šiʕal] *v:* • **1.** to ignite, light, set fire to – إشعِل شوَيَّة نار. الدِّنيا بارِدَة [ʔišʕil šwayya naːr. ʔiddinya baːrda] Light up a little fire. It's cold. إشعِل عُودَة شِخّاط وَباوُع هنا [ʔišʕil ʕuːdat šixxaːṭ wbaːwuʕ hna] Strike a match and look here. • **2.** to turn on (a light) – إشعِل الضُّوَة قَبُل ما تخُشّ [ʔišʕil ʔiððuwa gabul maː txušš] Turn on the light before you enter. المُدِير شِعَل أهلنا بالشُّغُل [ʔilmudiːr šiʕal ʔahlna biššuɣul] The director worked us to death.

اِشتِعَل [ʔištiʕal] *v:* • **1.** to catch fire, ignite, flare up, blaze, be or become on fire – تبَلِّلَت عُودَة الشِّخّاط وَبَعَد ما تِشتِعِل [tballilat ʕuːdat ʔiššixxaːṭ wabaʕad maː tištiʕil] The match got wet and won't light now. ظَلَّت النّار تِشتِعِل اللَّيل كُلَّه [ðallat ʔinnaːr tištiʕil ʔillayl kullah] The fire kept burning all night. يبَيِّن اِشتِعلَت بَيناتهُم. قامَوا يتصايحُون [yibayyin ʔištiʕlat baynaːthum. gaːmaw yitṣaːyħuːn] It seems like things have gotten hot between them. They've started to shout at each other.

شَعِل [šaʕil] *n:* • **1.** lighting, setting fire

شُعلَة [šuʕla] *n:* شُعلات [šuʕlaːt] *pl:* • **1.** flame – هُوَّ شُعلَة مِن النّار بالشُّغُل [huwwa šuʕla min ʔinnaːr biššuɣul] He is a real ball of fire.

مَشعَل [mašʕal] *n:* مشاعِيل [mšaːʕiːl] *pl:* • **1.** fireplace

مِشعَل [mišʕal] *n:* مَشاعِل [mašaːʕil] *pl:* • **1.** torch

شاعُول [šaːʕuːl] *n:* شَواعِيل [šawaːʕiːl] *pl:* • **1.** fire tender, fire-keeper, fireman

اِشتِعال [ʔištiʕaːl] *n:* • **1.** ignition

مِشتِعِل [mištiʕil] *adj:* • **1.** burning, ablaze, on fire

مَشعُول [mašʕuːl] *adj:* • **1.** burnt, on fire

ش ع و ذ

شَعوَذ [šaʕwað] *v:* • **1.** to practice jugglery or magic

مُشَعوِذ [mušaʕwið] *n:* • **1.** quack

شَعوَذَة [šaʕwaða] *n:* • **1.** jugglery, legerdemain, trickery, magic • **2.** practicing magic

ش ع و ط

شَعوَط [šaʕwaṭ] *v:* • **1.** to overheat, burn, scorch – شِيل الأكِل مِن النّار. مُو شَعوَطتَه [ši:l ʔilʔakil min ʔinna:r. mu: šaʕwaṭtah] Take the food off the fire. You've burned it! • **2.** to harass, torment, bedevil – شَعوَط أُمّه هوايَة مِن كان صغَيِّر [šaʕwaṭ ʔummah hwa:ya min ča:n ṣɣayyir] He gave his mother a lot of trouble when he was small.

تشَعوَط [tšaʕwaṭ] *v:* • **1.** to be burned, scorched – التِّمَّن تشَعوَط بِهَالنّار القَوِيَّة [ʔittimman tšaʕwaṭ bhanna:r ʔilqawiyya] The rice got burned on that hot fire.

شِعواط [šiʕwa:ṭ] *n:* • **1.** burning, scorching, overheating – دَأشتَم رِيحَة شِعواط [daʔaštam ri:ħat šiʕwa:ṭ] I smell something burning.

ش غ ب

شاغَب [ša:ɣab] *v:* • **1.** to make trouble, disturb the peace – دِير بالَك مِنّه. تَرَة يشاغِب عَلِيك [di:r ba:lak minnah. tara yša:ɣib ʕali:k] Watch out for him. He'll make trouble for you.

شَغَب [šaɣab] *n:* • **1.** trouble, strife, discord, dissension, unrest, commotion, controversy

مُشاغِب [muša:ɣib] *adj:* مُشاغِبِين [muša:ɣibi:n] *pl:* • **1.** troublemaker, agitator, mischief-maker

ش

ش غ ر

شِغَر [šiɣar] *v:* • **1.** to be vacant, free, unoccupied – الشَّهَر الجّاي راح تِشغر وَظِيفَة. قَدِّم عَلِيها [ʔiššahar ʔiǰǰa:y ra:ħ tišɣar waðˤi:fa. qaddim ʕali:ha] Next month a position will be open. Apply for it.

شُغُور [šuɣu:r] *n:* • **1.** vacancy (of a position)

شاغِر [ša:ɣir] *adj:* • **1.** free, vacant, unoccupied – مِتأَسِّفِين. ماكُو مُكان شاغِر [mitʔassifi:n. ma:ku muka:n ša:ɣir] We're sorry. There's no position open. • **2.** pl. شَواغِر [šawa:ɣir] vacancy, opening

ش غ ف

اِنشِغَف [ʔinšiɣaf] *v:* • **1.** to fall madly in love, be madly in love – شبِالعَجَل اِنشِغِفت بِيها [šbilʕaǰal ʔinšiɣafit bi:ha] I fell for her right off the bat!

ش غ ل

شِغَل [šiɣal] *v:* • **1.** to occupy, busy – كُلّما يزُورنِي بَالدّائِرَة، يشِغلنِي بِحَكيه وَشُغلِي يِتأَخَّر [kullma yzu:rni bidda:ʔira, yišɣilni bħačyah wšuɣli yitʔaxxar] Whenever he visits me in the office, he takes up my time talking and my work gets behind. غيبتَه شِغلَت فِكرِي [ɣi:btah šiɣlat fikri] His absence worried me. • **2.** to occupy, take up – الدِّراسَة شاغلَة كُلّ وَقتِي [ʔiddira:sa ša:ɣla kull wakti] Studying has taken up all my time. شِغَل وَضِيفتَين أَكثَر مِن سَنَة [šiɣal waðˤi:ftayn ʔakθar min sana] He held two jobs for more than a year.

شَغَّل [šaɣɣal] *v:* • **1.** to make or let work – ما يجُوز تشَغِّل المَساجِين [ma: yǰu:z tšaɣɣil ʔilmasa:ǰi:n] It isn't permitted to make the prisoners work. • **2.** to employ, provide employment – رُوح عَلِيه باكِر. بَلكِي يشَغّلَك [ru:ħ ʕali:h ba:čir. balki yšaɣɣlak] Go to him tomorrow. Maybe he'll employ you. • **2.** to make work, put to work, put in operation, make run, start – مِن أَشِيل إِيدِي، شَغِّل السَّيّارَة [min ʔaši:l ʔi:di, šaɣɣil ʔissayya:ra] When I raise my hand, you start the car. هَالمَكِينَة تِشتُغُل بِالبانزِين. ما تِقدَر تشَغِّلها بِالنَّفُط [halmaki:na tištuɣul bilbanzi:n. ma: tigdar tšaɣɣilha bilnafuṭ] This motor runs on gasoline. You can't operate it on kerosene. شَغِّل الرّادِيُو. خَلِّي نِسمَع الأَخبار [šaɣɣil ʔirra:dyu. xalli: nismaʕ ʔilʔaxba:r] Turn on the radio. Let's hear the news. إذا ما تشَغِّل العَصَى عَلَيهُم، ما يدِرسُون [ʔiða ma: tšaɣɣil ʔilʕaṣa ʕali:hum, ma: ydirsu:n] If you don't take a stick to them, they won't study. شَغَّل إيدَه عَلَيّا [šaɣɣal ʔi:dah ʕalayya] He beat me up. • **3.** to invest – شَغَّل فلُوسَه بِالتِّجارَة [šaɣɣal flu:sah bittiǰa:ra] He invested his money in commerce.

تشَغَّل [tšaɣɣal] *v:* • **1.** to employ

اِنشِغَل [ʔinšiɣal] *v:* • **1.** to be or become busy, occupied, engrossed, distracted – وَالله، جانِي خُطّار وَاِنشِغَلِت [wallah, ǰa:ni xuṭṭa:r wʔinšiɣalit] Really, I had company and got all tied up.

اِشتِغَل [ʔištiɣal] *v:* • **1.** to work, to be busy, engaged, occupied – شقَدّ صارلَك تِشتُغُل بِهَالدّائِرَة؟ [šgadd ṣa:rlak tištuɣul bhadda:ʔira?] How long have you been working in this office? اللّي يِشتُغُل بِالسِّياسَة، الشُّرطَة دائِماً وَراه [ʔilli yištuɣul bissiya:sa, ʔiššurṭa da:ʔiman wara:h] If anyone's engaged in politics, the police are always after him. • **2.** to operate, run, work, be in operation or motion – تِرَك السَّيّارَة تِشتُغُل ودِخَل لِلمَطعَم [tirak ʔissayya:ra tištuɣul wdixal lilmaṭʕam] He left the car running and went in the restaurant. هَالرّادِيُو يِشتُغُل عالباترِي [harra:dyu yištuɣul ʕalpa:tri] This radio operates by battery. أَشُو بَسّ دِست الزِّرّ، اِشتِغلَت المَكِينَة [ʔašu bass dist ʔizzirr, ʔištiɣlat ʔilmaki:na] It seems that the minute I pushed the button, the machine started. • **3.** to do business, to be in business – هَالمَخزَن يِشتُغُل خُوش شُغُل [halmaxzan yištuɣul xu:š šuɣul] This shop does a brisk business. دَيِشتُغُل عَلَى حسابَه [dayištuɣul ʕala ħsa:bah] He's in business for himself. هالمَطعَم يِشتُغُل لِنُص اللّيل [halmaṭʕam yištuɣul linuṣṣ ʔillayl] This restaurant is open until midnight. هَالفِلِم بَعدَه دَيِشتُغُل بِسِينَما الرَّشِيد [halfilim baʕdah dayištuɣul bsinama ʔirraši:d] This film is still playing at the Rashid theater.

شُغُل [šuɣul] *n:* أشغال [ʔašɣa:l] *pl:* • **1.** work, labor – سَيّارتَك يِنراد إلها شُغُل هوايَة [sayya:rtak yinra:d ʔilha šuɣul hwa:ya] Your car needs a lot of work. • **2.** workmanship – هَالزُّولِيَّة شُغُلها زين [hazzu:liyya šuɣulha zi:n] The workmanship on this

carpet is good. هَالسّاعَة شُغُل إيد [hassaːʕa šuɣul ʔiːd] This watch is hand made. • **3.** task, chore, thing to be done – دَزَّيت إبنِي بِشُغُل [dazziːt ʔibni bšuɣul] I sent my son on an errand. • **4.** business, concern – هَذا مُو شُغلَك [haːða muː šuɣlak] That's none of your business. • **5.** business, trade – واعَدتنِي عِشرِين مَرَّة وَمَا جَيت هَذا مُو شُغُل [waːʕadtni ʕišriːn marra wama ǰiːt haːða muː šuɣul] You made an appointment with me twenty times and didn't show up. That's no way to do things. • **6.** pl. أشغال work, job, occupation – أَخُوك عِندَه شُغُل وَإلّا بَطّال؟ [ʔaxuːk ʕindah šuɣul waʔilla baṭṭaːl?] Your brother---has he got a job or is he out of work? أَبُويَا بَعدَه بِالشُّغُل [ʔabuːya baʕdah biššuɣul] My father's still at work.
شَغلَة [šaɣla] *n:* شَغلات [šaɣlaːt] *pl:* • **1.** task, chore, something to be done – صارَت عِندِي شَغلَة. ما قِدَرت أَجِي [ṣaːrat ʕindi šaɣla. maː gidarit ʔaǰi] I had some work. I couldn't come. هاي شلُون شَغلَة! كُلّ المَخازِن معَزّلَة وَجِكايرِي خَلصانَة [haːy šluːn šaɣla! kull ʔilmaxaːzin mʕazzla wǰigaːyri xalṣaːna] This is a fine business! All the stores are closed and my cigarettes are all gone.
شَغلَة [šaɣla] *n:* • **1.** chore, task
مَشغَل [mašɣal] *n:* • **1.** workshop, workhouse
مشَغِّل [mšaɣɣil] *n:* • **1.** person who recruits workers, headhunter, recruiter
تَشغِيل [tašɣiːl] *n:* • **1.** employment, occupation, hiring, provision of work, • **2.** investment (of money) • **3.** production, manufacture
إشغال [ʔišɣaːl] *n:* • **1.** occupancy
شَغّال [šaɣɣaːl] *adj:* • **1.** working, being in operation • **2.** laborious
شاغِل [šaːɣil] *adj:* • **1.** incumbent, occupied
مشَغَّل [mšaɣɣal] *adj:* • **1.** recruited
شاغُول [šaːɣuːl] *adj:* شواغِيل [šwaːɣiːl] *pl:* • **1.** hard-working, industrious, diligent – عامِل شاغُول [ʕaːmil šaːɣuːl] a hard worker.
مَشغُول [mašɣuːl] *adj:* • **1.** busy, occupied, in use – آنِي مَشغُول هَسَّة [ʔaːni mašɣuːl hassa] I'm busy now. الخَطّ مَشغُول [ʔilxaṭṭ mašɣuːl] The line's busy.

ش ف

شافَى [šaːfaː] *v:* شافات [šaːfaːt] *pl:* • **1.** suppository

ش ف ت [1]

شِفت [šift] *n:* • **2.** shaft

ش ف ت [2]

شِفِت [šifit] *n:* شفُوت [šfuːt] *pl:* • **1.** tweezers

ش ف ج

شِفِج [šifiǰ] *n:* شفُوج [šfuːǰ] *pl:* • **1.** bull water buffalo

ش ف ر [1]

شَفرَة [šafra] *n:* شَفرات [šafraːt] *pl:* • **1.** a chisel-like knife with angled edge at the tip, a skew knife

ش ف ر [2]

شَفَّر [šaffar] *v:* • **1.** to code. As n: شَفَر [šafar] cipher, code
تَشفِير [tašfiːr] *n:* • **1.** coding, ciphering
مشَفَّر [mšaffar] *adj:* • **1.** coded, ciphered

ش ف ط

شُفَط [šufaṭ] *v:* • **1.** to suck, gulp • **2.** to sip
اِنشُفَط [ʔinšufaṭ] *v:* • **1.** to be sucked, to be gulped, to be sipped
شَفُط [šafuṭ] *n:* • **2.** sipping, gulping, sucking
شَفطَة [šafṭa] *n:* • **1.** sip
شَفّاطَة [šaffaːṭa] *n:* • **1.** siphon, شَفّاطَة الغُبار [šaffaːṭat ɣubaːr] vacuum cleaner
شَفّاط [šaffaːṭ] *adj:* • **1.** sucker • **2.** greedy
مَشفُوط [mašfuːṭ] *adj:* • **1.** sipped, sucked, gulped

ش ف ع

شِفَع [šifaʕ] *v:* • **1.** to put in a good word, intercede, intervene, plead – هَالمَرَّة ماكُو أَحَّد يِشفَعلَك؛ راح تِنطِرِد [halmarra maːku ʔaħħad yišfaʕlak; raːħ tinṭirid] This time there's no one to intercede for you; you're going to be fired.
تشَفَّع [tšaffaʕ] *v:* • **1.** to put in a good word, intercede, intervene, plead – إذا نطرَدِت مِنُو راح حيتشَفَّعلَك عِند الوَزِير [ʔiða ʔinṭiradit minu raːħ yitšaffaʕlak ʕind ʔilwaziːr] If you get fired, who will plead your case to the minister?
شَفاعَة [šafaːʕa] *n:* • **1.** intercession, mediation, advocacy
شَفِيع [šafiːʕ] *adj:* شُفَعاء [šufaʕaːʔ] *pl:* • **1.** mediator, intercessor, advocate
شافِعِي [šaːfiʕi] *adj:* • **1.** Shafiitic – المَذهَب الشّافِعِي [ʔilmaðhab ʔiššaːfiʕi] the Shafiitic school (of Moslem theology). • **2.** pl. شافِعِيِّين Shafiite, follower of al-Shafa'i

ش ف ف [1]

شِفَّة [šiffa] *n:* شِفّات، شفايِف [šiffaːt, šfaːyif] *pl:* • **1.** lip

ش ف ف [2]

شَفّاف [šaffaːf] *adj:* • **1.** thin, flimsy, transparent, translucent – لابسَة أَتَك جَوَّة فِستانها الشَّفّاف [laːbsah ʔatag ǰawwa fistaːnha ʔiššaffaːf] She's wearing a slip under her transparent dress. • **2.** candid, frank, open – صَدِيقَك يِعجِبنِي. هُوَّ شَفّاف هوايَة [ṣadiːqak yiʕǰibni. huwwa šaffaːf hwaːya] I like your friend. He's very frank.

ش ف ق

شِفَق [šifaq] *v:* • **1.** to take pity

ش

أَشفَق عَلَى [ʔašfaq ʕala] *v:* • **1.** to take pity – أَشفَق عَليه وَما طَلَّعه مِن الشُغُل [ʔašfaq ʕali:h wama ṭallaʕah min ʔiššuɣul] He took pity on him and didn't put him out of work.
شَفَقَة [šafaqa] *n:* • **1.** pity, compassion, sympathy, kindness, solicitude, tenderness, affection – قَلبَه ما بِيه ذَرَّة شَفَقَة [galbah ma: bi:h ðarrat šafaqa] He doesn't have a bit of pity in him.
شَفقَة [šafqa] *n:* شَفقات [šafqa:t] *pl:* • **1.** hat (with a brim)
إِشفاق [ʔišfa:q] *n:* • **1.** compassion, pity, sympathy
أَشفَق [ʔašfaq] *comparative adjective:* • **1.** more or most compassionate

ش ف ل ح

شِفَلَّح [šifallaḥ] *n:* • **1.** a kind of desert bush with red-centered flowers

ش ف و

شَفَوِي، شَفَهِي [šafawi:, šafahi] *adj:* • **1.** oral, spoken
شَفَهِيّاً، شَفَوِيّاً [šafahiyyan, šafawiyyan] *adverbial:* • **1.** orally

ش ف ي

شِفَى [šifa:] *v:* • **1.** to recuperate, convalesce, recover, get well, be healed – لَو ما مِستَعمِل هَالدُّوا، ما كان شِفَيت [law ma: mistaʕmil hadduwa:, ma: ča:n šifayt] If you hadn't used this medicine, you wouldn't have been cured.
شافَى [ša:fa:] *v:* • **1.** to cure, heal, restore to health – هَوا لُبنان شافاك [hawa lubna:n ša:fa:k] The Lebanese air cured you.
أَشفَى [ʔašfa:] *v:* • **1.** to provide a cure, to cure, heal, restore to health – هَالدُّوا يسَكِّن الوُجَع بَسّ ما يِشفِي [hadduwa ysakkin ʔilwujaʕ bass ma: yišfi] This medicine soothes the pain but won't cure. الله يِشفِيك [ʔallah yišfi:k] May God heal you.
تشافَى [tša:fa:] *v:* • **1.** as in شِفَى to recuperate, convalesce, recover, get well, be healed – الحَمد لاِل المَرِيض تشافَى [lħamd lʔallah] [ʔilmari:ð tša:fa:] Thank God, the patient recovered.
اِشتِفَى [ʔištifa:] *v:* • **1.** to take revenge, receive satisfaction, take it out – اِشتِفَيت بِيه مِن طِردوه، لِأَنّ هُوَّ سَبَب طَردِي [ʔištifi:t bi:h min ṭirdu:h, liʔann huwwa sabab ṭardi] I got a lot of satisfaction when they fired him, because he's the reason I was fired. زَفَّيتَه زَفَّة اِشتِفَيت مِنَّه بِيها [zaffaytah zaffa ʔištifi:t minnah bi:ha] I told him off and got even with him that way.
شِفاء، شَفاء [šifa:ʔ, šafa:ʔ] *n:* • **1.** recuperation, cure, healing, restoration, recovery
مُستَشفَى [mustašfa] *n:* مُستَشفَيات [mustašfaya:t] *pl:* • **1.** hospital

ش ق ر

اِشقَرّ [ʔišgarr] *v:* • **1.** to become blond – شَعَرها يِشقَرّ مِن تِلعَب بِالشَّمِس [šaʕarha yišgarr min tilʕab biššamis] Her hair becomes blond when she plays in the sun.
شَقار [šaga:r] *n:* • **1.** blondness
أَشقَر [ʔašgar] *adj:* شُقُر [šugur] *pl:* شَقرَة [šagra] *feminine:* • **1.** blond – شَعَر أَشقَر [šaʕar ʔašgar] blond hair.

ش ق ش ق

شَقشَق [šagšag] *v:* • **1.** to tear, rip repeatedly – الجّاهِل شَقشَق الخَرِيطَة وُصلَة وُصلَة [ʔiǰǰa:hil šagšag ʔilxari:ṭa wuṣla wuṣla] The child tore the map into little pieces.
تشَقشَق [tšagšag] *v:* • **1.** pass. of شَقشَق to be torn – الكِتاب تشَقشَق. لازم نجَلِّدَه [ʔilkita:b tšagšag. la:zim nǰallidah] The book got torn apart. We should bind it.

ش ق ف 1

شِقَف [šigaf] *n:* • **1.** (coll.) chip(s), fragment(s), shard(s)
شِقفَة [šigfa] *n:* شِقفات [šigfa:t] *pl:* • **1.** chip, fragment, shard

ش ق ف 2

شِقَف [šigaf] *n:* شِقَفات [šigafa:t] *pl:* • **1.** a net on a pole, used to catch birds

ش ق ق 1

شَقّ [šagg] *v:* • **1.** to tear, rip, rend – مِتأَسِّف! شَقَّيت ثُوبِك [mitʔassif! šaggayt θu:bič] I'm sorry! I tore your blouse. بَعَد ما قِرا المَكتُوب، شَقَّه وَذَبَّه [baʕad ma: qira: ʔilmaktu:b, šaggah wðabbah] After he read the letter, he tore it up and threw it away. آنِي أَرقع وَهُوَّ يشُقّ [ʔa:ni ʔargiʕ wahuwwa yšugg] I set things straight and he makes a shambles. • **2.** to dress, clean – لَهِّب البَطَّة قَبُل ما تشُقَّها [lahhib ʔilbaṭṭa gabul ma: tšuggha] Singe the duck before you dress it. • **3.** to cut through, put through, construct, build (a road or highway) – راح يشُقُّون شارِع عامّ بِهَالمَنطِقَة [ra:ħ yšuggu:n ša:riʕ ʕa:mm bhalmanṭiqa] They're going to cut a public street through this area.
شَقَّق [šaggag] *v:* • **1.** to tear to pieces, tear up – شَقَّق المَكتُوب قَبُل ما يِقراه [šaggag ʔilmaktu:b gabul ma: yiqra:h] He tore up the letter before he read it. • **2.** to wear out – لِيش ما تِلبَس غير قاط؟ مُو شَقَّقتَه لِلقاط الجِّدِيد [li:š ma: tilbas ɣi:r qa:ṭ? mu: šaggagtah lilqa:ṭ ʔiǰǰidi:d] Why don't you wear a different suit? You've worn out the new suit!
اِنشَقّ [ʔinšaqq] *v:* • **1.** to split off, break away, secede, separate, withdraw – اِنشَقُّوا عَن الحِزب وَشَكِّلوا حِزب غيرَه [ʔinšaqqaw ʕan ʔilħizib wšakkilaw ħizib ɣayrah] They broke with the party and formed a separate party.

شَقّ [šagg] *n:* شقُوق [šgu:g] *pl:* • **1.** rip, tear, slit
شَقّ [šag] *n:* شقُوق [šgu:g] *pl:* • **1.** crack
شِقَّة، شُقَّة [šiqqa, šuqqa] *n:* شُقَق [šuqaq] *pl:* • **1.** apartment, flat
شَقَّة [šugga] *n:* شُقّات [šugga:t] *pl:* • **1.** half of a butchered animal, a side of meat
مَشَقَّة [mašaqqa] *n:* • **1.** burden, trouble • **3.** discomfort • **2.** labor, difficulty, hardship, toil
شَقِيقَة [šaqi:qa] *n:* • **1.** migraine headache
اِنشِقاق [ʔinšiqa:q] *n:* • **1.** split, separation, dissension, discord, disunion
مشَقَّق [mšaggag] *adj:* • **1.** cracked, chapped (lips)
مُشتَقّ [muštaqq] *adj:* • **1.** deriving, derived (gram.)
مَشقُوق [mašgu:g] *adj:* • **1.** torn

ش ق ق 2
شَقّ [šaqq, šagg] *n:* • **1.** trouble, difficulty, hardship – ما حَصَّلناها إلّا بشَقّ الأنفُس [ma: ħaṣṣalna:ha ʔilla bšaqq ʔilʔanfus] We didn't get it except by extreme effort.
شاقّ [ša:qq] *adj:* • **1.** troublesome, toilsome, tiresome, tedious, arduous, onerous, difficult, hard – حِكَمَه سَنتَين بالأشغال الشّاقّة [ħikamah santayn bilʔašɣa:l ʔišša:qqa] He sentenced him to two years at hard labor.
أشَقّ [ʔašaqq] *comparative adjective:* • **1.** more or most troublesome, toilsome, tedious, arduous

ش ق ق 3
شِقَّة [šigga] *n:* شقاق [šga:g] *pl:* • **1.** a type of cheap rug

ش ق ل ب
شَقلَب، چَقلَب [čaqlab] *v:* • **1.** to send tumbling – دِفَعنِي وَچَقلَبنِي مِن فُوق الدَّرَج [difaʕni wčaqlabni min fu:g ʔiddaraǰ] He pushed me and sent me tumbling from the top of the stairs.
تشَقلَب، تچَقلَب [tčaqlab] *v:* • **1.** to tumble, fall head over heels – عِثَر بحجارَة وَتچَقلَب [ʕiθar bħja:ra witčaqlab] He tripped on a rock and took a tumble.
شُقلُمبَة، چُقلُمبَة [čuqlumba] *n:* شُقلُمبات، چُقلُمبات [čuqlumba:t] *pl:* • **1.** somersault, tumble

ش ق ن ق
شقَنَّق [šgannag] *n:* • **1.** (coll.) chips, broken pieces (of brick)
شقَنَّقَة [šgannaga] *n:* شقَنَّقات [šgannaga:t] *pl:* • **2.** coll. chips, broken pieces (of brick)

ش ق و
شاقَى [ša:qa:] *v:* • **1.** to tease, bait, needle, rib, kid, joke – لا تشاقِيه تَرَة يِزعَل بالعَجَل [la: tša:qi:h tara yizʕal bilʕaǰal] Don't tease him, because he gets mad quickly.
تشاقَى [tša:qa:] *v:* • **1.** to banter, joke with one another, kid around – تِقدَر تِتشاقَى ويّاه. يِعجِبَه الشَّقَا [tiqdar titša:qa: wiyya:h. yiʕiǰbah ʔiššaqa] You can kid around with him. He likes kidding.
شَقَا [šaqa] *n:* • **1.** badinage, banter, teasing, joking, kidding – هاي كِيميا، مُو شَقَا. لازِم تِدرُس [ha:y ki:mya, mu: šaqa. la:zim tidrus] This is chemistry, not play. You must study. ألفين دينار مُو شَقَا [ʔalfayn dina:r mu: šaqa] Two thousand dinars ain't hay.
شَقاء [šaqa:ʔ] *n:* • **1.** misery
شَقاوَة [šaqa:wa] *n:* • **1.** thuggery, hooliganism • **2.** brutality, savagery
شَقِي [šaqi] *adj:* / *n:* أشقِياء [ʔašqiya:ʔ] *pl:* • **1.** bandit, highwayman, thug, villain, scoundrel, rogue
شَقِيّ [šaqi] *adj:* أشقِياء [ʔašqiya:ʔ] *pl:* • **1.** thug, bully, tough guy • **2.** scoundrel, rogue
شَقايچِي، شَقّاچِي [šaqa:yči, šaqqa:či] *adj:* شَقّاچِيَّة [šaqqačiyya] *pl:* • **1.** joker, clown, tease

ش ق ي
See also: ش ق و

ش ك ر 1
شِكَر [šikar] *v:* • **1.** to thank, express gratitude to – أشكُركُم. هَذا لُطُف مِنكُم [ʔaškurkum. ha:ða luṭuf minkum] I thank you. That's nice of you.
تشَكَّر [tšakkar] *v:* • **1.** to be thankful, grateful, to express one's thanks – رُوح تشَكَّر مِنَّه عالهَدِيَّة [ru:ħ tšakkar minnah ʕalhadiyya] Go thank him for the gift.
شُكُر [šukur] *n:* • **1.** gratitude, gratefulness, thankfulness • **2.** thanks, acknowledgment – وَجّهُولَه كِتاب شُكُر عَلَى نَشاطَه [waǰǰihu:lah kita:b šukur ʕala naša:ṭah] They sent him a letter of appreciation for his zeal. الحَمدُ لله وَالشُّكُر [ʔilħamdu lilla:h wiššukur] Praise and thanks be to God.
شاكِر [ša:kir] *adj:* • **1.** thankful
مَشكُور [mašku:r] *adj:* • **1.** meritorious, laudable, praiseworthy, deserving thanks – هَذا عَمَل مَشكُور مِنَّك [ha:ða ʕamal mašku:r minnak] That was a laudable thing you did.
مِتشَكِّر [mitšakkir] *adj:* • **1.** grateful, thankful – إحنا مِتشَكّرِين كُلِّش [ʔiħna mitšakkri:n kulliš] We're very grateful.
شُكراً [šukran] *adverbial:* • **1.** thanks, thank you – شُكراً، ما أدَخِّن [šukran, ma: ʔadaxxin] Thanks, I don't smoke.

ش ك ر 2
شَكَّر [šakkar] *v:* • **1.** to turn to sugar, become sugar – الدِّبِس شَكَّر [ʔiddibis šakkar] The date molasses turned to sugar.
شَكَر [šakar] *n:* • **1.** sugar – رُوح الشَّكَر [ru:ħ ʔiššakar] saccharine. شَكَر دان [šakar da:n] sugar bowl.

شُكَّر [šukkar] *n:* • **1.** a variety of dates
شَكَرات [šakara:t] *n:* • **1.** (invar.) sweets, treats, goodies, sugar candy
شَكَرچي [šakarči] *n:* شَكَرچِيَّة [šakarčiyya] *pl:* • **1.** confectioner, man who makes and sells sweets
شَكَرايَة [šakara:ya] *n:* • **1.** candy
شَكَري، لَون شَكَري [šakari, lu:n šakari] *adj:* • **1.** light beige, creamy white
شَكَرلي، قَهوَة شَكَرلي [šakarli, gahwa šakarli] *adj:* • **1.** coffee with sugar

ش ك ر ل م

شَكَرلَمَة [šakarlama] *n:* • **1.** (coll.) a kind of sugar cookie
شَكَرلَمايَة [šakarlama:ya] *n:* شَكَرلَمايات [šakarlama:ya:t] *pl:* • **1.** a kind of sugary cookie

ش ك س

شاكَس [ša:kas] *v:* • **1.** to irritate, antagonize, contradict – ما صَحِيح تشاكِس المُعَلِّم [ma: ṣaḥi:ḥ tša:kis ʔilmuʕallim] It isn't proper to contradict the teacher.
تشاكَس [tša:kas] *v:* • **2.** to be irritated, antagonized, contradicted
شَكِس [šakis] *adj:* • **1.** ill-tempered, grumpy, unfriendly
مُشاكَسَة [muša:kasa] *n:* • **1.** quarrel
مُشاكِس [muša:kis] *adj:* • **1.** belligerent • **2.** quarrelsome

ش ك ش ك

شَكشَك [čakčak] *v:* • **1.** to stick, to pierce, to prick
تشَكشَك [tčakčak] *v:* • **1.** to be stuck, to be pricked, to be pierced
مشَكشَك [mčakčak] *n:* • **1.** sticked, pricked, pierced
تشِكشِيك [tčikči:k] *n:* • **1.** sticking

ش ك ك

شَكّ [čakk] *v:* • **1.** to prick, stick, pierce – شَكّنِي بِالدَّمبُوس [čakkni biddambu:s] He pricked me with a pin.
شَكّ [šakk] *v:* • **1.** to doubt – أشُكّ أن التَّجرُبَة راح تِنجَح [ʔašukk ʔan ʔittajruba ra:ḥ tinjaḥ] I doubt that the experiment is going to succeed. • **2.** to distrust, suspect – يشُكّ حَتَّى بِأصدِقائَه [yšukk ḥatta bʔaṣdiqa:ʔah] He suspects even his close friends. • **3.** to be skeptical, doubtful – آنِي أشُكّ. ما أعتِقِد الخَبَر صَحِيح [ʔa:ni ʔašukk. ma: ʔaʕtiqid ʔilxabar ṣaḥi:ḥ] I'm skeptical. I don't think the information is correct.
شَكَّك [šakkak] *v:* • **1.** to make someone doubt
اِنشَكّ [ʔinčakk] *v:* • **1.** to be pricked, to be stuck (as with a needle)
شُكّ، شُكّ مال نَدّاف [čukk, čukk ma:l nadda:f] *n:* • **1.** a short, heavy, wooden mallet used by the cotton teaser to strike his bow • **1.** large needle used for making mattresses

شَكّ [šakk] *n:* شُكُوك [šuku:k] *pl:* • **1.** doubt, uncertainty, suspicion, misgiving – بَلا شَكّ [bala šakk] without doubt, certainly. راح أشُوفَك بِالحَفلَة بَلا شَكّ [ra:ḥ ʔašu:fak bilḥafla bala šakk] I'll see you at the party without fail.
شَكَّة [čakka] *n:* • **1.** pricking
شَكّاك [šakka:k] *adj:* • **1.** skeptical, suspicious, uncertain
مَشكُوك [mašku:k] *adj:* • **1.** doubtful, dubious, uncertain – هَذا فَدّ شِي مَشكُوك بِيه [ha:ða fadd ši mašku:k bi:h] This sort of thing is unlikely.
شكُوكِي [šku:ki] *adj:* • **1.** suspicious

ش ك ل

See also: م ش ك ل
شِكَل [šikal] *v:* • **1.** to fetter, hobble – شكِل الطِّير حَتَّى لا يطِير [škil ʔiṭṭi:r ḥatta la: yṭi:r] Fetter the bird so he won't fly away.
شَكَّل [šakkal] *v:* • **1.** to form, fashion, shape, mold, create – شَكَّل وِزارَة جِدِيدَة [šakkal wiza:ra jidi:da] He formed a new cabinet. • **2.** to fasten, affix, pin – شَكِّلّي هالوَردَة بصَدري [šakkilli halwarda bṣadri] Pin this flower on my lapel for me. شَكَّل الجّامِلُّغ مُوَقَّتاً بِتِيل إلَى أن نُوصَل لِلكَراج [šakkil ʔičča:mulluɣ muʔaqqatan bti:l ʔila ʔan nu:ṣal lilgara:ǰ] Fasten the fender temporarily with wire till we reach the garage. • **3.** to catch, snag, become caught – شَكَّل ثَوبِي بِالبِسمار [šakkal θu:bi bilbisma:r] My shirt got caught on the nail. السّاعَة ما بِيها شِي، لَكِن المِيل دَيشَكِّل بِفَدّ شِي [ʔissa:ʕa ma: bi:ha ši, la:kin ʔilmi:l dayšakkil bfadd ši] There's nothing wrong with the watch, but the hand is catching on something. الرّادِيُو دَيِشتُغُل شوَيَّة وَيشَكِّل [ʔirra:dyu dayištuɣul šwayya wyišakkil] The radio works a little while and stops. • **4.** to join – وَلَو ماكِل، شَكِّل وِيّانا [walaw ma:kil, šakkil wiyya:na] Even though you've eaten, join us. شَكِّل وِيّانا. هَسَّة نُوصَل [šakkil wiyya:na. hassa nu:ṣal] Squeeze in with us. We'll be there in no time. • **5.** to diversify, vary, variegate, to make assorted, varied – أرِيد دُوندِرمَة، بَسّ شَكِّلِّي إيّاها [ʔari:d du:ndirma, bass šakkilli ʔiyya:ha] I want some ice cream, but make it several flavors for me. جِيبلِي ماعُون مشَكَّل [ǰi:bli ma:ʕu:n mšakkal] Bring me an assorted dish.
تشَكَّل [tšakkal] *v:* • **1.** pass. of شَكَّل to be shaped, formed, caught, joined, fastened
اِستَشكَل [ʔistaškal] *v:* • **1.** to have doubts about the religious propriety of – ما يخَلِّي فلُوسَه بِالبَنك. يِستَشكِل [ma: yxalli: flu:sah bilbang. yistaškil] He doesn't put his money in the bank. He feels it might be wrong religiously.
شِكِل [šikil] *n:* أشكال، شكُول [ʔaška:l, šku:l] *pl:* • **1.** outward appearance, looks – صَدِيقَك شلُون شِكلَه؟ [ṣadi:qak šlu:n šiklah?] What does your friend look like? شِكلَه شِكل الشّادِي [šiklah šikl ʔišša:di] He looks

like a monkey. عابتلك هَالشِّكِل [ʕa:bitlak haššikil] Your face is a disgrace! ولده غير شكول. ما بيهُم واحِد حِلو [wildah γi:r šku:l. ma: bi:hum wa:ħid ħilw] His children sure are ugly. Not a one of them is nice looking. قاطك بِشِكلِي [qa:ṭak bšikli] Your suit looks just like mine. • **2.** shape, form, configuration, pattern – الأوتيل بيه بار عَلَى شِكِل دائرَة بِنُصّ الغُرفَة [ʔilʔuti:l bi:h ba:r ʕala šikil da:ʔira bnuṣṣ ʔilγurfa] The hotel has a bar in the shape of a circle in the middle of the room. • **3.** sort, kind, variety, class, type – عِندِي أشكال هوايَة مِن الثِّياب [ʕindi ʔaška:l hwa:ya min ʔiθθiya:b] I have many kinds of shirts. هَالشِّكِل أوادِم ما يُعتَمَد عَلَيهُم [haššikil ʔawa:dim ma: yuʕtamad ʕali:hum] That kind of person isn't dependable. قِدّامِي يِحكِي شِكِل، وَوَرايَا غير شِكِل [gidda:mi yiħči šikil, wawra:ya γayr šikil] In my presence he says one thing, and in my absence something else. مُو هَالشِّكِل. لازِم تِرَخِّي البُرغِي أوَّل [mu: haššikil. la:zim traxxi ʔilburγi ʔawwal] Not that way. You have to loosen the screw first.

شَكِل [šakil] *n:* • **1.** fettering, hobbling

شكُول [šku:l] *n:* شكُولات [šku:la:t] *pl:* • **1.** looks, appearance – لا تعَيِّب عَليه. يَعنِي شكُولَك أحسَن؟ [la: tʕayyib ʕali:h. yaʕni šku:lak ʔaħsan?] Don't ridicule him. Do you think your appearance is better? • **2.** example, type – دَيمشِي ويّا شكُولات تلَعّب النَّفِس [dayimši wiyya šku:la:t tlaʕʕb ʔinnafis] He runs around with sickening types of people.

شِكّالَة [šikka:la] *n:* شِكّالات [šikka:la:t] *pl:* • **1.** clip, clasp, pin

مُشكِلَة [muškila] *n:* مَشاكِل [maša:kil] *pl:* • **1.** problem

إشكال [ʔiška:l] *n:* • **1.** problem, complication

تَشكِيل [taški:l] *n:* • **1.** forming, shaping

شاكلَة [ša:kila] *n:* • **1.** pattern • **2.** way

تَشكِيلَة [taški:la] *n:* تَشكِيلات [taški:la:t] *pl:* • **1.** assortment, selection, variety

شَكلِي، شِكلِي [šakli, šikli] *adj:* • **1.** formal, conventional, customary – هَذا شِي شِكلِي، لَكِن مَطلُوب [ha:ða ši šikli, la:kin maṭlu:b] This is a formality, but it's required. • **2.** pl. شَكلِيّات formality

مشَكَّل [mšakkal] *adj:* • **1.** assorted • **2.** diverse, different

ش ك و [1]

شِكَى [šika:] *v:* • **1.** to complain about – شِكالِي أمرَه [šika:li ʔamrah] He complained to me about his situation. • **2.** to suffer, have a complaint – إبنِي يِشكِي مِن مِعِدتَه [ʔibni yiški min miʕidtah] My son is suffering with his stomach.

شَكَّى [šakka:] *v:* • **1.** to make or let complain – المُدِير ما شَكّانِي [ʔilmudi:r ma: šakka:ni] The director wouldn't let me complain.

تشَكَّى [tšakka:] *v:* • **1.** to complain – لا تِبقَى تِتشَكَّى [la: tibqa: titšakka:] Don't keep on complaining. الطُّلّاب دَيِتشَكُّون هوايَة مِن الإمتِحانات [ʔiṭṭulla:b dayitšakku:n hwa:ya min ʔilʔimtiħa:na:t] The students are grumbling a lot about the exams.

اِشتِكَى [ʔištika:] *v:* • **1.** to suffer, have a complaint – بَعدَه يِشتِكِي مِن مِعِدتَه [baʕdah yištiki min miʕidtah] He is still suffering with his stomach. • **2.** to sue, bring to court – اِشتِكَى عَلَى الشَّرِكَة لِأَنّ المال طِلَع بِيه عِيب [ʔištika: ʕala ʔiššarika liʔann ʔilma:l ṭilaʕ bi:h ʕi:b] He sued the company because a defect showed up in the merchandise. • **3.** with عَلَى to raise, lodge, file a complaint about – اِشتِكَيت عَليه عِند المُدَرِّس [ʔištiki:t ʕali:h ʕind ʔilmudarris] I complained about him to the teacher. اِشتِكَيت عَليه بِالشُّرطَة [ʔištiki:t ʕali:h biššurṭa] I made a complaint against him to the police.

شَكوَى [šakwa:] *n:* شَكاوِي [šaka:wi] *pl:* • **1.** complaint, grievance • **2.** accusation

شَكِيَّة، شِكِيَّة [šakiyya, šikiyya] *n:* شِكِيّات [šikiyya:t] *pl:* • **1.** complaint, grievance • **2.** accusation

تَشَكِّي [tašakki] *n:* • **1.** gripe • **1.** complaint, grievance

شِكايَة [šika:ya] *n:* شِكايات [šika:ya:t] *pl:* • **1.** complaint, grievance • **2.** accusation

مِشتِكِي [mištiki] *n:* • **1.** complainant, plaintiff

ش ك و [2]

شِكوَة [šičwa] *n:* شِكوات [šičwa:t] *pl:* • **1.** a small skin in which cream is shaken to produce butter

ش ل ب

شِلِب [šilib] *n:* • **1.** field rice, rice before being processed for food

ش ل ب ه

تشَلبَه [tšalbah] *v:* • **1.** to climb up, ascend – البَزُّونَة دَتِتشَلبَه عَالحايِط [ʔilbazzu:na datitšalbah ʕalħa:yiṭ] The cat's climbing up the wall.

تِشِلبِه [tišilbih] *n:* • **1.** climbing

مِتشَلبِه [mitšalbih] *adj:* • **1.** climbing

ش ل ت

شَلتَة [šalta] *n:* شَلتات [šalta:t] *pl:* • **1.** pallet, thin mattress

ش ل ت غ

شَلتَغ [šaltaγ] *v:* • **1.** to deceive, cheat, lie – شَلتَغ عَليه وَأخَذ فلُوسَه [šaltaγ ʕali:h waʔaxað flu:sah] He tricked him and took his money.

ش ل ح

شَلَّح [šallaħ] *v:* • **1.** to undress, remove the clothing from the lower part of the body, uncover the legs – شَلِّحَتَه وَغِسلَت رِجلَيه [šalliħatah wγislat rijlayh] She undressed him and washed his legs. • **2.** to bare one's legs, disrobe, undress – شَلِّحَت وَراوَتنِي زرُورها [šalliħat wra:watni zru:rha] She lifted her dress and showed me her thighs. نَزِّلِي نَفنُوفِك. مُو عِيب تشَلِّحِين بِالشّارِع [nazzli

ش

nafnu:fič. mu: ʕi:b tšallhi:n biššaːriʕ] Lower your dress. It's shameful to expose yourself on the street! أخُوك مشَلَّح. قُلَّه يتغَطّى [ʔaxu:k mšallaħ. gullah yidɣaṭṭa:] Your brother is indecently exposed. Tell him to cover himself.
تشَلَّح [tšallaħ] *v:* • **1.** to undress, disrobe – سِدّ الشِّبّاك قبُل ما تِتشَلَّح [sidd ʔiššibba:č gabul ma: titšallaħ] Close the window before you undress.
مشَلَّح [mšallaħ] *adj:* • **1.** naked, disrobed

ش ل ع

شِلَع [šilaʕ] *v:* • **1.** to extract, remove, pull out, take out – إشلَع البِسمار مِن الحايِط [ʔišlaʕ ʔilbisma:r min ʔilħa:yiṭ] Pull the nail out of the wall. شِلعَوا الشِّبّاك وَدِخلَوا البَيت [šilʕaw ʔiššibba:č wdixlaw ʔilbayt] They removed the window and entered the house. راح الطَبِيب الأسنان حَتَّى يِشلَع سِنَّه [ra:ħ lṭabi:b ʔilʔasna:n ħatta yišlaʕ sinnah] He went to the dentist to get his tooth pulled. إبنِك شِلَع قَلبِي اليُوم [ʔibnič šilaʕ galbi ʔilyu:m] Your son gave me a hard time today. هالشُّغُل صَعُب يِشلَع القَلُب [haššuɣul ṣaʕub yišlaʕ ʔilgalub] This work is murder. • **2.** to leave, depart, go away hurriedly – أخَذ غَراضَه وَشِلَع [ʔaxað ɣara:ḍah wšilaʕ] He took his things and left.
شَلَّع [šallaʕ] *v:* • **1.** to shed baby teeth – الجَاهِل ما يِبكِي هوايَة مِن يِبدِي يشَلِّع [ʔijja:hil ma: yibči hwa:ya min yibdi yšalliʕ] The child doesn't cry much when he starts shedding his baby teeth. • **2.** intens. of to extract, remove, pull out, take out – شَلِّع كَم وُصلَة تَمُر مِن هَالحِلانَة [šalliʕ čam wuṣlat tamur min halħilla:na] Dig out some hunks of dates from this basket. قاعِد وَيشَلِّع بِشَعراتَه البِيض [ga:ʕid wyšalliʕ bšaʕra:tah ʔilbi:ḍ] He's sitting and plucking his gray hairs.
تشَلَّع [tšallaʕ] *v:* • **1.** to be pulled out, be removed – أوراق الكِتاب كُلّها تشَلّعَت [ʔawra:q ʔilkita:b kullha tšalliʕat] All the pages of the book were pulled out.
إنشِلَع [ʔinšilaʕ] *v:* • **1.** pass. of شِلَع to be extracted, removed, pulled out, taken out
شَلِع [šaliʕ] *n:* • **1.** pulling out, extracting, removing • **2.** leaving hurriedly
شَلعَة [šalʕa] *n:* • **1.** pulling out, extraction, removal • **2.** hurried departure
شلِيع [šli:ʕ] *n:* • **1.** going away hurriedly
مشَلَّع [mšallaʕ] *adj:* • **1.** ripped off, pulled off, removed
مَشلُوع [mašlu:ʕ] *adj:* • **1.** extracted, removed, pulled out

ش ل غ م

شَلغَم [šalɣam] *n:* • **1.** (coll.) turnips – راس شَلغَم [ra:s šalɣam] a turnip.
شَلغَمَة [šalɣama] *n:* شَلغَمات [šalɣama:t] *pl:* • **1.** turnip

ش ل ف

شِلَف [šilaf] *v:* • **1.** to eject, expel, get rid of – بُقَى بِالوَظِيفَة شَهرَين وَبَعدين شِلفُوه [buqa: bilwaḍi:fa šahrayn wbaʕdi:n šilfu:h] He stayed with the job for two months and then they kicked him out. إحكِي ويّاه شوَيَّة وَبَعدين إشلِفَه [ʔiħči wiyya:h šwayya wbaʕdi:n iišlfah] Talk to him a while and then get rid of him.
شَلِف [šalif] *n:* • **1.** ejection, expelling

ش ل ق

شِلِق [šilig] *n:* • **1.** a cucumber-shaped variety of melon

ش ل ك

شِلَك [čilak] *n:* • **1.** (coll.) strawberry(ies)
شِلكَة [čilka] *n:* شِلكات [čilka:t] *pl:* • **2.** strawberry

ش ل ل

شَلّ [šall] *v:* • **1.** to paralyze – ضِرَبَه أبرَة برجلَه وَشَلّها عَن الحَرَكَة [ðirabah ʔubra brijlah wšallha ʕan ʔilħaraka] He gave him a shot in his leg and paralyzed it.
انشَلّ [ʔinšall] *v:* • **1.** to be paralyzed – بَعَد حادِث السَّيّارَة، انشَلَّت إيدَه [baʕad ħa:diθ ʔissayya:ra, ʔinšallat ʔi:dah] After the auto accident, his hand became paralyzed.
شَلّ [šall] *n:* • **1.** paralysis, palsy
شَلَل [šalal] *n:* • **1.** paralysis, palsy – شَلَل الأطفال [šalal ʔilʔaṭfa:l] infantile paralysis, polio.
شِلَّة [šilla] *n:* • **1.** rice cooked to a thick, gummy consistency • **2.** a group of friends
شلِيل [šli:l] *n:* • **1.** pocket formed with the front of the robe – فُكّ شلِيلَك [fukk šli:lak] Hold up the front of your robe and form a basket. • **2.** pl. شلايِل [šla:yil] the tail of a horse
شَلّال [šalla:l] *n:* شَلّالات [šalla:la:t] *pl:* • **1.** waterfall, cataract
شِلِيلَة [šili:la] *n:* شِلِيلات [šili:la:t] *pl:* • **1.** a hank of yarn – شِلِيلَة وَضايِع راسها [šili:la wḍa:yiʕ ra:sha] Everything is all fouled up (lit., it's a hank of yarn and the end of it is lost).
مِنشَلّ [minšall] *adj:* • **1.** paralyzed
شَلّالِي [šalla:li] *adj:* • **1.** quick, hurried, sloppy – لا توَدِّي هدُومَك لِهَالأُوتچِي. شُغلَه شَلّالِي [la: twaddi: hdu:mak lihalʔu:tči. šuɣlah šalla:li] Don't take your clothes to that presser. His work is hurried and sloppy. • **2.** quickly, hurriedly – لا تحاوِل تعَلّمَه عالشُّغُل شلالِي [la: tħa:wil tʕallimah ʕaššuɣul šalla:li] Don't try to teach him the work too quickly.
مَشلُول [mašlu:l] *adj:* • **1.** paralyzed

ش ل م ن

شَلمَن [šalman] *v:* • **1.** to brag, exaggerate, talk big – لا تصَدِّق بيه؛ يشَلمِن هوايَة [la: tṣaddig bi:h; yšalmin hwa:ya] Don't believe him; he brags a lot.

شِيلمانَة [šilma:na] *n:* • **1.** girder(s), metal beam(s) • **2.** blustering, exaggerated talk, bragging – هَذا كُلَّه شَيلمان [ha:ða kullah šilma:n] That's all a lot of talk.
شَيلمانَة [ši:lma:na] *n:* شَيلمانات [šilmana:t] *pl:* • **1.** girder, steel beam
شَيلمَنجِي [šilmanči] *adj:* شَيلمَنجِيَّة [šilmančiyya] *pl:* • **1.** braggart, boaster

ش ل ن ف ص

شلُنفُص [šlunfuṣ] *adj:* شلُنفُصات [šlunfuṣa:t] *pl:* • **1.** harridan, hag, shrewish, bitchy woman

ش ل ه

شِلَه [šilah] *v:* • **1.** to run aground, to hit a snag – البَلَم شِلَه. لازم نجُرَّه [ʔilbalam šilah. la:zim nǰurrah] The boat has run aground. We'll have to pull it off.
شَلَّه [šallah] *v:* • **1.** to roll up (the sleeves or pants) – شَلَّه ردانَة وَخَشَّش إيدَه بالبِيب [šallah rda:na wxaššaš ʔi:dah bilpi:b] He rolled up his sleeve and plunged his hand into the barrel.
تشَلَّه [tšallah] *v:* • **1.** to roll up one's sleeves, pants, or robe – تشَلَّه ومِشَى بالمَيّ [tšallah wmiša: bilmayy] He rolled up his pants and waded into the water. • **2.** to proceed with vigor – إذا نِتشَلَّه إلها، نخَلِّصها بساع [ʔiða nitšallah ʔilha, nxalliṣha bsa:ʕ] If we plunge right into it, we'll finish it quickly. تشَلَّه وَخَلّي نخَلِّص الشُّغُل [tšallah wxalli: nxalliṣ ʔiššuɣul] Let's get going and finish the work.
شَلِه [šalih] *n:* • **1.** running aground, hitting a snag

ش ل ي ك

شِلّيك [šilli:g] *n:* • **1.** (coll.) strawberry(ies)
شِلّيكَة [šilli:ga] *n:* شِلّيكات [šilli:ga:t] *pl:* • **2.** strawberry

ش م ء ز

اِشمَئَزّ [ʔišmaʔazz] *v:* • **1.** to feel disgust, be disgusted – اِشمَأَزَّت نَفسَه مِن هَالحَياة [ʔišmaʔazzat nafsah min halħaya:t] He got disgusted with that life. هَالأَكِل تِشمِئِزّ النَّفس مِنَّه [halʔakil tišmiʔizz ʔinnafis minnah] This food is repulsive.
إشمِئزاز [ʔišmiʔza:z] *n:* • **1.** disgust, aversion, repugnance

ش م ب ن ز

شِمبانزي [šimba:nzi] *n:* • **1.** chimpanzee

ش م ت

شَمَّت [šammat] *v:* • **1.** to gloat, to rejoice at misfortune – إذا تِنحِبِس، راح تشَمِّت بِينا العِدوان [ʔiða tinħibis, ra:ħ tšammit bi:na ʔilʕidwa:n] If you go to jail, our enemies will rejoice at our misfortune.
تشَمَّت [tšammat] *v:* • **1.** to gloat, to rejoice at misfortune – مِن خِسَر كُلّهُم تشَمّتوا بِيه [min xiṣar kullhum tšammitaw bi:h] When he lost, they all gloated over his misfortune.
شَماتَة [šama:ta] *n:* • **1.** malicious joy, gloating
مِتشَمِّت [mitšammit] *adj:* • **1.** enjoying another's misfortune, malicious, gloating
شَمتان [šamta:n] *adj:* • **1.** enjoying another's misfortune, malicious, gloating

ش م ر

شُمَر [šumar] *v:* • **1.** to toss, cast, throw – آني أشمُر الكلاص وَإنتَ لُقفَه [ʔa:ni ʔašmur ʔilgla:ṣ wʔinta lugfah] I'll toss the glass and you catch it. راح أصعَد فُوق وَإنتَ إشمُرلِي الحَبِل [ra:ħ ʔaṣʕad fu:g wʔinta ʔišmurli ʔilħabil] I'll climb up and you throw me the rope. عَيِّنُوه بِبَغداد بَسّ بَعدين شُمرُوه لفَدّ قَريَة بعِيدَة [ʕayyinu:h bibayda:d bass baʕdi:n šumru:h lfadd qarya biʕi:da] They employed him in Baghdad but later sent him off to a distant village. • **2.** to go off, roam, range – شُمَر بعِيد [šumar biʕi:d] He went a long way off. مِن طلَعنا نصِيد، شُمَرنا بعِيد [min ṭlaʕna nṣi:d, šumarna biʕi:d] When we went out hunting, we roamed far afield.
شَمَّر [šammar] *v:* • **1.** to strew, throw around – إبنِك، مِن يرجَع مِن المَدرَسَة، يشَمُّر كُتبَه وَهدُومَه [ʔibnič, min yirǰaʕ min ʔilmadrasa, yšammur kutbah whdu:mah] When your son comes in from school, he throws his books and clothes around.
اِنشُمَر [ʔinšumar] *v:* • **1.** to be thrown, to lose conscience
شَمُر [šamur] *n:* • **1.** tossing, casting, throwing
شَمرَة [šamra] *n:* شَمرات [šamra:t] *pl:* • **1.** toss, cast, throw • **2.** manner, style, way (esp. of talking) – عِندَه شَمرَة بِالحَكِي ماخِذها مِن أَبُوه [ʕindah šamra bilħači ma:xiðha min ʔabu:h] He has a style of talking that he got from his father.
مَشمَر [mašmar] *n:* مشامِر [mša:mir] *pl:* • **1.** muffler, scarf
مشَمَّر [mšammar] *adj:* • **1.** scattered
مَشمُور [mašmu:r] *adj:* • **1.** thrown

ش م س

شَمَّس [šammas] *v:* • **1.** to expose to the sun, lay out in the sun – شَمِّس هدُومَك قَبُل ما تضُمّها [šammis hdu:mak gabul ma: dǒummha] Lay your clothes out in the sun before you store them.
تشَمَّس [tšammas] *v:* • **1.** to expose oneself to the sun, bask in the sun, sun oneself – يِعجبَك تِتشَمَّس اليُوم؟ [yiʕiǰbak titšammas ʔilyu:m?] Would you like to get some sun today?
شَمِس [šamis] *n:* شمُوس [šmu:s] *pl:* • **1.** (fem.) sun – وَرَق عَبّاد الشَّمِس [waraq ʕabba:d ʔiššamis] litmus paper. ضِرِبَتَه الشَّمِس [ḍirabatah ʔiššamis] He had a sunstroke. وَرِد عَين الشَّمِس [warid ʕi:n ʔiššamis] sunflower.

ش

شَمسِيَّة [šamsiyya] *n:* شَمسِيّات [šamsiyya:t] *pl:* • **1.** umbrella, parasol • **2.** awning

شَمسِي قَمَر [šamsi qamar] *n:* • **1.** sunflower • **2.** sunflower (seeds)

شَمسِي [šamsi] *adj:* • **1.** solar, sun- – تَصوِير شَمسِي [taṣwi:r šamsi] picture taken by a professional photographer (as opposed to one taken with a box camera).

مُشمِس [mušmis] *adj:* • **1.** sunny

ش م ش م

شَمشَم [šamšam] *v:* • **1.** to sniff – شُوف الكَلب دَيشَمشِم بالغَراض [šu:f ʔiččalib dayšamšim bilɣara:ð] Look at the dog sniffing at the things.

تشَمشَم [tšamšam] *v:* • **1.** to nose around, snoop – إجا يِتشَمشَم الأَخبار [ʔiǰa yitšamšam ʔilʔaxba:r] He came to sniff out the news.

ش م ع

شَمَّع [šammaʕ] *v:* • **1.** to wax – إذا تشَمِّع خيط السِّبحَة، يصِير أقوَى [ʔiða tšammiʕ xi:ṭ ʔissibħa, yṣi:r ʔaqwa] If you wax the string of the prayer beads, it'll be strong. مِن شافنِي جاي، شَمَّع الخيط [min ša:fni ǰa:y, šammaʕ ʔilxi:ṭ] When he saw me coming, he ran away.

شَمِع [šamiʕ] *n:* • **1.** wax • **2.** candle(s)

شَمعَة [šamʕa] *n:* شَمعات، شمُوع [šamʕa:t, šmu:ʕ] *pl:* • **1.** piece of wax • **2.** candle – كلُوب أَبُو سِتِّين شَمعَة [glu:b ʔabu sitti:n šamʕa] sixty watt light bulb.

شَمّاع [šamma:ʕ] *n:* شَمّاعَة [šamma:ʕa] *pl:* • **1.** maker and seller of candles

مشَمَّع [mšammaʕ] *n:* • **1.** as Adj, waxed • **2.** oilcloth • **3.** pl. مشَمَّعات raincoat • **4.** plastic sheet set on the floor on top of which food is set

شمَيعَة [šmayʕa] *n:* • **1.** little candle

شَمعدان [šamiʕda:n] *n:* شَمِعدانات [šamiʕda:na:t] *pl:* • **1.** candlestick, candelabrum

شِمّاعَة [šimma:ʕa] *adj:* شِمّاعات [šimma:ʕa:t] *pl:* • **1.** coat rack, hat rack

ش م غ

شُمُغ [šumuɣ] *n:* • **1.** man's head scarf

شماغ [šma:ɣ] *n:* • **1.** man's head scarf

ش م ل [1]

شِمَل [šimal] *v:* • **1.** to include, imply, implicate – التَّرفِيع شِمَل كُلّ المُوَظَّفِين [ʔittarfi:ʕ šimal kull ʔilmuwaððafi:n] The promotion included all the employees. التُّهمَة ما تشِملَك [ʔittuhma ma: tišimlak] The accusation doesn't include you. شِمَلنِي بِعَطفَه [šimalni bʕaṭfah] He was very kind to me. • **2.** to be included among the winners while not winning first place – البِطاقَة مالتِي ما ربحَت لَكِن شِملَت [ʔilbiṭa:qa ma:lti ma: ribħat la:kin šimlat] My ticket didn't win but it did get me something.

اِنشِمَل [ʔinšimal] *v:* • **1.** to be included

اِشتِمَل [ʔištimal] *v:* • **1.** with عَلَى to contain, comprise, include, be made up of – بَيتنا يِشتِمِل عَلَى أَربَع غُرَف ومَطبَخ [baytna yištimil ʕala ʔarbaʕ ɣuraf wmaṭbax] Our house consists of four rooms and a kitchen.

شَمِل [šamil] *n:* • **1.** uniting, gathering – اِجتِمَع شَمِلهُم [ʔiǰtimaʕ šamilhum] They got together, they united, they held a reunion. اِجتِمَع شَمِلهُم بَعَد اِنفِصال عَشِر سنِين [ʔiǰtimaʕ šamilhum baʕad ʔinfiṣa:l ʕašir sni:n] They had their reunion after a separation of ten years.

شمال [šma:l] *n:* شمالات [šma:la:t] *pl:* • **1.** the sanitary apparatus worn by women during menstruation

شُمُول [šumu:l] *n:* • **1.** thoroughness

مُشتَمَل [muštamal] *n:* مُشتَمَلات [muštamala:t] *pl:* • **1.** a large cottage built adjacent to a private home for rental purposes or servant quarters

شامِل [ša:mil] *adj:* • **1.** comprehensive, exhaustive, detailed – مَقال شامِل [maqa:l ša:mil] a detailed article.

مَشمُول [mašmu:l] *adj:* • **1.** included, contained, comprised

ش م ل [2]

شِمال [šima:l] *n:* • **1.** north

شِمالِي [šima:li] *adj:* • **1.** north, northern, northerly – القِسم الشِّمالِي [ʔilqism ʔiššima:li] the north section.

ش م م

شَمّ [šamm] *v:* • **1.** to smell, sniff – شِمّ هالوَردَة وشُوف شلُون ريحَة بيها [šimm halwarda wšu:f šlu:n ri:ħa bi:ha] Smell this flower and see what an odor it has.

شَمَّم [šammam] *v:* • **1.** to make or let smell – ما دَيقبَل يشَمِّمنِي الوَردَة [ma: dayiqbal yšammimni ʔilwarda] He won't let me smell the flower.

اِشتَمّ [ʔištamm] *v:* • **1.** to smell, sniff – سَوَّى عَمَلِيَّة بِخَشمَه وَبَعَد مَا يِشتَمّ زين [sawwa: ʕamaliyya bxašmah wabaʕad ma: yištamm zi:n] He had an operation on his nose and since then doesn't smell well.

شَمّ [šamm] *n:* • **1.** smelling, sniffing

شَمَّة [šamma] *n:* شَمّات [šamma:t] *pl:* • **1.** a smell, a sniff • **2.** whiff, slight odor

شِمّام [šimma:m] *n:* • **1.** (coll.) muskmelon(s)

شِمّامَة [šimma:ma] *n:* شِمّامات [šimma:ma:t] *pl:* • **1.** one/a muskmelon

ش ن ت ر

شَنتَر [šantar] *v:* • **1.** to prick up (for ears) • **2.** to show off, to behave in a crude, coarse, lowbrow or vulgar manner

تشنتر [tšantar] *v:* • **1.** to behave in a crude, coarse, low-brow or vulgar manner – الوَلَد يقُوم يتشَنتَر مِن يشُوف بَنات [ʔilwalad yguːm yitšantar min yšuːf banaːt] The boy begins to act up when he sees girls.
شَنتَرَة [šantara] *n:* • **1.** showing off
مشَنتِر [mšantir] *adj:* • **1.** crude, coarse, vulgar, unpolished, ill-bred

ش ن ج

تشَنَّج [tšannaǰ] *v:* • **1.** to contract, tighten up, stiffen – عَضَلات رِجلِي تشَنِّجَت [ʕaðalaːt rijli tšannijat] My leg muscles have tightened up.
تَشَنُّج [tašannuǰ] *n:* • **1.** cramp, contraction (of a muscle), twitch, jerk, convulsion, spasm, fit
مِتشَنِّج [mitšanniǰ] *adj:* • **1.** stiff

ش ن ع

شِنَع [šinaʕ] *v:* • **1.** to expose to disgrace, notoriety, or unwanted fame – إذا ما تِنطُونِي حُصَّة، أَشنَعكُم [ʔiða maː tinṭuːni ħuṣṣa, ʔašnaʕkum] If you don't give me a share, I'll expose you. غِلَطِت وقِتلَه رُبَحِت مِيَّة دِينار وَهُوَّ شِنَعنِي [ɣilaṭit wgitlah rubaħit miyyat dinaːr wahuwwa šinaʕni] I goofed and told him I won a hundred dinars and he gave me away.
شَنع [šaniʕ] *n:* • **1.** horridness, hideousness, frightfulness • **2.** notoriety, unwanted fame
شَنِيع [šaniːʕ] *adj:* • **1.** repugnant, repulsive, disgusting – عَمَل شَنِيع [ʕamal šaniːʕ] a disgraceful deed.
أَشنَع [ʔašnaʕ] *comparative adjective:* • **1.** more or most repugnant, disgusting

ش ن ق

شِنَق [šinaq] *v:* • **1.** to hang – شِنقُوه الفَجِر [šinquːh ʔilfaǰir] They hanged him at dawn.
شَنَّق [šannag] *v:* • **1.** to make (bread dough) into lumps or balls – شَنَّق العَجِين حَتَّى نُخبُز [šannag ʔilʕaǰiːn ħatta nuxbuz] Make the dough into balls so we can bake.
شَنِق [šaniq] *n:* • **1.** hanging – حِكمَوا عليه بِالشَّنِق [ħikmaw ʕaliːh biššaniq] He was sentenced to death by hanging.
شُنقَة [šunga] *n:* شُنَق [šunag] *pl:* • **1.** a ball of bread dough ready to be rolled out flat to make a loaf
مَشنَقَة [mašnaqa] *n:* مَشانِق [mašaːniq] *pl:* • **1.** gallows, hanging place

ش ن ك ل

شَنكَل [čangal] *v:* • **1.** to fasten together, hook together – شَنكِل الياخَة إِلَى أَن يصِير عِندِي وَقِت أَخَيِّط الدُّقمَة [čangil ʔilyaːxa ʔila ʔan yṣiːr ʕindi wakit ʔaxayyiṭ ʔiddugma] Pin the collar together until I have time to sew on the button. شَنكِل هَالفارقُونَين بمَكِينَة القِطار [čangil halfarguːnayn bmakiːnat ʔilqiṭaːr] Couple these two boxcars to the train engine.
شِنكال [čingaːl] *n:* شناكِيل [čnaːgiːl] *pl:* • **1.** fastener, catch, hook • **2.** safety pin • **3.** stevedore's hook, bale hook • **4.** fork (for eating)
مشَنكِل [mčangil] *n:* • **1.** hooked up, fastenened

ش ن ن

شَنّ [šann] *v:* • **1.** to launch an attack, make a raid – العَدُو شَنّ حَملَة قَوِيَّة عالقَريَة [ʔilʕadu šann ħamla qawiyya ʕalqarya] The enemy launched a strong campaign against the village. • **2.** to dilute yogurt to make a kind of drink – شِنّ هَاللِّبَن وَخَلِّي بِيه ثَلِج [šinn halliban wxalliː biːh θaliǰ] Dilute this yoghurt and put ice in it.
شَنّ [šann] *n:* • **1.** launch, start, setting up
شنان [šnaːn] *n:* • **1.** crude soap made from dried, crushed leaves of a kind of desert bush
شِنِينَة [šiniːna] *n:* • **1.** a kind of drink made of yogurt diluted with water

ش ن و [1]

شِنُو [šinu] *interrogative:* • **1.** (interrogative pronoun) what? what's this? what do you mean? – شِنُو هاي؟ [šinu haːy?] What's this? تُعرُف شِنُو اللِّي بَقّانِي هنا؟ [tuʕruf šinuː ʔilli baqqaːni hna?] Do you know what made me stay here? شِنُو ما سمَعتِنِي؟ آنِي حِكَيت بصُوت عالِي [šinu maː smaʕitni? ʔaːni ħičiːt bṣuːt ʕaːli] What do you mean you didn't hear me? I spoke in a loud voice.

ش ن و [2]

شناو [šnaːw] *n:* • **1.** push-ups – ياخُذ شناو [yaːxuð šnaːw] He does push-ups.

ش ه

شاه [šaːh] *adj:* شاهات [šaːhaːt] *pl:* • **1.** Shah, ruler • **2.** king (in chess)

ش ه ب

شِهاب [šihaːb] *n:* شُهُب [šuhub] *pl:* • **1.** meteor, shooting star
أَشهَب [ʔašhab] *adj:* شُهُب [šuhub] *pl:* شَهبَة [šahba] *feminine:* • **1.** light gray, ash-colored

ش ه د

شِهَد [šihad] *v:* • **1.** to witness, be a witness to – شُوفُوا، يا ناس! جَرّ عَلَيّا خَنجَر. شِهَدتُوا [šuːfuː, yaː naːs! ǰarr ʕalayya xanǰar. šihadtuː] Look, you people! He pulled a knife on me. You're witnesses. • **2.** with عَلَى to sign as a witness – شِهدَوا إِثنَين عالكَفالَة [šihdaw ʔiθnayn ʕalkafaːla] Two signed the bond as witnesses. • **3.** to testify, bear witness, give testimony – لا تدِير بال. راح أَشهَدلَك [laː ddiːr baːl. raːħ ʔašhadlak] Don't worry. I'll testify for you. تصَوَّر، صَدِيقِي شِهَد عَلَيّا بِالمَحكَمَة [tṣawwar, ṣadiːqi šihad ʕalayya bilmaħkama] Imagine, my friend testified against

ش

me in court. خَمِس مَرّات غِلَبتِني. أَشهَدلَك إنتَ أُستاذ بِالشِّطرَنج [xamis marra:t ɣilabitni. ʔašhadlak ʔinta ʔusta:ð biššiṭranǰ] Five times you beat me. I can vouch for your being a master at chess. إشهدُوا عَلَيّا. إذا ما أَبُسطَه، حَقكُم [ʔišhdu: ʕalayya. ʔiða ma: ʔabusṭah, ħaqqkum] Mark my words. If I don't beat him up, you can tell everyone. أَشهَد بِالله، أَشهَد ما بِالله [ʔašhad billa:h, ʔašhad ma: billa:h] I swear by God. أَشهَد ما بِالله خُوش وَلَد [ʔašhad ma: billa:h xu:š walad] I swear by God he's a good boy.

شَهَّد [šahhad] *v:* • **1.** to make or let testify, cause to give testimony – إذا ما تقُرّ، راح أَشَهِّد عَلِيك جَماعَة [ʔiða ma: tqurr, ra:ħ ʔašahhid ʕali:k ǰama:ʕa] If you don't confess, I'll have people testify against you.

شاهَد [ša:had] *v:* • **1.** to witness, see, watch, observe, view

تشاهَد [tša:had] *v:* • **1.** to recite the creed of Islam – مُعَلِّم الدِّين سِأَلنِي أَتشاهَد وَما عِرَفِت [muʕallim ʔiddi:n siʔalni ʔatša:had wma ʕirafit] The religion techer ask me to recite the creed and I didn't know it. • **2.** (by extension) to be near death – مِن شِفت السَّبِع قِدّامِي، تشاهَدِت [min šift ʔissabiʕ gidda:mi, tša:hadit] When I saw the lion in front of me, I said my last words. ظَلّ يِتشاهَد ساعَة إلَى أن مات [ðall yitša:had sa:ʕa ʔila ʔan ma:t] He struggled for life for an hour until he died.

اِستَشهَد [ʔistašhad] *v:* • **1.** to die as a martyr, give one's life – ثنَين مِن وِلِدها اِستَشهِدَوا بالمَعرَكَة [θnayn min wilidha ʔistašhidaw balmaʕraka] Two of her children gave their lives in the battle. • **2.** with ب to cite as authority, quote as evidence or support – بِدِفاعَه، اِستَشهَد بِعِدَّة حَوادِث [bdifa:ʕah, ʔistašhad biʕiddat ħawa:diθ] In his defense, he cited several incidents. بخِطابَه، اِستَشهَد بِأَبيات لعِدَّة شُعَراء [bxiṭa:bah, ʔistašhad bʔabya:t lʕiddat šuʕara:ʔ] In his speech, he quoted the lines of several poets.

مَشهَد [mašhad] *n:* مَشاهِد [maša:hid] *pl:* • **1.** scene (of an occurrence) • **2.** act, scene (in theater, entertainment)

مُشاهَدَة [muša:hada] *n:* • **1.** viewing, observing, watching, witnessing

اِستِشهاد [ʔistišha:d] *n:* • **1.** citation, quotation • **2.** martyrdom, death of a hero

شَهِيد [šahi:d] *adj:* شُهَداء [šuhada:ʔ] *pl:* • **1.** martyr

شاهِد [ša:hid] *n:* شُهُود [šuhu:d] *pl:* • **1.** witness – شاهِد عَيان [ša:hid ʕaya:n] eye-witness.

شَهادَة [šaha:da] *adj:* شَهادات [šaha:da:t] *pl:* • **1.** testimony, witness, evidence, deposition • **2.** certificate, certification, affidavit • **3.** degree, diploma, credentials • **4.** identification

شاهُود [ša:hu:d] *adj:* شواهِيد [šwa:hi:d] *pl:* • **1.** large bead on the end of a string of prayer beads

مَشهُود [mašhu:d] *adj:* • **1.** memorable, well-known, well-attended

ش ه ر

شِهَر [šihar] *v:* • **1.** to make well-known, renowned, famous, notorious – شِهَرنِي وَما خَلَّه أَحَّد ما قَلَّه [šiharni wma xallah ʔaħħad ma: gallah] He exposed me and didn't leave anyone that he didn't tell.

اِشتِهَر [ʔištihar] *v:* • **1.** to be or become famous, well-known, famed, celebrated, notorious – اِشتِهَر بَعَد ما نِشَر كِتابَه [ʔištihar baʕad ma: nišar kita:bah] He became famous after he published his book.

شَهَر [šahar] *n:* أَشهُر [ʔašhur] *pl:* • **1.** month – شَهَر العَسَل [šahar ʔilʕasal] honeymoon.

شَهر [šahir] *n:* • **1.** exposure, announcement, declaration • **2.** fame notoriety

شُهرَة [šuhra] *n:* • **1.** repute, reputation, renown, fame, famousness • **2.** notoriety

شَهرِيَّة [šahriyya] *n:* شَهرِيّات [šahriyya:t] *pl:* • **1.** monthly payment or salary

تَشهِير [tašhi:r] *n:* • **1.** public exposure

إشهار [ʔišha:r] *n:* • **1.** declaration, proclamation, announcement • **2.** public sale, auction, publicity, advertising

اِشتِهار [ʔištiha:r] *n:* • **1.** fame, repute, reputation, renown, celebrity, notoriety

شَهرِي [šahri] *adj:* • **1.** monthly, mensual – الاشتِراك الشَّهرِي بِالجَّرِيدَة [ʔilʔištira:k ʔiššahri bijǰari:da] the monthly subscription rate for the paper. إيجار شَهرِي [ʔi:ǰa:r šahri] monthly rent.

شَهِير [šahi:r] *adj:* • **1.** famous, well-known, celebrated, renowned – مُؤَلِّف شَهِير [muʔallif šahi:r] a famous writer. • **2.** notorious

مَشهُور [mašhu:r] *adj:* • **1.** famous, well-known, renowned, celebrated – مُلاكِم مَشهُور [mula:kim mašhu:r] a famous boxer. هَالبَطَل مَشهُور بشَجاعتَه [halbaṭal mašhu:r bšaǰa:ʕtah] That hero's known for his bravery. • **2.** notorious – شَقِي مَشهُور [šaqi mašhu:r] a notorious thug. • **3.** pl. مَشاهِير celebrity, famous

أَشهَر [ʔašhar] *comparative adjective:* • **1.** more or most famous, well-known

شَهرِيّاً [šahriyyan] *adverbial:* • **1.** monthly

ش ه ق

شِهَق [šihag] *v:* • **1.** to hiccup, have the hiccups – لا تِشرَب مَيّ مِن تِضحَك تَرَة تِشهَق [la: tišrab mayy min tiðħak tara tišhag] Don't drink water when you laugh or you'll get the hiccups.

شَهق [šahig] *n:* • **1.** hiccup(s)

شَهِيق [šahi:q] *n:* • **1.** breathing in, braying

شَهقَة [šahga] *n:* • **1.** hiccups

شِهَّيقَة [šihhi:ga] *n:* • **1.** hiccups – لِزمَتَه الشِّهَّيقَة مُدَّة [lizmatah ʔiššihhi:ga mudda] He had the hiccups for a while.

ش

ش ه م

شَهامَة [šaha:ma] *n:* • **1.** gallantry, gentlemanliness • **2.** decency, respectability

شَهم [šahim] *adj:* شَهمِين [šahimi:n] *pl:* • **1.** noble, gallant, decent, gentlemanly

ش ه و

شَهَّى [šahha:] *v:* • **1.** to cause hunger, desire, craving, to whet the appetite, be appetizing – رِيحَة الأَكِل تشَهِّي [ri:ħat ʔilʔakil tšahhi] The odor of food whets the appetite.

اِشتَهَى [ʔištiha:] *v:* • **1.** to wish, desire, crave, have an appetite for – لا تجِيبلِي أَكِل. ما أَشتِهِي [la: dji:bli ʔakil. ma: ʔaštihi] Don't bring me any food. I have no appetite. دَأَشتِهِي أَكلَة سِمَك [daʔaštihi ʔaklat simač] I feel like eating fish. تبَيِّن مِشتِهِي بَسِط [tbayyin mištihi baṣiṭ] It looks like you're asking for a spanking.

شَهوَة [šahwa] *n:* شَهوات [šahwa:t] *pl:* • **1.** lust, carnal appetite • **2.** orgasm

شَهِيَّة [šahiyya] *n:* • **1.** appetite

مُشَهِّي [mušahhi] *n:* مُشَهِّيّات [mušahhiyya:t] *pl:* • **1.** appetizer

شَهواني [šahwa:ni] *adj:* • **1.** lustful, sensuous • **2.** debauched, lewd

ش ه و ل

شاهُول [ša:hu:l] *n:* شواهِيل [šwa:hi:l] *pl:* • **1.** plumb line, plummet, plumb bob

ش ه ي

See also: ش ه و

ش ه ي ن

شاهِين [ša:hi:n] *n:* شواهِين [šwa:hi:n] *pl:* • **1.** a kind of falcon

ش و ت

شَوَّت [šawwat] *v:* • **1.** to kick a ball, shoot – إنتَ تشَوِّت كُلِّش زين بِالسِّباق [ʔinta tčawwit kulliš zi:n bissiba:q] You kicked well in the game. شُوف شلُون شَوَّتها لِلطُّوبَة عالِي [šu:f šlu:n šawwatha littu:ba ʕa:li] Look how high he kicked the ball.

شُوت [šu:t] *n:* شُوتات، شواتَة [šu:ta:t, šwa:ta] *pl:* • **1.** kick, shot – ضِرَب الطُّوبَة شُوت [ḍirab ʔiṭṭu:ba šu:t] He kicked the ball.

ش و ر

شار [ša:r] *v:* • **1.** to consult, take counsel with – شُور أَبُوك قَبُل ما تسافِر [šu:r ʔabu:k gabul ma: tsa:fir] Consult your father before you leave.

شَوَّر [šawwar] *v:* • **1.** to have the power to call divine vengeance – هَالسَّيِّد يشَوِّر [hassayyid yšawwir] This descendant of Mohammed has the power to call divine vengeance.

شاوَر [ša:war] *v:* • **1.** to whisper to – شاوُرنِي حَتَّى ما يِسمَع شتقُولِّي [ša:wurni ħatta ma: yismaʕ štgu:lli] Whisper to me so he won't hear what you tell me.

أشار [ʔaša:r] *v:* • **1.** with عَلَى to advise, give advice to – أَشار عَلِيه الطَّبِيب ياخُذ مُسهِل [ʔaša:r ʕali:h ʔiṭṭabi:b ya:xuð mushil] The doctor advised him to take a laxative.

تشاوَر [tša:war] *v:* • **1.** to whisper to each other – دَيِتشاوُرُون وَما دَأَفهَم شدَيقُولُون [dayitša:wru:n wma daʔafham šdaygu:lu:n] They're whispering to each other and I don't understand what they're saying.

اِستَشار [ʔistaša:r] *v:* • **1.** to ask advice, seek an opinion from – ما يسَوِّي شِي إذا ما يِستِشِيرَه بِالأَوَّل [ma: ysawwi: ši ʔiða ma: yistiši:rah bilʔawwal] He does nothing without first asking his advice. ماكُو داعِي تِستَشِيرَه. أَعتِقِد يِتِّفِق وِيّاك [ma:ku da:ʕi tistaši:rah. ʔaʕtiqid yittifiq wiyya:k] There's no need for you to get his opinion. I think he agrees with you.

شور [šawr, šu:r] *n:* • **1.** counsel, advice, suggestion

شُورَة [šu:ra] *n:* • **1.** white, salt-like deposit on lime or concrete in damp places

مُشِير [muši:r] *n:* مُشِيرِين [muši:ri:n] *pl:* • **1.** field marshal, general of the armies

شُورَى [šu:ra] *n:* • **1.** consultation, deliberation, taking council, advise

مِشوار [mišwa:r] *n:* • **1.** a while, time, interval – صارلِي مِشوار أَنتَظرَك [ṣa:rli mišwa:r ʔantaðrak] I've been waiting for you for some time. رُوح فَدّ مِشوار ساعَة وَتَعال [ru:ħ fadd mišwa:r sa:ʕa wataʕa:l] Go away for about an hour and then come.

مَشورَة [mašu:ra, mašwara] *n:* • **1.** counsel, advice, suggestion, consultation, deliberation

مُشاوِر [muša:wir] *n:* مُشاوِرِين [muša:wiri:n] *pl:* • **1.** counselor, adviser, consultant

تَشاوُر [taša:wur] *n:* • **1.** joint consultation, deliberation

مُشاوَرَة [muša:wara] *n:* • **1.** whispering • **2.** pl. مُشاوَرات conference, consultation

مُستَشار [mustaša:r] *n:* مُستَشارِين [mustaša:ri:n] *pl:* • **1.** adviser, counselor • **2.** chancellor

اِستِشارَة [ʔistiša:ra] *n:* اِستِشارات [ʔistiša:ra:t] *pl:* • **1.** advice, recommendation • **2.** consultation

اِستِشارِي [ʔistiša:ri] *adj:* • **1.** advisory – مَجلِس اِستِشارِي [majlis ʔistiša:ri] advisory council. • **2.** consultative

ش و ر ب

شُوربَة [šu:rba] *n:* • **1.** soup, broth

ش و ر ت

شُورت [šu:rt] *n:* شُورتات [šu:rta:t] *pl:* • **1.** shorts • **1.** (electrical) short circuit

ش

ش و ش

شَوَّش [šawwaš] *v:* • **1.** to muddle, confuse, disturb, upset – لا تشَوِّشني؛ خَلّي أفَكِّر [la: tšawwišni; xalli: ʔafakkir] Don't confuse me; let me think. إنتَ شَوَّشتَه هوايَة بهَالخَبَر [ʔinta šawwaštah hwa:ya bhalxabar] You upset him a lot with that news. • **2.** with عَلَى to interfere with, jam – أكُو مَحَطَّة إذاعَة دَتشَوِّش عَلَى مَحَطّتنا [ʔaku maħaṭṭat ʔiða:ʕa datšawwiš ʕala maħaṭṭatna] There's a broadcasting station interfering with our station.

تشَوَّش [tšawwaš] *v:* • **1.** to be confused, muddled – ما أدري لِيش تشَوَّشِت [ma: ʔadri li:š tšawwašit] I don't know why I was confused. • **2.** to be disturbed, upset, become uneasy, worried – عَلِي ما رِجَع لهَسَّة. فِكري تشَوَّش عَليه [ʕali ma: rijaʕ lhassa. fikri tšawwaš ʕali:h] Ali didn't return yet. I'm uneasy about him. ماكُو داعِي تِتشَوَّش. هُوَّ شوَيَّة راح يتأخَّر [ma:ku da:ʕi titšawwaš. huwwa šwayya ra:ħ yitʔaxxar] There's no reason to worry. He'll be a little bit late.

شاش [ša:š] *n:* • **1.** cheesecloth, gauze

شاشَة [ša:ša] *n:* شاشات [ša:ša:t] *pl:* • **1.** piece of muslin • **2.** (movie) screen

تشويش [tašwi:š] *n:* • **1.** confusion, confounding, muddling, disturbance, derangement

مشَوَّش [mšawwaš] *adj:* • **1.** muddled, confused

مِتشَوِّش [mitšawwiš] *adj:* • **1.** muddled

ش و ط

شاط [ša:ṭ] *v:* • **1.** (of food) to scorch, burn – التِّمَّن شاط. لازِم النّار كانَت عالية [ʔittimman ša:ṭ. la:zim ʔinna:r ča:nat ʕa:lya] The rice scorched. The fire must have been to high. • **2.** to be or become upset, worried, disturbed – راح أقُلَّك فَدّ شِي بَسّ لا تشُوط [ra:ħ ʔagullak fadd ši bass la: tšu:ṭ] I'm going to tell you something but don't get upset. شاطَت عَلَى إبِنها مِن سِمعَت الخَبَر [ša:ṭat ʕala ʔibinha min simʕat ʔilxabar] She got upset about her son when she heard the news.

شَوَّط [šawwaṭ] *v:* • **1.** to burn, scorch – طَفّي النّار. شَوَّطت التِّمَّن [ṭaffi ʔinna:r. šawwaṭit ʔittimman] Turn off the fire. You've burned the rice. • **2.** to upset, disturb, worry – راح تشَوُّطَه بهَالخَبَر. إسكُت أحسَنلَك [ra:ħ tšawwuṭah bhalxabar. ʔiskut ʔaħsanlak] You'll upset him with this news. It would be better for you to keep quiet.

شَوط [šu:ṭ] *n:* • **1.** being or becoming disturbed, anxious, worried • **2.** pl. شَوطات short circuit, electrical short • **3.** pl. أشواط race

شَوطَة [šu:ṭa] *n:* • **1.** (of food) scorch, burn

شواط [šwa:ṭ] *n:* • **1.** burn, scorch (of food) • **2.** anger

ش و ف

شاف [ša:f] *v:* • **1.** to see – لازِم أشُوف البَيت قَبُل ما أتَجِّرها [la:zim ʔašu:f ʔilbayt gabul ma: ʔaʔajjirha] I must see the house before I rent it. شِفِت هَالفِلِم قَبُل [šifit halfilim gabul] I've seen that film before. شِفتَه مَرّ مِن يَمّنا [šiftah marr min yammna] I saw him pass by us. شايِف شسَوّى بيّا؟ [ša:yif ššawwa: biyya?] Did you see what he did to me? رِحِت لِلمَعمَل حَتَّى أشُوف شلُون يرَكّبُون السَّيّارات [riħit lilmaʕmal ħatta ʔašu:f šlu:n yrakkibu:n ʔissayya:ra:t] I went to the factory to observe how they assemble cars. شُوف، دَأقُلَّك، آني ما أقبَل بهيكِي سِعِر [šu:f, daʔagullak, ʔa:ni ma: ʔaqbal bhi:či siʕir] Look, I'm telling you, I won't agree to such a price. لا تشُوفَه هِيكِي. هُوَّ أشطَن مِن إبلِيس [la: tšu:fah hi:či. huwwa ʔašṭan min ʔibli:s] Don't let his looks fool you. He's more clever than a devil. شِفِت فَرِق عَلَى هَالدُوا [šifit fariq ʕala hadduwa] I noticed an improvement with this medicine. مِن تِتجادَل ويّاه، يشُوف نَفسَه يفتِهِم [min tidja:dal wiyya:h, yšu:f nafsah yiftihim] When you argue with him, he sees himself understanding everything. هَذا يشُوف نَفسَه عَلَى طُول [ha:ða yšu:f nafsah ʕala ṭu:l] This guy is always thinking of himself. صَدِيقَك شايِف نَفسَه هوايَة [ṣadi:qak ša:yif nafsah hwa:ya] Your friend is very conceited. البارحَة شِفِت طَيف [ʔilba:rħa šifit ṭi:f] Last night I had a dream. • **2.** to experience, go through, sustain, suffer, to find, encounter – نِجَح رَغم الصُّعُوبات اللّي شافها [nijaħ raɣm ʔiṣṣuʕu:ba:t ʔilli ša:fha] He succeeded despite the hardships which he experienced. مُو عَجِيب يحكِي هِيكِي لِأنَّه ما شايِف [mu: ʕaji:b yiħči hi:či liʔannah ma: ša:yif] It isn't strange that he would talk like that because he's inexperienced. • **3.** to find, discover – دَأشُوف لَذَّة بهَالشُّغُل [daʔašu:f laðða bhʔaššuɣul] I find pleasure in this work. شُوفلَك فَدّ واحِد يساعدَك [šu:flak fadd wa:ħid ysa:ʕdak] Find yourself someone to help you. لازِم تشُوف فَدّ حَلّ لِهَالمُشكِلَة [la:zim tšu:f fadd ħall lihalmuškila] You must find some solution for this problem. • **4.** to find out, ascertain, determine – فُحَصَه الطَّبِيب وشاف ما بِيه شِي [fuħaṣah ʔiṭṭabi:b wša:f ma: bi:h ši] The doctor examined him and found there was nothing wrong with him. خابرَه وشُوف شِيريد [xa:brah wšu:f šiyri:d] Phone him and see what he wants. • **5.** to think, believe, be of the opinion that – شِتشُوف أرُوح لِبَغداد لَو لاء؟ [šitšu:f? ʔaru:ħ lbayda:d law la:??] What do you think? Should I go to Baghdad or not? آني أشُوف لَو تقُلَّه بيها أحسَن [ʔa:ni ʔašu:f law dgullah bi:ha ʔaħsan] It seems to me that it would be better if you tell him about it. • **6.** to sense, apperceive, feel, to have a hunch, a premonition, a feeling – آني أشُوف تالِيها راح يجِينا إيد مِن وَرا وَإيد مِن قِدّام [ʔa:ni ʔašu:f ta:li:ha ra:ħ yiji:na ʔi:d min wara waʔi:d min gidda:m] I have a hunch that in the end he'll come to us empty-handed.

شَوَّف [šawwaf] *v:* • **1.** to cause to see, let see, show – شَوَّفنِي كُلّ كُتبَه [šawwafni kull kutbah] He showed me all his books. تِقدَر تشَوُّفهُم الكُلِّيَّة؟ [tigdar tšawwufhum ʔilkulliyya?] Can you show them the college?

تشاوَف [tšaːwaf] *v:* • **1.** to see each other – خَلِّي نِتشاوَف. مُو تغِيب فَدّ مَرَّة [xalliː nitšaːwaf. muː tɣiːb fadd marra] Let's see one another. Don't just disappear altogether.
اِنشاف [ʔinšaːf] *v:* • **1.** to be seen – بيش مِلتِهي؟ أَشُو ما دَتِنشاف [biyš miltihi? ʔašu maː datinšaːf] What've you been up to? It seems you haven't been seen around. • **2.** to be worth seeing – هَالفِلِم ما يِنشاف. يلَعِّب النَّفِس [halfilim maː yinšaːf. ylaʕʕib ʔinnafis] This film isn't worth seeing. It's sickening.
شَوف [šawf] *n:* • **1.** seeing – أَشتِرِيها عالشَّوف [ʔaštiriːha ʕaššawf] I'll buy it on approval.
شَوفَة [šawfa] *n:* شَوفات [šawfaːt] *pl:* • **1.** sight, look, glance
مَشُوفَة [mašuːfa] *n:* مَشُوفات [mašuːfaːt] *pl:* • **1.** mirror, looking glass

ش و ق

شَوَّق [šawwaq] *v:* • **1.** to fill with longing, desire, nostalgia – شَوَّقتِني عَليه. راح أَشتِرِيه [šawwaqitni ʕaliːh. raːħ ʔaštiriːh] You have made me want it. I'm going to buy it. هَالرَّسِم يشَوُّقنِي لِلبنان [harrasim yšawwuqni lilabnaːn] This drawing makes me long for Lebanon.
اِشتاق [ʔištaːq, ʔištaːg] *v:* • **1.** to feel longing, yearning, craving, desire, nostalgia – اِشتاقيت لِإبنِي وِاِضطَرَّيت أَسافِرلَه [ʔištaːqayt liʔibni wʔiḍṭarrayt ʔasaːfirlah] I longed to see my son and had to go to him. أَشتاق لذِيك الأَيّام الحِلوَة [ʔaštaːq lðiːč lʔayyaːm ʔilħilwa] I yearn for those pleasant times. تِدرِي، دَأَشتاقلَه المَلعُون [tidri, daʔaštaːqlah ʔilmalʕuːn] You know, I miss the rascal.
شَوق [šuːq, šuːg] *n:* أَشواق [ʔašwaːq, ʔašwaːg] *pl:* • **1.** longing, desire, craving, yearning
تَشوِيق [tašwiːq] *n:* • **1.** arousing of desire, awakening of excitement, yearning, desire
اِشتِياق [ʔištiyaːq, ʔištiyaːg] *n:* • **1.** longing, yearning, craving, desire, nostalgia
شَيِّق [šayyiq] *adj:* • **1.** interesting, exciting, gorgeous, splendid
مِشتاق [mištaːq, mištaːg] *adj:* • **1.** longing, yearning, craving, desirous, nostalgic – مِشتاقلَك [mištaːqlak] I've been longing for you, I miss you
مِتشَوِّق [mitšawwiq] *adj:* • **1.** eager, craving, yearning
أَشوَق [ʔašwaq] *comparative adjective:* • **1.** more or most desirous, nostalgic

ش و ك

شَوك [šuːk] *n:* • **1.** thorn (s), spine (s), prickle (s) • **2.** thorny bush(es)
شُوكَة [šuːka] *n:* شُوكات [šuːkaːt] *pl:* • **1.** fork • **2.** thorn, spine, prickle
شَوكايَة [šawkaːya, šuːkaːya] *n:* شَوكايات [šuːkaːyaːt] *pl:* • **1.** thorn, spine, prickle
شائك [šaːʔik] *adj:* • **1.** thorny, also prickly, spiny, delicate, ticklish, critical, difficult

ش و ل

شَوّال [šawwaːl] *n:* • **1.** Shawwal, the tenth month of the Moslem calendar

ش و م ن

شَومِينَة [šawmiːna, šumiːna] *n:* شَومِينات [šawminaːt] *pl:* • **1.** fireplace • **2.** chimney

ش و ن د ر

شَوَندَر [šwandar, šwanðar] *n:* • **1.** (coll.) beet(s)
شَوَندَرَة [šwandara, šwanðara] *n:* شَوَندَر، شَوَنذَرات [šwandara, šwanðaraːt] *pl:* • **1.** beet

ش و ه

شَوَّه [šawwah] *v:* • **1.** to make ugly, to disfigure, deform, deface, distort, mar, mutilate – الجِّدرِي شَوَّه وِجهه [ʔijjidri šawwah wiččah] Smallpox marred his face. يشَوِّه الحَقايِق [yšawwih ʔilħaqaːyiq] He distorts the facts. شَوَّه سُمعَة أَهلَه بِسلُوكَه [šawwah sumʕat ʔahlah bsuluːkah] He debased the reputation of his family by his conduct.
تشَوَّه [tšawwah] *v:* • **1.** pass. of شَوَّه to be ugly, to be disfigured, deformed, defaced – تشَوَّه وِجهه بالعَمَلِيَّة [tšawwah wiččah bilʕamaliyya] His face was marred by the operation.
تَشَوُّه [tašawwuh] *n:* • **1.** ugliness, malformation
تَشوِيه [tašwiːh] *n:* • **1.** deformation, defacement, mutilation, defamation, crippledness
مُشَوَّه [mušawwah] *adj:* • **1.** disfigured, defaced
مِتشَوِّه [mitšawwih] *adj:* • **1.** disfigured, defaced

ش و ي

شُوَى [šuwaː] *v:* • **1.** to broil, roast, cook (esp. meat) – شُوَى اللَّحَم عالفَحَم [šuwaː ʔillaħam ʕalfaħam] He broiled the meat over the charcoal. الشَّمِس تِشوِي اليُوم [ʔiššamis tišwi ʔilyuːm] The sun's broiling hot today. شُوَتنِي الشَّمِس [šuwatni ʔiššamis] I got a sunburn. المُعَلِّم شُوانا بِالإِمتِحانات [ʔilmuʕallim šuwaːna bilʔimtiħaːnaːt] The teacher raked us over the coals in the tests.
اِنشُوَى [ʔinšuwaː] *v:* • **1.** to be broiled, roasted – اِنشُوَى اللَّحَم خُوش شَويَة [ʔinšuwaː ʔillaħam xuːš šawya] The meat got a good broiling.
شَوِي [šawy] *n:* • **1.** broiling, roasting
شاوِي، مَطِي شاوِي [šaːwi, maṭi šaːwi] *n:* • **1.** one of a breed of small donkeys
مَشوِي [mašwi] *adj:* • **1.** broiled, roasted, cooked – لَحَم مَشوِي [laħam mašwi] broiled meat.

ش ي

شاي [ča:y] *n:* شايات [ča:ya:t] *pl:* • **1.** tea – شاي دارسِين [ča:y da:rsi:n] cinnamon and hot water. • **2.** cup of tea

شايخانَة، شاي خانَة [čayxa:na, ča:y xa:na] *n:* • **1.** tea house

شَايجِي [čayači, ča:yači] *adj:* شَايجِيَّة [čayačiyya] *pl:* • **1.** tea shop owner

ش ي ء

شاء [ša:ʔ] *v:* • **1.** (used in a few phrases, of God) to want, wish, desire – إن شاء الله [ʔin ša:ʔ ʔallah] God willing, it is to be hoped, we hope إن شاء الله، سَنَة اللّخ نرُوح لِمَكَّة [ʔinša:llah, sanat ʔillux nru:ħ limakka] God willing, next year we'll go to Mecca. إن شاء الله ما بيك شِي [ʔinša:llah ma: bi:k ši] I hope there's nothing wrong with you. ما شاء الله [ma: ša:ʔ ʔallah] Great! or God bless!

شِي [ši] *n:* أشياء [ʔašya:ʔ] *pl:* • **1.** thing – شِي عَجِيب، عَبالِي ما تُمطُر بِالصَّيف [ši ʕaǰi:b, ʕaba:li ma: tumṭur biṣṣayf] That's strange. I thought it didn't rain in the summer. الشّي اللّي ما يعِجبَك، لا تاخذَه [ʔišši ʔilli ma: yʕiǰbak, la: ta:xðah] Whatever you don't want, don't take. ما عِندِي شِي مُهِمّ [ma: ʕindi ši muhimm] I don't have anything important. بَعض الشّي [baʕḍ ʔišši] to a certain extent, a little somewhat. صِحّتَه تحَسّنَت بَعض الشّي [ṣiħħtah tħassnat baʕḍ ʔišši] His health improved a little. شِي عَلَى شِي [ši ʕala ši] all in all, on the whole. شِي عَلَى شِي، هُوَّ خُوش وَلَد [ši ʕala ši, huwwa xu:š walad] On the whole, he's a pretty fine fellow. • **2.** something – غَطِّي الأكِل بِشِي حَتَّى لا يتوَسَّخ [ɣaṭṭi ʔilʔakil bši ħatta la: yitwassax] Cover the food with something so that it won't get dirty. اليُوم أبدَى شِي مِن النَّشاط [ʔilyu:m ʔabda: ši min ʔinnaša:ṭ] Today he showed some activity. أكُو بِيه شِي [ʔaku bi:h ši] There's something wrong with it. It has a defect in it.

مَشِيئَة [maši:ʔa] *n:* • **1.** volition

شوَيَّة [šwayya] *adj:* • **1.** a small amount, a little bit, a few, some – عِندِي شوَيَّة فلُوس [ʕindi šwayya flu:s] I have a little bit of money. اِشتِرِي مِن البَقّال! شوَيَّة بُرتُقال [ʔištiri min ʔilbagga:! šwayya purtuqa:l] Buy a few oranges from the grocer. • **2.** a short time, a little while – راح أرجَع بَعد شوَيَّة [ra:ħ ʔarǰaʕ baʕd šwayya] I'll be back in a little while. اِلزَم الباب شوَيَّة حَتَّى أشِدّ البُرغِي [ʔilzam ʔilba:b šwayya ħatta ʔašidd ʔilburɣi] Hold the door a minute so I can put the screw in. كان بَعد شوَيَّة تِسحَقَه السَّيّارَة [ča:n baʕd šwayya tisħagah ʔissayya:ra] The car was just about to hit him. إلّا شوَيَّة [ʔilla šwayya] almost, very nearly. حَصَّلِتها لِلسَّيّارَة إلّا شوَيَّة [ħaṣṣalitha lissayya:ra ʔilla šwayya] I almost got the car. • **3.** a little, a little bit, somewhat – هُوَّ شوَيَّة مسَخِّن [huwwa šwayya msaxxin] He's just a bit feverish. إرجَع شوَيَّة إلَى أن أقلَّك أوقف [ʔirǰaʕ šwayya ʔila ʔan ʔagullak ʔu:gaf] Back up a little until I tell you to stop.

ش ي ب

شاب [ša:b] *v:* • **1.** (of hair) to become gray, white – شَعرَه شاب بشَبابَه [šaʕrah ša:b bšaba:bah] His hair turned white in his youth. • **2.** (of a person) to grow old, become gray-haired – شاب وَبَعَد ما يقدَر يِشتُغُل [ša:b wabaʕad ma: yigdar yištuɣul] He's grown old and can't work any more. شاب قَبُل وَقتَه [ša:b gabul waktah] he got old before his time.

شَيَّب [šayyab] *v:* • **1.** (of hair) to become gray, white – راسَه شَيَّب بِالأربَعِين [ra:sah šayyab bilʔarbaʕi:n] His hair turned gray at forty • **2.** (of a person) to grow old, become gray-haired – شَيَّب مِن القَهَر [šayyab min ʔilqahar] He grew old from suffering.

شِيب [ši:b] *n:* • **1.** grayness of the hair, gray or white hair • **2.** old age

شِيبَة [ši:ba] *n:* شِيبات [ši:ba:t] *pl:* • **1.** streak or touch of gray hair

شايِب [ša:yib] *n:* شِيّاب [šiyya:b] *pl:* • **1.** old, aged • **2.** old man • **3.** king (in card games)

مشَيِّب [mšayyib] *adj:* • **1.** gray-haired

أشيَب [ʔašyab] *comparative adjective:* • **1.** more or most aged, old • **2.** more or most gray-haired, gray

ش ي خ

شاخ [ša:x] *v:* • **1.** to be or become self-important, pompous, to act like a big shot – أشُو مِن صار مُدِير، شاخ [ʔašu min ṣa:r mudi:r, ša:x] It seems since he became director, it's gone to his head. شايِخ عَلَيهُم بِفلُوسَه [ša:yix ʕali:hum bflu:sah] He lords it over them with his money. • **2.** to attain a venerated old age – مِن يشِيخ السَّبع، تِضحَك عليه الواوِيَّة [min yši:x ʔissabiʕ, tiðħak ʕali:h ʔilwa:wiyya] When the lion gets old the jackals laugh at him.

شَيخ [šayx] *n:* شيُوخ [šyu:x] *pl:* • **1.** sheikh, chieftain, patriarch, leader, elder (of a tribe) • **2.** venerated religious scholar or teacher

مَشيَخَة [mašyaxa] *n:* مَشايِخ [maša:yix] *pl:* • **1.** sheikhdom, territory ruled by a sheikh

شَيخُوخَة [šayxu:xa] *n:* • **1.** old age, senility

ش ي ر [1]

شِير [ši:r] *n:* • **1.** heads (side of a coin) – شِير لَو خَطّ؟ [ši:r law xaṭṭ?] Heads or tails? • **2.** pl. شيارَة faucet, tap, spigot

ش ي ر [2]

شِيرَة [ši:ra] *n:* • **1.** syrup

ش ي ر ج

شِيرَج [ši:raǰ] *n:* • **1.** sesame oil

ش ي ر ز

سِيرَز [si:raz] *v:* • **1.** to sew a border around the edge of (a garment) – عِد مَن راح تشِيرز عَباتَك؟ [ʕid man ra:ħ

tši:riz ʕaba:tak?] Who will you have sew the border on your aba? • **2.** to stitch together the pages in a book – هَالكِتاب مجَلَّد بَسّ مُو مشيرَز [halkita:b mǰallad bass mu: mši:raz] That book has a binder but it isn't sewn together at the ends.
شِيرازي، تِتِن شِيرَزَة [ši:ra:zi, titin ši:raza] *adj:* • **1.** a type of tobacco from Persia, especially for use in narghiles

ش ي ر س

شيرَس [ši:ras] *v:* • **1.** to put paste or glue on – إنتَ شيرِس الأَوراق وَأَني أَلزَقها [ʔinta ši:ris ʔilʔawra:q waʔa:ni ʔalzagha] You put paste on the papers and I'll stick them up.

ش ي ش

شاش [ša:š] *v:* • **1.** to be or become angry, furious – مِن سِمَع إبنَه اِنبُسَط، شاش وَطِلَع بَرَّة [min simaʕ ʔibnah ʔinbusaṭ, ša:š wṭilaʕ barra] When he heard that his son had been beaten up, he became furious and went out.
شَيَّش [šayyaš] *v:* • **1.** to skewer, put on a skewer – آنِي أَقُصّ اللَّحَم وَإنتَ شَيِّشَه [ʔa:ni ʔaguṣṣ ʔillaħam wʔinta šayyišah] I'll cut the meat and you put it on the skewer.
شِيش [ši:š] *n:* شياش [šya:š] *pl:* • **1.** skewer • **2.** metal rod or bar • **3.** knitting needle – عَلِي شِيش [ʕali ši:š] turkey (bird).
شَيش [šayš] *n:* • **1.** anger
شِيشَة [ši:ša] *n:* شِيَش [šiyaš] *pl:* • **1.** glass bottle or jar • **2.** globe enclosing the flame of a lantern
مشَيَّش [mšayyaš] *adj:* • **1.** skewered • **2.** (food) sealed in a jar or can

ش ي ط ن

شَيطَن [ši:ṭan] *v:* • **1.** to make obnoxiously clever, cause to become a wise-guy, a smart alec – العِيشَة بِبَغداد شَيطَنَتَه [ʔilʕi:ša bibaɣda:d šayṭnatah] Living in Baghdad made him a wise guy.
تشَيطَن [tšayṭan] *v:* • **1.** to become obnoxiously clever, become a wise guy, a smart alec – تشَيطَن وَبَعَد ما يِنقِدِر عَليه [tšayṭan wabaʕad ma: yingidir ʕali:h] He became a wise guy and couldn't be controlled any more.
شَيطَنَة [šayṭana] *n:* • **1.** deviltry, devilishness, mischief • **2.** obnoxious cleverness
شيطان [ši:ṭa:n] *n:* شياطِين [šya:ṭi:n] *pl:* • **1.** devil, demon, fiend – مخاط الشِّيطان [mxa:ṭ ʔišši:ṭa:n] cobweb (s). • **2.** rascal, mischief-maker • **3.** wise guy, smart alec, show-off, know-it-all
شَيطاني [šayṭa:ni] *adj:* • **1.** devilish
أَشطَن [ʔašṭan] *comparative adjective:* • **1.** more or most devilish, fiendish • **2.** more or most mischievous • **3.** more or most clever, sly

ش ي ع

شاع [ša:ʕ] *v:* • **1.** to spread, diffuse, become widespread – شاع خَبَر زَواجَه بِسُرعَة [ša:ʕ xabar zawa:ǰah bsurʕa] The news of his marriage spread quickly. شاع اِستِعمال التِّلِفِزيُون بِبَغداد [ša:ʕ ʔistiʕma:l ʔittalifizyu:n bibaɣda:d] The use of television has gotten widespread in Baghdad.
شَيَّع [šayyaʕ] *v:* • **1.** to spread, divulge, circulate, publicize – قامَت تشَيِّع عَليه يِرتِشِي [ga:mat tšayyiʕ ʕali:h yirtiši] She started spreading rumors about him taking bribes. • **2.** شَيَّع الجَنازَة [šayyaʕ ʔiǰǰana:za] to pay last respects, to attend a funeral ceremony
أَشاع [ʔaša:ʕ] *v:* • **1.** to spread, divulge, circulate, publicize (esp. rumors or gossip) – أَشاع عَلَيهُم يبِيعُون تِرياك [ʔaša:ʕ ʕali:hum ybi:ʕu:n tirya:k] He spread rumors that they sell opium.
تشَيَّع [tšayyaʕ] *v:* • **1.** to become a Shiite, a Shia, to adopt the Shiitic branch of Islam – تشَيَّع حَتَّى بِنتَه تاخُذ كُلّ الوِرث [tšayyaʕ ħatta bintah ta:xuð kull ʔilwiriθ] He became a Shiite so his daughter could get the entire inheritance.
شيع [ši:ʕ] *n:* • **1.** spread (of news), diffusion
إشاعَة [ʔiša:ʕa] *n:* • **1.** spreading, circulation (of news) • **2.** pl. إشاعات rumor, gossip
الشِيعَة [ʔišši:ʕa] *n:* • **1.** the Shia, the branch of Islam which recognizes Ali as the rightful successor of the prophet Mohammed and does not acknowledge the precepts of the sunna
الشِيُوعِيَّة [ʔiššiyu:ʕiyya] *n:* • **1.** communism, the communist ideology
تَشيِيع : تَشيِيع الجَنازَة [tašyi:ʕ : tašyi:ʕ ʔiǰǰana:za] *n:* • **1.** funeral, burial
شِيعِي [ši:ʕi] *adj:* • **1.** Shiitic • **2.** pl. شِيعَة Shiite, Shia, adherent of the Shiite branch of Islam
شايع [ša:yiʕ] *adj:* • **1.** widespread, common, well-known, general, universal, joint
شِيُوعِي [šiyu:ʕi] *adj:* • **1.** communist, communistic – المَبدَأ الشُّيُوعِي [ʔilmabdaʔ ʔiššuyu:ʕi] the communist ideology. • **2.** a communist

ش ي ف

شَيَّف [šayyaf] *v:* • **1.** to slice (fruit or vegetables) lengthwise – شَيِّف الرَّقِّيَّة وَقَسِّمها عَلينا [šayyif ʔirraggiyya wqassimha ʕali:na] Slice the watermelon and divide it among us.
شِيف [ši:f] *n:* شياف [šya:f] *pl:* • **1.** slice, piece (of fruit or vegetable)
مشَيَّف [mšayyaf] *adj:* • **1.** sliced (fruit or vegetables)

ش ي ك 1

شَكّ [čakk, ši:k] *n:* شَكّات، شكُوك [čakka:t, čku:k, či:ka:t] *pl:* • **1.** check
شِيك [ši:k] *n:* • **1.** chic

ش

ش ي ك 2

شَيَّك [čayyak] *v:* • **1.** to check

تشَيَّك [tčayyak] *v:* • **1.** to be checked

تَشييك [tačyi:k] *n:* • **1.** checking

ش ي ل

شال [ša:l] *v:* • **1.** to lift, raise, elevate, pick up – شال الكُرسِي الثَّقِيل بِفَدّ إيد [ša:l ʔilkursi ʔiθθigi:l bfadd ʔi:d] He lifted the heavy chair with one hand. شال الصَّنْدُوق عَلَى ظَهره وَصِعَد لِفُوق [ša:l ʔiṣṣandu:g ʕala ḍahrah wṣiʕad lifu:g] He lifted the trunk onto his back and went upstairs. ما شال عَينَه مِن عَليها [ma: ša:l ʕaynah min ʕali:ha] He didn't take his eyes off of her. شايِل خَشمَه عالنّاس [ša:yil xašmah ʕanna:s] He sticks up his nose at everyone. He is conceited. • **2.** to carry, convey, transport – هالباص يشِيل عَشِر رُكّاب [halpa:ṣ yši:l ʕašir rukka:b] This bus carries ten passengers. إذا ما يِدفَع أُجرَة، ما راح أشِيلَه [ʔiða ma: yidfaʕ ʔujra, ma: ra:ħ ʔaši:lah] If he doesn't pay a fare, I won't take him. • **3.** to carry on one's person, wear, bear – يشِيل مُسَدَّس [yši:l musaddas] He carries a revolver. شايِل فلوس ويّاك؟ [ša:yil flu:s wiyya:k?] Do you have any money on you? المُقَدَّم يشِيل تاج وَنَجمَة [ʔilmuqaddam yši:l ta:ǰ wnajma] The lieutenant colonel wears a crown and star. شايِل هَمّ. شلُون يرُوح ويترُك جَهالَه وَحّدهُم؟ [ša:yil hamm. šlu:n yiru:ħ wyitruk ǰaha:lah waħħadhum?] He is burdened with worry. How can he go and leave his children by themselves? شال خَطِيتَه [ša:l xaṭi:tah] He spoke unjustly about him. He accused him unjustly. • **4.** to move, change location, change residence – جيرانّا راح يشِيلُون اليُوم [ǰi:ra:nna ra:ħ yiši:lu:n ʔilyu:m] Our neighbors are going to move today. • **5.** to take, take away, remove – جاب كاري آس وشال كُلّ الميز [ǰa:b ka:ri ʔa:s wša:l kull ʔilmi:z] He got four aces and took the whole pot. البانزين يشِيل اللَّكَّة مِن الثُّوب [ʔilbanzi:n yši:l ʔillakka min ʔiθθu:b] Gasoline will remove the spot from the shirt. مِن سِمَع آني جاي، شالها [min simaʕ ʔa:ni ǰa:y, ša:lha] When he heard I was coming, he beat it. • **6.** to take hold, take effect – الجِّدري مالِي ما شال [ʔiǰǰidri ma:li ma: ša:l] My smallpox vaccination didn't take.

شَيَّل [šayyal] *v:* • **1.** to load, burden with – شَيَّل الحَمّال كُلّ الجُنَط [šayyal ʔilħamma:l kull ʔiǰǰinaṭ] He loaded the porter with all the suitcases. • **2.** to cause to move, change location, change residence – البَلَدِيَّة شَيِّلَتهُم مِن هَالبَيت [ʔilbaladiyya šayyilathum min halbayt] The city evicted them from this house.

اِنشال [ʔinša:l] *v:* • **1.** to be carried

شيل [šayl, ši:l] *n:* • **1.** picking up, raising

شيلَة [ši:la] *n:* شِيَل، شيلات [šiyal, ši:la:t] *pl:* • **1.** a long head-scarf worn by women

شَيّال [šayya:l] *n:* شَيّالات [šayya:la:t] *pl:* • **1.** (pair of) suspenders

شايِل [ša:yil] *adj:* • **1.** loaded, lifting, carying

مَشيُول [mašyu:l] *adj:* • **1.** carried out

ش ي م

شَيَّم [šayyam] *v:* • **1.** to praise for character, virtue, integrity, etc – شَيِّم المعِيدِي وَأُخُذ عَباتَه [šayyim ʔilmʕi:di wʔuxuð ʕaba:tah] Praise the peasant for his virtues and you can take the shirt off his back.

شامَة [ša:ma] *n:* شامات [ša:ma:t] *pl:* • **1.** freckle • **2.** skin blemish • **3.** mole, freckle, skin blemish

شِيمَة [ši:ma] *n:* • **1.** character, integrity, virtue, charity, honor – أهل الشِّيمَة [ʔahl ʔišši:ma] people of integrity, charity, honor, etc. أهل الشِّيمَة ما يترِكُون جارهُم وَحدَه إذا أَحَّد اِعتِدَى عَلِيه [ʔahl ʔišši:ma ma: ytirku:n ǰa:rhum waħdah ʔiða ʔaħħad ʔiʕtida: ʕali:h] People of character don't abandon their neighbor if someone assaults him. • **2.** disposition, character

مَشِيمَة [maši:ma] *n:* • **1.** placenta

ش ي ن 1

شين [ši:n] *adj:* • **1.** bad – أقبَلَه، زين شين [ʔaqbalah, zi:n ši:n] I'll take it, good or bad.

مُشين [muši:n] *adj:* • **1.** dishonorable, scandalous, disgraceful

ش ي ن 2

شين [ši:n] *n:* • **1.** name of the letter

ص

ص ب ب 1

صَبّ [ṣabb] *v:* • **1.** to pour, pour out – صُبّ شوَيَّة مَيّ عَلَى إيدِي رَجاءاً [ṣubb šwayyat mayy ʕala ʔiːdi rajaːʔan] Pour a little water on my hand please. صُبِّلِي اِستِكان شاي [ṣubbli ʔistikaːn čaːy] Pour me a cup of tea. لازِم تصُبّ الشّوربَة بِالجّمجَة [laːzim tṣubb ʔiššuːrba biččamča] You'll have to dish up the soup with the ladle. • **2.** to pour forth, shed, flow, empty – شَطّ العَرَب يصُبّ بِخَلِيج البَصرَة [šaṭṭ ʔilʕarab yṣubb bxaliːj ʔilbaṣra] The Shatt Al-Arab empties into the Gulf of Basra. • **3.** to pour, mold, cast – الحَدّاد صَبّ رِجلَين القَريُولَة مِن برنج [ʔilħaddaːd ṣabb rijlayn ʔilqaryuːla min prinj] The blacksmith cast the legs of the bed out of brass.

صَبّ [ṣabb] *n:* • **1.** pouring, pouring out

صَبَّة [ṣabba] *n:* صَبّات [ṣabbaːt] *pl:* • **1.** form, casting

مَصَبّ [maṣabb] *n:* مَصَبّات [maṣabbaːt] *pl:* • **1.** outlet, drain • **2.** mouth (of a river)

ص ب ب 2

صُبِّي [ṣubbi] *adj:* صُبَّة [ṣubba] *pl:* • **1.** a Mandaean, a Sabian

ص ب ح

صَبَّح [ṣabbaħ] *v:* • **1.** to start the day (doing something or in a certain condition or state) – سِقنا اللَّيل كُلَّه وَصَبَّحنا بِالبَصرَة [siqna ʔillayl kullah wṣabbaħna bilbaṣra] We drove all night and arrived in Basra in the morning. اللّي يصَبُّح بِوِجّهَك ما يشُوف الخير [ʔilli yṣabbuħ bwiččhak maː yšuːf ʔilxayr] Anyone who sees you first thing in the morning won't have any luck. يَومِيّاً دَأصَبُّح بوجهه [yuːmiyyan daʔaṣabbuħ bwiččah] Every morning I see him. صَبَّحكُم الله بِالخير [ṣabbaħkum ʔallah bilxiːr] Good morning.

أصبَح [ʔaṣbaħ] *v:* • **1.** to be, become – أصبَحنا لِعبَة بإيدهُم [ʔaṣbaħna liʕba bʔiːdhum] We've become a plaything in their hands. أصبَحَت الأُمُور بإيدَه [ʔaṣbaħat ʔilʔumuːr bʔiːdah] The business is in his hands now. أصبَح عالَة عَالمُجتَمَع [ʔaṣbaħ ʕaːla ʕalmujtamaʕ] He turned out to be a parasite.

صُبُح [ṣubuħ] *n:* أصباح [ʔaṣbaːħ] *pl:* • **1.** morning – يُقعُد مِن الصُّبُح [yugʕud min ʔiṣṣubuħ] He gets up early.

صُبحَة، يوم الصُبحَة [ṣubħa, yuːm ʔiṣṣubħa] *n:* • **1.** the morning after the consummation of a marriage (when gifts are brought to the new couple)

صَباح [ṣabaːħ] *n:* • **1.** morning (limited to set phrases) – صَباح الخير [ṣabaːħ ʔilxiːr] Good morning. هَلا بِهَالصَّباح [halaː bhaṣṣabaːħ] It's nice to see you this morning. الصَّباح رباح [ʔiṣṣabaːħ rbaːħ] The early bird gets the worm.

صُبحِيَّة [ṣubħiyya] *n:* صُبحِيّات [ṣubħiyyaːt] *pl:* • **1.** morning, forenoon

صَبَّحجِي [ṣabbaħči] *n:* صَبَّحجِيَّة [ṣabbaħčiyya] *pl:* • **1.** night watchman who relieves the evening guard

إصباح [ʔiṣbaːħ] *n:* • **1.** being, becoming

صَباحِي [ṣabaːħi] *adj:* • **1.** morning – الدَّوام الصَّباحِي [ʔiddawaːm ʔiṣṣabaːħi] the morning session.

ص ب ر

صُبَر [ṣubar] *v:* • **1.** to be patient, have patience, wait patiently – إذا تُصبُر، تحَصِّلها [ʔiða tuṣbur, tħaṣṣilha] If you have patience, you'll get it. صُبَر شَهَر عَالفلُوس [ṣubar šahar ʕalfluːs] He waited a month for the money. تِقدَر تُصبُر لإسبُوع لاخ؟ الفلُوس مُو حاضرَة [tigdar tuṣbur lʔisbuːʕ laːx? ʔilfluːs muː ħaːðra] Can you give me another week? The money isn't available now.

اِصطُبَر [ʔiṣṭubar] *v:* • **1.** to be patient, have patience – اِصطُبَر شوَيَّة؛ لا تِستَعجِل [ʔiṣṭubar šwayya; laː tistaʕjil] Be a little patient, don't hurry so. اِصطُبُرلِي فَدّ يومَين وانطِيك الفلُوس [ʔiṣṭuburli fadd yuːmayn wanṭiːk ʔilfluːs] Be patient with me just two days and I'll give you the money. أُصطُبُرلِي. آنِي أعَلّمَك [ʔuṣṭuburli. ʔaːni ʔaʕallmak] Just give me some time. I'll teach you. اِصطُبُر! خَلِّي نشُوف شَكُو هنا [ʔiṣṭubur! xalli: nšuːf šaku hna] Wait! Let's see what's going on here.

صَبُر [ṣabur] *n:* • **1.** patience, forbearance • **2.** a bitter substance made from aloes, applied to the nipples in order to wean an infant, hence: مُرّ صَبُر – مُرّ صَبُر [murr ṣabur] as bitter as aloes.

صبُور [ṣbuːr] *n:* • **1.** a kind of kippered fish

صُبِّير [ṣubbiːr] *n:* • **1.** (coll.) Indian fig(s)

صُبِّيرَة [ṣubbiːra] *n:* صُبِّيرات [ṣubbiːraːt] *pl:* • **1.** Indian fig • **2.** cactus

صابِر [ṣaːbir] *adj:* صَوابِر [ṣawaːbir] *pl:* • **1.** temple (anat.)

صَبُور [ṣabuːr] *adj:* • **1.** patient, enduring, perseverant, steadfast

ص ب ع

إصبع [ʔiṣbiʕ] *n:* أصابع [ʔaṣaːbiʕ] *pl:* • **1.** finger – هُوَّ إلَه إصبع بِالجَّريمَة [huwwa ʔilah ʔiṣbiʕ bijjariːma] He has a hand in the crime. مُو كُلّ أصابعَك سُوَة [muː kull ʔaṣaːbʕak suwa] No two people are alike. مِن قِتلَه، وُجَّه صار إصبِعتين [min gitlah, wuččah ṣaːr ʔiṣbiʕtiːn] When I told him, his face became pale. • **2.** toe • **3.** cylinder, stick – إصبع دِينامِيت [ʔiṣbiʕ dinamiːt] stick of dynamite. أصابع جِكايِر [ʔaṣaːbiʕ jigaːyir] empty, rolled cigarette papers.

ص ب غ

صُبَغ [ṣubaɣ] *v:* • **1.** to paint, dye, stain, tint, color – صُبَغ بَيتَه لُون أَخضَر [ṣubaɣ baytah luːn ʔaxðar] He painted his house green. هَذِي صُبغَت شَعَرها أَصفَر [haːði ṣubɣat šaʕarha ʔaṣfar] She dyed her hair blond. • **2.** to black, shine, polish (shoes) – لازِم تُصبُغ قُندَرتَك قَبُل ما ترُوح لِلحَفلَة [laːzim tuṣbuɣ qundartak gabul maː truːħ lilħafla] You'd better polish your shoes before you go to the party. • **3.** to compliment (idiomatic use)

اِنصُبَغ [ʔinṣubaɣ] *v:* • **1.** pass. of صُبَغ to be painted, colored, stained – البَيت اِنصُبَغ كُلّه بِفَدّ يوم [ʔilbayt ʔinṣubaɣ kullah bfadd yuːm] The house was all painted in one day.

صُبُغ [ṣubuɣ] *n:* أَصباغ [ʔaṣbaːɣ] *pl:* • **1.** paint • **2.** dye, coloring • **3.** (shoe) polish – راح أَرُوح عَليه وَأَطَيِّح صُبغَه [raːħ ʔaruːħ ʕaliːh waʔaṭayyiħ ṣubɣah] I'm going to go see him and give him hell. • **4.** courtesy • **5.** compliment

صَبُغ [ṣabuɣ] *n:* • **1.** paint, painting

صَبّاغ [ṣabbaːɣ] *n:* صَبّاغِين، صبابِيغ [ṣabbaːɣiːn, ṣbaːbiːɣ] *pl:* • **1.** painter • **2.** dyer • **3.** bootblack

صَبغَة [ṣabɣa] *n:* صَبغات [ṣabɣaːt] *pl:* • **1.** color, dye

مَصبَغَة [maṣbaɣa] *n:* • **1.** dye works, dyeing plant

صِباغَة [ṣibaːɣa] *n:* • **1.** art of dyeing or staining

مَصبُوغ [maṣbuːɣ] *adj:* مَصبُوغات [maṣbuwɣaːt] *pl:* • **1.** painted, dyed

ص ب ن

صُوبَن [ṣuːban] *v:* • **1.** to soap, put soap on – صُوبِن المواعِين وَأَنِي أَشطُفها [ṣuːbin ʔilimwaːʕiːn waʔaːni ʔašṭufha] You soap the dishes and I'll rinse them.

صابُون [ṣaːbuːn] *n:* • **1.** (coll.) soap

صابُونَة [ṣaːbuːna] *n:* صابُونات [ṣaːbuːnaːt] *pl:* • **1.** cake of soap • **2.** kneecap – صابُونَة رِجِل [ṣaːbuːnat rijil] kneecap.

ص ب ي

صَبِي [ṣabi] *n:* صِبيان [ṣibyaːn] *pl:* • **1.** youth, lad, boy

صِبياني [ṣibyaːni] *adj:* • **1.** childish, juvenile – أَعمال صِبيانِيَّة [ʔaʕmaːl ṣibyaːniyya] childish actions.

ص ج م

صَجَّم [ṣajjam] *v:* • **1.** to flirt, to harass

صَجِم [ṣačim] *n:* • **1.** (coll.) shot, pellet(s), B-B(s) – بُندُقِيَّة صَجِم [bunduqiyyat ṣačim] air rifle, pellet gun. تُفقَة صَجِم [tufgat ṣačim] air rifle, pellet gun.

صَجمَة [ṣačma] *n:* صَجمات [ṣačmaːt] *pl:* • **1.** pellet, shot

تَصجِيم [taṣčiːm] *n:* • **1.** insinuation • **2.** harassment, flirtation

ص ح ب

صاحَب [ṣaːħab] *v:* • **1.** to make friends with, to make up with – لازِم تصاحبَه لِأَنّ الصُّوج كان مالَك [laːzim tṣaːħbah liʔann ʔiṣṣuːč čaːn maːlak] You must make up with him because the fault was yours. • **2.** to associate with – كان يصاحِب جَماعَة مُو مِن سِنَّه [čaːn yṣaːħib jamaːʕa muː min sinnah] He was associating with a group not of his age.

تصاحَب [tṣaːħab] *v:* • **1.** to become friends, make up with each other – تصاحبَوا بَعَد ما كانَوا زَعلانِين إسبُوع [tṣaːħbaw baʕad maː čaːnaw zaʕlaːniːn ʔisbuːʕ] They made up after they'd been mad for a week.

صاحِب [ṣaːħib] *n:* أَصحاب [ʔaṣħaːb] *pl:* • **1.** friend, companion, associate – أَصحاب النَّبِي [ʔaṣħaːb ʔinnabi] the companions of Mohammed. • **2.** owner, holder, possessor – صاحِب مَحَل [ṣaːħib maħall] shop owner. هِيَّ صاحبَة أَحلَى عيُون [hiyya ṣaːħbat ʔaħlaː ʕyuːn] She has the prettiest eyes. صاحِب الجَّلالَة [ṣaːħib ʔijjalaːla] His Majesty. • **3.** rightful owner • **4.** the one who is in the right – صاحِب الزَّمان [ṣaːħib ʔizzamaːn] (Shiite) the Mahdi, the last imam who will come to purify Islam. هَذا صاحِب فَضَل عَلَيّا [haːða ṣaːħib faðal ʕalayya] He has done favors for me. • **5.** originator, inventor, author – صاحِب فِكرَة [ṣaːħib fikra] originator of an idea.

صُحبَة [ṣuħba] *n:* • **1.** friendship, companionship, comradeship, • **2.** company, escort, asscociation

صاحبَة [ṣaːħba] *n:* صاحبات [ṣaːħbaːt] *pl:* صاحبَة [ṣaːħba] *feminine:* • **1.** friend, companion, associate • **2.** originator, inventor, author • **3.** the one who is in the right • **4.** owner, holder, possessor • **5.** rightful owner

تَصاحُب [taṣaːħub] *n:* • **1.** making friends, palling around

مَصحُوب [maṣħuːb] *adj:* • **1.** /with b-/ accompanied by, associated with – مَصحُوب بِالسَّلامَة [maṣħuːb bissalaːma] Peace be with you. (said on bidding someone good-bye).

ص ح ح

صَحّ [ṣaħħ] *v:* • **1.** to be true, correct, factual, authentic – إذا صَحّ الخَبَر، قَضِيتَك راح تِنحَل [ʔiða ṣaħħ ʔilxabar, qaðiːtak raːħ tinħall] If the news was correct, your case will be solved. • **2.** to allow an opportunity, give a chance – تِعفِينِي، وَالله ما يصِحّلِي أَجِي [tiʕfiːni, wallah maː yṣiħħli ʔaji] Please excuse me, but I don't have the time to come. يِصَحّلَك ترُوح وِيّانا باكِر؟ [yiṣaħħlak truːħ wiyyaːna baːčir?] Will you have a chance to go with us tomorrow? آنِي مَشغُول هوايَة، وَما يصَحّلِي أَحُكّ راسِي [ʔaːni mašɣuːl hwaːya, wmaː yṣaħħli ʔaħukk raːsi] I'm awfully busy, and I don't have time to scratch my head.

صَحَّح [ṣaħħaħ] *v:* • **1.** to correct, grade, mark – أَربَع مُعَلِّمِين راح يصَحِّحُون دَفاتِر الامتِحان

[ʔarbaʕ muʕallimiːn raːħ yṣaħħihuːn dafaːtir ʔilʔimtihaːn] Four teachers are going to correct the exam books.

صَحّ [ṣaħħ] *n:* • **1.** correct, right, proper – جَواب المَسألَة كان صَحّ [ǰawaːb ʔilmasʔala čaːn ṣaħħ] The answer to the question was correct.

صِحَّة [ṣiħħa, ṣaħħa] *n:* • **1.** health – شلُون صِحّتَك؟ [šluːn ṣiħħtak?] How are you? وِزارَة الصِّحَّة [wizaːrat ʔiṣṣiħħa] Ministry of Health. • **2.** truth, validity, authenticity, genuineness • **3.** (with بـ) selection, choice, a drink to someone's health

مَصَحّ [maṣaħħ] *n:* مَصَحّات [maṣaħħaːt] *pl:* • **1.** sanatorium

تَصحِيح [taṣhiːħ] *n:* • **1.** correcting, correction

صِحِّي [ṣiħħi] *adj:* • **1.** wholesome, healthy, healthful – الأكِل بِالسِّجِن مُو صِحِّي [ʔilʔakil bissiǰin muː ṣiħħi] The food in prison isn't wholesome. • **2.** hygienic, sanitary – لا تِشرَب هَالمَيّ. مُو صِحِّي [laː tišrab halmayy. muː ṣiħħi] Don't drink this water. It isn't sanitary.

صَحِيح [ṣahiːħ] *adj:* • **1.** whole, complete, integral, perfect • **2.** proper, correct, right – زين قِتلَه قَبُل ما ترُوح، هَذا الشِّي الصَّحِيح [ziːn gitlah gabul maː truːħ, haːða ʔišši ʔiṣṣahiːħ] It's good that you told him before you left. That was the right thing (to do). • **3.** true, correct, right, authentic, reliable, credible – صَحِيح؟ صُدُق راح يِجِي؟ [ṣahiːħ? ṣudug raːħ yiǰi?] Is that right? He's really coming? حِلَف ما يقُول إلّا الصَّحِيح [ħilaf maː yguːl ʔilla ʔiṣṣahiːħ] He swore he wouldn't speak anything but what was true. أعتَقِد إنتَ صَحِيح، لَكِن ما تِقدَر تِثبِتها [ʔaʕtaqid ʔinta ṣahiːħ, laːkin maː tigdar tiθbitha] I think you're right, but you can't prove it.

أصَحّ [ʔaṣaħħ] *comparative adjective:* • **1.** more or most complete, perfect • **2.** more or most proper, correct • **3.** more or most authentic, reliable

ص ح ر

صَحراء [ṣahraːʔ, ṣahra] *n:* صَحارِي [ṣahaːri] *pl:* • **1.** desert

صَحراوِي [ṣahraːwi] *adj:* • **1.** desertic, desolate – أراضِي صَحراوِيَّة [ʔaraːði ṣahraːwiyya] desert lands.

ص ح ف

صَحَّف [ṣaħħaf] *v:* • **1.** to bind (a book) – شُغُلَه يصَحُّف القرائِين [šuɣulah yṣaħħuf ʔilqraːʔiːn] His job is binding Korans.

صُحُفِي، صُحفِي [ṣuhufi, ṣuhfi] *adj:* • **1.** relating to news or the press and media in general – مُؤتَمَر صُحُفِي [muʔtamar ṣuhufi] press conference. • **2.** as Noun, journalist, newspaperman, reporter

مَصحَف [maṣhaf] *n:* مَصاحِف [maṣaːhif] *pl:* • **1.** edition, copy (of the Koran)

صَحّاف [ṣaħħaːf] *n:* صَحّافة، صَحّافِين [ṣaħħaːfa, ṣaħħaːfiːn] *pl:* • **1.** bookbinder

صَحِيفَة [ṣahiːfa] *n:* صُحُف، صَحايِف [ṣahaːyif, ṣuhuf] *pl:* • **1.** page, leaf (of a book, etc.) – صَحِيفتَه بيضَة [ṣahiːftah biːða] He has a clean record. • **2.** pl. newspaper

صَحافَة [ṣahaːfa] *n:* • **1.** journalism, the newspaper business • **2.** the press – حُرِّيَّة الصَّحافَة [ħurriyyat ʔiṣṣahaːfa] freedom of the press.

ص ح ن

صَحِن [ṣahin] *n:* صُحُون [ṣuhuːn] *pl:* • **1.** plate, saucer • **2.** courtyard (of a shrine or a traditional Arab house)

ص ح و

صِحَى [ṣihaː] *v:* • **1.** to regain consciousness, come to, to wake up – السَّكران بَعَد ساعتِين ما يِصحَى [ʔissakraːn baʕad saːʕtayn maː yiṣhaː] The drunkard won't wake up for two hours. صِحَى عَلَى نَفسَه وَترَك الرَّيسِز [ṣihaː ʕala nafsah wtirak ʔirraysiz] He came to his senses and quit the races.

صَحَّى [ṣaħħaː] *v:* • **1.** to clear up, Become clear, bright – تَعال شُوف. صَحَّت الدِّنيا [taʕaːl šuːf. ṣaħħat ʔiddinya] Come see. The weather has cleared up. • **2.** to awaken, rouse, wake up – باكِر صَحِّينِي السّاعَة سَبعَة الصُّبُح [baːčir ṣaħħiːni ʔissaːʕa sabʕa ʔiṣṣubuħ] Wake me up tomorrow at seven A. M.

صَحو [ṣahw] *n:* • **1.** clearness, brightness (of the weather) • **2.** clear, bright, sunny weather

صَحوَة [ṣahwa] *n:* • **1.** consciousness – صَحوَة مُوت [ṣahwat muːt] a wakeful period between coma and death.

صاحِي [ṣaːhi] *adj:* • **1.** clear, bright, sunny • **2.** awake, conscious, aware • **3.** sober, clear-headed

مصَحِّي [mṣaħħi] *adj:* • **1.** clear, purified

ص خ ر

تصَخَّر [tṣaxxar] *v:* • **1.** to run errands • **2.** to become petrified

صَخَر [ṣaxar] *n:* • **1.** (coll.) rock(s), stone(s)

صَخرَة [ṣaxra] *n:* صَخرات [ṣaxraːt] *pl:* • **1.** a rock, a stone

تَصَخُّر [taṣaxxur] *n:* • **1.** petrification

مصَخرِج [mṣaxrij] *n:* • **1.** over-fired, fused bricks – أرِيد لورِي طابُوق مصَخرِج [ʔariːd luːri ṭaːbuːg mṣaxriǰ] I want a truckload of fused bricks.

صَخرِي [ṣaxri] *adj:* • **1.** stony, rocky – أراضِي صَخرِيَّة [ʔaraːði ṣaxriyya] rocky land.

صَخرَج [ṣaxraǰ] *adj:* • **1.** to be or become over-fired, fused – طَلِّع الطّابُوق مِن الكُورَة تَرَة يصَخرِج [ṭalliʕ ʔiṭṭaːbuːg min ʔilkuːra tara yṣaxriǰ] Take the bricks out of the kiln or they'll be overfired.

ص خ ل

صَخلَة [ṣaxla] *n:* صَخلات [ṣaxlaːt] *pl:* • **1.** female goat

صَخَل [ṣaxal] *n:* صخُول [ṣxuːl] *pl:* • **1.** goat(s)

ص د

صاد [ṣaːd] *n:* • **1.** name of the letter

ص د ء

صَدَّى [ṣaddaː] *v:* • **1.** to rust, oxidize – الحَدِيدَة صَدَّت مِن المَيّ [ʔilħadiːda ṣaddat min ʔilmayy] The piece of iron rusted from the water.
تصَدَّى [tṣaddaː] *v:* • **1.** to be or become rusty
صَدَأ [ṣadaʔ] *n:* • **1.** rust, oxidation, rust (plant disease)
مصَدِّي [mṣaddi] *adj:* • **1.** rusty

ص د د

صَدّ [ṣadd] *v:* • **1.** to ward off, deflect, parry, repel, throw back – إلزَم الدِّرقَة حَتَّى تصُدّ ضَربات السَّيف [ʔilzam ʔiddirga ħatta tṣudd ð̣arbaːt ʔissayf] Hold the shield so you can deflect the sword's blows. جَيشنا صَدّ هِجُوم العَدُو [ǰayšna ṣadd hijuːm ʔilʕadu] Our army repelled the enemy's attack. آنِي أَضرُب الطُّوبَة وَإنتَ صِدّها [ʔaːni ʔað̣rub ʔiṭṭuːba wʔinta ṣiddha] I'll hit the ball and you knock it back.
صَدّ [ṣadd] *n:* • **1.** repelling

ص د ر

صِدَر [ṣidar] *v:* • **1.** to originate, stem, arise, emanate – الأَمُر صِدَر مِن رَئِيس أَركان الجَّيش [ʔilʔamur ṣidar min raʔiːs ʔarkaːn ʔiǰǰayš] The order originated from the Army Chief of Staff. ما عَبالِي يِصدُر مِنَّك هِيكِي عَمَل [maː ʕabaːli yiṣdur minnak hiːči ʕamal] I didn't expect that sort of action from you. • **2.** to be issued, be handed down – سِجنوه بَعَد ما صِدَر الحُكُم ضِدَّه [siǰnawh baʕad maː ṣidar ʔilħukum ð̣iddah] They put him in prison after the sentence was pronounced against him. • **3.** to come out, be published – قَرار اللَّجنَة بَعَد ما صِدَر [qaraːr ʔillaǰna baʕad maː ṣidar] The committee's report hasn't been published yet. الجَّرِيدَة ما راح تِصدُر باكِر [ʔiǰǰariːda maː raːħ tiṣdur baːčir] The newspaper won't come out tomorrow. • **4.** to be sent out, go out, leave – المَكتُوب صِدَر اليُوم [ʔilmaktuːb ṣidar ʔilyuːm] The letter went out today.
صَدَّر [ṣaddar] *v:* • **1.** to send out, dispatch, forward, send off – صَدَّرنا المَكتُوب قَبِل إسبُوع [ṣaddarna ʔilmaktuːb gabil ʔisbuːʕ] We sent the letter a week ago. • **2.** to export – العِراق يصَدِّر كَمِّيَّة كَبِيرَة مِن التُّمُور [ʔilʕiraːq yṣaddir kammiyya kabiːra min ʔittumuːr] Iraq exports a large amount of dates. • **3.** to issue, bring out, put out, publish – الحُكُومَة صَدِّرَت تَعلِيمات جِدِيدَة لأَصحاب المَطاعِم [ʔilħukuːma ṣaddirat taʕliːmaːt ǰidiːda lʔaṣħaːb ʔilmaṭaːʕim] The government issued new regulations for restaurant owners. راح نصَدِّر عَدَد خاصّ بمُناسَبَة العِيد [raːħ nṣaddir ʕadad xaːṣṣ bmunaːsabat ʔilʕiːd] We're going to publish a special edition on the occasion of the holiday.
صادَر [ṣaːdar] *v:* • **1.** to seize, impound, confiscate – الحُكُومَة صادرَت أَملاكَه [ʔilħukuːma ṣaːdrat ʔamlaːkah] The government confiscated his property.
أَصدَر [ʔaṣdar] *v:* • **1.** to pass sentence • **2.** to publish, to issue
تصَدَّر [tṣaddar] *v:* • **1.** to be exported – كُلّ هَالحُنطَة راح تِتصَدَّر [kull halħunṭa raːħ titṣaddar] All this wheat is going to be exported. • **2.** to occupy the seat of honor, take the best seat (at a gathering) – هَذا دائِماً يِتصَدَّر المَجلِس [haːða daːʔiman yitṣaddar ʔilmaǰlis] He always sits in the best place in the group.
صَدِر [ṣadir] *n:* صدُور [ṣduːr] *pl:* • **1.** chest, breast, bosom, bust – عَشر رياجِيل ما يَوقفُون بِصَدرَه [ʕašr ryaːǰiːl maː yuːgfuːn bṣadrah] Ten men can't stop him. • **2.** seat of honor, best seat (at a gathering) – تفَضَّل، أُقعُد بِالصَّدِر [tfað̣ð̣al, ʔugʕud biṣṣadir] Go ahead, sit in the place of honor. • **3.** front seat (of an automobile) – أُقعُد بِالصَّدِر، يَمّ السّايِق [ʔugʕud biṣṣadir, yamm ʔissaːyiq] Sit in the front seat, next to the driver.
مَصدَر [maṣdar] *n:* مَصادِر [maṣaːdir] *pl:* • **1.** origin, source – مَصادِر تَقرِير [maṣaːdir taqriːr] reference works of a report. • **2.** verbal noun (gram.)
صُدُور [ṣuduːr] *n:* • **1.** release, emanation, coming out, appearance, publication
صَدرِيَّة [ṣadriyya] *n:* صَدرِيّات، صَدارِي [ṣadriyyaːt, ṣadaːri] *pl:* • **1.** bib, apron • **2.** laboratory coat
تَصدِير [taṣdiːr] *n:* • **1.** exporting, exportation, export – إجازَة تَصدِير [ʔiǰaːzat taṣdiːr] export license. • **2.** sending, dispatch, forwarding,
صَدارَة [ṣadaːra] *n:* • **1.** precedence, presidency, chairmanship • **2.** first place, pre-eminence
إصدار [ʔiṣdaːr] *n:* • **1.** issuance, edition, publication, bringing out
مُصادَرَة [muṣaːdara] *n:* • **1.** seizure, confiscation
صادِر [ṣaːdir] *n:* صادِرات [ṣaːdiraːt] *pl:* • **1.** exportation, export, yield
صَدرِي [ṣadri] *adj:* • **1.** pectoral, chest – مَرَض صَدرِي [marað̣ ṣadri] chest disease.
صادِر [ṣaːdir] *adj:* • **1.** emanating, originating • **2.** outbound, going out (letters, etc.) – كاتِب الصّادِرَة [kaːtib ʔiṣṣaːdira] correspondence dispatch clerk. • **3.** issued, published, put out
مُصَدِّر [muṣaddir] *n:* مُصَدِّرِين [muṣaddiriːn] *pl:* • **1.** exporter
مَصدُور [maṣduːr] *adj:* • **1.** affected with a pulmonary ailment, consumptive, tubercular

ص د ع

صَدَّع [ṣaddaʕ] *v:* • **1.** to trouble, bother, harass – صَدَّعناكُم بِهالجَّيَة [ṣaddaʕnaːkum bhaǰǰaya] I'm afraid we've inconvenienced you by coming now. • **1.** to cause a headache

تصَدَّع [tṣaddaʕ] *v:* • **1.** pass. of – صدَّع [ṣaddaʕ] تصَدَّعتُوا هوايَة. نِشكُركُم [tṣaddaʕtu: hwa:ya. niškurkum] You've been bothered a lot. We thank you. • **2.** to be troubled, bothered, harassed • **3.** to have a headache • **4.** to be cracked
صَدع [ṣadiʕ] *n:* • **1.** crack, break, crevice, fissure
صُداع [ṣuda:ʕ] *n:* • **1.** headache
مصَدِّع [mṣaddiʕ] *adj:* • **1.** having a headache
متصَدِّع [mitṣaddiʕ] *adj:* • **1.** cracked, broken

ص د ف

صِدَف [ṣidaf] *v:* • **1.** to happen by chance, occur unexpectedly – هِيكِي شِي ما يِصدُف إِلّا مَرَّة بِالسَّنَة [hi:či ši ma: yiṣduf ʔilla marra bissana] This sort of thing doesn't happen more than once a year. إذا صِدَف وشِفتَه قُلَّه خَلِّي يخابُرنِي [ʔiða ṣidaf wšiftah gullah xalli: yxa:burni] If it happens that you see him, have him call me.
صادَف [ṣa:daf] *v:* • **1.** to meet by chance, encounter unexpectedly – صادَفتَك مَرّتَين اليُوم [ṣa:daftak marrtayn ʔilyu:m] I've run into you twice today! صادَفنا صُعُوبات هوايَة [ṣa:dafna ṣuʕu:ba:t hwa:ya] We encountered many difficulties. ما مصادفَتنِي هِيكِي قَضِيَّة قَبُل [ma: mṣa:dfatni hi:či qaḍiyya gabul] I've never come across such a case before. مصادِف الخير [mṣa:dif ʔilxi:r] Good luck! • **2.** to coincide with, occur with, be coincident with, to fall on (a certain date) – سَفَرَه راح يصادِف يوم زَواجِي [safarah ra:ħ yṣa:dif yu:m zawa:ǰi] His trip will coincide with the day of my marriage. العِيد راح يصادِف يوم الجُمعَة [ʔilʕi:d ra:ħ yṣa:dif yu:m ʔiǰǰumʕa] The feast will fall on a Friday. • **3.** to happen by chance, occur unexpectedly – كُلّما أرِيد أطلَع لِلصِّيد، يصادِف مُطَر [kullma: ʔari:d ʔaṭlaʕ liṣṣi:d, yṣa:dif muṭar] Everytime I want to go hunting it rains.
تصادَف [tṣa:daf] *v:* • **1.** to happen upon, run into, meet each other unexpectedly – تصادَفِت ويّاه بالسُّوق [tṣa:dafit wiyya:h bissu:g] I ran into him in the market.
صَدَف [ṣadaf] *n:* • **1.** seas-hell(s) • **2.** mother-of-pearl • **3.** fish scale(s)
صَدفَة [ṣadfa] *n:* صَدفات [ṣadfa:t] *pl:* • **1.** seashell, mother-of-pearl, fish scale
صُدفَة [ṣudfa, ṣidfa] *n:* صُدَف [ṣudaf] *pl:* • **1.** chance, coincidence, unexpected concurrence – شِفتَه بِالصُّدفَة [šiftah bissudfa] I saw him by chance.
تَصادُف [taṣa:duf] *n:* • **1.** meeting unexpectedly, accidentally • **2.** happening upon, running into
مُصادَفَة [muṣa:dafa] *n:* مُصادَفات [muṣa:dafa:t] *pl:* • **1.** coincidence, unexpected concurrence
صَدَفِي [ṣadafi] *adj:* • **1.** mother-of-pearl (adj), nacreous
صُدفَةً [ṣudfatan] *adverbial:* • **1.** accidently, coincidentally, by chance, by coincidence – صُدفَةً هُوَّ هَمّ كان هناك [ṣudfatan huwwa hamm ča:n hna:k] It so happened that he was there also.

ص د ق

صِدَق [ṣidaq, ṣidag] *v:* • **1.** to be truthful, sincere, to tell the truth – إصدِقنِي. مِنُو قَلَّك بِيها؟ [ʔiṣdiqni. minu gallak bi:ha?] Tell me the truth. Who told you about it? طِلَع صادِق بِحكايتَه [ṭilaʕ ṣa:diq biħča:ytah] He turned out to be telling the truth in his story.
صَدَّق [ṣaddaq] *v:* • **1.** to consent, assent, approve, endorse, confirm, ratify, certify, substantiate – المَجلِس صَدَّق المُعاهَدَة [ʔilmaǰlis ṣaddaq ʔilmuʕa:hada] Parliament ratified the treaty. خَلِّي المُدِير يصَدِّق عَرِيضتَك وَجِيبها [xalli: ʔilmudi:r yṣaddiq ʕari:ðtak wǰi:bha] Let the director endorse your application and bring it. صَدَّق عَلَى كُلّ شِي اللِّي قالَه [ṣaddaq ʕala kull ši ʔilli ga:lah] He agreed to everything he said.
صَدَّق [ṣaddag] *v:* • **1.** to consider true, credible, to believe, to trust – صَدَّق كُلّ كِلمَة اللِّي قِلتلَه إيّاها [ṣaddag kull čilma ʔilli giltlah ʔiyya:ha] He believed every word I told him. صَدِّق، ما أعرُف [ṣaddig, ma: ʔaʕruf] Believe me, I don't know.
صادَق [ṣa:daq, ṣa:dag] *v:* • **1.** to be or become friends with – شبِالعَجَل صادَقتَه؟ [šbilʕaǰal ṣa:daqtah?] How'd you make friends with him so fast? • **2.** with عَلَى to approve, confirm, ratify, substantiate, endorse, authenticate, certify – المَجلِس صادَق عالمِيزانِيَّة [ʔilmaǰlis ṣa:daq ʕalmi:za:niyya] The parliament ratified the budget.
تصَدَّق [tṣaddaq] *v:* • **1.** pass. of صَدَّق: to be approved, endorsed, confirmed, ratified, certified, substantiated – المُعاهَدَة تصَدِّقَت اليُوم [ʔilmuʕa:hada tṣaddiqat ʔilyu:m] The treaty was ratified today. • **2.** to give alms – دائماً نِتصَدَّق عالفُقَراء [da:ʔiman nitṣaddig ʕalfuqara:ʔ] We always give to the poor.
تصَدَّق [tṣaddag] *v:* • **1.** to be credible, believable – حكايتَك ما تِتصَدَّق [ħča:ytak ma: titṣaddaq] Your story is unbelievable.
تصادَق [tṣa:daq, ʔitṣa:dag] *v:* • **1.** to be or become mutual friends, to form a friendship with each other – شُوف الجِّهال شِبساع تصادقوا [šu:f ʔiǰǰiha:l šibsa:ʕ tṣa:dqaw] Look at how fast the kids made friends.
صُدُق [ṣudug] *n:* • **1.** truth, verity, truthfulness – أنِصحَك تِحكِي الصُّدُق [ʔaniṣħak tiħči ʔiṣṣudug] I advise you to tell the truth. صُدُق نِجَح بِالإمتِحان؟ [ṣudug nijaħ bilʔimtiħa:n?] Is it true that he passed the exam? صُدُق هَذا غَبِي [ṣudug ha:ða ɣabi] He's really stupid. مِن صُدُق [min ṣudug] actually, really, truly. عَبالِي دَيِتشاقَى. طِلَع غالِب مِن صُدُق [ʕaba:li dayitša:qa:. ṭilaʕ ɣa:lib min ṣudug] I thought he was kidding. He really did win. زِعَل مِن صُدُق [ziʕal min ṣudug] He really got mad. صايِر رياضِي مِن صُدُق [ṣa:yir riya:ḍi min ṣudug] He has become a real athlete.

ص

صِدِق [ṣidiq] *n:* • **1.** truth, sincerity
صَدَقَة [ṣadaqa] *n:* صَدَقات [ṣadaqa:t] *pl:* • **1.** a charitable gift, alms – سَوِّيها صَدَقَة لِالله [sawwi:ha ṣadaqa l?allah] Do it as a charity for God. أصِيرلَك صَدَقَة [?aṣi:rlak ṣadaqa] I'll sacrifice myself for you. I'll do anything for you. لا تِشغِل فِكرَك؛ باكِر نِدَبُّر الفلُوس. أصِيرلَك صَدَقَة [la: tišɣil fikrak; ba:čir ndabbur ?ilflu:s. ?aṣi:rlak ṣadaqa] Don't fret yourself; tomorrow we'll get the money. I'll do all I can. • **2.** an expression of amazement or astonishment – صَدَقَة لِالله، شلُون عيُون عَليها [ṣadaqa l?allah, šlu:n ʕyu:n ʕali:ha] My God, what beautiful eyes she has! صَدَقَة! قام يمشِي [ṣadaqa! ga:m yimši] Glory be! He's started to walk!
صَدِيق [ṣadi:q, ṣadi:g] *n:* أصدِقاء، صِدقان [?aṣdiqa:?, ṣidqa:n] *pl:* • **1.** friend
صَداقَة [ṣada:qa] *n:* صَداقات [ṣada:qa:t] *pl:* • **1.** friendship • **2.** (invar.) friendly, good friends – صارَوا صَداقَة وِيّانا [ṣa:raw ṣada:qa wiyya:na] They became friendly with us.
تَصدِيق [taṣdi:q] *n:* • **1.** belief, faith • **2.** approval, confirmation, ratification, verification, authentication • **3.** consent, assent, agreement
مُصادَقَة [muṣa:dqa] *n:* • **1.** consent, agreement, approval, confirmation, ratification, verification, authentication
مِصداقِيَّة [miṣda:qiyya] *n:* • **1.** credibility, reliability
أصدَق [?aṣdaq, ?aṣdag] *comparative adjective:* • **1.** more or most truthful, sincere, honest
صادِق [ṣa:diq, ṣa:dig] *adj:* • **1.** true, truthful, sincere • **2.** reliable, accurate, genuine
مصَدِّق [mṣaddig] *adj:* • **1.** credible, believable, reliable, trustworthy
مُصَدَّق [muṣaddaq] *adj:* • **1.** certified, attested, authenticated, confirmed
مصادِق [mṣa:diq] *adj:* • **1.** having a girlfriend • **2.** in an intimate relationship with

ص

ص د م

صِدَم [ṣidam] *v:* • **1.** to dump, strike, hit, run into – صِدَمنِي بسَيّارتَه [ṣidamni bsayya:rtah] He ran into me with his car. صِدمَتنِي هَالأكلَة [ṣidmatni hal?akla] This meal didn't agree with me.
صادَم [ṣa:dam] *v:* • **1.** to clash, to bump, to strike, to dash, to bang, to knock
تصادَم [tṣa:dam] *v:* • **1.** to collide – القِطارَين تصادمَوا بوَقِت ما كان ضَباب كَثِيف [?ilqiṭa:rayn tṣa:dmaw bwaqit ma: ča:n ðaba:b kaθi:f] The two trains collided during a thick fog. • **2.** to clash, conflict – أخُوه تصادَم وِيّا المُحاسِب [?axu:h tṣa:dam wiyya ?ilmuħa:sib] His brother clashed with the accountant.
اِنصِدَم [?inṣidam] *v:* • **1.** to be shocked
اِصطِدَم [?iṣṭidam] *v:* • **1.** to clash, conflict – مُلاحِظنا اِصطِدَم وِيّا المُدِير الجِّدِيد [mula:ħiðna ?iṣṭidam wiyya ?ilmudi:r ?ijǰidi:d] Our supervisor clashed with the new director. • **2.** with بـ to bump into, hit, strike, collide with – السَّيّارَة اِصطِدمَت بالعَمُود [?issayya:ra ?iṣṭidmat bilʕamu:d] The car ran into the pole.
صَدِم [ṣadim] *n:* • **1.** shock, blow, jolt, push • **2.** hitting, running into
صَدمَة [ṣadma] *n:* صَدمات [ṣadma:t] *pl:* • **1.** jolt, shock, blow • **2.** (emotional) shock, blow, commotion
صِدام [ṣida:m] *n:* • **1.** clash, collision, breakdown, collapse
تَصادُم [taṣa:dum] *n:* • **1.** clash, collision, crash, impact
اِصطِدام [?iṣṭida:m] *n:* • **1.** collision, clash, impact, bounce – حادِث اِصطِدام [ħa:diθ ?iṣṭida:m] a collision, an accident.
مُصادَمَة [muṣa:dama] *n:* • **1.** collision, clash, impact
مَصدُوم [maṣdu:m] *adj:* • **1.** shocked, traumatized

ص د ي

تصَدَّى [tṣadda:] *v:* • **1.** with لـ to oppose, resist, fight against – بَسّ يِنتِقِد الوَضِع بخِطابَه الكُلّ راح يِتصَدُّولَه [bass yintiqid ?ilwaðiʕ bxiṭa:bah ?ilkull ra:ħ yitṣaddu:lah] As soon as he criticizes the situation in his speech, all will oppose him. • **2.** to bar the way of, stand in the path of – مِن يُمُرّ من هنا راح يِتصَدُّولَه وَيبُسطُوه [min yumurr min hina: ra:ħ yitṣaddu:lah wybuṣṭu:h] When he passes by here they're going to stand in his way and beat him up.
صَدَى [ṣada:] *n:* أصداء [?aṣda:?] *pl:* • **1.** echo, reverberation

ص ر ح

صَرَّح [ṣarraħ] *v:* • **1.** to make a statement, make an announcement – وَزِير الخارجِيَّة صَرَّح بأشياء مُهِمَّة [wazi:r ?ilxa:riǰiyya ṣarraħ b?ašya:? muhimma] The Foreign Minister made an announcement about some important things.
صارَح [ṣa:raħ] *v:* • **1.** to speak openly, frankly to – صارَحنِي بالقَضِيَّة وَعِرَفِت كُلّشِي [ṣa:raħni bilqaðiyya wʕirafit kullši] He spoke frankly to me about the matter and I found out everything. صارَحنِي بسِرَّه [ṣa:raħni bsirrah] He disclosed his secret to me.
تصارَح [tṣa:raħ] *v:* • **1.** to speak frankly, openly, candidly to each other – بالأخِير تصارَحنا وَواحِدنا رِضَى عَن الثّانِي [bil?axi:r tṣa:raħna wwa:ħidna riða: ʕan ?iθθa:ni] Finally we spoke frankly with each other and each of us was satisfied with the other.
صَراحَة [ṣara:ħa] *n:* • **1.** clearness, explicity, distinctness • **2.** frankness, openness, candor – أقُلَّك بصَراحَة، هِيَّ ما تحِبَّك [?agullak bṣara:ħa, hiyya ma: tħibbak] I'll tell you frankly, she doesn't love you.
تَصرِيح [taṣri:ħ] *n:* تَصرِيحات، تَصارِيح [taṣri:ħa:t, taṣa:ri:ħ] *pl:* • **1.** declaration, statement

تَصرِيحَة، تَصرِيحَة جُمرُكِيَّة [taṣri:ħa, taṣri:ħa gumrugiyya] *n:* • **1.** customs declaration

صَرِيح [ṣari:ħ] *adj:* • **1.** explicit, clear, unambiguous, unequivocal, manifest, plain • **2.** frank, open, candid, sincere

مُصَرَّح [muṣarraħ] *adj:* مُصَرَّحِين [muṣṣaraħi:n] *pl:* • **1.** authorized

ص ر خ

صِرَخ [ṣirax] *v:* • **1.** to scream, yell, shout, cry out, shriek – صِرَخ بكُلّ حيلَه مِن المجَبُّر جَبَّر رِجلَه [ṣirax bkull ħi:lah min ʔilmǰabbur ǰabbar rijlah] He screamed at the top of his lungs when the bonesetter set his leg. الجّاهِل لِيش دَيِصرَخ؟ [ʔiǰǰa:hil li:š dayiṣrax?] Why's the kid screaming? • **2.** to yell, bellow, roar – العَرِيف دائِماً يِصرَخ عَلَى الجُّنُود الجِّدَد [ʔilʕari:f da:ʔiman yiṣrax ʕala ʔiǰǰinu:d ʔiǰǰidad] The sergeant always yells at the new soldiers. لَمّا طلَبِت مِنَّه فلُوس، صِرَخ بوُجهِي وَطرَدني [lamma ṭlabit minnah flu:s, ṣirax bwujhi wṭiradni] When I asked him for money, he shouted in my face and threw me out.

صَرَّخ [ṣarrax] *v:* • **1.** intensive of – صرَخ صارلَك ساعَة تصَرِّخ بَسّ عاد [ṣa:rlak sa:ʕa tṣarrix bass ʕa:d] You've been bawling an hour. Knock it off! ظَلّ يصَرِّخ إِلَى أَن مات [ðall yṣarrix ʔila ʔan ma:t] He kept on screaming till he died.

صَرِخ [ṣarix] *n:* • **1.** screaming, shouting, yelling

صَرخَة [ṣarxa] *n:* صَرخات، صرِيخ، صراخ [ṣarxa:t, ṣri:x, ṣra:x] *pl:* • **1.** scream, cry, shriek, shout, yell • **2.** clamor, screaming, screams

صارُوخ [ṣa:ru:x] *n:* صَوارِيخ [ṣawa:ri:x] *pl:* • **1.** rocket – صارُوخ مُوَجَّه [ṣa:ru:x muwaǰǰah] guided missile.

صارِخ [ṣa:rix] *adj:* • **1.** blatant, noisy • **2.** flashy (color), bold (color)

ص ر ر

صَرّ [ṣarr] *v:* • **1.** to wrap in a cloth bundle – صَرّ كُلّ هدُومَه وَراح [ṣarr kull hdu:mah wra:ħ] He wrapped all his clothes in a bundle and left.

أَصَرّ [ʔaṣarr] *v:* • **1.** to make up one's mind, resolve, determine – أَصَرّ عَلَى أَن يِدرُس بأَمرِيكا [ʔaṣarr ʕala ʔan yidrus bʔamri:ka] He resolved that he would study in America. • **2.** to insist, be persistent – أَصَرّ يرُوح وِيّانا [ʔaṣarr yiru:ħ wiyya:na] He insisted on going with us.

صَرّ [ṣarr] *n:* • **1.** wrapping in a cloth bundle

صُرَّة [ṣurra] *n:* صُرّات، صُرَر [ṣurra:t, ṣurar] *pl:* • **1.** navel • **2.** belly, soft underside (of a fish) • **3.** cloth bundle, packet • **4.** the decorated portion of a quilt not covered by a protective sheet

إِصرار [ʔiṣra:r] *n:* • **1.** insistence, tenaciousness, perseverance

مُصِرّ [muṣirr] *adj:* • **1.** determined, persistent

ص ر ص ر

صُرصُر [ṣurṣur] *n:* صَراصِر [ṣara:ṣir] *pl:* • **1.** cricket • **2.** cockroach

ص ر ط

صِرَط [ṣiraṭ] *v:* • **1.** to gulp down, swallow whole – شال البَيضَة وَصِرَطها [ša:l ʔilbayða wṣiraṭha] He picked up the egg and swallowed it whole.

صَرُط [ṣaruṭ] *n:* • **1.** swallowing whole, gulping down

ص ر ع

صِرَع [ṣiraʕ] *v:* • **1.** to throw down, fell, to get a fall, to pin – صِرَعَه بأَخِر جَولَة [ṣiraʕah bʔaxir ǰawla] He pinned him in the last round.

صارَع [ṣa:raʕ] *v:* • **1.** to wrestle – إلمَن راح تصارِع اليُوم؟ [ʔilman ra:ħ tṣa:riʕ ʔilyu:m?] Who are you going to wrestle today?

تصارَع [tṣa:raʕ] *v:* • **1.** to wrestle each other – راح يِتصارَع وِيّا واحِد أَطوَل مِنَّه [ra:ħ yitṣa:raʕ wiyya wa:ħid ʔaṭwal minnah] He'll be wrestling with a taller man.

اِنصِرَع [ʔinṣiraʕ] *v:* • **1.** to be fallen, to be pinned, to be thrown – اِنصِرَع مَرّتَين [ʔinṣiraʕ marrtayn] He was pinned two times.

صَرَع [ṣaraʕ] *n:* • **1.** epilepsy

صَرِع [ṣariʕ] *n:* • **1.** throwing down

صَرعَة [ṣarʕa] *n:* صَرعات [ṣarʕa:t] *pl:* • **1.** an epileptic seizure, a fit

مُصرَع [muṣraʕ] *n:* مُصارِع [muṣa:riʕ] *pl:* • **1.** top (child's toy) • **2.** as Adjective: a very active and fast person

صِراع [ṣira:ʕ] *n:* • **1.** conflict • **2.** wrestling match • **3.** struggle

مُصارِع [muṣa:riʕ] *n:* مُصارِعِين [muṣa:riʕi:n] *pl:* • **1.** wrestler

تَصارُع [taṣa:ruʕ] *n:* • **1.** wrestling fight • **2.** fight

مُصارَعَة [muṣa:raʕa] *n:* • **1.** wrestling

مَصرُوع [maṣru:ʕ] *adj:* • **1.** thrown to the ground, pinned • **2.** epileptic • **3.** insane, mad, crazy

ص ر ف

صِرَف [ṣiraf] *v:* • **1.** to dismiss, send away – المُعَلِّم صِرَفنا بالعَجَل [ʔilmuʕallim ṣirafna bilʕaǰal] The teacher dismissed us quickly. جانِي لِلدّائِرَة لَكِن صِرَفتَه بالزَّينِيَّة [ǰa:ni lidda:ʔira la:kin ṣiraftah bizzayniyya] He came to the office, but I sent him away with a few pleasantries. صِرَف النَّظَر عَن [ṣiraf ʔinnaðar ʕan] to dismiss from one's mind, disregard, pay no attention to. صِرَف النَّظَر عَن مَشرُوع السَّفرَة [ṣiraf ʔinnaðar ʕan mašru:ʕ ʔissafra] He put the plan for the trip out of his mind. الحُكُومَة صِرفَت النَّظَر عَن مَشرُوع الجِّسِر [ʔilħuku:ma ṣirfat ʔinnaðar ʕan mašru:ʕ ʔiǰǰisir] The government dropped the idea of the bridge project. • **2.** to spend, pay out, expend – صِرَف هوايَة فلُوس بسَفرتَه [ṣiraf hwa:ya flu:s

ص

bsafirtah] He spent a lot of money on his trip. • **3.** to cash – بِأي بَنك أقدَر أصرُف هَالشّيك؟ [b?ay bang ?agdar ?aṣruf haččiːk?] Which bank can I cash this check in? • **4.** to gulp down, swallow whole – يِصرُف بيضَة وِحدَة عالرِّيق [yiṣruf biːḏa wiħda ʕarriːg] He swallows one egg before breakfast.

صَرَّف [ṣarraf] *v:* • **1.** to bring profit, be profitable, be of benefit – لَو يصَرُّف، كان بِعتَه بِدِينار [law yṣarruf, čaːn biʕtah bdinaːr] If it had been profitable, I would have sold it for a dinar. ما يصَرُّفلَك تبيعَه بِدينار [maː yṣarruflak tbiːʕah bdinaːr] It won't bring you any profit to sell it for a dinar. آني ما يصَرُّفلي هِيكِي حَكِي [?aːni maː yṣarrufli hiːči ħači] This sort of talk is of no benefit to me. • **2.** to dispose of, liquidate, sell, market – تِقدَر تصَرُّف البِضاعَة بِبَغداد [tigdar tṣarruf ?ilbiḏaːʕa bibaɣdaːd] You can market the goods in Baghdad. • **3.** to change (money) – أرجُوك، صَرُّفلي الدِّينار [?arǰuːk, ṣarrufli ?iddiːnaːr] Would you please change this dinar for me.

تصَرَّف [tṣarraf] *v:* • **1.** to act independently, freely, at one's own discretion – لا تِلتِزِم بِالتَّعلِيمات. تصَرَّف حَسَب الظّرُوف [laː tiltizim bittaʕliːmaːt. tṣarraf ħasab ?iḏḏuruːf] Don't stick too close to the instructions. Act according to the circumstances. قُل لَهُم شما قِتلَك. لا تِتصَرَّف بكَيفَك [gul lahum šma gitlak. laː titṣarraf bkayfak] Tell them what I told you. Don't add anything on your own. ما قِتلَك لا تِتصَرَّف بِالتَّرجُمَة؟ [maː gitlak laː titṣarraf bittarǰuma?] Didn't I tell you not to render the translation freely? ما كان لازم تِتصَرَّف بِالفلُوس [maː čaːn laːzim titṣarraf bilfiluːs] You weren't supposed to use the money as you wished. سِجنوه لِأنّ تصَرَّف بِمال الحُكُومَة [siǰnuːh li?ann tṣarraf bmaːl ?ilħukuːma] They put him in jail because he misappropriated government property. • **2.** to behave, act, conduct oneself, comport oneself – تصَرَّف بِصُورَة مُو لايقَة [tṣarraf bṣuːra muː laːyga] He behaved in an improper manner. ما يُعرُف يِتصَرَّف [maː yuʕruf yitṣarraf] He doesn't know how to behave.

اِنصِرَف [?inṣiraf] *v:* • **1.** to be spent – الفلُوس كُلّها اِنصُرفَت [?ilfluːs kullha ?inṣurfat] The money's all spent.

صَرُف [ṣaruf] *n:* • **1.** dismissing, sending away • **2.** spending

صَرّاف [ṣarraːf] *n:* صَرّافين [ṣarraːfiːn] *pl:* • **1.** money changer • **2.** spend-thrift, big spender

مَصرَف [maṣraf] *n:* مَصارِيف [maṣaːriːf] *pl:* • **1.** expenditure, expense, cost • **2.** (pl. مَصارُف) bank (in certain formal expressions:) – مَصرَف حُكُومي [maṣraf ħukuːmi] a government bank. مَصرَف الرافِدَين [maṣraf ?irraːfidiːn] The Rafidayn Bank. مَصرَف الرُّهُون [maṣraf ?irruhuːn] Security Deposit Bank. مَصرَف زِراعِي [maṣraf ziraːʕi] Agricultural Bank.

تَصَرُّف [taṣarruf] *n:* تَصَرُّفات [taṣarrufaːt] *pl:* • **1.** action, conduct, behavior, demeanor • **2.** free disposal, right of disposal – هَالمَقال مترَجَم بِتَصَرُّف [halmaqaːl mtarǰam btaṣarruf] This article is translated freely. تَحَت تَصَرُّف [taħat taṣarruf] at the disposal of, under control of. حَطّ سَيّارتَه تَحَت تَصَرُّفِي [ħaṭṭ sayyaːrtah taħat taṣarrufi] He put his car at my disposal. مُطلَق التَّصَرُّف [muṭlaq ?ittaṣarruf] invested with full power, having unrestricted control. • **3.** as in بِتَصَرُّف: freely, unrestrictedly

صِرفَة [ṣirfa] *n:* • **1.** solution, exit

صِرِيفَة [ṣiriːfa] *n:* صَرايِف [ṣaraːyif] *pl:* • **1.** hut, shack

صِرافَة [ṣraːfa] *n:* • **1.** change – عِندَك صِرافَة دِينار؟ [ʕindak ṣraːfat dinaːr?] Do you have change for a dinar?

مُتَصَرِّف [mutaṣarrif] *n:* مُتَصَرِّفين [mutaṣarrifiːn] *pl:* • **1.** governor of a province

مَصرُوف [maṣruːf] *n:* مَصرُوفات، مَصارِيف [maṣruːfaːt, maṣaːriːf] *pl:* • **1.** expense, expenditure, cost

صَيرَفَة [ṣayrafa] *n:* • **1.** exchange

تَصرِيف [taṣriːf] *n:* • **1.** disposal, disribution, sale, retail • **2.** change, alteration, distribution • **3.** inflection, declension, conjugation

صَرفِيّات [ṣarfiyyaːt] *n:* • **1.** (pl. only) expenses, expenditures, payments

صِرف [ṣirf] *adj:* • **1.** pure, unadulterated, unmixed – حَرِير صِرف [ħariːr ṣirf] pure silk. ماي صِرف [maːy ṣirf] plain water. تَعبِير بَغدادِي صِرف [taʕbiːr baɣdaːdi ṣirf] a pure Baghdadi expression.

أصرَف [?aṣraf] *comparative adjective:* • **1.** more or most profitable, beneficial, economical – اِشتِريها بِالنَّقدِي. أصرَفلَك [?ištiriːha binnaqdi. ?aṣraflak] Buy it for cash. It's more economical for you.

ص ر م 1

صُرمايَة [ṣurmaːya] *n:* • **1.** capital, financial assets • **2.** money

ص ر م 2

اِستَصرَم [?istaṣram] *v:* • **1.** to flirt, make passes, chase (girls) – كُلّ يوم يوقف يَمّ المَدرَسَة يِستَصرُم عَالبَنات [kull yuːm yuːgaf yamm ?ilmadrasa yistaṣrum ʕalbanaːt] Every day he stands near the school and makes passes at the girls. كان دَيِستَصرُم يَمّ السِّينَما [čaːn dayistaṣrum yamm ?issinama] He was trying to make a pick-up near the movie theater.

صُرُم [ṣurum] *n:* صرامَة [ṣraːma] *pl:* • **1.** (vulgar) rectum

ص ر م 3

صَرامَة [ṣaraːma] *n:* • **1.** sharpness, sternness, severity, rigor

صارِم [ṣaːrim] *adj:* • **1.** tough, harsh, hard, severe, stern

ص

ص ر م ب ر

صُرُمبارَة [ṣurumpa:ra] *n:* صُرُمبارِيَّة [ṣurumpa:riyya] *pl:* • **1.** wolf, womanizer, skirt-chaser • **2.** hoodlum, hooligan, ruffian, juvenile delinquent

ص ع ب

صِعَب [ṣiʕab] *v:* • **1.** to be or become difficult, hard, unpleasant – مِن تِثلِج، السَّفَر يِصعَب [min tiθlij, ʔissafar yiṣʕab] When it snows, traveling becomes difficult. تَحصِيل وَظِيفَة دَيِصعَب سَنَة عَلَى سَنَة [taħṣi:l waðʼi:fa dayiṣʕab sana ʕala sana] Getting a job is becoming more difficult year after year. يِصعَب عَلَيّا أَترُكهُم وَحَّدهُم [yiṣʕab ʕalayya ʔatrukhum waħħadhum] It's unpleasant for me to leave them by themselves.

صَعَّب [ṣaʕʕab] *v:* • **1.** to make difficult, hard – الكُلِّيَّة صَعَّبَت الامتِحان هالسَّنَة [ʔilkulliyya ṣaʕʕubat ʔilʔimtiħa:n hassana] The college has made the exam difficult this year.

تصَعَّب [tṣaʕʕab] *v:* • **1.** to be or become difficult, hard – لازِم نِتصَعَّب وِيّا الطُّلّاب هَالسَّنَة [la:zim nitṣaʕʕab wiyya ʔiṭṭulla:b hassana] We have to be tough on the students this year. لا تِتصَعَّب. هَذا خُوش سِعِر [la: titṣaʕʕab. ha:ða xu:š siʕir] Don't be difficult. This is a good price.

اِستَصعَب [ʔistaṣʕab] *v:* • **1.** to consider difficult, hard – لا تِستَصعُب الرَّوحَة لِلدُّكّان [la: tistaṣʕub ʔirrawħa liddukka:n] Don't make it sound so hard to go to the store.

صُعُوبَة [ṣuʕu:ba] *n:* صُعُوبات، مَصاعُب [ṣuʕuba:t, maṣa:ʕub] *pl:* • **1.** difficulty, hardship

صَعُب [ṣaʕub] *adj:* • **1.** difficult, hard, unpleasant – اِمتِحان صَعُب [ʔimtiħa:n ṣaʕub] a difficult exam. لا تِشتِري مِنَّه. صَعُب هوايَة [la: tištiri minnah. ṣaʕub hwa:ya] Don't buy from him. He's very hard to deal with.

أصعَب [ʔaṣʕab] *comparative adjective:* • **1.** more or most difficult, hard, unpleasant

ص ع د

صِعَد [ṣiʕad] *v:* • **1.** to ascend, rise, go upward – شوَقِت يِصعَد البالُون؟ [šwakit yiṣʕad ʔilba:lu:n?] What time does the balloon go up? خَلّي نِصعَد فُوق [xalli: niṣʕad fu:g] Let's go up. سِعِر الشَّكَر صِعَد [siʕir ʔiššakar ṣiʕad] The price of sugar went up. • **2.** (sometimes with عَلَى) to climb on, mount, scale – صِعَد عَالكُرسِي حَتَّى يشُوف [ṣiʕad ʕalkursi ħatta yšu:f] He got up on the chair so he could see. تِقدَر تِصعَد عَلَى هَالشَّجرَة؟ [tigdar tiṣʕad ʕala haššijra?] Can you climb this tree? حصانِي صِعَد فَرَسكُم [ħṣa:ni ṣiʕad faraskum] My horse mounted your mare.

صَعَّد [ṣaʕʕad] *v:* • **1.** to cause to rise, ascend, go up, to send up, to take up – صَعِّد جِنُطتِي لغُرُفتِي [ṣaʕʕid jinuṭti lɣurufti] Take my bag up to my room.

تصاعَد [tṣa:ʕad] *v:* • **1.** to drift upward, rise, ascend – الدُّخّان دَيتصاعَد مِن وَرا التَّلّ [ʔidduxxa:n dayitṣa:ʕad min wara ʔittall] The smoke's rising from behind the hill.

اِنصِعَد [ʔinṣiʕad] *v:* • **1.** sometimes with عَلَى to be ascended, climbed – هَالجِّبَل ما يِنصِعِد عَليه [hajjibal ma: yinṣiʕid ʕali:h] That mountain can't be climbed.

صَعدَة [ṣaʕda] *n:* صَعدات [ṣaʕda:t] *pl:* • **1.** climbing, ascending • **2.** upward slope, rise, ascent

مَصعَد [maṣʕad] *n:* مَصاعِد [maṣa:ʕid] *pl:* • **1.** elevator, lift

صَعِيد [ṣaʕi:d] *n:* • **1.** plateau, highland, upland • **2.** فِي صَعِيد وَاحِد on a common basis, on common ground, indiscriminately

صُعُود [ṣuʕu:d] *n:* • **1.** ascending, rising, lifting, take-off (of an airplane) • **2.** ascent, boom

صَعّادَة [ṣaʕʕa:da] *n:* صَعّادات [ṣaʕʕa:da:t] *pl:* • **1.** skyrocket (fireworks)

تَصعِيد [taṣʕi:d] *n:* • **1.** stepping up • **2.** increase, escalation

تَصاعُد [taṣa:ʕud] *n:* • **1.** escalation, growth, increase

صاعِد [ṣa:ʕid] *adj:* • **1.** on the ascent, ascending, rising, climbing – هَذا نَجمَه صاعِد [ha:ða najmah ṣa:ʕid] He's coming up in the world (lit., his star is rising). من هنا وصاعِد [min hina: wṣa:ʕid] from here on out, from now on. من هنا وصاعِد ماكُو تَدخِين بالغُرفَة [min hina: wṣa:ʕid ma:ku tadxi:n bilɣurfa] From now on there will be no smoking in the room.

تَصاعُدِي [taṣa:ʕudi] *adj:* • **1.** progressive, incremental

ص ع ق

صِعَق [ṣiʕaq] *v:* • **1.** to stun, to shake • **2.** to lose consciousness

اِنصِعَق [ʔinṣiʕaq] *v:* • **1.** to bowl over • **2.** to be stunned, to be struck

صاعِقَة [ṣa:ʕiqa] *n:* صَواعِق [ṣawa:ʕiq] *pl:* • **1.** bolt of lightning

صَعِق [ṣaʕiq] *adj:* • **1.** stunned, struck, thunderstruck, dumbfounded

ص ع ل ك

صَعلُوك [ṣaʕlu:k] *adj:* صَعالِيك [ṣaʕa:li:k] *pl:* • **1.** utterly destitute person, pauper, have-not • **2.** vagrant, bum, tramp, loafer

ص غ ر

صِغَر [ziɣar] *v:* • **1.** to be or become small, little – هَالقاط صِغَر عَلَيّا [halqa:ṭ ṣiɣar ʕalayya] This suit has gotten too small for me. صِغَر بعَينِي هوايَة مِن سَبّ أَبُوه [ṣiɣar bʕayni hwa:ya min sabb ʔabu:h] He grew a lot smaller in my eyes when he cursed his father.

صَغَّر [zaɣɣar] *v:* • **1.** to make smaller – جِيب هَالثُّوب كِبِير. تِقدَر تصَغّرَه؟ [ji:b haθθu:b čibi:r.

ص

tigdar tṣaɣɣrah?] The pocket of this shirt is big. Can you make it smaller? هَالقَنَفات صَغَّرَت الغُرفَة [halqanafa:t ṣaɣɣirat ʔilɣurfa] These couches made the room smaller. • **2.** to reduce, decrease – صَغَّرَت عُمُرها سَنتَين [ṣaɣɣrat ʕumurha santayn] She reduced her age two years.
تصَغَّر [tzaɣɣar] *v:* • **1.** to be made smaller – هَالنَّفنُوف ما يِتصَغَّر [hannafnu:f ma: yitṣaɣɣar] This dress can't be made smaller.
إستَصغَر [ʔistazɣar] *v:* • **1.** to consider small, little, insignificant, paltry – لا تِستَصغِرَه، تَرَة هُوَّ أَقوَى مِنَّك [la: tistaṣɣirah, tara huwwa ʔaqwa minnak] Don't underestimate him, because he's stronger than you.
صُغُر [zuɣur] *n:* • **1.** smallness, littleness – ما عِندِي بِسمار بِهَالصُّغُر [ma: ʕindi bisma:r bhaṣṣuɣur] I don't have a nail this small. • **2.** youth, childhood
صاغُور [za:ɣu:r] *n:* صُواغِير [zuwa:ɣi:r] *pl:* • **1.** small alley, hole
صغَيِّر [ṣɣayyir, zɣayyir] *adj:* • **1.** small, little – غُرفَة صغَيِّرَة [ɣurfa zɣayyra] a small room. • **2.** insignificant, minor, paltry – مُوَظَّف صغَيِّر [mwaððaf zɣayyir] a minor official. • **3.** young, juvenile, minor – جِرو صغَيِّر [ǰirw ṣɣayyir] a young puppy.
مصَغَّر [mṣaɣɣar, mzaɣɣar] *adj:* • **1.** reduced
صغَيرُون [ṣɣayru:n, zɣayru:n] *adj:* • **1.** tot
أَصغَر [ʔaṣɣar, ʔazɣar] *comparative adjective:* • **1.** smaller or smallest • **2.** younger or youngest
صُغراً، وَلا صُغراً بِ [zuɣran, wala ṣuɣran bi-] *adv:* • **1.** without belittling someone (introducing a criticism)

ص غ ل م

صَغلَم [ṣaɣlam] *adj:* • **1.** contraction of صاغ سَلِم safe and sound, in perfect condition

ص غ و

صِغَى [ṣiɣa:] *v:* • **1.** to heed, listen, pay attention – لازِم تِصغِي لِلمُعَلِّم [la:zim tiṣɣi lilmuʕallim] You should pay attention to the teacher.
إصغاء [ʔiṣɣa:ʔ] *n:* • **1.** listening, attention, attentiveness
مُصغِي [muṣɣi] *adj:* • **1.** listening, paying attention • **2.** as Noun, listener, hearer

ص غ ي

See also: ص غ و

ص ف ح

صافَح [ṣa:fah] *v:* • **1.** to shake hands with – كُلّنا صافَحنا الوَزِير [kullna ṣa:faħna ʔilwazi:r] We all shook hands with the minister.
تصَفَّح [tṣaffaħ] *v:* • **1.** to leaf through, thumb through – تصَفَّحت الِكتاب وَما شِفِت بِيه شِي [tṣaffaħt ʔilkita:b wama šifit bi:h ši] I leafed through the book and didn't see anything in it.
تصافَح [tṣa:faħ] *v:* • **1.** to shake hands with each other – لازِم تِتصافحُون قَبُل ما تِتلاكمُون [la:zim titṣa:fħu:n gabul ma: titla:kmu:n] You have to shake hands before you start fighting.
صَفحَة [ṣafħa] *n:* صَفحات [ṣafħa:t] *pl:* • **1.** page, leaf (of a book) – أُقلُب صَفحَة [ʔuglub ṣafħa] Change the subject! • **2.** pl. صَفحات, صِفاح side, face, facet – صَفحَة مِن صفاح المُكَعَّب لَونها فاهِي [ṣafħa min ṣfa:ħ ʔilmukaʕʕab lu:nha fa:hi] One of the sides of the cube is light-colored. يا صَفحَة تَوجعَك؟ [ya: ṣafħa tu:ǰʕak?] Which side hurts you? آنِي مِن صَفِحتَك [ʔa:ni min ṣafiħtak] I'm on your side. عَلَى صَفحَة [ʕala ṣafħa] aside, to one side. جَرِّيته عَلَى صَفحَة وحِكَيت وِيّاه [ǰarri:tah ʕala ṣafħa wħiči:t wiyya:h] I took him aside and talked with him. خَلِّي هَالشُّغُل عَلَى صَفحَة البَعدَين [xalli: haššuɣul ʕala ṣafħa lbaʕdi:n] Set this work aside for later. • **3.** direction, way – هَسَّة فاتَوا مِن هالصَّفحَة [hassa fa:taw min ha:lṣafħa] They just went that way. • **4.** pl. صُفاح ancestor – نَعلَة عَلَى صَفحَة صَفِحتَك [naʕla ʕala ṣafħat ṣafiħtak] Damn your ancestors' ancestors! نَعلَة عالصُفاح وَالرُواح [naʕla ʕaṣṣufa:ħ wirruwa:ħ] A curse upon you and your ancestors.
صفاح [ṣfa:ħ] *n:* • **1.** side, face, facet • **2.** sheet, leaf
تَصَفُّح [taṣaffuħ] *n:* • **1.** skimming through • **1.** browsing
صَفِيحَة [ṣafi:ħa] *n:* • **1.** can, jerry can, metal container, round metal plate • **2.** tin plate, tin sheet
تَصافُح [taṣa:fuħ] *n:* • **1.** handshaking, handshake
مُصافَحَة [muṣa:faħa] *n:* • **1.** hand shake
صَفُح [ṣafuħ] *adj:* • **1.** sideways, in a sidewise direction – الجِّنِّيب يِمشِي صَفُح [ʔiǰǰinni:b yimši ṣafuħ] The crab walks sideways.
مصَفَّح [mṣaffaħ] *adj:* • **1.** plated, armored • **2.** polygonal, many-faceted
صَفحاوي [ṣafħa:wi] *adj:* • **1.** toward the side, sideways

ص ف ر 1

صُوفَر [ṣu:far] *v:* • **1.** to whistle – مِن يِمشِي، لَو يصُوفِر لَو يغَنِّي [min yimši, law yṣu:fir law yɣanni] When he walks, he either whistles or sings.
صُفَر [ṣufar] *v:* • **1.** to whistle, make a whistling sound – القِطار يُصفُر قَبُل ما يِتحَرَّك [ʔilqiṭa:r yuṣfur gabul ma: yitħarrak] The train whistles before it moves.
صَفَّر [ṣaffar] *v:* • **2.** intens. of صِفَر – الشُّرطِي صَفَّرلَه حَتَّى يوقَف [ʔiššurṭi ṣaffarlah ħatta yu:gaf] The policeman whistled at him so he'd stop.
صَفُر [ṣafur] *n:* • **1.** whistling
صَفِير [ṣafi:r] *n:* • **1.** whistle • **2.** whistling
صافِرَة [ṣa:fira] *n:* صافِرات [ṣa:fira:t] *pl:* • **1.** whistle
صَفّارَة [ṣaffa:ra] *n:* صَفّارات [ṣaffa:ra:t] *pl:* • **1.** siren • **2.** whistle (of a referee in sports, of a locomotive)
صوفرَة [ṣu:fra] *n:* • **1.** a whistle

ص ف ر 2

اِصفَرّ [ʔiṣfarr] *v:* • **1.** to yellow, turn yellow – بالخَريف، أوراق الأشجار تِصفَرّ وَبَعدين تُوقَع [bilxari:f, ʔawra:q ʔilʔašja:r tiṣfarr wbaʕdi:n tu:gaʕ] In the fall the leaves of the trees turn yellow and then fall. • **2.** (of the face) to become pale, turn pale, pale – مِن شاف السَّبع، خاف وَاصفَرّ وِجهه [min ša:f ʔissabiʕ, xa:f wʔiṣfarr wiččah] When he saw the lion, he got scared and his face turned pale.

صُفرَة [ṣufra] *n:* • **1.** yellowness, yellow • **2.** pallor, paleness (of the face) • **3.** vertigo, motion sickness

صَفار [ṣafa:r] *n:* • **1.** yellowness, yellow • **2.** pallor, paleness • **3.** pl. صَفارات egg yolk

صُفار [ṣufa:r, ṣufa:r] *n:* صُفارات [ṣufa:ra:t, ṣafa:ra:t] *pl:* • **1.** egg yolk

صَفّار [ṣaffa:r] *n:* صَفَفير، صفافير [ṣafafi:r, ṣfa:fi:r] *pl:* • **1.** coppersmith

صِفرِيَّة [ṣifriyya] *n:* صِفرِيّات [ṣifriyya:t] *pl:* • **1.** a copper basin built into the floor of a public bath to heat water

صِفِر [ṣifir] *adj:* • **1.** brass • **2.** bronze • **3.** copper

أَصفَر [ʔaṣfar] *adj:* صُفُر، صَفرين [ṣufur, safri:n] *pl:* صَفرَة [ṣafra] *feminine:* • **1.** yellow • **2.** pale, pallid, sallow – وِجهه أصفَر مِن شُرُب التِّرياك [wiččah ʔaṣfar min šurub ʔittirya:k] His face is pale from smoking opium.

صَفراوي [ṣafra:wi] *adj:* • **1.** subject to motion sickness – ما أركَب بِالطَّيّارَة لِأَنّي صَفراوي [ma: ʔarkab biṭṭayya:ra liʔanni ṣafra:wi] I don't ride by airplane because I get motion sickness.

ص ف ر 3

تصَفَّر [tṣaffar] *v:* • **1.** to be empty, to be devoid, to be vacant, to be free (of)

صِفِر [ṣifir] *n:* صفارَة [ṣfa:ra] *pl:* • **1.** zero, naught – هَذا صِفِر بِالحِساب [ha:ða ṣifir bilħisa:b] He's a blank in arithmetic.

مصَفَّر [mṣaffar] *adj:* • **1.** empty-handed

ص ف ر 4

صَفَر [ṣafar] *n:* • **1.** Safar, name of the second month of the Moslem year

ص ف ص ف

صُفصاف [ṣufṣa:f] *n:* • **1.** (coll.) willow(s)

صُفصافَة [ṣufṣa:fa] *n:* صُفصافات [ṣufṣa:fa:t] *pl:* • **1.** a willow tree

ص ف ف

صَفّ [ṣaff] *v:* • **1.** to set in a row or line, line up, align, arrange, array, order – صُفّ التَّلاميذ قِدّام غُرُفتي [ṣuff ʔittala:mi:ð gidda:m ɣurufti] Line up the students in front of my office. صَفّ التَّلاميذ صَفّين [ṣaff ʔittala:mi:ð ṣaffayn] He lined the pupils up in two lines.

صَفَّف [ṣaffaf] *v:* • **1.** to arrange, array, set in order – دَتصَفُّف شَعَرها قِدّام المرايا [datṣaffuf šaʕarha gidda:m ʔilmra:ya] She is arranging her hair in front of the mirror.

اِنصَفّ [ʔinṣaff] *v:* • **1.** to keep close to, hug – اِنصَفّ بِالحايط حَتَّى يسَوّي طَريق لِلسَّيّارَة [ʔinṣaff bilħa:yiṭ ħatta ysawwi: ṭari:q lissayya:ra] He hugged the wall in order to make way for the car.

اِصطَفّ [ʔiṣṭaff] *v:* • **1.** to form a line or row, line up, fall into formation – الجِّنُود اِصطَفّوا أَربَعَة أَربَعَة [ʔiǰǰinu:d ʔiṣṭaffaw ʔarbaʕa ʔarbaʕa] The soldiers lined up in columns of four.

صَفّ [ṣaff] *n:* صفُوف [ṣfu:f] *pl:* • **1.** row, line, file, column, rank, queue • **2.** grade, form (in school) • **3.** course, class – ضابُط صَفّ [ḍa:buṭ ṣaff] non-commissioned officer. بِالباص، كانَت بصَفّي بنَيَّة حِلوَة [bilpa:ṣ, ča:nat bṣaffi bnayya ħilwa] On the bus, there was a cute girl right next to me. حُطّ الكُرسِي بصَفّ الباب [ħuṭṭ ʔilkursi bṣaff ʔilba:b] Put the chair right by the door.

تَصفيف [taṣfi:f] *n:* • **1.** hairstyling, hairdressing

اِصطِفاف [ʔiṣṭifa:f] *n:* • **1.** lineup

مَصفُوف [maṣfu:f] *adj:* • **1.** smooth, combed, flat (hair)

ص ف ق

صُفَق [ṣufag] *v:* • **1.** to slap, smack, slam, bang (a door) – صُفَقتَه بعِجِل دَوَّختَه [ṣufagtah bʕiǰil dawwaxtah] I slapped him on the head and made him dizzy. صُفَق الباب وَراه [ṣufag ʔilba:b wara:h] He slammed the door behind him. • **2.** to clap, flap

صَفَّق [ṣaffag] *v:* • **1.** to clap, to applaud, clap the hands – صَفِّق لِلبُوي حَتَّى يِجي [ṣaffug lilbu:y ħatta yiǰi] Clap for the waiter to come. مِن خَلَّص، صَفِّقُولَه هوايَة [min xallaṣ, ṣaffugu:lah hwa:ya] When he finished, they applauded him a lot.

تصَفَّق [tṣaffag] *v:* • **1.** to applaud • **2.** to clap (hands for somebody)

اِنصُفَق [ʔinṣufag] *v:* • **1.** to be slapped, to be slammed

صَفُق [ṣafug] *n:* • **1.** slapping, smacking

صَفقَة [ṣafqa] *n:* صَفقات [ṣafqa:t] *pl:* • **1.** transaction, deal, bargain • **2.** handclasp (in concluding a deal), conclusion of a contract

صَفقَة [ṣafga] *n:* صَفقات [ṣafga:t] *pl:* • **1.** slap, smack, clap • **2.** ovation, round of applause

تصُفُّق [tṣuffug] *n:* • **1.** applause • **2.** clapping

تَصفيق [taṣfi:g] *n:* • **1.** applause • **2.** hand clapping

ص ف ن

صُفَن [ṣufan] *v:* • **1.** to reflect, to ponder, muse, meditate, brood – أُصفُن زين. شكان لابِس؟ [ʔuṣfun zi:n. šča:n la:bis?] Think carefully. What was he wearing? صُفَنِت ساعَة لَكِن إسمَه ما جا عَلَى بالِي [ṣufanit sa:ʕa

ص

la:kin ʔismah ma: ǰa: ʕala ba:li] I pondered for an hour but his name didn't come to me. مِن أسألَه، يُصفُن قَبِل ما يجاوُب [min ʔasʔalah, yuṣfun gabil ma: yǰa:wub] When I question him, he reflects before he answers. آني دَأصفَن عَليه. شلُون يِكذِب عَلَيّا؟ [ʔa:ni daʔaṣfan ʕali:h. šlu:n yičðib ʕalayya?] I'm perplexed about him. How could he lie to me? • **2.** to stand with one foot slightly raised

صَفَّن [ṣaffan] *v:* • **1.** to daydream – ما يِقدَر يِفتِهِم الدَّرِس لِأَنَّه يصَفُّن [ma: yigdar yiftihim ʔiddaris liʔannah yṣaffun] He can't understand the lessons because he daydreams.

صَفُن [ṣafun] *n:* • **1.** daydreaming • **2.** meditation

صَفنَة [ṣufna] *n:* صَفنات [ṣufna:t] *pl:* • **1.** a period of daydreaming – أخذَتَه الصَّفنَة وَما إفتِهَم شقُلتلَه [ʔaxðatah ʔiṣṣafna wma ʔiftiham šgultlah] A blank look came over him and he didn't understand what I told him.

صافِن [ṣa:fin] *adj:* • **1.** thoughtful • **2.** meditating, pondering

ص ف و

صُفَى [ṣufa:] *v:* • **1.** to be or become clear, unpolluted, limpid, unclouded, pure – صُفَت الدِّنيا وَبَعَد ماكُو عَجاج [ṣufat ʔiddinya wabaʕad ma:ku ʕaǰa:ǰ] The weather cleared up and afterward there was no more dust. بَعَد ما يِصفَى المَيّ، إشرَب مِنَّه [baʕad ma: yiṣfa: ʔilmayy, ʔišrab minnah] After the water clears, drink some of it. • **2.** to remain, be left over – إذا أنطِيكُم خَمسَة خَمسَة، ما راح يِصفالِي شِي [ʔiða ʔanṭi:kum xamsa xamsa, ma: ra:ħ yiṣfa:li ši] If I give you each five, nothing will be left for me.

صَفَّى [ṣaffa:] *v:* • **1.** to make clear, unpolluted, limpid, unclouded, pure, to purify – يصَفُّون ماي الشَّطّ وَيضِخُّوه لِلبيُوت [yṣaffu:n ma:y ʔiššaṭṭ wyðixxu:h lilbyu:t] They purify the river water and pump it to the houses. • **2.** to refine – وين يصَفُّون نَفُط هَالمَنطِقَة؟ [wi:n yṣaffu:n nafuṭ halmanṭiqa?] Where do they refine the oil from this area? • **3.** to clear up, settle, straighten out – لازِم تصَفِّي شُغلَك قَبِل ما تسافِر [la:zim tṣaffi šuɣlak gabil ma: tsa:fir] You'll have to clear up your work before you leave town. صَفَّيت حسابَك وِيّا الشَّرِكَة؟ [ṣaffi:t ħsa:bak wiyya ʔiššarika?] Did you settle your account with the company? • **4.** to drain, pour off the water – بَعَد ما تصَفِّي التِّمَّن، خَلِّي عَليه دِهِن [baʕad ma: tṣaffi ʔittimman, xalli: ʕali:h dihin] After you drain the rice, put some oil on it.

تصَفَّى [tṣaffa:] *v:* • **1.** to be ironed out • **2.** to be purified

تصافَى [tṣa:fa:] *v:* • **1.** to settle up, become even, reach amiable terms with each other – إذا أنطِيك عَشِر دَنانِير، يكُون تصافينا [ʔiða ʔanṭi:k ʕašir dana:ni:r, yku:n tṣa:fi:na] If I give you ten dinars, we'll be even. ظَلَّوا زَعلانِين شَهَر وَبَعدين تصافَوا [ðallaw zaʕla:ni:n šahar wbaʕdi:n tṣa:faw] They stayed mad for a month and then made up.

اِصطِفَى [ʔiṣṭifa:] *v:* • **1.** same as تصافَى: to settle up, become even, reach amiable terms with each other – إنطِينِي فلُوسِي وَإنتَ رُوح اِصطِفِي وِيّاه [ʔinṭi:ni flu:si wʔinta ru:ħ ʔiṣṭifi wiyya:h] Give me my money and you go clear it up with him.

صَفُو [ṣafw] *n:* • **1.** clearness, purity, limpidity

مَصفِي [maṣfi] *n:* مَصافِي [maṣa:fi:] *pl:* • **1.** strainer, filter • **2.** sieve • **3.** colander

مَصفَة [maṣfa] *n:* مَصافِي [maṣa:fi] *pl:* • **1.** refinery

صَفاء [ṣafa:ʔ] *n:* • **1.** clearness, purity, limpidity

مِصفاة [miṣfa, miṣfa:t] *n:* • **1.** strainer, filter, sieve, colander

تَصفِيَة [taṣfiya] *n:* تَصفِيات [taṣfiya:t] *pl:* • **1.** purification, clarification, filtration • **2.** liquidation, clearance • **3.** elimination (also in sports)

صافِي [ṣa:fi] *adj:* • **1.** clear, limpid, pure, unpolluted, unmixed, unadulterated – السِّما صافيَة اليُوم [ʔissima: ṣa:fya ʔilyu:m] The sky is clear today. مَيّ النَّهَر صافِي [mayy ʔinnahar ṣa:fi] The river water's clear. رِبِح صافِي [ribiħ ṣa:fi] net profit. إجَّتَه صافيَة دافيَة [ʔiǰattah ṣa:fya da:fya] He got it with no effort at all.

مصَفَّى [mṣaffa] *adj:* • **1.** clear, purified

أصفَى [ʔaṣfa] *comparative adjective:* • **1.** more or most clear, pure, unpolluted

ص ق ر

صُوقَر [ṣu:gar] *v:* • **1.** to insure, to underwrite – راح أصُوقِر البِضاعَة مالتِي [ra:ħ ʔaṣawgir ʔilbiða:ʕa ma:lti] I'm going to insure my goods. • **2.** to ensure, assure, guarantee – إنطِينِي مُهلَة يومَين وَآنِي أصَوقِرلَك التَّرفِيع [ʔinṭi:ni muhla yu:mayn waʔa:ni ʔaṣu:girak ʔitttarfi:ʕ] Give me two day's time and I can assure you of the promotion. وُصُولَه اليُوم مصُوقَر [wuṣu:lah ʔilyu:m mṣu:gar] His arrival today is assured.

تصُوقَر [tṣu:gar] *v:* • **1.** to be insured – ماكُو حاجَة البَضايِع اللِّي ما تِحتِرِق تِتصُوقَر [ma:ku ħa:ǰa ʔilbaða:yiʕ ʔilli ma: tiħtirig titṣu:gar] There's no need for goods which won't catch fire to be insured. • **2.** to be ensured, guarantee – بَسّ يِوافِق المُدِير إجازتِي، تِتصُوقَر [bass yiwa:fiq ʔilmudi:r ʔiǰa:zti, titṣu:gar] As soon as the director approves my leave, it'll be guaranteed.

صقَر [ṣagur, ṣigar, ṣaqur, ṣaqir] *n:* صقُور [ṣgu:r, ṣqu:r] *pl:* • **1.** falcon

صَوقَرتَة [ṣu:garta] *n:* • **1.** insurance

مصوقَر [mṣu:gar] *adj:* • **1.** insured, underwritten • **2.** assured, ensured, guaranteed – مصُوقَر مِن أجِي لِبَغداد أمُرّ عَلَيكُم [mṣu:gar min ʔaǰi libayda:d ʔamurr ʕali:kum] Of course when I come to Baghdad I'll come to see you.

ص

ص ق ع

صِقَع [ṣigaʕ] *v:* • **1.** to slap on top of the head – الأمّ صِقعَت إبنها مِن فَشّر [ʔilʔumm ṣigʕat ʔibinha min faššar] The mother slapped her son on top of the head when he talked dirty. خُشّ لِلبَيت لا تصِقعَك الشّمِس [xušš lilbayt laː tṣigʕak ʔiššamis] Go in the house so you won't get sunstroke.

صَقِع [ṣagiʕ] *n:* • **1.** slapping on top of the head

صَقِيع [ṣaqiːʕ] *adj:* • **1.** loose-tongued, prattling, garrulous • **2.** foolish, silly – شلُون صَقِيع! صُرَف فلُوسَه وَهَسَّة ما عِندَه أُجُور المَدرَسَة [šluːn ṣaqiːʕ! ṣuraf fluːsah whassa maː ʕindah ʔujuːr ʔilmadrasa] How foolish! He spent his money and now he doesn't have tuition for school. لا تصِير صَقِيع. إذا تبَطِّل، تمُوت مِن الجُوع [laː tṣiːr ṣaqiːʕ. ʔiða tbaṭṭil, tmuːt min ʔijjuːʕ] Don't be foolish. If you quit, you'll starve. • **3.** as Noun: frost • **4.** cold (of a person), distant

ص ق ل

صِقَل [ṣiqal] *v:* • **1.** to smooth, polish, burnish – صِقَل الصِّينِيَّة بِجَلّافَة [ṣiqal ʔiṣṣiːniyya bǰallaːfa] He polished the tray with a scouring pad.

صَقِل [ṣaqil] *n:* • **1.** polishing, burnishing

صَقلَة [ṣagla] *n:* • **1.** a children's game, similar to jacks, played with pebbles

مَصقُول [maṣquːl] *adj:* • **1.** polished, burnished, smoothed • **2.** (coll.) sugar-coated almonds, Jordan almonds

مَصقُولَة [maṣquːla] *adj:* مَصقُولات [maṣquːlaːt] *pl:* • **1.** (unit noun of مَصقُول [maṣquːl] sugar-coated almond, Jordanian almond

ص ك ك [1]

صَكّ [ṣakk] *v:* • **1.** to clench, close tight – الجّاهِل صَكّ رِجلَيه مِن البَرِد [ʔijjaːhil ṣakk rijlayh min ʔilbarid] The kid closed his legs because of the cold. • **2.** to become hard, solid, to harden, set, solidify – لا تفُوت مِن هنا. الشّبِنتُو بَعدَه ما صَكّ [laː tfuːt min hina. ʔiččbintu baʕdah maː ṣakk] Don't go through here. The cement still hasn't hardened. المَيّ صَكّ بالكلاص [ʔilmayy ṣakk bilglaːṣ] The water froze in the glass.

ص ك ك [2]

صَكّ [ṣakk] *n:* صَكّات، صكُوك [ṣakkaːt, ṣkuːk] *pl:* • **1.** check, draft

ص ل

صالَة [ṣaːla] *n:* صالات [ṣaːlaːt] *pl:* • **1.** auditorium, assembly hall • **2.** large room

ص ل ب [1]

تصَلَّب [tṣallab] *v:* • **1.** to become hard, solid, firm, rigid – تصَلّبَت عِندَه الشّرايين ودِخَل المُستَشفَى [tṣallubat ʕindah ʔiššaraːyiːn wdixal ʔilmustašfa] His arteries hardened and he entered the hospital. تصَلَّب بمَوقِفَه وَما قِبَل يتفاهَم [tṣallab bimawqifah wamaː qibal yitfaːham] He took a rigid position and refused to listen to reason.

تَصَلُّب [taṣallub] *n:* • **1.** hardness, callousness, stiffness • **2.** hardening (especially of the arteries)

صَلابَة [ṣalaːba] *n:* • **1.** hardness, firmness, rigidity • **2.** intolerance, stubbornness, obstinacy, doggedness – تمَسَّك بِرَأيَه بِصَلابَة [tmassak braʔyah bṣalaːba] He stuck to his opinion stubbornly.

صَلِب [ṣalib] *adj:* • **1.** hard, firm, rigid • **2.** stubborn, dogged, tenacious

صلُبِي [ṣlubi] *adj:* صلُبَة [ṣluba] *pl:* • **1.** nomad, desert dweller

متصَلِّب [mitṣallib] *adj:* • **1.** inflexible, hard, tenacious, intolerant

أَصلَب [ʔaṣlab] *comparative adjective:* • **1.** more or most hard, firm, rigid • **2.** more or most stubborn, tenacious

ص ل ب [2]

صِلَب [ṣilab] *v:* • **1.** to crucify – المَسِيح، صِلبَوه عالصَّلِيب [ʔilmasiːħ, ṣilbawh ʕaṣṣaliːb] They crucified Christ on the cross. • **2.** to hang, execute – صِلبَوا القاتِل الفَجِر [ṣilbaw ʔilkaːtil ʔilfajir] They hanged the killer at dawn. • **3.** to keep (someone) waiting – صِلَبنِي ساعَة بِالمَحَطَّة [ṣilabni saːʕa bilmaħaṭṭa] He left me stranded at the station for an hour.

صَلُب [ṣalub] *n:* • **1.** crucifixion

صَلِيب [ṣaliːb] *n:* صُلبان [ṣulbaːn] *pl:* • **1.** cross – صَلِيب مَعكُوف [ṣaliːb maʕkuːf] swastika.

صَلّاب [ṣallaːb] *n:* صَلّابَة [ṣallaːba] *pl:* • **1.** hangman

صَلِيبِي، الحُرُوب الصَلِيبِيَّة [ṣaliːbi, ʔilħuruːb ʔiṣṣaliːbiyya] *n:* • **1.** The Crusades

ص ل ب خ

صَلبَخ [ṣalbax] *v:* • **1.** to be or become like stone, to petrify, calcify – التُّنقَة صَلبُخَت وَبَعَد ما تبَرِّد مَيّ [ʔittunga ṣalbuxat wabaʕad maː tbarrid mayy] The jar has calcified and won't cool water any more. هُوَّ مصَلبُخ وَدَمَّه ثِقِيل [huwwa mṣalbux wdammah θigiːl] He's got a stone face and he's a bore.

صَلبُوخ [ṣalbuːx] *n:* صلابِيخ [ṣlaːbiːx] *pl:* • **1.** stone, rock

ص ل ح

صِلَح [ṣilaħ] *v:* • **1.** to be proper, good, right, righteous, pious, godly – لا تطَفِّي الشّمعَة عالقَبُر. ما يِصلَح [laː ṭṭaffi ʔiššamʕa ʕalgabur. maː yiṣlaħ] Don't put out the candle on the grave. It isn't proper. هَذا فَدّ واحِد ما يِصلَح. عَليه ألف قَضِيَّة [haːða fadd waːħid maː yiṣlaħ. ʕaliːh ʔalf qaðiyya] He's a bad guy. He's got a thousand things against him. • **2.** to be useful, practicable, serviceable, suitable, fit –

ص

شُوف هَالقَلَم يِصلَحلَك [šu:f halqalam yiṣlaħlak] See if this pen suits you. هُوَّ ما يِصلَح يصِير مُدِير [huwwa ma: yiṣlaħ yṣi:r mudi:r] He isn't fit to be director.
صَلَّح [ṣallaħ] *v:* • **1.** to correct, set in order, adjust, settle – صَلَّح خَمسِين دَفتَر مِن دَفاتِر الامتِحان [ṣallaħ xamsi:n daftar min dafa:tir ʔilʔimtiħa:n] He corrected fifty of the examination booklets. • **2.** to repair, fix, mend, restore to usefulness – صَلَّح الرّاديُو لَو بَعَد؟ [ṣallaħ ʔirra:dyu law baʕad?] Did he fix the radio yet? لا تِشتِري الشَّربَة قَبُل ما يصَلّحلَك إيّاها [la: tištiri ʔiššarba gabul ma: yṣallaħlak ʔiyya:ha] Don't buy the clay jug before he patches it for you.
صالَح [ṣa:laħ] *v:* • **1.** to make peace, become reconciled, reach a settlement or compromise with – وَلَو صُوجَه، بَسّ راح أصالحَه [walaw ṣu:čah, bass ra:ħ ʔaṣa:lħah] Even though it is his fault, I'll make up with him.
أصلَح [ʔaṣlaħ] *v:* • **1.** to reform, improve, set right, amend, rectify – لازِم نِصلِح الأوضاع [la:zim niṣliħ ʔilʔawḍa:ʕ] We have to improve the conditions. • **2.** to act as a mediator, bring about peace, agreement, conciliation – دَزّوه حَتَّى يِصلِح بين القَبِيلتَين [dazzawh ħatta yiṣliħ bi:n ʔilqabi:ltayn] They sent him to make peace between the two tribes.
تصَلَّح [tṣallaħ] *v:* • **1.** to be repaired, to be fixed
تصالَح [tṣa:laħ] *v:* • **1.** to become reconciled, make peace with each other – تصالحَوا وَصارَوا أصدِقاء مَرَّة ثانيَة [tṣa:lħaw wṣa:raw ʔaṣdiqa:ʔ marra θa:nya] They made up and became friends again.
انصِلَح [ʔinṣilaħ] *v:* • **1.** to become a better person
اِصطِلَح [ʔiṣṭilaħ] *v:* • **1.** to make peace, become reconciled, reach an agreement or compromise – اِصطِلحَوا بَعَد زَعَل سَنَة [ʔiṣṭilħaw baʕad zaʕal sana] They made up after not speaking for a year. • **2.** to apply, assign – اِصطِلحَوا عَليها فَدّ إسِم غَرِيب [ʔiṣṭilħaw ʕali:ha fadd ʔisim ɣari:b] They applied a strange name to it. • **3.** with عَلَى to agree upon, accept, adopt – اِصطِلحَوا عَلَى هالإشارَة بَيناتهُم [ʔiṣṭilħaw ʕala halʔiša:ra bayna:thum] They agreed upon this signal between themselves.
صُلُح [ṣuluħ] *n:* • **1.** peace, reconciliation, settlement of differences – مَحكَمَة الصُّلح [maħkamat ʔiṣṣulħ] the lowest criminal court.
صلاح [ṣla:ħ] *n:* • **1.** patching material for pottery
مُصَلِّح [muṣalliħ] *n:* مُصَلّحِين [muṣalliħi:n] *pl:* • **1.** repairman, fixer, correcter, grader
صَلاح [ṣala:ħ] *n:* • **1.** good, proper or right condition • **2.** righteousness, probity, pious nature (of a person)
مَصلَحَة [maṣlaħa] *n:* مَصالِح [maṣa:liħ] *pl:* • **1.** benefit, interest, advantage, welfare • **2.** government administered agency, department, authority – مَصلَحَة نَقل الرُّكّاب [maṣlaħat naql ʔirrukka:b] public transit agency. • **3.** occupation, vocation, profession
إصلاح [ʔiṣla:ħ] *n:* إصلاحات [ʔiṣla:ħa:t] *pl:* • **1.** reform, correction, improvement, amelioration
مُصطَلَح [muṣṭalaħ] *n:* • **1.** generally accepted, agreed upon, conventional, customary • **2.** technical term • **3.** pl. مُصطَلَحات [muṣṭalaħa:t] idiomatic expressions
تَصلِيح [taṣli:ħ] *n:* • **1.** repair, repairing, fixing
تَصالُح [taṣa:luħ] *n:* • **1.** reconciliation, friendly settlement, amicable arrangement (jur.)
صَلاحِيَّة [ṣala:ħiyya] *n:* • **1.** suitability, fitness, appropriateness, aptness, applicability • **2.** usability, usefulness, use, practicability, worth • **3.** pl. صَلاحِيّات full power, authority, jurisdiction
اِصطِلاح [ʔiṣṭila:ħ] *n:* اِصطِلاحات [ʔiṣṭila:ħa:t] *pl:* • **1.** convention, agreement, practice, usage, thing agreed upon • **2.** (gram.) idiom, colloquial expression • **3.** technical term – اِصطِلاح فَنِّي [ʔiṣṭila:ħ fanni]
مُصالَحَة [muṣa:laħa] *n:* • **1.** reconciliation, peace, compromise, settlement
صالِح [ṣa:liħ] *adj:* • **1.** virtuous, pious, devout, godly • **2.** usable, practicable, suitable, appropriate, fitting, fit – هَالسَّيّارَة ما صالحَة لِلإستِعمال [hassayya:ra ma: ṣa:lħa lilʔistiʕma:l] This car isn't serviceable. ما صالِح لِلخِدمَة العَسكَرِيَّة [ma: ṣa:liħ lilxidma ʔilʕaskariyya] He isn't fit for military service. • **3.** pl. benefit, advantage, interest, good
إصلاحي [ʔiṣla:ħi] *adj:* • **1.** reformational, reform – مَدرَسَة إصلاحِيَّة [madrasa ʔiṣla:ħiyya] reform school, reformatory. سِياسَة إصلاحِيَّة [siya:sa ʔiṣla:ħiyya] policy of reform.
مَصلَحچي [maṣlaħči] *adj:* • **1.** opportunist
اِصطِلاحي [ʔiṣṭila:ħi] *adj:* • **1.** conventional, agreed upon • **2.** (gram.) idiomatic • **3.** technical – تَعبِير اِصطِلاحي [taʕbi:r ʔiṣṭila:ħi] technical term.
أصلَح [ʔaṣlaħ] *comparative adjective:* • **1.** more or most pious, virtuous, etc • **2.** more or most suitable, fitting, appropriate

ص ل ع

اِصلَعّ [ʔiṣlaʕʕ] *v:* • **1.** to be or become bald – اِصلَعّ بشَبابَه [ʔiṣlaʕʕ bšaba:bah] He became bald in his youth.
صَلَع [ṣalaʕ] *n:* • **1.** baldness
صَلعَة [ṣalʕa] *n:* صَلعات [ṣalʕa:t] *pl:* • **1.** bald head, bald spot
أصلَع [ʔaṣlaʕ] *adj:* صُلُع، صَلعِين [ṣuluʕ, ṣalʕi:n.] *pl:* صَلعَة [ṣalʕa] *feminine:* • **1.** bald, bald-headed • **2.** bald person

ص ل ف

صَلافَة [ṣala:fa] *n:* • **1.** boorishness, vainglory, rudeness
صَلِف [ṣalif] *adj:* صَلِفِين [ṣalifi:n] *pl:* • **1.** pompous, boorish, rude • **2.** boor

ص

ص ل ل

صَلّ [ṣall] *v:* • **1.** to be cold to the touch, to conduct coldness – الحَدِيد يصِلّ بِالشّتا هوايَة [ʔilħadiːd yṣill biššitaː hwaːya] Metal is very cold to the touch in the winter.

صِلّ [ṣill] *n:* صلال [ṣlaːl] *pl:* • **1.** small snake – لَئِيم مِثل الصِّلّ؛ بَسّ يحِبّ يأَذّي النّاس [laʔiːm miθl ʔiṣṣill; bass yħibb yʔaðði ʔinnaːs] He's as mean as a snake; he likes to hurt people.

ص ل و

صَلّى [ṣallaː] *v:* • **1.** to pray, perform the ritual of prayer – إبنِي يصَلّي وَيصُوم [ʔibni yṣalli wyṣuːm] My son prays and fasts. صَلّيت صَلاة الصُّبُح وَلّا بَعَد؟ [ṣalliːt ṣalaːt ʔiṣṣubuħ walla baʕad?] Have you performed the morning prayer yet?

صَلاة [ṣalaː(t)] *n:* صَلَوات [ṣalawaːt] *pl:* • **1.** praying, prayer – صَلَوات! الوَلَد قام يِمشِي [ṣalawaːt! ʔilwalad gaːm yimši] My! My! The boy's started to walk.

مَصلَى، مَصلَة [maṣla] *n:* مَصالِي [maṣaːli] *pl:* • **1.** place of prayer, oratory

مُصَلّي [muṣalli] *n:* • **1.** one who prays, worshiper

ص ل و ن

صالُون [ṣaːluːn] *n:* صالُونات [ṣaːluːnaːt] *pl:* • **1.** salon, parlor – صالُون حِلاقَة [ṣaːluːn ħilaːqa] barber shop. • **2.** sedan سَيّارَة صالُون

ص ل ي

صِلَة [ṣila] *n:* • **1.** to burn, scorch (fig.) – بالجَّول الشّمِس تِصلِي [biččawl ʔiššamis tiṣli] The sun is scorching hot in the desert. صِلانا بِهالأَسئِلَة الصَّعبَة [ṣilaːna bhalʔasʔila ʔiṣṣaʕba] He scorched us with these hard questions. • **2.** to rake, spray with gunfire – صِعَد عَالجِّبَل وَصِلاهُم بِرصاص الرَّشّاش [ṣiʕad ʕajǰibal wṣilaːhum birṣaːṣ ʔirraššaːš] He got up on the mountain and raked them with machine gun fire.

صَلِي [ṣaly] *n:* • **1.** burning, scorching (fig.) • **2.** spraying, raking

صَلَيَة [ṣalya] *n:* صَليات [ṣalyaːt] *pl:* • **1.** burst, volley

ص م ت

صامِت، فِلِم صامِت [ṣaːmit, filim ṣaːmit] *adj:* • **1.** silent movie

ص م خ

صُمَخ [ṣumax] *v:* • **1.** to endure, last, hold out, remain, survive – ما عَبالِي يُصمُخ هَالقَدّ [maː ʕabaːli yuṣmux halgadd] I never thought he'd stick it out so long. ما قِدَر يصمُخ بوَظِيفتَه الجِّدِيدَة [maː gidar yiṣmux bwaðiːftah ʔiǰǰidiːda] He couldn't bear to stay in his new position.

صَمُخ [ṣamux] *n:* • **1.** enduring, holding out, remaining, surviving

صماخ [ṣmaːx] *n:* صماخات [ṣmaːxaːt] *pl:* • **1.** head, dome • **2.** intellectual, egghead, brain

ص م د

صِمَد [ṣimad, ṣumad] *v:* • **1.** to hold out, stand up defiantly, resist stubbornly – إذا تصُمدُون، تحَقّقُون مَطالِيبكُم [ʔiða tṣumduːn, tħaqqiquːn maṭaːliːbkum] If you hold on stubbornly, your demands will be met. صُمدَوا بوِجه العَدُو [ṣumdaw bwijh ʔilʕadu] They held out in the face of the enemy.

صَمَّد [ṣammad] *v:* • **1.** to hoard, lay by, save (money) – دَيصَمِّد فلُوسَه حَتَّى يِشترِيلَه بَيت [dayṣammid fluːsah ħatta yištiriːlah bayt] He's hoarding his money to buy himself a house.

صَمِد [ṣamid] *n:* • **1.** resistance • **2.** as Adjective: tough, resistant

صُمُود [ṣumuːd] *n:* • **1.** steadfastness • **2.** remaining in power • **3.** resistance

صامِد [ṣaːmid] *adj:* • **1.** resistant

ص م غ

صَمَّغ [ṣammaɣ] *v:* • **1.** to put paste or glue on – صَمُّغ الصُّورَة حَتَّى أَلزَقها بِالكتاب [ṣammuɣ ʔiṣṣuːra ħatta ʔalzagha bilktaːb] Put some glue on the picture so I can paste it in the book.

صَمُغ [ṣamuɣ] *n:* صُمُوغ [ṣumuːɣ] *pl:* • **1.** mucilage, glue, paste

ص م م

صَمّ [ṣamm] *v:* • **1.** to close, shut – صُمّ إيدَك [ṣumm ʔiːdak] Close your hand.

صَمَّم [ṣammam] *v:* • **1.** to be determined, resolved, to make up one's mind, decide definitely – صَمَّمِت عالسَّفَر [ṣammamit ʕassafar] I made up my mind about traveling. صَمَّمِت أَرُوح [ṣammamit ʔaruːħ] I'm determined to go. • **2.** to design, plan – أَيّ مُهَندِس صَمَّم هالبِنايَة؟ [ʔayy muhandis ṣammam halbinaːya?] What engineer designed this building?

صَمّ [ṣamm] *n:* صمُوم [ṣmuːm] *pl:* • **1.** handful – صَمّ چُكلَيت [ṣamm čukliːt] a handful of candy.

صَمّام [ṣammaːm] *n:* صَمّامات [ṣammaːmaːt] *pl:* • **1.** valve, stopcock

مُصَمِّم [muṣammim] *n:* • **1.** designer

تَصمِيم [taṣmiːm] *n:* • **1.** design, designing • **2.** planning

صَمِيمِي [ṣamiːmi] *n:* • **1.** intimate • **2.** cordial, hearty

أَصَمّ [ʔaṣamm] *adj:* صُمّ [ṣumm] *pl:* • **1.** deaf

صَمِيم [ṣamiːm] *adj:* • **1.** true, genuine, authentic, through and through – عِراقِي صَمِيم [ʕiraːqi ṣamiːm] a true Iraqi. ضَربَة بِالصَّمِيم [ðarba biṣṣamiːm] a telling blow, effective hit. مِن صَمِيم القَلب [min ṣamiːm ʔilgalb] wholeheartedly. أَشكُرَك مِن صَمِيم قَلبِي

[ʔaškurak min ṣamiːm galbi] I thank you from the bottom of my heart.
مصَمِّم [mṣammim] *adj:* • **1.** determined
صَمّاء [ṣammaːʔ] *adj:* • **1.** deaf
مُصَمَّم [muṣammam] *adj:* • **1.** designed

ص م ن

صَمُّون [ṣammuːn] *n:* • **1.** (coll.) a kind of bread baked in large, oblong loaves, similar to French bread
صَمُّونَة [ṣammuːna] *n:* صَمُّونات [ṣammuːnaːt] *pl:* • **1.** a loaf of bread • **2.** nut (for a bolt or screw) • **3.** threaded joint in a pipe

ص ن ت

صِنَت [ṣinat] *v:* • **1.** to be or become silent, quiet, still – بَس ما دِخَل المُعَلِّم لِلصَّفّ، كُلّهُم صِنتَوا [bas maː dixal ʔilmuʕallim liṣṣaff, kullhum ṣinṭaw] As soon as the teacher entered the class, they all became silent.
تصَنَّت [tṣannat] *v:* • **1.** to eavesdrop, listen secretly – إسكُت. لا تِحكِي. أَعتِقِد أَكُو واحِد دَيِتصَنَّت [ʔiskut. laː tiħči. ʔaʕtiqid ʔaku waːħid dayitṣannaṭ] Hush. Don't talk. I think there's someone listening in.
صَنتَة [ṣanta] *n:* • **1.** quiet, silence, quietness, stillness – كُلّ الأشياء يسَوِّيها بِالصَّنتَة حَتَّى مَحَّد يِدرِي بِيه [kull ʔilʔašyaːʔ ysawwiːha biṣṣanṭa ħatta maħħad yidri biːh] He does everything quietly so that nobody'll know about it.
تَصَنُّت [taṣannut] *n:* • **1.** eavesdropping
صَنتاوي [ṣantaːwi] *adj:* • **1.** quiet, silent, taciturn, close-mouthed – حَصَّل عَلَى شُغُل بِالصَّنتاوي [ħaṣṣal ʕala šuɣul biṣṣanṭaːwi] He got a job without letting anyone know. • **2.** بِالصَّنتاوي quietly,silently, covertly, secretively, on the sly

ص ن د ق

صَندُوق [ṣanduːq] *n:* صَنادِيق [ṣnaːdiːq] *pl:* • **1.** place where money is kept, coffer, money box • **2.** treasurer – صَندُوق تَوفِير [ṣanduːq tawfiːr] postal savings. • **3.** cashier – صَندُوق الوِلايات [ṣanduːg ʔilwlaːyaːt] peep-show. صَندُوق يغَنّي [ṣanduːg yɣanni] gramophone, record player. • **4.** trunk (of an automobile), chest
صِندَقجَة [ṣindaqča] *n:* صِندَقجات [ṣindaqčaːt] *pl:* • **1.** small box, chest, trunk

ص ن د ل

صَندَل، صِندال [ṣandal, ṣindaːl] *n:* صَنادِل [ṣanaːdil] *pl:* • **1.** sandalwood • **2.** pl. صَنادِل (pair of) sandals

ص ن ص ل

صَنصَل [ṣanṣal] *v:* • **1.** to drip (water)
صَنصُول [ṣanṣuːl] *n:* • **1.** thin stream of water, small dripping of water • **2.** as Adj: skinny

ص ن ع

صِنَع [ṣinaʕ] *v:* • **1.** to manufacture, turn out, produce, make – هَالمَعمَل يِصنَع تايَرات [hallmaʕmal yiṣnaʕ taːyaraːt] This factory manufactures tires.
صَنَّع [ṣannaʕ] *v:* • **1.** to industrialize – الحُكُومَة راح تصَنِّع هَالمَنطِقَة [ʔilħukuːma raːħ tṣanniʕ halmanṭiqa] The government is going to industrialize this area. • **2.** to decorate, embellish – صَنّعَوا البِنايَة لِلعِيد [ṣannʕaw ʔilbinaːya lilʕiːd] They decorated the building for the holiday. • **3.** to apply cosmetics, to make up – صَنِّعَت نَفِسها قَبُل ما يِجُون الخُطّار [ṣanniʕat nafisha gabul maː yiǰuːn ʔilxuṭṭaːr] She made herself up before the guests came.
تصَنَّع [tṣannaʕ] *v:* • **1.** to behave in an artificial, affected, stilted manner – شدَعوَة تِتصَنَّع بِحَكيَك؟ [šdaʕwa titṣannaʕ bħačyak?] How come you're so affected in your speech? • **2.** to make oneself up, apply make-up – صارلِك ساعَة دَتِتصَنّعِين. ما تخَلّصِين عاد [ṣaːrlič saːʕa datitṣannʕiːn. maː txallṣiːn ʕaːd] You've been making up for an hour. Why don't you finish!
اِصطِنَع [ʔiṣṭinaʕ] *v:* • **1.** to fake, assume, put on, pretend, feign – اِصطِنَع الابتِسامَة حَتَّى يِخفِي خَجَلَه [ʔiṣṭinaʕ ʔilibtisaːma ħatta yixfi xaǰalah] He faked the smile to hide his embarrassment.
صَنِع [ṣaniʕ] *n:* • **1.** manufacturing, production, make
مَصنَع [maṣnaʕ] *n:* مَصانِع [maṣaːniʕ] *pl:* • **1.** plant, factory, works
صانِع [ṣaːniʕ] *n:* صِنّاع [ṣinnaːʕ] *pl:* • **1.** apprentice, helper • **2.** servant • **3.** a student under a mullah
صَنعَة [ṣanʕa] *n:* صَنعات، صَنايِع [ṣanʕaːt, ṣanaːyiʕ] *pl:* • **1.** trade, craft, occupation, technical or artistic skill
صِناعَة [ṣinaːʕa] *n:* صِناعات [ṣinaːʕaːt] *pl:* • **1.** industry, manufacturing
صَنِيعَة [ṣaniːʕa] *n:* • **1.** accomplishment • **2.** action, deed, favor
صَنعَة [ṣanʕa] *n:* صَنعَات [ṣanʕaːt] *pl:* • **1.** work, technical skill, occupation • **2.** craft, business, vocation
تَصنِيع [taṣniːʕ] *n:* • **1.** industrialization
مصَنَّع [mṣannaʕ] *adj:* • **1.** manufactured • **2.** industrialized
صِناعِي [ṣinaːʕi] *adj:* • **1.** industrial, manufacturing – مَنطِقَة صِناعِيَّة [manṭiqa ṣinaːʕiyya] an industrial area.
مَصنُوع [maṣnuːʕ] *adj: /n* مَصنُوعات [maṣnuːʕaːt] *pl:* • **1.** manufactured • 2. product, produced article
مُصطَنَع [muṣṭanaʕ] *adj:* • **1.** affected, sham, put-on, phony – ضِحكاتها كُلّها مُصطَنَعَة [ðiħkaːtha kullha muṣṭanaʕa] Her laughter is all phony.
متصَنِّع [mitṣanniʕ] *adj:* • **1** behaving in an affected or unnatural way • **2.** fake
اِصطِناعِي [ʔiṣṭinaːʕi] *adj:* • **1.** artificial, synthetic, imitation – رِجِل اِصطِناعِيَّة [riǰil ʔiṣṭinaːʕiyya] artificial leg. لاستِيك اِصطِناعِي [laːstiːk ʔiṣṭinaːʕi] synthetic rubber.

ص ن ف

صَنَّف [ṣannaf] *v:* • **1.** to classify, categorize, sort – الحُكومَة صَنِّفَت دافِعِين الضَّرائِب إلَى خَمِس أصناف [ʔilħuku:ma ṣannifat da:fʕi:n ʔiððara:ʔib ʔila xamis ʔaṣna:f] The government classified the taxpayers into five groups. صَنِّف البِضاعَة وَخَلّي عَلَى كُلّ صِنِف سِعِر [ṣannif ʔilbiða:ʕa wxalli: ʕala kull ṣinif siʕir] Sort the goods and put a price on each category. • **2.** with عَلَى to ridicule, mock, make fun of – ظَلّوا يصَنِّفُون عَليه مُدَّة إلَى أن زِعَل [ðallaw yṣannifu:n ʕali:h mudda ʔila ʔan ziʕal] They kept ridiculing him for some time until he got mad.

صِنِف [ṣinif] *n:* أصناف، صُنُوف [ʔaṣna:f, ṣunu:f] *pl:* • **1.** kind, sort, type • **2.** genus, species, class, category

تَصنِيف [taṣni:f] *n:* • **1.** classification, categorization, sorting • **2.** (pl. تَصنِيفات) farce, sham, mockery – شُغلِي شلَونَه؟ تَصنِيف. كُلّ شِي ما دَأسَوِّي [šuɣli šlu:nah? taṣni:f. kull ši ma: daʔasawwi:] How's my work? A farce. I don't do a thing.

مصَنِّفجِي [mṣannifči] *adj:* مصَنِّفجِيَّة [mṣannifčiyya] *pl:* • **1.** joker, buffoon, clown

ص ن م

صَنَم [ṣanam] *n:* أصنام [ʔaṣna:m] *pl:* • **1.** idol, image – واقُف مِثل الصَّنَم. ما يِتحَرَّك [wa:guf miθl ʔiṣṣanam. ma: yitħarrak] He's standing like a statue. He isn't moving.

ص ن ن

صَنَّن [ṣannan] *v:* • **1.** to smell of perspiration – فانِيلتَه صَنِّنَت مِن العَرَق [fa:ni:ltah ṣanninat min ʔilʕarag] His undershirt stank from perspiration.

صنان [ṣna:n] *n:* • **1.** body odor, odor from the armpits

مصَنِّن [mṣannin] *adj:* • **1.** stinky, malodorous

ص ن و ب ر

صِنُوبَر [ṣinu:bar] *n:* • **1.** pine tree(s) • **2.** pine nut(s)

صِنُوبرَة [ṣinu:bra] *n:* صنُوبَرات [ṣnu:bara:t] *pl:* • **1.** pine tree

ص ه ل

صِهَل [ṣihal] *v:* • **1.** to neigh, whinny – الحصان دَيِصهِل [ʔilħṣa:n dayiṣhil] The horse is neighing.

صِهِيل [ṣihi:l] *n:* • **1.** whinnying, neighing

ص ه ي ن

صَهيُون [ṣahyu:n] *n:* • **1.** Zion

صَهيُونِيَّة [ṣahyu:niyya] *n:* • **1.** Zionism

صَهيُونِي [ṣahyu:ni] *adj:* • **1.** Zionistic,(as n:) Zionist

ص و ب 1

صاب [ṣa:b] *v:* • **1.** to strike, afflict (principally the evil eye) – العين صابَتَه [ʔilʕi:n ṣa:batah] The evil eye fell on him. An evil spell was cast upon him. حاطَّة حِرز عَلَى صَدِر إبنها حَتَّى لا تصِيبَه العين [ħa:ṭṭa ħiriz ʕala ṣadir ʔibinha ħatta la: tṣi:bah ʔilʕayn] She's put an amulet on her son's chest so the evil eye won't affect him. صابَتَه بِعَين وَتوَجِّع [ṣa:batah bʕayn wtwaǰǰiʕ] She gave him the evil eye and he got sick. • **2.** to hit (a target)

صَوَّب [ṣawwab] *v:* • **1.** to aim, point – صَوَّب البُندُقِيَّة عَلَيّا [ṣawwab ʔilbunduqiyya ʕalayya] He aimed the rifle at me. • **2.** to hit (a target), to shoot – الشُّرطَة صَوُّبتَه برِجلَه [ʔiššurṭa ṣawwubatah brijlah] The police shot him in his leg.

أصاب [ʔaṣa:b] *v:* • **1.** to hit (a target) – ما تصِيب الهَدَف إذا ما تِتقَرَّب شوَيَّة [ma: tṣi:b ʔilhadaf ʔiða ma: titgarrab šwayya] You won't hit the target if you don't get a little closer. القَنابُل أصابَت الهَدَف [ʔilqana:bul ʔaṣa:bat ʔilhadaf] The bombs hit the target. • **2.** to befall, happen to, fall to the lot of – شقَدّ أصابَك مِن الوِرث؟ [šgadd ʔaṣa:bak min ʔilwiriθ?] How much did you get from the inheritance? حَظَّه مَرَّة يخطِي ومَرَّة يصِيب [ħaððah marra yixṭi wmarra yṣi:b] One time his luck misses and one time it holds. أصابَتَه خَسارَة كِبِيرَة [ʔaṣa:batah xasa:ra čibi:ra] He suffered a great loss. أصابَه غُبُن [ʔaṣa:bah ɣubun] He got a raw deal. • **3.** to strike, attack, afflict – لا تخُشّ بهَالغُرفَة. يصِيبَك مَرَض [la: txušš bhalɣurfa. yṣi:bak marað] Don't enter that room. You'll catch a disease. إذا تعَقِّم كُلّشِي، مِن الصَّعُب يصِيبَك مَرَض [ʔiða tʕaqqim kullši, min ʔiṣṣaʕub yṣi:bak marað] If you sterilize everything, it'll be difficult for a sickness to strike you. أصابَتَه اِنتِكاسَة بَعَد العَمَلِيَّة [ʔaṣa:batah ʔintika:sa baʕad ʔilʕamaliyya] He had a relapse after the operation.

تصَوَّب [tṣawwab] *v:* • **1.** to be hit (by a bullet), to be shot – تصَوَّب وَأخذَوه لِلمُستَشفَى [tṣawwab wʔaxðawh lilmustašfa] He got shot and they took him to the hospital.

اِنصاب [ʔinṣa:b] *v:* • **1.** to be stricken, afflicted, to catch (a disease) – اِنصاب بِالسِّلّ [ʔinṣa:b bissill] He was stricken by tuberculosis. • **2.** to be hit, be shot – اِنصاب بِطَلقَة بِكِتفَه الأيمَن [ʔinṣa:b bṭalqa bčitfah ʔilʔayman] He caught a bullet in his right shoulder.

اِستَصوَب [ʔistaṣwab] *v:* • **1.** to approve, sanction – اِستَصوَب الحَلّ مالِي لِلمُشكِلَة [ʔistaṣwab ʔilħall ma:li lilmuškila] He approved of my solution to the problem.

صوب [ṣawb] *n:* • **1.** side, bank (of a river) • **2.** direction, quarter • **3.** advantage, favor – مِن صوب [min ṣu:b] to the advantage of. هَالسِّعِر زين وَمِن صُوبَك [hassiʕir zi:n wmin ṣu:bak] This price is fair and to your advantage. طَبعاً تحِبَّه، لِأنّ يِحكِي مِن صُوبَك [ṭabʕan tħibbah, liʔann yiħči min ṣu:bak] Of course you like him, because he speaks in your favor.

صواب [ṣwa:b] *n:* • **1.** louse eggs • **2.** bullet wound • **3.** pl. صوابات hit, strike, blow

ص

صَواب [ṣawa:b] *n:* • **1.** reason
إصابَة [ʔiṣa:ba] *n:* إصابات [ʔiṣa:ba:t] *pl:* • **1.** score, goal – مَدرَستنا غُلبَتهُم بإصابتَين [madrasatna ɣulbathum bʔiṣa:bti:n] Our school beat them by two goals. • **2.** injury, wound, state of being afflicted (by a disease) – أَكُو إصابَة بالجِّدري بِهالمَنطَقَة [ʔaku ʔiṣa:ba bijjidri bhalmanṭaqa] There's a case of smallpox in that neighborhood. • **3.** (attack of) illness, sickness
مُصِيبَة [muṣi:ba] *n:* مُصايِب [muṣa:yib] *pl:* • **1.** tragedy, calamity, disaster, misfortune – هاي صُدُق مُصِيبَة. المِسكِين كُلّ ولدَه ماتَوا بالحادِث [ha:y ṣudug muṣi:ba. ʔilmiski:n kull wildah ma:taw bilħa:diθ] This is a real tragedy. All the poor man's sons died in the accident. • **2.** fuss, to-do, ado – سَوّيتها مُصِيبَة عاد [sawwi:tha muṣi:ba ʕa:d] You've made a big to-do out of it!
تَصويب [taṣwi:b] *n:* • **1.** aiming, pointing • **2.** correction, rectification
مُصِيب [muṣi:b] *adj:* • **1.** pertinent, apropos, correct, on the mark, to the point
مُصاب [muṣa:b] *adj:* مُصابِين [muṣa:bi:n] *pl:* • **1.** injured
مَصيُوب [maṣyu:b] *adj:* مَصيُوبِين، مصاوِيب [maṣyu:bi:n, mṣa:wi:b] *pl:* • **1.** casualty, wounded person
مِنصاب [minṣa:b] *adj:* • **1.** injured, wounded, sick, ill, • **2.** casualty, victim of an accident, wounded person
مِتصَوِّب [mitṣawwib] *adj:* مِتصَوِّبِين [mitṣawwibi:n] *pl:* • **1.** injured
أَصوَب [ʔaṣwab] *comparative adjective:* • **1.** more or most pertinent, apropos, correct

ص و ب 2

صُوبَة [ṣu:pa] *n:* صُوبات [ṣu:pa:t] *pl:* • **1.** kerosene heater

ص و ب ط

صُوباط [ṣu:ba:ṭ] *n:* صوابِيط [ṣwa:bi:ṭ] *pl:* • **1.** arbor, bower – صُوبَاط عِنَب [ṣu:ba:ṭ ʕinab] grape arbor.

ص و ت

صَوَّت [ṣawwat] *v:* • **1.** to vote, cast a ballot – ما يحُقّلَك تصَوِّت مَرّتَين [ma: yħuqqlak tṣawwit marrtayn] You aren't supposed to vote twice.
صُوت [ṣu:t, ṣawt] *n:* أَصوات [ʔaṣwa:t] *pl:* • **1.** sound, noise • **2.** voice • **3.** vote, ballot – الصُّوت، وَالله مالِي أَيّ عِلاقَة بِيه [ʔiṣṣu:t, wallah ma:li ʔayy ʕila:qa bi:h] Take it from me, I swear I have nothing to do with it. مِن تِهمُوه بالبوقَة، ساح الصُّوت وقال هُوَّ بَرِيء [min tihmu:h bilbu:ga, sa:ħ ʔiṣṣu:t wga:l huwwa bari:ʔ] When they accused him of the theft, he swore he was innocent.
صِيت [ṣi:t] *n:* • **1.** repute, standing, prestige • **2.** fame, renown – ذايِع الصِّيت [ða:yiʕ ʔiṣṣi:t] famous, celebrated, well-known. هُوَّ ذايِع الصِّيت بِالفَنّ [huwwa ða:yiʕ ʔiṣṣi:t bilfann] He is famous for his art. مِن غِلَب، طِلَع صِيتَه [min ɣilab, ṭilaʕ ṣi:tah] After he won, his fame spread.
تَصويت [taṣwi:t] *n:* • **1.** voting, polling, vote, balloting
صَوتي [ṣu:ti, ṣawti] *adj:* • **1.** sonant, sound-, sonic, acoustic, vocal – خُيُوط صَوتِيَّة [xuyu:ṭ sawtiyya] vocal chords.

ص و ج

صَوَّج [ṣawwač] *v:* • **1.** to accuse, blame – لُويش دَتصَوِّجنِي؟ آنِي شَعلَيّا [luwi:š dadṣawwični? ʔa:ni šaʕlayya] Why are you blaming me? I had nothing to do with it. • **2.** to convict, find guilty – المَحكَمَة صَوِّجَتَه [ʔilmaħkama ṣawwičatah] The court found him guilty.
تصَوَّج [tṣawwač] *v:* • **1.** pass. of صَوَّج: to be accused, blamed – لا تخُشّ لِلغُرفَة تَرَة تِتصَوَّج [la: txušš lilɣurfa tara titṣawwač] Don't enter the room or you'll be blamed.
صُوج [ṣu:č] *n:* • **1.** blame, fault, guilt – لا تذِبّ عَلَيّا الصُّوج. آنِي ما كِنِت مَوجُود [la: dðibb ʕalayya ʔiṣṣu:č. ʔa:ni ma: činit mawǰu:d] Don't throw the blame onto me. I wasn't there. صُوجَك. إنتَ اللّي إنطَيتَه مَجال يِحكِي [ṣu:čak. ʔinta ʔilli ʔinṭi:tah maǰa:l yiħči] It is your fault. You gave him a chance to talk.
مُصوِج [muṣwič] *adj:* • **1.** at fault, deserving of blame, guilty • **2.** one who is at fault, one who is to blame, guilty party

ص و د

صُودَة [ṣu:da] *n:* • **1.** soda, sodium carbonate • **2.** baking soda, sodium bicarbonate • **3.** soda water • **4.** carbonated beverage

ص و ر

صَوَّر [ṣawwar] *v:* • **1.** to represent, depict, portray – هَالرَّسِم يصَوِّر الحَياة بِالرِّيف العِراقِي [harrasim yṣawwir ʔilħaya:t birri:f ʔilʕira:qi] This drawing depicts life in the Iraq countryside.
تصَوَّر [tṣawwar] *v:* • **1.** to conceive, imagine, think – هَالسَّيّارَة مُو غالِيَة مِثلما تِتصَوَّر [hassayya:ra mu: ɣa:lya miθilma titṣawwar] This car's not as expensive as you imagine. تِتصَوَّر يِقدَر يرُوح لأُورُبّا بِلا مُوافقَة أَهلَه؟ [titṣawwar yigdar yiru:ħ lʔu:ruppa bila muwa:faqat ʔahlah?] Do you think he can go to Europe without his family's approval? هَذا شِي ما يِتصَوَّرَه العَقِل [ha:ða ši ma: yitṣawwarah ʔilʕaqil] That's inconceivable.
صُورَة [ṣu:ra] *n:* صُوَر [ṣuwar] *pl:* • **1.** image, likeness, picture • **2.** photograph • **3.** copy, duplicate • **4.** replica • **5.** sura, chapter or section of the Koran • **6.** way, manner – حِكاها بِصُورَة جِدِّيَّة [ħiča:ha bṣu:ra ǰiddiyya] He said it seriously. قُلّه إيّاه بِصُورَة ما يِزعَل بِيها

[gullah ʔiyya:h bṣu:ra ma: yizʕal bi:ha] Tell it to him in such a way that he won't get mad.
دَبِّرلِي فلُوس بأي صُورَة مِن الصُّوَر [dabbirli flu:s bʔay ṣu:ra min ʔiṣṣuwar] Get me some money any way possible. • **7.** as a special case, as an exception – قِبلوه بِالجّامِعَة بِصُورَة خاصَّة [qiblu:h bijja:miʕa bṣu:ra xa:ṣṣa] They admitted him to the university as a special case. • **8.** especially, particularly, in particular – دِير بالَك عالأوراق، وَبصُورَة خاصَّة، مَكاتِيب المُدِير [di:r ba:lak ʕalʔawra:q, wbṣu:ra xa:ṣṣa, maka:ti:b ʔilmudi:r] Take good care of the papers, and especially the director's correspondence.
بَغداد حِلوَة بِالرَّبِيع بِصُورَة خاصَّة [bayda:d ħilwa birrabi:ʕ bṣu:ra xa:ṣṣa] Baghdad is beautiful in springtime especially.
مُصَوِّر [muṣawwir] *n:* مُصَوِّرِين [muṣawwiri:n] *pl:* • **1.** photographer, cameraman
تَصَوُّر [taṣawwur] *n:* • **1.** imagination, impression, conception, concept • **2.** fancy, idea, fantasy
تَصوِير [taṣwi:r] *n:* • **1.** photography • **2.** representation, portrayal, depiction • **3.** pl. تَصاوِير photograph
تَصوِيرَة [taṣwi:ra] *n:* تَصاوِير [taṣa:wi:r] *pl:* • **1.** picture, image, illustration, pictorial representation • **2.** photo
تَصَوُّرِي [taṣawwuri] *adj:* • **1.** fantastic, fictitious, fancied • **2.** imaginary, existing in imagination only
تَصوِيرِي [taṣwi:ri] *adj:* • **1.** depictive, descriptive

ص و ص

صَوص [ṣu:ṣ] *n:* • **1.** sauce

ص و غ

صاغ [ṣa:ɣ] *v:* • **1.** to fashion, form, mold, create – يا صايِغ صاغلِك القلادَة؟ [ya: ṣa:yiɣ ṣa:ɣlič ʔilgla:da?] Which goldsmith fashioned your necklace for you?
صاغ لمَرتَه حِجِل ذَهَب [ṣa:ɣ lmartah ħijil ðahab] He had a gold anklet made for his wife.
صاغ [ṣa:ɣ] *v:* • **1.** to polish, refine, improve (literary style, etc.) – تِقدَر تصِيغ هَالجُملَة بِأسلُوب أحسَن؟ [tigdar tṣi:ɣ haljumla bʔuslu:b ʔaħsan?] Can you polish this sentence into a better style?
تصَوَّغ [tṣawwaɣ] *v:* • **1.** to shop for gifts to take home from a trip – أحتاج كَم دِينار أتصَوَّغ بِيها [ʔaħta:j čam dina:r ʔatṣawwaɣ bi:ha] I need a few dinars to buy gifts for my homecoming.
تصَيَّغ [tṣayyaɣ] *v:* • **1.** to contract a temporary marriage, marry for a limited period – راح لإيران وَتصَيَّغ مَرَة لِمُدَّة بَقائَه [ra:ħ liʔira:n wtṣayyaɣ mara limuddat baqa:ʔah] He went to Iran and married a woman for the term of his stay.
صُوغَة [ṣu:ɣa] *n:* صُوغات [ṣu:ɣa:t] *pl:* • **1.** a gift brought back from a journey
صايِغ [ṣa:yiɣ] *n:* صِيّاغ [ṣiyya:g] *pl:* • **1.** goldsmith, silversmith, jeweler
صِيغَة [ṣi:ɣa] *n:* • **1.** (literary) style, arrangement, wording • **2.** temporary marriage by contract
صِياغَة [ṣiya:ɣa] *n:* • **1.** goldsmithing, silversmithing, jewelry making • **2.** improvement, polishing • **3.** molding, drafting
صاغ [ṣa:ɣ] *adj:* • **1.** right, in order, proper, sound (in the expression:) – صاغ سَلِيم [ṣa:ɣ sali:m] safe and sound, in perfect condition. رِجَع مِن الحَرُب صاغ سَلِيم [rijaʕ min ʔilħarub ṣa:ɣ sali:m] He returned from the war safe and sound. اِستِلَمِت الرّاديُو صاغ سَلِيم [ʔistilamit ʔirra:dyu ṣa:ɣ sali:m] I received the radio in perfect condition. • **2.** pure, unadulterated – الذَّهَب الصّاغ غالِي [ʔiððahab ʔiṣṣa:ɣ ɣa:li] Pure gold is expensive.

ص و ف

صَوَّف [ṣawwaf] *v:* • **1.** to be or become woolly, fuzzy – مِن يصَوُّف الخُوخ، يكُون لاحِق [min yṣawwuf ʔilxu:x, yku:n la:ħig] When peaches get fuzzy, they're ripe.
صُوف [ṣu:f] *n:* أصواف [ʔaṣwa:f] *pl:* • **1.** wool
صُوفَة [ṣu:fa] *n:* صُوفات [ṣu:fa:t] *pl:* • **1.** piece of wool
صُوفِي [ṣu:fi] *adj:* • **1.** wool, woolen • **2.** wooly

ص و ك ر

صُوكَر [ṣu:gar, ṣawgar] *v:* • **1.** to guarantee
مصُوكَر [mṣu:gar, mṣawgar] *adj:* • **1.** guaranteed

ص و م

صام [ṣa:m] *v:* • **1.** to fast, to abstain from food, drink, and sexual intercourse – صام عَشرَة أيّام بَسّ وَفُطَر [ṣa:m ʕašrat ʔayya:m bass wfuṭar] He fasted for only ten days and stopped.
صَوَّم [ṣawwam] *v:* • **1.** to cause to fast, make observe the fast – أبُوه صَوَّمَه بَسّ الطَّبِيب فَطَّرَه [ʔabu:h ṣawwamah bass ʔiṭṭabi:b faṭṭarah] His father made him fast but the doctor stopped him.
صوم [ṣawm] *n:* • **1.** fast • **2.** fasting, observing a fast
صِيام [ṣiya:m] *n:* • **1.** fasting, observing a fast
صايِم [ṣa:yim] *adj:* صايِمِين، صِيّام [ṣa:yimi:n, ṣiyya:m] *pl:* • **1.** fasting, observing a fast • **2.** person observing a fast

ص و م ع

صَومَعَة [ṣawmaʕa] *n:* صَوامِع [ṣawa:miʕ] *pl:* • **1.** retreat, haven, hermitage hermitage, monastery • **2.** minaret

ص و ن

صان [ṣa:n] *v:* • **1.** to conserve, keep, preserve, retain, sustain
اِنصان [ʔinṣa:n] *v:* • **1.** to preserve • **2.** to become preserved, well protected, well kept

ص

صُون [ṣu:n] *n:* • **1.** preservation, keeping, conservation, guarding
صِيانَة [ṣiya:na] *n:* • **1.** preservation, conservation, care, servicing, maintenance
مَصُون [maṣu:n] *adj:* • **1.** well protected, well kept, well- guarded • **2.** virtuous (of women), also an epithet for women الحَرَم المَصُون [:ʔilħaram ʔalmaṣu:n] the respected wife

ص و ن د
صُوندَة [ṣu:nda] *n:* صُوندات [ṣu:nda:t] *pl:* • **1.** hose, rubber tube

ص و ي
مَصوي [maṣwi] *adj:* • **1.** thin, frail, skinny • **2.** thin person

ص ي ج
صاج [sa:ǰ] *n:* • **1.** teak, teakwood
صاج [ṣa:ǰ] *n:* صاجات، صُوج [ṣa:ǰa:t, ṣu:ǰ] *pl:* • **1.** a pan or tin used for baking bread or roasting coffee

ص ي ح
صاح [ṣa:ħ] *v:* • **1.** to call out, yell, shout – مِن ضِرَبتَه، صاح "آخ!" [min ḍirabtah, ṣa:ħ "ʔa:x!"] When I hit him he yelled 'Ouch!' الشُّرطِي صاح عَلَيّا مِن شافني دَأعبُر الشّارِع [ʔiššurṭi ṣa:ħ ʕalayya min ša:fni daʔaʕbur ʔišša:riʕ] The policeman shouted at me when he saw me crossing the street. لا ترُوحلَه قَبُل ما يصِيح إسمَك [la: tru:ħlah gabul ma: yṣi:ħ ʔismak] Don't go in to him before he calls your name. • **2.** to call, call out to, address – صِحتَك مِيَّة مَرَّة. إنتَ أطرَش؟ [ṣiħtak miyyat marra. ʔinta ʔaṭraš?] I called you a hundred times. Are you deaf? قالَتلِي "صِيحلِي مَرتَه" [ga:latli "ṣi:ħli martah"] She told me, "Call his wife for me." إسمَه كاظُم بَسّ يصِيحُوه أبُو جُواد " [ʔismah ka:ḍum bass yṣi:ħu:h ʔabu ǰuwa:d] His name is Kadhum but they call him Abu Juwad. صاح الدّاد [ṣa:ħ ʔidda:d] to become utterly disgusted, fed up, exasperated. الجِّيران صاحوا الدّاد مِن إبنَك [ʔiǰǰi:ra:n ṣa:ħaw ʔidda:d min ʔibnak] The neighbors are thoroughly fed up with your son.
صَيَّح [ṣayyaħ] *v:* • **1.** to call or shout repeatedly – مِنُو دَيصَيِّح بِالدَّرُب؟ [minu dayṣayyiħ biddarub?] Who's shouting out there on the street? صَيَّح الدّاد [ṣayyaħ ʔidda:d] to make utterly disgusted, fed up, exasperated. إبنِي صَيَّحنِي الدّاد بِكُثرَة مَصرَفَه [ʔibni ṣayyaħni ʔidda:d bkuθrat maṣrafah] My son has thoroughly exasperated me with his excessive spending.
تصايَح [tṣa:yaħ] *v:* • **1.** to shout at one another – أبُوك وأُمَّك دَيتصايحُون. شَكُو عِدهُم؟ [ʔabu:k wʔummak dayitṣa:yħu:n. šaku ʕidhum?] Your father and mother are shouting at each other. What's with them?
صِيحَة [ṣi:ħa] *n:* صِيحات [ṣi:ħa:t] *pl:* • **1.** yell, shout, cry • **2.** scream, shriek, wail
صِياح [ṣiya:ħ] *n:* • **1.** shouting • **2.** screaming, shrieking, wailing

ص ي د
صاد [ṣa:d] *v:* • **1.** to trap, catch – البَزُّونَة صادَت فارَة [ʔilbazzu:na ṣa:dat fa:ra] The cat caught a mouse. المُدِير صادني دَأقرا جَرِيدَة [ʔilmudi:r ṣa:dni daʔaqra: ǰari:da] The director caught me reading the paper. صادنِي بِهالسُّوال [ṣa:dni bhassuʔa:l] He trapped me with that question. • **2.** to hunt – راح لِلشِّمال يصِيد دِبَبَة [ra:ħ liššima:l yiṣi:d dibaba] He went up North to hunt bears. • **3.** to hunt down, to bag – صاد غزالَين بِبُندُقِيتِي [ṣa:d ɣaza:layn bbunduqi:ti] He bagged two gazelles with my rifle. • **4.** to fish – خَلِّي نرُوح نصِيد سِمَك [xalli: nru:ħ nṣi:d simač] Let's go fishing.
تصَيَّد [tṣayyad] *v:* • **1.** to stalk game, to go hunting – طِلَع يِتصَيَّد بالهُور [ṭilaʕ yitṣayyad bilhu:r] He went out stalking game in the swamp.
إنصاد [ʔinṣa:d] *v:* • **1.** to be trapped, be caught – نصادِينا؛ جَتّي الشُّرطَة [nṣa:di:na; ǰatti ʔiššurṭa] We're caught; the police have arrived.
صيد [ṣayd] *n:* • **1.** hunting – بُندُقِيَّة صَيد [bunduqiyyat ṣayd] shotgun. كُلّ يوم جُمعَة يِطلَع لِلصِّيد [kull yu:m ǰumʕa yiṭlaʕ liṣṣi:d] Every Friday he goes out hunting. واقُف عَلَى رِجل الصَّيد [wa:guf ʕala riǰl ʔiṣṣayd] He is on pins and needles. • **2.** fishing – صَيد السِّمَك [ṣayd ʔissimač] fishing.
صيدة [ṣi:da] *n:* صِيدات [ṣi:da:t] *pl:* • **1.** bag, catch, thing caught – إلَك حُصَّة بِهالصَّيدَة [ʔilak ħuṣṣa bhaṣṣi:da] You have a share in this catch. • **2.** find, bargain, rare opportunity – هِيكِي سَيّارَة ما تِحصَل كُلّ يوم. هاي صيدَة [hi:či sayya:ra ma: tiħṣal kull yu:m. ha:y ṣayda] Such a car won't come along every day. This is a real find.
صَيّاد [ṣayya:d] *n:* صَيّادِين [ṣayya:dai:n] *pl:* • **1.** hunter • **2.** fisherman
مَصيدَة، مِصيادَة [maṣyada, miṣya:da] *n:* مِصيادات [miṣya:da:t] *pl:* • **1.** trap, snare – مِصيادَة فار [miṣya:dat fa:r] mouse trap. • **2.** slingshot

ص ي د ل
صَيدَلَة [ṣaydala] *n:* • **1.** pharmacology, pharmacy, apothecary's trade
صَيدَلِي [ṣaydali] *n:* صَيادِلَة [ṣaya:dila] *pl:* • **1.** pharmacist, druggist
صَيدَلِيَّة [ṣaydaliyya] *n:* صَيدَلِيّات [ṣaydaliyya:t] *pl:* • **1.** pharmacy, drug store
صَيدَلانِيَّة [ṣaydala:niyya] *n:* صَيدَلانِيّات [ṣaydala:niyya:t] *pl:* • **1.** female pharmacist

ص ي ر
صار [ṣa:r] *v:* • **1.** to become, to come to be, turn out to be – إبنها صار طَبِيب [ʔibinha ṣa:r ṭabi:b] Her son

ص

became a doctor. أخُوك صارِ ما ينحِمِل [ʔaxu:k ṣar ma: yinħimil] Your brother has become unbearable. شعرَه صار أبيَض [šaʕrah ṣa:r ʔabyað̣] His hair turned grey. صِير خُوش وَلَد ورُوح لِلمَدرَسَة [ṣi:r xu:š walad wru:ħ lilmadrasa] Be a good boy and go to school. إذا يصِيرلَه مَكان، أرِيدَه بالغُرفَة [ʔiða yṣi:rlah maka:n, ʔari:dah bilɣurfa] If a place can be found for it, I want it in the room. صار الأكِل لَو بَعَد؟ [ṣa:r ʔilʔakil law baʕad?] Is the food ready yet? صار عَلِيك دِينارَين [ṣa:r ʕali:k dina:rayn] This makes two dinars charged against you. صارَت ساعَة خَمسَة [ṣa:rat sa:ʕa xamsa] It is five o'clock. صار وَقِت الأكِل لَو بَعَد؟ [ṣa:r waqit ʔilʔakil law baʕad?] It is time to eat yet? صار وَقِت الصَّلاة. خَلِّي نصَلِّي [ṣa:r waqit ʔiṣṣala:. xalli: nṣalli] It's time for prayer. Let's pray. صار مُدَّة ما شِفتَك [ṣa:r mudda ma: šiftak] I haven't seen you for some time. راح يصِير سِتّ أشهُر ما شايفَك [ra:ħ yṣi:r sitt ʔašhur ma: ša:yfak] It will be six months that I haven't seen you. صار مُدَّة دَأنتَظرَك [ṣa:r mudda daʔantað̣rak] I've been waiting for you quite a while. صارلَه يومَين مَرِيض [ṣa:rlah yu:mayn mari:ð̣] He's been sick two days. صارلَه شَهرَين بلا شُغُل [ṣa:rlah šahrayn bila šuɣul] He's been without a job for two months. شقَدّ صارلَك هنا؟ [šgadd ṣa:rlak hna?] How long have you been here? قَبِل شوَيَّة كان هنا. وين صار؟ [gabil šwayya ča:n hna. wi:n ṣa:r?] He was here a bit ago. Where did he get off to? دِير بالَك لا يصِير الصُّبُغ عَلَى هدُومَك [di:r ba:lak la: yṣi:r ʔiṣṣubuɣ ʕala hdu:mak] Be careful that the paint doesn't get on your clothes. صار وِيّايا ضِدَّه [ṣa:r wiyya:ya ð̣iddah] He sided with me against him. • **2.** to happen, occur, take place – شصار بِالدّائرَة اليُوم؟ [šṣa:r bidda:ʔira ʔilyu:m?] What happened at the office today? إذا ما دِفَعتِلَه اليُوم، شِيصِير؟ [ʔiða ma: difaʕitlah ʔilyu:m, ši:ṣi:r?] If I don't pay him today, what happens? إنتَ تُعرُف شدَيصِير؟ [ʔinta tuʕruf šdayṣi:r?] Do you know what's going on? صارَت ثَورَة بِالشِّمال [ṣa:rat θawra biššima:l] A revolution took place in the north. هَالسَّنَة ما صار فَيَضان [hassana ma: ṣa:r fayaða:n] This year there was no flood. طَقطَقَة الباب دَتصِير مِن الهَوَا [ṭagṭagat ʔilba:b datṣi:r min ʔilhawa] The banging of the door is happening because of the wind. القَضِيَّة راح تصِير بِهَالكَيفِيَّة [ʔilqað̣iyya ra:ħ tṣi:r bhalkayfiyya] The matter will be taken care of in this manner. صارَت بِيّا مَلاريا مَرّتَين [ṣa:rat biyya mala:rya: marrtayn] I had malaria twice. إذا تخَلِّيها عِندي، ما يصِير عَلِيها شِي [ʔiða txalli:ha ʕindi, ma: yṣi:r ʕali:ha ši] If you leave it with me, nothing will happen to it. شصار عَلِيك مِستَعجِل؟ [šṣa:r ʕali:k mistaʕjil?] What caused you to be in such a hurry? أخُويا، ما صارلَه شِي بحادِث السَّيّارَة [ʔaxu:ya, ma: ṣa:rlah ši bħa:diθ ʔissayya:ra] Nothing happened to my brother in the auto accident. • **3.** to develop, ensue, follow, result – شصار مِن قَضِيتَك؟ [šṣa:r min qað̣i:tak?] What resulted from that deal of yours? شصار ؟ كُلَّه تُطلُبنِي دِينار [šṣa:r? kullah tuṭlubni dina:r] What of it? All you have coming from me is a dinar. ما صارَت وِيّاك. ما قِتلَك لا تِلعَب بغَراضِي؟ [ma: ṣa:rat wiyya:k. ma: gitlak la: tilʕab bɣara:ð̣i?] It left no impression on you. Didn't I tell you not to play with my things? قِتلَك مِيَّة مَرَّة. ما صارَت وِيّاك عاد [gitlak miyyat marra. ma: ṣa:rat wiyya:k ʕa:d] I told you a hundred times. It did no good with you then! • **4.** to be possible, have a chance of occurrence – يصِير أجِي لِبَغداد وَما أشُوفكُم؟ [yṣi:r ʔaǰi libaɣda:d wma: ʔašu:fkum?] Could it happen that I'd come to Baghdad and not see you? يصِير آخذ القَلَم؟ [yṣi:r ʔa:xuð ʔilqalam?] Can I take the pencil? ما يصِير تِدخُل بلا بِطاقَة [ma: yṣi:r tidxul bila biṭa:qa] You can't get in without a ticket. ما يصِير يِقبَل هِيكِي سِعِر [ma: yṣi:r yiqbal hi:či siʕir] He would never accept such a price. ما يصِير. تكَلِّفنِي أكثَر [ma: yṣi:r. tkallifni ʔakθar] Nothing doing. It costs me more. أرجُوك ساعِد هَالرِّجّال! -- صار [ʔarǰu:k sa:ʕid harrijǰa:l! -- ṣa:r] Please help this man! --- O. K. • **5.** with لـ to come to, befall, be the lot of – صارلَه كَرِش [ṣa:rlah kariš] He developed a pot-belly. إذا تصِيرلَك حاجَة عِندَه، ما يعُرفَك [ʔiða tṣi:rlak ħa:ǰa ʕindah, ma: yʕurfak] If you should have a need for him, he won't know you. صارِلهُم سَنَة مِتزَوّجِين وَما صارِلهُم شِي [ṣa:rilhum sana midzawwǰi:n wma: ṣa:rilhum ši] They've been married a year and they've had no children. • **6.** with عِند to fall into the possession of – أنطِيك مِن تصِير عِندِي فلُوس [ʔanṭi:k min tṣi:r ʕindi flu:s] I'll give to you when some money comes my way. هَسَّة شقَدّ صار عِندَك؟ [hassa šgadd ṣa:r ʕindak?] How much do you have now? صار عِندَك خُردَة هَسَّة؟ [ṣa:r ʕindak xurda hassa?] Have you gotten any change yet?

صِير [ṣi:r] *n:* • **1.** becoming

مَصِير [maṣi:r] *n:* • **1.** fate, destiny, lot, future – اللُّجنَة اجتِمعَت حَتَّى تقَرِّر مَصِيرَه [ʔilluǰna ʔiǰtimʕat ħatta tqarrir maṣi:rah] The committee met to decide his fate. ما نِدرِي شلُون راح يصِير مَصِيرنا [ma: nidri šlu:n ra:ħ yṣi:r maṣi:rna] We don't know how our destiny will turn out. حَقّ تقرِير المَصِير [ħaqq taqri:r ʔilmaṣi:r] right of self-determination. • **2.** end, outcome, upshot, issue, result

مَصِيرِي [maṣi:ri] *adj:* • **1.** crucial

ص ي ف

صَيَّف [ṣayyaf] *v:* • **1.** to summer, spend the summer – هالسَّنَة راح أصَيِّف بسوِيسرا [hassana ra:ħ ʔaṣayyif bswi:sra] This year I'm going to spend the summer in

ص

Switzerland. • **2.** to wear summer clothing, put on summer clothes – اِحتَرَّت الدِّنيا. راح أَصَيِّف [ʔiħtarrat ʔiddinya. ra:ħ ʔaṣayyif] The weather has got hot. I'm going to switch to summer clothes.
اِصطاف [ʔiṣṭa:f] *v:* • **1.** to take a summer vacation, pass the summer – راح أَصطاف بسويسرا [ra:ħ ʔaṣṭa:f bswi:sra] I'm going to take a summer vacation in Switzerland.
صِيف [ṣayf, ṣi:f] *n:* أَصياف [ʔaṣya:f] *pl:* • **1.** summer, summertime
صَيفِيَّة [ṣayfiyya] *n:* صَيفِيّات [ṣayfiyya:t] *pl:* • **1.** summer, summer season
اِصطِياف [ʔiṣṭiya:f] *n:* • **1.** summer vacationing – مَوسِم الاصطِياف [mawsim ʔilʔiṣṭiya:f] resort season. حَرَكَة الاصطِياف [ħarakat ʔilʔiṣṭiya:f] resort activity.
مَصِيف [maṣi:f] *adj:* مَصايِف [maṣa:yif] *pl:* • **1.** summer resort
مصَيِّف [mṣayyif] *adj:* • **1.** wearing summer clothing, putting on summer clothes • **2.** summer vacationing
صِيفِي، صَيفِي [ṣi:fi, ṣayfi] *adj:* • **1.** summer, summery
مُصطاف [muṣṭa:f] *adj:* مُصطافِين [muṣṭa:fi:n] *pl:* • **1.** summer vacationer

ص ي ن

صِين [ṣi:n] *n:* • **1.** China
صِينِيَّة [ṣi:niyya] *n:* صواني [ṣwa:ni:] *pl:* • **1.** tray, brass round tray
صِينِي [ṣi:ni] *adj:* • **1.** Chinese • **2.** a Chinese

ص ي ه د

صَيهُود [ṣayhu:d] *n:* • **1.** drought, dry spell, period of low water

ض

ض ء ل

تضائَل [dǫa:ʔal] *v:* • **1.** to diminish, dwindle, wane, decline, decrease – صِحّتَه دَتِتضاءَل يوم عَلَى يوم [ṣiħħtah dadidǫʔal yu:m ʕala yu:m] His health is getting worse day after day.

ضَئيل [ǫaʔi:l] *adj:* • **1.** small, scanty, meager, sparse, slight – حَصَّل عَلَى رِبح ضَئيل مِن هَالصَّفقَة [ħaṣṣal ʕala ribiħ ǫaʔi:l min haṣṣafqa] He realized a very small profit from this transaction.

ض ب ب

ضَبّ [ǫabb] *v:* • **1.** to gather, bundle, tie together – ضَبّوا غَراضهُم وَخَلّوها بِاللّوري [ǫabbaw ɣara:ǫhum wxallawha billu:ri] They bundled their things together and put them on the truck. • **2.** to tighten – ضُبّ حزامَك حَتّى ما يِنزِل بَنطَرُونَك [ǫubb ħza:mak ħatta ma: yinzil panṭaru:nak] Tighten your belt so your pants won't fall. ضُبّ البُرغي بِهالدَّرنَفيس [ǫubb ʔilburɣi bhaddarnafi:s] Tighten the screw with this screwdriver. • **3.** to be firm, unyielding, steadfast with or toward – مِن يِجي يَمَّك، ضُبَّه [min yiǰi yammak, ǫubbah] When he comes around, be firm with him. المُدير ضَبَّه لعَلِي لِأَنّ ما كَمَّل الشُّغُل [ʔilmudi:r ǫabbah lʕali liʔann ma: kammal ʔiššuɣul] The director put the screws to Ali because he didn't finish the work. • **4.** to take seriously, work hard at – إِذا ما تضُبّ الشُّغُل ما نِستَفاد شِي [ʔiǫa ma: dǫubb ʔiššuɣul ma: nistafa:d ši] If you don't take the work seriously, we won't benefit a bit.

اِنضَبّ [ʔinǫabb] *v:* • **1.** to be tightened – هَالبُرغِي ما يِنضَبّ [halburɣi ma: yinǫabb] The screw can't be tightened.

ضَبّ [ǫabb] *n:* ضباب [ǫba:b] *pl:* • **1.** a variety of large lizard • **2.** bundle, gathering

ضَبّ [ǫabb] *n:* • **1.** bundling, gathering

ضَبَّة [ǫabba] *n:* ضَبّات [ǫabba:t] *pl:* • **1.** scolding, talking to • **2.** handful, bunch – ضَبَّة وَرِد [ǫabbat warid] bunch of flowers.

ضَباب [ǫaba:b] *n:* • **1.** fog, mist

مَضبُوب [maǫbu:b] *adj:* • **1.** tight

ض ب ر

ضَبَّر [ǫabbar] *v:* • **1.** to bind, tie up, wrap – ضَبَّر رِجلَه بِخِرقَة [ǫabbar riǰlah bxirga] He bound up his leg with a rag.

ضبارَة [ǫba:ra] *n:* ضبارات، أضابِير [ǫba:ra:t, ʔaǫa:bi:r] *pl:* • **1.** file, dossier

ض ب ض ب

ضَبضَب [ǫabǫab] *v:* • **1.** to tie up, bundle up, gather up – ضَبضُب الغَراض بِهَالحَبِل [ǫabǫub ʔilɣara:ǫ bhalħabil] Tie the things up with this rope.

تضَبضَب [dǫabǫab] *v:* • **1.** pass. of ضَبضَب: to be tied up, be bundled up, be gathered up

مضَبضَب [mǫabǫab] *adj:* • **1.** tied up

ض ب ط

ضُبَط [ǫubaṭ] *v:* • **1.** to control, maintain control over – المُعَلِّم ما دَيِقدَر يُضبُط الصَّفّ [ʔilmuʕallim ma: dayigdar yuǫbuṭ ʔiṣṣaff] The teacher can't control the class. أُضبُط نَفسَك ولَا تِحكِي شِي هَسَّة [ʔuḍbuṭ nafsak wla: tiħči ši hassa] Control yourself and don't say anything now. • **2.** to observe, check, watch closely – أُضبُط الوَقِت وشُوف شقَدّ أَطَوُّل جَوَّة المَيّ [ʔuǫbuṭ ʔilwaqit wšu:f šgadd ʔaṭawwul ǰawwa ʔilmayy] Check the time and see how long I last under water. • **3.** to keep track of, keep records of – أُضبُط كَمِّيَّة البَنزِين اللّي تِستَعمِلها يَومِيّاً [ʔuǫbuṭ kammiyyat ʔilbanzi:n ʔilli tistaʕmilha yawmiyyan] Keep track of the amount of gasoline you use daily. طُلبَت الشَّرِكَة واحِد يُضبُط حِساباتها [ṭulbat ʔiššarika wa:ħid yuǫbuṭ ħisa:ba:tha] The company asked for someone to keep its books. • **4.** to set, regulate, adjust – ضُبَط ساعتَه عَلَى ساعتِي [ǫubaṭ sa:ʕtah ʕala sa:ʕti] He set his watch by my watch. • **5.** to do precisely, exactly, meticulously, accurately – لازِم تُضبُط القِياس زين حَتّى نُعرُف شقَدّ نريد [la:zim tuǫbuṭ ʔilqiya:s zi:n ħatta nuʕruf šgadd nri:d] You must be precise about measuring so we will know how much we want.

تضَبَّط [dǫabbaṭ] *v:* • **1.** to be demanding, greedy (in bargaining) – أَبُوها قِبَل يزَوِّجها بَسّ أُمّها دَتِتضَبَّط [ʔabu:ha qibal yzawwiǰha bass ʔummaha datidǫabbaṭ] Her father agreed to marry her off but her mother is holding out for more dowry. لا تِتضَبَّط. هَذا خُوش سِعِر [la: tidǫabbaṭ. ha:ǫa xu:š siʕir] Don't be too demanding. This is a good price.

اِنضُبَط [ʔinǫubaṭ] *v:* • **1.** to be controled, to be observed, to be checked, to be recorded

ضَبُط [ǫabuṭ] *n:* • **1.** discipline, control, restraint • **2.** observation, checking • **3.** recording • **4.** regulation, adjustment • **5.** exactness, precision, accuracy – إِجا ساعَة خَمسَة بِالضَبُط [ʔiǰa sa:ʕa xamsa biǫǫabuṭ] He came at five o'clock on the dot. • **6.** exactly, precisely – اِنطاه خَمسِين دِينار ضَبُط [ʔinṭa:h xamsi:n dina:r ǫabuṭ] He gave him fifty dinars exactly.

ضابُط [ǫa:buṭ] *n:* ضُبّاط [ǫubba:ṭ] *pl:* • **1.** officer – ضابُط صَفّ [ǫa:buṭ ṣaff] noncommissioned officer.

مَضبَطَة [maǫbaṭa] *n:* مَضابُط [maǫa:buṭ] *pl:* • **1.** petition

ضَوابِط [ǫawa:biṭ] *n:* • **1.** restrictions

اِنضِباط [ʔinǫiba:ṭ] *n:* • **1.** discipline – لُجنَة الانضِباط

[luǰnat ʔilʔinðibaːṭ] disciplinary board. • **2.** اِنضِباطِيَّة military policeman – جُندِي اِنضِباط [ǰundi ʔinðibaːṭ] military policeman. دائِرَة الانضِباط [daːʔirat ʔilʔinðibaːṭ] military police headquarters.

مَضبُوط [maðbuːṭ] *adj:* • **1.** accurate, precise, exact, correct – حَكيَك كُلَّه مَضبُوط [ħačyak kullah maðbuːṭ] Everything you say is correct. مَواعِيدَه ما مَضبُوطَة [mawaːʕiːdah maː maðbuːṭa] He doesn't keep his appointments.

أَضبَط [ʔaðbaṭ] *comparative adjective:* • **1.** more or most precise, accurate, exact, correct – عَبالِي عَلِي كَذّاب. أَخُوه طِلَع أَضبَط [ʕabaːli ʕali čaððaːb. ʔaxuːh ṭilaʕ ʔaðbaṭ] I thought Ali was a liar. His brother proved to be even more so.

ض ب ع

ضَبُع [ðabuʕ] *n:* ضباع [ðbaːʕ] *pl:* • **1.** hyena

مِضِبعَة، كَلبَة مِضِبعَة [miðibʕa, čalba miðibʕa] *adj:* • **1.** bitch in heat • **2.** ferocious female dog

ض ج ج

ضَجّ [ðaǰǰ] *v:* • **1.** to clamor, shout, raise a hue and cry – مِن قال أَكُو دَوام باكِر، كُلّهُم ضَجّوا [min gaːl ʔaku dawaːm baːčir, kullhum ðaǰǰaw] When he said there would be working hours tomorrow, they all raised a ruckus.

ضَجّ [ðaǰǰ] *n:* • **1.** clamor, cry, noise

ضَجَّة [ðaǰǰa] *n:* ضَجّات [ðaǰǰaːt] *pl:* • **1.** uproar, din, clamor • **2.** crowd, noisy group

ضَجِيج [ðajiːǰ] *n:* • **1.** noise • **2.** uproar, din, clamor

ض ح ك

ضِحَك [ðiħak] *v:* • **1.** to laugh – الجّاهِل ضِحَك مِن دَغدَغتَه [ʔiǰǰaːhil ðiħak min daɣdaɣtah] The child laughed when I tickled him. • **2.** with عَلَى to mock, ridicule, deride, scorn – لا تصَدِّق بِيهُم. دَيضحَكُون عَلِيك [laː tṣaddig biːhum. dayiðħakuːn ʕaliːk] Don't believe them. They're making fun of you.

ضَحَّك [ðaħħak] *v:* • **1.** to cause to laugh – ضَحَّكنا هوايَة بِلَطايفه [ðaħħakna hwaːya blaṭaːyfah] He made us laugh a lot with his witticisms. خَلّانِي أَنشُر المَقال وَضَحَّك النّاس عَلَيّا [xallaːni ʔanšur ʔilmaqaːl wðaħħak ʔinnaːs ʕalayya] He let me publish the article and made the people laugh at me.

تضَحَّك [dðaħħak] *v:* • **1.** to amuse

تضاحَك [dðaːħak] *v:* • **1.** to laugh at – قُلُولِي عَلَى ويش دَتِتضاحكُون [guluːli ʕala wiːš datidðaːħkuːn] Tell me what you are laughing at. يِتضاحَك مِثل القَحبَة [yidðaːħak miθl ʔilgaħba] He laughs like a whore.

اِنضِحَك [ʔinðiħak] *v:* • **1.** with عَلَى to be gotten the best of – هَذا شِيطان. ما يِنضِحِك عَلَيه [haːða šiːṭaːn. maː yinðiħik ʕaliːh] He's a clever rascal. He can't be fooled.

ضِحِك [ðiħik] *n:* • **1.** laughing, laughter – قالها ضِحِك. ما قِصَدها [gaːlha ðiħik. maː qiṣadha] He said it jokingly. He didn't mean it. ضِحِك عالذُّقُون [ðiħik ʕaððiquːn] mockery, ridicule, derision. • **2.** بضِحِك jokingly

ضِحكَة [ðiħka] *n:* ضِحكات [ðiħkaːt] *pl:* • **1.** laugh

تَضحِيك [taðħiːk] *n:* • **1.** amusement

ضَحُوك [ðaħuːk] *adj:* • **1.** jolly, smiling, cheerful, gay – وِجِه ضَحُوك [wiǰih ðaħuːk] a pleasant face.

ضاحِك [ðaːħik] *adj:* ضَواحِك [ðawaːħik] *pl:* • **1.** laughing • **2.** pl. only ضَواحِك premolar teeth

مُضحِك [muðħik] *adj:* • **1.** comical, funny

مَضحَكَة [maðħaka] *adj:* • **1.** object of ridicule, laughing-stock

ض ح ل

ضَحِل [ðaħil] *adj:* • **1.** shallow, shoal • **2.** superficial, shallow – مَعلُوماتَه ضَحلَة [maʕluːmaːtah ðaħla] His knowledge is superficial. • **3.** (as n:) a shallow, a shoal • **4.** a frivolous person

ض ح و

ضَحَّى [ðaħħaː] *v:* • **1.** with ب to sacrifice, offer up, immolate – يضَحِّي بِكُلّشِي مِن أَجِلها [yðaħħi bikullši min ʔaǰilha] He sacrifices everything for her sake.

ضَحَى [ðaħaː] *n:* • **1.** (masc.) forenoon – الضَّحَى العالِي [ʔiððaħa ʔilʕaːli] late forenoon.

ضَحِيَّة [ðaħiyya] *n:* ضَحايا [ðaħaːyaː] *pl:* • **1.** blood sacrifice • **2.** victim – راح ضَحِيَّة الغَدِر وِالخِيانَة [raːħ ðaħiyyat ʔilɣadir wilxiyaːna] He was a victim of treachery and betrayal.

أَضحَى، عِيد الأَضحَى [ʔaðħa, ʕiːd ʔilʔaðħa] *n:* • **1.** a sacrificial feast observed on the tenth day of Zu'lhijja, lasting four days

ضاحِيَة [ðaːħiya] *n:* ضَواحِي [ðawaːħi] *pl:* • **1.** suburb, outlying area – سِباق ضاحيَة [sibaːq ðaːħya] cross-country foot race.

تَضحِيَة [taðħiya] *n:* • **1.** sacrifice

مضَحِّي [mðaħħi] *adj:* • **1.** sacrificing, sacrificer

مُضَحَّى [muðaħħa] *adj:* • **1.** with prep ب: sacrificed

ض خ خ

ضَخّ [ðaxx] *v:* • **1.** to pump

اِنضَخّ [ʔinðaxx] *v:* • **1.** to be pumped

ضَخّ [ðaxx] *n:* • **1.** pumping

مَضَخَّة [maðaxxa] *n:* مَضَخّات [maðaxxaːt] *pl:* • **1.** pump, pump station

ض خ م

ضَخَّم [ðaxxam] *v:* • **1.** to enlarge, expand, make huge, big, to exaggerate, amplify – دَتضَخُّم القَضِيَّة بِلا مُوجِب [dadðaxxum ʔilqaðiyya bila muːǰib] You're blowing the matter up without any reason.

تَضَخَّم [dðaxxam] *v:* • **1.** to be made huge, to swell, expand, distend – الكِبد مالَه تضَخَّم [ʔilkabid maːlah dðaxxam] His liver was distended.
تَضَخُّم [taðaxxum] *n:* • **1.** inflation – تَضَخُّم نَقدِي [taðaxxum naqdi] inflation (econ.).
ضَخامَة [ðaxaːma] *n:* • **1.** largeness, bigness, bulkiness, grossness, corpulence, obesity • **2.** greatness, pomp, splendor
تَضخِيم [taðxiːm] *n:* • **1.** exaggeration • **2.** inflation, inflating
ضَخُم [ðaxum] *adj:* • **1.** huge, enormous, vast, ample – بِنايَة هَالبَنك ضَخمَة [binaːyat halbang ðaxma] This bank building is enormous. ياخُذ راتِب ضَخُم [yaːxuð raːtib ðaxum] He gets a huge salary.
أضخَم [ʔaðxam] *comparative adjective:* • **1.** more or most enormous

ض د

ضاد [ðaːd] *n:* • **1.** name of the letter

ض د د

ضادَد [ðaːdad] *v:* • **1.** to contradict – كُلّما أقُول شِي، يضادِدنِي [kullma ʔaguːl ši, yðaːdidni] Everytime I say something, he contradicts me.
تضادَد [dðaːdad] *v:* • **1.** to oppose one another – إنتُو قَرايِب لِيش تِتضادُّون [ʔintu garaːyib liːš tidðaːdduːn?] You are relatives. Why are you opposed to each other?
ضِدّ [ðidd] *adj:* أضداد [ʔaðdaːd] *pl:* • **1.** opposite, contrast • **2.** adversary, opponent • **3.** antidote, antitoxin • **4.** against – دَيحكِي ضِدَّك بِالقَهاوِي [dayiħči ðiddak bilgahaːwi] He's talking against you in the cofés. نَقلَه مِن الشُّعبَة كان ضِدّ رَغبتِي [naqlah min ʔiššuʕba čaːn ðidd raɣibti] His transfer from this section was against my will. • **5.** anti-, -proof, impervious to – ضِدّ النّار [ðidd ʔinnaːr] fireproof. ضِدّ الماي [ðidd ʔilmaːy] waterproof. ضِدّ الكَسِر [ðidd ʔilkasir] shockproof, unbreakable.
مُضاد [muðaːdd] *adj:* مُضادّات [muðaːddaːt] *pl:* • **1.** opposed, anti- • **2.** (n: in Pl. form) the cons

ض ر ب

ضِرَب [ðirab] *v:* • **1.** to strike, hit, beat – ضِرَب الزُّمال بِالعَصا [ðirab ʔizzumaːl bilʕaṣaː] He hit the donkey with the stick. ضِرَبَه بِسِگّينَة بخاصِرتَه [ðirabah bsiččiːna bxaːṣirtah] He stabbed him with a knife in his side. ضِرَبَه بطَلقَة وِحدَة وَقِتَلَه [ðirabah bṭalqa wiħda wkitalah] He shot him with one bullet and killed him. كانَت المُمَرِّضَة تضُربَه أبرَة كُلّ أربَع ساعات [čaːnat ʔilmumarriða dðurbah ʔubra kull ʔarbaʕ saːʕaːt] The nurse was giving him a shot every four hours. ضرَبتِي الثُّوب مالِي أُوتِي؟ [ðrabti ʔiθθuːb maːli ʔuːti?] Did you iron my shirt? ضُربَتَه الشَّمِس [ðurbatah ʔiššamis] He had a sunstroke. يِضرُب جُلُق [yiðrub ǰuluq] He masturbates. ضِرَب دَبَّة وَما قِبَل يرُوح [ðirab dabba wmaː qibal yiruːħ] He got obstinate and refused to go. ضُربَوه ذَيل [ðurbawh ðayl] They fired him. بالمُناقَشَة مالتَه، كان يُضرُب هوايَة أمثِلَة [bilmunaːqaša maːltah, čaːn yuðrub hwaːya ʔamθila] In his argument, he was quoting a lot of proverbs. تلُومنِي لُويش أحكِي هِيكِي؟ خَلِّي أضرُبلَك مَثَل شسَوَّى بِيّا [tluːmni luwiːš ʔaħči hiːči? xalliː ʔaðrublak maθal ššawwaː biyya] You blame me for saying such a thing? Let me give you an example of what he did to me. أضرُب كَفّ، لا ترُوح تِغرَق [ʔuðrub čaff, laː truːħ tiɣrag] Keep paddling or you'll drown! أضرُبها قاط صُبُغ لاخ [ʔuðrubha qaːṭ ṣubuɣ laːx] Slap another coat of paint on it. دِير بالَك مِنَّه؛ يِضرُب جِيب [diːr baːlak minnah; yiðrub ǰiːb] Watch out for him; he picks pockets. أخُويَا ضِرَب الرَّقم القِياسِي بِالسِّبِح [ʔaxuːya ðirab ʔirraqm ʔilqiyaːsi bissibiħ] My brother broke the record in swimming. راحَت تِستِشِير واحِد يِضرُب بِالتَّخَت رَمُل [raːħat tistišiːr waːħid yiðrub bittaxat ramul] She went to consult a fellow who practices geomancy. راح أضرُب راسِي مُوس [raːħ ʔaðrub raːsi muːs] I'm going to shave my head. ضُربَوا الأكِل وطِلعَوا [ðurbaw ʔilʔakil wṭilʕaw] They bolted down the food and went out. الطّالِب ضِرَب الدَّرِس [ʔiṭṭaːlib ðirab ʔiddaris] The student cut the class. وِين المُحاسِب؟ ضِرَب الباب [wiːn ʔilmuħaːsib? ðirab ʔilbaːb] Where is the accountant? He just up and left. • **2.** to fire, go off – فُطرَوا بَعَد ما ضِرَب الطُّوب [fuṭraw baʕad maː ðirab ʔiṭṭuːb] They ended their fast after the cannon went off. • **3.** to multiply – أُضرُب هَالرَّقم بِخَمسَة [ʔuðrub harraqm bixamsa] Multiply this number by five. • **4.** to copulate, fornicate, have sexual intercourse with • **5.** to act severely toward – الوَزِير ضِرَب المُدِير بَعَد ما عِرَف عَنَّه يِرتِشِي [ʔilwaziːr ðirab ʔilmudiːr baʕad maː ʕiraf ʕannah yirtiši] The minister reassigned the director after he found out that he takes bribes. • **6.** to take dishonestly – ضِرَب الفلُوس عَلَيّا [ðirab ʔalfluːs ʕalayya] He cheated me out of the money.
ضَرَّب [ðarrab] *v:* • **1.** to strike repeatedly – لِيش دَتضَرُّب الجِّهال؟ [liːš dadðarrub ʔiǰǰihaːl?] Why are you hitting the children? • **2.** to breed, cross-breed – الفَلّاح ضَرَّب الغَنَم مالتَه ويّا نُوع أسبانِي [ʔilfallaːħ ðarrab ʔilɣanam maːltah wiyya nuːʕ ʔaspaːni] The farmer crossed his sheep with a Spanish breed.
أضرَب [ʔaðrab] *v:* • **1.** to go on strike, refuse to work – العُمّال أضرِبَوا [ʔilʕummaːl ʔaðribaw] The workers went on strike. المَسجُونِين أضرِبَوا عَن الطَّعام [ʔilmasǰuːniːn ʔaðribaw ʕan ʔiṭṭaʕaːm] The prisoners went on a hunger strike.
تضارَب [dðaːrab] *v:* • **1.** to exchange blows, hit each other – تشاتمَوا وَبَعدِين تضارَبوا [tšaːtmaw wbaʕdiːn

ض

dǫa:rbaw] They insulted each other and then exchanged blows. • **2.** to conflict, be in disagreement, contradict each other – أخبار الحادِث تضاربَت [ʔaxba:r ʔilħa:diθ dǫa:rbat] Reports of the accident conflicted.

اِنضُرَب [ʔinǫurab] *v:* • **1.** to be struck, hit – اِنضُرَب بِحجار براسَه [ʔinǫurab biħja:r bra:sah] He got hit on the head by a stone. الزَّرِع مالهُم اِنضُرَب كُلّه هالسَّنَة [ʔizzariʕ ma:lhum ʔinǫurab kullah hassana] Their crops were all stricken this year. بُخلَه، ينضُرَب بِيه المَثَل [buxlah, yinǫurab bi:h ʔilmaθal] Legends are told about his stinginess! صَدِيقِي اِنضُرَب ذَيل [ṣadi:qi ʔinǫurab ðayl] My friend got fired.

اِضطِرَب [ʔiǫṭirab] *v:* • **1.** to be or become agitated, upset, disturbed, in a state of turmoil – اِضطِرَبِت مِن سِمَعِت الأخبار [ʔiǫṭirabit min simaʕit ʔilʔaxba:r] I became upset when I heard the news. يبَيِّن الحالَة اِضطِربَت بِالشِّمال [yibayyin ʔilħa:la ʔiǫṭirbat biššima:l] It seems that the situation is in turmoil in the North.

ضَرُب [ǫarub] *n:* • **1.** striking, hitting, beating • **2.** multiplication – جَدوَل الضَّرُب [ǰadwal ʔiǫǫarub] the multiplication tables.

ضَربَة [ǫarba] *n:* ضَربات [ǫarba:t] *pl:* • **1.** a blow • **2.** a beating – ضَربَة الشَّمِس [ǫarbat ʔiššamis] sunstroke.

مَضرَب [maǫrab] *n:* مَضارِب [maǫa:rib] *pl:* • **1.** camp site, camp • **2.** spot – مَضرَب دِهِن [maǫrab dihin] a greasy spot, smear, stain.

ضَرِيبَة [ǫari:ba] *n:* ضَرائِب [ǫara:ʔib, ǫara:yib] *pl:* • **1.** imposition, excessive requirement • **2.** tax, duty – ضَرِيبَة الدَّخَل [ǫari:bat ʔiddaxal] income tax.

إضراب [ʔiǫra:b] *n:* إضرابات [ʔiǫra:ba:t] *pl:* • **1.** strike

اِضطِراب [ʔiǫṭira:b] *n:* اِضطِرابات [ʔiǫṭira:ba:t] *pl:* • **1.** trouble, unrest, commotion, tumult, disruption, disturbance

ضارِب [ǫa:rib] *adj:* • **1.** striking, hitting, beating, etc – لُون نَفنُوفها ضارِب لِلحُمرَة [lu:n nafnu:fha ǫa:rib lilħumra] The color of her dress has a reddish tint.

مضرَّب [mǫarrab] *adj:* • **1.** crossbred, mixed (derrog. when used for people) • **2.** beaten

مُضرِب [muǫrib] *adj:* مُضرِبِين [muǫribi:n] *pl:* • **1.** striking, on strike • **2.** (as n:) striker

مَضرُوب [maǫru:b] *adj:* • **1.** beaten, multiplied

مِضطِرِب [miǫṭirib] *adj:* • **1.** turbulent • **2.** unquiet, restive • **3.** confused

مِتضارُب [mitǫa:rub] *adj:* • **1.** different • **2.** conflicting, in conflict with

ضَرّاب : ضَرّاب جَيب [ǫarra:b, ǫarra:b ǰi:b] *n:* ضَرّابِين : ضَرّابِين جيُوب [ǫarra:bi:n : ǫarra:bi:n ǰyuwb] *pl:* • **1.** beater, hitter • **2.** in this specific idiom: pickpocket

أضرَب [ʔaǫrab] *comparative adjective:* • **1.** even more so, even more of a beater, hitter – هالمُعَلِّم شَدِيد لَكِن المُعَلِّم الجّاي أضرَب مِنَّه [halmuʕallim šadi:d la:kin ʔilmuʕallim ʔiǰǰa:y ʔaǫrab minnah] This teacher is strict but the next teacher is much more so than he. هَذا يِفتِهم بَسّ أبُوه أضرَب مِنَّه [ha:ða yiftihim bass ʔabu:h ʔaǫrab minnah] He is knowledgeable but his father is even more so than him. أخُوك أضرَب مِن صَدِيقِي بِاللَّطايِف [ʔaxu:k ʔaǫrab min ṣadi:qi billaṭa:yif] Your brother is far better than my friend at telling jokes.

ض ر ح

ضَرِيح [ǫari:ħ] *n:* ضَرايِح، أضرِحَة [ǫara:yiħ, ʔaǫriħa] *pl:* • **1.** tomb, mausoleum

ض ر ر

ضَرّ [ǫarr] *v:* • **1.** to be harmful, noxious, injurious, to harm, impair, damage, injure – لا تاكُل أكِل دِهِين تَرَة يضُرَّك [la: ta:kul ʔakil dihi:n tara yǫurrak] Don't eat greasy food because it's harmful to you. يضُرّ شِي إذا تروُح وَحدَك وَتسَوِّيها؟ [yǫurrši ʔiða tru:ħ waħdak wtsawwi:ha?] Will it do any harm if you go alone and do it? ضَرَّيتنِي هوايَة بِهالشَّروَة [ǫarraytni hwa:ya bihaššarwa] You caused me a great loss on this purchase.

تضَرَّر [dǫarrar] *v:* • **1.** to suffer, undergo harm, damage, loss – الحُكُومَة عَوَّضَت كُلّ مَن تضَرَّر بِالفَيَضان [ʔilħuku:ma ʕawwǫat kull man dǫarrar bilfayaǫa:n] The government compensated everyone who suffered damage in the flood. الزُّرّاع تضَرَّرَوا هوايَة مِن الحالُوب [ʔizzurra:ʕ dǫarriraw hwa:ya min ʔilħa:lu:b] The farmers suffered badly from the hail.

اِنضَرّ [ʔinǫarr] *v:* • **1.** to be harmed, damaged, injured, impaired – مَحَّد يِنضَرّ بِهالقانُون غير الفُقَراء [maħħad yinǫarr bihalqa:nu:n ɣi:r ʔilfuqara:ʔ] No one will be hurt by this law except the poor. اِنضَرَّيت هوايَة بِهالشَّراكَة [ʔinǫarrayt hwa:ya bhaššara:ka] I've been hurt badly in this partnership.

اِضطَرّ [ʔiǫṭarr] *v:* • **1.** to force, compel, coerce – اِضطَرّونِي أسَوِّيها [ʔiǫṭarru:ni ʔasawwi:ha] They forced me to do it. • **2.** to be forced, compelled, obliged – ما كان عِندِي فلُوس وإضطَرَّيت أرُوح مَشِي [ma: ča:n ʕindi flu:s wʔiǫṭarrayt ʔaru:ħ mašy] I had no money and was forced to go on foot.

ضَرّ [ǫarr] *n:* • **1.** harm, damage, detriment

ضَرَر [ǫarar] *n:* أضرار [ʔaǫra:r] *pl:* • **1.** harm, damage, loss • **2.** detriment, disadvantage

ضَرَّة [ǫarra] *n:* ضَرّات، ضَرايِر [ǫarra:t, ǫara:yir] *pl:* • **1.** an additional wife in a plural marriage • **2.** pl. ضَرّات an edible gland in the udder of a cow

مَضَرَّة [maǫarra] *n:* مَضَرّات، مَضارّ [maǫarra:t, maǫa:rr] *pl:* • **1.** harm, damage, detriment, loss, disadvantage

ضَرُورَة [ǫaru:ra] *n:* ضَرُورات [ǫaru:ra:t] *pl:* • **1.** necessity, need

ض

اِضطِرار [ʔiðṭira:r] *n:* • **1.** compulsion, coercion, necessity, exigency – عِند الاِضطِرار [ʕind ʔilʔiðṭira:r] in case of emergency.
مُضِرّ [muðirr] *adj:* • **1.** harmful, injurious, detrimental, noxious
ضَرير [ðari:r] *adj:* • **1.** blind • **2.** blind man
ضَرُوري [ðaru:ri] *adj:* • **1.** necessary, imperative, requisite – المِلح ضَرُوري بالأكِل [ʔilmiliħ ðaru:ri bilʔakil] Salt is necessary in food. • **2.** (pl. -iyya:t) necessity, obligatory thing(s)
مَضرُور [maðru:r] *adj:* • **1.** harmed, damaged, injured, having suffered loss – مَحَّد اِستَفاد. كُلّنا طِلَعنا مَضرُورين [maħħad ʔistafa:d. kullna ṭilaʕna maðru:ri:n] No one benefited. We all came out short. دايِنّي كَم دِينار حَتّى ألعَب وِيّاكُم. آني مَضرُور [da:yinni čam dina:r ħatta ʔalʕab wiyya:kum. ʔa:ni maðru:r] Lend me a few dinars so I can play with you. I'm busted.
مِتضَرِّر [mitðarrir] *adj:* • **1.** damaged • **2.** affected, harmed
اِضطِراري [ʔiðṭira:ri] *adj:* • **1.** compulsory, necessary, mandatory, obligatory – باب خُرُوج اِضطِراري [ba:b xuru:ǰ ʔiðṭira:ri] emergency exit.
أضَرّ [ʔaðarr] *comparative adjective:* • **1.** more or most harmful, injurious

ض ر س

ضِرِس [ðiris] *n:* أضراس [ʔaðra:s] *pl:* • **1.** molar, molar tooth

م ض ر ط ض ر ط

ضِرَط [ðiraṭ, ðuraṭ] *v:* • **1.** to break wind noisily, fart
ضَرَّط [ðarraṭ] *v:* • **1.** to break wind repeatedly, fart • **2.** to scare, cause to cower, cow – صاح عَليه صَيحَة وِحدَة ضَرَّطَه بيها [ṣa:ħ ʕali:h ṣayħa wiħda ðarraṭah bi:ha] He shouted at him once and cowed him.
اِستَضرَط [ʔistaðraṭ] *v:* • **1.** to have contempt for, to consider weak, cowardly – المُوَظَّفين اِستَضرطُوه لِلمُلاحِظ مِن عِرفُوه ضَعيف [ʔilmuwaððafi:n ʔistaðriṭu:h lilmula:ħið min ʕirfu:h ðaʕi:f] The employees had no respect for the supervisor when they found out he was weak.
ضَرطَة [ðarṭa] *n:* ضَرطات [ðarṭa:t] *pl:* • **1.** act of breaking wind, farting • **2.** (coll.) ضَرط farts
مَضرَط [maðraṭ] *n:* مَضارِط [maða:riṭ] *pl:* • **1.** rectum, anus (vulgar)
مضَرَّط [mðarraṭ] *adj:* مضارطَة [mða:rṭa] *pl:* • **1.** low, cowardly, sneaking, mean • **2.** ignoble, contemptible person
مَضرُوطَة [maðru:ṭa] *adj:* مَضرُوطات [maðru:ṭa:t] *pl:* • **1.** bitch, slut
أضرَط [ʔaðraṭ] *comparative adjective:* • **1.** more or most ignoble, lowly, contemptible

ض ر ع 1

تضَرَّع [dðarraʕ] *v:* • **1.** with لِ- to implore, beseech, beg – تضَرَّع لِرَبَّه يخَلِّصَه مِن هَالمُشكِلَة [dðarraʕ lirabbah yxalliṣah min halmuškila] He implored his God to deliver him from that problem.
ضَرِع [ðariʕ] *n:* ضرُوع [ðru:ʕ] *pl:* • **1.** udder
تَضَرُّع [taðarruʕ] *n:* • **1.** begging, imploring
مِتضَرِّع [mitðarriʕ] *adj:* • **1.** implorer, beggar (esp. before God)

ض ر ع 2

مُضارِع [muða:riʕ] *n:* • **1.** present • **2.** imperfect (gram.)

ض ر ق

ضِرَق [ðirag] *v:* • **1.** (of a bird or fowl) to defecate, drop excrement – ضِرَق الطَّير عَلَى سِترتَك [ðirag ʔiṭṭi:r ʕala sitirtak] The bird dropped something on your coat.
ضَرَّق [ðarrag] *v:* • **1.** to defecate repeatedly – الدِّجاج اللَّيل كُلَّه كان يضَرِّق عالميز [ʔiddiǰa:ǰ ʔillayl kullah ča:n yðarrig ʕalmi:z] The chickens were messing on the table all night long.
ضَرِق [ðarig] *n:* ضرُوق [ðru:g] *pl:* • **1.** bird dropping – ضرُوق خِشّاف [ðru:g xišša:f] bat guano.

ض ر م

اِضطِرَم [ʔiðṭiram] *v:* • **1.** to flare up
اِضطِرام [ʔiðṭira:m] *n:* • **1.** burning, conflagration

ض

ض ع ض ع

ضَعضَع [ðaʕðaʕ] *v:* • **1.** to undermine, weaken, ruin, upset – ضَعضَعِت الميز مِن قَدّ ما تهِزَّه [ðaʕðaʕit ʔilmi:z min gadd ma: thizzah] You've weakened the table by shaking it so much. خَلّيه قاعِد بمُكانَه. لا تضَعضِعَه [xalli:h ga:ʕid bimuka:nah. la: dðaʕðiʕah] Leave it sitting where it is. Don't disturb it.
تضَعضَع [dðaʕðaʕ] *v:* • **1.** to be undermined, weakened – صِحّتَه تضَعضِعَت مِن شُرُب التِّرياك [ṣiħħtah dðaʕðiʕat min šurub ʔittirya:k] His health was weakened by smoking opium.

ض ع ف 1

ضِعَف [ðiʕaf] *v:* • **1.** to be or become frail, slim, thin – إذا ما تاكُل زين، تِضعَف [ʔiða ma: ta:kul zi:n, tiðʕaf] If you don't eat well, you'll get weak. كان سِمين لٰكِن ضِعَف هَالصَّيف [ča:n simi:n la:kin ðiʕaf haṣṣayf] He was fat but he lost weight this summer. • **2.** to weaken, become weaker, diminish – مَركَزَه بالحِزِب ضِعَف [markazah bilħizib ðiʕaf] His position in the party weakened.
ضَعَّف [ðaʕʕaf] *v:* • **1.** to make frail, thin, slim, to weaken, enfeeble, debilitate
أضعَف [ʔaðʕaf] *v:* • **1.** to make frail, thin, slim, to weaken, enfeeble, debilitate

اِستَضعَف [ʔistaðˁʕaf] *v:* • **1.** to consider weak, feeble, to underestimate – لا تِستَضعِفَه تَرَة تِتنَدَّم [laː tistaðˁʕifah tara titnaddam] Don't think of him as weak or you'll be sorry.
ضُعُف [ðˁuʕuf] *n:* • **1.** slimness, frailty
تَضعِيف [taðˁʕiːf] *n:* • **1.** weakening
ضَعِيف [ðˁaʕiːf] *adj:* • **1.** frail, thin, emaciated • **2.** weak, feeble – ذاكِرتَه ضَعِيفَة [ðaːkirtah ðˁaʕiːfa] His memory is poor.
ضَعفان [ðˁaʕfaːn] *adj:* • **1.** weakened, enfeebled, thin, skinny, slim – يبَيِّن عَليك ضَعفان. ما دَتاكُل؟ [yibayyin ʕaliːk ðˁaʕfaːn. maː dataːkul?] You look thin. Aren't you eating?
ضعَيفُوني [ðˁʕayfuːni] *adj:* • **1.** slim, skinny
أَضعَف [ʔaðˁʕaf] *comparative adjective:* • **1.** more or most delicate, emaciated, feeble

ض ع ف 2

ضاعَف [ðˁaːʕaf] *v:* • **1.** to double, redouble, multiply, compound – إذا تضاعِف عَدَد الشُّرطَة، يصِير أَمان بالبَلَد [ʔiða dðˁaːʕif ʕadad ʔiššurṭa, yṣiːr ʔamaːn bilbalad] If you double the number of police there'll be safety in the city. ضاعَف ثَروتَه مِن أَسَّس هَالشَّرِكَة [ðˁaːʕaf θarwtah min ʔassas haššarika] He redoubled his wealth when he formed this company.
تضاعَف [dðˁaːʕaf] *v:* • **1.** pass. of ضاعَف: to be compounded, to be doubled – تضاعَف عَدَدهُم بمُدَّة قَصِيرَة [dðˁaːʕaf ʕadadhum bmudda qaṣiːra] Their number doubled in a short time. الأَلَم مالَه تضاعَف مِن فَكَّه البَنج [ʔilʔalam maːlah dðˁaːʕaf min fakkah ʔilbanǰ] His pain was redoubled when the anesthetic wore off.
ضِعِف [ðˁiʕif] *n:* أَضعاف [ʔaðˁʕaːf] *pl:* • **1.** double, twice as much • **2.** multiple, several times as much – رِبح هَاليُوم كان ثلَث أَضعاف رِبح البارحَة [ribiħ halyuːm čaːn tlaθ ʔaðˁʕaːf ribiħ ʔilbaːrħa] Today's profit was three times as much as yesterday's profit.
مُضاعَفات [muðˁaːʕafaːt] *n:* • **1.** pl. only exponentiation, increasing by any power (e.g. squaring, cubing)
مضاعَف [mðˁaːʕaf] *adj:* • **1.** doubled

ض غ ط

ضِغَط [ðˁiɣaṭ] *v:* • **1.** with عَلَى to exert pressure on, press on, bear down upon – لا تخَلِّي الإشداد يُضغُط هوايَة عَالجِّرح [laː txalli: ʔiliʔišdaːd yuðˁɣuṭ hwaːya ʕaǰǰariħ] Don't let the bandage press too tightly on the wound.
اِنضِغَط [ʔinðˁiɣaṭ] *v:* • **1.** to bear down • **2.** to be pressed
ضَغِط [ðˁaɣiṭ] *n:* • **1.** pressure – الضَّغط الجَّوِّي [ʔiðˁðˁaɣṭ ʔiǰǰawwi] atmospheric pressure. ضَغُط دَمّ [ðˁaɣuṭ damm] blood pressure. • **2.** emphasis, stress, oppression, suppression, tension
ضُغُوط [ðˁuɣuːṭ] *n:* ضُغُوطات [ðˁuɣuːṭaːt] *pl:* • **1.** pressure(s) • **2.** tension, oppression, stress
ضاغِطَة [ðˁaːɣiṭa] *n:* • **1.** compressor (tool)
ضاغِط [ðˁaːɣiṭ] *adj:* • **1.** compressing
مَضغُوط [maðˁɣuːṭ] *adj:* • **1.** compressed – هَوا مَضغُوط [hawa maðˁɣuːṭ] compressed air.

ض غ ن

ضَغِينَة [ðˁaɣiːna] *n:* • **1.** grudge, rancor, spite, malice, malevolence, ill will

ض ف ر

ضُفَر [ðˁufar] *v:* • **1.** to plait, braid (hair) – العَرُوس دَيضُفرُون قِصايِبها [ʔilʕaruːs dayðˁufruːn giṣaːyibha] They're plaiting the bride's braids. • **2.** to catch, grasp, lay one's hands on – بَسّ أَظُفرَه، أَعرُف شأَسَوِّي بِيه [bass ʔaðˁufrah, ʔaʕruf šʔasawwi: biːh] Once I catch him, I'll know what to do with him. • **3.** intertwine, interweave, interlace
ضَفُر [ðˁafur] *n:* • **1.** plait, braid
ضِفِيرَة [ðˁifiːra] *n:* ضَفايِر [ðˁafaːyir] *pl:* • **1.** adornment on the end of a girl's braid

ض ل ع

ضِلَع [ðˁilaʕ] *v:* • **1.** to take someone's side, to sympathize with someone, to make common cause with someone
ضِلِع [ðˁiliʕ] *n:* ضلُوع، أَضلاع [ðˁluːʕ, ʔaðˁlaːʕ] *pl:* • **1.** rib, chop, cutlet • **2.** side (of a triangle)
ضِلعَة [ðˁilʕa] *n:* ضِلعات [ðˁilʕaːt] *pl:* • **1.** a cut of meat from the ribs of an animal
مضَلَّع [mðˁallaʕ] *adj:* • **1.** polygonal • **2.** ribbed, supported

ض ل ف

ضِلِف [ðˁilif] *n:* أَضلاف [ʔaðˁlaːf] *pl:* • **1.** cloven hoof

ض ل ل

ضَلَّل [ðˁallal] *v:* • **1.** to mislead, misguide, fool, confuse – حَطّوا أَغصان أَشجار عَالدَّبّابات حَتَّى يضَلِّلُون العَدُو [ħaṭṭaw ʔaɣṣaːn ʔašǰaːr ʕaddabbaːbaːt ħatta yðˁallilu:n ʔilʕadu] They put tree branches on the tanks to mislead the enemy.
تَضلِيل [taðˁliːl] *n:* • **1.** misleading (someone), deceiving (someone)
ضَلالَة [ðˁalaːla] *n:* • **1.** error • **2.** loss
ضالّ [ðˁaːll] *adj:* • **1.** lost, astray

ض م ح ل

اِضمَحَلّ [ʔiðˁmaħall] *v:* • **1.** to disappear, vanish, dwindle, fade away, melt away; to decrease, become less
اِضمِحلال [ʔiðˁmiħlaːl] *n:* • **1.** disappearing, vanishing, evanescence

مُضمَحِلّ [muðmaħill] *adj:* • **1.** vanishing, evanescent, fading; damped

ض م د

ضَمَّد [ðammad] *v:* • **1.** to dress, bandage – رُوح لِلمُستَشفى حَتّى يضَمِّدُوا لَك الجَرِح [ru:ħ lilmustašfa ħatta yðammidu:lak ʔijjariħ] Go to the hospital so they can bandage the wound for you.
ضماد [ðama:d] *n:* ضَمادات [ðama:da:t] *pl:* • **1.** bandage
مُضَمِّد [muðammid] *n:* مُضَمِّدِين [muðammidi:n] *pl:* • **1.** hospital attendant who administers minor treatments, male nurse
مُضَمَّد [muðammad] *adj:* • **1.** bandaged

ض م ر

ضُمَر [ðumar] *v:* • **1.** to secrete, keep secret, conceal – أُضمُر عَدَد وَأَني أَحزِره [ʔuðmur ʕadad waʔa:ni ʔaħizrah] Think of a number and I'll guess what it is. • **2.** to harbor, entertain – اِتفاداه. هَذا دَيضمُرلَك الشَّرّ [ʔitfa:da:h. ha:ða dayiðmurlak ʔiššarr] Avoid him. He's holding a grudge against you.
ضَمُر [ðamur] *n:* • **1.** concealing, keeping secret
ضَمِير [ðami:r] *n:* ضَمائِر [ðama:ʔir, ðama:yir] *pl:* • **1.** conscience, scruples • **2.** personal pronoun (gram.)
ضُمُور [ðumu:r] *n:* • **1.** atrophy, wasting away

ض م ض م

ضَمضَم [ðamðam] *v:* • **1.** to be secretive, keep things to oneself – لا تضَمضُم عَلَيّا. قُلّي كُلّشِي [la: dðamðum ʕalayya. gulli kullši] Don't hide things from me. Tell me everything. شما تسَوِّي، أُمّها تضَمضُم إلها [šma tsawwi:, ʔummaha dðamðum ʔilha] Whatever she does, her mother covers up for her. دَيضَمضُم بفلُوسَه وَما يقُول لِأَحَّد [dayðamðum bflu:sah wma ygu:l lʔaħħad] He is hiding his money and doesn't tell anyone.
تضَمضَم [dðamðam] *v:* • **1.** to be concealed, be kept secret – القَضِيَّة اِنفُضحَت وَبَعَد ما تِتضَمضَم [ʔilqaðiyya ʔinfuðħat wabaʕad ma: tidðamðam] The matter has been disclosed and can't be covered up anymore.
مضَمضَم [mðamðam] *adj:* • **1.** hidden

ض م م

ضَمّ [ðamm] *v:* • **1.** to be secretive, to keep things to oneself – إحكِي! لا تضُمّ عَلَيّا [ʔiħči! la: dðumm ʕalayya] Speak up! Don't hide anything from me. • **2.** to hide, conceal, secrete – الجّاهِل ضَمّ القَلَم مالَه بمُكان ما نِندَلَّه [ʔijja:hil ðamm ʔilqalam ma:lah bmuka:n ma: nindallah] The child hid his pencil in a place we wouldn't find. • **3.** to put away for safekeeping, to save, to salt away – لا تُصرُف كُلّ راتبَك. ضُمّ مِنَّه شوَيَّة [la: tuṣruf kull ra:tbak. ðumm minnah šwayya] Don't spend all your salary. Put away a little of it. تِقدَر تضُمّلِي فلُوسِي عِندَك إلَى أَن أَرجَع؟ [tigdar dðummli flu:si ʕindak ʔila ʔan ʔarjaʕ?] Could you keep my money for me until I return? • **4.** to join, unite, add – آنِي أَضُمّ صُوتِي إلَى صَوتَك بالإحتِجاج [ʔa:ni ʔaðumm ṣu:ti ʔila ṣawtak bilʔiħtija:j] I'll add my voice to yours in the protest.
اِنضَمّ [ʔinðamm] *v:* • **1.** to hide oneself – مِن شاف الشُّرطِي جاي، اِنضَمّ مِنهُم [min ša:f ʔiššurṭi ja:y, ʔinðamm] When he saw the policeman coming, he hid himself. • **2.** with ل to enter, join – اِنضَمّ لِلحِزب بدُون مُوافَقَة أَهلَه [ʔinðamm lilħizib bidu:n muwa:faqat ʔahlah] He joined the (political) party without his family's consent.
ضَمّ [ðamm] *n:* • **1.** hiding, keeping secret, concealing, saving, joining
ضَمَّة [ðamma] *n:* • **1.** embrace, hug
اِنضِمام [ʔinðima:m] *n:* • **1.** entry, enrollment, affiliation (into an organization and the like)
مِنضَمّ [minððam] *adj:* • **1.** enrolled, affiliated • **2.** hidden
مَضمُوم [maðmu:m] *adj:* • **1.** hidden

ض م ن

ضُمَن [ðuman] *v:* • **1.** to guarantee, ensure, make sure, be certain – شلُون تِضمَن ما يعِيد نَفس الغَلطَة؟ [šlu:n tiðman ma: yʕi:d nafs ʔilɣalṭa?] How can you be sure that he won't repeat the same mistake? • **2.** to contract for the unharvested crop of (an orchard) – ضُمَن البُستان بمِيتَين دِينار [ðuman ʔilbusta:n bmi:tayn dina:r] He contracted for the orchard for two hundred dinars.
ضَمَّن [ðamman] *v:* • **1.** to sell the unharvested crop of (an orchard) – ما أَضَمُّن البُستان بأَقَلّ مِن مِيَّة دِينار [ma: ʔaðammun ʔilbusta:n bʔaqall min miyyat dina:r] I won't sell the orchard's crop for less than a hundred dinars.
تضَمَّن [dðamman] *v:* • **1.** to imply • **2.** to include, to contain
اِنضُمَن [ʔinðuman] *v:* • **1.** to be guaranteed, to be ensured
ضِمن، مِن ضِمن، بضِمن [ðimin, min ðimin, bðimin] *n:* • **1.** included in, among, belonging to, part of the group of – مِن ضِمن الأَشياء اللّي حِكالِي إيّاها قِصَّة السَّيّارَة [min ðimin ʔilʔašya:ʔ ʔilli ħiča:li ʔiyya:ha qiṣṣat ʔissayya:ra] Among the things he told me was the story about the car. هُوَّ مِن ضِمن الجَّماعَة اللّي اِعتِدَوا عَلَيّا [huwwa min ðimin ʔijjama:ʕa ʔilli ʔiʕtidaw ʕalayya] He is one of the group who attacked me. الضَّرِيبَة داخلَة بضِمن السِّعِر [ʔiððari:ba da:xla bðimin ʔissiʕir] The tax is included in the price.
ضَمّان [ðamma:n] *n:* ضَمّانَة [ðamma:na] *pl:* • **1.** landlord, man who owns an orchard and sells the unharvested crop

ضَمان [ð̣ama:n] *n:* • **1.** guarantee, insurance, warrant, security, assurance
تَضامُن [tað̣a:mun] *n:* • **1.** solidarity, mutuality, reciprocity, joint liability
ضامِن [ð̣a:min] *adj:* • **1.** guarantor
مَضمُون [mað̣mu:n] *adj:* • **1.** guaranteed
مِتضَمِّن [mitð̣ammin] *adj:* • **1.** including
مِتضامِن [mitð̣a:min] *adj:* • **1.** contracted • **1.** showing solidarity
أَضمَن [ʔað̣man] *comparative adjective:* • **1.** more or most vouchsafed, guaranteed, warranted, safe – أضمَنلَك تاخُذ ويّاك عَشِر دَنانِير زايدَة [ʔað̣manlak ta:xuð wiyya:k ʕašir dana:ni:r za:yda] It's safer for you to take ten dinars extra with you.

ض ن ك

ضِنَك [ð̣inak] *v:* • **1.** to place in straitened, impoverished circumstances – دَفع الإيجار ضِنكَنِي [dafiʕ ʔilʔi:ǰa:r ð̣inakni] Paying the rent put me in straitened circumstances.
اِنضِنَك [ʔinð̣inak] *v:* • **1.** to be placed in straitened circumstances – مِن اِشتِرَيت الحُوش، اِنضِنَقِت. فلُوسِي ما دَتكَفِّي [min ʔištirayt ʔilħu:š, ʔinð̣inakit. flu:si ma: datkaffi] When I bought the house, I put myself in a bind. My money isn't enough.
ضَنَك [ð̣anak] *n:* • **1.** poverty, distress, straits – عايِش بِضَنَك [ʕa:yiš bð̣anak] He's living in poverty.
مَضنُوك [mað̣nu:k] *adj:* • **1.** in financial straits – ما راح أقدَر أدفَع قِسط السَّيّارَة هَالشَّهَر. آنِي مَضنُوك [ma: ra:ħ ʔagdar ʔadfaʕ qisṭ ʔissayya:ra haššahar. ʔa:ni mað̣nu:k] I won't be able to pay the car payment this month. I'm in a bind.

ض ه د

اِضطِهَد [ʔið̣ṭihad] *v:* • **1.** to persecute, oppress, treat unjustly – اِستَولَوا عالبَلَد وَاِضطِهدَوا سُكّانَه [ʔistawlaw ʕalbalad wʔið̣ṭihdaw sukka:nah] They conquered the country and treated its inhabitants unjustly.
اِضطِهاد [ʔið̣ṭiha:d] *n:* • **1.** persecution, suppression, oppression, repression, maltreatemnt
مُضطَهَد [muð̣ṭahid] *adj:* • **1.** persecuted, oppressed, mistreated

ض ه ي

ضاهَى [ð̣a:ha:] *v:* • **1.** to resemble, be like, be comparable to, to match, equal – جَمالها ما يضاهِي أيّ جَمال [ǰama:lha ma: yð̣a:hi ʔayy ǰama:l] He beauty is like no other beauty. مَحَّد يضاهِيه بِالشِّعِر [maħħad yð̣a:hi:h biššiʕir] Nobody can come up to his level in poetry.
مُضاهاة [muð̣a:ha:t] *n:* • **1.** similarity, resemblance, likeness

ض و ج

ضاج [ð̣a:ǰ] *v:* • **1.** to become uneasy, upset, annoyed, disturbed, irritated – لا تجِيب طارِي الامتِحان تَرَة يضُوج [la: dji:b ṭa:ri ʔilʔimtiħa:n tara yð̣u:ǰ] Don't bring up the subject of the exam or he'll get upset. المُعَلِّم ضاج مِنَّه هوايَة [ʔilmuʕallim ð̣a:ǰ minnah hwa:ya] The teacher got extremely fed up with him. • **2.** to become restless, bored – ضِجِت وَحدِي بالغُرفَة [ð̣iǰit waħdi bilɣurfa] I got bored being alone in the room. إبنِكُم ضاج خُوش ضُوجَة عِدنا [ʔibinkum ð̣a:ǰ xu:š ð̣u:ǰa ʕidna] Your son got real bored at our place.
ضَوَّج [ð̣awwaǰ] *v:* • **1.** to upset, bother, disturb, annoy, irritate – يضَوِّج هوايَة بكَلامَه [yð̣awwiǰ hwa:ya bkala:mah] He annoys people a lot when he talks. • **2.** to bore – البَطالَة ضَوِّجَتنِي [ʔilbaṭa:la ð̣awwiǰatni] The idleness bored me.
تضَوَّج [dð̣awwaǰ] *v:* • **1.** pass. of ضَوَّج: [ð̣awwaǰ] to be bothered, to be disturbed, to be annoyed
ضوج [ð̣awǰ] *n:* • **1.** irritation, annoyance • **2.** boredom, restlessness
ضُوجَة [ð̣u:ǰa] *n:* ضَوجات [ð̣u:ǰa:t] *pl:* • **1.** irritation, annoyance, boredom, restlessness
ضواجَة [ð̣wa:ǰa] *n:* • **1.** boredom
تَضويج [tað̣wi:ǰ] *n:* • **1.** annoying, bothering, upsetting
مضَوِّج [mð̣awwiǰ] *adj:* • **1.** bothering someone
ضايِج [ð̣a:yiǰ] *adj:* • **1.** wretched • **2.** disturbed, annoyed, upset
ضَوَجان [ð̣awaǰa:n] *adj:* • **1.** bothersome, annoying, upsetting • **2.** boring – هَالشُّغُل ضَوَجان [haššuɣul ð̣awaǰa:n] This work is boring.

ض و ي

ضُوَى [ð̣uwa:] *v:* • **1.** to gleam, beam, radiate, shine – وِجهَها يضوِي مِثل البَدِر [wiččha yið̣wi miθl ʔalbadir] Her face shines like the full moon.
ضَوَّى [ð̣awwa:] *v:* • **1.** to light, light up, illuminate – گلُوب أبُو مِيَّة يضَوِّي الغُرفَة کُلِّش زين [glu:b ʔabu miyya yð̣awwi ʔilɣurfa kulliš zi:n] A hundred watt bulb lights the room very well. إشعِل الضُّوَة، وَضَوِّيلِي الطَّرِيق [ʔišʕil ʔið̣ð̣uwa, wað̣wwi:li ʔiṭṭari:q] Turn on the light and light up the road for me. • **2.** to provide light – ضَوِّيلِي حَتَّى أقدَر أقرا القُطعَة [ð̣awwi:li ħatta ʔagdar ʔaqra: ʔilquṭʕa] Give me some light so I can read the sign.
ضُوَة، ضُوَا [ð̣uwa] *n:* ضُوايات، أضوِيَة [ð̣uwa:ya:t, ʔað̣wiya] *pl:* • **1.** light – ضُوَا الشَّمِس [ð̣uwa ʔiššamis] sunlight.
ضَوِي [ð̣awiy] *n:* • **1.** shining, gleaming, beaming
إضاءَة [ʔið̣a:ʔa] *n:* • **1.** lighting
ضُوِي، ضاوِي [ð̣uwi, ð̣a:wi] *adj:* • **1.** bright, lighted, illuminated – غُرفَة ضويَّة [ɣurfa ð̣wiyya] a bright room. أُقعُد. الدِّنيا ضويَّة [ʔugʕud. ʔiddinya ð̣wiyya] Get up. It's daylight.

ضُويَّة [ḍuwiyya] *adj:* • **1.** bright, lighted
ضاوِيَة [ḍa:wiya] *adj:* • **1.** light • **2.** bright

ض ي ع

ضاع [ḍa:ʕ] *v:* • **1.** to be lost, get lost – البارحَة ضاعَت بِنتَه بالسُّوق [ʔilba:rħa ḍa:ʕat bintah bissu:g] Yesterday his daughter got lost in the marketplace. ضاع مِفتاح القاصَة [ḍa:ʕ mifta:ħ ʔilqa:ṣa] The key to the safe got lost. ضاع عَلَيّا الحساب؛ ما أدري شقَد أطُلبَه [ḍa:ʕ ʕalayya ʔilħsa:b; ma: ʔadri šgadd ʔaṭulbah] I lost count; I don't know how much he owes me. لِيش ما قَدَّمِت عَرِيضَة؟ الفُرصَة ضاعَت عَلِيك [li:š ma: qaddamit ʕari:ḍa? ʔilfurṣa ḍa:ʕat ʕali:k] Why didn't you submit an application? The opportunity has passed you by.
ضَيَّع [ḍayyaʕ] *v:* • **1.** to cause to get lost – عَبالنا يُعرُف البَيت، لَكِن فَوَّتنا بدَرابِين وَضَيَّعنا [ʕaba:lna yuʕruf ʔilbayt, la:kin fawwatna bdara:bi:n wḍayyaʕna] We thought he knew the house, but he sent us through alleys and got us lost. ضَيِّع نَفسَك فَدّ ساعَة حَتَّى ما يشُوفَك [ḍayyiʕ nafsak fadd sa:ʕa ħatta ma: yšu:fak] Make yourself scarce for an hour so he won't see you. • **2.** to lose – ضَيَّع ساعتَه بالسِّينَما [ḍayyaʕ sa:ʕtah bissinama] He lost his watch in the movie. ضَيِّع إبنَه بالإزدِحام [ḍayyʕ ʔibnah bilʔizdiħa:m] He lost his son in the crowd. • **3.** to waste, squander, spend uselessly – لا تضَيِّع وَقتَك بِاللِّعِب [la: dḍayyiʕ waktak billiʕib] Don't waste your time playing. ضَيَّعِت عَلَيّا الوَقت [ḍayyaʕit ʕalayya ʔilwakit] You've wasted my time. لا تضَيِّع الحكايَة. قُلّي إي لَو لا [la: dḍayyiʕ ʔilħča:ya. gulli: ʔi law la:] Don't beat around the bush. Tell me yes or no. • **4.** with عَلَى to cause to lose, miss – ضَيَّع الفُرصَة عَلَيّا [ḍayyaʕ ʔilfurṣa ʕalayya] He made me miss the opportunity.
ضيع [ḍi:ʕ] *n:* • **1.** loss
مَضيعَة [maḍyaʕa] *n:* • **1.** waste • **2.** perdition
ضايع [ḍa:yiʕ] *adj:* • **1.** lost
مضَيِّع [mḍayyiʕ] *adj:* • **1.** wasteful • **2.** absent minded

ض ي ف

ضاف [ḍa:f] *v:* • **1.** to add, subjoin, annex, attach – إذا تضيف هَالجُملَة، تِنفِهم القَضِيَّة [ʔiḍa dḍi:f hajjumla, tinfihim ʔilqaḍiyya] If you add this sentence, the matter will be understood.
ضَيَّف [ḍayyaf] *v:* • **1.** to take in (as a guest), receive hospitably – ضَيِّفُونا بِبَيتهُم إسبُوع [ḍayyifu:na bbaythum ʔisbu:ʕ] They took us into their house as guests for a week. إذا ترُوح عَلَيهُم، يضَيِّفُوك [ʔiḍa tru:ħ ʕali:hum, yḍayyifu:k] If you go to their house, they treat you like a guest.
انضاف [ʔinḍa:f] *v:* • **1.** to be added
اِستَضيَف [ʔistaḍyaf] *v:* • **1.** to invite to be a guest – يِستَضِيفُون أيّ واحِد يزُور البَلدَة [yistiḍi:fu:n ʔayy wa:ħid yzu:r ʔilbalda] They invite anyone visiting the city to stay with them.
اِستَضاف [ʔistaḍa:f] *v:* • **1.** to host
ضَيف [ḍayf] *n:* ضِيُوف [ḍiyu:f] *pl:* • **1.** guest
مُضِيف [muḍi:f] *n:* مُضايِف [muḍa:yif] *pl:* • **1.** hospice, guest house, hostel.
إضافَة [ʔiḍa:fa] *n:* إضافات [ʔiḍa:fa:t] *pl:* • **1.** addition, annexation, attachment, augmentation, supplementation – بالإضافَة إلَى ذَلِك [bilʔiḍa:fa ʔila ḍa:lik] In addition to that. . . . • **2.** genitive construction (gram.)
مُضَيِّفَة [muḍayyifa] *n:* مُضَيِّفات [muḍayyifa:t] *pl:* • **1.** stewardess, hostess, air hostess
ضِيافَة [ḍiya:fa] *n:* • **1.** hospitality, hospitable reception and entertainment • **2.** hospitable reception and entertainment
اِستِضافَة [ʔistiḍa:fa] *n:* • **1.** hospitality • **2.** Hosting
إضافِي [ʔiḍa:fi] *adj:* • **1.** additional, supplementary, auxiliary, extra, secondary – مَبلَغ إضافِي [mablaɣ ʔiḍa:fi] a supplementary amount.
ضاق [ḍa:g] *v:* • **1.** to be or become narrow, straitened, cramped, confining – يبَيِّن القاط ضاق عَلِيك [yibayyin ʔilqa:ṭ ḍa:g ʕali:k] It looks like the suit is too small for you. ضاقَت الدِّنيا بِيه [ḍa:gat ʔiddinya bi:h] He became depressed (lit., the world became too confining for him). ضاقَت الوَسعَة بِيه [ḍa:gat ʔilwasʕa bi:h] He became depressed. إذا ضاق خُلقِك، تذَكَّر أيّام عِرسِك [ʔiḍa ḍa:g xulgič, dḍakkir ʔayya:m ʕirsič] If you feel sad, remember the days of your wedding.
ضَيَّق [ḍayyaq] *v:* • **1.** with عَلَى to harass, beset, put pressure on – إذا تضَيِّق عَليه، يِنطِيك الفلُوس [ʔiḍa dḍayyiq ʕali:h, yinṭi:k ʔilflu:s] If you pressure him, he'll give you the money.
ضَيَّق [ḍayyag] *v:* • **1.** to make narrow, straiten, cramp, tighten – راح آخُذ البَنطَرُون لِلخَيّاط حَتَّى يضَيِّقَه [ra:ħ ʔa:xuḍ ʔilpanṭaru:n lilxayya:ṭ ħatta yḍayyigah] I'm going to take the pants to the tailor so he can make them tighter.
ضايَق [ḍa:yaq] *v:* • **1.** to vex, annoy, pester, harass, bother, disturb – دَيضايِقنِي هوايَة بمُخابَراتَه [dayḍa:yiqni hwa:ya bmuxa:bara:tah] He's bothering me a lot with his phone calls.
تضَيَّق [dḍayyag] *v:* • **1.** to become tight, to become narrowed
تضايَق [dḍa:yaq] *v:* • **1.** to be or become annoyed, irritated – يِتضايَق هوايَة مِن الزِّيارات [yidḍa:yaq hwa:ya min ʔizziya:ra:t] He gets very irritated at visits.
ضِيق [ḍi:q] *n:* • **1.** distress, need, want, lack, paucity, poverty – عايِش بضِيق [ʕa:yiš bḍi:q] He's living in

ض

poverty. أَقدَر أَساعدَك عِند الضِّيق [ʔagdar ʔasaːʕdak ʕind ʔiððiːq] I can help you in time of need.
مَضِيق [maðiːq] *n:* مَضايِق [maðaːyiq] *pl:* • **1.** narrow passage, straits – مَضِيق جَبَل طارِق [maðiːq ǰabal ṭaːriq] Straits of Gibraltar.
تَضيِيق [taðyiːg] *n:* • **1.** narrowing, tightening, restriction, limitation, oppression
مُضايَقَة [muðaːyaqa] *n:* مُضايَقات [muðaːyaqaːt] *pl:* • **1.** annoyance, disturbance, vexation, irritation, nuisance, harassment

ضَيِّق [ḍayyig] *adj:* • **1.** narrow – شارِع ضَيِّق [šaːriʕ ðayyig] a narrow street. • **2.** tight, cramped, confining – سِتِرتِي ضَيِّقَة عَلَيّا. ما أَقدَر أَتنَفَّس [sitirti ḍayyga ʕalayya. maː ʔagdar ʔatnaffas] My jacket is tight on me. I can't breathe. هَالبَيت صار ضَيِّق هوايَة عَلينا [halbayt ṣaːr ḍayyig hwaːya ʕaliːna] This house has gotten too small for us.
مِتضايِق [mitðaːyiq] *adj:* • **1.** bothered, annoyed, vexed • **2.** uncomfortable
أَضيَق [ʔaðyag] *comparative adjective:* • **1.** narrower, narrowest • **2.** more or most confining

ض

ط

ط ب ب

طَبّ [ṭabb] *v:* • **1.** to enter, go in – جيبِي صغَيِّر. إيدِي ما تطُبّ بِيه [ǰiːbi ṣɣayyir. ʔiːdi maː ṭṭubb biːh] My pocket's too small. My hand won't go in it. هَالبُرغِي ما يطُبّ بِالصَّمُّونَة [halburɣi maː yṭubb biṣṣammuːna] This bolt won't fit into the nut. شال دِشداشتَه وطَبّ يخُوض بِالماي [šaːl dišdaːštah wṭabb yxuːð̣ bilmaːy] He lifted his robe and went wading into the water. طَبّ عَلَيهُم وَشافهُم مَشغُولِين [ṭabb ʕaliːhum wšaːfhum mašɣuːliːn] He dropped in on them and found them busy. يطُبَّه مَرَض [yṭubbah marað̣] To hell with him! Plague take him! • **2.** to pat, tap lightly – طَبّ عَلَى كِتفِي وَإبتِسَم [ṭabb ʕala čitfi wʔibtisam] He patted my shoulder and smiled. • **3.** to slam, dash, bang – شالَه وَطَبَّه بِالقاع [šaːlah wṭabbah bilgaːʕ] He picked him up and slammed him on the ground.

طَبَّب [ṭabbab] *v:* • **1.** to cause to enter, bring in, take in – لِيش موَقُّف صَدِيقَك بَرَّة؟ طَبُّبَه لِلبَيت [liːš mwagguf ṣadiːqak barra? ṭabbubah lilbayt] Why are you keeping your friend outside? Bring him in the house. طَبُّب الوايَر مِن هَالزُّرُف [ṭabbub ʔilwaːyar min hazzuruf] Insert the wire through this hole. • **2.** to treat medically – أحسَن الدَّكاترَة طَبِّبُوه لَكِن ما صارَتلَه جارَة [ʔaħsan ʔiddakaːtra ṭabbibawh laːkin maː ṣaːratlah čaːra] The best doctors treated him but there was no cure for him.

تطَبَّب [tṭabbab] *v:* • **1.** to be entered, to be taken, to be treated

اِنطَبّ [ʔinṭabb] *v:* • **1.** to be entered – هَالغُرفَة ما ينطَبّ [halɣurfa maː yinṭabb] This room is not to be entered.

طِبّ [ṭibb] *n:* • **1.** medical treatment • **2.** medicine, medical science – طِبّ الأسنان [ṭibb ʔilʔasnaːn] dentistry, dental science.

مَطَبّ [maṭabb] *n:* مَطَبّات [maṭabbaːt] *pl:* • **1.** speed bump, bump

طَبَّة [ṭabba] *n:* • **1.** boom, rumbling

طَبِيب [ṭabiːb] *n:* أطِبّاء [ʔaṭibbaːʔ] *pl:* • **1.** doctor, physician – طَبِيب الأسنان [ṭabiːb ʔilʔasnaːn] dentist. طَبِيب بَيطَرِي [ṭabiːb bayṭari] veterinarian.

طِبابَة [ṭibaːba] *n:* • **1.** dispensary • **2.** medical profession, medical treatment

طِبِّي [ṭibbi] *adj:* • **1.** medical – فَحِص طِبِّي [faħiṣ ṭibbi] a medical examination.

ط ب خ

طُبَخ [ṭubax, ṭibax] *v:* • **1.** to cook, to prepare – لا تطُبخِين. راح أجِيب أكِل مِن المَطعَم [laː ṭṭubxiːn. raːħ ʔaǰiːb ʔakil min ʔilmaṭʕam] Don't cook anything. I'll bring some food from the restaurant. شطابخَة اليُوم؟ [šṭaːbxa ʔilyuːm?] What have you cooked today? خَلِّي أرُوح قَبلَك أطبُخها لِلقَضِيَّة [xalliː ʔaruːħ gablak ʔaṭbuxha lilqað̣iyya] Let me go ahead of you and get things ready. خَلِّي أرُوح أطبُخَه. بَلكِي يِقبَل يشُوفَك [xalliː ʔaruːħ ʔaṭubxah. balki yiqbal yšuːfak] Let me go soften him up. Perhaps he'll agree to see you.

اِنطُبَخ [ʔinṭubax] *v:* • **1.** to be cooked, prepared – هَاللَّحَم ما ينطُبُخ بِساع [hallaħam maː yinṭubux bsaːʕ] This meat can't be cooked quickly.

طَبُخ [ṭabux] *n:* • **1.** cooking, cuisine

طَبخَة [ṭabxa] *n:* طَبخات [ṭabxaːt] *pl:* • **1.** (cooked) meal, dish, food

طَبّاخ [ṭabbaːx] *n:* طَبّاخِين [ṭabbaːxiːn] *pl:* • **1.** cook • **2.** pl. kitchen stove, range

طِبِيخ [ṭibiːx] *n:* • **1.** cooked rice

مَطبَخ [maṭbax, muṭbax] *n:* مَطابِخ [maṭaːbix] *pl:* • **1.** kitchen • **2.** kitchen stove.

ط ب ر

طُبَر [ṭubar] *v:* • **1.** to hack, chop – طُبَر راسَه بِالسَّيف [ṭubar raːsah bissayf] He hacked his head with the sword.

طَبَّر [ṭabbar] *v:* • **1.** to hack, chop repeatedly or continuously – عِمَى السِّكِّينَة لِأنّ كان يطَبُّر الخِشبَة بِيها [ʕimaː ʔissiččiːna liʔann čaːn yṭabbur ʔilxišba biːha] He dulled the knife because he was chopping up the board with it.

طَبُر [ṭabur] *n:* • **1.** hacking, cutting

طُبَر [ṭubar] *n:* طبارَة، طبُور [ṭbaːra, ṭbuːr] *pl:* • **1.** axe, hatchet • **2.** pl. طبُور small stream

طَبرَة [ṭabra] *n:* طَبرات [ṭabraːt] *pl:* • **1.** hacking, cutting • **2.** mark, scar

ط ب ش

طَبَّش [ṭabbaš] *v:* • **1.** to splash, splatter, play (in water) – إبنَك يعِجبَه يطَبُّش بِالمَيّ [ʔibnak yiʕiǰbah yṭabbuš bilmayy] Your son likes to splash around in the water.

تَطبِيش [taṭbiːš] *n:* • **1.** splashing

مطَبِّش [mṭabbiš] *adj:* • **1.** splatter

ط ب ش ر

طَباشِير [ṭabaːšiːr, tabaːšiːr] *n:* • **1.** chalk

ط ب ط ب

طَبطَب [ṭabṭab] *v:* • **1.** to pat, tap lightly – طَبطَب إلها لِلبَزُّونَة حَتَّى سِكتَت [ṭabṭab ʔliha lilbazzuːna ħatta siktat] He patted the cat until it kept quiet. • **2.** to bounce, dribble – بكُرَة السَّلَّة، لازِم تطَبطُب الطُّوبَة مِن تِمشِي [bkurat ʔissalla, laːzim ṭṭabṭub ʔiṭṭuːba min timši] In basketball you have to dribble the ball when you move.

طَبطَبَة [ṭabṭaba] *n:* • **1.** pat

ط

ط ب ع

طِبَع [ṭibaʕ, ṭubaʕ] *v:* • **1.** to print – طِبعَوا المَناشِير بِمَطبَعَة سِرِّيَّة [ṭibʕaw ʔilmanaːšiːr bmaṭbaʕa sirriyya] They printed the hand bills with a secret press. • **2.** to type – أَرجُوك، إِطبَعلِي هَالمَكتُوب [ʔarǰuːk, ʔiṭbaʕli halmaktuːb] Please type this letter for me.

طَبَّع [ṭabbaʕ] *v:* • **1.** to imprint on, impress on, impart to – أُمَّه طَبُّعَتَه عَلَى أَشياء مَحبُوبَة هوايَة [ʔummah ṭabbuʕatah ʕala ʔašyaːʔ maħbuːba hwaːya] His mother imparted to him many endearing traits. لازِم تطَبُّعُون الوَلَد بإِطباعكُم [laːzim ttabbuʕuːn ʔilwalad bʔiṭbaːʕkum] You have to imprint your characteristics on the boy. • **2.** to accustom, condition, train – طَبَّع زَوجتَه عَلَى ذَوقه بِالأَكِل [ṭabbaʕ zawiǰtah ʕala ðawqah bilʔakil] He accustomed his wife to his taste in food. طَبَّع الكَلِب ياكُل وِيّا البَزُّونَة مالتَه [ṭabbaʕ ʔiččalib yaːkul wiyya ʔilbazzuːna maːltah] He trained the dog to eat with his cat.

تطَبَّع [tṭabbaʕ] *v:* • **1.** to be affected, influenced – رِجَع مُتطَبُّع بِطباع الأُورُبِّيِّين [riǰaʕ muttabbuʕ biṭbaːʕ ʔilʔurubbiyyiːn] He came back influenced by European customs. • **2.** to be trained, accustomed, conditioned – الغَزال ما يِتطَبَّع بِالعَجَل [ʔilɣazaːl maː yiṭṭabbaʕ bilʕaǰal] A gazelle can't be trained easily.

اِنطِبَع [ʔinṭibaʕ] *v:* • **1.** to be printed – هَالكِتاب وين اِنطِبَع؟ [halkitaːb wiːn ʔinṭibaʕ?] Where was this book printed? • **2.** to be typed – شُوف المَكتُوب اِنطِبَع لَو بَعَد [šuːf ʔilmaktuːb ʔinṭibaʕ law baʕad] Find out if the letter has been typed or not.

طَبُع [ṭabuʕ] *n:* • **1.** printing, typing – تَحت الطَّبُع [taħt ʔiṭṭabuʕ] being printed or typed, at the press, in press. • **2.** disposition, nature, temper, character • **3.** pl. أَطباع trait, characteristic, peculiarity • **4.** (with ب) بِالطَّبُع [biṭṭabuʕ] by nature naturally, of course

طَبّاع [ṭabbaːʕ] *n:* طَبّاعِين [ṭabbaːʕiːn] *pl:* • **1.** printer, typesetter

طابِع [ṭaːbiʕ] *n:* طَوابِع [ṭawaːbiʕ] *pl:* • **1.** (postage, etc.) stamp

طَبعَة [ṭabʕa] *n:* طَبعات [ṭabʕaːt] *pl:* • **1.** edition • **2.** printing • **3.** issue (of publication)

طَبِيعَة [ṭabiːʕa] *n:* طَبايِع [ṭabaːyiʕ] *pl:* • **1.** nature, character, constitution – طَبِيعَة المَنطَقَة جَبَلِيَّة [ṭabiːʕat ʔilmanṭaqa ǰabaliyya] The nature of the area is mountainous. • **2.** peculiarity, characteristic, trait – لازِم تجُوز مِن هَالطَّبِيعَة [laːzim dǰuːz min haṭṭabiːʕa] You should get away from this tendency. • **3.** nature – الطَّبِيعَة تجَهِّز الحَيوانات بوَسائِل الدِّفاع عَن النَّفِس [ʔiṭṭabiːʕa dǰahhiz ʔilħaywaːnaːt bwasaːʔil ʔiddifaːʕ ʕan ʔinnafis] Nature provides animals with the means of self-defense.

طَبِيعِي [ṭabiːʕi] *n:* • **1.** natural, of nature – تارِيخ طَبِيعِي [taːriːx ṭabiːʕi] natural history. • **2.** inborn, innate, inherent • **3.** normal, ordinary, usual – هَذا شِي طَبِيعِي [haːða ši ṭabiːʕi] That's natural.

مَطبَعَة [maṭbaʕa] *n:* مَطابِع [maṭaːbiʕ] *pl:* • **1.** printing press • **2.** print shop, printing office

طابِعَة [ṭaːbiʕa] *n:* • **1.** typing, typewriting – كاتِب طابِعَة [kaːtib ṭaːbiʕa] typist. • **2.** typewriter

طِباعَة [ṭibaːʕa] *n:* • **1.** art of printing, typography

اِنطِباع [ʔinṭibaːʕ] *n:* • **1.** impression

مَطبُوعات [maṭbuːʕaːt] *n:* • **1.** printed matter • **2.** publications

مَطبَعِي [maṭbaʕi] *adj:* • **1.** printing, printer's, typographical – غَلَط مَطبَعِي [ɣalaṭ maṭbaʕi] a printing error, a typo

مَطبُوع [maṭbuːʕ] *adj:* • **1.** printed

اِنطِباعِي [ʔinṭibaːʕi] *adj:* • **1.** impressionistic

طَبعاً [ṭabʕan] *adverbial:* • **1.** of course, certainly

ط ب ق

طُبُق سُوَة [ṭubag suwa] *v:* • **1.** to juxtapose, place alongside – أُطبُق هَالتِّرِيشَة وِيّا رِجل الكُرسِي حَتَّى تِتحَمَّل ثُقُل [ʔuṭbug hattiriːša wiyya riǰl ʔilkursi ħatta tiθħammal θugul] Put this slat alongside the leg of the chair so it can bear weight. أُطبُق هَالفَردَة القُندَرَة وِيّا هَالفَردَة وشُوف إِذا نَفس القِياس [ʔuṭbug halfardat ʔilqundara wiyya halfarda wšuːf ʔiða nafs ʔilqiyaːs] Put this shoe alongside that one and see if they're the same size. أُطبُق هَاللَّوحات وِحدَة وِيّا اللَّخ وسَوِّيها سَقُف لِلغُرفَة [ʔuṭbug hallawħaːt wiħda wiyya ʔillux wsawwiːha saguf lilɣurfa] Lay these boards one beside the other and make a ceiling for the room. إِنتَ أَخُويَا. شلُون تُطبُق وِيّاه عَلَيّا؟ [ʔinta ʔaxuːya. šluːn tuṭbug wiyyaːh ʕalayya?] You're my brother. How could you side with him against me? • **2.** to close, shut – أُطبُق الكِتاب [ʔuṭbug ʔilkitaːb] Close the book. مِن تِطلَع، أُطبُق الباب رَجاءاً [min tiṭlaʕ, ʔuṭbug ʔilbaːb raǰaːʔan] When you go out, close the door, please. • **3.** to pull over, to park

طَبَّق [ṭabbaq] *v:* • **1.** to apply, make applicable – تعتِقِد يقدرُون يطَبُّقُون القانُون بهَالمَنطِقَة؟ [tiʕtiqid yigidruːn yṭabbuquːn ʔilqaːnuːn bhalmanṭiqa?] Do you think they can make the law applicable in this area? • **2.** to apply one's knowledge, gain practical experience, to intern – لازِم يطَبُّق بِفَدّ مَدرَسَة قَبُل ما يِتخَرَّج مِن دار المُعَلِّمِين [laːzim yṭabbuq bfadd madrasa gabul maː yitxarraǰ min daːr ʔilmuʕallimiːn] He has to practice in a school before he graduates from teacher's college. • **3.** to intern – راح نِبدِي نطَبُّق مِن الإِسبُوع الجّاي [raːħ nibdi nṭabbuq min ʔilʔisbuːʕ ʔiǰǰaːy] We're going to begin our internship next week.

طَبَّق [ṭabbag] *v:* • **1.** to place a covering, layer over, to cover, superimpose, over-spread – القاع كُلّها مَحَفُّرَة. لازِم تطَبُّقها بالكاشِي [ʔilgaːʕ kullha mħaffura. laːzim ṭṭabbugha bilkaːši] The ground's all dug up. You should cover it with tile. • **2.** to fold, make layers of – طَبُّق الهِدُوم زين قَبُل ما تخَلِّيها بِالجُنطَة [ṭabbug ʔilhduːm ziːn gabul maː txalliːha biǰǰunṭa]

Fold the clothes well before you put them in the suitcase. • **3.** to smother, cover – طَبِّق الدِّجاج بِتِمِّن [ṭabbug ʔiddiǰa:ǰ btimman] Fix the chicken smothered in rice. عَشانا اليُوم سِمَك مطَبَّق [ʕaša:na ʔilyu:m simač mṭabbag] Our dinner today is fish smothered in rice. • **4.** (voice) to be or become hoarse, deep – طَبَّق حِسَّه مِن البَكِي [ṭabbag ħissah min ʔilbači] His voice became hoarse from crying.

طابَق [ṭa:baq] *v:* • **1.** to correlate, compare, contrast – طابَقِت جَوابِي وِيّاه وطِلعَوا نَفس الشّي [ṭa:baqit ǰawa:bi wiyya:h wṭilʕaw nafs ʔišši] I compared my answer with his and they came out the same thing. • **2.** to correspond, concur, agree, conform with – حكايتَه تطابُق حكايتَك [ħča:ytah ṭṭa:buq ħča:ytak] His story corresponds with your story.

تطبَّق [tṭabbaq] *v:* • **1.** to be applied – هَالقانُون ما يِتطَبَّق بسُهُولَة [halqa:nu:n ma: yiṭṭabbaq bsuhu:la] This law cannot be easily applied.

تطبَّق [tṭabbug] *v:* • **1.** to be covered – هَالغُرفَة راح تِتطَبَّق بكاشِي [halɣurfa ra:ħ tiṭṭabbag bka:ši] This room is going to be laid with tile.

تطابَق [tṭa:baq] *v:* • **1.** to be compared – هَالجَوابَين ما يِطّابقُون لِأنّ السُّوالَين يِختَلفُون [hajjawa:bayn ma: yiṭṭa:bqu:n liʔann ʔissuʔa:layn yixtalfu:n] These two answers can't be compared because the two questions are different. • **2.** to compare with one another – خَلّي نِتطابَق حَتّى نشُوف الغَلَط وِين [xalli: niṭṭa:baq ħatta nšu:f ʔilɣalaṭ wi:n] Let's compare with each other to see where the mistake is. • **3.** to correspond, conform – هَالمُثَلَّثَين ما يِتطابقُون واحِد وِيّا اللّاخ [halmuθallaθayn ma: yiṭṭa:bqu:n wa:ħid wiyya ʔilla:x] These two triangles do not correspond with each other.

اِنطِبَق [ʔinṭubaq] *v:* • **1.** to be applicable, apply – القاعِدَة ما تِنطُبُق عَلَى هَالجُملَة [ʔilqa:ʕida ma: tinṭubuq ʕala hajjumla] The rule doesn't apply to this sentence.

طِبق، صُورَة طِبق الأَصِل [ṭibq, ṣu:ra ṭibq ʔilʔaṣil] *n:* • **1.** exact copy, true replica

طُبَق [ṭubag, ṭabag] *n:* طباق [ṭba:g] *pl:* • **1.** a large bamboo basket • **2.** a basket-work tray, usually coated with asphalt

طَبُق، يَوم الطَبُق [ṭabug, yu:m ʔiṭṭabug] *n:* • **1.** the tenth day of muharram (a day of mourning)

طَبُق [ṭabug] *n:* • **1.** placing alongside • **2.** pulling over, parking

طَبَقَة [ṭabaqa] *n:* طَبَقات [ṭabaqa:t] *pl:* • **1.** layer, stratum • **2.** class (of society)

طابِق [ṭa:biq] *n:* طَوابِق [ṭawa:biq] *pl:* • **1.** floor, story (of a building)

تَطبِيق [taṭbi:q] *n:* • **1.** practical experience, practical application, internship

طابُوق [ṭa:bu:g] *n:* • **1.** (coll.) brick(s)

طُبّاقَة [ṭubba:ga] *n:* طُبّاقات [ṭubba:ga:t] *pl:* • **1.** snap, fastener (on clothing)

طابُوقَة [ṭa:bu:ga] *n:* طابُوقات، طوابِيق [ṭa:bu:ga:t, ṭwa:bi:g] *pl:* • **1.** a brick

اِنطِباق [ʔinṭiba:q] *n:* • **1.** correlation, attachment

مُطابَقَة [muṭa:baqa] *n:* • **1.** conformity

طَبقَة، طَبقَة وَرَق [ṭabga, ṭabgat waraq] *n:* طَبقات، طَبقات وَرَق [ṭabqa:t, ṭabqa:t waraq] *pl:* • **1.** a large sheet of paper of a standard size

مُطبِق [muṭbiǰ] *adj:* • **1.** side-by-side – تُفقَة صَيد مُطبِقَة [tufgat ṣi:d muṭibǰa] double-barreled shotgun. • **2.** (pl. مَطابِج) a double-tubed flute

مُطبَق، مُطَبَّق [muṭbag, muṭabbag] *adj:* مطابُق [mṭa:bug] *pl:* • **1.** a double-tubed flute

طَبَقِيَّة [ṭabaqiyya] *n:* • **1.** sectarian

مُطابِق [muṭa:biq] *adj:* • **1.** matching

مَطبُوق [maṭbu:g] *adj:* • **1.** attached

تَطبِيقِي [taṭbi:qi] *adj:* • **1.** practical, applied

ط ب ل

طَبَّل [ṭabbal] *v:* • **1.** to make a racket, cause a lot of noise – شقَدّ طَبَّل وَما فاد [šgadd ṭabbal wma: fa:d] He made so much noise and it served no purpose.

طَبُل [ṭabul] *n:* طُبُول [ṭubu:l] *pl:* • **1.** drum

طَبلَة [ṭabla] *n:* طَبلات [ṭabla:t] *pl:* • **1.** small table • **2.** ashtray – طَبلَة الإذِن [ṭablat ʔilʔiðin] eardrum. • **3.** drum

طَبّال [ṭabba:l] *n:* طَبّالَة، طَبّالِين [ṭabba:la, ṭabba:li:n] *pl:* • **1.** drummer

ط ب و ر

طابُور [ṭa:bu:r] *n:* طوابِير [ṭwa:bi:r] *pl:* • **1.** file, queue, line, column (esp. of soldiers)

ط ح ل

طِحَل، طحَل [ṭiħal, ṭħal] *v:* • **1.** to be filling, fill one up

اِنطِحَل [ʔinṭiħal] *v:* • **1.** to stuff oneself, eat too much – أَكَلِت هوايَة وَاِنطِحَلِت [ʔakalit hwa:ya wʔinṭiħalit] I ate a lot and made myself uncomfortable.

طَحِل [ṭaħil] *n:* • **1.** glut, excessive supply

طحال [ṭħa:l] *n:* طحالات [ṭħa:la:t] *pl:* • **1.** spleen

طحلَتني هَالأَكلَة [ṭiħlatni halʔakla] *n:* • **1.** This meal bloated me

ط ح ل ب

طُحلُب [ṭuħlub] *n:* طَحالِب [ṭaħa:lib] *pl:* • **1.** water moss

ط ح ن

طِحَن [ṭiħan] *v:* • **1.** to mill, grind, pulverize – طحَنّا نُصّ طَنّ حُنطَة [ṭħanna nuṣṣ ṭann ħunṭa] We milled a half ton of wheat.

اِنطِحَن [ʔinṭiħan] *v:* • **1.** to be milled, grinded, pulverized

طَحِن [ṭaħin] *n:* طَحنات [ṭaħna:t] *pl:* • **1.** grinding

طِحِين، طحِين [ṭiħi:n, ṭħi:n] *n:* • **1.** flour

طَحّان [ṭaħħa:n] *n:* طَحّانَة [ṭaħħa:na] *pl:* • **1.** miller
طحِينَة [ṭħi:na] *n:* • **1.** a thick sauce made from sesame seeds
مَطحَنَة [maṭħana] *n:* مَطاحِن [maṭa:ħin] *pl:* • **1.** grist mill • **2.** coffee grinder, coffee mill
طاحُونَة، طاحُونَة هَوائِيَّة [ṭa:ħu:na, ṭa:ħu:na hawa:ʔiyya] *n:* طَواحِين [ṭawa:ħi:n] *pl:* • **1.** mill, windmill
مَطحُون [maṭħu:n] *adj:* • **1.** ground, crushed

ط خ خ

طَخّ [ṭaxx] *v:* • **1.** to bump, strike, hit, touch – نَزِّل راسَك مِن تخُشّ حَتَّى لا يطُخّ [nazzil ra:sak min txušš ħatta la: yṭuxx] Duck your head when you enter so it won't bump. إيدِي تُوجَعنِي. بالله لا تطُخها [ʔi:di tu:ǰaʕni. ballah la: tṭuxxha] My hand hurts. Please don't touch it. طَخَّت السَّيّارَة بِباب الكَراج [ṭaxxat ʔissayya:ra biba:b ʔilgara:ǰ] The car bumped into the garage door. السُّرعَة زادَت شوَيَّة شوَيَّة إلَى أَن طَخَّت بِالمِيَّة [ʔissurʕa za:dat šwayya šwayya ʔila ʔan ṭaxxat bilmiyya] The speed increased little by little until it reached a hundred. رُوح طُخَّه. بَلكِي يداينَك كَم دِينار [ru:ħ ṭuxxah. balki yda:ynak čam dina:r] Go put the touch on him. Maybe he'll lend you a few dinars.
انطَخّ [ʔinṭaxx] *v:* • **1.** to be bumped, struck, hit – راسَه اِنطَخّ بِالباب [ra:sah ʔinṭaxx bilba:b] His head got bumped on the door.
طَخّ [ṭaxx] *n:* • **1.** bumping, striking, hitting, touching
طَخَّة [ṭaxxa] *n:* طَخّات [ṭaxxa:t] *pl:* • **1.** bumping, striking, hitting, touching
مَطخُوخ [maṭxu:x] *adj:* • **1.** bumped, struck

ط خ م

طَخُم [ṭaxum] *n:* طخُومَة [ṭxu:ma] *pl:* • **1.** set, group – طَخُم سنُون [ṭaxum snu:n] set of false teeth, dentures. طَخُم قَنَفات [ṭaxum qanafa:t] set of couches (consisting of two couches and four upholstered chairs).

ط ر ء

طِرَأ [ṭiraʔ] *v:* • **1.** to come, descend – هِيكِي شِي ما يِطرَأ عالبال [hi:či ši ma: yiṭraʔ ʕalba:l] Such a thing wouldn't come to mind.
طارِئ [ṭa:riʔ] *adj:* • **1.** having happened suddenly, newly added or arrived
طارِئ [ṭa:riʔ] *adj:* طَوارِي [ṭawa:ri] *pl:* • **1.** unforeseen event – حالَة الطَّوارِئ [ħa:la ʔiṭṭawa:riʔ] state of emergency.

ط ر ب

طِرَب، طرَب [ṭurab, ṭrab] *v:* • **1.** to be delighted, enraptured, filled with joy – البارحَة طرَبِت هوايَة عَلَى صَوت المُغَنِّيَة الجِّدِيدَة [ʔilba:rħa ṭrabit hwa:ya ʕala ṣawt ʔilmuɣanniya ʔiǰǰidi:da] Yesterday I was enraptured by the new singer's voice. • **2.** to delight, enrapture – المُغَنِيَّة طِربَت الكُلّ [ʔilmuɣaniyya ṭirbat ʔilkull] The singer delighted everyone.
أَطرَب [ʔaṭrab] *v:* • **1.** to delight, fill with joy, enrapture – الغِنَى مالَه يطرِب [ʔilɣina: ma:lah yiṭrib] His singing fills one with joy.
اِنطُرَب [ʔinṭurab] *v:* • **1.** to be delighted, enraptured
طَرَب [ṭarab] *n:* • **1.** joy, delight • **2.** music
مُطرِب [muṭrib] *adj:* • **1.** (also A) delightful, charming • **2.** (as n:) singer, vocalist

ط ر ب ش

طَربُوش [ṭarbu:š] *n:* طَرابِيش [ṭara:bi:š] *pl:* • **1.** fez, tarboosh

ط ر ب ق

طَربَق [ṭarbag] *v:* • **1.** to rattle • **2.** to rumble
طَربَقَة [ṭarbaga] *n:* • **1.** clatter

ط ر ح

طِرَح [ṭiraħ] *v:* • **1.** to lay flat, spread out, cause to lie down flat – الطَّبِيب طِرَح الجّاهِل عالميز وَضُرَبَه أبرَة [ʔiṭṭabi:b ṭiraħ ʔiǰǰa:hil ʕalmi:z wḍurabah ʔubra] The doctor laid the child on the table and gave him a shot. الشُّرطِي طِرَحَه عَالقاع وَدَوَّرَه [ʔiššurṭi ṭiraħah ʕalga:ʕ wdawwarah] The policeman got him down on the ground and searched him. • **2.** to subtract – إطرَح ثمانيَة مِن العَدَد [ʔiṭraħ θma:nya min ʔilʕadad] Subtract eight from the number. • **3.** to miscarry, have a miscarriage – زَوجتَه طِرحَت [zawiǰtah ṭirħat] His wife had a miscarriage.
طَرَّح [ṭarraħ] *v:* • **1.** to perform an abortion, cause to have a miscarriage – طَرَّحها الطَّبِيب وَما حَدّ دِرى بِيه [ṭarraħha ʔiṭṭabi:b wma ħadd dira: bi:h] The doctor performed an abortion on her and nobody knew about it.
اِنطِرَح [ʔinṭiraħ] *v:* • **1.** to lie down, prostrate oneself – اِنطِرَحِت عالفراش ساعتِين [ʔinṭiraħit ʕalifra:š sa:ʕtayn] I stretched out on the bed for two hours.
طَرِح [ṭariħ] *n:* • **1.** subtraction
طُرُح [ṭuruħ] *n:* طُرُحات [ṭuruħa:t] *pl:* • **1.** advantage – إنطَيتَه داس طُرُح يَالله لِعَب ويّايا [ʔinṭaytah da:s ṭuruħ yallah liʕab wiyya:ya] I gave him a one game advantage to get him to play with me.
طَرِح [ṭariħ] *n:* • **1.** spreading out, lying down flat, abortion, subtraction
أُطرُوحَة [ʔuṭru:ħa] *n:* أُطرُوحات [ʔuṭruwħa:t] *pl:* • **1.** thesis • **2.** thesis, dissertation
مَطرُوح [maṭru:ħ] *adj:* • **1.** laid down, spread out – مَطرُوح عَلَى ظَهر الباخِرَة [maṭru:ħ ʕala ðahir ʔilba:xira] loaded on board the ship. السِّعر عَشِر دَنانِير لِلطَّنّ الواحِد، مَطرُوح عَلَى ظَهر الباخِرَة [ʔissiʕir ʕašir dana:ni:r liṭṭann ʔilwa:ħid, maṭru:ħ ʕala

ðahir ʔilbaːxira] The price is ten dinars per single ton, loaded on board the ship. • 2. subtrahend – المَطرُوح بِيه [ʔilmaṭruːħ biːh] the minuend.

ط ر د

طِرَد [ṭirad] *v:* • 1. to drive away, chase away, banish, dismiss, expel, drive out, evict – أطرُد البَزُّونَة مِن المَطبَخ [ʔuṭrud ʔilbazzuːna min ʔilmaṭbax] Chase the cat out of the kitchen. خَلَّى الخادِم عِندَه يومَين وَبَعدين طِرَدَه [xallaː ʔilxaːdim ʕindah yuːmayn wbaʕdiːn ṭiradah] He kept the servant two days and then dismissed him. إذا تِرسِب مَرَّة لُخ، يطرُدُوك [ʔiða tirsib marra lux, yṭurduːk] If you fail once more, they'll expel you. طِرَد مَرتَه مِن البَيت [ṭirad martah min ʔilbayt] He threw his wife out of the house. الله يطرُد الشَّرّ عَنَّك [ʔallah yiṭrud ʔiššarr ʕannak] May God protect you from evil.
طَرَّد [ṭarrad] *v:* • 1. to kick out
طارَد [ṭaːrad] *v:* • 1. to run – إمشِي عَلَى كَيفَك. لا تطارِد [ʔimši ʕala kayfak. laː ṭṭaːrid] Walk slowly, Don't run. طارَد بِالشِّعِر [ṭaːrad biššiʕir] to play a game of composing lines of poetry. طارَدتَه بِالشِّعِر نُصّ ساعَة وَبَعدين غِلَبنِي [ṭaːradtah biššiʕir nuṣṣ saːʕa wbaʕdiːn ɣilabni] I matched him in a poetry composing contest for a half hour and then he beat me. • 2. to chase
تطارَد [tṭaːrad] *v:* • 1. to rival with – خَلِّي نِتطارَد بِالشِّعِر [xalli: nitṭaːrad biššiʕir] Let's match lines of poetry.
اِنطِرَد [ʔinṭirad] *v:* • 1. pass. of طِرَد to be driven away, to be chased away, to be banished, to be dismissed
طَرِد [ṭarid] *n:* • 1. banishment, dismissal, expulsion, eviction
طَردَة [ṭarda] *n:* طَردات [ṭardaːt] *pl:* • 1. banishment, dismissal, expulsion, eviction
طَرّاد [ṭarraːd] *n:* طَرّادات [ṭarraːdaːt] *pl:* • 1. cruiser (warship)
مُطارَدَة [muṭaːrada] *n:* • 1. chase • 2. pursuit
طَردِي، تَناسُب طَردِي [ṭardi, tanaːsub ṭardi] *n:* • 1. direct proportion (math.)
طَرّادَة [ṭurraːda] *adj:* طراريد [traːriːd] *pl:* • 1. dinghy, small rowboat
مَطرُود [maṭruːd] *adj:* • 1. dismissed

ط ر ر

طَرّ [ṭarr] *v:* • 1. (dawn) to break – ساعَة بيش يطُرّ الفَجِر؟ [saːʕa biyš yṭurr ʔilfajir?] What time does dawn break? • 2. to throw – لا تطُرّ حجار عالبَيت [laː ṭṭurr ħjaːr ʕalbayt] Don't throw stones at the house.
طَرّ [ṭarr] *n:* • 1. throwing, breaking (dawn)
طُرَّة [ṭurra] *n:* طُرّات [ṭurraːt] *pl:* • 1. blaze, mark on an animal's forehead • 2. heads (of a coin)
طَرار [ṭaraːr] *n:* طَرارات [ṭaraːraːt] *pl:* • 1. shaded veranda facing onto the main patio of an eastern-style house

ط ر ز

طَرَّز [ṭarraz] *v:* • 1. to embroider – تُعرُف تخَيِّط وتطَرِّز زين [tuʕruf txayyiṭ wṭṭarriz ziːn] She knows how to sew and embroider well.
تطَرَّز [tṭarraz] *v:* • 1. to be embroidered – هَالقُماش ثِخِين؛ ما يِتطَرَّز [halqumaːš θixiːn; maː yiṭṭarraz] This material is thick; it can't be embroidered.
طَرِز، طِراز [ṭariz, ṭiraːz] *n:* • 2. style, pattern – طَيّارات جَيشنا مِن أَحدَث طِراز [ṭayyaːraːt ǰayšna min ʔaħdaθ ṭiraːz] Our army's planes are the latest type. هَذا مُحامِي مِن الطِّراز الأَوَّل [haːða muħaːmi min ʔiṭṭiraːz ʔilʔawwal] That lawyer is first class. هالبِنايَة عالطِّراز العَرَبِي [halbinaːya ʕaṭṭiraːz ʔilʕarabi] This building is in the Arab style.
تَطرِيز [taṭriːz] *n:* • 1. embroidery
مطَرَّز [mṭarraz] *adj:* • 1. embroidered

ط ر ز ن

طَرَزِينَة [ṭaraziːna] *n:* طَرَزِينات [ṭaraziːnaːt] *pl:* • 1. self-propelled railroad car

ط ر ش 1

طَرَّش [ṭarraš] *v:* • 1. to make deaf, deafen – صَوت المَكِينَة دَيطَرِّش [ṣawt ʔilmakiːna dayṭarriš] The noise of the machine is deafening.
اِطرَشّ [ʔiṭrašš] *v:* • 1. to be or become deaf – طرَشَّت إذنِي مِن هَالصَّوت [traššat ʔiðni min haṣṣawṭ] I've been deafened by this noise.
طَرِش [ṭariš] *n:* • 1. (no pl.) herd (esp. of donkeys)
طَرَش [ṭaraš] *n:* • 1. deafness
طارِش [ṭaːriš] *n:* طوارِش، طراريش [ṭwaːriš, ṭraːriːš] *pl:* • 1. messenger
أَطرَش [ʔaṭraš] *adj:* طُرُش، طَرشِين [ṭuruš, ṭaršiːn] *pl:* طَرشَة [ṭarša] *feminine:* • 1. deaf • 2. deaf person
مطَرَّش [mṭarraš] *adj:* • 1. becoming deaf

ط ر ش 2

طُرشِي [ṭurši] *n:* • 1. pickles
طُرُشچِي [ṭuruščiː] *n:* طُرُشچِيَّة [ṭuruščiyya] *pl:* • 1. pickle vendor
طُرشِيَّة [ṭuršiyya] *n:* • 1. pickle • 2. a piece of pickle

ط ر ش ن

طِرشانَة [ṭiršaːna] *n:* • 1. dried apricots

ط ر ط ر

طَرطُور [ṭarṭuːr] *adj:* طَراطِير [ṭaraːṭiːr] *pl:* • 1. braggart, boaster, blow-hard • 2. coward

ط ر ف

تطَرَّف [tṭarraf] *v:* • 1. to go to extremes, hold a radical position or view – يِتطَرَّف هوايَة بِآرائِه [yiṭṭarraf hwaːya bʔaːraːʔih] He goes to extremes in his opinions.

ط

طَرَف [ṭaraf] *n:* أَطراف [ʔaṭra:f] *pl:* • **1.** extremity, end, tip, edge • **2.** corner (of the eye) • **3.** district, zone, region, area • **4.** with مِن means relative to, concerning, about • **5.** with مِن in favor of, on the side of
طَرفَة [ṭarfa] *n:* • **1.** tamarisk
تَطَرُّف [taṭarruf] *n:* • **1.** excess, extremism
طارِيف [ṭa:ri:f] *adj:* • **1.** (Jewish usage) not kosher – لَحَم طارِيف [laħam ṭa:ri:f] non-kosher meat.
مُتَطَرِّف [mutaṭarrif] *adj:* • **1.** extremist, radical
طَرفانِي [ṭarfa:ni] *adj:* • **1.** end-most, located at the farthest point – تِقدَر تُقعُد عَالكُرسِي الطَّرفانِي [tigdar tugʕud ʕalkursi ʔiṭṭarfa:ni] You can sit on the end chair.

ط ر ق

طِرَق [ṭirag] *v:* • **1.** to beat, whip (eggs, etc.) – إطرُق اللِّبَن بِالخاشُوقَة [ʔiṭrug ʔilliban bilxa:šu:ga] Beat the yogurt with the spoon.
طَرَّق [ṭarrag] *v:* • **1.** to fold, fold up – طَرِّق هالوُصلَة القُماش [ṭarrig halwuṣlat ʔilquma:š] Fold up this piece of cloth.
تطَرَّق [ṭṭarraq] *v:* • **1.** to stray, wander, digress – تطَرَّق إلَى مَوضُوع ما كان لازِم يِبحثَه [ṭṭarraq ʔila mawḏu:ʕ ma: ka:n la:zim ybiħθah] He wandered onto a subject he shouldn't have discussed.
اِنطِرَق [ʔinṭirag] *v:* • **1.** to be beaten, whipped (eggs, etc)
اِستَطرَق [ʔistaṭraq] *v:* • **1.** to pass, go, come – إذا يِستَطرِق من هنا، أوَقّفه [ʔiða yistaṭriq min hina, ʔawaggfah] If he passes by here, I'll stop him.
طَرِق [ṭarig] *n:* • **1.** beating, whipping (eggs, etc)
طَرَقَة [ṭaraqa] *n:* طَرَقات [ṭaraqa:t] *pl:* • **1.** firecracker
طَرِيق [ṭari:q] *n:* طُرُق [ṭuruq] *pl:* • **1.** way – راح آخذَك وِيّايا بِالسَّيّارَة حَتَّى تدَلِّينِي عَالطَّرِيق [ra:ħ ʔa:xðak wiyya:ya bissayya:ra ħatta ddalli:ni ʕaṭṭari:q] I'm going to take you with me in the car so that you can show me the way. بطَرِيقَك، مُرّ عالأُوتَجِي وَجِيب ثَوبِي [bṭari:qak, murr ʕalʔu:tači wji:b θawbi] On your way, pass by the cleaner's and bring my shirt. اِنحِرَف عَن الطَّرِيق مِن صادَق هَالجَّماعَة [ʔinħiraf ʕan ʔiṭṭari:q min ṣa:daq hajjama:ʕa] He turned away from the straight and narrow when he got friendly with that crowd. طِلَع عَن الطَّرِيق [ṭilaʕ ʕan ʔiṭṭari:q] He stepped out of line. سَوُّوا طَرِيق؛ خَلِّي السَّيّارَة تفُوت [sawwu: ṭari:q; xalli: ʔissayya:ra tfu:t] Make way; let the car pass. ماكُو أَيّ عَقَبَة بطَرِيق تَقَدُّم هالبَلَد [ma:ku ʔayy ʕaqaba bṭari:q taqaddum halbalad] There's no obstacle in the way of this country's progress. • **2.** road, highway – صارِلهُم سَنَة يِشتُغلُون بهَالطَّرِيق [ṣa:rilhum sana yištuɣlu:n bhaṭṭari:q] They've been a year working on this road.
تَطَرُّق [taṭarruq] *n:* • **1.** digression • **2.** mentioning (something)
طَرِيقَة [ṭari:qa] *n:* طُرُق [ṭuruq] *pl:* • **1.** manner, mode, means • **2.** way, method, procedure • **3.** religious brotherhood
طِرّاقَة [ṭirra:ga] *n:* طِرّاقات [ṭirra:ga:t] *pl:* • **1.** egg beater
مِطرَقَة [miṭraqa] *n:* • **1.** hammer
طَرِق، بطَرِق [ṭarig, bṭarig] *n:* • **1.** by itself, alone – آنِي ساكِن بطَرِق رُوحِي [ʔa:ni sa:kin bṭarig ru:ħi] I live alone. رِحت بطَرِق رُوحِي [riħt bṭarig ru:ħi] I went by myself. مِن ماتَت مَرتَه، بُقَى بطَرِق نَفسَه [min ma:tat martah, buqa: bṭarig nafsah] When his wife died, he was left alone. صرَفِت كُلّ فلُوسِي وَبُقَيت بطَرِق دِينار [ṣrafit kull flu:si wbuqi:t bṭarig dina:r] I spent all my money and was left with only a dinar. دَيعِيش بطَرِق راتبَه [dayʕi:š bṭarig ra:tbah] He's living on just his salary. شِفِتها بِطَرِق اللِّباس [šifitha bṭarig ʔilliba:s] I saw her in just her pants. هُوَّ بطَرِق الحَكِي؛ ما يسَوِّي شُغُل [huwwa bṭarig ʔilħači; ma: ysawwi: šuɣul] He only talks; he doesn't do any work.

ط ر ق ع

طَرقَع [ṭargaʕ] *v:* • **1.** to clatter, bang, make noise – سِمَعنا اللُّورِيّات تطَرقِع عَالجِّسِر [simaʕna ʔillu:riyya:t ṭṭargiʕ ʕajjisir] We heard the trucks making a big noise on the bridge.
طَرقَعَة [ṭargaʕa] *n:* • **1.** noise
طِرقاعَة [ṭirga:ʕa] *n:* طِرقاعات، طَراقِيع [ṭirga:ʕa:t, ṭara:gi:ʕ] *pl:* • **1.** problem, catastrophe

ط ر م

طَرمَة [ṭarma] *n:* طَرامِي، طَرمات [ṭara:mi, ṭarma:t] *pl:* • **1.** porch, veranda

ط ر م ب

طُرمبَة [ṭrumba] *n:* طرُمبات [ṭrumba:t] *pl:* • **1.** water outlet, hydrant • **2.** faucet

ط ر م ب ي ل

طرُمبِيل [ṭrumbi:l, ṭrambi:l] *n:* طرُمبِيل، طرَامبِيلات [ṭrumbi:l, ṭrambi:la:t] *pl:* • **1.** automobile
طرامبِيلچِي [ṭrambilči] *n:* طرامبِيلچِيَّة [ṭrambilčiyya] *pl:* • **1.** driver

ط ر ن ج

طرِنجَة [ṭrinǰa] *n:* طرنجات [ṭrinǰa:t] *pl:* • **1.** citron
طرِنج [ṭrinǰ] *adj:* • **1.** (coll.) citron(s)

ط ر ه ت

طُرَّهات [ṭurraha:t] *n:* • **1.** (invar.) no-good, worthless – هَالأَكِل طُرَّهات؛ ما يِسوَى [halʔakil ṭurraha:t; ma: yiswa:] This food is lousy; it's not worth anything. هُوَّ طُرَّهات بِالحِساب. يِسقُط عَلَى طُول [huwwa ṭurraha:t biliħsa:b. yisquṭ ʕala ṭu:l] He's no good at arithmetic. He continually fails.

ط ر و

See also: ط ر ي

طِرَى [ṭira:] *v:* • **1.** to be or become fresh, succulent, moist, tender – ضِيف عَليه شوَيَّة مَيّ حَتَّى يِطرَى [ði:f ʕali:h šwayyat mayy ħatta yiṭra:] Add a little water to it so it will be fresh.

طَراوَة [ṭara:wa] *n:* • **1.** freshness, softness, tenderness

إطراء [ʔiṭra:ʔ] *n:* • **1.** commendation, complimenting

طَرِي [ṭari] *adj:* • **1.** soft, tender, succulent, moist, juicy

أطرَى [ʔaṭra:] *comparative adjective:* • **1.** more or most tender, succulent

ط ر ي

See also: ط ر و

طاري [ṭa:ri] *n:* • **1.** matter, subject, topic (of someone) – لا تجِيب طاريَّه. هُوَّ ما مَوجُود هنا [la: dji:b ṭa:riyyah. huwwa ma: mawǰu:d hna] Don't bring up the subject of him. He's not here. كُلّما يجِيبُون طاري إبنَه اللّي مات، تاخذَه العَبرَة [kullma: yǰi:bu:n ṭa:ri ʔibnah ʔilli ma:t, ta:xðah ʔilʕabra] Every time they mention his dead son, he bursts into tears. كِنّا بِطاريَّك قَبِل شوَيَّة [činna bṭa:riyyak gabil šwayya] We were just talking about you a moment ago.

ط س س

طَسّ [ṭass] *v:* • **1.** to hit a bump, go over a rough place – مِن طَسَّت السَّيّارَة، راسَه دَقّ بِالسَّقُف [min ṭassat ʔissayya:ra, ra:sah dagg bissaguf] When the car hit a bump, his head hit the roof. إذا ما تِدرُس زين، تَرَة تطُسّ بِالإمتِحان [ʔiða ma: tidrus zi:n, tara ṭṭuss bilʔimtiħa:n] If you don't study well, you will mess up on the exam. • **2.** to drop in unannounced – أعتِقِد عَلِي بِالبَيت. خَلّي نرُوح نطُسَّه [ʔaʕtiqid ʕali bilbayt. xalli: nru:ħ nṭussah] I believe Ali's at home. Let's go surprise him.

طَسّ [ṭass] *n:* • **1.** bump

طَسَّة [ṭassa] *n:* طَسّات [ṭassa:t] *pl:* • **1.** bump, rough place in the road

ط ش ت

طَشِت [ṭašit] *n:* طشُوت [ṭšu:t] *pl:* • **1.** wash basin • **2.** wash tub

ط ش ر

طَشَّر [ṭaššar] *v:* • **1.** to spill, scatter accidentally – طَشَّر المِشمِش كُلَّه بِالقاع [ṭaššar ʔilmišmiš kullah bilga:ʕ] He spilled all the apricots on the ground.

تطَشَّر [tṭaššar] *v:* • **1.** to scatter, disperse – وُقَع وَتطَشَّرَت كُلّ الغَراض مِنَّه [wugaʕ wtṭašširat kull ʔilɣara:ð minnah] He fell down and all the things scattered away from him. مِن شافَوا الشُّرطَة جايِّين، تطَشَّرَوا [min ša:faw ʔiššurṭa ǰa:yyi:n, ṭṭašširaw] When they saw the police coming, they scattered.

مطَشَّر [mṭaššar] *adj:* • **1.** scattered

طَشّاري [ṭašša:ri] *adj:* • **1.** prevalent, spread out, widespread

ط ش ش

طَشّ [ṭašš] *v:* • **1.** to scatter, strew around – طُشّ شوَيَّة شعِير لِلدِّجاج [ṭušš šwayya šʕi:r liddiǰa:ǰ] Throw a little barley to the chickens. • **2.** to spill – دِير بالَك! لا تطُشّ الماي [di:r ba:lak! la: ṭṭušš ʔilma:y] Be careful! Don't spill the water. • **3.** to spread, disseminate – ما كان لازِم يطُشّ الخَبَر [ma: ča:n la:zim yṭušš ʔilxabar] He shouldn't have spread the news all around.

انطَشّ [ʔinṭašš] *v:* • **1.** to be scattered, strewed around

طَشّ [ṭašš] *n:* • **1.** scattering, strewing around

مَطشُوش [maṭšu:š] *adj:* • **1.** scattered, strewed around

ط ع ج

طِعَج [ṭiʕaǰ] *v:* • **1.** to bend, to twist, to flex

انطِعَج [ʔinṭiʕaǰ] *v:* • **1.** to dent • **2.** to be bended, to be twisted

طَعِج [ṭaʕiǰ] *n:* • **1.** bending

طَعجَة [ṭaʕǰa] *n:* • **1.** bending

مطَعَّج [mṭaʕʕaǰ] *adj:* • **1.** bended, twisted

مَطعُوج [maṭʕu:ǰ] *adj:* • **1.** bended, twisted, spoiled

ط ع م

طَعَّم [ṭaʕʕam] *v:* • **1.** to feed, give food to – الجّاهِل يِنرادلَه واحِّد يطَعِّمَه [ʔiǰǰa:hil yinra:dlah waħħid yiṭaʕʕimah] The child needs someone to feed him. جيرانّا طَعّمُونا سِمَك اليُوم [ǰi:ra:nna ṭaʕʕmu:na simač ʔilyu:m] Our neighbors brought us over some fish today. • **2.** to inoculate, vaccinate – المُمَرِّضَة طَعُّمَت الجّاهِل ضِدّ التِّيفو [ʔilmumarriða ṭaʕumat ʔiǰǰa:hil ðidd ʔitti:fu] The nurse inoculated the child against typhoid. • **3.** to inlay – طَعَّم الميز بِالصَّدَف [ṭaʕʕam ʔilmi:z biṣṣadaf] He inlaid the table with mother-of-pearl.

إستَطعَم [ʔistaṭʕam] *v:* • **1.** to enjoy, savor, relish the taste of – أكلَة البارحَة، اِستَطعَمتها هوايَة [ʔaklat ʔilba:rħa, ʔistaṭʕamitha hwa:ya] I enjoyed the taste of yesterday's meal a lot.

طَعَم، طَعُم [ṭaʕam, ṭaʕum] *n:* • **1.** (no pl.) taste, flavor – سَوّاها بِلا طَعُم. كُلّما يرِيد فلُوس، يِجي عَلَيّا [sawwa:ha bila ṭaʕum. kullma yri:d flu:s, yiji ʕalayya] He's gone too far. Every time he wants money, he comes to me.

طُعُم [ṭuʕum] *n:* • **1.** bait – طَلَّع دِينار وَراواه إيّاه. يِبَيِّن دَيذِبلَه طُعُم [ṭallaʕ dina:r wra:wa:h ʔiyya:h. yibayyin dayðibblah ṭuʕum] He took out a dinar and showed it to him. It looks like he's throwing out bait to him.

ط

طَعام [ṭaʕa:m] *n:* • **1.** food, nourishment • **2.** grain
مَطعَم [maṭʕam] *n:* مَطاعِم [maṭa:ʕim] *pl:* • **1.** restaurant
إطعام [ʔiṭʕa:m] *n:* • **1.** feeding
تَطعِيم [taṭʕi:m] *n:* • **1.** inoculation
مطعَّم [mṭaʕʕam] *adj:* • **1.** inlaid • **2.** flavoured • **3.** mixed

ط ع ن

طِعَن [ṭiʕan] *v:* • **1.** to stab, transfix, run through – طِعَنَه بالخَنجَر بقَلبَه [ṭiʕanah bilxanǰar bgalbah] He stabbed him in his heart with the dagger. • **2.** with ب to find fault with, discredit, defame – ما نِقدَر نِطعَن بحُكمَه [ma: nigdar niṭʕan biħukmah] We can't find any fault with his judgment. ما لازِم تِطعَن بيه. هُوَّ ما مَوجُود [ma: la:zim tiṭʕan bi:h. huwwa ma: mawǰu:d] You shouldn't cut him down. He isn't here.
اِنطِعَن [ʔinṭiʕan] *v:* • **1.** to be stabbed
طَعِن [ṭaʕin] *n:* • **1.** stab
طَعنَة [ṭaʕna] *n:* طَعنات [ṭaʕna:t] *pl:* • **1.** stab, thrust • **2.** stitch
طاعُون [ṭa:ʕu:n] *n:* طَواعِين [ṭawa:ʕi:n] *pl:* • **1.** plague – أُخُذ طاعُونك ورُوح. جَزَّعتُونِي [ʔuxuð ṭa:ʕu:nak wru:ħ. ǰazzaʕtu:ni] Take your kids and get out. You've made me sick.
طاعِن، طاعِن بِالسِّنّ [ṭa:ʕin, ṭa:ʕin bis-sinn] *adj:* • **1.** old, aged, advanced in years
مَطعُون [maṭʕu:n] *adj:* • **1.** lancinating, plague-infected • **2.** stabbed

ط غ ر

طغار [ṭɣa:r] *n:* طغارات [ṭɣa:ra:t] *pl:* • **1.** a unit of weight equal to 2000 kilograms

ط غ و

طِغَى [ṭiɣa:] *v:* • **1.** to overflow, leave its banks – النَّهَر طِغَى وغَرَّق البساتِين [ʔinnahar ṭiɣa: wɣarrag ʔilibsa:ti:n] The river overflowed and flooded the orchards. • **2.** to be or become tyrannical, despotic, cruel – مِن صار رَئِيس جَمهُورِيَّة، طِغَى [min ṣa:r raʔi:s ǰamhu:riyya, ṭiɣa:] When he became president, he became a tyrant. • **3.** with عَلَى to dominate, outweigh, overshadow – جَمالها طِغَى عَلَى كُلّ جَمال البَنات [ǰama:lha ṭiɣa: ʕala kull ǰama:l ʔilbana:t] Her beauty overshadowed all the girls' beauty.
طاغِي، طاغِيَّة [ṭa:ɣi, ṭa:ɣiyya] *adj:* طُغاة [ṭuɣa:t] *pl:* • **1.** tyrant, despot
أطغَى [ʔaṭɣa:] *comparative adjective:* • **1.** more or most tyrannical, despotic

ط ف ء

طَفَّى [ṭaffa:] *v:* • **1.** to put out, extinguish, smother – لا تنام قَبُل ما تطَفِّي النّار [la: tna:m gabul ma: ṭṭaffi ʔinna:r] Don't go to sleep until you put out the fire. • **2.** to turn off, switch off, put out – لا تطَفِّي الضَوَة. أرِيد أطالِع [la: ṭṭaffi ʔiððuwa. ʔari:d ʔaṭa:liʕ] Don't turn off the light. I want to study. • **3.** to quench – أرِيد كلاص مَيّ بارِد حَتَّى أطَفِّي العَطَش [ʔari:d gla:ṣ mayy ba:rid ħatta ʔaṭaffi ʔilʕaṭaš] I want a cold glass of water to quench the thirst.
تطَفَّى [ṭṭaffa:] *v:* • **1.** pass. of طَفَّى to be turned off, to be extinguished
اِنطُفَى [ʔinṭufa:] *v:* • **1.** to go out, die down, be extinguished – صار شَوط وإنطُفَى الضَوا [ṣa:r šu:ṭ wʔinṭufa: ʔiððuwa] There was a short circuit and the light went out.
مِطفَأة [miṭfaʔa] *n:* مَطافِئ [maṭa:fiʔ] *pl:* • **1.** fire extinguisher
إطفائِي [ʔiṭfa:ʔi] *adj:* إطفائِيَّة [ʔiṭfa:ʔi:yya] *pl:* • **1.** related to fire (as n:) اطفائچي [ʔiṭfa:ʔči] fireman
إطفائِيَّة [ʔiṭfa:ʔiyya] *n:* • **1.** fire department
مَطفِي [maṭfi] *adj:* • **1.** turned off, switched off – ضَوَا القُبَّة مَطفِي. لازِم ماكُو أحَّد بيها [ðuwa ʔilgubba maṭfi. la:zim ma:ku ʔaħħad bi:ha] The light in the room is off. There must not be anyone in it.

ط ف ح

طُفَح [ṭufaħ] *v:* • **1.** to become full to overflowing – السِّرداب طُفَح مَيّ [ʔassirda:b ṭufaħ mayy] The basement became filled with water. • **2.** to overflow, run over, flow over – طُفَح المَيّ مِن الطَّشِت [ṭufaħ ʔilmayy min ʔiṭṭašit] The water overflowed from the basin.
تطافَح [ṭṭa:faħ] *v:* • **1.** to overflow, run over, be too full – الجِّدِر مَليان ماي؛ دَيتطافَح [ʔiǰǰidir malya:n ma:y; dayiṭṭa:faħ] The cooking pot's full of water; it's overflowing.
طَفَح [ṭafaħ] *n:* • **1.** rash, skin eruption
طَفُح [ṭafuħ] *n:* • **1.** superabundance, overflowing
طافِح [ṭa:fiħ] *adj:* • **1.** flowing over

ط ف ر

طُفَر [ṭufar] *v:* • **1.** to jump – هَالرِّياضِي يُطفُر خَمِس أمتار [harriya:ði yuṭfur xamis ʔamta:r] This athlete jumps five meters. رُوحِي طُفرَت وَبَعَد ما أتحَمَّلَه [ru:ħi ṭufrat wabaʕad ma: ʔatħammalah] My very being rebelled and I can't stand him any more. إمشِي شَهَر وَلا تُطفُر نَهَر [ʔimši šahar wla: tuṭfur nahar] Don't take chances (lit., walk a month but don't jump a river). • **2.** with عَلَى to descend upon, to break into, burglarize – الحَرامِي طُفَر عَلَى بَيت جِيرانَّا [ʔilħara:mi ṭufar ʕala bayt ǰi:ra:nna] The thief got over the wall into our neighbors' house.
طَفَّر [ṭaffar] *v:* • **1.** to jump, bounce repeatedly – الجَّهال دَيطَفُّرُون عالرَّمُل [ʔiǰǰaha:l dayṭaffuru:n ʕarramul] The children are jumping in the sand. • **2.** to make, let, or help jump – طَفَّر صَدِيقَه مِن حايِط الحَدِيقة قَبُل ما تِجِي الشُّرطَة [ṭaffar ṣadi:qah min ħa:yiṭ ʔilħadi:qa gabul ma: tiǰi ʔiššurṭa] He helped his friend jump from the garden wall before the police came. • **3.** to cause to splash –

إذا تذِبّ هَالحجارَة بِالحوض، يطَفُّر عَلينا هوايَة مَيّ [ʔiða dðibb halħja:ra bilħu:ḍ, yṭaffur ʕali:na hwa:ya mayy] If you throw this rock in the pond, it'll splash a lot of water on us. • **4.** to skip over, omit, leave out – إقرا سَطِر وَطَفُّر سَطِر [ʔiqra saṭir wṭaffur saṭir] Read a line and skip a line. مِن قِرا القائِمَة، طَفَّر إسمِي [min qira: ʔilqa:ʔima, ṭaffar ʔismi] When he read the list, he missed my name.

تطَفَّر [tṭaffar] *v:* • **1.** to splash

تطافَر [tṭa:far] *v:* • **1.** to hold a jumping contest, compete with each other in jumping – خَلِّي نِطّافَر وشُوف ياهُو اللّي يُغلُب [xalli: niṭṭa:far wšu:f ya:hu ʔilli yuɣlub] Let's have a jumping contest and see who wins.

طَفُر [ṭafur, ṭafr] *n:* • **1.** jumping, leaping – طَفر العَرِيض [ṭafr ʔilʕari:ḍ] broad jumping.

طَفرَة [ṭafra] *n:* طَفرات [ṭafra:t] *pl:* • **1.** a jump, a leap

تَطَفُّر [taṭaffur] *n:* • **1.** splashing

طَفران [ṭafra:n] *adj:* • **1.** disgusted, fed up, sick and tired

ط ف ف

طَفِيف [ṭafi:f] *adj:* • **1.** small, slight, trivial, insignificant – أَلَم طَفِيف [ʔalam ṭafi:f] a slight pain.

ط ف ل

تطَفَّل [tṭaffal] *v:* • **1.** to intrude, butt in – لا تِتطَفَّل. مَحَّد سِألَك [la: tiṭṭaffal. maħhad siʔalak] Don't intrude. Nobody asked you.

طِفِل [ṭifil] *n:* أطفال [ʔaṭfa:l] *pl:* • **1.** infant, baby, child

تَطَفُّل [taṭafful] *n:* • **1.** intrusion • **2.** parasitism

طُفُولَة [ṭufu:la] *n:* • **1.** childhood, infancy

طُفَيلِي [ṭufayli] *adj:* طُفَيلِيِّين [ṭufayliyyi:n] *pl:* • **1.** parasite, free-loader, sponger, hanger-on

متطَفِّل [miṭṭaffil] *adj:* • **1.** parasitical

طُفُولِي [ṭufu:li] *adj:* • **1.** childish

ط ف و

طُفَى [ṭufa:] *v:* • **1.** to float, rise to the surface – المَيِّت طُفَى بِالنَّهَر [ʔilmayyit ṭufa: binnahar] The dead man floated in the river.

طَفُو [ṭafw] *n:* • **1.** float

ط ق س

طَقِس [ṭaqis] *n:* • **1.** weather, climate

طِقُوس [ṭiqu:s] *n:* • **1.** rite, religious custom

ط ق ط ق

طَقطَق [ṭagṭag] *v:* • **1.** to make a cracking, snapping, popping noise – الحَطَب، إذا ما يكُون يابِس، يطَقطِق هوايَة بِالنّار [ʔilħaṭab, ʔiða ma: yku:n ya:bis, yṭagṭig hwa:ya binna:r] If the firewood isn't dry, it crackles and snaps a lot in the fire. طَقطَق إصابعَه [ṭagṭag ʔiṣa:bʕah] He cracked his knuckles. • **2.** to rattle, clatter – هَالسَّيّارَة مجَرقِعَة. تطَقطِق هوايَة [hassayya:ra mčarqiʕa. tṭagṭig hwa:ya] This car is all worn out. It rattles a lot. سنُونِي دَتطَقطِق مِن البَرِد [snu:ni daṭṭagṭig min ʔilbarid] My teeth are chattering from the cold. لا تطَقطِق. أبُوك نايِم [la: tṭagṭig. ʔabu:k na:yim] Don't make noise. Your father is sleeping.

طَقطَقَة [ṭagṭaga] *n:* • **1.** cracking, snapping, popping • **2.** clattering, rattling

طِقطاقَة [ṭigṭa:ga] *n:* طِقطاقات [ṭigṭa:ga:t] *pl:* • **1.** noisemaker, rattle

طَقطُوقِيّات [ṭagṭu:giyya:t] *n:* • **1.** (pl. only) odds and ends, small things, remnants, scraps

ط ق ع

طَقَّع [ṭaggaʕ] *v:* • **1.** to stain, spot, splatter – الجّاهِل طَقَّع الشَرشَف بحِبِر [ʔijja:hil ṭaggaʕ ʔaččarčaf bħibir] The kid stained the tablecloth with ink. عِندَك قماش أبيَض مطَقَّع بأحمَر؟ [ʕindak qma:š ʔabyaḍ mṭaggaʕ bʔaħmar?] Do you have a white cloth spotted with red? • **2.** to become stained, spotted, splotched – أشُو مِن غِسَلِت القماش، طَقَّع [ʔašu: min ɣisalit ʔilqma:š, ṭaggaʕ] It seems when you washed the cloth, the colors ran. • **3.** to blanch, pale, show terror – مِن سِمَع حِسّ المَدافِع، طَقَّع [min simaʕ ħiss ʔilmada:fiʕ, ṭaggaʕ] When he heard the noise of the cannons, he blanched.

طَقعَة [ṭagʕa] *n:* طَقعات [ṭagʕa:t] *pl:* • **1.** person full of himself a big fart • **2.** act of breaking wind

طُقعَة [ṭugʕa] *n:* طُقَع [ṭugaʕ] *pl:* • **1.** stain, spot, splotch

طُقُوع [ṭugu:ʕ] *n:* • **1.** cowardice – هَذا ما يصِير جُندِي. طُقُوع [ha:ða ma: yṣi:r ǰundi. ṭugu:ʕ] He'll never be a soldier. He is chicken.

أطقَع [ʔaṭgaʕ] *comparative adjective:* • **1.** more or most cowardly

ط ق ق

طَقّ [ṭagg] *v:* • **1.** to explode, burst – بُطِل الصُّودا طَقّ وَجِرَح إيدِي [buṭil ʔiṣṣu:da ṭagg wǰiraħ ʔi:di] The bottle of soda burst and cut my hand. أبُو التّاكسِي طَقّ عِندَه تايَر [ʔabu ʔitta:ksi ṭagg ʕindah ta:yar] The taxi driver had a tire blow out. خَلُّوا ثَلِج بِالتّابُوت حَتَّى ما يطُقّ المَيِّت [xallaw θaliǰ bitta:bu:t ħatta ma: yṭugg ʔilmayyit] They put ice in the coffin so the dead man wouldn't burst. يا معَوَّد، خَلِّينِي أطُبّ أوَّل. راح تطُقّ بَولتِي [ya: mʕawwad, xalli:ni ʔaṭubb ʔawwal. ra:ħ ṭṭugg bu:lti] For heaven's sake, let me go in first. My bladder's about to pop. أرِيد أطلَع شوَيَّة بَرَّة؛ طَقَّت رُوحِي هنا [ʔari:d ʔaṭlaʕ šwayya barra; ṭaggat ru:ħi hna] I want to go outside for a little bit; I'm fed up in here. • **2.** to crack, split, break – طُقِّلِي بَيضتَين. أرِيد أترَيَّق [ṭuggli bayḍtayn. ʔari:d ʔatrayyag] Break me a couple of eggs. I want to have breakfast. طَقَّله بوطِل صُودا [ṭugglah buṭil ṣuːda] Open a bottle of soda pop for him! طَقِّلي صُورَة [ṭaggli ṣuːra] He snapped a picture of me. الجُندي طَقَّله سَلام لِلضابُط [ʔijjundi ṭagglah salaːm liððaːbuṭ] The soldier gave the officer a snappy salute.

طَقّ [ṭagg] *n:* • **1.** sudden noise, crash, bang, explosion

طَقَّة [ṭagga] *n:* طَقّات [ṭaggaːt] *pl:* • **1.** sudden noise, crash, bang • **2.** burst, explosion – عَلَى طَقَّة، واقفة عَلَى طَقَّة [ʕala ṭagga, waːgfa ʕala ṭagga] on the verge of exploding. ما يِندِرَى شوَقِت تصِير العَركَة. عَلَى طَقَّة [maː yindiraː šwakit tṣiːr ʔilʕarka. ʕala ṭagga] It's not known when the fight'll break out. Any little thing'll do it.

مُطقاقَة [muṭgaːga] *n:* مُطقاقات [muṭgaːgaːt] *pl:* • **1.** bottle opener • **2.** can opener

مَطقُوق [maṭguːq] *adj:* • **1.** crashed, banged, exploded

ط ق م

طَقُم [ṭaqum] *n:* • **1.** variant of طُخُم see under ط - خ - م • **2.** set, group

طاقِم [ṭaːqim] *n:* • **1.** crew (e.g. airplane)

ط ل ب

طِلَب [ṭilab] *v:* • **1.** to ask for, request, apply for – الطُّلّاب طِلبَوا مِن المُعَلِّم أَن يوَدِّيهُم لِلمَتحَف [ʔiṭṭullaːb ṭilbaw min ʔilmuʕallim ʔan ywaddiːhum lilmatħaf] The students asked the teacher to take them to the museum. العُمّال طِلبَوا زِيادَة رَواتِبهُم [ʔilʕummaːl ṭilbaw ziyaːdat rawaːtibhum] The workers asked for an increase in their salaries. طِلَب إيدها وَرُفضَت [ṭilab ʔiːdha wrufðat] He asked for her hand (in marriage) and she refused. أَقدَر أَطلُب السَّيّارَة مالتَّك يوم الجُمعَة؟ [ʔagdar ʔaṭlub ʔissayyaːra maːlttak yuːm ʔijjumʕa?] Can I borrow your car Friday? • **2.** to order – طلبنا مِيَّة تَلَفِيزيُون مِن أَمرِيكا [ṭlabna miyyat talafiːzyuːn min ʔamriːka] We ordered a hundred TV sets from America. • **3.** to be the creditor of, be owed money by – نِسِيت شقَدّ تُطلُبنِي [nisiːt šgadd tuṭlubni] I've forgotten how much I owe you. • **4.** to call, telephone, ring up – أُطلُب البَدّالَة وِينطُوك خَطّ [ʔuṭlub ʔilbaddaːla wyinṭuːk xaṭṭ] Ask the switchboard and they'll give you a line. أُطلُب النَّجَف وشُوف شَكُو [ʔuṭlub ʔinnajaf wšuːf šaku] Call up Najaf and see what's happening. مِنُو طِلَبنِي بِالتَّلَفُون؟ [minu ṭilabni bittalifuːn?] Who wanted me on the phone?

طالَب [ṭaːlab] *v:* • **1.** to make a demand, put forward a claim – العُمّال دَيطالبُون بِزِيادَة [ʔilʕummaːl dayṭaːlbuːn bziyaːda] The workers are asking for a raise. راح أَطالبَه بِالفلُوس مِن يِجِي [raːħ ʔaṭaːlbah bilfiluːs min yiji] I'll dun him for the money when he comes.

تطَلَّب [tṭallab] *v:* • **1.** to necessitate, demand, require, exact – النَّجاح يِتطَلَّب شُغُل هوايَة [ʔinnajaːħ yiṭṭallab šuɣul hwaːya] Success requires a lot of work.

تطالَب [tṭaːlab] *v:* • **1.** to be argumentative, quarrelsome, make undue demands – لِيش دائماً تِتطالَب وِيّا النّاس؟ [liːš daːʔiman tiṭṭaːlab wiyya ʔinnaːs?] Why do you always get into fights with people?

انطِلَب [ʔinṭilab] *v:* • **1.** pass. of طِلَب to be asked for, requested, applied for

طَلَب [ṭalab] *n:* طَلَبات [ṭalabaːt] *pl:* • **1.** demand, claim • **2.** request • **3.** application • **4.** demand (econ.)

طَلبَة [ṭulba, ṭilba] *n:* طُلبات [ṭulbaːt, ṭilbaːt] *pl:* • **1.** request, desire, wish – إلِي عِندَك طِلبَة. تسَوِّيها؟ [ʔili ʕindak ṭilba. tsawwiːha?] I have a favor to ask of you. Would you do it?

مَطلَب [maṭlab] *n:* مَطالِيب [maṭaːliːb] *pl:* • **1.** demand, claim

طالِب [ṭaːlib] *n:* طُلّاب [ṭullaːb] *pl:* • **1.** student, pupil

طَلَبِيَّة [ṭalabiyya] *n:* طَلَبِيّات [ṭalabiyyaːt] *pl:* • **1.** order, commission (com.)

طلابَة [ṭlaːba] *n:* طلايِب [ṭlaːyib] *pl:* • **1.** fuss, to-do, commotion – سَوِّيت طلابَة كبِيرَة عَلَى شِي ما يِسوَى [sawwiːt ṭlaːba čbiːra ʕala ši maː yiswaː] You've made a big fuss over something that doesn't matter.

مَطلُوب [maṭluːb] *n:* • **1.** requested, required, wanted • **2.** due, owed (money, etc.) • **3.** indebted – آنِي مَطلُوبلَك [ʔaːni maṭluːblak] I'm indebted to you. • **4.** pl. مَطالِيب wish, desire

مُطالَبَة [muṭaːlaba] *n:* مُطالَبات [muṭaːlabaːt] *pl:* • **1.** demand, claim – مُطالَبَة بدَين [muṭaːlaba bdayn] demand for repayment of a debt.

مُتَطَلَّبات [mutaṭallabaːt] *n:* • **1.** requirements

طَلّاب [ṭallaːb] *adj:* طَلّابَة [ṭallaːba] *pl:* • **1.** creditor, lender

طُلّابِي [ṭullaːbi] *adj:* • **1.** pertaining to students

ط ل س م

طِلِّسِم [ṭillisim] *n:* طَلاسِم [ṭalaːsim] *pl:* • **1.** talisman, charm, amulet – مَكتُوبَه مِثِل الطِّلِّسِم. ما يِنفِهِم مِنَّه شِي [maktuːbah miθl ʔiṭṭillisim. maː yinfihim minnah ši] His letter is mystifying. Nothing can be understood from it.

ط ل ع

طِلَع [ṭilaʕ] *v:* • **1.** to appear, show, come into view – راح تِطلَع الشَّمِس ساعَة سِتَّة باكِر [raːħ tiṭlaʕ ʔiššamis saːʕa sitta baːčir] The sun will appear at six o'clock tomorrow. طِلعَت حَبّايَة بِيدَه [ṭilʕat ħabbaːya biːdah] A sore came out on his hand. طِلَع إسمَك بِالجَّرِيدَة اليُوم [ṭilaʕ ʔismak bijjariːda ʔilyuːm] Your name appeared in the paper today. طِلَع نَفُط يَمّ المُوصِل [ṭilaʕ nafuṭ yamm ʔilmuːṣil] Oil was discovered near Mosul. السَّيّارَة، طِلَع بِيها مِيَّة عِيب [ʔissayyaːra, ṭilaʕ biːha miyyat ʕiːb] A hundred defects showed up in the car. طِلعَتلِي مُشكِلَة جِدِيدَة [ṭilʕatli muškila jidiːda] A new problem has come up for me. إذا ما طِلَعلَه صاحِب، يصِير مالَك [ʔiða maː ṭilaʕlah ṣaːħib, yṣiːr maːlak] If an owner doesn't turn up for it, it will be yours.

to be, prove to be – طِلَع أَوَّل عَلَى صَفَّه [ṭilaʕ ʔawwal ʕala ṣaffah] He came out first in his class. طِلَع نايِب مِن هَالمَنطِقَة [ṭilaʕ naːyib min halmanṭiqa] He became a representative from that area. طِلَعِت خَسران دِينار [ṭilaʕit xasraːn dinaːr] I came out a dinar in the hole. تُعرُف صَدِيقَه طِلَع جاسُوس؟ [tuʕruf ṣadiːqah ṭilaʕ ǰaːsuːs?] Do you know his friend turned out to be a spy? طِلَع مِن حَقّها [ṭilaʕ min ħaqqha] He was worthy of it. He was able to handle it. إنطُوه شَغلَة صَعبَة لَكِن طلَع مِن حَقّها [ʔinṭuːh šaɣla ṣaʕba laːkin ṭilaʕ min ħaqqha] They gave him a hard job, but he managed it. • **6.** to look, present an appearance, appear – طِلَع حِلو بِالرَّسِم [ṭilaʕ ħilw birrasim] He looks nice in the picture. طِلعَت فَلّة مِن لِبسَت النَّفنُوف الجِّدِيد [ṭilʕat falla min libsat ʔinnafnuːf ʔiǰǰidiːd] She looked terrific when she put on the new dress. إنتَ طالِع نَصبَة اليُوم [ʔinta ṭaːliʕ naṣba ʔilyuːm] You're looking sharp today. طِلَع عَلَى أَبُوه [ṭilaʕ ʕala ʔabuːh] He takes after his father. • **7.** to overtake, pass, move ahead of – إطلَعَه. دَيمشِي عَلَى كَيفَه [ʔiṭlaʕah. dayimši ʕala kiːfah] Pass him. He's just poking along. إطلَع السَّيّارَة اللِّي قِدّامَك حَتَّى نِقدَر نِسرِع [ʔiṭlaʕ ʔissayyaːra ʔilli giddaːmak ħatta nigdar nisriʕ] Pass the car in front of you so we can go fast.

طَلَّع [ṭallaʕ] *v:* • **1.** to remove, withdraw, take out – طَلِّع إيدَك مِن جِيبِي [ṭalliʕ ʔiːdak min ǰiːbi] Take your hand out of my pocket! دَيطَلّعُون الجُّثَّة مِن الشَّطّ [dayṭallʕuːn ʔiǰǰuθθa min ʔiššaṭṭ] They're taking the corpse out of the river. إذا ما ترُوح لِلمَدرَسَة، أَطَلِّع رُوحَك [ʔiða maː truːħ lilmadrasa, ʔaṭalliʕ ruːħak] If you don't go to school, I'll have your hide. يضَوِّجُوه بَالدّائِرَة وَبِاللَّيل يطَلِّع كُلّ دَردَه بمَرتَه [yðawwiǰuːh biddaːʔira wbillayl yṭalliʕ kull dardah bmartah] They give him trouble at the office and at night he takes all his troubles out on his wife. تُسكُت لَو أَجِي أَطَلِّع كُلّ دَرد الله بِيك [tuskut law ʔaǰi ʔaṭalliʕ kull dard ʔallah biːk] You shut up or I'll come and give you what for. • **2.** to obtain, acquire, get – لازم تطَلِّع إجازَة سِياقَة [laːzim tṭalliʕ ʔiǰaːzat siyaːqa] You'll have to get a driving permit. طَلَّع مُعَدَّل مُمتاز [ṭallaʕ muʕaddal mumtaːz] He got a fine average. دَيطَلِّع دِينار بِاليُوم [dayṭalliʕ dinaːr bilyuːm] He's making a dinar a day. • **3.** to put out, stick out – طَلِّع لِسانَك دَأفحَصَه [ṭalliʕ lisaːnak daʔafħaṣah] Stick out your tongue and let me examine it. ما دَأَطَلِّع راس وِيّاه؛ عَلَى طُول يُغلُبنِي [maː daʔaṭalliʕ raːs wiyyaːh; ʕala ṭuːl yuɣlubni] I'm not getting anywhere with him; he always beats me. • **4.** to eject, oust, dismiss, expel, evict, throw out – طَلّعُوه مِن شُغلَه [ṭallʕuːh min šuɣlah] They dismissed him from his job. طَلّعَه مِن البَيت لِأَنّ ما دِفَع الإيجار [ṭallaʕah min ʔilbayt liʔann maː difaʕ ʔilʔiːǰaːr] He evicted him from the house because he didn't pay the rent. • **5.** to produce, turn out, bring forth, give

طِلعَتلِي الجّائِزَة الأُولَى بالیانَصِيب [ṭilʕatli ʔiǰǰaːʔiza ʔilʔuːla bilyaːnaṣiːb] I got first prize in the lottery. لازِم آخُذلَك رَسم اللّاخ. هَالصُّورَة ما طِلعَت [laːzim ʔaːxuðlak rasm ʔillaːx. haṣṣuːra maː ṭilʕat] I have to take another picture of you. This photo didn't turn out. كُومَة الثِّياب، ما يِطلَع مِنها غير ثلاثَة زينَة [kuːmat ʔiθθiyaːb, maː yiṭlaʕ minha ɣiːr tlaːθa ziːna] No more than three good ones will come out of the pile of shirts. نَتائِج الامتِحان طِلعَت [nataːʔiǰ ʔilʔimtiħaːn ṭilʕat] The results of the exam are out. الإجازَة مالتَك ما تِطلَع هَاليُوم [ʔilʔiǰaːza maːltak maː tiṭlaʕ halyuːm] Your permit won't be issued today. أُترُكَه! هَذا ما يِطلَع شِي مِن وَراه [ʔuturkah! haːða maː yiṭlaʕ ši min waraːh] Leave him! Nothing good will ever come from him. مِن إجا أَبُوه، طِلعَت عَينَه وَقام يسِبّنا [min ʔiǰa ʔabuːh, ṭilʕat ʕaynah wgaːm ysibbna] When his father came, he got brave and began to insult us. • **2.** to come up, sprout, grow forth – بِدَت تِطلَعلَه سنُون [bidat tiṭlaʕlah snuːn] His teeth have started to come in. هَالقاع ما يِطلَع بِيها كُلّ زَرِع [halgaːʕ maː yiṭlaʕ biːha kull zariʕ] No plant will grow in the land. مَكان الجِّرِح ما يِطلَع بِيه شَعَر [makaːn ʔiǰǰariħ maː yiṭlaʕ biːh šaʕar] Hair won't grow on the wound. • **3.** to come out, go out, get out – الكِتاب عاصِي بجِيبِي. ما دَيطلَع [ʔilkitaːb ʕaːṣi bǰiːbi. maː dayiṭlaʕ] The book is caught in my pocket. It won't come out. الفارَة طِلعَت مِن الزَّرُف [ʔilfaːra ṭilʕat min ʔizzaruf] The mouse came out of the hole. وُقَع بوَرطَة ما يِطلَع مِنها [wugaʕ bwarṭa maː yiṭlaʕ minha] He fell into a mess that he won't get out of. هَسَّة طِلَع ويرجَع بَعَد نُصّ ساعَة [hassa ṭilaʕ wyirǰaʕ baʕad nuṣṣ saːʕa] He just went out and he'll be back in a half hour. ما تِطلَع إلّا ويّا أُخُوها [maː tiṭlaʕ ʔilla wiyya ʔaxuːha] She won't go out except with her brother. طلَعنا لِلصَّيد [ṭlaʕna liṣṣiːd] We went out hunting. إطلَع وَلا تِجِي بَعَد [ʔiṭlaʕ wla tiǰiː baʕad] Get out and don't come back! هَالدَّربُونَة ما تِطلَع [haddarbuːna maː tiṭlaʕ] This alley is a dead end. طِلَع حَلِيب أُمَّه مِن حَلقَه [ṭilaʕ ħaliːb ʔummah min ħalgah] He was thoroughly exasperated. He took more than he could bear. ما صار عُمرَه عَشِر سنِين حَتَّى طِلَع حَلِيب أُمِّي مِن خَشمِي [maː ṣaːr ʕumrah ʕašir sniːn ħatta ṭilaʕ ħaliːb ʔummi min xašmi] He wasn't ten years old before I'd had all I could take. • **4.** to exit, leave, depart – طِلَعِت مِن الشَّرِكَة، هَسَّة دَأشتُغُل عَلَى حسابِي [ṭilaʕit min ʔaššarika, hassa daʔaštuɣul ʕala ħsaːbi] I left the company and now I'm working on my own. قاعِد ببَيتنا صار خَمس سنِين وَما دَيطلَع [gaːʕid bbaytna ṣaːr xams sniːn wma dayiṭlaʕ] He's been living in our house for five years and won't leave. طِلعَت رُوحَه قَبُل ما يِجِي الطَّبِيب [ṭilʕat ruːħah gabul maː yiǰi ʔiṭṭabiːb] His soul departed before the doctor came. طِلعَت رُوحِي يَلّا قِدَرِت أَحَصِّل شُغُل [ṭilʕat ruːħi yalla gidarit ʔaħaṣṣil šuɣul] I almost died before I was able to find work. • **5.** to emerge, come out, turn out forth – هَالمَكِينَة تطَلّع ألف بِسمار بِالدَّقِيقَة [halmaki:na ṭṭalliʕ ʔalf bisma:r biddaqi:qa] This machine turns out a thousand nails per minute. هَالدَّورَة طَلّعَت أحسَن الضُبّاط [haddawra ṭallʕat ʔaħsan ʔiððubba:ṭ] This class produced the best officers. مَكِينَة السَّيّارَة دَتطَلّع دُخّان [maki:nat ʔissayya:ra daṭṭalliʕ duxxa:n] The car's motor is giving off smoke. الجّاهِل طَلّع سنُون [ʔijja:hil ṭallaʕ snu:n] The child has cut his teeth. مطَلّع حَبّايَة بِيدَه [mṭalliʕ ħabba:ya bi:dah] He's developed a wart on his hand. طَلّعلِي حَسبَة جِدِيدَة [ṭallaʕli ħasba ǰidi:da] He came up with a new problem for me. لا تطَلّعلَك حِجَّة. إنتَ ما ترِيد تِجِي [la: ṭṭalliʕlak ħiǰǰa. ʔinta ma: tri:d tiji] Don't make up an excuse for yourself. You just don't want to come. طَلّعلِي النِّسبَة المِئَوِيَّة [ṭalliʕli ʔinnisba ʔilmiʔawiyya] Find the percentage for me. طَلّع هَالكِلمَة بالقامُوس [ṭalliʕ haččilma bilqa:mu:s] Look up this word in the dictionary. • **6.** to expose, show, uncover, cause to appear – طَلّع صُرّتَه وَشِفنا بِيها وُسَخ [ṭallaʕ ṣurrtah wšifna bi:ha wuṣax] He showed his navel and we saw some lint in it. طَلّع كُلّ عيُوبَه. ما خَلّى شِي ما قالَه [ṭallaʕ kull ʕyu:bah. ma: xalla: ši ma: ga:lah] He exposed all of his faults. He didn't leave a thing unsaid. • **7.** to make cause to become – إذا تِنطِي فلُوس، يطَلّعُوك نايِب [ʔiða tinṭi flu:s, yṭalliʕu:k na:yib] If you contribute money, they'll make you a representative. طَلّعتنِي كَذّاب. لِيش قِلت عِندِي فلُوس؟ [ṭallaʕtni čaðða:b. li:š gilit ʕindi flu:s?] You made a liar of me. Why did you say I had money? الحاكِم طَلّعَه تَبرِيَة [ʔilħa:kim ṭallaʕah tabriya] The judge acquitted him.

طالَع [ṭa:laʕ] *v:* • **1.** to read seriously, peruse, study – دائِماً يطالِع كُتُب أجنَبِيَّة [da:ʔiman yiṭa:liʕ kutub ʔaǰnabiyya] He's always studying foreign books.

أطلَع [ʔaṭlaʕ] *v:* • **1.** to inform, apprise, notify, tell – أطلَعنِي عَلَى سِرَّه [ʔaṭlaʕni ʕala sirrah] He let me in on his secret.

اِطَّلَع [ʔiṭṭilaʕ] *v:* • **1.** to study, become acquainted, obtain information – اِطَّلع عَلَى أحدَث الأساليب بصِناعَة القُماش [ʔiṭṭilaʕ ʕala ʔaħdaθ ʔilʔasa:li:b bṣina:ʕat ʔilquma:š] He acquainted himself with the most modern methods of manufacturing cloth.

اِستَطلَع [ʔistaṭlaʕ] *v:* • **1.** to scout, reconnoiter – رِجَع بَعَد ما اِستَطلَع المَنطَقَة [riǰaʕ baʕad ma: ʔistaṭlaʕ ʔilmanṭaqa] He returned after he scouted the area. • **2.** to seek information, inquire, find out – أرِيد أستَطلِع رَأيَه عَن المَوضُوع [ʔari:d ʔastaṭliʕ raʔyah ʕan ʔilmawðu:ʕ] I want to find out his opinion on the case.

طَلع [ṭaliʕ, ṭuluʕ] *n:* • **1.** (no pl.) carbuncle, subcutaneous infection

طَلعَة [ṭalʕa] *n:* • **1.** going out • **2.** excursion, trip – عِندَك طَلعَة لِلسُّوق اليُوم؟ [ʕindak ṭalʕa lissu:g ʔilyu:m?] Are you going to the market today?

طِلّيع [ṭilli:ʕ] *n:* • **1.** pollen of the palm tree

مَطلَع [maṭlaʕ] *n:* • **1.** starting point, rise

تَطَلُّع [taṭalluʕ] *n:* • **1.** aspiration, aim

طُلوع [ṭulu:ʕ] *n:* • **1.** rising, going up

اِطّلاع [ʔiṭṭila:ʕ] *n:* • **1.** knowledge, review

طَلِيعَة [ṭali:ʕa] *n:* طَلائِع [ṭala:ʔiʕ] *pl:* • **1.** front row, avant-garde

مطَلّعجِي [mṭalliʕči] *n:* مطَلّعجِيَّة [mṭalliʕči:yya] *pl:* • **1.** customs broker or agent

مُطالَعَة [muṭa:laʕa] *n:* • **1.** review • **2.** reading, study

اِستِطلاع [ʔistiṭla:ʕ] *n:* • **1.** probing, investigation, research – حُبّ الاستِطلاع [ħubb ʔilʔistiṭla:ʕ] curiosity. • **2.** scouting, exploration, reconnaissance

طالِع [ṭa:liʕ] *adj:* • **1.** appearing, showing up

مطَلّع [mṭalliʕ] *adj:* • **1.** taking something or someone out

مطَلَّع [mṭallaʕ] *adj:* • **1.** dismissed

مِطّلِع [miṭṭiliʕ] *adj:* • **1.** familiar • **2.** aware

طَلائِعِي [ṭala:ʔiʕi] *adj:* • **1.** avant-garde

اِستِطلاعِي [ʔistiṭla:ʕi] *adj:* • **1.** exploratory, investigative

ط ل ق

طِلَق [ṭilag] *v:* • **1.** to be in labor – طَلّقها بَعَد ما صارَت ما تِنحِمِل [ṭallagha baʕad ma: ṣa:rat ma: tinħimil] He divorced her when she became unbearable.

طَلَّق [ṭallag, ṭallaq] *v:* • **1.** to repudiate • **2.** to get a divorce

أطلَق [ʔaṭlaq] *v:* • **1.** to release

تطَلَّق [ṭṭallag] *v:* • **1.** to be repudiated, divorced – سِمَعِت راح تِتطَلَّق [simaʕit ra:ħ tiṭṭallag] I heard she's going to be divorced.

اِنطِلَق [ʔinṭilaq] *v:* • **1.** to be launched, to be released, to be started

طَلقَة [ṭalqa] *n:* طَلقات [ṭalqa:t] *pl:* • **1.** bullet • **2.** shot

طَلاق [ṭala:g] *n:* طَلاقات [ṭala:ga:t] *pl:* • **1.** divorce

طُلُوقَة [ṭulu:ga] *n:* • **1.** labor pains, travail – جَتّها الطُّلُوقة [ǰattha ʔiṭṭulu:ga] She went into labor.

طِلاقَة [ṭilla:ga] *n:* طلالِيق [ṭla:li:g] *pl:* • **1.** one leaf of a double window or door

طَلاقَة [ṭala:qa] *n:* • **1.** fluency

إطلاق [ʔiṭla:g] *n:* • **1.** launching

اِنطِلاق [ʔinṭila:q] *n:* • **1.** outbreak, release, start, explosion

إطلاقَة [ʔiṭla:qa] *n:* • **1.** shooting, bullet

طالِق [ṭa:liq, ṭa:lig] *adj:* • **1.** divorced

مُطلَق [muṭlaq] *adj:* • **1.** absolute

مطَلَّق [mṭallag] *adj:* مطَلّقِين [mṭallgi:n] *pl:* • **1.** divorced

مُطَلَّقَة [muṭallaqa, muṭalliga] *adj:* مُطَلّقات [muṭalliqa:t, muṭalliga:t] *pl:* • **1.** divorcee, divorced woman

مِنطِلِق [minṭiliq] *adj:* • **1.** happy, excited

مُطلَقاً [muṭlaqan] *adverbial:* • **1.** never

ط ل ل

طَلّ [ṭall] *v:* • **1.** to look out, peep out (of or onto something), to appear
أَطلال [ʔaṭla:l] *n:* • **1.** ruins
مُطِلّ [muṭill] *adj:* • **1.** overlooking, facing

ط ل ي

طِلَى [ṭila:] *v:* • **1.** to plate, overlay, coat – يِطلِي الخواشِيك بِفُضَّة حَتَّى ما تزَنجِر [yiṭli ʔilxwa:ši:g bfuððða ħatta ma: dzanjir] He plates the spoons with silver so they won't rust.
طِلي [ṭili] *n:* طِليان [ṭilya:n] *pl:* • **1.** lamb, young sheep
طَلِي [ṭali] *n:* • **1.** plating
مَطلِي [maṭli] *adj:* • **1.** coated

ط م ء ن

طَمئَن [ṭamʔan] *v:* • **1.** to calm, pacify, soothe, assure – ما قِبلَت إلَى أَن طَمأَنتها عَن الشَّرِكَة [ma: qiblat ʔila ʔan ṭamʔantha ʕan ʔiššarika] She wouldn't agree until I set her mind at ease about the company.
طَمَّن [ṭamman] *v:* • **1.** var. of طَمأَن to calm, pacify, soothe, assure
اِطمَأَنّ [ʔiṭmaʔann] *v:* • **1.** to be calm, tranquil, at ease, relaxed, composed, assured, confident – إذا ما أَطمَئِنّ عَلَى صِحّتَك، ما أَطلَع [ʔiða ma: ʔaṭmaʔinn ʕala ṣiħħtak, ma: ʔaṭlaʕ] If I don't feel assured about your health, I won't leave.
طَمأنِينَة [ṭamʔani:na] *n:* • **1.** calm, peace of mind
مُطَمئِنّ [muṭamʔinn] *adj:* مُطمَئِنِّين [muṭmaʔinni:n] *pl:* • **1.** secure, calm, at ease

ط م ح

طِمَح [ṭumaħ] *v:* • **1.** with ب ,ل to aspire to, be ambitious for – يِطمَح بِمَناصِب عالِيَة [yiṭmaħ bmana:ṣib ʕa:lya] He's aspiring to high positions.
طُمُوح [ṭumu:ħ] *n:* • **1.** aspiration, striving
طَمُوح [ṭamu:ħ] *adj:* • **1.** aspiring, ambitious, striving, eager, craving, avid • **2.** ambitious person – الطَّمُوح يِتقَدَّم بِالحَياة [ʔiṭṭamu:ħ yitqaddam bilħaya:t] The ambitious person gets ahead in life.

ط م ر

طُمَر [ṭumar] *v:* • **1.** to cover over, bury – الطِّين طُمَر كُلّ الدّايات [ʔiṭṭi:n ṭumar kull ʔidda:ya:t] The mud buried all the seedlings.
طَمُر [ṭamur] *n:* • **1.** covering over, burying
مَطمُور [maṭmu:r] *adj:* • **1.** buried, covered over

ط م س

طُمَس [ṭumas] *v:* • **1.** to sink down, bog down, become immersed – دِير بالَك لا تُطمُس بِالطِّين [di:r ba:lak la: tuṭmus bitti:n] Be careful not to bog down in the mud. البِدُوِي طُمَس كُلَّه بِالرَّمُل النّاعِم [ʔilbduwi ṭumas kullah birramul ʔinna:ʕim] The Bedouin sank completely into the soft sand. آني طامُس لِلهامَة بِالشُّغُل [ʔa:ni ṭa:mus lilha:ma biššuɣul] I'm buried up to the top of my head in work. طُمَس بِالدَّين [ṭumas biddayn] He's up to his neck in debts. طُمَس بِامتِحان واحِد [ṭumas bʔimtiħa:n wa:ħid] He failed one exam. • **2.** to hide, cover up, obscure – بتَهرِيجاتهُم، دَيحاولُون يطمُسُون الحَقايِق [btahri:ja:thum, dayħa:wlu:n yṭumsu:n ʔilħaqa:yiq] They're trying to cover up the facts with their commotion.
طَمَّس [ṭammas] *v:* • **1.** to immerse, plunge, dip, sink, bury – طَمُّس المواعِين كُلّها بِالمَيّ الحارّ [ṭammus ʔilmwa:ʕi:n kullha bilmayy ʔilħa:rr] Plunge all the dishes in the hot water. طَمُّس الخُبزَة بالمَرَق حَتَّى تِنقَع زين [ṭammus ʔilxubza bilmarag ħatta tingaʕ zi:n] Dip the bread in the stew until it is well soaked. مِن كِنّا دَنِسبَح، طَمَّسني [min činna danisbaħ, ṭammasni] When we were swimming, he pulled me under. طَمَّسنِي بِالدَّين. كُلّ يوم يِشتِري شِي [ṭammasni biddayn. kull yu:m yištiri ši] He's buried me in debts. Every day he buys something.
انطُمَس [ʔinṭumas] *v:* • **1.** to be sunk down, be bogged down, be immersed
طَمُس [ṭamus] *n:* • **1.** sinking down, immersing
طَمسَة [ṭamsa] *n:* • **1.** dip, dipping • **2.** sinking down, immersing, dipping
طامِس [ṭa:mis] *adj:* • **1.** immersed, submerged
مَطمُوس [maṭmu:s] *adj:* • **1.** immersed, sunken

ط م ط

طَماطَة [ṭama:ṭa] *n:* • **1.** (coll.) tomato(es)
طَماطايَة [ṭama:ṭa:ya] *n:* طَماطايات [ṭama:ṭa:ya:t] *pl:* • **1.** tomato

ط م ط م

طَمطَم [ṭamṭam] *v:* • **1.** to hide, cover up, conceal – طَمطُمَوا القَضِيَّة وَما وُصلَت لِلشُّرطَة [ṭamṭumaw ʔilqaðiyya wma wuṣlat liššurṭa] They covered up the story and it didn't get to the police.
تطمطم [tṭumṭum] *n:* • **1.** hiding, covering, concealing
مطمطم [mṭamṭam] *adj:* • **1.** covered up, concealed, hidden

ط م ع

طُمَع [ṭumaʕ] *v:* • **1.** to be or become greedy, covetous, avaricious – لا تِطمَع؛ ما دام بِيها رِبِح، بِيع [la: tiṭmaʕ; ma: da:m bi:ha ribiħ, bi:ʕ] Don't be greedy; since there's profit in it, sell. • **2.** to aspire, be ambitious, yearn, long, wish – يِطمَع يصِير وَزِير [yiṭmaʕ yṣi:r wazi:r] His ambition is to become a minister. طُمَع بِالمَنصَب وَسَبَّب فَصل المُدِير [ṭumaʕ bilmanṣab wsabbab faṣl ʔilmudi:r] He was avid for the position and brought about the dismissal of the director. طُمَع بِيها وَأخَذها بِالقُوَّة [ṭumaʕ bi:ha wʔaxaðha bilguwwa] He wanted it and took it by force.

طَمَّع [ṭammaʕ] *v:* • **1.** to arouse greed, avarice, covetousness, avidity in – إنتَ دَتطَمُّعَه بهَالحَكِي مالَك [ʔinta daṭṭammuʕah bhalħači maːlak] You're making him greedy with this talk of yours.
اِستَطمَع [ʔistaṭmaʕ] *v:* • **1.** to become greedy – مِن قِبَلنا بالسِّعِر، اِستَطمَع وَقام يُطلُب أكثَر [min qibalna bissiʕir, ʔistaṭmaʕ wgaːm yuṭlub ʔakθar] When we agreed on the price, he became greedy and began to ask for more.
طَمَع [ṭamaʕ] *n:* • **1.** greed, greediness, avidity, covetousness, ambitious desire
طَمّاع [ṭammaːʕ] *adj:* • **1.** greedy, avid, avaricious, desirous – لا تصِير طَمّاع. مُو أَخَذِت حُصّتَك [laː tṣiːr ṭammaːʕ. muː ʔaxaðit ħuṣṣtak] Don't be greedy. You've had your share!

ط م غ

طُمَغ [ṭumaɣ] *v:* • **1.** to stamp, impress – أطمُغ عَريضتَه وَسَجِّلها [ʔuṭmuɣ ʕariːðtah wsajjilha] Stamp his application and register it.
طَمَّغ [ṭammaɣ] *v:* • **1.** to stamp repeatedly or frequently – شُغلَه يطَمُّغ طَوابِع مَكاتِيب بالبَرِيد [šuɣlah yṭammuɣ ṭawaːbiʕ makaːtib bilbariːd] His job is cancelling stamps on letters in the post office. أرِيد هَالأوراق كُلّها تِتطَمَّغ حالاً [ʔariːd halʔawraːq kullha tiṭṭammaɣ ħaːlan] I want all of these papers stamped immediately.
اِنطِمَغ [ʔinṭimaɣ] *v:* • **1.** to be stamped, impressed
طَمُغ [ṭamuɣ] *n:* • **1.** impression, imprint, stamp
طَمغَة [ṭamɣa] *n:* طَمغات [ṭamɣaːt] *pl:* • **1.** impression, imprint, stamp • **2.** cancellation stamp • **3.** stamp, rubber stamp • **4.** label, gummed label
مَطمُوغ [maṭmuːɣ] *adj:* • **1.** stamped

ط م م

طَمّ [ṭamm] *v:* • **1.** to bury, cover over – الجّاهِل طَمّ المِحبَس مالَه بالتُّراب [ʔijjaːhil ṭamm ʔilmiħbas maːlah bittiraːb] The child buried his ring in the dirt.
طَمّ [ṭamm] *n:* • **1.** burying, covering over
طَمَّة [ṭamma] *n:* طَمّات [ṭammaːt] *pl:* • **1.** city dump

ط ن ط ل

طَنطَل [ṭanṭal] *adj:* طَناطِل [ṭanaːṭil] *pl:* • **1.** giant • **2.** tall person

ط ن ط ن

طَنطَن [ṭanṭan] *v:* • **1.** to hum, buzz, drone – البَقّ يطَنطِن بالإذِن [ʔilbagg yṭanṭin bilʔiðin] Mosquitoes cause a humming noise in the ear.
طَنطَنَة [ṭanṭana] *n:* • **1.** buzzing, drone (of an insect)

ط ن

طَنّ [ṭann] *n:* أطنان [ʔaṭnaːn] *pl:* • **1.** ton
طَنِين [ṭaniːn] *n:* • **1.** buzzing, humming, drone

ط ه ر

طَهَّر [ṭahhar] *v:* • **1.** to clean, cleanse, purge, purify, chasten – الحُكُومَة الجِّدِيدَة راح تطَهِّر جِهاز الحُكُومَة مِن الفَساد [ʔilħukuːma ʔijjidiːda raːħ ṭṭahhir jihaːz ʔilħukuːma min ʔilfasaːd] The new government is going to purge the governmental system of corruption. • **2.** to circumcise – الدُّكتُور طَهَّر الوَلَد [ʔidduktuːr ṭahhar ʔilwalad] The doctor circumcised the boy.
تطَهَّر [ṭṭahhar] *v:* • **1.** pass. of طَهَّر to be clean, cleanse, purge, purify, chasten • **2.** to be circumcised
طُهُر [ṭuhur] *n:* • **1.** chastity
طهُور [ṭhuːr] *n:* • **1.** circumcision
طَهارَة [ṭahaːra] *n:* طَهايِر [ṭahaːyir] *pl:* • **1.** toilet, lavatory
تَطهِير [taṭhiːr] *n:* • **1.** purge
مطَهِّرچِي [mṭahhirči] *n:* مطَهِّرچِيَّة [mṭahhirčiyya] *pl:* • **1.** circumciser
طاهِر [ṭaːhir] *adj:* • **1.** religiously clean, pure • **2.** circumspect, exemplary, faultless – هَذا واحِد ذِمّتَه طاهرَة [haːða waːħid ðimmtah ṭaːhra] He is a man of unblemished character.
مُطَهِّر [muṭahhir] *n:* مُطَهِّرات [muṭahhiraːt] *pl:* • **1.** an antiseptic, a disinfectant
طوارنِي [ṭwaːrni] *n:* طوارنِيَّة [ṭwaːrniyya] *pl:* • **1.** wild pigeon, dove

ط و

طاوَة [ṭaːwa] *n:* طاوات [ṭaːwaːt] *pl:* • **1.** frying pan, skillet

ط و ب

طُوب [ṭuːb] *n:* طواب [ṭwaːb] *pl:* • **1.** cannon
طُوبَة [ṭuːba] *n:* طُوبات، طُوَب [ṭuːbaːt, ṭuwab] *pl:* • **1.** (rubber) ball
مطَوَّب [mṭawwub] *adj:* • **1.** registered

ط و ح

تَطَوطِح [taṭawṭiħ] *n:* • **1.** stagger

ط و خ

تطوَخ [tiṭwax] *v:* • **1.** to become dark in color, to darken – شُوف الصُّبُغ شلُون تطوَخ [šuːf ʔiṣṣubuɣ šluːn ṭṭwaxx] Look how the paint turned dark!
طُوَخ [ṭuwax] *v:* • **1.** to get dark, darken – لُون المِيز مِن يِبَس، طُوَخ [luːn ʔilmiːz min yibas, ṭuwax] When it dried, the color of the table got darker.
طاخ [ṭaːx] *v:* • **1.** to become serious, grave – طاخَت القَضِيَّة. جَرّ مُسَدَّس عَلَيه [ṭaːxat ʔilqaðiyya. jarr musaddas ʕaliːh] The matter got out of hand. He pulled a pistol on him. طاخَت عاد! كُلّ يوم تِجِي لِلبَيت سَكران وَمضَيِّع فلُوسَك

[ṭaːxat ʕaːd! kull yuːm tiǰi lilbayt sakraːn wmḍayyiʕ fluːsak] That's too much! Every day you come home drunk and with your money all squandered.
طَوَّخ [ṭawwax] *v:* • **1.** to make dark in color – لَو تطَوِّخ اللُّون، تِطلَع أَحلَى [law ṭṭawwix ʔilluːn, tiṭlaʕ ʔaħlaː] If you darken the color, it'll come out better. طَوُّخلِي الشاي مالِي [ṭawwuxli ʔiččaːy maːli] Make my tea stronger. • **2.** to make serious, grave – بَسّ، عاد! مُو طَوَّختها؟ [bass, ʕaːd! muː ṭawwaxtha?] Hold on, there! Haven't you already gone too far?
طوخ [ṭuːx] *adj:* • **1.** dark, deep – لُون طُوخ [luːn ṭuːx] a dark color. ثُوب أَخضَر طُوخ [θuːb ʔaxḍar ṭuːx] a dark green shirt. • **2.** deep, profound – بَيناتنا صَداقَة طُوخ [baynaːtna ṣadaːqa ṭuːx] There's a deep friendship between us.
مطَوَّخ [mṭawwax] *adj:* • **1.** darkened
أَطوَخ [ʔaṭwax] *comparative adjective:* • **1.** darker, darkest • **2.** more or most profound

ط و د

مِنطاد [minṭaːd] *n:* مَناطِيد [manaːṭiːd] *pl:* • **1.** balloon, dirigible, blimp

ط و ر

طَوَّر [ṭawwar] *v:* • **1.** to develop (something)
تطَوَّر [ṭṭawwar] *v:* • **1.** to evolve, be developed – كُلّشِي يِتطَوَّر. ما يِبقَى ثابِت [kullši yiṭṭawwar. maː yibqaː θaːbit] Everything evolves. It doesn't remain still. القَضِيَّة تطَوَّرَت ووُصلَت لِلشُّرطَة [ʔilqaḍiyya ṭṭawwurat wwuṣlat liššurṭa] The matter built up and got to the police.
طُور [ṭuːr] *n:* • **1.** time, period of time – قِضى ويّاها فَدّ طُور وَبَعدين تِرَكها [giḍaː wiyyaːha fadd ṭuːr wbaʕdiːn tirakha] He spent some time with her and then left her.
تَطَوُّر [taṭawwur] *n:* تَطَوُّرات [taṭawwuraːt] *pl:* • **1.** development
أطوار [ʔaṭwaːr] *n:* • **1.** behavior – غَرِيب الأَطوار [ɣariːb ʔilʔaṭwaːr] eccentric, having strange behavior.
تَطوِير [taṭwiːr] *n:* • **1.** development
مِتطَوِّر [miṭṭawwir] *adj:* • **1.** advanced, developed
تَطوِيرِي [taṭwiːri] *adj:* • **1.** developmental

ط و ر ب ي د

طُوربِيد [ṭuːrbiːd] *n:* طَوربِيدات [ṭuːrbiːdaːt] *pl:* • **1.** torpedo

ط و ز

طُوز [ṭuːz] *n:* • **1.** dust • **2.** powder

ط و س

طاس [ṭaːs] *n:* طاسات [ṭaːsaːt] *pl:* • **1.** (pair of) cymbals
طاسَة [ṭaːsa] *n:* طاسات، طُوس [ṭaːsaːt, ṭuːs] *pl:* • **1.** drinking bowl, cup
طاوُوس [ṭaːwuːs] *n:* طواوِيس [ṭwaːwiːs] *pl:* • **1.** peacock

ط و ط

طَوَّط [ṭawwaṭ] *v:* • **1.** to blow a horn, honk, toot – طَوُّطلَه حَتَّى يوَخِّر عَن السَّيّارَة [ṭawwuṭlah ħatta ywaxxir ʕan ʔissayyaːra] Blow the horn at him so he'll get out of the way of the car. • **2.** to vaunt, boast, brag – مقرَّبهُم، لِأَنّ يطَوّطُوله [mqarribhum, liʔann yṭawwṭuːlah] He's a close friend of theirs, because they brag about him. • **3.** to broadcast, spread, tell around – لا تقُلَّه بالخَبَر تَرَة يطَوُّط بِيه [laː tgullah bilxabar tara yṭawwuṭ biːh] Don't tell him the news or he will blab it around.
طُوّاطَة [ṭuwwaːṭa] *n:* طُوّاطات [ṭuwwaːṭaːt] *pl:* • **1.** bulb horn

ط و ط ح

تطوطَح [ṭṭuːṭaħ] *v:* • **1.** to stagger, reel, totter – دَيتطُوطَح مِثل السَّكران [dayiṭṭuːṭaħ miθl ʔissakraːn] He is tottering like a drunkard.

ط و ع

طاع [ṭaːʕ] *v:* • **1.** to obey, be obedient – إذا يطِيع أَبُوه، ينطِيه شما يرِيد [ʔiða yṭiːʕ ʔabuːh, yinṭi šma yriːd] If he obeys his father, he gives him whatever he wants.
طَوَّع [ṭawwaʕ] *v:* • **1.** to cause to obey, make obedient, discipline – ظَلّ يلاحِقهُم حَتَّى طَوَّعهُم [ðall ylaːħighum ħatta ṭawwaʕhum] He kept after them until he made them obey. إنقُل هَالتِّلمِيذ بصَفِّي وَأنِي أَطَوّعلَك إيّاه [ʔinqul hattilmiːð bṣaffi waʔaːni ʔaṭawwiʕlak ʔiyyaːh] Transfer this student to my class and I'll straighten him out for you. كان شَقِي لَكِن العَسكَرِيَّة طَوّعَته [čaːn šaqi laːkin ʔilʕaskariyya ṭawwʕatah] He was a tough guy but the military set him straight.
طاوَع [ṭaːwaʕ] *v:* • **1.** to comply with or accede to the wishes of – نَفسِي ما تطاوِعنِي عالغِشّ [nafsi maː ṭṭaːwiʕni ʕalɣišš] My nature doesn't allow me to cheat. نَفسَه تطاوعَه عَالكِذِب [nafsah ṭṭaːwʕah ʕaččiðib] His nature is quite amenable to lies.
تطَوَّع [ṭṭawwaʕ] *v:* • **1.** to volunteer – لَمّا ما حَصَّل شُغُل، تطَوَّع بِالجَيش [lamma maː ħaṣṣal šuɣul, ṭṭawwaʕ biǰǰayš] When he didn't find any work, he volunteered for the army.
اِنطاع [ʔinṭaːʕ] *v:* • **1.** to be obeyed – إذا يكُون قاسِي، ما ينطاع [ʔiða ykuːn qaːsi, maː yinṭaːʕ] If he is cruel, he won't be obeyed.
اِستَطاع [ʔistaṭaːʕ] *v:* • **1.** to be able, be in a position to do – ما يستَطِيع يدفَع هَالمَبلَغ [maː yistiṭiːʕ yidfaʕ halmablaɣ] He's not able to pay this amount.

ط

طاعَة [ṭaːʕa] *n:* • **1.** obedience, compliance, submission to
تَطَوُّع [taṭawwuʕ] *n:* • **1.** recruitment, volunteering
اِستِطاعَة [ʔistiṭaːʕa] *n:* • **1.** ability, capacity, capability, power, faculty, possibility
طايِع [ṭaːyiʕ] *adj:* • **1.** obedient
مُطِيع [muṭiːʕ] *adj:* • **1.** obedient
مِتطَوِّع [miṭṭawwiʕ] *n:* مِتطَوِّعِين [miṭṭawwiʕiːn] *pl:* • **1.** volunteer
مُستَطاع، قدِر المُستَطاع [mustaṭaːʕ, qdir ʔilmustaṭaːʕ] *adj:* • **1.** possible, feasible, practicable

ط و ف

طاف [ṭaːf] *v:* • **1.** to circumambulate, walk around – طاف الكَعبَة ثلَث مَرّات [ṭaːf ʔilkaʕba tlaθ marraːt] He circumambulated the Kaaba three times. • **2.** to tour, wander around, roam all about – طاف بَغداد كُلّها [ṭaːf baγdaːd kullha] He wandered all over Baghdad. • **3.** to float • **4.** to be or become inundated
طَوَّف [ṭawwaf] *v:* • **1.** to guide, show around – الحِجّاج دَيِنتَظرُون فَدّ واحِد يطَوُّفهُم [ʔilħijjaːǰ dayintaðruːn fadd waːħid yṭawwufhum] The religious pilgrims are waiting for someone to guide them around. • **2.** to float, rise, come to the surface – أُصبُر شوَيَّة. هَسَّة راح تطَوُّف الطُّوبَة [ʔuṣbur šwayya. hassa raːħ ṭṭawwuf ʔiṭṭuːba] Wait a minute. The ball will come to the surface now. • **3.** to float, cause to float – يخَلُّون هَوا بالباخِرَة الغَرقانَة حَتَّى يطَوُّفُوها [yixalluːn hawa bilbaːxira ʔilγargaːna ħatta yṭawwufuːha] They put air in the sunken ship to make it float. • **4.** to be or become flooded, inundated – سِدّ الماي. الحَدِيقَة طَوَّفَت [sidd ʔilmaːy. ʔilħadiːqa ṭawwfat] Cut off the water. The garden's flooded. • **5.** to build a wall around – طَوَّف البُستان بطِين [ṭawwaf ʔilbustaːn bṭiːn] He walled the orchard with mud.
طوف، طوفَة [ṭuːf, ṭuːfa] *n:* طوفات [ṭuːfaːt] *pl:* • **1.** mud wall
مطَوُّف [mṭawwuf] *n:* مطَوُّفِين [mṭawwufiːn] *pl:* • **1.** pilgrims' guide in Mecca
مَطاف [maṭaːf] *n:* • **1.** touring, traveling, riding about, itineration, circuit, tour, round trip
طَواف [ṭawaːf] *n:* • **1.** circumambulation of the Kaaba (as part of the Islamic pilgrimage ceremonies)
طَوّافَة [ṭawwaːfa] *n:* طَوّافات [ṭawwaːfaːt] *pl:* • **1.** float, buoy
طائِفَة [ṭaːʔifa] *n:* طائِفات، طَوائِف [ṭaːʔifaːt, ṭawaːʔif] *pl:* • **1.** religious sect, denomination, faction
طُوفان [ṭuːfaːn] *n:* • **1.** flood • **1.** deluge
طايِف [ṭaːyif] *adj:* • **1.** wandering, roving, itinerant • **2.** having made a circumambulation (esp. of the Kaaba) • **3.** floating • **4.** spare, excess, extra – أَحتاج فلُوس. عِندَك دِينار طايِف؟ [ʔaħtaːǰ fluːs. ʕindak dinaːr ṭaːyif?] I need money. Do you have an extra dinar? هَالمُوَظَّف طايِف ويمكِن يطَلّعُوه [hallmuwaððaf ṭaːyif wyimkin yṭalliʕuːh] That employee is unneeded and they might get rid of him. كُلّ واحِد أَخَذ كتاب وَأَنِي بقِيت طايِف لِأَنّ الكُتُب خِلصَت [kull waːħid ʔaxað ktaːb waʔaːni biqiːt ṭaːyif liʔann ʔilkutub xilṣat] Everyone took a book and I was left out because the books ran out.
طائِفِي [ṭaːʔifi] *adj:* • **1.** sectarian, denominational, factional

ط و ق [1]

طَوَّق [ṭawwaq] *v:* • **1.** to encircle, surround – الجِّنُود طَوِّقُوهُم وَبَعدين كُمشُوهُم [ʔiǰǰinuːd ṭawwiguːhum wbaʕdiːn kumšuːhum] The soldiers encircled them and then caught them.
تطَوَّق [ṭṭawwaq] *v:* • **1.** to be surrounded
طوق [ṭuːq] *n:* طواق [ṭwaːg] *pl:* • **1.** hoop, large ring
طاق [ṭaːg] *n:* طُوق [ṭuːg] *pl:* • **1.** arch • **2.** layer, stratum
طاقِيَّة، طاقيَة [ṭaːgiyya, ṭaːgya] *n:* طاقِيات، طاقِيّات [ṭaːgyaːt, ṭaːgiyyaːt] *pl:* • **1.** skullcap – اللّي يِحكِي الصُّدُق طاقِيتَه مَنقُوبَة [ʔilli yiħči ʔiṣṣudug ṭaːgiːtah manguːba] Anybody who tells the truth has got something wrong with him (lit., has a hole in his skullcap).
تَطوِيق [taṭwiːq] *n:* • **1.** encirclement, enclosure, surrounding
مطَوَّق [mṭawwag] *adj:* • **1.** surrounded

ط و ق [2]

طاق [ṭaːq] *v:* • **1.** to bear
اِنطاق [ʔinṭaːq] *v:* • **1.** to be bearable
مُطاق [muṭaːq] *adj:* • **1.** bearable

ط و ق [3]

طاقَة [ṭaːga] *n:* طاقات [ṭaːgaːt] *pl:* • **1.** unit of measure by which fine cloth is sold (approx. three yards)

ط و ل

طال [ṭaːl] *v:* • **1.** to last, last long – ما أَضُوج مِن هَالدَّرِس شقَدّ ما يطُول [maː ʔaðuːǰ min haddaris šgadd maː yṭuːl] I don't get bored with this class, no matter how long it lasts. طالَت غيبتَه [ṭaːlat γiːbtah] His absence was prolonged. شصار مِن قَضِيتَك؟ أَشُو طالَت [šṣaːr min qaðiːtak? ʔašu ṭaːlat] What happened to your case? It seems to have become long and drawn out.
طُوَل [ṭuwal] *v:* • **1.** to be or become long, to lengthen, grow longer – هَالحَبِل قصَيِّر. كَمّلَه وُصلَة اللّخ حَتَّى يِطوَل [halħabil gṣayyir. čammlah wuṣlat ʔillux ħatta yiṭwal] This rope is short. Add another piece to it so it'll be longer. • **2.** to become tall, grow tall – ما شاء الله، طُوَل بالعَجَل [maː šaːʔ ʔallah, ṭuwal bilʕaǰal] My goodness gracious, he's sure grown fast!

طَوَّل [ṭawwal] *v:* • **1.** to lengthen, elongate, extend, stretch, prolong, protract – تِقدَر تطَوِّلي البَنطَرُون؟ [tigdar ṭṭawwilli ʔilpanṭaruːn?] Can you lengthen the pants for me? دَيطَوِّل شَعرَه [dayṭawwil šaʕrah] He's letting his hair grow long. الله يطَوِّل عُمرَك [ʔallah yṭawwil ʕumrak] May God grant you long life. صار ساعَة يِحكِي. سالُوفَة قصَيِّرَة طَوَّلها [ṣaːr saːʕa yiħči. saːluːfa gṣayyra ṭawwalha] He's been talking for an hour. He's made a short story long and drawn out. بَسّ عاد، لا تطَوِّلها [bass ʕaːd, laː ṭṭawwilha] Okay, don't make a Federal case out of it! طَوِّل بالَك! راح أخَلِّص بَعَد دَقِيقَة [ṭawwil baːlak! raːħ ʔaxalliṣ baʕad daqiːqa] Hold your horses! I'll be through in a minute. • **2.** to make tall, make taller – هَالتَّمرِين يطَوِّل الواحِد [hattamriːn yṭawwil ʔilwaːħid] This exercise makes one taller. • **3.** to last, endure, continue – أُضبُط الوَقِت وشُوف شقَدّ أَطَوُّل جَوَّة المَيّ [ʔuðbuṭ ʔilwaqit wšuːf šgadd ʔaṭawwul ǰawwa ʔilmayy] Check the time and see how long I last under water. ضِجِت لِأنّ المُحاضَرَة طَوّلَت ساعتين [ðijit liʔann ʔilmuħaːðara ṭawwlat saːʕtayn] I became bored because the lecture lasted two hours.

تطَوَّل [tṭawwal] *v:* • **1.** to be lengthened – هَالردان ما تِتطَوَّل [halirdaːn maː tiṭṭawwal] This sleeve can't be lengthened.

تطاوَل [tṭaːwal] *v:* • **1.** to be insolent, fresh – لا تِتطاوَل عَلَيّا، تَرَة أكسِر خَشمَك [laː tiṭṭaːwal ʕalayya, tara ʔaksir xašmak] Don't be insolent to me, or I'll break your nose.

اِستَطوَل [ʔistaṭwal] *v:* • **1.** to consider long, too long – لا تِستَطوِل المُدَّة. هَذِي عَمَلِيَّة صَعبَة [laː tistaṭwil ʔilmudda. haːði ʕamaliyya ṣaʕba] Don't look at the time as being too long. This is a complicated operation.

طول [ṭuːl] *n:* • **1.** length – هَالبَنطَرُون بِيه طُول. لازِم أقَصّرَه [halpanṭaruːn biːh ṭuːl. laːzim ʔagaṣṣrah] These pants are a bit too long. I should shorten them. أخَذنِي طُول وعُرُض [ʔaxaðni ṭuːl wʕuruð] He took me completely by storm. He overwhelmed me. ما نطانِي فُرصَة أحكِي؛ أخَذنِي طُول وعُرُض [maː nṭaːni furṣa ʔaħči; ʔaxaðni ṭuːl wʕuruð] He didn't give me a chance to speak; just ran up one side and down the other. خَطّ الطُول [xaṭṭ ʔiṭṭuːl] geographical longitude, meridian. أَرِيد بِسمار بِطُول هَذا [ʔariːd bismaːr bṭuːl haːða] I want a nail the same length as this. الميز يِمكِن يخُشّ مِن الباب بِالطُول [ʔilmiːz yimkin yxušš min ʔilbaːb biṭṭuːl] The table will maybe go through the door lengthwise. • **2.** the whole length, all the way, to the end – إمشِي عَلَى طُول الشّارِع [ʔimši ʕala ṭuːl ʔiššaːriʕ] Go all the way down the street. آنِي ويّاك عَلَى طُول الخَطّ [ʔaːni wiyyaːk ʕala ṭuːl ʔilxaṭṭ] I'm with you all the way down the line. • **3.** all the time, continually, always, persistently, frequently, often – هُوَّ عَلَى طُول بِالقَهوَة [huwwa ʕala ṭuːl bilgahwa] He's always in the coffeeshop. إذا تظَلُّون تِتزاوِرُون عَلَى طُول، يِمكِن تِتزَوَّجها [ʔiða dðalluːn tidzaːwruːn ʕala ṭuːl, yimkin tidzawwaǰha] If you keep on visiting with each other frequently, perhaps you will marry her. زُورنا عَلَى طُول [zuːrna ʕala ṭuːl] Visit us often. • **4.** height, tallness, size • **5.** (prep.) all during, throughout – طُول اللَّيل [ṭuːl ʔillayl] all night long. طُول عُمرَك تِبقَى مجَدِّي [ṭuːl ʕumrak tibqaː mǰaddi] All your life you'll be a beggar.

طول [ṭuːl] *n:* طوال [ṭwaːl] *pl:* • **1.** bolt (of cloth)

طُولَة [ṭuːla] *n:* طُولات [ṭuːlaːt] *pl:* • **1.** stable

طِيلَة [ṭiːla] *n:* • **1.** the length, the whole, all – كانَت تنام عِندِي طِيلَة هَالمُدَّة [čaːnat tnaːm ʕindi ṭiːlat halmudda] She was sleeping with me all during this time.

تِطوالَة [tiṭwaːla] *n:* • **1.** extension

طوِيل [ṭuwiːl] *adj:* • **1.** long, lengthy – بِسمار طُوِيل [bismaːr ṭuwiːl] a long nail. إيدَه طوِيلَة [ʔiːdah ṭwiːla] He steals. He has sticky fingers. لسانَه طوِيل [lsaːnah ṭwiːl] He uses vulgar language. He has a dirty mouth. • **2.** tall, big – هَالرِّجّال شقَدّ طُوِيل [harriǰǰaːl šgadd ṭuwiːl] That man's really tall!

مُطَوَّل [muṭawwal] *adj:* • **1.** elaborate, detailed

طوالَة [ṭwaːla] *adj:* • **1.** (no pl.) an unnecessarily prolonged matter, affair – هاي طوالَة. ما تفِلّ بِيُوم أَو يومَين [haːy ṭwaːla. maː tfill byuːm ʔaw yuːmayn] It's a long, drawn-out affair. It can't be done in a day or two. ما تجُوز، عاد! مُو سَوَّيتها طوالَة [maː dǰuːz, ʕaːd! muː sawwiːtha ṭwaːla] Knock it off! You're making a mountain out of a molehill!

طُولانِي [ṭuːlaːni] *adj:* • **1.** running lengthwise, longitudinal – فَكَّوا شارِع طُولانِي جدِيد قَبُل كَم سَنَة [fakkaw šaːriʕ ṭuːlaːni ǰdiːd gabul čam sana] They cut through a new lengthwise street a few years ago.

مُستَطِيل [mustaṭiːl] *adj:* مُستَطِيلات [mustaṭiːlaːt] *pl:* • **1.** rectangle

متطاوِل [mitṭaːwil] *adj:* • **1.** arrogant, insolent

أطوَل [ʔaṭwal] *comparative adjective:* • **1.** longer, longest • **2.** taller, tallest

عَلَى طُول [ʕala ṭuːl] *adverbial:* • **1.** all of a sudden, suddenly – عَلَى بَغتَة سمَعنا عياط [ʕala baɣta smaʕna ʕyaːṭ] All of a sudden we heard shouting. بَغتَتاً الكَلِب قُمَز عَلَيّا [baɣtatan ʔiččalib gumaz ʕalayya] Suddenly the dog jumped at me.

طالَما [ṭaːlama] *subordinating conjunction:* • **1.** while, as long as – ما أَرِيد هِيكِي شِي يصِير بِالدّائِرَة طالَما آنِي مُدِير [maː ʔariːd hiːči ši yṣiːr biddaːʔira ṭaːlama ʔaːni mudiːr] I don't want such a thing to take place in the office as long as I'm director. طالَما مَوجُود، خَلّي نقُلَّه [ṭaːlamaː mawǰuːd, xalliː ngullah] While he's here, let's tell him.

ما طُول [maː ṭuːl] *subordinating conjunction:* • **1.** as long as, since, being that – ماطُولَك هنا، وَقِّع المَكاتِيب [maːṭuːlak hna, waqqiʕ ʔilmakaːtiːb] As long as you're here, sign the letters. ما طُول الأَكِل هوايَة، أُكُل ويّانا [maː ṭuːl ʔilʔakil hwaːya, ʔukul wiyyaːna] Since there's plenty of food, eat with us.

طُولات، إشطُولاتَه، شطولاتَه [ṭu:lat, ʔišṭu:la:tah, šṭu:la:tah] *n:* • **1.** Look at the size of it! – شُوف هَالرِّجّال شطُولاتَه. أَحسَنلَك ما تِتعارَك وِيّاه [šu:f harrijja:l šṭu:la:tah. ʔaħsanlak ma: titʕa:rak wiyya:h] Look how tall that guy is! It would be better for you not to fight with him. هَالحَبِل شطُولاتَه! ما يكفِي [halħabil šṭu:la:tah! ma: yikfi] Look how short this rope is! It isn't enough.

ط و ل ي

طاولي [ṭa:wli] *n:* • **1.** backgammon, trick-track • **2.** pl. طَولِيّات backgammon set

ط و ي

طِوَى [ṭiwa:] *v:* • **1.** to fold, fold up, roll up – أُطوِي الوَرَقَة طَويتَين [ʔuṭwi ʔilwaraqa ṭawi:tayn] Fold the paper twice. أُطوِي الزُّولِيَّة وشِيلها [ʔuṭwi ʔizzu:liyya wši:lha] Roll up the carpet and take it away.
طَوَّى [ṭawwa:] *v:* • **1.** var. of طِوَى to fold, fold up, roll up
اِنطِوَى [ʔinṭuwa:] *v:* • **1.** to be folded, to be rolled up
طَوِي [ṭawy] *n:* • **1.** Foldable
طَويَة، طَيَّة [ṭawya, ṭayya] *n:* طَويات [ṭawya:t] *pl:* • **1.** fold, pleat • **2.** hem (of a garment)
مَطوَة [maṭwa] *n:* مَطاوِي [maṭa:wi] *pl:* • **1.** a hoop used as a spool for yarn
مِنطَوِي [minṭawi] *adj:* • **1.** isolated, secluded

ط و ي ر ن ي

طوَيرني [ṭwi:rni] *n:* طوَيرنِيَّة [ṭwi:rniyya] *pl:* • **1.** wild pigeon, dove

ط ي ب

طاب [ṭa:b] *v:* • **1.** to be or become pleasant. nice, agreeable, enjoyable – شَهَر الجّاي الهَوا يطِيب [šahar ʔijja:y ʔilhawa yṭi:b] Next month the weather will be nice. طابَتلَه القَعدَة هنا [ṭa:batlah ʔilgaʕda hna] Staying here was pleasant for him. بِلا عَلِي ما تطِيب القَعدَة [bila ʕali ma: tṭi:b ʔilgaʕda] Without Ali the get-together won't be any fun.
طَيَّب [ṭayyab] *v:* • **1.** to cure, heal – ماكُو دُكتُور يِقدَر يطَيِّبَه [ma:ku duktu:r yigdar yṭayyibah] No doctor can cure him. يِمكِن هَالدُّوا يطَيّبَك [yimkin hadduwa yṭayybak] Perhaps this medicine will make you well. • **2.** to make delicious, tasty – الطَّماطَة تطَيِّب الأكِل [ʔiṭṭama:ṭa tṭayyib ʔilʔakil] Tomatoes make the meal delicious.
تطَيَّب [tṭayyab] *v:* • **1.** to perfume, scent oneself – هاك، تطَيَّب بِهَالرِّيحَة [ha:k, tṭayyab bharri:ħa] Here, perfume yourself with this scent.
اِستَطيَب [ʔistaṭyab] *v:* • **1.** to find nice, enjoyable, pleasant, delicious – آنِي أَستَطيِب طَبُخها [ʔa:ni ʔastaṭyib ṭabuxha] I enjoy her cooking.
طِيب [ṭi:b] *n:* • **1.** goodness – عَن طِيب خاطِر [ʕan ṭi:b xa:ṭir] gladly, with pleasure. سَوّا لِي إيّاها عَن طِيب خاطِر [sawwa: li: ʔiyya:ha ʕan ṭi:b xa:ṭir] He did it for me gladly.
طَيِّب [ṭayyib] *adj:* • **1.** pleasant, enjoyable, agreeable, nice – هَوا طَيِّب [hawa ṭayyib] pleasant weather. أَخلاق طَيِّبَة [ʔaxla:q ṭayyba] nice manners. • **2.** delicious, tasty, good – لَحَم الدِّجاج طَيِّب [laħam ʔiddija:j ṭayyib] Chicken is tasty. • **3.** well, in good health – أُمَّه ماتَت العام بَسّ أَبُوه طَيِّب [ʔummah ma:tat ʔilʕa:m bass ʔabu:h ṭayyib] His mother died last year but his father is well. • **4.** (as an answer or comment) fine, good, all right, O.K – طَيِّب! أَمُرّ عَلِيك مِن أَخَلِّص شُغلِي [ṭayyib! ʔamurr ʕali:k min ʔaxalliṣ šuɣli] O. K. ! I'll come see you when I finish my work.
أَطيَب [ʔaṭyab] *adj:* • **1.** more or most pleasant, enjoyable, etc • **2.** more or most tasty, delicious

ط ي ح

طاح [ṭa:ħ] *v:* • **1.** to be or become available – مِن تطِيح هِيكِي سَيّارَة، أخابرَك [min tṭi:ħ hi:či sayya:ra, ʔaxa:brak] When such a car is available, I'll call you. المِشمِش طاح بَسّ كُلّش غالِي [ʔilmišmiš ṭa:ħ bass kulliš ɣa:li] Apricots are in season but very expensive. لَو يطِيح بِيدِي، أَسَوِّي كُلّ ما ترِيد [law yṭi:ħ bi:di, ʔasawwi: kull ma: tri:d] If it were within my power I'd do whatever you want. • **2.** to fall, drop – طاح فَدّ شِي مِن اللُّورِي [ṭa:ħ fadd ši min ʔillu:ri] Something fell out of the truck. • **3.** to fall ill, become sick – أَبُوهُم طاح وَمَرِضتَه راح تطَوِّل [ʔabu:hum ṭa:ħ wmariðtah ra:ħ tṭawwil] Their father got sick and his illness will be prolonged.
طَيَّح [ṭayyaħ] *v:* • **1.** to drop, allow to fall, cause to fall – الجّاهِل طَيَّح الكلاص [ʔijja:hil ṭayyaħ ʔilgla:ṣ] The baby dropped the glass. طَيَّح صُبغَه [ṭayyaħ ṣubɣah] He blistered him (lit., caused his paint to fall). راح أَرُوح عَليه وَأطَيِّح صُبغَه [ra:ħ ʔaru:ħ ʕali:h waʔaṭayyiħ ṣubɣah] I'll go see him and give him hell.
طِيح [ṭi:ħ] *n:* • **1.** falling • **2.** dropping, becoming available • **3.** taking ill
طَيحَة [ṭi:ħa] *n:* طَيحات [ṭi:ħa:t] *pl:* • **1.** a fall
طايِح [ṭa:yiħ] *adj:* • **1.** fallen • **2.** run-down, dilapidated – بَيتهُم طايِح ويرِيدلَه تَعمِير [baythum ṭa:yiħ wyri:dlah taʕmi:r] Their house is run down and needs renovating. طايِح الصُّبُغ [ṭa:yħ ʔiṣṣubuɣ] ambitionless, listless. كُلّ وُلدَه دِخلَوا مَدرَسَة بَسّ واحِد مِنهُم طايِح صُبغَه [kull wuldah dixlaw madrasa bass wa:ħid minhum ṭa:yiħ ṣubɣah] All his sons went to school except one of them who has no ambition.
مطَيِّح [mṭayyiħ] *adj:* • **1.** dropping

ط ي ر

طار [ṭa:r] *v:* • **1.** to fly off, fly away, take off – الطِّير طار وحَطّ عَالشِّجرَة [ʔiṭṭi:r ṭa:r wħaṭṭ ʕaššijra]

The bird flew off and perched in the tree. الطَّيّارَة طارَت بوَقِت مِتأَخِّر [ʔiṭṭayyaːra ṭaːrat bwaqit mitʔaxxir] The airplane took off late. راح أَطِير السّاعَة سَبعَة مِن بَغداد [raːħ ʔaṭiːr ʔissaːʕa sabʕa min baɣdaːd] I'm going to take a plane at seven o'clock from Baghdad. لَك، دَطِير! إِنتَ شجابَك عالشِّطرَنج؟ [lak, daṭiːr! ʔinta šjaːbak ʕaššiṭranǰ?] Go on, beat it! What do you know about chess? طار مِن الفَرَح [ṭaːr min ʔilfaraħ] He was overjoyed. طار عَقلَه [ṭaːr ʕaqlah] He was astounded. • **2.** to fly up – نَفنُوفها طار مِن الهَوا وطِلعَت زرُورها [nafnuːfha ṭaːr min ʔilhawa wṭilʕat zruːrha] Her dress flew up because of the wind and her legs were exposed. • **3.** to fly, dash, rush, hurry – بَسّ قِتلَه أَبُوه رِجَع، طار لِلبَيت [bass gitlah ʔabuːh rijaʕ, ṭaːr lilbayt] The minute I told him his father had returned, he dashed home. • **4.** to fly past, fly away – شبِالعَجَل طار الوَقِت [šbilʕaǰal ṭaːr ʔilwakit] How fast the time passed! شِبساع طارَت فلُوسِي [šibsaːʕ ṭaːrat fluːsi] How quickly my money went! • **5.** to evaporate – قَبُّغها التَّنَكَة البَنزِين تَرَة كُلَّه يطِير [qappuɣha ltanakat ʔilbanziːn tara kullah yṭiːr] Cover up the container of gasoline or it will all evaporate.

طَيَّر [ṭayyar] *v:* • **1.** to cause to fly – قَبَّت هَويَة وطَيِّرَت كُلّشِي [gabbat hawya wṭayyirat kullši] A gust of wind came up suddenly and sent everything flying. الهَوا طَيَّر نَفنُوفها [ʔilhawa ṭayyar nafnuːfha] The wind blew her dress up. جَمالها يطَيِّر العَقِل [ǰamaːlha yṭayyir ʔilʕaqil] Her beauty drives one mad. Her beauty is astounding. • **2.** to fly – أَكُو خُوش هَوا. خَلِّي نطَيِّر طَيّاراتنا [ʔaku xuːš hawa. xalli: nṭayyir ṭayyaːraːtna] There's a good breeze. Let's fly our kites. المِطيَرجِي دَيطَيِّر طيُورَه [ʔilmiṭyarči dayṭayyir ṭyuːrah] The pigeon fancier's flying his pigeons. • **3.** to send flying, send packing, boot out – وَزِيرنا، أَعتِقِد راح يطَيّرُوه [waziːrna, ʔaʕtiqid raːħ yṭayyiruːh] I think they're going to fire our minister.

تطايَر [tṭaːyar] *v:* • **1.** to fly about, fly in all directions, to diffuse, spread, scatter – إِرجَع شوَيَّة. الشّرارات دَتِطّايَر مِن النّار [ʔirjaʕ šwayya. ššaraːraːt datiṭṭaːyar min ʔinnaːr] Back up a little. Sparks are flying out from the fire.

طير [ṭayr, ṭiːr] *n:* طيُور [ṭyuːr] *pl:* • **1.** bird • **2.** domestic pigeon

طَيّار [ṭayyaːr] *n:* طَيّارِين [ṭayyaːriːn] *pl:* • **1.** pilot, aviator, flyer

مَطار [maṭaːr] *n:* مَطارات [maṭaːraːt] *pl:* • **1.** airport, airfield

طَيّارَة [ṭayyaːra] *n:* طَيّارات [ṭayyaːraːt] *pl:* • **1.** aviatrix, woman pilot • **2.** airplane, aircraft • **3.** kite (toy)

طِيّارَة [ṭiyyaːra] *n:* طِيّارات [ṭiyyaːraːt] *pl:* • **1.** airplane, aircraft • **2.** kite (toy)

طَيَران [ṭayaraːn] *n:* • **1.** flying, flight • **2.** aviation

طائِرَة [ṭaːʔira] *n:* طائِرات [ṭaːʔiraːt] *pl:* • **1.** airplane, aircraft

تَطايِر [taṭaːyir] *n:* • **1.** flying, scattering

مطَيِّرجِي، مِطيَرجِي [mṭayyirči, miṭyarči] *adj:* مِطيَرجِيَّة [miṭyarčiyya] *pl:* • **1.** pigeon fancier, man who raises and trains domesticated pigeons

ط ي ز

طِيز [ṭiːz] *n:* • **1.** buttocks, rump

ط ي ش

طَيش [ṭayš, ṭiːš] *n:* • **1.** thoughtlessness

طايِش [ṭaːyiš] *adj:* • **1.** thoughtless

ط ي ع

See also: ط و ع

ط ي ف

طَيف [ṭiːf] *n:* أَطياف [ʔaṭyaːf] *pl:* • **1.** vision, apparition, phantasm (in a dream) – الطَّيف الشَّمسِي [ʔiṭṭiːf ʔiššamsi] the spectrum (phys.).

ط ي ن

طَيَّن [ṭayyan] *v:* • **1.** to cover or spatter with mud or clay – فات بالبِستان وَطَيَّن رِجلَيه [faːt bilbistaːn wṭayyan rijlayh] He passed through the orchard and got mud on his feet.

تطَيَّن [tṭayyan] *v:* • **1.** to become covered with mud – وُقَع بِالشّارِع وَتطَيِّنَت هدُومَه [wugaʕ biššaːriʕ wiṭṭayyinat hduːmah] He fell down in the street and his clothes got muddy.

طِين [ṭiːn] *n:* • **1.** mud, clay – طِين خاوَة [ṭiːn xaːwa] a white, clay-like substance commonly used to wash the hair. زاد الطِّين بَلَّة [zaːd ʔiṭṭiːn balla] He aggravated the situation. He made things worse.

طِينَة [ṭiːna] *n:* طِينات [ṭiːnaːt] *pl:* • **1.** a piece of mud or clay

مطَيَّن [mṭayyin] *adj:* • **1.** stained with mud • **2.** complicated

مِتطَيِّن [miṭṭayyin] *adj:* • **1.** stained with mud • **2.** complicated

ط

ظ

ظ ر ف

ظَرُف [ðaruf] *n:* ظرُوف [ðru:f] *pl:* • **1.** small leather container, bag, pouch • **2.** envelope • **3.** situation, condition, circumstance – أَقدَر أَصَلِّح الرّاديُو بظَرُف ساعَة [ʔagdar ʔaṣalliħ ʔirra:dyu bðaruf sa:ʕa] I can fix the radio within an hour.

مَظرُوف [maðru:f] *n:* مَظارِيف [maða:ri:f] *pl:* • **1.** envelope

أَظرَف [ʔaðraf] *comparative adjective:* • **1.** more elegant, more brilliant

ظ ف ر

إظفُر [ʔiðfir] *n:* أَظافِير، أَظافِر [ʔaða:fi:r, ʔaða:fir] *pl:* • **1.** fingernail, claw, talon

ظ ل ل

ظَلّ [ðall] *v:* • **1.** to stay, remain, last – ظَلّ ساعَة يِنتَظرَك [ðall sa:ʕa yintaðrak] He stayed an hour waiting for you. ظَلّ واقِف. بَلكِي يمُرّ [ðull wa:guf. balki yumurr] Stay here. Maybe he'll come by. شقَدّ ظَلَّت فلُوس عِندَك؟ [šgadd ðallat flu:s ʕindak?] How much money do you still have left? خَلّي نرُوح. ما ظَلّ وَقِت [xalli: nru:ħ. ma: ðall wakit] Let's go. There's no time left. • **2.** to continue, persist, persevere – ظَلَّت تُمطُر اللَّيل كُلّه [ðallat tumṭur ʔillayl kullah] It kept raining all night. إنتَ تظَلّ تشاغِب؟ [ʔinta dðall tša:ɣib?] Are you still stirring up trouble?

ظَلَّل [ðallal] *v:* • **1.** to shade, darken, add shadow to – ظَلِّل الصُّورَة بِهالقَلَم [ðallil ʔiṣṣu:ra bhalqalam] Shade the picture with this crayon.

ظِلّ [ðill] *n:* أظلال، ظِلال [ʔaðla:l, ðila:l] *pl:* • **1.** shade, shadow

ظَلّ [ðall] *n:* • **1.** staying, remaining

مَظَلَّة [maðalla] *n:* مَظَلّات [maðalla:t] *pl:* • **1.** umbrella, parasol, sunshade • **2.** parachute

مَظَلّي [maðalli] *n:* مَظَلِّيِّين [maðalliyyi:n] *pl:* • **1.** paratrooper • **2.** parachutist

مظَلَّل [mðallal] *adj:* • **1.** tinted, shadowed (glass)

ظ ل م

ظِلَم [ðilam] *v:* • **1.** to do wrong or evil, commit outrage, be tyrannical – هالمُدِير راح يُظلُم أكثَر مِن الأَوَّل [halmudi:r ra:ħ yuðlum ʔakθar min ʔilʔawwal] This director will be more tyrannical than the first one. • **2.** to wrong, ill-treat, unjustly – لِيش تُظلُمها لِلبنَيَّة وَتزَوِّجها لِهالشّايِب؟ [li:š tuðlumha lilbnayya wdzawwiǰha lhašša:yib?] Why are you being unfair to the girl and marrying her to this old man?

ظَلَّم [ðallam] *v:* • **1.** to be or become dark, gloomy, to darken – السّاعَة سِتَّة تظَلُّم الدِّنيا [ʔissa:ʕa sitta dðallum ʔiddinya] It gets dark at six o'clock.

تظَلَّم [dðallam] *v:* • **1.** to complain, make a complaint – راح يِتظَلَّم عِند الوَزِير عَلَى قَساوَتهُم [ra:ħ yitðallam ʕind ʔilwazi:r ʕala qasa:wathum] He's going to complain to the minister about their cruelties.

إنظِلَم [ʔinðilam] *v:* • **1.** to be wronged, treated unjustly – إنظِلَم هوايَة. المِسكِين ما مسَوِّي شِي [ʔinðilam hwa:ya. ʔilmiski:n ma: msawwi ši] He was treated very unjustly. The poor guy hasn't done a thing.

إظلَمّ [ʔiðlamm] *v:* • **1.** to become dark, gloomy, to darken – إجَت عَجَّة البارحَة وَاظلَمَّت الدِّنيا مِنها [ʔiǰat ʕaǰǰa ʔilba:rħa wʔiðlammat ʔiddinya minha] A dust storm came yesterday and the sky grew dark from it.

ظُلُم [ðulum] *n:* • **1.** unfairness, injustice, inequity • **2.** oppression, tyranny

ظَلام [ðala:m] *n:* • **1.** darkness, gloom, murkiness

مَظلَمَة [maðlama] *n:* مَظالِم [maða:lim] *pl:* • **1.** misdeed, wrong, iniquity, outrage, act of injustice

أَظلَم [ʔaðlam] *adj:* ظَلمَة [ðalma] *feminine:* • **1.** dark, gloomy, murky • **2.** more or most gloomy, murky, dusky

ظالِم [ða:lim] *adj:* ظُلّام [ðulla:m] *pl:* • **1.** unjust, unfair, iniquitous, tyrannical • **2.** harsh, severe • **3.** pl. ظُلّام tyrant, oppressor, evildoer, villain

مُظلِم [muðlim] *adj:* • **1.** darkened, lightless – غُرفَة مُظلِمَة [ɣurfa muðlima] darkroom.

مَظلُوم [maðlu:m] *adj:* • **1.** wronged, maltreated, unjustly treated, tyrannized – هَذا مَظلُوم بشُغلَه [ha:ða maðlu:m bšuɣlah] He's been discriminated against in his job.

أَظلَم [ʔaðlam] *comparative adjective:* • **1.** more or most unjust, unfair, tyrannical, iniquitous

ظُلماً [ðulman] *adverbial:* • **1.** wrongfully • **2.** unjustly

ظ ن ن

ظَنّ [ðann] *v:* • **1.** to think, believe, assume, presume, suppose – أَظُنّ راح يوصَل اليوم مِن بَغداد [ʔaðunn ra:ħ yu:ṣal ʔilyu:m min bayda:d] I think he'll arrive today from Baghdad. • **2.** to think capable of, to expect from – ما ظَنَّيتَك تخُونّي [ma: ðanni:tak txu:nni] I never expected you to betray me. • **3.** to be suspicious – آني أَظُنّ بيه [ʔa:ni ʔaðunn bi:h] I am suspicious of him.

ظَنّ [ðann] *n:* ظُنُون [ðunu:n] *pl:* • **1.** assumption, supposition, view, opinion, idea – خاب ظَنّي بِيك [xa:b ðanni bi:k] My opinion of you faltered. I was disappointed in you. حُسن الظَّنّ [ħusn ʔiððann] good opinion. أَشكُرَك عَلَى حُسن ظَنَّك بِيّا [ʔaškurak ʕala ħusn ðannak biyya] I thank you for your good opinion of me. أَغلَب الظَّنّ، أَكثَر الظَّنّ راح يِنتِقِل لِغَير مَدرَسَة [ʔaɣlab ʔiððann, ʔakθar ʔiððann ra:ħ yintiqil lɣi:r madrasa] Most probably he will transfer to another school. • **2.** to think, believe, assume, presume, suppose

ظ ه ر

ظِهَر [ðihar] *v:* • **1.** to show, appear, emerge, come into view – بَعَد ساعَة، يِظهَر القُمَر [baʕad saːʕa, yiðhar ʔilgumar] The moon will appear in an hour. هَسَّة ظِهرَت الحَقِيقَة [hassa ðihrat ʔilħaqiːqa] Now the truth is out. • **2.** to be or become apparent, clear, obvious, evident, manifest – ظِهَرلِي بَعدين فَدّ واحِد كَذّاب [ðiharli baʕdiːn fadd waːhid čaððaːb] It became apparent to me later that he was a liar. يِظهَر ما يريد يِبِيع البَيت [yiðhar maː yriːd yibiːʕ ʔilbayt] It seems he doesn't want to sell the house. عَلَى ما يِظهَر، حَسَب ما يِظهَر [ʕala maː yiðhar, ħasab maː yiðhar] according to the evidence, apparently, the way things look. عَلَى ما يِظهَر، ما راح يِجُون [ʕala maː yiðhar, maː raːħ yiǰuːn] Evidently they aren't coming.

ظَهَّر [ðahhar] *v:* • **1.** to endorse (a check, etc.) – ظَهِّر الشَيك قَبُل ما تِنطِيه [ðahhir ʔiččiːk gabul maː tinṭiːh] Endorse the check before you present it.

أظهَر [ʔaðhar] *v:* • **1.** to make visible, make apparent, show, present, demonstrate, bring to light, expose, divulge, disclose, reveal, make known – بِشَهادتَه، أظهَر الحَقّ [bšahaːdtah, ʔaðhar ʔilħaqq] By his testimony, he revealed the truth.

تظَهَّر [dðahhar] *v:* • **1.** to be endorsed – الشَيك، لازِم يِتظَهَّر قَبُل ما يِنصُرُف [ʔiččiːk, laːzim yitðahhar gabul maː yinṣuruf] The check must be endorsed before it can be cashed.

تظاهَر [dðaːhar] *v:* • **1.** to demonstrate, stage a public demonstration – الطُلّاب تظاهرَوا وَطالبَوا بإستِقالَة الوَزِير [ʔiṭṭullaːb dðaːhraw wṭaːlbaw bʔistiqaːlat ʔilwaziːr] The students demonstrated and demanded the resignation of the minister. • **2.** with ب to feign, affect, pretend, simulate, – تظاهَر بالحُبّ إلها [dtðaːhar bilħubb ʔilha] He pretended to be in love with her.

ظِهَر [ðihar] *n:* ظهُور، ظهُورَة [ðuhuːr, ðhuːra] *pl:* • **1.** back (anat.) – إجا ظَهرَه [ʔiǰa ðahrah] He reached sexual climax. He had an orgasm. طِلَع رِجّال. هَذا صُدُق مِن ظَهر أَبُوه [ṭilaʕ rijjaːl. haːða ṣudug min ðahir ʔabuːh] He proved to be a real man. He's really his father's seed. • **2.** back, rear, rear side, reverse side – ما يخاف؛ الوَزِير بظَهرَه [maː yxaːf; ʔilwaziːr bðahrah] He's not afraid; the minister's behind him. • **3.** deck – عَلَى ظَهر الباخِرَة [ʕala ðahir ʔilbaːxira] aboard the ship. • **4.** backing, support, advocacy – اللّي ما عِندَه ظَهر ما يحَصِّل وَظِيفَة [ʔilli maː ʕindah ðahir maː yħaṣṣil waðiːfa] Whoever doesn't have backing can't get a job. • **5.** generation – هُوَّ مِن الظَهَر السّابع لِلأُسرَة الحاكمَة [huwwa min ʔiððahar ʔissaːbiʕ lilʔusra ʔilħaːkima] He is from the seventh generation of the ruling family.

ظُهُر [ðuhur] *n:* ظَهاري [ðahaːri] *pl:* • **1.** noon, midday – راح أشُوفَه الظُهُر [raːħ ʔašuːfah ʔiððuhur] I'm going to see him at noon. بَعد الظُهُر [baʕd ʔiððuhur] afternoon, p. m.

ظُهُور [ðuhuːr] *n:* • **1.** appearance • **2.** visibility, conspicuousness • **3.** ostentation, show, splendor, pomp – حُبّ الظُهُور [ħubb ʔiððuhuːr] ostentatiousness, love of pomp and splendor.

مَظهَر [maðhar] *n:* مَظاهِر [maðaːhir] *pl:* • **1.** external appearance, looks • **2.** (pl. only) ostentatious displays, status symbols

ظاهِرَة [ðaːhira] *n:* ظَواهِر [ðawaːhir] *pl:* • **1.** phenomenon

تَظاهُر [taðaːhur] *n:* • **1.** dissimulation, pretending

مُظاهَرَة [muðaːhara] *n:* مُظاهَرات [muðaːharaːt] *pl:* • **1.** public demonstration, rally

ظاهِر [ðaːhir] *adj:* • **1.** visible, distinct, manifest, obvious, conspicuous, clear, evident, apparent – الظّاهِر [ʔiððaːhir] apparently, evidently, obviously. . . الظّاهِر طَلَّق مَرتَه [ʔiððaːhir ṭallag martah] Evidently he divorced his wife. حَسَب الظّاهِر [ħasab ʔiððaːhir] according to the evidence, the way things look, apparently. . . حَسَب الظّاهِر، ما راح يِجِي [ħasab ʔiððaːhir, maː raːħ yiǰi] Apparently he isn't going to come.

ظُهرِيَّة [ðuhriyya] *adj:* • **1.** noon, noontime

ظاهِري [ðaːhiri] *adj:* • **1.** superficial – عَمَلَه كان فَدّ شِي ظاهِري [ʕamalah čaːn fadd ši ðaːhiri] The thing he did was strictly for show.

مُتَظاهِر [mutaðaːhir] *adj:* مُتَظاهِرين [mutaðaːhiriːn] *pl:* • **1.** (public) demonstrator

ظاهِرِيَّة [ðaːhiriyya] *n:* • **1.** virtual appearance

ظ

ع

ع ب ء 1

عِبء [ʕibʔ] *n:* أعباء [ʔaʕbaːʔ] *pl:* • **1.** load, burden

تَعبِئَة [taʕbiʔa] *n:* • **1.** drafting, mobilization, conscription, filling, bottling

ع ب ء 2

عَبَة [ʕaba] *n:* عِبِي [ʕibi] *pl:* • **1.** عَبَة is a loose, flowing, robe-like outer garment, with arm holes instead of sleeves, worn by men and women

عَبايَة [ʕabaːya] *n:* عَبايات [ʕabaːyaːt] *pl:* • **1.** عَبايَة is a loose, flowing, robe-like outer garment, with arm holes instead of sleeves, worn by men and women

ع ب ب

عِبّ [ʕibb] *n:* عبُوب [ʕbuːb] *pl:* • **1.** shirt front • **2.** front of the دِشداشَة (traditional dress), above the belt (where objects may be carried) – ما يِنحَطّ بِالعِبّ [maː yinħaṭṭ bilʕibb] He can't be pushed around. He's no patsy. دَيِضحَك بِعِبَّه [dayiðħak bʕibbah] He's laughing up his sleeve.

ع ب ب خ ن

عَبَّخانَة، عَبَّة خانَة [ʕabbaxaːna, ʕabba xaːna] *n:* عَبَّخانات، عَبَّة خانات [ʕabbaxaːnaːt, ʕabba xaːnaːt] *pl:* • **1.** originally powerhouse, now, a quarter in Baghdad.

ع ب ث

عِبَث [ʕibaθ] *v:* • **1.** to cause disorder, confusion, wreak havoc – فَدّ أَحَّد عِبَث بِالأوراق مالتِي [fadd ʔaħħad ʕibaθ bilʔawraːq maːlti] Someone messed up my papers. الجَّيش دِخَل المَدِينَة وَعِبَث بِيها [ʔiǰǰayš dixal ʔilmadiːna wʕibaθ biːha] The army entered the city and caused havoc in it. الشُّرطَة لِزمَوه لِأَنّ عِبَث بِبنَيَّة صغَيِّرَة [ʔiššurṭa lizmawh liʔann ʕibaθ bibnayya zɣayyra] The police picked him up for molesting a little girl.

عَبَّث [ʕabbaθ] *v:* • **1.** same as عِبَث : to cause disorder, confusion, wreak havoc – ما يِقدَر إِلّا يعَبِّث ويأَذِّي الغَير [maː yigdar ʔilla yʕabbiθ wyʔaððiː ʔilɣiːr] He can't do anything except cause trouble and hurt others.

اِنعِبَث [ʔinʕibaθ] *v:* • **1.** pass. of عِبَث : to be disturbed – حُطّها بِالقاصَة حَتَّى ما يِنعِبَث بِيها [ħuṭṭha bilqaːṣa ħatta maː yinʕibaθ biːha] Put them in the safe so that they won't be disturbed.

عَبَث [ʕabaθ] *n:* • **1.** in vain, to no avail, uselessly, needlessly – تَعَبِي وِيّاه راح عَبَث [taʕabi wiyyaːh raːħ ʕabaθ] My efforts with him were of no avail. قَدَّمِت عَرِيضَة عَبَث [qaddamit ʕariːða ʕabaθ] I submitted an application uselessly. نَصِيحتَك إِلَه عَبَث [naṣiːħtak ʔilah ʕabaθ] Your advice to him is in vain.

ع ب د

عِبَد [ʕibad] *v:* • **1.** to worship – المَجُوس يِعبِدُون النّار [ʔilmaǰuːs yʕibduːn ʔinnaːr] The Magians worship fire. • **2.** to adore, venerate, worship – يِعبِد حَبِيبتَه [yiʕbid ħabiːbtah] He adores his sweetheart. يِعبِدُون الفلُوس [yiʕbiduːn ʔilfluːs] They worship money.

عَبَّد [ʕabbad] *v:* • **1.** to improve, develop (a road), to pave – الحُكُومَة دَتعَبِّد هَالطَّرِيق [ʔilħukuːma datʕabbid haṭṭariːq] The government is improving this road. البَلَدِيَّة راح تعَبِّد كُلّ هَالطُّرُق [ʔilbaladiyya raːħ tʕabbid kull haṭṭuruq] The city will pave all these roads.

تعَبَّد [tʕabbad] *v:* • **1.** to devote oneself to God – الرّاهِب مسَوِّيلَه مُكان بِالجِبَل يِتعَبَّد بِيه [ʔirraːhib msawwiːlah mukaːn biǰǰibal yitʕabbad biːh] The hermit has made himself a place on the mountain in which he devotes himself to worship.

اِستَعبَد [ʔistaʕbad] *v:* عَبِيد [ʕabiːd] *pl:* • **1.** to enslave, subjugate – اِستَولَوا عَلَيهُم وَاِستَعبِدُوهُم [ʔistawlaw ʕaliːhum wʔistaʕbiduːhum] They conquered and enslaved them.

عَبِد [ʕabid] *n:* عَبِيد [ʕabiːd] *pl:* • **1.** slave, serf • **2.** bondsman, servant • **3.** black man

عَبدَة [ʕabda] *n:* عَبدات [ʕabdaːt] *pl:* • **1.** female slave, bondswoman • **2.** black woman

مَعبَد [maʕbad] *n:* مَعابِد [maʕaːbid] *pl:* • **1.** temple, place of worship

تَعَبُّد [taʕabbud] *n:* • **1.** piety, devoutness, devotion • **2.** worship, hagiolatry

عِبادَة [ʕibaːda] *n:* • **1.** worship, adoration, veneration, • **2.** divine service, religious observances, acts of devotion

عُبُودِيَّة [ʕubuːdiyya] *n:* • **1.** slavery, serfdom • **2.** humble veneration, adoration, homage, worship

عَبّادان [ʕabbaːdaːn] *n:* • **1.** island and town in West Iran

اِستِعباد [ʔistiʕbaːd] *n:* • **1.** enslavement

عَبّاد، عَبّاد الشَّمِس [ʕabbaːd, ʕabbaːd ʔiššamis] *n:* • **1.** sunflower – وَرَق عَبّاد الشَّمِس [waraq ʕabbaːd ʔiššamis] litmus paper.

عابِد [ʕaːbid] *adj:* • **1.** enslaved • **2.** worshiper

مَعبُود [maʕbuːd] *adj:* • **1.** worshiped, adored

مِتعَبِّد [mitʕabbid] *adj:* • **1.** pious, devout • **2.** pious worshiper (Chr.)

مِستَعبِد [mistaʕbid] *adj:* • **1.** enslaved

ع ب ر

عُبَر [ʕubar] *v:* • **1.** to cross – خَلِّي نُعبُر الشّارِع [xalliː nuʕbur ʔiššaːriʕ] Let's cross the street. راح نِعبُر لِصُوب الكَرخ [raːħ niʕbur ʔilṣuːb ʔilkarx] We'll cross to the Karkh side. الكَلِب عُبَر عَالسِّياج وَوُقَع عالوَرد

[ʔiččalib ʕubar ʕassiya:ǰ wwugaʕ ʕalwarid] The dog jumped over the fence and fell on the flowers. النُّكتَة عُبرَت عَليه [ʔinnukta ʕubrat ʕali:h] He fell for the joke. ما يُعبُر عَليه شِي [ma: yuʕbur ʕali:h ši] You can't put anything over on him. ما عُبرَت بدَرس الكِيميا [ma: ʕubarit bdars ʔilki:mya] I didn't pass in chemistry.

عَبَّر [ʕabbar] *v:* • **1.** to express, voice, assert, state clearly – ما دَأقدَر أعَبُّر عَن قَصدِي [ma: daʔagdar ʔaʕabbur ʕan qaṣdi] I can't express what I mean. • **2.** to take across, send across, let across – الشُّرطِي عَبَّر الجَاهِل الشّارِع [ʔiššurṭi ʕabbar ʔiǰǰa:hil ʔiššaːriʕ] The policeman let the child cross the street. إسأل أبُو البَلَم. بَلكِي يعَبّرَك [ʔisʔal ʔabu ʔilbalam. balki yʕabbrak] Ask the boatman. Maybe he'll take you across. عَبُّرلَه دِينارَين وَيمَشِّيلَك إيّاها [ʕabburlah dina:rayn wymašši:lak ʔiyya:ha] Slip him two dinars and he'll take care of it for you.

اِنعِبَر [ʔinʕibar] *v:* • **1.** to be crossed – هَالشَّطّ عَرِيض، ما يِنعُبُر سِبِح [haššaṭṭ ʕari:ð̣, ma: yinʕubur sibiħ] The river is wide. It can't be crossed by swimming.

اِعتُبَر [ʔiʕtubar] *v:* • **1.** to learn a lesson, learn from experience – ما إعتِبَرت مِن اللِّي صار بأخُوك؟ [ma: ʔitʕibarit min ʔilli ṣa:r bʔaxu:k?] Didn't you learn a lesson from what happened to your brother? • **2.** to consider, regard as – اِعتُبَرناه واحِد مِن العائِلَة [ʔiʕtubarna:h wa:ħid min ʔilʕa:ʔila] We considered him one of the family. أعتَبرَه مُطِي [ʔaʕtabrah muṭi] I consider him a jackass. نِعتُبُر هَالعَمَل فَدّ شِي خَطِير [niʕtubur halʕamal fadd ši xaṭi:r] We regard this act as being serious. اِعتُبُرها صَدَقَة لِالله [ʔiʕtuburha ṣadaqa lʔallah] Look at it as a charity for God's sake. • **3.** to show regard, to respect, value – رِحتِلَه، لَكِن ما إعتُبَرنِي [riħitlah, la:kin ma: ʔiʕtubarni] I went to him, but he didn't show me any consideration.

عِبِر [ʕibir] *n:* • **1.** across, over – عِبر الشّارِع [ʕibr ʔiššaːriʕ] across the street.

عُبُر [ʕubur, ʕibir] *n:* • **1.** through, throughout

عَبرَة [ʕabra] *n:* • **1.** tears, crying – لِزمَتَه العَبرَة [lizmatah ʔilʕabra] He began to cry. تاخذَه العَبرَة [ta:xð̣ah ʔilʕabra] He bursts into tears.

عِبرَة [ʕibra] *n:* عِبرات، عِبَر [ʕibra:t, ʕibar] *pl:* • **1.** a crossing, an act of crossing

عِبرَة [ʕibra] *n:* عِبَر [ʕibar] *pl:* • **1.** warning, example, lesson, object lesson

مَعبَر [maʕbar] *n:* مَعابِر [maʕa:bir] *pl:* • **1.** crossing, place for crossing • **2.** ford • **3.** ferry landing, dock

عُبُور [ʕubu:r] *n:* • **1.** crossing, traversing, transit, passage

عَبِير [ʕabi:r] *n:* • **1.** fragrance, scent, perfume, aroma, bouquet (of wine)

عِبارَة [ʕiba:ra] *n:* عِبارات [ʕiba:ra:t] *pl:* • **1.** sentence, clause, phrase, expression – عِبارَة عَن [ʕiba:ra ʕan] actually, really, simply, merely. اللاسِلكِي عِبارَة عَن راديُو [ʔilla:silki ʕiba:ra ʕan ra:dyu] The wireless is simply a radio. لا تدِير بال. هِيَّ عِبارَة عَن خَمس دَنانِير [la: ddi:r ba:l. hiyya ʕiba:ra ʕan xams dana:ni:r] Don't worry. It's only a matter of five dinars.

عَبّارَة [ʕabba:ra] *n:* عَبّارات [ʕabba:ra:t] *pl:* • **1.** ferry, ferry boat

تَعبِير [taʕbi:r] *n:* تَعابِير [taʕa:bi:r] *pl:* • **1.** expression, mode of expression, way of putting it – بغَير تَعبِير، بتَعبِير آخَر [byayr taʕbi:r, btaʕbi:r ʔa:xar] in other words.

اِعتبار [ʔiʕtiba:r] *n:* • **1.** respect, regard, esteem – عِندَه إعتِبار بالسُّوق [ʕindah ʔiʕtiba:r bissu:g] He has a good credit rating in the market. • **2.** pl. اِعتِبارات consideration, regard – أخَذ بنَظَر الاعتِبار [ʔaxað bnað̣ar ʔilʔiʕtiba:r] to take into consideration. راح ياخذُون مَرَضَك بنَظَر الاعتِبار [ra:ħ ya:xðu:n marað̣ak bnað̣ar ʔilʔiʕtiba:r] They'll take your illness into consideration. بإعتِبار مَعرفتَك بالمِيكانِيك، إنتَ صَلِّحها [bʔiʕtiba:r maʕriftak bilmikani:k, ʔinta ṣalliħha] In consideration of your knowledge of mechanics, you fix it. إنتَ إحكِي ويّاها بإعتِبارَك تُعرُف إنكِلِيزِي [ʔinta ʔiħči wiyya:ha bʔiʕtiba:rak tuʕruf ʔingili:zi] You talk with her since you know English. بإعتِبارَه وَكِيل الوَزِير، فِتَح الجِّسِر [bʔiʕtiba:rah waki:l ʔilwazi:r, fitaħ ʔiǰǰisir] In his capacity as the minister's representative, he opened the bridge.

اِعتِباراً، اِعتِباراً مِن [ʔiʕtiba:ran, ʔiʕtiba:ran min] *adverbial:* • **1.** effective, beginning, starting with – اِعتِباراً مِن باكِر، لازِم نِجِي ساعَة ثمانيَة [ʔiʕtiba:ran min ba:čir, la:zim niǰi sa:ʕa θma:nya] Beginning tomorrow, we've got to come at eight.

عِبرِي [ʕibri] *adj:* • **1.** Hebrew, Hebraic – اللُّغَة العِبرِيَّة، العِبرِيَّة [ʔilluɣa ʔilʕibriyya, ʔilʕibriyya] the Hebrew language, Hebrew. • **2.** a Hebrew

عِبرِي [ʕibri] *adj:* عِبرِيَّة [ʕibriyya] *pl:* • **1.** passenger (paying) – راح عِبرِي [ra:ħ ʕibri] He went as a passenger. He went on public transportation.

عابِر [ʕa:bir] *adj:* • **1.** passing, crossing, traversing • **2.** fleeting (smile), transient, transitory, ephemereal, bygone, past • **3.** casual

مُعَبِّر [muʕabbir] *adj:* • **1.** expressive

مُعتَبَر [muʕtabar] *adj:* • **1.** highly regarded, well thought of, much praised – قماش مُعتَبَر [qma:š muʕtabar] cloth that is well thought of. مُعَلِّم مُعتَبَر [muʕallim muʕtabar] a highly regarded teacher.

عِبرانِي [ʕibra:ni] *adj:* • **1.** var. عِبرِي Hebrew, Hebraic

تَعبِيرِي [taʕbi:ri] *adj:* • **1.** expressional, expressive, emotive

ع ب س

عَبَّس [ʕabbas] *v:* • **1.** to frown, scowl, glower – عَبَّس مِن سِمَع الفلُوس تأخّرَت [ʕabbas min simaʕ ʔilflu:s

tʔaxxrat] He frowned when he heard the money had been delayed. عَبَّس بوجهي [ʕabbas bwičči] He scowled at me.
عابِس [ʕaːbis] *adj:* • **1.** frowning, gloomy
معَبِّس [mʕabbis] *adj:* • **1.** grim • **2.** frowning, gloomy
عَبُوس [ʕabuːs] *adj:* • **1.** sullen, grim
عَبّاسي [ʕabbaːsi] *adj:* • **1.** Abbaside, belonging to the Abbaside period, an Abbaside

ع ب ق ر

عَبقَرِيَّة [ʕabqariyya] *n:* • **1.** ingenuity, genius, cleverness
عَبقَري [ʕabqari] *adj:* عَباقِرَة [ʕabaːqira] *pl:* • **1.** ingenious, clever, gifted – قائِد عَبقَري [qaːʔid ʕabqari] an ingenious leader. حَلّ عَبقَري [ħall ʕabqari] an ingenious solution. • **2.** as Noun: genius

ع ب و

عَبَّى [ʕabbaː] *v:* • **1.** to stuff, pack – عَبِّي الجُكلَيت بِكِيسَين [ʕabbi ʔiččukliːt bčiːsayn] Pack the candy into two bags. شِفتَه يعَبِّي شَكَر بجِيبَه [šiftah yʕabbi šakar bjiːbah] I saw him stuffing candy in his pocket. • **2.** to fill, pack – عَبِّي هَالكِيس جُكلَيت [ʕabbi haččiːs čukliːt] Fill this sack with candy.
عَبوَة [ʕabwa] *n:* عَبوات [ʕabwaːt] *pl:* • **1.** booby trap • **2.** container, pack (of an article, of a commodity)
معَبَّى، معَبّايَة [mʕabba, mʕabbaːya] *adj:* • **1.** filled, loaded

ع ت ب

عِتَب [ʕitab] *v:* • **1.** to gripe, grumble, complain – عِتَب عَلَى مُعامَلتَك إلَه [ʕitab ʕala muʕaːmaltak ʔilah] He complained about your treatment of him. دَيِعتِب هوايَة كيف ما زِرناه [dayiʕtib hwaːya čiːf maː zirnaːh] He's grumbling a lot because we didn't visit him.
عَتَّب [ʕattab] *v:* • **1.** to blame, censure – إذا طِلَع مُو زين، لا تعَتِّبني [ʔiða ṭilaʕ muː ziːn, laː tʕattibni] If it turns out badly, don't blame me. إذا اِنهِزَم مِن المَدرَسَة، آني ما معَتَّب [ʔiða ʔinhizam min ʔilmadrasa, ʔaːni maː mʕattab] If he runs away from school, I'm not to blame.
عاتَب [ʕaːtab] *v:* • **1.** to scold, upbraid, censure, rebuke – راح أرُوح عَليه وَأعاتبَه عَلَى هَالعَمَل [raːħ ʔaruːħ ʕaliːh waʔaʕaːtbah ʕala halʕamal] I'm going to see him and scold him for that action.
تعاتَب [tʕaːtab] *v:* • **1.** to find fault with each other – تعاتَبنا شوَيَّة وَبَعدين كُلّشي قِعَد بمُكانَه [tʕaːtabna šwayya wbaʕdiːn kullši giʕad bimukaːnah] We argued a little and then everything was all right.
عَتَب [ʕatab] *n:* • **1.** censure, blame, rebuke, reprimand
عِتبَة [ʕitba] *n:* عِتبات [ʕitbaːt] *pl:* • **1.** window sill door step, threshhold, doorway, sill
عَتَبَة [ʕataba] *n:* عَتَبات [ʕatabaːt] *pl:* • **1.** shrine, tomb of a holy man – العَتَبات المُقَدَّسَة [ʔilʕatabaːt ʔilmuqaddisa] the holy shrines.
عِتاب [ʕitaːb] *n:* • **1.** blame
معاتَب [mʕaːtab] *n:* • **1.** blamed, rebuked, reproofed reprimanded

ع ت د

عِتاد [ʕitaːd] *n:* • **1.** war material, ammunition

ع ت ق

عِتَق [ʕitaq] *v:* • **1.** to grow old – ساعتِي عِتقَت، لَكِن بَعَدها تِشتُغُل زين [saːʕti ʕitgat, laːkin baʕadha tištuɣul ziːn] My watch has gotten old, but it still works well. قُوطِي كُلّها عِتقَت [quːṭi kullha ʕitgat] All my suits have gotten old.
عَتَّق [ʕattaq, ʕattag] *v:* • **1.** to age • **2.** to free, to emancipate • **3.** to ferment
تعَتَّق [tʕattaq, ʔitʕattaq] *v:* • **1.** to be fermented • **2.** to be aged
عَتِق [ʕatig] *n:* • **1.** growing old
عاتِق [ʕaːtiq] *n:* • **1.** shoulder – أخَذ المَشرُوع عَلَى عاتقَه [ʔaxað ʔilmašruːʕ ʕala ʕaːtqah] He took the project on. خَلِّيها عَلَى عاتقِي [xalliːha ʕala ʕaːtqi] Leave it to me.
عَتِيق [ʕatiːg] *adj:* عِتَّق [ʕittag] *pl:* • **1.** old – سَيّارَة عَتِيقَة [sayyaːra ʕatiːga] an old car. • **2.** obsolete, old-fashioned – طُرُق عَتِيقَة [ṭuruq ʕatiːga] old-fashioned methods. واوِي عَتِيق [waːwi ʕatiːg] a sly old fox.
معَتَّق [mʕattaq, mʕattag] *adj:* • **1.** aged, mellowed, ancient • **2.** fermented
أعتَق [ʔaʕtag] *comparative adjective:* • **1.** more or most aged – لَطايفَه أعتَق مِن اليَخني [laṭaːyfah ʔaʕtag min ʔilyaxni] His jokes are old as the hills.

ع ت ل

عَتَلَة [ʕatala] *n:* عَتَلات [ʕatalaːt] *pl:* • **1.** lever (phys.)

ع ت م

عَتَّم [ʕattam] *v:* • **1.** to darken, block out – عَتِّموا المَدِينَة مِن سِمعَوا حِسّ الطَّيّارات [ʕattimaw ʔilmadiːna min simʕaw ħiss ʔiṭṭiyyaːraːt] They blacked out the city when they heard the noise of airplanes.
تَعتِيم [taʕtiːm] *n:* • **1.** blackout
مِعتِم [miʕtim] *adj:* • **1.** dim • **2.** dark

ع ت ه

مَعتُوه [maʕtuːh] *adj:* • **1.** insane, crazy, idiotic • **2.** lunatic, insane person

ع

ع ت و

عِتوِي [ʕitwi] *n:* عتاوِي [ʕtaːwi] *pl:* • **1.** a big tom cat

ع ث ث

انعَث [ʔinʕaθθ] *v:* • **1.** to become moth-eaten – لا تخَلِّي قاطَك بِهَالصَّندُوق، تَرَة يِنعَثّ [laː txalli: qaːṭak bhaṣṣanduːg, tara yinʕaθθ] Don't leave your suit in this trunk or it'll get moths in it.

عِث [ʕiθθ] *n:* • **1.** (coll.) moth(s)

عِثَّة [ʕiθθa] *n:* عِثّات [ʕiθθaːt] *pl:* • **1.** moth

مَعثُوث [maʕθuːθ] *adj:* • **1.** moth-eaten – قَبُوط مَعثُوث [qappuːṭ maʕθuːθ] a moth-eaten overcoat.

ع ث ر

عِثَر [ʕiθar] *v:* • **1.** to trip, stumble – عِثَر بِبُورِي المَيّ وَوُقَع [ʕiθar bbuːri ʔilmayy wwugaʕ] He tripped over the water pipe and fell. • **2.** with عَلَى to come across, hit on, stumble onto – عِثَرت عَلَى خُوش قُمصان بِفَدّ مَخزَن [ʕiθarit ʕala xuːš qumṣaːn bfadd maxzan] I stumbled onto some terrific shirts in a store. • **3.** with ب to find, run into (someone)

عَثَّر [ʕaθθar] *v:* • **1.** to trip, make stumble – دِير بالَك عالعَتبَة، تَرَة تعَثّرَك [diːr baːlak ʕalʕatba, tara tʕaθθrak] Watch out for the door sill, or it'll trip you. • **2.** to trip up – تِدرِي إنتَ تعَثّرَه بأسئِلتَك؟ [tidri ʔinta tʕaθθirah bʔasʔiltak?] Do you realize you trip him up with your questions?

تعَثَّر [tʕaθθar] *v:* • **1.** to stumble, trip – يِتعَثَّر هوايَة مِن يِمشِي [yitʕaθθar hwaːya min yimši] He stumbles a lot when he walks. • **2.** to stutter, stammer, speak haltingly – يِتعَثَّر هوايَة بكَلامَه [yitʕaθθar hwaːya bkalaːmah] He stammers a lot in his speech.

عَثرَة [ʕaθra] *n:* • **1.** stumbling, tripping

عُثُور [ʕuθuːr] *n:* • **1.** discovery, detection

عاثُورَة [ʕaːθuːra] *n:* • **1.** something in the way, something underfoot

مِتعَثِّر [mitʕaθθir] *adj:* • **1.** stumbling, tripping, • **2.** stuttering, hesitating

ع ث ق

عِثِق [ʕiθig] *n:* عثُوق [ʕθuːg] *pl:* • **1.** bunch, cluster, stalk (of dates, bananas, etc.)

ع ث م ن

عُثماني [ʕuθmaːni] *adj:* • **1.** Ottoman

ع ج ب

عِجَب [ʕijab] *v:* • **1.** to please, delight, appeal to – البَيت الجِّدِيد عِجَبنِي كُلِّش [ʔilbayt ʔijjidiːd ʕijabni kulliš] The new house pleased me very much. يعجِبنِي أرُوح لِلسِّينَما [yiʕjibni ʔaruːħ lissiːnama] I'd like to go the movies.

عَجَّب [ʕajjab] *v:* • **1.** to amaze, astonish, surprise – مَوقِفَه يعَجِّب الواحِد [mawqifah yʕajjib ʔilwaːħid] His attitude is amazing.

تعَجَّب [tʕajjab] *v:* • **1.** to be surprised, amazed, astonished – تعَجَّب مِن قِتلَه [tʕajjab min gitlah] He was astonished when I told him. دَأتعَجَّب شلُون يِقدَر يِشتُغُل خمُسطَعَش ساعَة [daʔatʕajjab šluːn yigdar yištuɣul xmusṭaʕaš saːʕa] I'm amazed at how he can work fifteen hours! لُويش دَتِتعَجَّب؟ كُلّشِي مُمكِن [luwiːš datitʕajjab? kullši mumkin] Why are you surprised? Anything is possible.

عَجَب [ʕajab] *n:* • **1.** astonishment, amazement • **2.** wonder, oddity, strange occurrence – عَجَب ما دَيبَيِّن هنا [ʕajab maː daybayyin hna] It's odd he doesn't show up here. • **3.** then, in that case – شعَجَب ما إجا [šʕajab maː ʔijaː] I wonder why he didn't come. ما سِألِت عَنِّي. شعَجَب [maː siʔalit ʕanni. šʕajab] You didn't ask about me. I wonder why.

عِجبَة [ʕijba] *n:* • **1.** sensation, amazing thing, source of amazement

تَعَجُّب [taʕajjub] *n:* • **1.** as in عَلامَة تَعَجُّب : exclamation mark

إعجاب [ʔiʕjaːb] *n:* • **1.** admiration

تعجِيب [taʕjiːb] *n:* • **1.** rousing admiration, amazement

إعجُوبَة [ʔiʕjuːba] *n:* عَجايِب [ʕajaːjiːb] *pl:* • **1.** source of amazement, wondrous thing, sensation, unheard-of thing, miracle, marvel, wonder

عَجِيب [ʕajiːb] *adj:* • **1.** amazing, remarkable, strange, odd

أعجَب [ʔaʕjab] *comparative adjective:* • **1.** more or most astonishing, remarkable

مُعجَب [muʕjab] *adj:* • **1.** admirer (with بـ- of s.o or s.th), proud (of) – هَذا مُعجَب بِالرّاقِصَة [haːða muʕjab birraːqiṣa] He's an admirer of the dancer. مُعجَب بِنَفسَه [muʕjab bnafsah] vain, conceited.

عَجِيبَة [ʕajiːba] *n:* عَجايِب [ʕajaːyib] *pl:* • **1.** remarkable thing, oddity, curiosity, prodigy, marvel

عَجَباً، عَجَبا [ʕajaban, ʕajabaː] *adverbial:* • **1.** (approximately) I wonder, do you suppose – عَجَبا راح يِنطُونَه عُطلَة باكِر؟ [ʕajabaː raːħ yintuːna ʕuṭla baːčir?] Do you think they'll give him a holiday tomorrow? عَجَباً راح يِقبَل؟ [ʕajaban raːħ yiqbal?] Do you suppose he is going to accept?

عَجِب [ʕajib] *int:* • **1.** how come! why so!

ع ج ج

عَجّ [ʕajj] *v:* • **1.** to swarm, teem – باكِر المَطار راح يعِجّ بِالمُسافِرِين [baːčir ʔilmaṭaːr raːħ yʕijj bilmusaːfiriːn] Tomorrow the airport is going to be packed with travelers. • **2.** with بـ- to rage, to roar

ع

عَجَّج [ʕajjaj] *v:* • **1.** to raise the dust – إمشِي عَلَى كَيفَك. لا تعَجِّج [ʔimši ʕala kayfak. la: tʕajjij] Walk slowly. Don't raise the dust.
عَجّ [ʕajj] *n:* • **1.** swarming
عَجَّة [ʕajja] *n:* عَجّات [ʕajja:t] *pl:* • **1.** dust storm
عَجاج [ʕaja:j] *n:* • **1.** (swirling) dust

ع ج ر ف

تعَجرَف [tʕajraf] *v:* • **1.** to be arrogant, haughty, presumptuous – صارَت عِندَك شوَيَّة فلُوس وَقُمت تِتعَجرَف عالنّاس [ṣa:rat ʕindak šwayya flu:s wagumit titʕajraf ʕanna:s] You got a little money and then you began to be arrogant toward people.
متعَجرِف [mitʕajrif] *adj:* • **1.** arrogant, haughty – ظابُط مِتعَجرِف [ða:buṭ mitʕajrif] an arrogant officer.

ع ج ز

عِجَز [ʕijaz] *v:* • **1.** to be weak, lack strength, be incapable, unable – ظَلّيت أَلِحّ عَليه إِلَى أَن عِجزَت [ðalli:t ʔaliħħ ʕali:h ʔila ʔan ʕjazit] I kept insisting on it till I was exhausted. عِجَز عَن دَفع المَبلَغ وَباعَوا بيتَه [ʕijaz ʕan dafiʕ ʔilmablaɣ wba:ʕaw baytah] He was incapable of paying the amount and they sold his house. • **2.** to become sick, become tired – عِجَزت مِن أَكِل الدِّجاج [ʕijazit min ʔakil ʔiddija:j] I've gotten sick of eating chicken.
عَجَّز [ʕajjaz] *v:* • **1.** to age, grow old – عَجِّزَت وَما تِقدَر تِشتُغُل بَعَد [ʕajjizat wma tigdar tištuɣul baʕad] She has grown old and can't work any more. • **2.** to weaken, exhaust – عَجَّزتنِي بِأَسِلتَك [ʕajjaztni bʔasʔiltak] You've exhausted me with your questions.
تعاجَز [tʕa:jaz] *v:* • **1.** to be unwilling, to be unable to bother, to be lazy – مِن أَقُلَّك تسَوِّي شِي، لا تِتعاجَز [min ʔagullak tsawwi: ši, la: titʕa:jaz] When I tell you to do something, don't give me a hard time. يِتعاجَز يسَوِّي أَيّ شِي اللِّي أَطُلبَه مِنَّه [yitʕa:jaz ysawwi: ʔayy ši ʔilli ʔaṭulbah minnah] He can't be bothered doing anything I ask him.
عَجِز [ʕajiz] *n:* • **1.** shortage, deficit • **2.** incapacity, weakness
عَجِز [ʕajiz, ʕajuz] *n:* أَعجاز [ʔaʕja:z] *pl:* • **1.** posterior, rump, backside, buttocks
مُعجِزَة [muʕjiza] *n:* مُعجِزات [muʕjiza:t] *pl:* • **1.** miracle (esp. those performed by a prophet)
عَجُوز [ʕaju:z] *adj:* عَجَزَة [ʕajaza] *pl:* • **1.** old, elderly, aged – مَرَة عَجُوز [mara ʕaju:z] an old woman. • **2.** as Noun: old, elderly person, oldster • **3.** also as Noun: lazy person, sloth, stick-in-the-mud
عاجِز [ʕa:jiz] *adj:* • **1.** weak, feeble, powerless, incapable – رِجّال عاجِز [rijja:l ʕa:jiz] a feeble man.
عَجزان [ʕajza:n] *adj:* • **1.** sick and tired, fed up – عَجزان مِن الدِّراسَة [ʕajza:n min ʔiddira:sa] sick and tired of studying.
عَجُوزَة [ʕaju:za] *adj:* عَجُوزات، عَجايِز [ʕaju:za:t, ʕaja:yiz] *pl:* • **1.** old, elderly, aged woman
عجُوزِي [ʕju:zi] *adj:* عجُوزِيَّة [ʕju:ziyya] *pl:* • **1.** lazy, slothful, indolent • **2.** lazy person
متعاجِز [mitʕa:jiz] *adj:* • **1.** lazy, slothful, indolent

ع ج ع ج

عَجعَج [ʕajʕaj] *v:* • **1.** to stir up dust – إمشِي عَلَى كَيفَك. لا تعَجعِج [ʔimši ʕala kayfak. la: tʕajʕij] Walk slowly. Don't stir up the dust.
معَجعَج [mʕajʕaj] *adj:* • **1.** dusty

ع ج ل

عَجَّل [ʕajjal] *v:* • **1.** to hurry, rush, speed – عَجِّل شوَيَّة؛ ما بُقَى وَقِت [ʕajjil šwayya; ma: buqa: wakit] Hurry up a little bit; there isn't much time left. • **2.** to hurry, rush, urge, drive – ما أَقدَر أكتِب زين إذا تعَجِّلنِي [ma: ʔagdar ʔaktib zi:n ʔiða tʕajjilni] I can't write well if you rush me.
استَعجَل [ʔistaʕjal] *v:* • **1.** to hurry, rush, be in a hurry – لا تِستَعجِل. عِدنا وَقِت [la: tistaʕjil. ʕidna waqit] Don't hurry. We have time.
عَجَل، بالعَجَل [ʕajal, bilʕajal] *n:* • **1.** hurry, haste – تَعال هنا بالعَجَل [taʕa:l hna: bilʕajal] Come here, on the double! قُلَّه يرُوح بِالعَجَل [gullah yiru:ħ bilʕajal] Tell him to go immediately. هُوَّ يِتصَدَّق بِالعَجَل [huwwa yitṣaddag bilʕajal] He's easily convinced. • **2.** with بـ- : in a hurry, quickly, rapidly
عَجَلَة [ʕajala] *n:* • **1.** haste, hurry – العَجَلَة مِن الشَّيطان [ʔilʕajala min ʔišši:ṭa:n] Haste makes waste (lit. Haste is of the devil).
تَعجِيل [taʕji:l] *n:* • **1.** hurrying up, speeding up • **2.** expediting, acceleration
اِستِعجال [ʔistiʕja:l] *n:* • **1.** hurry, haste, precipitation
عَجُول [ʕaju:l] *adj:* • **1.** quick, fast, swift, speedy, rapid, hasty, rash – إذا ما تكُون عَجُول، تِقدَر تبِيعها بِسِعِر زين [ʔiða ma: tku:n ʕaju:l, tigdar tbi:ʕha bsiʕir zi:n] If you aren't in too much of a hurry, you can sell it for a good price.
عاجِل [ʕa:jil] *adj:* • **1.** urgent, immediate
مِستَعجِل [mistaʕjil] *adj:* • **1.** in a hurry, hurried – شصار عِندَك مِستَعجِل؟ [šṣa:r ʕindak mistaʕjil?] What are you in such a hurry about?
أَعجَل [ʔaʕjal] *comparative adjective:* • **1.** quicker, faster
عاجِلاً [ʕa:jilan] *adverbial:* • **1.** in the near future, soon, presently, before long, at once, immediately, instantly • **2.** as in عاجِلاً أَو آجِلاً : sooner or later
عِجِل [ʕijil] *n:* عِجُول، عجُول [ʕiju:l, ʕju:l] *pl:* • **1.** calf – لَحَم عِجِل [laħam ʕijil] veal. جِلد عِجِل [jilid ʕijil] calfskin. • **2.** slap (on the cheek or the back of the neck)

ع

ع ج م

مَعجَم [maʕjam] *n:* • **1.** dictionary, lexicon
عِجَيمي [ʕji:mi] *n:* • **1.** (invar.) a variety of grape, resembling Tokay
عَجَمي [ʕajami] *adj:* عَجَمِيَّة [ʕajamiyya] *pl:* • **1.** unlearned, unsophisticated, backward person • **2.** speaking incorrect Arabic, dumb, speechless
عَجمِي، عِجمِي [ʕajmi, ʕijmi] *adj:* عَجَم [ʕajam] *pl:* • **1.** Persian, a Persian • **2.** as in بلاد العَجَم : Persia

ع ج ن

عِجَن [ʕijan] *v:* • **1.** to knead (bread dough) – إنتي عِجني وَآني أَخبُز [ʔinti ʕijni wʔa:ni ʔaxbuz] You knead and I'll bake. آني عاجنَه وخابزَه [ʔa:ni ʕa:jnah wxa:bzah] I know him inside out (lit., I've kneaded him and baked him). • **2.** to make dough, mix up dough – عِجنَت عَشِر كِيلُوّات طحِين [ʕijnat ʕašir ki:luwwa:t ṭhi:n] She made dough from ten kilos of flour.
عَجَّن [ʕajjan] *v:* • **1.** to become doughy, soft – شُرّ الخُبُز حَتّى ما يعَجِّن [šurr ʔilxubuz ħatta ma: yʕajjin] Spread the bread out so it won't turn soft.
عَجِن [ʕajin] *n:* • **1.** mixing dough, kneading
عَجنَة [ʕajna] *n:* عَجنات [ʕajna:t] *pl:* • **1.** batch of bread dough
عَجِين [ʕaji:n] *n:* • **1.** (coll.) bread dough
عَجِينَة [ʕaji:na] *n:* عَجِينات [ʕaji:na:t] *pl:* • **1.** a piece of dough, ball of dough
مَعِجنَة [maʕijna, maʕjna] *n:* مَعاجِن [maʕa:jin, mʕa:jin] *pl:* • **1.** a large metal bowl usually used to make bread dough
مَعجُون [maʕju:n] *n:* • **1.** paste, cream – مَعجُون طَماطَة [maʕju:n ṭama:ṭa] tomato paste. مَعجُون أَسنان [maʕju:n ʔasna:n] toothpaste.
معجان، معجال [miʕja:n, miʕja:l] *n:* مَعَاجِين، مَعَاجِيل [maʕa:ji:n, maʕa:ji:l] *pl:* • **1.** sling • **2.** bowl
مُعَجَّنات [muʕajjana:t] *n:* • **1.** pastry, pasta

ع د د

عَدّ [ʕadd] *v:* • **1.** to count, reckon, enumerate – عُمرَه سِتّ سنِين وَيِقدَر يعِدّ لِلمِيَّة [ʕumrah sitt sni:n wyigdar yʕidd lilmiyya] He's six years old and can count to a hundred. • **2.** to consider, think, reckon – آني ما أَعِدَّه مِن الطُّلّاب الفاهمِين [ʔa:ni ma: ʔaʕiddah min ʔiṭṭulla:b ʔilfa:hmi:n] I don't consider him one of the bright students.
عَدَّد [ʕaddad] *v:* • **1.** to enumerate, count off – تِقدَر تعَدِّد أَسباب سُقُوط هَالمَملَكَة؟ [tigdar tʕaddid ʔasba:b suqu:ṭ halmamlaka?] Can you enumerate the reasons for the fall of this kingdom? الأَسباب تعَدِّدَت [ʔilʔasba:b tʕaddidat] The reasons increased. • **2.** Also تعَدَّد : to multiply, to proliferate, to increase
اِنعَدّ [ʔinʕadd] *v:* • **1.** to be counted
اِستَعَدّ [ʔistaʕadd] *v:* • **1.** to get ready, prepare oneself – لازِم أَستِعِدّ لِلإِمتِحان [la:zim ʔastiʕidd lilʔimtiħa:n] I must prepare for the exam. • **2.** to come to attention – لازِم تِستِعِدّ مِن يمُرّ الضّابُط [la:zim tistiʕidd min ymurr ʔiððða:buṭ] You must come to attention when the officer passes by.
عَدّ [ʕadd] *n:* • **1.** counting, count, enumeration, listing, calculation
عِدَّة [ʕidda] *n:* • **1.** several, a number of, many, numerous – عِدَّة مَرّات [ʕiddat marra:t] several times. • **2.** legally prescribed period during which a woman may not remarry after being widowed or divorced
عَدَد [ʕadad] *n:* أعداد [ʔaʕda:d] *pl:* • **1.** number, numeral • **2.** figure, quantity • **3.** number or issue of a newspaper
تَعَدُّد [taʕaddud] *n:* • **1.** variety, diversity, great number, multitude – تَعَدُّد الزَّوجات [taʕaddud ʔizzawja:t] polygamy.
تعداد [tiʕda:d] *n:* تعدادات [tiʕda:da:t] *pl:* • **1.** count, total
مُعِدّات [muʕidda:t] *n:* • **1.** (invar. pl.) gear, material, materiel, equipment – مُعِدّات حَربِيَّة [muʕidda:t ħarbiyya] war material.
إعداد [ʔiʕda:d] *n:* • **1.** preparation, readying, setting-up, arranging, drafting, making
إعتِداد [ʔiʕtida:d] *n:* • **1.** confidence, trust, reliance – إعتِداد بِنَفسَه [ʔiʕtida:d bnafsah] self-confidence, self-reliance.
إستِعداد [ʔistiʕda:d] *n:* • **1.** willingness, readiness, preparedness – ما عِندِي اِستِعداد أَصرُف عَليه فِلس واحِد [ma: ʕindi ʔistiʕda:d ʔaṣruf ʕali:h filis wa:ħid] I'm not prepared to spend one fils on him. عِندَك اِستِعداد تِشتُغُل ويّايا اليُوم؟ [ʕindak ʔistiʕda:d tištuɣul wiyya:ya ʔilyu:m?] Are you willing to work with me today? • **2.** preparation, preparedness – اِستِعداد لِلإِمتِحان [ʔistiʕda:d lilʔimtiħa:n] preparation for the examination.
إعدادِيَّة [ʔiʕda:diyya] *n:* • **1.** high school (from إعدادِي preparatory)
عَدِيد [ʕadi:d] *adj:* • **1.** numerous, many – مَشاكِل عَدِيدَة [maša:kil ʕadi:da] numerous problems.
مَعدُود [maʕdu:d] *adj:* • **1.** limited, few – أَصدِقائَه مَعدُودِين [ʔaṣdiqa:ʔah maʕdu:di:n] his friends are few.
مِتعَدِّد [mitʕaddid] *adj:* • **1.** numerous, varied, diverse – أَسباب مِتعَدِّدَة [ʔasba:b mitʕaddida] various reasons.
مستعِدّ [mistiʕidd] *adj:* • **1.** prepared, ready – آني ما مِستِعِدّ آكُل مَسَبَّة [ʔa:ni ma: mistiʕidd ʔa:kul masabba] I'm not about to take any insults.
إعدادِي [ʔiʕda:di] *adj:* • **1.** secondary, preparatory – مَدرَسَة إعدادِيَّة [madrasa ʔiʕda:diyya] secondary school. شَهادَة إعدادِيَّة [šaha:da ʔiʕda:diyya] secondary school degree.

ع

ع د س

عَدَس [ʕadas] *n:* • **1.** (coll.) lentil(s)

عَدَسَة [ʕadasa] *n:* عَدَسات [ʕadasa:t] *pl:* • **1.** lens • **2.** lentil (a grain of)

ع د ل

عِدَل [ʕidal] *v:* • **1.** with بَين to be impartial toward, not to discriminate between – إذا يِعدِل بينهُم، كُلّهُم يحُبُّوه [ʔiða yiʕdil bi:nhum, kullhum yħubbu:h] If he acts impartially toward them, they'll all like him. • **2.** with عَن to give up, drop, abandon – عِدَل عَن فِكرَة السَّفَر [ʕidal ʕan fikrat ʔissafar] He dropped the idea of traveling. • **3.** to straighten, straighten out, straighten oneself – شَعرَه مجَعَّد. شقَدّ ما يحُطلّه دِهِن، ما يِعدَل [šaʕrah mǰaʕʕad. šgadd ma: yħuṭṭlah dihin, ma: yiʕdal] His hair is kinky. No matter how much oil he puts on, it won't straighten out. هُوَّ مِثِل ذَيل الكَلِب. ما يِعدَل [huwwa miθil ðayl ʔiččalib. ma: yiʕdal] He's like a dog's tail. He won't straighten out. الكُردي وَلَو يحكِي عَرَبِي عِشرين سَنَة، لُغتَه ما تِعدَل [ʔilkurdi walaw yiħči ʕarabi ʕišri:n sana, luɣtah ma: tiʕdal] Even if the Kurd speaks Arabic for twenty years, his language won't improve.

عَدَّل [ʕaddal] *v:* • **1.** to straighten, make straight – عَدَّل السِّيم بِالجاكُوج [ʕaddal ʔissi:m bičča:ku:č] He straightened the wire with the hammer. عَدِّل الرَّسِم عَالحايِط [ʕaddil ʔirrasim ʕalħa:yiṭ] Straighten the picture on the wall. • **2.** to smooth, flatten, level – جابَوا رُولَة تعَدِّل القاع [ja:baw ru:la tʕaddil ʔilga:ʕ] They brought a roller to flatten the ground. • **3.** to amend, improve, change, alter – الحُكُومَة راح تعَدِّل القانُون [ʔilħuku:ma ra:ħ tʕaddil ʔilqa:nu:n] The government is going to amend the law. المُعَلِّم عَدَّل دَرَجتَه [ʔilmuʕallim ʕaddal darajtah] The teacher corrected his grade. • **4.** to get better, improve – أبُويا عَدَّل عَلَى هالهَوا [ʔabu:ya ʕaddal ʕala halhawa] My father got healthier in this climate. دَأشُوفَك معَدِّل هوايَة [daʔašu:fak mʕaddil hwa:ya] I see you're looking a lot healthier. • **5.** to put in order, straighten out, settle – ما عَدَّل أُمُورَه قَبُل ما مات [ma: ʕaddal ʔumu:rah gabul ma: ma:t] He didn't get his affairs in order before he died. عَدِّل حَكيَك. قِدّامَك آدَمِي [ʕaddil ħačyak. gidda:mak ʔa:dami] Watch your language. There's a gentleman in front of you.

عادَل [ʕa:dal] *v:* • **1.** to equal, be equal to, be the equal of – هَالجُندِي يعادِل خَمس جنُود بِالشَّجاعَة [hajjundi yʕa:dil xams ǰnu:d biššaǰa:ʕa] That soldier is equal to five soldiers in bravery. • **2.** to find the equivalent, evaluate – الوِزارَة راح تعادِل شَهادتِي [ʔilwiza:ra ra:ħ tʕa:dil šaha:dti] The ministry will evaluate my degree. • **3.** to match – ما عِندَه مانِع يعادِلها بِالفلُوس حَتَّى يِتزَوَّجها [ma: ʕindah ma:niʕ yʕa:dilha bilfilu:s ħatta yidzawwaǰha] He doesn't mind matching her weight in money in order to marry her.

تعَدَّل [tʕaddal] *v:* • **1.** to be straightened – هَالسِّيم ما يِتعَدَّل إلّا بِالجاكُوج [hassi:m ma: yitʕaddal ʔilla bičča:ku:č] This wire can only be straightened with a hammer. • **2.** to straighten oneself, straighten out – لِيش قاعِد أعوَج؟ تعَدَّل [li:š ga:ʕid ʔaʕwaǰ? tʕaddal] Why are you sitting crooked? Straighten up! • **3.** to be smoothed, flattened, leveled – القاع لازِم تِتعَدَّل قَبُل ما تِتبَلَّط [ʔilga:ʕ la:zim titʕaddal gabul ma: titballaṭ] The ground has to be leveled before it's paved. • **4.** to be put in order, be straightened out, be settled – بَعَد ما تِتعَدَّل الأمُور، كُلّ واحِد ياخُذ حَقَّه [baʕad ma: titʕaddal ʔilʔumu:r, kull wa:ħid ya:xuð ħaqqah] After matters are straightened out, everyone will get what's coming to him. • **5.** to be changed, amended – إذا يِتعَدَّل القانُون، يِشمِلنَا التَّرفِيع [ʔiða yitʕaddal ʔilqa:nu:m, yišmilna ʔittarfi:ʕ] If the law is amended, we'll be included in the promotions. • **6.** to be improved, be bettered – صِحّتَه تعَدّلَت بلُبنان [ṣiħħtah tʕaddlat blubna:n] His health improved in Lebanon. الأحوال راح تِتعَدَّل، إن شاء الله [ʔilʔaħwa:l ra:ħ titʕaddal, ʔinša:llah] Conditions will get better, I hope. إذا تاخُذ سَبعِين بِالإمتِحان تِتعَدَّل دَرَجتَك [ʔiða ta:xuð sabʕi:n bilʔimtiħa:n titʕaddal darajtak] If you get seventy on the test your grade will improve.

تعادَل [tʕa:dal] *v:* • **1.** to be equal – ضِيف خَمسَة حَتَّى تِتعادَل المُعادَلَة [ði:f xamsa ħatta titʕa:dal ʔilmuʕa:dala] Add five so the equation will be balanced. • **2.** to tie, tie each other, be tied – تعادلَوا الفَرِيقَين بِالسِّباق [tʕa:dlaw ʔilfari:qayn bissiba:q] The two teams tied in the game.

إعتَدَل [ʔiʕtidal] *v:* • **1.** to be or become moderate, temperate – راح يِعتِدِل الهَوا بَعَد فَدّ كَم يوم [ra:ħ yiʕtidil ʔilhawa baʕad fadd čam yu:m] The weather will be moderate in a few days. لازِم تِعتِدِل بِشُرب السِّجايِر [la:zim tiʕtidil bšurb ʔijjiga:yir] You've got to become moderate in smoking cigarettes.

إستَعدَل [ʔistaʕdal] *v:* • **1.** to straighten out – دَوِّر السِّكّان عاليِمنَى وَبَعدين إستَعدِل [dawwir ʔissikka:n ʕalyimna wbaʕdi:n ʔistaʕdil] Turn the wheel to the right and then straighten it out. إذا أترَفَّع عَلَى خَمسِين دِينار، أستَعدِل تَمام [ʔiða ʔatraffaʕ ʕala xamsi:n dina:r, ʔastaʕdil tama:m] If I get a payraise to fifty dinars, I'll be all straightened out.

عِدِل [ʕidil] *n:* عدُول [ʕdu:l] *pl:* • **1.** a large pair of bags slung on either side of a beast of burden

عَدِل [ʕadil] *n:* • **1.** justice, impartiality, fairness

عَدِيل [ʕadi:l] *n:* عُدالاء، عِدلان [ʕuda:la:ʔ, ʕidla:n] *pl:* • **1.** the husband of one's wife's sister • **2.** also used for 'brother-in-law' (husband of one's sister)

مُعَدَّل [muʕaddal] *n:* مُعَدَّلات [muʕaddala:t] *pl:* • **1.** (n.) average, average amount or sum

عُدُول [ʕudu:l] *n:* • **1.** giving up, dropping, refraining, desistance • **2.** renunciation, forgoing, abandonment

ع

عَدالَة [ʕada:la] *n:* • **1.** justice, fairness, impartiality • **2.** justice (different from عَدلِيَّة which refers to justice as administration of justice or jurisprudence)

تعديل [taʕdi:l] *n:* تَعدِيلات [taʕdi:la:t] *pl:* • **1.** change, amendment, modification, – تَعدِيل وِزارِي [taʕdi:l wiza:ri] cabinet reshuffle.

تَعادُل [taʕa:dul] *n:* • **1.** balance, equilibrium, equality • **2.** tie, draw (in sports)

مُعادَلَة [muʕa:dala] *n:* مُعادَلات [muʕa:dala:t] *pl:* • **1.** equation (math.)

إعتِدال [ʔiʕtida:l] *n:* • **1.** straightness, erectness, tenseness, evenness, symmetry, proportion

عَدِل [ʕadil] *adj:* • **1.** straight – بِسمار عَدِل [bisma:r ʕadil] a straight nail. أُوقَف عَدِل [ʔu:gaf ʕadil] Stand up straight. • **2.** straight, vertical, upright, plumb – شَجرَة عَدلَة [šajra ʕadla] a straight tree. الحايِط مُو عَدلَة [ʔilħa:yiṭ mu: ʕadla] The wall is not straight. • **3.** level, flat, smooth – قاع عَدلَة [ga:ʕ ʕadla] a level floor. أَراضِي عَدلَة [ʔara:ði ʕadla] flat land. شارِع عَدِل [ša:riʕ ʕadil] a smooth road. • **4.** upright, honest, fair, just – يِمشِي عَدِل [yimši ʕadil] He's honest. يحكِي عَدِل [yiħči ʕadil] He tells the truth. كاتِب العَدِل [ka:tib ʔilʕadil] civil servant in the legal system, holding functions of a notary public. • **5.** sound, whole, unbroken – طابُوقَة عَدلَة [ṭa:bu:ga ʕadla] a whole brick, an unbroken brick. • **6.** healthy, hale, alive – أَبُوه بَعدَه عَدِل [ʔabu:h baʕdah ʕadil] His father is still alive.

عَدلِي [ʕadli] *adj:* • **1.** legal, forensic, juristic – الطِّبّ العَدلِي [ʔiṭṭibb ʔilʕadli] forensic medicine. طَبِيب عَدلِي [ṭabi:b ʕadli] coroner.

عادِل [ʕa:dil] *adj:* • **1.** just, fair, equitable – عادِل بِحُكمَه [ʕa:dil biħukmah] just in his decisions. عادِل بِقِسمتَه [ʕa:dil bqisimtah] fair in his distribution.

عَدلِيَّة [ʕadliyya] *n:* • **1.** justice, administration of justice, jurisprudence – وَزِير العَدلِيَّة [wazi:r ʔilʕadliyya] Minister of Justice.

معتَدِل [miʕtadil] *adj:* • **1.** temperate, moderate – مُعتَدِل بِصَرف الفلُوس [muʕtadil bṣarf ʔilflu:s] moderate in spending money. • **2.** mild, clement – مَناخ مُعتَدِل [mana:x muʕtadil] mild weather.

مُعادِل [muʕa:dil] *adj:* • **1.** equivalent, equal, of equal status, having equal rights

متعادِل [mitʕa:dil] *adj:* • **1.** neutral • **2.** balanced

أَعدَل [ʔaʕdal] *comparative adjective:* • **1.** more or most just • **2.** straighter, straightest

ع د م

عِدَم [ʕidam] *v:* • **1.** to spoil, go bad – الأَكِل عِدَم ولازِم نذِبَّه [ʔilʔakil ʕidam wla:zim nðibbah] The food spoiled and we'll have to throw it out. • **2.** to ruin, spoil – الخَيّاط عِدَم القاط مالِي [ʔilxayya:ṭ ʕidam ʔilqa:ṭ ma:li] The tailor ruined my suit. • **3.** to execute – عِدمَوا الجّاسُوس اليُوم الفَجِر [ʕidmaw ʔijja:su:s ʔilyu:m ʔilfajir] They executed the spy today at dawn.

عَدَم [ʕadam] *n:* • **1.** nothing, nothingness • **2.** lack of, absence of – عَدَم التَّدخِين [ʕadam ʔittadxi:n] abstinence from smoking. عَدَم رَغبَة [ʕadam raɣba] lack of desire, lack of interest.

إعدام [ʔiʕda:m] *n:* • **1.** execution (as in حُكم بالإعدَام :death sentence) – عُقُوبَة الإعدام [ʕuqu:bat ʔilʔiʕda:m] the death penalty.

إنعِدام [ʔinʕida:m] *n:* • **1.** absence, lack, non existence

عَدِيم [ʕadi:m] *adj:* • **1.** devoid of, without,-less – عَدِيم الشُّعُور [ʕadi:m ʔiššuʕu:r] lacking feeling. عَدِيم الذَّوق [ʕadi:m ʔiððu:q] tasteless. سَقَط عَدِيم [saqaṭ ʕadi:m] worthless junk. أَشتِرِيها ولَو كانَت سَقَط عَدِيم [ʔaštiri:ha walaw ča:nat saqaṭ ʕadi:m] I'd buy it even if it was junk.

عادِم [ʕa:dim] *adj:* • **1.** non-existent, lost, unrestorable

مُعدَم [muʕdam] *adj:* • **1.** poor, destitute

مَعدُوم [maʕdu:m] *adj:* • **1.** ruined, spoiled – أَكِل مَعدُوم [ʔakil maʕdu:m] spoiled food. • **2.** denatured – كُحُول مَعدُوم [kuħu:l maʕdu:m] denatured alcohol. • **3.** executed • **4.** (as n:) executed person

ع د و

عِدَى [ʕida:] *v:* • **1.** to infect – لا تِشرَب مِن كلاصَه، تَرَة يعدِيك [la: tišrab min gla:ṣah, tara yiʕdi:k] Don't drink from his glass or he'll infect you. هَالمَرَض يِعدِي [halmarað yiʕdi:] This disease is infectious.

عَدَّى [ʕadda:] *v:* • **1.** to pass, let pass – الشُّرطِي عَدّانِي مِن الباب [ʔiššurṭi ʕadda:ni min ʔilba:b] The policeman let me by the door. شيعَدِّيك بِهالإزدِحام؟ [šyʕaddi:k bhalʔizdiħa:m?] How are you going to get through this crowd?

عادَى [ʕa:da:] *v:* • **1.** to treat as an enemy, regard as an enemy – آنِي أَعادِي كُلّ أَعداءَك [ʔa:ni ʔaʕa:di kull ʔaʕda:ʔak] I consider all your enemies as my enemies. • **2.** to turn against, fall out with – عادانِي لِأَنّ أَحكِي الصُّدُق [ʕa:da:ni liʔann ʔaħči ʔiṣṣudug] He turned against me because I tell the truth.

تعَدَّى [tʕadda:] *v:* • **1.** to pass, go by – أَخُوك هَسَّة تعَدَّى مِن هنا [ʔaxu:k hassa tʕadda: min hna] Your brother just now passed by here. • **2.** to be insulting, offer insult, give provocation – إنتَ تعَدَّيت عَليه بِهالكِلمَة [ʔinta tʕaddi:t ʕali:h bhaččilma] You insulted him with that remark. هُوَّ تعَدَّى عَلَيّا بِالأَوَّل [huwwa tʕadda: ʕalayya bilʔawwal] He provoked me in the first place. • **3.** to overstep, exceed – شَقاهُم تعَدَّى الحُدُود وواحِد قام يِسِبّ الثّانِي [šaqa:hum tʕadda: ʔilħudu:d wwa:ħid ga:m yisibb ʔiθθa:ni] Their teasing went too far and one began to curse the other. • **4.** to exceed – سِعِرها ما يِتعَدَّى العَشِر دَنانِير

ع

[siʕirha maː yitʕaddaː ʔilʕašir danaːniːr] Its price won't exceed ten dinars.
تعادَى [tʕaːdaː] *v:* • **1.** to be or become hostile to each other, be enemies – بَعَد الجِّدال، تعادَوا [baʕad ʔijjidaːl, tʕaːdaw] After the argument, they were hostile to each other. • **2.** to be or become hostile, inimical – عَلَى ويش تعادَيت ويّاه؟ سَوّالَك شِي؟ [ʕala wiːš tʕaːdiːt wiyyaːh? sawwaːlak ši?] Why'd you get mad at him? Did he do anything to you? مِن قال هَالكِلمَة تعادالّه [min gaːl haččilma tʕaːdaːlah] When he said this he turned hostile to him.
اِعتِدَى [ʔiʕtidaː] *v:* • **1.** to commit aggression, commit a hostile act, attack – هَالدَّولَة اِعتِدَت عَلَى جِيرانها [haddawla ʔiʕtidat ʕala jiːraːnha] This nation committed aggression against its neighbor. إذا تِعتِدِي عَليه يِشتِكِي عَلِيك بِالشُّرطَة [ʔiða tiʕtidi ʕaliːh yištiki ʕaliːk biššurṭa] If you attack him he'll complain to the police about you.
عَدُو [ʕadu] *n:* عاداء، عُدوان [ʕaːdaːʔ, ʕudwaːn] *pl:* • **1.** enemy
تَعَدِّي [taʕaddi] *n:* تَعَدِّيات [taʕaddiːyyaːt] *pl:* • **1.** assault, attack, provocation, insult • **2.** infraction, violation, transgression, infringement of the law
عَدوَى [ʕadwa] *n:* • **1.** infection
عَداوَة [ʕadaːwa] *n:* • **1.** enmity, hostility, animosity, antagonism • **2.** (invar.) inimical, enemies – كانَوا أصدِقاء، وبَعدين صارَوا عَداوَة [čaːnaw ʔaṣdiqaːʔ, wbaʕdiːn ṣaːraw ʕadaːwa] They were friends, but later became enemies. إحنا عَداوَة ويّاهُم [ʔiħna ʕadaːwa wiyyaːhum] We're enemies to them. هُوَّ عَداوَة ويّايا [huwwa ʕadaːwa wiyyaːya] He's an enemy to me.
اِعتِداء [ʔiʕtidaːʔ] *n:* اِعتِداءات [ʕtidaːʔaːt] *pl:* • **1.** attack, assault, aggression
مُعدِي [muʕdi] *adj:* • **1.** contagious, infectious – مَرَض مُعدِي [marað muʕdi] contagious disease.
مُعادِي [muʕaːdi] *adj:* • **1.** hostile, inimical, antagonistic
مِعتِدِي [miʕtidi] *adj:* • **1.** agressing • 2. (as n:) aggressor
عِدائِي [ʕidaːʔi] *adj:* • **1.** aggressive, hostile
مِتعَدِّي [mitʕaddi] *adj:* • **1.** violated • **2.** transitive
عِدوانِي [ʕidwaːni] *adj:* • **1.** hostile, aggressive
عَدا [ʕadaː] *invariable v:* • **1.** except, with the exception of – كُلّهُم عَدا واحِد [kullhum ʕadaː waːħid] all except one.

ع ذ ب

عَذَّب [ʕaððab] *v:* • **1.** to torture – عَذِّبُوه هوايَة حَتَّى اِعتِرَف [ʕaððibuːh hwaːya ħatta ʔiʕtiraf] They tortured him terribly until he confessed. • **2.** to torment, pain, afflict – الجّاهِل عَذَّب أُمَّه طُول النَّهار [ʔijjaːhil ʕaððab ʔummah ṭuːl ʔinnahaːr] The child tormented his mother all day long. • **3.** to punish (of God) – الله يعَذِّب اللّي ما يصَلُّون [ʔallah yʕaððib ʔilli maː yṣalluːn] God will punish those who don't pray.
تعَذَّب [tʕaððab] *v:* • **1.** to be tortured – إذا ما يتعَذَّب، ما يقُرّ [ʔiða maː yitʕaððab, maː yqurr] If he isn't tortured, he won't confess. • **2.** to suffer, have trouble – هَالمَرَة تعَذِّبَت هوايَة بتَربِيَة اِبنها [halmara tʕaððibat hwaːya btarbiyat ʔibinha] That woman suffered a lot in raising her son. باع سَيّارتَه بَعَد ما تعَذَّب بيها [baːʕ sayyaːrtah baʕad maː tʕaððab biːha] He sold his car after he'd had a lot of trouble with it.
عَذاب [ʕaðaːb] *n:* • **1.** torture, pain, torment, suffering
متعَذِّب [mitʕaððib] adj: • 1. suffering, agonizing
تَعذِيب [taʕðiːb] *n:* • **1.** affliction, tormenting, torturing, torture, punishment
عِذُوبَة [ʕiðuːba] *n:* • **1.** sweetness
عَذِب، مَيّ عَذِب [ʕaðib, mayy ʕaðib] *adj:* • **1.** sweet, fresh water
أعذَب [ʔaʕðab] *comparative adjective:* • **1.** sweeter, more pleasant, more agreeable

ع ذ ر

عِذَر [ʕiðar] *v:* • **1.** to excuse – المُعَلِّم ما يعُذرَك مِن الإمتِحان إذا ما تجِيب تَقرِير طِبِّي [ʔilmuʕallim maː yʕuðrak min ʔilʔimtiħaːn ʔiða maː djiːb taqriːr ṭibbi] The teacher won't excuse you from the exam if you don't bring a medical report. قُلّه "كِنِت مَرِيض" حَتَّى يعُذرَك [gullah "činit mariːð" ħatta yʕuðrak] Tell him "I was sick" so he'll excuse you. إعذُرنِي؛ ما أقدَر أرُوح [ʔiʕðurni; maː ʔagdar ʔaruːħ] I'm sorry; I can't go.
تعَذَّر [tʕaððar] *v:* • **1.** to be difficult, impossible – يتعَذَّر وُجُود أدَوات هَالسَّيّارَة [yitʕaððar wujuːd ʔadawaːt hassayyaːra] It's impossible to find parts for this car. يتعَذَّر عَلَيّا أساعدَك [yitʕaððar ʕalayya ʔasaːʕdak] It's impossible for me to help you. • **2.** to make excuses, excuse oneself, apologize – كُلّما أعزِمَه، يتعَذَّر [kullmaː ʔaʕizmah, yitʕaððar] Whenever I invite him to dinner he makes excuses. مُو صُوجِي. لُويش أتعَذَّر؟ [muː ṣuːči. luwiːš ʔatʕaððar?] I'm not to blame. Why should I apologize?
اِعتِذَر [ʔiʕtiðar] *v:* • **1.** to apologize, excuse oneself – رُوح اِعتِذِر مِنَّه [ruːħ ʔiʕtiðir minnah] Go apologize to him.
عُذُر [ʕuður] *n:* أعذار [ʔaʕðaːr] *pl:* • **1.** excuse – عُذُر غير مَشرُوع [ʕuður ɣiːr mašruːʕ] an illegitimate excuse, a poor excuse.
مَعذُور [maʕðuːr] *adj:* • **1.** excused, justified
اِعتِذار [ʔiʕtiðaːr] *n:* • **1.** apology, excuse, plea
عاذِر [ʕaːðir] *adj:* • **1.** forgiving • **2.** (as n:) forgiver
عَذراء [ʕaðraːʔ] *adj:* عَذارَى، عَذرات [ʕaðaːraː, ʕaðraːt] *pl:* • **1.** virgin, maiden
مِتعَذِّر [mitʕaððir] *adj:* • **1.** impossible, difficult, impracticable, unfeasible

ع ر ب

عَرَّب [ʕarrab] *v:* • **1.** to Arabicize, make Arabic – عَرَّبوا هَالكِلمَة وسَوَّوا فِعِل مِنها [ʕarrabaw haččilma wsawwaw fiʕil minha] They Arabicized this word and derived a verb from it. • **2.** to translate into Arabic – مِنُو عَرَّب هَالكِتاب؟ [minu ʕarrab halkitaːb?] Who translated this book into Arabic?

أعرَب [ʔaʕrab] *v:* • **1.** to express, to declare, to state clearly, to voice, to proclaim, to make known, to manifest

تعَرَّب [tʕarrab] *v:* • **1.** to become an Arab, adopt Arab customs, assimilate to the Arabs – عاش بين القَبائِل، وَتعَرَّب تَماماً [ʕaːš biːn qabaːʔil, wtʕarrab tamaːman] He lived among the tribes and adopted Arab customs completely.

عَرَبَة [ʕaraba] *n:* عَرَبات [ʕarabaːt] *pl:* • **1.** wagon, cart • **2.** car, coach (railroad) – عَرَبَة أطفال [ʕarabat ʔaṭfaːl] baby carriage.

عُرُوبَة [ʕuruːba] *n:* • **1.** Arabism, pan-Arabism

إعراب [ʔiʕraːb] *n:* • **1.** manifestation, expression, declaration, pronouncement, expression • **2.** desinential inflection (gram.)

عَرَبانَة [ʕarabaːna] *n:* عَرَبايِن [ʕarabaːyin] *pl:* • **1.** cart, wagon, horsecart, buggy, carriage

عَرَب [ʕarab] *adj:* • **1.** (coll.) Arabs

عَرَبِي [ʕarabi] *adj:* • **1.** Arab, Arabian • **2.** an Arab • **3.** (invar.) Arabic, the Arabic language

عُربِي، عُرُبِي [ʕurbi, ʕrubi] *adj:* عُربان [ʕurbaːn] *pl:* • **1.** man from a rural area, tribesman

مُعَرَّب [muʕarrab] *adj:* • **1.** translated into Arabic

عَرَبنجِي [ʕarabanči] *adj:* عَرَبَنجِيَّة [ʕarabančiyya] *pl:* • **1.** driver of an عَرَبانَة, cart driver

ع ر ب د

عَربَد [ʕarbad] *v:* • **1.** to shout angrily, to be noisy, riotous, to raise a din – دائماً يعَربِد عَلَى مَرتَه [daːʔiman yʕarbid ʕala martah] He continually raises cain with his wife.

عِربِيد [ʕirbiːd] *n:* عَرابِيد [ʕaraːbiːd] *pl:* • **1.** a large snake, a male snake

عَربَدَة [ʕarbada] *n:* • **1.** riot, noise, din, uproar

ع ر ب ن

عَرَبُون [ʕarabuːn] *n:* عَرابِين [ʕaraːbiːn] *pl:* • **1.** deposit, down payment

ع ر ج

عِرَج [ʕiraǰ] *v:* • **1.** to limp – دَيعرَج لِأَنّ رِجلَه مَضرُوبَة [dayiʕraǰ liʔann riǰlah maḍruːba] He is limping because his leg was hurt.

تعَرَّج [tʕarraǰ] *v:* • **1.** to be twisted

عَرَج [ʕaraǰ] *n:* • **1.** limping, lameness

تَعَرُّج [taʕarruǰ] *n:* • **1.** winding, twisting, zigzag

مِعراج، لَيلَة المِعراج [miʕraːǰ, laylat ʔilmiʕraːǰ] *n:* • **1.** the night of Mohammed's ascension to the seven heavens

أعرَج [ʔaʕraǰ] *adj:* عِرِج، عَرجِين [ʕiriǰ, ʕarǰiːn] *pl:* عَرجَة [ʕarǰa] *feminine:* • **1.** lame, limping, having a limp • **2.** lame person

معَرَّج [mʕarraǰ] *adj:* • **1.** corrugated – جِينكُو معَرَّج [čiːnku mʕarraǰ] corrugated galvanized sheet metal.

متعَرِّج [mitʕarriǰ] *adj:* • **1.** winding, twisting, tortuous, sinuous

ع ر س

عَرَّس [ʕarras] *v:* • **1.** to get married – عَرَّس عَلَى بِتّ عَمَّه قَبُل سَنتَين وَلِسَّه ما جاه طِفِل [ʕarras ʕala bitt ʕammah gabul santayn wlissah maː ǰaːh ṭifil] He married his cousin two years ago and still hasn't had a baby.

عِرِس [ʕiris] *n:* أعراس [ʔaʕraːs] *pl:* • **1.** marriage, wedding – أَبُو العِرِس [ʔabu ʔilʕiris] weasel.

عَرُوس، عرُوس [ʕaruːs, ʕruːs] *n:* عَرايِس [ʕaraːyis] *pl:* • **1.** bride

عِرِّيس [ʕirriːs] *n:* عَرارِيس [ʕaraːriːs] *pl:* • **1.** bridegroom

معَرِّس [mʕarris] *adj:* • **1.** married

ع ر ش

عَرِش [ʕariš] *n:* عُرُوش [ʕuruːš] *pl:* • **1.** throne, also used for 'tribe' occasionally

ع ر ص

عَرَصَة [ʕaraṣa] *adj:* عَرَصات [ʕaraṣaːt] *pl:* • **1.** a plot of land, a vacant lot, also land and the buildings on it, constituting mortmain endowment (wakf)

ع ر ض

عِرَض [ʕiraḍ] *v:* • **1.** to show, present, display, exhibit – راح يِعرِضُون هَالفِلم الإسبُوع الجّاي [raːħ yʕirḍuːn halfilm ʔilʔisbuːʕ ʔiǰǰaːy] They're going to show this film next week. عِرَضنا مَصنُوعاتنا بِالمَعرَض [ʕiraḍna maṣnuːʕaːtna bilmaʕraḍ] We exhibited our manufactures at the fair. • **2.** to submit, turn in, suggest, propose – هاي خُوش فِكرَة. راح أعرِضها عَالمُدِير [haːy xuːš fikra. raːħ ʔaʕriḍha ʕalmudiːr] That's a good idea. I'll submit it to the director. • **3.** to offer – إعرُض عَلَيّا سِعِر [ʔiʕruḍ ʕalayya siʕir] Make me an offer. عِرَض سَيّارتَه لِلبيع [ʕiraḍ sayyaːrtah lilbiːʕ] He offered his car for sale. عِرَض سَيّارتَه عَلَيّا بِألِف دِينار [ʕiraḍ sayyaːrtah ʕalayya bʔalif dinaːr] He offered his car to me for a thousand dinars. • **4.** to widen, broaden, become wide – النَّهَر، مِن يِطلَع مِن البَلدَة، يِعرَض [ʔinnahar, min yiṭlaʕ min ʔilbalda, yiʕraḍ] The river widens when it leaves the city. أَشُو كُلّما جالَك دَتِعرَض [ʔašu kullmaː ǰaːlak datiʕraḍ] It seems you're continually getting fatter.

ع

عَرَّض [ʕarrað̣] *v:* • **1.** to widen, broaden – الحُكُومَة راح تعَرِّض هَالشّارِع [ʔilħukuːma raːħ tʕarrið̣ haššaːriʕ] The government's going to widen this street. • **2.** to expose – لا تعَرِّض نفسَك لِلبَرِد [laː tʕarrið̣ nafsak lilbarid] Don't expose yourself to the cold. المُلازِم عَرَّض جِنُودَه لِلخَطَر [ʔilmulaːzim ʕarrað̣ ǰinuːdah lilxaṭar] The lieutenant exposed his troops to danger.

عارَض [ʕaːrað̣] *v:* • **1.** to oppose, object to – زُعَماء الحِزِب عارضَوا سِياستَه [zuʕamaːʔ ʔilħizib ʕaːrð̣aw siyaːstah] The party bosses opposed his policy.

تعَرَّض [tʕarrað̣] *v:* • **1.** to be widened – الشّارِع تعَرَّض السَّنَة اللّي فاتَت [ʔiššaːriʕ tʕarrað̣ ʔissana ʔilli faːtat] The street was widened last year. • **2.** to be exposed, expose oneself – طِلَع وَتعَرَّض لِلبَرِد [ṭilaʕ wtʕarrað̣ lilbarid] He went out and got exposed to the cold. • **3.** with ب to annoy, pester, accost, antagonize – دائِماً يوقَف بِالشّارِع ويِتعَرَّض بالبَنات [daːʔiman yuːgaf biššaːriʕ wyitʕarrað̣ bilbanaːt] He's always standing in the street pestering girls. هَذا شَقي؛ مَحَّد يِقدَر يِتعَرَّض بِيه [haːða šaqi; maħħad yigdar yitʕarrað̣ biːh] He's tough guy; no one can mess around with him.

تعارَض [tʕaːrað̣] *v:* • **1.** to conflict, be contradictory, be incompatible – هَالعَمَل يِتعارَض ويّا القانُون [halʕamal yitʕaːrað̣ wiyya ʔilqaːnuːn] That action is in conflict with the law. وَقتي يِتعارَض ويّا وَقتَك [waqti yitʕaːrað̣ wiyya waqtak] My schedule conflicts with yours. • **2.** to get sick, be taken ill, have an attack – أَبُوه تعارَض البارحَة وجابولَه الطَّبِيب [ʔabuːh tʕaːrað̣ ʔilbaːrħa wǰaːbuːlah ʔiṭṭabiːb] His father had an attack yesterday and they brought the doctor for him.

اِنعِرَض [ʔinʕirað̣] *v:* • **1.** to be submitted, turned in, proposed – طَلَبَك اِنعِرَض عاللُّجنَة [ṭalabak ʔinʕirað̣ ʕallujna] Your request was submitted to the committee.

اِعترَض [ʔiʕtirað̣] *v:* • **1.** to object, protest, oppose – مَحَّد اِعترَض عالإِقتِراح [maħħad ʔiʕtirað̣ ʕalʔiqtiraːħ] No one objected to the proposal. • **2.** to obstruct, block – رِدِت أَخُشّ بالبِنايَة، لَكِن الشُّرطِي اِعترَض طَرِيقي [ridit ʔaxušš bilbinaːya, laːkin ʔiššurṭi ʔiʕtirað̣ ṭariːqi] I wanted to enter the building but the policeman blocked the way.

اِستَعرَض [ʔistaʕrað̣] *v:* • **1.** to pass in review – راح تِستَعرِض وِيّا الجِّنُود وَإلّا لا؟ [raːħ tistaʕrið̣ wiyya ʔiǰǰinuːd waʔilla laː?] Are you going to pass in review with the troops or not? • **2.** to review, inspect – القائِد اِستَعرَض الجِّنُود [ʔilqaːʔid ʔistaʕrað̣ ʔiǰǰinuːd] The commander reviewed the troops.

عُرُض [ʕuruð̣] *n:* عُرُوض [ʕuruːð̣] *pl:* • **1.** width, breadth – قُصّ الخِشبَة بالعُرُض [guṣṣ ʔilxišba bilʕuruð̣] Cut the piece of wood crosswise. عَلَى كَيفَك! أَشُو أَخَذتنا طُول عُرُض [ʕala kayfak! ʔašuː ʔaxaðitna ṭuːl ʕuruð̣] Take it easy! You're not giving us a chance. • **2.** presentation, showing, displaying, offering • **3.** performance, display, exhibition, exposition, submission

عَرض، خَطّ العَرض [ʕarð̣, xaṭṭ ʔilʕarð̣] *n:* • **1.** degree or parallel of latitude – ساحَة العَرض [saːħat ʔilʕarð̣] parade ground. العَرض وَالطَّلَب [ʔilʕarð̣ wiṭṭalab] supply and demand.

عَرض [ʕarð̣] *n:* • **1.** honor, good repute – نَعلَة عَلَى عَرضَك [naʕla ʕala ʕarð̣ak] Damn you! (lit., a curse on your honor)

عَرَض [ʕarað̣] *n:* أعراض [ʔaʕraːð̣] *pl:* • **1.** symptom, manifestation (of a disease) • **2.** بِالعَرَض incidentally, by chance

عُرضَة [ʕurð̣a] *n:* • **1.** target, butt – عُرضَة لِلسَّبّ [ʕurð̣ah lissabb] a target for curses, exposed to censure. بِالعُرضَة [bilʕurð̣a] (approx.,) help yourself, you're welcome to it (a polite expression when a possession is praised, not expected to be taken literally).

مَعرَض [maʕrað̣] *n:* مَعارِض [maʕaːrið̣] *pl:* • **1.** showroom, also, used car lot • **2.** exhibition, show • **3.** fair, exposition

تَعَرُّض [taʕarruð̣] *n:* • **1.** exposure • **2.** objection

عَرِيضَة [ʕariːð̣a] *n:* عَرايِض [ʕaraːyið̣] *pl:* • **1.** application, petition – كاتِب عَرايِض [kaːtib ʕaraːyið̣] man who, for a fee, writes applications and official documents.

تَعارُض [taʕaːruð̣] *n:* • **1.** conflict, contradiction

عارِض، عارِضَة [ʕaːrið̣, ʕaːrið̣a] *n:* • **1.** model, as in عارِضَة أَزيَاء • **2.** exhibitor (at a fair), demonstrator, bidder (at an auction)

تَعرِيض [taʕriːð̣] *n:* • **1.** intimation, allusion, hint, indication

مُعارَضَة [muʕaːrað̣a] *n:* • **1.** opposition (esp. pol.) – حِزب المُعارَضَة [ħizb ʔilmuʕaːrað̣a] the opposition party.

اِعتِراض [ʔiʕtiraːð̣] *n:* • **1.** objection, protest, rebuttal

اِستِعراض [ʔistiʕraːð̣] *n:* اِستِعراضات [ʔistiʕraːð̣aːt] *pl:* • **1.** parade, review

عَرضَحالچِي، عَرضَحَلچِي [ʕarð̣aħaːlči, ʕarð̣aħalči] *n:* عَرضَحالچِيَّة، عَرضَحَلچِيَّة [ʕarð̣aħaːlčiyya, ʕarð̣aħalčiyya] *pl:* • **1.** man who sits outside public offices, and for a fee writes out applications

عَرِيض [ʕariːð̣] *adj:* • **1.** wide, broad – شارِع عَرِيض [šaːriʕ ʕariːð̣] a wide street.

عارِض [ʕaːrið̣] *n:* عَوارِض [ʕawaːrið̣] *pl:* • **1.** an unexpected delay, hindrance, or obstacle

مُعَرَّض [muʕarrað̣] *adj:* • **1.** exposed

عَرَضِي [ʕarað̣i] *adj:* • **1.** casual

مُعارِض [muʕaːrið̣] *n:* • **1.** opponent, antagonist, opposer

مِتعَرِّض [mitʕarrið̣] *adj:* • **1.** exposed, revealed

مَعرُوض [maʕruːð̣] *adj:* • **1.** shown, displayed

عَرضانِي [ʕarðaːni] *adj:* • **1.** transverse, crosswise – شارِع عَرضانِي [šaːriʕ ʕarðaːni] cross street.
اِستِعراضِي، فِلِم اِستِعراضِي [ʔistiʕraːðiː, filim ʔistiʕraːði] *adj:* • **1.** movie musical
أَعَرض [ʔaʕarð] *comparative adjective:* • **1.** wider

ع ر ض ح ل

عَرضَحال [ʕarðaħaːl] *n:* عَرضَحالات [ʕarðaħaːlaːt] *pl:* • **1.** application, petition

ع ر ف [1]

عِرَف [ʕiraf] *v:* • **1.** to know – عِرَفِت كُلّ الأَجوِبَة [ʕirafit kull ʔilʔajwiba] I knew all the answers. تُعرُف أَحَّد مِن المَوجُودِين؟ [tuʕruf ʔaħħad min ʔilmawjuːdiːn?] Do you know any of those present? أَعرُف شلُون أَطَلِّع فلُوس مِنَّه [ʔaʕruf šluːn ʔaṭalliʕ fluːs minnah] I know how to get money out of him. يُعرُف يِقرا وَيِكتِب [yuʕruf yiqraː wyiktib] He knows how to read and write. يُعرُف يِسبَح [yuʕruf yisbaħ] He knows how to swim. مَحَّد يُعرُف لِلرّادِيُو بقَدَّه [maħħad yuʕruf lirraːdyu bgaddah] No one knows radios like him. هُوَّ يُعرُفنِي إِلِي، مُو غير شَخِص [huwwa yuʕrufni ʔili, muː ɣiːr šaxiṣ] He'll come to me, not someone else. آنِي أَعُرفَه إِلَه. شَعلَيّا بالغير؟ [ʔaːni ʔaʕurfah ʔilah. šaʕlayya bilɣiːr?] He's the one I'll deal with. Why should I care about someone else? ما تُعرُف هَذا شقَدّ خُوش وَلَد [maː tuʕruf haːða šgadd xuːš walad] You can't imagine what a nice guy he is. يُعرُف نَفسَه. ما يِنغُلُب بِالشِّطرَنج [yuʕruf nafsah. maː yinɣulub biššiṭranj] He's self-confident. He can't be beaten in chess. • **2.** to recognize, tell – تُعرُف المَرِيض مِن وجهه [tuʕruf ʔilmariːð min wiččah] You can tell the sick man by his face. عِرَفتَه مِن حِسَّه [ʕiraftah min ħissah] I recognized him by his voice. • **3.** to see, realize, perceive, acknowledge, concede – هَسَّة عِرَفِت كُلّ حَكيَه كِذِب [hassa ʕirafit kull ħačyah čiðib] Now I realize all his talk is lies. إِنتَ دَتُعرُف شدَيصِير بَالدّائِرَة؟ [ʔinta datuʕruf šdayṣiːr biddaːʔira?] Are you aware of what's going on in the office? هَسَّة عِرَفِت فِكرتِي صَحِيحَة؟ [hassa ʕirafit fikirti ṣaħiːħa?] Now do you admit my idea is right? • **4.** to find out, figure out, discover – بَعدِين عِرَفِت مِنُو باق السّاعَة مالتِي [baʕdiːn ʕirafit minu baːg ʔissaːʕa maːlti] Later I found out who stole my watch. ما دَأَقدَر أَعرُف لُويش وُقفَت المَكِينَة [maː daʔagdar ʔaʕruf luwiːš wugfat ʔilmakiːna] I can't figure out why the motor stopped.
عَرَّف [ʕarraf] *v:* • **1.** to introduce – أَرِيد أَعَرّفَك بِالزُّوّار [ʔariːd ʔaʕarrfak bizzuwwaːr] I'd like to introduce you to the visitors. • **2.** to define – تِقدَر تعَرُّفلِي المُثَلَّث؟ [tigdar tʕarrufli ʔilmuθallaθ?] Can you define the triangle for me?
تعَرَّف [tʕarraf] *v:* • **1.** to be introduced, to meet, to get to know, to get acquainted – تعَرَّفِت عَلَى واحِد أَمرِيكِي [tʕarrafit ʕala waːħid ʔamriːki] I got acquainted with an American. لازِم تِتعَرَّف بِجَماعَة، إِلهُم نُفُوذ [laːzim titʕarraf bjamaːʕa, ʔilhum nufuːð] You've got to get acquainted with any group that has influence.
تعارَف [tʕaːraf] *v:* • **1.** to become acquainted – تعارَفنا بفَدّ مُناسَبَة [tʕaːrafna bfadd munaːsaba] We became acquainted at a celebration. تعارَفِت ويّاه البارحَة بِالحَفلَة [tʕaːrafit wiyyaːh ʔilbaːrħa bilħafla] I got acquainted with him yesterday at the party.
اِنعِرَف [ʔinʕiraf] *v:* • **1.** to be or become known, be discovered – هَسَّة اِنعِرَف سَبَب نَقلَه [hassa ʔinʕiraf sabab naqlah] Now the reason for his transfer is known. • **2.** to be recognized – حاوِل يِتنَكَّر لَكِن اِنعِرَف بساع [ħaːwil yitnakkar laːkin ʔinʕiraf bsaːʕ] He tried to disguise himself but he was recognized quickly.
اِعتِرَف [ʔiʕtiraf] *v:* • **1.** to confess, admit, acknowledge, own – اِعتِرَف بِالجَّرِيمَة بحُضُورِي [ʔiʕtiraf bijjariːma bħuðuːri] He confessed to the crime in my presence. أَعتِرِف هاي كانَت غَلطَة مِنِّي، لَكِن ما لِقِيت غير حَلّ [ʔaʕtirif haːy čaːnat ɣalṭa minni, laːkin maː ligiːt ɣiːr ħall] I admit this was a mistake on my part, but I couldn't find another solution. أَعتِرِف آنِي مقَصِّر بحَقَّك [ʔaʕtirif ʔaːni mqaṣṣir bħaqqak] I'm afraid I didn't do all I could for you. • **2.** with بـ- to recognize, give recognition to – ما كان لازِم نِعتِرِف بِهالحُكُومَة بسُرعَة [maː čaːn laːzim niʕtirif bhalħukuːma bsurʕa] We shouldn't have recognized this government so quickly.
مَعرِفَة [maʕrifa] *n:* مَعارِف [maʕaːrif] *pl:* • **1.** knowledge, learning, information • **2.** pl. only مَعارِف acquaintance, conversance – وَزِير المَعارِف [waziːr ʔilmaʕaːrif] minister of education.
تَعرِيف [taʕriːf] *n:* تَعارِيف [taʕaːriːf] *pl:* • **1.** definition, determination, identification, specification
تَعارُف [taʕaːruf] *n:* • **1.** getting acquainted – حَفلَة تَعارُف [ħaflat taʕaːruf] reception, get-acquainted party. • **2.** polite formalities, ceremony
عُرفان [ʕurfaːn] *n:* • **1.** cognition, knowledge, perception, recognition, acknowledgment
تَعرِيفَة، تَعرِيفَة جُمرُكِيَّة [taʕriːfa, taʕriːfa gumrugiyya] *n:* • **1.** tariff, price list • **2.** list of customs duties
اِعتِراف [ʔiʕtiraːf] *n:* اِعتِرافات [ʕitiraːfaːt] *pl:* • **1.** recognition, acceptance • **2.** confession, avowal, admission, acknowledgment • **3.** gratitude, thankfulness
عارِف [ʕaːrif] *adj:* عارفِين [ʕaːrfiːn] *pl:* • **1.** aware, familiar, conversant • **2.** acquainted (with) • **3.** connoisseur, expert
مَعرُوف [maʕruːf] *adj:* • **1.** known, well-known – مَعرُوف بِالشَّجاعَة [maʕruːf biššajaːʕa] known for courage. مُلاكِم مَعرُوف [mulaːkim maʕruːf] a well-known boxer.

مِعتِرِف [miʕtirif] *adj:* • **1.** confessing • **2.** confessor (in the hierarchy of saints)
مُعتَرَف [muʕtaraf] *adj:* • **1.** recognized, accepted, admitted, granted, approved-of, licensed, authorized
مُتَعارَف [mutaʕa:raf] *adj:* • **1.** customary, usual, common – الشّي المُتَعارَف [ʔišši ʔilmutaʕa:raf] the customary thing.
أعرَف [ʔaʕraf] *comparative adjective:* • **1.** more or most knowledgeable

ع ر ف 2

عُرُف [ʕuruf] *n:* • **1.** custom, convention, tradition, usage, practice, habit • **2.** pl. أعراف crest, comb (of a rooster) – عُرف الدِّيك [ʕurf ʔiddi:č] red flower shaped like a cockscomb.
عُرفِي، الأحكام العُرفِيَّة [ʕurfi, ʔilʔaħka:m ʔilʕurfiyya] *adj:* • **1.** martial, martial law

ع ر ف 3

عَرِيف [ʕari:f] *n:* عُرَفاء [ʕurafa:ʔ] *pl:* • **1.** sergeant – رَئِيس عُرَفاء [raʔi:s ʕurafa:ʔ] approx.: master sergeant. نائِب عَرِيف [na:ʔib ʕari:f] approx.: corporal.

ع ر ق

عِرَق [ʕirag] *v:* • **1.** to sweat, perspire – عِرَقِت هوايَة بِالسِّينَما [ʕiragit hwa:ya bissinama] I perspired a lot in the movie. قُصّتَه ما تِعرَق [guṣṣtah ma: tiʕrag] He's not ashamed of anything (lit. his forehead doesn't sweat).
عَرَّق [ʕarrag] *v:* • **1.** to cause to sweat – عَرَّق نَفسَه بالبُخار [ʕarrag nafsah bilbuxa:r] He got himself all sweaty in the steam.
تعَرَّق [tʕarraq] *v:* • **1.** to sweat freely or copiously – قَبُل ما تِغسِل لازِم تِتعَرَّق بالبُخار [gabul ma: tiɣsil la:zim titʕarrag bilbuxa:r] Before you wash you should sweat a lot in the steam. اِتغَطّى بالبَطّانِيَّة حَتَّى تِتعَرَّق شوَيَّة وَتطِيب [ʔitɣaṭṭa: bilbaṭṭa:niyya ħatta titʕarrag šwayya wiṭṭi:b] Cover yourself with the blanket so that you'll sweat a little and get well.
عِرِق [ʕirig] *n:* عُرُوق [ʕuru:g] *pl:* • **1.** root • **2.** stem, branch, cutting • **3.** vein • **4.** stock, descent, background, family – عِرق السُوس [ʕirg ʔissu:s] licorice root. (شَربَت) عِرق السُوس [(šarbat) ʕirg ʔissu:s] a beverage made of licorice. عِرق النِّسا [ʕirig ʔinnisa] sciatica (med.). عِرِق تُوت [ʕirig tu:t] a mulberry branch, and by extension, a strong man.
عَرَق [ʕarag] *n:* • **1.** sweat, perspiration • **2.** arrack, liquor
عَرقَة [ʕarga] *n:* عَرقات [ʕarga:t] *pl:* • **1.** a period of sweating
عرُوق [ʕru:g] *n:* • **1.** grain (in wood) • **2.** (coll) a kind of كَباب, small hamburgers made of ground meat, flour, parsley, and onions fried in oil
العِراق [ʔilʕira:q] *n:* • **1.** Iraq
عرُوقايَة [ʕru:ga:ya] *n:* عرُوقايات [ʕru:ga:ya:t] *pl:* • **1.** خُبز عرُوق bread with pieces of meat, onions, parsley, spices, etc. baked into it.
عَرِيق [ʕari:q] *adj:* • **1.** deep-rooted, ancient • **2.** from an old, respectable family, of noble descent, highborn
عِراقِي [ʕira:qi] *adj:* • **1.** Iraqi, from Iraq • **2.** Iraqi
عَرقان [ʕarga:n] *adj:* • **1.** sweaty – ثِياب عَرقانَة [θiya:b ʕarga:na] sweaty clothes.
عَرَقچِي [ʕaragči] *adj:* عَرَقچِيَّة [ʕaragči:yya] *pl:* • **1.** person who drinks a lot of arrack, hence, a drunkard

ع ر ق چ ن

عَرَقچِين [ʕaraqči:n] *n:* عَرَقچِينات [ʕaraqči:na:t] *pl:* • **1.** skullcap

ع ر ق ل

عَرقَل [ʕarqal] *v:* • **1.** to complicate, hinder, hamper, obstruct, delay – قَضِيتِي كانَت ماشيَة بَسّ إنتَ عَرقَلتها [qaðiːti ča:nat ma:šya bass ʔinta ʕarqaltha] My case was going well but you fouled it up.
تعَرقَل [tʕarqal] *v:* • **1.** pass. of عَرقَل – قَضِيَّة تَرفِيعِي تعَرقِلَت [qaðiyyat tarfi:ʕi tʕarqilat] The matter of my promotion was delayed.
عَرقَلَة [ʕarqala] *n:* عَراقِيل [ʕara:qi:l] *pl:* • **1.** obstacle, hindrance, impediment, difficulty, handicap

ع ر ك

عارَك [ʕa:rak] *v:* • **1.** to fight, contend with – يعارِكهُم عَلَى أقَلّ شِي [yʕa:rikhum ʕala ʔaqall ši] He argues with them about the least thing. • **2.** to cause to fight, stir up, provoke, incite – جِيب دِيكَك؛ خَلِّي نعاركَه ويّا دِيكِي [ǰi:b di:čak; xalli: nʕa:rkah wiyya di:či] Bring your cock; let's put it to fight with mine. يِقدَر يعارِكهُم بِحكايَة وِحدَة [yigdar yʕa:rikhum biħča:ya wiħda] He can get them fighting with one remark.
تعارَك [tʕa:rak] *v:* • **1.** to fight one another – جِيرانّا يِتعارکُون عَلَى طُول [ǰi:ra:nna yitʕa:rku:n ʕala ṭu:l] Our neighbors fight all the time.
عَركَة [ʕarka] *n:* عَركات [ʕarka:t] *pl:* • **1.** fight, struggle
عراك [ʕra:k] *n:* • **1.** conflict • **2.** fight, quarrel, squabble
مَعرَكَة [maʕraka] *n:* مَعارِك [maʕa:rik] *pl:* • **1.** battle, combat, battlefield
عَرّاك [ʕarra:k] *adj:* عَرّاكَة [ʕarra:ka] *pl:* • **1.** fighter, scrapper
معارَكچِي [mʕa:rakči] *adj:* معارَكچِيَّة [mʕa:rakči:yya] *pl:* • **1.** fighter, ruffian, person who picks fights

ع ر م ط

عَرمُوطَة [ʕarmu:ṭa] *n:* • **1.** pear

ع ر ن
عَرِين [ʕari:n] *n:* • **1.** den, lair (of a wild animal)

ع ر ن س
عَرْنُوس [ʕarnu:s] *n:* • **1.** ear (of corn), corncob

ع ر و
عُروَة [ʕurwa] *n:* عراوي [ʕra:wi] *pl:* • **1.** a closed, usually rounded, handle, e.g., of a cup, pitcher, teapot, basket, etc

ع ر ي
عَرَّى [ʕarra:] *v:* • **1.** to undress, disrobe, unclothe – عَرِّي الجّاهِل حَتَّى يِتشَمَّس [ʕarri ʔijja:hil ħatta yitšammas] Undress the baby so he can get some sun.
تعَرَّى [tʕarra:] *v:* • **1.** to undress oneself, get undressed – تعَرَّى حَتَّى يفُحصَه الطَّبِيب [tʕarra: ħatta yfuħṣah ʔiṭṭabi:b] He disrobed so the doctor could examine him.
اِعترَى [ʔiʕtira:] *v:* • **1.** to overcome, overwhelm – اِعتِراه الخَوف [ʔiʕtira:h ʔilxu:f] He was overcome by fear. اِعتِرَاتَه نوبَة عَصَبِيَّة [ʔiʕtira:tah nu:ba ʕaṣabiyya] He had a nervous breakdown.
عارِي [ʕa:ri] *adj:* • **1.** devoid, bereft – خَبَر عاري عَن الصِّحَّة [xabar ʕa:ri ʕan ʔiṣṣiħħa] news devoid of any truth.
عَريان [ʕarya:n] *adj:* عَريانِين، عرايا [ʕarya:ni:n, ʕra:ya] *pl:* • **1.** naked, nude, bare, undressed – نِسوان عرايَة [niswa:n ʕra:ya] naked women.
عارِيَّة [ʕa:riyya] *adj:* • **1.** (invar.) loosely, lightly, unsteadily, insecurely – العَمُود واقُف عارِيَّة [ʔilʕamu:d wa:guf ʕa:riyya] The pole is standing unsteadily. رِجل الكُرسِي مَحطُوط عارِيَّة [rijl ʔilkursi maħṭu:ṭ ʕa:riyya] The chair leg is insecurely attached. الرِّدِن مشَكَّلَة بِالسِّترَة عارِيَّة [ʔirridin mšakkilah bissitra ʕa:riyya] The sleeve is attached loosely to the coat. دِير بالَك تَرَة الكلاص مَحطُوط عارِيَّة [di:r ba:lak tara ʔilgla:ṣ maħṭu:ṭ ʕa:riyya] Be careful because the glass is unsteadily settled.

ع ز ب
عَزَّب [ʕazzab] *v:* • **1.** to be a guest, stay overnight – إذا تروح لِلنَّجَف، عَزِّب عِند أخُويَا [ʔiða tru:ħ linnajaf, ʕazzib ʕind ʔaxu:ya] If you go to Najaf, stay with my brother. • **2.** to give lodging to, give a place to stay, take in
عُزُوبَة [ʕuzu:ba] *n:* • **1.** bachelorhood, celibacy
عُزُوبِيَّة [ʕuzu:biyya] *n:* • **1.** bachelorhood, celibacy
عَزبَة [ʕazba] *adj:* عَزبات [ʕazba:t] *pl:* • **1.** elderly unmarried woman, spinster
أعزَب [ʔaʕzab] *adj:* عُزّاب [ʕuzza:b] *pl:* • **1.** unmarried, single, celibate • **2.** bachelor
معَزِّب [mʕazzib] *adj:* مَعازِيب [maʕa:zi:b] *pl:* • **1.** guest, visitor
عازِب [ʕa:zib] *adj:* • **1.** single, unmarried, celibate, bachelor

ع ز ر ء ل
عِزرَئيل [ʕizraʔi:l] *n:* • **1.** Azrael, the angel of death

ع ز ز
عَزّ [ʕazz] *v:* • **1.** to cherish, hold dear – آني أعِزَّك هوايَة [ʔa:ni ʔaʕizzak hwa:ya] I hold you very dear. • **2.** with عَلَى : to pain – يعِزّ عَلينا تسافِر [yʕizz ʕali:na tsa:fir] It pains us that you're leaving.
عَزَّز [ʕazzaz] *v:* • **1.** to strengthen, reinforce – الجَّيش دَيعَزِّز مَركَزَه [ʔijjayš dayʕazziz markazah] The army is fortifying its position.
تعَزَّز [tʕazzaz] *v:* • **1.** to take advantage of devotion – مَرتَه تِتعَزَّز عَليه هوايَة [martah titʕazzaz ʕali:h hwa:ya] His wife takes advantage of his devotion.
اِعتَزّ [ʔiʕtazz] *v:* • **1.** to be proud, boast, pride oneself – آني أعتَزّ بِكُلّ صَدِيق مُخلِص [ʔa:ni ʔaʕtazz bkull ṣadi:q muxliṣ] I am proud of every loyal friend.
عِزّ، أيّام العِزّ [ʕizz, ʔayya:m ʔilʕizz] *n:* • **1.** days of glory, the good old days, the days of prosperity – بِعِزّ شَبابَه [bʕizz šaba:bah] in the prime of his youth. • **2.** might, power, strength, intensity, prime, • **3.** honor, glory, high fame, renown
عَزّ [ʕazz] *n:* • **1.** cherishing, holding s.o or something dear
عِزَّة [ʕizza] *n:* • **1.** might, power, strength, honor, glory, fame, renown • **2.** pride, self-esteem
مَعَزَّة [maʕazza] *n:* • **1.** regard, esteem, affection, love
تَعزِيز [taʕzi:z] *n:* • **1.** support, consolidation, backing
اِعتِزاز [ʔiʕtiza:z] *n:* • **1.** with بـ : pride, esteem, regard
عَزِيز [ʕazi:z] *adj:* • **1.** strong – سُوق عَزِيز [su:g ʕazi:z] a strong market. • **2.** dear, beloved as in عَزِيزِي my dear, my old buddy
معتَزّ [miʕtazz] *adj:* • **1.** appreciative • **2.** proud
مَعزُوز [maʕzu:z] *adj:* • **1.** beloved, respected, highly regarded – مَعزُوز بين أهلَه [maʕzu:z bi:n ʔahlah] beloved by his family. مَعزُوز العَين [maʕzu:z ʔilʕayn] dear friend.
أعَزّ [ʔaʕazz] *comparative adjective:* • **1.** dearer or dearest

ع ز ف
عِزَف [ʕizaf] *v:* • **1.** to play (usually, on a musical instrument) – تعَلَّم يِعزِف عالكَمَنجَة [tʕallam yiʕzif ʕalkamanja] He learned to play the violin.
عَزِف [ʕazif] *n:* • **1.** performance, play (music)
عازِف [ʕa:zif] *n:* • **1.** player, performer (on a musical instrument)
مَعزُوفَة [maʕzu:fa] *n:* مَعزُوفات [maʕzu:fa:t] *pl:* • **1.** piece of music, musical selection

ع

ع ز ق

عَزَقَة [ʕazaqa] *n:* عَزَقات [ʕazaqa:t] *pl:* • **1.** bother, problem, headache

ع ز ل

عِزَل [ʕizal] *v:* • **1.** to isolate, set aside, separate, segregate, detach – عِزلوا المَسلُولِين مِن المَرضَى الباقِين [ʕizlaw ʔilmaslu:li:n min ʔilmarð̣a: ʔilba:qi:n] They isolated the tuberculosis patients from the rest. • **2.** to cull, to sort – عِزَلت الطَّماطَة لَو بَعَد؟ [ʕizalt ʔiṭṭama:ṭa law baʕad?] Have you sorted the tomatoes yet? • **3.** to discharge, dismiss, release, remove – عِزلوه مِن الوَظِيفَة لِأَنّ كان ياخُذ رَشوَة [ʕizlu:h min ʔilwað̣i:fa liʔann ča:n ya:xuð rašwa] They fired him from the job because he was taking bribes.
عَزَّل [ʕazzal] *v:* • **1.** to close, close down, close up – يوم الجُمعَة الكُلّ يعَزّلُون [yu:m ʔiǰǰumʕa ʔilkull yʕazzilu:n] On Friday they all close their businesses.
اِنعِزَل [ʔinʕizal] *v:* • **1.** pass. of عِزَل : to be isolated, to be sorted, to be discharged, to be dismissed, to be released, to be culled – هَالمَرِيض لازم يِنعِزِل وَإِلّا الكُلّ يِنصابُون [halmari:ð̣ la:zim yinʕizil waʔilla ʔilkull yinṣa:bu:n] This patient must be isolated or all will be infected. الطَّماطَة بَعَد ما تِنعِزِل، أَسعارها تِختِلِف [ʔiṭṭama:ṭa baʕad ma: tinʕizil, ʔasʕa:rha tixtilif] After the tomatoes are sorted, their prices will vary. بَعَد ما اِنعِزَل مِن الوَظِيفَة، قام يِبِيع جِكايِر [baʕad ma: ʔinʕizal min ʔilwað̣i:fa, ga:m yibi:ʕ ǰiga:yir] After he was discharged from his position, he started selling cigarettes. • **2.** to separate, to part company – بَعَد ما تزَوَّج، اِنعِزَل عَن أَهلَه [baʕad ma: dzawwaǰ, ʔinʕizal ʕan ʔahlah] After he got married, he separated from his family.
عَزِل [ʕazil] *n:* • **1.** isolation (also, used in case of contagious diseases) – مُستَشفى عَزِل [mustašfa ʕazil] quarantine hospital. • **2.** (invar.) culled, discarded – طَماطَة عَزِل [ṭama:ṭa ʕazil] culled tomatoes. • **3.** dismissal, separation, segregation
عُزلَة [ʕuzla] *n:* • **1.** seclusion, privacy, solitude • **2.** retreat, retirement, isolation
تَعزِيل [taʕzi:l] *n:* • **1.** cleaning • **2.** closing
أَعزَل [ʔaʕzal] *adj:* عُزُل، عُزَّل [ʕuzul, ʕuzzal] *pl:* عَزلَة [ʕazla] *feminine:* • **1.** defenseless, unarmed
عازِل [ʕa:zil] *adj:* • **1.** insulator, insulating
معَزِّل [mʕazzil] *adj:* • **1.** closed
مُعتَزِل [muʕtazil] *adj:* • **1.** withdrawn, living alone and in isolation
مَعزُول [maʕzu:l] *adj:* • **1.** isolated, insulated
مِنعِزِل [minʕizil] *adj:* مِنعَزِلِين [minʕizil, minʕizili:n] *pl:* • **1.** isolated, solitary, single
إِنعِزالِي [ʔinʕiza:li] *adj:* • **1.** isolationist, isolationistic

ع ز م

عِزَم [ʕizam] *v:* • **1.** to invite – عِزَم كُلّ أَصدِقائَه عالعَشا [ʕizam kull ʔaṣdiqa:ʔah ʕalʕaša] He invited all his friends to dinner.
عَزَّم [ʕazzam] *v:* • **1.** to intend to do, to try to do • **2.** to remove a charm, to tell the future
عَزِم [ʕazim] *n:* • **1.** determination, firm will, firm intention, decision, resolution
عازِم [ʕa:zim] *n:* • **1.** host
عَزِيمَة [ʕazi:ma] *n:* عَزايِم [ʕaza:yim] *pl:* • **1.** invitation • **2.** banquet, dinner party
معَزِّم [mʕazzim] *adj:* • **1.** determined, resolute • **2.** charm remover, diviner, seer
مَعزُوم [maʕzu:m] *adj:* • **1.** invited

ع ز و

عَزَّى [ʕazza:] *v:* • **1.** to comfort, console, offer condolences – خَلِّي نرُوح نعَزِّي بوَفاة أَبُوه [xalli: nru:ħ nʕazzi bwafa:t ʔabu:h] Let's go console him about the death of his father. • **2.** to charge, blame, upbraid, scold – أَرِيد أَرُوح لِيها وَأعَزِّيها عَلَى كِذبها [ʔari:d ʔaru:ħ li:ha wʔaʕazzi:ha ʕala čiðibha] I want to go call her to account for her lie. الله يعَزِّيك عَلَى هَالدَقَّة هاي [ʔallah yʕazzi:k ʕala haldagga ha:y] God will punish you for that dirty trick.
تعَزَّى [tʕazza:] *v:* • **1.** to be consoled – تعَزَّى مِن قِبَل الصَّدِيق وَالعَدُو [tʕazza: min qibal ʔiṣṣadi:q wilʕadu] He was consoled by friends and enemies both. • **2.** to have trouble, bad luck – هُوَّ تعَزَّى بِالزَّواج مالَه [huwwa tʕazza: bizzawa:ǰ ma:lah] He's had a bad time with his marriage.
عَزا [ʕaza] *n:* عَزايات، عِزيات [ʕaza:ya:t, ʕizya:t] *pl:* • **1.** wake, mourning ceremony • **2.** mourning procession, also a commemorative procession on the anniversary of a man's death
تَعزِيَة [taʕazya] *n:* تَعازِي [taʕa:zi] *pl:* • **1.** religious ceremony among Shiites observing the marytrdom of Husain
تَعزِيَة [taʕziya] *n:* تَعازِي [taʕa:zi:] *pl:* • **1.** comfort, consolation, solace • **2.** condolence
مُعَزِّي [muʕazzi] *adj:* • **1.** consoler, condoler, mourner
متعَزِّي [mitʕazzi] *adj:* • **1.** in mourning • **2.** stricken

ع س ر

عَسَّر [ʕassar] *v:* • **1.** to experience difficulty in giving birth – عَسِّرَت بِطِفِلها الأَوَّل وسَوّولها عَمَلِيَّة [ʕassirat bṭifilha ʔilʔawwal wsawwu:lha ʕamaliyya] She had trouble giving birth to her first child and they operated on her. • **2.** to experience trouble laying an egg – الدِّجاجَة دَتِتعَسِّر. لازم البَيضَة كبِيرَة [ʔiddiǰa:ǰa datitʕassir. la:zim ʔilbayð̣a čbi:ra] The chicken's having trouble laying. The egg must be too large.

عَسِر [ʕasir] *n:* • **1.** hard – ماي عَسِر [maːy ʕasir] hard water.
عَسِير [ʕasiːr] *adj:* • **1.** hard, difficult
مِتعَسِّر [mitʕassir] *adj:* • **1.** hard, difficult

ع س ك ر

عَسكَر [ʕaskar] *n:* عَساكِر [ʔasːkir] *pl:* • **1.** army, troops
عَسكَرِي [ʕaskari] *n:* • **1.** military, army related • **2.** soldier
مُعَسكَر [muʕaskar] *n:* مُعَسكَرات [muʕaskaraːt] *pl:* • **1.** army camp, camp
عَسكَرِيَّة [ʕaskariyya] *adj:* • **1.** military service, army

ع س ل

عَسَل [ʕasal] *n:* • **1.** honey – شَهَر العَسَل [šahar ʔilʕasal] the honeymoon.
معَسَّل [mʕassal] *n:* • **1.** honey sweet • **2.** a mild-tasting tobacco,flavored with honey,apple, etc.
عَسَلِي [ʕasali] *adj:* • **1.** honey-colored, amber, brownish – عيُون عَسَلِيَّة [ʕyuːn ʕasaliyya] brownish eyes.
مَعسُول [maʕsuːl] *adj:* • **1.** honeyed – كَلام مَعسُول [kalaːm maʕsuːl] sweet talk, honeyed words.

ع س ي

عَسَى [ʕasaː] *conjunction:* • **1.** /with pronominal ending/ may, let, I hope that – عَساهُم يمُوتُون [ʕasaːhum ymuːtuːn] I hope they die. عَساها بِكَسر الرُّقبَة [ʕasaːha bkasr ʔirrugba] I hope she breaks her neck. طِلَع بِالبَرِد وَما سِمَع كَلامِي. عَساه يِتمَرَّض [ṭilaʕ bilbarid wma simaʕ kalaːmi. ʕasaːh yitmarrað̣] He went out in the rain and wouldn't listen to me. I hope he gets sick. عَساك بأَمَرّ مِن هاي [ʕasaːk bʔamarr min haːy] I wish you worse than that.

ع ش ب

عِشِب [ʕišib] *n:* • **1.** grass, herbage, plants, pasture
عَشّاب [ʕaššaːb] *n:* • **1.** herbalist
عُشبِي [ʕušbi] *adj:* • **1.** herbaceous, herbal

ع ش ر

عاشَر [ʕaːšar] *v:* • **1.** to be on intimate terms with, associate closely with – عاشَرهُم مُدَّة لَكِن شافهُم مُو خُوش ناس [ʕaːšarhum mudda laːkin šaːfhum muː xuːš naːs] He associated with them a while but he found they were a bad lot. عاشَرها سَنَة وَبَعدين تِرَكها [ʕaːšarha sana wbaʕdiyn tirakha] He lived with her for a year and then left her.
تعاشَر [tʕaːšar] *v:* • **1.** to pal around, be friends with • **2.** to associate
عُشُر [ʕušur] *n:* أعشار [ʔaʕšaːr] *pl:* • **1.** one tenth, tenth part
عَشرَة [ʕašra] *n:* عَشرات [ʕašraːt] *pl:* • **1.** ten
عِشرَة [ʕišra] *n:* • **1.** companionship, relations, company
عَشِيرَة [ʕašiːra] *n:* عَشايِر [ʕašaːyir] *pl:* • **1.** family, kin-folk, close relatives • **2.** tribe, clan. العَشايِر the tribes – قانُون العَشايِر [qaːnuːn ʔilʕašaːyir] tribal law.
عاشُور [ʕaːšuːr] *n:* • **1.** name for the first Moslem calendar month, Muharram • **2.** عاشُورَة name of a voluntary fast day on the10th day of Muharram, a day of mourning sacred to the Shiites.
عِشرِين [ʕišriːn] *n:* • **1.** twenty
مُعاشِر [muʕaːšir] *n:* • **1.** companion, fellow, comrade
تَعاشُر [taʕaːšur] *n:* • **1.** companionship
مُعاشَرَة [muʕašara] *n:* • **1.** companionship • **2.** close social relations
عُشرِي [ʕušri] *adj:* • **1.** decimal – كَسِر عُشرِي [kasir ʕušri] decimal fraction.
عاشِر [ʕaːšir] *adj:* • **1.** tenth (ordinal)
عَشائِرِي [ʕašaːʔiri] *adj:* • **1.** tribal

ع ش ش

عَشَّش [ʕaššaš] *v:* • **1.** to build a nest, to nest – اللَّقلَق عَشَّش عالمَنارَة [ʔillaglag ʕaššaš ʕalmanaːra] The stork built a nest on the minaret.
عِشّ [ʕišš] *n:* عشُوش [ʕšuːš] *pl:* • **1.** nest – عِشّ عَنكَبُوت [ʕišš ʕankabuːt] cobweb, spider web.
معَشِّش [mʕaššiš] *adj:* • **1.** to have a nest, to take root, to become established, rooted

ع ش ع ش

عَشعَش [ʕašʕaš] *v:* • **1.** also عَشَّش to build a nest, to nest – أَكثَر الطِيُور تعَشعِش بِالرَّبِيع [ʔakθar ʔiṭṭiyuːr tʕašʕiš birrabiːʕ] Most birds build nests in the spring.
معَشعِش [mʕašʕiš] *adj:* • **1.** nestled

ع ش ق

عِشَق [ʕišag] *v:* • **1.** to love passionately, to fall passionately in love – عِشَقها وتزَوَّجها [ʕišagha wdzawwajha] He fell madly in love with her and married her.
عِشِق [ʕišig] *n:* • **1.** love, passion, ardor of love
عاشِق [ʕaːšig, ʕaːšiq] *adj:* عُشّاق [ʕuššaːg, ʕuššaːq] *pl:* عَشِيقَة، عَشِيقَات [ʕaːšiqa, ʕaːšiqaːt] *feminine:* • **1.** lover
مَعشُوق [maʕšuːg] *adj:* • **1.** lover, sweetheart • **2.** mistress

ع ش و

عِشَى [ʕišaː] *v:* • **1.** to be night-blind – عِثَر بِعتِبَة الباب البارحَة باللَّيل لِأَنّ يِعشِي [ʕiθar bʕitbat ʔilbaːb ʔilbaːrħa billayl liʔann yiʕši] He tripped over the door sill last night because he has night blindness. • **2.** to be extremely near-sighted – بَسّ ينزَع مَناظرَه، يقُوم يِعشِي [bass yinzaʕ manaːð̣rah, yguːm yiʕši] He only has to take off his glasses, and he can't see a thing.

عَشّى [ʕašša:] *v:* • **1.** to give someone a dinner, invite to dinner – بِدال ما عزَمتني عَلَى سِينَما راح أَعَشِّيك [bida:l ma: ʕzamtni ʕala sinama ra:ħ ʔaʕašši:k] In exchange for your inviting me to a movie, I'm going to treat you to dinner. • **2.** to feed, give someone his supper – قُولِيلها تعَشّي الجّاهِل وَتنَيِّمَه [gu:li:lha tʕašši ʔijja:hil wtnayymah] Tell her to give the child supper and put him to bed.

تعَشّى [tʕašša:] *v:* • **1.** to have supper, to dine – بَعَدما تِتعَشّى، خابُرنِي [baʕadma titʕašša:, xa:burni] After you have supper, call me.

عَشا [ʕaša] *n:* عَشاوات [ʕaša:wa:t] *pl:* • **1.** dinner, supper • **2.** evening, also, evening darkness – أَشُوفَك العَشا [ʔašu:fak ʔilʕaša] I'll see you this evening.

عَشِي، عَشُو [ʕašy, ʕašw] *n:* • **1.** night-blindness

مِتعَشّي [mitʕašši] *adj:* • **1.** having already eaten dinner

عَشوائي [ʕašwa:ʔi] *adj:* • **1.** random, without plan, happening at random, aimless, haphazard, blind

ع ص ب

عَصَّب [ʕaṣṣab] *v:* • **1.** to wrap the head with a brow band, sash or turban – الأُمّ عَصُّبَت إبنها المَرِيض [ʔilʔumm ʕaṣṣubat ʔibinha ʔilmari:ḍ] The mother tied a piece of cloth around the forehead of her sick son. • **2.** to wrap, bandage

تعَصَّب [tʕaṣṣab] *v:* • **1.** to wrap one's head, wear a headband – إذا ما تِتعَصَّب، راسها يوَجعها [ʔiða ma: titʕaṣṣab, ra:sha yu:jaʕha] If she doesn't wear a headband, her head hurts. • **2.** to be bigoted, fanatic – يِتعَصَّب هوايَة بمُعامَلتَه لِلمُوَظَّفِين [yitʕaṣṣab hwa:ya bmuʕa:maltah lilmuwaḍḍafi:n] He's bigoted in his treatment of the employees. • **3.** with لـ to cling fanatically to, support fanatically or obdurately – يِتعَصِّبُون لمَبادِي الحِزِب [yitʕaṣṣibu:n lmaba:di ʔilħizib] They support the party ideology dogmatically. يِتعَصَّب لِدِينَه [yitʕaṣṣab ldi:nah] He is fanatic about his religion.

عَصَب [ʕaṣab] *n:* أعصاب [ʔaʕṣa:b] *pl:* • **1.** nerve

عُصَب [ʕuṣab] *n:* • **1.** plastic – مِشِط عُصَب [mišiṭ ʕuṣab] a plastic comb.

عُصبَة [ʕuṣba] *n:* عُصَب [ʕuṣab] *pl:* • **1.** tendon, sinew • **2.** headband

تَعَصُّب [taʕaṣṣub] *n:* • **1.** bigotry, prejudice • **2.** fanaticism, ardent zeal

عِصابَة [ʕiṣa:ba] *n:* عِصابات [ʕiṣa:ba:t] *pl:* • **1.** gang, band

عصَابَة [ʕṣa:ba] *n:* عصَابات [ʕṣa:ba:t] *pl:* • **1.** headband

عَصَبِي [ʕaṣabi] *adj:* • **1.** nervous, neural – مَرَض عَصَبِي [marað ʕaṣabi] a nervous disorder. • **2.** nervous, high-strung, excitable – حصان عَصَبِي [ħṣa:n ʕaṣabi] a nervous horse. • **3.** mad, angry, irritable, bad-tempered – شَخِص عَصَبِي [šaxiṣ ʕaṣabi] an irritable person.

عَصِيب [ʕaṣi:b] *adj:* • **1.** crucial, hot, critical (time, stage, situation)

مِتعَصِّب [mitʕaṣṣub] *adj:* • **1.** dogmatic • **2.** bigot, fanatic, extremist

ع ص د

عَصِيدَة [ʕaṣi:da] *n:* • **1.** a thick porridge made of flour, oil or butter, and sugar

ع ص ر

عِصَر [ʕiṣar] *v:* • **1.** to wring out – إعصِر الثُّوب وَشُرُّه عَالحَبِل [ʔiʕṣir ʔiθθu:b wšurrah ʕalħabil] Wring out the shirt and hang it on the line. • **2.** to squeeze, press – عِصَر نُومِيَّة حامضَة عَالسِّمكَة [ʕiṣar nu:miyya ħa:mḍa ʕassimča] He squeezed a lemon on the fish. هَذا بَخِيل هوايَة. يِعصِر النِّخالَة، يطَلِّع مِنها دِهِن [ha:ða baxi:l hwa:ya. yiʕṣir ʔinnixa:la, yṭalliʕ minha dihin] He's very stingy. He squeezes wheat husks, and gets oil from them. دَيُعصُر هوايَة لِأَنّ بَطنَه قَبُض [dayuʕṣur hwa:ya liʔann baṭnah qabuð] He is straining hard because he is constipated. عِصَر إيدَه بقُوَّة [ʕiṣar ʔi:dah bguwwa] He clenched his fists.

عَصَّر [ʕaṣṣar] *v:* • **1.** intens. of عِصَر : to squeeze, press, to wring out – لا تعَصِّر الطَماطَة بإيدَك تَرَة تِتلَف [la: tʕaṣṣir ʔiṭṭama:ṭa bi:dak tara titlaf] Don't keep squeezing all the tomatoes or they'll spoil.

عَصِر [ʕaṣir] *n:* عُصُور [ʕuṣu:r] *pl:* • **1.** age, era, time – العَصر الحَجَري [ʔilʕaṣr ʔilħajari] the Stone Age. العَصر الحاضِر [ʔilʕaṣr ʔilħa:ðir] the present time. • **2.** afternoon, as in العَصِر in the afternoon • **3.** also صَلاة العَصِر afternoon prayer (Isl.Law)

عَصِر [ʕaṣir] *n:* • **1.** (act of) squeezing out, pressing (out) • **2.** (act of) wringing (out)

عَصِير [ʕaṣi:r] *n:* • **1.** juice

عصِير [ʕṣi:r] *n:* • **1.** date pulp remaining from date molasses-making, fed to livestock

عَصرِيَّة [ʕaṣriyya] *n:* عَصرِيّات [ʕaṣriyya:t] *pl:* • **1.** afternoon

عصّارَة [ʕaṣṣa:ra, ʕuṣṣa:ra] *n:* عصّارات [ʕaṣṣa:ra:t, ʕuṣṣa:ra:t] *pl:* • **1.** juicer, squeezer, press

إعصار [ʔiʕṣa:r] *n:* أعاصِير [ʔaʕa:ṣi:r] *pl:* • **1.** tornado, hurricane

معصارَة [miʕṣa:ra] *n:* • **1.** juicer, squeezer

عَصري [ʕaṣri] *adj:* • **1.** modern, recent, contemporary – مَجزَرَة عَصرِيَّة [majzara ʕaṣriyya] a modern slaughter-house.

عصارَة [ʕṣa:ra] *n:* • **1.** stinginess, a person who squeezes himself out to save

معاصِر [mʕa:ṣir] *adj:* • **1.** contemporary, modern

مَعصُور [maʕṣu:r] *adj:* • **1.** squeezed (out)

مِتعاصِر [mitʕa:ṣir] *adj:* • **1.** contemporary, modern

ع ص ص

تعاصَص [tʕaːṣaṣ] *v:* • **1.** to become caught in penis retentus, to get stuck together – الكِلاب يِتعاصَصُون أحياناً [ʔiččilaːb yitʕaːṣaṣuːn ʔaħyaːnan] Dogs get stuck together sometimes.

ع ص ع ص

تعصعَص [tʕasʕaṣ] *v:* • **1.** same as تعاصَص : to become difficult

عَصعُوص [ʕaṣʕuːṣ] *n:* عَصاعِيص، عصاعِص [ʕaṣaːʕiːṣ, ʕaṣaːʕiṣ] *pl:* • **1.** coccyx • **2.** (an insulting term of address, approximately:) jerk, asshole

ع ص ف

عِصَف [ʕiṣaf] *v:* • **1.** to storm, to blow

عاصِفَة [ʕaːṣifa] *n:* عَواصِف [ʕawaːṣif] *pl:* • **1.** storm, tempest, violent wind, hurricane, gale

عاصِف [ʕaːṣif] *adj:* • **1.** stormy, windy

ع ص ف ر

عِصفِر [ʕiṣfir] *n:* • **1.** safflower

عَصفُور [ʕaṣfuːr] *n:* عَصافِير [ʕaṣaːfiːr] *pl:* • **1.** sparrow • **2.** any small bird

ع ص م

معصَم [miʕṣam] *n:* مَعاصِم [maʕaːṣim] *pl:* • **1.** wrist

عاصِمَة [ʕaːṣima] *n:* عاصِمات، عَواصِم [ʕaːṣimaːt, ʕawaːṣim] *pl:* • **1.** capital city

اِعتِصام [ʔiʕtiṣaːm] *n:* • **1.** sit-in, strike, occupation esp. of university or other government buildings etc.

مَعصُوم [maʕṣuːm] *adj:* • **1.** infallible – ماكُو أحَّد مَعصُوم مِن الخَطَأ [maːku ʔaħħad maʕṣuːm min ʔilxaṭaʔ] No one's free of error.

عِصامِي [ʕiṣaːmi] *adj:* • **1.** independent, self-reliant, eminent, noble, self-made man

ع ص و [1]

عَصَّى [ʕaṣṣaː] *v:* • **1.** to become hard and fibrous – الفِجِل عَصَّى وَما ينكال [ʔilfijil ʕaṣṣaː wamaː yinkaːl] The radishes have gotten hard and can't be eaten.

ع ص و [2]

عَصا عُصَّة، عَصايَة [ʕaṣa, ʕuṣṣa, ʕaṣaːya] *n:* عُصِي، عِصِي [ʕuṣiː, ʕiṣiː] *pl:* • **1.** stick • **2.** blow with a stick

ع ص ي

عِصَى [ʕiṣaː] *v:* • **1.** to disobey, resist, oppose, defy – عِصَوا الجِّنُود عالضابُط وَما سَلّمَوا سلاحهُم إلّا بالقُوَّة [ʕiṣaw ʔijjinuːd ʕaðððaːbuṭ wma sallmaw slaːħhum ʔilla bilguwwa] The soldiers disobeyed the officer and wouldn't surrender their arms except by force. مِن تجُبرَك الحُكُومَة، ما تِقدَر تِعصِي [min dǰubrak ʔilħukuːma, maː tigdar tiʕṣi] When the government compels you, you can't resist. سافَر لبارِيس وعِصَى هناك [saːfar lpaːriːs wʕiṣaː hnaːk] He went to Paris and stayed there stubbornly. أَخَذ الطُّوبَة الجّاهِل وعِصَى بِيها [ʔaxað ʔiṭṭuːba ʔijjaːhil wʕiṣaː biːha] The child took the ball and hung on to it. هَالشَّخِص ما يِعصَى عَليه القَضِيَّة أبَداً [haššaxiṣ maː tiʕṣaː ʕaliːh ʔilqaðiyya ʔabadan] That guy never gets stuck with a problem. عِصَت التَّبَدُورَة بالبُوطِل [ʕiṣat ʔittabbaduːra bilbuṭil] The cork got stuck in the bottle.

اِستَعصَى [ʔistaʕṣaː] *v:* • **1.** to be difficult, hard – اِستَعصَت عَلَيهُم المُشكِلَة وَما يِدرُون شِيسَوُّون [ʔistaʕṣat ʕaliːhum ʔilmuškila wmaː yidruːn šiːsawwuːn] The problem was difficult for them and they don't know what to do. • **2.** to be malignant, incurable – اِستَعصَى المَرَض [ʔistaʕṣaː ʔilmarað] The disease was incurable.

عِصيان [ʕiṣyaːn] *n:* عِصيانات [ʕiṣyaːnaːt] *pl:* • **1.** insurrection, revolt, rebellion, mutiny • **2.** disobedience, insubordination

مَعصِيَة [maʕṣiya] *n:* مَعاصِي [maʕaːṣiː] *pl:* • **1.** disobedience to God, sin

عاصِي [ʕaːṣi] *adj:* • **1.** in revolt, revolting – عاصِي عَن الحُكُومَة [ʕaːṣi ʕan ʔilħukuːma] in revolt against the goverment. • **2.** stuck – عاصِي بِالبُوطِل [ʕaːṣi bilbuṭil] stuck in the bottle.

مُستَعصِي [mustaʕṣi] *adj:* • **1.** incurable – مَرَض مُستَعصِي [marað mustaʕṣi] an incurable disease.

ع ض ب

أعضَب [ʔaʕðab] *adj:* عُضُب، عَضبِين [ʕuðub, ʕaðbiːn] *pl:* عَضبَة [ʕaðba] *feminine:* • **1.** paralyzed in one hand or arm, having a deformed hand or arm • **2.** person with a paralyzed or deformed hand or arm

ع ض د

تعاضَد [tʕaːðad] *v:* • **1.** to stick together • **2.** to support one another • **3.** to assist or aid mutually, to cooperate (with)

عُضُد [ʕuðud] *n:* عُضُود [ʕuðuːd] *pl:* • **1.** stalk of a plant

مُعضَد [muʕðad] *n:* مَعاضِد [maʕaːðid] *pl:* • **1.** bracelet

تعاضُد [taʕaːðud] *n:* • **1.** mutual aid, mutual assistance, cooperation

عَضِيد [ʕaðiːd] *adj:* عُضَداء [ʕuðadaːʔ] *pl:* • **1.** backer, supporter

ع ض ض

عَضّ [ʕaðð] *v:* • **1.** to bite – اِبتِعِد عَن الكَلِب تَرَة يعَضَّك [ʔibtiʕid ʕan ʔiččalib tara yʕaððak] Stay away from the dog or he'll bite you. • **2.** to be sarcastic, biting – لا تعَضّ بحَكيَك [laː tʕaðð bħačyak] Don't be caustic in your talk.

ع

عَضّ [ʕaðð] *n:* • **1.** (act of) biting, bite
عَضَّة [ʕaðða] *n:* عَضّات [ʕaððaːt] *pl:* • **1.** bite

ع ض ع ض

عَضعَض [ʕaðʕað] *v:* • **1.** to chew, to keep biting – الطِّفِل دَيعَضعَض بإصبِعِي [ʔiṭṭifil dayʕaðʕað bʔiṣbiʕi] The baby is chewing on my finger.
تعَضعَض [tʕaðʕað] *v:* • **1.** to be snapped
عَضعَضَة [ʕaðʕaða] *n:* • **1.** snapping
معَضعَض [mʕaðʕað] *adj:* • **1.** uneven • **2.** bitten

ع ض ل

عَضَلَة [ʕaðala] *n:* عَضَلات [ʕaðalaːt] *pl:* • **1.** muscle
مُعضِلَة [muʕðila] *n:* مُعضِلات [muʕðilaːt] *pl:* • **1.** puzzle, enigma, tough problem
معَضِّل [mʕaððil] *adj:* • **1.** muscular
عُضال [ʕuðaːl] *adj:* • **1.** incurable (disease), chronic, inveterate
عَضَلِي [ʕaðali] *adj:* • **1.** muscular

ع ض و

عُضو [ʕuðw] *n:* أعضاء [ʔaʕðaːʔ] *pl:* • **1.** member, limb, organ (of the body) – أعضاء التَّناسُل [ʔaʕðaːʔ ʔittanaːsul] reproductive organs, genitals. • **2.** member (of an organization)
عُضوَة [ʕuðwa] *n:* عُضوات [ʕuðwaːt] *pl:* • **1.** female member
عُضويَّة [ʕuðwiyya] *n:* عُضويّات [ʕuðwiyyaːt] *pl:* • **1.** membership
عُضوي [ʕuðwi] *adj:* • **1.** organic – كِيمياء عُضويَّة [kiːmya ʕuðwiyya] organic chemistry.

ع ط ب

عَطَّب [ʕaṭṭab] *v:* • **1.** to char, be scorched – جُرّ الخاولِي مِن يَمّ النّار. قام يِعَطُّب [jurr ʔilxaːwli min yamm ʔinnaːr. gaːm yiʕaṭṭub] Pull the towel away from the fire. It's begun to char. عَطَّبِت مِن العَطَش [ʕaṭṭabit min ʔilʕaṭaš] I became parched from thirst. هَالجّاهِل عَطَّب قَلبِي [hajjaːhil ʕaṭṭab galbi] That kid has driven me to distraction.
عَطَب [ʕaṭab] *n:* أعطاب [ʔaʕṭaːb] *pl:* • **1.** damage, defect
عُطّاب [ʕuṭṭaːb, ʕiṭṭaːb] *n:* • **1.** burned or charred cloth – رِيحَة عُطّاب [riːħat ʕuṭṭaːb] smell of something burning.
عُطّابَة [ʕuṭṭaːba] *n:* عُطّابات [ʕuṭṭaːbaːt] *pl:* • **1.** a burning cloth, applied to the head to cauterize a head wound or to cure headache
معَطّب [mʕaṭṭib] *adj:* • **1.** damaged, defected, burnt

ع ط ر

عَطَّر [ʕaṭṭar] *v:* • **1.** to perfume, scent – عَطِّرَت شَعرها [ʕaṭṭirat šaʕarha] She perfumed her hair.
تعَطَّر [tʕaṭṭar] *v:* • **1.** to perfume oneself – العَرُوس دَتِتعَطَّر [ʔilʕaruːs datitʕaṭṭar] The bride is perfuming herself.
عِطِر [ʕiṭir] *n:* عُطُور [ʕuṭuːr] *pl:* • **1.** perfume, scent, essence
عَطّار [ʕaṭṭaːr] *n:* • **1.** dealer in non-perishable foodstuffs (spices, herbs, coffee, tea, soap, nuts --- anything except fresh foods)
مُعَطِّر [muʕaṭṭir] *n:* • **1.** deodorant, air freshener
معَطَّر [mʕaṭṭar] *adj:* • **1.** perfumed, scented, fragrant

ع ط ر د

عَطارِد [ʕaṭaːrid] *n:* • **1.** (the planet) Mercury

ع ط س

عِطَس [ʕiṭas] *v:* • **1.** to sneeze – عِطَس لَمّا باوَع بِالشَّمِس [ʕiṭas lamma baːwaʕ biššamis] He sneezed when he looked at the sun.
عَطَّس [ʕaṭṭas] *v:* • **1.** to sneeze, to sneeze a lot – دَيعَطِّس هوايَة مِن النَّشلَة [dayʕaṭṭis hwaːya min ʔinnašla] He sneezes a lot because of his cold.
عَطِس [ʕaṭis] *n:* • **1.** (act of) sneezing
عَطسَة [ʕaṭsa] *n:* عَطسات [ʕaṭsaːt] *pl:* • **1.** a sneeze
تِعِطِّس [tiʕiṭṭis] *n:* • **1.** sneezing

ع ط ش

عِطَش [ʕiṭaš] *v:* • **1.** to be or become thirsty – جِيبلِي شوَيَّة مَيّ. عِطَشِت [jiːbli šwayyat mayy. ʕṭašit] Bring me a little water. I've gotten thirsty.
عَطَّش [ʕaṭṭaš] *v:* • **1.** to make thirsty – الأكِل المالِح يعَطِّش [ʔilʔakil ʔilmaːliħ yʕaṭṭiš] Salty food makes one thirsty.
عَطَش [ʕaṭaš] *n:* • **1.** thirst
عَطشَة [ʕaṭša] *n:* عَطشات [ʕaṭšaːt] *pl:* • **1.** a thirst
عَطشان [ʕaṭšaːn] *adj:* عَطاشَة، عَطشانِين [ʕaṭaːša, ʕaṭšaːniːn] *pl:* • **1.** thirsty – عَطشان عَلَى كلاص مَيّ [ʕaṭšaːn ʕala glaːṣ mayy] thirsty for a glass of water. • **2.** anxious, desirous, craving – عَطشان عَلَى أخبار [ʕaṭšaːn ʕala ʔaxbaːr] anxious for news.
متعَطِّش [mitʕaṭṭiš] *adj:* • **1.** with عَلَى or لـ avid, craving for – مِتعَطِّش عالمَشرُوب [mitʕaṭṭiš ʕalmašruːb] anxious for a drink. مِتعَطِّش عالعِلِم [mitʕaṭṭiš ʕalʕilim] avid for knowledge. مِتعَطِّش لِلدَّمّ [mitʕaṭṭiš liddamm] bloodthirsty.

ع ط ط

عَطّ [ʕaṭṭ] *v:* • **1.** to spread, to permeate, to penetrate – رِيحَة البُصَل تعُطّ بالمَطبَخ [riːħat ʔilbuṣal tʕuṭṭ bilmaṭbax] The odor of onions is permeating the kitchen. • **2.** to be permeated, penetrated, to be redolent, to reek, to smell – سَيّارتَك تعُطّ بِرِيحَة البَنزِين [sayyaːrtak tʕuṭṭ briːħit ʔilbanziːn] Your car's filled with the smell of gasoline. البَيت يعُطّ بِالدُّخّان [ʔilbayt yʕuṭṭ bidduxxaːn] The house

is permeated with smoke. هِيَّ تعُطّ بالرِّيحَة [hiyya tʕuṭṭ birri:ħa] She reeks of perfume.
عَطّ [ʕaṭṭ] *n:* • **1.** (act of) spreading, penetrating, permeating
عاطّ [ʕa:ṭṭ] *adj:* • **1.** spread (out) • **2.** yelling, screaming

ع ط ف

عِطَف [ʕiṭaf] *v:* • **1.** to be compassionate, sympathetic – هُوَّ يِعطُف عالفَقِير [huwwa yiʕṭuf ʕalfaqi:r] He has compassion for the poor.
انعِطَف [ʔinʕiṭaf] *v:* • **1.** to curve
إستَعطَف [ʔistaʕṭaf] *v:* • **1.** to beseech, implore, plead with – إستَعطَف الوَزِير إلَى أن عِفَى عَنَّه [ʔistaʕṭaf ʔilwazi:r ʔila ʔan ʕifa: ʕannah] He pleaded with the minister until he pardoned him.
عَطُف [ʕaṭuf] *n:* • **1.** compassion, sympathy, mercy, attachment, liking (for)
مِعطَف [miʕṭaf] *n:* مَعاطِف [maʕa:ṭif] *pl:* • **1.** overcoat, topcoat
عاطِفة [ʕa:ṭifa] *n:* عَواطِف [ʕawa:ṭif] *pl:* • **1.** emotion, feeling, affection, attachment, kindness, sympathy
مُنعَطَف [munʕaṭaf] *n:* • **1.** curve, bend, twist (in road, path etc.)
تَعاطُف [taʕa:ṭuf] *n:* • **1.** mutual affection, sympathy
انعِطاف [ʔinʕiṭa:f] *n:* • **1.** curvature, bending
إستِعطاف [ʔistiʕṭa:f] *n:* • **1.** affection, sympathy
عَطُوف [ʕaṭu:f] *adj:* • **1.** very compassionate, kind, sympathetic
عاطِفِي [ʕa:ṭifi] *adj:* • **1.** emotional, sentimental – قَصِيدَة عاطِفِيَّة [qaṣi:da ʕa:ṭifiyya] an emotional poem. رِجّال عاطِفِي [rijja:l ʕa:ṭifi] a sentimental man.
مِتعاطِف [mitʕa:ṭuf] *adj:* • **1.** sympathetic to, kind, affectionate
أعطَف [ʔaʕṭaf] *comparative adjective:* • **1.** more or most sympathetic, compassionate

ع ط ل

عِطَل [ʕiṭal] *v:* • **1.** to tire, become tired – عِطلَت إيدَه مِن الشُّغُل [ʕiṭlat ʔi:dah min ʔiššuɣul] He became tired from the work. عِطَلِت مِن المَشِي [ʕiṭalit min ʔilmašy] I got tired walking. عِطَل لِساني مِن الحَكِي وِيّاه [ʕiṭal lisa:ni min ʔilħači wiyya:h] I got tired of talking with him. • **2.** to tire, weary, become sick and tired – عِطَلنا مِن هَالحَرُب [ʕiṭalna min halħarub] We've gotten tired of this war. عِطَل مِن القَعدَة [ʕiṭal min ʔilgaʕda] He got tired of idleness.
عَطَّل [ʕaṭṭal] *v:* • **1.** to delay, interrupt, hinder, hamper – لا تعَطِّلني. آنِي مِستَعجِل [la: ʔitʕaṭṭilni. ʔa:ni mistaʕjil] Don't delay me. I'm in a hurry. عَطَّل أوراقِي عَلَى المِيز مالَه [ʕaṭṭal ʔawra:qi ʕala ʔilmi:z ma:lah] He held up my papers on his desk. عَطِّلَوا الشُّغُل عَلَى حسابَه [ʕaṭṭilaw ʔiššuɣul ʕala ħsa:bah] They suspended the work on account of him. • **2.** to close up, close down, remain closed – دَوائِر الحُكُومَة تعَطِّل يوم الجُّمعَة [dawa:ʔir ʔilħuku:ma tʕaṭṭil yu:m ʔijjumʕa] Government offices are closed on Fridays. المَعمَل معَطِّل بِسَبَب الإضراب [ʔilmaʕmal mʕaṭṭil bisabab ʔilʔiðra:b] The factory is closed down because of the strike.
تعَطَّل [tʕaṭṭal] *v:* • **1.** to be late – اِنتِظِرنِي بالباب. آنِي ما راح أتعَطَّل [ʔintiðirni bilba:b. ʔa:ni ma: ra:ħ ʔatʕaṭṭal] Wait for me by the door. I won't be late. • **2.** to be stopped, interrupted – كُلّ الشُّغُل وَمَصالح النّاس تعَطّلَت بَعد هَالثَّورَة [kull ʔiššuɣul wamaṣa:liħ ʔinna:s tʕaṭṭilat baʕd haθθawra] All business and industry has been interrupted by this revolution. كُلّ شُغلَه ماشِي؛ ما تعَطّلَتلَه وَلا قَضِيَّة [kull šuɣlah ma:ši; ma: tʕaṭṭlatlah wala qaðiyya] His work's going well; nothing has been interrupted.
عَطَل [ʕaṭal] *n:* • **1.** tiredness, sickness, weariness
عُطلَة [ʕuṭla] *n:* عُطلات [ʕuṭla:t] *pl:* • **1.** holiday • **2.** vacation, recess – عُطلَة رَبِيعِيَّة [ʕuṭla rabi:ʕiyya] spring vacation.
تَعطِيل [taʕṭi:l] *n:* • **1.** obstruction, interruption, suspension (of activity)
عَطالَة [ʕaṭa:la] *n:* • **1.** (like بَطالَة) unemployment
عَطَلَة [ʕaṭala] *adj:* • **1.** (invar.) useless, worthless – وَلَد عَطَلَة [walad ʕaṭala] a useless boy.
عاطِل [ʕa:ṭil] *adj:* • **1.** idle, inactive, unemployed, out-of-work, jobless – مَكِينَة عاطلَة [maki:na ʕa:ṭla] an idle machine. عُمّال عاطلِين [ʕumma:l ʕa:ṭli:n] idled workers, unemployed workers. • **2.** worthless, useless – وَلَد عاطِل [walad ʕa:ṭil] a worthless boy. مُو عاطِل [mu: ʕa:ṭil] not bad. شِكِلها مُو عاطِل [šikilha mu: ʕa:ṭil] She's not bad looking. سَيّارَة مُو عاطلَة [sayya:ra mu: ʕa:ṭla] not a bad car.
معَطِّل [mʕaṭṭil] *adj:* • **1.** out on vacation

ع ط و

تعاطَى [tʕa:ṭa:] *v:* • **1.** to deal, to be engaged – إحنا ما نِتعاطَى بهِيكِي بِضاعَة [ʔiħna ma: nitʕa:ṭa: bhi:či biða:ʕa] We don't deal in such commodities. كُلّ أهلَه يتعاطُون بالتِّجارَة [kull ʔahlah ytʕa:ṭu:n bittija:ra] All his family is engaged in commerce.
إستَعطَى [ʔistaʕṭa:] *v:* • **1.** to beg, seek alms – المجَدِّي دَيِستَعطِي بِالقَهوَة [ʔilmgaddi dayistaʕṭi bilgahwa] The beggar is begging in the coffeehouse.
عَطا [ʕaṭa] *n:* عَطايات، عَطايا [ʕaṭa:ya:t, ʕaṭa:ya:] *pl:* • **1.** gift, present, reward (from God) – عَطا مِن الله [ʕaṭa min ʔallah] a gift from God. • **2.** giving – ماكُو أخِذ وَعَطا. السُّوق واقُف [ma:ku ʔaxið wʕaṭa:. ʔissu:g wa:guf] There's no buying and selling. The market's dead. أشُو ماكُو أخِذ وَعَطا بَيناتنا [ʔašu: ma:ku ʔaxið wʕaṭa bayna:tna] There doesn't seem to be any give and take between us.
عَطاء [ʕaṭa:ʔ] *n:* • **1.** bid (at an auction)
تعاطِي [taʕa:ṭi] *n:* • **1.** addiction, pursuit, practice

ع

عاطِي [ʕaːṭi] *adj:* • **1.** as Noun/Adj: giver (of), giving
مُعطِي [muʕṭi] *adj:* مُعطاة [muʕṭaːt] *feminine:* • **1.** Noun/Adj: giver, giving
مُعطَى [muʕṭa] *adj:* • **1.** given

ع ظ م

عَظَّم [ʕaðð̣am] *v:* • **1.** to magnify, enlarge – عَظَّم المُشكِلَة، وَكانَت بَسِيطَة [ʕaðð̣am ʔilmuškila, wčaːnat basiːṭa] He magnified the problem, but it was really nothing. شدَعوَة عَظَّمت القَضِيَّة [šdaʕwa ʕaðð̣amt ʔilqað̣iyya] You really blew the matter up out of all proportion! • **2.** to become skin and bones, become skinny, waste away – عَظَّم جِسمَه مِن السِّل [ʕaðð̣am ǰismah min ʔissill] His body wasted away from tuberculosis.
عَظُم، عَظَمَة [ʕað̣um, ʕað̣ma] *n:* عَظمات [ʕað̣maːt] *pl:* • **1.** (coll.) bone • **2.** piece of bone
عَظَمَة [ʕað̣ama] *n:* • **1.** arrogance, haughtiness – جُنُون العَظَمَة [ǰunuːn ʔilʕað̣ama] delusions of grandeur.
مُعظَم [muʕð̣am] *n:* • **1.** the majority, most of
عَظِيم [ʕað̣iːm] *adj:* عُظَماء [ʕuð̣amaːʔ] *pl:* • **1.** great, grand, magnificent – قائِد عَظِيم [qaːʔid ʕað̣iːm] a great leader. اِنتِصار عَظِيم [ʔintiṣaːr ʕað̣iːm] a great victory. • **2.** great, wonderful, tremendous – سَيّارَة عَظِيمَة [sayyaːra ʕað̣iːma] a wonderful car. • **3.** great person
أعظَم [ʔaʕð̣am] *comparative adjective:* • **1.** greater or greatest
عُظمَى [ʕuð̣ma] *comparative adjective:* • **1.** greater or greatest برِطانيا العُظمَى : [briṭaːnya ʔalʕuð̣ma] Great Britain

ع ف ر ت

تعَفرَت [tʕafrat] *v:* • **1.** to be a bully, to act tough, to act big – يِتعَفرَت عَلَى المُوَظَّفِين، لِأَنّ متزَوِّج بِتّ المُدِير [yitʕafrat ʕala ʔilmuwað̣ð̣afiːn, liʔann midzawwiǰ bitt ʔilmudiːr] He lords it over the employees because he's married to the director's daughter. • **2.** to be or become brave, bold – أَشُو مِن جا أَخُوك تعَفرَتِت [ʔašuː min ǰaː ʔaxuːk tʕafratit] I see you got brave when your brother came.
عِفرِيت [ʕifriːt] *n:* عَفارِيت [ʕafaːriːt] *pl:* • **1.** clever, capable • **2.** brave, bold • **3.** mighty, tough • **4.** imp, devil, demon

ع ف ر م

عَفارِم [ʕafaːrim] *adj:* • **1.** (an exclamation from Turkish origin) well done! good for you! bravo!

ع ف ص [1]

عِفَص [ʕifaṣ, ʕifas] *v:* • **1.** to wrinkle, rumple, crumple – لا تِعفَص الوَرَقَة [laː tiʕfaṣ ʔilwaraqa] Don't crumple the paper. عِفَصِت الثُّوب مالِي [ʕifaṣit ʔiθθuːb maːli] I wrinkled my shirt. • **2.** to irritate, anger – عِفَصنِي بِهَالكِلمَة [ʕifaṣni bhaččilma] He irritated me with that remark.
عَفَّص [ʕaffaṣ] *v:* • **1.** to wrinkle, rumple, crumple – الجّاهِل عَفَّص الكِتاب [ʔiǰǰaːhil ʕaffaṣ ʔilkitaːb] The kid wrinkled the pages in the book.
تعَفَّص [tʕaffaṣ] *v:* • **1.** to be or become wrinkled, crumpled – المَكتُوب تعَفَّص بجيبِي [ʔilmaktuːb tʕaffaṣ bǰiːbi] The letter got crumpled in my pocket.

ع ف ص [2]

عَفُص، عَفص [ʕafuṣ, ʕafṣ] *n:* • **1.** (coll.) gall tree(s), and gallnut(s) • **2.** wrinkle, crumple
عَفصَة [ʕafṣa] *n:* عَفصات [ʕafṣaːt] *pl:* • **1.** gall tree, gallnut

ع ف ط

عِفَط [ʕifaṭ] *v:* • **1.** to give a raspberry, to give a Bronx cheer – كُل ما أحكِي، يِعفُط [kull maː ʔaħči, yiʕfuṭ] Everytime I say something, he gives a Bronx cheer. عِفَطِتلَه مِن قام يِحكِي لَغوَة [ʕifaṭitlah min gaːm yiħči laɣwa] I gave him a Bronx cheer when he started to talk nonsense.
عَفُط [ʕafuṭ] *n:* • **1.** (act of) giving a Bronx cheer
عَفطَة [ʕafṭa] *n:* عَفطات، عفاط [ʕafṭaːt, ʕfaːṭ] *pl:* • **1.** Bronx cheer, raspberry – جِبتَه بعَفطَة [ǰibtah bʕafṭa] I gave him the raspberry. اِستَقبلُوه بعفاط [ʔistaqbiluːh bʕifaːṭ] They received him with Bronx cheers.
معَفُّط [mʕaffuṭ] *adj:* • **1.** giving a raspberry
عُفطِي [ʕufṭi] *adj:* • **1.** impertinent, jerk, asshole • **2.** playboy

ع ف ف

عَفّ [ʕaff] *v:* • **1.** to stop, quit, give up, abstain, refrain – ما عَفّ مِن البُوق إِلَى أَن الحُكُومَة فُصلَتَه [maː ʕaff min ʔilbuːg ʔila ʔan ʔilħukuːma fuṣlatah] He didn't quit stealing till the government fired him. مِن صار عُمرَه أَربَعِين سَنَة راح لِلحِجّ وَعَفّ عَن كُلّشِي [min ṣaːr ʕumrah ʔarbaʕiːn sana raːħ lilħiǰǰ wʕaff ʕan kullši] When he turned forty he went on the pilgrimage and gave up everything. • **2.** with عَن to leave alone, let alone
عِفَّة [ʕiffa] *n:* • **1.** virtuousness, virtue, decency • **2.** integrity, honesty, uprightness, probity • **3.** chastity, purity
عَفاف [ʕafaːf] *n:* • **1.** virtuousness, virtue, decency
عَفِيف [ʕafiːf] *adj:* • **1.** virtuous, decent, pure – مَرَة عَفِيفَة [mara ʕafiːfa] a virtuous woman. • **2.** honest, upright, righteous – مُوَظَّف عَفِيف [muwað̣ð̣af ʕafiːf] an honest official.
متعَفِّف [mitʕaffif] *adj:* • **1.** modest, virtuous, honest

ع ف ك

عِفَك [ʕifač] *n:* • **1.** 'Afaq, a city in Diwaniya Province

عِفكاوِي [ʕifča:wi] *adj:* • **1.** from 'Afaq, a native of 'Afaq • **2.** crooked, bent, twisted – عَصا عِفكاوِيَّة [ʕaṣa: ʕifča:wiyya] a crooked stick.

ع ف ن

عَفَّن [ʕaffan] *v:* • **1.** to rot, decay, putrefy, spoil – لِبّ الجُوز عَفَّن [libb ʔiǰǰu:z ʕaffan] The nut meats rotted. • **2.** to be or become moldy, mildewed – الخُبُز عَفَّن وذَبَّيناه [ʔilxubuz ʕaffan wðabbayna:h] The bread molded and we threw it out.
عَفَن [ʕafan] *n:* • **1.** rottenness, decay, spoiledness
عُفُونَة [ʕufu:na] *n:* • **1.** rottenness, decay, putridity, spoiledness • **2.** mildew, mold
عَفِن [ʕafin] *adj:* • **1.** rotten, decayed, spoiled, moldy, mildewed, musty – لوز عَفِن [lu:z ʕafin] a spoiled almond. بَيت عَفِن [bayt ʕafin] a musty house.
معَفِّن [mʕaffin] *adj:* • **1.** spoiled, decayed, rotten, putrid, musty, moldy, mildewed – لَحَم معَفِّن [laḥam mʕaffin] spoiled meat. جِثَّة معَفّنَة [ǰiθθa mʕaffna] a rotted corpse. مَرَة معَفّنَة [mara mʕaffna] a dirty woman, a smelly woman.
متعَفِّن [mitʕaffin] *adj:* • **1.** spoiled, decayed, rotten, putrid, musty, moldy, mildewed

ع ف و

عِفَى [ʕifa:] *v:* • **1.** to forgive, pardon – إعفِينِي هَالمَرَّة. بَعَد ما أسَوِّي [ʔiʕfi:ni halmarra. baʕad ma: ʔasawwi:] Forgive me this time. I won't do it again. بَعَد ما إعترِفوا، عِفَى عَنهُم [baʕad ma: ʔiʕtirfaw, ʕifa: ʕanhum] After they confessed, he pardoned them. رُفَق بِيه الحاكِم وَعِفَى عَنَّه [rufaq bi:h ʔilḥa:kim wʕifa: ʕannah] The judge took pity on him and let him off. • **2.** to excuse, exempt, free, relieve – عِفوه مِن العَسكَرِيَّة لِأنّ بِيه سِلّ [ʕifu:h min ʔilʕaskariyya liʔann bi:h sill] They exempted him from military service because he had tuberculosis. أرجُوك تِعفِينِي. ما أقدَر أجِي [ʔarǰu:k tiʕfi:ni. ma: ʔagdar ʔaǰi] Please excuse me. I can't come. المُدَرِّس عِفاه مِن الإمتِحان [ʔilmudarris ʕifa:h min ʔilimtiḥa:n] The teacher excused him from the examination.
عافَى [ʕa:fa:] *v:* • **1.** to grant or insure health – الله يعافِيك [ʔallah yʕa:fi:k] May God grant you good health (to a sick man or someone who has just eaten or drunk).
تعافَى [tʕa:fa:] *v:* • **1.** to recuperate, recover, regain health – مِن إن شاء الله، تِتعافَى ندزّك لِلُبنان [min ʔinša:llah, titʕa:fa: ndizzak lilubna:n] When, God willing, you regain your health, we'll send you to Lebanon.
عَفو [ʕafw] *n:* • **1.** pardon, forgiveness • **2.** amnesty – عَفو عامّ [ʕafw ʕa:mm] a general amnesty. • **3.** العَفو excuse me, pardon me • **4.** العَفو : don't mention it, it's nothing (an answer to أشكُرَك)
عَفيَة [ʕafya] *n:* • **1.** bravo! good! – عَفيَة عَلِيك! شلُون دَبَّرتها؟ [ʕafya ʕali:k! šlu:n dabbartha?] Bravo for you! How did you manage to do it?
عافيَة [ʕa:fya] *n:* عافيات، عَوافِي [ʕa:fya:t, ʕawa:fi] *pl:* • **1.** health, good health – ألف عافيَة [ʔalf ʕa:fya] many thanks. ألف عافيَة، لَكِن ما أقدَر أكُل بَعَد [ʔalf ʕa:fya, la:kin ma: ʔagdar ʔa:kul baʕad] Many thanks, but I can't eat any more. هَالكَيكة سَوَّيتها إلَك. ألف عافيَة [halkayka sawwi:tha ʔilak. ʔalf ʕa:fya] I made this cake for you. Eat it in health. هَذا قاطَك الجِّدِيد؟ إلبِسَه بِالعافيَة [ha:ða qa:ṭak ʔiǰǰidi:d? ʔilibsah bilʕa:fya] Is this your new suit? Wear it in health. قاطَك لَطِيف. تقَطِّعَه بِالعافيَة [qa:ṭak laṭi:f. tgaṭṭiʕah bilʕa:fya] Your suit is nice. Wear it out in good health. بِالعافيَة، آنِي شَبعان. إنتُو أكلُوا [bilʕa:fya, ʔa:ni šabʕa:n. ʔintu ʔuklu:] Thank you, I'm full. But you go ahead and eat.
عَفوِيَّة [ʕafawiyya] *n:* • **1.** spontaneity • **2.** with بِ automatically, involuntarily
إعفاء [ʔiʕfa:ʔ] *n:* • **1.** exemption, excuse, dispensation, discharge, dismissal
مَعفِي [maʕfi] *adj:* • **1.** exempt – بِضاعَة مَعفِيَّة مِن الرُّسُوم الجُّمرُكِيَّة [biḏa:ʕa maʕfiyya min ʔirrusu:m ʔilgumrugiyya] goods exempt from customs duties. مَعفِي مِن الخِدمَة العَسكَرِيَّة [maʕfi min ʔilxidma ʔilʕaskariyya] exempt from military service.
عَفوِي [ʕafawi] *adj:* • **1.** spontaneous, without design or interference from others • **2.** بصُورَة عَفوِيَّة accidently, unintentionally
عَفواً [ʕafwan] *adverbial:* • **1.** excuse me, pardon me • **2.** don't mention it, it's nothing (an answer to thank you)

ع ق ب

عِقَب [ʕiqab] *v:* • **1.** to follow, succeed – عِقبَوا وَزِير المَعارِف السّابِق وَزِيرَين قَدِيرَين [ʕiqbaw wazi:r ʔilmaʕa:rif ʔissa:biq wazi:rayn qadi:rayn] Two capable ministers succeeded the former minister of education.
عِقَب [ʕigab] *v:* • **1.** to pass – عِقَبتُوه لِلمَطعَم. صار وَراكُم [ʕigabtu:h lilmaṭʕam. ṣa:r wara:kum] You passed the restaurant. It's behind you now.
عَقَّب [ʕaqqab] *v:* • **1.** to follow, follow up, comment – عَقَّب عَلَى خِطاب الوَزِير بِتَعلِيق لَطِيف [ʕaqqab ʕala xiṭa:b ʔilwazi:r btaʕli:q laṭi:f] He followed up the minister's speech with a nice comment. عَقَّب عالمَقال الافتِتاحِي بمَقال شَدِيد [ʕaqqab ʕalmaqa:l ʔilʔiftita:ḥi bmaqa:l šadi:d] He commented on the editorial in a critical article. • **2.** to follow, pursue, trail – الشُّرطَة تعَقّبَوا القاتِل وما قِدرَوا يلِزمُوه [ʔiššurṭa tʕaqqibaw ʔilka:til wma gidraw yilizmu:h] The police followed the killer but they weren't able to catch him. لازِم تعَقِّب مُعامَلَة الباسبَورت بِنَفسَك [la:zim tʕaqqib muʕa:malat ʔilpa:spu:rt bnafsak] You must follow through the processing of the passport yourself.
عَقَّب [ʕaggab] *v:* • **1.** to save, leave – دَتعَقُّب شِي مِن راتبَك وَإلّا لا؟ [datʕaggub ši min ra:tbak waʔilla la:?] Are you saving anything out of your

ع

salary or not? أُكُل وَعَقُّبلي شوَيَّة [ʔukul waʕaggubli šwayya] Eat and save a little for me.
عاقَب [ʕaːqab] *v:* • **1.** to punish – المُعَلِّم عاقَبَه لِأَنّ ما كِتَب دَرسَه [ʔilmuʕallim ʕaːqabah liʔann maː kitab darsah] The teacher punished him because he didn't write his lesson.
تعَقَّب [tʕaggab] *v:* • **1.** to stay, remain – تعَقَّب لِأَنّ كان عِندَه شُغُل [tʕaggab liʔann čaːn ʕindah šuɣul] He remained behind because he's got work to do. تعَقَّب بِالبَيت [tʕaggab bilbayt] He stayed at home. • **2.** to be left over, be saved – راتبِي قَلِيل. ما يِتعَقَّب مِنَّه شِي [raːtbi qaliːl. maː yitʕaggab minnah ši] My salary's small. None of it is (ever) left over. الأَكِل طَيِّب. ما يِتعَقَّب مِنَّه شِي [ʔilʔakil ṭayyib. maː yitʕaggab minnah ši] The food's good. There's not going to be any of it left over.
تعاقَب [tʕaːqab] *v:* • **1.** to be punished – تعاقَبِت عَلَى فَدّ شِي آنِي ما مسَوِّيه أَبَداً [tʕaːqabit ʕala fadd ši ʔaːni maː msawwiːh ʔabadan] I was punished for something I never did.
تعاقَب [tʕaːgab] *v:* • **1.** to pass one another, miss each other – تعاقَبنَا بِالطَّرِيق وَما شِفتَه [tʕaːgabna biṭṭariːq wma šiftah] We passed each other on the way and I didn't see him.
عُقُب [ʕugub] *n:* • **1.** after – عُقُب الغَدا [ʕugub ʔilɣada] after lunch. عُقُب المَغرِب [ʕugub ʔilmaɣrib] after sundown. عُقُب كُلّ اللِّي سَوَّيتلَك إيّاه، شلُون تِحكِي عَلَيّا؟ [ʕugub kull ʔilli sawwiːtlak ʔiyyaːh, šluːn tiħči ʕalayya?] After all that I've done for you, how can you talk against me? عُقُب باكِر [ʕugub baːčir] the day after tomorrow. أَشُوفَك عُقُب باكِر [ʔašuːfak ʕugub baːčir] I'll see you day after tomorrow.
عَقُب [ʕagub] *n:* • **1.** passing (by s.o)
عَقِيب [ʕaqiːb] *n:* • **1.** one who, or that which succeeds or is subsequent • **2.** following, subsequent
عَقَبَة [ʕaqaba] *n:* عَقَبات [ʕaqabaːt] *pl:* • **1.** obstacle, difficulty
عُقبَة [ʕugba] *n:* • **1.** the day after tomorrow
عقاب [ʕgaːb] *n:* عُقبان [ʕugbaːn] *pl:* • **1.** eagle
تَعَقُّب [taʕaqqub] *n:* • **1.** pursuit, chase, investigation
عُقُوبَة [ʕuquːba] *n:* عُقُوبات [ʕuquːbaːt] *pl:* • **1.** punishment, penalty – عُقُوبات اِقتِصادِيَّة [ʕuquːbaːt ʔiqtiṣaːdiyya] economic sanctions. قانُون العُقُوبات [qaːnuːn ʔilʕuquːbaːt] penal code.
تَعقِيب [taʕqiːb] *n:* • **1.** comment, criticism • **2.** following, pursuit, following up • **3.** appeal (of a sentence, jur.)
عاقِبَة [ʕaːqiba] *n:* عَواقِب [ʕawaːqib] *pl:* • **1.** result, consequence, end, outcome, upshot, issue, effect.
العَقَبَة [ʔilʕaqaba] *n:* • **1.** Aqaba (city in Jordan)
مُعَقِّب [muʕaqqib] *n:* • **1.** an expediter, who for a fee, pushes an application or the like through the bureaucracy
متِعاقِب [mitʕaːqib] *adj:* • **1.** punished
عُقُب ما [ʕugub ma:] *subordinating conjunction:* • **1.** (conj.) after – عُقُب ما خَلَص أَكِل، تِركنا [ʕugub maː xallaṣ ʔakil, tirakna] After he finished eating, he left us.

ع ق ج

عِقَج [ʕiqač] *v:* • **1.** to wrinkle, crease – عِقَجِت السِّترَة مِن قَعدتَك [ʕiqačit ʔissitra min gaʕdtak] You've wrinkled your suit sitting down. وَخِّر إيدَك. عِقَجِت ياخَة القَمِيص [waxxir ʔiːdak. ʕiqačit yaːxat ʔilqamiːṣ] Move your hand. You've wrinkled the shirt collar. • **2.** to hurt, upset, crush – صَدِيقِي عِقَجنِي هوايَة مِن ما دايَنِّي فلُوس [ṣadiːqi ʕiqačni hwaːya min maː daːyanni fluːs] My friend crushed me when he wouldn't lend me any money. عِقَجِت لَك إيّاه عَقجَة زِينَة [ʕiqačit lak ʔiyyaːh ʕaqča ziːna] I cut him down to size.
عَقَّج [ʕaqqač] *v:* • **1.** to wrinkle – مِنُو قِعَد عَالسِّترَة مالتِي وَعَقَّجها؟ [minu giʕad ʔassitra maːlti wʕaqqačha?] Who sat on my coat and wrinkled it?
تعَقَّج [tʕaqqač] *v:* • **1.** to be wrinkled, to wrinkle – هالبَنطَرُون ما يِتعَقَّج بسهُولَة [halpanṭaruːn maː yitʕaqqač bsuhuːla] These pants don't wrinkle easily.
اِنعِقَج [ʔinʕiqač] *v:* • **1.** to be hurt, upset – اِنعِقَجِت مِن عاط عَلَيّا [ʔinʕiqačit min ʕaːṭ ʕalayya] I was hurt when he shouted at me.
عَقِج [ʕaqič] *n:* • **1.** wrinkle, crease
عُقجَة [ʕuqča] *n:* عُقَج [ʕuqač] *pl:* • **1.** heel (of a shoe) • **2.** a wrinkle, a crease
معَقَّج [mʕaqqač] *adj:* • **1.** wrinkled, crumpled – قاط معَقَّج [qaːṭ mʕaqqač] a wrinkled suit. وَرَق معَقَّج [waraq mʕaqqač] crumpled paper.
مَعقُوج [maʕquːč] *adj:* • **1.** dejected

ع ق د

عِقَد [ʕiqad] *v:* • **1.** to hold – رَئِيس الحِزب عِقَد جَلسَة سِرِّيَّة لِلَّجنَة المَركَزِيَّة [raʔiːs ʔilħizib ʕiqad ǰalsa sirriyya lillaǰna ʔilmarkaziyya] The party chief held a secret session of the central committee. عِقدَوا اِجتِماعهُم بِبَغداد [ʕiqdaw ʔiǰtimaːʕhum bibaɣdaːd] They held their meeting in Baghdad. عِقدَت الحُكُومَة اِتِّفاقات تِجارِيَّة وِيّا عِدَّة دُوَل [ʕiqdat ʔilħukuːma ʔittifaːqaːt tiǰaːriyya wiyya ʕiddat duwal] The government concluded trade agreements with several countries. راح يِجِي القاضِي ساعَة خَمسَة يِعقِد العَقِد [raːħ yiǰi ʔilqaːḍi saːʕa xamsa yiʕqid ʔilʕaqid] The judge is coming at five to formalize the contract. شوَقِت راح يِعقِد عَلِيها؟ [šwakit raːħ yiʕqid ʕaliːha?] When is he going to sign the marriage contract with her?
عِقَد [ʕigad] *v:* • **1.** to knot, tie – أُعقُد الخيط عُقدتَين [ʔuʕgud ʔilxiːṭ ʕugidtayn] Tie two knots in the string. عِقَد الحَبلَين واحِد بِاللّاخ [ʕigad ʔilħablayn waːħid billaːx] He tied the two ropes together.
عَقَّد [ʕaqqad] *v:* • **1.** to complicate, make difficult – لِيش تعَقِّد المُشكِلَة؟ [liːš tʕaqqid ʔilmuškila?] Why

complicate the problem? إِنتَ دَتعَقِّد الأشياء [ʔinta datʕaqqid ʔilʔašyaːʔ] You're complicating things.
عَقَّد [ʕaggad] *v:* • **1.** to knot, tangle – الجّاهِل لِعَب بِالكُبّابَة وَعَقَّد الخيط [ʔijjaːhil liʕab bilkubbaːba wʕaggad ʔilxiːṭ] The baby played with the ball and tangled the yarn. • **2.** to be or become lumpy, to coagulate – العَجين يِعَقِّد إذا ما تعِجنَه زين [ʔilʕajiːn yiʕaggid ʔiða maː tʕijnah ziːn] The dough 'll get lumpy if you don't knead it well. ضِيف مَيّ شوَيَّة شوَيَّة حَتَّى ما يعَقِّد اللِّبَن مِن تُمُردَه [ðiːf mayy šwayya šwayya ħatta maː yʕaggid ʔilliban min tumurdah] Add water gradually so the yoghurt won't get lumpy when you blend it. البنَيَّة ديُوسها تعَقِّد بِالثِّلطَعش، وَبَعدين تِكبَر [ʔilbnayya dyuːsha tʕaggid bittilaṭaʕš, wbaʕdiːn tikbar] The girl's breasts get hard at thirteen, and then enlarge.
تعَقَّد [tʕaqqad] *v:* • **1.** to be or become complicated – الأُمُور تعَقِّدَت [ʔilʔumuːr tʕaqqidat] Affairs became complicated.
تعَقَّد [tʕaggad] *v:* • **1.** to be or become tangled, knotted – أُخُذ الخيط مِن الوَلَد قَبُل ما يِتعَقَّد [ʔuxuð ʔilxiːṭ min ʔilwalad gabul maː yitʕaggad] Take the string away from the boy before it gets tangled.
تعاقَد [tʕaːqad] *v:* • **1.** to contract, make a contract – الحُكُومَة تعاقدَت ويّا شَركَة أجنَبِيَّة لِبِناء الجِّسِر [ʔilħukuːma tʕaːqdat wiyya šarika ʔajnabiyya lbinaːʔ ʔijjisir] The government contracted with a foreign company for building the bridge. • **2.** to agree, reach an agreement – البَلَدَين تعاقدَوا عَلَى رَفع الحَواجِز الجُّمرُكِيَّة [ʔilbaladayn tʕaːqdaw ʕala rafʕ ʔilħawaːjiz ʔilgumrugiyya] The two countries agreed on lifting the customs barriers.
اِنعقَد [ʔinʕiqad] *v:* • **1.** to be held – المؤتَمَر راح يِنعِقِد بِالإسبُوع القادِم [ʔilmuʔtamar raːħ yinʕiqad bilʔisbuːʕ ʔilqaːdim] The conference will be held next week.
اِنعقَد [ʔinʕigad] *v:* • **1.** to be or become knotted, tied – الخَيط اِنعِقَد؛ ما دَينفَكّ [ʔilxiːṭ ʔinʕigad; maː dayinfakk] The string has gotten knotted; it won't untie.
اِعتقَد [ʔiʕtiqad] *v:* • **1.** to believe – يِعتقِد بيه كُلِّش [yiʕtiqid biːh kulliš] He believes in him completely. أعتقِد هُوَّ ما راح يِجي اليُوم [ʔaʕtiqid huwwa maː raːħ yiji ʔilyuːm] I think he's not going to come today.
عَقِد [ʕaqid] *n:* عُقُود [ʕuquːd] *pl:* • **1.** contract – عَقد القِران [ʕaqd ʔilqiraːn] marriage contract, marriage. • **2.** holding
عَقِد [ʕagid] *n:* عقُود [ʕguːd] *pl:* • **1.** alley, narrow street, side street • **2.** knot
عُقدَة [ʕuqda] *n:* عُقَد [ʕuqad] *pl:* • **1.** quirk, complex, problem, entanglement (of a plot) – عُقَد نَفسِيَّة [ʕuqad nafsiyya] personality problems. • **2.** knot (also, nautical mile)
عَقِيد [ʕaqiːd] *n:* عُقَداء [ʕuqadaːʔ] *pl:* • **1.** colonel (mil.)
عُقدَة [ʕugda] *n:* عُقَد [ʕugad] *pl:* • **1.** knot • **2.** knot, lump, swelling, outgrowth • **3.** small bundle
عَقِيدَة [ʕaqiːda] *n:* عَقائِد [ʕaqaːʔid, ʕaqaːyid] *pl:* • **1.** (article of) faith, creed, belief, tenet, doctrine • **2.** creed, faith, belief • **3.** superstition – بعَقِيدتِي [bʕaqiːdti] according to my belief.
تَعقِيد [taʕqiːd] *n:* تَعقِيدات [taʕqiːdaːt] *pl:* • **1.** complication
تَعاقُد [taʕaːqud] *n:* • **1.** contract, agreement, treaty, contactual obligation
اِنعِقاد [ʔinʕiqaːd] *n:* • **1.** holding, meeting, convening – اِنعِقاد الجّلسَة [ʔinʕiqaːd ʔijjalsa] holding the session.
اِعتِقاد [ʔiʕtiqaːd] *n:* اِعتِقادات [ʔiʕtiqaːdaːt] *pl:* • **1.** belief, faith, trust, confidence, conviction • **2.** tenet, principle of faith
مُعَقَّد [muʕaqqad] *adj:* • **1.** complicated, involved, entangled, intricate, difficult – مَوضُوع مُعَقَّد [mawḍuːʕ muʕaqqad] a complicated subject. شَخص مُعَقَّد [šaxiṣ muʕaqqad] a mixed-up person.
معَقَّد [mʕaggad] *adj:* • **1.** knotted (for thread or wood)
مِتعاقِد [mitʕaːqid] *adj:* • **1.** under contract, contractual
أعقَد [ʔaʕqad] *comparative adjective:* • **1.** more or most complicated, difficult

ع ق ر

عِقَر [ʕigar] *v:* • **1.** to kick (on the leg) – عِقَرنِي مِن كِنّا دَنلِعَب طُوبَة، وَهَسَّة رجلِي تُوجَعني [ʕigarni min činna danilʕab ṭuːba, whassa rijli tuːjaʕni] He kicked me while we were playing ball, and now my leg hurts me.
اِنعِقَر [ʔinʕigar] *v:* • **1.** to be kicked (on the leg) – ما أقدَر ألعَب باكِر لِأنّ اِنعِقَرت بِالسِّباق اليُوم [maː ʔagdar ʔalʕab baːčir liʔann ʔinʕigarit bissibaːq ʔilyuːm] I can't play tomorrow, because I got kicked in the game today.
عِقِر [ʕagir] *n:* • **1.** kicking (on the leg)
عِقار [ʕiqaːr] *n:* عِقارات [ʕiqaːraːt] *pl:* • **1.** real estate, real property
عَقرَة [ʕagra] *n:* عَقرات [ʕagraːt] *pl:* • **1.** kick (on the leg)
عاقِر، عاقرَة [ʕaːqir, ʕaːqira, ʕaːgir, ʕaːgra] *adj:* • **1.** sterile, barren (women only) – مَرَة عاقِر [mara ʕaːqir] a sterile woman.
عِقارِي، البَنك العِقارِي [ʕiqaːri, ʔilbang ʔilʕiqaːri] *adj:* • **1.** real estate bank, a government supported bank which makes building loans

ع ق ر ب

عَقرَب [ʕagrab] *n:* عَقارُب [ʕagaːrub] *pl:* • **1.** scorpion • **2.** hand (on a clock or watch) – عَقرَب السّاعَة [ʕagrab ʔissaːʕa] the hour hand. عَقرَب الدَّقايِق [ʕagrab ʔiddaqaːyiq] the minute hand.

ع ق ر ق

عُقرُق [ʕugrug] *n:* • **1.** (coll.) frog(s)
عُقرُقَة [ʕugrugga] *n:* عُقرُقات [ʕugrugaːt] *pl:* • **1.** frog

ع

ع ق ع ق

عقعق [ʕagʕag] *n:* عَقاعِق [ʕaga:ʕig] *pl:* • **1.** magpie

ع ق ل

تعيقل [tʕi:qal] *v:* • **1.** to be self-important, to give oneself airs, to be fussy – ماكو حاجَة تِتعَيقَل؛ إذا يِعجبَك ترُوح لِلسِّينَما، يَالله قُوم [ma:ku ħa:ǰa titʕayqal; ʔiða yiʕiǰbak tru:ħ lissinama, yallah gu:m] There's no need to be a prima donna; if you'd like to go to the movies, come on. صَدِيقَك يِتعيقَل هوايَة وشايِف نَفسَه [ṣadi:qak yitʕayqal hwa:ya wša:yif nafsah] Your friend behaves very haughtily and is conceited. كُلَّما أَطلُب مِنَّه شِي، يقُوم يِتعيقَل بِراسِي [kullma: ʔaṭlub minnah ši, ygu:m yitʕi:qal bra:si] Whenever I ask him for something, he gives me a hard time. • **1.** to be a smart alec, braggart

عِقَل [ʕiqal, ʕigal] *v:* • **1.** to be sensible, to come to one's senses, get some sense – إعقَل وَإسمَع كَلام أَبُوك [ʔiʕqal wʔismaʕ kala:m ʔabu:k] Be sensible and listen to what your father says. إبنَه عِقَل وَقام ما يدَوُّر مكَسِّرات [ʔibnah ʕiqal wga:m ma: ydawwur mkassira:t] His son came to his senses and stopped dissipating. • **2.** to accept, credit, believe – هِيكِي شِي ما يِعقلَه أَسخَف شَخِص [hi:či ši ma: yiʕqalah ʔasxaf šaxiṣ] The stupidest person wouldn't believe such a thing. • **3.** to behave well, to act politely

عَقَّل [ʕaqqal] *v:* • **1.** to bring someone to his senses – يِظهَر المَدرَسَة عَقَّلَته [yiðhar ʔilmadrasa ʕaqqilatah] It appears that the school has brought him to his senses.

عَقَّل [ʕaggal] *v:* • **1.** to put a head-band (and head-cloth) on someone – أَبُوه عَقَّلَه وَوَدّاه لِلسُّوق [ʔabu:h ʕaggalah wawadda:h lissu:g] His father put a headband and headcloth on him and took him to the market.

تعَقَّل [tʕaggal] *v:* • **1.** to put on one's head-band – تعَقَّل وَلِبَس عَباتَه وَطِلَع [tʕaggal wlibas ʕaba:tah wṭilaʕ] He put on an agal and his aba and went out.

إعتِقَل [ʔiʕtiqal] *v:* • **1.** to intern, to imprison (for political reasons) – الحُكُومَة اعتِقلَت رَئِيس الحِزب [ʔilħuku:ma ʔiʕtiqlat raʔi:s ʔilħizib] The government jailed the party boss.

عَقِل [ʕaqil] *n:* • **1.** mind, intellect, intelligence, reason, sense – ما يِتصَوَّرها العَقِل [ma: yitṣawwarha ʔilʕaqil] It's unbelievable. جَمالها يطَيِّر العَقِل [ǰama:lha ytayyir ʔilʕaqil] Her beauty makes one's senses reel. عَلَى قَدّ عَقلَه [ʕala gadd ʕaqlah] according to his nature, in line with what he is. داريه عَلَى قَدّ عَقلَه [da:ri:h ʕala gadd ʕaqlah] Take him for what he is. كُلّ عَقلَه، بِكُلّ عَقلَه [kull ʕaqlah, bkull ʕaqlah] he's fully convinced, he sincerely believes. هِيَّ كُلّ عَقِلها راح يِتزَوَّجها [hiyya kull ʕaqilha ra:ħ yidzawwaǰha] She firmly believes he's going to marry her. إنتَ كُلّ عَقلَك أَقبَل بهيكِي سِعِر؟ [ʔinta kull ʕaqlak ʔaqbal bhi:či siʕir?] Do you really believe I will accept such a price? أَمراض عَقلِيَّة [ʔamra:ð ʕaqliyya] mental disorders.

عُقلَة [ʕuqla] *n:* عُقلات [ʕuqla:t] *pl:* • **1.** horizontal bar, used in gymnastics

عقال [ʕga:l] *n:* عُقُل [ʕugul] *pl:* • **1.** agal, head-band used to hold the كُوفِيَّة headgear in place

عَقلِيَّة [ʕaqliyya] *n:* • **1.** mentality, mental attitude

عَقِيلَة [ʕaqi:la] *n:* عَقِيلات [ʕaqi:la:t] *pl:* • **1.** wife, spouse

مُعتَقَل [muʕtaqal] *n:* مُعتَقَلات [muʕtaqala:t] *pl:* • **1.** concentration camp • **2.** internment camp, detention center (for political prisoners)

عاقُول [ʕa:gu:l] *n:* • **1.** a low spiny shrub found on waste land and in the desert, camel's-thorn

تعَيقُل [tʕayqul] *n:* • **1.** strut, swagger

عَقلِي [ʕaqli] *adj:* • **1.** mental

عاقِل [ʕa:qil] *adj:* • **1.** wise, polite

مَعقُول [maʕqu:l] *adj:* • **1.** reasonable, sensible, rational – جَواب مَعقُول [ǰawa:b maʕqu:l] a reasonable answer. • **2.** plausible, comprehensible, conceivable – مَعقُول يجِي وَما يقُلّي؟ [maʕqu:l yiǰi wama: ygulli?] Is it conceivable he'd come without telling me? عُذُر مُو مَعقُول [ʕuður mu: maʕqu:l] an implausible excuse.

عَقلانَة [ʕaqla:na] *adj:* • **1.** sensible, dignified, serious – مال عَقلانَة [ma:l ʕaqla:na] sensible, dignified, serious. لِبسَه عَقلانَة [libsah ʕaqla:na] He's moderate in his dress. لابِس هِدُوم مال عَقلانَة [la:bis hidu:m ma:l ʕaqla:na] He is wearing tasteful, conservative clothes.

متعَيقِل [mitʕi:qil] *adj:* • **1.** smart aleck, braggart

أَعقَل [ʔaʕqal] *comparative adjective:* • **1.** more or more sensible

ع ق م

عَقَّم [ʕaqqam] *v:* • **1.** to disinfect, sterilize – عَقِّم إيدَك قَبُل ما تجِيس الجَّرح [ʕaqqim ʔi:dak gabul ma: dgi:s ʔiǰǰariħ] Disinfect your hands before you touch the wound. إذا يعَقِّمُون الحَلِيب، يِبقَى مُدَّة طوِيلَة [ʔiða yʕaqqimu:n ʔilħali:b, yibqa: mudda ṭwi:la] If they sterilize the milk, it keeps a long time.

تعَقَّم [tʕaqqam] *v:* • **1.** to be sterilized, disinfected – الأبرَة تعَقَّمَت وَإلّا بَعَد؟ [ʔilʔubra tʕaqqmat waʔilla baʕad?] Is the needle sterilized yet?

عُقُم [ʕuqum] *n:* • **1.** barrenness, sterility

مُعَقِّم [muʕaqqim] *n:* • **1.** disinfectant

تَعقِيم [taʕqi:m] *n:* • **1.** sterilization

عَقِيم [ʕaqi:m] *adj:* • **1.** sterile (of men) – زوجها عَقِيم [zu:ǰha ʕaqi:m] Her husband's sterile. • **2.** useless, futile, ineffectual, ineffective – طُرُق عَقِيمَة [ṭuruq ʕaqi:ma] ineffective methods.

مُعَقَّم [muʕaqqam] *adj:* • **1.** sterilized, disinfected – أُبرَة مَعَقَّمَة [ʔubra mʕaqqama] a sterilized needle. حَلِيب معَقَّم [ħali:b mʕaqqam] sterilized milk (heated to a higher temperature and having better keeping properties than pasteurized milk.)

ع ك ر

عَكَّر [ʕakkar] *v:* • **1.** to make bumpy or rough, to rut – العَرَبايِن عَكِّرَت الشّارِع [ʔilʕaraba:yin ʕakkirat ʔišša:riʕ] The carts have made the road rough.

تعَكَّر [tʕakkar] *v:* • **1.** to be or become rough, bumpy, or rutted – الشّارِع تعَكَّر مِن اللّوريّات [ʔišša:riʕ tʕakkar min ʔillu:riyya:t] The street has gotten rutted from the trucks.

عُكرَة [ʕukra] *n:* عُكرات، عُكَر [ʕukra:t, ʕukar.] *pl:* • **1.** bump, lump, projection • **2.** (pl. عُكَر an irritating or objectionable person, a hard person to deal with, an unpleasant-looking person.

معَكَّر [mʕakkar] *adj:* • **1.** rough, bumpy – شارِع معَكَّر [ša:riʕ mʕakkar] a bumpy road.

ع ك ز

تعَكَّز [tʕakkaz] *v:* • **1.** to lean, support oneself – مِن كِسَر رِجلَه، قام يِتعَكَّز بعِكّازتَين مِن يِمشِي [min kisar rijlah, ga:m yitʕakkaz bʕikka:ztayn min yimši] Since he broke his leg, he's been walking on crutches. هَالأعرَج يِتعَكَّز عَلَى عِكّازَة وِحدَة [halʔaʕraj yitʕakkaz ʕala ʕikka:za wiħda] This lame man uses one crutch. إذا تخاف تُوقَع، تعَكَّز بِيّا [ʔiða txa:f tu:gaʕ, tʕakkaz biyya] If you're afraid of falling, hang onto me. • **2.** to lean, to depend – ماكُو حاجَة تِتعَكَّز بأبُوك. إذا عِندَك شُغُل، رُوح إقضِيه وحدَك [ma:ku ħa:ja titʕakkaz bʔabu:k. ʔiða ʕindak šuɣul, ru:ħ ʔigði:h wħdak] There's no need to depend on your father. If you've got something to do, go attend to it by yourself.

عِكّازَة [ʕikka:za] *n:* عِكّازات [ʕikka:za:t] *pl:* • **1.** crutch • **2.** staff, cane

ع ك س

عِكَس [ʕikas] *v:* • **1.** to reflect – المرايَة تِعكِس الضُّوَة [ʔilmra:ya tiʕkis ʔiððuwa] The mirror reflects light. • **2.** to reverse – مَحكَمَة الاستِئناف عِكسَت القَرار وَبَرَّت المُتَّهَم [maħkamat ʔilisti:na:f ʕiksat ʔilqara:r wbarrat ʔilmuttaham] The Court of Appeals reversed the decision and cleared the accused. • **3.** to block, stop – عِكَس قَضِيَّة تَرفِيعي حَتَّى يرَفِّع أخُوه [ʕikas qaðiyyat tarfi:ʕi ħatta yraffiʕ ʔaxu:h] He blocked my promotion so as to give his brother a raise. مُو كُلّنا نرِيد نرُوح لِلسِّينَما. لا تِعكِسها [mu: kullna nri:d nru:ħ lissinama. la: tiʕkisha] Look, all of us want to go to the movies. Don't screw it up.

عاكَس [ʕa:kas] *v:* • **1.** to oppose, contradict – يعاكِسنِي بكُلّ اِقتِراحاتِي [yʕa:kisni bkull ʔiqtira:ħa:ti] He opposes me on all my suggestions. كُلّشِي اللّي أقُولَه، يعاكسَه [kullši ʔilli ʔagu:lah, yʕa:ksah] He contradicts everything I say. • **2.** to molest, tease, harass – لا تعاكس الجّاهِل. خَلِّيه يِلعَب [la: tʕa:kis ʔijja:hil. xalli:h yilʕab] Don't tease the baby. Let him play. المُوَظَّف الجِّدِيد كُلّهُم يعاكسُوه لأنّ سَخِيف [ʔilmuwaððaf ʔijjidi:d kullhum yʕa:ksu:h liʔann saxi:f] They all harass the new official because he's stupid.

اِنعِكَس [ʔinʕikas] *v:* • **1.** to be reversed, inverted – هَسَّة الأمُور اِنعِكسَت. آنِي المُدِير هَسَّة [hassa ʔilʔumu:r ʔinʕiksat. ʔa:ni ʔilmudi:r hassa] Now the tables are turned. I'm the director now. • **2.** to be blocked, stopped – قَضِيَّة التَّرفِيع اِنعِكسَت [qaðiyyat ʔitttarfi:ʕ ʔinʕiksat] The promotion was blocked. • **3.** to be reflected, be mirrored – صُورتِي اِنعِكسَت بالمَيّ [ṣu:rti ʔinʕiksat bilmayy] My image was reflected in the water.

عكِس [ʕakis] *n:* • **1.** opposite, contrast, contrary, reverse – هُوَّ عَكِس أبُوه [huwwa ʕakis ʔabu:h] He's the opposite of his father. هُوَّ بعَكسَك، كُلِّش ذَكِي [huwwa bʕaksak, kulliš ðaki] He's the opposite of you, very smart. بالعَكِس، سَيّارتِي أغلَى مِن هَالسَّيّارَة [bilʕakis, sayya:rti ʔaɣla min hassayya:ra] On the contrary, my car's more expensive than this one. آنِي، بالعَكِس، أحِبّ أساعدَك [ʔa:ni, bilʕakis, ʔaħibb ʔasa:ʕdak] I, on the contrary, would like to help you. بعَكِس ما تظِنّ، هَذا يحِبَّك [bʕakis ma: tðinn, ha:ða yħibbak] Contrary to what you think, he likes you. سَوَّى عَكِس ما قِتلَه [sawwa: ʕakis ma: gitlah] He did the opposite of what I told him. • **2.** bad luck • **3.** pl. عكُوسَة photograph • **4.** reflection

عكِس [ʕikis] *n:* عكُوس [ʕku:s] *pl:* • **1.** elbow, elbow joint – عِكِس غَنَم [ʕikis ɣanam] lamb shank. • **2.** elbow (plumbing and elec.)

عَكّاسَة [ʕakka:sa] *n:* عَكّاسات [ʕakka:sa:t] *pl:* • **1.** camera

اِنعِكاس [ʔinʕika:s] *n:* • **1.** reflection • **2.** reaction, repercussion

مُعاكَسَة [muʕa:kasa] *n:* • **1.** harassment

عَكسِي [ʕaksi] *adj:* • **1.** inverse – تَناسُب عَكسِي [tana:sub ʕaksi] inverse proportion. يِتناسَب تَناسُب عَكسِي وِيّا العُمُر [yitna:sab tana:sub ʕaksi wiyya ʔilʕumur] It's inversely proportional to age.

عَكّاس [ʕakka:s] *adj:* عَكّاسَة [ʕakka:sa] *pl:* • **1.** photographer

معاكَس، خِشَب معاكَس [mʕa:kas, xišab mʕa:kas] *adj:* • **1.** plywood

مُعاكِس [muʕa:kis] *adj:* • **1.** opposed, adverse, counter-, contra-, anti-

منعِكِس [minʕikis] *adj:* • **1.** reflected, reflex

ع ك ف

عِكَف [ʕikaf] *v:* • **1.** to turn, bend – رُوح قُبَل وَبَعدين أعكُف عاليِمنَة [ru:ħ gubal wbaʕdi:n ʔuʕkuf ʕalyimna] Go straight ahead and then turn to the right. الطَّرِيق يُعكُف عاليِمنَة بَعَد مَسافَة مِيل [ʔiṭṭari:q yuʕkuf ʕalyimna baʕad masa:fat mi:l] The road turns to the right after a mile.

ع

عَكَّف [ʕakkaf] *v:* • **1.** to screw up, twist up – لا تعَكُّف وِجهَك. هَسَّة أسَوِّيلَك إيّاها [la: tʕakkuf wiččak. hassa ʔasawwi:lak ʔiyya:ha] Don't twist up your face. I'll do it for you now.
عَكُف [ʕakuf] *n:* • **1.** bending, turning
عَكفَة [ʕakfa] *n:* عَكفات [ʕakfa:t] *pl:* • **1.** turn bend (in a road)
مُعتَكَف [muʕtakaf] *n:* • **1.** site of worship, place of veneration of God
عاكِف [ʕa:kif] *adj:* • **1.** intent (on), busily engaged, completely focused
مَعكُوف، صَلِيب مَعكُوف [maʕku:f, ṣali:b maʕku:f] *adj:* • **1.** swastika
مِعتِكِف [miʕtikif] *adj:* • **1.** isolated

ع ك م

عَكّام [ʕakka:m] *adj:* عَكّامَة [ʕakka:ma] *pl:* • **1.** man who makes all arrangements and leads groups of pilgrims to Mecca

ع ك ن ش

عَكنَش [ʕaknaš] *v:* • **1.** to wrinkle
تعَكنَش [tʕaknaš] *v:* • **1.** to wrinkle
تِعكنِش [tʕikniš] *n:* • **1.** making a wrinkle

ع ل ب

عَلَّب [ʕallab] *v:* • **1.** to can, tin – هَالمَعمَل يعَلِّب مِشمِش وخَوخ بَسّ [halmaʕmal yʕallib mišmiš wxawx bass] This factory cans apricots and peaches only.
عِلبَة [ʕilba] *n:* عِلَب [ʕilab] *pl:* • **1.** wooden container, flat and round, used mostly for storing yogurt – لِبَن عِلبَة [liban ʕilba] a type of yoghurt, made and stored in a tin or wooden container. • **2.** can, tin
تَعلِيب [taʕli:b] *n:* • **1.** canning – مَعمَل تَعلِيب [maʕmal taʕli:b] canning factory.
عِلبَة، عِلباة [ʕilba, ʕilba:t] *n:* • **1.** (no pl.) nape, scruff of the neck – ضِرَبتَه عِجِل عَلَى عِلباتَه [ðirabtah ʕijil ʕala ʕilba:tah] I hit him a whack on the back of his neck. • **2.** jowl, side of the jaw
مُعَلَّب [muʕallab] *adj:* • **1.** canned, packaged – جِبِن مُعَلَّب [jibin muʕallab] packaged cheese. فَواكِه مُعَلَّبَة [fawa:kih muʕallaba] canned fruit. مُعَلَّبات [muʕallaba:t] canned goods.

ع ل ج [1]

عالَج [ʕa:laǰ] *v:* • **1.** to treat (a patient, a disease, or a subject) – عالَجَه الطَّبِيب مُدَّة إسبُوعَين [ʕa:lajah ʔiṭṭabi:b muddat ʔisbu:ʕayn] The doctor treated him for two weeks. يعالِج النَّشلَة بِالوِيسكِي [yʕa:liǰ ʔinnašla bilwiski] He treats a cold with whisky. لازِم تعالِج المَوضُوع بِفَدّ صُورَة مَعقُولَة [la:zim tʕa:liǰ ʔilmawðu:ʕ bfadd ṣu:ra maʕqu:la] You should treat the subject in a reasonable manner. • **2.** to undergo death throes, to be in the last agony – ما مات. بَعدَه دَيعالِج [ma: ma:t. baʕdah dayʕa:liǰ] He didn't die. He's still in his last agony.
تعالَج [tʕa:laǰ] *v:* • **1.** to be treated, cured, healed
عِلاج [ʕila:ǰ] *n:* عِلاجات [ʕila:ǰa:t] *pl:* • **1.** treatment • **2.** cure
مُعالِج [muʕa:liǰ] *n:* مُعالِجين [muʕa:liǰi:n] *pl:* • **1.** therapist, (male)nurse, processor
مُعالَجَة [muʕa:laǰa] *n:* مُعالَجات [muʕa:laǰa:t] *pl:* • **1.** treatment (of patient also of a subject), nursing (of a patient)

ع ل ج [2]

عَلِيجَة [ʕali:ǰa] *n:* • **1.** feed-bag

ع ل س

عِلَس [ʕilas] *v:* • **1.** to chew – إعلِس الخُبزَة زين قَبُل ما تبِلَعها [ʔiʕlis ʔilxubza zi:n gabul ma: tiblaʕha] Chew the bread well before you swallow it. الجّاهِل دَيعلِس بثُوبَه [ʔijǰa:hil dayiʕlis bθu:bah] The kid is chewing on his shirt. • **2.** to pigeonhole, postpone action indefinitely – أشُو صاحبَك عِلَسها لِلقَضِيَّة [ʔašu ṣa:ħbak ʕilasha lilqaðiyya] It seems your friend has decided to forget about the matter.
اِنعِلَس [ʔinʕilas] *v:* • **1.** to be killed, to be ignored, to be kidnapped, to be chewed
عَلِس [ʕalis] *n:* • **1.** postponing an action, chewing
مَعلُوس [maʕlu:s] *adj:* • **1.** kidnapped, killed, finished done • **2.** chewed (food)

ع ل ف

عِلَف [ʕilaf] *v:* • **1.** to feed – إعلِف الخَيل قَبُل ما تطَلِّعها [ʔiʕlif ʔilxayl gabul ma: ṭṭalliʕha] Feed the horses before you take them out.
عَلَف [ʕalaf] *n:* • **1.** feed, fodder, forage, provender
عَلِف [ʕalif] *n:* • **1.** feeding
مَعلَف [maʕlaf] *n:* مَعالِف [mʕa:lif] *pl:* • **1.** manger, feeding trough, feeding place, feeding area – يحَضِّر المَعلَف قَبِل الحِصان [yħaððir ʔilmaʕlaf gabil ʔilħiṣa:n] He puts the cart before the horse. (lit., he prepares the manger before he has a horse).

ع ل ق

عِلَق [ʕilag] *v:* • **1.** to stick – الفِكرَة عِلقَت بذِهنِي [ʔilfikra ʕilqat bðihni] The idea stuck in my mind.
عِلَق [ʕilag] *v:* • **1.** to light, ignite, set on fire – هاك الشِّخّاطَة وَإعلِق الحَطَب [ha:k ʔiššixxa:ṭa waʔiʕlig ʔilħaṭab] Take the matches and light the firewood. تجادلُوا شوَيَّة وَبَعدين عِلقَت بَيناتهُم [dǰa:dlaw šwaya wbaʕdi:n ʕilgat bayna:thum] They argued a little and then really got mad at each other.
عَلَّق [ʕallaq] *v:* • **1.** to comment, make comments – مَحَّد عَلَّق عالخِطاب مالَه [maħħad ʕallaq ʕalxiṭa:b ma:lah] Nobody made any comment on his speech.

عَلَّق [ʕallag] *v:* • **1.** to hang, suspend, attach, fasten – عَلَّق سِترتَه بالبِسمار [ʕallag sitirtah bilbismaːr] He hung his coat on the nail. عَلَّق صُورتَه يَمّ صُورَة أبُوه [ʕallag ṣuːrtah yamm ṣuːrat ʔabuːh] He hung his picture next to his father's picture. إذا تُقتِلها، يعَلّقُوك [ʔiða tuktilha, yʕallguːk] If you kill her, they'll hang you. • **2.** to flee, escape, run away – أخَذ الفلُوس وعَلَّق [ʔaxað ʔilfluːs wʕallag] He took the money and beat it.
تعَلَّق [tʕallaq] *v:* • **1.** to be attached, devoted, fond – هُوَّ مِتعَلِّق بأُمَّه هوايَة [huwwa mitʕallaq bʔummah hwaːya] He's very attached to his mother. • **2.** to depend, be dependent – دُخُولي الجّامعَة مِتعَلِّق عالقَبُول [duxuːli ʔijjaːmiʕa mitʕalliq ʕalqabuːl] My entrance into college depends on acceptance. قَضِيتِي مِتعَلِّقَة قَضِيّتَك [qaðiyyti mitʕalliqa bqaðiyytak] My case is dependent on your case.
انعِلَق [ʔinʕilag] *v:* • **1.** to be lighted
اعتِلَق [ʔiʕtilag] *v:* • **1.** to be lit, to catch fire
عَلَق [ʕalag] *n:* • **1.** (coll.) larva(e) of mosquito
عَلِق [ʕalig] *n:* • **1.** lighting, sticking, setting on fire, igniting
عَلقَة [ʕalga] *n:* عَلقات [ʕalgaːt] *pl:* • **1.** larva(e) of mosquito • **2.** fight
عِلقَة [ʕilga] *n:* عِلقات [ʕilgaːt] *pl:* • **1.** tinder, kindling
تَعَلُّق [taʕalluq] *n:* • **1.** attachment, relationship, devotion
عِلاقَة [ʕilaːqa] *n:* عِلاقات [ʕilaːqaːt] *pl:* • **1.** relationship, association • **2.** connection, relevance
تَعليق [taʕliːq] *n:* • **1.** remark(s), comment, commentary
عِلّاقَة [ʕillaːga] *n:* عِلّاقات، علاليق [ʕillaːgaːt, ʕilaːliːg] *pl:* • **1.** basket • **2.** coat hanger
مِعلاق [miʕlaːg] *n:* معاليق [mʕaːliːg] *pl:* • **1.** liver (as food) • **2.** liver, heart, lungs and windpipe
تِعلاقَة [tiʕlaːga] *n:* تِعلاقات [tiʕlaːgaːt] *pl:* • **1.** coat hanger, hanger
مُعَلِّق [muʕalliq] *n:* • **1.** commentator (radio and press)
مُعَلَّق [muʕallaq] *adj:* • **1.** suspended, hanging – جِسِر مُعَلَّق [jisir muʕallaq] suspension bridge. • **2.** pending, in abeyance, undecided – قَضِيتَه مُعَلَّقَة [qaðiːtah muʕallaqa] His case is pending.
عالِق [ʕaːlig] *adj:* • **1.** stuck, attached (to), devoted (to)
مِتعَلِّق [mitʕallig] *adj:* مِتعَلقات [mitʕalgaːt] *pl:* • **1.** hung, suspended
مُتعَلِّق [mutʕalliq] *adj:* مُتعَلقات [mutʕallqaːt] *pl:* • **1.** devoted, fond (of), attached • **2.** with بـ pertaining, concerning, connected
مَعلُوقَة [maʕluːga] *adj:* • **1.** lighted, lit

ع ل ك

عِلَك [ʕilač] *v:* • **1.** to chew (gum) – يِعلِك بَعَد كُلّ وَجبَة أكِل [yiʕlič baʕad kull wajbat ʔakil] He chews gum after every meal.
عَلَّك [ʕallač] *v:* • **1.** to talk as if chewing gum, to talk from the corner of one's mouth – هَالرِّجّال يعَلِّك بحَكيَه [harrijjaːl yʕallič bħačyah] That man distorts his speech.
تعَلَّك [tʕallač] *v:* • **1.** to be or become chewy – هَالنُّوجَة تِتعَلَّك بالحَلِق [hannuːga titʕallač bilħalig] This nougat becomes chewy in the mouth.
عِلك [ʕilič] *n:* • **1.** gum, chewing gum
عَلك [ʕalič] *n:* • **1.** (act of) chewing (gum)
عِلّاجي [ʕillaːči, ʕallaːči] *adj:* • **1.** chewy – تَمُر عِلّاكِي [tamur ʕillaːči] chewy dates. حَلقُوم عِلّاكي [ħalquːm ʕillaːči] chewy Turkish delight.
عالُوكِي [ʕaluːči] *adj:* • **1.** chewy

ع ل ل

عَلَّل [ʕallal] *v:* • **1.** to justify, explain – شِتعَلِّل عَدَم رَغبتَه بالسَّفَر؟ [šitʕallil ʕadam raɣibtah bissafar?] What reason can you give for his aversion to travel?
تعَلَّل [tʕallal] *v:* • **1.** to gather in the evening for socializing – راح نِتعَلَّل ببَيت صَدِيقِي [raːħ nitʕallal bibayt ṣadiːqi] We will spend the evening after dinner at my friend's house.
عِلَّة [ʕilla] *n:* عِلّات [ʕillaːt] *pl:* • **1.** defect, fault, deficiency – عِلَّة بقَلبَك [ʕilla bgalbak] Damn you! عِلَّة بقَلُب عَدُوَّك [ʕilla bgalub ʕaduwwak] Long life to you! عَلَى عِلّات [ʕala ʕillaːt] /plus pronominal suffix/ at face value, as is. أخَذ الجَّواب عَلَى عِلّاتَه [ʔaxað ʔijjawaːb ʕala ʕillaːtah] He accepted the answer at face value. أقبَل المَكِينَة عَلَى عِلّاتها [ʔaqbal ʔilmakiːna ʕala ʕillaːtha] I'll accept the machine as is.
تَعليل [taʕliːl] *n:* • **1.** argumentation, entertainment
تَعلُولَة [taʕluːla] *n:* تَعلُولات [taʕluːlaːt] *pl:* • **1.** a social gathering after the evening meal • **2.** the period after the evening meal, when friends normally gather
عَلِيل [ʕaliːl] *adj:* • **1.** sick, ill, ailing, weak • **2.** sick person

ع ل م

عِلَم [ʕilam] *v:* • **1.** to know – الله يِعلَم شقَدّ آني أحِبَّك [ʔallah yiʕlam šgadd ʔaːni ʔaħibbak] God knows how I love you. يِعلَم بالغيب [yiʕlam bilɣiːb] He's clairvoyant.
عَلَّم [ʕallam] *v:* • **1.** to teach, instruct – هُوَّ عَلَّمنِي أركَب بايسِكِل [huwwa ʕallamni ʔarkab paːysikil] He taught me to ride a bike. • **2.** to mark, designate – عَلِّم الصَّنادِيق اللّي تِرُوح البَصرَة [ʕallim ʔiṣṣanaːdiːg ʔilli truːħ ʔilbaṣra] Put a mark on the boxes going to Basra.
تعَلَّم [tʕallam] *v:* • **1.** to learn, study – وِين تعَلَّمت فَرَنسِي؟ [wiːn tʕallamit faransi?] Where'd you learn French?
استَعلَم [ʔistaʕlam] *v:* • **1.** to inquire, ask – خَلِّي نِستَعلِم عَنَّه [xalliː nistaʕlim ʕannah] Let's inquire about him.

ع

عِلِم [ʕilim] *n:* • **1.** information, knowledge • **2.** pl. عُلُوم science

عَلَم [ʕalam] *n:* أَعلام [ʔaʕlaːm] *pl:* • **1.** flag, banner • **2.** dignitary, luminary, authority

عالَم [ʕaːlam] *n:* عِلّام، عُلَمَة [ʕillaːm, ʕulama] *pl:* • **1.** world • **2.** people • **3.** (pl. only) عُلَمَا, عِلّام religious authority

عالِم [ʕaːlim] *n:* عُلَماء [ʕulamaːʔ] *pl:* • **1.** scholar, scientist – عُلَماء الدِّين [ʕulamaːʔ ʔiddiːn] the religious authorities.

مُعَلِّم [muʕallim] *n:* • **1.** teacher, instructor

معَلِّم [mʕallim] *n:* • **1.** functionary of the Jewish religion, one of whose chief functions is over-seeing the slaughtering of animals

عَلّامَة [ʕallaːma] *n:* • **1.** (invar.) high authority, most learned man – عَلّامَة بِالرِّياضِيّات [ʕallaːma birriyaːđiyyaːt] an expert in mathematics.

عَلامَة [ʕalaːma] *n:* عَلامات، عَلائِم [ʕalaːmaːt, ʕalaːʔim] *pl:* • **1.** mark – عَلامَة فارِقَة [ʕalaːma faːriqa] a distinguishing mark. عَلامَة مُسَجَّلَة [ʕalaːma musaǰǰala] registered trade mark. عَلامَة اِستِفهام [ʕalaːmat ʔistifihaːm] question mark.

مَعالِم [maʕaːlim] *n:* • **1.** (pl. only) sights, curiosities

مَعلُوم [maʕluːm] *n:* مَعلُومات [maʕluːmaːt] *pl:* • **1.** known, acknowledged, accepted – شِي مَعلُوم [ši maʕluːm] a known fact. بَعَد ما مَعلُوم شوَقِت أرُوح [baʕad maː maʕluːm šwakit ʔaruːħ] It's still undecided when I'll go. ما مَعلُوم شوَقِت يِجِي [maː maʕluːm šwakit yiǰi] Nobody knows what time he'll come. • **2.** (an affirmative reply) of course! naturally! certainly! sure! • **3.** (pl. only) مَعلُومات data, information

تَعلِيم [taʕliːm] *n:* تَعالِيم، تَعلِيمات [taʕaːliːm, taʕliːmaːt] *pl:* • **1.** teaching, instruction, training, schooling, education, apprenticeship • **2.** (pl.only) instructions, directions, directives, announcements

إعلام [ʔiʕlaːm] *n:* • **1.** media, information, annoucement, advertisement

مَعلُومَة [maʕluːma] *n:* مَعلُومات [maʕluːmaːt] *pl:* • **1.** known or given fact, piece of data, piece of information

اِستِعلام [ʔistiʕlaːm] *n:* اِستِعلامات [ʔstiʕlamaːt] *pl:* • **1.** inquiry – مَكتَب الاستِعلامات [maktab ʔilʔistiʕlaːmaːt] information desk.

عِلمانِيَّة [ʕilmaːniyya] *n:* • **1.** laicism, secularism

عِلمِي [ʕilmi] *adj:* • **1.** scientific – طَرِيقَة عِلمِيَّة [ṭariːqa ʕilmiyya] scientific method.

عَلِيم [ʕaliːm] *adj:* • **1.** knowledgeable

عالَمِي [ʕaːlami] *adj:* • **1.** world (adj.) – بَطَل عالَمِي [baṭal ʕaːlami] a world champion. المَعرَض العالَمِي [ʔilmaʕrađ ʔilʕaːlami] the World's Fair.

متعَلِّم [mitʕallim] *adj:* • **1.** educated, schooled

عالَمِي [ʕaːlami] *adj:* عالَمِيَّة [ʕaːlamiyya] *feminine:* • **1.** international

إعلامِي [ʔiʕlaːmi] *adj:* • **1.** informative, relating to communication • **2.** computer-related

عِلمانِي [ʕilmaːni] *adj:* • **1.** secular, laic

تَعلِيمِي [taʕliːmi] *adj:* • **1.** educational, instructional, pedagogical

أَعلَم [ʔaʕlam] *comparative adjective:* • **1.** more or most knowledgeable, learned

عالَمِيّاً [ʕaːlamiyyan] *adverbial:* • **1.** internationally

ع ل ن

أعلَن، عِلَن [ʔaʕlan, ʕilan] *v:* • **1.** to announce, disclose, declare – راح نِعلِن أسماء الفائِزِين بِالجَّرِيدَة وَالرّادِيُو [raːħ niʕlin ʔasmaːʔ ʔilfaːʔiziːn biǰǰariːda wirraːdyu] We'll announce the winners' names in the newspapers and on the radio. هالبَلَد راح يِعلِن الحَرُب عَلينا [halbalad raːħ yiʕlin ʔilħarub ʕaliːna] That country will declare war on us. • **2.** to advertise, publicize, proclaim – عِلنوا بِالجَّرِيدَة عَن مُنتَجاتهُم [ʕilnaw biǰǰariːda ʕan muntaǰaːthum] They advertised their products in the newspaper.

اِنعِلَن [ʔinʕilan] *v:* • **1.** to be advertised

إعلان [ʔiʕlaːn] *n:* إعلانات [ʔiʕlaːnaːt] *pl:* • **1.** notice, statement • **2.** لَوحَة الإعلانات [lawħat ʔalʔiʕlaːnaːt] bulletin board • **3.** advertisement, ad

عَلَنِي [ʕalani] *adj:* • **1.** public, open, overt, public, evident, patent – مَزاد عَلَنِي [mazaːd ʕalani] public auction. جَلسَة عَلَنِيَّة [ǰalsa ʕalaniyya] open session.

مُعلَن [muʕlan] *adj:* • **1.** announced

عَلَناً [ʕalanan] *adverbial:* • **1.** openly, overtly, publicly – قالها عَلَناً وَما إستِحَى [gaːlha ʕalanan wmaː ʔistiħaː] He said it openly and wasn't ashamed.

ع ل و 1

عِلَى [ʕilaː] *v:* • **1.** to rise, get high (sound, in pitch and volume) – شُوف الطَّيّارَة دَتِعلَى [šuːf ʔiṭṭiyyaːra datiʕlaː] Look at the airplane climbing. شُوف البِنايَة شلُون دَتِعلَى يوم عَلَى يوم [šuːf ʔilbinaːya šluːn datiʕlaː yuːm ʕala yuːm] Notice how the building's getting higher every day. كُلّما تِعلَى دَرَجتَه، يِتكَبَّر أَزيَد [kullma tiʕlaː daraǰtah, yitkabbar ʔazyad] The higher his position gets, the more supercilious he gets. • **2.** to rise, ascend – حِسَّك عِلَى هوايَة. الجِّيران راح ينزَعجُون [ħissak ʕila hwaːya. ʔiǰǰiːraːn raːħ yinzaʕǰuːn] You've raised your voice too much. The neighbors will be annoyed.

عَلَّى [ʕallaː] *v:* • **1.** to raise – عَلِّي إيدَك شوَيَّة حَتَّى أنُوش [ʕalli ʔiːdak šwayya ħatta ʔanuːš] Raise your hand a little so I can reach you. عَلِّي حِسَّك؛ ما دَأسمَع [ʕalli ħissak; maː daʔasmaʕ] Raise your voice; I can't hear. • **2.** to render ritually clean by dipping three times in clear water – إغسِل الماعُون وَعَلِّيه. الكَلِب أكَل بِيه [ʔiɣsil ʔilmaːʕuːn wʕalliːh. ʔiččalib ʔakal biːh] Wash the dish and make it ritually clean. The dog ate out of it.

تعَلَّى [tʕallaː] *v:* • **1.** to be ritually cleansed – كُلّ هَالمواعِين لازم تِتعَلَّى قبِل ما يِتخَلَّى بيها أكِل [kull halmwaːʕiːn laːzim titʕallaː gabil maː yitxallaː biːha ʔakil] All these dishes have to be ritually cleansed before food is put in them. • **2.** to be raised, lifted – كُرسِي الحَلاق شلُون يِتعَلَّى؟ [kursi ʔilħallaːq šluːn yitʕallaː?] How's the barber's chair raised?

عِلُو [ʕilw] *n:* • **1.** height – شقَدّ عِلو النَّخلَة؟ [šgadd ʕilw ʔinnaxla?] How high is the palm tree? • **2.** level, volume (of a sound)

عال [ʕaːl] *n:* • **1.** excellent, first-class, outstanding, of top quality – قماش عال [qmaːš ʕaːl] top quality cloth. عال العال [ʕaːl ʔilʕaːl] the very best, the finest, the highest quality. • **2.** (exclamation) excellent! fine! very good!

عَلوَة [ʕalwa] *n:* عَلاوِي [ʕalaːwi] *pl:* • **1.** a high place • **2.** a farmers' market, where farmers and grain merchants bring their goods for wholesale marketing

عَلوجِي [ʕalawči] *n:* عَلوجِيَّة [ʕalawčiyya] *pl:* • **1.** proprietor of a farmers' market

مَعالِي [maʕaːli] *n:* • **1.** highness, excellency • **2.** excellency

عَلاوَة [ʕalaːwa] *n:* • **1.** addition, raise, bonus, extra pay • **2.** with عَلَى, in addition to

عالِي [ʕaːli] *adj:* • **1.** high, tall, elevated – شِجرَة عالِيَة [šiǰra ʕaːlya] a tall tree. مُكان عالِي [mukaːn ʕaːli] a high place. • **2.** (by extension) high, inflated – أسعار عالِيَة [ʔasʕaːr ʕaːlya] high prices. هَالتّاجِر يُضرُب بالعالِي [hattaːǰir yuđrub bilʕaːli] That merchant charges high prices. ماكُو حاجَة تُضرُب بالعالِي. يَعنِي إلّا تِركَب بكادِلاك؟ [maːku ħaːǰa tuđrub bilʕaːli. yaʕni ʔilla tirkab bkaːdilaːk?] There's no need to demand the best. Do you have to ride in a Cadillac? • **3.** high, strong – هَوا عالِي [hawa ʕaːli] a high wind. ضَغِط عالِي [đaɣiṭ ʕaːli] high pressure. • **4.** high – مَناصِب عالِيَة [manaːṣib ʕaːlya] high positions. رُتبَة عالِيَة [rutba ʕaːlya] high rank. دَرَجات عالِيَة [daraǰaːt ʕaːlya] high grades. الضَّحَى العالِي [ʔiđđaħa ʔilʕaːli] late forenoon (around 11 a. m.).

معَلِّي [mʕalli] *adj:* • **1.** upgraded, elevated

أعلَى [ʔaʕla] *comparative adjective:* • **1.** more or most elevated

عَلَى [ʕala] *preposition:* • **1.** on, upon, on top of – عالميز [ʕalmiːz] on the table. واحِد عَاللّاخ [waːħid ʕallaːx] one on top of the other. سَجِّلها عَلَى حسابِي [saǰǰilha ʕala ħsaːbi] Put it on my bill. عَلَى عينِي، عَلَى راسِي، عَلَى عينِي وَراسِي، عالعين وَالرّاس [ʕala ʕiːni, ʕala raːsi, ʕala ʕiːni wraːsi, ʕalʕiːn wʔirraːs] Gladly, with pleasure. عَلَى الله [ʕala ʔallah] Not bad (answer to شلُونَك؟) • **2.** about, on, concerning – حِكَى عَالمَوضُوع ساعَة [ħičaː ʕalmawđuːʕ saːʕa] He talked about the subject for an hour. آني شَعلَيّا بَعَد؟ [ʔaːni šaʕlayya baʕad?] What concern of mine is it then? What's it to me then? Why should I care then? عَلَى حساب [ʕala ħsaːb] on account of, on behalf of. هَالتَّنَقُّلات عَلَى حساب إبن الوَزِير [hattanaqqulaːt ʕala ħsaːb ʔibin ʔilwaziːr] These transfers are on behalf of the minister's son. عَلَى شَرَف [ʕala šaraf] in honor of. عَلَى شَرَف صَدِيقَه [ʕala šaraf ṣadiːqah] in his friend's honor. • **3.** for, over, about – يمُوت عالتُّفّاح [ymuːt ʕattiffaːħ] He's crazy about apples. ما عِندَه مانِع يُقتُل عَلَى فلِس [maː ʕindah maːniʕ yuqtul ʕala filis] He wouldn't mind killing for a fils. لا شُكر عَلَى واجِب [laː šukr ʕala waːǰib] Don't bother to thank me. عَلَى دَقِيقَة بَعَد كان أغلُبَه [ʕala daqiːqa baʕad čaːn ʔaɣulbah] With one more minute, I'd have beaten him. • **4.** against – سَجَّل شَكِيَّة عَليه بِالمَحكَمَة [saǰǰal šakiyya ʕaliːh bilmaħkama] He filed a complaint against him in court. يِحكِي عَليك بِغيابَك [yiħči ʕaliːk bɣiyaːbak] He talks about you behind your back. يِحكِي عَالرّايِح وَالجاي [yiħči ʕarraːyiħ wʔiǰǰaːy] He talks everybody down. • **5.** in accordance with, according to, by – كُلّشِي صار عَالمَرام [kullši ṣaːr ʕalmaraːm] Everything went as desired. كُلّ تَصَرُّفاتَه عالأُصُول [kull taṣarrufaːtah ʕalʔuṣuːl] All his actions are as they should be. عَلَى قَولَك القَضِيَّة خَلصانَة بَسّ لِسَّة ما بَيَّن شِي [ʕala guːlak ʔilqađiyya xalṣaːna bass lissa maː bayyan ši] By your account the matter's finished, but nothing's appeared so far. عَلَى أن [ʕala ʔan] provided that, providing. وافَق يِشتِرِيها عَلَى أن ينطُوه تَخفِيض خَمسَة بِالمِيَّة [waːfaq yištiriːha ʕala ʔan yinṭuːh taxfiːđ xamsa bilmiyya] He agreed to buy it providing they gave him a five percent discount. عَلَى كُلّ حال [ʕala kull ħaːl] at any rate, anyhow, anyway. عَلَى كُلّ حال، خَلِّي نِنساها [ʕala kull ħaːl, xalliː ninsaːha] At any rate, let's forget it. • **6.** عَلَى اللّي, عَلَى ما plus following verb: as, according to, what, from what – عَلَى ما تقُول، ما نِقدَر نسَوِّيها [ʕala maː dguːl, maː nigdar nsawwiːha] From what you say, we can't do it. عَلَى ما أعرُف، ما أعتِقِد القَضِيَّة راح تصِير [ʕala maː ʔaʕruf, maː ʔaʕtiqid ʔilqađiyya raːħ tṣiːr] According to what I know, I don't think that will come about. عَلَى ما يظهَر [ʕala maː yiđhar] evidently, as it appears. عَلَى ما يِظهَر، ما راح يسَوُّوها [ʕala maː yiđhar, maː raːħ yisawwuːha] Evidently, they're not going to do it.

ع ل و ²

عَلَوّا [ʕalawwa] *subordinating conjunction:* • **1.** (exclamation of hope, approx.:) it would be good if, it would be nice if, I wish, I hope – عَلَوّا تِجِي وِيّايا [ʕalawwaː tiǰi wiyyaːya] Wish you were coming with me!

ع ل ي

See also ع ل و

ع ل ي ش ي ش

عَلِي شِيش [ʕališiːš] *n:* • **1.** turkey

ع

ع م ب

عَمبَة [ʕamba] *n:* • **1.** (coll.) pickled mangoes, mango pickles

عَمبايَة [ʕamba:ya] *n:* عَمبايات [ʕamba:ya:t] *pl:* • **1.** pickled mango, mango pickle

ع م ب ر

عَنبَر، عَمبَر [ʕanbar, ʕambar] *n:* • **1.** a variety of rice • **2.** pleasant smell • **3.** ambergris

عَمبار [ʕamba:r] *n:* • **1.** shed

ع م د

عَمَّد [ʕammad] *v:* • **1.** to baptize, christen – يُوحَنّا المُعَمِّدان عَمَّد المَسِيح [yu:ħanna: ʔilmuʕammida:n ʕammad ʔilmasi:ħ] John the Baptist baptized Christ.

تعَمَّد [tʕammad] *v:* • **1.** to intend, to do on purpose, to do intentionally – تعَمَّد يقُولها قِدّامَه [tʕammad ygu:lha gidda:mah] He intentionally said it in front of him. تعَمَّد وَرَسَّب نَفسَه حَتَّى يِطلَع مِن المَدرَسَة [tʕammad wrassab nafsah ħatta yiṭlaʕ min ʔilmadrasa] He acted intentionally to flunk himself to get out of school. • **2.** to be baptized – الجّاهِل تعَمَّد إسبُوع اللِّي فات [ʔiǰǰa:hil tʕammad ʔisbu:ʕ ʔilli fa:t] The baby was baptized last week.

إعتِمَد [ʔiʕtimad] *v:* • **1.** to rely, depend – أقدَر أعتِمِد عَليه بهَالقَضِيَّة [ʔagdar ʔaʕtimid ʕali:h bhalqaðiyya] I can depend on him in this case.

عَمِد، عَن عَمِد [ʕamid, ʕan ʕamid] *n:* • **1.** on purpose, intentionally, deliberately – ما سَوّاها عَن عَمِد [ma: sawwa:ha ʕan ʕamid] He didn't do it on purpose.

عَمِيد [ʕami:d] *n:* عُمَداء [ʕumada:ʔ] *pl:* • **1.** dean – عَمِيد الكُلِّيَّة [ʕami:d ʔilkulliyya] dean of the college. عَمِيد السِّلك السِّياسِي [ʕami:d ʔissilk ʔissiya:si] dean of the diplomatic corps. • **2.** military rank, approx.: general

عَمُود، عامُود [ʕamu:d, ʕa:mu:d] *n:* عَوامِيد [ʕawa:mi:d] *pl:* • **1.** post • **2.** pole (esp. electric or telephone) • **3.** (newspaper or magazine) column – العَمُود الفَقَرِي [ʔilʕamu:d ʔilfaqari] the spinal column.

تَعَمُّد [taʕammud] *n:* • **1.** intention, intent, design, resolution, determination, purpose

تعمِيد [taʕmi:d] *n:* • **1.** baptism

إعتِماد [ʔiʕtima:d] *n:* • **1.** reliance, dependence, confidence, trust – الإعتِماد عَن النَّفِس [ʔiliʕtima:d ʕan ʔinnafis] self-reliance. أوراق الإعتِماد [ʔawra:q ʔiliʕtima:d] credentials (of diplomats).

عَمدِي [ʕamdi] *adj:* • **1.** intentional, deliberate – شِي عَمدِي [ši ʕamdi] something intentional. • **2.** premeditated, willful – قَتِل عَمدِي [qatil ʕamdi] willful murder.

عَمُودِي [ʕamu:di] *adj:* • **1.** vertical, perpendicular, upright – دِنقَة عَمُودِيَّة [dinga ʕamu:diyya] an upright column. طَيّارَة عَمُودِيَّة [ṭiyya:ra ʕamu:diyya] helicopter.

مُعتَمَد [muʕtamad] *adj:* • **1.** reliable, dependable, authorized

مِعتِمِد [miʕtimid] *adj:* • **1.** dependent

عَمداً [ʕamdan] *adverbial:* • **1.** intentionally, deliberately – سَوّاها عَمداً حَتَّى يأذِينِي [sawwa:ha ʕamdan ħatta yʔaðði:ni] He did it on purpose to hurt me.

ع م ر

عُمَر [ʕumar] *v:* • **1.** to thrive, prosper – عُمَر بَيتَك، إن شاء الله [ʕumar baytak, ʔinša:llah] May your household be prosperous! (said by a guest when leaving. A common answer is: الله يُحفظَك [ʔallah yuħfiðak]) • **2.** to be or become populated, built up – هَالمَنطِقَة عُمرَت، وصارَت بِيها بيُوت وَمَدارِس [halmanṭiqa ʕumrat, wṣa:rat bi:ha byu:t wmada:ris] This area has been developed, and acquired houses and schools.

عَمَّر [ʕammar] *v:* • **1.** to repair, overhaul, restore, refurbish, rebuild – راح أعَمُّر البَيت إسبُوع الجّاي [ra:ħ ʔaʕammur ʔilbayt ʔisbu:ʕ ʔiǰǰa:y] I'm going to have the house repaired next week. اِشتِرَيت هالسَّيّارَة رخِيص، وَعَمَّرتها [ʔištirayt hassayya:ra rxi:ṣ, wʕammaritha] I bought this car cheap, and repaired it. • **2.** to build up, develop – الحُكُومَة بِنَت سَدَّة هنا وَعَمَّرَت المَنطَقَة كُلها [ʔilħuku:ma binat sadda hna: wʕammrat ʔilmanṭaqa kullha] the government built a dam here and developed the whole area. • **3.** to prepare, arrange, set up – بالله ما تعَمِّرلِي النَّرقِيلَة؟ [ballah ma: tʕammirli ʔinnargi:la?] Would you please fix the narghile for me? عَمِّرلِي فَدّ بِيك نَفِيس [ʕammirli fadd pi:k nafi:s] Fix me a real good drink.

تعَمَّر [tʕammar] *v:* • **1.** to be repaired, rebuilt, renovated – البَيت تعَمَّر مَرّتَين هَالسَّنَة [ʔilbayt tʕammar marrtayn hassana] The house has been fixed twice this year. • **2.** to be built – هالسَّنَة هوايَة بيُوت تعَمرَت بهَالمِحَلَّة [hassana hwa:ya byu:t tʕammrat bhalimħalla] A lot of houses have been built in this neighborhood this year. • **3.** to be developed, built up – كُلّ هَالمَنطِقَة راح تِتعَمَّر [kull halmanṭiqa ra:ħ titʕammar] All this area will be developed.

إستَعمَر [ʔistaʕmar] *v:* • **1.** to hold as a colony, exploit – الإنكلِيز اِستَعمِرَوا الهِند مُدَّة طُويلَة [ʔilʔingili:z ʔistaʕmiraw ʔilhind mudda ṭuwi:la] The British dominated India for a long time. • **2.** to make into a colony – الدُّوَل الكُبرَى اِستَعمِرَت الشَّرق الأوسَط بَعد الحَرُب [ʔidduwal ʔilkubra ʔistaʕmirat ʔiššarq ʔilʔawsaṭ baʕd ʔilħarub] The Great Powers turned the Middle East into colonies after the war.

عُمُر [ʕumur] *n:* أعمار [ʔaʕma:r] *pl:* • **1.** life, lifetime, life span – الأعمار بإيد الله [ʔilʔaʕma:r bʔi:d ʔallah] I'll take my chances. • **2.** age (of a person)

عَمّار [ʕamma:r] *n:* عَمّارَة [ʕamma:ra] *pl:* • **1.** designer, builder

عِمارَة [ʕimaːra] *n:* عِمارات، عِمايِر [ʕimaːraːt, ʕimaːyir] *pl:* • **1.** building, edifice, structure
عُمران [ʕumraːn] *n:* • **1.** development, building – حَرَكَة العُمران [ħarakat ʔilʕumraːn] construction activity. • **2.** built-up area – أُسطَة عُمران [ʔusṭa ʕumraːn] variety of fresh dates.
معمار [miʕmaːr] *n:* • **1.** builder, contractor, designer, architect
تَعمير [taʕmiːr] *n:* • **1.** repair, overhaul, restoration, overhauling, refurbishing, reconditioning – مَحَلّ تَعمِير سَيّارات [maħall taʕmiːr sayyaːraːt] an auto repair shop.
إعمار [ʔiʕmaːr] *n:* • **1.** development • **2.** construction
عَمّارِيَّة [ʕammaːriyya] *n:* عَمّارِيّات [ʕammaːriyyaːt] *pl:* • **1.** a frame of palm stalks, in which a thorny shrub عاقُول is compressed, and soaked to provide a rudimentary air cooler and humidifier.
اِستِعمار [ʔistiʕmaːr] *n:* • **1.** colonialism, imperialism • **2.** imperialistic exploitation • **3.** establishment of imperialistic control
مُستعمَرَة [mustaʕmara] *n:* مُستَعمَرات [mustaʕmaraːt] *pl:* • **1.** colony, settlement
عامِر [ʕaːmir] *adj:* • **1.** built-up – مَنطِقَة عامرَة [manṭiqa ʕaːmra] a built-up area. • **2.** well-stocked, well-furnished – مَكتَبَة عامرَة [maktaba ʕaːmra] a well-furnished library. بار عامرَة [baːr ʕaːmra] a well-stocked bar. جيبَه عامِر [ǰiːbah ʕaːmir] He's loaded. He's flush. • **3.** lively, enjoyable, pleasant – لَيلَة عامرَة [layla ʕaːmra] an enjoyable evening.
معَمَّر [mʕammar] *adj:* • **1.** renovated, refurbished
عُمراني [ʕumraːni] *adj:* • **1.** development, construction – مَشاريع عُمرانِيَّة [mašaːriːʕ ʕumraːniyya] development projects.
مِعماري [miʕmaːri] *adj:* • **1.** architectural, structural, building – مُهَندِس مِعماري [muhandis miʕmaːri] architect.
مُستَعمِر [mustaʕmir] *n:* • **1.** colonialist, imperialist
اِستِعماري [ʔistiʕmaːri] *adj:* • **1.** colonialist, imperialist, imperialistic – أغراض اِستِعمارِيَّة [ʔaɣraːð̣ ʔistiʕmaːriyya] colonial, imperialist intentions.
أعمَر [ʔaʕmar] *comparative adjective:* • **1.** more or most populous, developed

ع م ش

أعمَش [ʔaʕmaš] *adj:* عِمِش، عَمشِين [ʕimiš, ʕamšiːn] *pl:* عَمشَة [ʕamša] *feminine:* • **1.** myopic • **2.** squint-eyed

ع م ق

تعَمَّق [tʕammaq] *v:* • **1.** to deepen, to be deep, to immerse
عُمُق [ʕumuq] *n:* أعماق [ʔaʕmaːq] *pl:* • **1.** depth, deepness • **2.** depth, profoundness, profundity • **3.** bottom (of river, sea)
عَمِيق [ʕamiːq] *adj:* • **1.** deep – نَهَر عَمِيق [nahar ʕamiːq] a deep river. • **2.** deep, profound – تَفكِير عَمِيق [tafkiːr ʕamiːq] profound thought.
أعمَق [ʔaʕmaq] *comparative adjective:* • **1.** deeper, deepest

ع م ل

عِمَل [ʕimal] *v:* • **1.** to pull a prank, to do something bad – عِمَل عَملَة كِبِيرَة وَطِردُوه مِن العَشِيرَة [ʕimal ʕamla čibiːra wṭirduːh min ʔilʕašiːra] He did something very bad and they threw him out of the tribe. عِمَلها بِيّا [ʕimalha biyya] He did me a dirty deed. He fouled me up.
عَمَّل [ʕammal] *v:* • **1.** to work, be effective, give results – البَسُط ما يعَمِّل بِيه [ʔilbasuṭ maː yʕammil biːh] Beating doesn't work with him. • **2.** to fester, be or become infected – الجَّرِح عَمَّل [ʔiǰǰariħ ʕammal] The wound became infected.
عامَل [ʕaːmal] *v:* • **1.** to treat, handle, deal with – عامَلني مُعامَلَة لَطِيفَة [ʕaːmalni muʕaːmala laṭiːfa] He treated me well. • **2.** to bargain with, haggle with – عامَلتَه لَكِن ما نَزَّل السِّعِر [ʕaːmaltah laːkin maː nazzal ʔissiʕir] I bargained with him but he didn't lower the price.
تعامَل [tʕaːmal] *v:* • **1.** to deal, trade – إحنا ما نتعامَل ويّا هَالشَّرِكَة [ʔiħna maː nitʕaːmal wiyya haššarika] We don't deal with this company. • **2.** to bargain, haggle – صاحِب هَالدُّكّان أَبَداً ما يِتعامَل [ṣaːħib hadddukkaːn ʔabadan maː yitʕaːmal] The owner of this store never bargains.
اِستَعمَل [ʔistaʕmal] *v:* • **1.** to use, employ, utilize – اِشتِرَيت شَمسِيَّة بَسّ بَعَد ما اِستَعمَلتها [ʔištirayt šamsiyya bass baʕad maː ʔistaʕmalitha] I bought an umbrella but I haven't used it yet.
عَمَل [ʕamal] *n:* عَملَة [ʕamla] *feminine:* • **1.** work, employment • **2.** (pl. أعمال) act, action • **3.** bowel movement • **4.** عَملَة a prank, a bad action, an evil deed
عُملَة [ʕumla] *n:* عُملات [ʕumlaːt] *pl:* • **1.** currency, cash, money
عِملَة [ʕimla] *n:* • **1.** bargaining, haggling
عَمِيل [ʕamiːl] *n:* عُمَلاء [ʕumalaːʔ] *pl:* • **1.** agent, hireling, lackey – عَمِيل اِستِعمار [ʕamiːl ʔistiʕmaːr] an agent of imperialism.
عَمّال [ʕammaːl] *n:* عَمّالَة [ʕammaːla] *pl:* • **1.** bricklayer's helper, builder's helper
مَعمَل [maʕmal] *n:* مَعامِل [maʕaːmil] *pl:* • **1.** factory, mill, plant, works – مَعمَل الألبان [maʕmal ʔilʔalbaːn] dairy.
عامِل [ʕaːmil] *n:* عَوامِل، عُمّال [ʕawaːmil, ʕummaːl] *pl:* • **1.** factor, element – عامِل مُساعِد [ʕaːmil musaːʕid] catalyst (chem.). • **2.** pl. عُمّال laborer, worker
عَمَلِيَّة [ʕamaliyya] *n:* عَمَلِيّات [ʕamaliyyaːt] *pl:* • **1.** operation, process • **2.** operation (med.) – غُرفَة العَمَلِيّات [ɣurfat ʔilʕamaliyyaːt] operating room.

ع

مَعمِيل [maʕmiːl, miʕmiːl] *n:* مَعامِيل [maʕaːmiːl] *pl:* • **1.** customer
عُمُولَة [ʕumuːla] *n:* عُمُولات [ʕumuːlaːt] *pl:* • **1.** commission, brokerage
عَمّالَة [ʕammaːla] *n:* • **1.** (invar.) bricklayer's helper, builder's helper • **2.** road worker
مَعمُول [maʕmuːl] *n:* • **1.** manufactured, made – مَعمُول بِيه [maʕmuːl biːh] effective, valid, in force, in effect. القانُون مَعمُول بِيه بِجَمِيع أنحاء البَلَد [ʔilqaːnuːn maʕmuːl biːh bǰamiːʕ ʔanħaːʔ ʔilbalad] The law is effective in all sections of the country. • **2.** a kind of sweet pastry
عَمالَة [ʕamaːla] *n:* • **1.** employment
تَعامُل [taʕaːmul] *n:* • **1.** trade, trade dealings, trade relations, transactions, business
مُعامَلَة [muʕaːmala] *n:* • **1.** behavior, conduct, treatment, social intercourse – مُعامَلتَه لِلنّاس طَيِّبَة [muʕaːmaltah linnaːs ṭayyba] He treats people well. • **2.** matter, affair, case – بِالمُعامَلَة [bilmuʕaːmala] in the works. • **3.** pl. مُعامَلات business dealings
إستِعمال [ʔistiʕmaːl] *n:* • **1.** use, usage • **2.** operation, handling – لاستِيك إستِعمال [laːstiːk ʔistiʕmaːl] prophylactic, condom.
عَمَلِي [ʕamali] *adj:* • **1.** practical – حَلّ عَمَلِي [ħall ʕamali] a practical solution.
عُمّالِي [ʕummaːli] *adj:* • **1.** labor (adj.) – نَشاط عُمّالِي [naṣaːṭ ʕummaːli] labor activity.
مُستَعمَل [mustaʕmal] *adj:* • **1.** used, employed, in use, applied • **2.** not new, secondhand
عَمَلِيّاً [ʕamaliyyan] *adverbial:* • **1.** practically

ع م ل ق

عِملاق [ʕimlaːq] *n:* عَمالِقَة [ʕamaːliqa] *pl:* • **1.** (as adj:) gigantic, huge • **2.** a giant

ع م م

عَمّ [ʕamm] *v:* • **1.** to be or become general, common, prevalent, to prevail – بزَمَن الحَرُب الغَلاء عَمّ بِكُلّ البَلَد [bzaman ʔilħarub ʔilɣalaːʔ ʕamm bkull ʔilbalad] During the war high prices prevailed in the whole country. • **2.** to cause trouble, inconvenience – بِضِحِكتَك بِالصَّفّ عَمَّيت عَلينا وَخَلَّيت المُعَلِّم يِزعَل [bðiħiktak biṣṣaff ʕammiːt ʕaliːna wxalliːt ʔalmuʕallim yizʕal] By your laughter in class you have caused us all trouble and made the teacher mad. مِتأَسِّف، آنِي عَمَّيت عَلِيك وَحرَمتَك مِن الرَّواح لِلسِّينَما [mitʔassif, ʔaːni ʕammiːt ʕaliːk wħramtak min ʔirrawaːħ lissinama] I'm sorry I caused you trouble and deprived you of going to the movie.
عَمَّم [ʕammam] *v:* • **1.** to make generally known, to make universally known and applicable – عَمِّم هَالبَيان عالمُوَظَّفِين [ʕammim halbayaːn ʕaːlmuwaððafiːn] Circulate this notice to the employees. المُدِير العامّ عَمَّم الأَمُر عَلَى جَمِيع الشُّعَب [ʔilmudiːr ʔilʕaːmm ʕammam ʔilʔamur ʕala ǰamiːʕ ʔiššuʕab] The director general made the order applicable to all the sections. • **2.** to put a turban on someone – عَمَّم إبنَه وأَخَذَه ويّاه لِلجّامِع [ʕammam ʔibnah wʔaxaðah wiyyaːh lijǰaːmiʕ] He put a turban on his son and took him with him to the mosque.
عَمّ [ʕamm] *n:* عمام، عمومَة [ʕmaːm, ʕmuːma.] *pl:* • **1.** father's brother, paternal uncle – إبِن العَمّ [ʔibin ʔilʕamm] cousin (on the father's side). بِنت العَمّ [bint ʔilʕamm] female cousin (on the father's side). • **2.** (by extension) father-in-law
عَمُّو [ʕammu] *n:* • **1.** (term of address) عَمِّي my uncle, uncle • **2.** (to a friend or a youngster, approx.:) buddy, pal
عَمَّة [ʕamma] *n:* عَمّات [ʕammaːt] *pl:* • **1.** paternal aunt
عُمُوم [ʕumuːm] *n:* • **1.** whole, totality, aggregate. • **2.** with ال the public, the people.
عامَّة [ʕaːmma] *n:* • **1.** generality, the masses, the people – عامَّة النّاس [ʕaːmmat ʔinnaːs] the populace. • **2.** عامَّتاً in general, generally, commonly, altogether.
عمامَة [ʕmaːma] *n:* عمامات، عمايِم [ʕmaːmaːt, ʕmaːyim] *pl:* • **1.** turban
تَعمِيم [taʕmiːm] *n:* • **1.** circulation, distribution, dissemination, diffusion, propagation. • **2.** generalization, popularization, democratization.
عامّ [ʕaːmm] *adj:* • **1.** public – الرَّأي العامّ [ʔirraʔy ʔilʕaːmm] public opinion. • **2.** general – مُدِير عامّ [mudiːr ʕaːmm] director general.
عامِّي [ʕaːmmi] *adj:* عَوامّ [ʕawaːmm] *pl:* • **1.** common man, ordinary person, man in the street • **2.** ordinary citizen (without official position)
عامِّي [ʕaːmmi] *adj:* • **1.** colloquial – عِراقِي عامِّي [ʕiraːqi ʕaːmmi] colloquial Iraqi. اللُّغَة العامِّيَّة [ʔilluɣa ʔilʕaːmmiyya] the colloquial language.
مُعَمَّم [muʕammam] *adj:* • **1.** turbaned man, i.e., a religious functionary
عُمُومِي [ʕumuːmi] *adj:* • **1.** public – تِلِفُون عُمُومِي [tilifuːn ʕumuːmi] a public telephone.
العامِّيَّة [ʔilʕaːmmiyya] *adj:* • **1.** colloquial, the colloquial language • **2.** dialectal language, dialect

ع م ن

عَمّان [ʕammaːn] *n:* • **1.** Amman

ع م ي

عِمَى [ʕimaː] *v:* • **1.** to go blind – إنصاب بِالتِّراخوما وَبَعدين عِمَى [ʔinṣaːb bittiraːxuːma wbaʕdiyn ʕimaː] He was attacked by trachoma and later went blind. عِمَت عيُونها مِن البَكِي [ʕimat ʕyuːnha min ʔilbači] She cried her heart out. • **2.** to be dulled, become dull – المِنشار كان كُلِّش حاد، وَإستَعمَلتَه هوايَة وَعِمَى [ʔilminšaːr čaːn kulliš ħaːd, wʔistaʕmaltah hwaːya wʕimaː] The saw was very sharp, but I used it a lot, and it got dull. • **3.** to dull – الجّاهِل عِمَى السِّكِّينَة [ʔijja:hil ʕima: ʔissičči:na] The kid dulled the knife. • **4.** to blind – بِالزَّمان القَدِيم كانَوا يِعمُون المُجرِمِين [bizzama:n ʔilqadi:m ča:naw yiʕmu:n ʔilmujrimi:n] In olden times they used to blind criminals. هَالضُوَة القَوِي عِمَى عيُونِي لمُدَّة دَقِيقَة وِحدَة [haðđuwa ʔilqawi ʕima: ʕyu:ni ʔilmuddat daqi:qa wiħda] That strong light blinded me for a minute.

اِنعِمَى [ʔinʕima:] *v:* • **1.** to be blinded – اِحتِرَق شوَيَّة بِالنّار وَانعِمَت عيُونَه [ʔiħtirag šwayya binna:r wʔinʕimat ʕyu:nah] He got burned somewhat in the fire and was blinded.

عَمَة، عِمَة [ʕama, ʕima] *n:* • **1.** blindness – عَمَة بِقَلبَك [ʕama bgalbak] Go to hell! عَمَة بِطِيزَه [ʕama bţi:zah] To hell with him!

أعمَى [ʔaʕma] *adj:* عِمِي، عِميان، عِمِّين [ʕimi, ʕimya:n, ʕimyi:n] *pl:* عَميَة [ʕamya] *feminine:* • **1.** blind – مجَدِّي أعمَى [mgaddi ʔaʕma] a blind beggar. • **2.** blind person • **3.** dull – سِكِّينَة عَميَة [sičči:na ʕamya] a dull knife. هَالجّاهِل أعمَى القَلُب. المَدرَسَة ما تفِيدَه [hajja:hil ʔaʕma ʔilgalub. ʔilmadrasa ma: tfi:dah] That kid is stupid. School won't do him any good.

مَعمِي [maʕmi] *adj:* • **1.** blinded

ع ن

عَن [ʕan] *preposition:* • **1.** from, away from, off – أقعُد بِعِيد عَن النّار [ʔugʕud biʕi:d ʕan ʔinna:r] Sit a long way from the fire. قَعِّد الجّاهِل بالفَيّ عَن الشَّمِس [gaʕʕid ʔijja:hil bilfayy ʕan ʔiššamis] Put the baby in the shade away from the sun. لا تُخرُج عَن المَوضُوع [la: tuxruj ʕan ʔilmawđu:ʕ] Don't get off the subject. • **2.** against, as protection from – شايِل حِرز عَن العَين [ša:yil ħiriz ʕan ʔilʕayn] He carries a talisman against the evil eye. لابِس مَناظِر عَن الشَّمِس [la:bis mana:đir ʕan ʔiššamis] He's wearing glasses as protection from the sun. • **3.** about, on – يِحكِي عَنَّك دائِماً [yiħči ʕannak da:ʔiman] He always talks about you. قرَيت مَقال عَن هَالمَوضُوع [qrayt maqa:l ʕan halmawđu:ʕ] I read an article on this subject. • **4.** for, per – ناخُذ دِينار عَن كُلّ نَفَر [na:xuð dina:r ʕan kull nafar] We charge a dinar for each person. لازِم تِدفَع فِلسَين عَن كُلّ يوم إذا ما ترَجِّع الكِتاب بالوَقِت [la:zim tidfaʕ filsayn ʕan kull yu:m ʔiða ma: trajjiʕ ʔilkita:b bilwakit] You have to pay 2 fils for each day, if you don't return the book on time. • **5.** out of, due to – قِتلَك بِيها عَن إخلاص [gitlak bi:ha ʕan ʔixla:ṣ] I told you about it out of sincere concern. سَوّاها عَن رَغبَة [sawwa:ha ʕan rayba] He did it willingly. • **6.** for, in behalf of – دِفَعِت عَنَّه قِسط السَّيّارَة [difaʕit ʕannah qisṭ ʔissayya:ra] I payed the installment on the car for him. وَزّعَوا فلُوس عَالفُقَراء عَن رُوح المَرحُوم [wazzʕaw flu:s ʕalfuqara:ʔ ʕan ru:ħ ʔilmarħu:m] They distributed money to the poor for the soul of the deceased. • **7.** after, on, upon – يوم عَن يوم دَيِسمَن [yu:m ʕan yu:m dayisman] Day after day he's getting fatter. سَنَة عَن سَنَة دَيصِير زَنكِين [sana ʕan sana dayṣi:r zangi:n] Year after year he gets richer. عَن طَرِيق [ʕan ṭari:q] via, by way of, through. راح البَصرَة عَن طَرِيق الكُوت [ra:ħ ʔilbaṣra ʕan ṭari:q ʔilku:t] He went to Basra by way of Kut. تعَرَّفِت عَلَيه عَن طَرِيق عَلِي [tʕarrafit ʕali:h ʕan ṭari:q ʕali] I met him through Ali.

ع ن ب

عِنَب [ʕinab] *n:* • **1.** (coll.) grape(s)

عِنّاب [ʕinna:b] *n:* • **1.** jujube(s) (bot.) • **2.** (its fruit) jujube(s)

عِنّابَة [ʕinna:ba] *n:* عِنّابات [ʕinna:ba:t] *pl:* • **1.** Unit name of عِنّاب : a jujube fruit • **2.** clitoris

عِنبايَة [ʕinba:ya] *n:* عِنبايات [ʕinba:ya:t] *pl:* • **1.** grape – عِنَب الثَّعلَب [ʕinab ʔiθθaʕlab] black nightshade (bot.).

ع ن ب ر [1]

عَنبَر [ʕanbar] *n:* • **1.** ambergris – حُوت العَنبَر [ħu:t ʔilʕanbar] sperm whale. تِمَّن عَنبَر [timman ʕanbar] a variety of rice of good quality (with a distinctive odor to it).

ع ن ب ر [2]

عَنبَر [ʕanbar] *n:* عَنابِر [ʕana:bir] *pl:* • **1.** warehouse, storehouse

عُنبار [ʕunba:r] *n:* عُنبارات [ʕunba:ra:t] *pl:* • **1.** ambergris, a wax-like substance from the sperm whale used for making perfume

ع ن ت

مِتعَنِّت [mitʕannit] *adj:* • **1.** uncompromising, obstinate, stubborn, pigheaded

ع ن ت ر

عَنتَر [ʕantar] *v:* • **1.** to become distended, to become erected (of the penis)

عَنتَر [ʕantar] *n:* • **1.** Antar, a heroic historical figure and writer, and by extension, a hero, a strong man

عَنترِيَّة [ʕantiriyya] *adj:* عَنترِيّات [ʕantiriyya:t] *pl:* • **1.** boastful promises, boastful threats, big talk

ع ن ت ك

تعَنتَك [tʕantak] *v:* • **1.** to show off, to act up – لا تِتعَنتَك وِيّايا، تَرَة أَنَذّيك [la: titʕantak wiyya:ya, tara ʔaʔaðði:k] Don't get funny with me or you'll be sorry. البارحَة خَشّ عَالمُدِير وَتعَنتَك براسَه إلَى أن زَعَّلَه [ʔilba:rħa xašš ʕalmudi:r watʕantak bira:sah ʔila ʔan zaʕʕalah] Yesterday he went in to see the director and gave him a hard time until he made him mad.

ع

آني أعرُف لُويش دَيتعَنتك براسكُم [ʔaːni ʔaʕruf luwiːš dayitʕantak braːskum] I know why he is being critical and acting superior toward you.

عَنتَكَة [ʕantaka] *n:* • **1.** bullying, boastfulness

عَنتيكَة، إنتيكَة [ʕantiːka, ʔintiːka] *adj:* عَنتيكات [ʕantiːkaːṭ] *pl:* • **1.** unusual, strange, rare – وَرِد عَنتيكَة [warid ʕantiːka] rare flowers. كَلِب عَنتيكَة [čalib ʕantiːka] an unusual dog. • **2.** odd, peculiar, eccentric, funny – وَلَد عَنتيكَة [walad ʕantiːka] a funny guy. • **3.** old hand, experienced person, wise old man • **4.** pl عَنتيكات, عَناتيك antique, old hand, experienced person, wise old man

ع ن ج ر

عَنجَر [ʕanǰar] *v:* • **1.** to beat, beat up – عَنجرُوه مِن البَسِط [ʕanǰiruːh min ʔilbasiṭ] They beat him black and blue.

تعَنجَر [tʕanǰar] *v:* • **1.** to be beaten, be beaten up – تعَنجَر عَنجَرَة زينَة [tʕanǰar ʕanǰara ziːna] He really got his lumps. • **2.** to get a bump

عَنجُور [ʕanǰuːr] *n:* عَنجُورَة [ʕanǰuːra] *feminine:* • **1.** small, unripe melon(s) • **2.** small, unripe apricot(s) • **3.** عَنجُورَة (pl. -ات) unit noun of عَنجُور

عُنجُرَّة [ʕunǰurra] *n:* عُنجُرّات، عَناجير [ʕunǰurraːt, ʔanaːǰiːr] *pl:* • **1.** lump, swelling (from a blow, esp on the head)

معَنجِر [mʕanǰir] *adj:* • **1.** beaten, beaten up • **2.** person who has been beaten up • **3.** person who is hard to get along with

ع ن ج ص

عِنجاص [ʕinǰaːṣ] *n:* • **1.** (coll.) plum(s) – عِنجاص مَيَبِّس [ʕinǰaːṣ myabbis] prune (s).

عِنجاصَة [ʕinǰaːṣa] *n:* عِنجاصات [ʕinǰaːṣaːt] *pl:* • **1.** plum(s), prune(s)

ع ن د

عانَد [ʕaːnad] *v:* • **1.** to disobey, resist, oppose – لا تعانِد أبُوك وَأُمَّك [laː tʕaːnid ʔabuːk wʔummak] Don't disobey your father and mother. • **2.** to be or become stubborn, to insist – عانَد وَما قِبَل يرُوح [ʕaːnad wma qibal yiruːħ] He got stubborn and wouldn't go. عانَد إلّا يرُوح لِلسِّينَما [ʕaːnad ʔilla yiruːħ lissinama] He insisted on going to the movies.

تعانَد [tʕaːnad] *v:* • **1.** to disagree (stubbornly) – تعانَدوا عَلَى فَدّ شِي تافِه [tʕaːndaw ʕala fadd ši taːfih] They got stubborn with each other over a trivial thing.

عِند، عِدّ [ʕind, ʕidd] *n:* • **1.** (عِند before vowel) (عِدّ before cons.) at, near, by, with – عِند الحَلّاق [ʕind ʔilħallaːq] at the barber's. باتَت عِدنا [baːtat ʕidna] She stayed overnight with us. عِند الامتِحان، يُكرَم المَرء أو يُهان [ʕind ʔilʔimtiħaːn, yukram ʔilmarʔ ʔaw yuhaːn] When it comes to the test, you'll come through or catch hell. عِند الحاجَة، عِند الضَّرُورَة [ʕind ʔilħaːǰa, ʕind ʔiððaruːra] in case of need, in an emergency. عِند الحاجَة، طَلِّع فلُوسَك مِن البَنك [ʕind ʔilħaːǰa, ṭalliʕ fluːsak min ʔilbank] If you need to, draw your money out of the bank. إذا تِحتاج فلُوس، آني عِندَك [ʔiða tiħtaːǰ fluːs, ʔaːni ʕindak] If you need any money, I'm at your service. • **2.** /plus pronominal suffix, signifies possession:/ – عِندَك قَلَم زايِد؟ [ʕindak qalam zaːyid?] Do you have an extra pencil? ما عِندِي شِي مُهِمّ [maː ʕindi ši muhimm] I don't have anything important (to say, discuss, bring up, etc.). تَعالُوا عِدنا باكِر [taʕaːluː ʕidna baːčir] Come to our place tomorrow. هَسَّة جِيت مِن عِدهُم [hassa ǰiːt min ʕidhum] I just now came from their house. مِن عِند [min ʕind] from, of. أخِذت الكِتاب مِن عِندَه [ʔaxiðt ʔilkitaːb min ʕindah] I got the book from him. وهذا دِينار مِن عِندِي [whaːða dinaːr min ʕindi] And here's a dinar from me. هَذا كان تَصَرُّف أحمَق مِن عِندَه [haːða čaːn taṣarruf ʔaħmaq min ʕindah] That was foolish of him. مِن عِند القَرايِب، يِتصَعَّب [min ʕind ʔilgaraːyib, yitṣaʕʕab] When it comes to his relatives, he's real uncooperative.

عناد [ʕnaːd] *n:* • **1.** resistance, stubbornness

عَنُود [ʕanuːd] *adj:* • **1.** stubborn, obstinate, pigheaded • **2.** stubborn person

عَنِيد [ʕaniːd] *adj:* • **1.** very stubborn

عنادي [ʕnaːdi] *adj:* • **1.** stubborn, obstinate, pig-headed

عنُودِي [ʕnuːdi] *adj:* • **1.** stubborn, obstinate, pigheaded

معانِد [mʕaːnid] *adj:* • **1.** uncompromising • **2.** stubborn

أعنَد [ʔaʕnad] *comparative adjective:* • **1.** more or most stubborn, obstinate

ع ن ز

عَنز [ʕanz] *n:* • **1.** goat(s) – دِيس العَنز [diːs ʔilʕanz] a kind of grape, long, sweet, and light green in color.

عَنزَة [ʕanza] *n:* • **1.** goat

ع ن س

عانِس [ʕaːnis] *adj:* عَوانِس [ʕawaːnis] *pl:* • **1.** old maid

ع ن ص ر

عُنصُر [ʕunṣur] *n:* عَناصِر [ʕanaːṣir] *pl:* • **1.** race, stock, breed, ethnic origin • **2.** ethnic element • **3.** element (chem. and pol.)

عُنصُريَّة [ʕunṣuriyya] *n:* • **1.** racism, ethnic bigotry

ع ن ف

عُنُف [ʕunuf] *n:* • **1.** violence, roughness, harshness, ruggedness, vehemence, fierceness

عُنفُوان [ʕunfuwaːn] *n:* • **1.** vigor, prime, bloom • **2.** عُنفُوان شَبابَه in the prime of his youth.

عَنِيف [ʕaniːf] *adj:* • **1.** fierce, tough, bitter – مُقاوَمَة عَنِيفَة [muqaːwama ʕaniːfa] fierce resistance.

ع ن ق

اِعتِنَق [ʔiʕtinaq] *v:* • **1.** to adopt, embrace, take up – اِعتِنَق الدِّين الإسلامِي [ʔiʕtinaq ʔiddiːn ʔilʔislaːmi] He adopted the Islamic religion.
عُنِق [ʕunig, ʕuniq] *n:* عنُوق [ʕnuːg] *pl:* • **1.** neck
اِعتِناق [ʔiʕtinaːq] *n:* • **1.** adoption, acceptance, embracement

ع ن ق د

عَنقُود [ʕanguːd] *n:* عَناقِيد [ʕanaːgiːd] *pl:* • **1.** bunch, cluster (esp. of grapes)

ع ن ك ب و ت

عَنكَبُوت [ʕankabuːt] *n:* عَنكَبُوتات [ʕankabuːtaːt] *pl:* • **1.** spider – بَيت العَنكَبُوت، عِشّ العَنكَبُوت [bayt ʔilʕankabuːt, ʕišš ʔilʕankabuːt] spider web.

ع ن و

عِنّاوَة [ʕinnaːwa] *n:* عِنّاوات [ʕinnaːwaːt] *pl:* • **1.** clitoris

ع ن و ن

عَنوَن [ʕanwan] *v:* • **1.** to address – عَنوِن المَكتُوب بِاسِم الشَّرِكَة وَهُوَّ يَوصَلِّي [ʕanwin ʔilmaktuːb bism ʔiššarika wahuwwa yuːṣalli] Address the letter with the company's name and it will reach me.
عِنوان [ʕinwaːn] *n:* • **1.** address • **2.** title – كَلِمَة بِعِنوان [kalima bʕinwaːn] an address entitled. . . . تَبدِيل عِنوان [tabdiːl ʕinwaːn] change of (job) title.
معَنوَن [mʕanwan] *adj:* • **1.** addressed, inscribed, entitled

ع ن ي

عِنَى [ʕinaː] *v:* • **1.** to concern, interest – هِيكِي شِي ما يِعنِيك. لا تِتدَخَّل [hiːči ši maː yiʕniːk. laː tiddaxxal] That thing doesn't concern you. Don't interfere. مَشاكِلهُم ما تِعنِينِي؛ عِندِي مَشاكِلِي الخاصَّة [mašaːkilhum maː tiʕniːni; ʕindi mašaːkli ʔilxaːṣṣa] Their problems don't interest me; I have my own. سِلُوك إبنِي بِالمَدرَسَة يِعنِينِي هوايَة [siluːk ʔibni bilmadrasa yiʕniːni hwaːya] My son's behavior in school concerns me greatly. • **2.** to mean, to have in mind – شتِعنِي بهَذا؟ [štiʕni bhaːða?] What do you mean by that? شتِعنِي هَالكَلِمَة؟ [štiʕni haččilma?] What's this word mean? ما يِعنِيك بهَالتَّعلِيق [maː yiʕniːk bhattaʕliːq] He didn't have you in mind with that remark.
يَعنِي [yaʕni] *v:* • **1.** that is, in other words, in fact, then. – يَعنِي ما ترِيد تِجِي وِيّانا [yaʕni maː triːd tiǰi wiyyaːna] In other words, you don't want to come with us. يَعنِي، ما أرِيدَك تِحكِي وِيّاه [yaʕni, maː ʔariːdak tiħči wiyyaːh] In short, I don't want you to talk with him. يَعنِي، قُول ما ترِيد تبِيعَه [yaʕni, guːl maː triːd tbiːʕah] Well then, say you don't want to sell it. • **2.** (a parenthetical remark, approx.:) then. – شِنُو، يَعنِي؟ بَسّ إلِي ما تِنطِينِي؟ [šinu, yaʕni? bass ʔili maː tinṭiːni?] What then? I'm the only one you don't give any to? لِيش، يَعنِي، ما جا؟ [liːš, yaʕni, maː ǰaː?] Why didn't he come then? • **3.** (a somewhat noncommital answer, expressing reservations:) so-so, sort of. – يِعجبَك هَالجَوّ؟ --- يَعنِي [yiʕiǰbak haǰǰaww? yaʕni] Do you like this weather? Well, sort of.
عانَى [ʕaːnaː] *v:* • **1.** to suffer, bear, endure, undergo – عانَى هوايَة إلَى أن تخَرَّج [ʕaːnaː hwaːya ʔila ʔan txarraǰ] He went through a lot before he graduated.
تعَنَّى [tʕannaː] *v:* • **1.** to trouble oneself – لا تِتعَنَّى عَلَى مُودِي [laː titʕannaː ʕala muːdi] Don't trouble yourself for my sake.
اِعتِنَى [ʔiʕtinaː] *v:* • **1.** to take care – اِعتِنِي بقاطَك الجِّدِيد [ʔiʕtini bqaːṭak ʔiǰǰidiːd] Take care of your new suit.
مَعنَى [maʕna] *n:* مَعانِي [maʕaːni] *pl:* • **1.** sense, meaning – شِنُو مَعناها؟ [šinuː maʕnaːha?] What's it mean? بكُلّ مَعنى الكَلِمَة [bkull maʕnaː ʔiččilma] in every sense of the word. شمَعنَى ترُوح وَما تقُلِّي؟ [šmaʕna truːħ wma dgulli?] What do you mean going and not telling me? زَعَلَك ما إلَه مَعنى [zaʕalak maː ʔilah maʕna] There's no reason for your anger.
عِنايَة [ʕinaːya] *n:* • **1.** care, caring, taking care of – عِنايَة بِالمَرضَى [ʕinaːya bilmarða] caring for patients. • **2.** care, pains, carefulness – بِعِنايَة [bʕinaːya] carefully. بَلا عِنايَة [bala ʕinaːya] carelessly. • **3.** concern, solicitude, heed, notice, regard, attention
اعتِناء [ʔiʕtinaːʔ] *n:* • **1.** care, nursing • **2.** attention, carefulness, painstaking
مُعاناة [muʕaːnaːt] *n:* • **1.** suffering, effort, toil, hardship, distress
مَعنَوِيّات [maʕnawiyyaːt] *n:* • **1.** morale, spirit
مَعنِي [maʕni] *adj:* • **1.** concerned, affected, interested
مَعنَوِي [maʕnawi] *adj:* • **1.** pertaining to meaning, • **2.** abstract, mental, spiritual
مِعتِنِي [miʕtini] *adj:* • **1.** concerned • **2.** taken care of

ع ه د

تعَهَّد [tʕahhad] *v:* • **1.** to take on oneself, to guarantee – أتعَهَّدلَك بِالفلُوس [ʔatʕahhadlak bilfiluːs] I'll guarantee you the money. • **2.** to undertake, to bind oneself, to pledge oneself, to obligate oneself – النَّجّار تعَهَّد يخَلِّص الشُّغُل بيومَين [ʔinnaǰǰaːr tʕahhad ʔiːxallis ʔiššuɣul byawmayn] The carpenter undertook to finish the work in two days. • **3.** to promise – تعَهَّدلِي ما يسَوِّيها [tʕahhadli maː ysawwiːha] He promised me he wouldn't do it.

ع

تعاهَد [tʕa:had] *v:* • **1.** to make a mutual pledge – تعاهَدوا يِبقُون أصدِقاء [tʕa:hdaw yibqu:n ʔaṣdiqa:ʔ] They vowed to remain friends.

عَهَد [ʕahad] *n:* • **1.** knowledge: – عَهدِي بِيه [ʕahdi bi:h] to my knowledge, as far as I know. عَهدِي بِيه، ما يبُوق [ʕahdi bi:h, ma: ybu:g] To my knowledge, he doesn't steal. • **2.** pledge, promise • **3.** time, epoch, era – وَلِي العَهَد [wali ʔilʕahad] the crown prince, heir apparent.

عُهدَة، عَلَى عُهدَة [ʕuhda, ʕala ʕuhda] *n:* • **1.** in the charge of, under the care of – راح آخُذ هَالقَضيِّة عَلَى عُهُدتِي [ra:ħ ʔa:xuð halqaðiyya ʕala ʕuhudti] I'll take this matter on myself. • **2.** بعُهدَة, عَلَى عُهدَة at the charge of – سافَر المُدِير وَخَلَّى كُلّشِي بِعُهدَة المُعاوِن مالُه [sa:far ʔilmudi:r wxalla: kullši bʕuhdat ʔilmuʕa:win ma:lah] The director went off and left everything in his assistant's charge.

مَعهَد [maʕhad] *n:* مَعاهِد [maʕa:hid] *pl:* • **1.** (public) institute or institution • **2.** institute

تَعَهُّد [taʕahhud] *n:* • **1.** promise, pledge, commitment • **2.** engagement, obligation, liability

مُعاهَدَة [muʕa:hada] *n:* مُعاهَدات [muʕa:hada:t] *pl:* • **1.** treaty, accord, agreement, pact

مِتعَهِّد [mitʕahhid] *adj:* • **1.** contractor, supplier

مَعهُود [maʕhu:d] *adj:* • **1.** well-known, trusted • **2.** entrusted

ع ه ر

عاهِرَة [ʕa:hira] *n:* عاهِرات [ʕa:hira:t] *pl:* • **1.** whore, prostitute

ع و ج

عِوَج [ʕiwaǰ] *v:* • **1.** to bend, twist – دِير بالَك لا تِعوِج السِّيم [di:r ba:lak la: tiʕwiǰ ʔissi:m] Be careful not to bend the wire. • **2.** to turn off, to turn aside – فُوت شوَيَّة وَبَعدين إعوِج عَاليِمنَى [fu:t šwayya wbaʕdi:n ʔiʕwiǰ ʕalyimna] Go ahead a little way and then bear to the right.

عَوَّج [ʕawwaǰ] *v:* • **1.** to bend, twist – عَوَّج التَّيل بِالكَلّابتين [ʕawwaǰ ʔittayl biččilla:btayn] He bent the wire with the pliers.

تعَوَّج [tʕawwaǰ] *v:* • **1.** to buckle • **2.** to be bent, twisted

اِنعِوَج [ʔinʕiwaǰ] *v:* • **1.** to be or become bent, twisted – دَعّامِيَّة السَّيّارَة اِنعِوجَت بحادِث الاصطِدام [daʕʕa:miyyat ʔissayya:ra ʔinʕiwǰat bħa:diθ ʔilʔiṣṭida:m] The car's bumper got bent in the collision.

عاج [ʕa:ǰ] *n:* • **1.** ivory

عَوَج [ʕawaǰ] *n:* • **1.** bending, twistedness, curvature • **2.** deviation

عواج [ʕawa:ǰ] *n:* • **1.** bending, twisting

تعَوُّج [tʕawwuǰ] *n:* • **1.** bending, twisting

عُوجِيَّة [ʕu:čiyya] *n:* عُوجِيّات [ʕu:čiyya:t] *pl:* • **1.** cane, walking stick

عاجِي [ʕa:ǰi] *adj:* • **1.** ivory (adj.) – تَماثِيل عاجِيَّة [tama:θi:l ʕa:ǰiyya] ivory statues. • **2.** ivory, ivorylike – عَليها سِيقان عاجِيَّة [ʕali:ha si:qa:n ʕa:ǰiyya] She has ivory legs. أَسنان عاجِيَّة [ʔasna:n ʕa:ǰiyya] ivory-like teeth.

أعوَج [ʔaʕwaǰ] *adj:* عُوج [ʕu:ǰ] *pl:* عوجَة [ʕu:ǰa] *feminine:* • **1.** bent, crooked, twisted – بِسمار أعوَج [bisma:r ʔaʕwaǰ] a bent nail. حَلِق أعوَج [ħalig ʔaʕwaǰ] a twisted mouth. أُقعُد أعوَج وَإحكِي عَدِل [ʔugʕud ʔaʕwaǰ wʔiħči ʕadil] Feel at ease but tell the truth. • **2.** winding, twisting, tortuous – طَرِيق أعوَج [ṭari:q ʔaʕwaǰ] a winding road. • **3.** lopsided

معوَّج [mʕawwaǰ] *adj:* • **1.** bended, twisted, bent

مَعوُوج [maʕwu:ǰ] *adj:* • **1.** bended, twisted, lopsided

متعَوِّج [mitʕawwiǰ] *adj:* • **1.** bended, twisted

ع و د

عاد [ʕa:d] *v:* • **1.** to return, come back – اللُّجنَة عادَت مِن جَولَتها [ʔilluǰna ʕa:dat min ǰawlatha] The committee returned from its tour.

عاد [ʕa:d] *v:* • **1.** to repeat – عِيد هَالجُملَة مَرَّة ثانيَة [ʕi:d haǰǰumla marra θa:nya] Repeat this sentence again. ما حُفَظ الكِلمَة إلّا لَمّا عادها عِدَّة مَرّات [ma: ħufaḍ ʔiččilma ʔilla lamma ʕa:dha ʕiddat marra:t] He didn't memorize the word until he repeated it several times. لا تعِيدها بَعَد، تَرَة أزعَل [la: tʕi:dha baʕad, tara ʔazʕal] Don't do it again, or I'll get mad. يَعنِي كُلّ يوم نعِيد وَنُصقُل؟ [yaʕni kull yu:m nʕi:d wnuṣqul?] You mean we have to go through this day in and day out? المَحكَمَة عادَت النَّظَر بِالقَضيِّة [ʔilmaħkama ʕa:dat ʔinnaḍar bilqaḍiyya] The court reconsidered the case. • **2.** to return, give back, send back – عادَوا الأَوراق لِلُّجنَة [ʕa:daw ʔilʔawra:q lilluǰna] They returned the papers to the committee. عادَوه لِلوَظِيفَة [ʕa:dawh lilwaḍi:fa] They sent him back to his regular job.

عَوَّد [ʕawwad] *v:* • **1.** to accustom, condition, teach the habit – عَوِّدَوا اِبنهُم عالنَّظافَة [ʕawwidaw ʔibinhum ʕannaḍa:fa] They trained their son to be tidy. لا تعَوِّد لِسانَك عالحَكِي الوَسِخ [la: tʕawwid lisa:nak ʕalħači ʔilwasix] Don't get into the habit of using dirty words.

عاوَد [ʕa:wad] *v:* • **1.** to revert, resume – إذا يعاوِد، أبُسطَه [ʔiða yʕa:wid, ʔabusṭah] If he does it again, I'll beat him up.

أعاد [ʔaʕa:d] *v:* • **1.** to repeat – أعاد الشِّعِر لِأَنّ ما سمَعتَه [ʔaʕa:d ʔiššiʕir liʔann ma: smaʕtah] He repeated the poetry because I didn't hear it. الوِزارَة راح تعِيد النَّظَر بقَضِيتَه [ʔilwiza:ra ra:ħ tʕi:d ʔinnaḍar bqaḍi:tah] The ministry is going to reconsider his case. • **2.** to reorganize, revise – الشُّرطَة أعادَت تَنظِيم حَرَكَة المُرُور [ʔiššurṭa ʔaʕa:dat tanḍi:m ħarakat ʔilmuru:r] The police reorganized the traffic regulations.

تعوّد [tʕawwad] *v:* • **1.** to get acccustomed to, to accustom oneself – تعوّد ينام مِن وَقِت [tʕawwad yinaːm min wakit] He got accustomed to going to sleep early.
انعاد [ʔinʕaːd] *v:* • **1.** to be returned, to be brought back, to be taken back, to be sent back – راح ينعاد لوَظيفتَه [raːħ yinʕaːd lwaðiːftah] He'll be returned to his job. • **2.** to be repeated, to be done over – الامتِحان راح ينعاد لأنّ اِكتِشفَوا الأسئلة مَبيُوقة [ʔilʔimtiħaːn raːħ yinʕaːd liʔann ʔiktišfaw ʔilʔasʔila mabyuːga] The examination will be repeated because they found the questions stolen. راح ينعاد طَبع الكِتاب لأنّ أكو بيه سَهو [raːħ yinʕaːd ṭabʕ ʔilkitaːb liʔann ʔaku biːh sahw] Typing the letter will be done over because there is a mistake in it.
اعتاد [ʔiʕtaːd] *v:* • **1.** to be or become accustomed, used – لازم تِعتاد عَلَى الدِّراسَة باللَّيل [laːzim tiʕtaːd ʕala ʔiddiraːsa billayl] You must get used to studying at night.
استَعاد [ʔistaʕaːd] *v:* • **1.** to recover • **2.** to regain
عُود [ʕuːd] *n:* أعواد [ʔaʕwaːd] *pl:* • **1.** lute • **2.** (an interjection, approx.:) well, then – عُود مِن يِجي، أقُلّه [ʕuːd min yiji, ʔagullah] Well, when he comes, I'll tell him. درُوح هَسَّة، عُود مِن ترُدّ أنطِيك إيّاها [daruːħ hassa, ʕuːd min trudd ʔanṭiːk ʔiyyaːha] Go ahead now, and then when you come back I'll give it to you.
عُودَة [ʕuːda] *n:* عُودات، عُوَد [ʕuːdaːt, ʕuwad] *pl:* • **1.** splinter • **2.** match, matchstick – عُودَة شِخّاط [ʕuːdat šixxaːṭ] matchstick. • **3.** stick
مُعيد [muʕiːd] *n:* • **1.** teaching assistant, graduate assistant • **2.** (esp. in the law school) failed in annual examination, person who failed and needed to take the exam again – طِلَع مُعِيد [ṭilaʕ muʕiːd] He failed his exams.
عَودَة [ʕawda] *n:* • **1.** return
تَعَوُّد [taʕawwud] *n:* • **1.** habituation
عادَة [ʕaːda] *n:* • **1.** habit, custom, practice – العادَة السِّرِّيَّة [ʔilʕaːda ʔissirriyya] masturbation, onanism. جِرَت العادَة أن يزُورُون مَرّتَين بالإسبُوع [ǰirat ʔilʕaːda ʔan yizzawruːn marrtayn bilʔisbuːʕ] It became customary for them to visit each other twice a week. حَسَب العادَة [ħasab ʔilʕaːda] as usual, according to custom. راح يعَيِّد جِيرانا حَسَب العادَة [raːħ yiʕayyid ǰiːraːna ħasab ʔilʕaːda] He went to congratulate his neighbors on the feast as is customary. • **2.** period, menstruation – جَتّها العادَة [ǰattha ʔilʕaːda] She got her period.
عِيادَة [ʕiyaːda] *n:* عِيادات [ʕiyaːdaːt] *pl:* • **1.** clinic • **2.** doctor's office
تَعوِيد [taʕwiːd] *n:* • **1.** accustomation, acclamation, habituation
إعادَة [ʔiʕaːda] *n:* • **1.** repetition • **2.** giving back, sending back
اِستِعادَة [ʔistiʕaːda] *n:* • **1.** recovery, regaining, reconquest, retrieval, recuperation.

عادِي [ʕaːdi] *adj:* • **1.** ordinary, run-of-the-mill, common – قماش عادِي [qmaːš ʕaːdi] ordinary cloth. • **2.** (by extension) cheap, common, vulgar – فَدّ واحِد عادِي [fadd waːħid ʕaːdi] a vulgar person.
مَعَوَّد [mʕawwad] *adj:* • **1.** accustomed, used – مَعَوَّد عالعِيشَة بالجِبال [mʕawwad ʕalʕiːša biǰǰibaːl] accustomed to life in the mountains. • **2.** (a term of address, often implying a degree of impatience, irritation, or dismay, approx.:) Mac, buster, buddy, man – مَعَوَّد، لَحِّقلَه. راح يغرق [mʕawwad, laħħiglah. raːħ yiɣrig] Get him, Mac. He's going to drown. يا مَعَوَّد، آني شَعلَيَّا؟ [yaː mʕawwad, ʔaːni šaʕlayya?] Look man, what's it to me? ما تجُوز، يا مَعَوَّد! هَذا شماعَرّفَه إنكِلِيزِي؟ [maː dǰuːz, yaː mʕawwad! haːða šmaʕarrfah ʔingiliːzi?] Knock it off, Mac! What does he know about English? لا، يا مَعَوَّد! شوَقِت مات؟ [laː, yaː mʕawwad! šwakit maːt?] No, man! When did he die?
مُعاد [muʕaːd] *adj:* • **1.** recycled • **2.** repeated
عائد [ʕaːʔid] *adj:* • **1.** pertinent • **2.** returning • **3.** revenue
متعَوِّد [mitʕawwid] *adj:* • **1.** used, accustomed – مِتعَوِّد يتأخَّر باللَّيل [mitʕawwid yitʔaxxar billayl] used to staying out late. مِتعَوِّد عالرَّزالَة [mitʕawwid ʕarrazaːla] used to being called on the carpet.
مُعتاد، حَسب المُعتاد، كَالمُعتاد [muʕtaːd, ħasb ʔilmuʕtaːd, kalmuʕtaːd] *adj:* • **1.** as usual • **2.** used, accustomed (to)
اِعتِيادِي [ʔiʕtiyaːdi] *adj:* • **1.** usual, customary, habitual – الطَّرِيق الاعتِيادِي [ʔiṭṭariːq ʔilʔiʕtiyaːdi] the usual way, route. • **2.** normal, usual, commonplace – مَنظَر اِعتِيادِي [manðar ʔiʕtiyaːdi] a commonplace sight. شِي اِعتِيادِي بِالمُستَشفى [ši ʔiʕtiyaːdi bilmustašfa] a common thing in hospitals.
عُودَين [ʕuːdayn] *adv:* • **1.** (an interjection, approx:) well, then
عادَةً [ʕaːdatan] *adverbial:* • **1.** usually, customarily
عاد [ʕaːd] *int:* • **1.** (an exclamation of emphasis used with commands, approx.:) now, mind you, dammit – بَسّ عاد [bass ʕaːd] That's enough now! يَزِّي عاد [yazzi ʕaːd] Quit it, dammit! لا تثَخّنها عاد [laː tθaxxinha ʕaːd] Don't push your luck too far! عاد، خَلِّي نرُوح [ʕaːd, xalliː nruːħ] Dammit, let's go! • **2.** (an exclamation of emphasis used in denying or rejecting a statement or proposal, approx.:) but, well, even – عاد هَذا أحسَن وَلَد. ما يسَوِّي هِيكِي شِي [ʕaːd haːða ʔaħsan walad. maː ysawwiː hiːči ši] But he's a good boy. He wouldn't do such a thing. عاد لَو يِنطِينِي مِليَون دِينار، ما أبِيع [ʕaːd law yinṭiːni milyuːn dinaːr, maː ʔabiːʕ] Even though he gives me a million dinars, I won't sell. عاد وَلا أبِيع [ʕaːd wala ʔabiːʕ] I'll never sell. عاد مُو بِالحَيف [ʕaːd muː bilħayf] Not on your life.

ع

ع و ذ

عاذ، أَعُوذُ بِالله [ʕaːð, ʔaʕuːðu bʔallaːh] *v:* • **1.** (used when something shameful, distasteful, or evil is mentioned or encountered, approx.:) God forbid! Heaven forbid! God save me . . ., God deliver me. . – أعُوذ بِالله مِن هَالخِلقَة [ʔaʕuːð billaːh min halxilqa] God save me from this face! أعُوذ بِالله مِن الصُّوت [ʔaʕuːð billaːh min ʔiṣṣuːt] God deliver me from that voice!

عُوذَة [ʕuːða] *n:* عُوذات، عُوَذ [ʕuːðaːt, ʕuwað] *pl:* • **1.** talisman, charm, amulet • **2.** (by extension) something very small • **3.** (an exclamation invoking protection from something dirty, ritually unclean, or distasteful.) – عُوذَة، عُوذَة! لا توَسِّخ هدُومِي [ʕuːða, ʕuːða! laː twassix hduːmi] Get away! Don't dirty my clothes. عُوذَة! شلُون خِلقَة عَليه [ʕuːða! šluːn xilqa ʕaliːh] God forbid! What a face he's got!

عِياذ، عِياذ بِالله [ʕiyaːð, ʕiyaːð billaːh] *n:* • **1.** God forbid! God save us! God protect us! – عِياذ بِالله مِن هَالوِلِد [ʕiyaːð billaːh min halwilid] God save us from those kids!

تَعوِيذَة [taʕwiːða] *n:* تَعوِيذات [taʕwiːðaːt] *pl:* • **1.** talisman, charm, amulet

مَعاذ، مَعاذ الله [maʕaːð, maʕaːð ʔillaːh] *int:* • **1.** god forbid

ع و ر

عَوَّر [ʕawwar] *v:* • **1.** to hurt, to injure – عَوَّرتنِي بِهَالضَربَة [ʕawwaritni bhaððarba] You hurt me with this blow. دِفعَه عَالسِّياج وَعَوَّرَه [difaʕah ʕassiyaːǰ wʕawwarah] He pushed him against the fence and injured him.

أعار [ʔaʕaːr] *v:* • **1.** to lend – تِقدَر تعِيرنِي كتابَك هاللَّيلَة؟ [tigdar tʕiːrni ktaːbak hallayla?] Can you lend me your book this evening?

تعَوَّر [tʕawwar] *v:* • **1.** to be hurt, get hurt – وُقَع مِن الدَّرَج وَتعَوَّر [wugaʕ min ʔiddaraj wtʕawwar] He fell from the ladder and was hurt.

اِستَعار [ʔistaʕaːr] *v:* • **1.** to borrow – اِستَعار مِنِّي عِدَّة أَشياء وَما رَجَّعها [ʔistaʕaːr minni ʕiddat ʔašyaːʔ wama rajǰaʕha] He borrowed several things from me and didn't return them.

عَورَة [ʕawra] *n:* عَورات [ʕawraːt] *pl:* • **1.** genitals, pudendum • **2.** crotch, genital area

إعارَة [ʔiʕaːra] *n:* • **1.** lending – الإعارَة وَالتَّأجِير [ʔilʔiʕaːra wittaʔǰiːr] lend-lease. إعارَة خَدَمات [ʔiʕaːrat xadamaːt] lending the services of personnel.

اِستِعارَة [ʔistiʕaːra] *n:* • **1.** borrowing, lending

أَعوَر [ʔaʕwar] *adj:* عُور، عُوران، عَورِين [ʕuːr, ʕuːraːn, ʕuːriːn] *pl:* عُورَة [ʕuːra] *feminine:* • **1.** one-eyed, blind in one eye • **2.** one-eyed man – المُصران الأعوَر [ʔilmuṣraːn ʔilʔaʕwar] the vermiform appendix.

عَوارَة، عوارَة [ʕawaːra, ʕwaːra] *adj:* عوارات [ʕwaːraːt] *pl:* • **1.** fault, defect

مِتعَوِّر [mitʕawwir] *adj:* • **1.** hurt, injured

مُستَعار [mustaʕaːr] *adj:* • **1.** false, artificial – شَعَر مُستَعار [šaʕar mustaʕaːr] wig, toupee, hairpiece. إسِم مُستَعار [ʔisim mustaʕaːr] pseudonym, assumed name.

مِستِعِير [mistiʕiːr] *adj:* • **1.** borrowing, borrower

ع و ز

عاز [ʕaːz] *v:* • **1.** to be needed by, to be lacking – آنِي مِكتِفِي وَما يعُوزنِي شِي [ʔaːni miktifi wmaː yʕuːzni ši] I am satisfied and lacking nothing. هَالسَّيّارَة مُمتازَة. ما يعُوزها غير باترِي جِدِيد [hassayyaːra mumtaːza. maː yʕuːzha γiːr paːtri ǰidiːd] This is an excellent car. It needs only a new battery. كُلشِي عِدهُم؛ بَسّ عايزهُم تَلَفزيُون [kullši ʕidhum; bass ʕaːyizhum talafizyuːn] They have everything but a television set.

عَوز [ʕawz] *n:* • **1.** poverty

عازَة [ʕaːza] *n:* • **1.** need, necessity, exigency

عوازَة [ʕwaːza] *n:* • **1.** extra, in addition, more – نُصّ يارِدَة عوازَة [nuṣṣ yaːrda ʕwaːza] half a yard more. قُرصَة خُبُز عوازَة [gurṣat xubuz ʕwaːza] an extra loaf of bread.

مِعتاز [miʕtaːz] *adj:* • **1.** lacking, in need of – مِعتازَة تايَرات [miʕtaːza taːyaraːt] in need of tires.

ع و س ج

عَوسَج [ʕuːsaǰ, ʕawsaǰ] *n:* • **1.** boxthorn, boxthorn plant – حِرِش عَوسَج [ħiriš ʕuːsaǰ] boxthorn bush.

ع و ش

عَوَّش [ʕawwaš] *v:* • **1.** to be or become dispirited, listless – أشُو مِن خَلِّينا البِلبِل بِالقُفَص، عَوَّش [ʔašu min xalliːna ʔilbilbil bilqufaṣ, ʕawwaš] It seems when we put the nightingale in the cage, he drooped visibly. شبِيه أبُوك؟ أشُو مِعَوِّش اليُوم [šbiːh ʔabuːk? ʔašu mʕawwiš ʔilyuːm] What's the matter with your father? He seems down in the mouth today.

مِعَوِّش [mʕawwiš] *adj:* • **1.** dispirited, listless

ع و ص

عِوَص [ʕiwaṣ] *v:* • **1.** with عَين to squint – عَلَى ويش دَتِعوِص عينَك؟ [ʕala wiːš datiʕwiṣ ʕaynak?] Why are you squinting? عِوَص عَينَه وَنَيشَن البُندُقِيَّة [ʕiwaṣ ʕaynah wanayšan ʔilbunduqiyya] He squinted and aimed the rifle.

عَوَّص [ʕawwaṣ] *v:* • **1.** with عَين means to squint

عَوِص [ʕawiṣ] *n:* • **1.** squinting

أَعوَص [ʔaʕwaṣ] *adj:* عُوص، عَوصِين [ʕuːṣ, ʕuːṣiːn] *pl:* عوصَة [ʕawṣa] *feminine:* • **1.** squinting, squinted – عَينَه عوصَة [ʕaynah ʕawṣa] His eye is squinted. • **2.** person with a narrowed eye, person who squints

عَوِيص [ʕawiːṣ] *adj:* • **1.** difficult, hard to comprehend, abstruse, obscure – مُشكِلَة عَوِيصَة [muškila ʕawiːṣa] a difficult problem.

ع و ض

عَوَّض [ʕawwað̣] *v:* • **1.** to substitute, replace, take the place – خَلّي يرُوح. آني أعَوُّض عَنّه [xalli: yiru:ħ. ʔaːni ʔaʕawwuð̣ ʕannah] Let him go. I'll substitute for him. • **2.** to recompense, compensate – الحُكومَة عَوّضَت الفَلّاحين عَن خَسايرهُم [ʔilħuku:ma ʕawwð̣at ʔilfalla:ħi:n ʕan xasa:yirhum] The government compensated the peasants for their losses. إذا تِخسَر، أعَوُّضَك [ʔiða tixsar, ʔaʕawwuð̣ak] If you lose, I'll make it up to you. الله يعَوُّض [ʔallah yʕawwuð̣] God will provide (an expression of hope for the future, after a loss).

اِستَعاض [ʔistaʕa:ð̣] *v:* • **1.** to replace, exchange, substitute – تِقدَر تِستَعيض عَنّه بمُوَظَّف آخَر [tigdar tistaʕi:ð̣ ʕannah bmuwað̣ð̣af ʔa:xar] You can replace him with another employee.

عِوَض [ʕiwað̣] *n:* • **1.** compensation, recompense, indemnity

تَعويض [taʕwi:ð̣] *n:* • **1.** compensation, indemnification, reparation – طالَب بالتَّعويض [ṭa:lab bittaʕwi:ð̣] He requested compensation.

تَعويضي [taʕwi:ð̣i] *adj:* • **1.** compensative, compensatory, reparative

عِوَضاً [ʕiwað̣an] *adverbial:* • **1.** as a substitute for, in replacement of

ع و ع ي

عَوعَى [ʕu:ʕa:] *v:* • **1.** to crow – ديكنا يعَوعي مِن يِسمَع حِسّ ديكِكُم [di:čna yʕu:ʕi min yismaʕ ħiss di:čkum] Our rooster crows when he hears your rooster.

ع و ف

عاف [ʕa:f] *v:* • **1.** to desert, abandon – طَلَّق مَرتَه وَعاف ولدَه [ṭallag martah wʕa:f wildah] He divorced his wife and deserted his children. • **2.** to leave, also with عَن to leave alone, let alone, let be – يعُوف سَيّارتَه قِدّام البَيت [yʕu:f sayya:rtah gidda:m ʔilbayt] He leaves his car in front of the house. إذا تعيف كُتُبَك هنا، تِنباق [ʔiða tʕi:f kutubak hna, tinba:g] If you leave your books here, they'll get stolen. ما تعيفني! مُو راح تخَبُّلني [ma: tʕi:fni! mu: ra:ħ txabbulni] Let me alone! You're going to drive me to distraction! ما تعُوف عَنّه عاد [ma: tʕu:f ʕannah ʕa:d] Leave him alone, for God's sake! ما تعُوفنا! مِن عِندَه فلوس؟ [ma: tʕu:fna! min ʕindah flu:s?] Come off it! Who's got any money? ما تعُوفنا مِن هَالحَكي [ma: tʕu:fna min halħači] Spare us that talk!

اِنعاف [ʔinʕa:f] *v:* • **1.** to be left (alone), to be deserted

عيف [ʕayf, ʕi:f] *n:* • **1.** abandonment, desertion

عَوف [ʕawf, ʕu:f] *n:* • **1.** abandonment, desertion

عُوفَة، عيفَة [ʕu:fa, ʕi:fa] *n:* • **1.** abandonment, desertion

مَعيُوف [maʕyu:f] *adj:* • **1.** abandoned, left

ع و ق

عاق [ʕa:q] *v:* • **1.** to hinder, prevent – ماكو شي يعُوقني عَن المَجيئ [ma:ku ši yʕu:qni ʕan ʔilmaji:ʔ] Nothing can prevent me from coming.

عَوَّق [ʕawwag] *v:* • **1.** to hinder, delay – صارلي ساعَة أنتَظرَك. ما تقُلّي شِنُو اللّي عَوَّقَك؟ [ṣa:rli sa:ʕa ʔantað̣rak. ma: tgulli šinu ʔilli ʕawwagak?] I've been waiting an hour for you. Why don't you tell me what delayed you? • **2.** to save, to keep, to leave – لا تُصرُف راتبَك كُلّه. عَوِّق شوَيَّة مِنّه [la: tuṣruf ra:tbak kullah. ʕawwig šwayya minnah] Don't spend all your salary. Save a little of it. أكُل وَعَوِّقلي شوَيَّة [ʔukul wʕawwugli šwayya] Eat and leave a little bit for me.

تعَوَّق [tʕawwaq, tʕawwag] *v:* • **1.** to be delayed – لا تِنتَظرُوني بالعَشا. راح أتعَوَّق شوَيَّة [la: tintað̣ru:ni bilʕaša:. ra:ħ ʔatʕawwag šwayya] Don't wait dinner for me. I'll be delayed a little while. • **2.** to be saved, be kept, be left over – ما تعَوَّق شي مِن الرّاتِب هَالشَّهَر [ma: tʕawwag ši min ʔirra:tib haššahar] Nothing was left over from my salary this month. • **3.** to stay, remain (behind) – تعَوَّق لِلغَدا [tʕawwag lilɣada] He stayed there for lunch.

عايق [ʕa:yiq] *n:* عَوايق، مُعَوِّقات [ʕawa:yiq, muʕawwiqa:t] *pl:* • **1.** obstacle, stumbling block, obstacle

إعاقَة [ʔiʕa:qa] *n:* • **1.** hindering, preventing • **2.** hindrance, obstacle, impediment

مُعَوَّق [muʕawwaq] *adj:* • **1.** handicapped

ع و ل

عَوَّل [ʕawwal] *v:* • **1.** to rely, depend, count on – مُو عَوَّلنا عَليك، وَقُلنا إنتَ تسَوّيها؟ [mu: ʕawwalna ʕali:k, wgulna ʔinta tsawwi:ha?] Didn't we depend on you and say you would do it? • **2.** to expect – إنتَ معَوِّل تحَصِّل هيكي دَرَجَة؟ [ʔinta mʕawwil tħaṣṣil hi:či daraja?] Did you really expect to get such a grade?

عال، أعال [ʕa:l, ʔaʕa:l] *v:* • **1.** to support, provide for – إذا يمُوت أبُوهُم، مِنُو يعُولهُم؟ [ʔiða ymu:t ʔabu:hum, minu yʕu:lhum?] If their father dies, who'll provide for them?

عيال [ʕya:l] *n:* • **1.** in-laws, especially the husband's family • **2.** dependents – صاحِب عيال [ṣa:ħib ʕiya:l] supporter of a large family.

مَعوَل [maʕwal] *n:* مَعاوِل [maʕa:wil] *pl:* • **1.** pick, pick-ax, mattock

مُعيل [muʕi:l] *n:* • **1.** provider for a family, sole support of someone (and therefore exempt from military service)

إعالَة [ʔiʕa:la] *n:* • **1.** supporting a family (as an excuse for avoiding military service)

عائلَة [ʕa:ʔila] *n:* عَوائِل [ʕawa:ʔil] *pl:* • **1.** family

ع

عالَة [ʕaːla] *adj:* • **1.** (invar.) burden, dependent – عالَة عَالمُجتَمَع [ʕaːla ʕalmuǰtamaʕ] a burden on society.
معَوِّل [mʕawwil] *adj:* • **1.** dependent (on)
عائِلي [ʕaːʔili] *adj:* • **1.** family-related – قَضِيَّة عائِلِيَّة [qaðiyya ʕaːʔiliyya] a family matter. • **2.** domestic

ع و م

عام [ʕaːm] *v:* • **1.** to float, to swim
عام، العام [ʕaːm, ʔilʕaːm] *n:* • **1.** last year – العام قِضَينا الصَّيف بأورُبّا [ʔilʕaːm giðayna ʔiṣṣayf bʔuːruppa] Last year we spent the summer in Europe.
عوم [ʕuːm] *n:* • **1.** swimming
عَوّامَة [ʕawwaːma] *n:* • **1.** buoy, float, raft, pontoon
عايِم [ʕaːyim] *adj:* • **1.** floating – جِسِر عايِم [ǰisir ʕaːyim] pontoon bridge.

ع و ن

عاوَن [ʕaːwan] *v:* • **1.** to aid, assist, help – تِقدَر تعاوِنِي أَلِمّ الغَراض؟ [tigdar tʕaːwinni ʔalimm ʔilɣaraːð?] Can you help me gather up the things?
عان [ʕaːn] *v:* • **1.** to aid, assist, support – الله يعِين الفَقِير [ʔallah yʕiːn ʔilfaqiːr] God helps the poor.
تعاوَن [tʕaːwan] *v:* • **1.** to help each other, cooperate – لَو تِتعاوَنُون، تخَلّصُون الشُّغُل بساع [law titʕaːwanuːn, txallṣuːn ʔiššuɣul bsaːʕ] If you help each other, you'll finish the work quickly. لِيش ما تِتعاوَن وِيّانا؟ [liːš maː titʕaːwan wiyyaːna?] Why don't you cooperate with us?
اِستَعان [ʔistaʕaːn] *v:* • **1.** to seek help – كُلّما يريد يسَوّي شِي يِستِعِين بِيّا [kullma yriːd ysawwiː ši yistiʕiːn biyya] Whenever he wants to do something, he comes to me for help.
عَون، عُون [ʕawn, ʕuːn] *n:* • **1.** help, aid, assistance, support (in a few expressions:) – الله يكُون بعَونَه [ʔallah ykuːn bʕawnah] He'll want divine assistance for that. جِبتَه عون طِلَعلِي فِرعون [ǰibtah ʕawn ṭilaʕli firʕawn] I brought him for support and he turned out a tyrant. • **2.** pl. أعوان helper, supporter, henchman • **3.** good fortune, good luck – عَونَه اللِي يرُوح لأورُبّا [ʕuːnah ʔilli yruːħ lʔuːruppa] He's lucky to go to Europe.
عانَة [ʕaːna] *n:* عانات [ʕaːnaːt] *pl:* • **1.** five fils coin – راح ناخُذ عاناتنا مِن المُحاسِب اليوم [raːħ naːxuð ʕaːnaːtna min ʔilmuħaːsib ʔilyuːm] We're going to get our pittance from the accountant today. • **2.** pubes, pubic area
إعانَة [ʔiʕaːna] *n:* إعانات [ʔiʕaːnaːt] *pl:* • **1.** contribution, aid, help, assistance, donation
تَعاوُن [taʕaːwun] *n:* • **1.** cooperation
مُعاوِن [muʕaːwin] *n:* • **1.** assistant • **2.** police lieutenant
مَعُونَة [maʕuːna] *n:* • **1.** help, aid, assistance
مُعاوَنَة [muʕaːwana] *n:* • **1.** aid, assistance, help
اِستِعانَة [ʔistiʕaːna] *n:* • **1.** (act or instance of) seeking help, • **2.** with ب- : making use of, with the help of
مُعِين، الله المُعِين [muʕiːn, ʔallah ʔilmuʕiːn] *adj:* • **1.** God will provide – يا الله يا مُعِين [yaː ʔallah yaː muʕiːn] said when lifting a weight, pushing an object, or otherwise exerting effort, or when in need of divine help.
تَعاوُني [taʕaːwuni] *adj:* • **1.** cooperative – جَمعِيَّة تَعاوُنِيَّة [ǰamʕiyya taʕaːwuniyya] cooperative society. • **2.** with cooperative spirit, community spirit
مِتعاوِن [mitʕaːwin] *adj:* • **1.** cooperative

ع و ه

عاهَة [ʕaːha] *n:* عاهات [ʕaːhaːt] *pl:* • **1.** defect, handicap

ع و ي

عِوَى [ʕiwaː] *v:* • **1.** to howl (dog, wolf, jackal) – الذِّيب كان يِعوِي وَما قدَرِت أنام [ʔiððiːb čaːn yiʕwi wma gdarit ʔanaːm] The wolf was howling and I couldn't sleep.
عَوَّى [ʕawwaː] *v:* • **1.** to howl
عَوِي [ʕawi] *n:* • **1.** howling (of dog, wolf, jackal)
تعُوِّي [tʕuwwi] *n:* • **1.** howling, whining, yelping

ع ي ب

عاب، عاب وِجّهَك، عاب هَالجِهرَة، عابَتلِك هَالشِّكِل [ʕaːb, ʕaːb wiččak, ʕaːb halčihra, ʕaːbatlič haššikil] *v:* • **1.** Damn you! Go to hell!
عَيَّب [ʕayyab] *v:* • **1.** to find fault, criticize – ما قِبَل يِلبَس السِّترَة بَعَد، لِأَنّ عَيِّبَوا عَليها [maː qibal yilbas ʔissitra baʕad, liʔann ʕayyibaw ʕaliːha] He wouldn't wear the jacket any more because they criticized it. • **2.** to mimic, make fun of – لا تعَيِّب! بَسّ آني عَرجَة؟ [laː tʕayyib! bass ʔaːni ʕarǰa?] Don't poke fun! Am I the only one with a limp? شُوف الجّاهِل دَيعَيِّب عَلَى أُختَه [šuːf ʔiǰǰaːhil dayʕayyib ʕala ʔuxtah] Look at the kid making faces at his sister.
اِنعاب [ʔinʕaːb] *v:* • **1.** to be or become defective – اِنعابَت القُندَرَة وَما تِنلِبِس بَعَد [ʔinʕaːbat ʔilqundara wamaː tinlibis baʕad] The shoes became unsuitable for wearing any more.
عيب [ʕiːb] *n:* عيُوب [ʕyuːb] *pl:* • **1.** fault, defect, flaw • **2.** vice, failing, weakness • **3.** sin, disgrace, shame, embarrassment – عِيب عَلِيك [ʕiːb ʕaliːk] Shame on you!
مَعيُوب [maʕyuːb] *adj:* • **1.** defective, shameful

ع

ع ي ث

عاث [ʕaːθ] *v:* • **1.** with فَساد to cause havoc, run amuck, ravage – الجِّنُود عاثوا فَساد بالأرض [ʔijjinuːd ʕaːθaw fasaːd bilʔarð̣] The soldiers ravaged the countryside.

عيث [ʕayθ, ʕiːθ] *n:* • **1.** ravage, havoc

ع ي د

عَيَّد [ʕayyad] *v:* • **1.** to celebrate or observe a feast – راح نعَيِّد بِبَغداد [raːħ nʕayyid bibaɣdaːd] We'll celebrate the feast day in Baghdad.

عيد [ʕiːd] *n:* أعياد [ʔaʕyaːd] *pl:* • **1.** feast, feast day, holiday – عِيد الاستِقلال [ʕiːd ʔilʔistiqlaːl] Independence Day. عِيد الكِبير؛ عِيد الإضحَى [ʕiːd ʔiččibiːr; ʕiːd ʔilʔiđ̣ħa] Greater Bairam. عِيد الصغَيِّر؛ عِيد الفِطِر؛ عِيد رَمَضان [ʕiːd ʔizzɣayyir; ʕiːd ʔilfiṭir; ʕiːd ramađ̣aːn] Lesser Bairam. العِيد [ʔilʕiːd] either of the two major Muslim holy days.

ع ي ر

عار [ʕaːr] *v:* • **1.** to attach, attribute – لا تعِيرلَه وَزِن. هُوَّ فَدّ واحِد تافِه [laː tʕiːrlah wazin. huwwa fadd waːħid taːfih] Don't attach any importance to him. He's an insignificant fellow.

عَيَّر [ʕayyar] *v:* • **1.** to rebuke, reproach, blame, condemn – دِيعَيّرُوه بأخُوه لأنَّه جَبان [dayʕayyruh bʔaxuːh liʔannah jabaːn] They throw his brother up to him because he's a coward. بِنتَك عَيِّرَتنِي البارحَة عَلَى لِبسِي [bintak ʕayyiratni ʔilbaːrħa ʕala libsi] Your daughter gave me a hard time about my clothes yesterday. • **2.** to weigh – عَيِّرلِي كِيلُو خيار [ʕayyirli kiːlu xyaːr] Weigh out a kilo of cucumbers for me.

عير [ʕiːr] *n:* عيُورَة [ʕyuːra] *pl:* • **1.** penis

عِيار [ʕiyaːr] *n:* • **1.** weight, measure – عيارَه ناقِص [ʕyaːrah naːgiṣ] He gives short weight. • **2.** (pl. عيَارَات) weight (used on a scale)

مِعيار [miʕyaːr] *n:* معايِير [maʕaːyiːr] *pl:* • **1.** standard • **2.** measuring standard, yardstick

عار [ʕaːr] *n:* • **1.** shame, disrepute, bad behaviour

عارسِزّ [ʕaːrsizz] *adj:* • **1.** shameless, without honor

ع ي س

عِيسَى [ʕiːsa] *n:* • **1.** Jesus

ع ي ش

عاش [ʕaːš] *v:* • **1.** to live, be alive – عاش مِيَّة سَنَة [ʕaːš miyyat sana] He lived a hundred years. زَوجتَه، خَطِيَّة، ما يعِيش إلها [zawijtah, xaṭiyya, maː yʕiːš ʔilha] His wife, poor thing, all her children have died. عايِش عِيشَة تَعسَة [ʕaːyiš ʕiːša taʕsa] He's leading a miserable life. • **2.** to exist, make a living – ما دَنُعرُف منِين دَيعِيش [maː danuʕruf mniːn dayʕiːš] We don't know how he makes his living. يعِيش عالبُوق [yiʕiːš ʕalbuːg] He lives by stealing. • **3.** to dwell, reside – عِشنا بِبَغداد خَمس سنِين، وسِكَنّا بِبَيت كِبِير [ʕišna bibaɣdaːd xams sniːn, wsikannaː bbayt čibiːr] We lived in Baghdad five years, in a large house. الأكراد يعِيشُون بالشّمال [ʔilʔakraːd yʕiːšuːn biššimaːl] The Kurds live in the North. يَعِيش المَلِك [yaʕiːš ʔilmalik] Long live the King! عاش مِن شافِك [ʕaːš min šaːfič] It's real nice to see you again (a standard greeting to someone one hasn't seen for some time).

عَيَّش [ʕayyaš] *v:* • **1.** to support, provide for – عَيَّشنا سَنَة كامْلَة [ʕayyašna sana kaːmla] He helped us with living expenses for a full year. مات زوجها وَما حَدّ راح يعَيِّشها [maːt zuːjha wma ħadd raːħ yʕayyišha] Her husband died and no one will take her in.

تعَيَّش [tʕayyaš] *v:* • **1.** to eke out a living, barely make ends meet – دَيتعَيَّش براتِب قلِيل [dayitʕayyaš braːtib qaliːl] He's barely getting by on a small salary.

إنعاش [ʔinʕaːš] *v:* • **1.** with بـ to be lived in – هَالقَريَة ما ينعاش بيها [halqarya maː yinʕaːš biːha] It's not possible to live in this town.

عيش [ʕayš, ʕiːš] *n:* • **1.** life, living – ماكُو عِيشَة هنا [maːku ʕiːša hna] Things aren't so good here.

مَعاش [maʕaːš] *n:* • **1.** salary, pay

عِيشَة [ʕiːša] *n:* عِيشَات [ʕiːšaːt] *pl:* • **1.** existence • **2.** sort of life, way or (mode) of life

مَعِيشَة [maʕiːša] *n:* مَعِيشات [maʕiːšaːt] *pl:* • **1.** life, living

إعاشَة [ʔiʕaːša] *n:* • **1.** supply, supplying, provisioning – ضابُط إعاشَة [đ̣aːbuṭ ʔiʕaːša] supply officer. مُدِيرِيَّة الإعاشَة [mudiːriyyat ʔilʔiʕaːša] quartermaster section, supply directorate.

عايِش [ʕaːyiš] *adj:* • **1.** living • **2.** well off, alive

ع ي ط

عاط [ʕaːṭ] *v:* • **1.** to yell, scream – عاطَت مِن شافَت إبنها وُقَع بالشَّطّ [ʕaːṭat min šaːfat ʔibinha wugaʕ biššaṭṭ] She screamed when she saw her son fall in the river. كُلّما أحكِي وِيّاك، تعِيط عَلَيّا [kullmaː ʔaħči wiyyaːk, tʕiːṭ ʕalayya] Whenever I speak with you, you yell at me.

عَيَّط [ʕayyaṭ] *v:* • **1.** intens. of عاط to yell, to scream – المَرَة عَيّطَت مِن سِمعَت إبنها مات [ʔilmara ʕayyṭat min simʕat ʔibinha maːt] The woman screamed when she heard her son died. عَلَى مَن دَتعَيِّط؟ [ʕala man datʕayyiṭ?] Who do you think you're shouting at?

تعايَط [tʕaːyaṭ] *v:* • **1.** to shout at each other, to yell at each other, – ماكُو حاجَة تِتعايطُون. خَلّي نشُوف شبِيكُم [maːku ħaːja titʕaːyṭuːn. xalliː nšuːf šbiːkum] There's no need to yell at each other. Let's see what your trouble is. يَومِيّاً تِتعايَط وِيّا الجِّيران [yawmiyyan titʕaːyaṭ

wiyya ʔijjiːraːn] Every day she exchanges shouts with the neighbors.
عيط [ʕiːṭ] *n:* • **1.** yelling, shouting
عِياط [ʕiyaːṭ, ʕyaːṭ] *n:* • **1.** shouting, yelling, screaming
عيطَة [ʕiːṭa] *n:* عيطات [ʕiːṭaːt] *pl:* • **1.** a shout, a yell, a scream

ع ي ق

عَيَّق [ʕayyaq] *v:* • **1.** to shout, yell, scream (invective) – بَسّ تجيسها، تقُوم تعَيِّق عَليك [bass dgiːsha, dguːm tʕayyiq ʕaliːk] Just touch her and she begins to shout at you.
عايقَة [ʕaːyqa] *adj:* عايقات [ʕaːyqaːt] *pl:* • **1.** bitchy woman, fish-wife • **2.** gad-about, woman who neglects her house to roam about and gossip

ع ي ل

عال [ʕaːl] *v:* • **1.** to start, cause, instigate, incite, provoke, stir up – إذا تعِيل مَرَة ثانيَة، تاكُلها [ʔiða tʕiːl mara θaːnya, taːkulha] If you start trouble again, you'll get it. اللّي يعِيل، ينبُسُط [ʔilli yʕiːl, yinbuṣuṭ] Whoever starts a fight, gets beat up. • **2.** with ب ,عَلي to irritate, anger, provoke, stir up – إنتَ عِلِت بيه بهَالكِلمَة [ʔinta ʕilit biːh bhaččilma] You irritated him with that remark. بُسَطتَه لِأنّ عال بإبني [busaṭṭah liʔann ʕaːl bʔibni] I hit him because he provoked my son.
عايِل [ʕaːyil] *adj:* • **1.** troublemaker, instigator, cause of trouble, the one at fault

ع ي ن

عَيَّن [ʕayyan] *v:* • **1.** to specify, designate – عَيِّنلي الأشياء اللّي تريدها وَآني أجيبلَك إيّاها [ʕayyinli ʔilʔašyaːʔ ʔilli triːdha waʔaːni ʔajiːblak ʔiyyaːha] Specify the things you want and I'll bring them to you. • **2.** to fix, appoint, schedule, stipulate – عَيِّنلي السّاعَة وآني أجي عالوَقِت [ʕayyinli ʔissaːʕa wʔaːni ʔaji ʕalwakit] Set me a time and I'll be on time. • **3.** to nominate, appoint, assign – الحُكُومَة عَيّنتَه مُدِير زراعَة [ʔilħukuːma ʕayynatah mudiːr ziraːʕa] The government appointed appointed him an agricultural director.
عايَن [ʕaːyan] *v:* • **1.** to look, see – تَعال عايِن هنا وشُوف شَكُو [taʕaːl ʕaːyin hna wšuːf šaku] Come and look over here and see what's going on! لا تعايِن عَليها تَرَة هِيَّ تِخجَل [laː tʕaːyin ʕaliːha tara hiyya tixjal] Don't look at her or she'll get embarrassed. شَكُو عِندَك دَتعايِن بجيبي؟ [šaku ʕindak datʕaːyin bjiːbi?] What are you doing looking in my pocket? آني بَعَد ما أعايِن بوجهَه أبَداً [ʔaːni baʕad maː ʔaʕaːyin bwiččah ʔabadan] I don't ever want to look at his face again.
تعَيَّن [tʕayyan] *v:* • **1.** to be appointed, assigned – تعَيَّنِت بدائِرَة البَرِيد [tʕayyanit bdaːʔirat ʔilbariːd] I got an appointment in the post office department. • **2.** to be set, fixed, designated – مَوعِد الاِجتِماع لهَسَّة ما تعَيَّن [mawʕid ʔilʔijtimaːʕ lhassa maː tʕayyan] The date for the meeting hasn't been set yet.
عين [ʕayn] *n:* أعيان [ʔaʕyaːn] *pl:* • **1.** senator – مَجلِس الأعيان [majlis ʔilʔaʕyaːn] senate. عَين الشِّي [ʕayn ʔišši] the same thing.
عين [ʕayn, ʕiːn] *n:* عيُون [ʕyuːn] *pl:* • **1.** eye – عينِي [ʕayni] means: my dear, darling, old friend, old buddy – عَلَى عينِي وَراسِي [ʕala ʕiːni wraːsi] gladly, with pleasure (a reply to a request). هُوَّ بعَينَه [huwwa bʕiːnah] he himself personally, none other than he. مِنُو طَلّع عينَك؟ [minu ṭallaʕ ʕaynak?] Who gave you that impudence? • **2.** evil eye, envious eye – حَطّوا نَعَل عَالباب عَن العَين [ħaṭṭaw naʕal ʕalbaːb ʕan ʔilʕayn] They put a horseshoe over the door against the evil eye. يلبَس هِدُوم رخِيصَة عَن العَين [yilbas hiduːm rixiːṣa ʕan ʔilʕayn] He wears cheap clothes to avoid the envious eye. • **3.** spring (of water) • **4.** burner – طَبّاخ أبُو ثلاث عيُون [ṭabbaːx ʔabu tlaθ ʕyuːn] a three burner stove. • **5.** عُوَينات [ʕuwaynaːt] (lit. small eyes) eyeglasses, spectacles • **6.** name of the letter ع
عَينَة [ʕayna] *n:* عَينات [ʕaynaːt] *pl:* • **1.** mirror
مَعين [maʕiːn] *n:* مَعينات [maʕiːnaːt] *pl:* • **1.** rhombus (gem.)
عَيان، شاهِد عَيان [ʕayaːn, šaːhid ʕayaːn] *n:* • **1.** eyewitness
تَعيين [taʕyiːn] *n:* • **1.** specification, designation – بِدُون تَعيين [biduːn taʕyiːn] at random. • **2.** pl. تَعيينات appointment, assignment, nomination
مُعايَنَة [muʕaːyana] *n:* مُعايَنات [muʕaːyanaːt] *pl:* • **1.** examination (by a doctor)
عِينَة [ʕiːna] *adj:* • **1.** the best, the pick – عِينَة الطَّماطَة [ʕiːnat ʔiṭṭamaːṭa] the best of the tomatoes.
مُعَيَّن [muʕayyan] *adj:* • **1.** fixed, designated, set, prescribed – وَقِت مُعَيَّن [waqit muʕayyan] a set time. • **2.** nominated, appointed – مُوَظَّف مُعَيَّن جِدِيد [muwwaððaf muʕayyan jidiːd] a newly appointed employee. • **3.** rhombus (geom.)
معَيَّن [mʕayyan] *adj:* • **1.** hired, recruited

ع ي ي

إعياء [ʔiʕyaːʔ] *n:* • **1.** exhaustion

غ

غ ب ر

غَبَر [ɣbarr] *v:* • **1.** to make (s.t.) dusty – الدِّنيا تِغبَرّ مِن يصِير هَوا [ʔiddinya tiɣbarr min yṣiːr hawa] The weather gets dusty when it's windy.

غَبَّر [ɣabbar] *v:* • **1.** to become dusty – هَمّ الدِّنيا غَبَّرِت [hamm ʔiddinya ɣabbarit] The weather's gotten dusty again.

غُبار [ɣubaːr] *n:* • **1.** dust

أَغبَر [ʔaɣbar] *adj:* غُبُر، غُبرِين [ɣubur, ɣubriːn.] *pl:* غَبرَة [ɣabra] *feminine:* • **1.** dusty – يوم أَغبَر [yuːm ʔaɣbar] a dusty day. دِنيا غَبرَة [dinya ɣabra] dusty weather. • **2.** dull, slow, not quick-witted, not quick on the uptake • **3.** dull person

أَغبَر [ʔaɣbar] *comparative adjective:* • **1.** more or most slow-witted

غ ب ش

غَبَّش [ɣabbaš] *v:* • **1.** to be early, to come, or go, early in the morning – إذا ما تغَبُّش، ما تحَصِّل مُكان بِالقِطار [ʔiða maː tɣabbuš, maː tħaṣṣil mukaːn bilqiṭaːr] If you don't come at dawn you won't get a seat on the train.

غُبشَة [ɣubša] *n:* • **1.** early morning • **2.** in the early morning – راح ناخُذ الطَّيّارَة باكِر غُبشَة [raːħ naːxuð ʔiṭṭayyaːra baːčir ɣubša] We're going to take the plane tomorrow at dawn.

مغَبِّش [mɣabbiš] *adj:* • **1.** early

غ ب ط

غُبَط [ɣubaṭ] *v:* • **1.** to envy – آني أَغُبطَك عَلَى هالعِيشَة [ʔaːni ʔaɣubṭak ʕala halʕiːša] I envy you for that life.

غُبُط [ɣabuṭ] *n:* • **1.** envy

غ ب ن

غَبَن [ɣuban] *v:* • **1.** to cheat, shortchange, treat unjustly – الحُكُومَة غِبنَتنِي بِهالرّاتِب [ʔilħukuːma ɣibnatni bharraːtib] The government treated me unfairly with that salary.

غُبُن [ɣubun] *n:* • **1.** cheating, unfair treatment – أَصابَه غُبُن [ʔaṣaːbah ɣubun] He got a raw deal. He was treated unfairly.

مَغبُون [maɣbuːn] *adj:* • **1.** wronged, injured, unfairly treated – مَغبُون بِالتَّرفِيع [maɣbuːn bittarfiːʕ] wronged as to his raise. حَقَّه مَغبُون [ħaqqah maɣbuːn] His rights were infringed upon.

غ ب ي

تغابَى [tɣaːbaː] *v:* • **1.** to pretend to be ignorant, stupid

غَباء [ɣabaːʔ] *n:* • **1.** ignorance • **2.** stupidity

غَباوَة [ɣabaːwa] *n:* • **1.** ignorance, foolishness, stupidity

غَبِي [ɣabi] *adj:* أَغبِياء [ʔaɣbiyaːʔ] *pl:* • **1.** stupid, ignorant, foolish • **2.** stupid person

أَغبَى [ʔaɣbaː] *comparative adjective:* • **1.** more or most ignorant, foolish, stupid

غ ت ر

غُترَة [ɣutra] *n:* غُتَر [ɣuṭar] *pl:* • **1.** head-cloth

غ ث ث

غَثّ [ɣaθθ] *v:* • **1.** to trouble, upset, bother – قُلّي شبِيك. مِنُو غَثَّك؟ [gulli šbiːk. minu ɣaθθak?] Tell me what's wrong. Who upset you? لا تغُثّ نَفسَك بِتَصلِيح هالمَكِينَة [laː tɣuθθ nafsak btaṣliːħ halmakiːna] Don't bother yourself with fixing this machine. لَو تغُثّ نَفسَك بِالدِّراسَة، تِنجَح [law tɣuθθ nafsak biddiraːsa, tinǰaħ] If you'll stir yourself and study, you'll pass.

انغَثّ [ʔinɣaθθ] *v:* • **1.** to be or become upset, disturbed – انغَثّ مِن حكايتِي [ʔinɣaθθ min ħčaːyti] He got upset at what I said.

غَثّ [ɣaθθ] *n:* • **1.** leanness

غِثَّة [ɣiθθa] *n:* • **1.** bother, nuisance, trouble

مَغَثَّة [maɣaθθa] *n:* • **1.** bother • **2.** torment, troubling feelings

غَثِيث [ɣaθiːθ] *adj:* • **1.** bothersome, pesky • **2.** bothersome person, pest

غ ج ر

غَجَري [ɣaǰari] *adj:* • **1.** gypsy

غ د د

غُدَّة [ɣudda] *n:* • **1.** gland (zool)

غ د ر

غِدَر [ɣidar] *v:* • **1.** to act treacherously toward, to double-cross – لا توثِق بِيهُم. أَكُو اِحتِمال يِغدرُوك [laː tuːθiq biːhum. ʔaku ʔiħtimaːl yɣidruːk] don't trust them. They will likely turn on you. • **2.** to be unfair to, to wrong – المُعَلِّم غِدَرنِي بِالتَّصلِيح [ʔilmuʕallim ɣidarni bittaṣliːħ] The teacher was unfair to me on grading.

غادَر [ɣaːdar] *v:* • **1.** to depart, leave

انغِدَر [ʔinɣidar] *v:* • **1.** to be deceived, betrayed

غَدِر [ɣadir] *n:* • **1.** betrayal • **2.** doublecross • **3.** disloyalty

غدِير، عِيد الغَدِير [ɣadiːr, ʕiːd ʔilɣadiːr] *n:* • **1.** annual Shiite feast celebrating the naming of Ali as successor by Mohammed

غَدّارَة [ɣaddaːra] *n:* غَدّارات [ɣaddaːraːt] *pl:* • **1.** sub-machine gun, Tommy gun

غ

مُغادَرَة [muɣa:dara] *n:* • **1.** departure
غَدّار [ɣadda:r] *adj:* • **1.** disloyal, deceitful
مَغدُور [maɣdu:r] *adj:* • **1.** betrayed

غ د و 1

غَدَّى [ɣadda:] *v:* • **1.** to give lunch, feed – شوَقِت راح تغَدِّي الجّهَال؟ [šwakit ra:ħ tɣaddi ʔijjaha:l?] When are you going to give the children lunch? • **2.** to buy lunch for, treat to lunch – إذا تساعِدنِي، أغَدِّيك اليُوم [ʔiða tsa:ʕidni, ʔaɣaddi:k ʔilyu:m] If you will help me, I'll treat you to lunch today.
تغَدَّى [tɣadda:] *v:* • **1.** to have lunch – إمشِي تغَدَّى ويّايا [ʔimši tɣadda: wiyya:ya] Come on and have lunch with me.
غَدا [ɣada] *n:* غدايات، غِديات [ɣada:ya:t, ɣidya:t] *pl:* • **1.** lunch

غ د و 2

غادانِي [ɣa:da:ni] *adj:* • **1.** far, distant – الكِتاب الغادانِي [ʔilkita:b ʔilɣa:da:ni] the book on the far end.
غاد [ɣa:d] *adv:* • **1.** yonder, over there – واقُف غاد بذاك الصُّوب [wa:guf ɣa:d bða:k ʔiṣṣu:b] He's standing over there on the other bank. رُوح غاد! خَلِّينِي أشتُغُل [ru:ħ ɣa:d! xalli:ni ʔaštuɣul] Get away! Let me work. ما يُعرُف شَكُو هنا. جاي مِن الغاد [ma: yuʕruf šaku hna. ǰa:y min ʔilɣa:d] He doesn't know what's going on here. He's from out-of-town.
غادِي [ɣa:di] *adv:* • **1.** far, yonder, over there

غ د و 3

غِدا [ɣida:] *v:* • **1.** to become, turn into (in certain expressions:) – شِرَب حَتَّى غِدا طَبُل [širab ħatta ɣida: ṭabul] He drank until his head pounded (lit., he drank until he became a drum). غديت مَيّ مِن العَرَق [ɣdi:t mayy min ʔilʕarag] I got soaking wet with perspiration (lit., I became water).
غَدي [ɣady] *n:* • **1.** turning into

غ ذ و

غَذَى [ɣaðða:] *v:* • **1.** to support, back (with money) – مِنُو دَيغَذِّي هالحَرَكَة؟ [minu dayɣaðði halħaraka?] Who's supporting this movement?
تغَذَى [tɣaðða:] *v:* • **1.** to be fed, be nourished, get nourishment – الطِّفِل يِتغَذَّى بحَلِيب أُمَّه أحسَن مِن حَلِيب البُوطِل [ʔiṭṭifil yidɣaðða: bħali:b ʔummah ʔaħsan min ħali:b ʔilbu:ṭil] the child is better nourished by his mother's milk than bottled milk. النَّبات تغَذَّى مِن السَّماد [ʔinnaba:t tɣaðða: min ʔissma:d] The plants get nourishment from fertilizer.
غِذاء [ɣiða:ʔ] *n:* • **1.** nourishment, nutriment, food value • **2.** pl. only أغذِيَة food, foodstuffs, victuals
تغذِيَة [taɣðiya] *n:* • **1.** nourishment
مُغَذِّي [muɣaðði] *adj:* • **1.** nourishing, nutritious – أكِل مُغَذِّي [ʔakil muɣaððí] nourishing food.
غِذائي [ɣiða:ʔi] *adj:* • **1.** nourishing, nutritive, nutritional – مَوادّ غِذائِيَّة [mawa:dd ɣiða:ʔiyya] nourishing substances.

غ ر ب

غِرَب [ɣurab] *v:* • **1.** to set (of the sun) – شوَقِت راح تُغرُب الشَّمِس؟ [šwakit ra:ħ tuɣrub ʔiššamis?] What time will the sun set?
غَربَل [ɣarbal] *v:* • **1.** to sift, sieve – غَربِل الحُنطَة [ɣarbil ʔilħunṭa] Sift the wheat. • **2.** to purge, shake up – أكُو إشاعَة الوَزِير راح يغَربِل المُوَظَّفِين [ʔaku ʔiša:ʕa ʔilwazi:r ra:ħ yɣarbil ʔilmuwaððafi:n] There's a rumor that the minister is going to sift the deadwood from the employees.
تغَرَّب [tɣarrab] *v:* • **1.** to go to a foreign country, to emigrate – أبقى بِبَغداد. لُويش تَرُوح تِتغَرَّب؟ [ʔubqa: bibaɣda:d. luwi:š tru:ħ tidɣarrab?] Stay in Baghdad. Why go and leave the country?
اِستَغرَب [ʔistaɣrab] *v:* • **1.** to be surprised – لا تِستَغرُب إذا سمَعِت هَذا صار وَزِير [la: tistaɣrub ʔiða smaʕit ha:ða ṣa:r wazi:r] Don't be surprised if you hear he's become a minister. آنِي دَأستَغرِب مِن تَصَرُّفَه [ʔa:ni daʔastaɣrib min taṣarrufah] I'm surprised by his behavior. • **2.** to be frightened, shy – الجّاهِل دَيِستَغرُب مِن الخُطّار [ʔijja:hil dayistaɣrub min ʔilxuṭṭa:r] The baby's afraid of the guests.
غَرب [ɣarb] *n:* • **1.** west
غُربَة [ɣurba] *n:* غِربان [ɣirba:n] *pl:* • **1.** absence from one's homeland
مُغرُب، مِغرِب [muɣrub, miɣrib] *n:* • **1.** sunset • **2.** sunset, sundown • **3.** at sunset – خَيَّمنا المُغرُب [xayyamna ʔilmuɣrub] We made camp at sunset.
غراب [ɣra:b] *n:* • **1.** crow, raven
غُرُوب [ɣuru:b] *n:* • **1.** setting (of the sun)
غِربِيل [ɣirbi:l, ɣarbi:l] *n:* غَرابِيل [ɣara:bi:l] *pl:* • **1.** a coarse sieve
المَغرِب [ʔilmaɣrib] *n:* • **1.** northwest Africa • **2.** Morocco
غُرُوبِيَّة [ɣuru:biyyya] *n:* • **1.** dusk time
مَغرِبِيَّة [maɣribiyya] *n:* • **1.** evening
اِستِغراب [ʔistiɣra:b] *n:* • **1.** astonishment, surprise
غَربِي [ɣarbi] *adj:* • **1.** western, westerly, west – هَوا غَربِي [hawa ɣarbi] a west wind. • **2.** occidental, Western, European – رِجّال غَربِي [rijja:l ɣarbi] a Westerner. • **3.** Westerner, European
غَرِيب [ɣari:b] *adj:* غُرَباء، غُربَة [ɣuraba:ʔ, ɣurba.] *pl:* • **1.** strange, foreign – وَلَد غَرِيب [walad ɣari:b] a stranger, a foreigner. • **2.** strange, odd, queer – لِبِس غَرِيب [libis ɣari:b] strange clothing. غَرِيب الشِّكِل [ɣari:b ʔiššikil] strange-looking. • **3.** strange, amazing, astonishing – قُصَّة غَرِيبَة [quṣṣa ɣari:ba] an amazing story. • **4.** stranger, foreigner, alien, outsider

أغرَب [ʔaɣrab] *adj:* • **1.** more or most unusual, strange, etc
مَغرِبي [maɣribi] *adj:* مَغارِبَة [maɣa:riba] *pl:* • **1.** North African • **2.** person from North Africa • **3.** Moroccan, from Morocco • **4.** person from Morocco
غَربَلَة [ɣarbala] *adj:* غَربَلات [ɣarbala:t] *pl:* • **1.** sifting • **2.** shake-up, purge, reorganization
غَرِيبَة [ɣari:ba] *adj:* • **1.** strange

غ ر د

غَرَّد [ɣarrad] *v:* • **1.** to sing, twitter – البلبل دَيغَرِّد [ʔilbilbil dayɣarrid] The nightingale is singing.
تَغرِيد [taɣri:d] *n:* • **1.** singing, warbling
مغَرِّد [mɣarrid] *adj:* • **1.** singing, twittering

غ ر ر

غَرّ [ɣarr] *v:* • **1.** to deceive, mislead – لا يغُرَّك المَظهَر مالَه، تَرَة ما يفهَم شِي [la: yɣurrak ʔilmaðhar ma:lah, tara ma: yifham ši] Don't let his appearance fool you, because he doesn't know a thing.
اِغتَرّ [ʔiɣtarr] *v:* • **1.** to be or become conceited – يغتَرّ هوايَة بنَفسَه [yiɣtarr hwa:ya bnafsah] He's very taken with himself.
اِنغَرّ [ʔinɣarr] *v:* • **1.** to be deceived, misled, decoyed
غُرَّة، غُرَّة الشَهَر [ɣurra, ɣurrat ʔiššahar] *n:* • **1.** the first day of the month
غُرُور [ɣuru:r] *n:* • **1.** deception, delusion
مغتَرّ [mɣtarr] *adj:* • **1.** conceited, vain • **2.** having the head covered with a veil
مَغرُور [maɣru:r] *adj:* • **1.** conceited, vain – مَغرُور بنَفسَه [maɣru:r bnafsah] very much taken with himself.

غ ر ز

غِرزَة [ɣirza] *n:* • **1.** stitch
غَرِيزَة [ɣari:za] *n:* غَرائِز [ɣara:ʔiz] *pl:* • **1.** instinct, natural impulse
غَرِيزِي [ɣari:zi] *adj:* • **1.** natural, native • **2.** instinctive

غ ر س

غِرَس [ɣiras] *v:* • **1.** to plant – غِرسَوا أشجار بِبَعَض الشّوارِع [ɣirsaw ʔašja:r bibaʕað ʔiššawa:riʕ] They planted trees along some of the streets.
غَرِس [ɣaris] *n:* • **1.** planting
مَغرُوس [maɣru:s] *adj:* • **1.** planted

غ ر ش

غَرشَة [ɣarša] *n:* غَرشات، غراش [ɣarša:t, ɣra:š] *pl:* • **1.** narghile

غ ر ض

تغَرَّض [tɣarrað] *v:* • **1.** to be biased, prejudiced – رَئِيسِي تغَرَّض وِيّايا وَما رَفَّعني [raʔi:si tɣarrað wiyya:ya wama raffaʕni] My boss was prejudiced toward me and didn't promote me. المُعَلِّم تغَرَّضلَه وسِقَط بالإمتِحان [ʔilmuʕallim tɣarrað̣lah wsiqaṭ bilʔimtiḥa:n] The teacher was biased toward him and he failed the exam.
غَرَض [ɣarað] *n:* أغراض [ʔaɣra:ð] *pl:* • **1.** intention, design, purpose – مالَه غَرَض [ma:lah ɣarað] he doesn't care, he's not concerned. رُوح؛ شما تسَوِّي، آني ما إلِي غَرَض [ru:ḥ; šma tsawwi:, ʔa:ni ma: li ɣarað] Go ahead; whatever you do, I'm not concerned. • **2.** pl. غَراض possession, belonging, thing

غ ر غ ر

تغَرغَر [tɣarɣar] *v:* • **1.** to gargle – تغَرغَر بمَيّ ومِلِح [tɣarɣar bmayy wmiliḥ] He gargled with water and salt.
غَرغَرَة [ɣarɣara] *n:* غَرغَرات [ɣarɣara:t] *pl:* • **1.** gargle

غ ر ف

غِرَف [ɣiraf] *v:* • **1.** to dip up, ladle, scoop – إنطِينِي شِي أغرُف الماي بِيه [ʔinṭi:ni ši ʔaɣruf ʔilma:y bi:h] Give me something to dip up the water with. • **2.** to paddle (a boat) – هَذا يغرُف البَلَم كُلِّش سَرِيع [ha:ða yuɣruf ʔilbalam kulliš sari:ʕ] He paddles the boat very fast. غُرَفَه لِلبَلَم غَرُفتَين وَطَيِّرَه [ɣurafah lilbalam ɣaruftayn wṭayyarah] He paddled the boat two strokes and sent it flying.
اِنغِرَف [ʔinɣiraf] *v:* • **1.** to be ladled
غَرُف [ɣaruf] *n:* • **1.** scooping, dipping
غُرفَة [ɣurfa] *n:* غُرَف [ɣuraf] *pl:* • **1.** room, chamber – غُرفَة التِّجارَة [ɣurfat ʔittija:ra] chamber of commerce.
غَرفَة [ɣarfa] *n:* غَرفات [ɣarfa:t] *pl:* • **1.** the act of dipping up, a scoop • **2.** a stroke of the paddle
غُرّافَة [ɣurra:fa] *n:* غُرّافات، غِراريف [ɣurra:fa:t, ɣira:ri:f] *pl:* • **1.** scoop • **2.** paddle
مِغرَفَة [miɣrafa] *n:* مِغرَفات، مَغارِيف [miɣrafa:t, maɣa:ri:f] *pl:* • **1.** large spoon, ladle, scoop
مُغرافَة [muɣra:fa] *n:* مُغرافات [muɣra:fa:t] *pl:* • **1.** paddle

غ ر ق

غِرَق [ɣirag] *v:* • **1.** to sink – الباخِرَة غِرقَت بعاصِفَة [ʔilba:xira ɣirgat bʕa:ṣifa] The boat sank in a storm. • **2.** to be immersed, submerged, flooded – مَزرَعتِي غِرقَت مِن المُطَر [mazraʕti ɣirgat min ʔilmuṭar] My farm was flooded by the rain. • **3.** to go under, be drowned – فَدّ وَلَد غِرَق بالشَّطّ [fadd walad ɣirag biššaṭṭ] A boy drowned in the river. • **4.** to be immersed, swamped, snowed under – لِقَيتَه غارِق بالشُّغُل [ligaytah ɣa:rig biššuɣul] I found him swamped with work. • **5.** to be lost, wholly engaged, absorbed – شبِيك غارِق بالتَّفكِير؟ [šbi:k ɣa:rig bittafki:r?] What's making you so lost in thought?
غَرَّق [ɣarrag] *v:* • **1.** to sink, cause to sink – الغَوّاصَة غَرِّقَت ثلَث بَواخِر [ʔilɣawwa:ṣa ɣarrigat tlaθ

غ

bawa:xir] The submarine sank three ships. • **2.** to submerge, immerse, flood – المُطَر غَرَّق شارِعنا [ʔilmuṭar ɣarrag ša:riʕna] The rain flooded our street. رُشّ القاع بَسّ لا تغَرِّقها [rušš ʔilga:ʕ bass la: dɣarrigha] Sprinkle the ground but don't flood it. • **3.** to drown, cause to drown – خَلّي أسبَح. راح تغَرِّقنِي [xalli: ʔasbaħ. ra:ħ tɣarrigni] Let me swim. You're going to drown me. هالمَيّ قَوِي. يغَرِّق [halmayy qawi. yɣarrig] This water's swift. It'll drown you.

تغَرَّق [tɣarrag] *v:* • **1.** to shower • **2.** to sink

اِستَغرَق [ʔistaɣraq] *v:* • **1.** to take, last, dure (an amount of time)

تغِرِّق [tɣirrig] *n:* • **1.** sinking, drowning

غارِق [ɣa:rig] *adj:* • **1.** swamped, snowed under – غارِق بِالشُّغُل [ɣa:rig biššuɣul] swamped with work.

غَرِيق [ɣari:q] *adj:* • **1.** drowning

غَرقان [ɣarga:n] *adj:* • **1.** sunk, sunken • **2.** submerged, flooded • **3.** drowned • **4.** swamped, snowed under

مِستَغرِق [mistaɣriq] *adj:* • **1.** immersed, engrossed • **2.** spent

غ ر م

غَرَّم [ɣarram] *v:* • **1.** to fine, impose a fine – الحاكِم غَرَّمَه دِينارَين [ʔilħa:kim ɣarramah dina:rayn] The judge fined him two dinars. • **2.** to dock, to charge – المُدِير غَرَّمَه راتِب يومَين [ʔilmudi:r ɣarramah ra:tib yu:mayn] The boss docked him two days' pay. إذا تِكسِر شِي، يغَرِّمُوك [ʔiða tiksir ši, yɣarrimu:k] If you break anything, they'll charge you for it.

تغَرَّم [tɣarram] *v:* • **1.** to be fined, to be docked, to be charged – تغَرَّم دِينار لأَنّ ذَبّ زِبِل بِالشّارِع [tɣarram dina:r liʔann ðabb zibil biššariʕ] He was fined a dinar because he threw trash in the street.

غرام [ɣra:m] *n:* غرامات [ɣra:ma:t] *pl:* • **1.** gram

غَرام [ɣara:m] *n:* • **1.** infatuation, love, passion

غَرامَة [ɣara:ma] *n:* غَرامات [ɣara:ma:t] *pl:* • **1.** fine • **2.** penalty • **3.** charge for breakage

غَرامِيّات [ɣara:miyya:t] *n:* • **1.** romance, love – بَيناتهُم غَرامِيّات [bi:na:thum ɣara:miyya:t] There's a romantic interest between them. دَيبِيع غَرامِيّات بِراسها [daybi:ʕ ɣara:miyya:t bra:sha] He's thrusting his affections upon her.

مُغرَم [muɣram] *adj:* • **1.** in love, enamored, infatuated

غَرامِي [ɣara:mi] *adj:* • **1.** passionate, erotic, amorous, love – قُصَص غَرامِيَّة [quṣaṣ ɣara:miyya] love stories. مَكتُوب غَرامِي [maktu:b ɣara:mi] love letter.

غ ر و

أغرَى [ʔaɣra:] *v:* • **1.** to entice, allure, tempt – قِدَر يِغرِيها بِفلُوسَه [gidar yiɣri:ha bflu:sah] He was able to attract her with his money.

غرا [ɣira:, ɣara:] *n:* • **1.** glue

إغراء [ʔiɣra:ʔ] *n:* • **1.** temptation, enticement, seduction

مُغرِي [muɣri] *adj:* • **1.** tempting, enticing, alluring, seductive – لِبِس مُغرِي [libis muɣri] seductive clothing. حَلِق مُغرِي [ħalig muɣri] a tempting mouth. • **2.** attractive, tempting – راتِب مُغرِي [ra:tib muɣri] an attractive salary. شُرُوط مُغرِيَة [šuru:ṭ muɣriya] attractive conditions. • **3.** enviable – مَنصَب مُغرِي [manṣab muɣri] an enviable position.

غ ز

غاز [ɣa:z] *n:* غازات [ɣa:za:t] *pl:* • **1.** gas

غ ز ر

غَزَّر [ɣazzar] *v:* • **1.** to be appreciative, to appreciate, to show appreciation – كُلّ الأكِل اللّي أكّلتَه إيّاه، ما دَيغَزِّر [kull ʔilʔakil ʔilli ʔakkaltah ʔiyya:h, ma: dayɣazzir] All the meals I've fed him, and he isn't appreciative. شما تسَوِّيلَه، ما يغَزِّر بعَينَه [šma tsawwi:lah, ma: yɣazzir bʕaynah] Whatever you do for him he doesn't show any appreciation.

غَزارَة [ɣaza:ra] *n:* • **1.** abundance, profusion – المُطَر دَينزِل بغَزارَة [ʔilmuṭar dayinzil bɣaza:ra] The rain is coming down heavily.

غَزِير [ɣazi:r] *adj:* • **1.** plentiful, copious, abundant – مُطَر غَزِير [muṭar ɣazi:r] plentiful rainfall. مَعلُومات غَزِيرَة [maʕlu:ma:t ɣazi:ra] a boundless store of information.

غ ز ل

غِزَل [ɣizal] *v:* • **1.** to spin – غِزلَت صُوفَة الخَرُوف كُلّها [ɣizlat ṣu:fat ʔilxaru:f kullha] She spun all the sheep's wool.

غازَل [ɣa:zal] *v:* • **1.** to court, flirt with – بَسّ تعَرَّف عَليها قام يغازِلها [bass tʕarraf ʕali:ha ga:m yɣa:zilha] As soon as he met her he began courting her.

تغَزَّل [tɣazzal] *v:* • **1.** to celebrate in love poems – تغَزَّل بجَمالها بِالقَصِيدَة اللّي هِضَمها [dɣazzal bǰama:lha bilqaṣi:da ʔilli hiðamha] He celebrated her beauty in a poem he wrote. يِتغَزَّل بِشِعرَه بِكُلّ المُناسَبات [yidɣazzal bšiʕrah bkull ʔilmuna:saba:t] He puts amour into his poetry on every occasion.

غَزِل [ɣazil] *n:* • **1.** spinning • **2.** yarn, spun thread

غَزَل [ɣazal] *n:* • **1.** flirtation, flirtatiousness, flirtatious remarks • **2.** love poetry, erotic poetry

غَزَلِي [ɣazali] *n:* • **1.** amorous, erotic, love – قَصِيدَة غَزَلِيَّة [qaṣi:da ɣazaliyya] a love poem.

غزال [ɣaza:l] *n:* غِزلان [ɣizla:n] *pl:* • **1.** gazelle

غَزالَة [ɣaza:la] *n:* غَزالات [ɣaza:la:t] *pl:* female gazelle

مَغزَل [maɣzal] *n:* مَغازِل [maɣa:zil] *pl:* • **1.** a spindle used in wool spinning

مغَيزِل، مغَيزِل بابا، مغَيزِل دادَة [mɣayzil, mɣayzil ba:ba, mɣayzil da:da] *n:* • **1.** a kind of sand spider found in the desert

غ ز و

غزا [ɣiza:] *v:* • **1.** to raid, attack, invade – هَالقَبِيلَة راح تِغزِيهُم وَتاخُذ كُلّ ما عِدهُم [halqabi:la ra:ħ tiɣzi:hum wta:xuð kull ma: ʕidhum] That tribe will raid them and take all they have. البَضائِع اليابانِيَّة راح تِغزِي السُّوق [ʔilbaða:ʔiʕ ʔilya:ba:niyya ra:ħ tiɣzi ʔissu:g] Japanese goods will invade the market.

غَزُو [ɣazw] *n:* • **1.** invasion, inroad

غَزوَة [ɣazwa] *n:* غَزوات [ɣazwa:t] *pl:* • **1.** raid, attack

مَغزَى [maɣza:] *n:* مَغازِي [maɣa:zi] *pl:* • **1.** sense, meaning, import, significance

غ س ل

غِسَل [ɣisal, xisal] *v:* • **1.** to wash – إغسِل إيدَك بمَيّ حارّ [ʔigsil ʔi:dak bmayy ħa:rr] Wash your hands in hot water. آنِي غاسِل إيدِي مِن إبنِي [ʔa:ni ɣa:sil ʔi:di min ʔibni] I've no hope for my son. حَماتَه غِسلَتَه خُوش غَسلَة [ħama:tah ɣislatah xu:š ɣasla] His mother-in-law gave him a good scolding. • **2.** to develop (film, prints) – بالله إغسِل الفِلِم وَراوِينا إيّاه [ballah ʔiɣsil ʔilfilim wra:wi:na ʔiyya:h] Please develop the film and show it to me.

غَسَّل [ɣassal, xassal] *v:* • **1.** to wash thoroughly – رُوح غَسِّل. الأكِل حاضِر [ru:ħ ɣassil. ʔilʔakil ħa:ḍir] Go wash. The food is ready. • **2.** to wash (a corpse) – غَسِّلَوا المَيِّت بِسُرعَة وَدِفنُوه [ɣassilaw ʔilmayyit bsurʕa wdifnu:h] They bathed the corpse quickly and buried it.

انغِسَل [ʔinɣisal, ʔinxisal] *v:* • **1.** to bathe • **2.** to be washed

اغتِسَل [ʔiɣtisal, ʔixtisal] *v:* • **1.** to perform major ritual ablution (i.e. to wash the whole body after intercourse) – لازِم تِغتِسِل قَبُل ما يطُرّ الفَجِر حَتَّى تصَلِّي [la:zim tiɣtisil gabul ma: yṭurr ʔilfajir ħatta tṣalli] You must cleanse yourself before dawn breaks in order to pray.

غَسِل [ɣasil, xasil] *n:* غَسلات [ɣasla:t] *pl:* • **1.** washing

مَغسَل، مَغسَلَة [maɣsal, maɣsala, maxsal, maxsala] *n:* مَغاسِل [maɣa:sil] *pl:* • **1.** washbowl, sink

مغيسِل [mɣi:sil] *n:* • **1.** bath-house for the dead

غَسّالَة [ɣassa:la, xassa:la] *n:* غَسّالات [ɣassa:la:t] *pl:* • **1.** washer • **2.** washerwoman, washing machine

تَغسِيل [taɣsi:l, taxsi:l] *n:* • **1.** washing

غاسِل [ɣa:sil, xa:sil] *adj:* • **1.** washed, clean • **2.** bathed

مغَسَّل [mɣassil, mxassil] *adj:* • **1.** washed

مَغسُول [maxsu:l] *adj:* • **1.** washed

غ ش ش

غَشّ [ɣašš] *v:* • **1.** to cheat, act dishonestly – ما يِنجَح إذا ما يغُشّ [ma: yinjaħ ʔiða ma: yɣušš] He won't pass if he doesn't cheat. • **2.** to cheat, swindle – لا تِشتِرِي مِنَّه، تَرَة يغُشَّك [la: tištiri minnah, tara yuɣuššak] Don't buy from him or he'll cheat you. • **3.** to deceive, fool, take in – لا تغُشَّك هدُومَه، تَرَة هَذا زَنكِين [la: tɣuššak hdu:mah, tara ha:ða zangi:n] Don't let his clothes fool you, because he is rich. • **4.** to adulterate, dilute – صاحِب المَطعَم يغِشّ الأكِل مالَه [ṣa:ħib ʔilmaṭʕam yɣišš ʔilʔakil ma:lah] The restaurant owner adulterates his food.

انغَشّ [ʔinɣašš] *v:* • **1.** to be cheated, taken, swindled – اِنغَشَّيت بِهالسَّيّارَة [ʔinɣaššayt bhassayya:ra] I got taken on this car. • **2.** to be deceived, fooled, taken in – اِنغَشَّيت بِحَكيَه؛ عَبالِي هَذا آدَمِي [ʔinɣaššayt bħačyah; ʕaba:li ha:ða ʔa:dami] I was fooled by his talk; I thought he was a gentleman. • **3.** to be adulterated – الدِّهِن يِنغِشّ بسُهُولَة [ʔiddihin yinɣišš bsuhu:la] Oil is easily adulterated.

غِشّ [ɣišš] *n:* • **1.** cheating, fraud, swindling

غَشّاش [ɣašša:š] *adj:* غَشّاشَة [ɣašša:ša] *pl:* • **1.** cheater, cheat, swindler

مَغشُوش [maɣšu:š] *adj:* • **1.** adulterated – دِهِن مَغشُوش [dihin maɣšu:š] adulterated oil.

غ ش م

غَشَّم [ɣaššam] *v:* • **1.** with نفس or رُوح to feign ignorance, innocence, or inexperience – نَغّها لِلبنَيَّة وَغَشَّم رُوحَه [naɣɣha lilbnayya wɣaššam ru:ħah] He poked the girl and pretended to be innocent. تُعرُفها كُلِّش زين. لا تغَشِّم نَفسَك [tuʕrufha kulliš zi:n. la: dɣaššim nafsak] You know all about it. Don't pretend to be naive.

غَشِيم [ɣaši:m] *adj:* غِشمَة، غُشَّم [ɣišma, ɣuššam] *pl:* • **1.** inexperienced, green, new – غَشِيم بِالمَصلَحَة [ɣaši:m bilmaṣlaħa] new at the business. • **2.** greenhorn, bumpkin

غ ش و

تغَشَّى [tɣašša:] *v:* • **1.** to veil oneself, wear a veil – بِتّها سفُور بَسّ هِيَّ تِتغَشَّى [bittha sufu:r bass hiyya tidɣašša:] Her daughter doesn't wear a veil but she veils herself.

غشاء [ɣiša:ʔ, ɣiša] *n:* أغشِيَة [ʔaɣšiya] *pl:* • **1.** membrane – غِشاء مُخاطِي [ɣiša:ʔ muxa:ṭi] mucous membrane. غِشاء البَكارَة [ɣiša:ʔ ʔilbaka:ra] hymen, maidenhead.

غَشاوَة [ɣaša:wa] *n:* • **1.** filmy covering of the eyes, cataract • **2.** veil

غ ص ب

غِصَب [ɣiṣab] *v:* • **1.** to force, compel, coerce – لا تُغصُبنِي. ما أشتِهِي آكُل [la: tuɣṣubni. ma: ʔaštihi ʔa:kul] Don't force me. I have no appetite to eat.

انغِصَب [ʔinɣiṣab] *v:* • **1.** to be forced, compelled – اِنغِصَبِت أرُوح وِيّاه لِلسِّينَما [ʔinɣiṣabit ʔaru:ħ wiyya:h

غ

lissinama] I had to go with him to the movies. اِنغِصَب يِفتَح القاصَة [ʔinɣiṣab yiftaħ ʔilqaːṣa] He was forced to open the safe.

اِغتِصَب [ʔiɣtiṣab] *v:* • **1.** to rape, ravish, violate – بَعَد ما اِغتِصَبها اِضطَرّ يِتزَوَّجها [baʕad maː ʔiɣtiṣabha ʔiḍṭarr yidzawwajha] After he had her he had to marry her.

غَصُب [ɣaṣub] *n:* • **1.** force, compulsion, coercion • **2.** with Prep - بـ, by force, forcibly

غَصباً [ɣaṣban] *adverbial:* • **1.** by force, forcibly – غَصباً عَليه [ɣaṣban ʕaliːh] against his will, in defiance of him. غَصباً عَنَّه [ɣaṣban ʕannah] against his will, in defiance of him. راح أَشتِريها غَصباً عَليك [raːħ ʔaštiriːha ɣaṣban ʕaliːk] I'm going to buy it in spite of you. المُدير عَيَّنَه غَصباً عَلَى أَنفَك [ʔilmudiːr ʕayyanah ɣaṣban ʕala ʔanfak] The director appointed him in spite of you.

غ ص ص

غَصّ [ɣaṣṣ] *v:* • **1.** to choke – دِير بالَك، لا تغُصّ بِالسِّمَك [diːr baːlak, laː tɣuṣṣ bissimač] Look out you don't choke on the fish. لا تاكُل بِسُرعَة تَرَة تغُصّ [laː taːkul bsurʕa tara tɣuṣṣ] Don't eat fast or you'll choke. • **2.** to be or become choked, jammed, packed, congested – السِّينَما غَصَّت بِالنّاس البارحَة [ʔissinama ɣaṣṣat binnaːs ʔilbaːrħa] The movie theater was choked with people yesterday.

اِنغَصّ [ʔinɣaṣṣ] *v:* • **1.** to be choked

غَصّ [ɣaṣṣ] *n:* • **1.** choking

غَصَّة [ɣaṣṣa] *n:* غَصّات [ɣaṣṣaːt] *pl:* • **1.** choking spell

غ ص ن

غُصُن [ɣuṣun] *n:* أَغصان، غُصُون [ʔaɣṣaːn, ɣuṣuːn] *pl:* • **1.** branch, bough, limb (of a tree)

غُصِن [ɣuṣin] *n:* أَغصان، غُصُون [ʔaɣṣaːn, ɣuṣuːn] *pl:* • **1.** branch, bough, limb (of a tree)

غ ض ب

غِضَب [ɣiḍ̣ab] *v:* • **1.** to be or become angry, cross, irritated, exasperated, furious – أَبُوها يِغضَب عَلَى أَقَلّ شِي [ʔabuːha yiɣḍ̣ab ʕala ʔaqall ši] Her father gets mad at the least thing.

غَضَّب [ɣaḍ̣ḍ̣ab] *v:* • **1.** to make angry

أَغضَب [ʔaɣḍ̣ab] *v:* • **1.** to annoy, exasperate, anger, enrage, infuriate – الطّالِب أَغضَب المُعَلِّم بتَصَرُّفَه [ʔiṭṭaːlib ʔaɣḍ̣ab ʔilmuʕallim btaṣarrufah] The student angered the teacher with his behavior.

غَضَب [ɣaḍ̣ab] *n:* • **1.** rage, fury, wrath – غَضَب الله عَلَيهُم. رُفعَوا الأَسعار بِلا سَبَب [ɣaḍ̣ab ʔallah ʕaliːhum. rufʕaw ʔilʔasʕaːr bila sabab] May the wrath of Allah be on them. They raised the prices without any reason. • **2.** anger, exasperation, indignation – غَضَب مال الله [ɣaḍ̣ab maːl ʔallah] a holy terror, a real menace.

غَضبان [ɣaḍ̣baːn] *adj:* • **1.** angry, exasperated, furious, infuriated – غَضبان عَلَى أَخُوه [ɣaḍ̣baːn ʕala ʔaxuːh] mad at his brother. غَضبان مِنِّي [ɣaḍ̣baːn minni] mad at me.

مَغضُوب [maɣḍ̣uːb] *adj:* • **1.** with عَلَى means object of anger

غ ض ر

غُضرُوف [ɣuḍ̣ruːf] *n:* غَضاريف [ɣaḍ̣aːriːf] *pl:* • **1.** cartilage, gristle

غُضرُوفِي [ɣuḍ̣ruːfi] *adj:* • **1.** cartilaginous – عُضُو غُضرُوفِي [ʕuḍ̣w ɣuḍ̣ruːfi] a cartilaginous organ.

غ ض ض

غَضّ [ɣaḍ̣ḍ̣] *v:* • **1.** with النَظَر to overlook, ignore, forget – إذا تِدهِن إيدَه، يغُضّ النَّظَر عَنها [ʔiða tidhin ʔiːdah, yuɣuḍ̣ḍ̣ ʔinnaḍ̣ar ʕanha] If you grease his palm, he'll overlook it. يُغُضّ النَّظَر مِن يشُوف شِي مُو صحِيح [yuɣuḍ̣ḍ̣ ʔinnaḍ̣ar min yšuːf ši muː ṣħiːħ] He avoids noticing anything not right.

غَضّ [ɣaḍ̣ḍ̣] *n:* • **1.** overlooking, ignoring

غ ض و

تغاضَى [tɣaːḍ̣aː] *v:* • **1.** with عَن or عَلَى to disregard, ignore, pretend not to see – هُوَّ يِتغاضَى عَن كُلّ الأَغلاط اللِّي يسَوِّيها [huwwa yidɣaːḍ̣aː ʕan kull ʔilʔaɣlaːṭ ʔilli ysawwiːha] He ignores all the mistakes that he makes.

تغاضِي [taɣaːḍ̣i] *n:* • **1.** overlooking, disregard

غ ط ر س

تغَطرَس [tɣaṭras] *v:* • **1.** to be haughty, arrogant, snobbish, conceited – هَذا ما يِستَحِقّ يكُون مُدِير. يِتغَطرَس هوايَة [haːða maː yistaħiqq ykuːn mudiːr. yidɣaṭras hwaːya] He doesn't deserve to be director. He's extremely arrogant. يِتغَطرَس بمَشِيتَه [yidɣaṭras bmašiːtah] He has a haughty bearing. He swaggers.

غَطرَسَة [ɣaṭrasa] *n:* • **1.** arrogance, snobbishness

مِتغَطرِس [mitɣaṭris] *adj:* • **1.** haughty, arrogant, snobbish, conceited

غ ط س

غِطَس [ɣiṭas] *v:* • **1.** to sink – غِطَس الماعُون بِالحوض [ɣiṭas ʔilmaːʕuːn bilħawḍ̣] The plate sank in the pool.

غَطَّس [ɣaṭṭas] *v:* • **1.** to dip, plunge, immerse – غَطِّس القُماش بِالمَيّ عِدَّة مَرّات [ɣaṭṭis ʔilqumaːš bilmayy ʕiddat marraːt] Dip the cloth in the water several times.

غَطِس [ɣaṭis] *n:* • **1.** sinking

غَطّاس [ɣaṭṭaːs] *n:* • **1.** diver

غاطِس [ɣaːṭis] *adj:* • **1.** sunk, immersed, disappeared from sight

غَطسان [ɣaṭsaːn] *adj:* • **1.** sunk, immersed, disappeared from sight

غ

غ ط ط

غطّ [ɣaṭṭ] *v:* • **1.** to plunge, dive – غطّ لِكَعب النَّهَر [ɣaṭṭ lčaʕb ʔinnahar] He dived to the bottom of the river. باوِع هَالبَطَّة. هَسَّة راح تغُطّ [baːwiʕ halbaṭṭa. hassa raːħ tɣuṭṭ] Watch this duck. It's about to dive. بَس ما خَلَّى راسَه عالِمخَدَّة، غَطّ بالنَّوم [bas maː xallaː raːsah ʕalimxadda, ɣaṭṭ binnuːm] As soon as he put his head on the pillow, he sank into sleep. • **2.** to disappear – أشُو غَطَّيت! صار إلنا ساعتين ننتِظِر [ʔašu gaṭṭayt! ṣaːr ʔilna saːʕtayn nintiðir] You must have been swallowed up by the earth! We've been waiting two hours. غَطّ سَنتَين وَما حَدّ دِرى وين [ɣaṭṭ santayn wma ħadd diraː wiːn] He disappeared for two years and no one knew where he was.

غَطَّط [ɣaṭṭaṭ] *v:* • **1.** to plunge, dip, dunk, immerse – غَطِّط الماعُون بِالمَيّ مَرّتَين وجيبَه [ɣaṭṭiṭ ʔilmaːʕuːn bilmayy marrtayn wjiːbah] Plunge the plate in the water twice and bring it here. إذا ما تفُكّ ياخَة مِنّي تَرَة أغَطِّطَك [ʔiða maː tfukk yaːxa minni tara ʔaɣaṭṭiṭak] If you don't leave me alone, I'm going to dunk you.

غطّ [ɣaṭṭ] *n:* • **1.** plunge, dive

غَطَّة [ɣaṭṭa] *n:* غطّات [ɣaṭṭaːt] *pl:* • **1.** dive • **2.** disappearance – هاي وين هَالغَطَّة؟ صار إلنا يومَين ما شِفناك [haːy wiːn halɣaṭṭa? ṣaːr ʔilna yuːmayn maː šifnaːk] Where've you been so long? We haven't seen you for two days.

غ ط و

غَطّى [ɣaṭṭaː] *v:* • **1.** to cover – غَطّي الجِّدِر حَتّى يفُور المَيّ بِسُرعَة [ɣaṭṭi ʔijjidir ħatta yfuːr ʔilmayy bsurʕa] Cover the pot so that the water will boil quickly. عِندَك بُولَين آچُغ. غَطِّيهُم [ʕindak puːlayn ʔaːčuɣ. ɣaṭṭiːhum] You've two pieces unguarded. Cover them. شما تسَوّي مِن نامَربُوطِيّات، أُمّها تغَطّيلها [šma tsawwiː min naːmarbuːṭiyyaːt, ʔummaha tɣaṭṭiːlha] Whatever mischievious things she does, her mother covers up for her. خِطابَه غَطّى عالكُلّ [xiṭaːbah ɣaṭṭaː ʕalkull] His speech stood out above all the others.

تغَطّى [tɣaṭṭaː] *v:* • **1.** to be or become covered – تغَطّينا بِالتُّراب مِن عَجاج البارحَة [tɣaṭṭayna bitturaːb min ʕajaːj ʔilbaːrħa] We got covered with dust in the dust storm yesterday. • **2.** to cover oneself, cover up – البارحَة تغَطّيت بثلَث بَطّانيّات يَالله دِفيت [ʔilbaːrħa tɣaṭṭayt btlaθ baṭṭaːniyyaːt yallah difayt] Yesterday I covered up with three blankets before I got warm.

غطا [ɣaṭa, ɣiṭa] *n:* أغطِيَة [ʔaɣṭiya] *pl:* • **1.** cover, wrap, wrapper • **2.** covers, bed clothing • **3.** cover, lid

مغَطّى [mɣaṭṭa] *adj:* • **1.** veiled, obscure – حَكِي مغَطّى [ħači mɣaṭṭa] veiled talk.

غ ف ر

غفَر [ɣufar] *v:* • **1.** to forgive, grant pardon, remit – الله يغُفرلَك ذنُوبَك [ʔallah yuɣfurlak ðnuːbak] May God pardon your sins for you.

اِغتَفَر [ʔiɣtifar] *v:* • **1.** to ask for forgiveness

اِستَغفَر [ʔistaɣfar] *v:* • **1.** to seek forgiveness, to ask someone's pardon – أستَغفِر الله [ʔastaɣfir ʔallah] I ask God's forgiveness.

غُفران [ɣufraːn] *n:* • **1.** pardon, forgiveness, remission – عِيد الغُفران [ʕiːd ʔilɣufraːn] Yom Kippur, Day of Atonement.

مَغفِرَة [maɣfira] *n:* • **1.** pardon, forgiveness

اِستِغفار [ʔistiɣfaːr] *n:* • **1.** forgiveness • **2.** plea for pardon

غَفُور [ɣafuːr] *adj:* • **1.** much-forgiving (esp of God)

غَفّار [ɣaffaːr] *adj:* • **1.** much-forgiving (esp of God)

مَغفُور، المَغفُور لَهُ [maɣfuːr, ʔilmaɣfuːr lahu] *adj:* • **1.** the deceased, the late departed (of public figures)

غ ف ل

غِفَل [ɣufal] *v:* • **1.** to neglect, ignore, be forgetful, be unmindful – دِير بالَك عَالجّاهِل. لا تُغفُل عَنَّه [diːr baːlak ʕajjaːhil. laː tuɣful ʕannah] Watch the kid. Don't let your attention off of him.

تغافَل [tɣaːfal] *v:* • **1.** to overlook, disregard, pretend not to notice – تغافَلِت عَنَّه هالمَرَّة، لَكِن ثانِي مَرَّة أعاقبَه [tɣaːfalit ʕannah halmarra, laːkin θaːni marra ʔaʕaːqbah] I overlooked it this time, but next time I'll punish him. آني أدري هُوَّ مُهمِل، بَسّ دَأتغافَل [ʔaːni ʔadri huwwa muhmil, bass daʔadɣaːfal] I know he is negligent, but I'm pretending not to notice. • **2.** to be inattentive – إذا تِتغافَل بِالدَّرِس، شلُون تِفهَم المَوضُوع؟ [ʔiða tidɣaːfal biddaris, šluːn tifham ʔilmawðuːʕ?] If you're inattentive in class, how can you understand the subject? • **3.** to be neglectful – لا تِتغافَل بِالشُّغُل تَرَة يِتكَوَّم عَليك [laː tidɣaːfal biššuɣul tara yitkawwam ʕaliːk] Don't be neglectful of your work or it'll pile up on you.

غَفُل [ɣaful] *n:* • **1.** by surprise, unawares, unprepared, unexpecting – أخَذني غَفُل [ʔaxaðni ɣaful] He took me by surprise.

غَفلَة، عَلَى غَفلَة [ɣafla, ʕala ɣafla] *n:* • **1.** all of a sudden, unawares, unexpectedly – طَبَّيت عَليه عَلَى غَفلَة وشِفتَه نايم [ṭabbiːt ʕaliːh ʕala ɣafla wšiftah naːyim] I burst in on him unexpectedly and found him sleeping.

مُغَفَّل [muɣaffal] *adj:* • **1.** inattentive, absent-minded • **2.** absent-minded person

غافُل [ɣaːful] *adj:* • **1.** absent-minded

غَفلان [ɣaflaːn] *adj:* • **1.** unaware, uninformed – كِنِت غَفلان عَنَّه [činit ɣaflaːn ʕannah] I wasn't aware of it.

غ

غ ف و

غَفَى [ɣufaː] *v:* • **1.** to doze off, fall asleep – بَسّ اِنطِرَح عالفراش، غُفَى [bass ʔinṭirah ʕalfraːš, ɣufaː] As soon as he lay down on the bed, he was out.
غَفّى [ɣaffaː] *v:* • **1.** to doze, to nod, to nap – كان يِغَفّي بِالصَّفّ [čaːn yiɣaffi biṣṣaff] He was dozing in class.
غَفُو [ɣafw] *n:* • **1.** nap, doze
غَفَّة [ɣaffa] *n:* غَفّات [ɣaffaːt] *pl:* • **1.** nap, cat nap, doze
غَفوَة [ɣafwa] *n:* غَفوات [ɣafwaːt, ɣaffa] *pl:* • **1.** doze
غَفيَة [ɣafya] *n:* • **1.** doze, nap

غ ل ب

غِلَب [ɣilab] *v:* • **1.** to win, triumph, be victorious – صارلَه يومَين يُغلُب بِالقمار [ṣaːrlah yuːmayn yuɣlub bilqmaːr] He's been winning at gambling for two days. فَريق مَدرَستنا غِلَب بِسِباق كُرَة القَدَم [fariːq madrasatna ɣilab bsibaːq kurat ʔilqadam] Our school team won the soccer game. • **2.** to beat, defeat – مَحَّد يغُلبَه بِالسِّبِح [maħħad yɣulbah bissibiħ] Nobody beats him at swimming. • **3.** to get the better, get the best, to best – البَزّاز غِلَبَك بِهَالقاط [ʔilbazzaːz ɣilabak bhalqaːṭ] The clothing material dealer got the best of you on this suit.
تغَلَّب [tɣallab] *v:* • **1.** to overcome, surmount, master – بِمُساعَدتَك أقدَر أتغَلَّب عَلَى جَميع الصُّعُوبات [bmusaːʕadtak ʔagdar ʔadɣallab ʕala ǰamiːʕ ʔiṣṣuʕuːbaːt] With your help, I can overcome all the difficulties.
تغالَب [tɣaːlab] *v:* • **1.** to compete with each other – إبنِي وَإبنَك تغالبَوا بِالرِّكِض البارحَة [ʔibni waʔibnak tɣaːlbaw birrikið ʔilbaːrħa] My son and your son raced each other yesterday.
اِنغِلَب [ʔinɣilab] *v:* • **1.** to be defeated
غَلبَة [ɣalba] *n:* غَلبات [ɣalbaːt] *pl:* • **1.** victory
تَغَلُّب [taɣallub] *n:* • **1.** overcoming
مغالَب [mɣaːlab] *n:* • **1.** contest, race – ياكُل بسُرعَة، عَبالَك القَضِيَّة مغالَب [yaːkul bsurʕa, ʕabaːlak ʔilqaðiyya mɣaːlab] He eats so fast, you'd think it was a matter of racing.
أغلَبِيَّة [ʔaɣlabiyya] *n:* • **1.** majority, greater portion
غالِبِيَّة [ɣaːlibiyya] *n:* • **1.** majority, greater portion
غالُب [ɣaːlub] *n:* • **1.** winner, victor • **2.** (as adj:) victorious, winning
غالِب، عَالغالِب [ɣaːlib, ʕalɣaːlib] *adj:* • **1.** mostly, usually, for the most part – عالغالِب، يِجِي المُغرُب [ʕalɣaːlib, yiǰi ʔilmuɣrub] Mostly, he comes about sunset.
مَغلُوب [maɣluːb] *adj:* • **1.** beaten, defeated – الفَريق المَغلُوب [ʔilfariːq ʔilmaɣluːb] the losing team.
غَلبان [ɣalbaːn] *adj:* • **1.** most, majority • **2.** in a winning position
أغلَب [ʔaɣlab] *comparative adjective:* • **1.** the majority, the greater portion, most – عَالأغلَب يِجِي ساعَة ثمانيَة [ʕalʔaɣlab yiǰi saːʕa θmaːnya] Usually he comes at eight.
غالِباً [ɣaːliban] *adverbial:* • **1.** frequently

غ ل ر ي

غالِيري [galiːri] *n:* غالِيريّات [galiriyyaːt] *pl:* • **1.** gallery (in a theater)

غ ل س

غَلَّس [ɣallas] *v:* • **1.** to feign inattention, to pretend not to hear – يِسمَع ويغَلِّس [yismaʕ wiyɣallis] He hears and shows no sign of it. دَأحكِي ويّاك. لا تغَلِّس [daʔaħči wiyyaːk. laː tɣallis] I'm talking to you. Don't pretend you didn't hear.
تغَلَّس [tɣallas] *v:* • **1.** to try to get away with, to try to get out of (doing), to ignore
تَغلِيس [taɣliːs] *n:* • **1.** pretending not to hear
مغَلِّس [mɣallis] *adj:* • **1.** pretending not to hear

غ ل ط

غِلَط [ɣilaṭ] *v:* • **1.** to make a mistake, foul up, goof – تِدرِي، غِلَطِت غير غَلطَة! دَزّيتِلهُم أسعار أقَلّ مِن التَّكليف [tidri, ɣilaṭit ɣiːr ɣalṭa! dazziːtilhum ʔasʕaːr ʔaqall min ttakliːf] You know, I made a bad mistake! I sent them prices that are below cost. غِلَطِت بالسّوال الثّانِي مال الامتِحان [ɣilaṭit bissuʔaːl ʔiθθaːni maːl ʔilʔimtiħaːn] I made a mistake on the second question of the exam. وَين ما ترُوح، تِغلُط [wiːn maː truːħ, tiɣluṭ] You foul up everywhere you go. غِلَطِت غَلطَة فِشَلِت مِنها هوايَة [ɣilaṭit ɣalṭa fišalit minha hwaːya] I goofed and was very embarassed about it. • **2.** to tell inadvertently, give away – دِير بالَك لا تِغلَط بِالحكايَة [diːr baːlak laː tiɣlaṭ bilħčaːya] Watch out you don't spill the story.
غَلَّط [ɣallaṭ] *v:* • **1.** to cause someone to make a mistake – بِحَكيَك غَلَّطتِنِي بِحَلّ المَسألَة [bħačyak ɣallaṭtini bħall ʔilmasʔala] With your talk you made me make a mistake in solving the problem.
تغَلَّط [tɣallaṭ] *v:* • **1.** to make mistakes – يِتغَلَّط هوايَة بالقِراءَة [yidɣallaṭ hwaːya bilqiraːʔa] He makes lots of mistakes in reading.
غَلَط [ɣalaṭ] *n:* • **1.** (coll.) error(s), mistake(s) • **2.** pl. أغلاط errors, mistakes
غلِط [ɣaliṭ] *n:* • **1.** clot • **2.** teasing, bothering
غَلطَة [ɣalṭa] *n:* غَلطات، أغلاط [ɣalṭaːt, ʔaɣlaːṭ] *pl:* • **1.** error, mistake
مُغالَطَة [muɣaːlaṭa] *n:* مُغالَطات [muɣaːlaṭaːt] *pl:* • **1.** falsification, distortion
غَلَط [ɣalaṭ] *adj:* • **1.** wrong, incorrect – جَواب غَلَط [ǰawaːb ɣalaṭ] a wrong answer.
غَلطان [ɣalṭaːn] *adj:* • **1.** wrong, mistaken, in error, erring • **2.** erring person

غ ل ظ

غِلَظ [ɣilað (a ɣalið)] *v:* • **1.** to become thick – لِفّ كَم خيط عَلَى هَالحَبِل حَتَّى يِغلَظ [liff čam xiːṭ ʕala

halħabil ħatta yiɣlað̣] Wind some strings around this rope so it'll be thicker.
غُلُظ [ɣuluð̣] *n:* • **1.** thickness
غَليظ [ɣaliːð̣] *n:* • **1.** thick – حَبِل غَلِيظ [ħabil ɣaliːð̣] a thick rope. الأمعاء الغَلِيظَة [ʔilʔamʕaːʔ ʔilɣaliːð̣a] the large intestine. • **2.** deep, rough, gruff – صُوت غَلِيظ [ṣuːt galiːð̣] a deep voice.
أَغلَظ [ʔaɣlað̣] *comparative adjective:* • **1.** thicker or thickest

غ ل غ ل

تغَلغَل [tɣalɣal] *v:* • **1.** to penetrate, pass through – تغَلغَل بصُفُوف العَدُو وعِرَف كُلّشِي [tɣalɣal bṣufuːf ʔilʕadu wʕiraf kullši] He penetrated into the enemy lines and found out about everything.
تَغَلغُل [taɣalɣul] *n:* • **1.** penetration, passing through
متغَلغِل [mitɣalɣil] *adj:* • **1.** penetrated, deeply embedded

غ ل ف 1

غَلَّف [ɣallaf] *v:* • **1.** to put in a cover, envelope, or case – غَلِّف الكِتاب حَتَّى ما يتمَزَّق [ɣallif ʔilkitaːb ħatta maː yitmazzag] Put a cover on the book so it won't get worn out. • **2.** to wrap, cover – غَلَّف الباكَيت وَدَزَّه بالبَرِيد [ɣallaf ʔilpaːkiːt wdazzah bilbariːd] He wrapped the package and mailed it. غَلِّف الدَّعّامِيّات قَبُل ما تُصبُغ السَّيّارَة [ɣallif ʔiddaʕʕaːmiyyaːt gabul maː tuṣbuɣ ʔissayyaːra] Mask the bumpers before you paint the car.
غِلاف [ɣilaːf] *n:* أَغلِفَة [ʔaɣlifa] *pl:* • **1.** covering, wrapper, casing • **2.** cover, book jacket
مُغَلَّف [muɣallaf] *adj:* • **1.** wrapped, covered • **2.** enveloped

غ ل ف 2

غُولف [guːlf] *n:* • **1.** golf

غ ل ق

غِلَق [ɣilaq, ɣilag] *v:* • **1.** to close, shut – أُغلُق الكِتاب وجِيبَه لِهنا [ʔuɣlug ʔilkitaːb wǰiːbah lihna] Close the book and bring it here. • **2.** to latch, fasten, secure – مِن تسِدّ الباب بالله إغلُقها [min tsidd ʔilbaːb ballah ʔiɣluqha] When you close the door please latch it. أُغلُق الباب بَسّ لا تُقفُلها [ʔuɣlug ʔilbaːb bass laː tuqfulha] Close the door but don't lock it.
غَلَّق [ɣallag] *v:* • **1.** to close, shut, fasten, latch – غَلِّق الشِّبابِيك قَبُل ما تِطلَع [ɣallig ʔiššibaːbiːč gabul maː titlaʕ] Latch the windows before you go out. • **2.** to become hoarse – اِنّشَل البارحَة وَغَلَّق حِسَّه [ʔinnišal ʔilbaːrħa wɣallag ħissah] He caught cold yesterday and it made his voice hoarse.
غَلِق [ɣaliq, ɣalig] *n:* • **1.** shutting, closing
مُغلَق [muɣlaq] *adj:* • **1.** closed
مِنغِلِق [minɣiliq] *adj:* • **1.** closed, isolated

غ ل ل

غَلّ [ɣall] *v:* • **1.** to nudge, poke – صاحبَك ما دَينتِبِه. غُلّه [ṣaːħbak maː dayintibih. ɣullah] Your friend isn't paying attention. Poke him.
اِستَغَلّ [ʔistaɣall] *v:* • **1.** to make a profit, invest profitably, utilize – الحُكُومَة دَتِستَغِلّ مَصادِر البَلَد بمَشارِيع العُمران [ʔilħukuːma datistaɣill maṣaːdir ʔilbalad bmašaːriːʕ ʔilʕumraːn] The government is utilizing the country's resources in the development projects. • **2.** to exploit, take advantage of – اِستَغَلّ بَساطتَه وَغشَّه [ʔistaɣall baṣaːṭtah wɣaššah] He took advantage of his simplicity and cheated him. لا تِتشارَك وِيّاه تَرَة يِستَغِلَّك [laː titšaːrak wiyyaːh tara yistaɣillak] Don't go partners with him or he'll take advantage of you.
غَلّ [ɣall] *n:* • **1.** nudge, poke
اِستِغلال [ʔistiɣlaːl] *n:* • **1.** utilization, expoitation
مَغلُول، إيدَه مَغلُولَة [maɣluːl, ʔiːdah maɣluːla] *adj:* • **1.** fettered, shackled, inactive • **2.** thrifty, cheapskate
مُستَغِلّ [mustaɣill] *adj:* • **1.** exploiter, utilizer • **2.** exploiting, utilizing
مُستَغَلّ [mustaɣall] *adj:* • **1.** yield, crops, proceeds, profit • **2.** taken advantage of, exploited
اِستِغلالِي [ʔistiɣlaːli] *adj:* • **1.** exploitative

غ ل ن

غَلَن [galan] *n:* غَلَنات [galanaːt] *pl:* • **1.** container
غالُون [gaːluːn] *n:* • **1.** gallon

غ ل و

غِلا [ɣilaː] *v:* • **1.** to be or become expensive, high priced – بأيّام الحَرُب كُلّشِي غِلا [bʔayyaːm ʔilħarub kullši ɣilaː] During the war everything became expensive.
غَلَّى [ɣallaː] *v:* • **1.** to raise the price of – سمَعِت راح يغَلُّون أسعار الحُبُوب [smaʕit raːħ yɣalluːn ʔasʕaːr ʔilħubuːb] I heard they're going to raise grain prices.
غَلا، غَلاء [ɣala, ɣalaːʔ] *n:* • **1.** inflation, period of high prices
مُغالاة [muɣaːlaːt] *n:* • **1.** exaggeration
غالِي [ɣaːli] *adj:* • **1.** expensive, high priced – قُوط غالِيَة [quːṭ ɣaːlya] expensive suits. بِناء البَيت يكَلِّف غالِي [binaːʔ ʔilbayt ykallif ɣaːli] Building a house costs a lot. هَالتّاجِر يبِيع غالِي [hattaːǰir yibiːʕ ɣaːli] This merchant charges a lot.
أَغلَى [ʔaɣla] *comparative adjective:* • **1.** more or most expensive, costly

غ ل و ن

غَلوَن [ɣalwan] *v:* • **1.** to galvanize – إذا تغَلوَن الحَدِيد، ما يزَنجِر [ʔiða dɣalwan ʔilħadiːd, maː yzanǰir] If you galvanize the metal, it won't rust.

غ

غ ل ي

غَلَى [ɣila:] *v:* • **1.** to boil, bubble – طَفّي النّار. المَيّ دَيِغلِي [ṭaffi ʔinna:r. ʔilmayy dayiɣli] Turn off the fire. The water is boiling. • **2.** to boil, cause to boil, make boil – إغلِي الحَلِيب قَبُل ما تشُربَه [ʔiɣli ʔilħali:b gabul ma: tšurbah] Boil the milk before you drink it.

غَلَيان [ɣalaya:n] *n:* • **1.** boiling

غ م ر

غُمَر [ɣumar] *v:* • **1.** to flood, inundate – المَيّ غُمَر أراضِينا [ʔilmayy ɣumar ʔara:ḏi:na] The water covered our lands.

غامَر [ɣa:mar] *v:* • **1.** to be adventurous, to have adventures – غامَر هوايَة مِن كان شَباب [ɣa:mar hwa:ya min ča:n šaba:b] He was very adventurous when he was a youth. • **2.** with ب to venture, risk – غامَرِت بِثَرُوتِي وحَصَّلِت هوايَة [ɣa:marit bθarwwti wħaṣṣalit hwa:ya] I risked my fortune and got a lot back. ما عِندَه مانِع يغامِر بِحَياتَه مِن أجل الحِزب [ma: ʕindah ma:niʕ yɣa:mir bħaya:tah min ʔajl ʔilħizib] He doesn't mind risking his life for the sake of the party.

غَمُر [ɣamur] *n:* • **1.** flooding

مُغامَرَة [muɣa:mara] *n:* مُغامَرات [muɣa:mara:t] *pl:* • **1.** adventure

مَغمُور [maɣmu:r] *adj:* • **1.** sunken

مغامِر [mɣa:mir] *adj:* • **1.** adventurous

غ م ز

غُمَز [ɣumaz] *v:* • **1.** to signal, make a sign, beckon, wink – غُمَزلَه بعَينَه حَتَّى ما يِحكِي [ɣumazlah bʕaynah ħatta ma: yiħči] He winked at him so he wouldn't say anything. أغمُز إلها. بَلكِي تلِحقَك [ʔuɣmuz ʔilha. balki tliħgak] Give her a come-on. Maybe she'll follow you.

غَمُز [ɣamuz] *n:* • **1.** winking

غَمزَة [ɣamza] *n:* غمزات [ɣamza:t] *pl:* • **1.** come-on, wink, flirtatious gesture

غ م س

غَمَّس [ɣammas] *v:* • **1.** to dip, dunk – دَيغَمُّس الخُبُز بالمَرَق [dayɣammus ʔilxubuz bilmarag] He's dunking the bread in the stew.

غمُوس [ɣmu:s] *n:* • **1.** anything eaten with bread

غ م ض

غُمَض [ɣumaḏ] *v:* • **1.** to close (of the eye) – اللَّيل كُلَّه ما غُمضَت عينِي [ʔillayl kullah ma: ɣumḏat ʕayni] My eyes didn't close all night.

غَمَّض [ɣammaḏ] *v:* • **2.** to close, shut (of the eye) – غَمُّض عَين وَفَتِّح عَين مِن تبَوِّع بِالدَّربِين [ɣammuḏ ʕayn wfattiħ ʕayn min tbawwiʕ biddarbayn] Close one eye and open one eye when you look through the telescope.

تغَمَّض [tɣammaḏ] *v:* • **1.** to be closed (of the eye)

غُمُوض [ɣumu:ḏ] *n:* • **1.** ambiguity, abstruseness

غَمضَة [ɣamḏa] *n:* • **1.** blink

غُمَّيضَة [ɣummi:ḏa] *n:* • **1.** children's game similar to blindman's buff

غامِض [ɣa:miḏ] *adj:* • **1.** obscure, dark, ambiguous – سِرّ غامِض [sirr ɣa:miḏ] deep, dark, hidden secret.

مغَمُّض [mɣammuḏ] *adj:* • **1.** having closed eyes

غ م ق

غَمَّق [ɣammag] *v:* • **1.** to deepen, increase the depth of – هاك المِسحا. غَمُّق النُّقرَة بِيها [ha:k ʔilmisħa. ɣammug ʔinnugra bi:ha] Here's the spade. Deepen the hole with it. • **2.** to deepen, darken (color) – إذا ترِيد تغَمُّق لونَه لِلثُّوب، أُصبَغَه فَدّ مَرّتَين لُخ [ʔiða tri:d tɣammug lu:nah lilθu:b, ʔuṣbaɣah fadd marrtayn lux] If you want to deepen the color of the shirt, dye it a couple more times. • **3.** to go too far, to over-step the bounds – غَمَّق ويّايا بِالشَّقَة وَزَعَّلنِي [ɣammag wiyya:ya biššaqa wzaʕʕalni] He went too far in joking with me, and irritated me. لا تغَمُّق ويّاه بِالحَكِي تَرَة تِتنَدَّم [la: tɣammug wiyya:h bilħači tara titnaddam] Don't go too far talking with him or you'll be sorry.

غُمُق [ɣumug] *n:* • **1.** depth, deepness • **2.** depth, darkness (of color)

غُمِق [ɣumiǰ] *n:* • **1.** depth

غَمِيق [ɣami:g] *adj:* • **1.** deep – بِير غَمِيقَة [bi:r ɣami:ga] a deep well. • **2.** deep, dark – لُون غَمِيق [lu:n ɣami:g] a dark color.

غامِق [ɣa:mig] *adj:* • **1.** dark

أَغمَق [ʔaɣmag] *comparative adjective:* • **1.** deeper or deepest • **2.** darker or darkest (color)

غ م م

غَمّ [ɣamm] *v:* • **1.** to express exasperation with someone by a wave of the hand, as if pushing him away – مِن ما عِرَف يجاوُب، غَمَّتَه أُمَّه [min ma: ʕiraf yǰa:wub, ɣammatah ʔummah] When he didn't know the answer, his mother waved her hand at him in disgust.

اِغتَمّ [ʔiɣtamm] *v:* • **1.** to be distressed, be worried – اِغتَمّ هوايَة عَن قَضِيَّة إبنَه [ʔiɣtamm hwa:ya ʕan qaḏiyyat ʔibnah] He worries a lot about his son's situation.

اِنغَمّ [ʔinɣamm] *v:* • **1.** to be distressed, be worried

غَمّ [ɣamm] *n:* • **1.** expressing exasperation with someone by a wave of the hand, as if pushing him away • **2.** grief, sadness

غَمَّة [ɣamma] *n:* • **1.** a gesture of pushing someone away, usually as a result of displeasure

غُمَّة [ɣumma] *n:* • **1.** grief, sadness, sorrow

غ م ي

غِمَى [ɣima:] *v:* • **1.** to faint • **2.** with عَلَى to overcome – بِالحَرّ، يِغمَى عَليه [bilħarr, yiɣma: ʕali:h] In the heat, he is overcome.

غ ن م

اِغتَنَم [ʔiɣtinam] *v:* • **1.** to seize, take advantage of – راح أَغتِنِم فُرصَة وُجُود الطَّبِيب هنا وَأَسأَلَه عَن صِحّتِي [raːħ ʔaɣtinim furṣat wuʒuːd ʔiṭṭabiːb hna wʔasʔalah ʕan ṣiħħti] I'm going to seize the opportunity of the doctor's presence here and ask him about my health.

غَنَم [ɣanam] *n:* أَغنام [ʔaɣnaːm] *pl:* • **1.** Coll. sheep – لَحم الغَنَم [laħm ʔilɣanam] lamb, mutton. قَطِيع غَنَم [qaṭiːʕ ɣanam] herd of sheep.

غَنّام [ɣannaːm] *n:* غَنّامَة [ɣannaːma] *pl:* • **1.** shepherd, shepherdess • **2.** sheep owner

غَنِيمَة [ɣaniːma] *n:* غَنايِم [ɣanaːyim, ganaːʔim] *pl:* • **1.** spoils, booty, loot

غانِم، سالِم وَغانِم [ɣaːnim, saːlim waɣaːnim] *adj:* • **1.** safe and sound – وُصَل سالِم وَغانِم [wuṣal saːlim wɣaːnim] He arrived safe and sound.

غ ن ي

غِنَى [ɣinaː] *v:* • **1.** to enrich, make rich, make free from want – الله يِغنِيك [ʔallah yiɣniːk] May God enrich you. لا يِغنِيك وَ لايخَلِّيك تجَدِّي [laː yiɣniːk wlaː yxalliːk tʒaddi] He gives you no way out (lit. he won't make you rich and won't let you beg).

غَنَّى [ɣannaː] *v:* • **1.** to sing – مِنُو راح يغَنِّي بالحَفلَة اليُوم؟ [minu raːħ yɣanni bilħafla ʔilyuːm?] Who's going to sing at the party today?

تغَنَّى [tɣannaː] *v:* • **1.** with ب to extol, praise, sing the praises of – الكُلّ يِتغَنُّون بجَمالها [ʔilkull yidɣannuːn bʒamaːlha] They all sing the praises of her beauty.

اِغتِنَى [ʔiɣtinaː] *v:* • **1.** to become rich – بواسطَة أَبُوها، اِغتِنَى هوايَة [bwaːsṭat ʔabuːha, ʔiɣtinaː hwaːya] With the influence of her father, he became very rich.

اِستَغنَى [ʔistaɣnaː] *v:* • **1.** with عَن to spare, dispense with, manage, or do, without – آنِي ما أَقدَر أَستَغنِي عَن الخَدّامَة [ʔaːni maː ʔagdar ʔastaɣni ʕan ʔilxaddaːma] I can't get along without the maid.

غِنَى [ɣinaː] *n:* • **1.** wealth, riches • **2.** singing, song

غَنُّوَة، غُنُّوَة [ɣannuwwa, ɣunnuwwa] *n:* غُنُّوات [ɣunnuwwaːt] *pl:* • **1.** song

مُغَنِّي [muɣanni] *n:* مُغَنِّين [muɣanniːn] *pl:* • **1.** singer, vocalist

غِناء [ɣinaːʔ] *n:* • **1.** singing

أُغنِيَة [ʔuɣniya] *n:* أُغنيات، أَغانِي [ʔuɣniyaːt, ʔaɣaːni] *pl:* • **1.** song

مُغَنِّيَة [muɣanniya] *n:* مُغَنِّيات [muɣanniyaːt] *pl:* • **1.** (female) singer, vocalist, songstress

غَنِي [ɣani] *adj:* أَغنِياء [ʔaɣniyaːʔ] *pl:* • **1.** prosperous, well-to-do, wealthy, rich

غِنائِي [ɣinaːʔi] *adj:* • **1.** singing, song, vocal – حَفلَة غِنائِيَّة [ħafla ɣinaːʔiyya] song recital, concert of vocal music.

غ و ث

أَغاث [ʔaɣaːθ] *v:* • **1.** to help, go to the aid of – إذا مَحَّد يغِيثهُم كُلّهُم يمُوتُون [ʔiða maħħad yɣiːθhum kullhum ymuːtuːn] If no one goes to their aid, they'll all die.

اِستَغاث [ʔistaɣaːθ] *v:* • **1.** to appeal for help, to seek the aid – دَيِستَغِيثُون بِينا. خَلِّي نرُوح نساعِدهُم [dayistaɣiːθuːn biːna. xalliː nruːħ nsaːʕidhum] They're calling to us for help. Let's go help them. بِمَن تِستَغِيث؟ كُلّهُم عِدوان [biman tistaɣiːθ? kullhum ʕidwaːn] Whom can you call on for help? They're all enemies.

غَوث [ɣawθ, ɣuːθ] *n:* • **1.** call for help, aid, help

إغاثَة [ʔiɣaːθa] *n:* • **1.** help, aid,succor

اِستِغاثَة [ʔistiɣaːθa] *n:* • **1.** help, aid, succor

مُغِيث [muɣiːθ] *adj:* • **1.** helper (esp of God), deliverer from distress

غ و ر

غار [ɣaːr] *v:* • **1.** with عَلَى to raid, attack, fall upon – القَبِيلَة غارَت عَالبَلدَة [lqabiːla ɣaːrat ʕalbalda] The tribe invaded the city.

غار [ɣaːr] *n:* • **1.** (invar.) laurel, bay – زَيت الغار [zayt ʔilɣaːr] laurel oil.

غار [ɣaːr] *n:* • **1.** burrow, hole (of an animal) • **2.** pl. غارات [ɣaːraːt] cave, cavern

غارَة [ɣaːra] *n:* غارات [ɣaːraːt] *pl:* • **1.** raid, foray, attack, predatory excursion

مَغارَة [maɣaːra] *n:* مَغارات [maɣaːraːt] *pl:* • **1.** cavern, cave, grotto

مِغوار [migwaːr] *n:* • **1.** wooden weapon

إغارَة [ʔiɣaːra] *n:* • **1.** (with عَلَى) attack, raid, invasion

مُغوار [muɣwaːr] *adj:* مغاوِير [mɣaːwiːr] *pl:* • **1.** courageous

غ و ر ل

غورِيلّا [ɣuriːlla] *n:* غورِيلّات [ɣuriːllaːt] *pl:* • **1.** gorilla

غ و ش

غَوَّش [ɣawwaš] *v:* • **1.** to go out of focus, to blur – راح لِلطَّبِيب لِأَنّ عيُونَه دَتغَوِّش [raːħ liṭṭabiːb liʔann ʕyuːnah dadɣawwiš] He went to the doctor because his eyes are blurry.

مغَوَّش [mɣawwaš] *adj:* • **1.** out of focus, blurred, unclear, fuzzy – صُورَة مغَوِّشَة [ṣuːra mɣawwiša] a fuzzy picture.

غ و ص

غاص [ɣaːṣ] *v:* • **1.** to submerge, dive, plunge – يِقدَر يغُوص لِكَعب البَحَر [yigdar yɣuːṣ lčaʕb ʔilbaħar] He can dive to the bottom of the sea.

غَوص [ɣawṣ] *n:* • **1.** diving

غ

غَوّاص [ɣawwaːṣ] *n:* غَوّاصِين [ɣawwaːṣiːn] *pl:* • **1.** diver

غَوّاصَة [ɣawwaːṣa] *n:* غَوّاصات [ɣawwaːṣaːt] *pl:* • **1.** submarine

غ و غ ء

غَوغاء [ɣawɣaːʔ] *n:* • **1.** mob

غَوغائِي [ɣawɣaːʔi] *adj:* • **1.** demagogic

غ و ل [1]

اِغتال [ʔiɣtaːl] *v:* • **1.** to assassinate

مُغتال [muɣtaːl] *n:* • **1.** assassin

اِغتِيال [ʔiɣtiyaːl, ʔixtiyaːl] *n:* • **1.** snatching away, kidnapping • **2.** assassination

غ و ل [2]

غُول [ɣuːl] *n:* غِيلان [ɣiːlaːn] *pl:* • **1.** ghoul, demon, giant, ogre

غ و ي

تغاوَى [tɣaːwaː] *v:* • **1.** to put on airs – زَنكِين هوايَة. لُويش ما يتغاوَى؟ [zangiːn hwaːya. luwiːš maː yidɣaːwaː?] He's very rich. Why doesn't he put on airs?

غُوَة [ɣuwa] *n:* • **1.** snobbishness

إغواء [ʔiɣwaːʔ] *n:* • **1.** seduction

غاوِي [ɣaːwi] *adj:* • **1.** dabbler, dilettante; seducer

غ ي ب

غاب [ɣaːb] *v:* • **1.** to be absent, be or stay away, absent oneself – التِّلمِيذ غاب عَن المَدرَسَة شَهرَين [ʔittilmiːð ɣaːb ʕan ʔilmadrasa šahrayn] The student was absent from school for two months. • **2.** to set, go down – بُردَت الدِّنيا بَعَد ما غابَت الشَّمِس [burdat ʔiddinya baʕad maː ɣaːbat ʔiššamis] It got cold after the sun went down.

غَيَّب [ɣayyab] *v:* • **1.** to keep away – مُدِير المَدرَسَة غَيَّب الطُّلّاب عَن المُظاهَرَة [mudiːr ʔilmadrasa ɣayyab ʔiṭṭullaːb ʕan ʔilmuḍaːhara] The school principal kept the students away from the demonstration. شغَيَّبَك عَنها؟ [šɣayyabak ʕanha?] What kept you away from her?

تغَيَّب [tɣayyab] *v:* • **1.** to be absent, be away, stay away – إذا تِتغَيَّب هوايَة، ما تِتعَلَّم [ʔiða tidɣayyab hwaːya, maː titʕallam] If you stay absent a lot you won't learn.

اِغتاب [ʔiɣtaːb] *v:* • **1.** to slander – عَلَى طُول يِغتابُون أَصدِقائهُم [ʕala ṭuːl yiɣtaːbuːn ʔaṣdiqaːʔhum] They always talk behind their friends' backs.

اِستَغاب [ʔistaɣaːb] *v:* • **1.** to slander

غيب، الغيب [ɣayb, ʔilɣayb] *n:* • **1.** the unknown, the supernatural – يِعلَم بالغيب [yiʕlam bilɣayb] He's clairvoyant.

غابَة [ɣaːba] *n:* غابات [ɣaːbaːt] *pl:* • **1.** forest, wood • **2.** jungle

غَيبَة [ɣayba, ɣiːba] *n:* غَيبات [ɣiːbaːt] *pl:* • **1.** absence

غِيبَة [ɣiːba] *n:* • **1.** slander, harmful talk about someone

غِياب [ɣiyaːb] *n:* • **1.** being away • **2.** pl. غِيابات absences

غَيبُوبَة [ɣaybuːba] *n:* • **1.** unconsciousness, faint, fainting spell

غايِب [ɣaːyib] *adj:* • **1.** absent – غايِب مِن الدَّرِس [ɣaːyib min ʔiddaris] absent from class. • **2.** person who is absent – الغايِب [ʔilɣaːyib] the sum agreed upon in a marriage contract to be paid by a man in case he divorces his wife.

غِيابِي، حُكُم غِيابِي [ɣiyaːbi, ħukum ɣiyaːbi] *adj:* • **1.** sentencing in absentia – مُحاكَمَة غِيابِيَّة [muħaːkama ɣiyaːbiyya] trial in absentia.

غِيابِيّاً [ɣiyaːbiyyan] *adverbial:* • **1.** in absentia – حُكمَوه غِيابِيّاً [ħukmawh ɣiyaːbiyyan] They tried him in absentia.

غ ي ر

غار [ɣaːr] *v:* • **1.** to be jealous – يغار مِن أَخُوه الصِّغَيِّر [yɣaːr min ʔaxuːh ʔizziɣayyir] He's jealous of his little brother. • **2.** to be zealous – يغار عَلَى وَطَنَه [yɣaːr ʕala waṭanah] He's earnestly concerned with his country, he's a zealous patriot. • **3.** to be ticklish – شُوفَه يغار لَو لا [šuːfah yɣaːr law laː] Tickle him and see whether he's ticklish or not.

غَيَّر [ɣayyar] *v:* • **1.** to change, alter, modify, make different – لا تغَيِّر أَيّ شِي بِالمِسوَدَّة [laː tɣayyir ʔayy ši bilmiswadda] Don't change anything in the draft. إذا الله اِنطاه العافيَة راح يغَيِّر هَوا بأُورُبّا [ʔiða ʔallah ʔinṭaːh ʔilʕaːfya raːħ yɣayyir hawa bʔuːruppa] If God grants him good health, he is going to take a change of climate to Europe. هالسَّنَة غَيِّرَوا شوَيَّة بالمَنهَج الدِّراسِي [hassana ɣayyiraw šwayya bilmanhaǰ ʔiddiraːsi] This year they changed a few things in the study program. • **2.** to change, exchange, replace – لازم نغَيِّر التّايِر [laːzim nɣayyir ʔittaːyir] We've got to change the tire. إذا ما تِعجبَك، يغَيِّرلَك إيّاها [ʔiða maː tʕiǰbak, yɣayyirlak ʔiyyaːha] If you don't like it, he'll exchange it for you. • **3.** to make jealous – لابسَة يغَيِيلَك الجِّدِيد؛ دَتغَيِّر صَدِيقَتها [laːbsah nafnuːfha ʔiǰǰidiːd; dadɣayyir ṣadiːqatha] She's wearing her new dress; making her friend jealous.

تغَيَّر [tɣayyar] *v:* • **1.** to be replaced – مُدِيرنا راح يِتغَيَّر الشَّهَر الجّاي [mudiːrna raːħ yidɣayyar ʔiššahar ʔiǰǰaːy] Our director will be replaced next month.

غير [ɣayr, ɣiːr] *n:* • **1.** other, another, different – غير ثُوب [ɣiːr θuːb] another shirt. غير يوم [ɣiːr yuːm] another day. غير واحِد [ɣiːr waːħid] someone else. • **2.** (someone or something) other than, except, else – دَيتخورَد عالبنَيّة بفلُوس غيرَه [dayitxawrad ʕalbnayya bflu:s ɣayrah] He's showing off for the girl with someone else's money. خَلّي يِجي واحِد غيرَك يِحكِي وِيّاها [xalli: yiǰi wa:ħid ɣi:rak yiħči wiyya:ha] Let someone besides you come to talk to her. ما عِدكُم غير الأَقمِشَة الصُّوفِيَّة؟ [ma: ʕidkum ɣi:r ʔilʔaqmiša ʔiṣṣu:fiyya?] Don't you have anything but wool cloth? الغَير شَعلِيه؟ [ʔilɣayr šaʕli:h?] What does he care about anyone else? • **3.** (an interrogative used in replying to a question or statement, approx.:) what else but, could it be anything but, wasn't it – غير هُوَّ راد يأَذّيك؟ [ɣi:r huwwa ra:d yʔaððī:k?] What else but that he wanted to hurt you? غير مِن طَرَف الفلُوس مالتِي؟ [ɣi:r min ṭaraf ʔilflu:s ma:lti?] Could it be anything else but concerning my money? غير إنتَ ما قبَلِت تِشتِري؟ هُوَّ راد يبِيع [ɣi:r ʔinta ma: qbalit tištiri? huwwa ra:d yibi:ʕ] Wasn't it you that wouldn't buy? He wanted to sell. غير إنتَ اللّي قِتلِي هاي خُوش سَيّارَة وخَلَّيتنِي أَشتِريها؟ [ɣi:r ʔinta ʔilli gittli ha:y xu:š sayya:ra wxallaytni ʔaštiri:ha?] Didn't you yourself tell me this was a good car and let me buy it? • **4.** were it not that, except that, but for the fact that – غَير الحاكِم قَرايبَه، وَإلّا كان انحِكَم [ɣi:r ʔilħa:kim gara:ybah, waʔilla ča:n ʔinħikam] If it weren't for the fact that the judge is related to him, he'd have been found guilty. غير لِقِينا الطَّرِيق مَسدُود، وَإلّا كان وُصَلنا ساعَة خَمسَة [ɣi:r ligi:na ʔiṭṭari:q masdu:d, waʔilla ča:n wuṣalna sa:ʕa xamsa] If we hadn't found the road closed, we'd have arrived at five. كان جاوَبت الأَسئِلَة كُلّها غير هِيَّ مُو مِن الكِتاب [ča:n ǰa:wabt ʔilʔasʔila kullha ɣi:r hiyya mu: min ʔilkita:b] I'd've answered all the questions except that they weren't from the book. • **5.** (an intensifying particle, approx.:) real, quite a, such a, what a, really, quite, so – بُسَطتَه غير بَسطَة [busaṭṭah ɣi:r basṭa] I gave him a real beating. نِجَح غير نَجاح [nijaħ ɣi:r naja:ħ] What a success he achieved! هَذا غير مُطِي [ha:ða ɣi:r muṭi] He's a real dope! بِنتَه غير حِلوَة [bintah ɣi:r ħilwa] His daughter's really pretty! • **6.** not, non- – غير قانُونِي [ɣi:r qa:nu:ni] illegal, not legal. غير مَعقُول [ɣi:r maʕqu:l] unreasonable, not reasonable.

غيرَة [ɣi:ra] *n:* • **1.** jealousy
تَغيِير [taɣyi:r] *n:* تَغيِيرات [taɣyi:ra:t] *pl:* • **1.** change
غَيُور [ɣayu:r] *adj:* • **1.** jealous
غَيّار [ɣayya:r] *adj:* • **1.** jealous
غَيران [ɣayra:n] *adj:* • **1.** jealous
مِتغَيِّر [mitɣayyir] *adj:* • **1.** changed

غ ي ض

غاض [ɣa:ð] *v:* • **1.** to anger, make angry – لا تقُلَّه هِيكِي شِي تَرَة تغِيضَه [la: tgullah hi:či ši tara dɣi:ð̣ah] Don't tell him such a thing or you'll anger him.
اِغتاض [ʔiɣta:ð] *v:* • **1.** to be or become angry, to get mad – لا تِغتاض مِنَّه. هُوَّ أَخُوك [la: tiɣta:ð̣ minnah. huwwa ʔaxu:k] Don't get angry at him. He's your brother.
غَيض [ɣayð, ɣi:ð̣] *n:* • **1.** anger

غ ي م

غَيَّم [ɣayyam] *v:* • **1.** to be or become cloudy, to cloud up – الدِّنيا ساعَة تغَيِّم وساعَة تصَحِّي [ʔiddinya sa:ʕa tɣayyim wsa:ʕa tṣaħħi] The sky gets cloudy one hour and then clears up the next. شبِيه أَخُوك؟ أَشُو وِجهه مغَيِّم [šbi:h ʔaxu:k? ʔašu: wiččah mɣayyim] What's with your brother? He seems glum.
غيم [ɣaym, ɣi:m] *n:* • **1.** (coll.) cloud(s)
غيمَة [ɣayma, ɣi:ma] *n:* غيُوم [ɣyu:m] *pl:* • **1.** cloud
مغَيِّم [mɣayyim] *adj:* • **1.** cloudy

غ ي ن

غين [ɣayn] *n:* • **1.** name of the letter

غ ي ي

غايَة [ɣa:ya] *n:* غايات [ɣa:ya:t] *pl:* • **1.** object, objective, end, intention, intent, purpose – هالقَضِيَّة مُهِمَّة لِلغايَة [halqaḍiyya muhimma lilɣa:ya] This matter is extremely important. غايَة بـ [ɣa:ya bi] extremely, extraordinarily. هِيَّ غايَة بِالجَّمال [hiyya ɣa:ya bijǰama:l] She is extraordinarily beautiful. هَذا غايَة بِالذَّكاء [ha:ða ɣa:ya biððaka:ʔ] He's extremely intelligent.

غ

ف

ف

فاء [faːʔ] *n:* • **1.** name of the letter

ف ء

فِئَة [fiʔa] *n:* فِئات [fiʔaːt] *pl:* • **1.** group, gang, party, faction • **2.** price, denomination – طَوابِع فِئَة خَمس فلُوس [ṭawaːbiʕ fiʔat xams fluːs] five fils stamps.

ف ء د

أُفَاد، إفّاد [ʔuffaːd, ʔiffaːd] *n:* • **1.** heart, chest – إفّادَه يِلزَمَه [ʔifaːdah yilzamah] His chest hurts him. ضِرَبَه بِدَفرَة وَقِطَع إفادَه [ðirabah bdafra wgiṭaʕ ʔiffaːdah] He kicked him and hurt him something awful. حكايتَه بَعدها تُنقُر بِأُفَادِي [ħčaːytah baʕadha tungur bʔuffaːdi] His remark is still gnawing at my heart. هالشُّغُل دَيِشلَع أُفَادِي [haššuɣul dayišlaʕ ʔuffaːdi] This work is wearing me out. لا تاكُل راس أُفَادِي [laː taːkul raːs ʔuffaːdi] Don't give me a hard time.

ف ء ل [1]

تفاءَل [tfaːʔal] *v:* • **1.** to be optimistic – آنِي مِتفائِل بِهالصَّفقَة [ʔaːni mitfaːʔil bhaṣṣafqa] I'm optimistic about this deal. أتفائَلَك بِالنَّجاح [ʔatfaːʔallak binnajaːħ] I predict success for you. • **2.** with ب to regard as a good omen, regard as auspicious – أتفاءَل بِالبِلبِل [ʔatfaːʔal bilbilbil] I always regard the nightingale as a good sign.

فال، أخَذ فال، فِتَح فال [faːl, ʔaxað faːl, fitaħ faːl] *n:* • **1.** to tell fortunes, predict the future – فِتَح فال [fitaħ faːl] to tell fortunes, predict the future. فِتَحلِي فال [fitaħli faːl] He told my fortune. إنطِيه عَشِر فلُوس حَتَّى ياخُذلَك فال [ʔintiːh ʕašir fluːs ħatta yaːxuðlak faːl] Give him ten fils so he will tell your fortune. فَتّاح فال [fattaːħ faːl] fortuneteller. رُوح بِفالَك [ruːħ bfaːlak] Go on. Go ahead. Do what you want.

فَوّال [fawwaːl] *n:* فَوّالِين [fawwaːliːn, -a] *pl:* • **1.** fortune-teller

تفاؤُل [tafaːʔul] *n:* • **1.** optimism

مِتفائِل [mitfaːʔil] *adj:* • **1.** optimist

ف ء ل [2]

فالَة [faːla] *n:* فالات [faːlaːt] *pl:* • **1.** fish gig, trident

ف ت ت

فَتّ [fatt] *v:* • **1.** to break – إبنِك ما يِنحِمِل وَيفِتّ القَلُب [ʔibnič maː yinħimil wyfitt ʔilgalub] Your son is unbearable, and he gets on one's nerves.

فَتَّت [fattat] *v:* • **1.** to crumble, break into small pieces – فَتِّت الخُبزَة وَإنطِيها لِلعَصافِير [fattit ʔilxubza waʔinṭiːha lilʕaṣaːfiːr] Crumble the bread and give it to the birds.

تفَتَّت [tfattat] *v:* • **1.** to crumble, disintegrate, break up into fragments – هَالكلَيجَة تِتفَتَّت بالإيد [halkliːča titfattat bilʔiːd] These cookies fall apart in the hand. أُفّادها تفَتَّت مِن البَكِي [ʔuffaːdha tfattat min ʔilbačy] She cried her heart out.

إنفَتّ [ʔinfatt] *v:* • **1.** to be anguished, be beside oneself – اِنفَتَّت عَلَى موت أَبُوها [ʔinfattat ʕala muːt ʔabuːha] She was anguished by her father's death. اِنفَتّ مِن سِمَع تَرَفَّعِت [ʔinfatt min simaʕ traffaʕit] He was beside himself when he heard I got promoted. اِنفَتّ قَلبِي مِن تَصَرُّفَه [ʔinfatt galbi min taṣarrufah] I was all torn up about his behavior.

فتاتَة [ftaːta] *n:* فتات [ftaːt] *pl:* • **1.** crumb(s), (small) piece(s) – فَتات خُبُز [fataːt xubuz] bread crumbs.

تَفتيت [taftiːt] *n:* • **1.** dismemberment, partition, crumbling

فِتيت [fitiːt] *adj:* • **1.** falling apart, overcooked, cooked to shreds – لَحَم فِتِيت [laħam fitiːt] overcooked meat.

ف ت ح

فِتَح [fitaħ] *v:* • **1.** to open – فِتَحِت بُوطِل صُودَا جِدِيد [fitaħit buṭil ṣuːda jidiːd] I opened a new bottle of soda. الله يِفتَحلَك [ʔallah yiftaħlak] God bless you (lit. God open the door to riches for you). • **2.** (by extension) to open, start – راح أَفتَح حساب بهالبَنك [raːħ ʔaftaħ ħsaːb bhalbang] I'm going to open an account in this bank. فِتَحلَه مَخزَن بِشارِع الرَّشِيد [fitaħlah maxzan bšaːriʕ ʔirrašiːd] he opened a store on Rashid Street. فِتحَوا شارِع جِدِيد هنا [fitħaw šaːriʕ jidiːd hna] They opened a new street here. • **3.** to open, inaugurate – رَئِيس الوُزَراء راح يِفتَح الشّارِع الجِّدِيد [raʔiːs ʔilwuzaraːʔ raːħ yiftaħ ʔiššaːriʕ ʔijjidiːd] The prime minister will officially open the new street. • **4.** to turn on – فِتَحت الرّادِيُو مِن دِخَلِت الغُرفَة [fitaħt ʔirraːdyu min dixalit ʔilɣurfa] I turned on the radio when I entered the room. فِتَح المَيّ وَخَلّاه [fitaħ ʔilmayy wxallaːh] He turned on the water and left it on. إفتَح الضُّوَة مِن تخُشّ [ʔiftaħ ʔiððuwa min txušš] Turn on the light when you go in. الطُّرشِي يِفتَح الشَّهِيَّة [ʔiṭṭurši yiftaħ ʔiššahiyya] Pickles stimulate the appetite. إنطِينِي إيدَك؛ خَلِّي أَفتَحلَك فال [ʔinṭiːni ʔiːdak; xalliː ʔaftaħlak faːl] Give me your hand, let me tell your fortune. • **5.** to conquer, capture – القائِد فِتَح المَدِينَة بَعَد مُقاوَمَة عَنِيفَة [ʔilqaːʔid fitaħ ʔilmadiːna baʕad muqaːwama ʕaniːfa] The commander captured the city after a fierce battle.

فَتَّح [fattaħ] *v:* • **1.** to open (something) – لا تفَتِّح عينَك إِلَى أَن أَقُولَّك [la: tfattiħ ʕaynak ʔila ʔan ʔaguːllak] Don't open your eyes till I tell you. شوَقِت تفَتِّح كُلّ يوم؟ [šwakit tfattiħ kull yuːm?] What time do you open each day? هَذا يفَتِّح بِاللِّبَن [haːða yfattiħ billiban] You can't pull the wool over his eyes. • **2.** (of flowers) to open, to bloom – الوَرِد كُلّه فَتَّح [ʔilwarid kullah fattaħ] The flowers have all bloomed.

فاتَح [faːtaħ] *v:* • **1.** to approach, speak to – راح أَفاتحَه بِالمَوضُوع [raːħ ʔafaːtħah bilmawðuːʕ] I'll bring the subject up with him. ما دَأعرُف شلُون أَفاتحَه بِالمَوضُوع [maː daʔaʕruf šluːn ʔafaːtħah bilmawðuːʕ] I don't know how I'll approach him about the subject.

تفاتَح [tfaːtaħ] *v:* • **1.** to feel out, sound out – ما أَقدَر أَفاتحَه هَسَّة لِأَنّ زَعلان [maː ʔagdar ʔafaːtħah hassa liʔann zaʕlaːn] I can't sound him out now since he's mad. تفاتَحنا بِالقَضِيَّة وَاتِّفَقنا [tfaːtaħna bilqaðiyya wʔittifaqna] We felt each other out on the matter and we agreed.

اِنفَتَح [ʔinfitaħ] *v:* • **1.** to be opened – شوَقِت اِنفِتَح هَالبُطُل؟ [šwakit ʔinfitaħ halbuṭul?] When was this bottle opened? هالمَخزَن شوَقِت اِنفِتَح؟ [halmaxzan šwakit ʔinfitaħ?] When did this store open?

اِفتِتَح [ʔiftitaħ] *v:* • **1.** to open, inaugurate – اِفتِتَح الحَفلَة بِكَلِمَة قَصِيرَة [ʔiftitaħ ʔilħafla bkalima qaṣiːra] He opened the ceremony with a few words.

اِستَفتَح [ʔistaftaħ] *v:* • **1.** to start, to begin – بَعَد ما اِستَفتَحِت. ما عِندِي خُردَة [baʕad maː ʔistaftaħit. maː ʕindi xurda] I haven't done any business yet. I haven't got any change. • **2.** to start doing business

فَتِح [fatiħ] *n:* • **1.** opening, introduction, commencement, beginning

فَتحَة [fatħa] *n:* • **1.** the vowel point 'a' (gram.) • **2.** a card game, roughly similar to rummy • **3.** opener (of the gates of sustenance and profit)

فَتّاح، فَتّاح الفال [fattaːħ, fattaːħ ʔilfaːl] *n:* • **1.** fortune teller • **2.** opener (of the gates of sustenance an profit • **3.** opener (of the gates of sustenance and profit

مِفتاح [miftaːħ] *n:* مَفاتِيح [mafaːtiːħ] *pl:* • **1.** key • **2.** opener, can opener, bottle opener

فاتِحَة [faːtiħa] *n:* فَواتِح [fawaːtiħ] *pl:* • **1.** a recitation of the opening sura of the Koran

فاتحَة [faːtħa] *n:* فاتحات [faːtħaːt] *pl:* • **1.** a commemorative service for a dead man • **2.** funeral

اِفتِتاح [ʔiftitaːħ] *n:* • **1.** opening, inauguration, introduction – حَفلَة الاِفتِتاح [ħaflat ʔilʔiftitaːħ] the opening ceremony. • **2.** getting early earnest money

اِستِفتاح [ʔistiftaːħ] *n:* • **1.** start, beginning • **2.** getting early earnest (opener) money

فاتِح [faːtiħ] *adj:* • **1.** conqueror, victor • **2.** light (color) – نَفنُوف أَخضَر فاتِح [nafnuːf ʔaxðar faːtiħ] a light green dress.

مفَتِّح [mfattiħ] *adj:* • **1.** open, opened – لِسّاعَة شقَدّ تظَلّ مفَتِّح؟ [lissaːʕa šgadd tðall mfattiħ?] What hour will you be open to? ما تِقدَر تغُلبَه. هُوَّ مفَتِّح بِاللِّبَن [maː tigdar tɣulbah. huwwa mfattiħ billiban] You can't get the best of him. He has eyes in the back of his head (he can see through yoghurt).

فَتّاحَة [fattaːħa] *adj:* فَتّاحات [fattaːħaːt] *pl:* • **1.** opener, can opener, bottle opener • **2.** corkscrew

مَفتُوح [maftuːħ] *adj:* • **1.** open, opened – كِتاب مَفتُوح [kitaːb maftuːħ] an open book. • **2.** open, open for business – المَخزَن مَفتُوح [ʔilmaxzan maftuːħ] The store's open. • **3.** on – الماي مَفتُوح [ʔilmaːy maftuːħ] The water is on.

اِفتِتاحِي [ʔiftitaːħi] *adj:* • **1.** opening, introductory, preliminary, prefatory – كَلِمَة اِفتِتاحِيَّة [kalima ʔiftitaːħiyya] opening address. مَقال اِفتِتاحِي [maqaːl ʔiftitaːħi] leading article, leader, editorial.

اِفتِتاحِيَّة [ʔiftitaːħiyya] *adj:* اِفتِتاحِيّات [ʔiftitaːħiyyaːt] *pl:* • **1.** editorial, leader, leading article • **2.** overture (mus.)

أَفتَح [ʔaftaħ] *comparative adjective:* • **1.** lighter or lightest (color)

ف ت ر

فِتَر [fitar] *v:* • **1.** to lose interest, cool off – حَضَّر كُلّشِي لِلزّواج، أَشُو بَعدين فِتَر [ħaððar kullši lizzawaːǰ, ʔašu baʕdiːn fitar] He got everything ready for the wedding, but it seems he lost interest after that. بِالأَوَّل كان مِتحَمِّس لِلقَضِيَّة بَسّ بَعدين فِتَر [bilʔawwal čaːn mitħammis lilqaðiyya bass baʕdiːn fitar] At first he was enthusiastic about the matter but later he lost interest. • **2.** to measure (by the span of thumb to index finger) – اِفتِر المِيز وَقُلّي شقَدّ عُرضَه وَطُولَه [ʔiftir ʔilmiːz wgulli šgadd ʕurðah wṭuːlah] Measure the table with your hand and tell me its width and length.

فَتَّر [fattar] *v:* • **1.** to let up, let up on (speed), lower (speed) – فَتَّر السُّرعَة مِن وُصَل لِلجِّسِر [fattar ʔissurʕa min wuṣal lijjisir] He let up on the speed when he reached the bridge. فَتِّر شوَيَّة. أَكُو ناس دَيعُبرُون الشّارِع [fattir šwayya. ʔaku naːs dayʕubruːn ʔiššaːriʕ] Slow down a little. There are people crossing the street. • **2.** to lower, reduce – فَتِّر حَرَكَة الفانُوس حَتَّى ينام الجّاهِل [fattir ħarakat ʔilfaːnuːs ħatta ynaːm ʔijǰaːhil] Turn down the lantern wick so the child can sleep. فَتِّر الطَّبّاخ؛ اِحتِرَق الأَكِل [fattir ʔittabbaːx; ʔiħtirag ʔilʔakil] Turn the oven down; the food's gotten burned.

فِتِر [fitir] *n:* فتار [ftaːr] *pl:* • **1.** a unit of measurement equal to the span of the extended thumb and index finger

فَترَة [fatra] *n:* فَترات [fatraːt] *pl:* • **1.** period, pause, interval of time, spell, while

فاتِر [faːtir] *adj:* • **1.** tepid, lukewarm – مَيّ فاتِر [mayy faːtir] lukewarm water.

ف

ف ت ش

فَتَّش [fattaš] *v:* • **1.** to search – الشُّرطَة فَتِّشَتَه وَعِثرَت عَلَى مُسَدَّس [ʔiššurṭa fattišatah wʕiθrat ʕala musaddas] The police searched him and found a pistol. • **2.** to inspect, make an inspection – نَظُّم الميز. المُدِير راح يِجِي يفَتِّش [naðð̣um ʔilmi:z. ʔilmudi:r ra:ħ yiǰi yfattiš] Straighten up the desk. The director is coming to inspect. • **3.** to take attendance, check attendance – كُلّ يوم الصُّبُح، المُعَلِّم يفَتِّش [kull yu:m ʔiṣṣubuħ, ʔilmuʕallim yfattiš] Every morning the teacher takes attendance.

تفَتَّش [tfattaš] *v:* • **1.** to be searched, checked

مُفَتِّش [mufattiš] *n:* • **1.** inspector, supervisor

تَفتِيش [tafti:š] *n:* • **1.** search, searching • **2.** inspection • **3.** taking, or checking, attendance

تَفتِيشِي [tafti:ši] *adj:* • **1.** investigational, investigatory, examining, examinatory

ف ت ق

فِتَق [fitag] *v:* • **1.** to slit, or split open, a seam, to undo the stitching – إفتِق القُونِيَّة وطَلِّع شوَيَّة تِمَّن [ʔiftig ʔilgu:niyya wṭalliʕ šwayya timman] Split the seam on the gunny sack and take out a little rice. فِتَقلِي فَتِق كِبِير [fitagli fatig čibi:r] He really got me into trouble. • **2.** to break out, break through (liquids) – المَيّ فِتَق وغَرَّق الأَراضِي [ʔilmayy fitag wɣarrag ʔilʔara:ð̣i] The water broke through and flooded the land.

فَتَّق [fattag] *v:* • **1.** intens. of فِتَق to slit, split open – فَتِّق الكِيَاس كُلّها وَإنطِينِي نَمُونَة مِنها [fattig ʔilkya:s kullha wʔinṭi:ni namu:na minha] Open the seam on each of the sacks and give me a sample from it.

تفَتَّق [tfattag] *v:* • **1.** to tear at the seams, split at the seams, be torn – بَسّ تِلبَس هَالسِّترَة، تِتفَتَّق [bass tilbas hassitra, titfattag] Just put on this coat, and it will tear.

اِنفِتَق [ʔinfitag] *v:* • **1.** to be split at the seams – مِن شال إيدَه اِنفِتقَت سِترتَه مِن جَوَّة الأُبُط [min ša:l ʔi:dah ʔinfitgat sitirtah min ǰawwa ʔilʔubuṭ] When he lifted his arm his coat split a seam under the armpit. • **2.** to be broken, ruptured – السَّدَّة اِنفِتقَت والماي غَرَّق المَزارِع [ʔissadda ʔinfitgat wilma:y ɣarrag ʔilmaza:riʕ] The dam broke and the water flooded the farms.

فَتِق [fatiq] *n:* فُتُوق [futu:q] *pl:* • **1.** hernia, rupture (med.)

فَتِق [fatig] *n:* • **1.** split seam – فَتِق رِيح [fatig ri:ħ] hernia. • **2.** crack, fissure, break

مَفتُوق [maftu:g] *adj:* • **1.** open • **2.** split open

ف ت ك

فِتَك [fitak] *v:* • **1.** with ب to destroy, annihilate – أَهل القَريَة فِتكَوا بِالحَيوانات بهَالمَنطِقَة [ʔahl ʔilqarya fitkaw bilħaywa:na:t bhalmanṭiqa] The villagers have destroyed the animal life in this area. العَدُو فِتَك بِيهُم [ʔilʕadu fitak bi:hum] The enemy annihilated them.

فَتِك [fatik] *n:* • **1.** lethality, annihilation, destruction

فَتّاك [fatta:k] *adj:* • **1.** deadly, lethal, murderous • **2.** as a Noun, dangerous person

ف ت ل

فِتَل [fital] *v:* • **1.** to twist together – إفتِل هالخَيطَين حَتَّى تصِيرُون أَقوَى [ʔiftil halxayṭayn ħatta tṣi:ru:n ʔaqwa] Twist these two strings together so they'll be stronger. • **2.** to braid, plait – إفتِل هَالخيُوط وسَوِّيها حَبِل [ʔiftil halxyu:ṭ wsawwi:ha ħabil] Braid these threads and make a rope out of them.

تفَتَّل [tfattal] *v:* • **1.** to lounge around • **2.** to wander around

فَتِل [fatil] *n:* • **1.** twisting, braiding

تَفَتُّل [tafattul] *n:* • **1.** traveling, wandering around

فِتِيلَة [fiti:la] *n:* فِتِيلات، فَتايِل [fiti:la:t,, fata:yil] *pl:* • **1.** wick (of a lamp or candle) • **2.** mantle (of a gasoline lantern) • **3.** fuse • **4.** rectal suppository

فَتّالَة [fatta:la] *n:* فَتّالات [fatta:la:t] *pl:* • **1.** dust devil, whirlwind

فَتلَبِيج [fatlapi:č] *n:* فَتلَبِيجات [fatlapi:ča:t] *pl:* • **1.** trick, prank

ف ت ن

فِتَن [fitan] *v:* • **1.** to inform, denounce, tell, tattle – إذا ما تجُوز، تَرَة أَفتِن عَلِيك عِند المُعَلِّم [ʔiða ma: dǰu:z, tara ʔaftin ʕali:k ʕind ʔilmuʕallim] If you don't stop it, I'll tell on you to the teacher.

فَتَّن [fattan] *v:* • **1.** to be in the habit of tattling, informing, to bear tales – إنتَ شگَدّ تفَتِّن عَلَى أَصدِقائَك [ʔinta šgadd tfattin ʕala ʔaṣdiqa:ʔak] My, how you carry tales on your friends!

فِتنَة [fitna] *n:* • **1.** tattling, tale bearing • **2.** discord, dissension, riot, sedition

فَتّان [fatta:n] *adj:* • **1.** as an Adj: captivating, enchanting, charming, fascinating – جَمال فَتّان [ǰama:l fatta:n] captivating beauty. • **2.** as a Noun: tattletale, tale-bearer, informer

ف ت و

فِتَى [fita:] *v:* • **1.** to give a formal legal opinion – العالِم الدِّينِي راح يِفتِي بِيها [ʔilʕa:lim ʔiddi:ni ra:ħ yifti bi:ha] The religious authority will give a religious opinion on it.

فَتوَة [fatwa] *n:* فَتاوِي [fata:wi:] *pl:* • **1.** a formal legal opinion (Islamic law), a formal ruling on a religious matter

مُفتِي [mufti] *n:* مُفتِيِّين [muftiyyin] *pl:* • **1.** mufti, official interpreter of Islamic law

إفتاء [ʔifta:ʔ] *n:* • **1.** deliverance of formal legal opinions

اِستِفتاء [ʔistifta:ʔ] *n:* • **1.** plebiscite • **2.** request for a formal legal opinion, consulting • **3.** referendum

ف

ف ت و ر

فاتُورَة [fatu:ra] *n:* فَواتِير [fawa:ti:r] *pl:* • **1.** bill, invoice

ف ت ي

فاتيَة [fa:tya] *n:* فاتيات، فواتِي [fa:tya:t, fwa:ti] *pl:* • **1.** drawer

ف ج ء

فاجَئ [fa:ǰaʔ] *v:* • **1.** to surprise, take by surprise – فاجَأته بالخَبَر [fa:ǰaʔtah bilxabar] I surprised him with the news.

تفاجَئ [tfa:ǰaʔ] *v:* • **1.** to be surprised, be taken by surprise – تفاجَئِت وَما كِنِت أدري [tfa:ǰaʔit wama činit ʔadri] I was taken by surprise and didn't know.

مُفاجَأة [mufa:ǰaʔa] *n:* مُفاجَآت [mufa:ǰaʔa:t] *pl:* • **1.** surprise – دِخَل عَلينا مُفاجَأة [dixal ʕali:na mufa:ǰaʔa] He came in on us unexpectedly. • **1.** *Adverbial* مُفاجَأةً: [mufa:ǰaʔatan] by surprise

فُجائِي [fuǰa:ʔi] *adj:* • **1.** unexpected, sudden – مَرَض فُجائِي [marað fuǰa:ʔi] an unexpected illness. حَرّ فُجائِي [ħarr fuǰa:ʔi] an unexpected heat wave. هِجُوم فُجائِي [hiǰu:m fuǰa:ʔi] a sudden attack.

مُفاجِئ [mufa:ǰiʔ] *adj:* • **1.** sudden, unexpected, surprising – هِجُوم مُفاجِئ [hiǰu:m mufa:ǰiʔ] a sudden attack.

فُجأة، فُجأةً [fuǰʔa, fuǰʔatan] *adverbial:* • **1.** suddenly, unexpectedly – مات فُجأة [ma:t fuǰʔa] He died suddenly.

ف ج ج

فَجّ [faǰǰ] *v:* • **1.** to cut, slice, split, cleave – فَجّ راسَه بالعُودَة [faǰǰ ra:sah bilʕu:da] He split his head open with the stick. الباخِرَة تفجّ المَيّ مِن تِمشي [ʔilba:xira tfiǰǰ ʔilmayy min timši] The ship cuts the water as it goes along.

فَجّ [faǰǰ] *n:* • **1.** cleavage

فِجَّة [fiǰǰa] *n:* فِجَج [fiǰaǰ] *pl:* • **1.** piece of cloth • **2.** small carpet, rug

ف ج ر

فِجَر [fiǰar] *v:* • **1.** to lance, prick – ما أرِيد أفجِرلَك هَالدِّمبِلَة إلَى أن تِلحَق [ma: ʔari:d ʔafǰirlak haddimbila ʔila ʔan tilħag] I don't want to lance that boil for you till it's ready. الطَّبِيب فِجَرلي البُطباتَة [ʔiṭṭabi:b fiǰarli ʔilbuṭba:ta] The doctor opened the blister for me.

فَجَّر [faǰǰar] *v:* • **1.** to explode – الشُّرطَة وَدّوا القُنبُلَة لِلجَوْل وَفَجّروها [ʔiššurṭa waddaw ʔilqumbula liččuːl wfaǰǰiru:ha] The police took the bomb to the desert and exploded it.

تفَجَّر [tfaǰǰar] *v:* • **1.** to gush out, spurt forth, erupt, burst out – شُوف المَيّ شلُون دَيِتفَجَّر مِن هَالعَين [šu:f ʔilmayy šlu:n dayitfaǰǰar min halʕi:n] Look at how the water is bursting forth from this spring.

اِنفِجَر [ʔinfiǰar] *v:* • **1.** to explode, burst, go off – ذَبّوا قُنبُلَة عَالسَّيّارَة لَكِن ما اِنفِجرَت [ðabbaw qunbula ʕassayya:ra la:kin ma: ʔinfiǰrat] They threw a bomb at his car but it didn't explode. الدِّمبلَة اِنفِجرَت باللَّيل [ʔiddimbila ʔinfiǰrat billayl] The boil burst during the night.

فَجِر [faǰir] *n:* • **1.** dawn, daybreak

فَجِر [faǰir] *n:* • **1.** (act of) lancing

فَجرِيَّة [faǰriyya] *n:* • **1.** dawn time

تَفجِير [tafǰi:r] *n:* • **1.** (act of) detonating, exploding • **2.** (act of) exploding

اِنفِجار [ʔinfiǰa:r] *n:* اِنفِجارات [ʔinfiǰa:ra:t] *pl:* • **1.** explosion, detonation, eruption

مُتَفَجِّرَة [mutafaǰǰira] *n:* مُتَفَجِّرات [mutafaǰǰira:t] *pl:* • **1.** explosive device

فاجِر [fa:ǰir] *adj:* فُجّار، فَجَرَة [fuǰǰa:r, faǰara.] *pl:* • **1.** libertine, debauchee, rake, adulterer, sinner

فَاجِرَة [fa:ǰira] n: فاجِرات [fa:ǰira:t] pl: • 1. adulteress, whore, harlot, loose woman

مَفجُور [mafǰu:r] *adj:* • **1.** detonated, exploded

مِتفَجِّر [mitfaǰǰir] *adj:* • **1.** detonated, exploded

ف ج ع

فِجَع [fiǰaʕ] *v:* • **1.** to inflict suffering and grief (by bereaving someone) – الله فِجَعَه بِبِنتَه [ʔallah fiǰaʕah bbintah] God took his daughter away.

اِنفِجَع [ʔinfiǰaʕ] *v:* • **1.** to be stricken (with grief, by the death of someone) – اِنفِجَعِت بمُوتَة صَدِيقِي [ʔinfiǰaʕit bmu:tat ṣadi:qi] I was stricken by my friend's death. اِنفِجَع بوَلَدَه [ʔinfiǰaʕ bwaladah] He was stricken by his son's death.

فَجِع [faǰiʕ] *n:* • **1.** act of inflicting suffering and grief

فاجِعَة [fa:ǰiʕa] *n:* فَواجِع [fawa:ǰiʕ] *pl:* • **1.** calamity, disaster, tragedy

مُفجِع [mufǰiʕ] *adj:* • **1.** tragic, calamitous, disastrous

مَفجُوع [mafǰu:ʕ] *adj:* • **1.** afflicted, distressed, stricken (by a tragedy)

ف ج ل

فِجِل [fiǰil] *n:* • **1.** radish(es)

فِجلايَة [fiǰla:ya] *n:* • **1.** radish

ف ج و

فَجوَة [faǰwa] *n:* فَجوات [faǰwa:t] *pl:* • **1.** gap, opening, hole, aperture, breach

ف ح ح

فَحّ [faħħ] *v:* • **1.** to hiss (snake)

فَحِيح [faħi:ħ] *n:* • **1.** hissing, hiss

ف ح ش

فاحِشَة [faːħiša] *n:* فاحِشات، فَواحِش [faːħišaːt, fawaːħiš] *pl:* • **1.** whore, prostitute • **2.** lewdness, misconduct, obscenity • **3.** vile deed, adultery, fornication

ف ح ص

فُحَص [fuħaṣ] *v:* • **1.** to examine, check – إفحَص الكَبريتَر؛ يبَيِّن بيها وُسَخ [ʔifħaṣ ʔilkabriːtar; yibayyin biːha wuṣax] Check the carburetor; it seems to have dirt in it. الدُّكتور فُحَصني وَقالّي ما بيك شي [ʔidduktuːr fuħaṣni wgaːlli maː biːk ši] The doctor examined me and told me I was OK.

تفَحَّص [tfaħħaṣ] *v:* • **1.** to examine closely, scrutinize, check closely – لازِم تتفَحَّص السَّيّارَة أوَّل [laːzim titfaħħaṣ ʔissayyaːra ʔawwal] You'd better examine the car carefully first. دَيتفَحَّص بيها زين قَبُل ما يِشتِريها [dayitfaħħaṣ biːha ziːn gabul maː yištiriːha] He's scrutinizing it well before he buys it.

انفُحَص [ʔinfuħaṣ] *v:* • **1.** to be examined – مِنُو يريد ينفُحِص أوَّل؟ [minu yriːd yinfuħiṣ ʔawwal?] Who wants to be examined first?

فَحِص [faħiṣ] *n:* فُحوص، فُحوصات [fuħuːṣ, fuħuːṣaːt] *pl:* • **1.** checkup, examination, physical or medical examination

ف ح ل

اِستفحَل [ʔistafħal] *v:* • **1.** to become serious, get out of control – الغَلاء اِستفحَل وَالحُكُومَة ما تُعرُف شِتسَوّي – [ʔilɣalaːʔ ʔistafħal wilħukuːma maː tuʕruf šitsawwiː] Inflation has gotten out of control and the government doesn't know what to do. اِستَفحَل المَرَض [ʔistafħal ʔilmarað̣] The disease got out of control.

فَحَل [faħal] *n:* فحُول [fħuːl] *pl:* • **1.** male – طِلَع فَحَل عَلَى أبُوه [ṭilaʕ faħal ʕala ʔabuːh] He turned out to be a real man just like his father. فَحَل شبُوَّة [faħal šbuwwa] stud. • **2.** (leaf) spring (automobile)

فُحُولَة [fuħuːla] *n:* • **1.** virility

اِستِفحال [ʔistifħaːl] *n:* • **1.** getting out of control, seriousness, gravity

مِستَفحِّل [mistafħħil] *adj:* • **1.** terrible, dreadful, very serious

ف ح م

فَحَّم [faħħam] *v:* • **1.** to char, burn to a crisp – نِسَوا الأكِل عَالنّار إلَى أن فَحَّم [nisaw ʔilʔakil ʕannaːr ʔila ʔan faħħam] They forgot the food on the fire until it got burned. فَحَّمِت مِن العَطَش [faħħamit min ʔilʕaṭaš] I'm dried out from thirst.

أفحَم [ʔafħam] *v:* • **1.** to dumbfound, strike dumb, astound – أفحَمهُم بخِطابَه المُمتاز [ʔafħamhum bxiṭaːbah ʔilmumtaːz] He dumbfounded them with his excellent speech.

فَحَم [faħam] *n:* • **1.** (coll.) charcoal, coal(s)

فَحمَة [faħma] *n:* فَحمات [faħmaːt] *pl:* • **1.** lump of coal, piece of charcoal

فَحّام [faħħaːm] *n:* فَحّامَة [faħħaːma] *pl:* • **1.** coal dealer

فَحمِي [faħmi] *adj:* • **1.** dark black, coal black • **2.** coal-black

ف ح و

فَحوَى [faħwa] *n:* • **1.** sense, meaning, signication, tenor (of a report, speech, discussion) • **2.** essence, main meaning, purport (of a speech, etc.)

ف خ ت ي

فُختِيَّة [fuxtiyya] *n:* فُختِيّات، فُخاتِي [fuxtiyyaːt, fuxaːti] *pl:* • **1.** turtledove

فُختايَة [fuxtaːya] *n:* فُختايات [fuxtaːyaːt] *pl:* • **1.** turtledove

ف خ ج

فاخَج [faːxaǰ] *v:* • **1.** to walk with legs wide apart – يمشِي ويفاخِج لِأنَّه مطَهَّر [yimši wyfaːxiǰ liʔannah mṭahhar] He walks with his legs spread apart because he has been circumcised.

فَخَّج [faxxaǰ] *v:* • **1.** to walk with legs wide apart – لُويش دَيفَخِّج هَذا؟ [luwiːš dayfaxxiǰ haːða?] Why's that fellow walking with his legs apart? إذا تفَخِّج، ما تِقدَر تِمشِي سَريع [ʔiða tfaxxij, maː tigdar timši sariːʕ] If you spread your legs you can't walk fast.

ف خ خ

فَخَّخ [faxxax] *v:* • **1.** to booby trap (e.g. a car)

فَخّ [faxx] *n:* أفخاخ [ʔafxaːx] *pl:* • **1.** snare, trap, booby trap

مفَخَّخ [mfaxxax] *adj:* • **1.** trapped, booby trapped

ف خ ذ

فُخُذ [fuxuð] *n:* أفخاذ [ʔafxaːð] *pl:* • **1.** thigh • **2.** leg (of meat) • **3.** subdivision (of a tribe)

ف خ ر

فُخَر [fuxar] *v:* • **1.** to be proud, pride oneself – يفخَر بابِنَه لِأنّ ينجَح بإمتِياز [yifxar bʔibnah liʔann yinǰaħ bʔimtiyaːz] He's proud of his son because he passes with flying colors. آني أفخَر بيك لِأنَّك فَدّ صَدِيق مُخلِص وَكَرِيم [ʔaːni ʔafxar biːk liʔannak fadd ṣadiːq muxliṣ wkariːm] I am proud of you because you are a sincere and generous friend. • **2.** to fire, bake – إذا ما تفُخرُون التُّنَك، تمُوع بِالمَيّ [ʔiða maː tfuxruːn ʔittunag, tmuːʕ bilmayy] If you don't bake the clay jugs, they'll fall apart in water.

فاخَر [faːxar] *v:* • **1.** to boast – حَتَّى لَو صُدُق، ما لازِم تفاخِر لِهَالحَدّ [ħatta law ṣudug, maː

la:zim tfa:xir lihalħadd] Even though it's true, you shouldn't boast so much.
تفاخَر [tfa:xar] *v:* • **1.** to boast – دَيتفاخرُون بأجدادهُم اللّي صارَوا تراب [dayitfa:xru:n bʔajda:dhum ʔilli ṣa:raw tra:b] They are boasting about their ancestors who have become dust.
اِفتِخَر [ʔiftixar] *v:* • **1.** to be proud, pride oneself – إحنا نِفتِخِر بكُلّ واحِد يأدّي خِدمَة لِلجَمعِيَّة [ʔiħna niftixir bkull wa:ħid yʔaddi xidma lijjamʕiyya] We are proud of each one who contributes a service to the association.
فَخَر [faxar] *n:* • **1.** glory, honor, credit • **2.** someone or something to be proud of – إنتَ فَخَرنا وَكُلّنا نِعتَزّ بيك [ʔinta faxarna wkullna niʕtazz bi:k] You are the object of our pride and we all are proud of you. تِجي عَليه بالبَسكُوت وَتبُطحَه. هَذا مُو فَخَر [tiji ʕali:h bilbasku:t wtbuṭħah. ha:ða mu: faxar] You sneak up on him and throw him. That's no accomplishment.
فَخّار [faxxa:r] *n:* • **1.** pottery, earthenware, crockery
فَخري [faxri] *adj:* • **1.** honorary – رَئيس فَخري [raʔi:s faxri] honorary chairman.
فاخِر [fa:xir] *adj:* • **1.** superb, magnificent, – أكِل فاخِر [ʔakil fa:xir] superb food.
مَفخَرَة [mafxara] *adj:* مَفاخِر [mafa:xir] *pl:* • **1.** object of pride, glorious deed, exploit • **2.** someone or something to be proud of
فَخّاري [faxxa:ri] *adj:* • **1.** made out of clay, earthen, ceramic
أفخَر [ʔafxar] *comparative adjective:* • **1.** more or most superb

ف خ ف خ

فَخفَخَة [faxfaxa] *n:* • **1.** luxury, splendor • **2.** ostentation, showiness

ف خ م

فَخَّم [faxxam] *v:* • **1.** to praise extravagantly, glorify, build up – يفَخِّم بأجدادَه [yfaxxim bʔajda:dah] He makes his ancestors out to have been something special. دَيفَخِّم هوايَة بأعمال الحُكُومَة [dayfaxxim hwa:ya bʔaʕma:l ʔilħuku:ma] He's really glorifying the actions of the government.
فَخامَة [faxa:ma] *n:* • **1.** (title of respect for a prime minister) Excellency – فَخامَة رَئيس الوُزَراء [faxa:mat raʔi:s ʔilwuzara:ʔ] His Excellency the Prime Minister.
فَخِم [faxim] *adj:* • **1.** impressive, stately, magnificent – قَصِر فَخِم [qaṣir faxim] a magnificent palace.

ف د ح

فادِح [fa:diħ] *adj:* • **1.** excessive, serious

ف د د

فَدّ [fadd] *adv:* • **1.** one, a single, the same – أكُو فَدّ طَريقَة لِحَلّ هَالمُشكِلَة [ʔaku fadd ṭari:qa lħall halmuškila] There's one way to solve this problem. أكُو فَدّ واحِد بَسّ يُعرُف الجَّواب [ʔaku fadd wa:ħid bass yuʕruf ʔijjawa:b] There's only one person who knows the answer. أقدَر أمَوّتَه بفَدّ بُوكس [ʔagdar ʔamawwtah bfadd bu:ks] I can kill him with one punch. سَوَّيت كُلّ هالشُّغُل بفَدّ يوم؟ [sawwayt kull haššuɣul bfadd yu:m?] Did you do all this work in one day? خَلّينا كُلّ الغَراض بفَدّ مُكان [xalli:na kull ʔilɣara:ð̣ bfadd muka:n] We put all the things in the same place. هَذا وَصَديقَه يلبسُون مَلابِس فَدّ شِكِل [ha:ða wṣadi:qah ylibsu:n mala:bis fadd šikil] He and his friend wear the same kind of clothes. كُلَّه فَدّ شِي بالنِّسبَة إلي [kullah fadd ši binnisba ʔili] It's all the same to me. فَدّ مَرَّة شِفتَه ويّا بنَيَّة حِلوَة [fadd marra šiftah wiyya bnayya ħilwa] Once I saw him with a pretty girl. • **2.** a, an – عِندَك فَدّ نُصّ دِينار تدايِنّي؟ [ʕindak fadd nuṣṣ dina:r dda:yinni?] Do you have a half dinar to lend me? تعَرَّفِت عَلَى فَدّ أمريكِي اليُوم [tʕarrafit ʕala fadd ʔamri:ki ʔilyu:m] I got acquainted with an American today. تُعرُف فَدّ شِي عَن هَالقَضِيَّة؟ [tuʕruf fadd ši ʕan halqaḍiyya?] Do you know anything about this matter? بِعتلَه فَدّ كَم حاجَة عَتيقَة [biʕitlah fadd čam ħa:ja ʕati:ga] I sold him a few old things. أقدَر آخُذ فَدّ شوَيَّة مِن هَالعِنَب؟ [ʔagdar ʔa:xuð fadd šwayya min halʕinab?] May I take a few of these grapes? فَدّ شوَيَّة وأمُرّ عَليك [fadd šwayya wʔamurr ʕali:k] Just a little while and I'll come to your place. • **3.** one, a real, quite the – ذُولَة فَدّ ناس. ما ينحِكِي ويّاهُم [ðu:la fadd na:s. ma: yinħiči wiyya:hum] They're some people. You can't talk to them. هَذا فَدّ بَلاء. ما ينقِدِر عَليه [ha:ða fadd bala:ʔ. ma: yingidir ʕali:h] He's one smart cookie. You can't get around him. هَالمُوَظَّف فَدّ زمال. لا يحِلّ وَلا يربُط [halmuwaḍḍaf fadd zma:l. la: yħill wala yirbuṭ] That official's a real jerk. He can't do anything. • **4.** some, some sort of – كُلّما أقُلّه عَلَى شِي يطَلّعلي فَدّ حِجَّة [kullma: ʔagullah ʕala ši yṭalliʕli fadd ħijja] Whenever I tell him anything, he comes up with some sort of excuse. هُوَّ يعِيش بفَدّ قَريَة مَحَّد يندَلّها [huwwa yiʕi:š bfadd qarya maħħad yindallha] He lives in some village no one can find. قَلّي فَدّ شِي لكِن نِسَيتَه [galli fadd ši la:kin nisi:tah] He told me something but I forgot it. خَلّي نرُوح لفَدّ مُكان وَنِسكَر سُوَة [xalli: nru:ħ lfadd muka:n wniskar suwa] Let's go somewhere and get drunk together. • **5.** some, a few – سِألتَه وَجاوَبني فَدّ أجوبَة سَخيفَة [siʔaltah wja:wabni fadd ʔajwiba saxi:fa] I asked him and he gave me some silly answers. اِشتِرَيت فَدّ أشياء جِديدَة اليُوم [ʔištirayt fadd ʔašya:ʔ jidi:da ʔilyu:m] I bought some new things today. سَمَّعنِي فَدّ حَكِي ما سامعَه قَبُل [sammaʕni fadd ħači ma: sa:mʕah gabul] He let me in on some talk I hadn't heard before. • **6.** some, about, approximately – مَسافَة فَدّ خَمسِين مِيل [masa:fat fadd xamsi:n mi:l] a distance of some fifty miles. كانَوا فَدّ عِشرِين واحِد [ča:naw fadd ʕišri:n wa:ħid] There were about twenty

ف

people. اِنتِظَرتَه فَدّ نُصّ ساعَة وَما جا [ʔintiðartah fadd nuṣṣ saːʕa wma ǰaː] I waited for him about a half hour and he didn't come. • **7.** simply, only, just – كان فَدّ يِريد يِتخَلَّص مِنَّك [čaːn fadd yiriːd yitxallaṣ minnak] He only wanted to get rid of you. هَمَّه، فَدّ يِجمَع فلُوس [hammah, fadd yiǰmaʕ fluːs] His goal is just to get money. فَدّ قُلَّه بِإسمِي وَما عَلَيك [fadd gullah biʔismi wma ʕaliːk] Just mention my name to him and you'll have no trouble. فَدّ تِضحَك عَلَى أَبُوه؛ يبُسطَك [fadd tiðħak ʕala ʔabuːh; ybusṭak] Just laugh at his father; he'll hit you. هَذا يِحكِي فَدّ حَكِي. لا تصَدِّق بِيه [haːða yiħči fadd ħači. laː tṣaddig biːh] He's just talking. Don't believe him. • **8.** the minute, as soon as – فَدّ وُصَلِت، شَوَّفنِي الغَراض [fadd wuṣalit, šawwafni ʔilɣaraːð] The minute I arrived, he showed me the things. فَدّ ذَكَّرتَه بِالقَضِيَّة، سَوّاها [fadd ðakkartah bilqaðiyya, sawwaːha] As soon as I reminded him of the matter, he took care of it. مُو فَدّ شِي [muː fadd ši] nothing, no great thing. تَصلِيح هَالرّاديُو مُو فَدّ شِي [taṣliːħ harraːdyu muː fadd ši] Repairing this radio is nothing. • **9.** any

فَدّ مَرَّة [fadd marra] *adv:* • **1.** might as well – خُو، فَدّ مَرَّة، قُول آنِي كَذّاب [xuː, fadd marra, guːl ʔaːni čaððaːb] Well, you might as well say I'm a liar. • **2.** completely – سَوَّى نَفسَه فَدّ مَرَّة ما يُعرُف شِي [sawwaː nafsah fadd marra maː yuʕruf ši] He pretended not to know anything. فَدّ نوب [fadd nawb] completely. فَدّ نَوب ما يُعرُف شِي [fadd nuːb maː yuʕruf ši] He really doesn't know anything.

ف د ن

فَدّان [faddaːn] *n:* فدادِين [fdaːdiːn] *pl:* • **1.** simple, animal-drawn plow

ف د ي

فِدَى [fidaː] *v:* • **1.** to sacrifice to – الجِّنُود فِدَوا الوَطَن بِأنفُسهُم [ʔiǰǰinuːd fidaw ʔilwaṭan bʔanfushum] The soldiers sacrificed themselves to the fatherland. كُلّنا نِفدِيك بِأَرواحنا [kullna nifdiːk bʔarwaːħna] We all sacrifice our souls for you.

تفادَى [tfaːdaː] *v:* • **1.** to avoid – حاوِل تِتفادَى الخَطَر بسَفِرتَك [ħaːwil titfaːdaː ʔilxaṭar bsafirtak] Try to avoid danger on your trip. أحاوِل أتفادَى الشَّقَا [ʔaħaːwil ʔatfaːdaː ʔiššaqa] I try to avoid teasing anyone.

فِديَة [fidya] *n:* • **1.** ransom

فِداء [fidaːʔ] *n:* • **1.** sacrifice

فِدائِي [fidaːʔi] *n:* فِدائِيِّين، فِدائِيَّة [fidaːʔiyyiːn, fidaːʔiyya.] *pl:* • **1.** fighter who risks his life recklessly • **2.** commando, guerrilla, member of the fedayeen

تَفادِي [tafaːdi] *n:* • **1.** avoidance

ف ذ ل ك

فَذلَكَة [faðlaka, fatlaka] *n:* فَذلَكات [faðlakaːt,fatlakaːt] *pl:* • **1.** a new one, something new, a new twist, a new angle – أَبُو الكَراج طَلَّعلِي فَدّ فتلَكَة ويرِيد دِينارَين بَعَد [ʔabu ʔilgaraːǰ ṭallaʕli fadd fatlaka wyriːd dinaːrayn baʕad] The garageman brought out something new on me and wants two more dinars. ترِيدهُم يوافقُون؟ جِيبِلهُم فَدّ فَتلَكَة [triːdhum ywaːfquːn? ǰiːbilhum fadd fatlaka] You want them to give in? Bring up some new angle.

ف ر

فار [faːr] *n:* فِيران [fiːraːn] *pl:* • **1.** (coll.) mouse (mice) – غاب القِطّ إلعَب يا فار [ɣaːb ʔilqiṭṭ ʔilʕab yaː faːr] When the cat's away the mice will play.

فارَة [faːra] *n:* فارات، فِيران [faːraːt, fiːraːn] *pl:* • **1.** mouse • **2.** any of the muscles of the lamb shank, as meat

ف ر ت

الفُرات [ʔilfuraːt] *n:* • **1.** Euphrates (river in Iraq)

ف ر ج

فَرَج [furaǰ] *v:* • **1.** to dispel, drive away (grief, worries, etc) – لا تِهتَمّ. الله يِفرِجها [laː tihtamm. ʔallah yifriǰha] Don't worry. Allah will ease the situation.

فِرَج [firaǰ] *v:* • **1.** with عَن to release, to set free

فَرَّج [farraǰ] *v:* • **1.** to show – مِن رِحِت لِبَغداد عَمِّي فَرَّجنِي عَلَى مُكانات هوايَة [min riħit lbaɣdaːd ʕammi farrajni ʕala mukaːnaːt hwaːya] When I went to Baghdad my uncle showed me around many places.

أفرَج [ʔafraǰ] *v:* • **1.** to release • **2.** with عَن to release, to set free

تفَرَّج [tfarraǰ] *v:* • **1.** to watch, observe – مُو شَرط تِلعَب. تِقدَر تِتفَرَّج بَسّ [muː šarṭ tilʕab. tigdar titfarraǰ bass] You don't have to play. You can just watch.

اِنفرَج [ʔinfiraǰ] *v:* • **1.** with عَن to be released

فَرج [fariǰ] *n:* فرُوج [fruːǰ] *pl:* • **1.** external female genitals, vulva

فَرَج [faraǰ] *n:* • **1.** relief from suffering

فُرجَة [furǰa] *n:* • **1.** (no pl.) sight, spectacle – إمشُوا من هنا! قابِل عِدنا فُرجَة؟ [ʔimšuː min hna! qaːbil ʕidna furǰa?] Get away from here! Do you think we're holding a sideshow here? خِلقتَه صارَت فُرجَة لِلنّاس [xiliqtah ṣaːrat furǰa linnaːs] His looks were an object of curiosity for the people.

فَرُّوج [farruːǰ] *n:* • **1.** (coll.) pullet(s), young hen esp. one less than one year old

فَرُّوجَة [farruːǰa] *n:* فرارِيج [fraːriːǰ] *pl:* • **1.** chick, young chicken, a young hen, less than one year old.

إفراج [ʔifraːǰ] *n:* • **1.** release, liberation, freeing

اِنفِراج [ʔinfiraːǰ] *n:* • **1.** relaxation, relaxedness

ف

مِتفَرِّج [mitfarrij] *adj:* مِتفَرِّجين [mitfarriji:n] *pl:* • **1.** spectator • **2.** viewer, watcher

ف ر ج ل

فِرجال [firja:l] *n:* فَراجيل [fara:ji:l] *pl:* • **1.** compass, dividers

ف ر ح

فِرَح [firaħ] *v:* • **1.** to be glad, happy – فِرَحِت مِن شِفتَه [firaħit min šiftah] I was pleased when I saw him.

فَرَّح [farraħ] *v:* • **1.** to gladden, make happy, delight – خَبَر نَجاحَك فَرَّحني هوايَة [xabar naja:ħak farraħni hwa:ya] The news of your success delighted me very much.

فَرَح [faraħ] *n:* • **1.** happiness, gladness, joy, gaiety, mirth, merriment – طار مِن الفَرَح [ṭa:r min ʔilfaraħ] He was beside himself with happiness. He jumped for joy. • **2.** pl. أفرَاح celebration, joyous occasion, feast of rejoicing, wedding (feast) – إن شاء الله، دائماً بالأفراح [ʔinša:llah, da:ʔiman bilʔafra:ħ] I hope you'll always be happy.

مُفرِح [mufriħ] *adj:* • **1.** delightful, cheerful, festive

فَرحان [farħa:n] *adj:* • **1.** joyful, happy, glad, delighted – شبيك هَالقَدّ فَرحان؟ [šbi:k halgadd farħa:n?] How come you're so joyful?

ف ر خ

فَرَّخ [farrax] *v:* • **1.** to have young ones (of birds) – طيُورنا فَرَّخوا [ṭyu:rna farrixaw] Our birds had a covey of young.

فَرِخ [farix] *n:* فرُوخ [fru:x] *pl:* • **1.** fledgeling, young bird. فَرُّوج - فَرارِيج is also used.

تَفريخ، مَكينَة تَفريخ [tafri:x] *n:* • **1.** hatching • **2.** brooder

فَريخات [frayxa:t] *n:* • **1.** hens, chicks, children • **2.** lesbians (derog.)

فَرخجي [faraxči, farixči] *adj:* فَرخجيَّة، فَرخجيِّين [farixčiyya, farixčiyyi:n] *pl:* • **1.** pedophile, man who likes young boys

ف ر د

فِرَد [firad] *v:* • **1.** to separate, isolate, segregate – إفرِد الطَّماطَة الدُّونيَّة مِن الزَّينَة [ʔifrid ʔiṭṭama:ṭa ʔiddu:niyya min ʔizzayna] Separate the bad tomatoes from the good ones. إفرِد الدِّيك عَن الدِّجاج [ʔifrid ʔiddi:č ʕan ʔiddija:j] Isolate the rooster from the chickens.

اِنفِرَد [ʔinfirad] *v:* • **1.** to withdraw, move or walk away, to isolate oneself – لا تِنفِرد عَن الجَّماعَة [la: tinfirid ʕan ʔijjama:ʕa] Don't isolate yourself from the group. راح أنفِرِد بيه وَأقُلّه [ra:ħ ʔanfirid bi:h wagullah] I will get him alone and tell him.

فَرِد [farid] *n:* • **1.** odd number. • **2.** one, a single, the same. • **3.** a, an • **4.** one, a real, quite the • **5.** some, some sort of • **6.** some, a few • **7.** pl. أفراد odd, uneven

فَرِد [farid] *n:* • **1.** separation, isolation

فَردَة [farda] *n:* • **1.** one part, one of a pair – فَردَة قُندَرَة [fardat qundara] a shoe. فَردَة تَمُر [fardat tamur] a date. فَردَة وفَردَة [farda wfarda] unmatched. لابِس الجواريب فَردَة وفَردَة [la:bis ʔajwa:ri:b farda wfarda] He's wearing unmatched socks.

مُفرَد [mufrad] *n:* مُفرَدات [mufrada:t] *pl:* • **1.** item, single unit – ما نبيع بالمُفرَد [ma: nbi:ʕ bilmufrad] We don't sell retail. • **2.** with ب retail

فراد [fra:d] *n:* • **1.** heavy cloth sack usually used as a packsaddle on draft animals or beasts of burden

اِنفِراد [ʔinfira:d] *n:* • **1.** solitude, isolation, loneliness, seclusion

فَردِي [fardi] *adj:* • **1.** single, individual, pertaining to a single person – عَدَد فَردِي [ʕadad fardi] odd number. • **2.** odd, uneven • **3.** singles (in tennis)

مِنفِرِد [minfirid] *adj:* • **1.** isolated, detached, separated, lone, alone, solitary

فَريد [fari:d] *adj:* • **1.** singular, precious, unique, matchless, unrivaled, incomparable

إنفِرادِي [ʔinfira:di] *adj:* • **1.** individualistic, isolationistic

ف ر د و س

الفِردَوس [ʔilfirdaws] *n:* • **1.** Paradise

ف ر ر

فَرّ [farr] *v:* • **1.** to flee, run off, run away, escape – ثلاث مَساجين فَرّوا مِن السِّجِن [tlaθ masa:ji:n farraw min ʔissijin] Three prisoners escaped from the prison. • **2.** to spin – فَرّ المُصرَع وَخَلّاه ينوعِر [farr ʔilmuṣraʕ wxalla:h ynawʕir] He spun the top and made it hum. • **3.** to whirl, swing, spin, circle – فَرّ المِعكال قَبُل ما يضرُب [farr ʔilmiʕča:l gabul ma: yiðrub] He swung the sling before he threw the rock. فَرّ بيدَه مِن قِتلَه شِي ما عِجَبَه [farr bi:dah min gitlah ši ma: ʕijabah] He waved his hand when I told him something he didn't like. ظَلّ يفُرّ براسَه وَما يِدري شِيسَوّي [ðall yfurr bira:sah wama yidri šiysawwi:] He kept shaking his head and didn't know what to do. • **4.** to take around, show around, take on a tour – فَرّنا بَغداد بسَيّارتَه [farrna baɣda:d bsayya:rtah] He showed us Baghdad in his car. • **5.** to greet warmly – مِن طَبّيت عَليه، فَرّ بيّا [min ṭabbayt ʕali:h, farr biyya] When I went in to see him, he greeted me warmly.

فَرَّر [farrar] *v:* • **1.** to show around – أخُذ الجَّهّال وَفَرِّرهُم بحَديقَة الحَيوانات [ʔuxuð ʔijjahha:l wfarrirhum bħadi:qat ʔilħaywa:na:t] Take the kids and show them around the zoo.

اِفتَرّ [ʔiftarr] *v:* • **1.** to spin, turn – المُصرَع بَعدَه دَيفتَرّ [ʔilmuṣraʕ baʕdah dayiftarr] The top is still spinning. • **2.** to wander about – شَكُو عِندَك تِفتَرّ هنا؟ [šaku ʕindak tiftarr hna?] What are you doing wandering around here?

ف

اِنفَرّ [ʔinfarr] *v:* • **1.** to swing around • **2.** to be swung, to be spun
فَرّ [farr] *n:* • **1.** to flee, run off, run away, escape
فَرَّة [farra] *n:* فَرّات [farra:t] *pl:* • **1.** turn, spin • **2.** circuit, turn, spin, swing – أُخُذلَك فَدّ فَرَّة بالسُّوق، بَلكِي تشُوفه [ʔuxuðlak fadd farra bissu:g, balki tšu:fah] Take a look around the marketplace, and maybe you'll see him.
إفرار، أفرار [ʔifra:r, ʔafra:r] *n:* إفرارِيَّة [ʔifra:riyya] *pl:* • **1.** fugitive (esp. from military service)
فُرّارَة [furra:ra] *n:* فُرّارات [furra:ra:t] *pl:* • **1.** merry-go-round • **2.** small propeller on a stick played with by children • **3.** a gambling game played with a hexagonal or octagonal stick, differently colored on each side
مَفَرّ، ما مِنها مَفَرّ *n:* [mafarr, ma: minha mafarr] • **1.** flight, escape • **2.** ما مِنهَا مَفَرّ It is unavoidable. There's no way out.
فِرار [fira:r] *n:* • **1.** flight, escape

ف ر ز

فُرَز [furaz] *v:* • **1.** to separate, set apart, detach, isolate – راح نِفرِز نُصّ القاع وَنِعرُضها لِلبيع [ra:ħ nifriz nuṣṣ ʔilga:ʕ wniʕruðha lilbi:ʕ] We're going to detach half the lot and offer it for sale. أفرُز البُتَيتَة الكبار [ʔufruz ʔilputayta ʔilkba:r] Separate the large potatoes. • **2.** to secrete, excrete, discharge – المَرارَة تِفرِز مادَّة تذَوِّب الشَّحُوم [ʔilmara:ra tifriz ma:dda dðawwub ʔiššħu:m] The gall bladder secretes a substance which dissolves fats.
فَرِز [fariz] *n:* • **1.** separation, setting apart, sorting, screening, sifting, selection, selecting
مَفرَزَة [mafraza] *n:* مَفرَزات [mafraza:t] *pl:* • **1.** detachment, group, squad
فارِزَة [fa:riza] *n:* فَوارِز [fawa:riz] *pl:* • **1.** comma
مفَرَّز [mfarraz] *adj:* • **1.** excreted, discharged • **2.** selected, screened

ف ر ز ن

ف

فَرزَن [farzan] *v:* • **1.** to see clearly, to see details, to see differences, to distinguish things – نَظَرَه ضَعِيف. ما يِقدَر يفَرزِن [naðarah ðaʕi:f. ma: yigdar yfarzin] His eyesight is weak. He can't distinguish things. • **2.** to distinguish, tell the difference, see the difference – ما يِقدَر يفَرزِن بَعض الألوان [ma: yigdar yfarzin baʕð ʔilʔalwa:n] He can't distinguish some colors. ما أقدَر أفَرزِنهُم لِأَنَّهُم توم [ma: ʔagdar ʔafarzinhum liʔannhum tawm] I can't tell the difference between them because they are twins. تِقدَر تفَرزَن هَاللُّون مِن ذاك؟ [tigdar tfarzan hallu:n min ða:k?] Can you distinguish this color from that? هَالتُّوم ما تِقدَر تفَرزِن بَيناتهُم [hattu:m ma: tigdar tfarzin bayna:thum] You can't tell the difference between these two twins.
تفَرزَن [tfarzan] *v:* • **1.** to be distinguished, be told apart – هَالتُّوم ما يِتفَرزنُون [hattu:m ma: yitfarzinu:n] Those twins can't be told apart.

ف ر س

فَرَس [faras] *n:* أفراس، فرُوسَة [ʔafra:s, fru:sap] *pl:* • **1.** mare – فَرَس الماء [faras ʔilma:ʔ] hippopotamus. • **2.** knight (chess)
فارِس [fa:ris] *n:* فُرسان، فَوارِس [fursa:n, fawa:ris] *pl:* • **1.** horseman, rider, knight, cavalier
فَرِيسَة [fari:sa] *n:* فَرِيسات، فَرايِس [fari:sa:t, fara:yis] *pl:* • **1.** prey, kill (of a wild animal)
فُرُوسِيَّة [furu:siyya] *n:* • **1.** horsemanship, equitation, • **2.** chivalry, knighthood
مُفتَرِس [muftaris] *adj:* • **1.** predatory, rapacious (animal) – حَيوان مُفتَرِس [ħaywa:n muftaris] a beast of prey.
فارسِي [fa:rsi] *adj:* • **1.** Persian, Iranian نَمِل فارسِي [namil fa:rsi] a sort of large ants. خَطّ فارسِي [xaṭṭ fa:rsi] Farsi script. • **2.** a Persian, an Iranian • **3.** the Persian language

ف ر ش

فُرَش [furaš] *v:* • **1.** to spread, spread out – أفرُش هَالزُّولِيَّة بغُرفَة الخُطّار [ʔufruš hazzu:liyya byurfat ʔilxuṭṭa:r] Spread this carpet in the guest room. • **2.** to cover – فُرشَوا الغُرفَة بِزوالِي [furšaw ʔilyurfa bizwa:li] They covered the room with carpets. • **3.** to make a bed, spread out the bedding, prepare a bed – فُرشَت لِإبِنها المَرِيض حَتَّى ينام [furšat liʔibinha ʔilmari:ð ħatta yna:m] She prepared the bed for her sick son so he could sleep.
فَرَّش [farrač] *v:* • **1.** to brush – يفَرِّش سنُونَه قَبُل ما ينام [yfarrič snu:nah gabul ma: yna:m] He brushes his teeth before retiring. فَرِّش سِترتَك. بِيها عَجاج هوايَة [farriš sitirtak. bi:ha ʕaja:j hwa:ya] Brush your coat. There's a lot of dust on it.
اِنفُرَش [ʔinfuraš] *v:* • **1.** to be covered, spread
فُرُش [faruš] *n:* • **1.** spreading, covering, making a bed • **2.** spread, cover, blanket, mattress, bed
فِرشَة [firča] *n:* فِرَش [firač] *pl:* • **1.** فِرشَت البُطِل brush for cleaning bottles • **2.** a plant resembling a bottle brush – راح تِلمَع القُندَرَة مِن تُضرُبها فِرشَة [ra:ħ tilmaʕ ʔilqundara min tuðrubha firča] The shoes will shine when you brush them.
فراش [fra:š] *n:* فراشات [fra:ša:t] *pl:* • **1.** mattress, bedding • **2.** bed
فَرّاش [farra:š] *n:* فَرّاشِين، فرارِيش [farra:ši:n, fra:ri:š] *pl:* • **1.** errand boy, handy man, and janitor, in an office or school
فَرّاش [farra:š] *n:* • **1.** butterfly (butterflies) • **2.** moth(s)

فَرّاشَة [farraːša] *n:* فَرّاشات [farraːšaːt] *pl:* • **1.** a butterfly, a moth
تَفرِيش [tafriːč] *n:* • **1.** brushing • **2.** sitting down on the ground

ف ر ص

فُرصَة [furṣa] *n:* فُرَص [furaṣ] *pl:* • **1.** opportunity, chance, auspicious moment – اِنتِهِز الفُرصَة [ʔintihiz ʔilfurṣa] Seize the opportunity. • **2.** recess (between classes)

ف ر ض

فُرَض [furað̣] *v:* • **1.** to impose – الحُكُومَة راح تُفرُض ضَرايِب عالأراض الزِّراعِيَّة [ʔilħukuːma raːħ tufruð̣ ð̣araːyib ʕalʔaraːð̣ ʔizziraːʕiyya] The government will impose taxes on farm lands. ما تِقدَر تُفرُض إرادتَك عَلَيّا [maː tigdar tufruð̣ ʔiraːdtak ʕalayya] You can't force your will on me. • **2.** to suppose, assume – أُفرُض ما يريد يُقُلَّك. شتِقدَر تسَوِّي؟ [ʔufruð̣ maː yriːd yugullak. štigdar tsawwiː?] Suppose he doesn't want to tell you. What can you do?
اِنفُرَض [ʔinfurað̣] *v:* • **1.** to be imposed
اِفتِرَض [ʔiftirað̣] *v:* • **1.** to assume, presuppose – دَيِفتِرِض أشياء ما مُمكِن تصِير [dayiftirið̣ ʔašyaːʔ maːmumkin tṣiːr] He is assuming things which aren't possible.
فَرِض [farið̣] *n:* فُرُوض [furuːð̣] *pl:* • **1.** order, injunction, duty • **2.** any of the five obligatory prayers of the day • **3.** assumption, supposition, hypothesis
فَرَضِيَّة [farað̣iyya] *n:* فَرَضِيّات [farað̣iyyaːt] *pl:* • **1.** theory, hypothesis
فَرِيضَة [fariːð̣a] *n:* فَرايِض [faraːyið̣] *pl:* • **1.** religious duty, religious obligation
مَفرُوض [mafruːð̣] *adj:* • **1.** supposed, assumed, premised • **2.** (pl. مَفرُوضات duties, obligations
فَرضاً [farð̣an] *adverbial:* • **1.** suppose (that), what if..

ف ر ط

فَرَّط [farraṭ] *v:* • **1.** to break the seeds apart – إكسِر الرُّمّانَة وَفَرِّطها [ʔiksir ʔirrummaːna wfarriṭha] Break open the pomegranate and take the seeds out.
تفَرَّط [tfarraṭ] *v:* • **1.** to break apart – وُقعَت القلادَة وَتفَرِّطَت [wugʕat ʔilglaːda wtfarriṭat] The necklace fell and scattered apart.
إفراط [ʔifraːṭ] *n:* • **1.** excess • **2.** بإفراط to excess
فَرُط [faruṭ] *adj:* • **1.** loose, unpackaged, by the piece, individually – تبِيعهُم فَرُط لَو بالكُومَة؟ [tbiːʕhum faruṭ law bilkuːma?] Do you sell them individually or by the pile?

ف ر ع

فَرَّع [farraʕ] *v:* • **1.** to branch, put out branches – الأشجار تفَرِّع بالرَّبِيع [ʔilʔašjaːr tfarriʕ birrabiːʕ] The tress grow branches in the spring. • **2.** to uncover, bare (the head) – فَرِّع الجّاهِل. الدِّنيا حارَّة [farriʕ ʔijjaːhil. ʔiddinya ħaːrra] Uncover the kid's head. The weather's hot.
تفَرَّع [tfarraʕ] *v:* • **1.** to branch, branch off, branch out – النَّخلَة ما تِتفَرَّع [ʔinnaxla maː titfarraʕ] The palm tree doesn't branch. النَّهَر يِتفَرَّع إلَى فَرعَين [ʔinnahar yitfarraʕ ʔila farʕayn] The river branches into two streams. هَالجّادَّة تِتفَرَّع مِنها عِدَّة شَوارِع [hajjaːdda titfarraʕ minha ʕiddat šawaːriʕ] Several streets branch off from this avenue. • **2.** to uncover (one's head), to take off one's hat – تفَرَّع وَنزَع سِترتَه وَقام يلعَب [tfarraʕ wnizaʕ sitirtah wgaːm yilʕab] He uncovered his head and took off his coat and began to play.
فَرِع [fariʕ] *n:* فرُوع [fruːʕ] *pl:* • **1.** twig, branch • **2.** branch, branch office
فَرعِي [farʕi] *adj:* • **1.** branch, subsidiary, secondary, tributary, sub- – شَرِكَة فَرعِيَّة [šarika farʕiyya] subsidiary company. دائِرَة فَرعِيَّة [daːʔira farʕiyya] branch office. نَهَر فَرعِي [nahar farʕi] tributary. لَجنَة فَرعِيَّة [lajna farʕiyya] sub-committee.
فارِع [faːriʕ] *adj:* • **1.** tall, lofty, slender, slim • **2.** beautiful, handsome, pretty
مفَرَّع [mfarraʕ] *adj:* • **1.** ramified, branched
مِتفَرِّعَة [mitfarriʕa] *adj:* مِتفَرِّعات [mitfarriʕaːt] *pl:* • **1.** branched, unveiled • **2.** (plural noun:) secondary things

ف ر ع ن

تفَرعَن [tfarʕan] *v:* • **1.** to act with arrogance (lit. to act like a Pharaoh)
فِرعَون [firʕawn] *n:* • **1.** Pharaoh
مِتفَرعِن [mitfarʕin] *adj:* • **1.** snob, snobby, arrogant
فِرعَونِي [firʕawni] *adj:* • **1.** pharaonic

ف ر غ

فُرَغ [furaɣ] *v:* • **1.** to be or become empty – تانكِي الماي فُرَغ [taːnki ʔilmaːy furaɣ] The water tank went dry. ظَلّ يِصرُف فلُوس حَتَّى فُرَغ جيبَه [ð̣all yiṣruf fluːs ħatta furaɣ jiːbah] He kept on spending money until his pockets were empty. • **2.** to be or become vacant – البَيت فُرَغ البارحَة. ترِيدَه هَسَّة؟ [ʔilbayt furaɣ ʔilbaːrħa. triːdah hassa?] The house was vacated yesterday. Do you want it now? • **3.** to be or become free, get done – أسَوِّيلَك إيّاها لَمّا أفرَغ [ʔasawwiːlak ʔiyyaːha lamma ʔafraɣ] I'll do it for you when I get free.
فَرَّغ [farraɣ] *v:* • **1.** to empty – فَرِّغِي السَّلَّة؛ أرِيد أرُوح أتسَوَّق [farriɣi ʔissalla; ʔariːd ʔaruːħ ʔatsawwag] Empty the basket; I want to go shopping. فَرِّغ كُلّ جيُوبَك [farriɣ kull jyuːbak] Empty all your pockets. فَرَّغ مُسَدَّسَه براسَه [farraɣ musaddasah braːsah] He emptied his pistol into

his head. راح يفَرِّغ وَبَعدَه بِالخَلاء [raːħ yfarriɣ wbaʕdah bilxalaːʔ] He went to relieve himself and he's still in the toilet. • **2.** to vacate, make empty, evacuate – فَرِّغولهُم البَيت حَتَّى يِنتَقلُون [farriɣuːlhum ʔilbayt ħatta yintaqluːn] They vacated the house for them so they could move. • **3.** to unload – فَرِّغوا الباخِرَة مِن الحِمِل [farriɣaw ʔilbaːxira min ʔilħimil] They unloaded the ship of its cargo. ثنينّا راح نفَرِّغ الفَرقون [θnaynna raːħ nfarriɣ ʔilfarguːn] Two of us will unload the boxcar. • **4.** to pour out – فَرِّغلِي شوَيَّة شوربَة [farriɣli šwayya šuːrba] Pour me out a little soup.

تفَرَّغ [tfarraɣ] *v:* • **1.** to be emptied – لازم جيُوبَك كُلّها تِتفَرَّغ قَبُل ما يِنضُرُب القاط أُوتِي [laːzim ǰyuːbak kullha titfarraɣ gabul maː yinðurub ʔilqaːṭ ʔuːti] Your pockets all have to be emptied before the suit is ironed. • **2.** to devote (oneself), apply (oneself) – أريدَك تِتفَرَّغ النَّهار كُلَّه لِهَالشَّغلَة [ʔariːdak titfarraɣ ʔinnahaːr kullah lihaššaɣla] I want you to devote the whole day to this job. • **3.** to have time – بَسّ أتفَرَّغ لها، أخَلِّصها بساعَة [bass ʔatfarraɣ laha, ʔaxalliṣha bsaːʕa] As soon as I have free time for it, I'll finish it in an hour.

فَرغَة [farɣa] *n:* فَرغات [farɣaːt] *pl:* • **1.** free time, free period – أسَوِّيها عالفَرغَة [ʔasawwiːha ʕalfarɣa] I'll do it when I get a little free time. • **2.** عالفَرغَة [ʕalfarɣa] at leisure

فَراغ [faraːɣ] *n:* فَراغات [faraːɣaːt] *pl:* • **1.** void, vacuum, space • **2.** power vacuum, vacuum (pol.) • **3.** empty space, emptiness, lack (fig.) – موتَه تِرَك فَراغ كِبِير [muːtah tirak faraːɣ čibiːr] His death left a great lack. • **4.** free time, leisure

مُفَرِّغَة [mufarriɣa] *n:* • **1.** ventilator

فارِغ [faːriɣ] *adj:* • **1.** empty, void – جِيب فارِغ [ǰiːb faːriɣ] an empty pocket. حَكِي فارِغ [ħači faːriɣ] empty talk. فَدّ واحِد فارِغ [fadd waːħid faːriɣ] an empty-headed person, an ignorant person. • **2.** vacant, unoccupied – بَيت فارِغ [bayt faːriɣ] a vacant house. • **3.** free, at leisure, not busy, unoccupied – إذا فارِغ تَعال عاونِّي [ʔiða faːriɣ taʕaːl ʕaːwinni] If you're free, come and help me.

مفَرَّغ [mfarraɣ] *adj:* • **1.** empty, vacant, vacated

مَفرُوغ، مَفرُوغ مِنَّه [mafruːɣ, mafruːɣ minnah] *adj:* • **1.** finished, settled, a foregone conclusion – نَجاحَه بِالإمتِحان مَفرُوغ مِنَّه لَكِن ما أعتِقِد راح يِطلَع أوَّل [naǰaːħah bilʔimtiħaːn mafruːɣ minnah laːkin maː ʔaʕtiqid raːħ yiṭlaʕ ʔawwal] His passing is a foregone conclusion but I don't think he'll come out in first place. إدخال المَرِيض بِالمُستَشفى فَدّ شِي مَفرُوغ مِنَّه [ʔidxaːl ʔilmariːð bilmustašfa fadd ši mafruːɣ minnah] Placing of the sick man in the hospital is a must. أخِذ الامتِحان الشّامِل فَدّ شِي مَفرُوغ مِنَّه [ʔaxið ʔilʔimtiħaːn ʔiššaːmil fadd ši mafruːɣ minnah] You can't get out of taking the comprehensive exam.

متفَرِّغ [mitfarriɣ] *adj:* • **1.** available

أفرَغ [ʔafraɣ] *comparative adjective:* • **1.** emptier

ف ر ف ر [1]

فَرفَر [farfar] *v:* • **1.** to cry one's heart out, to become exhausted from crying – إبنِك فَرفَر مِن البَكِي [ʔibnič farfar min ʔilbači] Your son has worn himself out from crying. طَبَّت عَلينا تفَرفِر. أخُوها سِحقَتَه سَيّارَة [ṭabbat ʕaliːna tfarfir. ʔaxuːha siħgatah sayyaːra] She came in to us distraught. A car ran over her brother.

فَرفَرَة [farfara] *n:* • **1.** wandering around

ف ر ف ر [2]

فَرفُوري [farfuːri] *n:* • **1.** china, fine porcelain

ف ر ق

فِرَق [firaq] *v:* • **1.** to differ, be different – هَذا مُو مِثلَه؛ يِفرُق هوايَة [haːða muː miθlah; yifruq hwaːya] That's not the same; it differs quite a bit. • **2.** to make a difference – ما تُفرُق عِندِي [maː tufruq ʕindi] It makes no difference to me. خُو اِمتِحِن هَسَّة! شتُفرُق؟ [xuː ʔimtiħin hassa! štufruq?] So take the exam now! What's the difference? إذا تِشتِرِيها مِن المَعمَل رأساً، تُفرُقلَك خَمس دَنانِير [ʔiða tištiriːha min ʔilmaʕmal raʔsan, tufruqlak xams danaːniːr] If you buy it direct from the factory, it will save you five dinars. • **3.** to recognize – ضَعفانَة هوايَة! ما فِرَقتِك [ðaʕfaːna hwaːya! maː firaqtič] You've gotten very thin. I didn't recognize you.

فُرَق [furag] *v:* • **1.** to part (the hair) – أخُذ المِشِط وَأفرُقلِي شَعرِي [ʔuxuð ʔilmišiṭ wʔufrugli šaʕri] Take the comb and part my hair for me.

فَرَّق [farraq, farrag] *v:* • **1.** to divide – فَرِّق --- تَسُد [farriq tasud] Divide and rule. • **2.** to disperse, scatter – الشُّرطَة فَرِّقت المُتَظاهِرِين [ʔiššurṭa farriqat ʔilmutaðaːhiriːn] The police dispersed the demonstrators. • **3.** to distinguish – هَل قَدّ ما يِتشابهُون ما أقدَر أفَرِّق بينهُم [hal gadd maː yitšaːbhuːn maː ʔagdar ʔafarriq biːnhum] They're so alike I can't distinguish between them. ما يِقدَر يفَرِّق الأحمَر مِن الأخضَر [maː yigdar yfarriq ʔilʔaħmar min ʔilʔaxðar] He can't distinguish red from green. • **4.** to make a difference, to make a saving – إذا تِشتِري كُلّشِي بِالجُملَة، يفَرِّقلَك هوايَة [ʔiða tištiri kullši bijǰumla, yfarriqlak hwaːya] If you buy everything in quantity, it'll make a big difference for you. ما إشتِرَى السَّيّارَة إلَى أن فَرَّقها شوَيَّة [maː ʔištiraː ʔissayyaːra ʔila ʔan farraqha šwayya] He didn't buy the car until he came down on the price.

فَرَّق [farrag] *v:* • **1.** to distribute, dispense – بالعِيد يفَرِّقُون فلُوس عَالفُقَراء [bilʕiːd yfarriguːn fluːs ʕalfuqaraːʔ] On the holiday they distribute money to the poor.

تفَرَّق [tfarraq, tfarrag] *v:* • **1.** to disperse, dissolve, break up – المُظاهَرَة تفَرِّقَت [ʔilmuðaːhara tfarriqat] The demonstration broke up. المُتَظاهِرِين تفَرِّقوا مِن إجَوا الشُّرطَة

[ʔilmutaðaːhiriːn tfarriqaw min ʔiǰaw ʔiššurṭa] The demonstrators dispersed when the police came.
تفارَق [tfaːrag] *v:* • **1.** to part • **2.** to separate
اِنفِرَق [ʔinfiraq, ʔinfurag] *v:* • **1.** to be distinguished (from) – و لا يِنفرقُون واحِد عَن اللّاخ [wala yinfarquːn waːhid ʕan ʔillaːx] They can't be distinguished from each other.
اِفتِرَق [ʔiftiraq] *v:* • **1.** to split up, to separate – ظَلَّوا أصدِقاء سَنَة وَبَعدين اِفتِرقوا [ðallaw ʔaṣdiqaːʔ sana wbaʕdiːn ʔiftirqaw] They remained friends for a year and then split up.
فَرِق [fariq] *n:* فُرُوق [furuːq] *pl:* • **1.** difference • **2.** difference (math.) • **3.** change (esp. one for the better)
فَرِق [farig] *n:* فرُوق [fruːg] *pl:* • **1.** part (in hair)
فِرقَة، فَرِيق [firqa, fariːq] *n:* فِرَق [firaq] *pl:* • **1.** team • **2.** band, orchestra • **3.** division (mil.)
فَرِيق [fariːq] *n:* فُرَقاء [furaqaːʔ] *pl:* • **1.** team • **2.** lieutenant general
فِرقَة [firga] *n:* فِرقات [firgaːt] *pl:* • **1.** act of giving alms to the poor, or of distributing gifts to neighbors
فراق [fraːg] *n:* • **1.** separation, farewell
مُفتَرَق [muftaraq] *n:* • **1.** crossroads, intersection
فارِق [faːriq] *adj:* • **1.** distinguishing, distinctive – عَلامَة فارِقَة [ʕalaːma faːriqa] trademark, identifying mark. • **2.** difference, distinction
مَفرَق [mafrag] *adj:* مَفارِق [mafaːrig] *pl:* • **1.** junction (railroad) • **2.** fork, crossroads, highway intersection
مِتفَرِّق [mitfarriq] *adj:* • **1.** separated
مِفتِرِق [miftiriq] *adj:* • **1.** separated, dispersed, scattered
مِتفارِق [mitfaːrig] *adj:* • **1.** separated, apart

ف ر ق س

فَرقَس [fargas] *v:* • **1.** to become blistered – إيدِي فَرقِسَت مِن الجِّدِف [ʔiːdi fargisat min ʔiǰǰadif] My hands got blistered from rowing. • **2.** to become inflamed, become infected and swollen – اِنجِرَح إصبِعِي وبَعَدما غسَلتَه بالماي فَرقَس [ʔinǰirah ʔiṣibʕi wbaʕadmaː ɣsaltah bilmaːy fargas] My finger got cut and when I rinsed it in water it became inflamed. اِحتِرَق إصبِعِي وَبَعدين فَرقَس [ʔiħtirag ʔiṣibʕi wbaʕdiyn fargas] My finger got burned and later inflamed.
تفَرقَس [tfargas] *v:* • **1.** to become blistered – تفَرقِسَت رِجلِي مِن القُندَرَة [tfargisat riǰli min ʔilqundara] My feet got swollen and sore from the shoes.
فُرقاس [furgaːs] *n:* • **1.** (coll.) inflammation, infection, swelling, sore(s) – هُوَّ فُرقاس ما يِنقاس [huwwa furgaːs maː yingaːs] He's so sensitive he can't be touched.
فُرقاسَة [furgaːsa] *n:* فُرقاسات، فَراقِيس [furgaːsaːt, faraːgiːs] *pl:* • **1.** blister • **2.** unit name of فُرغَاس: a blister

ف ر ق ع

فَرقَع [fargaʕ] *v:* • **1.** to heat clarified butter to boiling – فَرقِع شوَيَّة دِهِن لِلتِّمَّن [fargiʕ šwayya dihin littimman] Heat some ghee for the rice.
فِرقاعَة [firgaːʕa] *n:* • **1.** boiling clarified butter (for pouring over rice, etc.)

ف ر ق ن

فَرقُون [farguːn] *n:* فَرقُونَات، فَراقِين [farguːnaːt, faraːgiːn] *pl:* • **1.** railroad car

ف ر ك

فُرَك [furak] *v:* • **1.** to rub – لا تُفرُك عينَك تَرَة تِحمَرّ [laː tufruk ʕaynak tara tiħmarr] Don't rub your eye or it'll get red. أفرُك الطِّينَة بإيدَك وشُوفها شلَونها [ʔufruk ʔiṭṭiːna biːdak wšuːfha šluːnha] Rub the clay between your fingers and see how it is. إذا تِحكِي زايِد أفرُك خَشمَك [ʔiða tiħči zaːyid ʔafruk xašmak] If you talk any more I'll mash your nose.
فَرَّك [farrak] *v:* • **1.** to rub, massage – فَرّكِيلِي كتافِي؛ تُوجَعنِي [farrkiːli čtaːfi; tuːǰaʕni] Massage my shoulders. They're hurting me. يَزِّي تفَرِّك بخَشمَك [yazzi tfarrik bxašmak] Stop rubbing your nose!
فَرِك [farik] *n:* • **1.** act of rubbing, rub
فَركَة [farka] *n:* • **1.** time, time enough – إذا تِنطِينِي فَركَة أسَوِّي لَك إيّاها [ʔiða tinṭiːni farka ʔasawwiː lak ʔiyyaːha] If you'll just give me enough time, I'll do it for you. أرِيد أصَلِّح الرّاديُو بَسّ ماكُو فَركَة [ʔariːd ʔaṣalliħ ʔirraːdyu bass maːku farka] I want to fix the radio but I don't have time.
تَفرِيك [tafriːk] *n:* • **1.** rubbing, massaging
مفَرَّك [mfarrak] *adj:* • **1.** rubbed, massaged

ف ر ك ت

فُركَيتَة [furkiːta] *n:* فُركَيتات [furkiːtaːt] *pl:* • **1.** hair pin, bobby pin – دَمبُوس فُركَيتَة [dambuːs furkiːta] safety pin.

ف ر ن

فِرِن [firin] *n:* أفران [ʔafraːn] *pl:* • **1.** oven
فِرنِي [firni] *n:* • **1.** a pudding made of milk, rice flour, and sugar also called محَلَّبِي [mħallabi]
فَرّان [farraːn] *n:* • **1.** baker

ف ر ن ج 1

فرَنجِي [franǰi] *adj:* • **1.** European – هدُوم فرَنجِيَّة [hduːm franǰiyya] European clothes. مِرحاض فرَنجِي [mirhaːð franǰi] European style toilet. • **2.** a European • **3.** (loosely) French • **4.** Frenchman

ف ر ن ج 2

فرِنجِي [frinǰi] *n:* • **1.** syphilis – مِلِح فرِنجِي [miliħ fringi] Epsom salts.

ف

ف ر ن س

فَرَنسا [faransa] *n:* • **1.** France
فَرَنسِي [faransi] *adj:* • **1.** French
فَرَنساوِي [faransa:wi] *adj:* • **1.** French

ف ر ه

فَره [farih] *adj:* • **1.** wide, spacious, ample, uncrowded – غُرفَة فَرهَة [ɣurfa farha] a spacious room. وِلايَة فَرهَة [wila:ya farha] an uncrowded city.
أَفرَه [ʔafrah] *comparative adjective:* • **1.** wider, ampler, more spacious, less crowded

ف ر ه د

فَرهَد [farhad] *v:* • **1.** to loot, steal
فَرهُود [farhu:d] *n:* • **1.** looter, act of looting

ف ر و

فَرْو [farw] *n:* • **1.** (coll.) (fur(s), pelt(s), skin(s) – قَبُّوط فَرو [qappu:ṭ farw] fur coat.
فَروَة [farwa] *n:* فَروات، فراوِي [farwa:t, fra:wi] *pl:* • **1.** فَروَة الرَّاس scalp • **2.** a long sheep-skin coat with the wool on the inside • **3.** fur, pelt, skin

ف ر ي [1]

اِفتِرَى [ʔiftira:] *v:* • **1.** to lie, to slander
اِفتِراء [ʔiftira:ʔ] *n:* • **1.** lie, slander, calumny, falsehood

ف ر ي [2]

فِرَى [fira:] *v:* • **1.** to break, burst – إفري البُطباطَة بإصبِعَك [ʔifri ʔilbuṭba:ṭa bʔiṣibʕak] Break the blister with your fingers. دِير بالَك. لا تِفري المرارَة مِن تشُقّ السِّمكَة [di:r ba:lak. la: tifri ʔilmra:ra min tšugg ʔissimča] Be careful. Don't break the gall bladder when you clean the fish.
اِنفِرَى [ʔinfira:] *v:* • **1.** to be or become broken, to burst – اِنفِرَت المرارَة وصارَت السِّمكَة مُرَّة [ʔinfirat lumra:ra wṣa:rat ʔissimča murra] The gall bladder got broken and the fish became bitter.
فَرِي [fari] *n:* • **1.** putting pressure on oneself, torturing oneself, burning (figuratively, as in with anger or jealousy)

ف ر ي [3]

فارَى [fa:ra:] *v:* • **1.** to coo (pigeon) – هَذا حِسّ فَرخ الحَمَام ديفَارِي [ha:ða ħiss farx ʔilħama:m dayfa:ri:] That's the sound of the male pigeon cooing.

ف ز ز

فَزّ [fazz] *v:* • **1.** to be startled, to start – مِن خَشّيت، قُمَز بِوجهي وفَزّيت [min xašši:t, gumaz bwiǰhi wfazzi:t] When I came in, he jumped in front of me and I was startled. قُمزَت البَزّونَة مِن عَالحايِط وفَزّيت مِن النُّوم [gumzat ʔilbazzu:na min ʕalħa:yiṭ wfazzi:t min ʔinnu:m] The cat jumped down off the wall and I woke up with a start. • **2.** to wake up – السّاعَة بيش فَزّيت البارحَة؟ [ʔissa:ʕa biyš fazzi:t ʔilba:rħa?] What time did you wake up yesterday?
فَزَّز [fazzaz] *v:* • **1.** to startle – فَزَّزني بعَطِستَه [fazzazni bʕaṭistah] He startled me with his sneeze. • **2.** to wake, wake up, awaken – فَزَّزني مِن النُّوم مِن وَقِت [fazzazni min ʔannu:m min wakit] He woke me up early.
تفَزَّز [tfazzaz] *v:* • **1.** to be startled, alarmed
اِستَفَزّ [ʔistafazz] *v:* • **1.** to agitate, excite, stir up – إنتَ دَتِستِفِزَّه بهيكي حَكي [ʔinta datistifizzah bhi:či ħači] You are getting him all worked up with that talk.
فَزّ [fazz] *n:* • **1.** to be startled, to startle
فَزَّة [fazza] *n:* • **1.** a startle, a scare
اِستِفزاز [ʔistifza:z] *n:* اِستِفزازات [ʔistifza:za:t] *pl:* • **1.** instigation, agitation, provocation, incitement
فازّ [fa:zz] *adj:* • **1.** startled, alarmed, scared
اِستِفزازي [ʔistifza:zi] *adj:* • **1.** inflammatory, rabble-rousing, provocative, incendiary – أعمال اِستِفزازِيَّة [ʔaʕma:l ʔistifza:ziyya] inflammatory acts.

ف ز ع

فِزَع [fizaʕ] *v:* • **1.** with لـ to go to someone's aid, to help, go to help someone – بَسّ تمِدّ إيدَك عَليه، أَخُوه يفزَعلَه [bass tmidd ʔi:dak ʕali:h, ʔaxu:h yifzaʕlah] As soon as you lay your hand on him, his brother comes to his aid. فِزعَوله فَدّ فَزعَة [fizʕawlah fadd fazʕa] They came to his aid at once.
فَزَّع [fazzaʕ] *v:* • **1.** to frighten, scare, terrify – صُوت الأَسَد يفَزِّع الواحِد [ṣu:t ʔilʔasad yfazziʕ ʔilwa:ħid] The lion's roar terrifies a person.
فَزِع [faziʕ] *n:* • **1.** (urgent/alarmed) help, aid
فَزَع [fazaʕ] *n:* • **1.** scare • **2.** fear
فَزعَة [fazʕa] *n:* • **1.** group, gang
فَزّاع [fazza:ʕ] *n:* فَزّاعَة [fazza:ʕa] *pl:* • **1.** rescuer • **2.** scarecrow
مَفزُوع [mafzu:ʕ] *adj:* • **1.** startled, frightened, alarmed

ف س

فاس [fa:s] *n:* فاسات، فُوس [fa:sa:t, fu:s] *pl:* • **1.** adze, axelike tool for cutting away the surface of wood.

ف س ت ق

فِستِق [fistiq] *n:* • **1.** (coll.) pistachio nut(s) – فِستِق عَبِيد [fistiq ʕabi:d] peanut (s).
فِستِقَة [fistiqa, fistiqa:ya] *n:* فِستِقايات [fistiqa:ya:t] *pl:* • **1.** pistachio nut
فُستِقِي [fistiqi] *adj:* • **1.** (invar.) pistachio (color) – لُون فِستِقِي [lu:n fistiqi] pistachio colored.

ف س ت ن

فِستان [fista:n] *n:* فِساتِين [fisa:ti:n] *pl:* • **1.** (woman's) dress

ف س ح

فِسَح [fisaħ] *v:* • **1.** to give, allow, provide – فِسَحِتلَه الفُرصَة مَرّتَين وَما إستَفاد مِنها [fisaħitlah ʔilfurṣa marrtayn wma ʔistafa:d minha] I gave an opportunity twice and he didn't take advantage of it. لا تِفسَحلَه المَجال تَرَة بَعدين يِنكُت بِيك [la: tifsaħlah ʔilmaǰa:l tara baʕdi:n yinkut bi:k] Don't give him free rein or he will double-cross you.

اِنفِسَح [ʔinfisaħ] *v:* • **1.** to be given, allowed, provided – اِنفِسَحلِي المَجال عِدَّة مَرّات أصِير مُدِير وَما قبَلِت [ʔinfisaħli ʔilmaǰa:l ʕiddat marra:t ʔaṣi:r mudi:r wma qbalit] I was given a chance to be director on several occasions and I didn't accept.

فَسحَة [fasħa] *n:* • **1.** room, space, roominess, spaciousness – ما بِيه فَسحَة [ma: bi:h fasħa] It's not roomy.

فَسِيح [fasi:ħ] *adj:* • **1.** wide, ample, spacious, roomy, broad

ف س خ

فُسَخ [fusax] *v:* • **1.** to dislocate, put out of joint, sprain – لُوَى إيدِي حيل وَفُسَخها [luwa: ʔi:di ħi:l wfusaxha] He twisted my arm hard and dislocated it. • **2.** to dissolve, cancel, void – فُسَخ العَقِد [fusax ʔilʕaqid] He broke the contract. تعارگوا وفُسخَوا الخُطبَة [tʕa:rkaw wfusxaw ʔilxuṭba] They argued and broke the engagement.

فَسَّخ [fassax] *v:* • **1.** to tear apart, break apart – فَصَّخ فُخذ الخَرُوف [faṣṣax fuxð ʔilxaru:f] He broke the leg of lamb apart. فَصِّخ الدِّجاجَة لِلجِهّال حَتَّى ياكلُون [faṣṣix ʔiddija:ja lijjiha:l ħatta ya:klu:n] Split the chicken apart for the children so they can eat. • **2.** to take apart, disassemble – فَصَّخ مَكِينَة السَّيّارَة [faṣṣax maki:nat ʔissayya:ra] He took the car's motor apart. فَصَّخ القَنَفَة حَتَّى يدَخِّلها بالغُرفَة [faṣṣax ʔilqanafa ħatta ydaxxilha bilɣurfa] He took the couch apart to get it into the room.

تفَسَّخ [tfassax] *v:* • **1.** to come apart • **2.** to be dislocated, be put out of joint, be sprained

تفاسَخ [tfa:sax] *v:* • **1.** to split up, to dissolve an association – ظَلّوا شَراكَة سَنَة وِحدَة وبَعدين تفاسخَوا [ðallaw šara:ka sana wiħda wbaʕdi:n tfa:sxaw] They remained partners for one year and then split up.

اِنفُسَخ [ʔinfusax] *v:* • **1.** to be dislocated, be put out of joint, be sprained – ضرَبتَه بُوكس وإنفُسَخ إصبِعِي [ðrabtah bu:ks wʔinfusax ʔiṣibʕi] I hit him with my fist and my finger got dislocated.

فَسِخ [fasix] *n:* • **1.** dislocation, sprain – مُكان الفَسِخ [muka:n ʔilfaṣix] sprained place.

تَفَسُّخ [tafassux] *n:* • **1.** (act of) coming apart • **2.** dislocation, sprain

مفَسَّخ [mfassax] *adj:* • **1.** apart • **2.** dislocated, separated

متفَسِّخ [mitfassix] *adj:* • **1.** decayed • **2.** degenerate

مَفسُوخ [mafsu:x] *adj:* • **1.** out of joint • **2.** dislocated

ف س د

فِسَد [fisad] *v:* • **1.** to spoil, go bad, become rotten, decayed, putrid – فِسَد البَيض كُلَّه مِن الحَرّ [fisad ʔilbi:ð kullah min ʔilħarr] The eggs all spoiled from the heat. • **2.** to be or become bad, corrupt, depraved – إذا يظَلّ يِمشِي ويّا هِيكِي ناس راح يِفسَد [ʔiða yðall yimši wiyya hi:či na:s ra:ħ yifsad] If he keeps running around with those people he will turn rotten. • **3.** to be or become bad, go to pieces, turn out badly – القَضِيَّة فِسدَت عَلينا [ʔilqaðiyya fisdat ʕali:na] The affair turned out badly for us.

فَسَّد [fassad] *v:* • **1.** to spoil, ruin, corrupt, deprave – فَسِّدَتها صَدِيقَتها [fassidatha ṣadi:qatha] Her girl friend corrupted her. • **2.** to spoil, ruin, mess up – كِنّا نِحكِي بَيناتنا المَوضُوع، وَخَشّ عَلينا واحِد فَسَّد كُلْشِي [činna niħči bayna:tna ʔilmawðu:ʕ, wxašš ʕali:na wa:ħid fassad kullši] We were talking the matter over between us and a guy came over to us and messed it all up.

فَساد [fasa:d] *n:* • **1.** rottenness, spoiledness • **2.** depravity, corruption – يدَوُّر فَساد [ydawwur fasa:d] He's depraved.

مَفسَدَة [mafsada] *n:* • **1.** place of immorality, place of depravity • **2.** cause of evil, scandalous deed

فاسِد [fa:sid] *adj:* فَسّاد [fassa:d] *pl:* • **1.** bad, spoiled, rotten putrid – بيضَة فاسدَة [bi:ða fa:sda] a rotten egg. • **2.** stale, impure, polluted – هَوا فاسِد [hawa fa:sid] stale air. • **3.** wicked, immoral, depraved – وَلَد فاسِد [walad fa:sid] a bad guy. فاسِد مِن البَيض [fa:sid min ʔilbi:ð] immoral right from the start.

أفسَد [ʔafsad] *comparative adjective:* • **1.** more or most immoral, corrupt, depraved

ف س ر

فَسَّر [fassar] *v:* • **1.** to explain, interpret – شلُون تفَسِّر هَالتَّطَوِّرات؟ [šlu:n tfassir hattaṭawwira:t?] How do you explain these developments? بالله ما تفَسِّرلِي هَالجُملَة [ballah ma: tfassir li hajjumla] Please explain to me what this sentence means. بَعَض الأُدَباء الأجانِب فَسِّروا القُرآن [baʕað ʔilʔudaba:ʔ ʔilʔaǰa:nib fassiraw ʔilqurʔa:n] Some foreign literary critics interpreted the Koran. • **2.** to be able to see well, to have good eyesight (usually negative) – عيُونَه ضَعِيفَة؛ ما تفَسِّر مِن بِعِيد [ʕyu:nah ðaʕi:fa; ma: tfassir min biʕi:d] His eyes are weak; he can't see anything at a distance. • **3.** to break, break up – ضِرَب المِيز ضَربَة وِحدَة، وَفَسَّرَه كُلَّه [ðirab ʔilmi:z ðarba wiħda, wfassarah kullah] He hit the table with a single blow and splintered it.

تفَسَّر [tfassar] *v:* • **1.** to be explained, interpreted – هَذا الشِّعِر صَعُب وَما يِتفَسَّر [haːða ʔišsiʕir ṣaʕub wma yitfassar] This poem is difficult and can't be explained. • **2.** to be broken up, to be broken to pieces, to be smashed – إذا تخَلّي البُطِل عَلَى النّار مُدَّة طُويلَة، يِتفَسَّر [ʔiða txalliː ʔilbuṭil ʕala ʔinnaːr mudda ṭuwiːla, yitfassar] If you leave the bottle on the fire a long time, it'll get broken.

اِستَفسَر [ʔistafsar] *v:* • **1.** to inquire, ask – استَفسِر عَن القَضِيَّة [ʔastafsar ʕan ʔilqaḍiyya] He asked about the matter. راح استَفسِر مِن عَلِي [raːħ ʔastafsir min ʕali] I'm going to ask Ali. راح أستَفسِرلَك وأشُوف شِنُو القُصَّة [raːħ ʔastafsirlak wʔašuːf šinu ʔilquṣṣa] I'm going to inquire for you and find out what the story is.

تَفسِير [tafsiːr] *n:* • **1.** explanation, interpretation • **2.** pl. تَفاسِير a book interpreting and commenting on the Koran

اِستِفسار [ʔistifsaːr] *n:* • **1.** inquiry, question, query

مفَسِّر [mfassir] *adj:* مفَسِّرين [mfassiriːn] *pl:* • **1.** interpreter, commentator (esp. on the Koran) – مفَسِّر الأحلام [mfassir ʔilʔaħlaːm] interpreter of dreams.

مُستَفسِر [mustafsir] *adj:* • **1.** questioning, questioner

ف س ف ر

فُسفُور [fusfuːr] *n:* • **1.** phosphorus

فِسفُورَة [fisfuːra] *n:* فِسفُورات [fisfuwraːt] *pl:* • **1.** flashing signs

فِسفُورِي [fisfuwri] *adj:* • **1.** phosphorescent, glimmering

ف س ق

فاسِق [faːsiq] *adj:* • **1.** sinful, depraved, dissolute, wanton • **2.** as Noun: sinner, adulterer, offender, a person who is not righteous.

ف س ق ن

فَسقان [fasgaːn] *adj:* • **1.** silly, light-headed, lame-brained, unreliable – هُوَّ فَدّ واحِد فَسقان. ما يِدرِي شَكُو بِهَالدِّنيَة [huwwa fadd waːħid fasgaːn. maː yidri šaku bhaddinya] He's a dopey guy. He doesn't know what's going on in the world.

ف س ل

فِسِيل [fisiːl] *n:* • **1.** (coll.) palm shoot(s), palm seedling(s)

فِسِيلَة [fisiːla] *n:* فِسِيلات، فِسايِل [fisiːlaːt, fisaːyil] *pl:* • **1.** palm shoot, palm seedling

ف س و

فِسَى [fisaː] *v:* • **1.** to break wind noiselessly – صار وجهه أحمَر لِأنّ فِسَى [ṣaːr wiččah ʔaħmar liʔann fisaː] His face became red because he broke wind.

فَسَّى [fassaː] *v:* • **1.** intens. of فِسَى to break wind – إذا تاكُل حُمُّص، تفَسِّي هوايَة [ʔiða taːkul ħummuṣ, tfassi hwaːya] If you eat peas, you'll be passing a lot of gas.

فَسُو [fasw] *n:* • **1.** (coll.) (soundless) breaking wind

فَسوَة [faswa] *n:* فَسوات [faswaːt] *pl:* • **1.** Unit noun of the act of soundless breaking wind

ف ش

فاشِي [faːši] *adj:* • **1.** formal equivalent of • **2.** fascist (Adj and Noun)

فاشِيَّة [faːšiyya] *n:* • **1.** fascist (fem. Adj. form) • **2.** fascism

ف ش خ

فِشَخ [fišax, fičax, fišag] *v:* • **1.** to hit (on the head), to injure (the head) – فِشَخ راسَه بِالشّماغ [fičax raːsah biččimaːɣ] He laid his head open with the club. فِشَخِت راسَه بالحجارَة [fičaxit raːsah bilħijaːra] I gashed his head with a rock. فِشَخنِي وشِرَد [fičaxni wširad] He beaned me and ran away.

فَشَّخ [faččax, faššax] *v:* • **1.** intens. of فِشَخ to hit (on the head), to injure (the head) – خَطِيَّة، فَشَّخُوه الجَّهال [xaṭiyya, faččixuːh ʔijjahaːl] Poor guy, the kids plastered him with rocks.

اِنفِشَخ [ʔinfičax, ʔinfišax] *v:* • **1.** to be hit, injured

فَشِخ [fačix, fašix] *n:* • **1.** hitting (on the head), injuring (the head)

فَشخَة [fačxa, fašxa] *n:* فَشخات [fačxaːt, fašxaːt] *pl:* • **1.** a head wound caused by a blow

مَفشُوخ [mafšuːx, mafšuːg] *adj:* • **1.** injured (head)

ف ش ر

فَشَّر [faššar] *v:* • **1.** to curse in a vulgar way, to make insulting, off-color remarks – ماكُو حاجَة تفَشِّر عَلِيه؛ وَلا حِكَى عَلِيك [maːku ħaːja tfaššir ʕaliːh; wala ħičaː ʕaliːk] There's no need to curse him; he never said anything against you. حَلقَه زَفِر وَيفَشِّر هوايَة [ħalgah zafir wyfaššir hwaːya] His mouth is filthy and he curses people a lot. تِفلَت بوجهَه لِأنّ فَشَّر عَليها [tiflat bwiččah liʔann faššar ʕaliːha] She spit in his face because he insulted her.

فشار [fšaːr] *n:* • **1.** profanity, cursing, off-color insults

فَشُّورَة [faššuːra] *n:* فَشُّورات [faššuːraːt] *pl:* • **1.** off-color word or phrase

ف ش س ت

فاشِستِي [faːšisti] *adj:* • **1.** fascist, fascistic • **2.** a fascist فاشِستِيَّة [faːšistiyya] n: • **1.** fascism

ف ش ش

فَشّ [fašš] *v:* • **1.** to cause to go down, to deflate – هَالدُّوا يفِشّ الوَرَم [hadduwaː yfišš ʔilwarum]

This medication will reduce the swelling.
فِشّ الجُوب قَبُل ما تلِحمَه [fišš ʔiččuːb gabul maː tliħmah] Deflate the tube before you patch it. • **2.** to go down, deflate – النُّفّاخَة انزُرفَت وَفَشَّت [ʔinnuffaːxa ʔinzurfat wfaššat] The balloon got a hole in it and deflated. • **3.** to shrink back, subside, be deflated – مِن تصِيح بوجهَه، يفِشّ [min tṣiːħ bwiččah, yfišš] When you yell in his face, he becomes timid.
فَشّ [fašš] *n:* • **1.** act of deflating, going flat
مفشُوش [mafšuːš] *adj:* • **1.** deflated, emptied, exhausted of air
فاشُوش [faːšuːš] *adj:* • **1.** worthless, (figuratively) empty

ف ش ف ش

فِشافِيش [fišaːfiːš, fašaːfiːš] *n:* • **1.** (invar.) liver broiled on a skewer

ف ش ق 1

فِشقِي [fišqi] *n:* • **1.** horse manure (when used for fertilizer)

ف ش ق 2

فِشَق [fišag] *v:* • **1.** to cut in two, split in two, halve – فِشَق اللّوحَة بِالفاس [fišag ʔilluːħa bilfaːs] He split the board with the adze.
فَشَّق [faššag] *v:* • **1.** intens. of فِشَق to cut in two, split in two, halve – فَشِّق الرَّقّي وَخَلِّيه بِالصُّوانِي [faššig ʔirraggi wxalliːh biṣṣuwaːni] Halve the watermelons and put them on the trays. فَشِّق الكَرَب حَتَّى نشِعلَه [faššig ʔilkarab ħatta nšiʕlah] Split up the palm stems so we can burn them.
فَشِق [fašig] *n:* • **1.** act of spliting in two
فِشقَة [fišga] *n:* فِشقات، فِشَق [fišgaːt, fišag] *pl:* • **1.** half, a half (of something) • **2.** cartridge, round, bullet

ف ش ل

فِشَل [fišal] *v:* • **1.** to fail, be unsuccessful – فِشَل بِالإمتِحان وَبَطَّل [fišal bilʔimtiħaːn wbaṭṭal] He failed on the exam and quit. • **2.** to be or become embarrassed – فِشَلِت مِن مَجِيد لِأنّ راد مِنِّي دِينار وماعِندِي [fišalit min majiːd liʔann raːd minni dinaːr wmaːʕindi] I was embarrassed by Majid because he wanted to borrow a dinar and I didn't have it.
فَشَّل [faššal] *v:* • **1.** to fail, cause to fail – المُعَلِّم فَشَّلَه بِالإمتِحان [ʔilmuʕallim faššalah bilʔimtiħaːn] The teacher flunked him in the exam. • **2.** to embarrass, ridicule – ما لازِم تفَشّلَه قِدّام النّاس [maː laːzim tfaššlah giddaːm ʔinnaːs] You shouldn't embarrass him in front of people. خَلِّي يِحكِي. لا تفَشّلَه [xalliː yiħči. laː tfaššlah] Let him talk. Don't give him a hard time. يا معَوَّد، إبذِل جَهدَك. لا تفَشِّلنِي [yaː mʕawwad, ʔibðil jahdak. laː tfaššilni] For gosh sakes, exert yourself. Don't disappoint me.
تفَشَّل [tfaššal] *v:* • **1.** to be embarrassed – ما يِتفَشَّل بِالعَجَل [maː yitfaššal bilʕajal] He's not easily embarrassed. تَرَة إذا يِسألُوك، تِتفَشَّل [tara ʔiða yisʔaluːk, titfaššal] I tell you, if they ask you, you will be embarrassed.
تفاشَل [tfaːšal] *v:* • **1.** to embarrass each other, to agitate each other – هاي قَضِيَّة بَسِيطَة ما تِسوَى نِتفاشَل عَليها [haːy qaðiyya basiːṭa maː tiswaː nitfaːšal ʕaliːha] This is a simple matter which isn't worth getting ourselves all in an uproar about.
فَشَل [fašal] *n:* • **1.** failure, fiasco, flop, disappointment
فَشلَة [fašla] *n:* فَشلات [fašlaːt] *pl:* • **1.** embarrassment, disgrace – لازِم تسَلِّم عَليه. فَشلَة [laːzim tsallim ʕaliːh. fašla] You must greet him. It's disgraceful not to.
فاشِل [faːšil] *adj:* • **1.** unsuccessful, failing – مُحاوَلَة فاشلَة [muħaːwala faːšla] an unsuccessful attempt. نداء فاشِل [nidaːʔ faːšil] an uncompleted phone call.
فَشلان [fašlaːn] *adj:* • **1.** embarrassed, unsuccessful

ف ش و

فِشَى [fišaː] *v:* • **1.** with ب to reveal, let out – ما يِفشِي بِأيّ سِرّ حَتَّى لَو تبُسطَه [maː yifši bʔay sirr ħatta law tbusṭah] He won't reveal any secret even if you beat him.
تفَشَّى [tfaššaː] *v:* • **1.** to spread – إذا تفَشَّى المَرَض، مِن الصَّعُب السَّيطَرَة عَليه [ʔiða tfaššaː ʔilmarað, min ʔiṣṣaʕub ʔissayṭara ʕaliːh] If the disease spreads, it'll be hard to control it.
فَشِي [fašy] *n:* • **1.** act of disclosing, divulging, revealing, spreading
تَفَشِّي [tafašši] *n:* • **1.** spreading, outbreak
إفشاء [ʔifšaːʔ] *n:* • **1.** act of disclosing, circulation, revealing, spread

ف ص ح 1

فَصاحَة [faṣaːħa] *n:* • **1.** purity of the language, fluency, eloquence
فَصِيح [faṣiːħ] *adj:* • **1.** pure, classical, literary (language), eloquent – عَرَبِي فَصِيح [ʕarabi faṣiːħ] classical Arabic.
أفصَح [ʔafṣaħ] *comparative adjective:* فُصحَى [fuṣħa] *feminine:* • **1.** more or most classical, literary – الفُصحَى، اللُّغَة الفُصحَى، العَرَبِيَّة الفُصحَى [ʔilfuṣħa, ʔilluga ʔilfuṣħa, ʔilʕarabiyya ʔilfuṣħa] classical Arabic.

ف ص ح 2

فُصِح، عِيد الفُصِح [fuṣiħ, ʕiːd ʔilfuṣiħ] *n:* • **1.** Easter • **2.** Passover

ف ص د

فُصَد [fuṣad] *v:* • **1.** to bleed, perform blood-letting – الطَّبِيب فُصَد العِرق اللّي برِجلِي [ʔiṭṭabiːb fuṣad ʔilʕirig ʔilli brijli] The doctor took some blood out of the vein in my leg.

ف

فَصِد [faṣid] *v:* • **1.** act of bleeding s.o, performing bloodletting

ف ص ص

فُصّ [fuṣṣ] *n:* فصُوص [fṣu:ṣ] *pl:* • **1.** stone (of a ring) • **2.** lump, chunk, clump, glob – فُصّ مِلِح [fuṣṣ miliħ] lump of salt. فُصّ تَمُر [fuṣṣ tamur] chunk of dates.
مفَصّص [mfaṣṣaṣ] *adj:* • **1.** lumpy

ف ص ل

فُصَل [fuṣal] *v:* • **1.** to separate – إذا ما تُفصِل العِجِل عَن أمَّه، ما تحَصِّل حَلِيب [ʔiða ma: tufṣil ʔilʕijil ʕan ʔummah, ma: tħaṣṣil ħali:b] If you don't separate the calf from his mother, you won't get any milk. • **2.** to discharge, dismiss, fire – فِصلوه مِن الوَظِيفَة لِأنّ كان يبُوق [fiṣlawh min ʔilwaðiːfa liʔann ča:n ybu:g] They fired him from the job because he was stealing. • **3.** to ensure a killer's safety by paying the victim's family – فُصلَوا القاتِل بمِيَة دِينار حَتَّى ما يِتعَرِّضُوله [fuṣlaw ʔilka:til bmiyat dina:r ħatta ma: yitʕarriðu:lah] To ensure the killer's safety they paid the victim's family a hundred dinars so they wouldn't hurt him.
فَصَّل [faṣṣal] *v:* • **1.** to cut out, tailor, make to measure – فَصِّل هَالقاط عَلَى قاط أخُويَا [faṣṣil halqa:ṭ ʕala qa:ṭ ʔaxu:ya] Cut this coat like my brother's. فَصَّلِت ساك صُوف عِند الخَيّاط [faṣṣalit sa:k ṣu:f ʕind ʔilxayya:ṭ] I had a woolen jacket made at the tailor's. • **2.** to cut up, cut into sections, cut into pieces – راح أقُصّلَك شوَيَّة لَحَم بَعَد ما أفَصِّل الفُخُذ كُلَّه [ra:ħ ʔaguṣṣlak šwayya laħam baʕad ma: ʔafaṣṣil ʔilfuxuð kullah] I'll cut you some meat after I cut up all this leg. • **3.** to cut up, cut to pieces – قِتَلَه لِعَدُوَّه وفَصَّلَه تَفصِيل [kitalah lʕaduwwah wfaṣṣalah tafṣi:l] He killed his enemy and cut him to pieces.
اِنفُصَل [ʔinfuṣal] *v:* • **1.** to separate oneself, to disassociate oneself, to quit, to leave – عِرَف أغلاط الحِزِب، واِنفُصَل مِنَّه [ʕiraf ʔaɣla:ṭ ʔilħizib, wʔinfuṣal minnah] He realized the party's mistakes, and left it. اِنفُصَل عَنهُم وفِتَح مَخزَن عَلَى بِدَّه [ʔinfuṣal ʕanhum wfitaħ maxzan ʕala biddah] He disassociated himself from them and opened a shop on his own. • **2.** to cut oneself off, isolate onself – تزَوَّج وِحدَة أجنَبِيَّة واِنفُصَل مِن كُلّ أهلَه واصدِقائَه [dzawwaǰ wiħda ʔaǰnabiyya wʔinfuṣal min kull ʔahlah waṣdiqa:ʔah] He married a foreign girl and cut himself off from all his family and friends. • **3.** to be fired, discharged – اِنفُصَلِت مِن وَظِيفتِي لِأنّ اِشتِرَكِت بمُظاهَرات ضِدّ الحُكُومَة [ʔinfuṣalit min waði:fti liʔann ʔištirakit bmuða:hara:t ðidd ʔilħuku:ma] I was sacked from my job because I took part in anti-government demonstrations. • **4.** to be suspended – اِنفُصَل مِن المَدرَسَة إسبُوعَين [ʔinfuṣal min ʔilmadrasa ʔisbu:ʕayn] He was suspended from school for two weeks.
اِفتِصَل [ʔiftiṣal] *v:* • **1.** to settle accounts, to settle up – آني آخُذ حَقِّي وَإنتَ اِفتِصِل وِيّاه [ʔa:ni ʔa:xuð ħaqqi wʔinta ʔiftiṣil wiyya:h] I'll take what's mine and you settle up with him.
فَصِل [faṣil] *n:* • **1.** discharge, dismissal • **2.** wergild, money paid by a killer's family to the victim's family to prevent a blood feud • **3.** (pl. فُصُول) chapter • **4.** season • **5.** term, semester
فَصِيل، فَصِيلَة [faṣi:l, faṣi:la] *n:* فَصايِل، فَصائل [faṣa:yil, faṣa:ʔil] *pl:* • **1.** platoon, squadron
مَفصَل [mafṣal] *n:* مَفاصِل [mafa:ṣil] *pl:* • **1.** joint, articulation – مَفصَل إيد [mafṣal ʔi:d] knuckle. مَفصَل القُصبَة [mafṣal ʔilguṣba] section of bamboo.
فصال [fṣa:l] *n:* • **1.** cutting, cutting out • **2.** cut (of a garment) • **3.** argumentative discussion
تفصِيل [tafṣi:l] *n:* تَفاصِيل [tafa:ṣi:l] *pl:* • **1.** cut (of a garment) • **2.** detail, بالتَّفصِيل [bittafṣi:l] in detail
تفصال [tifṣa:l] *n:* • **1.** design, style, cut (of a garment)
فَصلِي [faṣli] *adj:* • **1.** term, semester – اِمتِحان فَصلِي [ʔimtiħa:n faṣli] semester exam, final exam.
فاصِل [fa:ṣil] *adj:* • **1.** separatory, separating, dividing, conclusive, decisive • **2.** بلا فاصِل [bila fa:ṣil] without interruption
مُفَصَّل [mufaṣṣal] *adj:* • **1.** detailed
مَفصُول [mafṣu:l] *adj:* • **1.** detached, separated, disconnected, dismissed
منفصِل [minfiṣil] *adj:* • **1.** separated, isolated
تَفصِيلِي [tafṣi:li] *adj:* • **1.** main, detailed
تَفصِيلِياً [tafṣi:liyyan] *adverbial:* • **1.** in detail, elaborately, minutely, circumstantially

ف ص و ل

فاصُولِيَا، فاصُولِيَّة [fa:ṣu:lya, fa:ṣu:liyya] *n:* فاصُولِيّات [fa:ṣu:liyya:t] *pl:* • **1.** (coll.) bean(s)

ف ض ح

فُضَح [fuðaħ] *v:* • **1.** to expose, to disclose or uncover someone's faults or offenses – الجَّرِيدَة فُضحَتهُم [ʔiǰǰari:da fuðħathum] The newspaper exposed them.
اِنفُضَح [ʔinfuðaħ] *v:* • **1.** to be exposed, to be shamed, to be humiliated
اِفتِضح [ʔiftiðiħ] *v:* • **1.** to come to light, to be made public – هَالحَرامِيَّة اِفتِضَح أمُرهُم بِالعَجَل [halħara:miyya ʔiftiðaħ ʔamurhum bilʕaǰal] Those criminals' racket was exposed quickly.
فَضِح [faðiħ] *n:* • **1.** exposure, humiliation, disgracing, dishonoring
فَضِيحَة [faði:ħa] *n:* فَضايِح [faða:yiħ] *pl:* • **1.** scandal, disgrace, dishonor
مَفضُوح [mafðu:ħ] *adj:* • **1.** exposed, compromised • **2.** covered with shame, dishonored, infamous • **3.** embarrassing

ف

ف ض ض

فَضّ [faðð] *v:* • **1.** to finish up, conclude – تِقدَر تفُضّلِي هَالقَضِيَّة بِالعَجَل، رَجاءاً؟ [tigdar tfuððli halqaðiyya bilʕajal, raja:ʔan?] Can you finish this matter up for me quickly, please? فُضّنِي. أرِيد أرُوح [fuððni. ʔari:d ʔaru:ħ] Finish my business. I want to go. • **2.** to solve, settle – فَضّ المُشكِلَة مالتِي بِالعَجَل [faðð ʔilmuškila ma:lti bilʕajal] He solved my problem quickly.

اِنفَضّ [ʔinfaðð] *v:* • **1.** to be solved, settled – هَالقَضِيَّة ما تِنفَضّ إلّا إذا تِحكِي ويّا المُدِير [halqaðiyya ma: tinfaðð ʔilla ʔiða tiħči wiyya ʔilmudi:r] This problem can't be solved unless you talk with the director. • **2.** to be adjourned, concluded, closed – الاجتِماع اِنفَضّ بَعَد ساعتِين [ʔilʔijtima:ʕ ʔinfaðð baʕad sa:ʕtayn] The meeting was adjourned after two hours. اِنفَضَّت الجَّلسَة بِدُون قَرار [ʔinfaððat ʔijjalsa bidu:n qara:r] The session was adjourned without a decision.

اِفتَضّ [ʔiftaðð] *v:* • **1.** فَضّ, اِفتَضّ with بَكارَة to deflower

فَضّ [faðð] *n:* • **1.** opening, breaking, undoing

فُضَّة [fuðða] *n:* • **1.** silver

فُضّي [fuðði] *n:* • **1.** silver, silvery – صِينِيَّة فُضِّيَّة [ṣi:niyya fuððiyya] a silver tray. لُون فُضّي [lu:n fuðði] silver color.

ف ض ل

فُضَل [fuḍal] *v:* • **1.** to be left over, remain – فُضَل عِندِي دِينار واحِد [fuḍal ʕindi dina:r wa:ħid] I only have one dinar left. بَعَد العَزِيمَة، فُضَل أكِل هوايَة [baʕad ʔilʕazi:ma, fuḍal ʔakil hwa:ya] After the banquet, a lot of food was left over.

فَضَّل [faððal] *v:* • **1.** to prefer – أفَضّل السَّفَر بِالقِطار عَلَى السَّفَر بِالطَّيّارَة [ʔafaððil ʔissafar bilqiṭa:r ʕala ʔissafar biṭṭayya:ra] I prefer traveling by train to traveling by plane. أفَضّل أجَدّي مِن أن أشتُغُل قَوّاد [ʔafaððil ʔagaddi min ʔan ʔaštuɣul gawwa:d] I prefer to beg rather than work as a pimp. • **2.** to allow to remain, leave, leave behind, leave over – بَعَد ما ياكُل، يفَضّل هوايَة [baʕad ma: ya:kul, yfaððil hwa:ya] After he eats, he leaves a lot.

فاضَل [fa:ðal] *v:* • **1.** with بين to compare – إذا تفاضِل بينهُم، أعتِقِد تاخُذ الكِبِيرَة [ʔiða tfa:ðil bi:nhum, ʔaʕtiqid ta:xuð ʔiččibi:ra] If you compare them, I think you'll take the big one.

تفَضَّل [tfaððal] *v:* • **1.** (as imperative, approx.:) please, feel free, be my guest, go ahead, come in – تفَضَّل. اِستَعمِل القَلَم مالِي [tfaððal. ʔistaʕmil ʔilqalam ma:li] Go ahead. Use my pencil. الأكِل حاضِر؛ تفَضّلُوا [ʔilʔakil ħa:ðir; tfaððlu:] The food's ready; help yourselves. تفَضَّل، إشرَب قَهوَة [tfaððal, ʔišrab gahwa] Here, have some coffee. الباب مَفكُوك؛ تفَضَّل [ʔilba:b mafku:k; tfaððal] The door's open; come on in. • **2.** with عَلَى to honor, favor – يِمكِن تِتفَضَّل عَلينا بِالزِّيارَة؟ [yimkin titfaððal ʕali:na bizziya:ra?] Would you be kind enough to honor us with a visit?

تفاضَل [tfa:ðal] *v:* • **1.** to take liberties, behave incorrectly – هَذا الرِّجّال تفاضَل بِيّا [ha:ða ʔirrijja:l tfa:ðal biyya] That man made a pass at me. ما لازِم تِتفاضَل بِفلُوس غيرَك [ma: la:zim titfa:ðal bflu:s ɣi:rak] You shouldn't take liberties with other people's money.

فَضِل [faðil] *n:* أفضال [ʔafða:l] *pl:* • **1.** favor – تِقدَر تسَوِّي فَضِل عَلَيّا وَجِيبلِي قَمِيص ويّاك؟ [tigdar tsawwi: faðil ʕalayya wji:bli qami:ṣ wiyya:k?] Could you do a favor for me and bring me a shirt with you? صاحِب الفَضِل [ṣa:ħib ʔilfaðil] person who has done one a favor. مِن فَضلَك [min faðlak] please.

فَضلَة [faðla] *n:* فَضلات [faðla:t] *pl:* • **1.** remainder, residue, rest, leftover, waste • **2.** busy-body, meddler

فَضِيلَة [faði:la] *n:* فَضايِل [faða:yil] *pl:* • **1.** virtue, merit • **2.** excellence, used preceding the title of sheikh, an official Islamic authority

أفضَلِيَّة [ʔafðaliyya] *n:* • **1.** precedence, priority – هَالمَشرُوع إلَه أفضَلِيَّة عَلَى الكُلّ [halmašru:ʕ ʔilah ʔafðaliyya ʕala ʔilkull] This project takes precedence over all others.

فاضِل [fa:ðil] *adj:* • **1.** remaining, left – فلُوس فَضلَة [flu:s fa:ðla] remaining money. • **2.** eminent, distinguished, respected – رِجّال فاضِل [rijja:l fa:ðil] man of culture and refinement.

مُفَضَّل [mufaððal] *adj:* • **1.** preferred, favored

فُضُولِي [fuðu:li] *adj:* • **1.** nosy, curious, inquisitive

أفضَل [ʔafðal] *comparative adjective:* • **1.** more or most desirable

ف ض و

فَضاء [faða:ʔ] *n:* • **1.** space, cosmos – رائِد الفَضاء [ra:ʔid ʔilfaða:ʔ] astronaut, cosmonaut.

فَضوَة [faðwa] *n:* فَضوات [faðwa:t] *pl:* • **1.** open space, open area, square

فاضِي [fa:ði] *adj:* • **1.** empty, vacant – مُكان فاضِي [muka:n fa:ði] a vacant seat.

ف ط ر

فُطَر [fuṭar] *v:* • **1.** to crack – الزِّلزال فُطَر حِيطان البيُوت [ʔizzilza:l fuṭar ħi:ṭa:n ʔilbyu:t] The earthquake cracked the walls of the houses. • **2.** to break one's fast, eat and drink after a fast – الصّايِم فُطَر عَلَى شُوربَة بَسّ [ʔiṣṣa:yim fuṭar ʕala šu:rba bass] The faster broke his fast on just soup. نصُوم، وَنُفطُر عَلَى جِرِّيَّة [nṣu:m, wnufṭur ʕala jirriyya] We work and save and nothing works out (lit., we fast, and then break our fast with catfish).

فَطَّر [faṭṭar] *v:* • **1.** intens. of فُطَر to crack, to break one's fast, eat and drink after a fast – المَيّ الحارّ فَطَّر كُلّ الكوابَة [ʔilmayy ʔilħa:rr faṭṭar kull ʔilkwa:ba] The hot water cracked all the cups. • **2.** to allow someone to break

his fast – الطَّبِيب فَطَّرَه بِسَبَب صِحّتَه [ʔiṭṭabiːb faṭṭarah bsabab ṣiħħtah] The doctor excused him from fasting because of his health.
تفَطَّر [tfaṭṭar] *v:* • **1.** to be cracked, be split, be broken – صَبَّت الشّبِنتُو تفَطِّرَت لِأَنّ كان أَكُو نُوا بِيها [ṣabbat ʔiččbintu tfaṭṭirat liʔann čaːn ʔaku nuwa biːha] The cement form cracked because there were some date pits in it.
اِنفُطَر [ʔinfuṭar] *v:* • **1.** to be cracked, be split, be broken – اِنفُطَر راسِي مِن الوُجَع [ʔinfuṭar raːsi min ʔilwujaʕ] I had a splitting headache.
فَطِر [faṭir] *n:* فطُور [fṭuːr] *pl:* • **1.** crack, split, rupture, fissure, cleavage
فِطِر، عِيد الفِطِر [fiṭir, ʕiːd ʔilfiṭir] *n:* • **1.** Lesser Bairam, feast at the end of Ramadan, breaking the fast
فطِرّ [fṭirr] *n:* • **1.** (coll.) mushroom(s)
فِطرَة [fiṭra] *n:* • **1.** nature, instinct – الطِّفِل يحِبّ أُمَّه بالفِطرَة [ʔiṭṭifil yħibb ʔummah bilfiṭra] A child loves his mother instinctively. البَدو بَعَدهُم عالفِطرَة [ʔilbadw baʕadhum ʕalfiṭra] The Bedouins are still unspoiled. • **2.** بالفِطرَة by nature, by instinct, instinctively • **3.** (pl. فِطرات) obligation incurred by failing to observe the fast during Ramadan, repaid by fasting or by giving alms
فطُور [fṭuːr] *n:* • **1.** breaking one's fast at sundown during Ramadan • **2.** pl. the first meal after the daily fast in Ramadan
فطِرَّة [fṭirra] *n:* فطِرّات [fṭirraːt] *pl:* • **1.** mushroom
فَطارَة [faṭaːra] *n:* فَطارات [faṭaːraːt] *pl:* • **1.** nonsense, idiocy, rubbish
إفطار [ʔifṭaːr] *n:* • **1.** act of breaking the fast during the month of Ramadan
فُطِير، فطِير [fuṭiːr, fṭiːr] *adj:* • **1.** unleavened – خُبُز فُطِير [xubuz fuṭiːr] unleavened bread, also, bread baked before having time to rise. • **2.** unripe, green – رَقِّيَّة فُطِيرَة [raggiyya fuṭiːra] an unripe watermelon. • **3.** dope, jerk • **4.** pl. فُطّار foolish, silly, dopey, childish
مُفطِر [mufṭir] *adj:* مُفطِرِين، مُفاطِير [mufṭiriːn, mufaːṭiːr] *pl:* • **1.** person who does not observe a fast
مفَطَّر [mfaṭṭar] *adj:* • **1.** cracked
مَفطُور [mafṭuːr] *adj:* • **1.** cracked
أَفطَر [ʔafṭar] *comparative adjective:* • **1.** more or most foolish, childish

ف ط س

فُطَس [fuṭas] *v:* • **1.** (contemptuous) to die – المُجرِم فُطَس وَخلَصنا مِنَّه [ʔilmujrim fuṭas wxlaṣna minnah] The criminal died and we were rid of him. فُطَسنا مِن الضِّحِك [fuṭasna min ʔiððiħik] We nearly died laughing.
فَطَّس [faṭṭas] *v:* • **1.** to slaughter, slay – لا تِتحارَش بِيه تَرَة يفَطِّسَك [laː titħaːraš biːh tara yfaṭṭisak] Don't provoke him or he'll slaughter you. شِفنا فِلِم فَطَّسنا مِن الضِّحِك [šifna filim faṭṭasna min ʔiððiħik] We saw a film that really slew us.
فَطِس [faṭis] *n:* • **1.** (contemptuous) death
فَطِيسَة [fuṭiːsa] *n:* فَطايِس [fuṭaːyis] *pl:* • **1.** dead animal, animal carcass, carrion
أَفطَس [ʔafṭas] *adj:* • **1.** flat and wide (nose) – خَشِم أفطَس [xašim ʔafṭas] a flat nose. واحِد أفطَس [waːħid ʔafṭas] person with a flat nose.

ف ط ف ط

فَطفَط [faṭfaṭ] *v:* • **1.** to gurgle, bubble, make a sucking noise – مِن يحكِي، يظِلّ التِّفال يفَطفُط مِن حَلقَه [min yiħči, yðill ʔittifaːl yfaṭfuṭ min ħalgah] When he talks, the saliva bubbles from his mouth. • **2.** to decompose, rot (fish) – الحَرّ فَطفَط السِّمَك [ʔilħarr faṭfaṭ ʔissimač] The heat decomposed the fish.
مفَطفُط [mfaṭfuṭ] *adj:* • **1.** decomposed, rotted – سِمَك مفَطفُط [simač mfaṭfuṭ] rotted fish.

ف ط م

فُطَم [fuṭam] *v:* • **1.** to wean – راح تُفطُم إبنها بَعَد كَم يوم [raːħ tufṭum ʔibinha baʕad čam yuːm] She will wean her son in a few days.
فَطُم، فِطام [faṭum, fiṭaːm] *n:* • **1.** weaning

ف ط ن

فُطَن [fuṭan] *v:* • **1.** with عَلَى to be aware of, notice – هَالجّاهِل يِفطُن عَلَى كُلشِي [hajjaːhil yifṭun ʕala kullši] That kid notices everything. ما دَيِفطُن عَلَى اللّي دَأقُولَه [maː dayifṭun ʕala ʔilli daʔaguːlah] He isn't aware of what I am talking about. • **2.** to recall, remember – لهَسَّة يِفطُن عَلَى زَمَن الحَرب [lhassa yifṭun ʕala zaman ʔilħarb] He still recalls the time of the war.
فِطَن [fiṭan] *v:* • **1.** to grasp, to comprehend, to realize, become aware
فَطَّن [faṭṭan] *v:* • **1.** to remind, to make s.o realize, understand – أرجُوك باكِر فَطِّنِّي عَليها [ʔarjuːk baːčir faṭṭinni ʕaliːha] Please remind me of it tomorrow.
تفَطَّن [tfaṭṭan] *v:* • **1.** to think, to think back, to try to recall – تفَطَّن! بَلكِي تِلقِي واحِد يدايِنِّي [tfaṭṭan! balki tilgi waːħid ydaːyinni] Think! Maybe you can find someone to lend me money.
فَطِين [faṭiːn] *adj:* • **1.** clever, smart, bright, intelligent

ف ظ ع

فَظاعَة [faðaːʕa] *n:* • **1.** ugliness, abominableness, atrocity, horridness
فَظِيع [faðiːʕ] *adj:* • **1.** abominable, hideous, repulsive, disgusting, heinous, atrocious, horrid, horrible – جَرائِم فَظِيعَة [jaraːʔim faðiːʕa] hideous crimes.
أَفظَع [ʔafðaʕ] *comparative adjective:* • **1.** more or most hideous, disgusting, horrible

ف ع ص

فْعَص [fuʕaṣ] *v:* • **1.** to dent – داس عاللّعّابَة وَفْعَصها [daːs ʕallaʕʕaːba wfuʕaṣha] He stepped on the doll and dented it.
فَعَص [faʕaṣ] *n:* • **1.** dent
فَعصَة [faʕṣa] *n:* فَعصات [faʕṣaːt] *pl:* • **1.** a dent

ف ع ل

فِعَل [fiʕal] *v:* • **1.** to do, act, perform some activity
تفاعَل [tfaːʕal] *v:* • **1.** to react, combine – الذَّهَب ما يِتفاعَل ويّا الحامُض [ʔiððahab maː yitfaːʕal wiyya ʔilħaːmuð̣] Gold doesn't react with acid.
اِنفِعَل [ʔinfiʕal] *v:* • **1.** to be or become excited, agitated, upset – ماكُو داعِي تِنفِعِل. آنِي شقِلِت؟ [maːku daːʕi tinfiʕil. ʔaːni šgilit?] There's no reason to get excited. What did I say?
فِعِل [fiʕil] *n:* أَفعال [ʔafʕaːl] *pl:* • **1.** act, action, deed • **2.** effect, impact – بالفِعِل! أَحِبهُم كُلِّش زين [bilfiʕil! ʔaħibbhum kulliš ziːn] Yes indeed! I like them very much. قَرَّر يرُوح، وَبالفِعِل، راح [qarrar yiruːħ, wbilfiʕil, raːħ] He decided to go, and sure enough, he did! بالفِعِل، راح وحِكَى ويّاه وَقِبَل [bilfiʕil, raːħ wħičaː wiyyaːh wqibal] Actually, he went and talked with him and he agreed. • **3.** verb (gram.)
مَفعُول [mafʕuːl] *n:* مَفعُولات، مَفاعِيل [mafʕuːlaːt, mafaːʕiːl] *pl:* • **1.** effect, impact • **2.** with به passive participle – إسِم مَفعُول [ʔisim mafʕuːl] passive participle.
تَفاعُل [tafaːʕul] *n:* • **1.** reaction, interaction, interplay
فَعّالِيَّة [faʕʕaːliyya] *n:* فَعّالِيّات، [faʕʕaːliyyaːt] *pl:* • **1.** activity, event
فَعّال [faʕʕaːl] *adj:* • **1.** active, participating – عُضو فَعّال [ʕuð̣w faʕʕaːl] an active member.
فاعِل [faːʕil] *adj:* فاعِلِين، فَواعِل [faːʕiliːn, fauːʕil] *pl:* • **1.** perpetrator • **2.** pl. فَواعِل active subject of a verbal clause – إسِم فاعِل [ʔisim faːʕil] active participle.
فِعلِي [fiʕli] *adj:* • **1.** actual, real
مِنفِعِل [minfiʕil] *adj:* • **1.** irritable • **2.** excited, agitated
فِعلاً [fiʕlan] *adverbial:* • **1.** in effect, actually, really, sure enough • **2.** بِالفِعِل [bilfiʕil] actually, in effect, really – وَفِعلاً، سَجَّل ودِخَل اِمتِحان [wfiʕlan, sajjal wdixal ʔimtiħaːn] Actually, he registered and took an exam.

ف ف و ن

فافُون [faːfuːn] *n:* • **1.** aluminum – طاسَة فافُون [ṭaːsa faːfuːn] an aluminum bowl.

ف ق د

فُقَد [fuqad] *v:* • **1.** to lose – فُقَد ساعتَه بِالسِّينَما [fuqad saːʕtah bissinama] He lost his watch in the movie. أَيّ شِي تخَلِّيه بِالمَيّ يُفقُد شوَيَّة مِن وَزنَه [ʔayy ši txalliːh bilmayy yufqud šwayya min waznah] Anything you put in water loses a little of its weight. فُقَد شعُورَه وَقام يِحكِي مِثِل المخابِيل [fuqad šuʕuːrah wgaːm yiħči miθl ʔilmxaːbiːl] He lost his senses and began talking crazily. ما يبَطِّل الشُّرُب إلَى أَن يِفقِد [maː ybaṭṭil ʔaššurub ʔila ʔan yifqid] He doesn't stop drinking till he loses consciousness.
تفَقَّد [tfaqqad] *v:* • **1.** to keep up on, keep up with, keep tabs on, keep in touch with, show concern for – دائِماً يِتفَقَّد أَصدِقائَه [daːʔiman yitfaqqad ʔaṣdiqaːʔah] He always shows concern for his friends.
اِنفُقَد [ʔinfuqad] *v:* • **1.** to be or become lost – اِنفُقَد مِنَّك شِي بالسُّوق؟ [ʔinfuqad minnak ši bissuːg?] Did you lose anything in the market place?
اِفتِقَد [ʔiftiqad] *v:* • **1.** to miss – اِفتِقدُوه كُلّ أَصدِقائَه مِن سافَر [ʔiftiqduːh kull ʔaṣdiqaːʔah min saːfar] All his friends missed him when he went away. اِفتِقَدناه بوَقِت حَرِج [ʔiftiqadnaːh bwaqit ħarij] We missed him at a crucial time.
فَقِد [faqid] *n:* • **1.** loss, bereavement
فَقِيد [faqiːd] *n:* • **1.** deceased, dead • **2.** dead man
تَفَقُّد [tafaqqud] *n:* • **1.** check, inspection, visit
فُقدان [fuqdaːn] *n:* • **1.** loss (of something)
تَفَقُّدِيَّة [tafaqqudiyya] *n:* • **1.** inspectorate
فَقدِي [faqdi] *adj:* • **1.** credit – هَالبَقّال يبِيع بِالنَّقدِي والفَقدِ [halbaggaːl yibiːʕ binnaqdi wilfaqdi] This grocer sells for cash and credit.
فاقِد [faːqid] *adj:* • **1.** devoid, destitute, deprived – فاقِد الشُّعُور، فاقِد الإحساس [faːqid ʔiššuʕuːr, faːqid ʔilʔiħsaːs] unconscious.
مَفقُود [mafquːd] *adj:* مَفقُودات [mafquːdaːt] *pl:* • **1.** lost, lacking, wanting, missing person

ف ق ر

فُقَر [fugar] *v:* • **1.** to jinx, to bring bad luck – فُقَرتنِي بِحَكيَك وخَلَّيتنِي أَخسَر [fugaritni bħačyak wxalliːtni ʔaxsar] You put a jinx on me with what you said and made me lose.
فَقَّر [faqqar] *v:* • **1.** to make poor, impoverish – زَوجتَه فَقَّرَته بِمَصارِيفها الهِوايَة [zawijtah faqqratah bmaṣaːriːfha ʔilhwaːya] His wife made him poor with her large expenditures.
اِفتِقَر [ʔiftiqar] *v:* • **1.** with ل to need, lack, require, be in need of – هَالمَعمَل يِفتِقِر إلَى عُمّال ماهرِين [hallmaʕmal yiftiqir ʔila ʕummaːl maːhriːn] This factory is in need of skilled workers.
فُقِر، [fuqir] *n:* • **1.** need, lack, want فُقر دَمّ [fuqr damm] anemia
فُقُر [fuqur] *n:* • **1.** poverty
فُقُر [fugur] *n:* • **1.** (invar.) poor – كُلّنا فُقُر وَما عِدنا سَيّارات [kullna fugur wma ʕidna sayyaːraːt] We are all poor and we don't have cars.
فَقِر [fagir] *n:* • **1.** bad luck, jinx
فَقَرَة [faqara] *n:* فَقَرات [faqaraːt] *pl:* • **1.** vertebra • **2.** section, paragraph

اِفتِقار [ʔiftiqa:r] *n:* • **1.** need, requirement, lack (of), want

فَقَري [faqari] *adj:* • **1.** spinal, vertebral, – عَمُود فَقَري [ʕamu:d faqari] spinal column. حَيوان فَقَري [ħaywa:n faqari] vertebrate.

فَقِير [faqi:r] *adj:* فُقَراء، فُقرَة [fuqara:ʔ, fuqra] *pl:* • **1.** poor, poverty stricken • **2.** quiet, gentle, well-mannered, nice

أَفقَر [ʔafqar] *comparative adjective:* • **1.** poorer, poorest

ف ق س

فُقَس [fugas] *v:* • **1.** to hatch – بَعَد يومَين وَتُفقُس البَيضَة [baʕad yu:mayn wtufgus ʔilbayð̣a] Two more days and the egg will hatch. • **2.** to fall through, fail, fail to work – قَضِيتَك فُقسَت [qað̣i:tak fugsat] Your case didn't pan out. • **3.** to ruin, wreck, mess up – بِحكايتَه، فُقَسها لِلقَضِيَّة [biħča:ytah, fugasha lilqað̣iyya] By his remark he threw a monkey wrench into the case. فُقَسها غير فَقسَة [fugasha ɣi:r fagsa] He really messed it up good. إذا ما تِنطِينِي فلُوسِي أَفقُس عينَك وَأَخُذها [ʔiða ma: tinṭi:ni flu:si ʔafgus ʕaynak wʔa:xuðha] If you don't give me my money, I'll claw your eyes out and take it.

فَقَّس [faggas] *v:* • **1.** to hatch • **2.** to ruin, wreck, mess up • **3.** to fall through, fail, fail to work

فَقِس [fagis] *n:* • **1.** hatching • **2.** failing, failure

مَفقَس [mafqas] *n:* مَفاقِس [mafa:qis] *pl:* • **1.** incubator

ف ق ط

فَقَط [faqaṭ] *adv:* • **1.** only – أَرِيد باكَيت واحِد فَقَط [ʔari:d pa:ki:t wa:ħid faqaṭ] I want only one package. هَالجِّسر لِلسَّيّارات فَقَط [hajjisir lissayya:ra:t faqaṭ] This bridge is for cars only.

ف ق ع

فُقّاعَة [fuqqa:ʕa] *n:* فُقّاعات [fuqqa:ʕa:t] *pl:* • **1.** bubble

ف ق م

تفاقَم [tfa:qam] *v:* • **1.** to become grave, serious

فَقمَة [faqma] *n:* فقمات [faqma:t] *pl:* • **1.** seal (zool.)

تَفاقُم [tafa:qum] *n:* • **1.** aggravation, increasing gravity

ف ق ه

فِقه [fiqih] *n:* • **1.** systematic theology (Islam)

فَقِيه [faqi:h] *n:* فُقَهاء [fuqaha:ʔ] *pl:* • **1.** theologian, expert and scholar on فِقه [fiqh]

ف ك ر

فَكَّر [fakkar] *v:* • **1.** to reflect, meditate, think over, contemplate, consider – لا تفَكِّر. هَذِي خُوش شَروَة [la: tfakkir. ha:ði xu:š šarwa] Don't think it over. This is a good buy. إذا تفَكِّر زين، تِقدَر تحِلّ المَسأَلَة [ʔiða tfakkir zi:n, tigdar tħill ʔilmasʔala] If you think hard, you can solve the problem.

اِفتِكَر [ʔiftikar] *v:* • **1.** to think, to be of the opinion – أَفتِكِر راح يوصَل باكِر [ʔaftikir ra:ħ yu:ṣal ba:čir] I think he will arrive tomorrow. اِفتِكَرتَك تُعرُف إنكِلِيزِي [ʔiftikartak tuʕruf ʔingili:zi] I had the idea you knew English.

فِكِر [fikir] *n:* • **1.** thinking, reflection, meditation, speculation, contemplation – يَعنِي، شفِكرَك؟ تِتداين وَما تِدفَع؟ [yaʕni, šfikrak? tidda:yan wma tidfaʕ?] Well, what's the big idea? You borrow and don't pay back? خَلِّيه بِفِكرَه. لا تِقتِرِح شِي [xalli:h bfikrah. la: tiqtiriħ ši] Leave him to his own opinion. Don't suggest anything. فِكرَه بِالعَرَق والقمار [fikrah bilʕarag wilqma:r] His mind is on liquor and gambling. لا يضَلّ فِكرَك. لازِم يُوصَل اليُوم [la: yð̣all fikrak. la:zim yu:ṣal ʔilyu:m] Don't worry. He has to arrive today. كُلّ فِكرِي راح يساعِدنا [kull fikri ra:ħ ysa:ʕidna] I really believe he will help us.

فِكرَة [fikra] *n:* فِكرات، فِكِر، أَفكار [fikra:t, fikir, ʔafka:r.] *pl:* • **1.** idea, concept, thought, notion

مُفَكَّرَة [mufakkara] *n:* مُفَكَّرات [mufakkara:t] *pl:* • **1.** notebook, datebook • **2.** diary, journal

تَفكِير [tafki:r] *n:* • **1.** thinking, cogitation, reflection, meditation, contemplation, thought

فِكرِي [fikri] *adj:* • **1.** speculative, mental, requiring thinking – أَسئِلَة فِكرِيَّة [ʔasʔila fikriyya] questions requiring thought.

مُفَكِّر [mufakkir] *n:* • **1.** thinker

ف ك ف ك

فَكفَك [fakfak] *v:* • **1.** to open up – شَكُو عِندَك دَتفَكفُك بِالجِّنَط؟ [šaku ʕindak datfakfuk bijjinaṭ?] Why are you opening up all the suitcases? فَكفَكها لِلسّاعَة وُصلَة وُصلَة وَما قِدَر يعَمُّرها [fakfakha lissa:ʕa wuṣla wuṣla wma gidar yʕammurha] He took the watch all to pieces and couldn't put it back together.

فَكفَكَة [fakfaka] *n:* • **1.** disconnecting, separating

مفَكفَك [mfakfak] *adj:* • **1.** disassembled, disjointed, disconnected

ف ك ك

اِفتَكّ [ʔiftakk] *v:* • **1.** to open, be opened – إدفَع الباب حيل، بَلكِي تِفتَكّ [ʔidfaʕ ʔilba:b ħi:l, balki tiftakk] Push hard on the door and maybe it will open. • **2.** to be released, set free, let go – شوَقِت إبنَك راح يِفتَكّ مِن السِّجِن؟ [šwakit ʔibnak ra:ħ yiftakk min ʔissijin?] When will your son be freed from prison?

فَكّ [fakk] *v:* • **1.** to open (also fig.) – فَكّ الباب وَخَشّ بِالقُبَّة [fakk ʔilba:b wxašš bilgubba] He opened the door and entered the room. فُكّ عينَك زين، تَرَة هَذا يُغُشَّك [fukk ʕaynak zi:n, tara ha:ða yɣuššak] Keep your eyes open, or he'll cheat you. فَكّ دُكّان بِالشّورجَة [fakk dukka:n biššu:rǰa] He opened a shop in the Shorja district. أَيّ ساعَة يفُكّ المَخزَن مالَه؟ [ʔayy sa:ʕa yfukk ʔilmaxzan ma:lah?] What time does he open up his store? فَكّ حِساب بالبَنك [fakk ħisa:b bilbang] He opened an account in the bank. بإقتِراحَك هَذا فَكّيت إلنا فَدّ باب شيسِدّها بَعَد [bʔiqtira:ħak ha:ða fakki:t ʔilna fadd ba:b šysiddha baʕad] With this suggestion of yours, you have started something for us that we can't stop. القَعدَة عَالشَّطّ تفُكّ القَلب [ʔilgaʕda ʕaššatt tfukk ʔilgalub] Sitting by the river is a relaxing experience (lit., opens up the heart). • **2.** to turn on – فَكّ الماي وَفَيَّضها لِلحَدِيقَة [fakk ʔilma:y wfayyaðha lilħadi:qa] He turned on the water and flooded the garden. بالله ما تفُكّ الرّاديُو؟ [ballah ma: tfukk ʔirra:dyu?] Would you please turn on the radio? فُكّ الضَّوَة [fukk ʔiððuwa] Turn on the light. فَكّ عَليه التَّلِفُون وَرَزّلَه [fakk ʕali:h ʔittalifu:n warazzalah] He called him on the phone and bawled him out. • **3.** to untie, unfasten, undo – فُكّ العُقدَة [fukk ʔilʕugda] Undo the knot. فُكّ الحَبِل مِن رِجل الميز [fukk ʔilħabil min rijl ʔilmi:z] Untie the rope from the table leg. فُكّ سِترتَك [fukk sitirtak] Unbutton your jacket. فُكّي الدِّقَم مال ثُوبِك [fukki ʔiddigam ma:l θu:bič] Undo the buttons of your blouse. • **4.** to pull out, remove, loosen – فُكّ البسامِير يَالله تِقدَر تعَدِّل الميز [fukk ʔilbsa:mi:r yallah tigdar tʕaddil ʔilmi:z] Pull the nails out so you can straighten the table. • **5.** to unscrew, loosen – إذا تفُكّ هَالبُرغِي، تِقدَر تشِيل الكَبريتَر [ʔiða tfukk halburɣi, tigdar tši:l ʔilkabri:tar] If you unscrew this screw, you can take the carburetor off. • **6.** to free, set free, let go, release – المَسجُون راح يفُكُّوه باكِر [ʔilmasǰu:n ra:ħ yfukku:h ba:čir] They're going to free the prisoner tomorrow. لَمّا شافَوا ما عَلَيه شِي، فَكُّوه [lamma ša:faw ma: ʕali:h ši, fakku:h] When they saw he had nothing to do with it, they let him go. لا تفُكَّه مِن الوَظِيفَة إلَى أن يِجِي الخَلَف مالَه [la: tfukkah min ʔilwaði:fa ʔila ʔan yiji ʔilxalaf ma:lah] Don't release him from his assignment until his replacement arrives. إذا ترُوح وَما تقُلّه، شِيفُكَّك مِنَّه [ʔiða tru:ħ wma tgullah, šyifukkak minnah] If you go and don't tell him, nothing will save you from him. جُوز مِنَّه؛ لا تفُكّ حَلقَه [ǰu:z minnah; la: tfukk ħalgah] Leave him alone; don't get him started talking. عِندَه أُخت تفُكّ المَصلُوب [ʕindah ʔuxut tfukk ʔilmaşlu:b] He has a sister who is amazingly beautiful (lit., that could release a man condemned to death). فُكّنا! هَذا شمعَلّمَه فرَنسِي؟ [fukkna! ha:ða šmaʕallmah fransi?] Get off our back! What does he know about French? فَكّ ياخَة مِن [fakk ya:xa min] to let go of, get away from, leave alone. صاحِب البَيت ما دَيفُكّ مِنّي ياخَة [şa:ħib ʔilbayt ma: dayfukk minni ya:xa] The landlord won't get off my back (lit. --- won't let go of my collar).

• **7.** to divorce – أعتِقِد راح يفُكّ مَرتَه [ʔaʕtiqid ra:ħ yfukk martah] I think he's going to divorce his wife. • **8.** to leave, go away – مِن يكَلِّب بِيه وُجَع الرّاس ما يفُكَّه أبَداً [min yčallib bi:h wuǰaʕ ʔirra:s ma: yfukkah ʔabadan] When he gets a headache, it never goes away. البَنج فَكَّه [ʔilbanǰ fakka] The anesthetic wore off him. أُخُذ هَالحَبّ حَتّى تفُكَّك السُخُونَة [ʔuxuð halħabb ħatta tfukkak ʔişşuxu:na] Take these pills in order to break the fever. • **9.** to pay off, pay up, settle up – فَكّ الرَّهِن عَلَى بَيتَه [fakk ʔirrahin ʕala baytah] He paid off the mortgage on his house. لا تِشتِرِي شِي بَعَد قَبُل ما تفُكّ ديُونَك [la: tištiri ši baʕad gabul ma: tfukk dyu:nak] Don't buy anything more before you pay off your debts.

فَكَّك [fakkak] *v:* • **1.** to take to pieces, take apart, disassemble – يِقدَر يفَكِّك المَكِينَة وَيشِدّها مِن جِدِيد [yigdar yfakkik ʔilmaki:na wyšiddha min ǰidi:d] He can tear the machine down and put it back together again.

فاكَك [fa:kak] *v:* • **1.** to separate, break up – دِخَل بِيناتهُم وفاكَكهُم [dixal bayna:thum wfa:kakhum] He stepped in between them and separated them.

تفاكَك [tfa:kak] *v:* • **1.** to separate, move apart from each other – ظَلّوا يِتعارکُون عَشِر دَقايِق وَبَعدين تفاكَكَوا مِن كَيفهُم [ðallaw yitʕa:rku:n ʕašir daqa:yiq wbaʕdi:n tfa:kakaw min kayfhum] They kept on fighting for ten minutes and finally separated by themselves. بَعَد ما أنطِيك دِينار يكُون تفاكَكنا [baʕad ma: ʔanţi:k dina:r yku:n tfa:kakna] After I give you a dinar we won't owe each other anything.

انفَكّ [ʔinfakk] *v:* • **1.** to open, be opened – الباب ما تِنفَكّ [ʔilba:b ma: tinfakk] The door won't open. • **2.** to come out, be removed – البُرغِي ما يِنفَكّ بِهَالدَّرنَفِيس [ʔilburɣi ma: yinfakk bhaddarnafi:s] The screw won't come out with this screwdriver. • **3.** to be released, set free, let go – انفَكّ مِن الحَبِس البارحَة [ʔinfakk min ʔilħabis ʔilba:rħa] He was let out of jail yesterday. راح يِنفَكّ مِن الوَظِيفَة باكِر [ra:ħ yinfakk min ʔilwaði:fa ba:čir] He'll be released from the assignment tomorrow. انفَكّ بِمَرتَه غير فَكَّة [ʔinfakk bmartah ɣi:r fakka] He flew off the handle at his wife. مِن قِتلَه، انفَكّ عَليّا وَقام يصَيِّح نُصّ ساعَة [min gitlah, ʔinfakk ʕalayya wga:m yşayyiħ nuşş sa:ʕa] When I told him, he exploded at me and kept shouting a half hour.

فَكّ [fačč] *n:* فكُوك [fču:č] *pl:* • **1.** jaw, jawbone

فَكّ [fakk] *n:* • **1.** opening • **2.** untying • **3.** turning on

فَكَّة [fakka] *n:* فَكّات [fakka:t] *pl:* • **1.** opening, opportunity, break, chance – إذا ما تِنطِينِي فَكَّة، ما راح أقدَر أخَلِّص [ʔiða ma: tinţi:ni fakka, ma: ra:ħ ʔagdar ʔaxalliş] If you don't let me alone for a minute, I won't be able to finish.

مَفَكَّة [mafakka] *n:* • **1.** a rest, a moment's peace – ما نطانا مَفَكَّة حَتّى أخَذها [ma: nţa:na mafakka ħatta ʔaxaðha] He didn't give us any reprieve until he got it.

فكاكَة [fka:ka] *n:* • **1.** loose, slack – حَلقَه فكاكَة [ħalgah fka:ka] His mouth is slack. حَكيَه فكاكَة [ħačyah fka:ka] His speech is sloppy.
مَفكُوك [mafku:k] *adj:* • **1.** loose – بُرغِي مَفكُوك [burɣi mafku:k] a loose screw. شبيه دَيمشِي هَالشِّكِل؟ بَرَاغِيه مَفكُوكَة؟ [šbi:h dayimši haššikil? bara:ɣi:h mafku:ka?] What's wrong with him, walking that way? Is he falling apart?

ف ك ه
فُكاهَة [fuka:ha] *n:* فُكاهات [fuka:ha:t] *pl:* • **1.** joking, fun-making, jesting
فاكِهَة [fa:kiha] *n:* فَواكِه [fawa:kih] *pl:* • **1.** fruit
فُكاهِي [fuka:hi] *adj:* • **1.** comical • **2.** humorous

ف ل ت 1
فِلَت [filat] *v:* • **1.** to get loose, come loose, get away, escape – فِلَت العَصفُور مِن إيد الجَاهِل [filat ʔilʕaṣfu:r min ʔi:d ʔiǰǰa:hil] The sparrow slipped out of the child's hand. شِدّ الحَبِل زين حَتَّى ما يِفلِت [šidd ʔilħabil zi:n ħatta ma: yiflit] Tie the rope well so it won't come loose.
فَلَّت [fallat] *v:* • **1.** with نفس to get free, free, loose – فَلَّت نَفسَه مِن يِدَّين الشُّرطَة [fallat nafsah min yiddayn ʔiššurṭa] He wrested himself from the hands of the police.
فِلِت، فليت [filit, fli:t] *n:* • **1.** insecticide, bug spray
فَلِت [falit] *n:* • **1.** escaping, getting loose
فَلتَة [falta] *n:* فَلتات [falta:t] *pl:* • **1.** slip, oversight, error – فَلتَة لِسان [faltat lisa:n] a slip of the tongue. • **2.** freak • **3.** extraordinary, exceptional person
فالِت [fa:lit] *adj:* • **1.** loose, escaping
فَلتان [falta:n] *adj:* • **1.** loose, escaped

ف ل ت 2
فلات [fla:t] *adj:* • **1.** flat, out of control

ف ل ت 3
فولت [fu:lt] *n:* • **1.** volt

ف ل ت 4
فالتُون [fa:ltu:n] *n:* • **1.** chaos

ف ل ت ن
فِلتان [filta:n] *n:* • **1.** see فلان: so-and-so, particular person not needing to be specified.

ف ل ج
فالَج [fa:laǰ, fa:liǰ] *n:* • **1.** semiparalysis

ف ل ح
فِلَح [filaħ] *v:* • **1.** to plow, till, cultivate – راح يِفلَح وُصلَة القاع مالتَه [ra:ħ yiflaħ wuṣlat ʔilga:ʕ ma:ltah] He is going to cultivate his piece of land. • **2.** to prosper, thrive – اللّي يِعتِمِد عَلَى الله يِفلَح [ʔilli yiʕtimid ʕala ʔallah yiflaħ] He who depends on Allah prospers.
فَلِح [faliħ] *n:* • **1.** cultivation, tillage
فَلّاح [falla:ħ] *n:* فَلّاحِين، فلالِيح [falla:ħi:n, fla:li:ħ] *pl:* • **1.** farmer, peasant, fellah
فَلاح [fala:ħ] *n:* • **1.** prosperity, success, salvation, welfare
فلاحَة [fla:ħa] *n:* • **1.** cultivation, tillage – لا تاخُذنا فلاحَة ملاكَة. خَلِّي نِحكِي [la: ta:xuðna fla:ħa mla:ča. xalli: niħči] Don't monopolize everything. Let us talk.
فالِح [fa:liħ] *adj:* • **1.** lucky, successful
فَلّاحِي [falla:ħi] *adj:* • **1.** agricultural, rustic

ف ل ز
فِلِزّ [filizz] *n:* فِلِزّات [filizza:t] *pl:* • **1.** (nonprecious) metal

ف ل س
فَلَّس [fallas] *v:* • **1.** to be or become broke, go broke – ما أقدَر أداينَك --- فَلَّسِت [ma: ʔagdar ʔada:ynak fallasit] I can't loan you anything --- I'm flat broke. • **2.** to shell (beans or peas) – فَلِّس الباقِلَّة وحُطّها بِالجِّدِر [fallis ʔilba:gilla wħuṭṭha bǰǰidir] Shell the horse beans and put them in the pot.
اِستَفلَس [ʔistaflas] *v:* • **1.** to go broke – اِستَفلَس وَباع سَيّارتَه [ʔistaflas wba:ʕ sayya:rtah] He ran out of money and sold his car.
فِلِس [filis] *n:* فلاس، فِلسان [fla:s, filsa:n] *pl:* • **1.** one fils coin • **2.** (fish) scales
فلُوس [flu:s] *n:* • **1.** money • **2.** pl. of فِلِس [fils] 1/1000 dinar
إفلاس [ʔifla:s] *n:* • **1.** bankruptcy, insolvency
تَفلِيس [tafli:s] *n:* • **1.** going broke, declaration of bankruptcy
فلَيسات [flaysa:t] *n:* • **1.** money
مِفلِس [miflis] *adj:* مَفالِيس [mafa:li:s] *pl:* • **1.** bankrupt, insolvent, broke – شَرِكَة مِفلِسَة [šarika miflisa] an insolvent company. آنِي مِفلِس اليُوم [ʔa:ni miflis ʔilyu:m] I'm broke today.
مفَلِّس [mfallis] *adj:* • **1.** bankrupt, insolvent, broke
فلَيس، أَبُو فلَيس [flays, ʔabu flays] *adj:* (a small filis) • **1.** greedy • **2.** miserly, stingy

ف ل س ط ي ن
فَلَسطِين [falasṭi:n] *n:* • **1.** Palestine
فَلَسطِينِي [falasṭi:ni] *adj:* • **1.** Palestinian • **2.** a Palestinian

ف ل س ف
تفَلسَف [tfalsaf] *v:* • **1.** to philosophize, to pretend to be a philosopher – يِتفَلسَف بِحَكيَه [yitfalsaf bħačyah] He

philosophizes in his talk. لا تِتفَلسَف بِراسِي [laː titfalsaf braːsi] Don't pretend to be such a philosopher with me. Don't give me any of your guff.
فَلسَفَة [falsafa] *n:* • **1.** philosophy
فَيلَسُوف [faylasuːf] *n:* فَلاسِفَة [falaːsifa] *pl:* • **1.** philosopher
فَلسَفِي [falsafi] *adj:* • **1.** philosophical

ف ل ش 1

فَلَّش [fallaš] *v:* • **1.** to tear down, demolish – البَلَدِيَّة فَلَّشَت أَربَع دكاكِين [ʔilbaladiyya fallišat ʔarbaʕ dkaːkiːn] The city tore down four shops.
تفَلَّش [tfallaš] *v:* • **1.** to be torn down, demolished – هالبِناية راح تِتفَلَّش [halbinaːya raːħ titfallaš] This building's going to be torn down. • **2.** to be dissolved, broken up – شَراكَتهُم تفَلَّشَت [šaraːkathum tfallišat] Their partnership was dissolved.
تَفلِيش [tafliːš] *n:* تَفلِيشات [tafliːšaːt] *pl:* • **1.** disassembling
مفَلَّش [mfallaš] *adj:* • **1.** collapsed

ف ل ش 2

فلاش [flaːš] *n:* فلاشات [flaːšaːt] *pl:* • **1.** condom

ف ل ط ح

مفَلطَح [mfalṭaħ] *adj:* • **1.** flat, flattened – خَشمَه مفَلطَح [xašmah mfalṭaħ] His nose is flattened.
مِتفَلطِح [mitfalṭiħ] *adj:* • **1.** flat, flattened

ف ل ع

فِلَع [filaʕ] *v:* • **1.** to crack open
فَلَّع [fallaʕ] *v:* • **1.** to crack open, split open, cause to split open – الحَرّ فَلَّع البَطِّيخ [ʔilħarr fallaʕ ʔilbaṭṭiːx] The heat caused the melon to crack open.
اِنفِلَع [ʔinfilaʕ] *v:* • **1.** to split open, crack open, be split open – الرُّمّان إذا يُبقَى بِالشِّجرَة هوايَة، يِنفِلِع [ʔirrummaːn ʔiða yubqaː biššijra hwaːya, yinfiliʕ] If the pomegranate stays on the tree too long it splits.
فَلِع [faliʕ] *n:* فلُوع [fluːʕ] *pl:* • **1.** crack, split
مَفلُوع [mafluːʕ] *adj:* • **1.** cracked, split
مِتفَلِّع [mitfalliʕ] *adj:* • **1.** cracked, split

ف ل ف ل

فِلفِل، فِلفِلَة [filfil, filfila] *n:* • **1.** pepper • **2.** green pepper(s), hot pepper(s)
فَلافِل [falaːfil] *n:* • **1.** falafel (fried bean patty)
فِلفِلَة [filifla] *adj:* فِلفلات [filflaːt] *pl:* • **1.** pepper, green pepper, hot pepper • **2.** unit noun of فِلفِل pepper

ف ل ق

فِلَق [filaq] *v:* • **1.** to split • **2.** to crack
فَلَّق [fallaq] *v:* • **1.** to administer the bastinado – المُلّا فَلَّقَه لِأَنّ ما خَلَّص وَظِيفتَه [ʔilmulla fallaqah liʔann maː xallaṣ waðiːftah] The Mullah switched him on the soles of his feet because he didn't do his homework.
اِنفِلَق [ʔinfilaq] *v:* • **1.** to be split (apart)
فَلِق [faliq] *n:* • **1.** splitting
فَلَقَة [falaqa] *n:* فَلَقات [falaqaːt] *pl:* • **1.** a stick with a rope on it used for holding the feet of the delinquent during the bastinado • **2.** punishment by bastinado – أَكَل فَلَقتَين اليُوم [ʔakal falaqtayn ʔilyuːm] He got two bastinados today.
فَيلَق [faylaq] *n:* فَيالِق [fayaːliq] *pl:* • **1.** a large military unit, army corp • **2.** فَيلَق السِّلم [faylaq ʔissilm] Peace Corps

ف ل ك

فَلَك [falak] *n:* أَفلاك [ʔaflaːk] *pl:* • **1.** orbit, circuit – عِلم الفَلَك [ʕilm ʔilfalak] astronomy.
فِلكَة [filka] *n:* فِلكات [filkaːt] *pl:* • **1.** circle, traffic circle • **2.** riverboat
فَلَكِي [falaki] *adj:* • **1.** astronomical • **2.** astronomer

ف ل ل

فَلّ [fall] *v:* • **1.** to untie, undo – فِلّ هَالعُقُدتَين اللّي بِالخِيط [fill halʕugudtayn ʔilli bilxiːṭ] Unite these two knots in the string. فَلّ الصُّرَّة وَطَلَّع خاولِي مِنها [fall ʔiṣṣurra wṭallaʕ xaːwli minha] He opened the bundle and pulled a towel out of it. • **2.** to finish up, take care of – فَلَّت الحَسبَة بنُصّ ساعَة [fallat ʔilħasba bnuṣṣ saːʕa] The matter was taken care of in a half hour. فِلّها، عاد [fillha, ʕaːd] Get it over with, for heaven's sake!
مَفَلّ [mafall] *n:* مَفَلّات [mafallaːt] *pl:* • **1.** screwdriver
فلُول [filuːl] *n:* • **1.** pl. only remnants, followers
فَلَّة [falla] *n:* فَلّات [fallaːt] *pl:* • **1.** wonderful, amazing, tremendous, terrific – هُوَّ فَلَّة بِالرِّياضِيّات [huwwa falla birriyaːðiyyaːt] He's terrific in mathematics. جَمالها فَلَّة [jamaːlha falla] Her beauty is terrific. • **2.** loose, unpackaged – جُكلَيت فَلَّة [čukliːt falla] unpackaged candies.

ف ل م

فِلِم [filim] *n:* أَفلام [ʔaflaːm] *pl:* • **1.** film, roll of film • **2.** movie, motion picture, film

ف ل ن

فلان [flaːn] *n:* فلانَة [flaːn] *feminine:* • **1.** indefinite or unnamed person or thing, so-and-so, such-and-such – لا تِعتِمِد عَلَى فلان وَفِلتان؛ سَوِّيها بنَفسَك [laː tiʕtimid ʕala flaːn wfiltaːn; sawwiːha bnafsak] Don't depend on this and that person; do it yourself.
فلانِي [flaːni, fulaːni] *adj:* • **1.** Adjective of فلان related to an unknown (or not to be mentioned) person or thing – القَضِيَّة الفُلانِيَّة [ʔilqaðiyya ʔilfulaːniyya] such and such a matter. فلان الفُلانِي [flaːn ʔilfulaːni] John Doe.

ف ل و
فِلو [filw] *n:* فلاوَى [flaːwa] *pl:* • **1.** colt, foal, young horse • **2.** young man, young buck

ف ل و ن ز
فلاوَنزا [flawanza, ʔinflawanza] *n:* • **1.** influenza (highly contagious cold related disease), flu

ف ل ي
فَلّى [fallaː] *v:* • **1.** to delouse, search for lice – دَتفَلّي راس إبِنها [datfalli raːs ʔibinha] She is delousing her son's head. • **2.** to preen (of a bird) – الطَّير دَيتفَلّى بِالشَّمِس [ʔiṭṭiːr dayitfallaː biššamis] The bird is sitting in the sun picking and fluffing at its feathers with its beak.
تفَلّى [tfallaː] *v:* • **1.** to be deloused, to get rid of lice • **2.** exhume

ف ل ي ن
فِلّين [filliːn] *n:* • **1.** (coll.) cork
فِلّينَة [filliːna] *n:* فِلّينات [filliːnaːt] *pl:* • **1.** a cork

ف ن ج ن
فِنجان [finǰaːn] *n:* فناجين [fnaːǰiːn] *pl:* • **1.** small porcelain cup • **2.** coffee cup

ف ن د ق 1
فُندُق [funduq] *n:* فَنادِق [fanaːdiq] *pl:* • **1.** hotel, inn
فُندُقِيَّة [fundugiyya] *n:* • **1.** hotel-management, hospitality management

ف ن د ق 2
فِندِق [findiq] *n:* فَنادِق [fanaːdiq] *pl:* • **1.** (coll.) variant of بُندُق pine nut

ف ن ر
فَنَر [fanar] *n:* فَنَرات [fanaraːt] *pl:* • **1.** paper lantern, luminario, Chinese lantern • **2.** steel shutter, roll-up shop front
فَنار [fanaːr] *n:* فَنارات [fanaːraːt] *pl:* • **1.** lighthouse

ف ن ن
تفَنَّن [tfannan] *v:* • **1.** to be inventive, to be versatile, to vary – هِيَّ تِتفَنَّن بِاللِّبِس [hiyya titfannan billibis] She varies her clothes a lot. مَرتَه تِتفَنَّن بِالطَّبُخ [martah titfannan biṭṭabux] His wife is very versatile at cooking.
فَنّ، فِنّ [fann, finn] *n:* فِنون، فُنُون [finuːn, funuːn] *pl:* • **1.** art – الفُنُون الجَّمِيلَة [ʔilfunuːn ʔiǰǰamiːla] the fine arts. فَنّ التَّجمِيل [fann ʔittaǰmiːl] the art of cosmetics. • **2.** (with pronominal suffix) just let (him), I dare (him) – فِنَّك ترُوح وَما تقُلّي [finnak truːħ wma dgulli] Just you try to go and not tell me. فِنَّك تخُشّ بالمَقبَرَة باللَّيل [finnak txušš bilmaqbara billayl] I dare you to go into the cemetery at night. فِنَّه يِشتِكِي عَلَيّا بِالمَحكَمَة. وَالله أَقتلَه [finnah yištiki ʕalayya bilmaħkama. wʔallah ʔakutlah] He better not complain about me to the court. By golly, I'll kill him.
فَنّان [fannaːn] *n:* • **1.** artist
فَنّانَة [fannaːna] *n:* فَنّانات [fannaːnaːt] *pl:* • **1.** fem. of فَنّان artiste, night club dancer
فَنِّي [fanni] *adj:* • **1.** technical – مَوضُوع فَنِّي [mawḍuːʕ fanni] a technical subject. • **2.** artistic – لَوحَة فَنِّيَّة [lawħa fanniyya] an artistic work. • **3.** as a Noun, a technician

ف ن و س
فانُوس [faːnuːs] *n:* فوانِيس [fwaːniːs] *pl:* • **1.** lantern

ف ن ي
فِنَى [finaː] *v:* • **1.** to annihilate, destroy, ruin – العَدُو فِنَى المَدِينَة عَن آخِرها [ʔilʕadu finaː ʔilmadiːna ʕan ʔaːxirha] The enemy destroyed the city completely. • **2.** to be consumed, lose oneself – إحنا نِتفانَى بِحُبّ وَطَنّا [ʔiħna nitfaːnaː bħubb waṭanna] We are consumed with our love of our nation.
اِنفِنَى [ʔinfinaː] *v:* • **1.** to be annihilated, destroyed, wiped out – الفِرقَة اِنفِنَت بِكامِلها بِالمَعرَكَة [ʔilfirqa ʔinfinat bkaːmilha bilmaʕraka] The division was totally wiped out in the battle.
فَني [fany] *n:* • **1.** destruction, ruin, perdition, annihilation • **2.** passing away
فَناء [fanaːʔ] *n:* • **1.** passing away, extinction, vanishing • **2.** destruction, annihilation. perdition, ruin
تَفاني [tafaːni] *n:* • **1.** dedication, sacrifice
فانِي [faːni] *adj:* • **1.** vain, ephemeral, mortal

ف ن ي ل
فانيلَة [faniːla] *n:* • **1.** flannel • **2.** pl. فانِيلات undershirt, tee-shirt – فانِيلَة أُمّ عِلّاقَة [faniːla ʔumm ʕillaːga] brief undershirt, sleeveless undershirt.

ف ه د
فَهَد [fahad] *n:* فُهُود [fuhuːd] *pl:* • **1.** leopard, panther

ف ه ر س
فِهرَس، فِهرَست [fihras, fihrast] *n:* فَهارِس [fahaːris] *pl:* • **1.** table of contents, index

ف ه م
فِهَم [fiham] *v:* • **1.** to understand – ما دَ أَقدَر أَفهَمَك [maː da ʔagdar ʔafhamak] I can't understand you.
فَهَّم [fahham] *v:* • **1.** to make someone understand or see, to instruct, to explain to – فَهَّمتَه مَعنى هَالجُملَة

[fahhamtah maʕna hajǰumla] I explained the meaning of the sentence to him. فَهِّمني شقَلَّك [fahhimni šgallak] Explain to me what he told you.
تفاهَم [tfa:ham] *v:* • **1.** to communicate with each other – ما يِحكِي عَرَبِي. شلُون تفاهَمتُوا؟ [ma: yiħči ʕarabi. šlu:n tfa:hamtu:?] He doesn't speak Arabic. How did you communicate? • **2.** to reach an understanding, come to an agreement, come to terms – خَلِّي نُقعُد سُوَة وَنِتفاهَم [xalli: nugʕud suwa wnitfa:ham] Let's sit down together and come to an understanding. كانَوا مِتخاربِين، وَبَعدين تفاهمَوا [ča:naw mitxa:rbi:n, wbaʕdi:n tfa:hmaw] They were on bad terms, but finally they reached an understanding. هَذا واحِد ما يِتفاهَم [ha:ða wa:ħid ma: yitfa:ham] That's one guy who won't listen to you.
اِنفِهَم [ʔinfiham] *v:* • **1.** to be understood – هَالكِتاب ما يِنفِهِم [halkita:b ma: yinfihim] This book is incomprehensible.
اِفتِهَم [ʔiftiham] *v:* • **1.** to understand, comprehend – اِفتِهَمتَه لِلسُّؤال؟ [ʔiftihamtah lissuʔa:l?] Did you understand the question? • **2.** to be or become aware of something – هَالمُعَلِّم يِفتِهِم [halmuʕallim yiftihim] That teacher knows what he's doing. اِفتِهَمِت شِي عَن القَضِيَّة لَو بَعَد؟ [ʔiftihamit ši ʕan ʔilqaðiyya law baʕad?] Did you find out anything about the matter yet?
اِستَفهَم [ʔistafham] *v:* • **1.** to inquire, ask – لازِم نِستَفهِم عَن ماضِيه [la:zim nistafhim ʕan ma:ḍi:h] We'll have to inquire about his past.
فَهِم [fahim, fihim] *n:* أفهام [ʔafha:m] *pl:* • **1.** understanding, comprehension, grasp, discernment, insight – سُوء فَهِم [su:ʔ fahim] a misunderstanding. بَطِيئ الفَهِم [baṭi:ʔ ʔilfahim] slow to understand.
تَفَهُّم [tafahhum] *n:* • **1.** understanding, comprehension, grasping, grasp
تَفاهُم [tafa:hum] *n:* • **1.** mutual understanding, mutual agreement, accord
اِستِفهام [ʔistifha:m] *n:* • **1.** inquiry, question – عَلامَة اِستِفهام [ʕala:mat ʔistifha:m] question mark.
فَهِيم [fahi:m] *adj:* • **1.** intelligent • **2.** intelligent person
فاهِم [fa:him] *adj:* • **1.** knowledgeable, competent – مُحامِي فاهِم [muħa:mi fa:him] a knowledgeable lawyer.
فِهِيم [fihi:m] *adj:* • **1.** sensible, intelligent
مَفهُوم [mafhu:m] *adj:* • **1.** understood, understandable, comprehensible – شِي مَفهُوم [ši mafhu:m] an accepted fact. • **2.** also means: granted, certainly, of course, fine, sure – مَفهُوم، بَسّ هَذا مُو عُذُر [mafhu:m, bass ha:ða mu: ʕuður] I know, but that's no excuse. • **3.** (pl. مَفاهِيم [mafa:hi:m]) conception, concept, idea – المَفهُوم [ʔilmafhu:m] it is said, it is reported that. . . المَفهُوم إنُّو الوِزارَة راح تِستَقِيل [ʔilmafhu:m ʔinnu ʔilwiza:ra ra:ħ tistaqi:l] It's rumored the cabinet will resign.
مِتفَهِّم [mitfahhim] *adj:* • **1.** understanding • **2.** reasonable
مِتفاهِم [mitfa:him] *adj:* • **1.** understanding
اِستِفهامِي [ʔistifha:mi] *adj:* • **1.** interrogative
أفهَم [ʔafham] *comparative adjective:* • **1.** better or best informed, versed

ف ه و

فَهاوَة [faha:wa] *n:* • **1.** weakness, tastelessness, flatness
فاهِي [fa:hi] *adj:* • **1.** (invar.) weak, tasteless, flat – شاي فاهِي [ča:y fa:hi] weak tea. شَربَت فاهِي [šarbat fa:hi] flat-tasting fruit drink. حَكِي فاهِي [ħači fa:hi] dainty, prissy speech.

ف و ت 1

فات [fa:t] *v:* • **1.** to pass, go by – فات وَقِت تَقدِيم الطَّلَبات [fa:t wakit taqdi:m ʔiṭṭalaba:t] The time for submitting requests has passed. اِلبَس بِالعَجَل قَبِل ما يفُوت عَلِيك الوَقِت [ʔilbas bilʕaǰal gabil ma: yfu:t ʕali:k ʔilwakit] Dress quickly before it's too late. آنِي ما يفُوت عَلَيّا شِي. أعرُف شَكُو ماكُو [ʔa:ni ma: yfu:t ʕalayya ši. ʔaʕruf šaku ma:ku] Nothing gets by me. I know what's happening. فاتَتنِي غير فُوتَة [fa:tatni γi:r fu:ta] What a chance I missed! السَّنَة اللِّي فاتَت [ʔissana ʔilli fa:tat] the past year, the year just passed, last year. • **2.** to go, pass – هَسَّة فات مِن هنا [hassa fa:t min hna] He just went by here. تِقدَر تفُوت. ماكُو حاجَة تطُقّ الباب [tigdar tfu:t. ma:ku ħa:ǰa ṭṭugg ʔilba:b] You can come in. There's no need to knock on the door. فُوت لِلبَيت وَلَو آنِي مُو هناك [fu:t lilbayt walaw ʔa:ni mu: hna:k] Go in the house even if I'm not there. الثَّعلَب فات بِالغار [ʔiθθaʕlab fa:t bilγa:r] The fox went into the hole. صِحِت بِيه "فُوت" [ṣiħit bi:h "fu:t"] I yelled at him 'Scram.'
فَوَّت [fawwat] *v:* • **1.** to cause to go, cause to pass, put – فَوِّت السِّيم بِالزُّرُف [fawwit ʔissi:m bizzuruf] Insert the wire in the hole. • **2.** to cause to go by, cause to pass – إنتَ فَوَّتِت عَلَيّا الفُرصَة [ʔinta fawwatit ʕalayya ʔilfurṣa] You made me miss the opportunity. • **3.** to allow to pass, allow to go by – بَسّ قُول بِإسمِي وَهُوَّ يفَوّتَك [bass gu:l biʔismi wahuwwa yfawwtak] Just mention my name and he'll let you in. • **4.** to let by, let go, overlook – هُوَّ ما يفَوِّت شِي بِالأكِل [huwwa ma: yfawwit ši bilʔakil] He doesn't miss anything when he's eating. راح أفَوّتلَك إيّاها هالمَرَّة، بَسّ لا تعِيدها [ra:ħ ʔafawwtlak ʔiyya:ha halmarra, bass la: tʕi:dha] I'll let it go this time, but don't do it again.
تفاوَت [tfa:wat] *v:* • **1.** to differ, be different – أوقات مَجِيئنا دَتِتفاوَت [ʔawqa:t maǰi:ʔna datitfa:wat] Our arrival times differ.
فَوت [fawt, fu:t] *n:* • **1.** passing by, entering
تَفاوُت [tafa:wut] *n:* • **1.** difference, dissimilarity, contrast

ف

فَوات [fawaːt] *adj:* • **1.** passing, lapse – لازِم تُوصَل قَبِل فَوات الوَقِت [laːzim tuːṣal qabil fawaːt ʔilwaqit] You must arrive before it's too late.
فايِت [faːyit] *adj:* • **1.** past, elapsed • **2.** inner, ingoing, penetrating

ف و ت 2

فُوت [fuːt] *n:* فُوتات، فِيتات [fuːtaːt, fiːtaːt] *pl:* • **1.** foot (unit of measure)

ف و ج

فاج [faːǰ] *v:* • **1.** to swim – تُعرُف تفُوج وَإلّا لا؟ [tuʕruf tfuːǰ waʔilla laː?] Do you know how to swim or not?
فاوَج [faːwaǰ] *v:* • **1.** to swim with the breast stroke – إذا تريد تعَلّمَه يِسبَح، خَلِّيه يفاوِج [ʔiða triːd tʕallmah yisbaħ, xalliːh yfaːwiǰ] If you want to teach him to swim, let him do the breast stroke.
فَوج [fawǰ] *n:* أفواج [ʔafwaːǰ] *pl:* • **1.** regiment (mil.)
فواجَة [fwaːǰa] *n:* • **1.** swimming
مُفاوَجَة [mufaːwaǰa] *n:* • **1.** breast stroke

ف و ح

فاح [faːħ] *v:* • **1.** to spread, diffuse, emanate (odor) – رِيحَة المَرَق فاحَت مِن فتَحتَه [riːħat ʔilmarag faːħat min ftaħtah] The fragrance of the stew came out when you opened it.
فوح [fawħ, fuːħ] *n:* • **1.** water left over after rice is boiled in it • **2.** emanation (odor)

ف و خ

فاخ [faːx, fuːx] *v:* • **1.** to ease, relax – الوُجَع مال الجَّرِح ما فاخ لهَسَّة [ʔilwuǰaʕ maːl ʔiǰǰariħ maː faːx lhassa] The pain from the wound hasn't gone away yet. ما فُخِت إلّا لَمّا سِجنوه [maː fuxit ʔilla lamma siǰnuːh] I didn't feel at ease until they imprisoned him.
فَوَّخ [fawwax] *v:* • **1.** to ease, relieve – هالمَرهَم راح يفَوِّخ الوُجَع [halmarham raːħ yfawwix ʔilwuǰaʕ] This ointment will relieve the pain. فَوَّختِني هوايَة بهَالخَبَر [fawwaxtni hwaːya bhalxabar] You've relieved me a great deal with this news. بُسَطتَه بَسطَة فَوَّخِت قَلبِي بِيها [busaṭṭah basṭa fawwaxit galbi biːha] I gave him a beating that set my heart at ease.
فوخ [fuːx] *n:* • **1.** ease, relaxation

ف و ر

فار [faːr] *v:* • **1.** to boil, bubble – سَوِّي شوَيَّة شاي. المَيّ دَيفُور [sawwiː šwayya čaːy. ʔilmayy dayfuːr] Make a little tea. The water is boiling. • **2.** to effervesce, to fizz – إذا تخَلّي قُرصَين مِن هَالدُّوا بالمَيّ، المَيّ يقُوم يفُور [ʔiða txalliː qurṣayn min hadduwaː bilmayy, ʔilmayy yguːm yfuːr] If you put two tablets of this medicine in water, the water will start to fizz.
فَوَّر [fawwar] *v:* • **1.** to cause to boil, to boil – فَوِّر الحَلِيب قَبِل ما تشرُبَه [fawwir ʔilħaliːb gabil maː tšurbah] Boil the milk before you drink it. • **2.** to boil furiously – الرّادِيتَر دَتفَوِّر [ʔirraːdiːtar datfawwir] The radiator is boiling over.
تفَوَّر [tfawwar] *v:* • **1.** to be boiled, to be brought to a boil – المَيّ لازِم يِتفَوَّر قَبُل ما تخَلّي بِيه التِّمَّن [ʔilmayy laːzim yitfawwar gabul maː txalliː biːh ʔittimman] The water has to be boiling before you put the rice in it.
فَور، عَالفَور [fawr, ʕalfawr] *n:* • **1.** at once, immediately, right away, instantly, without delay, promptly, directly – إذا ما تسَوِّيها عالفَور، يفُصلُوك [ʔiða maː tsawwiːha ʕalfawr, yfuṣluːk] If you don't do it right away, they'll fire you. إذا ما يطُمغُون العَرِيضَة "عَلَى الفَور"، تِتعَطَّل [ʔiða maː yṭumɣuːn ʔilʕariːḍa "ʕala ʔilfawr", titʕaṭṭal] If you don't stamp the application "rush" it'll get delayed.
فور [fawr, fuːr] *n:* • **1.** boiling, simmering, bubbling
فَورَة [fuːra, fawra] *n:* فورات [fawraːt] *pl:* • **1.** a boiling
فَوران [fawraːn] *n:* • **1.** boiling, ebullition
تفوِير [tafwiːr] *n:* • **1.** boiling
فَورِي [fawri] *adj:* • **1.** instant, immediate, direct, prompt, instantaneous – صُوَر فَورِيَّة [ṣuwar fawriyya] pictures while you wait. الوِحدَة الفَورِيَّة [ʔilwiħda ʔilfawriyya] immediate union.
مفَوَّر [mfawwar] *adj:* • **1.** boiled, steamed
فَوراً [fawran] *adverbial:* • **1.** at once, right away, immediately, directly – راح أرُوح عَليه فَوراً وَأَقُلَّه [raːħ ʔaruːħ ʕaliːh fawran waʔagullah] I am going over to him right now and tell him. الشُّرطَة إجَوا لِمَكان الحادِث فَوراً بَعَد ما خابَرناهُم [ʔiššurṭa ʔiǰaw limakaːn ʔilħaːdiθ fawran baʕad maː xaːbarnaːhum] The police came to the scene of the accident immediately after we called them.

ف و ز

فاز [faːz] *v:* • **1.** to win, triumph, be victorious – ما أعتقِد راح يفُوز بهَالحَملَة الانتِخابِيَّة [maː ʔaʕtiqid raːħ yfuːz bhalħamla ʔilʔintixaːbiyya] I don't think he will win this election campaign. أيّ فَرِيق فاز بالسِّباق؟ [ʔayy fariːq faːz bissibaːq?] Which team won the game?
فَوز [fawz] *n:* فوزات [fuːzaːt] *pl:* • **1.** victory, triumph, success
فائِز [faːʔiz] *adj:* • **1.** successful, victorious, triumphant • **2.** victor, winner

ف و ص

فوصَة [fuːṣa] *adj:* فوصات [fuːṣaːt] *pl:* • **1.** quarrelsome woman

ف و ض

فَوَّض [fawwaḍ] *v:* • **1.** to authorize, empower – آني فَوَّضتَه يبِيع البَيت [ʔaːni fawwaḍtah yibiːʕ ʔilbayt] I authorized him to sell the house.

فاوَض [faːwað̣] *v:* • **1.** to negotiate with – راح يفاوِض الشَّرِكَة عَلَى قَضِيَّة بِناء الجِّسِر [raːħ yfaːwið̣ ʔiššarika ʕala qað̣iyyat binaːʔ ʔijjisir] He will negotiate with the company about building the bridge.
تفاوَض [tfaːwað̣] *v:* • **1.** to negotiate – دَيتفاوَضُون عَلَى مُعاهَدَة جِدِيدَة [dayitfaːwað̣uːn ʕala muʕaːhada jidiːda] They're negotiating for a new agreement. دَزّوا وَفِد يِتفاوَض ويّا الحُكُومَة [dazzaw wafid yitfaːwað̣ wiyya ʔilħukuːma] They sent a delegation to negotiate with the government.
فَوضَى [fawð̣a] *n:* • **1.** disorder, confusion, chaos • **2.** anarchy
مُفَوَّض [mufawwað̣] *n:* مُفَوَّضِين [mufawwað̣iːn] *pl:* • **1.** rank in the police force above sergeant but below lieutenant
مُفاوِض [mufaːwið̣] *n:* • **1.** negotiating partner
تَفوِيض [tafwiːð̣] *n:* • **1.** authorization, charging, mandate, procuration, proxy
تَفاوُض [tafaːwuð̣] *n:* • **1.** negotiation
فَوضَوِي، فَوضَوِيَّة [fawð̣awi, fawð̣awiyya] *adj:* • **1.** anarchic, chaotic • **2.** (n:) anarchist, anarchism
مُفَوَّضِيَّة [mufawwað̣iyya] *n:* مُفَوَّضِيّات [mufawwað̣iyyaːt] *pl:* • **1.** legation, commissariat

ف و ط

تفَوَّط [tfawwaṭ] *v:* • **1.** to put on a shawl or scarf – ما تِطلَع مِن البَيت إذا ما تِتفَوَّط [maː titlaʕ min ʔilbayt ʔiða maː titfawwaṭ] She doesn't go out of the house without putting on a long scarf.
فُوطَة [fuːṭa] *n:* فُوَط [fuwaṭ] *pl:* • **1.** woman's head scarf or kerchief

ف و ق

فاق [faːq] *v:* • **1.** to surpass, excel – فاق أُخوتَه بِالدِّراسَة [faːq ʔuxwutah biddiraːsa] He beat his brothers in school studies.
فاق [faːq, faːg] *v:* • **1.** to awake, wake up – فاق مِن النُّوم السّاعَة سَبعَة الصُّبُح [faːq min ʔinnuːm ʔissaːʕa sabʕa ʔiṣṣubuħ] He woke up at seven o'clock in the morning. • **2.** to come to, regain consciousness – يِرّادلَه ساعَة حَتَّى يفِيق مِن غَيبُوبتَه [yirraːdlah saːʕa ħatta yfiːq min ɣaybuːbtah] He'll need an hour to come out of his unconsciousness.
فَوَّق [fawwaq] *v:* • **1.** to give preference to, to favor – المُدِير فَوَّق إبنَه عَلَى باقِي الطُّلّاب [ʔilmudiːr fawwaq ʔibnah ʕala baːqi ʔiṭṭullaːb] The principal set his son above the rest of the students. • **2.** to consider superior, to prefer – أفَوِّق هَالقُماش عَلَى ذاك [ʔafawwuq halqumaːš ʕala ðaːk] I rate this material higher than that.
تفَوَّق [tfawwaq] *v:* • **1.** with عَلَى to excel, surpass, be superior to – تفَوَّق عَلَى أَصدِقائَه بِاللُّغَة الإنكِلِيزِيَّة [tfawwaq ʕala ʔaṣdiqaːʔah billuɣa ʔilʔingiliːziyya] He surpasses his friends at English.
فَوق [fawg, fuːg, fawq, fuːq] *n:* • **1.** (adv.) up, upstairs, on top, above – خَلّي نِصعَد فُوق [xalliː niṣʕad fuːg] Let's go upstairs. صَعِّد البَنطَرُون مالَك فُوق [ṣaʕʕid ʔilpanṭaruːn maːlak fuːg] Pull your pants up. ماكُو حاجَة تِنزِل؛ تِقدَر تِحكِي مِن فُوق [maːku ħaːja tinzil; tigdar tiħči min fuːg] No need to come down; you can talk from up there. تنَقَّعِت مِن فُوق لِجَوَّة [tnaggaʕit min fuːg lijawwa] I got wet from top to bottom. مِن تُصبُغ الحايِط؛ إبدِي مِن فُوق [min tuṣbuɣ ʔilħaːyiṭ; ʔibdi min fuːg] When you paint the wall start from the top. سَجِّل إسمَك لِفُوق [sajjal ʔismak lifuːg] Sign your name at the top. • **2.** (prep.) above, over – الطِّيّارَة طارَت فُوق الغَيم [ʔiṭṭayyaːra ṭaːrat fuːg ʔilɣaym] The plane flew above the clouds. فُوق المُلاحِظ أَكُو مُدِير [fuːg ʔilmulaːħið̣ ʔaku mudiːr] Above the supervisor there's a director. • **3.** on, on top of – ذِبّ فُوق الأَكِل شوَيَّة مِلِح [ðibb fuːg ʔilʔakil šwayya miliħ] Sprinkle some salt on top of the food. وَقِّع فُوق الطّابِع [waqqiʕ fuːg ʔiṭṭaːbiʕ] Sign on the stamps. خَلّي هَالجُّنطَة فُوق السَّيّارَة [xalliː hajjunṭa fuːg ʔissayyaːra] Put this suitcase on top of the car. • **4.** beyond, more than – فُوق المِيَة واحِد إجَوا [fuːg ʔilmiyat waːħid ʔijaw] More than one hundred people came. سَيّاراتنا أَسعارها مِن مِيتَين دِينار وفُوق [sayyaːraːtna ʔasʕaːrha min mitayn dinaːr wfuːg] The prices of our cars are 200 dinars and up. فُوق البَنَفسَجِي [fuːg ʔilbanafsaji] ultraviolet. الأَشِعَّة الفَوق البَنَفسَجِي [ʔilʔašiʕʕa ʔilfuːg ʔilbanafsaji] ultraviolet rays.
تَفَوُّق [tafawwuq] *n:* • **1.** superiority, preponderance, predominance, ascendancy
إفاقَة [ʔifaːqa] *n:* • **1.** awakening, recovery
متفَوِّق [mitfawwiq] *adj:* • **1.** successful, top-rated
فوقاني [fuːgaːni, fawqaːni] *adj:* • **1.** higher, upper – الطّابِق الفوقاني [ʔiṭṭaːbiq ʔilfuːgaːni] the upper floor.
فوقاها [fuːgaːha] *int:* • **1.** in addition to that, furthermore, besides – رَكّبتَه بالسَّيّارَة وفُوقاها يريدنِي أَشِيل غَراضَه [rakkabtah bissayyaːra wfuːgaːha yriːdni ʔašiːl ɣaraːð̣ah] I gave him a ride in the car, and on top of that he wants me to carry his stuff. سَوِّيت كُلّ هَذا، وفُوقاها هُوَّ زَعلان [sawwiːt kull haːða, wfuːgaːha huwwa zaʕlaːn] I did all that and still he got mad.

ف و ل

فاوُل [faːwul] *n:* • **1.** foul, error (in sports)
فُول، راح فُول [fuːl, raːħ fuːl] *adj:* • **1.** at full speed, very fast

ف و ل ذ

فُولاذ [fuːlaːð] *n:* • **1.** steel
فُولاذِي [fuːlaːði] *adj:* • **1.** stainless steel

ف

ف و م

فَوَّم [fawwam] *v:* • **1.** to soap, suds, lather – فَوُّم المواعِين بِالصّابُون وَبَعدين إغسِلهُم [fawwum ʔilmwaːʕiːn bisṣaːbuːn wbaʕdiːn ʔiɣsilhum] Suds the dishes in the soap and then rinse them.
فوم [fuːm] *n:* فوامَة [fwaːma] *pl:* • **1.** sudsing, soaping, lathering

ف و ه

تفوَّه [tfawwah] *v:* • **1.** with ب to pronounce, utter, voice, say – إذا تِتفَوَّه بكِلمَة وِحدَة بَعَد، يبُسطَك [ʔiða titfawwah bčilma wiħda baʕad, ybusṭak] If you utter one more word, he'll clobber you.
فَوهَة، فَوهَة حَرِيق [fawha, fawhat ħariːq] *n:* • **1.** fire hydrant

ف ي ت

فِيتَة [fiːta] *n:* • **1.** roll-up tape measure (steel or cloth)

ف ي ت ر

فِيتَر [fiːtar] *n:* فِيتَريَّة [fiːtariyya] *pl:* • **1.** (automotive) mechanic
فِيتَرچِي [fitarči] *n:* فِيتَرچِيَّة [fitarčiyya] *pl:* • **1.** (automotive) mechanic

ف ي ت م ي ن

فِيتامِين [fitamiːn] *n:* فِيتامِينات [fitamynaːt] *pl:* • **1.** vitamin

ف ي د

فاد [faːd] *v:* • **1.** to benefit, help, be of use, be useful, helpful, beneficial – هَالكِتاب فادني هوايَة بِالامتِحان [halkitaːb faːdni hwaːya bilʔimtiħaːn] This book helped me a lot in the exam. شما تِحكِي ويّاه ما يفِيد [šma tiħči wiyyaːh maː yfiːd] No matter what you say to him it doesn't do any good. خَلِّيه عِندَك، تَرَة يفِيدَك بالمُستَقبَل [xalliːh ʕindak, tara yfiːdak bilmustaqbal] Keep it with you because it will be of use to you in the future. • **2.** to notify, advise, inform, let know – تقُول ما يبُوق؟ لَعَد خَلِّي أفِيدَك بشِي [dguːl maː ybuːg? laʕad xalliː ʔafiːdak bši] You say he doesn't steal? Well, let me enlighten you about something.
أفاد [ʔafaːd] *v:* • **1.** to inform – أفادِني بِمَعلُومات مُهِمَّة [ʔafaːdni bmaʕluːmaːt muhimma] He let me in on some important bits of information.
اِستَفاد [ʔistafaːd] *v:* • **1.** to profit, benefit – ما إستَفاديت مِن هَالمُعَلِّم أبَداً [maː ʔistafaːdiːt min halmuʕallim ʔabadan] I didn't benefit at all from that teacher. لازِم تِستِفِيد مِن شَبابَك [laːzim tistifiːd min šabaːbak] You should make good use of your youth.
فود [fuːd] *n:* • **1.** use, usefulness. benefit – هَذا ما بِيه فُود [haːða maː biːh fuːd] He's useless.
إفادَة [ʔifaːda] *n:* إفادات [ʔifaːdaːt] *pl:* • **1.** notice, notification, statement, message
فائدَة، فايدَة [faːʔida, faːyda] *n:* فَوائِد، فَوايِد [fawaːiːd, fawaːʔid] *pl:* • **1.** usefulness, benefit, advantage – شِنُو الفايدَة؟ [šinu ʔilfaːyda?] What's the use? ما أرِيد أتشارَك لِأنّ هَالشَّغلَة ما بِيها فايدَة [maː ʔariːd ʔatšaːrak liʔann haššaɣla maː biːha faːyda] I don't want to become a partner because there's no profit in this business. هَالقُصَّة بِيها فائدَة إلَك [halquṣṣa biːha faːʔida ʔilak] There is a moral in this story for you.
إيفاد [ʔiːfaːd] *n:* • **1.** work assignment
اِستِفادَة [ʔistifaːda] *n:* • **1.** benefit, utility, advantage
مُفِيد [mufiːd] *adj:* • **1.** useful, beneficial, advantageous – قامُوس مُفِيد [qaːmuːs mufiːd] a useful dictionary.
مستَفاد [mistafaːd] *adj:* • **1.** beneficiary
مُستَفِيد [mustafiːd] *adj:* • **1.** beneficiary
أفيَد [ʔafyad] *comparative adjective:* • **1.** more or most useful, beneficial

ف ي ر ز

فَيرُوز [fayruːz] *n:* • **1.** turquoise

ف ي ر س

فَيرُوس [fiːruːs] *n:* • **1.** virus

ف ي ز [1]

فايِز [faːyiz] *adj:* • **1.** see under فَايِض [faːyiz] abundant • **2.** (as n:) interest, dividends

ف ي ز [2]

فِيزَة [fiːza] *n:* • **1.** visa

ف ي ز ي

فِيزِيا، فِيزِياء [fiːziya, fiːziyaːʔ] *n:* • **1.** physics
فِيزِيائي، فِيزِياوِي [fiːziyaːʔi, fiːziyaːwi] *adj:* فِيزِيائِيِّين [fiːzyaːʔiyyiːn] *pl:* • **1.** physical • **2.** physicist

ف ي ش

فِيشَة [fiːša] *n:* فِيَش [fiyaš] *pl:* • **1.** token, chip, poker chip

ف ي ض

فاض [faːð̣] *v:* • **1.** to overflow, flow over, run over – سِدّ المَيّ. الحَوض فاض [sidd ʔilmayy. ʔilħawð̣ faːð̣] Turn off the water. The pool's run over. ظَلّ ساعَة يعالِج وَبَعدين فاضَت رُوحَه [ðall saːʕa yʕaːliǰ wbaʕdiːn faːð̣at ruːħah] He kept struggling with death for an hour and then gave up the ghost.

فَيَّض [fayyaðˌ] *v:* • **1.** same as فَاض: [fa:ðˌ] to overflow, flow over – يَزِّي عاد! مُو فَيَّضتَه لِلجِدِر [yazzi ʕa:d! mu: fayyaðˌtah lijjidir] Hold it, man! You've overflowed the pot.
تفَيَّض [tfayyaðˌ] *v:* • **1.** to be flooded, to be inundated • **2.** to get so wet
فَيَضان [fayaðˌa:n] *n:* فَيَضانات [fayaðˌa:na:t] *pl:* • **1.** flood, flooding
فايِض، فائِض [fa:yiðˌ, fa:ʔiðˌ, fa:ʔiz] *adj:* • **1.** usury, interest (on money) – يِنطِي فلُوس بِالفايِض [yinṭi flu:s bilfa:yiðˌ] He lends money on interest. • **2.** بِالفَايِض on interest
مفَيِّض [mfayyiðˌ] *adj:* • **1.** overflowing, effusive

ف ي ل 1

فِيل [fi:l] *n:* فيال [fya:l] *pl:* • **1.** elephant • **2.** bishop (in chess)

ف ي ل 2

فايِل [fa:yil] *n:* • **1.** dossier, file (فايلات [fa:yla:t] pl:)

ف ي ن

فِينَة [fi:na] *n:* فِيَن [fiyan] *pl:* • **1.** fez, a conical red cap worn by men in some Muslim countries

ف ي ي

فَيَّى [fayya:] *v:* • **1.** to shade, to afford shade – الشَّمِس ما تِنحِمِل. فَيِّيلِي شوَيَّة حَتَّى أَشتُغُل [ʔiššamis ma: tinħimil. fayyi:li šwayya ħatta ʔaštuɣul] The sun is unbearable. Shade me a little so I can work.
فَيّ [fayy] *n:* • **1.** shade, shadow • **2.** (by extension) protection, patronage, benevolence – إحنا عايشِين بِفَيَّه [ʔiħna ʕa:yši:n bfayyah] We are living under his protection.

ق

ق ب

قاب [qa:b] *n:* قابات [qa:ba:t] *pl:* • **1.** plate, dish
قَبَة [qaba] *n:* • **1.** enormous, excessive – مَصرَف قَبَة [maṣraf qaba] an excessive expenditure. • **2.** gross, crude, ugly – سَيّارَة قَبَة [sayya:ra qaba] an ugly car. صَوت قَبَة [ṣawt qaba] an unpleasant voice.

ق ب ب

قَبّ [gabb] *v:* • **1.** to spring, jump, leap – بَسّ اِنتِقَد واحِد مِنهُم، كُلّهُم قَبّوا عَليه [bass ʔintiqad wa:ħid minhum, kullhum gabbaw ʕali:h] As soon as he criticized one of them they all jumped on him. إنطِيني أسبِرين. قَبّ عَلَيّا راسِي [ʔinṭi:ni ʔaspiri:n. gabb ʕalayya ra:si] Give me an aspirin. I've got an overwhelming headache. • **2.** to come up, spring up – قَبَّت هَويَة وطَيِّرَت الأوراق [gabbat hawya wṭayyirat ʔilʔawra:q] A breeze came up suddenly and sent the papers flying. • **3.** to blow
قَبَّب [gabbab] *v:* • **1.** to raise, stir up – سِدّ الشِّبّاك. راح تفُوت الخَيل وَتقَبُّب عَجاج [sidd ʔiššibba:k. ra:ħ tfu:t ʔilxayl wtgabbub ʕaǰa:ǰ] Close the window. The horses are going to go by and stir up the dust.
قَبّ [gabb] *n:* • **1.** leaping, jumping, leap, jump
قُبَّة [qubba] *n:* قُبَب [qubab] *pl:* • **1.** dome – سَوّى مِن الحَبَّة قُبَّة [sawwa: min ʔlħabba qubba] He's made a mountain out of a molehill (lit. he made a dome from a seed).
قُبَّة [gubba] *n:* قُبَب [gubab] *pl:* • **1.** room – اِشتِرَيت بَيت بِيه أربَع قُبَب [ʔištirayt bayt bi:h ʔarbaʕ gubab] I bought a four-room house. • **2.** pl. قباب dome (of a building), cupola

ق ب ح

قَبَّح [qabbaħ] *v:* • **1.** to make (s.o or s.th) physically or morally ugly, repulsive, disfigured – قَبَّح الله وُجهَه! آني ما قِلت هِيكِي شِي [qabbaħ ʔallah wuččah! ʔa:ni ma: gilit hi:či ši] God damn him! I never said such a thing.
قَبَّح [gabbaħ] *v:* • **1.** to be unpleasant, disgraceful, mean – قَبَّح وِيّا كُلّ النّاس. ما بِقَى عِندَه صَدِيق [gabbaħ wiyya kull ʔinna:s. ma: biqa: ʕindah ṣadi:q] He was nasty with everybody. He hasn't a friend left.
تقابَح [tga:baħ] *v:* • **1.** to be insulting – ما عِندِي مانِع أتقابَح وِيّاه وَأسِبَّه [ma: ʕindi ma:niʕ ʔatga:baħ wiyya:h wʔasibbah] I don't mind being insulting with him and cursing him.
قَباحَة [qaba:ħa] *n:* • **1.** ugliness • **2.** shamefulness, infamy, ignonimy
قَبِيح [qabi:ħ] *adj:* • **1.** ugly, repulsive – شِكِل قَبِيح [šikil qabi:ħ] ugly looks. وِجِه قَبِيح [wiǰih qabi:ħ] an ugly face. • **2.** shameful, disgraceful, foul, base, mean – عَمَل قَبِيح [ʕamal qabi:ħ] a dirty deed.
أقبَح [ʔaqbaħ] *comparative adjective:* • **1.** uglier, ugliest • **2.** more or most infamous • **3.** fouler, viler

ق ب ر

قَبُر [gabur] *n:* قبُور [gbu:r] *pl:* • **1.** grave, tomb
مَقبَرَة [maqbara, magbara] *n:* مَقابِر [maga:bir, maga:bur] *pl:* • **1.** cemetery, graveyard

ق ب ر ز

قِبرِيزي [qibri:zi] *n:* • **1.** horse of doubtful lineage, horse which is not pure Arabian

ق ب ر ص

قِبرِص [qibriṣ, qubruṣ] *n:* • **1.** Cyprus
قِبرِصِي [qibriṣi, qubruṣi] *adj:* • **1.** Cyprian, Cypriote, from Cyprus • **2.** a Cypriote

ق ب س

اِقتِبَس [ʔiqtibas] *v:* • **1.** to borrow, adopt – راح لأمرِيكا وَاِقتِبَس بَعض العادات الأمرِيكِيَّة [ra:ħ lʔamri:ka wʔiqtibas baʕð̣ ʔilʕa:da:t ʔilʔamri:kiyya] He went to America and adopted some American customs. اِقتِبَس المَوضُوع مِن مَجَلَّة عالَمِيَّة [ʔiqtibas ʔilmawð̣u:ʕ min maǰalla ʕa:lamiyya] He borrowed the topic from an international magazine.
اِقتِباس [ʔiqtiba:s] *n:* • **1.** learning, acquisition (of knowledge) • **2.** adaptation (of a literary text or passage) • **3.** quotation, citation (of another's literary work)

ق ب ض

قُبَض [qubað̣] *v:* • **1.** to receive, collect – قُبَض الدَّين مالَه [qubað̣ ʔiddayn ma:lah] He collected the debt owed him. شوَقِت تُقبُض راتبَك؟ [šwakit tuqbuð̣ ra:tbak?] When do you get your pay? عِزرائِيل يُقبُض الأرواح [ʕizra:ʔi:l yuqbuð̣ ʔilʔarwa:ħ] Azrael gathers souls. إنطَيتَه عَشِر دَنانِير وراح أقبُض مِن دَبَش [ʔinṭi:tah ʕašir dana:ni:r wra:ħ ʔaqbuð̣ min dabaš] I gave him ten dinars and don't expect to get it back. • **2.** to constipate – الشاي يُقبُض البَطِن [ʔičča:y yuqbuð̣ ʔilbaṭin] Tea constipates. • **3.** to dispirit, depress – القَعدَة وِيّاه تُقبُض الرُّوح [ʔilgaʕda wiyya:h tuqbuð̣ ʔirru:ħ] Sitting with him depresses you. هَالغُرفَة تُقبُض الرُّوح [halɣurfa tuqbuð̣ ʔirru:ħ] This room is too confining. • **4.** with عَلَى to seize, arrest, apprehend – الشُّرطَة قُبضَت عَليه [ʔiššurṭa qubð̣at ʕali:h] The police arrested him.
اِنقُبَض [ʔinqubað̣] *v:* • **1.** to be or become constipated –

بَطنَه اِنقُبضَت مِن شُرُب الشّاي [baṭnah ʔinqubðat min šurub ʔiččaːy] He's constipated from drinking tea. • 2. to be or become dispirited, depressed – نَفسِي تِنقُبُض مِن أحكِي وِيّاه [nafsi tinqubuð min ʔaħči wiyyaːh] I'm depressed when I talk with him.
قَبُض [qabuð] *n:* • 1. apprehension, arrest – أمُر بِإلقاء القَبُض عَليه [ʔamur bʔilqaːʔ ʔilqabuð ʕaliːh] a warrant for his arrest. • 2. receiving, receipt, collection • 3. constipation – ماكُو قَبُض [maːku qabuð] There's no result. أشُو تِزمُط وَماكُو قَبُض [ʔašu tizmuṭ wmaːku qabuð] You're always bragging but nothing seems to come of it. لَا تكَلّفَه لِهذا. كُلّ قَبُض ماكُو مِنَّه [laː tkallfah lhaːða. kull qabuð maːku minnah] Don't ask him. You'll get no results from him.
قَبضَة [qabða] *n:* قَبضات [qabðaːt] *pl:* • 1. fist, closed hand – قَبضَة إيد [qabðat ʔiːd] grip. • 2. grip, hold, clasp, grasp
اِنقِباض [ʔinqibaːð] *n:* • 1. low spirits, depression, anxiety, dejectedness, anguish, gloom
قابُض [gaːbuð] *adj:* • 1. receiver, recipient • 2. distressing, grievous, embarassing • 3. catcher, tongs, holder, gripper, clamp, claw
مُقبِض [muqbið] *adj:* • 1. depressing
مَقبُوض [maqbuːð] *adj:* • 1. with عَلَى (Adj) arrested, (Noun) person under arrest • 2. sad, worried, dejected, depressed, ill at ease

ق ب ط 1

قَبَّط [qabbaṭ, qappaṭ] *v:* • 1. to be full, filled up – ما أقدَر أشرَب بَعَد. قَبَّطِت [maː ʔagdar ʔašrab baʕad. qappaṭit] I can't drink anymore. I'm filled up. بَعَد فَدّ راكِب وَتقَبُّط السَّيّارَة [baʕad fadd raːkib wtqappuṭ ʔissayyaːra] One more passenger and the car will be full. • 2. to fill, fill up – أقدَر أقَبُّط السَّيّارَة بِمُدَّة ساعَة [ʔagdar ʔaqappuṭ ʔissayyaːra bmuddat saːʕa] I can fill the car in an hour.
تقَبَّط [tqabbaṭ, tqappaṭ] *v:* • 1. to be filled
مقَبُّط [mqabbuṭ, mqappuṭ] *adj:* • 1. filled, crowded

ق ب ط 2

قُبطِي [qubṭi] *adj:* أقباط [ʔaqbaːṭ] *pl:* • 1. Copt, Coptic • 2. a Copt

ق ب ط 3

قبطان [qabṭaːn] *n:* قبطانِيَّة [qabṭaːniyya] *pl:* • 1. captain (of a ship, etc.)

ق ب ط 4

قَبُّوط [qappuːṭ, qabbuːṭ] *n:* قَبُّوطات، قبابِيط [qappuːṭaːt, qpaːpiːṭ, qabbuːṭaːt, qbaːbiːṭ] *pl:* • 1. overcoat

ق ب ع

قُبَّعَة [qubbaʕa] *n:* قُبَّعات [qubbaʕaːt] *pl:* • 1. hat, cap

ق ب غ

قَبَّغ [qabbaɣ] *v:* • 1. to cap, cover with a cap – بمَعمَل الصُّودا أكُو مَكِينَة تقَبُّغ بطالَة [bmaʕmal ʔiṣṣuːda ʔaku makiːna tqabbuɣ bṭaːla] In the soda pop factory there's a machine that caps bottles.
تقَبَّغ [tqabbaɣ] *v:* • 1. pass. of قبَّغ [qabbaɣ] to be covered, to be capped
قَبَغ [qabaɣ] *n:* قَبَغات [qabaɣaːt] *pl:* • 1. cap, cover, top, lid

ق ب غ ل

قَبَغلِي، قُندَرَة قَبَغلِي [qabaɣli, qundara qabaɣli] *adj:* • 1. a sort of high-heeled slip-on shoe

ق ب ق ب

قَبقَب [gabgab] *v:* • 1. to swell – الحَبّايَة قَبقُبَت هوايَة [ʔilħabbaːya gabgubat hwaːya] The sore swelled up very much. • 2. to bulge – سِترتَك مقَبقُبَة. شايِل شِي جَوّاها؟ [sitirtak mgabguba. šaːyil ši ǰawwaːha?] Your jacket is bulging. Are you carrying something under it?
قُبقاب [qubqaːb] *n:* قَباقِيب، قباقِب [qabaːqiːb, qbaːqib] *pl:* • 1. (pair of) wooden clogs
مقَبقُب [mgabgub] *adj:* • 1. swollen – إيد مقَبقُبَة [ʔiːd mgabguba] a swollen hand. • 2. bulging – عِلبَة مقَبقُبَة [ʕilba mgabguba] a bulging can.

ق ب ك

قَبَك، قَبِك [qabač, qabič] *n:* • 1. a kind of partridge

ق ب ل 1

قِبَل [qibal] *v:* • 1. to accept – قِبَل الهَدِيَّة مِنّي [qibal ʔilhadiyya minni] He accepted the gift from me. أهلَه خِطبُولَه بنَيَّة وَقِبَلها مِن غير شُوف [ʔahlah xiṭbuːlah bnayya wqibalha min ɣiːr šuːf] His family betrothed him to a girl and he accepted her without seeing her. الحُكُومَة ما قِبلَت أوراق اِعتِماد السَّفِير [ʔilħukuːma maː qiblat ʔawraːq ʔiʕtimaːd ʔissafiːr] The government wouldn't accept the credentials of the ambassador. عِرضَوا عَليه وَظِيفَة زينَة وَما قِبَلها [ʕirðaw ʕaliːh waðiːfa ziːna wma qibalha] They offered him a good job but he didn't accept it. قِبَل كُلّ الحَكِي اللّي قِتلَه إيّاه [qibal kull ʔilħači ʔilli gitlah ʔiyyaːh] he accepted everything I said to him. لا تُبسُط المجَدّي. الله ما يِقبَل [laː tubsuṭ ʔilmgaddi. ʔallah maː yiqbal] Don't hit the beggar. God won't accept such a thing. • 2. to acquiesce, agree, consent, assent – المَحكَمَة قَسِّمَت الوِرث بَيناتهُم، لَكِن الأخّ الكِبير ما قِبَل بِالتَّقسِيم [ʔilmaħkama qassimat ʔilwiriθ baynaːthum, laːkin ʔilʔaxx ʔiččibiːr maː qibal bittaqsiːm] The court divided the inheritance among them, but the older brother didn't agree to the division. قِبَل عَالشُّرُوط اللّي قُلتِلَه بِيها [qibal ʕaššuruːṭ ʔilli gultillah biːha] He agreed to the terms I told him about. قِبَل يصِير شَرِيكي [qibal yṣiːr šariːki] He agreed to become my partner. آني ما أقبَل بهيكِي بَيت [ʔaːni maː ʔaqbal bhiːči bayt] I'm not satisfied with such a house. • **3.** to admit – قِبلُوني بكُلِّيَّة الصَّيدَلَة [qibluːni bkulliyyat ʔiṣṣaydala] They admitted me to the college of pharmacy.

قَبَّل [qabbal] *v:* • **1.** to cause to accept – قَبَّلَه إيّاها لِلسَّيّارَة بمِيتَين دِينار [qabbalah ʔiyyaːha lissayyaːra bmiːtayn dinaːr] He sold him the car for two hundred dinars.

قابَل [qaːbal, gaːbal] *v:* • **1.** to face, be opposite – وزارَتنا تقابِل سِينَما [wizaːratna tgaːbil sinama] Our ministry is just opposite a movie theatre. • **2.** to meet, receive – قابَلني بوُجِه بَشُوش [qaːbalni bwuǰih bašuːš] He met me with a friendly smile. • **3.** to call on – السَّفِير راح يقابِل وَزِير الخارِجِيَّة اليُوم [ʔissafiːr raːħ yqaːbil waziːr ʔilxaːriǰiyya ʔilyuːm] The ambassador's going to call on the foreign minister today. • **4.** to meet with, get together with – لازِم أقابِل المُدِير عَلَى هالمُشكِلَة [laːzim ʔaqaːbil ʔilmudiːr ʕala halmuškila] I'll have to see the director about this problem. • **5.** to interview – اللُّجنَة تقابِل عَشِر طُلّاب كُل ساعَة [ʔilluǰna tgaːbil ʕašir ṭullaːb kull saːʕa] The committee interviews ten students every hour. • **6.** to return, repay, requite – قابَل زَينِيتِي بمُو زَينِيَّة [qaːbal zayniːti bmuː zayniyya] He repaid my good deed with a bad one.

قابَل [gaːbal] *v:* • **1.** to be or stand opposite – النَّهار كُلَّه مقابُل الشِّبّاك وَيتفَرَّج عالشّارِع [ʔinnahaːr kullah mgaːbul ʔiššibbaːk wyitfarraǰ ʕaššaːriʕ] All day he sits facing the window and looking at the street.

تقَبَّل [tqabbal] *v:* • **1.** to receive, accept – تقَبَّل اِقتِراحِي بِرَحابَة صَدِر [tqabbal ʔiqtiraːħi braħaːbat ṣadir] He accepted my suggestion patiently. الله يِتقَبَّل دُعاك [ʔallah yitqabbal duʕaːk] May God accept your prayers.

تقابَل [tqaːbal, tgaːbal] *v:* • **1.** to meet, encounter – تقابَلتَه بِالشّارِع اليُوم [tqaːbaltah biššaːriʕ ʔilyuːm] I ran into him on the street today. • **2.** to meet, get together, have a meeting – تقابَل وِيّا المُدِير نُصّ ساعَة [tqaːbal wiyya ʔilmudiːr nuṣṣ saːʕa] He met with the director for a half hour. • **3.** to fight, engage in combat – حِمَت المَعرَكَة، وَتقابلَوا بِالسِّلاح الأبيَض [ħimat ʔilmaʕraka, wtqaːblaw bissilaːħ ʔilʔabyaḍ] The battle got hot and they fought with bayonets. الحَرامِي تقابَل وِيّا الشُّرطَة إلَى أن خِلَص رصاصَه [ʔilħaraːmi tqaːbal wiyya ʔiššurṭa ʔila ʔan xilaṣ rṣaːṣah] The thief fought with the police until his ammunition ran out.

تقابَل [tgaːbal] *v:* • **1.** to face each other – لا تدِير ظَهرَك عَلَيه. تقابلُوا [laː ddiːr ḍahrak ʕaliːh. tgaːbluː] Don't turn your back on him. Face each other. • **2.** to get together, team up – تقابَلنا عَلَيها ثنينّا وَخلَّصناها بنُصّ ساعَة [tgaːbalna ʕaliːha θniːnna wxallaṣnaːha bnuṣṣ saːʕa] Two of us teamed up on it and finished it in a half hour.

اِنقِبَل [ʔinqibal] *v:* • **1.** to be accepted – اِنقِبَلِت بِالكُلِّيَّة [ʔinqibalit bilkulliyya] I was accepted by the college. الهَدِيَّة ما انقِبلَت [ʔilhadiyya maː ʔinqiblat] The gift was not accepted.

اِستَقبَل [ʔistaqbal] *v:* • **1.** to meet, to go to meet – راح نِستَقبلَه بِالمَطار [raːħ nistaqbalah bilmaṭaːr] We are going to meet him at the airport. • **2.** to receive – اِستَقبَلنِي كُلِّش زين [ʔistaqbalni kulliš ziːn] He received me very nicely.

قَبُل [gabul, qabil] *n:* • **1.** (adv.) previously, formerly, earlier, before – ما شايفَه قَبُل [maː šaːyfah gabul] I haven't seen him before. آنِي جِيت قَبُل [ʔaːni ǰiːt gabul] I came first. بزَمَن قَبُل، ما كان أكُو سَيّارات [bzaman gabul, maː čaːn ʔaku sayyaːraːt] In past times, there were no cars. هَذا مِن أهَل قَبُل [haːða min ʔahal gabul] He's old-fashioned. He's from a past generation. • **2.** (prep.) before – شراح نسَوِّي قَبِل العَشا؟ [šraːħ nsawwiː gabil ʔilʕaša?] What are we going to do before dinner? قَبِل ما تقُول أيّ شِي، خَلِّي أقرالَك المَكتُوب [gabil maː dguːl ʔayy ši, xalliː ʔaqraːlak ʔilmaktuːb] Before you say anything, let me read you the letter.

قِبلَة [qibla] *n:* • **1.** ‘Kiblah’, direction Muslims turn to pray (toward the Kaaba) • **2.** recess in a mosque indicating the direction of the Kaaba, prayer niche

قَبُول [qabuːl] *n:* قَبُولات [qabuːlaːt] *pl:* • **1.** an informal party, informal gathering (of either men or women) • **2.** reception, welcome, acceptance, admission (e.g., for university study)

قُبُول [qubuːl] *n:* • **1.** acceptance

قبِيل [qabiːl] *n:* • **1.** kind, sort, species – مِن هالقَبِيل [min halqabiːl] of this kind, like this, such. عِندَه أشياء هوايَة مِن هالقَبِيل [ʕindah ʔašyaːʔ hwaːya min halqabiːl] He has many things of this sort.

قبال [gbaːl] *n:* • **1.** in front of, opposite, across from – قبال البَيت [gbaːl ʔilbayt] in front of the house. حاطّ رَسِم مَرتَه قبالَه وَيباوِع عَلَيها طُول النَّهار [ħaːṭṭ rasim martah gbaːlah wybaːwiʕ ʕaliːha ṭuːl ʔinnahaːr] He put his wife's picture in front of him and looks at it all day. صارلَك ساعَة قاعِد قبالِي. شتِرِيد؟ [ṣaːrlak saːʕa gaːʕid gbaːli. šitriːd?] You've been sitting opposite me an hour. What do you want? بَيت عَمِّي يِسكنُون قبالنا [bayt ʕammi ysiknuːn gbaːlna] My uncle's family lives across the way from us.

قَبِيلَة [qabiːla] *n:* قَبائِل [qabaːʔil] *pl:* • **1.** tribe

قِبالَة [qibaːla] *n:* • **1.** midwifery, obstetrics

إقبال [ʔiqbaːl] *n:* • **1.** attention, response, responsiveness • **2.** with عَلَى : concern, interest, demand

قابلَة [qaːbila] *n:* قابِلات، قَوابِل [qaːbilaːt, qawaːbil] *pl:* • **1.** midwife

مُقابِل [muqaːbil] *n:* • **1.** opposite, facing – مُقابِل لِلسِّينَما [muqaːbil lissinama] opposite the movie theatre. • **2.** equivalent, recompense, remuneration, wages • **3.** interviewer

قبالَة [gbaːla] *n:* • **1.** by the job, on a job-rate – أخَذِت هَالشَّغلَة قبالَة [ʔaxaðit haššaɣla gbaːla] I took this work on a job-rate basis. إذا ياخذُون الشُّغُل قبالَة يحَصّلُون أكثَر

ق

[ʔiða yaːxðuːn ʔiššuɣul gbaːla yħaṣṣluːn ʔakθar] If they take the work by the job they'll make more.
مُقابَلَة [muqaːbala] *n:* مُقابَلات [muqaːbalaːt] *pl:* • **1.** encounter, meeting • **2.** interview • **3.** fight, battle
قابلِيَّة [qaːbliyya] *n:* قابلِيّات [qaːbliyyaːt] *pl:* • **1.** faculty, ability, capacity, disposition, receptivity
مُستَقبَل [mustaqbal] *n:* • **1.** future • **2.** مُستَقبَلاً [mustaqbalan] in the future
اِستِقبال [ʔistiqbaːl] *n:* اِستِقبالات [ʔistiqbaːlaːt] *pl:* • **1.** reception, receiving – حَفلَة اِستِقبال [ħaflat ʔistiqbaːl] a reception.
قُبَل [gubal] *adj:* • **1.** forward, straight ahead – إمشِي قُبَل خَمس دَقايِق وَتِلقِي الجّامِع عَلَى يَمِينَك [ʔimši gubal xamis daqaːyiq wtilgi ʔiǰǰaːmiʕ ʕala yamiːnak] Go straight for five minutes and you'll find the mosque on your right.
قابِل [qaːbil] *adj:* • **1.** appropriate, acceptable, suitable – هَالقاط قابِل لِلحَفلَة؟ [halqaːṭ qaːbil lilħafla?] Is this suit appropriate for the party? يِلبَس ألوان مُو قابلَة [yilbas ʔalwaːn muː qaːbla] He wears unsuitable colors. البارحَة شِفتَك تغُشّ؛ هَذِي مُو قابلَة مِنَّك [ʔilbaːrħa šiftak tɣušš; haːði muː qaːbla minnak] Yesterday I saw you cheating; now that's not acceptable behavior of you. • **2.** /as a scathing question/ do you mean to say, do you suppose – إنتَ ما دَتسَوِّي شِي. قابِل دَنِلعَب هنا؟ [ʔinta maː datsawwiː ši. qaːbil danilʕab hna?] You're not doing anything. You think we just play here? قابِل ما راح تُمطُر السَّنَة كُلّها؟ [qaːbil maː raːħ tumṭur ʔissana kullha?] Do you mean it's not going to rain for the whole year? يَعنِي قابِل يرِيد يِلعَب براسِي؟ [yaʕni qaːbil yiriːd yilʕab braːsi?] You mean he thinks he can just make a fool out of me? يَعنِي قابِل هُوَّ الله؟ [yaʕni qaːbil huwwa ʔallah?] You mean we should accept him as God? Who does he think he is, God?
مَقبُول [maqbuːl] *adj:* • **1.** accepted • **2.** admitted, accepted (at a school) • **3.** acceptable, reasonable – تَصَرُّفات ما مَقبُولَة [taṣarrufaːt maː maqbuːla] improper conduct.
مُستَقبِل [mustaqbil] *adj:* مُستَقبِلِين [mustaqbiliːn] *pl:* • **1.** welcomer, greeter

ق ب ل 2

قُبلَة [qubla] *n:* قُبلات [qublaːt] *pl:* • **1.** kiss
تَقبِيل [taqbiːl] *n:* • **1.** kissing

ق ب ل 3

مُقبِل [muqbil] *adj:* • **1.** coming, next (e.g., month, year)

ق ب ل ن م

قِبلَنامَة [qiblanaːma] *n:* قِبلَنامات [qiblanaːmaːt] *pl:* • **1.** compass

ق ب ل و

قابلُو [qaːblu] *n:* قابلُوات [qaːbluwaːt] *pl:* • **1.** cable

ق ب ن

قَبَّن [gabban] *v:* • **1.** to weigh (with a steel-yard) – قَبُّن كياس التِّمَن وَقُلِّي شقَدّ وَزِنها [gabbun kyaːs ʔittimman wgulli šgadd wazinha] Weigh the sacks of rice and tell me their weight
قُبّان [gubbaːn] *n:* قُبابِين [gubaːbiːn] *pl:* • **1.** steelyard, large balance scale • **2.** carpenter's level

ق ب و

قَبُو [qabw] *n:* أقبِيَة [ʔaqbiya] *pl:* • **1.** vault, vaulted or arched ceiling, room or hall with a vault, cellar

ق ت ر

قَتَّر [qattar] *v:* • **1.** to be stingy – دَيقَتِّر عَلَى نَفسَه حَتَّى يِجمَع فلُوس السَّيّارَة [dayqattir ʕala nafsah ħatta yiǰmaʕ fluːs ʔissayyaːra] He's being stingy with himself so that he can save money for a car.
تَقتِير [taqtiːr] *n:* • **1.** stinginess, parsimony

ق ت ل

قِتَل [kital] *v:* • **1.** to kill, slay, murder – قِتلَوه وَأخَذَوا فلُوسَه [kitlawh wʔaxaðaw fluːsah] They murdered him and took his money. ما عِدنا شُغُل. دَنُقتِل وَقِت [maː ʕidna šuɣul. danuktil wakit] We have nothing to do. We're killing time. قِتَل كُلّ الفلُوس بِالقمار [kital kull ʔilfluːs bilqmaːr] He went through all the money gambling. قِتَل نَفسَه عَلَى هَالوَظِيفَة لَكِن ما حَصَّلها [kital nafsah ʕala halwaðiːfa laːkin maː ħaṣṣalha] He went all out for this job but he didn't get it. رِيحَة البَلُّوعَة تُقتِل [riːħat ʔilballuːʕa tuktil] The smell from the sewer is killing. • **2.** to beat up, whip severely – الجّاهِل قِتَل أُختَه وخَلّاها تِبكِي [ʔiǰǰaːhil kital ʔuxtah wxallaːha tibči] The kid beat up his sister and made her cry.
قَتَّل [kattal] *v:* • **1.** with بِ- to slaughter, massacre, butcher – دَيقَتّلُون بِهَالنّاس وَماكُو [daykattiluːn bihannaːs wmaːku] They're slaughtering those people and there's no end to it.
تقَتَّل [tkattal] *v:* • **1.** pass. of قَتَّل [kattal] to be killed – هوايَة ناس راح يِتقَتّلُون بِهَالثَّورَة [hwaːya naːs raːħ yitkattluːn bhaθθawra] Many people will be killed in this revolution.
تقاتَل [tkaːtal] *v:* • **1.** to engage in mortal combat, slay each other – ما دَنُعرُف عَلَى ويش القَبائِل دَتِتقاتَل [maː danuʕruf ʕala wiːš ʔilqabaːʔil datitkaːtal] We don't know why the tribes are killing each other. ماكُو حاجَة تِتقاتلُون. المَخزَن بِيه ساعات كافيَة لِلكُلّ [maːku ħaːǰa titkaːtluːn. ʔilmaxzan biːh saːʕaːt kaːfya lilkull] There's no reason for fighting each other. The store has enough watches for everyone.
اِنقِتَل [ʔinkital] *v:* • **1.** to be killed, murdered – أبُوها اِنقِتَل بِالحَرُب [ʔabuːha ʔinkital bilħarub] Her father was killed in the war.
قَتِل [qatil] *n:* • **1.** murder, killing – حادِث قَتِل [ħaːdiθ qatil] a murder.

ق

قاتِل [qa:til] *n:* قاتِلين، قَتَلَة [qa:tili:n, qatala] *pl:* • **1.** killer, murderer
قِتال [qita:l] *n:* • **1.** fight, struggle, combat, strife • **2.** battle (e.g., ساحَة القِتال battlefield)
مُقاتِل [muqa:til] *n:* • **1.** fighter, soldier, warrior, combatant
قَتّال [katta:l] *adj:* • **1.** deadly • **2.** lethal, murderous
مَقتُول [maktu:l] *adj:* مَقتُولين [maktu:li:n] *pl:* • **1.** murdered • **2.** victim of murder, murdered one
قِتالِي [qita:li] *adj:* • **1.** fighting, battle (in compounds)
مِستَقتِل [mistaqtil] *adj:* • **1.** desperate • **2.** persevering, painstaking, persistent • **3.** independent, autonomous

ق ت م

قاتِم [qa:tim] *adj:* • **1.** dark – لُون قاتِم [lu:n qa:tim] a dark color. أحمَر قاتِم [ʔaħmar qa:tim] dark red.

ق ج غ

قَجَّغ [qaǰǰaɣ] *v:* • **1.** to take without cost, cadge, sponge, bum – دَيقَجِّغ جِكايِر مِن الرّايِح وَالجاي [dayqaččiɣ ǰiga:yir min ʔirra:yiħ wʔiǰǰa:y] He's bumming cigarettes from everyone. لا، ما إشتِريتَه لِهَالثُّوب. قَجَّغتَه مِن عَلي [la:, ma: ʔistiri:tah lhaθθu:b. qaččaɣtah min ʕali] No, I didn't buy this shirt. I took it off Ali.
قَجَغ [qaǰaɣ] *n:* • **1.** smuggling • **2.** (invar.) smuggled, contraband – بِضاعَة قَجَغ [biđa:ʕa qačaɣ] smuggled goods. مِلِح قَجَغ [miliħ qačaɣ] bootlegged salt. رِكَب قَجَغ بِالباص [rikab qačaɣ bilpa:ṣ] He rode the bus without paying. • **3.** contraband, smuggled goods
قَجَغجِي [qaǰaɣǰi] *n:* قَجَغجِيَّة [qaǰaɣǰiyya] *pl:* • **1.** smuggler

ق ج ل غ

قِيجَلُغ [gi:ǰaluɣ] *n:* قِيجَلُغات [gi:ǰaluɣa:t] *pl:* • **1.** nightgown

ق ج م

أقجَم [ʔaqčam] *adj:* قَجمِين [qačmi:n] *pl:* قَجمَة [qačma] *feminine:* • **1.** pug-nosed – سَيّارَة قَجمَة [sayya:ra qačma] Jeep and other small military vehicles.

ق ح ب

تقَحَّب [tgaħħab] *v:* • **1.** to sleep around, whore around – دَتقَحُّب وَما حَدّ يدري بيها [datgaħħub wma ħadd yidri bi:ha] She's whoring around and nobody knows about it.
اِستَقحَب [ʔistagħab] *v:* • **1.** to become a whore, prostitute
قَحبَة [gaħba] *n:* قحاب [għa:b] *pl:* • **1.** prostitute, whore, harlot
قَحبَجي [gaħabči] *adj:* قَحَبجِيَّة [gaħabčiyya] *pl:* • **1.** man who frequently patronizes prostitutes
مَقحَبَة [magħaba] *adj:* • **1.** brothel
قَحباوِي [gaħba:wi] *adj:* • **1.** flashy, ostentatious, loud, colorful – لِبِس قَحباوِي [libis gaħba:wi] flashy clothes. سَيّارَة قَحباوِيَّة [sayya:ra gaħba:wiyya] a fancy car. • **2.** effeminate, sissified, queer – مَشِيتَه قَحباوِيَّة [maši:tah gaħba:wiyya] His walk is effeminate.

ق ح ح

قَحّ [gaħħ] *v:* • **1.** to cough – وَدِّيه لِلطَّبِيب. أَشُو دَيقُحّ هوايَة [waddi:h liṭṭabi:b. ʔašu dayguħħ hwa:ya] Take him to the doctor. He seems to be coughing a lot.
قَحَّة، كَحَّة [gaħħa] *n:* • **1.** coughing, cough • **2.** pl. قَحّات gaħħa:t cough
قُحّ [quħħ] *adj:* • **1.** (invar.) pure, unmixed, unadulterated – عَرَبِي قُحّ [ʕarabi quħħ] a pure Arab.

ق ح ط

قِحَط [qiħaṭ] *v:* • **1.** to be scarce – يَعنِي بِكُلّ بَغداد ماكُو طَماطَة. قابِل قِحطَت؟ [yaʕni bkull baɣda:d ma:ku ṭama:ṭa. qa:bil qiħṭat?] You mean in all Baghdad there aren't any tomatoes. Do you mean they're that scarce?
قَحَّط [qaħħaṭ] *v:* • **1.** to withhold, to be stingy – لا تقَحِّطها عَلينا. هاي ما تِكفِي [la: tqaħħiṭha ʕali:na. ha:y ma: tikfi] Don't be stingy with us. That isn't enough.
قَحَط [qaħaṭ] *n:* • **1.** drought
قَحَط [qaħaṭ] *n:* • **1.** drought, dryness • **2.** famine • **3.** scarcity, sth. scarce – راوِينا إيّاها عاد! قَحَط؟ [ra:wi:na ʔiyya:ha ʕa:d! qaħaṭ?] Show it to us then! Is it something so precious?

ق ح ف

قِحَف [giħaf] *v:* • **1.** to walk, trudge, slog (expresses a distaste for walking) – ما لَحَّقت بِالباص. رِحِت أَقحَف لِلبَيت [ma: laħħagit bilpa:ṣ. riħit ʔagħaf lilbayt] I didn't catch the bus. I had to go walking home.
ما تحِبّ تِركَب ويّانا؟ لَعَد رُوح إقحَف [ma: tħibb tirkab wiyya:na? laʕad ru:ħ ʔigħaf] You wouldn't like to ride with us? Then go walk.
قَحَّف [gaħħaf] *v:* • **1.** to dry out, get stale – لِفّ الخُبُز لا يقَحِّف [liff ʔilxubuz la: ygaħħif] Wrap up the bread so it won't dry out.
قَحُف [gaħuf, gaħif] *n:* • **1.** walking, on foot – إجِينا لِلمَدرَسَة قَحُف [ʔiji:na lilmadrasa gaħuf] We came to school on foot.
قِحِف [giħif] *n:* قحُوف [għu:f] *pl:* • **1.** piece of broken pottery, pot shard • **2.** worthless person

ق ح ل

قاحِل [qa:ħil] *adj:* • **1.** barren • **2.** dry, arid

ق ح م

قِحَم [giħam] *v:* • **1.** to overcome, best, beat – مَحَّد يِقحَمَه بِالشِّطرَنج [maħħad yigħamah biššiṭranǰ] No one can beat him at chess. هَالامتِحان صَعُب. شيِقحَمَه؟ [halʔimtiħa:n ṣaʕub. šyigħamah?] This exam is hard. How can one get through it?

انقحم [ʔingiħam] *v:* • **1.** to be overcome, beaten – الإطفائي اضطرّ يطلع مِن القبّة لأنّ النّار ما تِنقُحُم [ʔilʔiṭfa:ʔi ʔiðṭarr yiṭlaʕ min ʔilgubba liʔann ʔinna:r ma: tinguħum] The fireman had to leave the room because the fire couldn't be brought under control. هَذا فَدّ واحِد بَلاء. ما ينقُحُم [ha:ða fadd wa:ħid bala:ʔ. ma: yinguħum] He's an extraordinary fellow. He can't be beaten.

اقتحم [ʔiqtiħam] *v:* • **1.** to break in, intrude, invade

قَحُم [gaħum] *n:* • **1.** involving oneself in an affair, sticking one's nose (into) • **2.** intruding

اقتحام [ʔiqtiħa:m] *n:* • **1.** breaking in, intrusion, incursion, invasion

ق د ح

قدَح [qidaħ, ǰidaħ] *v:* • **1.** to spark, make sparks – هَالنّوع مِن الحَجَر ما يقدَح زين [hannu:ʕ min ʔalħaǰar ma: yigdaħ zi:n] This kind of flint doesn't make sparks well.

قَدِح [ǰadiħ, qadiħ] *n:* • **1.** sparking, striking fire (with a flint)

قدّاح [qidda:ħ] *n:* • **1.** (coll.) blossom of citrus tree – وَردَة قدّاح [wardat qidda:ħ] a citrus blossom.

قدّاحَة [qidda:ħa, ǰidda:ħa] *n:* قدّاحات [qidda:ħa:t, ǰidda:ħa:t] *pl:* • **1.** cigarette lighter, flint (for striking sparks)

ق د د

قَدّ [gadd] *n:* • **1.** capable of, equal to – هَذا قَدّ الوَظيفَة [ha:ða gadd ʔilwaði:fa] He's equal to the job. إذا بيك خير تصارَع ويّا واحِد بقَدّك [ʔiða bi:k xi:r tṣa:raʕ wiyya wa:ħid bgaddak] If you're the man you think you are, fight with someone your own size. عَلَى قَدّ [ʕala gadd] commensurate with, according to, in proportion to. عِدنا أكِل عَلَى قَدّ المَعزومين بَسّ [ʕidna ʔakil ʕala gadd ʔilmaʕzu:mi:n bass] We've enough food for only those invited. أحسَن شي وأستَر شي واحِد يُصرُف عَلَى قَدّ فلوسَه [ʔaħsan ši wʔastar ši wa:ħid yuṣruf ʕala gadd flu:sah] The best and most proper thing is for one to spend according to the amount of money he has. هَالثّوب مُو عَلَى قَدّك [haθθu:b mu: ʕala gaddak] This shirt isn't your size. مِن قَدّ ما يلغي، ما خَلّانا نفتهم [min gadd ma: yilɣi, ma: xalla:na niftihim] He talked nonsense so much, we couldn't understand him. • **2.** with ب- : equal in size, commensurate with, in proportion to

هَالقَدّ [halgadd] *n:* • **1.** so much – لا تحكي هَالقَدّ [la: tiħči halgadd] Don't talk so much. تَقديرهُم ما كان هَالقَدّ مَضبوط [taqdi:rhum ma: ča:n halgadd maðbu:ṭ] Their estimate wasn't so very correct. هَل قَدّ ما سمَن، هدومَه ما قامَت ترهَم عليه [hal gadd ma: siman, hdu:mah ma: ga:mat tirham ʕali:h] He got so fat, his clothes wouldn't fit him.

شقدّوتة [šgaddu:ta] *adj:* • **1.** how small, how tiny (usually followed by a Personal Pronoun) – شقدّوتَه ويحكي كبار [šgaddu:tah wyiħči kba:r] Look how tiny he is and he talks so big! شوف هَالسَّيّارَة الأجنَبيّة شقدّوتها [šu:f hassayya:ra ʔilʔaǰnabiyya šgaddu:tha] Look at how tiny this foreign car is!

شقَدّ [šgadd] *interrogative:* • **1.** how much, how many – شقَدّ عَدَدكُم بالصَّفّ؟ [šgadd ʕadadkum biṣṣaff?] How many of you are there in the class? شقَدّ تريد عَلَى هَالسّاعَة؟ [šgadd tri:d ʕala hassa:ʕa?] How much do you want for this watch? شقَدّ صارلَك ببَغداد؟ [šgadd ṣa:rlak bibaɣda:d?] How long have you been in Baghdad? • **2.** how much, so much, so many – شقَدّ قِتلَه "لا تروح"، لَكِن راح [šgadd gitlah "la: tru:ħ", la:kin ra:ħ] So many times I told him 'Don't go', but he went. شقَدّ وَصّيتَه يشتري بَيض ونسَى [šgadd waṣṣi:tah yištiri bayð wnisa:] As many times as I told him to buy eggs and he forgot! شوفَه شقَدّه ويحكي كبار [šu:fah šgaddah wyiħči kba:r] Look at his size and he still talks big! شقَدّ ما أحكي ويّاه ما يفيد [šgadd ma: ʔaħči wiyya:h ma: yfi:d] No matter how much I talk to him, it does no good.

ق د ر 1

قدَر [gidar] *v:* • **1.** to be able, to be capable of – ما قِدَر يسافِر البارحَة [ma: gidar ysa:fir ʔilba:rħa] He couldn't leave yesterday. ما أقدَر أصبُر [ma: ʔagdar ʔaṣbur] I can't wait. • **2.** to have power, be master – لا أبوه وَلا أمَّه يقدرون عليه [la: ʔabu:h wala ʔummah ygidru:n ʕali:h] Neither his father nor his mother can control him. مَحَّد يقدَرلَه لهذا غيري [maħħad yigdarlah lha:ða ɣayri] No one can handle him but me.

قَدَّر [qaddar] *v:* • **1.** to estimate, evaluate – شقَدّ تقَدِّر قيمَة هَالسّاعَة؟ [šgadd tqaddir qi:mat hassa:ʕa?] How much do you estimate the value of this watch to be? الأستاذ قَدَّرلي دَرَجَة وَما إمتِحَنت [ʔilʔusta:ð qaddarli daraǰa wama: ʔimtiħanit] The professor just estimated my grade and I didn't take an exam. • **2.** to appreciate, to think highly of – هُوَّ ما يقَدِّر هيكي نوع مِن الهَدايا [huwwa ma: yqaddir hi:či nu:ʕ min ʔilhada:ya] He doesn't appreciate that kind of presents. كُلّهُم يحترمُوه ويقَدّرُوه [kullhum yiħtarmu:h wyqaddiru:h] They all respect him and think highly of him. • **3.** (of God) to ordain, decree – إذا الله قَدَّر وَمُطرَت، الزَّرع ما يموت [ʔiða ʔallah qaddar wmuṭrat, ʔizzariʕ ma: ymu:t] If God decides to make it rain, the crops won't die. إذا --- الله لا يقَدِّر --- مِتِت، منو يهتَمّ بينا؟ [ʔiða ʔallah la: yqaddir mitit, minu yihtamm bi:na?] If --- God forbid --- you died, who would care for us?

قَدَّر [gaddar] *v:* • **1.** to try, measure, fit – قَدِّر البَردَة عالشِّبّاك [gaddir ʔilparda ʕaššibba:k] Measure the curtains to the window. قَدِّر هَالقُندَرَة، شوفها إذا عَلَى قَدَّك [gaddir halqundara, šu:fha ʔiða ʕala gaddak] Try on these shoes and see if they're your size. قَدِّر القُماش عَلَيّا [gaddir ʔilquma:š ʕalayya] Fit the cloth to me. هَذا شمقَدّرَه يتصارَع ويّا عَلي؟ عَلي أقوَى هوايَة [ha:ða šmgaddrah yitṣa:raʕ wiyya ʕali? ʕali ʔaqwa hwa:ya] How could he possibly wrestle with Ali? Ali is much stronger.

تقَدَّر [tqaddar] *v:* • **1.** to be appraised

ق

إنقدر [ʔingidar] *v:* • **1.** with عَلَى to be beaten, bested, overcome – هَذا عِفريت. ما ينقدِر عَليه [haːða ʕifriːt. maː yingidir ʕaliːh] He is very strong. He can't be beaten. • **2.** with لـ to be managed – إبنَك وَقيح. ما ينقدِرلَه [ʔibnak wakiːħ. maː yingidirlah] Your son is a bad boy. He can't be controlled.

قدِر [gadir, qadir] *n:* • **1.** prestige, regard – لَيلَة القَدِر [laylat ʔilqadir] night of the 26th of Ramadan, celebrating the revealing of the Koran to Mohammed. قَدَر الإمكان، عَلَى قَدَر الإمكان [qadar ʔilʔimkaːn, ʕala qadar ʔilʔimkaːn] as much as possible. راح أصبُر قَدَر الإمكان [raːħ ʔaṣbur qadar ʔilʔimkaːn] I'll be patient as long as possible. وُصلَة القُماش كانَت عالقِدَر [wuṣlat ʔilqumaːš čaːnat ʕalgidar] The piece of cloth was just right. بقدِر ما تسَوّي ويّاه زين، يسِبَّك [bqadir maː tsawwiː wiyyaːh ziːn, ysibbak] To the same extent that you treat him well, he'll insult you.

قَدَر [qadar] *n:* أقدار [ʔaqdaːr] *pl:* • **1.** divine foreordainment, fate, destiny – مات قَضاء وَقَدَر [maːt qaðaːʔ wqadar] He died of natural causes. إذا صار قَدَر بِالسَّيّارَة، شراح نسَوّي؟ [ʔiða ṣaːr qadar bissayyaːra, šraːħ nsawwiː?] If something goes wrong with the car, what will we do?

قدِر [gadar, gadir] *n:* • **1.** measure, measurement

قُدرَة [qudra] *n:* • **1.** capacity, ability, capability, aptitude – عِندَه قُدرَة عَلَى هالشُّغُل الصَّعُب [ʕindah qudra ʕala haššuɣul ʔiṣṣaʕub] He has the ability for this difficult work. طاب بقُدرَة الله [ṭaːb bqudrat ʔallah] He got well by the power of God. عايِش بِالقُدرَة [ʕaːyiš bilqudra] He's living by the will of God.

مُقدِّر [muqaddir] *adj:* • **1.** considerate

مِقدار [miqdaːr] *n:* مَقادِير [maqaːdiːr] *pl:* • **1.** period, extent of time • **2.** amount, scope, extent, rate, range, quantity

تَقدِير [taqdiːr] *n:* تَقدِيرات [taqdiːraːt] *pl:* • **1.** estimate, calculation, valuation – عَلَى أقَلّ تَقدِير [ʕala ʔaqall taqdiːr] at least. عَلَى أكثَر تَقدِير [ʕala ʔakθar taqdiːr] at most.

مُقدار، مِقدار [mugdaːr, migdaːr] *n:* مِقدارات [migdaːraːt] *pl:* • **1.** amount, quantity

مَقدِرَة [maqdira] *n:* • **1.** ability, capacity, aptitude, capability

اِقتِدار [ʔiqtidaːr] *n:* • **1.** ability, capability, capacity – كُلّ مَن يتبَرَّع عَلَى قَدّ اِقتِدارَه [kull man yitbarraʕ ʕala gadd ʔiqtidaːrah] Everyone donates according to his means. ما عِندي اِقتِدار أشتِري بَيت [maː ʕindi ʔiqtidaːr ʔaštiri bayt] I'm not able to buy a house. ساعَة يَالله يطبَع صَحيفَة. اِقتِدارَه هَالقَدّ [saːʕa yallah yitbaʕ ṣaħiːfa. ʔiqtidaːrah halgadd] It takes him a whole hour to type a page. That's all he's capable of.

مقَدَّر [mqaddar] *adj:* • **1.** estimated, appreciated • **2.** decreed, predestined

قادِر [qaːdir] *adj:* • **1.** capable, possessing power or stength

مُقتَدِر [muqtadir] *adj:* • **1.** well to do

تَقدِيرِي [taqdiːri] *adj:* • **1.** estimated

أقدَر [ʔaqdar] *comparative adjective:* • **1.** more or most capable

ق د ر 2

جِدِر، قِدِر [ǰidir] *n:* جدُور، جدُورَة [ǰduːr, ǰduːra] *pl:* • **1.** pot, cooking vessel

ق د س

قَدَّس [qaddas] *v:* • **1.** to hold sacred, venerate, revere – أهل القَريَة يقَدِّسُون هالعالِم الدِّيني [ʔahl ʔilqarya yqaddisuːn halʕaːlim ʔiddiːni] The people of the village venerate this religious authority. البارحَة كمشُوه بِالدَّربُونَة وَقَدّسُوه [ʔilbaːrħa kumšuːh biddarbuːna wqaddisuːh] Yesterday they caught him in the alley and beat him up.

قُدُس، القُدُس [qudus, ʔilqudus] *n:* • **1.** Jerusalem – رُوح القُدُس، الرُّوح القُدُس [ruːħ ʔilqudus] the Holy Ghost.

قُدّاس [quddaːs] *n:* قُدّاسات، قَدادِيس [quddaːsaːt, qadaːdiːs] *pl:* • **1.** Mass

قِدِّيس [qiddiːs] *n:* قِدِّيسِين [qiddiːsiːn] *pl:* • **1.** saint (Christian)

قَداسَة [qadaːsa] *n:* • **1.** holiness – قَداسَة البّابا [qadaːsat ʔilbaːbaː] His Holiness the Pope.

تَقدِيس [taqdiːs] *n:* • **1.** sanctification, consecration (as part of the Roman Catholic Mass)

مُقَدَّس [muqaddas] *adj:* • **1.** holy, sacred – الكِتاب المُقَدَّس [ʔilkitaːb ʔalmuqaddas] The Holy Bible. بمُقَدَّساتي، ما أعرُف عَنَّه شي [bmuqaddasaːti, maː ʔaʕruf ʕannah ši] By all the things I hold to be holy, I don't know anything about it.

قُدسِيَّة [qudsiyya] *n:* • **1.** holiness, sacredness, sanctity

ق د غ

قَدَغَة [qadaɣa] *n:* • **1.** bother, trouble, pain-in-the-neck, headache

ق د ف

قَدِيفَة [qadiːfa] *n:* • **1.** velvet (cloth) – عير قَدِيفَة [ʕiːr qadiːfa] dildo.

ق د م

قَدَّم [qaddam] *v:* • **1.** to offer, proffer, tender, extend, present – قَدِّمُولنا كَيك وَشاي [qaddimuːlna kayk wčaːy] They offered us cake and tea. قَدِّمتِلَه كُلّ مُساعَدَة مُمكِنَة [qaddamitlah kull musaːʕada mumkina] I offered him all possible assistance. قَدِّملي هَدِيَّة حِلوَة [qaddamli hadiyya ħilwa] He presented me with a nice gift. أريد أقَدِّملَك صَدِيقي [ʔariːd ʔaqaddimlak ṣadiːqi] I want to present my friend to you. إسمَحلي أقَدِّم نَفسِي [ʔismaħli ʔaqaddim nafsi] Let me introduce myself.

ق

قِدّام [gidda:m] *n:* • **1.** in front of – لا تذبّ الزّبل قِدّام البَيت [la: dðibb ʔizzibil gidda:m ʔilbayt] Don't throw the trash in front of the house. اِنطاه الفلُوس قِدّامِي [ʔinṭa:h ʔilflu:s gidda:mi] He gave him the money in my presence.

تَقَدُّم [taqaddum] *n:* • **1.** development, advancement, advance, progression, progress

قَدَمِيَّة [qadamiyya] *n:* • **1.** extra charge by a doctor for a house call

مُقَدِّمَة، مُقَدَّمَة [muqaddima, muqaddama] *n:* مُقَدِّمات [muqaddama:t] *pl:* • **1.** bow (of a ship), nose (of an airplane) • **2.** advance guard, vanguard, van • **3.** foreword, preface, introduction, prologue, preamble – قُولّي شتِرِيد. ماكُو حاجَة لِلمُقَدِّمات [gulli šitri:d. ma:ku ħa:ja lilmuqaddima:t] Tell me what you want. There's no reason for beating around the bush.

لِقِدّام [ligidda:m] *prepositional:* • **1.** to the front, forward – مِن تسُوق، باوِع لِقِدّام [min tsu:q, ba:wiʕ ligidda:m] When you drive, look to the front. خَلّي نُقعُد لِقِدّام [xalli: nugʕud ligidda:m] Let's sit down front. • **2.** in advance, beforehand, ahead of time – أخَذ عِشرِين دِينار لِقِدّام [ʔaxað ʕišri:n dina:r ligidda:m] He took twenty dinars in advance. أَقُلَّك لِقِدّام لازم تِشتِري بِطاقة [ʔagullak ligidda:m la:zim tištiri biṭa:qa] I'll tell you ahead of time, you have to buy a ticket.

تَقدِيم [taqdi:m] *n:* • **1.** applying, submission, offering, dedication

أَقدَمِيَّة [ʔaqdamiyya] *n:* • **1.** seniority

قَدِيم [qadi:m] *adj:* قُدَماء [qudama:ʔ] *pl:* • **1.** old, ancient – التّارِيخ القَدِيم [ʔitta:ri:x ʔilqadi:m] ancient history. صَدِيق قَدِيم [ṣadi:q qadi:m] an old friend. • **2.** former, previous, old – مَرتَه القَدِيمَة [martah ʔilqadi:ma] his former wife. مِن قَدِيم مِن قَدِيم [min qadi:m min qadi:m] from time immemorial. هالعائِلَة تُسكُن بِبَغداد مِن قَدِيم [halʕa:ʔila tuskun bibaɣda:d min qadi:m] This family has lived in Baghdad for generations.

قادِم [qa:dim] *adj:* • **1.** coming, next – لِلإسبُوع القادِم [lilʔisbu:ʕ ʔilqa:dim] next week, for the coming week

مِتقَدِّم [mitqaddim] *adj:* • **1.** in front, ahead – مِتقَدِّم عَلَى جَماعتَه [mitqaddim ʕala jama:ʕtah] ahead of his group. طالِب مِتقَدِّم [ṭa:lib mitqaddim] an advanced student.

أَقدَم [ʔaqdam] *comparative adjective:* • **1.** more or most ancient – هُوَّ أَقدَم مِنَّك بِهالدّائِرَة [huwwa ʔaqdam minnak bhadda:ʔira] He has seniority over you in this office.

مُقَدَّماً [muqaddaman] *adverbial:* • **1.** in advance, beforehand, first of all – دِفَعِت عَشِر دَنانِير مُقَدَّماً [difaʕit ʕašir dana:ni:r muqaddaman] I paid ten dinars in advance. مُقَدَّماً، أَقُلَّك ما تصِير [muqaddaman, ʔagullak ma: tṣi:r] First of all, I tell you it'll never happen.

قَدَّم تَقرِير عَن زِيارتَه لِلمَعمَل [qaddam taqri:r ʕan ziya:rtah lilmaʕmal] He presented a report on his visit to the factory. • **2.** to place (someone) at the head, ahead of – قَدَّم إبنَه عَلَى باقِي الطُّلّاب [qaddam ʔibnah ʕala ba:qi ʔiṭṭulla:b] He placed his son ahead of the rest of the students. قَدَّمتَه عَلَى نَفسِي [qaddamtah ʕala nafsi] I let him get ahead of me. • **3.** to give priority to – لا تقَدِّم أيّ شِي عَلَى هالشُّغُل [la: tqaddim ʔayy ši ʕala haššuɣul] Don't give anything priority over this job. • **4.** to apply – قَدَّم عَلَى قَبُول بِثلَث كُلِّيّات [qaddam ʕala qabu:l biθlaθ kulliyya:t] He applied for admission to three colleges. • **5.** to set ahead (a watch) – راح نقَدِّم ساعاتنا ساعَة وحدَة [ra:ħ nqaddim sa:ʕa:tna sa:ʕa wiħda] We're going to set our watches ahead an hour. • **6.** to gain, to be fast (a watch) – ساعتِي قَدّمَت خَمِس دَقايِق اليُوم [sa:ʕti qaddmat xamis daqa:yiq ʔilyu:m] My watch gained five minutes today.

قَدَّم [qaddam, gaddam] *v:* • **1.** to make or let precede – أُخُذهُم بِالسِّرَة. لا تقَدِّم واحِد عَاللّاخ [ʔuxuðhum bissira. la: tqaddim wa:ħid ʕalla:x] Take them in order. Don't put one ahead of the other. • **2.** to move up, move forward, advance – قَدِّم الماعُون يَمَّك حَتَّى ما يُوقَع الأكِل عَالقاع [gaddim ʔilma:ʕu:n yammak ħatta ma: yu:gaʕ ʔilʔakil ʕalga:ʕ] Move the dish close to you so that the food won't fall on the floor.

أَقدَم [ʔaqdam] *v:* • **1.** with عَلَى to have the audacity to – ما يِقدِم عَلَى هِيكِي عَمَل إلّا المَجنُون [ma: yiqdim ʕala hi:či ʕamal ʔilla ʔilmajnu:n] Nobody would have the audacity for such a deed except a crazy person.

تقَدَّم [tqaddam] *v:* • **1.** to go forward, advance – جَيشنا تقَدَّم خَمِس كِيلُومَترات [jayšna tqaddam xamis ki:lu:matra:t] Our army advanced five kilometers. • **2.** to progress, make progress – الصِّناعَة هوايَة تقَدّمَت [ʔiṣṣina:ʕa hwa:ya tqaddmat] Industry has progressed a lot. • **3.** to be served – الأكِل راح يِتقَدَّم ساعَة خَمسَة [ʔilʔakil ra:ħ yitqaddam sa:ʕa xamsa] The food will be served at five.

تقَدَّم [tqaddam, tgaddam] *v:* • **1.** to move forward, advance – لا تِتقَدَّم يَمّ الكَلِب تَرَة يعَضَّك [la: titgaddam yamm ʔiččalib tara yʕaððak] Don't go near the dog or he'll bite you. بَسّ تِتقَدَّم! أَبُسطَك [bass titgaddam! ʔabusṭak] Just take one more step! I'll clobber you.

اِستَقدَم [ʔistaqdam] *v:* • **1.** to ask to come, summon – الحُكُومَة راح تِستَقدِم خَبِير أمرِيكِي بِالدِّباغَة [ʔilħuku:ma ra:ħ tistaqdim xabi:r ʔamri:ki biddiba:ɣa] The government is going to bring in an American expert in tanning.

قِدَم [qidam] *n:* • **1.** seniority

قَدَم [qadam] *n:* أقدام [ʔaqda:m] *pl:* • **1.** foot – أَثَر قَدَم [ʔaθar qadam] a footprint. • **2.** foot (as a unit of measure)

مُقَدَّم [muqaddam] *n:* مُقَدَّمات [muqaddama:t] *pl:* • **1.** bow (of a ship) • **2.** nose (of an airplane, etc.) • **3.** (no pl.) portion of the bridal price paid in advance

ق

ق د و

اِقتَدَى [ʔiqtida:] *v:* • **1.** to imitate, copy, emulate, follow someone's example – لازِم تِقتِدُون بِيه [la:zim tiqtidu:n bi:h] You should follow his example.
اِقتِداء [ʔiqtida:ʔ] *n:* • **1.** imitation, emulation • **2.** with ب following the model or example (of)
قُدوَة، قِدوَة [qudwa, qidwa] *adj:* قُدوات [qudwa:t] *pl:* • **1.** model, pattern, example

ق ذ ر

قَذارَة [qaða:ra] *n:* • **1.** dirtiness, filthiness, squalor
قاذُورَة [qa:ðu:ra] *n:* قاذُورات [qa:ðu:ra:t] *pl:* • **1.** dirt, filth • **2.** قاذُورات trash, rubbish, garbage
قَذِر [qaðir] *adj:* • **1.** dirty, filthy – ماعُون قَذِر [ma:ʕu:n qaðir] a filthy plate. • **2.** vile, depraved, filthy • **3.** vile person
أقذَر [ʔaqðar] *comparative adjective:* • **1.** more or most filthy, vile

ق ذ ف

قِذَف [qiðaf] *v:* • **1.** to ejaculate (semen) • **2.** to vomit – نَفسَه لِعبَت وَقِذَف [nafsah liʕbat wqiðaf] He got nauseated and vomited. • **3.** to fling, to hurl (e.g., a bomb)
قَذِف [qaðif] *n:* • **1.** ejaculation, emission, discharge • **2.** act of hurling, throwing
قَذّاف [qaðða:f] *n:* • **1.** howitzer (military)
قَذِيفَة [qaði:fa] *n:* قَذائِف [qaða:ʔif, qaða:yif] *pl:* • **1.** projectile, artillery shell
قاذِفَة، قاذِفَة قَنابِل [qa:ðifa, qa:ðifat qana:bil] *adj:* • **1.** bomber (airplane) – قاذِفَة لَهَب [qa:ðifat lahab] flame thrower.

ق ذ ل

قُذلَة [guðla] *n:* قُذَل [guðal] *pl:* • **1.** forelock

ق ر ء

قِرا، قِرَأ [qira:, qiraʔ] *v:* • **1.** to recite, declaim, chant – مِنُو راح يِقرا قُرآن بِالرّادِيُو اليُوم؟ [minu ra:ħ yiqra: qurʔa:n birra:dyu ʔilyu:m?] Who is going to recite the Koran on the radio today? السّاحِر قِرا عالكَفِّيَّة وَانقُلبَت أَرنَب [ʔissa:ħir qira: ʕalčaffiyya wʔingulbat ʔarnab] The magician recited magic words over the handkerchief and it turned into a rabbit. أَيّ كتاب يَوقَع بِايد عَلِي بَعَد ما تشُوفَه. إقرا عَلَيه السَّلام [ʔayy kta:b yu:gaʕ bʔi:d ʕali baʕad ma: tšu:fah. ʔiqra ʕali:h ʔissala:m] Any book that falls into Ali's hands you won't see again. Kiss it good-by. • **2.** to read – قِريت جَرِيدَة اليُوم؟ [qiri:t ǰari:dat ʔilyu:m?] Have you read today's paper? شِمعَرّفَك؟ قابِل تِقرا المَمحِي؟ [šimʕarrfak? qa:bil tiqra: ʔilmamħi?] How do you know? Do you mean to tell me you can divine the unknown? • **3.** to study – إذا تِقرا زين، تِنجَح بِالإمتِحان [ʔiða tiqra: zi:n, tinǰaħ bilʔimtiħa:n] If you study well, you'll pass the exam.
قَرَّى [qarra:] *v:* • **1.** to cause to read – أَشُو المُعَلِّم ما دَيقَرِّينِي [ʔašu ʔilmuʕallim ma: dayqarri:ni] It seems the teacher doesn't ever ask me to read. • **2.** to teach, tutor – هَالمُعَلِّم يقَرِّينا حساب [halmuʕallim yqarri:na ħsa:b] This teacher teaches us arithmetic. قَرِّيت إبنِي درُوسَه [qarri:t ʔibni dru:sah] I helped my son with his lessons.
تقَرّا [tqarra:] *v:* • **1.** to be taught – هَالمواضِيع ما تِتقَرّا بصفُوف بِيها بَنات [halmwa:ði:ʕ ma: titqarra: bṣfu:f bi:ha bana:t] These subjects aren't taught in classes where there are girls.
اِنقِرَى [ʔinqira:] *v:* • **1.** to be recited – القَصِيدَة اِنقِرَت لَو بَعَد؟ [ʔilqaṣi:da ʔinqirat law baʕad?] Has the poem been recited yet? • **2.** to be read – هَالكِتابَة ما تِنقِرِي [halkita:ba ma: tinqiri] This writing can't be read.
قُرآن [qurʔa:n, qurʕa:n] *n:* قرائِين [qara:ʔi:n, qara:ʕi:n] *pl:* • **1.** Koran, holy book of the Moslems
قارِي، قارِئ [qa:ri, qa:riʔ] *n:* قارِيِّن، قُرّاء [qa:riyyin, qurra:ʔ] *pl:* • **1.** reader • **2.** reciter (of the Koranic text) • **3.** قِرَاءَات manner of recitation, punctuation and vocalization of the Koranic text
قِراءَة، قِرايَة [qira:ʔa, qira:ya] *n:* قِرايات [qira:ya:t] *pl:* • **1.** recitation, recital • **2.** reading • **3.** قِراءات attested manner of recitation of the Koran with attested punctuation and vocalization.
قرايَة [qra:ya] *n:* قرايات [qra:ya:t] *pl:* • **1.** mourning ceremony (Shiite)
قُرآنِي [qurʔa:ni] *adj:* • **1.** Koranic, or pertaining to the Koran

ق ر ب

قِرَب [qirab, girab] *v:* • **1.** to draw near, approach – الامتِحان قِرَب. لازِم نِتحَضَّرلَه [ʔilʔimtiħa:n girab. la:zim nitħaððarlah] The examination is near. We must get ready for it. • **2.** to be related (as in قَرابَة kinship, family relationship) – هَذا ما يِقرَبلِي [ha:ða ma: yigrabli] He isn't related to me.
قَرَّب [qarrab] *v:* • **1.** to cause or allow to come near or get close – الحادِث قَرَّب بين العائِلتَين [ʔilħa:diθ qarrab bi:n ʔilʕa:ʔiltayn] The accident brought the two families closer together. • **2.** to take as a protege, take under one's wing, to favor – المُدِير الجِّدِيد قَرَّب عَلِي إلَه [ʔilmudi:r ʔiǰǰidi:d qarrab ʕali ʔilah] The new director took Ali under his wing.
قارَب [qa:rab] *v:* • **1.** to come close, get close, approach – حسابنا قارَب المِيَة دِينار [ħsa:bna qa:rab ʔilmiyat dina:r] Our account came close to a hundred dinars.
تقَرَّب [tqarrab, tgarrab] *v:* • **1.** to approach, come or get near, near, come close, get close – لا تِتقَرَّب، تَرَة الكَلِب يعَضّك [la: titqarrab, tara ʔiččalib yʕaððak] Don't get too close or the dog will bite you. لا تِتقَرَّب مِنِّي [la: titqarrab minni] Don't come near me. إذا بَردان، تقَرَّب يَمّ النّار

[ʔiða barda:n, tqarrab yamm ʔinna:r] If you're cold get close to the fire. ظَلّ يِتقَرَّب عَلَيّا إِلَى أن وَقَّعنِي بِالشَّطّ [ðall yitqarrab ʕalayya ʔila ʔan waggaʕni biššaṭṭ] He kept getting closer to me till he knocked me into the river. • **2.** with إِلَى to curry favor with, to seek to gain someone's favor – شُوف شلُون دَيِتقَرَّب لِلمُدِير [šu:f šlu:n dayitqarrab lilmudi:r] Look how he's carrying favor with the boss. دَيِتصَدَّق عَالفُقَراء حَتَّى يِتقَرَّب لِالله [dayitṣaddaq ʕalfuqara:ʔ ħatta yitqarrab lʔallah] He's giving charity to the poor to endear himself to God.

تقارَب [tqa:rab] *v:* • **1.** to be or become near each other, approach one another – نُوّاب المُعارَضَة بِدَوا يِتقارِبُون بآراءهُم وِيّا الحُكُومَة [nuwwa:b ʔilmuʕa:raða bidaw yitqa:rbu:n bʔa:ra:ʔhum wiyya ʔilħuku:ma] The opposition deputies have begun to get close to the government in their opinions.

اِقتِرَب [ʔiqtirab] *v:* • **1.** to approach, get close – الصَّيف اِقتِرَب. حَضِّر هدُومَك [ʔiṣṣayf ʔiqtirab. ħaððir hdu:mak] Summer is getting near. Get your clothes ready. جيش العَدُو اِقتِرَب مِن مَواضِعنا [jayš ʔilʕadu ʔiqtirab min mawa:ðiʕna] The enemy army approached our positions.

اِستقرَب [ʔistagrab, ʔistaqrab] *v:* • **1.** to find near, regard as near – أدرِي هَالمَحَلّ غالِي بَسّ اِستَقرَبتَه [ʔadri halmaħall ɣa:li bass ʔistagrabtah] I realize this place is expensive but I figured it was nearer. • **2.** to drop in, come by (someone's house) – لِيش دَترُوح لِلبَيت؟ اِستَقرُب اليُوم وَتغَدَّى وِيّانا، ما دام صار وَقت الأكِل [li:š datru:ħ lilbayt? ʔistaqrub ʔilyu:m widɣadda: wiyya:na, ma: da:m ṣa:r wakit ʔilʔakil] Why are you going home? Come on and have dinner with us today, since it's time to eat. اِستَقرُب. اليُوم عِدنا سِمَك [ʔistaqrub. ʔilyu:m ʕidna simač] Drop by on your way and eat with us. We're having fish today.

قُرُب [qurub, gurub] *n:* • **1.** near, close to – وُصَل لِلمَدرَسَة قُرب الظُّهُر [wuṣal lilmadrasa qurb ʔiððuhur] He got to the school near noon. ما عَبالِي المَدرَسَة هَالقُرُب [ma: ʕaba:li ʔilmadrasa halqurub] I didn't realize the school was this close. تِعتِقِد راح يِجِي بِهَالقُرُب؟ [tiʕtiqid ra:ħ yiji bhalqurub?] Do you think he'll come in the near future?

قَرِيب [qari:b, gari:b] *n:* • **1.** near, close, nearby – قَرِيب مِن البَيت [qari:b min ʔilbayt] near the house. قَرِيب عَالسَّيّارَة [qari:b ʕassayya:ra] close to the car. مَكان قَرِيب [maka:n qari:b] a nearby place. • **2.** about to – هُوَّ قَرِيب يصِير مُدِير عامّ [huwwa qari:b yṣi:r mudi:r ʕa:mm] He's about to become director general. • **3.** pl. أقرِباء relative, relation (biological or by marriage)

قِربَة [girba] *n:* قِرَب [girab] *pl:* • **1.** water skin • **2.** water bag made of canvas, desert cooler • **3.** clay water jug

قراب [gra:b] *n:* قرابات [gra:ba:t] *pl:* • **1.** sheath or scabbard (for a knife or sword) – قراب مُسَدِّس [gra:b musaddis] holster.

قارِب [qa:rib] *n:* قَوارِب [qawa:rib] *pl:* • **1.** boat, skiff

تَقَرُّب [taqarrub] *n:* • **1.** approach, approximation

قَرابَة [qara:ba, gara:ba] *n:* • **1.** relation, relationship, kinship

قُربان [qurba:n] *n:* قَرابِين [qara:bi:n] *pl:* • **1.** sacrifice

قُرّابَة [qurra:ba] *n:* قُرّابات [qurra:ba:t] *pl:* • **1.** carboy, demijohn

تَقرِيب [taqri:b] *n:* • **1.** approximation

اِقتِراب [ʔiqtira:b] *n:* • **1.** approach, approximation

قَرِيب، قرَيِّب [qari:b, qrayyib, giri:b, grayyib] *adj:* • **1.** close, near, nearby place – هَل كَراج قرَيِّب. خَلِّي نوَدِّي السَّيّارَة لَه [hal gara:ǰ grayyib. xalli: nwaddi: ʔissayya:ra lah] That garage is near by. Let's take the car to it. • **2.** about to

مُقَرَّب [muqarrab] *adj:* • **1.** intimate, close

مُقارِب [muqa:rib] *adj:* • **1.** mediocre, borderline – دَرَجَة مُقارِبَة [daraǰa muqa:riba] a borderline grade. • **2.** almost, close to, approaching – عَدَدهُم كان مُقارِب لِلمِيَّة [ʕadadhum ča:n muqa:rib lilmiyya] Their number was almost a hundred. إذا ما عِندَك قاط أسوَد اِلبَس قاط مُقارِب لِلأسوَد [ʔiða ma: ʕindak qa:ṭ ʔaswad ʔilbas qa:ṭ muqa:rib lilʔaswad] If you don't have a black suit, wear a suit that is almost black.

قَرايِب [gara:yib] *adj:* • **1.** (invar.) relative – عَلِي قَرايبِي [ʕali gara:ybi] Ali is my relative.

تَقرِيبِي [taqri:bi] *adj:* • **1.** approximate, approximative

مِتقارِب [mitqa:rib] *adj:* • **1.** similar, close together

أقرَب [ʔaqrab, ʔagrab] *comparative adjective:* • **1.** more or most near, close, etc. (also fig.)

قَرِيباً [qariyiban] *adverbial:* • **1.** soon, before long, shortly, in the near future

تَقرِيباً [taqri:ban] *adverbial:* • **1.** roughly, about, approximately, almost, nearly – راتبَه مِيَّة دِينار تَقرِيباً [ra:tbah miyyat dina:r taqri:ban] His salary is nearly a hundred dinars.

ق ر ب ز

مُقُربَاز [muqurba:z] *n:* مُقُربَازِيَّة [muqurba:ziyya] *pl:* • **1.** cheater, swindler, crook • **2.** juggler

ق ر ج

قَرَج [qarač] *adj:* قَرايِج [qara:yic] *pl:* • **1.** loud, brazen, insolent • **2.** when a Noun: brazen woman

ق ر ح

تقَرَّح [tqarraħ] *v:* • **1.** to be ulcerated, be covered with ulcers

اِقتِرَح [ʔiqtiraħ] *v:* • **1.** to suggest, recommend, to propose, to suggest – أَقتِرِح عَلِيك تخابُرنِي قَبِل ما تِشتِرِيها [ʔaqtiriħ ʕali:k txa:burni gabil ma: tištiri:ha] I suggest that you call me before you buy it.

قُرحَة [qurħa] *n:* قُرَح، قُرحات [qurah, qurħa:t] *pl:* • **1.** ulcer

قَرِيحَة [qari:ħa] *n:* • **1.** genius, talent, gift, faculty

ق

مُقتَرَح [muqtaraħ] *n:* • **1.** proposal, suggestion, proposition
اِقتِراح [ʔiqtira:ħ] *n:* اِقتِراحات [ʔiqtira:ħa:t] *pl:* • **1.** suggestion, proposal
مِتقَرِّح [mitqarriħ] *adj:* • **1.** covered with ulcers

ق ر د 1

قِرد [qird] *n:* قُرُود [quru:d] *pl:* • **1.** ape, monkey, chimpanzee, simian

ق ر د 2

قَرَّد [garrad] *v:* • **1.** to hang on, to hold back – قَرَّد عَلَيّا وَما خَلّانِي أرُوح [garrad ʕalayya wama xalla:ni ʔaru:ħ] He hung on and didn't let me go. • **2.** to get in the way, to interfere – قَرَّد عَلَيّا وَحِرَمنِي مِن التَّرفِيع [garrad ʕalayya wħiramni min ʔittarfi:ʕ] He got in my way and kept me from being promoted. بمُخالَفتَك لِلتَّعليمات قَرَّدِت عَلينا وَما نِقدَر نوَقُّف السَّيّارَة هنا بَعَد [bmuxa:laftak littaʕli:ma:t garradit ʕali:na wma nigdar nwagguf ʔissayya:ra hna baʕad] By your violation of the rules, you loused things up for us and we can't park here anymore.
قِرِد [girid] *n:* • **1.** hard luck – مِن قَردَه، خَطِيَّة، يِنفُصِل [min gardah, xaṭiyya, yinfuṣil] It's his hard luck, poor fellow, to get fired.
قَراد [gara:d] *n:* • **1.** (coll.) tick, ticks (zool.)
قَرادَة [gara:da] *n:* قَرادات [gara:da:t] *pl:* • **1.** a tick (zool.)
مَقرُود [magru:d] *adj:* مقارِيد [mga:ri:d] *pl:* • **1.** pitiful, harmless, insignificant • **2.** a pitiful person

ق ر د ل

قُرديلَة [qurdi:la] *n:* قُرديلات [qurdi:la:t] *pl:* • **1.** ribbon, hair ribbon, bow

ق ر ر 1

قَرّ [qarr] *v:* • **1.** to confess, admit – ظَلّوا يِبسطُون بِيه حَتَّى قَرّ [ðallaw yibusṭu:n bi:h ħatta qarr] They kept beating on him until he confessed.
قَرَّر [qarrar] *v:* • **1.** to assign, stipulate, approve, decide on – وِزارَة المَعارِف قَرَّرَت هَالكِتاب [wiza:rat ʔilmaʕa:rif qarrarat halkita:b] The ministry of education assigned this book. • **2.** to decide – قَرَّرِت تِجي وِيّانا وَإلّا لا؟ [qarrarit tiji wiyya:na waʔilla la:?] Have you decided to come with us or not? • **3.** to lecture – بَعَد ما يقَرِّر المُدَرِّس الدَّرِس، تصِير مُناقَشَة [baʕad ma: yqarrir ʔilmudarris ʔiddaris, tṣi:r muna:qaša] After the teacher lectures to the class, there'll be a discussion. إسكُت! الأُستاذ دَيقَرِّر [ʔiskut! ʔalʔusta:ð dayqarrir] Be quiet! The professor is lecturing. • **4.** to interrogate, grill, cross-examine – الشُّرطَة ظَلَّت تقَرِّر بِيه إلَى أن اِعتِرَف [ʔiššurṭa ðallat tqarrir bi:h ʔila ʔan ʔiʕtiraf] The police kept grilling him until he confessed. المَحكَمَة قَرَّرَت المَسجُون [ʔilmaħkama qarrarat ʔilmasju:n] The court cross-examined the prisoner.
تقَرَّر [tqarrar] *v:* • **1.** to be decided – تقَرَّر نَقلَه لِلبَصرَة [tqarrar naqlah lilbaṣra] It was decided he'd be transferred to Basra.
اِستَقَرّ [ʔistaqarr] *v:* • **1.** to settle down, become settled, take up residence – ما دَيِستَقِرّ بمُكان [ma: dayistaqirr bmuka:n] He won't settle down in one place. • **2.** to settle, stabilize, become stabilized – الوَضِع اِستَقَرّ بالشِّمال [ʔilwaðiʕ ʔistaqarr biššima:l] The situation has calmed down in the North. فِكرَه ما اِستَقَرّ عَلَى شِي بَعَد [fikrah ma: ʔistaqarr ʕala ši baʕad] His mind hasn't settled on anything yet. His mind isn't made up yet.
مَقَرّ [maqarr] *n:* مَقَرّات [maqarra:t] *pl:* • **1.** headquarters, center of operations
قَرار [qara:r] *n:* قَرارات [qara:ra:t] *pl:* • **1.** decision, resolution – قَرار الحُكُم [qara:r ʔilħukum] the sentence, decision of the court.
قارَّة [qa:rra] *n:* قارّات [qa:rra:t] *pl:* • **1.** continent
تَقرِير [taqri:r] *n:* تَقارِير [taqa:ri:r] *pl:* • **1.** (official) report, account – تَقرِير المَصِير [taqri:r ʔilmaṣi:r] self-determination.
إقرار [ʔiqra:r] *n:* إقرارات [ʔiqra:ra:t] *pl:* • **1.** confession, admission
مُستَقَرّ [mustaqarr] *n:* • **1.** settlement • **2.** resting place
مُقَرَّرات [muqarrara:t] *n:* • **1.** (pl. only) decisions
اِستِقرار [ʔistiqra:r] *n:* • **1.** settledness, steadiness, stabilization, stability
مقَرَّر [mqarrar] *adj:* • **1.** decided
مُستَقِرّ [mustaqirr] *adj:* • **1.** same as قارّ [qa:rr] stable • **2.** settled

ق ر ر 2

قَرّ [garr] *v:* • **1.** with عَين [ʕayn] to congratulate – خَلّي نرُوح نقُرّ عَينها لِأمّ عَلي. إبِنها نِجَح بالإمتِحان [xalli: nru:ħ ngurr ʕaynha lʔumm ʕali. ʔibinha nijaħ bilʔimtiħa:n] Let's go congratulate Ali's mother. Her son passed the exam.
قُرَّة، قُرَّة عَينَك [gurra, gurrat ʕaynak] *n:* • **1.** congratulations! – قُرَّة عينَك! سِمَعِت إبنَك صار طَبِيب [gurrat ʕaynak! simaʕit ʔibnak ṣa:r ṭabi:b] congratulations! I heard your son became a doctor.

ق ر ز

قرِيز [gri:z] *n:* • **1.** grease

ق ر ش

قارَش [qa:raš] *v:* • **1.** to cope, compete, keep up – إذا تِتدَرَّب قَبُل ما تِلعَب وِيّاه، تِعتِقِد تِقدَر تقارِش؟ [ʔiða tiddarrab gabul ma: tilʕab wiyya:h, tiʕtiqid tigdar tqa:riš?] If you practice before you play him, do you think you can compete on equal terms? لا تِلعَب وِيّاه طاولي تَرَة ما تِقدَر تقارِش [la: tilʕab wiyya:h ṭa:wli tara ma: tigdar tqa:riš] Don't play backgammon with him because you don't have a chance. • **2.** to bother, pester, plague, annoy, interfere with – لا تقارشه. خَلّيه يِشتُغُل [la: tqa:ršah. xalli:h yištuɣul] Don't bother him. Let him work. مَحَّد قارَشَه؛ قام يِبكِي مِن كيفه [maħħad qa:rašah; ga:m yibči min ki:fah] No one did a thing to him; he just started crying on his own.

تقارَش [tqa:raš] *v:* • **1.** with ب to bother, annoy – آني ما أتقارَش ويّاه بِهالشُّغُل [ʔa:ni ma: ʔatqa:raš wiyya:h bhaššuɣul] I can't compare with him at this job. لا تِتقارَش بِيه تَرَة يبُسطَك [la: titqa:raš bi:h tara ybusṭak] Don't bother him or he'll beat you up.

قِرش [qiriš] *n:* قُرُوش [quru:š] *pl:* • **1.** piaster – صِرَفِت كُلّ فلُوسي؛ ما بِقَى عِندِي وَلا قِرش [ṣirafit kull flu:si; ma: biqa: ʕindi wala qiriš] I spent all my money; I don't even have a penny left. هَالسَّيّارَة ما تِسوَى قِرش [hassayya:ra ma: tiswa: qiriš] This car isn't worth a penny.

قارِش، قارِش وارِش [qa:riš, qa:riš wa:riš] *adj:* • **1.** hanky panky, funny business

ق ر ص

قِرَص [giraṣ] *v:* • **1.** to pinch – الجّاهِل قِرَص أُختَه وخَلّاها تبكِي [ʔijja:hil giraṣ ʔuxtah wxalla:ha tibči] The child pinched his sister and made her cry. • **2.** to bite, sting – قِرصَتَه بَقَّة [girṣatah bagga] A bug bit him.

قَرَّص [garraṣ] *v:* • **1.** intens. of قِرَص : to pinch, to bite, sting – دَيقَرِّص بِخدُودها [daygarriṣ bixdu:dha] He's pinching her cheeks.

اِنقِرَص [ʔingiraṣ] *v:* • **1.** to be pinched – اِنقِرصَت بِرِجلها بالإزدِحام [ʔingirṣat brijilha bilʔizdiħa:m] She was pinched on her leg in the crowd.

قُرُص [quruṣ] *n:* أقراص [ʔaqra:ṣ] *pl:* • **1.** plate, disk, discus – رَمي القُرُص [ramy ʔilquruṣ] discus throwing. • **2.** tablet, lozenge, pastille – دُوا عَلَى شِكِل أقراص [duwa ʕala šikil ʔaqra:ṣ] medicine in tablet form. • **3.** dial (of telephone)

قَرِص [gariṣ] *n:* • **1.** pinch, act of pinching

قُرصَة [gurṣa] *n:* قُرَص [guraṣ] *pl:* • **1.** flat round loaf (of bread)

قَرصَة [garṣa] *n:* قَرصات [garṣa:t] *pl:* • **1.** pinch – قَرصَة بَرِد [garṣat barid] a bit of cold, a nip in the air. • **2.** bite, sting (of an insect)

قِرّاصَة [qirra:ṣa] *n:* قِرّاصات [qirra:ṣa:t] *pl:* • **1.** clothespin

قارِص [ga:riṣ] *n:* قارِصات [ga:riṣa:t] *pl:* • **1.** bedbug

ق ر ص غ

قُرصاغ [qurṣa:ɣ] *n:* • **1.** patience, forbearance, endurance

ق ر ص ن

قَرصَنَة [qarṣana] *n:* • **1.** piracy

قُرصان [qurṣa:n] *adj:* قَراصِنَة [qara:ṣina] *pl:* • **1.** pirate

ق ر ض

قِرَض [qiraḍ] *v:* • **1.** to kill off, annihilate – الدِّكتاتُور قَصدَه يُقرُضهُم [ʔiddikta:tu:r qaṣdah yuqruḍhum] The dictator's purpose is to annihilate them. • **2.** to talk behind someone's back, to cut down, cut to pieces – قاعدِين بِالقَهوَة يقُرضُون النّاس [ga:ʕdi:n bilgahwa yqurḍu:n ʔinna:s] They're sitting in the coffeeshop cutting people to pieces.

قِرَض [giraḍ] *v:* • **1.** to gnaw, nibble, bite – الفارَة دَتُقرُض سِترتَك [ʔilfa:ra datugruḍ sitirtak] The mouse is gnawing on your jacket. • **2.** to smash, mangle – الحَدِيدَة وُقعَت عَلَى إيدِي وقِرضَت إصبِعِي [ʔilħadi:da wugʕat ʕala ʔi:di wgirḍat ʔiṣibʕi] The piece of iron fell on my hand and mashed my finger. • **3.** to punch, perforate – التِّيتِي نِسَى يقرُض التِّكِت مالِي [ʔitti:ti nisa: yigruḍ ʔittikit ma:li] The conductor forgot to punch my ticket. • **4.** to gossip, talk behind one's back – قُرضوك البارحَة بِالقَهوَة [gurḍu:k ʔilba:rħa bilgahwa] They cut you down behind your back yesterday in the café. • **5.** to get thick, thicken – نِسِيت المُرقَة عَالنّار وقِرضَت [nisi:t ʔilmurga ʕanna:r wgirḍat] I left the gravy on the fire and it got thick. خَلِّي القَهوَة تُقرُض [xalli: ʔilgahwa tugruḍ] Let the coffee get stronger.

قَرَّض [qarraḍ] *v:* • **1.** to loan, lend, advance (money) – قَرِّضني فَدّ كَم دِينار لِباكِر [qarriḍni fadd čam dina:r lba:čir] Lend me a few dinars until tomorrow.

قَرَّض [garraḍ] *v:* • **1.** to gnaw, nibble – دَأسمَع حِسّ الفار يقَرِّض بِالهدُوم [daʔasmaʕ ħiss ʔilfa:r ygarruḍ bilhdu:m] I hear the mice gnawing on the clothes. • **2.** to smash, mangle – قَرَّض أصابعَه كُلّها بِالجاكُوج [garraḍ ʔaṣa:bʕah kullha bičča:ku:č] He smashed all his fingers with the hammer. • **3.** to loan, lend, advance (money) – قِتلَه يقَرِّضني فَدّ دِينار [gitlah ygarriḍni fadd dina:r] I asked him to lend me a dinar.

تقَرَّض [tqarraḍ] *v:* • **1.** to borrow – أقدَر أتقَرَّض نُصّ دِينار مِنَّك؟ [ʔagdar ʔatqarraḍ nuṣṣ dina:r minnak?] Can I borrow a half dinar from you?

تقَرَّض [tgarraḍ] *v:* • **1.** to be gnawed, chewed – ما قِتلَك أكُو جرِيدِيَّة هنا. شُوف سِترتِي شلُون تقَرَّضَت [ma: gitlak ʔaku ǰri:diyya hna šu:f sitirti šlu:n dgarriḍat] I told you there were mice here. Look how my jacket got gnawed up. • **2.** to borrow (money) – راح أتقَرَّضلِي كَم فِلِس مِنَّه [ra:ħ ʔatgarraḍli čam filis minnah] I'm going to borrow some money from him.

اِنقِرَض [ʔinqiraḍ] *v:* • **1.** to become extinct, to die out – الدَّينَصَور اِنقِرَض [ʔiddaynaṣu:r ʔinqiraḍ] The dinosaur has become extinct.

اِنقِرَض [ʔingiraḍ] *v:* • **1.** to be smashed, mangled – الجاكُوك وُقَع عَلَى إيدِي وَإصبِعِي اِنقِرَض [ʔičča:ku:č wugaʕ ʕala ʔi:di waʔisibʕi ʔingiraḍ] The hammer fell on my hand and my finger got mashed. • **2.** to be or become frayed – الحَبِل اِنقِرَض [ʔilħabil ʔingiraḍ] The rope was frayed.

اِقتِرَض [ʔiqtiraḍ] *v:* • **1.** to borrow – اِقتِرَض مِنِّي دِينارَين وَما إنطانِي إيّاها [ʔiqtiraḍ minni dina:rayn wama ʔinṭa:ni ʔiyya:ha] He borrowed two dinars from me and didn't give them back to me.

ق

اِستَقرَض [ʔistaqrað̣] *v:* • **1.** to ask for a loan – ما أقدر أشتريها بَلا ما أستقرِض فلوس مِنّه [maː ʔagdar ʔaštiriːha bala maː ʔastaqrið̣ fluːs minnah] I can't buy it unless I ask for money from him.
قَرض [qarið̣] *n:* قرُوض [qruːð̣] *pl:* • **1.** loan – سَنَد قَرض [sanad qarið̣] (government) bond.
قَرض [garið̣] *n:* قرُوض [gruːð̣] *pl:* • **1.** hole, gnawed place
قراضَة [qraːð̣a] *n:* • **1.** (invar.) worn-out – الرّاديُو مالَك ما يفِيد. قراضَة [ʔirraːdyu maːlak maː yfiːd. graːð̣a] Your radio is no good. It's worn out. اِنحال لِلتَّقاعُد لِأَنَّه صار قراضَة [ʔinħaːl littaqaːʕud liʔannah ṣaːr graːð̣a] He got retired because he became old and worn out. • **2.** shreds, scraps
مُقراضَة [muqraːð̣a, mugraːð̣a] *n:* مُقراضات [muqraːð̣aːt, mugraːð̣aːt] *pl:* • **1.** nail clipper
قُرضَة [qurð̣a] *adj:* • **1.** as a loan – إنطِينِي مِيَّة فِلِس قُرضَة [ʔinṭiːni miyyat filis qurð̣a] Give me a hundred fils as a loan.
مُنقَرِض [munqarið̣] *adj:* • **1.** extinct – حَيوان مُنقَرِض [ħaywaːn munqarið̣] an extinct animal.

ق ر ض م

تقَرضَم [tgarð̣am] *v:* • **1.** to be burnt up
تقُرضُم [tgurð̣um] *n:* • **1.** burning up • **2.** being eaten up

ق ر ط

قِرَط [giraṭ] *v:* • **1.** to chew, chew up, to munch, nibble – الزّمال قِرَط قِشِر الرَّقِّيَّة [ʔizzumaːl giraṭ gišir ʔirraggiyya] The donkey chewed up the watermelon rind. لا تُقرُط حَبّ الشِّجَر، كَرِّزَه [laː tugruṭ ħabb ʔiššijar, karrizah] Don't chew up the pumpkin seeds, open them up and take the hearts out. يِقرُط بسنُونَه مِن ينام [yigruṭ bsnuːnah min ynaːm] He gnashes his teeth in his sleep. صِحّتَه مُو زينَة، يبَيِّن راح يقرُط الحَبل [ṣiħħtah muː ziːna, yibayyin raːħ yigruṭ ʔilħabil] His health is bad. It seems he's going to die. • **2.** to waste, squander, lose – وُقعَتلَه خُوش فلوس لَكِن قِرَطها كُلّها [wugʕatlah xuːš fluːs laːkin giraṭha kullha] He came into a good sum of money but he went through it all. قِرَط راسها لِبِتّ النّاس [giraṭ raːsha libitt ʔinnaːs] He was responsible for the girl's death. قِرَط فلُوسِي كُلّها [giraṭ fluːsi kullha] He took me for all my money.
قَرَّط [garraṭ] *v:* • **1.** to munch away, chew away, nibble away – الجّاهِل دَيقَرُّط بِالخيار [ʔijjaːhil daygarruṭ bʔilxyaːr] The child is munching on the cucumbers.
اِنقِرَط [ʔingiraṭ] *v:* • **1.** to be nibbled, munched – الخُبُز اِنقِرَط [ʔilxubuz ʔingiraṭ] The bread's been nibbled. هَالبنَيَّة شقَدّ حِلوَة! تِنقِرِط [halbnayya šgadd ħilwa! tingiriṭ] How pretty this girl is! She looks good enough to eat.
قَرُط [garuṭ] *n:* • **1.** chewing, munching, nibbling • **2.** the sound of munching • **3.** a sort of wild clover
قَرِط [gariṭ] *n:* • **1.** chewing, nibbling, munching; wasting
قرِيط [griːṭ] *n:* • **1.** chewing, munching, nibbling

ق ر ط س

قِرطاسِيَّة [qirṭaːsiyya] *n:* • **1.** stationery

ق ر ط ف

قَرطَف [garṭaf] *v:* • **1.** to trim, clip – قَرطِفَوا جناح الطِّير حَتَّى ما يطِير [garṭifaw ǰnaːħ ʔiṭṭiːr ħatta maː yṭiːr] They trimmed the bird's wings so he won't fly away. الحَلّاق قَرطَف شَعرِي زايِد [ʔilħallaːq garṭaf šaʕri zaːyid] The barber clipped too much off my hair. ظَلّوا يقَرطِفُون بالمِيزانِيَّة إِلَى أَن ما بِقَى بِيها شِي [ð̣allaw ygarṭifuːn bilmiːzaːniyya ʔila ʔan maː biqaː biːha ši] They kept trimming the budget till there's no more left of it.
تقَرطَف [tgarṭaf] *v:* • **1.** to be trimmed, clipped – لا تقُصّ بَعَد. مُو شَعرِي تقَرطَف [laː tguṣṣ baʕad. muː šaʕri dgarṭaf] Don't cut more. My hair has been clipped too much!
مقَرطَف [mgarṭaf] *adj:* • **1.** stingy, tight-fisted, scrimpy • **2.** miser, skin-flint, tightwad

ق ر ع

قِرَع [graʕʕ] *v:* • **1.** to get ringworm – راسَه قرَع. لازِم إنوَدِّيه لِلطَّبِيب [raːsah graʕʕ. laːzim ʔinwaddiːh liṭṭabiːb] He's gotten ringworm. We've got to take him to the doctor.
قَرَّع [garraʕ] *v:* • **1.** to scalp, make bald – لا تقُصّ شَعرِي بَعَد. قَرَّعتَه لراسِي [laː tguṣṣ šaʕri baʕad. garraʕtah lraːsi] Don't cut any more of my hair. You've made me bald-headed. راح أَنطِيه فلُوسَه وأخلَص مِنَّه. قَرَّعَه لراسِي [raːħ ʔanṭiːh fluːsah wʔaxlaṣ minnah. garraʕah lraːsi] I'm going to give him his money and get rid of him. He pestered me a lot. شأسَوِّي؟ قَرَّعنِي عَلِيها [šʔasawwiː? garraʕni ʕaliːha] What could I do? He kept insisting on it.
قَرَع [garaʕ] *n:* • **1.** ringworm • **2.** baldness
قُرعَة [qurʕa] *n:* قُرَع [quraʕ] *pl:* • **1.** lot drawing, lottery – سَوَّوا قُرعَة [sawwaw qurʕa] They drew lots. • **2.** conscription, recruitment (by lot) – قُرعَة عَسكَرِيَّة [qurʕa ʕaskariyya] draft, draft call.
قَرعَة [garʕa] *n:* قَرعات [garʕaːt] *pl:* • **1.** a bald spot (on the head) • **2.** a head infected by ringworm • **3.** mangy head
أقرَع [ʔagraʕ] *adj:* قَرعِين [garʕiːn] *pl:* قَرعَة [garʕa] *feminine:* • **1.** infected with ringworm, person with ringworm • **2.** bald, bald person – القَرعَة تباهِي بِشَعَر أُختها [ʔilgarʕa tbaːhi bšaʕar ʔuxutha] The man who lacks something boasts of someone else's (lit., the bald girl brags about her sister's hair).

ق ر ف 1

قِرِف [girif] *n:* قرُوف [gruːf] *pl:* • **1.** hoof of a butchered animal
قِرفَة [girfa] *n:* • **1.** ilk, type (always derogatory) – مِن نَفِس القِرفَة [min nafis ʔilgirfa] of the same type.

عَلَى هَالقِرفَة [ʕala halgirfa] of that ilk. أُخُذ قِرفَة [ʔuxuð girfa] Let's face it/Let's face the facts. • **2.** stingy, tight, miserly – لا تِدّايَن مِنَّه. هَذا فَدّ واحِد قِرفَة [la: tidda:yan minnah. ha:ða fadd wa:ħid girfa] Don't borrow from him. He's a stingy guy.

ق ر ف 2

مُقرِف [muqrif] *adj:* • **1.** disgusting, loathsome
قَرفان [qarfa:n] *adj:* • **1.** disgusted, sick and tired, nauseated

ق ر ق

قُرُق، حَمّام قُرُق [quruq, ħamma:m quruq] *adj:* • **1.** a reserved bathhouse.

ق ر ق ر

قَرقَر [qarqar] *v:* • **1.** to rumble, growl – بَطني تقرقِر. جُوعان [baṭni tqarqir. ǰu:ʕa:n] My stomach is growling. I'm hungry.
قَرقَرَة [qarqara] *n:* قَرقَرات [qarqara:t] *pl:* • **1.** growl, rumble (of the stomach)
قَرقَري [gargari] *n:* • **1.** a type of candy, similar to taffy

ق ر ق ش

قَرقَش [qarqaš] *v:* • **1.** to hit (someone) for money, to demand money from – عَلِي يبَيِّن زَنكِين اليُوم. خَلِّي نرُوح نقَرقِشَه [ʕali yibayyin zangi:n ʔilyu:m. xalli: nru:ħ nqarqišah] Ali appears to be rich today. Let's go get some money from him. • **2.** to give, to enrich – يوم المَعاش أَبُويَا يقَرقِشنِي بِدِينار [yu:m ʔilmaʕa:š ʔabu:ya yqarqišni bdina:r] On payday my father gives me a dinar.
قَرقَش [gargaš] *v:* • **1.** to chew, gnaw, munch – دَيقَرقِش قشُور رَقّي [daygargiš gšu:r raggi] He's gnawing on watermelon rinds.
قَرقُوش، حُكُم قَرَقُوش [qaraqu:š, ħukum qaraqu:š] *n:* • **1.** arbitrary rule – شلُون تِقدَر تفصُلنِي؟ لِيش، ماكُو قانُون؟ قابِل حُكُم قَرَقُوش؟ [šlu:n tigdar tufṣulni? li:š, ma:ku qa:nu:n? qa:bil ħukum qaraqu:š?] How can you fire me? Isn't there any law? Do you imagine there's anarchy?

ق ر ق ع

قَرقَع [gargaʕ] *v:* • **1.** to thunder – دَتقَرقِع وَيمكِن راح تُمطُر [dadgargiʕ wyimkin ra:ħ tumṭur] It's thundering and it might rain. • **2.** to shake, rock (fig.) – قَرقَع المَجلِس بخِطابَه [gargaʕ ʔilmaǰlis bxiṭa:bah] He rocked the parliament with his speech. هُوَّ يقَرقِع بالمَجلِس [huwwa ygargiʕ bilmaǰlis] He's a powerful man in the parliament. • **3.** to frighten, scare, terrify – قَرقَعَه بِهَالتَّهدِيد [gargaʕah bhattahdi:d] He terrified him with that threat.
تقَرقَع [tgargaʕ] *v:* • **1.** to be scared – تقُول إنتَ سَبِع؟ أَشُو تقَرقَعِت بَسّ صاح بِيك فَدّ صَيحَة [dgu:l ʔinta sabiʕ? ʔašu tgargaʕit bass ṣa:ħ bi:k fadd ṣayħa] You claim you're brave? I see that you were scared when he shouted at you only once.
قَرقَعَة [gargaʕa] *n:* • **1.** thundering • **2.** pl. قَراقِيع clap of thunder
قَرقُوعَة [gargu:ʕa] *n:* قَراقِيع [gara:gi:ʕ] *pl:* • **1.** clap of thunder

ق ر ق ف

قَرقَف [gargaf] *v:* • **1.** to become encrusted – كَعَب الجِّدِر قَرقَف. حُكَّه بِالجَّلّافَة [čaʕab ʔiǰǰidir gargaf. ħukkah biǰǰalla:fa] The bottom of the pot has a crust formed on it. Scour it with the steel wool. وِجه الجّاهِل مقَرقِف [wičč ʔiǰǰa:hil mgargif] The kid's face is crusted with dirt.
مقَرقُف [mgarguf] *adj:* • **1.** dry

ق ر ق و ز

قَرقُوز [qaraqu:z] *n:* قَرقَوزات [qaraqu:za:t] *pl:* • **1.** puppet

ق ر م

قِرَم [giram] *v:* • **1.** to blunt, dull, break – قِرَم راس السِّكِّينَة [giram ra:s ʔissičči:na] He blunted the point of the knife.
قَرَّم [garram] *v:* • **1.** to cripple – سَيّارَة ضُربَتَه وَقَرّمَتَه [sayya:ra ðurbatah wgarrmatah] A car hit him and crippled him.
تقَرَّم [tgarram] *v:* • **1.** to be or become crippled – وُقَع مِن السَّطِح وَتقَرَّم [wugaʕ min ʔissaṭiħ wtgarram] He fell off the roof and became crippled.
انقِرَم [ʔingiram] *v:* • **1.** to be dulled, blunted, broken – راس السِّكِّينَة اِنقِرَم [ra:s ʔissičči:na ʔingiram] The point of the knife was broken off.
قَرُم [garum] *n:* • **1.** furrowing, breaking
قِرمَة [qirma] *n:* قِرَم [qiram] *pl:* • **1.** pleat
قِرّامَة [girra:ma] *n:* • **1.** (exclamation of surprise or astonishment, approx.:) My God! – قِرّامَة شقَدّ حِلوَة [girra:ma šgadd ħilwa] My God, how beautiful she is! قِرّامَة عَلَى هَالعيُون [girra:ma ʕala halʕyu:n] My God, those eyes! قامَت تِحكِي. قِرّامَة [ga:mat tiħči. girra:ma] She started to speak. Good God!
مقَرَّم [mqarram] *adj:* • **1.** pleated – تَنُّورَة مقَرَّمَة [tannu:ra mgarrama] a pleated skirt.
مقَرَّم [mgarram] *adj:* • **1.** crippled, lame – مقَرَّم مِن صُغرَه [mgarram min ṣuɣrah] He's been crippled from childhood. • **2.** pl. مقَرَّمِين : a cripple (person who is crippled) – المقَرَّم ما يِقدَر يِمشِي [ʔilmgarram ma: yigdar yimši] The cripple can't walk.

ق ر م ب ر

قُرُمبَرَة [qurumpara, qurumbara] *n:* قُرُمبَرِيَّة [qurumpariyya, qurumbariyya] *pl:* • **1.** pederast, pedophile

ق

ق ر م د 1

قِرمِيد [girmiːd] *n:* • **1.** brick, tile

ق ر م د 2

قرمِيد [qirmiːd, girmiːd] *adj:* • **1.** stingy

ق ر م ز

قِرمِزي [qirmizi] *adj:* • **1.** crimson, carmine, scarlet – الحُمَّة القِرمِزِيَّة [ʔilħumma ʔilqirmiziyya] scarlet fever.

ق ر م ط

قَرمَط [garmaṭ] *v:* • **1.** to cut down, cut back, withhold – قَرمِطُوه لمَنهَج الحَفلَة. لا راح يجِيبُون راقِصَة وَلا مُغَنِّيَة [karmiṭuːh lmanhaǰ ʔilħafla. laː raːħ yǰiːbuːn raːqiṣa wala muɣanniya] They cut down the program for the party. They're not going to bring a dancer or a singer. إنطِينِي بَعَد شوَيَّة. لا تقَرمُطها [ʔinṭiːni baʕad šwayya. laː tqarmuṭha] Give me a little more. Don't cut down the amount.

قَرمَط [garmaṭ] *v:* • **1.** to nibble, munch, chew – الصَّخلَة دَ تقَرمُط بقِشر الرَّقِّي [ʔiṣṣaxla da tgarmuṭ bgišr ʔirraggi] The goat is munching on the watermelon rinds. زَوجِتَه قَرمُطَت فلُوسَه [zawiǰtah garmuṭat fluːsah] His wife got all his money bit by bit. قَرمَط كُلّ الفلُوس اللِّي حَصَّلها بِالقمار [garmaṭ kull ʔilfluːs ʔilli ħaṣṣalha bilqmaːr] He frittered away all the money he won at gambling.

ق ر ن

قارَن [qaːran] *v:* • **1.** with بَين to compare – قارِن بين اللُّغَة الأَسبانِيَّة وَاللُّغَة البُرتُغالِيَّة [qaːrin biːn ʔilluɣa ʔilʔaspaːniyya willuɣa ʔilpurtuɣaːliyya] Compare the Spanish language and the Portuguese language.

قَرِن [qarin] *n:* قُرُون [quruːn] *pl:* • **1.** century – القُرُون الوُسطَى [ʔilquruːn ʔilwusṭa] the Middle Ages.

قِرِن [girin] *n:* قرُون [gruːn] *pl:* • **1.** pl. قرُون horn (of an animal) • **2.** أَبُو قرُون [ʔabu gruːn] cuckold, pimp

قِران، عَقِد قِران [qiraːn, ʕaqid qiraːn] *n:* • **1.** marriage contract

قران [qraːn, graːn] *n:* قرانات [qraːnaːt] *pl:* • **1.** term for the twenty fils coin

قَرِين [qariːn] *n:* • **1.** companion, mate • **2.** husband, spouse, consort

مقَرِّن [mgarrin] *n:* • **1.** pimp, cuckold

قَرَنِيَّة [qaraniyya] *n:* قَرَنِيّات [qaraniyyaːt] *pl:* • **1.** cornea (anat. of eye)

قَرِينَة [qariːna] *n:* قَرِينات [qariːnaːt] *pl:* • **1.** formal term for wife

مُقارَنَة [muqaːrana] *n:* مُقارَنات [muqaːranaːt] *pl:* • **1.** comparison – بِالمُقارَنَة طِلعَوا يِتشابهُون هوايَة [bilmuqaːrana ṭilʕaw yitšaːbhuːn hwaːya] In comparison, they turned out to be very similar.

مَقرُون [maqruːn] *adj:* • **1.** connected, joined, linked • **2.** combined, associated

ق ر ن ب ط

قَرنَبِيط [qarnabiːṭ] *n:* • **1.** cauliflower

ق ر ن ص

قَرنَص [qarnaṣ] *v:* • **1.** to scallop, to make a deckle-edge, to pink – قَرنُص حاشيَة، القُماش، حَتَّى ما تِتسَلَّت الخِيُوط [qarnuṣ ħaːšyat ʔilqumaːš ħatta maː titsallat ʔilxiyuːṭ] Pink the edge of the cloth, so the threads won't come loose. قَرنَص حاشيَة التَّصوِير بالمُقَصّ [qarnaṣ ħaːšyat ʔittaṣwiːr bilmugaṣṣ] He scalloped the edge of the photo with scissors.

مقَرنَص [mqarnaṣ] *adj:* • **1.** having scalloped edges/ sides

ق ر ن ف ل

قَرنُفُل [grunful, qrinfil] *n:* • **1.** clove • **2.** (coll.) carnation(s)

قُرُنفِلَة [qurunfila] *n:* قُرُنفِلات [qurunfilaːt] *pl:* • **1.** a carnation

ق ر و

قَروَة، قرِيوَة [garwa, griːwa] *n:* قريوات [griːwaːt] *pl:* • **1.** a cyst

ق ر و ن

قَروانَة [qarawaːna] *n:* قَروانات، قَرَوايِن [qarawaːnaːt, qarawaːyin] *pl:* • **1.** large round shallow metal serving bowl

ق ر ي

قَريَة [qarya] *n:* قُرَى [quraː] *pl:* • **1.** village

قَرَوِي [qurawi] *adj:* • **1.** rural, relating-to- village – حَياة قُرَوِيَّة [ħayaːt qurawiyya] village life. • **2.** as Noun: a villager

ق ر ي ل

قَريُولَة [qaryuːla] *n:* قَريُولات [qaryuːlaːt] *pl:* • **1.** steel cot – قَريُولَة سَفَرِيَّة [qaryuːla safariyya] folding camp cot.

ق ز ح

قَزَح، قوز قَزَح [qazaħ, quːz qazaħ] *n:* • **1.** rainbow

قَزَحِيَّة [qazaħiyya] *n:* قَزَحِيّات [qazaħiyyaːt] *pl:* • **1.** iris (of the eye)

ق ز ز 1

قَزّ [qazz] *v:* • **1.** to be disgusted, nauseated – نَفسِي قَزَّت مِنَّه، هَل قَدّ ما وَسِخ [nafsi qazzat minnah, hal gadd maː waṣix] I was nauseated by him, he was so dirty.

قَزَّز [qazzaz] *v:* • **1.** to disgust, nauseate – مَنظَرَه يقَزِّز النَّفس [manð̣arah yqazziz ʔinnafis] The sight of him disgusts you.

تقَزَّز [tqazzaz] *v:* • **1.** to be disgusted, nauseated – آني تقَزَّزت مِنّه [ʔaːni tqazzazit minnah] I was disgusted with him.
قَزّ، دُودَة القَزّ [qazz, duːdat ʔilqazz] *n:* • **1.** silkworm
قَزّ [gazz] *n:* • **1.** raw silk
قَزّاز [qazzaːz] *n:* قَزّازَة [qazzaːza] *pl:* • **1.** silk merchant
قِزاز، قزيز [gizaːz, gziːz] *n:* • **1.** glass
تقَزُّز [taqazzuz] *n:* • **1.** disgust
مُقَزِّز [muqazziz] *adj:* • **1.** disgusting

ق ز ز 2

قِزَّة [qizza] *n:* قِزّات، قِزَز [qizzaːt, qizaz] *pl:* • **1.** queen, in non-western card games
قِزَّة [gizza] *n:* قِزّات [gizzaːt] *pl:* • **1.** nip, playful bite

ق ز ق ز

قَزقَز [gazgaz] *v:* • **1.** to gnash one's teeth, grit one's teeth – مِن يُحمَق عَلَى إبنَه يقَزقِز [min yuħmaq ʕala ʔibnah ygazgiz] When he gets mad at his son, he gnashes his teeth.
قَزقُوزَة [gazguːza] *n:* قَزقُوزات، قَزاقِيز [gazguːzaːt, gazaːgiːz.] *pl:* • **1.** well proportioned girl with a good figure

ق ز ل

قِزَل [gizal] *v:* • **1.** to limp, have a stiff leg – يِقزِل مِن يِمشِي [yigzil min yimši] He limps when he walks.
قَزِل [gazil] *n:* • **1.** limping
قَزلَة [gazla] *n:* قَزلات [gazlaːt] *pl:* • **1.** limp, stiff leg

ق ز ل ق ر ط

قُزُلقُرط [quzzulqurṭ] *int:* • **1.** (exclamation of exasperation, lit., the black wolf, approx.:) Shut up! Drop dead! Go to hell!

ق ز م

قَزَم، قِزِم [qazam, qizim] *n:* أقزام [ʔaqzaːm] *pl:* • **1.** dwarf, midget, pygmy • **2.** little fellow, shrimp
قَزمَة [qazma] *n:* قَزمات [qazmaːt] *pl:* • **1.** pick, mattock

ق ز ن

قَزان [qazaːn] *n:* قَزانات [qazaːnaːt] *pl:* • **1.** kettle, caldron, large metal pot for heating water

ق ز و

قَزوَة [gazwa] *n:* قَزوات [gazwaːt] *pl:* • **1.** slingshot

ق ز و ن

قَزوِين، بَحَر قَزوِين [qazwiːn, baħar qazwiːn] *n:* • **1.** Caspian Sea

ق س ب

قَسَّب [gassab] *v:* • **1.** to make crisp – إنطِينِي إيّاها وَأقَسِّبلَك إيّاها بالفِرِن [ʔinṭiːni ʔiyyaːha waʔagassiblak ʔiyyaːha bilfirin] Give it to me and I'll make it crisp for you in the oven. • **2.** to be or become crisp – خَلِّي الخُبُز يقَسِّب زين قَبِل ما تطَلّعَه [xalliː ʔilxubuz ygassib ziːn gabil maː ṭṭallʕah] Let the bread get good and crisp before you take it out.
قَسِب [gasib, ǰasib] *n:* • **1.** dried dates
مقَسِّب [mgassib, mǰassib] *adj:* • **1.** crisp

ق س س

قِسّ، قَسّ، قِسِّيس [qiss, qass, qissiːs] *n:* قِسِّيسِين، قَساوِسَة، قسُوس [qissiːsiːn, qasaːwisa, qsuːs] *pl:* • **1.** clergyman, priest, minister, parson, pastor (Christian)

ق س ط

قَسَّط [qassaṭ] *v:* • **1.** to distribute, spread out (payments) – إذا تقَسِّطلِي قِيمَة التَّلِفزيُون كُلّ أربَعَة أشهُر عَشِر دَنانِير، أشتِري مِنَّك [ʔiða tqassiṭli qiːmat ʔittalifizyuːn kull ʔarbaʕat ʔašhur ʕašir danaːniːr, ʔaštiri minnak] If you spread out the price of the television, ten dinars every four months, I'll buy from you. • **2.** to pay in installments – راح أقَسِّط المَبلَغ عَلَى أربَع أقساط [raːħ ʔaqassiṭ ʔilmablaɣ ʕala ʔarbaʕ ʔaqsaːṭ] I'm going to pay the amount in four installments.
قُسُط [qusuṭ, qisiṭ] *n:* أقساط [ʔaqsaːṭ] *pl:* • **1.** payment – اِشتِرَيناه بالأقساط [ʔištiraynaːh bilʔaqsaːṭ] We bought it by installments. • **2.** with بـ- and pl. أقسَاط : installment
تَقسِيط، بِالتَقسِيط [taqsiːṭ, bittaqsiːṭ] *n:* • **1.** in installments, gradually – نبِيع بِالتَّقسِيط [nbiːʕ bittaqsiːṭ] We sell on installment.

ق س م

قِسَم [qisam] *v:* • **1.** to divide, split – قِسَم الكَيكَة قِسمَين [qisam ʔilkayka qismayn] He divided the cake in two. هُوَّ قِسَم الغُرفَة إلَى غُرُفتَين [huwwa qisam ʔilɣurfa ʔila ɣuruftayn] He partitioned the room into two rooms. • **2.** to destine, fore-ordain, will – الله قِسَملَه هِيكِي [ʔallah qisamlah hiːči] God willed it this way for him.
قِسَم [qisam] *v:* • **1.** to take an oath, swear – قِسَم بِالله مالَه عِلاقَة بِالمَوضُوع [qisam bʔallah maːlah ʕilaːqa bilmawðuːʕ] He swore by God he had nothing to do with the matter.
قَسَّم [qassam] *v:* • **1.** to divide – قَسِّم عَشرَة عَلَى ثنَين [qassim ʕašra ʕala θnayn] Divide ten by two. • **2.** to divide, distribute – قَسَّم الفلُوس عَلينا [qassam ʔilfluːs ʕaliːna] He divided the money among us. • **3.** with عَلَى to play (a stringed instrument) – حِلو يقَسِّم عَلعُود [ħilw yqassim ʕalʕuːd] He plays the lute nicely.
قاسَم [qaːsam] *v:* • **1.** to divide (in shares) • **2.** to share

ق

أَقسَم [ʔaqsam] *v:* • **1.** to swear, take an oath – أَقسَم ما يِحكِي ويّاك بَعَد [ʔaqsam maː yiħči wiyyaːk baʕad] He swore he wouldn't talk to you any more.
تقَسَّم [tqassam] *v:* • **1.** to be divided – هَالعَدَد ما يِتقَسَّم عَلَى ثنَين [halʕadad maː yitqassam ʕala θnayn] This number can't be divided by two. الطُّلّاب تقَسّمَوا إِلَى قِسمَين [ʔiṭṭullaːb tqassmaw ʔila qismayn] The students were divided into two groups. تقاسمَوا الفلُوس [tqaːsmaw ʔilfluːs] They split the money.
تقاسَم [tqaːsam] *v:* • **1.** to share
اِنقِسَم [ʔinqisam] *v:* • **1.** to be divided – الجَّيش اِنقِسَم إِلَى قِسمَين [ʔiǰǰayš ʔinqisam ʔila qismayn] The army was divided into two parts.
قِسِم [qisim] *n:* أقسام [ʔaqsaːm] *pl:* • **1.** part, section, share • **2.** some, part, portion • **3.** section, department
قَسَم [qasam] *n:* أقسام [ʔaqsaːm] *pl:* • **1.** oath
قِسمَة [qisma] *n:* • **1.** dividing, division, distribution, allotment, apportionment • **2.** (math.) division • **3.** pl. قِسَم lot, destiny, fate
قَسِيمَة [qasiːma] *n:* قَسايِم [qasaːyim] *pl:* • **1.** coupon
تقسِيم [taqsiːm] *n:* تَقسِيمات، تَقاسِيم [taqsiːmaːt, taqaːsiːm] *pl:* • **1.** (elec.) plug with several female sides • **2.** pl. تقسيمات division, subdivision, partition, splitting – تَقسِيمات إِدارِيَّة [taqsiːmaːt ʔidaːriyya] administrative divisions. • **3.** pl. تقسيمات portioning, distribution, allotment • **4.** pl. تَقاسِيم facial features • **5.** pl. تَقاسِيم solo recital (mus.)
مُقاسَمَة [muqaːsama] *n:* • **1.** partnership, participation, sharing
اِنقِسام [ʔinqisaːm] *n:* • **1.** division,split, breakup, schism
قاسِم [qaːsim] *n:* • **1.** divisor, denominator (math.) – القاسِم المُشتَرَك الأَعظَم [ʔilqaːsim ʔilmuštarak ʔilʔaʕḍam] largest common denominator (lit. highest common denominator).
مقَسَّم [mqassam] *adj:* • **1.** divided, partitioned
مَقسُوم [magsuːm] *adj:* • **1.** divided • **2.** with ال/ share, income
مِنقِسِم [minqisim] *adj:* • **1.** split • **2.** divided
قَسَماً [qasaman] *adverbial:* • **1.** I swear! – قَسَماً بِالله، راح أَمَوّتَك إِذا ما تِسكُت [qasaman billaːh, raːħ ʔamawwtak ʔiða maː tiskut] By God, I'll kill you if you don't shut up!

ق س و

قِسَى [qisaː] *v:* • **1.** to be harsh, cruel – إِذا تِقسِي بِمُعامَلتَك إِلهُم، يكُرهُوك [ʔiða tiqsi bmuʕaːmaltak ʔilhum, ykurhuːk] If you're harsh in your treatment of them, they'll hate you.
قاسَى [qaːsaː] *v:* • **1.** to undergo, suffer, endure, bear, stand – قاسَى هوايَة بِشَبابَه [qaːsaː hwaːya bšabaːbah] He suffered a lot in his youth.
قَسوَة [qaswa] *n:* • **1.** harshness, severity, cruelty, mercilessness
قَساوَة [qasaːwa] *n:* • **1.** harshness, severity, cruelty, mercilessness
قاسِي [qaːsi] *adj:* قُساة [qusaːt] *pl:* • **1.** harsh, stern, severe, cruel – حاكِم قاسِي [ħaːkim qaːsi] a harsh judge.
أَقسَى [ʔaqsa] *comparative adjective:* • **1.** more or most stern, severe, etc

ق ش ب

قِشَب [qišab] *v:* • **1.** to gossip
قَشِب [qašib] *n:* • **1.** gossip

ق ش ر

قِشَر [gišar] *v:* • **1.** to scrape, scratch, pick, chip – خَلِّي الحَبّايَة تطِيب. لا تُقشُرها [xalliː ʔilħabbaːya ṭṭiːb. laː tugšurha] Let the sore heal. Don't scratch at it. أُقشُر الجُّصّ مِن الطّابُوقَة [ʔugšur ʔiǰǰuṣṣ min ʔiṭṭaːbuːga] Chip the mortar off the brick.
قَشَّر [gaššar] *v:* • **1.** to peel, pare, shell, skin, scale – قَشِّر الخيارَة قَبُل ما تِثرُمها [gaššir ʔilxyaːra gabul maː tiθrumha] Peel the cucumber before you chop it up. قَشِّر السِّمكَة قَبُل ما تشُقّها [gaššir ʔissimča gabul maː tšuggha] Scrape the scales off the fish before you gut it.
تقَشَّر [tgaššar] *v:* • **1.** pass. of قَشَّر to be peeled – الخيارَة لازِم تِتقَشَّر قَبِل ما تِنثُرُم [ʔilxyaːra laːzim titgaššar gabil maː tinθurum] The cucumber must be peeled before it's cut up.
قِشِر [gišir] *n:* قشُور [gšuːr] *pl:* • **1.** peel, rind, skin • **2.** shell • **3.** bark (of a tree)
قِشرَة [gišra] *n:* • **1.** dandruff
قَشرات [gašraːt] *n:* • **1.** (pl. only) scraps, meat scraps
أَقشَر [ʔagšar] *adj:* أَقشَرِين [ʔagšariːn] *pl:* قَشرَة [gašra] *feminine:* • **1.** quite a, a real, some – لاعُوب شِطرَنج أَقشَر [laːʕuːb šiṭranǰ ʔagšar] quite a chess player. كَذّاب أَقشَر [čaððaːb ʔagšar] a real liar. ساعَة قَشرَة [saːʕa gašra] an evil hour. كانَت ساعَة قَشرَة تعَرَّفِت عَلِيه بِيها [čaːnat saːʕa gašra tʕarrafit ʕaliːh biːha] I wish I'd never met him (lit., it was an ill-fated moment in which I met him).

ق ش ش

قَشّ [gašš] *v:* • **1.** to collect, gather up, pick up – قُشّ قصاقِيص الوَرَق اللّي عالقاع [gušš gṣaːgiːṣ ʔilwaraq ʔilli ʕalgaːʕ] Sweep up the shreds of paper on the floor. • **2.** to skim, take off the top – قُشّ القِشوَة قَبُل ما تِشرَب الحَلِيب [gušš ʔilgišwa gabul maː tišrab ʔilħaliːb] Skim off the top before you drink the milk. أُوزِنلِي كِيلُو تمُر بَسّ قُشّلِي مِن راس الطَّبَق [ʔuːzinli kiːlu tamur bass guššli min raːs ʔiṭṭubag] Weigh me a kilo of dates but take them off the top of the basket. • **3.** to lift, move, budge – مِن يرُوح بمُكان ماكُو شِي يقُشَّه. يظَلّ النَّهار كُلَّه [min yiruːħ bmukaːn maːku ši ygušsah. yðall ʔinnahaːr kullah] When he goes someplace, there is nothing that can budge him. He stays all day.

ق

اِنقَشّ [ʔingašš] *v:* • **1.** to leave, take off – أَكَل وَشِرَب يَالله اِنقَشّ [ʔakal wširab yallah ʔingašš] He ate and drank and then took off.
قَشّ [gašš] *n:* • **1.** collecting, gathering up
قِشّايَة [giššaːya] *n:* قِشّايات [giššaːyaːt] *pl:* • **1.** small twig
قشاش [gšaːš] *adj:* • **1.** chips, refuse, sweepings

ق ش ط

قِشَط [gišaṭ] *v:* • **1.** to scratch, nick, gouge – الطَّلقَة قِشطَت كِتفَه [ʔiṭṭalqa gišṭat čitfah] The bullet grazed his shoulder. قِشَط الميز بمُكانَين [gišaṭ ʔilmiːz bmukaːnayn] He gouged the table in two places. • **2.** to scratch off, scrape off, pick at – قِشَط الحَبّايَة وَطِلَع الدَّمّ [gišaṭ ʔilħabbaːya wṭilaʕ ʔiddamm] He picked at the sore and it bled.
قَشَّط [gaššaṭ] *v:* • **1.** to scratch, pick at – الجّاهِل دَيقَشِّط الحَبّايَة [ʔiǰǰaːhil daygaššiṭ ʔilħabbaːya] The kid is picking at the sore. • **2.** to peel, flake off – هَالصُّبُغ مُو زين. يقَشِّط بِالعَجَل [haṣṣubuɣ muː ziːn. ygaššiṭ bilʕaǰal] This paint isn't good. It begins to peel fast.
تقَشَّط [tgaššaṭ] *v:* • **1.** to be peeled off, scraped off – الصُّبُغ العَتيق لازِم يِتقَشَّط قَبُل ما يِنصُبُغ الحايِط [ʔiṣṣubuɣ ʔilʕatiːg laːzim yitgaššaṭ gabul maː yinṣubuɣ ʔilħaːyiṭ] The old paint must be peeled off before the wall is painted.
اِنقِشَط [ʔingišaṭ] *v:* • **1.** to be scratched, nicked – لا تخَلّي شي عالميز لا يرُوح يِنقِشِط [laː txalliː ši ʕalmiːz laː yruːħ yingišiṭ] Don't put anything on the table or it might get scratched.
قَشِط [gašiṭ] *n:* • **1.** scratch, nick, gouge
قِشطَة [gišṭa] *n:* قِشطات [gišṭaːt] *pl:* • **1.** chip, piece (of a dish, etc.)

ق ش ع

اِنقِشَع [ʔinqišaʕ] *v:* • **1.** to dissipate
اِنقِشاع [ʔinqišaːʕ] *n:* • **1.** dissipation, scattering

ق ش ع ر

قَشعَرِيرَة [qašʕariːra] *n:* • **1.** chill

ق ش ل

قِشلَة [qišla] *n:* قِشَل [qišal] *pl:* • **1.** barracks

ق ش م ر

قَشمَر [qašmar] *v:* • **1.** to deceive, fool – قَشمَرني وَباعِلي ساعَة ما تِشتُغُل [qašmarni wbaːʕli saːʕa maː tištuɣul] He deceived me and sold me a watch that doesn't run. • **2.** to joke, chaff, banter, poke fun – لا تقَشمُر. يَعني قابِل سَيّارتَك أحسَن [laː tqašmur. yaʕni qaːbil sayyaːrtak ʔaħsan] Don't make fun of it. Do you mean to say your car is better? ظَلّوا يقَشمُرُون عَليه وَما شِعَر [ðallaw yqašmuruːn ʕaliːh wma šiʕar] They kept pulling his leg and he never realized.
تقَشمَر [tqašmar] *v:* • **1.** to be deceived, fooled – هَالوَلَد ما يِتقَشمَر [halwalad maː yitqašmar] This guy can't be fooled.
قَشمَرَة [qašmara] *n:* • **1.** deception, fooling • **2.** joking, chaffing, banter, poking fun • **3.** a joke, a laughing stock, a travesty
قَشمِريّات [qašmiriyyaːt] *n:* • **1.** deception, trickery • **2.** joking, banter
قَشمَر [qašmar] *n:* قَشامِر [qašaːmir, qašaːmra] *pl:* • **1.** fool, ass, idiot, jerk • **2.** laughing stock, butt of jokes, person who is not to be taken seriously

ق ش و

قِشوَة [gišwa] *n:* قِشوات [gišwaːt] *pl:* • **1.** the thin skin that forms on top of heated milk

ق ص

قاصَة [qaːṣa] *n:* قاصات [qaːṣaːt] *pl:* • **1.** safe, vault

ق ص ب

قُصَب، قِصَب [guṣab, giṣab] *v:* • **1.** to cut meat, cut up (a slaughtered animal) – صارلَه سَنَة وَبَعدَه ما يُعرُف يُقصُب [ṣaːrlah sana wbaʕdah maː yuʕruf yugṣub] It's been a year and he still doesn't know how to cut meat. لا تِشتِري مِن هَالبَقّال، تَرَة يُقصُب [laː tištiri min halbaggaːl, tara yugṣub] Don't buy from that grocer, because he charges an arm and a leg.
قُصَب [guṣab] *n:* • **1.** (coll.) reed(s), cane(s)
قَصُب [gaṣub] *n:* • **1.** cutting up (a slaughtered animal)
قَصَبَة، القَصَبَة الهَوائِيَة [qaṣaba, ʔilqaṣaba ʔilhawaːʔiyya] *n:* • **1.** the respiratory tract bronchial tubes, windpipe
قُصبَة [guṣba] *n:* قُصبات [guṣbaːt] *pl:* • **1.** unit.n: of قُصَب [quṣab, guṣab] a reed, a cane
قَصّاب [qaṣṣaːb, gaṣṣaːb] *n:* قَصّابين، قصاصِيب [gaṣṣaːbiːn, gṣaːṣiːb] *pl:* • **1.** butcher, meat cutter
قصابَة [gṣaːba] *n:* • **1.** the butcher's trade, butchering, meat cutting
قصيبَة [gṣiːba] *n:* قِصايِب [giṣaːyib] *pl:* • **1.** pigtail, braid
مقَصَّب [mgaṣṣab] *adj:* • **1.** embroidered with gold and silver thread, brocaded, trimmed with brocade – عِقال مقَصَّب [ʕigaːl mgaṣṣab] a brocaded head band.

ق ص د

قِصَد [qiṣad] *v:* • **1.** to intend, aim, mean – ما قِصَد يزَعّلَك [maː qiṣad yzaʕʕlak] He didn't mean to make you mad. • **2.** to mean, try to say – شتُقصُد بِهَالعِبارَة؟ [štuqṣud bhalʕibaːra?] What do you mean by that expression?
تقَصَّد [tqaṣṣad] *v:* • **1.** to decide, set one's mind, make up one's mind – هَالتِّلميذ مُجتَهِد لَكِن المُعَلِّم تقَصَّد وَسَقَّطَه [hattilmiːð muǰtahid laːkin ʔilmuʕallim tqaṣṣad wsaqqaṭah] This student is a good one but the teacher had set his mind on failing him. • **2.** to mean, try to say – يِتقَصَّد بِكُلّ كِلمَة يقُولها عَلَيّا [yitqaṣṣad bkull čilma yguːlha ʕalayya] He means every word he says against me.

ق

اِنقِصَد [ʔinqiṣad] *v:* • **1.** to mean
اِقتِصَد [ʔiqtiṣad] *v:* • **1.** to economize, be economical, thrifty – ما تِقدَر تِشترِي سَيّارَة إذا ما تِقتِصِد [maː tigdar tištiri sayyaːra ʔiða maː tiqtiṣid] You can't buy a car if you don't economize. • **2.** to save – بِدال ما أَركَب باص دَأَرُوح مَشِي لِلدّائِرَة وأَقتِصِد عَشِر فلُوس [bidaːl maː ʔarkab paːṣ daʔaruːħ mašy liddaːʔira wʔaqtiṣid ʕašir fluːs] Instead of taking the bus I walk to the office and save ten fils.
قَصِد [qaṣid] *n:* • **1.** intention, intent • **2.** design, purpose – عَن قَصِد [ʕan qaṣid] intentionally, purposely. بَلا قَصِد، عَن غير قَصِد [bala qaṣid, ʕan ɣiːr qaṣid] unintentionally, inadvertently.
قَصِيد، بَيت القَصِيد [qaṣiːd, biːt ʔilqaṣiːd] *n:* • **1.** the essence, the gist
مَقصَد [maqṣad] *n:* مَقاصِد [maqaːṣid] *pl:* • **1.** intention, intent • **2.** design, purpose
قَصِيدَة [qaṣiːda] *n:* قَصائِد [qasaːʔid] *pl:* • **1.** poem, piece of poetry
اِقتِصاد [ʔiqtiṣaːd] *n:* • **1.** economization, economy • **2.** economics
قاصِد [qaːṣid, gaːṣid] *adj:* • **1.** aiming, meaning, direct, straight (way)
قَصدَنِي [qaṣdani] *adj:* • **1.** intentionally, on purpose – سَوّاها قَصدَنِي حَتَّى يخَجِّلنِي [sawwaːha qaṣdani ħatta yxaǰǰilni] He did it on purpose to embarrass me.
مَقصُود [maqṣuːd] *adj:* • **1.** deliberate, intended, intentional, meant, aimed at
مِقتِصِد [miqtiṣid] *adj:* • **1.** conservative
اِقتِصادِي [ʔiqtiṣaːdi] *adj:* • **1.** saving, thrifty, provident – مَرتِي كُلِّش اِقتِصادِيَّة [marti kulliš ʔiqtiṣaːdiyya] My wife is very thrifty. • **2.** economical – سَيّارَة اِقتِصادِيَّة [sayyaːra ʔiqtiṣaːdiyya] an economical car. • **3.** economic – الحالَة الاقتِصادِيَّة [ʔilħaːla ʔilʔiqtiṣaːdiyya] the economic situation. • **4.** economist, political economist
قَصداً [qaṣdan] *adverbial:* • **1.** on purpose

ق ص د ر

قَصدِير [qaṣdiːr] *n:* • **1.** zinc

ق ص ر

قِصَر [giṣar] *v:* • **1.** to be or become short, shorter – البنَيَّة كُبرَت وَكُلّ نَفانِيفها قِصرَت عَلِيها [ʔilbnayya kubrat wkull nafaːniːfha giṣrat ʕaliːha] The girl grew and all her dresses are too short for her. اللَّيل قِصَر هوايَة بهالشَّهَر [ʔillayl giṣar hwaːya bhaššahar] The nights have grown short this month.
قَصَّر [qaṣṣar, gaṣṣar] *v:* • **1.** to shorten, make shorter, curtail – قَصَّر الله بعُمرَك [qaṣṣar ʔallah bʕumrak] May God shorten your life! • **2.** to stint, to be sparing – ما يقَصِّر ويّا إبنَه. كُلّ ما يُطلُب مِنَّه ينطِيه [maː yqaṣṣir wiyya ʔibnah. kull maː yuṭlub minnah yinṭi] He doesn't stint his son. Anything he asks for he gives him. إنتَ ما دَتقَصِّر ويّاه. دَتساعدَه هوايَة [ʔinta maː datqaṣṣir wiyyaːh. datsaːʕdah hwaːya] You aren't sparing anything with him. You're helping him a lot. • **3.** to be lax, negligent, neglectful – قَصَّرت ما قُتلَه عَليها [qaṣṣarit maː gutlah ʕaliːha] You were neglectful not to tell him about it. لازِم كان تِشتِرِيها؛ قَصَّرت [laːzim čaːn tištiriːha; qaṣṣarit] You should have bought it; you made a mistake. • **4.** to lose (time) – ساعتِي تقَصِّر [saːʕti tqaṣṣir] My watch loses time. هَالسّاعَة تقَصِّر خَمِس دَقايِق بِاليُوم [hassaːʕa tqaṣṣir xamis daqaːyiq bilyuːm] This watch loses five minutes a day.
تقَصَّر [tgaṣṣar] *v:* • **1.** to be shortened – هالبَنطَرُون ما يِتقَصَّر [halpanṭaruːn maː yitgaṣṣar] These pants can't be shortened.
اِقتِصَر [ʔiqtiṣar] *v:* • **1.** to be limited, restricted, confined – راح تِقتِصِر حَفلَة الزَّواج عَلَى الأَقارِب بَسّ [raːħ tiqtiṣir ħaflat ʔizzawaːǰ ʕala ʔilʔaqaːrib bass] The marriage celebration will be restricted to relatives only.
قَصِر [qaṣir] *n:* قصُور [qṣuːr] *pl:* • **1.** palace, mansion
قُصُر [quṣur, guṣur] *n:* • **1.** shortness – قُصُر نَظَر [quṣur naðar] nearsightedness. عِندَه قُصُر نَظَر؛ يِحتاج مَناظِر [ʕindah quṣur naðar; yiħtaːǰ manaːðir] He's near-sighted; he needs glasses.
قُصُور [quṣuːr] *n:* • **1.** deficiency, inadequacy, shortcoming, lacking, insufficiency • **2.** slackness, laxity, negligence, neglectfulness, inefficiency
قصُور [qṣuːr] *n:* • **1.** change (left after buying something)
تَقصِير [taqṣiːr] *n:* • **1.** neglect, dereliction, laxity, slackness, negligence • **2.** shortcoming, fault, defect
تَقصِير [taqṣiːr, tagṣiyr] *n:* • **1.** shortening, making shorter
مَقصُورَة [maqṣuːra] *n:* مَقصُورات [maqṣuːraːt] *pl:* • **1.** box, box seat, loge
قَصِير [gaṣiːr] *adj:* • **1.** short – عُودَة قَصِيرَة [ʕuːda qaṣiːra] a short stick. • **2.** small, short, low – رِجّال قَصِير [riǰǰaːl qaṣiːr] a short man. شِجرَة قَصِيرَة [šiǰra qaṣiːra] a low tree. نَهار قَصِير [nahaːr qaṣiːr] a short day.
قاصِر [qaːṣir] *adj:* قاصِرِين، قُصَّر [qaːṣiriːn, quṣṣar] *pl:* • **1.** legally minor, underage • **2.** (idiom.) – مَسحُوق قاصِر، قاصِر أَلوان [masħuːq qaːṣir, qaːṣir ʔalwaːn] bleaching agent (chem.).
قصَيِّر [gṣayyir] *adj:* قصار [gṣaːr] *pl:* قصَيِّرَة [gṣayyira] *feminine:* • **1.** short – جُملَة قصَيِّرَة [ǰumla gṣayyra] a short sentence. بَردَة قصَيِّرَة [parda gṣayyra] a short curtain.
مقَصَّر [mgaṣṣar] *adj:* • **1.** shortened • **2.** having shortcomings, falling short of
أَقصَر [ʔagṣar] *comparative adjective:* • **1.** shorter or shortest

ق ص ص

قَصّ [qaṣṣ] *v:* • **1.** to relate, narrate, tell – شِفتَه قاعِد يقُصّ عَلَيهُم إيش شاف بأُورُبّا [šiftah gaːʕid yquṣṣ ʕaliːhum ʔiːš šaːf bʔuːruppa] I saw him sitting telling them what he saw in Europe.

قَصّ [gaṣṣ] *v:* • **1.** to cut, cut off, clip – دِير بالَك، لا تقُصّ إيدَك بالسِّكِّين [diːr baːlak, laː tguṣṣ ʔiːdak bissiččiːn] Look out, don't cut your hand with the knife. قُصّ هَاللَّحمَة ثلاث وُصَل [guṣṣ hallaħma tlaθ wuṣal] Cut this piece of meat into three pieces. جِيب المِنشار وَقُصّ الخِشبَة [jiːb ʔilminšaːr wguṣṣ ʔilxišba] Bring the saw and saw the piece of wood. ما تقُصّ أظافرَك! صارَوا طوال [maː tguṣṣ ʔaðaːfrak! ṣaːraw ṭwaːl] Why don't you clip your fingernails! They've gotten long. الطَّبِيب قال لازِم يقُصُّون رِجلَه اليِسرَى [ʔiṭṭabiːb gaːl laːzim yguṣṣuːn rijlah ʔilyisra] The doctor said they have to amputate his left leg. إذا عِرَفِت تسَوِّيها لِهاي، أقُصّها لإيدِي [ʔiða ʕirafit tsawwiːha lhaːy, ʔaguṣṣha lʔiːdi] If you know how to do that, I'll cut off my hand! إذا تِحكِي كِلمَة اللُّخ، أجِي أقُصَّه الشّارباك [ʔiða tiħči čilmat ʔillux, ʔaji ʔaguṣṣah lšaːrbak] If you say another word, I'll cut your mustache off! راح يقُصُّون شارِع جِدِيد هنا [raːħ yguṣṣuːn šaːriʕ jidiːd hna] They're going to cut a new street through here. خَلِّي نقُصّ مِن البِستان حَتَّى يقصَر الطَّرِيق [xalliː nguṣṣ min ʔilbistaːn ħatta yigṣar ʔiṭṭariːq] Let's cut through the orchard so that it'll be shorter. إذا ترِيد تُعبُر الشَّطّ عَدِل، لازِم تقُصّ قَصّ [ʔiða triːd tuʕbur ʔiššaṭṭ ʕadil, laːzim dguṣṣ gaṣṣ] If you want to cross the river straight, you have to cut diagonally across the current. الهَوا بارِد يقُصّ [ʔilhawa baːrid yguṣṣ] The wind is cold and cutting. صَدِيقَك قَصَّك اليُوم بالدّائرَة [ṣadiːqak gaṣṣak ʔilyuːm biddaːʔira] Your friend cut you down today in the office. لا تِشترِي مِن هَالبَقّال تَرَة يقُصّ [laː tištiri min halbaggaːl tara yguṣṣ] Don't buy from this grocer, because he overcharges. اليُوم قَصَّيت قاطَين [ʔilyuːm gaṣṣayt qaːṭayn] Today I bought material for two suits. تِقدَر تقُصّلِي بِطاقَة وِيّاك؟ أخاف ما راح ألَحِّق عالفِلِم [tigdar dguṣṣli bitaːqa wiyyaːk? ʔaxaːf maː raːħ ʔalaħħig ʕalfilim] Would you buy a ticket for me? I'm afraid I won't be on time for the movie. إذا ما تبَيِّض الجِدِر يقُوم يقُصّ [ʔiða maː tbayyið ʔijjidir yguːm yguṣṣ] If you don't tin the copper pot, it'll react with what's put in it.

قاصَص [qaːṣaṣ] *v:* • **1.** to punish – المُعَلِّم قاصَصَه لِأنّ ما مسَوِّي وَظِيفتَه [ʔilmuʕallim qaːṣaṣah liʔann maː msawwi waðiːftah] The teacher punished him because he didn't do his homework.

اِقتَصّ [ʔiqtaṣṣ] *v:* • **1.** to avenge, revenge oneself, take vengeance – لازِم أقتَصّ مِنَّه عَلَى هَالدَّقَّة [laːzim ʔaqtaṣṣ minnah ʕala haldagga] I'll have to get revenge on him for that dirty deed.

اِنقَصّ [ʔingaṣṣ] *v:* • **1.** to be or become cut – الخِشبَة لازِم تِنقَصّ هنا [ʔilxišba laːzim tingaṣṣ hna] The piece of wood must be cut here.

قَصّ [gaṣṣ] *n:* • **1.** cutting – رَقِّي مالَت قَصّ السِّكِّين [raggi maːlat gaṣṣ ʔissiččiːn] watermelon cut open for inspection. • **2.** لَحَم قَصّ broiled mutton, cut in thin slices and arranged conically on a vertical skewer (also known as شَوَرمَة) – لَحَم قَصّ [laħam gaṣṣ] broiled mutton, cut in thin slices and arranged conically on a vertical skewer.

قَصّ [qaṣṣ] *n:* • **1.** narration

قِصَّة [quṣṣa, qiṣṣa] *n:* قِصَص [qiṣaṣ] *pl:* • **1.** story, tale – شِنُو قُصَّة أخُوك؟ يبَيِّن عَلِيه زَعلان [šinu quṣṣat ʔaxuːk? yibayyin ʕaliːh zaʕlaːn] What's the story with your brother? He seems mad.

قَصَّة [gaṣṣa] *n:* • **1.** height, size – فَدّ قَصَّة [fadd gaṣṣa] the same height. هَالطُّلّاب كُلهُم فَدّ قَصَّة [haṭṭullaːb kullhum fadd gaṣṣa] All these students are the same height.

قُصَّة [guṣṣa] *n:* قُصَص [guṣaṣ] *pl:* • **1.** forehead

مُقص، مقصّ، مقاصَة [mugaṣ, mugaṣṣ, mgaːṣa] *n:* مُقَصّات، مقاصِيص [mugaṣṣaːt, mgaːṣiːṣ] *pl:* • **1.** scissors, shears • **2.** tin snips

قَصاص [qaṣaːṣ] *n:* • **1.** punishment

قصاصَة [gṣaːṣa] *n:* • **1.** diagonally across – خَلِّي نِسبَح قصاصَة حَتَّى ما نِنحِدِر [xalliː nisbaħ gṣaːṣa ħatta maː ninħidir] Let's swim into the current so we won't be swept down-stream.

ق ص ط ر

قَصطُور [qasṭuːr] *n:* • **1.** a kind of cloth, resembling karakul, used for overcoats

ق ص ع

قِصَع [giṣaʕ] *v:* • **1.** to mash, squash, crush – مِن شاف القَملَة قِصَعها [min šaːf ʔilgamla giṣaʕha] When he saw the louse, he squashed it with his thumbnail. قاعِد صَنتَة مِثل القَملَة المَقصُوعَة [gaːʕid ṣanta miθl ʔilgamla ʔilmagṣuːʕa] He's sitting silent as a squashed louse. • **2.** to squelch, squash – قِصَعَه بِهالحكايَة [giṣaʕah bhalħčaːya] He stopped him short by saying that.

قَصَّع [gaṣṣaʕ] *v:* • **1.** to crush repeatedly – ما عِندَه شُغُل بَسّ يقَصِّع قَمُل [maː ʕindah šuɣul bass ygaṣṣiʕ gamul] He's got nothing to do but crush lice.

قَصِع [gaṣiʕ] *n:* • **1.** mashing, squashing, crushing

قُصعَة [guṣʕa] *n:* قُصَع [guṣaʕ] *pl:* • **1.** a large bowl or kettle, used for carrying food to the troops, and by extension, an army meal – وَقِت القُصعَة [wakit ʔilquṣʕa] chow time. شِنُو قُصعَتنا اليُوم؟ [šinu quṣʕatna ʔilyuːm?] What's for chow today? البُوقِي دَيدُقّ القُصعَة [ʔilbuːqi daydugg ʔilquṣʕa] The bugler's playing chow call.

ق ص ف

قُصَف [quṣaf] *v:* • **1.** to shatter, to smash, to break – الله يُقصُف عُمرَك عَلَى هَالدَّقَّة [ʔallah yuqṣuf ʕumrak ʕala haddagga] Damn you for doing that. • **2.** to bomb, to thunder (cannon), to roar, to grumble, to peal (thunder) – الطَّيّارات قُصفَت مَعمَلَين بالمَدِينَة [ʔiṭṭayyaːraːt quṣfat maʕmalayn bilmadiːna] The airplanes bombed two factories in the city.

قِصَف [giṣaf] *v:* • **1.** to shorten, cut down, cut short – الله يُقصُف عُمرَك [ʔallah yugṣuf ʕumrak] Drop dead (lit., may God cut short your life)! • **2.** to be or become

small – السِّترَة قِصفَت عَلِيك [ʔissitra giṣfat ʕaliːk] The jacket has become too small for you.
قَصَّف [gaṣṣaf] *v:* • **1.** to narrow, cut down – بَنطَرُوني عَرِيض. قَصِّفَه شوَيَّة [panṭaruːni ʕariːð̣. gaṣṣfah šwayya] My pants are too big. Narrow them down a bit.
تقَصَّف [tgaṣṣaf] *v:* • **1.** to be narrowed, cut down – هَالبَنطَرُون ما يِتقَصَّف [halpanṭaruːn maː yitgaṣṣaf] These pants can't be narrowed.
اِنقُصَف [ʔinquṣaf] *v:* • **1.** to be bombed – هالمَدِينَة ما اِنقُصفَت بأيّام الحَرُب [halmadiːna maː ʔinquṣfat bʔayyaːm ʔilħarub] This city didn't get bombed during the war.
اِنقِصَف [ʔingiṣaf] *v:* • **1.** to be cut short, shortened – اِنقِصَف عُمرَك! ما تُقعُد راحَة [ʔingiṣaf ʕumrak! maː tugʕud raːħa] Drop dead! Why don't you be good.
قُصُف [guṣuf] *n:* • **1.** narrowness
قَصُف [gaṣuf] *n:* • **1.** shortening, cutting down
قَصُف [qaṣuf] *n:* • **1.** thunder, roar (e.g., of cannon) • **2.** bombing, bombardment
قِصِيف [giṣiːf] *adj:* • **1.** narrow – شارِع قِصِيف [šaːriʕ giṣiːf] a narrow street.
مقَصَّف [mgaṣṣaf] *adj:* • **1.** narrowed, cut down, shortened
مَقصُوف [maqṣuːf] *adj:* • **1.** bombed, attacked, bombarded, blown away • **2.** attacked, bombed, blown away
قاصِفَة [qaːṣifa] *adj:* • **1.** (also n:) bomber

ق ص ق ص

قَصقَص [gaṣgaṣ] *v:* • **1.** to cut up, cut to pieces – قَصقِص اللَّحَم بِالسِّكِّينَة [gaṣgiṣ ʔillaħam bissiččiːna] Cut the meat into pieces with the knife. الجّاهِل بِيدَه المُقَصّ وَدَيقَصقِص بِالوَرَق [ʔijjaːhil biːdah ʔilmugaṣṣ wadaygaṣgiṣ bilwaraq] The child has the scissors in his hand and is shredding the paper.
تقَصقَص [tgaṣgaṣ] *v:* • **1.** to be cut up, be cut to pieces – هَالوَرَق لازِم يِتقَصقَص [halwaraq laːzim yidgaṣgaṣ] This paper must be cut up.
تقِصقِص [tgiṣgiṣ] *n:* • **1.** act of cutting
قَصقُوصَة [gaṣguːṣa] *n:* قِصاقِيص [giṣaːgiːṣ] *pl:* • **1.** piece, shred, scrap
مقَصقَص [mgaṣgaṣ] *adj:* • **1.** shredded

ق ص و 1

أَقصَى، إِلَى أَقصَى حَدّ [ʔaqṣa, ʔila ʔaqṣa ħadd] *comparative adjective:* • **1.** to the extreme limit, to the utmost – بِذَل جُهدَه إِلَى أَقصى حَدّ لمُساعَدتِي [biðal ǰuhdah ʔila ʔaqṣa ħadd lmusaːʕadti] He exerted himself to the utmost limit to help me. الشَّرق الأَقصَى [ʔiššarq ʔilʔaqṣa] the Far East.

ق ص و 2

قِصا [giṣaː] *v:* • **1.** to harm, hurt – إِنتَ صَدِيقي. ما أَقصِي بِيك [ʔinta ṣadiːqi. maː ʔagṣi biːk] You're my friend. I can't hurt you.

تقَصَّى [tqaṣṣaː] *v:* • **1.** to search, to examine, to study, to investigate
قَصي [gaṣy] *n:* • **1.** harm, hurt
تَقَصِّي [taqaṣṣi] *n:* • **1.** investigation, examination

ق ص و 3

اِستِقصاء [ʔistiqṣaːʔ] *n:* • **1.** thorough investigation, close study, fathoming • **2.** search

ق ض ب

قِضَب [giðab] *v:* • **1.** to seize, catch, find – الشُّرطِي قِضَبَه دَيبُوق [ʔiššurṭi giðabah daybuːg] The policeman apprehended him stealing. قِضبَوه دَيغُشّ بِالإمتِحان [giðbawh dayɣušš bilʔimtiħaːn] They caught him cheating on the exam. • **2.** to hold, hold on to, hang on to – اِقضَب راس الحَبِل [ʔigðab raːs ʔilħabil] Hold the end of the rope. قِضَبِتلَك مَكان يَمِّي بِالسِّينَما [giðabitlak makaːn yammi bissinama] I saved a place for you near me in the movie theater. الجُنطَة ما تِقضَب كُلّ هدُومِي [ʔijjunṭa maː tigðab kull hduːmi] The suitcase won't hold all my clothes. اِقضَب إِيدَك! فلُوسَك راح تِخلَص [ʔigðab ʔiːdak! fluːsak raːħ tixlaṣ] Hold it! Your money is about gone.
اِنقِضَب [ʔingiðab] *v:* • **1.** to be seized, caught – الحَرامِي اِنقضَب بِالسِّرداب [ʔilħaraːmi ʔingiðab bissirdaːb] The thief was caught in the basement. • **2.** to have a seizure, fit – خَطِيَّة اِنقضَب بَالدّائِرَة اليُوم [xaṭiyya ʔingiðab biddaːʔira ʔilyuːm] The poor guy had a fit in the office today.
قَضُب [gaðub] *n:* • **1.** seizing, catching, finding
قَضِيب [qaðiːb] *n:* قُضبان [quðbaːn] *pl:* • **1.** wand, rod • **2.** by extension, phallus, penis
مقَضَّب [mgaððab] *n:* • **1.** stiff – جِسمِي مقَضَّب؛ ما دَأقدَر أَتحَرَّك [ǰismi mgaððab; maː daʔagdar ʔatħarrak] My body is stiff; I can't move.

ق ض و

قَضَوِيَّة [qaðawiyya] *n:* قَضَوِيّات [qaðawiyyaːt] *pl:* • **1.** red fez wrapped with white cloth, worn by Moslem religious functionaries

ق ض ي

قِضَى [qiðaː, giðaː] *v:* • **1.** to spend, pass – راح يِقضِي الصَّيف بِالشَّمال [raːħ yiqði ʔiṣṣayf biššimaːl] He'll spend the summer in the north. • **2.** with عَلَى to stamp out, annihilate, eradicate – هَالدُّوا يِقضِي عَلَى مَرَض البَلهارزيا [hadduwa yiqði ʕala marað ʔilbalharizya] This medicine will stamp out schistosomiasis.
قَضَّى [gaððaː] *v:* • **1.** intensive قِضى [qiðaː, giðaː] of to spend – قَضَّى أُمرَه بالحِيلَة وَالسَّختَة [gaððaː ʔumrah bilħiːla wissaxta] He spent his life playing tricks. دَنلِعَب وَرَق حَتَّى نقَضِّي وَقِت [danilʕab waraq ħatta ngaðði wakit] We're playing cards to pass time.

تقضّى [tgaðða:] *v:* • **1.** to get along, get by, make do – لازم نتقضّى عَلَى هَالفلوس إلَى راس الشَّهَر [la:zim nitgaðða: ʕala halfilu:s ʔila ra:s ʔiššahar] We have to get along on this money until the end of the month.

تقاضَى [tqa:ða:] *v:* • **1.** to deal, reckon – خَلّي يسَوّي شما يريد وَأني بَعدين أتقاضَى ويّاه [xalli: ysawwi: šma: yri:d waʔa:ni baʕdi:n ʔatqa:ða: wiyya:h] Let him do as he pleases and later I'll reckon with him.

انقضَى [ʔingiða:] *v:* • **1.** to come to an end, cease, stop – تِنقِضي. ما تظَلّ الأمُور هِيكِي [tingiði. ma: tðall ʔilʔumu:r hi:či] It'll come to an end. Things can't go on like this. • **2.** to pass, go by, run out – اِنقِضَى النَّهار وَبَعدَه ما جا [ʔingiða: ʔinnaha:r wbaʕdah ma: ja:] The day is gone and he hasn't come yet.

اقتضَى [ʔiqtiða:] *v:* • **1.** to necessitate, require – إذا تِقتِضي القَضِيَّة عراك، أتعارَك [ʔiða tiqtiði ʔilqaðiyya ʕra:k, ʔatʕa:rak] If the matter requires fighting, I'll fight. أصرُف حَسَب ما تِقتِضي الحاجَة [ʔuṣruf ħasab ma: tiqtiði ʔilħa:ja] Spend as necessity requires. ما تِقتِضي تِزعَل [ma: tiqtiði tizʕal] There's no need to get mad. إذا اِقتِضَى، أجي [ʔiða ʔiqtiða:, ʔaji] If it's necessary, I'll come. كُلّما يِقتِضيلَك شي، إحنا حاضرين [kullma: yiqtiði:lak ši, ʔiħna ħa:ðri:n] Whenever you need something, we're ready.

قَضا, قَضاء [qaða, qaða:ʔ] *n:* • **1.** fate – القَضاء وَالقَدَر [ʔilqaða:ʔ wilqadar] fate and divine decree. • **2.** stamping out, eradication – القَضاء عالأُمِّيَّة [ʔilqaða:ʔ ʕalʔummiyya] the eradication of illiteracy. • **3.** pl أقضِيَة [ʔaqðiya] district, sub-province

قَضِيَّة [qaðiyya] *n:* قَضايا [qaða:ya] *pl:* • **1.** (legal) case, legal affair • **2.** matter, affair – شصار مِن قَضِيَّة سَفَرَك لأورُبّا؟ [šša:r min qaðiyyat safarak lʔu:ruppa?] What happened to the plans for your trip to Europe? راح أشُوفَك وَأقُولّك بِالقَضِيَّة مِن أوَّلها لِتاليها [ra:ħ ʔašu:fak waʔagullak bilqaðiyya min ʔawwalha lta:li:ha] I'll see you and tell you about the story from beginning to end. • **3.** question, problem, issue – شِنُو قَضِيتَك؟ أشُو طَوَّلتها [šinu qaði:tak? ʔašu ṭawwaltha] What's the matter with you? You seem to have taken a long time about it.

قاضِي [qa:ði] *n:* قُضاة [quða:t] *pl:* • **1.** judge of religious based law • **2.** as Adj: mortal, lethal – ضَربَة قاضيَة [ðarba qa:ðya] a mortal blow.

قاضِي [ga:ði] *adj:* • **1.** finished, done for – رَجُل قاضِي [rajul ga:ði] an old man. مَكِينَة قاضيَة [maki:na ga:ðya] a worn-out engine.

قَضيان [gaðya:n] *adj:* • **1.** finished, done for – حَسبتَه قَضيانَة [ħasbtah gaðya:na] He's all worn out.

قَضائي [qaða:ʔi] *adj:* • **1.** judicial – السُّلطَة القَضائِيَّة [ʔissulṭa ʔilqaða:ʔiyya] judicial branch.

ق ط ب

قُطب [quṭub] *n:* أقطاب [ʔaqṭa:b] *pl:* • **1.** pole – القُطب الشَّمالِي [ʔilquṭb ʔiššima:li] the North Pole. القُطب الجِّنُوبِي [ʔilquṭb ʔijjinu:bi] the South Pole. قُطب سالِب [quṭub sa:lib] negative pole, cathode. قُطب مُوجَب [quṭub mu:jab] positive pole, anode.

قُطبِي [quṭbi] *adj:* • **1.** polar – المَنطِقَة القُطبِيَّة [ʔilmanṭiqa ʔilquṭbiyya] the Polar region.

ق ط ر

قَطَّر [qaṭṭar, gaṭṭar] *v:* • **1.** to drop, drip, let fall in drops – تِقدَر تقَطِّر بعَينِي فَدّ قَطرتَين؟ [tigdar tqaṭṭir bʕi:ni fadd qaṭirtayn?] Could you drop a couple of eyedrops in my eye? • **2.** to distill – لازِم نقَطِّر الماي قَبِل ما نِشرَبَه [la:zim nqaṭṭir ʔilma:y gabil ma: nišrabah] We must distill the water before we drink it. • **3.** to line up – قَطِّر سلال المخَضَّر قِدّام الدُّكّان حَتَّى يشُوفُوها النّاس [qaṭṭir sla:l ʔilmxaððar gidda:m ʔiddukka:n ħatta yšu:fu:ha ʔinna:s] Line up the baskets of vegetables in front of the store so that the people will see them.

تقَطَّر [tqaṭṭar] *v:* • **1.** to be distilled – الماي لازم يِتقَطَّر قَبُل ما يِنشِرُب [ʔilma:y la:zim yitqaṭṭar gabul ma: yinšurub] The water should be distilled before it's drunk. • **2.** to be lined up – الوُلِد تقَطّرَوا بِالباب [ʔilwulid tqaṭṭiraw bilba:b] The boys were lined up at the door.

قَطَر [qaṭar] *n:* قَطَرات [qaṭara:t] *pl:* • **1.** a line (of things) – لِيش واقفين قَطَر؟ [li:š wa:gfi:n qaṭar?] Why are you standing in a line?

قُطُر [quṭur] *n:* أقطار [ʔaqṭa:r] *pl:* • **1.** region, quarter, area – أقطار الدِّنيا [ʔaqṭa:r ʔiddinya] the four corners of the world. هَذا مِفتَرّ أقطار الدِّنيا [ha:ða miftarr ʔaqṭa:r ʔiddinya] This man has toured the countries of the world. • **2.** diameter – نُصف القُطُر [nuṣf ʔilquṭur] radius (of a circle).

قَطرَة [qaṭra, gaṭra] *n:* قَطرات [qaṭra:t, gaṭra:t] *pl:* • **1.** drop (also as a medicine)

قِطار [qiṭa:r] *n:* قِطارات [qiṭa:ra:t] *pl:* • **1.** train

تِقِطِّر [tiqiṭṭir, tigiṭṭir] *n:* • **1.** stinginess

قَطّارَة [qaṭṭa:ra, gaṭṭa:ra] *n:* قَطّارات [qaṭṭa:ra:t, gaṭṭa:ra:t] *pl:* • **1.** dropper, eyedropper

تقطِير [taqṭi:r] *n:* • **1.** distilling, distillation, refining, filtering

مقَطَّر [mqaṭṭar] *adj:* • **1.** distilled, filtered, refined – ماي مقَطَّر [ma:y mqaṭṭar] distilled water.

ق ط ط

قَطّ [qaṭṭ] *v:* • **1.** to sharpen, point – قُطّ القَلَم [quṭṭ ʔilqalam] Sharpen the pencil.

انقَطّ [ʔinqaṭṭ] *v:* • **1.** to be sharpened – القَلَم اِنقَطّ [ʔilqalam ʔinqaṭṭ] The pencil was sharpened.

قَطّ [qaṭṭ] *n:* • **1.** sharpening

مِقطاطَة [miqṭa:ṭa] *n:* مِقطاطات [miqṭa:ṭa:t] *pl:* • **1.** sharpener, pencil sharpener

مَقطُوط [maqṭu:ṭ] *adj:* • **1.** sharpened, sharp – قَلَم مَقطُوط [qalam maqṭu:ṭ] a sharp pencil.

ق

ق ط ع

قطع [giṭaʕ] *v:* • **1.** to cut, cut off, break off – الوَلَد دَيقطَع الوَرِد [ʔilwalad dayigṭaʕ ʔilwarid] The boy is picking the roses. الهَوا قِطَع خيط الطَّيّارَة [ʔilhawa giṭaʕ xiːṭ ṭayyaːra] The wind broke the kite string. قِطَع تِكِت، قِطَع بِطاقَة [giṭaʕ tikit, giṭaʕ biṭaːqa] He bought a ticket. إقطَعلي تِكِت ويّاك [ʔigṭaʕli tikit wiyyaːk] Get me a ticket too. قطَعِت أفادي [gṭaʕit ʔuffaːdi] You've given me a hard time. • **2.** to break off, sever – العَلاقات مَقطوعَة بين الدَّولتَين [ʔilʕalaːqaːt magṭuːʕa biːn ʔiddawiltayn] Relations have been severed between the two countries. • **3.** to cut off, interrupt, stop – إذا ما تِدفَع الفلوس، راح نِقطَع الكَهرَباء [ʔiða maː tidfaʕ ʔilfluːs, raːħ nigṭaʕ ʔilkahrabaːʔ] If you don't pay the money, we'll cut off the electricity. قِطعَوا عَنَّه المُخَصَّصات [giṭʕaw ʕannah ʔilmuxaṣṣaṣaːt] They cut off the allowances to him. إذا ما تداوُم، يقطَعُون راتبَك [ʔiða maː ddaːwum, yigṭaʕuːn raːtbak] If you don't show up at work, they'll cut off your salary. لُويش دَتِحكي عَلَيّا؟ تريد تِقطَع خُبزتي؟ [luwiːš datiħči ʕalayya? triːd tigṭaʕ xubuzti?] Why are you talking about me? Do you want to cut off my livelihood? ما رَجَّعلي كُلّ الفلوس. قِطعني دِينارَين [maː rajjaʕli kull ʔilfluːs. giṭaʕni dinaːrayn] He didn't return all the money to me. He short-changed me two dinars. • **4.** to block, stop, cut off, intercept – حَرِّك سَيّارتَك من هنا؛ قِطَعِت المُرُور [ħarrik sayyaːrtak min hna giṭaʕit ʔilmuruːr] Move your car away from here; you've blocked traffic. الجَّيش قِطَع عَلينا خَطّ الرَّجعَة [ʔijjayš giṭaʕ ʕaliːna xaṭṭ ʔirrajʕa] The army cut off our return route. قِطَع نَفَسَه نُصّ دَقيقَة [giṭaʕ nafasah nuṣṣ daqiːqa] He held his breath for half a minute. • **5.** to interrupt, break into – قِطَعِت عَلَيّا سِلسِلَة أفكاري [giṭaʕt ʕalayya silsilat ʔafkaːri] You broke into my train of thought. • **6.** to conclude, come to agreement on, agree on, settle – صار إلنا ساعَة نِتعامَل؛ خَلّي نِقطَع السِّعِر [ṣaːr ʔilna saːʕa nitʕaːmal; xalliːnigṭaʕ ʔissiʕir] We've been bargaining for an hour; let's set the price. صَدِيقي قِطَع مَهَر ويمكِن يتزَوَّج بالصَّيف [ṣadiːqi giṭaʕ mahar wyimkin yidzawwaj bissayf] My friend concluded the marriage contract and perhaps will get married this summer. • **7.** to cover, traverse – السَّبّاح قِطَع المَسافَة بدَقيقَة ونُصّ [ʔissabbaːħ giṭaʕ ʔilmasaːfa bdaqiːqa wnuṣṣ] The swimmer covered the distance in a minute and a half. قِطَع المَسافَة بثنَعَش دَقيقَة [giṭaʕ ʔilmasaːfa biθnaʕaš daqiːqa] He covered the distance in twelve minutes. قِطَع الأمَل [giṭaʕ ʔilʔamal] He gave up hope. قِطَعت الأمَل مِن رَجعتَه [giṭaʕt ʔilʔamal min rajiʕtah] I gave up hope of his returning. قِطَع عَقلَه [giṭaʕ ʕaqlah] He made up his mind. يقطَع عَقلي مَا أرُوح لِلشُّغُل [yigṭaʕ ʕaqli maː ʔaruːħ liššuɣul] I've got a good mind not to go to work. عَقلَه قِطَع بيها. بَعَد مَحَّد يقدَر يبَدِّل فِكرَه [ʕaqlah giṭaʕ biːha. baʕad maħħad yigdar ybaddil fikrah] His mind is made up. No one can change his idea. عَقلي مَا دَيقطَع بهالسَّيّارَة [ʕaqli maː dayigṭaʕ bhassayyaːra] I've decided not to buy this car.

قطّع [gaṭṭaʕ] *v:* • **1.** to cut off, break off, pick – قَطِّعلي شوَيَّة عِنَب [gaṭṭiʕli šwayya ʕinab] Pick me a few grapes. • **2.** to break, snap, sever (intens.) – الوَلَد قَطَّع الخيط وُصلَة وُصلَة [ʔilwalad gaṭṭaʕ ʔilxiːṭ wuṣla wuṣla] the boy broke the string into a lot of pieces. • **3.** to tear up, wear out – ما تِلبَس غير قاط؟ مُو قَطَّعتَه لِهذا [maː tilbas ɣiːr qaːṭ? muː gaṭṭaʕtah lhaːða] Why don't you wear another suit? You've worn that one out.

قاطع [qaːṭaʕ] *v:* • **1.** to boycott – لازم نقاطِع البِضاعَة الأجنَبِيَّة [laːzim nqaːṭiʕ ʔilbiðaːʕa ʔilʔajnabiyya] We have to boycott foreign goods. • **2.** to interrupt – لا تقاطِعني مِن أحكي [laː tqaːṭiʕni min ʔaħči] Don't interrupt me when I'm talking. • **3.** to trade, exchange (chess) – يقاطِع هوايَة بأوَّل اللِّعِب [yqaːṭiʕ hwaːya bʔawwal ʔilliʕib] He exchanges a lot in the beginning of the game.

تقطّع [tgaṭṭaʕ] *v:* • **1.** to be or become broken – هَالخَيط يِتقَطَّع بسُهُولَة [halxayṭ yitgaṭṭaʕ bsuhuːla] This string gets broken easily.

تقاطع [tqaːṭaʕ] *v:* • **1.** to trade with each other – تقاطَعِت ويّاه بالوَزير [tqaːṭaʕit wiyyaːh bilwaziːr] I exchanged queens with him.

إنقطع [ʔingiṭaʕ] *v:* • **1.** to break, tear, snap – لا تحُطّ هدُوم هوايَة؛ الحَبِل يِنقِطِع [laː tħuṭṭ hiduːm hwaːya; ʔilħabil yingiṭiʕ] Don't put too many clothes on. The rope will break. • **2.** to stop – حُطّ هَالدُّوا عالجَرِح حَتَّى يِنقِطِع الدَّمّ [ħuṭṭ hadduwa ʕajjariħ ħatta yingiṭiʕ ʔiddamm] Put this medicine on the wound so that it'll stop bleeding. اِنقِطَع خَمِس أيّام مِن المَدرَسَة [ʔingiṭaʕ xamis ʔayyaːm min madrasa] He stopped coming to school for five days.

إقتطع [ʔiqtiṭaʕ] *v:* • **1.** to deduct, subtract – خَلّي المُحاسِب يقتِطِعها مِن راتبي [xalliːʔilmuħaːsib yiqtiṭiʕha min raːtbi] Let the accountant take it out of my salary.

إستقطع [ʔistaqṭaʕ] *v:* • **1.** to deduct – راح أستَقطِع خَمس دَنانير مِن الفلوس اللّي تُطلُبني إيّاها [raːħ ʔastaqṭiʕ xams danaːniːr min ʔilfluːs ʔilli tuṭlubni ʔiyyaːha] I'll deduct five dinars from the money I owe you.

قطع [qaṭiʕ, gaṭiʕ] *n:* • **1.** cutting off

قطعة [qiṭʕa] *n:* قِطَع [qiṭaʕ] *pl:* • **1.** piece, fragment, lump, chunk • **2.** piece, selection – قِطعَة مُوسِيقِيَّة [qiṭʕa muːsiːqiyya] a musical selection. • **3.** license plate, number plate • **4.** signboard, shingle • **5.** pl. قطعات, قِطَع plot, piece, lot – قِطعَة الباصات [qiṭʕat ʔilpaːṣaːt] bus depot, bus terminal.

قطيع [qaṭiːʕ] *n:* قِطعان [qiṭʕaːn] *pl:* • **1.** herd, flock, drove

مقطع [maqṭaʕ] *n:* مَقاطِع [maqaːṭiʕ] *pl:* • **1.** cross-section, section, division, passage, extract • **2.** Pl. مَقاطِع selections (from a musical piece or a literary work)

ق

قاطِع [qaːṭiʕ] *n:* قَواطِع [qawaːṭiʕ] *pl:* • **1.** partition, screen • **2.** divider • **3.** mugger, highway robber, holdup man
قَطّاع [qaṭṭaːʕ] *n:* • **1.** (stone- or wood-) cutter
قَطِيعَة [qaṭiːʕa] *n:* قَطِيعات [qaṭiːʕaːt] *pl:* • **1.** separation, legal separation
إقطاع [ʔiqṭaːʕ] *n:* • **1.** feudal estate, land held by feudal tenure
تَقاطُع [taqaːṭuʕ] *n:* • **1.** intersection, crossing, junction
مُقاطَعَة [muqaːṭaʕa] *n:* مُقاطَعات [muqaːṭaʕaːt] *pl:* • **1.** boycott • **2.** feudal estate, large land holding
إقطاعِي [ʔiqṭaːʕi] *n:* إقطاعِيِّين [ʔiqṭaːʕiːyyiːn] *pl:* • **1.** feudal • **2.** feudal landlord, large landholder
اِنقِطاع [ʔinqiṭaːʕ] *n:* • **1.** separation, disjunction, intrruption, break, cessation, stoppage, termination
تَقطِيعَة [taqṭiːʕa] *n:* تَقطِيعات، تَقَاطِيع [taqṭiːʕaːt, taqaːṭiːʕ] *pl:* • **1.** feature
مَقطُوعَة [maqṭuːʕa] *n:* مَقاطِع [maqaːṭiʕ] *pl:* • **1.** piece • **2.** piece (of music)
اِستِقطاع [ʔistiqṭaːʕ] *n:* • **1.** deduction (e.g., from a salary)
قَطعِي [qaṭʕi] *adj:* • **1.** final, definite – جَواب قَطعِي [ǰawaːb qaṭʕi] a definite answer.
مقَطَّع [mqaṭṭaʕ, mgaṭṭaʕ] *adj:* • **1.** broken, broken in many places – فِلِم مقَطَّع [filim mgaṭṭaʕ] a much broken reel of film.
قاطِع [gaːṭiʕ] *adj:* • **1.** separated from someone
مَقطُوع [maqṭuːʕ, magṭuːʕ] *adj:* • **1.** decided, settled, finished, done with – سِعِر مَقطُوع [siʕir maqṭuːʕ] a fixed price.
مِنقِطِع [mingiṭiʕ, minqiṭiʕ] *adj:* • **1.** separated, cut off
مِتقَطِّع [mitqaṭṭiʕ, mitgaṭṭiʕ] *adj:* • **1.** cut, disconnected, discontinuous, ruptured, interrupted,
مِتقاطِع [mitgaːṭiʕ] *adj:* • **1.** separated from someone
مِتقاطِع [mitqaːṭiʕ] *adj:* • **1.** crossed, intersected
قَطعاً [qaṭʕan] *adverbial:* • **1.** absolutely, decidedly, definitely, emphatically
قَطعِيّاً [qaṭʕiyyan] *adverbial:* • **1.** absolutely – ما سَوَّيتها قَطعِيّاً [maː sawwiːtha qaṭʕiyyan] I absolutely didn't do it. ما أرِيدَك تِحكِي وِيّاه قَطعِيّاً [maːʔariːdak tiħči wiyyaːh qaṭʕiyyan] I don't want you to talk to him at all.

ق ط ف

قِطَف [giṭaf] *v:* • **1.** to duck – أُقطُف راسَك؛ الباب ناصِي [ʔugṭuf raːsak; ʔilbaːb naːṣi] Duck your head; the door is low. • **2.** to throw, toss – أُقطُف الكِتاب؛ أَقدَر أَلُقفَه [ʔugṭuf ʔilkitaːb; ʔagdar ʔalugfah] Throw the book; I can catch it.
قَطَّف [gaṭṭaf] *v:* • **1.** to throw around – الجّاهِل دَيقَطُّف بالمَلاعِيب مالتَه [ʔiǰǰaːhil daygaṭṭuf bilmalaːʕiːb maːltah] The kid is throwing his toys around.
قُطُف [guṭuf] *n:* قطُوف [gṭuːf] *pl:* • **1.** butt – قُطُف سِجارَة [guṭuf sigaːra] cigarette butt.
قَطفَة [gaṭfa] *n:* قَطفات [gaṭfaːt] *pl:* • **1.** throw, toss
مُقتَطَف [muqtaṭaf] *adj:* • **1.** selected or select piece

ق ط م

قِطَم [giṭam] *v:* • **1.** to cut, cut off – ضِرَب البَزُّونَة بالفاسَة وَقِطَم ذَيلها [ðirab ʔilbazzuːna bilfaːsa wgiṭam ðiːlha] He hit the cat with the axe and cut off its tail. • **2.** to break, break off – قِطَم الخيارَة بِيدَه [giṭam ʔilxyaːra biːdah] He snapped the cucumber in two in his hand. • **3.** to cut short – قِطَم القُصَّة لِأنّ ما كان عِندَه وَقِت [giṭam ʔilquṣṣa liʔann maː čaːn ʕindah wakit] He cut the story short because he didn't have time.
قَطَّم [gaṭṭam] *v:* • **1.** to cut off – هَالمَكِينَة تقَطُّم رُؤوس الدِّجاج وَتنَظُّفها [halmakiːna tgaṭṭum ruʔuːs ʔiddiǰaːǰ wtnaððufha] This machine cuts off the chickens' heads and cleans them.
اِنقِطَم [ʔingiṭam] *v:* • **1.** to be cut off – اِنقُطمَت إيدَه بالمِنشار الكَهرَبائِي [ʔinguṭmat ʔiːdah bilminšaːr ʔilkahrabaːʔi] His hand was cut off by the electric saw.
قَطُم [gaṭum] *n:* • **1.** cutting off
قُطمَة [guṭma] *n:* قُطَم [guṭam] *pl:* • **1.** fragment, piece, shard
مقَطَّم [mgaṭṭam] *adj:* • **1.** unknown, obscure, without family background • **2.** person with no background
مَقطُوم [magṭuːm] *adj:* • **1.** trimmed, cut

ق ط م ر

قَطمَر [qaṭmar] *adj:* • **1.** extreme, complete, real – كَذّاب قَطمَر [čaððaːb qaṭmar] a real liar. شيُوعِي قَطمَر [šyuːʕi qaṭmar] a confirmed communist. • **2.** (bot.) double, having more than one row of petals – بَتُونيا قَطمَر [patuːnya qaṭmar] double petunias. شَبُّو قَطمَر [šabbu qaṭmar] double stock, double gillyflower.

ق ط ن

قَطَّن [gaṭṭan] *v:* • **1.** to mold, mildew, be or become moldy – الخُبُز قَطَّن [ʔilxubuz gaṭṭan] The bread got moldy.
قُطُن، قُطِن [guṭun, guṭin] *n:* • **1.** cotton
قطِين [qṭiːn, gṭiːn] *n:* • **1.** (coll.) squash, gourd – قطِين أَحمَر [gṭiːn ʔaħmar] pumpkin.
قَطّان، قِطّان [gaṭṭaːn, giṭṭaːn] *n:* • **1.** a kind of edible fresh-water fish
قَطّان [gaṭṭaːn] *n:* • **1.** cotton manufacturer, cotton merchant
قِيطان [qiːṭaːn] *n:* قياطِين [qyaːṭiːn] *pl:* • **1.** lace, string, cord
قطِينَة [qṭiːna, gṭiːna] *n:* قطِينات [qṭiːnaːt, gṭiːnaːt] *pl:* • **1.** a squash, a gourd
قُطنِي [quṭni] *adj:* • **1.** made of cotton, of cotton material

ق ط ي

قِطَة [giṭa] *n:* • **1.** (coll.) sand grouse
قِطايَة [giṭaːya] *n:* قِطايات [giṭaːyaːt] *pl:* • **1.** a sand grouse

ق

ق ع د

قعد [giʕad] *v:* • **1.** to sit down, take a seat – أُقعُد؛ اِستِريح [ʔugʕud; ʔistiriːħ] Sit down; take a load off your feet! تعاتَبنا شوَيَّة وَبَعدين كُلّ شِي قِعَد بِمُكانَه [tʕaːtabna šwayya wbaʕdiːn kull ši giʕad bimukaːnah] We argued for a little while and then everything was straightened out. ما تُقعُد راحَة؟ مُو ضَوَّجتِني [maː tugʕud raːħa? muː ḍawwajtni] Why don't you quit it? Haven't you pestered me enough already? باكِر راح أقعُد الصُّبُح. عِندي شُغُل [baːčir raːħ ʔagʕud ʔiṣṣubuħ. ʕindi šuɣul] I'm going to take the morning off tomorrow. I have something to do. • **2.** to sit, be sitting – وين تحِب تِقعُد؟ [wiːn tħibb tigʕud?] Where do you want to sit? قِعَدنا بِالقَهوَة نُصّ ساعَة نِنتَظرَك [giʕadna bilgahwa nuṣṣ saːʕa nintaḍ̣rak] We've been sitting in the coffee house a half hour waiting for you. هالقاط قِعَد حِلو عَليك [halqaːṭ giʕad ħilw ʕaliːk] This suit fits you well. لَو تُصبُغ السَّيّارَة وَتِشتِريلها تايَرات، تُقعُد [law tuṣbuɣ ʔissayyaːra wtištiriːlha taːyaraːt, tugʕud] If you paint the car and buy tires for it, it'll look nice. • **3.** to remain, stay, dwell, live – قِعَدنا سَنَة وِحدَة بالكَرخ، وَبَعدين حَوَّلنا لِلأعظَميَّة [giʕadna sana wiħda bilkarx, wbaʕdiːn ħawwalna lilʔaʕḍ̣amiyya] We lived in the Karkh area a year, and then moved to Adhamiya. قاعدِين بِالكَرّادَة [gaːʕdiːn bilkarraːda] We live in Karraada. زِرتَه يوم واحِد ورَجَّع الزِّيّارَة بَعَد شَهَر، لَكِن قِعَد عَلَى أُفّادِي ثلَث أَسابيع [zirtah yuːm waːħid wrajjaʕ ʔizziyyaːra baʕad šahar, laːkin giʕad ʕala ʔuffaːdi tlaθ ʔasaːbiːʕ] I visited him for a day, and he returned the visit after a month, but he plagued me for three weeks.

قَعَّد [gaʕʕad] *v:* • **1.** to make sit down, make sit, seat – الرِّجّال قَعَّدنا لِقِدّام [ʔirrijjaːl gaʕʕadna ligiddaːm] The man seated us down front. سَنَة اللُّخ راح يصِير عُمرَه سَبع سنِين وَنقَعّدَه بِالمَدرَسَة [sanat ʔillux raːħ yṣiːr ʕumrah sabʕ sniːn wngaʕʕdah bilmadrasa] Next year he'll be seven years old and we'll enter him in school. رَئِيس الوُزَراء قَعّدَه قبال مَرتَه كيف عارَضَه [raʔiːs ʔilwuzaraːʔ gaʕʕadah gbaːl martah čiːf ʕaːraḍ̣ah] The Prime Minister sent him home because he opposed him. هَالصُّبُغ راح يقَعِّدها لِلسَّيّارَة [haṣṣubuɣ raːħ ygaʕʕidha lissayyaːra] This paint will make the car look nice. • **2.** to wake, wake up, awaken – قَعِّدني مِن النُّوم ساعَة خَمسَة [gaʕʕidni min ʔannuːm saːʕa xamsa] Wake me up at five. يِنرادلِي فَدّ كُوب قَهوَة أَقَعِّد راسِي بِيه [yinraːdli fadd kuːb gahwa ʔagaʕʕid raːsi biːh] I need a cup of coffee to wake myself up.

تقَعَّد [tgaʕʕad] *v:* • **1.** to be awakened

تقاعَد [tqaːʕad] *v:* • **1.** to be pensioned off, retire – أَخُويا تقاعَد السَّنَة اللِّي فاتَت [ʔaxuːya tqaːʕad ʔissana ʔilli faːtat] My brother retired last year.

تقاعَد [tgaːʕad] *v:* • **1.** to confer, consult – تقاعَدنا ويّاهُم وَانحَلَّت المُشكِلَة [tgaːʕadna wiyyaːhum wʔinħallat ʔilmuškila] We conferred with them and the problem was solved.

انقِعَد [ʔingiʕad] *v:* • **1.** with ب to be lived in, be occupied – هَالبَيت عَتِيق ما ينقِعِد بيه [halbayt ʕatiːg maː yingiʕid biːh] This house is old. It can't be lived in.

اِستَقعَد [ʔistagʕad] *v:* • **1.** to take as a mistress – اِستَقعَدلَه وِحدَة مِن كان بِالبَصرَة [ʔistagʕadlah wiħda min čaːn bilbaṣra] He took a mistress when he was in Basra.

قِعدَة، ذُو القِعدَة [qiʕda, ðulqiʕda] *n:* • **1.** Zu'lkadah, eleventh month of the Moslem calendar

مَقعَد [maqʕad] *n:* مَقاعِد [maqaːʕid] *pl:* • **1.** seat, chair • **2.** seat cushion, pad • **3.** backside, seat, buttocks

قَعدَة [gaʕda] *n:* • **1.** sitting • **2.** get together, session – قَعدَة بُوكَر [gaʕdat puːkar] a session of poker.

قُعُود [guʕuːd] *n:* • **1.** sitting down

قَعّادَة [qaʕʕaːda] *n:* قَعّادات [qaʕʕaːdaːt] *pl:* • **1.** bedpan • **2.** potty

تَقاعُد [taqaːʕud] *n:* • **1.** pension, retirement fund – راح أَحِيل نَفسِي عالتَّقاعُد [raːħ ʔaħiːl nafsi ʕattaqaːʕud] I'm going to go on pension.

قاعِدَة [qaːʕida] *n:* قَواعِد [qawaːʕid] *pl:* • **1.** base, pedestal, support • **2.** base (mil.) – قاعِدَة جَوِّيَّة [qaːʕida jawwiyya] air base. • **3.** precept, rule, principle – قَواعِد اللُّغَة [qawaːʕid ʔilluɣa] grammar. حَسَب القاعِدَة [ħasab ʔilqaːʕida] as usual. حَسَب القاعِدَة، جا مِتأَخِّر [ħasab ʔilqaːʕida, jaː mitʔaxxir] As usual, he came late.

قاعِد [gaːʕid] *adj:* • **1.** idle, unemployed – أَخُوك بَعدَه قاعِد لَو اِشتِغَل؟ [ʔaxuːk baʕdah gaːʕid law ʔištiɣal?] Is your brother still idle or did he get a job? • **2.** in the process of, engaged in – المَكِينَة قاعِد تِشتُغُل بِالبُوش [ʔilmakiːna gaːʕid tištuɣul bilbuːš] The motor's running in neutral.

مُقعَد [muqʕad] *adj:* • **1.** crippled, lame, disabled, invalid, infirm

مُتَقاعِد [mutaqaːʕid] *adj:* مُتقاعِدِين [mutqaːʕidiːn] *pl:* • **1.** retired

ق ع ر

قَعَر [qaʕar] *n:* • **1.** bottom – قَعر البَحَر [qaʕr ʔilbaħar] bottom of the sea.

مُقَعَّر [muqaʕʕar] *adj:* • **1.** hollow, dished, concave – عَدَسَة مُقَعَّرَة [ʕadasa muqaʕʕara] concave lens.

ق ع س

تقاعَس [tqaːʕas] *v:* • **1.** to be aloof, stand-offish – ساعِد أَصدِقائَك. لا تِتقاعَس [saːʕid ʔaṣdiqaːʔak. laː titqaːʕas] Help your friends. Don't be aloof.

ق ف

قاف [qaːf] *n:* • **1.** name of the letter ق

ق ف ز 1

قِفَز [qifaz] *v:* • **1.** to jump – أَخُوك يِقفِز أَعلَى مِنِّي [ʔaxuːk yiqfiz ʔaʕla minni] Your brother jumps higher than I do.

قَفِز [qafiz] *n:* • **1.** jumping – القَفز العالِي [qafz ʔilʕaːli] high jump. القَفز العَرِيض [qafz ʔilʕariːð̣] broad jump.
قَفزَة [qafza] *n:* قَفزات [qafzaːt] *pl:* • **1.** jump, leap, spring

ق ف ز [2]

قُفَز [kufaz] *v:* • **1.** to mount, cover – خَرُوفنا قُفَز نَعجَتهُم [xaruːfna kufaz naʕǯathum] Our ram mounted their ewe.
قَفَّز [kaffaz] *v:* • **1.** intens. of قُفَز to mount, cover – هَالصَّخَل جايبِيه حَتَّى يقَفُّز صَخلاتهُم [haṣṣaxal ǯaːybiːh ħatta ykaffuz ṣaxlaːthum] They've brought this billy goat to breed their female goats.
قَفُز [kafuz] *n:* • **1.** mounting, covering

ق ف ص

قُفَص [qufaṣ] *v:* • **1.** to catch – قُفَصِت طَير بِيدِي [qufaṣit ṭiːr biːdi] I caught a bird with my hands. قُفصَوا لِلمُجرِم بِبَيتَه [qufṣaw lilmuǯrim bibaytah] They captured the criminal at home. قُفَصتَه لعَلِي يِلعَب بكُتبَك [qufaṣtah lʕali yilʕab bkutbak] I caught Ali playing with your books.
قَفَّص [qaffaṣ] *v:* • **1.** to fasten, secure – آنِي أَرَكُّب البُورِيات عَالحايِط وَإنتَ قَفُّصها [ʔaːni ʔarakkub ʔilbuːriyaːt ʕalħaːyiṭ wʔinta qaffuṣha] I'll lay the pipes against the wall and you fasten them in place.
اِنقُفَص [ʔinqufaṣ] *v:* • **1.** to be caught – الجّرِيدِي خَشّ بِالمُصيادَة وَانقُفَص [ʔiǯǯriːdi xašš bilmuṣyaːda wʔinqufaṣ] The rat went into the trap and got caught. ظَلّ يبُوق غَراض إلَى أن انقُفَص [ð̣all ybuːg ɣaraːð̣ ʔila ʔan ʔinqufaṣ] He kept on stealing things until he was caught.
قَفَص [qafaṣ, qufaṣ] *n:* قُفَصات، قفاص [qufaṣaːt, qfaːṣ] *pl:* • **1.** cage – القَفَص الصَّدرِي [ʔilqafaṣ ʔiṣṣadri] the rib cage, the thorax. قَفَص الاَتِّهام [qafaṣ ʔilʔittihaːm] (prisoner's) dock. • **2.** basket, crate (of palm fronds)
قَفِيص [qafiːṣ] *n:* قَفِيصات [qafiːṣaːt] *pl:* • **1.** (metal) strap, band

ق ف ع

قُفَع [gufaʕ] *v:* • **1.** to peel, to flake – الشّبِنتُو قُفَع مِن الحايِط [ʔiččbintu gufaʕ min ʔilħaːyiṭ] The plaster peeled off of the wall.
قَفَّع [gaffaʕ] *v:* • **1.** to peel, flake – المِشَق مال إيدَه بدا يقَفُّع لِأَنّ ما خَلّاها دِهِن فازلِين [ʔilmišag maːl ʔiːdah bidaː ygaffuʕ liʔann maː xallaːha dihin fazaliːn] The chapped place on his hand started to peel because he didn't put vaseline on it.
قَفُع [gafuʕ] *n:* • **1.** peel, flake

ق ف ف

قُفَّة [guffa] *n:* قُفَف [gufaf] *pl:* • **1.** large basket • **2.** coracle, a round, asphalt covered straw boat

ق ف ق ف

قَفقَف [gafgaf] *v:* • **1.** to set – قَفقُفَت الدِّجاجَة عالبَيض كُلَّه وَماكُو بيضَة تبَيِّن [gafgufat ʔiddiǯaːǯa ʕalbayð̣ kullah wmaːku bayð̣a tbayyin] The hen settled herself over all the eggs and not one is visible.

ق ف ل also ز ق ف ل

قُفَل [qufal] *v:* • **1.** to lock – أُقفُل الباب بَعَد ما تِطلَع [ʔuqful ʔilbaːb baʕad maː tiṭlaʕ] Lock the door after you go out.
قَفَّل [qaffal] *v:* • **1.** to lock up – قَفَّلنا كُلّ الأَبواب [qaffalna kull ʔilʔabwaːb] We locked up all the doors.
اِنقُفَل [ʔinqufal] *v:* • **1.** to be locked – الباب ما دَينقِفِل [ʔilbaːb maː dayinqifil] The door can't be locked.
قُفُل [quful] *n:* قفال، قفالة [qfaːl, qfaːla] *pl:* • **1.** lock • **2.** safety (on a gun)
قافِلَة [qaːfila] *n:* قَوافِل [qawaːfil] *pl:* • **1.** caravan, convoy
زُقفالَة [zuqfaːla] *n:* زُقفالات [zugfaːlaːt] *pl:* • **1.** catch, latch
قافُل [qaːful] *adj:* • **1.** stubborn
مقَفَّل [mqaffal] *adj:* • **1.** locked up • **2.** plaid, having vertical and horizontal stripes
مَقفُول [maqfuːl] *adj:* • **1.** locked
مزَقفُلَة [mzaqfula] *adj:* • **1.** locked

ق ف و

قَفَّى [qaffaː] *v:* • **1.** to rhyme, put into rhyme – إقرا كَم بَيت وَآنِي أقَفِّي [ʔiqra čam bayt waʔaːni ʔaqaffi] Recite a few lines and I'll put rhymes to them. إنتَ مُو كُلّما أَحكِي تقَفِّيلِي؟ [ʔinta muː kullma ʔaħči tqaffiːli?] Every time I speak, why must you interrupt and finish what I'm trying to say?
قُفا [gufa] *n:* • **1.** back, reverse, wrong side – عَلَى قُفاه [ʕala gufaːh] inside out لابِس البلُوز عَلَى قُفاه [laːbis ʔilbluːz ʕala gufaːh] He's wearing the sweater inside out. يِحكِي بالقُفا [yiħči bilgufa] He talks behind one's back. يِحكِي بِقُفا النّاس [yiħči bgufa ʔinnaːs] He talks behind people's backs.
قافِيَة [qaːfiya] *n:* قَوافِي [qawaːfi] *pl:* • **1.** rhyme

ق ك و

قَكاوَة [qačaːwa] *n:* قَكاوات [qačaːwaːt] *pl:* • **1.** camel litter for females, seat for riding on a camel (howdah)

ق ل ب

قِلَب [qilab, gilab] *v:* • **1.** to change – كان لونَه أَحمَر حِلو لَكِن قِلَب [čaːn luːnah ʔaħmar ħilw laːkin gilab] It used to be a nice red color, but it changed. • **2.** to go back on one's word, to change one's mind – قَلِّي راح يبِيع السَّيّارَة وَقِلَب عَلَيّا [galli raːħ ybiːʕ ʔissayyaːra wgilab ʕalayya] He told me he was going to sell the car and then changed his mind on me. وافَق يبِيعها بِدِينار وَبَعدين قِلَب [waːfaq yibiːʕha bdinaːr wbaʕdiyn gilab] He agreed to sell it for a dinar and afterwards he went back on his word.

ق

قَلِب، قَلب [qalib, qalb] *v:* • **1.** bad, counterfeit – فلُوس قَلب [flu:s qalb] counterfeit money. • **2.** inconstant, fickle, variable, changeable • **3.** fickle person • **4.** insincere – حَكيَه قَلب [ħačyah qalb] His talk is insincere. أعمالَه قَلب [ʔaʕma:lah qalb] His actions are insincere.

قِلَب [gilab] *v:* • **1.** to turn, turn over – أُقلُب الصَّفحَة. أَرِيد أَشُوف الرَّسِم [ʔuglub ʔiṣṣafħa. ʔari:d ʔašu:f ʔirrasim] Turn the page. I want to see the picture. • **2.** to turn upside down, turn over – خَلِّي نِقلُب الصَّندُوق. بَلكِي الكِتابَة عالكَعب [xalli: niglub ʔiṣṣandu:g. balki ʔilkita:ba ʕaččaʕb] Let's turn the trunk upside down. Perhaps the writing is on the bottom. قِلَب الدِّنيا [gilab ʔiddinya] He raised heaven and earth. He made a big racket. لِيش قالُب خِلِقتَك؟ [li:š ga:lub xiliqtak?] What's wrong with you? Why the long face? داخ وَقِلَب مِن راسَه [da:x wgilab min ra:sah] He got dizzy and vomited. • **3.** to overturn, upset, topple – البَزُّونَة قِلبَت الجِّدِر [ʔilbazzu:na gilbat ʔijjidir] The cat upset the pot. • **4.** to invert, reverse – الخَيّاط غِلَب القَولَة مالَت ثَوبِي [ʔilxayya:ṭ ɣilab ʔilqawla ma:lat θu:bi] The tailor turned the collar of my shirt. • **5.** to change, switch, alter, convert – راح يقُلبُون الكَهرَباء مِن دِي سِي إِلَى أَيّ سِي [ra:ħ ygulbu:n ʔilkahraba:ʔ min di si ʔila ʔayy si] They are going to convert the electricity from D. C. to A. C. يَزِّي عاد! أُقلُب صَفحَة [yazzi ʕa:d! ʔuglub ṣafħa] That's enough! Change the subject. لُويش تُقلُب الحكايَة؟ آني ما قِلِت هِيك [luwi:š tuglub ʔilħča:ya? ʔa:ni ma: gilit hi:č] Why do you twist what's said? I didn't say that. • **6.** to tumble, turn somersaults – هَذا الطَّير يُقلُب [ha:ða ʔiṭṭi:r yuglub] This bird turns somersaults. • **7.** to change color, run – هَالقماش، مِن تغِسلَه، يُقلُب [halqma:š, min tɣislah, yuglub] When you wash this material, the colors run.

قَلَّب [gallab] *v:* • **1.** to turn, turn over – تِقدَر تقَلُّب الكَباب بالجَّطَل [tigdar tgallub ʔilkaba:b biččaṭal] You can turn the hamburgers with the fork. • **2.** to stir – بالله قَلُّب المَرَق حَتَّى ما يِحتِرِق [ballah gallub ʔilmarag ħatta ma: yiħtirig] Please stir up the stew so that it won't burn. • **3.** to rummage, ransack, rake, poke around – صارلَك ساعَة تقَلُّب وَما إِشتِرَيت شِي [ṣa:rlak sa:ʕa tgallub wma ʔištirayt ši] You've been rummaging around for an hour and haven't bought anything.

تقَلَّب [tqallab, tgallab] *v:* • **1.** to vary, change, swing – يِتقَلَّب حَسَب الظُّرُوف [yitqallab ħasab ʔiððuru:f] He changes according to circumstances. يِتقَلَّب ويّا الهَوا [yitqallab wiyya ʔilhawa] He swings with the wind. • **2.** to fluctuate – الأَسعار ما ثابتَة. دَتِتقَلَّب عَلَى طُول [ʔilʔasʕa:r ma: θa:bta. datitqallab ʕala ṭu:l] Prices are not stable. They are fluctuating all the time.

انقلَب [ʔingilab] *v:* • **1.** to turn over – اِنقلَب الماعُون مِن إِيدَه وَوُقَع اللَّحَم [ʔingilab ʔilma:ʕu:n min ʔi:dah wwugaʕ ʔillaħam] The plate turned over in his hand and the meat fell. • **2.** to change into, turn into, become – سمَعنا فَدّ رِجّال اِنقِلَب مرَيَّة [smaʕna fadd rijja:l ʔingilab mrayya] We heard that a man turned into a woman. • **3.** to turn – كان صَدِيقِي لَكِن اِنقِلَب عَلَيّا [ča:n ṣadi:qi la:kin ʔingilab ʕalayya] He was my friend but he turned on me.

قَلُب [galub] *n:* قلُوب [glu:b] *pl:* • **1.** heart – حِكاها مِن كُلّ قَلبَه [ħiča:ha min kull galbah] He said it from the bottom of his heart, he said it wholeheartedly. إِذا تسافِر، أُمَّك يظَلّ قَلُبها عَلِيك [ʔiða tsa:fir, ʔummak yðull galubha ʕali:k] If you go on a trip, your mother will worry. طَلَّع هَالحكايَة مِن قَلبَه [ṭallaʕ halħča:ya min galbah] He made up this talk out of his imagination. شِلَع قَلبِي إِبنَك. أُخذَه [šilaʕ galbi ʔibnak. ʔuxðah] Your son has pestered me to death. Take him. أَكَل قَلبِي [ʔakal galbi] He annoyed me, he got on my nerves. نِشكُرِك، قَلبِي [niškurič, galbi] Thank you, dearie.

قَلُب [galub] *n:* • **1.** turnover, reversal

قَلِب [qalib] *n:* • **1.** reversal, changing

قَلبَة [qalba, galba] *n:* قَلبات [qalba:t] *pl:* • **1.** a breach of promise

قالَب [qa:lab] *n:* قَوالِب، قوالِب [qawa:lib, qwa:lib.] *pl:* • **1.** form • **2.** mold • **3.** cake, block – قالَب صابُون [qa:lab ṣa:bu:n] cake of soap, bar of soap. قالَب ثَلِج [qa:lab θalij] block of ice. قالَب طَباشِير [qa:lab taba:ši:r] stick of chalk.

تَقَلُّب [taqallub] *n:* تَقَلُّبات [taqalluba:t] *pl:* • **1.** fluctuation, change

قَلبَة [galba] *n:* • **1.** (pants) cuff • **2.** French cuff • **3.** (shirt) collar • **4.** lapels (of a coat.)

قَلّاب [galla:b] *n:* • **1.** dumper, tip wagon

مَقلَب، مُقلاب [maglab, mugla:b] *n:* • **1.** dump, garbage dump, refuse pile

تَقلِيب [taqli:b, tagli:b] *n:* • **1.** leafing through • **2.** changing, transforming, reshaping

اِنقِلاب [ʔinqila:b] *n:* اِنقِلابات [ʔinqila:ba:t] *pl:* • **1.** overthrow, coup d'etat

قَلبِي [qalbi] *adj:* • **1.** of the heart, heart – الأَمراض القَلبِيَّة [ʔilʔamra:ð ʔilqalbiyya] heart diseases.

مَقلُوب [maglu:b] *adj:* • **1.** upside down – مَوَقَّف الكلاص بِالمَقلُوب [mwaggaf ʔilgla:ṣ bilmaglu:b] The glass is set upside down. • **2.** wrong side out – أَشُو لابِس جوارِيبَك بِالمَقلُوب [ʔašu la:bis jwa:ri:bak bilmaglu:b] Looks like you're wearing your socks inside out. • **3.** backwards, wrong way around – طَبّ عَلينا لابِس وجهه بِالمَقلُوب [ṭabb ʕali:na la:bis wiččah bilmaglu:b] He came in on us wearing a sour face.

مِتقَلِّب [mitqallib, mitgallub] *adj:* • **1.** changeable, variable, inconstant

ق ل ب ل غ

قَلَبالَغ [qalaba:liɣ] *n:* • **1.** crowd, throng • **2.** commotion

ق ل ج

قُلّاج [gulla:j] *n:* • **1.** (coll.) flat, disk-shaped capsules that can be filled with a pharmaceutical compound

قُلّاجَة [gulla:ja] *n:* قُلّاجات [gulla:ja:t] *pl:* • **1.** flat, disk-shaped capsules that can be filled with a pharmaceutical compound

ق ل د

قَلَّد [qallad] *v:* • **1.** to copy, ape, imitate – تِقدَر تقَلِّد هَالمُمَثِّل؟ [tigdar tqallid halmumaθθil?] Can you imitate this actor? اليابانِيِّين يُعرُفُون شلُون يقَلّدُون البَضايِع الأَجنَبِيَّة [ʔilya:ba:niyyi:n yuʕrufu:n šlu:n yqallidu:n ʔilbaðaːyiʕ ʔilʔajnabiyya] The Japanese know how to imitate foreign products. • **2.** with عَلَى to mock, make fun of – لا تقَلِّد عَلَيه. يَعنِي قابِل إنتَ أَحسَن؟ [la: tqallid ʕali:h. yaʕni qa:bil ʔinta ʔaħsan?] Don't make fun of him. Do you think you're better? قام يقَلِّد عَليه وَخَلّانا نِضحَك [ga:m yqallid ʕali:h wxalla:na niðħak] He began to mock him and made us laugh.
تقَلَّد [tqallad] *v:* • **1.** to be imitated – ضِحِكتَه ما تِتقَلَّد [ðiħiktah ma: titqallad] His laugh can't be imitated.
تَقلِيد [taqli:d] *n:* تَقالِيد [taqa:li:d] *pl:* • **1.** imitation, copying • **2.** convention, custom, usage
قلادَة [gla:da] *n:* قلادات، قلايِد [gla:da:t, gla:yid] *pl:* • **1.** necklace – قلادَة لِيلُو [gla:da li:lu] a pearl necklace.
مقَلَّد [mqallad] *adj:* • **1.** fake • **2.** false, ingenuine
تَقلِيدِي [taqli:di] *adj:* • **1.** traditional, customary, usual – عَمَل تَقلِيدِي [ʕamal taqli:di] routine job.

ق ل ص

قَلَّص [qallaṣ] *v:* • **1.** to contract, draw together – قَلَّص عَضَلات إيدَه [qallaṣ ʕaðala:t ʔi:dah] He flexed the muscles in his arm. • **2.** to decrease, cut down – الوِزارَة راح تقَلِّص عَدَد مُوَظَّفِيها [ʔilwiza:ra ra:ħ tqalliṣ ʕadad muwaððafi:ha] The ministry will decrease the number of its employees.
تقَلَّص [tqallaṣ] *v:* • **1.** to contract, shrink – الحَدِيد يِتقَلَّص مِن تِنخُفُض دَرَجَة الحَرارَة [ʔilħadi:d yitqallaṣ min tinxufuð darajat ʔilħara:ra] Metal contracts as the temperature decreases.
تَقَلُّص [taqalluṣ] *n:* تَقَلُّصات [taqalluṣa:t] *pl:* • **1.** contraction, shrinking
مِتقَلِّص [mitqalliṣ] *adj:* • **1.** shrunken

ق ل ط غ

قُلطُغ [qulṭuɣ] *n:* قُلطُغات، قَلاطِغ [qulṭuɣa:t, qala:ṭiɣ] *pl:* • **1.** over-stuffed chair, easy chair

ق ل ع

قِلَع [qilaʕ] *v:* • **1.** to pull out by the roots, uproot, tear out, extract – إقلَع شِجرَة المِشمِش وَإزرَعها بالبِستان [ʔiqlaʕ šijrat ʔilmišmiš wʔizraʕha bilbista:n] Pull up the apricot tree and plant it in the orchard. طَبِيب الأَسنان راح يِقلَع سِنَّه [ṭabi:b ʔilʔasna:n ra:ħ yiqlaʕ sinnah] The dentist will pull his tooth. • **2.** to quarry – دَيِقلِعُون الصَّخَر مِن هَالمَنطِقَة [dayiqilʕu:n ʔiṣṣaxar min halmanṭiqa] They're quarrying stone from this area. • **3.** to budge, move, dislodge – هَذا مِن يزُور أَحَّد ماكُو شِي يِقلَعَه [ha:ða min yzu:r ʔaħħad ma:ku ši yiqlaʕah] When he visits someone, there's nothing that'll dislodge him.
اِنقِلَع [ʔinqilaʕ, ʔingilaʕ] *v:* • **1.** to budge, move, be dislodged – قاعِد بغُرُفتِي ما دَيِنقِلِع [ga:ʕid byurufti ma: dayinqiliʕ] He sits in my room and can't be budged. اِنقِلِع مِن قِدّامِي تَرَة أَمَوِّتَك [ʔinqiliʕ min gidda:mi tara ʔamawwtak] Get out of here or I'll kill you. اِنقِلِع، مِن كُلّ عَقلَك يبِيعلَك البَيت؟ [ʔinqiliʕ, min kull ʕaglak ybi:ʕlak ʔilbayt?] Come off it! Do you really think he'll sell you the house?
قَلع [qaliʕ, galiʕ] *n:* • **1.** rooting out • **2.** extracting
قَلعَة [qalʕa] *n:* قِلاع [qila:ʕ] *pl:* • **1.** castle, fortress • **2.** rook, castle (chess)
مَقلَع [maqlaʕ] *n:* مَقالِع [maqa:liʕ] *pl:* • **1.** stone quarry

ق ل ف

قَلافَة [qala:fa] *n:* قَلافات [qala:fa:t] *pl:* • **1.** build, physique • **2.** appearance

ق ل ق

قِلَق [qilaq] *v:* • **1.** to be or become uneasy, disquieted, apprehensive, anxious, upset, troubled, disturbed – قِلَق هوايَة عَلَى صِحَّة إبنَه [qilaq hwa:ya ʕala ṣiħħat ʔibnah] He was very worried about his son's health. • **2.** to trouble, worry, alarm, disturb, upset – هالأخبار قِلقَتنِي [halʔaxba:r qilqatni] This news disturbed me. حَماتِي دَتِقلِق راحتِي [ħama:ti datiqliq ra:ħti] My mother-in-law is disturbing my rest.
قَلَّق [gallag] *v:* • **1.** to dirty, soil
أَقلَق [ʔaqlaq] *v:* • **1.** to trouble, worry, alarm, disturb, upset – هَالخَبَر أَقلَقنِي هوايَة [halxabar ʔaqlaqni hwa:ya] That news upset me a lot.
اِنقِلَق [ʔinqilaq] *v:* • **1.** to be or become uneasy, disquieted, apprehensive, anxious, upset, troubled, disturbed – لا تِنقِلِق. ماكُو شِي عَالوَلَد [la: tinqiliq. ma:ku ši ʕalwalad] Don't worry. There's nothing wrong with the boy.
قَلَق [qalaq] *n:* • **1.** anxiety, worry
مقَلَّق [mgallag] *adj:* • **1.** dirtied, befouled, filthy
قَلقان [qalqa:n] *adj:* • **1.** worried

ق ل ق ل

قَلقَل [galgal] *v:* • **1.** to move, to shake, wiggle – قَلقِل البِسمار حَتَّى يِنشِلِع بسُهُولَة [galgil ʔilbisma:r ħatta yinšiliʕ bsuhu:la] Wiggle the nail so it can be removed easily. • **2.** to disturb, trouble, harass – جابلِي فَدّ خَبَر، قَلقَل دَماغِي بِيه [ja:bli fadd xabar, galgal dama:ɣi bi:h] He brought me some news which disturbed me. إبنَك ما ينحِمِل. يقَلقِل المُخّ [ʔibnak ma: yinħimil. ygalgil ʔilmuxx] Your son is unbearable. He gives you a headache.
تقَلقَل [tgalgal] *v:* • **1.** to be moved, shaken, wiggled – سِنِّي يِتقَلقَل. راح أَشِلعَه [sinni yitgalgal. ra:ħ ʔašilʕah]

ق

My tooth is loose. I'm going to pull it. • **2.** to move – لا تبيع غراضك وَلا تِتقلقل مِن بَيتَك. هَالشّغلَة مُو أكِيدَة [la: tbi:ʕ ɣara:ðak wala titgalgal min baytak. haššaɣla mu: ʔaki:da] Don't sell your things or move out of your house. That job isn't definite.
قَلاقِل [qala:qil] *n:* • **1.** unrest
قَلاقِيل [qala:qi:l] *n:* • **1.** things, odds and ends, junk • **2.** private parts, genitals – هَذا شايِب؛ قَلاقِيلَه واقعَة [ha:ða ša:yib; qala:qi:lah wa:gʕa] He's old and falling apart.
قُلقُلِي [gulguli] *adj:* • **1.** pink (color)
مقَلقَل [mgalgal] *adj:* • **1.** shaky

ق ل ل

قَلّ [qall] *v:* • **1.** to decrease, diminish, to be or become less, littler, smaller, fewer – فلُوسنا قَلَّت هوايَة بِسَبَب السَّفرَة [flu:sna qallat hwa:ya bsabab ʔissafra] Our money dwindled a lot as a result of the trip. عِندَه ثَروَة؛ ما تقِلّ عَن المِليُون دينار [ʕindah θarwa; ma: tqill ʕan ʔilmilyu:n dina:r] He has a fortune; not less than a million dinars. قَلَّت قيمتَه بنَظَري [qallat qi:mtah bnaðari] His worth decreased in my eyes. قَلَّت قيمتَه بعَمَلَه هَذا [qallat qi:mtah bʕamalah ha:ða] He lost some respect because of what he did.
قَلَّل [qallal] *v:* • **1.** to diminish, lessen, decrease, reduce – إذا تقَلِّل السِّعِر تبيع هوايَة [ʔiða tqallil ʔissiʕir tbi:ʕ hwa:ya] If you'll reduce the price, you'll sell a lot more. قَلِّل بأكلَك حَتّى ينزِل وَزنَك [qallil bʔaklak ħatta yinzil waznak] Cut down what you eat so your weight will go down. أشُو أخُوك قَلَّل مِن جَيّاتَه لِينا [ʔašu ʔaxu:k qallal min ǰayya:tah li:na] It seems your brother has reduced the frequency of his visits to us.
تقَلَّل [tqallal] *v:* • **1.** to be diminished, lessened, decreased, reduced – هَالسِّعِر ما يِتقَلَّل بَعَد أكثَر مِن هَذا [hassiʕir ma: yitqallal baʕad ʔakθar min ha:ða] The price can't be reduced any more than that. الضَّغط ما يِتقَلَّل بَعَد [ʔiððaɣiṭ ma: yitqallal baʕad] The pressure can't be lowered more.
اِستَقَلّ [ʔistaqall] *v:* • **1.** to be or become independent – خَمِس بُلدان اِستَقَلَّت هالسَّنَة [xamis bulda:n ʔistaqallat hassana] Five countries became independent this year. بَعَد ما تزَوَّج اِستَقَلّ عَن أهلَه [baʕad ma: dzawwaǰ ʔistaqall ʕan ʔahlah] After he married he lived independently from his family.
قَلّ [qall] *n:* • **1.** diminishing, decreasing
قِلَّة [qilla] *n:* • **1.** shortage, scarcity, lack – قِلَّة إدراك [qillat ʔidra:k] lack of understanding, lack of realization. قِلَّة حَياء، قِلَّة أدَب [qillat ħaya:ʔ, qillat ʔadab] shamelessness, impudence, insolence. هاي قِلَّة حَياء مِنَّك. شلُون تشَتِّم أبُوك؟ [ha:y qillat ħaya:ʔ minnak. šlu:n tšattim ʔabu:k?] This is shameless of you. How could you insult your father? مِن قِلَّة الخَيل شَدّوا عالكِلاب سرُوج [min qillat ʔilxayl šaddaw ʕaččila:b sru:ǰ] Any port in a storm (lit., due to the shortage of horses, they saddled the dogs).
قُلَّة [gulla] *n:* قُلَل [gulal] *pl:* • **1.** cannonball. – رَمي القُلَّة [ramy ʔilgulla] shotput. • **2.** Indian club. • **3.** mosquito net
تَقلِيل [taqli:l] *n:* • **1.** decrease, diminution, reduction
اِستِقلال [ʔistiqla:l] *n:* • **1.** independence
قَلِيل [qali:l] *adj:* • **1.** few – الكُتُب المُهِمَّة قَلِيلَة بالمَكتَبَة [ʔilkutub ʔilmuhimma qali:la bilmaktaba] The important books in the library are few. • **2.** small, scant, scanty, spare, sparse, meager, insufficient – هَذا قَلِيل. أرِيد بَعَد [ha:ða qali:l. ʔari:d baʕad] This is insufficient. I want more. الفلُوس اللّي عِندي قَلِيلَة. ما تكَفّي [flu:s ʔilli ʕindi qali:la. ma: tkaffi] My money is insufficient. It isn't enough. يُومِيتي قَلِيلَة. تِقدَر تزَيِّدها؟ [yu:mi:ti qali:la. tigdar dzayyidha?] My daily wage is small. Can you raise it? هَذا قَلِيل بِحَقَّه. يِستاهِل أزيَد [ha:ða qali:l bħaqqah. yista:hil ʔazyad] That's less than his share. He deserves more. كان بالقَلِيل قِتلَه آني قَرايبَك [ča:n bilqali:l gitlah ʔa:ni gara:ybak] You could have at least told him that I'm your relative. قَلِيل الارتِفاع [qali:l ʔilʔirtifa:ʕ] of low elevation, not very high. هَالجِّبَل قَلِيل الارتِفاع؛ تِقدَر تِصعَدَه [hajǰibal qali:l ʔilʔirtifa:ʕ; tigdar tiṣʕadah] This mountain is of low elevation; you can climb it. قَلِيل الاهتِمام [qali:l ʔilʔihtima:m] inattentive. هَالمُوَظَّف قَلِيل الاهتِمام بواجِباتَه [hallmuwaððaf qali:l ʔilʔihtima:m bwa:ǰiba:tah] This employee is slack in his duties. • **3.** scarce, rare – الأصدِقاء المُخلِصِين قَلِيلِين [ʔilʔaṣdiqa:ʔ ʔilmuxliṣi:n qali:li:n] Good friends are rare. • **4.** seldom, rarely, very little – قَلِيل يِجِي هنا [qali:l yiǰi hna] he rarely comes here. قَلِيل الأدَب، قَلِيل الحَيا، قَلِيل الحَياء [qali:l ʔilʔadab, qali:l ʔilħaya, qali:l ʔiħaya:ʔ] lacking in manners, lacking modesty. اِبنَك قَلِيل الأدَب [ʔibnak qali:l ʔilʔadab] Your son has no manners. هِيَّ قَلِيلَة الحَياء. تفَشِّر [hiyya qali:lat ʔiħaya:ʔ. tfaššir] She is shameless. She talks dirty.
قلِيل، قلَيِّل [gili:l, glayyil] *adj:* • **1.** few, small, scant, scanty, spare, sparse, meager, insufficient, scarce, rare • **2.** seldom, rare, very little
أقَلِّيَّة [ʔaqalliyya] *n:* أقَلِّيّات [ʔaqalliyya:t] *pl:* • **1.** minority
مُستَقِلّ [mustaqill] *adj:* • **1.** independent • **2.** separate – بَيت مُستَقِلّ [bayt mustaqill] a separate house.
أقَلّ [ʔaqall] *comparative adjective:* • **1.** less, least – يِزعَل عَلَى أقَلّ شِي [yizʕal ʕala ʔaqall ši] He gets angry at the least little thing. أقَلّ شِي يصِير بالوَلَد، إنتَ مَسؤول [ʔaqall ši yṣi:r bilwalad, ʔinta masʔu:l] If anything happens to the boy, you're responsible. عالأقَلّ [ʕalʔaqall] at least. إذا ما ترُوح ويّايا، عالأقَلّ دَلّيني [ʔiða ma: tru:ħ wiyya:ya, ʕalʔaqall dalli:ni] If you aren't going with me, at least show me how to get there. أقَلّ ما [ʔaqall ma:] the least that. أقَلّ ما يسَوّي يحكِي عَلِيك [ʔaqall ma: ysawwi: yiħči ʕali:k] The least he'll do is talk against you. أقَلّ ما بِيهُم يِملُك ألف دِينار [ʔaqall ma: bi:hum yimluk ʔalf dina:r] The least among them has a thousand dinars.
أقَلّها [ʔaqallaha] adj: • 1. at least – أقَلّها كان اِشترَيتلي نفنُوف [ʔaqallaha ča:n ʔištiri:tli nafnu:f] You could have at least bought me a dress.

أَقَلّاً [ʔaqallan] *adverbial:* • **1.** at least – أَقَلّاً كان جِيت شِي لِلجِّهال [ʔaqallan čaːn ǰibit ši liǰǰihaːl] At least you could've brought something for the children.
قَلَّ، قَلَّما [qalla, qallama] *n:* • **1.** seldom, rarely – هَذا قَلَّما يِنشاف بِهالقَهوَة [haːða qallama yinšaːf bhalgahwa] He is seldom seen in this café.

ق ل م

قَلَّم [qallam] *v:* • **1.** to trim, prune – قَلِّم هرُوش الوَرِد [qallim hruːš ʔilwarid] Trim the rose bushes. • **2.** to stripe – قَلِّم وُصلَة القُماش بأَحمَر وَأَخضَر [qallim wuṣlat ʔilqumaːš bʔaħmar wʔaxḍar] Stripe the cloth with red and green.
قَلَّم [gallam] *v:* • **1.** to string – قَلَّمتِي البامِيَة وَإِلّا بَعَد؟ [gallamti ʔilbaːmya waʔilla baʕad?] Did you string up the okra for drying yet?
تقَلَّم [tqallam] *v:* • **1.** to be trimmed, pruned – الهرُوش لازِم تِتقَلَّم [ʔilhruːš laːzim titqallam] The bushes must be trimmed. • **2.** to be striped – هَالقُماش، إذا يِتقَلَّم، ما يِصِير حِلو [halqumaːš, ʔiða yitqallam, maː yṣiːr ħilw] If this cloth were striped, it wouldn't look right.
قَلَم [qalam] *n:* أقلام [ʔaqlaːm] *pl:* • **1.** pen – قَلَم حِبِر، قَلَم باندان [qalam ħibir, qalam paːndaːn] fountain pen. قَلَم حِبِر جاف [qalam ħibir ǰaːf] ballpoint pen. قَلَم بَصمَة [qalam başma] pencil, lead pencil. رُؤُوس أَقلام [ruʔuːs ʔaqlaːm] notes. • **2.** stripe, streak, line • **3.** section, department • **4.** slip, cutting (bot.) – دِشداشَة مقَلَّمَة بأَحمَر [dišdaːša mqallma bʔaħmar] a red-striped robe.
تَقلِيم [taqliːm] *n:* • **1.** clipping, trimming
مِقلَمَة [miqlama] *n:* • **1.** pen case
مقَلَّم [mqallam] *adj:* • **1.** striped, streaked

ق ل و

قِلَى [gilaː] *v:* • **1.** to fry – إقلِيها لِلسِّمكَة [ʔigliːha lissimča] Fry the fish.
قَلَّى [gallaː] *v:* • **1.** same as قِلَى : to fry – قَلِّيلِي بَيضتَين [galliːli bayḍtayn] Fry me two eggs.
تقَلَّى [tgallaː] *v:* • **1.** to fry, be fried – خَلِّي البَيتِنجان يِتقَلَّى شوَيَّة [xalliː ʔlbiːtinǰaːn yitgallaː šwayya] Let the eggplant fry a while. العَصفُور يِتفَلَّى والصَّيّاد يِتقَلَّى [ʔilʕaṣfuːr yitfallaː wiṣṣayyaːd yitgallaː] He's enjoying himself and the other stewing in his own juice (lit., the sparrow relaxes and the hunter fries).
قَلي [galy] *n:* • **1.** frying
مقَلَّى [mgallaː] *adj:* • **1.** fried

ق ل ي

قَلّاي [qallaːy] *n:* • **1.** tin (used in tinning copper pots)

ق م ب ص

قَمبَص [gambaṣ] *v:* • **1.** to squat, hunker down – الجّاهِل قَمبَص عَلَى رِجلَيه [ʔiǰǰaːhil gambaṣ ʕala rijlayh] The kid sat on his haunches. لِيش مقَمبُص؟ [liːš mgambuṣ?] Why are you squatting?
مقَمبُص [mgambuṣ] *adj:* • **1.** squatting

ق م ج ي

قَمجِي [qamči] *n:* قماجِي [qmaːči] *pl:* • **1.** hose for a narghile • **2.** whip, lash, quirt • **3.** blow with a whip, lash

ق م ر [1]

قامَر [qaːmar] *v:* • **1.** to gamble, to wager, to stake, to bet on – حِلَف بَعَد ما يقامِر [ħilaf baʕad maː yqaːmir] He swore he wouldn't gamble any more.
قَمر، قَمر الدِين [qamr, qamr ʔiddiːn] *n:* • **1.** a hard, translucent confection made in thin sheets from finely ground apricots
قُمَر [gumar] *n:* قمارَة، أقمار [gmaːra, ʔaqmaːr] *pl:* • **1.** moon
قمار [qmaːr] *n:* • **1.** gambling – يِلعَب قمار [yilʕab qumaːr] He gambles.
قَمرَة [gamra] *n:* • **1.** moonlight – عايِش بِقَمرَة وَرِبِيعَة. الله رَبَّه [ʕaːyiš bgamra wribiːʕa. ʔallah rabbah] He's living the life of Riley. God looks out for him.
قَمَرِيَّة [qamariyya] *n:* قَمَريّات [qamariyyaːt] *pl:* • **1.** arbor, trellis – قَمَرِيَّة عِنَب [qamariyyat ʕinab] grape arbor.
قَمَرجِي، قُمَرجِي، قُمارجِي [qamarči, qumarči, qumaːrči] *n:* قُمَرجِيَّة، قُمارجِيَّة [qumarčiyya, qumaːrčiyya] *pl:* • **1.** gambler
قَمارَة [qamaːra] *n:* قَمارات [qamaːraːt] *pl:* • **1.** private compartment (in a public bath-house) – سَيّارَة قَمارَة [sayyaːra qamaːra] sedan.
قَمرِيَّة [gamriyya] *n:* قَمرِيّات [gamriyyaːt] *pl:* • **1.** moonlight
مُقامَرَة [muqaːmara] *n:* • **1.** gambling
قَمَرِي [qamari] *adj:* • **1.** lunar

ق م ر [2]

قَمَرِي [qamari] *n:* • **1.** penny

ق م ز

قُمَز [gumaz] *v:* • **1.** to jump – لا تُقمُز مِن السَّطِح تَرَة تِكسِر رِجلَك [laː tugmuz min ʔissaṭiħ tara tiksir riǰlak] Don't jump from the roof or you'll break your leg. مِن صاحَوا إسمَه قُمَز وَركَض بسُرعَة [min ṣaːħaw ʔismah gumaz wrikaḍ bsurʕa] When they called his name, he jumped up and ran quickly. • **2.** to bounce – هالطُّوبَة تُقمُز زين [haṭṭuːba tugmuz zayn] This ball bounces well. • **3.** to increase, jump, skip – راتبَه شلُون قُمَز مِن عِشرِين إلَى خَمسِين دِينار؟ [raːtbah šluːn gumaz min ʕišriːn ʔila xamsiːn dinaːr?] How did his salary jump from twenty to fifty dinars?

ق

قَمَّز [gammaz] *v:* • **1.** to jump around, bounce up and down – الجِّهال دَيقَمِّزُون عالقَنَفَة [ʔijǰaha:l daygammzu:n ʕalqanafa] The children are bouncing up and down on the couch. • **2.** to shift around, switch around – دَيقَمُّز مِن وَظِيفَة لوَظِيفَة لِأَنّ أَبُوه وَزِير [daygammuz min waðiːfa lwaðiːfa liʔann ʔabu:h wazi:r] He's shifting from job to job because his father is a minister. • **3.** to increase, make increase by jumps – قَمِّزَوه مِن رُتبَة عَرِيف إِلَى مُلازِم ثانِي [gammizawh min rutbat ʕari:f ʔila mula:zim θa:ni] They jumped him from the rank of sergeant to second lieutenant.
اِنقُمَز [ʔingumaz] *v:* • **1.** to be jumped, to be skipped, to be increased – هالسَّطِح يِنقُمُز مِنَّه لِأَنّ ناصِي [hassatiħ yingumuz minnah liʔann na:ṣi] This roof can be jumped from because it's low.
قَمُز [gamuz] *n:* • **1.** jumping
قَمزَة [gamza] *n:* قَمزات [gamza:t] *pl:* • **1.** jump • **2.** increase, jump (in wages, rank, etc.) • **3.** shift, jump (from job to job)
قَمّاز [gamma:z] *adj:* • **1.** jumper

ق م ش

قماش [qma:š] *n:* قماشات، أَقمِشَة [qma:ša:t, ʔaqmiša] *pl:* • **1.** cloth, fabric

ق م ص

قَمِيص [qami:ṣ] *n:* قُمصان [qumṣa:n] *pl:* • **1.** shirt • **2.** white cotton cloth

ق م ص ل

قَمصَلَة [qamṣala] *n:* قَمصَلات، قَماصِل [qamṣala:t, qama:ṣil] *pl:* • **1.** jacket, windbreaker

ق م ط

قَمَّط [gammaṭ] *v:* • **1.** to swaddle – أَكثَر الأُمَّهات يقَمُّطُون أَطفالهُم [ʔakθar ʔilʔummaha:t ygammuṭu:n ʔaṭfa:lhum] Most mothers swaddle their children.
تقَمَّط [tgammaṭ] *v:* • **1.** to be swaddled – الجّاهِل لازِم يِتقَمَّط [ʔijja:hil la:zim yitgammaṭ] The baby has to be swaddled.
قَمُط [gamuṭ] *n:* • **1.** mating (with), (having) intercourse
قماط [gma:ṭ] *n:* قماطات [gma:ṭa:t] *pl:* • **1.** swaddling clothes, swaddle

ق م ع

قِمَع [gumaʕ] *v:* • **1.** to cause death (by bringing bad luck) – قُصّتَه شَرّ. إِسبُوع وَرا ما اِنولَد، قُمَع أَبُوه [guṣṣtah šarr. ʔisbu:ʕ wara ma: ʔinwilad, gumaʕ ʔabu:h] He brings bad luck. A week after he was born, he brought death to his father. أَقمَع إِبنِي، ما أَدرِي [ʔagmaʕ ʔibni, ma: ʔadri] May I be responsible for my son's death if I know. I don't know.
قِمَع [qimaʕ] *v:* • **1.** to restrain, check, suppress, to tame, to curb
قَمَّع [gammaʕ] *v:* • **1.** to cut off the stem end – قَمُّع الباميَة بِهالسِّكِّينَة [gammuʕ ʔilba:mya bhassiččiːna] Cut the stem ends off the okra with this knife.
اِنقُمَع [ʔingumaʕ] *v:* • **1.** to be dead (by bad luck) – اِنقُمَعِت! ما تُقعُد راحَة [ʔingumaʕit! ma: tugʕud ra:ħa] Drop dead! Why don't you be quiet?
اِنقِمَع [ʔinqimaʕ] *v:* • **1.** to be restrained
قُمُع [gumuʕ] *n:* قمُوع [gmu:ʕ] *pl:* • **1.** sip • **2.** stem (esp. of an okra pod)
قَمِع [qamiʕ] *n:* • **1.** repression, suppression, curbing, taming, prevention
قَمُع [gamuʕ] *n:* • **1.** causing death
مَقمُوع [magmu:ʕ] *adj:* • **1.** dead (by bad luck)

ق م ق م

قُمقُم [qumqum, gumgum] *n:* قماقُم [qma:qum, gma:gum] *pl:* • **1.** large copper coffeepot

ق م ل

قَمَّل [gammal] *v:* • **1.** to be or become lice-infested – ما تِغسِل راسَك! مُو راح تقَمُّل مِن الوُسَخ [ma: tiɣsil ra:sak! mu: ra:ħ tgammul min ʔilwusax] Why don't you take a bath? You're going to become lice-infested from the filth.
قَمُل [gamul] *n:* • **1.** (coll.) lice
قَملَة [gamla] *n:* قَملات [gamla:t] *pl:* • **1.** louse

ق م م

قِمَّة [qimma, qumma] *n:* قِمَم [qimam, qumam] *pl:* • **1.** peak, summit, top
قُمامَة [quma:ma] *n:* • **1.** garbage

ق م و س

قامُوس [qa:mu:s] *n:* قَوامِيس [qawa:mi:s] *pl:* • **1.** dictionary

ق ن ب

قِنَّب [ginnab] *n:* • **1.** hemp

ق ن ب ر

قُمبُرَة [qumbura, gunubra] *n:* قَنابِر [qana:bir, gna:bir] *pl:* • **1.** lark (zool. type of birds)
قَمبُور [qambu:r, qanbu:r] *n:* قَنبُورِين [qanbu:ri:n, qambu:ri:n] *pl:* • **1.** hunchback
قَمبُورَة، قَنبُورَة [qambu:ra, qanbu:ra] *n:* قَنبُورات [qanbu:ra:t] *pl:* • **1.** hump, hunch – أَبُو قَمبُورَة [ʔabu qambu:ra] hunchback.

ق ن ب ل

قُنبُلَة، قُمبُلَة [qunbula, qumbula] *n:* قَنابُل [qana:bul] *pl:* • **1.** bomb • **2.** shell

ق ن ت

قَناة [qana:t] *n:* قَنَوات [qanawa:t] *pl:* • **1.** canal (e.g., in TV programs)

ق ن د

قَنْد [qand] *n:* • **1.** rock sugar

ق ن د ر

قُندَرَة [qundara] *n:* قَنادِر [qana:dir] *pl:* • **1.** shoe
قُندَرجِي [qundarči] *n:* قُندَرجِيَّة [qundarčiyya] *pl:* • **1.** shoemaker

ق ن د غ

قُنداغ [qunda:ɣ, qinda:ɣ] *n:* • **1.** very weak tea • **2.** hot water and sugar

ق ن د ل

قَندَل [qandal] *v:* • **1.** to glow – هَفِّي لِلفَحَم حَتَّى يقَندِل كُلَّه [haffi lilfaħam ħatta yqandil kullah] Fan the coal until it all glows. • **2.** to be or become tipsy, to get a glow on – شِرَبلَه بِيك واحِد وَقَندَل [širablah pi:k wa:ħid wqandal] He had one drink and became tipsy.
قَندِيل [qandi:l] *n:* قَنادِيل [qana:di:l] *pl:* • **1.** hanging lamp, or light fixture using candles or oil
مقَندِل [mqandil] *adj:* • **1.** tipsy, warmed, flushed – مقَندِل مِن الشُّرُب [mqandil min ʔiššurub] flushed with drink. • **2.** short-tempered, hot under the collar – لا تِحكِي ويّاه تَرَة هُوَّ مقَندِل اليوم [la: tiħči wiyya:h tara huwwa mqandil ʔilyu:m] Don't talk to him because he is short-tempered today.

ق ن ز

قَنزَة، قَنزَة وَنزَة [qanza, qanza wanza] *n:* • **1.** (invar.) a trick, a fast one – وافق يبِيعَه بَسّ بَعدين طَلَّع إلنا قَنزَة وَنزَة [wa:faq ybi:ʕah bass baʕdi:n ṭallaʕ ʔilna qanza wanza] He agreed to sell it but later he pulled a fast one on us. جابلَه خُوش قَنزَة وَنزَة وَأَخَذ مِنَّه ضِعف السِّعِر [ǰa:blah xu:š qanza wanza waʔaxað minnah ðiʕf ʔissiʕir] He pulled a real shady trick on him and got double the price from him. مِن تِتعامَل وِيّاه، يجِيبلَك مِيَّة قَنزَة وَنزَة [min titʕa:mal wiyya:h, yiǰi:blak miyyat qanza wanza] When you bargain with him, he comes up with a hundred unexpected tricks.

ق ن ص

قِنَص [ginaṣ] *v:* • **1.** to lie in ambush – راح يِقنُص لِلبَطّ بهالمُكان [ra:ħ yignuṣ lilbaṭṭ bhalmuka:n] He will lie in wait for the ducks right here.
تقَنَّص [tgannaṣ] *v:* • **1.** to lie in wait for, lay for – شايِل خَنجَر وَدَيتقَنَّص عَلِي [ša:yil xanǰar wadayitgannaṣ ʕali] He's carrying a dagger and laying for Ali.
قَنِص [ganiṣ] *n:* • **1.** lying in ambush, lying in wait (for)
قَنّاص [qanna:ṣ] *n:* • **1.** sniper

ق ن ص ل

قُنصُلِيَّة [qunṣuliyya] *n:* قُنصُلِيّات [qunṣuliyya:t] *pl:* • **1.** consulate
قُنصُل [qunṣul] *n:* قَناصِل [qana:ṣil] *pl:* • **1.** consul
قُنصُلِي [qunṣuli] *adj:* • **1.** consular – سُلطَة قُنصُلِيَّة [sulṭa qunṣuliyya] consular authority.

ق ن ط

قُنُوط [qunu:ṭ] *n:* • **1.** despair, despondency, desperateness, hopelessness

ق ن ط ر [1]

قَنطَرَة، قُنتَرَة [ganṭara, guntara] *n:* قَنطَرات [ganṭara:t] *pl:* • **2.** small bridge (i.e. over a stream)
قَنطَرَة [qanṭara] *n:* قَناطِر [qana:ṭir] *pl:* • **1.** arched bridge, stone bridge • **2.** arch, arch-way, span
قَنطَور [qanṭu:r, kantu:r] *n:* قَنطَورات [kanṭu:ra:t] *pl:* • **1.** wardrobe, movable clothes closet

ق ن ط ر [2]

قُنطَرجِي [qunṭarči] *n:* قُنطَرجِيَّة [qunṭarčiyya] *pl:* • **1.** contractor

ق ن ع

قِنَع [qinaʕ] *v:* • **1.** to be or become convinced, persuaded – شقَدّ حكَيت وِيّاه وَما دَيِقنَع [šgadd ħči:t wiyya:h wma dayiqnaʕ] I talked with him so much and he won't become convinced. • **2.** to convince, persuade – حِكالِي القُصَّة وَقِنَعنِي [ħiča:li ʔilquṣṣa wqinaʕni] He told me the story and convinced me.
قَنَّع [qannaʕ] *v:* • **1.** to persuade, convince – قَنَّعتَه يِشتُغُل وِيّايا [qannaʕtah yištuɣul wiyya:ya] I persuaded him to work with me. قِدَر يقَنِّعها بعَشِر دَنانِير [gidar yqanniʕha bʕašir dana:ni:r] He was able to persuade her with ten dinars.
أقنَع [ʔaqnaʕ] *v:* • **1.** to convince, to persuade
تقَنَّع [tqannaʕ] *v:* • **1.** to be persuaded, convinced – هَذا شلُون عنادِي. ما يِتقَنَّع [ha:ða šlu:n ʕna:di. ma: yitqannaʕ] How stubborn he is. He can't be persuaded.
اِقتِنَع [ʔiqtinaʕ] *v:* • **1.** to be or become satisfied, content – المُدِير اِقتِنَع بِالعُذُر مالِي [ʔilmudi:r ʔiqtinaʕ bilʕuður ma:li] The principal was satisfied with my excuse. • **2.** to be or become convinced – هَسَّة اِقتِنَعِت ماكُو عِلاقَة بَيناتهُم [hassa ʔiqtinaʕit ma:ku ʕila:qa bayna:thum] Now am convinced there is no relationship between them.
قِناع [qina:ʕ] *n:* أَقنِعَة [ʔaqniʕa] *pl:* • **1.** mask, veil
قَناعَة [qana:ʕa] *n:* • **1.** content, contentment • **2.** conviction • **3.** moderation, temperance
إقناع [ʔiqna:ʕ] *n:* • **1.** persuasion, convincing, conviction • **2.** satisfaction
تَقنِيع [taqni:ʕ] *n:* • **1.** persuasion
اِقتِناع [ʔiqtina:ʕ] *n:* • **1.** conviction, convincing • **2.** satisfaction, contentment
قَنُوع [qanu:ʕ] *adj:* • **1.** frugal, modest, temperate – صِير قَنُوع. اِقبَل بِهالرّاتِب وَاِسكُت [ṣi:r qanu:ʕ. ʔiqbal bharra:tib wʔiskut] Be satisfied. Accept this salary and keep quiet.

ق

قانِع [qa:niʕ] *adj:* • **1.** satisfied, convinced • **2.** with بـ content
مُقنِع [muqniʕ] *adj:* • **1.** convincing, satisfying
مُقَنَّع [muqannaʕ] *adj:* مُقَنَّعِين [muqannaʕa:t] *pl:* • **1.** masked

ق ن ع ر

تقنعَر [tqanʕar] *v:* • **1.** to put on airs, give oneself airs – "دُولَة اللّي يتقنعَرُون يقُولُون، "بَنات فلان أَدَبسِزِّيَات [ðu:la ʔilli yitqanʕaru:n ygu:lu:n, "bana:t fla:n ʔadabsizziyya:t"] The people who like to show off their erudition say "So and so's daughters are lacking in manners. " لا تِتقَنعَر براسِي. إذا ما يعِجبَك الوَضِع وَالرّاتِب، بَطِّل [la: titqanʕar bra:si. ʔiða ma: yʕiǰbak ʔilwaðiʕ wirra:tib, baṭṭil] Don't complain to me. If you don't like the position and the salary, quit.
قَنعَرَة [qanʕara] *n:* • **1.** putting on airs, giving oneself airs

ق ن ف

قَنَفَة [qanafa] *n:* قَنفات [qanafa:t] *pl:* • **1.** couch, sofa

ق ن ف ذ

قُنفُذ [qunfuð, gunfuð] *n:* قَنافِذ [qana:fuð, gana:fið] *pl:* • **1.** hedgehog, porcupine

ق ن ق ن

قَنَقِينَة [qanaqi:na] *n:* • **1.** quinine • **2.** unpleasant person, a pill

ق ن ل

قَنال [qana:l] *n:* قَنالات [qana:la:t] *pl:* • **1.** canal

ق ن ن

قانُون [qa:nu:n] *n:* قَوانِين [qawa:ni:n] *pl:* • **1.** law – قانُون أَساسِي [qa:nu:n ʔasa:si] constitution. • **2.** a musical instrument resembling the zither
قانُونجِي [qanu:nči] *n:* قانُونجِيَّة [qanu:nčiyya] *pl:* • **1.** one who knows the law, person well versed in the law • **2.** one who plays the zither (musical instrument)
القانُونِيَّة [ʔilqa:nu:niyya] *n:* • **1.** legality
قانُونِي [qa:nu:ni] *adj:* • **1.** legal – غير قانُونِي [ɣayr qa:nu:ni] illegal.
قانُوناً [qa:nu:nan] *adverbial:* • **1.** by law
قانُونِيّاً [qa:nu:niyyan] *adverbial:* • **1.** legally

ق ه ر

قِهَر [qihar] *v:* • **1.** to annoy, irritate, anger, upset – البارحَة صَدِيقَك قِهَرنِي هوايَة [ʔilba:rħa ṣadi:qak qiharni hwa:ya] Yesterday your friend annoyed me a lot. راح أراوِي بايسِكلِي لِعَلِي وأقِهرَه [ra:ħ ʔara:wi pa:ysikli lʕali wʔaqihrah] I'm going to show my bicycle to Ali and make him jealous. • **2.** to sadden, to grieve – مَنظَر المَرِيض يِقهَر [manðar ʔilmari:ð yiqhar] The sick man is a saddening sight.
انِقهَر [ʔinqihar] *v:* • **1.** to be or become annoyed, irritated, angry, upset – لا تقُلَّه بِيها تَرَة يِنقِهِر [la: tgullah bi:ha tara yinqihir] Don't tell him about it or he'll get upset. • **2.** to be or become saddened, grieved – انِقهَر عَلَى إبنَه اللّي مات بِالحَرِيق [ʔinqihar ʕala ʔibnah ʔilma:t bilħari:q] He became morose over his son who died in the fire.
قَهَر [qahar] *n:* • **1.** grief • **2.** annoyance, irritation
قَهرَة [qahra] *n:* • **1.** grief, sorrow
القاهِرَة [ʔilqa:hira] *n:* • **1.** Cairo (Egypt)
مَقهُور [maqhu:r] *adj:* • **1.** defeated, devastated

ق ه ق ر

تقَهقَر [tqahqar] *v:* • **1.** to retreat, withdraw – تقَهقَرَوا أَمام العَدُو [tqahqaraw ʔama:m ʔilʕadu] They retreated in front of the enemy.

ق ه و

مَقهَى [maqha] *n:* مَقاهِي [maqa:hi] *pl:* • **1.** coffee house
قَهوَة [gahwa] *n:* • **1.** coffee • **2.** coffee-house, coffee shop, café • **3.** pl. قَهاوِي coffee, cup of coffee, café, coffee house, coffee shop.
قَهوَجِي، قَهوجِي [gahwači, gahawči] *n:* قَهَوجِيَّة [gahawčiyya] *pl:* • **1.** coffeehouse owner, proprietor of a café, coffeehouse
قَهوائِي [qahwa:ʔi] *adj:* • **1.** coffee-colored – رباط قَهوائِي [rba:ṭ qahwa:ʔi] a coffee-colored tie.

ق و ب ي

قُوبايَة [gu:ba:ya] *n:* قُوبايات [gu:ba:ya:t] *pl:* • **1.** cold sore • **2.** pimple

ق و ت

قُوت [qu:t] *n:* • **1.** nourishment, nutriment, aliment

ق و د

قاد [qa:d, ga:d] *v:* • **1.** to lead, command – أيّ ضابُط قادهُم بِالمَعرَكَة؟ [ʔayy ða:buṭ qa:dhum bilmaʕraka?] Which officer led them in the battle?
قَوَّد [gawwad] *v:* • **1.** to procure, pander, pimp – الخادِم مالَه يقَوِّدلَه [ʔilxa:dim ma:lah ygawwidlah] His servant procures for him. دَيقَوِّد عَليها بالبارات [daygawwid ʕali:ha bilba:ra:t] He's pimping for her in the bars.
انقاد [ʔinqa:d, ʔinga:d] *v:* • **1.** to be led, to be guided
قائِد [qa:ʔid] *n:* قُوّاد [quwwa:d] *pl:* • **1.** commander, leader
قَوّاد [gawwa:d] *n:* قواوِيد [gwa:wi:d] *pl:* • **1.** pander, pimp, procurer • **2.** قَوّادَة [gawwa:da] madam, brothel manager
قِيادَة [qiya:da] *n:* • **1.** leadership, command, control • **2.** pl. قِيادات command

قوادة [gwaːda] *n:* • **1.** pimping, procurement • **2.** pl. قوادات fee for procurement or pimping
قَوّادَة [gawwaːda] *n:* قَوّادات [gawwaːdaːt] *pl:* • **1.** madam, manager of a brothel
اِنقِياد [ʔinqiyaːd] *n:* • **1.** obedience, compliance
مقَوِّد [mgawwid] *adj:* • **1.** with عَلَى pimping • **2.** pimp

ق و ر م

قاوَرمَة [qaːwarma, qaːwirma] *n:* • **1.** chunks of meat fried with tomatoes and onions

ق و ر م ش

قُرمامِش [gurmaːmiš] *n:* قُرمَامشِيَّة [gurmaːmšiyya] *pl:* • **1.** crude person, clod, rube, hick – شلُون قُورمامِش! بَسّ حَطّوا الأكِل عالميز هِجَم عَليه [šluːn guːrmaːmiš! bass ħaṭṭaw ʔilʔakil ʕalmiːz hiǰam ʕaliːh] What a clod! When food is put on the table he attacks it.

ق و ر ي

قُوري [quːri] *n:* قُوريّات، قواري [quːriːyyaːt, qwaːri] *pl:* • **1.** teapot

ق و ز

قوز [guːz] *n:* قوزات [guːzaːt] *pl:* • **1.** bow, long-bow – قوز كَمَنجَة [guːz kamanǰa] violin bow. قوز النَّدّاف [guːz ʔinnaddaːf] teasing bow used to fluff cotton.

ق و ز غ

قوزَغ [quːzaɣ] *v:* • **1.** to give someone the shaft, to shaft, to cheat – باعلَه راديُو ما يِشتُغُل؛ قوزَغه بيه [baːʕlah raːdyu maː yištuɣul; quːzaɣah biːh] He sold him a radio that doesn't work; he put the shaft to him with it.
تقوزَغ [tquːzaɣ] *v:* • **1.** to be given the shaft, be shafted, be cheated
قازُوغ [qaːzuːɣ] *n:* قَوازِيغ [qawaːziːɣ] *pl:* • **1.** the shaft, the royal shaft, the dirty end of the stick – ضِرَبَه قازُوغ [ðirabah qaːzuːɣ] He gave him the shaft. ضِرَبنِي قازُوغ بِهالشَّروَة [ðirabni qaːzuːɣ bhaššarwa] He gave me the royal shaft on this purchase.

ق و ز ي

قُوزي [quːzi] *n:* قوازِي [qwaːziː] *pl:* • **1.** baby lamb • **2.** a dish consisting of rice with roasted mutton on top and sometimes raisins and almonds

ق و س

تقَوَّس [tqawwas] *v:* • **1.** to be bent, to be curved
قوس، قوز [quːs, qaws, guːz] *n:* أَقواس، قُوزَات [ʔaqwaːs, quːzaːt] *pl:* • **1.** bow, long-bow – قُوس قَزَح [quːs qazaħ] rainbow. • **2.** arc (geom.) • **3.** arch, vault (arch.; of a bridge)
قَوّاس [qawwaːs] *n:* قَوّاسِين [qawwaːsiːn] *pl:* • **1.** guard, doorman, watchman • **2.** messenger, porter, handyman (in an office)
مُقَوَّس [muqawwas] *adj:* • **1.** curved, crooked, bent, arched • **2.** bent, arched
مِتقَوِّس [mitqawwis] *adj:* • **1.** bent • **2.** curved, crooked, arched

ق و ش

قاوُوش [qaːwuːš] *n:* قَواوِيش [qawaːwiːš] *pl:* • **1.** ward (in a hospital) • **2.** squad bay, bay (in barracks) • **3.** large cell (in a prison)

ق و ش ر

قوشَر [guːšar] *n:* قواشِر [gwaːšir] *pl:* • **1.** large two-handled basket, woven of palm leaves • **2.** small handle-less basket

ق و ط

قاط [qaːṭ] *n:* قُوط [quːṭ] *pl:* • **1.** suit (of clothes) • **2.** coat, layer (of paint, etc.) • **3.** floor, story, level – باص أَبُو قاطَين [paːṣ ʔabu qaːṭayn] double-decker bus. • **4.** time, instance, once – قاط لاخ [qaːṭ laːx] again, once more.

ق و ط ي

قُوطِيَّة [quːṭiyya] *n:* قواطِي [qwaːṭiː] *pl:* • **1.** tin, tin box, rectangular tin can • **2.** small box

ق و ع

قاع [qaːʕ] *n:* • **1.** bottom (of the sea, river, etc.)
قاع [gaːʕ] *n:* قِيعان [giʕaːn] *pl:* • **1.** ground, earth • **2.** land • **3.** floor
قاعَة [qaːʕa] *n:* قاعات [qaːʕaːt] *pl:* • **1.** hall, large room – قاعَة الطَّعام [qaːʕat ʔiṭṭaʕaːm] dining hall. • **2.** auditorium
قويعَة [gwiːʕa] *n:* • **1.** a spot, a small piece of land
قاعِيَّة [gaːʕiyya] *adj:* قاعِيّات [gaːʕiyyaːt] *pl:* • **1.** background (painting) • **2.** pot (poker) • **3.** ante (poker) • **4.** pouch (of a slingshot or sling)

ق و ق

قُوقَة [guːga] *n:* قُوقات [guːgaːt] *pl:* • **1.** rear top part of the head

ق و ك

قَوك [qawč, quːč] *n:* • **1.** a children's game similar to jacks, played with pebbles

ق و ل [1]

قال، قال وَقِيل [qaːl, qaːl wqiːl] *v:* • **1.** gossip, rumors
قال [gaːl] *v:* • **1.** to speak, say, tell – قال ما راح يِجِي لِلدّائِرَة اليُوم [gaːl maː raːħ yiǰi liddaːʔira ʔilyuːm] He said he isn't going to come to the office

today. ما دَأفهَم شدَتقُول [maː daʔafham šdatguːl] I don't understand what you're saying. ما يِقدَر يقُول حَرف العَين [maː yigdar yiguːl ħarf ʔilʕayn] He can't pronounce the letter 'ayn.

قاوَل [qaːwal] *v:* • **1.** to make a deal, strike a bargain with (someone) – قاوَلتَه يجِيب الغَراض لبَيتِي [qaːwaltah yǰiːb ʔilgaraːḍ lbiːti] I made a deal with him to bring the things to my house.

تقاوَل [tqaːwal] *v:* • **1.** to make a contract – تقاوَلنا يجَهِّزنا بكُلّ الطّابُوق اللّي نِحتاجَه [tqaːwalna yǰahhizna bkull ʔiṭṭaːbuːg ʔilli niħtaːǰah] We made a contract that he'd supply us with all the bricks we need.

اِنقال [ʔingaːl] *v:* • **1.** to be said – ما أريد هَالشّي ينقال مَرَّة لُخ [maː ʔariːd hašši yingaːl marra lux] I don't want this thing said again.

قَول [gawl] *n:* أقوال [ʔaqwaːl] *pl:* • **1.** word, promise – بَعدِي عَلَى قَولِي [baʕdi ʕala qawli] I'm still keeping my word.

مَقال، مَقالَة [maqaːl, maqaːla] *n:* مَقالات [maqaːlaːt] *pl:* • **1.** article, paper – مَقال اِفتِتاحِي [maqaːl ʔiftitaːħi] editorial, leading article.

قَولَة [gawla] *n:* • **1.** statement – قَولتَك إنتَ --- مِنو أبُو باكِر؟ [gawltak ʔinta minu ʔabu baːčir?] As you say --- who knows what tomorrow will bring? قَولَة المَثَل دَوِّر، تِلقِي [gawlat ʔilmaθal dawwir, tilgi] As the proverb says --- seek and you will find.

مُقاوِل [muqaːwil] *n:* مُقاوِلِين [muqaːwiliːn] *pl:* • **1.** contractor

مُقاوَلَة [muqaːwala] *n:* مُقاوَلات [muqaːwalaːt] *pl:* • **1.** contract

ق و ل 2

قُولَة [quːla] *n:* • **1.** (invar.) French cuffs – ثُوب أبُو القُولَة [θuːb ʔabu ʔilquːla] shirt with French cuffs. • **2.** collar

ق و ل ن

قُولُون [quːluːn] *n:* • **1.** colon

ق و م

ق

قام [qaːm] *v:* • **1.** to perform, do, carry out, execute – هُوَّ خُوش عامِل؛ دَيقُوم بواجبَه [huwwa xuːš ʕaːmil; dayquːm bwaːǰbah] He's a good worker; he carries out his duties. يقُوم بأعمال مُخزيَة [yquːm bʔaʕmaːl muxziya] He does shameful things.

قام [gaːm] *v:* • **1.** to get up, stand up, rise – قام عَلَى رِجلَه وبِدا يمشِي [gaːm ʕala riǰlah wbidaː yimši] He got up on his feet and started to walk. قام مِن مُكانَه وَقَعَّد أبُوه [gaːm min mukaːnah wgaʕʕad ʔabuːh] He got up from his place and seated his father. لَك دقُوم! هَذا شمفَهّمَه بالكِيمياء؟ [lak daguːm! haːða šmfahhmah bilkiːmya?] Oh, go away! What does he know about chemistry? • **2.** to wake up, get up, rise – شوَقِت قُمِت مِن النُّوم البارحَة؟ [šwakit gumit min ʔinnuːm ʔilbaːrħa?] What time did you wake up yesterday? • **3.** to flare up, break out – الحَرُب قامَت بين القَبِيلتَين عَلَى شِي تافِه [ʔilħarub gaːmat biːn ʔilqabiːltayn ʕala ši taːfih] War broke out between the two tribes over a trifling matter. قامَت ثَورَة بالشّمال [gaːmat θawra biššimaːl] A revolt broke out in the North. • **4.** to begin, start – مِن خابَرتَه قام يعاتِبنِي [min xaːbartah gaːm yiʕatibni] No sooner had I called him than he began upbraiding me. لا تقُوم تِحكِي عَليه. هُوَّ ما مَوجُود [laː tguːm tiħči ʕaliːh. huwwa maː mawǰuːd] Don't start talking about him. He isn't here. • **5.** to be used up, to be gone – الأكِل قام بخَمِس دَقايِق [ʔilʔakil gaːm bxamis daqaːʔiq] The food was gone in five minutes. الياخَة قامَت؛ بَعَد الثُّوب ما ينلِبِس [ʔilyaːxa gaːmat; baʕad ʔiθθuːb maː yinlibis] The collar has had it; the shirt can't be worn anymore. • **6.** with عَلَى to rise against, revolt, rebel against, turn on, attack – الحَرامِي قام عَلَى صاحِب البَيت بالسِّكِّينَة [ʔilħaraːmi gaːm ʕala ṣaːħib ʔilbayt bissiččiːna] The thief attacked the owner of the house with a knife. القَبائِل قامَت عالحُكُومَة [ʔilqabaːʔil gaːmat ʕalħukuːma] The tribes rose up against the government. مِن بِدا يِتحَدَّى الحاضرِين قاملَه واحِد وَزَفَّه خُوش زَفَّة [min bidaː yitħaddaː ʔilħaːðriːn gaːmlah waːħid wzaffah xuːš zaffa] When he began challenging the audience a man stood up against him and gave him a piece of his mind. قام عَليه سِنَّه [gaːm ʕaliːh sinnah] His tooth began bothering him. بيش قام عَلِيك القاط؟ [biyš gaːm ʕaliːk ʔilqaːṭ?] How much did the suit cost you?

قَوَّم [gawwam] *v:* • **1.** to make or cause to rise, make stand up, make get up – قَوَّمَه مِن مُكانَه بالقُوَّة [gawwamah min mukaːnah bilguwwa] He got him out of his seat by force. • **2.** to be or become sexually aroused – مِن شافها مسَلِّخَة، قَوَّم [min šaːfha msallixa, gawwam] When he saw her nude, he became sexually aroused. • **3.** to finish, use up, wear out, ruin – قَوَّم ياخَة الثُّوب هَل قَدّ ما غِسَلَه [gawwam yaːxat ʔiθθuːb hal gadd maː ɣisalah] He wore out the shirt collar by washing it so much. قَوَّم گير السَّيّارَة [gawwam giːr ʔissayyaːra] He wrecked the car's gearbox.

قاوَم [qaːwam] *v:* • **1.** to resist, oppose – مَحَّد يقدَر يقاومَه [maħħad yigdar yqaːwmah] No one can stand up against him. • **2.** to fight, combat – المَلاريا اِنتِشرَت بالصَّيف وَوَزارَة الصِّحَّة بدَت تقاوُمها [ʔilmalaːrya ʔintišrat biṣṣayf wwazaːrat ʔiṣṣiħa bidat tqaːwumha] Malaria spread during the summer and the Ministry of Health started to combat it. • **3.** to hold up, hold out, last, stand up – هَالقُندَرَة ما قاومَت شَهَر [halqundara maː qaːwmat šahar] These shoes didn't last a month. شقَدّ ما تصِير صَبُور، ما تِقدَر تقاوُم ويّا هالمُدِير [šgadd maː tṣiːr ṣabuːr, maː tigdar tqaːwum wiyya halmudiːr] No matter how patient you are, you won't be able to stomach this director. جَيشهُم ما قِدَر يقاوِم أكثَر مِن يومَين [ǰayšhum maː gidar yqaːwim ʔakθar min yuːmayn] Their army couldn't stand more than two days.

أَقام [ʔaqa:m] *v:* • **1.** to live, reside, dwell, remain, stay – راح يقِيم بِبَغداد سَنتَين [ra:ħ yqi:m bibaɣda:d santayn] He will reside in Baghdad for two years. • **2.** to lodge, file (complaint, suit, legal proceedings) – أَقام عَليه دَعوَة بالمَحكَمَة [ʔaqa:m ʕali:h daʕwa bilmaħkama] He filed a complaint against him in court.

تقَوَّم [tgawwam] *v:* • **1.** to be made to rise

اِستَقام [ʔistaqa:m] *v:* • **1.** to be or become right, correct, proper, to straighten out – شقَدّ ما يِحكِي أَبُوه ويّاه، ما يِستِقِيم [šgadd ma: yiħči ʔabu:h wiyya:h, ma: yistiqi:m] No matter how much his father talks to him, he doesn't straighten out. • **2.** to remain, endure, keep on – ما أَعتِقِد هَالحايِط راح يِستِقِيم هوايَة [ma: ʔaʕtiqid halħa:yiṭ ra:ħ yistiqi:m hwa:ya] I don't believe that this wall will last long. الدِّنيا ما تِستِقِيم لأَحَّد [ʔiddinya ma: tistiqi:m lʔaħħad] The world won't stand still for anybody.

قَوم [gu:m] *n:* • **1.** (invar.) unfriendly, inimical, enemy, enemies – هُمَّ قُوم [humma gu:m] They're enemies. آنِي قُوم ويّاه [ʔa:ni gu:m wiyya:h] I'm an enemy to him. • **2.** performance, execution

قامَة [qa:ma] *n:* قامات [qa:ma:t] *pl:* • **1.** a short, broad, double-edged sword – جِيبِي ضارُب قامَة [ǰi:bi ðа:rub qa:ma] I'm flat broke. • **2.** ضارُب قامَة He's broke

مَقام [maqa:m] *n:* مَقامات [maqa:ma:t] *pl:* • **1.** standing, position, rank, dignity – صاحِب مَقام [ṣa:ħib maqa:m] dignitary, holder of a high position. طَبعاً أَحتَرمَه. هَذا بِمَقام أَبُويَا [ṭabʕan ʔaħtarmah. ha:ða bmaqa:m ʔabu:ya] Of course I respect him. He is to me like my father. إذا يسافِر، مِنُو راح يكُون بمَقامَه؟ [ʔiða ysa:fir, minu ra:ħ yku:n bmaqa:mah?] If he goes away, who will take over his duties? • **2.** shrine, sacred place, tomb of a saint • **3.** a style of music with several sub-categories, also a song in this style

قِيمَة [qi:ma] *n:* قِيَم [qiyam] *pl:* • **1.** price • **2.** value, worth – حَكيَه ما إلَه كُلّ قِيمَة [ħačyah ma: ʔilah kull qi:ma] His talk doesn't amount to anything. خَلِّي يِنتِقِد. شِنُو قِيمتَه؟ [xalli: yintiqid. šinu: qi:mtah?] Let him criticize. What does he matter? هَالنّائِب إلَه قِيمتَه بالمَجلِس [hanna:ʔib ʔilah qi:mtah bilmaǰlis] This representative is respected in the senate. • **3.** finely ground or chopped meat • **4.** a stew made from chopped meat and peas

قامَة [qa:ma, ga:ma] *n:* قامات [qa:ma:t, ga:ma:t] *pl:* • **1.** fathom (measure of length, approx. six feet)

مُقِيم [muqi:m] *n:* مُقِيمِين [muqi:mi:n] *pl:* • **1.** resident, dweller

قِيام [qiya:m] *n:* • **1.** performance, execution

قَومَة [gu:ma] *n:* • **1.** up rising, revolt, rising

قَوام [qawa:m] *n:* • **1.** support, basis • **2.** figure

قَوّام [qawwa:m] *n:* • **1.** manager, director, caretaker

قَومِيَّة [qawmiyya] *n:* • **1.** ethnic pride, ethnic nationalism

قِيامَة [qiya:ma] *n:* • **1.** resurrection – عِيد القِيامَة [ʕi:d ʔilqiya:ma] Easter. يوم القِيامة [yu:m ʔilqiya:ma] Judgement Day.

تَقوِيم [taqwi:m] *n:* تَقاوِيم [taqa:wi:m] *pl:* • **1.** estimation, rating, valuation • **2.** survey, surveying • **3.** calendar

إقامَة [ʔiqa:ma] *n:* • **1.** stay, sojourn – دائِرَة الإقامَة [da:ʔirat ʔilʔiqa:ma] Alien Residents' Office. دَفتَر الإقامَة [daftar ʔilʔiqa:ma] temporary residence permit.

قائِمَة [qa:ʔima] *n:* قَوائِم [qawa:ʔim] *pl:* • **1.** list, roster, table, schedule; bill, invoice; menu

مُقاوَمَة [muqa:wama] *n:* • **1.** resistance, opposition, fight, struggle, battle – مُقاوَمَة ضِدّ الأَمراض [muqa:wama ðidd ʔilʔamra:ð] resistance to disease. مُقاوَمَة شَعبِيَّة [muqa:wama šaʕbiyya] popular resistance, i.e., national guard.

اِستِقامَة [ʔistiqa:ma] *n:* • **1.** straightness • **2.** honesty, integrity, uprightness

قَيمَقامِيَّة [qaymaqa:miyya] *n:* • **1.** residence of the governor of a sub-province

قائِم مَقام، قَيِّم مَقام [qa:ʔim maqa:m, qayyim maqa:m] *n:* • **1.** governor of a sub-province,

قَيِّم [qayyim] *adj:* • **1.** valuable, responsible • **2.** as Noun: caretaker

قَومِي [qawmi] *adj:* • **1.** nationalist, nationalistic • **2.** a nationalist

قَوام [qawa:m] *adj:* • **1.** greasy – مَرَق قَوام [marag qawa:m] greasy stew.

قائِم [qa:ʔim] *adj:* • **1.** right, upright, erect – زاوِيَة قائِمَة [za:wiya qa:ʔima] right angle. قائِم الزّاوِيَة [qa:ʔim ʔizza:wiya] right-angled. مُثَلَّث قائِم الزّاوِيَة [muθallaθ qa:ʔim ʔizza:wiya] right triangle. قائِم بِالأَعمال [qa:ʔim bilʔaʕma:l] charge d'affaires (dipl.).

قايِم [ga:yim] *adj:* • **1.** worn out – ياخَة قايمَة [ya:xa ga:yma] a worn-out collar.

مقَوُّم [mgawwum] *adj:* • **1.** erected

مُقاوُم [muqa:wum] *adj:* • **1.** resistant

مُستَقِيم [mustaqi:m] *adj:* • **1.** straight, upright, erect, – خَطّ مُستَقِيم [xaṭṭ mustaqi:m] a straight line.

القَيُّوم [ʔilqayyu:m] *adj:* • **1.** the Everlasting, the Eternal (God)

ق و ن

قَوان [qawa:n] *n:* • **1.** (coll.) record(s), phonograph record(s) • **2.** (coll.) cartridge case(s), shell(s)

قَوانَة [qawa:na] *n:* قَوانات [qawa:na:t] *pl:* • **1.** tale, story, strange tale – هاي صارَت قَوانَة. يِعجبَك تِجِي ويّانا لَو لا؟ [ha:y ṣa:rat qawa:na. yiʕiǰbak tiǰi wiyya:na law la:?] You're giving me the same old story. Do you want to go with us or not? • **2.** fuss, to do – سَوّالَه قَوانَة البارحَة [sawwa:lah qawa:na ʔilba:rħa] He made a big fuss yesterday. سَوَّيتها قَوانَة [sawwi:tha qawa:na] You made a big issue out of it. • **3.** record, phonograph record • **4.** cartridge case, shell • **5.** a musical disk

ق و ن ي

قُونِيَّة [gu:niyya] *n:* قُونِيّات، قوانِي [gu:niyya:t, gwa:ni] *pl:* • **1.** gunny sack, burlap bag

قُونيَة [gu:nya] *n:* قُونيات [gu:nya:t] *pl:* • **1.** sack

ق

ق و ي

قِوَى [qiwaː, quwaː] *v:* • **1.** to be or become strong – كُل سَنَة الشَّجَرَة تِقوَى [kull sana ʔiššajara tiqwaː] The tree gets stronger every year. دُقّ هَالخِشِبتَين عالصَّندُوق حَتَّى يُقوَى [dugg halxišibtayn ʕaṣṣanduːg ħatta yuqwaː] Nail these two boards onto the crate so it will be strong. • **2.** to increase in power, gain ascendency – هالوَزِير بِدا يِقوَى [halwaziːr bidaː yiqwaː] That minister has begun to gain power.

قَوَّى [qawwaː] *v:* • **1.** to make strong, strengthen – الحُكُومَة قَوَّت الجَّيش بِشِراء الطَّيّارات [ʔilħukuːma qawwat ʔijjayš bširaːʔ ʔiṭṭiyyaːraːt] The government strengthened the army by buying the airplanes. هَالدُّوا يقوِّي البَدَن [hadduwa yqawwi ʔilbadan] This medicine builds up the body.

تقَوَّى [tqawwaː, tgawwaː] *v:* • **1.** to be or become strong – جَيشنا تقَوَّى هوايَة خِلال العَشر سنِين الأَخِيرَة [ǰayšna tqawwaː hwaːya xilaːl ʔilʕašr sniːn ʔilʔaxiːra] Our army became much stronger during the last ten years. دَيِتقَوَّى بأَقارِبَه [dayitqawwaː bʔaqaːrbah] He derives strength from his relatives.

تقاوَى [tqaːwaː] *v:* • **1.** to compete in strength – لا تِتقاوَى ويّايا تَرَة أَذِّيك [laː titqaːwaː wiyyaːya tara ʔaʔaððiːk] Don't match strength with me or I'll hurt you.

قُوَّة [quwwa, guwwa] *n:* قُوّات [quwwaːt] *pl:* • **1.** strength • **2.** power, force • **3.** قُوّات armed forces • **4.** squad (of police) • **5.** القُوَّة الجَّوِّيَّة air force

تَقوِيَة [taqwiya] *n:* • **1.** strengthening, encouragement

مقَوّايَة [mqawwaːya] *n:* مقَوّايات [mqawwaːyaːt] *pl:* • **1.** cardboard, corrugated cardboard

قَوِي [qawi, guwi] *adj:* قواي، أَقوِياء، قَوِيِّين [qwaːy, ʔaqwiyaːʔ, qawiyyiːn] *pl:* • **1.** strong, powerful – رِجّال قَوِي [rijaːl qawi] a strong man. • **2.** firm, solid, hardy, sturdy – سَقُف قَوِي [saguf qawi] a sturdy ceiling. جُوزَة قَوِّيَّة [juːza qawwiyya] a tough nut. • **3.** intense, violent, vehement – قَصِيدَة قَوِيَّة [qaṣiːda qawiyya] a strongly-worded poem.

مُقَوِّي [muqawwi] *adj:* مُقَوِّيّات [muqawwiyyaːt] *pl:* • **1.** tonic, restorative

مقَوَّى [mqawwa] *adj:* • **1.** (coll.) cardboard, corrugated cardboard

أَقوَى [ʔaqwa] *comparative adjective:* • **1.** stronger, strongest

ق ي ء

تقَيَّ [tqayya] *v:* • **1.** to vomit – داخ وَتقَيَّ [daːx wtqayya] He got dizzy and vomited.

ق ي ث ر

قِيثارَة [qiːθaːra] *n:* قِيثارات [qiːθaːraːt] *pl:* • **1.** harp • **2.** lyre • **3.** guitar

ق ي ح

قَيَّح [qayyaħ] *v:* • **1.** to fester – مُكان الجَّرِح وُرَم وَتقَيَّح [mukaːn ʔijjariħ wuram wtqayyaħ] The wound swelled up and festered.

تقَيَّح [tqayyaħ] *v:* • **1.** to fester

قِيح [qiːħ] *n:* • **1.** pus

تَقَيُّح [taqayyuħ] *n:* • **1.** suppuration • **2.** pus festering

ق ي د

قَيِّد [qayyad, qayyid] *v:* • **1.** to restrict, limit, confine – لا تقَيِّدنِي. خَلِّينِي أَرُوح وَأَجِي بكَيفِي [laː tqayyidni. xalliːni ʔaruːħ wʔaji bkayfi] Don't restrict me. Let me go and come as I wish. • **2.** to write, write down, record, list, enter – قَيِّد إِسمَه هنا [qayyid ʔismah hna] List his name here. قَيِّد كُلّ شِي اللِّي تبِيعَه بِالدَّفتَر [qayyid kull ši ʔilli tbiːʕah biddaftar] Enter everything that you sell in the notebook. • **3.** to charge, debit – ما عِندِي فلُوس هَسَّة. قَيِّدها عَلَيّا [maː ʕindi fluːs hassa. qayyidha ʕalayya] I don't have money now. Charge it to me.

تقَيَّد [tqayyad] *v:* • **1.** to take care, look after, be careful – تقَيَّد عالكُتُب زين [tqayyad ʕalkutub ziːn] Take good care of the book. • **2.** to be careful, watch out – تقَيَّد عَلِي! الجّاهِل راح يوقَع [tqayyad ʕali! ʔijjaːhil raːħ yuːgaʕ] Watch out Ali! The kid's going to fall. إذا ما تِتقَيَّد بأَكلَك تِتمَرَّض [ʔiða maː titqayyad bʔaklak titmarrað̣] If you don't watch what you eat, you'll get sick. هُوَّ فَدّ واحِد خَبِيث. تقَيَّد مِنَّه [huwwa fadd waːħid xabiːθ. tqayyad minnah] He's a mean one. Be careful of him.

قِيد [qiːd] *n:* قُيُود [qiyuːd] *pl:* • **1.** cord(s), band(s), thong(s) • **2.** restriction, limitation, reservation – قِبَل يرَجِّعها بِلا قِيد وَلا شَرط [qibal yrajjiʕha bila qiːd wala šarṭ] He agreed to return it without any reservations. شما تسَوِّي بكَيفها. أُمَّها ما عِدها قِيد [šma tsawwiː bkayfha. ʔummaha maː ʕiddha qiːd] Whatever she does is up to her. Her mother has no concern. أَبُوه بَعدَه عَلَى قِيد الحَياة [ʔabuːh baʕdah ʕala qiːd ʔilħayaːt] His father is still living. • **3.** pl. قُيُود tally, count, list, record

قِيدَة [qiːda] *n:* قيدات [qiːdaːt] *pl:* • **1.** unit noun of قيد : a cord, band, thong • **2.** razor blade

تَقيِيد [taqyiːd] *n:* • **1.** registering, registration

مِتقَيِّد [mitqayyid] *adj:* • **1.** restricted • **2.** uneasy • **3.** registered

ق ي ر

قَيَّر [gayyar, ǰayyar] *v:* • **1.** to cover with asphalt, to pave with asphalt – جَيِّرُوا الطَّرِيق كُلَّه [ǰayyiraw ʔilṭariːq kullah] They paved the entire road with asphalt. • **2.** to tar – طَبُّقَوا السَّطِح وَقَيِّرُوه [ṭabbugaw ʔissaṭiħ wgayyiruːh] They laid tiles on the roof and put asphalt on it. • **3.** to pave – عِدنا مَكِينَة تقَيِّر الشَّوارِع [ʕidna makiːna dgayyir ʔiššawaːriʕ] We have a machine that paves streets.

تقيَّر [tgayyar] *v:* • **1.** to be tarred – السَّطِح لازم يِتقَيَّر عَن المُطَر [ʔissaṭiħ la:zim yitgayyar ʕan ʔilmuṭar] The roof has to be tarred to keep out the rain. • **2.** to be paved – ما نِخلَص مِن الطِّين إلّا إذا تقَيَّر الشّارِع [ma: nixlaṣ min ʔiṭṭi:n ʔilla ʔiða dgayyar ʔišša:riʕ] We won't be rid of the mud unless the street is paved.

قير [gi:r, ǰi:r] *n:* • **1.** asphalt, tar – قير سَيّال [gi:r sayya:l] a naturally liquid type of asphalt, used as waterproofing agent.

مِقيار [migya:r] *n:* مِقيارات [migya:ra:t] *pl:* • **1.** a club with a heavy knob of asphalt on the end, used as a black-jack

مقَيَّر [mgayyar, mǰayyar] *adj:* • **1.** paved, asphalted

ق ي ر ج

قِيراج [qi:ra:ǰ] *adj:* • **1.** diagonal

ق ي ر ط

قِيراط [qi:ra:ṭ] *n:* قِيراطات [qi:ra:ṭa:t] *pl:* • **1.** a weight

ق ي ز

قاز [ga:z] *adverbial:* • **1.** on edge, edgewise – وَقِّف الجّامَة قاز عالميز [waggif ʔiǰǰa:ma ga:z ʕalmi:z] Set the pane of glass on its edge on the table. نِزلَت الطِّيّارَة قاز عالسَّطِح [nizlat ʔiṭṭayya:ra ga:z ʕaṣṣaṭiħ] The kite crashed nose-down onto the roof.

ق ي س

قاس [qa:s] *v:* • **1.** to measure, take the measurements of – قِيس طُول وَعُرُض الغُرفَة وَقُلّي شقَدّ [qi:s ṭu:l wʕuruð ʔilɣurfa wgulli šgadd] Measure the length and width of the room and tell me how much it is. • **2.** to weigh, judge, measure – ما تِقدَر تقِيس نَفسَك بغَيرَك [ma: tigdar tqi:s nafsak bɣi:rak] You can't judge yourself by someone else. وقِيس عَلَى ذَلِك [wqi:s ʕala ða:lik] and along with that..., similarly, analogously, along that line also.

اِنقاس [ʔinqa:s] *v:* • **1.** to be measured – هَالقاع كبِيرَة. ما تِنقاس بِالسِنتِيمَتِر [halga:ʕ čibi:ra. ma: tinqa:s bilsintimatir] This plot is large. It can't be measured by the centimeter. • **2.** to be compared – هَذا ما يِنقاس بهَذا [ha:ða ma: yinqa:s bha:ða] This can't be compared with that.

مَقاس [maqa:s] *n:* • **1.** size, measuring, gauging, measurement, dimension

قِياس [qiya:s] *n:* قِيَاسَات [qiya:sa:t] *pl:* • **1.** measurement, measure, dimension

مِقياس [miqya:s] *n:* مَقايِيس [maqa:yi:s] *pl:* • **1.** measure, tape measure • **2.** gauge, measuring instrument – مِقياس النَّهَر [miqya:s ʔinnahar] stream gauge. مِقياس الكَهرَباء [miqya:s ʔilkahraba:ʔ] electric meter. مِقياس المَيّ [miqya:s ʔilmayy] water meter. • **3.** scale (on a map) • **4.** standard, criterion

قِياسِي، رَقَم قِياسِي [qiya:si, raqam qiya:si] *adj:* • **1.** a record (in swimming, racing, etc.)

ق ي ش [1]

قَيَّش [gayyaš] *v:* • **1.** to wade – تِعتِقِد تقَيِّش بِهَالجَدوَل؟ [tiʕtiqid dgayyiš bhalǰadwal?] Do you think you can wade in this creek?. • **2.** to run a ground – البَلَم قَيَّش. إنزِل إدفَع [ʔilbalam gayyaš. ʔinzil ʔidfaʕ] The boat ran a ground. Get out and push. • **3.** to keep up, to compete, to keep one's head above water – ما تقَيِّش ويّاه بِالكِيمياء [ma: tgayyiš wiyya:h bilki:mya] You can't surpass him in chemistry. هَالصَّفّ قَوِي. ما أقَيِّش بِيه [haṣṣaff qawi. ma: ʔagayyiš bi:h] This class is tough. I can't keep up. • **4.** to bag, to sack, to put (dates) in a skin bag – قَيِّشَوا التَّمُر كُلَّه وَدَزّوا لِبَغداد [gayyišaw ʔittamur kullah wdazzu: libaɣda:d] They put all the dates in skin bags and sent them to Baghdad.

قايَش [ga:yaš] *v:* • **1.** to equal, compete with – مَحَّد يقايِش ويّا هَذا بِالرِّكِض [maħħad yga:yiš wiyya ha:ða birrikið] No one can compete with him in running.

قيش [gi:š] *n:* • **1.** shallow water, shoal, place where one can wade – إمشِي، خَلِّي نُعبُر. الشَّطّ كُلَّه كَيش [ʔimši, xalli: nuʕbur. ʔiššaṭṭ kullah gi:š] Come on, let's go across. The river isn't over your head anywhere. إنزِل بِالمَيّ وَراوِينِي الكَيش لوين واصِل [ʔinzil bilmayy wra:wi:ni ʔilgi:š liwi:n wa:ṣil] Get in the water and show me where someone can stand without swimming.

قياش [gya:š] *n:* • **1.** same meaning as قيش : shallow water, shoal, place where one can wade

قِيشَة [gi:ša] *n:* قِيَش [giyaš] *pl:* • **1.** date container made from a tanned lamb or goat skin, skin bag

ق ي ش [2]

قايِش [qa:yiš] *n:* قايِشات، قَوايِش [qa:yiša:t, qawa:yiš] *pl:* • **1.** leather thong, strap • **2.** strop • **3.** belt – قايِش مال البَرَوانَة [qa:yiš ma:l ʔilparawa:na] fan belt. • **4.** trick, prank

ق ي ص ر

قَيصَر [qayṣar] *n:* قَياصِر، قَياصِرَة [qaya:ṣir, qaya:ṣira] *pl:* • **1.** czar

قَيصَرِيَّة [qayṣariyya] *n:* • **1.** caesarean, c-section • **2.** strip mall

ق ي ظ

قَيَّظ [gayyað] *v:* • **1.** to put on summer clothes, change to summer dress – لُويش قَيَّظِت؟ الدِّنيا بَعَدها بارِدَة [luwi:š gayyaðit? ʔiddinya baʕadha ba:rda] Why have you switched to summer clothes? The weather's still cold.

قيظ [gi:ð] *n:* قيظات [gi:ða:t] *pl:* • **1.** summer, esp. a very hot one

ق

ق ي ل

أقال [ʔaqa:l] *v:* • **1.** to dismiss, discharge – رَئِيس الجُمهُورِيَّة أقال ثلاث وُزَراء [raʔi:s ʔiǰǰumhu:riyya ʔaqa:l θla:θ wuzara:ʔ] The president of the republic dismissed three ministers.

اِستَقال [ʔistaqa:l] *v:* • **1.** to resign – نِقَم عَالوَضِع واستَقال [niqam ʕalwaðiʕ wʔistaqa:l] He got disgusted at the situation and resigned.

إقالَة [ʔiqa:la] *n:* • **1.** dismissal, discharge

اِستِقالَة [ʔistiqa:la] *n:* اِستِقالات [ʔistiqa:la:t] *pl:* • **1.** resignation

مُستَقِيل [mustaqi:l, mistaqi:l] *adj:* • **1.** resigned

ق ي م

قَيَّم [qayyam] *v:* • **1.** to estimate, assess, appraise, value, rate – بيش تقَيِّم هَالزُّولِيَّة؟ [biyš tqayyim hazzu:liyya?] What price would you put on this carpet?

تَقيِيم [taqyi:m] *n:* • **1.** evaluation, appraisal

ق ي م ر

قَيمَر [gaymar] *n:* • **1.** Devonshire cream (clotted)

ق ي و

قِيوَة [gi:wa] *n:* قيوات [gi:wa:t] *pl:* • **1.** (pair of) cotton slippers, cloth shoes

ق ي ي

قَيّ [gayy] *n:* • **1.** money put up by a bridegroom to furnish his bride's new home

ق

ك

ك 1

ك [ka--] *conjunction:* • **1.** as, in the capacity of – هُوَّ، كَمُعَلِّم، فاخِر، بَسّ كَشُرطِي، مُو زين [huwwa, kamuʕallim, faːxir, bass kašurṭi, muː ziːn] He, as a teacher, is great, but as a policeman, no good.

ك 2

ك [-- ak (mas), --ač (fem.)] *pronoun:* • **1.** (suffix) second person pronoun (you)

ك ء ب

كَئِيب [kaʔiːb] *adj:* • **1.** depressed

ك ء س

كَأس، كاس [kaʔs, kaːs] *n:* كُؤوس [kuʔuːs] *pl:* • **1.** trophy cup – مَدرَستَنا أَخذَت الكَأس بكُرَة السَّلَّة [madrasatna ʔaxðat ʔilkaʔs bkurat ʔissalla] Our school won the trophy cup in basketball.

ك ء ن

كَنّ contracted form of كَأَنّ [čann–] *pseudo-verb:* • **1.** like – حِسَّه كَنَّه حِسّ أَبُوك [ħissah čannah ħiss ʔabuːk] His voice is like your father's voice. قَصِير وَمدَحدَح كَنَّه جِكّ مال نَدّاف [qaṣiːr wimdaħdaħ čannah čikk maːl naddaːf] He's short and pudgy like a cotton-teaser's mallet. • **2.** it seems as though, it looks as if, it appears that – كَنّها تاهَت بِالطَّرِيق [čannha taːhat bittariːq] It looks as though she got lost on the way. كَنَّك ما تريد ترُوح [čannak maː triːd truːħ] It looks as though you don't want to go. كَنَّه عَلِي بِالباب [čannah ʕali bilbaːb] It seems to be Ali at the door. • **3.** (followed by pronominal suffixes): as though, as if – يصَيِّح كَنَّه زُمال [yṣayyiħ čannah zumaːl] He shouts as though he were a donkey. يِمشِي كَنَّه طاوُوس [yimši čannah ṭaːwuːs] He walks like a peacock. قاعِدِين كَنّهُم مُلُوك [gaːʕidiːn čannhum muluːk] They're sitting as though they were kings.

ك ب ب

كَبّ [čabb, kabb] *v:* • **1.** to pour out – كِبّ هَالمَيّ الوَسِخ بَرَّة [čibb halmayy ʔilwasix barra] Pour this dirty water outside. • **2.** to spill – دِير بالَك لا تكِبّ الشّاي مالِي [diːr baːlak laː tčibb ʔiččaːy maːli] Careful, don't spill my tea. • **3.** to ejaculate to come (semen)
اِنكَبّ [ʔinčabb, ʔinkabb] *v:* • **1.** to be spilled, to get poured out – اِنكَبّ الحَلِيب كُلَّه [ʔinčabb ʔilħaliːb kullah] All the milk was spilled. • **2.** (impolite) to shut up, be quiet, quit talking – اِنكَبّ! لا تِحكِي شِي بَعَد [ʔinčabb! laː tiħči ši baʕad] Shut up! Don't say anything else.
كَبّ [čabb, kabb] *n:* • **1.** pouring out
كُبَّة [kubba] *n:* • **1.** meatballs made from meat with rice or cracked wheat and spices
كَباب [kabaːb] *n:* • **1.** (coll.) meatball(s) broiled on a skewer
كُبّايَة [kubbaːya] *n:* كُبّايات [kubbaːyaːt] *pl:* • **1.** a meatball made from meat with rice or cracked wheat and spices
كَبَبجِي، كُبابجِي [kababči, kubaːbči] *n:* كَبَبجِيَّة، كُبابجِيَّة [kababčiyya, kubaːbčiyya] *pl:* • **1.** man who makes and sells kabobs
كَبابَة [kabaːba] *n:* • **1.** cubeb (bot.) (a kind of pepper)
كُبّابَة، كَبُّوبَة [kubbaːba, kabbuːba] *n:* كَبُّوبات [kabbuːbaːt] *pl:* • **1.** ball of yarn
كَبابايَة [kabaːbaːya] *n:* كَبابايات [kabaːbaːyaːt] *pl:* • **1.** meatball broiled on a skewer
مِنكَبّ [minčabb, minkabb] *adj:* • **1.** spilled, poured out • **2.** silent, quiet (impolite) because intent on or totally engaged in
مَكبُوب [mačbuːb, makbuːb] *adj:* • **1.** spilled, poured out

ك ب د

تكَبَّد [tkabbad] *v:* • **1.** to suffer, bear, endure, undergo (e.g., losses or hardships)
كَبَد [kabad, kabid] *n:* أَكباد [ʔakbaːd] *pl:* • **1.** liver
كِبدَة [kibda] *n:* • **1.** liver
تَكَبُّد [takabbud] *n:* • **1.** suffering, enduring, sustaining, undergoing

ك ب ر

كُبَر [kubar] *v:* • **1.** to grow, enlarge, become big – إِبنَك كُبَر هوايَة [ʔibnak kubar hwaːya] Your son's grown a lot. الدِّمبِلَة كُبرَت هوايَة. لازِم ترُوح لِلطَّبِيب [ʔiddimbila kubrat hwaːya. laːzim truːħ littabiːb] The sore has become too large. You'd better go to the doctor. شدَعوَة كُبَر راسَك؟ [šdaʕwa kubar raːsak?] How come you feel so important?
كَبَّر [kabbar] *v:* • **1.** to make big, large, to enlarge, magnify, aggrandize, to expand, amplify, extend, widen – لا تكَبُّر النُّقرَة هوايَة [laː tkabbur ʔinnugra hwaːya] Don't make the hole too big. كَبُّرلِي هَالصُّورَة [kabburli haṣṣuːra] Enlarge this picture for me. لا تكَبُّر راسَه هَالقَدّ [laː tkabbur raːsah halgadd] Don't give him such a swelled head. • **2.** to praise, glorify (esp. God) – كَبِّرَوا وَحِمدُوه الله [kabbiraw wħimdaw ʔallah] They praised and thanked God. • **3.** to say الله أَكبَر [ʔallahu ʔakbar] God is greater
تكَبَّر [tkabbar] *v:* • **1.** to be enlarged – هَالصُّورَة ما تِتكَبَّر [haṣṣuːra maː titkabbar] This picture can't be enlarge. • **2.** to be proud, haughty, to feel

self-important – لا تِتكَبَّر عالنّاس [la: titkabbar ʕanna:s] Don't look down on people. • **3.** to be vain

كُبُر [kubur] *n:* • **1.** size, magnitude, largeness – عِندَك ماعُون بِكُبُر هَذا؟ [ʕindak ma:ʕu:n bkubur ha:ða?] Do you have a dish of this size? • **2.** age – إبنِي عُمرَه سَبع سنِين؛ إبنَك شكُبرَه؟ [ʔibni ʕumrah sabʕ sni:n; ʔibnak škubrah?] My son is seven years old; how old is your son? • **3.** old age – ذاكِرتَه ضُعفَت بِكُبرَه [ða:kirtah ðuʕfat bkubrah] His memory failed in his old age. • **4.** growth

مُكَبِّرَة [mukabbira] *n:* مُكَبِّرات [mukabbira:t] *pl:* • **1.** magnifying glass • **2.** loudspeaker

تَكبِير [takbi:r] *n:* • **1.** enlargement, increase, magnification • **2.** chanting, saying اللهُ أكبَر [ʔallahu ʔakbar] (God is greater)

كِبرِياء [kibriya:ʔ] *n:* • **1.** arrogance, haughtiness • **2.** pride

مُكابَرَة [muka:bara] *n:* • **1.** haughtiness, obstinacy, selfimportance

كِبِير [čibi:r, kibi:r] *adj:* كبار [kba:r] *pl:* • **1.** big, large – خَلِّي نُقعُد بالغُرفَة الكِبِيرَة [xalli: nugʕud bilɣurfa ʔilčibi:ra] Let's sit in the big room. • **2.** old, aged – إبنِي الكِبِير دُكتُور [ʔibni ʔilčibi:r duktu:r] My oldest son is a doctor.

كَبرَة، نار كَبرَة [kabra, na:r kabra] *adj:* • **1.** ball of fire, human dynamo, an energetic, dynamic, vigorous person – إبن الجِّيران نار كَبرَة [ʔibn ʔijji:ra:n na:r kabra] The neighbor's boy is a real tornado.

مُكَبَّر [mukabbar] *adj:* • **1.** enlarged, magnified – سَوِّيلِي نُسخَة مُكَبَّرَة مِن كُل صُورَة [sawwi:li nusxa mukabbara min kull ṣu:ra] Make me an enlargement of each picture.

مِتكَبُّر [mitkabbur] *adj:* • **1.** conceited • **2.** proud

كَبران [kabra:n] *adj:* • **1.** grown-up • **2.** growing older, becoming older • **3.** growing larger (as in clothes)

أكبَر [ʔakbar] *comparative adjective:* • **1.** bigger, biggest, larger, largest • **2.** older, oldest • **3.** more or most in rank • **4.** more, most important

الكُبرَى [ʔilkubra:] comparative adjective: • 1. largest, biggest most important

ك ب ر ت

كِبرِيت [kibri:t] *n:* • **1.** sulphur, matches • **2.** عِين كِبريت a sulphur spring

كابرِيتَة [kabri:ta] *n:* • **1.** carburetor

ك ب س

كِبَس [kibas, čibas] *v:* • **1.** to pack, press tightly together – يكِبسُون التَّمُر قَبُل ما يصَدِّرُوه [ykibsu:n ʔittamur gabul ma: yṣaddru:h] They pack the dates tightly before they export them. • **2.** to raid, take by surprise – الشُّرطَة كِبسَتهُم بِهالبَيت [ʔiššurṭa kibsathum bihalbi:t] The police raided them in this house. • **3.** to spike a ball (in volleyball) – هَاللّاعِب يِكبِس كُلِّش زين [halla:ʕib yikbis kulliš zi:n] That player spikes the ball very well.

اِنكِبَس [ʔinkibas, ʔinčibas] *v:* • **1.** to be pressed – التَّمُر لازِم يِنكِبِس قَبُل ما يِتعَبَّى بِقواطِي [ʔittamur la:zim yinkibis gabul ma: yitʕabba: bqwa:ṭi] The dates must be pressed before they're packed in crates.

كَبِس [kabis, čabis] *n:* • **1.** pressure, squeeze • **2.** packing, pressing tightly together

مَكبَس [makbas, mačbas] *n:* مَكابِس [mača:bis, maka:bis] *pl:* • **1.** packing house (usually for dates)

كَبسَة [kabsa] *n:* • **1.** surprise, kind of food

كِبّاسَة [čibba:sa] *n:* كِبّاسات [čibba:sa:t] *pl:* • **1.** weight put on top of food while frying it

كابُوس [ka:bu:s] *n:* كَوابِيس [kawa:bi:s] *pl:* • **1.** nightmare, incubus

كابسَة [ka:bisa] *n:* كابسات [ka:bisa:t] *pl:* • **1.** stapler

كَبِيسَة، سَنَة كَبِيسَة [kabi:sa, sana kabi:sa] *n:* • **1.** leap year

مَكبُوس [makbu:s, mačbu:s] *adj:* • **1.** pressed, packed tightly

ك ب س ل

كَبسَل [kabsal] *v:* • **1.** to take narcotics, drugs, pills

كَبسُولَة [kabsu:la] *n:* كَبسُول [kabsu:l] *pl:* • **1.** capsule, cap, snap fastener

ك ب س ن

كَبسُونَة [kabsu:na] *n:* كَبسُونات [kabsu:na:t] *pl:* • **1.** percussion cap • **2.** bullet

ك ب ش

كَبِش [kabiš] *n:* أكباش [ʔakba:š] *pl:* • **1.** ram, male sheep

ك ب ك ب

كَبكَب [čabčab] *v:* • **1.** to splash, slop – الجّاهِل دَيكَبكِب مَيّ عَلَى هدُومَه [ʔijja:hil dayčabčib mayy ʕala hdu:mah] The baby's splashing water on his clothes. تِرَس القِدِر مَيّ وظَلّ يِتكَبكَب [tiras ʔilgidir mayy wðall yitčabčab] He overfilled the pot with water and it kept spilling out.

تكَبكَب [tčabčab] *v:* • **1.** to slosh out, spill over

كَبكَبَة [kabkaba] *n:* • **1.** pomp, ceremony, splendor – شدَعوَة هَالكَبكَبَة؛ قابِل هُوَّ مَلِك؟ [šdaʕwa halkabkaba; qa:bil huwwa malik?] Why all this fuss and bother; is he a king?

ك ب ن

كَبَّن [čabban] *v:* • **1.** to be or become matted, thick – شَعرِي مكَبِّن، يرِيدلَه غَسِل [šaʕri mčabbin, yri:dlah ɣasil] My hair is snarled. It needs washing. دَماغَه مكَبِّن [dama:ɣah mčabbin] or راسَه مكَبِّن [ra:sah mčabbin] He's got a thick head. He's terribly slow-witted.

كِبَن [čiban] *n:* • **1.** a felt material used for saddle blankets
كِبنَة [čibna] *n:* كِبنات [čibna:t] *pl:* • **1.** saddle blanket, felt pad
مكَبِّن [mčabbin] *adj:* • **1.** matted, thick

ك ب ن ت
كبِنتُو، شبِنتُو [čbintu, šbintu] *n:* • **1.** cement • **2.** plaster, mortar

ك ب ن ك
كَبَنك [kabang, kabank] *n:* كَبَنكات [kabanka:t] *pl:* • **1.** roll-up store front, a shutter across the front of a store with no doors – بَعَد نُصّ ساعَة راح أنَزِّل الكَبَنك [baʕad nuṣṣ sa:ʕa ra:ħ ʔanazzil ʔilkabang] After half an hour, we'll call it a day.

ك ب ي ن
كابِينَة [ka:bi:na] *n:* كابِينات [ka:bi:na:t] *pl:* • **1.** cabinet

ك ت
كَتَة [čata] *adj:* • **1.** (invar.) undisciplined, helterskelter, disorganized, a mess – الدَّوام بِهالدّائِرَة كَتَة. كُلّ مَن يرُوح ويِجِي بكَيفَه [ʔiddawa:m bhadda:ʔira čata. kull man yiru:ħ wyiǰi bkiyfah] Working hours in this office are loose and informal. Everyone goes and comes as he pleases. • **2.** pl. كَتَوات undisciplined person, slacker, idler, goof-off – ما يدِير بال لِلشُّغُل. هَذا كَتَة [ma: ydi:r ba:l liššuɣul. ha:ða čata] He doesn't pay attention to work. He's a goof-off. حَتَّى لَو تكُون كَتَة بِالصَّفّ، ينَجِّحَك [ħatta law tku:n čata biṣṣaff, ynaǰǰiħak] Even if you're a lazy slacker in class, he'll promote you.

ك ت ب
كِتَب [kitab] *v:* • **1.** to write, to write down, record, inscribe – إكتِب أسماء التَّلامِيذ الغايبِين [ʔiktib ʔasma:ʔ ʔittala:mi:ð ʔilɣa:ybi:n] Write down the names of the students who are absent. كِتَبِتلَه مَكتُوب البارحَة [kitabitlah maktu:b ʔilba:rħa] I wrote him a letter yesterday.
كَتَّب [kattab] *v:* • **1.** to make write – المُعَلِّم كَتَّبنا صَفُحتَين [ʔilmuʕallim kattabna ṣafuħtayn] The teacher made us write two pages.
تكاتَب [tka:tab] *v:* • **1.** to write to each other, exchange correspondence – صار إلنا سَنَة نِتكاتَب [ṣa:r ʔilna sana nitka:tab] We have kept up a correspondence for a year. • **2.** to enter into a written agreement – تكاتبَوا عَلَى كُلّ شِي قِدّام القاضِي [tka:tbaw ʕala kull ši gidda:m ʔilqa:ḍi] They settled a written agreement about everything before the judge. • **3.** to join forces – تكاتبَوا ويّا قَبِيلَة قَويَّة [tka:tbaw wiyya qabi:la qawiyya] They joined forces with a strong tribe.
انكِتَب [ʔinkitab] *v:* • **1.** pass. of كِتَب to be writen – إذا تغِيب، إسمَك ينكِتِب بدَفتَر الغِيابات [ʔiða tɣi:b, ʔismak yinkitib bdaftar ʔilɣiya:ba:t] If you are absent, your name will be written down in the absentee log.
كِتاب [kita:b] *n:* كُتُب [kutub] *pl:* • **1.** book • **2.** an official correspondence • **3.** business letter
مَكتَب [maktab] *n:* مَكاتِب [maka:tib] *pl:* • **1.** office • **2.** bureau
كاتِب [ka:tib] *n:* كُتّاب [kutta:b] *pl:* • **1.** writer • **2.** clerk, clerical employee – كاتِب طابِعَة [ka:tib ṭa:biʕa] typist.
كُتَيِّب [kutayyib] *n:* • **1.** pamphlet, booklet (a small book)
كِتابَة [kita:ba] *n:* كِتابات [kita:ba:t] *pl:* • **1.** writing, handwriting, penmanship
كَتِيبَة [kati:ba] *n:* كَتائِب [kata:ʔib] *pl:* • **1.** battalion
مَكتَبَة [maktaba] *n:* مَكتَبات [maktaba:t] *pl:* • **1.** library – أَرِيد أرُوح أدرُس بالمَكتَبَة [ʔari:d ʔaru:ħ ʔadrus bilmaktaba] I want to go study in the library. • **2.** bookstore – مِن يا مَكتَبَة اِشتِرَيت هَالكِتاب؟ [min ya: maktaba ʔištiri:t halkita:b?] From which bookstore did you buy this book? • **3.** bookshelf – النَّجّار راح يسَوِّيلِي مَكتَبَة [ʔinnaǰǰa:r ra:ħ ysawwi:li maktaba] The carpenter is going to make me a bookshelf.
مَكتُوب [maktu:b] *n:* مَكاتِيب [maka:ti:b] *pl:* • **1.** (pl. مَكاتِيب) letter, missive, note • **2.** as Noun: fate, destiny
مُكاتَبَة [muka:taba] *n:* • **1.** correspondence
كِتابِي [kita:bi] *adj:* • **1.** clerical – وَظِيفَة كِتابِيَّة [waḍi:fa kita:biyya] clerical position.
مَكتُوب [maktu:b] *adj:* • **1.** written, written down, recorded • **2.** subscribed • **3.** fated, foreordained, destined – مَكتُوبلَه يصِير بِيه هِيكِي شِي [maktu:blah yṣi:r bi:h hi:či ši] It was destined for such a thing to happen to him.

ك ت ت
كَتّ [katt] *v:* • **1.** to express, let forth (an emotion) – كَتّ كُلّ اللِّي بِقَلبَه مِن قَهرَه [katt kull ʔilli bgalbah min qahrah] He poured out his heart in his distraction. • **2.** (liquid) to pour, gush forth – المُطَر دَيكُتّ اليُوم [ʔilmuṭar daykutt ʔilyu:m] The rain is pouring down today. المَيّ دَيكُتّ مِن السَّطلَة [ʔilmayy daykutt min ʔissaṭla] The water is pouring from the bucket.
كَتّ [katt] *n:* • **1.** pouring (liquid), expressing (an emotion), spending (money)

ك ت د ر ء ي
كاتِدرائِيَّة [katidra:ʔiyya] *n:* • **1.** cathedral

ك ت ف
كَتَّف [čattaf, kattaf] *v:* • **1.** to bind, tie up – كَتِّفَوا المُجرِم وَحطَّوه بِالسَّيّارَة [čattifaw ʔilmuǰrim wħaṭṭawh bissayya:ra] They bound up the criminal and put him

in the car. المُدير الجِّدِيد كَتَّفني. ما يخَلِّيني أمضِي وَلا مَكتُوب [ʔilmudi:r ʔijjidi:d čattafni. ma: yxalli:ni ʔamḍi wala maktu:b] The new director's tied my hands. He won't let me sign even a single letter.

تكَتَّف [tčattaf, tkattaf] *v:* • **1.** to fold one's arms – تكَتَّف ووُقَف قِدّامِي [tčattaf wwugaf gidda:mi] He folded his arms and stood in front of me.

تكاتَف [tka:taf] *v:* • **1.** to support one another, to stand together

كِتِف [čitif, kitif] *n:* كتاف، كتافات [čta:f, čta:fa:t, kta:f, kta:fa:t] *pl:* • **1.** shoulder – اِنطاه كِتِف [ʔinṭa:h čitif] He helped him. He gave him a hand.

تكاتُف [taka:tuf] *n:* • **1.** solidarity

كَتّافِيَّة [čatta:fiyya, katta:fiyya] *n:* كَتّافِيّات [čatta:fiyya:t, katta:fiyya:t] *pl:* • **1.** shoulder pad (in clothing)

مُكَتَّف [mukattaf] *adj:* • **1.** concentrated, intensified

مكَتَّف [mčattaf, mkattaf] *adj:* • **1.** with hands tied up • **2.** with arms crossed, with folded hands • **3.** tied up, bound, unable to act

ك ت ك ت

كَتكَت [katkat] *v:* • **1.** to flow, pour, gush forth – المَيّات دَتكَتكِت مِن التُّنَق [ʔilmayya:t datkatkit min ʔittunag] The water is pouring out of the jars.

ك ت ل

كَتَّل [kattal] *v:* • **1.** to gather (something) into a mass, press into a lump – خَلِّي مَيّ عَالطِّين وَكَتِّله [xalli: mayy ʕaṭṭi:n wkattilah] Put water with the mud and press it into a lump.

تكَتَّل [tkattal] *v:* • **1.** to cluster, clot, agglomerate, gather into a mass – مِن تكَتِّلوا، الشُّرطَة فَرِّقَتهُم [min tkattilaw, ʔiššurṭa farriqathum] When they massed themselves, the police dispersed them.

كُتلَة [kutla] *n:* كُتَل [kutal] *pl:* • **1.** lump, hunk, clod, clot – الكُتلَة الشَّرقِيَّة [ʔilkutla ʔiššarqiyya] The Eastern Bloc (of nations). • **2.** bloc, block

ك ت ل ك

كَتالُوك [katalu:k, katalu:g] *n:* • **1.** catalogue

ك ت ل ي

كِتلِي [kitli] *n:* كِتلِيّات، كتالِي [kitliyya:t, kta:li] *pl:* • **1.** teakettle

ك ت م

كِتَم [kitam] *v:* • **1.** to conceal, keep secret (something) – ما يِقدَر يِكتِم سِرّ [ma: yigdar yiktim sirr] He can't keep a secret.

تكَتَّم [tkattam] *v:* • **1.** to be secretive, keep silent – يِتكَتَّم وَما يِحكِي شِي [yitkattam wma yiħči ši] He keeps quiet and won't say a thing. ماكُو حاجَة تِتكَتَّم بِكُلّ اللّي تسَوِّي [ma:ku ħa:ja titkattam bkull ʔilli tsawwi:] There's no reason to be secretive about everything that you do.

مَكتُوم [maktu:m] *n:* • **1.** a variety of fresh dates

كِتمان [kitma:n] *n:* • **1.** secrecy, secretiveness, concealment

كاتِم [ka:tim] *adj:* • **1.** act od keeping secret, concealed, hidden • **2.** silencer, confidant, keeper of secrets

كَتُوم [katu:m] *adj:* كَتُومِين [katuwmi:n] *pl:* • **1.** discreet, reserved, secretive, uncommunicative

مَكتُوم [maktu:m] *adj:* • **2.** hidden, concealed, kept, preserved (secret) • **3.** a type of palm dates

ك ت ن

كِتّان [kitta:n] *n:* • **1.** flax, linen

ك ث ب

كَثِيب [kaθi:b] *adj:* كُثبَان [kuθba:n] *pl:* • **1.** dune

ك ث ث

كَثّ [kaθθ] *adj:* • **1.** thick, dense

ك ث ر

كِثَر [kiθar, čiθar] *v:* • **1.** to increase, multiply, grow – طُلّاب مَدرَستنا كِثَر عَدَدهُم [ṭulla:b madrasatna kiθar ʕadadhum] The number of students in our school increased. • **2.** to be plentiful – الرَّقِّي يِكثَر بِالصَّيف [ʔirraggi yikθar biṣṣayf] Watermelon becomes plentiful in the summer.

كَثَّر [kaθθar, čaθθar] *v:* • **1.** to make more of, to increase, augment, compound, multiply – هَالكَمِّيَّة ما تِكفِي. كَثِّرها شوَيَّة [halkammiyya ma: tikfi. kaθθirha šwayya] This amount isn't enough. Increase it a little. الله يكَثِّر مِن أمثالَك [ʔallah ykaθθir min ʔamθa:lak] God should allow more of the likes of you. • **2.** to overdo (something), to go to excessive lengths – إسأله بَس. لا تكَثِّر ويّاه [ʔisʔalah bass. la: tkaθθir wiyya:h] Just ask him. Don't go to any length with him.

تكاثَر [tka:θar] *v:* • **1.** to multiply, grow in number, increase – الأرانِب تِتكاثَر بِسُرعَة [ʔilʔara:nib titka:θar bsurʕa] Rabbits multiply quickly.

اِستَكثَر [ʔistakθar] *v:* • **1.** to consider excessive, regard as too much – اِستَكثَرَه لِلسِّعِر [ʔistakθarah lissiʕir] He thought the price was too much.

كُثُر [kuθur] *n:* • **1.** amount – قُلِّي شكُثُر ترِيد وآنِي أنطِيك [gulli škuθur tri:d wʔa:ni ʔanṭi:k] Tell me how much you want and I'll give it to you.

كُثرَة [kuθra, kaθra] *n:* • **1.** abundance, copiousness, numerosity, frequency, multiplicity, plurality – هالسَّنَة التِّفّاح مِتوَفِّر بِكُثرَة [hassana ʔittiffa:ħ mitwaffir bkuθra] This year the apples are available in abundance. الكُثرَة تُغلُب الشَّجاعَة [ʔilkuθra tuɣlub ʔiššaja:ʕa] Numbers beat bravery.

تَكاثُر [taka:θur] *n:* • **1.** growth, increase, multiplication, proliferation, propagation
أَكثَرِيَّة [ʔakθariyya] *n:* • **1.** majority – الأَكثَرِيَّة موافقِين عالإقتِراح [ʔilʔakθariyya mwa:fqi:n ʕa:lʔiqtira:ħ] The majority are in agreement with the proposal.
كِثِير [kiθi:r, čiθi:r] *adj:* • **1.** much, many, numerous, abundant, plentiful, copious
مِتكاثِر [mitka:θir] *adj:* • **1.** multiplied, increased • **2.** numerous, extensive, multiple
أَكثَر [ʔakθar] *comparative adjective:* • **1.** more, most – شوَقِت راح تمُرّ عَليه؟ . . . عالأَكثَر باكِر الصُّبُح [šwakit ra:ħ tmurr ʕali:h? . . . ʕalʔakθar ba:čir ʔiṣṣubuħ] When are you going to stop and see him? . . . It'll most likely be tomorrow morning.

ك ث ف

كَثَّف [kaθθaf] *v:* • **1.** to thicken, condense, concentrate – عِدهُم مَكِينَة تكَثِّف البُخار [ʕidhum maki:na tkaθθif ʔilbuxa:r] They have a machine to condense vapor. حَلِيب مُكَثَّف [ħali:b mukaθθaf] condensed milk.
كَثافَة [kaθa:fa] *n:* • **1.** density – كَثافَة السُّكّان بهَالبَلَد عالية [kaθa:fat ʔissukka:n bhalbalad ʕa:lya] The density of population in this country is high. • **2.** thickness, solidity, heaviness
كَثِيف [kaθi:f] *adj:* كثاف [kθa:f] *pl:* • **1.** thick, dense • **2.** heavy, viscous

ك ج ر

كُجَرات، شاي كُجَرات [kuǰara:t, ča:y kuǰara:t] *n:* • **1.** tea made from zedoary leaves, a red, sour, and aromatic beverage

ك ح ح

كَحّ [gaħħ] *v:* • **1.** to cough
كَحَّة [gaħħa] *n:* • **1.** coughing, cough

ك ح ك ح

كَحكَح [gaħgaħ] *v:* • **1.** to cough – شبِيه صَدرَك؟ صارلَك ساعَة تقَحقِح [šbi:h ṣadrak? ṣa:rlak sa:ʕa tgaħgiħ] What's the matter with your chest? You've been coughing for an hour.

ك ح ل

كَحَّل [kaħħal] *v:* • **1.** to beautify (eyes) with kohl – ما تِطلَع بَرَّة إذا ما تكَحِّل عيُونها [ma: tiṭlaʕ barra ʔiða ma: tkaħħil ʕyu:nha] She won't go out without putting kohl on her eyes. جا يكَحِّلها وَعماها [ǰa: ykaħħilha wʕima:ha] He was supposed to improve the situation and he made it worse.
تكَحَّل [tkaħħal] *v:* • **1.** to beautify one's eyes with kohl – واقفَة قِدّام المرايَة وَدتِتكَحَّل [wa:gfa gidda:m ʔilmra:ya wadatitkaħħal] She's standing in front of the mirror and putting on eye makeup.
كُحُل [kuħul] *n:* • **1.** a preparation of pulverized antimony used as eye cosmetic
كُحُول [kuħu:l] *n:* • **1.** alcohol
كاحِل [ka:ħil] *n:* كَواحِل [kawa:ħil] *pl:* • **1.** anklebone
مَكحَلَة [makħala] *n:* مَكحَلات، مَكاحِل [makħala:t, maka:ħil] *pl:* • **1.** a long-necked jar for kohl (black eye dye or coloring)
تَكحِيل [takħi:l] *n:* • **1.** treatment of the eyes with kohl
كحيلان [kħi:la:n] *n:* • **1.** a strain of Arabian horses
مكَحَّل [mkaħħal] *adj:* • **1.** wearing (black) eyeliner
كُحُولِي [kuħu:li] *adj:* • **1.** alcoholic
كحيلَة [kħi:la] *n:* كحيلات [kħi:la:t] *pl:* • **1.** thoroughbred mare, horse of the finest breeding
مِتكَحِّل [mitkaħħil] *adj:* • **1.** wearing eyeliner

ك د ح

كِدَح [kidaħ] *v:* • **1.** to apply oneself diligently, to work hard – ظَلّ يكدَح إلَى أن حَصَّلَه شُغُل [ðall yikdaħ ʔila ʔan ħaṣṣallah šuɣul] He kept applying himself diligently until he found himself a job.
كادِح [ka:diħ] *adj:* • **1.** hard-working, diligent (worker)

ك د د

كَدّ [kadd] *v:* • **1.** to work hard, toil, labor, exert oneself – يكُدّ وَفلُوسَه يتِلفُوها ولِدَه [ykudd wflu:sah ytilfu:ha wildah] He works hard and his children waste his money. يكُدّ مِثِل الدّابَّة وَشُغلَه ضايِع [ykudd miθl ʔidda:bba wšuɣlah ða:yiʕ] He works like a mule and his effort is wasted. • **2.** to wear, last – ثُوب النّايلَون يكُدّ هوايَة [θu:b ʔinnaylu:n ykudd hwa:ya] A nylon shirt lasts a long time.
كَدّ [kadd] *n:* • **1.** hard work, labor
كادُود [ka:du:d] *adj:* كوادِيد [kwa:di:d] *pl:* • **1.** hard-working, diligent • **2.** hard worker

ك د ر 1

كِدَر [kidar] *v:* • **1.** to worry, to trouble, to annoy, to disturb
تكَدَّر [tkaddar] *v:* • **1.** to take offense • **2.** to be annoyed, to be worried
مِتكَدِّر [mitkaddir] *adj:* • **1.** worried, annoyed, sad

ك د ر 2

كادِر [ka:dir] *n:* كَوادِر [kawa:dir] *pl:* • **1.** staff, high officials

ك د س

كَدَّس [kaddas] *v:* • **1.** to pile up, heap up, amass, accumulate – دَيِشتِري بِهالبَضايِع وَيكَدِّس بِيها [dayištiri

bhalbaḍa:yiʕ wykaddis bi:ha] He is buying up those commodities and stockpiling them.
تكَدَّس [tkaddas] *v:* • **1.** pass. of كَدَّس : to be piled up – تكَدِّسَت بِهَالمَخزَن أكثَر القُمصان [tkaddisat bhalmaxzan ʔakθar ʔilqumṣa:n] Most of the shirts are stocked in this store.
تَكَدُّس [takaddus] *n:* • **1.** piling up, overcrowding, accumulation
مكَدَّس [mkaddas] *adj:* • **1.** overstocked, stacked, piled up

ك د ش

كَدَّش [kaddaš] *v:* • **1.** (horse) to be or become useless, worthless – حصانَه كَدَّش. راح يبيعَه [ḥṣa:nah kaddaš. ra:ḥ ybi:ʕah] His horse has become useless. He'll sell it.
كِديش [kidi:š] *adj:* كِدّش، كِدشان [kiddaš, kidša:n] *pl:* • **1.** nag, worthless horse – المُوَظَّف الجِّدِيد كِدِيش [ʔilmuwaḍḍaf ʔijjidi:d kidi:š] The new employee is a dope. • **2.** a dope, a dumb person

ك د م

كِدَم [čidam] *n:* • **1.** (coll.) sandstone
كَدمَة [kadma] *n:* كَدَمات [kadama:t] *pl:* • **1.** bruise, contusion, wound caused by a bite
كِدمايَة [čidma:ya] *n:* كِدمايات [čidma:ya:t] *pl:* • **1.** piece of sandstone

ك ذ

كَذا وَكذا [kaða: wkaða:] *n:* • **1.** such-and-such, so-and-so – قال عَنَّك كَذا وَكَذا [ga:l ʕannak kaða: wkaða:] He said such-and-such about you.

ك ذ ب

كِذَب [čiðab, kiðab] *v:* • **1.** to lie, tell a lie – لا تصَدِّق بيه. يكذِب هوايَة [la:tṣaddig bi:h. yičðib hwa:ya] Don't believe him. He lies a lot.
كَذَّب [čaððab, kaððab] *v:* • **1.** to tell lies, prevaricate, speak untruthfully – إحكِي الصُّدُق. لا تكَذِّب [ʔiḥči ʔiṣṣudug. la: tčaððib] Tell the truth. Don't tell lies. • **2.** to deny, refute, disprove – كَذّبَوا خَبَر زَواجَه [čaððibaw xabar zawa:jah] They denied the news of his marriage. ما كَذَّب خَبَر [ma: čaððab xabar] He didn't hesitate. He wasted no time. قِتلَه لِلمُجامَلَة "إذا تِحتاج فلُوس، آني عِندَك" ماكَذَّب خَبَر وَطِلَب دِينارَين [gitlah lilmuja:mala "ʔiða tiḥta:j flu:s, ʔa:ni ʕindak" ma: čaððab xabar wṭilab dina:rayn] I told him out of politeness 'If you need money, I'm at your service.' He took me at my word and asked for two dinars.
كِذِب [čiðib, kiðib] *n:* • **1.** a lie
كِذبَة [čiðba, kiðba] *n:* كِذبات، أكاذِيب [čiðba:t, kiðba:t, ʔaka:ði:b] *pl:* • **1.** lie, untruth, falsehood
تَكذِيب [takði:b] *n:* • **1.** denial
إكذُوبَة [ʔikðu:ba] *n:* أكاذِيب، إكذُوبات [ʔaka:ði:b, ʔikðu:ba:t] *pl:* • **1.** lie
كَذّاب [čaðða:b, kaðða:b] *adj:* كَذّابِين [čaðða:bi:n, kaðða:bi:n] *pl:* • **1.** liar, prevaricator
كاذِب [ka:ðib, ča:ðib] *adj:* • **1.** liar • **2.** lying
أكذَب [ʔačðab, ʔakðab] *comparative adjective:* • **1.** more or most untruthful – هَذا أكذَب الكُلّ [ha:ða ʔačðab ʔilkull] He's the biggest liar of all.

ك ر

كار [ka:r] *n:* كارات [ka:ra:t] *pl:* • **1.** vocation, trade, profession, occupation, business – راح أترُك النِّجارَة لِأَنّ هَالكار ما بيه عِيشَة [ra:ḥ ʔatruk ʔinnija:ra liʔann halka:r ma: bi:h ʕi:ša] I'm going to quit carpentry because there's no living in this trade. إذا بُسَطَك، آني مالِي كار [ʔiða busaṭak, ʔa:ni ma:li ka:r] If he beats you, it's none of my business.

ك ر ب

كِرَب [kirab] *v:* • **1.** to plow, till – أكرُب القاع زين قَبُل ما تِزرَعها [ʔukrub ʔilga:ʕ zi:n gabul ma: tizraʕha] Plow up the ground well before you plant it.
كَرَّب [karrab] *v:* • **1.** to trim nodules from a palm tree – يِقدَر يكَرُّب النَّخلَة بنُص ساعَة [yigdar ykarrub ʔinnaxla bnuṣṣ sa:ʕa] He can trim the bumps off a palm tree in a half hour. • **2.** to overburden – دَيكَرُّبنا بشُغُل هوايَة [daykarrubna bšuɣul hwa:ya] He loads us down with a lot of work. يدفَعلَه مِيَّة فِلس بِاليُوم وَيكَرُّب عَليه طُول النَّهار [yidfaʕlah miyyat filis bilyu:m wykarrub ʕali:h ṭu:l ʔinnaha:r] He pays him hard all day long.
اِنكِرَب [ʔinkirab] *v:* • **1.** to be plowed – القاع كُلّها لازِم تِنكُرُب اليُوم [ʔilga:ʕ kullha la:zim tinkurub ʔilyu:m] All of this land must be plowed today.
كَرَب [karab] *n:* • **1.** (coll.) nodules on the trunk of a palm tree from which the fronds grow
كَراب [kara:b] *n:* • **1.** hard work, toil, drudgery
كَربَة [karba] *n:* كَربات [karba:t] *pl:* • **1.** nodules on the trunk of a palm tree from which the fronds grow
مَكرُوب [makru:b] *adj:* • **1.** depressed, over-worked, sad, worried, distressed

ك ر ب ج

كُرباج، كِرباج [kurba:č, kurba:g, kirba:j] *n:* كَرابِيج [kara:bi:č] *pl:* • **1.** whip, riding crop, kurbash

ك ر ب س

كَربَس [karbas] *v:* • **1.** to push into an inescapable situation – كَربَسنِي بِهَالسَّيّارَة اللّي مُو زِينَة [karbasni bhassayya:ra ʔilli mu: zi:na] He stuck me with this no-good car.

تكربس [tkarbas] *v:* • **1.** to fall or be pushed into an inescapable situation – تكربَس المِحبَس بيدِي وَما دَيطلَع [tkarbas ʔilmiħbas biːdi wma dayiṭlaʕ] The ring got stuck on my hand and won't come off.

ك ر ب و ن

كاربُون [karbuːn] *n:* • **1.** carbon – وَرَق كَربُون [waraq karbuːn] carbon paper.

ك ر ت

كَرتَة [karata] *n:* كَرتات [karataːt] *pl:* • **1.** shoehorn
كارت [kaːrt] *n:* • **1.** card

ك ر ت و ن

كَرتُون [kartuːn] *n:* • **1.** (coll.) thin cardboard, heavy paper
كَرتُونَة [kartuːna] *n:* كَرتُونات [kartuːnaːt] *pl:* • **1.** a sheet of cardboard, heavy paper

ك ر ث

اِكتِرَث [ʔiktiraθ] *v:* • **1.** with ل to heed, pay attention to, care about, take an interest in – آنِي ما أكتِرِثلَه. خَلّي يِحكِي شما يرِيد [ʔaːni maː ʔaktiriθlah. xalli: yiħči šma yriːd] I don't care about him. Let him say whatever he wants.
كُرّاث [kurraːθ] *n:* • **1.** a variety of leek
كارِثَة [kaːriθa] *n:* كَوارِث [kawaːriθ] *pl:* • **1.** disaster, calamity, catastrophe – سُقُوط الطَّيّارَة كان كارِثَة كِبِيرَة [suquːṭ ʔiṭṭiyyaːra čaːn kaːriθa čibiːra] The airplane crash was a terrible disaster.
مُكتَرِث [muktariθ] *adj:* • **1.** attentive, interested

ك ر ج

كَراج [garaːǰ] *n:* كَراجات [garaːǰaːt] *pl:* • **1.** garage

ك ر خ

كِرَخ [kirax] *v:* • **1.** to dredge, clean out (a river, etc.) – الحُكُومَة راح تِكرُخ النَّهَر يَمّ بَغداد [ʔilħukuːmma raːħ tikrux ʔinnahar yamm baɣdaːd] The government's going to dredge the river near Baghdad.
اِنكِرَخ [ʔinkirax] *v:* • **1.** pass. of كِرَخ : to be cleaned, to be dredged – النَّهَر اِنكِرَخ السَّنَة اللّي فاتَت [ʔinnahar ʔinkirax ʔissana ʔilli faːtat] The river was dredged last year.
كَرِخ [karix] *n:* • **1.** cleaning out (a river, etc), dredging, dredge
كَرّاخَة [karraːxa] *n:* كَرّاخات [karraːxaːt] *pl:* • **1.** dredge
كراخَة [kraːxa] *n:* • **1.** cleaning out (a river, etc), dredge

ك ر خ ل

كَرخَلَة [čarxala] *n:* كَرخَلات [čarxalaːt] *pl:* • **1.** a spin, turn, revolution – إنطِي الأَرقام كَرخَلَة زينَة قَبُل ما تجُرّ [ʔinṭi ʔilʔarqaːm čarxala ziːna gabul maː dǰurr] Give the numbers a good spin before you draw. خَلّي ناخذ إلنا فَدّ جَرخَلَة بالسُّوق بَلكِي نِلقِيه [xalli: naːxuð ʔilna fadd čarxala bissuːg balki nilgiːh] Let's take ourselves a spin around the marketplace and perhaps we'll find him.

ك ر خ ن

كَرخانَة [karxaːna] *n:* كَرخانات، كَرخايِن [karxaːnaːt, karxaːyin] *pl:* • **1.** factory, workshop • **2.** brothel, whore-house
كَرخَنجِي [karxanči] *adj:* كَرخَنجِيَّة [karxančiyya] *pl:* • **1.** pimp, panderer, procurer

ك ر د

كَرِد [čarid] *n:* كرُود [čruːd] *pl:* • **1.** cigar
كُردِي [kurdi] *adj:* أكرَاد [ʔakraːd] *pl:* • **1.** Kurdish • **2.** (pl. كُرِد [kurid] أكرَاد) Kurd, person from Kurdistan

ك ر د غ

كِرداغ [čirdaːɣ] *n:* كَرادِيغ [čaraːdiːɣ] *pl:* • **1.** summer cabin, a hut built on the river

ك ر ر [1]

كَرَّر [karrar] *v:* • **1.** to repeat, reiterate, do again, do repeatedly – كَرِّر كُلّ كِلمَة أَقُولها [karrir kull čilma ʔaguːlha] Repeat each word I say.
تكَرَّر [tkarrar] *v:* • **1.** to be repeated, to recur – أَواعدَك هالغَلطَة بَعَد ما تِتكَرَّر [ʔawaːʕdak halɣalṭa baʕd maː titkarrar] I promise you this error won't recur any more.
تِكرار [tikraːr] *n:* • **1.** repetition
مُكَرَّر [mukarrar] *adj:* • **1.** repeated, reiterated – رَقَم تَلِفُونَه خَمسَة، مُكَرَّر أَربَعَة، ثنين، واحِد [raqam talifuːnah xamsa, mukarrar ʔarbaʕa, θnayn, waːħid] Our phone number is five, four, four, two, one.
مِتكَرِّر [mitkarrir] *adj:* • **1.** recurring, repeated

ك ر ر [2]

تكرِير [takriːr] *n:* • **1.** refinery (oil) • **2.** cooking or roasting twice

ك ر ز

كَرَّز [karraz, čarraz] *v:* • **1.** to eat seeds or small nuts by cracking them and separating the hulls in the mouth – عِيب تكَرِّز حَبّ بالسِّينَما [ʕiːb tčarriz ħabb bissinama] Shame on you eating seeds in the movie theater.
كَرَز [karaz, čaraz] *n:* كَرَزات [čarazaːt] *pl:* • **1.** mixed nuts, seeds – مَحَلّ كَرَزات [maħall čarazaːt] nut store.
كَرَز [karaz, čaraz] *n:* • **1.** cherry, cherries • **2.** nuts
كَرَزَة [karaza] *n:* كَرزات [karzaːt] *pl:* • **1.** cherry
كَرَزات [karazaːt, čarazaːt] *n:* • **1.** generic term for edible nuts

ك

ك ر س

كَرَّس [čarras] *v:* • **1.** to daydream, be distracted, let one's attention wander – طَبعاً ما تُعرُف إذا تكَرِّس بِالصَّفّ [ṭabʕan maː tuʕruf ʔiða tčarris biṣṣaff] Of course you won't know if you daydream in class.
كَرَّس [karras] *v:* • **1.** to devote, consecrate, dedicate
كُرسِي [kursi] *n:* كَراسِي [karaːsi] *pl:* • **1.** chair
كُورس [kuːrs] *n:* • **1.** course
كُرّاسَة [kurraːsa] *n:* كُرّاسات [kurraːsaːt] *pl:* • **1.** a penmanship book traditionally used to teach school children to write Arabic • **2.** pamphlet, brochure
تَكرِيس [takriːs] *n:* • **1.** devoting, dedication, consecration
كَرسِي [čarsi] *adj:* كَرسِيَّة [čarsiyya] *pl:* • **1.** daydreamer • **2.** absentminded person

ك ر س ت

كَرَستَة [karasta] *n:* • **1.** (invar.) the solid material of which anything is constructed, foundation substance – اِستَعمِلَوا خُوش كَرَستَة بِبِناء هَالبَيت [ʔistaʕmilaw xuːš karasta bbinaːʔ halbayt] They used good materials in building this house. • **2.** solid, well-built, soundly constructed – السَّيّارات الألمانِيَّة كَرَستَة [ʔissayyaːraːt ʔilʔalmaːniyya karasta] German automobiles are solidly constructed.

ك ر س ي

كُورسِي [kuːrsi] *n:* كُورسِيات [kursiyyaːt] *pl:* • **1.** corset (closely fitting undergarment worn by women for support)

ك ر ش

كَرِش [kariš] *n:* كرُوش [kruːš] *pl:* • **1.** pot belly, bay window, paunch – صار عِندَه كَرِش مِن قَدّ ما ياكُل تِمَّن [ṣaːr ʕindah kariš min gadd maː yaːkul timman] He got a pot belly from eating so much rice.
كِرشَة، كَرشَة [kirša, karša] *n:* كِرَش [kiraš] *pl:* • **1.** stomach (of an animal), tripe • **2.** calf (of the leg)

ك ر ع

كراع [kraːʕ] *n:* كراعِين، كراعات، كِرعان [kraːʕiːn, kraːʕaːt, kirʕaːn] *pl:* • **1.** lower leg and foot of a cow or sheep (esp. as food)

ك ر ف

كِرَف [kiraf] *v:* • **1.** to pick up, scoop up (something) and take it away – أكرُف الرَّمُل وذِبَّه بِاللُّوري [ʔukruf ʔirramul wðibbah billuːri] Scoop up the sand and throw it in the truck. أكرُف التِّراب كُلَّه [ʔukruf ʔittiraːb kullah] Gather up all the dirt and take it out. جَت الشُّرطَة وَكِرفَتهُم كُلّهُم [ǰat ʔiššurṭa wkirfathum kullhum] The police came and picked them all up and took them away.
اِنكِرَف [ʔinkiraf] *v:* • **1.** pass. of كِرَف : to be picked up – هَالتِراب ما ينكِنِس؛ لازم ينكُرُف بالإيد [halʔitraːb maː yinkinis; laːzim yinkuruf bilʔiːd] This dirt can't be swept; it must be gathered up by hand.
كَرُف [karuf] *n:* • **1.** picking up, scooping up and taking away • **2.** in a bunch, as a group – نبِيع المِشمِش كَرُف، مُو مِستَنقَى [nbiːʕ ʔilmišmiš karuf, muː mistanga] We sell apricots in lots, not singly.
مُكرافَة [mukraːfa] *n:* مُكرافات [mukraːfaːt] *pl:* • **1.** scooping device • **2.** dust pan

ك ر ف ت

كَرفَت [karfat] *v:* • **1.** to shove, force, cram, crowd – دَيكَرفِت الجَّهّال بِالباص وَمابُقَى مُكان [daykarfit ʔiǰǰahhaːl bilpaːṣ wma buqaː mukaːn] He's cramming the kids into the bus and there's no room left. كَرفِتوه بِالسِّجِن [karfituːh bissiǰin] They threw him in prison.

ك ر ف س

كرَفُس [krafus] *n:* • **1.** celery

ك ر ك 1

كِرَك [kirak] *v:* • **1.** (fowl) to brood, quit laying, go into lethargy – دِجاجَتنا راح تُكرُك بَعَد يومَين [diǰaːǰatna raːħ tukruk baʕad yaymayn] Our hen will be brooding in two days. • **2.** (fowl) to brood, sit on or incubate (eggs), to dwell on
كَرَّك [karrak] *v:* • **1.** same as كِرَك, (fowl) to brood, sit on or incubate (eggs), to dwell on – دِجاجنا كُلَّه كَرَّك [diǰaːǰna kullah karrak] All our chickens quit laying.
كُرُك [kuruk] *n:* • **1.** brooding, incubating (eggs)
كُرَكجِي [čurakči] *n:* • **1.** baker

ك ر ك 2

كَرَك [karak] *n:* كَرَكات [karakaːt] *pl:* • **1.** shovel, scoop

ك ر ك 3

كارَك [čaːrak] *n:* كوارِيك [čwaːriːk] *pl:* • **1.** one-fourth, a quarter – كارَك ساعَة [čaːrak saːʕa] a quarter hour. • **2.** one-fourth – اِشتِرِي كارَك شعِير لِلدِّجاج [ʔištiri čaːrak šʕiːr liddiǰaːǰ] Buy six kilograms of barley for the chickens.

ك ر ك 4

كُرَك [čurak] *n:* • **1.** (coll.) a kind of bread, shaped like a pretzel
كُركَة، كُركايَة [čurka, čurkaːya] *n:* كُركات [čurkaːt] *pl:* • **1.** kind of bread
كُرُك [čuruk] *adj:* • **1.** (invar.) bad, no good, undesirable – هَالرّاديُو طِلَع كُرُك [harraːdyuː ṭilaʕ čuruk] This radio has turned out to be a bad one. هَالبِنَيَّة كُرُك؛ عَليها حَكِي هوايَة [halbnayya čuruk; ʕaliːha

ك

ħači hwa:ya] That girl's no good; there's a lot of talk about her.

ك ر ك ب

كَركَب [čarčab] *v:* • **1.** to put into a frame, to frame – كَركَب الصُّورَة وخَلّاها عالميز [čarčab ʔiṣṣu:ra wxalla:ha ʕalmi:z] He framed the picture and put it on the table.

كَركُوبَة [čarču:ba] *n:* كَركُوبات، كَراكِيب [čarču:ba:t, čara:či:b] *pl:* • **1.** picture frame

ك ر ك د ن

كَركَدَن، حَيوان الكَركَدَن [karkadan, ħaywa:n ʔilkarkadan] *n:* • **1.** rhinoceros

ك ر ك ر

كَركَر [karkar] *v:* • **1.** to laugh noisily, guffaw – كَركَر هوايَة عالنُّكتَة مالتَك [karkar hwa:ya ʕannukta ma:ltak] He guffawed a lot over your joke. • **2.** to giggle – البَنات ظَلَّوا يكَركِرُون [ʔilbana:t ðallaw ykarkiru:n] The girls kept on giggling.

تكَركِر [tkirkir] *n:* • **1.** laughing noisily, guffawing

كَركَرَة [karkara] *n:* • **1.** laughing noisily, guffawing

مكَركِر [mkarkir] *adj:* • **1.** laughing (person)

ك ر ك ش

كَركُوشَة [karku:ša] *n:* كَراكِيش [kara:ki:š] *pl:* • **1.** tassel – عِندي خاولِي بيه كَراكِيش طويلَة [ʕindi xa:wli bi:h kara:ki:š ṭwi:la] I've got a towel that has long tassels on it.

ك ر ك م

كُركُم [kurkum] *n:* • **1.** turmeric

ك ر م

كِرَم [kiram] *v:* • **1.** to be generous – آنِي ما إشتِرَيت هَالكِتاب. صَدِيقي كِرَملِي إيّاه [ʔa:ni ma: ʔištiri:t halkita:b. ṣadi:qi kiramli ʔiyya:h] I didn't buy this book. My friend gave it to me. تِقدَر تِكرُمنِي سَيّارتَك مُوَقَّتاً؟ [tigdar tikrumni sayya:rtak muwaqqatan?] Could you lend me your car for a short time?

كَرَّم [karram] *v:* • **1.** to honor, venerate, treat with deference – العَرَب يكَرِّمُون الضَّيف [ʔilʕarab ykarrimu:n ʔiððayf] The Arabs treat their guests with great deference. مُدَّة بَقائِي بِبَغداد كَرَّمنِي وَعَزَّزنِي كُلِّش [muddat baqa:ʔi bibaɣda:d karramni wʕazzazni kulliš] During my stay in Baghdad, he was extremely nice to me.

تكَرَّم [tkarram] *v:* • **1.** to show generosity – تكَرَّم عَلينا بِرَأيَك [tkarram ʕali:na braʔyak] Honor us with your opinion.

كَرَم [karam] *n:* • **1.** generosity, magnanimity, liberality, munificence

كَرامَة [kara:ma] *n:* • **1.** nobility, honor, dignity • **2.** respect, esteem, standing, prestige

مَكرَمَة [makrama] *n:* • **1.** noble deed, reward, bonus

تَكرِيم [takri:m] *n:* • **1.** honoring, tribute

إكرامِيَّة [ʔikra:miyya] *n:* إكرامِيّات [ʔikra:miyya:t] *pl:* • **1.** bonus • **2.** tangible token of gratitude

كَرِيم [kari:m] *adj:* كُرَماء [kurama:ʔ] *pl:* • **1.** generous, munificent, liberal, magnanimous, beneficent • **2.** noble, distinguished, eminent

أكرَم [ʔakram] *comparative adjective:* • **1.** more or most generous

ك ر م ش

كَرمَش [karmaš] *v:* • **1.** to become wrinkled – وُجَّه كَرمَش مِن الكُبُر [wuččah karmaš min ʔilkubur] His face became wrinkled from old age.

كَرمَشَة [karmaša] *n:* • **1.** wrinkle

مكَرمُش [mkarmuš] *adj:* • **1.** wrinkled

ك ر ن

كرَين [krayn] *n:* • **1.** crane

ك ر ن ت ي

كَرَنتِي [garanti] *n:* كَرَنتِيّات [garantiyya:t] *pl:* • **1.** guarantee

ك ر ن ق

قرُنقَة [črunga, srunga] *n:* كرُنجات [črunqa:t, srunqa:t] *pl:* • **1.** syringe, hypodermic syringe. Also written جرُنقَة [črunga]

ك ر ه

كِرَه [kirah] *v:* • **1.** to hate, detest, loathe, abhor – لُويش تِكرَه أبُوك؟ [luwi:š tikrah ʔabu:k?] Why do you hate your father?

كَرَّه [karrah] *v:* • **1.** to make hate, cause to hate – ظَلّ يذِمّ التَّدخِين إلَى أن كَرَّهنِي إيّاه [ðall yðimm ʔittadxi:n ʔila ʔan karrahni ʔiyya:h] He kept saying bad things about smoking until he made me hate it. كَرَّه نَفسَه بِإنتِقاداتَه [karrah nafsah bʔintiqa:da:tah] He made himself hated with his criticisms.

أكرَه [ʔakrah] *v:* • **1.** to force, compel, coerce – أكرَهنِي عَلَى هَالعَمَل [ʔakrahni ʕala halʕamal] He forced me into this deed.

تكارَه [tka:rah] *v:* • **1.** to hate each other – كانَوا أصدِقاء، لَكِن مِن شِهَد ضِدَّه، تكارهَوا [ča:naw ʔaṣdiqa:ʔ, la:kin min šihad ðiddah, tka:rhaw] They were friends, but since he testified against him, they hate each other.

اِنكِرَه [ʔinkirah] *v:* • **1.** pass. of كِرَه : to be detested, to be hated – اِنكِرَه مِن كُلّ النّاس [ʔinkirah min kull ʔinna:s] He was hated by everyone.

كُرُه [kuruh] *n:* • **1.** hate, hatred, detestation, aversion, repugnance, loathing

ك

كَراهَة [kara:ha] *n:* • **1.** dislike, aversion, antipathy, detestation,abhorrence • **2.** hate, hatred
كَراهِيَّة [kara:hiyya] *n:* كَراهِيّات [kara:hiyya:t] *pl:* • **1.** aversion, antipathy, dislike, distaste, disgust, repugnance,
كَرِيه [kari:h] *adj:* • **1.** loathsome, repugnant, offensive, disgusting, odious
مَكرُوه [makru:h] *adj:* • **1.** offensive, hated, detested, disgusting, repugnant • **1.** unpleasant, distasteful, disagreeable, reprehensible

ك ر و
كِرا [kira:] *v:* • **1.** to dig
كُرَة [kura] *n:* كُرات [kura:t] *pl:* • **1.** ball, globe, sphere – كُرَة القَدَم [kurat ʔilqadam] soccer (game). الكُرَة الأَرضِيَّة [ʔilkura ʔilʔarðiyya] the world globe.
كُرَيَّة [kurayya] *n:* كُرَيّات [kurayya:t] *pl:* • **1.** small ball, globule • **2.** corpuscle
كَرَوِي [kurawi] *adj:* • **1.** global, spherical, ball-shaped

ك ر و ب
كارُوب [ka:ru:b] *n:* • **1.** a large, beetle-like insect

ك ر و ت
كَرَوِيتَة [karawi:ta] *n:* كَرَوِيتات [karawita:t] *pl:* • **1.** couch, sofa

ك ر و ك
كارُوك [ka:ru:k] *n:* كوارِيك [kwa:ri:k] *pl:* • **1.** baby cradle

ك ر و م
كرُوم [kru:m] *n:* • **1.** chromium

ك ر ي 1
كِرَى [kira:] *v:* • **1.** to rent, lease, hire out – هَالمَحَلّ يِكرِي بايسِكلات [halmaħall yikri pa:ysikla:t] This place rents out bicycles. • **2.** to rent, lease, hire – راح أَكرِي بايسِكِل ساعَة وِحدَة [ra:ħ ʔakri pa:ysikil sa:ʕa wiħda] I will hire a bicycle for one hour. • **3.** to dredge, deepen, dig out (a canal, river, etc.) – الحُكُومَة راح تِكرِي هَالجَدوَل [ʔilħuku:ma ra:ħ tikri hajjadwal] The government will dredge out this canal.
كَري [kary] *n:* • **1.** renting, leasing, hiring out
كَروَة [karwa] *n:* كَروات، كَراوِي [karwa:t, kara:wi] *pl:* • **1.** fare, charge, fee, rent, rental fee

ك ر ي 2
كاري [ka:ri] *n:* • **1.** (in poker) four of a kind

ك ر ي 3
مكارِي [mča:ri] *n:* مكارِيَّة [mča:riyya] *pl:* • **1.** muleteer, donkey driver

ك ر ي 4
كارِي [ka:ri] *n:* • **1.** curry, curry powder

ك ر ي م
كريم [kri:m] *n:* • **1.** cream, cold cream
كريمَة [kri:ma] *n:* كريمات [kri:ma:t] *pl:* • **1.** a pudding made of milk, eggs, and sugar

ك ز ب ر
كَزبَر [kazbar] *v:* • **1.** to cause a creepy sensation – شِكِلها يكَزبُر الجِّلِد [šikilha ykazbur ʔijjilid] Her looks make your skin crawl.
كُزبَرَة [kuzbara] *n:* • **1.** coriander

ك ز ز 1
كَزّ [čazz] *v:* • **1.** to mark over, cross out – ما عِندِي مَسّاحَة. تِقدَر تكِزّ الكِلمَة بالقَلَم [ma: ʕindi massa:ħa. tigdar tčizz ʔiččilma bilqalam] I don't have an eraser. You can cross out the word with the pencil. • **2.** to squeak – قُندَرتِي الجِّدِيدَة تكِزّ [qundarti ʔijjidi:da tčizz] My new shoes squeak.

ك ز ز 2
كزّاز [gazza:z, guzza:z] *n:* • **1.** tetanus

ك ز ك ت
كازكِيتَة [gazgi:ta] *n:* كازكِيتات [ga:zgi:ta:t] *pl:* • **1.** gasket

ك ز ن و
كازِينُو [gazi:nu] *n:* كازِينَوات، كازِينات [gazi:nawa:t, gazi:na:t] *pl:* • **1.** night club, casino

ك س
كاسَة [ka:sa] *n:* كاسات [ka:sa:t] *pl:* • **1.** bowl

ك س ب
كِسَب [kisab] *v:* • **1.** to win, gain – كِسَب هوايَة بِالبُوكَر البارحَة [kisab hwa:ya bilpu:kar ʔilba:rħa] He won a lot at poker yesterday. • **2.** to acquire, to earn
كَسَّب [kassab] *v:* • **1.** to beat, win out over – لِعَب وِيّانا مَرَّة وِحدَة وَكَسَّبنا كُلّنا [liʕab wiyya:na marra wiħda wkassabna kullna] He played with us one time and won all our money. • **2.** to win, gain – إبنِي كَسَّب هوايَة بلِعب الدُعبُل [ʔibni kassab hwa:ya bliʕb ʔidduʕbul] My son won a lot playing marbles.
تكَسَّب [tkassab] *v:* • **1.** to earn a living, work for profit (esp. in a private business) – دَيِتكَسَّب عَلَى باب الله [dayitkassab ʕala ba:b ʔallah] He is making a living by the grace of God.
اِكتِسَب [ʔiktisab] *v:* • **1.** to acquire, obtain, take on – اِكتِسَب العِلِم بِالجّامِعَة [ʔiktisab ʔilʕilim bijja:miʕa] He acquired the knowledge at the university.

كِسِب [kisib] *n:* • **1.** gain, profit, winnings – كِسِبهُم بِالقمار كان شوَيَّة [kisibhum bilqmaːr čaːn šwayya] Their winnings at gambling were small. إذا أبيعها بمِيَة دِينار، ما بِيها كِسِب [ʔiða ʔabiːʕha bmiyat dinaːr, maː biːha kisib] If you sell it for a hundred dinars, there won't be a profit in it.

كِسبَة [kisba] *n:* • **1.** oil cake, meal from vegetables after they have been dehydrated

مَكسَب [maksab] *n:* مَكاسِب [makaːsib] *pl:* • **1.** earnings • **2.** gain, profit

اِكتِساب [ʔiktisaːb] *n:* • **1.** acquisition, gaining, winning

كاسِب [kaːsib] *adj:* كَسَبَة [kasaba] *pl:* • **1.** winner • **2.** earner, provider • **3.** independent businessman

مِكتِسِب [miktisib] *adj:* • **1.** acquired, gained

ك س ت م

كُوستِم [kustiːm] *n:* كُوستِمات [kustimaːt] *pl:* • **1.** (woman's) attire, outfit, get-up

ك س ت ن

كستانَة [kistaːna, kastaːna] *n:* • **1.** chestnut(s)

كِستانايَة [kistaːnaːya] *n:* كَستَنايات [kastanaːyaːt] *pl:* • **1.** chestnut

كَستَنائِي [kastanaːʔi] *adj:* • **1.** chestnut (color)

ك س ح

كَسَّح [kassaħ] *v:* • **1.** to throw out, get rid of, chuck out, bounce – اِنطِيه الكِتاب وَكَسّحَه [ʔinṭi ʔilkitaːb wkassħah] Give him the book and get rid of him. بُقَى بِالوَظِيفَة مُدَّة شَهَر وَبَعدين كَسِّحُوه [buqaː bilwaðiːfa muddat šahar wbaʕdiːn kassiħuːh] He remained in the position for a month and then they sacked him.

تكَسَّح [tkassaħ] *v:* • **1.** to leave, get out, beat it – تكَسَّح! إحنا ما نخاف مِنَّك [tkassaħ! ʔiħna maː nxaːf minnak] Scram! We're not afraid of you. اِنطِيه فلُوس وَخَلِّيه يِتكَسَّح [ʔinṭi fluːs wxalliːh yitkassaħ] Give him some money and let him get lost.

اِكتِسَح [ʔiktisaħ] *v:* • **1.** to overrun, sweep across, spread over – الجَّيش اِكتِسَح الجَّزِيرَة [ʔijjayš ʔiktisaħ ʔijjaziːra] The army overran the island. المَرَض اِكتِسَح الجُّنُوب كُلَّه [ʔilmarað ʔiktisaħ ʔijjunuːb kullah] The disease spread over the whole South. • **2.** to flood, inundate, sweep across – ماي الفَيَضان اِكتِسَح الوِلايَة [maːy ʔilfayaðaːn ʔiktisaħ ʔilwilaːya] The flood waters swept over the city.

كُساح، مَرَض الكُساح [kusaːħ, marað ʔilkusaːħ] *n:* • **1.** rickets (bone-softening disease of children, caused by a vitamin D deficiency).

كاسِح [kaːsiħ] *adj:* • **1.** overwhelming, sweeping everything away

كَسِيح [kasiħ] *adj:* • **1.** lame, palsied, paralyzed

ك س د

كِسَد [kisad] *v:* • **1.** to sell badly, move slowly, find no market – هَالبَضايِع إذا ما نباعَت بالمَوسِم، تِكسَد [halbaðaːyiʕ ʔiða maː nbaːʕat bilmawsim, tiksad] If these goods aren't sold in season, there won't be a market for them.

كَسَّد [kassad] *v:* • **1.** with عَلَى to hurt, injure, damage – لَو ما تِحكِي ويّاها، كان دَترُوح ويّايا. إنتَ كَسَّدِت عَلَيّا [law maː tiħči wiyyaːha, čaːn datruːħ wiyyaːya. ʔinta kassadit ʕalayya] If you hadn't talked with her, she would have gone with me. You spoiled it for me. إذا يفَتِّح قبالنا، راح يكَسِّد علينا [ʔiða yfattiħ gbaːlna, raːħ ykassid ʕaliːna] If he opens up across from us, he will ruin our business.

كَساد [kasaːd] *n:* • **1.** depression, recession, slump, economic stagnation. slow day – اليُوم كَساد. ما بِعنا كُلّ شِي [ʔilyuːm kasaːd. maː biʕna kull ši] There's no business today. We haven't sold a thing.

كاسِد [kaːsid] *adj:* • **1.** selling badly, listless (market)

ك س ر

كِسَر [kisar] *v:* • **1.** to break, shatter, fracture – الجّاهِل كِسَر الماعُون [ʔijjaːhil kisar ʔilmaːʕuːn] The child broke the plate. راح يكِسرُون السَّدَّة شِمال بَغداد [raːħ yikisruːn ʔissadda šimaːl baɣdaːd] They are going to break the levee north of Baghdad. • **2.** to break (fig.) – كِسَر وَعدَه ويّايا [kisar waʕdah wiyyaːya] He broke his promise to me. كِسَر الرَّقم القِياسِي بِركض المِيَة مَتِر [kisar ʔirraqm ʔilqiyaːsi brikð ʔilmiyat matir] He broke the record in the 100-meter dash. المُعَلِّم كِسَر مُعَدَّلِي بِهالدَّرَجَة [ʔilmuʕallim kisar muʕaddali bhaddaraja] The teacher ruined my average with that grade. حالتَه تِكسِر القَلُب [ħaːltah tiksir ʔilgalub] His situation is heartbreaking. هَالسَّيّارَة كِسرَت عينِي. بَعَد ما أشتِري سَيّارَة مُستَعمَلَة أبَداً [hassayyaːra kisrat ʕiːni. baʕad maː ʔaštiri sayyaːra mustaʕmila ʔabadan] This car's been a pain in the neck to me. I'll never buy a used car again. مَحَّد كِسَر عَين هالمُلاحِظ إلّا المُدِير الجِّدِيد [maħħad kisar ʕayn halmulaːħið ʔilla ʔilmudiːr ʔijjidiːd] No one put the supervisor in his place except the new director. ما يِسكُت إلّا لَمّا أكسِر عَينَه [maː yiskut ʔilla lamma ʔaksir ʕaynah] He won't shut up until I take him down a peg. • **3.** to defeat, rout – الدِّيك مالِي كِسَر دِيك عَلِي [ʔiddiːč maːli kisar diːč ʕali] My rooster defeated Ali's rooster. ولد محَلّتنا كِسرَوا ولد محَلّتكُم [wild mħallatna kisraw wild mħallatkum] The kids in our neighborhood beat up the kids in your neighborhood. • **4.** to bankrupt, to break – إذا يظَلُّون يبِيعُون رِخِيص راح يكِسرُونا [ʔiða yðalluːn ybiːʕuːn rixiːṣ raːħ ykisruːna] If they keep on selling cheap they're going to break us. • **5.** to break open, cut open – إكسِر رَقِّيَّة وِحدَة بَسّ

[ʔiksir raggiyya wiħda bass] Cut only one watermelon.
كَسَّر [kassar] *v:* • **1.** to break up – دَيكَسِّر جُوز وَياكُل اللُّب [daykassir ǰuːz wyaːkul ʔillibb] He is breaking walnuts and eating the meats. كَسِّر هالخِشَب حَتَّى نشِعلَه بِالشِّتا [kassir halxišab ħatta nšiʕlah biššita] Cut up this wood so we can burn it during the winter. • **2.** to shatter, smash – ضِرَب الكُوب عَالحايِط وَكَسَّرَه [ðirab ʔilkuːb ʕalħaːyiṭ wkassarah] He threw the cup against the wall and smashed it. • **3.** to calculate, figure out – هَسَّة أكَسِّرلك إيّاها [hassa ʔakassirlak ʔiyyaːha] Now I'll calculate it for you.
كاسَر [kaːsar] *v:* • **1.** to pit against each other, to set against each other – جِيب الدِّيك مالَك حَتَّى نكاسرَه وِيّا دِيكِي [ǰiːb ʔiddiːč maːlak ħatta nkaːsrah wiyya diːči] Bring your cock so we can fight him with my cock. بِالشِّمال يكاسرُون القَبِك [biššimaːl ykaːsruːn ʔilqabič] In the North they pit quail against each other. • **2.** to dilute, cut – ما أقدَر أشرَب العَرَق سادَة. كاسِرلي إيّاه بمَيّ [maː ʔagdar ʔašrab ʔilʕarag saːda. kaːsirli ʔiyyaːh bmayy] I can't drink arrack straight. Cut it with water for me. كاسِر المَيّ حَتَّى أقدَر أغسِل بِيه [kaːsir ʔilmayy ħatta ʔagdar ʔaɣsil biːh] Dilute the hot water with some cold water so I can wash with it.
تكَسَّر [tkassar] *v:* • **1.** to be or become broken, shattered, smashed – الماعُون وُقَع مِن إيدِي وَتكَسَّر. صار مِيَّة وُصلَة [ʔilmaːʕuːn wugaʕ min ʔiːdi wtkassar. ṣaːr miyyat wuṣla] The dish fell from my hand and shattered. It's in a hundred pieces. هَالكلاصات تِتكَسَّر بِالعَجَل [halglaːṣaːt titkassar bilʕaǰal] These glasses get broken quickly.
اِنكِسَر [ʔinkisar] *v:* • **1.** to be or become broken – وُقَع الكلاص وَاِنكِسَر [wugaʕ ʔilglaːṣ wʔinkisar] The glass fell and got broken. مُوجَة الحَرّ اِنكِسرَت [muːǰat ʔilħarr ʔinkisrat] The heat wave was broken. قَلبِي اِنكِسَر مِن شِفتَه يِشتُغُل بِالحَرّ [galbi ʔinkisar min šiftah yištuɣul bilħarr] It broke my heart to see him working in the heat. اِنكِسَر خاطرِي عَليه وَاِنطَيتَه دِينار [ʔinkisar xaːṭri ʕaliːh waʔinṭiːtah dinaːr] I took pity on him and gave him a dinar. مِن أكَل ذِيك البَسطَة، اِنكِسرَت عَينَه. بَعَد ما يِلعَب بِالسَّيّارَة [min ʔakal ðiːč ʔalbaṣṭa, ʔinkisrat ʕaynah. baʕad maː yilʕab bissayyaːra] Since he got that beating, he's learned his lesson. He won't play with the car again. اِنكِسرَت عينَك لَو أجِي أبُسطَك بَعَد؟ [ʔinkisrat ʕaynak law ʔaǰi ʔabusṭak baʕad?] Have you had enough or do I have to beat you up again? أدَبسِز. ما تِنكِسِر عَينَه [ʔadabsizz. maː tinkisir ʕaynah] He's got no manners. He can't be shamed. • **2.** to be defeated, be destroyed – اِنكِسَر جيش العَدُو بَعَد مُقاوَمَة قَلِيلَة [ʔinkisar ǰayš ʔilʕadu baʕad muqaːwama qaliːla] The enemy army was defeated after a slight resistance. • **3.** to be bankrupted, be broken – ثلَث تُجّار اِنكِسرَوا هَالشَّهَر [tlaθ tuǰǰaːr ʔinkisraw haššahar] Three merchants went bankrupt this month.
كَسِر [kasir] *n:* كسُور [ksuːr] *pl:* • **1.** break, breach, fracture – كَسِر بِالرِّجِل [kasir birriǰil] a fracture of the leg. • **2.** fraction (arith.) – كَسِر عِشرِي [kasir ʕišri] decimal fraction. يِملُك ألف دِينار وَكسُور [yimluk ʔalf dinaːr wksuːr] He is worth a thousand and some odd dinars. • **3.** bankruptcy – التّاجِر طِلَع كَسِر [ʔittaːǰir ṭilaʕ kasir] The merchant went bankrupt.
كَسرَة [kasra] *n:* كَسرات [kasraːt] *pl:* • **1.** break, breach, fracture
كِسرَة، كَسرَة [kisra, kasra] *n:* كَسرات، كِسَر [kasraːt, kisar] *pl:* • **1.** piece, fragment, chunk
كَسّار [kassaːr] *n:* كَسّارِين [kassaːriːn] *pl:* • **1.** woodcutter • **2.** (wood) cutter
كَسّارَة [kassaːra] *n:* كَسّارات [kassaːraːt] *pl:* • **1.** nutcracker – كَسّارَة جُوز [kassaːrat ǰuːz] walnut cracker. • **2.** crusher – كَسّارَة صَخَر [kassaːrat ṣaxar] rock crusher.
كَسرِيَّة [kasriyya] *n:* • **1.** shotgun, rifle
تكسِير [taksiːr] *n:* • **1.** breaking, fracturing, shattering
اِنكِسار [ʔinkisaːr] *n:* • **1.** breaking, rout • **2.** to go bankrupt
كاسِر [kaːsir] *adj:* • **1.** breaking, shattering – حَيوان كاسِر [ħaywaːn kaːsir] beast of prey. طَير كاسِر [ṭiːr kaːsir] bird of prey. • **2.** predatory (animal), savage, ferocious, rapacious
مكَسَّر [mkassar] *adj:* • **1.** broken, fragmented, shattered, smashed • **2.** broken (also, for language)
مَكسُور [maksuːr] *adj:* • **1.** broken
مِتكَسِّر [mitkassir] *adj:* • **1.** broken
مِنكِسِر [minkisir] *adj:* • **1.** bankrupt • **2.** broken (emotionally)
مكَسِّرات [mkassiraːt, mkassaraːt] *adj:* • **1.** (pl. only) sins, immoral conduct, loose living – عُمرَه خَمسِين سَنَة وَبَعدَه يدَوُّر مكَسِّرات [ʕumrah xamsiːn sana wbaʕdah ydawwur mkassiraːt] He's fifty years old and still leading a wild life.

ك س س

كُسّ [kuss] *n:* كساسَة [ksaːsa] *pl:* • **1.** vulva, vagina • **2.** (by extension; vulgar) woman, girl
كسَيِّس [ksayyis] *n:* • **1.** diminutive of كُسّ : (small) vulva, vagina • **1.** sissy
كَسّاسِي [kassaːsi] *adj:* • **1.** sexy cloth, attractive cloth • **2.** sissy, effeminate

ك س ف

كِسَف [kisaf] *v:* • **1.** to be eclipsed – مِن تِكسِف الشَّمِس، تِظلَمّ الدِّنيا [min tiksif ʔiššamis, tiðlamm ʔiddinya] When the sun is eclipsed, the sky grows dark.
كَسَّف [kassaf] *v:* • **1.** to upbraid, berate, tell off, chew out – راحلَه لِلبَيت وَكَسَّفَه [raːħlah lilbayt wkassafah] He went to him at home and berated him.
تكَسَّف [tkassaf] *v:* • **1.** to be humiliated –

ك

تكَسَّف قِدّام المُوَظَّفِين لِأَنّ شُغلَه طِلَع كُلَّه غَلَط [tkassaf gidda:m ʔilmuwaððafi:n liʔann šuɣlah ṭilaʕ kullah ɣalaṭ] He was humiliated in front of the employees because his work turned out to be all wrong. • **2.** to get into trouble, get in a jam – تكَسَّف بِلَندَن. صِرَف كُلّ فلُوسَه وبُقى مِفلِس [tkassaf blandan. ṣiraf kull flu:sah wbuqa: miflis] He got into trouble in London. He spent all his money and ended up broke. لَك درُوح، تكَسَّف! إِنتَ شِمقَدّرَك تُغلُبنِي بِالشِّطرَنج؟ [lak dru:ħ, tkassaf! ʔinta šimgaddrak tuɣlubni biššiṭranǰ?] Aw go on, beat it! How could you beat me in chess?
كَسافَة [kasa:fa] *n:* كَسافات [kasa:fa:t] *pl:* • **1.** misery, nightmare, fright – العِيشَة بهالقَريَة كَسافَة. لا أَكُو مَطاعِم وَلا كَهرَباء [ʔilʕi:ša bha:lqarya kasa:fa. la: ʔaku maṭa:ʕim wala: kahraba:ʔ] Living in this village is misery. There are neither restaurants nor electricity. الشُّغُل بِهالدّائِرَة كَسافَة [ʔiššuɣul bhadda:ʔira kasa:fa] Working in this office is a nightmare.
كَسِيف [kasi:f] *adj:* • **1.** bad, horrible, horrid, terrible – لُون كَسِيف [lu:n kasi:f] a terrible color. جُملَة كَسِيفَة [ǰumla kasi:fa] a horrible sentence. • **2.** useless, worthless – واحِد كَسِيف [wa:ħid kasi:f] a useless person. حَكِي كَسِيف [ħači kasi:f] idle talk.
كُسُوف [kusu:f] *adj:* • **1.** solar eclipse, eclipse of the sun

ك س ك ت

كَسكِيتَة [kaski:ta] *n:* كَسكِيتات [kaski:ta:t] *pl:* • **1.** cap with a visor

ك س ك ن

كَسكَن [kaskan] *v:* • **1.** to be or become angry, irritated, annoyed – هَذا عَصَبِي؛ يكَسكِن بِالعَجَل [ha:ða ʕaṣabi; ykaskin bilʕaǰal] He's irritable; he gets annoyed quickly. • **2.** to be or become aroused, excited, get hot – يكَسكِن عَلَى هَالحَكِي [ykaskin ʕala halħači] He gets a charge out of that talk.
كَسكِين [kaski:n] *adj:* • **1.** strong – تِتِن كَسكِين [titin kaski:n] strong tobacco. شاي كَسكِين [ča:y kaski:n] strong tea. • **2.** spicy, hot – أَكِل كَسكِين [ʔakil kaski:n] spicy food. • **3.** sharp – حَكِي كَسكِين [ħači kaski:n] sharp words.

ك س ل

كَسَّل [kassal] *v:* • **1.** to make lazy – جَوّ البَصرَة يكَسِّل الواحِد [ǰaww ʔilbaṣra ykassil ʔilwa:ħid] The weather in Basra makes one lazy.
تكاسَل [tka:sal] *v:* • **1.** to be lazy, sluggish, indolent, become discouraged – لا تِتكاسَل. خَلِّص شُغلَك [la: titka:sal. xalliṣ šuɣulak] Don't be lazy. Finish your work. المَسافَة طُوِيلَة وماعِندِي سَيّارَة. تكاسَلِت [ʔilmasa:fa ṭuwi:la wma:ʕindi sayya:ra. tka:salit] It's a long way and I don't have a car. I just decided it wasn't worth it.
كَسَل [kasal] *n:* • **1.** laziness, idleness, inactivity, indolence, loafing
كَسلَة [kasla] *n:* كَسلات [kasla:t] *pl:* • **1.** traditional outing, group picnic
كَسلان [kasla:n] *adj:* كَسالَة، كَسلانِين [kasla:ni:n, kasa:la] *pl:* • **1.** lazy, indolent – تِلمِيذ كَسلان [tilmi:ð kasla:n] a lazy student. الحَيوان الكَسلان، حَيوان الكَسلان [ʔilħaywa:n ʔilkasla:n, ħaywa:n ʔilkasla:n] sloth, tree sloth. • **2.** lazy person
أَكسَل [ʔaksal] *comparative adjective:* • **1.** more or most indolent, lazy

ك س م

كِسَم [kisam] *v:* • **1.** to shape, fashion (something)
كَسِم [kasim] *n:* • **1.** cut, style (of a dress) clothing, clothes, costume, fashion, form, shape, manner, mode
تكسِيم [tagsi:m] *n:* • **1.** forming, shaping, fashioning, molding
مكَسَّم [mgassam] *adj:* • **1.** well-shaped, shapely

ك س و

كِسوَة [čiswa] *n:* كِسوات، كِسَو [čiswa:t, čisaw] *pl:* • **1.** bathing suit, swimming trunks

ك س ي

كَسَّى [čassa:] *v:* • **1.** to lose one's nerve, become frightened, back down, turn tail – هِجَم عَلَيّا بالخَنجَر، وَمِن شاف بِيدِي مُسَدَّس، كَسَّى [hiǰam ʕalayya bilxanǰar, wamin ša:f bi:di musaddas, čassa:] He attacked me with a dagger, but when he saw the pistol in my hand, he lost his enthusiasm. الكَلِب رِكَض عَلَيّا لَكِن مِن شِلت العُودَة، كَسَّى [ʔiččalib rikað ʕalayya la:kin min šilt ʔilʕu:da, čassa:] The dog ran at me, but when I picked up the stick, he cringed away. • **2.** to quiet down, shut up, be quiet, be still – ما تكَسِّي عاد؟ مُو ضَوَّجتنا؟ [ma: tčassi ʕa:d? mu: ðawwaǰtina?] Why don't you shut up? Haven't you annoyed us enough? • **3.** to become tired, worn out, run down – مِشَى مِيلَين وَكَسَّى [miša: mi:layn wčassa:] He walked two miles and got pooped out. الباترِي دَيكَسِّي عِندِي [ʔilpa:tri dayčassi: ʕindi] The battery is going dead on me.

ك ش ت ب ن

كُشتُبان [kuštuba:n, kištiba:n, kišitba:n] *n:* كِشِتبانات [kišitba:na:t] *pl:* • **1.** thimble

ك ش خ

كِشَخ [kišax] *v:* • **1.** to show off, be boastful, boast, brag – كِشَخ بسَيّارتَه الجِّدِيدَة [kišax bsayya:rtah ʔiǰǰidi:da] He showed off with his new car. لا تِكشَخ براسِي. آنِي أَعُرفَك شِنُو إِنتَ [la: tikšax bra:si.

ʔaːni ʔaʕurfak šinuː ʔinta] Don't go showing off to me. I know what you are. • **2.** with بـ to waste, squander – كِشَخ بِالفلُوس اللّي تدايَنها [kišax bilfiluːs ʔilli ddaːyanha] He squandered the money he borrowed.

كَشخَة [kašxa] *n:* • **1.** showing off, bragging, boasting – يِحكِي كَشخَة. كُلّ حَكيَه بالمَلايِين [yiħči kašxa. kull ħačyah bilmalaːyiːn] He talks big. Everything is millions with him. عَلَى وَيش هَالكَشخَة؟ يَعنِي مَحّد عِندَه بايسِكِل؟ [ʕala wiːš halkašxa? yaʕni maħħad ʕindah paːysikil?] Why this showing off? Are you the only one who has a bicycle? • **2.** fine, impressive, sharp – سَيّارَة كَشخَة [sayyaːra kašxa] an impressive car. بَيت كَشخَة [bayt kašxa] a fine house. اليُوم إنتَ طالِع كَشخَة بِهَالبَدلَة [ʔilyuːm ʔinta ṭaːliʕ kašxa bhalbadla] Today you are looking sharp in that suit.

كَشّاخ [kaššaːx] *adj:* كَشّاخِين، كَشّاخَة [kaššaːxiːn, kaššaːxa] *pl:* • **1.** show-off, braggart

كاشِخ [kaːšix] *adj:* • **1.** elegant

ك ش د

كَشِيدَة [kašiːda] *n:* كَشايِد [kašaːyid] *pl:* • **1.** fez wrapped with a thick, colored cloth

ك ش ر

كَشَّر [kaššar] *v:* • **1.** to bare one's teeth – إذا يكَشِّر البَزُّون يَعنِي غَضبان [ʔiða ykaššir ʔilbazzuːn yaʕni ɣaðbaːn] If a cat shows its teeth, it means he's mad.

كِشرَة [kišra] *n:* • **1.** grimace

تَكشِيرَة [takšiːra] *n:* • **1.** a flash of the teeth

ك ش ش

كَشّ [kašš] *v:* • **1.** to shoo, shoo away – كِشّ الدِّجاج. راح ياكلُون التِّمَّن كُلَّه [kišš ʔiddijaːj. raːħ yaːkluːn ʔittimman kullah] Shoo the chickens. They're going to eat all the rice. • **2.** (in chess) to check – راح أكِشّ المَلِك [raːħ ʔakišš ʔilmalik] I'm going to check the king.

اِنكَشّ [ʔinkašš] *v:* • **1.** to be shooed, be shooed away – الذِّبّان ما دَينكَشّ. أكُشَّه ويرجَع [ʔiððibbaːn maː dayinkašš. ʔakuššah wyirjaʕ] The flies can't be shooed away. I shoo them off and they come back. ظَلّ يِحكِي وَما إنكَشّ إلَى نُصّ اللَّيل [ðall yiħči wamaː ʔinkašš ʔila nuṣṣ ʔillayl] He kept talking and didn't leave until midnight.

كَشّ [kašš] *n:* • **1.** shooing away

كَشَّة [kašša] *n:* كَشّات [kaššaːt] *pl:* • **1.** a shooing, shooing off, shooing away

كِشّ [kišš] *n:* • **1.** shooing, shooing off, shooing away • **2.** checking, check (chess) – كِشّ مات [kišš maːt] checkmate.

مَكشُوش [makšuːš] *adj:* • **1.** checked, in check (chess)

ك ش ف

كِشَف [kišaf] *v:* • **1.** to uncover, unveil, remove a covering – كِشفَت وُجهها حَتَّى تشُوف السِّمَك زين [kišfat wuččha ħatta tšuːf ʔissimač ziːn] She uncovered her face to see the fish well. • **2.** to disclose, reveal – أرجُوك، إكِشفِلِي وَرَقَك [ʔarjuːk, ʔikšifli waraqak] Show me your cards, please. • **3.** to examine (medically) – الطَّبِيب كِشَف عَلَيّا بَسّ ما لِقَى شِي [ʔiṭṭabiːb kišaf ʕalayya bass maː ligaː ši] The doctor examined me but didn't find anything. • **4.** to fade – هَالقُماش يِكشِف؟ [halqumaːš yikšif?] Does this cloth fade? هَالثُّوب لونَه كاشِف [haθθuːb luːnah kaːšif] This shirt has faded. • **5.** with عَلَى to study, scrutinize, investigate, examine – اللُّجنَة راح تِجِي تِكشِف عالبِناء [ʔillujna raːħ tiji tikšif ʕalbinaːʔ] The committee is going to come inspect the building.

كَشَّف [kaššaf] *v:* • **1.** to uncover – لا تنام مكَشَّف، لا ترُوح تُبرَد [laː tnaːm mkaššaf, laː truːħ tubrad] Don't sleep uncovered or you'll catch cold. عِيب، لا تكَشّفِين وُجهك بِالشّارِع [ʕiːb, laː tkaššfiːn wujhič biššaːriʕ] For shame, don't uncover your face on the street!

تكَشَّف [tkaššaf] *v:* • **1.** to uncover oneself – إذا مِحتَرّ ليش ما تِتكَشَّف؟ [ʔiða miħtarr liːš maː titkaššaf?] If you're hot why don't you throw off the covers?

تكاشَف [tkaːšaf] *v:* • **1.** to show to each other, reveal to each other – ماكُو حاجَة نضُمّ واحِد عَاللاخ. خَلِّي نِتكاشَف ونشُوف شِتريد [maːku ħaːja nðumm waːħid ʕallaːx. xalli: nitkaːšaf winšuːf šitriːd] There's no need to conceal things from each other. Let's be frank with each other and see what you want. تكاشفُوا حَتَّى نُعرُف مِنُو الغالُب [tkaːšfuː ħatta nuʕruf minu ʔilɣaːlub] Show your cards to each other so we'll know who is the winner.

اِنكِشَف [ʔinkišaf] *v:* • **1.** to be disclosed, be revealed – هَسَّة الحَقِيقَة اِنكِشفَت [hassa ʔilħaqiːqa ʔinkišfat] Now the truth is revealed.

اِكتِشَف [ʔiktišaf] *v:* • **1.** to discover, find out, detect – اِكتِشَف جَزِيرَة صغَيرَة بالمُحِيط الهِندِي [ʔiktišaf jaziːra zɣayyra bilmuħiːṭ ʔilhindi] He discovered a small island in the Indian Ocean.

اِستَكشَف [ʔistakšaf] *v:* • **1.** to discover, to explore

كَشِف [kašif] *n:* • **1.** inspecting, examining • **2.** inspection, inspection tour • **3.** pl. كُشُوف (medical) examination, check-up • **4.** uncovering

كَشّاف [kaššaːf] *n:* كَشّافَة [kaššaːfa] *pl:* • **1.** scout, boy scout • **2.** flare • **3.** search light

مُكتَشِف [muktašif] *n:* مُكتَشِفِين [muktašifiːn] *pl:* • **1.** explorer, discover

كَشّافَة [kaššaːfa] *n:* • **1.** scout organization

كَشفِيَّة [kašfiya] *n:* • **1.** medical check fee

اِكتِشاف [ʔiktišaːf] *n:* اِكتِشافات [ʔiktišaːfaːt] *pl:* • **1.** discovery

مُستَكشِف [mustakšif] *n:* • **1.** explorer, discover

اِستِكشاف [ʔistikšaːf] *n:* • **1.** discovery, exploration

ك

• **2.** reconnaissance, reconnoitering, scouting – طِيّارَة اِستِكشاف [ṭiyya:rat ʔistikša:f] a reconnaissance plane.
كاشِف [ka:šif] *adj:* • **1.** faded – لُون كاشِف مِن الغَسِل [lu:n ka:šif min ʔilɣasil] a color faded by washing.
• **2.** pale, light – لُون أَخضَر كاشِف [lu:n ʔaxḍar ka:šif] a light green color.
مكَشَّف [mkaššaf] *adj:* • **1.** uncovered, exposed
مَكشُوف [makšu:f] *adj:* • **1.** uncovered, open, evident – وَرَقَة مَكشُوفَة [waraqa makšu:fa] a card lying face-up. بُوكَر مَكشُوف [pu:kar makšu:f] stud poker. حَكِي مَكشُوف [ħači makšu:f] frank talk. عيُوب مَكشُوفَة [ʕyu:b makšu:f] obvious defects. راح أرُوح أحكِي وِيّاه عالمَكشُوف [ra:ħ ʔaru:ħ ʔaħči wiyya:h ʕalmakšu:f] I'm going to go talk with him openly.
أكشَف [ʔakšaf] *comparative adjective:* • **1.** more or most pale, faded

ك ش ك 1
كَشكَة [kaška] *n:* • **1.** a dish made from cracked wheat, chickpeas, and noodles

ك ش ك 2
كُشُك [kušuk] *n:* • **1.** stall, stand, newspaper stand, small store

ك ش ك ش
كَشكَش [kaškaš] *v:* • **1.** to shoo, shoo away, scare away – الجّاهِل دَيكَشكِش الدِّجاج [ʔijǰa:hil daykaškiš ʔiddija:ǰ] The kid is scaring the chickens away.
كَشكَش [kaškaš] *adj:* • **1.** pleated – تَنُّورَة كَشكَش [tannu:ra kaškaš] a pleated skirt. • **2.** ruffles, pleats

ك ش ك ل
كَشكُول [kašku:l] *n:* كَشكُولات [kašku:la:t] *pl:* • **1.** beggar's bag • **2.** catch-all

ك ش م ش
كِشمِش [kišmiš] *n:* • **1.** (coll.) raisin(s)
كِشمِشَة [kišmiša] *n:* كِشمِشات [kišmiša:t] *pl:* • **1.** unit noun of كِشمِش, raisin • **2.** dried grapes

ك ش م ي ر
كَشمِير [kašmi:r] *n:* • **1.** cashmere

ك ش ن
كُشِن [kušin] *n:* كُشِنات، كُشنات [kušina:t, kušna:t] *pl:* • **1.** seat, seat cushion (of an automobile)

ك ش و ن
كَشوانِي [kašwa:ni] *n:* • **1.** shoes keeper in mosque
كَشوانِيَّة [kašwa:niyya] *n:* • **1.** shoes keeping place

ك ش ي
كاشِي [ka:ši] *n:* • **1.** (coll.) tile(s)
كاشِيَّة [ka:šiyya] *n:* كاشِيّات [ka:šiyya:t] *pl:* • **1.** tile, piece of tiling

ك ظ ظ
كَظّ [kaðð] *v:* • **1.** to seize, catch – أركُض وَراه وَكُظَّه [ʔurkuð wara:h wkuððah] Run after him and grab him.
• **2.** to hold, hold fast to – كُظّ إيد الجّاهِل حَتَّى ما يُوقَع [kuðð ʔi:d ʔijǰa:hil ħatta ma: yu:gaʕ] Hold onto the kid's hand so he won't fall.
اِنكَظّ [ʔinkaðð] *v:* • **1.** to be caught, be seized – الطِّير ما ينكَظّ بالإيد [ʔiṭṭi:r ma: yinkaðð bilʔi:d] The bird can't be caught with the hand.
اِكتَظّ [ʔiktaðð] *v:* • **1.** to be over-full, be packed, be chock-full – اِكتَظَّت السِّينَما بالنّاس [ʔiktaððat ʔissinama binna:s] The movie theater was packed with people.
كَظّ [kaðð] *n:* • **1.** catching

ك ع ب
كَعَّب [čaʕʕab] *v:* • **1.** to speak boldly, speak roughly – كُلّنا نخاف نِحكِي وِيّاه. بَسّ عَلِي يكَعِّبلَه [kullna nxa:f niħči wiyya:h. bass ʕali yčaʕʕiblah] All of us are afraid to talk to him. Only Ali tells him off. شِفتَه شلُون كَعَّبلَه؟ ما اِنطاه فُرصَة يجاوُب [šiftah šlu:n čaʕʕablah? ma: ʕinṭa:h furṣa yǰa:wub] Did you see how he raked him over the coals? He didn't give him a chance to answer.
كَعَّب [kaʕʕab] *v:* • **1.** to cube – كَعِّب هَالرَّقَم [kaʕʕib harraqam] Cube this number.
كَعَب [čaʕab] *n:* كعُوب [čʕu:b] *pl:* • **1.** bottom, lower part – أَكُو شَكَر باقِي بكَعب الكُوب [ʔaku šakar ba:qi bčaʕb ʔilku:b] There's still some sugar in the bottom of the cup. • **2.** end, last part – كَعَب شَهَر وماعِندِي فلُوس [čaʕab šahar wma:ʕindi flu:s] It's the end of the month and I don't have any money. • **3.** back, rear part – بِالصَّفّ ما يقعُد إلّا بالكَعَب [bişşaff ma: yigʕud ʔilla biččaʕab] In class he doesn't sit anywhere except in the back. • **4.** a bone from the lower leg of the sheep, in the form of a truncated cone, cleaned, often dyed, and used in boys' games
كَعبَة [kaʕba] *n:* • **1.** the Kaaba (in Mecca, Saudi Arabia)
كَعبِيَّة [čaʕbiyya] *n:* كَعبِيّات [čaʕbiyya:t] *pl:* • **1.** the portion in the bottom, in the rear, at the end, the tailings, the last portion – كَعبِيَّة الدَّونديرمَة تكُون جامدَة أكثَر [čaʕbiyyat ʔiddu:ndirma tku:n ǰa:mda ʔakθar] The ice cream in the bottom is more solid.
مُكَعَّب [mukaʕʕab] *adj:* • **1.** cube-shaped, cubic – مَتِر مُكَعَّب [matir mukaʕʕab] cubic meter. • **2.** cube, cubed – رَقَم مُكَعَّب [raqam mukaʕʕab] a cubed number. • **3.** pl. مُكَعَّبات blocks, toy blocks
تكعيبِي، الجَذر التَّكعيبِي [takʕi:bi, ʔiǰǰaðir ʔittakʕi:bi] *adj:* • **1.** cubic root (math.)

ك

ك ع ب ر

كَعبَر [kaʕbar] *v:* • **1.** to crumple up – كَعبَر الوَرَقَة وَذَبّها بِالسَلَّة [kaʕbar ʔilwaraqa waðabbha bissalla] He crumpled up the paper and threw it into the waste basket.

تكَعبَر [tkaʕbar] *v:* • **1.** to be crumpled up

مكَعبَر [mkaʕbar] *adj:* • **1.** crumpled, wrinkled – وَرَق مكَعبَر [waraq mkaʕbar] crumpled papers. • **2.** mis-shapen, gnarled – راس مكَعبَر [raːs mkaʕbar] a mis-shapen head.

ك ع د

كِعِد [kiʕid] *n:* كُعُود [kuʕuːd] *pl:* • **1.** barge, cargo boat (without motor)

ك ع ك

كَعَك [kaʕak] *n:* • **1.** (coll.) a type of pretzel-like pastry, sometimes in the form of cookies

كَعكَة [kaʕka] *n:* كَعكات [kaʕkaːt] *pl:* • **1.** a type of pretzel-like pastry, sometimes in the form of cookies

ك ع ك ل

كَعكَل [kaʕkal] *v:* • **1.** to curl

تكَعكَل [tkaʕkal] *v:* • **1.** to curl

كَعكُولَة [kaʕkuːla] *n:* كَعكُولات [kaʕkuːlaːt] *pl:* • **1.** cowlick, pompadour • **2.** crest (of a bird)

ك غ د

كاغَد [kaːɣad, qaːɣad] *n:* كَواغِد [kawaːɣid] *pl:* • **1.** (coll.) paper – كاغَد سُمبادَة [kaːɣad sumbaːda] sandpaper. بَعدَه بالكاغَد. مَحَّد اِستَعمَلَه [baʕdah bilkaːɣad. maħħad ʔistaʕmalah] It's still brand new (lit., it's still in the wrappers). No one has used it.

كاغَدَة [kaːɣada] *n:* كاغَدات، كواغِد، [kaːɣadaːt, kwaːɣid] *pl:* • **1.** sheet, piece of paper

ك ف

كاف [kaːf] *n:* • **1.** name of the letter

ك ف ء

كافَأ [kaːfaʔ, kaːfaː] *v:* • **1.** to reward – إذا تِشتُغُل زين، يكافئَك بِفَدّ شِي [ʔiða tištuɣul ziːn, ykaːfʔak bfadd ši] If you work well, he'll reward you with something.

كَفاءَة [kafaːʔa] *n:* • **1.** efficiency, capability, ability, competence

تَكافُؤ [takaːfuʔ] *n:* • **1.** equivalence, sameness

مُكافَأة [mukaːfaʔa] *n:* • **1.** reward, indemnity, remuneration, compensation

كُفُو [kufu, kafu] *adj:* • **1.** equal, a match, comparable – ما زَوجوه إيّاها لِأَنّ مُو كُفو إلها [maː zawwjuːh ʔiyyaːha liʔann muː kufu ʔilha] They didn't marry her to him because he isn't a match for her. • **2.** qualified, capable, able, competent – كُفو عَلَى دَفِع المَبلَغ [kufu ʕala dafiʕ ʔilmablaɣ] capable of paying the amount. هَذا مُو كُفو لهيكِي وَظِيفَة [haːða muː kufu lhiːči waḏiːfa] He's not qualified for such a position.

كَفِيء، كُفُء [kafiʔ, kufuʔ] *adj:* أَكِفّاء [ʔakiffaːʔ] *pl:* • **1.** qualified, capable, able, competent – مُوَظَّف كُفِء [mwaḏḏaf kufiʔ] a capable employee.

كَفوء [kafuːʔ] *adj:* • **1.** efficient • **2.** eligible • **3.** competent

مُكافِئ [mukaːfiʔ, mukaːfi] *adj:* • **1.** equivalent

متكافِئ [mitkaːfiʔ, mitkaːfi] *adj:* • **1.** equivalent, equal, commensurate, corresponding

أكفَأ [ʔakfaʔ, ʔakfa] comparative adjective: • **1.** more or most capable, able, competent, efficient

ك ف ت

كِفَت [čifat] *v:* • **1.** to crowd, cram, jam, stuff, force – أَخَذ الفلوس وَكِفَتها بِجَيبَه [ʔaxað ʔilfluːs wčifatha bjiːbah] He took the money and stuffed it down into his pocket. إكفِت الكِتاب بين بَقِيَّة الكُتُب [ʔičfit ʔilkitaːb biːn baqiyyat ʔilkutub] Jam the book in among the rest of the books. إكفِت كُلّ الجِّهال بِالحوض الوَراني [ʔičfit kull ʔijjihaːl bilħuːḏ ʔilwaraːni] Stick all the kids in the back seat. كِفتُوه بِالسِّجِن [čiftuːh bissijin] They stuck him in jail. • **2.** to intrude, burst in, to enter suddenly – دُقّ الباب بِالأَوَّل. لا تِكفِت [dugg ʔilbaːb bilʔawwal. laː tičfit] Knock on the door first. Don't burst in. كِفتَوا فَدّ كَفتَة [čiftaw fadd čafta] They burst right in. • **3.** to spring, pounce, jump suddenly – كِفَت عَليه الكَلِب وَمَلَّخَه [čifat ʕaliːh ʔiččalib wmallaxah] The dog pounced on him and ripped him up. • **4.** to hit – كِفَتَه بِلَكمَة وَوَقّعَه [čifatah blakma wwaggaʕah] He hit him a blow and knocked him down. الحاكِم كِفَتَه بسَنَتَين حَبِس [ʔilħaːkim čifatah bsantayn ħabis] The judge hit him with a two-year sentence. المُدِير كِفتَه بِغَرامَة يومَين [ʔilmudiːr čifatah byaraːma yuːmayn] The director docked him two days pay.

تكافَت [tčaːfat] *v:* • **1.** to clash, exchange blows – تشاتمَوا بِالأَوَّل وَبَعدين تكافتَوا [tšaːtmaw bilʔawwal wbaʕdiːn tčaːftaw] First they exchanged insults and then they got into a fist fight.

كَفِت [čafit] *n:* • **1.** act of crowding, cramming, jamming, stuffing

كُفتَة [kufta] *n:* • **1.** a dish composed mainly of meatballs, with spices, tomato sauce, and sometimes rice

كَفتَة، فَدّ كَفتَة [čafta, fadd čafta] *adj:* • **1.** intruder, interloper • **2.** brash person, brazen person – أَخَذ رَواتبَه كُلّها فَدّ كَفتَة [ʔaxað rawaːtbah kullha fadd čafta] He took all his earnings in one lump sum. • **3.** فَدّ كَفتَة all at once

ك ف ت ر ي
كافِتِيريا [kafiti:rya] *n:* • **1.** cafeteria, coffee shop

ك ف ح
كافَح [ka:fah] *v:* • **1.** to combat, to fight against, struggle against – كافحَوا المَرَض مُدَّة حَتَّى قِضَوا عَليه [ka:fhaw ʔilmarað mudda ħatta qiðaw ʕali:h] They struggled with the disease for some time until they conquered it.
كِفاح [kifa:ħ] *n:* • **1.** struggle, fight, battle
مُكافَحَة [muka:faħa] *n:* • **1.** fight • **2.** countering, struggle • **3.** section of security service • **4.** control (e.g, pest, diseases, illiteracy)
كِفاحِي [kifa:ħi] *adj:* • **1.** battle (in compounds) • **2.** relating to battle or struggle

ك ف ر
كُفَر [kufar] *v:* • **1.** to be irreligious, be an infidel, not to believe – لِيش تقُول ماكُو الله؟ دَتُكفُر [li:š dgu:l ma:ku ʔallah? datukfur] Why do you say there's no God? You're blaspheming. لُويش دَتُكفُر؟ ما تخاف مِن الله؟ [luwi:š datukfur? ma: txa:f min ʔallah?] Why are you being so sacrilegious? Have you no respect for God? قابِل كُفَرِت جِبت إسمَه قِدّامَك؟ [qa:bil kufarit jibit ʔismah gidda:mak?] Is it so awful I brought up his name in your presence?
كَفَّر [kaffar] *v:* • **1.** to curse, to blaspheme – ظَلّ يِسِبّ وَيكَفُّر مِن غَضَبَه [ðall yisibb wykaffur min ɣaðabah] He kept cursing and blaspheming in his anger. • **2.** to exasperate, madden, infuriate – ظَلّ يلِحّ عَلَيّا إلَى أن كَفَّرنِي [ðall yliħħ ʕalayya ʔila ʔan kaffarni] He kept insisting until he made me want to curse. كَفَّرتنِي. لا تحكِي عاد [kaffartni. la: tiħči ʕa:d] You're driving me nuts! Can't you shut up! مُو كَفَّرتِني! مَحَّد يغلَط؟ [mu: kaffartni! maħħad yiɣlaṭ?] Don't give me a hard time! Doesn't anyone else make mistakes? • **3.** with عَن to atone, make amends, do penance – وَزَّع فلُوس عالفُقَرَة حَتَّى يكَفُّر عَن ذِنُوبَه [wazzaʕ flu:s ʕalfuqara ħatta ykaffur ʕan ðinu:bah] He gave out money to the poor to atone for his sins.
كُفُر [kufur] *n:* • **1.** unbelief, infidelity, profanity, blasphemy
كَفّارَة [kuffa:ra] *n:* • **1.** penance, atonement
تَكفِير [takfi:r] *n:* • **1.** expiation, charge of unbelief
كافِر [ka:fir] *adj:* كَفَرَة، كُفّار [kafara, kuffa:r] *pl:* • **1.** infidel, unbeliever, atheist

ك ف ش
كَفشَة [kafša] *n:* • **1.** tuft
مَكفُوش [makfu:š] *adj:* • **1.** tangled

ك ف ف 1
كَفّ [kaff] *v:* • **1.** to hem, edge – نَفنُوفها طوِيل؛ راح تكُفَّه [nafnu:fha ṭwi:l; ra:ħ tkuffah] Her dress is too going to hem it. • **3.** with عَن to leave alone, let alone – كُفّ عَنِّي. مُو ضَوَّجتنِي [kuff ʕanni. mu: ðawwajitni] Get off my back. You're bothering me!
اِنكَفّ [ʔinkaff] *v:* • **1.** to cease, stop, desist, abstain • **2.** with عَن : to avert
كَفّ [kaff] *n:* • **1.** hem
كافَّة [ka:ffa] *n:* • **1.** all, all of – كافَّة أهِل بَغداد [ka:ffat ʔahil baɣda:d] all the people of Baghdad. كافَّة الطُّلّاب [ka:ffat ʔiṭṭulla:b] all the students.
كَفِيف [kafi:f] *adj:* • **2.** blind
مَكفُوف [makfu:f] *adj:* مَكافِيف [maka:fi:f] *pl:* • **1.** blind, blind person

ك ف ف 2
كَفّ [čaff] *n:* كفُوف [čfu:f] *pl:* • **1.** inside part of the hand, palm • **2.** handful • **3.** glove • **4.** ضَرُب كَفّ to swim with an overhand stroke – اليُوم راح أعَلّمَك تُضرُب كَفّ [ʔilyu:m ra:ħ ʔaʕallmak tuðrub čaff] Today I'm going to teach you to swim with an overhand stroke. • **5.** ضَرُب كَفّ to work hard – صارلِي ساعَة دَأضرُب كَفّ بهالشُّغُل وَما خَلَّصِت [ṣa:rli sa:ʕa daʔaðrub čaff bhaššuɣul wma xallaṣit] I've been battling this work for an hour and haven't finished.
كَفِّيَّة [čaffiyya] *n:* كفافِي، كَفِّيّات [čfa:fi, čaffiyya:t] *pl:* • **1.** handerchief

ك ف ل
كِفَل [kifal] *v:* • **1.** to vouch for, answer for, go bail for, to guarantee, cosign for – ما سِمحُولَه يطلَع لِأنّ ماكُو واحِد يكفلَه [ma: simħuwlah yiṭlaʕ liʔann ma:ku wa:ħid yikfalah] They didn't permit him to get out because no one would go bail for him. آنِي أكِفلَه. داينَه الفلُوس [ʔa:ni ʔakiflah. da:ynah ʔilflu:s] I'll stand good for him. Lend him the money. العَصفُور كِفَل الزَّرزُور وَإثنَينهُم طَيّارَة [ʔilʕaṣfu:r kifal ʔizzarzu:r wʔiθnaynhum ṭayya:ra] The sparrow vouched for the starling and they're both slippery characters (lit., good flyers-- maybe also liars).
كَفَّل [kaffal] *v:* • **1.** to ask to be a guarantor, to get as guarantor
تكَفَّل [tkaffal] *v:* • **1.** to cosign for, guarantee, be a guarantor for, be responsible for – البَنك ما يداينِّي الفلُوس إلّا إذا فَدّ واحِد تكَفَّلنِي [ʔilbank ma: yda:yinni ʔilflu:s ʔilla ʔiða fadd wa:ħid tkaffalni] The bank won't lend me the money unless someone cosigns for me. إنتَ إدفَع دِينارَين وَآنِي أتكَفَّل الباقِي [ʔinta ʔidfaʕ dina:rayn waʔa:ni ʔatkaffal ʔilba:qi] You pay two dinars and I'll be responsible for payment of the rest. هُوَّ رَجلِك مُو مِتكَفّلَه؟ [huwwa ra:jlič mu: mitkafflah?] Isn't your husband sponsoring him (acting as surety for him) ?
اِنكِفَل [ʔinkifal] *v:* • **1.** to be guaranteed
كَفالَة [kafa:la] *n:* كَفالات [kafa:la:t] *pl:* • **1.** pledge, deposit, surety, collateral • **2.** bail –

طِلَع مِن السِّجِن بِكَفالَة [ṭilaʕ min ʔissijin bkafaːla] He got out of jail on bail.
كَفيل [kafiːl] *adj:* كُفَلاء [kufalaːʔ] *pl:* • **1.** guarantor, co-signer – إذا تِتدايَن فلُوس، إلمَن راح تكَفِّل؟ [ʔiða tiddaːyan fluːs, ʔilman raːħ tkaffil?] If you borrow money, who will you get for a guarantor?
مَكفُول [makfuːl] *adj:* • **1.** covered, guaranteed

ك ف ن
كَفَّن [čaffan] *v:* • **1.** to wrap in a winding sheet (for dead people) – كَفِّنَوا المَيِّت بخام أبيَض [čaffinaw ʔilmayyit bxaːm ʔabyað] They wrapped the corpse in a white cloth.
كِفَن [čifan] *n:* كفانَة [čfaːna] *pl:* • **1.** winding sheet • **2.** winding sheet (for the dead), shroud

ك ف و ر
كافُور [kaːfuːr] *n:* • **1.** camphor

ك ف ي 1
كِفَى [kifaː] *v:* • **1.** to be enough, be sufficient, suffice – هَالمَبلَغ يِكفِينِي شَهرَين [halmablaɣ yikfiːni šahrayn] This amount will be enough for me for two months. يِكفِي عاد تِتبَجَّح [yikfi ʕaːd titbajjaħ] That's enough bragging for now!
كَفَّى [kaffaː] *v:* • **1.** same as كِفَى : to be enough, be sufficient, suffice
اِكتِفَى [ʔiktifaː] *v:* • **1.** to be content, to content oneself – المُعَلِّم اِكتِفَى بإنذارَه، وَما قاصَصَه هَالمَرَّة [ʔilmuʕallim ʔiktifaː bʔinðaːrah, wama qaːṣaṣah halmarra] The teacher was satisfied with a threat and didn't punish him this time. اِكتِفيت؛ ما أقدَر آكُل بَعَد [ʔiktifiːt; maː ʔagdar ʔaːkul baʕad] I've had enough; I can't eat any more.
كَفِي [čafy] *n:* • **1.** saving, sparing from (e.g., disease, evil), protecting
كِفايَة [kifaːya] *n:* • **1.** sufficient amount – أُخُذ كِفايَتَك مِن الماي وَالبانزِين قَبُل ما تسافِر [ʔuxuð kifaːytak min ʔilmaːy wilbanziːn gabul maː tsaːfir] Take all the water and gas you'll need before you start.
إكتِفاء [ʔiktifaːʔ] *n:* • **1.** contentedness, contentment, self-satisfaction
كافِي [kaːfi] *adj:* • **1.** sufficient, enough, adequate – تِعتِقِد هَالمَبلَغ كافِي؟ [tiʕtiqid halmablaɣ kaːfi?] Do you think this amount is enough?
مِكتِفِي [miktifi] *adj:* • **1.** sufficient • **2.** contented

ك ف ي 2
كِفَى [čifaː, kifaː] *v:* • **1.** to save, spare from – إكفِينِي شَرَّك تَرَة أمَوّتَك [ʔičfiːni šarrak tara ʔamawwtak] Spare me your unpleasantness or I'll murder you. الله يِكفِيك شَرَّه [ʔallah yičfiːk šarrah] God protect you from him. • **2.** to turn over, invert, turn upside down – مِن كِفَوه عَلَى وجهه، شافَوا السِّكِّينَة بِظَهرَه [min čifawh ʕala wiččah, šaːfaw ʔissiččiːna bðahrah] When they turned him over on his stomach, they saw the knife in his back. إكفِي الماعُون عَلَى وجهه [ʔičfi ʔilmaːʕuːn ʕala wiččah] turn the dish upside down. • **3.** to spread out, stretch out, flatten – ضِرَبتَه بَند وَكِفَيتَه عَلَى وجهه [ðirabtah band wčifiːtah ʕala wiččah] I tripped him and sent him sprawling. الطَّبِيب كِفاه عَلَى وجهه [ʔiṭṭabiːb čifaːh ʕala wiččah] The doctor laid him face down.
تكَفَّى [tčaffaː] *v:* • **1.** to avoid, keep away from – خَلِّي نِتكَفَّى الشَّرّ وَنفُوت مِن هنا [xalliː nitčaffaː ʔiššarr wanfuːt minhna] Let's avoid trouble and go this way.
انكِفَى [ʔinčifaː] *v:* • **1.** to be inverted, get turned over – اِنكِفَى الجِّدِر وَراح كُلّ الأكِل [ʔinčifaː ʔijjidir wraːħ kull ʔilʔakil] The pot got turned over and all the food spilled. • **2.** to fall flat, to sprawl – الجّاهِل كُلّ ساع يِنكِفِي عَلَى وجهه [ʔijjaːhil kull saːʕ yinčifi ʕala wiččah] The baby falls on his face all the time. ما قِبَل يِنكِفِي عَلَى وجهه، وَخَلَّى العَريف يِزعَل [maː qibal yinčifi ʕala wiččah, wxallaː ʔilʕariːf yizʕal] He refused to stretch out on his belly, and made the sergeant mad.

ك ق و ك
كاكُوك [čaːquːč] *n:* كاكُوكات [čaːquːčaːt] *pl:* • **1.** hammer

ك ك ل ك
كُكلُك [kukluk] *n:* كَكالِك [kakaːlik] *pl:* • **1.** a kind of game bird resembling the partridge

ك ك و
كاكاو [kakaw] *n:* • **1.** cocoa

ك ل
كالَة [kaːla] *n:* كالات [kaːlaːt] *pl:* • **1.** (pair of) soft, quarterless slipper(s), usually made of felt

ك ل ب
كِلَب [čilab] *v:* • **1.** to ruin, spoil – هِيَّ اللِّي كِلبَت إبِنها، هَل قَدّ ما دَلِّلَتَه [hiyya ʔilli čilbat ʔibinha, hal gadd maː dallilatah] She's the one who ruined her son, she's spoiled him so much. الفلُوس كِلبَتَه. اِشتِرَالَه ثلاث سَيّارات [ʔilfluːs čilbatah. ʔištiraːlah tlaθ sayyaːraːt] The money has spoiled him. He bought himself three cars. • **2.** to make a swine of – الوَظِيفَة الجِّدِيدَة كِلبَتَه. ما قام يِنجِرِع بَعَد [lwaðiːfa ʔijjidiːda čilbatah. maː gaːm yinjiriʕ baʕad] The new position's made a swine of him. He's no longer bearable.
كَلَّب [čallab] *v:* • **1.** to stick, cling, hold on – طَيّارَة الجّاهِل خَرَّت وكَلِّبَت بِالشَّجرَة [ṭayyaːrat ʔijjaːhil xarrat wčallibat biššijra] The kid's kite nose dived and hung up in the tree. أكُو خَيط مكَلِّب بسِترتَك [ʔaku xiːṭ mčallib bsitirtak] There's a thread hanging on your

coat. شُوف الجّاهِل مكَلِّب بِالعَرَبانَة [šu:f ʔiǰǰa:hil mčallib bilʕaraba:na] Look at the kid hanging onto the carriage! هِدّنِي! شَكُو عِندَك مكَلِّب بِيّا [hiddni! šaku ʕindak mčallib biyya] Turn me loose! Why are you holding onto me? شكَلِّبِت بِيّا مِثِل القَرادَة؟ مُو قِتلَك ما عِندِي فلُوس أنطِيك [ʔiščallabit biyya miθil ʔilgara:da? mu: gitlak ma: ʕindi flu:s ʔanṭi:k] Why are you hanging on like a leech? I told you I've got no money to give you. شيخَلصَك مِنَّه؟ غَرقان وَمكَلِّب بِسِبّاحَة [šyxallṣak minnah? ɣarga:n wmčallib bsibba:ħa] How can you get away from him? He's a drowning man grasping at a float. • **2.** to insist – كَلِّب بِيّا إلّا أتغَدّى وِيّاه [čallab biyya ʔilla ʔadɣadda: wiyya:h] He insisted that I have lunch with him. مكَلِّب إلّا يرُوح وِيّاهُم [mčallib ʔilla yiru:ħ wiyya:hum] He's insisting on going with them. كَلِّب بِيّا أرُوح وِيّاه [čallab biyya ʔaru:ħ wiyya:h] He insisted I go with him.
تكالَب [tča:lab] *v:* • **1.** to assail one another, to grapple with, fight each other – تشاتَموا وَتكالبَوا وَبَعدين فاكَكناهُم [tša:tmaw wtča:lbaw wbaʕdi:n fa:kakna:hum] They exchanged insults and grappled with each other and then we separated them.
اِنكِلَب [ʔinčilab] *v:* • **1.** to become swell-headed, get too big for one's breeches – اِنكِلَب مِن صارَت عِندَه فلُوس. يرِيد يِتزَوَّج بِنت المَلِك [ʔinčilab min ṣa:rat ʕindah flu:s. yri:d yidzawwaǰ bint ʔilmalik] He got big ideas when he became rich. He wants to marry the king's daughter. • **2.** to become a swine – أشُو مِن تزَنكَن، اِنكِلَب [ʔašu: min dzangan, ʔinčilab] It seems since he became rich, he's lost his manners. • **3.** to be seized by hydrophobia – كَلِبنا اِنكِلَب [čalibna ʔinčilab] Our dog got rabies.
كَلِب [čalib, kalib] *n:* كلاب [čla:b, kla:b] *pl:* • **1.** dog – فطِرّ كلاب [fṭirr čla:b] poisonous mushroom, toadstool.
كَلبَة [čalba, kalba] *n:* كَلبات [čalba:t, kalba:t] *pl:* • **1.** female dog, bitch
كَلَبِي [čalabi] *n:* كَلَبِيَّة [čalabiyya] *pl:* • **1.** man from a wealthy class of merchants and landlords • **2.** dignitary
كِلّاب [čilla:b] *n:* كلالِيب [čla:li:b] *pl:* • **1.** hook • **2.** safety pin
كَلبَشَة [kalbaša, kalbaǰa] *n:* • **1.** handcuffing
كَلَبِيَّة [čalabiyya] *adj:/n:* كَلَبِيّات [čalabiyya:t] *pl:* • **1.** tall, slender, and attractive girl
كِلّابتَين [čilla:btayn] *n:* كِلّابتَينات [čilla:btina:t] *pl:* • **1.** pliers
كِلِّيب [čilli:b] *adj:* • **1.** stubborn, persistent person
مَكلُوب [mačlu:b] *adj:* • **1.** infected with hydrophobia, rabid, mad • **2.** rabid dog • **3.** madman, lunatic
أكلَب [ʔačlab] *comparative adjective:* • **1.** more or most uncivilized

ك ل ب ت و ز

كالِبتُوز [kalibtu:z] *n:* • **1.** (coll.) eucalyptus (Bot.)
كالِبتَوزايَة [ka:libtu:za:ya] *n:* كالِبتَوزايات [ka:libtu:za:ya:t] *pl:* • **1.** a eucalyptus tree

ك ل ب د و ن

كَلَبدُون [kalabdu:n] *n:* • **1.** gold thread – شَعَرها أصفَر كَلَبدُون [šaʕarha ʔaṣfar kalabdu:n] Her hair is golden yellow.

ك ل ب ش

كَلبَش [kalbač] *v:* • **1.** to handcuff – كَلبِشَوه وأخذوه لِمَركَز الشُّرطَة [kalbičawh wʔaxðawh limarkaz ʔiššurṭa] They handcuffed him and took him to the police station. كَلبِشُونِي بِهالشُّغُل فُوق كُلّ شُغلِي [kalbiču:ni bhaššuɣul fu:g kull šuɣli] They saddled me with this job in addition to all my own work.
تكَلبَش [tkalbač] *v:* • **1.** to be handcuffed – هَذا لازِم يِتكَلبَش تَرَة يِنهِزِم [ha:ða la:zim yitkalbač tara yinhizim] He has to be handcuffed or he'll escape.
كَلَبشَة [kalabča] *n:* كَلَبشات [kalabča:t] *pl:* • **1.** handcuffs

ك ل ج

كلَج [klač] *n:* • **1.** clutch

ك ل خ ن

كُلخان [kulxa:n] *n:* كُلخانات [kulxa:na:t] *pl:* • **1.** firepit under a Turkish bath
كُلخَنجِي [kulxanči] *adj:* كُلخَنجِيَّة [kulxančiyya] *pl:* • **1.** fireman who stokes the fire in a public bath

ك ل س

كَلَّس [kallas] *v:* • **1.** to deflate – راح يكَلّسُون الرِّيَّة مالتَه [ra:ħ ykallisu:n ʔirriyya ma:ltah] They're going to deflate his lung.
تكَلَّس [tkallas] *v:* • **1.** to be calcified
كِلس [kils] *n:* • **1.** lime (stone)
تَكَلُّس [takallus] *n:* • **1.** calcification
كِلسِي [kilsi] *adj:* • **1.** basic, alkaline – أرض كِلسِيَّة [ʔarḍ kilsiyya] alkaline soil.
مِتكَلِّس [mitkallis] *adj:* • **1.** calcified

ك ل س ك

كلاسِيكِي [kla:si:ki] *n:* • **1.** classic, classical
كلاسِيك [kla:si:k] *adj:* • **1.** classic

ك ل ش

كلاش [kla:š] *n:* كلاشات [kla:ša:t] *pl:* • **1.** a sort of quarterless slipper
كلِيشَة [kili:ša, kali:ša] *n:* كِلِيشات، كِلايِش [kili:ša:t, kila:yiš] *pl:* • **1.** engraving, engraved plate • **2.** rubber stamp • **3.** cliche, trite phrase

ك

ك ل ش ن ك ف

كلاشينكوف [klašniku:f] *n:* • **1.** kalashnikov, rifle (AK-47)

ك ل ص

كلاص [gla:ṣ] *n:* كلاصات [gla:ṣa:t] *pl:* • **1.** glass, drinking cup – كلاص بِسكِت مال دوندِرمَة [gla:ṣ biskit ma:l du:ndirma] a cone (for icecream).

ك ل ف

كَلَّف [kallaf] *v:* • **1.** to cost – القاط شقَدّ كَلَّفَك؟ [ʔilqa:ṭ šgadd kallafak?] How much did the suit cost you? قاطِي كَلَّفنِي عِشرِين دِينار [qa:ṭi kallafni ʕišri:n dina:r] My suit cost me twenty dinars. • **2.** to assign, require, ask, have – إذا تِحتاج شِي مِن السُّوق، رُوح اِشتِرِي. لا تكَلِّف أَحَّد [ʔiða tiħta:ǰ ši min ʔissu:g, ru:ħ ʔištiri. la: tkallif ʔaħħad] If you need something from the market, go buy it. Don't ask someone else. دَأَقُلَّك صِحّتِي مبَنجِرَة. كَلِّف غيرِي يسَوِّيها [daʔagullak ṣiħħti mpančira. kallif γayri ysawwi:ha] I tell you my health's run down. Have somebody else do it. • **3.** to bother, trouble, inconvenience – أَقدَر أَكَلّفَك بشِي؟ [ʔagdar ʔakallfak bši?] Could I trouble you for something? لا تكَلِّف نَفسَك عَلَى مُودِي [la: tkallif nafsak ʕala mu:di] Don't trouble yourself on my account. كَلَّفتنِي أَلف كُلفَة اليُوم [kallaftni ʔalf kulfa ʔilyu:m] You've imposed on me a thousand times today.

تكَلَّف [tkallaf] *v:* • **1.** to put oneself out, go to a lot of trouble – تكَلَّف هوايَة اليُوم عَلَى مُودِي [tkallaf hwa:ya ʔilyu:m ʕala mu:di] He went to a lot of trouble today for my sake. • **2.** to be unnatural, affected, pretentious – يِتكَلَّف هوايَة بكَلامَه [yitkallaf hwa:ya bkala:mah] He puts on airs with his talk. • **3.** with عَلَى, ب to cost – هَالبَيت تكَلَّف عَلَيّا بأَلفَين دِينار [halbayt tkallaf ʕalayya bʔalfi:n dina:r] This house cost me 2000 dinars.

كُلفَة [kulfa] *n:* كُلَف [kulaf] *pl:* • **1.** cost, expense, expenditure, outlay • **2.** assignment, requisition, request, task • **3.** trouble, inconvenience, imposition

تَكَلُّف [takalluf] *n:* • **1.** unnaturalness of manner, mannerisms, airs, affectation, affected behavior

تكلِيف [takli:f] *n:* تَكالِيف [taka:li:f] *pl:* • **1.** cost – تكالِيف المَعِيشَة [taka:li:f ʔilmaʕi:ša] the cost of living. • **2.** request, task • **3.** imposition, bother

تَكلُفَة [taklufa] *n:* • **1.** cost, costs, expenses, expenditure • **2.** inconvenience, trouble

مُكَلَّف [mukallaf] *adj:* • **1.** liable to the draft, eligible for the draft • **2.** person who is eligible for the draft • **3.** obligated, under obligation, liable

مكَلِّف [mkallif] *adj:* • **1.** costing, expensive

مِتكَلِّف [mitkallif] *adj:* • **1.** responsible, concerned, burdened, put out – إذا يرِيد يرُوح، آنِي ما مِتكَلِّف بِيه [ʔiða yri:d yiru:ħ, ʔa:ni ma: mitkallif bi:h] If he wants to go, it's no skin off my neck. لا تِجِي عَلَيّا بَعَد. آنِي ما مِتكَلِّف بهَالقَضِيَّة [la: tiǰi ʕalayya baʕad. ʔa:ni ma: mitkallif bhalqaðiyya] Don't come to me again. I'm not concerned with this matter. وَالله، مِتكَلِّف [wallah, mitkallif] You poor overburdened thing! صرَفِت مِيَّة دِينار بأُورُبّا؟ وَالله مِتكَلِّف! آنِي صرَفِت أَلف [ṣrafit miyyat dina:r bʔu:ruppa? wallah mitkallif! ʔa:ni ṣrafit ʔalf] You spent a hundred dinars in Europe? You poor guy! I spent a thousand.

ك ل ك 1

كَلَّك [kallak] *v:* • **1.** to trick, deceive, fool – كَلِّكَه لِجّاهِل وَخَلِّيه يِجِي وِيّاك [kallikah lijǰa:hil wxalli:h yiǰi wiyya:k] Fool the kid and make him come with you.

كَلَك [kalak, čalač] *n:* كَلَكات [kalaka:t] *pl:* • **1.** trick, fast one – عَبَّر عَلَيه فَدّ كَلَك واخَذها مِنَّه [ʕabbar ʕali:h fadd kalak wʔaxaðha minnah] He put one over on him and took it away from him.

كَلَكچِي [kalakči] *n:* كَلَكچِيَّة [kalakčiyya] *pl:* • **1.** trickster, tricky person, smooth operator

ك ل ك 2

كَلَك [kalak] *n:* كَلَكات [kalaka:t] *pl:* • **1.** raft of inflated skins

كَلَّك [kallak] *adj:* كَلَّكِين [kallaki:n] *pl:* • **1.** operator of a raft, raftsman

ك ل ل 1

كَلّ [kall] *v:* • **1.** to be or become tired, fatigued, weary, exhausted – ظَلَّيت أَتوَسَّل بِيه حَتَّى كَلَّيت [ðalli:t ʔatwassal bi:h ħatta kalli:t] I kept pleading with him until I was exhausted.

كُلَّة [kulla] *n:* كُلّات، كُلَل [kulla:t, kulal] *pl:* • **1.** mosquito net

كَلَل [kalal] *n:* • **1.** exhaustion, extreme fatigue

إكلِيل [ʔikli:l] *n:* أَكالِيل [ʔaka:li:l] *pl:* • **1.** wreath, garland

ك ل ل 2

كُلّ [kull] *n:* • **1.** whole, entire, all – كُلّنا راح نرُوح [kullna ra:ħ nru:ħ] We're all going. بِقَوا هناك كُلّ اليُوم [biqaw hna:k kull ʔilyu:m] They stayed there all day. كُلّ التَّلامِيذ سَوُّوا إضراب [kull ʔittala:mi:ð sawwaw ʔiðra:b] All the students went on strike. آنِي شبِيدِي عَلِيك؟ هُوَّ الكُلّ بالكُلّ [ʔa:ni šbi:di ʕali:k? huwwa ʔilkull bilkull] What have I got to do for you? He's the one person with authority. • **2.** /followed by indefinite noun/ every – كُلّ تِلمِيذ لازِم يِحضَر [kull tilmi:ð la:zim yiħðar] Every student has to be present. كُلّ واحِد يُعرُف هَذا [kull wa:ħid yuʕruf ha:ða] Everyone knows that. كُلّ شِي صار عَالمَرام [kull ši ṣa:r ʕalmara:m] Everything went well. كُلّ بيضَة بعَشِر فلُوس [kull bi:ða bʕašir flu:s] The eggs are 10 fils each. يَعنِي كُلّ يوم نعِيد وَنُصقُل؟ [yaʕni kull yu:m nʕi:d wnuṣqul?] You mean we have to go through this day in and day out? عَلَى كُلّ حال، ما راح نِجتِمِع إِلَى أَن يِجِي [ʕala kull ħa:l, ma: ra:ħ nijtimiʕ ʔila ʔan yiji] At any rate, we're not going to meet until he comes. • **3.** /with negative particle/ any, a single, the least – ما أَعرُف كُلّ شِي عَنَّه [ma: ʔaʕruf kull ši ʕannah] I don't know anything about it. ما يسَوِّي كُلّ شِي بَالدّائِرَة [ma: ysawwi: kull ši bidda:ʔira] He doesn't do a single thing in the office. ما إِلَك كُلّ فِلِس عَلَيّا [ma: ʔilak kull filis ʕalayya] I don't owe you a single penny. • **4.** الكُلّ all of them, everyone, every one – خَبُّر الكُلّ [xabbur ʔilkull] Tell everyone. الكُلّ نظاف؛ بَسّ هَالماعُون وَسِخ شوَيَّة [ʔilkull nða:f; bass halma:ʕu:n waṣix šwayya] They're all clean; just this dish is a bit dirty.

كُلّ مَن [kull man] *n:* • **1.** everyone who, whoever (grammatically, a quantifier noun) – كُلّ مَن يِشتُغُل بِهَالدّائِرَة لازِم يجِيب شَهادَة صِحِّيَّة [kull man yištuɣul bhadda:ʔira la:zim yji:b šaha:da ṣiħħiyya] Everyone who works in this office must bring a health certificate. • **2.** everyone – كُلّ مَن ياخُذ حَقَّه [kull man ya:xuð ħaqqah] Everyone will get his share.

كُلٍّ، عَلَى كُلٍّ [kullin, ʕala kullin] *n:* • **1.** anyway, anyhow, at any rate – عَلَى كُلٍّ، أَرِيدَك تِحكِي وِيّاه وَتِنسَى المَوضُوع [ʕala kullin, ʔari:dak tiħči wiyya:h wtinsa: ʔilmawðu:ʕ] At any rate, I want you to talk to him, and forget the matter.

كُلّ ما، كُلَّما [kull ma:, kullma] *subordinating conjunction:* • **1.** كُلّ مَا [kull ma:] everything that, all that, whatever – الحَرامِي أَخَذ كُلّ ما عِندِي [ʔilħara:mi ʔaxað kull ma: ʕindi] The thief took everything I had. هُوَّ يوافِق كُلّ أَسَوِّي [huwwa ywa:fiq kullma: ʔasawwi:] He agrees to whatever I do. • **2.** كُلّما [kullma], كُلّ مَن [kullman] ... whenever – كُلّما أخابرَه، التَّلِفُون مَشغُول [kullma: ʔaxa:brah, ʔittalifu:n mašɣu:l] Whenever I call him, the phone's busy.

كُلّشِي [kullši, kull ši] *n:* • **1.** everything

كُلِّيَة [kulliya] *n:* • **1.** college, school (e.g., school of Arts)

كُلِّي [kulli] *adj:* • **1.** entire, complete, overall, comprehensive, complete – خُسُوف كُلِّي [xusu:f kulli] total eclipse. مَجمُوع كُلِّي [majmu:ʕ kulli] total, sum total.

كُلَّة [kullat] *adj:* • **1.** /plus pronominal suffix/ all of.

كُلِّيَة [kulliyat] *adj:* • **1.** all, whole, entirety – كُلِّيَتهُم ماتَوا [kulliyyathum ma:taw] All of them died. كُلّتنا راح نرُوح وِيّاك [kullitna ra:ħ nru:ħ wiyya:k] All of us will go with you. نِكَر مَعرِفتِي بِالكُلِّيَّة [nikar maʕrifti bilkulliyya] He denied knowing me entirely.

كُلِّيّاً [kulliyyan] *adverbial:* • **1.** entirely • **2.** completely

ك ل ل 3

كَلَّة [kalla] *n:* كَلّات، كلال [kalla:t, kla:l] *pl:* • **1.** head • **2.** sugar loaf, loaf of sugar

كَلَّجِي [kallači] *n:* كَلَّجِيَّة [kallačiyya] *pl:* • **1.** seller of sheep heads and lights • **2.** person who frequents the red-light district

كَلَّجِيَّة [kallačiyya] *adj:* • **1.** former neighborhood in Baghdad where a red-light district was maintained • **2.** (by extension) any red-light district

ك ل ل ش

كُلِّش [kulliš] *adj:* • **1.** (invar.) very, extremely, highly – مَسأَلَة كُلِّش مُهِمَّة [masʔala kulliš muhimma] a very important question. هَالسَّيّارَة كُلِّش غالية [hassayya:ra kulliš ɣa:lya] This car is very expensive. • **2.** very much, at all – أَحِبّها كُلِّش [ʔaħibbha kulliš] I like her very much. الفِلِم عِجَبنِي كُلِّش [ʔilfilim ʕijabni kulliš] I liked the film very much. لا تسَوِّي نَفسَك كُلِّش ما تُعرُف [la: tsawwi: nafsak kulliš ma: tuʕruf] Don't make as though you don't know at all. عِندِي أَمَل كُلِّش يِجِي باكِر [ʕindi ʔamal kulliš yiji ba:čir] I have high hopes he'll come tomorrow. كُلِّش! مَيِّت عَليها [kulliš! mayyit ʕali:ha] Very much so! He's wild about her!

ك ل م 1

كَلَّم [kallam] *v:* • **1.** to talk to, speak with – كَلَّمته بِيها وَأَعتِقِد راح يِقبَل [kallamtah bi:ha wʔaʕtiqid ra:ħ yiqbal] I talked to him about it and I think he will agree.

تكَلَّم [tkallam] *v:* • **1.** to talk, speak – لا تِتكَلَّم. خَلِّي المُعَلِّم يدَرِّس [la: titkallam. xalli: ʔilmuʕallim ydarris] Don't talk. Let the teacher teach.

كَلِمَة [kalima, kilma, čilma] *n:* كَلِمات [kalima:t, čilma:t] *pl:* • **1.** word • **2.** speech, address

كَلام [kala:m] *n:* • **1.** talking, speaking – كَلام فارِغ [kala:m fa:riɣ] idle talk, prattle, nonsense. • **2.** words, word, statement, remark – إذا تِسمَع كَلام أَبُوك، تِتوَفَّق [ʔiða tismaʕ kala:m ʔabu:k, titwaffaq] If you listen to what your father says, you will do well. • **3.** promise, word, assurance – إنطانِي كَلام باكِر يسَوِّيلِي إيّاها [ʔinṭa:ni kala:m ba:čir ysawwi:li ʔiyya:ha] He gave me his word he would do it for me tomorrow.

مُكالَمَة [muka:lama] *n:* مُكالَمات [muka:lama:t] *pl:* • **1.** conversation (especially, on the telephone)

مِتكَلِّم [mitkallim] *adj:* • **1.** speaker

ك ل م 2

كَلَم [kalam] *n:* • **1.** kohlrabi, a variety of cabbage

ك ل و 1

كِلوَة [čilwa] *n:* كِلوات، كَلاوِي [čilwa:t, čala:wi] *pl:* • **1.** kidney

ك ل و 2

كلاو [kla:w] *n:* كلاوات [kla:wa:t] *pl:* • **1.** cap with no brim or visor – لابِس كلاو الخَنّاس [la:bis kla:w ʔilxanna:s] He's invisible (lit., he's wearing the devil's cap). لازِم أَشُوفَه. قابِل لابِس كلاو الخَنّاس؟ [la:zim ʔašu:fah. qa:bil la:bis kla:w ʔilxanna:s?] I should see him. Do you suppose he's made himself invisible?

ك

لَبَّسَه كلاو [labbasah kla:w] He took him. He cheated him. He pulled the wool over his eyes. صاحِب المَخزَن لَبَّسَه خُوش كلاو [ṣa:ħib ʔilmaxzan labbasah xu:š kla:w] The storekeeper really took him to the cleaners. • **2.** (pl. only) poppy-cock, baloney, bull – لا تِهتَمّ باللِّي يقُولُوا. هَذا كُلّها كلاوات [la: tihtamm billi ygu:lu:. ha:ða kullha kla:wa:t] Don't be concerned about what they say. That's all baloney.
كلاوچي [kla:wči] *n:* كلاوچِيَّة [kla:wčiyya] *pl:* • **1.** confidence man, con artist. • **2.** a man who cannot be trusted, deceptive person, devious person

ك ل و ب

كلُوب [glu:b] *n:* كلُوبات [glu:ba:t] *pl:* • **1.** light bulb

ك ل و ر

كلُور [klu:r] *n:* • **1.** chlorine

ك ل و ش

كالُوش [ka:lu:š] *n:* كالُوشات، كواليش [ka:lu:ša:t, kwa:li:š] *pl:* • **1.** galoshes, rubber overshoes • **2.** a kind of slipper without quarter

ك ل و ص

كلَوص [glu:ṣ] *n:* • **1.** gross, in bulk, in big(ger) amounts

ك ل ي ج

كلَيجَة [kli:ča] *n:* • **1.** (coll.) a cookie-like pastry
كليجايَة [kli:ča:ya] *n:* كليجايات [kli:ča:ya:t] *pl:* • **1.** cookie-like pastry

ك م

كام، خِشَب كام [ča:m, xišab ča:m] *n:* • **1.** an inexpensive, light-colored, light-weight wood used for boxes, shelves, cheap furniture, etc
كَم [čam] *interrogative:* • **1.** how many? how much? – كَم وَلَد عِندَك؟ [čam walad ʕindak?] How many boys do you have? • **2.** so many! so much! – كَم مَرَّة قِتلَه وَما فاد [čam marra gitlah wma fa:d] I told him so many times and it did no good! • **3.** some, a few – أَعتِقِد القِطار راح يوصَل بَعَد كَم دَقيقَة [ʔaʕtiqid ʔilqiṭa:r ra:ħ yu:ṣal baʕad čam daqi:qa] I think the train will arrive in a few minutes. إنطِيني فَدّ كَم دينار؛ أَريد أَتسَوَّق [ʔinṭi:ni fadd čam dina:r; ʔari:d ʔatsawwag] Give me a few dinars; I want to go shopping.

ك م ب ر

كُمبار [kumba:r] *n:* • **1.** bast, a plant fiber used for making rugs

ك م ب ي ل

كُمبِيالَة [kumpiya:la, kumbiya:la] *n:* كُمبِيالات [kumpiya:la:t, kumbiya:la:t] *pl:* • **1.** promissory note, IOU

ك م خ

كَمَخ [kumax] *v:* • **1.** to cover with a cloth – أكمُخ الطَّماطَة الخَضرَة حَتَّى تصِير حَمرَة [ʔukmux ʔiṭṭama:ṭa ʔilxaðra ħatta tṣi:r ħamra] Cover the green tomatoes with a cloth, so they'll turn red.
كَمَّخ [kammax] *v:* • **1.** same as كَمَخ : to cover with a cloth – نَزِّل حَرَكَة الطَّبّاخ وَكَمُّخ الجِّدِر [nazzil ħarakat ʔiṭṭabba:x wkammux ʔijjidir] Turn down the stove and cover up the pot with a cloth.
كَمُخ [kamux] *n:* • **1.** act of covering (s.th.)
كماخ [kma:x] *adj:* كماخات [kma:xa:t] *pl:* • **1.** important person, V.I.P., big shot

ك م د

كَمّادَة [kamma:da] *n:* كَمّادات [kamma:da:t] *pl:* • **1.** compress, pack

ك م ر [1]

كُمَر [kumar] *v:* • **1.** to cover – كُمَر الطَّماطَة حَتَّى تِلحَق [kumar ʔiṭṭama:ṭa ħatta tilħag] He covered up the tomatoes so they'd ripen.
كَمُر [kamur] *n:* • **1.** act of covering (s.th.)

ك م ر [2]

كِمري [čimri] *n:* • **1.** dates, picked green and ripened artificially

ك م ش

كُمَش [kumaš] *v:* • **1.** to seize, grasp, grip, clutch – أُكمُش راس الحَبِل [ʔukmuš ra:s ʔilħabil] Grab the end of the rope. كُمَش إيدِي وَما خَلّانِي أَضُربَه [kumaš ʔi:di wma xalla:ni ʔaðurbah] He grabbed my hand and wouldn't let me hit him. أُكمُشَه؛ باق جِزداني [ʔukumšah; ba:g jizda:ni] Grab him; he stole my wallet! الجّاهِل دَيُركُض. رُوح أُكمُشَه [ʔijja:hil dayurkuḍ. ru:ħ ʔukumšah] The baby's running off. Go catch him. أُكمُشلِي مُكان يَمَّك بالسِّينَما [ʔukmušli muka:n yammak bissinama] Save me a seat next to you at the movies. قَلبِي كُمَشنِي [galbi kumašni] I got a pain in the chest. كُمَشنِي دَمار برِجلِي [kumašni dama:r brijli] I got a cramp in my leg. • **2.** to catch, take hold, take root – الجِّدري مالِي كُمَش [ʔijjidri ma:li kumaš] My smallpox vaccination took. يبَيِّن شَتِل الوَرِد كُمَش [yibayyin šatil ʔilwarid kumaš] Looks like the rose bush has taken hold. • **3.** to hold, hold back – لا تُكمُشنِي. خَلِّي أَرُوح أَعَلّمَه [la: tukmušni. xalli: ʔaru:ħ ʔaʕallmah] Don't hold me. I'll show him. أُكمُش إيدَك! فلُوسَك راح تِخلَص [ʔukmuš ʔi:dak! flu:sak ra:ħ tixlaṣ] Hold on! Your money's going to run out. • **4.** to contain, hold – هَالصَّندُوق ما يُكمُش كُلّ هَالغَراض [haṣṣandu:g ma: yukmuš kull halɣara:ḍ] This trunk won't hold all these things.

كَمَّش [kammaš] *v:* • **1.** to catch, collect, round up – الجِّهال دَيكَمّشون الغَنَم، يحُطّوها بِاللّوري [ʔijjiha:l daykammšu:n ʔilɣanam, yħuṭṭu:ha billu:ri] The boys are catching the sheep and putting them on the truck. الشُّرطَة دَتكَمُّش كُلّ المُتَظاهِرين [ʔiššurṭa datkammuš kull ʔilmutaðˤa:hiri:n] The police are picking up all the demonstrators.
اِنكُمَش [ʔinkumaš] *v:* • **1.** to be caught, be seized – اِنكُمَش قَبُل ما يِطلَع مِن البِنايَة [ʔinkumaš gabul ma: yiṭlaʕ min ʔilbina:ya] He was caught before he left the building. قَلبِي يِنكُمُش بِهالمَكان [galbi yinkumuš bhalmaka:n] I feel cooped up in this place. • **2.** to shrink – هالقِماش يِنكِمِش مِن تِغِسلَه [halqima:š yinkimiš min tɣislah] This material shrinks when you wash it.
كَمُش [kamuš] *n:* • **1.** grabbing, catching • **2.** (adj:) ignorant, stupid
كَمشَة [kamša] *n:* كَمشات [kamša:t] *pl:* • **1.** grasp, grip • **2.** handful
اِنكِماش [ʔinkima:š] *n:* • **1.** shrinking, absorption, preoccupation
كامُش [ka:muš] *adj:* • **1.** holding, grabbing

ك م ع

كَمعَة [kamʕa] *n:* كَمعات [kamʕa:t] *pl:* • **1.** sip, taste

ك م ك ش

كَمكَش [kamkaš] *v:* • **1.** to grope, feel one's way – يبَيِّن ما دَيشُوف بِالظَلمَة؛ شُوفَه دَيكَمكِش [yibayyin ma: dayšu:f biðˤðˤalma; šu:fah daykamkiš] Apparently he can't see in the dark; look at him groping about.
تكَمكَش [tkamkaš] *v:* • **2.** same as كَمكَش : to grope, feel one's way

ك م ل

كِمَل [kimal] *v:* • **1.** to be finished, done, completed, accomplished – البَيت راح يِكمَل بَعَد شَهَر [ʔilbayt ra:ħ yikmal baʕad šahar] The house will be completed in a month. كُلّ الغَراض اللّي رِدتها كِملَت [kull ʔilɣara:ðˤ ʔilli riditha kimlat] All the things you wanted are ready. عَلِي جا؛ كِملَت السِّبحَة [ʕali ǰa:; kimlat ʔissibħa] Ali is here; it's all set.
كَمَّل [čammal] *v:* • **1.** to add a bit extra, to put some more in – هَالشُّوربَة ثخِينَة. كَمّلها شوَيَّة مَيّ [haššu:rba θixi:na. čammilha šwayyat mayy] This soup is thick. Add a little more water to it. الخَبّاز كَمَّلّي كَم صَمُّونَة [ʔilxabba:z čammalli čam ṣammu:na] The baker threw in a few extra loaves for me.
كَمَّل [kammal] *v:* • **1.** to complete, finish, finish up – كَمِّل هالجُمَل بِكَلِمات مِن عِندَك [kammil hajǰumal bkalima:t min ʕindak] Complete these sentences in your own words. راح يكَمِّل دِراستَه بأُورُبّا [ra:ħ ykammil dira:stah bʔu:ruppa] He will complete his studies in Europe. كَمِّل شُغلَك وَتَعال [kammil šuɣlak wataʕa:l] Finish your work and come on.
تكَمَّل [tkammal] *v:* • **1.** to be completed, finished – هَالبَيت ما يِتكَمَّل بشَهَر [halbayt ma: yitkammal bšahar] This house can't be completed in a month.
كَمِل [kamil] *n:* • **1.** finishing, completing, accomplishing
كَمال [kama:l] *n:* • **1.** perfection, completeness – الله مَوصُوف بِالكَمال [ʔallah mawṣu:f bilkama:l] God is described as perfection.
كمالَة [čma:la] *n:* كمالات [čma:la:t] *pl:* • **1.** extra portion, a bit more – أَبُوه بُسَطَه وَإنتَ بُسَطَه كمالَة [ʔabu:h buṣaṭah wʔinta buṣaṭah čma:la] His father beat him and you beat him more yet. إذا تِشتِري خَمِس كَيلُوات خيار، ينطِيك خيارتَين كمالَة [ʔiða tištiri xamis kiluwa:t xya:r, yinṭi:k xya:rtayn čma:la] If you buy five kilograms of cucumbers, he'll give you two extra cucumbers. • **2.** complement, addition, supplement
تَكامُل [taka:mul] *n:* • **1.** integration
تَكمِلَة [takmila] *n:* • **1.** supplement, complement
كمال [kma:l] *adj:* كمالِيَّة [kma:liyya] *pl:* • **1.** incomplete, obligated to take a make-up examination – اِمتِحان الإكمال [ʔimtiħa:n ʔilʔikma:l] make-up exam. طِلَع كمال بِالرِّياضِيّات [ṭilaʕ kma:l birriya:ðˤiyya:t] He ended up having to take a make-up exam in mathematics.
كامِل [ka:mil] *adj:* • **1.** complete, full – اِستَعمِلَوا فَوج كامِل بِالمَعرَكَة [ʔistaʕmilaw fawǰ ka:mil bilmaʕraka] They used an entire regiment in the fight. القَريَة بكامِلها اِستَقبِلَتَه [ʔilqarya bka:milha ʔistaqbilatah] The whole village received him. • **2.** whole, entire – إذا دَرزَن الإقلام ما كامِل ما آخذَه [ʔiða darzan ʔilʔiqla:m ma: ka:mil ma: ʔa:xðah] If the dozen of pencils isn't complete, I won't take them.
مُكَمَّل [mukammal, mkammal] *adj:* • **1.** finished, completed – بَيت مُكَمَّل [bayt mukammal] a complete house. مُطبَخ مُكَمَّل [muṭbax mukammal] a well-equipped kitchen. • **2.** perfect, excellent, fine – سايِق مُكَمَّل [sa:yiq mukammal] an excellent driver. طَبّاخ مُكَمَّل [ṭabba:x mukammal] a fine cook. إنكِلِيزِي مُكَمَّل [ʔingili:zi mukammal] perfect English. إبنَك أَدَبسِزّ بَسّ إبنَه مكَمَّل [ʔibnak ʔadabsizz bass ʔibnah mkammal] Your son has no manners but his son is faultless.
كَمالِي [kama:li] *adj:* • **1.** luxury, luxurious – أَشياء كَمالِيَّة [ʔašya:ʔ kama:liyya] luxury items. • **2.** (pl. only كَمالِيّات) luxuries
مِتكامِل [mitka:mil] *adj:* • **1.** integrative, integral, integrated • **2.** perfect • **3.** total, complete
تَكمِيلِي [takmi:li] *adj:* • **1.** completing, complementing, complementary, supplementary

ك م م 1

كَمِّيَّة [kammiyya] *n:* كَمِّيّات [kammiyya:t] *pl:* • **1.** amount, quantity

ك م م 2

كَمَّم [kammam] *v:* • **1.** to gag

تكَمَّم، تكِمَّم [tkammam, tkimmim] *v:* • **1.** to be gagged
كمّامَة [kamma:ma] *n:* كمّامات [kamma:ma:t] *pl:* • **1.** muzzle • **2.** face cover, surgical gauze mask • **3.** gas mask
تَكمِيم [takmi:m] *n:* • **1.** gagging

ك م ن 1
كَمِين [kami:n] *n:* • **1.** ambush • **2.** trap – الشُّرطَة نُصبَتلَه كَمِين [ʔiššurṭa nuṣbatlah kami:n] The police set a trap for him.
كامِن [ka:min] *adj:* • **1.** hidden, concealed, latent

ك م ن 2
كَمان [kama:n] *n:* • **1.** violin

ك م ن 3
كَمُّون [kammu:n] *n:* • **1.** cumin, cumin seed

ك م ن ج
كَمَنجَة [kamanǰa] *n:* كَمَنجات [kamanǰa:t] *pl:* • **1.** violin, fiddle

ك م ي
كِمَة [čima] *n:* • **1.** (coll.) truffle(s)
كِمايَة [čima:ya] *n:* كِمايات [čima:ya:t] *pl:* • **1.** truffle

ك م ي ء
كِيميا، كِيمِياء [ki:mya, ki:mya:ʔ] *n:* • **1.** chemistry • **2.** alchemy – هَالتِّجارَة كِيميا [hattiǰa:ra ki:mya] This trade is a gold mine.
كِمِيائي، كِيمياوي [kimya:ʔi, kimya:wi] *adj:* • **1.** chemical – صِناعَة كِيميائِيَّة [ṣina:ʕa ki:mya:ʔiyya] chemical industry. • **2.** chemist

ك م ي ر
كامِيرَة [kami:ra] *n:* كامِيرات [kamira:t] *pl:* • **1.** camera

ك ن ت ر
كَنتُور [kantu:r] *n:* كَنتورات [kantu:ra:t] *pl:* • **1.** wardrobe, movable clothes closet
كاوِنتَر [kawintar] *n:* • **1.** drawer

ك ن ت ي ن
كِنتِيانَة [čintiya:na] *n:* كِنتِيانات [čintiya:na:t] *pl:* • **1.** short, double-edged sword

ك ن د
كُندَة [kunda] *n:* كُندات، كُنَد [kunda:t, kunad] *pl:* • **1.** buttocks, bottom

ك ن ر ي
كَنارِي [kana:ri] *n:* • **1.** canary

ك ن ز
كِنَز [kinaz] *v:* • **1.** to pile up, amass, hoard (money) – دَيِكنُز فلُوس. صار مِليُونِير [dayiknuz flu:s. ṣa:r milyu:ni:r] He's piling up money. He became a millionaire.
كَنز [kanz] *n:* كُنُوز [kunu:z] *pl:* • **1.** treasure (especially buried treasure)

ك ن س
كِنَس [kinas] *v:* • **1.** to sweep – كِنسَت البَيت كُلَّه [kinsat ʔilbayt kullah] She swept the whole house.
اِنكِنَس [ʔinkinas] *v:* • **1.** to be swept – البارحَة اِنكِنسَت القُبَّة. شِبساع وُصَّختها [ʔilba:rḥa ʔinkinsat ʔalgubba. šibsa:ʕ wuṣṣaxtha] The room was swept yesterday. You certainly got it dirty fast!
كَنّاس [kanna:s] *n:* كَنّاسِين، كنانِيس [kanna:si:n, kna:ni:s] *pl:* • **1.** sweeper, street-sweeper
كَنِيسَة [kani:sa, kini:sa] *n:* كَنايِس [kana:yis] *pl:* • **1.** church – راح تِرُوح لِلكَنِيسَة هَالأَحَّد؟ [ra:ḥ tru:ḥ lilkani:sa halʔaḥḥad?] Are you going to church this Sunday?
كانُوس [ka:nu:s] *n:* كوانِيس [kwa:ni:s] *pl:* • **1.** sweeper
مَكنَسَة [maknasa] *n:* مكانِس [mka:nis] *pl:* • **1.** broom
مَكنُوس [maknu:s] *n:* • **1.** swept
مُكناسَة [mukna:sa] *n:* مُكناسات، مُكانِيس [mukna:sa:t, muka:ni:s] *pl:* • **1.** broom – هَالمُكناسَة العَتِيقَة ما تنَظُّف زين [halmukna:sa ʔilʕati:ga ma: tnaḍḍuf zi:n] This old broom doesn't clean well.

ك ن غ ر
كَنغَر [kanɣar] *n:* • **1.** kangaroo – حَيوان الكَنغَر [ḥaywa:n ʔilkanɣar] kangaroo.

ك ن ك ر ن
كَنكَرِين [gangari:n] *n:* • **1.** gangrene

ك ن ك ر ي ت
كَنكري، كُنكرِيت [kankari, kunkri:t] *n:* • **1.** concrete (mixture of gravel, sand, cement and water)

ك ن ن 1
كَنَّة [čanna] *n:* كنايِن [čna:yin] *pl:* • **1.** daughter-in-law • **2.** loosely, woman married to any junior member of a household

ك ن ن 2
اِستَكَنّ [ʔističann] *v:* • **1.** to settle down, make a home – رَح أَشتِري هَالبَيت وَإستَكِنّ بِيه [raḥ ʔaštiri halbayt wʔastačinn bi:h] I'm going to buy this house and settle down in it.

ك ن و ن
كانُون، كانُون الأَوَّل [ka:nu:n, ka:nu:n ʔilʔawwal] *n:* • **1.** December

كانُون الثّاني [ka:nu:n ʔiθθa:ni] *n:* • **1.** January

ك ن ي ك

كَونياك [ku:nya:k] *n:* • **1.** cognac

ك ن ي ن

كِنِين [kini:n] *n:* • **1.** quinine

ك ه ر ب

كَهرَب [kahrab] *v:* • **1.** to shock, give a shock – هَالبَنكَة تكَهرُبَك إذا تِلعَب بِيها [halpanka tkahrubak ʔiða tilʕab bi:ha] This fan will give you a shock if you play with it.

تكَهرَب [tkahrab] *v:* • **1.** to get a shock, be given a shock – تكَهرَب وَمات [tkahrab wma:t] He got electrocuted.

كَهرَب [kahrab] *n:* • **1.** amber • **2.** made of amber, amber – سِبحَة كَهرَب [sibħa kahrab] amber worry beads.

كَهرَباء [kahraba:ʔ] *n:* • **1.** electricity – راح يجُرُّون إلنا كَهرَباء اليُوم [ra:ħ yiǰurru:n ʔilna kahraba:ʔ ʔilyu:m] They're going to bring in our electricity today. أبُو الكَهرَباء [ʔabu ʔilkahraba:ʔ] electrician.

كَهرَبائِي [kahraba:ʔi] *n:* • **1.** electric, electrical – أُوتِي كَهرَبائِي [ʔu:ti kahraba:ʔi] an electric iron. • **2.** electrician

ك ه ف

كَهَف [kahaf] *n:* كُهُوف [kuhu:f] *pl:* • **1.** cave

ك ه ل

كَهَل [kahal] *adj:* كُهُول [kuhu:l] *pl:* • **1.** middle-aged • **2.** middle-aged person • **3.** very old, aged • **4.** aged person

ك ه ن

تكَهَّن [tkahhan] *v:* • **1.** to predict, foretell, prophesy – لا تاخُذ كَلامَه راس. هُوَّ دَيِتكَهَّن [la: ta:xuð kala:mah ra:s. huwwa dayitkahhan] Don't take what he says seriously. He's just guessing.

كاهِن [ka:hin] *n:* كَهَنَة [kahana] *pl:* • **1.** priest, religious leader

تَكَهُّن [takahun] *n:* • **1.** prediction, prophecy

كَهَنُوت [kahanu:t] *n:* • **1.** priesthood

كَهنُوتِيَّة [kahnu:tiyya] *n:* • **1.** priesthood

متكَهِّن [mitkahhin] *adj:* / *n:* • **1.** diviner, fortuneteller

كَهنُوتِي [kahnu:ti] *adj:* • **1.** priestly

ك ه ي

كاهِي [ka:hi] *n:* • **1.** (coll.) a light, flaky pastry topped with syrup

كاهِيَّة [ka:hiyya] *n:* كاهِيّات [ka:hiyya:t] *pl:* • **1.** a cake similar to a sweet croissant

كاهَجِي [ka:hači] *adj:* كاهَجِيَّة [kahači:yya] *pl:* • **1.** man who makes and sells 'kaahi'

ك و ب

كُوب [ku:b] *n:* كواب، كوابَة [kwa:b, kwa:ba] *pl:* • **1.** cup

كُوبَة [ku:pa] *n:* • **1.** hearts (suit in cards)

ك و ب ن

كُوبُون [kupu:n, kubu:n] *n:* • **1.** coupon

ك و ت

كَوَّت [čawwat] *v:* • **1.** to add bluing (to laundry), to whiten – راح تِغسِل القَمِيص وِتكَوِّتَه [ra:ħ tiɣsil ʔilqami:ṣ witčawwitah] She will wash the shirt and blue it.

ك و ت ر

كُوترَة [gu:tra] *n:* • **1.** (invar.) undifferentiated, unsorted – أبِيعَ كُوترَة، الكَوم بمِيَة فلِس [ʔabi:ʕa gu:tra, ʔilkawm bmiyat filis] I'm selling them as is, a hundred fils per pile. • **2.** anarchy, disorder – شِنُو، قابِل كُوترَة؟ ماكُو حُكُومَة؟ [šinu, qa:bil gu:tra? ma:ku ħuku:ma?] What, is it the rule of the jungle? Is there no government?

ك و ج

كَوجَة [gawǰa] *n:* • **1.** (coll.) a kind of large, light-colored plum-like fruit

كَوجايَة [gawǰa:ya] *n:* كَوجايات [gawǰa:ya:t] *pl:* • **1.** a kind of large, light-colored, plum-like fruit

ك و خ

كَوَّخ [kawwax] *v:* • **1.** to be or become bent over, stooped, round-shouldered – جِدِّي كَوَّخ بآخِر أيّامَه [ǰiddi kawwax biʔa:xir ʔayya:mah] My grandfather became stooped toward the end of his life. • **2.** to be worn out, be run down – كَوَّخ مِن الكُبُر [kawwax min ʔilkubur] He's run-down from age. مِن صار عُمرَه أربَعِين سَنَة، كَوَّخ [min ṣa:r ʕumrah ʔarbaʕi:n sana, kawwax] By the time he was forty years old, he was all run down.

كُوخ، [ku:x, x] *n:* أكواخ، كواخَة [kwa:x, kwa:xa] • 1. hut, shack . Also, جَرداغ ,جَرادِيغ [čarda:ɣ čara:diɣ] pl:

ك و د 1

كاد، بِالكاد [ka:d, bilka:d] *n:* • **1.** hardly, scarcely, not quite – راتبَه بِالكاد يكفِيه [ra:tbah bilka:d yikfi:h] His salary is hardly enough for him.

ك و د 2

كُودَة [ku:da] *n:* • **1.** a tax on livestock, levied at the markets

ك و ر

كَوَّر [kawwar] *v:* • **1.** to round off

تكَوَّر [tkawwar] *v:* • **1.** to become round
كُورَة [ku:ra] *n:* كُوَر [kuwar] *pl:* • **1.** forge • **2.** kiln, furnace – كُورَة طابُوق [ku:rat ṭa:bu:g] brick kiln. كُورَة نُورَة [ku:rat nu:ra] lime kiln. كُورَة زَنَابِير [ku:rat zana:bi:r] wasp nest.
تكوِير [takwi:r] *n:* • **1.** pelletizing
مكَوَّر [mkawwar] *adj:* • **1.** All together, rounded up, added together – مَجمُوعَة مكَوَّر صار عِدنا عِشرِين دِينار [majmu:ʕa mkawwar ṣa:r ʕidna ʕišri:n dina:r] All together we've gotten twenty dinars. • **2.** round, ball-shaped, globular

ك و ر س

كَورَس [kawras, ku:ris] *n:* • **1.** choir

ك و ر ن ي ش

كَورنِيش [ku:rni:š] *n:* كَورنِيشات [ku:rni:ša:t] *pl:* • **1.** corniche, road along a river or sea

ك و ز

كُوز [ku:z] *n:* كواز، كوازَة [kwa:z, kwa:za.] *pl:* • **1.** clay urn for storing water • **1.** corn cob

ك و س

كُوس [ku:s] *n:* • **1.** thin, sparse (beard) – لِحيتَه كُوسَة [liħi:tah ku:sa] His beard grows only on his chin.

ك و س ج

كَوسَج [ku:saǰ] *n:* كَواسِج، كواسِج [kawa:siǰ, kwa:siǰ] *pl:* • **1.** shark

ك و ف

الكُوفَة [ʔilku:fa] *n:* • **1.** Kufa (city in Iraq)
كُوفِي [ku:fi] *adj:* • **1.** Kufic, Kufi – كِتابَة كُوفِيَّة [kita:ba ku:fiyya] Kufic script, Kufic calligraphy.

ك و ك

كَوَّك [kawwak] *v:* • **1.** to baste, baste together – الخَيّاط يكَوُّك السِّترَة قَبُل ما يخَيِّطها [ʔilxayya:ṭ yikawwuk ʔissitra gabul ma: yxayyiṭha] The tailor bastes the jacket together before he sews it. • **2.** to wind, wind up – وُقفَت السّاعَة. كَوُّكها [wugfat ʔissa:ʕa. kawwukha] The watch stopped. Wind it.
تكَوَّك [tkawwak] *v:* • **1.** to be basted • **2.** to be influenced
كُوك [ku:k] *n:* • **1.** spring mechanism, spring drive – سَيّارَة الجّاهِل تِشتُغُل بكُوك [sayya:rat ʔiǰǰa:hil tištuɣul bku:k] The child's car runs by being wound up.
مَكُوك [maku:k] *n:* مواكِيك [mwa:ki:k] *pl:* • **1.** bobbin (of a sewing machine)
كواكَة [kwa:ka] *n:* • **1.** basting, long stitches
تكوِيك [takwi:k] *n:* • **1.** winding – بُرغِي تَكوِيك [burɣi takwi:k] winding stem. اللّعّابَة تِشتُغُل بالتَّكوِيك [ʔillaʕʕa:ba tištuɣul bittakwi:k] The toy is spring driven. The toy winds up.
مكَوَّك [mkawwak] *adj:* • **1.** influenced

ك و ك ب

كَوكَب [kawkab] *n:* كَواكِب [kawa:kib] *pl:* • **1.** star – كَوكَب سِينَمائِي [kawkab si:nama:ʔi] movie star. كَوكَب سَيّار [kawkab sayya:r] planet.
كَوكَبَة [kawkaba] *n:* كَوكَبات [kawkaba:t] *pl:* • **1.** squadron (mounted police, cavalry, armor)

ك و ك ت ي ل

كُوكتيل [ku:kti:l] *n:* • **1.** cocktail – حَفلَة كُوكتَيل [ħaflat ku:kti:l] cocktail party.

ك و ك و ك

كاوكُوك [ka:wču:k] *n:* • **1.** rubber, caoutchouc

ك و ل 1

كاولِي [ka:wli] *adj:* كاولِيَّة، كاوَلِيَّة [ka:wliyya, kwaliyya.] *pl:* • **1.** gypsy

ك و ل 2

كُول [gu:l] *n:* • **1.** goal

ك و ل س

كَولِيس [kawli:s] *n:* كَوالِيس [kawa:li:s] *pl:* • **1.** coulisse, opening at the side of a stage

ك و ل و ن ي

كُولُونيا [kulu:nya, qulu:nya] *n:* • **1.** cologne, perfume

ك و ل ي ر

كُولِيرا [ku:li:ra] *n:* • **1.** cholera

ك و م

كَوَّم [kawwam] *v:* • **1.** to heap, pile up, stack up – كَوَّم الغَراض كُلّها بنُصّ الغُرفَة [kawwam ʔilɣara:ð kullha bnuṣṣ ʔilɣurfa] He piled all the things in the center of the room. كَوَّمَه ببُوكس واحِد [kawwamah bibu:ks wa:ħid] He knocked him flat with one punch.
تكَوَّم [tkawwam] *v:* • **1.** to pile up, pile on – تكَوُّمَوا عَليه مِثِل الذِّبّان [tkawwumaw ʕali:h miθil ʔiððibba:n] They piled on it like flies.
كُوم [ku:m] *n:* كُوام [kuwam] *pl:* • **1.** heap, pile • **2.** بالكُوم in quantity, in large quantities – البُرتَقال مَوجُود بالكَوم اليُوم بالسُّوق [ʔilpurtaqa:l mawǰu:d bilkawm ʔilyu:m bissu:g] There are plenty of oranges at the market today. المُعَلِّم ينطِي دَرَجات عالِيَة بالكَوم [ʔilmuʕallim yinṭi daraǰa:t ʕa:lya bilkawm] The teacher gives out good grades left and right. يبِيع بالكَوم [yibi:ʕ bilkawm] He sells wholesale.

كَومَة، كُومَة [kawma, ku:ma] *n:* كُوَم، كَومات، كُومات، أكوام [kuwam, ku:ma:t, ʔakwa:m] *pl:* • **1.** heap, pile, stack
مكوَّم [mkawwam] *adj:* • **1.** piled, abundant
مِتكَوُّم [mitkawwum] *adj:* • **1.** piled, abundant

ك و م د

كُومَدِي [ku:madi] *n:* • **1.** locker, cabinet

ك و ن

كَوَّن [kawwan] *v:* • **1.** to produce, create, bring into being, form – هَذا كَوَّنلَه عِصابَة [ha:ða kawwanlah ʕiṣa:ba] He formed a gang. إذا تِبقَى مُدَّة شَهَر، تِقدَر تكَوِّنلَك أصدِقاء [ʔiða tibqa: muddat šahar, tigdar tkawwinlak ʔaṣdiqa:ʔ] If you stay a month, you can make yourself some friends.
تكَوَّن [tkawwan] *v:* • **1.** to be formed – المُطَر يِتكَوَّن مِن الغيم [ʔilmuṭar yitkawwan min ʔilɣi:m] Rain is formed from clouds.
تكاوَن [tka:wan] *v:* • **1.** to engage in argument, dispute, controversy – لُويش تِتكاوَن ويّا الجِّيران عَلَى طُول؟ [luwi:š titka:wan wiyya ʔiǰǰi:ra:n ʕala ṭu:l?] Why do you continually fight with the neighbors?
مَكان [maka:n, muka:n] *n:* مُكانات، أماكِن، أمكِنَة [muka:na:t, ʔama:kin, ʔamkina] *pl:* • **1.** place, site, spot, location – مُكان الحادِث [muka:n ʔilħa:diθ] scene of the incident. بكُلّ مُكان [bkull muka:n] everywhere. • **2.** place, seat – وَخِّر! هالمُكان مالِي [waxxir! halmuka:n ma:li] Move out of the way! This seat is mine. غَيِّر مُكانَك. الشَّمِس جَتِّي [ɣayyir muka:nak. ʔiššamis ǰatti] Change your seat. The sun has come around. • **3.** room, space – ما إلَك مُكان بالسَّيّارَة [ma: ʔilak muka:n bissayya:ra] There's no room for you in the car. إذا أكُو مَكان بالغُرفَة، خَلّي الأثاث بِيه [ʔiða ʔaku maka:n bilɣurfa, xalli: ʔilʔaθa:θ bi:h] If there is space in the room, put the furniture in it. • **4.** place, position, stead – مِنُو راح يِحتَلّ مَكانَه إذا نُقلَوه؟ [minu ra:ħ yiħtall maka:nah ʔiða nuqlu:h?] Who will fill his position if they transfer him? لَو آنِي بمُكانَك، كان سَوَّيتها [law ʔa:ni bmuka:nak, ča:n sawwi:tha] If I were in your place, I would have done it. لَو تخَلِّي نَفسَك بمُكانِي، كان عِرَفِت شلُون هَالمُشكِلَة صَعبَة [law txalli: nafsak bmuka:ni, ča:n ʕirafit šlu:n halmuškila ṣaʕba] If you put yourself in my place, you would know how difficult this problem is.
كائِن [ka:ʔin] *n:* • **1.** a being, entity, creation, creature • **2.** as Adj: existing
مُكَوِّن [mukawwin] *n:* • **1.** constituent, component, element
الكَون [ʔilkawn] *n:* • **1.** the world, the universe – ماكُو مِثلَه بالكَون [ma:ku miθlah bilkawn] There's none like it in the world.
مَكانَة [maka:na] *n:* مَكانات [maka:na:t] *pl:* • **1.** position, standing, rank, influence, authority – هالوَزِير، مَكانتَه بالبَلَد مَعرُوفَة [halwazi:r, maka:ntah bilbalad maʕru:fa] This minister's standing in the country is well-known. اللُّغَة الإنكِلِيزِيَّة إلها مَكانَتها [ʔilluɣa ʔilʔingili:ziyya ʔilha maka:natha] The English language has considerable importance.
تَكوِين [takwi:n] *n:* • **1.** forming, creation, formation
مُكَوَّن [mukawwan] *adj:* • **1.** with مِن composed of, consisting of
مِتكَوِّن [mitkawwin] *adj:* • **1.** composed of, contains
كان [ka:n, ča:n] *auxiliary verb:* • **1.** to be – الوَفِد راح يكُون هنا باكِر [ʔilwafid ra:ħ yiku:n hna: ba:čir] The delegation will be here tomorrow. البارحَة كِنِت مَرِيض بَسّ اليُوم شوَيَّة أحسَن [ʔilba:rħa činit mari:ð̣ bass ʔilyu:m šwayya ʔaħsan] Yesterday I was sick but today I'm a bit better. أتزَوَّجَه شما يكُون [ʔadzawwaǰah šma: yku:n] I'll marry him whatever he is. كان أكُو هوايَة ناس بالحَفلَة [ča:n ʔaku hwa:ya na:s bilħafla] There were a lot of people at the party. كان عِندِي دِينار واحِد بَسّ [ča:n ʕindi dina:r wa:ħid bass] I had only one dinar. • **2.** (as an auxiliary verb:) • **2.a.** in perfect tense with following imperfect verb, denotes past progressive tense – كِنِت دَألبَس قُندَرتِي مِن دَقّ التِّلِفون [činit daʔalbas qundarti min dagg ʔittilifu:n] I was putting on my shoes when the phone rang. وُقعَت مِن كانَت دَتِركَب الباص [wugʕat min ča:nat datirkab ʔilpa:ṣ] She fell as she was getting on the bus. كان دَياكُل مِن وُصَلنا [ča:n daya:kul min wuṣalna] He was eating when we arrived. مَناظرَه العَتِيقَة كانَت دَتسَبِّبلَه وُجَع راس [mana:ð̣rah ʔilʕati:ga ča:nat datsabbiblah wuǰaʕ ra:s] His old glasses were causing him headaches. كان يِدَلغُم كُلّما يشُوفنِي أطلَع [ča:n yidalɣum kullma: yšu:fni ʔaṭlaʕ] He would frown every time he saw me go out. ما كان يسِدّ الثَّلاّجَة بَعَد ما يطَلِّع مِنها شِي [ma: ča:n ysidd ʔiθθilla:ǰa baʕad ma: yṭalliʕ minha ši] He wouldn't close the refrigerator after he took something out of it. كِنِت أدُقّ كَمان مِن كِنِت صغَيِّر [činit ʔadugg kama:n min činit ṣɣayyir] I used to play the violin when I was small. كان يحُطّ هوايَة فِلفِل بالأكِل [ča:n yħuṭṭ hwa:ya filfil bilʔakil] He used to put a lot of pepper in the food. كانَت تِرسِم زين [ča:nat tirsim zi:n] She used to draw well. • **2.b.** in perfect tense with following active participle, denotes past perfect tense – لَمّا وُصَلنا لِلسِّينَما، الفِلِم كان بادِي [lamma wuṣalna lissinama, ʔilfilim ča:n ba:di] When we got to the theater, the film had started. كان باقِيلَه يوم يصِير دُكتُور [ča:n ba:qaylah yu:m yṣi:r duktu:r] There was one day remaining for him to become a doctor. كانَوا مقَشمرِينِي مُدَّة طوِيلَة [ča:naw mqašmuri:ni mudda ṭwi:la] They had been making fun of me for a long time. كان حاطّ الفلُوس بجِيبَه [ča:n ħa:ṭṭ ʔilflu:s bǰi:bah] He had put the money in his pocket. • **3.** (invar, with following verb as result statement of an implied or stated conditional, approx:) would have, could have, should have

ك و ن ت ي س

كونتيسَة [ku:nti:sa] *n:* • **1.** countess

ك و ن ي

كُونِيَة [ku:niya] *n:* كُونيات [ku:niya:t] *pl:* • **1.** (carpenter's) square • **2.** triangle (drafting)

ك و و ش

كاوُوش [ča:wu:š] *n:* كواويش [čwa:wi:š] *pl:* • **1.** crew boss, foreman

ك و ي

كُوَى [čuwa:] *v:* • **1.** to burn, sear, scald – المَيّ الحارّ كُوَى إيدَه [ʔilmayy ʔilħa:rr čuwa: ʔi:dah] The hot water scalded his hand. • **2.** to cauterize – إذا تِكوِي الجَّرِح، يطِيب بِساع [ʔiða tičwi ʔiǰǰariħ, yṭi:b bsa:ʕ] If you cauterize the wound, it will heal quickly. كُوَى الحَبّايَة اللّي بوجّه بِجِكارَة [čuwa: ʔilħabba:ya ʔilli bwiččah bǰiga:ra] He burned the pimple on his face with a cigarette. • **3.** to brand – بأمرِيكا، يِكوُون الهُوش بِعَلامات خاصَّة حَتَّى ما تِنباق [bʔamri:ka, yičwu:n ʔilhu:š bʕala:ma:t xa:ṣṣa ħatta ma: tinba:g] In America, they brand cattle with personal markings so they won't get stolen.

كُوَى [kuwa:] *v:* • **1.** to iron, press – مِنُو راح يِكوِي قمِيصَك؟ [minu ra:ħ yikwi qami:ṣak?] Who will press your shirt? • **2.** to curl (with a curling iron) – تُكوِي شَعَرها [tukwi šaʕarha] She curls her hair.

كَوَّى [čawwa:] *v:* • **1.** same as كُوَى : to burn, sear, scald, to cauterize, to brand

اِنكُوَى [ʔinčuwa:] *v:* • **1.** to be burned, be seared, be scalded – الجّاهِل اِنكُوَى بالسَّماوَر [ʔiǰǰa:hil ʔinčuwa: bissama:war] The child got burned on the samovar.

كَوي [kawy] *n:* • **1.** ironing

كَوي [čawy] *n:* • **1.** burning

كَويَة [čawya] *n:* كَويات [čawya:t] *pl:* • **1.** burn • **2.** burn scar • **3.** brand

مَكوِي [makwi] *n:* مَكاوِي [maka:wi] *pl:* • **1.** pressing shop, cleaner's

كاويَة [ka:wya] *n:* كاويات [ka:wya:t] *pl:* • **1.** soldering iron

مَكوَجِي [makwaǰi, makwači] *n:* • **1.** ironing worker, person who irons clothes

ك و ي ت

الكُويت [ʔilkuwi:t] *n:* • **1.** Kuwait

ك و ي ل

كُويل [ku:yil] *n:* كَويلات [ku:yla:t] *pl:* • **1.** coil (auto.)

ك ي ب

كِيبايَة [ki:ba:ya] *n:* كِيبايات [ki:ba:ya:t] *pl:* • **1.** boiled lamb's stomach stuffed with ground lamb, rice, almonds and spices (a kind of Iraqi haggis)

ك ي ب ل

كَيبُل [kaybul] *n:* • **1.** cable

ك ي ت

كَيَّت [čayyat] *v:* • **1.** to plunge, dive, jump – لا تجَيِّت بِالمَيّ تَرَة مُو غَميج [la: tčayyit bilmayy tara mu: ɣami:ǰ] Don't plunge into the water in case it isn't deep. • **2.** to burst in – دُقّ الباب عَليه. مُو تكَيِّت [dugg ʔilba:b ʕali:h. mu: tčayyit] Knock at the door for him. Don't just burst in.

كِيت [či:t] *n:* • **1.** an inexpensive, lightweight cotton cloth

كَيت، كَيت وَ كَيت [ki:t, ki:t wki:t] *n:* • **1.** such and such – قال عَنَّه كَيت وَ كَيت [ga:l ʕannah ki:t w ki:t] He said such and such about him.

ك ي ج

كَيج [gayǰ] *n:* • **1.** gauge

ك ي س

كَيَّس [čayyas] *v:* • **1.** to scrub with a coarse cloth mitten – الأمّ كَيِّسَت رِجلَين إبنها [ʔilʔumm čayyisat riǰlayn ʔibinha] The mother scrubbed her son's legs. • **2.** to bog down, get stuck – كَيِّسِت بِالطِّين إلَى رُكُبتِي [čayyasit biṭṭi:n ʔila rukubti] I bogged down in the mud to my knees. سَيّارتِي كَيِّسَت بالطِّين [sayya:rti čayyisat biṭṭi:n] My car got stuck in the mud. سِمَعِت عَلِي كَيَّس بالإمتِحان [simaʕit ʕali čayyas bilʔimtiħa:n] I heard Ali failed on the exam.

كِيس [či:s, ki:s] *n:* كِياس [čiya:s] *pl:* • **1.** bag, sack, pouch, purse, pocket • **2.** a mitten made of coarse, heavy cloth, used to scrub the skin

ك ي ف

كَيَّف [kayyaf] *v:* • **1.** to fit, modify, adjust, adapt – تِقدَر تكَيِّف هَالقُصَّة حَسَب ما تريد [tigdar tkayyif halquṣṣa ħasab ma: tri:d] You can adapt the story however you wish • **2.** to condition – اِشتِرَينا جِهاز يكَيِّف الهَوا [ʔištirayna ǰiha:z yikayyif ʔilhawa] We bought an appliance that conditions the air. • **3.** to be amused, pleased, delighted – الجّاهِل كَيَّف بالهَدِيَّة [ʔiǰǰa:hil kayyaf bilhadiyya] The child was pleased with the gift. • **4.** with ل to enjoy, take pleasure in – هُوَّ كَيِّف لِهِيكِي حَكِي [huwwa kayyif lhi:či ħači] He enjoys such talk.

تكَيَّف [tkayyaf] *v:* • **1.** to adapt oneself, adjust oneself – أكثَر الحَيوانات تِتكَيَّف حَسَب المُحِيط [ʔakθar ʔilħaywa:na:t titkayyaf ħasab ʔilmuħi:ṭ] Most animals adapt themselves according to the environment.

كَيف [kayf] *n:* • **1.** mood, humor, state of mind, frame of mind – شلُون كَيفَك اليُوم؟ [šlu:n kayfak ʔilyu:m?] How do you feel today? • **2.** well-being, good humor, high spirits, pleasure, delight – مالَه كَيف اليُوم [ma:lah kayf ʔilyu:m] He's not feeling well today. مِن حَصَّل الجّائِزَة، طار مِن الكَيف [min ħaṣṣal ʔiǰǰa:ʔiza, ṭa:r min ʔilkayf] When he won the prize, he jumped with joy. • **3.** discretion, option, will – كُلّ شِي صار عَلَى كَيفَك [kull ši ṣa:r ʕala kayfak] Everything went the way you wanted it. إذا ما تريد ترُوح ويّايا، كَيفَك [ʔiða ma: tri:d tru:ħ wiyya:ya, kayfak] If you don't want to go with me, that's up to you. بكَيفَك. إذا تريد ترُوح، آني أجي ويّاك [bkayfak. ʔiða tri:d tru:ħ, ʔa:ni ʔaǰi wiyya:k] As you wish. If you want to go, I'll come with you. سُوق عَلَى كَيفَك. تِقدَر تخَلّص [su:q ʕala kayfak. tigdar txalliṣ] Drive slowly. You can make it. ظَلّوا يتعاركُون عَشِر دَقايِق وَبَعدين تفاكِكَوا مِن كَيفهُم [ðallaw yitʕa:rku:n ʕašir daqa:yiq wbaʕdi:n tfa:kikaw min kayfhum] They kept on fighting for ten minutes and finally separated by themselves. • **4.** pl. كَيفات party, celebration – البارحَة كان عِدّهُم كَيف [ʔilba:rħa ča:n ʕiddhum kayf] Yesterday they had a party with singing and dancing.

تَكَيُّف [takayyuf] *n:* • **1.** adaptation, adjustment

كَيفِيَّة [kayfiyya] *n:* كَيفِيّات [kayfiyya:t] *pl:* • **1.** manner, mode, fashion

مُكَيِّفَة [mukayyifa] *n:* مُكَيِّفات [mukayyifa:t] *pl:* • **1.** air conditioner

تَكيِيف [takyi:f] *n:* • **1.** forming, shaping, air conditioning

كَيفِي [kayfi] *adj:* • **1.** arbitrary – عَمَل كَيفِي [ʕamal kayfi] an arbitrary action. فَصِل كَيفِي [faṣil kayfi] an arbitrary dismissal.

مكَيِّف [mkayyif] *adj:* • **1.** excited • **2.** happy, satisfied

كَيفجِي [ki:fči] *adj:* كَيفجِيَّة [ki:fčiyya] *pl:* • **1.** good-time Charlie, continuous party goer, party boy

كيف [či:f] *adv:* • **1.** because, since – ما أقدَر أرُوح لِلسِّينَما كيف ما عِندِي فلُوس [ma: ʔagdar ʔaru:ħ lissi:nama či:f ma: ʕindi flu:s] I can't go to the movies because I haven't got any money.

ك ي ك

كاك [ča:k] *n:* • **1.** (invar.) base down, the winning position (said of the كَعَب, the bone used to play a popular children's game). – الكَعَب مالِي وُقَف كاك [ʔaččaʕab ma:li wugaf ča:k] My bone landed base down. شلُون ما تذِبَّه، يُوقُف كاك [šlu:n ma: dðibbah, yu:guf ča:k] No matter what happens, he comes out all right.

كاك [ka:k] *n:* كاكات [ka:ka:t] *pl:* • **1.** valve, faucet, tap, cock – كاك بُورِي الدُّوش [ka:k bu:ri ʔiddu:š] the shower faucet. كاك مال البُورِي العُمُومِي [ka:k ma:l ʔilbu:ri ʔilʕumu:mi] the valve on the main.

كيك [kayk] *n:* • **1.** (coll.) cake(s)

كيكَة [kayka] *n:* كَيكات [kayka:t] *pl:* • **1.** unit noun of cake

ك ي ل

كال [ča:l] *v:* • **1.** to measure out – كِيلِّي كَيلتَين إذرَة [či:lli čayltayn ʔiðra] Measure out two ladles of corn for me.

كَيَّل [čayyal] *v:* • **1.** to stockpile, store up – كُلّ رِبيع يكَيّلُون حُنطَة تكَفِّيهُم السَّنَة كُلّها [kull ribi:ʕ yčayylu:n ħunṭa tkaffi:hum ʔissana kullha] Every spring they buy up enough wheat to last them the whole year.

كيلَة [čayla] *n:* كيلات [čayla:t] *pl:* • **1.** a container of no standard size used by merchants to measure out grain, etc • **2.** bullet • **3.** gunshot

كَيّال [čayya:l] *n:* كَيّالَة [čayya:la] *pl:* • **1.** measurer, person who measures out grain

مكيال [mičya:l] *n:* • **1.** measure of capacity, dry measure of grain

ك ي ل م ت ر

كِيلُومَتر [kilumatr] *n:* كِيلُومَترات [kilumatra:t] *pl:* • **1.** kilometer • **2.** speedometer

ك ي ل ن

كَيلُون [kaylu:n, ki:lu:n] *n:* كَيلُونات [kaylu:na:t] *pl:* • **1.** large key • **2.** (door) lock

ك ي ل و

كَيلُو [ki:lu:] *n:* كَيلُوات [ki:lu:wa:t] *pl:* • **1.** kilo, kilogram

ك ي م س

كِيمُوس [ki:mu:s] *n:* • **1.** gastric juice

ك

ل

ل [1]

لي، ليها [li, liːha] *pronoun:* • **1.** see under عَلَى

ال [ʔil] *determiner:* • **1.** (definite article) the

ل [2]

لِ-، ل [li-, la-] *preposition:* • **1.** for – إذا تشُوف عَلِي، قُلَّه إلَه مَكتُوب عِندِي [ʔiða tšuːf ʕali, gullah ʔilah maktuːb ʕindi] If you see Ali, tell him I've got a letter for him. إلَك عِندِي خَمس دَنانِير [ʔilak ʕindi xams danaːniːr] I owe you five dinars. أريدها لِنَفسِي [ʔariːdha lnafsi] I want it for myself. مالَه أيّ مُكان بَالسَّيّارَة [maːlah ʔayy mukaːn bissayyaːra] There's no room for him in the car. ما إلَك أيّ حَقّ تِستَعمِل غُرُفتِي [maː ʔilak ʔayy ħaqq tistaʕmil ɣurufti] You've got no right to use my room. لازِم إلَه سَبَب [laːzim ʔilah sabab] There must be a reason for it. أكُو عِدَّة أسباب لِسقُوطَه [ʔaku ʕiddat ʔasbaːb lisiquːṭah] There are many reasons for his failure. إلَه يومَين زَعلان [ʔilah yawmayn zaʕlaːn] He's been mad two days. حَذَّرتَه لِلمَرَّة الثّانيَة وَما إعتِقِد يفِيد [ħaððartah lilmarra ʔiθθaːnya wma ʔiʕtiqid yfiːd] I warned him for the second time but I don't think it did any good. • **2.** for, to the benefit of, on behalf of, in favor of – رُوح اِشتِكِي وَأنِي أشهَدلَك [ruːħ ʔištiki waʔaːni ʔašhadlak] Go file a complaint and I'll testify for you. سَوِّيت لَك إيّاها لأنَّك صَدِيقِي [sawwiːt lak ʔiyyaːha liʔannak ṣadiːqi] I did it for you because you're my friend. اِنحاز لجانِب الحُكُومَة [ʔinħaːz ljaːnib ʔilħukuːma] He sided with the government. • **3.** for, for the purpose of – هَالمَيّ ما يصلَح لِلشُّرُب [halmayy maː yiṣlaħ liššurub] This water isn't suitable for drinking. هَالسَّيّارَة زينَة لِلسِّباق [hassayyaːra ziːna lissibaːq] This car is good for racing. • **4.** to (of the dative) – قُلِّي شتِرِيد [gulli šitriːd] Tell me what you want. جِبتها إلَك [jibitha ʔilak] I brought it to you. رُشّلَه مِلِح لِلأكِل [ruššlah miliħ lilʔakil] Add salt to the food. تبَرَّع بدِينار لِلمَدرَسَة [tbarraʕ bdiːnaːr lilmadrasa] He donated a dinar to the school. ما مَسمُوح لَهُم ياخذُون الكُتُب [maː masmuːħ lahum yaːxðuːn ʔilkutub] They're not permitted to take the books. أمرِي لِلّه [ʔamri lʔallah] My destiny is up to God. • **5.** because of, due to, owing to – لِكُثرَة المُطَر بهالمَنطَقَة، ما نِقدَر نِزرَع حُنطَة [lkuθrat ʔilmuṭar bhalmanṭaqa, maː nigdar nizraʕ ħunṭa] Due to the large amount of rain in this area, we can't grow wheat. ما سَوّوا لَه العَمَليَّة لكُبُر سِنَّه [maː sawwaːw lah ʔilʕamaliyya ʔilkubur sinnah] They didn't perform the operation on him because of his age. • **6.** paraphrases the genitive – هالشّادِي ما إلَه ذَيل [haššaːdi maː ʔilah ðayl] This monkey has no tail. هَالمَرَّة إلَك. مَرَّة الثّانيَة ما أسامحَك [halmarra ʔilak. marrat ʔiθθaːnya maː ʔasaːmħak] This time is gratis. Next time I won't pardon you. • **7.** (var. of إلَى [ʔila]) (which see under) • **8.** to, toward (denoting direction or destination) – راح أرُوح لِلبَيت [raːħ ʔaruːħ lilbayt] I'm going to the house. شوَقِت راح ترجَع لِبَغداد؟ [šwakit raːħ tirjaʕ lbaɣdaːd?] When will you return to Baghdad? • **9.** to, up to, until – لِليوم ما أعرُف السَّبَب [lilyuːm maː ʔaʕruf ʔissabab] To this day I don't know the reason. ما شِفتَه لهَسَّة [maː šiftah lhassa] I haven't seen him up to now. بقينا هناك لِنُصّ اللَّيل [biqiːna hnaːk linuṣṣ ʔillayl] We stayed there until midnight. لا تبالِغ لِهالدَّرَجَة [laː tbaːliɣ lhaddaraja] Don't exaggerate to such an extent. • **10.** (introduces a post-stated object (in a frequently used, specifically Iraqi syntactic structure.) – ما يحِبَّه لعَلِي [maː yħibbah lʕali] He doesn't like Ali. صَلَّحِتها لِلسَّيّارَة [ṣallaħitha lissayyaːra] I have repaired the car. • **11.** supports the otherwise unaccented accusative suffix for the purpose of emphasis – رادنِي إلِي [raːdni ʔili] He wanted me. رادنِي إليّا [raːdni ʔiliyya] He wanted me. شِفتَك إلَك بِالمَحَطَّة، مُو أخُوك [šiftak ʔilak bilmaħaṭṭa, muː ʔaxuːk] I saw you in the station, not your brother.

ل [3]

لا [laː] *negative particle:* • **1.** no – ما أرِيد أرُوح [laː ʔariːd ʔaruːħ] No. I don't want to go. • **2.** there is not, there is no – لا إلَاه إلّا الله [laː ʔilaːh ʔilla ʔallah] There is no god but God. لا بُدّ يِسمَع الخَبَر [laː budd yismaʕ ʔilxabar] He's bound to hear the news. لا بَأس [laː baʔas] there is no objection, there's nothing wrong. هَالسَّيّارَة لا بَأس بيها، وَلَو عَتيقَة [hassayyaːra laː baʔas biːha, walaw ʕatiːga] There's nothing wrong with this car, even though it's old. لا بَأس تِجِي وِيّانا [laː baʔas tiji wiyyaːna] There's no objection to your coming with us. لا شَكّ [laː šakk] there is no doubt, undoubtedly. لا شَكّ تُعرُف شدَيسَوّي [laː šakk tuʕruf šdaysawwiː] You undoubtedly know what he's up to. لا. . . وَلا [laː. . . wala] neither. . . nor. . . . ما يُملُك --- لا سَيّارَة وَلا بَيت [maː yumluk laː sayyaːra walaː bayt] He owns nothing --- neither a car nor a house. لا حِكَى وَلا ضِحَك [laː ħičaː wala ḍiħak] He neither spoke nor laughed. • **3.** (with shortened vowel and following verb, expressing negative imperative) don't, don't let it happen that – لا يكُون ترُوح وَما تقُلِّي [laː ykuːn truːħ wma dgulli] You mustn't go and not tell me. لا يهِمَّك. آنِي عِندَك [laː yhimmak. ʔaːni ʕindak] Don't let it bother you. I'm with you. لا يقَشمُرَك، تَرَة ما عِندَه فلُوس [laː yqašmurak, tara maː ʕindah fluːs] Don't let him fool you, because he doesn't have any money. *Editor's Note: There are some syntactically complex uses of* لا *which could not be included in this dictionary.*

ل

ل ء م 1

لائَم [laːʔam] *v:* • **1.** to agree with, be good for, suit, accommodate – جَوّ البَصرَة ما يلائِم صِحّتَه [ǰaww ʔilbaṣra maː ylaːʔim ṣiħħtah] The weather of Basra doesn't agree with his health.

تلائَم [tlaːʔam] *v:* • **1.** to agree, fit in, go well – لُون البَردَة ما يِتلائَم ويّا لُون الحِيطان [luːn ʔilparda maː yitlaːʔam wiyya luːn ʔalħiːṭaːn] The color of the curtain doesn't go well with the color of the walls. • **2.** to get along well, fit in – طَلّعَه مِن الصَّفّ لِأَنّ ما يِتلائَم ويّا الطُّلّاب [ṭallaʕah min ʔiṣṣaff liʔann maː yitlaːʔam wiyya ʔiṭṭullaːb] He expelled him from the class because he doesn't fit in with the students.

مُلائَمَة [mulaːʔama] *n:* • **1.** suitability, fitness (physical), adequacy

مُلائِم [mulaːʔim] *adj:* • **1.** appropriate, fitting, suitable, proper, favorable – هالفُرصَة مُلائِمَة لمُفاتَحتَه بِالمَوضُوع [halfurṣa mulaːʔima lmufaːtaħtah bilmawðuːʕ] This is a favorable occasion for approaching him about the matter.

مِتلائِم [mitlaːʔim] *adj:* • **1.** appropriate, fitting, suitable, proper, favorable

ل ء م 2

اِلتِئَم [ʔiltiʔam] *v:* • **1.** to heal, mend – الجَّرِح راح يِلتِئِم خِلال إسبُوع [ʔiǰǰariħ raːħ yiltiʔim xilaːl ʔisbuːʕ] The wound will heal within a week.

اِلتِئام [ʔiltiʔaːm] *n:* • **1.** healing

ل ء م 3

لُؤُم [luʔum] *n:* • **1.** meanness, wickedness, evil, ignobility, baseness, iniquity

لآمَة [laʔaːma] *n:* • **1.** meanness, ignobility, wickedness, evil, baseness, iniquity

لَئِيم [laʔiːm] *adj:* لَئِيمِين، لُؤَماء [laʔiːmiːn, luʔamaːʔ] *pl:* • **1.** mean, ignoble, evil, wicked, depraved • **2.** mean, base, sordid person

أَلأَم [ʔalʔam] *comparative adjective:* • **1.** more or most ignoble, wicked

ل ب ب

لِبّ [libb] *n:* • **1.** (coll.) core, kernel, meat (of nuts, fruit, etc.) – لِبّ جُوز [libb ǰuːz] nut meats. لِبّ غراش [libb ɣraːš] coconut. • **2.** prime, best part – أَحِبّ إبن إبنِي لِأَنّ هُوَّ لِبّ اللِّبّ [ʔaħibb ʔibin ʔibni liʔann huwwa libb ʔillibb] I love my grandson because he's the best of the best.

لِبَّة [libba] *n:* لِبّات [libbaːt] *pl:* • **1.** لِبّات unit n: of لِبّ: [libb] core, kernel, meat (of nuts, fruit, etc) • **2.** prime, best part • **3.** heart, core, center

ل ب خ

لِبَخ [libax] *v:* • **1.** to plaster

لَبُخ [labux] *n:* • **1.** plaster, cataplasm

لَبّاخ [labbaːx] *n:* • **1.** plasterer

ملَبَّخ [mlabbax] *adj:* • **1.** covered, plastered

مَلبُوخ [malbuːx] *adj:* • **1.** covered, plastered

ل ب س

لِبَس [libas] *v:* • **1.** to put on, to get dressed, clothe oneself – إلبَس هدُومَك. صار الوَقِت [ʔilbas hduːmak. ṣaːr ʔilwakit] Put on your clothes. It's time. يِقدَر يِلبَس بخَمِس دَقايِق [yigdar yilbas bxamis daqaːyiq] He can dress in five minutes. • **2.** to wear, be dressed in – حَتَّى بِالصَّيف يِلبَس قَبُّوط [ħatta bişşayf yilbas qappuːt] Even in the summer he wears an overcoat. لا تدِيرلَه بال؛ إلبسَه بِرِجلَك [laː ddiːrlah baːl; ʔilibsah briǰlak] Don't pay him any attention; ignore him.

لَبَّس [labbas] *v:* • **1.** to clothe, dress, garb – لَبّسِي الجّاهِل لا يِبرَد [labbsi ʔiǰǰaːhil laː yibrad] Dress the child so he doesn't get cold. • **2.** to put on, slip on – الصّايِغ لَبَّس المِحبَس بإصبِعِي [ʔiṣṣaːyiɣ labbas ʔilmiħbas bʔiṣbiʕi] The jeweler put the ring on my finger. لَبَّسَه كلاو [labbasah klaːw] He pulled the wool over his eyes. He duped him. دِير بالَك مِنَّه هَذا يلَبِّس كلاوات [diːr baːlak minnah haːða ylabbis klaːwaːt] Watch out for him. He'll con you. • **3.** to cover – لِيش ما تلَبِّس القَنَفَة الجِّدِيدَة بوُجِه؟ [liːš maː tlabbis ʔilqanafa ʔiǰǰidiːda bwuǰih?] Why don't you cover the new sofa with a slip cover? • **4.** to cover, coat, plate – يلَبّسُون الحَدِيد بالفُضَّة [ylabbisuːn ʔilħadiːd bilfuððа] They plate the iron with silver. هالمِحبَس ملَبَّس بذَهَب [halmiħbas mlabbas bðahab] This ring is gold plated. • **5.** to have sexual intercourse

تلابَس [tlaːbas] *v:* • **1.** to be the same size as, to be able to wear each other's clothes – آنِي وَأُختِي نِتلابَس [ʔaːni wʔuxti nitlaːbas] My sister and I can wear each other's clothes. لِبَسِت قاط أَخُويَا لِأَنّ آنِي ويّاه نِتلابَس [libasit qaːṭ ʔaxuːya liʔann ʔaːni wiyyaːh nitlaːbas] I wore my brother's suit because we're the same size.

اِنلِبَس [ʔinlibas] *v:* • **1.** to be worn – هَالنَّفنُوف ما يِنلِبِس باللَّيل [hannafnuːf maː yinlibis billayl] This dress isn't worn at night. • **2.** to be ignored

اِلتِبَس [ʔiltibas] *v:* • **1.** to become obscure, dubious, ambiguous, equivocal, confusing – اِلتِبسَت عَلَيّا الأُمُور [ʔiltibsat ʕalayya ʔilʔumuːr] The events have gotten confusing to me. • **2.** to mistake, confuse with someone else – العَفو، اِلتِبَست بِيك [ʔilʕafw, ʔiltibasit biːk] Sorry, I mistook you for someone else.

لَبِس [labis] *n:* • **1.** confusion, uncertainty, ambiguity, muddle

لِبِس [libis] *n:* • **1.** cloth, apparel, dress

لِباس [libaːs] *n:* لِبسان، لِباسات [libsaːn, libaːsaːt] *pl:* • **1.** pants, panties • **1.** (men's) drawers, underpants

مَلابِس [malaːbis] *n:* • **1.** (pl. only) clothes, clothing

ل

مَلبُوس [malbu:s] *adj:* • **1.** worn, used • **2.** underwear
اِلتِباس [ʔiltiba:s] *n:* • **1.** confusion, ambiguity, doubt, uncertainty
تَلبِيسَة [talbi:sa] *n:* • **1.** paneling
ملَبَّس [mlabbas] *adj:* • **1.** covered, coated, plated • **2.** chunks of candy, bonbons
لابِس [la:bis] *adj:* • **1.** wearing
مِتلَبِّس [mitlabbis] *adj:* • **1.** in the act, red-handed – الشُرطَة لِزمَوه مِتلَبِّس [ʔiššurṭa lizmawh mitlabbis] The police caught him in the act.
مِلتِبِس [miltibis] *adj:* • **1.** confused, mistaken – لازِم إنتَ مِلتِبِس [la:zim ʔinta miltibis] You must be mistaken.

ل ب ط

لُبَط [lubaṭ] *v:* • **1.** to wiggle, wriggle, thrash about – هَالسِّمَك تازَة وَبَعدَه يِلبُط [hassimač ta:za wbaʕdah yilbuṭ] These fish are fresh and still wiggling.
لَبُط [labuṭ] *n:* • **1.** wiggling

ل ب ق

لَباقَة [laba:qa] *n:* • **1.** cleverness, smartness, slyness, subtlety, adroitness
لَبِق [labiq] *adj:* • **1.** clever, sly, smart, skilled, elegant, suave

ل ب ل ب

لَبلَب [lablab] *v:* • **1.** to extract the core, meat, best part from – لَبلِب الرَّقِّيَّة وذِبّ القشُور بَرَّة [lablib ʔirraggiyya wđibb ʔilgšu:r barra] Take the meat out of the watermelon and throw the rinds outside. • **2.** to summarize, condense, prepare an extract, make a summary – مِن ترُوح تواجِه المُدِير، لَبلِبلَه القَضِيَّة بحِكايتَين [min tru:ħ twa:ǰih ʔilmudi:r, labliblah ʔilqađiyya bihča:ytayn] When you go to see the director, summarize the matter in two sentences for him. لَبلَبِتلَه المَوضُوع وَإنطَيته إيّاه [lablabitlah ʔilmawđu:ʕ wʔinṭaytah ʔiyya:h] I prepared a concise summary of the subject and gave it to him. • **3.** to edit, revise, refine, polish – المُحَرِّر لَبلَب المَقال وَنِشَرَه [ʔilmuħarrir lablab ʔilmaqa:l wnišarah] The editor polished up the article and published it.
لَبلَبِي [lablabi] *n:* • **1.** boiled chick peas
لَبلَبان [lablaba:n] *adj:* لَبلَبانِيَّة [lablaba:niyya] *pl:* • **1.** smooth talker, convincing speaker – هَذا غير لَبلَبان. مِنُو يِقدَرلَه؟ [ha:ða ɣi:r lablaba:n. minu yigdarlah?] He's a real talker. Who can get the better of him? • **2.** talkative person, chatterbox – هاي غير لَبلَبان. حَلقها ما يُوقَف وَلا دَقِيقَة [ha:y ɣi:r lablaba:n. ħaligha ma: yu:gaf wala daqi:qa] She's a real chatterbox. Her mouth doesn't stop for a minute.

ل ب ن

لِبَن [liban] *n:* • **1.** yogurt, coagulated sour milk • **2.** pl. ألبان milk product, dairy product – مَعمَل ألبان [maʕmal ʔalba:n] dairy.
لِبِن [libin] *n:* • **1.** (coll.) adobe(s), dried mud brick(s)
لِبنَة [libna] *n:* لِبنات [libna:t] *pl:* • **1.** yogurt • **2.** adobe, dried mud brick
لَبّان [labba:n] *n:* لَبّانَة [labba:na] *pl:* • **1.** dairy or yogurt vendor
لُبنان [lubna:n] *n:* • **1.** Lebanon
لُبناني [lubna:ni] *adj:* • **1.** Lebanese, from Lebanon – لَهجَة لُبنانِيَّة [lahǰa lubna:niyya] a Lebanese accent. • **2.** a Lebanese

ل ب و

لَبوَة [labwa] *n:* لَبوات [labwa:t] *pl:* • **1.** lioness

ل ت ر

لِتِر [latir, litir] *n:* • **1.** liter

ل ت ي ن

لاتِينِي [lati:ni] *adj:* • **1.** Latin

ل ث غ

لِثَغ [liθaɣ] *v:* • **1.** to lisp
لَثِغ [laθiɣ] *n:* • **1.** lisp, lisping
لَثغَة [laθɣa] *n:* • **1.** lisp

ل ث م

لَثَّم [laθθam] *v:* • **1.** to cover the lower part of the face – لَثَّم إبنَه مِن قَبَّت العَجَّة [laθθam ʔibnah min gabbat ʔilʕaǰǰa] He covered his son's face when the dust storm came.
تلَثَّم [tlaθθam] *v:* • **1.** to cover the lower part of one's face – الحَرامِي تلَثَّم حَتَّى ما يِنعُرُف [ʔilħara:mi tlaθθam ħatta ma: yinʕuruf] The thief masked himself so he wouldn't be recognized.
لِثام [liθa:m] *n:* لِثامات [liθa:ma:t] *pl:* • **1.** veil, covering the lower part of the face • **2.** mask
متلَثِّم [mitlaθθim] *adj:* مُتلَثِّمِين [mitlaθθimi:n] *pl:* • **1.** masked

ل ث و

لَثَّة [laθθa] *n:* لَثّات [laθθa:t] *pl:* • **1.** gum

ل ج ء

لِجَا، لِجَأ [liǰa:, liǰaʔ] *v:* • **1.** to take refuge, resort, have recourse
اِلتِجَا، اِلتِجَأ [ʔiltiǰa:, ʔiltiǰaʔ] *v:* • **1.** to resort • **2.** to seek refuge from someone
مَلجَأ [malǰaʔ] *n:* • **1.** place of refuge, shelter
لِجُوء [liǰu:ʔ] *n:* • **1.** asylum (usually لِجُوء سِياسِي political asylum)

اِلتِجاء [ʔiltiǰa:ʔ] *n:* • **1.** resorting, recourse to, seeking refuge

لاجِئ [la:ǰiʔ] *adj:* • **1.** seeking refuge, refugee

ل ج ج

لَجّ [laǰǰ] *v:* • **1.** to be insistent, persistent – أصبُر شوَيَّة. لا تلجّ [ʔuṣbur šwayya. la: tliǰǰ] Be a little patient. Don't be so insistent. لا تلجّ عَليه. خَلّيه عَلى كيفَه [la: tliǰǰ ʕali:h. xalli:h ʕala ki:fah] Don't nag him. Leave him alone.

لَجّ [laǰǰ] *n:* • **1.** insistence

لَجُوج [laǰu:ǰ] *adj:* لَجُوجِين [laǰu:ǰi:n] *pl:* • **1.** insistent, pestering, bothersome, intrusive • **2.** insistent person

ل ج م

لِجَم [liǰam] *v:* • **1.** to bridle, put the bridle on – لا تِلجِم الحِصان قَبُل ما توَكّله [la: tilǰim ʔilħiṣa:n gabul ma: twakklah] Don't bridle the horse before you feed him. • **2.** to muzzle, silence – لِجَم الشُّرطِي بِخَمس دنانير [liǰam ʔiššurṭi bxams dna:ni:r] He muzzled the cop with five dinars.

لَجَّم [laǰǰam] *v:* • **1.** same as لِجَم : to bridle, put the bridle on, to muzzle, silence

اِنلِجَم [ʔinliǰam] *v:* • **1.** to be muzzled, kept quiet, and, by extension, to remain silent – شبيك اِنلِجَمِت؟ ما تِحكِي؟ [šbi:k ʔinliǰamit? ma: tiħči?] Why are you silent? Can't you speak?

لَجِم [laǰim] *n:* • **1.** act of putting the bridle on

لجام [lǰa:m] *n:* لجامات [lǰa:ma:t] *pl:* • **1.** bridle • **2.** bit, mouthpiece of a bridle

ل ج ن

لُجنَة [luǰna] *n:* لِجان [liǰa:n, luǰa:n] *pl:* • **1.** committee, board, council

ل ح ح

لَحّ [laħħ] *v:* • **1.** to persist, be persistent, insist – إذا تلِحّ هوايَة بِأكل العِنجاص، يصِير عِندَك إسهال [ʔiða tliħħ hwa:ya bʔakl ʔilʕinǰa:ṣ, yṣi:r ʕindak ʔisha:l] If you keep on continually eating prunes, you'll get diarrhea. لا تلِحّ. ما أقدَر أرُوح [la: tliħħ. ma: ʔagdar ʔaru:ħ] Don't be so persistent. I can't go. • **2.** with عَلى to pester, harass, keep after – إذا ما تلِحّ عَليه، ما يِنطِيك فلُوسَك [ʔiða ma: tliħħ ʕali:h, ma: yinṭi:k flu:sak] If you don't keep after him, he won't give you your money.

لَحّ [laħħ] *n:* • **1.** act of insisting

مَلَحَّة [malaħħa] *n:* مَلَحّات [malaħħa:t] *pl:* • **1.** harassment, pestering, insisting – بَعَد المَلَحَّة خَلّانِي أستَعمِل سَيّارتَه [baʕad ʔilmalaħħa xalla:ni ʔastaʕmil sayya:rtah] After a lot of pestering he let me use his car.

إلحاح [ʔilħa:ħ] *n:* • **1.** insistence, earnest request, urgent solicitation

لَحُوح [laħu:ħ] *adj:* • **1.** insistent, stubborn, persistent

ل ح د

إلحاد [ʔilħa:d] *n:* • **1.** atheism • **2.** apostacy, heresy

مُلحِد [mulħid] *adj:* • **1.** atheist, apostate, heretic

ل ح س

لِحَس [liħas] *v:* • **1.** to lick – الهايشَة دَتِلحَس راس عِجِلها [ʔilha:yša datilħas ra:s ʕiǰilha] The cow is licking her calf's head.

اِنلِحَس [ʔinliħas] *v:* • **1.** to be licked • **1.** to be idiotic

لَحِس [laħis] *n:* • **1.** licking

مَلحُوس [malħu:s] *adj:* • **1.** licked • **2.** idiotic

ل ح ظ

لاحَظ [la:ħað] *v:* • **1.** to notice, perceive, observe, be aware of – لاحَظِت عَليه أيّ تَغَيُّر؟ [la:ħaðit ʕali:h ʔayy tayayyur?] Have you noticed any change in him? دَتلاحِظ شلُون دَتِتطَوَّر الأشياء؟ [datla:ħið šlu:n datiṭṭawwar ʔilʔašya:ʔ?] Do you see how things are shaping up? • **2.** to watch, pay attention to – لاحظَه زين تَرَة يبُوق [la:ħðah zi:n tara ybu:g] Watch him well because he steals.

لَحظَة [laħða] *n:* لَحظات [laħða:t] *pl:* • **1.** moment, instant – اِنتِظِرني لَحظَة [ʔintiðirni laħða] Wait for me a moment. • **2.** بلَحظَة in a moment, instantly

مُلاحِظ [mula:ħið] *n:* مُلاحِظِين [mula:ħiði:n] *pl:* • **1.** superintendent, supervisor (a rank in the Iraqi civil service below that of director)

مُلاحَظَة [mula:ħaða] *n:* مُلاحَظات [mula:ħaða:t] *pl:* • **1.** observation, remark, comment • **2.** note, post-script (on a letter)

مَلحُوظَة [malħu:ða] *n:* مَلحُوظات [malħu:ða:t] *pl:* • **1.** observation, remark, comment • **2.** note

مَلحُوظ [malħu:ð] *adj:* • **1.** noticeable, noteworthy, remarkable – تَقَدُّم مَلحُوظ [taqaddum malħu:ð] noticeable progress.

ل ح ف

لحاف [lħa:f] *n:* لِحِف، لِحفان [liħif, liħfa:n] *pl:* • **1.** bedcover, blanket, quilt, comforter, wrap

ل ح ق

لُوحَق [lu:ħag] *v:* • **1.** to chase, try to catch – الكَلِب دَيلُوحِق البَزُّونَة وَين ما ترُوح [ʔiččalib daylu:ħig ʔilbazzu:na wi:n ma: tru:ħ] The dog's chasing the cat wherever it goes. صارلَه إسبُوع ملَوحِقنِي عَالفلُوس [ṣa:rlah ʔisbu:ʕ mlawħigni ʕalflu:s] He's been after me for a week for the money.

لِحَق [liħaq] *v:* • **1.** to attach, connect, join, annex, append – الغُرفَة مُلحَقَة بِهالقاعَة [ʔilyurfa mulħaqa bhalqa:ʕa] The room is connected to this hall. لِحقوا مُدِيريَّة السِّكَك بوُزارَة المُواصَلات [liħqaw mudi:riyyat ʔissikak bwuza:rat ʔilmuwa:ṣala:t] They attached the Directorate of Railroads to the Communications Ministry.

ل

لِحَق [liħag] *v:* • **1.** to follow, trail after – فَدّ رِجّال لِحَق بِنتِي مِن المَدرَسَة [fadd rijja:l liħag binti min ʔilmadrasa] Some man followed my daughter from the school. • **2.** to chase, pursue – الشُّرطِي لِحَق الحَرامِي وَلِزَمَه [ʔiššurṭi liħag ʔilħara:mi wlizamah] The policeman chased the thief and caught him. • **3.** to ripen, become ripe – كُمَر الطَّماطَة حَتَّى تِلحَق [kumar ʔiṭṭama:ṭa ħatta tilħag] He covered the tomatoes so they'd ripen. • **4.** to become ready – أُكُلَّك شوَيَّة لِبَن حَتَّى يِلحَق الأَكِل [ʔukullak šwayyat liban ħatta yilħag ʔilʔakil] Have a little yoghurt until the food gets ready. • **5.** with لِ- to rush to the aid of

لَحَّق [laħħag] *v:* • **1.** to have time for, have a chance to – ما أَلَحِّق أَرُوح لِلسُّوق وأَرجَع بساعَة وِحدَة [ma: ʔalaħħig ʔaru:ħ lissu:g wʔarjaʕ bsa:ʕa wiħda] I don't have time to go to the market and back in one hour. ما لَحَّقِت حَتَّى أَسَلِّم عَليه. كان مِستَعجِل [ma: laħħagit ħatta ʔasallim ʕali:h. ča:n mistaʕjil] I didn't even have time to greet him. He was in a hurry. • **2.** to ready, make ready – راح أَلَحِّقلَك القاط بِتلَث أَيّام [ra:ħ ʔalaħħiglak ʔilqa:ṭ bitlaθ ʔayya:m] I'll have the suit ready for you in three days. • **3.** to ripen, make ripe – هالحَرّ راح يلَحِّق التَّمُر [halħarr ra:ħ ylaħħig ʔittamur] This heat will ripen the dates. • **4.** to unbalance, cause to be mentally disturbed – ظَلَّوا يِتشاقُون وَيصَنِّفُون عَليه إِلَى أَن لَحَّقوه [ḍallaw yitša:qu:n wyṣannifu:n ʕali:h ʔila ʔan laħħigu:h] They kept poking fun at him and teasing him until they drove him nutty. • **5.** with ب to catch up with, overtake – لَحَّقنا بِيهُم يَمّ الحُدُود [laħħagna bi:hum yamm ʔilħudu:d] We overtook them near the border. تَرَفَّعِت قَبلَه لَكِن بَعَد سَنَة لَحَّق بِيّا [traffaʕit gablah la:kin baʕad sana laħħag biyya] I was promoted before him but after a year he caught up with me. لَحِّق تَرَة الأَكِل راح يِخلَص [laħħig tara ʔilʔakil ra:ħ yixlaṣ] Hurry up or the food will be all gone. • **6.** with ل to hammer, pelt – لَحَّقلَه ضَربَة وَرا ضَربَة، وَلا إِنطاه فُرصَة يشِيل إِيدَه [laħħaglah ḍarba wara ḍarba, wala ʔinṭa:h furṣa yši:l ʔi:dah] He threw blow after blow at him, and didn't give him a chance to raise his fist. لَحَّقلَه بأَسئِلَة حَتَّى خَربَطَه [laħħaglah bʔasʔila ħatta xarbaṭah] He pelted him with questions until he got him all confused. • **7.** with ب- or عَلَى to be on time for – إذا آخُذ الطَّيّارَة هَسَّة، أَلَحِّق عَلَى مَوعِد الإجتِماع [ʔiða ʔa:xuð ʔiṭṭiyya:ra hassa, ʔalaħħig ʕala mawʕid ʔilʔijtima:ʕ] If I take a plane now, I can be on time for the meeting. خَلِّي ناخُذ تاكسِي تَرَة ما نلَحِّق بِالطَّيّارَة [xalli: na:xuð ta:ksi tara ma: nlaħħig biṭṭayya:ra] Let's take a taxi or we won't catch the plane.

لاحَق [la:ħig] *v:* • **1.** to chase, follow, track

تلَحَّق [tlaħħag] *v:* • **2.** with لِ- to rush to the aid of – كان مات لَو ما يِتلَحَّقُوا لَه [ča:n ma:t law ma: yitlaħħigu:lah] He'd have died if they hadn't rushed to his aid.

تلاحَق [tla:ħag] *v:* • **1.** to catch up with

اِنلِحَق [ʔinliħag] *v:* • **1.** to be followed, pursued – أَفتِكِر اِنلِحَقنا [ʔaftikir ʔinliħagna] I think we've been followed. • **2.** with بِيه to be overtaken, caught – هَذا يِركُض كُلِّش سَرِيع. أَبَد ما يِنلِحِق بِيه [ha:ða yirkuḍ kulliš sari:ʕ. ʔabad ma: yinliħiq bi:h] He runs very fast. He'd never be caught.

اِلتِحَق [ʔiltiħaq] *v:* • **1.** with ب to enter, join, enroll in, become a part of – أَكثَر خِرِّيجِين هَالكُلِّيَّة يِلتِحقُون بِخِدمَة الحُكُومَة [ʔakθar xirri:ji:n halkulliyya yiltiħqu:n bxidmat ʔilħuku:ma] Most of the graduates of this college join the government service.

لِحِق [laħig] *n:* • **1.** chasing, pursuing, pursuit

إِلحاق [ʔilħa:q] *n:* • **1.** appending, annexing, connecting, attaching, joining,

مُلاحَقَة [mula:ħaqa] *n:* • **1.** chase, pursuit

مُلحَق [mulħaq] *adj:* مَلاحِق [malaħiq] *pl:* • **1.** attached, affixed, annexed, appended – مُلحَق بالبِنايَة [mulħaq bilbina:ya] attached to the building. مُلحَق بهالقِسِم [mulħaq bhalqisim] attached to this section. • **2.** supplement, extra section • **3.** appendix • **4.** annex • **5.** pl. مُلحَقِين attaché, affiliate, assistant

لاحِق [la:ħig] *adj:* • **1.** ready – الأَكِل لاحِق لَو بَعَد؟ [ʔilʔakil la:ħig law baʕad?] Is the food ready yet? • **2.** ripe – لا تِقطَع البُرتَقال؛ بَعدَه ما لاحِق [la: tigṭaʕ ʔilpurtaqa:l; baʕdah ma: la:ħig] Don't pick the oranges; they aren't ripe yet. عَقلَه لاحِق [ʕaqlah la:ħig] He's got a screw loose. He's a bit crazy.

مِلتِحِق [miltiħiq] *adj:* • **1.** joined

مُلاحَق [mula:ħaq] *adj:* • **1.** followed

ل ح م

لِحَم [liħam] *v:* • **1.** to mend, patch – الفِيتَرجِي لِحَم الجُوب [ʔalfitarči liħam ʔičču:b] The mechanic patched the tube. • **2.** to weld, solder – رِجل القَريُولَة اِنكِسرَت. لازِم تِلحَمها [rijl ʔilqaryu:la ʔinkisrat. la:zim tilħamha] The leg on the bed broke. You'll have to weld it. • **3.** to heal – الجَّرِح لِحَم [ʔijjariħ liħam] The wound healed.

اِنلِحَم [ʔinliħam] *v:* • **1.** to be welded, to be soldered

اِلتِحَم [ʔiltiħam] *v:* • **1.** to mend, patch, to heal

لَحَم [laħam] *n:* لُحُوم [luħu:m.] *pl:* • **1.** meat, flesh

لَحِم [laħim] *n:* • **1.** soldering

لَحمَة [laħma] *n:* لَحمات [laħma:t] *pl:* • **1.** a piece of meat

لِحمَة [liħma] *n:* لِحمات [liħma:t] *pl:* • **1.** warp (of fabric) – تخَيَّط القاط وَما زاد شِي مِن القماش طِلعَت سِدها بِلِحمَتها [txayyaṭ ʔilqa:ṭ wma za:d ši min ʔilquma:š. ṭilʕat sida:ha bliħmatha] The suit was made and no cloth was left over. It came out right on the nose.

لِحِيم [liħi:m] *n:* • **1.** welding material • **2.** solder

لَحّام [laħħa:m] *n:* لَحّامِين [laħa:mi:n] *pl:* • **1.** welder, solderer • **2.** butcher

لَحمَجي [laħamǰi] *n:* لَحمَجِيَّة [laħimǰiyya] *pl:* • **1.** welder, solderer • **2.** butcher

اِلتِحام [ʔiltiħaːm] *n:* • **1.** closeness, union, cohesion

لَحمِي [laħmi] *adj:* • **1.** flesh-colored – لابسَة جواريب لَونها لَحمِي [laːbsah ǰwaːriːb luːnha laħmi] She's wearing flesh-colored hose.

مَلحَم [malħam] *adj:* • **1.** healing ointment, salve

ل ح ن

لَحَّن [laħħan] *v:* • **1.** to compose music – مِنُو لَحَّن هالأغنِيَة؟ [minu laħħan halʔuɣniya?] Who wrote the music for this song?

لَحِن [laħin] *n:* ألحان [ʔalħaːn] *pl:* • **1.** song, tune, melody

مُلَحِّن [mulaħħin] *n:* مُلَحِّنِين [mulaħħiniːn] *pl:* • **1.** composer (of music)

تَلحِين [talħiːn] *n:* • **1.** musical composition

ل ح و

See also: ل ح ي

ل ح ي

لِحيَة [liħya] *n:* لِحايَة، لِحَى [liħaːya, liħa] *pl:* • **1.** beard – صَدِيقِي دَيرَبِّي لِحيَة [ṣadiːqi dayrabbi lihya] My friend is growing a beard.

مِلتَحِي [miltaħi] *adj:* • **1.** bearded, having a beard

ل خ خ

لَخَّة [laxxa] *n:* لَخّات [laxxaːt] *pl:* • **1.** crowd, throng (of people) – السُّوق اليُوم لَخَّة ما ينطَبّ بيه [ʔissuːg ʔilyuːm laxxa maː yinṭabb biːh] The market today is crowded. You can't get in.

ل خ ص

لَخَّص [laxxaṣ] *v:* • **1.** to summarize, sum, compress

تلَخَّص [tlaxxaṣ] *v:* • **1.** to summarize, sum

مُلَخَّص [mulaxxaṣ] *n:* • **1.** summary, gist, extract, rundown

تَلخِيص [talxiːṣ] *n:* • **1.** summary, resumé, epitome, abstract

ل خ م

لَخمَة [laxma] *n:* • **1.** same as لَكمَة : punch, blow with the fist • **2.** shutting someone up

ل د د

لَدُود [laduːd] *adj:* • **1.** bitter, grim, tough, mortal

ل د غ

لِدَغ [lidaɣ] *v:* • **1.** to sting – لِدَغنِي العَقرَب [lidaɣni ʔilʕagrab] The scorpion stung me.

لَدِغ [ladiɣ] *n:* • **1.** biting, sting

لَدغَة [ladɣa] *n:* لدغات [ladɣaːt] *pl:* • **1.** a sting, a bite (by a snake or scorpion)

ل ذ ذ

لَذّ [laðð] *v:* • **1.** to become delightful, pleasant, enjoyable, delicious – لَذَّتلِي العِيشَة بِبَغداد وَلا أَطلَع مِنها [laððatli ʔilʕiːša bibaɣdaːd wala ʔaṭlaʕ minha] Life in Baghdad is pleasant for me now and I won't ever leave it.

تلَذَّذ [tlaððað] *v:* • **1.** with ب to enjoy, relish, savor, take delight in – الجّاهِل يِتلَذَّذ بأكل السّاهُون [ʔiǰǰaːhil yitlaððað bʔakl ʔissaːhuːn] The child enjoys eating peanut brittle.

اِستَلَذّ [ʔistalaðð] *v:* • **1.** with ب to find delightful, take pleasure in, enjoy – اِستِلَذَّيت كُلِّش بِهالأَكلَة [ʔistilaððiːt kulliš bhalʔakla] I really enjoyed this meal.

لَذَّة [laðða] *n:* لَذّات [laððaːt] *pl:* • **1.** delight, joy, bliss, pleasure – هالأَكِل لَذَّة [halʔakil laðða] This food is delicious. سِمَعنا أخبار لَذَّة [simaʕna ʔaxbaːr laðða] We heard some delightful news. • **2.** orgasm, climax

مَلَذَّة [malaðða] *n:* • **1.** joy, delightfulness, enjoyment, delectation

لَذِيذ [laðiːð] *adj:* • **1.** enjoyable, pleasant – أَكِل الدَّوندرمَة لَذِيذ [ʔakil ʔidduːndirma laðiːð] Eating ice cream is enjoyable. • **2.** delicious, delightful – الكِمَة لَذِيذ [ʔiččima laðiːð] Truffles are delicious.

مِتلَذِّذ [mitlaððið] *adj:* • **1.** loving fine food and drink • **2.** epicure

أَلَذّ [ʔalaðð] *comparative adjective:* • **1.** more or most enjoyable, pleasant, delightful, delicious

ل ذ ع

لاذِع [laːðiʕ] *adj:* • **1.** acid • **2.** burning, pungent, acrid, biting, sharp

ل ز ق

لِزَق [lizag] *v:* • **1.** to adhere, stick, cling – هالطّابِع ما دَيلزَق [haṭṭaːbiʕ maː dayilzag] This stamp won't stick. لِزَق بيّا. ما فارَقنِي وَلا لَحظَة [lizag biyya. maː faːragni wala laħḍa] He stuck to me. He didn't leave me for a minute. • **2.** to affix, paste, stick – إلزَق الطّابِع بَعَد ما تِكتِب العِنوان [ʔilzag ʔiṭṭaːbiʕ baʕad maː tiktib ʔilʕinwaːn] Paste the stamp on after you write the address.

لَزَّق [lazzag] *v:* • **1.** intens. of لِزَق to adhere, stick, cling – العِلِك يلَزِّق بالإيد [ʔilʕilič ylazzig bilʔiːd] Gum really sticks to the hand. دَيقُصّ صُوَر مِن المَجَلَّة وَيلَزّقها بالدَّفتَر [dayguṣṣ ṣuwar min ʔilmaǰalla wylazzigha biddaftar] He cuts pictures out of the magazine and pastes them in a notebook.

تلَزَّق [tlazzag] *v:* • **1.** to be stuck, pasted – هالحايِط ما يِتلَزَّق عَلَيه شِي لأَنّ بَعدَه مبَلَّل [halħaːyiṭ maː yitlazzag ʕaliːh ši liʔann baʕdah mballal] Nothing can be stuck to this wall because it's still wet.

اِنلِزَق [ʔinlizag] *v:* • **1.** to be stuck, pasted – الحَدِيد ما يِنلِزِق عَلَيه شِي [ʔilħadiːd maː yinlizig ʕaliːh ši] Nothing can be pasted to iron.

ل

لَزِق [lazig] *n:* • **1.** adhering, sticking, clinging
لَزْقَة [lazga] *n:* لَزقات [lazga:t] *pl:* • **2.** stupe, plaster, poultice • **3.** adhering, sticking, clinging
لِزَّيق [lizzi:g] *n:* • **1.** adhesive tape
تَلْزِيق [talzi:g] *n:* • **1.** patchwork • **2.** adhesion • **3.** accomplishing a task imperfectly
لَزْقِي [lazgi] *adj:* • **1.** sloppy, slap-dash – يُضرُب بِالعالِي وَشُغلَه لَزقِي [yuðrub bilʕa:li wšuɣlah lazgi] He charges high prices and his work is sloppy. • **2.** pl. لَزقِيّات odd job, piecework – عايِش بِاللَّزقِيّات [ʕa:yiš billazgiyya:t] He's making a living at anything he can find.
لازِق [la:zig] *adj:* • **1.** stuck, glued
مَلزُوق [malzu:g] *adj:* • **1.** stuck, glued, plastered

ل ز م

لِزَم [lizam] *v:* • **1.** to catch, seize, grab, get hold of – بَسّ أَلزِمَه، أَزِفَّه خُوش زَفَّة [bass ʔalizmah, ʔaziffah xu:ṣ zaffa] When I get hold of him, I'm going to give him hell. لِزَموه وَهُوَّ دَينطِي فلُوس قَلب [lizmawh wahuwwa dayinṭi flu:s qalb] They caught him as he was passing counterfeit money. لِزَموه مَرّتَين وَانهِزَم [lizmawh marrtayn wʔinhizam] They caught him twice and he got away. لِزَم القَلَم وَقام يشَطِّب [lizam ʔilqalam wga:m yšaṭṭub] He grabbed the pen and started crossing things out. الجِّنُود لِزَموا الدَّرُب. أَيّ واحِد يمُرّ، يفَتّشُوه [ʔijjinu:d lizmaw ʔaddarub. ʔayy wa:ħid yumurr, yifattišu:h] The soldiers seized the road. Anyone who passes, they search. لِزَم خُوش قُنطَرات [lizam xu:š qunṭara:t] He hooked a good contract. ما لِزَموا عَليه شِي [ma: lizmaw ʕali:h ši] They didn't get anything on him. • **2.** to befall, set upon, descend upon – لِزمَتنِي المَطرَة [lizmatni ʔilmaṭra] I got caught in the rain. بَسّ طارَت الطَّيّارَة، لِزمَتَه الدَّوخَة [bass ṭa:rat ʔiṭṭiyya:ra, lizmatah ʔiddawxa] As soon as the plane took off, dizziness overcame him. كُلّ لَيلَة تِلزَمَه السُّخُونَة [kull layla tilzamah ʔissuxu:na] Every night he gets a fever. • **3.** to take effect, take hold – لُقاح الجِّدري مالِي ما لِزَم [luqa:ħ ʔijjidri ma:li ma: lizam] My smallpox vaccination didn't take. • **4.** to hold, hold on to, keep a hold on – رَجاءاً اِلزَم كُتبِي حَتَّى أَلبَس سِترتِي [raja:ʔan ʔilzam kutbi ħatta ʔalbas sitirti] Please hold my books so I can put on my coat. الجّاهِل لازِم الطِّير مِن رِجلَيه [ʔijja:hil la:zim ʔiṭṭayr min rijlayh] The kid's holding the bird by its leg. إذا اِنهِزَم بَالسَّيّارَة، آنِي إلمَن أَلزَم؟ [ʔiða ʔinhizam bissayya:ra, ʔa:ni ʔilman ʔalzam?] If he runs off with the car, who can I hold responsible? تعَطَّلنا لِأَنّ لِزَمنا عالعَشا [tʕaṭṭalna liʔann lizamna ʕalʕaša] We were late because he kept us for dinner. اِلزَم هَالطَّرِيق تُوصَل لِلجِّسِر [ʔilzam haṭṭari:q tu:ṣal lijjisir] Stay on this road and you'll come to the bridge. آنِي لازِم قَلبِي. خاف تكُون الأَسئِلَة صَعبَة [ʔa:ni la:zim galbi. xa:f tku:n ʔilʔasʔila ṣaʕba] I'm very apprehensive. I'm afraid the questions will be hard. • **5.** to hold, cling, adhere – الشّبِنتُو ما يِلزَم زين لِأَنّ بِيه رَمُل هوايَة [ʔiččbintu ma: yilzam zi:n liʔann bi:h ramul hwa:ya] The cement won't hold well because there is too much sand in it. وُقَع الطّابُوق كُلَّه لِأَنّ الشّبِنتُو ما لِزَم [wugaʕ ʔiṭṭa:bu:g kullah liʔann ʔiččbintu ma: lizam] All the bricks fell because the cement didn't hold. • **6.** to hold, contain, keep in one place – هَالصَّندُوق ما يِلزَم كُلّ غراضِي [haṣṣandu:g ma: yilzam kull ɣara:ði] This trunk won't hold all my things. اِلزَم إيدَك [ʔilzam ʔi:dak] Hold it! Stop! That's enough! اِلزَم إيدَك. اِنتِرسَت العِلّاقَة [ʔilzam ʔi:dak. ʔintirsat ʔilʕilla:ga] Hold it. The basket is full. اِلزَم إيدَك. أَكُو جاهِل دَيمُرّ [ʔilzam ʔi:dak. ʔaku ja:hil daymurr] Hold up a minute. There's a child coming by. لِزَم النَّفِس [lizam ʔinnafis] to control oneself. exercise restraint. إذا تِلزَم نَفسَك فَدّ شَهَر، تِقدَر تبَطِّل التَّدخِين [ʔiða tilzam nafsak fadd šahar, tigdar tbaṭṭil ʔittadxi:n] If you control yourself for a month, you can quit smoking. لِزَم حِساب [lizam ħisa:b] to keep count, maintain an accounting. آنِي أَقرا الأَرقام وَإِنتَ اِلزَم حِساب [ʔa:ni ʔaqra: ʔilʔarqa:m wʔinta ʔilzam ħisa:b] I'll read the numbers and you keep count. لِزَم وَقِت [lizam waqit] to time, keep time. لِزَمنالَه وَقِت مِن رِكَض [lizamna:lah waqit min rikað] We kept time for him when he ran. لِزَم المِعدَة [lizam ʔilmiʕda] to calm, settle the stomach. إذا نَفسَك دَتِلعَب، اِشرَب شاي. يِلزَم المِعدَة [ʔiða nafsak datilʕab, ʔišrab ča:y. yilzam ʔilmiʕda] If you're nauseated, drink tea. It settles the stomach. ما يِلزَم، لِقِيت قَلَمِي [ma: yilzam, ligi:t qalami] Never mind, I found my pen.
لَزَّم [lazzam] *v:* • **1.** to cause to take hold of – بَعَدما ينطِيك دَرس بِالسِّياقَة، يلَزِّمَك السُّكّان [baʕadma: yinṭi:k daris bissiya:qa, ylazzimak ʔissukka:n] After he gives you a driving lesson, he turns the wheel over to you. إذا ما ترِيدَه لِهالعامِل، لَزِّمَه الباب [ʔiða ma: tri:dah lhalʕa:mil, lazzmah ʔilba:b] If you don't want this worker, give him the gate.
لازَم [la:zam] *v:* • **1.** to hold onto, cling, adhere to, maintain a hold on – المَرَض لازَمَه مُدَّة طُويلَة [ʔilmarað la:zamah mudda ṭuwi:la] The sickness stayed with him a long time.
تلازَم [tla:zam] *v:* • **1.** to grapple with each other – تشاتمَوا وَتلازمَوا، بَسّ إحنا فاكَكناهُم [tša:tmaw wtla:zmaw, bass ʔiħna fa:kakna:hum] They exchanged insults and grappled with each other, but we separated them.
اِنلِزَم [ʔinlizam] *v:* • **1.** to be held – رُمّانتَين بِفَدّ إيد ما تِنلِزَم [rumma:ntayn bfadd ʔi:d ma: tinlizam] You can't do two things at once (lit., two pomegranates can't be held in one hand).
اِلتِزَم [ʔiltizam] *v:* • **1.** to assume responsibility for, to take on as one's own responsibility or duty – اِلتِزَم يِدفَع كُلّ ما صِرفَوا عَليه [ʔiltizam yidfaʕ kull ma: ṣirfaw ʕali:h] He took the responsibility for paying all they spent on him. لَو ما يِلتِزمنِي، ما كان ترَفَّعِت

[law maː ʔiltizimni, maː čaːn traffaʕit] If he hadn't been behind me, I wouldn't have been promoted. • **2.** to secure a monopoly on, get control of – اِلتِزَم البُستان [ʔiltizam ʔilbustaːn] He secured a contract on the orchard.
اِستَلزَم [ʔistalzam] *v:* • **1.** to require
لَزِم [lazim] *n:* • **1.** adherence to, persisting, sticking to, keeping close to.
لَزمَة [lazma] *n:* لَزمات [lazmaːt] *pl:* • **1.** grip, handhold, thing to hold on to – شقَدّ ما تِتجادَل وِيّاه، ما يِنطِيك لَزمَة [šgadd maː tidǰaːdal wiyyaːh, maː yinṭiːk lazma] No matter how much you argue with him, he won't give you anything you can get your teeth into.
لُزوم [luzuːm, lizuːm] *n:* • **1.** necessity, exigency, need – ماكو لُزوم تِجي. تِقدَر تخابُر [maːku luzuːm tiǰi. tigdar txaːbur] There's no need for you to come. You can call. عِند اللُّزوم [ʕind ʔilluzuːm] in case of need, as necessary. آخُذ مِن البَنك فلوس عِند اللُّزوم [ʔaːxuð min ʔilbang fluːs ʕind ʔilluzuːm] I take money out of the bank as it is necessary. مالِي لُزوم بِيه [maːli luzuːm biːh] I have no concern with it. It isn't important to me. شما يِعجِبَك، سَوّي؛ آني مالِي لِزوم [šmaː yiʕiǰbak, sawwiː ; ʔaːni maːli lizuːm] Do whatever you like; It's of no concern to me.
مَلزَم [malzam] *n:* مَلازِم [malaːzim] *pl:* • **1.** grip, handhold, place to hold on to
مَلزَمَة [malzama] *n:* مَلازِم [malaːzim] *pl:* • **1.** section, signature of a book (printing)
لَوازِم [lawaːzim] *n:* • **1.** (pl. only) necessities, exigencies, requisites
مُلازِم [mulaːzim] *n:* مُلازِمين [mulaːzimiːn] *pl:* • **1.** lieutenant – مُلازِم أوَّل. مُلازِم ثانِي [mulaːzim ʔawwal. mulaːzim θaːni] first lieutenant. second lieutenant.
اِلتِزام [ʔiltizaːm] *n:* • **1.** commitment, obligation, duty
إلزامِيَّة [ʔilzaːmiyya] *n:* • **1.** obligation, compulsion, requirement
مُستَلزَمات [mustalzamaːt] *n:* • **1.** pl. only requirements, requisites, necessities, obligations
لازِم [laːzim] *adj:* • **1.** necessary, requisite, imperative, required, obligatory – كُلّ جُندي لازِم عَليه يِطِيع الأوامِر [kull ǰundi laːzim ʕaliːh yiṭiːʕ ʔilʔawaːmir] Every soldier is required to obey orders. لازِم تروح وِيّايا [laːzim truːħ wiyyaːya] You have to go with me. كُلّ واحِد لازِم يصَلّي خَمِس مَرّات بالِيوم، بَسّ بَعضهُم ما يصَلّون [kull waːħid laːzim yṣalli xamis marraːt bilyuːm, bass baʕaðhum maː yṣalluːn] Everyone is supposed to pray five times a day but some of them don't pray. ما لازِم تسَوّي هِيكِي شي بَعَد [maː laːzim tsawwiː hiːči ši baʕad] You shouldn't do that any more. كان لازِم تِسألَه [čaːn laːzim tisʔalah] You should have asked him. ما لازِم. لِقيت واحِد [maː laːzim. ligiːt waːħid] Never mind. I found one. ما لازِم! بَسّ إنتَ عِندَك سَيّارَة؟ [maː laːzim! bass ʔinta ʕindak sayyaːra?] Forget it! Do you think you're the only one with a car? • **2.** (invar.) it must be that – لازِم تَصليح السَّيّارَة كَلَّفَك هوايَة [laːzim taṣliːħ ʔissayyaːra kallafak hwaːya] Repairing the car must have cost you a lot. لازِم هالكلُوب مَحرُوق. بَدِّلَه [laːzim halgluːb maħruːg. baddilah] This bulb must be burned out. Change it. بلازِم [blaːzim] in need of. آني بِلازِم فلُوس [ʔaːni blaːzim fluːs] I need money. مالَه لازِم [maːlah laːzim] It's none of his concern. It doesn't concern him. مالَك لازِم. العَركَة بِينَه وبَين مَرتَه [maːlak laːzim. ʔilʕarka biːnah wbiːn martah] It's none of your business. The fight is between him and his wife.
مَلزُوم [malzuːm] *adj:* • **1.** obligated, under obligation – آني ما مَلزُوم أنتَظرَك ساعتين وَما تِجي [ʔaːni maː malzuːm ʔantaðrak saːʕtayn wma tiǰi] I'm not obligated to wait for you two hours when you don't come. إذا صار عَليك شي، آني ما مَلزُوم [ʔiða ṣaːr ʕaliːk ši, ʔaːni maː malzuːm] If anything happens to you, I'm not responsible.
مِلتِزِم [miltizim] *adj:* • **1.** engaged, committed • **2.** religious, strict
إلزامِي [ʔilzaːmi] *adj:* • **1.** compulsory, required – التَّعلِيم إلزامِي بِالعِراق [ʔittaʕliːm ʔilzaːmi bilʕiraːq] Education is compulsory in Iraq.

ل س ت ك

لاستيك [lastiːk] *n:* لاستِيكات [lastiːkaːt] *pl:* • **1.** elastic • **2.** rubber • **3.** لَستِيكات rubber band • **4.** garter. • **5.** condom.

ل س س

لِسَّة [lissa] *adv:* • **1.** not yet, still not – لِسَّة بَيَّن شِي [lissa bayyan ši] Nothing has appeared so far.

ل س ل ك

لاسِلكِي [laːsilki] *adj:* • **1.** wireless, radio

ل س ن

تلاسَن [tlaːsan] *v:* • **1.** to argue
لسان [lsaːn] *n:* لسانات، ألسِنَة [lsaːnaːt, ʔalsina] *pl:* • **1.** tongue – إسمَه عَلَى راس لِساني [ʔismah ʕala raːs lisaːni] His name is on the tip of my tongue. لا تِحكِي وِيّاه. هَذا لسانَه وَسِخ [laː tiħči wiyyaːh. haːða lsaːnah waṣix] Don't talk to him. He uses vulgar language. شلُون لسان عِندَه [šluːn lsaːn ʕindah] What a talker he is. إذا تِجيه بلسان طَيِّب، يوافُق [ʔiða tiǰi blsaːn ṭayyib, ywaːfuq] If you approach him in a nice way, he'll agree. • **2.** language • **3.** bolt (of a lock)
مُلاسَنَة [mulaːsana] *n:* • **1.** argument

ل ش ش

لَشَّة [lašša] *n:* لَشّات، لشاش [laššaːt, lšaːš] *pl:* • **1.** carcass, animal body dressed for food • **2.** (contemptuous) human carcass, corpse, cadaver, dead body • **3.** (contemptuous) torso, body, physique

ل

ل ش ي

لاشَى [la:ša:] *v:* • **1.** to tease, bait, stir up, encourage to argue – لا تلاشِيه. هَذا أَدَبسِزّ [la: tla:ši:h. ha:ða ʔadabsizz] Don't encourage him. He's got no manners.

تلاشَى [tla:ša:] *v:* • **1.** to disappear, fade away, vanish – الغَيم تلاشَى بِسُرعَة بَعد المُطَر [ʔilɣi:m tla:ša: bsurʕa baʕd ʔilmuṭar] The clouds vanished quickly after the rain. • **2.** to engage in inane, petty argument – هَالمَرَة تِتلاشَى وِيّا أَيّ واحِد [halmara titla:ša: wiyya ʔayy wa:ħid] This woman will argue with anyone.

تَلاشِي [tala:ši] *n:* • **1.** disappearance, annihilation

ملاشاة [mla:ša] *n:* • **1.** annihilation, evanescence, ruin, waning, decline

مِتلاشِي [mitla:ši] *adj:* • **1.** evanescent, disappeared, waning, faded

ل ص ق

مُلصَق [mulṣaq] *n:* مُلصَقات [mulṣaqa:t] *pl:* • **1.** poster, sticker

لاصِق [la:ṣiq] *n:* • **1.** sticker • **2.** adhesive

ل ض م

لِضَم [liðam] *v:* • **1.** to thread, string – أُلضُم الخِرَز بِهَالخَيط [ʔulðum ʔilxiraz bhalxi:ṭ] String the beads onto this string. هاك الأُبرَة. أُلضُم بِيها خيط [ha:k ʔilʔubra. ʔulðum bi:ha xi:ṭ] Here's the needle. Run a thread through it.

لَضّم [laððam] *v:* • **1.** to string, string up – آنِي أَقَمُّع الباميَة وَإنتَ لَظُّمها [ʔa:ni ʔagammuʕ ʔilba:mya wʔinta laððumha] I'll take the heads off the okra and you string it up.

اِنلِضَم [ʔinliðam] *v:* • **1.** to be strung, to be packed closely together, to be threaded

لَضُم [laðum] *n:* • **1.** threading, stringing together

مَلضُوم [malðu:m] *adj:* • **1.** strung, strung up • **2.** packed closely together, in tight formation – مَلظُوم لَضُم [malðu:m laðum] jam-packed, very crowded. السِّينَما مَلظُومَة لَضُم بِالنّاس [ʔissinama malðu:ma laðum binna:s] The movie theater is packed full with people.

ل ط خ

لِطَخ [liṭax] *v:* • **1.** to stain, soil, spot – لِطَخ الباب بحِبِر [liṭax ʔilba:b bħibir] He spattered the door with ink. لِطَخ وُجَّه بِطِين [liṭax wuččah bṭi:n] He got his face splotched with mud. • **2.** to slam, smash, throw down hard – شالَه وَلِطَخَه بِالقاع [ša:lah wliṭaxah bilga:ʕ] He picked him up and threw him on the ground.

لَطَّخ [laṭṭax] *v:* • **1.** intens. of لِطَخ to stain, soil, spatter, spot – اِنجِرَح وَلَطَّخ ثوبَه بِالدَّم [ʔinǰirah wlaṭṭax θu:bah bʔiddamm] He got wounded and spattered his shirt with blood.

تلَطَّخ [tlaṭṭax] *v:* • **1.** to become stained, spattered, spotted – تلَطِّخَت سِترِتِي بِالبويَة [tlaṭṭixat sitirti bilbu:ya] My jacket got spattered by the paint.

لَطِخ [laṭix] *n:* • **1.** staining, spattering, spotting

لَطخَة [laṭxa] *n:* لَطخات [laṭxa:t] *pl:* • **1.** stain, smear, spot, blemish

ملَطَّخ [mlaṭṭax] *adj:* • **1.** stained, sullied, blotched

ل ط ش

لِطَش [liṭaš] *v:* • **1.** var. of لِطَخ: to slam, smash, strike

اِنلِطَش [ʔinliṭaš] *v:* • **1.** to be struck, slammed

لَطشَة [laṭša] *n:* • **1.** stike, hit

تَلطِيش [talṭi:š] *n:* • **1.** patchwork • **2.** tinkering • **3.** patching

ل ط ط

لَطّ [laṭṭ] *v:* • **1.** to slap – مِن فَشَّر عَليها، لَطَّتَه عَلَى حَلقَه [min faššar ʕali:ha, laṭṭatah ʕala ħalgah] When he insulted her, she slapped him on his mouth. • **2.** to slam, bang, throw – لَطِّيتَه بِالقاع مَرّتَين وَما إنكِسَر [laṭṭi:tah bilga:ʕ marrtayn wama ʔinkisar] I slammed it on the ground twice and it didn't break. مِن أَشُوفَه، أَلُطّ حكايتَه بوِجَّه [min ʔašu:fah, ʔaluṭṭ ħča:ytah bwiččah] When I see him, I'll make him eat his words.

اِنلَطّ [ʔinlaṭṭ] *v:* • **1.** to be slapped – اِنلَطّ عَلَى وُجَّه مَرّتَين [ʔinlaṭṭ ʕala wuččah marrtayn] He was slapped in the face twice.

لَطّ [laṭṭ] *n:* • **1.** act of slapping

ل ط ع

لِطَع [liṭaʕ] *v:* • **1.** to lick, lap up – البَزّونَة لِطعَت الحَلِيب كُلَّه مِن الماعُون [ʔilbazzu:na liṭʕat ʔilħali:b kullah min ʔilma:ʕu:n] The cat lapped up all the milk from the dish.

لَطَّع [laṭṭaʕ] *v:* • **1.** to lick repeatedly – الجّاهِل دَخَّل إصبِعَه بِالمرَبَّى وَقام يلَطِّع بِيه [ʔiǰǰa:hil daxxal ʔiṣibʕah bilmrabba wga:m yilaṭṭiʕ bi:h] The child stuck his finger in the jam and started licking away at it.

اِنلِطَع [ʔinliṭaʕ] *v:* • **1.** to be licked – شِيشَة المرَبَّى اِنلِطعَت كُلّها [ši:šat ʔalmrabba: ʔinliṭʕat kullha] The jam jar was licked clean.

لَطِع [laṭiʕ] *n:* • **1.** licking, lapping up

لَطعَة [laṭʕa] *n:* لَطعات [laṭʕa:t] *pl:* • **1.** a lick

ل ط ف

لَطَّف [laṭṭaf] *v:* • **1.** to make pleasant, enjoyable, nice – المُطَر يلَطُّف الجَّوّ [ʔilmuṭar ylaṭṭuf ʔiǰǰaww] The rain makes the weather nice. لَطَّفلَه السَّفَر لأُورُبّا وَإقتِنَع [laṭṭaflah ʔissafar lʔu:ruppa wiqtinaʕ] He made travelling to Europe sound pleasant to him, and he decided on it.

لاطَف [la:ṭaf] *v:* • **1.** to joke with, tease, kid – دَألاطفَك. لا تِزعَل [daʔala:ṭfak. la: tizʕal] I'm just kidding you. Don't get mad.

تلَطَّف [tlaṭṭaf] *v:* • **1.** to become pleasant, enjoyable, nice – لَو تُمطُر، يِتلَطَّف الجَّوّ [law tumṭur, yitlaṭṭaf ʔiǰǰaww] If it rains, the weather will get nice. • **2.** to be kind, do a favor – تلَطَّف عَلينا وَتَعال زُورنا [tlaṭṭaf ʕali:na wataʕa:l zu:rna] Do us the kindness to come and visit us.

تلاطَف [tla:ṭaf] *v:* • **1.** to joke with each other – لا تِزعَل. دَيِتلاطَف وِيّاك [la: tizʕal. dayitla:ṭaf wiyya:k] Don't get mad. He's just kidding around with you.

اِستَلطَف [ʔistalṭaf] *v:* • **1.** to find pleasant, agreeable, enjoyable, to enjoy, like – اِستَلطَفِت الأَكِل وَطلَبِت بَعَد [ʔistalṭafit ʔilʔakil wiṭlabit baʕad] I thought the food was delicious and asked for more.

لُطُف [luṭuf] *n:* ألطاف [ʔalṭa:f] *pl:* • **1.** kindness, benevolence, friendliness, courtesy, politeness, civility – أشكُرَك، هَذا لُطُف مِنَّك [ʔaškurak, ha:ða luṭuf minnak] Thank you, that's kind of you. حِكَى بِلُطُف وِيّايا [ħiča: biluṭuf wiyya:ya] He spoke gently to me.

لَطِيفَة [laṭi:fa] *n:* لَطايِف [laṭa:yif] *pl:* • **1.** favor, kindness • **2.** polite, nice thing to do – مُو لَطِيفَة مِنَّك تمُرّ عَليه وَما تسَلِّم [mu: laṭi:fa minnak tmurr ʕali:h wma tsallim] It's not a nice thing for you to pass by him and not speak. • **3.** witticism, quip – خَلِّي أحكِيلكُم وِحدَة مِن لَطايفَه [xalli: ʔaħči:lkum wiħda min laṭa:yfah] Let me tell you one of his witty remarks.

تَلطِيف [talṭi:f] *n:* • **1.** pleasing, making pleasant, kind

مُلاطَفَة [mula:ṭafa] *n:* • **1.** amiable treatment, friendliness, kindness, politeness

لَطِيف [laṭi:f] *adj:* لَطِيفِين [laṭi:fi:n] *pl:* • **1.** pleasant, agreeable, pleasing, enjoyable, nice – شلُون مَنظَر لَطِيف [šlu:n manðar laṭi:f] What a beautiful view! المُوَظَّف الجِّدِيد شقَدّ لَطِيف وَحَبُّوب [ʔilmuwaððaf ʔiǰǰidi:d šgadd laṭi:f wħabbu:b] How nice and likeable the new employee is! لَطِيف! هَذا خُوش جَواب [laṭi:f! ha:ða xu:š ǰawa:b] Splendid! That's a fine answer. لَطِيف، لَطِيف! لَعَد غِلَبنا [laṭi:f, laṭi:f! laʕad ɣilabna] Great, great! So we won!

مُلَطِّف [mulaṭṭif] *adj:* • **1.** sedative, soothing

لَطِيفجِي [laṭi:fči] *adj:* لَطِيفجِيَّة [laṭi:fčiyya] *pl:* • **1.** wit, humorist, wag, comic

ألطَف [ʔalṭaf] *comparative adjective:* • **1.** more or most enjoyable, pleasant

لُطفاً [luṭfan] *adverbial:* • **1.** please – لُطفاً أقدَر أستِعِير قَلَمَك فَدّ دَقِيقَة؟ [luṭfan ʔagdar ʔastiʕi:r qalamak fadd daqi:qa?] Could I please borrow your pencil a moment?

ل ط ل ط

لَطلَط [laṭlaṭ] *v:* • **1.** to slosh, slop – لا تِترِس الجِّدِر تَمام حَتَّى ما يلَطلِط الحَلِيب [la: titris ʔiǰǰidir tama:m ħatta ma: ylaṭliṭ ʔilħali:b] Don't fill the pot completely so the milk won't slosh over.

ملَطلَط [mlaṭlaṭ, mlaṭliṭ] *adj:* • **1.** sloshed, slopped • **2.** as Noun: a person who is childish or foolish his/her behavior

ل ط م

لِطَم [liṭam] *v:* • **1.** to slap, strike with the hand – مِن فَشَّر عَليها، لِطمَتَه عَلَى حَلقَه [min faššar ʕali:ha, liṭmatah ʕala ħalgah] When he talked dirty to her, she slapped him on his mouth. قامَت تبكِي وَتُلطُم عَلَى إبِنها المَيِّت [ga:mat tibči wtulṭum ʕala ʔibinha ʔilmayyit] She began to cry and slap herself over her dead son.

لَطِم [laṭim] *n:* • **1.** slap, blow with the hand (esp. on the face)

لَطمَة [laṭma] *n:* لَطمات [laṭma:t] *pl:* • **1.** slap, blow with the hand (esp. on the face)

لَطمِيَّة [laṭmiyya] *n:* • **1.** Shiite mourning tradition involving pounding of the chest • **2.** sad or exaggerated event

ل ع ب

لِعَب [liʕab] *v:* • **1.** to play – الجّاهِل دَيِلعَب بَرَّة [ʔiǰǰa:hil dayilʕab barra] The child is playing outside. لِعبَوا كُرَة القَدَم ساعَة وَنُصّ [liʕbaw kurat ʔilqadam sa:ʕa wnuṣṣ] They played soccer for an hour and a half. • **2.** to toy, play around, fool around – رَكُّب البلَكّات بَسّ لا تِلعَب بالكابرَيتَة [rakkub ʔilplakka:t bass la: tilʕab bilkabri:ta] Install the spark plugs but don't mess with the carburetor. لا تِلعَب بخَشمَك [la: tilʕab bxašmak] Don't pick at your nose. هَذا زَنكِين. يِلعَب بِالفلُوس [ha:ða zangi:n. yilʕab bilfilu:s] He's wealthy. He has money to burn. فِرقَتنا لِعبَت بِيهُم شاطِي باطِي [firqatna liʕbat bi:hum ša:ṭi ba:ṭi] Our team played circles around them. لِعَب براسَه [liʕab bira:sah] He made a fool of him. يَعنِي قابِل يرِيد يِلعَب براسِي؟ [yaʕni qa:bil yiri:d yilʕab bra:si?] You mean he thinks he wants to make a fool of me? يِلعَب على حَبلَين [yilʕab ʕala ħablayn] He plays both sides of the fence. هَذا يِلعَب عَلَى مِيَّة حَبِل [ha:ða yilʕab ʕala miyyat ħabil] That guy has a hundred angles. • **3.** to play, wager – لِعَبِت دِينارَين عَلَى حصانَك [liʕabit dina:rayn ʕala ħṣa:nak] I played two dinars on your horse. • **4.** to act, play, perform – لِعَب دَور رَئِيسِي بالمُفاوَضات [liʕab dawr raʔi:si bilmufa:waða:t] He played a leading role in the negotiations. • **5.** to be loose, have play in it, wiggle, move, stir – سِنِّي دَيِلعَب [sinni dayilʕab] My tooth is loose. هَذا العَمُود مِن تدِفعَه، يِلعَب [ha:ða ʔilʕamu:d min ddifʕah, yilʕab] When you push this pole, it moves. مِن يِحكِي، إذنَه تِلعَب [min yiħči, ʔiðnah tilʕab] When he talks, his ear moves. الهَوا دَيِلعَب اليَوم [ʔilhawa dayilʕab ʔilyu:m] It's windy today. عَقلَه لِعَب [ʕaqlah liʕab] He went crazy. His mind slipped. نَفسَه دَتِلعَب [nafsah datilʕab] He's nauseated. He's sick at his stomach. لَمّا أفتَرّ، نَفسِي تقُوم تِلعَب [lamma ʔaftarr, nafsi dgu:m tilʕab] When I spin around, I begin to get nauseated. لِعبَت نَفسِي مِن هالشُّغُل [liʕbat nafsi min haššuɣul] I got sick of this job.

ل

لَعَّب [laʕʕab] *v:* • **1.** to make or let play – ما دَيلَعِّبُونِي ويّاهُم [ma: daylaʕʕibu:ni wiyya:hum] They won't let me play with them. لَعِّبِي الجّاهِل إلَى أن أرجَع [laʕʕibi ʔijja:hil ʔila ʔan ʔarjaʕ] Keep the kid busy until I return. • **2.** to wiggle, jiggle, cause to move – لا تلَعِّب الميز. دَأكتِب [la: tlaʕʕib ʔilmi:z. daʔaktib] Don't jiggle the table. I'm writing. لَعِّبلها حواجبَه [laʕʕabilha ħwa:jbah] He wiggled his eyebrows at her. لَعَّب نَفسَه [laʕʕab nafsah] It nauseated him. It made him sick at his stomach. لُون سَيّارتَك يلَعِّب النَّفِس [lu:n sayya:rtak ylaʕʕib ʔinnafis] The color of your car is sickening. لَعَّب إيدَه [laʕʕab ʔi:dah] He gave a bribe (lit., waggled his hand). لَعِّب إيدَك حَتَّى أسمَحلَك [laʕʕib ʔi:dak ħatta ʔasmaħlak] Grease my palm and I'll let you go. ما خَلّاه الشُّرطِي يمُرّ إلّا بَعَد ما لَعَّب إيدَه [ma: xalla:h ʔiššurṭi yumurr ʔilla baʕad ma: laʕʕab ʔi:dah] The cop wouldn't let him pass until he'd come across with a bribe. لَعَّب مُخَّه [laʕʕab muxxah] It addled his brain. هَالامتِحان لَعَّب مُخِّي [halʔimtiħa:n laʕʕab muxxi] This examination drove me crazy.

لاعَب [la:ʕab] *v:* • **1.** to play with, play around with – لاعبَت إبنها مُدَّة وَبَعدين نَيِّمَته [la:ʕbat ʔibinha mudda wbaʕdi:n nayyimatah] She played with her son a while and then put him to sleep.

تلاعَب [tla:ʕab] *v:* • **1.** to toy, play around, meddle, tamper – التُّجّار دَيتلاعبُون بأسعار الحُنطَة [ʔittujja:r dayitla:ʕbu:n bʔasʕa:r ʔilħunṭa] The merchants are meddling with wheat prices. الكاتِب تلاعَب بالِحساب [ʔilka:tib tla:ʕab biliħsa:b] The clerk juggled the accounts.

اِنلِعَب [ʔinliʕab] *v:* • **1.** pass. of لِعَب: to be played, to be performed, to be moved, to be wiggled – ساحَة التَّنِس ما مخَطَّطَة. ما ينلِعِب بيها [sa:ħat ʔittanis ma: mxaṭṭiṭa. ma: yinliʕib bi:ha] The tennis court is unlined. It can't be played on.

لِعِب [liʕib] *n:* ألعاب [ʔalʕa:b] *pl:* • **1.** play – ألعاب رِياضِيَّة [ʔalʕa:b riya:ḍiyya] athletics, sports. ألعاب سِحرِيَّة [ʔalʕa:b siħriyya] magic, sleight of hand. ألعاب سُويدِيَّة [ʔalʕa:b suwi:diyya] calisthenics. ألعاب نارِيَّة [ʔalʕa:b na:riyya] fireworks. • **2.** game

لِعبَة [liʕba] *n:* لِعبات، ألعاب، مَلاعِيب [liʕba:t, ʔalʕa:b, mala:ʕi:b] *pl:* • **1.** game • **2.** trick, catch, subterfuge – لِيش دَيبِيع سَيّارتَه بمِيَة دِينار؟ لازِم هاي بيها لِعبَة [li:š daybi:ʕ sayya:rtah bmiyat dina:r? la:zim ha:y bi:ha liʕba] Why is he selling his car for a hundred dinars? There must be a catch in this somewhere. هَالقَضِيَّة بيها لِعبَة [halqaḍiyya bi:ha liʕba] There's something shady about this affair. • **3.** toy

مَلعَب [malʕab] *n:* مَلاعِب [mala:ʕib] *pl:* • **1.** athletic field • **2.** playground

لاعِب [la:ʕib] *n:* • **1.** playing • **2.** sportsman • **3.** pl. لاعِبِين [la:ʕibi:n] player, participant in a game

لُعاب [luʕa:b] *n:* • **1.** saliva

لَعّابَة [laʕʕa:ba] *n:* لَعّابات [laʕʕa:ba:t] *pl:* • **1.** doll

تمِلعِب [tmilʕib] *n:* • **1.** playing around, fooling around

تَلاعُب [tala:ʕub] *n:* • **1.** game, gamble, manipulation, elbow-room, latitude

مَلاعِيب [mala:ʕi:b] *n:* • **1.** (pl. only) toys, playthings

لِعبِي [liʕbi] *adj:* • **1.** playful, light-headed, not serious • **2.** tricky, deceitful, untrustworthy – دِير بالَك مِنَّه، تَرَة هَذا لِعبِي [di:r ba:lak minnah, tara ha:ða liʕbi] Watch out for him, because he's pretty tricky.

ملَعَّب [mlaʕʕab] *adj:* • **1.** playful, prankish, waggish • **2.** undependable, unreliable – شلُون ملَعَّب! ما تِقدَر تِعتِمِد عَلَيه؛ يقُلَّك شِي ويسَوِّي شِي [šlu:n mlaʕʕab! ma: tigdar tiʕtimid ʕali:h; yugullak ši wysawwi: ši] What an undependable person! You can't depend on him; he tells you something and does something else. هَذا فَدّ واحِد ملَعَّب. لا تاخُذ كَلامَه مِيَّة بِالمِيَّة [ha:ða fadd wa:ħid mlaʕʕab. la: ta:xuð kala:mah miyya bilmiyya] That guy is always fooling around. Don't take what he says completely.

لَعُوب [laʕu:b] *adj:* • **1.** playful

لاعُوب [la:ʕu:b] *adj:* لواعِيب [lwa:ʕi:b] *pl:* • **1.** player, participant in a game • **2.** sportsman

لِعبان، لِعبان نَفِس [liʕba:n, liʕba:n nafis] *adj:* • **1.** nausea

مَلعُوب [malʕu:b] *adj:* • **1.** covered with spittle • **2.** decoy, trick, ruse, artifice

ل ع ث م

تلَعثَم [tlaʕθam] *v:* • **1.** to hesitate, falter, stutter, stammer

تلِعثِم [tliʕθim] *n:* • **1.** hesitation, stuttering, stammering

ل ع د

لَعَد [laʕad] *conjunction:* • **1.** then, so, in that case – لَعَد ما راح تِنطِينِي الفلُوس اليُوم؟ [laʕad ma: ra:ħ tinṭi:ni ʔilflu:s ʔilyu:m?] So you're not going to give me the money today? لِيش لَعَد أخُويَا أخَذ وُصلَة؟ [li:š laʕad ʔaxu:ya ʔaxað wuṣla?] Why did my brother get a piece then? إذا هَذا ما يعِجبَك، شيعِجبَك، لَعَد؟ [ʔiða ha:ða ma: yʕijbak, šyʕijbak, laʕad?] If this doesn't please you, what will then? لَعَد شأقُلَّه إذا سِأل؟ [laʕad šʔagullah ʔiða siʔal?] So what do I tell him if he asks? لَعَد أبقَى عَشِر ساعات بِلا أكِل؟ [laʕad ʔabqa: ʕašir sa:ʕa:t bila ʔakil?] You mean I should go ten hours without anything to eat? • **2.** well? what else? what of it? – خَلَّصِت شُغلَك كُلَّه بنُصّ ساعَة بَسّ؟ --- لَعَد؟ [xallaṣit šuγlak kullah bnuṣṣ sa:ʕa bass? laʕad?] You finished all your work in just a half hour? --- What do you expect? تِنطِي بَالسَّيّارَة مِيَّة دِينار بَسّ؟ --- لَعَد شقَدّ؟ [tinṭi bissayya:ra miyyat dina:r bass? laʕad šgadd?] You'll only give a hundred dinars for the car? --- What else?

ل ع ل

لَعَلّ [laʕalla] *pseudo-verb:* • **1.** /usually with formal pronominal suffix attached/ perhaps, maybe – اِنتِظِر شوَيَّة، لَعَلّه يِجِي [ʔintiðir šwayya, laʕallah yiǰi] Wait a while and perhaps he'll come.

ل ع ل ع

لَعلَع [laʕlaʕ] *v:* • **1.** to make an irritatingly loud noise – البارحَة كان صَوت الرَّصّاص يلَعلِع [ʔilba:rħa ča:n ṣu:t ʔirraṣṣa:ṣ ylaʕliʕ] Yesterday the sound of the gunfire was terribly noisy.

تلعلِع [tliʕliʕ] *n:* • **1.** making an irritatingly loud noise

ملَعلِع [mlaʕliʕ] *adj:* • **1.** in between, undetermined

ل ع ن see also ل ع ن

لِعَن [liʕan] *v:* • **1.** to damn, to curse

اِنلِعَن [ʔinliʕan] *v:* • **1.** to be cursed, damned

لَعِن [laʕin] *n:* • **1.** cursing, malediction

لَعنَة [laʕna] *n:* • **1.** curse

لَعِين [laʕi:n] *adj:* • **1.** damned, cursed, abominable, outcast

مَلعُون [malʕu:n] *adj:* • **1.** cursed, damned, outcast • **2.** witty, playful

ل غ د

لَغَّد [laɣɣad] *v:* • **1.** to grow a double chin, to get fat – لَغَّد عَلَى هَالأكِل وَهالهَوَا [laɣɣad ʕala halʔakil whalhawa] He's gotten fat on this food and this climate.

لُغُد [luɣud] *n:* لغُود [lɣu:d] *pl:* • **1.** double chin, flesh at the throat and under the chin

ملَغِّد [mlaɣɣid] *adj:* • **1.** one who has a double chin, one who has a fold of skin under the chin

ل غ ز

لُغُز [luɣuz] *n:* ألغاز [ʔalɣa:z] *pl:* • **1.** riddle, puzzle, brain-teaser

ل غ م

لِغَم [liɣam] *v:* • **1.** to mine, to plant mines, explosives

لَغَّم [laɣɣam] *v:* • **1.** to mine, to plant explosives

اِنلِغَم [ʔinliɣam] *v:* • **1.** to be mined, filled with explosives

لَغَم [laɣam, luɣum] *n:* ألغام [ʔalɣa:m] *pl:* • **1.** mine, explosive, booby-trap

ملَغَّم [mlaɣɣam] *adj:* • **1.** mined, filled with explosives

مِتلَغُّم [mitlaɣɣum] *adj:* • **1.** filled with explosives, mined

مَلغُوم [malɣu:m] *adj:* • **1.** filled with explosives, mined

ل غ م ط

لَغمَط [laɣmaṭ] *v:* • **1.** to cover, strew, spray, smear – لَغمَط هدُومَه بِالصُّبُغ [laɣmaṭ hdu:mah biṣṣubuɣ] He got his clothes covered with paint. لَغمُط العَجِينَة بِالطِّحِين حَتَّى ما تِلزَق بإيدَك [laɣmuṭ ʔilʕaǰi:na biṭṭiħi:n ħatta ma: tilzag bi:dak] Cover the dough with flour so it won't stick to your hands. • **2.** to cover up, obscure, hide – لَغمُطَوا القَضِيَّة حَتَّى ما يِنعُرُف صُوج مَن [laɣmuṭaw ʔilqaðiyya ħatta ma: yinʕuruf ṣu:č man] They covered up the affair so it wouldn't be known whose fault it was. • **3.** to obscure, blur, make indistinct – إحكِي عَلَى كَيفَك وَلا تلَغمُط الحكايَة [ʔiħči ʕala kayfak wla tlaɣmuṭ ʔilħča:ya] Talk slowly and don't mumble the words.

تلَغمَط [tlaɣmaṭ] *v:* • **1.** to be blurred, smeared – الكِتابَة كُلّها تلَغمُطَت مِن هالحِبِر [ʔilkita:ba kullha tlaɣmuṭat min halħibir] The writing all became smeared because of this ink.

ل غ و

لِغَى [liɣa:] *v:* • **1.** to prattle, chatter, talk incessantly – مِن تِفتَح المَوضُوع ويّاه، يِلغِي هوايَة [min tiftaħ ʔilmawðu:ʕ wiyya:h, yilɣi hwa:ya] When you bring up the subject to him, he talks on and on endlessly. • **2.** to invalidate, abolish, eliminate, do away with, cancel – وزارَة المَعارِف لِغَت هَالكِتاب [wiza:rat ʔilmaʕa:rif liɣat halkita:b] The Ministry of Education stopped the use of this book. الحُكُومَة الجِّدِيدَة لِغَت بَعَض المَشارِيع القَدِيمَة [ʔilħukuma ʔiǰǰidi:da liɣat baʕað ʔilmaša:ri:ʕ ʔilqadi:ma] The new government cancelled some of the old projects.

ألغَى [ʔalɣa:] *v:* • **1.** to cancel, to call off

تلاغَى [tla:ɣa:] *v:* • **1.** to engage in heated discussion, have an argument with each other – هُوَّ وأَبُوه تلاغَوا الصُّبُح [huwwa wʔabu:h tla:ɣaw ʔiṣṣubuħ] He and his father argued this morning. البارحَة تلاغَى وِيّا مَرتَه [ʔilba:rħa tla:ɣa: wiyya martah] Yesterday he had words with his wife.

اِنلِغَى [ʔinliɣa:] *v:* • **1.** to be nullified, canceled – أمُر نَقلِي اِنلِغَى [ʔamur naqli ʔinliɣa:] My transfer order was cancelled.

لُغَة [luɣa] *n:* لُغات [luɣa:t] *pl:* • **1.** language

لَغُو [laɣw] *n:* • **1.** talking incessantly

لُغَوِي [luɣawi] *n:* • **1.** linguistic, lexicographic, philological • **2.** a linguist, lexicographer, philologist

لَغوَة [laɣwa] *n:* لَغوات، لَغاوِي [laɣwa:t, laɣa:wi:] *pl:* • **1.** stir, fuss, uproar, disturbance • **2.** bother, headache, trouble • **3.** argument, heated discussion • **4.** aimless chatter, babbling, nonsense

إلغاء [ʔilɣa:ʔ] *n:* • **1.** cancellation, abrogation, repeal

لَغوِي [laɣwi] *adj:* • **1.** loquacious, talkative, garrulous • **2.** talkative person, chatterbox, prattler

لاغِي [la:ɣi] *adj:* • **1.** abolished, abrogated, repealed, canceled, null and void

مَلغِي [malɣi] *adj:* • **1.** abolished, canceled, annulled, invalid, abrogated, null and void

لَغوَجي [laɣawči, laɣwači] *adj:* لَغوَجِيَّة [laɣwačiyya] *pl:* • **1.** talkative person, chatterbox

مُلغَى [mulɣaː] *adj:* • **1.** cancelled, abrogated, repealed, annulled, void, abolished, expired, suppressed

ل ف ت

لِفَت، لِفَت النَظَر [lifat, lifat ʔinnaðar] *v:* • **1.** to catch one's eye, attract attention – بوينباغه لِفَت نَظَري [buːyinbaːɣah lifat naðari] His tie caught my eye. • **2.** to give warning, to call attention, point out – لِفَتنا نَظَرَك هَالمَرَّة؛ لَكِن مَرَّة اللُّخ نفُصلَك [lifatna naðarak halmarra; laːkin marrat ʔillux nfuṣlak] This time we warned you; next time we'll fire you.

تلَفَّت [tlaffat] *v:* • **1.** to look around, direct one's gaze here and there – شَكُو عِندَك تِتلَفَّت؟ دَتِنتِظِر واحِد يِجِي؟ [šaku ʕindak titlaffat? datintiðir waːħid yiji?] Why are you looking around? Are you waiting for someone to come?

اِلتِفَت [ʔiltifat] *v:* • **1.** to pay attention – إذا تِلتِفِت زين لِشُغُلَك، تِترَفَّع [ʔiða tiltifit ziːn lišuɣulak, titraffaʕ] If you pay good attention to your work, you'll be promoted. • **2.** to turn, turn one's attention – اِلتِفَت عَلَيّا وَضِحَك [ʔiltifat ʕalayya wðiħak] He looked around at me and laughed.

لافِتَة [laːfita] *n:* لافِتات [laːfitaːt] *pl:* • **1.** sign, signboard (bearing an inscription)

إلفات [ʔilfaːt] *n:* • **1.** calling attention, catching one's eye, attracting attention • **2.** warning, calling people's attention

اِلتِفات [ʔiltifaːt] *n:* • **1.** turn, turning with the neck • **2.** inclination, attention, care, solicitude

اِلتِفاتَة [ʔiltifaːta] *n:* • **1.** turn of the face or eyes, glance, side glance • **2.** care, solicitude, consideration

مُلفِت، مُلفِت لِلنَظَر [mulfit, mulfit lilnaðar] *adj:* • **1.** attracting attention, striking, eye catching

ل ف ح

لِفَح [lifaħ] *v:* • **1.** to sear, burn – هَوا السُّمُوم يِلفَح الوُجِه [hawa ʔissumuːm yilfaħ ʔalwujih] The dry, hot desert wind burns the face.

لَفِح [lafiħ] *n:* • **1.** burning, scorching

لافِح [laːfiħ] *adj:* • **1.** blazing, burning, scorching

ل ف ظ

لُفَظ [lufað] *v:* • **1.** to enunciate, articulate, pronounce – لُفَظها غَلَط لِلكِلمَة [lufaðha ɣalaṭ liččilma] He pronounced the word wrong.

تلَفَّظ [tlaffað] *v:* • **1.** same as لُفَظ : to pronounce

لَفُظ [lafuð] *n:* ألفاظ [ʔalfaːð] *pl:* • **1.** expression, term, word, wording

تَلَفُّظ [talaffuð] *n:* • **1.** pronunciation, articulation

مَلفُوظ [malfuːð] *adj:* • **1.** pronounced, emitted, ejected

ل ف ف

لَفّ [laff] *v:* • **1.** to wrap, envelop, cover, swathe – تريد ألِفّ القَمِيص لَو تاخذَه هِيكِي؟ [triːd ʔaliff ʔilqamiːṣ law taːxðah hiːči?] Do you want me to wrap up the shirt or will you take it like that? لِفّ رُقُبتَك بهالوُصلَة [liff rugubtak bhalwuṣla] Wrap your neck with this cloth. لِفّ الجاهِل بِقَبُّوطَك حَتَّى يِدفَى [liff ʔijjaːhil bqappuːṭak ħatta yidfaː] Wrap your overcoat around the kid so he'll keep warm. الشُرطَة لَفَّت كُلّ المُتَظاهِرين بلوريّين [ʔiššurṭa laffat kull ʔilmutaðaːhiriːn bluːriyayn] The police bundled all the demonstrators into two trucks. • **2.** to roll, wind up, coil, reel – لِفّ هَالخَيط عالبَكَرَة [liff halxiːṭ ʕaːlbakra] Roll this string up on the spool. بالله لِفّلِي فَدّ سِجارَة [ballah liffli fadd sigaːra] Please roll me a cigarette. • **3.** to twist together, join, connect – لِفّ راسَين الوايَر وَسَوِّيه حَلَقَة [liff raːsiːn ʔilwaːyar wsawwiːh ħalaqa] Connect the two ends of the wire and make a ring. • **4.** to make off with, abscond with, swipe, steal – لَفّ الفلُوس كُلّها [laff ʔilfluːs kullha] He swiped all the money. هُوَّ يلِفّهُم كُلّهُم [huwwa yliffhum kullhum] He gets the best of all of them.

اِلتَفّ [ʔiltaff] *v:* • **1.** to wind, twist, coil oneself – اِلتَفَّت الحَيَّة حَول رُقُبتَه [ʔiltaffat ʔilħayya ħawil rugubtah] The snake wrapped itself around his neck. • **2.** to intertwine, become tangled, snarled – اِلتَفَّت الخِيُوط وَ ما دَأقدَر ألِفّها عالبَكَرَة [ʔiltaffat ʔilxiyuːṭ wma daʔagdar ʔaliffha ʕalbakra] The strings got tangled and I can't wind them on the spool.

لَفّ [laff] *n:* • **1.** wrapping, covering, winding, folding

لَفَّة [laffa] *n:* لَفّات [laffaːt] *pl:* • **1.** reel, spool • **2.** roll • **3.** turban • **4.** a sandwich made by rolling up a piece of Arabic bread with filling inside

مَلَفّ، مَلَفَّة [malaff, malaffa] *n:* مَلَفّات [malaffaːt] *pl:* • **1.** portfolio, folder, dossier, file

لَفّاف [laffaːf] *n:* لَفّافات [laffaːfaːt] *pl:* • **1.** binding, bandage • **2.** scarf, muffler

لفيفَة [lfiːfa] *n:* لفايف [lfaːyif] *pl:* • **1.** a cut of meat from near the backbone of a camel

لَفّ، سِجارَة لَفّ [laff, jigaːra laff] *adj:* • **1.** hand-rolled cigarette

ملتَفّ [miltaff] *adj:* • **1.** winding, twisting, rolled up

مَلفُوف [malfuːf] *adj:* • **1.** wrapped up, coiled, rolled up

ل ف ق

لَفَّق [laffaq] *v:* • **1.** to fabricate, to concoct, to contrive, to piece together

تَلفِيق [talfiːq] *n:* • **1.** fibbing, falsification, fabrication

ملَفَّق [mlaffaq] *adj:* • **1.** fabricated, phony

ل ف ل ف

لَفلَف [laflaf] *v:* • **1.** to grab up, snatch up – هُوَّ يلَفلِف كُلشِي يوقَع بِيدَه [huwwa ylaflif kullši yuːgaʕ biːdah] He grabs up everything that falls into his hands. • **2.** to wrap up, bundle up – لَفلِف نَفسَك زين تَرَة الدِّنيا بارِدَة [laflif nafsak ziːn tara ʔiddinya baːrda] Wrap yourself up well because it's cold.

تلفلف [tlaflaf] *v:* • **1.** to wrap oneself up, cover oneself – تلَفلَف قَبُل ما تِطلَع مِن الحَمّام [tlaflaf gabul maː titlaʕ min ʔilħammaːm] Wrap yourself up before you leave the bathroom.

لِفليف [lifliːf] *adj:* لِفليفين [lifliːfiːn] *pl:* • **1.** efficient, clever fellow • **2.** opportunist

ملفلف [mlaflaf] *adj:* • **1.** wrapped, rounded

ل ف ي

لِفى [lifaː] *v:* • **1.** to spend one's time, hang around, be found – يَومِيّاً يِلفي بِالقَهوَة [yawmiyyan yilfi bilgahwa] He's in the coffeeshop every day. صارلَه إسبُوع لافي بِبَيتنا [ṣaːrlah ʔisbuːʕ laːfi bibaytna] He's been at our house for a week. إذا ما يحِبُّوك، لُويش تِلفي عَلَيهُم؟ [ʔiða maː yħibbuːk, luwiːš tilfi ʕaliːhum?] If they don't like you, why do you go see them?

لَفّى [laffaː] *n:* • **1.** to cause to spend one's time, allow to spend one's time – هَذا شِيلَفِّيه بِالبَيت؟ النَّهار كُلَّه يِفتَرّ بِالشَّوارِع [haːða šiylaffiːh bilbayt? ʔinnahaːr kullah yiftarr biššawaːriʕ] What can keep him at home? All day he roams the streets. لَو ما عَمَّه الوَزير، وَلا يلِفُّوه يوم بِهَالدّائِرَة [law maː ʕammah ʔilwaziːr, wala yliffuːh yuːm bhaddaːʔira] If his uncle weren't the minister, they wouldn't let him stay in this office one day. إذا أَبُوه طِرَدَه، مِنُو راح يلَفِّيه؟ [ʔiða ʔabuːh ṭiradah, minu raːħ ylaffiːh?] If his father kicked him out, who'll take him in?

تلافى [tlaːfaː] *v:* • **1.** to avoid, to prevent

تَلافي [talaːfi] *n:* • **1.** preventing, avoiding • **2.** repair, correction, removal (of a danger or deficiency)

ل ق ب

لَقَب [laqab] *n:* أَلقاب [ʔalqaːb] *pl:* • **1.** surname, last name, family name • **2.** honorific or title at the end of one's name

ل ق ح

لَقَّح [laqqaħ] *v:* • **1.** to vaccinate, to inoculate • **1.** to fertilize, to impregnate • **2.** to gaft, to bud (a tree)

تلَقَّح [tlaqqaħ] *v:* • **1.** to be vaccinated, fertilized, grafted

لُقاح [luqaːħ] *n:* لُقاحات [luqaːħaːt] *pl:* • **1.** vaccine

تَلقيح [talqiːħ] *n:* • **1.** vaccination, impregnation

مِتلَقِّح [mitlaqqiħ] *adj:* • **1.** vaccinated

ل ق ط

لِقَط [ligaṭ] *v:* • **1.** to glean, pick out, pick up – إلقُط الحَصو مِن التِّمَّن [ʔilguṭ ʔilħaṣw min ʔittimman] Pick the small gravel out of the rice. لا تقُول هِيكِي أَشياء قِدّام الجّاهِل، لِأَنّ يِلقُط الحَكي بِالعَجَل [laː tguːl hiːči ʔašyaːʔ giddaːm ʔiǰǰaːhil, liʔann yilguṭ ʔilħači bilʕaǰal] Don't say such things in front of the child, because he picks words up fast. • **2.** to pick over – صارلِها مُدَّة تِلقُط التِّمَّن [ṣaːrilha mudda tilguṭ ʔittimman] She's been quite a while picking over the rice. • **3.** to sew around the edges, to sew overcast stitches – بَعَد ما تِلقُط حاشيَة البَنطَرُون، إثنِيها [baʕad maː tilguṭ ħaːšyat ʔilpanṭaruːn, ʔiθniːha] After you sew the edges of the pants, hem them.

لَقَّط [laggaṭ] *v:* • **1.** to pick out, pick up – لَقَّط الخِرَز الحُمُر وِحدَة وِحدَة [laggaṭ ʔilxiraz ʔilħumur wiħda wiħda] He picked out the red beads one by one. الشُّرطَة لَقَّطَت كُلّ المقادي وَخَلَّتهُم بِبَيت خاص [ʔiššurṭa laggiṭat kull ʔilmgaːdi wxallathum bibayt xaːṣṣ] The police gathered up all the beggars and put them in a special house. • **2.** to pick over – بَعَد ما تلَقّطِين التِّمَّن، غِسلِيه [baʕad maː tlaggṭiːn ʔittimman, ɣisliːh] After you pick over the rice, wash it.

لُقُط [luguṭ] *n:* • **1.** cracked grain, pieces of grain • **2.** bird food – خَلّيتَه يِغلُبني اليُوم حَتّى أذِبلَه لُقط وِيلعَب وِيّايا بَعَد [xalliːtah yuɣlubni ʔilyuːm ħatta ʔaðibblah lugaṭ wyilʕab wiyyaːya baʕad] I let him beat me today in order to entice him to play with me again.

لُقطَة [lagṭa, lugṭa] *n:* لُقطات [lagṭaːt, lugṭaːt] *pl:* • **1.** (lucky) find, bargain – زين إشتِرَيت هَالرّاديُو. كان خُوش لُقطَة [ziːn ʔištirayt harraːdyu. čaːn xuːš lugṭa] It's good you bought this radio. It was a good bargain.

لَقطَة [laqṭa] *n:* لَقطات [laqṭaːt] *pl:* • **1.** shot (photography)

مِلقَط [milqaṭ] *n:* مَلاقِط [malaːqiṭ] *pl:* • **1.** tongs • **2.** tweezers

لاقِطَة [laːqiṭa] *n:* • **1.** apparatus for recording sound waves. search device (techn.)

تَلقيط [talgiːṭ] *n:* • **1.** picking up • **2.** tweezing

اِلتِقاط [ʔiltiqaːṭ] *n:* • **1.** gathering, collection, picking up • **2.** reception, interception

ل ق ف

لِقَف [ligaf] *v:* • **1.** to catch, seize, snatch, grab – شلُون ما تِشمُرلَه الطُّوبَة، يِلقُفها [šluːn maː tišmurlah ʔiṭṭuːba, yilgufha] However, you throw him the ball, he catches it. بَسّ أَلقُفَه، أَدَمُّرَه [bass ʔalugfah, ʔadammurah] As soon as I catch him, I'll tear him apart. المُعَلِّم لِقَفني أَحكِي بِالصَّفّ [ʔilmuʕallim ligafni ʔaħči biṣṣaff] The teacher caught me talking in class. • **2.** to breathe laboriously, gasp for breath – ظَلّ يِلقُف حَوالِي رُبُع ساعَة قَبُل ما يمُوت [ðall yilguf ħawaːli rubuʕ saːʕa gabul maː ymuːt] He kept gasping for about a quarter hour before he died.

لَقَّف [laggaf] *v:* • **1.** to keep catching – هَالبَهلَوان راكُب عالبايسِكِل وَيلَقُّف أَربَع طُوَب [halpahlawaːn

ل

ra:kub ʕalpa:ysikil wylagguf ʔarbaʕ ṭuwab] That acrobat's riding a bicycle and juggling four balls.
تلاقف [tla:gaf] *v:* • **1.** to descend upon, pounce on, jump, catch – الجّهال تلاقفوا السَّكران بالحجار [ʔijǰaha:l tla:gfaw ʔissakra:n bilḥǰa:r] The children pounced on the drunkard with rocks. بَسّ تِنزِل هالثِّياب لِلسُّوق، النّاس يِتلاقفوها [bass tinzil haθθiya:b lissu:g, ʔinna:s yitla:gfawha] The minute these shirts go on sale in the market, the people will pounce on them.
انلِقَف [ʔinligaf] *v:* • **1.** to be caught – يبَيِّن هالمَرَّة اِنلِقَفنا. الشُّرطَة حاطوا البَيت [yibayyin halmarra ʔinligafna. ʔiššurṭa ḥa:ṭaw ʔilbayt] It looks like this time we're caught. The police have surrounded the house.
لَقُف [laguf] *n:* • **1.** grabbing, catching, snatching
لاقُف [la:guf] *adj:* • **1.** catching

ل ق ق

لَقّ [lagg] *v:* • **1.** to lick – الكَلِب دَيلُقّ رِجلَه المَجرُوحَة [ʔiččalib daylugg rijlah ʔilmajru:ḥa] The dog is licking its wounded leg.
لَقّ [lagg] *n:* • **1.** licking

ل ق ل ق

لَقلَق [laglag, laqlaq] *v:* • **1.** to talk nonsense – هَذا دَيلَقلِق. لا تدِيرلَه بال [ha:ða daylaqliq. la: ddi:rlah ba:l] He's just babbling. Don't pay any attention to him.
لَقلَق [laglag] *n:* لَقالِق [laga:lig] *pl:* • **1.** stork
لِقلاقِي [liqla:qi] *adj:* • **1.** prattler, babbler

ل ق م

لَقَّم [laggam] *v:* • **1.** to cadge, sponge, bum, free-load – النَّهار كُلَّه يلَقُّم بِبيُوت الجِّيارِين [ʔinnaha:r kullah ylaggum bibyu:t ʔijǰiya:ri:n] All day he bums his meals at the neighbors' houses.
لُقُم [luqum] *n:* • **1.** Turkish delight, a jelly-like confection, usually dusted with sugar
لُقمَة [lugma] *n:* لِقَم [ligam] *pl:* • **1.** bite, mouthful – خَلِّي نفُوت بِهالمَطعَم ناكُل لُقمَة [xalli: nfu:t biha:lmaṭʕam na:kul lugma] Let's go into this restaurant and get a bite to eat.
لَقّام [lagga:m] *n:* لَقّامَة [lagga:ma] *pl:* • **1.** cadger, sponger, free-loader, bum

ل ق ن

لَقَّن [laqqan] *v:* • **1.** to teach, instruct in, inculcate – هاي مِنُو لَقَّنَك هالحَكِي؟ [ha:y minu laqqanak halḥači?] Who taught you these words? • **2.** to prompt – ما يِقدَر يِحكِي عَالمَسرَح إذا ما يلَقِّنَه واحِد [ma: yigdar yiḥči ʕalmasraḥ ʔiða ma: ylaqqinah wa:ḥid] He can't talk on a stage if someone doesn't prompt him.
لِقَن [ligan] *n:* لِقَنات [ligana:t] *pl:* • **1.** large metal wash basin
تَلقِين [talqi:n] *n:* • **1.** instruction, direction • **2.** insinuation, suggestion, prompting
مُلَقِّن [mulaqqin] *n:* ملَقِّنِين [mulaqqani:n] *pl:* • **1.** prompter

ل ق و

لَقو [lagaw] *n:* • **1.** a dice game similar to chuck-a-luck

ل ق ي

لِقَى [liga:] *v:* • **1.** to find – لِقيت دِينار بِالشّارِع [ligi:t dina:r biššaːriʕ] I found a dinar on the street. لِقَيتلَك خُوش سَيّارَة رِخِيصَة [ligi:tlak xu:š sayya:ra rixi:ṣa] I found you a good cheap car. • **2.** to encounter, meet, run into, come across – ما لِقيت صُعُوبَة بِالمَوضُوع [ma: ligi:t ṣuʕu:ba bilmawḏu:ʕ] I didn't encounter any difficulty in the matter. اللّي يسَوِّي زين يِلقِي زين [ʔilli ysawwi: zi:n yilgi zi:n] He who does good reaps good. بَيت، وَسَيّارَة، وَفلُوس --- وين لاقِيها؟ [bayt, wsayya:ra, wiflu:s wi:n la:gi:ha?] A house, a car, and money --- where can one come across these things?
لَقَّى [lagga:] *v:* • **1.** to find, locate – مُمكِن تلَقِّيلَه شَغلَة أَحسَن مِن هاي؟ [mumkin tlaggi:lah šayla ʔaḥsan min ha:y?] Could you find him a better job than this? • **2.** (of God) to punish – الله يلَقِّيك إيّاها بوُلدَك [ʔallah ylaggi:k ʔiyya:ha bwuldak] May God take it out on you through your children.
لاقَى [la:ga:] *v:* • **1.** to encounter, meet with – لاقيتَه لعَلِي بالسُّوق [la:gaytah lʕali bissu:g] I ran into Ali in the market. • **2.** to meet – لاقَينا الخُطّار بِالباب [la:gayna ʔilxuṭṭa:r bilba:b] We met the guests at the door. إن شاء الله تلاقِي كُلّ الخير [ʔinša:llah tla:gi kull ʔilxi:r] I hope that you may meet with only good fortune.
تلَقَّى [tlaqqa:] *v:* • **1.** to receive – رِحنا نِتلَقّاه بِالمَطار [riḥna nitlagga:h bilmaṭa:r] We went to receive him at the airport. تلَقّى! جَتَّك الطّابُوقَة [tlagga:! ǰattak ʔiṭṭa:bu:ga] Catch! Here comes the brick. • **2.** to get, obtain – ناس تاكُل بِالدِّجاج، وَناس تِتلَقَّى العَجاج [na:s ta:kul biddija:ǰ, wna:s titlagga: ʔilʕaǰa:ǰ] Some people eat chicken, and others get dust. إن شاء الله تِتلَقّاها بعُمرَك [ʔinša:llah titlagga:ha bʕumrak] I hope you get your comeuppance sometime in your life.
تلاقَى [tla:ga:] *v:* • **1.** to come together, get together, join each other, meet each other – خَلّي نِتلاقَى بالمَسبَح السّاعَة سَبعَة [xalli: nitla:ga: bilmasbaḥ ʔissa:ʕa sabʕa] Let's meet at the beach at seven o'clock. تلاقيت وِيّاه بدائِرَة البَرِيد [tla:gayt wiyya:h bda:ʔirat ʔilbari:d] I ran into him in the post office.
اِنلِقَى [ʔinliga:] *v:* • **1.** to be found – هالبُحَيرَة ما يِنلِقِي بِيها سِمَك [halbuḥayra ma: yinligi bi:ha simač] Fish cannot be found in this lake. • **2.** to be encountered, be met with – هَذا ما يِنلِقِي باللَّيل [ha:ða ma: yinligi billayl] You never see that guy at night.

ل

اِلتِقَى [ʔiltiga:] *v:* • **1.** to be available, obtainable, be found – اِشتِرِيها. هِيكِي سِترَة ما تِلتِقِي عَلَى طُول [ʔištiri:ha. hi:či sitra ma: tiltigi ʕala ṭu:l] Buy it. Such a jacket isn't always available. دائِماً يِلتِقِي بِالبار [da:ʔiman yiltigi bilba:r] He can always be found in the bar.
لَقِي [lagy] *n:* • **1.** finding
لِقيَة [ligya] *n:* لِقيات [ligya:t] *pl:* • **1.** find, something found – مبارَك! هاي خُوش لِقيَة [mba:rak! ha:y xu:š ligya] Congratulations! That's a good find.
لِقاء [liqa:ʔ] *n:* • **1.** meeting, encounter, get together, reunion
مَلقَى [malga:] *n:* • **1.** (the way of) welcoming, receiving (a guest) • **2.** receiving (guest) • **3.** reception
إلقاء [ʔilqa:ʔ] *n:* • **1.** presentation, throwing, casting • **2.** elocution, diction, art of speech • **3.** arrest as in إلقاء القَبض [ʔiqa:ʔ ʔilqabð̣]
مُلتَقَى [multaqa:] *n:* • **1.** gathering point, meeting place, rendezvous
تَلاقِي [tala:qi] *n:* • **1.** meeting, encounter
اِلتِقاء [ʔiltiqa:ʔ] *n:* • **1.** meeting, reunion

ل ك

لَك [mas. lak, fem. lič] *preposition plus clitic pronoun:* • **1.** (emphatic particle, approx.:) look, hey you, say – لَك دِوَلّي! شِمقَدرَك تِغلُبَه؟ [lak diwalli! šimgaddrak tɣulbah?] Oh go on! How could you beat him? لَك، ما قِتلَك لا تِحكِي وِيّاه بَعَد؟ [lak, ma: gitlak la: tiħči wiyya:h baʕad?] Look, haven't I told you not to talk with him anymore? لَك ما عليكُم، تَرَة مَسؤُولِيَّة [lak ma: ʕli:kum, tara masʔu:liyya] Look, keep out of it, or you'll get in trouble! لَك شُوف! إذا ما ترَجِّعلِي فلُوسِي، أشتِكِي عَلِيك [lak šu:f! ʔiða ma: trajjiʕli flu:si, ʔaštiki ʕali:k] Look here you! If you don't return my money, I'll sue you. لَك وَالله، اللّي يطُخَّه أمَوّتَه [lak wallah, ʔilli yṭuxxah ʔamawwtah] By God, I'll kill anyone who touches it! لَك، لَك، لا تِشلَع الوَرِد [lak, lak, la: tišlaʕ ʔilwarid] Hey you, don't pick the flowers. لَك خاطِر الله، ساعدُونِي [lak xa:ṭir ʔallah, sa:ʕdu:ni] Hey, for the love of God, help me! لَك يابَة، هَذا شلُون جَمال [lak ya:ba, ha:ða šlu:n ǰama:l] Hey man, that's real beauty!
وِلَك [wilak] وِلكُم [wilkum] *pl:*
وِلِك [wilič] *feminine:* • **1.** look, hey you, say

ل ك ك [1]

لَكّ [lakk] *v:* • **1.** to seal, fasten securely, secure – لُكّ المَكتُوب حَتَّى مَحَّد يفتَحَه [lukk ʔilmaktu:b ħatta maħħad yiftaħah] Seal the letter so nobody will open it. الشُّرطَة لَكُّوها لِلقاصَة [ʔiššurṭa lakku:ha lilqa:ṣa] The police sealed the safe. • **2.** to poke in the ribs – لُكَّه حَتَّى يِلتِفِت عَلِيك [lukka ħatta yiltifit ʕali:k] Poke him in the ribs so he'll look around at you.
لُكّ [lukk] *n:* • **1.** sealing wax

لَكَّة [lakka] *n:* لَكّات [lakka:t] *pl:* • **1.** spot, stain, smudge • **2.** a poke in the ribs

ل ك ك [2]

لُكّ [lukk] *n:* • **1.** a great number, a large, but vague, amount. – لُكّ مَرَّة قِتلَه ونِسَى [lukk marra gitlah wnisa:] I told him a million times and he forgot.

ل ك ل ك

لَكلَك [laklak] *v:* • **1.** to spatter, spot, stain – دِير بالَك. لا تلَكلِك ثُوبَك [di:r ba:lak. la: tlaklik θu:bak] Be careful. Don't stain your shirt. • **2.** to roll, form into a ball or lump – لَكلِك الطِّينَة وشِيلها [laklik ʔiṭṭi:na wši:lha] Roll the piece of mud into a ball and pick it up. • **3.** to poke repeatedly in the ribs – لا تلَكلِك! دَأسمَعَك [la: tlaklik! daʔasmaʕak] Don't poke at me! I hear you.
لَكلُوكَة، لُكلُكَّة [laklu:ka, luklukka] *n:* لَكلُوكات، لُكلُكّات، لَكالِيك [laklu:ka:t, luklukka:t, laka:li:k] *pl:* • **1.** ball, lump, hunk

ل ك م

لِكَم [likam, ličam] *v:* • **1.** to hit, strike – الوَلَد مطَهَّر. دِير بالَك لا تلِكمَه [ʔilwalad mṭahhar. di:r ba:lak la: tličmah] The boy's been circumcised. Be careful not to hit him.
لِكَم [likam] *v:* • **1.** to punch, strike with the fist – لِكَمَه عَلَى خَشمَه وَوَقَّعَه [likamah ʕala xašmah wwaggaʕah] He punched him on the nose and knocked him down.
لاكَم [la:kam] *v:* • **1.** to box, engage in a fist fight with – شِفِت حَيوان الكَنغَر يلاكِم صاحبَه [šifit ħaywa:n ʔilkanɣar yila:kim ṣa:ħbah] I saw a kangaroo boxing with its owner.
تلاكَم [tla:kam] *v:* • **1.** as in لاكَم : to box • **2.** to be punched
اِنلِكَم [ʔinličam] *v:* • **1.** to be hit, struck – لا تِلعَب ويّا الوُلِد لا ترُوح تِنلِكِم [la: tilʕab wiyya ʔilwulid la: tru:ħ tinličim] Don't play with the boys and you won't get hit.
لَكِم [lakim] *n:* • **1.** punching, boxing
لَكِم [lačim] *n:* • **1.** hitting, striking
لَكمَة [lakma] *n:* لَكمات [lakma:t] *pl:* • **1.** punch, blow with the fist
مُلاكِم [mula:kim] *n:* مُلاكِمِين [mula:kmi:n] *pl:* • **1.** boxer, pugilist
تَلاكُم [tala:kum] *n:* • **1.** boxing
مُلاكَمَة [mula:kama] *n:* • **1.** boxing, fist fighting

ل ك ن

لَكِن [la:kin] *conjunction:* • **1.** but, however – آنِي شِفتَه الأخُوك لَكِن ما قُتلَه عَلِيها [ʔa:ni šiftah ʔilaxu:k la:kin ma: gutlah ʕali:ha] I saw your brother but I didn't tell him about it. ترِيد تجاوُب لَكِنَّك ما تُعرُف [tri:d

ل

ďja:wub lakinnak ma: tuʕruf] You want to answer but you don't know. لَكِن إذا جِيت وَما لقيتنِي، خَلّي خَبَر عِند أَخُويَا [la:kin ʔiða ǰi:t wma lgi:tni, xalli: xabar ʕind ʔaxu:ya] However, if you come and don't find me, leave word with my brother.

ل ك ن د

لوكَندَة، لاكُندَة [lu:kanda, la:kunda also lu:qanṭa, la:qunṭa] *n:* لاكُندات، لوكَندات [la:kunda:t, lu:kanda:t also lu:qanṭa:t, la:qunṭa:t] *pl:* • **1.** restaurant • **2.** boardinghouse, inn

ل ل ن ك

لالَنكي [lalangi] *n:* • **1.** (coll.) tangerine(s)
لالَنكيَّة [lalangiyya] *n:* لالَنكيّات [lalangiyya:t] *pl:* • **1.** tangerine

ل ل ي

لالَى [la:la:] *v:* • **1.** to shine, glow, beam, radiate – هَالبِنَيَّة الحِلوَة وِجهَها يلالِي [halʔibnayya ʔilħilwa wiččha yla:li] That pretty girl's face really glows. جِلَف الصِّينِيَّة وخَلّاها تلالِي [ǰilaf ʔiṣṣi:niyya wxalla:ha tla:li] He scoured the tray and made it shine.
لالَة [la:la] *n:* لالات [la:la:t] *pl:* • **1.** lantern, lamp with a candle inside

ل م

لَمّا [lamma] *subordinating conjunction:* • **1.** when, as, at the time that – لَمّا ترُوح لِلسُّوق، لا تِنسَى تِشتِرِي شَكَر [lamma tru:ħ lissu:g, la: tinsa: tištiri šakar] When you go to market, don't forget to buy sugar. لا تِكتِب إلّا لَمّا أَقُلَّك [la: tiktib ʔilla lamma ʔagullak] Don't write until I tell you. • **2.** until, the time when – خَلّيهَا عِندَك لَمّا يِجِي [xalli:ha ʕindak lamma yiǰi] Keep it with you until he comes. • **3.** since, whereas – ماكُو داعِي تِدفَع لَمّا ما عِندَك فلُوس هَسَّة [ma:ku da:ʕi tidfaʕ lamma ma: ʕindak flu:s hassa] There's no need to pay since you don't have any money now.

ل م ب

لَمبَة [lamba] *n:* لَمبات [lamba:t] *pl:* • **1.** kerosene lamp • **2.** radio tube

ل م ح

لِمَح [limaħ] *v:* • **1.** to glimpse, catch sight of – لمَحتَه دَيِعبُر الشّارِع [lmaħtah dayiʕbur ʔišša:riʕ] I caught a glimpse of him crossing the street.
لَمَّح [lammaħ] *v:* • **1.** to intimate, insinuate, hint, allude, refer – لَمَّحلِي بِرَغبتَه لِلسَّفَر لأُورُبّا [lammaħli brayibtah lissafar lʔu:ruppa] He hinted to me of his desire to go to Europe.
لَمِح [lamiħ] *n:* • **1.** glimpse

لَمحَة [lamħa] *n:* لَمحات [lamħa:t] *pl:* • **1.** glance, glimpse, quick look – شِفتَه شدَيسَوِّي بِلَمحَة وِحدَة [šiftah šdaysawwi: blamħa wiħda] I saw what he was up to in one glance.
مَلامِح [mala:miħ] *n:* • **1.** (pl. only) features, outward appearance, looks
تلمِيح [talmi:ħ] *n:* تَلامِيح [tala:mi:ħ] *pl:* • **1.** insinuation
تَلمِيحَة [talmi:ħa] *n:* • **1.** hint • **2.** sign

ل م س

لِمَس [limas] *v:* • **1.** to touch, feel, handle – مِن لمَسِت قُصّتَه، فَزّ مِن النُّوم [min lmasit guṣṣtah, fazz min ʔinnu:m] When I touched his forehead, he woke up. • **2.** to feel, sense, have a hunch – لمَسِت عِندَه تَعَصُّب دِينِي [lmasit ʕindah taʕaṣṣub di:ni] I felt that he had religious prejudice.
تلَمَّس [tlammas] *v:* • **1.** to feel, palpate, examine by touch – تلَمَّس هَالقماش وشُوف شقَدّ ناعِم [tlammas halqma:š wšu:f šgadd na:ʕim] Feel this cloth and see how smooth it is.
اِلتِمَس [ʔiltimas] *v:* • **1.** to ask, request – ما دام الوَزِير صَدِيقَك ليش ما تِلتِمِس مِنَّه يعَيِّن إبنَك [ma: da:m ʔilwazi:r ṣadi:qak li:š ma: tiltimis minnah yʕayyin ʔibnak] Since the minister is your friend, why don't you ask him to appoint your son. • **2.** to make an urgent request, to implore, beseech, beg – اِلتِمَس مِنَّه بَلكِي يِقبَل [ʔiltimas minnah balki yiqbal] He begged him to accept if he could. التَمسَك تِجِي تِتعَشَّى عِدنا [ʔaltamsak tiǰi titʕašša: ʕidna] Please come have dinner with us.
لَمِس [lamis] *n:* • **1.** touching, feeling
مَلمَس [malmas] *n:* مَلامِس [mala:mis] *pl:* • **1.** place of touch, spot touched, touch, contact • **2.** texture
اِلتِماس [ʔiltima:s] *n:* اِلتِماسات [ʔiltima:sa:t] *pl:* • **1.** request, solicitation • **2.** plea, entreaty
مَلمُوس [malmu:s] *adj:* • **1.** touched, felt • **2.** tangible, palpable, noticeable – أَكُو تَحَسُّن مَلمُوس بِصِحّتَه [ʔaku taħassun malmu:s bṣiħħtah] There's a noticeable improvement in his health.

ل م ع

لِمَع [limaʕ] *v:* • **1.** to gleam, glisten, shine – المِحبَس مالَك دَيِلمَع [ʔilmiħbas ma:lak dayilmaʕ] Your ring is shining. هَذا الوَرَق يِلمَع. ما يِصلَح لِلمَكاتِيب [ha:ða ʔilwaraq yilmaʕ. ma: yiṣlaħ lilmaka:ti:b] This paper is glossy. It's no good for letters.
لَمَّع [lammaʕ] *v:* • **1.** to shine, make shine, impart a shine to – لَمِّع الدُّقَم والنَّجمات [lammiʕ ʔiddugam winnaǰma:t] Shine the buttons and the stars. هَالدِّهِن يلَمِّع القَنادِر [haddihin ylammiʕ ʔilqana:dir] This polish will make the shoes shine.
لَمِع [lamiʕ] *n:* • **1.** shining, shine, lustre, shimmer, gleam, gloe, brightness

لَمعَة [lamʕa] *n:* لَمعات [lamʕaːt] *pl:* • **1.** shine, sparkle, gloss, gleam, luster
لَمَعان [lamaʕaːn] *n:* • **1.** flash • **2.** shining, gleaming, shimmering, glossing
تَلمِيع [talmiːʕ] *n:* • **1.** polishing
لَمّاع [lammaːʕ] *adj:* • **1.** bright, shiny, glistening, sparkling, glossy
لامِع [laːmiʕ] *adj:* • **1.** shimmering, shiny • **2.** famous, brilliant, splendid
مِتلَمِّع [mitlammiʕ] *adj:* • **1.** radiant, brilliant

ل م ل م

لَملَم [lamlam] *v:* • **1.** to collect, gather, gather up – يَاللهْ! لَملِم غَراضَك وَإطلَع [yallah! lamlim ɣaraːđak wʔiṭlaʕ] Come on! Gather up your things and get out!
تلَملَم [tlamlam] *v:* • **1.** to gather oneself together – لَو تِتلَملَم بقَعِدتَك، يصِيرلِي مَكان [law titlamlam bgaʕidtak, yṣiːrli makaːn] If you don't sit sprawled out, there'll be room.
لَملُوم [lamluːm] *adj:* • **1.** gang, bunch (esp. of thieves, etc.) – دَيمشِي ويّا فَدّ لَملُوم ما بِيهُم خير [dayimši wiyya fadd lamluːm maː biːhum xiːr] He runs around with a nogood bunch of riffraff.

ل م م

لَمّ [lamm] *v:* • **1.** to collect, gather together, assemble – لِمّ الغَراض وَحُطّها بالجُنطَة [limm ʔilɣaraːđ wħuṭṭha bijjunṭa] Gather the things and put them in the suitcase. الطُّلّاب دَيلِمُّون تَبَرُّعات [ʔiṭṭullaːb daylimmuːn tabarruʕaːt] The students are collecting donations. صارلِي سَنَة أَلِمّ فلُوس حَتَّى أشتِري بايسِكِل [ṣaːrli sana ʔalimm fluːs ħatta ʔaštiri paːysikil] I have been saving money a year to buy a bicycle. الشُّرطَة لَمَّت كُلّ المَشبُوهِين [ʔiššurṭa lammat kull ʔilmašbuːhiːn] The police rounded up all the suspects. لِمّ الرَّبُع حَتَّى نِلعَب طُوبَة [limm ʔirrabuʕ ħatta nilʕab ṭuːba] Get the gang together so we can play ball. المُحتَكِر لَمّ كُلّ الشَّكَر اللِّي بِالسُّوق [ʔilmuħtakir lamm kull ʔiššakar ʔilli bissuwg] The monopolist cornered all the sugar in the market. البَزُّونَة لَمَّت نَفِسها وَكُمزَت عَالطِّير [ʔilbazzuːna lammat nafisha wgumzat ʕaṭṭiːr] The cat drew itself up and pounced on the bird.
اِنلَمّ [ʔinlamm] *v:* • **1.** to be collected, gathered – الطِّحِين ما يِنلَم بِالإيد [ʔiṭṭiħiːn maː yinlamm bilʔiːd] The flour can't be gathered up by hand.
اِلتَمّ [ʔiltamm] *v:* • **1.** to come together, assemble, unite, gather – اِلتَمّوا كُلّهُم يَمّ مُكان الحادِث [ʔiltammaw kullhum yamm mukaːn ʔilħaːdiθ] They all gathered near the scene of the accident. اِلتَمّوا عَلَيّا عِشرِين واحِد [ʔiltammaw ʕalayya ʕišriːn waːħid] Twenty guys ganged up on me. كانَت عايزَة اِلتَمَّت [čaːnat ʕaːyza ʔiltammat] It was one thing right on top of another. It was more than one could bear. كانَت عايزَة اِلتَمَّت. الصُّبُح بَيتِي اِحترَق، تالِي طَلّعونِي مِن شُغلِي، وَهَسَّة حصانِي مات [čaːnat ʕaːyza ʔiltammat. ʔiṣṣubuħ bayti ʔiħtirag, taːli ṭallʕuːni min šuɣli, whassa ħṣaːni maːt] It was a chain of catastrophes. This morning my house caught on fire, then they fired me from work, and now my horse died.
لَمّ [lamm] *n:* • **1.** collecting, gathering, putting together
لَمَّة [lamma] *n:* لَمّات [lammaːt] *pl:* • **1.** gathering, assembly, crowd
مَلمُوم [malmuːm] *adj:* • **1.** collected, gathered, assembled • **2.** compact

ل م ن

لَمَّن [lamman] *subordinating conjunction:* • **1.** var. of لَمّا : when

ل ن ك

لَنكَة [langa] *n:* لَنكات [langaːt] *pl:* • **1.** bale (of cotton, etc.) • **2.** compartment, section of a container

ل ه ب

لِهَب [lihab] *v:* • **1.** to burn, flame, blaze – الفانُوس دَيلهَب. نَزِّل الفِتيلَة [ʔilfaːnuːs dayilhab. nazzil ʔilftiːla] The lantern's blazing. Turn down the wick. • **2.** to catch fire, ignite, blaze – لا تحُطّ نار يَمّ البانزِين تَرَة يِلهَب بِالعَجَل [laː tħuṭṭ naːr yamm ʔilbanziːn tara yilhab bilʕajal] Don't put the fire near the gasoline because it catches fire easily.
لَهَّب [lahhab] *v:* • **1.** to singe, burn – لَهِّب البَطَّة زين قَبُل ما تشُقّها [lahhib ʔilbaṭṭa ziːn gabul maː tšuggha] Singe the duck well before you dress it.
اِلتِهَب [ʔiltihab] *v:* • **1.** to flame, flare up, burn brightly – اِلتِهبَت النِّيران بالمَعمَل [ʔiltihbat ʔinniːraːn bilmaʕmal] The flames blazed up in the factory. • **2.** to become inflamed – اِلتِهبَت اللّوزَتَين عِندَه [ʔiltihbat ʔillawzatayn ʕindah] His tonsils became inflamed.
لَهَب [lahab, lahib] *n:* • **1.** flare, blaze, flame
لَهبَة [lahba] *n:* لَهبات [lahbaːt] *pl:* • **1.** flame, blaze
اِلتِهاب [ʔiltihaːb] *n:* • **1.** inflammation – اِلتِهاب الحُنجَرَة [ʔiltihaːb ʔilħunjara] tonsilitis. اِلتِهاب المَفاصِل [ʔilthaːb ʔilmafaːṣil] arthritis.
مِلتِهِب [miltihib] *adj:* • **1.** burning, flaming • **2.** inflamed

ل ه ت

لَهات [lahaːt] *n:* لَهاتات [lahaːtaːt] *pl:* • **1.** velum, soft palate, rear portion of the roof of the mouth

ل ه ث

لِهَث [lihaθ] *v:* • **1.** to pant, gasp, be out of breath – لُويش تُركُض زايِد وَبَعدين تقُوم تِلهَث؟ [luwiːš turkuđ zaːyid wbaʕdiːn tguːm tilhaθ?] Why do you run so much that you begin to pant?
لَهِث [lahiθ] *n:* • **1.** gasp, pant
مَلهُوث [malhuːθ] *adj:* • **1.** breathless, out of breath

ل

ل ه ج

لَهجَة [lahǰa] *n:* لَهجات [lahǰa:t] *pl:* • **1.** dialect

ل ه س

اِستَلهَس [ʔistalhas] *v:* • **1.** to develop a desire, craving – لا تِنطِي الجّاهِل بَعَد تَرَة يِستَلهِس [la: tinṭi ʔiǰǰa:hil baʕad tara yistalhis] Don't give the kid any more or he'll get to wanting more and more. مِن شاف أكُو بَنات بِالحَفلَة اِستَلهَس وبُقى لنُصّ اللَّيل [min ša:f ʔaku bana:t bilħafla ʔistalhas wbuqa: lnuṣṣ ʔillayl] When he saw there were girls at the party he got interested and stayed until midnight.

ل ه ق

مَلهُوق [malhu:g, malhu:q] *adj:* • **1.** eager, avid – شبيك مَلهُوق؟ ما تِنتِظِر شوَيَّة؟ [šbi:k malhu:g? ma: tintiðir šwayya?] How come you're so eager? Can't you wait a little?

ل ه م

لِهَم [liham] *v:* • **1.** to devour, gobble up, swallow up – مِن حَطّينا الأكِل قِدّامَه، لِهَمَه بدَقِيقَة [min ħaṭṭi:na ʔilʔakil gidda:mah, lihamah bdaqi:qa] When we put the food before him, he devoured it in a minute.

لَهِم [lahim] *n:* • **1.** gulping, devouring, gobbling up

لَهمَة [lahma] *n:* لَهمات [lahma:t] *pl:* • **1.** bite – أُخذلَك لَهمَة مِن هَالسِّمسِم [ʔuxuðlak lahma min hassimsim] Take a bite of this sesame.

لهُوم [lhu:m] *n:* • **1.** a confection made of ground chickpeas and sugar

إلهام [ʔilha:m] *n:* • **1.** inspiration • **2.** instinct

مُلهَم [mulham] *adj:* • **1.** inspired • **2.** gifted

ل ه ن

لَهّانَة، لَهانَة [lahha:na, laha:na] *n:* • **1.** cabbage

ل ه و

لَهَّى [lahha:] *v:* • **1.** to amuse, divert, distract – لَهِّي الجّاهِل إلَى أن يِجِي أبُوه [lahhi ʔiǰǰa:hil ʔila ʔan yiǰi ʔabu:h] Entertain the child until his father comes. التَّلَفِزيُون يلَهِّي الواحِد. النَّهار يِنقِضِي وَلا تحِسّ بيه [ʔittalafizyu:n ylahhi ʔilwa:hid. ʔinnaha:r yingiði wala tħiss bi:h] Television passes one's time. The day goes and you never know it. لَهّانِي عَن شُغلِي [lahha:ni ʕan šuɣli] He distracted me from my work. الرِّياضَة ملَهِّيتَه، وَلا دَيِدرُس [ʔirriya:ða mlahhi:tah, wala dayidrus] Sports have engrossed him, and he won't do any studying. لَهِّي الشُّرطِي حَتَّى أخُشّ جَوَّة [lahhi ʔiššurṭi ħatta ʔaxušš ǰawwa] Hold the policeman's attention so I can go in.

تلَهَّى [tlahha:] *v:* • **1.** to amuse oneself, pass the time, occupy oneself – تلَهَّى بهالشَغلَة إلَى أن تِلقِيلَك أحسَن مِنها [tlahha: bhalšaɣla ʔila ʔan tilgi:lak ʔaħsan minha] Pass the time with this job, until you find something better. ما عِدنا فلُوس نِشتِرِيلَك بايسِكِل جِدِيد. تلَهَّى بهَذا [ma: ʕidna flu:s ništiri:lak pa:ysikil ǰidi:d. tlahha: bha:ða] We don't have the money to buy you a new bike. Occupy yourself with this one.

اِلتِهَى [ʔiltiha:] *v:* • **1.** to occupy oneself, devote one's time or attention – اِلتِهِي بهالشَّغلَة حَتَّى نشُوفلَك شَغلَة أحسَن [ʔiltihi bhaššaɣla ħatta nšu:flak šaɣla ʔaħsan] Keep busy with this job until we can find you a better one. اِلتِهَى بِاللِّعب وَتِرَك درُوسَه [ʔiltiha: billiʕib wtirak dru:sah] He spent all his time playing and abandoned his studies. بيش مِلتِهِي هَالأيّام؟ [biyš miltihi halʔayya:m?] What have you been doing these days?

لَهُو [lahw] *n:* • **1.** amusement, fun, entertainment • **2.** diversion, pastime

مَلهَى [malha] *n:* مَلاهِي [mala:hi] *pl:* • **1.** night club, cabaret

لَهاة [laha:t] *n:* • **1.** uvula

تَلهِيَة [talhiya] *n:* • **1.** distraction, diversion

مِلتِهِي [miltihi] *adj:* • **1.** unfocused, distracted, occupied, busy

ل و

لَو [law, lu:] *subordinating conjunction:* • **1.** if (introducing a conditional or hypothetical clause) – لَو ساحقَه القِطار، كان صِرت مَسؤُول [law sa:ħgah ʔilqiṭa:r, ča:n ṣirit masʔu:l] If the train had run over him, you would have been responsible. أشُوف لَو تاخُذ وِيّاك أكِل، أصرَفلَك [ʔašu:f law ta:xuð wiyya:k ʔakil, ʔaṣraflak] It seems to me that it would be cheaper for you if you take some food with you. يا معَوَّد! لَو قايِلَّه لأنّ ما يِدرِي [ya: mʕawwad! law ga:yillah liʔann ma: yidri] Good Lord! If only you'd told him, because he doesn't know. لِيش دِفَعتَه؟ لَو واقِع؟ [li:š difaʕtah? law wa:giʕ?] Why did you push him? What if he'd fallen? لَو ما [law ma:] if it weren't for. . ., except for the fact that. . . . لَو ما القاط غالِي، كان اِشتِرَيتَه [law ma: ʔilqa:ṭ ɣa:li, ča:n ʔištiraytah] If the suit weren't so expensive, I'd have bought it. لَو ما المُعَلِّم أخُوه، ما كان يِنجَح [law ma: ʔilmuʕallim ʔaxu:h, ma: ča:n yinǰaħ] If the teacher weren't his brother, he wouldn't have passed. لَو ما جاي، كان ترَزَّلِت [law ma: ǰa:y, ča:n trazzalit] If you hadn't come, I'd have been in a mess. • **2.** or – ياهِي أحسَن، سَيّارتِي لَو سَيّارتَك؟ [ya:hi ʔaħsan, sayya:rti law sayya:rtak?] Which is better, my car or your car? لَو. . . لَو [law. . . law] either. . . or. . . . لَو هَذا لَو هَذا [law ha:ða...law ha:ða] Either this or that. لَو يِجِي لَو ما يِجِي [law yiǰi law ma: yiǰi] Either he'll come or he won't come. لَو بَعَد [law baʕad] yet, or not. خَلَّصِت لَو بَعَد؟ [xallaṣit law baʕad?] Have you finished yet?

ل و ب ي

لُوبيَة [lu:bya] *n:* • **1.** (coll.) cowpea(s), black-eyed

pea(s) • **2.** green beans, string beans
لوبيايَة [luːbyaːya] *adj:* لوبيايات [luːbyaːyaːt] *pl:* • **1.** cowpea, bean

ل و ث

لَوَّث [lawwaθ] *v:* • **1.** to dust, sprinkle dust on – لَوِّث الصِّينِيَّة بِالطِّحِين قَبُل ما تخَلِّي عَليها العَجِين [lawwiθ ʔiṣṣiːniyya biṭṭiħiːn gabul maː txalliː ʕaliːha ʔilʕajiːn] Dust the tray with flour before you put the dough on it.
لواث [lwaːθ] *n:* • **1.** fine layer of flour on a pan to prevent sticking
تَلَوُّث [talawwuθ] *n:* • **1.** pollution
مُلَوَّث [mulawwaθ] *adj:* • **1.** stained, blotted, polluted
متِلَوِّث [mitlawwiθ] *adj:* • **1.** contaminated

ل و ح

لاح [laːħ] *v:* • **1.** to hit (a target) – تِقدَر تلُوح الشَّجرَة بالحجارَة مِن هَالمُكان؟ [tigdar tluːħ ʔiššijra bilħjaːra min halmukaːn?] Can you hit the tree with the rock from here?
لَوَّح [lawwaħ] *v:* • **1.** to sign, to wave, to make a sign • **2.** to throw at, to hit
انلاح [ʔinlaːħ] *v:* • **1.** to be hit – الطِّير ما ينلاح مِن هَالبُعُد [ʔiṭṭiːr maː yinlaːħ min halbuʕud] The bird can't be hit from this distance.
لَوح [luːħ] *n:* • **1.** hitting (a target) • **2.** (coll.) slab(s), sheet(s), plate(s) • **3.** board(s), plank(s) • **4.** pl. لواح plot, patch, section – قَسَّم حَدِيقتَه إلَى ألواح [qassam ħadiːqtah ʔila ʔalwaːħ] He divided his garden into small plots.
لَوحَة [lawħa, luːħa] *n:* لَوحات، ألواح، لواح [luːħaːt, lawħaːt, ʔalwaːħ, lwaːħ] *pl:* • **1.** board, plank (of wood) • **2.** sheet, slab, pane, plate, panel (of glass, etc.) • **3.** board, blackboard, slate • **4.** (artist's) canvas – لَوحَة فَنِّيَّة [lawħa fanniyya] painting.
لائِحَة [laːʔiħa] *n:* لَوائِح، لائِحات [lawaːʔiħ, laːʔiħaːt] *pl:* • **1.** bill, motion (in parliament)
تَلوِيح [talwiːħ] *n:* • **1.** beckoning, waving, sign, signal

ل و خ

لاخ [laːx] *v:* • **1.** to make a mess of, mess up, cause to go wrong – صاحبَك لاخها بِتَدَخُّلَه [ṣaːħbak laːxha btadaxxulah] Your friend messed it up with his intervention.
لَوَّخ [lawwax] *v:* • **1.** to soil, stain, besmudge, make dirty – الجّاهِل لَوَّخ إيدَه بِالطِّين [ʔijjaːhil lawwax ʔiːdah biṭṭiːn] The kid got his hands dirty in the mud.
تلَوَّخ [tlawwax] *v:* • **1.** to become soiled, get dirty – دِير بالَك لا تُوقَع وَتلَوَّخ هدُومَك [diːr baːlak laː tuːgaʕ wtlawwax hduːmak] Be careful not to fall or your clothes will get dirty.
تلاوَخ [tlaːwax] *v:* • **1.** to fight with each other – عَلِي تلاوَخ وِيّا المُعَلِّم [ʕali tlaːwax wiyya ʔilmuʕallim] Ali mixed it up with the teacher.
لَوخ [laux, luːx] *n:* • **1.** messing up

ل و ر ي

لَورِي [luːri] *n:* • **1.** truck

ل و ز

لُوز [luːz] *n:* • **1.** (coll.) almond(s) • **2.** (an expression of enthusiastic approval) excellent! splendid! – الأكِل مُمتاز! لوز [ʔilʔakil mumtaːz! luːz] The food is excellent. Really good! شلُون بنَيَّة! لوز [šluːn bnayya! luːz] What a girl! Wow!
لُوزَة [luːza] *n:* لُوزات [luːzaːt] *pl:* • **1.** almond • **2.** (pl. only) tread – لَوزات تايَر [luːzaːt taːyar] the tread of a tire.
لَوزَة [lawza] *n:* لَوزَتَين، لَوزات [luːzatiːn, lawzaːt] *pl:* • **1.** tonsil

ل و ص

لاص [laːṣ] *v:* • **1.** to make a mess of, mess up – مِن كان يِستَنقِي، لاص الطَّماطَة كُلّها [min čaːn yistangi, laːṣ ʔiṭṭamaːṭa kullha] When he was choosing, he ruined all the tomatoes. تدَخَل وَلاصها لِلقَضِيَّة [ddaxal wlaːṣha lilqaðiyya] He interfered and messed up the matter.
لَوَّص [lawwaṣ] *v:* • **1.** to exaggerate, talk through one's hat – هَذا دَيلَوِّص. ماكُو هِيكِي شِي [haːða daylawwiṣ. maːku hiːči ši] He's exaggerating. There's no such thing.
انلاص [ʔinlaːṣ] *v:* • **1.** to be made a mess of, be messed up – يبَيِّن الوَضِع انلاص بِالشِّمال [yibayyin ʔilwaðiʕ ʔinlaːṣ biššimaːl] It seems the situation in the north has gotten all messed up.
لَوص [lawṣ, luːṣ] *n:* • **1.** complications
مَليُوص [malyuːṣ] *adj:* • **1.** messed up, complicated

ل و ف

لاف [laːf] *v:* • **1.** to turn, change course, take a different direction – مِن تُوصَل لراس الشّارِع، لُوف عاليمنَى [min tuːṣal lraːs ʔiššaːriʕ, luːf ʕalyimna] When you get to the end of the block, turn right.
التاف [ʔiltaːf] *v:* • **1.** to turn, turn around, swing around – بَعدين التاف عَليه وَسَبَّه [baʕdiːn ʔiltaːf ʕaliːh wsabbah] Then he turned around to him and cursed him.
لَوف [lawf, luːf] *n:* • **1.** turn, curve, change of direction
لَوفَة [lawfa] *n:* • **1.** turn, curve, change of direction – هَالطَّرِيق بِيه لُوفات هوايَة [haṭṭariːq biːh luːfaːt hwaːya] This road's got a lot of curves in it. • **2.** detour – سَوَّوا بِالطَّرِيق لُوفَة لأنّ أكُو تَصلِيحات بِيه [sawwaw biṭṭariːq luːfa liʔann ʔaku taṣliːħaːt biːh] They made a detour in the road because they are mending it. • **3.** way around, way out, expedient – القَضِيَّة صَعبَة. لازِم نشُوف إلها فَدّ لُوفَة [ʔilqaðiyya ṣaʕba. laːzim nšuːf ʔilha fadd luːfa] The situation is difficult. We'll have to find some way around it.

ل

ل و ك س

لُوكس [luːks] *n:* • **1.** (invar.) deluxe, of the best quality – هَذا شلُون ثُوب! لُوكس [haːða šluːn θuːb! luːks] What a shirt. Top quality!

ل و ل

لُولَة [luːla] *n:* لُوَل [luwal] *pl:* • **1.** cylinder, tube, pipe • **2.** large cylindrical pillow

ل و ل ب

لَولَب [lawlab] *n:* • **1.** spiral • **2.** loop (contraceptive)

لَولَبِي [lawlabi] *adj:* • **1.** spiral

ل و ل ي

لُولَى [luːlaː] *v:* • **1.** to sing a lullaby – إبنِي ما ينام إذا ما تلُولِيلَه أُمَّه [ʔibni maː ynaːm ʔiða maː tluːliːlah ʔummah] My son won't go to sleep if his mother doesn't sing him a lullaby.

ل و م

لام [laːm] *v:* • **1.** to blame, censure, rebuke, chide, reproach – لا تدَخِّل نفسَك تَرَة بَعدين يلُومَك [laː ddaxxil nafsak tara baʕdiːn yluːmak] Don't interfere or later he'll blame you.

لَوَّم [lawwam] *v:* • **1.** same as لام : to blame, censure, rebuke, chide, reproach – حَتَّى لَو مَا تسَاعِدَه، مَحَّد يلَوِّمَك [ħatta law maː tsaːʕidah, maħħad ylawwimak] Even if you don't help him, no one will blame you.

تلاوَم [tlaːwam] *v:* • **1.** to blame each other – ظَلّوا يتلاومُون وَما حَدّ عِرَف صُوج مَن [ðallaw yitlaːwmuːn wamaː ħadd ʕiraf ṣuːč man] They kept on blaming each other and nobody knew whose fault it was.

اِنلام [ʔinlaːm] *v:* • **1.** to be blamed, censured, reproached – المُدِير ما ينلام بيه. هَذا يستاهِل الطَّرِد [ʔilmudiːr maː yinlaːm biːh. haːða yistaːhil ʔiṭṭarid] The director can't be blamed for it. This man deserves to be fired. ما ينلام عَلَى قَساوتَه. يستاهلُون [maː yinlaːm ʕala qasaːwtah. yistaːhluːn] He can't be taken to task for his cruelty. They deserve it.

لَوم [lawm, luːm] *n:* • **1.** blame • **2.** rebuke, reproach

مَلام، مَلامَة [malaːm, malaːma] *n:* • **1.** blame, rebuke, reproof

مُلام [mulaːm] *adj:* • **1.** blamed, censured

ل و ن [1]

لَوَّن [lawwan] *v:* • **1.** to color, add color to – مِن ترسِم البَيت، لَوِّن الباب أخضَر [min tirsim ʔilbayt, lawwin ʔilbaːb ʔaxðar] When you draw the house, color the door green.

تلَوَّن [tlawwan] *v:* • **1.** to be colored – الرَّسِم ما يتلَوَّن بسُهُولَة عَلَى هَالنَّوع مِن الوَرَق [ʔirrasim maː yitlawwan bsuhuːla ʕala hannuːʕ min ʔilwaraq] The picture can't be colored easily on this type of paper. • **2.** to change colors, shift with the wind, be changeable – هَذا يتلَوَّن حَسَب الظُّرُوف [haːða yitlawwan ħasab ʔiððuruːf] He shifts his position according to the circumstances.

لَون [lawn, luːn] *n:* ألوان [ʔalwaːn] *pl:* • **1.** color, hue, tint, shade, complexion • **2.** kind, sort, variety, species – قَدِّمُولنا ألوان وَأشكال مِن الأكِل [qaddimuːlna ʔalwaːn wʔaškaːl min ʔilʔakil] They offered us all sorts of food.

تلوِين [talwiːn] *n:* • **1.** coloring

مُلَوَّن [mulawwan] *adj:* • **1.** colored, tinted – أقلام مُلَوَّنَة [ʔaqlaːm mulawwana] colored pencils. فِلِم ملَوَّن [filim mlawwan] a color film, color movie.

مِتلَوِّن [mitlawwin] *adj:* • **1.** changeable, inconstant, unreliable, fickle – هَذا واحِد مِتلَوِّن. لا تِعتمِد عَليه [haːða waːħid mitlawwin. laː tiʕtimid ʕaliːh] He's changeable. Don't depend on him.

ل و ن [2]

شلَون ما، إشلَون ما [šluːn maː, ʔišluːn maː] *subordinating conjunction:* • **1.** however, howsoever – أقدَر أصبُغلَك السَّيّارَة شلَون ما ترِيد [ʔagdar ʔaṣbuɣlak ʔissayyaːra šluːn maː triːd] I can paint the car for you any way you want.

شلَون، إش لَون [šluːn, ʔiš luːn, šuːn, ʔišuːn] *interrogative:* • **1.** how, in what manner, in what way – ما يُعرُف شلُون يجاوُب [maː yuʕruf šluːn yǰaːwub] He doesn't know how to answer. • **2.** how, in what condition, in what state – شلُونَك اليُوم؟ [šluːnak ʔilyuːm?] How are you today? • **3.** how could it be that, for what reason, why – شلُون تقُلَّه ما كِنِت مَوجُود هنا؟ [šluːn dgullah maː činit mawǰuːd hna?] How could you tell him I wasn't here? شلُون ما شِفتَه لهَسَّة؟ [šluːn maː šiftah lhassa?] How come you haven't seen him yet? مُو عَلَّمتَك؟ شلُون ما تُعرُف الجَّواب؟ [muː ʕallamtak? šluːn maː tuʕruf ʔiǰǰawaːb?] Didn't I teach you? What do you mean you don't know the answer? • **4.** what, what sort of, what kind of, what a – شلُون؟ إنتِي اللّي ما قبلِت [šluːn? ʔinti ʔilli maː qbalit] What? You're the one that refused. شلُون مُعامَلَة هاي؟ هُوَّ مُو كَلِب [šluːn muʕaːmala haːy? huwwa muː čalib] What kind of treatment is that? He's not a dog. هَسَّة شلُون وِيّاك؟ ما تِجِي وِيّايا؟ [hassa šluːn wiyyaːk? maː tiji wiyyaːya?] Now what's the matter with you? Aren't you coming with me? أدرِي شلُون وِجِه يلَعِّب النَّفِس عَليه [ʔadri šluːn wijih ylaʕʕib ʔinnafis ʕaliːh] I realize what a sickening face he has. شلُون عيُون عَليها! فَلَّة [šluːn ʕyuːn ʕaliːha! falla] What gorgeous eyes she has! They're gorgeous!

شلُون [šluwn] *interrogative:* • **1.** how

ل و ي

لُوَى [luwaː] *v:* • **1.** to bend, flex – تِقدَر تِلوِي هَالشِّيش الغَلِيظ؟ [tigdar tilwi haššiːš ʔilɣaliːð?] Can you bend this thick

rod? • **2.** to twist, contort, wrench, warp – لَوَى إيدَه وَأخَذ الفلُوس مِنَّه [luwa: ʔi:dah wʔaxað ʔilflu:s minnah] He twisted his arm and took the money from him. • **3.** to turn aside, avert, hang – لُوَى راسَه مِن الخَجَل مِن المُعَلِّم رَزَّلَه [luwa: ra:sah min ʔilxajal min ʔilmuʕallim razzalah] He hung his head in embarrassment when the teacher scolded him.
تلَوَّى [tlawwa:] *v:* • **1.** to writhe, wriggle, squirm – البَزُّونَة وُقعَت وقامَت تِتلَوَّى مِن الوُجَع [ʔilbazzu:na wugʕat wga:mat titlawwa: min ʔilwujaʕ] The cat fell and began to writhe in pain. الحَيَّة، مِن تِمشِي، تِتلَوَّى [ʔilħayya, min timši, titlawwa:] When the snake moves, he wriggles.
تلاوَى [tla:wa:] *v:* • **1.** to arm wrestle, Indian wrestle – أرِيد أتلاوَى ويّا واحِد إيدَه قَوِيَّة [ʔari:d ʔatla:wa: wiyya wa:ħid ʔi:dah qawwiyya] I want to Indian wrestle with someone whose arm is strong.
انلُوَى [ʔinluwa:] *v:* • **1.** to be bent, be flexed – هَالشِّيش ما يِنلُوِي [hašši:š ma: yinluwi:] This rod can't be bent.
التُوَى [ʔiltuwa:] *v:* • **1.** to warp, twist, become bent, crooked, contorted out of shape – اللُّوحَة اِلتُوَت مِن الرُّطُوبَة [ʔillu:ħa ʔiltuwat min ʔirruṭu:ba] The board warped from the dampness. رِجل الكَلِب اِلتُوَت [rijl ʔiččalib ʔiltuwat] The dog's leg became twisted.
لَوي [lawy] *n:* • **1.** twisting, coil, winding – سِبرِنقات لَوِي [sipringa:t lawy] coil springs.
لِواء [liwa:ʔ] *n:* ألوِيَة [ʔalwiya] *pl:* • **1.** province, district • **2.** brigade (mil.) – أمِير لِواء [ʔami:r liwa:ʔ] major general.
لَويَة [lawya] *n:* • **1.** bend, curve, twist
مَلوِيَّة [malwiyya] *n:* • **1.** a minaret near Samarra with a spiral path leading up the outside to the top
اِلتِواء [ʔiltiwa:ʔ] *n:* • **1.** curvedness, twist, bend, curve
مَلوِي [malwi] *adj:* مَلاوِي [mala:wi] *pl:* • **1.** spiral • **2.** bent, curved, coiled, twisted • **3.** as a Noun, (pl. مَلاوِي) twisted metal band
مِلتُوِي [miltuwi] *adj:* • **1.** same as مَلوِي : tortuous, involved – لا تِحكِي بِصُورَة مِلتَوِيَة [la: tiħči bṣu:ra miltawya] Don't beat around the bush. • **2.** bent, curved, coiled, twisted, spiral, winding

ل ي ت

لِيت [li:t] *pseudo-verb:* • **1.** vari. of رِيت : would that!, would God!, I wish!, if only

ل ي خ

لاخ [la:x] *v:* • **1.** to leave in a hurry, depart hurriedly, beat it – لِيخ قَبُل ما يكُمشُوك [li:x gabul ma: ykumšu:k] Scram before they catch you! تَرَة مِن ياخُذ الفلُوس، يلِيخ [tara min ya:xuð ʔilflu:s, yli:x] As soon as he gets the money, he will beat it.
ليخ [layx, li:x] *n:* • **1.** leaving in a hurry

ل ي ر

لِيرَة [li:ra] *n:* لَيرات [li:ra:t] *pl:* • **1.** lira

ل ي س

لِيسَة [li:sa] *n:* لِيسات [li:sa:t] *pl:* • **1.** unborn lamb

ل ي ش

لِيش، لُويش، إلوِيش [li:š, luwi:š, ʔilwi:š] *interrogative:* • **1.** why, for what reason, what for – لِيش ما تِجِي وِيّانا؟ [li:š ma: tiji wiyya:na?] Why don't you come with us? ما أدرِي لوَيش [ma: ʔadri lwi:š] I don't know why. لُويش ما قِلتِلِي البارحَة؟ [luwi:š ma: gilitli ʔilba:rħa?] Why didn't you tell me yesterday? سألتَه لُويش ما خابَر [sʔaltah luwi:š ma: xa:bar] I asked him why he didn't phone.

ل ي ط

لِيطَة [li:ṭa] *n:* لِيطات، لِيَط [li:ṭa:t, liyaṭ] *pl:* • **1.** thin, flexible stick • **2.** thorn

ل ي ف

لَيَّف [layyaf] *v:* • **1.** to scrub with a luffa – إذا ما تلَيِّف زين، ما يِطلَع الوُسَخ [ʔiða ma: tlayyif zi:n, ma: yiṭlaʕ ʔilwusax] If you don't scrub well, the dirt won't come off. مُمكِن تلَيِّفلِي شوَيَّة؟ [mumkin tlayyifli šwayya?] Could you scrub me a little?
لِيف [li:f] *n:* • **1.** (coll.) bast, plant fiber(s)
لِيفَة [li:fa] *n:* لِيفات، لِيَف [li:fa:t, liyaf] *pl:* • **1.** luffa, a pad of plant fibers, commonly used as a scouring pad or bath sponge
ملَيِّف [mlayyif] *adj:* • **1.** scrubbed

ل ي ق

لاق [la:g] *v:* • **1.** with ل to suit, be fitting for, be just the right thing for – هَذا يلُوق لِهالوَظِيفَة [ha:ða ylu:g lhalwaḍi:fa] He's the right man for this position. الماوِي يلُوقلِك [ʔilma:wi ylu:glič] The color blue becomes you. هَالثنَين واحِد يلُوق لِلّاخ [haθθnayn wa:ħid ylu:g lilla:x] These two are made for each other.
لِياقَة [liya:qa] *n:* • **1.** propriety, suitableness, decency • **2.** fitness (physical)
لايِق [la:yig, la:yiq] *adj:* • **1.** appropriate, suitable, proper, suited, fit

ل ي ل

لَيل [layl, li:l] *n:* • **1.** night, nighttime
لَيلَة [laila, li:la] *n:* لَيلات، لَيالِي [layla:t, laya:li] *pl:* • **1.** night • **2.** evening
لَيلِي [layli] *adj:* • **1.** night, evening – مَدرَسَة لَيلِيَّة [madrasa layliyya] night school.

لَيلَكِي [laylaki] *adj:* • **1.** lilac
لَيلِيّاً [layliyyan] *adverbial:* • **1.** nightly, each night

ل ي ل و

لِيلُو، لُولِي [li:lu, lu:li] *n:* • **1.** (coll.) pearl(s)
لِيلُوَّة [li:luwwa] *n:* لِيلُوّات [li:luwwa:t] *pl:* • **1.** a pearl
لَيلُوَّة [layluwwa] *n:* لَيلُوّات [layluwwa:t] *pl:* • **1.** lullaby

ل ي م ن

لَيمُون [laymu:n, li:mu:n] *n:* • **1.** lemon

ل ي ن

لان [la:n] *v:* • **1.** to become soft, pliable, flexible, supple – جِلِد هَالقُندَرَة قَوِي لَكِن يلِين بالإستِعمال [ǰilid halqundara qawi la:kin yli:n bilʔistiʕma:l] The leather of this shoe is stiff but it'll soften with use. • **2.** to yield, give in – إذا تِحكِي ويّاه بلسان طَيِّب، يلين [ʔiða tiħči wiyya:h blsa:n ṭayyib, yli:n] If you talk to him nicely, he'll give in. • **3.** to soften, become gentle, tender – قَلبَه لان مِن شافَه يِبكِي [galbah la:n min ša:fah yibči] His heart softened when he saw him cry.
لَيَّن [layyan] *v:* • **1.** to soften, make soft, supple, pliable – تِقدَر تلَيِّنها لِلطِّينَة بِشوَيَّة مَيّ [tigdar tlayyinha litti:na bišwayyat mayy] You can soften the mud with a little water.
لِين [li:n] *n:* • **1.** tenderness, gentleness, kindness – إذا تِجِي ويّاه بِاللِّين، يِقبَل [ʔiða tiǰi wiyya:h billi:n, yiqbal] If you approach him nicely, he'll agree.
لِيُونَة [liyu:na] *n:* • **1.** flexibility, softness, tenderness
لَيِّن [layyin] *adj:* • **1.** soft, flexible, pliable, pliant, supple, resilient • **2.** gentle, tender-hearted
مُلَيِّن [mulayyin] *adj:* مُلَيِّنات [mulayyina:t] *pl:* • **1.** softener, softening agent, emollient • **2.** mild laxative
أَلين [ʔalyan] *comparative adjective:* • **1.** softer, more tender

ل ي و ن

لِيوان [li:wa:n] *n:* لُواوِين [luwa:wi:n] *pl:* • **1.** a covered, paved area, open to the air, facing on a courtyard

ل ي ي

لِيَّة [liyya] *n:* لِيّات [liyya:t] *pl:* • **1.** tail (of a fat-tailed sheep, the fat of which is used in cooking)

ل

م

م[1]

ما [maː] *negative particle:* • **1.** /negating prefix used with verbs, participles, and prepositions in equational phrases/ not – ما ضَنَّيت إِنَّك مَشغُول [maː ðanniːt ʔinnak mašɣuːl] I didn't think you were busy. ما أَقدَر أَجِي السّاعَة خَمسَة [maː ʔagdar ʔaǰi ʔissaːʕa xamsa] I can't come at five o'clock. إِذا ما تِستَعجِل، ما راح تخَلِّص شُغلَك [ʔiða maː tistaʕǰil, maː raːħ txalliṣ šuɣlak] If you don't hurry, you won't finish your work. هاي سَفرَة ما تِتفَوَّت [haːy safra maː titfawwat] This is a trip that isn't to be passed up. آني ما بايِت هنا قَبُل [ʔaːni maː baːyit hna gabul] I haven't spent the night here before. وِلدِك بَعَدهُم ما ماكلِين [wildič baʕadhum maː maːkliːn] Your children still haven't eaten. إبنِي الصَّغَيِّر ما مِتزَوِّج [ʔibni ʔiṣṣɣayyir maː midzawwiǰ] My youngest son is not married. لازِم أَشُوفلِي شِقَّة ما مُؤَثَّثَة [laːzim ʔašuːfli šiqqa maː muʔaθθaθa] I've got to find myself an unfurnished apartment. لا، آنِي ما تَعبان [laː, ʔaːni maː taʕbaːn] No, I'm not tired. ماكُو حاجَة تخابرَه [maːku ħaːǰa txaːbrah] There's no need to phone him. ماكُو عُطلَة هَالإِسبُوع [maːku ʕuṭla halʔisbuːʕ] There isn't any holiday this week. الصَّندُوق فارِغ؛ ما بِيه شِي [ʔiṣṣanduːg faːriɣ; maː biːh ši] The box is empty; there's nothing in it. هَالفِكرَة، ما بِيها فايدَة [halfikra, maː biːha faːyda] There is no advantage to this idea. هَالقماش، ما عَلَيه طَلَب هوايَة [halqmaːš, maː ʕaliːh ṭalab hwaːya] There isn't a lot of demand for this cloth. ما عِندِي فلُوس كافيَة [maː ʕindi fluːs kaːfya] I don't have enough money.

مُو [muː] *negative particle:* • **1.** (particle of negation) not – هَذا مُو شُغلِي [haːða muː šuɣli] That's not my business. هَذا مُو الكِتاب اللِّي قِتلَك عَليه [haːða muː ʔilkitaːb ʔilli gitlak ʕaliːh] This isn't the book that I told you about. هَالقُصَّة مُو صَحِيحَة؛ لا تصَدِّق بيها [halquṣṣa muː ṣaħiːħa; laː tṣaddig biːha] This story isn't true; don't believe it. أَبُويَا مُو بالبَيت؛ بَعدَه بالشُّغُل [ʔabuːya muː bilbayt; baʕdah biššuɣul] My father isn't at home; he's still at work. هَالمَكتُوب مُو إِلَك [halmaktuːb muː ʔilak] This letter isn't for you. هُوَّ اللِّي سَوّاها، مُو آنِي [huwwa ʔilli sawwaːha, muː ʔaːni] He's the one who did it, not I. اِنطِيه فلُوس، بَسّ مُو أَكثَر مِن عَشِر دَنانِير [ʔinṭi fluːs, bass muː ʔakθar min ʕašir danaːniːr] Give him some money, but not more than ten dinars. أَرِيدَك تسَوِّيها اليُوم، مُو باكِر [ʔariːdak tsawwiːha ʔilyuːm, muː baːčir] I want you to do it today, not tomorrow.

م[2]

ما [maː] *subordinating conjunction:* • **1.** suffix forming a conjunction from a preposition, interrogative, comparative, and certain other forms (see under first constituent) – خَلِّي نخَلِّص شُغُلنا قَبِل ما يِجِي المُدِير [xalliː nxalliṣ šuɣulna gabil maː yiǰi ʔilmudiːr] Let's finish our work before the director comes. سَوِّيها شلُون ما ترِيد [sawwiːha šluːn maː triːd] Do it any way you like. سَوِّي شما يِعجبَك [sawwiː šma yiʕiǰbak] Do whatever you like. هَذا أَحسَن ما عِندَك؟ [haːða ʔaħsan maː ʕindak?] Is that the best you've got? كُلّما أَشُوفَه، هُوَّ سَكران [kullma ʔašuːfah, huwwa sakraːn] Whenever I see him, he's drunk.

م ء ق

مُوق [muːg] *n:* مواقَة [mwaːga] *pl:* • **1.** inner corner of the eye • **2.** target hole in boys' marble games

م ء ن

مُؤنَة، مَؤُونَة [maʔuːna, muːna] *n:* مُؤَن [muʔan] *pl:* • **1.** provision, food, stock, supply, burden

م ء و

مِيَّة [miyya] *n:* مِيّات، مِيايَة [miyyaːt, miyaːya] *pl:* • **1.** one hundred percent • **2.** totally, completely – قِتلَك مِيَّة مَرَّة، لا تسَوِّي هِيكِي [gitlak miyyat marra, laː tsawwiː hiːči] I've told you a hundred times, don't do that! ياخُذ خَمسَة بالمِيَّة دلالَة [yaːxuð xamsa bilmiyya dlaːla] He gets a five percent auction fee.

مِئَوِي [miʔawi] *adj:* • **1.** centigrade – دَرَجَة حَرارَة الغُرفَة ثلاثِين مِئَوِيَّة [daraǰat ħaraːrat ʔilɣurfa tlaːθiːn miʔawiyya] The room temperature is 30° centigrade. نِسبَة مِئَوِيَّة [nisba miʔawiyya] percentage. عِيد مِئَوِي [ʕiːd miʔawi] hundredth anniversary, centennial.

م ب ي ن

مابَين [maːbayn] *n:* مابَينات [maːbaynaːt] *pl:* • **1.** anteroom, entryway, hall

م ت ر

مَتِر، مِتِر، مَترَة [matir, mitir, matra] *n:* أَمتار، مَترات [ʔamtaːr, matraːt] *pl:* • **1.** meter (39.34 inches)

م ت ع

مَتَّع [mattaʕ] *v:* • **1.** with ب to make enjoy – مَتِّع عينَك بهَالجَّمال [mattiʕ ʕaynak bhaǰǰamaːl] Feast your eyes upon this beauty.

تمَتَّع [tmattaʕ] *v:* • **1.** with ب to enjoy, savor, relish – تمَتَّع بحَياتَك ما دامَك شَباب [tmattaʕ bħayaːtak maː daːmak šabaːb] Enjoy your life while you're still young.

مِتعَة، مُتعَة [mitʕa, mutʕa] *n:* • **1.** enjoyment, pleasure, delight, gratification • **2.** زَواج المُتعَة temporary marriage for the purpose of sexual gratification

م

تَمَتُّع [tamattuʕ] *n:* • **1.** enjoyment, delight, gratification, pleasure

مُمتِع [mumtiʕ] *adj:* • **1.** pleasant, delicious, enjoyable, delightful

م ت ن

مِتَن [mitan] *v:* • **1.** to become thick, stout, strong, heavy – هَالشِّجرَة دَتِمتَن سَنَة عَلَى سَنَة [haššijra datimtan sana ʕala sana] This tree is getting thicker year after year. • **2.** to dislocate the shoulder – لا تجُرّ إيد الوَلَد تَرَة تِمتِنها [la: ďjurr ʔi:d ʔilwalad tara timtinha] Don't tug on the boy's arm or you'll dislocate his shoulder.

مَتِن [matin] *n:* مْتُون [mtu:n] *pl:* • **1.** shoulder

مِتِن [mitin] *n:* • **1.** thickness, heaviness • **2.** gauge (of wire)

مِتِين [miti:n] *adj:* • **1.** thick, stout, heavy, strong – دَيجُرّ البَلَم بحَبِل مِتِين [dayǰurr ʔilbalam bħabil miti:n] He's pulling the boat with a thick rope.

مَمتُون [mamtu:n] *adj:* • **1.** having a sprained or dislocated shoulder

أمتَن [ʔamtan] *comparative adjective:* • **1.** thicker or thickest, stronger or strongest

م ت ي

يَمتَى [yamta] *adverbial:* • **1.** when

م ث ل

مَثَّل [maθθal] *v:* • **1.** to act, play (a role) – أيّ دَور ينطُوه، يمَثّلَه كُلّش زين [ʔayy dawr yinṭu:h, ymaθθilah kulliš zi:n] Any role they give him, he plays very well. ما يُعرُف يمَثّل أدوار هَزَلِيَّة [ma: yuʕruf ymaθθil ʔadwa:r hazaliyya] He doesn't know how to play comedy roles. • **2.** to show, demonstrate – هَالمَشاريع الضَّخمَة تمَثّل إخلاص الحُكُومَة [halmaša:ri:ʕ ʔiððaxma tmaθθil ʔixla:ṣ ʔilħuku:ma] These vast projects show the government's sincerity. • **3.** to represent – منُو راح يمَثّل الوِزارَة بهاللُّجنَة؟ [minu ra:ħ ymaθθil ʔilwiza:ra bhalluǰna?] Who's going to represent the ministry on this committee? • **4.** to liken, compare – أمَثّل خَشمَه بخَرطُوم الفِيل [ʔamaθθil xašmah bxarṭu:m ʔilfi:l] I would compare his nose to an elephant's trunk.

تمَثَّل [tmaθθal] *v:* • **1.** to be represented

امتِثَل [ʔimtiθal] *v:* • **1.** with لـ to obey, carry out – الجُندي يمتِثِل لِلأوامِر العَسكَرِيَّة [ʔiǰǰundi yimtiθil lilʔawa:mir ʔilʕaskariyya] The soldier obeys military orders.

مِثِل [miθil] *n:* • **1.** like, similar to, just like, the same as – هُوَّ فَدّ خُوش وَلَد. ما كُو مِثلَه [huwwa fadd xu:š walad. ma: ku: miθlah] He's a real fine fellow. There's none like him. لَعَد مِثلَك؟ أصرُف كُل راتبي؟ [laʕad miθlak? ʔaṣruf kul ra:tbi?] You mean I should be like you? Spend all my salary? تِقدَر تِكتِب حَرف العَين مِثلِي؟ [tigdar tiktib ħarf ʔilʕayn miθli?] Can you write the letter 'ayn the way I do? أشُو مِثِل حِسّها [ʔašu miθil ħissha] It sounds like her voice. بالمِثِل [bilmiθil] in kind, in the same manner, likewise. عاملَه بالمِثِل [ʕa:mlah bilmiθil] Treat him the same way. • **2.** pl. أمثال similar thing, thing of the same kind – هُوَّ وَأمثالَه [huwwa wʔamθa:lah] He and all his kind.

مَثَل [maθal] *n:* أمثال [ʔamθa:l] *pl:* • **1.** proverb, adage • **2.** example • **3.** warning, example, object lesson

مثال [miθa:l] *n:* أمثِلَة [ʔamθila] *pl:* • **1.** example • **2.** model, exemplar

مَثِيل [maθi:l] *n:* • **1.** equal, match – ما إلَه مَثِيل [ma: ʔilah maθi:l] It has no equal. It's incomparable.

مُمَثّل [mumaθθil] *n:* مُمَثّلِين [mumaθθili:n] *pl:* • **1.** actor, stage performer • **2.** agent, representative

تِمثال [timθa:l] *n:* تَماثِيل [tama:θi:l] *pl:* • **1.** statue

تَمثِيل [tamθi:l] *n:* • **1.** acting

مُمَثّلَة [mumaθθila] *n:* مُمَثّلات [mumaθθila:t] *pl:* • **1.** actress

تَماثُل [tama:θul] *n:* • **1.** analogy • **2.** matching, similarity, symmetry, similitude, likeness

مُمَثّلِيَّة [mumaθθiliyya] *n:* • **1.** agency, representation • **2.** pl. مُمَثّلِيّات diplomatic mission

امتِثال [ʔimtiθa:l] *n:* • **1.** obedience, compliance, submission

تَمثِيلِيَّة [tamθi:liyya] *n:* تَمثِيلِيّات [tamθi:liyya:t] *pl:* • **1.** play, stage presentation – تَمثِيلِيَّة هَزَلِيَّة [tamθi:liyya hazaliyya] a comedy.

مِثالِي [miθa:li] *adj:* • **1.** model, exemplary – أبُوه مُعَلِّم مِثالِي [ʔabu:h muʕallim miθa:li] His father is an exemplary teacher.

مُماثِل [muma:θil] *adj:* • **1.** similar, comparable, corresponding, analogous

أمثَل [ʔamθal] *comparative adjective:* • **1.** best, perfect, exemplary

مَثَلاً [maθalan] *adverbial:* • **1.** for example, for instance

مِثلما [miθilma] *subordinating conjunction:* • **1.** just as, like, the same as – راح أسَوّي مِثلما تقُول [ra:ħ ʔasawwi: miθilma: dgu:l] I'll do just as you say.

م ث ن

مَثانَة [maθa:na] *n:* مَثانات [maθa:na:t] *pl:* • **1.** (urinary) bladder

م ج ج

مَجّ، مَيّ مَجّ [maǰǰ, mayy maǰǰ] *adj:* • **1.** hard water, water with high mineral content • **2.** brackish, bad-tasting water

م ج د

مَجَّد [maǰǰad] *v:* • **1.** with بـ to praise, laud, extol, glorify (esp. God) – المُوَذِّن قَبِل الفَجِر يمَجِّد وَبَعدين يوَذِّن

[ʔilmuwaððin gabil ʔilfajir ymajjid wbaʕdiːn ywaððin] Before dawn the muezzin praises God and then gives the call to prayer. دائِماً يمَجِّد بأجدادَه [daːʔiman ymajjid bʔajdaːdah] He's always glorifying his ancestors.

مَجد [majd] *n:* • **1.** splendor, glory

مَجِيد [majiːd] *adj:* • **1.** glorious, illustrious, exalted – القُرآن المَجِيد [ʔilqurʔaːn ʔilmajiːd] the glorious Koran. وَالقُرآن المَجِيد ما أعرُف [wilqurʔaːn ʔilmajiːd maː ʔaʕruf] I swear I don't know.

ماجِد [maːjid] *adj:* • **1.** praised

م ج ر

المَجَر [ʔilmajar] *n:* • **1.** Hungary

مَجَري [majari] *adj:* • **1.** Hungarian • **2.** a Hungarian

م ج ن

ماجِينَة [maːjiːna] *n:* • **1.** a children's holiday, similar to Halloween, observed during the month of Ramadan

مَجّاني [majjaːni] *adj:* • **1.** free, no cost

مَجّاناً [majjaːnan] *adverbial:* • **1.** free of charge – الدُّخُول بِالحَدِيقَة مَجّاناً [ʔidduxuːl bilħadiːqa majjaːnan] Entrance to the park is free.

م ج و س

مَجُوس [majuːs] *n:* • **1.** Magi, adherents of Mazdaism

مَجُوسِي [majuːsi] *adj:* • **1.** Magian • **2.** a Magian

مَجُوسِيَّة [majuːsiyya] *adj:* • **1.** Mazdaism

م ح ر

مَحّار [maħħaːr] *n:* • **1.** (coll.) sea shell(s), oyster shell(s), snail shell(s)

مَحّارَة [maħħaːra] *n:* مَحّارات [maħħaːraːt] *pl:* • **1.** sea shell, oyster shell, snail shell

م ح ض

مَحض [maħð̣] *adj:* • **1.** absolute, pure, unadulterated, genuine

م ح ل

مَحَل [maħal] *n:* • **1.** dearth, famine, drought, barrenness

م ح ل ق

مَحلَقُو [maħlaqu] *n:* • **1.** children's game similar to hopscotch

م ح ن

مَحَّن [maħħan] *v:* • **1.** to leave stranded – أخَذ سَيّارتي وَمَحَّنّي [ʔaxað sayyaːrti wmaħħanni] He took my car and left me stranded.

اِمتِحَن [ʔimtiħan] *v:* • **1.** to examine, test – المُعَلِّم راح يمتِحِنّا بِالإنكِلِيزي باكِر [ʔilmuʕallim raːħ yimtiħinna bilʔingiliːzi baːčir] The teacher is going to test us in English tomorrow. • **2.** to take an examination – لازِم تِمتِحِن قَبُل ما يقبَلُوك [laːzim timtiħin gabul maː yiqbaluːk] You'll have to take an examination before they'll accept you.

مِحنَة [miħna] *n:* مِحَن [miħan] *pl:* • **1.** severe trial, tribulation, ordeal, hardship, distress, misfortune – مَرضَة أبُويا خَلّتنا بِمِحنَة [marð̣at ʔabuːya xallatna bmiħna] My father's sickness left us under a strain.

اِمتِحان [ʔimtiħaːn] *n:* اِمتِحانات [ʔimtiħaːnaːt] *pl:* • **1.** examination, test

م ح و

مِحَى [miħaː] *v:* • **1.** to erase, rub out, wipe off – إمحِي هَالكِلمَة وَإكتِبها مَرَّة لُخ [ʔimħi haččilma wʔiktibha marra lux] Erase this word and write it again. • **2.** to wipe out, eradicate, exterminate – الجَّيش مِحاهُم عَن آخِرهُم [ʔijjayš miħaːhum ʕan ʔaːxirhum] The army wiped them out to the last man.

مَحَّى [maħħaː] *v:* • **1.** to erase repeatedly – الوَرقَة صارَت سُودَة مِن قَدّ ما يمَحّي [ʔilwarqa ṣaːrat suːda min gadd maː ymaħħi] The page turned black from his erasing so much.

اِنمِحَى [ʔinmiħaː] *v:* • **1.** to be wiped out, obliterated – آثارهُم اِنمِحَت؛ مَحَّد يُعرُف شصار مِنهُم [ʔaːθaːrhum ʔinmiħat; maħħad yuʕruf šṣaːr minhum] Their traces were wiped out; no one knows what happened to them.

مَحِي [maħy] *n:* • **1.** erasing, wiping off

مَحّايَة [maħħaːya] *n:* مَحّايات [maħħaːyaːt] *pl:* • **1.** pencil eraser

مَمحِي [mamħi] *adj:* • **1.** place where something has been erased – ما يُعبُر عَليه شِي. يقرا المَمحِي [maː yuʕbur ʕaliːh ši. yiqraː ʔilmamħi] Nothing gets past him. He's very clever (lit., reads what's been erased).

م خ خ

مُخّ [muxx] *n:* مخاخ، مخُوخَة [mxaːx, mxuːxa] *pl:* • **1.** brain • **2.** mind, intelligence • **3.** medulla, marrow

مُخَسِّز [muxxsizz] *adj:* • **1.** brainless, senseless – المَدرَسَة ما تفِيدَه. هُوَّ مُخَسِّز [ʔilmadrasa maː tfiːdah. huwwa muxxsizz] School does him no good. He's brainless.

م خ ط

مُخَط [muxaṭ] *v:* • **1.** to blow one's nose – عَلِّم إبنَك يمخُط بِالكَفِّيَّة [ʕallim ʔibnak yumxuṭ biččaffiyya] Teach your son to blow his nose with a handkerchief.

مَخَّط [maxxaṭ] *v:* • **1.** to blow one's nose frequently – مَنشُول وَدَيمَخُّط هوايَة [manšuːl wadaymaxxuṭ hwaːya] He's got a cold and he's blowing his nose a lot. • **2.** to cause to blow the nose – مَخِّطَت إبنها وَمِسحَت خَشمَه [maxxiṭat ʔibinha wmisħat xašmah] She made her son blow and wiped his nose.

مَخِط [maxiṭ] *n:* • **1.** blowing the nose

مَخطَة [maxṭa] *n:* مَخطات [maxṭaːt] *pl:* • **1.** a blowing of the nose

م

مُخطَة [muxṭa] *n:* مُخطات [muxṭa:t] *pl:* • **1.** blob of mucus, piece of snot
مخاط [mxa:ṭ] *n:* • **1.** nasal mucus, snot – مخاط الشَّيطان [mxa:ṭ ʔišši:ṭa:n] gossamer, cobwebs.
مُخطان [muxṭa:n] *n:* مخاطِين [mxa:ṭi:n] *pl:* • **1.** coll pl. مخاطِين nasal mucus, snot – مُخطان الشَّيطان [muxṭa:n ʔišši:ṭa:n] cobwebs, gossamer.
مُخطانَة [muxṭa:na] *n:* مُخطانات [muxṭa:na:t] *pl:* • **1.** un.n. of مُخطَان : nasal mucus, snot
مُخاطِي [muxa:ṭi] *adj:* • **1.** mucous – أغشِيَة مُخاطِيَّة [ʔaɣšiya muxa:ṭiyya] mucous membranes.

م خ ط ر

تمَخطَر [tmaxṭar, tmaxtar] *v:* • **1.** to walk with a graceful, swinging gait

م خ ل م

مَخلَمَة [maxlama] *n:* مَخلَمات [maxlama:t] *pl:* • **1.** omelette • **2.** meat and vegetable omelette

م خ و ذ

ماخُوذ [ma:xu:ð] *n:* مُواخِيذ [muwa:xi:ð] *pl:* • **1.** club, bludgeon, bat • **2.** also used as a euphemism for male or female genitals

م د ح

مدَح [midaħ] *v:* • **1.** to commend, praise, laud, extol – مِدَحَه بقَصِيدَة رَنّانَة [midaħah bqaṣi:da ranna:na] He praised him in a resounding poem.
انمِدَح [ʔinmidaħ] *v:* • **1.** pass. of مِدَح to be praised • **2.** to be commended, lauded
مدِح [madiħ] *n:* • **1.** praise, commendation, laudation, glorification

م د د

مَدّ [madd] *v:* • **1.** to extend, stretch, stretch out – راح أقعُد هنا حَتَّى أقدَر أمِدّ رِجلَيَّا [ra:ħ ʔagʕud hna ħatta ʔagdar ʔamidd rijlayya] I'll sit here so I can stretch out my legs. مَدّلِي إيدَه [maddli ʔi:dah] He extended his hand to me. • **2.** to spread, spread out, lay, lay out – الشَّرِكَة دَتمِدّ أنابِيب نَفُط من هنا لِبَغداد [ʔiššarika datmidd ʔana:bi:b nafuṭ min hna libayda:d] The company is laying oil pipes from here to Baghdad. • **3.** to provide, supply – قِدَر يدرُس بالخارِج، لِأنّ أبُوه كان يمِدَّه بالفلُوس [gidar yidrus bilxa:rij, liʔann ʔabu:h ča:n ymiddah bilfilu:s] He was able to study abroad because his father was supplying him with money.
مَدَّد [maddad] *v:* • **1.** to stretch out, spread out – مَدِّدُوه عَالقاع وَدَوّرَوا جيُوبَه [maddidu:h ʕalga:ʕ wdawwraw jyu:bah] They stretched him out on the ground and went through his pockets. • **2.** to extend, distend, elongate, expand – الحَرارَة تمَدِّد المَعادِن [ʔilħara:ra tmaddid ʔilmaʕa:din] Heat expands metals. • **3.** to lengthen, extend, protract, prolong – راح أمَدِّد إجازتِي شَهَر لاخ [ra:ħ ʔamaddid ʔija:zti šahar la:x] I am going to extend my leave another month. مَدَّدلِي مُدَّة دَفع الدَّين شَهرَين [maddadli muddat dafiʕ ʔiddayn šahrayn] He extended the payment time of the debt two months for me.
تمَدَّد [tmaddad] *v:* • **1.** to be extended, prolonged – وَقِت الامتِحان تمَدَّد إلَى يوم الخَمِيس [wakit ʔilʔimtiħa:n tmaddad ʔila yu:m ʔilxami:s] The exam time has been put off until Thursday. • **2.** to lengthen, expand, distend, extend, stretch, spread – ترِكَوا هَالشقُوق بِالجِسِر لِأنّ يِتمَدَّد بالحَرارَة [tirkaw halšgu:g biljisir liʔann yitmaddad bilħara:ra] They left these cracks in the bridge because it expands in the heat. • **3.** to stretch oneself out, sprawl – البارحَة تمَدَّدِت بِالفراش وَنِمِت هوايَة [ʔilba:rħa tmaddadit bilfra:š wnimit hwa:ya] Yesterday I stretched out on the bed and slept quite a while.
امتَدّ [ʔimtadd] *v:* • **1.** to extend, run, stretch (over a distance) – هَالطَّرِيق يمتَدّ مِن بَيتنا لِلشَّطّ [haṭṭari:q yimtadd min baytna liššaṭṭ] This road extends from our house to the river.
استَمَدّ [ʔistamadd] *v:* • **1.** to draw, derive, get – يِستِمِدّ قُوّتَه مِن الحِزب [yistimidd quwwtah min ʔilħizib] He derives his power from the party.
مَدّ [madd] *n:* • **1.** extension, stretching – عَلَى مَدّ البَصَر [ʕala madd ʔilbaṣar] as far as the eye can see. أكُو أشجار عَلَى مَدّ البَصَر [ʔaku ʔašja:r ʕala madd ʔilbaṣar] There are trees as far as the eye can see. • **2.** lengthening, protraction – آنِي وِيّاك عَلَى مَدّ الله [ʔa:ni wiyya:k ʕala madd ʔallah] In time I'll show you! • **3.** tide, flood tide – هَالسَّفِينَة ما راح ترُوح إلّا لَمّا يِجِي المَدّ [hassifi:na ma: ra:ħ tru:ħ ʔilla lamma yiji ʔilmadd] This ship won't depart until the tide comes in.
مُدَّة [mudda] *n:* مُدَد [mudad] *pl:* • **1.** period of time, interval – بِمُدَّة شَهَر تعَلَّم كُلّ شِي [bmuddat šahar tʕallam kull ši] In the period of a month he learned everything. • **2.** while – اِنتِظَرتَه مُدَّة لَكِن ما جا [ʔintiðartah mudda la:kin ma: ja:] I waited for him a while but he didn't come. صارلِي مُدَّة طوِيلَة ما شايفَك [ṣa:rli mudda ṭwi:la ma: ša:yfak] It's been a long time since I saw you. • **3.** limited time, term
مَدَد [madad] *n:* أمداد [ʔamda:d] *pl:* • **1.** advantage, handicap (in a contest, etc.) – إنطِينِي مَدَد خَمس أمتار وأتغالَب وِيّاك [ʔinṭi:ni madad xams ʔamta:r wʔadɣa:lab wiyya:k] Give me a five-meter handicap and I'll race you.
مادَّة [ma:dda] *n:* مَوادّ [mawa:dd] *pl:* • **1.** material, matter, substance – مَوادّ أوَّلِيَّة [mawa:dd ʔawwaliyya] raw materials. مَوادّ حَربِيَّة [mawa:dd ħarbiyya] war materiel. • **2.** subject, field of study – هَالمادَّة ما مَطلُوبَة بالامتِحان [halma:dda ma: maṭlu:ba bilʔimtiħa:n] This subject isn't required in the exam. • **3.** article, paragraph of a legal document) – اِنحِكَم حَسَب المادَّة الخامِسَة مِن القانُون

م

[ʔinhikam ħasab ʔilmaːdda ʔilxaːmisa min ʔilqaːnuːn] He was sentenced according to article five of the law.
مَدَّة [madda] *n:* • **1.** carpet, rug
مادَّة [maːdda] *n:* • **1.** pus, purulent matter
إمداد [ʔimdaːd] *n:* إمدادات [ʔimdaːdaːt] *pl:* • **1.** provision, supply
تَمدِيد [tamdiːd] *n:* • **1.** extension, prolongation, lengthening, elongation

م د ل
مَدالِيَة [madaːlya] *n:* مَداليات [madaːlyaːt] *pl:* • **1.** medal, decoration

م د ل ي و ن
مَدالِيَون [madaːlyuːn] *n:* مَدالِيَونات [madaːlyuːnaːt] *pl:* • **1.** pendant, locket, medallion

م د م
مَدام، مَدامَة [madaːm, madaːma] *n:* مَدامات [madaːmaːt] *pl:* • **1.** madam, lady (polite form of address or term for a non Arab woman) – لابسَة لِبس طالعَة بِيه مَدام [laːbsa libis ṭaːlʕa biːh madaːm] She looks like a fashionable foreigner in those clothes she's wearing.

م د ن
مَدَّن [maddan] *v:* • **1.** to civilize, urbanize, refine – هَالمِعدان، شيمَدِّنهُم؟ [halmiʕdaːn, šyimaddinhum?] How could these yokels ever be civilized?
تمَدَّن [tmaddan] *v:* • **1.** to become urbanized, civilized, modernized – العِراق تمَدَّن هوايَة بَعد الحَرُب [ʔilʕiraːq tmaddan hwaːya baʕd ʔilħarub] Iraq became quite modern after the war. شُوف عَلِي، شلُون تمَدَّن! اِشتِرَى راديُو وحَطّ بِبَيتَه تِلِفُون [šuːf ʕali, šluːn tmaddan! ʔištiraː raːdyu wħaṭṭ bibaytah tilifuːn] Look how urbanized Ali's gotten! He bought a radio and put a telephone in his house.
مَدِينَة [madiːna] *n:* مُدُن [mudun] *pl:* • **1.** city, town
مَدَنِي [madani] *adj:* • **1.** civic, civil, city – مَركَز مَدَنِي [markaz madani] civic center. • **2.** civilian (as opposed to military) – مَلابِس مَدَنِيَّة [malaːbis madaniyya] civilian clothes. • **3.** a civilian
مَدَنِيَّة [madaniyya] *adj:* • **1.** civilization
متمَدِّن [mitmaddin] *adj:* • **1.** civilized

م د ي
تمادَى [tmaːdaː] *v:* • **1.** to persist • **2.** to continue something, keep or go on doing something, to go far, go to extremes
مَدَى [madaː] *n:* • **1.** range, extension, expanse, stretch, spread, compass, scope
تَمادِي [tamaːdi] *n:* • **1.** persistence, going too far in something

م د ي ل
مُوديل [muːdiːl] *n:* مُوديلات [muːdiːlaːt] *pl:* • **1.** model

م ر ء
مَرَة [mara] *n:* • **1.** woman • **2.** wife • **3.** This word doesn't have a plural. نِسوَان is the commonly used plural form.
مرَيَّة [mrayya] *n:* مرَيّات [mrayyaːt] *pl:* • **1.** var. of مَرَة woman
مرُوَّة، مرُوءَة [mruwwa, mruːʔa] *n:* • **1.** the best virtues of mankind, especially compassion, generosity, and a sense of honor – هَالقَصّاب يبِيع غالِي. ما عِندَه مرُوَّة [halgaṣṣaːb yibiːʕ ɣaːli. maː ʕindah mruwwa] This butcher charges too much. He has no heart. أهل المرُوَّة جِمعُولَه فلُوس وَمَشّوه لأهلَه [ʔahl ʔilmruwwa ǰimʕuwlah fluːs wmaššuːh lʔahlah] The kind-hearted people collected money for him and sent him to his family. مرُوتَك! خَلِّصنِي مِن هَالرِّجّال [mruːtak! xalliṣni min harriǰǰaːl] By your honor! Save me from this man! إنتَ وَمرُوتَك. شما تِنطِينِي، أقبَل [ʔinta wmruːtak. šma tinṭiːni, ʔaqbal] I leave it to your conscience. Whatever you give me, I'll accept.
مَرِيء [mariːʔ] *n:* • **1.** esophagus, gullet
مَرِيئاً [mariːʔan] *adverbial:* • **1.** approx: may it do you good, May you enjoy it.(food) – أُكُلها هَنِيئاً ء مَرِيئاً [ʔukulha haniːʔan mariːʔan] Eat it in good health.

م ر ج ح
مَرجَح [marǰaħ] *v:* • **1.** to swing
تمَرجَح [tmarǰaħ] *v:* • **1.** to swing, pendulate – خَلِّي الجّاهِل يِتمَرجَح بِهَالمَرجِيحَة [xalliː ʔiǰǰaːhil yitmarǰaħ bhalmarǰiːħa] Let the child swing in this swing.
تمِرجِح، مَرجَهَة [tmirǰiħ, marǰaħa] *n:* • **1.** swinging
مُرجِيحَة، مَرجُوحَة [murǰiːħa, marǰuːħa] *n:* مَراجِيح [maraːǰiːħ] *pl:* • **1.** swing

م ر ج ن
مَرجان [marǰaːn, mirǰaːn] *n:* • **1.** coral
مَرجانِي [marǰaːni] *adj:* • **1.** coralline, coral-like, coral-red

م ر ح
مَرَح [maraħ] *n:* • **1.** joy, cheerfulness, mirth, glee, gaiety, merriment
مَرِح [mariħ] *adj:* مَرحِين [marħiːn] *pl:* • **1.** joyful, lively, merry, glad, happy

م ر خ
المِرِّيخ [ʔilmirriːx] *n:* • **1.** the planet Mars

م ر د
مُرَد [murad] *v:* • **1.** to crush, squash, mash – عَلَى كَيفَك، مُرَدت الطَّماطَة [ʕala kayfak, muradt

ʔiṭṭama:ṭa] Take it easy, you've crushed the tomatoes. السَّيّارَة داسَت الكَلِب وَمُردَتَه [ʔissayya:ra da:sat ʔiččalib wmurdatah] The car ran over the dog and squashed him. أمرُد الطَّماطَة قَبِل ما تخَلِّيها بِالجِّدِر [ʔumrud ʔiṭṭama:ṭa gabil ma: txalli:ha bǰǰidir] Mash the tomatoes before you put them in the pot. وَالله أمُردَك إذا تِحكِي كِلمَة [wʔallah ʔamurdak ʔiða tiħči čilma] By God, I'll smash you if you say a word! الحَرّ مُرَدنِي [ʔilħarr muradni] The heat took a lot out of me. • **2.** to waste, squander, fritter away – مُرَد كُلّ فلُوسَه بِالقمار [murad kull flu:sah bilqma:r] He squandered all his money on gambling.
مَرَّد [marrad] *v:* • **1.** to smash, crush up – لا تِستَنقِي بَعَد. مَرَّدت العِنجاص [la: tistangi baʕad. marradt ʔilʕinǰa:ṣ] Don't choose any more. You've squashed all the plums.
تمَرَّد [tmarrad] *v:* • **1.** to be crushed, squashed, mashed – تمَرِّدَوا تَحَت رِجلَين النّاس [tmarridaw taħat riǰlayn ʔinna:s] They were crushed under the people's feet. تمَرَّد قَلبِي [tmarrad galbi] My heart ached (lit., was crushed). تمَرَّد قَلبِي عَلَى هَالمِسكِين [tmarrad galbi ʕala halmiski:n] I was very sorry for that poor fellow. • **2.** to be refractory, recalcitrant, unruly, rebellious – قِسِم مِن الجيش تمَرَّد [qisim min ʔiǰǰayš tmarrad] A part of the army rebelled.
اِنمُرَد [ʔinmurad] *v:* • **1.** to be crushed, squashed – اِنمُرَد الخُوخ كُلَّه [ʔinmurad ʔilxu:x kullah] All the peaches got squashed. قَلبِي اِنمُرَد [galbi ʔinmurad] My heart ached (lit., was crushed). قَلبِي اِنمُرَد مِن سِمعِت خَبَر وَفاتَه [galbi ʔinmurad min simaʕit xabar wafa:tah] My heart sank when I heard the news of his death. اِنمُرَدِت بِالإمتِحان [ʔinmuradit bilʔimtiħa:n] I did badly in the exam. • **2.** to be wasted, squandered, frittered away – هَالعَصرِيَّة اِنمُرَدَت عَلينا وَما سَوَّينا شِي [halʕaṣriyya ʔinmurdat ʕali:na wma sawwi:na ši] This afternoon was wasted for us and we didn't do a thing.
مَرِد [marid] *n:* • **1.** crushing, squashing, mashing, pulping
مَرد [mard] *n:* • **1.** var. of مَردانَة man, esp one possessing the knightly virtues of manliness, chivalrousness, and honor see م-ر-د-ن
مَردِي [mardi] *n:* مَرادِي [mara:di] *pl:* • **1.** punting pole, long wooden pole used by boatmen
مَردَة [marda] *n:* مَردات [marda:t] *pl:* • **1.** punting pole, long wooden pole used by boatmen
مُرِيدَة [muri:da] *n:* • **1.** pulp, mash

م ر د ش و ر

مَردَشُور [mardašu:r] *adj:* مَردَشُورِيَّة [mardašu:riyya] *pl:* • **1.** rapacious, grasping, greedy person • **2.** parasite, free-loader

م ر د ن

مَردانَة [marda:na] *adj:* • **1.** man or women esp. one possessing the knightly virtues of manliness, chivalrousness, and honor – هَالخُردَفَرُوش يبِيع غَراض مال زَنانَة وَمال مَردانَة [halxurdafaru:š yibi:ʕ ɣara:ð ma:l zana:na wma:l marda:na] This variety store sells articles for women and for men. إذا ما أخَذِت حَيفِي مِنَّك، آني مُو مَردانَة [ʔiða ma: ʔaxaðit ħayfi minnak, ʔa:ni mu: marda:na] If I don't get my revenge on you, I'm not a man! طِلَع مَردانَة. ما خَلَّى أحَّد يِعتِدِي عالمَرَة [ṭilaʕ marda:na. ma: xalla: ʔaħħad yiʕtidi ʕalmara] He proved himself a real man. He didn't let anyone assault the woman. دَقَّة مَردانَة [dagga marda:na] a gentlemanly, chivalrous, gallant deed. دَقَّت وِيّايا دَقَّة مَردانَة وَما داعَتنِي بِالدَّين [daggat wiyya:ya dagga marda:na wama da:ʕatni biddayn] She was very gracious to me and didn't ask me for the debt.

م ر ر 1

مَرّ [marr] *v:* • **1.** to pass, elapse, go by – مَرَّت أيّام بَلا ما نِسمَع مِنَّه [marrat ʔayya:m bala ma: nismaʕ minnah] Days passed without us hearing from him. العَمَلِيَّة مَرَّت بسَلام [ʔilʕamaliyya marrat bsala:m] The operation went well. • **2.** to pass, go, come, walk – كُلّ يوم عِدَّة بَواخِر تمُرّ مِن القَنال [kull yu:m ʕiddat bawa:xir tmurr min ʔilqana:l] Every day several ships pass through the canal. قَبُل شوَيَّة مَرّ من هنا [gabul šwayya marr min hna] A while ago he passed by here. الفَراشَة، بِتَطَوُّر حَياتها، تمُرّ بِعِدَّة أدوار [ʔilfara:ša, btaṭawwur ħaya:tha, tmurr biʕiddat ʔadwa:r] During the development of its life, the butterfly goes through several stages. آنِي أمُرّ عَلِيك بِالبَيت [ʔa:ni ʔamurr ʕali:k bilbayt] I'll drop in on you at home. مَرَّت عَلَيّا أيّام قاسيَة [marrat ʕalayya ʔayya:m qa:sya] Hard times came my way. ما مَرَّت عَلَيّا هِيكِي قَضِيَّة قَبُل [ma: ma:rrat ʕalayya hi:či qaðiyya gabul] I've never had experience with such a matter before. عَرِيضتِي مَرَّت عَلَى عِدَّة أشخاص [ʕari:ðti marrat ʕala ʕiddat ʔašxa:ṣ] My application has gone through several people. مُرّلِي مِن تُفرَغ [murrli min tufraɣ] Drop by and see me when you are free.
مَرَّر [marrar] *v:* • **1.** to let pass – هالجِّسر ما يمَرِّرُون عَليه لَورِيّات [haǰǰisir ma: ymarriru:n ʕali:h lu:riyya:t] They won't let trucks cross over this bridge. • **2.** to pass, cause to pass – لا تمَرِّر إيدَك عَلَى شَعرِي [la: tmarrir ʔi:dak ʕala šaʕri] Don't run your hand over my hair.
اِنمَرّ [ʔinmarr] *v:* • **1.** to be passed – هَالطَّرِيق ما يِنمَرّ مِنَّه [haṭṭari:q ma: yinmarr minnah] This road is impassable.
اِستَمَرّ [ʔistamarr] *v:* • **1.** to last, endure, continue – المُطَر اِستِمَرّ عَشِر ساعات [ʔilmuṭar ʔistimarr ʕašir sa:ʕa:t] The rain continued for ten hours. • **2.** to continue, persist, persevere, keep on – اِستِمِرّ عَلَى دِراستَك وَتِنجَح بِالإمتِحان [ʔistimirr ʕala dira:stak wtinǰaħ bilʔimtiħa:n] Go on with your studies and pass the exam.
مَرّ [marr] *n:* • **1.** passing, transit, traversal, coming or going • **2.** pl. مرار hoe, tool shaped like a hoe and used to move dirt • **3.** pl. مِرار [mira:r] sometimes

مَرَّة [marra] *n:* مَرّات [marra:t] *pl:* • **1.** time, instance – لِعَبنا بُوكَر مَرَّة وِحدَة [liʕabna pu:kar marra wiħda] We played poker once. قِتلَك ألف مَرَّة، لا تسَوِّي هِيكِي [gitlak ʔalf marra, la: tsawwi: hi:či] I've told you a thousand times, don't do that. مَرَّة يِركَب الباص ومَرَّة يِجِي بيادَة [marra yirkab ʔilpa:ṣ wmarra yiǰi pya:da] Sometimes he rides the bus and sometimes he comes on foot. مَرَّة عَلَى مَرَّة [marra ʕala marra] time after time, continually. مَرَّة مِن المَرّات [marra min ʔilmarra:t] one of these times, sometime. مَرَّة هَذا، مَرَّة ذاك [marra ha:ða, marra ða:k] Sometimes this, sometimes that. فَدّ مَرَّة، بِالمَرَّة [fadd marra, bilmarra] completely, absolutely, entirely. آني مِفلِس فَدّ مَرَّة [ʔa:ni miflis fadd marra] I'm completely broke. طِلَع زمال فَدّ مَرَّة [ṭilaʕ zma:l fadd marra] He turned out to be a complete ass. هَذا فَدّ مَرَّة ما يِفتِهِم [ha:ða fadd marra ma: yiftihim] He doesn't know at all. مالِي عِلاقَة بِيه بِالمَرَّة [ma:li ʕila:qa bi:h bilmarra] I haven't any connections with him at all. وأشُو فَدّ مَرَّة [wʔašu: fadd marra] and it seemed all at once. . . , and suddenly. . .

مَمَرّ [mamarr] *n:* مَمَرّات [mamarra:t] *pl:* • **1.** passageway, corridor

مُرُور [muru:r] *n:* • **1.** passing, passage • **2.** traffic – شُرطَة المُرُور [šurṭat ʔilmuru:r] traffic police.

اِستِمرار [ʔistimra:r] *n:* • **1.** continuing • **2.** permanence

اِستِمرارِيَّة [ʔistimra:riyya] *n:* • **1.** continuity

مارّ [ma:rr] *adj:* مارَّة [ma:rra] *pl:* • **1.** passer-by • **2.** pedestrian

مِستِمِرّ [mistimirr] *adj:* • **1.** lasting, permanent, continual, uninterrupted, incessant, continuous, constant

م ر ر 2

مَرارَة [mara:ra] *n:* • **1.** bitterness • **2.** hardship, difficulty, tribulation • **3.** pl. مَرارات gall bladder

مُرّ [murr] *adj:* • **1.** bitter – القَهوَة مُرَّة. جِيبلِي شوَيَّة شَكَر [ʔilgahwa murra. ǰi:bli šwayya šakar] The coffee is bitter. Bring me some sugar. شاف المُرّ، ضاق المُرّ [ša:f ʔilmurr, ða:g ʔilmurr] He's experienced hardship. He's had a hard time.

أمَرّ [ʔamarr] *comparative adjective:* • **1.** more or most bitter • **2.** worse, worst, more or most terrible – قاسَيت الأمَرَّين مِن إيدَه [qa:si:t ʔilʔamarrayn min ʔi:dah] I went through terrible hardship because of him. • **3.** الأمَرَّين originally, the two worst things, poverty and old age) great hardship, tribulation, difficulty

م ر س

مارَس [ma:ras] *v:* • **1.** to pursue, exercise, practice (a profession) – مارَس مِهنَة الطِّبّ مُدَّة طوِيلَة [ma:ras mihnat ʔiṭṭibb mudda ṭwi:la] He practiced medicine for a long time.

مُمارَسَة [muma:rasa] *n:* • **1.** practice, exercise, pursuit

مِتمَرِّس [mitmarris] *adj:* • **1.** practiced, experienced

مُمارِس [muma:ris] *adj:* • **1.** practicing, experiencing

م ر ش ل

مارشال [ma:rša:l] *n:* • **1.** same as مُشِير: [muši:r] marshal (milit.)

م ر ض

مُرَض [murað] *v:* • **1.** to become sick – مُرَض مَرّتَين هالسَّنَة [murað marrtayn hassana] He got sick twice this year.

مَرَّض [marrað] *v:* • **1.** to make sick – أكلَة البارحَة مَرِّضَتها [ʔaklat ʔilba:rħa marriðatha] The food yesterday made her sick.

تمَرَّض [tmarrað] *v:* • **1.** to get sick, be made sick – هُوَّ ضَعِيف البُنيَة وَ يِتمَرَّض بسُرعَة [huwwa ðaʕi:f ʔilbunya w yitmarrað bsurʕa] He has a weak constitution and gets sick easily.

تمارَض [tma:rað] *v:* • **1.** to feign illness, malinger – التِّلمِيذ تمارَض حَتَّى ما يرُوح لِلمَدرَسَة [ʔittilmi:ð tma:rað ħatta ma: yru:ħ lilmadrasa] The student feigned illness so he wouldn't have to go to school.

مَرَض [marað] *n:* أمراض [ʔamra:ð] *pl:* • **1.** disease, ailment • **2.** sickness, illness

مَرضَة [marða] *n:* مَرضات [marða:t] *pl:* • **1.** bout of sickness, siege of illness

مَرِيض [mari:ð] *n:* مُرضَة [murða] *pl:* • **1.** sick, ill, ailing – عَمِّي بَعدَه مَرِيض وَنايِم بِالفراش [ʕammi baʕdah mari:ð wna:yim bilfra:š] My uncle's still stick and staying in bed.

مُمَرِّض [mumarrið] *n:* مُمَرِّضات، مُمَرِّضِين [mumarriða:t, mumarriði:n] *pl:* مُمَرِّضَة [mumarriða] *feminine:* • **1.** nurse, male nurse

تَمرِيض [tamri:ð] *n:* • **1.** nursing, caring for the sick

مَرِيض [mari:ð] *adj:* مَرِيضِين [mari:ðyin] *pl:* • **1.** sick, ill • **2.** as Noun: patient

مَرَضِي [maraði] *adj:* • **1.** pathological, relating to sickness or disease, morbid

مِتمَرِّض [mitmarrið] *adj:* • **1.** out of health, sickly, unwell

م ر غ

مَرَّغ [marraɣ] *v:* • **1.** to massage, rub – طِلَب مِن إبنَه يمَرِّغلَه ظَهرَه [ṭilab min ʔibnah ymarriɣlah ðahrah] He asked his son to massage his back for him.

م ر غ ل

مَرغَل [marɣal] *v:* • **1.** to roll, roll around – حَتَّى يأذِّيه، مَرغَل شَفقتَه بِالتِّراب [ħatta yʔaððiːh, marɣal šafiqtah bittira:b] To hurt him he rolled his hat around in the dirt. مَرغَل زِرّ الدِّجاجَة بِالطِّحِين قَبُل ما يقَلِّيه [marɣal zirr ʔiddiǰa:ǰa biṭṭhi:n gabul ma: ygalli:h] He rolled the chicken leg in flour before he fried it.

تمَرغَل [tmarɣal] *v:* • **1.** to wallow, roll around – الكَلِب تمَرغَل بِالتِّراب [ʔiččalib tmarɣal bittira:b] The dog wallowed in the dirt.

مَرغَلَة [marɣala] *n:* • **1.** rolling around

م

م ر ق

مَرَق [marag] *n:* • **1.** gravy • **2.** stew, goulash
مَرقَة [marga] *n:* مَرقات [marga:t] *pl:* • **1.** stew – مَرقَة إسبيناغ [margat ʔispi:na:ɣ] spinach stew. مَرقَة بيتِنجان [margat bi:tinǰa:n] eggplant stew.

ر ق ص see also م ر ق ص

تمَرقَص [tmargaṣ] *v:* • **1.** to mince, move with a mincing gait, move daintily – يتمَرقَص مِن يِمشِي. عَبالَك بنَيَّة. [yitmargaṣ min yimši. ʕaba:lak bnayya] He walks with a mincing gait. He looks like a girl.
مَرقَص [marqaṣ] *n:* مَراقِص [mara:qiṣ] *pl:* • **1.** dance hall, ballroom

م ر ك

ماركَة [ma:rka] *n:* ماركات [ma:rka:t] *pl:* • **1.** brand, make – أيّ ماركَة هَالسّاعَة؟ [ʔayy ma:rka hassa:ʕa?] What brand of watch is this?

م ر ك ش

مَرّاكِش [marra:kiš] *n:* • **1.** Marrakech (city in western Morocco) • **2.** Morocco
مَرّاكِشِي [marra:kiši] *adj:* • **1.** from or of Marrakech • **2.** Moroccan • **3.** a native of Marrakech • **4.** a Moroccan

م ر م ر [1]

مَرمَر [marmar] *v:* • **1.** to exasperate, vex – الجّاهِل مَرمَر أُمَّه بِالبَكِي مالَه [ʔijǰa:hil marmar ʔummah bilbači ma:lah] The kid exasperated his mother with his crying.
تمُرمُر [tmurmur] *n:* • **1.** agony

م ر م ر [2]

مَرمَر [marmar] *n:* • **1.** marble • **2.** coll. marbles (game)
مَرمَرايَة [marmara:ya] *n:* مَرمَرايات [marmara:ya:t] *pl:* • **1.** marble

م ر ن

مَرَّن [marran] *v:* • **1.** to train, drill (someone) – المُعَلِّم مَرَّنهُم هوايَة قَبِل السِّباق [ʔilmuʕallim marranhum hwa:ya gabil ʔissiba:q] The teacher drilled them a lot before the game. • **2.** to accustom, condition, season, get used – دَيمَرِّن نَفسَه عَالكِتابَة بِيدَه اليِسرَى [daymarrin nafsah ʕalkita:ba bi:dah ʔilyisra] He's accustoming himself to writing with his left hand.
تمَرَّن [tmarran] *v:* • **1.** to exercise, practice, train, rehearse – لازِم تِتمَرَّن هوايَة قَبِل ما تُدخُل السِّباق [la:zim titmarran hwa:ya gabil ma: tudxul ʔissiba:q] You've got to practice a lot before you enter the game. المُلاكِم دَيتمَرَّن ساعتين كُلّ يوم [ʔilmula:kim dayitmarran sa:ʕtayn kull yu:m] The boxer is training two hours every day. المُمَثِّلين دَيتمَرِّنُون عَلَى أدوارهُم [ʔilmumaθθili:n dayitmarrinu:n ʕala ʔadwa:rhum] The actors are rehearsing their roles.
تمرين [tamri:n] *n:* تَمرينات، تَمارِين [tamri:na:t, tama:ri:n] *pl:* • **1.** exercise, practice, training
مُرُونَة [muru:na] *n:* • **1.** flexibility, elasticity, pliability
مَرِن [marin] *adj:* • **1.** reasonable, flexible – تِقدَر تِتفاهَم ويّاه. هُوَّ فَدّ واحِد مَرِن [tigdar titfa:ham wiyya:h. huwwa fadd wa:ħid marin] You can reach an understanding with him. He's a flexible person.

م ر و ن

مارُونِي [ma:ru:ni] *adj:* • **1.** maroon

م ر ي ل

مَريول [maryu:l] *n:* مَريولات [maryu:la:t] *pl:* • **1.** apron • **2.** smock

م ز ج

مِزَج [mizaǰ] *v:* • **1.** to mix, blend – دَيمِزجُون شَحَم ويّا الزّيت وَيبِيعُوه [daymizǰu:n šaħam wiyya ʔizzi:t wybi:ʕu:h] They're mixing fat with vegetable oil and selling it. • **2.** to combine, consolidate – ماكُو مُعَلِّم لِهَالصَّفّ. إمزِج الصَّفَّين [ma:ku muʕallim lihaṣṣaff. ʔimziǰ ʔiṣṣaffayn] There's no teacher for this class. Consolidate the two classes.
اِنمِزَج [ʔinmizaǰ] *v:* • **1.** to be mixed, mingled
اِمتِزَج [ʔimtizaǰ] *v:* • **1.** to mix, mingle – آنِي ما أمتِزِج ويّا هِيچِي ناس [ʔa:ni ma: ʔamtiziǰ wiyya hi:či na:s] I don't mingle with that kind of people.
مَزِج [maziǰ] *n:* • **1.** mixing, blending
مِزاج [miza:ǰ] *n:* أمزِجَة [ʔamziǰa] *pl:* • **1.** temperament, disposition, nature • **2.** frame of mind, mood, humor • **3.** taste, discernment – هَذا صاحِب مِزاج؛ ما عِندَه مانِع يُصرُف فلُوس أزيَد عالعَرَق الزّين [ha:ða ṣa:ħib miza:ǰ; ma: ʕindah ma:niʕ yuṣruf flu:s ʔazyad ʕalʕarag ʔizzi:n] He has taste; he doesn't mind spending more money for good arrack.
مَزِيج [mazi:ǰ] *adj:* مَزيجات [mazi:ǰa:t] *pl:* • **1.** mixture, blend • **2.** compound, combination

م ز ز

مَزَّة [mazza] *n:* مَزّات [mazza:t] *pl:* • **1.** appetizers, hors d'oeuvres (when served with alcoholic beverages)

م ز ق

مِزَق [mizaq] *v:* • **1.** to tear, rip, rend – البايسِكِل مِزَق بَنطَرُونِي [ʔilpa:ysikil mizag panṭaru:ni] The bicycle tore my pants. مِزَق وَرقَة الدَّفتَر [mizag warqat ʔiddaftar] He tore a page of the notebook.
مَزَّق [mazzaq] *v:* • **1.** to humiliate, degrade, disgrace – مَزِّقُوه قِدّام أصدِقائَه [mazziqu:h gidda:m ʔaṣdiqa:ʔah] They humiliated him in front of his friends.
مَزَّق [mazzag] *v:* • **1.** with ب to tear up, rip up, to tear to bits – الجّاهِل دَيمَزِّق بِكتابِي [ʔijǰa:hil daymazziq

bikta:bi] The kid is tearing my book up.
تمَزَّق [tmazzag] *v:* • **1.** to be or become torn to shreds – تمَزِّقت هدُومَه مِن العَركَة [tmazziqat hdu:mah min ʔilʕarka] His clothes were all torn up in the fight.
اِنمزَق [ʔinmizag] *v:* • **1.** to be torn – تَنتَة السَّيّارَة اِنمِزقَت [tantat ʔissayya:ra ʔinmizqat] The convertible car top got torn.
مَزِق [mazig] *n:* • **1.** tearing, ripping, rending • **2.** pl. مزُوق tear, rip, torn place
مَزقَة [mazga] *n:* مَزقات [mazga:t] *pl:* • **1.** tear, rip

م ز ل ق

مَزلَق [mazlag] *v:* • **1.** to make slip – دِير بالَك مِن الثَّلِج تَرَة يمَزلِقَك [di:r ba:lak min ʔiθθalij tara ymazligak] Watch out for the ice or it'll make you slip and fall. المُحامِي مَزلَق المُتَّهَم بأسئِلتَه [ʔilmuħa:mi mazlag ʔilmuttaham bʔasʔiltah] The lawyer made the defendant slip with his questions.
تمَزلَق [tmazlag] *v:* • **1.** to slip, slide, be slippery – الماعُون تمَزلَق مِن إيدي وَوُقَع [ʔilma:ʕu:n tmazlag min ʔi:idi wwugaʕ] The dish slipped from my hand and fell. الصّابُونَة تِتمَزلَق بالإيد [ʔiṣṣa:bu:na titmazlag bilʔi:d] Soap is slippery in the hand.
مزليقَة [mizli:ga] *n:* مِزليقات [mizli:ga:t] *pl:* • **1.** slick spot, slippery place

م ز ن

مِزنَة [mizna] *n:* مِزَن [mizan] *pl:* • **1.** rain, shower

م ز ي

مَزِيَّة [maziyya] *n:* مَزايا [maza:ya] *pl:* • **1.** merit, virtue

م ز ي ق

مَزِيقَة [mazi:qa] *n:* • **1.** music

م س ت ك

مَستَكي [mastaki] *adj:* • **1.** mastic, resin of the mastic tree • **2.** a confection containing a small amount of mastic

م س ح

مِسَح [misaħ] *v:* • **1.** to wipe, wipe off, clean – إمسَح الميز قَبُل ما تحُطّ عليه شِي [ʔimsaħ ʔilmi:z gabul ma: tħuṭṭ ʕali:h ši] Wipe off the table before you put anything on it. • **2.** to wipe out, rub out, erase – مِسحَوا إسمَك مِن قائمَة التَّرفِيع [misħaw ʔismak min qa:ʔimat ʔitttarfi:ʕ] They struck your name off the promotion list. مِسَح العار عَن عائِلتَه [misaħ ʔilʕa:r ʕa:n ʕa:ʔiltah] He wiped out the shame on his family.
تمَسَّح [tmassaħ] *v:* • **1.** with ب to rub up against – البَزُّون دَيتمَسَّح بيّا [ʔilbuzzu:n dayitmassaħ biyya] The cat is rubbing up against me. • **2.** to wipe, cleanse oneself – الإسلام يِتشَطِّفُون وَالمَسِيحِيِّين يِتمَسِّحُون [ʔilʔisla:m yitšaṭṭifu:n wʔilmasi:ħiyyi:n yitmassiħu:n] The Moslems wash themselves and the Christians wipe themselves.
انمسَح [ʔinmisaħ] *v:* • **1.** to be erased, rubbed out – الحِبِر ما يِنمِسِح بِالمِسّاحَة [ʔilħibir ma: yinmisiħ bilmissa:ħa] Ink can't be erased with the eraser.
مَسِح [masiħ] *n:* • **1.** wiping, wiping off, cleaning
مَسحَة [masħa] *n:* مَسحات [masħa:t] *pl:* • **1.** rubbing, wiping
مَسّاح [massa:ħ] *n:* مَسّاحِين [massa:ħi:n] *pl:* • **1.** land surveyor
تمِسِّح [tmissiħ] *n:* • **1.** rubbing against something
مِساحَة [missa:ħa] *n:* مِسّاحات [missa:ħa:t] *pl:* • **1.** eraser
مَساحَة [masa:ħa] *n:* مَساحات [masa:ħa:t] *pl:* • **1.** area, surface extent – مَساحَة دائِرَة [masa:ħat da:ʔira] area of a circle. • **2.** surveying, survey – مُدِيرِيَّة المَساحَة [mudi:riyyat ʔilmasa:ħa] Directorate of Survey.
ماسِحَة [ma:siħa] *n:* ماسِحات [ma:siħa:t] *pl:* • **1.** mop, windshield wiper
مَمسَحَة [mamsaħa, mimsaħa] *n:* • **1.** mop, dust cloth, dust rag, washcloth, dishrag
المَسِيح [ʔilmasi:ħ] *n:* • **1.** Christ, the Messiah
مَسِيحِيَّة [masi:ħiyya] *n:* • **1.** Christianity
مَسِيحِي [masi:ħi] *adj:* • **1.** Christian • **2.** a Christian

م س د

مَسَّد [massad] *v:* • **1.** to rub, stroke (esp. an animal) – مَسَّد إلها لِلبَزُّونَة حَتَّى هِدأت [massad ʔilha lilbazzu:na ħatta hidʔat] He stroked the cat until it calmed down.

م س س

مَسّ [mass] *v:* • **1.** to come into contact with, to touch, to palpate
اِنمَسّ [ʔinmass] *v:* • **1.** to come into contact with • **2.** to become insane (because touched by a djinn) • **3.** to be touched
مَسّ [mass] *n:* • **1.** touching, touch, contact, misfortune, calamity • **2.** insanity, madness, frenzy, possession, violation
مَمسُوس [mamsu:s] *adj:* • **1.** insane, mentally deranged, posessed

م س ط ر

مَسطَر [masṭar] *v:* • **1.** to rule, draw straight lines – مَسطِر الدَّفتَر كُلَّه قَبُل ما تدَخِّل الحساب [masṭir ʔiddaftar kullah gabul ma: ddaxxil ʔilħsa:b] Rule off the whole notebook before you enter the amounts.

م س ك

مِسَك [misak] *v:* • **1.** to begin fasting (during Ramadan) – صارَت ساعَة خَمسَة. لازم تِمسِك [ṣa:rat sa:ʕa xamsa. la:zim timsik] It is five o'clock. You have to start fasting. • **2.** to hold

أَمسَك [ʔamsak] *v:* • **1.** same as مِسَك to hold, to start fasting
تمَسَّك [tmassak] *v:* • **1.** to cling, adhere, hold fast – دَيتِمَسَّك بِرَأيَه وَما يِتنازَل [dayitmassak braʔyah wama: yitna:zal] He's sticking to his opinion and won't come off it.
مَسك، مَسك الدَفاتِر [mask, mask ʔiddafa:tir] *n:* • **1.** book-keeping, accounting
تمَسُّك [tamassuk] *n:* • **1.** adherence, devotedness, devotion, attachment
مَسكَة [maska] *n:* • **1.** grip
إمساك [ʔimsa:k] *n:* • **1.** the time of day for beginning the Ramadan fast • **2.** (med.) constipation – بَطنِي تُوجَعنِي لِأَنّ عِندِي إمساك [baṭni tu:ǰaʕni liʔann ʕindi ʔimsa:k] My stomach hurts because I'm constipated.
تَماسُك [tama:suk] *n:* • **1.** holding together, cohesiveness, cohesion, coherence
مُستَمسَك [mustamsak] *n:* مُستَمسَكات [mustamsaka:t] *pl:* • **1.** document of proof (e.g. deed, birth certificate, license, etc.)
إمساكِيَّة [ʔimsa:kiyya] *n:* إمساكِيّات [ʔimsa:kiyya:t] *pl:* • **1.** a calendar showing times for sunrise and sunset used for fasting during Ramadan
مَمسَك [mamsak] *adj:* • **1.** something to hold on to, grip, handhold – ما علَيه أَيّ مَمسَك [ma: ʕli:h ʔayy mamsak] I can't get anything on him.
متمَسِّك [mitmassik] *adj:* • **1.** holding fast, hanging on, clinging, adhering
مُتَماسِك [mutama:sik] *adj:* • **1.** holding fast, hanging on, clinging, withholding

م س ك ن

تمَسكَن [tmaskan] *v:* • **1.** to become poor, be reduced, to poverty, to pretend to be poor • **2.** to be submissive, fawning, servile, slavish
مَسكَنة [maskana] *n:* • **1.** poverty, misery, humbleness, humility, submissiveness
مِسكِين [miski:n] *adj:* مَساكِين [masa:ki:n] *pl:* • **1.** poor, wretched, miserable person

م س م ر

مِسمار [misma:r] *n:* • **1.** same as بِسمار : nail
مِسمارِي [misma:ri] *adj:* • **1.** cuneiform

م س و

مَسَّى [massa:] *v:* • **1.** to spend the evening – صَبَّحنا بِبَغداد وَمَسَّينا بِالبَصرَة [ṣabbaħna bibaɣda:d wmassi:na bilbaṣra] In the morning we were in Baghdad and in the evening we were in Basra. يصَبُّح بِالسَّبّ وَيمَسِّي بِالسَّبّ [yṣabbuħ bʔissabb wymassi bissabb] He spends the morning and the evening in cursing.
أَمِس [ʔamis] *n:* • **1.** yesterday – أَوَّل أَمِس [ʔawwal ʔamis] day before yesterday.
مَسا، مَساء [masa:, masa:ʔ] *n:* • **1.** (no pl.) evening – مَساء الخير [masa:ʔ ʔilxi:r] Good evening!
أُمسِيَّة [ʔumsiyya] *n:* أُمسِيّات [ʔumsiyya:t] *pl:* • **1.** evening
مَسائِي [masa:ʔi] *adj:* • **1.** evening – جَرِيدَة مَسائِيَّة [ǰari:da masa:ʔiyya] an evening newspaper.

م س ي ق

مَوسِيقَى [musi:qa] *n:* • **1.** music

م ش

ماش [ma:š] *n:* • **1.** green gram, a leguminous grain plant
ماشَة [ma:ša] *n:* ماشات [ma:ša:t] *pl:* • **1.** tongs, pincers • **2.** bobby pin, hair pin • **3.** fork (of a bicycle)

م ش ش

مَشّ [mašš] *v:* • **1.** to wipe, wipe off – مِشّ الميز بهالوُصلَة [mišš ʔilmi:z bhalwuṣla] Wipe the table with this cloth. مِشّ بُوزَك. ماكُو تَرفِيعات [mišš bu:zak. ma:ku tarfi:ʕa:t] Forget it (lit., wipe your mouth). There aren't any promotions.
مَشّ [mašš] *n:* • **1.** wiping off

م ش ط

مَشَّط [maššaṭ] *v:* • **1.** to comb – دَتمَشِّط شَعَرها قِدّام المرايَّة [datmaššiṭ šaʕarha ǰidda:m ʔilmra:yya] She's combing her hair in front of the mirror. مَشِّطِي الصُّوف قَبُل ما تِغزلِيه [maššiṭi ʔiṣṣu:f gabul ma: tɣizli:h] Comb the wool before you spin it.
تمَشَّط [tmaššaṭ] *v:* • **1.** to be combed – شَعرَك وَسِخ وَما يِتمَشَّط [šaʕrak waṣix wma yitmaššaṭ] Your hair is dirty and cannot be combed.
مِشِط [mišiṭ] *n:* مشاط، مشُوطَة [mša:ṭ, mšu:ṭa] *pl:* • **1.** comb • **2.** clip (of bullets)

م ش ق

مَشَّق [maššag] *v:* • **1.** to become rough and chapped – إِيدِي مَشَّقَت مِن البَرِد [ʔi:di maššigat min ʔilbarid] My hands became chapped from the cold. • **2.** to break, to tear up (skin), become chapped
مِشَق [mišag] *n:* • **1.** chapping • **2.** chapped skin • **3.** dry skin

م ش ك ل

مَشكَل [maškal] *v:* • **1.** to place in a quandary, to cause problems, trouble – قُلِّي ترُوح لَو لا لا تمَشكِلنِي [gulli tru:ħ law la: la: tmaškilni] Tell me whether you're going or not. Don't cause me trouble.
تمَشكَل [tmaškal] *v:* • **1.** to have trouble – اِشتِرَى سَيّارَة عَتِيقَة وَتمَشكَل بِيها [ʔištira: sayya:ra ʕati:ga wtmaškal bi:ha] He bought an old car and had trouble with it. • **2.** to get in trouble

م ش م ش

مِشمِش [mišmiš] *n:* • **1.** (coll.) apricot(s) • **2.** apricot tree(s)

مِشمِشَة [mišmiša] *n:* مِشمِشات، مِشمِش [mišmiša:t, mišmiš] *pl:* • **1.** apricot • **2.** apricot tree

مِشمِشايَة [mišmiša:ya] *n:* • **1.** apricot

م ش ي

مِشَى [miša:] *v:* • **1.** to walk, go on foot – الجّاهِل بِدا يِمشِي [ʔijǰa:hil bida: yimši] The child has begun to walk. • **2.** to go – باكِر راح أَمشِي لِلمَوصِل [ba:čir ra:ħ ʔamši lilmu:ṣil] Tomorrow I'm going to go to Mosul. القِطار مِشَى ساعَة خَمسَة [ʔilqiṭa:r miša: sa:ʕa xamsa] The train left at five o'clock. • **3.** to move along, proceed – إمشِي! لا تُوقَف هنا [ʔimši! la: tu:gaf hna] Move along! Don't stand here. لازِم تِمشُون عَلَى خِطَّة مُعَيَّنَة [la:zim timšu:n ʕala xiṭṭa muʕayyana] You should follow a specific plan. • **4.** to run around, associate, keep company – لا تِمشِي ويّا السَّرسَرِيَّة تَرَة تصِير مِثلهُم [la: timši wiyya ʔissarsariyya tara tṣi:r miθilhum] Don't run around with bums or you'll become like them. رباطَك ما يِمشِي ويّا هَالقاط [riba:ṭak ma: yimši wiyya halqa:ṭ] Your tie doesn't go with this coat. • **5.** to run, operate, work – سَيّارتِي ما دَتِمشِي؛ يِمكِن البَنزِين خِلَص [sayya:rti ma: datimši; yimkin ʔilbanzi:n xilaṣ] My car won't run; maybe it's out of gas. الفلُوس الإنكِليزِيَّة ما تِمشِي هنا [ʔilflu:s ʔilʔingili:ziyya ma: timši hna] English money doesn't work here. الخَطرانِيَّة ما تِمشِي بهَالدّائِرَة [ʔilxaṭra:niyya ma: timši bhadda:ʔira] Favoritism doesn't go in this office. الحِيلَة مِشَت عَليه [ʔilħi:la mišat ʕali:h] The trick worked on him. مِشَت بَطنَك اليُوم؟ [mišat baṭnak ʔilyu:m?] Did your bowels move today? • **6.** to succeed – مِشيت بِامتِحان الكِيميا [miši:t bʔimtiħa:n ʔilki:mya] I passed the chemistry exam. هَالجِّگايِر الجِّدِيدَة مِشَت؛ كُلّ النّاس دَيِشترُوها [hajjiga:yir ʔijjidi:da mišat; kull ʔinna:s dayištiru:ha] These new cigarettes went over; all the people are buying them. يِبَيِّن قَضِيَّة تَرفِيعَك ما راح تِمشِي [yibayyin qaðiyyat tarfi:ʕak ma: ra:ħ timši] It seems that the matter of your promotion isn't going through.

مَشَّى [maššaː] *v:* • **1.** to walk, make or let walk – خَلِّي نطَلِّع الجّاهِل بَرَّة ونمَشّيه [xalli: nṭalliʕ ʔijǰa:hil barra wnmašši:h] Let's take the child out and walk him. • **2.** to make or let go, send – إنطِيه فلُوسَه وَمَشّيه [ʔinṭi:h flu:sah wmašši:h] Give him his money and let him go. راح يمَشِّي إبنَه لِبَغداد [ra:ħ ymašši ʔibnah libayda:d] He's going to send his son to Baghdad. • **3.** to pass, run – مَشّي إيدَك عَليها وشُوفها شلُون ناعمَة [mašši ʔi:dak ʕali:ha wšu:fha šlu:n na:ʕma] Run your hand across it and see how smooth it is. • **4.** to advance, further, promote – كُلّ واحِد يرِيد يمَشِّي مَصلَحتَه [kull wa:ħid yri:d ymašši maṣlaħtah] Everyone wants to further his own interests. دَيسَوِّيلها دِعايَة لِلبِيرَة حَتَّى يمَشِّيها [daysawwi:lha diʕa:ya lilbi:ra ħatta ymašši:ha] He's running advertising for the beer in order to push it. مَشّي الشُّغُل؛ لا تعَطّلَه [mašši ʔiššuɣul; la: tʕaṭṭlah] Get the work going; don't delay it. مَشّينِي، يا معَوَّد! آنِي مِستَعجِل [mašši:ni, ya: mʕawwad! ʔa:ni mistaʕǰil] Hurry up with me, for gosh sakes; I'm in a hurry. مَشّي وَعَبّي بِالخُرج [mašši wʕabbi bilxuriǰ] Don't take pains. Don't be so fussy (lit., let things go and fill the saddlebags). • **5.** to allow to advance, to promote, pass – ما جاوَب زين بالامتِحان لَكِن راح أَمَشّيه [ma: ǰa:wab zi:n bilʔimtiħa:n la:kin ra:ħ ʔamašši:h] He didn't answer very well on the exam but I'm going to pass him. • **6.** to relieve, loosen (the bowels) – الرَّقِّي يمَشّي البَطِن [ʔirraggi ymašši ʔilbaṭin] Watermelon relieves the bowels.

ماشَى [ma:ša:] *v:* • **1.** to get along with, stay on good terms with, go along with, humor – إذا ترِيد تِتزَوَّجها، لازِم تماشِي أَبُوها [ʔiða tri:d tidzawwaǰha, la:zim tma:ši ʔabu:ha] If you want to marry her, you'll have to get along with her father. ماشِيه فَدّ كَم إسبُوع. هُوَّ مَنقُول [ma:ši:h fadd čam ʔisbu:ʕ. huwwa manqu:l] Go along with him for a few weeks. He's being transferred.

تمَشَّى [tmašša:] *v:* • **1.** to take a walk, to stroll, promenade – يِعجبَك نرُوح نِتمَشّى شوَيَّة؟ [yiʕiǰbak nru:ħ nitmašša: šwayya?] Would you like to go for a little stroll?

اِنمِشَى [ʔinmiša:] *v:* • **1.** pass. of مِشَى to walk – الغُرفَة مَليانَة غَراض ما ينمِشِي بِيها [ʔilɣurfa malya:na ɣara:ð ma: yinmiši bi:ha] The room is so full of things you can't walk in it.

مَشِي [mašy] *n:* • **1.** walking

مَشيَة [mašya] *n:* مَشيات [mašya:t] *pl:* • **1.** manner of walking, gait, step • **2.** trip, journey

مَمشَى [mamša:] *n:* مَماشِي [mama:ši] *pl:* • **1.** walkway, passageway, aisle, corridor • **2.** footpath, pathway

ماشِيَة [ma:šiya] *n:* مَواشِي [mawa:ši] *pl:* • **1.** livestock, cattle

ماشِي [ma:ši] *adj:* مُشات [muša:t] *pl:* • **1.** walking, going – جِيت ماشِي مِن المَحَطَّة لِلبَيت [ǰi:t ma:ši min ʔilmaħaṭṭa lilbayt] I came home on foot from the station. • **2.** foot soldier, infantryman • **3.** pl ماشِين (as n:) pedestrian • **4.** pl. n: مُشاة [muša:t] infantry

م ص خ

مُصَخ [muṣax] *v:* • **1.** to upbraid, scold, shame, humiliate – أَبُوه مُصَخَه تَمام [ʔabu:h muṣaxah tama:m] His father scolded him good and proper. مُصَخ أَحوالَه [muṣax ʔaħwa:lah] He really told him off. He scolded him harshly. راح أَشُوفَه اليُوم وَأَمصُخلَك أَحوالَه [ra:ħ ʔašu:fah ʔilyu:m wʔamṣuxlak ʔaħwa:lah] I'm going to see him today and tell him off but good.

مَصَّخ [maṣṣax] *v:* • **1.** to make dirty, to soil, stain – الجّاهِل لِعَب بِالطّين ومَصَّخ هدُومَه [ʔijǰa:hil liʕab biṭṭi:n wmaṣṣax hdu:mah] The kid played in the mud and got his clothes all dirty. يَزِّي عاد! مُو مَصَّختها [yazzi ʕa:d! mu:

maṣṣaxitha] Enough now! You've already gone too far! مَصَّخ أحوالَه [maṣṣax ʔaħwa:lah] He really told him off. He scolded him harshly. عَلي تعارَك ويّا سامِي ومَصَّخ أحوالَه [ʕali tʕa:rak wiyya sa:mi wmaṣṣax ʔaħwa:lah] Ali had an argument with Sami and really told him off.
تمَصَّخ [tmaṣṣax] *v:* • **1.** pass. of مَصَّخ : to be stained – لا تخَلّي الجّاهِل يلعَب بالطّين. هدُومَه تمَصّخَت [la: txalli: ʔijja:hil yilʕab bitti:n. hdu:mah tmaṣṣxat] Don't let the kid play in the mud. His clothes got dirty.
مَصاخَة [maṣa:xa] *n:* • **1.** a humiliating, dirty, unpleasant thing – الشّغُل بهالمَعمَل مَصاخَة [ʔiššuɣul bhalmaʕmal maṣa:xa] Working in this factory is an unpleasant thing.
ماصِخ [ma:ṣix] *adj:* • **1.** flat, tasteless, needing salt – أكِل ماصِخ [ʔakil ma:ṣix] tasteless food. شقَدّ ما أخَلّي مِلح بيه، بَعدَه ماصِخ [šgadd ma: ʔaxalli: miliħ bi:h, baʕdah ma:ṣix] No matter how much salt I add to it, it's still flat.

م ص ر

مِصِر [miṣir, maṣir] *n:* • **1.** Egypt
مِصري [miṣri, maṣri] *adj:* • **1.** Egyptian • **2.** an Egyptian

م ص ر ن

مُصران [muṣra:n] *n:* مَصارين [maṣa:ri:n] *pl:* • **1.** intestine, gut

م ص ص

مَصّ [maṣṣ] *v:* • **1.** to suck – الجّاهِل دَيمُصّ إبهامَه [ʔijja:hil daymuṣṣ ʔibha:mah] The child is sucking his thumb. • **2.** to soak up, absorb – وَرَق نِشّاف يمُصّ الحِبر [waraq niššа:f ymuṣṣ ʔilħibir] Blotter paper soaks up ink. • **3.** to sip – إذا توَصِّل المُصّاصَة لِكَعب الكلاص، تِقدَر تمُصّ الشَّربَة كُلّه [ʔiδa twaṣṣil ʔilmuṣṣa:ṣa lčaʕb ʔilgla:ṣ, tigdar tmuṣṣ ʔiššarbat kullah] If you stick a straw to the bottom of the glass, you can sip the whole drink.
اِنمَصّ [ʔinmaṣṣ] *v:* • **1.** to be sucked – هَالحَبّايَة لازِم تِنمَصّ؛ ما تِنبِلِع [halħabba:ya la:zim tinmaṣṣ; ma: tinbiliʕ] This pill has to be sucked; it can't be swallowed.
اِمتَصّ [ʔimtaṣṣ] *v:* • **1.** to soak up, absorb – ذِبّ الخِرقَة عَالمَيّ حَتّى تِمتَصّه [δibb ʔilxirga ʕalmayy ħatta timtaṣṣah] Throw the rag on the water so it'll soak it up.
مَصّ [maṣṣ] *n:* • **1.** sucking, sucking up, soaking up • **2.** sipping
مَصَّة [maṣṣa] *n:* مَصّات [maṣṣa:t] *pl:* • **1.** sucking, suck, suction, sip
مُصّاصَة [muṣṣa:ṣa] *n:* مُصّاصات [muṣṣa:ṣa:t] *pl:* • **1.** sucker, lollipop • **2.** drinking straw • **3.** something to suck, pacifier
اِمتِصاص [ʔimtiṣa:ṣ] *n:* • **1.** suction
مَمصُوص [mamṣu:ṣ] *adj:* • **1.** lean, emaciated, skinny – شُوفَه شلُون مَمصُوص! عَبالَك صارلَه شَهَر ما ماكِل شِي [šu:fah šlu:n mamṣu:ṣ! ʕaba:lak ṣa:rlah šahar ma: ma:kil ši] Look at how skinny he is! As though he's not eaten anything in a month.

م ص ط ب

مَصطَبَة [maṣṭaba, muṣṭaba] *n:* مَصاطُب، مَصطَبات [maṣa:ṭub, maṣṭaba:t] *pl:* • **1.** bench

م ص ل

مَصَّل [maṣṣal] *v:* • **1.** to water, salivate – مِن شِفتَه ياكُل طُرشِي، مَصَّل حَلقِي [min šiftah ya:kul ṭurši, maṣṣal ħalgi] When I saw him eating pickles, my mouth watered.
مَصِل [maṣil] *n:* أمصال [ʔamṣa:l] *pl:* • **1.** serum • **2.** plasma

م ص م ص

مَصمَص [maṣmaṣ] *v:* • **1.** to suck – لَمّا خِلَص اللَّحَم، بِدَوا يمَصمُصُون بالعظام [lamma xilaṣ ʔillaħam, bidaw ymaṣumṣu:n biliʕδa:m] When the meat was gone, they started sucking on the bones. • **2.** (mostly humorous) to kiss – حَطّها بِالسَّيّارَة وبِدا يمَصمُص بيها [ħaṭṭha bissayya:ra wbida: ymaṣmuṣ bi:ha] He got her in the car and started smooching her.
تمُصمُص [tmuṣmuṣ] *n:* • **1.** sucking • **2.** kissing (making out)

م ض ر ط

تمَضرَط [tmaδraṭ] *v:* • **1.** (impolite) to make an ass of oneself – يِتمَضرَط بحَكيَه [yitmaδraṭ bħačyah] He makes an ass of himself when he talks.
مَضرَطَة [maδraṭa] *n:* • **1.** speaking nonsense

م ض ض

مَضّ [maδδ] *v:* • **1.** to affect, have an effect, take effect – الطَّلقَة العادِيَّة ما تمُضّ بِالتِّمساح [ʔiṭṭalqa ʔilʕa:diyya ma: tmuδδ bittimsa:ħ] An ordinary bullet won't have any effect on a crocodile. الحَيَّة ما يمُضّ بيها السِّمّ [ʔilħayya ma: ymuδδ bi:ha ʔissimm] Poison won't affect a snake. البَسِط ما يمُضّ بيه [ʔilbasiṭ ma: ymuδδ bi:h] Beating doesn't affect him.
مَضّ [maδδ] *n:* • **1.** taking effect, having an effect, impact
ماضّ [ma:δδ] *adj:* • **1.** penetrating, effective, trenchant
أمَضّ [ʔamaδδ] *comparative adjective:* • **1.** more or most penetrating, effective, trenchant

م ض م ض

مَضمَض [maδmaδ] *v:* • **1.** to rinse out (the mouth) – مَضمُض حَلقَك بِهالدُّوا [maδmuδ ħalgak bhadduwa] Rinse out your mouth with this medicine.

تمضمض [tmaðmað] *v:* • **1.** to rinse out one's mouth – تمضمض بَعَد ما تفرّك سنُونَك [tmaðmað baʕad maː tfarrič snuːnak] Rinse out your mouth after you brush your teeth.
متمضمض [mitmaðmuð] *adj:* • **1.** rinsed (mouth)

م ض ي

مُضَى [muðaː] *v:* • **1.** to pass, go by, elapse – مُضَت مُدَّة وَما دِفَع الإيجار [muðat mudda wma difaʕ ʔilʔiːǰaːr] Quite a while passed and he didn't pay the rent.
مَضّى [maððaː] *v:* • **1.** to pass, spend – دَنلِعَب وَرَق حَتَّى نمَضّي وَقِت [danilʕab waraq ħatta nmaðði waqit] We're playing cards to kill time. • **2.** to cause to sign, make sign – لا تِنسَى تمَضّيه قَبُل ما تِنطِيه فلُوس [laː tinsaː tmaððiːh gabul maː tinṭiːh fluːs] Don't forget to make him sign before you give him any money.
مُضي [muðiy] *n:* • **1.** moving on • **2.** signing one's name, affixing one's signature
إمضاء [ʔimðaːʔ] *n:* إمضاآت [ʔimðaːʔaːt] *pl:* • **1.** signature
ماضي [maːði] *adj:* • **1.** past, bygone – السَّنَة الماضيَة [ʔissana ʔilmaːðya] last year. • **2.** (as Noun) past life, history – هَذا الرِّجّال مَعرُوف ماضِيه [haːða ʔirriǰǰaːl maʕruːf maːðiːh] This man's past is well-known. • **3.** (as Noun) the past – إحنا ما عَلَينا بِالماضِي. هَسَّة شراح نسَوِّي؟ [ʔiħna maː ʕaliːna bilmaːði. hassa šraːħ nsawwiː?] We don't care about the past. What will we do now? • **4.** (as Noun) the past tense (gram.)

م ض ي ق

تمَضيَق [tmaðyag] *v:* • **1.** to behave in an unnatural, affected manner – يِتمَضيَق بِحَكيَه [yitmaðyag bħačyah] He has an affected manner of speaking.
مَضيَقَة [maðyaga] *n:* • **1.** behaving in an unnatural, affected manner
تمِضييق [tmiðyiːg] *n:* • **1.** behaving in an unnatural, affected manner

م ط ر [1]

مُطَر [muṭar] *v:* • **1.** to rain – البارحَة مُطرَت مُدَّة ساعتَين [ʔilbaːrħa muṭrat muddat saːʕtayn] Yesterday it rained for two hours.
مَطَّر [maṭṭar] *v:* • **1.** to rain – يِبَيِّن راح تمَطِّر باكِر [yibayyin raːħ tmaṭṭir baːčir] It looks like it's going to rain tomorrow. • **2.** to cause to rain – بَلكِي الله يمَطِّرها وَينتِعِش الزَّرِع [balki ʔallah ymaṭṭirha wyintiʕiš ʔizzariʕ] Perhaps God will make it rain and the crops will be rejuvenated.
مُطَر [muṭar] *n:* أمطار [ʔamṭaːr] *pl:* • **1.** rain
مَطرَة [maṭra] *n:* مَطرات [maṭraːt] *pl:* • **1.** downpour, shower
مَطّارَة [maṭṭaːra] *n:* مَطّارات [maṭṭaːraːt] *pl:* • **1.** canteen, flask
مُمطِر [mumṭir] *adj:* • **1.** rainy – جَوّ مُمطِر [ǰaww mumṭir] rainy weather.
ماطِر [maːṭir] *adj:* • **1.** rainy
مَطَري [maṭari] *adj:* • **1.** rainy

م ط ر [2]

مَطران [maṭraːn] *n:* مَطارنَة [maṭaːrna] *pl:* • **1.** bishop

م ط ر ل و ز

مَطرِلّوز [maṭrilluːz] *n:* مَطرِلّوزات [maṭrilluːzaːt] *pl:* • **1.** machine gun

م ط ط

مَطّ [maṭṭ] *v:* • **1.** to expand by pulling, to strech something
مَطّى [maṭṭaː] *v:* • **1.** to stretch, strain – لا تمَطّي الجِّلِد زايد تَرَة يِتمِزِق [laː tmaṭṭi ʔiǰǰilid zaːyid tara yitmizig] Don't stretch the hide too much or it'll tear. • **2.** to extend push out, stick out – مَطّى شِفَّتَه [maṭṭaː šifftah] He stuck out his lip.
تمَطّى [tmaṭṭaː] *v:* • **1.** to stretch, extend – هَالجواريب تِتمَطّى [halǰwaːriːb titmaṭṭaː] These socks are stretchable.
مَطّاط [maṭṭaːṭ] *n:* • **1.** rubber tree, rubber • **2.** rubber
تُمُطّي [tumuṭṭi] *n:* • **1.** stretching
مَطّاطِي [maṭṭaːṭi] *adj:* • **1.** rubbery, of rubber

م ط ق

مَطِّق [maṭṭag] *v:* • **1.** to smack one's lips
تمُطِّق [tmuṭṭig] *v:* • **1.** to smack one's lips
تَمطِيق [tamṭiːg] *n:* • **1.** act of smacking one's lips

م ط ل

مُطَل [muṭal] *v:* • **1.** to throw down (in wrestling) – هُوَّ أكبَر مِنّي بَسّ أقدَر أمُطلَه [huwwa ʔakbar minni bass ʔagdar ʔamuṭlah] He's bigger than me but I can throw him down.
ماطَل [maːṭal] *v:* • **1.** to wrestle, wrestle with – ماطلَه، وَإذا تُغلُب، تاخُذ جائِزَة [maːṭlah, wʔiðaː tuɣlub, taːxuð ǰaːʔiza] Wrestle him, and if you win, you'll get a prize. • **2.** to stall, put off – ظَلّ شَهرَين يماطِلني قَبُل ما يرَجِّعلي الفلُوس [ðall šahrayn ymaːṭilni gabul maː yraǰǰiʕli ʔilfluːs] He kept putting me off for two months before he returned the money to me.
تماطَل [tmaːṭal] *v:* • **1.** to wrestle, wrestle with each other – شُوف الجّاهِل وأخُوه دَيِتماطلُون عَالثَّيِّل [šuːf ʔiǰǰaːhil wʔaxuːh dayitmaːṭluːn ʕaθθayyil] Look at the kid and his brother wrestling on the lawn.
مَطِل [maṭil] *n:* • **1.** act of throwing (s.o) down (in wrestling)
مُطّال [muṭṭaːl] *n:* • **1.** (coll.) dried dung chips used for fuel
مُطّالَة [muṭṭaːla] *n:* مُطّالات [muṭṭaːlaːt] *pl:* • **1.** unit noun of مُطّال [muṭṭaːl] dried dung chip used for fuel

م

مُماطَلَة [muma:ṭala] *n:* • **1.** stalling, putting off – لازِم تِنطِيني الفلوس باكِر، بِلا مُماطَلَة [la:zim tinṭi:ni ʔilflu:s ba:čir, bila muma:ṭala] You've got to give me the money tomorrow, without stalling.

م ط و ر

ماطُور [maṭu:r] *n:* ماطُورات [maṭu:ṭu:ra:t] *pl:* • **1.** motor, engine • **2.** launch, motor boat, motor barge • **3.** motorcycle

م ط و ر س ك ل

ماطُورسِكِل [maṭu:rsikil] *n:* ماطُورسِكِلات [maṭu:rsikila:t] *pl:* • **1.** motorcycle

م ط ي

مُطِي [muṭy] *n:* مطايا [mṭa:ya] *pl:* • **1.** donkey, ass – لا تصِير مُطِي [la: tṣi:r muṭi] Don't be a jackass!

م ع

مَعَ [maʕa] *preposition:* • **1.** (in a few set phrases) with – مَعَ الأسَف [maʕa ʔilʔasaf] with regrets, regretfully, unfortunately. مَعَ الأسَف، ما أقدَر أجِي [maʕa ʔilʔasaf, ma: ʔagdar ʔaǰi] Unfortunately, I can't come. مَعَ العِلم [maʕa ʔilʕilm] with knowledge, knowingly, deliberately, intentionally. مَعَ المَمنُونِيَّة [maʕa ʔilmamnu:niyya] with pleasure, gladly. مَعَ هَذا [maʕa ha:ða] despite that, nevertheless, notwithstanding, even so. مَعَ هَذا ما كان لازِم تقُلَّه [maʕa ha:ða ma: ča:n la:zim dgullah] Nevertheless, you shouldn't have told him.

م ع د 1

مِعدَة [miʕda] *n:* مِعدات، مِعَد [miʕda:t, miʕad] *pl:* • **1.** stomach

م ع د 2

معِيدِي [mʕi:di] *n:* مِعدان [miʕda:n] *pl:* • **1.** peasant, yokel, rube, hick, redneck

م ع د ن

مَعدَن [maʕdan] *n:* مَعادِن [maʕa:din] *pl:* • **1.** metal • **2.** mineral – جِدِر مَعدَن [ǰidir maʕdan] enamelware pot. أثِق بِيه لأنّ المَعدَن مالَه زين [ʔaθiq bi:h liʔann ʔilmaʕdan ma:lah zi:n] I trust him because he's made of good stuff.

مَعدَنِي [maʕdani] *adj:* • **1.** mineral – مَوادّ مَعدَنِيَّة [mawa:dd maʕdaniyya] mineral substances. مِياه مَعدَنِيَّة [miya:h maʕdaniyya] mineral waters.

م ع د ن و س

مَعدَنُوس [maʕdanu:s] *n:* • **1.** parsley

م ع ض

امتِعَض [ʔimtiʕað̣] *v:* • **1.** to be angry, annoyed

امتِعاض [ʔimtiʕa:ð̣] *n:* • **1.** anger, annoyance

ممتِعِض [mimtiʕið̣] *adj:* • **1.** annoyed, angry

م ع ك ر و ن

مَعكَرُونَة [maʕkaru:na, makaru:na] *n:* • **1.** macaroni

م ع ك ل

مِعكال [miʕča:l] *n:* معاكِيل [mʕa:či:l] *pl:* • **1.** sling, slingshot

م ع م ع

مَعمَع [maʕmaʕ] *v:* • **1.** to bleat – هَالصَّخَل يمَعمِع هوايَة [haṣṣaxal ymaʕmiʕ hwa:ya] This billy goat bleats a lot.

مَعمَعَة [maʕmaʕa] *n:* • **1.** bleating • **2.** confusion

م ع ن

تمَعَّن [tmaʕʕan] *v:* • **1.** to look closely, check carefully – تمَعَّن بِالقَضِيَّة قَبُل ما تقَرِّر شِي [tmaʕʕan bilqað̣iyya gabul ma: tqarrir ši] Look into the matter carefully before you decide anything.

تَمَعُّن [tamaʕʕun] *n:* • **1.** close examination, careful study, scrutiny

ماعُون [ma:ʕu:n] *n:* مواعِين [mwa:ʕi:n] *pl:* • **1.** plate, dish • **2.** (pl. only) dishes, tableware

إمعان [ʔimʕa:n] *n:* • **1.** close examination, careful study, scrutiny

م ع و

مِعي [miʕy] *n:* أمعاء [ʔamʕa:ʔ] *pl:* • **1.** intestines, gut, bowels

مِعَوِي [miʕawi] *adj:* • **1.** of or pertaining to the intestines, intestinal

م غ ص

مُغَص [muɣaṣ] *v:* • **1.** to cause gripes, renal colic

انمُغَص [ʔimuɣaṣ] *v:* • **1.** to have gripes, colic • **2.** to suffer from colic

مَغَص [maɣaṣ] *n:* • **1.** gripes, colic

مَمغُوص [mamɣu:ṣ] *adj:* • **1.** having gripes, suffering from colics

م غ ط

تمَغَّط [tmaɣɣaṭ] *v:* • **1.** to stretch, stretch one's limbs – البارحَة ما نام هوايَة. دَيتثاوب وَيتمَغَّط [ʔilba:rħa ma: na:m hwa:ya. dayitθa:wab wyitmaɣɣaṭ] He didn't sleep much yesterday. He's yawning and stretching.

م غ ن ط ي س

مِغناطِيس [miɣna:ṭi:s] *n:* • **1.** magnetism • **2.** pl. مِغناطِيسات magnet

م

م ق ل ج

تمقلَج [tmaqlač] *v:* • **1.** to be strained, act in an unnatural manner – يِتمَقلَج بِحَكيَه [yitmaqlač bħačyah] He talks in an unnatural manner.

تمِقلِج [tmiqlič] *n:* • **1.** acting in an unnatural manner

م ك

ماكَة [maːča] *n:* ماكات [maːčaːt] *pl:* • **1.** spade (suit in cards)

م ك ر

مَكِر [makir] *n:* • **1.** cunning, slyness

مَكّار [makkaːr] *adj:* • **1.** cunning, sly, crafty, wily

م ك ر ف و ن

مِكرَفُون [mikrafuːn] *n:* مِكرَفُونات [mikrafuːnaːt] *pl:* • **1.** microphone • **2.** loudspeaker, speaker (in a radio, etc.)

م ك ك

مَكُّوك [makkuːk] *n:* مَكُّوكات [makkuːkaːt] *pl:* • **1.** bobbin (of a sewing machine)

م ك ن 1

يِمكِن [yimkin] *v:* • **1.** (no perfect form) it may be..., probably

مَكَّن [makkan] *v:* • **1.** to enable, put in a position, afford the possibility, make possible – صِحّتي ما تمَكِّني أسافِر [ṣiħħti maː tmakkinni ʔasaːfir] My health doesn't allow me to travel.

أمكَن [ʔamkan] *v:* • **1.** to be possible – ما أمكَنّي أجي [maː ʔamkanni ʔaǰi] It wasn't possible for me to come. ما يِمكِن تِترَفَّع قَبُل نِهايَة السَّنَة [maː yimkin titraffaʕ gabul nihaːyat ʔissana] It's impossible for you to be promoted before the end of the year. سَوِّيت كُلّ اللّي يِمكِن أسَوّي [sawwiːt kull ʔilli yimkin ʔasawwiː] I did all that I possibly could do. يِمكِن [yimkin] it's possible, possibly, perhaps, maybe. يِمكِن يكُون مَوجُود [yimkin ykuːn mawǰuːd] Maybe he's there. يِمكِن راح تُمطُر [yimkin raːħ tumṭur] Maybe it'll rain.

تمَكَّن [tmakkan] *v:* • **1.** to be in a position, be able – ما تمَكَّنِت أجي لِلحَفلَة [maː tmakkanit ʔaǰi lilħafla] I can't come to the party.

تَمَكُّن [tamakkun] *n:* • **1.** power, ability, mastery, capability

إمكان [ʔimkaːn] *n:* • **1.** power, capacity, capability – مُو بِإمكانِي أساعدَه [muː bʔimkaːni ʔasaːʕdah] It isn't in my power to help him. مُو بِإمكانِي أسَوّيها [muː bʔimkaːni ʔasawwiːha] I'm not in a position to do it. • **2.** possibility – رَح أمِدَّك بِالفلُوس حَسَب الإمكان [raħ ʔamiddak bilfiluːs ħasab ʔilʔimkaːn] I'll provide you with as much money as I can. راح أساعدَك عَلَى قَدَر الإمكان [raːħ ʔasaːʕdak ʕala qadr ʔilʔimkaːn] I'll help you as much as possible. عِند الإمكان [ʕind ʔilʔimkaːn] When and if possible. أخابرَك عِند الإمكان [ʔaxaːbrak ʕind ʔilʔimkaːn] I'll call you if I have a chance. • **3.** حَسب الإمكان, بالإمكان, بقدر الإمكان, عَلَى قدر الإمكان : [ħasb ʔilʔimkaːn, bilʔimkaːn, biqadr ʔilʔimkaːn, ʕala qadr ʔilʔimkaːn] it's possible, possibly, maybe, perhaps

إمكانيَّة [ʔimkaːniyya] *n:* إمكانيّات [ʔimkaːniyyaːt] *pl:* • **1.** possibility – تبَرَّع بِأقَلّ مِن إمكانِيتَه [tbarraʕ bʔaqall min ʔimkaːniːtah] He donated less than he could have.

مُمكِن [mumkin] *adj:* • **1.** possible – هَذا شِي مُمكِن [haːða ši mumkin] That's possible. • **2.** possibly, perhaps, maybe – مُمكِن أسافِر باكِر [mumkin ʔasaːfir baːčir] Maybe I'll leave tomorrow.

متمَكِّن [mitmakkin] *adj:* • **1.** in a secure position, having everything under control – بِهالحَرَكَة، راح أكُون مِتمَكِّن عَليك [bhalħaraka, raːħ ʔakuːn mitmakkin ʕaliːk] With this move, I'll have the upper hand on you. • **2.** well-to-do, well-off, wealthy – يِدرُس بِأورُبّا لِأنّ أبُوه مِتمَكِّن [yidrus bʔuːruppa liʔann ʔabuːh mitmakkin] He studies in Europe because his father is well-to-do.

م ك ن 2

مَكِينَة [makiːna] *n:* مَكايِن [makaːyin] *pl:* • **1.** machine – مَكِينَة ماي [makiːnat maːy] water pump. مَكِينَة حِلاقَة [makiːnat ħilaːqa] razor, shaver. • **2.** works, movement (of a watch) • **3.** mill, grist mill • **4.** motor, engine

م ك ي ج

تمَكيَج [tmakyaǰ] *v:* • **1.** to put on make up

مِكياج [mikyaːǰ] *n:* • **1.** make-up • **2.** greasepaint

مِتمَكيجَة [mitmakyǰa] *adj:* • **1.** made-up, wearing makeup (for female)

م ل ء

اِنملَى [ʔinmilaː] *v:* • **1.** to be filled – الرّاديتَر اِنمِلَت مَيّ [ʔirraːdiːtar ʔinmilat mayy] The radiator was filled with water.

اِمتِلَى [ʔimtilaː] *v:* • **1.** to fill up, become full – الجِّدِر اِمتِلَى. وِين أحُطّ بَقِيَة التِّمَّن؟ [ʔiǰǰidir ʔimtilaː. wiːn ʔaħuṭṭ baqiyat ʔittimman?] The pot is full. Where should I put the rest of the rice?

مَلي [maly] *n:* • **1.** act of filling (s.th.)

مَملي [mamli] *adj:* • **1.** filled up, loaded

مَليان [malyaːn] *adj:* • **1.** full, filled

م ل ج

مِلَج [milaǰ] *v:* • **1.** to spread with a trowel – خَلّي الجُّصّ عَليه وَإملِجَه [xalliː ʔiǰǰuṣṣ ʕaliːh wʔimilǰah] Put the mortar on it and spread it with a trowel. • **2.** to mix – إملِج شوَيَّة جُصّ [ʔimliǰ šwayya ǰuṣṣ] Mix up a little mortar.

مَلِج [maliǰ] *n:* • **1.** spreading with a trowel

مالَج [maːlaǰ] *n:* موالِج [mwaːliǰ] *pl:* • **1.** trowel

م ل ح

مَلَّح [mallaħ] *v:* • **1.** to salt – بَعَد ما تمَلِّح البَيتِنجان، قَلِّيه [baʕad maː tmalliħ ʔilbiːtinǰaːn, galliːh] After you salt the eggplant, fry it.
مِلِح [miliħ] *n:* أملاح [ʔamlaːħ] *pl:* • **1.** salt
مَلّاح [mallaːħ] *n:* ملاليح [mlaːliːħ] *pl:* • **1.** crew • **2.** sailor, seaman, mariner
مَملَحَة [mamlaħa] *n:* مَملَحات، مَمالح [mamlaħaːt, mamaːliħ] *pl:* • **1.** salina, place where salt is obtained • **2.** salt shaker, salt-cellar
مَوالِح [mawaːliħ] *n:* • **1.** salted nuts, peanuts, almonds
مِلُوحَة [miluːħa] *n:* • **1.** saltiness, salt taste
مِلاحَة [milaːħa] *n:* • **1.** navigation, shipping
أملَح [ʔamlaħ] *adj:* مِلِح [miliħ] *pl:* مَلحَة [malħa] *feminine:* • **1.** grey, salt-colored – رِباط أملَح [ribaːṭ ʔamlaħ] a gray tie.
مالِح [maːliħ] *adj:* • **1.** salty – المُرقَة مالحَة اليُوم [ʔilmurga maːlħa ʔilyuːm] The stew is salty today.
أملَح [ʔamlaħ] *comparative adjective:* • **1.** more or most salty

م ل خ

مِلَخ [milax] *v:* • **1.** to tear, rip, to tear a piece out of – البَزّونَة مِلخَت ثَوبي [ʔilbazzuːna milxat θawbi] The cat tore a piece out of my shirt. • **2.** to hit hard, strike violently – مِلَخَه ببُوكس كَسَّر سنُونَه [milaxah bibuːks kassar snuːnah] He struck him a blow that broke his teeth. • **3.** to run away, flee – أَخَذ الفلُوس مِنَّه وَمِلَخ [ʔaxað ʔilfluːs minnah wmilax] He took the money from him and fled. • **4.** to exaggerate – شقَدّ يِملخ بِحَكيَه [šgadd yimlix bħačyah] He sure does talk big!
مَلَّخ [mallax] *v:* • **1.** to tear up, rip up, tear to shreds – عَلَى كَيفَك! مَلَّختَه لِلكتاب [ʕala kayfak! mallaxtah lilktaːb] Take it easy! You've torn up the book. • **2.** to beat up, give a severe beating to – إبنَك، مَلّخُوه مِن البَسِط [ʔibnak, mallixuːh min ʔilbasiṭ] They beat your son to a bloody pulp. • **3.** to exaggerate – الشُرطَة ما صَدِّقَت بيه لِأنّ يمَلِّخ عَلَى طُول [ʔiššurṭa maː ṣaddigat biːh liʔann ymallix ʕala ṭuːl] The police wouldn't believe him because he's always telling wild tales.
تمَلَّخ [tmallax] *v:* • **1.** to be torn to shreds, ripped to pieces – جواريبها تمَلّخَت مِن الغَسِل [ǰwaːriːbha tmallixat min ʔilɣasil] Her stockings became shredded from washing.
تمالَخ [tmaːlax] *v:* • **1.** to have a violent fight, fight with each other – عَلِي تمالَخ وِيّا الشُرطِي [ʕali tmaːlax wiyya ʔiššurṭi] Ali fought it out with the policeman.
مَلِخ [malix] *n:* • **1.** tearing • **2.** hitting hard • **3.** exaggeration
تمِلِّخ [tmillix] *n:* • **1.** tearing off, ripping
مَلخِيّات [malxiyyaːt] *n:* • **1.** (pl. only) wild talk, tall tales, nonsense – ما تخَلّينا مِن هالمَلخِيّات؟ [maː txalliːna min halmalxiyyaːt?] How about sparing us all that nonsense? قُلنالَه إنتَ خُوش آدَمِي وَتساعِد الأَصدِقاء وَمِن هالمَلخِيّات [gulnaːlah ʔinta xuːš ʔaːdami wtsaːʕid ʔilʔaṣdiqaːʔ wmin halmalxiyyaːt] We told him you're a good guy and help friends and all that baloney.
مِتمَلِّخ [mitmallix] *adj:* • **1.** torn, beaten

م ل ر ي

مَلاريا [malaːrya] *n:* • **1.** malaria

م ل س

أملَس [ʔamlas] *adj:* مِلِس، مَلسِين [milis, malsiːn] *pl:* مَلسَة [malsa] *feminine:* • **1.** smooth, sleek

م ل ص

مِلَص [milaṣ] *v:* • **1.** to slide, slip – مِلَص المِحبَس مِن إصبِعها [milaṣ ʔilmiħbas min ʔiṣbiʕha] He slipped the ring off of her finger. إسكُت، تَرَة أَجِي أملُص رُقبتَك [ʔiskut, tara ʔaǰi ʔamluṣ rugubtak] Shut up, or I'll come and take your head off. • **2.** to sneak off, slip away, escape – آنِي أَلَهِّي الجّاهِل وَإنتَ أُملُص [ʔaːni ʔalahhi ʔiǰǰaːhil wʔinta ʔumluṣ] I'll amuse the kid and you slip away.
تمَلَّص [tmallaṣ] *v:* • **1.** with مِن to squirm out of, shirk, dodge, evade – يِتمَلَّص مِن المَسؤُولِيَّة عَلَى طُول [yitmallaṣ min ʔilmasʔuːliyya ʕala ṭuːl] He dodges responsibilities all the time.
إنمُلَص [ʔinmulaṣ] *v:* • **1.** to slide, slip – المِحبَس إنمُلَص مِن إصبِعِي وَوُقَع بالمَيّ [ʔilmiħbas ʔinmulaṣ min ʔiṣibʕi wwugaʕ bilmayy] The ring slipped off my finger and fell in the water.
مَلِص [maliṣ] *n:* • **1.** slipping, sliding
تَمَلُّص، تمِلِّص [tamalluṣ, tmilliṣ] *n:* • **1.** slipping away, escaping, escape

م ل ط

مِلَط [milaṭ] *v:* • **1.** to shave, to wax
مَلِط [maliṭ] *n:* • **1.** removing hair from root
مالطَة [maːlṭa] *n:* • **1.** Malta (the Island of Malta)
أملَط [ʔamlaṭ] *adj:* مُلُط، مَلطِين [muluṭ, malṭiːn] *pl:* مَلطَى [malṭa] *feminine:* • **1.** hairless • **2.** hairless person

م ل ق

تمَلَّق [tmallaq] *v:* • **1.** with لِ to flatter – تِتمَلَّق لِرَجِلها حَتَّى يِشترِيلها هدُوم [titmallaq lirraǰilha ħatta yištiriːlha hduːm] She flatters her husband so he'll buy clothes for her.
تَمَلُّق [tamalluq] *n:* • **1.** same also as مَلَق : flattery • **2.** adulation
مِتمَلِّق [mitmalliq] *adj:* • **1.** flatterer

م ل ك

مِلَك [milak] *v:* • **1.** to possess, own, have, be the owner of – يِملُك قِيعان وَبيُوت [yimluk giːʕaːn wbyuːt] He owns land and houses. ما أملُك وَلا فِلِس [maː ʔamluk

wala filis] I don't have even a penny. • **2.** to dominate, control, be master of – إذا تِنطِيه دينارَين، تِمُلكَه بيها [ʔiða tinṭiːh dinaːrayn, timulkah biːha] If you give him two dinars, you can control him with it.
مَلَّك [mallak] *v:* • **1.** to make the owner of – الحُكُومَة مَلِّكَت العُمّال البِيُوت اللّي ساكنين بيها [ʔilħukuːma mallikat ʔilʕummaːl ʔilbiyuːt ʔilli saːkniːn biːha] The government deeded the workers the houses they were living in. • **2.** to gain ownership of
تمالَك [tmaːlak] *v:* • **1.** to control, restrain oneself (an emotion, etc) – ما يِقدَر يِتمالَك أعصابَه [maː yigdar yitmaːlak ʔaʕṣaːbah] He can't control his temper.
امتِلَك [ʔimtilak] *v:* • **1.** to possess
اِستَملَك [ʔistamlak] *v:* • **1.** to acquire by purchase, buy – البَلَدِيَّة اِستَملِكَت كُلّ هالدَّكاكِين [ʔilbaladiyya ʔistamlikat kull haddakaːkiːn] The municipality bought up all those shops. • **2.** to take possession of, assume ownership of – إذا تِدفَع نُصّ قِيمَة البَيت، تِستَملكَه [ʔiða tidfaʕ nuṣṣ qiːmat ʔilbayt, tistamlikah] If you pay half the price of the house, you can take possession.
مُلُك [muluk] *n:* أملاك [ʔamlaːk] *pl:* • **1.** property, possessions, fortune • **2.** real estate, landed property – هَالبَيت إيجار لَو مُلُك؟ [halbayt ʔiːjaːr law muluk?] Do you rent this house or own it? كانَت تُرقُص بالمُلُك [čaːnat turguṣ bilmuluk] She was dancing in the raw.
مَلِك [malik] *n:* مُلُوك [muluːk] *pl:* مَلِكَة، مَلِكات [malika, malikaːt] *feminine:* • **1.** king, queen
مَلَك [malak] *n:* مَلائِكَة [malaːʔika] *pl:* • **1.** angel
مَلّاك [mallaːk, mallaːč] *n:* مَلّاكِين [mallaːkiːn, mallaːka, mallaːča, mallaːčiːn] *pl:* • **1.** real estate tycoon • **2.** landlord, landowner
مالِك، مالِك الحَزِين [maːlik, maːlik ʔilħaziːn] *n:* • **1.** possessor, in possession • **2.** heron
مَلاكَة [malaːča] *n:* • **1.** owner's fee, landlord's share (in share-cropping) – صاحِب القاع ياخُذ رُبع الحاصِل ملاكَة [ṣaːħib ʔilgaːʕ yaːxuð rubʕ ʔilħaːṣil mlaːča] The land owner gets a fourth of the crop for rent.
مَلَكِيَّة [malakiyya] *n:* • **1.** monarchy, kingship
مَملَكَة [mamlaka] *n:* مَمالِك [mamaːlik] *pl:* • **1.** kingdom
تَملِيك [tamliːk] *n:* • **1.** transfer of ownership, conveyance of property
مِلكِيَّة [milkiyya, mulkiyya] *n:* • **1.** ownership (legal proof of), deed
مَلَكُوت [malakuːt] *n:* • **1.** (usually divine or God's) realm, kingdom, empire
مُلُوكِيَّة [muluːkiyya] *n:* • **1.** royalty, regality • **2.** monarchic rule
اِمتِلاك [ʔimtilaːk] *n:* • **1.** taking possession, occupancy
مَلَكِي [malaki] *adj:* • **1.** royal, kingly, regal – حَرَس مَلَكِي [ħaras malaki] royal guard.
مُلكِي [mulki] *adj:* • **1.** civil, civilian (as opposed to military) – يِلبَس مُلكِي [yilbas mulki] He wears civilian clothing.
مالِك [maːlik] *n:* مُلّاك [mullaːk] *pl:* • **1.** owner, landlord
مالِكِي [maːliki] *adj:* • **1.** belonging to the Malikite school of Moslem theology • **2.** a Maliki
مَملُوك [mamluːk] *adj:* مَمالِيك [mamaːliːk] *pl:* • **1.** white slave, mameluke
مَلَكُوتِي [malakuːti] *adj:* • **1.** divine, heavenly

م ل ل

مَلّ [mall] *v:* • **1.** to be or become tired, bored, impatient, fed up – مَلِّيت مِن أكِل الدِّجاج [malliːt min ʔakil ʔiddijaːj] I've gotten tired of eating chicken.
مَلّ [mall] *n:* • **1.** weary, tired, fed up
مُلَّة [mulla] *n:* مُلالِي [mulaːli] *pl:* • **1.** tutor, usually an older man who holds classes for children in his home
مَلَل [malal] *n:* • **1.** tiredness, boredom
مِلَّة [milla] *n:* مِلَل [milal] *pl:* • **1.** sect, religious community • **2.** religion, creed, faith, confession, denomination
مُلّايَة [mullaːya] *n:* مُلّايات [mullaːyaːt] *pl:* • **1.** woman who sings at weddings, funerals, etc • **2.** tutor, usually an older woman who holds classes for children in her home
مُمِلّ [mumill] *adj:* • **1.** boring, tiresome, tedious

م ل و

مِلَى [milaː] *v:* • **1.** to fill – إملِي القَلَم بحِبِر أخضَر [ʔimliː ʔilqalam bħibir ʔaxðar] Fill the pen with green ink. مِلَى الأكِل مِلِح [milaː ʔilʔakil miliħ] He put too much salt in the food. • **2.** to fill out – إقرا التَّعلِيمات قَبُل ما تِملِي الاستِمارَة [ʔiqra ʔittaʕliːmaːt gabul maː timliː ʔilʔistimaːra] Read the instructions before you fill out the application.
مَلَّى [mallaː] *v:* • **1.** to dictate – المُعَلِّم مَلّانا قُصَّة مِن الكِتاب [ʔilmuʕallim mallaːna quṣṣa min ʔilkitaːb] The teacher dictated a story from the book to us.
أملَى [ʔamlaː] *v:* • **1.** to dictate – المُعَلِّم أملَى عَلينا قُصَّة مِن الكِتاب [ʔilmuʕallim ʔamlaː ʕaliːna quṣṣa min ʔilkitaːb] The teacher dictated a story from the book to us.
إملاء ، إملا [ʔimlaːʔ, ʔimla] *n:* • **1.** dictation

م ل ي

مِليم [milliːm] *n:* مِلِّم [millim] *pl:* • **1.** millimeter (mm)

م ل ي ر

مِليار [milyaːr] *n:* • **1.** billion

م م ب ر

مُمبار [mumbaːr] *n:* • **1.** large intestine of the lamb, used in making a kind of sausage

م م ي

مَمَّة، مَمِّيَّة [mamma, mammiyya] *n:* مَمِّيّات [mammiyyaːt] *pl:* • **1.** nipple (for a bottle) • **2.** nursing bottle

م ن [1]

مِنُو ما [minu maː] • **1.** whoever

مَن [man] *interrogative:* • **1.** (interrogative pronoun suffix) who? whom? whose? (see also – ببَيت مَن نِمِت البارحَة؟ [bbayt man nimit ʔilbaːrħa?] Whose house did you stay in last nigh? إلمَن تريدِني أنطِي المَكتُوب؟ [ʔilman triːdni ʔanṭi ʔilmaktuːb?] Who do you want me to give the letter to? بِمَن تعَرَّفت بِالحَفلَة؟ [biman tʕarrafit bilħafla?] Who'd you meet at the party? عَلَى مَن دَتِحكِي؟ [ʕala man datiħči?] Who are you talking about? مِن مَن أخِذت الفلُوس؟ [min man ʔaxiðt ʔilfluːs?] Who'd you get the money from? هَالرَّسِم مال مَن؟ [harrasim maːl man?] Whose picture is this?

مِنُو [minu] *interrogative:* • **1.** who – مِنُو عَلَّمَك عالسِّياقَة؟ [minu ʕallamak ʕassiyaːqa?] Who taught you driving?

م ن [2]

مِنَّا، مِن هنا [min hna, minna] *preposition:* • **1.** from here, from this place [minna] is the pronunciation of three different (and not to be confused) complex words : (a) 'here, from here' مِن هَنا (b) 'from us' مِنَّا [minna] and (c) 'from him' مِنَّه [minna(h)]

م ن ح

مِنَح [minaħ] *v:* • **1.** to grant, give, award – مِنحُوه إجازَة نُصّ شَهَر [minħuːh ʔijaːza nuṣṣ šahar] They granted him a half a month leave.

مَنِح [maniħ] *n:* • **1.** giving, granting, donation, bestowal, award(ing)

مِنحَة [minħa] *n:* مِنَح [minaħ] *pl:* • **1.** gift, present, donation, benefaction, grant • **2.** allowance, remuneration, scholarship

مَمنُوح [mamnuːħ] *adj:* • **1.** granted

م ن ع

مِنَع [minaʕ] *v:* • **1.** to hinder, prevent, stop – هَالمادَّة تِمنَع الزِّنجار [halmaːdda timnaʕ ʔizzinjaːr] This material prevents rust. هَالدِّهِن يِمنَع سُقُوط الشَّعَر [haddihin yimnaʕ suquːṭ ʔiššaʕar] This oil stops loss of hair. • **2.** to forbid, prohibit – مِنعَوا التَّدخِين بِالسِّينَما [minʕaw ʔittadxiːn bissinama] They prohibited smoking in the movie. الحُكُومَة مِنعَتَه مِن السَّفَر خارِج البَلَد [ʔilħukuːma minʕatah min ʔissafar xaːrij ʔilbalad] The government prohibited him from traveling outside the country. الطَّبِيب مِنَعَه مِن الأكل المالِح [ʔiṭṭabiːb minaʕah min ʔilʔakl ʔilmaːliħ] The doctor restricted him from salty food.

مانَع [maːnaʕ] *v:* • **1.** to be opposed, to put up resistance, act in opposition – مانَع هوايَة بِدُخُول بِنتَه لِلمَدرَسَة [maːnaʕ hwaːya bduxuːl bintah lilmadrasa] He was strongly opposed to his daughter's entering school.

تمَنَّع [tmannaʕ] *v:* • **1.** to refrain, abstain – تمَنَّع هوايَة قَبِل ما يبِيعها [tmannaʕ hwaːya gabil maː ybiːʕha] He held off a long time before he sold it.

إنمِنَع [ʔinminaʕ] *v:* • **1.** to be hindered, prevented, stopped

إمتِنَع [ʔimtinaʕ] *v:* • **1.** with مِن to refrain from, abstain from, stop, cease – إمتِنَع مِن التَّدخِين [ʔimtinaʕ min ʔittadxiːn] He stopped smoking.

مَنِع [maniʕ] *n:* • **1.** prevention, obstruction, hindering, stop

مانِع [maːniʕ] *n:* مَوانِع [mawaːniʕ] *pl:* • **1.** hindrance, obstacle, obstruction – سِباق قَفز المَوانِع [sibaːq qafz ʔilmawaːniʕ] hurdles race. • **2.** preventive, preventative – مانِع لِلزِّنجار [maːniʕ lizzinjaːr] rust preventative. مانِع لِلتَّجَمُّد [maːniʕ littajammud] anti-freeze. مانِع لِلرُّطُوبَة [maːniʕ lirruṭuːba] moisture protection. • **3.** contraceptive • **4.** objection – ماكُو مانِع تِجِي وِيّانا [maːku maːniʕ tiji wiyyaːna] There's no objection to your coming with us. ما عِندِي مانِع [maː ʕindi maːniʕ] I don't mind.

مَناعَة [manaːʕa] *n:* • **1.** immunity

مانِعَة [maːniʕa] *n:* • **1.** lightning rod

مُمانَعَة [mumaːnaʕa] *n:* • **1.** opposition, resistance • **2.** revolt, rebellion

إمتِناع [ʔimtinaːʕ] *n:* • **1.** refraining from, abstinence, abstention, refusal

مَمنُوعات [mamnuːʕaːt] *n:* • **1.** prohibited, banned, forbidden things (e.g., drugs)

مَنِيع [maniːʕ] *adj:* • **1.** strong, powerful, well-fortified • **2.** unapproachable, inaccessable, impenetrable, impregnable

مَمنُوع [mamnuːʕ] *adj:* • **1.** forbidden, prohibited, banned

ممتِنِع [mimtiniʕ] *adj:* • **1.** refrained, abstained, stopped, ceased

م ن ك س

مِنكاسَة [minčaːsa] *n:* مناكِيس [mnaːčiːs] *pl:* • **1.** bowl

م ن ك ن

مَنكَنَة [mangana] *n:* مَنكَنات [manganaːt] *pl:* • **1.** vise

م ن ل ج

مَنلُوج [manuluːg] *n:* مَنلُوجات [manuluːgaːt] *pl:* • **1.** monologue • **2.** (cabaret) act, skit, sketch • **3.** ballad, satirical song

م ن ن

مَنّ [mann] *v:* • **1.** to yearn, be covetous, desire the return – إنطانِي ساعَة وَبَعدين مَنّ بِيها [ʔinṭaːni saːʕa wbaʕdiːn mann biːha] He gave me a watch and then wanted it back.

مَنّ، مَنّ السِما [mann, mann ʔissima] *n:* • **1.** manna

مَنّ [mann] *n:* منان [mnaːn] *pl:* • **1.** a measure of weight, approximately 24 kilograms – سِتّ حُقَق تسَوِّي مَنّ. أربَعَة منان تسَوِّي وَزنَه [sitt ħugag tsawwi: mann. ʔarbaʕa mnaːn tsawwi: waznah] Six

م

huggas equal one mann. Four manns equal one wazna.
مِنِّيَّة [minniyya] *n:* مِنِّيَات [minniyya:t] *pl:* • **1.** favor or good deed – وحَمَّلني مِنِّيَّة [wħammalni minniyya] He helped me with demanding repayment. عاونّي بالشُّغُل [ʕa:wanni biššuɣul] the work and imposed an obligation on me. لا آخُذ مِنَّه شِي وَلا أرِيد مِنِّيتَه [la: ʔa:xuð minnah ši wla: ʔari:d minniyytah] I don't take anything from him and I don't want to owe him anything.
إمتِنان [ʔimtina:n] *n:* • **1.** gratitude
مَمنُونِيَّة [mamnu:niyya] *n:* • **1.** gratefulness, obligation • **2.** pleasure, gladness – أساعدَك بِكُلّ مَمنُونِيَّة [ʔasa:ʕdak bkull mamnu:niyya] I'd be most pleased to help you.
ممتَنّ [mimtann] *adj:* • **1.** indebted, obliged, grateful, thankful – مِمتَنِّين مِنَّه لِأنَّه تبَرَّع بِمَبلَغ ضَخُم [mimtanni:n minnah liʔannah tbarraʕ bmablaɣ ḍaxum] Were grateful to him because he donated a great amount. • **2.** gratified, satisfied, pleased – المُعَلِّم ممتَنّ هوايَة مِن إبنَك [ʔilmuʕallim mimtann hwa:ya min ʔibnak] The teacher is very satisfied with your son.
مَمنُون [mamnu:n] *adj:* • **1.** indebted, obliged, grateful, thankful – إذا تصَلِّح الرّاديُو، تسَوِّيني هوايَة مَمنُون [ʔiða tṣallih ʔirra:dyu, tsawwi:niy hwa:ya mamnu:n] If you fix the radio, I'll be very much obliged. • **2.** gratified, satisfied, pleased – المُعَلِّم هوايَة مَمنُون مِنَّك [ʔilmuʕallim hwa:ya mamnu:n minnak] The teacher is very satisfied with you. • **3.** (in answer to a request) Gladly! With pleasure! • **4.** (as a reply to أشكُرَك) You're welcome!

م ن ي

تمَنّى [tmanna:] *v:* • **1.** to wish – أتمَنّى أكُون بِبَغداد [ʔatmanna: ʔaku:n bibaɣda:d] I wish I were in Baghdad. تمَنِّيتَه مَوجُود حَتّى يشُوف بعَينَه [tmanni:tah mawǰu:d ħatta yšu:f bʕaynah] I wished he was present so he could see with his own eyes. نِتمَنّالَك النَّجاح بالإمتِحان [nitmanna:lak ʔinnaǰa:ħ bilʔimtiħa:n] We wish you success on the exam.
مَنِيّ [maniyy] *n:* • **1.** semen, sperm
مُنيَة [munya] *n:* مُنيات [munya:t] *pl:* • **1.** desire, object of desire, objective, goal – مُنِيتَه بِالحَياة يصِير مُعَلِّم [muni:tah bilħaya:t yṣi:r muʕallim] His goal in life is to become a teacher.
مَنِيَّة، مِنيَّة [maniyya, miniyya] *n:* • **1.** death
تِمَنّي [tamanni] *n:* • **1.** wishing
أُمنِيَّة [ʔumniyya] *n:* أماني [ʔama:ni] *pl:* • **1.** wish, desire, object of desire, goal

م ه د

مَهَّد [mahhad] *v:* • **1.** to smooth, level, pave – أبُوه مَهَّدلَه الطَّرِيق حَتّى يسَوِّيه وَزِير [ʔabu:h mahhadlah ʔiṭṭari:q ħatta ysawwi:h wazi:r] His father paved the way for him to become a minister.
تمَهَّد [tmahhad] *v:* • **1.** pass. of مَهَّد : to be smoothed, to be paved – هَسَّة الطَّرِيق تمَهَّد. خَلّي نرُوح نِحكِي وِيّاه [hassa ʔiṭṭari:q tmahhad. xalli: nru:ħ niħči wiyya:h] Now the way is prepared. Let's go talk to him.
مَهَد [mahad] *n:* مهُود [mhu:d] *pl:* • **1.** cradle, baby's crib
تَمهِيد [tamhi:d] *n:* • **1.** paving, pavement • **2.** preface, foreword, introduction, preliminaries • **3.** facilitation, easing, preparation
تَمهِيدِي [tamhi:di] *adj:* • **1.** preparatory, preliminary, introductory

م ه ر [1]

مَهَر [mahar] *n:* • **1.** dower, bridal price – قِطَع المَهَر [giṭaʕ ʔilmahar] to conclude the marriage contract. قِطَعنا المَهَر اليُوم، لَكِن راح نِتزَوَّج بَعَد شَهرَين [giṭaʕna ʔilmahar ʔilyu:m, la:kin ra:ħ nidzawwaǰ baʕad šahrayn] We made the marriage agreement today, but we won't consummate the marriage for two months.
مُهرَة [muhra] *n:* مُهرات [muhra:t] *pl:* • **1.** filly
مَهارَة [maha:ra] *n:* • **1.** skillfulness, adroitness, dexterity, skill, expertness, proficiency, adeptness
ماهِر [ma:hir] *adj:* • **1.** skillful, adroit, proficient, adept, expert – زَوجتَه ماهرَة بِالطَّبُخ [zawiǰtah ma:hra biṭṭabux] His wife is skillful at cooking.
أمهَر [ʔamhar] *comparative adjective:* • **1.** more or most skillful, adroit, proficient, adept, expert

م ه ر [2]

مُهَر [muhar] *v:* • **1.** to stamp with a personal seal – خَلّي يُمهُر العَرِيضَة قَبُل ما تجِيبها [xalli: yumhur ʔilʕari:ḍa gabul ma: dǰi:bha] Have him put his seal on the petition before you bring it.
مُهُر [muhur] *n:* مهُور، مهار [mhu:r, mha:r] *pl:* • **1.** signet, personal seal, stamp used by illiterates as a signature • **2.** سَرمُهُر, سِرمُهُر seal, that which secures – لا تِشتِري الدُّوا إذا ما يكُون سِرمُهُر [la: tištiri ʔidduwa: ʔiða ma: yku:n sirmuhur] Don't buy the medicine if it isn't sealed. • **3.** colt, foal

م ه ر ج ن

مَهرَجان [mahraǰa:n] *n:* مَهرَجانات [mahraǰa:na:t] *pl:* • **1.** festival, celebration, gala, jamboree

م ه ل

مِهَل [mihal] *v:* • **1.** to allow time, grant a delay – الشَّرِكَة راح تِمهِلنِي شَهَر لِأنّ ما عِندِي فلُوس [ʔiššarika ra:ħ timhilni šahar liʔann ma: ʕindi flu:s] The company is going to grant me a month's delay because I don't have money.
أمهَل [ʔamhal] *v:* • **1.** same as مِهَل : to allow time, grant a delay
تمَهَّل [tmahhal] *v:* • **1.** to take one's time, proceed slowly and deliberately – إذا يِتمَهَّل بشُغلَه، كُلّشِي يطلَع زين [ʔiða yitmahhal bšuɣlah, kullši yitlaʕ zi:n] If he takes his time about his work, everything comes out well.
تماهَل [tma:hal] *v:* • **1.** same as تمَهَّل : to take one's time,

م

proceed slowly and deliberately – لَا تِتماهَل بشُغلَك تَرَة تِنضَرّ [la: titma:hal bšuɣlak tara tinðarr] Don't be too slow in your work or you'll get in trouble.
مَهَل [mahal] *n:* • **1.** slowness, leisureliness – عَلَى مَهلَك [ʕala mahlak] Take your time. Take it easy. إذا تِمشِي عَلَى مَهلَك، ما تِزلَق [ʔiða timši ʕala mahlak, ma: tizlag] If you walk at an easy pace, you won't slip.
مُهلَة [muhla] *n:* مُهلات [muhla:t] *pl:* • **1.** respite, delay, period of grace
تَمَهُّل [tamahhul] *n:* • **1.** slowness, deliberateness
إمهال [ʔimha:l] *n:* • **1.** allowing, extending time, granting a delay
متمَهِّل [mitmahhil] *adj:* • **1.** slow, unhurried
مِتماهِل [mitma:hil] *adj:* • **1.** lax • **2.** comfortable, easy, unhurried, slow

م ه م

مَهما [mahma] *subordinating conjunction:* • **1.** whatever, no matter what – لا تصَدِّق بِيه مَهما يُقُلَّك [la: tṣaddig bi:h mahma: yugullak] Don't believe him, whatever he tells you. • **2.** no matter how much – راح أسَوِّي هَذا، مَهما كَلَّف [ra:ħ ʔasawwi: ha:ða, mahma: kallaf] I'm going to do that, no matter what it costs.

م ه ن 1

اِمتِهَن [ʔimtihan] *v:* • **1.** to degrade, humiliate, abuse
مِهنَة [mihna] *n:* مِهَن [mihan] *pl:* • **1.** job, work, occupation, profession, vocation, trade, business
اِمتِهان [ʔimtiha:n] *n:* • **1.** degradation, humiliation, contempt, abuse, misuse, improper treatment
مِهَنِي [mihani] *adj:* • **1.** vocational, trade- – التَّعلِيم المِهَنِي [ʔittaʕli:m ʔilmihani] vocational education.

م ه ن 2

مُهِين [muhi:n] *adj:* • **1.** despised, despicable, contemptible, vile

م و ب ي ل ي

مُوبِيليا [mubi:lya] *n:* مُوبِيليات [mubi:lya:t] *pl:* • **1.** furniture

م و ت

مات [ma:t] *v:* • **1.** to die, become dead – مات بسَكتَة قلبِيَّة [ma:t bsakta qalbiyya] He died of a heart attack. أَحِبَّه لمَجِيد. أَمُوت عَلَيه [ʔaħibbah lmaǰi:d. ʔamu:t ʕali:h] I like Majid. I would die for him. ما راح تحَصِّل فلُوسَك مِنّه. يبَيِّن الخَمس دَنانِير ماتَت عَلِيك [ma: ra:ħ tħaṣṣil flu:sak minnah. yibayyin ʔilxams dana:ni:r ma:tat ʕali:k] You're not going to collect your money from him. It looks like you're stuck for five dinars. مات بِيدِي الدُّوشَيش [ma:t bi:di ʔiddu:ši:š] I'm stuck with the double six. I can't play the double six.
مَوَّت [mawwat] *v:* • **1.** to kill – ظَلّ يُضرُب البَزُّونَة بِالعَصا حَتَّى مَوَّتها [ðall yuðrub ʔilbazzu:na bilʕaṣa: ħatta mawwatha] He kept beating the cat with the stick until he killed it. ماكُو حاجَة تمَوِّت نَفسَك مِن الشُّغُل [ma:ku ħa:ǰa tmawwit nafsak min ʔiššuɣul] There's no reason to kill yourself working. مَوَّت نَفسَه عَالوَظِيفَة [mawwat nafsah ʕalwaði:fa] He almost killed himself for the position. الثَّعلَب، مِن يشُوف السَّبِع، يمَوِّت نَفسَه [ʔiθθaʕlab, min yšu:f ʔissabiʕ, ymawwit nafsah] When the fox sees the lion, he plays dead. المُعَلِّم جاب إلنا أَسئِلَة تمَوِّت [ʔilmuʕallim ǰa:b ʔilna ʔasʔila tmawwit] The teacher gave us some awfully tough questions.
اِستَمات [ʔistama:t] *v:* • **1.** to defy death, risk one's life – الجِّنُود اِستَماتَوا بِالمَعرَكَة [ʔiǰǰinu:d ʔistama:taw bilmaʕraka] The soldiers defied death on the battlefield.
موت [mawt, mu:t] *n:* • **1.** death – موت! مُو عِيب تخاف؟ [mu:t! mu: ʕi:b txa:f?] Shame on you! Aren't you ashamed of being afraid? • **2.** For shame! Shame on you!
مَيِّت [mayyit] *n:* أموات، مَوتَى، مياتَة [ʔamwa:t, mawta, mwa:ta] *pl:* • **1.** dead, deceased, lifeless, inanimate person
مَوتَة [mu:ta] *n:* مَوتات [mu:ta:t] *pl:* • **1.** death (act of dying), demise, passing
مَيِّت [mayyit] *adj:* مَيِّتِين [mayyti:n] *pl:* • **1.** dead, deceased, lifeless, inanimate
مُمِيت [mumi:t] *adj:* • **1.** deadly, lethal, fatal, mortal

م و ج

تمَوَّج [tmawwaǰ] *v:* • **1.** to rise in waves – مِن يكُون هَوا عالِي، مَيّ البَحَر يِتمَوَّج [min yku:n hawa ʕa:li, mayy ʔilbaħar yitmawwaǰ] When there's a strong wind, the sea becomes covered with waves.
موج [mawǰ, mu:ǰ] *n:* • **1.** seas, billows, breakers • **2.** waves • **3.** ripples
موجَة [mawǰa, mu:ǰa] *n:* موجات [mawǰa:t, mu:ǰa:t] *pl:* • **1.** sea, billow, breaker • **2.** wave – مَوجَة قَصِيرَة [mawǰa qaṣi:ra] short wave (radio). مَوجَة حَرّ [mawǰat ħarr] heat wave, hot spell.
تَمَوُّج [tamawwuǰ] *n:* • **1.** wave, undulation • **2.** vibration
أَمواج [ʔamwa:ǰ] *n:* • **1.** seas, billows, waves, ripples • **2.** waves, ripples
مُمَوَّج [mumawwaǰ] *adj:* • **1.** wavy, undulatory
مِتمَوِّج [mitmawwiǰ] *adj:* • **1.** wavy, undulatory

م و د 1

مُود، عَلَى مُود [mu:d, ʕala mu:d] *n:* • **1.** on behalf of, for the sake of – تعارَك وِيّاهُم عَلَى مُودَك [tʕa:rak wiyya:hum ʕala mu:dak] He fought with them for your sake. • **2.** about, concerning – حِكَيت وِيّاه عَلَى مُود الإيجار؟ [ħiči:t wiyya:h ʕala mu:d ʔilʔi:ǰa:r?] Did you talk to him about the rent?

م و د 2

مُودَة [mu:da] *n:* مُودات [mu:da:t] *pl:* • **1.** mode, fashion, style – مزَوِّج مَرَة عَالمُودَة [mzawwiǰ mara ʕalmu:da] He's married a fashionable lady. قاصَّة شَعَرها عَالمُودَة [ga:ṣṣa šaʕarha ʕalmu:da] She's cut her hair according to the latest fashion. هَالبنَيَّة طالعَة عَالمُودَة [halbnayya ṭa:lʕa ʕalmu:da] That girl is dressed fashionably.

م و ر ي

مُورِي [mu:ri] *adj:* • **1.** purple

م و ز

موز [mawz, mu:z] *n:* موزات [mawza:t, mu:za:t] *pl:* موزَة [mawza, mu:za] *feminine:* • **1.** (coll.) banana(s)
موزَة [mawza, mu:za] *n:* موزات [mawza:t, mu:za:t] *pl:* • **1.** banana

م و س

مُوس [mu:s] *n:* مواس، مواسَة [mwa:s, mwa:sa] *pl:* • **1.** straight razor • **2.** razor blade

م و س ق

مُوسِيقِي [musi:qi] *adj:* • **1.** musical – حَفلَة مَوسِيقِيَّة [ħafla musi:qiyya] concert. • **2.** a musician (pl. مُوسِيقِيِّن)
مُوسِيقار [musi:qa:r] *adj:* مُوسِيقارِيَّة [musi:qa:riyya] *pl:* • **1.** musician

م و ص ل [1]

مَوصَل [mu:ṣal] *v:* • **1.** to blow a whistle – الجّاهِل صارلَه مُدَّة دَيمَوصِل بِالماصُولَة مالَه [ʔijǰa:hil ṣa:rlah mudda daymawṣil bilma:ṣu:la ma:lah] The kid has been blowing his whistle for quite a while.
ماصُول [ma:ṣu:l] *n:* مواصِيل [mwa:ṣi:l] *pl:* • **1.** toy whistle, reed whistle
ماصُولَة [ma:ṣu:la] *n:* ماصُولات [ma:ṣu:la:t] *pl:* • **1.** toy whistle, reed whistle

م و ص ل [2]

مَصلاوِي، مُصلاوِي [maṣla:wi, muṣla:wi] *adj:* مصلاوِيِّين [mṣla:wiyyi:n] *pl:* • **1.** native to Mosul, coming from Mosul • **2.** person (or people) from Mosul (pl. مصالوَة، مواصلَة – (مصَالوَة, مَواصلَة [mṣa:lwa, mwa:ṣla] person from Mosul.

م و ل

مَوَّل [mawwal] *v:* • **1.** to finance – عَمَّه كان يمَوِّلَه عَلَى طُول بِتِجارتَه [ʕammah ča:n ymawwilah ʕala ṭu:l btija:rtah] His uncle was always financing him in his dealings.
مال [ma:l] *n:* أموال [ʔamwa:l] *pl:* • **1.** property, possessions, chattels, goods • **2.** wealth, fortune, estate • **3.** (a euphemism for the genitals, approx.:) private parts • **4.** particle indicating possession or ownership – وين الكِتاب مالِي؟ [wi:n ʔilkita:b ma:li?] Where's my book? هَالسَّيّارَة مالَت مَن؟ [hassayya:ra ma:lat man?] Who does this car belong to? • **5.** for, for the purpose of – هَالقماش مال ثياب [halqma:š ma:l θya:b] This material is for shirts. هَذا مُو مال مُعَلِّم [ha:ða mu: ma:l muʕallim] He could never be a teacher. • **6.** in the realm of, having to do with – ثُوب بدِينار؟ مال بَلاش [θu:b bdi:na:r? ma:l bala:š] A shirt for one dinar? That's dirt cheap. إسكُت! مال الوُجَع [ʔiskut! ma:l ʔilwuǰaʕ] Shut up! Plague be your lot.
مالِيَّة [ma:liyya] *n:* • **1.** monetary affairs, finance – وِزارَة المالِيَّة [wiza:rat ʔilma:liyya] Ministry of Finance.
تَموِيل [tamwi:l] *n:* • **1.** financing
مالِي [ma:li] *adj:* • **1.** monetary, financial • **2.** fiscal – سَنَة مالِيَّة [sana ma:liyya] fiscal year.
مُمَوِّل [mumawwil] *adj:* • **1.** **financed** • **2.** **(as n:)** financier
متمَوِّل [mitmawwil] *adj:* • **1.** wealthy, rich, well-to-do – تزَوَّجها لِأَنّ أَبُوها متمَوِّل [dzawwaǰha liʔann ʔabu:ha mitmawwil] He married her because her father is well-to-do.

م و ن

مان [ma:n] *v:* • **1.** to be a good friend, on close terms – أَقدَر أَطلُب مِنَّه هَالشَّي لِأَنّ آني أَمُون عَليه [ʔagdar ʔaṭlub minnah hašši liʔann ʔa:ni ʔamu:n ʕali:h] I can request such a thing from him because I'm close to him.
مَوَّن [mawwan] *v:* • **1.** to provision, supply provisions – راح يمَوِّنُون الطُّلّاب بجَمِيع ما يحتاجُوه مِن الأكِل [ra:ħ ymawwinu:n ʔiṭṭulla:b bǰami:ʕ ma: yiħta:ǰu:h min ʔilʔakil] They're going to provide the students with all the food they need.
تمَوَّن [tmawwan] *v:* • **1.** to store up provisions, provision oneself – تمَوَّنّا بِكُلّشِي لِلسَّفرَة [tmawwanna bikullši lissafra] We supplied ourselves with everything for the trip.
مُونَة [mu:na] *n:* • **1.** provisions, • **2.** ammunition • **3.** nourishment, richness – هَالشُّوربَة ما بِيها مُونَة [haššu:rba ma: bi:ha mu:na] This soup has no nourishment in it.
مَيانَة [maya:na] *n:* مَيانات [maya:na:t] *pl:* • **1.** close friendship • **2.** (invar.) intimate, close – صِرنا مَيانَة مِن اِشتِغَلنا سُوَة [ṣirna maya:na min ʔištiɣalna suwa] We became close when we worked together.
تَموِين [tamwi:n] *n:* • **1.** ration, food supply, provision

م و ه

مَوَّه [mawwah] *v:* • **1.** to camouflage, feign
تمَوَّه [tmawwah] *v:* • **1.** to camouflage, feign
تَموِيه [tamwi:h] *n:* • **1.** camouflage, act of feigning distorting the truth)
مَيّ [mayy] *n:* • **1.** same as مَاي [ma:y]: water – مَيّ وَرِد [mayy warid] rose water, and, loosely, any similar perfume made from blossoms. دِجاج مَيّ [dija:ǰ mayy] coot. خُبُز مَيّ [xubuz mayy] plain bread as opposed to bread with meat, etc., baked into

م

it). • **2.** liquid, fluid • **3.** juice – مَيّ الرُّمّان [mayy ʔirrumma:n] pomegranate juice.
ماي [ma:y] *n:* • **1.** var. of مَيّ [mayy] water
مائِي [ma:ʔi] *adj:* • **1.** water, aquatic – حَيوانات مائِيَّة [ħaywa:na:t ma:ʔiyya] aquatic animals.

م و ه ²

مَيّخانَة [mayyxa:na] *n:* مَيّخانات [mayyxa:na:t] *pl:* • **1.** bar (slightly derogatory)
مَيّخَنچي [mayyxanči] *n:* مَيّخَنچِيَّة [mayyxančiyya] *pl:* • **1.** bartender, barkeeper • **2.** barfly

م ي ج ن

مَيجَنَة [mayǰana] *n:* مَيجَنات، مَياجِن [mi:ǰana:t, maya:ǰin] *pl:* • **1.** a large wooden pestle used to grind grain in a mortar

م ي د ن

مِيدان [mi:da:n] *n:* مَيادِين [maya:di:n] *pl:* • **1.** square, open place • **2.** field (of contest), arena
مِيدانلِي [mida:nli] *n:* مِيدانلِيَّة [mida:nliyya] *pl:* • **1.** loafer, idler

م ي ز ¹

مَيَّز [mayyaz] *v:* • **1.** to consider better – آنِي أَمَيِّزَه عَنهُم بِاللُّغَة الإنكلِيزِيَّة [ʔa:ni ʔamayyizah ʕanhum billuɣa ʔilʔingili:ziyya] I feel he's better than they are in English. • **2.** to prefer – آنِي أَمَيِّز بارِيس عَلَى أَيّ مَدِينَة بأورُبّا [ʔa:ni ʔamayyiz pa:ri:s ʕala ʔayy madi:na bʔu:ruppa] I prefer Paris above any city in Europe. • **3.** to distinguish, differentiate – ما أَقدَر أَمَيِّز بين القَبُوطَين. ياهُو مالَك؟ [ma: ʔagdar ʔamayyiz bi:n ʔilqappu:ṭayn. ya:hu ma:lak?] I can't distinguish between the two coats. Which one's yours? • **4.** to appeal to a higher court – راح أَمَيِّز الدَّعوَة [ra:ħ ʔamayyiz ʔiddaʕwa] I'm going to appeal the case.
تمَيَّز [tmayyaz] *v:* • **1.** to be distinguished, to stand out – هَالوَلَد يِتمَيَّز بذَكاءَه [halwalad yitmayyaz bðaka:ʔah] This boy is distinguished by his intelligence.
اِمتاز [ʔimta:z] *v:* • **1.** to distinguish oneself, to stand out, be marked – مِن كِنِت بالكُلِّيَّة، اِمتازِت بمَعرِفَة ثلَث لُغات [min činit bilkulliyya, ʔimta:zit bmaʕrifat tlaθ luɣa:t] When I was in college, I distinguished myself by learning three languages. هَالبَلَدَة تِمتاز بنَظافَتها وَبشَوارِعها الواسعَة [halbalda timta:z bnaða:fatha wibšawa:riʕha ʔilwa:sʕa] This city stands out for its cleanness and its wide streets. • **2.** with عَلَى to excel, surpass, outdo, be better than – اِمتاز عَلينا بالرِّياضِيّات [ʔimta:z ʕali:na birriya:ḍiyya:t] He surpassed us in mathematics.
مِيزَة [mi:za] *n:* مِيزات [mi:za:t] *pl:* • **1.** peculiarity, distinguishing feature, characteristic, essential property • **2.** prerogative, priority right – إنتَ شِنُو مِيزتَك عَنَّه؟ [ʔinta šinu: mi:ztak ʕannah?] What makes you any better than he?
تَميِيز [tamyi:z] *n:* • **1.** preference, preferring • **2.** differentiation • **3.** appeal (jur.) – مَحكَمَة التَّمييز [maħkamat ʔittamyi:z] court of cassation, highest appeal court.
مُمَيِّزَة [mumayyiza] *n:* مُمَيِّزات [mumayyiza:t] *pl:* • **1.** distinguishing mark, feature, advantage
اِمتِياز [ʔimtiya:z] *n:* اِمتِيازات [ʔimtiya:za:t] *pl:* • **1.** distinction, honor – نِجَح بِاِمتِياز [nijaħ bʔimtiya:z] He passed with distinction. • **2.** special right, privilege • **3.** concession, license, franchise
مُمَيَّز [mumayyaz] *adj:* مُمَيَّزِين [mumayyazi:n] *pl:* • **1.** supervisor, overseer, superintendent
متمَيِّز [mitmayyiz] *adj:* متمَيِّزِين [mitmayyizi:yn] *pl:* • **1.** distinguished
مُمتاز [mumta:z] *adj:* • **1.** outstanding, superior, excellent, exceptional, first-rate – الأَكِل بِهالمَطعَم مُمتاز [ʔilʔakil biha:lmaṭʕam mumta:z] The food in this restaurant is excellent!

م ي ز ²

مَيز [mayz] *n:* مِيُوزَة [myu:za] *pl:* • **1.** table • **2.** desk • **3.** pot (in poker)

م ي س

مايِس [ma:yis] *n:* • **1.** May

م ي ش

مِيش [mi:š] *n:* • **1.** a kind of a thin, soft leather. • **2.** highlights (hair)

م ي ع

ماع [ma:ʕ] *v:* • **1.** to melt, dissolve, become liquefied – ماع الثَّلج كُلَّه بالمَيّ [ma:ʕ ʔiθθalij kullah bilmayy] All the ice melted in the water. خَلِّي الحَبّايَة تمُوع بحَلقَك [xalli: ʔilħabba:ya tmu:ʕ bħalgak] Let the pill dissolve in your mouth. ماعَت رُوحَه [ma:ʕat ru:ħah] He fell unconscious. مِن شاف الدَّم، ماعَت رُوحَه [min ša:f ʔiddamm, ma:ʕat ru:ħah] When he saw the blood, he passed out.
مَوَّع [mawwaʕ] *v:* • **1.** to melt, dissolve, liquefy – مَوِّع الرِّصاص وَصُبَّه بالقالَب [mawwiʕ ʔirriṣa:ṣ wṣubbah bilqa:lab] Melt the lead and pour it in the mold. مَوِّع المِلِح قَبُل ما تخَلِّيه بالجِّدِر [mawwiʕ ʔilmiliħ gabul ma: txalli:h bǰǰidir] Dissolve the salt before you put it in the pot.
مَوع [mu:ʕ] *n:* • **1.** act of melting, dissolving, becoming liquefied
مَوعَة [mu:ʕa] *n:* مَوعات [mu:ʕa:t] *pl:* • **1.** dissolving, melting, liquefying, unconsciousness – لِزمَتَه المَوعَة [lizmatah ʔilmu:ʕa] Unconsciousness overcame him. لِزمَتَه المُوعَة مِن الحَرّ [lizmatah ʔilmu:ʕa min ʔilħarr] He fainted from the heat.
مايِع [ma:yiʕ] *adj:* • **1.** melted, dissolved, liquid • **2.** pl. مايعِين sissy, softy, pantywaist

م ي ك ر و ب

ميكروب [mikruːb] *n:* ميكرُوبات [mikruːbaːt] *pl:* • **1.** microbe, germ

م ي ل 1

مال [maːl] *v:* • **1.** to bend, bend down, lean over – الشِّجرَة مالَت مِن الهَوَا [ʔiššiǰra maːlat min ʔillhawa] The tree bent in the wind. • **2.** to incline, tend, be favorably disposed, have a predilection, liking, or propensity – النّاس هَسَّة يمِيلُون لِلسَّيّارات الصّغار [ʔinnaːs hassa ymiːluːn lissayyaːraːt ʔiṣṣɣaːr] People now are more in favor of small cars. إذا تعامِل الجَاهِل بلُطُف، يمِيللَك [ʔiða tʕaːmil ʔiǰǰaːhil bluṭuf, ymiːllak] If you treat the child gently, he'll get to like you. • **3.** to incline, tend, have a tendency – لُون نَفنُوفها يمِيل لِلحُمرَة [luːn nafnuːfha ymiːl lilħumra] The color of her dress tends toward red.

مَيَّل [mayyal] *v:* • **1.** to incline, tip, tilt, bend, bow – مَيِّل نَفسَك شوَيَة حَتَّى يصِير راسَك بالفَيّ [mayyil nafsak šwaya ħatta yṣiːr raːsak bilfayy] Bend over a little so that your head will be in the shade. • **2.** to make inclined, favorably disposed, sympathetic – اِنطاه لِلجّاهِل جُكلَيت حَتَّى يمَيِّلَه إلَه [ʔinṭaːh liǰǰaːhil čukliːt ħatta ymayyilah ʔilah] He gave the kid some candy to win his favor.

تمايَل [tmaːyal] *v:* • **1.** to sway, swing – شُوف البنَيَّة دَتِتمايَل بِمَشيها [šuːf ʔilbnayya datitmaːyal bmašyha] Look at the girl swaying as she walks.

اِستَمال [ʔistamaːl] *v:* • **1.** to attract, win over, bring to one's side, to gain favor with, win the affection of – الوَزِير حاوَل يِستَمِيل بَعض السِّياسِيِّين [ʔilwaziːr ħaːwal yistimiːl baʕð ʔissiyaːsiyyiːn] The minister tried to win over some of the politicians.

مَيل، ميلان [mayl, miːl, maylaːn] *n:* مِيُول [miyuːl] *pl:* • **1.** propensity, disposition, bent, leaning, inclination

مايِل [maːyil] *adj:* • **1.** bent • **2.** inclined

م ي ل 2

ميل [miːl] *n:* أَميال، ميال [ʔamyaːl, myaːl] *pl:* • **1.** mile

م ي ل 3

ميل [miːl] *n:* ميالَة [myaːla] *pl:* • **1.** Indian club, a heavy wooden weight used in body-building exercises • **2.** stick applicator (for cosmetics) • **3.** needle, indicator (of a gauge) • **4.** hand (of a watch)

م ي ن 1

مِينَة [miːna] *n:* • **1.** glaze, glazing • **2.** enamel coating • **3.** face, dial (of a watch or clock)

م ي ن 2

مِيناء [miːnaːʔ, miːna] *n:* مَوانِئ [mawaːniʔ] *pl:* • **1.** port, harbor

م ي و 1

مايُو [maːyu] *n:* مايُوهات [maːyuːhaːt] *pl:* • **1.** woman's bathing suit

م ي و 2

مِيوَة [miːwa] *n:* • **1.** fruit

ن

ن ب ء

تنَبَّأ [tnabbaʔ] *v:* • **1.** to prognosticate, foretell, forecast, predict – بمَقالَه، تنَبَّأ راح تصِير حَرُب [bmaqa:lah, tnabbaʔ ra:ħ tṣi:r ħarub] In his article, he predicted there was going to be a war.

نَبأ [nabaʔ] *n:* أنباء [ʔanba:ʔ] *pl:* • **1.** news • **2.** news, tidings, report, information, announcement, news item

تَنَبُّؤ [tanabbuʔ] *n:* تَنَبُّؤات [tanabbuʔa:t] *pl:* • **1.** prediction, prophecy

نُبوءَة [nubu:ʔa] *n:* نُبوءآت [nubu:ʔa:t] *pl:* • **1.** prediction, prophecy

ن ب ت

نِبَت [nibat] *v:* • **1.** to grow – هَالقاع ما ينبِت بيها أيّ زَرِع [halga:ʕ ma: yinbit bi:ha ʔayy zariʕ] No crop grows in this land. راحَة الإيد، ما ينبِت بيها شَعَر [ra:ħat ʔilʔi:d, ma: yinbit bi:ha šaʕar] Hair won't grow in the palm of the hand. • **2.** to stick, become rooted, firmly implanted – نَيشِن عالخِشبَة وذِبّ السِّكّينَة حيل حَتَّى تِنبِت بيها [nayšin ʕalxišba wðibb ʔissičči:na ħi:l ħatta tinbit bi:ha] Aim at the board and throw the knife hard so that it'll stick in it. نِبَت بهالمُكان وَما قِبَل يرُوح [nibat bha:lmuka:n wma qibal yru:ħ] He's gotten rooted in this place and wouldn't think of leaving.

نَبَّت [nabbat] *v:* • **1.** to sprout, germinate – البَزر اللّي زِرَعته إسبُوع اللّي فات كُلّه نَبَّت [ʔilbazr ʔilli ziraʕtah ʔisbu:ʕ ʔilli fa:t kullah nabbat] The seeds I planted last week have all sprouted. • **2.** to plant, implant, embed, stick – تِقدَر تنَبِّت السِّكّينَة بالحايِط؟ [tigdar tnabbit ʔissičči:na bilħa:yiṭ?] Can you stick the knife in the wall?

نَبِت [nabit] *n:* • **1.** growth

نَبتَة [nabta] *n:* نَبتات [nabta:t] *pl:* • **1.** plant

نَبات [naba:t] *n:* • **1.** plants, vegetation – عِلم النَّبات [ʕilm ʔinnaba:t] botany. • **2.** pl. نَباتات plant, vegetable organism • **3.** rock candy • **4.** pl. نَباتات [naba:ta:t] plant, vegetable organism

مَنبَت [manbat] *n:* مَنابِت [mana:bit] *pl:* • **1.** plantation, nursery, arboretum • **2.** birthplace, hotbed, origin

نَباتي [naba:ti] *adj:* • **1.** vegetarian • **2.** material of a vegetal source

ن ب ح

نِبَح [nibaħ] *v:* • **1.** to bark – لا تخاف مِن هَالكَلِب. هُوَّ بَسّ ينبَح [la: txa:f min haččalib. huwwa bass yinbaħ] Don't be afraid of this dog. He only barks.

تنابَح [tna:baħ] *v:* • **1.** to bark at each other – هَالكَلبَين صارِلهُم مُدَّة يتنابحُون [haččalbayn ṣa:rilhum mudda yitna:bħu:n] Those two dogs have been barking at each other for quite a while.

نَبِح [nabiħ] *n:* • **1.** barking

نَبحَة [nabħa] *n:* نَبحات [nabħa:t] *pl:* • **1.** a bark, a yelp

نِباح [niba:ħ] *n:* • **1.** barking

ن ب ذ

نِبَذ [nibað] *v:* • **1.** to reject, spurn with disdain – كُلّ أصدِقائَه نِبذَوه بِسَبَب أخلاقَه [kull ʔaṣdiqa:ʔah nibðawh bsabab ʔaxla:qah] All his friends rejected him because of his manners.

نَبِذ [nabið] *n:* • **1.** throwing away, discarding • **2.** rejection, disavowal, repudiation

نُبذَة [nubða] *n:* نُبَذ، نُبذات [nubað, nubða:t] *pl:* • **1.** (printed) article, story, report • **2.** summary, synopsis, abstract

نَبِيذ [nabi:ð] *n:* • **1.** wine

مَنبُوذ [manbu:ð] *adj:* مَنبُوذِين [manbu:ði:n] *pl:* • **1.** outcast, pariah, untouchable

ن ب ر

مَنبَر [manbar] *n:* مَنابِر [mana:bir] *pl:* • **1.** pulpit • **2.** rostrum, platform, dais

مِنبار [mimba:r] *n:* مِنبارات [mimba:ra:t] *pl:* • **1.** intestine, gut (used for sausage)

ن ب س

نِبَس [nibas] *v:* • **1.** to utter, say, speak – وَلا نِبَس بكِلمَة [wala nibas bčilma] He didn't even utter one word.

نَبِس [nabis] *n:* • **1.** uttering, speech

ن ب ش

نِبَش [nibaš] *v:* • **1.** to dig up, unearth, disinter – الشُّرطَة نِبشَت القَبُر وَفُحصَت المَيِّت [ʔiššurṭa nibšat ʔilgabur wfuħṣat ʔilmayyit] The police dug up the grave and examined the dead man. • **2.** to scratch, poke around, rummage – الدِّجاجَة دَتِنبِش بِالتِّراب [ʔiddiǰa:ǰa datinbiš bittira:b] The chicken's scratching in the dirt. • **3.** to stir, stir up – نِبَش الفَحَم حَتَّى يحتِرِق زين [nibaš ʔilfaħam ħatta yiħtirig zi:n] He stirred up the coal so that it would burn better.

نَبَّش [nabbaš] *v:* • **1.** to keep digging up, keep unearthing – ظَلّ ينَبِّش عَلَيّا حَتَّى حَطِّمني [ðall yinabbiš ʕalayya ħatta ħaṭṭamni] He kept digging up things against me until he ruined me. • **2.** same as نِبَش: to scratch, poke around, rummage – ظَلّ ينَبِّش بخَشمَه حَتَّى طِلَع الدَّمّ [ðall yinabbiš bxašmah ħatta ṭilaʕ ʔiddamm] He kept picking his nose until it bled. لِيش دَتنَبِّش بالأوراق مالتِي؟ [li:š datnabbiš bilʔawra:q ma:lti?] Why are you rummaging through my papers?

اِنتِبَش [ʔintibaš] *v:* • **1.** to go to the grave, be buried (said of someone disliked) – اِنتِبَش وَخِلَصنا مِنَّه

[ʔintibaš wxilaṣna minnah] He's dead and gone to hell and we're rid of him.
نَبِش [nabiš] *n:* • **1.** digging up, excavation, unearthing • **2.** نَبِش القَبُر desecration

ن ب ص

نُبَص [nubaṣ] *v:* • **1.** to turn up • **2.** to interfere, to meddle with
نَبُص [nabuṣ] *n:* • **1.** interference, intrusion

ن ب ض

نُبَض [nubaδ̣] *v:* • **1.** to beat, pulsate – قَلبِي دَينبُض بسُرعَة [galbi dayinbuδ̣ bsurʕa] My heart's beating fast.
نَبُض [nabuδ̣] *n:* • **1.** pulsation, beating, throb • **2.** pulse, heartbeat – جَسّ نَبضَه الطَّبِيب وشاف عِندَه سخُونَة [ǰass nabδ̣ah ʔiṭṭabi:b wša:f ʕindah sxu:na] The doctor felt his pulse and saw he had a fever. إجا يجِسّ النَّبُض حَتَّى يُعرُف شِيسَوِّي [ʔiǰa yǰiss ʔannabuδ̣ ħatta yuʕruf šiysawwi:] He came to feel out the situation so he would know what to do.
نابُض [na:buδ̣] *adj:* • **1.** beating, pulsating, throbbing, palpitating

ن ب ع

نِبَع [nibaʕ] *v:* • **1.** to spring, issue, originate, flow – هَالمَيّ يِنبَع مِن الجِّبال [halmayy yinbaʕ min ʔiǰǰiba:l] This water comes from the mountains. • **2.** to appear, burst forth, grow – بِالرَّبِيع، أَوراق الأَشجار تِنبَع [birrabi:ʕ, ʔawra:q ʔilʔašǰa:r tinbaʕ] In spring, the tree leaves appear.
نَبَّع [nabbaʕ] *v:* • **1.** to gush out, pour forth – ظَلّ أُحفُر إِلَى أَن يِنَبِّع الماي [δ̣all ʔuħfur ʔila ʔan yinabbiʕ ʔilma:y] Keep digging until water gushes out. • **2.** to leaf, put forth leaves – جا الرِّبِيع والأَشجار بِدَت تنَبِّع [ǰa: ʔirribi:ʕ wilʔašǰa:r bidat tnabbiʕ] Spring has come and the trees have started to leaf.
نَبِع [nabiʕ] *n:* • **1.** spring, source • **2.** growth, shoots
مَنبَع [manbaʕ] *n:* مَنابِع [mana:biʕ] *pl:* • **1.** spring, well, fountainhead, springhead source, origin
يَنبُوع [yanbu:ʕ] *n:* يَنابِيع [yana:bi:ʕ] *pl:* • **1.** spring, source, well
نابِع [na:biʕ] *adj:* • **1.** with مِن flowed (from), originated (from), gushed

ن ب غ

نِبَغ [nibaɣ] *v:* • **1.** to become renowned, become an outstanding figure – نِبَغ بِالشِّعِر بَعَد سِنّ العِشرِين [nibaɣ biššiʕir baʕad sinn ʔilʕišri:n] He became an outstanding figure in poetry after the age of twenty.
نُبُوغ [nubu:ɣ] *n:* • **1.** genius, distinction, giftedness, talent
نابِغَة [na:biɣa] *n:* نَوابِغ [nawa:biɣ] *pl:* • **1.** talented, famous, or outstanding person
نابِغ [na:biɣa] *adj:* نَوابِغ [nawa:biɣ] *pl:* • **1.** talented, brilliant, outstanding

ن ب ق

نُبَق [nubag] *v:* • **1.** to jump up (out of water) – شُوف هَالسِّمكَة نُبقَت مِن هناك [šu:f hassimča nubgat min hna:k] Look at that fish that jumped up over there. شُوف البَطَّة دَتغُطّ وَتُنبُق بِالمَيّ [šu:f ʔilbaṭṭa dadɣuṭṭ wtunbug bilmayy] Look at the duck diving under and coming up in the water. • **2.** to speak up suddenly, to butt in – إحنا دَنِحكِي وَحَدنا. إنتَ لُويش دَتُنبُق وِتجاوُب؟ [ʔiħna daniħči waħadna. ʔinta luwi:š datunbug wdǰa:wub?] We're talking among ourselves. Why are you butting in and answering?
نَبُق [nabug] *n:* • **1.** jujube(s) • **2.** jujube tree(s) • **3.** jumping up (out of the water), speaking up suddenly
نَبقَة [nabga] *n:* نَبقات [nabga:t] *pl:* • **1.** jujube

ن ب ل

نَبَّل [nabbal] *v:* • **1.** to point, sharpen to a point – نَبِّل العُودَة حَتَّى تِقدَر تُزرُف بِيها [nabbil ʔilʕu:da ħatta tigdar tuzruf bi:ha] Sharpen the stick so you can poke a hole with it.
نُبُل [nubul] *n:* • **1.** nobleness, high-mindedness – نُبلَه ما يخَلِّيه يِحكِي عالنّاس [nublah ma: yxalli:h yiħči ʕanna:s] His nobleness keeps him from talking about people.
نَبلَة، نِبالَة [nabla, niba:la] *n:* نَبلات، نِبالات [nabla:t, niba:la:t] *pl:* • **1.** point, tip
نَبِيل [nabi:l] *adj:* • **1.** aristocratic, highborn, patrician, distinguished – هُوَّ مِن عائِلَة نَبِيلَة [huwwa min ʕa:ʔila nabi:la] He's from a distinguished family.
منَبَّل [mnabbal] *adj:* • **1.** sharp-tipped
أَنبَل [ʔanbal] *comparative adjective:* • **1.** nobler, more noble-minded, more generous

ن ب ه

نَبَّه [nabbah] *v:* • **1.** to inform, notify, alert – ما دَيدري شدَيصِير بَالدّائِرَة. لازِم إنّبّهَه [ma: dayidri šdayṣi:r bidda:ʔira. la:zim ʔinnabbihah] He doesn't know what's happening in the office. We'd better put him wise. • **2.** to remind – لا تِنسَى تنَبِّهنِي عَلَى قَضِيتَك [la: tinsa: tnabbihni ʕala qaδ̣i:tak] Don't forget to remind me about your matter. مِن يصِير الوَقِت، نَبِّهنِي [min yṣi:r ʔilwakit, nabbihni] When the time comes, remind me.
تنَبَّه [tnabbah] *v:* • **1.** to notice, note, realize, become aware – ما يِتنَبَّه إلّا واحِد يِنَبّهَه [ma: yitnabbah ʔilla wa:ħid yinabbhah] He won't notice unless someone informs him.
اِنتِبَه [ʔintibah] *v:* • **1.** to understand, realize, grasp, comprehend – ما اِنتِبَهت لِلنُّكتَة مالتَك [ma: ʔintibahit linnukta ma:ltak] I didn't get your joke. • **2.** to pay attention – إذا تِنتِبِه بِالصَّفّ، تِفهَم الدَّرِس [ʔiδa tintibih biṣṣaff, tifham ʔiddaris] If you pay attention in class, you'll understand the lesson. اِنتِبِه عَلَى نَفسَك، تَرَة فلُوسَك راح تِخلَص [ʔintibih ʕala nafsak, tara flu:sak ra:h tixlaṣ] Come to your senses or your money will be gone.

ن

نَباهَة [naba:ha] *n:* • **1.** awareness, alertness • **2.** intelligence

إنتِباه [ʔintiba:h] *n:* • **1.** attention, attentiveness, alertness, vigilance

مُنَبِّه [munabbih] *adj:* • **1.** awakening, arousing – ساعَة مُنَبِّهَة [sa:ʕa munabbiha] alarm clock. • **2.** stimulant – دُوا مُنَبِّه [duwa: munabbih] a stimulant (medicine). • **3.** pl. مُنَبِّهات stimulants, stimulative agents, excitants

نَبِيه [nabi:h] *adj:* • **1.** alert, aware, eminent, superior • **2.** understanding, judicious, discerning, sensible

مِتنَبِّه [mitnabbih] *adj:* • **1.** alert, awake, watchful

مِنتبِه [mintibih] *adj:* • **1.** alert, awake, careful

ن ب و

نَبِي [nabi] *n:* أنبِياء [ʔanbiya:ʔ] *pl:* • **1.** prophet • **2.** النَّبِي the Prophet Mohammad

نُبُوَّة [nubuwwa] *n:* • **1.** prophethood

نَبَوِي [nabawi] *adj:* • **1.** prophetic, pertaining to the Prophet Mohammed

ن ت ج

نِتَج [nitaǰ] *v:* • **1.** with مِن or عَن: to result, ensue, arise, be a result – ما نِتَج شِي مِن هالإجتِماع [ma: nitaǰ ši min halʔiǰtima:ʕ] Nothing resulted from that meeting.

أنتَج [ʔantaǰ] *v:* • **1.** to produce, yield, bring forth, make – إذا تسَمِّد القاع زين، تِنتِج أكثَر [ʔiða tsammid ʔilga:ʕ zi:n, tintiǰ ʔakθar] If you fertilize the ground well, it'll yield more. العِراق يِنتِج حُبُوب وتُمُور بكَثرَة [ʔilʕira:q yintiǰ ħubu:b wtumu:r bkaθra] Iraq produces grain and dates in abundance.

إستَنتَج [ʔistantaǰ] *v:* • **1.** to conclude, infer, deduce, gather – إستَنتَجِت مِن كَلامَه يحِبّ يِدرُس [ʔistantaǰit min kala:mah yħibb yidrus] I concluded from his talk that he likes to study. منين جِبت هالمَعلُومات؟ لازِم إستَنتَجِتها مِن التَّقرِير [mni:n ǰibit halmaʕlu:ma:t? la:zim ʔistantaǰitha min ʔittaqri:r] Where did you get this information? You must have deduced it from the report.

مُنتَج [muntaǰ] *n:* مُنتَجات [muntaǰa:t] *pl:* • **1.** produce, product

نَتِيجَة [nati:ǰa] *n:* نَتائِج [nata:ʔiǰ] *pl:* • **1.** result, outcome, upshot, consequence – نَتائِج الامتِحان ما طِلعَت لهَسَّة [nata:ʔiǰ ʔilʔimtiħa:n ma: ṭilʕat lhassa] The results of the exam haven't come out yet. إجَوا الشُّرطَة. خَلّي نشُوف النَّتِيجَة [ʔiǰaw ʔiššurṭa. xalli: nšu:f ʔinnati:ǰa] The police have come. Let's see what happens. هَذا نَتِيجتَه يرُوح لِلسِّجِن [ha:ða nati:ǰtah yiru:ħ lissiǰin] He'll end up going to jail. النَّتِيجَة وِيّاك؟ ما قِتلَك مِيَّة مَرَّة لا تِلعَب بغَراضِي؟ [ʔinnati:ǰa wiyya:k? ma: gitlak miyyat marra la: tilʕab byara:ḍi?] What's going to come of you? Haven't I told you a hundred times not to play with my things? بِالنَّتِيجَة، ما حَصَّلنا شِي [binnati:ǰa, ma: ħaṣṣalna ši] In the end, we gained nothing.

إنتاج [ʔinta:ǰ] *n:* • **1.** producing, manufacturing, making • **2.** production • **3.** output

إستِنتاج [ʔistinta:ǰ] *n:* إستِنتاجات [ʔistinta:ǰa:t] *pl:* • **1.** inference, conclusion

إنتاجِيَّة [ʔinta:ǰiyya] *n:* • **1.** productivity

مُنتِج [muntiǰ] *adj:* • **1.** fruitful, productive, prolific • **2.** pl. مُنتِجِين producer, maker, manufacturer

ناتِج [na:tiǰ] *adj:* • **1.** resultant, resulting, proceeding, deriving

مَنتُوج [mantu:ǰ] *adj:* مَنتُوجات [mantu:ǰa:t] *pl:* • **1.** product, creation

إنتاجِي [ʔinta:ǰi] *adj:* • **1.** productive, related to production

ن ت ر

نِتَر [nitar] *v:* • **1.** to snap, shout, bark, speak sharply – مِن شافنِي ألعَب بالرّاديُو، نِتَر بِيّا [min ša:fni ʔalʕab birra:dyu, nitar biyya] When he saw me playing with the radio, he shouted at me.

نَتِر [natir] *n:* • **1.** shouting, yelling, speaking sharply and loud • **2.** speaking abruptly or sharply, shouting

نَترَة [natra] *n:* نَترات [natra:t] *pl:* • **1.** yell, yelling, shout, shouting, act of speaking sharply,

ن ت ر و ج ن

نِترُوجِين [nitruǰi:n] *n:* • **1.** nitrogen

ن ت ش

نِتَش [nitaš] *v:* • **1.** to snatch, grab away – فَدّ وَلَد نِتَش الخُبُز مِن إيدِي [fadd walad nitaš ʔilxubuz min ʔi:di] Some boy snathed the bread from my hand.

إنِّتَش [ʔinnitaš] *v:* • **1.** pass. of نِتَش: to be snatched, to be grabbed away

نَتِش [natiš] *n:* • **1.** snatching, grabbing away

ن ت ف

نِتَف [nitaf] *v:* • **1.** to pluck, pull out, tear out – نِتَف كَم رِيشَة مِن الدِّجاج [nitaf čam ri:ša min ʔiddiǰa:ǰ] He plucked some feathers from the chicken. • **2.** to strike, hit – نِتَفَه ببُوكس وَوَقَّعَه [nitafah bibu:ks wwaggaʕah] He punched him and knocked him down. الأستاذ نِتَفنِي بخوش دَرَجَة [ʔilʔusta:ð nitafni bxu:š daraǰa] The professor fixed me up with a good grade. • **3.** to deal harshly with, be stern with – الوَزِير الجِّدِيد نِتَفَه لِلمُلاحِظ مالنَا و سَوّاه كاتِب [ʔilwazi:r ʔiǰǰidi:d nitafah lilmula:ħið ma:lna w sawwa:h ka:tib] The new minister dealt harshly with our supervisor and made him a clerk. نِتَفَه خُوش نَتفَة [nitafah xu:š natfa] He really told him off.

نَتَّف [nattaf] *v:* • **1.** to pluck, pull out, tear out – الجّاهِل نَتَّف ذَيل الطَّير [ʔiǰǰa:hil nattaf ðayl ʔiṭṭayr] The child pulled out the bird's tail.

تنَتَّف [tnattaf] *v:* • **1.** to be plucked, pulled out – رِيش الدِّجاجَة يِتنَتَّف بسُهُولَة [ri:š ʔiddiǰa:ǰa yitnattaf bsuhu:la] The chicken's feathers can be plucked easily.

ن

تناتف [tnaːtaf] *v:* • **1.** to exchange (blows) – ظَلّوا يِتناتفون بُوكسات ساعَة زَمان [ðallaw yitnaːtfuːn buːksaːt saːʕa zamaːn] They kept on exchanging punches for a whole hour.
نَتف [natif] *n:* • **1.** pulling out, tearing out
نِتفَة [nitfa] *n:* نِتفات [nitfaːt] *pl:* • **1.** pinch, dash, small amount
مَنتُوف [mantuːf] *adj:* مَنتُوفِين [mantuːfiːn] *pl:* • **1.** plucked • **2.** pl. مَنتُوفِين rascal, bounder, rogue

ن ت ل
نِتَل [nital] *v:* • **1.** to jerk, tug at – اِنتِل الطَّيّارَة حَتَّى تِعلَى [ʔintil ʔiṭṭayyaːra ħatta tiʕlaː] Jerk the kite so it will go up. إذا البِسمار ما يِنشِلِع، اِنتِلَه حيل [ʔiða ʔilbismaːr maː yinšiliʕ, ʔinitlah ħiːl] If the nail won't come out, jerk it hard. • **2.** to snag, hook, catch – نِتَل ثوبَه بِالبِسمار [nital θuːbah bilbismaːr] He snagged his shirt on the nail. • **3.** to shock, give an electrical shock – دِير بالَك لا يِنتِلَك الوايَر [diːr baːlak laː ynitlak ʔilwaːyar] Be careful the wire doesn't shock you. • **4.** (of fish) to bite, take bait – لا تِتحَرَّك تَرَة السِّمكَة دَتِنتِل [laː titħarrak tara ʔissimča datintil] Don't move; the fish is biting.
نَتَّل [nattal] *v:* • **1.** to jerk hard, tug repeatedly – شقَدّ ما تنَتِّل، ما يفِيد. الهَوا واقُف [šgadd maː tnattil, maː yfiːd. ʔilhawa waːguf] No matter how much you jerk it won't help. The wind's stopped.
اِنّتَل [ʔinnital] *v:* • **1.** to become snagged, be caught – اِنِتلَت عَباتَه بِالبِسمار [ʔinitlat ʕabaːtah bilbismaːr] His aba got snagged on the nail. • **2.** to be shocked, get a shock – اِنِتلِت مِن كِنِت أشِدّ الكلُوب [ʔinitalit min činit ʔašidd ʔilgluːb] I got a shock as I was replacing the bulb.
نَتِل [natil] *n:* • **1.** jerking, tugging at
نَتلَة [natla] *n:* نَتلات [natlaːt] *pl:* • **1.** jerk, quick tug, pull • **2.** electrical shock
نَتّالَة [nattaːla] *n:* نَتّالات [nattaːlaːt] *pl:* • **1.** small fish-hook and line

ن ث ث
نَثّ [naθθ] *v:* • **1.** to rain lightly, sprinkle, drizzle – ما كان يِجري مَيّ هوايَة بِالشّوارِع لِأَنّ كانَت تنِثّ [maː čaːn yiǰri mayy hwaːya biššawaːriʕ liʔann čaːnat tniθθ] There wasn't much water flowing in the streets because it was just sprinkling.
نَثّ [naθθ] *n:* • **1.** raining lightly, sprinkling

ن ث ر
نِثَر [niθar] *v:* • **1.** to scatter, strew, sprinkle – نِثرَوا وَرِد عَليه [niθraw warid ʕaliːh] They scattered flowers on him. نِثرَت شَعَرها وقامَت تُرقُص [niθrat šaʕarha wgaːmat turguṣ] She let her hair down and started dancing.
تناثَر [tnaːθar] *v:* • **1.** to be scattered about, be strewn around – شَقّ المُخَدَّة وَتناثَر الرِّيش مِنها [šagg ʔilmuxadda wtnaːθar ʔirriːš minha] He tore the pillow and the feathers scattered out of it.
اِنّثَر [ʔinniθar] *v:* • **1.** to be strewn, be scattered – جُنطِتي وُقعَت مِن السَّيّارَة وَكُلّ غَراضِي اِنّثرَت بِالقاع [ǰunițti wugʕat min ʔissayyaːra wkull γaraːði ʔinniθrat bilgaːʕ] My suitcase fell from the car and all my things got scattered on the ground.
نَثِر [naθir] *n:* • **1.** scattering, strewing about • **2.** prose
نَثرِيّات [naθriyyaːt] *n:* • **1.** (pl. only) incidentals, sundries, miscellany – مَصارِيف نَثرِيَّة [maṣaːriːf naθriyya] incidental expenses.
نَثري [naθri] *adj:* نَثرِيّات [naθriyyaːt] *pl:* • **1.** prose, prosaic • **2.** small, little, insignificant, trifling
مَنثُور [manθuːr] *adj:* • **1.** scattered, dispersed
مِتناثِر [mitnaːθir] *adj:* • **1.** scattered, dispersed

ن ث ي
نِثيَة [niθya] *n:* نثايا [nθaːya] *pl:* • **1.** female

ن ج ب
نَجابَة [naǰaːba] *n:* • **1.** nobility, nobleness, high-mindedness, distinction
نَجِيب [naǰiːb] *adj:* نَجِيبِين، نُجَباء [naǰiːbiːn, nuǰabaːʔ] *pl:* • **1.** noble, high-minded, distinguished

ن ج ح
نِجَح [niǰaħ] *v:* • **1.** to succeed, be successful – نِجَح بِهَالشّغلَة لِأَنّ كان عِندَه صُرمايَة زينَة [niǰaħ bhaššaγla liʔann čaːn ʕindah ṣurmaːya ziːna] He succeeded in this business because he had a good amount of capital. الطَّبِيب قلّي العَمَلِيَّة نِجحَت وَبَعَد ماكُو خَطَر عَليه [ʔiṭṭabiːb galli ʔilʕamaliyya niǰħat wabaʕad maːku xaṭar ʕaliːh] The doctor told me the operation was a success and that he was no longer in danger. • **2.** to pass – لَمّا نِجَح، أَبُوه هِداله ساعَة [lamma niǰaħ, ʔabuːh hidaːlah saːʕa] When he passed, his father presented him with a watch. إبنَك نِجَح لِلصَّفّ الثّانِي [ʔibnak niǰaħ lișșaff ʔiθθaːni] Your son passed to the second grade.
نَجَّح [naǰǰaħ] *v:* • **1.** to pass, promote – نَجَّح إبنَك بِدُون اِستِحقاق [naǰǰaħ ʔibnak biduːn ʔistiħqaːq] He passed your son without justification.
نَجاح [naǰaːħ] *n:* • **1.** success • **2.** passing – دَرَجَة نَجاح [daraǰat naǰaːħ] a passing grade.
ناجِح [naːǰiħ] *adj:* • **1.** successful, passing, having passed (examination)

ن ج د
نِجَد [niǰad] *v:* • **1.** to assist, help, aid, support
اِستَنجَد [ʔistanǰad] *v:* • **1.** to appeal for aid, seek help – مِن حاصَرهُم العَدُو، اِستَنجِدَوا بِينا [min ħaːṣarhum ʔilʕadu, ʔistanǰidaw biːna] When the enemy encircled them, they appealed to us for aid.

نَجْدَة [najda] *n:* نَجدات [najda:t] *pl:* • **1.** support, aid, help, assistance – شُرطَة النَّجدَة [šurṭat ʔinnajda] police rescue squad.
اِستِنجاد [ʔistinja:d] *n:* • **1.** seeking help, appealing for aid

ن ج ر 1

نِجَر [nijar] *v:* • **1.** to hew, hack, chop – جِيب الفاس وَإنجِر هَالخِشبَة [ji:b ʔilfa:s wʔinjir halxišba] Bring the hatchet and chop this piece of wood. اِلتَمّوا عَليه وَنِجرُوه خُوش نَجرَة [ʔiltammaw ʕali:h wnijru:h xu:š najra] They ganged up on him and gave him a good beating. مُعَلِّم الكِيميا نِجَرني بِصِفِر [muʕallim ʔilki:mya nijarni bṣifir] The chemistry instructor gave me a zero.
نَجِر [najir] *n:* • **1.** chopping, carpentry
نَجرَة [najra] *n:* نَجرات [najra:t] *pl:* • **1.** chopping, hacking • **2.** beating
نَجّار [najja:r] *n:* نَجّارِين [najja:ri:n] *pl:* • **1.** carpenter, cabinet maker
نِجارَة [nija:ra, nja:ra] *n:* • **1.** carpentry, the carpenter's trade – مَعمَل نِجارَة [maʕmal nija:ra] cabinet shop. • **2.** wood shavings

ن ج ر 2

نَجِر [načir] *adj:* • **1.** skittish, wary, timid – ما تِقدَر تأكِّل هَالعَصفُور مِن إيدَك لِأَنّ نَجِر [ma: tigdar tʔakkil halʕaṣfu:r min ʔi:dak liʔann načir] You can't feed this bird from your hand because he's timid. • **2.** shy, bashful – لا تصِير نَجِر. إطلَع أقعُد ويّا الخُطّار [la: tṣi:r načir. ʔiṭlaʕ ʔugʕud wiyya ʔilxuṭṭa:r] Don't be shy. Go out and sit with the guests.

ن ج ز

نِجَز [nijaz] *v:* • **1.** to complete, to carry out, to accomplish, to fulfill
اِنجاز [ʔinja:z] *n:* اِنجازات [ʔinja:za:t] *pl:* • **1.** achievement, realization, implementation, accomplishment
مُنجَزات [munjaza:t] *n:* • **1.** pl. only accomplishments, achievements, successes
مُنجَز [munjaz] *adj:* • **1.** completed, finished

ن ج س

نِجَس [nijas, nigas] *v:* • **1.** to become ritually unclean, become impure – إذا الكَلِب ياكُل بِالماعُون، الماعُون يِنجَس [ʔiða ʔiččalib ya:kul bilma:ʕu:n, ʔilma:ʕu:n yingas] If the dog eats from the plate, the plate becomes unclean.
نَجَّس [najjas, naggas] *v:* • **1.** to taint, foul, make dirty – الكَلِب، إذا يِمشِي بِالمَيّ، يِنَجّسَه [ʔiččalib, ʔiða yimši bilmayy, yinaggsah] If the dog walks in the water, he makes it dirty. • **2.** to foul oneself, soil oneself – إبنِك نَجَّس. بَدِّلِيلَه [ʔibnič naggas. baddili:lah] Your son has dirtied his pants. Change him.
تنَجَّس [tnaggas] *v:* • **1.** to become ritually unclean, become impure – لا تِمشِي مِن هنا تَرَة تِتنَجَّس [la: timši min hina: tara titnaggas] Don't walk through here or you'll be made unclean. أَتنَجَّس أحكِي ويّا واحِد مِثلَك [ʔatnaggas ʔaħči wiyya wa:ħid miθlak] I'd be dirtying myself speaking to someone like you.
اِستَنجَس [ʔistangas] *v:* • **1.** to consider ritually unclean – يِستَنجِس يِشرَب بِكلاص غَيرَه [yistangis yišrab bigla:ṣ ɣayrah] He feels it's dirty to drink out of somebody else's glass. هُوَّ يِستَنجِس مِن الكِلاب [huwwa yistangis min ʔiččila:b] He considers dogs dirty.
نَجاسَة [naja:sa, naga:sa] *n:* • **1.** impurity
نَجِس [najis, nagis] *adj:* • **1.** ritually unclean, impure • **2.** dirty, filthy, tainted – هَالمَيّ نَجِس. لا تِغسِل بِيه [halmayy nagis. la: tiɣsil bi:h] This water is filthy. Don't wash in it. هَذا فَدّ واحِد نَجِس. ما أَثِق بِيه [ha:ða fadd wa:ħid nagis. ma: ʔaθiq bi:h] He's a loathsome fellow. I don't trust him.
مِنَجِّس [mnaggis] *adj:* • **1.** defiled, excreted
أَنجَس [ʔangas] *comparative adjective:* • **1.** more or most filthy, dirty

ن ج ف

نَجَف [najaf] *n:* • **1.** Najaf is a town in central Iraq
نَجَفِي [najafi] *adj:* • **1.** Najafite, from Najaf

ن ج ل 1

مِنجَل [minjal] *n:* مَناجِل [mana:jil] *pl:* • **1.** sickle • **2.** scythe

ن ج ل 2

نَجِل [najil] *n:* • **1.** son, scion

ن ج م

نَجَّم [najjam] *v:* • **1.** to soar, fly up, rise high – شُوف الطَّيّارَة شلُون نَجَّمَت [šu:f ʔiṭṭiyya:ra šlu:n najjimat] Look how high the kite has soared!
نَجِم [najim] *n:* نُجُوم [nuju:m] *pl:* • **1.** star • **2.** lucky star, fortune – نَجمَه دَيِصعَد يوم عَلَى يوم [najmah dayiṣʕad yu:m ʕala yu:m] His lucky star is climbing higher day after day. • **3.** motion picture star
نَجمَة [najma] *n:* نَجمات [najma:t] *pl:* • **1.** star • **2.** asterisk • **3.** female motion picture star
مَنجَم [manjam] *n:* مَناجِم [mana:jim] *pl:* • **1.** mine (for minerals)
مُنَجِّم [munajjim] *n:* مُنَجِّمِين [munajjimi:n] *pl:* • **1.** astrologer
تَنجِيم [tanji:m] *n:* • **1.** astrology

ن ج ن

نجانَة [nja:na] *n:* نجانات [nja:na:t] *pl:* • **1.** basin

ن ج و

نِجا [nija:] *v:* • **1.** to escape, be saved, be rescued – نِجا مِن المَوت بِإعجُوبَة [nija: min ʔilmawt bʔiʕju:ba] He escaped death by a miracle.

ن

نَجّا [najja:] *v:* • **1.** to rescue, deliver, save – الله نَجّاه مِن المَوت [ʔallah najja:h min ʔilmawt] God saved him from death. مِنُو يِقدَر يِنَجّيك مِنّي؟ [minu yigdar ynajji:k minni?] Who can rescue you from me?
ناجَى [na:ja:] *v:* • **1.** to confide in, entrust a secret to – يُقعُد نُصّ اللّيل يصَلّي وَيناجي رَبّه [yugʕud nuṣṣ ʔillayl yṣalli wyna:ji rabbah] He sits half the night praying and confiding in his God. • **2.** to take into one's confidence, converse confidentially, exchange secrets
نَجاة [naja:t] *n:* • **1.** escape, deliverance, salvation – كُلّنا هَنّيناه بِنَجاته بحادِث الطَّيّارَة [kullna hanni:na:h bnaja:tah bħa:diθ ʔiṭṭayya:ra] We all congratulated him on his escape from the plane crash.
مُناجاة [muna:ja:t] *n:* • **1.** secret conversation, confidentail talk, dialogue with God

ن ح ت
نِحَت [niħat] *v:* • **1.** to hew, carve, chisel, sculpture – نِحَت إسمَه عَلى صَخرَة [niħat ʔismah ʕala ṣaxra] He chiseled his name on a rock. الفَنّان نِحَت تِمثال لرَئِيس الجَمهُورِيَّة [ʔilfanna:n niħat timθa:l lraʔi:s ʔijjamhu:riyya] The artist sculptured a statue of the president of the republic.
نَحِت [naħit] *n:* • **1.** stonework, stonecutting • **2.** sculpturing, sculpture
نَحّات [naħħa:t] *adj:* نَحّاتَة، نَحّاتِين [naħħa:ta, naħħa:ti:n] *pl:* • **1.** stonecutter, stonemason • **2.** sculptor
مَنحُوت [manħu:t] *adj:* • **1.** sculpted

ن ح ر
نِحَر [niħar] *v:* • **1.** to slaughter, to kill
اِنتِحَر [ʔintiħar] *v:* • **1.** to commit suicide – اِنتِحَر لِأنّ ما حَبَّته [ʔintiħar liʔann ma: ħabbatah] He committed suicide because she didn't love him.
نَحِر [naħir] *n:* • **1.** slaughtering, killing, butchering
اِنتِحار [ʔintiħa:r] *n:* اِنتِحارات [ʔintiħa:ra:t] *pl:* • **1.** suicide
مِنتِحِر [mintiħir] *adj:* • **1.** person who committed suicide

ن ح س
نِحَس [niħas] *v:* • **1.** to be in a bad mood, to become grumpy • **2.** to make unhappy, to bring bad luck
نُحاس [nuħa:s] *n:* • **1.** copper – نُحاس أصفَر [nuħa:s ʔaṣfar] brass.
نَحاسَة [naħa:sa] *n:* • **1.** grumpiness, surliness, cloudiness, moodiness
نَحِس [naħis] *adj:* • **1.** temperamental, moody – شلُون نَحِس! لا يِتصادَق وِيّا أَحَّد وَلا يِحكِي شِي [šlu:n naħis! la: yitṣa:daq wiyya ʔaħħad wala yiħči ši] How moody he is! He doesn't make friends with anyone and he doesn't say anything. إبني نَحِس. يِبكِي عَلَى طُول وَما يِنطِي شِي لِأَخُوه [ʔibni naħis. yibči ʕala ṭu:l wma yinṭi: ši lʔaxu:h] My son is temperamental. He cries all the time and doesn't give his brother anything. • **2.** unlucky, luckless, disastrous, calamitous
نُحاسِي [nuħa:si] *adj:* • **1.** copper, made of copper – تَماثِيل نُحاسِيَّة [tama:θi:l nuħa:siyya] copper statues.
مَنحُوس [manħu:s] *adj:* • **1.** luckless, ill-fated, unfortunate, ominous, unlucky
أَنحَس [ʔanħas] *comparative adjective:* • **1.** more or most temperamental

ن ح ل
نَحَل [naħal] *n:* • **1.** (coll.) bee(s)
نَحلَة [naħla] *n:* نَحلات [naħla:t] *pl:* • **1.** bee
مَنحَل [manħal] *n:* مَناحِل [mana:ħil] *pl:* • **1.** beehive, apicultural station
نِحُول [niħu:l] *n:* • **1.** skinniness, thinness, slimness, slenderness,
اِنتِحال [ʔintiħa:l] *n:* • **1.** undue assumption, arrogation • **2.** literary theft, plagiarism • **3.** act of assuming a name, alias, pseudonym
نَحِيل [naħi:l] *adj:* • **1.** skinny, lean, slender, slim
مِنتِحِل [mintiħil] *adj:* • **1.** plagiarizing, plagiarist • **2.** impersonating, (as n:) impersonator
مِنتِحَل [mintiħal] *adj:* • **1.** usurped; plagiarized

ن ح و
تنَحَّى [tnaħħa:] *v:* • **1.** to quit, to step aside, to walk away, withdraw (from)
نَحْو [naħw] *n:* • **1.** syntax, grammar
تَنَحّي [tanaħħi] *n:* • **1.** stepping aside, withdrawing, moving away
ناحِيَة [na:ħiya] *n:* نَواحِي [nawa:ħi] *pl:* • **1.** viewpoint, standpoint, aspect, facet – دِرَسنا القَضِيَّة مِن جَمِيع نَواحِيها [dirasna ʔilqaḍiyya min jami:ʕ nawa:ħi:ha] We studied the matter in all its aspects. • **2.** subdivision of a subprovince قَضاء roughly comparable to a precinct or municipality • **3.** with مِن with regard to, in respect to, as for, concerning, on the part of – مِن ناحِيتِي، ما عِندِي مانِع [min na:ħi:ti, ma: ʕindi ma:niʕ] As for me, I have no objection. • **4.** with مِن on the one hand, for one thing – مِن ناحِيَة تِحكِي عَلِيه، وَكُلّ يوم تِطلَع وِيّاه [min na:ħiya tiħči ʕali:h, wkull yu:m tiṭlaʕ wiyya:h] On the one hand you talk against him, and then every day you go out with him.
تَنحِيَة [tanħiya] *n:* • **1.** elimination, removal
نَحَوِي [naħawi] *adj:* • **1.** syntactical, grammatical
نَحو [naħw] *preposition:* • **1.** towards, approximately

ن خ ب
نَخَّب [naxxab] *v:* • **1.** to make holes in, riddle with holes – الزِّنجار نَخَّب التَّنَكَة [ʔizzinja:r naxxab ʔittanaka] The rust ate holes in the can. هَالكِيس منَخَّب وَدَيُوقَع مِنَّه الطَّحِين [hačči:s mnaxxab wadayu:gaʕ minnah ʔiṭṭiħi:n] This bag has holes in it and the flour is falling out of it.

اِنتِخَب [ʔintixab] *v:* • **1.** to select, pick, choose – كُلّها بنَفِس السِّعِر. اِنتِخِب ياهُو اللّي تِعجِبَك [kullha bnafis ʔissiʕir. ʔintixib ya:hu ʔilli tiʕijbak] They're all the same price. Select any one you like. • **2.** to elect, to vote for – اِنتِخبَوه رَئِيس لحِزِبهُم [ʔintixbawh raʔi:s lħizibhum] They elected him head of their party.
نُخبَة [nuxba] *n:* • **1.** selected piece, selected item, group • **2.** the pick, elite, cream
ناخِب [na:xib] *n:* • **1.** voter, elector, consistuent
مُنتَخِب [muntaxib] *n:* • **1.** voter, elector, consistuent
مُنتَخَب [muntaxab] *n:* • **1.** representative, selected team (in sport), national team
اِنتِخاب [ʔintixa:b] *n:* اِنتِخابات [ʔintixa:ba:t] *pl:* • **1.** election • **2.** choice, selection
مُنتَخَب [muntaxab] *adj:* • **1.** chosen, elected, selected
اِنتِخابِي [ʔintixa:bi] *adj:* • **1.** election • **2.** electoral – حَملَة اِنتِخابِيَّة [ħamla ʔintixa:biyya] election campaign.

ن خ ر

نِخَر [nixar] *v:* • **1.** to decompose, to spoil, to crumble, to desintegrate
مَنخَر [manxar] *n:* مَناخِر [mana:xir] *pl:* • **1.** nostril
مِنخار [minxa:r] *n:* مَناخِير [mana:xi:r] *pl:* • **1.** nostril
مَنخُور [manxu:r] *adj:* • **1.** wormy, worm-eaten • **2.** decayed, rotten

ن خ ل

نِخَل [nixal] *v:* • **1.** to sift – نِخلَت الطِّحِين قَبُل ما تعِجنَه [nixlat ʔiṭṭiħi:n gabul ma: tʕijnah] She sifted the flour before she made dough from it. • **2.** sieve out
اِنّخَل [ʔinnixal] *v:* • **1.** pass. of نِخَل: to be sifted
نَخَل [naxal] *n:* • **1.** (coll.) date palm(s)
نَخلَة [naxla] *n:* نَخلات [naxla:t] *pl:* • **1.** date palm
مُنخُل [munxul] *n:* مَناخِل [mana:xil] *pl:* • **1.** sifter, sieve
نَخِيل [naxi:l] *n:* • **1.** (coll.) palm tree
نخالَة [nxa:la] *n:* • **1.** the residue left after sifting • **2.** bran

ن خ و

نِخا [nixa:] *v:* • **1.** to appeal to the pride of, awaken the sense of honor – إذا تِنخِيه، يساعدَك [ʔiða tinxi:h, ysa:ʕdak] If you arouse his sense of honor, he'll help you.
نَخّى [naxxa:] *v:* • **1.** same as نِخَى: to appeal to the pride of, awaken the sense of honor
اِنّخَى [ʔinnixa:] *v:* • **1.** pass. of نِخَى to have one's pride appealed to, to have one's sense of honor aroused – شقَدّ ما تِتوَسَّل بِيه، ما يِنّخِي [šgadd ma: titwassal bi:h, ma: yinnixi] No matter how much you beg of him, his sense of honor won't be aroused.
نَخوَة [naxwa] *n:* • **1.** pride, dignity, sense of honor, self-respect – هَذا صاحِب نَخوَة. إذا شاف مَرَة تِحتاج مُساعَدَة يساعِدها [ha:ða ṣa:ħib naxwa. ʔiða ša:f mara tiħta:ǰ musa:ʕada ysa:ʕidha] He's an honorable man. If he saw a woman who needs help, he'd help her.

ن د ب

نِدَب [nidab] *v:* • **1.** to mourn, lament, bewail
نَدِب [nadib] *n:* • **1.** weeping, wailing, lamentation
ندبَة [nidba] *n:* أنداب، ندُوب [ʔanda:b, ndu:b] *pl:* • **1.** scar, cicatrice, scabby wound
مَندُوب [mandu:b] *n:* مَندُوبِين [mandu:bi:n] *pl:* • **1.** delegate, representative
اِنتِداب [ʔintida:b] *n:* • **1.** appointment, deputation, charging, assignment, • **2.** mandate (over a territory)
مُنتَدَب [muntadab] *adj:* • **1.** deputized, delegated, authorized, appointed, entrusted, assigned

ن د د

نِدّ [nidd] *n:* أنداد [ʔanda:d] *pl:* • **1.** match • **2.** peer, equal

ن د ر 1

نِدَر [nidar] *v:* • **1.** to become rare, become scarce – التِّفّاح يِندُر بِهَالمَوسِم [ʔittiffa:ħ yindur bhalmawsim] Apples get scarce at this season.
تنَدَّر [tnaddar] *v:* • **1.** to be clever, display one's cleverness – مِن ما تُعرُف شِي، تُسكُت؛ بَسّ مِن تُعرُف شوَيَّة، تِتنَدَّر [min ma: tuʕruf ši, tuskut; bass min tuʕruf šwayya, titnaddar] When you don't know anything, you remain silent; but when you know a little, you make yourself look good. لا تِتنَدَّرِين. قُومِي سَوِّيلِي أكِل [la: titnaddiri:n. gu:mi sawwi:li ʔakil] Don't act smart. Go make me some food. • **2.** to be industrious, work diligently – النَّهار كُلَّه ما تِشتُغُل. مِن يِجِي رَجِلها تِتنَدَّر [ʔinnaha:r kullah ma: tištuɣul. min yiǰi raǰilha titnaddar] All day she doesn't work. When her husband comes she makes herself busy.
نُدرَة [nudra] *n:* • **1.** rareness, rarity
نَدارَة [nada:ra] *n:* • **1.** cleverness, efficiency • **2.** diligence, industriousness
نادِر [na:dir] *adj:* • **1.** rare, infrequent, uncommon – لَو ما الألماس نادِر، ما كان صار غالِي [law ma: ʔilʔalma:z na:dir, ma: ča:n ṣa:r ɣa:li] If diamonds weren't rare, they wouldn't be expensive. • **2.** diligent, industrious, able – مَرتَك أمّ بَيت نادرَة [martak ʔumm bayt na:dra] Your wife is an industrious housekeeper.
نادِراً [na:diran] *adverbial:* • **1.** rarely, seldom – نادِراً تُمطُر بِهالشَّهَر [na:diran tumṭur bhaššahar] It rarely rains in this month.

ن د ر 2

مَندَر [mindar, mandar] *n:* مَنادِر [mana:dir.] *pl:* • **1.** cushion

ن

ن د ف

نَدَف [nidaf] *v:* • **1.** to tease, fluff (cotton) – نِدَف القُطِن مال الدُّواشِك [nidaf ʔilguṭin maːl ʔidduwaːšig] He fluffed the mattress cotton.
نَدِف [nadif] *n:* • **1.** teasing, fluffing (cotton)
نَدّاف [naddaːf] *n:* نَدّافين، نداديف [naddaːfiːn, ndaːdiːf] *pl:* • **1.** cotton teaser, a man who renovates mattresses by fluffing the cotton in them
ندافة [ndaːfa] *n:* • **1.** teasing, fluffing (cotton)

ن د م

نِدَم [nidam] *v:* • **1.** to be sorry – لا تِشتِريها تَرَة تِندَم بَعدين [laː tištiriːha tara tindam baʕdiːn] Don't buy it or you'll be sorry later. نِدَم عَلَى تَصَرُّفَه [nidam ʕala taṣarrufah] He regretted his behavior.
تنَدَّم [tnaddam] *v:* • **1.** same as نِدَم: to be sorry
نَدَم [nadam] *n:* • **1.** regret, remorse
نَدامَة [nadaːma] *n:* • **1.** regret, remorse, repentance
نادِم [naːdim] *adj:* • **1.** remorseful, regretful, repentant
ندمان [nadmaːn] *adj:* • **1.** remorseful, regretful, repentant
مِتنَدِّم [mitnaddim] *adj:* • **1.** remorseful, regretful, repentant

ن د ه

نِدَه [nidah] *v:* • **1.** to call, call to, shout at – بالله، ما تِندَه أَبُويَا مِن يَمَّك؟ [ballah, maː tindah ʔabuːya min yammak?] Please, would you call to my father from where you are?
نَدِه [nadih] *n:* • **1.** calling, calling to
نَدهَة [nadha] *n:* نَدهات [nadhaːt] *pl:* • **1.** pl. ندهات instance noun of ندِه a call

ن د و

نَدَّى [naddaː] *v:* • **1.** to make wet, to moisten
نادَى [naːdaː] *v:* • **1.** to call, to shout, to announce, to call together
نَدَة [nada] *n:* • **1.** dampness • **2.** dampness, wetness, moisture, moistness
نداء [nidaːʔ] *n:* نِداءات [nidaːʔaːt] *pl:* • **1.** appeal, call, summons • **2.** telephone call • **3.** حَرف نِداء interjection (gram.)
نادِي [naːdi] *n:* نَوادِي [nawaːdi] *pl:* • **1.** club, circle, clubhouse, social organization
مُنتَدَى [muntadaː] *n:* مُنتَدَيات [muntadayaːt] *pl:* • **1.** gathering place, assembly room, club
منادِي [mnaːdi] *n:* • **1.** caller
مُناداة [munaːdaːt] *n:* • **1.** calling, shouting, call
منَدِّي [mnaddi] *adj:* • **1.** wet, damp, moist, humid
منادَى [mnaːda] *adj:* • **1.** with عَلَى called, summoned

ن ذ ر

نِذَر [niðar] *v:* • **1.** to pledge (a sacrifice) to God – نِذرَت خَرُوف إِذا يطِيب إِبنها [niðrat xaruːf ʔiða yṭiːb ʔibinha] She vowed to sacrifice a sheep if her son got well. • **2.** to notify, give notice, give a warning – نِذرونا نِطلَع مِن البَيت قَبُل نِهايَة الشَّهَر [niðrawna niṭlaʕ min ʔilbayt gabul nihaːyat ʔiššahar] They gave us notice to vacate the house before the end of the month. • **3.** to warn, caution, admonish – هَالمَرَّة نِذَرناه؛ مَرَّة اللُّخ نفُصلَه [halmarra niðarnaːh; marrat ʔillux nfuṣlah] This time we gave him a warning; next time we'll fire him.
أنذَر [ʔanðar] *v:* • **1.** to notify, issue a warning or notice to – الحُكُومَة أَنذِرَته إِذا ما يسَلِّم، يحاكمُوه غِيابِيّاً [ʔilħukuːma ʔanðiratah ʔiða maː ysallim, yħaːkmuːh ɣiyaːbiyyan] The government warned him if he doesn't give up, they'll sentence him in absentia.
اِنِّذَر [ʔinniðar] *v:* • **1.** to be warned, cautioned, admonished – اِنِّذَر مَرّتَين وَما تاب [ʔinniðar marrtayn wma taːb] He was warned twice and didn't reform.
نِذِر [niðir] *n:* نذُور [nðuːr] *pl:* • **1.** sacrificial offering (to God) • **2.** vow, solemn pledge
نَذِير [naðiːr] *n:* • **1.** consecrated to God • **2.** vowed, solemnly pledged • **3.** warner, herald
إنذار [ʔinðaːr] *n:* إنذارات [ʔinðaːraːt] *pl:* • **1.** admonition • **2.** warning – صَفّارَة الإنذار [ṣaffaːrat ʔilʔinðaːr] siren. • **3.** (military) alert
ناذِر [naːðir] *adj:* • **1.** one who has made a vow
مَنذُور [manðuːr] *adj:* • **1.** solemnly pledged, vowed, consecrated to God

ن ذ ل

نَذالَة [naðaːla] *n:* • **1.** lowness, baseness, depravity
نَذِل [naðil] *adj:* أَنذال [ʔanðaːl] *pl:* • **1.** low, base, depraved • **2.** depraved person

ن ر ج س

نَرجِس [narǰis] *n:* • **1.** daffodil, narcissus (bot.)
نَرجِسَة [narǰisa] *n:* نَرجِسات [narǰisaːt] *pl:* • **1.** daffodil, narcissus (bot.)
نَرجِسِي [narǰisi] *adj:* • **1.** narcissistic • **2.** brown color of the eye (iris)

ن ر ف ز

نَرفَز [narfaz] *v:* • **1.** to make someone tense, edgy, nervous
نَرفَزَة [narfaza] *n:* • **1.** tautness, tenseness, strain, tension
مِتنَرفِز [mitnarfiz] *adj:* • **1.** nervous, tense, strained, edgy

ن ر م د

نُرمادَة [nurmaːda] *n:* نُرمادات [nurmaːdaːt] *pl:* • **1.** hinge

ن ر ن ج

نارَنج [naːranǰ, naːrinǰ] *n:* • **1.** (coll.) bitter orange(s)
نارَنجَة [naːranǰa] *n:* نارَنجات [naːranǰaːt] *pl:* • **1.** bitter orange

ن ر و ج

نَرويج [narwiːǰ] *n:* • **1.** Norway

نَرويجِي [narwiːǰi] *adj:* • **1.** Norwegian • **2.** a Norwegian

ن ز ح

نِزَح [nizaħ] *v:* • **1.** to empty, drain, clean out – المِرحاض مَليانَة. لازِم نجِيب واحِد يِنزَحها [ʔilmirħaːð̣ malyaːna. laːzim nǰiːb waːħid yinzaħha] The septic tank is full. We've got to get some-one to empty it.

نِزَح [nizaħ] *v:* • **1.** to be far off, to immigrate, emigrate from, depart, leave

نَزِح [naziħ] *n:* • **1.** scooping out, emptying, draining, drainage

نَزّاح [nazzaːħ] *n:* نَزّاحِين، نزازِيح [nazzaːħiːn, nzaːziːħ] *pl:* • **1.** man who empties septic tanks

نِزُوح [nizuːħ] *n:* • **1.** migration, emigration

نازِح [naːziħ] *adj:* • **1.** far-off, distant, going away from home, moving to other lands, leaving for distant shores

ن ز ز

نَزّ [nazz] *v:* • **1.** to start, jump, twitch – بَسّ تنُغزَه، ينِزّ [bass tnuɣzah, ynizz] You just poke him and he jumps. • **2.** to seep, ooze, leak – مِن يزِيد الشَّطّ، القاع تنِزّ [min yziːd ʔiššaṭṭ, ʔilgaːʕ tnizz] When the river rises, the ground oozes water.

نَزّ [nazz] *n:* • **1.** starting, jumping, twitching

نِزِيز [niziːz] *n:* • **1.** seepage

ن ز ع

نِزَع [nizaʕ] *v:* • **1.** to remove, take off – نِزَع قُندَرتَه قَبُل ما خَشّ لِلجّامِع [nizaʕ qundartah gabul maː xašš lijǰaːmiʕ] He took off his shoes before he entered the mosque. نِزَع جِلد السِّمكَة [nizaʕ ǰild ʔissimča] He skinned the fish. • **2.** to disrobe, get undressed – إنزَع وَجَيِّت بِالمَيّ [ʔinzaʕ wčayyit bilmayy] Take off your clothes and jump in the water.

نَزَّع [nazzaʕ] *v:* • **1.** to disrobe, undress, remove the clothes from – نَزّعَته هدُومَه لِلطِّفِل وَغِسلَتلَه [nazzʕatah hduːmah liṭṭifil wɣislatlah] She undressed the child and washed him.

نازَع [naːzaʕ] *v:* • **1.** to fight, to contend, dispute with – نازَعهُم هوايَة عَلَى قَضِيَّة القاع [naːzaʕhum hwaːya ʕala qað̣iyyat ʔilgaːʕ] He fought with them a lot over the land deal.

اِنْزَع [ʔinnizaʕ] *v:* • **1.** to be removed, taken off – هَالثُّوب لازِق بِجِلدِي وَما دَيِنِّزِع [haθθuːb laːzig bǰildi wamaː dayinniziʕ] This shirt is stuck to my skin and can't be removed.

نَزِع [naziʕ] *n:* • **1.** taking off, removing • **2.** removal, withdrawal

نَزعَة [nazʕa] *n:* نَزعات [nazʕaːt] *pl:* • **1.** inclination, tendency, leaning – نَزعَة طائِفِيَّة [nazʕa ṭaːʔifiyya] religious prejudice.

مَنزَع [manzaʕ] *n:* مَنازِع [manaːziʕ] *pl:* • **1.** dressing room

نِزاع [nizaːʕ] *n:* نِزاعات [nizaːʕaːt] *pl:* • **1.** fight, struggle, strife

تَنازُع [tanaːzuʕ] *n:* • **1.** fight, struggle

نِزاع [nizaːʕ] *n:* • **1.** removal, withdrawal, elimination • **2.** controversy, dispute, contest

مَنزُوع [manzuːʕ] *adj:* • **1.** removed, taken away • **2.** conflicting, clashing

مِتنازِع [mitnaːziʕ] *adj:* • **1.** contested, disputed • **2.** conflicting, clashing

ن ز ف

نِزَف [nizaf] *v:* • **1.** to lose much blood, bleed profusely, bleed to death

اِستَنزَف [ʔistanzaf] *v:* • **1.** to exhaust, drain, deplete

نَزِف [nazif] *n:* • **1.** exhaustion, draining, emptying • **2.** bleeding, loss of blood, hemorrhage, hemophilia

نَزِيف [naziːf] *n:* • **1.** bleeding, hemorrhage

اِستِنزاف [ʔistinzaːf] *n:* • **1.** exhaustion, drainage, attrition (of powers, material)

نازِف [naːzif] *adj:* • **1.** bleeding, draining

ن ز ك

نَيزَك [nayzak] *n:* نَيازِك [nayaːzik] *pl:* • **1.** shooting star, meteor

نَزاكَة [nazaːka] *n:* • **1.** daintiness, delicateness, fragility • **2.** kindness, gentleness, tenderness, compassion

نازِك [naːzik] *adj:* • **1.** dainty, delicate, frail, fragile – هَالبنَيَّة شقَدّ نازكَة؛ مِن أقَلّ شِي تِتأَذَّى [halbnayya šgadd naːzka; min ʔaqall ši titʔaððaː] How delicate this girl is; the least thing can hurt her! • **2.** kind, gentle, tender, compassionate

ن ز ل

نِزَل [nizal] *v:* • **1.** to descend, go down, come down, move down – اِنتِظِرنِي؛ هَسَّة أنزِل [ʔintið̣irni; hassa ʔanzil] Wait for me; I'll come right down. نِزَل بِالبَرَشُوت [nizal bilparašuːt] He parachuted down. عَلَى غَفلَة بَيَّن، عَبالَك بِالدّائِرَة السِّما [ʕala ɣafla bayyan, ʕabaːlak nizal min ʔissima] All of a sudden he appeared as if he descended from the sky. • **2.** to get down, get off, alight, dismount, disembark – بأَي مَوقِف راح تِنزِل؟ [bʔay mawqif raːħ tinzil?] Which stop will you ge off at? الجِّنُود نِزلَوا لِلبَرّ بنُقطَتَين [ʔijǰinuːd nizlaw lilbarr bnuquṭṭayn] The soldiers went ashore at two points. • **3.** to come down, let down, land – الطِّيّارَة نِزلَت قَبُل ساعَة [ʔiṭṭiyyaːra nizlat gabul saːʕa] The plane landed an hour ago. • **4.** to fall – هَالمَنطِقَة، ما ينِزِل بِيها ثَلِج [halmanṭiqa, maː yinzil biːha θalij] Snow doesn't fall in this area. • **5.** to fall, sink, drop, go down – الأسعار نِزلَت هوايَة [ʔilʔasʕaːr nizlat hwa:ya] Prices have gone down a lot. • **6.** to go down, abate, subside, let up – إيدي بَعَدها تُوجَعني لَكِن الوَرَم نِزَل [ʔi:di baʕadha tuǰaʕni la:kin ʔilwaram nizal] My hand is still hurting me but the swelling went down. هَوا التّايَر نِزَل [hawa ʔitta:yar nizal] The air in the tire is low. • **7.** to stop over, stay, put up, take lodging – نِزَل عِدنا مِن كان بِبَغداد [nizal ʕidna min ča:n bibaɣda:d] He stayed with us when he was in Baghdad. مِن اِنتِقلَوا لِبَغداد، نِزلَوا يَمّنا [min ʔintiqlaw lbaɣda:d, nizlaw yammna] When they moved to Baghdad, they took a house near us. • **8.** to come, appear, come in season – الرَّقّي راح يِنزِل لِلسُّوق إسبُوع الجّاي [ʔirraggi ra:ħ yinzil lissu:g ʔisbu:ʕ ʔiǰǰa:y] Watermelons will come into the market next week. التُّكّي راح يِنزِل هَالشَّهَر [ʔittukki ra:ħ yinzil haššahar] Mulberries will come in season this month. • **9.** to play, put down (a card) – إذا البِلّي بإيدَك، نِزلَه [ʔiða ʔalbilli bi:dak, nizlah] If you have the ace in your hand, play it. • **10.** with عَلَى to fall upon, attack, assault, assail – نِزَل عَليه بِالسَّبّ [nizal ʕali:h bissabb] He fell upon him with insults. البارحَة نِزَل عَلينا حَرامِي [ʔilba:rħa nizal ʕali:na ħara:mi] Yesterday a thief broke into our house.

نَزَّل [nazzal] *v:* • **1.** to take down, bring down, to put down, let down, lower – نَزِّل كُلّ الكَراسِي جَوَّة [nazzil kull ʔilkara:si ǰawwa] Take all the chairs downstairs. نَزِّل الجّاهِل مِن عالحصان. راح يُوقَع [nazzil ʔiǰǰa:hil min ʕalħṣa:n. ra:ħ yu:gaʕ] Take the child down from the horse. He's going to fall. نَزِّل راسَك حَتَّى تِقدَر تطُب مِن الشِّبّاك [nazzil ra:sak ħatta tigdar ṭṭubb min ʔiššibba:č] Duck your head so you can get through the window. الله نَزَّل عَلَيهُم غَضَبَه [ʔallah nazzal ʕali:hum ɣaðabah] God sent his wrath down upon them. • **2.** to unload – نَزِّلُوا الكَراسِي مِن اللُّورِي [nazzlu: ʔilkara:si min ʔillu:ri] Unload the chairs from the truck. نَزَّل لِلسُّوق [nazzal lissu:g] to take to market, to put on the market. راح أنَزِّل الحُنطَة لِلسُّوق إسبُوع الجّاي [ra:ħ ʔanazzil ʔilħunṭa lissu:g ʔisbu:ʕ ʔiǰǰa:y] I'm going to take the wheat to market next week. • **3.** to cause to dismount, disembark, get off – نَزِّل الرُّكّاب حَتَّى نبَدِّل التّايَر [nazzil ʔirrukka:b ħatta nbaddil ʔitta:yar] Have the passengers get off so we can change the tire. • **4.** to land, put ashore (troops) – نَزّلوا ألف جُندِي بِالجَزيرَة [nazzlaw ʔalf ǰundi bilǰazi:ra] They landed a thousand soldiers on the island. • **5.** to lower, decrease, lessen, diminish, reduce – نَزِّلوا رُتُبتَه مِن عَريف إلَى نائِب عَريف [nazzilaw rutubtah min ʕari:f ʔila na:ʔib ʕari:f] They demoted him from sergeant to corporal. • **6.** to take in, put up, lodge, accommodate – مِن كِنّا بِبَغداد، نَزِّلونا عِدهُم [min činna bibaɣda:d, nazzilu:na ʕidhum] When we were in Baghdad, they put us up at their house.

تنَزَّل [tnazzal] *v:* • **1.** to lower oneself, stoop, condescend – ما أتنَزَّل أحكِي ويّاه [ma: ʔatnazzal ʔaħči wiyya:h] I won't lower myself to talk to him.

تنازَل [tna:zal] *v:* • **1.** to give in, yield, concede – دَيتِمَسَّك بِرَأيَه وَما يِتنازَل [dayitmassak braʔyah wama: yitna:zal] He's sticking to his opinion and won't give in. • **2.** with عَن to relinquish, surrender, give up – تنازَلّي عَن حُصّتَه [tna:zalli ʕan ħuṣṣtah] He gave up his share to me. تنازَل عَن العَرش لإبنَه [tna:zal ʕan ʔilʕarš lʔibnah] He gave up the throne to his son. • **3.** same as تنَزَّل: to lower oneself, stoop, condescend

اِنّزَل [ʔinnizal] *v:* • **1.** pass. of نِزَل to be descended from (lineage), gone down, come down, moved down – هَالسِّرداب ما بِيه دَرَج؛ ما يِنِّزِلَّه [hassirda:b ma: bi:h daraǰ; ma: yinnizillah] This basement has no stairs; it can't be gotten down into.

نُزُول [nuzu:l] *n:* • **1.** descending, descent • **2.** dismounting, alighting, getting down

مَنزِل [manzil] *n:* مَنازِل [mana:zil] *pl:* • **1.** inn, hostel

نَزلَة [nazla] *n:* • **1.** bronchitis, flu • **2.** descent, decline, drop,falling • **3.** countdown

مَنزِلَة [manzila] *n:* • **1.** status, prestige, standing – ما بُقتَله أيّ مَنزِلَة [ma: buqatlah ʔayy manzila] He had no prestige left.

إنزال [ʔinza:l] *n:* إنزالات [ʔinza:la:t] *pl:* • **1.** (military) landing, invasion

مَنزُول [manzu:l] *n:* • **1.** red-light district

تنازُل [tana:zul] *n:* • **1.** condescension, yielding

تنزِيل [tanzi:l] *n:* تَنزِيلات [tanzi:la:t] *pl:* • **1.** sending down, reduction, bringing down • **2.** pl. only تَنزِيلات [tanzi:la:t] sale

نازِل [na:zil] *adj:* • **1.** sloping, sloped, downward, inclined, descending, slanted

منَزَّل [mnazzal] *adj:* • **1.** send down from heaven, revealed

مَنزِلِي [manzili] *adj:* • **1.** domestic, local

مِتنازِل [mitna:zil] *adj:* • **1.** resigning, abdicating • **2.** renouncing, relinquishing, ceding

نزُول [nzu:l] *int:* • **1.** fall, drop, descending, descent, landing • **2.** pain, affliction – ما تِتحَرَّك؟ شبِيك، نزُول؟ [ma: titħarrak? šbi:k, nzu:l?] Can't you move? Are you crippled or something? نزُول عَلَى قَلبَك! لُويش ضِرَبتَه [nzu:l ʕala galbak! luwi:š ðirabtah] Plague take you! Why did you hit him? • **3.** Interjection or exclamative form (e.g., my God!, Damn it! and the like – نزُول، واحِد أوقَح مِن اللّاخ [nzu:l, wa:ħid ʔawkaħ min ʔilla:x] My God, one's worse than the other! نزُول! ما تُقعُد راحَة عاد؟ [nzu:l! ma: tugʕud ra:ħa ʕa:d?] Damn it! Can't you let up for just a minute?

ن ز ه

نَزَّه [nazzah] *v:* • **1.** to deem or declare honest, respectable, honorable, innocent of guilt – فَدّ واحِد تِهمُه ا بِالبوقَة بَسّ كُلّ المُوَظَّفِين نَزّهوه [fadd wa:ħid tihmu bilbu:ga bass kull ʔilmuwaððafi:n nazzihu:h] Someone accused him of the theft but all the employees said he was above it. شلُون تِقدَر تنَزَّهَه؟ الكُلّ دَيقُولُون هَذا مِشتِرِك بِالبوقَة

ن

[šlu:n tigdar tnazzahah? ʔilkull daygu:lu:n ha:ða mištirik bilbu:ga] How can you say he's above it? Everyone is saying that he took part in the theft. لا تنَزِّه نَفسَك هَسَّة. مَحَّد يِغَيِّر فِكرَه عَنَّك [la: tnazzih nafsak hassa. maћћad yiɣayyir fikrah ʕannak] Don't claim to be honest now. Nobody will change his idea of you.

تنَزَّه [tnazzah] *v:* • **1.** to enjoy the out-of-doors, to take an outing, go for a stroll, promenade – طلَعنا نِتنَزَّه بِحَدايِق بَغداد [ṭlaʕna nitnazzah bћada:yiq baɣda:d] We went out to enjoy ourselves in Baghdad's parks.

نُزهَة [nuzha] *n:* نُزهات [nuzha:t] *pl:* • **1.** outing, excursion, pleasure trip, stroll • **2.** recreation, amusement, fun, diversion

نَزاهَة [naza:ha] *n:* • **1.** honesty, purity, righteousness, integrity

مُنتَزَه [muntazah] *n:* مُنتَزَهات [muntazaha:t] *pl:* • **1.** recreation ground, park

نَزِيه [nazi:h] *adj:* • **1.** pure, blameless, above reproach, respectable – هالمُوَظَّفِين ما بِيهُم واحِد نَزِيه [halmuwaððafi:n ma: bi:hum wa:ћid nazi:h] There's not one of these employees who's above reproach. • **2.** honest, righteous, impartial

مُنَزَّه [munazzah] *adj:* • **1.** infallible

ن س

ناس [na:s] *n:* • **1.** people

ن س و

See also: ن س ء

ن س ب

نِسَب [nisab] *v:* • **1.** to ascribe, attribute, impute – نِسَب بَيت الشِّعِر إلَى شاعِر مَشهُور [nisab bayt ʔiššiʕir ʔila ša:ʕir mašhu:r] He attributed the line of poetry to a famous poet.

نَسَّب [nassab] *v:* • **1.** to deem or declare more appropriate, suitable, or proper, to recommend – آنِي أنَسِّب ترُوح تِحكِي ويّاه شَخصِياً [ʔa:ni ʔanassib tru:ћ tiћči wiyya:h šaxṣiyyan] I think it best you go talk with him personally.

ناسَب [na:sab] *v:* • **1.** to be appropriate, suitable, fitting, proper – هَذا عِندَه دِكتُوراه. ما يناسِب يِنطُوه وَظِيفَة كاتِب [ha:ða ʕindah diktu:ra:h. ma: yna:sib yinṭu:h waði:fat ka:tib] He has a doctor's degree. It isn't fitting that they give him a position as clerk. راتبَه ما يناسِب شُغلَه [ra:tbah ma: yna:sib šuɣlah] His salary isn't commensurate with his job. لَو تناسِب، كان بِعِتلَك إيّاها بهَالسِّعِر [law tna:sib, ča:n biʕitlak ʔiyya:ha bhassiʕir] If it were profitable, I would have sold it to you at that price. • **2.** to become, befit, behoove – هَالحَكِي أبَداً ما يناسبَك [halћači ʔabadan ma: yna:sbak] This kind of talk isn't like you at all. • **3.** to become related by marriage to – دَيرِيد يناسِبهُم لأَنّهُم زَناكِين [dayri:d yina:sibhum liʔannhum zana:gi:n] He wants to marry into their family because they're wealthy.

تناسَب [tna:sab] *v:* • **1.** to be related by marriage – راح نِتناسَب ويّا عائِلَة مِن البَصرَة [ra:ћ nitna:sab wiyya ʕa:ʔila min ʔilbaṣra] We are going to be related by marriage to a family from Basra. • **2.** to be proportionate, match, fit – قُوَّتَه ما تِتناسَب ويّا حَجمَه [quwwtah ma: titna:sab wiyya ћaǰmah] His strength isn't proportionate to his size.

انتِسَب [ʔintisab] *v:* • **1.** with إلى to become affiliated, associated with, to join – انتِسَب إلَى جَمعِيَّة خَيرِيَّة [ʔintisab ʔila ǰamʕiyya xayriyya] He joined a charitable organization.

نَسَب [nasab] *n:* أنساب [ʔansa:b] *pl:* • **1.** lineage, ancestry – نَسَبهُم يرجَع لِلنَّبِي [nasabhum yirǰaʕ linnabi] Their lineage goes back to the Prophet. إبِن حَسَب ونَسَب [ʔibin ћasab wnasab] person from an esteemed old family.

نِسبَة [nisba] *n:* نِسَب [nisab] *pl:* • **1.** relationship, affinity, connection, link – ماكُو نِسبَة بين شُغُل هَالمِيز وَهالمِيز [ma:ku nisba bi:n šuɣul halmi:z whalmi:z] There's no comparison between the workmanship in this table and this one. • **2.** rate – نِسبَة المُوت [nisbat ʔilmu:t] death rate. • **3.** proportion – نِسبَة الكُحُول بالبِيرَة قَلِيلَة [nisbat ʔilkuћu:l bilbi:ra qali:la] The proportion of alcohol in beer is small. نِسبَة مِئَوِيَّة [nisba miʔawiyya] percentage. بالنِّسبَة إلَى [binnisba ʔila] with regard to, regarding, in connection with, concerning. بالنِّسبَة إلِي، ما عِندِي مانِع [binnisba ʔili, ma: ʕindi ma:niʕ] As far as I'm concerned, I have no objection.

نِسِيب [nisi:b] *n:* نِسبان، نِسابَة [nisba:n, nisa:ba] *pl:* • **1.** in-law, relative by marriage

مِنتِسِب [mintasib] *n:* • **1.** employee, associate member, affiliation

تَناسُب [tana:sub] *n:* • **1.** proportion

مُناسَبَة [muna:saba] *n:* مُناسَبات [muna:saba:t] *pl:* • **1.** suitability, appropriateness, aptness, fitness • **2.** relationship, affinity • **3.** (pl. مُناسَبات) relation, reference, relevancy, bearing, pertinence, link, connection • **4.** occasion – راح يسَوُّون حَفلَة بِمُناسَبَة رُجُوعَه [ra:ћ ysawwu:n ћafla bimuna:sabat ruǰu:ʕah] They are going to give a party on the occasion of his return. مُناسَبَة يِزعَل؛ حَكِيِّي كُلَّه صُدُق [muna:saba yizʕal; ћačiyi kullah ṣudug] He has nothing to be mad about; all my remarks are true. بالمُناسَبَة، يِعجبَك ترُوح ويّانا لِلسِّينَما؟ [bilmuna:saba, yiʕiǰbak tru:ћ wiyya:na lissinama?] Incidentally, would you like to go to the movies with us?

انتِساب [ʔintisa:b] *n:* • **1.** relation, connection, membership, affiliation

نِسبِي [nisbi] *adj:* • **1.** relative, proportionate, proportional – رُطُوبَة نِسبِيَّة [ruṭu:ba nisbiyya] relative humidity.

مَنسُوب [mansu:b] *adj:* • **1.** ascribed, attributed, imputed • **2.** (water) level – مَنسُوب مَيّ النَّهَر نازِل [mansu:b mayy ʔinnahar na:zil] The water level of the river is low.
مُناسِب [muna:sib] *adj:* • **1.** suitable, fitting, appropriate, proper – راح أحكِي ويّاه بوَقِت مُناسِب [ra:ħ ʔaħči wiyya:h bwakit muna:sib] I'll talk to him at an appropriate time. سِعِر هَالسَّيّارَة مناسِب [siʕir hassayya:ra mna:sib] The price of this car is reasonable.
مِتناسِب [mitna:sib] *adj:* • **1.** proportionate, properly proportioned
أنسَب [ʔansab] *comparative adjective:* • **1.** more or most suitable, proper, appropriate, etc
نِسبِيّاً [nisbiyyan] *adverbial:* • **1.** comparatively, comparatively speaking

ن س ت ل

نَستَلَة [nastala] *n:* نَساتِل [nasa:til] *pl:* • **1.** candy bars

ن س ج

نِسَج [nisaǰ] *v:* • **1.** to weave, to knit
نَسِج [nasiǰ] *n:* • **1.** weaving, fabric, texture
نَسِيج [nasi:ǰ] *n:* أنسِجَة [ʔansiǰa] *pl:* • **1.** texture, tissue • **2.** woven fabric, textile
نَساج [nasa:ǰ] *n:* • **1.** weaver
مَنسُوج [mansu:ǰ] *n:* مَنسُوجات [mansu:ǰa:t] *pl:* • **1.** woven fabric, texture

ن س خ

نِسَخ [nisax] *v:* • **1.** to copy, transcribe
اِستَنسَخ [ʔistansax] *v:* • **1.** to copy, transcribe something
نَسِخ [nasix] *n:* • **1.** copying, transcription
نُسخَة [nusxa] *n:* نُسَخ [nusax] *pl:* • **1.** transcript, copy – عِندَك النُّسخَة العَرَبِيَّة مِن التَّقرِير؟ [ʕindak ʔinnusxa ʔilʕarabiyya min ʔittaqri:r?] Do you have the Arabic copy of the report? يِشبَه أبُوه بِالضَبُط؛ نُسخَة طِبق الأصِل [yišbah ʔabu:h biððabuṭ; nusxa ṭibq ʔilʔaṣil] He looks exactly like his father; an exact copy of the original.
نَسّاخ [nassa:x] *n:* نَسّاخِين [nassa:xi:n] *pl:* • **1.** copyist, transcriber, scribe
اِستِنساخ [ʔistinsa:x] *n:* • **1.** copying, transcription
مَنسُوخ [mansu:x] *adj:* • **1.** copied, written
مُستَنسَخ [mustansax] *adj:* • **1.** copied, written

ن س ر

نِسِر [nisir] *n:* نسُور [nsu:r] *pl:* • **1.** eagle
ناسُور [na:su:r] *n:* نواسِير [nwa:si:r] *pl:* • **1.** fistula • **2.** hemorrhoid

ن س ف

نِسَف [nisaf] *v:* • **1.** to demolish, blow up, blast to bits – نِسفَوا المَعمَل بقُمبُلَة مُوَقَّتَة [nisfaw ʔilmaʕmal bqumbula muwaqqata] They blew up the factory with a time bomb. ما بُقَى شِي مِن الأكِل. نِسفُوه كُلّه [ma: buqa: ši min ʔilʔakil. nisfu:h kullah] Nothing was left of the food. They demolished it.
نَسَّف [nassaf] *v:* • **1.** to winnow – نَسِّف التِّمَّن. بِيه تراب هوايَة [nassif ʔittimman. bi:h tra:b hwa:ya] Winnow the rice. There's a lot of dirt in it.
اِنسَف [ʔinnisaf] *v:* • **1.** pass. of نِسَف: to be demolished, blown up – الجِّسِر الجِّدِيد اِنِّسَف [ʔiǰǰisir ʔiǰǰidi:d ʔinnisaf] The new bridge was blown up.
نَسِف [nasif] *n:* • **1.** blowing up, blasting, demolition, destruction
ناسِف [na:sif] *adj:* • **1.** explosive, dynamite
مَنسُوف [mansu:f] *adj:* • **1.** blown-up, destroyed, demolished

ن س ق

نَسَّق [nassaq] *v:* • **1.** to dispose, set in proper order, rearrange – المُدِير نَسَّق المُوَظَّفِين بَالدّائِرَة مالتَه [ʔilmudi:r nassaq ʔilmuwaððafi:n bidda:ʔira ma:ltah] The director shuffled the employees in his office. • **2.** to let go, fire – نَسِّقوا عِدَّة مُوَظَفِين بِوِزارَة الزِّراعَة [nassiqaw ʕiddat muwaðafi:n bwiza:rat ʔizzira:ʕa] They fired several employees in the Agricultural Ministry.
تَنسِيق [tansi:q] *n:* • **1.** ordering, arrangement, distribution, coordination
تَناسُق [tana:suq] *n:* • **1.** uniformity • **2.** order, symmetry, harmony
مَنَسَّق [mnassaq] *adj:* • **1.** well-ordered, well-arranged
مِتناسِق [mitna:siq] *adj:* • **1.** well-ordered, well-arranged, regular, symmetrical

ن س ل

تناسَل [tna:sal] *v:* • **1.** to breed, multiply, propagate, reproduce – الأرانِب، إذا يخَلُّوها تِتناسِل بِحُرِّيَّة، يِكثَر عَدَدها [ʔilʔara:nib, ʔiða yxallu:ha titna:sil bħurriyya, yikθar ʕadadha] If they let rabbits breed freely, their number increases.
نَسِل [nasil] *n:* • **1.** progeny, issue, offspring – تَحدِيد النَّسِل [taħdi:d ʔinnasil] birth control.
تَناسُل [tana:sul] *n:* • **1.** sexual propagation, reproduction, procreation – أعضاء التَّناسُل [ʔaʕḍa:ʔ ʔittana:sul] sexual organs, genitals.
تَناسُلِي [tana:suli] *adj:* • **1.** reproductive, venereal, sexual, genital

ن س م

نَسمَة [nasma] *n:* نَسمات [nasma:t] *pl:* • **1.** breeze – نَسمَة هَوا [nasmat hawa] a breath of fresh air.
نَسِيم [nasi:m] *n:* نِسام [nisa:m] *pl:* • **1.** wind, breeze

ن س ن س

نَسناس [nasna:s] *n:* نسانِيس [nsa:ni:s] *pl:* • **1.** long-tailed monkey

ن

ن س و

نِساء [nisaːʔ] *n:* نِسوان [niswaːn] *pl:* • **1.** women (always a plural)

نِسائِي [nisaːʔi] *adj:* • **1.** female, feminine, womanly – مَلابِس نِسائِيَّة [malaːbis nisaːʔiyya] women's apparel.

ن س ي

نِسَى [nisaː] *v:* • **1.** to forget – لا تِنسَى مَوعِدنا [laː tinsaː mawʕidna] Don't forget our date.

نَسَّى [nassaː] *v:* • **1.** to cause to forget – ظَلّ يِحكِي وِيّايا إلَى أن نَسّانِي عِندِي اِجتِماع [ðall yiħči wiyyaːya ʔila ʔan nassaːni ʕindi ʔiǰtimaːʕ] he kept on talking with me till he made me forget I had a meeting.

تنَسَّى [tnassaː] *v:* • **1.** to have a craving for strange food (usually common among pregnant women) – مَرتِي دَتِتنَسَّى. ترِيد رَقِّي بِالشِّتا [marti datitnassaː. triːd raggi biššita] My wife is craving strange foods. She wants water-melon in the winter.

تناسَى [tnaːsaː] *v:* • **1.** to be or become oblivious to, ignore – حاوِل تِتناسَى المَوضُوع [ħaːwil titnaːsaː ʔilmawðuːʕ] Try to ignore the matter.

اِنّسَى [ʔinnisaː] *v:* • **1.** to be forgotten – كُلّ الأشياء اللِّي سَوَّيتها اِنّسَت [kull ʔilʔašyaːʔ ʔilli sawwiːtha ʔinnisat] Everything I did has been forgotten.

نِسيان [nisyaːn] *n:* • **1.** forgetfulness – مَرَض النِّسيان [marað ʔinnisyaːn] amnesia.

مَنسِي [mansi] *adj:* • **1.** forgotten

ن ش ء

نِشَأ [nišaʔ] *v:* • **1.** to grow up – نِشَأ بِبِيئَة فَقِيرَة [nišaʔ bbiːʔa faqiːra] He grew up in a poor environment.

أنشَأ [ʔanšaʔ] *v:* • **1.** to found, establish, institute, set up, organize – الحُكُومَة أنشِأت المَعامِل بِعِدَّة ألوِيَة [ʔilħukuːma ʔanšiʔat ʔilmaʕaːmil biʕiddat ʔalwiya] The government set up factories in several provinces.

مَنشَأ [manšaʔ] *n:* مَناشِئ [manaːšiʔ] *pl:* • **1.** place of origin

نَشأَة [našʔa] *n:* • **1.** growing up, upgrowth, growth, early life, youth

نُشُوء، نِشُوء [nušuːʔ, nišuːʔ] *n:* • **1.** growing up

ناشِئ [naːšiʔ] *n:* • **1.** beginner (in sports), junior

إنشاء [ʔinšaːʔ] *n:* إنشاءات [ʔinšaːʔaːt] *pl:* • **1.** setting up, establishment, institution, organization, installation • **2.** essay, composition, treatise

مُنشَأة [munšaʔa] *n:* مُنشَآت [munšaʔaːt] *pl:* • **1.** establishment, foundation, installation, institution • **2.** growing up, upgrowth, growth

ناشِئ [naːšiʔ, naːši] *adj:* • **1.** growing, growing up • **2.** arising, budding, proceeding, emanating, resulting from

إنشائِي [ʔinšaːʔi] *adj:* • **1.** creative, constructive, relating to construction or composition

ن ش ب [1]

نِشّاب [niššaːb] *n:* • **1.** (coll.) arrow(s)

نِشّابَة [niššaːba] *n:* نِشّابات [niššaːbaːt] *pl:* • **1.** arrow

ن ش ب [2]

نِشَب [nišab] *v:* • **1.** to break out (war), to flare up (flame) • **2.** to flare up (flame)

نُشُوب [nušuːb] *n:* • **1.** outbreak

ن ش ت ر

نَشتَر، ضُرَب نَشتَر [naštar, ðurab naštar] *n:* • **1.** to lance, cut open

ن ش د

نِشَد [nišad] *v:* • **1.** to seek information, inquire, ask – ما عِدنا قُمصان بَسّ تِقدَر تِنشِد بِذاك الدُّكّان [maː ʕidna qumṣaːn bass tigdar tinšid bðaːk ʔiddukkaːn] We don't have shirts but you can inquire in that store.

ناشَد [naːšad] *v:* • **1.** to implore, adjure – الحُكُومَة ناشدَت الأهالِي ما يسَوُّون مُظاهَرات [ʔilħukuːma naːšdat ʔilʔahaːli maː ysawwuːn muðaːharaːt] The government appealed to the people not to demonstrate.

نَشِد [našid] *n:* • **1.** inquiring, seeking, appealing, requesting

نِشدَة [nišda] *n:* نِشدات [nišdaːt] *pl:* • **1.** request for information – خَلِّي نِسأَل أَحَّد؛ النِّشدَة مُو عِيب [xalliː nisʔal ʔaħħad; ʔinnišda muː ʕiːb] Let's ask someone; there's nothing wrong with asking. • **2.** information, answer to a request for information – ما يِنطِي نِشدَة [maː yinṭi nišda] He won't volunteer any information.

نَشِيد [našiːd] *n:* • **1.** anthem, song

مَنشُود [manšuːd] *adj:* • **1.** sought, aspired, desired, pursued (aim, objective)

ن ش ر

نِشَر [nišar] *v:* • **1.** to spread around, publicize, broadcast – نِشَر الحكايَة بالولايَة [nišar ʔilħčaːya bilwlaːya] He spread the story around town. • **2.** to publish – نِشَر القُصَّة بِمَجَلَّة أجنَبِيَّة [nišar ʔilquṣṣa bmaǰalla ʔaǰnabiyya] He published the story in a foreign magazine. الجَّرِيدَة راح تِنشُرلَه مَقال باكِر [ʔiǰǰariːda raːħ tinšurlah maqaːl baːčir] The paper's going to print an article by him tomorrow.

نَشَّر [naššar] *v:* • **1.** to exorcise evil by burning African rue – نَشَّرتلَه حَتَّى تُطرُد الشَّرّ عَنَّه [naššaritlah ħatta tuṭrud ʔiššarr ʕannah] She burned African rue to drive evil away from him.

اِنّشَر [ʔinnišar] *v:* • **1.** to be published – الكِتاب راح يِنّشَر الشَّهَر الجّاي [ʔilkitaːb raːħ yinnišar ʔiššahar ʔiǰǰaːy] The book will be published next month.

اِنتِشَر [ʔintišar] *v:* • **1.** to spread – المَرَض اِنتِشَر [ʔilmarað ʔintišar] The disease spread. • **2.** to spread

out, scatter – لا تظلّون متكتّلين هنا. اِنتَشرُوا [la: dðallu:n mitkattili:n hna. ʔintašru:] Don't stay bunched up here. Spread out.
نَشِر [našir] *n:* • **1.** spreading, publication, propagation, diffusion
نَشرَة [našra] *n:* نَشرات [našra:t] *pl:* • **1.** announcement, proclamation, notice • **2.** (radio) broadcast • **3.** publication, periodical • **4.** bulletin board
ناشِر [na:šir] *n:* ناشِرين [na:širi:n] *pl:* • **1.** publisher
نِشارَة [niša:ra] *n:* • **1.** sawdust, wood shavings
مِنشار [minša:r] *n:* مِناشِير [mina:ši:r] *pl:* • **1.** saw
اِنتِشار [ʔintiša:r] *n:* • **1.** circulation • **2.** spreading, diffusion
مَنشُور [manšu:r] *adj:* • **1.** spread abroad, made public, published • **2.** extra edition (of a newspaper) • **3.** pl. مَناشِير leaflet, pamphlet, circular
مِنتِشِر [mintišir] *adj:* • **1.** widespread, current, rife – الإشاعَة مِنتِشرَة بالوِلايَة [ʔilʔiša:ʕa mintišra bilwila:ya] The rumor's widespread in the city.

ن ش ز

نَشاز [naša:z] *n:* • **1.** dissonance, discord • **2.** dissonant, off key – لَو ما يغَنّي ويّاهُم أحسَن. غِناه نَشاز [law ma: yɣanni wiyya:hum ʔaħsan. ɣina:h naša:z] It'd be better if he didn't sing with them. His singing is off key.
ناشِز [na:šiz] *adj:* نَواشِز [nawa:šiz] *pl:* • **1.** recalcitrant, disobedient – مَرَة ناشِز [mara na:šiz] a recalcitrant woman, a shrew.

ن ش ش

نَشّ [našš] *v:* • **1.** to shoo away, drive away – الدِّجاج دَياكُل التِّمَّن. نِشّه [ʔiddiǰa:ǰ daya:kul ʔittimman. niššah] The chickens are eating the rice. Shoo them away.
نَشّ [našš] *n:* • **1.** driving away, shooing away

ن ش ط

نِشَط [nišaṭ] *v:* • **1.** to be or become strong or energetic – ضِيف هالخَيطَين عَلَى هَالخَيط حَتَّى يِنشَط [ði:f halxayṭayn ʕala halxi:ṭ ħatta yinšaṭ] Add these two strings to this string so it will be strong.
نَشَّط [naššaṭ] *v:* • **1.** to invigorate, energize – الدُّوش البارِد ينَشِّط الجِّسِم [ʔiddu:š ʔilba:rid ynaššiṭ ʔiǰǰisim] A cold shower invigorates the body.
تنَشَّط [tnaššaṭ] *v:* • **1.** same as نِشَط: to be energized – لِيش مَا تِتمَشّى حَتَّى تِتنَشَّط [li:š ma: titmašša ħatta titnaššaṭ] Why don't you walk around so you'll get some energy.
نَشاط [naša:ṭ] *n:* • **1.** energy, enthusiasm
ناشِط [na:šiṭ] *n:* • **1.** lively, energetic, active • **2.** activist
نَشِط [našiṭ] *adj:* • **1.** energetic, active, busy, bustling – هَالوَلَد كُلِّش نَشِط [halwalad kulliš našiṭ] This boy is very energetic. • **2.** boisterous, obstreperous, aggressive – إبنكُم كُلِّش نَشِط. الوِلِد يخافُون مِنَّه [ʔibinkum kulliš našiṭ. ʔilwilid yixa:fu:n minnah] Your son is very aggressive. All the kids are afraid of him.
نَشِيط [naši:ṭ] *adj:* • **1.** energetic, active, busy, bustling – المُوَظَّف الجِّدِيد مُو نَشِيط [ʔilmuwaðða ʔiǰǰidi:d mu: naši:ṭ] The new employee isn't energetic.
مُنَشِّط [munaššiṭ] *adj:* مُنَشِّطات [munaššiṭa:t] *pl:* • **1.** activating, inciting, enlivening, stimulating
ناشِط [na:šiṭ] *adj:* • **1.** energetic, active
أنشَط [ʔanšaṭ] *comparative adjective:* • **1.** more or most energetic, active

ن ش ف

نِشَف [nišaf] *v:* • **1.** to be dry, become dry – لا تفُوت إلّا لَمّا تِنشَف القاع [la: tfu:t ʔilla lamma tinšaf ʔilga:ʕ] Don't go in until the floor dries.
نَشَّف [naššaf] *v:* • **1.** to dry, make dry, blot dry – أخُذ الخاولِي وَنَشِّف الجّاهِل [ʔuxuð ʔilxa:wli wnaššif ʔiǰǰa:hil] Take the towel and dry the kid. الحِبِر بَعدَه ما ناشِف. نَشِّف المَكتُوب قَبُل ما تحُطَّه بِالظَرُف [ʔilħibir baʕdah ma: na:šif. naššif ʔilmaktu:b gabul ma: tħuṭṭah biððaruf] The ink isn't dry yet. Blot the letter before you put it in the envelope.
تنَشَّف [tnaššaf] *v:* • **1.** to dry oneself – إنطِينِي المَنشَفَة دَأتنَشَّف بِيها [ʔinṭi:ni ʔilmanšafa daʔatnaššaf bi:ha] Give me the bath towel so I can dry myself off with it.
نَشِف [našif] *n:* • **1.** dryness
نِشّاف، نِشِّيف : وَرَق نِشّاف، نِشِّيف [nišša:f, nišši:f waraq nišša:f, nišši:f] *n:* • **1.** blotting paper
نِشّافَة [nišša:fa] *n:* نِشّافات [nišša:fa:t] *pl:* • **1.** blotter, blotting pad
مِنشَفَة، مَنشَفَة [minšafa, manšafa] *n:* مَناشِف [mana:šif] *pl:* • **1.** towel, bath towel
نَواشِف [nawa:šif] *n:* • **1.** pl. only pieces of fried food without sauce
ناشِف [na:šif] *adj:* • **1.** dry • **2.** hard, tough, stiff

ن ش ل

نِشَل [nišal] *v:* • **1.** to cause to catch a cold – الهَوا البارِد نِشَلنِي [ʔilhawa ʔilba:rid nišalni] The cold weather gave me a cold. آني مَنشُول وَما راح أرُوح لِلمَدرَسَة [ʔa:ni manšu:l wma ra:ħ ʔaru:ħ lilmadrasa] I have a cold and I'm not going to go to school.
اِنّشَل [ʔinnišal] *v:* • **1.** to catch a cold – اِنّشَلِت نَشلَة قَوِيَّة [ʔinnišalit našla qawiyya] I caught a bad cold.
نَشِل [našil] *n:* • **1.** cold, catarrh
نَشلَة [našla] *n:* نَشلات [našla:t] *pl:* • **1.** cold, catarrh
نَشّال [našša:l] *n:* نَشّالِين [našša:li:n] *pl:* • **1.** pickpocket
مَنشُول [manšu:l] *adj:* • **1.** suffering from a (common) cold

ن

ن ش م

نَشمِي [našmi] *adj:* نِشامَة [niša:ma] *pl:* • **1.** helpful, willing to be of service • **2.** helpful person

ن ش ن

نَيشَن [nayšan] *v:* • **1.** to mark, inscribe, assign an identifying mark to – نَيشِن الصَّفحَة حَتَّى ما تضَيِّعها [nayšin ʔiṣṣafħa ħatta ma: ayyiʕha] Mark the page so you won't lose track of it. • **2.** to aim, point – نَيشَن بِالتُّفقَة عَلَيّا [nayšan bittufga ʕalayya] He pointed the gun at me. نَيشِن عَلَى مَركَز الدّائِرَة [nayšin ʕala markaz ʔidda:ʔira] Aim at the bull's-eye. • **3.** to send a gift with a proposal of marriage to – إبِن الوَزِير نَيشَن بنَيَّة مِن قَرايبِي [ʔibin ʔilwazi:r nayšan bnayya min gara:ybi] The minister's son sent a gift proposing marriage to one of my relatives. مَعَ الأَسَف، بِتّنا منَيشنَة [maʕa ʔilʔasaf, bittna mni:šna] Unfortunately, our girl is promised.

نِيشان [ni:ša:n] *n:* • **1.** aim – أُخُذ نِيشان زين قَبُل ما ترمِي [ʔuxuð ni:ša:n zi:n gabul ma: tirmi] Take good aim before you fire. • **2.** pl. نياشِين mark, sign, identifying character • **3.** a personal gift sent to a girl, the acceptance of which implies consent to marriage medal, decoration, badge of honor

نِيشَنجِي، نِيشانجِي *pl:* • **1.** marksman, sharp shooter

ن ش ن ش

نَشنَش [našnaš] *v:* • **1.** to feel unfettered, free, to enjoy oneself – اليُوم مَعاش؛ راح أَنَشنِش [ʔilyu:m maʕa:š; ra:ħ ʔanašniš] Today is payday; I'll be able to live again. بِهالتَّرفِيع، راح أَنَشنِش [bhattarfi:ʕ, ra:ħ ʔanašniš] With this promotion, I'll be on easy street. هُوَّ ينَشنِش هوايَة بالبِيرَة [huwwa ynašniš hwa:ya bilbi:ra] He really enjoys himself on beer.

منَشنِش [mnašniš] *adj:* • **1.** happy, comfortable, healthy

ن ش و

نَشَّى [našša:] *v:* • **1.** to starch – قُول لِلمكَوِّي ينَشِّيلَك ياخَة القَمِيص [gu:l lilmkawwi ynašši:lak ya:xat ʔilqami:ṣ] Tell the cleaner to starch the shirt collar for you.

تنَشَّى [tnašša:] *v:* • **1.** to be starched – هَالثُّوب ما يِتنَشَّى [haθθu:b ma: yitnašša:] This shirt can't be starched.

اِنتِشَى [ʔintiša:] *v:* • **1.** to become intoxicated – يِنتِشِي بِكلاص بِيرَة واحِد [yintiši bigla:ṣ bi:ra wa:ħid] He gets high on one glass of beer.

نِشا [niša] *n:* • **1.** starch

نَشوَة [našwa] *n:* • **1.** intoxication, drunkenness – شِرَب رُبُع بُوطِل عَرَق وصارَت عِندَه نَشوَة [širab rubuʕ buṭil ʕarag wṣa:rat ʕindah našwa] He drank a quarter of a bottle of arrack and got high. بَعدَه بِنَشوَة الانتِصار [baʕdah bnašwat ʔilintiṣa:r] He's still drunk with victory.

ن ش ي

See also: ن ش و

ن ص ب

نِصَب [niṣab] *v:* • **1.** to erect, set up, put up, install, set in place – راح ينِصبُون تِمثال بِهالسّاحَة [ra:ħ yniṣbu:n timθa:l bhassa:ħa] They're going to erect a statue in this square. • **2.** to strike a pose – مِن تِحكِي ويّاه، يطَلِّع صَدرَه وَينِصُب مِثل الدِّيك [min tiħči wiyya:h, yṭalliʕ ṣadrah wyinṣub miθl ʔiddi:č] When you talk to him he sticks out his chest and poses like a cock. • **3.** to look one's best, put one's best foot forward – ما يِجِي لِلحَفلَة إذا ما يُنصُب تَمام [ma: yiji lilħafla ʔiða ma: yunṣub tama:m] He won't come to the party if he isn't looking his best. • **4.** to brag, boast, put on airs – ماكُو حاجَة تِنصُب بِراسِي [ma:ku ħa:ja tinṣub bra:si] There's no reason for you to do all this boasting to me. • **5.** to set – أنصُب ساعتَك عَلَى ساعتِي [ʔunṣub sa:ʕtak ʕala sa:ʕti] Set your watch by mine. • **6.** to wind – أنصُب السّاعَة وشُوف إذا تِشتُغُل وَإلّا لا [ʔunṣub ʔissa:ʕa wšu:f ʔiða tištuɣul waʔilla la:] Wind the watch and see if it's working or not.

نَصَّب [naṣṣab] *v:* • **1.** to appoint, install – نَصُّبَوه بوَظِيفَة وَهُوَّ مُو قَدّها [naṣṣubawh bwaḍi:fa wahuwwa mu: gaddha] They fixed him up with a position and he couldn't handle it.

تنَصَّب [tnaṣṣab] *v:* • **1.** to behave domineeringly, despotically – طِلعَت مِن البَيت لِأَنّ أَخُوها يِتنَصَّب عَلِيها [ṭilʕat min ʔilbayt liʔann ʔaxu:ha yitnaṣṣab ʕali:ha] She left the house because her brother was bossing her around.

اِنتِصَب [ʔintiṣab] *v:* • **1.** to rise up, stand erect

نَصُب [naṣub] *n:* • **1.** setting up, installation

نَصبَة [naṣba] *n:* نَصبات [naṣba:t] *pl:* • **1.** posture, position, pose • **2.** bearing, carriage, demeanor • **3.** appearance – اليُوم إنتَ طالِع نَصبَة [ʔilyu:m ʔinta ṭa:liʕ naṣba] You're dressed smartly today. • **4.** (act of) bragging, boasting, putting on airs – عَلَى مَن هَالنَّصبَة؟ قابِل إحنا ما نعُرفِك إنتِي مِنُو؟ [ʕala man hannaṣba? qa:bil ʔiħna ma: nʕurfič ʔinti minu?] Who are you putting on airs for? Do you think we don't know who you are? • **5.** setting, adjustment (of a clock) • **6.** winding (a clock)

نِصاب [niṣa:b] *n:* • **1.** minimum number or amount, quorum

نَصِيب [naṣi:b] *n:* • **1.** share, portion – شقَدّ نَصِيبَك مِن وِرث أَبُوك؟ [šgadd naṣi:bak min wirθ ʔabu:k?] What's your share of your father's legacy? • **2.** lot, fate, destiny • **3.** luck, chance

ن

مَنصِب [manṣab] *n:* مَناصِب [manaːṣib] *pl:* • **1.** position, post, rank, office
نَصّاب [naṣṣaːb] *n:* • **1.** cheater, scammer
مَنصُوب [manṣuːb] *adj:* • **1.** accusative or subjunctive • **2.** erect

ن ص ح

نِصَح [niṣaħ] *v:* • **1.** to advise, counsel, give sincere advice to – أنصحَك لا تِمشِي ويّا هِيكِي ناس [ʔaniṣħak laː timši wiyya hiːči naːs] I advise you not to run around with such people. إنصحَه قبُل ما يسَوِّي جَرِيمَة [ʔiniṣħah gabul maː ysawwi ǰariːma] Set him straight before he commits a crime. • **2.** to be sincere, to mean well, to try to do the right thing – هَالقَصّاب يِنصَح بِمُعامَلتَه [halgaṣṣaːb yinṣaħ bmuʕaːmaltah] That butcher is sincere in his dealings.
نُصُح [nuṣuħ] *n:* • **1.** advice, exhortation, admonition
نَصِيحَة [naṣiːħa] *n:* نَصايِح [naṣaːyiħ] *pl:* • **1.** (sincere) advice
نَصاحَة [naṣaːħa] *n:* • **1.** smartness
ناصِح [naːṣiħ] *adj:* • **1.** sincere, well-meaning • **2.** good, beneficial, useful – هَالجَوز ما بِيه وِحدَة ناصحَة [halǰuːz maː biːh wiħda naːṣħa] Not one of these walnuts is any good.

ن ص ر

نِصَر [niṣar] *v:* • **1.** to grant victory to, to allow to triumph – الله يِنصُر العَرَب [ʔallah yinṣur ʔilʕarab] May God make the Arabs victorious.
ناصَر [naːṣar] *v:* • **1.** to stand by, to support, to defend
تناصَر [tnaːṣar] *v:* • **1.** to stand by somebody's side
اِنتِصَر [ʔintiṣar] *v:* • **1.** to triumph, be victorious – الحُلَفاء اِنتِصرَوا بالحَرُب [ʔilħulafaːʔ ʔintiṣraw bilħarub] The allies won the war. جَيشنا اِنتِصَر عَلَى جَيش العَدُو [ǰayšna ʔintiṣar ʕala ǰayš ʔilʕadu] Our army triumphed over the enemy's army.
نَصِر [naṣir] *n:* • **1.** victory, triumph
نَصِير [naṣiːr] *n:* • **1.** benefactor • **2.** helper, supporter, defender, protector
تَناصُر [tanaːṣur] *n:* • **1.** collaboration, cooperation
اِنتِصار [ʔintiṣaːr] *n:* اِنتِصارات [ʔintiṣaːraːt] *pl:* • **1.** victory, triumph مِنتِصِر [mintiṣir] *adj:* • 1. victorious, triumphant
نَصرانِيَّة [naṣraːniyya] *n:* • **1.** Christianity
مِتنَصِّر [mitnaṣṣir] *adj:* • **1.** converted to Christianty, Christianized
مِنتِصِر [mintiṣir] *adj:* • **1.** victorious, triumphant
نَصراني [naṣraːni] *adj:* نَصارَى [naṣaːra] *pl:* • **1.** Christian

ن ص ص 1

نَصّ [naṣṣ] *v:* • **1.** with عَلَى to stipulate, specify, provide for – القانُون يِنُصّ عَلَى هَالشِّي [ʔilqaːnuːn ynuṣṣ ʕala haššiː] The law calls for this.
نَصّ [naṣṣ] *n:* نصُوص [nṣuːṣ] *pl:* • **1.** text – هَالكَلِمَة ما مَوجُودَة بِنَصّ القانُون [halkalima maː mawǰuːda bnaṣṣ ʔilqaːnuːn] This word isn't present in the text of the law. • **2.** wording – بِالنَّصّ إقرالِي التَّقرِير [ʔiqraːli ʔittaqriːr binnaṣṣ] Read me the report verbatim. • **3.** بِالنَصّ [binnaṣṣ] verbatim
مَنَصَّة [manaṣṣa] *n:* مَنَصّات [manaṣṣaːt] *pl:* • **1.** platform, dais, podium

ن ص ص 2

نَصَّة [naṣṣa] *n:* نَصّات [naṣṣaːt] *pl:* • **1.** depression, dip, low place (see also n-ṣ-y)
نصَيِّص [nṣayyiṣ] *adj:* • **1.** low – يِكتِب عَلَى مَيز نصَيِّص [yiktib ʕala miːz nṣayyiṣ] He writes on a low table. دِير بالَك. آنِي مُو حايِط نصَيِّص [diːr baːlak. ʔaːni muː ħaːyiṭ nṣayyiṣ] Watch it. I'm not something to be dismissed easily. هَذا حايِط نصَيِّص. ياهُو اللِّي يِيجِي يصَيِّح عَليه [haːða ħaːyiṭ nṣayyiṣ. yaːhu ʔilli yiǰi yṣayyiħ ʕaliːh] He's a nothing. Everyone shouts at him.
أنَصّ [ʔanaṣṣ] *adj:* • **1.** lower or lowest

ن ص ص 3

نُصّ [nuṣṣ] *n:* نصاص [nṣaːṣ] *pl:* • **1.** (نُصّ is an alternative form of نُصف) half – خابَرنِي بِنُصّ اللَّيل [xaːbarni bnuṣṣ ʔillayl] He called me in the middle of the night. • **2.** middle

ن ص ف

نِصَف [niṣaf] *v:* • **1.** to be just, act fairly, treat without discrimination – المُعَلِّم ما نِصَف ويّايا بهَالدَّرَجَة [ʔilmuʕallim maː niṣaf wiyyaːya bhaddaraǰa] The teacher wasn't fair with me on this grade.
ناصَف [naːṣaf] *v:* • **1.** same as نِصَف: to be just, act fairly, treat without discrimination – ناصَف وِيّاه واِنطَاه كُلّ حَقَّه [naːṣaf wiyyaːh wʔinṭaːh kull ħaqqah] He was just with him and gave him all he deserved.
نِصِف [nisif] *n:* أنصاف [ʔanṣaːf] *pl:* • **1.** half
إنصاف [ʔinṣaːf] *n:* • **1.** justice, fairness
مُناصَفَة [munaːṣafa] *n:* • **1.** fairness, justice, just treatment • **2.** in equal shares, half and half – قَسَّمنا الرِّبِح مُناصَفَة [qassamna ʔirribiħ munaːṣafa] We divided the profits fifty-fifty.
نِصفي [nişfi] *adj:* • **1.** half-, semi-, hemi- (in compounds) – تِمثال نِصفي [timθaːl nişfi] bust. شَلَل نِصفي [šalal nişfi] hemiplegia.
مُنصِف [munṣif] *adj:* مُنصِفِين [munṣifiːn] *pl:* • **1.** fair, just, righteous • **2.** a righteous man
مِنتَصِف [mintaṣif] *adj:* • **1.** middle, halfway
أنصَف [ʔanṣaf] *comparative adjective:* • **1.** more or most fair, just
اِنصافاً [ʔinṣaːfan] *adverbial:* • **1.** in all fairness, to be truthful – اِنصافاً، عَلِي خُوش وَلَد [ʔinṣaːfan, ʕali xuːš walad] In fairness, Ali is a good boy.

ن

ن ص و

نِصَى [niṣa:] *v:* • **1.** to sink down, become low – الحايِط دَينصَى لِأَنّ القاع مُو قَوِيَّة [ʔilħa:yiṭ dayinṣa: liʔann ʔilga:ʕ mu: qawiyya] The wall is sinking because the ground isn't solid. حِسّهُم دَينصَى. يبَيِّن راح ينامُون [ħisshum dayinṣa:. yibayyin ra:ħ yna:mu:n] Their voices are getting lower. It seems they're going to sleep.

نَصَّى [naṣṣa:] *v:* • **1.** to lower – لِيش حاطّ الرَّسِم عالِي؟ نَصِّي شوَيَّة [li:š ħa:ṭṭ ʔirrasim ʕa:li? naṣṣi šwayya] Why did you put the picture up so high? Lower it a little. إذا ما تنَصِّي راسَك ما تِقدَر تخُشّ [ʔiða ma: tnaṣṣi ra:sak ma: tigdar txušš] If you don't duck your head, you can't go in. نَصِّي حِسَّك؛ الجِّهال نايمِين [naṣṣi ħissak; ʔiǰǰiha:l na:ymi:n] Lower your voice; the children are sleeping. • **2.** to squat down, bend down – نَصِّي شوَيَّة حَتَّى أَشُوف شَكُو فُوق راسَك [naṣṣi šwayya ħatta ʔašu:f šaku fu:g ra:sak] Squat down a little so I can see what's on top of your head.

تنَصَّى [tnaṣṣa:] *v:* • **1.** to be lowered – هَالخَرِيطَة ما تِتنَصَّى لِأَنّ لازقَة بِالحايِط [halxari:ṭa ma: titnaṣṣa: liʔann la:zga bilħa:yiṭ] This map can't be lowered because it is stuck to the wall.

نَصيَة [naṣya] *n:* • **1.** sinking down, becoming low

تنِصِّي [tniṣṣi] *n:* • **1.** sinking down, becoming low

ناصِي [na:ṣi] *adj:* • **1.** low – دِيلاب ناصِي [di:la:b na:ṣi] a low cabinet.

أَنصَى [ʔanṣa:] *comparative adjective:* • **1.** lower or lowest

ن ض ح

نِضَح [niðaħ] *v:* • **1.** to wet, moisten, splash, leak, flow over

نَضِح [naðiħ] *n:* • **1.** splashing

نِضُوح [niðu:ħ, nðu:ħ] *n:* • **1.** leak

ن ط ح

نِطَح [niṭaħ] *v:* • **1.** to butt – الصَّخَل نِطَح الشِّجرَة وَانكِسرَت قرُونَه [ʔiṣṣaxal niṭaħ ʔiššiǰra wʔinkisrat gru:nah] The goat butted the tree and his horns broke.

تناطَح [tna:ṭaħ] *v:* • **1.** to butt each other – شُوف هَذُولَك الغِزلان دَيتناطحُون [šu:f haðu:lak ʔilɣizla:n dayitna:ṭħu:n] Look at those gazelles butting each other.

نَطِح [naṭiħ] *n:* • **1.** butting

نَطحَة [naṭħa] *n:* نَطحات [naṭħa:t] *pl:* • **1.** butting (i.e. heads)

ناطِحَة : ناطِحَة السَحاب [na:ṭiħa, na:tiħat ʔissaħa:b] *adj:* ناطِحات [na:ṭiħa:t] *pl:* • **1.** skyscraper

ن ط ر

نِطَر [niṭar] *v:* • **1.** to stand guard, keep watch – مِنُو راح يِنطُر هاللَّيلَة؟ [minu ra:ħ yinṭur hallayla?] Who's going to keep watch tonight? • **2.** to await, wait for – إنتَ خَلِّص شُغلَك وَأَنِي أَنطرَك هنا [ʔinta xalliṣ šuɣlak waʔa:ni ʔaniṭrak hna] You finish your work and I'll wait for you here.

تنَطَّر [tnaṭṭar] *v:* • **1.** to lie in wait, hide in ambush – تنَطَّرلَه يَمّ الجِّسِر وَمِن فات، ضِرَبَه بطَلقَة [tnaṭṭarlah yamm ʔiǰǰisir wamin fa:t, ðirabah bṭalqa] He lay in wait for him near the bridge and when he passed, he shot him.

ناطُور [na:ṭu:r] *n:* نواطِير [nwa:ṭi:r] *pl:* • **1.** watchman, guard

ن ط ط

نَطّ [naṭṭ] *v:* • **1.** to jump in, butt in – مَحَّد سِأَلَك. لِيش نَطِّيت مِن يَمَّك؟ [maħħad siʔalak. li:š naṭṭi:t min yammak?] No one asked you. Why did you butt in? ما أَداينَك لَو تنُطّ [ma: ʔada:ynak law tnuṭṭ] I won't make you a loan no matter what you do.

نَطّ [naṭṭ] *n:* • **1.** jumping

ن ط ق

نِطَق [niṭaq] *v:* • **1.** to speak, utter – قِعَد وِيّانا ساعَة وَما نِطَق بوَلا كِلمَة [giʕad wiyya:na sa:ʕa wama: niṭaq bwala: čilma] He sat with us for an hour and didn't say one word. • **2.** to pronounce – شلُون تِنطُق هالحَرُف؟ [šlu:n tinṭuq halħaruf?] How do you pronounce this letter?

نَطَّق [naṭṭaq] *v:* • **1.** to cause to speak – الله نَطَّقَه وحِكَى الصِّدُق [ʔallah naṭṭaqah wħiča: ʔiṣṣudug] Allah moved him to speak and he told the truth.

اِنطَق [ʔinniṭaq] *v:* • **1.** to be pronounced

اِستَنطَق [ʔistanṭaq] *v:* • **1.** to question, interrogate, cross-examine – بَعَد ما اِستَنطِقوه، عِرفَوا القُصَّة [baʕad ma: ʔistanṭiqawh, ʕirfaw ʔilquṣṣa] After they interrogated him, they knew the story.

نُطُق [nuṭuq] *n:* • **1.** utterance, pronunciation

نِطاق [niṭa:q] *n:* نِطاقات، أَنطِقَة [niṭa:qa:t, ʔanṭiqa] *pl:* • **1.** scope, range, field, extent, sphere – لا تُخرُج عَن نِطاق المُجادَلَة [la: tuxruǰ ʕan niṭa:q ʔilmuǰa:dala] Don't go outside the sphere of the debate. • **2.** a wide belt worn by the military

مَنطِق [manṭiq] *n:* • **1.** logic

مَنطِقَة [manṭiqa, manṭaqa] *n:* مَناطِق [mana:ṭiq, mana:ṭig] *pl:* • **1.** area • **2.** district, zone – قَصَّيت مَنطِقتَين بِالباص [gaṣṣi:t manṭiqti:n bilpa:ṣ] I bought a two-zone ticket on the bus. • **3.** neighborhood

ناطِق [na:ṭiq] *adj:* • **1.** talking, speaking – فِلِم ناطِق [filim na:ṭiq] sound film. • **2.** spokesman, speaker

مَنطِقِي [manṭiqi] *adj:* • **1.** logical

مَنطُوق [manṭu:q] *adj:* • **1.** pronounced, uttered, articulated • **2.** wording, arrangement • **3.** text (of a document)

مَنطِقِيّاً [manṭiqiyyan] *adverbial:* • **1.** logically

ن

ن ط و

نطى [niṭaː] *v:* • **1.** to give – إنطَيت الكِتاب لِلوَلَد [ʔinṭiːt ʔilkitaːb lilwalad] I gave the book to the boy. إنطِيني المُدِير. أرِيد أحكِي وِيّاه [ʔinṭiːni ʔilmudiːr. ʔariːd ʔaħči wiyyaːh] Give me the boss. I want to talk with him. هُوَّ ما ياخُذ وَينطِي. ما تِقدَر تِتفاهَم وِيّاه [huwwa maː yaːxuð wyinṭi. maː tigdar titfaːham wiyyaːh] He won't give and take. you can't negotiate with him. • **2** to give up, give away – عَلِي خِطَب بِتّهُم لَكِن ما انطَاوها [ʕali xiṭab bitthum laːkin maː nṭuːha] Ali asked to marry their daughter but they wouldn't give her up. • **3** to afford, allow – ما إنطَانِي مَجال أحكِي [maː ʔinṭaːni majaːl ʔaħči] He didn't give me a chance to speak. • **4** to grant, permit – نِجحَت العَمَلِيَّة وَالله إنطاه عُمُر جِدِيد [nijħat ʔilʕamaliyya wʔallah ʔinṭaːh ʕumur jidiːd] The operation was successful and God granted him a new life. • **5.** to offer – اِنطَيتَه ألف دِينار بَالسَّيّارَة وَما باع [ʔinṭaytah ʔalf dinaːr bissayyaːra wmaː baːʕ] I offered him a thousand dinars for the car and he wouldn't sell. • **6.** to give off, emit, shed, yield – العِكِس مال البُورِي دَينطِي مَيّ [ʔilʕikis maːl ʔilbuːri dayinṭi mayy] The elbow of the pipe is leaking water.

اِنّطى [ʔinniṭaː] *v:* • **1.** to be given – هَالغَراض ما يصِير تِنّطِي لِلجّاهِل [halɣaraːð maː yṣiːr tinniṭi lijjaːhil] These things shouldn't be given to children. هِيكِي أشياء ما تِنّطِي؛ لازم تِنباع [hiːči ʔašyaːʔ maː tinniṭi; laːzim tinbaːʕ] Those things aren't to be given away; they should be sold.

نَطِي [naṭy] *n:* • **1.** giving

مِنطِي [minṭi] *adj:* • **1.** given

ن ظ ر

نِظَر [niðar] *v:* • **1.** with ب to take under consideration, look into, examine – اللُّجنَة راح تِنظُر بِالمَوضُوع [ʔillujna raːħ tinður bilmawðuːʕ] The committee will look into the matter.

اِنتِظَر [ʔintiðar] *v:* • **1.** to expect, anticipate – ما اَنتِظِر أيّ رِبِح مِن هَذا [maː ʔantiðir ʔayy ribiħ min haːða] I don't expect any profit from this. • **2.** to await, wait for – اِنتِظِرنِي بَرَّة [ʔintiðirni barra] Wait for me outside.

اِستَنظَر [ʔistanðar] *v:* • **1.** same as اِنتِظَر: to wait for

نَظَر [naðar] *n:* أنظار [ʔanðaːr] *pl:* • **1.** consideration, contemplation, examination, perusal – اللُّجنَة قَرَّرَت إعادَة النَّظَر بِالمَوضُوع [ʔillujna qarrarat ʔiʕaːdat ʔinnaðar bilmawðuːʕ] The committee decided to resume consideration of the matter. حالتَه الصِّحِّيَّة، أخذُوها بِنَظَر الاعتِبار [ħaːltah ʔiṣṣiħħiyya, ʔaxðuːha bnaðar ʔilʔiʕtibaːr] They took his state of health into consideration. القَضِيَّة بِيها نَظَر [ʔilqaðiyya biːha naðar] The matter's under consideration. إلفات نَظَر [ʔilfaːt naðar] letter of reprimand. • **2.** eyesight, vision – بِعِيد النَّظَر [biʕiːd ʔinnaðar] farsighted. قُصُر نَظَر [quṣur naðar] short-sightedness. ضِرَب نَظَر [ðirab naðar] to stare. بَسّ عاد تُضرُب نَظَر عَالبَنات [bass ʕaːd tuðrub naðar ʕalbanaːt] Stop staring at the girls! • **3.** out-look, prospect • **4.** aspect, view • **5.** opinion, point of view – بنَظَري، هذا مُو صَحِيح [bnaðari, haːðaː muː ṣaħiːħ] In my opinion, that's not true. إسأله؛ بَلكِي عِندَه وُجهَة نَظَر بِالمَوضُوع [ʔisʔalah; balki ʕindah wujhat naðar bilmawðuːʕ] Ask him; maybe he has an opinion about the subject.

نَظرَة [naðra] *n:* نَظرات [naðraːt] *pl:* • **1.** look, glance

نَظِير [naðiːr] *n:* نُظَراء [nuðaraːʔ] *pl:* • **1.** similar, like, equal, match, corresponding, equivalent, comparable – هَالمَرَة ما إلها نَظِير [halmara maː ʔilha naðiːr] This woman has no equal.

مَنظَر [manðar] *n:* مَناظِر [manaːðir] *pl:* • **1.** sight, view, panorama • **2.** scene (of a play)

نَظَرِيَّة [naðariyya] *n:* نَظَرِيّات [naðariyyaːt] *pl:* • **1.** theory, hypothesis

نَظّارَة [naððaːra] *n:* نَظّارات [naððaːraːt] *pl:* • **1.** (pair of) eye-glasses, spectacles • **2.** (pair of) goggles

ناظُور [naːðuːr] *n:* نُواظِير [nuwaːðiːr] *pl:* • **1.** field glasses, binoculars • **2.** telescope, spyglass

مَنظَرَة [manðara] *n:* مَناظِر [manaːðir] *pl:* • **1.** (pair of) eye-glasses, spectacles, goggles

مِنظار [minðaːr] *n:* مِنظارات، مَناظِير [minðaːraːt, manaːðiːr] *pl:* • **1.** telescope

مَناظِر [manaːðir] *n:* • **1.** eyeglasses

اِنتِظار [ʔintiðaːr] *n:* • **1.** waiting, wait, expectation

نَظّاراتي [naððaːraːti] *n:* نَظّاراتِيِّين [naððaːraːtiyyiːn] *pl:* • **1.** optician

نَظَرِي [naðari] *adj:* • **1.** optical, visual • **2.** theoretical, hypothetical, speculative – هَذا حَلّ نَظَرِي لِلمُشكِلَة [haːða ħall naðari lilmuškila] This is a theoretical solution to the problem.

ناظِر [naːðir] *adj:* • **1.** looking • **2.** **(as n:)** supervisor, observer, overseer

مِنتَظِر [mintaðir] *adj:* • **1.** expected

مُنتَظَر [muntaðar] *adj:* • **1.** prospective

نَظَرِيّاً [naðariyyan] *adverbial:* • **1.** theoretically – نَظَرِيّاً، تِقدَر تسَوِّيها هِيكِي [naðariyyan, tigdar tsawwiːha hiːči] Theoretically, you can do it that way.

ن ظ ف

نِظَف [niðaf] *v:* • **1.** to be or become clean – إغسِل إيدَك إلَى أن تِنظَف زين [ʔiɣsil ʔiːdak ʔila ʔan tinðaf ziːn] Wash your hands until they are very clean.

نَظَّف [naððaf] *v:* • **1.** to clean, cleanse, make clean – هَالصّابُون ينَظُّف زين [haṣṣaːbuːn ynaððuf ziːn] This soap cleans well. ما يطلَع مِن الدّائِرَة قَبِل ما ينَظُّف المِيز مالَه، وَما يخَلِّي عَلَيه وَلا وَرقَة [maː yiṭlaʕ min ʔiddaːʔira gabil maː ynaððuf ʔilmiːz maːlah, wamaː yxalliː ʕaliːh wala warqa] He won't leave the office before the clears his desk,

ن

and he won't leave one paper on it. الوَزِير الجِّدِيد راح ينَظُّف الوزارَة مِن أَمثال هَالمُوَظَّف [ʔilwaziːr ʔijjidiːd raːħ ynaððuf ʔilwizaːra min ʔamθaːl hallmuwaððaf] The new minister is going to clean up the ministry from the likes of this official.

تنَظَّف [tnaððaf] *v:* • **1.** pass. of نَظَّف: to be cleaned – هَالثَّوب كُلِّش وَسِخ. ما يِتنَظَّف [haθθuːb kulliš waṣix. maː yitnaððaf] This shirt is very dirty. It can't be cleaned.

نَظافَة [naḍaːfa] *n:* • **1.** cleanliness

تَنظِيف [tanḍiːf] *n:* • **1.** cleaning

نَظِيف [naḍiːf] *adj:* • **1.** clean – ثُوب نَظِيف [θuːb naḍiːf] a clean shirt.

مُنَظِّف [munaððif] *adj:* مُنَظِّفات [munaððifaːt] *pl:* • **1.** **(as n:)** cleanser, cleaning agent

أَنظَف [ʔanḍaf] *comparative adjective:* • **1.** cleaner or cleanest

ن ظ م

نِظَم [niðam] *v:* • **1.** to compose (poetry), versify – الشّاعِر نِظَم قَصِيدَة رائِعَة عَن تارِيخ بَغداد [ʔiššaːʕir niðam qaṣiːda raːʔiʕa ʕan taːriːx baɣdaːd] The poet composed a splendid poem about the history of Baghdad.

نَظَّم [naððam] *v:* • **1.** to organize, arrange, put in order – نَظُّم الفايلات حَسَب الحُرُوف [naððum ʔilfaːylaːt ħasab ʔilħuruːf] Arrange the files in alphabetical order. إذا ما تنَظُّم الغُرفَة، مَحَّد يأَجِّرها [ʔiða maː tnaððum ʔilɣurfa, maħħad yʔajjirha] If you don't straighten up the room, nobody will rent it. • **2.** to regulate, adjust, make regular – إذا تنَظُّم وَقِت أَكلَك، صِحَّتَك تِتحَسَّن [ʔiða tnaððum waqit ʔaklak, ṣiħħtak titħassan] If you regulate your meal times, your health will improve. • **3.** to put together, make ready, prepare – نَظّمَوا قَوائِم الرَّواتِب وَإلّا بَعَد؟ [naððumaw qawaːʔim ʔirrawaːtib waʔilla baʕad?] Did they make out the payroll yet?

تنَظَّم [tnaððam] *v:* • **1.** pass.of نَظَّم [naððam] to be organized, arranged, put in order – هالفايلات ما تِتنَظَّم [halfaːylaːt maː titnaððam] These files can't be arranged.

اِنتِظَم [ʔintiðam] *v:* • **1.** to be well organized, orderly, well arranged – إذا تحُطّ المِيز يَمّ الباب، الغُرفَة تِنتِظِم [ʔiða tħuṭṭ ʔilmiːz yamm ʔilbaːb, ʔilɣurfa tintiðum] If you put the table next to the door, the room will be well arranged. ما اِنتِظَم الشُّغل بِهالدّائِرَة إلّا بَعَد ما نِقلَوا عَلِي [maː ʔintiðam ʔiššuɣul bhaddaːʔira ʔilla baʕad maː niqlaw ʕali] The work in this office wasn't well organized until after they transferred Ali.

نُظُم [nuðum] *n:* • **1.** order, arrangement, system, regulation

نِظام [niðaːm] *n:* أَنظِمَة [ʔanḍima] *pl:* • **1.** order, regular arrangement • **2.** system • **3.** statute, law

ناظُم [naːðum] *n:* نَواظُم [nawaːðum] *pl:* • **1.** barrage, dam

مُنَظَّمَة [munaððama] *n:* مُنَظَّمات [munaððamaːt] *pl:* • **1.** organization – مُنَظَّمَة الطُّلّاب العَرَب [munaððamat ʔiṭṭullaːb ʔilʕarab] Arab Student Organization.

تَنظِيم [tanḍiːm] *n:* • **1.** organization, arrangement, regulation, reorganization

اِنتِظام [ʔintiðaːm] *n:* • **1.** regularity, orderliness – دَيِجِينا البَرِيد بِانتِظام [dayijiːna ʔilbariːd bʔintiðaːm] The mail comes to us regularly. دِراستَه دَتِمشِي بِانتِظام [diraːstah datimši bʔintiðaːm] His studies are proceeding normally.

مَنظُومَة [manḍuːma] *n:* • **1.** system

نِظامِي [niðaːmi] *adj:* • **1.** methodical, orderly, systematic • **2.** regular – جيش نِظامِي [ǰayš niðaːmi] regular army.

مِنتِظِم [mintiðim] *adj:* • **1.** well-organized, orderly, systematic

تَنظِيمِي [tanḍiːmi] *adj:* • **1.** regulatory

أَنظَم [ʔanḍam] *comparative adjective:* • **1.** more or most orderly, systematic, well-organized

نِظامِيّاً [niðaːmiyyan] *adverbial:* • **1.** systematic, regular, orderly

ن ع ت

نِعَت [niʕat] *v:* • **1.** to describe

ن ع ج

نَعجَة [naʕja] *n:* نَعجات، نعاج [naʕjaːt, nʕaːǰ] *pl:* • **1.** ewe, female sheep

نعيج، نعيج المَيّ [nʕiːǰ, nʕiːǰ ʔilmayy] *n:* • **1.** sea gull(s)

ن ع ر

نَوعَر [nawʕar] *v:* • **1.** to whine, scream, roar

نِعَر [niʕar] *v:* • **1.** to whine, scream, roar – اللُّورِي دَيِصعَد الجِّبَل يِنعُر [ʔilluːri dayiṣʕad ʔijjibal yinʕur] The truck's roaring up the mountain. المُصرَع مالِي يِنعُر زين [ʔilmuṣraʕ maːli yinʕur ziːn] My top hums nicely.

نَعِير [naʕiːr] *n:* • **1.** shouting, clamor

ناعُور [naːʕuːr] *n:* نُواعِير [nuwaːʕiːr] *pl:* • **1.** noria, water wheel • **2.** whistling top

ن ع س

نِعَس [niʕas] *v:* • **1.** to become drowsy, sleepy – دَيِتثاوَب. يبَيِّن نِعَس [dayitθaːwab. yibayyin niʕas] He's yawning. He must've gotten sleepy.

نَعَّس [naʕʕas] *v:* • **1.** same as نِعَس: to be drowsy, sleepy – مِن تصِير ساعَة تِسعَة باللَّيل، أَنَعِّس [min tṣiːr saːʕa tisʕa billayl, ʔanaʕʕis] When it gets nine p. m., I get sleepy. • **2.** to cause to be drowsy, sleepy – هالجَوّ ينَعِّس الواحِد [hajjaww ynaʕʕis ʔilwaːħid] This weather makes one drowsy.

نَعسَة [naʕsa] *n:* نَعسات [naʕsaːt] *pl:* • **1.** doze, nap, slumber

ن

نُعاس [nuʕa:s] *n:* • **1.** sleep, sleepiness, drowsiness
مْنَعِّس [mnaʕʕis] *adj:* • **1.** sleepy, drowsy
نَعسان [naʕsa:n] *adj:* • **1.** sleepy, drowsy

ن ع ش

أنعَش [ʔanʕaš] *v:* • **1.** to refresh, invigorate, stimulate, arouse, enliven – هالهَوا يِنعِش البَدَن [halhawa yinʕiš ʔilbadan] This climate invigorates the body.
اِنتِعَش [ʔintiʕaš] *v:* • **1.** to revive, come to new life, be strengthened – الزَّرِع اِنتِعَش بالمُطَر [ʔizzariʕ ʔintiʕaš bilmuṭar] The crops were rejuvenated by the rain. • **2.** to be refreshed, invigorated – أُخُذ دُوش وَانتِعِش [ʔuxuð du:š wʔintiʕiš] Take a shower and refresh yourself.
نَعِش [naʕiš] *n:* نعُوش [nʕu:š] *pl:* • **1.** bier
اِنتِعاش [ʔintiʕa:š] *n:* • **1.** refreshment, recreation
مُنعِش [munʕiš] *adj:* • **1.** refreshing, invigorating, restorative

ن ع ل [1]

نَعَّل [naʕʕal] *v:* • **1.** to shoe, furnish with shoes – راح أنَعِّل الحِصان [ra:ħ ʔanaʕʕil ʔilħiṣa:n] I'm going to shoe the horse.
نَعَل [naʕal] *n:* نَعلات [naʕla:t] *pl:* • **1.** horseshoe • **2.** sandal • **3.** sole (of a shoe) – نَعَل كامِل [naʕal ka:mil] full sole. نُصّ نَعَل [nuṣṣ naʕal] half sole. جِلِد نَعَل [ǰilid naʕal] a grade of leather used for shoe soles, harness, etc.
نَعال [naʕa:l] *n:* نعالات، نِعِل، نِعلان، نعُولَة [nʕa:la:t, niʕil, niʕla:n, nʕu:la] *pl:* • **1.** (pair of) sandals
نَعَلجَة [naʕalča] *n:* نَعَلجات [naʕalča:t] *pl:* • **1.** tap, metal plate on a shoe

ن ع ل [2]

نِعَل [niʕal] *v:* • **1.** same as لِعَن: to curse, damn, execrate – شسَوَّى حَتَّى تِنعَل أبُوه؟ [ššawwa: ħatta tinʕal ʔabu:h?] What did he do that you'd curse his father? نِعَل أصلَه وَفصلَه [niʕal ʔaṣlah wfaṣlah] He really cussed him out (lit., damned his ancestors and his pedigree). بهالشُّغُل، نِعَل سَلفَة سَلفايا [bhaššuɣul, niʕal salfat salfa:ya] He really gave me hell on this job (lit., cursed the ancestors of my ancestors).
نَعَّل [naʕʕal] *v:* • **1.** same as لَعَّن: to curse, damn, execrate • **2.** intensive of نِعَل: to curse, damn, execrate – بَسّ تسَوِّي شِي ما يِعجبَه، يقُوم ينَعِّل [bass tsawwi ši ma: yʕiǰbah, ygu:m ynaʕʕil] Just do something that doesn't please him and he starts cursing up and down.
نَعِل [naʕil] *n:* • **1.** same as لِعِن: [liʕan] cursing, damning
نَعلَة [naʕla] *n:* نَعلات [naʕla:t] *pl:* • **1.** same as لَعنَة: cursing, curse, damning, damnation – نَعلَة الله عَلِيك [naʕlat ʔallah ʕali:k] The curse of God on you!
مَنعُول [manʕu:l] *adj:* • **1.** same as مَلعُون: damned, cursed

ن ع م

نِعَم [niʕam] *v:* • **1.** to be or become fine, powdery – دُقها لِلقَهوَة زين. بَلكِي تِنعَم بَعَد [duggha lilgahwa zi:n. balki tinʕam baʕad] Pound the coffee well. Perhaps it'll become still finer. • **2.** to soften, to be or become smooth, soft – اِستَعمِلِي هَالدُّوا حَتَّى جِلدِك يِنعَم [ʔistaʕmili hadduwa: ħatta ǰildič yinʕam] Use this medicine so that your skin will get soft.
نَعَّم [naʕʕam] *v:* • **1.** to grind, pulverize, powder – هَالمَكِينَة ما تنَعِّم القَهوَة زين [halmaki:na ma: tnaʕʕim ʔilgahwa zi:n] This grinder doesn't pulverize the coffee well. إذا ما تِنكَبّ، أجِي أنَعِّم ضلُوعَك [ʔiða ma: tinčabb, ʔaǰi ʔanaʕʕim ðlu:ʕak] If you don't shut up, I'll come beat you to a pulp (lit., pulverize your ribs). • **2.** to soften, to make smooth, soft – هَالمادَّة تنَعِّم القُماش بِالغَسِل [halma:dda tnaʕʕim ʔilquma:š bilɣasil] This stuff'll soften the cloth during washing.
أنعَم [ʔanʕam] *v:* • **1.** (of God) to be bountiful, bestow favors – الله أنعَم عَليه [ʔallah ʔanʕam ʕali:h] God was good to him. الله يِنعَم عَلِيك [ʔallah yinʕam ʕali:k] (lit., may God bestow his favor upon you) the standard reply to نَعِيماً
تنَعَّم [tnaʕʕam] *v:* • **1.** to live in luxury, lead a life of ease – هَذا مِتنَعِّم بِحَياتَه [ha:ða mitnaʕʕim bħaya:tah] He's lived in luxury during his lifetime. • **2.** with ب to enjoy – تنَعَّم بِحَياتَك ما طُول عِندَك فلُوس [tnaʕʕam bħaya:tak ma: ṭu:l ʕindak flu:s] Enjoy your life while you still have money.
نِعمَ [niʕma] *n:* • **1.** /followed by a noun with definite article/ what a wonderful...! such a perfect...! – نِعمَة الصَّدِيق [niʕma ʔiṣṣadi:q] He's truly a fine friend!
نِعمَة [niʕma] *n:* نِعَم [niʕam] *pl:* • **1.** boon, benefaction, blessing, benefit, grace, kindness – مِن نِعمَة الله، ما مِحتاج شِي [min niʕmat ʔallah, ma: miħta:ǰ ši] By the grace of God, I'm not in need of anything. إبن نِعمَة [ʔibin niʕma] man from a wealthy family. هَذا إبن نِعمَة؛ نَفسَه ما تِدنى عَلَى شِي [ha:ða ʔibin niʕma; nafsah ma: tidna ʕala ši] He was born with a silver spoon in his mouth; he isn't hurting for anything. • **2.** food
نَعام [naʕa:m] *n:* نَعام [naʕa:m] *pl:* نَعامَة، نَعامَات [naʕa:ma, naʕa:ma:t] *feminine:* • **1.** (coll.) ostrich(es)
نَعِيم [naʕi:m] *n:* • **1.** amenity, comfort, ease, happiness – هَذا عايِش بِنَعِيم [ha:ða ʕa:yiš bnaʕi:m] He's living in comfort
نُعُومَة [nuʕu:ma] *n:* • **1.** smoothness, fineness, daintiness
ناعِم [na:ʕim] *adj:* • **1.** pulverized, powdery, fine – شَكَر ناعِم [šakar na:ʕim] fine sugar. • **2.** soft, silky – هَالقُماش ناعِم [halquma:š na:ʕim] This cloth is soft. • **3.** smooth – النَّجّار رَندَج اللَّوحَة وصارَت ناعمَة [ʔinnaǰǰa:r randaǰ ʔillawħa wṣa:rat na:ʕma] The carpenter planed the board and it became smooth.

ن

مَكِينَة الزِيان الكَهرَبائِيَّة ما تزَيِّن ناعِم [maki:nat ʔilziya:n ʔilkahraba:ʔiyya ma: dzayyin na:ʕim] Electric shavers don't shave close. • **4.** small, tender (vegetables, etc.) • **5.** trim, lean, slim – رَجِلها ناعِم لِأَنّ يدِير بالَه عَلَى أَكلَه [rajilha na:ʕim liʔann ydi:r ba:lah ʕala ʔaklah] Her husband is trim because he is careful about what he eats.

نُوَيعِم [nuwayʕim] *adj:* • **1.** tiny, little • **2.** soft, dainty

نِعِيماً [naʕi:man] *adverbial:* • **1.** a standard polite expression said to someone after a bath or haircut

نَعَم [naʕam] *int:* • **1.** yes, certainly, to be sure – نَعَم، أَعُرفَه [naʕam, ʔaʕurfah] Yes, I know him. • **2.** yes? what did you say? I beg your pardon? – نَعَم؟ ما سِمَعِت شقلِت [naʕam? ma: simaʕit šgilit] Pardon? I didn't hear what you said.

ن ع ن ع

نِعناع [niʕna:ʕ] *n:* • **1.** a variety of mint – قُرُص نِعناع [quruṣ niʕna:ʕ] mint candy.

ن غ ب ش

نَغبَش [nayˤbaš] *v:* • **1.** to dig, search, paw around – لا تنَغبِش بِالجُنطَة مالتِي [la: tnaɣbiš bijjunṭa ma:lti] Don't paw through my suitcase. • **2.** to dig around, poke around, pry – ظَلّ يِنَغبُش عَلَيّا إِلَى أَن نِقلونِي [ðall yinaɣbuš ʕalayya ʔila ʔan niqlu:ni] He continued to undermine me until they transferred me.

ن غ ز

نِغَز [niɣaz] *v:* • **1.** to prick, stick, scratch – نِغَزنِي بالأُبرَة [niɣazni bilʔubra] He pricked me with the needle. إِنتَ عَلَى طُول تِنغُز بِحَكيَك [ʔinta ʕala ṭu:l tinɣuz bħačyak] You're always making cutting remarks.

نَغَّز [naɣɣaz] *v:* • **1.** to prick, stick, scratch – بَطّانِيّات الصُوف الرِّخِيص تنَغِّز [baṭṭa:niyya:t ʔiṣṣu:f ʔirrixi:ṣ tnaɣɣiz] Blankets of cheap wool scratch.

تنَغَّز [tnaɣɣaz] *v:* • **1.** to be pricked, scratched – مِن كان يقَطِّع وَرِد، تنَغَّزَت إِيدَه [min ča:n ygaṭṭiʕ warid, tnaɣɣzat ʔi:dah] When he was picking roses, his hand got pricked.

اِنّغَز [ʔinniɣaz] *v:* • **1.** to be pricked – اِنّغَز بإِصِبعَه مَرّتَين بالشَّوكَة [ʔinniɣaz bʔiṣibʕah marrtayn biššawka] He got stuck on his finger two times by the thorn.

نَغِز [naɣiz] *n:* • **1.** sticking, pricking

نِغّيز [niɣɣi:z] *n:* • **1.** (coll.) thorn(s)

نَغزَة [naɣza] *n:* نَغزات [naɣza:t] *pl:* • **1.** prick, scratch

نِغّيزَة [niɣɣi:za] *n:* نِغّيزات [niɣɣi:za:t] *pl:* • **1.** a thorn

ن غ ص

نَغَّص [naɣɣaṣ] *v:* • **1.** to spoil, disturb, make miserable – نَغَّص عَلَيّا السَّفرَة وَما توَنَّسِت [naɣɣaṣ ʕalayya ʔissafra wma twannasit] He spoiled the trip for me and I didn't have a good time. نَغَّص عَلَيّا عِيشتِي [naɣɣaṣ ʕalayya ʕi:šti] He made life miserable for me.

تنَغَّص [tnaɣɣaṣ] *v:* • **1.** to be disturbed, feel uneasy, be unable to enjoy oneself – تنَغَّصِت بِالحَفلَة لِأَنّ إِبنِي كان يِبكِي [tnaɣɣaṣit bilħafla liʔann ʔibni ča:n yibči] I didn't enjoy the ceremony because my son was crying.

متنَغِّص [mitnaɣɣiṣ] *adj:* • **1.** disturbed, annoyed

ن غ غ

نَغّ [naɣɣ] *v:* • **1.** to poke, jab – مِن نَغّنِي، صِحِت "آخ" [min naɣɣni, ṣiħit "ʔa:x"] When he poked me, I yelled 'Ouch'.

نَغّ [naɣɣ] *n:* • **1.** poking, jabbing

نَغَّة [naɣɣa] *n:* نَغّات [naɣɣa:t] *pl:* • **1.** poke

ن غ ل

نَغَل [naɣal] *n:* نغُولَة [nɣu:la] *pl:* • **1.** illegitimate child, bastard

منَغَّل [mnaɣɣal] *adj:* • **1.** illegitimate, bastardized

ن غ م

نَغَم [naɣam] *v:* • **1.** to hum softly in an even rhythm

نَغمَة [naɣma] *n:* أَنغام [ʔanɣa:m] *pl:* • **1.** melody, tune, air

ن غ م ش

نَغمَش [naɣmaš] *v:* • **1.** to cause a tickling sensation – النَّملَة دَتنَغمِش بظَهرِي [ʔinnamla datnaɣmiš bðahri] The ant is making my back itch.

ن غ ي

ناغَى [na:ɣa:] *v:* • **1.** to coo, sing, speak softly – فَحَل الحَمام دَيناغِي لِلنّتيَة [faħal ʔilħama:m dayna:ɣi linniθya] The male pigeon is cooing at the female. الأُمّ دَتناغِي لإِبنها [ʔilʔumm datna:ɣi lʔibinha] The mother is singing softly to her son.

ن ف ث

نَفّاثَة، طِيّارَة نَفّاثَة [naffa:θa, ṭiyya:ra naffa:θa] *n:* • **1.** jet airplane

ن ف ث ل ي ن

نَفثَلِين [naftali:n] *n:* • **1.** naphthalene • **2.** moth balls

ن ف خ

نُفَخ، نِفَخ [nufax, nifax] *v:* • **1.** to blow up, inflate, fill with air – أُنفُخ الجُوب حَتَّى نُعرُف إذا ينَفِّس [ʔunfux ʔiččuːb ħatta nuʕruf ʔiða ynaffis] Inflate the tube so we can tell whether it leaks. • **2.** to blow, puff, breathe on or into – نُفَخ الشّاي حَتَّى يُبرُد [nufax ʔičča:y ħatta yubrud] He blew on the tea so it would cool. • **3.** to boast, brag – لا تصَدِّق كُلّ ما يقُول تَرَة يُنفَخ هوايَة [la: tṣaddig kull ma: yigu:l tara yunfax hwa:ya] Don't believe all he says because he brags a lot. • **4.** to hiss, spit – هَالبَزُّونَة، مِن تِتقَرَّب يَمّها، تِنفُخ [halbazzu:na, min titqarrab yammha, tinfux] When you come near this cat, it spits.

اِنُّفَخ [ʔinnufax] *v:* • **1.** to be blown up, inflated – شُوف النُّفّاخَة اِنُّفخَت بِالعَجَل [šu:f ʔinnuffa:xa ʔinnufxat bilʕajal] Look how fast the balloon got inflated! • **2.** to become puffed up, filled with pride – اِنُّفَخ مِن صار مُدِير [ʔinnufax min ṣa:r mudi:r] He's gotten puffed up since he became director.

اِنتُفَخ [ʔintufax] *v:* • **1.** to swell, puff up, become bloated, inflated – الجُثَّة اِنتُفخَت وَطافَت عَالمَيّ [ʔijjuθθa ʔintufxat wṭa:fat ʕalmayy] The corpse swelled up and floated on the water. بَطنَه اِنتُفخَت مِن الأكِل [baṭnah ʔintufxat min ʔilʔakil] His stomach puffed out because of the meal.

نَفُخ [nafux] *n:* • **1.** blowing up

نَفخَة [nafxa] *n:* نَفخات [nafxa:t] *pl:* • **1.** blow, puff, breath

نُفّاخَة [nuffa:xa] *n:* نُفّاخات [nuffa:xa:t] *pl:* • **1.** balloon

نافُوخ، يافُوخ [na:fu:x, ya:fu:x] *n:* • **1.** top of the head

مِنفاخ [minfa:x] *n:* مَنافِيخ [mana:fi:x] *pl:* • **1.** bellows

اِنتِفاخ [ʔintifa:x] *n:* • **1.** bulge, swelling, protuberance • **2.** inflation, distension

مَنفُوخ [manfu:x] *adj:* • **1.** puffed up, self-important, conceited – شدَعوَة مَنفُوخ هَالقَدّ؟ [šdaʕwa manfu:x halgadd?] How come you're so puffed up?

مِنتُفُخ [mintufux] *adj:* • **1.** blown up, puffed up

ن ف ذ 1

نِفَذ [nifað] *v:* • **1.** with مِن to get through, pass through, penetrate – الشِّبّاك بَعدَه يِنفِذ مِنَّه هَوا [ʔiššubba:č baʕdah yinfið minnah hawa] The window still has air leaking through it.

نَفَّذ [naffað] *v:* • **1.** to carry out, execute, accomplish, put into effect, discharge, fulfill – نَفّذَوا حُكم الإعدام بِيه اليُوم الصُّبُح [naffiðaw ħukm ʔilʔiʕda:m bi:h ʔilyu:m ʔiṣṣubuħ] They carried out the death sentence on him at dawn today.

تنَفَّذ [tnaffað] *v:* • **1.** pass. of نَفَّذ: to be carried out, to be executed – لِيش أوامري ما دَتِتنَفَّذ؟ [li:š ʔawa:mri ma: datitnaffað?] Why aren't my orders being carried out?

اِستَنفَذ [ʔistanfað] *v:* • **1.** to exhaust

نُفُوذ [nufu:ð] *n:* • **1.** penetration, permeation, leakage • **2.** influence, authority, prestige

مَنفَذ [manfað] *n:* مَنافِذ [mana:fið] *pl:* • **1.** opening, vent, outlet

تَنفِيذ [tanfi:ð] *n:* • **1.** carrying out, implementation, enforcement, execution

اِستِنفاذ [ʔistinfa:ð] *n:* • **1.** exhaustion

نافِذ [na:fið] *adj:* • **1.** valid, in effect • **2.** effective, operative

مستَنفِذ [mistanfið] *adj:* • **1.** exhausted

تَنفِيذِي [tanfi:ði] *adj:* • **1.** executive

ن ف ذ 2

نِفَذ [nifað] *v:* • **1.** to sew, to stitch

نِفذَة [nifða] *n:* نِفذات [nifða:t] *pl:* • **1.** stitch

ن ف ر

نُفَر [nufar] *v:* • **1.** to shy away, stay away, keep clear – الجّاهِل دَيُنفُر مِن الضّيُوف [ʔijja:hil dayunfur min ʔiððiyu:f] The baby's shying away from the guests.

نَفَر [nafar] *n:* نَفَرات، أنفار [nafara:t, ʔanfa:r] *pl:* • **1.** person, individual – كانَوا مسَوِّين أكِل يكَفِّي مِيَّة نَفَر [ča:naw msawwi:n ʔakil ykaffi miyyat nafar] They had prepared enough food for a hundred people. جَرپايَة أمّ نَفَرَين [čarpa:ya ʔumm nafarayn] double bed. • **2.** pl. أنفار private, recruit (mil.)

نَفُر [nafur] *n:* • **1.** shying, staying away

نُفرَة [nufra] *n:* نُفرات [nufra:t] *pl:* • **1.** aversion, dislike, antipathy

نفِير، نَفِير عامّ [nafi:r, nafi:r ʕa:mm] *n:* • **1.** general call to arms, general alarm

نافُورَة [na:fu:ra] *n:* نافُورات، نَوافِير [na:fu:ra:t, nawa:fi:r] *pl:* • **1.** fountain

ن ف س

نِفَس [nifas] *v:* • **1.** to look upon with envy and spoil the possessor's enjoyment of it, to put the evil eye on – إنطِيه شوَيَّة مِن الأكِل قَبُل ما ينفِسَه [ʔinṭi:h šwayya min ʔilʔakil gabul ma: ynifsah] Give him a bit of the food before he ruins it with his envious eyes.

نَفَّس [naffas] *v:* • **1.** to leak, let out air – الجُوب دَينَفِّس [ʔičču:b daynaffis] The tube's leaking. • **2.** to unburden oneself, relax, take things easy – رُوح توَنَّس وَنَفِّس عَن نَفسَك [ru:ħ twannas wnaffis ʕan nafsak] Go have a good time and relax.

نافَس [na:fas] *v:* • **1.** to compete, vie, fight with – مِنُو راح ينافسَك عالبُطُولَة؟ [minu ra:ħ yna:fsak ʕalbuṭu:la?] Who's going to compete with you for the championship?

تنَفَّس [tnaffas] *v:* • **1.** to breathe, inhale and exhale – بَعدَه دَيتنَفَّس [baʕdah dayitnaffas] He's still breathing. • **2.** to take a breather, have a rest break – أرِيد المُدِير يِطلَع حَتَّى أتنَفَّس شوَيَّة [ʔari:d ʔilmudi:r yiṭlaʕ ħatta ʔatnaffas šwayya] I wish the director'd go out so I could take a breather.

تنافَس [tna:fas] *v:* • **1.** to compete with each other – صارِلهُم مُدَّة دَيتنافسُون عَالوَظِيفَة [ṣa:rilhum mudda dayitna:fsu:n ʕalwaði:fa] They've been competing for the position for some time.

اِنّفَس [ʔinnifas] *v:* • **1.** pass. of نِفَس to be looked upon with envy thereby spoiling the possessor's enjoyment of it, to be given the evil eye – كِنِت أَتأَمَّل حصاني يُغلُب، لَكِن اِنّفَس [činit ʔatʔammal ħṣa:ni yuɣlub, la:kin ʔinnifas] I was expecting my horse would win, but he got the evil eye.

نَفِس [nafis] *n:* نُفُوس، أَنفُس [nufu:s, ʔanfus] *pl:* • **1.** soul, psyche, id, spirit, subjective tendencies or qualities, nature, essence – نَفسَه دِنِيَّة [nafsah diniyya] He's self-indulgent. جا مِن نَفسَه. مَحَّد جُبَرَه [ǰa: min nafsah. maħħad ǰubarah] He came of his own accord. No one forced him. عِلم النَّفِس [ʕilm ʔinnafis] psychology. • **2.** self, personal identity – لازِم تِعتِمِد عَلَى نَفسَك [la:zim tiʕtimid ʕala nafsak] You've got to depend on yourself. رِحِتلَه بنَفسِي وحِكَيت وِيّاه عَنَّك [riħitlah bnafsi wħiči:t wiyya:h ʕannak] I personally went to him and talked to him about you. بنَفسِي، أَشتِرِي سَيّارَة، بَسّ ما عِندِي فلُوس [bnafsi, ʔaštiri sayya:ra, bass ma: ʕindi flu:s] If it were up to me, I'd buy a car, but I don't have any money. • **3.** animate being, living creature, human being, person, individual – إِنتُو كَم نَفِس ساكنِين هنا؟ [ʔintu čam nafis sa:kni:n hna?] How many of you are there living here? مُدِيرِيَّة النُّفُوس [mudi:riyyat ʔinnufu:s] census bureau. نُفُوس العِراق أَكثَر مِن ثلاثِين مَليُون [nufu:s ʔilʕira:q ʔakθar min θla:θi:n malyu:n] The population of Iraq is seven million. • **4.** /followed by a noun in the construct state/ the same, the very same – هَذا نَفس الرِّجّال اللِّي شِفتَه البارحَة [ha:ða nafs ʔirrijǰa:l ʔilli šiftah ʔilba:rħa] That's the same man I saw yesterday. أَرِيدها بنَفِس اللُّون [ʔari:dha bnafis ʔillu:n] I want it in the same color.

نَفَس [nafas] *n:* نَفَسات، أَنفاس [nafasa:t, ʔanfa:s] *pl:* • **1.** breath • **2.** puff (from a cigarette, etc.)

نِفاس [nifa:s] *n:* • **1.** confinement for childbirth • **2.** child-bed, puerperium

تَنَفُّس [tanaffus] *n:* • **1.** respiration, breathing

نَفاسَة [nafa:sa] *n:* • **1.** preciousness, costliness, value

تَنفِيس [tanfi:s] *n:* • **1.** ventilation, airing

تَنافُس [tana:fus] *n:* • **1.** mutual competition, rivalry

مُتَنَفَّس [mutanaffas] *n:* • **1.** place to breathe freely, breathing space, free scope, atmosphere, escape, way out

مُنافَسَة [muna:fasa] *n:* • **1.** competition, emulation

نَفسِي [nafsi] *adj:* • **1.** psychological, mental – حالتَه النَّفسِيَّة مُو زينَة [ħa:ltah ʔinnafsiyya mu: zi:na] His psychological condition isn't good.

نِفسَة [nifsa] *adj:* • **1.** abed with child, confined to childbed – أُمَّك نِفسَة. إِنتِي سَوِّي شُغُل البَيت [ʔummič nifsa. ʔinti sawwi: šuɣul ʔilbayt] Your mother is in childbed. You do the housework.

نَفِيس [nafi:s] *adj:* نَفائِس [nafa:ʔis] *pl:* • **1.** precious, valuable, priceless • **2.** magnificent, excellent – هاي شلُون قلادَة نَفِيسَة [ha:y šlu:n gla:da nafi:sa] What a magnificent necklace!

مُنافِس [muna:fis] *adj:* مُنافِسِين [muna:fisi:n] *pl:* • **1.** rival, competitor

تَنَفُّسِي [tanaffusi] *adj:* • **1.** respiratory

نَفسانِي، عالِم نَفسانِي [nafsa:ni, ʕa:lim nafsa:ni] *adj:* • **1.** psychologist

ن ف س ك

نَفِسكَة، نَفسُوك [nafiska, nafsu:k] *adj:* • **1.** covetous, greedy – شلُون نَفِسكَة! بَسّ يشُوف جُكلَيت يرِيدَه [šlu:n nafiska! bass yšu:f čukli:t yiri:dah] How greedy he is! The minute he sees candy he wants it.

ن ف ش

نِفَش [nifaš] *v:* • **1.** to puff up, swell out, to ruffle its feathers – الطَّير مِن ينفِش نَفسَه، يبَيِّن كِبِير [ʔiṭṭi:r min yinfiš nafsah, yibayyin čibi:r] When the bird ruffles its feather, it looks big.

نَفَّش [naffaš] *v:* • **1.** to tease, fluff up – نَفِّشِي الصُّوف قَبُل ما تغزلِيه [naffiši ʔiṣṣu:f gabul ma: tɣizli:h] Fluff up the wool before you spin it.

اِنّفَش [ʔinnifaš] *v:* • **1.** to become puffed up, self-important – مِن صار مُدِير، اِنّفَش [min ṣa:r mudi:r, ʔinnifaš] When he became director, he got a swelled head.

اِنتِفَش [ʔintifaš] *v:* • **1.** to ruffle its feathers, to strut, swagger – الدِّيك اِنتِفَش مِن شاف الدِّجاجَة [ʔiddi:č ʔinnifaš min ša:f ʔiddiǰa:ǰa] The cock ruffled his feathers when he saw the chicken.

نَفِش [nafiš] *n:* • **1.** puffing, swelling

مَنفُوش [manfu:š] *adj:* • **1.** disheveled – أَشُو شَعرَك مَنفُوش. ما تمَشِّط [ʔašu: šaʕrak manfu:š. ma: tmaššiṭ] I see your hair is disheveled. Why don't you comb it.

ن ف ض

نُفَض [nufað] *v:* • **1.** to shake, shake out, dust off – أُنفُض البَردَة. بِيها عَجاج هوايَة [ʔunfuð ʔilparda. bi:ha ʕaǰa:ǰ hwa:ya] Shake out the curtain. There's a lot of dust in it. • **2.** to shake up, shock – إِذا ما تنُفضَه زين، ما يتأَدَّب [ʔiða ma: tnufðah zi:n, ma: yitʔaddab] If you don't shake him up good, he won't behave. • **3.** to hit suddenly or unexpectedly – نُفَضتَه ببُوكس وَقَّعتَه [nufaðtah bibu:ks waggaʕtah] I hit him with a punch that knocked him down.

نَفَّض [naffað] *v:* • **1.** to shake out, dust off – دَينَفُّضُون الزُّوالِي بَرَّة [daynaffuðu:n ʔizzuwa:li barra] They're shaking out the carpets outside. خَلِّي أَنَفُّض كِتفَك؛ عَلِيه تراب [xalli: ʔanaffuð čitfak; ʕali:h tra:b] Let me brush off your shoulder; there's dust on it.

اِنتُفَض [ʔintufað] *v:* • **1.** to be shaken, upset, shocked – اِنتُفَض مِن سِمَع إِبنَه اِنجِرَح بِالحادِث [ʔintufað min simaʕ ʔibnah ʔinǰirah bilħa:diθ] He was shaken up when he heard that his son was injured in the accident.

نَفُض [nafuð̣] *n:* • **1.** shaking • **2.** scolding
نَفضَة [nafð̣a] *n:* نَفضات [nafð̣a:t] *pl:* • **1.** pl. نَفَضات instnace noun of نَفُض a shake
نُفّاضَة [nuffa:ð̣a] *n:* نُفّاضات [nuffa:ð̣a:t] *pl:* • **1.** ashtray • **2.** fit of chills and fever, ague, malaria attack

ن ف ط

نَفُط [nafuṭ] *n:* • **1.** petroleum, oil – نَفُط أَسوَد [nafuṭ ʔaswad] crude oil. نَفُط أَبيَض [nafuṭ ʔabyað̣] kerosene.
نَفطِي [nafṭi] *adj:* • **1.** oily

ن ف ع

نِفَع [nifaʕ] *v:* • **1.** to benefit, to be useful, beneficial, of use to – هَالدُّوا هوايَة نِفَعني [hadduwa: hwa:ya nifaʕni] That medicine did me a lot of good. ضُمّ قِسِم مِن فلوسَك. يِجِي يوم تِنفَعَك [ð̣umm qisim min flu:sak. yiǰi yu:m tinfaʕak] Save part of your money. A day will come when it'll be useful to you. هَالحَكِي ما يِنفَع [halħači ma: yinfaʕ] That talk won't help.
نَفَّع [naffaʕ] *v:* • **1.** to cause to benefit, gain, profit – عَلِي نَفَّعنِي مِيَّة دِينار [ʕali naffaʕni miyyat dina:r] Ali gained me a hundred dinars.
تنَفَّع [tnaffaʕ] *v:* • **1.** to profit, gain, benefit – أَهَل هَالولايَة يِتنَفَّعُون هوايَة مِن الزُّوار [ʔahal halwla:ya yitnaffuʕu:n hwa:ya min ʔizzuwa:r] The people of this city benefit a lot from the visitors.
اِنتِفَع [ʔintifaʕ] *v:* • **1.** same as تنَفَّع: to benefit from – دَانتِفِع مِنهُم زَرنِيخ [daʔantifiʕ minhum zarni:x] I'm benefiting from them a lot.
نَفِع [nafiʕ] *n:* • **1.** use, avail, benefit, profit, gain, advantage – لَك، إِنتَ ما بِيك لا نَفِع وَلا دَفِع [lak, ʔinta ma: bi:k la: nafiʕ wala: dafiʕ] You're good for nothing and you can't do anything.
نَفعِي [nafʕi] *n:* • **1.** self-interested, devoted to personal gain • **2.** opportunist, profiteer
مَنفَعَة [manfaʕa] *n:* مَنافِع [mana:fiʕ] *pl:* • **1.** use, avail, benefit, profit, gain, advantage
نافِع [na:fiʕ] *adj:* • **1.** useful, beneficial, advantageous, profitable
أَنفَع [ʔanfaʕ] *comparative adjective:* • **1.** more or most useful, beneficial

ن ف ف

نَفّ [naff] *v:* • **1.** to drizzle
نَفّ [naff] *n:* • **1.** drizzle

ن ف ق

نافَق [na:faq] *v:* • **1.** to play the hypocrite, feign honesty, innocence – إِنتَ شقَدّ تنافِق [ʔinta šgadd tna:fiq] You play the hypocrite so much! • **2.** to inform, bear tales – نافَق عَلَيّا عِند المُدِير [na:faq ʕalayya ʕind ʔilmudi:r] He informed on me to the director.
نَفَقَة [nafaqa] *n:* نَفَقات [nafaqa:t] *pl:* • **1.** expense, expenditure, outlay – دَيدرُس عَلَى نَفَقَة الحُكُومَة [dayidrus ʕala nafaqat ʔilħuku:ma] He's studying at government expense. • **2.** alimony • **3.** child support
نِفاق [nifa:q] *n:* • **1.** hypocrisy
مُنافِق [muna:fiq] *adj:* مُنافِقِين [muna:fiqi:n] *pl:* • **1.** hypocrite

ن ف ن ف

نَفنُوف [nafnu:f] *n:* نَفانِيف [nafa:ni:f] *pl:* • **1.** (woman's) dress, gown

ن ف ي

نِفَى [nifa:] *v:* • **1.** to exile, banish, expatriate – الحُكُومَة نِفَتَه لِقُبرُص [ʔilħuku:ma nifatah lqubruṣ] The government exiled him to Cyprus. • **2.** to rebut, deny – الحُكُومَة نِفَت الخَبَر بِالجَّرِيدَة [ʔilħuku:ma nifat ʔilxabar biǰǰari:da] The government denied the news story in the newspaper.
نافَى [na:fa:] *v:* • **1.** to contradict, be contrary to – تصَرُّفَه ينافِي الآداب [tṣarrufah yna:fi ʔilʔa:da:b] His conduct is contrary to good manners.
تنافَى [tna:fa:] *v:* • **1.** to contradict each other – تَصَرُّفَه بهَالقَضِيَّة يِتنافَى ويّا تَصَرُّفَه بقَضِيَّة مُشابِهَة [taṣarrufah bhalqað̣iyya yitna:fa: wiyya taṣarrufah bqað̣iyya muša:biha] His action in this matter is contrary to his action in a similar matter.
اِنَّفَى [ʔinnifa:] *v:* • **1.** to be denied – الخَبَر بَعَد ما اِنَّفَى [ʔilxabar baʕad ma: ʔinnifa:] The news hasn't been denied yet.
نَفِي [nafy]*n:* • **1.** negative, disavowal, denial – جَوابَه كان كُلَّه بِالنَّفِي [ǰawa:bah ča:n kullah bʔinnafy] His answers were all in the negative. • **2.** exile, deportation, banishment • **3.** negation (gram.)
مَنفَى [manfa] *n:* مَنافِي [mana:fi] *pl:* • **1.** place of exile • **2.** exile, banishment – بُقَى بالمَنفَى عَشِر سنِين قَبُل ما يِرجَع لوَطَنَه [buqa: bilmanfa: ʕašir sni:n gabul ma: yirǰaʕ lwaṭanah] He stayed in exile for ten years before he returned to his native land.
نِفايَة [nifa:ya] *n:* نِفايات [nifa:ya:t] *pl:* • **1.** cast-off, discarded thing • **2.** remnant • **3.** bit, piece, scrap (of dirt, lint, etc.) – أَكُو نِفايات قُطِن عَلَى راسَك [ʔaku nifa:ya:t guṭin ʕala ra:sak] There are some bits of cotton on your head.
مَنفِي [manfi] *adj:* • **1.** exiled, deported, banned

ن ق ب 1

نَقِيب [naqi:b] *n:* نُقَباء [nuqaba:ʔ] *pl:* • **1.** leader of a union, etc
نِقاب [niqa:b] *n:* • **1.** face veil, a veil that covers the whole face (and parts of the whole) body

ن

نَقابَة [naqa:ba] *n:* نَقابات [naqa:ba:t] *pl:* • **1.** union, guild, association – نَقابَة عُمّال [naqa:bat ʕumma:l] labor union. نَقابَة المُحامِين العِراقِيِّين [naqa:bat ʔilmuħa:mi:n ʔilʕira:qiyyi:n] The Iraqi Bar Association.
مَنقَبَة، مَنقَبَة نَبَوِيَّة [manqaba, manqaba nabawiyya] *n:* مَناقِب [mana:qib] *pl:* • **1.** a chanting of commendations and praises to the Prophet in poetry
تَنقِيب [tanqi:b] *n:* • **1.** excavation, digging, excavation
مُنَقَّب [munaqqab] *adj:* • **1.** masked, veiled

ن ق ب 2

نِقَب [nigab] *v:* • **1.** to pierce, perforate, make a hole in – نِقَب القُوطِيَّة بِالبِسمار [nigab ʔilqu:ṭiyya bilbisma:r] He punched a hole in the container with the nail. • **2.** to deflower, deprive of virginity – نِقَبها وَتوَرَّط بِيها [nigabha wtwarraṭ bi:ha] He deflowered her and got into trouble over it.
نَقَّب [naggab] *v:* • **1.** intensive of نِقَب: to pierce, perforate, make a hole in – نَقَّب الجِّدِر و سَوّاه مَصفِي [naggab ʔiǰǰidir w sawwa:h maṣfi] He punched holes in the pot and made a strainer out of it.
اِنَّقَب [ʔinnigab] *v:* • **1.** to be pierced, perforated – الجِّدِر اِنَّقَب [ʔiǰǰidir ʔinnigab] The pot's got a hole in it.
نَقُب، نُقُب [nagub, nugub] *n:* نقُوب [ngu:b] *pl:* • **1.** perforation, hole • **2.** (vulgar) anus

ن ق ب ر

نَقبَر [nagbar] *v:* • **1.** to pick (e.g., one's nose)
تنُقبُر [tnugbur] *n:* • **1.** to pick • **2.** picking, searching

ن ق د

نِقَد [niqad] *v:* • **1.** to review, make a critique of – نِقَد الكِتاب مالِي بِالجَّرِيدَة [niqad ʔilkita:b ma:li biǰǰari:da] He reviewed my book in the newspaper.
نَقَّد [naqqad] *v:* • **1.** to pay or give cash to – أَبُوه نَقَّدَه عَشِر فلُوس [ʔabu:h naqqadah ʕašir flu:s] His father gave him ten fils.
نَقَّد [naggad] *v:* • **1.** (of dates) to begin to ripen, show first signs of ripeness – الخلال نَقَّد وَراح يصِير رُطَب [ʔilxla:l naggad wra:ħ yṣi:r ruṭab] The green dates have begun to ripen and are about to become fresh. • **2.** to become mentally unbalanced – مِن يِجِي الصَّيف، هَذا ينَقِّد [min yiǰi ʔiṣṣayf, ha:ða ynaggid] When summer comes, he goes off his rocker. • **3.** to throw stones (at)
اِنتِقَد [ʔintiqad] *v:* • **1.** to criticize, find fault with – يِنتِقِدنِي عَلَى أَيّ شِي [yintiqidni ʕala ʔayy ši] He criticizes me about any little thing.
نَقِد [naqid] *n:* • **1.** criticism, reviewing (literary) • **2.** pl. نُقُود cash, ready money, coins
ناقِد [na:qid] *n:* نُقّاد [nuqqa:d] *pl:* • **1.** critic, reviewer
اِنتِقاد [ʔintiqa:d] *n:* • **1.** criticism
نَقدِي [naqdi] *adj:* • **1.** monetary, pecuniary, cash – تَضَخُّم نَقدِي [taðaxxum naqdi] inflation. هالبَقّال يبِيع بِالنَّقدِي بَسّ [halbagga:l yibi:ʕ binnaqdi bass] This grocer sells for cash only.
مُنتَقِد [muntaqid] *adj:* • **1.** critical
نَقداً [naqdan] *adverbial:* • **1.** cash • **2.** in cash

ن ق ذ

نِقَذ [niqað] *v:* • **1.** to rescue, deliver, save
إنقاذ [ʔinqa:ð] *n:* • **1.** saving, rescue, salvaging, deliverance, salvation, recovery, relief
مُنقِذ [munqið] *n:* • **1.** rescuer, savior, life-saver

ن ق ر 1

نَقّارَة [naqqa:ra] *n:* نَقّارات [naqqa:ra:t] *pl:* • **1.** small metal drum – سَوّالِي نَقّارَة [sawwa:li naqqa:ra] He caused me a lot of trouble.

ن ق ر 2

نِقَر [nigar] *v:* • **1.** to peck – الدِّيك نِقَر الجّاهِل بإيدَه [ʔiddi:č nigar ʔiǰǰa:hil bʔi:dah] The rooster pecked the boy on his hand. • **2.** to pick up, grab off, make off with – نِقَرها لِلجّائِزَة الأولَى [nigarha liǰǰa:ʔiza ʔilʔu:la] He grabbed the first prize. • **3.** to tap, beat, drum with the tips of the fingers – دَينقُر عالدُّمبُك نَقِر خَفِيف [dayingur ʕaddumbug nagir xafi:f] He's beating the drum lightly with the tips of his fingers. • **4.** to pick at, nag, harass – ظَلَّت تُنقُر بِراس رَجِلها حَتَّى سِمَع كَلامها [ðallat tungur bra:s raǰilha ħatta simaʕ kala:mha] She kept nagging her husband until he did what she wanted. قُصّتَك تُنقُر بأفادِي [quṣṣtak tungur bʔuffa:di] Your story makes me very sad. حكايتَه ظَلَّت تُنقُر بأفادِي وَما إرتاحَيت إلّا لَمّا سَبَّيتَه [ħča:ytah ðallat tungur bʔuffa:di wma ʔirtaħit ʔilla lamma sabbaytah] His remark kept bothering me and I couldn't rest until I'd told him off.
نَقَّر [naggar] *v:* • **1.** to peck repeatedly – الدِّجاج دَينَقِّر بالشِّعِير [ʔiddiǰa:ǰ daynaggir biššiʕi:r] The chickens are pecking at the barley.
تناقَر [tna:gar] *v:* • **1.** to bicker, to quarrel with one another – عَلِي وَأُختَه يِتناقرُون النَّهار كُلَّه [ʕali wʔuxtah yitna:gru:n ʔinnaha:r kullah] Ali and his sister are at each other's throats all day. جِيرانَّتنا تِتناقَر ويّا رَجِلها هوايَة [ǰi:ra:natna titna:gar wiyya raǰilha hwa:ya] The lady next door argues with her husband a lot.
نَقِر [nagir] *n:* • **1.** pecking
نَقرَة [nagra] *n:* نَقرات [nagra:t] *pl:* • **1.** peck • **2.** light blow, tap, rap – إنطِيها نَقرَة صغَيِّرَة بِالجاكُوج [ʔinṭi:ha nagra ṣɣayyra bičča:ku:č] Give it a little tap with the hammer.
نُقرَة [nugra] *n:* • **1.** bickering, wrangling, argument – ما دَأعرُف عَلَى ويش هَالنُّقرَة بَيناتكُم [ma: daʔaʕruf ʕala wi:š hannugra bayna:tkum] I can't understand why there's

this bickering between you. • **2.** pl. نُقَر hole, pit, cavity – راح يحفرُولَه نُقرَة وَيسَبِّبُون فَصلَه [raːħ yħufruːlah nugra waysabbibuːn faṣlah] They're going to lay a trap for him and cause him to get fired.

مِنقار [mingaːr] *n:* مناقِير [mnaːgiːr] *pl:* • **1.** beak, bill (of a bird)

مناقَرَة [mnaːgara] *n:* • **1.** bickering

نُقرِي [nugri] *adj:* • **1.** nagging, argumentative • **2.** **(n:)** nagger

ن ق ز

نَقَّز [naggaz] *v:* • **1.** to jump, hop, leap – شَكَّيتَه بالأبرَة وَقام ينَقِّز [čakkiːtah bilʔubra wgaːm ynaggiz] I pricked him with the needle and he began to jump up and down.

نَقّازَة، تِمَّن نَقّازَة [naggaːza, timman naggaːza] *adj:* • **1.** a kind of broad-grained rice

ن ق ش

نِقَش [niqaš] *v:* • **1.** to carve, engrave, sculpture, chisel – نِقَش إسمَه عالرَّحلَة [niqaš ʔismah ʕarraħla] He carved his name on the desk.

نَقَّش [naqqaš, naggaš] *v:* • **1.** to daub, paint, cover with bright colors – نَقَّش البَيض لِلحَفلَة [naqqaš ʔilbayð lilħafla] He painted the eggs for the party. • **2.** to decorate, embellish – صاحِب المَحَلّ نَقَّش الجّامخانَة [ṣaːħib ʔilmaħall naqqaš ʔiǰǰaːmxaːna] The shop owner decorated the show window. تُسكُت لَو أنَقِّشلَك؟ [tuskut law ʔanaqqišlak?] Are you going to shut up or shall I tell you off? • **3.** to eat a small amount as a courtesy – وَلَو شَبعان، راح أنَقِّش وِيّاكُم [walaw šabʕaːn, raːħ ʔanaqqiš wiyyaːkum] Even though I'm full, I'll eat a little bit with you.

ناقَش [naːqaš] *v:* • **1.** to debate with, argue with – آني رَئِيسَك؛ لا تناقِشني [ʔaːni raʔiːsak; laː tnaːqišni] I'm your boss; don't argue with me. • **2.** to talk, consult with – لازِم أناقشَك بِهالمَوضُوع حَتَّى أنطِيك رَأيِي [laːzim ʔanaːqšak bhalmawðuːʕ ħatta ʔanṭiːk raʔyi] I need to discuss this matter with you so I can give you my opinion.

تناقَش [tnaːqaš] *v:* • **1.** to argue, debate, discuss with each other – أرِيد أتناقَش وِيّاك عَلَى فَدّ نُقطَة مُهِمَّة [ʔariːd ʔatnaːqaš wiyyaːk ʕala fadd nuqṭa muhimma] I want to discuss an important point with you.

نَقِش [naqiš] *n:* نُقُوش [nuquːš] *pl:* • **1.** engraving, inscription • **2** design, embellishment, decoration • **3.** جاب نَقِش he was lucky, he pulled a trick – جاب نَقِش مُمتاز وَأخَذ فلُوسها [ǰaːb naqiš mumtaːz wʔaxað fluːsha] He pulled a clever trick and took her money. لَو ما يِجِيب نَقِش، ما كان غِلَبنِي بِالطّاولِي [law maː yǰiːb naqiš, maː čaːn ɣilabni bittaːwli] If he had been lucky he wouldn't have beat me in backgammon. دَيجِيب خُوش نَقِش. بِكُلّ اِمتِحان، يِطلَع أوَّل [dayǰiːb xuːš naqiš. bkull ʔimtiħaːn, yiṭlaʕ ʔawwal] He's having a streak of luck. He comes out first on every exam.

نِقاش [niqaːš] *n:* نِقاشات [niqaːšaːt] *pl:* • **1.** controversy, dispute, argument, debate

نَقشَة [naqša] *n:* نَقشات [naqšaːt] *pl:* • **1.** pattern

مِنقاش [minqaːš, mingaːš] *n:* مَناقِيش [manaːqiːš, mnaːgiːš] *pl:* • **1.** tweezers

مُناقَشَة [munaːqaša] *n:* مُناقَشات [munaːqašaːt] *pl:* • **1.** debate, argument • **2.** discussion

مَنَقَّش [mnaqqaš] *adj:* • **1.** colored, dappled, painted, engraved, decorated

مَنقُوش [manquːš] *adj:* • **1.** colored, dappled, painted, engraved

ن ق ص

نِقَص [nigaṣ, niqaṣ] *v:* • **1.** to decrease, diminish, become less – فلُوسَه نِقصَت شوَيَّة [fluːsah nigṣat šwayya] His money dwindled somewhat. بهَالقَضِيَّة، نِقَص قَدرَه [bhalqaðiyya, nigaṣ qadrah] With this affair, his prestige has suffered. • **2.** to be lacking, deficient, insufficient, inadequate – المُواعِين راح تُنقُص لِأنّ الخُطّار جابَوا جَهالهُم وِيّاهُم [ʔilmuwaːʕiːn raːħ tunquṣ liʔann ʔilxuṭṭaːr ǰaːbaw ǰahaːlhum wiyyaːhum] The dishes won't go around because the guests brought their children with them. • **3.** to be missing, absent from, be lacking in – كُلّ غَراض الكُبَّة عِندِي؛ بَسّ يُنقُصنِي الكِشمِش [kull ɣaraːð ʔilkubba ʕindi; bass yunguṣni ʔilkišmiš] I have all the stuff for the kubba; the raisins are all I'm lacking. شيُنقُصها؟ بنَيَّة حِلوَة وَمُثَقَّفَة [šyunguṣha? bnayya ħilwa wmuθaqqafa] What is lacking in her? She's a nice-looking, educated girl.

نَقَّص [naggaṣ, naqqaṣ] *v:* • **1.** to decrease, diminish, lessen – المَكِينَة دَتُركُض؛ نَقِّصها [ʔilmakiːna daturkuð; naggiṣha] The engine's racing; slow it down. • **2.** to reduce, curtail – الشَّرِكَة نَقِّصَت حُصَّتنا هَالمَرَّة [ʔiššarika naggiṣat ħuṣṣatna halmarra] The company reduced our quota this time.

تناقَص [tnaːgaṣ] *v:* • **1.** to decline

اِستَنقَص [ʔistangaṣ, ʔistanqaṣ] *v:* • **1.** to consider insufficient, deficient, lacking – رُفَض الطَّلَب لِأنّ اِستَنقَص الكَمِّيَّة [rufað ʔiṭṭalab liʔann ʔistanqaṣ ʔilkammiyya] He rejected the order because he considered the quantity insufficient.

نَقِص [naqiṣ, naquṣ] *n:* • **1.** deficiency, lack, want, shortage, deficit – المُحاسِب اِكتِشَف نَقِص بحسابَه [ʔilmuħaːsib ʔiktišaf naqiṣ bħsaːbah] The paymaster discovered a shortage in his accounts. التَّقرِير كامِل شامِل. ما بِيه أيّ نَقِص [ʔittaqriːr kaːmil šaːmil. maː biːh ʔayy naqiṣ] The report is complete and comprehensive. It lacks nothing. • **2.** imperfection, inferiority, defect, shortcoming, failing, fault – مُرَكَّب نَقُص [murakkab naquṣ] inferiority complex. يِتصَرَّف هِيكِي لِأنَّه يِشعُر بِنَقُص [yitṣarraf hiːči liʔannah yišʕur bnaquṣ] He behaves that way because he feels inferior.

نُقصان [nuqṣaːn] *n:* • **1.** shortage, lack

ن

نَقِيصَة [naqiːṣa] *n:* نَقائِص [naqaːʔiṣ] *pl:* • **1.** deficit, shortage, lack • **2.** defect, shortcoming, fault
تَنقِيص [tangiːṣ] *n:* • **1.** diminution, lessening, lowering, decrease
تَناقُص [tanaːguṣ] *n:* • **1.** decrease, diminution, decrement
مُناقَصَة [munaːqaṣa] *n:* مُناقَصات [munaːqaṣaːt] *pl:* • **1.** invitation for bids on a contract – الحُكُومَة راح تِعلِن مُناقَصَة عَلَى بِناء جِسِر [ʔilħukuːma raːħ tiʕlin munaːqaṣa ʕala binaːʔ ǰisir] The government is going to announce an invitation for bids on building a bridge.
ناقِص [naːqiṣ] *adj:* ناقِصِين، نُوَاقِيص [naːqiṣiːn, nuwaːqiːṣ] *pl:* • **1.** inferior, lowly, mean – هُوَّ فَدّ واحِد أَدبسِزّ وَناقِص [huwwa fadd waːħid ʔadabsizz wnaːqiṣ] He's boorish and inferior. • **2.** pl. نَواقِص something lacking – اِشتِرَيت عِدَّة أَشياء بَسّ بَعَد أَكُو نَواقِص [ʔištirayt ʕiddat ʔašyaːʔ bass baʕad ʔaku nawaːqiṣ] I bought several thing but there are still some things lacking. لِيش ما تِتزَوَّجها؟ بنَيَّة جاهلَة وَحِلوَة. شناقِصها؟ [liːš maː tidzawwaǰha? bnayya ǰaːhla wħilwa. šnaːqiṣha?] Why don't you marry her? She's young and beautiful. What's wrong with her?
أَنقَص [ʔangaṣ] *comparative adjective:* • **1.** more or most deficient, lacking – المَيّ اليُوم أَنقَص مِن البارحَة [ʔilmayy ʔilyuːm ʔangaṣ min ʔilbaːrħa] The water is lower today than yesterday.

ن ق ض ¹

نِقَض [niqað̣] *v:* • **1.** to cancel, abolish, repeal, revoke, nullify, annul, invalidate, rescind – مَحكَمَة الاستِئناف نِقضَت الحُكُم [maħkamat ʔalʔistiʔnaːf niqð̣at ʔilħukum] The Appeals Court reversed the decision.
ناقَض [naːqað̣] *v:* • **1.** to contradict, be contrary, opposite to, be in conflict, inconsistent with – يِقُول شِي وَبَعدين يناقِض نَفسَه [yiguːl ši wbaʕdiːn yinaːqið̣ nafsah] He says something and afterwards contradicts himself.
تناقَض [tnaːqað̣] *v:* • **1.** to contradict each other – اللِّي دَتقُولَه هَسَّة يتناقَض ويّا حَكيَك مال البارحَة [ʔilli datguːlah hassa yitnaːqað̣ wiyya ħačyak maːl ʔilbaːrħa] What you're saying now is contrary to what you said yesterday.
نَقِض [naqið̣] *n:* • **1.** violation, refutation, invalidation • **2.** reversal, appeal, repeal
نَقِيض [naqiːð̣] *n:* • **1.** opposition, contrast, antithesis • **2.** as Adj: opposed, opposite, contrary
أَنقاض [ʔanqaːð̣] *n:* • **1.** debris, rubble
تَناقُض [tanaːquð̣] *n:* • **1.** mutual contradiction, inconsistency • **2.** conflict
مِتناقِض [mitnaːqið̣] *adj:* • **1.** contradictory

ن ق ض ²

نِقَض [nigað̣] *v:* • **1.** to become tired, weary, exhausted – اِشتِغَلِت بِالحَدِيقَة وَنِقَضِت. لازِم أَرتاح [ʔištiɣalit bilħadiːqa wnigað̣it. laːzim ʔartaːħ] I worked in the garden and got tired. I've got to rest.
نَقَّض [naggað̣] *v:* • **1.** to tire, make tired – رَكَّضتَه لِلحصان إِلَى أَن نَقَّضتَه [rakkað̣tah lilħṣaːn ʔila ʔan naggað̣tah] I ran the horse till I'd tired him out.
نَقِض [nagið̣] *n:* • **1.** exhaustion, fatigue, tiredness
نَقضان [nagð̣aːn] *adj:* • **1.** tired, weary, exhausted – هَذا شايِب نَقضان؛ هَالشَّغلَة يِنرادِلها واحِد قَوِي [haːða šaːyib nagð̣aːn; haššaɣla yinraːdilha waːħid qawi] He's a worn-out old man; this job needs a strong person.

ن ق ط

نَقَّط [naqqaṭ] *v:* • **1.** to point, put in diacritical marks – العَرَب ما كانَوا ينَقِّطُون الحُرُوف [ʔilʕarab maː čaːnaw ynaqqituːn ʔilħuruːf] The Arabs didn't used to put dots on the letters of the alphabet. • **2.** to spot, dot, put in dots – نَقِّط هَالجِهَة بِالرَّسِم حَتَّى تبَيِّن [naqqiṭ halǰiha birrasim ħatta tbayyin] Put dots on this side of the diagram so it will show up clearly.
نَقَّط [naggaṭ] *v:* • **1.** to spot, dot, dab, speckle, dapple – صُبَغ الصَّندُوق أَبيَض وَنَقَّطَه بأَحمَر [ṣubaɣ ʔiṣṣanduːg ʔabyað̣ wnaggaṭah bʔaħmar] He painted the box white and speckled it with red. فِستانها أَبيَض منَقَّط بأَحمَر [fistaːnha ʔabyað̣ mnaggaṭ bʔaħmar] Her dress is white with red polka dots. • **2.** to drip, fall in drops – المَيّ دَينَقِّط مِن الحَنَفِيَّة [ʔilmayy daynaggiṭ min ʔilħanafiyya] The water is dripping from the faucet. • **3.** to drip, let fall in drops – الحَنَفِيَّة دَتنقِّط [ʔilħanafiyya datnaggiṭ] The faucet's dripping.
نُقطَة [nuqṭa] *n:* نُقَط [nuqaṭ] *pl:* • **1.** dot, point, speck, spot • **2.** period • **3.** point, subject, detail, item • **4.** (mil.) post, base, position
نُقطَة [nugṭa, nuqṭa] *n:* نُقَط [nugaṭ, nuqaṭ] *pl:* • **1.** spot, dot • **2.** stain • **3.** drop (of liquid) – هالكلاص ما بِيه نُقطَة مَيّ [halglaːṣ maː biːh nugṭat mayy] This glass doesn't have a drop of water in it.
ناقُوط [naːguːṭ] *n:* • **1.** water which has dripped from a porous clay water jug – ناقُوط الحِبّ صافِي وَبارِد [naːguːṭ ʔilħibb ṣaːfi wbaːrid] The water which has dripped from the water jug is clear and cold. حَسبَة الصَّرُف عَالسَّيّارَة ما تِخلَص؛ مِثِل ناقُوط الحِبّ [ħasbat ʔiṣṣaruf ʕassayyaːra maː tixlaṣ; miθil naːguːṭ ʔilħibb] The business of spending on the car never ends, like the water that drips from the water jug. • **2.** pl. نُواقِيط a small container for collecting droplets from a clay water jug

ن ق ع

نِقَع [nigaʕ] *v:* • **1.** to soak up moisture, to become thoroughly soaked – خَلِّي الحُمُّص بِالماي ساعتِين إِلَى أَن يِنقَع زِين [xalliː ʔilħummuṣ bilmaːy saːʕtayn ʔila ʔan yingaʕ ziːn] Put the chickpeas in water for two hours until they're well soaked. رُشّ القاع حَتَّى تِنقَع تَمام [rušš ʔilgaːʕ ħatta tingaʕ tamaːm] Sprinkle the ground until it's thoroughly wet.

نَقَّع [naggaʕ] *v:* • **1.** to soak, steep – نَقَّع القُماش بِالمَيّ حَتَّى يخُشّ [naggaʕ ʔilquma:š bilmayy ħatta yxušš] He soaked the cloth in water so it would shrink. ظَلّيت أَلُومَه إِلَى أَن نَقَّعتَه [ðalli:t ʔalu:mah ʔila ʔan naggaʕtah] I kept blaming him until I got him all worked up. • **2.** to cause to sweat, to make nervous, embarrass

تنَقَّع [tnaggaʕ] *v:* • **1.** to become soaked – تنَقَّعِت بالمُطَر [tnaggaʕit bilmuṭar] I got soaked in the rain.

نَقِع [nagiʕ] *n:* • **1.** soaking

نقُوع [ngu:ʕ] *n:* • **1.** dried whole apricots

مُستَنقَع [mustanqaʕ] *n:* • **1.** marsh, swamp

ناقِع [na:giʕ] *adj:* • **1.** soaked, wet

منَقَّع [mnaggaʕ] *adj:* • **1.** soaked, wet

مَنقُوع [mangu:ʕ] *adj:* • **1.** macerated, soaked

متنَقِّع [mitnaggiʕ] *adj:* • **1.** soaking wet

أَنقَع [ʔangaʕ] *comparative adjective:* • **1.** more or most soaked, wet

ن ق ق

نَقّ [nagg] *v:* • **1.** to croak (frog), cackle, cluck (hen)

نَقّ [nagg] *n:* • **1.** croaking, cackling, gabbling, babbling

نَقّاق [nagga:g] *adj:* • **1.** surly person, gruff man, grumbler, griper

ن ق ل

نِقَل [niqal, nigal] *v:* • **1.** to transport, transmit, convey – جابَوا لوري وَنِقلَوا كُلّ غَراضهُم [ǰa:baw lu:ri wniqlaw kull ɣara:ðhum] They brought a truck and moved all their things. • **2.** to transfer, shift – المُدِير نِقَلَه إِلَى وَظِيفَة جِدِيدَة [ʔilmudi:r niqalah ʔila waði:fa ǰidi:da] The director transferred him to a new job. نِقلُولَه دَمّ [niqlu:lah damm] They gave him a blood transfusion. • **3.** to copy – نِقَل عَلَيّا بِالإِمتِحان [niqal ʕalayya bilʔimtiħa:n] He copied from me during the examination. أُنقُل المَجمُوع مِن القَوائِم إِلَى دَفتَر الحساب [ʔunqul ʔilmaǰmu:ʕ min ʔilqawa:ʔim ʔila daftar ʔilħsa:b] Copy the total from the bills into the ledger. • **4.** to pass on, relate, report – حِكَينا قِدّامَه وَنِقَل كُلّ حَكِينا لعَلِي [ħiči:na gidda:mah wniqal kull ħačyna lʕali] We talked in front of him and he related everything we said to Ali. • **5.** to relay – راح ينِقلُون حَفلَة غِناء لمَحَطَّة بَغداد حَتَّى نِسمَعها [ra:ħ yniqlu:n ħaflat ɣina:ʔ lmaħaṭṭat bayda:d ħatta nismaʕha] They will relay a concert to a Baghdad station so we can hear it. • **6.** to spread, communicate – الذِّبّان يُنقُل هوايَة أَمراض [ʔiððibba:n yunqul hwa:ya ʔamra:ð] Flies spread many diseases.

تنَقَّل [tnaqqal] *v:* • **1.** to rove, roam, travel around – يعجبَه يِتنَقَّل مِن بَلدَة لِبَلدَة [yʕiǰbah yitnaqqal min balda lbalda] He likes to move around from town to town. قِضى شَهَر يِتنَقَّل بين عَواصِم أُورُبّا [giða: šahar yitnaqqal bi:n ʕawa:ṣim ʔu:ruppa] He spent a month traveling between the capitals of Europe.

تناقَل [tna:qal] *v:* • **1.** to be circulated, transported

اِنِّقَل [ʔinniqal] *v:* • **1.** to be transferred – عَلِي اِنِّقَل لبَغداد [ʕali ʔinniqal lbayda:d] Ali was transferred to Baghdad.

اِنتِقَل [ʔintiqal] *v:* • **1.** to pass on, be transferred, conveyed – بَعَد موتَه، مُلكِيَّة البَيت اِنتِقلَت إِلَى اِبنَه [baʕad mu:tah, mulkiyyat ʔilbayt ʔintiqlat ʔila ʔibnah] After his death, ownership of the house passed to his son. • **2.** to move, change residence – راح نِنتِقِل مِن هالمحَلَّة [ra:ħ nintiqil min halmħalla] We're going to move from this neighborhood. • **3.** to be spread, communicated – هَالمَرَض يِنتِقِل بِالماي [halmarað yintiqil bilma:y] This disease is communicated by water.

نَقِل [naqil, nagil] *n:* • **1.** transportation, transmission, conveyance

مَنقَل، مَنقَلَة [manqal, manqala] *n:* مَناقِل [mana:qil] *pl:* • **1.** brazier • **2.** grill (charcoal)

ناقِل [na:qil] *n:* ناقِلِين [na:qili:n] *pl:* • **1.** carrier, bearer

تَنَقُّل [tanaqqul] *n:* • **1.** change of position or place, traveling, migration, transmission

نَقلَة [naqla] *n:* • **1.** transmission, migration, move, change of residence or locality

نَقلِيَّة [naqliyya] *n:* نَقلِيّات [naqliyya:t] *pl:* • **1.** (usually pl.) transportation, transport, portage • **2.** freight company • **3.** moving company – آمِر النَّقلِيّات العَسكَرِيَّة [ʔa:mir ʔinnaqliyya:t ʔilʕaskariyya] Commander of Military Transport. • **4.** freight, freight charge, cartage – أَخذَوا دِينار نَقلِيَّة عالغَراض [ʔaxðaw dina:r naqliyya ʕalɣara:ð] They charged a dinar freight fee for the stuff.

ناقِلَة [na:qila] *n:* ناقِلات [na:qila:t] *pl:* • **1.** transport, transport vessel – ناقِلَة نَفُط [na:qilat nafuṭ] oil tanker.

نَقّالَة [naqqa:la] *n:* • **1.** stretcher, ambulance, lorry, truck, transport vehicule

نَقلِيّات [naqliyya:t] *n:* • **1.** transportation

اِنتِقال [ʔintiqa:l] *n:* • **1.** transition, move, change of locality

نَقّال [naqqa:l] *adj:* • **1.** mobile

مُتَنَقِّل، مِتنَقِّل [mutanaqqil, mitnaqqil] *adj:* • **1.** mobile • **2.** roving, roaming, itinerant, migrant

مَنقُول [manqu:l] *adj:* • **1.** carried, transported, transmitted, copied

اِنتِقالي [ʔintiqa:ly] *adj:* • **1.** transitional, transitive

ن ق م

نِقَم [niqam] *v:* • **1.** to become angry, disgusted, fed up – نِقَم عَالوَضِع وِاستَقال [niqam ʕalwaðiʕ wʔistaqa:l] He got disgusted with the situation and resigned.

اِنتِقَم [ʔintiqam] *v:* • **1.** to take revenge, avenge oneself – الله يِنتِقِم مِنَّك [ʔallah yintiqim minnak] God will get revenge on you.

نِقمَة، نَقمَة [niqma, naqma] *n:* نَقمات [naqma:t] *pl:* • **1.** affliction, adversity, misfortune

اِنتِقام [ʔintiqa:m] *n:* • **1.** revenge, vengeance

ن

ناقِم [na:qim] *adj:* • **1.** angry, disgusted – هُوَّ ناقِم عَلَيهُم كُلّهُم [huwwa na:qim ʕali:hum kullhum] He's disgusted at all of them.
مِنتَقِم [mintiqim] *adj:* مِنتَقمِين [mintaqmi:n] *pl:* • **1.** avenger, vindictive, revengeful
اِنتِقامِي [ʔintiqa:mi] *adj:* • **1.** revengeful, vindicative

ن ق ن ق

نَقنَق [naqnaq, nagnag] *v:* • **1.** to mumble to oneself in discontent, to become disgruntled, grumpy, peevish – لا تقُوم تنَقنِق. هَسَّة أرَجِّعلَك القَلَم [la: tgu:m tnaqniq. hassa ʔarajjiʕlak ʔilqalam] Don't get grumpy. I'll give the pencil back to you right away.
نَقنَق [nagnag] *v:* • **1.** to eat a small amount – وَلَو شَبعان، تَعال نَقنِق ويّانا [walaw šabʕa:n, taʕa:l nagnig wiyya:na] Even though you're full, come on and have a bite with us.
نِقناقِي [nigna:gi, niqna:qi] *adj:* • **1.** disgruntled, grumpy, peevish
نِقناقِيَّة [niqna:qiyya] *n:* • **1.** nag

ن ق ه

نَقاهَة [naqa:ha] *n:* • **1.** convalescence, recovery – دَور النَّقاهَة [dawr ʔinnaqa:ha] convalescent stage.

ن ق و

نَقّى [naqqa:] *v:* • **1.** to purify, clean, cleanse – هَالدُّوا ينَقِّي الدَّم [hadduwa ynaqqi ʔiddamm] This medicine purifies the blood.
اِستَنقى [ʔistanga:] *v:* • **1.** to pick out, select, choose – اِستَنقِي اللّي يِعجبَك [ʔistangi: ʔilli yiʕijbak] Pick the one you like.
نَقاوَة [naqa:wa] *n:* • **1.** purity
نَقِي [naqi] *adj:* • **1.** pure, clean • **2.** clear, limpid – ماي نَقِي [ma:y naqi] clear water.
مِستَنقى [mistanga] *adj:* • **1.** picked, chosen, selected – طَماطَة هَالبَقّال مِستَنقى [ṭama:ṭat halbagga:l mistanga:] This grocer's tomatoes are select. يبِيع مِستَنقى [yibi:ʕ mistanga:] He lets customers pick and choose.

ن ق و س

ناقُوس [na:qu:s] *n:* نَواقِيس [nawa:qi:s] *pl:* • **1.** bell (church)

ن ق ي

See also: ن ق و

ن ك ب

نِكَب [nikab] *v:* • **1.** to make unhappy, make miserable, afflict, distress – الحَرُب نِكبَتهُم. ماتَوا خَمسَة مِن وِلِدهُم [ʔilħarub nikbathum. ma:taw xamsa min wilidhum] The war caused them great suffering. Five of their sons died. إبنِي نِكَبنِي. اِشتِرَى هوايَة غَراض بِالدَّين وَهَسَّة ما دَنِقدَر نسَدِّد الفلُوس [ʔibni nikabni. ʔištira: hwa:ya ɣara:ð biddayn whassa ma: danigdar nsaddid ʔilflu:s] My son has caused me a lot of trouble. He bought a lot of things on credit and now we can't pay the money.
تنَكَّب [tnakkab] *v:* • **1.** to shoulder, place on one's shoulder – الجِّنُود اِتنَكّبَوا السِّلاح قَبُل ما يمُرّ وَزِير الدِّفاع [ʔijjinu:d ʔitnakkibaw ʔissila:ħ gabul ma: yumurr wazi:r ʔiddifa:ʕ] The soldiers shouldered their weapons before the Defense Minister passed.
اِنّكَب [ʔinnikab] *v:* • **1.** pass. of نِكَب: to be distressed (by) – اِنّكبَوا بمُوتَة أبُوهُم [ʔinnikbaw bmu:tat ʔabu:hum] They were distressed by the death of their father. المِسكِين اِنِكَب. كُلّ ولدَه ماتَوا بِالحَرِيق [ʔilmiski:n ʔinikab. kull wildah ma:taw bilħari:q] The poor guy has really had troubles. All his sons died in the fire.
نَكِب [nakib] *n:* • **1.** distress, affliction
نَكبَة [nakba] *n:* نَكبات [nakba:t] *pl:* • **1.** misfortune, calamity, disaster, catastrophe
مَنكُوب [manku:b] *adj:* • **1.** unhappy, unfortunate, miserable • **2.** as Noun, victim (of a disaster) – مَنكُوبِين الفَيَضان [manku:bi:n ʔilfayaḍa:n] the flood victims.

ن ك ت

نِكَت [nikat] *v:* • **1.** to play a prank, play a trick – عَلِي نِكَت بِيّا. قَلّي اليُوم عُطلَة وَخَلّانِي ما أرُوح لِلمَدرَسَة [ʕali nikat biyya. galli ʔilyu:m ʕuṭla wxalla:ni ma: ʔaru:ħ lilmadrasa] Ali played a trick on me. He told me today was a day off and caused me not to go to school. • **2.** to renege, go back on a promise – واعَد يدايِنّي فلُوس وَنِكَت [wa:ʕad yida:yinni flu:s wnikat] He promised to lend me money and then reneged. إذا تواعِد، لا تِنكُت [ʔiða twa:ʕid, la: tinkut] If you make a promise, don't break it. نِكَت بِيّا وَحَيَّرنِي [nikat biyya wħayyarni] He went back on his word to me and left me all confused. نِكَت بِيّا بِالمَحكَمَة. جا يِشهَد، قال "ما أعُرفَه" [nikat biyya bilmaħkama. ja: yišhad, ga:l "ma: ʔaʕurfah"] He double-crossed me in court. When he came to testify he said, "I don't know him. "
نَكَّت [nakkat] *v:* • **1.** to be witty, crack jokes, tell amusing stories – ضيفنا نَكَّت هوايَة البارحَة [ði:fna nakkat hwa:ya ʔilba:rħa] Our guest told a lot of jokes last night. • **2.** with عَلَى to mock, ridicule, poke fun at – خَلّوه بِالنُّصّ وقامَوا ينَكّتُون عليه [xallu:h binnuṣṣ wga:maw ynakkitu:n ʕali:h] They got him in the center and began to poke fun at him.
اِنّكَت [ʔinnikat] *v:* • **1.** with ب to be tricked, duped – هَذا شِيطان؛ ما يِنّكِت بِيه [ha:ða ši:ṭa:n; ma: yinnikit bi:h] He's a tricky fellow; he can't be humbugged.
نَكِت [nakit] *n:* • **1.** playing a trick or prank
نُكتَة [nukta] *n:* نُكَت [nukat] *pl:* • **1.** joke, witticism, wise-crack, pun • **2.** prank, trick, practical joke
منَكِّت [mnakkit] *n:* • **1.** witty
تَنكِيت [tanki:t] *n:* • **1.** humor

ن ك ث

نِكَث [nikaθ] *v:* • **1.** to break, violate (an obligation) – نِكَث العَهَد بِساع [nikaθ ʔilʕahad bsaːʕ] He broke the pledge right away. • **2.** (of moisture) to fall, come down – بَعَدها دَتِنكُث. يِبَيِّن راح تُمطُر النَّهار كُلَّه [baʕadha datinkuθ. yibayyin raːħ tumṭur ʔinnahaːr kullah] It's still coming down. It looks like it's going to rain all day. • **3.** to drip – طَبّ لِلقُبَّة يِنكُث عَرَق [ṭabb lilgubba yinkuθ ʕarag] He entered the room dripping sweat. • **4.** to shake, shake out, wave violently – إنكُث السِّترَة. يجُوز بِيها فلُوس [ʔinkuθ ʔissitra. yǰuːz biːha fluːs] Shake the coat. Maybe there are some coins in it.

نَكِث [nakiθ] *n:* • **1.** violation (an obligation), breaking

ن ك ح

نِكَح [nikaħ] *v:* • **1.** to marry, to get married (formal use)

نِكاح [nikaːħ] *n:* • **1.** marriage, matrimony – عَقد النِّكاح [ʕaqd ʔinnikaːħ] marriage contract.

ن ك ر

نِكَر [nikar] *v:* • **1.** to deny, disclaim, disavow – نِكَر كُلّشِي قِدّام الحاكِم [nikar kullši giddaːm ʔilħaːkim] He denied everything before the judge. نِكَر الدَّين عَلَيّا [nikar ʔiddayn ʕalayya] He denied owing me the debt.

تنَكَّر [tnakkar] *v:* • **1.** to assume a disguise, to mask, disguise oneself – بَطَل الرُّوايَة تنَكَّر وَخَشّ لِلحَفلَة [baṭal ʔirruwaːya tnakkar wxašš lilħafla] The hero of the story masked himself and went in to the party.

اِستَنكَر [ʔistankar] *v:* • **1.** to denounce, protest, disapprove of – كُلّهُم اِستَنكِرَوا العُدوان عالبَلَد [kullhum ʔistankiraw ʕilʕudwaːn ʕalbalad] They all denounced the aggression against the country.

نَكِر [nakir] *n:* • **1.** disclaiming, denial, disavowal

تَنَكُّر [tanakkur] *n:* • **1.** disguise

نُكران [nukraːn] *n:* • **1.** denial – نُكران الذّات [nukraːn ʔiðđaːt] self-denial. نُكران الجَّمِيل [nukraːn ʔiǰǰamiːl] ingratitude.

إنكار [ʔinkaːr] *n:* • **1.** denial

تَنَكُّرِي، حَفلَة تَنَكُّرِيَّة [tanakkuri, ħafla tanakkuriyya] *adj:* • **1.** masquerade party, costume ball

مِتنَكِّر [mitnakkir] *adj:* • **1.** disguised – مِن لِزمَتَه الشُّرطَة طِلَع رِجّال مِتنَكِّر بِزَيّ مَرَة [min lizmatah ʔiššurṭa ṭilaʕ rijǰaːl mitnakkir bzayy mara] When the police caught him he turned out to be a man disguised as a woman.

ن ك س

نَكَّس [nakkas] *v:* • **1.** to lower to half-mast, fly at half-mast – مِن مات المَلِك، نَكِّسَوا الأعلام [min maːt ʔilmalik, nakkisaw ʔilʔaʕlaːm] When the King died, they flew the flags at half-mast. • **2.** to bow, hang, bend – نَكَّس راسَه مِن الخَجَل [nakkas raːsah min ʔilxaǰal] He bowed his head from shame.

تنَكَّس [tnakkas] *v:* • **1.** pass. of نَكَّس to be lowered to half-mast, to be bowed, to be bent – الأعلام راح تِتنَكَّس مُدَّة إسبُوع [ʔilʔaʕlaːm raːħ titnakkas muddat ʔisbuːʕ] The flags will be flown at half-mast for a week.

اِنتِكَس [ʔintikas] *v:* • **1.** to suffer a relapse – صِحّتَه كانَت دَتِتحَسَّن لَكِن أخَذ بَرِد وَانتِكَس [ṣiħħtah čaːnat datitħassan laːkin ʔaxað barid wʔintikas] His health was improving but he caught a cold and had a relapse. اِنتِكسَت صِحّتَه مِن خَربَط بالأكِل [ʔintiksat ṣiʕʕtah min xarbaṭ bilʔakil] He had a relapse when he didn't follow instructions in his diet.

اِنتِكاسَة [ʔintikaːsa] *n:* اِنتِكاسات [ʔintikaːsaːt] *pl:* • **1.** relapse

مَنكُوس [mankuːs] *adj:* • **1.** inverted, reversed, relapsing

مِنتِكِس [mintikis] *adj:* • **1.** relapsing

ن ك ف

اِستَنكَف [ʔistankaf] *v:* • **1.** to look down on, feel too good for, to disdain, scorn – يِستَنكِف يِشتُغُل بِهالمَصلَحَة [yistankif yištuɣul bhalmaṣlaħa] He feels that he's above working in this occupation. يَعنِي تِستَنكِف تِحكِي ويّايا؟ [yaʕni tistankif tiħči wiyyaːya?] Do you mean you consider it degrading to talk with me? • **2.** with عَن to spurn, reject contemptuously – جِيت أبَلّغَه لَكِن اِستَنكَف عَن التَّبلِيغ [ǰiːt ʔaballɣah laːkin ʔistankaf ʕan ʔittabliːɣ] I went to present him with the summons but he contemptuously refused the summons.

نُكاف [nukaːf] *n:* • **1.** mumps – ما راح لِلمَدرَسَة لِأنّ عِندَه نُكاف [maː raːħ lilmadrasa liʔann ʕindah nukaːf] He didn't go to school because he has mumps.

ن ك ه

نكهَة [nakha, nukha] *n:* نكهات [nakhaːt, nukhaːt] *pl:* • **1.** aroma, scent, smell • **2.** flavor

ن م ذ ج

نمُوذَج [numuːðaǰ, namuːðaǰ] *n:* نَماذِج [namaːðiǰ] *pl:* • **1.** model • **2.** sample, specimen • **3.** exemplar, example

نَمُوذَجِي [namuːðaǰi] *adj:* • **1.** model, exemplary – هَذا رِياضِي نَمُوذَجِي [haːða riyaːđi namuːðaǰi] He's an ideal sportsman.

ن م ر 1

نِمِر [nimir] *n:* نُمُور [numuːr] *pl:* • **1.** tiger • **2.** leopard

ن م ر 2

نَمَّر [nammar] *v:* نُمَر [numar] *pl:* • **1.** to number, assign numbers to, put numbers on – نَمُّر الصَّفحات حَتَّى ما تِتخَربَط [nammur ʔiṣṣafħaːt ħatta maː titxarbaṭ] Number the pages so they won't get mixed up.

ن

ن م س

النّمسا [ʔannamsa:, ʔinnimsa:] *n:* • **1.** Austria

نمساوِي [namsa:wi] *adj:* • **1.** Austrian • **2.** an Austrian

ن م ش

نَمَش [namaš] *n:* • **1.** freckles, skin discolorations

منَمِّش [mnammiš] *adj:* • **1.** freckled

ن م ط

نَمَط [namaṭ] *n:* أنماط [ʔanma:ṭ] *pl:* • **1.** fashion • **2.** mode, form, shape, style

نَمَطِي [namaṭi] *adj:* • **1.** formal, rigid, stiff

ن م ل

نَمَّل [nammal] *v:* • **1.** to tingle, prickle, be numb, be asleep – أشُو إيدِي دَتنَمِّل [ʔašu ʔi:di datnammil] I think my hand is asleep.

نَمِل [namil] *n:* • **1.** (coll.) ant(s)

نَملَة [namla] *n:* نَملات [namla:t] *pl:* • **1.** ant

منَمِّل [mnammil] *adj:* • **1.** asleep • **2.** numb, creepy

ن م ن

نمُونَة [nimmu:na, nammu:na] *n:* نَمَايِن [nama:yin] *pl:* • **1.** sample, specimen

ن م ن م

نِمنِم [nimnim] *n:* • **1.** (coll.) small bead(s) – لابسَة قلادَة نِمنِم [la:bsah gla:da nimnim] She's wearing a necklace of small beads.

نِمنِمَة [nimnima] *n:* نِمنِمات [nimnima:t] *pl:* • **1.** small bead

منَمنَم [mnamnam] *adj:* • **1.** small, diminutive – شِتسَوِّي بهيكِي بَيت كِبِير؟ شُوفلَك بَيت صغَيِّر منَمنَم [šitsawwi: bhi:či bayt čibi:r? šu:flak bayt ṣɣayyir mnamnam] What'll you do with such a big house? Find yourself a small, compact house. تزَوَّج بنَيَّة حِلوَة منَمنِمَة [dzawwaǰ bnayya ħilwa mnamnima] He married a pretty, petite girl.

ن م و

نِمَى [nima:] *v:* • **1.** to grow, expand – الشَّرِكَة نِمَت وصار إلها فرُوع هوايَة [ʔiššarika nimat wṣa:r ʔilha furu:ʕ hwa:ya] The company grew and acquired many branch offices.

نَمَّى [namma:] *v:* • **1.** to cause to grow – هالسّماد ينَمّي الوَرِد بسُرعَة [hassma:d ynammi ʔilwarid bsurʕa] This fertilizer will make the flowers grow fast.

نُمُو [numuw] *n:* • **1.** growing

تنمِيَة [tanmiya] *n:* • **1.** growth, expansion • **2.** progress

إنماء [ʔinma:ʔ] *n:* • **1.** expansion, promotion, advancement, increase, augmentation

نامِي [na:mi] *adj:* • **1.** being in state of growth and development

إنمائِي [ʔinma:ʔi] *adj:* • **1.** serving growth and development, developmental

ن م و س

نامُوس [na:mu:s] *n:* • **1.** honor, integrity – ما عِندَك نامُوس؟ شلُون تخَلِّي مَرتَك تِخدِم الرِّياجِيل؟ [ma: ʕindak na:mu:s? šlu:n txalli: martak tixdim ʔirriya:ǰi:l?] Haven't you got any honor? How can you let your wife work as a servant to men? راح أخَلِّي القَضِيَّة يَمّ نامُوسَك [ra:ħ ʔaxalli: ʔilqaðiyya yamm na:mu:sak] I'll leave the matter up to your integrity. بنامُوسَك، آنِي صُدُق قِتلَك هِيكِي؟ [bna:mu:sak, ʔa:ni ṣudug gitlak hi:či?] On your honor, did I really tell you that? بنامُوسَك، ما يِصِير. خَلِّي آنِي أدفَع [bna:mu:sak, ma: yṣi:r. xalli: ʔa:ni ʔadfaʕ] By your honor, I won't allow it. Let me pay. وَنامُوسَك، راح أسَوِّيها باكِر [wna:mu:sak, ra:ħ ʔasawwi:ha ba:čir] I assure you, I'm going to do it tomorrow.

ن م ي

See also: ن م و

اِنتمَى [ʔintima:] *v:* • **1.** to become a member – راح أنتِمِي لِهَالحِزب [ra:ħ ʔantimi lhalħizib] I'm going to join this party. • **2.** to trace one's ancestry, to be descended – يِنتِمِي لِعائِلَة شَرِيفَة [yintimi lʕa:ʔila šari:fa] He is descended from a noble family.

اِنتماء [ʔintima:ʔ] *n:* • **1.** membership, commitment, affiliation

منتَمِي إلَى [mintimi ʔila] *adj:* • **1.** descended (from) • **2.** member, belonging (to)

ن ه ب

نِهَب [nihab] *v:* • **1.** to steal, plunder, take by force – وَقُفوه بِالطَّرِيق وَنِهبَوا كُلّ ما عِندَه [waggufawh bittari:q wnihbaw kull ma: ʕindah] They stopped him on the road and stole all he had. لا تِشتِرِي مِن هالبَقّال تَرَة يِنهَبَك [la: tištiri min halbagga:l tara yinhabak] Don't buy from this grocer or he'll rob you.

اِنّهَب [ʔinnihab] *v:* • **1.** to be stolen

نَهِب [nahib] *n:* • **1.** plunder

نِهِيبَة [nihi:ba] *n:* • **1.** stealing, plundering, pillage, looting

نَهّاب [nahha:b] *adj:* نَهّابَة [nahha:ba] *pl:* • **1.** robber, looter, plunderer – هَالتُّجّار كُلّهُم نَهّابَة [hattuǰǰa:r kullhum nahha:ba] These merchants are all robbers.

مَنهُوب [manhu:b] *adj:* • **1.** stolen, looted • **2.** robbed

ن ه ت

نِهَت [nihat] *v:* • **1.** to pant, gasp, breathe heavily – ظَلّ مُدَّة عَشِر دَقايِق يِنهَت مِن الرِّكِض [ðall muddat ʕašir daqa:yiq yinhat min ʔirrikið] He kept panting for ten minutes after running.

نَهت [nahit] *n:* • **1.** breathing heavily, gasping (for air)

ن ه ج

نِهَج [nihaǰ] *v:* • **1.** to proceed, to pursue

مَنهَج [manhaǰ, minha:ǰ] *n:* مَناهِج [mana:hiǰ] *pl:* • **1.** program, schedule of events

مِنهاج [minha:ǰ] *n:* • **1.** program, schedule of events

مَنهَجِي [manhaǰi] *adj:* • **1.** methodological

ن ه د

تنهَّد [tnahhad] *v:* • **1.** to sigh

نَهِد [nahid] *n:* نهُود [nhu:d] *pl:* • **1.** bosom, female (swelling) breast

تَنَهُّد [tanahhud] *n:* • **1.** sighing

تَنهِيد [tanhi:d] *n:* • **1.** sighing

ن ه ر

نَهَر [nahar] *n:* أنهار [ʔanha:r] *pl:* • **1.** river

نَهار [naha:r] *n:* نَهارات [naha:ra:t] *pl:* • **1.** day, daytime, the daylight hours

نَهرِي [nahri] *adj:* • **1.** river – السِّمَك النَّهرِي أطيَب مِن السِّمَك البَحرِي [ʔissimač ʔinnahri ʔaṭyab min ʔissimač ʔilbaħri] River fish are tastier than ocean fish.

نَهارِي [naha:ri] *adj:* • **1.** day, daytime – تِلمِيذ نَهارِي [tilmi:ð naha:ri] day student. حَفلَة نَهارِيَّة [ħafla naha:riyya] matinee.

ن ه ز

اِنتِهَز [ʔintihaz] *v:* • **1.** to seize, take advantage of – اِنتِهِز الفُرصَة وَلا تخَلِّيها تفُوتَك [ʔintihiz ʔilfurṣa wla: txalli:ha tfu:tak] Seize the opportunity and don't let it pass you by.

اِنتِهاز [ʔintiha:z] *n:* • **1.** taking advantage of

اِنتِهازِي [ʔintiha:zi] *adj:* اِنتِهازِيِّين [ʔintiha:ziyyi:n] *pl:* • **1.** opportunist

ن ه ش

نِهَش [nihaš] *v:* • **1.** to mangle, tear to pieces – الكِلاب اِلتَمَّت عَليه وَنِهشَت لَحمَه [ʔiččila:b ʔiltammat ʕali:h wnihšat laħmah] The dogs ganged up on him and tore his flesh to pieces.

نَهِش [nahiš] *n:* • **1.** snapping, biting, mangling, tearing to pieces

ن ه ق

نِهَق [nihag] *v:* • **1.** to bray – الزُّمال دَينهَق [ʔizzuma:l dayinhag] The donkey's braying. • **2.** to pant – تَعبان مِن الرِّكِض. دَينهَق [taʕba:n min ʔirrikið. dayinhag] He's tired of running. He's panting.

نَهِيق [nahi:g] *n:* • **1.** braying (donkey)

ن ه ك

أنهَك [ʔanhak] *v:* • **1.** to exhaust, wear out, enervate – هالشُّغُل أنهَكنِي [haššuɣul ʔanhakni] That work exhausted me.

اِنتِهَك [ʔintihak] *v:* • **1.** to violate, defile, abuse, profane, desecrate – اِنتِهَك حُرمَة الجامِع [ʔintihak ħurmat ʔiǰǰa:miʕ] He violated the sanctity of the mosque. حِبسوه لِأنَّه اِنتِهَك أعراض النّاس [ħibsu:h liʔannah ʔintihak ʔaʕra:ð ʔinna:s] They jailed him because he desecrated the honor of the people.

اِنِّهَك [ʔinnihak] *v:* • **1.** to be exhausted, run down, worn out

اِنتِهاك [ʔintiha:k] *n:* • **1.** exhaustion, weakening, enervation • **2.** abuse, misuse, violation,profanation, desecration

مُنهِك [munhik] *adj:* • **1.** exhausting

مِنتَهِك [mintahik] *adj:* • **1.** abusive

مُنتَهَك [muntahak] *adj:* • **1.** abused

مَنهُوك [manhu:k] *adj:* • **1.** exhausted

ن ه م

نَهِم [nahim] *adj:* • **1.** glutton, greedy, insatiable, gourmand

ن ه ي

نِهَى [niha:] *v:* • **1.** to prohibit, ban, forbid, interdict – ألف مَرَّة نهَيتَك مِن اللِّعب هنا [ʔalf marra nhi:tak min ʔilliʕib hna] I've told you a thousand times not to play here.

أنهَى [ʔanha:] *v:* • **1.** to bring to an end, terminate, finish, conclude, complete – لا ترُوح قَبُل ما تِنهِي كُلّ شُغلَك [la: tru:ħ gabul ma: tinhi kull šuɣlak] Don't go before you finish all your work.

اِنتِهَى [ʔintiha:] *v:* • **1.** to come to an end, draw to a close, to be terminated, concluded, finished, done with – السِّباق يِنتِهِي السّاعَة أربَعَة [ʔissiba:q yintihi ʔissa:ʕa ʔarbaʕa] The race ends at four o'clock. كُلّشِي بَيناتهُم اِنتِهَى [kullši bayna:thum ʔintiha:] Everything's all over between them.

نَهي [nahy] *n:* • **1.** forbidding, prohibiting, prohibition

نِهايَة [niha:ya] *n:* نِهايات [niha:ya:t] *pl:* • **1.** end • **2.** termination, conclusion • **3.** outcome, result – بالنِّهايَة، حَصَّل عَلَى دَرَجَة الدُّكتُورا [bʔinniha:ya, ħaṣṣal ʕala daraǰat ʔidduktura] Finally, he obtained his doctoral degree.

إنهاء [ʔinha:ʔ] *n:* • **1.** finishing, termination, completion, conclusion

اِنتِهاء [ʔintiha:ʔ] *n:* • **1.** end, termination, conclusion, completion

لا نِهايَة [la: niha:ya] *n:* • **1.** infinity

نِهائِي [niha:ʔi] *adj:* • **1.** final, last – اِمتِحان نِهائِي [ʔimtiħa:n niha:ʔi] final exam.

مِنتِهِي [mintihi] *adj:* • **1.** finished, done

نِهائِيّاً [niha:ʔiyyan] *adverbial:* • **1.** at all, whatsoever – ماكُو أيّ عِلاقَة بَيناتهُم نِهائِيّاً [ma:ku ʔayy ʕila:qa bayna:thum niha:ʔiyyan] There is no relationship between them at all.

ن و ب

ناب [naːb] *v:* • **1.** to act as representative, stand in, substitute, act as proxy – الوَزِير ما قِدَر يِجِي. آنِي أنُوب عَنَّه [ʔilwaziːr maː gidar yiǰi. ʔaːni ʔanuːb ʕannah] The minister couldn't come. I represent him. مِنُو يِنُوب عَنَّه مِن يغِيب؟ [minu ynuːb ʕannah min yɣiːb?] Who substitutes for him when he is absent?

نَوَّب [nawwab] *v:* • **1.** to appoint as representative, agent, or substitute – إلمَن راح ينَوُّب هَالمَرَّة؟ [ʔilman raːħ ynawwub halmarra?] Who will he appoint to fill in this time?

تناوَب [tnaːwab] *v:* • **1.** to take turns, alternate – إذا تِتناوبُون بِالشُّغُل، ما تِتعَبُون [ʔiða titnaːwbuːn biššuɣul, maː titʕabuːn] If you take turns at the work, you won't get tired.

نوبَة [nawba nuːba] *n:* نوبات [nuːbaːt] *pl:* • **1.** turn – هَسَّة نُوبَة مَن؟ [hassa nuːbat man?] Whose turn is it now? راح نُنطُر البُستان بالنَّوبَة [raːħ nunṭur ʔilbustaːn binnuːba] We're going to guard the orchard by shifts. • **2.** time, instance – خابَرتَك نَوبتَين لَكِن ما كان أَكُو جَواب [xaːbartak nawbtayn laːkin maː čaːn ʔaku ǰawaːb] I called you two times but there was no answer. هَالنَّوبَة إِلَك. نَوبَة اللَّخ أَبُسطَك [hannawba ʔilak. nawbat ʔillux ʔabusṭak] This time is for free. Next time I'll bust you. نوبات يِرجَع سَكران [nawbaːt yirǰaʕ sakraːn] Sometimes he comes back drunk. • **3.** fit, spell, attack, paroxysm – أحياناً تِلزمَه نوبَة عَصَبِيَّة [ʔaħyaːnan tilizmah nawba ʕaṣabiyya] Occasionally he has a nervous spell. • **4.** swamp fever, malaria

نائِب، نايِب [naːʔib, naːyib] *n:* نُوّاب [nuwwaːb] *pl:* • **1.** representative – أَخُويَا طِلَع نائِب مِن هَالمَنطِقَة [ʔaxuːya ṭilaʕ naːʔib min halmanṭiqa] My brother became a representative for this district. مَجلِس النُّوّاب [maǰlis ʔinnuwwaːb] house of representatives, lower house of parliament. • **2.** vice- – نائِب قُنصُل [naːʔib qunṣul] vice-consul. نائِب عَرِيف [naːʔib ʕariːf] corporal. نائِب ضابُط [naːʔib ḍaːbuṭ] warrant officer. • **3.** deputy

نِيابَة [niyaːba] *n:* • **1.** representation, substitution, deputyship, proxy – بِالنِّيابَة عَن [binniyaːba ʕan] in place of, in lieu of. إنتَ وَقِّع بِالنِّيابَة عَنَّه [ʔinta waqqiʕ binniyaːba ʕannah] You sign in his place.

تَناوُب [tanaːwub] *n:* • **1.** alternation, rotation • **2.** with بـ- by rotation, in shifts

مُناوَبَة [munaːwaba] *n:* • **1.** alternation, rotation

فَدّ نَوبَة [fadd nawba] *n:* • **1.** at one time, all at once, in one bunch – كُلّكُم تَعالُوا فَدّ نوبَة [kullkum taʕaːluː fadd nawba] All of you come at the same time. • **2.** /usually with imperative/ might as well, just go ahead and – فَدّ نوبَة قُول كُلّشِي ما يِفتِهِم [fadd nawba guːl kullši maː yiftihim] You might as well say he doesn't understand anything. • **3.** too much, to excess – سَوّاها فَدّ نوبَة. مُو حَقِّي أَزعَل؟ [sawwaːha fadd nawba. muː ħaqqi ʔazʕal?] He went too far. Don't I have a right to get mad?

نَوبَجِي [nawbači] *adj:* نَوبَجِيَّة [nawbačiyya] *pl:* • **1.** guard, watchman

نِيابِي [niyaːbi] *adj:* • **1.** representative – حُكُومَة نِيابِيَّة [ħukuːma niyaːbiyya] representative government.

مناوِب [mnaːwib] *adj:* • **1.** on duty

مِتناوِب [mitnaːwib] *adj:* • **1.** rotational

ن و ح

ناح [naːħ] *v:* • **1.** to give a mournful cry, make a sorrowful sound – يقُولُون الحَمام يِنُوح [yiguːluːn ʔilħamaːm ynuːħ] They say that the pigeon gives a mournful cry. دَتنُوح عَلَى وِلِدها اللِّي ماتَوا [datnuːħ ʕala wilidha ʔilli maːtaw] She is mourning for her dead children.

نياح [nyaːħ] *n:* • **1.** loud weeping • **2.** lamentation, wailing, mourning

مَناحَة [manaːħa] *n:* • **1.** lamentation, wailing, mourning

ن و خ

نَوَّخ [nawwax] *v:* • **1.** to kneel down – النّاقَة نَوُّخَت بِالعَجَل [ʔinnaːga nawwuxat bilʕaǰal] The camel kneeled down quickly. • **2.** to make kneel down – نَوُّخ الجِّمَل حَتَّى أَركَب عَليه [nawwux ʔiǰǰimal ħatta ʔarkab ʕaliːh] Make the camel kneel down so I can get on him.

مَناخ [manaːx] *n:* • **1.** climate, weather

مَناخَة [manaːxa] *n:* مَناخات [manaːxaːt] *pl:* • **1.** parking area for caravans

ن و خ ذ

نوخذَة [nuːxða] *n:* نوخذات [nuːxðaːt] *pl:* • **1.** captain of a sailing vessel (Persian term, not very common)

ن و ر

نَوَّر [nawwar] *v:* • **1.** to enlighten – نَوِّرنا بِآرائَك [nawwirna bʔaːraːʔak] Enlighten us with your opinions.

تنَوَّر [tnawwar] *v:* • **1.** to be enlightened – أُدخُل المَدرَسَة حَتَّى تِتنَوَّر بِالعِلِم [ʔudxul ʔilmadrasa ħatta titnawwar bilʕilim] Enter the school so you'll become enlightened by knowledge.

نار [naːr] *n:* نِيران [niːraːn] *pl:* • **1.** fire – الأَسعار اليُوم نار [ʔilʔasʕaːr ʔilyuːm naːr] Prices today are unbearable. عيُونَه دَتِجدَح نار مِن الغَضَب [ʕyuːnah datiǰdaħ naːr min ʔilɣaḍab] His eyes are shooting fire from anger. لا تِحكِي ويّاه تَرَة صايِر نار [laː tiħči wiyyaːh tara ṣaːyir naːr] Don't speak to him 'cause he's infuriated. • **2.** gunfire

نُور [nuːr] *n:* • **1.** light, illumination – الغُرفَة ما بِيها نُور كافِي [ʔilɣurfa maː biːha nuːr kaːfi] The room doesn't have enough light in it. نُور كَشّاف [nuːr kaššaːf] searchlight.

ن

نُورَة [nu:ra] *n:* • **1.** lime, quicklime
مَنوَر [manwar] *n:* • **1.** light hole (in a wall), skylight
مَنارَة [mana:ra] *n:* مَنايِر [mana:yir] *pl:* • **1.** minaret
إنارَة [ʔina:ra] *n:* • **1.** lighting, illumination, enlightenment
تَنوِير [tanwi:r] *n:* • **1.** flare, flowering, illumination, lighting
مُناوَرَة [muna:wara] *n:* مُناوَرات [muna:wara:t] *pl:* • **1.** (military) maneuver • **2.** often deceptive planned or controlled action
نارِي [na:ri] *adj:* • **1.** fiery, igneous, fire- – أَلعاب نارِيَّة [ʔalʕa:b na:riyya] fireworks. أسلِحَة نارِيَّة [ʔasliħa na:riyya] firearms.
منَوِّر [mnawwir] *adj:* • **1.** lighted, illuminated, enlightened
مِتنَوِّر [mitnawwir] *adj:* • **1.** lighted, illuminated, enlightened
نُورانِي [nu:ra:ni] *adj:* • **1.** luminous

ن و ش

ناش [na:š] *v:* • **1.** to reach, get to – ما يِقدَر يِنُوش السَّبُّورَة لِأَنَّه قَصِير [ma: yigdar yinu:š ʔissabbu:ra liʔannah qaṣi:r] He can't reach the blackboard because he's short. البَطّانِيَّة ناشها مَيّ. شُرها بِالشَّمِس [ʔilbaṭṭa:niyya na:šha mayy. šurha biššamis] Water has gotten to the blanket. Hang it out in the sun. إذا قال يسَوِّيها، اِعتُبُرها خَلصانَة، لِأَنّ هَذا إيدَه تنُوش [ʔiða ga:l ysawwi:ha, ʔiʕtuburha xalṣa:na, liʔann ha:ða ʔi:dah tnu:š] If he said he'd do it, consider it done, because he's a capable fellow.
ناوَش [na:waš] *v:* • **1.** to hand, pass – ناوشِنِي الكِتاب حَتّى أَخَلِّيه عَالرَّفّ [na:wišni ʔilkita:b ħatta ʔaxalli:h ʕarraff] Hand me the book so I can put it on the shelf.
تناوَش [tna:waš] *v:* • **1.** to take, seize, grab, take into one's hand – تناوَش الكِتاب. إيدِي تِعبَت [tna:waš ʔilkita:b. ʔi:di tiʕbat] Take the book. My hand is tired. تناوَش السّاعَة وضِرَبنِي بِيها [tna:waš ʔissa:ʕa wḍirabni bi:ha] He grabbed the clock and hit me with it. • **2.** to attack, set upon, engage in a skirmish with – مِن مَرّ، تناوشُوه الجُّهّال بالحجار [min marr, tna:wšu:h ʔijjaha:l bilħja:r] When he passed by, the children attacked him with rocks. بَسّ خَشّ لِلغُرفَة، تناوَشناه [bass xašš lilɣurfa, tna:wašna:h] The minute he entered the room, we lit into him.
نوش [nawš nu:š] *n:* • **1.** reaching, getting to
مُناوَشَة [muna:waša] *n:* مُناوَشات [muna:waša:t] *pl:* • **1.** hostile encounter, exchange, skirmish
مناوِشچِي [mna:wišči] *adj:* مناوِشچِيَّة [mna:wiščiyya] *pl:* • **1.** bricklayer's helper

ن و ط

نُوط [nu:ṭ] *n:* نواط [nwa:ṭ] *pl:* • **1.** bank note, bill – نُوط أَبُو العَشِر دَنانِير [nu:ṭ ʔabu ʔilʕašir dana:ni:r] a ten-dinar bill. • **2.** medal of honor
نَوطَة [nu:ṭa] *n:* نَوطات [nu:ṭa:t] *pl:* • **1.** musical note • **2.** sheet music – ما أَقدَر أَدُقّ كَمَنجَة بَلا نُوطَة [ma: ʔagdar ʔadugg kamanǰa bala nu:ṭa] I can't play a violin without sheet music.

ن و ع

نَوَّع [nawwaʕ] *v:* • **1.** to make different, diversify, variegate, add variety to – يِنَوِّع بِأَحادِيثَه --- مَرَّة أَخبار، مَرَّة قُصَص، مَرَّة فَلسَفَة [yinawwiʕ bʔaħa:di:θah marra ʔaxba:r, marra quṣaṣ, marra falsafa] He inserts variety in his speeches --- one time current events, then stories, then philosophy. لَو الشَّرِكَة تنَوِّع الحاجات اللِّي تِشترِيها مِن الخارِج، كان يصِير عَلِيها إقبال [law ʔiššarika tnawwiʕ ʔilħa:ǰa:t ʔilli tištiri:ha min ʔilxa:riǰ, ča:n yṣi:r ʕali:ha ʔiqba:l] If the company diversified the goods that it buys from abroad, there would be a demand for them.
تنَوَّع [tnawwaʕ] *v:* • **1.** pass. of نَوَّع to be different, diversified, variegated – كُلّما تِتنَوَّع بِضاعَتنا، شُغُلنا يِتحَسَّن [kullma titnawwaʕ biḍa:ʕatna, šuɣulna yitħassan] The more diversified our goods are, the more our business improves.
نوع [nu:ʕ] *n:* أنواع [ʔanwa:ʕ] *pl:* • **1.** kind, sort, type, species
تَنَوُّع [tanawwuʕ] *n:* • **1.** variety, diversity
نَوعِيَّة [nawʕiyya] *n:* نَوعِيّات [nawʕiyya:t] *pl:* • **1.** quality – الكَمِّيَّة قَلِيلَة بَسّ النَّوعِيَّة زينَة [ʔilkammiyya qali:la bass ʔinnawʕiyya zi:na] The quantity is small but the quality is good.
تَنوِيع [tanwi:ʕ] *n:* • **1.** change, alteration, modification • **2.** diversification
مُنَوَّع [munawwaʕ] *adj:* • **1.** miscellaneous, varied
مُتَنَوِّع [mutanawwiʕ] *adj:* • **1.** diversified, different, various • **2.** Pl. مُتَنَوِّعات sundries, miscellany
نَوعاً ما [nawʕan ma:] *subordinating conjunction:* • **1.** somewhat, to a certain degree, in a way – المَرِيض نَوعاً ما أَحسَن اليُوم [ʔilmari:ḍ nawʕan ma: ʔaħsan ʔilyu:m] The patient is somewhat better today.

ن و ق [1]

ناقَة [na:ga] *n:* ناقات، نُوق [na:ga:t, nu:g] *pl:* • **1.** female camel

ن و ق [2]

نُوقَة [nu:ga] *n:* • **1.** nougat

ن و ل

تناوَل [tna:wal] *v:* • **1.** to take, seize, grasp, grab, attack (s.th.)
نُول [nu:l] *n:* أنوال [ʔanwa:l] *pl:* • **1.** loom
مِنوال [minwa:l] *n:* • **1.** way, manner
تَناوُل [tana:wul] *n:* • **1.** eating, taking (a meal) • **2.** ingesting, comprehending, grasping

متناوَل [mitna:wal] *n:* • **1.** availability, reach, attainableness, range

ن و م

نام [na:m] *v:* • **1.** to sleep – آني أنام سَبع ساعات بِاليُوم [ʔa:ni ʔana:m sabiʕ sa:ʕa:t bilyu:m] I sleep seven hours per night. • **2.** to retire, go to bed – صار نُصّ اللَّيل؛ خَلّي نرُوح نِنام [ṣa:r nuṣṣ ʔillayl; xalli nru:ћ nina:m] It's midnight; let's go to bed. • **3.** to lie, lie down – نام عَلَى بَطنَك حَتَّى أمَرِّخ ظَهرَك [na:m ʕala baṭnak ћatta ʔamarrix ð̣ahrak] Lie on your stomach so I can massage your back. حُطّ دِهِن بِشَعرَك حَتَّى ينام [ћuṭṭ dihin bišaʕrak ћatta yna:m] Put oil on your hair so that it'll stay in place.

نَوَّم، نَيَّم [nawwam, nayyam] *v:* • **1.** to put to bed, put to sleep – وَكّلِي الجّاهِل وَنَيِّمِيه [wakkili ʔijǰa:hil wnayyimi:h] Feed the child and put him to sleep. وين راح نَنَيِّمهُم؟ عِدنا غُرفَة نُوم وِحدَة [wi:n ra:ћ nnayyimhum? ʕidna ɣurfat nu:m wiћda] Where are we going to bed them down? We have only one bedroom. • **2.** to make lie down – هَالدِّهِن ينَيِّم الشَّعَر [haddihin ynayyim ʔiššaʕar] This cream makes the hair lie down. • **3.** to hypnotize – نَوَّمَه وَقام يِسأَلَه أسئِلَة [nawwamah wga:m yisʔalah ʔasʔila] He hypnotized him and began asking him questions.

اِنّام [ʔinna:m] *v:* • **1.** pass. of نام to be slept (in) – هَالغُرفَة بارِدَة؛ ما يِنّام بِيها [halɣurfa ba:rda; ma: yinna:m bi:ha] This room is cold; it can't be slept in.

نُوم [nu:m, nawm] *n:* • **1.** sleeping, sleep – غُرفَة نُوم [gurfat nu:m] bedroom.

نَومَة [nawma] *n:* نُومات [nu:ma:t] *pl:* • **1.** sleeping, sleep

مَنام [mana:m] *n:* • **1.** sleeping, sleep

تَنوِيم [tanwi:m] *n:* • **1.** hypnotism, hypnosis (e.g., تَنوِيم مُغنَطِيسِي)

مُنَوِّم [munawwim] *adj:* • **1.** hypnotist (e.g., مُنَوِّم مُغنَطِيسِي)

نايِم [na:yim] *adj:* • **1.** sleeping

ن و م ي

نُومِي بَصرَة [nu:mi baṣra] *n:* • **1.** dried lemons imported from Muscat, through the port of Basra • **2.** a condiment made from dried lemons – نُومِي حِلو [nu:mi ћilw] sweet lemon(s), a thin-skinned citrus fruit resembling the orange, but having a yellow skin. نُومِي حامُض [nu:mi ћa:muð] lemon(s).

نُومايِي [nu:ma:yi] *adj:* • **1.** lemon yellow – لُون نُوماي [lu:n nu:ma:yi] lemon yellow.

ن و ن

نُون [nu:n] *n:* • **1.** name of the letter 'n'

نُونَة [nu:na] *n:* نُونات [nu:na:t] *pl:* • **1.** beauty spot on the forehead, applied artificially by women

ن و ه

نَوَّه [nawwah] *v:* • **1.** to hint, allude, intimate, imply

تَنوِيه [tanwi:h] *n:* • **1.** hinting, alluding, implying, intimating

تَنوِيهَة [tanwi:ha] *n:* • **1.** hint, allusion

ن و ي

نَوَى [nuwa:] *v:* • **1.** to intend, propose, plan, have in mind – يِنوُون يِبنُون مُستَشفى بِهَالمَنطَقَة [yinwu:n yibnu:n mustašfa bhalmanṭaqa] They plan to build a hospital in this neighborhood.

نُوَة [nuwa] *n:* • **1.** (coll.) pit(s), stone(s) (of fruit).

نِيَّة [niyya] *n:* نِيّات [niyya:t] *pl:* • **1.** intention, intent, purpose, plan, design, scheme – ما كانَت عِندِي نِيَّة أشتِرِيها بَسّ إنتَ رَغَّبتِنِي عَلَيها [ma: ča:nat ʕindi niyya ʔaštiri:ha bass ʔinta raɣɣabtini ʕali:ha] I had no intention of buying it but you got me enthusiastic about it. إنتَ شنِيَّتَك؟ ما تخَلِّينِي أشتُغُل؟ [ʔinta šniyytak? ma: txalli:ni ʔaštuɣul?] What are you up to? Why don't you let me work? حُسُن النِّيَّة [ћusun ʔinniyya] good intention, good will, sincerity. سَوّاها بحُسُن نِيَّة [sawwa:ha bћusun niyya] He did it with good intentions. سَلِيم النِّيَّة [sali:m ʔinniyya] guileless, sincere. يعجِبنِي لِأنَّه شَخص سَلِيم النِّيَّة [yiʕǰibni liʔannah šaxiṣ sali:m ʔinniyya] I like him because he is a sincere person. سُوء النِّيَّة [su:ʔ ʔinniyya] evil intent, malice, insincerity, deceit.

نوايَة [nwa:ya] *n:* نوايات [nwa:ya:t] *pl:* • **1.** pit, stone (of a fruit)

نَوَوِي [nawawi, nuwawi] *adj:* • **1.** nuclear, atomic – أسلِحَة نُوَوِيَّة [ʔasliћa nuwawiyya] nuclear weapons.

ن ي ء

نَيّ [niyy] *adj:* • **1.** raw, uncooked – المعالِيق بَعَدها نِيَّة [ʔilmʕa:li:g baʕadha niyya] The livers are still raw.

ن ي ب

ناب [na:b] *n:* أنياب [ʔanya:b] *pl:* • **1.** fang • **2.** eye-tooth • **3.** tusk

ن ي س ن

نِيسان [ni:sa:n] *n:* • **1.** April

ن ي ك

ناك [na:č] *v:* • **1.** (vulgar) to have sexual intercourse (with)

نَيَّك [nayyič] *v:* • **1.** to perform the female role in sexual intercourse

تناَيَك [tna:yač] *v:* • **1.** to copulate, have sexual intercourse with each other

نَيك [nayč] *n:* • **1.** copulating, having sexual intercourse

ن

نَيكَة [ni:ča] *n:* • **1.** unit n: of نِيك [nayk, ni:k] an instance of sexual intercourse
مِناك [mina:č] *adj:* • **1.** person upon whom sexual acts are performed
منَيِّك [mnayyič] *adj:* • **1.** screwed, sexually abused
مَنيُوك [manyu:k, manyu:č] *adj:* مَناوِيك [mana:wi:č] *pl:* • **1.** asshole, jerk • **2.** screwed up, sexually abused

ن ي ل 1
النِيل [ʔinni:l] *n:* • **1.** the Nile

ن ي ل 2
نيل [ni:l] *n:* • **1.** indigo • **2.** indigo plant
نِيلِي [ni:li] *n:* • **1.** blue, dark blue – اِشتِريت قاط نِيلِي [ʔištiraytli qa:ṭ ni:li] I bought a dark blue suit.

ن ي ل ن
نايلون [na:ylu:n] *n:* • **1.** nylon

ن ي م
نَيَّم [nayyam] *v:* • **1.** to sate oneself with food, to eat one's fill – البارحَة نَيَّمت زين بِالعَزِيمَة [ʔilba:rħa nayyamit zi:n bilʕazi:ma] I really ate my fill at the dinner party yesterday.

ن ي ي
ناي [na:y] *n:* نايات [na:ya:t] *pl:* • **1.** a kind of flute

ه

ه 1

هذاك [haðaːka] *demonstrative:* هَذُولَة، هَذُولاك [haðuːka, haðuːlaːka] *pl:* هَذِيك [haðiːča] *feminine:* • **1.** that one, that person • **2.** that, those

ها [haː] *int:* • **1.** (an interjection used in address, approx.:) well, so, yes, okay – ها عَلِي! شلُونَك اليُوم؟ [ha ʕali! šluːnak ʔilyuːm?] Well Ali! How are you today? ها عَمِّي! شِتريد؟ [ha ʕammi! šitriːd?] Yes uncle! What can I do for you? ها ها، كُلّ مَن يِقُول يا رُوحِي [ha ha, kull man yiguːl yaː ruːħi] Well, well, everyone looks out for himself. ها ها! اِفتِهَمِت [ha ha! ʔiftihamit] Oh yeah! Now I understand. • **2.** (in surprise or amazement) oh? really? what? – ها؟ تزَوّج وَما حَدّ دِرى بِيه؟ [ha? dzawwaǰ wma ħadd diraː biːh?] Oh? He got married and no one knew about it? ها؟ مات؟ لا [ha? maːt? laː] What? He died? Oh, no! • **3.** (in reply to a half-heard question) huh? what? – ها؟ وَالله ما أدري وين راح [ha? wallah maː ʔadri wiːn raːħ] Huh? Golly, I don't know where he went.

ه 2

هَ- [ha-] *demonstrative:* • **1.** /plus definite article and noun/ this, this particular – هَالمَرَّة دُورَك [halmarra duːrak] This time it's your turn. هَالرَّسِم مُو حِلو [harrasim muː ħilw] This painting isn't very pretty.

ه ب ب

هَبّ [habb] *v:* • **1.** to blow – الهَوا، إذا يهِبّ مِن هَالجِهَة، يجِيب عَجاج [ʔilhawa, ʔiða yhibb min halǰiha, yǰiːb ʕaǰaːǰ] If the wind blows from this direction, it brings dust.

هَبّ رِيح [habb riːħ] *n:* هَبِّين رِيح [habbiːn riːħ] *pl:* هَبّات، هَبّات رِيح [habbaːt, habbaːt riːħ] *feminine:* • **1.** refreshing, friendly person • **2.** capable, willing worker

هَبّ [habb] *n:* • **1.** blowing, gust

ه ب ش

هَبَّش [habbaš] *v:* • **1.** to polish, mill – راح نهَبِّش الشِّلِب كُلّه قَبِل ما نبِيعَه [raːħ nhabbiš ʔiššilib kullah gabil maː nbiːʕah] We're going to polish all the field rice before we sell it. سِعِر التِّمّن المهَبَّش دِينار وَنُصّ [siʕir ʔittimman ʔilmhabbaš dinaːr wnuṣṣ] The price of polished rice is a dinar and a half.

هَبّاشَة [habbaːša] *n:* هَبّاشات [habbaːšaːt] *pl:* • **1.** rice-polishing machine

ه ب ط

هُبَط [hubaṭ] *v:* • **1.** to drop, sink, fall downward – هُبطَت دَرَجَة الحَرارَة لَيلَة البارحَة [hubṭat daraǰat ʔilħaraːra laylat ʔilbaːrħa] The temperature went down last night. هُبَط قَلبِي [hbaṭ galbi] My heart sank. مِن قَلّي بِالقَضِيَّة، هُبَط قَلبِي [min galli bilqaðiyya, hbaṭ galbi] When he told me about the thing, my heart sank. هُبَطِت. عَبالِي الفلُوس ضاعَت [hubaṭit. ʕabaːli ʔilfluːs ðaːʕat] I was scared. I thought the money was gone.

هَبَّط [habbaṭ] *v:* • **1.** to cause to sink, drop, fall downward – مَسح قُصَّة المَرِيض بالكُحُول يهَبُّط دَرَجَة الحَرارَة [masiħ guṣṣat ʔilmariːð bilkuħuːl yihabbuṭ daraǰat ʔilħaraːra] Rubbing a sick person's forehead with alcohol reduces the fever. هَبَّط قَلبَه [habbaṭ galbah] He made his heart sink. طِلَعلِي مِن وَرا الباب وَهَبَّط قَلبِي [ṭilaʕli min wara ʔilbaːb whabbaṭ galbi] He came out from behind the door and scared me.

اِنهُبَط [ʔinhubaṭ] *v:* • **1.** to be scared

هَبُط، هُبُوط [habuṭ, hubuːṭ] *n:* • **1.** dropping, sinking

هَبطَة [habṭa] *n:* • **1.** dropping, sinking – هُبَط قَلبِي فَدّ هَبطَة [hbaṭ galbi fadd habṭa] My heart really sank.

هبِيط [hibiːṭ] *n:* • **1.** a meat dish prepared and given to the poor as a sacrifice in gratitude for good fortune bestowed by God

هابُط [haːbuṭ] *adj:* • **1.** falling, dropping, sinking, descending

مَهبُوط [mahbuːṭ] *adj:* • **1.** emaciated, skinny

ه ب ل

هِبِل [hibil] *adj:* • **1.** idiot

أهبَل [ʔahbal] *comparative adjective:* هَبلاء [hablaːʔ] *feminine:* • **1.** idiotic

ه ت ر

اِستَهتَر [ʔistahtar] *v:* • **1.** to have little respect, attach little importance – هُوَّ يِستَهتِر بِالقَوانِين [huwwa yistahtir bilqawaːniːn] He has little respect for laws.

اِستِهتار [ʔistihtaːr] *n:* • **1.** recklessness

مِستَهتِر [mistahtir] *adj:* • **1.** wanton, unrestrained, uninhibited – الكُلّ يُعرفُوها مِستَهتِرَة. مَحَّد دَيتزَوَّجها [ʔilkull yuʕurfuːha mistahtira. maħħad dayitzawwaǰha] Everyone knows she's a bit loose. No one's going to marry her.

ه ت ف

هِتَف [hitaf] *v:* • **1.** with ل or ب to cheer, hail, acclaim, applaud – الجَّماهِير هِتفَت لِلزَّعِيم مِن مَرّ مِن هنا [ʔiǰǰamaːhiːr hitfat lizzaʕiːm min marr min hina] The crowds cheered the leader when he passed by here. هِتفَوا ثلَث مَرّات بِحَياة رَئِيس الجُّمهُورِيَّة [hitfaw tlaθ marraːt bħayaːt raʔiːs ʔiǰǰumhuːriyya] They gave three cheers for the life of the president of the republic. • **2.** with ضِد to boo, jeer – مِن كان يِخطُب قام واحِد وَهِتَف ضِدَّه

ه

[min ča:n yixṭub ga:m wa:ħid whitaf ðiddah] As he was speaking, someone stood up and booed him.
هتاف [hita:f] *n:* هتافات [hita:fa:t] *pl:* • **1.** boo, jeer • **2.** cheering, shouting
هاتف [ha:tif] *n:* هاتفين [ha:tifi:n] *pl:* • **1.** caller, shouter, rejoicer
هاتفي [ha:tifi] *adj:* • **1.** via telephone

ه ت ك

هتك [hitak] *v:* • **1.** to expose, reveal, bare, disclose – هتكهم كُلّهم بالجَريدَة [hitakhum kullhum bijjari:da] He exposed them all in the newspaper. • **2.** to disgrace, bring shame to – الجاهِل هتكنا قِدّام الجِّيران [ʔijja:hil hitakna gidda:m ʔijji:ra:n] The kid disgraced us in front of the neighbors. هتك عَرضَه [hitak ʕarðah] He disgraced his honor. • **3.** to ruin – إبنهُم صَرّاف؛ هتك أهلَه [ʔibinhum ṣarra:f; hitak ʔahlah] Their son is a spendthrift; he ruined his family.
تهتّك [thattak] *v:* • **1.** to behave in a disgraceful, shameless manner – هيَّ تتهتّك بلِبسها [hiyya tithattak blibsha] She's shameless in her way of dressing.
انهتك [ʔinhitak] *v:* • **1.** to be disgraced – رِقصَت ويّا واحِد ما تعُرفَه وانهتكَت [rigṣat wiyya wa:ħid ma: tʕurfah wʔinhitkat] She danced with someone she didn't know and was disgraced. • **2.** to be ruined – انهتك؛ خِسَر كُلّ فلُوسَه بالقمار [ʔinhitak; xiṣar kull flu:sah bilqma:r] He was ruined; he lost all his money in gambling.
هتك [hatik] *n:* • **1.** ruin, exposure, disgrace
هتيكة [hati:ka] *n:* هتيكات [hati:ka:t] *pl:* • **1.** scandal, disgrace
مهتوك [mahtu:k] *adj:* • **1.** exposed, scandalized, shamed, disgraced • **2.** ruined, penniless – شلُون أداينَك فلُوس؟ آني مَهتوك [šlu:n ʔada:ynak flu:s? ʔa:ni mahtu:k] How could I lend you money? I'm flat broke.
متهتّك [mithattik] *adj:* • **1.** shameless, dishonorable

ه ت ل ف

مهتلف [mhatlaf] *adj:* • **1.** bum • **2.** maltreated, oppressed, miserable, disorderly, neglected • **3.** derelict

ه ج ج

هجّ [hajj] *v:* • **1.** to flee, run away – كان هنا، لكِن مِن شافكُم جايّين، هجّ [ča:n hna, la:kin min ša:fkum ja:yyi:n, hajj] He was here, but when he saw you coming, he beat it. هجّ مِن حَرّ بَغداد [hajj min ħarr bayda:d] He escaped from the heat of Baghdad. راح أهِجّ مِن إيدَك [ra:ħ ʔahijj min ʔi:dak] I'm going to leave because of the things you do.
هجّج [hajjaj] *v:* • **1.** to cause to flee – راح تهجّجني إذا تِبقى تسَوّي هيكي [ra:ħ thajjijni ʔiða tibqa: tsawwi hi:či] You're going to drive me away if you keep on doing that.
هَجيج، الهَجيج [haji:j, ʔilhaji:j] *n:* • **1.** I'm leaving! I'm getting out of here! – الهَجيج ! ما ينعاش بهالبَيت [ʔilhaji:j ! ma: yinʕa:š bihalbayt] I'm leaving! It's impossible to live in this house.

ه ج ر

هِجَر [hijar] *v:* • **1.** to abandon, forsake, leave behind, give up – هِجَرها لمَرتَه وتزَوَّج وِحدَة لُخ [hijarha lmartah widzawwaj wiħda lux] He abandoned his wife and married someone else.
هاجَر [ha:jar] *v:* • **1.** to emigrate – هاجَر لأمريكا [ha:jar lʔamri:ka] He emigrated to America.
انهجَر [ʔinhijar] *v:* • **1.** to be deserted, to be left behind
هجر [hajir] *n:* • **1.** abandonment, leaving, separation
هِجرَة [hijra] *n:* هِجرات [hijra:t] *pl:* • **1.** emigration, exodus
مَهجَر [mahjar] *n:* • **1.** emigration (to the Western Hemisphere) • **2.** the emigrant community (esp. in America) – أمّها بلُبنان بَسّ أبُوها بالمَهجَر [ʔummaha blubna:n bass ʔabu:ha bilmahjar] Her mother is in Lebanon but her father is in America.
هجران [hijra:n] *n:* • **1.** abandonment, leaving, separation
هِجري [hijri] *adj:* • **1.** pertaining to the Hegira – سَنَة هِجريَّة [sana hijriyya] year in the Moslem era.
مُهاجِر [muha:jir] *n:* مُهاجرين [muha:jiri:n] *pl:* • **1.** emigrant • **2.** immigrant
مَهجُور [mahju:r] *adj:* • **1.** abandoned – بِنايَة مَهجُورَة [bina:ya mahju:ra] abandoned building, condemned building.

ه ج ع

هِجَع [hijaʕ] *v:* • **1.** to become calm, still, silent – إبني، شقَدّ تِبكي. ما تِهجَع عاد؟ [ʔibni, šgadd tibči. ma: tihjaʕ ʕa:d?] Son, you're crying so much. Why don't you calm down? • **2.** to sleep peacefully – سِنّي كان يوجَعني البارحَة. ما هجَعت إلّا قَريب الصُّبُح [sinni ča:n yu:jaʕni ʔilba:rħa. ma: hjaʕit ʔilla qari:b ʔiṣṣubuħ] My tooth was hurting me yesterday. I didn't get to sleep until almost morning.
هَجَّع [hajjaʕ] *v:* • **1.** to make calm, still, silent
انهِجَع [ʔinhijaʕ] *v:* • **1.** to be calm, still, silent
مَهجُوع [mahju:ʕ] *adj:* • **1.** calm, still, silent

ه ج م

هِجَم [hijam] *v:* • **1.** with عَلَى to attack, assault, storm, assail – السَّبِع هِجَم عالصَّيّاد [ʔissabiʕ hijam ʕaṣṣayya:d] The lion attacked the hunter. هِجَم عَلينا الحَرّ فَدّ مَرَّة [hijam ʕali:na ʔilħarr fadd marra] The heat was upon us all Why don't you quiet down. هِجَم بَيتَه [hijam baytah] He ruined him (lit., destroyed his house).

ه

هِجمَت بَيتِي بِهالمَصرَف القَبَة [hijmat bayti bhalmaṣraf ʔilqaba] She ruined me with that excessive expense.
هاجَم [haːǰam] *v:* • **1.** to attack, assault, assail, charge – هاجمَوا العَدُو الفَجِر [haːǰmaw ʔilʕadu ʔilfaǰir] They attacked the enemy at dawn. • **2.** to rush, pounce upon – هاجمَه وَأُخذ الطُّوبَة مِنَّه [haːǰmah wʔuxð ʔiṭṭuːba minnah] Move in on him and take the ball away from him. • **3.** to attack, assail, criticize severely – هاجَمهُم بِالجَّرِيدَة [haːǰamhum bijǰariːda] He attacked them in the newspaper.
تهَجَّم [thaǰǰam] *v:* • **1.** to assume the offensive, to be aggressive, behave hostilely – ماكُو حاجَة تِتهَجَّم عَليه [maːku ħaːǰa tithaǰǰam ʕaliːh] There's no reason for you to be so hostile toward him.
تهاجَم [thaːǰam] *v:* • **1.** to attack
إنهِجَم [ʔinhiǰam] *v:* • **1.** pass. of هِجَم to have a trajedy inflicted upon, to be destroyed, to be ruined • **2.** with preposition عَلَى to be attacked, assaulted, stormed, assailed
هُجُوم [huǰuːm] *n:* • **1.** assault, attack, charge – هِجُوم مُعاكِس [hiǰuːm muʕaːkis] counterattack. • **2.** forward line, forward positions (in soccer, etc.)
هَجمَة [haǰma] *n:* • **1.** attack
مُهاجَمَة [muhaːǰama] *n:* • **1.** assault, attack, charge
هُجُومِي [huǰuːmi] *adj:* • **1.** offensive, aggressive – خِطَّة هُجُومِيَّة [xiṭṭa huǰuːmiyya] offensive plan.
مُهاجِم [muhaːǰim] *n:* مُهاجِمِين [muhaːǰimiːn.] *pl:* • **1.** attacker, assailant, aggressor • **2.** forward (in soccer, etc.)

هـ ج ن

هَجّانَة، شُرطَة هَجّانَة [haǰǰaːna, šurṭa haǰǰaːna] *adj:* • **1.** mounted police, a force which patrols the desert on camels

هـ ج و

هِجَى [hiǰaː] *v:* • **1.** to satirize, mock, ridicule (esp. in poetry) – هالشّاعِر يِهجِي كُلّ مَن ما يِنطِيه فلُوس [haššaːʕir yihǰi kull man maː yinṭiːh fluːs] This poet satirizes everyone who doesn't give him money. هِجاه بقَصِيدَة قَوِيَّة [hiǰaːh bqaṣiːda qawiyya] He made fun of him in a strongly worded poem.
تهَجَّى [thaǰǰaː] *v:* • **1.** to spell – شلُون تِتهَجَى هَالكِلمَة؟ [šluːn tithaǰǰah haččilma?] How do you spell this word?
هِجاء [hiǰaːʔ] *n:* • **1.** satire, derision, ridicule • **2.** alphabet, successive order of letters
هِجائِي [hiǰaːʔi] *adj:* • **1.** satirical – قَصِيدَة هِجائِيَّة [qaṣiːda hiǰaːʔiyya] satirical poem. • **2.** alphabetical

هـ د ء

هِدَأ [hidaʔ] *v:* • **1.** to become calm, calm down – الجّاهِل بِكَى مُدَّة وَبَعدِين هِدَأ [ʔiǰǰaːhil bičaː mudda wbaʕdiːn hidaʔ] The kid cried a while and then calmed down. • **2.** to subside, abate, die down, let up – العاصِفَة هِدأَت [ʔilʕaːṣifa hidʔat] The storm died down.
هَدَّئ [haddaʔ, haddaː] *v:* • **1.** to quiet, calm, tranquilize, make still – رُوح هَدَّأه. هَالأخبار قِلّقاتَه [ruːħ haddiʔah. halʔaxbaːr qillqaːtah] Go calm him down. These news upset him. هَالحَبّ يهَدِّي الأَعصاب [halħabb yhaddiː ʔilʔaʕṣaːb] These pills calm the nerves.
هُدُوء [huduːʔ, hidu] *n:* • **1.** tranquility, stillness, quiet, calmness – يِشتُغُل بهدُوء وَبِدِقَّة [yištuɣul bhiduːʔ wibdiqqa] He works quietly and with precision.
هُدُوء [huduːʔ, hudu] *n:* • **1.** calmness
هادِي [haːdi] *adj:* • **1.** calm, still, tranquil, quiet – المُحِيط الهادِي [ʔilmuħiːṭ ʔilhaːdi] The Pacific Ocean.
مُهَدِّئ [muhaddiʔ] *adj:* مُهَدِئات [muhadiʔaːt] *pl:* • **1.** tranquilizer
هادِئ [haːdiʔ] *adj:* • **1.** calm
أهدَأ [ʔahdaʔ, ʔahda] *comparative adjective:* • **1.** more or most tranquil

هـ د ب

هِدِب، هَدَب [hidib, hadab] *n:* أهداب [ʔahdaːb] *pl:* • **1.** eyelashes

هـ د د

هَدّ [hadd] *v:* • **1.** to release, let go of, turn loose, set free – الشُّرطِي هَدَّه بَعَد ما شاف هَوِيتَه [ʔiššurṭi haddah baʕad maː šaːf hawiːtah] The policeman released him after seeing his identification. هِدّ إيدِي [hidd ʔiːdi] Let go of my hand! هَدّ عَلَيّا الكَلِب [hadd ʕalayya ʔiččalib] He turned the dog loose on me. لا ترُوح لِلحَدِيقَة؛ الكَلِب مَهدُود [laː truːħ lilħadiːqa; ʔiččalib mahduːd] Don't go in the garden; the dog's been turned loose. • **2.** to tear down, wreck, raze – لِيش دَيهِدُّون هَالحايِط؟ [liːš dayhidduːn halħaːyiṭ?] Why are they wrecking this wall?
هَدَّد [haddad] *v:* • **1.** to threaten – هَدَّدَه حَتَّى يوافِق [haddadah ħatta ywaːfiq] He threatened him so he'd accept. هُوَّ هَدَّدنِي بالقَتِل [huwwa haddadni bilqatil] He threatened me with death.
اِنهَدّ [ʔinhadd] *v:* • **1.** to be released, get loose – الكَلِب اِنهَدّ مِن إيدِي [ʔiččalib ʔinhadd min ʔiːdi] The dog got loose from me. بَسّ سِمَع صَوتِي بِالتَّلِفُون، اِنهَدّ عَلَيّا فَدّ هَدَّة [bass simaʕ ṣuːti bittalifuːn, ʔinhadd ʕalayya fadd hadda] As soon as he heard my voice on the phone, there came a torrent of abuse at me. • **2.** to be destroyed, wrecked – الكَراج اِنهَدّ بِالعاصِفَة [ʔilgaraːǰ ʔinhadd bilʕaːṣifa] The garage was wrecked in the storm.
هَدّ [hadd] *n:* • **1.** release, letting go, turning loose, setting free
هَدَّة [hadda] *n:* • **1.** insults, abuse – اِنهَدّ عَلينا فَدّ هَدَّة [ʔinhadd ʕaliːna fadd hadda] There came a torrent of insults at us.
تَهدِيد [tahdiːd] *n:* • **1.** threat
مهَدَّد [mhaddad] *adj:* • **1.** threatened
منهَدّ [minhadd] *adj:* • **1.** exhausted, destroyed, ruined

هـ

مَهدُود [mahdu:d] *adj:* • **1.** weakened, exhausted • **2.** released

ه د ر

هِدَر [hidar] *v:* • **1.** to waste
اِنهِدَر [ʔinhidar] *v:* • **1.** to be wasted
هَدِر [hadir] *n:* • **1.** waste
هَدِير [hadi:r] *n:* • **1.** roar • **2.** surge, raging
مَهدُور [mahdu:r] *adj:* • **1.** useless, spilled and unavenged (blood)

ه د ر و ج ي ن

هَيدرُوجِين [haydruǰi:n] *n:* • **1.** hydrogen – قُنبُلَة هَيدرُوجِينِيَّة [qumbula haydruǰi:niyya] hydrogen bomb.

ه د ف

هِدَف [hidaf] *v:* • **1.** to aim, endeavor, strive – الحُكُومَة تِهدِف إِلَى القَضاء عالأُمِّيَّة [ʔilħuku:ma tihdif ʔila ʔilqaða:ʔ ʕa:lʔummiyya] The government is aiming at the abolition of illiteracy.
هَدَّف [haddaf] *v:* • **1.** to shoot (a ball toward the goal in sports) – هَاللّاعِب يهَدِّف مُمتاز [halla:ʕib yhaddif mumta:z] That player shoots very well.
اِستَهدَف [ʔistahdaf] *v:* • **1.** to have as one's aim or goal, to strive for, work toward, reach for – بهَالمَشرُوع، الحُكُومَة تِستَهدِف رَفع مُستَوَى الفَلّاح [bhalmašru:ʕ, ʔilħuku:ma tistahdif rafiʕ mustawa: ʔilfalla:ħ] With this project, the government is striving for an elevation of the farmer's standard.
هَدَف [hadaf] *n:* أَهداف [ʔahda:f] *pl:* • **1.** object, goal, aim, purpose • **2.** target • **3.** goal (in sports)
اِستِهداف [ʔistihda:f] *n:* • **1.** targeting, aiming
هَدّاف [hadda:f] *adj:* هَدّافِين [hadda:fi:n] *pl:* • **1.** good shot, sharp-shooter, dead-eye (esp. in sports)

ه د ل

هِدَل [hidal] *v:* • **1.** to sag, droop, hang down – خالّة سُتيان حَتَّى ما تِهدِل ديُوسها [xa:lla sutya:n ħatta ma: tihdil dyu:sha] She's got on a bra so her breasts won't sag. الكِتِف اليِسرَة مال السِّترَة دَيِهدِل. راح أَحُطلَه كَتّافِيَّة [ʔiččatif ʔilyisra ma:l ʔissitra dayihdil. ra:ħ ʔaħuṭṭlah čatta:fiyya] The left shoulder of the jacket droops. I'm going to put in a shoulder pad.
تهَدَّل [thaddal] *v:* • **1.** to strip to the waist, take off one's shirt – تهَدَّل وَقِعَد بِالشَّمِس [thaddal wgiʕad biššamis] He stripped to the waist and sat in the sun.
هَدِل [hadil] *n:* • **1.** sagging, drooping, hanging down
هادِل [ha:dil] *adj:* • **1.** sagging, drooping, hanging down – شخالّ بجَيبَك؟ أَشُو هادِل [šxa:ll bǰi:bak? ʔašu: ha:dil] What have you put in your pocket? It's sagging.
مهَدِّل [mhaddil] *adj:* • **1.** saggy, droopy, hanging down
متهَدِّل [mithaddil] *adj:* • **1.** saggy, droopy, hanging down

ه د م

هِدَم [hidam] *v:* • **1.** to tear down, raze, wreck, demolish, destroy – البَلَدِيَّة هِدمَت كَم بَيت وَسَوَّت بمُكانهُم ساحَة [ʔilbaladiyya hidmat čam bayt wsawwat bmuka:nhum sa:ħa] The city razed several houses and made an open square in their place.
هَدَّم [haddam] *v:* • **1.** to tear down, raze, demolish, wreck, destroy – دَيهَدِّمُون الأُوتيل وَيبنُون واحِد غيرَه [dayhaddimu:n ʔilʔuti:l wyibnu:n wa:ħid ɣayrah] They're tearing down the hotel and building another one. العَرَق هَدَّم صِحّتَه [ʔilʕarag haddam ṣiħħtah] Arrack destroyed his health.
تهَدَّم [thaddam] *v:* • **1.** to fall down, collapse, fall apart – تهَدَّم البَيت مِن المُطَر [thaddam ʔilbayt min ʔilmuṭar] The house collapsed because of the rain. • **2.** to be torn down, razed, wrecked, demolished, destroyed
اِنهِدَم [ʔinhidam] *v:* • **1.** to be demolished, wrecked, ruined – البِنايَة اِنهِدمَت بِالعاصِفَة [ʔilbina:ya ʔinhidmat bilʕa:ṣifa] The building was destroyed by the storm.
هِدِم، هدُوم [hidim, hdu:m] *n:* • **1.** clothes, clothing
هَدِم [hadim] *n:* • **1.** demolition
تَهدِيم [tahdi:m] *n:* • **1.** demolition, wrecking, destruction
هَدّام [hadda:m] *adj:* • **1.** destructive – الشِّيُوعِيَّة مَبداها هَدّام [ʔiššiyu:ʕiyya mabda:ha hadda:m] Communism is a destructive ideology.
هادِم [ha:dim] *adj:* • **1.** destroying, demolishing
مهَدَّم [mhaddam] *adj:* • **1.** destroyed, demolished
مَهدُوم [mahdu:m] *adj:* • **1.** torn down, demolished, wrecked, destroyed
مِتهَدِّم [mithaddim] *adj:* • **1.** destroyed, demolished

ه د ن

هُدنَة [hudna] *n:* هُدنات، هُدَن [hudna:t, hudan] *pl:* • **1.** armistice, truce

ه د ه د

هُدهُد [hudhud, hidhid] *n:* هَداهِد [hada:hid] *pl:* • **1.** hoopoe (a type of birds)

ه د ي

هِدَى [hida:] *v:* • **1.** to lead on the right path – بَلكِي الله يِهدِيه وَيجُوز مِن قمار [balki ʔallah yihdi:h wi:ǰu:z min qma:r] Perhaps God will guide him and he will give up gambling.
اِنهِدَى [ʔinhida:] *v:* • **1.** to be guided to the right way • **2.** to be given a gift
هَدِيَّة [hadiyya] *n:* هَدايَة [hada:ya] *pl:* • **1.** gift, present
إِهداء [ʔihda:ʔ] *n:* • **1.** donation, dedication
هِدايَة [hida:ya] *n:* • **1.** guidance
مِهتِدِي [mihtidi] *adj:* • **1.** rightly guided

ه ذ

هَذا، هَذِي، هاي [ha:ða, ha:ði, ha:y] *demonstrative:* هَذُولَة هَذُول، ذُولَة ، ذُول [ðu:l, ðu:la, haðu:l, haðu:la] *pl:* • **1.** this, this one – هاي مَرتِي [ha:y marti] This is my wife. هَذُولَة وِلدِي [haðu:la wildi] These are my sons. أُخُذ اللّاخ؛ هَذا مالِي [ʔuxuð ʔilla:x; ha:ða ma:li] Take the other one; this one is mine. طَبعاً أَعُرفَه؛ هَذا عَمِّي [ṭabʕan ʔaʕurfah; ha:ða ʕammi] Of course I know him; he's my uncle. هَذا بايسِكلَك طِلَع ما يِشتُغُل [ha:ða pa:ysiklak ṭilaʕ ma: yištuɣul] This bicycle of yours, it turns out, doesn't work. صَدِيقِي هَذا يِقُول سَيّارتَك ما تِسوَى [ṣadi:qi ha:ða yigu:l sayya:rtak ma: tiswa:] My friend here says your car's no good. هَذُولَة شَعلَيهُم؟ آنِي كسَرِت الجّام [haðu:la šaʕli:hum? ʔa:ni ksarit ʔiǰǰa:m] What do these people have to do with it? I broke the glass. شِنُو هاي؟ شدَتسَوِّي؟ [šinu: ha:y? šdatsawwi:?] What's this? What are you doing? هاي هِيَّ. لا تجِيب بَعَد [ha:y hiyya. la: tǰi:b baʕad] That's it. Don't bring any more. مَعَ هَذا [maʕa ha:ða] nevertheless, even so. حَصَّلِتلَه شُغُل زين وَمَع هَذا ما قابِل [ħaṣṣalitlah šuɣul zi:n wmaʕa ha:ða ma: qa:bil] I got him a good job and still he's not satisfied.

ه ذ ب

هَذَّب [haððab] *v:* • **1.** to educate, instruct, edify – المَدرَسَة تهَذِّب أَبنائنا [ʔilmadrasa thaððib ʔabna:ʔna] School educates our sons.

تهَذَّب [thaððab] *v:* • **1.** to become educated – لازِم تُدخُل مَدرَسَة حَتَّى تِتهَذَّب [la:zim tudxul madrasa ħatta tithaððab] You have to enter a school to become educated.

تَهذِيب [tahði:b] *n:* • **1.** education, instruction • **2.** politeness, discipline

مهَذَّب [mhaððab] *adj:* • **1.** educated, well-mannered

ه ذ ي

هِذَى [hiða:] *v:* • **1.** to babble, jabber, rave, talk irrationally – السَّكران دَيهذِي وَما يُعرُف شدَيقُول [ʔissakra:n dayihði wma: yuʕruf šdaygu:l] The drunk is talking irrationally and doesn't know what he's saying.

هَذَيان [haðaya:n] *n:* • **1.** drivel, nonsense, jabbering

ه ر ب

هِرَب [hirab] *v:* • **1.** to flee, run away, escape – واحِد مِن المَساجِين هِرَب [wa:ħid min ʔilmasa:ǰi:n hirab] One of the prisoners escaped. هِرَب مِن الجُّندِيَّة [hirab min ʔiǰǰundiyya] He deserted from military service.

هَرَّب [harrab] *v:* • **1.** to smuggle – هَرَّب كَمِّيَّة حَشِيش لِلعِراق [harrab kammiyyat ħaši:š lilʕira:q] He smuggled a quantity of hashish into Iraq.

تهَرَّب [tharrab] *v:* • **1.** with مِن to shirk, evade, dodge, get away from – لِيش تِتهَرَّب مِن المَسؤُولِيَّة؟ [li:š titharrab min ʔilmasʔu:liyya?] Why do you dodge responsibility?

هرُوب [huru:b] *n:* • **1.** escape

تَهَرُب [taharub] *n:* • **1.** evasion, shirking

تَهرِيب [tahri:b] *n:* • **1.** smuggling

هارِب [ha:rib] *adj/ n:* • **1.** fleeing, fugitive, runaway • **2.** deserter • **3.** pl. هارِبين fugitive, runaway

مُهَرِّب [muharrib] *n:* مُهَرِّبين [muharribi:n] *pl:* • **1.** smuggler

مُهَرَّب [muharrab] *adj:* • **1.** smuggled

هَربان [harba:n] *adj:* • **1.** run away, fugitive

ه ر ج

هِرَج [hiraǰ] *v:* • **1.** to disturb, disrupt, agitate – نَصِّي الرّاديُو. حِسَّه هِرَج البَيت [naṣṣi ʔirra:dyu. ħissah hiraǰ ʔilbayt] Turn down the radio. Its noise has disturbed the whole house.

هَرَّج [harraǰ] *v:* • **1.** to talk loudly, shout – إحكِي يَواش. لا تهَرِّج [ʔiħči yawa:š. la: tharriǰ] Speak softly. Don't shout. هَذا شجابَه عالوَطَنِيَّة؟ بَسّ يهَرِّج [ha:ða šǰa:bah ʕalwaṭaniyya? bass yiharriǰ] What does he have to do with nationalism? He just talks loud. إذا تِبقَى تهَرِّج حَقِيقتَك راح تِنعُرُف [ʔiða tibqa: tharriǰ ħaqi:qtak ra:ħ tinʕuruf] If you keep on making a racket, your true nature will be exposed.

هَرَج، سُوق الهَرَج [haraǰ, su:g ʔilharaǰ] *n:* • **1.** auction marketplace, (by extension) any place of great confusion

هَرَج [haraǰ] n: • 1. commotion, noise, disorder, tumult

هَرجَة [harǰa] *n:* هَرجات [harǰa:t] *pl:* • **1.** noise, racket, commotion, din, clamor

مُهَرِّج [muharriǰ] *n:* • **1.** clown

تَهرِيج [tahri:ǰ] *n:* • **1.** clowning, buffoonery

ه ر ر

هِرّ [hirr] *n:* • **1.** cat

ه ر س

هِرَس [hiras] *v:* • **1.** to crush, squash, mash – عَلَى كَيفَك! مُو هِرَست الطَّماطَة [ʕala kayfak! mu: hirast ʔiṭṭama:ṭa] Take it easy! You're squashing the tomatoes! السَّيّارَة هِرسَت رِجلَه [ʔissayya:ra hirsat riǰlah] The car crushed his leg.

انهِرَس [ʔinhiras] *v:* • **1.** to become soft, mushy – شِيل التِّفّاح مِن عالنّار. انهِرَس [ši:l ʔittiffa:ħ min ʕanna:r. ʔinhiras] Take the apples off the fire. They've gotten soft.

هَرِس [haris] *n:* • **1.** crushing, squashing

هَرِيسَة [hari:sa] *n:* • **1.** a dish consisting of wheat and meat boiled to the consistency of pudding

مَهرُوس [mahru:s] *adj:* • **1.** mashed

ه

ه ر ش

هَرَش [hiraš] *v:* • **1.** to scratch, claw – دَقّ جِدري وظَلّ يِهرِش بيه [dagg ǰidri wð̣all yihriš biːh] He got a smallpox vaccination and kept scratching at it. الكَلِب هِرَش رِجلِي [ʔiččalib hiraš riǰli] The dog scratched my leg with his claws.
هِرِش [hiriš] *n:* هرُوش [hruːš] *pl:* • **1.** plant, bush, vine
هَرِش [hariš] *n:* • **1.** scratching
مَهرُوش [mahruːš] *adj:* • **1.** worn out, battered • **2.** greedy

ه ر ط م ن

هُرطُمان [hurṭumaːn, huruṭmaːn] *n:* • **1.** oats

ه ر ف

هَرفِي [harfi] *adj:* • **1.** newborn, young – لَحم الطِّلِي الهَرفِي يِستُوِي بِالعَجَل [laħm ʔiṭṭili ʔilharfi yistuwi bilʕaǰal] The meat of young lamb cooks quickly.

ه ر م

هَرَم [haram] *n:* أهرام [ʔahraːm] *pl:* • **1.** pyramid

ه ر م و ن ي ك

هارمَونِيكا [harmuniːka] *n:* • **1.** harmonica

ه ر ن

هُورِن [huːrin] *n:* هُورِنات [huːrnaːt] *pl:* • **1.** horn (car), horns (animal)
هِيرُوين [hiruwiːn] *n:* • **1.** heroin

ه ر و ل

هَروَل [harwal] *v:* • **1.** to jog, trot, run at a medium pace – خَلّانا الضّابُط نهَرول بمُكانّا نُصّ ساعَة [xallaːna ʔiðð̣aːbuṭ nharwil bmukaːnna nuṣṣ saːʕa] The officer made us run in place for a half hour.
مهَروِل [mharwil] *adj:* • **1.** hurrying, speeding, in a hurry

ه ر ي

هِرَى [hiraː] *v:* • **1.** to break open, lacerate – هِرَى جِلدَه بالقَمجِي وَقام يِنزِل دَمّ [hiraː ǰildah bilqamči wgaːm yinzil damm] He lacerated his skin with the whip and he began to bleed. التِّيزاب هِرَى إيدَه [ʔittiːzaːb hiraː ʔiːdah] The nitric acid burned his hand. هِرَى جِلدَه [hiraː ǰildah] He thrashed him soundly. المُعَلِّم هِرَى جِلدَه بِالعَصا [ʔilmuʕallim hiraː ǰildah bilʕaṣa] The teacher thrashed him soundly with the stick.
تهَرَّى [tharraː] *v:* • **1.** to become worn out, threadbare – تهَرَّت سِترتِي مِن الغَسِل [tharrat sitirti min ʔilɣasil] My jacket's gotten worn out from washing.
اِنهِرَى [ʔinhiraː] *v:* • **1.** to become worn out, threadbare
هَرِي [hary] *n:* • **1.** laceration, breaking open
مِنهِرِي [minhiri] *adj:* • **1.** worn out

ه ز ء

هِزَأ [hizaʔ] *v:* • **1.** to scoff, jeer, laugh, make fun – يِهزَأ مِن أقُلّه ما تِقدَر تسَوِّيها [yihzaʔ min ʔagullah maː tigdar tsawwiːha] He scoffs when I tell him you can't do it.
اِستَهزَأ [ʔistahzaʔ] *v:* • **1.** to scoff, jeer, laugh, to consider ridiculous – لا تِستَهزأ بِاللِّي يقُولَه [laː tistahziʔ billiː yguːlah] Don't scoff at what he says.
هَزِء [haziʔ] *n:* • **1.** laughing, making fun
اِستِهزاء [ʔistihzaːʔ] *n:* • **1.** mockery, redicule
مِستَهزِئ [mistahziʔ, mistahzi] n: • **1.** mocker, scoffer

ه ز ر

هَزار [hazaːr] *n:* هَزارات [hazaːraːt] *pl:* • **1.** nightingale

ه ز ز

هَزّ [hazz] *v:* • **1.** to shake, jiggle – هِزّ الشِّجرَة حَتَّى يَوقَع التُّكِّي [hizz ʔiššiǰra ħatta yuːgaʕ ʔittukki] Shake the tree so the mulberries will fall. مِن هَزّ كِتفَه، عِرَفِت ما يِهتَمّ [min hazz čitfah, ʕirafit maː yihtamm] When he shrugged his shoulder, I knew he didn't care. • **2.** to wave, sway, swing – البَزُّونَة مِن تضُوج تهِزّ ذَيلها [ʔilbazzuːna min tð̣uːǰ thizz ðaylha] When the cat gets mad, it switches its tail. • **3.** to rock, jog – هِزِّي الكارُوك. الجّاهِل دَيِبكِي [hizzi ʔilkaːruːk. ʔiǰǰaːhil dayibči] Rock the cradle. The kid is crying. • **4.** to shake, jiggle, wriggle – هَالرّاقِصَة خُوش تهِزّ [harraːqiṣa xuːš thizz] That dancer shakes nicely. مِن يجاوُب، ما يِحكِي. بَسّ يهِزّ براسَه [min yǰaːwub, maː yiħči. bass yhizz biraːsah] When he answers, he doesn't speak. He just shakes his head. مِن يُقعُد، يهِزّ برجلَه [min yugʕud, yhizz briǰlah] When he's sitting down, he jiggles his leg.
اِنهَزّ [ʔinhazz] *v:* • **1.** to be shaken, rocked – مِن فاتَت الطِّيّارَة، اِنهَزَّت البِنايَة [min faːtat ʔiṭṭiyyaːra, ʔinhazzat ʔilbinaːya] When the plane went by, the building was shaken.
اِهتَزّ [ʔihtazz] *v:* • **1.** to shake, tremble, quake, quiver – اِهتَزَّت البيُوت مِن صُوت المَدفَع [ʔihtazzat ʔilbyuːt min ṣuːt ʔilmadfaʕ] The houses shook from the noise of the cannon.
هَزّ [hazz] *n:* • **1.** tremor, shake • **2.** jiggling
هَزَّة [hazza] *n:* هَزّات [hazzaːt] *pl:* • **1.** tremor, shake – هَزَّة أرضِيَّة [hazza ʔarð̣iyya] earthquake.
هِزَّة [hizza] *n:* هِزّات، هِزَز [hizzaːt, hizaz] *pl:* • **1.** a large cloth slung on the shoulder by workmen to carry sand, etc
اِهتِزاز [ʔihtizaːz] *n:* اِهتِزازات [ʔihtizaːzaːt] *pl:* • **1.** vibration
مِهتَزّ [mihtazz] *adj:* • **1.** shaken, unstable, unsteady
هَزّاز [hazzaːz] *adj:* • **1.** shaking, swinging

ه

مَهزُوز [mahzu:z] *adj:* • **1.** shaken, unstable, unsteady

ه ز ل

هِزَل [hizal] *v:* • **1.** to joke, banter, speak jokingly – كان يهزَل مِن طِلَب مِنَّك الفلوس [ča:n yihzal min ṭilab minnak ʔilflu:s] He was joking when he asked you for the money. يِهزَل بِكُلّ كَلامَه [yihzal bkull kala:mah] He never talks seriously.

هَزَل [hazal] *n:* • **1.** joking – لا تُعتُبُر اللي أَقُلَّك إيّاه فَدّ شِي هَزَل [la: tuʕtubur ʔilli ʔagul lak ʔiyya: fadd ši hazal] Don't take what I tell you as a joke.

مَهزَلَة [mahzala] *n:* مَهازِل [maha:zil] *pl:* • **1.** farce, comedy

هَزَلِي [hazali] *adj:* • **1.** funny, comical – رُوايَة هَزَلِيَّة [ruwa:ya hazaliyya] a comedy. مُمَثِّل هَزَلِي [mumaθθil hazali] comedian.

ه ز م

هِزَم [hizam] *v:* • **1.** to defeat, vanquish – فِرقَتنا هِزمَتهُم بِسِباقَين [firqatna hizmathum bsiba:qayn] Our team defeated them in two games.

هَزَّم [hazzam] *v:* • **1.** to help or allow to escape – وَقِّفوه لِلشُّرطِي لِأَنّ هَزَّم واحِد مَسجُون [waggifawh liššurṭi liʔann hazzam wa:ħid masǰu:n] They arrested the policeman because he helped a prisoner escape. • **2.** to rout, put to flight, chase away – الامتِحانات الهوايَة هَزِّمَته مِن المَدرَسَة [ʔilʔimtiħa:na:t ʔilhwa:ya hazzimatah min ʔilmadrasa] The numerous examinations drove him away from the school. لِيش قِتلَه بِهالسِّعِر؟ مُو هَزَّمتَه [li:š gitlah bhassiʕir? mu: hazzamtah] Why did you quote this price to him? You've scared him away!

تهَزَّم [thazzam] *v:* • **1.** to be evasive, to hedge, temporize – كُلّما يِطِّلبُون مِنَّه يزُورهُم، يِتهَزَّم [kullma: yiṭulbu:n minnah yzu:rhum, yithazzam] Every time they ask him to visit them, he hedges. • **2.** to escape, shrink, stay clear, stay away – هَالمُوَظَّف يذِبّ الشُّغُل عَلَى غيرَه وَيِتهَزَّم مِن المَسؤُولِيَّة [hallmuwaððaf yðibb ʔiššuɣul ʕala ɣayrah wyithazzam min ʔilmasʔu:liyya] This official pushes off work on others and evades responsibility. ظَلّ يِتهَزَّم مِن المَدرَسَة إِلَى أَن طِردوه [ðall yithazzam min ʔilmadrasa ʔila ʔan ṭirdawh] He kept playing truant from school until they expelled him.

انهِزَم [ʔinhizam] *v:* • **1.** to be defeated, vanquished – بَعَد مَعرَكَة قَوِيَّة، انهِزَم جيش العَدُو [baʕad maʕraka qawiyya, ʔinhizam ǰayš ʔilʕadu] After a fierce battle, the enemy army was vanquished. • **2.** to run away, flee – الجّاهِل اِنهِزَم مِن شاف الكَلب [ʔiǰǰa:hil ʔinhizam min ša:f ʔiččalib] The child ran away when he saw the dog. • **3.** to escape – اِنهِزَم مِن السِّجِن باللَّيل [ʔinhizam min ʔissiǰin billayl] He escaped from the jail by night.

هَزِم [hazim] *n:* • **1.** defeat

هَزِيمَة [hazi:ma] *n:* هَزايِم [haza:yim] *pl:* • **1.** defeat, rout

اِنهِزام [ʔinhiza:m] *n:* • **1.** defeat

هَزّام، هَلَة بِالهَزّام [hazza:m, hala bilhazza:m] *adj:* • **1.** (a greeting to a friend one hasn't seen for a long time, approx.:) Hi, stranger!

مِنهِزِم [minhizim] *adj:* • **1.** defeated • **2.** escaped

مَهزُوم [mahzu:m] *adj:* • **1.** defeated, escaped

اِنهِزامِي [ʔinhiza:mi] *adj:* • **1.** defeatist

ه س ت و

هَستَوّا [hastawwa] *adv:* • **1.** /with pronoun suffix/ now, right this moment – هَستَوَّة طِلَع [hastawwa ṭilaʕ] He just this minute went out.

ه س س

هَسَّة [hassa] *adv:* • **1.** now, right this moment – أَرِيد فلُوسِي هَسَّة [ʔari:d flu:si hassa] I want my money now. المَتحَف راح يكُون مَفتُوح مِن هَسَّة إِلَى ساعَة خَمسَة [ʔilmatħaf ra:ħ yiku:n maftu:ħ min hassa ʔila sa:ʕa xamsa] The museum will be open from now until five o'clock. هَسَّة شلُون؟ [hassa šlu:n?] Now what do we do? • **2.** right away, in just a moment, soon – تفَضَّل اِستِرِيح وَهَسَّة يشُوفَك الطَّبِيب [tfaððal ʔistiri:ħ whassa yšu:fak ʔiṭṭabi:b] Please have a seat and the doctor will see you in a moment. هَسَّة يِجِي وَأَقُلَّه [hassa yiǰi wagullah] He'll be coming soon and I'll tell him. • **3.** just this moment, just a moment ago – هَسَّة فات مِن هنا [hassa fa:t min hina] He just now passed by here.

ه ش ش 1

هِشّ [hišš] *int:* • **1.** to shoo, scare away – هَشّ الطُّيُور مِن الشِّعِير [hašš ʔiṭṭuyu:r min ʔiššiʕi:r] He shooed the birds away from the barley. • **2.** hush! shush! – هِشّ! لا تِحكِي بَعَد [hišš! la: tiħči baʕad] Hush! Don't say any more.

ه ش ش 2

هَشاشَة [haša:ša] *n:* • **1.** crispness, weakness, softness

هَشّ [hašš] *adj:* • **1.** crisp – هَالخِيار تازَة وَهَشّ [halixya:r ta:za whašš] These cucumbers are fresh and crisp.

ه ش م

هَشَّم [haššam] *v:* • **1.** to smash – أَهَشِّم راسَك إِذا تِحكِي بَعَد [ʔahaššim ra:sak ʔiða tiħči baʕad] I'll smash your head if you say any more.

مهَشَّم [mhaššam] *adj:* • **1.** smashed, crushed, destroyed

مِتهَشِّم [mithaššim] *adj:* • **1.** smashed, crushed, destroyed

 adj, adjective; adv, adverb; int, interjection; n, noun; pl, plural; v, verb

ه ض م

هِضَم [hiðam] *v:* • **1.** to digest – هَالدُّوا يِهضُم الأَكِل [hadduwaː yihðum ʔilʔakil] This medicine digests the food. • **2.** to upset, distress, cause grief to – هِضَمنِي هوايَة بِهالحكايَة [hiðamni hwaːya bhalħčaːya] He really upset me by that remark.

اِنهِضَم [ʔinhiðam] *v:* • **1.** to be upset, distressed – اِنهِضَمِت مِنَّه هوايَة لِأَنّ باع السَّيّارَة بَلا ما يقُلّي [ʔinhiðamit minnah hwaːya liʔann baːʕ ʔissayyaːra bala maː ygulli] I was very upset by him because he sold the car without telling me. • **2.** to be sorry, feel bad, feel regret – اِنهِضَم عَلَى بَيعَة السَّيّارَة بِهالسِّعِر [ʔinhiðam ʕala bayʕat ʔissayyaːra bhassiʕir] He regretted selling the car for that price.

اِستَهضَم [ʔistahðam] *v:* • **1.** to become upset, distressed – حَقَّه الواحِد يِستَهضُم إذا ضاعلَه شِي [ħaggah ʔilwaːhid yistahðum ʔiða ðaːʕlah ši] A person has a right to get upset if he loses something. اِستَهضَمِت عَلَى عَلِي مِن سِمَعِت فِصلَوه [ʔistahðamit ʕala ʕali min simaʕit fiṣlawh] I was sorry for Ali when I heard they fired him.

هَضُم [haðum] *n:* • **1.** digestion

هَضِيمَة [haðiːma] *n:* هَضايِم [haðaːyim] *pl:* • **1.** injustice, wrong, outrage – هَضِيمَة يزَوّجُوها لهِيكِي واحِد [haðiːma yzawwjuːha lhiːči waːħid] It's a crime they're marrying her off to that guy.

مَهضُوم [mahðuːm] *adj:* • **1.** oppressed, outraged • **2.** digested

مِنهِضِم [minhiðim] *adj:* • **1.** oppressed

ه ط ر

هِطَر [hiṭar] *v:* • **1.** to beat, beat up, thrash soundly – لِزمَوه بشارِع أَظلَم وَهِطرُوه زين [lizmawh bšaːriʕ ʔaðlam whiṭruːh ziːn] They caught him in a dark street and beat him up good.

اِنهِطَر [ʔinhiṭar] *v:* • **1.** to be beaten, beaten up – صاحبَك اِنهِطَر خُوش هَطرَة [ṣaːħbak ʔinhiṭar xuːš haṭra] Your buddy was beaten up real good.

هَطِر [haṭir] *n:* • **1.** beating

هَطرَة [haṭra] *n:* هَطرات [haṭraːt] *pl:* • **1.** beating – أَكَل خُوش هَطرَة مِن الشُّرطَة [ʔakal xuːš haṭra min ʔiššurṭa] He took a good beating from the police.

مَهطُور [mahṭuːr] *adj:* • **1.** beaten

ه ف ت

هِفَت [hifat] *v:* • **1.** to abate, subside, die down – بِلَعت الحَبّايَة وَوُجَع سِنِّي هِفَت [bilaʕt ʔilħabbaːya wwujaʕ sinni hifat] I took the pill and my toothache subsided. هِفَت الوَرَم [hifat ʔilwaram] The swelling went down. لا تخَلّي النّار تِهفِت. ذِبّلها حَطَب [laː txalli: ʔinnaːr tihfit. ðibblha ħaṭab] Don't let the fire die. Throw some wood on it.

هَفَّت [haffat] *v:* • **1.** to cause to abate, subside – أَرِيد فَدّ دُوا يهَفِّت الوُجَع [ʔariːd fadd duwa yhaffit ʔilwujaʕ] I want some medicine to relieve the pain.

هُفُوت [hufuːt] *n:* • **1.** extinction

ه ف ف

هَفّ [haff] *v:* • **1.** to hit, strike, slap, smack – هَفَّه بحجارَة براسَه [haffah bħjaːra braːsah] He hit him on the head with a rock. مِن سَبَّه، هَفَّه براشدِي [min sabbah, haffah braːšdi] When he insulted him he slapped him on the side of his head. هَفَّه بدَمغَة [haffah bdamɣa] He whacked him on top of the head. • **2.** to fire, sack – المُدير الجِّدِيد هَفّ نُصّ المُوَظّفِين وبُقوا بلا شُغُل [ʔilmudiːr ʔijjidiːd haff nuṣṣ ʔilmuwaððafiːn wbuqaw bila šuɣul] The new director canned half the employees and they were left without work. • **3.** to bolt, gulp down, polish off – هَفّ دِجاجَة كاملَة وَماعُونَين تِمَّن [haff dijaːja kaːmla wmaːʕuːnayn timman] He downed a whole chicken and two dishes of rice. يهِفّ كُلّشِي بالأَكِل [yihiff kullši bilʔakil] He'll eat anything. • **4.** to seize, grab, snatch – هَفّ الفلُوس وَانهِزَم [haff ʔilfluːs wʔinhizam] He snatched the money and fled. • **5.** to have sexual relations with • **6.** to blurt out, come out with – هَفّها لِلحكايَة بدُون تَفكِير [haffha lilħčaːya biduːn tafkiːr] He blurted out the remark without thinking.

اِنهَفّ [ʔinhaff] *v:* • **1.** to be fired, sacked – سِمَعِت مُدِير الذّاتِيَّة اِنهَفّ [simaʕit mudiːr ʔiððaːtiyya ʔinhaff] I heard the personnel supervisor was fired.

هَفّ [haff] *n:* • **1.** hit, strike, slap, smack • **2.** bolt, gulp down, polish off • **3.** have sexual relations with

ه ف و

هَفوَة [hafwa] *n:* هَفوات [hafwaːt] *pl:* • **1.** slip, lapse, mistake, error – كانَت هَفوَة مِنّي وَسامِحنِي عَلِيها [čaːnat hafwa minni wsaːmiħni ʕaliːha] It was a slip on my part and please forgive me for it.

ه ف ي [1]

هَفَّى [haffaː] *v:* • **1.** to fan – هَفّي النّار حَتَّى يِستِوِي اللَّحَم [haffi ʔinnaːr ħatta yistiwi ʔillaħam] Fan the fire so that the meat will get done. الدِّنيا حارَّة. هَفّي لِلجّاهِل [ʔiddinya ħarra. haffi lijjaːhil] It's hot. Fan the child.

تهَفَّى [thaffaː] *v:* • **1.** to fan oneself – هاك مهَفّتِي. تهَفَّى بِيها [haːk mhaffti. thaffaː biːha] Here, take my fan. Fan yourself with it.

مهَفَّة [mhaffa] *n:* مهَفّات، مهافِيف [mhaffaːt, mhaːfiːf] *pl:* • **1.** hand fan • **2.** manually operated overhead fan

ه ف ي [2]

مَهفِي [mahfi] *adj:* • **1.** famished, starved • **2.** greedy, over-eager

ه ك

هاك [haːk, haːč] *demonstrative:* هاكُم [haːkum] *pl:* • **1.** here, here you are – هاك دِينار؛ اِشتِرِيلَك نَفنُوف حِلو [haːč dinaːr; ʔištiriːlič nafnuːf ħilw] Here's a dinar;

ه

buy your- self a nice dress. هاك، أُخُذها [ha:k, ʔuxuðha] Here, take it!

هكلك

هُكلُك [hukluk] *n:* هَكالِك [haka:lik] *pl:* • **1.** a kind of bird similar to the partridge

هكم

تَهَكَّم [thakkam] *v:* • **1.** to scoff, mock, jeer, make fun – لا تِتهَكَّم عَليه. قابِل إنتَ أَحسَن مِنَّه؟ [la: tithakkam ʕali:h. qa:bil ʔinta ʔaħsan minnah?] Don't make fun of him. Do you think you're better than he is? لا تِتَهَكَّم. يِجِي يوم أَغْلبَك بِالشِّطرَنج [la: tithakkam. yiǰi yu:m ħaɣulbak biššiṭranǰ] Don't laugh. The day'll come when I'll beat you in chess.

تَهَكُّم [tahakkum] *n:* • **1.** mockery, derision, scorn

متهَكِّم [mithakkim] *adj:* • **1.** sarcastic • **2.** mocking

هل[1]

هَل [hal] *interrogative:* • **1.** interrogative particle introducing a question – هَل هُوَّ باقِي وَإلّا لا؟ [hal huwwa ba:qi waʔilla la:?] Is he still there or not?

هل[2]

هَل-، هَ [hal-, ha-] *demonstrative:* • **1.** plus definite article/ – هالكَلِب [haččilib] This dog - هالدِّينار [haddi:na:r] This dinar.

هلب

هِلِب [hilib] *adj:* • **1.** light, downy hair

هلس

هِلَس [hilas] *v:* • **1.** to pluck, pull out – الوَلَد هِلَس كُلّ رِيش الطَّير [ʔilwalad hilas kull ri:š ʔiṭṭi:r] The boy plucked all the bird's feathers. • **2.** to scrape, remove the hair from – شُغلَه يِهلِس جلُود بالمَدبَغَة [šuɣlah yihlis ǰlu:d bilmadbaɣa] His job is to scrape hides in the tannery.

هَلَّس [hallas] *v:* • **1.** to pluck, pull out – قاعِد وَيهَلِّس الشَّعَر مِن رِجلَيه [gaːʕid wyhallis ʔiššaʕar min riǰlayh] He's sitting and plucking hair from his legs.

تهَلَّس [thallas] *v:* • **1.** to fall out – مِن تمَرَّض، تهَلَّس شَعرَه كُلَّه [min tmarrað̣, thallas šaʕrah kullah] When he got sick, all his hair fell out.

هَلِس [halis] *n:* • **1.** plucking, pulling out

مَهلوس [mahlu:s] *adj:* • **1.** plucked • **2.** hairless, featherless • **3.** broke, penniless – شتِدّاين مِنَّه؟ ما دَتشُوفَه مَهلُوس؟ [štidda:yan minnah? ma: datšu:fah mahlu:s?] What can you borrow from him? Don't you see he's been picked clean?

منهِلِس [minhilis] *adj:* • **1.** plucked

هلك

هِلَك [hilak] *v:* • **1.** to perish, die – راح أَقعُد شوَيَّة. هِلَكِت مِن المَشِي [ra:ħ ʔagʕud šwayya. hilakit min ʔilmašy] I'm going to sit down a while. I'm dead from walking. إِبِنها هِلَك مِن البَكِي [ʔibinha hilak min ʔilbačy] Her son about died from crying. • **2.** with عَلَى to crave, want badly – هِلَك عالوَظِيفَة [hilak ʕalwaḍi:fa] He wanted the job very much. • **3.** to ruin, destroy, annihilate – إذا ما تقُلِّي، أَهلِكَك [ʔiða ma: tgulli, ʔahilkak] If you don't tell me, I'll ruin you. هِلَكنِي الحَرّ [hilakni ʔilħarr] The heat wilted me. جاوُب، عاد! مُو هِلَكتِنِي [ǰa:wub, ʕa:d! mu: hilakitni] Answer, man! You've made me sick to death

اِستَهلَك [ʔistahlak] *v:* • **1.** to wear out – تايَرات السَّيّارَة اِستَهلِكَت [ta:yara:t ʔissayya:ra ʔistahlikat] The car's tires are worn out. • **2.** to consume, use up, exhaust – السَّيّارَة تِستَهلِك بَنزِين هوايَة [ʔissayya:ra tistahlik banzi:n hwa:ya] The car uses a lot of gasoline.

هَلِك [halik] *n:* • **1.** perdition

هَلاك [hala:k] *n:* • **1.** perdition

مَهلَكَة [mahlaka] *n:* مَهالِك [maha:lik] *pl:* • **1.** dangerous situation, perilous predicament

تَهلُكَة [tahluka] *n:* • **1.** jeopardy, danger, peril

اِستِهلاك [ʔistihla:k] *n:* • **1.** consumption, usage – ضَرِيبَة اِستِهلاك [ḍari:bat ʔistihla:k] consumption tax, a wholesale tax paid on farm produce.

هَلكان [halka:n] *adj:* • **1.** ruined – دايِنِّي كَم دِينار. آنِي هَلكان [da:yinni čam dina:r. ʔa:ni halka:n] Lend me a few dinars. I'm broke.

مُستَهلِك [mustahlik] *n:* مُستَهلِكِين [mustahliki:n] *pl:* • **1.** consumer, buyer, user

اِستِهلاكي [ʔistihla:ki] *adj:* • **1.** related to consumption or consumers, consumer (in compounds)

هلل

هَلّ [hall] *v:* • **1.** to begin (lunar month) – باكِر يهِلّ الشَّهَر [ba:čir yhill ʔiššahar] Tomorrow the lunar month begins.

اِستَهَلّ [ʔistahall] *v:* • **1.** to begin, start – اِستَهَلّ خِطابَه بِشُكر الحاضِرِين [ʔistahall xiṭa:bah bšukr ʔilħa:ḍiri:n] He began his speech with thanks to those present.

هَلّ [hall] *n:* • **1.** coming

هِلال [hila:l] *n:* • **1.** first quarter of the moon, new moon • **2.** crescent, half-moon – الهِلال الأَحمَر [ʔilhila:l ʔilʔaħmar] The Red Crescent, Middle Eastern branch of the International Red Cross.

مُستَهَلّ [mustahall] *adj:* • **1.** beginning

هِلالِي [hila:li] *adj:* • **1.** lunate, crescent-shaped

هلهل

هَلهَل [halhal] *v:* • **1.** to make a trilling sound with the voice (on joyous occasions such as wedings) –

شُوف هَالمَرَة دَتهَلهِل بعِرِس إبِنها [šuːf halmara dathalhil bʕiris ʔibinha] Look at that woman trilling at her son's wedding ceremony.
مهَلهَل [mhalhal] *n:* • **1.** miserable
هَلهُولَة [halhuːla] *n:* هَلاهِل [halaːhil] *pl:* • **1.** a burst of trilling

ه ل و

هَلُو [halaw] *int:* • **1.** hello – هَلَو سَعِيد. شلَونَك؟ [halaw saʕiːd. šluːnak?] Hello, Sa'id. How are you? • **2.** (an expression of enthusiastic approbation, approx.:) great, wow, say, hey – هَلَو ياب! طَلَّع كُول اللاّخ [halaw yaːb! ṭallaʕ guːl ʔillaːx] Great, man! He made another goal.

ه ل و س

هَلوَس [halwas] *v:* • **1.** to hallucinate, have illusions
هَلوَسَة [halwasa] *n:* • **1.** hallucination

ه ل ي ل ج

هلَيلَج [hliːlaǰ] *n:* • **1.** myrobalan, a black astringent plum-like fruit from a variety of palm tree used in tanning

ه م ج

هَمَجِي [hamaǰi] *adj:* • **1.** barbaric, savage

ه م ز

هَمزَة [hamza] *n:* هَمزات [hamzaːt] *pl:* • **1.** glottal stop

ه م س

هِمَس [himas] *v:* • **1.** to whisper – هِمَس بإذنَه کَم كِلمَة ضَحَّكَه بِيها [himas bʔiðnah čam čilma ðaħħakah biːha] He whispered a few words in his ear, which made him laugh.
تهامَس [thaːmas] *v:* • **1.** to whisper to each other – شكُو عِدهُم، دَيتهامسُون؟ [šaku ʕidhum, dayithaːmsuːn?] What are they up to, whispering to each other?
هَمس [hams] *n:* • **1.** whispering
هَمسَة [hamsa] *n:* هَمسات [hamsaːt] *pl:* • **1.** whisper

ه م ش

هِمَش [himaš] *v:* • **1.** to seize, grab, take a grip on – الكَلِب هِمَشَه مِن زِرَّه [ʔiččalib himašah min zirrah] The dog seized him by the leg. لا تِهمِش أيّ شِي تشُوفَه عالميز [laː tihmiš ʔayy ši tšuwfah ʕalmiːz] Don't grab up anything you see on the table.
هَمَّش [hammaš] *v:* • **1.** to gesture, gesticulate – لا تهَمِّش بِإيدَيك! إحكِي [laː thammiš biːdiːk! ʔiħči] Don't wave your hand around! Speak up!
هَمِش [hamiš] *n:* • **1.** take a grip on
هامِش [haːmiš] *n:* هَوامِش [hawaːmiš] *pl:* • **1.** margin, border, space around the edge – هَذِي حكايَة عالهامِش [haːði hčaːya ʕalhaːmiš] This is an incidental remark.

ه م ك

اِنهِمَك [ʔinhimik] *v:* • **1.** to be engrossed, be completely engaged, be dedicated
اِنهِماك [ʔinhimaːk] *n:* • **1.** wholehearted dedication, abandon, engrossment

ه م ل

هِمَل [himal] *v:* • **1.** to neglect – لُويش دَتِهمِل واجباتَك؟ [luwiːš datihmil waːǰibaːtak?] Why are you neglecting your duties? • **2.** to ignore – إذا تِهمَلَه، يِسكُت مِن كيفَه [ʔiða tihmalah, yiskut min kiːfah] If you ignore him, he'll shut up of his own accord.
اِنهِمَل [ʔinhimal] *v:* • **1.** to be neglected – الجِّهال اِنهِملَوا. مَحَّد دَيدارِيهُم [ʔiǰǰihaːl ʔinhimlaw. maħħad daydaːriːhum] The children were neglected. No one is looking after them.
إهمال [ʔihmaːl] *n:* • **1.** neglect, oversight, carelessness
هامِل [haːmil] *adj:* هامِلِين [haːmiliːn] *pl:* • **1.** neglectful, irresponsible
مُهمَل [muhmal] *adj:* • **1.** neglected, disregarded – سَلَّة المُهمَلات [sallat ʔilmuhmalaːt] wastebasket.
مُهمِل [muhmil] *adj:* • **1.** neglectful, irresponsible

ه م م 1

هَمّ [hamm] *v:* • **1.** to concern, affect, preoccupy – صِحَّة أبُويا تهِمّنِي هوايَة [ṣiħħat ʔabuːya thimmni hwaːya] My father's health concerns me a lot. • **2.** to be important, of consequence, to matter – ما يهِمّ. مِن يِجِي، أقُلَّه [maː yhimm. min yiǰi, ʔagullah] It doesn't matter. When he comes I'll tell him. • **3.** to make threatening gestures – سَبَّه وهَمّ عَلِيه بِالسِّچِّينَة [sabbah whamm ʕaliːh bissiččiːna] He insulted him and made threatening motions at him with the knife.
اِنهَمّ [ʔinhamm] *v:* • **1.** to become distressed, concerned, worried – مِن سِمَع إبنَه سِقَط، اِنهَمّ هوايَة [min simaʕ ʔibnah siqaṭ, ʔinhamm hwaːya] When he heard his son failed, he was very unhappy.
اِهتَمّ [ʔihtamm] *v:* • **1.** to worry, be concerned – خَلّي يفُصلُونِي! مِنُو يِهتَمّ؟ [xalli yfuṣluːni! minu yihtamm?] Let them fire me! Who cares? اِهتَمّ بِقَضِيتَك هوايَة [ʔihtamm biqaðiːtak hwaːya] He was very concerned about your case. • **2.** to go to great trouble, be very solicitous – اِهتَمُّوا بِينا هوايَة وَدارَونا [ʔihtammaw biːna hwaːya wdaːruːna] They went to great lengths on our behalf and took care of us. • **3.** to pay attention, to take notice – لا تِهتَملَه. هُوَّ فَدّ واحِد سَخِيف [laː tihtamlah. huwwa fadd waːħid saxiːf] Don't pay any attention to him. He's a foolish fellow.
هَمّ [hamm] *n:* هُمُوم [humuːm] *pl:* • **1.** anxiety, concern, worry – شايِل هَمّ. شلُون يرُوح ويترُك جَهالَه وَحَدهُم؟ [šaːyil hamm. šluːn yiruːħ wyitruk ǰahaːlah waħħadhum?] He's burdened with worry. How can he go and leave his children by themselves? • **2.** sorrow, grief, distress – ماتَت مِن الهَمّ وَالحُزُن [maːtat min

ه

ʔilhamm wilħuzun] She died from distress and grief. • **3.** concern, interest – كُلّ هَمَّه يصِير وَزِير [kull hammah yṣiːr waziːr] His only concern is to become a minister.
هِمَّة [himma] *n:* • **1.** enthusiasm
أهَمِّيَّة [ʔahammiyya] *n:* • **1.** importance, significance, consequence
اِهتِمام [ʔihtimaːm] *n:* • **1.** concern, interest
هامّ [haːmm] *adj:* • **1.** important, significant, momentous – راح يِلقِي خِطاب هامّ بالمُؤتَمَر [raːħ yilqi xiṭaːb haːmm bilmuʔtamar] He will deliver an important speech in the convention.
مُهِمّ [muhimm] *adj:* • **1.** important, significant, momentous – عِندَك شِي مُهِمّ؟ [ʕindak ši muhimm?] Do you have anything important to do?
هِمِيم [himiːm] *adj:* • **1.** eager, energetic – مَجِيد كُلِّش هِمِيم. مِن تكَلّفَه بشِي يِركُضلَك [majiːd kulliš himiːm. min tkallfah bši yirkuðlak] Majid is very eager. When you ask him to do something he puts himself out for you.
مُهِمَّة [muhimma] *adj:* مُهِمّات، مَهامّ [muhimmaːt, mahaːmm] *pl:* • **1.** important thing • **2.** important task, mission
مِهتَمّ [mihtamm] *adj:* • **1.** interested
مَهمُوم [mahmuːm] *adj:* • **1.** in low spirits • **2.** concerned, worried, distressed
أهَمّ [ʔahamm] *comparative adjective:* • **1.** more or most important

ه م م 2
هَمّ، هَمَّين، هَمَّينَة [hamm, hammayn, hammayna] *adv:* • **1.** also, too, in addition – إنتَ هَمّ تِدرُس هنا؟ [ʔinta hamm tidrus hna?] Do you also study here? عَلِي هَمَّينَة زَعلان مِنَّك [ʕali hammayna zaʕlaːn minnak] Ali too is mad at you. أخَذ دِينارَين وَهَمَّينا يرِيد بَعَد [ʔaxað dinaːrayn whammayna yriːd baʕad] He got two dinars and wants more in addition. • **2.** again, once more – هَمّ قامَت تُمطُر [hamm gaːmat tumṭur] It's started to rain again. هَمَّينَة حِكَيت. ما قِتلَك لا تِحكِي؟ [hammayna ħičiːt. maː gitlak laː tiħči?] You spoke again. Didn't I tell you not to speak?

ه م م 3
هُمَّة [humma] *pronoun:* • **1.** they

ه م ه م
هَمهَم [hamham] *v:* • **1.** to growl
هَمهَمَة [hamhama] *n:* • **1.** growl
تهِمهِم [thimhim] *n:* • **1.** growling

ه م ي ن
هَمايُون [hamaːyuːn] *n:* • **1.** large bolt, or sheet, of cloth

ه ن
هنا، هنانَة [hna, hnaːna] *adv:* • **1.** here, in this place – ماكُو أحَّد هنا [maːku ʔaħħad hna] There's no one here. اِنتِظِرنِي هنانَة [ʔintiðirni hnaːna] Wait for me here.
هناك، هناكَة [hnaːk, hnaːka] *adv:* • **1.** there, in that place – ما لقَيتَه هناك [maː lgiːtah hnaːk] I didn't find him there.
هنايَة [hnaːya] *adv:* • **1.** here

ه ن ء
هَنَّى [hannaː] *v:* • **1.** to congratulate, felicitate, express good wishes to – أهَنِّيك عالنَّجاح [ʔahanniːk ʕannajaːħ] Congratulations on your success. رِحنا نهَنِّيهُم بالعِيد [riħna nhanniːhum bilʕiːd] We went to give them our best wishes on the occasion of the holiday. • **2.** to grant happiness, to delight – الله يهَنِّيك بعُمرَك [ʔallah yhanniːk bʕumrak] May God grant you happiness in your life.
تهَنَّى [thannaː] *v:* • **1.** to take pleasure – أكُل عَلَى كَيفَك وَتهَنَّى بأكلَك [ʔukul ʕala kayfak wthannaː bʔaklak] Eat slowly and enjoy your food.
تَهنِيَة، تَهنِئَة [tahniya, tahniʔa] *n:* تَهانِي [tahaːni] *pl:* • **1.** congratulation, felicitation
مُهَنِّئ [muhanniʔ] *adj:* مُهَنِّئِين [muhanniʔiːn] *pl:* • **1.** congratulator, well-wisher
هَنِيئاً، هَنِيئاً مَرِيئاً [haniːʔan, haniːʔan mariːʔan] *adverbial:* • **1.** (polite expression said to someone who has just eaten, or drunk water) May you enjoy it! May it bring you good health!

ه ن ج ل
هَنجَل [hanjal] *v:* • **1.** to jump up and down on one foot, to hop on one foot – تعَوُّرَت رِجلَه وَقام يهَنجِل [tʕawwurat rijlah wgaːm yhanjil] His foot got hurt and he began jumping up and down. خَلِّي نهَنجِل لِلمَدرَسَة وَنشُوف ياهُو يُغلُب [xalliː nhanjil lilmadrasa winšuːf yaːhu yuɣlub] Let's hop to school on one foot and see who wins. • **2.** to bounce – يهَنجِل بمَشِيتَه [yhanjil bmašiːtah] He bounces when he walks.

ه ن د
الهِند [ʔilhind] *n:* • **1.** India – جُوز هِند [juːz hind] coconut. تَمُر هِند [tamur hind] tamarind.
هِندِي [hindi] *adj:* هنُود [hinuːd, hunuːd] *pl:* • **1.** Indian – السَّفارَة الهِندِيَّة [ʔissafaːra ʔilhindiyya] the Indian Embassy.

ه ن د ب ر ي ك
هاندبرَيك [haːndbrayk] *n:* • **1.** emergency brake

ه ن د ر
هِندِر [hindir] *n:* هِندِرات [hindiraːt] *pl:* • **1.** crank handle

ه ن د س 1
هَندَس [handas] *v:* • **1.** to design, engineer – مِنُو هَندَسلَك البَيت؟ [minu handaslak ʔilbayt?] Who designed the house for you?

هَندَسَة [handasa] *n:* • **1.** (technical) design, engineering • **2.** architecture • **3.** geometry
مُهَندِس [muhandis] *n:* مُهَندِسِين [muhandisi:n] *pl:* • **1.** technical designer, engineer • **2.** architect
هَندَسِي [handasi] *adj:* • **1.** engineering, technical

ه ن د س 2
هِندِس [hindis] *adj:* • **1.** (invar.) pitch black, completely devoid of light – القُبَّة ظَلمَة هِندِس [ʔilqubba ðalma hindis] The room is pitch black.

ه ن د س 3
هِندُوس [hindu:s] *adj:* • **1.** (coll.) Hindu(s)
هِندُوسِي [hindu:si] *adj:* • **1.** Hindu

ه ن د م
هَندَم [handam] *v:* • **1.** to dress up, spruce up, attire smartly – صارلَه ساعَة يهَندِم نَفسَه [ṣa:rlah sa:ʕa yhandim nafsah] He's spent an hour sprucing up.
تهَندَم [thandam] *v:* • **1.** to dress oneself smartly – لازِم تِتهَندَم قَبُل ما تشُوفها لِلبنَيَّة [la:zim tithandam gabul ma: tšu:fha lilbnayya] You have to get dressed up before you see the girl.
هِندام [hinda:m] *n:* • **1.** neatness, tidiness (of attire) • **2.** appearance, looks
مهَندَم [mhandam] *adj:* • **1.** neat

ه و ج
أهوَج [ʔahwaǰ] *adj:* هُوج، هَوجِين [hu:ǰ, hu:ǰi:n] *pl:* هُوجَة [hu:ǰa] *feminine:* • **1.** foolish, rash, thoughtless, harebrained • **2.** thoughtless person
هُوجَة [hu:ǰa] *adj:* • **1.** foolish, rash, thoughtless, harebrained • **2.** thoughtless person

ه و د
هَوَّد [hawwad] *v:* • **1.** to abate, subside, calm down, quiet down – بِكَى مُدَّة وَبَعدين هَوَّد [biča: mudda wbaʕdi:n hawwad] He cried for a while and then was quiet. هَوَّد الوِجَع بَعَد نُصّ ساعَة [hawwad ʔilwijaʕ baʕad nuṣṣ sa:ʕa] The pain subsided after a half hour. • **2.** to cause to abate, subside, to soothe, calm, quiet – هَالحَبّ يهَوِّد وُجَع لراس [halḥabb yhawwid wujaʕ lra:s] These pills will relieve a headache.
تَهوِيد [tahwi:d] *n:* • **1.** Judaization
مهاوَدَة [mha:wada] *n:* • **1.** complaisance, obligingness
مِتهاوِد [mitha:wid] *adj:* • **1.** moderate (price)

ه و د ج
هُودَج [hu:daǰ] *n:* هُوادِج [huwa:diǰ] *pl:* • **1.** howdah, camel litter

ه و ر
هَوَّر [hawwar] *v:* • **1.** to stretch, become too large – قُندَرتِي ظَلَّت تِكبَر بِالإستِعمال إِلَى أَن هَوّرَت [qundarti ðallat tikbar bilʔistiʕma:l ʔila ʔan hawwrat] My shoes kept getting larger from use until they got too big.
تهَوَّر [thawwar] *v:* • **1.** to rash, reckless, heedless – يِتهَوَّر بِكُلّ أَعمالَه [yithawwar bkull ʔaʕma:lah] He's rash in everything he does. • **2.** to speak disrespectfully, to show disrespect – يِتهَوَّر عالمُعَلِّم عَلَى طُول [yithawwar ʕalmuʕallim ʕala ṭu:l] He shows disrespect toward the teacher all the time.
تهَوَّر [thawwar] *v:* • **1.** to act careless
اِنهار [ʔinha:r] *v:* • **1.** to collapse, fall down, fall apart – اِنهارَت البِنايَة عَلَيهُم [ʔinha:rat ʔilbna:ya ʕali:hum] The building fell down on them. اِنهارَت أَعصابَه [ʔinha:rat ʔaʕṣa:bah] He lost control of himself.
هُور [hu:r] *n:* أهوار [ʔahwa:r] *pl:* • **1.** marsh, swamp
هُورَة [hu:ra] *n:* • **1.** small marsh, bog – راحَت بُولَة بهورَة [ra:ḥat bu:la bhu:ra] It was all wasted.
اِنهيار [ʔinhiya:r] *n:* • **1.** collapse, breakdown
مِتهَوِّر [mithawwir] *adj:* • **1.** careless, hasty
مِنهار [minha:r] *adj:* • **1.** rundown

ه و ر ن
هُورِن [hu:rin] *n:* هَورِنات [hu:rina:t] *pl:* • **1.** horn (auto.)

ه و س
هَوَّس [hawwas] *v:* • **1.** to chant slogans – قِسِم مِن المُتَضاهِرِين كانَوا يهَوِّسُون [qisim min ʔilmutaða:hiri:n ča:naw yhawwisu:n] Some of the demonstrators were chanting slogans. • **2.** to make a commotion, raise an uproar, be noisy – مِن قالِلهُم أكُو دَوام اليُوم، هَوِّسَوا [min ga:llhum ʔaku dawa:m ʔilyu:m, hawwisaw] When he told them they had to work today, they raised a ruckus. أكُو عِرِس اليُوم وَالفَلّاحِين دَيهَوِّسُون [ʔaku ʕiris ʔilyu:m wilfalla:ḥi:n dayhawwisu:n] There is a marriage today and the peasants are being rowdy.
هَوسَة [hawsa hu:sa] *n:* هَوسات [hawsa:t] *pl:* • **1.** slogan, chant • **2.** din, clamor, commotion, uproar

ه و ش 1
هُوش [hu:š] *n:* • **1.** (coll.) cattle – لَحَم هَوش [laḥam hu:š] beef.
هايشَة [ha:yša] *n:* هوايِش [hwa:yiš] *pl:* • **1.** cow

ه و ش 2
تهاوَش [tha:waš] *v:* • **1.** to quarrel
تَهاوُش [taha:wuš] *n:* • **1.** quarrel
مِتهاوِش [mitha:wiš] *adj:* • **1.** quarreled

ه و ش 3
مهَوَّش [mhawwaš] *adj:* • **1.** winnowed

ه و ع
تهَوَّع [thawwaʕ] *v:* • **1.** to gag

تهوُّع [thuwwuʕ] *n:* • **1.** retching, gagging

ه و ل

هَوَّل [hawwal] *v:* • **1.** to exaggerate, over-emphasize, magnify – لا تصَدِّق بِحَكيَه عَلَى طُول. يهَوِّل كُلْشِي [la: tṣaddig bħačyah ʕala ṭu:l. yhawwil kullši] Don't believe everything he says. He exaggerates everything. لا تهَوِّل القَضِيَّة لِهَدَرَجَة [la: thawwil ʔilqaðiyya lhaddaraǰa] Don't magnify the matter to such a degree.

هُول [hu:l] *n:* • **1.** (no pl.) family room, rumpus room (where the family lives, as opposed to the parlor, where guests are received)

هالَة [ha:la] *n:* هالات [ha:la:t] *pl:* • **1.** halo • **2.** nimbus – اِرتِفاع هَالجَّبَل هائِل [ʔirtifa:ʕ haǰǰibal ha:ʔil] The height of this mountain is tremendous.

تَهوِيل [tahwi:l] *n:* • **1.** exaggeration

مُهَوِّل [muhawwil] *adj:* • **1.** exaggerated

هائِل [ha:ʔil] *adj:* • **1.** appalling, stupendous, huge, amazing, enormous – اِرتِفاع هَالجَّبَل هائِل [ʔirtifa:ʕ haǰǰibal ha:ʔil] The height of this mountain is tremendous.

ه و ل ن د

هَولَندا [hu:landa] n: • 1. Holland, The Netherlands

هَولَندِي [hu:landi] *adj:* • **1.** Dutch

ه و م

هامَة [ha:ma] *n:* هامات [ha:ma:t] *pl:* • **1.** vertex, crown (of the head)

ه و ن 1

هان [ha:n] *v:* • **1.** to become easy, simple, facile – إذا يِجي وِيّانا واحِد لاخ، يهُون الشُّغُل [ʔiða yiǰi wiyya:na wa:ħid la:x, yhu:n ʔiššuɣul] If one more comes with us, the work will be easy. • **2.** to humble, abase, humiliate, treat with contempt – هانَه قِدّام النّاس [ha:nah gidda:m ʔinna:s] He humiliated him in front of the people. لا ترُوح عَليه تَرَة يِهينَك [la: tru:ħ ʕali:h tara yihi:nak] Don't go see him or he'll humiliate you.

هَوَّن [hawwan] *v:* • **1.** to make easy, simple, facile – هَالقامُوس يهَوِّن عَلَيّا الدِّراسَة [halqa:mu:s yhawwin ʕalayya ʔiddira:sa] This dictionary makes studying easier for me.

أهان [ʔaha:n] *v:* • **1.** to insult

تهاوَن [tha:wan] *v:* • **1.** to be negligent, careless, lax – إذا تِتهاوَن بِشُغلَك، يفُصلُوك [ʔiða titha:wan bišuɣlak, yfuṣlu:k] If you're lax in your work, they'll fire you. إذا تِتهاوَن عَلَى طُول، تاكُلها بَعدين [ʔiða titha:wan ʕala ṭu:l, ta:kulha baʕdi:n] If you take thing easy all the time, you'll really catch it later.

اِنهان [ʔinha:n] *v:* • **1.** to be humiliated, abased, insulted – اِنبُسَط وَإنهان [ʔinbuṣaṭ wʔinha:n] He was beaten up and humiliated.

اِستَهان، اِستَهوَن [ʔistaha:n, ʔistahwan] *v:* • **1.** to consider easy, simple, to esteem lightly, underrate, underestimate – لا تِستِهِين هَالشَّغلَة [la: tistihi:n haššaɣla] Don't think this job is easy. لا تِستَهوِن بِقُوّتَه [la: tistahwin biqu:tah] Don't take his strength lightly.

هُون [hu:n] *n:* • **1.** easiness, facility

مَهانَة [maha:na] *n:* • **1.** humiliation, degradation, abasement, disgrace

إهانَة [ʔiha:na] *n:* إهانات [ʔiha:na:t] *pl:* • **1.** insult

تَهاوُن [taha:wun] *n:* • **1.** laxity • **2.** disesteem, disdain

اِستِهانَة [ʔistiha:na] *n:* • **1.** neglect, disdain, disesteem, scorn, contempt

هَيِّن [hayyin] *adj:* • **1.** easy, simple, facile – هالشُّغُل هَيِّن وَما بيه تَعَب [haššuɣul hayyin wma bi:h taʕab] This work is easy and requires no exertion.

مِتهاوِن [mitha:win] *adj:* • **1.** negligent, remiss, lax, indifferent

مِستِهين [mistiyhi:n] *adj:* • **1.** apathetic, uncaring

أهيَن، أهوَن [ʔahyan, ʔahwan] *comparative adjective:* • **1.** more or most facile, etc

ه و ن 2

هاوَن [ha:wan] *n:* هاوَنات [ha:wana:t] *pl:* • **1.** mortar (vessel) – مَدفَع الهاوَن [madfaʕ ʔilha:wan] mortar (weapon). • **2.** large bowl

ه و و

هُوَّ [huwwa] *pronoun:* • **1.** he, it – هَذا هُوَّ! خَلِّيه يِزعَل [ha:ða huwwa! xalli:h yizʕal] That's the way it is! Let him get mad. راح أزَيِّد دِينار اللّاخ وهذا هُوَّ [ra:ħ ʔazayyid dina:r ʔilla:x wha:ða huwwa] I'm going to raise another dinar and that's it. وين عَلِي؟ ما هُوَّ [wi:n ʕali? ma: huwwa] Where's Ali? He's not here.

ه و ي 1

هَوَّى [hawwa:] *v:* • **1.** to ventilate, air – هَوِّي الغُرفَة حَتَّى يِطلَع العَجاج [hawwi ʔilɣurfa ħatta yiṭlaʕ ʔalʕaǰa:ǰ] Air out the room so the dust will go away.

تهَوَّى [thawwa:] *v:* • **1.** to be ventilated, to be refreshed

هَوا [hawa] *n:* • **1.** air • **2.** wind, breeze, draft – الهَوا شال نَفنُوفها [ʔilhawa ša:l nafnu:fha] The wind lifted her dress. اليُوم الدِّنيا بِيها هَوا شوَيَّة [ʔilyu:m ʔiddinya bi:ha hawa šwayya] Today the weather's a little bit windy. • **3.** weather, climate – سافَر لِسّويسرا حَتَّى يغَيِّر هَوا [sa:far lisswi:sra: ħatta yɣayyir hawa] He travelled to Switzerland to get a change of climate.

هَويَة [hawya] *n:* هَويات [hawya:t] *pl:* • **1.** gust of wind, breeze

هَوِيَّة [hawiyya] *n:* هَوِيّات [hawiyya:t] *pl:* • **1.** identity • **2.** identification papers

هاوِيَة [ha:wiya] *n:* هاويات [ha:wya:t] *pl:* • **1.** pit, chasm, abyss (used figuratively as in:) – وِقَع بِالهاوِيَة [wiqaʕ bilha:wya] He fell for the trap.

ه

تهوِيَة [tahwiya] *n:* • **1.** airing, ventilation
هاوي [ha:wi] *adj:* هُواة [huwa:t] *pl:* • **1.** amateur, fan
هَوائي [hawa:ʔi] *adj:* • **1.** air-, pneumatic – مَضَخَّة هَوائي [maðaxxa hawa:ʔi] air pump. • **2.** flighty, capricious, unpredictable – لا تِعتَمدِين عَليه بِالزَّواج. هَذا وَلَد هَوائي. يبَدِّل رأيَه كُلّ دَقيقَة [la: tiʕtamdi:n ʕali:h bizzawa:ǰ. ha:ða walad hawa:ʔi. ybaddil raʔyah kull daqi:qa] Don't depend on him to marry. He's a capricious boy. He changes his mind every minute.
هِوايَة [hiwa:ya] *adv:* هِوايات [hiwa:ya:t] *pl:* • **1.** hobby, spare time activity

ه و ي 2
هوايَة [hwa:ya] *adj:* • **1.** much, many, numerous – عِندِي فلُوس هوايَة [ʕindi flu:s hwa:ya] I've got a lot of money. هوايَة ناس يزُورُون هَالمَتحَف [hwa:ya na:s yzu:ru:n halmatħaf] Many people visit this museum. • **2.** too much, excessive – هَالقماش هوايَة عَلَيّا؛ راح يزُود مِنَّه [halqma:š hwa:ya ʕalayya; ra:ħ yzu:d minnah] This is too much cloth for me; there will be some of it left over. إذا تاكُل هوايَة، تِسمَن [ʔiða ta:kul hwa:ya, tisman] If you eat too much, you'll get fat. • **3.** very, extremely – آنِي مَمنُون هوايَة [ʔa:ni mamnu:n hwa:ya] I'm very grateful. هالبِنايَة عالِي هوايَة [halbina:ya ʕa:li hwa:ya] This building is very tall. • **4.** often, frequently – يتَرَدَّد هوايَة عَلَى هَالمَحَلّ [yitraddad hwa:ya ʕala halmaħall] He comes back to this spot frequently. • **5.** for a long time – ظَلّ يباوِع بِالصُّورَة هوايَة [ðall yba:wiʕ bʔiṣṣu:ra hwa:ya] He kept looking at the picture a long time.

ه ي
هاء ها [ha:ʔ, ha:] *n:* • **1.** name of the letter

ه ي ء
هَيَّأ [hayyaʔ] *v:* • **1.** to prepare, make ready, put in readiness – هَيِّئ مُكان لِأَربَعَة أَشخاص [hayyiʔ muka:n liʔarbaʕa ʔašxa:ṣ] Prepare a place for four people.
تهَيَّئ [thayyaʔ] *v:* • **1.** to get ready, prepare oneself – تهَيّئُوا! الزَّعِيم دَيِجِي [thayyʔu:! ʔizzaʕi:m dayiǰi] Get ready! The leader is coming.
هَيئَة [hayʔa] *n:* هَيئات [hayʔa:t] *pl:* • **1.** appearance, mien, bearing • **2.** state, condition • **3.** group, organization, association, body – هَيئَة الأُمَم المُتَّحِدَة [hayʔat ʔilʔumam ʔilmuttaħida] The United Nations Organization. هَيئَة دِبلُوماسِيَّة [hayʔa diplima:siyya] diplomatic corps.
تهَيُّؤ [tahayyuʔ] *n:* • **1.** preparation
مُهَيَّأ [muhayyaʔ] *adj:* • **1.** prepared
مِتهَيِّأ [mithayyiʔ] *adj:* • **1.** prepared

ه ي ب
هاب [ha:b] *v:* • **1.** to respect – هُوَّ ما يهاب أَيّ واحِد [huwwa ma: yha:b ʔayy wa:ħid] He's not awed by any one. المُعَلِّم لازِم يهابَه كُلّ طالِب [ʔilmuʕallim la:zim yha:bah kull ṭa:lib] Every student should respect the teacher. آنِي أَهاب القانُون [ʔa:ni ʔaha:b ʔilqa:nu:n] I have a healthy respect for the law. • **2.** to be awed by, stand in awe of
تهَيَّب [thayyab] *v:* • **1.** to be filled with awe – مِن يدخُل عالوَزِير يِتهَيَّب هوايَة [min yidxul ʕalwazi:r yithayyab hwa:ya] When he goes in to see the minister he feels great awe.
هَيبَة [hayba, hi:ba] *n:* • **1.** fear, respect
مَهابَة [maha:ba] *n:* • **1.** fear, respect
مَهيُوب [mahyu:b] *adj:* • **1.** respectful
أَهيَب [ʔahyab] *comparative adjective:* • **1.** more or most awesome, venerable

ه ي ج
هاج [ha:ǰ] *v:* • **1.** to be in a state of agitation, turmoil, commotion, excitement – العاصِفَة خَلَّت البَحَر يهِيج [ʔilʕa:ṣifa xallat ʔilbaħar yihi:ǰ] The storm made the sea roll and toss. • **2.** to become furious, angry, indignant – مِن سِمَع بهَالخَبَر، هاج [min simaʕ bhalxabar, ha:ǰ] When he heard that news, he exploded.
هَيَّج [hayyaǰ] *v:* • **1.** to provoke, incite, stir up, agitate – خِطابَه هَيَّج الطُّلّاب [xiṭa:bah hayyaǰ ʔiṭṭulla:b] His speech stirred up the students. • **2.** to arouse, excite, awaken – مَشيها يهَيِّج [mašyha yihayyiǰ] Her way of walking is provocative.
تهَيَّج [thayyaǰ] *v:* • **1.** to become aroused, excited – ماكُو حاجَة تِتهَيَّج وَتصَيِّح [ma:ku ħa:ǰa tithayyaǰ wtṣayyiħ] There's no reason for you to get excited and shout. ما يِقرا كُتُب جِنسِيَّة لِأَنّ يِتهَيَّج بسُرعَة [ma: yiqra: kutub ǰinsiyya liʔann yithayyaǰ bsurʕa] He doesn't read sexy books because he gets excited quickly. • **2.** to become agitated, stirred up, excited
تهَيُّج [tahayyuǰ] *n:* • **1.** disturbance, commotion, excitement
هَيَجان [hayaǰa:n] *n:* • **1.** excitement
هايِج [ha:yiǰ] *adj:* • **1.** furious, rough, heaving (sea, waves), excited, angry, impassioned
مهَيِّج [mhayyiǰ] *adj:* • **1.** exciting, stirring
مِتهَيِّج [mithayyiǰ] *adj:* • **1.** agitated, upset, excited, impassioned • **2.** sexually excited, horny

ه ي ر و غ ل ف
الهِيرُوغلِيفِيَّة [ʔilhi:ruɣli:fiyya] *n:* • **1.** hieroglyphics

ه ي س
هَيَّس [hayyas] *v:* • **1.** to feel, sense, be aware, cognizant – رِجلَه مَيِّتَة وَما يهَيِّس إذا تِنغُزها [riǰlah mayyta wma yhayyis ʔiða tinɣuzha] His leg is dead and he doesn't feel if you prick it. طَبّ لِلبَيت وَما حَدّ هَيَّس بيه

ه

[ṭabb lilbayt wma ħadd hayyas bi:h] He got in the house and no one realized it.

ه ي ض

هَيضَة [hayð̣a] *n:* • **1.** Asiatic cholera

ه ي ك

هيكِي، هِيك [hi:či:, hi:č] *adv:* • **1.** such, this, that, this kind of, that kind of – شلُون تِمشِي ويّا هِيكِي ناس؟ [šlu:n timši wiyya hi:či na:s?] How could you run around with such people? شلُون تِحكِي هِيكِي؟ ما تِستِحِي؟ [šlu:n tiħči hi:či? ma: tistiħi?] How could you say that? Aren't you ashamed? هِيَّ هِيكِي الصَّداقَة؟ [hiyya hi:či ʔiṣṣada:qa?] Is that the way friendship is? مِن هِيكِي ما دَيحكِي ويّايا [min hi:či ma: dayiħči wiyya:ya] That's why he isn't talking to me. أَخُوك راح هِيك قَبُل خَمِس دَقايِق [ʔaxu:k ra:ħ hi:č gabul xamis daqa:yiq] Your brother went that way five minutes ago. • **2.** so, thus – إرسِمها هِيكِي [ʔirsimha hi:či] Draw it like this. بِالأَوَّل أمُرّ عَليه وَبَعدين نِجِي عَليك. مُو هِيك؟ [bilʔawwal ʔamurr ʕali:h wbaʕdi:n niǰi ʕali:k. mu: hi:č?] First I go by his place and then we come to yours. Isn't that it?

ه ي ك ل

هَيكَل [haykal] *n:* • **1.** temple, pagan place of worship • **2.** framework • **3.** skeleton – هَيكَل عَظمِي [haykal ʕað̣mi] skeleton. • **4.** chassis (of an automobile) • **5.** shape, looks, appearance

ه ي ل [1]

هال [ha:l] *v:* • **1.** to pour, strew – هالَوا التِّراب عَلَى قَبُر المَيِّت [ha:law ʔittira:b ʕala gabur ʔilmayyit] They threw the dirt onto the dead man's grave.

اِنهال [ʔinha:l] *v:* • **1.** to rain down – اِنهالَت عالوَزِير بَرقِيّات الاحتِجاج [ʔinha:lat ʕalwazi:r barqiyya:t ʔilʔiħtiǰa:ǰ] Telegrams of protest deluged the minister.

ه ي ل [2]

هَيل [hi:l] *n:* • **1.** cardamom

ه ي م

هام [ha:m] *v:* • **1.** to roam, wander, rove – هام بِالبَرّ [ha:m bilbarr] He wandered in the desert. اِنهِزَم مِن أَبُوه وَهام عَلَى وِجهَه [ʔinhizam min ʔabu:h wha:m ʕala wiǰhah] He fled from his father and wandered aimlessly about. • **2.** to fall in love – هام بِيها [ha:m bi:ha] He fell in love with her.

هِيم [hi:m] *n:* هِيَم [hiyam] *pl:* • **1.** crowbar, pry-bar

هَيم [haym hi:m] *n:* • **1.** roam

هَيمَة [hayma, hi:ma] *n:* • **1.** wilderness, desert

هيام [hiya:m] *n:* • **1.** passionate love

هَيمان [hayma:n] *adj:* • **1.** madly in love

ه ي و

See also: ه ي ي

ه ي ي

هِيَّ [hiyya] *pronoun:* • **1.** she, it – آنِي ما ضِرَبِتها؛ هِيَّ ضِربَتنِي [ʔa:ni ma: ð̣irabitha; hiyya ð̣irbatni] I didn't hit her; she hit me. هاي هِيَّ! لَو تِجِي وِيّايا لَو ما أَرُوح [ha:y hiyya! law tiǰi wiyya:ya law ma: ʔaru:ħ] That's it! Either you come with me or I won't go.

ه

و

و

و [w] *conjunction:* • **1.** and, plus – اِنطانِي القَلَم وَالكتاب [ʔinṭa:ni ʔilqalam wilkta:b] He gave me the pencil and the book. تَعال ساعَة خَمسَة وَنُصّ [taʕa:l sa:ʕa xamsa wnuṣṣ] Come at five-thirty. ثنَين وإثنَين يسَوِّي أربَع [θnayn wʔiθnayn ysawwi: ʔarbaʕ] Two plus two equals four. • **2.** while, as, when – التِّلِفُون دَقّ وَآنِي بِالحَمّام [ʔittalifu:n dagg wʔa:ni bilħamma:m] The telephone rang when I was in the bath. باقَوا الفلُوس مِنَّه وَهُوَّ نايِم [ba:gaw ʔilflu:s minnah wahuwwa na:yim] They stole the money from him while he was asleep. • **3.** (in an oath or exclamation) by – والله، ما أدري [wʔallah, ma: ʔadri] By God, I don't know.

و ب ء

وَباء [waba:ʔ] *n:* • **1.** infectious disease, epidemic

وَبائِي [waba:ʔi] *adj:* • **1.** infectious, contagious, epidemic

مَوبُوء [mawbu:ʔ] *adj:* • **1.** infected, poisoned, contaminated

و ب خ

وَبَّخ [wabbax] *v:* • **1.** to reprimand, rebuke, censure, scold – المُعَلِّم وَبَّخ الطّالِب عَلَى كَسَلَه [ʔilmuʕallim wabbax ʔiṭṭa:lib ʕala kasalah] The teacher reprimanded the student for his laziness.

توَبَّخ [twabbax] *v:* • **1.** pass. of وَبَّخ to be rebuked, to be censured – توَبَّخ عَلَى فَدّ شِي ما مسَوِّيه [twabbax ʕala fadd ši ma: msawwi:h] He was scolded for something he hadn't done.

توبِيخ [tawbi:x] *n:* • **1.** reprimand, rebuke, reproach

و ب ر

وَبَر [wabar, wubar] *n:* • **1.** camel hair

و ب ش

وَبش [wabš] *n:* أوباش [ʔawba:š] *pl:* • **1.** trash, rubbish

و ت د

وَتَد [watad] *n:* أوتاد [ʔawta:d] *pl:* • **1.** stake, peg, pin

و ت ر

وَتَّر [wattar] *v:* • **1.** to stretch, draw tight, pull taut, tighten, strain – لا توَتِّر الخيط زايِد تَرَة يِنقِطِع [la: twattir ʔilxi:ṭ za:yid tara yingiṭiʕ] Don't stretch the string too tight or it'll break. وَتَّر إيدَه حَتَّى يراوِينا عَضَلاتَه [wattar ʔi:dah ħatta yra:wi:na ʕaðala:tah] He tightened his hand in order to show us his muscles.

توَتَّر [twattar] *v:* • **1.** to become strained, tense – توَتَّرَت العِلاقات بَينِنا وَبَينهُم [twattirat ʔilʕila:qa:t baynna wbaynhum] Relations between us and them became strained.

وَتَر [watar] *n:* أوتار [ʔawta:r] *pl:* • **1.** string (of a bow or musical instrument) – وَتَر حَسّاس [watar ħassa:s] a sensitive area, tender spot, sore spot. ضِرَب عَلَى وَتَر حَسّاس؛ ظَلّ يذَكِّرها بِإبِنها اللِّي مات بِالحَرُب [ðirab ʕala watar ħassa:s; ðall yðakkirha bʔibinha ʔilli ma:t bilħarub] He touched a sore spot; he kept reminding her of her son who died in the war. • **2.** hypotenuse (geom.)

تَوَتُّر [tawattur] *n:* • **1.** tension, friction, strain

وَتِيرَة [wati:ra] *n:* • **1.** method, mode, way, manner

مَوتُور [mawtu:r] *adj:* مَوتُورِين [mawtu:ri:n] *pl:* • **1.** filled with hate, hostile, malevolent • **2.** vengeful person

مِتوَتَّر [mitwattir] *adj:* • **1.** taut, drawn tight, strained (nerves, situation, relations)

و ث ق

وِثَق [wiθaq] *v:* • **1.** with بـ to trust, place confidence in, depend upon, rely on – وِثَق بِيه وانطاه فلُوس [wiθaq bi:h wʔinṭa:h flu:s] He trusted him and gave him money. يُوثَق بنَفسَه هوايَة [yu:θaq bnafsah hwa:ya] He has a lot of self-confidence.

وَثَّق [waθθaq] *v:* • **1.** to strengthen, make firm, cement, consolidate – الزَّواج راح يوَثِّق العِلاقات بين العائِلتَين [ʔizzawa:ǰ ra:ħ ywaθθiq ʔilʕila:qa:t bi:n ʔilʕa:ʔiltayn] The marriage will cement relations between the two families.

توَثَّق [twaθθaq] *v:* • **1.** to be strengthened, consolidated, firmly established – توَثَّقَت العِلاقات بين هَالبَلَدَين [twaθθiqat ʔilʕila:qa:t bi:n halbaladayn] Relations have been strengthened between these two countries. • **2.** to have confidence, be confident, assured – توَثَّق لَو أعرُف، كان قِتلَك [twaθθaq law ʔaʕruf, ča:n gitlak] Rest assured that if I knew, I would have told you.

اِنوِثَق [ʔinwiθaq] *v:* • **1.** with بـ to be trusted, be relied on – هَذا ما ينوثِق بِيه [ha:ða ma: yinwiθiq bi:h] He can't be trusted.

ثِقَة [θiqa] *n:* • **1.** trust, confidence, faith • **2.** (pl. ثِقات) reliable, trustworthy – مَصدَر ثِقَة [maṣdar θiqa] a reliable source.

وُثُوق [wuθu:q] *n:* • **1.** confidence, self-assurance, firm attitude

وِثاق [wiθa:q] *n:* • **1.** tie, bond, fetter, chain

وَثِيقَة [waθi:qa] *n:* وَثايِق [waθa:yiq] *pl:* • **1.** document, certificate, record • **2.** transcript (of school grades)

مِيثاق [mi:θa:q] *n:* مَواثِيق [mawa:θi:q] *pl:* • **1.** pact, covenant, treaty, agreement

و

تَوثِيق [tawθiːq] *n:* • **1.** consolidation, strengthening
وَثِيق [waθiːq] *adj:* • **1.** firm, solid, strong – أَكُو عِلاقَة وَثِيقَة بَينِي وَبَين الوَزِير [ʔaku ʕilaːqa waθiːqa bayni wbayn ʔilwaziːr] There's a firm friendship between me and the minister.
واثِق [waːθiq] *adj:* • **1.** trusting, confident, certain, sure
مُوَثَّق [muwaθθaq] *adj:* • **1.** verified • **2.** certified, documented
مَوثُوق [mawθuːq] *adj:* • **1.** trusted
وَثائِقِي [waθaːʔiqi] *adj:* • **1.** documented • **2.** related to documentation
أَوثَق [ʔawθaq] *comparative adjective:* • **1.** more or most trusting, confident, sure • **2.** more or most firm, strong, solid • **3.** more or most dependable, reliable

و ث ن

وَثَن [waθan] *n:* أَوثان [ʔawθaːn] *pl:* • **1.** idol, graven image
وَثَنِي [waθani] *adj:* وَثَنِيَّة [waθaniyya] *pl:* • **1.** idolater, heathen, pagan • **2.** pagan, idolatrous

و ج ب

وِجَب [wiǰab] *v:* • **1.** to become obligatory, requisite, a duty – ما دام طاب، وِجبَت عَليه الصَّلاة [maː daːm ṭaːb, wiǰbat ʕaliːh ʔiṣṣalaː] Since he has recovered, it is his duty to pray.
وَجَّب [waǰǰab] *v:* • **1.** to be very hospitable toward – مِن زِرِتهُم، وَجِّبُونِي هوايَة [min zirithum, waǰǰibuːni hwaːya] When I visited them, they showed me every possible courtesy.
اِستَوجَب [ʔistawǰab] *v:* • **1.** to deserve, merit, be worthy of – القَضِيَّة ما تِستَوجِب هَالتَّعقِيدات [ʔilqaḍiyya maː tistawǰib hattaʕqiːdaːt] The matter doesn't merit these complexities. الجَّرِيمَة ما كانَت تِستَوجِب هِيكِي حُكُم [ʔaǰǰariːma maː čaːnat tistawǰib hiːči ḥukum] The crime didn't call for such a sentence.
وَجبَة [waǰba] *n:* وَجبات [waǰbaːt] *pl:* • **1.** portion, part (of a larger group) – وَجبَة تخُشّ وَوَجبَة تِطلَع. القاعَة مَليانَة [waǰba txušš wwaǰba tiṭlaʕ. ʔilqaːʕa malyaːna] A group goes in and a group comes out. The hall's still full. جابَوا وَجبَة مَساجِين جِدِيدَة [ǰaːbaw waǰba masaːǰiːn ǰidiːda] They brought a new shipment of prisoners. • **2.** meal, repast
واجِب [waːǰib] *n:* • **1.** binding, obligatory, necessary, incumbent • **2.** (pl. واجِبات) duty • **3.** assignment, task
مُوجِب [muːǰib] *n:* • **1.** positive (elec.) – القُطب المُوجِب [ʔilquṭb ʔilmuːǰib] the positive terminal. • **2.** (pl. مُوجِبات) cause, reason, motive – هَذا ما إِلَه مُوجِب [haːða maː ʔilah muːǰib] This is uncalled for.
وُجُوب [wuǰuːb] *n:* • **1.** necessity, obligation, duty
إِيجاب، بِالإِيجاب [ʔiːǰaːb, bilʔiːǰaːb] *n:* • **1.** in the affirmative – جانا جَواب بالإِيجاب [ǰaːna ǰawaːb bilʔiːǰaːb] We got an affirmative answer.
تَوجِيب [tawǰiːb] *n:* • **1.** priority
مُستَوجِب [mustawǰib] *adj:* • **1.** deserving
إِيجابِي [ʔiːǰaːbi] *adj:* • **1.** positive

و ج ج

وِجّ [wičč] *n:* • **1.** var. of وُجِه face (see under w - j - h)

و ج د

وُجَد [wuǰad] *v:* • **1.** to find – الشُّرطَة وُجدَت آثار أَقدام بِالحَدِيقَة [ʔiššurṭa wuǰdat ʔaːθaːr ʔaqdaːm bilḥadiːqa] The police found footprints in the garden. • **2.** to be found, exist – هَالسّاعَة ما يُوجَد مِثِلها بِالدِّنيا [hassaːʕa maː yuːǰad miθilha biddinya] You can't find a watch like this anywhere. بَصمَة أَصابعَك اِنوُجدَت عالقاصَة [baṣmat ʔaṣaːbʕak ʔinwuǰdat ʕalqaːṣa] Your fingerprints were found on the safe.
وَجَّد [waǰǰad] *v:* • **1.** to confirm, make sure about • **2.** to find out for sure – ما دَأَقدَر أَوَجِّد مَكانه [maː daʔagdar ʔawaǰǰid makaːnah] I can't locate him exactly.
تواجَد [twaːǰad] *v:* • **1.** to be available
اِنوجَد [ʔinwiǰad] *v:* • **1.** to be found
وُجُود [wuǰuːd] *n:* • **1.** existence, being
وُجدان [wuǰdaːn] *n:* • **1.** conscience – هَذا صاحِب وُجدان. ما يِغدُر أَحَّد [haːða ṣaːḥib wuǰdaːn. maː yiɣdur ʔaḥḥad] He has a conscience. He won't cheat anyone. بوُجدانَك، آنِي قِلِت شِي؟ [bwuǰdaːnak, ʔaːni gilit ši?] Honestly, did I say anything?
تَواجُد [tawaːǰud] *n:* • **1.** availability, existence
واجِد [waːǰid] *adj:* • **1.** much, plenty, a lot of – عِدنا أَكِل واجِد [ʕidna ʔakil waːǰid] We've got a lot of food.
مَوجُود [mawǰuːd] *adj:* • **1.** available, on hand, existent • **2.** present, in attendance, around – خابَرتَه، لَكِن قالُولِي ما مَوجُود بِالبَيت [xaːbartah, laːkin gaːluːli maː mawǰuːd bilbayt] I called him, but they told me he's not at home. • **3.** pl. مَوجُودات stock, supply, store
وِجدانِي [wiǰdaːni] *adj:* • **1.** emotional, affective
مِتواجِد [mitwaːǰid] *adj:* • **1.** available, present

و ج ع

وُجَع [wuǰaʕ, wiǰaʕ] *v:* • **1.** to pain, hurt – بَطنِي دَتُوجَعنِي لِأَنّ أَكَلِت هوايَة [baṭni datuːǰaʕni liʔann ʔakalit hwaːya] My stomach is hurting me because I ate too much. راسِي دَيُوجَعنِي [raːsi dayuːǰaʕni] I have a headache.
وَجَّع [waǰǰaʕ] *v:* • **1.** to hurt, cause pain – الضَّربَة مالتَك توَجِّع [ʔiḍḍarba maːltak twaǰǰiʕ] Your punch hurts a lot. • **2.** to make sick, cause to be sick – لا تاخُذ حَمّام بارِد تَرَة يوَجّعَك [laː taːxuð ḥammaːm baːrid tara yiwaǰǰʕak] Don't take a cold bath or it'll make you sick.

توَجَّع [twaǰǰaʕ] *v:* • **1.** to become sick – لا تخَلِّي الجّاهِل يِلعَب بِالمَيّ تَرَة يِتوَجَّع [la: txalli: ʔiǰǰa:hil yilʕab bilmayy tara yitwaǰǰaʕ] Don't let the child play in the water or he'll get sick.

وُجَع [wuǰaʕ, waǰaʕ, wiǰaʕ] *n:* أوجاع [ʔawǰa:ʕ] *pl:* • **1.** pain, ache • **2.** ailment, sickness, disease – وُجَع! ما تِسكُت عاد [wuǰaʕ! ma: tiskut ʕa:d] Damn it! Why don't you shut up!

توَجُّع [tawaǰǰuʕ] *n:* • **1.** pain, ache

وَجعان [waǰʕa:n] *adj:* وَجعانِين، وجاعَة [waǰʕa:ni:n, wǰa:ʕa] *pl:* • **1.** sick, ill

مَوجُوع [mawǰu:ʕ] *adj:* • **1.** feeling pain, in pain, aching, suffering

و ج غ

وجاغ [wǰa:ɣ, ʔuǰa:ɣ] *n:* أوجاغات [ʔuǰa:ɣa:t] *pl:* • **1.** hearth, fireplace • **2.** range, cook-stove

و ج ن

وَجنَة [waǰna] *n:* وَجنات [waǰna:t] *pl:* • **1.** the area of flesh covering the cheekbone just below the eye

و ج ه

وَجَّه [waǰǰah] *v:* • **1.** to turn, direct, aim, level, point – وَجِّهَوا مَدافِعهُم عالولايَة [waǰǰihaw mada:fiʕhum ʕalwla:ya] They pointed their artillery on the city. • **2.** to direct, give directions to, give orders to – الأُستا وَجَّه عُمّالَه وَبِدَوا يِشتَغلُون [ʔilʔusta waǰǰah ʕumma:lah wabidaw yištaɣlu:n] The boss gave orders to his workers and they went to work. • **3.** to counsel, advise – ما أعرُف شأسَوِّي. وَجِّهني [ma: ʔaʕruf šʔasawwi:. waǰǰihni] I don't know what to do. Advise me. • **4.** to address, direct, send – أرِيد أوَجِّه سُؤال لِلرَّئِيس [ʔari:d ʔawaǰǰih suʔa:l lirraʔi:s] I'd like to direct a question to the president. نوَجِّه النِّداء لكُلّ وَطَني يِشعُر بِالمَسؤُولِيَّة [nwaǰǰih ʔinnida:ʔ likull waṭani yišʕur bilmasʔu:liyya] We address the call to each patriot who feels the responsibility. وَجِّهُولَه إلفات نَظَر [waǰǰihu:lah ʔilfa:t naðar] They sent him a letter of reprimand. • **5.** to display, show, arrange attractively – إذا توَجِّه الخيار، يِنباع بِسِعِر أعلَى [ʔiða twaǰǰih ʔilxya:r, yinba:ʕ bsiʕir ʔaʕla] If you arrange the cucumbers nicely, they'll sell for a higher price.

واجَه [wa:ǰah] *v:* • **1.** to be opposite, facing, across from – بَيتنا يواجِه الوِزارَة [baytna ywa:ǰih ʔilwiza:ra] Our house is directly facing the ministry. • **2.** to see personally, have an audience interview with – راح أواجِه المُدِير عالتَّرفِيع [ra:ħ ʔawa:ǰh ʔilmudi:r ʕattarfi:ʕ] I'm going to see the director about the promotion. • **3.** to face, meet, stand up to, counter, withstand – لازِم تواجِه المُشكِلَة بِصَبُر [la:zim twa:ǰih ʔilmuškila bṣabur] You should face the problem with patience.

توَجَّه [twaǰǰah] *v:* • **1.** to be directed, aimed, pointed – الأضوِيَة كُلّها توَجِّهَت عَالمَسرَح [ʔilʔaðwiya kullha twaǰǰihat ʕalmasraħ] All the lights were directed onto the stage. • **2.** to turn, head, go – خَلِّي نتوَجَّه لِلحَبّانِيَّة [xalli: nitwaǰǰah lilħabba:niyya] Let's head for Habbaniyya.

تواجَه [twa:ǰah] *v:* • **1.** to meet face to face – تواجَهت وِيّا المُدِير [twa:ǰahit wiyya ʔilmudi:r] I met with the director.

اتِّجَه [ʔittiǰah] *v:* • **1.** to turn, head, go – خَمسَة مِن طَيّارات العَدُو اتِّجهَت إلَى مَواضِعكُم [xamsa min ṭayya:ra:t ʔilʕadu ʔittiǰhat ʔila mawa:ðiʕkum] Five enemy planes are headed toward your positions. • **2.** to lead, go – هَالطَّرِيق يِتِّجِه إلَى بَغداد [haṭṭari:q yittiǰih ʔila baɣda:d] This road leads to Baghdad.

جِهَة [ǰiha] *n:* جِهات [ǰiha:t] *pl:* • **1.** direction – بيا جِهَة مِشَوا؟ [bya: ǰiha mišaw?] Which direction did they go? • **2.** side – هَالجِهَة مِن البِنايَة بَعَدها ما مَصبُوغَة [hajǰiha min ʔilbina:ya baʕadha ma: maṣbu:ɣa] This side of the building isn't painted yet. • **3.** point of view, aspect, angle, side. Also, mostly with مِن about, concerning, with regard to – لازِم تِدرُس القَضِيَّة مِن كُلّ الجِّهات [la:zim tidrus ʔilqaðiyya min kull ʔiǰǰiha:t] You have to study the matter from all sides. مِن جِهتِي، آني ما عِندِي مانِع [min ǰihti, ʔa:ni ma: ʕindi ma:niʕ] For my part, I have no objection. مِن جِهَة. . . وَمِن جِهَة ثانيَة [min ǰiha. . . wamin ǰiha θa:nya] On the one hand. . . and on the other. . . . مِن جِهَة [min ǰihat] about, concerning, with regard to. أرِيد أحكِي وِيّاك مِن جِهَة الوَظِيفَة [ʔari:d ʔaħči wiyya:k min ǰihat ʔilwaði:fa] I want to speak to you with regard to the position. • **4.** area, section, part, region – ماكُو حَيايَة بِهَالجِّهات [ma:ku ħaya:ya bhaǰǰiha:t] There are no snakes in these parts.

وُجِه، وِجّ [wuǰih, wičč] *n:* • **1.** face, countenance – قَلَّه إيّاه بوُجهَه [gallah ʔiyya:h bwuččah] He told it to him to his face. He told him about it brazenly. حِكَى بوجَّه [ħiča: bwiččah] He talked back to him. ما يصِير تِحكِي بوُجِه أبُوك [ma: yṣi:r tiħči bwuǰih ʔabu:k] You mustn't talk back to your father. • **2.** front, face, facade • **3.** front, front side (of a fabric) – بلُوز أبُو وجّهَين [blu:z ʔabu wičči:n] reversible sweater. • **4.** slipcover, upholstery covering • **5.** embroidered pillow cover • **6.** meaning, sense, point – شِنُو وجِه النُّكتَة بهَالقُصَّة مالتَك؟ [šinu: wiǰih ʔinnukta bhalquṣṣa ma:ltak?] What's the point of the joke in this story of yours? • **7.** aspect, facet – بِحَثنا المُشكِلَة مِن كُلّ الوُجُوه [biħaθna ʔilmuškila min kull ʔilwuǰu:h] We studied the problem from all angles. • **8.** عَلَى وُجِه one way or the other, in a definite manner

وجهَة [wiǰha, wuǰha] *n:* وجهات [wiǰha:t, wuǰha:t] *pl:* • **1.** objective, goal, intention • **2.** destination • **3.** وُجهَة نَظَر point of view, viewpoint, standpoint

و

وَجاهَة [waǯa:ha] *n:* • **1.** prestige, eminence, esteem, standing, distinction • **2.** validity, legitimacy, soundness
اِتِّجاه [ʔittiǯa:h] *n:* اِتِّجاهات [ʔittiǯa:ha:t] *pl:* • **1.** direction, heading, course
واجِهَة [wa:ǯiha] *n:* واجِهات [wa:ǯiha:t] *pl:* • **1.** face, front (of a battle) • **2.** outside • **3.** facade
تَوجِيه [tawǯi:h] *n:* • **1.** directing, guiding, guidance, orientation (toward a goal)
مُواجَهَة [muwa:ǯaha] *n:* مُواجَهات [muwa:ǯaha:t] *pl:* • **1.** face to face encounter, meeting • **2.** audience, interview
وَجِيه [waǯi:h] *adj:* وُجَهاء [wuǯaha:ʔ] *pl:* • **1.** notable, eminent, distinguished • **2.** eminent man, notable • **3.** acceptable, sound – أَسباب وَجِيهَة [ʔasba:b waǯi:ha] acceptable reasons.
مُوَجَّه [muwaǯǯah] *adj:* • **1.** guided, directed, planned, crontolled
مِتِّجِه [mittiǯih] *adj:* • **1.** directed, tending, aiming (in a direction)
مُواجِه [muwa:ǯih] *adj:* • **1.** facing, opposed • **2.** (as a Noun) antagonist, opponent
تَوجِيهِي [tawǯi:hi] *adj:* • **1.** instructive • **2.** directing, guiding
أَوجَه [ʔawǯah] *comparative adjective:* • **1.** more or most eminent, notable, distinguished • **2.** more or most valid, sound, reasonable • **3.** more or most acceptable, proper, correct, suitable

و ح د

See also: ء ح د
وَحَّد [waħħad] *v:* • **1.** to unify, unite, make one – حِزبنا يريد يوَحِّد الدُّوَل العَرَبِيَّة [ħizibna yri:d yiwaħħid ʔidduwal ʔilʕarabiyya] Our party wants to unite the Arab countries. • **2.** to standardize – الحُكُومَة ترِيد توَحِّد الأوزان [ʔilħuku:ma tri:d twaħħid ʔilʔawza:n] The government wants to standardize weights. وَحَّد الله [waħħad ʔallah] Declare God to be one, proclaim the soleness of God.
توَحَّد [twaħħad] *v:* • **1.** to be unified, united – جُيُوش الدَّولتَين توَحّدَت [ǯuyu:š ʔiddawiltayn twaħħdat] The armies of the two countries were unified.
اِتَّحَد [ʔittiħad] *v:* • **1.** to unite, combine, join together, form a union – الدَّولتَين اِتِّحدَوا [ʔiddawiltayn ʔittiħdaw] The two countries united.
حِدَة، عَلَى حِدَة [ħida, ʕala ħida] *n:* • **1.** alone, apart, separate, detached, isolated – حُطّ كُلّ غَراضِي عَلَى حِدَة [ħuṭṭ kull ɣara:ḍ̣i ʕala ħida] Put all my things to one side.
وِحدَة [wiħda] *n:* • **1.** oneness, singleness, unity – الوِحدَة العَرَبِيَّة [ʔilwiħda ʔilʕarabiyya] Arab unity. • **2.** solitude, loneliness, solitariness, isolation – الوِحدَة قِتلَتنِي هنا [ʔilwiħda kitlatni hna] I'm dying of loneliness here. • **3.** (mus.) beat • **4.** pl. وِحدات unit, single group – وِحدَة عَسكَرِيَّة [wiħda ʕaskariyya] military unit. • **5.** fem. of واحِد
واحِد [wa:ħid] *n:* وِحدَة [wiħda] *feminine:* • **1.** one (numeral) • **2.** a person, someone, somebody – واحِد سِأَل عَنَّك [wa:ħid siʔal ʕannak] Someone asked about you. الواحِد ما يِدري وين يرُوح باللَّيل [ʔilwa:ħid ma: yidri wi:n yiru:ħ billayl] One doesn't know where to go at night.
اِتِّحاد [ʔittiħa:d] *n:* اِتِّحادات [ʔittiħa:da:t] *pl:* • **1.** unity, union, consolidation, amalgamation, merger, fusion • **2.** (pl. اِتِّحادات) union, confederation, league, federation, alliance, association
تَوحِيد [tawħi:d] *n:* • **1.** unification
وَحَّد [waħħad] *adj:* • **1.** alone, by oneself – رِحِت لِلسِّينَما وَحّدِي [riħit lissinama waħħdi] I went to the movies alone. راح ترُوحُون وَحَّدكُم؟ [ra:ħ tru:ħu:n waħħadkum?] Are you going by yourselves? كُلّ البِقاقِيل يِتعامِلُون. يَعنِي بَسّ إنتَ وَحَّد [kull ʔilbga:gi:l yitʕa:mlu:n. yaʕni bass ʔinta waħħad] All the grocers bargain. In other words, you're the only one who's different. • **2.** aside, apart, to one side – حُطّ البَيض وَحَّد [ħuṭṭ ʔilbi:ḍ̣ waħħad] Put the eggs to one side. هَذا وَحَّد؛ إحنا هَسَّة دَنِحكِي عالإمتِحان [ha:ða waħħad; ʔiħna hassa daniħči ʕalʔimtiħa:n] That's something else; now we're talking about the exam.
وَحد، عَلَى وَحد [waħd-, ʕala waħd-] *adj:* • **1.** /plus pronominal suffix/ alone, by oneself – بُقيت بِالبَيت وَحدِي [buqi:t bilbayt waħdi] I stayed in the house by myself.
وَحِيد [waħi:d] *adj:* • **1.** alone – بُقيت وَحِيد طُول النَّهار [buqi:t waħi:d ṭu:l ʔinnaha:r] I was alone all day. • **2.** solitary, lonely, lonesome – عَقلِي طار؛ بِقَيت وَحِيد بِهالوِلايَة بَلا أَصدِقاء [ʕaqli ṭa:r; biqi:t waħi:d bhalwla:ya bala ʔaṣdiqa:ʔ] I went out of my mind; I was lonely in that city without friends. • **3.** sole, only, exclusive – هَذا اللّاعِب الوَحِيد اللِّي أَبَداً ما خِسَر [ha:ða ʔilla:ʕib ʔilwaħi:d ʔilli ʔabadan ma: xisar] This is the only player who never was defeated. هَذا وَحِيد لأَهلَه [ha:ða waħi:d lʔahlah] He's an only child.
مُتَّحِد [muttaħid] *adj:* • **1.** united, combined, consolidated, amalgamated – الأُمَم المُتَّحِدَة [ʔilʔumam ʔilmuttaħida] the United Nations.
مُوَحَّد [muwaħħad] *adj:* • **1.** united, unified
مِتوَحِّد [mitwaħħid] *adj:* • **1.** united
أَوحَد [ʔawħad] *comparative adjective:* • **1.** singular, unique

و ح ش

وَحَش [waħaš] *v:* • **1.** to miss, to grieve by one's absence, cause to feel lonely – وُحَشتنا بِغِيابَك [wuħaština bɣiya:bak] We missed you a lot.
توَحَّش [twaħħaš] *v:* • **1.** to be or become wild, savage – لا توَدِّي الدُّبّ لِلغابَة، تَرَة يِتوَحَّش [la: twaddi ʔiddubb

و

lilɣa:ba, tara yitwaħħaš] Don't take the bear to the woods, or he'll become wild. مِن يِتعارَك، يِتوَحَّش [min yitʕa:rak, yitwaħħaš] When he fights, he goes wild.
اِستوَحَش [ʔistawħaš] *v:* • **1.** to feel lonely – آنِي أَستوحِش بِهالبَيت وَحدِي [ʔa:ni ʔastawħiš bihalbi:t waħdi] I feel lonely in this house by myself. • **2.** with لـ to miss, feel lonely, saddened without – اِستوَحَشنالَه مِن كان ببَيرُوت [ʔistawħašna:lah min ča:n bbayru:t] We missed him when he was in Beirut. • **3.** with مِن to have an aversion to, feel a distaste for – إبنِي يِستوَحِش مِن الغَرِيب [ʔibni yistawħiš min ʔilɣari:b] My son has an aversion to strangers.
وَحِش [waħiš] *n:* وُحُوش [wuħu:š] *pl:* • **1.** wild animal, wild beast
وَحشَة [waħša] *n:* • **1.** loneliness, forlornness, desolation – إبنِي إلَه وَحشَة. أتمَنَّى يِجِي [ʔibni ʔilah waħša. ʔatmanna: yiǰi] I miss my son. I hope he comes.
وَحشِيَّة [waħšiyya] *n:* • **1.** savagery, brutality
وَحشِي [waħši] *adj:* • **1.** wild, untamed – حَيوانات وَحشِيَّة [ħaywa:na:t waħšiyya] wild animals. هَالجّاهِل شلُون وَحشِي [hajǰa:hil šlu:n waħši] What a wild kid! إبنِي وَحشِي. ما يِتصادَق وِيّا النّاس [ʔibni waħši. ma: yitṣa:daq wiyya ʔinna:s] My son is shy. He doesn't make friends with people.
مُوحِش [mu:ħiš] *adj:* • **1.** desolate, dreary, deserted, forlorn, lonely – هَالبَيت الكِبِير كُلِّش مُوحِش [halbayt ʔiččibi:r kulliš mu:ħiš] This big house is very lonely. البَيت بِمَنطِقَة مُوحِشَة [ʔilbayt bmanṭiqa mu:ħiša] The house is in a desolate area.
مِتوَحِّش [mitwaħħiš] *adj:* • **1.** wild, untamed, barbarous, barbaric, savage • **2.** pl. مِتوَحِّشِين barbarian, savage • **3.** (as a Noun) a barbarian, a savage
مِستوحِش [mistawħiš] *adj:* • **1.** wild, savage • **2.** lonesome, unhappy, lonely, shy
أوحَش [ʔawħaš] *comparative adjective:* • **1.** more or most untamed • **2.** more or most savage, ferocious

و ح ل

وَحَل [waħal] *n:* وُحُول، أوحال [wuħu:l, ʔawħa:l] *pl:* • **1.** slough, morass, mire

و ح ي

وُحَى [wuħa:] *v:* • **1.** to inspire • **2.** to reveal
أوحَى [ʔawħa:] *v:* • **1.** to inspire
اِنوُحَى [ʔinwuħa:] *v:* • **1.** to inspire
وَحِي [waħy] *n:* • **1.** inspiration, revelation (theol.)
إيحاء [ʔi:ħa:ʔ] *n:* • **1.** suggestion, inspiration

و خ ر

وَخَّر [waxxar] *v:* • **1.** to remove, clear away, move aside – وَخِّر كُتُبَك شوَيَّة حَتَّى يصِير مَكان لِكُتبِي [waxxir kutubak šwayya ħatta yṣi:r maka:n likutbi] Move your books over a little so there'll be room for my books. وَخِّرَوه مِن هَالوَظِيفَة وخَلُّوه بوَظِيفَة أُخرَى [waxxirawh min halwaði:fa wxallu:h bwaði:fa ʔuxra] They took him out of this position and put him in another one. • **2.** to move aside, get out of the way – وَخِّر حَتَّى السَّيّارَة تفُوت [waxxir ħatta ʔissayya:ra tfu:t] Get out of the way so the car can pass.
توَخَّر [twaxxar] *v:* • **1.** to be moved aside, to be out of the way – وَخِّر حَتَّى أقُصّ بِطاقَة [waxxir ħatta ʔaguṣṣ biṭa:qa] He moved out of the way so I could get a ticket.
موَخِّر [mwaxxir] *n:* • **1.** moving aside, getting out of the way
موَخَّر [mwaxxar] *adj:* • **1.** moved aside

و خ م

وِخَم [wixam] *v:* • **1.** to be unhealthy, unwholesome, heavy
وَخَم [waxam] *n:* • **1.** unhealthy air, dirt, filth
وَخامَة [waxa:ma] *n:* • **1.** unhealthness, unwholesomeness (air, dust, filth)
وَخِم [waxim] *adj:* • **1.** unhealthy, unwholesome, heavy
وَخِيم [waxi:m] *adj:* • **1.** unhealthy, indigestible • **2.** grave, bad, evil, dangerous

و د د

وَدّ [wadd] *v:* • **1.** to like, be fond of, care for – آنِي أوِدَّك كثِير [ʔa:ni ʔawiddak kθi:r] I like you a lot. • **2.** to want, wish, desire – أوِدّ أَجِي وِيّاكُم [ʔawidd ʔaǰi wiyya:kum] I would like to come with you.
وِدّ [widd] *n:* • **1.** affection, amity • **2.** wish, desire
مَوَدَّة [mawadda] *n:* • **1.** friendship, love
وِدِّي [widdi] *adj:* • **1.** friendly, amicable – العَلاقات بين الدَّولتَين وِدِّيَّة [ʔilʕala:qa:t bi:n ʔiddawiltayn widdiyya] The relations between the two countries are friendly.

و د ع

وَدَّع [waddaʕ] *v:* • **1.** to bid farewell, say goodbye to – جِيت أوَدّعَك لِأنّ راح أسافِر باكِر [ǰi:t ʔawaddʕak liʔann ra:ħ ʔasa:fir ba:čir] I came to say goodbye to you because I'm going away tomorrow. لازِم نرُوح لِلمَطار نوَدّعَه [la:zim nru:ħ lilmaṭa:r nwaddʕah] We should go to the airport to see him off. • **2.** to deposit, leave for safekeeping – وَدَّع فلُوسَه بصَندُوق التَّوفِير [waddaʕ flu:sah bṣandu:g ʔittawfi:r] He deposited his money in the postal savings system.
أودَع [ʔawdaʕ] *v:* • **1.** to deposit
توادَع [twa:daʕ] *v:* • **1.** to bid each other farewell – تَعال نِتوادَع، لِأنّ الطَّيّارَة راح تطِير [taʕa:l nitwa:daʕ, liʔann ʔiṭṭiyya:ra ra:ħ ṭṭi:r] Come, let's say goodbye to each other, because the plane is going to leave.

و

وداع [widaːʕ, wadaːʕ] *n:* • **1.** farewell, leave-taking, adieu • **2.** مُوَدِّعِين .مُوَدِّع, ق‌ل person saying goodbye

مُوَدِّع [muwaddiʕ] *n:* مُوَدِّعِين [mwaddiʕiːn] *pl:* • **1.** person who is saying goodbye; depositor

وَدِيعَة [wadiːʕa] *n:* • **1.** consignment, s.th. entrusted to s.o.'s custody

إيداع [ʔiːdaːʕ] *n:* • **1.** depositing, consigning, deposition, deposit

تَودِيع [tawdiːʕ] *n:* • **1.** farewell, saying goodbye

مُستَودَع [mustawdaʕ] *n:* مُستَودَعات [mustawdaʕaːt] *pl:* • **1.** warehouse, depot (mil.)

وَداعِيَّة [wadaːʕiyya] *n:* • **1.** farewell party

اِستِيداع [ʔistiːdaːʕ] *n:* • **1.** depositing, consigning

وَدِيع [wadiːʕ] *adj:* • **1.** gentle, calm, peaceable, mild-tempered

و د ي

وَدَّى [waddaː] *v:* • **1.** to convey, transfer, take – راح أَوَدِّي السَّيّارَة لِلكَراج [raːħ ʔawaddi ʔissayyaːra lilgaraːǰ] I'm going to take the car to the garage. بَيتكُم بِعِيد. شيوَدِّينِي عَلَيه؟ [baytkum biʕiːd. šywaddiːni ʕaliːh?] Your house is far away. How will I get to it? هَالأَكِل هوايَة. وِين أَوَدِّيه؟ [halʔakil hwaːya. wiːn ʔawaddiːh?] This is a lot of food. Where am I going to put it? • **2.** to send – مِن تزَوَّج، وَدَّينالَه هَدِيَّة [min tzawwaǰ, waddaynaːlah hadiyya] When he got married, we sent him a gift. وَدِّيتلَه خَبَر وَإلّا لا؟ [waddiːtlah xabar waʔilla laː?] Did you send him news or not?

وادِي [waːdi] *n:* وِديان [widyaːn] *pl:* • **1.** wadi, valley, river valley

مَوَدِّي [mwaddi] *adj:* • **1.** delivering, sending

و ر ث

وُرَث [wuraθ] *v:* • **1.** to inherit – وُرَث كُلّ هَالأَملاك مِن أَبُوه [wuraθ kull halʔamlaːk min ʔabuːh] He inherited all this property from his father.

وَرَّث [warraθ] *v:* • **1.** to will, leave, bequeath – أَبُوه ما وَرَّثَه شِي لِأَنّ ما يحِبَّه [ʔabuːh maː warraθah ši liʔann maː yħibbah] His father didn't leave him anything because he didn't like him. مات مِفلِس وَما وَرَّث لِإبنَه شِي [maːt miflis wma warraθ lʔibnah ši] He died penniless and left nothing to his son. • **2.** to light – إنطِينِي شِخاطتَك حَتَّى أَوَرِّث جِيكارتِي [ʔinṭiːni šixxaːṭtak ħatta ʔawarriθ ǰigaːrti] Give me your matches so I can light my cigarette. • **3.** to be lit, catch fire – الجِّكارَة المبَلِّلَة ما توَرِّث بسُهُولَة [ʔiǰǰigaːra ʔilmballila maː twarriθ bsuhuːla] Wet cigarettes won't light easily. أَشُو مِن سِمَع الخَبَر، وَرَّث [ʔašu min simaʕ ʔilxabar, warraθ] When he heard the news, he exploded.

اِستَورَث [ʔistawraθ] *v:* • **1.** to inherit, receive as a legacy – اِستَورَث مِن أَبُوه بَيتَين [ʔistawraθ min ʔabuːh baytayn] He inherited two houses from his father.

إرث [ʔiriθ] *n:* • **1.** (var.of وِرث under و-ر-ث) inheritance, legacy

وِرث [wiriθ] *n:* • **1.** (var. of إرث under ء-ر-ث) inheritance, legacy

وارِث [wariːθ] *n:* وَرَثَة [waraθa] *pl:* • **1.** heir, inheritor

تُراث [turaːθ] *n:* • **1.** heritage, legacy • **2.** legacy

وِراثَة [wiraːθa] *n:* • **1.** heredity, hereditary transmission

مِيراث [miːraːθ] *n:* مَوارِيث [mawaːriːθ] *pl:* • **1.** inheritance, legacy, heritage

تَوارُث [tawaːruθ] *n:* • **1.** heredity

وِراثِي [wiraːθi] *adj:* • **1.** hereditary – مَرَض وِراثِي [marað̣ wiraːθi] a hereditary disease.

تُراثِي [turaːθi] *adj:* • **1.** pertaining to (cultural) heritage

مَورُوث [mawruːθ] *adj:* • **1.** inherited

مُتَوارَث [mutawaːraθ] *adj:* • **1.** inherited

و ر د [1]

وُرَد [wurad] *v:* • **1.** to drink, take water – وَدِّي الخيل لِلشَّطّ خَلِّي تُورِد [waddi ʔilxiːl liššaṭṭ xalliː tuːrid] Take the horses to the river and let them drink. • **2.** to water, take or lead to water – صار المِغرِب. رُوح أُورِدها لِلخَيل [ṣaːr ʔilmiɣrib. ruːħ ʔuːridha lilxayl] It's evening. Go water the horses.

اِنوُرَد [ʔinwurad] *v:* • **1.** to be watered – الخيل اِنوُردَت لَو بَعَد؟ [ʔilxiːl ʔinwurdat law baʕad?] Have the horses been watered yet?

اِستَورَد [ʔistawrad] *v:* • **1.** to import – اِستَورَدنا كَمِّيَّة كِبِيرَة مِن التّايَرات [ʔistawradna kammiyya čibiːra min ʔittaːyaraːt] We imported a large quantity of tires.

وَرِيد [wariːd] *n:* أَورِدَة [ʔawrida] *pl:* • **1.** vein

مَورِد [mawrid] *n:* مَوارِد [mawaːrid] *pl:* • **1.** income, revenue

وارِد [waːrid] *n:* وارِدات [waːridaːt] *pl:* • **1.** revenue, income • **2.** proceeds, return, take • **3.** import

وُرُود [wuruːd] *n:* • **1.** watering, drinking, taking, going to water

إيراد [ʔiːraːd] *n:* إيرادات [ʔiːraːdaːt] *pl:* • **1.** revenue, income – خَشُّوا بإيراد وَمَصرَف. هاي بَعَد شِيفُضّها؟ [xaššaw bʔiːraːd wmaṣraf. haːy baʕad šiyfuð̣ð̣ha?] They've gotten into a fruitless discussion. How'll that ever end?

اِستِيراد [ʔistiːraːd] *n:* اِستِيرادات [ʔistiːraːdaːt] *pl:* • **1.** import, importation

مُستَورِد [mustawrid] *n:* مُستَورِدِين [mustawridiːn] *pl:* • **1.** importer

و ر د [2]

وَرَّد [warrad] *v:* • **1.** to blossom, be in bloom – هِرش القَرُنفُل وَرَّد [hirš ʔilgrunful warrad] The clove plant bloomed. • **2.** to make rosy, pink – الشَّمِس وَرِّدَت خدُودها [ʔiššamis warridat xduːdha] The

sun made her cheeks rosy. • **3.** to become pink, rosy – وَرِّدَت خدُودها مِن هَوا لُبنان [warridat xdu:dha min hawa lubna:n] Her cheeks grew rosy from the Lebanese climate.
وَرِد [warid] *n:* • **1.** flower(s), blossom(s), bloom(s) • **2.** rose(s) • **3.** (exclamation) great! fine! excellent! – وَرِد! عَلِي صار مُدِيرنا [warid! ʕali ṣa:r mudi:rna] Great! Ali became our director.
وَردَة [warda] *n:* وَردات، وُرُود، وَرِد [warda:t, wuru:d, warid] *pl:* • **1.** flower
وَردِي [wardi] *adj:* • **1.** pink, rosy, rose-colored
مْوَرَّد [mwarrad] *adj:* • **1.** flowered, embellished with flowers – قماش مُوَرَّد [qma:š muwarrad] flowered material.
مُستَورَد [mustawrad] *adj:* • **1.** imported

و ر ط

وَرَّط [warraṭ] *v:* • **1.** to put in an unpleasant situation, get into a bad fix, entangle, embroil, involve – وَرَّطتِني ويّا المُدِير. لِيش قِتلَه جِيت لِلشُّغُل مِتأَخِّر؟ [warraṭitni wiyya ʔilmudi:r. li:š gitlah ǰi:t liššuɣul mitʔaxxir?] You got me into a bad fix with the director. Why did you tell him I came to work late? ما أرُوح؛ لا توَرِّطنِي [ma: ʔaru:ħ; la: twarriṭni] I'm not going to go; don't try to get me into something. وَرَّطنِي بِهَالسَّيّارَة وطِلعَت ما تِسوَى [warraṭni bhassayya:ra wṭilʕat ma: tiswa:] He got me involved with this car and it turned out to be worthless.
توَرَّط [twarraṭ] *v:* • **1.** to get oneself into a mess, get into trouble, become entangled, involved – توَرَّطِت. عَبالِي أكُو قِطار بَعَد نُصّ اللَّيل وتبَيَّن ماكُو [twarraṭit. ʕaba:li ʔaku qiṭa:r baʕad nuṣṣ ʔillayl wtbayyan ma:ku] I'm in a fix. I thought there was a train after midnight and it turned out there wasn't. لا تِشتِري هَالسَّيّارَة تَرَة تِتوَرَّط بِيها [la: tištiri hassayya:ra tara titwarraṭ bi:ha] Don't buy this car or you'll get stuck with it.
ورطَة [warṭa, wurṭa] *n:* ورطات [warṭa:t, wurṭa:t] *pl:* • **1.** plight, difficulty, predicament, dilemma, fix, jam – أخُويا وَرَّطنِي هَالوُرطَة الكِبِيرَة [ʔaxu:ya warraṭni halwurṭa ʔiččibi:ra] My brother got me into this big mess.
مْوَرَّط [mwarraṭ] *adj:* • **1.** implicated, involved
مِتوَرِّط [mitwarriṭ] *adj:* • **1.** implicated, involved

و ر ع

توَرَّع [twarraʕ] *v:* • **1.** to hesitate, be cautious, take time to think – مِن يسَوِّي شِي، ما يِتوَرَّع [min ysawwi: ši, ma: yitwarraʕ] When he does something, he doesn't pause to think. توَرَّع وَدِير بالَك [twarraʕ wdi:r ba:lak] Size up the situation and be careful.
وَرِع [wariʕ] *adj:* • **1.** pious, god-fearing, godly – رَجُل دِينِي وَرِع [rağul di:ni wariʕ] a pious man of God.

و ر ق

وَرَّق [warraq] *v:* • **1.** to leaf, put forth leaves – الأشجار كُلّها توَرِّق بِالرَّبِيع [ʔilʔašǰa:r kullha twarriq birrabi:ʕ] All the trees burst into leaf in the spring. • **2.** to leaf, thumb – وَرِّق بِالكتاب. بَلكِي تِلقِي الرَّسِم [warriq bilkta:b. balki tilgi ʔirrasim] Leaf through the book. Maybe you'll find the picture.
وَرَق [waraq, warag] *n:* • **1.** (coll.) foliage, leafage, leaves • **2.** (coll.) paper • **3.** cards, playing cards – يِلعَب وَرَق [yilʕab waraq] He plays cards.
وَرَقَة، وَرقَة [waraqa, warqa, waraga, warga] *n:* وَرقات [warqa:t] *pl:* • **1.** leaf • **2.** sheet of paper, piece of paper • **3.** note, paper, document • **4.** bank note

و ر ك

وِرِك [wirik] *n:* ورُوك [wru:k] *pl:* • **1.** hip • **2.** buttock

و ر م

وُرَم [wuram] *v:* • **1.** to swell up, become swollen – لِدَغه العَقرَب وَوُرمَت إيدَه [lidaɣah ʔilʕagrab wawurmat ʔi:dah] The scorpion stung him and his hand swelled up.
وَرَّم [warram] *v:* • **1.** to cause to swell, (and by extension) to bruise, hurt – بُسَطَه بَسطَة وَرَّمَه بِيها [buṣaṭah basṭa warramah bi:ha] He beat him black and blue. تُسكُت لَو أجِي أوَرّمَك [tuskut law ʔaǰi ʔawarrmak] You shut up or I'll come and beat you up. وَرَّمتَه بِالشِّطرَنج [warramtah biššiṭranǰ] I beat him badly at chess. المُعَلِّم وَرَّمنا بِأسِئلتَه الصَّعبَة [ʔilmuʕallim warramna bʔasʔiltah ʔiṣṣaʕba] The teacher tortured us with his hard questions. • **2.** same as وُرَم, to swell up, become swollen – وُجَّه وَرَّم مِن كان وَجعان [wuččah warram min ča:n waǰʕa:n] His face became swollen when he was sick.
توَرَّم [twarram] *v:* • **1.** to be hurt (esp. figuratively) – توَرَّمِت بِالرَّيسز البارحَة. خِسَرِت كُلّ فلُوسِي [twarramit birraysiz ʔilba:rħa. xisarit kull flu:si] I took a beating at the races yesterday. I lost all my money. توَرَّمِت. كُلّ رُوحَة لِلطَّبِيب تكَلِّف دِينار [twarramit. kull ru:ħa liṭṭabi:b tkallif dina:r] I've had it. Every visit to the doctor costs a dinar.
وَرَم [waram] *n:* أورام [ʔawra:m] *pl:* • **1.** swelling • **2.** swollen place
وارُم، وارِم [wa:rum, wa:rim] *adj:* • **1.** swollen
مْوَرَّم، مْوَرُّم [mwarram, mwarrum] *adj:* • **1.** swollen

و ر ن ش

وَرنِيش [warni:š] *n:* • **1.** varnish

و ر و ر

وَروَر [warwar] *n:* وَراوِر [wara:wir] *pl:* • **1.** pistol, hand gun

و

و ر ي

وَرا [wara] *n:* • **1.** behind, in the rear of, at the back of – أوقَف وَرا الشَّجرَة عَن الشَّمس [ʔuːgaf wara ʔiššiǰra ʕan ʔiššamis] Stand behind the tree away from the sun. تَعال لِقِدّام. لِيش واقُف وَرا الكُلّ؟ [taʕaːl ligiddaːm. liːš waːguf wara ʔilkull?] Come to the front. Why are you standing behind everyone? • **2.** from behind from the back of – خَشّ مِن وَرا القَنَفَة [xašš min wara ʔilqanafa] He came out from behind the sofa. • **3.** by means of, through, by, because of – هَالبَلاوي كُلّها جَتّنا مِن وَراك [halbalaːwi kullha ǰattna min waraːk] All these troubles came to us because of you. • **4.** to, in, proceeding from, resultant from – الزَّواج، ما وَراه غير المَشاكِل [ʔizzawaːǰ, maː waraːh ɣiːr ʔilmašaːkil] There is nothing to marriage except problems. هالحكِي ما وَراه نَتيجَة [halħači maː waraːh natiːǰa] This talk will lead nowhere. تَعَبَك ما وَراه نَتيجَة، لِأَنّ عَيّنَوا واحِد [taʕabak maː waraːh natiːǰa, liʔann ʕayynaw waːħid] Your efforts will be useless because they already appointed someone. • **5.** after – طَبّوا واحِد وَرا اللّاخ [ṭabbaw waːħid wara ʔillaːx] They came in one after the other. راح يِجُون وَرايَا بَعَد ساعَة [raːħ yiǰuːn waraːya baʕad saːʕa] They will come after me in an hour. • **6.** behind, in the rear, at the back – إنتَ أُقعُد قِدّام وَخَلّي الجّاهِل يُقعُد وَرا [ʔinta ʔugʕud giddaːm wxalliː ʔiǰǰaːhil yugʕud wara] You sit in front and let the kid sit in back. إرجَع لوَرا [ʔirǰaʕ lwara] Back up.

وَرّاني [warraːni] *adj:* • **1.** rear, back, hind – الدَّعامِيَّة الوَرّانِيَّة مَعوُوجَة [ʔiddaʕʕamiyya ʔilwarraːniyya maʕwuːǰa] The rear bumper is bent. رِجلَين الأرنَب الوَرّانِيَّة أَطوَل من القِدّامِيَّة [riǰlayn ʔilʔarnab ʔilwarraːniyya ʔaṭwal min ʔilgiddaːmiyya] The rabbit's hind legs are longer than the front ones.

وَرا ما [wara maː] *subordinating conjunction:* • **1.** after – وَرا ما تخَلّص، مُرّ عَلَيّا [wara maː txalliṣ, murr ʕalayya] After you finish, drop in on me.

و ز ر 1

وَزَّر [wazzar] *v:* • **1.** to wrap a loincloth around – وَزِّر الجّاهِل قَبُل ما يخُشّ لِلحَمّام [wazzir ʔiǰǰaːhil gabul maː yxušš lilħammaːm] Wrap something around the child's waist before he enters the bath.

توَزَّر [twazzar] *v:* • **1.** to put on or wear a loincloth – إذا ما عِندَك كِسوَة، توَزَّر وَإسبَح [ʔiða maː ʕindak čiswa, twazzar wʔisbaħ] If you don't have a swimming suit, put on a loincloth and go swimming.

وَزرَة [wazra, wizra] *n:* وَزرَة وِزرات [wazra, wizraːt] *pl:* • **1.** loincloth

و ز ر 2

إستَوزَر [ʔistawzar] *v:* • **1.** to appoint or install as a minister – رَئِيس الوِزارَة إستَوزَر إثنَين عِدهُم شَهادَة دُكتَورا [raʔiːs ʔilwizaːra ʔistawzar ʔiθnayn ʕidhum šahaːdat duktura] The prime minister appointed as ministers two men with doctorate degrees.

وَزير [waziːr] *n:* وُزَراء [wuzaraːʔ, wuzaraː] *pl:* • **1.** minister – رَئِيس الوُزَراء [raʔiːs ʔilwuzaraːʔ] prime minister. • **2.** cabinet member – مَجلِس الوُزَراء [maǰlis ʔilwuzaraːʔ] cabinet, council of ministers.

وِزارَة [wizaːra] *n:* وِزارات [wizaːraːt] *pl:* • **1.** ministry • **2.** cabinet, government. – رَئِيس وِزارَة [raʔiːs wizaːra] prime minister.

إستيزار [ʔistiːzaːr] *n:* • **1.** installation of a cabinet – حَفلَة إستيزار [ħaflat ʔistiːzaːr] cabinet inauguration ceremony.

وِزاري [wizaːri] *adj:* • **1.** ministerial • **2.** cabinet

و ز ز 1

وَزّ [wazz] *v:* • **1.** to incite, arouse, stir up, set – هَذا ما يِتعارَك. لازِم واحِد وَزّه [haːða maː yitʕaːrak. laːzim waːħid wazzah] He never fights. Someone must've incited him. حَماتَه وَزّتَه ويّا مَرتَه وَخَلّتهُم يِتعاركُون [ħamaːtah wazzatah wiyya martah wxallathum yitʕaːrkuːn] His mother-in-law got him irritated with his wife and made them fight.

انوَزّ [ʔinwazz] *v:* • **1.** to be incited, stirred up – ما ينوَزّ بِالعَجَل [maː yinwazz bilʕaǰal] He can't be aroused quickly.

وُزَّة [wuzza] *n:* • **1.** agitation, inciting

و ز ز 2

وَزّ [wazz] *n:* • **1.** (coll.) goose, geese – إبِن الوَزّ عَوّام [ʔibin ʔilwazz ʕawwaːm] Like father like son (lit., the goose's son is a swimmer).

وَزّة [wazza] *n:* وَزّات [wazzaːt] *pl:* • **1.** goose

و ز ع

وَزَّع [wazzaʕ] *v:* • **1.** to distribute, pass out, deal out – الوَزير وَزَّع الجَّوائِز عَالفائِزين [ʔilwaziːr wazzaʕ ʔiǰǰawaːʔiz ʕalfaːʔiziːn] The minister distributed the awards to the winners. وَزِّع الوَرَق [wazziʕ ʔilwaraq] Deal the cards! • **2.** to deliver – شُغلِي أَوَزِّع بَريد بهالمَنطَقَة [šuɣli ʔawazziʕ bariːd bhalmanṭaqa] My job is delivering mail in this area.

توَزَّع [twazzaʕ] *v:* • **1.** to be distributed – الجَّوائِز راح تِتوَزَّع اليُوم [ʔiǰǰawaːʔiz raːħ titwazzaʕ ʔilyuːm] The awards will be distributed today.

مُوَزِّع، مُوَزِّع بَريد [muwazziʕ, muwazziʕ bariːd] *n:* • **1.** mailman, postman

تَوزيع [tawziːʕ] *n:* • **1.** distribution • **2.** delivery

متوَزِّع [mitwazziʕ] *adj:* مِتوَزِعين [mitwazziʕiːn] *pl:* • **1.** distributed, delivered

و ز ن

وُزَن [wuzan] *v:* • **1.** to weigh, weigh out – وُزَنلي القَصّاب كِيلُو لَحَم [wuzanli ʔilgaṣṣaːb kiːlu laħam] The butcher weighed out a kilo of meat for me.

وازَن [wa:zan] *v:* • **1.** to balance, equilibrate, poise – تِقدَر توازِن المَسطرَة عَلَى راس القَلَم؟ [tigdar twa:zin ʔilmasṭara ʕala ra:s ʔilqalam?] Can you balance the ruler on the tip of the pencil? • **2.** with بين to compare, compare with, make a comparison between, weigh against – وازِن بين هَالوَظِيفَة وَوَظِيفتَك السّابقَة قَبُل ما تِنتِقِل [wa:zin bi:n halwaðiːfa wwaðiːftak ʔissa:bqa gabul ma: tintiqil] Compare this position with your last job before you were transferred. لازِم توازِن بين راتبَك وَمَصرَفَك [la:zim twa:zin bi:n ra:tbak wmaṣrafak] You have to weigh your salary against your expenses.

اِتّزَن [ʔittizan] *v:* • **1.** to behave in a poised, sedate, dignified manner – اِتِّزِن بِحَكيَك. عِيب عَليك [ʔittizin bħačyak. ʕi:b ʕali:k] Be careful what you say. Shame on you!

توازَن [twa:zan] *v:* • **1.** to counterbalance each other, be of the same weight – الجِهَتَين مِن المَسطَرَة ما دَتِتوازَن [ʔiǰǰihatayn min ʔilmasṭara ma: datitwa:zan] The two sides of the ruler don't balance.

اِنوُزَن [ʔinwuzan] *v:* • **1.** to be weighed – لا تاخُذ هَالكِيس. بَعَد ما يِنوُزَن [la: ta:xuð halči:s. baʕad ma: yinwuzan] Don't take this bag. It hasn't been weighed yet.

وَزِن، بِالوَزِن [wazin, bilwazin] *n:* أوزان، بِالأوزان [ʔawza:n, bilʔawza:n] *pl:* • **1.** weight – وَزِن نَوعِي [wazin nawʕi] specific gravity. لا تديرلَه بال. ما إلَه كُلّ وَزِن بَالدّائِرَة [la: ddi:rlah ba:l. ma: ʔilah kull wazin bidda:ʔira] Don't pay any attention to him. He carries no weight in the office. • **2.** poetic meter and rhyme – حَمام عَلَى وَزِن تَمام [ħama:m ʕala wazin tama:m] ħama:m (pigeon) rhymes with tama:m (fine). • **3.** conjugation, verb pattern • **4.** weight, weight class (e.g., in boxing)

وَزنَة [wazna] *n:* وَزنات [wazna:t] *pl:* • **1.** a unit of weight roughly equal to one hundred kilograms

وَزّان [wazza:n] *n:* وَزّانَة [wazza:na] *pl:* • **1.** scale operator

ميزان [mi:za:n] *n:* مِيازِين، مَوازِين [miya:zi:n, mawa:zi:n] *pl:* • **1.** scales, balance • **2.** Libra (astron.)

تَوازُن [tawa:zun] *n:* • **1.** balancing, balance, equilibrium, poise

اِتِّزان [ʔittiza:n] *n:* • **1.** balance, equilibrium, poise

مُوازَنَة [muwa:zana] *n:* • **1.** balance, equilibrium • **2.** comparison, parallel

ميزانِيَّة [mi:za:niyya] *n:* ميزانِيّات [mi:za:niyya:t] *pl:* • **1.** balance, equilibrium • **2.** budget • **3.** (tech.) adjustment, setting • **4.** meter, measuring device – ميزانِيَّة مَيّ [mi:za:niyyat mayy] water meter.

مَوزُون [mawzu:n] *adj:* • **1.** balanced, in equilibrium, evenly poised • **2.** weighed • **3.** metrically balanced (poetry)

و ز ي

وازَى [wa:za:] *v:* • **1.** to parallel, be parallel to – الشّارِع يوازِي النَّهَر [ʔišša:riʕ ywa:zi ʔinnahar] The street runs parallel to the river. • **2.** to encourage, embolden, urge on – لا توازِينِي تَرَة ألعَب عَشِر دَنانِير عَلَى هَالحِصان [la: twa:zi:ni tara ʔalʕab ʕašir dana:ni:r ʕala halħiṣa:n] Don't push me or I'll play ten dinars on that horse. وازانِي عَالزَّواج وَتزَوَّجِت وَأكَلتها [wa:za:ni ʕazzawa:ǰ wdzawwaǰit wʔakaltha] He talked me into marriage and I got married and got myself in a mess.

توازَى [twa:za:] *v:* • **1.** to be parallel – هَالخَطَّين يِتوازُون [halxaṭṭayn yitwa:zu:n] These two lines are parallel. • **2.** to become enthusiastic, get excited – مِن يشُوف الوَرَق، يِتوازَى ويرِيد يِلعَب بُوكَر [min yšu:f ʔilwaraq, yitwa:za: wyri:d yilʕab pu:kar] When he sees the cards he becomes excited and wants to play poker. البارحَة توازيت وَرِدت أشتِرِي البَيت إلّا شوَيَّة [ʔilba:rħa twa:zi:t wridt ʔaštiri ʔilbayt ʔilla šwayya] Yesterday I got all worked up and wanted to buy the house. • **3.** to work up one's courage – فَدّ يوم راح أتوازَى وأبَطِّل مِن هالشُّغُل [fadd yu:m ra:ħ ʔatwa:za: wʔabaṭṭil min haššuɣul] Some day I'm going to get fed up and quit this job.

تَوازِي [tawa:zi] *n:* • **1.** equal distance, parallelism, equivalence

مُوازاة [muwa:za:t] *n:* • **1.** equal distance, parallelism

مُوازِي [muwa:zi] *adj:* • **1.** parallel, equivalent

مُتَوازِي [mutawa:zi] *adj:* • **1.** parallel, similar – مُتَوازِي الأضلاع [mutawa:zi ʔilʔaðla:ʕ] parallelogram. • **2.** enthusiastic, excited, all worked up

و س خ

وَسَّخ [wassax] *v:* • **1.** to dirty, soil, foul – وَسَّخ إيدَه مِن كان يِلعَب [wassax ʔi:dah min ča:n yilʕab] He got his hands dirty when he was playing.

توَسَّخ [twassax] *v:* • **1.** to become dirty – شبِالعَجَل توَسَّخ الثُّوب [šbilʕaǰal twassax ʔiθθu:b] The shirt sure got dirty fast!

وُسَخ [wusax] *n:* • **1.** dirt, filth

وَساخَة [wasa:xa] *n:* • **1.** dirtiness, filthiness

أوساخ [ʔawsa:x] *n:* • **1.** refuse, filth, dirt • **2.** dirts

وَسِخ [wasix] *adj:* • **1.** dirty, filthy, foul – رُوح، إغسِل إيدَيك؛ وَسخَة [ru:ħ, ʔiɣsil ʔi:di:k; wasxa] Go wash your hands; they're dirty! لا تِحكِي ويّاه تَرَة لسانَه وَسِخ [la: tiħči wiyya:h tara lsa:nah waṣix] Don't talk with him, because his tongue is filthy.

موَسَّخ [mwassax] *adj:* • **1.** soiled

متوَسِّخ [mitwassix] *adj:* • **1.** soiled, dirty, filthy

و س ط

وَسَّط [waṣṣaṭ] *v:* • **1.** to place in the center, to center – إدفَع المِيز شوَيَّة وَوَسِّطَه بالغُرفَة [ʔidfaʕ ʔilmi:z šwayya wwaṣṣiṭah bilɣurfa] Push the table over a bit and center it in the room. • **2.** to cause to intercede, have act as agent – وَسَّطِت أبُوك عِند الوَزِير [waṣṣaṭit ʔabu:k ʕind ʔilwazi:r] I got your father to intercede with the minister.

و

تَوَسَّط [twaṣṣaṭ] *v:* • **1.** to be in the middle or center of – توَسَّط الصَّفّ الأمامي بِالمَسِيرَة [twaṣṣaṭ ʔiṣṣaff ʔilʔama:mi bilmasi:ra] He was in the middle of the front row in the procession. • **2.** to intercede, use one's good offices or influence – أَبُوك توَسَّطلي بِالقَضِيَّة [ʔabu:k twaṣṣaṭli bilqaðiyya] Your father interceded for me in the matter.

وَسَط [waṣaṭ] *n:* • **1.** middle, center • **2.** center (of a soccer team) • **3.** medium, average – حَجِم وَسَط [ħaǰim waṣaṭ] an average size. أَرِيدَه حَجِم وَسَط [ʔari:dah ħaǰim waṣaṭ] I want it medium size. • **4.** intermediate – لازِم نِلقي حَلّ وَسَط لِلمُشكِلَة [la:zim nilgi ħall waṣaṭ lilmuškila] We've got to find a compromise solution to the problem.

وَسطَة [waṣṭa] *n:* • **1.** middle, center

وَسِيط [waṣi:ṭ] *n:* • **1.** intermediary, middle, intermediate, medial, median • **2.** intermediary (person), mediator, go-between, broker

وَسطِيَّة [waṣṭiyya] *n:* • **1.** middle, center – هاي شجابها بِالوَسطِيَّة؟ إحنا دَنِحكي عَالفلُوس [ha:y šǰa:bha bilwaṣṭiyya? ʔiħna daniħči ʕalflu:s] What brought this up? We're talking about money.

وَساطَة [waṣa:ṭa] *n:* • **1.** intercession, good offices, recommendation • **2.** influence, patronage, favoritism

واسطَة [wa:ṣṭa] *n:* وَسائِط، وَسايِط [waṣa:ʔiṭ, waṣa:yiṭ] *pl:* • **1.** means, medium, mode – وَسائِط النَّقِل [waṣa:ʔiṭ ʔinnaqil] means of transportation. • **2.** interceder, intermediary, reference, sponsor, patron

أوسَط [ʔawṣaṭ] *adj:* وُسطَى [wuṣṭa:] *feminine:* • **1.** middle, central – الشَّرق الأوسَط [ʔiššarq ʔilʔawṣaṭ] the Middle East.

وَسَطِي [waṣaṭi] *adj:* • **1.** centrally • **2.** central

مُتَوَسِّط [mutawaṣṣiṭ, mitwaṣṣiṭ] *adj:* • **1.** middle, medium – مَوجَة مِتوَسّطَة [mawǰa mitwaṣṣṭa] medium wave (radio). • **2.** medial, intermediate – شَهادَة مُتَوَسِّطَة [šaha:dat mutawaṣṣiṭa] an intermediate school certificate. • **3.** central, centrally located – البَحَر الأبيَض المُتَوَسِّط [ʔilbaħar ʔilʔabyað ʔilmutawaṣṣiṭ] The Mediterranean Sea. • **4.** average, mediocre – دَرَجاتَك مُتَوَسِّطَة [daraǰa:tak mutawaṣṣiṭa] Your grades are mediocre.

وَسطانِي [waṣṭa:ni] *adj:* • **1.** middle, central, medial – حُطّ الأوراق عَالرَّفّ الوَسطانِي [ħuṭṭ ʔilʔawra:q ʕarraff ʔilwaṣṭa:ni] Put the papers on the middle shelf. حَطَّيناه وَسطانِي [ħaṭṭayna:h waṣṭa:ni] We ganged up on him. • **2.** medium, medium-sized – عِندَك بِسمار وَسطانِي؟ [ʕindak bisma:r waṣṭa:ni?] Do you have a medium-sized nail?

و س ع

وِسَع [wisaʕ] *v:* • **1.** to hold, accommodate, have room for, be large enough for – الصَّفّ يُوسَع خَمسِين تِلمِيذ [ʔiṣṣaff yu:saʕ xamsi:n tilmi:ð] The classroom will hold fifty pupils. الصَّفّ يِسَعنا كُلّنا [ʔiṣṣaff yisaʕna kullna] The classroom will hold us all.

وَسَّع [wassaʕ] *v:* • **1.** to make roomy, spacious, to enlarge, expand, extend – راح نوَسِّع الحَدِيقَة [ra:ħ nwassaʕ ʔilħadi:qa] We're going to enlarge the garden. • **2.** with عَلَى to be generous toward, to make wealthy – إذا الله يوَسِّع عَلينا، نِقدَر نِشتِري بَيت [ʔiða ʔallah ywassiʕ ʕali:na, nigdar ništiri bayt] If God is generous to us, we can buy a house.

تَوَسَّع [twassaʕ] *v:* • **1.** to become wider, more extensive, to expand, grow larger – أشغالنا توَسّعَت [ʔašɣa:lna twassʕat] Our business has expanded. • **2.** to expand, enlarge, expatiate – إذا نِتوَسَّع هوايَة بِالمَوضُوع، ما يهضمُوه [ʔiða nitwassaʕ hwa:ya bilmawðu:ʕ, ma: yhuðmu:h] If we expand on the topic too much, they won't digest it.

اِتَّسَع [ʔittisaʕ] *v:* • **1.** to grow larger, wider, more extensive – إذا اِتِّسَع الشَّقّ، بَعَد ما ينراف [ʔiða ʔittisaʕ ʔiššagg, baʕad ma: yinra:f] If the rip gets wider, it can't be darned any more.

سِعَة [siʕa] *n:* • **1.** capacity, holding capacity, volume

وَسعَة [wasʕa] *n:* • **1.** spaciousness, roominess – ضاقَت الوَسعَة بِيهُم [ða:gat ʔilwasʕa bi:hum] They became depressed.

تَوَسُّع [tawassuʕ] *n:* • **1.** extension, enlargement

إتِّساع [ʔittisa:ʕ] *n:* • **1.** breadth, expanse, extent, extending, extension, extensiveness, wideness

مَوسُوعَة [mawsu:ʕa] *n:* مَوسُوعات [mawsu:ʕa:t] *pl:* • **1.** encyclopedia

واسِع [wa:siʕ] *adj:* • **1.** spacious, vast, wide, extensive – قاعَة واسِعَة [qa:ʕa wa:sʕa] a spacious hall. عِندَك مَجال واسِع لوَقت الامتِحان [ʕindak maǰa:l wa:siʕ lwaqt ʔilʔimtiħa:n] You have plenty of time before the exam. الله واسِع الرَّحمَة [ʔallah wa:siʕ ʔirraħma] God is abounding in mercy.

مُوَسَّع [muwassaʕ] *adj:* • **1.** widened, extended

تَوَسُّعِي [tawassuʕi] *adj:* • **1.** expansionist

أوسَع [ʔawsaʕ] *comparative adjective:* • **1.** more or most spacious, extensive

و س ك ي

وِيسكِي [wiski] *n:* • **1.** whisky

و س ل

تَوَسَّل [twassal] *v:* • **1.** with بـ to plead with, implore, beseech, entreat – تَوَسَّل بِالشُّرطِي يهِدَّه [twassal biššurṭi yhiddah] He pleaded with the policeman to let him go.

وَسِيلَة [wasi:la] *n:* وَسائِل [wasa:ʔil] *pl:* • **1.** means, medium • **2.** device, expedient

تَواسِيل، تَوسِّل [tiwa:si:l, twissil] *n:* • **1.** imploring, beseeching, begging

و س م

تَوَسَّم، تَوَسَّم بِالخير [twassam, twassam bilxayr] *n:* • **1.** to see promising signs in someone, have high expectations of someone – نِتوَسَّم بِيه الخير [nitwassam bi:h ʔilxi:r] We expect him to do great things.

سِمَة [sima] *n:* سِمات [sima:t] *pl:* • **1.** visa
وِسام [wisa:m] *n:* أَوسِمَة [ʔawsima] *pl:* • **1.** medal, decoration
مَوسِم [mawsim] *n:* مَواسِم [mawa:sim] *pl:* • **1.** season, time of the year
وَسِيم [wasi:m] *adj:* • **1.** comely, handsome, pretty – وِجهَه وَسِيم [wiččah wasi:m] He has a nice-looking face.
مَوسِمِي [mawsimi] *adj:* • **1.** seasonal

و س و س

وَسوَس [waswas] *v:* • **1.** to whisper – ما تِحكِي حيل؟ لُويش دَتوَسوِس بإذنَه؟ [ma: tiħči ħi:l? luwi:š datwaswis bʔiðnah?] Can't you speak up? Why are you whispering in his ear? • **2.** to incite to evil, tempt – ظَلّيت توَسوِس إلَى أَن خَلّيتَه يطَلِّق مَرتَه [ðalli:t twaswis ʔila ʔan xalli:tah yṭallig martah] You kept talking evil until you made him divorce his wife. • **3.** to worry, feel uneasy, be apprehensive – دَزَّيتلَه الفلُوس بإيد أُخويَا الصّغَيِّر، لَكِن ظَلّيت أوَسوِس لا يضَيِّعها [dazzaytlah ʔilflu:s bʔi:d ʔaxu:ya ʔiṣṣɣayyir, la:kin ðallayt ʔawaswis la: yðayyiʕha] I sent the money to him by my little brother, but I kept worrying he might lose it.
وِسواس [wiswa:s] *n:* وَساوِس [wasa:wis] *pl:* • **1.** temptation, devilish insinuation, wicked thoughts
مُوَسوِس [muwaswis] *adj:* • **1.** obsessed with delusions

و س ي

See also: ء س و

و ش ع

وشِيعَة [wši:ʕa] *n:* وشايِع [wša:yiʕ] *pl:* • **1.** skein, reel, spool, bobbin

و ش ق

واشَق [wa:šag] *v:* • **1.** to compare – واشِق هَالبوينباغين وشُوف إذا يِتشابهُون [wa:šig halbu:yinba:ɣayn wšu:f ʔiða yitša:bhu:n] Compare these two ties and see if they are similar. • **2.** to match, go well with – ضَيَّعِت تَكّ مِن هَالقُندَرَة وَدَأدَوُّر وِحدَة تواشِقها [ðayyaʕit takk min halqundara wadaʔadawwur wiħda twa:šigha] I lost one of these shoes and I'm looking for one to match it.
تواشَق [twa:šag] *v:* • **1.** to match, go together – عِندِي عِشرِين جُوراب لَكِن ما بِيها ثنَين تِتواشَق [ʕindi ʕišri:n ǰu:ra:b la:kin ma: bi:ha θnayn titwa:šag] I have twenty socks but there are no two of them that match.

و ش ك

وَشَك، عَلَى وَشَك [wašak, ʕala wašak] *n:* • **1.** on the verge of, about to – القَضِيَّة عَلَى وَشَك تِخلَص [ʔilqaðiyya ʕala wašak tixlaṣ] The matter is about to be settled.

و ش ل

وَشَّل [waššal] *v:* • **1.** to empty, become empty – الحِبّ وَشَّل وَما بِيه قَطرَة مَيّ [ʔilħibb waššal wama: bi:h gaṭrat mayy] The jug's gone dry and there's not a drop of water in it. وَشَّلِت وماعِندِي وَلا فِلِس [waššalit wma ʕindi wala filis] I'm broke and don't have a single cent. • **2.** to drain, empty – أُقلُب التّانكِي وَوَشّلَه مِن المَيّ [ʔuglub ʔitta:nki wwaššilah min ʔilmayy] Turn the tank over and drain the water out of it. هالمَصرَف القَبَة وَشَّلنِي [halmaṣraf ʔilqaba waššalni] This enormous expense has drained me.
توَشَّل [twaššal] *v:* • **1.** same as وَشَّل to empty, become empty • **2.** to drain, empty

و ش م

وَشِم [wašim] *n:* • **1.** tattoo, tattoo markings

و ش و ش

وَشوَش [wašwaš] *v:* • **1.** to whisper (in someone's ear)
وَشوَشَة [wašwaša] *n:* • **1.** buzz • **2.** whispering, whisper

و ش ي

وُشَى [wuša:] *v:* • **1.** to inform, tell – قِتلَوه لِأَنّ وُشَى بِيهُم [kitlawh liʔann wuša: bi:hum] They killed him because he informed on them.
اِنوُشَى [ʔinwuša:] *v:* • **1.** pass. of وُشَى to be informed, to be told
وَشِي [wašy] *n:* • **1.** telling, informing
وِشايَة [wiša:ya, wuša:ya] *n:* • **1.** defamation, slander, calomny
واشِي [wa:ši] *adj:* واشِين، وُشاة [wa:ši:n, wuša:t] *pl:* • **1.** informer, tattletale, stool pigeon

و ص ف

وُصَف [wuṣaf] *v:* • **1.** to describe, depict, picture – وُصَف الوِلايَة خُوش وَصُف [wuṣaf ʔilwila:ya xu:š waṣuf] He gave an excellent description of the town. • **2.** to credit, praise – وُصَفَه بالشَّجاعَة وَالكَرَم [wuṣafah biššaǰa:ʕa wilkaram] He praised him for bravery and generosity. • **3.** to prescribe (a medicine) – الطَّبِيب وُصَفلِي دِهن الخِروع [ʔiṭṭabi:b wuṣafli dihn ʔilxirwiʕ] The doctor prescribed castor oil for me.
وَصَّف [waṣṣaf] *v:* • **1.** to give directions, to explain where something is – ما يِقدَر يوَصُّف بدُون ما يأشِّر [ma: yigdar ywaṣṣuf bidu:n ma: yiʔaššir] He can't give directions without waving his hands. ماكُو داعِي تِجِ وِيّايا وَصُّفلِي [ma:ku da:ʕi tiji wiyya:ya wuwṣufli] There's no need to come with me. Just show me where. تِقدَر توَصُّفلِي وِين صايرَة المَحَطَّة؟ [tigdar twaṣṣufli wi:n ṣa:yra ʔilmaħaṭṭa?] Can you tell me where the station is?
اِتَّصَف [ʔittiṣaf] *v:* • **1.** to be marked, characterized, known – هَالرِّجّال يِتِّصِف بالكَرَم [harriǰǰa:l yittiṣif bilkaram] This man is known for generosity.

و

اِنوُصَف [ʔinwuṣaf] *v:* • **1.** (pass. of وُصَف) to be described, depicted, pictured
صِفَة [ṣifa] *n:* صِفات [ṣifaːt] *pl:* • **1.** attribute, trait, quality, characteristic • **2.** (gram.) adjective
وَصُف [waṣuf] *n:* • **1.** description, depiction, portrayal
وَصفَة [waṣfa] *n:* وَصفات [waṣfaːt] *pl:* • **1.** description, depiction • **2.** medical prescription • **3.** recipe
وَصِيف [waṣiːf] *n:* وَصايِف [waṣaːyif] *pl:* وَصِيفَة [waṣiːfa] • **1.** slave woman • **2.** fem.form used for: servant girl • **3.** bride's maid, maid of a miss (in a beauty contest)
مُواصَفَة [muwaːṣafa] *n:* مُواصَفات [muwaːṣafaːt] *pl:* • **1.** detailed description • **2.** explanation • **3.** specification
مُستَوصَف [mustawṣaf] *n:* مُستَوصَفات [mustawṣafaːt] *pl:* • **1.** clinic, dispensary
مِتّصِف [mittiṣif] *adj:* • **1.** characterized, depicted. portrayed
مَوصُوف [mawṣuːf] *adj:* • **1.** described, depicted, portrayed

و ص ل

وُصَل [wuṣal] *v:* • **1.** to arrive – شوَقِت يُوصَل القِطار؟ [šwakit yuːṣal ʔilqiṭaːr?] What time does the train arrive? المَكتُوب وُصَل اليُوم [ʔilmaktuːb wuṣal ʔilyuːm] The letter got here today. وُصَلَّك المَكتُوب وَإلّا لا؟ [wuṣallak ʔilmaktuːb waʔilla laː?] Did you receive the letter or not? المَيّ وُصَل لِحَدّ الخَطَر [ʔilmayy wuṣal liħadd ʔilxaṭar] The water has reached the danger level. يَزّي عاد، تَرَة وُصلَت لِحَدّها [yazzi ʕaːd, tara wuṣlat liħaddha] Take it easy there now, because it's gone far enough. تباحَثنا بِالمَوضُوع ساعَة لَكِن ما وُصَلنا لِأَي نَتِيجَة [tbaːħaθna bilmawðuːʕ saːʕa laːkin maː wuṣalna lʔay natiːǰa] We deliberated on the matter for an hour but didn't reach any result.
وَصَّل [waṣṣal] *v:* • **1.** to get, take, bring – مِنُو راح يوَصِّلَّه الخَبَر؟ [minu raːħ ywaṣṣillah ʔilxabar?] Who is going to give him the news? لا تِحكِي شِي قِدّامَه تَرَة هَذا يوَصِّل حَكِي لِلمُدِير [laː tiħči ši giddaːmah tara haːða ywaṣṣil ħači lilmudiːr] Don't say anything in his presence or he'll take what is said to the director. ظَلّ يزَيِّد عالرّاديُو إلَى أن وَصَّل سِعرَه لِلخَمسِين دِينار [ðall yzayyid ʕarraːdyu ʔila ʔan waṣṣal siʕrah lilxamsiːn dinaːr] He kept bidding on the radio until he brought its price up to fifty dinars. • **2.** to take, carry, convey – أَقدَر أوَصّلَك بسَيّارتي لِلمَطار [ʔagdar ʔawaṣṣlak bsayyaːrti lilmaṭaːr] I can take you in my car to the airport. • **3.** to reach – هَالحَبِل ما يوَصِّل لِلشِّبّاك الثّاني [halħabil maː ywaṣṣil liššubbaːč ʔiθθaːni] This rope doesn't reach to the other window. ما أعتِقِد السَّيّارَة راح توَصِّل لِلبانزِين خانَة [maː ʔaʕtiqid ʔissayyaːra raːħ twaṣṣil lilbanziːn xaːna] I don't think the car will make it to the filling station.
واصَل [waːṣal] *v:* • **1.** to continue, proceed with, go on with – اِستَراحِينا شوَيَّة وَبَعدين واصَلنا السَّفَر [ʔistaraːħiːna šwayya wbaʕdiːn waːṣalna ʔissafar] We rested a little and then continued the trip. واصلَه شوَيَّة شوَيَّة حَتَّى تُوفي كُلّ الدَّين [waːṣlah šwayya šwayya ħatta tuːfi kull ʔiddayn] Keep paying him bit by bit until you repay the whole debt.
أَوصَل [ʔawṣal] *v:* • **1.** to conduct (electricity, heat, etc.) – البلاتِين يُوصِل الكَهرَباء زين [ʔilplaːtiːn yuːṣil ʔilkahrabaːʔ ziːn] Platinum conducts electricity well.
توَصَّل [twaṣṣal] *v:* • **1.** to obtain access, get through – لا تخاف عَليه. هَذا يُعرُف شلُون يِتوَصَّل لِلوُزَراء [laː txaːf ʕaliːh. haːða yuʕruf šluːn yitwaṣṣal lilwuzaraːʔ] Don't worry about him. He knows how to get to the ministers. • **2.** to attain, arrive, reach – ما عِندَه مانِع يِكذِب وَيبُوق حَتَّى يِتوَصَّل لِغايَتَه [maː ʕindah maːniʕ yikðib wybuːg ħatta yitwaṣṣal liɣaːyatah] He doesn't mind lying and stealing in order to achieve his goals.
اِنوُصَل [ʔinwuṣal] *v:* • **1.** (pass. of وُصَل) to be arrived (at), to be reached – هالمُكان ما اِنوُصِلَّه بفَدّ يوم [halmukaːn maː yinwuṣillah bfadd yuːm] This place can't be reached in one day.
اِتَّصَل [ʔittiṣal] *v:* • **1.** to get in touch, make contact – اِتّصَل بِيّا بِالتَّلِفُون قَبُل يومَين [ʔittiṣal biyya bittalifuːn gabul yuːmayn] He contacted me by telephone two days ago. راح أتِّصِل بِيه وَأقُلَّه [raːħ ʔattiṣil biːh wagullah] I'll get in touch with him and tell him. • **2.** to join, contact, connect – البَحر الأَبيَض مِتّصِل بالبَحر الأَحمَر عَن طَرِيق قَناة السِّويس [ʔilbaħr ʔilʔabyað mittiṣil bilbaħr ʔilʔaħmar ʕan ṭariːq qanat ʔissiwiːs] The Mediterranean Sea is connected to the Red Sea by the Suez Canal. • **3.** to have a relationship – يبَيِّن كان مِتّصِل بِيها قَبِل الزَّواج [yibayyin čaːn mittiṣil biːha gabil ʔizzawaːǰ] It seems that he had had a relationship with her before the marriage.
صِلَة [ṣila] *n:* صِلات [ṣilaːt] *pl:* • **1.** connection, link, tie, bond • **2.** relationship • **3.** kinship – إلنا صِلَة رَحَم خَفِيفَة ويّا هَالعائِلَة [ʔilna ṣilat raħam xafiːfa wiyya halʕaːʔila] We have a slight family connection with that family.
وَصِل [waṣil] *n:* وُصُولات [wuṣuːlaːt] *pl:* • **1.** receipt, voucher
وُصلَة [wuṣla] *n:* وُصَل [wuṣal] *pl:* • **1.** piece, fragment (esp. of cloth)
وُصُول [wuṣuːl] *n:* • **1.** arrival
تَوَصُّل [tawaṣṣul] *n:* • **1.** arrival, reunion
تَواصُل [tawaːṣul] *n:* • **1.** staying in contact keeping in touch • **2.** continuance, continuity
تَوصِيل [tawṣiːl] *n:* • **1.** transfer, connection
اِتّصال [ʔittiṣaːl] *n:* • **1.** connection, contact
تَوصِيلَة [tawṣiːla] *n:* • **1.** ride • **2.** power connection
مُواصَلات [muwaːṣalaːt] *n:* • **1.** lines of communication, communications • **2.** means of transportation,

transportation – وزارَة المُواصَلات [wiza:rat ʔilmuwa:ṣala:t] Ministry of Communications and Transportation.
مُوصِل [mu:ṣil] *adj:* • **1.** (elec.) conductor
مُتَّصِل [muttaṣil] *adj:* • **1.** connected • **2.** (as Noun) caller
وُصُولِي [wuṣu:li] *adj:* • **1.** upstart, parvenu, overly ambitious, aspiring person
مِتواصِل [mitwa:ṣil] *adj:* • **1.** continuous

و ص م

وُصَم [wuṣam] *v:* • **1.** to brand
اِنوُصَم [ʔinwuṣam] *v:* • **1.** to be disgraced
وَصُم [waṣum] *n:* • **1.** disgrace

و ص و ص

وَصوَص [waṣwaṣ] *v:* • **1.** to chirp, squeak – فَرخ العَصفُور دَيوَصوُص [farx ʔilʕaṣfu:r daywaṣwuṣ] The baby sparrow is chirping. • **2.** to peep
وَصوَصَة [waṣwaṣa] *n:* • **1.** peep

و ص ي

وَصَّى [waṣṣa:] *v:* • **1.** to request, ask, order – شقَدّ وَصّيتَه يِشتِري بَيض ونِسَى [šgadd waṣṣi:tah yištiri bayð̣ wnisa:] How many times I told him to buy eggs and he forgot! المُلاحِظ وَصّاني أطبَع هَالمَكتُوب قَبُل ما أَطلَع [ʔilmula:ħið̣ waṣṣa:ni ʔaṭbaʕ halmaktu:b gabul ma: ʔaṭlaʕ] The supervisor asked me to type this letter before I leave. • **2.** to charge, commission – لا توَصِّيه بشِي تَرَة ما يجِيبلَك إيّاه [la: twaṣṣi:h bši tara ma: yǰi:blak ʔiyya:h] Don't ask him to get anything because he won't bring it for you. بَعَد ما أوَصِّيك عَن هَالقَضِيَّة [baʕad ma: ʔawaṣṣi:k ʕan halqað̣iyya] I won't ask you to take care of this matter any more. • **3.** to advise, counsel, recommend – الدّكتُور وَصّاني آكُل بَسّ سِمَك وَدِجاج [ʔiddiktu:r waṣṣa:ni ʔa:kul bass simač wdiǰa:ǰ] The doctor advised me to eat only fish and chicken. • **4.** to make a will – مات وَما وَصَّى [ma:t wama waṣṣa:] He died and didn't make a will. • **5.** with عَلَى to order, place on order for – وَصَّيت عَلَى بَردات جِدِيدَة [waṣṣi:t ʕala parda:t ǰidi:da] I ordered new curtains. هَسَّة وَصَّيتَلك عَلَى قَهوَة [hassa waṣṣi:tlak ʕala gahwa] I just ordered you a cup of coffee. • **6.** with ب to enjoin, urge, impress, make incumbent upon – الإسلام يوَصِّي بِالحِشمَة [ʔilʔisla:m ywaṣṣi bilħišma] Islam urges propriety. • **7.** with ب to will, bequeath, leave – وَصَّى بِكُلّ فلُوسَه لمَرتَه [waṣṣa: bkull flu:sah lmartah] He willed all of his money to his wife.
توَصَّى [twaṣṣa:] *v:* • **1.** with ب to be urged to take care of someone or something
وَصِيّ [waṣiyy] *n:* أَوصِياء [ʔawṣiyya:ʔ] *pl:* • **1.** guardian • **2.** regent
وَصِيَّة [waṣiyya, wuṣiyya] *n:* وُصِيّات، وَصايا [wuṣiyya:t, waṣa:ya:] *pl:* • **1.** request, order – آني رايِح لِبَغداد. عِندَك وَصِيَّة؟ [ʔa:ni ra:yiħ lbaɣda:d. ʕindak waṣiyya?] I'm going to Baghdad. Do you have any errands? مِن ترُوح لِلبَصرَة، وُصِيَّتِي الوَحِيدَة تزُور أَخُويا [min tru:ħ lilbaṣra, wuṣiyyti ʔilwaħi:da dzu:r ʔaxu:ya] When you go to Basra, my only request is that you visit my brother. • **2.** advice, counsel, recommendation • **3.** will, testament
تَوصِيَة [tawṣiya] *n:* تَوصِيات [tawṣiya:t] *pl:* • **1.** (commercial) order, commission • **2.** with بـ to order, on commission • **3.** (same a وَصِيَّة) advice, counsel, recommendation • **4.** (same a وَصِيَّة) will, testament
تُوصاة [tu:ṣa:] *n:* • **1.** (invar.) custom made, made to order – بُسَطِتلَك إيّاه بَسطَة تُوصاة [buṣaṭitlak ʔiyya:h basṭa tu:ṣa:] I beat him up for you just the way you wanted. قَنادرَه كُلّها تُوصاة لِأَنّ رِجلَيه كبار [qana:drah kullha tu:ṣa: liʔann riǰlayh kba:r] All his shoes are custom made because his feet are big.
وِصايَة [wiṣa:ya] *n:* • **1.** guardianship • **2.** trusteeship
موَصّي [mwaṣṣi] *adj:* • **1.** ordered, recommended

و ض ء

توَضَّى [twað̣ð̣a:] *v:* • **1.** to perform the ritual ablution before prayer – يَالله توَضَّى حَتَّى نرُوح نصَلِّي [yallah twað̣ð̣a: ħatta nru:ħ nṣalli] Hurry up and wash yourself so we can go pray.
وُضُوء [wuð̣u:ʔ] *n:* • **1.** ritual cleanliness, purity • **2.** ritual ablution before prayer

و ض ح

وُضَح [wuð̣aħ] *v:* • **1.** to become clear, plain, manifest, obvious, evident – الدَّرس وُضَح بَعَد ما اِستَعمَل المُعَلِّم أَمثِلَة هوايَة [ʔiddaris wuð̣aħ baʕad ma: ʔistaʕmal ʔilmuʕallim ʔamθila hwa:ya] The lesson became clear after the teacher used many examples.
وَضَّح [wað̣ð̣aħ] *v:* • **1.** to make plain, clear, to explain, elucidate, expound, illustrate – طِلبَوا مِنَّه يوَضِّح السُّؤال قَبُل ما يجاوبُون [ṭilbaw minnah ywað̣ð̣iħ ʔissuʔa:l gabul ma: yǰa:wbu:n] They asked him to clear up the question before they answered.
توَضَّح [twað̣ð̣aħ] *v:* • **1.** (pass. of وَضَّح) to be cleared, to be explained, to be elucidated
اِتَّضَح [ʔittið̣aħ] *v:* • **1.** to become clear – بَعَد ما سِألهُم كَم سُؤال، اِتِّضَحلَه إنهُم ما يعرفُون شِي [baʕad ma: siʔalhum čam suʔa:l, ʔittið̣ aħlah ʔinhum ma: yʕirfu:n ši] After he asked them several questions, it became clear to him that they didn't know anything.
وَضِح [wað̣iħ] *n:* • **1.** light, brightness, luminosity
وُضُوح [wuð̣u:ħ] *n:* • **1.** clarity, clearness, plainness • **2.** (with بـ) clearly, plainly, distinctly
تَوضِيح [tawð̣i:ħ] *n:* تَوضِيحات [tawð̣i:ħa:t] *pl:* • **1.** clarification, elucidation, explanation, explication
إيضاح [ʔi:ð̣a:ħ] *n:* • **1.** showing, explanation, clarification
واضِح [wa:ð̣iħ] *adj:* • **1.** clear, plain • **2.** obvious, evident, manifest

مِتَّضِح [mittaðiħ] *adj:* • **1.** plain, obvious, manifest
أوضَح [ʔawðah] *comparative adjective:* • **1.** more or most clear, plain

و ض ع

وُضَع [wuðaʕ] *v:* • **1.** to lay, set, put in place – الوَزير وُضَع الحَجَر الأَساسِي لِهَالبِنايَة [ʔilwazi:r wuðaʕ ʔilħajar ʔilʔasa:si lhalbina:ya] The minister laid the cornerstone for this building. • **2.** وُضَع يَدَ لِ to put a stop to, cause an end to – لازِم نُوضَع حَدّ لِلأَشياء اللّي دَتصِير بَالدّائِرَة [la:zim nu:ðaʕ ħadd lilʔašya:ʔ ʔilli datṣi:r bidda:ʔira] We have to put an end to the things that are happening in the office. • **3.** وُضَع حَدّعَلَى to seize, lay hold of – الحُكُومَة وُضعَت اليَدّ عَلَى أَملاكَه [ʔilħuku:ma wuðʕat ʔilyadd ʕala ʔamla:kah] The government seized his property.
تواضَع [twa:ðaʕ] *v:* • **1.** to behave humbly and modestly – لِيش ما تِتواضَع شوَيَّة؟ [li:š ma: titwa:ðaʕ šwayya?] Why don't you be a bit modest? ما عِندَه مانِع يِتواضَع وَيسَلِّم هُوَّ بالأَوَّل [ma: ʕindah ma:niʕ yitwa:ðaʕ wysallim huwwa bilʔawwal] He has no objection to being humble and saying hello first.
وَضِع [waðiʕ] *n:* أوضاع [ʔawða:ʕ] *pl:* • **1.** laying, setting, placing • **2.** situation, condition, set of circumstances – كُلّ يوم يجُون لِلدّائِرَة مِتأَخّرِين. هَذا مُو وَضِع [kull yu:m yiju:n lidda:ʔira mitʔaxxri:n. ha:ða mu: waðiʕ] Every day they come to the office late. This is no way to do things! • **3.** pl. أوضاع position, stance, bearing, posture, attitude
مَوضِع [mawðiʕ] *n:* مَواضِع [mawa:ðiʕ] *pl:* • **1.** place, location
مَوضُوع [mawðu:ʕ] *n:* مَواضِيع [mawa:ði:ʕ] *pl:* • **1.** subject, topic, theme • **2.** matter, affair • **3.** problem, issue, question
تَواضُع [tawa:ðuʕ] *n:* • **1.** modesty, humility, humbleness
وَضعِيَّة [waðʕiyya] *n:* وَضعِيّات [waðʕiyya:t] *pl:* • **1.** pose • **2.** position, situation
وَضِيع [waði:ʕ] *adj:* وَضِيعِين، وُضَعاء [waði:ʕi:n, wuðaʕa:ʔ] *pl:* • **1.** lowly, base, vulgar, common • **2.** common, vulgar person
مَوضِعِي [mawðiʕi] *adj:* • **1.** local
مَوضُوعِي [mawðu:ʕi] *adj:* • **1.** objective
مِتواضِع [mitwa:ðiʕ] *adj:* • **1.** humble • **2.** modest

و ط ء

وَطّى [waṭṭa:] *v:* • **1.** to lower – وَطّي صَوتَك. دَنِقرَا [waṭṭi ṣawtak. daniqra] Lower your voice. We're reading.
وَطأَة [waṭʔa] *n:* • **1.** gravity, seriousness
مَوطِئ، مَوطَأ [mawṭiʔ, mawṭaʔ] *n:* • **1.** footing, foothold, place where the foot is set down, place where one lives
وُطِيَّة [wuṭiyya] *adj:* • **1.** ground, earth, terra firma
واطِي [wa:ṭi] *adj:* • **1.** low – المَيّ دَيرُوح لِلقاع الواطيَة [ʔilmayy dayru:ħ lilga:ʕ ʔilwa:ṭya] The water is flowing into the low ground. هُوَّ فَدّ واحِد واطِي. مَحَّد يحِبَّه [huww fadd wa:ħid wa:ṭi. maħħad yħibbah] He's a low-down character. Nobody likes him.
أَوطا [ʔawṭa] *comparative adjective:* • **1.** lower or lowest

و ط د

وَطَد [waṭad] *v:* • **1.** to make firm, strong or stable
توَطَّد [twaṭṭad] *v:* • **1.** to be made firm
تَوطِيد [tawṭi:d] *n:* • **1.** strengthening, consolidation, reinforcement
وَطِيد [waṭi:d] *adj:* • **1.** firm • **2.** strong, solid

و ط ن

إستَوطَن [ʔistawṭan] *v:* • **1.** to settle in, make a home in, take up residence in – هَالقَبِيلَة هاجرَت مِن الجِّنُوب وَإستَوطِنَت العِراق [halqabi:la ha:jrat min ʔijjinu:b wʔistawṭinat ʔilʕira:q] This tribe migrated from the South and settled in Iraq.
وَطَن [waṭan] *n:* أَوطان [ʔawṭa:n] *pl:* • **1.** homeland, fatherland, native country – حُبّ الوَطَن [ħubb ʔilwaṭan] patriotism.
مَوطِن [mawṭin] *n:* • **1.** residence, native place
وَطَنِيَّة [waṭaniyya] *n:* • **1.** patriotism • **2.** national sentiment, nationalism (esp. one-country, as opposed to Pan-Arab)
مُواطِن [muwa:ṭin] *n:* مُواطِنِين [muwa:ṭini:n] *pl:* • **1.** citizen, countryman
تَوطِين [tawṭi:n] *n:* • **1.** naturalization, giving permanent residence • **2.** resettlement
وَطَنِي [waṭani] *adj:* • **1.** indigenous, domestic – مَصنُوعات وَطَنِيَّة [maṣnu:ʕa:t waṭaniyya] domestic manufactures. • **2.** patriotic • **3.** nationalistic • **4.** patriot, nationalist
مِستَوطِن [mistawṭin] *adj:* • **1.** resident, native, deep-rooted

و ظ ب

واظَب [wa:ðab] *v:* • **1.** to persevere, to do persistently, keep doing, continue to do
مُواظَبَة [muwa:ðaba] *n:* • **1.** diligence, assiduity, persistence, perseverance

و ظ ف

وَظَّف [waððaf] *v:* • **1.** to appoint to a position, to employ, hire – الحُكُومَة ما توَظِّف أَجانِب [ʔilħuku:ma ma: twaððuf ʔaja:nib] The government doesn't employ foreigners.
توَظَّف [twaððaf] *v:* • **1.** to be hired, get a job – سِمَعِت عَلِي توَظَّف بدائِرَة البَرِيد [simaʕit ʕali twaððaf bda:ʔirat ʔilbari:d] I heard that Ali was hired by the Post Office.

و

مُوَظَّف [muwaððaf] *n:* مُوَظَّفِين [muwaððafi:n] *pl:* • **1.** appointee, official, employee (esp. of the government), civil servant
وَظِيفَة [waði:fa] *n:* وَظايِف [waða:yif] *pl:* • **1.** assignment, task, duty • **2.** homework assignment • **3.** office, position, post, job
تَوظِيف [tawði:f] *n:* • **1.** employment, appointment (to an office)
مِتوَظُّف [mitwaððuf] *adj:* • **1.** employed

و ع ب

اِستَوعَب [ʔistawʕab] *v:* • **1.** to comprehend, understand, to be able to take in, to grasp
اِستِيعاب [ʔisti:ʕa:b] *n:* • **1.** full comprehension, grasp
مُستَوعَب [mustawʕab] *adj:* • **1.** comprehended, understood

و ع د

وُعَد [wuʕad] *v:* • **1.** to make a promise, to promise – وُعَدنِي بِصُوغَة وَما جابلِي [wuʕadni bṣu:ɣa wama ǰa:bli] He promised me a present from his trip and didn't bring it to me.
واعَد [wa:ʕad] *v:* • **1.** to make an appointment, set a meeting with – واعَدنِي مَرّتَين وَما جا [wa:ʕadni marrtayn wama ǰa:] He made an appointment with me twice and didn't come. • **2.** to make a promise, to promise – واعَدنِي يِنطِينِي البَنكَة مِن يسافِر [wa:ʕadni yinṭi:ni ʔilpanka min ysa:fir] He promised me he'd give me the fan when he left. • **3.** to assure, to state confidently – آنِي أواعدَك هَسَّة، راح يسافِر وَما يقُولّ إلنا [ʔa:ni ʔawa:ʕdak hassa, ra:ħ ysa:fir wma ygull ʔilna] I'll tell you for sure now, he'll leave and not tell us. أواعدَك إذاما [ʔawa:ʕdak ʔiðama...] I assure you that. . . , mark my words that. . . . أواعدَك إذاما عَيّنوه [ʔawa:ʕdak ʔiðama ʕayynu:h] I assure you that they will appoint him. آنِي أواعدَك إذاما نِكَت بِينا [ʔa:ni ʔawa:ʕdak ʔiðama nikat bi:na] I'm sure he'll get us in a mess.
توَعَّد [twaʕʕad] *v:* • **1.** to threaten – خاف مِنَّه بَعَد ما توَعَّدَه [xa:f minnah baʕad ma: twaʕʕadah] He got scared of him after he threatened him.
تواعَد [twa:ʕad] *v:* • **1.** to make an appointment – تواعَدنا بِالقَهوَة [twa:ʕadna bilgahwa] We agreed to meet in the café. خَلِّي نِتّفِق بِالأَوَّل وَبَعدين نِتواعَد عالإجتِماع [xalli: nittifiq bilʔawwal wbaʕdi:n nitwa:ʕad ʕalʔiǰtima:ʕ] Let's agree first and then we'll set a date for the meeting.
اِنوُعَد [ʔinwuʕad] *v:* • **1.** pass. of وُعَد to be promised
وَعَد [waʕad] *n:* وُعُود [wuʕu:d] *pl:* • **1.** promise • **2.** appointed time, appointment
وَعدَة [waʕda] *n:* • **1.** term (of a loan)
مَوعِد، مِيعاد [mawʕid, mi:ʕa:d] *n:* مَواعِيد [mawa:ʕi:d] *pl:* • **1.** appointment, date, rendezvous • **2.** appointed time, deadline
مَوعُود [mawʕu:d] *adj:* • **1.** promised – آنِي مَوعُود بِتَرفِيع [ʔa:ni mawʕu:d btarfi:ʕ] I have been promised promotion. • **2.** booked, scheduled – آنِي اليُوم مَوعُود وماأقدَر أجِي [ʔa:ni ʔilyu:m mawʕu:d wmaʔagdar ʔaǰi] I have an appointment today and can't come.
مِتواعِد [mitwa:ʕid] *adj:* • **1.** having an appointment or date

و ع ر

وَعِر [waʕir] *adj:* • **1.** rough, rocky, uneven, rugged – الأَراضِي بِالشِّمال وَعرَة [ʔilʔara:ði biššima:l waʕra] The terrain in the north is rugged.

و ع ز

وُعَز [wuʕaz] *v:* • **1.** to give orders, give directions – المُدِير وُعَزلهُم يبقُون وَرا الدّوام وَيدِرسُون القَضِيَّة [ʔilmudi:r wuʕazilhum yibqu:n wara ʔiddawa:m wydirsu:n ʔilqaðiyya] The boss directed them to stay after hours and study the matter. • **2.** to suggest, make a suggestion – لَو ما تُوعِزلَه، ما كان سَوَّى هِيكِي شِي [law ma: tu:ʕizlah, ma: ča:n sawwa: hi:či ši] If you hadn't put him up to it, he wouldn't have done such a thing.
إيعاز [ʔi:ʕa:z] *n:* • **1.** advice, suggestion, order

و ع ظ

وُعَظ [wuʕað] *v:* • **1.** to preach, to admonish, exhort – الإمام يوعِظ بَعد الصَّلاة [ʔilʔima:m yu:ʕið baʕd ʔiṣṣala] The Imam preaches after the prayer.
اِتّعِظ [ʔittiʕið] *v:* • **1.** to learn a lesson, be admonished or warned – هالخَسارَة لازِم تخَلِّيك تِتِّعِظ [halxasa:ra la:zim txalli:k tittiʕið] This loss should teach you a lesson.
اِنوُعَظ [ʔinwuʕað] *v:* • **1.** to be given advice • **2.** to be learned (through experience)
وَعِظ [waʕið] *n:* • **1.** preaching, admonition
واعِظ [wa:ʕið] *n:* واعِظِين، وُعّاظ [wa:ʕiði:n, wuʕʕa:ð] *pl:* • **1.** preacher
مَوعِظَة [mawʕiða] *n:* مَواعِظ [mawa:ʕið] *pl:* • **1.** (religious) exhortation, sermon

و ع ي

وُعَى [wuʕa:] *v:* • **1.** to become aware, pay attention – إذا ما تُوعَى عَلَى زَمانَك، تَرَة بَعدين تِتنَدَّم [ʔiða ma: tu:ʕa: ʕala zama:nak, tara baʕdi:n titnaddam] If you don't pay attention to what's around you, then later you'll regret it. وُعَى عَلَى نَفسَه [wuʕa: ʕala nafsah] It dawned on him that. . . وُعَى عَلَى نَفسَه وعِرَف دُولَة مصادقِيه عَلَى فلُوسَه [wuʕa: ʕala nafsah wʕiraf ðu:la mṣa:dqi:h ʕala flu:sah] It dawned on him and he knew they befriended him for his money. • **2.** to awaken, wake up – بَعدَه ما وُعَى مِن النُّوم [baʕdah ma: wuʕa: min ʔannu:m] He hasn't woken up yet.
وَعَّى [waʕʕa:] *v:* • **1.** to wake, awaken – أرجُوك وَعِّينِي السّاعَة ثمانيَة [ʔarǰu:k waʕʕi:ni ʔissa:ʕa θma:nya] Please wake me up at eight o'clock.

تَوَعَّى [twaʕʕa:] *v:* • **1.** to arouse
وَعِي [waʕy] *n:* • **1.** consciousness, awareness, wakefulness – فُقَد وَعيَه [fuqad waʕyah] He fainted.
تَوعِيَة [tawʕiya] *n:* • **1.** enlightenment (people), consciousness raising
واعِي [wa:ʕi] *adj:* • **1.** awake, conscious – ظَلّيت واعِي لِسّاعَة ثِنتَين الصُّبُح [ðalli:t wa:ʕi lissa:ʕa θintayn ʔiṣṣubuḥ] I stayed awake until two o'clock in the morning.

و غ ف
وَغَّف [waɣɣaf] *v:* • **1.** to foam up, froth, make suds – الصّابُون اللّي إنطيتنِي إيّاه ما يوَغُّف زين [ʔiṣṣa:bu:n ʔilli ʔinṭi:tni ʔiyya:h ma: ywaɣɣuf zi:n] The soap that you gave me doesn't suds well.
وَغَف [waɣaf] *n:* • **1.** foam, froth, suds • **2.** jerk, unpleasant person
وَغفَة [waɣfa] *n:* وَغفات [waɣfa:t] *pl:* • **1.** pl. وَغفات unit noun of وَغَف foam, froth, suds

و غ و غ
وُغواغَة [wuɣwa:ɣa] *n:* وُغواغات [wuɣwa:ɣa:t] *pl:* • **1.** toy noisemaker

و ف د
أَوفَد [ʔawfad] *v:* • **1.** to appoint to a delegation – الحُكُومَة أَوفِدَته يِدرُس الغَلاء بِهالمَنطِقَة [ʔilḥuku:ma ʔawfidatah yidrus ʔilɣala:ʔ bhalmanṭiqa] The government appointed him to study the inflation in this area.
وَفِد [wafid] *n:* وُفُود [wufu:d] *pl:* • **1.** delegation

و ف ر
وَفَّر [waffar] *v:* • **1.** to save, lay by, put by, hoard – إذا تَوَفُّر فلُوس كافيَة، تِقدَر تِشتِري بَيت [ʔiða twaffur flu:s ka:fya, tigdar tištiri bayt] If you save enough money, you can buy a house. • **2.** to save, avoid expenditure of – المَكِينَة راح تَوَفُّر عَلينا هوايَة تَعَب وَوَكِت [ʔilmaki:na ra:ḥ twaffur ʕali:na hwa:ya taʕab wwakit] The machine will save us a lot of effort and time.
تَوَفَّر [twaffar] *v:* • **1.** to be saved – راتبِي، ما يِتوَفَّر مِنَّه وَلا فِلِس [ra:tbi, ma: yitwaffar minnah wala filis] Not a single fils can be saved out of my salary. • **2.** to abound, be plentiful, abundant, ample – السِّمَك يِتوَفَّر بِالرَّبِيع [ʔissimač yitwaffar birrabi:ʕ] Fish are plentiful in the spring. • **3.** to be met, fulfilled – إذا تُعبُر هَالامتِحان، الشُّرُوط تِتوَفَّر بِيك [ʔiða tuʕbur halʔimtiḥa:n, ʔiššuru:ṭ titwaffar bi:k] If you get by this exam, you will have met the conditions. ما قِبلَوه لِأَنّ الشُّرُوط ما مِتوَفُّرَة بِيه [ma: qiblawh liʔann ʔiššuru:ṭ ma: mitwaffura bi:h] They didn't accept him because he didn't fulfill the requirements.
وُفرَة [wufra] *n:* • **1.** abundance, profusion, plenty – السِّمَك مَوجُود بوُفرَة بِدِجلَة [ʔissimač mawǰu:d bwufra bdijla] Fish are in good supply in the Tigris.
تَوَفُّر [tawaffur] *n:* • **1.** availability • **2.** abundance
تَوفِير [tawfi:r] *n:* • **1.** savings – صَنْدُوق التَّوفِير [ṣandu:q ʔittawfi:r] postal savings bank.
مُوَفَّر [muwaffar] *adj:* • **1.** available, abundant, plentiful
وافِر [wa:fir] *adj:* • **1.** abundant, plentiful, available (in big quantities)
مِتوَفِّر [mitwaffir] *adj:* • **1.** ample, abundant • **2.** available, in stock, on hand

و ف ق
وَفَّق [waffaq] *v:* • **1.** to allow prosperity, grant success – إذا الله وَفَّقنِي، أفتَح مَحَلّ عَلَى حسابِي [ʔiða ʔallah waffaqni, ʔaftaḥ maḥall ʕala ḥsa:bi] If God grants me prosperity, I will open a shop on my own. • **2.** with بَين to reconcile, make consistent – ما يِقدَر يوَفِّق بين الشُّغُل وَالدِّراسَة [ma: yigdar ywaffiq bi:n ʔiššuɣul widdira:sa] He can't reconcile working with studying.
وافَق [wa:faq] *v:* • **1.** to suit, be agreeable to, be consistent with one's interests – ما قِبَل يِبِيع لِأَنّ السِّعِر ما وافَقَه [ma: qibal yibi:ʕ liʔann ʔissiʕir ma: wa:faqah] He wouldn't consent to sell because the price did suit him. الحِكايَة وافقَتَه هوايَة [ʔilḥča:ya wa:fqatah hwa:ya] The story pleased him a great deal. • **2.** to agree, concur, be of like mind with – آنِي ما أَوافقَك بِهالرَّأي [ʔa:ni ma: ʔawa:fqak bharraʔy] I don't agree with you on this idea. • **3.** to agree with, be beneficial for – يبَيِّن هَوا لُبنان وافَقَه [yibayyin hawa lubna:n wa:faqah] It seems that the Lebanese weather agrees with him. • **4.** to coincide with – الزَّواج راح يوافِق يوم العِيد [ʔizzawa:ǰ ra:ḥ ywa:fiq yu:m ʔilʕi:d] The wedding will coincide with the holiday. • **5.** to consent, agree, give one's consent – وافَق يِجِي وِيّايا لِلسِّينَما [wa:faq yiǰi wiyya:yalissinama] He agreed to come with me to the movies. • **6.** with عَلَى to approve, authorize, sanction, ratify – المُدِير وافَق عالإجازَة [ʔilmudi:r wa:faq ʕalʔiǰa:za] The director approved the leave.
تَوَفَّق [twaffaq] *v:* • **1.** to prosper, be successful – صَدِيقِي تَوَفَّق بِهالشَّغلَة، وَسَوَّى فلُوس هوايَة [ṣadi:qi twaffaq bhaššaɣla, wsawwa: flu:s hwa:ya] My friend prospered in this job and made a lot of money.
توافَق [twa:faq] *v:* • **1.** to agree with each other, to get along together – إبنِي وَإبنَك ما يِتوافقُون أَبَداً [ʔibni wʔibnak ma: yitwa:fqu:n ʔabadan] My son and yours don't get along at all.
اِتَّفَق [ʔittifaq] *v:* • **1.** to agree, reach an agreement – ما اِتَّفقوا عَلَى أَيّ حَلّ لهَسَّة [ma: ʔittifqaw ʕala ʔayy ḥall lhassa] They've not agreed on any solution yet. ما أَعرُف كِيميا، اِتَّفقنا، لَكِن أَعرُف إنكِلِيزِي [ma: ʔaʕruf ki:mya, ʔittifaqna, la:kin ʔaʕruf ʔingili:zi] I don't know chemistry, we agree, but I do know English.
تَوفِيق [tawfi:q] *n:* • **1.** success, prosperity
اِتِّفاق [ʔittifa:q] *n:* اِتِّفاقات [ʔittifa:qa:t] *pl:* • **1.** agreement, treaty – اِتِّفاق تِجارِي [ʔittifa:q tiǰa:ri] commercial agreement.

و

مُوافَقَة [muwaːfaqa] *n:* • **1.** agreement • **2.** consent, authorization, approval

مُوَافَقِيَّة [muwaːfagiyya] *n:* • **1.** success

اِتِّفاقِيَّة [ʔittifaːqiyya] *n:* اِتِّفاقِيّات [ʔittifaːqiyyaːt] *pl:* • **1.** agreement, pact, treaty

مُوَفَّق [muwaffaq] *adj:* • **1.** successful, prospering, fortunate

مِتَّفِق [mittifiq] *adj:* • **1.** agreed upon

مُوافِق [muwaːfiq] *adj:* • **1.** suitable, fit, appropriate

أوفَق [ʔawfaq] *comparative adjective:* • **1.** more or most suitable, appropriate, pleasing, acceptable

و ف ي

وُفَى [wufaː] *v:* • **1.** to be loyal, faithful, true – هَذا أَبَد ما وُفَى لأَحَّد [haːða ʔabad maː wufaː lʔaħħad] He was never faithful to anyone. • **2.** with ب to live up to, fulfill, keep, meet, carry out – وُفَى بوَعدَه [wufaː bwaʕdah] He kept his promise.

وَفَّى [waffaː, wuffaː] *v:* • **1.** to repay – لهَسَّة ما وَفَّى ديُونَه [lhassa maː waffaː dyuːnah] He hasn't repaid his debts so far.

توَفَّى [twaffaː] *v:* • **1.** to die, pass away – أَبُوه توَفَّى قَبُل شَهَر وَخَلَّف ثلَث يتامَى [ʔabuːh twaffaː gabul šahar wxallaf tlaθ ytaːma] His father passed away a month ago and left behind three surviving children.

توافَى [twaːfaː] *v:* • **1.** to settle accounts, settle in full – هاك نُصّ دِينار وَهَسَّة توافينا [haːk nuṣṣ dinaːr whassa twaːfiːna] Here's a half-dinar and now we're even.

اِستَوفَى [ʔistawfaː] *v:* • **1.** to obtain repayment of – راح أَستَوفِي المَبلَغ مِنَّه [raːħ ʔastawfi ʔilmablaɣ minnah] I'll get back the full amount from him. ما أَطُلبَه شِي. اِستَوفَيت حَقِّي [maː ʔaṭulbah ši. ʔistawfayt ħaqqi] He doesn't owe me a thing. I got what was due me.

وُفا، وُفاء [wufa, wafaːʔ] *n:* • **1.** loyalty, faithfulness, fidelity • **2.** fulfillment, keeping, meeting (of a promise, etc.)

وَفاة [wafaː, wafaːt] *n:* وَفايات، وَفيات [wafaːyaːt, wafiyyaːt] *pl:* • **1.** demise, death

وَفِيَّة [wafiyya] *n:* • **1.** death, decease • **2.** (Pl.) mortality, death rate

وَفِي [wafi] *adj:* أَوفياء [ʔawfiyaːʔ] *pl:* • **1.** loyal, faithful, reliable, true – إِنتَ صَدِيق وَفِي [ʔinta ṣadiːq wafi] You're a true friend.

وافِي [waːfi] *adj:* • **1.** ample, abundant

مِتوَفِّي [mitwaffi] *adj:* • **1.** late, deceased, dead

أوفَى [ʔawfa] *comparative adjective:* • **1.** more or most faithful, loyal

و ق ت

وَقَّت [waqqat] *v:* • **1.** to set – لازِم نُقعُد مِن الصُّبُح. لا تِنسَى توَقِّتها لِلسّاعَة [laːzim nugʕud min ʔiṣṣubuħ. laː tinsaː twaqqitha lissaːʕa] We have to get up early in the morning. Don't forget to set the clock.

وَقِت [waqit, wakit] *n:* أَوقات [ʔawqaːt] *pl:* • **1.** time, period of time, time span – أَوقات يُمُرّ عَلينا وَأَوقات بَسّ يخابُر [ʔawqaːt yumurr ʕaliːna wʔawqaːt bass yxaːbur] At times he comes by to see us and sometimes he just phones. شوَقِت؟ [šwakit?] when? what time? الوَقِت [ʕalwakit] on time, at the proper time. مِن وَقِت [min waqit] early, ahead of time. لازِم نِطلَع الصُّبُح مِن وَقِت [laːzim niṭlaʕ ʔiṣṣubuħ min waqit] We have to leave early in the morning. آنِي راح أَركُض وَإِنتَ إِلزَملِي وَقِت [ʔaːni raːħ ʔarkuḍ wʔinta ʔilzamli waqit] I'm going to run and you keep time for me.

تَوقِيت [tawqiːt] *n:* تَواقِيت [tawaːqiːt] *pl:* • **1.** setting (of a clock, etc) – حَسَب تَوقِيت بَغداد [ħasab tawqiːt baɣdaːd] according to Baghdad time. • **2.** timing, reckoning of time, time • **3.** تَوقِيت صَيفِي [tawqiːt ṣayfi] daylight saving time

مَواقِيت [mawaːqiːt] *n:* • **1.** times (as in times for prayer)

وَقتِي [waqti] *adj:* • **1.** temporary, transient, transitional, passing – هَذا تَرتِيب وَقتِي [haːða tartiːb waqti] This is a temporary arrangement.

مُوَقَّت [muwaqqat] *adj:* • **1.** scheduled, set for a given time – قُنبُلَة مُوَقَّتَة [qunbula muwaqqata] time bomb. • **2.** effective for a given period of time, temporal, temporary, interim, provisional, passing – هاي تَرتِيبات مُوَقَّتَة [haːy tartiːbaːt muwaqqata] These are temporary arrangements.

مَوقُوت [mawquːt] *adj:* • **1.** timed

مُوَقَّتاً [muwaqqatan] *adverbial:* • **1.** for the present • **2.** temporarily

وَقِت ما [wakit maː] *subordinating conjunction:* • **1.** whenever

شوَقِت [šwakit] *interrogative:* • **1.** when

و ق ح

وَقَّح [wakkaħ] *v:* • **1.** to make insolent, impudent, disrespectful – جَماعتَه وَقُّحُوه وصار أَدَبسِزّ [ǰamaːʕtah wakkħuːh wṣaːr ʔadabsizz] His gang made a smart aleck out of him and he has no manners anymore.

توَقَّح [twakkaħ] *v:* • **1.** to become insolent, impudent, disrespectful – لا تخَلِّي إِبنَك يلعَب ويّا هَالوَلَد تَرَة يتوَقَّح [laː txalliː ʔibnak yilʕab wiyya halwalad tara yitwakkaħ] Don't let your son play with this boy or he'll become disrespectful.

اِستَوقَح [ʔistawkaħ] *v:* • **1.** to become insolent, impudent – مِن شاف أَبُوه، اِستَوقَح [min šaːf ʔabuːh, ʔistawkaħ] When he saw his father, he became bolder.

وَقاحَة [wakaːħa] *n:* • **1.** insolence, impudence, boldness – إِنتَ دَتسَوِّي وَكاحَة هوايَة. راح أَقُلَّه لأَبُوك [ʔinta datsawwiː wakaːħa hwaːya. raːħ ʔagullah lʔabuːk] You're being very naughty. I'm going to tell your father.

وَقِح [wakiħ] *adj:* • **1.** awful • **2.** impudent, shameless, arrogant

وَقِيح [wakiːħ] *adj:* وُقَّح [wukkaħ] *pl:* • **1.** brash, insolent, impudent, bold – كُلّ وِلدها ما بِيهُم واحِد وَقِيح

[kull wilidha ma: bi:hum wa:ħid waki:ħ] Not one of her sons is impudent. • **2.** tough, rowdyish, ruffianly – لا تِتحارَش بِهَالبِنَيَّة تَرَة عِدها أُخوَة وُقّح [la: titħa:raš bhalbnayya tara ʕidha ʔuxwa wukkaħ] Don't make passes at that girl because she has some tough brothers.
أوقح [ʔawkaħ] *comparative adjective:* • **1.** more or most brash, insolent, bold

و ق د

موقد [mu:qad, mu:gad] *n:* مواقِد [mwa:qid, mwa:gid] *pl:* • **1.** fireplace, hearth (esp. for cooking)
وُقود [wuqu:d] *n:* • **1.** fuel

و ق ر

وَقَّر [waqqar] *v:* • **1.** to respect, honor, treat with reverence – عِزمُوه وَوَقِّرَوه وبَعدين طِلَع مُو خُوش آدَمِي [ʕizmu:h wwaqqirawh wbaʕdi:n ṭilaʕ mu: xu:š ʔa:dami] They invited him and treated him with respect and later he turned out to be a bad sort of person.
وقار [waqa:r, wiqa:r] *n:* • **1.** dignity, gravity, dignified conduct
وَقُور، وَقِر [waqu:r, waqir] *adj:* • **1.** dignified, venerable, deserving respect
مُوَقَّر [muwaqqar] *adj:* • **1.** respected, held in respect, venerable, reverend
أَوقَر [ʔawqar] *comparative adjective:* • **1.** more or most dignified, respectable, venerable

و ق ع 1

وَقَّع [waqqaʕ] *v:* • **1.** to sign, affix one's signature to – المُدِير وَقَّع المَكتُوب لَو بَعَد؟ [ʔilmudi:r waqqaʕ ʔilmaktu:b law baʕad?] Has the director signed the letter yet? • **2.** to cause to sign, affix a signature – أُخُذ العَرِيضَة وَوَقِّعهُم كُلّهُم [ʔuxuð ʔilʕari:ða wwaqqiʕhum kullhum] Take the petition and have them all sign.
واقَع [wa:qaʕ] *v:* • **1.** to have sexual intercourse with – الطَّبِيب مِنَعَه يواقِع زَوجِتَه مُدَّة شَهَر [ʔiṭṭabi:b minaʕah ywa:qiʕ zawiǰtah muddat šahar] The doctor forbade him to have sexual intercourse with his wife for a month.
توَقَّع [twaqqaʕ] *v:* • **1.** to expect, anticipate – أَتوَقَّع يِجِي باكِر [ʔatwaqqaʕ yiǰi ba:čir] I expect him to come tomorrow.
مَوقِع [mawqiʕ] *n:* مَواقِع [mawa:qiʕ] *pl:* • **1.** place, location, site • **2.** position (mil.)
واقِع، الواقِع [wa:qiʕ, ʔilwa:qiʕ] *n:* • **1.** the facts, the truth – إحكِيلِي الواقِع [ʔiħči:li ʔilwa:qiʕ] Tell me the facts. الواقع، مالِي عِلاقَة بِهَالمَوضُوع [ʔilwa:qiʕ, ma:li ʕila:qa bhalmawḍu:ʕ] Actually, I have nothing to do with this matter.
تَوَقُّع [tawaqquʕ] *n:* • **1.** expectation, anticipation
توقِيع [tawqi:ʕ] *n:* تَواقِيع [tawa:qi:ʕ] *pl:* • **1.** signature
إيقاع [ʔi:qa:ʕ] *n:* • **1.** rhythm, percussion (musi.)

واقِعَة [wa:qiʕa] *n:* • **1.** fact, case of (birth, death), event, happening, accident, mishap
واقِع [wa:giʕ] *adj:* • **1.** fallen • **2.** down, down on one's luck – مِسكِين يِبَيِّن واقِع، حَتَّى فلُوس أكِل ما عِندَه [miski:n yibayyin wa:giʕ, ħatta flu:s ʔakil ma: ʕindah] It seems the poor guy's gone under. He doesn't even have money to eat.
مُوَقَّع [muwaqqaʕ] *adj:* • **1.** signed
واقِعِي [wa:qiʕi] *adj:* • **1.** real, actual, true – هاي قُصَّة واقِعِيَّة [ha:y quṣṣa wa:qiʕiyya] This is a true story.

و ق ع 2

وُقَع [wugaʕ] *v:* • **1.** to fall – هالسَّنَة وُقَع ثَلِج هوايَة بِالشِّمال [hassana wugaʕ θaliǰ hwa:ya biššima:l] This year a lot of snow fell in the north. بَسّ يوَقَع بِيدِي، أَمَوّتَه [bass yu:gaʕ bi:di, ʔamawwtah] If only he falls into my hands, I'll murder him. هِيكِي سَيّارَة ما تُوقَع بالإيد كُلّ وَقِت [hi:či sayya:ra ma: tu:gaʕ bilʔi:d kull wakit] Such a car doesn't come along every time. • **2.** to fall down, drop – الكِتاب وُقَع مِن إيدِي [ʔilkita:b wugaʕ min ʔi:di] The book fell from my hand. طَيّارَة وُقعَت يَمّ بَغداد [ṭiyya:ra wugʕat yamm baɣda:d] A plane went down near Baghdad. شَعرِي دَيُوقَع [šaʕri dayu:gaʕ] My hair is falling out. • **3.** to come in season, ripen, become available – الرُّمّان يوقَع بالخَرِيف [ʔirrumma:n yu:gaʕ bilxari:f] Pomegranates ripen in the fall. • **4.** to fall, pounce – اِلتَمَوا عَلَيه وَوُقعَوا بيه دَقّ [ʔiltamaw ʕali:h wwugʕaw bi:h dagg] They ganged up on him and beat him up. وُقَع بِالدِّجاج دَقّ وَخَلّصَه كُلَّه [wugaʕ biddiǰa:ǰ dagg wxallaṣah kullah] He dug into the chicken and finished it completely. يَوقَع مِن قَدَر [yu:gaʕ min qadar] to detract from the standing of, degrade, lower. يَعنِي يَوقَع مِن قَدرَك إذا تناوِشنِي المِلِح؟ [yaʕni yu:gaʕ min qadrak ʔiða tna:wišni ʔilmiliħ?] Do you think it'll degrade you if you pass me the salt?
• **5.** with عَلَى to be humble to, beg the pardon of – أَبُوك زَعلان عَلَيك. رُوح أوقَع عَلَيه وَصالحَه [ʔabu:k zaʕla:n ʕali:k. ru:ħ ʔu:gaʕ ʕali:h wṣa:lħah] Your father is angry at you. Go beg his pardon and make up with him. • **6.** with عَلَى or لـ to fall to, befall, come to, happen to – وُقَعلَه بَيت وَألِف دِينار [wugaʕlah bayt wʔalif dina:r] A house and a thousand dinars fell into his lap.
وَقَّع [waggaʕ] *v:* • **1.** to cause to fall – دِفَعنِي ووَقَّعنِي عَالقاع [difaʕni wwaggaʕni ʕalga:ʕ] He pushed me and knocked me down on the ground. وَقَّعنا طِيّارتَين لِلعَدُو [waggaʕna ṭiyya:rtayn lilʕadu] We downed two enemy planes. الله لا يوَقِّع أَحَّد بإيد هَالطَّبِيب [ʔallah la: ywaggiʕ ʔaħħad bʔi:d haṭṭabi:b] God forbid that anyone should fall into the hands of this doctor. راح يوَقِّع نَفسَه بوَرطَة [ra:ħ ywaggiʕ nafsah bwarṭa] He's going to get himself into a jam. • **2.** to drop – الخادمَة وَقّعَت الماعُون [ʔilxa:dma waggʕat ʔilma:ʕu:n] The maid dropped the dish.
توَقَّع [twaggaʕ] *v:* • **1.** to lower, humble, debase oneself – لِيش تِتوَقَّع عالنّاس؟ إذا الشُّرُوط مِتوَفرَة بِيك، يوَظّفُوك

[liːš titwaggaʕ ʕannaːs? ʔiða ʔiššuruːṭ mitwaffra biːk, ywaðððfuːk] Why do you lower yourself to people? If you meet the qualifications, they'll employ you.
وَقع، وُقُوع [waqiʕ, wuquːʕ] *n:* • **1.** falling
وَقعَة [wagʕa] *n:* وَقعات [wagʕaːt] *pl:* • **1.** a fall

و ق ف

وُقَف [wugaf] *v:* • **1.** to stop, halt, come to a standstill – لِيش السَّيّارَة وُقفَت؟ [liːš ʔissayyaːra wugfat?] Why did the car stop? الباص وين يوقَف؟ [ʔilpaːṣ wiːn yuːgaf?] Where does the bus stop? ساعتِي وُقفَت [saːʕti wugfat] My watch stopped. لَو أكُو فَدّ شِي بِالرّاديُو لَو المَحَطَّة وُقفت [law ʔaku fadd ši birraːdyu law ʔilmaħaṭṭa wugfat] Either there's something wrong with the radio or the station shut down. أُوقَف، خَلِّي أقُلَّك شِي [ʔuːgaf, xalliː ʔagullak ši] Wait, let me tell you something. • **2.** to stand up, rise, get up – لازِم تُوقَف مِن تِحكِي وِيّا الضّابُط [laːzim tuːgaf min tiħči wiyya ʔiððaːbuṭ] You must stand up when you talk with the officer. • **3.** to stand, take a position, place oneself, post oneself – أُوقَف بِباب الدُّكّان وَإنتَظرَه [ʔuːgaf bibaːb ʔiddukkaːn wʔintaðrah] Stand by the door of the shop and wait for him. أُوقفُوا إثنَين إثنَين [ʔuːgfuː ʔiθnayn ʔiθnayn] Stand two by two. وُقَف عَلَى راسِي. ما راح إلَى أن خَلَّصِت [wugaf ʕala raːsi. maː raːħ ʔila ʔan xallaṣit] He stood right over me. He didn't go away until I finished. كُلّما أرِيد أسَوِّي شِي، يوقَف بوجهِي [kullma ʔariːd ʔasawwiː ši, yuːgaf bwičči] Every time I want to do something, he stands in my way. • **4.** to come, fall, devolve – هَسَّة القَضِيَّة وُقفَت عَلِيك [hassa ʔilqaðiyya wugfat ʕaliːk] Now the matter is in your hands. المُزايدَة وُقفت عَلَيّا بِألِف دِينار [ʔilmuzaːyda wugfat ʕalayya bʔalif dinaːr] The bidding rested with me at a thousand dinars. البَيت وُقَف عَلَيّا بِألِف دِينار [ʔilbayt wugaf ʕalayya bʔalif dinaːr] The house fell to me for a thousand dinars. القَضِيَّة وُقفَت عَلَى فلُوس الطَّوابِع؛ مَحَّد دَيِدفَعها [ʔilqaðiyya wugfat ʕala fluːs ʔiṭṭawaːbiʕ; maħħad dayidfaʕha] The matter has halted over the money for the stamps; no one is paying it. • **5.** with لـ to stand up for, take a position in favor of, back, support – كُلّما تصِير عِندِي مُشكِلَة، يُوقفلِي [kullma tṣiːr ʕindi muškila, yuːgafli] Every time I have a problem, he stands up for me.
وِقَف [wagaf] *v:* • **1.** to stop, to stand
وَقَّف [waqqaf] *v:* • **1.** to detain, hold in custody, arrest – الشُّرطَة وَقّفت خَمِس طُلّاب [ʔiššurṭa waqqifat xamis ṭullaːb] The police detained five students.
وَقَّف [waggaf, wagguf] *v:* • **1.** to stop, halt, bring to a standstill – وَقُّف السَّيّارَة [wagguf ʔissayyaːra] Stop the car! أكُو دُوا يوَقُّف النَّزِيف؟ [ʔaku duwa ywagguf ʔinnaziːf?] Is there any medicine that can stop the bleeding? لا تخَلِّيه يِلغِي؛ وَقفَه عِند حَدَّه [laː txalliːh yilɣi; waggfah ʕind ħaddah] Don't let him go on talking; put him in his place. • **2.** to park – خَلِّي نوَقُّف السَّيّارَة هنا [xalliː nwagguf ʔissayyaːra hna] Let's park the car here. • **3.** to cause to stand, to place in an upright position – وَقُّف الجّاهِل وَخَلِّيه يمشِي [wagguf ʔijǰaːhil wxalliːh yimši] Stand the child up and let him walk. وَقُّف التَّلامِيذ حَسَب الطُّول [wagguf ʔittalaːmiːð ħasab ʔiṭṭuːl] Stand the students up according to height. • **4.** to post, position, station, place – قَبُل ما نخُشّ لِلبَيت وَقَّف شُرطِي بِالباب الوَرّانِي حَتَّى لا حَدّ يِنهِزِم [gabul maː nxušš lilbayt waggaf šurṭi bilbaːb ʔilwarraːni ħatta laː ħadd yinhizim] Before we enter the house put a policeman at the back door so no one can escape.
توَقَّف [twaqqaf] *v:* • **1.** to be detained, arrested – خَمِس مُتَظاهِرِين توَقفَوا [xamis mutaðaːhiriːn twaqqfaw] Five demonstrators were arrested. • **2.** to depend, be dependent, conditional – تِتوَقَّف القَضِيَّة عَلَى مُوافقتَه [titwaqqaf ʔilqaðiyya ʕala muwaːfaqtah] The matter depends on his approval. بَقائَه بِالحُكُم مِتوَقُّف عَلَى نَتِيجَة الانتِخابات [baqaːʔah bilħukum mitwaqquf ʕala natiːǰat ʔilʔintixaːbaːt] His remaining in power is dependent on the result of the election.
تواقَف [twaːgaf] *v:* • **1.** to reach a stand-off, tie, draw with each other – لِعَبنا الشِّطرَنج طُول اللَّيل وَبالأخِير تواقفنا [liʕabna ʔiššiṭranǰ ṭuːl ʔillayl wbilʔaxiːr twaːgafna] We played chess all evening long and in the end we reached a stand-off. • **2.** to argue, have a dispute – تواقفِت وِيّاه عَلَى دِينار [twaːgafit wiyyaːh ʕala dinaːr] I argued with him over a dinar.
انوُقَف [ʔinwugaf, ʔinwuqaf] *v:* • **1.** pass. of وُقَف to be stopped – هَالكُرسِي مِتعَتَع. ما يِنوُقُف عَلِيه [halkursi mtaʕtaʕ. maː yinwuguf ʕaliːh] This chair is wobbly. It can't be stood upon. الشَّمِس حارَّة ما يِنوُقُف جَوّاها [ʔiššamis ħaːrra maː yinwuguf ǰawwaːha] The sun is so hot one can't stand in it.
وَقُف [waquf] *n:* أوقاف [ʔawqaːf] *pl:* • **1.** wakf, religious endowment • **2.** unalienable property – خَلِّينا نِلعَب. قابِل السّاحَة وَقُف عَلِيك؟ [xalliːna nilʕab. qaːbil ʔissaːħa waquf ʕaliːk?] Let us play. Do you think the court is yours alone?
مَوقِف [mawqif] *n:* مَواقِف [mawaːqif] *pl:* • **1.** position, stand, opinion, attitude • **2.** stopping place, bus stop • **3.** detention cell, place of temporary custody
وَقفَة [wagfa, waqfa] *n:* وَقفات [wagfaːt, waqfaːt] *pl:* • **1.** stop, halt • **2.** stance, position, posture • **3.** stand, position, stance – وُقَفلِي خُوش وَقفَة وَما جاز إلّا حَصَّلّي التَّرفِيع [wugafli xuːš wagfa wama ǰaːz ʔilla ħaṣṣalli ʔittarfiːʕ] He took a strong stand for me and didn't let up until he'd got me the raise. • **4.** market place, open square for vendors
وَقّاف [waggaːf] *n:* وَقّافَة [waggaːfa] *pl:* • **1.** attendant, functionary at a reception or celebration
تَوَقُّف [tawaqquf] *n:* • **1.** stop, standstill, pause, stopover, cessation • **2.** hesitation
وُقُوف [wuguːf, wuquːf] *n:* • **1.** parking • **2.** standing, stopping, halting

و

إيقاف [ʔiqaːf] *n:* • **1.** stopping, halting • **2.** arresting, arrest
تَوقِيف [tawqiːf] *n:* • **1.** imprisonment, stopping, arresting • **2.** detention, arrest
واقِف [waːgif] *adj:* • **1.** standing, upright, erect • **2.** standing still, motionless, at rest • **3.** pl. واقفِين bystander, spectator
موَقَّف [mwaqqaf] *adj:* • **1.** under arrest
مَوقُوف [mawquːf] *adj:* • **1.** arrested, detained, held in custody • **2.** prisoner, person under arrest
مِتوَقُّف [mitwaqquf] *adj:* • **1.** arrested, held • **2.** contingent (upon)

و ق ي 1

توَقَّى [twaqqaː] *v:* • **1.** to protect oneself, be on guard, be wary – توَقَّى تَرَة يِحكِي بقُفاك [twaqqaː tara yiħči bgufaːk] Beware of him because he'll say things behind your back. توَقَّى مِنَّه تَرَة هذا بِيه سِل [twaqqaː minnah tara haːðaː biːh sill] Protect yourself from him, because he has tuberculosis.
اِتَّقَى [ʔittiqaː] *v:* • **1.** to avoid, beware of – اِتِّقِي الشَّرّ. لا تِحكِي وِيّاه [ʔittiqi ʔiššarr. laː tiħči wiyyaːh] Stay out of trouble. Don't talk to him. اِتِّقِي شَرَّه لِهذا [ʔittiqi šarrah lhaːða] Keep away from that guy. • **2.** to fear (God) – اِتِّقِي الله وَلا تسَوِّي هِيكِي [ʔittiqi ʔallah wlaː tsawwiː hiːči] Fear God and don't do that. • **3.** to protect oneself, be on guard, be wary
وُقَة [wuga] *n:* وُقات [wugaːt] *pl:* • **1.** a pad or block of wood put on the head when carrying objects
تَقوَى [taqwa] *n:* • **1.** piety, devoutness, godliness
وِقايَة [wiqaːya] *n:* • **1.** protective covering • **2.** prevention, protection, precaution
تَقِي [taqi] *adj:* • **1.** devout, pious, God-fearing
وِقائِي [wiqaːʔi] *adj:* • **1.** preventive • **2.** protective
أَتقَى [ʔatqaː] *comparative adjective:* • **1.** more or most devout, pious

و ق ي 2

وقِيَّة، أُوقِيَّة [wgiyya, ʔuːgiyya] *n:* وقِيّات، وقايَة، أواق [wgiyyaːt, wgaːya, ʔawaːg] *pl:* • **1.** حُقَّة [ħuqqa] an oka, a unit of weight now equal to 1.28 kilograms (approx. 2.75 lbs.), now standardized at one kilogram – وقِيَّة إسطَنبُول [wgiyyat ʔistạnbuːl] an Istanbul oka, equal to approx. 320 grams (.7 lb.).

و ك ء

تَكَّى [taččaː] *v:* • **1.** to lean, prop up – تَكِّي كِيس التِّمَّن عَلَى فَدّ شِي حَتَّى ما يُوقَع [tačči kiːs ʔittimman ʕala fadd ši ħatta maː yuːgaʕ] Lean the sack of rice against something so it won't fall over. تَكِّيلَه لِلمَرِيض حَتَّى يُفحَصَه الطِّبِيب [taččiːlah lilmariːḍ ħatta yufħạṣah ʔiṭṭabiːb] Support the sick man so the doctor can examine him.
وَكَّى [waččaː] *v:* • **1.** to dock, berth, tie up – الماطُور راح يوَكِّي يَمّ البَلَم [ʔilmaːṭuːr raːħ ywačči yamm ʔilbalam] The motor barge is going to dock next to the sailing barge. • **2.** to camp, make camp – البَدو وَكُّوا بَرَّة الوِلايَة [ʔilbadw waččaw barra ʔilwlaːya] The Bedouins camped outside the town. • **3.** to come to rest, perch, alight, roost – الطَّير طار وَوَكَّى عَلَى شِجرَة عالِيَة [ʔiṭṭiːr ṭaːr wwaččaː ʕala šijra ʕaːlya] The bird flew up and perched in a high tree.
توَكَّى [twaččaː] *v:* • **1.** to lean, support oneself – ما يِقدَر يقُوم إذا ما يِتوَكَّى عَلَى شِي [maː yigdar yguːm ʔiða maː yitwaččaː ʕala ši] He can't get up if he doesn't support himself on something. ما يِقدَر يِمشِي إذا ما يِتوَكَّى عَلَى عوجِيَّة [maː yigdar yimši ʔiða maː yitwaččaː ʕala ʕuːčiyya] He can't walk without leaning on a cane.
اِنتِكَى [ʔintičaː] *v:* • **1.** to lean, rest one's weight – ما يِقدَر يوقَف؛ لازِم يِنتِكِي عَالحايِط [maː yigdar yuːgaf; laːzim yintiči ʕalħaːyiṭ] He can't stand up; he'll have to lean against the wall. خَلِّي المُخَدَّة وَراك وَانتِكِي عَليها [xalliː lumxadda waraːk wʔintiči ʕaliːha] Put the pillow behind you and lean back against it.
تَكوَة [tačwa] *n:* تَكوات [tačwaːt] *pl:* • **1.** prop, support, stay • **2.** back (of a seat)
توَكِّي [twičči] *n:* • **1.** leaning
مِتوَكِي [mitwači] *adj:* • **1.** leaning (on), supporting oneself

و ك ب

مَوكِب [mawkib] *n:* مَواكِب [mawaːkib] *pl:* • **1.** (religious) procession, cortege, pageant, parade

و ك د

See also: ء ك د

و ك ر

وَكَّر [wakkar] *v:* • **1.** to light, perch, come to rest – طَيرنا وَكَّر عَلَى سَطِحكُم [ṭiːrna wakkar ʕala saṭiħkum] Our pigeon lit on your roof.
وَكِر [wakir] *n:* أَوكار [ʔawkaːr] *pl:* • **1.** bird's nest, nest, den
موَكِّر [mwakkir] *adj:* • **1.** settled, nested

و ك س

وِكَس [wikas] *v:* • **1.** to reduce the probability of – وِكَس قَضِيَّة تَرفِيعِي [wikas qaðiyyat tarfiːʕi] He scuttled my chances for promotion.
وَكِس [wakis] *n:* • **1.** degrading, humiliating
وَكسَة [waksa] *n:* وَكسات [waksaːt] *pl:* • **1.** degrading, humiliating, shameful deed
مَوكُوس [mawkuːs] *adj:* • **1.** Unsuccessful

و ك ل

وَكَّل [wakkal] *v:* • **1.** to appoint as agent, authorize, empower – وَكَّلنِي أَبِيع البَيت مالَه [wakkalni ʔabiːʕ

ʔilbayt maːlah] He authorized me to sell his house. • **2.** to engage as counsel – راح توَكِّل مُحامِي وَإلّا لا؟ [raːħ twakkil muħaːmi waʔilla laː?] Will you engage a lawyer or not?

توَكَّل [twakkal] *v:* • **1.** to act as counsel – ماكُو مُحامِي يِقبَل يِتوَكَّل عَنَّه [maːku muħaːmi yiqbal yitwakkal ʕannah] There's no lawyer that'll agree to represent him. • **2.** with عَلَى to trust in, put one's confidence in – توَكَّل عَلَى الله [twakkal ʕala ʔallah] Trust in God.

اِتِّكَل [ʔittikal] *v:* • **1.** to rely, depend, place one's trust – آنِي أتِّكِل عَليك بهالقَضِيَّة [ʔaːni ʔattikil ʕaliːk bhalqaðiyya] I'm depending on you in this matter.

اِنتِكَل [ʔintikal, ʔintičal] *v:* • **1.** to rely (on), depend (on), place one's trust (in)

وَكِيل [wakiːl] *n:* وُكَلاء [wukalaːʔ] *pl:* • **1.** deputy, vice- – وَكِيل وَزِير [wakiːl waziːr] deputy minister, under-secretary of a ministry. • **2.** agent, representative – وَكِيلَك الله، هَذا حَقَّك [wakiːlak ʔallah, haːða ħaqqak] As God is your witness, this is your right.

وَكالَة [wakaːla] *n:* وَكالات [wakaːlaːt] *pl:* • **1.** power of attorney • **2.** agency • **3.** deputyship, proxy – وَزِير بِالوَكالَة [waziːr bilwakaːla] minister in the interim, acting minister.

مِتِّكِل [mittikil] *adj:* • **1.** dependent

و ل د

وِلَد [wilad] *v:* • **1.** to give birth, bear a child – البارحَة، مَرتِي وِلدَت بِالمُستَشفى [ʔilbaːrħa, marti wildat bilmustašfa] Yesterday, my wife had a baby in the hospital.

وَلَّد [wallad] *v:* • **1.** to generate – يوَلِّدُون كُلّ الكَهرَباء اللّي تِستَعمِلها المَدِينَة بِهالمَعمَل [ywalliduːn kull ʔilkahrabaːʔ ʔilli tistaʕmilah ʔilmadiːna bhalmaʕmal] They generate all the electricity used by the city in this plant. • **2.** to engender, breed, cause – هَالقَضِيَّة راح توَلِّد نَتايِج مُو زينَة [halqaðiyya raːħ twallid nataːyiǰ muː ziːna] This affair's going to produce unfavorable results. • **3.** to deliver, assist in childbirth – يا جِدَّة وَلِّدَتها؟ [yaː ǰiddah wallidatha?] Which midwife delivered her? هَالجِّدَّة وَلِّدَتنا كُلّنا [haǰǰidda wallidatna kullna] This midwife delivered us all.

توَلَّد [twallad] *v:* • **1.** to be engendered, caused, occasioned – الطّاعُون يِتوَلَّد مِن الفار [ʔiṭṭaːʕuːn yitwallad min ʔilfaːr] Plague is caused by mice.

توالَد [twaːlad] *v:* • **1.** to propagate, reproduce, multiply – الجِّرِيدِيَّة تِتوالَد بسُرعَة [ʔiǰǰiriːdiyya titwaːlad bsurʕa] Rodents multiply quickly.

اِنوِلَد [ʔinwilad] *v:* • **1.** to be born – اِنوِلَد يوم الجُّمعَة الظُّهُر [ʔinwilad yuːm ʔiǰǰumʕa ʔiððuhur] He was born Friday at noon.

وَلَد [walad] *n:* وُلِد، وِلِد، أولاد [wulid, wilid, ʔawlaːd] *pl:* • **1.** son, child, descendant, offspring • **2.** boy • **3.** knave, jack (in cards)

والِد [waːlid] *n:* وَالِدَين [waːlidayn] *pl:* • **1.** parent, father • **2.** الوَالِدَين one's parents

مُوَلِّد [muwallid] *n:* مُوَلِّدات [muwallidaːt] *pl:* • **1.** generator, dynamo

وِلادَة [wilaːda] *n:* • **1.** childbirth, delivery, birth – تاريخ الوِلادَة [taːriːx ʔilwilaːda] date of birth.

مِيلاد [miːlaːd] *n:* مَوالِيد [mawaːliːd] *pl:* • **1.** birth • **2.** time of birth, birthday, nativity – عِيد مِيلاد [ʕiːd miːlaːd] birthday celebration. عِيد المِيلاد [ʕiːd ʔilmiːlaːd] Christmas. قَبل المِيلاد [qabl ʔilmiːlaːd] before Christ, B. C.

والِدَة [waːlida] *n:* والِدات [waːlidaːt] *pl:* • **1.** mother

تَولِيد [tawliːd] *n:* • **1.** begetting, generating, producing • **2.** midwifery, obstetrics

مَوالِيد [mawaːliːd] *n:* • **1.** birthday

مَولُود [mawluːd] *adj:* مَوالِيد [mawaːliːd] *pl:* • **1.** born • **2.** (pl. only) those born on a given year, members of an age group. – وزارَة الدِّفاع دِعَت ما والِيد سَنَة أَلِف وَتِسِع مِيَّة وتِسعِين لخِدمَة العَلَم [wizaːrat ʔiddifaːʕ diʕat maː waːliːd sanat ʔalif wtisiʕ miyya witisʕiːn lxidmat ʔilʕalam] The Ministry of Defense called the 1990 age group to service of the flag. • **3.** as Noun: newborn baby, infant

مِيلادِي [miːlaːdi] *adj:* • **1.** birthday- • **2.** relating to the birth of Christ • **3.** after Christ, A.D – سَنَة أَلِف وَتِسِع مِيَّة وَثمانيَة وتِسعِين مِيلادِي [sanat ʔalif wtisiʕ miyya wθmaːnya witisʕiːn miːlaːdi] the year 1998 A. D.

و ل ع

توَلَّع [twallaʕ] *v:* • **1.** to be or become passionately fond, madly in love – مِن شاف جَمالها وَسِمَع حَكيها، توَلَّع بيها [min šaːf ǰamaːlha wsimaʕ ħačiːha, twallaʕ biːha] When he saw her beauty and heard her talk, he fell madly in love with her.

وَلَع [walaʕ] *n:* • **1.** passion, ardent love or desire – عِندَه وَلَع بِالمُوسِيقَى [ʕindah walaʕ bilmuːsiːqa] He has a passion for music.

تَوَلُّع [tawalluʕ] *n:* • **1.** passionate love, ardent desire, craving, passion

مُولَع [muːlaʕ] *adj:* • **1.** passionately fond, enamored – هُوَّ مُولَع بِالنَّحِت [huwwa muːlaʕ binnaħit] He's terribly fond of sculpture.

مِتوَلِّع [mitwalliʕ] *adj:* • **1.** in love, crazy with love, infatuated

و ل م

والَم [waːlam] *v:* • **1.** to suit, fit, match, be appropriate for – دُولَة واحِد والَم اللّاخ. ثنَينهُم خَرا [ðuːla waːħid waːlam ʔillaːx. θnaynhum xara] Each of them is a good match for the other. They're both scum. • **2.** to suit, be agreeable to – إذا الوَضِع ما دَيوالمَك، لِيش ما تِستَقِيل؟ [ʔiða ʔilwaðiʕ maː daywaːlmak, liːš maː tistiqiːl?] If the situation isn't agreeable to you, why don't you resign? هَالدُّوا ما دَيوالِمنِي [hadduwa maː daywaːlimni] This medicine doesn't agree with me.

توالَم [twaːlam] *v:* • **1.** to get along, go well, fit in with each other – جَارنَا وَمَرتَه ما يِتوالمُون [ǰaːrna wmartah maː yitwaːlmuːn] Our neighbor and his wife don't get along with each other.

وَلِيمَة [waliːma] *n:* وَلائِم [walaːʔim] *pl:* • **1.** banquet

مُوالَمَة [muwaːlama] *n:* • **1.** appropriateness, properness

مُوالِم [muwaːlim] *adj:* • **1.** harmonious, fit

متوالِم [mitwaːlim] *adj:* • **1.** harmonious

و ل و

وَلَو [walaw] *int:* • **1.** although, even though – ما راح أكُل هَسَّة وَلَو جُوعان [maː raːħ ʔakul hassa walaw ǰuːʕaːn] I'm not going to eat now even though I'm hungry.

و ل ي

ولِى [wilaː] *v:* • **1.** to catch, corner, gain ascendency over, get the upper hand over, get in one's power – وُلَيتَه يوم المَعاش وأخَذِت فلُوسِي مِنَّه [wuliːtah yuːm ʔilmaʕaːš wʔaxaðit fluːsi minnah] I cornered him on payday and took my money from him. هَالمَرَّة خَلَّصِت، لَكِن أولِيك غير مَرَّة [halmarra xallaṣit, laːkin ʔawliːk ɣiːr marra] You got away this time, but I'll catch you another time. إذا يولِي واحِد، ما يهِدَّه [ʔiða yuːli waːħid, maː yhiddah] If he ever gets someone in his power, he won't leave him alone. اِضطَرّيت أدفَع هَالسِّعِر لِأنّ ولانِي غير ولِيَة [ʔiðṭarriːt ʔadfaʕ hassiʕir liʔann wilaːni ɣayr wilya] I had to pay that price because he left me without any choice.

وَلَّى [wallaː] *v:* • **1.** to get out, leave, go away – جِيبِيلِي وُصلَة خُبُز وَإستِكان شاي حَتَّى أوَلِّي [ǰiːbiːli wuṣlat xubuz wʔistikaːn čaːy ħatta ʔawalli] Bring me a piece of bread and a cup of tea so I can get out of here. بُقَوا نُصّ ساعَة وَبَعدين وَلّوا [buqaw nuṣṣ saːʕa wbaʕdiːn wallaw] They stayed a half hour and then went away. كان يلاحِق البنَيَّة وَقالَتلَه "لِيش ما توَلِّي؟" [čaːn ylaːħig ʔilbnayya wgaːlatlah "liːš maː twalli? "] He was following the girl and she said to him 'Why don't you get lost? ' • **2.** to appoint as governor, ruler, administrator – السُّلطان وَلَّى واحِد مِن أقرِبائَه عالخِلافَة [ʔissulṭaːn wallaː waːħid min ʔaqribaːʔah ʕalxilaːfa] The sultan appointed one of his relatives to the caliphate.

توَلَّى [twallaː] *v:* • **1.** to assume control of, to take charge of – توَلَّى الحُكُم مِن كان عُمرَه واحِد وَعِشرِين سَنَة [twallaː ʔilħukum min čaːn ʕumrah waːħid wʕišriːn sana] He took over the rule when he was twenty-one years old. فَصِيلنا يِتوَلَّى الحِراسَة هاللَّيلَة [faṣiːlna yitwallaː ʔilħiraːsa hallayla] Our platoon is in charge of guard duty tonight.

توَالَى [twaːlaː] *v:* • **1.** to follow in succession, come one after the other – توالَت عَليه المَصايِب [twaːlat ʕaliːh ʔilmaṣaːyib] Misfortunes befell him, one immediately after the other.

انولَى [ʔinwilaː] *v:* • **1.** to be caught, be cornered – اِنولَى بالبِستان مِن كان دَيِشتُغُل وَما شايِل سلاح [ʔinwilaː bilbistaːn min čaːn dayištuɣul wma šaːyil slaːħ] He was cornered in the orchard when he was working, and was unarmed.

اِستَولَى [ʔistawlaː] *v:* • **1.** to seize control, get control, take possession of – الجَّيش اِستَولَى عالحُكُم [ʔiǰǰayš ʔistawlaː ʕalħukum] The army seized power. اِستَولَوا عَالمَدِينَة [ʔistawlaw ʕalmadiːna] They captured the city. اِستَولَت الحُكُومَة عَلَى أملاكَه [ʔistawlat ʔilħukuːma ʕala ʔamlaːkah] The government confiscated his property.

وَلِيّ [waliyy] *n:* • **1.** custodian, sponsor, legally responsible person

ولِيَة [wilya] *n:* • **1.** advantage, opportunity for power, authority, control – لِزَم ولِيَة [lizam wilya] to seize the advantage, get the upper hand. لِزَم ولِيَة وراد دِينارَين عَلَيها [lizam wilya wraːd dinaːrayn ʕaliːha] He got the upper hand and wanted two dinars for the thing. شدَعوَة الكِيلُو بِدينار؟ هَذِي ولِيَة لِأنّ تُعرُف ماكُو غير مَخزَن هنا [šdaʕwa ʔilkiːlu bdinaːr? haːði wilya liʔann tuʕruf maːku ɣiːr maxzan hna] What do you mean a dinar per kilo? That's taking advantage just because you know there's no other store here.

مَولَى [mawla] *n:* • **1.** master, lord • **2.** /with possessive suffix/ مَولانَا , مَولايَا a sarcastic form of address – مَولانا، إذا تِتلاكَم ويّايا، ما تقاوُم أكثَر مِن جَولَة وحدَة [mawlaːna, ʔiða titlaːkam wiyyaːya, maː tqaːwum ʔakθar min ǰawla wiħda] My dear sir, if you box with me, you won't last more than one round.

والِي [waːli] *n:* وِلاة [willaːt] *pl:* • **1.** governor

وَلاء [walaːʔ] *n:* • **1.** friendship, amity, loyalty

وِلايَة، ولايَة [wilaːya, wlaːya] *n:* ولايات [wlaːyaːt, wilaːyaːt] *pl:* • **1.** sovereignty • **2.** state – الوِلايات المُتَّحِدَة [ʔilwilaːyaːt ʔilmuttaħida] the United states. • **3.** city, municipality, or other administrative district headed by a وَالِي

أولَوِيَّة [ʔawlawiyya] *n:* • **1.** priority

مُوالاة [muwaːlaːt] *n:* • **1.** friendship, constancy

اِستِيلاء [ʔistiːlaːʔ] *n:* • **1.** appropriation, taking possession, capture, conquest

مِتوَلِّي [mitwalli] *adj:* • **1.** entrusted, in charge, having responsibility • **2.** pl. مِتوَلِّيَّة administrator of a religious endowment

أولَى [ʔawla] *comparative adjective:* • **1.** more or most worthy, deserving

و م س

مُومِس [muːmis, muːmisa] *n:* مُومِس، مُومِسات [muːmis, muːmisaːt] *pl:* • **1.** prostitute

و م ض

وُمَض [wumað̣] *v:* • **1.** to lighten, to glow, to flash, to gleam

وَمِيض [wamiːð̣] *n:* • **1.** sparkle, twinkle, brightness • **2.** lightning

و

و م ي

أومَى [ʔawma:] *v:* • **1.** to signal, beckon, motion – أومِيلَه حَتَّى يوقَف [ʔu:mi:lah ħatta yu:gaf] Signal to him to stop. ما يقُول شِي. بَسّ يُومِي براسَه [ma: ygu:l ši. bass yu:mi bra:sah] He won't say anything. He just nods his head. • **2.** to indicate, point out – ما دَأشُوفَه. أومِيلِي وينَه [ma: daʔašu:fah. ʔu:mi:li wi:nah] I don't see him. Point out where he is for me.

و ن ن

وَنّ [wann] *v:* • **1.** to moan, groan – المَرضَى كُلّهُم دَيوِنُّون [ʔilmarḍa kullhum daywinnu:n] All the sick people are moaning.

وَنّ [wann] *n:* • **1.** groan

وَنَّة [wanna] *n:* وَنّات [wanna:t] *pl:* • **1.** moan, groan

وِنين [wini:n] *n:* • **1.** groan

و ن و ن

وَنوَن [wanwan] *v:* • **1.** to moan, repeatedly or continually – شبيه دَيوَنوِن؟ أكُو شِي يُوجعَه؟ [šbi:h daywanwin? ʔaku ši yu:ǰʕah?] What's he moaning about? Is something hurting him?

و ه ب

وِهَب [wihab] *v:* • **1.** to donate, grant, give, make a gift of – صَدِيقَه بين مُدَّة وَمُدَّة يُوهِبلَه فَدّ شِي [ṣadi:qah bi:n mudda wmudda yu:hiblah fadd ši] From time to time his friend makes him a present of something.

هِبَة [hiba] *n:* هِبات [hiba:t] *pl:* • **1.** gift, present, donation – هَالسّاعَة هُوَّ ما إشتِراها. إجَتَّه هِبَة [hassa:ʕa huwwa ma: ʔištira:ha. ʔiǰattah hiba] He didn't buy this watch. It came to him as a gift.

مَوهِبَة [mawhiba] *n:* مَواهِب [mawa:hib] *pl:* • **1.** talent, gift – عِندَه مَوهِبَة بِالرَّسِم [ʕindah mawhiba birrasim] He has a talent for drawing.

واهِب [wa:hib] *adj:* • **1.** giver, donor

وَهّابِي [waha:bi] *adj:* • **1.** Wahabite, Wahabi (religious sect in Saudi Arabia)

مَوهُوب [mawhu:b] *adj:* • **1.** talented, gifted – فَنّان مَوهُوب [fanna:n mawhu:b] a talented artist.

و ه د ن

وَهدَن [wahdan] *v:* • **1.** to mislead, lead astray – ظَلّ يمدَح السَّيّارَة إلَى أن وَهدَنِّي وَخَلانِي أشتِريها [ðall yimdaħ ʔissayya:ra ʔila ʔan wahdanni wxalla:ni ʔaštiri:ha] He kept on praising the car until he misled me and made me buy it. أبُويا وَهدَنِّي بِالزَّواج [ʔabu:ya wahdanni bizzawa:ǰ] My father conned me into marriage. • **2.** to confuse – إنتَ، مِن حِكِيت، وَهدَنِتنِي [ʔinta, min ħiči:t, wahdanitni] When you spoke up, you made me lose track.

توَهدَن [twahdan] *v:* • **1.** to be confused – آنِي عَلَى طُول أتوَهدَن بِالإمتِحان [ʔa:ni ʕala ṭu:l ʔatwahdan bilʔimtiħa:n] I always get mixed up on the exam. • **2.** to make a mistake – لا يكُون تِتوَهدَن وتروح لِهالطَّبِيب تَرَة ما يِفتِهِم [la: yku:n titwahdan wtru:ħ lihaṭṭabi:b tara ma: yiftihim] Don't make the mistake of going to this doctor because he doesn't know his business. إشخُط هالعِبارَة. آنِي توَهدَنِت [ʔišxuṭ halʕiba:ra. ʔa:ni twahdanit] Cross out this phrase. I made a mistake. لا تِشتِريها تَرَة تِتوَهدَن بِيها [la: tištiri:ha tara titwahdan bi:ha] Don't buy it or you'll get stuck with it.

مِتوَهدِن [mitwahdin] *adj:* • **1.** confused

و ه س

وَهَّس [wahhas] *v:* • **1.** to worry, feel uneasy, have doubts – لا توَهِّس؛ ماكُو شِي عَلَى إبنَك [la: twahhis; ma:ku ši ʕala ʔibnak] Don't worry; nothing will happen to your son.

واهِس، وَهِس [wa:his, wahis] *n:* • **1.** concern, interest, yen, desire – مِن أقعُد يَمّها، يصِيرلِي واهِس [min ʔagʕud yammha, yṣi:rli wa:his] When I sit near her, I feel desire. إلَك واهِس ترُوح لِلسِّينَما؟ [ʔilak wa:his tru:ħ lissinama?] Are you interested in going to the movies? إبنَك واهسَه بِاللِّعِب، مُو بِالدِّراسَة [ʔibnak wa:hsah billiʕib, mu: biddira:sa] Your son's interest is in playing, not in studying. تِقدَر تسَوِّيلَه واهِس يِرُوح وِيّانَا؟ [tigdar tsawwi:lah wa:his yiru:ħ wiyya:na?] Can you talk him into going with us? بِحَكيَك هَذا، سَوَّيتلِي واهِس. راح أشتِريها [bħačyak ha:ða, sawwaytli wa:his. ra:ħ ʔaštiri:ha] With that talk you've given me the urge. I'll buy it.

و ه م

تِهَم [tiham] *v:* • **1.** to accuse, charge – لِيش دَتِتهِم صَدِيقَك؟ [li:š datithim ṣadi:qak?] Why are you accusing your friend? الشُّرطَة تِهمَتَه بِالبوقَة [ʔiššurṭa tihmatah bilbu:ga] The police charged him with the theft. راد يشُوف اللِّي تاهمَه [ra:d yšu:f ʔilli ta:hmah] He wanted to see whoever accused him.

وَهَّم [wahham] *v:* • **1.** to confuse, disorient – ما عِرَفت البَيت لِأنّ صُبغَه الجِّدِيد وَهَّمنِي [ma: ʕiraft ʔilbayt liʔann ṣubɣah ʔiǰǰdi:d wahhamni] I didn't recognize the house because its new paint fooled me. خَلِّينِي أحسِب الفلُوس. لا توَهِّمنِي [xalli:ni ʔaħsib ʔilflu:s. la: twahhimni] Let me count the money. Don't confuse me. آنِي كِنت أعرُف الجَّواب، لَكِن اللِّي وَرايا وَهَّمنِي [ʔa:ni čint ʔaʕruf ʔiǰǰawa:b, la:kin ʔilli wara:ya wahhamni] I knew the answer, but the guy behind me mixed me up.

توَهَّم [twahham] *v:* • **1.** to make a mistake, get the wrong idea, become confused – لا يكُون تِتوَهَّم وَتِقبَل الوَظِيفَة [la: yku:n titwahham wtiqbal ʔilwaḍi:fa] Beware of making a mistake and taking the job. توَهَّمِت وَدَخَّلِت هَالمَبلَغ بِحسابَك [twahhamit wdaxxalit halmablaɣ biħsa:bak] I made an error and entered this amount in your account. العَفو. توَهَّمِت بِيك. عَبالِي صَدِيقِي [ʔilʕafw. twahhamit bi:k. ʕaba:li ṣadi:qi] Pardon me. I made a mistake. I thought you were my friend.

اِنتِهَم [ʔintiham] *v:* • **1.** to be accused, charged – اِنتِهَم بالقَتِل [ʔintiham bilqatil] He was accused of murder.

و

اِتَّهَم [ʔittiham] *v:* • **1.** to accuse, charge – اِتَّهَم كُلّ المُوظَّفِين اللّي يِشتُغلُون وِيّاه [ʔittiham kull ʔilmuwaððafiːn ʔilli yištuɣluːn wiyyaːh] He accused all the officials who work with him. اِتِّهموُه بِالبوقَة [ʔittihmuːh bilbuːga] They accused him of the theft.
وَهَم [waham] *n:* أَوهام [ʔawhaːm] *pl:* • **1.** delusion, fancy, erroneous impression • **2.** hallucination
تُهمَة [tuhma] *n:* تُهَم [tuham] *pl:* • **1.** accusation, charge
وَهمَة [wihma] *n:* وِهمات [wihmaːt] *pl:* • **1.** mistake, error – رَجِّع الغَراض. صارَت وِهمَة [rajjiʕ ʔilɣaraːð. ṣaːrat wihma] Bring back the things. There's been a mix-up.
اِتِّهام [ʔittihaːm] *n:* اِتِّهامات [ʔittihaːmaːt] *pl:* • **1.** accusation, charge • **2.** indictment
تَوَهُّم [tawahhum] *n:* • **1.** suspicion, imagination
وَهمِي [wahmi] *adj:* • **1.** imaginary – خَطّ الاستِواء خَطّ وَهمِي [xaṭṭ ʔilʔistiwaːʔ xaṭṭ wahmi] The equator is an imaginary line. • **2.** fictitious – طَرزان شَخِص وَهمِي [ṭarzaːn šaxiṣ wahmi] Tarzan is a fictitious person.
مُتَّهَم [muttaham] *adj:* • **1.** accused, charged • **2.** indicted
تاهِم [taːhim] *adj:* • **1.** accusing • **2.** accuser
وَهمان [wahmaːn] *adj:* • **1.** confused, mixed up, mistaken
مَتهُوم [mathuːm] *adj:* • **1.** suspected, charged (with a crime)
مِتوَهِّم [mitwahhim] *adj:* • **1.** mistaken

و ه و س

وَهوَس [wahwas] *v:* • **1.** to hesitate, vacillate, feel doubtful, uncertain, unsure – اِشتِرِيها. لا تَوَهوِس [ʔištiriːha. laː twahwis] Buy it. Don't be indecisive. لا توَهوِس، السَّيّارَة ما بِيها شِي [laː twahwis, ʔissayyaːra maː biːha ši] Don't worry, there's nothing wrong with the car.
وِهواسِي [wihwaːsi] *adj:* • **1.** doubtful, unsure • **2.** as Noun, a person who is unable to make decisions

و ه و ه

توَهوَه [twahwah] *v:* • **1.** to hesitate, have doubts – لا تِتوَهوَه؛ لَو تِجِي وِيّانا لَو خَلِّينا نرُوح [laː titwahwah; law tiji wiyyaːna law xalliːna nruːħ] Make up your mind; either go with us or let us go. شبِيك مِتوَهوِه؟ قُلِّي شتِرِيد [šbiːk mitwahwih? gulli šitriːd] Why are you hesitating? Tell me what you want.
مِتوَهوِه [mitwahwih] *adj:* • **1.** timid

و و

واو [waːw] *n:* • **1.** name of the letter

و و ي

واوِي [waːwi] *n:* واوِيَّة [waːwiyya] *pl:* • **1.** jackal

و ي ح

واحَة [waːħa] *n:* واحات [waːħaːt] *pl:* • **1.** oasis

و ي ر

وايَر [waːyar] *n:* وايَرات [waːyaraːt] *pl:* • **1.** wire

و ي ص

واص [waːṣ] *v:* • **1.** to chirp, peep – فَرخ الدِّجاجَة يوِيص مِن يِطلَع مِن البَيضَة [farx ʔiddijaːja ywiːṣ min yiṭlaʕ min ʔilbayða] The baby chick chirps when it comes out of the egg.
وَيص [wiːṣ] *n:* • **1.** peeping

و ي ل [1]

ويل [wayl, wiːl] *n:* • **1.** distress, woe – ويلِي عَلَيه، أَويلِي عَلَيه [wiːli ʕaliːh, ʔawiːli ʕaliːh] Poor fellow, I'm so sorry for him!
أَوَيلاه، أَوَيلاخ [ʔawaylaːh, ʔawaylaːx] *int:* • **1.** Oh, Misery! Woe is me! – أَوَيلاه! شلُون أَقدَر أَعِيش بِلا أَصدِقاء؟ [ʔawaylaːh! šluːn ʔagdar ʔaʕiːš bila ʔaṣdiqaːʔ?] Woe is me! How can I ever live without friends?

و ي ل [2]

وِيل [wiːl] *n:* وِيلات [wiːlaːt] *pl:* • **1.** wheel

و ي ل [3]

وايِل [waːyil] *n:* • **1.** voile, a kind of sheer cloth

و ي ن

وين ما [wiːn maː] *subordinating conjunction:* • **1.** wherever – وَين ما يِسمَع أَكُو حَفلَة، يِرُوحِلها [wiːn maː yismaʕ ʔaku ħafla, yiruːħilha] Wherever he hears there's a party, he goes to it.
وين [wiːn] *interrogative:* • **1.** where, what place – وين المِفتاح؟ [wiːn ʔilmiftaːħ?] Where is the key? ما أَدرِي وين خَلِّيتها [maː ʔadri wiːn xalliːtha] I don't know where I put it. وين رِحتُوا البارحَة؟ [wiːn riħtuː ʔilbaːrħa?] Where did you all go yesterday? هاي وَينَك؟ صار إِسبُوع ما شِفتَك [haːy wiːnak? ṣaːr ʔisbuːʕ maː šiftak] Where have you been? I haven't seen you in i a week. لِوَين رايِح؟ [lwayn raːyiħ?] Where are you going? مِن وين، منِين [min wayn, mniːn] from where? منِينلَك هَالفِلُوس؟ [mniːnlak halfiluːs?] Where did you get this money? هَذا وين وذاك وين [haːða wayn wðaːk wiːn] This is nothing like that!
إمنِين، منِين، مِن وَين [ʔimniːn, mniːn, min wiːn] *interrogative:* • **1.** which see under • **2.** where

و ي ي

وِيّا [wiyya] *preposition:* • **1.** with – ترِيد تِجِي وِيّايا؟ [triːd tiji wiyyaːya?] Do you want to come with me? إِذا تعارِض هَالإِقتِراح، آنِي وِيّاك [ʔiða tʕaːrið halʔiqtiraːħ, ʔaːni wiyyaːk] If you oppose this suggestion, I'm with you. ماكُو أَحَّد بَالدّائِرَة، بَسّ آنِي وِيّاك [maːku ʔaħħad biddaːʔira, bass ʔaːni wiyyaːk] There's no one in the office, just you and I.

و

ي

ي

ياء [yaːʔ] *n:* • **1.** name of the letter

يا [yaː] *particle:* • **1.** (vocative and exclamatory particle) oh – يا إبن الحَرام [yaː ʔibin ʔalħaraːm] You bastard! يا ناس! شايفين هيكي شي؟ [yaː naːs! šaːyfiːn hiːči ši?] Hey, people! Have you ever seen such a thing? يا رَبّي، شراح أسَوّي؟ [yaː rabbi, šraːħ ʔasawwiː?] Oh God! What am I going to do? ثوب بِرُبُع دينار؟ يا بَلاش [θuːb brubuʕ dinaːr? yaː balaːš] A shirt for a quarter dinar? That's cheap, man! • **2.** var. of أي which, what

أيا [ʔayaː] *int:* • **3.** hey you – أيا حَيّال، شمَدريك؟ [ʔayaː ħayyaːl, šmadriːk?] Hey, you sly guy! How did you know? أيا مِسكين! تَوّة تزَوَّج [ʔayaː miskiːn! tawwa dzawwaǰ] Oh, poor guy! He just got married.

ي ء س

يأس [yiʔas] *v:* • **1.** to despair, give up hope – لا تيأس بالعَجَل. حاوِل مِن جِديد [laː tiːʔas bilʕaǰal. ħaːwil min ǰidiːd] Don't give up right away. Try again. يأسِت مِنّه؛ أبَد ما يتعَلَّم [yiʔasit minnah; ʔabad maː yitʕallam] I've given up hope in him; he'll never learn. يأس مِن الحَياة وقِتَل نَفسَه [yiʔas min ʔilħayaːt wkital nafsah] He lost all hope in life and killed himself.

يأّس [yaʔʔas] *v:* • **1.** to deprive of all hope, to discourage, dissuade – ما قِبَل يرجَع إلّا لَمّا يَأّستَه [maː qibal yirǰaʕ ʔilla lamma yaʔʔastah] He wouldn't agree to return until I gave him no other hope. ما تِقدَر تيَأّسني بسُهولَة. عِندي أمَل قَويّ [maː tigdar tyaʔʔisni bsuhuːla. ʕindi ʔamal qawiyy] You can't discourage me easily. I have high hopes.

يأس [yaʔas, yaʔis] *n:* • **1.** despair, hopelessness – سِنّ اليَأس [sinn ʔilyaʔs] female menopause.

يائس [yaːʔis] *adj:* • **1.** without hope, desperate

مَيؤوس، مَيؤوس مِن [mayʔuːs, mayʔuːs min] *adj:* • **1.** lost, hopeless – صِحّتَه مَيؤوس مِنها [ṣiħħtah mayʔuːs minha] His health is a hopeless case.

ي ب س

يِبَس [yibas] *v:* • **1.** to dry, become dry – الهِدوم يبسَت كُلّها [ʔilhduːm yibsat kullha] The clothes all got dry. يِبَس حَلقَه مِن العَطَش [yibas ħalgah min ʔilʕaṭaš] His mouth dried up from thirst.

يَبَّس [yabbas] *v:* • **1.** to make dry, to dry – هالصَّيف يَبَّسنا بامية هوايَة [haṣṣayf yabbasna baːmya hwaːya] This summer we dried a lot of okra. • **2.** to stiffen, make hard, rigid – البَرد يَبَّسَه [ʔilbarid yabbasah] The cold petrified him.

تيَبَّس [tyabbas] *v:* • **1.** to be dried – القُطُن لازم يتيَبَّس قَبُل ما ينوزِن [ʔilguṭun laːzim yityabbas gabul maː yinwizin] The cotton has to be dried before it's weighed.

يَبِس [yabis] *n:* • **1.** dryness

يَباس [yabaːs] *n:* • **1.** dryness

يابِس [yaːbis] *adj:* • **1.** dry, dried out, arid – خُبُز يابِس [xubuz yaːbis] stale bread. شِدّ الجَرح مالَك؛ بَعدَه ما يابِس [šidd ʔiǰǰariħ maːlak; baʕdah maː yaːbis] Bandage your wound; it still hasn't healed. • **2.** stiff, hard, firm – لا تمشي عالقير؛ بَعدَه ما يابس [laː timši ʕalgiːr; baʕdah maː yaːbis] Don't walk on the asphalt; it hasn't hardened yet. هَذا خَشمَه يابِس؛ لا تسألَه تَرَة ما يجاوبَك [haːða xašmah yaːbis; laː tsiʔlah tara maː yǰaːwbak] He's a snob; don't ask him because he won't answer you. • **3.** stingy, miserly – هُوَّ فَدّ واحِد يابِس؛ ما يتبَرَّع بشي [huwwa fadd waːħid yaːbis; maː yitbarraʕ bši] He's a stingy person; he wouldn't donate anything.

مَيَبِّس [myabbis] *adj:* • **1.** stingy, dried

متيَبِّس [mityabbis] *adj:* • **1.** dried up

أيبَس [ʔaybas] *comparative adjective:* • **1.** more or most dessicated • **2.** more or most rigid • **3.** more or most miserly

ي ب ن

اليابان [ʔilyabaːn] *n:* • **1.** Japan

ياباني [yaːbaːni] *adj:* • **1.** Japanese • 2. a Japanese

ي ت م

يَتَّم [yattam] *v:* • **1.** to deprive of a father – الحَرب يَتِّمَت هَالجاهِل [ʔilħarub yattimat hajǰaːhil] The war left this child fatherless. • **2.** to orphan, deprive of parents – حادِث السَّيّارَة يَتَّمَه مِن أُمَّه وأبوه [ħaːdiθ ʔissayyaːra yattamah min ʔummah wʔabuːh] The car accident left him motherless and fatherless.

تيَتَّم [tyattam] *v:* • **1.** to become an orphan, to be deprived of one's father – تيَتَّم وعُمرَه خَمس سنين [tyattam wʕumrah xams sniːn] He became an orphan when he was five years old.

مَيتَم [maytam] *n:* مَياتِم [mayaːtim] *pl:* • **1.** orphanage

يَتيم [yatiːm] *adj:* يتامَة، أيتام [ytaːma, ʔaytaːm] *pl:* • **1.** fatherless child • **2.** orphan

ي خ

ياخَة [yaːxa] *n:* ياخات [yaːxaːt] *pl:* • **1.** collar (of a garment) • **2.** lapel (of a jacket)

ي خ ن ي

يَخني [yaxni] *n:* • **1.** a thin stew made of meat, onions and chick-peas – سِمَعنا هالقِصَّة مِيَّة مَرَّة. صارَت يَخني [simaʕna halqiṣṣa miyyat marra. ṣaːrat yaxni] We've heard this story a hundred times. It's gotten worn out. • **2.** worn out

ي

ي د ق

يَدَق [yadag] *n:* يَدَقات [yadaga:t] *pl:* • **1.** extra, spare, reserve – أُخُذ سبانتَين حَتَّى تِبقَى وِحدَة عِندَك يَدَق عَلَى طُول [ʔuxuð spa:nti:n ħatta tibqa: wiħda ʕindak yadag ʕala ṭu:l] Take two wrenches so you can always have one as a spare.

ي د و

يَدّ [yadd] *n:* • **1.** hand – إِلَه يَدّ بِيها [ʔilah yadd bi:ha] He had a hand in it.

إيد [ʔi:d] *n:* إيدَين، إيدِينات [ʔi:di:n, ʔi:di:na:t] *pl:* • **1.** hand – شِفتهُم إيد بإيد [šifithum ʔi:d bʔi:d] I saw them hand in hand. مالَه إيد بِالقَضِيَّة [ma:lah ʔi:d bilqaðiyya] He has no hand in the matter. إذا وُقَع بِيديهُم يمَوّتُوه [ʔiða wugaʕ bidi:hum yimawwtu:h] If he falls into their hands they'll kill him. الطَّماطَة ما تُوقَع بِالإيد بِالشِّتا [ʔiṭṭama:ṭa ma: tu:gaʕ bilʔi:d biššita] Tomatoes aren't available in winter. هِيكِي راديُو بهَالسِّعِر ما يُوقَع بِالإيد عَلَى طُول [hi:či ra:dyu bhassiʕir ma: yu:gaʕ bilʔi:d ʕala ṭu:l] Such a radio for this price can't be gotten all the time. ساعَة إيد [sa:ʕat ʔi:d] wrist watch. إيد مِن وَرا وَإيد مِن قِدّام [ʔi:d min wara waʔi:d min gidda:m] empty-handed. لَعِّب إيدَك [laʕʕib ʔi:dak] Pay up! إيدَه خَفِيفَة [ʔi:dah xafi:fa] He's a fast worker. آخ مِن إيدَك، مَوِّتتنِي [ʔa:x min ʔi:dak, mawwatitni] Darn you, you'll be the death of me! هَذا كُلَّه مِن إيدَك [ha:ða kullah min ʔi:dak] This is all your doing. This is all your fault. كُلّهُم يِشتُغلُون جَوَّة إيدِي [kullhum yištuɣlu:n ǰawwa ʔi:di] They all work under my supervision. أَكُو جَوَّة إيدَك مِيَّة دِينار؟ [ʔaku ǰawwa ʔi:dak miyyat dina:r?] Do you have one hundred dinars at hand? هَالسَّيّارَة شُغُل إيد [hassayya:ra šuɣul ʔi:d] This car is hand made. • **2.** arm – إيدَه مَقطُوعَة مِن الكِتِف [ʔi:dah magṭu:ʕa min ʔiččitif] His arm is cut off at the shoulder. إيدَيهُم طُويلَة [ʔi:dayhum ṭuwi:la] They're light-fingered. • **3.** handle

يَدَّة [yadda] *n:* يَدّات [yadda:t] *pl:* • **1.** handle – كُرسِي أَبُو يَدّات [kursi ʔabu yadda:t] armchair.

يَدَوِي [yadawi] *adj:* • **1.** manual, hand- – عَمَل يَدَوِي [ʕamal yadawi] manual labor. قُنبُلَة يَدَوِيَّة [qumbula yadawiyya] hand grenade.

ي ر د

يَردَة [yarda] *n:* يَردات [yarda:t] *pl:* • **1.** yard (measure of length)

ي ز د ي

اليَزِيدِيَّة [ʔilyazi:diyya] *n:* • **1.** the Yezidi religion, a religion of Kurdistan which includes Devil worship

يَزِيدِي [yazi:di] *adj:* • **1.** Yezidi, belonging to the Yezidi religion

ي ز ي

يَزِي، يَزِّي [yazi, yazzi] *adj:* • **1.** (invar., an exclamation, approx.:) wait, hold on, that's enough – يَزِّي عاد [yazzi ʕa:d] Now just one minute!

ي س

ياس [ya:s] *n:* • **1.** privet (hedge shrub)

ي س ر

يَسَّر [yassar] *v:* • **1.** to make easy, facilitate – الله يِيَسِّر أُمُورَك [ʔallah yiyassir ʔumu:rak] May God make things easy for you!

تيَسَّر [tyassar] *v:* • **1.** to be or become available, easy to find – هَالنَّوع مِن القُماش ما يِتيَسَّر بالسُّوق [hannu:ʕ min ʔalquma:š ma: yityassar bissu:g] This type of cloth is not available in the market.

يُسُر [yusur] *n:* • **1.** a kind of semi-precious black stone

يَسار، يِسار [yasa:r, yisa:r] *n:* • **1.** left, left side – إمشِي قُبَل وديور لِليَسار بثانِي شارِع [ʔimši gubal wdi:wir lilyasa:r bθa:ni ša:riʕ] Go straight and turn to the left at the second street.

أَيسَر [ʔaysar] *adj:* يِسرَة [yisra] *pl:* يِسرَة [yisra] *feminine:* • **1.** left, located to the left – إيدَه اليِسرَى مَكسُورَة [ʔi:dah ʔilyisra maksu:ra] His left arm is broken.

يِسرَة [yisra] *adj:* • **1.** left

يِسارِي [yisa:ri] *adj:* • **1.** leftist, left-wing – عِندَه مِيُول يِسارِيَّة [ʕindah miyu:l yisa:riyya] He has leftist leanings.

مَيسُور، مِتيَسِّر [maysu:r, mityassir] *adj:* • **1.** available, easy to find

يِسراوِي [yisra:wi] *adj:* • **1.** left-handed – إبنَك يِسراوِي [ʔibnak yisra:wi] Your son is left-handed.

أَيسَر [ʔaysar] *comparative adjective:* • **1.** more or most easy

ي س م ن

ياسمِين [ya:smi:n] *n:* • **1.** jasmine

ي س و ع

اليَسُوع [ʔilyasu:ʕ] *n:* • **1.** Jesus

يَسُوعِي [yasu:ʕi] *adj:* • **1.** Jesuit – الآباء اليَسُوعِيِّين [ʔilʔa:ba:ʔ ʔilyasu:ʕiyyi:n] the Jesuit fathers.

ي ش م غ

يَشماغ [yašma:ɣ] *n:* يَشامِيغ [yaša:mi:ɣ] *pl:* • **1.** a man's headdress or kerchief of white cloth with red or black diamond-shaped embroidery

ي ص غ

يَصَّغ [yaṣṣaɣ] *v:* • **1.** to outlaw, make unlawful, illegal – الحُكُومَة راح تيَصِّغ الصَّيد بِالرَّبِيع [ʔilħuku:ma ra:ħ tyaṣṣiɣ ʔiṣṣayd birrabi:ʕ] The government is going to outlaw hunting in the spring.

ي غ د ن

ياغدان [ya:ɣda:n] *n:* ياغدانات [ya:ɣda:na:t] *pl:* • **1.** oilcan

ي ف و خ

يافوخ [ya:fu:x] *n:* • **1.** top of the head, crown of the head

ي ق ن

يَقَّن [yaqqan] *v:* • **1.** to be convinced, sure, certain – ما يَقَّن إِلّا لَمّا رَوَّيتَه إِيّاها [ma: yaqqan ʔilla lamma rawwi:tah ʔiyya:h] He wasn't convinced until I showed it to him. شما قُلَّك، ما تيَقِّن [šma gullak, ma: tyaqqin] No matter what I tell you, you don't believe it.

تيَقَّن [tyaqqan] *v:* • **1.** to ascertain, make sure, assure oneself – أَرِيد أَتيَقَّن زين قَبُل ما أَخابرَه [ʔari:d ʔatyaqqan zi:n gabul ma: ʔaxa:brah] I want to be very sure before I phone him.

يَقِين، عَلَى يَقِين [yaqi:n, ʕala yaqi:n] *n:* • **1.** certain, sure, positive – إِذا إِجا لِبَغداد، يَقِين يُمُرّ عَلَيهُم [ʔiða ʔiǰa libaɣda:d, yaqi:n yumurr ʕali:hum] If he comes to Baghdad, he'll surely drop in on them. كُون عَلَى يَقِين آنِي ما أَحكِي بقُفاك [ku:n ʕala yaqi:n ʔa:ni ma: ʔaħči bgufa:k] You can be sure I won't talk behind your back.

متيَقِّن [mityyaqqin] *adj:* • **1.** confident

ي ق و ت

ياقُوت [ya:qu:t] *n:* • **1.** (coll.) ruby(ies)

ياقُوتَة [ya:qu:ta] *n:* ياقُوتات [ya:qu:ta:t] *pl:* • **1.** ruby

ي ك ك

يَكّ [yakk] *n:* • **1.** one, a single unit (used in set expressions) – كُلّها يَكّ حَساب عَلَيّا [kullha yakk ħasa:b ʕalayya] It's all the same to me.

ي ل ك

يَلَك [yalag] *n:* يَلَكات [yalaga:t] *pl:* • **1.** vest, waistcoat

ي م

ياما، وياما [ya:ma, wya:ma] *int:* • **1.** How often!, how many times!

ي م ت

يَمتَى ما [yamta ma:] *subordinating conjunction:* • **1.** whenever, any time – يَمتَى ما تريد، آنِي حاضِر [yamta ma: tri:d, ʔa:ni ħa:ðir] Whenever you want, I'm ready.

يَمتَى [yamta] *interrogative:* • **1.** When? – آنِي يَمتَى قِلتَلَك هِيكِي؟ [ʔa:ni yamta: gilitlak hi:či?] When did I ever tell you that? يَمتَى تزُورنا؟ [yamta: dzu:rna?] When will you visit us?

ي م م [1]

تيَمَّم [tyammam] *v:* • **1.** to resort to sand, to substitute sand for water in ritual ablutions – إِيدَك مَجرُوحَة. ما تِقدَر تِتوَضَّى. تيَمَّم [ʔi:dak majru:ħa. ma: tigdar titwaððaː. tyammam] Your hand is cut. You can't wash yourself. Use sand to prepare for prayer.

ي م م [2]

يَمّ [yamm] *preposition:* • **1.** beside, next to, near – تَعال أُقعُد يَمِّي؛ أَرِيد أَقُلَّك فَدّ شِي [taʕa:l ʔugʕud yammi; ʔari:d ʔagullak fadd ši] Come here and sit next to me; I want to tell you something. حُطّها يَمّ الرّاديُو [ħuṭṭha yamm ʔirra:dyu] Put it next to the radio. بَيتنا صايِر يَمّ مَحَطَّة القِطار [baytna ṣa:yir yamm maħaṭṭat ʔilqiṭa:r] Our house is near the railroad station. رِحِت يَمَّه فَدّ ساعَة وَحكَيت وِيّاه [riħit yammah fadd sa:ʕa wħči:t wiyya:h] I went to see him for an hour and talked with him. • **2.** in the care of, in the hands of – أَقدَر أَخَلِّي ساعتِي يَمَّك حَتَّى أَسبَح؟ [ʔagdar ʔaxalli: sa:ʕti yammak ħatta ʔasbaħ?] Can I leave my watch with you so I can swim? لا تدِير بال. خَلِّيها يَمّ الله [la: ddi:r ba:l. xalli:ha yamm ʔallah] Don't worry. Leave it in God's hands. خَلِّيها يَمِّي [xalli:ha yammi] Leave it to me. • **3.** with مِن to the advantage of, in the interest of – إِذا بِنَوا جِسِر هنا، هاي مِن يَمِّي لِأَنّ قاعِي سِعِرها يزِيد [ʔiða binaw ǰisir hna, ha:y min yammi liʔann ga:ʕi siʕirha yzi:d] If they build a bridge here, it'll be in my favor because the price of my land will go up. هاي صارَت مِن يَمَّك [ha:y ṣa:rat min yammak] That's a real break for you! • **4.** with مِن on the part of, from the point of view of – مِن يَمِّي، ما عِندِي مانِع [min yammi, ma: ʕindi ma:niʕ] For my part, I have no objection.

ي م ن

يِمنَة [yimna] *n:* • **1.** right, right side – فُوت عاليمنَى [fu:t ʕalyimna] Go to the right.

يَمَنِي [yamani] *n:* يَمَنِيّات [yamani:ya:t] *pl:* • **1.** a kind of slipper

يَمِين [yami:n] *n:* أَيمان [ʔayma:n] *pl:* • **1.** oath – حِلَف يَمِين ما يِلعَب قمار بَعَد [ħilaf yami:n ma: yilʕab qma:r baʕad] He took an oath he wouldn't gamble any more. هَذا يَمِين، ما أَعرُف شِي [ha:ða yami:n, ma: ʔaʕruf ši] I swear I don't know anything.

يَمِين [yami:n] *n:* • **1.** right, right side – فُوت بِالشّارِع اللِّي عَاليَمِين [fu:t biššaːriʕ ʔilli ʕalyami:n] Turn into the street on the right.

اليَمَن [ʔilyaman] *n:* • **1.** Yemen

أَيمَن [ʔayman] *adj:* يِمنَى [yimna] *feminine:* • **1.** right, right side – الجّناح الأيمَن مال الطَّير مَكسُور [ʔiǰǰna:ħ ʔilʔayman ma:l ʔiṭṭi:r maksu:r] The bird's right wing is broken. العَين اليِمنَى ضَعِيفَة [ʔilʕayn ʔilyimna: ðaʕi:fa] The right eye is weak.

يَمِينِي [yami:ni] *adj:* • **1.** rightist, right-wing – هَذا يَمِينِي بِسِياستَه [ha:ða yami:ni bsiya:stah] He's rightist in his politics.

يَمانِي [yama:ni] *adj:* • **1.** from Yemen, Yemenite • **2.** a Yemeni, a Yemenite

يِمناوِي [yimna:wi] *adj:* • **1.** right-handed – نفَضِّل لاعُوب يِمناوِي [nfaððil la:ʕu:b yimna:wi] We prefer a right-handed player.

ي ن س ن

يانسُون [ya:nsu:n] *n:* • **1.** anise, aniseed

ي ن ص ب

يانَصِيب [ya:naṣi:b] *n:* يانَصِيبات [yana:ṣi:ba:t] *pl:* • **1.** lottery

ي ه و

ياهُو، ياهِي [ya:hu, ya:hi] *interrogative:* ياهُم، ياهُمَّ [ya:humma] *pl:* • **1.** which, what, who among them, whoever – يا هُوَّ، يا هِيَّ، يا هُمَّ [ya: huwwa, ya: hiyya, ya: humma] which, who among them, whoever. ياهُو اللِّي يقُولَّك، لا تصَدِّق بِيه [ya:hu ʔilli ygu:llak, la: tṣaddig bi:h] Whoever tells you, don't believe him. ياهُو مِنهُم سَبَّك؟ [ya:hu minhum sabbak?] Which of them insulted you? البَيت مالَه وَالفلُوس فلُوسَه، ياهِي مالتَك؟ [ʔilbayt ma:lah wilflu:s flu:sah, ya:hi ma:ltak?] The house is his and the money is his money; what concern is it of yours?

ي ه و د

يَهُود [yahu:d] *n:* • **1.** (coll.) Jew(s)

يَهُودِي [yahu:di] *adj:* يَهُودِيِّين، يَهُود [yahu:diyyi:n, yahu:d] *pl:* يَهُودِيَّة [yahu:diyya] *feminine:* • **1.** Jewish • **2.** Jew

يَهُودِيَّة [yahu:diyya] *adj:* • **1.** Judaism

ي و ح ن

يُوحَنّا [yu:ħanna] *n:* • **1.** John

ي و د

يَود [yu:d] *n:* • **1.** iodine – تَنتَر يَود [tantar yawd] tincture of iodine.

ي و س ف

يُوسِف [yu:sif] *n:* • **1.** Joseph

ي و ش

يَواش [yawa:š] *adj:* • **1.** slow, slowly – نَزِّل الصَّنُدُوق يَواش حَتَّى لا تِتكَسَّر المواعِين [nazzil ʔiṣṣandu:g yawa:š ħatta la: titkassar ʔilmwa:ʕi:n] Let the crate down slowly so the dishes don't get broken. مِن فَضلَك، إحكِي يَواش. ما أفهَمَك زين [min faðlak, ʔiħči yawa:š. ma: ʔafhamak zi:n] Please speak slowly. I don't understand you very well. مِدّ إيدَك يَواش يَواش وَأكمُش الطِّير [midd ʔi:dak yawa:š yawa:š wʔukmuš ʔiṭṭi:r] Extend your hand very slowly and grab the bird. يَواشَك! راح تُمرُد الطَّماطَة [yawa:šak! ra:ħ tumrud ʔiṭṭama:ṭa] Take it easy there! You'll mash the tomatoes!

ي و ل

يَوَلّ [yawall] *n:* يَوَلُّو [yawallu] *pl:* يَوَلِّي [yawalli] *feminine:* • **1.** (emphatic particle, approx.:) look, hey you, buddy, mac, man – يَوَلّ، أبقَى أعَلِّم بِيك وَما تِتعَلَّم؟ [yawall, ʔabqa: ʔaʕallim bi:k wma titʕallam?] Look, am I going to have to go on teaching you and you won't learn? يَوَلّ، لا تِتداخَل بهِيكِي قَضايا [yawall, la: tidda:xal bhi:či qaḍa:ya] Look, don't get involved in that sort of thing! جا الامتِحان. لازِم تِدرُس، يَوَلّ [ǰa: ʔilʔimtiħa:n. la:zim tidrus, yawall] The exam's getting close. You'd better study, man!

ي و م

يوم [yawm, yu:m] *n:* أيّام [ʔayya:m] *pl:* • **1.** day – قضَينا خُوش أيّام بِالبَصرَة [gḍi:na xu:š ʔayya:m bilbaṣra] We spent some wonderful days in Basra. الأسعار اِرتِفعَت هوايَة بأيّام الحَرُب [ʔilʔasʕa:r ʔirtifʕat hwa:ya bʔayya:m ʔilħarub] Prices went up a lot during war time. بَنات هَاليُوم وريحُون لِلمَدارِس [bana:t halyu:m yiri:ħu:n lilmada:ris] The girls nowadays go to schools. ما كان هنا اليُوم [ma: ča:n hna: ʔilyu:m] He wasn't here today.

يَومِيَّة [yawmiyya] *n:* يَومِيّات [yawmiyya:t] *pl:* • **1.** daily, every day – يَومِيّاً يخابُرني [yawmiyyan yxa:burni] He calls me every day. هَالمجَدِّي يَومِيَة الفَرد ياخُذ مِنِّي عَشِر فلُوس [halmgaddi yawmiyyi ʔilfarid ya:xuð minni ʕašir flu:s] Every single day this beggar gets ten fils from me. • **2.** daily wages, day's pay – أشتُغُل النَّهار كُلَّه ويَومِيّتِي رُبُع دِينار [ʔaštuɣul ʔinnaha:r kullah wyawmiyyti rubuʕ dina:r] I work all day and my day's pay is a quarter dinar. أبُويَا ما نطانِي ويومِيّتِي بَعَد [ʔabu:ya ma: nṭa:ni yawmiyyti baʕad] My father hasn't given me my daily allowance yet. • **3.** daily work, daily task • **4.** diary, journal, daybook, calendar

يَومِي [yawmi] *adj:* • **1.** daily – جَدوَل الدَّوام اليَومِي [ǰadwal ʔiddawa:m ʔilyawmi] daily attendance record.

يَومِيّاً [yawmiyyan] *adverbial:* • **1.** daily, every day

ي و ن ن

اليُونان [ʔilyu:na:n] *n:* • **1.** Greece

يُونانِي [yu:na:ni] *adj:* • **1.** Greek • 2. a Greek

ي ي

ياي [ya:y] *n:* يايات [ya:ya:t] *pl:* • **1.** switch-blade knife – سِكِّينَة أمّ ياي [sičči:na ʔumm ya:y] switch-blade knife.

إيّا [ʔiyya:] *particle:* • **1.** /particle serving as stem for pronominal suffix, e.g. إيّاك، إيّاها etc. – القَلَم مالَك بَعدَه عِندَه لَو رَجَّع لَك إيّاه؟ [ʔilqalam ma:lak baʕdah ʕindah law rajjaʕ lak ʔiyya:h?] Does he still have your pencil or did he return it to you?

ي

Part – II

ENGLISH–ARABIC

A

a • **1.** Do you have a stamp and an envelope? عِندَك طابِع وَظَرُف؟ [ʕindak ṭaːbiʕ wð̣aruf?] • **2.** فَدّ [fadd] There is a man at the door. أَكُو فَدّ رِجّال بِالباب [ʔaku fadd rijjaːl bilbaːb] • **3.** ال [ʔil] These eggs are fifty fils a dozen. هَالبَيض الدَّرزَن بِخَمسِين فِلس [halbiːð̣ ʔaddarzan bxamsiːn filis]

to abbreviate • **1.** اِختِصَر [ʔixtiṣar] اِختِصار [ʔixtiṣaːr] *vn: sv* i. The British Broadcasting Corporation is abbreviated B. B. C. مَصلَحَة الإذاعَة البَرِيطانِيَّة مُختَصَرَة إلَى "بِيه بِيه سِي" [maṣlaħat ʔilʔiðaːʕa ʔilbariːṭaːniyya muxtaṣara ʔila "biːh biːh si"]

ability • **1.** قابلِيَّة [qaːbliyya] قابلِيّات [qaːbliyyaːt] *pl:* اِقتِدار [ʔiqtidaːr] I don't doubt his ability. ما أَشُكّ بِقابلِيتَه [maː ʔašukk bqaːbliːtah]

able • **1.** مُقتَدِر [muqtadir] كُفُو [kufu, kafu] I'm sure he's an able officer. آنِي مِتأَكِّد هُوَّ ضابُط كَفُو [ʔaːni mitʔakkid huwwa ð̣aːbuṭ kafu]

to be able • **1.** قِدَر [gidar] مَقدِرَة، قُدرَة [maqdira, qudra] *vn: sv* a. Will you be able to come? راح تِقدَر تِجِي؟ [raːħ tigdar tiji?]

aboard • **1.** عَلَى [ʕala] We went aboard the boat an hour before it sailed. صعَدنا عالمَركَب ساعَة قَبُل ما مِشَى [ṣʕadna ʕalmarkab saːʕa gabul maː mišaː]

*** all aboard! (ship)** • **1.** كُلكُم اِصعِدُوا عَالمَركَب [kullkum ʔiṣiʕduː ʕalmarkab]

to abolish • **1.** لِغَى ن [liɣaː] إلغاء [ʔilɣaːʔ] *vn:* اِنلِغَى [ʔinliɣaː] *p:* When was slavery abolished in the United States? شوَقِت اِنلِغَت العُبُودِيَّة بأَمرِيكا؟ [šwakit ʔinliɣat ʔilʕubuːdiyya bʔamriːka?]

abortion • **1.** تَطرِيح [taṭriːħ] تَطرِيحات [taṭriːħaːt] *pl:* Abortion is against the law. التَّطرِيح ضِدّ القانُون [ʔittaṭriːħ ð̣idd ʔilqaːnuːn]

to perform an abortion on • **1.** طَرَّح [ṭarraħ] تَطرِيح [taṭriːħ] *vn:* تطَرَّح [tṭarraħ] *p:* He was arrested for performing an abortion on a young girl. توَقَّف لِأَنّ طَرَّح بنَيَّة صغَيِّرَة [twaqqaf liʔann ṭarraħ bnayya ṣɣayyra]

about • **1.** حَوالِي [ħawaːli] تَقرِيباً [taqriːban] There were about thirty people present. كان أَكُو حَوالِي ثلاثِين واحِد [čaːn ʔaku ħawaːli tlaːθiːn waːħid] It's about the same. تَقرِيباً نَفس الشِّي [taqriːban nafs ʔišši] • **2.** عَلَى وَشَك [ʕala wašak] Lunch is about ready. الغَدا عَلَى وَشَك يِحضَر [ʔilɣadaː ʕala wašak yiħð̣ar] He was about to leave when the phone rang. كان عَلَى وَشَك يِطلَع مِن دَقّ التِّلِفُون [čaːn ʕala wašak yiṭlaʕ min dagg ʔittilifuːn] • **3.** عَن [ʕan] عَلَى [ʕala] They were talking about the war. كانَوا يِحكُون عَن الحَرُب [čaːnaw yiħčuːn ʕann ʔilħarub] • **4.** ب [b] My husband is very particular about his food. رَجلِي هوايَة دِقداقِي بأَكلَه [rajli hwaːya diqdaːqi bʔaklah]

*** It's about time you got here.** • **1.** مايَاللّه عاد ؟ وين ظَلِّيت [mayallah ʕaːd ? wiːn ð̣alliːt]

what ... about • **1.** عَلَى وَيش [ʕala wiːš] What are you talking about? إنتَ عَلَى وَيش دَتِحكِي؟ [ʔinta ʕala wiːš datiħči?] What are you talking about? إنتَ شدَتِحكِي؟ [ʔinta šdatiħči?]

what about • **1.** رَأي [raʔy] آراء [ʔaːraːʔ] *pl:* شِتقُول [šitguːl] What about this one? شرَأيَك بهَذا؟ [šraʔyak bhaːða?]

to be about • **1.** عَلَى وَيش [ʕala wiːš] What's it all about? عَلَى وَيش هَذا كُلَّه؟ [ʕala wiːš haːða kullah?] What's it all about? شصار؟ [šṣaːr?] What's it all about? شَكُو؟ [šaku?] • **2.** عَلَى [ʕala] It's about the money he owes me. هاي عالفلُوس اللِّي أَطلُب إيّاه [haːy ʕalfluːs ʔilli ʔaṭlubh ʔiyyaːh] • **3.** كان يرِيد [čaːn yriːd] I was about to send for you. كِنِت دَأرِيد أَدِزّ عَلِيك [činit daʔariːd ʔadizz ʕaliːk] • **4.** عَلَى وَشَك [ʕala wašak] She was about to burst into tears. كانَت عَلَى وَشَك تِبكِي [čaːnat ʕala wašak tibči]

above • **1.** فَوق [fawg fuːq] He is above average height. طُولَه فُوق المُعَدَّل [ṭuːlah fuːg ʔilmuʕaddal] • **2.** بِالسّابِق [bissaːbiq] As already mentioned above. مِثلما اِنذِكَر بِالسّابِق [miθilmaː ʔinðikar bissaːbiq]

above all • **1.** وِالأَهَمّ [wilʔahamm] لا سِيَّما [laː siyyama] عَلَى الأَخَصّ [ʕala ʔalʔaxaṣṣ] خُصُوصاً [xuṣuːṣan] Above all, remember to be on time. وِالأَهَمّ، تذَكَّر لازِم تكُون عالوَقِت [wilʔahamm, ðdakkar laːzim tkuːn ʕalwakit] Above all, remember to be on time. لا سِيَّما، لا تِتأَخَّر [laː siyyama, laː titʔaxxar]

to be above • **1.** أَعلَى مِن [ʔaʕla min] أَرفَع مِن [ʔarfaʕ min] فَوق [fuːg, fuːq] She's above such petty things. هِيَّ أَرفَع مِن هَالأَشياء الطَّفِيفَة [hiyya ʔarfaʕ min halʔašyaːʔ ʔiṭṭafiːfa] He's above suspicion. هُوَّ فُوق الشُّبهات [huwwa fuːg ṣiššubhaːt]

abroad • **1.** خارِج [xaːrij] Are you going abroad this summer? إنتَ مسافِر لِلخارِج هَالصَّيف؟ [ʔinta msaːfir lilxaːrij haṣṣiːf?] He lives abroad. هُوَّ يِعِيش بالخارِج [huwwa yiʕiːš bilxaːrij] At home and abroad. . . بِالوَطَن وَبِالخارِج [bilwaṭan wbilxaːrij]

abrupt • **1.** يابِس [yaːbis] He has a very abrupt manner. عِندَه أَخلاقَه هوايَة يابسَة [ʕindah ʔaxlaːqah hwaːya ya:bsa] • **2.** فُجائي [fuja:ʔi] We noticed an abrupt change in his attitude. لاحَظنا تَغَيُّر فُجائي بِمَوقِفَه [la:ħaðna taɣayyur fuja:ʔi bmawqifah]

abruptly • **1.** بِجَفاف [bjafa:f] He treated me rather abruptly. عامَلني بِجَفاف [ʕa:malni bjafa:f]

absence • **1.** غِياب [ɣiya:b] No one noticed his absence. مَحَّد لاحَظ غِيابَه أَصلاً [maħħad la:ħað ɣiya:bah ʔaṣlan]

absent • **1.** غايِب [ɣa:yib] Three members were absent because of illness. ثلاث أعضاء كانوا غايبين بِسَبَب المَرَض [tlaθ ʔaʕða:ʔ ča:naw ɣa:yibi:n bisabab ʔilmarað]

absent-minded • **1.** فِكر شارِد [fikr ša:rid] دالغَجي [da:lɣači] دالغَجِيَّة [da:lɣači:yya] *pl:* He's very absent-minded. هَذا كُلِّش فِكرَه شارِد [ha:ða kulliš fikrah ša:rid] He's very absent-minded. هُوَّ كُلِّش دالغَجي [huwwa kulliš da:lɣači]

absolute • **1.** خالِص [xa:liṣ] صِرف [ṣirf] مَحض [maħð] That's the absolute truth. هَذا الصُّدُق الخالِص [ha:ða ʔiṣṣudug ʔilxa:liṣ] That's an absolute fact. هَذِيك الحَقِيقَة المَحضَة [haði:č ʔilħaqi:qa ʔilmaħða] • **2.** مُطلَق [muṭlaq] The dictator exercised absolute power. الدِّكتاتور مارَس سُلطَة مُطلَقَة [ʔiddikta:tu:r ma:ras sulṭa muṭlaqa]

absolutely • **1.** قَطعاً [qaṭʕan] He's absolutely right. الحَقّ وِيّاه قَطعاً [ʔilħaqq wiyya:h qaṭʕan]

to absorb • **1.** مَصّ [maṣṣ] مَصّ [maṣṣ] *vn:* اِنمَصّ [ʔinmaṣṣ] *p:* The sponge absorbed the water quickly. الإسفَنجَة مَصَّت الماي بالعَجَل [ʔilʔisfanja maṣṣat ʔilma:y bilʕajal] • **2.** هِضَم [hiðam] هَضُم [haðum] *vn:* اِنهِضَم [ʔinhiðam] *p:* You can't absorb all that material in a single lesson. ما تِقدَر تُهضُم كُلّ هالمَعلُومات بِفَدّ دَرِس [ma: tigdar tuhðum kull halmaʕlu:ma:t bfadd daris]

to be absorbed • **1.** اِنهِمَك [ʔinhimak] اِنهِماك [ʔinhima:k] *vn: sv* i. He was so absorbed in his book, he didn't hear me come in. كان هَالقَدّ مِنهِمِك بالقِرايَة ما حَسّ بيّا مِن خَشَّيت [ča:n halgadd minhimik biliqra:ya ma: ħass biyya min xašši:t]

to abuse • **1.** أساء [ʔasa:ʔ] إساءَة [ʔisa:ʔa] *vn:* اِنساء [ʔinsa:ʔ] *p:* He's abusing his authority. دَيسِيئ اِستِعمال سُلطتَه [daysi:ʔ ʔistiʕma:l ṣulṭtah] • **2.** أساء [ʔasa:ʔ] إساءَة [ʔisa:ʔa] *vn:* اِنساء [ʔinsa:ʔ] *p:* He abuses his wife. هُوَّ يسِيئ مُعامَلَة مَرتَه [huwwa ysi:ʔ muʕa:malat martah]

academic • **1.** دِراسِي [dira:si] The academic year. السَّنَة الدِّراسِيَّة [ʔissana ʔiddira:siyya] • **2.** نَظَري [naðari] This is an academic matter. هَذِي قَضِيَّة نَظَرِيَّة [ha:ði qaðiyya naðariyya]

academy • **1.** مَجمَع [majmaʕ] مَجامِع [maja:miʕ] *pl:* Scientific academy. مَجمَع عِلمِي [majmaʕ ʕilmi]

accelerator • **1.** أكسَلَيتَة [ʔaksali:ta] The accelerator's broken. الأكسَلَيتَة مَكسُورَة [ʔilʔaksali:ta maksu:ra]

accent • **1.** لَكنَة [lakna] لَهجَة [lahja] لَهجات [lahja:t] *pl:* He speaks with a German accent. يِحكي بِلَكنَة أَلمانِيَّة [yiħči blakna ʔalma:niyya] • **2.** تَشدِيد [tašdi:d] تَشدِيدات [tašdi:da:t] *pl:* Where is the accent in this word? وين التَّشدِيد بِهَالكِلمَة؟ [wi:n ʔittašdi:d bhalkilma?]

to accept • **1.** قِبَل [qibal] قُبُول [qubu:l] *vn:* اِنقِبَل [ʔinqibal] *p:* Are you going to accept that position? راح تِقبَل هَذِيك الوَظِيفَة؟ [ra:ħ tiqbal haði:č ʔilwaði:fa?]

access • **1.** اِستِعمال [ʔistiʕma:l] Access to the files is restricted to supervisors. اِستِعمال الفايلات مَقصُور عالمُلاحِظِين [ʔistiʕma:l ʔilfa:yla:t maqṣu:r ʕalmula:ħiði:n] • **2.** مَخرَج [maxraj] مَخارِج [maxa:rij] *pl:* Iraq has access to the sea through the Shatt-al-Arab. العِراق عِندَه مَخرَج لِلبَحَر عَن طَرِيق شَطّ العَرَب [ʔilʕira:q ʕindah maxraj lilbaħar ʕan ṭari:q šaṭṭ ʔilʕarab]

to have access to • **1.** قِدَر يِستَعمِل [gidar yistaʕmil] *sv* a. He has access to the files. هُوَّ يِقدَر يِستَعمِل الإضبارات [huwwa yigdar yistaʕmil ʔilʔiðba:ra:t] • **2.** قِدَر [gidar] *sv* a. She has access to the minister of interior. تِقدَر تُوصَل لِوَزِير الدّاخِلِيَّة [tigdar tuwṣal lwazi:r ʔidda:xiliyya]

accident • **1.** حادِثَة [ħa:diθa] حَوادِث [ħawa:diθ] *pl:* قَدَر [qadar] أقدار [ʔaqda:r] *pl:* When did the accident happen? شوَقِت صارَت الحادِثَة؟ [šwakit ṣa:rat ʔilħa:diθa?]

by accident • **1.** بالصِّدفَة [biṣṣidfa] I found it out by accident. اِكتِشَفتها بالصِّدفَة [ʔiktišafitha biṣṣidfa] • **2.** مِن كَيف [min ki:f] That didn't happen by accident. هَذِيك ما صارَت مِن كَيفها [haði:č ma: ṣa:rat min ki:fha]

accidentally • **1.** بِلا تَعَمُّد [bila taʕammud] I dropped the plate accidentally. وَقَّعِت الماعُون بِلا تَعَمُّد [waqqaʕit ʔilma:ʕu:n bila taʕammud] • **2.** صُدفَةً [ṣudfatan] I accidentally learned the truth. عِرَفِت الصُّدُق صُدفَةً [ʕirafit ʔiṣṣudug ṣudfatan]

to accommodate • **1.** لائَم [la:ʔam]

*** We can accommodate three more people.**

• **1.** نِقدَر نهَيِّء مَكان لِثلَث أَشخاص بَعَد [nigdar nhayyiʔ maka:n litlaθ ʔašxa:ṣ baʕad] عِدنَا مَكان لِثلاثَة بَعَد [ʕidna maka:n litla:θa baʕad]

accommodating • **1.** خَدُوم [xadu:m] The manager was very accommodating. المُدِير كان كُلِّش خَدُوم [ʔilmudi:r ča:n kulliš xadu:m]

accompaniment • **1.** عَزف [ʕazif] Who's going to play the accompaniment? مِنُو راح يقُوم بِالعَزف؟ [minu raːħ yquːm bilʕazif?]

to accompany • **1.** رافَق [raːfaq] مُرافَقَة [muraːfaqa] *vn:* *sv* i. صاحَب [ṣaːħab] مُصاحَبَة [muṣaːħaba] *vn:* *sv* i. He accompanied her on the lute. هُوَّ رافَقها عَلعُود [huwwa raːfaqha ʕalʕuːd] I played the lute and Ali accompanied me on the flute. آني دَقَّيت عُود وعَلِي صاحَبنِي عالنّاي [ʔaːni daggiːt ʕuːd wʕali ṣaːħabni ʕannaːy] • **2.** راح [raːħ] *sv* u. We'll accompany you to Damascus. نرُوح ويّاك لِلشّام [nruːħ wiyyaːk liššaːm]

to accomplish • **1.** خَلَّص [xallaṣ] تَخلِيص [taxliːṣ] *vn:* تخَلَّص [txallaṣ] *p:* كَمَّل [kammal] تكمِيل [takmiːl] *vn:* تكَمَّل [tkammal] *p:* He accomplished what he set out to do. خَلَّص الشِّي اللي بِدَا بِيه [xallaṣ ʔišši ʔilli bidaː biːh] He accomplished what he set out to do. كَمَّل اللي رَاد يسَوِّيه [kammal ʔilli raːd ysawwiːh] • **2.** طَلَّع [ṭallaʕ] تَطلِيع [taṭliːʕ] *vn:* تطَلَّع [tṭallaʕ] *p:* For one day he accomplished quite a lot. طَلَّع هوايَة شُغُل بفَدّ يوم [ṭallaʕ hwaːya šuɣul bfadd yuːm] • **3.** حَقَّق [ħaqqaq] تَحقِيق [taħqiːq] *vn:* تحَقَّق [tħaqqaq] *p:* He's accomplished a good deal in his life. حَقَّق هوايَة غايات بحَياتَه [ħaqqaq hwaːya ɣaːyaːt bħayaːtah] • **4.** توَصَّل [twaṣṣal] تَوَصُّل [tawaṣṣul] *vn:* *sv* a. Did you accomplish anything in Washington? توَصَّلِت لشِي بواشِنطِن؟ [twaṣṣalit liššiy bwaːšinṭin?]

accomplished • **1.** ماهِر [maːhir] He's an accomplished musician. هُوَّ مُوسِيقِي ماهِر [huwwa musiːqi maːhir]
  * **Mission accomplished.** • **1.** المَطلُوب صار [ʔilmaṭluːb ṣaːr] الغَرَض تحَقَّق [ʔilɣaraḍ tħaqqaq]

accomplishment • **1.** صَنِيعَة [ṣaniːʕa] صَنايِع [ṣanaːyiʕ] *pl:* His mother was proud of his accomplishments. أُمَّه كانَت فَخُورَة بصَنايعَه [ʔummah čaːnat faxuːra bṣanaːyʕah] *Feminine:* • **2.** عَمَل [ʕamal] عَملَة [ʕamla] Really, that was no small accomplishment. صُدُق، كان عَمَل مُو شَقَا [ṣudug, čaːn ʕamal muː šaqaː]

accord • **1.** إتِّفاق [ʔittifaːq] They acted in complete accord with him. تصَرِّفوا بِاتِّفاق كامِل ويّاه [tṣarrifaw bʔittifaːq kaːmil wiyyaːh] • **2.** كَيف [kayf] He did it of his own accord. سَوّاها مِن كيفَه [sawwaːha min kiːfah]

in accordance with • **1.** حَسَب [ħasab] مُوجِب [muːǰib] In accordance with your request we are sending you three more copies حَسَب طَلَبَك إحنا دازِّينلَك ثلَث نُسَخ بَعَد [ħasab ṭalabak ʔiħna daːzziːnlak tlaθ nusax baʕad]

accordingly • **1.** عَلَى هَالأساس [ʕala halʔasaːs] I acted accordingly. تصَرَّفِت عَلَى هَالأساس [tṣarrafit ʕala halʔasaːs] • **2.** بِناءاً عَلَى [binaːʔan ʕala] Accordingly, I wrote him a check for the full amount. بِناءاً عَليه، كِتَبِتلَه شَكّ بالمَبلَغ كُلَّه [binaːʔan ʕaliːh, kitabitlah čakk bilmablaɣ kullah]

according to • **1.** حَسَب [ħasab] Everything was carried out according to instructions. كُلشِي تنَفَّذ حَسَب التَّعلِيمات [kullši tnaffað ħasab ʔittaʕliːmaːt]

account • **1.** حساب [ħsaːb] I have an account in this bank. عِندِي حساب بهالبَنك [ʕindi ħsaːb bhalbang] • **2.** تَقرير [taqriːr] تَقارير [taqaːriːr] *pl:* وَصُف [waṣuf] His account of the accident isn't clear. تَقرِيرَه عَالحادِثَة مُو واضِح [taqriːrah ʕalħaːdiθa muː waːḍiħ] His account of the accident isn't clear. وَصفَه لِلحادِثَة مُو واضِح [waṣfah lilħaːdiθa muː waːḍiħ]
  on account of • **1.** عَلَى أساس [ʕala ʔasaːs] بسَبَب [bsabab] The game was postponed on account of rain. اللِّعِب تأَجَّل بِسَبَب المُطَر [ʔilliʕib tʔaǰǰal bisabab ʔilmuṭar]
  on no account • **1.** بأَي حال [bʔay ħaːl] مَهما صار [mahma ṣaːr] On no account must you open this drawer. إنتَ ما لازِم تفُكّ هالمِجَرّ بأَي حال [ʔinta maː laːzim tfukk halmiǰarr bʔayy ħaːl] On no account must you open this drawer. ما لازِم تفُكّ هالمِجَرّ مَهما صار [maː laːzim tfukk halmiǰarr mahma ṣaːr]
  to call to account • **1.** حاسَب [ħaːsab] مُحاسَبَة [muħaːsaba] *vn:* تحاسَب [tħaːsab] *p:* I'll call him to account. راح أحاسبَه [raːħ ʔaħaːsbah]
  to give an account of • **1.** بَيَّن [bayyan] تَبيِين [tabyiːn] *vn:* تبَيَّن [tbayyan] *p:* You have to give me an account of every penny you spend. لازِم تبَيِّنلِي كُلّ فِلس التُّصرُفَه وين يرُوح [laːzim tbayyinli kull filis ʔiltuṣurfah wiːn yiruːħ]
  * **Give me an account of what happened.** • **1.** إحكِيلِي اللّي صار [ʔiħčiːli ʔilli ṣaːr] أُوصِفلِي اللّي صار [ʔuːṣifli ʔilli ṣaːr]
  to take into account • **1.** أخَذ بنَظَر الاعتِبار [ʔaxað bnaḍar ʔilʔiʕtibaːr] You have to take all the facts into account. لازِم تاخُذ كُلّ الحَقايِق بنَظَر الاعتِبار [laːzim taːxuð kull ʔilħaqaːyiq bnaḍar ʔilʔiʕtibaːr]
  to account for • **1.** عَلَّل [ʕallal] تَعلِيل [taʕliːl] *vn:* تعَلَّل [tʕallal] *p:* How do you account for that? شلُون تعَلِّل هَذا؟ [šluːn tʕallil haːða?] • **2.** بَرَّر [barrar] تَبرِير [tabriːr] *vn:* *sv* i. You'll have to account for your actions. لازِم تبَرِّر أعمالَك [laːzim tbarrir ʔaʕmaːlak]

to be accountable for • **1.** تحاسَب عَن [tħaːsab ʕan] تَحاسُب [taħaːsub] *vn:* *sv* a. You alone will be accountable for the materials. إنتَ وَحدَك راح تِتحاسَب عَن هالمَوادّ [ʔinta waħdak raːħ titħaːsab ʕan halmawaːdd]

accountant • **1.** مُحاسِب [muħaːsib] مُحاسِبِين [muħaːsibiːn] *pl:*

accurate • **1.** دَقِيق [daqiːq] She's very accurate in her work. هِيَّ كُلِّش دَقِيقَة بشُغُلها [hiyya kulliš daqiːqa

A

bšuɣulha] • **2.** مَضبُوط [maðbu:ṭ] Is that watch accurate? هَالسّاعَة مَضبُوطَة؟ [hassa:ʕa maðbu:ṭa?]

accurately • 1. بِالضَبُط [biððabuṭ] بصُورَة مَضبُوطَة [bṣu:ra maðbu:ṭa] بدِقَّة [bdiqqa] She figured it out accurately. حِسبَتها بِالضَبُط [ħisbatha biððabuṭ]

to accuse • 1. تِهَم [tiham] إتِّهام [ʔittiha:m] *vn:* اِنتِهَم [ʔintiham] *p:* You can't accuse me of being lazy. ما تِقدَر تِتهِمنِي بِالكَسَل [ma: tigdar tithimni bilkasal] He was accused of theft. اِنتِهَم بِبَوقَة [ʔintiham bibawga]

accustomed • 1. مِتعَوِّد عَلَى [mitʕawwid ʕala] She's not accustomed to that. هِيَّ ما مِتعَوِّدَة عَلَى هَذا [hiyya ma: mitʕawwda ʕala ha:ða]

to get accustomed to • 1. تعَوَّد عَلَى [tʕawwad ʕala] تَعَوُّد [taʕawwud] *vn: sv* a. He can't get accustomed to the strict discipline. هُوَّ ما يِقدَر يِتعَوَّد عالنِّظام الدَّقِيق [huwwa ma: yigdar yitʕawwad ʕanniða:m ʔiddaqi:q]

ace • 1. آس [ʔa:s] آسات [ʔa:sa:t] *pl:* He has all four aces. هُوَّ عِندَه الأربَع آسات [huwwa ʕindah ʔilʔarbaʕ ʔa:sa:t]

to ache • 1. وُجَع [wujaʕ, wijaʕ] وُجَع [wujaʕ] *vn: sv* a. My ear aches. إذنِي تُوجَعنِي [ʔiðni tu:jaʕni]

to achieve • 1. حَقَّق [ħaqqaq] تَحقِيق [taħqi:q] *vn:* تحَقَّق [tħaqqaq] *p:* He achieved his purpose. حَقَّق مَرامَه [ħaqqaq mara:mah]

acid • 1. حامُض [ħa:muð] Bring me that bottle of acid. جِيبلِي ذاك بُطل الحامُض [ǰi:bli ða:k buṭul ʔilħa:muð] • **2.** لاذِع [la:ðiʕ] He made a few acid remarks. عَلَّق شوَيَّة تَعلِيقات لاذعَة [ʕallaq šwayyat taʕli:qa:t la:ðʕa]

to acknowledge • 1. اِعتِرَف [ʔiʕtiraf] اِعتِراف [ʔiʕtira:f] *vn: sv* i. We acknowledge receipt of your letter dated. . . نعتِرِف بِإستِلام مَكتُوبَك المُؤَرَّخ [niʕtirif bʔistila:m maktu:bak ʔilmuʔarrax]

acknowledged • 1. مُعتَرَف [muʕtaraf] He is an acknowledged expert. هُوَّ خَبِير مُعتَرَف بِيه [huwwa xabi:r muʕtaraf bi:h]

acorn • 1. بَلُّوطَة [ballu:ṭa] بَلُّوطات، بَلُّوط [ballu:ṭa:t, ballu:ṭ] *pl:* بَلُّوط [ballu:ṭ] *Collective*

to acquaint • 1. أطلَع [ʔaṭlaʕ] إطلاع [ʔiṭla:ʕ] *vn: sv* i. عَرَّف ب [ʕarraf b] تَعرِيف [taʕri:f] *vn: sv* u. First I want to acquaint you with the facts of the case. أَوَّلاً أرِيد أطلِعَك عَلَى حَقايِق القَضِيَّة [ʔawwalan ʔari:d ʔaṭliʕak ʕala ħaqa:yiq ʔilqaðiyya]

to acquaint oneself • 1. تعَرَّف [tʕarraf] تَعَرُّف [taʕarruf] *vn: sv* a. اِطَّلَع [ʔiṭṭilaʕ] إطِّلاع [ʔiṭṭila:ʕ] *vn: sv* i. It'll take me a week to acquaint myself with all the problems. يِنرادلِي إسبُوع حَتَّى أتعَرَّف عَلَى كُلّ المَشاكِل [yinra:dli ʔisbu:ʕ ħatta ʔatʕarraf ʕala kull ʔilmaša:kil]

to get acquainted with • 1. تعَرَّف عَلَى [tʕarraf ʕala] تَعَرُّف [taʕarruf] *vn: sv* a. You two should get acquainted with each other. لازِم إنتُو الثنَين تِتعَرّفُون عَلَى بَعَضكُم [la:zim ʔintu liθnayn titʕarrfu:n ʕala baʕaðkum]

acquaintance • 1. واحِد مِن المَعارِف [wa:ħid min ʔilmaʕa:rif] He's an old acquaintance of mine. هُوَّ واحِد مِن مَعارِفِي العِتَّق [huwwa wa:ħid min maʕa:rfi ʔilʕittag] • **2.** مَعرِفَة [maʕrifa] مَعارِف [maʕa:rif] *pl:* I am pleased to make your acquaintance. آنِي فَرحان بِمَعرِفتَك [ʔa:ni farħa:n bmaʕriftak]

to acquire • 1. حَصَّل [ħaṣṣal] حُصُول [ħuṣu:l] *vn:* تحَصَّل [tħaṣṣal] *p:* We acquired the house when our uncle died. حَصَّلنا عَالبَيت مِن مات عَمّنا [ħaṣṣalna ʕalbayt min ma:t ʕammna] • **2.** اِكتِسَب [ʔiktisab] اِكتِساب [ʔiktisa:b] *vn: sv* i. He's acquired considerable skill in tennis. اِكتِسَب هوايَة مَهارَة بِالتَّنِس [ʔiktisab hwa:ya maha:ra bittanis]

to acquit • 1. بَرَّأ [barraʔ] تَبرِئَة [tabriʔa] *vn:* تبَرَّى [tbarra:] *p:* The judge acquitted him. الحاكِم بَرّاه [ʔilħa:kim barra:h]

across • 1. بصَوب اللاخ [bṣu:b ʔilla:x] The station is across the river. المَحَطَّة بِصَوب اللّاخ مِن الشَّطّ [ʔilmaħaṭṭa bṣu:b ʔilla:x min ʔiššaṭṭ]

across the street • 1. قبال [gba:l] He lives across the street from us. هُوَّ يِسكُن قبالنا [huwwa yiskun gba:lna]

to go across • 1. عُبَر [ʕubar] عُبُور [ʕubu:r] *vn:* اِنعُبَر [ʔinʕubar] *p:* Let's go across the bridge. خَلِّي نُعبُر الجِّسِر [xalli nuʕbur ʔiǰǰisir]

*** This bus goes right across town.**

• **1.** هَالباص يِجتاز الولايَة عَلَى طُول [halpa:ṣ yiǰta:z ʔilwla:ya ʕala ṭu:l]

act • 1. عَمَل [ʕamal] عَملَة [ʕamla] *Feminine:* فِعِل [fiʕil] أفعَال [ʔafʕa:l] *pl:* That wasn't a selfish act. هَذا ما كان عَمَل أنانِي [ha:ða ma: ča:n ʕamal ʔana:ni] • **2.** فَصِل [faṣil] I don't want to miss the first act. ما أرِيد يفُوتنِي الفَصل الأوَّل [ma: ʔari:d yfu:tni ʔilfaṣl ʔilʔawwal]

*** Don't put on an act! • 1.** لا تِتصَنَّع [la: titṣannaʕ]

to act • 1. تصَرَّف [tṣarraf] تَصَرُّف [taṣarruf] *vn: sv* a. He's been acting like a child. كان يِتصَرَّف مِثل الزَّعطُوط [ča:n yitṣarraf miθl ʔizzaʕṭu:ṭ] • **2.** مَثَّل [maθθal] تَمثِيل [tamθi:l] *vn:* تمَثَّل [tmaθθal] *p:* She's going to act in that new play. راح تمَثِّل بذِيك التَّمثِيلِيَّة الجِّدِيدَة [ra:ħ tmaθθil bði:č ʔittamθi:liyya ʔiǰǰidi:da]

to act on • 1. اِتَّخَذ [ʔittixað] اِتِّخاذ [ʔittixa:ð] *vn: sv* i. They're going to act on our proposal tomorrow.

i, interjection; p, passive; pl, plural; sv, stem vowel; vn, verbal noun

راح يتّخذون إجراء بإقتِراحنا باكِر [raːħ yittaxðuːn ʔiǰraːʔ bʔiqtiraːħna baːčir]

action • **1.** حادِث، حادِثَة [ħaːdiθ, ħaːdiθa] حَوادِث [ħawaːdiθ] *pl:* The action of the novel takes place in Turkey. حَوادِث القُصَّة تِجري بتُركِيا [ħawaːdiθ ʔilquṣṣa tiǰri bturkiyaː] • **2.** إجراء [ʔiǰraːʔ] إجراءات [ʔiǰraːʔat] *pl:* This situation requires firm action. هَالوَضِع يتطَلَّب إجراء حازِم [halwaḍiʕ yiṭṭallab ʔiǰraːʔ ħaːzim] • **3.** تَصَرُّف [taṣarruf] تَصَرُّفات [taṣarrufaːt] *pl:* His actions are hard to understand. تَصَرُّفاته صَعُب تِنفِهِم [taṣarrufaːtah ṣaʕub tinfihim]

in action • **1.** مَعرَكَة [maʕraka] مَعارِك [maʕaːrik] *pl:* He was killed in action. اِنقِتَل بالمَعرَكَة [ʔinkital bilmaʕraka]

to bring action against • **1.** قام [qaːm] إقامَة [ʔiqaːma] *vn:* إنقام [ʔinqaːm] *p:* They will bring action against him. راح يقيمُون عَليه دَعوَة [raːħ yqiːmuːn ʕaliːh daʕwa]

to take action • **1.** أَخَذ مِن، أَخَذ عَلَى [ʔaxað min, ʔaxað ʕala] أَخِذ [ʔaxið] *vn:* اِنأخَذ [ʔinʔixað] *p:* Has any action been taken on my case? اِنأخَذ أيّ إجراء بقَضِيتي؟ [ʔinʔixað ʔayy ʔiǰraːʔ bqaḍiːti?]

active • **1.** عامِل [ʕaːmil] Are you an active member? إنتَ عُضو عامِل؟ [ʔinta ʕuḍw ʕaːmil?] • **2.** نَشِيط [našiːṭ] He's still very active for his age. بَعدَه كُلَّش نَشِيط بالنِّسبَة لعُمرَه [baʕdah kulliš našiːṭ binnisba lʕumrah] • **3.** فَعّال [faʕʕaːl] He has always been very active in our club. هُوَّ كان وَلحَدّ الآن كُلَّش فَعّال بنادِينا [huwwa čaːn walħadd ʔilʔaːn kulliš faʕʕaːl bnaːdiːna]

activity • **1.** نَشاط [našaːṭ] He had to give up all physical activity for a while. اِضطَرّ يترُك كُلّ النَّشاط الجِّسمِي فَدّ مُدَّة [ʔiḍṭarr yitruk kull ʔinnašaːṭ ʔiǰǰismi fadd mudda] • **2.** حَرَكَة [ħaraka] There's not much activity around here on Sunday. ماكُو هوايَة حَرَكَة هنا يوم الأحَّد [maːku hwaːya ħaraka hna yuːm ʔilʔaħħad] • **3.** عَمَل [ʕamal] عَملَة [ʕamla] *Feminine:* She engages in a lot of social activity. تِشتِرِك بهوايَة أعمال اِجتِماعِيَّة [tištirik bhwaːya ʔaʕmaːl ʔiǰtimaːʕiyya]

feverish activity • **1.** خَبصَة [xabṣa] خَبصات [xabṣaːt] *pl:* What's all that feverish activity over there? شِنُو هَالخَبصَة هناك؟ [šinuː halxabṣa hnaːk?]

actor • **1.** مُمَثِّل [mumaθθil] مُمَثِّلِين [mumaθθiliːn] *pl:*

actress • **1.** مُمَثِّلَة [mumaθθila] مُمَثِّلات [mumaθθilaːt] *pl:*

actual • **1.** حَقِيقِي [ħaqiːqi] فِعلِي [fiʕli] The actual reason was something entirely different. السَّبَب الحَقِيقِي كان فَدّ شِي يختِلِف تَماماً [ʔissabab ʔilħaqiːqi čaːn fadd ši yixtilif tamaːman] • **2.** أصلِي [ʔaṣli] She works here, but her actual office is on the second floor. هِيَّ تِشتُغُل هنا لَكِن مَحَلّ شُغُلها الأصلِي بالطّابِق الثّانِي [hiyya tištuɣul hna laːkin maħall šuɣulha ʔilʔaṣli biṭṭaːbiq ʔiθθaːni]

actually • **1.** حَقِيقَةً [ħaqiːqatan] فِعلاً [fiʕlan] صُدُق [ṣudug] Do you actually believe that story? إنتَ صُدُق تِعتِقِد بهَذِيك الحِكايَة؟ [ʔinta ṣudug tiʕtiqid bhaðiːč ʔilħčaːya?] • **2.** صَحِيح [ṣaħiːħ] Did he actually write this letter? صَحِيح كِتَب هَالمَكتُوب؟ [ṣaħiːħ kitab halmaktuːb?]

acute • **1.** حادّ [ħaːdd] He has acute dysentery. عِندَه دَزَنتَرِي حادّ [ʕindah dazantari ħaːdd] This triangle has two acute angles. هَالمُثَلَّث بِيه زاوِيتَين حادَّة [halmuθallaθ biːh zaːwiːtayn ħaːdda] • **2.** شَدِيد [šadiːd] If the pain becomes acute, call the doctor. إذا صار الألَم شَدِيد خابُر الطَّبِيب [ʔiða ṣaːr ʔilʔalam šadiːd xaːbur ʔiṭṭabiːb] • **3.** قَوِي [qawi, guwi] قَواي، أقوِياء، قَوِيِّين [qwaːy, ʔaqwiyaːʔ, qawiyyiːn] *pl:* Dogs have an acute sense of smell. الكِلاب عِدها حاسَّة شَمّ قَوِيَّة [ʔiččilaːb ʕidha ħaːssat šamm qawiyya]

ad • **1.** إعلان [ʔiʕlaːn] إعلانات [ʔiʕlaːnaːt] *pl:* I'd like to put in an ad. أريد أنشُر إعلان [ʔariːd ʔanšur ʔiʕlaːn]

to adapt • **1.** تكَيَّف [tkayyaf] تَكَيُّف [takayyuf] *vn:* *sv* a. She adapts easily to new social situations. هِيَّ تِتكَيَّف بسُهُولَة عَلَى الحالَة الاجتِماعِيَّة الجِّدِيدَة [hiyya titkayyaf bsuhuːla ʕala ʔilħaːla ʔiliǰtimaːʕiyya ʔiǰǰidiːda] • **2.** تلاءَم [tlaːʔam] تَلاؤُم [talaːʔum] *vn:* *sv* a. This method will adapt well to my purposes. هَالطَّرِيقَة تِتلاءَم زين ويّا أغراضِي [haṭṭariːqa titlaːʔam ziːn wiyya ʔaɣraːḍi] • **3.** كَيَّف [kayyaf] تكييف [takyiːf] *vn:* تكَيَّف [tkayyaf] *p:* He adapts himself easily. هُوَّ يكَيِّف نَفسَه بسُهُولَة [huwwa ykayyif nafsah bsuhuːla]

to add • **1.** زاد [zaːd] زيادَة [zyaːda] *vn:* *sv* i. You'll have to add some sugar. ينرادلَك تزِيد شوَيَّة شَكَر [yinraːdlak dziːd šwayyat šakar] • **2.** ضاف [ḍaːf] إضافَة [ʔiḍaːfa] *vn:* اِنضاف [ʔinḍaːf] *p:* I've nothing to add to that. ما عِندِي شي أضِيف لهَذا [maː ʕindi ši ʔaḍiːf lhaðaː] • **3.** جِمَع [ǰimaʕ] جَمِع [ǰamiʕ] *vn:* اِنجِمَع [ʔinǰimaʕ] *p:* Add up these figures. إجمَع هالأرقام [ʔiǰmaʕ halʔarqaːm]

to add up to • **1.** صار [ṣaːr] *sv* i. How much will the bill add up to? شقَدّ راح تصِير القائِمَة؟ [šgadd raːħ tṣiːr ʔilqaːʔima?]

addition • **1.** جَمِع [ǰamiʕ] Is my addition correct? جَمعِي صَحِيح؟ [ǰamʕi ṣaħiːħ?] • **2.** مُلحَق [mulħaq] مَلاحِق [malaħiq] *pl:* They're building an addition on that building. دَيبنُون مُلحَق لهَذِي البِنايَة [dayibnuːn mulħaq lihaːði ʔilbinaːya] • **3.** زِيادَة [ziyaːda] The addition of turpentine will thin the paint. زِيادَة التَّربَنتِين راح تخَفِّف الصُّبُغ [ziyaːdat ʔittarbantiːn raːħ txaffif ʔiṣṣubuɣ]

in addition • **1.** كمالَة [čmaːla] كمالات [čmaːlaːt] *pl:* فَوق [fuːg, fuːq] In addition he asked for ten dollars. كمالَة طِلَب عَشِر دُولارات [čmaːla ṭilab ʕašir dulaːraːt]

in addition to • **1.** بالإضافَة إلَى [bilʔiḍaːfa ʔila] In addition to his fixed salary he gets commissions. بالإضافَة عَلَى مَعاشَه ياخُذ عُمُولَة [bilʔiḍaːfa ʕala maʕaːšah yaːxuð ʕumuːla]

A

additional • **1.** إضافِي [ʔiðaːfi] He gave me an additional amount for incidentals. اِنطانِي فَدّ مَبلَغ إضافِي لِمَصارِيف نَثرِيَّة [ʔinṭaːni fadd mablaɣ ʔiðaːfi lmaṣaːriːf naθriyya] • **2.** أزيَد [ʔazyad] An additional dollar gives you better quality. فَدّ دُولار أزيَد يِنطِيك نُوع أحسَن [fadd dulaːr ʔazyad yinṭiːk nawʕ ʔaħsan]

address • **1.** عِنوان [ʕinwaːn] Send these books to this address. دِزّ هالكُتُب لهَذا العِنوان [dizz halkutub lhaðaː ʔilʕinwaːn] • **2.** خِطاب [xiṭaːb] خِطابات [xiṭaːbaːt] *pl:* The President delivered an important address. الرَّئِيس ألقَى خِطاب مُهِمّ [ʔirraʔiːs ʔalqaː xiṭaːb muhimm]

to address • **1.** عَنوَن [ʕanwan] تعَنوَن [tʕanwan] *p:* Address this letter to the manager. عَنوِن هَذا المَكتُوب لِلمُدِير [ʕanwin haːða ʔilmaktuːb lilmudiːr] • **2.** خاطَب [xaːṭab] مُخاطَبَة [muxaːṭaba] *vn: sv* u. How shall I address him? شلُون أخاطبَه؟ [šluːn ʔaxaːṭbah?] • **3.** وَجَّه [wajjah] تَوجِيه [tawjiːh] *vn:* توَجَّه [twajjah] *p:* I would like to address a question to the speaker. أحِبّ أوَجِّه سُؤال لِلمُتَكَلِّم [ʔaħibb ʔawajjih suʔaːl lilmutakallim]

adhesive tape • **1.** شَرِيط لِزَّيق [šariːṭ lizziːg]

adjective • **1.** صِفَة [ṣifa] صِفات [ṣifaːt] *pl:*

to adjoin • **1.** تحِدّ [tħidd] *sv* i. My garden adjoins his. حَدِيقتِي تحِدّ حَدِيقتَه [ħadiːqti tħidd ħadiːqtah] • **2.** جاوَر [jaːwar] مُجاوَرَة [mujaːwara] *vn: sv* i. Their garage adjoins the house. كَراجهُم يجاوِر البَيت [garaːjhum yjaːwir ʔilbayt]

to adjourn • **1.** فضّ [faðð] فضّ [faðð] *vn:* اِنفضّ [ʔinfaðð] *p:* He adjourned the meeting. هُوَّ فضّ الاِجتِماع [huwwa faðð ʔilʔijtimaːʕ]

to adjust • **1.** ضُبَط [ðubaṭ] ضَبُط [ðabuṭ] *vn:* اِنضُبَط [ʔinðubaṭ] *p:* The mechanic adjusted the carburetor. المِيكانِيكِي ضُبَط الكَبرِيتَر [ʔilmiːkaːniːki ðubat ʔilkabriːtar] • **2.** صَحَّح [ṣaħħaħ] تَصحِيح [taṣħiːħ] *vn:* تصَحَّح [tṣaħħaħ] *p:* The manager will adjust your bill. المُدِير راح يصَحِّح قائِمتَك [ʔilmudiːr raːħ yṣaħħiħ qaːʔimtak] • **3.** عَدَّل [ʕaddal] تَعدِيل [taʕdiːl] *vn:* تعَدَّل [tʕaddal] *p:* She adjusted her clothing. عَدِّلَت هدُومها [ʕaddilat hduːmha] • **4.** كَيَّف [kayyaf] تَكيِيف [takyiːf] *vn:* تكَيَّف [tkayyaf] *p:* I can't adjust myself to the climate here. ما أقدَر أكَيِّف نَفسِي لهَالجَوّ [maː ʔagdar ʔakayyif nafsi lhaljaww]

adjustable • **1.** مِتحَرِّك [mitħarrik] Is this seat adjustable? هَذا المَقعَد مِتحَرِّك؟ [haːða ʔilmaqʕad mitħarrik?]

to administer • **1.** دار [daːr] إدارَة [ʔidaːra] *vn:* اِندار [ʔindaːr] *p:* Who's administering his estate? مِنُو دَيدِير تَركاتَه؟ [minu daydiːr tarikaːtah?] • **2.** سَوَّى [sawwaː] *sv* i. He showed us how he administers artificial respiration. راوانا شلُون يسَوِّي تَنَفُّس اِصطِناعِي [raːwaːna šluːn ysawwi tanaffus ʔiṣṭinaːʕi]

administration • **1.** إدارَة [ʔidaːra]

admiral • **1.** أمِيرال [ʔamiraːl] أمِيرالات، أمِيرالِيَّة [ʔamiralaAt, ʔamiraliyya] *pl:*

admiration • **1.** إعجاب [ʔiʕjaːb] He got the admiration of all his friends. نال إعجاب كُلّ أصدِقائَه [naːl ʔiʕjaːb kull ʔaṣdiqaːʔah]

to admire • **1.** كان مُعجَب ب [kaːn muʕjab b-] I admire her beauty. آنِي مُعجَب بجَمالها [ʔaːni muʕjab bjamaːlha]
* **I admire your patience.** • **1.** يعجِبنِي صَبرَك [yiʕjibni ṣabrak]

admission • **1.** دُخُول [duxuːl] How much is the admission? بيش الدُّخُول؟ [biyš ʔidduxuːl?] • **2.** قُبُول [qubuːl] I have an appointment with the Director of Admissions. عِندِي مَوعِد ويّا مُدِير القُبُول [ʕindi mawʕid wiyya mudiːr ʔilqubuːl] • **3.** اِعتِراف [ʔiʕtiraːf] اِعتِرافات [ʕitiraːfaːt] *pl:* His admission proved my innocence. اِعتِرافَه أثبَت بَرائتِي [ʔiʕtiraːfah ʔaθbat baraːʔti]

admission charge • **1.** أُجرَة دُخُول [ʔujrat duxuːl] There's no admission charge. ماكُو أُجرَة دُخُول [maːku ʔujrat duxuːl]

to admit • **1.** دَخَّل [daxxal] تَدخِيل [tadxiːl] *vn:* تدَخَّل [tdaxxal] *p:* خَشَّش [xaššaš] تَخشِيش [taxšiːš] *vn:* تخَشَّش [txaššaš] *p:* Give this card to the doorman and he'll admit you. اِنطِي هَالكَرت لِلبَوّاب وَهُوَّ يدَخّلَك [ʔinṭi halkart lilbawwaːb wahuwwa ydaxxlak] • **2.** قِبَل [qibal] قُبُول [qubuːl] *vn:* اِنقِبَل [ʔinqibal] *p:* We can't admit this type of student. ما نِقدَر نِقبَل هِيكِي تِلمِيذ [maː nigdar niqbal hiːči tilmiːð] • **3.** قَرّ ب [qarr b-] إقرار [ʔiqraːr] *vn: sv* u. The accused finally admitted his guilt. المُتَّهَم أخِيراً قَرّ بذَنبَه [ʔilmuttaham ʔaxiːran qarr bðanbah] • **4.** اِعتِرَف [ʔiʕtiraf] اِعتِراف [ʔiʕtiraːf] *vn: sv* i. I admit I was wrong. أعتِرِف كِنِت غَلطان [ʔaʕtirif činit ɣalṭaːn]

to adopt • **1.** تبَنَّى [tbannaː] تَبَنِّي [tabanniː] *vn: sv* a. My friend has adopted a small boy. صَدِيقِي تبَنَّى وَلَد صغَيِّر [ṣadiːqi tbannaː walad ṣɣayyir] • **2.** اِعتِنَق [ʔiʕtinaq] اِعتِناق [ʔiʕtinaːq] *vn: sv* i. They adopted Islam toward the end of the first century. اِعتِنقَوا الإسلام بأواخِر القَرن الأوَّل [ʔiʕtinqaw ʔilʔislaːm biʔawaːxir ʔilqarn ʔilʔawwal] • **3.** اِتِّخَذ [ʔittixað] اِتِّخاذ [ʔittixaːð] *vn: sv* i. They adopted the measure unanimously. اِتِّخذَوا القَرار بالإجماع [ʔititixðaw ʔilqaraːr bilʔijmaːʕ] • **4.** اِتِّبَع [ʔittibaʕ] اِتِّباع [ʔittibaːʕ] *vn: sv* i.

Better results could be obtained if we adopted this method. نِتوَصَّل إِلَى نَتائِج أَحسَن إِذا اِتِّبَعنا هَالطَّرِيقَة [nitwaṣṣal ʔila nata:ʔiǰ ʔaḥsan ʔiða ʔittibaʕna haṭṭari:qa]

adult • **1.** كِبِير [čibi:r, kibi:r] كبار [kba:r] *pl:* There was milk for the children and coffee for the adults. كان أَكُو حَلِيب لِلصِّغار وقَهوَة لِلكِبار [ča:n ʔaku ħali:b liṣṣiɣa:r wgahwa lilikba:r]

advance • **1.** تَقَدُّم [taqaddum] تَرَقِّي [taraqqi] Great advances have been made in medicine during the last few years. هوايَة تَقَدُّم صار بِالطِّبّ بِالسِّنِين الأَخِيرَة [hwa:ya taqaddum ṣa:r biṭṭibb bissini:n ʔilʔaxi:ra] • **2.** سُلفَة [sulfa] سُلَف [sulaf] *pl:* Can you give me an advance? تِقدَر تِنطِينِي سُلفَة؟ [tigdar tinṭi:ni sulfa?]

in advance • **1.** لِقِدّام [ligidda:m] Let me know in advance if you're coming. قُلِّي لِقِدّام إِذا راح تِجِي [gulli ligidda:m ʔiða ra:ħ tiǰi]

to advance • **1.** تَرَقَّى [traqqa:] تَرَقِّي [taraqqi] *vn: sv* a. He advanced rapidly in the company. تَرَقَّى بِالعَجَل بِالشَّرِكَة [traqqa: bilʕaǰal biššarika] • **2.** رَفَّع [raffaʕ] تَرفِيع [tarfi:ʕ] *vn:* تَرَفَّع [traffaʕ] *p:* They just advanced him to assistant manager. تَوّهُم رَفِّعُوه إِلَى مُعاوِن مُدِير [tawwhum raffiʕu:h ʔila muʕa:win mudi:r] He was advanced to chief clerk. تَرَفَّع إِلَى رَئِيس كُتّاب [traffaʕ ʔila raʔi:s kutta:b] • **3.** قَدَّم [qaddam] تَقدِيم [taqdi:m] *vn:* تقَدَّم [tqaddam] *p:* They advanced the date of the lecture. قَدّمَوا تارِيخ المُحاضَرَة [qaddmaw ta:ri:x ʔilmuħa:ðara] • **4.** تقَدَّم [tqaddam] تَقَدُّم [taqaddum] *vn: sv* a. Our army advanced twenty miles. جَيشنا تقَدَّم عِشرِين مِيل [ǰayšna tqaddam ʕišri:n mi:l] • **5.** سَلَّف [sallaf] تَسلِيف [tasli:f] *vn: sv* i. The bank advanced him one thousand dinars. البَنك سَلَّفَه أَلف دِينار [ʔilbank sallafah ʔalf dina:r]

advantage • **1.** فائِدَة [fa:ʔida] فَوائِد [fawa:ʔid] *pl:* This method has advantages and disadvantages. هَالطَّرِيقَة بِيها فَوائِد وَعيُوب [haṭṭari:qa bi:ha fawa:ʔid wʕiyu:b]

an advantage over • **1.** أَفضَلِيَّة عَلَى [ʔafðaliyya ʕala] Your technical education gives you an advantage over me. ثَقافتَك الفَنِّيَّة تِنطِيك أَفضَلِيَّة عَلَيّا [θaqa:ftak ʔilfanniyya tinṭi:k ʔafðaliyya ʕalayya]

to one's advantage • **1.** لمَصلَحَة أَحَّد [lmaṣlaħat ʔaħħad] This is to your advantage. هَذا لمَصلَحتَك [ha:ða lmaṣlaħtak]

to take advantage of • **1.** اِنتِهَز [ʔintihaz] اِنتِهاز [ʔintiha:z] *vn: sv* i. He takes advantage of every opportunity. يِنتِهِز كُلّ فُرصَة [yintihiz kull furṣa] • **2.** اِستَغَلّ [ʔistaɣall] اِستِغلال [ʔistiɣla:l] *vn: sv* i. Don't let people take advantage of you. لا تخَلِّي النّاس يِستِغِلُّوك [la: txalli ʔinna:s yistiɣillu:k]

advantageous • **1.** مُفِيد [mufi:d] نافِع [na:fiʕ]

adventure • **1.** مُخاطَرَة [muxa:ṭara] مُخاطَرات [muxa:ṭara:t] *pl:* مُجازَفَة [muǰa:zafa] مُجازَفات [muǰa:zafa:t] *pl:* مُغامَرَة [muɣa:mara] مُغامَرات [muɣa:mara:t] *pl:*

adverb • **1.** ظَرُف [ðaruf] ظرُوف [ðru:f] *pl:*

to advertise • **1.** أَعلَن، عِلَن [ʔaʕlan, ʕilan] إِعلان [ʔiʕla:n] *vn:* اِنعِلَن [ʔinʕilan] *p:* The store advertised a sale. المَخزَن عِلَن تَنزِيلات [ʔilmaxzan ʕilan tanzi:la:t]

advertisement • **1.** إِعلان [ʔiʕla:n] إِعلانات [ʔiʕla:na:t] *pl:*

advertising • **1.** دِعايَة [diʕa:ya] إِعلان [ʔiʕla:n] إِعلانات [ʔiʕla:na:t] *pl:* Our company spends a lot on advertising. شَرِكَتنا تُصرُف هوايَة عالدِّعايَة [šarikatna tuṣruf hwa:ya ʕaddiʕa:ya]

advice • **1.** نَصِيحَة [naṣi:ħa] نَصايِح [naṣa:yiħ] *pl:* My advice is that you leave immediately. نَصِيحتِي أَن ترُوح حالاً [naṣi:ħti ʔan tru:ħ ħa:lan]

to ask advice • **1.** اِستَشار [ʔistaša:r] اِستِشارَة [ʔistiša:ra] *vn: sv* i. طِلَب [ṭilab] *sv* u. I asked his advice. اِستَشَرتَه [ʔistišartah] I asked his advice. طلَبِت نَصِيحتَه [ṭlabit naṣi:ħtah]

to give advice • **1.** نِصَح [niṣaħ] اِنِّصَح [ʔinniṣaħ] *p:* نِطَى [niṭa:] نَطِي [naṭi] *vn: sv* i. It is hard to give advice in this matter. صَعُب واحِد يِنصَح بِهَالمَوضُوع [ṣaʕub wa:ħid yinṣaħ bhalmawðu:ʕ] It is hard to give advice in this matter. صَعَب واحِد يِنطِي نَصِيحَة بِهَالمَوضُوع [ṣaʕab wa:ħid yinṭi naṣi:ħa bhalmawðu:ʕ]

advisable • **1.** أَعقَل [ʔaʕqal] I think it's advisable for you to stay home today. أَشُوف الأَعقَل تِبقَى بِالبَيت اليُوم [ʔašu:f ʔilʔaʕqal tibqa: bilbayt ʔilyu:m] • **2.** مُستَحسَن [mustaħsan] Would that be an advisable step to take? تِعتِقِد هالخَطوَة مُستَحسَنَة؟ [tiʕtiqid halxaṭwa mustaħsana?]

to advise • **1.** نِصَح [niṣaħ] اِنِّصَح [ʔinniṣaħ] *p:* شار عَلَى [ša:r ʕala] اِنشار [ʔinša:r] *p:* What do you advise me to do? شتِنصَحنِي أَسَوِّي؟ [štinṣaħni ʔasawwi?]

adviser • **1.** مُشاوِر عَدلِي [muša:wir ʕadli] • **2.** مُستَشار سِياسِي [mustaša:r siya:si] • **3.** مُرشِد [muršid] مُرشِدِين [muršidi:n] *pl:*

advisory • **1.** اِستِشارِي [ʔistiša:ri]

aerial • **1.** أَرِيَل [ʔaryal] أَرِيَلات [ʔaryala:t] *pl:* The aerial on the radio isn't connected. الأَيرِيَل مال الرّادِيُو ما مِتَّصِل [ʔilʔi:ryal ma:l ʔirra:dyu ma: mittiṣil]

aerial warfare • **1.** حَرُب جَوِّيَّة [ħarub ǰawwiyya]

A

affair • **1.** أَمُر [ʔamur] أَوامِر [ʔawaːmir] *pl:* I don't meddle in his affairs. ما أَتدَخَّل بأُمُورَه [maː ʔaddaxxal bʔumuːrah] • **2.** شُغُل [šuɣul] أشغال [ʔašɣaːl] *pl:* That's your affair. هذا شُغلَك إنت [hðaː šuɣlak ʔinta] • **3.** شَأن [šaʔn] شُؤُون [šuʔuːn] *pl:* He handled the affairs of the company badly. دار شُؤُون الشَّرِكَة بصُورَة مخَربطَة [daːr šuʔuːn ʔiššarika bṣuːra mxarubṭa] • **4.** مُناسَبَة [munaːsaba] مُناسَبات [munaːsabaːt] *pl:* Her party was a real nice affair. حَفلَتها كانَت مُناسَبَة لَطِيفَة جِدّاً [ħaflatha čaːnat munaːsaba laṭiːfa ǰiddan] • **5.** عِلاقَة [ʕilaːqa] عِلاقات [ʕilaːqaːt] *pl:* The cook had an affair with the chauffeur. الطَّبّاخَة صار عِدها عِلاقَة (غرامِيَّة) ويّا السّايِق [ʔiṭṭabbaːxa ṣaːr ʕidha ʕilaːqa (ɣaraːmiyya) wiyya ʔissaːyiq]

to affect • **1.** أَثَّر عَلَى [ʔaθθar ʕala] تَأثِير [taʔθiːr] *vn: sv* i. That damp climate affected his health. هَذاك الطَّقس الرَّطِب أَثَّر عَلَى صِحَّتَه [haðaːk ʔiṭṭaqis ʔirraṭib ʔaθθar ʕala ṣiħħtah] • **2.** تظاهَر [dðaːhar] تَظاهُر [taðaːhur] *vn: sv* a. He has affected an Egyptian accent. يِتظاهَر عِندَه لَكنَة مَصرِيَّة [yitðaːhar ʕindah lakna maṣriyya]

to be affected • **1.** تأثَّر ب [tʔaθθar b-] تَأثُّر [taʔaθθur] *vn: sv* a. His vision was affected by his illness. نَظَرَه تأثَّر بمَرَضَه [naðarah tʔaθθar bmaraðah]

affected • **1.** مُصطَنَع [muṣṭanaʕ] She's terribly affected. هِيَّ كُلِّش مِتصَنِّعَة [hiyya kulliš mitṣanniʕa] • **2.** مِتكَلِّف [mitkallif] Is his style in writing always that affected? إسلُوبَه بالكِتابَة دائِماً هِيكِي مِتكَلِّف؟ [ʔisluːbah bilkitaːba daːʔiman hiːči mitkallif?]

to afford • **1.** تمَكَّن [tmakkan] تَمَكُّن [tamakkun] *vn: sv* a. We can't afford to buy a car. ما نِتمَكَّن نِشتِري سَيّارَة [maː nitmakkan ništiri sayyaːra] We can't afford to buy a car. ما إلنا قابلِيَّة سَيّارَة [maː ʔilna qaːbliyyat sayyaːra]

*** I can't afford that much.** • **1.** هَذا غالِي عَلَيَّ [haːða ɣaːli ʕalayya]

*** You can afford to laugh.** • **1.** حَقَّك تِضحَك [ħaqqak tiðħak] إضحَك لَيش لا [ʔiðħak liːš laː]

Afghanistan • **1.** أفغانِستان [ʔafɣaːnistaːn]

to be afraid • **1.** خِشَى [xišaː] خِشيَة [xišya] *vn: sv* a. I'm afraid its going to rain. أَخشَى راح تُمطُر [ʔaxšaː raːħ tumṭur]

to be afraid of • **1.** n خاف مِن [xaːf min] خَوف [xuːf] *vn: sv* a. He's not afraid of anyone. ما يخاف مِن أَحَّد [maː yxaːf min ʔaħhad]

Africa • **1.** أفرِيقيا [ʔafriːqya]

African • **1.** أفرِيقِي [ʔafriːqi]

after • **1.** بَعَد [baʕad] Can you call me after supper? تِقدَر تخابُرني بَعد العَشا؟ [tigdar txaːburni baʕd ʔilʕaša?] • **2.** وَرا [wara] • **3.** عَلَى [ʕala] Day after day, his health is improving. يوم عَلَى يوم صِحَّتَه دَتِتحَسَّن [yuːm ʕala yuːm ṣiħħtah datitħassan] He named his son after his grandfather. سَمَّى إبنَه عَلَى إسِم جِدَّه [sammaː ʔibnah ʕala ʔisim ǰiddah] • **4.** عَلَى أَثَر [ʕala ʔaθar] After the death of my father, I had to quit school. عَلَى أَثَر وَفاة أَبُويَا اِضطَرَّيت أَبَطِّل مِن المَدرَسَة [ʕala ʔaθar wafaːt ʔabuːya ʔiðṭarriːt ʔabaṭṭil min ʔilmadrasa]

after all • **1.** مَهما يكُون [mahma ykuːn] Why shouldn't I help him? After all, he's my friend. لُوِيش ما أَساعدَه؟ مَهما يكُون هُوَّ صَدِيقِي [luwiːš maː ʔasaːʕdah? mahmaː ykuːn huwwa ṣadiːqi] • **2.** تالِي [taːli] تُوالِي [tuwaːli] *pl:* You are right, after all. تالِيها الحَقّ ويّاك [taːliːha ʔilħaqq wiyyaːk]

after this • **1.** مِن هِنَا و غادِي [minhna wɣaːdi] After this, please let us know in advance. مِن هِنَا وَغادِي إنطِينا خَبَر لِقِدّام [minna wɣaːdi ʔinṭiːna xabar ligiddaːm]

to be after • **1.** دَوَّر عَلَى [dawwar ʕala] تَدوِير [tadwiːr] *vn: sv* u. The police have been after him for two weeks. الشُّرطَة دَتدَوُّر عَليه مِن مُدَّة إسبُوعَين [ʔiššurṭa daddawwur ʕaliːh min muddat ʔisbuːʕayn]

afternoon • **1.** عَصرِيَّة [ʕaṣriyya] عَصرِيّات [ʕaṣriyyaːt] *pl:* I would like to see you one afternoon. يعجِبنِي أَشُوفَك فَدّ عَصرِيَّة [yiʕǰibni ʔašuːfak fadd ʕaṣriyya]

in the afternoon • **1.** بَعد الظُّهُر [baʕd ʔiððuhur] وَرا الظُّهُر [wara ʔiððuhur] عَصِر [ʕaṣir] I never drink coffee in the afternoon. آنِي أَبَد ما أَشرَب قَهوَة وَرا الظُّهُر [ʔaːni ʔabad maː ʔašrab gahwa wara ʔiððuhur]

this afternoon • **1.** اليَوم العَصِر [ʔilyuːm ʔilʕaṣir] Can you come this afternoon. تِقدَر تِجِي اليُوم العَصِر؟ [tigdar tiǰi ʔilyuːm ʔilʕaṣir?]

afterwards • **1.** بَعدِين [baʕdiːn]

again • **1.** مَرَّة لُخ [marra lux] مَرَّة اللُّخ [marrt ʔillux] مَرَّة ثانيَة [marra θaːnya] I'll tell him again. راح أَقُلَّه مَرَّة لُخ [raːħ ʔagullah marra lux] • **2.** مِن جِهَة اللُّخ [min ǰiht ʔillux] Again, we should study the other proposal, too. مِن جِهَة اللُّخ، هَمّ لازِم ندرُس الاقتِراح الثّانِي [min ǰihat ʔillux, hamm laːzim nidrus ʔilʔiqtiraːħ ʔiθθaːni] • **3.** بَعَد [baʕad] He never made that mistake again. هُوَّ ما سَوَّى ذِيك الغَلطَة بَعَد [huwwa maː sawwaː ðiːč ʔilɣalṭa baʕad]

again and again • **1.** مَرَّة وَرا مَرَّة [marra wara marra] ياما وياما [yaːma wyaːma,] I warned him again and again. حَذَّرتَه مَرَّة وَرا مَرَّة [ħaððartah marra wara marra]

over and over again • **1.** مَرّات هوايَة [marraːt hwaːya] He tried over and over again. هُوَّ حاوَل مَرّات هوايَة [huwwa ħaːwal marraːt hwaːya]

then again • **1.** هَمِّين [hammiːn] But then again, that's not always true. لَكِن هَمِّين، هذا مُو دائِماً صَحِيح [laːkin hammiːn, hðaː muː daːʔiman ṣaħiːħ]

A

against • **1.** بصَفّ [bşaff] Move this table over against the wall. حُطّ هَالميز بصَفّ الحايط [ħuṭṭ halmi:z bşaff ʔilħa:yiṭ] • **2.** ضِدّ [ðidd] أضداد [ʔaðda:d] *pl:* We had to swim against the current. اِضطَرَّينا نِسبَح ضِدّ المَي [ʔiðṭarri:na nisbaħ ðidd ʔilmayy] He voted against me. هُوَّ صَوَّت ضِدّي [huwwa şawwat ðiddi] • **3.** عَلَى [ʕala] He was leaning against the house. كان مِنتِكي عَالبَيت [ča:n mintiči ʕalbayt]

as against • **1.** مُقابِل [muqa:bil] Fifty ships went through the canal as against thirty five last month. خَمسِين سَفِينَة مَرَّت مِن القَنال مُقابِل خَمسَة وَثلاثِين بِالشَّهر اللّي فات [xamsi:n safi:na marrat min ʔilqana:l muqa:bil xamsa wtla:θi:n biššahr ʔilli fa:t]

age • **1.** عُمُر [ʕumur] أعمار [ʔaʕma:r] *pl:* سِنّ [sinn] أسنان [ʔasna:n] *pl:* He's about my age. هُوَّ تَقرِيباً بعُمري [huwwa taqri:ban bʕumri] He's about my age. هُوَّ تَقرِيباً بِسِنّي [huwwa taqri:ban bsinni] • **2.** عَصِر [ʕaşir] عُصُور [ʕuşu:r] *pl:* This is the atomic age. هَذا عَصر الذَّرَّة [ha:ða ʕaşr ʔiððarra]

in ages • **1.** مِن زَمان [min zama:n] We haven't seen them in ages. ما شِفناهُم مِن زَمان [ma: šifna:hum min zama:n]

of age • **1.** بالِغ سِنّ الرُّشُد [ba:liɣ sinn irrušud] He'll come of age next year. راح يِبلُغ سِنّ الرُّشُد السَّنَة الجّايَّة [ra:ħ yibluɣ sinn ʔirrušud ʔissana ʔijja:yya]

old age • **1.** كُبُر [kubur] He died of old age. مات مِن الكُبُر [ma:t min ʔilkubur]

to age • **1.** شَيَّب [šayyab] *sv* i. He's aged a great deal lately. شَيَّب هوايَة بالأيّام الأخِيرَة [šayyab hwa:ya bilʔayya:m ʔilʔaxi:ra] • **2.** عَتَّق [ʕattaq] تَعتِيق [taʕti:q] *vn:* تعَتَّق [tʕattaq] *p:* The brewery aged the beer ninety days. مَعمَل البيرَة عَتَّق البِيرَة تِسعِين يوم [maʕmal ʔilbi:ra ʕattaq ʔilbi:ra tisʕi:n yu:m] • **3.** تعَتَّق [tʕattaq, ʔitʕattag] *sv* a. They left the wine to age for a number of years. خَلّوا الشَّراب يِتعَتَّق كَم سَنَة [xallaw ʔiššara:b yitʕattaq čam sana]

agency • **1.** وَكالَة [waka:la] وَكالات [waka:la:t] *pl:* Our company has an agency in Beirut. شَرِكتنا عِدها وَكالَة بِبَيرُوت [šarikatna ʕidha waka:la bibayru:t] • **2.** دائِرَة [da:ʔira] دَوائِر [dawa:ʔir] *pl:* Government agencies submit their budgets this month. دَوائِر الحُكُومَة يقَدّمُون مِيزانِيّاتهُم هَالشَّهَر [dawa:ʔir ʔilħuku:ma yqaddimu:n mi:za:niyya:thum haššahar]

agent • **1.** وَكِيل [waki:l] وُكَلاء [wukala:ʔ] *pl:* Your agent called on me yesterday. وَكِيلَك جانِي البارحَة [waki:lak ja:ni ʔilba:rħa] • **2.** عَمِيل [ʕami:l] عُمَلاء [ʕumala:ʔ] *pl:* He is said to be a communist agent. الشّايِع عَنَّه هُوَّ عَمِيل شِيُوعِي [ʔišša:yiʕ ʕannah huwwa ʕami:l šiyu:ʕi] • **3.** مُمَثِّل [mumaθθil] مُمَثِّلِين [mumaθθili:n] *pl:* The insurance company sent its agent to the accident site. شَرِكَة التّأمِين دَزَّت وَكِيلها لمُكان الحادِث [šarikat ʔittaʔmi:n dazzat waki:lha lmuka:n ʔilħa:diθ] • **4.** سِرِّي [sirri] *pl:* -iyyiin. I think he's a police agent. أعتِقِد هُوَّ سِرِّي مِن الشُّرطَة [ʔaʕtiqid huwwa sirri min ʔiššurṭa] • **5.** عامِل [ʕa:mil] عَوامِل، عُمّال [ʕawa:mil, ʕumma:l] *pl:* This is a strong chemical agent. هَذا عامِل كِيمياوِي فَعّال [ha:ða ʕa:mil ki:mya:wi faʕʕa:l]

to aggravate • **1.** زَهَّق [zahhag] تزهِّق، تَزهِيق [tzihhig, tazhi:g] *vn:* تزَهَّق [tzahhag] *p:* His bragging really aggravated me. التَّبَجُّح مالَه زَهَّقني هوايَة [ʔittabajjuħ ma:lah zahhagni hwa:ya] • **2.** أزَّم [ʔazzam] تَأزُّم [taʔazzum] *vn:* تأزَّم [tʔazzam] *p:* The border incident aggravated the situation. حادِث الحُدُود أزَّم الوَضِع [ħa:diθ ʔilħudu:d ʔazzam ʔilwaðiʕ] • **3.** زَيَّد [zayyad] تَزيِيد [tazyi:d] *vn:* تزَيَّد [tzayyad] *p:* Scratching will aggravate the inflammation. الحَكّ راح يزَيِّد الالتِهاب [ʔilħakk ra:ħ yzayyid ʔilʔiltiha:b]

aggravation • **1.** إزعاج [ʔizʕa:j] Her nagging is a source of constant aggravation. إلحاحها مَصدَر إزعاج مُستَمِرّ [ʔilħa:ħha maşdar ʔizʕa:j mustamirr] • **2.** مِتأزِّم [mitʔizzim] تَدَهوُر [tadahwur] Any aggravation of the situation may lead to war. أيّ تَأزُّم بِالحالَة يِمكِن يأدّي إلَى حَرُب [ʔayy taʔazzum bilħa:la yimkin yʔaddi ʔila ħarub]

ago • **1.** قَبُل [gabul, qabil] I was there two months ago. كِنت هناك، قَبُل شَهرَين [čint hna:k, gabul šahrayn]

a while ago • **1.** قَبُل مُدَّة [gabul mudda] He left a while ago. راح قَبُل مُدَّة [ra:ħ gabul mudda]

agony • **1.** تُمُرمُر [tumurmur] عَذاب [ʕaða:b] I can't bear this agony. ما أقدَر أتحَمَّل هَالتُّمُرمُر [ma: ʔagdar ʔatħammal hattumurmur]

to agree • **1.** اِتَّفَق [ʔittifaq] اِتِّفاق [ʔittifa:q] *vn:* *sv* i. Their opinions never agree. آرائهُم أبَد ما تِتَّفِق [ʔara:ʔhum ʔabad ma: tittifiq] • **2.** وافَق عَلَى [wa:faq ʕala] مُوافَقَة [muwa:faqa] *vn:* *sv* i. He agreed to buy the radio. وافَق عَلَى أن يِشتِري الرّاديُو [wa:faq ʕala ʔan yištiri ʔirra:dyu]

to agree on • **1.** اِتَّفَق عَلَى [ʔittifaq ʕala] اِتِّفاق [ʔittifa:q] *vn:* *sv* i. We've agreed on everything. إحنا اِتَّفَقنا عَلَى كُلشِي [ʔiħna ʔittifaqna ʕala kullši]

to agree to • **1.** وافَق عَلَى [wa:faq ʕala] مُوافَقَة [muwa:faqa] *vn:* *sv* u. Do you agree to these terms? توافُق عَلَى هَالشّرُوط؟ [twa:fuq ʕala haššru:ṭ?]

to agree with • **1.** اِتَّفَق ويّا [ʔittifaq wiyya] اِتِّفاق ويّا [ʔittifa:q wiyya] *vn:* *sv* i. Do you agree with me? تِتَّفِق ويّايا؟ [tittifiq wiyya:ya?] • **2.** لائَم [la:ʔam] مُلائَمَة [mula:ʔama] *vn:* تلائَم [tla:ʔam] *p:* والَم [wa:lam] مُوالَمَة [muwa:lama] *vn:* توالَم [twa:lam] *p:* This weather doesn't agree with me at all. هَالجَوّ ما يوالِمنِي أبَداً [haljaww ma: ywa:limni ʔabadan]

agreeable • **1.** سَمِح [samiħ] She has an agreeable disposition. عِدها فَدّ طَبُع سَمِح [ʕidha fadd ṭabuʕ

A

samiħ] • **2.** مَقبُول [maqbu:l] These terms are not agreeable. هَالشُّرُوط ما مَقبُولَة [haššuru:ṭ ma: maqbu:la]

to be agreeable • **1.** وافَق [wa:faq] مُوافَقَة [muwa:faqa] *vn: sv* u. Is he agreeable to that? هُوَّ يوافُق عَلَى هَذا؟ [huwwa ywa:fuq ʕala ha:ða?]

agreement • **1.** اِتِّفاقِيَّة [ʔittifa:qiyya] اِتِّفاقِيّات [ʔittifa:qiyya:t] *pl:* The agreement has to be ratified by Parliament. الاتِّفاقِيَّة لازِم تِتصَدَّق مِن مَجلِس الأُمَّة [ʔilʔittifa:qiyya la:zim tiṭṣaddaq min majlis ʔilʔumma] • **2.** اِتِّفاق [ʔittifa:q] اِتِّفاقات [ʔittifa:qa:t] *pl:* The contract was extended by mutual agreement. المُقاوَلَة تمَدِّدَت بِاتِّفاق الطَّرَفَين [ʔilmuqa:wala tmaddidat bʔittifa:q ʔiṭṭarafayn]

to be in agreement • **1.** اِتِّفَق [ʔittifaq] اِتِّفاق [ʔittifa:q] *vn: sv* i. This is definitely not in agreement with the original terms of the contract. هَذا قَطعِيّاً ما يِتِّفِق ويّا شُرُوط المُقاوَلَة الأَصلِيَّة [ha:ða qaṭʕiyyan ma: yittifiq wiyya šuru:ṭ ʔilmuqa:wala ʔilʔaṣliyya] Are you in agreement with me? إِنتَ مِتِّفِق ويّايا؟ [ʔinta mittifiq wiyya:ya?]

to come to an agreement • **1.** وُصَل إِلَى اِتِّفاق [wuṣal ʔila ʔittifa:q] وُصُول إِلَى اِتِّفاق [wuṣu:l ʔila: ʔittifa:q] *vn: sv* a. We came to an agreement on that point. وُصَلنا إِلَى اِتِّفاق حَول هَذِيك النُّقطَة [wuṣalna ʔila ʔittifa:q ħawil haði:č ʔinnuqṭa]

agricultural • **1.** زِراعِي [zira:ʕi]

agriculture • **1.** زِراعَة [zira:ʕa] Inquire at the Department of Agriculture. إِسأَل بِوِزارَة الزِّراعَة [ʔisʔal bwiza:rat ʔizzira:ʕa] There isn't much agriculture in this region. ماكُو هوايَة زِراعَة بِهَالمَنطَقَة [ma:ku hwa:ya zira:ʕa bhalmanṭaqa]

ahead • **1.** مِتقَدِّم [mitqaddim] He's ahead of everybody in his studies. هُوَّ مِتقَدِّم عَلَى الكُلّ بدِراستَه [huwwa mitqaddim ʕala ʔilkull bdira:stah] I'm way ahead in my work. آني هوايَة مِتقَدِّم بِشُغلِي [ʔa:ni hwa:ya mitqaddim bšuɣli] • **2.** قَبُل [gabul, qabil] Are you next? No, he's ahead of me. هَسَّة سِراك؟ لا، هُوَّ قَبلِي [hassa sira:k? la:, huwwa gabli] • **3.** سابِق [sa:biq] غالُب [ɣa:lub] My horse was ahead during the race. حصاني كان غالُب وَقِت السِّباق [ħṣa:ni ča:n ɣa:lub wakit ʔissiba:q] • **4.** قِدّام [gidda:m] أَمام [ʔama:m] The soldiers marched ahead of the sailors in the parade. الجِّنُود مِشَوا قِدّام البَحّارَة بالإِستِعراض [ʔijjinu:d mišaw gidda:m ʔilbaħħa:ra bilʔistiʕra:ð̣]

straight ahead • **1.** قُبَل [gubal] عَدِل [ʕadil] Go straight ahead. فُوت قُبَل [fu:t gubal]

to get ahead • **1.** تقَدَّم [tqaddam] تَقَدُّم [taqaddum] *vn: sv* a. He doesn't seem to get ahead. ما دَيبَيِّن عَليه يِتقَدَّم [ma: daybayyin ʕali:h yitqaddam]

to go ahead • **1.** مِشَى [miša:] *sv* i. Just go ahead, don't mind me. إِمشِي بِفالَك ما علَيك مِنِّي [ʔimši bfa:lak ma: ʕli:k minni] • **2.** راح [ra:ħ] *sv* u. You go ahead, I'll follow you later. رُوح قَبلِي، آني أَلحقَك بَعدين [ru:ħ gabli, ʔa:ni ʔaliħgak baʕdi:n] • **3.** اِستَمَرّ [ʔistamarr] اِستِمرار [ʔistimra:r] *vn: sv* i. داوَم [da:wam] مُداوَمَة [muda:wama] *vn: sv* u. Just go ahead with your work, don't let me stop you. اِستِمِرّ بِشُغلَك، لا تخَلّينِي أَعَطّلَك [ʔistimirr bšuɣlak, la: txalli:ni ʔaʕaṭṭlak]

*** Go ahead and take it!** • **1.** تفَضَّل أُخُذَه [tfað̣ð̣al ʔuxuðah]

*** Go ahead and tell him.** • **1.** يا الله قُلَّه [ya: ʔallah gullah] / ما يخالِف، قُلَّه [ma: yxa:lif, gullah]

aid • **1.** إِسعاف [ʔisʕa:f] إِسعافات [ʔisʕa:fa:t] *pl:* I gave him first aid. سَوَّيتلَه إِسعاف أَوَّلِي [sawwi:tlah ʔisʕa:f ʔawwali] • **2.** مُساعَدَة [musa:ʕada] مُساعَدات [musa:ʕada:t] *pl:* That country received quite a bit of economic aid. هَالدَّولَة اِستِلمَت كَمِّيَّة كبِيرَة مِن المُساعَدات الاقتِصادِيَّة [haddawla ʔistilmat kammiyya kbi:ra min ʔilmusa:ʕada:t ʔilʔiqtiṣa:diyya]

to aid • **1.** ساعَد [sa:ʕad] مُساعَدَة [musa:ʕada] *vn:* تساعَد [tsa:ʕad] *p:* عاوَن [ʕa:wan] مُعاوَنَة [muʕa:wana] *vn:* تعاوَن [tʕa:wan] *p:* Can I aid you in any way? أَقدَر أَساعدَك بأَيّ طَرِيقَة؟ [ʔagdar ʔasa:ʕdak bʔayy ṭari:qa?]

aide • **1.** مُرافِق [mura:fiq] مُرافِقِين [mura:fiqi:n] *pl:* The British general and his aide went to Iraq. الجَّنَرال البَرِيطانِي وَمُرافقه راحوا لِلعِراق [ʔijjanara:l ʔilbari:ṭa:ni wmura:fqah ra:ħaw lilʕira:q] • **2.** مُعاوِن [muʕa:win] مُساعِد [musa:ʕid] مُساعِدِين [musa:ʕidi:n] *pl:* The minister consulted his top aides. الوَزِير اِستَشار أَكبَر مُعاوِنِيَه [ʔilwazi:r ʔistaša:r ʔakbar muʕa:wini:h]

ailing • **1.** مَرِيض [mari:ð̣] مُرضَة [murð̣a] *pl:* وَجعان [wajʕa:n] وَجعانِين، وجاعَة [wajʕa:ni:n, wja:ʕa] *pl:* She's always ailing. هِيَّ عَلَى طُول مَرِيضَة [hiyya ʕala ṭu:l mari:ð̣a]

aim • **1.** غايَة [ɣa:ya] غايات [ɣa:ya:t] *pl:* مَقصَد [maqṣad] مَقاصِد [maqa:ṣid] *pl:* غَرَض [ɣarað̣] أَغراض [ʔaɣra:ð̣] *pl:* هَدَف [hadaf] أَهداف [ʔahda:f] *pl:* His aim is to become a good doctor. غايتَه يصِير طَبِيب زين [ɣa:ytah yṣi:r ṭabi:b zi:n] • **2.** نِيشان [ni:ša:n] He took careful aim and fired. أَخَذ نِيشان زين وَضِرَب [ʔaxað ni:ša:n zi:n wð̣irab]

to aim • **1.** نَيشَن [nayšan] *sv* i. He aimed at a rabbit. نَيشَن عَلَى أَرنَب [nayšan ʕala ʔarnab] • **2.** نَوَى [nuwa:] نِيَّة [niyya] *vn: sv* i. What do you aim to do this afternoon? شتِنوِي تسَوِّي هَالعَصرِيَّة؟ [štinwi tsawwi halʕaṣriyya?] • **3.** وَجَّه [wajjah] تَوجِيه [tawji:h] *vn:* توَجَّه [twajjah] *p:* He aimed an insult at me. وَجَّه مَسَبَّة إِلي [wajjah masabba ʔili]

*** You're aiming too high!** • **1.** إِنتَ دَتُضرُب بِالعالِي [ʔinta datuð̣rub bilʕa:li] الجَنَّة أَقرَب [ʔijjanna ʔagrab] دَتُطلُب مُطَر [datuṭlub muṭar]

air • **1.** هَوا [hawa] The air in this room is bad. الهَوا بهَالغُرفَة مُو زين [ʔilhawa bhalɣurfa mu: zayn]

• **2.** جَوّ [ǰaww] أجواء [ʔaǰwaːʔ] *pl:* The meeting was surrounded by an air of mystery. الاجتِماع كان مُحاط بجَوّ غامُض [ʔilʔiǰtimaːʕ čaːn muħaːṭ bǰaww ɣaːmuð̣] • **3.** جَوِّي [ǰawwi] Send us a letter by air mail. دِزّ إِلْنَا مَكتُوب بِالبَرِيد الجَوِّي [dizz ʔilnaː maktuːb bilbariːd ʔiǰǰawwi]

*** He's continually putting on airs.**

• **1.** هُوَّ دائِماً يِتظاهَر عَلَى غير حَقِيقتَه [huwwa daːʔiman yitð̣aːhar ʕala ɣiːr ħaqiːqtah]

to be on the air • **1.** ذاع [ðaːʕ] إذاعَة [ʔiðaːʕa] *vn: sv* i. The president will be on the air this evening. الرَّئِيس راح يذِيع هاللَّيلَة [ʔirraʔiːs raːħ yðiːʕ halliːla]

to air • **1.** هَوَّى [hawwaː] تَهوِيَة [tahwiya] *vn:* تهَوَّى [thawwaː] *p:* Would you please air the room while I'm out? أَرجُوك هَوِّي الغُرفَة لَمّا أَكُون بَرَّة [ʔarǰuːk hawwi ʔilɣurfa lamma ʔakuːn barra] • **2.** شَرّ [šarr] شَرّ [šarr] *vn:* اِنشَرّ [ʔinšarr] *p:* I have to air the blanket this morning. لازِم أَشُرّ البَطّانِيَّة هَالصُّبُح [laːzim ʔašurr ʔilbaṭṭaːniyya haṣṣubuħ]

*** Don't air your personal problems in public.**

• **1.** لا تِطلِع النّاس عَلَى مَشاكلَك الشَّخصِيَّة [laː tiṭliʕ ʔinnaːs ʕala mašaːklak ʔiššaxṣiyya]

air base • **1.** قاعِدَة [qaːʕida] قَواعِد [qawaːʕid] *pl:*

aircraft carrier • **1.** حامِلَة طائِرات [ħaːmilat ṭaːʔiraːt]

airfield • **1.** مَطار [maṭaːr] مَطارات [maṭaːraːt] *pl:* Let's meet at the airfield. خَلِّي نِتلاقَى بِالمَطار [xalli nitlaːgaː bilmaṭaːr]

air force • **1.** قُوَّة جَوِّيَّة [quwwa ǰawwiyya] قُوَى جَوِّيَّة [quwaː ǰawwiyya] *pl:*

air line • **1.** خُطُوط جَوِّيَّة [xuṭuːṭ ǰawwiyya] شَرِكَة طَيَران [šarikat ṭayaraːn]

air mail • **1.** بَرِيد جَوِّي [bariːd ǰawwi] Send the package by air mail. دِزّ الرُّزمَة بِالبَرِيد الجَوِّي [dizz ʔirruzma bilbariːd ʔiǰǰawwi]

airplane • **1.** طِيّارَة [ṭiyyaːra] طِيّارات [ṭiyyaːraːt] *pl:* How long does it take by airplane? شقَدّ يطَوُّل بِالطِّيّارَة؟ [šgadd yṭawwul biṭṭayyaːra?]

airport • **1.** مَطار [maṭaːr] مَطارات [maṭaːraːt] *pl:*

air raid • **1.** غارَة جَوِّيَّة [ɣaːra ǰawwiyya] غارات جَوِّيَّة [ɣaːraːt ǰawwiyya] *pl:*

air sick • **1.** * He gets air sick every time he flies تِلزِمَه الصُّفرَة كُلَّما يطِير [tilizmah ʔiṣṣufra kullmaː yṭiːr]

aisle • **1.** مَمشَى [mamša] مَماشِي [mamaːši] *pl:* مَمَرّ [mamarr] مَمَرّات [mamarraːt] *pl:* He had to stand in the aisle. اِضطَرّ يوقَف بِالمَمشَى [ʔið̣ṭarr yuːgaf bilmamša]

ajar • **1.** مَفكُوك شوَيَّة [mafkuːk šwayya] The door was ajar. الباب كانَت مَفكُوك شوَيَّة [ʔilbaːb čaːnat mafkuːk šwayya]

alarm • **1.** جَرَس إنذار [ǰaras ʔinðaːr] Who turned in the alarm? مِنُو دَقّ جَرَس الإنذار؟ [minu dagg ǰaras ʔilʔinðaːr?] • **2.** خَوف [xuːf] She was full of alarm. كانَت كُلّها خَوف [čaːnat kullha xuːf] • **3.** مُنَبِّه [munabbih] Set the alarm for six. أنصُب المُنَبِّه عالسّاعَة سِتَّة [ʔunṣub ʔilmunabbih ʕassaːʕa sitta]

to alarm • **1.** خَرَّع [xarraʕ] تَخرِيع [taxriːʕ] *vn:* تخَرَّع [txarraʕ] *p:* فَزَّز [fazzaz] تَفزِيز [tafziːz] *vn:* تفَزَّز [tfazzaz] *p:* Her screams alarmed the whole building. عياطها خَرَّع كُلّ البِنايَة [ʕyaːṭha xarraʕ kull ʔilbinaːya] • **2.** شَوَّش [šawwaš] تَشوِيش [tašwiːš] *vn:* تشَوَّش [tšawwaš] *p:* The news report alarmed me. النَّشرَة الإخبارِيَّة شَوِّشَتنِي [ʔinnašra ʔlʔixbaːriyya šawwišatni]

to be alarmed • **1.** اِختِرَع [ʔixtiraʕ] *sv* i. Don't be alarmed! لا تِختِرِع [laː tixtiriʕ]

alarm clock • **1.** ساعَة مُنَبِّهَة [saːʕa munabbiha] ساعات مُنَبِّهَة [saːʕaːt munabbiha] *pl:* I bought myself a new alarm clock yesterday. اِشتِرَيتلِي ساعَة مُنَبِّهَة جِدِيدَة البارحَة [ʔištiriːtli saːʕa munabbiha ǰidiːda ʔilbaːrħa]

album • **1.** أَلبَوم [ʔalbuːm] أَلبَومات [ʔalbuːmaːt] *pl:* He gave me a photograph album. اِنطانِي أَلبُوم تَصاوِير [ʔinṭaːni ʔalbuːm taṣaːwiːr]

alcohol • **1.** كُحُول [kuħuːl] سبِيرتُو [spiːrtu] The medicine has alcohol in it. الدَّوا بِيه كُحُول [ʔiddawa biːh kuħuːl] She started the fire with alcohol. شِعلَت النّار بِالإسبِيرتُو [šiʕlat ʔinnaːr bilʔispiːrtuː]

Aleppo • **1.** حَلَب [ħalab]

alert • **1.** مِتيَقِّظ [mityaqqið̣] مِتنَبِّه [mitnabbih] He's an alert fellow. هُوَّ فَدّ واحِد مِتيَقِّظ [huwwa fadd waːħid mityaqqið̣]

on alert • **1.** تَحت الإنذار [taħt ʔilʔinðaːr] The defense minister put the army on alert. وَزِير الدِّفاع خَلَّى الجَّيش تَحت الإنذار [waziːr ʔiddifaːʕ xallaː ʔiǰǰiːš taħt ʔilʔinðaːr]

to be on the alert • **1.** توَقَّع [twaqqaʕ] تَوَقُّع [tawaqquʕ] *vn: sv* a. تحَضَّر [tħað̣ð̣ar] تَحَضُّر [taħað̣ð̣ur] *vn: sv* a. Be on the alert for a call from me. توَقَّع نِداء مِنِّي [twaqqaʕ nidaːʔ minni]

to alert • **1.** حَضَّر [ħað̣ð̣ar] تَحذِير [taħðiːr] *vn:* تحَذَّر [tħaððar] *p:* They alerted us about the coming of a storm. حَضَّرُونا بمَجِيء عاصِفَة [ħað̣ð̣iruːna bmaǰiːʔ ʕaːṣifa]

A

Alexandria • **1.** الإسكَندَرِيَّة [ʔilʔiskandariyya]

Algeria • **1.** الجَزائِر [ʔilǰaza:ʔir]

Algerian • **1.** جَزائِري [ǰaza:ʔiri]

Algiers • **1.** مَدِينَة الجَزائِر [madi:nat ʔilǰaza:ʔir]

alien • **1.** مُقِيم أَجنَبِي [muqi:m ʔaǰnabi:] مُقِيمِين أَجانِب [muqi:mi:n ʔaǰa:nib] *pl:* مُقِيمَة أَجنَبِيَّة [muqi:ma ʔaǰnabiyya] *Feminine:* مُقِيمات أَجنَبِيّات [muqi:ma:t ʔaǰnabiyya:t] *Feminine pl:*

alike • **1.** فَدّ شِكِل [fadd šikil] فَدّ شِي [fadd ši] These tables are all alike. هَالمِيوزَة كُلّها فَدّ شِكِل [halmyu:za kullha fadd šikil] • **2.** سُوَة، سُوا [suwa, suwa:] We treat all customers alike. إحنا نعامِل كُلّ المَعامِيل سُوَة [ʔiħna nʕa:mil kull ʔilmaʕa:mi:l suwa]

alive • **1.** حَيّ [ħayy] أحياء [ʔaħya:ʔ] *pl:* عَدِل [ʕadil] طَيِّب [ṭayyib] This fish is still alive. هَالسِّمكَة لهَسَّة حَيَّة [hassimča lhassa ħayya]

*** The atmosphere was alive with tension.**
• **1.** الجَوّ كان مَشحُون بِالتَوَتُّر [ʔiǰǰaww ča:n mašħu:n bittawattur]

*** This marsh is alive with snakes.** • **1.** هَالهَور كُلّه حَيايَة [halhu:r kullah ħaya:ya]

to be alive with • **1.** عَجّ [ʕaǰǰ] *sv* i. The pantry is alive with ants. الكِلَر يعِجّ بِالنَّمِل [ʔilkilar yʕiǰǰ binnamil]

to keep alive • **1.** ظَلّ [ðall] *sv* a. It's a wonder they kept alive. المُعجِزَة ظَلّوا طَيِّبِين [ʔilmuʕǰiza ðallaw ṭayybi:n]
• **2.** بُقَى [buqa:] بَقاء [baqa:ʔ] *vn: sv* a. How can you keep alive on this salary? شلُون تِقدَر تِبقَى عايِش بِهَالمَعاش؟ [šlu:n tigdar tibqa: ʕa:yiš bhalmaʕa:š?] • **3.** خَلَّى [xalla:] *sv* i. The doctor kept him alive for two weeks. الطَّبِيب خَلّاه عايِش إسبُوعَين [ʔiṭṭabi:b xalla:h ʕa:yiš ʔisbu:ʕayn]

all • **1.** كُلّ [kull] Did you all go? كُلّكُم رِحتُوا؟ [kullkum riħtu:?] This will upset all my plans. هَذا راح يخَربُط كُلّ مَشارِيعِي [ha:ða ra:ħ yxarbuṭ kull maša:ri:ʕi] The bread's all gone. الخُبُز كُلّه خِلَص [ʔilxubuz kullah xilaṣ] • **2.** طُول [ṭu:l] I've been waiting all day. صارلِي دَأنتِظِر طُول النَّهار [ṣa:rli daʔantiðir ṭu:l ʔinnaha:r] • **3.** جَمِيع [ǰami:ʕ] He took a vote of all the officers. أَخَذ أَصوات جَمِيع الضَّبّاط [ʔaxað ʔaṣwa:t ǰami:ʕ ʔiððabba:ṭ]

*** That's all.** • **1.** هَذا هُوَّ [ha:ða huwwa]

*** If that's all there is to it, I'll do it.**
• **1.** إذا بِهَالسُّهُولَة، راح أَسَوِّيها [ʔiða: bhassuhu:la, ra:ħ ʔasawwi:ha] إذا هِيكِي سَهل، راح أَسَوِّيها [ʔiða: hi:či sahla, ra:ħ ʔasawwi:ha]

*** The captain's all for starting now.**
• **1.** القَبطان يفَضِّل نِبدِي هَسَّة [ʔilqabṭa:n yfaððil nibdi hassa]

*** He isn't all there.** • **1.** هُوَّ مَشخُوط [huwwa mašxu:ṭ]

all along • **1.** عَلَى طُول [ʕala ṭu:l] دائماً [da:ʔiman] We've suspected him all along. إحنا عَلَى طُول كِنّا نشُكّ بِيه [ʔiħna ʕala ṭu:l činna nšukk bi:h]

all hours • **1.** أَيّ وَقِت [ʔayy wakit] He comes home to lunch at all hours. يِجِي لِلبَيت يِتغَدَّى أَيّ وَقِت كان [yiǰi lilbayt yidɣadda: ʔayy wakit ča:n]

all in • **1.** تَلفان [talfa:n] The kids are all in from playing. الجَّهال تَلفانِين مِن اللِّعِب [ʔiǰǰaha:l talfa:ni:n min ʔilliʕib]

all in all • **1.** شِي عَلَى شِي [ši ʕala ši] All in all, the movie was good. شِي عَلَى شِي، الفِلِم كان زِين [ši ʕala ši, ʔilfilim ča:n zi:n]

all of a sudden • **1.** عَلَى غَفلَة [ʕala ɣafla] All of a sudden it got dark. صارَت ظَلمَة عَلَى غَفلَة [ṣa:rat ðalma ʕala ɣafla]

all over • **1.** كُلّ مَكان [kull maka:n] They came from all over. إجَوا مِن كُلّ مَكان [ʔiǰaw min kull maka:n] He traveled all over the country. سافَر لكُلّ مَكان بالبَلَد [sa:far lkull maka:n bilbalad] • **2.** كُلّ [kull] He trembled all over from fright. رِجَف كُلّه مِن الخَوف [riǰaf kullah min ʔilxawf] He has pimples all over his face عِندَه دَنابِل بِكُلّ وِجّه [ʕindah dana:bil bkull wiččah] • **3.** مِن جِدِيد [min ǰidi:d] You have to do it all over. لازِم تسَوِّيها مِن جِدِيد [la:zim tsawwi:ha min ǰidi:d]

*** He came back after the war was all over.**
• **1.** رِجَع بَعَد ما اِنتِهَت الحَرُب [riǰaʕ baʕad ma: ʔintihat ʔilħarub]

all right • **1.** تَمام [tama:m] ماشِي [ma:ši] مُشات [muša:t] *pl:* Is everything all right? كُلّشِي ماشِي؟ [kullši ma:ši?] Is everything all right? كُلّشِي تَمام؟ [kullši tama:m?] I'd like to go, all right, but it's impossible. تَمام أَرِيد أَرُوح، بَسّ هَذا مُستَحِيل [tama:m ʔari:d ʔaru:ħ, bass ha:ða mustaħi:l] He knows why, all right. هُوَّ تَمام يُعرُف لُويش [huwwa tama:m yuʕruf luwi:š] He knows why, all right. هُوَّ زين يُعرُف لُويش [huwwa zi:n yuʕruf luwi:š] • **2.** طَيِّب [ṭayyib] زين [zi:n, zayn] All right, I'll do it. طَيِّب، راح أَسَوِّيها [ṭayyib, ra:ħ ʔasawwi:ha] All right, I'll do it. زين، راح أَسَوِّيها [zi:n, ra:ħ ʔasawwi:ha]

*** Is that all right with you?** • **1.** ما عِندَك مانِع؟ [ma: ʕindak ma:niʕ?]

all set • **1.** حاضِر [ħa:ðir] مِتحَضِّر [mitħaððir] We were all set to leave. كِنّا مِتحَضّرِين نرُوح [činna mitħaððri:n nru:ħ]

all the better • **1.** بَعَد أَحسَن [baʕad ʔaħsan] If that is so, all the better. لَو هِيكِي، بَعَد أَحسَن [law hi:či, baʕad ʔaħsan]

all the same • **1.** فَدّ شِي [fadd ši] نَفس الشِّي [nafs ʔišši] That's all the same to me. كُلّها فَدّ شِي بِالنِّسبَة إلِي [kullha fadd ši binnisba ʔili] • **2.** وَلَو [walaw] مَعَ هَذا [maʕa ha:ða:] عَلَى كُلّ حال [ʕala kull ħa:l] All the same, you didn't have to do it. وَلَو، ما كان لازِم تسَوِّيها [walaw, ma: ča:n la:zim tsawwi:ha]

all the time • **1.** عَلَى طُول [ʕala ṭuːl] دائماً [daːʔiman] كُلّ وَقت [kull wakit] She's complaining all the time. هِيَّ كُلّ وَقت تِتشَكّى [hiyya kull wakit titšakkaː]
all told • **1.** شِي عَلَى شِي [ši ʕala ši] All told, he's not a bad fellow. شِي عَلَى شِي، هُوَّ خُوش وَلَد [ši ʕala ši, huwwa xuːš walad]
above all • **1.** عَلَى ا لأَخَصّ [ʕala ʔilʔaxaṣṣ] أَهَمّ شِي [ʔahamm ši] Above all, don't get discouraged. عَلَى الأَخَصّ لا تِفتَر عَزِيمتَك [ʕala ʔilʔaxaṣṣ laː tiftar ʕaziːmtak]
at all • **1.** أَبَد [ʔabad] أَبَداً [ʔabadan] مَرَّة [marra] مَرّات [marraːt] *pl:* أَصلاً [ʔaṣlan] He has no patience at all. ما عِندَه صَبُر أَبَداً [maː ʕindah ṣabur ʔabadan]
in all • **1.** كُلّ بالكُلّ [kull bilkull] How many are there in all? شقَدّ أَكُو كُلّ بالكُلّ؟ [šgadd ʔaku kull bilkull?]

Allah • **1.** الله [ʔallah]

alley • **1.** دَربُونَة [darbuːna] درابِين [draːbiːn] *pl:* عَقِد [ʕagid] عقُود [ʕguːd] *pl:*

alliance • **1.** حِلِف [ħilif] أَحلاف [ʔaħlaːf] *pl:* The two countries formed an alliance. الدَّولتَين شَكّلَوا حِلِف [ʔiddawiltayn šakklaw ħilif]

to allow • **1.** سِمَح [simaħ] سَماح [samaːħ] *vn:* اِنسِمَح [ʔinsimaħ] *p:* He won't allow that. ما يِسمَح بهَذا [maː yismaħ bhaːðа] He doesn't allow himself a minute's rest. ما يِسمَح لِنَفسَه وَلا دَقِيقَة راحَة [maː yismaħ lnafsah wala daqiːqa raːħa] • **2.** حِسَب [ħisab] حساب [ħsaːb] *vn:* اِنحِسَب [ʔinħisab] *p:* How much will you allow me for my old car? بيش راح تِحسِب سَيّارتِي العَتِيقَة؟ [biyš raːħ tiħsib sayyaːrti ʔilʕatiːga?] • **3.** خَلّى [xallaː] تخَلّى [txallaː] *p:* How much should I allow for traveling expenses? شقَدّ لازِم أَخَلّي لِمَصارِيف السَّفَر؟ [šgadd laːzim ʔaxalli lmaṣaːriːf ʔissafar?] • **4.** رَخَّص [raxxaṣ] تَرخِيص [tarxiːṣ] *vn:* ترَخَّص [traxxaṣ] *p:* They're not allowed to sell beer after midnight. ما مرَخَّصِين يبِيعُون بِيرَة بَعَد نُصّ اللَّيل [maː mraxxaṣiːn ybiːʕuːn biːra baʕad nuṣṣ ʔillayl]

allowance • **1.** خَرجِيَّة [xarǰiyya] Do you give your son an allowance? تِنطِي لإِبنَك خَرجِيَّة؟ [tinṭi lʔibnak xarǰiyya?] • **2.** مُخَصَّصات [muxaṣṣaṣaːt] In addition to the regular salary, there is a cost of living allowance. بِالإِضافَة إِلَى الرّاتِب الاعتِيادِي أَكُو مُخَصَّصات غَلاء المَعِيشَة [bilʔiðaːfa ʔila ʔirraːtib ʔilʔiʕtiyaːdi ʔaku muxaṣṣaṣaːt ɣalaːʔ ʔilmaʕiːša]
to make allowance for • **1.** حِسَب حسَاب لِ [ħisab ħsaːb li-] *sv* i. You've got to make allowance for his inexperience. لازِم تِحسِب حِساب لِقِلَّة خِبرتَه [laːzim tiħsib ħisaːb liqillat xibirtah]

ally • **1.** حَلِيف [ħaliːf] They are our allies. هُمَّ حُلَفائنا [humma ħulafaːʔna]

to ally oneself • **1.** تحالَف [tħaːlaf] تَحالُف [taħaːluf] *vn: sv* a. They allied themselves with a neighboring country. تحالفَوا ويّا فَدّ دَولَة مُجاوِرَة [tħaːlfaw wiyya fadd dawla muǰaːwira]

almond • **1.** لُوزَة [luːza] لُوزات [luːzaːt] *pl:* لَوز [lawz] *Collective*

almost • **1.** تَقرِيباً [taqriːban] I'm almost finished. آنِي تَقرِيباً خَلَّصِت [ʔaːni taqriːban xallaṣit] • **2.** عَلَى وَشَك [ʕala wašak] We were almost ready to surrender. كِنّا عَلَى وَشَك نسَلِّم [činna ʕala wašak nsallim] • **3.** إِلّا شوَيَّة [ʔilla šwayya] The glass almost broke when I dropped it. الكلاص اِنكِسَر إِلّا شوَيَّة مِن وَقَّعتَه [ʔilglaːṣ ʔinkisar ʔilla šwayya min waggaʕtah]

alms • **1.** صَدَقَة [ṣadaqa] صَدَقات [ṣadaqaːt] *pl:*

alone • **1.** وَحد، عَلَى وَحد [waħd-, ʕala waħd-] Do you live alone? تُسكُن وَحدَك؟ [tuskun waħdak?] • **2.** بَسّ [bass] You alone can help me. بَسّ إِنتَ تِقدَر تساعِدنِي [bass ʔinta tigdar tsaːʕidni]
all alone • **1.** وَحِيد [waħiːd] He seems to be all alone in the world. يبَيِّن وَحِيد بِالدِّنيا [yibayyin waħiːd biddinya]
to leave alone • **1.** **n** جاز مِن [ǰaːz min] *sv* u. عاف [ʕaːf] *sv* u. Leave the radio alone! جُوز مِن الرّادِيُو [ǰuːz min ʔirraːdyu] Leave the radio alone! عُوف الرّادِيُو [ʕuːf ʔirraːdyu]

along • **1.** وِيّا [wiyya] Do you want to come along with me? ترِيد تِجِي وِيّايا؟ [triːd tiǰi wiyyaːya?] How much baggage should I take along. شقَدّ غَراض لازِم آخُذ وِيّايا [šgadd ɣaraːð laːzim ʔaːxuð wiyyaːya] • **2.** بمُحاذاة [bmuħaːðaːt] وِيّا [wiyya] We walked along the railroad tracks. مشَينا بمُحاذاة سِكَّة القِطار [mšiːna bmuħaːðaːt siččat ʔilqiṭaːr] • **3.** عَلَى طُول [ʕala ṭuːl] بجانِب [bǰaːnib] صَفّ [ṣaff] صفُوف [ṣfuːf] *pl:* We have flowers planted along the walk. عِدنا أُرُود مَزرُوعَة عَلَى طُول المَمشَى [ʕidna ʔuwruːd mazruːʕa ʕala ṭuːl ʔilmamšaː] • **4.** صَفّ [ṣaff] صفُوف [ṣfuːf] *pl:* وِيّا [wiyya] He parked his car along the wall. وَقَّف سَيّارتَه بصَفّ الحايِط [waggaf sayyaːrtah bṣaff ʔilħaːyiṭ] • **5.** حِبلَة [ħibla] حِبلات [ħiblaːt] *pl:* My wife is four months along. مَرتِي أَربَعَة أَشهُر حِبلَة [marti ʔarbaʕat ʔašhur ħibla]
all along • **1.** دائماً [daːʔiman] I said so all along. كِنِت دائماً أَقُول هَذا [činit daːʔiman ʔaguːl haːða] • **2.** عَلَى طُول [ʕala ṭuːl] We saw rabbits all along the road. شِفنا أَرانِب عَلَى طُول الطَّرِيق [šifna ʔaraːnib ʕala ṭuːl ʔiṭṭariːq]

alphabet • **1.** أَلِف باء [ʔalif baːʔ] أَلِف بَ [ʔalif ba]

alphabetical • **1.** حَسَب الأَلِف بَي [ħasab ilʔalif ba]

A

already • **1.** قَبُل [gabul, qabil] Haven't you been through this line already? إنتَ ما كِنِت بِهالسِّرَة قَبُل؟ [ʔinta maː činit bhassira gabul?] • **2.** They had already left when we arrived. كانَوا رايحِين لَمّا وصَلنا [čaːnaw raːyħiːn lamma wṣalna] I've eaten already. آني ماكِل [ʔaːni maːkil] It's already time to eat. صار وَقِت الأكِل [ṣaːr wakit ʔilʔakil] So you'll already be there by the time I arrive? لَعَد راح تكُون هناك بوَقت اللّي أوصَل؟ [laʕad raːħ tkuːn hnaːk bwakt ʔilli ʔuːṣal?]

also • **1.** هَمّ [hamm] هَمَّين [hammiːn] أيضاً [ʔayð̣an] We also discussed the test. وَهَمَّين بحَثنا الامتِحان [whammiːn bħaθna ʔilʔimtiħaːn]

altar • **1.** مِحراب [miħraːb] مَحاريب [maħaːriːb] *pl:*

to alter • **1.** بَدَّل ب [baddal b-] تَبديل [tabdiːl] *vn:* تبَدَّل [ɣayyar b-] *p:* غَيَّر ب [ɣayyar b-] تَغيير [taɣyiːr] *vn:* تغَيَّر [tɣayyar] *p:* عَدَّل [ʕaddal] تَعدِيل [taʕdiːl] *vn:* تعَدَّل [tʕaddal] *p:* صَلَّح [ṣallaħ] تَصليح [taṣliːħ] *vn:* تصَلَّح [tṣallaħ] *p:* The tailor is going to alter my suit. الخَيّاط راح يبَدِّل بقاطِي [ʔilxayyaːṭ raːħ ybaddil bqaːṭi]

alteration • **1.** تَعدِيل [taʕdiːl] تَعدِيلات [taʕdiːlaːt] *pl:* تَبدِيل [tabdiːl] تَغيير [taɣyiːr] تَغييرات [taɣyiːraːt] *pl:* تَصليح [taṣliːħ] The alterations are free. التَّعدِيلات بَبلاش [ʔittaʕdiːlaːt bibalaːš] We'll have to make a few alterations in the text of the speech. لازِم نسَوِّي شوَيَّة تَغييرات بنُصّ الخِطاب [laːzim nsawwi šwayya taɣyiːraːt bnuṣṣ ʔilxiṭaːb]

alternative • **1.** خِيار [xiyaːr] They left us no alternative. ما تِركَوا إلنّا خِيار [maː tirkuː ʔilnnaː xiyaːr] • **2.** جارَة [čaːra] جارات [čaːraːt] *pl:* You'll have to go. There's no alternative. لازِم ترُوح ماكُو جارَة [laːzim truːħ maːku čaːra] • **3.** غير [ɣiːr] I don't see any alternative solution. ما دَأشُوف غير حَلّ [maː daʔašuːf ɣiːr ħall]

although • **1.** وَلَو [walaw] I'll be there, although I have very little time. راح أكُون هناك، وَلَو وَقتِي كُلِّش ضَيِّق [raːħ ʔakuːn hnaːk, walaw wakti kulliš ð̣ayyiq]

altitude • **1.** اِرتِفاع [ʔirtifaːʕ] اِرتِفاعات [ʔirtifaːʕaːt] *pl:* عِلُو [ʕilw] The plane was flying at a very high altitude. الطَّيّارَة كانَت طايرَة عَلَى اِرتِفاع عالِي [ʔiṭṭiyyaːra čaːnat ṭaːyra ʕala ʔirtifaːʕ ʕaːli]

altogether • **1.** شِي عَلَى شِي [ši ʕala ši] كُلّ بالكُلّ [kull bilkull] مَجمُوع [majmuːʕ] Altogether there are thirty books. كُلّ بالكُلّ أكُو ثلاثِين كتاب [kull bilkull ʔaku tlaːθiːn ktaːb] • **2.** بصُورَة عامَّة [bṣuːra ʕaːmma] Altogether, this plan is good. بصُورَة عامَّة هالخُطَّة زينَة [bṣuːra ʕaːmma halxuṭṭa ziːna] • **3.** مَرَّة [marra] مَرّات [marraːt] *pl:* فَدّ مَرَّة [fadd marra] These prices are altogether too high. هَالأسعار عالِيَة بِالمَرَّة [halʔasʕaːr ʕaːlya bilmarra] • **4.** تَماماً [tamaːman] You're altogether right. إنتَ صَحِيح تَماماً [ʔinta ṣaḥiːħ tamaːman]

aluminum • **1.** فافُون [faːfuːn] ألَمنيَوم [ʔalaminyuːm]

always • **1.** دائِماً [daːʔiman] عَلَى طُول [ʕala ṭuːl] I'm always at home. آني دائِماً بِالبَيت [ʔaːni daːʔiman bilbayt] She's always been rich. هِيَّ كانَت زَنكِينَة عَلَى طُول [hiyya čaːnat zangiːna ʕala ṭuːl] She's always been rich. طُول عُمُرها كانَت زَنكِينَة [ṭuːl ʕumurha čaːnat zangiːna]

amateur • **1.** هاوِي [haːwi] هُواة [huwaːt] *pl:* For an amateur he paints quite well. كَهاوِي يرسِم كُلِّش زين [kahaːwi yirsim kulliš ziːn]

to amaze • **1.** عَجَّب [ʕajjab] تَعجِيب [taʕjiːb] *vn:* تعَجَّب [tʕajjab] *p:* He amazed us with his magic tricks. عَجَّبنا بِألعابَه السِّحرِيَّة [ʕajjabna bʔalʕaːbah ʔissiħriyya]
to be amazed • **1.** اِستَغرَب [ʔistaɣrab] اِستِغراب [ʔistiɣraːb] *vn:* *sv* i. I was amazed at his lack of concern. اِستَغرَبِت مِن عَدَم اِهتِمامَه [ʔistaɣrabit min ʕadam ʔihtimaːmah]

amazing • **1.** عَجِيب [ʕajiːb] مُدهِش [mudhiš]

ambassador • **1.** سَفِير [safiːr] سُفَراء [sufaraːʔ] *pl:*

amber • **1.** كَهرَب [kahrab]

ambergris • **1.** عَنبَر [ʕanbar]

ambiguous • **1.** غامِض [ɣaːmið̣]

ambiguity • **1.** غُمُوض [ɣumuːð̣]

ambition • **1.** طمُوح [ṭmuːħ] He has no ambition. ما عِندَه طمُوح [maː ʕindah ṭumuːħ]

ambitious • **1.** طمُوح [ṭmuːħ]

ambulance • **1.** سَيّارَة إسعاف [sayyaːrat ʔisʕaːf] This man is hurt! Call an ambulance! هَالرِّجّال مِتعَوِّر خابُر عَلَى سَيّارَة إسعاف [harrijjaːl mitʕawwir xaːbur ʕala sayyaːrat ʔisʕaːf]

ambush • **1.** كَمِين [kamiːn] They set up an ambush for him. نِصبُولَه كَمِين [niṣbuːlah kamiːn]
to be ambushed • **1.** وُقَع [wugaʕ] وُقُوع [wuguːʕ] *vn:* *sv* a. The patrol was ambushed outside the village. الدَّورِيَّة وِقعَت بكَمِين خارِج القَريَة [ʔiddawriyya wigʕat bkamiːn xaːrij ʔilqarya]
*** They ambushed the caravan.**
• **1.** هِجمَوا عَالقافِلَة عَلَى غَفلَة [hijmaw ʕalqaːfila ʕala ɣafla]

America • **1.** أَميركا [ʔami:rika] أمريكا [ʔamri:ka, ʔamiri:ka]

American • **1.** أَميركي [ʔamri:ki] أمريكِي [ʔamri:ki] أمريكان [ʔamri:ka:n] *pl:* أمريكاني [ʔamri:ka:ni] أمريكان [ʔamri:ka:n] *pl:*

Amman • **1.** عَمّان [ʕamma:n]

ammunition • **1.** عِتاد [ʕita:d] ذَخِيرَة [ðaxi:ra] ذَخايِر [ðaxa:yir] *pl:* مُونَة [mu:na]

amnesia • **1.** داء النِسيان [da:ʔ ʔinnisya:n] مَرَض النِسيان [marað̣ ʔinnisya:n]

amnesty • **1.** عَفو عامّ [ʕafw ʕa:mm]

among • **1.** بَين [bayn] You're among friends. إنتَ بين أصدقاء [ʔinta bi:n ʔaṣdiqa:ʔ] Look among the papers! باوِع بين الوَرَق [ba:wiʕ bi:n ʔilwaraq] • **2.** بينات [bi:na:t] بَين [bi:n] We decided it among ourselves. قَرَّرنا بَيناتنا [qarrarna bayna:tna] There were many nice people among them. كان أَكُو بَيناتهُم خُوش أوادِم هوايَة [ča:n ʔaku bayna:thum xu:š ʔawa:dim hwa:ya] • **3.** مِن [min] He's popular among most of the people. هُوَّ مَحبُوب مِن أَكثَر النّاس [huwwa maħbu:b min ʔakθar ʔinna:s] • **4.** عَلَى [ʕala] Pass the leaflets out among the crowd. وَزِّع المَناشِير عالحاضرِين [wazziʕ ʔilmana:ši:r ʕalħa:ð̣ri:n] • **5.** ويّا [wiyya] بَين [bayn] نُصّ [nuṣṣ] نصاص [nṣa:ṣ] *pl:* He lived four years among the Bedouins. عاش أربَع سنِين ويّا البَدو [ʕa:š ʔarbaʕ sni:n wiyya ʔilbadw]

among other things • **1.** مِن جُملَة الأشياء [min ǰumlat ʔilʔašya:ʔ] مِن ضِمن الأشياء [min ð̣imn ʔilʔašya:ʔ] Among other things he collects stamps. مِن جُملَة الأشياء يجَمِّع طَوابِع [min ǰumlat ʔilʔašya:ʔ yǰammiʕ ṭawa:biʕ]

amount • **1.** مَبلَغ [mablaɣ] مَبالِغ [maba:liɣ] *pl:* Write a check for the full amount. إكتِب شَكّ بِالمَبلَغ كُلّه [ʔiktib čakk bilmalbaɣ kullah] • **2.** كَمِّيَّة [kammiyya] كَمِّيّات [kammiyya:t] *pl:* مِقدار [miqda:r] مَقادِير [maqa:di:r] *pl:* We bought a large amount of coffee. اِشتِرينا كَمِّيَّة كَبِيرَة مِن القَهوَة [ʔištiri:na kammiyya kabi:ra min ʔilgahwa] • **3.** مَجمُوع [majmu:ʕ] Add up these numbers and tell me the amount. إجمَع هَالأرقام وَقُلّي بالمَجمُوع [ʔiǰmaʕ halʔarqa:m wgulli bilmajmu:ʕ]

to amount to • **1.** سَوَّى [sawwa:] *sv* i. صار [ṣa:r] *sv* i. How much does the bill amount to? شقَدّ تسَوِّي القائِمَة؟ [šgadd tsawwi ʔilqa:ʔima?] • **2.** سُوَة، سُوا [suwa, suwa:] *sv* a. He doesn't amount to much. هُوَّ ما يِسوَى شِي [huwwa ma: yiswa: ši]

to amputate • **1.** بِتَر [bitar] بَتِر [batir] *vn:* اِنبِتَر [ʔinbitar] *p:* قَصّ [gaṣṣ] قَصّ [gaṣṣ] *vn:* اِنقَصّ [ʔingaṣṣ] *p:* قِطَع [giṭaʕ] قَطِع [gaṭiʕ] *vn:* اِنقِطَع [ʔingiṭaʕ] *p:* The doctor amputated his leg. الطَّبِيب بِتَر رِجلَه [ʔiṭṭabi:b bitar riǰlah]

amulet • **1.** حِرِز [ħiriz] حرُوز [[ħru:z] *pl:*

to amuse • **1.** وَنَّس [wannas] توَنَّس [twannas] *p:* That amuses me very much. هَذا يوَنِّسنِي هوايَة [ha:ða ywannisni hwa:ya] • **2.** لَهَّى [lahha:] تلَهَّى [tlahha:] *p:* سَلَّى [salla:] تَسلِيَة [tasliya] *vn:* تسَلَّى [tsalla:] *p:* He amuses himself by reading. يلَهِّي نَفسَه بالقِرايَة [ylahhi nafsah biliqra:ya] • **3.** ضَحَّك [ð̣aħħak] تَضحِيك [tað̣ħi:k] *vn:* تضَحَّك [tð̣aħħak] *p:* The comedian amused the audience. الهَزَلِي ضَحَّك الحاضرِين [ʔilhazali ð̣aħħak ʔilħa:ð̣ri:n]

amusement • **1.** تَسلِيَة [tasliya] تَسلِيات [tasliya:t] *pl:* لَهُو [lahw] وَنسَة [wansa] He paints for amusement only. يِرسِم لِلتَّسلِيَة فَقَط [yirsim littasliya faqaṭ]

amusement tax • **1.** ضَرِيبَة مَلاهِي [ð̣ari:bat mala:hi]

amusing • **1.** مُمتِع [mumtiʕ] I read an amusing article in the paper today. قَرَيت مَقال مُمتِع بِالجَّرِيدَة اليَوم [qrayt maqa:l mumtiʕ biǰǰari:da ʔilyu:m]

anarchist • **1.** فَوضَوِي [fawð̣awi] فَوضَوِيِّين [fawð̣awiyyi:n] *pl:*

anarchy • **1.** فَوضَوِي، فَوضَوِيَّة [fawð̣awi, fawð̣awiyya]

analogous • **1.** مُشابِه [muša:bih] مُماثِل [muma:θil]

analogy • **1.** تَماثُل [tama:θul] تَشابُه [taša:buh]

analysis • **1.** تَحلِيل [taħli:l] تَحلِيلات، تَحالِيل [taħli:la:t, taħa:li:l] *pl:* They made a chemical analysis during class. سَوّوا تَحلِيل كِيمياوِي وَقِت الدَّرِس [sawwa:w taħli:l ki:mya:wi wakit ʔiddaris]

to analyze • **1.** حَلَّل [ħallal] تَحلِيل [taħli:l] *vn:* تحَلَّل [tħallal] *p:* First of all, analyze the problem. أَوَّل شِي، حَلِّل المُشكِلَة [ʔawwal ši, ħallil ʔilmuškila]

anatomical • **1.** تَشرِيحِي [tašri:ħi]

anatomy • **1.** عِلم التَّشرِيح [ʕilm ʔittašri:ħ] He studies anatomy at Cairo University. يِدرُس عِلم التَّشرِيح بِجامِعَة القاهِرَة [yidrus ʕilm ʔittašri:ħ bǰa:miʕat ʔilqa:hira] • **2.** تَركِيب جِسمِي [tarki:b ǰismi:] We dissected the rabbit and studied its anatomy. شَرَّحنا الأرنَب وَدِرَسنا تَركِيبَه الجِّسمِي [šarraħna ʔilʔarnab wdirasna tarki:bah ʔiǰǰismi]

ancestor • **1.** جِدّ [ǰidd] جدُود، أَجداد [ǰdu:d, ʔaǰda:d] *pl:* سَلَف [salaf]

A

anchor • 1. أَنقَر [ʔangar] أَناقِر [ʔana:gir] *pl:* The boat lost its anchor in the storm. ضاع أَنقَر المَركَب بِالعاصِفَة [ða:ʕ ʔangar ʔilmarkab bilʕa:ṣifa]

* **Our boat lay at anchor in the harbor.** • **1.** مَركَبنا كان راسِي بِالمِيناء [markabna ča:n ra:si bilmi:na:ʔ]

to drop anchor • 1. ذَبّ أَنقَر [ðabb ʔangar] *vn:* اِنذَبّ [ʔinðabb] *p:* The ship dropped anchor in the bay. الباخِرَة شال ذَبَّتْ بِالخَلِيج [ʔilba:xira [ša:l ʔangar bilxali:ǰ]

to weigh anchor • 1. شال أَنقَر [ša:l ʔangar] شَيل [ši:l] *vn:* اِنشال [ʔinša:l] p: رُفَع [rufaʕ] رَفُع [rafuʕ] *vn:* اِنرُفَع [ʔinrufaʕ] *p:* جَرّ [ǰarr] جَرّ [ǰarr] *vn:* اِنجَرّ [ʔinǰarr] *p:* We weighed anchor after the storm passed. شِلنا الأَنقَر بَعَد ما مَرَّت العاصِفَة [šilna lʔangar baʕad ma: marrat ʔilʕa:ṣifa]

to anchor • 1. رِسَى [risa:] رَسُو [rasu] *vn:* اِنرِسَى [ʔinrisa:] *p:* They anchored the ship out in the bay. رِسَوا الباخِرَة بِالخَلِيج [risaw ʔilba:xira bilxali:ǰ] • **2.** ثَبَّت [θabbat] تَثبِيت [taθbi:t] *vn:* تثَبَّت [tθabbat] *p:* They anchored the telephone pole in cement. ثَبّتَوا عَمُود التِّلِفُون بِالشِّبَينتُو [θabbitaw ʕamu:d ʔittilifu:n biččibi:ntu:]

* **He stood there as if he were anchored to the spot.** • **1.** وُقَف عَبالَك مبَسمَر بمُكانَه [wugaf ʕaba:lak mbasmar bmuka:nah]

ancient • 1. قَدِيم [qadi:m] قُدَماء [qudama:(ʔ)] *pl:* This is the palace of the ancient kings of Babylon. هَذا قَصِر مِلُوك بابِل القُدَماء [ha:ða qaṣir milu:k ba:bil ʔilqudama:ʔ] • **2.** عَتِيق [ʕati:g] عِتَّق [ʕittag] *pl:* Why did you invest so much money in that ancient building? لِيش حَطَّيت هَالقَدّ فلُوس عَلَى ذِيك البِنايَة العَتِيقَة؟ [li:š ħaṭṭi:t halgadd flu:s ʕala ði:č ʔilbina:ya ʔilʕati:ga?] I'm very much interested in ancient statues. آنِي كُلِّش مُولَع بِالتَّماثِيل القَدِيمَة [ʔa:ni kulliš mu:laʕ bittama:θi:l ʔilqadi:ma]

and • 1. و [w] They sell books and stationery. يبِيعُون كُتُب وَقِرطاسِيَّة [ybi:ʕu:n kutub waqirṭa:siyya]

and so forth (and so on) • 1. وما أَشبَه [wma: ʔašbah] / وَإِلَى آخِره [waʔila ʔa:xirih] I need paper, ink, and so forth. أَرِيد وَرَق، حِبر، و ما أَشبَه [ʔari:d waraq, ħibir, w ma: ʔašbah]

anesthetic • 1. بَنج [banǰ]

angel • 1. مَلَك [malak] مَلائِكَة [mala:ʔika] *pl:*

anger • 1. غَضَب [ɣaðab] زَعَل [zaʕal] In his anger, he said a lot of things he didn't mean. بِغَضَبَه، قال هوايَة أَشياء ما يِقصُدها [bɣaðabah, ga:l hwa:ya ʔašya:ʔ ma: yiqṣudha]

to anger • 1. زِعَل [ziʕal] زَعَل [zaʕal] *vn: sv* a. غِضَب [ɣiðab] غَضَب [ɣaðab] *vn: sv* a. He doesn't anger easily. ما يِزعَل بِالعَجَل [ma: yizʕal bilʕaǰal] • **2.** زَعَّل [zaʕʕal] تَزعِيل [tazʕi:l] *vn:* تزَعَّل [tzaʕʕal] *p:* أَغضَب [ʔaɣðab] إِغضاب [ʔiɣða:b] *vn: sv* i. His remarks angered me. حكاياتَه زَعَّلَتنِي [ħča:ya:tah zaʕʕalatni]

angle • 1. زاوِيَة [za:wiya] زَوايا [zawa:ya:] *pl:* Measure each angle of the triangle. قِيس كُلّ زاوِيَة مِن زَوايا المُثَلَّث [qi:s kull za:wiya min zawa:ya: ʔilmuθallaθ] • **2.** وُجِه [wuǰih] وُجُوه [wuǰu:h] *pl:* ناحِيَة [na:ħiya] نَواحِي [nawa:ħi] *pl:* We considered the matter from all angeles. بحَثنا المَوضُوع مِن كُلّ الوُجُوه [bħaθna ʔilmawðu:ʕ min kull ʔilwuǰu:h]

angry • 1. زَعلان [zaʕla:n] زَعلانِين، زعالَة [zaʕla:ni:n, zʕa:la] *pl:* غَضبان [ɣaðba:n] I haven't seen him angry very often. ما شِفتَه زَعلان إِلّا قَلِيل [ma: šiftah zaʕla:n ʔilla qali:l]

to be angry • 1. زِعَل [ziʕal] زَعَل [zaʕal] *vn: sv* a. غِضَب [ɣiðab] غَضَب [ɣaðab] *vn: sv* a. Please don't be angry with me! أَرجُوك لا تِزعَل مِنِّي [ʔarǰu:k la: tizʕal minni] Are you angry at him? إِنتَ زَعلان عَليه؟ [ʔinta zaʕla:n ʕali:h?] Are you angry at him? إِنتَ غَضبان عَليه؟ [ʔinta ɣaðba:n ʕali:h?]

to make angry • 1. زَعَّل [zaʕʕal] تَزعِيل [tazʕi:l] *vn: sv* i. غَضَّب [gaððab] تَغضِيب [taɣði:b] *vn: sv* i. That remark must have made him very angry. هَالمُلاحَظَة لازِم هوايَة زَعَّلَتَه [halmula:ħaða la:zim hwa:ya zaʕʕlatah]

animal • 1. حَيوان [ħaywa:n] حَيوانات [ħaywa:na:t] *pl:* Don't feed the animals. لا تأَكِّل الحَيوانات [la: tʔakkil ʔilħaywa:na:t]

Ankara • 1. أَنقَرَة [ʔanqara]

ankle • 1. مَفصَل قَدَم [mafṣal qadam]

anniversary • 1. ذِكرَى سَنَوِيَّة [ðikra: sanawiyya] The bank is celebrating the anniversary of its foundation. البَنك دَيِحتِفِل بِالذِّكرَى السَّنَوِيَّة لِتَأسِيسَه [ʔilbank dayiħtifil biððikra: ʔissanawiyya ltaʔsi:sah]

to announce • 1. ذاع [ða:ʕ] إِذاعَة [ʔiða:ʕa] *vn: sv* i. They announced the results on the radio. ذاعَوا النَّتائِج بِالرّادِيُو [ða:ʕaw ʔinnata:ʔiǰ birra:dyu] • **2.** عِلَن [ʕilan] إِعلان [ʔiʕla:n] *vn: sv* i. They announced their engagement last night. عِلنَوا خُطبَتهُم البارحَة بِاللِّيل [ʕilnaw xuṭbathum ʔilba:rħa billi:l]

announcement • 1. بَيان [baya:n] بَيانات [baya:na:t] *pl:* The government issued an announcement on their new policy. الحُكُومَة أَصدرَت بَيان عَن سِياسَتها الجِّدِيدَة [ʔilħuku:ma ʔaṣdirat baya:n ʕan siya:satha ʔiǰǰidi:da] • **2.** إِعلان [ʔiʕla:n] إِعلانات [ʔiʕla:na:t] *pl:* An announcement of their engagement was in the paper last night. إعلان خُطبَتهُم كان بِالجَّرِيدَة البارحَة باللَّيل [ʔiʕlaːn xuṭbathum čaːn bijjariːda ʔilbaːrħa billiːl]

announcer • **1.** مُذِيع [muðiːʕ] The announcer has a pleasant voice. المُذِيع عِندَه صَوت حِلو [ʔilmuðiːʕ ʕindah ṣawt ħilw]

to annoy • **1.** زِعَج [ziʕaj] إزعاج [ʔizʕaːj] *vn:* اِنزِعَج [ʔinziʕaj] *p:* أزعَج [ʔazʕaj] إزعاج [ʔizʕaːj] *vn: sv* i. ضَوَّج [ḍawwaj] تَضوِيج [taḍwiːj] *vn:* تضَوَّج [tḍawwaj] *p:* He annoyed me all morning. أزعَجنِي طُول الصُّبُح [ʔazʕajni ṭuːl ʔiṣṣubuħ]

to get annoyed • **1.** اِنزِعَج [ʔinziʕaj] اِنزِعاج [ʔinziʕaːj] *vn: sv* i. ضاج [ḍaːj] ضَوَجان [ḍawajaːn] *vn: sv* u. I got very annoyed at her. اِنزِعَجِت مِنها هوايَة [ʔinziʕajit minha hwaːya]

annoying • **1.** مُزعِج [muzʕij] That's very annoying. هَذا كُلِّش مُزعِج [haːða kulliš muzʕij]

another • **1.** لاخ [laːx] ثانِي [θaːni] Give me another cup of coffee please. إنطِينِي فِنجان قَهوَة لاخ رَجاءاً [ʔinṭiːni finjaːn gahwa laːx rajaːʔan] • **2.** غير [ɣiːr] ثانِي [θaːni] Show me another pattern. راوِينِي غير تُفصال [raːwiːni ɣiːr tufṣaːl] • **3.** بَعَد [baʕad] I don't want to hear another word about it. ما أرِيد أسمَع كِلمَة بَعَد عَنها [maː ʔariːd ʔasmaʕ čilma baʕad ʕanha]

one another • **1.** واحِد عَاللّاخ [waːħid ʕallaːx] We depend on one another. نِعتِمِد واحِد عَاللّاخ [niʕtimid waːħid ʕallaːx] • **2.** واحِد وِيّا اللاخ [waːħid wiyya ʔillaːx] Those two are always fighting with one another. هَالثّنَين يِتعارکُون واحِد وِيّا اللّاخ عَلَى طُول [halθnayn yitʕaːrkuːn waːħid wiyya ʔillaːx ʕala ṭuːl] • **3.** واحِد بِاللاخ [waːħid billaːx] They don't trust one another. ما يِثِقُون واحِد بِاللّاخ [maː yθiquːn waːħid billaːx]

answer • **1.** جَواب [jawaːb] أجوِبَة [ʔajwiba] *pl:* I'm waiting for an answer to my letter. دَأنتِظِر جَواب لِمَكتُوبِي [daʔantiḍir jawaːb lmaktuːbi] • **2.** حَلّ [ħall] حِلُول [ħiluːl] *pl:* How did you arrive at this answer? شلُون توَصَّلِت لِهالحَلّ [šluːn twaṣṣalit lihʔalħall]

to answer • **1.** جاوَب [jaːwab] مُجاوَبَة [mujaːwaba] *vn:* تجاوَب [tjaːwab] *p:* رَدّ [radd] رَدّ [radd] *vn:* اِنرَدّ [ʔinradd] *p:* He answered my question without any hesitation. جاوَب عَلَى أسئِلتِي بِدُون تَرَدُّد [jaːwab ʕala ʔasʔilti biduːn taraddud]

ant • **1.** نَملَة [namla] نَملات [namlaːt] *pl:* نَمِل [namil] *Collective*

antelope • **1.** غَزال [ɣazaːl] غِزلان [ɣizlaːn] *pl:*

antenna • **1.** أرِيَل [ʔaryal] أرِيَلات [ʔaryalaːt] *pl:*

anthem • **1.** نَشِيد [našiːd] أناشِيد [ʔanaːšiːd] *pl:* They played the national anthem before the game started. عِزفَوا النَّشِيد الوَطَنِي قَبُل ما يِبدَأ اللِّعِب [ʔizfaw ʔinnašiːd ʔilwaṭani gabul maː yibdaʔ ʔilliʕib]

antic • **1.** تَهرِيج [tahriːj] تَهرِيجات [tahriːjaːt] *pl:* His antics were very amusing. تَهرِيجاتَه كانَت هوايَة تضَحِّك [tahriːjaːtah čaːnat hwaːya dḍaħħik]

to anticipate • **1.** توَقَّع [twaqqaʕ] تَوَقُّع [tawaqquʕ] *vn: sv* a. The attendance was larger than we had anticipated. الحاضرِين كانَوا أزيَد مِن ما توَقَّعنا [ʔilħaːḍriːn čaːnaw ʔazyad min maː twaqqaʕna]

antidote • **1.** دُوا (ضِدّ التَسَمُّم) [duwa (ḍidd ʔittasammum)] What is the antidote for arsenic poisoning? شِنُو الدُّوا ضِدّ التَّسَمُّم مِن الزَّرنِيخ؟ [šinu ʔidduwaː ḍidd ʔittasammum min ʔizzarniːx?]

Antioch • **1.** أنطاكيا [ʔanṭaːkya]

antique • **1.** أنتِيك [ʕantiːk] He bought a very expensive antique watch. اِشتِرَى ساعَة أنتِيكَة كُلِّش غالِيَة [ʔištiraː saːʕa ʔantiːka kulliš ɣaːlya] • **2.** قَدِيم [qadiːm] قُدَماء [qudamaːʔ] *pl:* We visited some antique ruins yesterday. زِرنا بَعَض الأثار القَدِيمَة البارحَة [zirna baʕaḍ ʔilʔaaθaːr ʔilqadiːma ʔilbaːrħa]

anxiety • **1.** قَلَق [qalaq]

anxious • **1.** قَلِق [qaliq] We spent several anxious minutes waiting for their return. قضَينا عِدَّة دَقايِق قَلقَة بإنتِظار رُجُوعهُم [gḍiːna ʕiddat daqaːyiq qalqa bʔintiḍaːr rujuːʕhum]

to be anxious • **1.** مِتحَمِّس [mitħammis] مِشتاق [mištaːq, mištaːg] I'm anxious to see the new book. آنِي مِتحَمِّس أشُوف الكِتاب الجِّدِيد [ʔaːni mitħammis ʔašuːf ʔilkitaːb ʔijjidiːd] • **2.** قَلِق [qaliq] He's very anxious about his future. هُوَّ قَلِق عَلَى مُستَقبَلَه [huwwa qaliq ʕala mustaqbalah]

anxiously • **1.** اِشتِياق [ʔištiyaːq, ʔištiyaːg] They waited anxiously about an hour until the news came in. ظَلَّوا يِنتَظرُون بإشتِياق حَوالِي ساعَة إلَى أن وُصلَت الأخبار [ḍallaw yintaḍruːn bʔištiyaːq ħawaːli saːʕa ʔila ʔan wuṣlat ʔilʔaxbaːr]

any • **1.** أيّ [ʔayy] Did you find any books there? لِقِيت أيّ كُتُب هناك؟ [ligiːt ʔayy kutub hnaːk?] Any mechanic can fix that. أيّ مِيكانِيكِي يِقدَر يصَلِّح هَذا [ʔayy miːkaːniːki yigdar yṣalliħ haːða] • **2.** شِي [ši] أشياء [ʔašyaːʔ] *pl:* Don't eat any of it. لا تاكُل شِي مِنَّه [laː taːkul ši minnah]

not .... any • **1.** ما كُلّ [maː kull] ما أيّ [maː ʔayy] There isn't any bread. ماکُو كُلّ خُبُز [maːku kull xubuz]

A

anybody • **1.** أَحَّد [ʔaħħad] Was anybody at home? كان أَحَّد بِالبَيت؟ [ča:n ʔaħħad bilbayt?] • **2.** أَيّ واحِد [ʔayy wa:ħid] Anybody can do that. أَيّ واحِد يِقدَر يسَوِّي هَذا [ʔayy wa:ħid yigdar ysawwi ha:ða]

*** If he's anybody at all in this town, I'd know him.** • **1.** لَو كان شَخصِيَّة بهَالبَلَد، كان عِرَفتَه [law ča:n šaxṣiyya bhalbalad, ča:n ʕiraftah]

*** We can't take just anybody.** • **1.** ما نِقدَر نعَيِّن ياهُو الكان [ma: nigdar nʕayyin ya:hu ʔičča:n]

anyhow • **1.** عَلَى أَيّ حال [ʕala ʔayy ħa:l] عَلَى كُلّ حال [ʕala kull ħa:l] I would have gone anyhow. آنِي كان رِحِت، عَلَى كُلّ حال [ʔa:ni ča:n riħit, ʕala kull ħa:l]

anyone • **1.** أَحَّد [ʔaħħad] أَيّ واحِد [ʔayy wa:ħid] If anyone needs help, send him to me. إِذا أَحَّد يِحتاج مُساعَدَة دِزَّه عَلَيّا [ʔiða ʔaħħad yiħta:ǰ musa:ʕada dizzah ʕalayya] Anyone can do that. أَيّ واحِد يِقدَر يسَوِّي هَذا [ʔayy wa:ħid yigdar ysawwi ha:ða]

anything • **1.** أَيّ شِي [ʔayyši] فَدّ شِي [fadd ši] شِي [ši] أَشياء [ʔašya:ʔ] *pl:* Is there anything for me here? أَكُو أَيّ شِي إِلِي هنا؟ [ʔaku ʔayy ši ʔili hna?] Did he say anything? قال شِي؟ [ga:l ši?]

*** I wouldn't do that for anything.** • **1.** ما أَسَوِّي هَذا مَهما كان [ma: ʔasawwi ha:ða mahma ča:n]

*** I was anything but pleased with his work.** • **1.** ما كِنِت مِرتاح مِن عَمَلَه أَبَداً [ma: činit mirta:ħ min ʕamalah ʔabadan]

anything but • **1.** كُلّشِي بَسّ [kullši bass] You can do anything but that. تِقدَر تسَوِّي كُلّشِي بَسّ هَذا [tigdar tsawwi kullši bass ha:ða]

anyway • **1.** عَلَى كُلّ حال [ʕala kull ħa:l] She didn't want to come anyway. ما رادَت تِجِي عَلَى كُلّ حال [ma: ra:dat tiǰi ʕala kull ħa:l] I didn't go anyway. ما رِحِت عَلَى كُلّ حال [ma: riħit ʕala kull ħa:l]

anywhere • **1.** فَدّ مُكان [fadd muka:n] فَدّ مَحَلّ [fadd maħall] Are you going anywhere today? رايِح فَدّ مُكان اليُوم؟ [ra:yiħ fadd muka:n ʔilyu:m?] • **2.** وين ما [wi:n ma:] Anywhere you look there's dust. وَين ما تباوِع أَكُو عَجاج [wi:n ma: tba:wiʕ ʔaku ʕaǰa:ǰ]

not ... anywhere • **1.** ما أَيّ مَكان [ma: ʔayy makaan] ما أَيّ مَحَلّ [ma: ʔayy maħall] I couldn't find him anywhere. ما قِدَرت أَلقاه بأَيّ مُكان [ma: gidarit ʔalga:h bʔayy muka:n]

*** That won't get you anywhere.** • **1.** هَذِي ما راح توَصِّلَك لِفَدّ نَتِيجَة [ha:ði ma: ra:ħ twaṣṣilak lfadd nati:ǰa]

apart • **1.** مفَصَّخ [mfaṣṣax] Is my watch still apart? ساعَتِي لهَسَّة مفَصَّخَة؟ [sa:ʕati lhassa mfaṣṣixa?] • **2.** مِفتِرِق [miftiriq] They were apart for two weeks. كانَوا مِفتِرقِين لِمُدَّة إِسبُوعَين [ča:naw miftirqi:n lmuddat ʔisbu:ʕayn] • **3.** مِنفِصِل [minfiṣil] They've been living apart since their quarrel. كانَوا عايشِين مِنفَصلِين مِن وَقِت عراكهُم [ča:naw ʕa:yši:n minfaṣli:n min wakit ʕra:khum] • **4.** عَلَى حِدَة [ʕala ħida] Let's consider each argument apart from the others. خَلِّي نُنظُر بِكُلّ حِجَّة عَلَى حِدَة عَن الحِجَج الأُخرَى [xalli nunður bkull ħiǰǰa ʕala ħida ʕan ʔilħiǰaǰ ʔilʔuxra:]

*** The two buses will leave five minutes apart.** • **1.** الباصَين يِطلَعُون خَمَس دَقايِق واحِد وَرا اللاخ [ʔilpa:ṣayn yiṭlaʕu:n xamas daqa:yiq wa:ħid wara ʔilla:x]

apart from this • **1.** ما عَدا هاي [ma:ʕada: ha:y] Apart from this, he's a good man. ما عَدا هاي، هُوَّ خُوش رِجّال [ma: ʕada: ha:y, huwwa xu:š riǰǰa:l]

apartment • **1.** شِقَّة [šiqqa] شِقَق [šiqaq] *pl:* We're looking for an apartment. دَندَوِّر عَلَى شِقَّة [dandawwir ʕala šiqqa]

apartment house • **1.** عِمارَة لِلسَكَن [ʕima:ra lissakan] عِمارات لِلسَكَن [ʕima:ra:t lissakan] *pl:* They're building an apartment house on our street. دَيِبنُون عِمارَة لِلسَّكَن بِشارِعنا [dayibnu:n ʕima:ra lissakan bša:riʕna]

ape • **1.** شادِي [ša:di] شوادِي [šwa:di] *pl:* قِرد [qird] قُرُود [quru:d] *pl:* We saw an ape at the zoo. شِفنا فَدّ شادِي بحَدِيقَة الحَيوانات [šifna fadd ša:di bħadi:qat ʔilħaywa:na:t]

apiece • **1.** كُلّ واحِد [kull wa:ħid] كُلّ مَن [kull man] My brother and I earned six dollars apiece. آنِي واخُويَة حَصَّلنا كُلّ واحِد سِتّ دُولارات [ʔa:ni waxu:ya ħaṣṣalna kull wa:ħid sitt dula:ra:t]

to apologize • **1.** طِلَب العَفو، إِعتِذَر، تعَذَّر [ṭilab ʔilʕafw, ʔiʕtiðar, tʕaððar] طَلَب العَفو [ṭalab ʔilʕafw] *vn: sv* u. إِعتِذَر [ʔiʕtiðar] إِعتِذار [ʔiʕtiða:r] *vn: sv* i. تعَذَّر [tʕaððar] تَعَذُّر [taʕaðður] *vn: sv* a. I apologize. أَطلُب العَفو [ʔaṭlub ʔilʕafw] I apologize. آنِي أَعتِذِر [ʔa:ni ʔaʕtiðir]

to apologize to • **1.** تعَذَّر مِن [tʕaððar min] *sv* a. إِلَى [ʔila] إِعتِذَر مِن [ʔiʕtiðar min] *sv* i. إِلَى [ʔila] Did you apologize to her? إِعتِذَرِت إِلها؟ [ʔiʕtiðarit ʔilha?]

apology • **1.** إِعتِذار [ʔiʕtiða:r] مَعذُور [maʕðu:r]

apostrophe • **1.** عَلامَة إِختِصار [ʕala:mat ʔixtiṣa:r] عَلامات إِختِصار [ʕala:mata:t ʔixtiṣa:r] *pl:* عَلامَة إِضافَة [ʕala:mat ʔiḍa:fa] عَلامات إِضافَة [ʕala:mata:t iḍa:fa] *pl:*

apostle • **1.** الرَّسُول [ʔirrasu:l] حَوارِي [ħawa:ri]

apostolic • **1.** رَسُولِي [rasu:li] Could you direct me to the Apostolic Legation? تِقدَر تدَلِّينِي عَالقَصادَة الرَّسُولِيَّة [tigdar ddalli:ni ʕalqaṣa:da ʔirrasu:liyya]

apparatus • **1.** جهاز [ǰiha:z] أجهزَة [ʔaǰhiza] *pl:*

apparent • **1.** مبَيِّن [mbayyin] ظاهِر [ð̣a:hir] واضِح [wa:ð̣iħ] It's apparent that he didn't understand the question. مبَيِّن ما إفتِهَم السُّؤال [mbayyin ma: ʔiftiham ʔissuʔa:l]

apparently • **1.** عَلَى ما يظهَر [ʕala ma: yið̣har] حَسَبما يظهَر [ħasabma: yið̣har] He has apparently changed his mind. عَلَى ما يِظهَر غَيَّر فِكرَه [ʕala ma: yið̣har ɣayyar fikrah]

appeal • **1.** إستِئناف [ʔistiʔna:f] The appeal was denied. الاستِئناف إنرُفَض [ʔilʔistiʔna:f ʔinrufað̣] • **2.** طَلَب [ṭalab] طَلَبات [ṭalaba:t] *pl:* The United Nations got many appeals for help this year. الأُمَم المُتَّحِدَة إستِلمَت عِدَّة طَلَبات مُساعَدَة هالسَّنَة [ʔilʔumam ʔilmuttaħida ʔistilmat ʕiddat ṭalaba:t musa:ʕada hassana] • **3.** جاذِبِيَّة [ǰa:ðibiyya] She's got a lot of sex appeal. عِدها جاذِبِيَّة جِنسِيَّة هوايَة [ʕidha ǰa:ðibiyya ǰinsiyya hwa:ya]

to appeal • **1.** عِجَب [ʕiǰab] إعجاب [ʔiʕǰa:b] *vn: sv* i. It doesn't appeal to me. ما تِعجِبنِي [ma: tiʕǰibni] • **2.** توَسَّل [twassal] تَوَسُّل [tawassul] *vn: sv* a. He appealed to the president to pardon his son. توَسَّل مِن الرَّئِيس يعفِي عَن إبنَه [twassal min ʔirraʔi:s yiʕfi ʕan ʔibnah] • **3.** إستَأنَف [ʔistaʔnaf] إستِئناف [ʔistiʔna:f] *vn: sv* i. The lawyer decided to appeal the case. المُحامِي قَرَّر يِستَأنِف الدَّعوَة [ʔilmuħa:mi qarrar yistaʔnif ʔiddaʕwa] • **4.** إستَنجَد [ʔistanǰad] إستِنجاد [ʔistinǰa:d] *vn: sv* i. إستَغاث [ʔistaɣa:θ] إستِغاثَة [ʔistiɣa:θa] *vn: sv* i. During the flood, the country appealed for help from the neighboring countries. بوَقِت الفَيَضان، البَلَد إستَنجَد مُساعَدَة مِن البِلاد المُجاوِرَة [bwakit ʔilfayaða:n, ʔilbalad ʔistanǰad musa:ʕada min ʔilbila:d ʔilmuǰa:wira]

to appear • **1.** بَيَّن [bayyan] تبيِّن [tbiyyin] *vn:* تبَيَّن [tbayyan] *p:* He appeared at the last moment. بَيَّن بآخِر لَحظَة [bayyan biʔa:xir laħð̣a] • **2.** طِلَع [ṭilaʕ] طُلُوع [ṭulu:ʕ] *vn: sv* a. This paper appears every Thursday. هَالجَرِيدَة تِطلَع كُلّ خَمِيس [halǰari:da tiṭlaʕ kull xami:s] • **3.** ظِهَر [ð̣ihar] ظُهُور [ð̣uhu:r] *vn:* إنظِهَر [ʔinð̣ihar] *p:* A ship appeared on the horizon. فَدّ سَفِينَة ظِهرَت عالأُفُق [fadd safi:na ð̣ihrat ʕalʔufuq]

appearance • **1.** ظُهُور [ð̣uhu:r] It's his first appearance on the stage. هَذا أَوَّل ظُهُورَه عَالمَسرَح [ha:ða ʔawwal ð̣uhu:rah ʕalmasraħ] • **2.** مَظهَر [mað̣har] مَظاهِر [mað̣a:hir] *pl:* You have to pay more attention to your appearance. لازِم تِهتَمّ بمَظهَرَك أَزيَد [la:zim tihtamm bmað̣harak ʔazyad] Appearances are deceiving. بمَظاهِر خَدّاعَة [bmað̣a:hir xadda:ʕa]

appendicitis • **1.** إلتِهاب المُصران الأعوَر [ʔiltiha:b ʔilmuṣra:n ʔilʔaʕwar] إلتِهاب الزائِدَة الدُّودِيَّة [ʔiltiha:b ʔizza:ʔida ʔiddu:diyya]

appendix • **1.** الزّائِدَة الدُّودِيَّة [ʔizza:ʔida ʔiddu:diyya] المُصران الأعوَر [ʔilmuṣra:n ʔilʔaʕwar] They took his appendix out when he was five years old. قَصّولَه الزّائِدَة الدُّودِيَّة مِن كان عُمرَه خَمس سنِين [gaṣṣu:lah ʔizza:ʔida ʔiddu:diyya min ča:n ʕumrah xams sni:n] • **2.** مُلحَق [mulħaq] مَلاحِق [malaħiq] *pl:* Perhaps it's in the appendix. يمكِن هَذا بِالمُلحَق [yimkin ha:ða bilmulħaq]

appetite • **1.** شَهِيَّة [šahiyya] Our boy has a good appetite. إبنَنا عِندَه شَهِيَّة زينَة [ʔibinna ʕindah šahiyya zi:na] • **2.** رَغبَة [raɣba] رَغبات [raɣba:t] *pl:* He has a tremendous appetite for knowledge. عِندَه هوايَة رَغبَة بِالعِلِم [ʕindah hwa:ya raɣba bilʕilim]

appetizer • **1.** مُشَهِّي [mušahhi] مُشَهّيات [mušahhya:t] *pl:*

appetizing • **1.** مُشَهِّي [mušahhi] مُشَهِّيّات [mušahhiyya:t] *pl:*

to applaude • **1.** صَفَّق [ṣaffag] تَصفِيق، تصُفُّق [taṣfi:g, tṣuffug] *vn:* تصَفَّق [tṣaffag] *p:* We applauded heartily. صَفَّقنا مِن كُلّ قَلُبنا [ṣaffagna min kull galubna]

applause • **1.** تَصفِيق [taṣfi:g] تصُفُّق [tṣuffug] They met him with applause. إستَقبِلُوه بِالتَّصفِيق [ʔistaqbilu:h bittaṣfi:g]

apple • **1.** تِفّاحَة، تُفّاحَة [tiffa:ħa] تِفّاحات، تُفّاحات [tiffa:ħa:t, tuffa:ħa:t] *pl:* تِفّاح، تُفّاح [tiffa:ħ, tuffa:ħ] *Collective*

appliance • **1.** جِهاز [ǰiha:z] أجهزَة [ʔaǰhiza] *pl:* We carry all kinds of electrical appliances. نِتعاطَى جَمِيع الأجهزَة الكَهرَبائِيَّة [nitʕa:ṭa: ǰami:ʕ ʔilʔaǰhiza lkahraba:ʔiyya] This place sells household appliances. هَالمَحَلّ يبِيع أجهزَة بَيتِيَّة [halmaħall yibi:ʕ ʔaǰhiza bayiyya]

application • **1.** إستِمارَة [ʔistima:ra] إستِمارات [ʔistima:ra:t] *pl:* Fill in this application and forward it to the university. إملِي هَالاستِمارَة وَدِزّها لِلجامِعَة [ʔimli: halʔistima:ra wdizzha liǰǰa:miʕa] • **2.** عَرِيضَة [ʕari:ð̣a] عَرايِض [ʕara:yið̣] *pl:* He forwarded his application to the manager. قَدَّم عَرِيضتَه لِلمُدِير [qaddam ʕari:ð̣tah lilmudi:r] • **3.** تَطبِيق [taṭbi:q] The application of his theory wasn't practical. تَطبِيق نَظَرِيتَه ما كان عَمَلِي [taṭbi:q nað̣ari:tah ma: ča:n ʕamali] • **4.** طَلَب [ṭalab] طَلَبات [ṭalaba:t] *pl:* His application was rejected. طَلَبَه إنرُفَض [ṭalabah ʔinrufað̣] • **5.** قاط [qa:ṭ] قُوط [qu:ṭ] *pl:* طَبَقَة [ṭabaqa] طَبَقات [ṭabaqa:t] *pl:* You'll have to give it another application after this coat dries. لازِم تُضرُبها قاط لاخ بَعَد ما يَبَس هَالقاط [la:zim tuð̣rubha qa:ṭ la:x baʕad ma: yi:bas halqa:ṭ]

to apply • **1.** قَدَّم [qaddam] تَقدِيم [taqdi:m] *vn:* تقَدَّم [tqaddam] *p:* I'd like to apply for the job. أَحِبّ أقَدِّم عَالوَظِيفَة [ʔaħibb ʔaqaddim ʕalwað̣i:fa] • **2.** طَبَّق [ṭabbaq] تَطبِيق

A

[taṭbi:q] *vn:* تطَبَّق [ʔiṭṭabbaq] *p:* You've applied this rule incorrectly. طَبَّقِت هَالقاعِدَة غَلَط [ṭabbaqit halqa:ʕida ɣalaṭ] • **3.** حَطّ [ħaṭṭ] حَطّ [ħaṭṭ] *vn:* اِنحَطّ [ʔinħaṭṭ] p: اِستَعمَل [ʔistaʕmal] اِستِعمال [ʔistiʕma:l] *vn: sv* i. Apply a hot compress every two hours. حُطّ ضَمادَة حارَّة كُلّ ساعتِين [ħuṭṭ ðama:da ħa:rra kull sa:ʕtayn] I had to apply all my strength. اِضطَرَّيت أَحُطّ كُلّ قُوتِي [ʔiðṭarri:t ʔaħuṭṭ kull qu:ti] • **4.** طِلَب [ṭilab] طَلَب [ṭalab] *vn:* اِنطِلَب [ʔinṭilab] *p:* My father applied for a loan. أَبُويَا طِلَب دَين [ʔabu:ya ṭilab dayn] • **5.** حَطّ [ħaṭṭ] حَطّ [ħaṭṭ] *vn:* اِنحَطّ [ʔinħaṭṭ] *p:* خَلَّى [xalla:] تخِلِّي [txilli] *vn:* تخَلَّى [txalla:] *p:* She applied another coat of polish to her fingernails. حَطَّت قاط صُبُغ ثانِي عَلَى أَظافِرها [ħaṭṭat qa:ṭ ṣubuɣ θa:ni ʕala ʔaða:firha] • **6.** شِمَل [šimal] شِمُول [šimu:l] *vn:* اِنشِمَل [ʔinšimal] *p:* اِنطُبَق عَلَى [ʔinṭubaq ʕala] اِنطِباق [ʔinṭiba:q] *vn: sv* u. سِرَى [sira:] سَريان [sarya:n] *vn: sv* i. This order applies to everybody. هَالأَمُر يِشمِل الكُلّ [halʔamur yišmil ʔilkull]

to apply oneself • **1.** بِذَل جَهِد [biðal ǰihid] بَذِل [baðil] *vn:* اِنبِذَل [ʔinbiðal] *p:* He's smart but he doesn't apply himself. هُوَّ شاطِر لَكِن ما يِبذِل جَهدَه [huwwa ša:ṭir la:kin ma: yibðil ǰahdah]

to appoint • **1.** عَيَّن [ʕayyan] تَعيين [taʕyi:n] *vn:* تعَيَّن [tʕayyan] *p:* The ministry appointed five new engineers. الوُزارَة عَيِّنَت خَمِس مُهَندِسِين جِدَّد [ʔilwuza:ra ʕayyinat xamis muhandisi:n ǰiddad]

appointment • **1.** تَعيين [taʕyi:n] Congratulations on your appointment. التَّهانِي عَلَى تَعيينَك [ʔittaha:ni ʕala taʕyi:nak] • **2.** مَوعِد [mawʕid] مَواعِيد [mawa:ʕi:d] *pl:* I had to cancel all appointments for tomorrow. اِضطَرَّيت أَلغِي كُلّ المَواعِيد مال باكِر [ʔiðṭarri:t ʔalɣi kull ʔilmawa:ʕi:d ma:l ba:čir] I have an appointment with him. عِندِي مَوعِد وِيّاه [ʕindi mawʕid wiyya:h]

to make an appointment • **1.** تواعَد [twa:ʕad] تواعُد [twa:ʕud] *vn: sv* a. I made an appointment with Ali for five-o-clock. تواعَدِت وِيّا عَلِي السّاعَة خَمسَة [twa:ʕadit wiyya ʕali ʔissa:ʕa xamsa]

appraisal • **1.** تَقدِير [taqdi:r] تَقدِيرات [taqdi:ra:t] *pl:* تَثمِين [taθmi:n] تَثمِينات [taθmi:na:t] *pl:* A careful appraisal of the property showed that. . . تَقدِير المُلك بِصُورَة دَقِيقَة بَيَّن أَن [taqdi:r ʔilmuluk bṣu:ra daqi:qa bayyan ʔan]

to appraise • **1.** حَلَّل [ħallal] تَحلِيل [taħli:l] *vn:* تحَلَّل [tħallal] *p:* We want you to appraise the situation and give us your opinion. نرِيدَك تحَلِّل الوَضِع وَتِنطِينا رَأيَك [nri:dak tħallil ʔilwaðiʕ wtinṭi:na raʔayak] • **2.** قَدَّر [qaddar] تَقدِير [taqdi:r] *vn:* تقَدَّر [tqaddar] *p:* ثَمَّن [θamman] تَثمِين [taθmi:n] *vn:* تثَمَّن [tθamman] *p:* A broker's coming to appraise the house. فَدّ دَلّال راح يِجِي يقَدِّر البَيت [fadd dalla:l ra:ħ yiǰi yqaddir ʔilbayt]

to appreciate • **1.** كان مِمتَنِن، كان مَمنُون [ča:n mimtann, ča:n mamnu:n] *sv* u. مَمنُون [mamnu:n] I would appreciate it, if you could come. أَكُون مَمنُون إِذا تِقدَر تِجِي [ʔaku:n mamnu:n ʔiða tigdar tiǰi] • **2.** قَدَّر [qaddar] تَقدِير [taqdi:r] *vn:* تقَدَّر [tqaddar] *p:* She doesn't appreciate what we've done for her. ما دَتقَدِّر اللِّي سَوَّينا لها إيّاه [ma: datqaddir ʔilli sawwi:na lha ʔiyya:h] He doesn't appreciate good music. ما يقَدِّر المُوسِيقَى الرّاقيَة [ma: yqaddir ʔilmusi:qa ʔirra:qya] • **3.** عِرَف [ʕiraf] اِنعِرَف [ʔinʕiraf] *p:* I quite appreciate that it can't be done overnight. أَعرُف زين هَذا ما مُمكِن يِخلَص بِفَدّ يوم [ʔaʕruf zi:n ha:ða ma:mumkin yixlaṣ bfadd yu:m]

appreciation • **1.** تَقدِير [taqdi:r] تَقدِيرات [taqdi:ra:t] *pl:* I don't expect any appreciation. ما أَتوَقَّع أَيّ تَقدِير [ma: ʔatwaqqaʕ ʔayy taqdi:r] She has no appreciation for art. ما عِدها تَقدِير لِلفَنّ [ma: ʕidha taqdi:r lilfann]

appreciative • **1.** مَمنُون [mamnu:n] He doesn't seem very appreciative. يبَيِّن عَليه مُو مَمنُون [yibayyin ʕali:h mu: mamnu:n]

apprentice • **1.** صانع (تَحت التَدرِيب) [ṣa:niʕ (taħt ʔittadri:b)] صُنّاع (تَحت التَدرِيب) [ṣunna:ʕ (taħt ʔittadri:b)] *pl:* عامِل (تَحت التَدرِيب) [ʕa:mil (taħt ʔittadri:b)] عُمّال (تَحت التَدرِيب) [ʕumma:l (taħt ʔittadri:b)] *pl:*

approach • **1.** مَدخَل [madxal] مَداخِل [mada:xil] *pl:* They're repairing the approaches to the bridge. دَيصَلّحُون مَداخِل الجِّسِر [dayṣallħu:n mada:xil ʔiǰǰisir] • **2.** طَرِيقَة [ṭari:qa] طُرُق [ṭuruq] *pl:* Am I using the right approach? دَأَستَعمِل الطَّرِيقَة الصَّحِيحَة؟ [daʔastaʕmil ʔiṭṭari:qa ʔiṣṣaħi:ħa?]

to approach • **1.** تقَرَّب [tqarrab, tgarrab] تَقَرُّب [taqarrub] *vn: sv* a. They approached the enemy's camp cautiously. تقَرّبَوا مِن مُعَسكَر العَدُوّ بحَذَر [tgarrbaw min muʕaskar ʔilʕadu bħaðar] • **2.** فاتَح [fa:taħ] مُفاتَحَة [mufa:taħa] *vn:* تفاتَح [tfa:taħ] *p:* I'm going to approach my boss about a raise. راح أَفَتِّح الرَّئِيس مالِي بِالتَّرفِيع [ra:ħ ʔafattiħ ʔirraʔi:s ma:li bittarfi:ʕ] • **3.** عالَج [ʕa:laǰ] مُعالَجَة [muʕa:laǰa] *vn:* تعالَج [tʕa:laǰ] *p:* How would you approach the problem? شلُون تعالِج المُشكِلَة؟ [šlu:n tʕa:liǰ ʔilmuškila?]

appropriate • **1.** مُناسِب [muna:sib] مُلائِم [mula:ʔim] لايِق [la:yig] This gift is very appropriate. هَذِي الهَدِيَّة كُلِّش مُناسِبَة [ha:ði ʔilhadiyya kulliš muna:siba]

to appropriate • **1.** اِستَولَى [ʔistawla:] اِستِيلاء [ʔisti:la:ʔ] *vn: sv* i. My son has appropriated all my ties. إِبنِي اِستَولَى عَلَى كُلّ أَربِطتِي [ʔibni ʔistawla: ʕala kull ʔarbitti] • **2.** خَصَّص [xaṣṣaṣ] تَخصِيص [taxṣi:ṣ] *vn:* تخَصَّص [txaṣṣaṣ] *p:* The city has appropriated fifty thousand dinars to build a new library. البَلَدِيَّة خَصِّصَت خَمسِين أَلف دِينار لِبِنايَة مَكتَبَة جِدِيدَة

[ʔilbaladiyya xaṣṣiṣat xamsiːn ʔalf dinaːr libinaːyat maktaba ǰidiːda]

approval • **1.** مُوافَقَة [muwaːfaqa] مُصادقَة [muṣaːdqa] You'll have to get his approval on it. لازِم تاخُذ مُوافَقتَه عَليها [laːzim taːxuð muwaːfaqtah ʕaliːha]

*** This color will not meet her approval.** • **1.** ما راح توافِق عَلَى هَاللَّون [maː raːħ twaːfiq ʕala halluːn]

on approval • **1.** عَلَى شَرط المُوافَقَة [ʕala šarṭ ʔilmuwaːfaqa] They sent me the book on approval. دَزّولِي الكِتاب عَلَى شَرط المُوافَقَة [dazzuːli ʔilkitaːb ʕala šarṭ ʔilmuwaːfaqa]

to approve • **1.** وافَق [waːfaq] مُوافَقَة [muwaːfaqa] *vn:* توافَق [twaːfaq] *p:* Do you approve of my suggestion? توافُق عَلَى اِقتِراحِي؟ [twaːfuq ʕala ʔiqtiraːħi?] He doesn't approve of his son staying out late at night. ما يوافُق عَلَى إبنَه يِتأخَّر باللَّيل [maː ywaːfuq ʕala ʔibnah yitʔaxxar billayl] • **2.** صادَق [ṣaːdaq, ṣaːdag] مُصاداقَة [muṣaːdaːqa] *vn:* تصادَق [tṣaːdaq] *p:* وافَق [waːfaq] مُوافَقَة [muwaːfaqa] *vn:* توافَق [twaːfaq] *p:* The president approved the housing project. الرَّئِيس صادَق عَلَى مَشرُوع الإسكان [ʔirraʔiːs ṣaːdaq ʕala mašruːʕ ʔilʔiskaːn] The National Assembly approved the new constitution. المَجلِس الوَطَنِي صادَق عَلَى الدُستُور الجِّدِيد [ʔilmaǰlis ʔilwaṭani ṣaːdaq ʕala ʔiddustuːr ʔiǰǰidiːd]

approvingly • **1.** بإستِحسان [bʔistiħsaːn] She nodded her head approvingly. هَزَّت راسها بإستِحسان [hazzat raːsha bʔistiħsaːn]

approximate • **1.** تَقرِيبِي [taqriːbi] The approximate speed of the new planes is six-hundred miles an hour. السُّرعَة التَّقرِيبِيَّة لِلطَّيّارات الجِّدِيدَة سِتّ مِيَّة مِيل بِالسّاعَة [ʔissurʕa ʔittaqriːbiyya liṭṭiyyaːraːt ʔiǰǰidiːda sitt miyyat miːl bissaːʕa]

approximately • **1.** حَوالِي [ħawaːli] تَقرِيباً [taqriːban] He left approximately a month ago. سافَر قَبُل شَهَر تَقرِيباً [saːfar gabul šahar taqriːban]

apricot • **1.** مِشمِشَة [mišmiša] مِشمِشات، مِشمِش [mišmišaːt, mišmiš] *pl:* مِشمِش [mišmiš] *Collective*

April • **1.** نِيسان [niːsaːn]

apron • **1.** صَدرِيَّة [ṣadriyya] صَدريّات، صَداري [ṣadriyyaːt, ṣadaːri] *pl:*

apt • **1.** مُناسِب [munaːsib] مَكانَة [makaːna] مَكانات [makaːnaːt] *pl:* That was a very apt remark. هَذِي كانَت مُلاحَظَة كُلِّش مُناسِبَة [haːði čaːnat mulaːħaða kulliš munaːsiba] • **2.** مُحتَمَل [muħtamal] I'm apt to be out when you call. مُحتَمَل أكُون بَرَّة لَمّا تخابُر [muħtamal ʔakuːn barra lamma txaːbur] • **3.** مِن المُتوَقَّع [min ʔilmutwaqqaʕ] When he's drunk, he's apt to do anything. لَمّا يكُون سَكران، مِن المِتوَقَّع يسَوِّي أيّ شِي [lamma ykuːn sakraːn, min ʔilmitwaqqaʕ ysawwi ʔayy ši] • **4.** جاز [ǰaːz] It's apt to be two o'clock before we get home. يجُوز تكُون السّاعَة ثِنتَين قَبُل ما نُوصَل البَيت [yǰuːz tkuːn ʔissaːʕa θintayn gabul maː nuːṣal ʔilbayt]

*** He is an apt pupil.** • **1.** يِلقُط بِلعَجِل [yilguṭ bilʕaǰil]

Aqaba • **1.** العَقَبَة [ʔilʕaqaba]

Arab • **1.** عَرَبِي [ʕarabi] عَرَب [ʕarab] Collective

arabesque • **1.** زُخرُف [zuxruf] زَخارِف [zaxaːrif] *pl:* He's very good at arabesque. هُوَّ كُلِّش زين بِالزُّخرُف [huwwa kulliš ziːn bizzuxruf] • **2.** زُخرُفِي [zuxrufi] There's a beautiful arabesque engraving on the wall. أكُو نَقِش زُخرُفِي جَمِيل عَالحايِط [ʔaku naqiš zuxrufi ǰamiːl ʕalħaːyiṭ]

Arab League • **1.** الجامِعَة العَرَبِيَّة [ʔiǰǰaːmiʕa ʔilʕarabiyya]

Arabian Peninsula • **1.** الجَزِيرَة العَرَبِيَّة [ʔiǰǰaziːra ʔilʕarabiyya]

Arabian Sea • **1.** البَحر العَرَبِي [ʔilbaħr ʔilʕarabi] • **1.** عَرَبِي [ʕarabi] اللُّغَة العَرَبِيَّة [ʔilluɣa ʔilʕarabiyya]

Arabic • **1.** عَرَبِي [ʕarabi] اللُّغَة العَرَبِيَّة ʔilluɣa ʔilʕarabiyya

Arabist • **1.** مُستَشرِق [mustašriq] مُستَشرِقِين [mustašriqiːn] *pl:*

Aramaic • **1.** اللُّغَة الآرامِيَّة [ʔilluɣa ʔilʔaːraːmiyya]

arch • **1.** طاق [ṭaːg] طُوق [ṭuːg] *pl:* That bridge has a tremendous arch. هَذاك الجِّسِر بِيه فَدّ طاق ضَخُم [haðaːk ʔiǰǰisir biːh fadd ṭaːg ḍaxum]

fallen arches • **1.** فلات فُوت [flaːt fuːt] أقدام مُسَطَّحَة [ʔaqdaːm musaṭṭaħa] He has fallen arches. عِندَه فلات فُوت [ʕindah flaːt fuːt]

to arch • **1.** حِنَى [ħinaː] اِحناء [ʔiħinaːʔ] *vn:* اِنحِنَى [ʔinħinaː] *p:* The cat arched its back. البَزُّونَة حِنَت ظَهَرها [ʔilbazzuːna ħinat ḍaharha]

arched • **1.** مطَوَّق [mṭawwag] The church's ceiling is arched. سَقُف الكَنِيسَة مطَوَّق [saguf ʔilkaniːsa mṭawwag]

architect • **1.** مُهَندِس مِعمارِي [muhandis miʕmaːri] مُهَندِسِين مِعمارِيِّين [muhandisiːn miʕmaːriyyiːn] *pl:*

architecture • **1.** هَندَسَة مِعمارِيَّة [handasa miʕmaːriyya]

A

area • **1.** مَنطِقَة [manṭiqa] مَناطِق [mana:ṭiq] *pl:* The area around Baghdad is densely populated. المَنطِقَة حَوالِي بَغداد كُلِّش مِزدَحمَة بِالسُّكّان [ʔilmanṭiqa ħawa:li baɣda:d kulliš mizdaħma bissukka:n] • **2.** مَساحَة [masa:ħa] مَساحات [masa:ħa:t] *pl:* The area of the city is four square miles. مَساحَة المَدِينَة أَربَع أَميال مُرَبَّعَة [masa:ħat ʔilmadi:na ʔarbaʕ ʔamya:l murabbaʕa]

Argentina • **1.** الأَرجَنتِين [ʔilʔarǰanti:n]

to argue • **1.** جادَل [ǰa:dal] جَدَل، مُجادَلَة [muǰa:dala, ǰadal] *vn:* تجادَل [tǰa:dal] *p:* ناقَش [na:qaš] مُناقَشَة، نِقاش [muna:qaša, niqa:š] *vn:* تناقَش [tna:qaš] *p:* حاجَج [ħa:ǰaǰ] مُحاجَجَة [muħa:ǰaǰa] *vn:* تحاجَج [tħa:ǰaǰ] *p:* Don't argue with me. لا تجادِلنِي [la: dǰa:dilni] I won't argue that point. ما أَجادِل عَلَى هَالنُّقطَة [ma: ʔaǰa:dil ʕala hannuqṭa] That's something that can't be argued. هَذا فَدّ شِي ما يِتجادَل بِيه [ha:ða fadd ši ma: yidǰa:dal bi:h]

to argue (with someone) • **1.** تجادَل [dǰa:dal] تَجادُل [taǰa:dul] *vn: sv* a. تحاجَج [tħa:ǰaǰ] تَحاجُج [taħa:ǰuǰ] *vn: sv* a. تناقَش [tna:qaš] تَناقُش [tana:quš] *vn: sv* a. He'll argue with anyone about anything. يِتجادَل وِيّا أَيّ شَخِص عَلَى أَيّ شِي كان [yidǰa:dal wiyya ʔayy šaxiṣ ʕala ʔayy ši ka:n] They argue all the time. يِتجادلُون عَلَى طُول [yidǰa:dlu:n ʕala ṭu:l]

argument • **1.** حِجَّة [ħiǰǰa] حِجّات، حِجَج [ħiǰǰa:t, ħiǰaǰ] *pl:* They presented very convincing arguments. قَدِّمَوا حِجَج كُلِّش مُقنِعَة [qaddimaw ħiǰaǰ kulliš muqniʕa] • **2.** خِلاف [xila:f] خِلافات [xila:fa:t] *pl:* نِزاع [niza:ʕ] It was just a small argument. كان فَدّ خِلاف بَسِيط [ča:n fadd xila:f basi:ṭ] • **3.** لَغوَة [laɣwa] لَغوات، لَغاوِي [laɣwa:t, laɣa:wi:] *pl:* لَغاوِي [laɣa:wi] لَغوات [laɣwa:t] *pl:* We had a violent argument. صارَت بَيناتنا لَغوَة [ṣa:rat bayna:tna laɣwa]

to arise • **1.** ظِهَر [ðihar] ظُهُور [ðuhu:r] *vn: sv* a. The problem arose some time ago. المُشكِلَة ظِهرَت قَبُل مُدَّة [ʔilmuškila ðihrat gabul mudda] • **2.** قِعَد [giʕad] قُعُود [guʕu:d] *vn:* اِنقِعَد [ʔingiʕad] *p:* I arose at six this morning. قِعَدِت الصُّبُح ساعَة سِتَّة [giʕadit ʔiṣṣubuħ sa:ʕa sitta] • **3.** قام [ga:m] قوم [gu:m] *vn: sv* u. He arose from his chair and left the room. قام مِن الكُرسِي مالَه وَتِرَك الغُرفَة [ga:m min ʔilkursi ma:lah wtirak ʔilɣurfa] • **4.** سِنَح [sinaħ] سِنُوح [sinu:ħ] *vn: sv* a. As soon as the opportunity arises. . . أَوَّل ما تِسنَح الفُرصَة [ʔawwal ma: tisnaħ ʔilfurṣa]

arithmetic • **1.** حساب [ħsa:b]

arm • **1.** ذراع [ðra:ʕ] ذراعات، ذِرعان، أَذرُع [ðra:ʕa:t, ðirʕa:n, ʔaðruʕ] *pl:* He broke his arm. كِسَر ذراعَه [kisar ðra:ʕah] • **2.** يَدَّة [yadda] يَدّات [yadda:t] *pl:* The arms on this chair are too low. يَدّات هَالسكَملِي كُلِّش ناصيَة [yadda:t halskamli kulliš na:ṣya] • **3.** سلاح [sla:ħ] أَسلِحَة [ʔasliħa] *pl:* All arms have to be turned over to the police. كُلّ الأَسلِحَة لازِم تِتسَلَّم لِلشُّرطَة [kull ʔilʔasliħa la:zim titsallam liššurṭa]

underarm • **1.** أُبُط [ʔubuṭ] أباط [ʔuba:ṭ] *pl:*

under arms • **1.** تَحت السِّلاح [taħt ʔissila:ħ] All ablebodied men were under arms. كُلّ الرِّجال المُقتَدرِين كانَوا تَحت السِّلاح [kull ʔirriǰa:l ʔilmuqtadri:n ča:naw taħt ʔissila:ħ]

to be up in arms • **1.** هاج [ha:ǰ] هَيَجان [hayaǰa:n] *vn: sv* i. Everybody was up in arms. كُلّ واحِد كان هايِج [kull wa:ħid ča:n ha:yiǰ]

to arm • **1.** سَلَّح [sallaħ] تَسلِيح [tasli:ħ] *vn:* تسَلَّح [tsallaħ] *p:* The company armed its guards. الشَّرِكَة سَلِّحَت حُرّاسها [ʔiššarika salliħat ħurra:sha]

to be armed • **1.** تسَلَّح [tsallaħ] تَسَلُّح [tasalluħ] *vn: sv* a. The policeman is always armed with a revolver. الشُّرطِي دائِماً يِتسَلَّح بِمُسَدَّس [ʔiššurṭi da:ʔiman yitsallaħ bmusaddas] The gang is armed. العِصابَة مِتسَلّحَة [ʔilʕiṣa:ba mitsallħa]

armchair • **1.** كُرسِي أَبُو اليَدّات [kursi ʔabu ʔilyadda:t] كَراسِي أُمَّهات اليَدّات [kara:si ʔummaha:t ʔilyadda:t] *pl:*

armistice • **1.** هُدنَة [hudna] هُدنات، هُدَن [hudna:t, hudan] *pl:*

armor • **1.** دِرِع [diriʕ] درُوع [dru:ʕ] *pl:* These shells can't penetrate the heavy armor of a battleship. هَالقَنابِل ما تِختِرِق دِرع البارِجَة الحَربِيَّة [halqana:bil ma: tixtiriq dirʕ ʔilba:riǰa ʔilħarbiyya] • **2.** مصَفَّحَة [mṣaffaħa] مصَفَّحات [mṣaffaħa:t] *pl:* Armor doesn't operate well in this mountainous terrain. المُصَفَّحات ما تِشتُغُل زِين بِهَالمَنطِقَة الجَّبَلِيَّة [ʔilmuṣaffaħa:t ma: tištuɣul zi:n bhalmanṭiqa ʔiǰǰabaliyya]

armored • **1.** مصَفَّح [mṣaffaħ] Those tanks are heavily armored. هَذِي الدَّبّابات مصَفّحَة كُلِّش [ha:ði ʔiddabba:ba:t mṣaffaħa kulliš]

army • **1.** جَيش [ǰayš, ǰi:š] جِيُوش [ǰiyu:š] *pl:* Did you serve in the army or the navy? خِدَمِت بِالجَيش لَو بِالبَحرِيَّة؟ [xidamit biǰǰayš law bilbaħriyya?]

around • **1.** قَرِيب [qari:b, gari:b] He lives right around here. يِسكُن قَرِيب مِن هنا [yiskun qari:b min hna] • **2.** حَوالِي [ħawa:li] I have around twenty dinars. عِندِي حَوالِي عِشرِين دِينار [ʕindi ħawa:li ʕišri:n dina:r] • **3.** دايِر [da:yir] He tied the rope around the barrel. لَفّ الحَبَل دايِر البَرمِيل [laff ʔilħabal da:yir ʔilbarmi:l] • **4.** ب [b] There are some good movies around town this week. أَكُو فَدّ أَفلام زينَة بِالولايَة هَالإِسبُوع [ʔaku fadd ʔafla:m zi:na bilwila:ya halʔisbu:ʕ]

*** Is there anybody around?** • **1.** أَكُو أَحَّد هنا؟ [ʔaku ʔaħħad hna?]

*** The racetrack is a half mile around.** • **1.** فَرَّت السّاحَة نُصّ مِيل [farrat ʔissa:ħa nuṣṣ mi:l]

to arouse • **1.** فَزَّز [fazzaz] تفزيز، تفزِّز [tafzi:z, tfizziz] *vn:* تفزَّز [tfazzaz] *p:* A barking dog aroused me in the middle of the night. فَدّ كَلِب يِنبَح فَزَّزني بِنُصّ اللَّيل [fadd čalib yinbaħ fazzazni bnuṣṣ ʔillayl] • **2.** أثار [ʔaθa:r] إثارَة [ʔiθa:ra] *vn:* اِنثار [ʔinθa:r] *p:* Her strange behavior aroused my suspicion. تَصَرُّفها الغَريب أثار شَكّي [taṣarrufha ʔilɣari:b ʔaθa:r šakki] • **3.** وَعَّى [waʕʕa:] توَعِّي، تَوعِيَة [twiʕʕi, tawʕiya] *vn:* توَعَّى [twaʕʕa:] *p:* What time shall I arouse you? السّاعَة بيش أوَعِّيك؟ [ʔissa:ʕa biyš ʔawaʕʕi:k?]

arrack • **1.** عُشبِي [ʕušbi]

to arrange • **1.** سَفَّط [saffaṭ] تَسفِيط [tasfi:ṭ] *vn:* تسَفَّط [tsaffaṭ] *p:* رَتَّب [rattab] تَرتِيب [tarti:b] *vn:* ترَتَّب [trattab] *p:* Who arranged the books? مِنُو سَفَّط الكُتُب؟ [minu saffaṭ ʔilkutub?] • **2.** رَتَّب [rattab] تَرتِيب [tarti:b] *vn:* ترَتَّب [trattab] *p:* They arranged the room in two hours. رَتِّبَوا الغُرفَة بِساعتَين [rattibaw ʔilɣurfa bsa:ʕtayn] • **3.** دَستَر [dastar] إدِّستِر [ʔiddistir] *vn:* تدَستَر [tdastar] *p:* دَبَّر [dabbar] تَدبِير [tadbi:r] *vn:* تدَبَّر [tdabbar] *p:* رَتَّب [rattab] تَرتِيب [tarti:b] *vn:* ترَتَّب [trattab] *p:* I arranged with the guard to smuggle cigarettes to the prisoners. دَستَرتها ويّا الحارِس حَتَّى يخَشِّش جِكايِر لِلمَساجِين [dastaritha wiyya ʔilħa:ris ħatta yxaššiš ǰiga:yir lilmasa:ǰi:n]

arrangement • **1.** تَرتِيب [tarti:b] تَدبِير [tadbi:r] تَدابِير [tada:bi:r] *pl:* How do you like this arrangement? يِعجبَك هَالتَّرتِيب؟ [yiʕiǰbak hattarti:b?]

arrest • **1.** إلقاء قَبُض [ʔilqa:ʔ qabuḏ] The arrest was made at his home. إلقاء القَبُض صار بِبَيتَه [ʔilqa:ʔ ʔilqabuḏ ṣa:r bibaytah]

under arrest • **1.** مَوقُوف [mawqu:f] مَوَقَّف [mwaqqaf] He's been under arrest for two days. كان موَقَّف يومَين [ča:n mwaqqaf yawmayn]

to hold under arrest • **1.** وَقَّف [waqqaf] تَوقِيف [tawqi:f] *vn:* توَقَّف [twaqqaf] *p:* They held him under arrest at the police station. وَقِّفُوه بمَركَز الشُّرطَة [waqqufu:h bmarkaz ʔiššurṭa]

to arrest • **1.** قُبَض عَلَى [qubaḏ ʕala] قَبُض [qabuḏ] *vn:* اِنقُبَض [ʔinqubaḏ] *p:* They arrested him and released him on bail. قُبضَوا عَلَيه وَفَكُّوه بكَفالَة [qubḏaw ʕali:h wfakku:h bkafa:la]

arrival • **1.** وُصُول [wuṣu:l] His arrival caused a lot of enthusiasm. وُصُولَه سَبَّب حَماس هوايَة [wuṣu:lah sabbab ħama:s hwa:ya]

to arrive • **1.** وُصَل [wuṣal] وُصُول [wuṣu:l] *vn: sv* a. When did the train arrive? شوَقِت وُصَل القِطار؟ [šwakit wuṣal ʔilqiṭa:r?] • **2.** توَصَّل [twaṣṣal] تَوَصُّل [tawaṣṣul] *vn: sv* a. Did they arrive at a decision? توَصَّلَوا لِفَدّ قَرار؟ [twaṣṣalaw lfadd qara:r?] • **3.** اِنولَد [ʔinwilad] *sv* i. The baby arrived at three this morning. الطِّفِل اِنولَد السّاعَة ثلاثَة الصُّبُح [ʔiṭṭifil ʔinwilad ʔissa:ʕa tla:θa ʔiṣṣubuħ]

arrow • **1.** سَهَم [saham] أسهُم [ʔashum] *pl:* The arrow points north. السَّهِم يأشِّر لِلشِّمال [ʔissahim yiʔaššir liššima:l] • **2.** نِشّابَة [nišša:ba] نِشّابات [nišša:ba:t] *pl:* نِشاب [niša:b] *Collective:* He killed the rabbit with an arrow. قِتَل الأرنَب بِنِشّابَة [kital ʔilʔarnab bnišša:ba]

arsenic • **1.** زَرنِيخ [zarni:x]

art • **1.** فَنّ [fann] He knows a lot about art. يُعرُف هوايَة عَن الفَنّ [yuʕruf hwa:ya ʕan ʔilfann] There's an art to it. يرِيدِلها فَدّ فَنّ [yri:dilha fadd fann]

work of art • **1.** قِطعَة فَنِّيَّة [qiṭʕa fanniyya] قِطَع فَنِّيَّة [qiṭaʕ fanniyya] *pl:* This building contains many works of art. هالبِنايَة تِحوِي قُطَع فَنِّيَّة هوايَة [halbina:ya tiħwi quṭaʕ fanniyya hwa:ya]

art gallery • **1.** مَتحَف فِنُون [matħaf finu:n] مَتاحِف فِنُون [mata:ħif finu:n] *pl:*

arthritis • **1.** اِلتِهاب المَفاصِل [ʔiltiha:b ʔilmafa:ṣil]

article • **1.** مَقال [maqa:l] مَقالَة [maqa:la] مَقالات [maqa:la:t] *pl:* There was a good article about it in the newspaper. كان أكُو مَقال زين عَنَّه بِالجَّرِيدَة [ča:n ʔaku maqa:l zi:n ʕannah bijǰari:da] • **2.** مادَّة [ma:dda] مَوادّ [mawa:dd] *pl:* Please read article three of the constitution. رَجاءاً إقرا المادَّة الثّالثَة مِن الدَّستُور [raǰa:ʔan ʔiqra: ʔilma:dda ʔiθθa:lθa min ʔiddastu:r] • **3.** شِي [ši] أشياء [ʔašya:ʔ] *pl:* مادَّة [ma:dda] مَوادّ [mawa:dd] *pl:* Many valuable articles were stolen. هوايَة أشياء ثَمِينَة اِنباقَت [hwa:ya ʔašya:ʔ θami:na ʔinba:gat]

definite article • **1.** أداة التَّعرِيف [ʔada:t ʔittaʕri:f]

artificial • **1.** اِصطِناعِي [ʔiṣṭina:ʕi] Are those flowers artificial? هَالوَرد اِصطِناعِي؟ [halwarid ʔiṣṭina:ʕi?] She has an artificial smile. عِدها اِبتِسامَة اِصطِناعِيَّة [ʕidha ʔibtisa:ma ṣṭina:ʕiyya]

artillery • **1.** مَدفَعِيَّة [madfaʕiyya]

artist • **1.** فَنّان [fanna:n] He is a famous artist. هُوَّ فَنّان مَشهُور [huwwa fanna:n mašhu:r]

as • **1.** عَلَى ما [ʕala ma:] Leave it as it is. خَلِّيهَا عَلَى ما هِيَّ [xalli:ha ʕala ma: hiyya] • **2.** مِثِل ما [miθil ma:] Do as you please. سَوِّي مِثِلما يِعجبَك [sawwi miθilma: yiʕiǰbak] Everything stands as it was. كُلّشِي باقِي مِثِلما كان [kullši ba:qi miθilma: ča:n] • **3.** عَلَى [ʕala] حَسَب [ħasab] He's late, as usual. هُوَّ مِتأخِّر، حَسَب العادَة [huwwa mitʔaxxir, ħasab ʔilʕa:da]

A

• **4.** ما دام [maː daːm] لأَن [liʔan] As he is leaving tomorrow, we must hurry. ما دام هُوَّ ماشِي باكِر، لازِم نِستَعجِل [maː daːm huwwa maːši baːčir, laːzim nistaʕǰil] • **5.** و [w] Did you see anyone as you came in? شِفِت أَحَّد وَإِنتَ داخِل [šifit ʔaħħad wʔinta daːxil] • **6.** كَ [ka--] مِثِل [miθil] I think of him as a brother. أَعتَبرَه كَأَخ [ʔaʕtabrah kaʔax] He used his coat as a pillow. اِستَعمَل سِترتَه كَمخَدَّة [ʔistaʕmal sitirtah kamxadda] • **7.** ب [b] His house is as big as ours. بَيتَه بكُبُر بَيتنا [baytah bkubur baytna]

*** I work as a clerk for them.** • **1.** أَشتُغُل كاتِب عِدهُم [ʔaštuɣul kaːtib ʕidhum]

*** I regard it as important.** • **1.** أَعتَبرَه مُهِمّ [ʔaʕtabrah muhimm]

as far as • **1.** حَدّ [ħadd] حُدُود [ħuduːd] *pl:* The train goes as far as Nasriyya. القِطار يرُوح لِحَدّ النّاصرِيَّة [ʔilqiṭaːr yiruːħ liħadd ʔinnaːṣriyya] • **2.** حَسَبما [ħasabmaː] عَلَى ما [ʕala maː] As far as I can see, he's right. حَسَب ما أَشُوف، هُوَّ صَحِيح [ħasab maː ʔašuːf, huwwa ṣaħiːħ] • **3.** عَلَى مَدّ [ʕala madd] The fields extend as far as you can see. المَزارِع تِمتَدّ عَلَى مَدّ البَصَر [ʔilmazaːriʕ timtadd ʕala madd ʔilbaṣar]

as far as he's concerned • **1.** بِالنِسبَة إِلَه [binnisba ʔilah] مِن ناحِيَتَه [min naːħiyatah] As far as he's concerned it's all right. بِالنِّسبَة إِلَه، زينَة [binnisba ʔilah, ziːna]

as for • **1.** أَمّا [ʔamma] مِن طَرَف [min ṭaraf] بِ النِسبَة لِ [binnisba li-] مِن ناحِيَة [min naːħya (t)] As for him, it's all right. أَمّا هُوَّ، ما عِندَه مانِع [ʔamma huwwa, maː ʕindah maːniʕ]

as if • **1.** عَبالَك [ʕabaːlak] كَأَن [kaʔan] He acts as if he were the director himself. دَيِتصَرَّف عَبالَك المُدِير نَفسَه [dayitṣarraf ʕabaːlak ʔilmudiːr nafsah]

as soon as • **1.** أَوَّل ما [ʔawwal maː] حالما [ħaːlmaː] Let me know as soon as you geet here. خَبُّرنِي أَوَّل ما تُوصَل هنا [xabburni ʔawwal maː tuːṣal hna]

as yet • **1.** لِحَدّ الآن [lħadd ʔalʔaːn] لِهَسَّة [lihassa] لِلآن [lilʔaːn] بَعَد [baʕad] Nothing has happened as yet. ما صار شِي لِحَدّ الآن [maː ṣaːr ši liħadd ʔalʔaːn]

asbestos • **1.** أَزبَست [ʔazbast] سبَستُوس [spastus]

ascetic • **1.** مِتزَهِّد [mitzahhid]

to be ashamed • **1.** خِجَل [xiǰal] خَجَل [xaǰal] *vn: sv* a. Don't be ashamed of this job. لا تِخجَل مِن هالشُغُل [laː tixǰal min haššuɣul] • **2.** اِختِزَى [ʔixtizaː] خِزي [xizi] *vn: sv* i. He's not ashamed of anything. ما يِختِزِي مِن أَيّ شِي [maː yixtizi min ʔayy ši] • **3.** اِستَحَى [ʔistaħaː] مِستَحاة [mistaħaː (t)] *vn: sv* i. He was ashamed to show his grades to his father. اِستَحَى يراوِي دَرَجاتَه لأَبُوه [ʔistaħaː yiraːwi daraǰaːtah lʔabuːh]

ash can • **1.** تَنَكَة زِبِل [tanakat zibil] تَنَكات زِبِل [tanakaːt zibil] *pl:*

ashes • **1.** رَماد رماد [ramaːd, rmaːd]

ashore • **1.** بَرّ [barr] ساحِل [saːħil] سَواحِل [sawaːħil] *pl:* We weren't allowed to go ashore. ما كان مَسمُوح إِلنا نِنزِل لِلبَرّ [maː čaːn masmuːħ ʔilna ninzil lilbarr]

ashtray • **1.** طَبلَة [ṭabla] طَبلات [ṭablaːt] *pl:* نُفّاضَة [nuffaːḍ̣a] نُفّاضات [nuffaːḍ̣aːt] *pl:*

Asia Minor • **1.** آسِيا الصُغرَى [ʔaːsyaː ʔiṣṣuɣra]

aside • **1.** عَلَى صَفحَة [ʕala ṣafħa] عَلَى جِهَة [ʕala ǰiha] I have to put a little money aside for the trip. لازِم أَخَلِّي شوَيَّة فلُوس عَلَى صَفحَة لِلسَّفرَة [laːzim ʔaxalli šwayya fluːs ʕala ṣafħa lissafra]

aside from • **1.** بغَضّ النَظَر عَن [bɣaḍ̣ḍ̣ ʔinnaḍ̣ar ʕan] Aside from the paint, it's a good car. بغَضّ النَّظَر عَن الصُّبُغ هِيَّ خُوش سَيّارَة [bɣaḍ̣ḍ̣ ʔinnaḍ̣ar ʕan ʔiṣṣubuɣ hiyya xuːš sayyaːra] • **2.** ما عَدا [maː ʕadaː] Aside from that, I have nothing else to add. ما عَدا هَذا، ما عِندِي شِي أَضِيفَه [maː ʕadaː haːða, maː ʕindi ši ʔaḍ̣iːfah]

to ask • **1.** سِأَل [siʔal] سُؤال [suːʔaːl] *vn:* اِنسِأَل [ʔinsiʔal] *p:* I'll ask him right away. راح أَسأَلَه حالاً [raːħ ʔasʔalah ħaːlan] Ask at the ticket office in the railroad station. إِسأَل بشِبّاك بَيع التَّذاكِر بمَحَطَّة القِطار [ʔisʔal bšibbaːč biːʕ ʔittaðaːkir bmaħaṭṭat ʔilqiṭaːr] • **2.** طِلَب [ṭilab] طَلَب [ṭalab] *vn:* اِنطِلَب [ʔinṭilab] *p:* He asked for help. طِلَب مُساعَدَة [ṭilab musaːʕada] • **3.** طِلَب [ṭilab] طَلَب [ṭalab] *vn:* اِنطِلَب [ʔinṭilab] *p:* راد [raːd] رَيد [riːd] *vn:* اِنراد [ʔinraːd] *p:* How much did he ask for washing the car? شقَدّ طِلَب عَلَى غَسِل السَّيّارَة؟ [šgadd ṭilab ʕala ɣasil ʔissayyaːra?]

asleep • **1.** نُوم [nawm, nuːm] I must have been asleep. لازِم كِنِت نايِم [laːzim činit naːyim] • **2.** خَدران [xadraːn] منَمِّل [mnammil] My leg's asleep. رِجلِي خَدرانَة [riǰli xadraːna]

to fall asleep • **1.** غُفَى [ɣufaː] غَفو [ɣafw] *vn: sv* i. I fell asleep about three o'clock. غُفَيت حَوالِي السّاعَة ثلاثَة [ɣufiːt ħawaːli ʔissaːʕa tlaːθa]

aspect • **1.** ناحِيَة [naːħiya] نَواحِي [nawaːħi] *pl:* We studied the problem from every aspect. دِرَسنا المُشكِلَة مِن كُلّ نَواحِيها [dirasna ʔilmuškila min kull nawaːħiːha] • **2.** مَظهَر [maḍ̣har] مَظاهِر [maḍ̣aːhir] *pl:* This is one of the aspects of Iraqi life. هَذا مَظهَر مِن مَظاهِر الحَياة العِراقِيَّة [haːða maḍ̣har min maḍ̣aːhir ʔilħayaːt ʔilʕiraːqiyya]

asphalt • **1.** قِير [giːr, ǰiːr] زِفِت [zifit] أَسفَلت [ʔasfalt]

A

aspirin • **1.** أسبرِينَة [ʔaspiriːna] أسبرِينات [ʔaspiriːnaːt] *pl:* أسبرِين [ʔaspiriːn] *Collective*

ass • **1.** زمال [zmaːl] زمايِل [zmaːyil] *pl:* حمار [ħmaːr] حَمِير، حمايِر [ħamiːr, ħmaːyir] *pl:*

to assassinate • **1.** اِغتال [ʔiɣtaːl] اِغتِيال [ʔiɣtiyaːl] *vn: sv* a. His former friends assassinated him. أصدِقائَه السّابقِين اِغتالوه [ʔaṣdiqaːʔah ʔissaːbqiːn ʔiɣtaːluːh]

assault • **1.** هُجُوم [hujuːm] The assault on the island began at five o'clock. الهُجُوم عالجَّزِيرَة بِدَت السّاعَة خَمسَة [ʔilhujuːm ʕajjaziːra bidat ʔissaːʕa xamsa] • **2.** تَعَدّي [taʕaddi] تَعَدِّيات [taʕaddiːyyaːt] *pl:* He was charged with assault. اِنتِهَم بِالتَّعَدّي [ʔintiham bittaʕaddi]

to assault • **1.** تعَدّى [tʕaddaː] تَعَدّي [taʕaddi] *vn: sv* a. That man assaulted me. تعَدّى عَلَيّا ذاك الرِّجّال [tʕaddaː ʕalayya ðaːk ʔirrijjaːl] • **2.** هِجَم عَلَى [hijam ʕala] هُجُوم [hujuːm] *vn:* اِنهِجَم [ʔinhijam] *p:* هاجَم [haːjam] مُهاجَمَة [muhaːjama] *vn: sv* i. They assaulted the enemy position with everything they had. هِجمَوا عَلَى مَوقِع العَدُو بِكُلّ ما عِدهُم [hijmaw ʕala mawqiʕ ʔilʕadu bkullma ʕidhum]

to assemble • **1.** تجَمَّع [djammaʕ] تَجَمُّع [tajammuʕ] *vn: sv* a. اِلتَمّ [ʔiltamm] اِلتِمام [ʔiltimaːm] *vn: sv* a. The pupils assembled in the auditorium. التَّلامِيذ تجَمّعَوا بالقاعَة [ʔittalaːmiːð djammʕaw bilqaːʕa] • **2.** اِجتِمَع [ʔijtimaʕ] اِجتِماع [ʔijtimaːʕ] *vn: sv* i. تجَمَّع [djammaʕ] تَجَمُّع [tajammuʕ] *vn: sv* a. The lawyers will assemble to discuss the case tomorrow morning. المُحامِين راح يِجتَمعُون لِبَحث القَضِيَّة باكِر الصُّبُح [ʔilmuħaːmiːn raːħ yijtamʕuːn libaħθ ʔilqaðiyya baːčir ʔiṣṣubuħ] • **3.** جِمَع [jimaʕ] جَمِع [jamiʕ] *vn:* اِنجِمَع [ʔinjimaʕ] *p:* You'll have to give me enough time to assemble the information. لازِم تِنطِينِي وَقِت كافِي حَتّى أجمَع المَعلُومات [laːzim tinṭiːni wakit kaːfi ħatta ʔajmaʕ ʔilmaʕluːmaːt] • **4.** رَكَّب [rakkab] تَركِيب [tarkiːb] *vn:* ترَكَّب [trakkab] *p:* He assembles airplane engines. يرَكُّب مَكايِن طَيّارات [yrakkub makaːyin ṭayyaːraːt]

assembly • **1.** جَماعَة [jamaːʕa] جَماعات [jamaːʕaːt] *pl:* حِشَد [ħišad] جَمهُور [jamhuːr] جَماهِير [jamaːhiːr] *pl:* He spoke before a large assembly of lawyers. خِطَب قِدّام جَماعَة كبِيرَة مِن المُحامِين [xiṭab giddaːm jamaːʕa čbiːra min ʔilmuħaːmiːn] • **2.** جَمعِيَّة [jamʕiyya] جَمعِيّات [jamʕiyyaːt] *pl:* The General Assembly of the United Nations rejected the proposal. الجَّمعِيَّة العامَّة لِلأُمَم المُتَّحِدَة رُفضَت الاقتِراح [ʔijjamʕiyya ʔilʕaːmma lilʔumam ʔilmuttaħida rufðat ʔilʔiqtiraːħ] • **3.** قِسِم [qisim] أقسام [ʔaqsaːm] *pl:* جُزُء [juzuʔ] أجزاء [ʔajzaːʔ] *pl:* We'll have to remove this entire assembly. لازِم نشِيل هَالقِسِم كُلَّه [laːzim nšiːl halqisim kullah] pl. ʔajzaaʔ.

assembly line • **1.** خَطّ تَركِيب [xaṭṭ tarkiːb] خَطّ تَجمِيع [xaṭṭ tajmiːʕ] I work on the assembly line in an automobile factory. أشتُغُل بِخَطّ التَّركِيب مال مَعمَل السَّيّارات [ʔaštuɣul bxaṭṭ ʔittarkiːb maːl maʕmal ʔissayyaːraːt]

to assign • **1.** عَيَّن [ʕayyan] تَعيِين [taʕyiːn] *vn:* تعَيَّن [tʕayyan] *p:* نِطَى [niṭaː] نَطِي [naṭi] *vn:* اِنِّطَى [ʔinniṭa] *p:* The teacher assigned us a composition. المُعَلِّم اِنطانا إنشاء [ʔilmuʕallim ʔinṭaːna ʔinšaːʔ] • **2.** خَصَّص [xaṣṣaṣ] تَخصِيص [taxṣiːṣ] *vn:* تخَصَّص [txaṣṣaṣ] *p:* عَيَّن [ʕayyan] تَعيِين [taʕyiːn] *vn:* تعَيَّن [tʕayyan] *p:* He assigned two men to guard the prisoner. خَصَّص رَجّالَين لِحِراسَة المَسجُون [xaṣṣaṣ rajjaːlayn liħiraːsat ʔilmasjuːn]

assignment • **1.** وَظِيفَة [waðiːfa] وَظايِف [waðaːyif] *pl:* واجِب [waːjib] Our teacher gave us a difficult assignment. مُعَلِّمنا اِنطانا واجِب صَعُب [muʕallimna ʔinṭaːna waːjib ṣaʕub] • **2.** شَغلَة [šaɣla] شَغلات [šaɣlaːt] *pl:* وَظِيفَة [waðiːfa] وَظايِف [waðaːyif] *pl:* مُهِمَّة [muhimma] مُهِمّات، مَهام [muhimmaːt, mahaːm] *pl:* The boss gave me an interesting assignment. المُدِير اِنطانِي فَدّ شَغلَة لَطِيفَة [ʔilmudiːr ʔinṭaːni fadd šaɣla laṭiːfa] • **3.** تَوزِيع [tawziːʕ] تَعيِين [taʕyiːn] تَقسِيم [taqsiːm] تَقسِيمات، تَقاسِيم [taqsiːmaːt, taqaːsiːm] *pl:* The assignment of jobs only took ten minutes. تَوزِيع الأشغال أخَذ عَشِر دَقايِق [tawziːʕ ʔilʔašɣaːl ʔaxað ʕašir daqaːʔiq]

to assist • **1.** ساعَد [saːʕad] مُساعَدَة [musaːʕada] *vn: sv* i. عاوَن [ʕaːwan] مُعاوَنَة [muʕaːwana] *vn: sv* i. Who assisted you? مِنُو عاوَنَك؟ [minu ʕaːwanak?]

assistance • **1.** مُساعَدَة [musaːʕada] مُساعَدات [musaːʕadaːt] *pl:* مُعاوَنَة [muʕaːwana] He did it without any assistance. سَوّاها بلا أي مُساعَدَة [sawwaːha bilaʔayya musaːʕada]

assistant • **1.** مُساعِد [musaːʕid] مُساعِدِين [musaːʕidiːn] *pl:* مُعاوِن [muʕaːwin]

associate • **1.** زَمِيل [zamiːl] زُمَلاء [zumalaːʔ] *pl:* رَفِيق [rafiːq] رُفَقاء [rufaqaːʔ] *pl:* He's been my associate for many years. صارلَه زَمِيلي سنِين هوايَة [ṣaːrlah zamiːli sniːn hwaːya]

associate judge • **1.** نائِب حاكِم [naːʔib ħaːkim] نُوّاب حُكّام [nuwwaːb ħukkaːm] *pl:*
associate member • **1.** عَضُو مُسانِد [ʕaðu musaːnid] أعضاء مُسانِدِين [ʔaʕðaːʔ musaːnidiːn] *pl:*
associate professor • **1.** أستاذ مُساعِد [ʔustaːð musaːʕid] أساتِذَة مُساعِدِين [ʔasaːtiða musaːʕidiːn] *pl:*
to associate • **1.** خالَط ويّا، اِختِلَط ويّا، عاشَر، تعاشَر [xaːlaṭ wiyya, ʔixtilaṭ wiyya, ʕaːš ar, tʕaːš ar] مُخالَطَة عُشرَة، مُعاشَرَة، تَعاشُر [muxaːlaṭa, ʕušra, muʕaːšra, taʕaːš ur] *vn: sv* i. اِختِلَط [ʔixtilaṭ] اِختِلاط [ʔixtilaːṭ] *vn: sv* i. عاشَر [ʕaːšar] عِشرَة،

A

مُعاشَرَة [ʕišra, muʕa:šara] *vn: sv* i. تعاشَر [tʕa:šar] تَعاشُر [taʕa:šur] *vn: sv* a. He doesn't like to associate with them. ما يعجبَه يخالِطهُم [ma: yʕijbah yxa:liṭhum] • **2.** رُبَط [rubaṭ] رَبُط [rabuṭ] *vn: sv* u. I always associate big cars with rich people. آني دائِماً أربُط عِلاقَة بين السَّيّارات الكِبِيرَة وَالزَّناكِين [ʔa:ni da:ʔiman ʔarbuṭ ʕila:qa bi:n ʔissayya:ra:t ʔiččibi:ra wizzana:gi:n]

*** He was associated with them for ten years.** • **1.** كانَت إلَه عَلاقَة ويّاهُم مِن عَشر سنين [ča:nat ʔilah ʕala:qa wiyya:hum min ʕašr sni:n]

association • **1.** جَمعِيَّة [jamʕiyya] جَمعِيّات [jamʕiyya:t] *pl:* I don't think I'll join the association. ما أعتِقِد راح أشتِرِك بِالجَمعِيَّة [ma: ʔaʕtiqid ra:ħ ʔaštirik bijjamʕiyya] • **2.** عِلاقَة [ʕila:qa] عِلاقات [ʕila:qa:t] *pl:* I wouldn't ever make that particular association. آني أبَد ما أسَوّي ذِيك العَلاقَة الخاصَّة [ʔa:ni ʔabad ma: ʔasawwi ði:č ʔilʕala:qa ʔilxa:ṣṣa]

assorted • **1.** مشَكَّل [mšakkal] منَوَّع [mnawwaʕ] I want one kilo of assorted chocolates. أرِيد كِيلُو جكلَيت مشَكَّل [ʔari:d ki:lu čkli:t mšakkal]

assortment • **1.** تَشكِيلَة [taški:la] تَشكِيلات [taški:la:t] *pl:* They've got a large assortment of ties. عِدهُم تَشكِيلَة كبِيرَة مِن الأربطَة [ʕidhum taški:la čbi:ra min ʔilʔarbiṭa]

to assume • **1.** توَقَّع [twaqqaʕ] تَوَقُّع [tawaqquʕ] *vn: sv* a. قَدَّر [qaddar] تَقدِير [taqdi:r] *vn: sv* i. I assume that he'll be there too. أتوَقَّع راح يكُون هناك أيضاً [ʔatwaqqaʕ ra:ħ yku:n hna:k ʔayðan] I assume the price will be less than twenty dinars. أقَدِّر السِّعِر يكُون أقَلّ مِن عِشرِين دِينار [ʔaqaddir ʔissiʕir yku:n ʔaqall min ʕišri:n dina:r] • **2.** تحَمَّل [tħammal] تَحَمُّل [taħammul] *vn: sv* a. I can't assume any responsibility for what happened. ما أقدَر أتحَمَّل أيّ مَسؤُولِيَّة عَن اللّي صار [ma: ʔagdar ʔatħammal ʔayy masʔu:liyya ʕan ʔilli ṣa:r] • **3.** اِستِعباد [ʔistiʕba:d] تَظاهُر [taða:hur] *vn: sv* a. Don't assume such an air of innocence! لا تِتظاهَر بِسَلامَة النِّيَّة [la: titða:har bsala:mat ʔinniyya] • **4.** فُرَض [furað] فَرِض [farið] *vn:* اِنفُرَض [ʔinfurað] *p:* For example, let's assume birds can't fly. مَثَلاً، خَلّي نُفرُض الطِّيُور ما تِقدَر تطِير [maθalan, xalli nufruð ʔiṭṭiyu:r ma: tigdar ʔiṭṭi:r]

assurance • **1.** تَعَهُّد [taʕahhud] تَأكِيد [taʔki:d] تأكِيدات [taʔki:da:t] *pl:* He gave me his assurance that he'd pay. اِنطانِي تَعَهُّد راح يِدفَع [ʔinṭa:ni taʕahhud ra:ħ yidfaʕ] pl. -aat.

to assure • **1.** أكَّد [ʔakkad] تَأكِيد [taʔki:d] *vn:* تأكَّد [tʔakkad] *p:* تعَهَّد [tʕahhad] تَعَهُّد [taʕahhud] *vn: sv* a. He assured us that he would be there. أكَّد إلنا راح يكُون هناك [ʔakkad ʔilna ra:ħ yku:n hna:k]

asthma • **1.** تَنَق نِفَس [tanag nifas] ضِيق نِفَس [ði:g nifas] رَبُو [rabw]

at • **1.** ب [b] I'll wait for you at the entrance. راح أنتَظرَك بالباب [ra:ħ ʔantaðrak bilba:b] I did it at his request. سَوَّيتها بِرَغبتَه [sawwi:tha braɣubtah] I did it at his request. سَوَّيتها حَسَب رَغبتَه [sawwi:tha ħasab raɣubtah] The children are at school. الأطفال بِالمَدرَسَة [ʔilʔaṭfa:l bilmadrasa] It happened at night. صارَت باللّيل [ṣa:rat billayl] He came at three o'clock. إجا بِالثّلاثَة [ʔija bittila:θa] He came at three o'clock. جا السّاعَة بِالثّلاثَة [ja: ʔissa:ʕa bittila:θa] He came at three o'clock. جا السّاعَة ثلاثَة [ja: ʔissa:ʕa tla:θa] • **2.** عِند [ʕind] عِد [ʕid] We were at the tailor's. كِنّا عِند الخَيّاط [činna ʕind ʔilxayya:ṭ] I met him at the dentist's. قابَلتَه عِد طَبِيب الأسنان [qa:baltah ʕid ṭabi:b ʔilʔasna:n] • **3.** مِن [min] I was astonished at the size of the city. اِندِهَشِت مِن كُبر الوِلايَة [ʔindihašit min kubr ʔilwila:ya] • **4.** إلَى [ʔila] We haven't arrived at a decision yet. ما توَصَّلنا إلَى فَدّ قَرار لِحَدّ الآن [ma: twaṣṣalna ʔila fadd qara:r liħadd ʔilʔaan] • **5.** عَلَى [ʕala] He aimed at the target. نَيشَن عالهَدَف [nayšan ʕalhadaf] • **6.** عَلَى [ʕala] مِن [min] Don't get angry at me. لا تِزعَل عَلَيّا [la: tizʕal ʕalayya] Don't get angry at me. لا تِزعَل مِنّي [la: tizʕal minni]

at all • **1.** أبَد [ʔabad] أبَداً [ʔabadan] أصلاً [ʔaṣlan] بِ المَرَّة [bilmarra] I haven't got any money at all. ما عِندِي فلُوس أبَداً [ma: ʕindi flu:s ʔabadan] I haven't got any money at all. أبَد ما عِندِي أيّ فلُوس [ʔabad ma: ʕindi ʔayy flu:s]

at all costs • **1.** بأيّ ثَمَن [bʔayy θaman] We must get it at all costs. لازِم ناخذَه بأيّ ثَمَن [la:zim na:xðah bʔayy θaman]

at first • **1.** بِالبِدايَة [bilbida:ya] أوَّل [ʔawwal] أوائِل [ʔawa:ʔil] *pl:* أولَى [ʔuwla] *Feminine:* أوَّلاً [ʔawwalan] At first we didn't like the town. بِالبِدايَة ما حَبَّينا الوِلايَة [bilbida:ya ma: ħabbayna ʔilwila:ya]

at last • **1.** أخِيراً [ʔaxi:ran] بِالتّالِي [bitta:li:] تالِيها [ta:li:ha] He came at last. أخِيراً جا [ʔaxi:ran ja:]

at least • **1.** أقَلّ [ʔaqall] There were at least a hundred people present. كانوا عَالأقَلّ مِيَّة واحِد حاضرِين [ča:naw ʕalʔaqall miyyat wa:ħid ħa:ðri:n] • **2.** أقَلّاً [ʔaqallan] At least, mention my name to him. أقَلّاً، إذكُرلَه إسمِي [ʔaqallan, ʔiðkurlah ʔismi]

at most • **1.** أكثَر شِي [ʔakθar ši] At most the bill will come to twenty dinars. أكثَر شِي راح توَصِّل القائِمَة لعِشرين دِينار [ʔakθar ši ra:ħ twaṣṣil ʔilqa:ʔima lʕišri:n dina:r]

at once • **1.** حالاً [ħa:lan] هَسَّة [hassa] Do it at once. سَوِّيها حالاً [sawwi:ha ħa:lan] • **2.** بفَدّ وَقِت [bfadd wakit] بفَدّ مَرَّة [bfadd marra] I can't do everything at once. ما أقدَر أسَوّي كُلّشِي بفَدّ مَرَّة [ma: ʔagdar ʔasawwi kullši bfadd marra]

at that • **1.** شِكِل [šikil] أشكال، شكُول [ʔaška:l, šku:l] *pl:* عِند هَالحَدّ [ʕind halħadd] عَلَى ما هُوّ [ʕala ma: huwwa] Let's leave it at that. خَلّي نِترُكها بِهَالشِّكِل [xalli: niturkha bhaššikil]

at times • **1.** دَورَة [dawra] دورات [dawra:t] *pl:* أَحياناً [ʔaħya:nan] نوبَة [nu:ba] نوبات [nu:ba:t] *pl:* مَرَّة [marra] مَرّات [marra:t] *pl:* At times I'm doubtful. دَورات أَشُكّ [du:ra:t ʔašukk]

at will • **1.** مِثِلما يريد [miθilma: yri:d] حَسَبما يريد [ħasabma: yri:d] كَيف [kayf] They come and go at will. يِرحُون ويِجُون مِثِلما يِردُون [yirħu:n wyiǰu:n miθilma: yirdu:n] They come and go at will. يِسرَحُون وَيِمرَحُون [yisraħu:n wyimraħu:n]

atheism • **1.** إلحاد [ʔilħa:d]

atheist • **1.** مُلحِد [mulħid] مُلحِدِين [mulħidi:n] *pl:*

athlete • **1.** رِياضِي [riya:ð̣i] رِياضِيِّين [riya:ð̣iyyi:n] *pl:*

athletic • **1.** رِياضِي [riya:ð̣i]

athletics • **1.** رِياضَة [riya:ð̣a]

Atlantic • **1.** المُحِيط الأَطلَسِي [ʔilmuħi:ṭ ʔilʔaṭlasi] أَطلَنطِيكِي [ʔaṭlanṭi:ki] أَطلَنطِي [ʔaṭlanṭi]

atlas • **1.** أَطلَس [ʔaṭlas] أَطالِس [ʔaṭa:lis] *pl:* We're going to take the atlas with us on the trip. راح ناخُذ الأَطلَس ويّانا بِالسَّفرَة [ra:ħ na:xuð ʔilʔaṭlas wiyya:na bissafra]

atmosphere • **1.** جَوّ [ǰaww] أَجواء [ʔaǰwa:ʔ] *pl:* The atmosphere contains oxygen. الجَّوّ يِحتوِي عَلَى أُوكسِيجِين [ʔiǰǰaww yiħtiwi ʕala ʔu:ksiǰi:n] We work in a very nice atmosphere. نِشتُغُل بجَوّ كُلِّش زين [ništuɣul bǰaww kulliš zi:n]

atmospheric • **1.** جَوِّي [ǰawwi]

atom • **1.** ذَرَّة [ðarra] ذَرّات [ðarra:t] *pl:* We live in the age of the atom. نعِيش بِعَصر الذَّرَّة [nʕi:š bʕaṣr ʔiððarra]

atomic • **1.** ذَرِّي [ðarri]

atrocity • **1.** جَرِيمَة [ǰari:ma] جَرايِم [ǰara:yim] *pl:* The enemy committed many atrocitics during the war. العَدُو اِرتِكَب جَرائِم هوايَة أَثناء الحَرُب [ʔilʕadu ʔirtikab ǰara:ʔim hwa:ya ʔaθna:ʔ ʔilħarub]

to attach • **1.** شَكَّل [šakkal] تَشكِيل [taški:l] *vn:* تشَكَّل [tšakkal] *p:* Please attach the envelope to the letter with a pin. رَجاءاً شَكِّل الظَّرُف بِالمَكتُوب بِدَمبُوس [raǰa:ʔan šakkil ʔiððaruf bilmaktu:b bdambu:s] • **2.** رُفَق [rufaq] إرفاق [ʔirfa:q] *vn:* اِنرُفَق [ʔinrufaq] *p:* Don't forget to attach a picture with your application. لا تِنسَى تِرفِق صُورَة بِعَرِيضتَك [la: tinsa: tirfiq ṣu:ra bʕari:ð̣tak] • **3.** حَجَز [ħiǰaz] حَجِز [ħaǰiz] *vn:* اِنحِجَز [ʔinħiǰaz] *p:* We can attach his salary if he doesn't pay up. نِقدَر نِحجِز راتبَه إذا ما يِدفَع [nigdar niħǰiz ra:tbah ʔiða ma: yidfaʕ] • **4.** عَلَّق [ʕallaq] تَعلِيق [taʕli:q] *vn:* تعَلَّق [tʕallaq] *p:* You attach too much importance to money. تعَلِّق أَهَمِّيَّة هوايَة عَالفلُوس [tʕalliq ʔahammiyya hwa:ya ʕalflu:s]

to be attached to • **1.** تعَلَّق ب [tʕallaq b] تَعَلُّق [taʕalluq] *vn: sv* a. I've become attached to this child. آنِي تعَلَّقِت بِهالطِّفِل [ʔa:ni tʕallaqit bhaṭṭifil] I've become attached to this child. صِرِت مِتعَلِّق بِهالطِّفِل [ṣirit mitʕalliq bhaṭṭifil]

attache • **1.** مُلحَق [mulħaq] مَلاحِق [malaħiq] *pl:*

attached • **1.** مِلتِحِق [miltiħiq] He's attached to the embassy. هُوَّ مِلتِحِق بِالسَّفارَة [huwwa miltiħiq bissafa:ra]

attachments • **1.** مُلحَق [mulħaq] مَلاحِق [malaħiq] *pl:* I bought a vacuum cleaner with all its attachments. اِشتِرَيت مُكناسَة كَهرَبائِيَّة ويّا كُلّ مُلحَقاتها [ʔištiri:t mukna:sa kahraba:ʔiyya wiyya kull mulħaqa:tha] • **2.** مُرفَق [murfaq] There are five attachments to the letter. أَكُو خَمِس مُرَفَّقات ويّا المَكتُوب [ʔaku xamis muraffaqa:t wiyya ʔilmaktu:b]

attack • **1.** هَجمَة [haǰma] هَجمات [haǰma:t] *pl:* هُجُوم [huǰu:m] *Collective:* The attack was beaten back. الهَجمَة اِنرَدَّت [ʔilhaǰma ʔinraddat]

to attack • **1.** هِجَم [hiǰam] هَجُوم [haǰu:m] *vn:* اِنهِجَم [ʔinhiǰam] *p:* They attacked the castle in the middle of the night. هِجمَوا عالقَلعَة بِنُصّ اللَّيل [hiǰmaw ʕalqalʕa bnuṣṣ ʔillay] • **2.** هاجَم [ha:ǰam] مُهاجَمَة [muha:ǰama] *vn:* تهاجَم [tha:ǰam] *p:* He attacked them in the newspaper. هاجمُوهُم بِالجَّرِيدَة [ha:ǰmu:hum biǰǰari:da] • **3.** تناوَل [tna:wal] تَناوُل [tana:wul] *vn: sv* i. Let's attack this problem from a slightly different angle. خَلِّي نِتناوِل هَالمُشكِلَة مِن جِهَة تِختِلِف شوَيَّة [xalli nitna:wil halmuškila min ǰiha tixtilif šwayya]

heart attack • **1.** سَكتَة قَلبِيَّة [sakta qalbiyya] سَكتات قَلبِيَّة [sakta:t qalbiyya] *pl:* He died from a heart attack. مات بِالسَّكتَة القَلبِيَّة [ma:t bissakta ʔilqalbiyya]

attempt • **1.** مُحاوَلَة [muħa:wala] مُحاوَلات [muħa:wala:t] *pl:* At least make an attempt! عَالأَقَلّ سَوِّي فَدّ مُحاوَلَة [ʕalʔaqall sawwi fadd muħa:wala]

to attempt • **1.** حاوَل [ħa:wal] مُحاوَلَة [muħa:wala] *vn:* تحاوَل [tħa:wal] *p:* Don't attempt to do too much at one time. لا تحاوِل تسَوِّي أَشياء هوايَة بِفَدّ وَقِت [la: tħa:wil tsawwi ʔašya:ʔ hwa:ya bfadd wakit]

to attend • **1.** حِضَر [ħið̣ar] حُضُور [ħuð̣u:r] *vn:* اِنحِضَر [ʔinħið̣ar] *p:* Did you attend the meeting? حِضَرت الاِجتِماع؟ [ħið̣art ʔilʔiǰtima:ʕ?] • **2.** داوَم [da:wam] مُداوَمَة [muda:wama] *vn:* تداوَم [tda:wam] *p:* I attended business school. داوَمِت بِمَدرَسَة تِجارَة [da:wamit bmadrasat tiǰa:ra] • **3.** راجَع [ra:ǰaʕ] مُراجَعَة [mura:ǰaʕa] *vn:* تراجَع [tra:ǰaʕ] *p:* عالَج [ʕa:laǰ] What doctor attended you? يا طَبِيب راجَعَك؟ [ya: ṭabi:b ra:ǰaʕak?]

to attend to • **1.** باشَر [ba:šar] مُباشَرَة [muba:šara] *vn: sv* i. عالَج [ʕa:laǰ] عِلاج، مُعالَجَة [ʕila:ǰ, muʕa:laǰap] *vn:* تعالَج [tʕa:laǰ] *p:* I still have some things to attend to. بَعَد عِندي بَعَض الأشياء لازِم أباشِرها [baʕad ʕindi baʕaḍ ʔilʔašya:ʔ la:zim ʔaba:širha]

attendance • **1.** حُضُور [ħuḍu:r] Attendance is compulsory. الحُضُور إجبارِي [ʔilħuḍu:r ʔiǰba:ri]

attention • **1.** إنتِباه [ʔintiba:h] I tried to attract his attention. حاوَلت أجلِب إنتِباهَه [ħa:walit ʔaǰlib ʔintiba:hah]

to call attention • **1.** لِفَت [lifat] لَفِت [lafit] *vn:* اِنلِفَت [ʔinlifat] *p:* I've called attention to that repeatedly. لِفَتِت النَّظَر لِلذّاك عِدَّة مَرّات [lifatit ʔinnaḍar liððaːk ʕiddat marra:t]

to pay attention • **1.** اِنتِبَه [ʔintibah] اِنتِباه [ʔintiba:h] *vn: sv* i. دار بَال [da:rba:l] دَورَة [dawra] *vn: sv* i. Please pay attention! اِنتِبِه مِن فَضلَك [ʔintibih min faḍlak]

attentively • **1.** اِنتِباه [ʔintiba:h] The children listened attentively. الجَّهال تصَنَّتَوا بانتِباه [ʔiǰǰaha:l tṣanntaw bʔintiba:h]

attitude • **1.** وَضِع [waḍiʕ] أوضَاع [ʔawḍa:ʕ] *pl:* I don't like his attitude in class. ما يعجِبنِي وَضعَه بِالصَّفّ [ma: yiʕǰibni waḍʕah bişşaff] • **2.** مَوقِف [mawqif] مَواقِف [mawa:qif] *pl:* I don't understand your attitude towards religion. ما دَأفتِهِم مَوقِفَك مِن الدِّين [ma: daʔaftihim mawqifak min ʔiddi:n]

attorney • **1.** مُحامِي [muħa:mi] مُحامِين [muħa:mi:n] *pl:* Who's your attorney? مِنُو مُحامِيك؟ [minu muħa:mi:k?]

to attract • **1.** جاب [ǰa:b] جَيب [ǰayb] *vn:* إنجاب [ʔinǰa:b] *p:* What's attracting the flies here? شدَيجِيب الذِّبّان هنا؟ [šdayǰi:b ʔiððabba:n hna?] • **2.** جِذَب [ǰiðab] جَذِب [ǰaðib] *vn:* اِنجِذَب [ʔinǰiðab] *p:* Magnets attract nails. المَغانِط تِجذِب البسامِير [ʔilmaɣa:niṭ tiǰðib ʔilbsa:mi:r] • **3.** جِلَب [ǰilab] جَلِب [ǰalib] *vn:* اِنجِلَب [ʔinǰilab] *p:* Be quiet! You're attracting attention. إسكُت، دَتِجلِب النَّظَر [ʔiskut, datiǰlib ʔinnaḍar]

attraction • **1.** جاذِبِيَّة [ǰa:ðibiyya] The attraction of the moon causes the tides. جاذِبِيَّة القُمَر تسَبِّب المَدّ وَالجَزر [ǰa:ðibiyyat ʔilgumar tsabbib ʔilmadd wilǰazir] • **2.** مُغرِي [muɣri] What's the big attraction around this town? شِنُو المُغرِي بِهَالوِلايَة؟ [šinu ʔilmuɣri bhalwla:ya?]

attractive • **1.** جَذّاب [ǰaðða:b] She is very attractive. هِيَّ كُلِّش جَذّابَة [hiyya kulliš ǰaðða:ba] • **2.** مُغرِي [muɣri] He made me a very attractive offer. عِرَض عَلَيّا فَدّ عَرِض كُلِّش مُغرِي [ʕirað ʕalayya fadd ʕarið kulliš muɣri]

auction • **1.** مَزاد [maza:d] مَزادات [maza:da:t] *pl:*

audience • **1.** الحاضرِين [ʔilħa:ðri:n] The audience was enthusiastic. الحاضرِين كانَوا مِتحَمّسِين [ʔilħa:ðri:n ča:naw mitħammsi:n]

August • **1.** آب [ʔa:b]

aunt • **1.** عَمَّة [ʕamma] عَمّات [ʕamma:t] *pl:*

Austria • **1.** نَمسا [namsa]

Austrian • **1.** نَمساوِي [namsa:wi] نَمساوِيِّين [namsa:wi:yyi:n] *pl:*

authentic • **1.** حَقِيقِي [ħaqi:qi] He wrote an authentic account of the war. كِتَب وَصُف حَقِيقِي لِلحَرُب [kitab waṣuf ħaqi:qi lilħarub] • **2.** أصلِي [ʔaṣli] حَقِيقِي [ħaqi:qi] This is an authentic Babylonian vase. هَذِي مَزهَرِيَّة بابِلِيَّة أصلِيَّة [ha:ði mazhariyya ba:biliyya ʔaṣliyya]

author • **1.** مُؤَلِّف [muʔallif] مُؤَلِّفِين [muʔallifi:n] *pl:* He always wanted to be an author. دائِماً كان يرِيد يصِير مُؤَلِّف [da:ʔiman ča:n yri:d yṣi:r muʔallif] • **2.** صاحِب [ṣa:ħib] أصحاب [ʔaṣħa:b] *pl:* The prime minister is the author of the plan. رَئِيس الوُزَراء صاحِب هَالخُطَّة [raʔi:s ʔilwuzara:ʔ ṣa:ħib halxuṭṭa]

authorities • **1.** سُلطَة [sulṭa] سُلطات [sulṭa:t] *pl:* مَرجِع [marǰiʕ] مَراجِع [mara:ǰiʕ] *pl:* The local authorities condemned the building. السُّلطات المَحَلِّيَّة أمرَت بِهَدم البِنايَة [ʔissulṭa:t ʔilmaħaliyya ʔumrat bihadm ʔilbina:ya]

authority • **1.** صَلاحِيَّة [ṣala:ħiyya] تَخوِيل [taxwi:l] He has no authority to sign the check. ما عِندَه صَلاحِيَّة يوَقِّع الصَّكّ [ma: ʕindah ṣala:ħiyya ywaqqiʕ ʔiṣṣakk] Do you have the authority to sign this contract for him? عِندَك تَخوِيل توَقِّع عَنَّه هَالعَقِد؟ [ʕindak taxwi:l twaqqiʕ ʕannah halʕaqid?] • **2.** سُلطَة [sulṭa] سُلطات [sulṭa:t] *pl:* The police have no authority over diplomats. الشُّرطَة ما عِدها سُلطَة عَالدِّبلُماسِيِّين [ʔiššurṭa ma: ʕidha sulṭa ʕaddibluma:siyyi:n] • **3.** حُجَّة [ħuǰǰa] حُجَج [ħuǰaǰ] *pl:* He's an authority on the Koran. هُوَّ حُجَّة بالقُرآن [huwwa ħuǰǰa bilqurʔa:n]

to authorize • **1.** خَوَّل [xawwal] تَخوِيل [taxwi:l] *vn:* تخَوَّل [txawwal] *p:* Who authorized you to spend that money? مِنُو خَوَّلَك تُصرُف هَالفلُوس؟ [minu xawwalak tuṣruf halfilu:s?]

A

authorized • **1.** مُخَوَّل [muxawwal] He's authorized to sign the receipts. هُوَّ مخَوَّل يوَقِّع الوُصُولات [huwwa mxawwal ywaqqiʕ ʔilwuṣu:la:t]

automatic • **1.** مُسَدَّس [musaddas] مُسَدَّسات [musaddasa:t] *pl:* وَرْوَر [warwar] وَراوِر [wara:wir] *pl:* Officers carry automatics. الضُّبّاط شايلِين مُسَدَّسات [ʔiððubba:ṭ ša:yli:n musaddasa:t] • **2.** أوتوماتِيكي [ʔutumati:ki] Is this an automatic pump? هَالمَضَخَّة أوتوماتِيكِيَّة؟ [halmaðaxxa ʔu:tu:ma:ti:kiyya?]

automatically • **1.** بصُورَة تِلقائِيَّة [bṣu:ra tilqa:ʔiyya] بصُورَة أوتوماتِيكِيَّة [bṣu:ra ʔutumati:kiyya] بلَيّا شُعُور [blayya: šuʕu:r] He picked up the phone automatically. شال التِّلِفُون بِصُورَة تِلقائِيَّة [ša:l ʔittilifu:n bṣu:ra tilqa:ʔiyya]

automobile • **1.** سَيّارَة [sayya:ra] سَيّارات [sayya:ra:t] *pl:*

autopsy • **1.** تَشرِيح [tašri:ħ]

autumn • **1.** خَرِيف [xari:f] I hope to stay through the autumn. أتأمَّل أبقى لِنِهايَة الخَرِيف [ʔatʔammal ʔabqa: linniha:yat ʔilxari:f]

available • **1.** مَوجُود [mawǰu:d] They used all available cars. اِستَعمِلَوا كُلّ السَّيارات المَوجُودَة [ʔistaʕmilaw kull ʔissaya:ra:t ʔilmawǰu:da] Is this pen available in red? هَالقَلَم الباندان مَوجُود عَلَى أحمَر؟ [halqalam ʔilpa:nda:n mawǰu:d ʕala ʔaħmar?] • **2.** جَوَّة الإيد [ǰawwa ʔilʔi:d] I have two houses available. عِندِي بَيتَين جَوَّة الإيد [ʕindi baytayn ǰawwa ʔilʔi:d] • **3.** فارِغ [fa:riɣ] When will the director be available? شوَقِت المُدِير يكُون فارِغ؟ [šwakit ʔilmudi:r yku:n fa:rig?] • **4.** مَيسُور [maysu:r] مِتيَسِّر [mityassir] Vegetables are available in the market. المُخَضّرات مِتيَسِّرَة بالسُّوق [ʔilmuxaððra:t mityassira bissu:g]

avenue • **1.** شارِع [ša:riʕ] شَوارِع [šawa:riʕ] *pl:*

average • **1.** بمُعَدَّل [muʕaddal] مُعَدَّلات [muʕaddala:t] *pl:* He has a good average in school. عِندَه خُوش مُعَدَّل بِالمَدرَسَة [ʕindah xu:š muʕaddal bilmadrasa] • **2.** مُستَوَى اِعتِيادِي [mustawa: ʔiʕtiya:di] He's of average intelligence. مُستَوَى ذَكائَه اِعتِيادِي [mustawa: ðaka:ʔah ʔiʕtiya:di]

on the average • **1.** بِمُعَدَّل [bmuʕaddal] مُعَدَّلات [muʕaddala:t] *pl:* I go to the movies on the average of once a week. أرُوح لِلسِّينَما بِمُعَدَّل مَرَّة بالإسبُوع [ʔaru:ħ lissinama bmuʕaddal marra bilʔisbu:ʕ]

to average • **1.** طَلَّع مُعَدَّل [ṭallaʕ muʕaddal] تَطلِيع مُعَدَّل [taṭli:ʕ muʕaddal] *vn: sv* i. He averages sixty dollars a week. يطَلِّع مُعَدَّل سِتِّين دُولار بالإسبُوع [yṭalliʕ muʕaddal sitti:n dula:r bilʔisbu:ʕ]

to avoid • **1.** تحاشَى [tħa:ša:] تحاشِي [tħa:ši] *vn: sv* a. تجَنَّب [dǰannab] تَجَنُّب [taǰannub] *vn: sv* i. Why is he avoiding me? لُويش دَيتحاشانِي؟ [luwi:š dayitħaša:ni?]

to await • **1.** اِنتِظَر [ʔintiðar] اِنتِظار [ʔintiða:r] *vn: sv* i. ترَقَّب [traqqab] تَرَقُّب [taraqqub] *vn: sv* a. توَقَّع [twaqqaʕ] تَوَقُّع [tawaqquʕ] *vn: sv* a. They were ordered to await the signal. جاهُم أمُر يِنتَظرُون الإشارَة [ǰa:hum ʔamur yintaðru:n ʔilʔiša:ra]

awake • **1.** صاحِي [ṣa:ħi] قاعِد [ga:ʕid] Are you awake? إنتَ صاحِي؟ [ʔinta ṣa:ħi?]

to awake • **1.** صِحَى [ṣiħa:] صَحُو [ṣaħw] *vn: sv* i. قِعَد [giʕad] قعِد [gaʕid] *vn: sv* u. فاق [fa:q] فِيق [fi:q] *vn: sv* i. I awoke at seven o'clock. قعَدِت السّاعَة سَبعَة [gʕadit ʔissa:ʕa sabʕa]

to awaken • **1.** قَعَّد [gaʕʕad] تقِعِّد [tgiʕʕid] *vn:* تقَعَّد [tgaʕʕad] *p:* صَحَّى [ṣaħħa:] تصِحِّي [tṣiħħi] *vn:* تصَحَّى [tṣaħħa:] *p:* فَيَّق [fayyaq] تفِيِّق [tfi yyiq] *vn:* تفَيَّق [tfayyaq] *p:* A noise awakened me. فَدّ حِسّ صَحّانِي [fadd ħiss ṣaħħa:ni]

aware • **1.** عارِف [ʕa:rif] دارِي [da:ri] عِندَه خَبَر [ʕindah xabar] I'm aware of the difficulties involved in the subject. آنِي عارِف بِالصُّعُوبات الدّاخلَة بِالمَوضُوع [ʔa:ni ʕa:rif bissuʕu:ba:t ʔidda:xla bilmawðu:ʕ] He's not aware of his brother's death yet. لهَسَّة ما عِندَه خَبَر بمُوتَة أخُوه [lhassa ma: ʕindah xabar bmu:tat ʔaxu:h] • **2.** حاسّ [ħa:ss] He was aware of movements behind him. كان حاسِس بحَرَكات وَراه [ča:n ħa:sis bħaraka:t wara:h]

away • **1.** غايِب [ɣa:yib] Have you been away? كِنِت غايِب؟ [činit ɣa:yib?]

to be away • **1.** غاب [ɣa:b] غِياب [ɣiya:b] *vn: sv* i. He was away from school for a week. غاب عَن المَدرَسَة لِمُدَّة إسبُوع [ɣa:b ʕan ʔilmadrasa limuddat ʔisbu:ʕ]

*** The station is far away from our house.** • **1.** المَحَطَّة كُلِّش بعِيدَة مِن بَيتنا [lmaħaṭṭa kulliš bʕi:da min baytna]

*** Park the car away from the house.** • **1.** وَقِّف السَّيّارَة بعِيد عَنّ البَيت [waggif ʔissayya:ra bʕi:d ʕann ʔilbayt]

awful • **1.** فَظِيع [faði:ʕ] It was an awful accident. كان حادِث فَظِيع [ča:n ħa:diθ faði:ʕ] • **2.** قَبِيح [qabi:ħ] That coat is awful. هَالسِّترَة قَبِيحَة [hassitra qabi:ħa] • **3.** وَكِح [wakiħ] The kids have been awful today. الجِّهال كانوا وَكحِين اليُوم [ʔiǰǰaha:l ča:naw wakħi:n ʔilyu:m]

*** It's been an awful day.** • **1.** كان يَوم أسوَد [ča:n yu:m ʔaswad]

awfully • **1.** كُلِّش [kulliš] هوايَة [hwa:ya] I'm awfully tired. آنِي كُلِّش تَعبان [ʔa:ni kulliš taʕba:n]

awhile • **1.** فَترَة [fatra] فَترات [fatra:t] *pl:* شوَيَّة [šwayya] He was here awhile this afternoon. كان هنا فَدّ فَترَة اليُوم العَصِر [ča:n hna fadd fatra ʔilyu:m ʔilʕaṣir] I want to think about it awhile. أَرِيد أفَكِّر بِيها شوَيَّة [ʔari:d ʔafakkir bi:ha šwayya]

awkward • **1.** مخَربَط [mxarbaṭ] Why is he so awkward in everything he does? لُويش هُوَّ هِيكِي مخَربَط بِكُلَّشِي اللِّي يسَوِّيه؟ [luwi:š huwwa hi:či mxarbaṭ bkullši ʔilli ysawwi:h?] • **2.** مُخرِج [muħrij] It was an awkward situation. كانَت فَدّ وَضعِيَّة مُحرِجَة [ča:nat fadd waðʕiyya muħrija]

awning • **1.** شَمسِيَّة [šamsiyya] شَمسِيّات [šamsiyya:t] *pl:* شَماسِي [šama:si] شَمسِيّات [šamsiyya:t] *pl:*

axe • **1.** فاس [fa:s] فاسات، فُوس [fa:sa:t, fu:s] *pl:*

axis • **1.** مِحوَر [miħwar] مَحاوِر [maħa:wir] *pl:* The world turns on its axis once a day. الأَرض تدُور حَول مِحوَرها مَرَّة بِاليُوم [ʔilʔarð ddu:r ħawil miħwarha marra bilyu:m]

axle • **1.** أَكسِل [ʔaksil] أَكسِلات [ʔaksila:t] *pl:* The axle is broken. الأَكسِل مَكسُور [ʔilʔaksil maksu:r]

B

baby • **1.** طِفِل [ṭifil] أطفال [ʔaṭfa:l] *pl:* The baby is crying. الطِّفِل دَيبكِي [ʔiṭṭifil dayibči] They treat me like a baby. يعاملُونِي مِثِل طِفِل [yʕa:mlu:ni miθil ṭifil] • **2.** جاهِل [ǰa:hil] جَهَلَة [ǰahala] *pl:* My sons are still babies. وِلدِي بَعَدهُم جِهّال [wildi baʕadhum ǰihha:l]

to baby • **1.** دَلَّل [dallal] تَدلِيل [tadli:l] *vn: sv* i. You baby your children more than necessary. إنتَ تدَلِّل جِهّالَك أكثَر مِن اللّازِم [ʔinta ddallil ǰihha:lak ʔakθar min ʔilla:zim]

to baby oneself • **1.** دارَى نَفِس [da:ra: nafis] مُداراة نَفِس [muda:ra:t nafis] *vn: sv* i. He babies himself very much. هُوَّ يداري نَفسَه كُلِّش هواية [huwwa yda:ri nafsah kulliš hwa:ya]

baby carriage • **1.** عَرَبانَة مال جاهِل [ʕaraba:na ma:l ǰa:hil] عَرَباين مال جَهال [ʕaraba:yin ma:l ǰaha:l] *pl:*

bachelor • **1.** أعزَب [ʔaʕzab] عُزّاب [ʕuzza:b] *pl:* My older brother is still a bachelor. أخُويَا الكِبِير بَعدَه أعزَب [ʔaxu:ya ʔiččibi:r baʕdah ʔaʕzab]

back • **1.** ظِهَر [ðihar] ظُهُور، ظهُورَة [ðuhu:r, ðhu:ra] *pl:* He was lying on his back. كان مِنجِطِل عَلَى ظَهرَه [ča:n minǰiṭil ʕala ðahrah] This chair has a high back. هَالسكَملِي ظَهرَه عالي [hasskamli ðahrah ʕa:li] My back aches. ظَهرِي يوجَعنِي [ðahri yu:ǰaʕni] • **2.** وَرّانِي [warra:ni] The back rooms are dark. القُبَب الوَرّانِيَّة ظَلمَة [ʔilgubab ʔilwarra:niyya ðalma]

*** They did it behind my back.** • **1.** سَوّاها بِلا حِسِّي [sawwa:ha bala ħissi]

*** He walked back and forth in the room.** • **1.** ظَلّ يرُوح ويِجِي بِالقُبَّة [ðall yru:ħ wyiǰi bilgubba]

in back • **1.** لوَرا [liwara] I prefer to sit in back. أفَضِّل أقعُد لوَرا [ʔafaððil ʔagʕud lwara]

in back of • **1.** وَرا [wara] There's a garden in back of the house. أكُو حَدِيقَة وَرا البَيت [ʔaku ħadi:qa wara ʔilbayt] I wonder who is in back of this plan? عِجِبَة مِنُو وَرا هَالمَشرُوع؟ [ʕiǰiba minu wara halmašru:ʕ?]

in the back of • **1.** آخِر [ʔa:xir] أواخِر [ʔawa:xir] *pl:* You'll find it in the back of the book. راح تِلقاها بآخِر الكِتاب [ra:ħ tilga:ha bʔa:xir ʔilkita:b]

*** I have had it in the back of my mind to tell you for a long time.** • **1.** هاي صارِلها مُدَّة بفِكرِي أرِيد أقُلَّك إيّاها [ha:y ṣa:rilha mudda bfikri ʔari:d ʔagullak ʔiyya:ha]

to be back • **1.** رِجَع [riǰaʕ] رُجُوع [ruǰu:ʕ] *vn: sv* a. He isn't back yet. لِهَسَّة بَعَد ما رِجَع [lihassa baʕad ma: riǰaʕ]

to come back • **1.** رِجَع [riǰaʕ] رُجُوع [ruǰu:ʕ] *vn: sv* a. When is he coming back? شوَقِت راح يرجَع؟ [šwakit ra:ħ yirǰaʕ?]

to go back • **1.** رِجَع [riǰaʕ] رُجُوع [ruǰu:ʕ] *vn: sv* a. When are you going back to Basra? شوَقِت راح تِرجَع لِلبَصرَة؟ [šwakit ra:ħ tirǰaʕ lilbaṣra?]

to go back over • **1.** راجَع [ra:ǰaʕ] مُراجَعَة [mura:ǰaʕa] *vn: sv* i. He went back over his work in order to find his mistakes. راجَع شغلَه حَتَّى يلقِي غلطَه [ra:ǰaʕ šuɣlah ħatta yilgi ɣaliṭṭah]

to step back • **1.** رِجَع لوَرا [riǰaʕlwara] رُجُوع لوَرا [ruǰu:ʕ lwara] *vn: sv* a. Step back a bit. إرجَع شوَيَّة لوَرا [ʔirǰaʕ šwayya lwara] • **2.** توَخَّر [twaxxar] تَوَخُّر [tawaxxur] *vn: sv* a. Please step back out of the way. بالله وَخِّر عَن الطَّرِيق [ballah waxxir ʕan ʔiṭṭari:q]

to back • **1.** أيَّد [ʔayyad] تَأيِيد [taʔyi:d] *vn:* تأيَّد [tʔayyad] *p:* All parties are backing him. كُلّ الأحزاب تأيِّدَه [kull ʔilʔaħza:b tʔayydah]

to back down • **1.** تراجَع [tra:ǰaʕ] تَراجُع [tara:ǰuʕ] *vn: sv* a. He finally backed down and admitted his error. أخِيراً تراجَع وَإعترَف بِغَلطتَه [ʔaxi:ran tra:ǰaʕ wʔiʕtiraf byaliṭṭah]

to back up • **1.** رِجَع لوَرا [riǰaʕ lwara] *sv* a. I still can't back up. آنِي بَعَدنِي ما أقدَر أرجَع لوَرا [ʔa:ni baʕadni ma: ʔagdar ʔarǰaʕ lwara] • **2.** سانَد [sa:nad] مُسانَدَة [musa:nada] *vn: sv* i. He backs me up in all my decisions. يسانِدنِي بِكُلّ قَراراتِي [ysa:nidni bkull qara:ra:ti] • **3.** رَجَّع [raǰǰaʕ] تَرجِيع، ترجِّع [tarǰi:ʕ, triǰǰiʕ] *vn: sv* i. Back up your car a little. رَجِّع سَيّارتَك لوَرا شوَيَّة [raǰǰiʕ sayya:rtak lwara šwayya]

backbone • **1.** عَمُود فَقَرِي [ʕamu:d faqari] أعمِدَة فَقَرِيَّة [ʔaʕmida faqariyya] *pl:* They performed an operation on her backbone. سَوَّوا عَمَلِيَّة بالعَمُود الفَقَرِي مالها [sawwa:w ʕamaliyya bilʕamu:d ʔilfaqari ma:lha] • **2.** جُرأة [ǰurʔa] If only he had a little backbone he'd tell her to shut up. لَو كان عِندَه شوَيَّة جُرأة كان قَال إلها "يَزِّي عاد" [law ča:n ʕindah šwayyat ǰurʔa ča:n ga:l ʔilha "yazzi ʕa:d"]

background • **1.** قاعِيَّة [ga:ʕiyya] قاعِيّات [ga:ʕiyya:t] *pl:* The cloth has a black background with white dots. القماش قاعِيتَه سُودَة وَمنَقَّط بأبيَض [ʔilgma:š ga:ʕi:tah su:da wmnaggaṭ bʔabyað] • **2.** خِبرَة [xibra] خِبرات، خِبَر [xibra:t, xibar] *pl:* We want someone with a wide background for this job. نرِيد واحِد عِندَه خِبرَة واسِعَة لِهَالوَظِيفَة [nri:d wa:ħid ʕindah xibra wa:sʕa lihalwaðī:fa]

in the background • **1.** بِالصُفُوف الخَلفِيَّة [biṣṣufu:f ʔilxalfiyya] His father remained in the background throughout the elections. أبُوه ظَلّ بِالصُّفُوف الخَلفِيَّة خِلال الانتِخابات [ʔabu:h ðall biṣṣufu:f ʔilxalfiyya xila:l ʔilintixa:ba:t] His father remained in the background throughout the elections. أبُوه ما بَيَّن نَفسَه خِلال الانتِخابات [ʔabu:h ma: bayyan nafsah xila:l ʔilintixa:ba:t]

B

back talk • **1.** جَسارَة [ǰasa:ra] تَجاسُر [taǰa:sur] I won't listen to any back talk. ما راح أسمَع بأيّ تَجاسُر [ma: ra:ħ ʔasmaʕ bʔayy taǰa:sur]

backward • **1.** مِتأَخِّر [mitʔaxxir] The people there are very backward. النّاس هناك هوايَة مِتأَخِّرين [ʔinna:s hna:k hwa:ya mitʔaxxiri:n] • **2.** بَلِيد [bali:d] بَلِيدِين، بُلَداء [bali:di:n, bulada:ʔ] *pl:* Her son is a bit backward. إبنها شوَيَّة بَلِيد [ʔibinha šwayya bali:d]

backward(s) • **1.** لِوَرا [lwara] He fell backwards. وِقَع لوَرا [wiqaʕ lwara] • **2.** بالمَقلُوب [bilmaglu:b] You've got that sweater on backwards. إنتَ لابِس هالبلُوز بِالمَقلُوب [ʔinta la:bis halblu:z bilmaglu:b]

*** He knows the lesson backwards and forwards.** • **1.** يُعرُف الدَرِس كِلمَة عَلَى كِلمَة [yuʕruf ʔiddaris čilma ʕala čilma]

bad • **1.** بَطّال [batta:l] مُو زين [mu: zi:n] سَيِّئ [sayyiʔ] He has a bad reputation. عِندَه سُمعَة مُو زينَة [ʕindah sumʕa mu: zi:na] • **2.** قَوِي [qawi, guwi] قَوَاي، أقوِياء، قَوِيِّين [ʔaqwiya:ʔ, qawiyyi:n] *pl:* I have a bad cold today. عِندِي فَدّ نَشلَة قَوِيَّة اليُوم [ʕindi fadd našla qawiyya ʔilyu:m] • **3.** لا بَأس ب [la:baʔs b-] • **4.** ما [ma:] He has bad eyes. عيُونَه ما تشُوف زين [ʕyu:nah ma: tšu:f zi:n] He has bad eyes. نَظَرَه ضَعِيف [naðarah ðaʕi:f] I feel bad today. آنِي مُو زين هَاليُوم [ʔa:ni mu: zi:n halyu:m] I feel bad today. مالِي خُلُق اليُوم [ma:li xulug ʔilyu:m] • **5.** شِين [ši:n] We have to take the good with the bad. لازِم نِرضَى بِالزَّين وِالشّين [la:zim nirða: bizzi:n wišši:n]

*** His business is going from bad to worse.** • **1.** شغلَه دَيتدَهوَر [šɣlah dayitdahwar]

too bad • **1.** مُؤسِف [muʔsif] That's too bad! هَذا شِي مُؤسِف [ha:ða ši muʔsif] • **2.** مَع الأَسَف [maʕ ʔilʔasaf] Too bad that you couldn't come. مَعَ الأسَف إنتَ ما قِدَرت تِجي [maʕa ʔilʔasaf ʔinta ma: gidarit tiǰi]

to feel bad • **1.** تأثَّر [tʔaθθar] تَأثُّر [taʔaθθur] *vn: sv* a. Now he feels very bad about what happened. هُوَّ هَسَّة كُلِّش مِتأثِّر مِن اللّي جِرَى [huwwa hassa kulliš mitʔaθθir min ʔilli ǰira:]

bag • **1.** كِيس [či:s, ki:s] كِياس [čiya:s] *pl:* Put these apples in a bag. حُطّ هَالتُّفّاح بِكِيس [ħutt hattiffa:ħ bči:s] • **2.** جُنطَة [ǰunta] جُنَط، جَنطات [ǰunat, ǰanta:t] *pl:* She took some change out of her bag. طَلّعَت شوَيَّة خُردَة مِن جَنطَتها [tallʕat šwayya xurda min ǰantatha] Where can I check my bag? وين أَئمِّن جَنطَتِي؟ [wi:n ʔagdar ʔaʔammin ǰantati?] • **3.** قُونِيَّة [gu:niyya] قُونِيّات، قوانِي [gu:niyya:t, gwa:ni] *pl:* كِيس [či:s, ki:s] كِياس [čiya:s] *pl:* Have them put the bags of rice in the truck. خَلِّيهُم يحُطُّون قوانِي التِّمَّن بِاللُّورِي [xalli:hum yħuttu:n gwa:ni ʔittimman billu:ri]

*** He has the money and I'm left holding the bag.** • **1.** هُوَّ يِضرُب بِالدِجاج وانِي أتلَقَّى العَجاج [huwwa yiðrub biddiǰa:ǰ wa:ni ʔatlagga: ʔilʕaǰa:ǰ] / النّاس تاكُل بِالتَّمُر وَأنِي النُّوايا حِصَّتِي [ʔinna:s ta:kul bittamur waʔa:ni ʔinnuwa:ya ħissati]

*** They moved in on us, bag and baggage.** • **1.** إجَوا كُلّهُم فَدّ نَوبَة وقِعدَوا عَلَى قلُوبنا [ʔiǰaw kullhum fadd nawba wgiʕdaw ʕala glu:bna]

baggage • **1.** غَرَض [ɣarað] أغراض [(ʔa)ɣra:ð] *pl:* I want to send my baggage on ahead. أرِيد أدِزّ غَراضِي لِقِدّام [ʔari:d ʔadizz ɣara:ði ligidda:m]

bail • **1.** كَفالَة [kafa:la] كَفالات [kafa:la:t] *pl:* The court fixed his bail at two thousand dinars. المَحكَمَة قَرَّرَت أن تكُون كَفالتَه بألفَين دِينار [ʔilmaħkama qarrarat ʔan tku:n kafa:ltah bʔalfayn dina:r]

to put up bail • **1.** كِفَل [kifal] كَفالَة [kafa:la] *vn:* اِنكِفَل [ʔinkifal] *p:* Who is going to put up bail for him? مِنُو راح يِكفَلَه؟ [minu ra:ħ yikfalah?]

to bail out • **1.** غِرَف [ɣiraf] غَرُف [ɣaruf] *vn:* اِنغِرَف [ʔinɣiraf] *p:* We used our helmets to bail the water out of the boat. اِستَعمَلنا خُوَذنا حَتَّى نُغرُف الماي مِن البَلَم [ʔistaʕmalna xuwaðna ħatta nuɣruf ʔilma:y min ʔilbalam] • **2.** طُفَر [tufar] طَفُر [tafur] *vn: sv* u. I had to bail out of my plane at an elevation of five thousand feet. آنِي اِنجُبَرت أطفُر مِن طِيّارتِي مِن علو خَمسَة آلاف قَدَم [ʔa:ni ʔinǰubarit ʔatfur min tiyya:rti min ʕilu xamsat ʔa:la:f qadam]

bait • **1.** طُعُم [tuʕum] He put bait on the hook so he could catch himself a fish. خَلَّى طُعُم بالشُّصّ حَتَّى يصِيدلَه سِمكَة [xalla: tuʕum biššuss ħatta ysi:dlah simča]

to bake • **1.** خُبَز [xubaz] خَبُز [xabuz] *vn:* اِنخُبَز [ʔinxubaz] *p:* My mother baked bread yesterday. أُمِّي خُبزَت البارحَة [ʔummi xubzat ʔilba:rħa] • **2.** سَوَّى [sawwa:] *sv* i. She baked the baklava in the oven. سَوَّت البَقلاوَة بِالفِرن [sawwa:t ʔilbaqla:wa bilfirin]

baker • **1.** خَبّاز [xabba:z] خَبّازِين، خبابِيز [xabba:zi:n, xba:bi:z] *pl:* كُرَكجِي [čurakči] كُرَكجِيَّة [čurakčiyya] *pl:* This baker has good bread. هَالخَبّاز عِندَه خُوش خُبُز [halxabba:z ʕindah xu:š xubuz]

bakery • **1.** مَخبَز [maxbaz] مَخابِز [maxa:biz] *pl:* فِرن [firin] أفران [ʔafra:n] *pl:* The bakery is around the corner. المَخبَز بلُوفَة الشّارِع [ʔilmaxbaz blu:fat ʔišša:riʕ]

baking powder • **1.** بَيكِن باودَر [baykin pa:wdar]

baking soda • **1.** صَودَة مال كَيك [su:da ma:l kayk] بَيكِن صَودَة [baykin su:da] صَودَة خُبُز [su:dat xubuz]

balance • **1.** مِيزان [mi:za:n] مَوازِين [mawa:zi:n] *pl:* The jeweler put the bracelets on the balance and weighed them.

الصّايغ حَطّ السوارات بالمِيزان وَوُزَنهُم [ʔiṣṣaːyiɣ ħaṭṭ ʔisswaːraːt bilmiːzaːn wawuzanhum] • **2.** مُوازَنَة [muwaːzana] I lost my balance. اِختَلَّت مُوازَنتِي [ʔixtallat muwaːzanti] • **3.** باقِي [baːqi] Pay one-third down and the balance in monthly installments. إنطِي ثِلث القِيمَة لِقِدّام والباقِي بأقساط شَهرِيَّة [ʔinṭi θilθ ʔilqiːma ligiddaːm wilbaːqi bʔaqsaːṭ šahriyya]

*** His life hung in the balance.** • **1.** تعَلَّق بَين إلحَيات والمَوت [tʕallag biːn ʔilħayaːt wilmawt]

to balance • **1.** وازَن [waːzan] مُوازَنَة [muwaːzana] *vn:* توازَن [twaːzan] *p: sv* i. Can you balance a stick on your forehead? تِقدَر توازِن عُودَة عَلَى قُصّتَك؟ [tigdar twaːzin ʕuːda ʕala guṣṣtak?] Our bookkeeper balances his books at the end of each month. مُحاسِبنا يوازِن دَفاتره بنِهايَة كُلّ شَهَر [muħaːsibna ywaːzin dafaːtrah bnihaːyat kull šahar] • **2.** طابَق [ṭaːbaq] مُطابَقَة [muṭaːbaqa] *vn: sv* u. Does the account balance? الحساب دَيطابُق؟ [ʔilħsaːb dayṭaːbuq?]

balcony • **1.** بَلكُون [balkuːn] بَلكُونات [balkuːnaːt] *pl:* I have an apartment with a balcony. عِندِي شِقَّة بِيها بَلكُون [ʕindi šiqqa biːha balkuːn] • **2.** غالِيري [gaːliːri] غالِيرِيّات [galiriyyaːt] *pl:* We had seats in the first balcony. كان عِدنا مَقاعِد بأوَّل غالِيري [čaːn ʕidna maqaːʕid bʔawwal galiːri]

bald • **1.** أصلَع [ʔaṣlaʕ] صُلُع، صَلعِين [ṣuluʕ, ṣalʕiːn.] *pl:* صَلعَة [ṣalʕa] *Feminine:* He was bald at thirty. كان أصلَع بالثّلاثِين [čaːn ʔaṣlaʕ bittilaːθiːn]

bald spot • **1.** صَلعَة [ṣalʕa] صَلعات [ṣalʕaːt] *pl:* He has a small bald spot. عِندَه صَلعَة صغَيّرَة [ʕindah ṣalʕa ṣɣayyra]

ball • **1.** طُوبَة [ṭuːba] طُوبات، طُوَب [ṭuːbaːt, ṭuwab] *pl:* They played ball all afternoon. لِعبَوا طُوبَة العَصِر كُلّه [liʕbaw ṭuːba ʔilʕaṣir kullah] • **2.** كُبّابَة، كَبُّوبَة [kubbaːba, kabbuːba] كَبُّوبات [kabbuːbaːt] *pl:* I'd like a ball of white wool. أرِيد كَبُّوبَة صُوف أبيَض [ʔariːd kabbuːbat ṣuːf ʔabyað] • **3.** كُرَة [kura] كُرات [kuraːt] *pl:* He butted the ball with his head. نقر القُرَة براسَه [nigar ʔilkuːra braːsah]

balled up • **1.** مخَربَط [mxarbaṭ] I found everything all balled up. لِقيت كُلّشِي مخَربَط [ligiːt kullši mxarbaṭ] • **2.** مِرتِبِك [mirtibik] He was all balled up. كان كُلّش مِرتِبِك [čaːn kulliš mirtibik]

balloon • **1.** بالُون [baːluːn] بالُونات [baːluːnaːt] *pl:* نُفّاخَة [nuffaːxa] نُفّاخات [nuffaːxaːt] *pl:*

ballot • **1.** وَرَقَة اِنتِخاب [waragat ʔintixaːb] أوراق اِنتِخاب [ʔawraːq ʔintixaːb] *pl:* Have all the ballots been counted? كُلّ أوراق الانتِخاب تعَدَّت؟ [kull ʔawraːq ʔilʔintixaːb tʕaddat?]

secret ballot • **1.** اِنتِخاب سِرِّي [ʔintixaːb sirri]

ballroom • **1.** قاعَة مال رِقِص [qaːʕa maːl rigiṣ] قاعات مال رِقِص [qaːʕa ːt maːl rigiṣ] *pl:*

Baltic Sea • **1.** بَحر البَلطِيق [baħr ʔilbalṭiːq]

bamboo • **1.** خَيزَران [xayzaraːn]

to ban • **1.** مِنَع [minaʕ] مَنع [maniʕ] *vn:* اِنمِنَع [ʔinminaʕ] *p:* The government has banned the sale of narcotics. الحُكُومَة مِنعَت بَيع المُخَدَّرات [ʔilħukuːma minʕat biːʕ ʔilmuxaddaraːt]

banana • **1.** موزَة [mawza, muːza] موزات [mawzaːt, muːzaːt] *pl:* مَوز [mawz] *Collective*

band • **1.** جَوق [ǰawq] أجواق [ʔaǰwaːq] *pl:* The band played dance music all evening. الجَّوق دَقّ مُوسِيقَى رِقِص طُول اللَّيل [ʔiǰǰawq dagg musiːqat rigiṣtuːl ʔillayl] • **2.** شَرِيط [šariːṭ] أشرِطَة، شَرائِط [ʔašriṭa, šaraːyiṭ] *pl:* The Christians tie a black band on their arm in mourning. المَسِيحِيِّين يشِدُّون شَرِيط أسوَد عَلَى إيدهُم لِلحِزن [ʔilmasiːħiyyiːn yšidduːn šariːṭ ʔaswad ʕala ʔiːdhum lilħizin] • **3.** عِصابَة [ʕiṣaːba] عِصابات [ʕiṣaːbaːt] *pl:* The police caught the leader of the bank of smugglers. الشُّرطَة لِزمَت رَئِيس عِصابَة المُهَرِّبِين [ʔiššurṭa lizmat raʔiːs ʕiṣaːbat ʔilmuharribiːn] • **4.** موجَة [mawǰa, muːǰa] مَوجات [mawǰaːt, muːǰaːt] *pl:* You can get that station on the 25 meter band. تِقدَر تحَصِّل هالمَحَطَّة عَلَى مَوجَة خَمسَة وعِشرِين [tigdar tħaṣṣil halmaħaṭṭa ʕala mawǰa xamsa wʕišriːn]

bandage • **1.** لَفّاف [laffaːf] لَفّافات [laffaːfaːt] *pl:* Don't undo the bandage. لا تفُكّ اللَّفّاف [laː tfukk ʔillaffaːf]

to bandage • **1.** لَفّ بلَفّاف [laff bilaffaːf] *sv* i. You'd better bandage the cut at once. أحسَنلَك تلِفّ الجَّرِح بلَفّاف هَسَّة [ʔaħsanlak tliff ʔiǰǰariħ blaffaːf hassa]

bandit • **1.** حَرامِي [ħaraːmi] حَرامِيَّة [ħaraːmiyya] *pl:* سَلّاب [sallaːb] سَلّابَة [sallaːba] *pl:*

bang • **1.** طَقَّة [ṭagga] طَقّات [ṭaggaːt] *pl:* The loud bang startled her. الطَّقَّة العالِيَة جَفّلَتها [ʔiṭṭagga ʔilʕaːlya ǰafflatha]

to bang • **1.** ضِرَب [ðirab] ضَرُب [ðarub] *vn: sv* u. He banged his shoe on the table. ضِرَب قُندَرته عالمِيز [ðirab qundartah ʕalmiːz]

to banish • **1.** أبعَد [ʔabʕad] إبعاد [ʔibʕaːd] *vn: sv* i. They banished the troublemakers from the capital for two years. أبعِدَوا المُشاغِبِين مِن العاصِمَة لِمُدَّة سَنتَين [ʔabʕidaw ʔilmušaːɣibiːn min ʔilʕaːṣima limuddat santayn] • **2.** نِفَى [nifaː] نَفِي [nafy] vn: اِنّفَى [ʔinnifaː] *p:* They banished the party leaders from the country. نِفَوا زُعَماء الحِزب مِن البِلاد [nifaw zuʕamaːʔ ʔilħizib min ʔilbilaːd]

banister • **1.** محَجَّر [mħaǰǰar] محَجَّرات [mħaǰǰaraːt] *pl:* Hold on to the banister. إلزَم المحَجَّر [ʔilzam ʔilmħaǰǰar]

B

bank • **1.** بَنك [bank] بُنُوك [bunu:k] *pl:* I keep my money in the bank. آني أضُمّ فلوسي بالبَنك [ʔa:ni ʔaðumm flu:si bilbang] • **2.** شاطِي [ša:ṭi] شواطِي [šwa:ṭi] *pl:* He swam to the nearby bank. سِبَح لِلشَّط القَرِيب [sibaħ liššaṭ ʔilqiri:b]

to bank on • **1.** اِعتِمَد عَلَى [ʔiʕtimad ʕala] اِعتِماد [ʔiʕtima:d] *vn: sv* i. You can bank on that. تِقدَر تِعتِمِد عَلَى ذاك [tigdar tiʕtimid ʕala ða:k]

banker • **1.** صَرّاف [ṣarra:f] صَرّافِين [ṣarra:fi:n] *pl:*

bankrupt • **1.** مِفلِس [miflis] مَفالِيس [mafa:li:s] *pl:* مِنكِسِر [minkisir] He is bankrupt. هُوَّ مِفلِس [huwwa miflis] • **2.** كَسِر [kasir] كسُور [ksu:r] *pl:* The company went bankrupt. الشَّرِكَة طِلعَت كَسِر [ʔiššarika ṭilʕat kasir]

to go bankrupt • **1.** فَلَّس [fallas] إفلاس [ʔifla:s] *vn: sv* a. اِنكِسَر [ʔinkisar] اِنكِسار [ʔinkisa:r] *vn: sv* i. He went bankrupt. فَلَّس [fallas]

bankruptcy • **1.** إفلاس [ʔifla:s] كَسِر [kasir] كسُور [ksu:r] *pl:* The firm had to announce its bankruptcy. الشَّرِكَة اِنجُبرَت تِعلِن إفلاسها [ʔiššarika ʔinǰubrat tiʕlin ʔifla:sha]

banner • **1.** بَيرَق [bayraq] بَيارِق [baya:riq] *pl:* عَلَم [ʕalam] أعلام [ʔaʕla:m] *pl:*

banquet • **1.** عَزِيمَة [ʕazi:ma] عَزايِم [ʕaza:yim] *pl:* حَفلَة [ħafla] حَفلات [ħafla:t] *pl:*

to baptize • **1.** عَمَّد [ʕammad] تَعمِيد [taʕmi:d] *vn:* تعَمَّد [tʕammad] *p:* He baptized him in the Jordan River. عَمَّدَه بنَهر الأُردُن [ʕammadah bnahr ʔilʔurdun]

bar • **1.** قالَب [qa:lab] قَوالِب، قوالِب [qawa:lib, qwa:lib.] *pl:* Here's a bar of soap. هاك هَذا قالَب صابُون [ha:k ha:ða qa:lab ṣa:bu:n] • **2.** شِيش [ši:š] شياش [šya:š] *pl:* We are going to need more iron bars to finish this foundation. راح نِحتاج بَعَد شِيش حَتَّى نصَلِّح هَالأساس [ra:ħ niħta:ǰ baʕad ši:š ħatta nṣalliħ halʔasa:s] • **3.** بار [ba:r] بارات [ba:ra:t] *pl:* Let's meet in the bar in an hour. خَلّي نِتلاقَى بالبار بَعَد ساعَة [xalli nitla:ga: bilba:r baʕad sa:ʕa] Let's have a drink at the bar. خَلّي نِشرَب إلنا فَدّ شِي بالبار [xalli nišrab ʔilna fadd ši bilba:r] • **4.** مَيخانَة [mayyxa:na] مَيخانات [mayyxa:na:t] *pl:* There was a fight in this cheap bar last night. صارَت عَركَة بهاي المَيخانَة البارحَة باللَّيل [ṣa:rat ʕarka bha:y ʔilmayxa:na ʔilba:rħa billi:l] • **5.** فاصلَة [fa:ṣla] فاصلات [fa:ṣla:t] *pl:* He played a few bars of the tune. دَقّ كَم فاصلَة مِن النَّغمَة [dagg čam fa:ṣla min ʔinnaɣma] • **6.** نَقابَة المُحامِين [naqa:bat ʔilmuħa:mi:n] When were you admitted to the bar? شوَقِت اِنقِبَلِت بنَقابَة المُحامِين؟ [šwakit ʔinqibalit bnaqa:bat ʔilmuħa:mi:n?] • **7.** جَسرَة [ǰasra] جَسرات [ǰasra:t] *pl:* Let's swim out to the bar. خَلّي نِسبَح لِلجَّسرَة [xalli nisbaħ liǰǰasra]

to bar • **1.** سَدّ [sadd] سَدّ [sadd] *vn:* اِنسَدّ [ʔinsadd] *p:* He forgot to bar the stable door. نِسَى يسِدّ باب الطَّولَة [nisa: ysidd ba:b ʔiṭṭawla] • **2.** مِنَع [minaʕ] مَنع [maniʕ] *vn:* اِنمِنَع [ʔinminaʕ] *p:* They posted soldiers at the entrances to bar people from entering. حَطّوا جُنُود بالمَداخِل حَتَّى يمنَعُون النّاس مِن الدُّخُول [ħaṭṭaw ǰunu:d bilmada:xil ħatta yimnaʕu:n ʔinna:s min ʔiddixu:l]

barbed wire • **1.** سِلك شائِك [silk ša:ʔik] أسلاك شائِكَة [ʔasla:k ša:ʔika] *pl:*

barber • **1.** مزَيِّن [mzayyin] مزَيِّنِين [mzayyini:n] *pl:* حَلّاق [ħalla:q] حَلّاقِين [ħalla:qi:n] *pl:* Is there a good barber in town? أكُو مزَيِّن زين بالولايَة؟ [ʔaku mzayyin zi:n bilwila:ya?]

barber shop • **1.** صالُون حِلاقَة [ṣa:lu:n ħila:qa] صالُونات حِلاقَة [ṣa:lu:na:t ħila:qa] *pl:* دُكّان مزَيِّن [dukka:n mzayyin] دَكاكِين مال زيان [daka:ki:n ma:l zya:n] *pl:*

bare • **1.** مسَلَّخ [msallax] مسَلَّخِين، مسالِيخ [msallaxi:n, msa:li:x] *pl:* عَريان [ʕarya:n] عَريانِين، عرايا [ʕarya:ni:n, ʕra:ya] *pl:* Little kids are always swimming bare. الوُلِد الصِّغار دائِماً يِسبَحُون مسالِيخ [ʔilwulid ʔiṣṣiɣa:r da:ʔiman yisbaħu:n msa:li:x] • **2.** مكَشَّف [mkaššaf] Don't go out in the sun with your head bare. لا تِطلَع بَرَّة بالشَّمِس مكَشَّف الرّاس [la: tiṭlaʕ barra biššamis mkaššaf ʔirra:s] • **3.** خالِي [xa:li] I looked in the cupboard and found the shelves were bare. باوَعِت بالدِّيلاب وَلِقِيت الرُّفُوف كانَت خالِيَة [ba:waʕit biddi:la:b wligi:t ʔirrufu:f ča:nat xa:lya] These are the bare facts. هَذِي هِيَّ الحَقايِق خالِيَة مِن كُلّ رتُوش [ha:ði hiyya ʔilħaqa:yiq xa:lya min kull ritu:š]

to bare • **1.** كَشَّف [kaššaf] تكِشِّف [tkiššif] *vn:* تكَشَّف [tkaššaf] *p:* The nurse told me to bare my right arm. المُمَرِّضَة قالَتلِي أكَشِّف ذراعِي اليَمِين [ʔilmumarriđa ga:latli ʔakaššif ðra:ʕi ʔilyami:n] • **2.** تفَرَّع [tfarraʕ] تَفَرُّع [tafarruʕ] *vn: sv* a. The men bared their heads when the flag passed. الرِّياجِيل تفَرّعَوا مِن مَرّ العَلَم [ʔirriya:ǰi:l tfarrʕaw min marr ʔilʕalam]

barefoot • **1.** حافِي [ħa:fi] حِفّاي [ħiffa:y] *pl:* Children, don't play barefoot. صغار، لا تِلعَبُون حِفّاي [ṣɣa:r, la: tilʕabu:n ħiffa:y]

barely • **1.** دُوب [du:b] يا دُوب [ya: du:b] He's barely ten. هُوَّ دُوب عَشِر سنِين [huwwa du:b ʕašir sni:n] I barely had time to finish the book. الوَقت اللِّي كان عِندِي يا دُوب كَفَّى أخَلِّص الكِتاب [ʔilwakt ʔilli ča:n ʕindi ya: du:b kaffa: ʔaxalliṣ ʔilkita:b] • **2.** بالكاد [bilka:d] He barely managed it. بالكاد دَبَّرها [bilka:d dabbarha]

bargain • **1.** شَروَة [šarwa] شَروات [šarwaːt] *pl:* This book was a good bargain. هَالكِتاب كان خُوش شَروَة [halkitaːb čaːn xuːš šarwa] • **2.** صَفقَة [ṣafqa] صَفقات [ṣafqaːt] *pl:* That's just part of the bargain. ذاك فَدّ قِسِم مِن الصَّفقَة [ðaːk fadd qisim min ʔiṣṣafqa] • **3.** اِتِّفاق [ʔittifaːq] اِتِّفاقات [ʔittifaːqaːt] *pl:* According to our bargain you were to pay half. حَسَب اِتِّفاقنا كان لازِم تِدفَع النُّصّ [ħasab ʔittifaːqna čaːn laːzim tidfaʕ ʔinnuṣṣ]

*** All right, it's a bargain!** • **1.** زَين، صار [zayn, ṣaːr] زَين، موافِق / زين، موافِق [zayn, mwaːfiq] / [ziːn, mwaːfiq]

to bargain • **1.** تعامَل [tʕaːmal] عِملَة [ʕimla] *vn: sv* a. She bargains for hours with the shopkeepers. تِتعامَل ساعات ويّا الدُّكّانچِيَّة [titʕaːmal saːʕaːt wiyya ʔiddukkaːnčiyya] • **2.** فاوَض [faːwað̣] مُفاوَضَة [mufaːwað̣a] *vn: sv* i. The workmen are bargaining with their employer for a raise. العُمّال دَيفاوضُون مُستَخدِمهُم حَول زِيادَة بالأُجُور [ʔilʕummaːl dayfaːwð̣uːn mustaxdimhum ħawil ziyaːda bilʔujuːr]

*** He got more than he bargained for.** • **1.** حَصَّل أكثَر مِن ما توَقَّع [ħaṣṣal ʔakθar min maː twaqqaʕ]

bark • **1.** قِشرَة [gišra] The eucalyptus trees have a thin bark. أشجار اليُوكالِبتُس إلها قِشرَة خَفِيفَة [ʔašjaːr ʔilyuːkaːliptus ʔilha gišra xafiːfa] • **2.** نَبحَة [nabħa] نَبحات [nabħaːt] *pl:* The dog's bark is worse than his bite. نَبحَة الكَلِب أنجَس مِن عَضتَه [nabħat ʔiččalib ʔangas min ʕað̣ð̣tah]

to bark • **1.** نِبَح [nibaħ] نباح [nibaːħ] *vn: sv* a. عِوَى [ʕiwaː] عَوِي [ʕawi] *vn: sv* i. The dog barked loudly. الكَلِب عَوَّى بِصَوت عالِي [ʔiččalib ʕawwaː bṣuːt ʕaːli]

barley • **1.** شِعِير [šiʕiːr]

barometer • **1.** بَرَومَتِر [barawmatir] بَرومَترات [barumatraːt] *pl:*

barrack(s) • **1.** ثَكَنَة [θakana] ثَكَنات [θakanaːt] *pl:* مُعَسكَر [muʕaskar] مُعَسكَرات [muʕaskaraːt] *pl:* Our barracks were built of concrete. ثَكَنَتنا مَبنِيَّة بِسِمَنت [θakanatna mabniyya bsimant]

barrel • **1.** بَرمِيل [barmiːl] بَرامِيل [baraːmiːl] *pl:* We used up a whole barrel of oil. اِستَعمَلنا بَرمِيل كامِل مِن الدِّهَن [ʔistaʕmalna barmiːl kaːmil min ʔiddihan] • **2.** سَبَطانَة [sabaṭaːna] سَبَطانات [sabaṭaːnaːt] *pl:* Show the boy how to clean the barrel of his gun. راوِي الوَلَد شلُون يِنَظِّف سَبَطانَة بُندِقِيتَه [raːwi ʔilwalad šluːn ynað̣ð̣uf sabaṭaːnat bundiqiːtah]

barren • **1.** قاحِل [qaːħil] Except for a strip along the river, all the land is barren. بِاستِثناء وُصلَة مُحاذِيَة لِلنَّهَر، كُلّ الأراضِي قاحلَة [bistiθnaːʔ wuṣla muħaːð̣iya linnahar, kull ʔilʔaraːð̣i qaːħla] • **2.** عاقِر [ʕaːqir] He divorced his wife because she is barren. طَلَّق مَرتَه لِأنّها عاقِر [ṭallag martah liʔanh ʕaːqir]

barricade • **1.** مانِع [maːniʕ] مَوانِع [mawaːniʕ] *pl:* The rebels set up barricades in the streets. الثُّوّار نِصبَوا مَوانِع بِالشَّوارِع [ʔiθθuwwaːr niṣbaw mawaːniʕ biššawaːriʕ]

to barricade • **1.** سَدّ [sadd] سَدّ [sadd] *vn:* اِنسَدّ [ʔinsadd] *p:* قِطَع [giṭaʕ] قَطِع [gaṭiʕ] *vn:* اِنقِطَع [ʔingiṭaʕ] *p:* They barricaded all the roads into the area. سَدّوا كُلّ الطُّرُق اللّي تفُوت لِلمَنطِقَة [saddaw kull ʔiṭṭuruq ʔilli tfuːt lilmanṭiqa]

base • **1.** قاعِدَة [qaːʕida] قَواعِد [qawaːʕid] *pl:* The base of the statue was still standing. قاعِدَة التِّمثال كانَت بَعَدها باقيَة [qaːʕidat ʔittimθaːl čaːnat baʕadha baːqya] The planes returned to their base. الطَّيّارات رِجعَت لِقاعِدَتها [ʔiṭṭiyyaːraːt rijʕat liqaːʕidatha] • **2.** أساس [ʔasaːs] أساسات [ʔasaːsaːt] *pl:* The water pipe passes under the base. بُورِي الماي يفُوت جَوَّة الأساس [buːri ʔilmaːy yfuːt jawwa ʔalʔasaːs]

*** Paint the bathroom walls with an oil-base paint.** • **1.** أصبُغ حِيطان الحَمّام بدِهِن [ʔuṣbuɣ ħiːṭaːn ʔilħammaːm bdihin]

to base • **1.** بِنَى [binaː] بِناء [binaːʔ] *vn:* اِنبِنَى [ʔinbinaː] *p:* On what do you base your figures? عَلَى ويش بنَيت حسابَك؟ [ʕala wiːš bnayt ħsaːbak?] • **2.** سَوَّى [sawwaː] تَسوِيَة [taswiya] *vn: sv* i. The company decided to base its operations in Basra. الشَّرِكَة قَرَّرَت تسَوِّي مَركَزها بِالبَصرَة [ʔiššarika qarrarat tsawwi markazha bilbaṣra]

basement • **1.** سِرداب [sirdaːb] سَرادِيب [saraːdiːb] *pl:*

bashful • **1.** خَجُول [xajuːl] She is very bashful. هِيَّ فَدّ وِحدَة كُلِّش خَجُولَة [hiyya fadd wiħda kulliš xajuːla]

to be bashful • **1.** خِجَل [xijal] خَجَل [xajal] *vn: sv* a. اِستِحَى [ʔistiħaː] اِستِحاء [ʔistiħaːʔ] *vn: sv* i. She is bashful with people. تِستِحِي مِن النّاس [tistiħi min ʔinnaːs] Don't be bashful, ask him. لا تِخجَل، إسألَه [laː tixjal, ʔisʔalah]

basic • **1.** رَئِيسِي [raʔiːsi] أساسِي [ʔasaːsi] جَوهَري [jawhari] He earns enough money for his basic needs. يحَصِّل فلُوس تكَفِّي حاجاتَه الرَّئِيسِيَّة [yħaṣṣil fluːs tkaffi ħaːjaːtah ʔirraʔiːsiyya] The argument came up because of a basic difference of opinion. النِّقاش صار بِسَبَب خِلاف رَئِيسِي بِالرَّأي [ʔinniqaːš ṣaːr bisabab xilaːf raʔiːsi birraʔy]

basically • **1.** جَوهَرِيّاً [jawhariyyan] There is nothing basically wrong with your idea. فِكِرتَك ما بِيها عِيب جَوهَرِيّاً [fikirtak maː biːha ʕiːb jawhariyyan]

basil • **1.** ريحان [riħaːn]

B

basin • **1.** نجانَة [nǰa:na] نجانات [nǰa:na:t] *pl:* Please bring me a basin of warm water. أَرجُوك جِيبلِي نجانَة ماي دافِي [ʔarǰu:k ǰi:bli nǰa:na ma:y da:fi] • **2.** حَوض [ħawð] أَحواض [ʔaħwa:ð̣] *pl:* وادِي [wa:di] وِديان [widya:n] *pl:* The basin of the Tigris and Euphrates is the most fertile in Iraq. حَوض نَهر دِجلَة وَالفُرات أَخصَب أَرض بِالعِراق [ħawð̣ nahr diǰla wilfura:t ʔaxṣab ʔarð̣ bilʕira:q]

basis • **1.** أَساس [ʔasa:s] أَساسات [ʔasa:sa:t] *pl:* We can't continue on this basis. ما نِقدَر نِستِمِرّ عَلَى هَالأَساس [ma: nigdar nistimirr ʕala halʔasa:s]

basket • **1.** سَلَّة [salla] سلال، سَلّات [sla:l, salla:t] *pl:* Put the clothes in the basket. حُطّ الهدُوم بِالسَّلَّة [ħuṭṭ ʔilhdu:m bissalla]

basketball • **1.** كُرَة السَلَّة [kurat ʔissalla] باسكِت بال [ba:skit ba:l]

to baste • **1.** كَوَّك [kawwak] تَكوِيك [tkuwwuk, takwi:k] *vn:* تكَوَّك [tkawwak] *p:* It's better to baste the hem first. أَوَّل لَو تكَوُّك الطَّوِيَة أَحسَن [ʔawwal law tkawwuk ʔiṭṭawya ʔaħsan] • **2.** ساقَى [sa:qa:] مُساقاة [musa:qa: (t)] *vn: sv* i. Baste the chicken with the oil from time to time while it's cooking. ساقِي الدِّجاجَة بِالدِّهِن مِن حِين الآخَر لَمّا تِنطُبُخ [sa:qi ʔiddiǰa:ǰa biddihin min ħi:n ʔilʔa:xar lamma tinṭubux]

bat • **1.** خَفّاش اللَّيل [xaffa:š, xuffa:š] خَفافِيش اللَّيل [xafa:fi:š ʔillayl, xufa:fi:š ʔillayl] *pl:* خَشّاف اللَّيل [xašša:f ʔillayl] خَشاشِيف اللَّيل [xaša:ši:f ʔillayl] *pl:* I'm afraid of bats. آنِي أَخاف مِن خَفافِيش اللَّيل [ʔa:ni ʔaxa:f min xafa:fi:š ʔillayl]

to bat • **1.** ضِرَب [ð̣irab] *sv* u. طَفَّر [ṭaffar] *sv* u. He batted the ball over the fence. ضِرَب الطُّوبَة الخارِج السِّياج [ð̣irab ʔiṭṭu:ba lxa:riǰ ʔissiya:ǰ]

*** He really went to bat for me.** • **1.** صُدُق وُقَفلِي [ṣudug wugafli]

*** He told his story without batting an eye.** • **1.** حِكَى حكايتَه بَلا ما تِطرُفلَه عَين [ħiča: ħča:ytah bala: ma: tiṭruflah ʕi:n]

batch • **1.** خَبطَة [xabṭa] خَبطات [xabṭa:t] *pl:* This batch of cement won't be enough. هَالخَبطَة مِن الشِمَنتُو ما راح تكَفِّي [halxabṭa min ʔiččimantu ma: ra:ħ tkaffi] • **2.** جَوق [ǰawq] أَجواق [ʔaǰwa:q] *pl:* The second batch of pilgrims will arrive tomorrow. الجُوقَة الثّانِيَة مِن الحِجّاج راح تُوصَل باكِر [ʔiǰǰu:ga ʔiθθa:nya min ʔilħiǰǰa:ǰ ra:ħ tu:ṣal ba:čir] • **3.** تَنُّور [tannu:r] تنانِير [tna:ni:r] *pl:* تَنُّورَة [tannu:ra] تَنُّورات [tannu:ra:t] *pl:* How many batches of bread do you bake a day? كَم تَنُّور خُبُز تُخبُز بِاليُوم؟ [čam tannu:r xubuz tuxbuz bilyu:m?] • **4.** بَطِن [baṭin] بطُون [bṭu:n] *pl:* This is the biggest batch of kittens our cat has ever had. هاي أَكبَر بَطِن جابَتَه بَزُّونَتنا [ha:y ʔakbar baṭin ǰa:batah bazzu:natna]

bath • **1.** حَمّام [ħamma:m] حَمّامات [ħamma:ma:t] *pl:* I'd like to take a hot bath. دَأَرِيد آخُذ حَمّام حارّ [daʔari:d ʔa:xuð ħamma:m ħa:rr] Have you a room with bath? عِندَك غُرفَة بِيها حَمّام؟ [ʕindak ɣurfa bi:ha ħamma:m?]

to bathe • **1.** غِسَل [ɣisal, xisal] غَسِل [ɣasil] *vn:* اِنغِسَل [ʔinɣisal] *p:* Bathe the baby in lukewarm water. إغسِل الطِّفِل بماي دافِي [ʔiɣsil ʔiṭṭifil bma:y da:fi] We usually bathe at the public bathhouse. إحنا عادَةً نِغسِل بِالحَمّام العُمُومِي [ʔiħna ʕa:datan niɣsil bilħamma:m ʔilʕumu:mi] • **2.** سِبَح [sibaħ] سِبِح [sibiħ] *vn:* اِنسِبَح [ʔinsibaħ] *p:* We went bathing in the river almost every day. سِبَحنا بِالشَّطّ تَقرِيباً كُلّ يوم [sibaħna biššaṭṭ taqri:ban kull yu:m]

bathhouse • **1.** حَمّام عام [ħamma:m ʕa:mm] حَمّامات عامَّة [ħamma:ma:t ʕa:mma] *pl:* There are many public bathhouses in the city. أَكُو هوايَة حَمّامات عامَّة بِالوِلايَة [ʔaku hwa:ya ħamma:ma:t ʕa:mma bilwila:ya] • **2.** مَنزَع [manzaʕ] مَنازِع [mana:ziʕ] *pl:* There is a bathhouse at the beach where we can change our clothes. أَكُو مَنزَع بالمَسبَح نِقدَر نِنزَع هدُومنا بِيه [ʔaku manzaʕ bilmasbaħ nigdar ninzaʕ hdu:mna bi:h]

bathing suit • **1.** مايُو [ma:yu] مايُوهات [ma:yu:ha:t] *pl:* (for women), كِسوَة [čiswa] كِسَو [čisaw] pl: (for men)

bathrobe • **1.** رُوب [ru:b] رواب رواَبة ، [rwa:b, rwa:ba] *pl:* بُرنُص [burnuṣ] بَرانِص [bara:niṣ] *pl:*

bathroom • **1.** حَمّام [ħamma:m] حَمّامات [ħamma:ma:t] *pl:* I'm looking for the toilet not the bathroom. دَأدَوِّر عالمِرحاض مُو الحَمّام [daʔadawwur ʕalmirħa:ð̣ mu: ʔilħamma:m]

bath towel • **1.** مَنشَفَة [manšafa] مَناشِف [mana:šif] *pl:*

bathtub • **1.** بانيُو [ba:nyu] بانيُوات [ba:nyuwa:t] *pl:*

batter • **1.** عَجِينَة [ʕaǰi:na] عَجِينات [ʕaǰi:na:t] *pl:* Is the batter for the cake mixed? العَجِينَة مال الكَيك مَخبُوطَة؟ [ʔilʕaǰi:na ma:l ʔilki:k maxbu:ṭa?]

to batter in • **1.** كَسَّر [kassar] تَكسِير [taksi:r] *vn:* تكَسَّر [tkassar] *p:* The firemen battered in the door and saved the man. رجال الإطفاء كَسّرَوا الباب وَخَلّصَوا الرِّجّال [riǰa:l ʔilʔiṭfa:ʔ kassraw ʔilba:b wxallṣaw ʔirriǰǰa:l]

battered-up • **1.** مهَشَّم [mhaššam] He bought a battered-up old car. اِشتِرَى سَيّارَة عَتِيقَة مُهَشَّمَة [ʔištira: sayya:ra ʕati:ga muhaššama]

battery • **1.** باترِي [pa:tri] باترِيّات [pa:triyya:t] *pl:* My car has to have a new battery. سَيّارتِي يِنرادِلها باترِي جدِيد [sayya:rti yinra:dilha pa:tri ǰdi:d]

battle • **1.** مَعرَكَة [maʕraka] مَعارِك [maʕa:rik] *pl:*

battlefield • **1.** ساحَة المَعرَكَة [sa:ħat ilmaʕraka] مِيدان [mi:da:n] مَيادِين [maya:di:n] *pl:*

battle ship • **1.** بارجَة [ba:riǰa] بَوارِج [bawa:riǰ] *pl:*

to bawl • **1.** صِرَخ [ṣirax] صراخ [ṣra:x] *vn: sv* u. عَيَّط [ʕayyaṭ] عياط [ʕya:ṭ] *vn:* The child has been bawling for an hour. الطِّفِل صارلَه ساعَة دَيُصرُخ [ʔiṭṭifil ṣa:rlah sa:ʕa dayuṣrux]

to bawl out • **1.** رَزَّل [razzal] تَرزِيل، ترِزِّل [tarzi:l, trizzil] *vn:* تَرَزَّل [trazzal] *p:* Why did he bawl you out? لُويش رَزَّلَك؟ [luwi:š razzalak?]

bay • **1.** خَلِيج [xali:ǰ] خِلجان [xilǰa:n] *pl:* There's a steamship anchored out in the bay. أَكُو باخِرَة راسِيَة بِالخَلِيج [ʔaku ba:xira ra:siya bilxali:ǰ]

bayonet • **1.** حَربَة [ħarba] حِراب [ħira:b] *pl:* حراب [ħra:b] حرابات [ħra:ba:t] *pl:*

to be • **1.** كان [ča:n] Are you planning to be there? بنِيتَك تكُون هناك؟ [bni:tak tku:n hna:k?] When will you be at home? شوَقِت راح تكُون بِالبَيت؟ [šwakit ra:ħ tku:n bilbayt?] Where have you been? وين كِنِت؟ [wi:n činit?] I was planning to go with you. كِنِت ناوِي أرُوح وِيّاك [činit na:wi ʔaru:ħ wiyya:k] I wasn't at home when you phoned me. ما كِنِت بِالبَيت مِن خابَرتِني [ma: činit bilbayt min xa:baritni] He had climbed that hill when he was a child. كان متسَلِّق هَالتَّلّ مِن كان جاهِل [ča:n mitsalliq hattall min ča:n ǰa:hil] When I got to the office, he was about to leave. لَمّا وُصَلت الدّائِرَة، كان دَيِطلَع [lamma wuṣalt ʔidda:ʔira, ča:n dayiṭlaʕ] His children were playing with ours. جَهالَه كانَوا دَيلِعبُون ويّا جَهّالنا [ǰaha:lah ča:naw dayilʕabu:n wiyya ǰahha:lna] • **2.** صار [ṣa:r] صَيرَة [ṣayra] *vn: sv* i. Be good while I'm away, children. يا جَهال، صِيرُوا عُقّال بغِيابِي [ya: ǰaha:l, ṣi:ru: ʕuqqa:l bɣiya:bi] Don't be rude! لا تصِير خَشِن [la: tṣi:r xašin] He wants to be an engineer. يرِيد يصِير مُهَندِس [yri:d yṣi:r muhandis] How much is it going to be? شقَدّ راح يصِير؟ [šgadd ra:ħ yṣi:r?] Would it be all right if we used this room? يصِير نِستَعمِل هَالغُرفَة؟ [yṣi:r nistaʕmil halɣurfa?] How much will that be? شقَدّ صار؟ [šgadd ṣa:r?] If that were true, we'd all be rich. لَو هَذا صُدُق، كان كُلّنا صِرنا زَناكِين [law ha:ða ṣudug, ča:n kullna ṣirna zana:gi:n] He has been climbing that hill everyday for years. صارلَه سنِين يِتسَلَّق ذاك التَّلّ كُلّ يوم [ṣa:rlah sni:n yitsallaq ða:k ʔittall kull yu:m] He had already been there a month when he resigned. كان صارلَه شَهَر هناك مِن قَرَّر يِستِقِيل [ča:n ṣa:rlah šahar hna:k min qarrar yistiqi:l] • **3.** How much is this? هَذا بيش؟ [ha:ða biyš?] The man is a merchant. الرِّجّال هُوَّ تاجِر [ʔirriǰǰa:l huwwa ta:ǰir] The man is a merchant. الرِّجّال فَدّ واحِد تاجِر [ʔirriǰǰa:l fadd wa:ħid ta:ǰir] His name is Salih. إسمَه صالِح [ʔismah ṣa:liħ] They are all company employees. كُلّهُم مُستَخدَمِين بِالشَّرِكَة [kullhum mustaxdami:n biššarika] He is ill. هُوَّ مَرِيض [huwwa mari:ð̣] He seems to be ill. يبَيِّن (هُوَّ) مَرِيض [yibayyin (huwwa) mari:ð̣] The children are playing in the street. الجِّهال دَيلِعبُون بِالدَّرُب [ʔiǰǰiha:l dayilʕabu:n biddarub] If I were you, I'd forget the whole thing. لَو آنِي بمَكانَك، أنسَى كُلّشِي [law ʔa:ni bmaka:nak, ʔansa: kullši]

there is, are • **1.** أَكُو [ʔaku] There are five men at the door. أَكُو خَمس رِياجِيل بِالباب [ʔaku xams riya:ǰi:l bilba:b]

there isn't, aren't • **1.** ماكُو [ma:ku] There isn't anyone at home. ماكُو أَحَّد بِالبَيت [ma:ku ʔaħħad bilbayt]

there was, were • **1.** كان أَكُو [ča:n ʔaku] There were many people ahead of me. كان أَكُو هوايَة ناس قَبلِي [ča:n ʔaku hwa:ya na:s gabli]

there wasn't, weren't • **1.** ما كان أَكُو [ma: ča:n ʔaku] There wasn't anyone at the door. ما كان أَكُو أَحَّد بِالباب [ma: ča:n ʔaku ʔaħħad bilba:b]

beach • **1.** بلاج [bila:ǰ] بِلاجات [bila:ǰa:t] *pl:* We built a fire on the beach. شعَلنا نار عالبِلاج [šʕalna na:r ʕalbila:ǰ]

bead • **1.** خِرزَة [xirza] خِرزات، خِرَز [xirza:t, xiraz] *pl:* How many beads are there on this string? كَم خِرزَة أَكُو بهَالخَيط؟ [čam xirza ʔaku bhalxi:ṭ?] • **2.** حَبَّة [ħabba] حَبّات [ħabba:t] *pl:* Beads of sweat covered his forehead. حَبّات العَرَق غَطَّت قُصّتَه [ħabba:t ʔilʕarag ɣaṭṭat guṣṣṭah]

beads • **1.** قلادَة [gla:da] قلادات، قلايِد [gla:da:t, gla:yid] *pl:* قلايِد [gla:yid] قلادات [gla:da:t] *pl:* She lost her beads on the way home from the party. ضَيّعَت قلادَتها بطَرِيقها لِلبَيت مِن الحَفلَة [ð̣ayyʕat gla:datha bṭari:qha lilbayt min ʔilħafla]

prayer beads • **1.** سِبحَة [sibħa] سِبَح [sibaħ] *pl:* I never saw him without his prayer beads in his hand. أَبَد ما شِفتَه مِن غير سِبحَة بإيدَه [ʔabad ma: šiftah min ɣayr sibħa bʔi:dah]

beam • **1.** جِسِر [ǰisir] جسُور، جسُورَة [ǰsu:r, ǰsu:ra] *pl:* The roof was supported by strong beams. السَّقُف كان مَسنُود بجسُور قَوِيَّة [ʔissaguf ča:n masnu:d biǰsu:r qawiyya] • **2.** شَيلمانَة [šaylma:na] شَيلمانات [šaylmana:t] *pl:* شَيلمان [ši:lma:n] *Collective:* The warehouse has a framework of steel beams. المَخزَن هَيكَلَه مِن شَيلمان [ʔilmaxzan haykalah min šaylma:n] • **3.** شُعاع [šuʕa:ʕ] أَشِعَّة [ʔašiʕʕa] *pl:* Throw a beam of light on it. وَجِّه شُعاع ضُوَا عَلَيه [wajǰih šuʕa:ʕ ð̣uwa ʕali:h]

to beam • **1.** أَشرَق [ʔašraq] إشراق [ʔišra:q] *vn: sv* u. Her face beams every time he talks to her. يِشرُق وِجهها كُلّما يحكِي وِيّاها [yišruq wiččha kullma yiħči wiyya:ha] • **2.** شَعّ [šaʕʕ] إشعاع [ʔišʕa:ʕ] *vn: sv* i. The face of the pious man beams with light. وُجِه الرِّجّال الصّالِح يشِعّ نُور [wučč ʔirriǰǰa:l ʔiṣṣa:liħ yšiʕʕ nu:r] • **3.** وَجَّه [wajǰah] تَوجِيه [tawǰi:h] *vn: sv* i.

B

This program is being beamed to the Middle East. هالمَنهَج موَجَّه إِلَى الشَّرق الأَوسَط [halmanhaǰ mwaǰǰah ʔila ʔiššarq ʔilʔawṣaṭ]

beans • **1.** فاصُولِيّات [faṣu:lya, faṣuliyya] فاصُولِيَا، فاصُولِيَّة [faṣuliyya:t] *pl:*
broad beans • **1.** باقِلّاية [ba:gilla:ya] با قِلّايات [ba:gilla:ya:t] *pl:* باقِلّاء [ba:gilla] *Collective*

bear • **1.** دُبّ [dubb] دِبَبَة، دباب [dibaba, dba:b] *pl:* Are there any bears in this forest? أَكُو دِبَبَة بِهالغابَة؟ [ʔaku dibaba bhalɣa:ba?]
to bear • **1.** تحَمَّل [tħammal] تَحَمُّل [taħammul] *vn: sv* a. I can't bear the suspense any longer. ما أَقدَر أَتحَمَّل هالغُمُوض بَعَد [ma: ʔagdar ʔatħammal halɣumu:ð̣ baʕad] He has to bear all the responsibility himself. هُوَّ وَحدَه لازِم يِتحَمَّل كُلّ المَسؤُلِيَّة [huwwa waħdah la:zim yitħammal kull ʔilmasʔuliyya] • **2.** شال [ša:l] شَيل [šayl] *vn:* اِنشال [ʔinša:l] *p:* This date tree didn't bear last year. هالنَّخلَة ما شالَت السَّنَة اللِّي فاتَت [hannaxla ma: ša:lat ʔissana ʔilli fa:tat] • **3.** وِلَد [wilad] وِلادَة [wila:da] *vn:* اِنوِلَد [ʔinwilad] *p:* She bore her first child when she was eighteen. وِلدَت أَوَّل طِفِلها مِن كان عُمُرها ثمَنطَعَش [wildat ʔawwal ṭifilha min ča:n ʕumurha θmanṭaʕaš]
to bear down • **1.** داس [da:s] دَوس [daws] *vn:* اِنداس [ʔinda:s] *p:* Don't bear down so hard on the pencil, it might break. لا تدُوس عالقَلَم حيل، تَرَة يِنكِسِر [la: ddu:s ʕalqalam ħi:l, tara yinkisir] • **2.** توَجَّه [twaǰǰah] *sv* i. The car bore down upon us at a terrible speed. السَّيّارَة توَجّهَت عَلينا بسُرعَة هائلَة [ʔissayya:ra twaǰǰhat ʕali:na bsurʕa ha:ʔla] • **3.** ضِغَط [ð̣iɣaṭ] ضَغِط [ð̣aɣiṭ] *vn:* اِنضِغَط [ʔinð̣iɣaṭ] *p:* The boss is beginning to bear down on us more everyday. المُدِير قام يُضغُط عَلينا أَكثَر يوم عَلَى يوم [ʔilmudi:r ga:m yuð̣ɣuṭ ʕali:na ʔakθar yu:m ʕala yu:m]
to bear fruit • **1.** أَثمَر [ʔaθmar] إِثمار [ʔiθma:r] *vn: sv* i. The apricot trees did not bear much fruit this year. أَشجار المِشمِش ما أَثمِرَت هالسَّنَة [ʔašǰa:r ʔilmišmiš ma: ʔaθmirat hassana] After many years, his efforts finally bore fruit. بَعَد هواية سنِين، جُهُودَه أَخِيراً أَثمِرَت [baʕad hwa:ya sni:n, ǰuhu:dah ʔaxi:ran ʔaθmirat]

bearable • **1.** مُمكِن اِحتِمالَه [mumkin ʔiħtima:lah] It is bearable for a while, but not continually. هَذا مُمكِن اِحتِمالَه فترَة بَسّ مُو عَلَى طُول [ha:ða mumkin ʔiħtima:lah fatra bass mu: ʕala ṭu:l]
to be bearable • **1.** اِنطاق [ʔinṭa:q] إِطاقَة [ʔiṭa:qa] *vn: sv* a. اِنحِمَل [ʔinħimal] اِنحِمال [ʔinħima:l] *vn: sv* i. The heat is still bearable. الحَرّ بَعدَه يِنحِمِل [ʔilħarr baʕdah yinħimil]

beard • **1.** لِحيَة [liħya] لِحايَة، لِحَى [liħa:ya, liħa] *pl:* He has a long beard. هُوَّ مطَوِّل لَه لِحيَة [huwwa mṭawwil lah liħya] I'm letting my beard grow. دَأَرَبِّي لِحِيتي [daʔarabbi liħi:ti]

bearing • **1.** بير [bi:r] بيارَة، آبار [bya:r, ʔa:ba:r] *pl:* This motor needs new bearings. هالمَكِينَة يِنرادِلها بَيرِنات جِدِيدَة [halmaki:na yinra:dilha bi:rina:t ǰidi:da]
to get one's bearing • **1.** عَيَّن [ʕayyan] تَعيِين [taʕyi:n] *vn:* تعَيَّن [tʕayyan] *p:* First let's get our bearings. خَلّي أَوَّل نعَيِّن مَوقِعنا [xalli ʔawwil nʕayyin mawqiʕna]
to have bearing on • **1.** إِلَه عَلاقَة ب [ʔilah ʕala:qa b-] What bearing does that have on what we're doing? هَذاك شلَه عِلاقَة بِالشِّي اللِّي دَنسَوِّيه [haða:k šilah ʕila:qa biššī ʔilli dansawwi:h]

beast • **1.** دابَّة [da:bba] دَوابّ [dawa:bb] *pl:* The horse, the donkey and the mule are beasts of burden. الحصان وَالزُّمال وَالبَغَل دَوابّ [ʔilħṣa:n wizzuma:l wilbaɣal dawa:bb] • **2.** حَيوان [ħaywa:n] حَيوانات [ħaywa:na:t] *pl:* حَواوِين [ħawa:wi:n] حَيوانات [ħaywa:na:t] *pl:* He paced up and down in the room like a caged beast. راح وَجا بالغُرفَة مِثل الحَيوان المَحصُور [ra:ħ wǰa: bilɣurfa miθl ʔilħaywa:n ʔilmaħṣu:r]

beat • **1.** نَبُض [nabuð̣] His heartbeat has become stronger. نَبُض قَلبَه صار أَقوَى [nabuð̣ galbah ṣa:r ʔaqwa:] • **2.** دَقَّة [dagga] دَقّات [dagga:t] *pl:* ضَربَة [ð̣arba] ضَربات [ð̣arba:t] *pl:* Count the heartbeats. إِحسِب دَقّات القَلب [ʔiħsib dagga:t ʔilgalub]
to beat • **1.** ضِرَب [ð̣irab] ضَرُب [ð̣arub] *vn:* اِنضِرَب [ʔinð̣irab] *p:* بُسَط [busaṭ] بَسِط [baṣiṭ] *vn:* اِنبُسَط [ʔinbuṣaṭ] *p:* If you keep on throwing stones at my car, I'll beat you up. إِذا تظَلّ تذِبّ حجار عَلَى سَيّارتي، تَرَة أَبُسطَك [ʔiða dð̣all dð̣ibb ħǰa:r ʕala sayya:rti, tara ʔabusṭak] • **2.** دَقّ [dagg] دَقّ [dagg] *vn:* اِندَقّ [ʔindagg] *p:* If you want to beat your drum, go outside. إِذا ترِيد تدُقّ طَبلَك، إِطلَع بَرَّة [ʔiða tri:d tdugg ṭablak, ʔiṭlaʕ barra] Her heart was beating wildly from fear. قَلبها كان دَيدُقّ حيل مِن الخُوف [galubha ča:n daydugg ħi:l min ʔilxu:f] • **3.** طِرَق [ṭirag] طَرِق [ṭarig] *vn:* اِنطِرَق [ʔinṭirag] *p:* Beat two eggs. أُطرُق بَيضتَين [ʔuṭrug bayð̣tayn] • **4.** غِلَب [ɣilab] غُلُب [ɣulub] *vn:* اِنغِلَب [ʔinɣilab] *p:* We beat them in today's game. إِحنا غلَبناهُم بِاللِّعِب اليُوم [ʔiħna ɣlabna:hum billiʕib ʔilyu:m] • **5.** سِبَق [sibaq] سَبِق [sabiq] *vn:* اِنسِبَق [ʔinsibaq] *p:* He beats me to work every day. يِسبِقنِي لِلشُّغُل كُلّ يوم [yisbiqni liššuɣul kull yu:m]
to beat down • **1.** قَصّ [gaṣṣ] قَصّ [gaṣṣ] *vn:* اِنقَصّ [ʔingaṣṣ] *p:* I was able to beat down the price 10 Dinars. قِدَرِت أَقُصّ عَشِر دَنانِير مِن السِّعِر [gidarit ʔaguṣṣ ʕašir dana:ni:r min ʔissiʕir]
to beat in • **1.** خُبَط [xubaṭ] خَبُط [xabuṭ] *vn:* اِنخُبَط [ʔinxubaṭ] *p:* مِزَج [mizaǰ] مَزِج [maziǰ] *vn:* اِنمِزَج [ʔinmizaǰ] *p: sv* i. Beat the eggs into the mixture. أُخبُطي البَيض بِهالخَلِيط [ʔuxubṭi ʔilbayð̣ bhalxali:ṭ]
to beat off • **1.** طِرَد [ṭirad] طَرِد [ṭarid] *vn:* تطَرَّد [ʔiṭṭarrad] *p:* I beat off the dogs with a club. طَرَّدِت الكِلاب بتُوثِيَّة [ṭarradit ʔiččila:b btu:θiyya]

to beat up • **1.** بُسَط [busaṭ] بَسِط [basiṭ] *vn:* اِنبُسَط [ʔinbusaṭ] *p:* ضِرَب [ðirab] ضَرُب [ðarub] *vn:* اِنضِرَب [ʔinðirab] *p:* قِتَل [kital] قِتِل [katil] *vn:* اِنقِتَل [ʔinkital] *p:* They beat him up. بُسطَوه [busṭawh]
*** Beat it!** • **1.** وَلّي [walli]

beautician • **1.** أخِصّائي بِالتَّجمِيل [ʔaxiṣṣa:ʔi bittaǰmi:l] أخِصّائِيِّين بِالتَّجمِيل [ʔaxiṣṣa:ʔiyyi:n bittaǰmi:l] *pl:*

beautiful • **1.** حِلو [ħilw] جَمِيل [ǰami:l] بَدِيع [badi:ʕ] What a beautiful day! شلُون نَهار حِلو [šlu:n naha:r ħilw] The bride is a beautiful girl. العَرُوس بنَيَّة حِلوَة [ʔilʕaru:s bnayya ħilwa] • **2.** بَداعَة [bada:ʕa] مُمتاز [mumta:z] He did a beautiful job on that. سَوَّى شَغلَة بَداعَة بهٰذا [sawwa: šaɣla bada:ʕa bha:ða]

beautifully • **1.** كُلِّش زَين [kulliš zayn] Your daughter sews beautifully. بِنتَك تخَيِّط كُلِّش زين [bintak txayyiṭ kulliš zi:n]

to beautify • **1.** جَمَّل [ǰammal] تَجمِيل [taǰmi:l] *vn:* تجَمَّل [tǰammal] *p:* The plans for beautifying the city are almost finished. خِطَط تَجمِيل المَدِينَة عَلَى وَشَك أن تِنتِهي [xiṭaṭ taǰmi:l ʔilmadi:na ʕala wašak ʔan tintihi]

beauty • **1.** جَمال [ǰama:l] They stood there a long time enjoying the beauty of the sunset. وُقفوا هناك مُدَّة طُويلَة يتمَتَّعُون بجَمال الغُرُوب [wugfaw hna:k mudda ṭuwi:la yitmattaʕu:n bǰama:l ʔilɣuru:b] • **2.** بَداعَة [bada:ʕa] فَلَّة [falla] فَلّات [falla:t] *pl:* She's a real beauty! هِيَّ بَداعَة [hiyya bada:ʕa] She's a real beauty! هِيَّ صُدُق فَلَّة [hiyya ṣudug falla] The fish we caught were beauties. السِّمَك إلِّي صِدناه كان فَلَّة [ʔissimač ʔilli ṣidna:h ča:n falla]

beauty parlor • **1.** صالُون تَجمِيل [ṣa:lu:n taǰmi:l] صالُونات تَجمِيل [ṣa:lu:na:t taǰmi:l] *pl:*

because • **1.** لِأن [liʔan] سَبَب [sabab] أسباب [ʔasba:b] *pl:* He didn't come because he was sick. ما جا لِأنَّ كان مَرِيض [ma: ǰa: liʔann ča:n mari:ð] I didn't buy it because the price wasn't agreeable to me. ما إشتِرَيتَه لِأنَّ السِّعِر ما وافَقني [ma: ʔištiri:tah liʔann ʔissiʕir ma: wa:faqni]
because of • **1.** لِأن [liʔan] سَبَب [sabab] أسباب [ʔasba:b] *pl:* Ali, I'm going to be late because of you. يا عَلِي، آني راح أتأخَّر بسَبَبَك [ya: ʕali, ʔa:ni ra:ħ ʔatʔaxxar bsababak] • **2.** عَلَى مُود [ʕala mu:d] خاطِر [xa:ṭir] I did it because of her. سَوَّيتَه عَلَى مُودها [sawwi:tah ʕala mu:dha] I don't want you to do it just because of me. ما أرِيدَك تسَوِّيها بَسّ لِخاطِري [ma: ʔari:dak tsawwi:ha bass lixa:ṭiri]

to become • **1.** صار [ṣa:r] *sv* i. أصبَح [ʔaṣbaħ] *sv* a. What became of them? شصار مِنهُم؟ [šṣa:r minhum?] What became of them? وين أصبِحَوا؟ [wi:n ʔaṣbiħaw?] What has become of my purse? جِزداني وِين صار؟ [ǰizda:ni wi:n ṣa:r?] It has become a matter of 'pull'. القَضِيَّة أصبَحَت واسطَة [ʔilqaðiyya ʔaṣbaħat wa:sṭa]

to be becoming • **1.** لاق [la:g] *sv* u. That color is very becoming to you. هَاللَّون هوايَة يلُوقلِك [hallu:n hwa:ya ylu:gič]

bed • **1.** فراش [fra:š] فراشات [fra:ša:t] *pl:* I want a room with two beds. أرِيد غُرفَة بِيها فراشَين [ʔari:d ɣurfa bi:ha fra:šayn] My bed hasn't been made. فراشي ما مسَوَّى [fra:ši ma: msawwa] • **2.** سَرِير [sari:r] سرايِر [sra:yir] *pl:* The government is building a new hospital with 80 beds. الحُكُومَة دَتِبنِي مُستَشفى جِدِيد بيه ثمانِين سَرِير [ʔilħuku:ma datibni mustašfa: ǰidi:d bi:h θma:ni:n sari:r] • **3.** جُربايَة [čurpa:ya] جُربايات، جَرابِي [čurpa:ya:t, čara:pi] *pl:* Where was this bed (stead) made? هَالجَّربايَة وِين مَعمُولَة؟ [haččarpa:ya wi:n maʕmu:la?] • **4.** I want you to weed the rose beds today. أرِيدَك تِشلَع الحَشِيش مِن جَوَّة الوَرد اليُوم [ʔari:dak tišlaʕ ʔilħaši:š min ǰawwa ʔilwarid ʔilyu:m] • **5.** قاعِيَّة [ga:ʕiyya] قاعِيّات [ga:ʕiyya:t] *pl:* Put the box in the middle of the truck bed. حُطّ الصَّندُوق بنُصّ قاعِيَة اللُّورِي [ħuṭṭ ʔiṣṣandu:g bnuṣṣ ga:ʕi:at ʔillawri]
*** He must have gotten up on the wrong side of the bed today.** • **1.** هُوَّ ما أدري بوجه مَن مصَبُّح هَاليَوم [huwwa ma: ʔadri bwiǰǰ man mṣabbuħ halyu:m]
to go to bed • **1.** نام نَوم [na:m, nawm] I went to bed late. نِمِت مِتأخِّر [nimit mitʔaxxir]
to put to bed • **1.** نَوَّم [nawwam] تَنوِيم [tanwi:m] *vn:* تنَوَّم [tnawwam] *p:* نَيَّم [nayyam] تَنوِيم [tanwi:m] *vn:* تنَيَّم [tnayyam] *p:* *sv* i. Tell the nurse to put the children to bed early. قُول لِلمُرَبِّيَة تنَيِّم الجُّهال مِن وَقِت [gu:l lilmurabbiya tnayyim ʔiǰǰaha:l min wakit]
to stay in bed • **1.** بُقَى بِالفراش، ظَلّ بِالفراش [buqa: bilifra:š, ðall bilifra:š] *sv* a. ظَلّ [ðall] *sv* a. He still has to stay in bed. بَعدَه لازِم يبقَى بِالفراش [baʕdah la:zim yibqa: bilfra:š]

bed bug • **1.** بَقَّة الفراش [baggat ʔilifra:š]

bed clothes • **1.** شَرشَف [čarčaf] شَراشِف [čara:čif] *pl:*

bedding • **1.** الفُرش وِالشَّراشِف [ʔilfuriš wiččara:čif] Air the bedding today. هَوِّي الفِرش وَالشَّراشِف هَاليُوم [hawwi ʔilfiriš wiččara:čif halyu:m]

Bedouin • **1.** بَدوِي [badwi, bdiwi, badawi] بَدو [badw] *Collective*

bed pan • **1.** قَعّادَة [qaʕʕa:da] قَعّادات [qaʕʕa:da:t] *pl:*

bed rock • **1.** الطَّبَقَة الصَّخرِيَّة [ʔiṭṭabaqa ʔiṣṣaxriyya]

B

bed room • **1.** غُرفَة نَوم [ɣurfat nawm] غُرَف نَوم [ɣuraf nawm] *pl:* قُبَّة [gubba] قُبَب [gubab] *pl:* قباب نَوم [gba:b nu:m] قُبَب نَوم [gubab nu:m] *pl:*

bedspread • **1.** شَرشَف [čarčaf] شَراشِف [čara:čif] *pl:* غِطا مال فراش [ɣiṭa: ma:l fra:š] شَراشِف [čara:čif] *pl:*

bedstead • **1.** سَرِير [sari:r] سرَايِر [sra:yir] pl: (wooden) جَربايَة [čarba:ya] (metal)

bee • **1.** نَحلَة [naħla] نَحلات [naħla:t] *pl:* زَنبُور [zanbu:r] زنابِير [zna:bi:r] *pl:*

beech tree • **1.** زان [za:n]

beef • **1.** لَحَم هَوش [laħam hu:š] Do you like beef? تحِبّ لَحم الهُوش؟ [tħibb laħm ʔilhu:š?]

beehive • **1.** كُورَة نَحَل [ku:rat naħal] كُوَر نَحَل [kuwar naħal] *pl:* كُورَة زَنابِير [ku:rat zana:bi:r] كُوَر زَنابِير [kuwar zana:bi:r] *pl:*

beer • **1.** بِيرَة [bi:ra] بيرات [bi:ra:t] *pl:* I'd like a glass of beer, please. أرِيد فَدّ كلاص بِيرَة، رَجاءاً [ʔari:d fadd gla:ṣ bi:ra, raǰa:ʔan]

beet • **1.** شوَندَرَة [šwandara, šwanðara] شوَنذَرات [šwandara, šwanðara:t] *pl:* شوَندَر [šwandar] *Collective*

beetle • **1.** خَنفَس [xanfas] خُنفُسان [xunfusa:n] *Collective:* The beetles have eaten all the leaves. الخُنفُسان أكلَوا كُلّ وَرَق الشَّجَر [ʔilxunǰusa:n ʔaklaw kull waraq ʔiššaǰar]

before • **1.** قَبُل [gabul, qabil] I'll be there before two o'clock. راح أكُون هناك قَبل السّاعَة ثنَين [ra:ħ ʔaku:n hna:k gabil ʔissa:ʕa θnayn] The telegram should be there before evening. البَرقِيَّة لازم تُوصَل هناك قَبل المَغرُب [ʔilbarqiyya la:zim tu:ṣal hna:k gabil ʔilmaɣrub] Call me up before you come. خابُرنِي قَبُل ما تِجي [xa:burni gabul ma: tiji]

*** Business before pleasure.** • **1.** الشُغُل قَبل اللِّعِب [ʔiššuɣul gabl ʔilliʕib]

before long • **1.** بَعد شوَيَّة [baʕd šwayya] Before long he'll be able to help you. راح يِقدَر يعاونَك بَعد شوَيَّة [ra:ħ yigdar yʕa:wnak baʕd šwayya] • **2.** ظَلّ شوَيَّة [ðall šwayya] Before long the money we've been saving will come to a hundred dinars. ظَلّ شوَيَّة والفلُوس اللي دَنلِمها تصِير مِيَّة دِينار [ðall šwayya wilflu:s ʔilli danlimmha tṣi:r miyyat dina:r]

never ... before • **1.** ما [ma:] بعُمر ما [bʕumr ma:] I've never been there before. آني ما رايح لِهناك قَبُل أبَد [ʔa:ni ma: ra:yiħ lihna:k gabul ʔabad] I've never been there before. بعُمري ما رِحت لِهناك [bʕumri ma: riħit lihna:k]

the day before • **1.** قَبل بيوم [gabl byu:m] It had rained the day before. مُطرَت قَبِل بِيُوم [muṭrat gabil byu:m] • **2.** اليُوم السابِق ل [ʔalyu:m ʔissa:biq l-] I didn't get my passport until the day before I left. ما حَصَّلِت باسبَورتِي لِليوم السّابِق لِسَفَري [ma: ħaṣṣalit pa:ṣpu:rti lilyu:m ʔissa:biq lisafari]

the day before yesterday • **1.** أوَّل البارحَة [ʔawwal ʔilba:rħa] He was here the day before yesterday. كان هنا أوَّل البارحَة [ča:n hna ʔawwal ʔilba:rħa]

beforehand • **1.** لِقِدّام [ligidda:m] I knew it beforehand. آنِي عرَفِتها لِقِدّام [ʔa:ni ʕrafitha ligidda:m]

to beg • **1.** جَدَّى [ǰadda:] جِديَة [ǰidya] *vn: sv* i. He spends most of his day begging in the market. يِقضِي مُعظَم يَومَه يجَدِّي بالسُّوق [yigði muʕðam yu:mah yǰaddi bissu:g] • **2.** توَسَّل ب [twassal b-] توسِّل، تَوَسُّل [twissil, tawassul] *vn: sv* a. The children begged their father for some money. الأطفال توَسّلَوا بأبُوهُم عَلَى كَم فِلِس [ʔilʔaṭfa:l twasslaw bʔabu:hum ʕala čam filis] They begged us to help them. توَسّلَوا بِينا نساعِدهُم [twasslaw bi:na nsa:ʕidhum]

beggar • **1.** مجَدِّي [mǰaddi, mgaddi] مجادِي [mǰa:di, mga:di] *pl:* There's a beggar at the door. أكُو مجَدِّي بِالباب [ʔaku mǰaddi bilba:b]

*** Beggars can't be choosers.** • **1.** لازِم نِرضَى بِالمَقسُوم [la:zim nirða: bilmaqsu:m] / البُطَر مُو زين [ʔilbuṭar mu: zi:n]

to begin • **1.** بِدا [bida:] بَدوَة، بِدايَة [badwa, bida:ya] *vn:* اِنبِدا [ʔinbida:] *p:* When did you begin working in your present job? شوَقِت بِدَيت تِشتُغُل بوَظِيفتَك الجِّدِيدَة؟ [šwakit bidi:t tištuɣul bwaði:ftak ʔiǰǰidi:da?] • **2.** بَلَّش [ballaš] تَبلِيش [tabli:š] *vn:* تبَلَّش [tballaš] *p:* The oil company has begun drilling. شَرِكَة النَّفُط بَلّشَت بِالحَفُر [šarikat ʔinnafuṭ ballšat bilħafur] As soon as they met on the street, they began to curse one another. مِن تلاقَوا بِالشّارِع بَلّشَوا يشَتّمُون واحِد عَاللّاخ [min tla:gaw biššа:riʕ ballšaw yšattmu:n wa:ħid ʕalla:x] • **3.** قام [ga:m] قِيام [qiya:m] *vn: sv* u. All at once, the donkey began to bray. فُجأَةً، الزمال قام يجَوعِر [fuǰʔatan, ʔizzima:l ga:m yǰawʕir]

to begin with • **1.** أوَّلاً [ʔawwalan] قَبُل كُلّشِي [gabul kullši] To begin with, we haven't got enough money. أوَّلاً، ما عِدنا فلُوس كافيَة [ʔawwalan, ma: ʕidna flu:s ka:fya]

beginner • **1.** مُبتَدِئ [mubtadiʔ] مُبتَدِئِين [mubtadiʔi:n] *pl:* He's still a beginner. بَعدَه مُبتَدِئ [baʕdah mubtadiʔ]

beginning • **1.** بِدايَة [bida:ya] بِدايات [bida:ya:t] *pl:* The box office remains open until 10 minutes after the beginning of the film. مَحَلّ البِطاقات يِبقَى مَفتُوح عَشِر دَقايِق بَعَد بِدايَة الفِلِم [maħall ʔilbiṭa:qa:t yibqa: maftu:ħ ʕašir daqa:yiq baʕad bida:yat ʔilfilim]

B

to begrudge • **1.** حِسَد [ħisad] حَسَد [ħasad] *vn: sv* i. Why should he begrudge me my job? لِيش يِحسِدنِي عَلَى وَظِيفتِي؟ [liːš yiħsidni ʕala waðiːfti?] I don't begrudge him his success, he deserves it. ما أَحِسدَه عَلَى نَجاحَه، هُوَّ يِستَحِقَّه [maː ʔaħisdah ʕala najaːħah, huwwa yistaħiqqah]

on behalf of • **1.** بالنِيابَة عَن [binniyaːba ʕan] I want to thank you on behalf of our organization. أَحِبّ أَشكُرَك بِالنِّيابَة عَن مُؤَسَّستنا [ʔaħibb ʔaškurak binniyaːba ʕan muʔassasatna]

to behave • **1.** تصَرَّف [tṣarraf] تَصَرُّف [taṣarruf] *vn: sv* a. He doesn't know how to behave. ما يُعرُف شلُون يِتصَرَّف [maː yuʕruf šluːn yitṣarraf] • **2.** تأَدَّب [tʔaːddab] تَأَدُّب [taʔaddub] *vn: sv* a. حَسَّن [ħassan] تَحسِين [taħsiːn] *vn:* تحَسَّن [tħassan] *p:* Behave yourself! تأَدَّب، حَسِّن سِلُوكَك [tʔaddab, ħassin siluːkak] Behave yourself! صِير خُوش وَلَد [ṣiːr xuːš walad]

behind • **1.** وَرا [wara] There's a garage behind the house. أَكُو كَراج وَرا البَيت [ʔaku garaːǰ wara ʔilbayt] The attack came from behind. إجا الهُجُوم مِن وَرا [ʔiǰa ʔilhuǰuːm min wara]

to be behind • **1.** تأَخَّر [tʔaxxar] تَأَخُّر، تَأخِير [taʔaxxur, taʔxiːr] *vn: sv* a. My watch is always ten minutes behind. ساعَتِي دائِماً مِتأَخرَة عَشِر دَقايِق [saːʕati daːʔiman mitʔaxxra ʕašir daqaːyiq] • **2.** أَيَّد [ʔayyad] تَأيِيد [taʔyiːd] *vn:* تأَيَّد [tʔayyad] *p:* All the people are behind the president of the republic. كُلّ النّاس يأَيِّدُون رَئِيس الجَّمهُورِيَّة [kull ʔinnaːs yʔayyiduːn raʔiːs ʔiǰǰamhuːriyya] • **3.** وَرا [wara] Who's behind this project? مِنُو وَرا هَالمَشرُوع؟ [minu wara halmašruːʕ?]

to fall behind • **1.** تأَخَّر [tʔaxxar] تَأَخُّر [taʔaxxur] *vn: sv* a. He has fallen behind in his work. هُوَّ مِتأَخِّر بِشُغلَه [huwwa mitʔaxxir bšuɣlah]

to leave behind • **1.** تِرَك [tirak] تَرك [tarik] *vn:* اِنتِرَك [ʔintirak] *p:* We had to leave our trunk behind. اِضطَرَّينا نِترُك صَندُوقنا [ʔiðṭarriːna nitruk ṣanduːgna] • **2.** خَلَّى [xallaː] *sv* i. We left the dog behind to watch the house. خَلِّينا الكَلِب يدِير بالَه عَالبَيت [xalliːna ʔiččalib ydiːr baːlah ʕalbayt]

belch • **1.** تَريُوعَة [taryuːʕa] تَريُوعات [taryuːʕaːt] *pl:*

to belch • **1.** تتَريَع [ttaryaʕ, ʔittaryaʕ] ترِيِيع [tiryiːʕ] *vn: sv* a. He ate radishes and began belching a lot. أَكَل فِجِل وَقام يِتَّريَع هواية [ʔakal fiǰil wgaːm yittaryaʕ hwaːya]

Belgian • **1.** بَلجِيكِي [balǰiːki] بَلجِيكِيِّين [balǰiːkiyyiːn] *pl:*

Belgium • **1.** بَلجِيكا [balǰiːka]

belief • **1.** إيمان [ʔiːmaːn] My belief in him was seriously shaken. إيمانِي بِيه ضِعَف كُلِّش هوايَة [ʔiːmaːni biːh ðiʕaf kulliš hwaːya] • **2.** اِعتِقاد [ʔiʕtiqaːd] إعتِقادات [ʔiʕtiqaːdaːt] *pl:* Belief in superstitions is wide-spread among illiterates. الاعتِقاد بِالخُرافات شايِع بين الأُمِّيِّين [ʔilʔiʕtiqaːd bilxuraːfaːt šaːyiʕ bayn ʔilʔummiyyiːn]

to believe • **1.** صَدَّق [ṣaddag] تَصدِيق [taṣdiːg] *vn:* تصَدَّق [tṣaddag] *p:* Don't believe anything he says. لا تصَدِّق أَيّ شِي اللِّي يقُولَه [laː tṣaddig ʔayy ši ʔilli yguːlah] • **2.** اِعتِقَد [ʔiʕtiqad] اِعتِقاد [ʔiʕtiqaːd] *vn: sv* i. I don't believe he did it. آنِي ما أَعتِقِد هُوَّ سَوّاها [ʔaːni maː ʔaʕtiqid huwwa sawwaːha]

to believe in • **1.** آمَن ب [ʔaːman b-] *sv* i. Do you believe in his sincerity? إِنتَ تآمِن بإخلاصَه؟ [ʔinta tʔaːmin bʔixlaːṣah?]

bell • **1.** جَرَس [ǰaras] أجراس [ʔaǰraːs] *pl:* The bell doesn't work. الجَّرَس ما يِشتُغُل [ʔiǰǰaras maː yištuɣul]

belligerent • **1.** مُشاكِس [mušaːkis] مُشاكِسِين [mušaːkisiːn] *pl:* He is always belligerent and rude to the people that work with him. هُوَّ دائِماً مُشاكِس وَخَشِن وِيّا النّاس اللِّي يِشتَغلُون وِيّاه [huwwa daːʔiman mušaːkis wxašin wiyya ʔinnaːs ʔilli yištaɣluːn wiyyaːh] • **2.** مِتحارُب [mitħaːrub] مِتحارُبِين [mitħaːrubiːn] *pl:* They have arranged a truce between the two belligerent nations. دَبّرَوا هُدنَة بين الدَّولتَين المِتحارُبتَين [dabbiraw hudna bayn ʔiddawiltayn ʔilmitħaːrubtayn] • **3.** مِتخاصُم [mitxaːṣum] مِتخاصُمِين [mitxaːṣumiːn] *pl:* The leaders of both the belligerent parties have been arrested. زُعَماء الفَرِيقَين المِتخاصمَين توَقفَوا [zuʕamaːʔ ʔilfariːqayn ʔilmitxaːṣmayn twaqqfaw]

bellows • **1.** مِنفاخ [minfaːx] مَنافِيخ [manaːfiːx] *pl:* Where can I buy a pair of bellows? وِين أَقدَر أَشتِرِي مِنفاخ؟ [wiːn ʔagdar ʔaštiri minfaːx?] • **2.** جراب [ǰraːb] جُربان [ǰurbaːn] *pl:* The bellows on my camera is ripped. Can you fix it? الجّراب مال كامَيرتِي مَشقُوق، تِقدَر تصَلّحَه؟ [ʔiǰǰraːb maːl kamiraːti mašguːg, tigdar tṣallħah?]

belly • **1.** بَطِن [baṭin] بطُون [bṭuːn] *pl:* This strap goes around the horse's belly. هَالسِّير يِلتَفّ عَلَى بَطن الحِصان [hassiːr yiltaff ʕala baṭn ʔilħiṣaːn] The plane made a forced landing and slid two hundred meters on its belly. الطَّيّارَة نِزلَت نِزُول اِضطِرارِي وَزِحفَت عَلَى بَطِنها مِيتَين مَتِر [ʔiṭṭiyyaːra nizlat nizuːl ʔiðṭiraːri wziħfat ʕala baṭinha mitayn matir] • **2.** كَرِش [kariš] كرُوش [kruːš] *pl:* He has a very big belly. عِندَه كَرِش كِبِير [ʕindah kariš čibiːr]

to belong to • **1.** عاد ل- [ʕaːd li-] *sv* u. This building belongs to the oil company. هَالبِنايَة تعُود لِشَركَة النَّفُط [halbinaːya tʕuːd lišarikat ʔinnafuṭ] • **2.** خَصّ [xaṣṣ] *sv* u. These files belong to the Personnel Section. هالفايلات تخُصّ شُعبَة الذّاتِيَّة [halfaːylaːt txuṣṣ šuʕbat ʔiððaːtiyya] • **3.** مال [maːl] أَموال [ʔamwaːl] *pl:* Who does this car belong to? هَالسَّيّارَة مال مَن؟

B

[hassayya:ra ma:l man?] • **4.** عُضُو ب [ʕuðw b-] He also belongs to the club. هُوَّ هَمّ عُضُو بِالنّادِي [huwwa hamm ʕuðw binna:di]

below • **1.** جَوَّة [ǰawwa] The temperature here seldom gets below zero. دَرَجَة الحَرارَة هنا نادِر تِنزِل جَوَّة الصِّفِر [darajat ʔilħara:ra hna na:dir tinzil ǰawwa ʔiṣṣifi r] • **2.** تَحت [taħit, taħat] The Dead Sea is below sea-level. البَحَر المَيِّت تَحَت مُستَوَى البَحَر [ʔilbaħar ʔilmayyit taħat mustawa ʔilbaħar]

belt • **1.** حزام [ħza:m] حِزِم [ħizim] *pl:* Do you wear a belt? تِلبَس حزام؟ [tilbas ħza:m?] • **2.** قايِش [qa:yiš] قايِشات، قَوايِش [qa:yiša:t, qawa:yiš] *pl:* My pump needs a new belt. مَكِينتِي يِراد إلها قايِش جِدِيد [maki:nti yira:d ʔilha ga:yiš ǰidi:d]

*** He's got a few under his belt.** • **1.** شِربلَه كَم بَيك [širablah čam pi:k]

*** That's hitting below the belt.** • **1.** هَذِي نَذالَة [ha:ði naða:la]

bench • **1.** مَسطَبَة [masṭaba] مَسطَبات [masṭaba:t] *pl:* مَصطَبَة [maṣṭaba, muṣṭaba] مَصاطِب، مَصطَبات [maṣa:ṭub, maṣṭaba:t] *pl:* The benches were just painted. المَسطَبات تَوّها مَصبُوغَة [ʔilmasṭaba:t tawwha maṣbu:ɣa]

bend • **1.** لَوفَة [lawfa] لَوِيَة [lawya] لَويات [lawya:t] *pl:* We can cross the river at the bend. نِقدَر عُوَّج الشَّطّ بِاللَّوفَة [nigdar nuʕbur ʔiššaṭṭ billawfa]

to bend • **1.** عِوَج [ʕiwaǰ] عَوَج [ʕawaǰ] *vn:* اِنعُوَج [ʔinʕuwaǰ] *p:* لُوَى [luwa:] لَوِي [lawy] *vn:* اِنلُوَى [ʔinluwa:] *p: sv* i. He bent the wire. عُوَّج السِّيم [ʕuwwaǰ ʔissi:m] • **2.** مال [ma:l] مَيل، مَيَلان [mayl, mayala:n] *vn: sv* i. The tree bends when the wind blows. الشَّجَرَة تمِيل مِن يهِبّ الهَوا [ʔiššaǰara tmi:l min yhibb ʔilhawa] • **3.** حِنَى [ħina:] حَنِي [ħany] *vn:* اِنحِنَى [ʔinħina:] *p:* Bend your head forward. إحنِي راسَك لِقِدّام [ʔiħni ra:sak ligidda:m]

*** We must bend every effort.** • **1.** لازِم نِبذِل كُلّ مَجهُود [la:zim nibðil kull majhu:d]

to bend down • **1.** نَصَّى [naṣṣa:] تَنصِيَة [tanṣiya] *vn:* تنَصَّى [tnaṣṣa:] *p:* I can't bend down. آنِي ما أقدَر أنَصِّي [ʔa:ni ma: ʔagdar ʔanaṣṣi]

beneath • **1.** جَوَّة [ǰawwa] He was buried beneath the tree. هُوَّ اِندِفَن جَوَّة الشَّجَرَة [huwwa ʔindifan ǰawwa ʔiššaǰara] I put it beneath all the other papers. خَلِّيتها جَوَّة كُلّ الأوراق الأُخرَى [xalli:tha ǰawwa kull ʔilʔawra:q ʔilʔuxra:] • **2.** أنزَل [ʔanzal] That's beneath his level. هَذِيك أنزَل مِن مُستَواه [haði:č ʔanzal min mustawa:h]

benefactor • **1.** نَصِير [naṣi:r] نُصَراء [nuṣara:ʔ] *pl:* عَضِيد [ʕaði:d] عُضَداء [ʕuðada:ʔ] *pl:* He was both a friend and a benefactor to me. كانلِي صَدِيق وَعَضِيد [ča:nli ṣadi:q wʕaði:d]

beneficial • **1.** مُفِيد [mufi:d] مُفِيدِين [mufi:di:n] *pl:* نافِع [na:fiʕ] نافِعِين [na:fiʕi:n] *pl:* The new treatment has proved very beneficial to my back. العِلاج الجِّدِيد أثبَت كَونَه جِدّاً مُفِيد لِظَهرِي [ʔilʕila:ǰ ʔiǰǰidi:d ʔaθbat kawnah ǰiddan mufi:d lǒðahri]

beneficiary • **1.** مُستَفِيد [mustafi:d] مُستَفِيدِين [mustafi:di:n] *pl:* He made me the beneficiary of his life insurance policy. سَوّانِي المُستَفِيد مِن عَقد التَّأمِين عَلَى حَياتَه [sawwa:ni ʔilmustafi:d min ʕagd ʔittaʔmi:n ʕala ħaya:tah]

benefit • **1.** فائِدَة [fa:ʔida] فَوائِد [fawa:ʔid] *pl:* I don't expect to get any benefit out of it. ما أتوَقَّع أحَصِّل أيّ فائِدَة مِنها [ma: ʔatwaqqaʕ ʔaħaṣṣil ʔayy fa:ʔida minha]

to benefit • **1.** فاد [fa:d] فائِدَة [fa:ʔida] *vn:* إنفاد [ʔinfa:d] *p: sv* i. The trip did not benefit us much. السَّفرَة ما فادَتنا هوايَة [ʔissafra ma: fa:datna hwa:ya]

bent • **1.** مِنحِنِي [minħini] He is bent with age. هُوَّ مِنحِنِي مِن الكُبُر [huwwa minħini min ʔilkubur] • **2.** أعوَج [ʔaʕwaǰ] عُوج [ʕu:ǰ] *pl:* عوجَة [ʕu:ǰa] *Feminine:* The nail is bent. البِسمار أعوَج [ʔilbisma:r ʔaʕwaǰ] • **3.** مايِل [ma:yil] The tree is bent from the force of the wind. الشَّجَرَة مايلَة مِن قُوَّة الهَوا [ʔiššaǰara ma:yla min quwwat ʔilhawa] • **4.** مِتقَوِّس [mitqawwis] مُقَوَّس [muqawwas] His leg is bent this way because he had rickets when he was young. رِجلَه مقَوَّسَة هِيكِي لِأنّ صار بِيه مَرَض الكُساح مِن كان جاهِل [rijlah mqawwsa hi:či liʔann ṣa:r bi:h marað ʔilkusa:ħ min ča:n ǰa:hil]

bent out of shape • **1.** مَعوُوج [maʕwu:ǰ] The pan is all bent out of shape. الجِّدِر كُلّه مِتعَوِّج [ʔiǰǰidir kullah mitʕawwiǰ]

berry • **1.** no generic equivalent; see specific kinds

berth • **1.** مَنام [mana:m] فراش [fra:š] فُرِش [furiš] *pl:* I couldn't get a berth in the late train. ما قِدَرت أحَصِّل عَلَى مَنام بِالقِطار الأخِير [ma: gidarit ʔaħaṣṣil ʕala mana:m bilqiṭa:r ʔilʔaxi:r]

*** Whenever I see her I try to give her a wide berth.** • **1.** كُلّ ما أشُوفها أحاوِل أتجَنَّبها [kull ma: ʔašu:fha ʔaħa:wil ʔatǰannabha]

beside • **1.** يَمّ [yamm] Please put this trunk beside the other one. أرجُوك حُطّ هَالصَّندُوق يَمّ الصَّندُوق اللّاخ [ʔarǰu:k ħuṭṭ haṣṣandu:q yamm ʔiṣṣandu:q ʔilla:x] Who's that standing beside your father? مِنو ذاك الواقُف يَمّ أبُوك؟ [minu: ða:k ʔilwa:guf yamm ʔabu:k?]

*** That's beside the point.** • **1.** هَذِي وَحَّد [ha:ði waħħad]

to be beside oneself • **1.** تخَبَّل [txabbal] خبال [xba:l] *vn: sv* a. He was beside himself when he heard the news. تخَبَّل خبال مِن سِمَع الخَبَر [txabbal xba:l min simaʕ ʔilxabar] He was beside himself with rage.

كان مِتخَبُّل مِن الغَضَب [čaːn mitxabbul min ʔilɣaðab] She was beside herself with grief. كانَت مِتخَبّلَة مِن الحِزن [čaːnat mitxabbla min ʔilħizin]

besides • **1.** بالإضافَة إلَى [bilʔiðaːfa ʔila] Besides his being a large landowner, he has a soap factory. بالإضافَة إلَى كَومَة مَزارِع عِندَه مَعمَل صابُون [bilʔiðaːfa ʔila kawma mazaːriʕ ʕindah maʕmal ṣaːbuːn] • **2.** عَلاوَة عَلَى [ʕalaːwa ʕala] He's a good worker, and besides, everybody likes him. هُوَّ شاغُول وَعَلاوَة عَلَى ذاك كُلّ واحِد يحِبَّه [huwwa šaːɣuːl wʕalaːwa ʕala ðaːk kull waːħid yħibbah] • **3.** كمالَة [čmaːla] كمالات [čmaːlaːt] *pl:* And besides, he is not related to me. وَكمالَة، هُوَّ مُو قَرايبِي [wačmaːla, huwwa muː garaːybi] • **4.** فوق [fuːg] Besides his wages, he gets tips. فُوق أُجُورَه يحَصِّل بَخشِيش [fuːg ʔujuːrah yħaṣṣil baxšiːš]

best • **1.** أَحسَن [ʔaħsan] We don't want anything but the best. إحنا ما نرِيد غير الأَحسَن [ʔiħna maː nriːd ɣiːr ʔilʔaħsan] I work best in the morning. الصُّبُح أَحسَن وَقِت أَقدَر أَشتُغُل بِيه [ʔiṣṣubuħ ʔaħsan wakit ʔagdar ʔaštuɣul biːh] I think this is the best way. أَعتِقِد هَذِي أَحسَن طَرِيقَة [ʔaʕtiqid haːði ʔaħsan ṭariːqa] • **2.** أَعَزّ [ʔaʕazz] He's my best friend. هُوَّ أَعَزّ أَصدِقائِي [huwwa ʔaʕazz ʔaṣdiqaːʔi] • **3.** أَزيَد شِي [ʔazyad ši] I like your hair best this way. شَعرِك يعجِبنِي هِيكِي أَزيَد شِي [šaʕrič yiʕjibni hiːči ʔazyad ši]

*** Perhaps it's all for the best.** • **1.** بَلكِي بِيها الخَير [balki biːha ʔilxayr]

at best • **1.** مَهما يكُون [mahma ykuːn] شما يكُون [šmaː ykuːn] At best, potatoes are a very poor substitute for rice. مَهما تكُون، البُتَيتَة مُو خُوش بَدَل لِلتِّمَّن [mahmaː tkuːn, ʔilputayta muː xuːš badal littimman]

to get the best of • **1.** قَشمَر [qašmar] قَشمَرَة [qašmara] *vn:* تقَشمَر [tqašmar] *p:* We have to be careful that he doesn't get the best of us. لازِم ندِير بالنّا حَتَّى لا يقَشمُرنا [laːzim ndiːr baːlna ħatta laː yqašmurna] • **2.** غِلَب [ɣilab] غُلُب [ɣulub] *vn: sv* u. I think we got the best of this bargain. أَعتِقِد غلَبنا بِهَالصَّفقَة [ʔaʕtiqid ɣlabna bhaṣṣafqa]

*** This cold will get the best of me.** • **1.** هَالنَّشلَة ما راح تخَلِّي بِيّا حَيل [hannašla maː raːħ txalli biyya]

to make the best of • **1.** رِضَى ب [riðaː b-] رَضِي [raði] *vn: sv* a. We don't like our new apartment, but we'll have to make the best of it. ما عِجبَتنا شُقَّتنا الجِّدِيدَة لَكِن لازِم نِرضَى بِيها [maː ʕijbatna šuqqatna ʔijjidiːda laːkin laːzim nirðaː biːha]

bet • **1.** رَهَن [rahan] رُهُون [ruhuːn] *pl:* When are you going to pay me the bet? شوَقِت راح تِدفَعلِي الرَّهَن؟ [šwakit raːħ tidfaʕli ʔirrahan?]

*** That's your best bet.** • **1.** هَذاك أَحسَن شِي إلَك [haðaːk ʔaħsan ši ʔilak]

to bet • **1.** تراهَن عَلَى [traːhan ʕala] تَراهُن [taraːhun] *vn: sv* a. Want to bet? تِتراهَن؟ [titraːhan?] • **2.** راهَن [raːhan] مُراهَنَة [muraːhana] *vn: sv* i. I'll bet you haven't seen anything like this before. أَراهنَك إنتَ ما شايِف شِي مِثِل هَذا قَبُل [ʔaraːhnak ʔinta maː šaːyif ši miθil haːða gabul]

to bet on • **1.** لِعَب عَلَى [liʕab ʕala] لِعِب [liʕib] *vn:* انلِعَب [ʔinliʕab] *p:* تراهَن عَلَى [traːhan ʕala] *sv* a. I bet five dinars on the black horse. آنِي أَلعَب خَمس دَنانِير عالحصان الأَسوَد [ʔaːni ʔalʕab xams danaːniːr ʕalħṣaːn ʔilʔaswad]

to betray • **1.** خان [xaːn] خانات [xaːnaːt] *pl:* خِيانَة [xiyaːna] *vn:* اِنخان [ʔinxaːn] *p:* He betrayed his best friend. خان أَحسَن أَصدِقائَه [xaːn ʔaħsan ʔaṣdiqaːʔah] • **2.** خَيَّب [xayyab] تَخيِيب [taxyiːb] *vn: sv* i. She betrayed my confidence. هِيَّ خَيِّبَت ثِقتِي [hiyya xayybat θiqati]

better • **1.** أَحسَن [ʔaħsan] Don't you have a better room? ما عِندَك غُرفَة أَحسَن؟ [maː ʕindak ɣurfa ʔaħsan?] They got better after they had practiced a little. صارَوا أَحسَن بَعَد ما تمَرّنَوا شوَيَّة [ṣaːraw ʔaħsan baʕad maː tmarrnaw šwayya] Do you feel better? تِشعُر أَحسَن؟ [tišʕur ʔaħsan?] We'd better go before it rains. أَحسَن نرُوح قَبُل ما تُمطُر [ʔaħsan nruːħ gabul maː tumṭur] You'd better go. أَحسَنلَك لَو ترُوح [ʔaħsanlak law truːħ]

to be better off • **1.** أَحسَن لِ [ʔaħsan l-] We'll be better off if we move to another house. أَحسَن إلنا إذا نِتحَوَّل لِغير بَيت [ʔaħsan ʔilna ʔiða nitħawwal lɣayr bayt] • **2.** أَحسَن [ʔaħsan] We used to be better off before the war. حالَتنا كانَت أَحسَن قَبِل الحَرُب [ħaːlatna čaːnat ʔaħsan gabil ʔilħarub] We'd have been better off without his help. كان أَحسَن إلنا بِلا مُساعَدَة مِنَّه [čaːn ʔaħsan ʔilna bila musaːʕada minnah]

to get the better of • **1.** غِلَب [ɣilab] غُلُب [ɣulub] *vn:* اِنغِلَب [ʔinɣilab] *p:* He tried to get the better of you. راد يغُلبَك [raːd yɣulbak]

between • **1.** بَين [bayn, biːn] We'll meet between six and seven. راح نِتلاقَى بين السِّتَّة وَالسَّبعَة [raːħ nitlaːgaː biːn ʔissitta wissabʕa] • **2.** بِينات [biːnaːt] بَين [bayn] This is just between you and me. هَذِي بَينِي وبينَك [haːði bayni wbiːnak] Just between us, it's his own fault. الحَكِي بَيناتنا، تَرَة صُوجَه [ʔilħači baynaːtna, tara ṣuːčah]

*** Honest people are few and far between.** • **1.** الخَوش أوادِم قَلِيلِين ونادِر يِلتِقُون [ʔilxawš ʔawaːdim qaliːliːn wnaːdir yiltiguːn]

beverage • **1.** مَشرُوب [mašruːb] مَشارِيب [mašaːriːb] *pl:* • **2.** مُرَطِّبات [murattibaːt]

to beware of • **1.** تقَيَّد مِن [tqayyad min] تَقَيُّد [taqayyud] *vn: sv* a. Beware of him! تقَيَّد مِنَّه [tqayyad minnah] • **2.** تقَيَّد مِن [tqayyad min] تَقَوُّد مِن [taqayyud min] *vn: sv* i. Beware of pickpockets! دِير بالَك مِن ضَرّابِين الجِّيُوب [diːr baːlak min ðarraːbiːn ʔijjiyuːb]

B

to bewilder • **1.** تحَيَّر [tħayyar] تَحَيُّر [taħayyur] *vn: sv* a. I was completely bewildered. تحَيَّرت تماماً [tħayyarit tama:man]

beyond • **1.** غادِي [ɣa:di] The house is beyond the river. البَيت غادِي مِن الشَّطّ [ʔilbayt ɣa:di min ʔiššaṭṭ] • **2.** وَرا [wara] The house is right beyond the hospital. البَيت وَرا المُستَشفى تَماماً [ʔilbayt wara ʔilmustašfa tama:man] • **3.** أكثَر مِن [ʔakθar min] فَوق [fu:g] We are living beyond our means. دَنُصرُف أكثَر مِن طاقَتنا [danuṣruf ʔakθar min ṭa:qatna] Our neighbors are living beyond their means. جيرانّا دَيعيشُون فُوق مُستَواهُم [ǰi:ra:nna dayʕi:šu:n fu:g mustawa:hum]

*** He is beyond help.** • **1.** ما تصِيرلَه چارَة [maṭṣi:rla ča:ra]

to go beyond • **1.** فاق [fa:q, fa:g] *sv* u. That goes beyond my authority. هَذا يفُوق سُلُطتِي [ha:ða yfu:q suluṭṭi]

biased • **1.** مِتحَيِّز [mitħayyiz] مُغرِض [muɣrið] He is very biased. هُوَّ كُلِّش مِتحَيِّز [huwwa kulliš mitħayyiz]

Bible • **1.** الكِتاب المُقَدَّس [ʔilkita:b ʔilmuqaddas]

bicarbonate of soda • **1.** كاربُون [karbu:n]

bicycle • **1.** بايسِكِل [pa:ysikil, ba:ysikil] بايسِكِلات [pa:ysikila:t, ba:ysikila:t] *pl:* دَرّاجَة [darra:ǰa] دَرّاجات [darra:ǰa:t] *pl:* My bicycle needs fixing. البايسِكِل مالِي يِرّادلَه تَصليح [ʔilpa:ysikil ma:li yirra:dlah taṣli:ħ]

bid • **1.** عَطاء [ʕaṭa:ʔ] عَطاءآت [ʕaṭa:ʔa:t] *pl:* All the bids for the new building must be in by the fifteenth of the month. كُلّ العَطاءات لِلبِنايَة الجِّدِيدَة لازم تكُون هنا قَبِل خمُسطَعَش بِالشَّهَر [kull ʔilʕaṭa:ʔa:t lilbina:ya ʔiǰǰidi:da la:zim tku:n hna: gabil xmusṭaʕaš biššahar]

to bid • **1.** زايَد [za:yad] مُزايَدَة [muza:yada] *vn: sv* i. He bid ten dinars for the rug. زايَد عَشِر دَنانِير عالسِّجّادَة [za:yad ʕašir danani:r ʕassiǰǰa:da]

big • **1.** كِبِير [čibi:r, kibi:r] كبار [kba:r] *pl:* The live in a big house. يسُكنُون بِبَيت كِبِير [ysuknu:n bibayt čibi:r] Her father is a big lawyer. أبُوها مُحامِي كبِير [ʔabu:ha muħa:mi čbi:r] He talks big. يِحكِي كبار [yiħči kba:r]

*** He's a big shot now.** • **1.** صار شَخصِيَّة هَسَّة [ṣa:r šaxṣiyya hassa]

bill • **1.** قائِمَة [qa:ʔima] قَوائِم [qawa:ʔim] *pl:* We have to pay this bill today. لازِم نِدفَع هالقائِمَة اليُوم [la:zim nidfaʕ halqa:ʔima ʔilyu:m] • **2.** نُوط [nu:t] نواط [nwa:t] *pl:* Give me some small bills, please. أرجُوك إنطِينِي نواط صغَيّرَة [ʔarǰu:k ʔinṭi:ni nwa:ṭ ṣɣayyra] • **3.** لائِحَة [la:ʔiħa] لَوائِح، لائِحات [lawa:ʔiħ, la:ʔiħa:t] *pl:* The bill was passed. اللّائِحَة تصَدّقَت [ʔilla:ʔiħa tṣaddqat] • **4.** مِنقار [minga:r] مناقِير [mna:gi:r] *pl:* Storks have long bills. اللَّقالِق عِدها مَناقِير طويلَة [ʔillaga:lig ʕidha mna:gi:r ṭwi:la] • **5.** إعلان [ʔiʕla:n] إعلانات [ʔiʕla:na:t] *pl:* Posting bills is forbidden here. لَصق الإعلانات مَمنُوع هنا [laṣq ʔilʔiʕla:na:t mamnu:ʕ hna]

to fill the bill • **1.** وُفَى بِالمَرام [wufa: bilmara:m] وَفاء بِالمَرام [wafa:ʔ bilmara:m] *vn: sv* i. I don't think that these will fill the bill. ما أظُنّ هَذولَة يُوفُون بالمَرام [ma: ʔaðunn haðu:la yu:fu:n bilmara:m]

to foot the bill • **1.** دِفَع [difaʕ] دَفِع [dafiʕ] *vn: sv* a. Who's going to foot the bill for all this? مِنُو راح يِدفَع كُلّ هَذا الحساب؟ [minu ra:ħ yidfaʕ kull ha:ða ʔilħsa:b?]

to bill • **1.** دَزّ قائِمَة [dazz qa:ʔima] *sv* i. Bill me for the account. دِزّلِي قائِمَة بِالحِساب [dizzli qa:ʔima biliħsa:b]

billboard • **1.** لَوحَة إعلان [lawħat ʔiʕla:n] لَوحات إعلان [lu:ħa:t ʔiʕla:n] *pl:*

billfold • **1.** جِزدان [ǰizda:n] جِزدانات، جَزادِين [ǰizda:na:t, ǰaza:di:n] *pl:*

billiards • **1.** بِليارد [bilya:rd] Let's play a game of billiards. خَلِّي نِلعَب فَدّ جَيم بِليارد [xalli nilʕab fadd gi:m bilya:rd]

billion • **1.** بِليَون [bilyu:n] بَلايِين [bala:yi:n] *pl:* That runs into billions. هَذا يُوصَل إلَى بَلايِين [ha:ða yu:ṣal ʔila bala:yi:n]

to bind • **1.** جَلَّد [ǰallad] تَجلِيد [taǰli:d] *vn:* تجَلَّد [tǰallad] *p: sv* i. Can you bind these magazines for me? تِقدَر تجَلّدلِي هالمَّجَلات؟ [tigdar dǰallidli halmaǰalla:t?] • **2.** حِصَر [ħiṣar] حَصِر [ħaṣir] *vn: sv* i. This coat binds a little under the arms. Can you let it out? هَالسِّترَة تِحصِرنِي شوَيَّة جَوَّة الأُبُط تِقدَر تكَبُّرها؟ [hassitra tiħṣirni šwayya ǰawwa ʔilʔubuṭ tigdar tkabburha?] • **3.** لِزَم [lizam] *sv* i. Your signature binds you to fulfill the contract on time. تَوقِيعَك يلِزمَك بِإنجاز العَقِد عالوَقِت [tawqi:ʕak ylizmak bʔinǰa:z ʔilʕaqid ʕalwakit] • **4.** شَدّ [šadd] شَدّ [šadd] *vn: sv* i. رُبَط [rubaṭ] رَبُط [rabuṭ] *vn: sv* u. The police bound the thief's hands with his handkerchief. الشُّرطَة شَدّوا إيدَين الحَرامِي بكَفِّيتَه [ʔiššurṭa šaddaw ʔi:dayn ʔilħara:mi bčaffi:tah] Put glue on both surfaces and bind them together tightly with wire. حُطّ غِيرَة عالصَّفحَتَين وَشِدّهُم سُوَة بتَيل حيل [ħuṭṭ ɣi:ra ʕaṣṣafiħti:n wšiddhum suwa bitayl ħi:l]

to bind up • **1.** ضَمَّد [ðammad] تَضمِيد [taðmi:d] *vn: sv* i. Bind up his wounds and give him two aspirins with some water. ضَمِّد جرُوحَه وَانطِيه أسبرِينتَين ويّا شوَيَّة ماي [ðammid ǰru:ħah waʔinṭi:h ʔaspiri:ntayn wiyya šwayya ma:y]

binder • **1.** مُجَلِّد [muǰallid] مُجَلِّدِين [muǰallidi:n] *pl:* The newspapers are at the binder's. الجَّرايِد عِند المُجَلِّد [ʔiǰǰara:yid ʕind ʔilmujallid] • **2.** مَحفَظَة [maħfaða] مَحفَظات، مَحافِظ [maħfaða:t, maħa:fið] *pl:* You'd better buy a binder for those loose papers. أَحسَن لَو تِشتِري مَحفظَة لِهالأَوراق المَفلُولَة [ʔaħsan law tištiri maħfaða lhalʔawra:q ʔilmaflu:la]

bindery • **1.** مَحَل تَجلِيد الكُتُب [maħall tajli:d ʔilkutub] مَحَلات تَجلِيد الكُتُب [maħalla:t tajli:d ʔilkutub] *pl:*

binding • **1.** تَجلِيد [tajli:d] تَجلِيدات [tajli:da:t] *pl:* The binding is damaged. التَّجلِيد تَلفان [ʔittajli:d talfa:n]

to be binding • **1.** مُلزَم [mulzam] This contract is binding on both parties. هَالعَقِد مُلزِم عالطَّرَفين [halʕaqid mulzim ʕaṭṭarafi:n]

binoculars • **1.** دَوربِين [du:rbi:n] دَوربِينات [du:rbi:na:t] *pl:* ناظُور [na:ðu:r] نَواظِير [nuwa:ði:r] *pl:*

bird • **1.** طير [ṭayr, ṭi:r] طيُور [ṭyu:r] *pl:* What kind of bird is this? شِنُو نُوع هالطَير؟ [šinu nu:ʕ haṭṭi:r?]

*** A bird in the hand is worth two in the bush.**

• **1.** عَصفُور بِالإيد أَحسَن مِن عَشرَة عَالشَجَرَة [ʕaṣfu:r bilʔi:d ʔaħsan min ʕašra ʕaššajara]

*** He killed two birds with one stone.**

• **1.** ضِرَب عَصفُورَين بِحجارَة [ðirab ʕaṣfu:rayn biħja:ra]

birth • **1.** مِيلاد [mi:la:d] مَوالِيد [mawa:li:d] *pl:* وِلادَة [wila:da] وِلادات [wila:da:t] *pl:* They announced the birth of their son. عِلنَوا مِيلاد إبِنهُم [ʕilnaw mi:la:d ʔibinhum] • **2.** وِلادَة [wila:da] جَيبُوبَة [jaybu:ba] جَيبُوبات [jaybu:ba:t] *pl:* This time it was an easy birth. هَالمَرَّة الوِلادَة كانَت سَهلَة [halmarra ʔilwila:da ča:nat sahla]

by birth • **1.** وِلادَة [wila:da] Are you an American by birth? إنتَ أَمرِيكِي بالوِلادَة؟ [ʔinta ʔamri:ki bilwila:da?]

date of birth • **1.** تارِيخ الوِلادَة [ta:ri:x ʔilwila:da] You forgot to put down your date of birth? نِسِيت تحُطّ تارِيخ وِلادتَك [nisi:t tħuṭṭ ta:ri:x wila:dtak]

place of birth • **1.** مَحَلّ الوِلادَة [maħall ʔilwila:da] My place of birth is Bagdad. مَحَلّ وِلادتِي بَغداد [maħall wila:dti bayda:d]

birth control • **1.** تَحدِيد النَّسِل [taħdi:d ʔinnasil]

birthday • **1.** عِيد مِيلاد [ʕi:d mi:la:d] We are celebrating our son's birthday today. دَنِحتِفِل بعِيد مِيلاد إبِنَنا اليُوم [daniħtifil bʕi:d mi:la:d ʔibinna ʔilyu:m]

birthday party • **1.** حَفلَة عِيد المِيلاد [ħaflat ʕi:d ʔilmi:la:d] My wife is giving a birthday party tomorrow for our daughter. Can you come? مَرتِي دَتسَوِّي حَفلَة عِيد مِيلاد لِبِنتنا باكِر، تِقدَر تِجِي؟ [marti datsawwi ħaflat ʕi:d mi:la:d lbinitna ba:čir, tigdar tiji?]

birth rate • **1.** نِسبَة الوِلادَة [nisbat ʔilwila:da] The government is concerned about the rapid rise in the birth rate. الحُكُومَة مَقلُوقَة مِن الزِّيادَة الكِبِيرَة بِنِسبَة الوِلادَة [ʔilħuku:ma maqlu:qa min ʔizziya:da ʔiččibi:ra bnisbat ʔilwila:da]

bishop • **1.** مَطران [maṭra:n] مَطارنَة [maṭa:rna] *pl:* His uncle is a bishop. عَمَّه مُطران [ʕammah muṭra:n] • **2.** فِيل [fi:l] فيال [fya:l] *pl:* You've already lost one bishop and the game has just begun. اِنقِتَل عِندَك فِيل واللِّعب تَوَّة بِدا [ʔinkital ʕindak fi:l walliʕib tawwa bida:]

bit • **1.** لجام [lja:m] لجامات [lja:ma:t] *pl:* The horse's mouth has been injured by the bit. حَلق الحِصان مَجرُوح مِن اللِّجام [ħalg ʔilħiṣa:n majru:ħ min ʔillija:m] • **2.** شوَيَّة [šwayya] The tea is a bit strong. الشاي شوَيَّة طُوخ [ʔičča:y šwayya ṭu:x] I'm sorry but you'll have to wait a bit longer. مِتأَسِّف لَكِن لازِم تِنتِظِر بَعَد شوَيَّة [mitʔassif la:kin la:zim tintiðir baʕad šwayya] • **3.** نِتفَة [nitfa] نِتفات [nitfa:t] *pl:* There's a bit of lint on your coat. أَكُو نِتفَة قُطِن عَلَى سِترتَك [ʔaku nitfat guṭin ʕala sitirtak]

*** That's going a bit too far.** • **1.** ثَخَّنِتها [θaxxanitha]

*** That doesn't make a bit of difference.** • **1.** ما يهِمّ أَبَدَاً [ma: yhimm ʔabadan]

bit by bit • **1.** شوَيَّة شوَيَّة [šwayya šwayya] We learned the story bit by bit. عِرَفنا الحكايَة شوَيَّة شوَيَّة [ʕirafna ʔilħča:ya šwayya šwayya]

not a bit • **1.** وَلا شوَيَّة [wala: šwayya] أَبَداً [ʔabadan] وَلا وُصلَة [wala wuṣla] There's not a bit left. ما باقِي وَلا شوَيَّة [ma: ba:qi wala šwayya] There isn't a bit of bread in the house. ماكُو وَلا وُصلَة خُبُز بالبَيت [ma:ku wala wuṣlat xubuz bilbayt]

bite • **1.** عَضَّة [ʕaðða] عَضّات [ʕaðða:t] *pl:* The bite itches. العَضَّة تحُكّ [ʔilʕaðða tħukk] He took a bite out of the apple. أَخَذلَه فَدّ عَضَّة مِن التُّفّاحَة [ʔaxaðlah fadd ʕaðða min ʔittiffa:ħa] • **2.** وُصلَة [wuṣla] وُصَل [wuṣal] *pl:* We haven't a bite left. ما بُقَى عِدنا وَلا وُصلَة [ma: buqa: ʕidna wala wuṣla] • **3.** لُقمَة [lugma] لِقَم [ligam] *pl:* Won't you have a bite with us? ما تاكُلّك فَدّ لُقمَة ويّانا؟ [ma: ta:kullak fadd lugma wiyya:na?]

to bite • **1.** عَضّ [ʕaðð] عَضّ [ʕaðð] *vn:* اِنعَضّ [ʔinʕaðð] *p:* Will the dog bite? الكَلب يعَضّ؟ [ʔiččalib yʕaðð?] • **2.** نِقَر [nigar] نَقِر [nagir] *vn: sv* u. The fish are biting well today. السِّمَك دَيُنقُر زين هَاليُوم [ʔissimač dayungur zi:n halyu:m]

*** I tried twice but he didn't bite.**

• **1.** نِصَبِتلَه فَخّ مَرتَين لَكِن ما وُقَع [niṣabitlah faxx martayn la:kin ma: wugaʕ] / ذَبَّيتلَه طُعُم مَرَّتَين لَكِن ما نصاد [ðabbi:tlah ṭuʕum marrtayn la:kin ma: nṣa:d]

biting • **1.** قَصّ [gaṣṣ] قَصّ [gaṣṣ] *vn: sv* u. It's a biting wind. هَذا فَدّ هَوا يقُصّ [ha:ða fadd hawa yguṣṣ]

B

bitter • **1.** That tastes bitter. ذاك طَعمَه مُرّ [ðaːk ṭaʕmah murr] He has had some bitter experiences. مَرّ بتَجارُب مُرَّة [marr btaǰaːrub murra] • **2.** قاسِي [qaːsi] قُساة [qusaːt] *pl:* شَدِيد [šadiːd] It was bitter cold. كان البَرِد قاسِي [čaːn ʔilbarid qaːsi] • **3.** لَدُود [laduːd] أَلِدّاء [ʔaliddaːʔ] *pl:* They are bitter enemies. هُمَّ أَعداء أَلِدّاء [humma ʔaʕdaːʔ ʔaliddaːʔ]

 * **They fought to the bitter end.** • **1.** حاربَوا لِلمَوت [ħaːrbaw lilmuːt]

bitterly • **1.** بحُرقَة [bħurga] أَلَم [ʔalam] آلام [ʔaːlaːm] *pl:* مَرارَة [maraːra] He complained to me bitterly. إشتَكالِي بحُرقَة [ʔištakaːli bħurga]

black • **1.** أَسوَد [ʔaswad] سُود [suːd] *pl:* سُودَة [suːda] *Feminine:* His hair is black. شَعرَه أَسوَد [šaʕrah ʔaswad] • **2.** زَنجِي [zanǰi] زُنُوج [zunuːǰ] *pl:* He has become a leader of the black people. صايِر زَعِيم الزُّنُوج [ṣaːyir zaʕiːm ʔizzunuːǰ]

 to turn black • **1.** إسوَدّ [ʔiswadd] *sv* a. The sky turned black before the storm. الدِّنيا سوَدَّت قَبِل العاصِفَة [ʔiddinya swaddat gabil ʔilʕaːṣifa]

black bird • **1.** زَرزُور [zarzuːr] زَرازِير [zaraːziːr] *pl:*

blackboard • **1.** سَبُّورَة [sabbuːra] سَبُّورات [sabbuːraːt] *pl:* لَوحَة [lawħa, luːħa] لَوحات، أَلواح، لواح [luːħaːt, lawħaːt, ʔalwaːħ, lwaːħ] *pl:* Write it on the blackboard. إكِتبها عالسَّبُّورَة [ʔikitbha ʕassabbuːra]

to blacken • **1.** سَوَّد [sawwad] تَسوِيد [taswiːd] *vn:* تسَوَّد [tsawwad] *p:* The smoke from the fire blackened the ceiling. الدُّخّان مِن النّار سَوَّد السَّقُف [ʔidduxxaːn min ʔinnaːr sawwad ʔissaguf]

black market • **1.** السُّوق السَّوداء [ʔissuːq ʔissawdaːʔ]

blackness • **1.** سَواد [sawaːd]

blackout • **1.** تَعتِيم [taʕtiːm] The army is going to carry out a trial blackout tomorrow. الجَّيش راح يقُوم بتَمرِين تَعتِيم باكِر [ʔiǰǰiːš raːħ yquːm btamriːn taʕtiːm baːčir]

 to black out • **1.** عَتَّم [ʕattam] تَعتِيم [taʕtiːm] *vn:* تعَتَّم [tʕattam] *p:* The government has decided to blackout the city for ten minutes. الحُكُومَة قَرَّرَت تعَتِّم المَدِينَة لِمُدَّة عَشِر دَقايِق [ʔilħukuːma qarrarat tʕattim ʔilmadiːna limuddat ʕašir daqaːyiq]

Black sea • **1.** البَحر الأَسوَد [ʔilbaħr ʔilʔaswad]

blacksmith • **1.** حَدّاد [ħaddaːd] حَدّادِين [ħaddaːdiːn] *pl:*

bladder • **1.** مَثانَة [maθaːna] مَثانات [maθaːnaːt] *pl:*

blade • **1.** مُوس [muːs] مواس، مواسَة [mwaːs, mwaːsa] *pl:* راس حادّ [raːs ħaːdd] رُؤُوس حادَّة [ruʔuːs ħaːdda] *pl:* I need a knife with two blades. أَحتاج سِچِّينَة أُمّ راسَين [ʔaħtaːǰ siččiːna ʔumm raːsayn] These blades don't fit my razor. هَالمواس ما يِرهَمُون عَلَى مَكِينَة الزِّيان مالتِي [halmwaːs maː yirhamuːn ʕala makiːnat ʔizziyaːn maːlti]

blame • **1.** مَسؤُولِيَّة [masʔuːliyya] مَسؤُولِيّات [masʔuːliyyaːt] *pl:* He took the blame for their mistake. أَخَذ مَسؤُولِيَّة غَلطَتهُم عَلَى نَفسَه [ʔaxað masʔuːliyyat ɣalṭathum ʕala nafsah] • **2.** لَوم [lawm] Don't put the blame on me! لا تذِبّ اللَّوم عَلَيّا [laː dðibb ʔillawm ʕalayya]

 to blame • **1.** لام [laːm] لَوم [lawm] *vn:* انلام [ʔinlaːm] *p:* بِلَى [bilaː] بَلوَة [balwa] *vn:* انبِلَى [ʔinbilaː] *p:* Don't blame me. لا تبِلِينِي إلِي [laː tibliːni ʔili] Under these circumstances I could hardly blame her. بِهالحالَة كُلِّش صَعُب أَقدَر أَلُومها [bhalħaːla kulliš ṣaʕub ʔagdar ʔaluːmha] This child can't be blamed for anything. هَذا طِفِل ما يِنلام عَلَى شِي [haːða ṭifil maː yinlaːm ʕala ši]

 to be to blame for • **1.** كان مُصوِچ ب [čaːn muṣwič b-] Who's to blame for the collision? مِنُو المُصوِچ بالإصطِدام؟ [minu ʔilmuṣwič bilʔiṣṭidaːm?]

blank • **1.** إستِمارَة [ʔistimaːra] إستِمارات [ʔistimaːraːt] *pl:* Would you help me to fill out this blank form? تِقدَر تساعِدنِي بتَرِس هَالاستِمارَة؟ [tigdar tsaːʕidni btaris halʔistimaːra?] • **2.** فَراغ [faraːɣ] فَراغات [faraːɣaːt] *pl:* Fill in all blanks. حَشِّي كُلّ الفَراغات [ħašši kull ʔilfaraːɣaːt] • **3.** أَبيَض [ʔabyað̣] بِيض [biːð̣] *pl:* بَيضَة [biːð̣a] *Feminine:* The envelope contained only a blank sheet of paper. الظَّرُف ما بِيه غير وَرقَة بيضَة [ʔið̣ð̣aruf maː biːh ɣiːr warqa biːð̣a] • **4.** خالِي [xaːli] Did you notice her blank expression? لاحَظِت شلُون وِجِهها خالِي مِن كُلّ تَعبِير؟ [laːħaðit šluːn wiččha xaːli min kull taʕbiːr?]

 * **My mind is a complete blank.** • **1.** فِكرِي واقُف تَماماً [fikri waːguf tamaːman]

blanket • **1.** بَطّانِيَّة [baṭṭaːniyya] بَطّانِيّات [baṭṭaːniyyaːt] *pl:* Take another blanket and you won't be cold any more. أُخُذ بَطّانِيَّة لُخ وَبَعَد ما تُبرَد [ʔuxuð baṭṭaːniyya lux wabaʕad maː tubrad] • **2.** شامِل [šaːmil] He made a blanket statement which satisfied no one. صَرَّح تَصرِيح شامِل ما رَضَّى أَحَّد [ṣarraħ taṣriːħ šaːmil maː rað̣ð̣aː ʔaħħad]

 to blanket • **1.** غَطّة [ɣaṭṭa] غَطّات [ɣaṭṭaːt] *pl:* تغِطِّي، تَغطِيَة [tɣiṭṭi, taɣṭiya] *vn:* *sv* i. A thick fog blanketed the airfield. ضَباب كَثِيف غَطَّى المَطار [ð̣abaːb kaθiːf ɣaṭṭaː ʔilmaṭaːr]

blast • **1.** إنفِجار [ʔinfiǰaːr] إنفِجارات [ʔinfiǰaːraːt] *pl:* You can hear the blast for miles. تِقدَر تِسمَع الإنفِجار مِن بُعُد أَميال [tigdar tismaʕ ʔilʔinfiǰaːr min buʕud ʔamyaːl]

 full blast • **1.** لَيل [layl, liːl] بكُلّ طاقَة [bkull ṭaːqa] The plant is going full blast. المَعمَل دَيِشتُغُل لَيل نَهار [ʔilmaʕmal dayištuɣul layl nahaːr]

to blast • **1.** فَجَّر [fajjar] تفجِّر، تَفجِير [tfijjir, tafji:r] *vn:* تفَجَّر [tfajjar] *p: sv* i. They're blasting a tunnel. دَيفَجّرُون نَفَق [dayfajjru:n nafaq] • **2.** نِسَف [nisaf] نَسِف [nasif] *vn:* اِنّسَف [ʔinnisaf] *p: sv* i. The guerrillas blasted the bridge last night. الفِدائِيِّن نِسفَوا الجِّسِر البارحَة باللَّيل [ʔilfida:ʔiyyin nisfaw ʔijjisir ʔilba:rħa billayl]

blaze • **1.** حَرِيق [ħari:q] حَرايِق [ħara:yiq] *pl:* The blaze destroyed a whole block. الحَرِيق دَمَّر كُلّ المَنطَقَة اللِّي بَين الشّارعَين [ʔilħari:q dammar kull ʔilmanṭaqa ʔilli bayn ʔišša:rʕayn] • **2.** نار [na:r] نِيران [ni:ra:n] *pl:* Come and warm your hands over the blaze. تَعال ودَفِّي إيدَيك عَالنّار [taʕa:l wdaffi ʔi:di:k ʕanna:r]

to blaze (up) • **1.** اِلتِهَب [ʔiltihab] اِلتِهاب [ʔiltiha:b] *vn: sv* i. Don't put kerosene in the brazier or the fire will blaze up. لا تحُطّ نَفُط بالمَنقَل تَرَة النّار تِلتِهِب [la: tħuṭṭ nafuṭ bilmanqal tara ʔinna:r tiltihib]

blazing • **1.** لافِح [la:fiħ] We had to stand for half an hour in the blazing sun. اِضطَرّينا نوقَف حَوالِي نُصّ ساعَة جَوَّة الشَّمس اللّافحَة [ʔiđṭarri:na nu:gaf ħawa:li nuṣṣ sa:ʕa jawwa ʔiššams ʔilla:fħa]

to bleach • **1.** كِشَف [kišaf] كَشِف [kašif] *vn: sv* i. The wash is bleaching in the sun. الهدُوم دَتِكشِف بِالشَّمِس [ʔilhdu:m datikšif biššamis]

to bleed • **1.** نِزَف [nizaf] نَزف [nazif] *vn: sv* i. My nose is bleeding. خَشمِي دَينزِف [xašmi dayinzif]

to bleed to death • **1.** مات مِن النَّزِيف [ma:t min ʔannazi:f] مَوت مِن النَّزِيف [mu:t min ʔannazi:f] *vn: sv* u. He nearly bled to death. مات مِن النَّزِيف إلّا شوَيَّة [ma:t min ʔinnazi:f ʔilla šwayya]

blend • **1.** خَبطَة [xabṭa] خبطات [xabṭa:t] *pl:* خَلِيط [xali:ṭ] مَزِيج [mazi:j] مَزِيجات [mazi:ja:t] *pl:* I make the blend I smoke myself. آنِي أسَوِّي الخَبطَة اللِّي أدَخِّنها بِيدِي [ʔa:ni ʔasawwi ʔilxabṭa ʔilli ʔadaxxinha bi:di]

to bless • **1.** بارَك [ba:rak] مُبارَكَة [muba:raka] *vn:* تبارَك [tba:rak] *p:* May God bless you! بارَك الله فِيك [ba:rak ʔallah fi:k]

blessing • **1.** بَرَكَة [baraka] رَحمَة [raħma] It was really a blessing that she came. جَيّتها كانَت فَدّ رَحمَة مِن الله [jayyatha ča:nat fadd raħma min ʔallah] Go with my blessing! رُوح بِالبَرَكَة [ru:ħ bilbaraka]

blind • **1.** Shall I pull up the blinds? أصَعِّد القِيمات؟ [ʔaṣaʕʕid ʔilqi:ma:t?] • **2.** أعمَى [ʔaʕma] عِمِي، عِميان، عِميِّن [ʕimi, ʕimya:n, ʕimyi:n] *pl:* عَميَة [ʕamya] *Feminine:* بَصِير [baṣi:r] This building is a home for the blind. هالبِنايَة هِيَّ دار لِلعِميان [halbina:ya hiyya da:r lilʕimya:n] We helped the blind man across the street. عاوَنّا الرِّجّال الأعمَى حَتَّى يُعبُر الشّارِع [ʕa:wanna: ʔirrijja:l ʔilʔaʕma: ħatta yuʕbur ʔišša:riʕ] • **3.** غافُل [ɣa:ful] I'm not blind to her faults. آنِي مُو غافِل عَن غَلطاتها [ʔa:ni mu: ɣa:fil ʕan ɣalṭa:tha]

blind (in one eye) • **1.** أعوَر [ʔaʕwar] عُور، عُوران، عَورِين [ʕu:r, ʕu:ra:n, ʕu:ri:n] *pl:* عُورَة [ʕu:ra] *Feminine:* He's been blind in one eye from birth. كان أعوَر مِن الوِلادَة [ča:n ʔaʕwar min ʔilwila:da]

to go blind • **1.** عِمَى [ʕima:] عَمَى [ʕama:] *vn: sv* a. I hope he's not going to go blind. أتأمَّل هُوَّ ما يِعمَى [ʔatʔammal huwwa ma: yiʕma:]

to blind • **1.** عَمَى [ʕama:, ʕima:] عَمي [ʕamy] *vn:* اِنعِمَى [ʔinʕima:] *p:* The sun is blinding me. الشَّمِس دَتِعمِينِي [ʔiššamis datiʕmi:ni]

blind alley • **1.** دَربُونَة ما تِطلَع [darbu:na ma: tiṭlaʕ] دَرابِين ما تِطلَع [dara:bi:n ma: tiṭlaʕ] *pl:* I drove into a blind alley and had to back all the way out. خَشَّيت بِدَربُونَة ما تِطلَع وإضطَرَّيت أرجَع باك [xašši:t bdarbu:na ma: tiṭlaʕ wʔiđṭarri:t ʔarjaʕ ba:k]

to blink • **1.** رِمَش [rimaš] رَمِش [ramiš] *vn: sv* i. He blinked his eyes when I turned the light on. رِمَش عَينَه مِن شِعَلت الضُّوَة [rimaš ʕaynah min šiʕalt ʔiđđuwa] • **2.** شِعَل وطَفَّى [šiʕal wṭaffa:] Blink your lights to attract his attention. إشعِل وَطَفِّي اللّايت مالَك حَتَّى تِجلِب اِنتِباهَه [ʔišʕil wṭaffi ʔilla:yt ma:lak ħatta tijlib ʔintiba:hah]

blister • **1.** بُطباطَة [buṭba:ṭa] بُطباطات، بَطابِيط [buṭba:ṭa:t, baṭa:bi:ṭ] *pl:* He has a blister on his foot. عِندَه بُطباطَة برِجلَه [ʕindah buṭba:ṭa brijlah]

blizzard • **1.** عاصِفَة ثَلجِيَّة [ʕa:ṣifa θaljiyya] عَواصِف ثَلجِيَّة [ʕawa:ṣif θaljiyya] *pl:* This is the worst blizzard we've had in ten years. هَذِي أرذَل عاصِفَة ثَلجِيَّة مَرَّت عَلينا بِخِلال عَشِر سنِين [ha:ði ʔarzal ʕa:ṣifa θaljiyya marrat ʕali:na bxila:l ʕašir sni:n]

bloc • **1.** كُتلَة [kutla] كُتَل [kutal] *pl:* There are a number of political blocs in Parliament. أكُو عِدَّة كُتَل سِياسِيَّة بالبَرلَمان [ʔaku ʕiddat kutal siya:siyya bilparlama:n]

block • **1.** قِطعَة [qiṭʕa] قِطَع [qiṭaʕ] *pl:* What do you plan to do with these blocks of wood? شراح تسَوِّي بِهالقِطَع خِشَب؟ [šra:ħ tsawwi bhalqiṭaʕ xišab?] • **2.** مُكَعَّب [mukaʕʕab] Jamil, put your blocks away. جَمِيل، ضُمّ المُكَعَّبات مالتَك [jami:l, đumm ʔilmukaʕʕaba:t ma:ltak] • **3.** شارِع [ša:riʕ] شَوارِع [šawa:riʕ] *pl:* Walk three blocks and then turn right. إمشِي ثَلاث شَوارِع وَبَعدين دُور لِليمنَى [ʔimši tlaθ šawa:riʕ wbaʕdiyn du:r lilyimna]

*** The fire destroyed the whole block.** • **1.** الحَرِيق دَمَّر كُلّ البِنايات بَين هَالشَّوارِع الأربَعَة [ʔilħari:q dammar kull ʔilbina:ya:t bayn haššawa:riʕ ʔilʔarbaʕa]

B

to block • **1.** سَدّ [sadd] سَدّ [sadd] *vn:* اِنسَدّ [ʔinsadd] *p:* قِطَع [qiṭaʕ] قَطِع [qaṭiʕ] *vn:* اِنقِطَع [ʔinqiṭaʕ] *p:* *sv* a. The road is blocked. الطَّرِيق مَسدُود [ʔiṭṭari:q masdu:d] • **2.** حَطّ [ħaṭṭ] اِنحَطّ [ʔinħaṭṭ] *p:* I'd like to have my old hat blocked. أَرِيد شَفقِتي العَتِيقَة تِنحَطّ بِقالَب [ʔari:d šafiqti ʔilʕati:ga tinħaṭṭ bqa:lab]

blond • **1.** أَشقَر [ʔašgar] شُقُر [šugur] *pl:* شَقرَة [šagra] *Feminine:* She has blond hair. عِدها شَعَر أَشقَر [ʕidha šaʕar ʔašgar]

blonde • **1.** شَقرَة [šagra] شَقرات [šagra:t] *pl:* Who's that good-looking blonde over there? مِنُو هَذِيك الشَّقرَة الحِلوَة هناك؟ [minu haði:č ʔiššagra ʔilħilwa hna:k?]

blood • **1.** دَمّ [damm] دِماء [dima:ʔ] *pl:* دِماء [dima:ʔ] دمُوم [dmu:m] *pl:* The doctor took a sample of my blood. الدِّكتُور أَخَذ نُمُوذَج مِن دَمِّي [ʔiddiktu:r ʔaxað numu:ðaǰ min dammi] She fainted at the sight of all the blood on the floor. خُربَت مِن شافَت الدمُوم بِالقاع [xurbat min ša:fat ʔildmu:m bilga:ʕ]

*** Blood is thicker than water.**

• **1.** آنِي وأَخُويَا عَلَى إِبن عَمِّي وآنِي وإِبن عَمِّي عَلَى الغَرِيب [ʔa:ni wʔaxu:ya ʕala ʔibin ʕammi wʔa:ni wʔibin ʕammi ʕala ʔilɣari:b]

in cold blood • **1.** بَلا رَحمَة [bala: raħma] They were murdered in cold blood. اِنقِتلَوا بَلا رَحمَة [ʔinkitlaw bala raħma]

*** He shot them in cold blood.**

• **1.** رِماهُم بِالرِصاص وَلا عِندَه بِالقَيد [rima:hum birriṣa:ṣ wala: ʕindah bilqi:d]

blood poisoning • **1.** تَسَمُّم الدَمّ [tasammum ʔiddamm]

blood pressure • **1.** ضَغِط دَمّ [ðaɣiṭ damm] He has high blood pressure. عِندَه ضَغِط دَمّ عالِي [ʕindah ðaɣiṭ damm ʕa:li]

blood shed • **1.** إِراقَة الدِماء [ʔira:qat ʔildima:ʔ] We must avoid blood-shed at all costs. لازِم نِتفادَى إِراقَة الدِّماء بأَيّ ثَمَن [la:zim nitfa:da: ʔira:qat ʔiddima:ʔ bʔayy θaman]

blood shot • **1.** مَحَمَّر [mħammar] His eyes are bloodshot from loss of sleep. عيُونَه مِحمَرَّة مِن قِلَّة النَّوم [ʕyu:nah miħmarra min qillat ʔinnawm]

blood stain • **1.** لَكَّة دَمّ [lakkat damm] لَكّات دَمّ [lakka:t damm] *pl:* The bloodstains on my shirt will not come out. لَكّات الدَّمّ عَلَى ثَوبِي ما تِطلَع [lakka:t ʔiddamm ʕala θu:bi ma: tiṭlaʕ]

blood type • **1.** نَوع دَمّ [nawʕ damm] أَنواع دَمّ [ʔanwa:ʕ damm] *pl:*

bloody • **1.** مدَمَّى [mdamma] His handkerchief was all bloody. كَفِّيتَه كانَت كُلّها مدَمّايَة [čaffi:tah ča:nat kullha mdamma:ya] • **2.** دَمَوِي [damawi] Did you hear the rumors about the bloody battle between the tribes. سمَعت الإِشاعات عَن المَعرَكَة الدَّمَوِيَّة بين العَشايِر [smaʕt ʔilʔiša:ʕa:t ʕan ʔilmaʕraka ʔiddamawiyya bi:n ʔilʕaša:yir]

bloom • **1.** وَردَة [warda] وَردات، وُرُود، وَرِد [warda:t, wuru:d, warid] *pl:* وَرِد [warid] *Collective:* She picked the choicest blooms in the garden for us. قُطفَت إِلنا أَحسَن وَرِد اللِّي بِالبِستان [guṭfat ʔilna ʔaħsan warid ʔilli bilbista:n] • **2.** شَرِخ [šarix] He died in the bloom of his youth. مات بِشَرِخ شَبابَه [ma:t bšarix šaba:bah]

in bloom • **1.** موَرَّد [mwarrad] The apricot trees are now in bloom. أَشجار المِشمِش هَسَّة موَرِّدَة [ʔašǰa:r ʔilmišmiš hassa mwarrda]

to bloom • **1.** وَرَّد [warrad] تَورِيد [tawri:d] *vn:* *sv* i. My roses didn't bloom well last year. الوَرِد مالِي ما وَرَّد زين السَّنَة اللِّي فاتَت [ʔilwarid ma:li ma: warrad zi:n ʔissana ʔilli fa:tat]

blossom • **1.** وَردَة [warda] وَردات، وُرُود، وَرِد [warda:t, wuru:d, warid] *pl:* وَرِد [warid] *Collective:* The blossoms are falling off the pomegranate bushes. الوَرِد دَيُوقَع مِن شَجَرَة الرُّمّان [ʔilwarid dayu:gaʕ min šaǰarat ʔirrumma:n] • **2.** قِدّاح [qidda:ħ] The scent from the orange blossoms filled the whole garden. رِيحَة القِدّاح تِرسَت الحَدِيقَة [ri:ħat ʔilqidda:ħ tirsat ʔilħadi:qa]

to blossom • **1.** وَرَّد [warrad] تَورِيد [tawri:d] *vn:* *sv* i. The carnations will start to blossom next week. القَرُنفُل راح يِبدِي يوَرِّد إِسبُوع الجّاي [ʔiqrunful ra:ħ yibdi ywarrid ʔisbu:ʕ ʔiǰǰa:y]

blot • **1.** لَكَّة [lakka] لَكّات [lakka:t] *pl:* The page is full of blots. الصَّفحَة كُلّها لَكّات [ʔaṣṣafħa kullha lakka:t]

to blot • **1.** نَشَّف [naššaf] تَنشِيف [tanši:f] *vn:* تنَشَّف [tnaššaf] Blot the signature before you fold the letter. نَشِّف الإِمضاء قَبُل ما تِطوِي المَكتُوب [naššif ʔilʔimða:ʔ gabul ma: tiṭwi ʔilmaktu:b]

to blot out • **1.** سَدّ [sadd] سَدّ [sadd] *vn:* *sv* i. The trees blot out the view. الأَشجار تسِدّ المَنظَر [ʔilʔašǰa:r tsidd ʔilmanðar]

to blot up • **1.** نَشَّف [naššaf] تَنشِيف [tanši:f] *vn:* *sv* i. Blot up the ink with a blotter. نَشِّف الحِبِر بِالنَّشِّيف [naššif ʔilħibir binnišši:f]

blotch • **1.** طُقعَة [ṭugʕa] طُقَع [ṭugaʕ] *pl:* What caused these red blotches on your face? شسَبَّب هالطُّقعَة الحَمرَة بِوِجهَك؟ [šsabbab haṭṭugaʕa ʔilħamra bwiččak?]

blotter • **1.** نِشِّيفَة [nišši:fa] نِشِّيفات [nišši:fa:t] *pl:* نِشِّيف [nišši:f] *Collective:* نِشّافَة [nišša:fa] نِشّافات [nišša:fa:t] *pl:*

نِشِّيف [niššiːf] *Collective:* Quick, give me a blotter! إنطِينِي نِشِّيف بِالعَجَل [ʔinṭiːni niššiːf bilʕaǰal]

blotting paper • **1.** وَرَقَة نِشّاف [waraqa niššaːf] وَرَق نِشّاف [waraq niššaːf] *pl:* أوراق نِشّاف [ʔawraːq niššaːf] *Collective:* I'd like three sheets of blotting paper. أرِيد ثلَث وَرَقات نِشّاف [ʔariːd tlaθ waraqaːt niššaːf]

blow • **1.** ضَربَة [ð̣arba] ضَربات [ð̣arbaːt] *pl:* That was a hard blow. ذِيك كانَت فَدّ ضَربَة قَوِيَّة [ðiːč čaːnat fadd ð̣arba qawiyya] That blow struck home. ذِيك الضَّربَة جَتّي بمَكانها [ðiːč ʔið̣ð̣arba ǰatti bmakaːnha] That blow struck home. هَالدَّقَّة ضِربَت بِالدَّمار [haldagga ð̣irbat biddamaːr]

to blow • **1.** هَبّ [habb] هَبّ [habb] *vn: sv* i. The wind is blowing from the North. الهَوا دَيهِبّ مِن الشِّمال [ʔilhawa dayhibb min ʔiššimaːl] • **2.** قَبّ [gabb] قَبّ [gabb] *vn: sv* u. Last night a severe sandstorm blew in on Baghdad. البارحَة قَبَّت عَجَّة قَوِيَّة عَلَى بَغداد [ʔilbaːrħa gabbat ʕaǰǰa qawiyya ʕala baɣdaːd] • **3.** دَقّ [dagg] دَقّ [dagg] *vn: sv* u. When do they blow taps? شوَقِت يدُقُّون بُوق النَّوم؟ [šwakit ydugguːn buːq ʔinnuːm?] • **4.** دَقّ [dagg] دَقّ [dagg] *vn: sv* u. طَوَّط [ṭawwaṭ] تطُوُّط [tṭuwwuṭ] *vn:* تطَوَّط [ʔiṭṭawwaṭ] *p:* Blow the horn three times. دُقّ الهَورن ثلَث دَقّات [dugg ʔilhuːrin tlaθ daggaːt] • **5.** صُوفَر [ṣuːfar] مصَوفرَة [mṣuːfra] *vn:* تصَوفَر [tṣuːfar] *p:* The umpire blew his whistle three times. الحَكَم صَوفَر بصافِرتَه ثلاث مَرّات [ʔilħakam ṣuːfar bṣaːfirtah tlaθ marraːt] • **6.** نُفَخ [nufax] نَفُخ [nafux] *vn: sv* u. Blow on the coffee, if you want to cool it. أُنفُخ عالقَهوَة إذا ترِيد تبَرِّدها [ʔunfux ʕalgahwa ʔiða triːd tbarridha]

to blow away • **1.** طار [ṭaːr] *sv* i. The paper blew away. الوَرقَة طارَت [ʔlwarga ṭaːrat] • **2.** طَيَّر [ṭayyar] تطِيِّر [tṭiyyir] *vn: sv* i. The wind blew the papers away. الهَوا طَيَّر الوَرَق [ʔilhawa ṭayyar ʔilwaraq]

to blow one's nose • **1.** مُخَط [muxaṭ] مَخِط [maxiṭ] *vn: sv* u. I have to blow my nose. لازِم أمخُط [laːzim ʔamxuṭ]

to blow out • **1.** طَفَّى [ṭaffaː] تَطفِيَة [taṭfiya] *vn: sv* i. Take a deep breath and blow out the candle. أُخُذ نَفَس طُوِيل وَطَفّي الشَّمعَة [ʔuxuð nafas ṭuwiːl wṭaffi ʔiššamʕa] • **2.** طَقّ [ṭagg] طَقّ [ṭagg] *vn: sv* u. The old tire blew out. التّايَر العَتِيق طَقّ [ʔittaːyir ʔilʕatiːg ṭagg] • **3.** فَكّ [fakk] *sv* u. Blow out the clogged tube. فُكّ البُورِي المَسدُود بِواسِطَة الهَوا [fukk ʔilbuːri ʔilmasduːd bwaːsiṭa ʔilhawa] • **4.** حِرَق [ħirag] حَرِق [ħarig] *vn: sv* i. Be careful you don't blow out the fuse. دِير بالَك لا تحرِق الفيُوز [diːr baːlak laː taħrig ʔilfyuːz]

to blow over • **1.** هِدَى [hidaː] هِدُوء [hiduːʔ] *vn: sv* a. The storm will blow over soon. العاصِفَة راح تِهدَأ بَعَد شوَيَّة [ʔilʕaːṣifa raːħ tihdaʔ baʕad šwayya] • **2.** بُرَد [burad] *sv* a. Her anger will soon blow over. غَضَبها راح يِبرَد بَعَد شوَيَّة [ɣað̣abha raːħ yibrad baʕad šwayya]

to blow up • **1.** اِنفِجَر [ʔinfiǰar] اِنفِجار [ʔinfiǰaːr] *vn: sv* i. The powder plant blew up. مَعمَل البارُود اِنفِجَر [maʕmal ʔalbaːruːd ʔinfiǰar] • **2.** نِسَف [nisaf] نَسِف [nasif] *vn: sv* i. The enemy blew up all the bridges. العَدُو نِسَف كُلّ الجِّسُور [ʔilʕadu nisaf kull ʔiǰǰisuːr] • **3.** نُفَخ [nufax] نَفُخ [nafux] *vn: sv* u. Blow up the balloons for the children. إنفُخ النُّفّاخات لِلجُّهّال [ʔinfux ʔinnuffaːxaːt liǰǰihhaːl]

blowout • **1.** پَنچَر [pančar] We had a blowout on the way home. بطَرِيقنا لِلبَيت صار عِدنا پَنچَر [bṭariːqna lilbayt ṣaːr ʕidna pančar]

blue • **1.** أزرَق [ʔazrag] زُرُق، زَرقِين [zurug, zargiːn] *pl:* زَرقَة [zarga, zarqa] *Feminine:* She has beautiful blue eyes. عِدها عيُون زُرُق حِلوَة [ʕidha ʕyuːn zurug ħilwa] • **2.** مَقهُور [maqhuːr] She looks blue this morning. يبَيِّن عَليها مَقهُورَة هوايَة اليُوم [yibayyin ʕaliːha maqhuːra hwaːya ʔilyuːm]

* **He arrived out of the blue.** • **1.** نِزَل عَلَينا مِن السِما [nizal ʕaliːna min ʔissima]

to get the blues • **1.** اِنقُبَض [ʔinqubað̣] اِنقِباض [ʔinqibaːð̣] *vn: sv* u. I get the blues when it rains. إنقُبَض مِن تُمطُر [ʔinqubað̣ min tumṭur]

to turn blue • **1.** اِزرَقّ [ʔizragg] *sv* a. Your face has turned blue with cold. وِجهَك ازرَقّ مِن البَرِد [wiččak ʔizragg min ʔilbarid]

blueing • **1.** كُوَى [čuwaː] كُويت [čuwiːt]

blueness • **1.** زَراق [zaraːg]

blue print • **1.** خَرِيطَة [xariːṭa] خَرايِط [xaraːyiṭ] *pl:* تَصمِيم [taṣmiːm] Show him how to read the blueprint. راوِيه شلُون يِقرا الخَرِيطَة [raːwiːh šluːn yiqraː ʔilxariːṭa]

bluff • **1.** جُرُف عالِي [ǰuruf ʕaːli] جرُوف عالِيَة [ǰruːf ʕaːlya] *pl:* He's building his house on a bluff overlooking the river. دَيِبني بَيتَه عَلَى جُرُف عالِي يطِلّ عَالشَّطّ [dayibni baytah ʕala ǰuruf ʕaːli yṭill ʕaššaṭṭ] • **2.** قَشمَرَة [qašmara] بَلفَة [balfa] بَلفات [balfaːt] *pl:* That's only a bluff. هَذِي مُو أكثَر مِن فَدّ بَلفَة [haːði muː ʔakθar min fadd balfa]

to bluff • **1.** قَشمَر [qašmar] قَشامِر قَشمَرَة [qašmara] *vn:* تقَشمَر [tqašmar] *p:* He's only bluffing. هَذا دَيقَشمُر [haːða dayqašmur] • **2.** بِلَف [bilaf] بَلِف [balif] *vn:* When he took another card, I knew he was bluffing. مِن أخَذ وَرقَة اللُّخ عِرَفِت دَيِبلِف [min ʔaxað warqat ʔillux ʕirafit dayiblif]

* **If I were you, I'd have called his bluff.** • **1.** لَو كِنت بمَكانَك كان خَلَّيتَه يكشِف لِعبتَه [law čint bmakaːnak čaːn xalliːtah yikšif liʕibtah]

blunder • **1.** غَلطَة [ɣalṭa] غَلطات، أغلاط [ɣalṭaːt, ʔaɣlaːṭ] *pl:* I made an awful blunder. آنِي سَوَّيت فَدّ غَلطَة فَظِيعَة [ʔaːni sawwiːt fadd ɣalṭa faðiːʕa]

B

blunt • **1.** أعمَى [ʔaʕma] عَميَة [ʕamya] *Feminine:* This knife is too blunt. هَالسِّكّينَة كُلّش عَميَة [hassiččiːna kulliš ʕamya]

*** Said is awfully blunt.** • **1.** سَعِيد يطُقّ الحِكايَة بوُجّ الواحِد [saʕiːd yṭugg ʔilħčaːya bwučč ʔilwaːħid]

bluntly • **1.** * He told me the truth very bluntly. طَقّ الحَقِيقَة بوُجهي [ṭagg ʔilħaqiːqa bwučči]

to blush • **1.** اِحمَرّ [ʔiħmarr] اِحمِرار [ʔiħmiraːr] *vn:* *sv* a. She blushes easily. هِيَّ تِحمَرّ بالعَجَل [hiyya tiħmarr bilʕaǰal]

board • **1.** لَوحَة [lawħa, luːħa] لَوحات، ألواح، لواح [luːħaːt, lawħaːt, ʔalwaːħ, lwaːħ] *pl:* لَوح [luːħ] *Collective:* We need some large boards. نِحتاج كَم لَوحَة كبِيرَة [niħtaːǰ čam luːħa čbiːra] Write it on the board. إكِتبها عَاللَّوحَة [ʔikitbha ʕalluːħa] • **2.** أكِل [ʔakil] My board costs me more than my room. أكِلي يكَلّفنِي أزيَد مِن إيجارِي [ʔakli ykallifni ʔazyad min ʔiːǰaːri]

on board (ship) • **1.** مَركَب [markab] مَراكِب [maraːkib] *pl:* There was a famous actress on board ship with us. كان أكُو مُمَثِّلَة مَشهُورَة بالمَركَب ويّانا [čaːn ʔaku mumaθθila mašhuːra bilmarkab wiyyaːna]

on board (train) • **1.** بالقِطار [bilqiṭaːr] Is everybody on board the train? الكُلّ رِكبَوا بالقِطار؟ [ʔilkull rikbaw bilqiṭaːr?]

room and board • **1.** غُرفَة مَعَ أكِل [ɣurfa maʕa ʔakil] How much do you pay for room and board? شقَدّ تِدفَع عَن الغُرفَة مَعَ الأكِل؟ [šgadd tidfaʕ ʕann ʔilɣurfa maʕa ʔilʔakil?]

to board • **1.** أكَل [ʔakal] *sv* u. I would like to arrange to board with an Iraqi family. أرِيد أسَوّي تَرتِيب ويّا عائِلَة عِراقِيَّة حَتَّى آكُل عِدهُم بفلُوس [ʔariːd ʔasawwi tartiːb wiyya ʕaːʔila ʕiraːqiyya ħatta ʔaːkul ʕidhum bfluːs] • **2.** رِكَب [rikab] رُكُب [rukub] *vn:* اِنرِكَب [ʔinrikab] *p:* We boarded the train in Washington. رِكَبنا القِطار بواشِنطِن [rikabna ʔilqiṭaːr bwaːšinṭin]

boarder • **1.** * Do you take in boarders? عِدكُم تَرتِيب النّاس ياكلُون بِبَيتكُم بفلُوس؟ [ʕidkum tartiːb ʔinnaːs yaːkluːn bibaytkum bifluːs?]

board of health • **1.** دائِرَة الصِّحَّة [daːʔirat ʔiṣṣiħħa]

to boast • **1.** تبَجَّح [tbaǰǰaħ] تَبَجُّح [tabaǰǰuħ] *vn:* *sv* a. Stop boasting! ما يَزِي تِتبَجَّح [maː yaziː titbaǰǰaħ] • **2.** تباهَى [tbaːhaː] تَباهِي [tabaːhi] *vn:* *sv* a. He is always boasting about how much influence his family has. عَلَى طُول يِتباهَى بنُفُوذ عائِلتَه [ʕala ṭuːl yitbaːhaː bnufuːð ʕaːʔiltah]

boat • **1.** بَلَم [balam] أبلام [(ʔa)blaːm] *pl:* We went fishing in his boat. رِحنا نصِيد سِمَك بالبَلَم مالَه [riħna nṣiːd simač bilbalam maːlah] • **2.** مَركَب [markab] مَراكِب [maraːkib] *pl:* باخِرَة [baːxira] بَواخِر [bawaːxir] *pl:* This boat goes to Australia. هالمَركَب يرُوح لأستراليا [halmarkab yiruːħ liʔustraːlya]

*** We're all in the same boat.** • **1.** كُلّنا فِي الهَوا سَوا [kullna fi ʔilhawa sawa]

bobby pin • **1.** فُركَيتَة [furkayta] فُركَيتات [furkaytaːt] *pl:* ماشَة مال شَعَر [maːša maːl šaʕar] ماشات مال شَعَر [maːšaːt maːl šaʕar] *pl:*

body • **1.** جِسِم [ǰisim] أجسام [ʔaǰsaːm] *pl:* جَسَد [ǰasad] أجساد [ʔaǰsaːd] *pl:* He has a rash on his body. عِندَه شِرَة بجِسمَه [ʕindah šira bǰismah] There are solid, liquid, and gaseous bodies. أكُو أجسام صَلبَة، وسائلَة وغازِيَّة [ʔaku ʔaǰsaːm ṣalba, wsaːʔla wɣaːziyya] • **2.** لَشَّة [lašša] لَشّات، لشاش [laššaːt, lšaːš] *pl:* جِثَّة [ǰiθθa] جِثَث [ǰiθaθ] *pl:* The body of the dog is still lying in the middle of the road. لَشَّة الكَلِب بَعَدها مَذبُوبَة بنُصّ الشّارِع [laššat ʔiččalib baʕadha maðbuːba bnuṣṣ ʔiššaːriʕ] The body was cremated. الجُثَّة اِنحِرقَت [ʔiǰǰuθθa ʔinħirgat]

*** They barely manage to keep body and soul together.** • **1.** ما عِدهُم عَشا اللَّيلَة [maː ʕidhum ʕaša ʔillayla]

in a body • **1.** بجَوقَة [bǰawga] بجَماعَة [bǰamaːʕa] They left the hall in a body. طِلعَوا مِن القاعَة بِجَوقَتهُم [ṭilʕaw min ʔilqaːʕa bǰawgathum]

bodyguard • **1.** حارِس [ħaːris] حُرّاس [ħurraːs] *pl:*

to bog down • **1.** طُمَس [ṭumas] طَمُس [ṭamus] *vn:* اِنطُمَس [ʔinṭumas] *p:* The car bogged down in the mud. السَّيّارَة طُمسَت بالطِّين [ʔissayyaːra ṭumsat biṭṭiːn] • **2.** طَمَّس [ṭammas] تطُمُّس [tṭummus] *vn:* تطَمَّس [ʔiṭṭammas] *p:* This illness bogged me down financially. هَالمَرَض طَمَّسنِي بالدَّين [halmarað ṭammasni biddayn]

boil • **1.** دِنبِلَة [dimbila] دنابِل [dnaːbil] *pl:* He has a boil on his neck. عِندَه دِمبِلَة برُقُبتَه [ʕindah dimbila brugubtah] • **2.** أُخُت [ʔuxut] أخوات، خوات [ʔaxwaːt, xwaːt] *pl:* That round scar on his face is a Baghdad boil. هَالنَّدبَة المدَوَّرَة بوُجهَه أُخُت [hannadba ʔilmdawwra bwuččah ʔuxut]

to boil • **1.** فار [faːr] فِيران [fiːraːn] *vn:* *sv* u. غِلَى [ɣilaː] غَلَيان [ɣalayaːn] *vn:* اِنغِلَى [ʔinɣilaː] *p:* The water is boiling. الماي دَيفُور [ʔilmaːy dayfuːr] • **2.** فَوَّر [fawwar] تَفوِير، تفُوُّر [tafwiːr, tfuwwur] *vn:* تفَوَّر [tfawwar] *p:* Boil the water before you give it to the baby. فَوِّر الماي قَبُل ما تِنطِيه لِلجّاهِل [fawwar ʔilmaːy gabul maː tintiːh liǰǰaːhil] Boil the vegetables in salted water. فَوِّر الخُضرَوات بماي ومِلح [fawwar ʔilxuðrawaːt bmaːy wmiliħ] • **3.** سِلَق [silag] سَلِق [salig] *vn:* اِنسِلَق [ʔinsilag] *p:* Please boil the eggs two minutes.

باللّه إسلُق البَيض دَقيقتَين [ballah ʔislug ʔilbiːð̣ daqiːqtayn]
to boil with rage • **1.** غِلَى من الغضَب [gilaː mnilɣað̣ab] He was boiling with rage. كان دَيغِلي مِن الغضَب [čaːn dayigli min ʔilɣað̣ab] He was boiling with rage. كان صايِر نار [čaːn ṣaːyir naːr]

boiler • **1.** بَويلَر [bawylar] بَويلَرات [bawlaraːt] *pl:* قَزان [qazaːn] قَزانات [qazaːnaːt] *pl:* The boiler exploded. طَقّ البَويلَر [ṭagg ʔilbawylar]

bold • **1.** جَسِر [ǰasir] جَرِيئ [ǰariːʔ] جَرِيئِين [ǰariːʔiːn] *pl:* That was a bold statement. هٰذا تَصريح جَرِيئ [haːða taṣriːħ ǰariːʔ]

bolt • **1.** بُرغِي [burɣi] بَراغِي [baraːgi] *pl:* This nut doesn't fit the bolt. هَالصَّمُّونَة ما تِرهَم عَالبُرغِي [haṣṣammuːna maː tirham ʕalburɣi] • **2.** طُول [ṭuːl] طوال [ṭwaːl] *pl:* There are only ten yards of material left in this bolt. بُقَت بَسّ عَشِر ياردات قماش بِهَالطُّول [buqat bass ʕašir yaːrdaːt qmaːš bhaṭṭuːl] • **3.** لسان [lsaːn] لسانات، ألسِنَة [lsaːnaːt, ʔalsina] *pl:* سِقّاطَة [siqqaːṭa, saqqaːṭa] سِقّاطات [siqqaːṭaːt, saqqaːṭaːt] *pl:* Did you push the bolt shut? سَدَّيت اللِّسان [saddiːt ʔillisaːn] • **4.** صاعِقَة [ṣaːʕiqa] صَواعِق [ṣawaːʕiq] *pl:* The news came like a bolt from the blue. ذِيك الأخبار نِزلَت مِثل الصّاعِقَة [ðiːč ʔilʔaxbaːr nizlat miθl ʔiṣṣaːʕiqa]
to bolt • **1.** حَطّ [ħaṭṭ] *sv* u. You forgot to bolt the garage door. إنتَ نِسِيت تحُطّ السَقّاطَة بِباب الكَراج [ʔinta nisiːt tħuṭṭ ʔiṣṣaqqaːṭa bibaːb ʔilgaraːǰ] • **2.** شَدّ [šadd] شَدّ [šadd] *vn: sv* i. رَكَّب [rakkab] *sv* i. Bolt the plate onto the work bench. شِدّ الرّاسطَة عالتِّزقَة [šidd ʔirraːsṭa ʕattizgaː] • **3.** جِمَح [ǰimaħ] جمُوح [ǰmuːħ] *vn: sv* a. Suddenly the horse shied and bolted. عَلَى غَفلَة جِفَل الحصان وَجِمَح [ʕala ɣafla ǰifal ʔilħṣaːn wǰimaħ]

bomb • **1.** قُنبُلَة [qunbula] قَنابِل [qanaːbil] *pl:* بَمبَة [bamba] بَمبات [bambaːt] *pl:* The whole district has been destroyed by bombs. المَنطِقَة كُلّها كانَت مدَمَّرَة بالقَنابُل [ʔilmanṭiqa kullha čaːnat mdammra bilqanaːbul]
to bomb • **1.** قِصَف [giṣaf] قَصُف [qaṣuf] *vn:* اِنقِصَف [ʔinqiṣaf] *p:* The planes bombed the factory again during the night. الطَّيّارات قُصفَت المَعمَل مَرَّة لُخ باللَّيل [ʔiṭṭiyyaːraːt quṣfat ʔilmaʕmal marra lux billayl]

bomber • **1.** قاصِفَة [qaːṣifa] قاصِفات [qaːṣifaːt] *pl:* The Air Force is using a new type of long-range bomber. القُوَّة الجَوِّيَّة دَتِستَعمِل نُوع جِدِيد مِن القاصِفات بِعِيدَة المَدَى [ʔilquwwa ʔiǰǰawwiyya datistaʕmil nuːʕ ǰidiːd min ʔilqaːṣifaːt biʕiːdat ʔilmada]

bond • **1.** سَنَد [sanad] سَنَدات [sanadaːt] *pl:* He invested all his money in stocks and bonds. كُلّ فلُوسَه شَغَّلها بالأسهُم والسَّنَدات [kull fluːsah šaɣɣalha bilʔashum wʔissanadaːt] • **2.** رابِطَة [raːbiṭa] رَوابِط [rawaːbiṭ] *pl:* There's a firm bond between the two friends. أكُو فَدّ رابِطَة قَوِيَّة بين الصَّدِيقَين [ʔaku fadd raːbiṭa qawiyya biːn ʔiṣṣadiːqayn]

bone • **1.** عَظمَة [ʕað̣ma] عَظمات [ʕað̣maːt] *pl:* عَظُم [ʕað̣um] عظام [ʕð̣aːm] *pl:* Give the dog a bone. اِنطِي لِلكَلِب فَدّ عَظمَة [ʔinṭi liččalib fadd ʕað̣ma] He's nothing but skin and bones. هُوَّ بَسّ جِلد وَعَظُم [huwwa bass ǰild wʕað̣um] This fish has an awful lot of bones. هَالسِّمكَة مَليانَة عظام [hassimča malyaːna ʕð̣aːm]
*** He made no bones about his intentions.** • **1.** هُوَّ ما حاوَل يسَوِّي شِي جَوَّة العَباة [huwwa maː ħaːwal ysawwi ši ǰawwa lʕaba]
*** I feel chilled to the bone.** • **1.** دَأحِسّ جِمدَت عظامِي [da ʔaħiss ǰimdat ʕð̣aːmi]

bonfire • **1.** نار [naːr] نِيران [niːraːn] *pl:*

bonnet • **1.** كلاو [klaːw] كلاوات [klaːwaːt] *pl:*

bonus • **1.** عَلاوَة [ʕalaːwa] مِنحَة [minħa] مِنَح [minaħ] *pl:* The employees here get a bonus at the end of each year. المُستَخدَمِين هنا ياخذُون علاوَة بنِهايَة كُلّ سَنَة [ʔilmustaxdamiːn hna yaːxðuːn ʕlaːwa bnihaːyat kull sana]

book • **1.** كِتاب [kitaːb] كُتُب [kutub] *pl:* Did you like the book? عِجَبَك الكِتاب؟ [ʕiǰabak ʔilkitaːb?]

bookbindery • **1.** مَحَلّ تَجلِيد الكُتُب [maħall taǰliːd ʔilkutub] مَحَلّات تَجلِيد الكُتُب [maħallaːt taǰliːd ʔilkutub] *pl:*

bookcase • **1.** دِيلاب [diːlaːb] دوالِيب [dwaːliːb] *pl:* مَكتَبَة [maktaba] مَكتَبات [maktabaːt] *pl:* Close the bookcase. سِدّ الدِّيلاب مال الكُتُب [sidd ʔiddiːlaːb maːl ʔilkutub] Close the bookcase. سِدّ باب المَكتَبَة [sidd baːb ʔilmaktaba]

book end • **1.** سَنّادَة مال كُتُب [sannaːda maːl kutub] سَنّادات مال كُتُب [sannaːdaːt maːl kutub] *pl:*

bookkeeper • **1.** مُحاسِب [muħaːsib] مُحاسِبِين [muħaːsibiːn] *pl:*

bookkeeping • **1.** مُحاسَبَة [muħaːsaba] مُحاسَبات [muħaːsabaːt] *pl:* مَسِك الدَفاتِر [masik ʔiddafaːtir]

booklet • **1.** كُرّاسَة [kurraːsa] كُرّاسات [kurraːsaːt] *pl:*

bookstore • **1.** مَكتَبَة [maktaba] مَكتَبات [maktabaːt] *pl:* Were you in this bookstore? إنتَ خاشّ بِهَالمَكتَبَة؟ [ʔinta xaːšš bhalmaktaba?]

boom • **1.** دَويَة [dawya] دَويات [dawyaːt] *pl:* You can hear the boom of the cannon. تِقدَر تِسمَع دَويَة المَدفَع [tigdar tismaʕ dawyat ʔilmadfaʕ] • **2.** وَقت النِعمَة [wakt ʔinniʕma]

B

وَقت الخَير [wakt ʔilxiːr] He made all his money in the boom during the war. حَصَّل كُلّ فلُوسَه بوَقِت النِّعمَة أثناء الحَرُب [ħaṣṣal kull fluːsah bwakit ʔinniʕma ʔaθnaːʔ ʔilħarub] How do you explain this sudden boom? شلُون تفَسِّر هَالخَير اِش صار عَلَى غَفلَة؟ [šluːn tfassir halxiːr ʔiṣṣaːr ʕala ɣafla?]

to boom • **1.** لَعلَع [laʕlaʕ] لَعلَعَة [laʕlaʕa] *vn: sv* i. دُوا [duwaː] دُويات، أدويَة [duwyaːt, ʔadwiya] *pl:* دَوي [dawi] *vn: sv* i. He has a booming voice. عِندَه صُوت يلَعلِع [ʕindah ṣuːt ylaʕliʕ] • **2.** راج [raːǰ] رَواج [rawaːǰ] *vn: sv* u. اِزدِهَر [ʔizdihar] اِزدِهار [ʔizdihaːr] *vn: sv* i. Our business is booming now. شُغلنا هَسَّة رايج [šuɣlna hassa raːyiǰ]

to boost • **1.** صَعَّد [ṣaʕʕad] تَصعِيد [taṣʕiːd] *vn:* تصَعَّد [tṣaʕʕad] *p:* The drought has boosted the prices of wheat. قِلَّة المُطَر صَعِّدَت أسعار الحُنطَة [qillat ʔilmuṭar ṣaʕʕidat ʔasʕaːr ʔilħunṭa]

boot • **1.** جُزمَة [ǰuzma, čazma] جُزَم [ǰuzam, čuzam] *pl:* When I go fishing I wear high boots. لَمّا أرُوح الصَّيد السِّمَك ألبَس جُزمَة [lamma ʔaruːħ ʔiṣṣiːd ʔissimač ʔalbas ǰuzma] • **2.** بُسطال [busṭaːl] بَساطِيل [basaːṭiːl] *pl:* Soldiers wear black boots. الجِّنُود يلبَسُون بَساطِيل سُود [ʔiǰǰinuːd yilbasuːn psaːṭiːl suːd]

to boot • **1.** كمالَة [čmaːla] علاوَة [ʕlaːwa] He paid me for my work and gave me five dinars to boot. دِفَعلِي حَقِّي وَإنطانِي خَمس دَنانِير كمالَة [difaʕli ħaqqi wʔinṭaːni xams danaːniːr čmaːla]

to boot • **1.** جَلَّق [čallaq] تَجلِيق [tačliːq] *vn:* تجَلَّق [tčallaq] *p:* They booted him out of the coffee house. جَلِّقَوه مِن القَهوَة [čalliqawh min ʔilgahwa]

bootblack • **1.** صَبّاغ قَنادِر [ṣabbaːɣ qanaːdir] صَبابِيغ قَنادِر [ṣabaːbiːɣ qanaːdir] *pl:*

booth • **1.** مَحَلّ [maħall] مَحَلّات [maħallaːt] *pl:* There were many display booths at the fair. كان أكُو هوايَة مَحَلّات عَرِض بالمَعرَض [čaːn ʔaku hwaːya maħallaːt ʕariđ bilmaʕrađ] • **2.** مَقصُورَة [maqṣuːra] مَقصُورات [maqṣuːraːt] *pl:* I'm calling from a phone booth. دَاخابُر مِن مَقصُورَة تِلِفُون [daxaːbur min maqṣuːrat tilifuːn]

border • **1.** حَدّ [ħadd] حُدُود [ħuduːd] *pl:* When do we reach the border? شوَقِت نُوصَل لِلحِدُود؟ [šwakit nuːṣal lilħiduːd?] • **2.** حاشيَة [ħaːšiya] حَواشِي [ħawaːši] *pl:* The border of this rug is getting worn. حاشيَة هَالزُّولِيَّة سايفَة [ħaːšyat hazzuːliyya saːyfa]

to be bordered by • **1.** اِنحَدّ [ʔinħadd] *sv* a. مَحدُود ب [maħduːd b-] Holland is bordered on the south by Belgium. هَولَندَة مَحدُودَة مِن الجِنُوب بِبَلجِيكا [huːlanda maħduːda min ʔilǰinuːb bibalǰiːka]

to border on • **1.** كاد يُوصَل لِ [kaːd yuːṣal li-] *sv* a. That borders on the ridiculous. هَذا يكاد يُوصَل لِدَرَجَة السَّخافَة [haːđa ykaːd yuːṣal lidaraǰat ʔissaxaːfa]

border line • **1.** حِدُود [ħiduːd] The border line of my property is marked by a row of trees. حِدُود مُلكِي معَيَّن بقَطَر أشجار [ħiduːd mulki mʕayyan bqaṭar ʔašǰaːr] • **2.** بَين بَين [bayn bayn] That is a border line case. هَالقَضِيَّة بَين بَين [halqađiyya bayn bayn]

to bore • **1.** زِرَف [ziraf] زُرُف [zuruf] *vn:* اِنزِرَف [ʔinziraf] *p:* We'll have to bore a hole through the wall. إحنا لازِم نِزرُف زُرُف بِالحايِط [ʔiħna laːzim nizruf zuruf bilħaːyiṭ] • **2.** ضَوَّج [đawwaǰ] تضُوُّج، تَضويج [tđuwwuǰ tađwiːǰ] *vn:* تضَوَّج [tđawwaǰ] *p:* His speech bored me. الحَدِيث مالَه ضَوَّجنِي [ʔilħadiːθ maːlah đawwaǰni]

to be bored • **1.** مَلّ [mall] مَلَل [malal] *vn:* اِنمَلّ [ʔinmall] *p:* ضاج [đaːǰ] ضَوج، ضَوَجان [đuːǰ, đawaǰaːn] *vn: sv* u. I'm bored of always seeing the same faces. مَلِّيت مِن شُوفَة نَفس الوُجُوه [malliːt min šuːfat nafs ʔilwuǰuːh]

boredom • **1.** ضواجَة [đwaːǰa] I almost died of boredom. مِتِت مِن الضُّواجَة إلّا شوَيَّة [mitit min ʔiđđuwaːǰa ʔilla šwayya]

boric acid • **1.** حامِض البَورِيك [ħaːmiđ ʔilburiːk]

to be born • **1.** اِنولَد [ʔinwilad] *p: sv* i. جا لِلدُّنيَا [ǰaː liddunya] جَيَّة لِلدُّنيَا [ǰayya liddunya] *vn: sv* i. مَولُود [mawluːd] مَوالِيد [mawaːliːd] *pl:* Where were you born? إنتَ وين اِنولَدِت؟ [ʔinta wiːn ʔinwiladit?] She was born blind. جَتّي لِلدِّنيا عَميَة [ǰatti liddinya ʕamya] My grandfather was born in Basra. أبُو جِدِّي اِنولَد بِالبَصرَة [ʔabu ǰiddi ʔinwilad bilbaṣra]

to borrow • **1.** اِتدايَن [ʔiddaːyan] *p: sv a.* طِلَب [ṭilab] طَلَب [ṭalab] *vn: sv* u. She borrowed the book from him. طُلبَت مِنَّه الكِتاب [ṭulbat minnah ʔilkitaːb]

bosom • **1.** صَدِر [ṣadir] صدُور [ṣduːr] *pl:*

* **They are bosom pals.** • **1.** ذَولَة أصدِقاء طَوخ [đawla ʔaṣdiqaːʔ ṭuːx]

boss • **1.** رَئِيس [raʔiːs] رُؤَساء [ruʔasaː, ruʔasaːʔ] *pl:* Do you know my boss? تُعرُف الرَّئِيس مالِي؟ [tuʕruf ʔirraʔiːs maːli?] • **2.** الكُلّ بالكُلّ [ʔilkull bilkull] Talk to his wife, she's the boss. إحكِي ويّا مَرتَه هِيَّ الكُلّ بالكُلّ [ʔiħči wiyya martah hiyya ʔilkull bilkull]

* **Who wouldn't want to be his own boss?** • **1.** مِنُو ما يريد يصِير مَلِك نَفسَه؟ [minu maː yriːd yṣiːr malik nafsah?]

B

to boss (around) • **1.** تأمَّر [tʔammar] تأمُّر [taʔammur] *vn: sv* a. Who gave him the right to boss me around? مِنُو اِنطاه سُلطَة يِتأمَّر عَلَيّا؟ [minu ʔinṭa:h sulṭa yitʔammar ʕalayya?]

to botch up • **1.** خَربَط [xarbaṭ] خَربَطَة [xarbaṭa] *vn:* تخَربَط [txarbaṭ] *p:* Your workman botched the job up and you'll have to repair it. صانعَك خَربَط الشَّغلَة وَاِنتَ لازِم تصَلِّحها [ṣa:nʕak xarbaṭ ʔiššaɣla wʔinta la:zim tṣalliħha]

both • **1.** ثنَين [θnayn] ثنَينات [θnayna:t] *pl:* Both brothers are in the navy. الأُخوَة الثّنَين بِالبَحرِيَّة [ʔilʔuxwa ʔiθθinayn bilbaħriyya] We both visited him. إحنا ثنَينّا زِرناه [ʔiħna θniynna zirna:h] I like to do both equally well. يِعجِبنِي أسَوِّي الثّنَين بدُون تَفضِيل [yiʕǰibni ʔasawwi liθnayn bdu:n tafðị:l]

bother • **1.** تَكلُفَة [taklufa] It's no bother at all. I'm always at your service. ماكُو أيّ كُلفَة، آنِي دائِماً بِالخِدمَة [ma:ku ʔayy kulfa, ʔa:ni da:ʔiman bilxidma] • **2.** دَوخَة راس [dawxat ra:s] Getting ready for the holiday is a big bother. الاستِعداد لِلعِيد دَوخَة راس كبِيرَة [ʔilʔistiʕda:d lilʕi:d dawxat ra:s čibi:ra] His constant questions are getting to be a bother. أسئِلتَه المِتكَرِّرَة صارَت دَوخَة راس [ʔasʔiltah ʔilmitkarrira ṣa:rat du:xat ra:s] • **3.** مَغَثَّة [maɣaθθa] This job is all bother and strain with no profit in it. هَالشَّغلَة ما بِيها غير المَغَثَّة وَشلِعان القَلب وما مِن وَراها فائِدَة [haššaɣla ma: bi:ha ɣi:r ʔilmaɣaθθa wšilʕa:n ʔilgalub wma: min wara:ha fa:ʔida] • **4.** إزعاج [ʔizʕa:ǰ] Pardon the bother, but I have to see you. أرجُو المَعذِرَة عَن إزعاجَك، لَكِن لازِم أشُوفَك [ʔarǰu: ʔilmaʕðira ʕan ʔizʕa:ǰak, la:kin la:zim ʔašu:fak]

to bother • **1.** زِعَج [ziʕaǰ] إزعاج [ʔizʕa:ǰ] *vn:* اِنزِعَج [ʔinziʕaǰ] *p:* Please don't bother me! أرجُوك لا تِزعِجنِي [ʔarǰu:k la: tizʕiǰni] Does my cigarette smoke bother you? الدُّخّان مال جِيكارتِي دَيزِعجَك؟ [ʔidduxxa:n ma:l ǰiga:rti dayziʕǰak?] Does the cough bother you much? الكَحَّة دَتزِعجَك هوايَة؟ [ʔilgaħħa dadziʕǰak hwa:ya?] • **2.** دَوَّخ [dawwax] تدُوُّخ، تَدوِيخ [tduwwux, tadwi:x] *vn:* تدَوَّخ [tdawwax] *p:* I really hate to bother you. آنِي ما أرِيد أدَوِّخ راسَك [ʔa:ni bilħaqi:qa ma: ʔari:d ʔadawwux ra:sak] I can't bother with that. ما أقدَر أدَوِّخ راسِي بذِيك [ma: ʔagdar ʔadawwux ra:si bði:č] • **3.** غَثّ [ɣaθθ] غَثّ [ɣaθθ] *vn:* اِنغَثّ [ʔinɣaθθ] *p:* What's bothering you? شِنُو اللِّي غاثَّك؟ [šinu: ʔilli ɣa:θθak?] What's bothering you? إنتَ مِن أيش مَغثُوث؟ [ʔinta min ʔi:š maɣθu:θ?] What's bothering you? شدَيغُثَّك؟ [šdayyuθθak?] • **4.** أنَّب [ʔannab] تأنِيب [taʔni:b] *vn: sv* i. His conscience bothered him. ضَمِيرَه أنَّبَه [ðami:rah ʔannabah]

to bother oneself • **1.** تكَلَّف [tkallaf] تكَلُّف [takalluf] *vn: sv* a. Please don't bother yourself on my account. أرجُوك لا تِتكَلَّف عَلَى مُودِي [ʔarǰu:k la: titkallaf ʕala mu:di]

bottle • **1.** بُطِل [buṭul] بطُولَة [bṭu:la] *pl:* شِيشَة [ši:ša] شِيَش [šiyaš] *pl:* Shall I get a few bottles of beer? تِردُون أجِيب كَم بُوطِل بِيرَة؟ [tirdu:n ʔaǰi:b čam buṭul bi:ra?] I'd like a bottle of ink. أرِيد شِيشَة حِبر [ʔari:d ši:šat ħibir]

bottle neck • **1.** عَقَبَة [ʕaqaba] عَقَبات [ʕaqaba:t] *pl:* The only bottle neck on Rashid Street is the Mirjan mosque. العَقَبَة الوَحِيدَة بشارِع الرَّشِيد هِيَّ جامِع مِرجان [ʔilʕaqaba ʔilwaħi:da bša:riʕ ʔirraši:d hiyya ǰa:miʕ mirǰa:n] • **2.** عَرقَلَة [ʕarqala] عَراقِيل [ʕara:qi:l] *pl:* The main bottle neck in the Post Office is the sorting section العَرقَلَة الرَّئِيسِيَّة بدائِرَة البَرِيد، شُعبَة التَّفرِيق [ʔilʕarqala ʔirraʔi:siyya bda:ʔirat ʔilbari:d, šuʕbat ʔittafri:q]

bottom • **1.** كَعَب [čaʕab] كعُوب [čʕu:b] *pl:* He found it at the bottom of the trunk. لِقاه بكَعب الصَّندُوق [liga:h bčaʕb ʔiṣṣandu:g] Bottoms up! - كَعب أبيَض [čaʕb ʔabyað] • **2.** أساس [ʔasa:s] أساسات [ʔasa:sa:t] *pl:* We have to get to the bottom of this affair. إحنا لازِم نُعرُف أساس هَالقَضِيَّة [ʔiħna la:zim nuʕruf ʔasa:s halqaðiyya] • **3.** عُمُق [ʕumuq] أعماق [ʔaʕma:q] *pl:* I thank you from the bottom of my heart. أشكُرَك مِن أعماق قَلبِي [ʔaškurak min ʔaʕma:q galbi] • **4.** جَوّانِي [ǰawwa:ni] Your shirts are in the bottom drawer. ثِيابَك بِالمَجَرّ الجَّوّانِي [θya:bak bilmaǰarr ʔiǰǰawwa:ni]

from top to bottom • **1.** مِن فَوق لِجَوَّة [min fawg liǰawwa] They searched the house from top to bottom. دَوّرَوا البَيت مِن فُوق لِجَوَّة [dawwraw ʔilbayt min fu:g liǰawwa] • **2.** مِن الراس لِلكَعَب [min ʔirra:s liččaʕab] The policeman searched me from top to bottom. الشُّرطِي فَتَّشنِي مِن الرّاس لِلكَعَب [ʔiššurṭi fattašni min ʔirra:s liččaʕab]

to reach rock bottom • **1.** وُصَل لأسفَل دَرَك [wuṣal ʔil ʔasfal darak] *sv* a. We've reached rock bottom! Things can't get worse. وصَلنا لأسفَل الدَّرَك الحالَة ما مُمكِن تصِير أتعَس [wṣalna lʔasfal ʔiddarak ʔilħa:la ma: mumkin tṣi:r ʔatʕas]

to touch bottom • **1.** قَيَّش [gayyaš] قيش [gi:š] *vn: sv* i. Can you touch bottom here? تِقدَر تقَيِّش هنا [tigdar dgayyiš hna] The boat has touched bottom. البَلَم قَيَّش [ʔilbalam gayyaš]

to bounce • **1.** قُمَز [gumaz] قَمُز [gamuz] *vn: sv* u. This ball doesn't bounce. هالطُّوبَة ما تُقمُز [haṭṭu:ba ma: tugmuz] • **2.** قَمَّز [gammaz] تَقمِيز، تقُمُّز [tagmi:z, tgummuz] *vn:* تقَمَّز [tgammaz] *p:* He bounced the ball. هُوَّ قَمَّز الطُّوبَة [huwwa gammaz ʔiṭṭu:ba]

to get (or be) bounced • **1.** اِنطِرَد [ʔinṭirad] *sv* i. He was bounced yesterday. اِنطِرَد البارحَة [ʔinṭirad ʔilba:rħa]

bound • **1.** مُكَتَّف [mukattaf] We found the man bound with a sheet. لِقينا الرِّجّال مكَتَّف بشَرشَف [liqi:na ʔirriǰǰa:l mčattaf bčarčaf] • **2.** مُجَلَّد [muǰallad] I bought a book bound in red leather. اِشتِرَيت كتاب مجَلَّد بجِلِد أَحمَر [ʔištiriːt ktaːb mǰallad bǰilid ʔaħmar] • **3.** مِرتِبُط [mirtibuṭ] I am bound by contract to finish this building in two months. آني مِرتِبِط بعَقِد أَخَلِّص هَالبِنايَة بشَهرَين [ʔaːni mirtibiṭ bʕaqid ʔaxalliṣ halbinaːya bšahrayn]

to be bound (for) • **1.** توَجَّه إِلَى [twaǰǰah ʔila] *sv* i. That boat is bound for America. هالمَركَب مِتوَجِّه إِلَى أَمريكا [halmarkab mitwaǰǰih ʔila ʔamriːka]

*** She's bound to be late.** • **1.** تَرَة راح تِتأَخَّر مِن كُلّ بُدّ [tara raːħ titʔaxxar min kull budd]

*** It was bound to happen sooner or later.** • **1.** هَذا أَوَّل وتالِي ما كان مِنَّه مَفَرّ [haːða ʔawwal wtaːli maː čaːn minnah mafarr]

boundary • **1.** حَدّ [ħadd] There is no boundary separating his property and mine. ماكُو حَدّ فاصِل بين مُلكَه وَمُلكِي [maːku ħadd faːṣil biːn mulkah wmulki]

to be bounded by • **1.** مَحدُود ب [maħduːd b-] Germany is bounded on the south by Switzerland. أَلمانيَا مَحدُودَة مِن الجِنُوب بسويسرا [ʔalmaːnya maħduːda min ʔilǰinuːb bswiːsra]

boundless • **1.** ما لَه حَدّ [maː lah ħadd] He has boundless selfconfidence. ثِقَتَه بنَفسَه ما إِلها حَدّ [θiqatah bnafsah maː ʔilha ħadd]

bounds • **1.** حَدّ [ħadd] حُدُود [ħuduːd] *pl:* His greed knows no bounds. طَمَعَه مالَه حَدّ [ṭamaʕah maːlah ħadd]

out of bounds • **1.** فَوق حَدّ [fuːg ħadd] The price he is asking is way out of bounds. السِّعر اللِّي دَيطُلبَه فُوق كُلّ حَدّ [ʔissiʕr ʔilli dayṭulbah fuːg kull ħadd] • **2.** آوت [ʔaːwt] The ball went out of bounds. الطُّوبَة طِلعَت آوت [ʔiṭṭuːba ṭilʕat ʔaːwt]

within the bounds • **1.** ضِمِن حِدُود [ðimin ħiduːd] I don't care what you do so long as you stay within the bounds of decency. ما أَدِير بال شما تسَوِّي طُول ما تِبقَى ضِمِن حِدُود النَّزاهَة [maː ʔadiːr baːl šma tsawwi ṭuːl maː tibqaː ðimin ħiduːd ʔinnazaːha]

bouquet • **1.** شَدَّة [šadda] شَدّات [šaddaːt] *pl:* باقَة [baːqa, baːga] باقات [baːgaːt] *pl:* Where did you get that beautiful bouquet of roses? منَينلَك هَالشَّدَّة الوَرِد الحِلوَة؟ [mniːnlak haššaddat ʔilwarid ʔilħilwa?]

bow • **1.** صَدِر [ṣadir] صدُور [ṣduːr] *pl:* I like to stand at the bow of the ship. يعجِبنِي أُوقَف بصَدِر المَركَب [yiʕǰibni ʔuːgaf bṣadr ʔilmarkab] • **2.** حَنيَة [ħanya] حَنيات [ħanyaːt] *pl:* He greeted me with a polite bow of the head. حَيّانِي بحَنيَة راس مُؤَدَّبَة [ħayyaːni bħanyat raːs muʔaddaba]

to bow • **1.** اِنحِنَى [ʔinħinaː] *sv* i. He bowed and left the stage. اِنحِنَى وَتِرَك المَسرَح [ʔinħinaː wtirak ʔilmasraħ] • **2.** حِنَى [ħinaː] حَني [ħany] *vn:* اِنحِنَى [ʔinħinaː] *p:* He bowed his head in shame. حِنَى راسَه مِن الخَجَل [ħinaː raːsah min ʔilxaǰal] • **3.** خِضَع [xiðaʕ] خُضُوع [xuðuːʕ] *vn: sv* a. He bowed to his father's wishes. خِضَع لِرَغبَة أَبُوه [xiðaʕ liraɣbat ʔabuːh]

bow • **1.** قوس، قوز [quːs, qaws, guːz] أَقواس، قُوزات [ʔaqwaːs, quːzaːt] *pl:* قوز [guːz] قوزات [guːzaːt] *pl:* Boys like to play with bows and arrows. الوِلِد يحِبُّون يلِعبُون بالقُوس وَالنِّشّاب [ʔilwilid yħibbuːn yliʕbuːn bilguːz winniššaːb] • **2.** قُردِيلَة [qurdiːla] قُرديلات [qurdiːlaːt] *pl:* She had a pretty bow in her hair. كانَت لابسَة قُردَيلَة حِلوَة بشَعَرها [čaːnat laːbsah qurdiːla ħilwa bšaʕarha] • **3.** قَوس [qaws] أَقواس [ʔaqwaːs] *pl:* The violinist is tightening the strings of his bow. الكَمَنجاتِي دَيضُبّ خيُوط القَوس مالَه [ʔilkamanǰaːti dayðubb xyuːṭ ʔilqaws maːlah] • **4.** عَواج [ʕawaːǰ] عَواجات [ʕawaːǰaːt] *pl:* This pole has a bow in it. Find me a straight one. هالعَمُود بيه عَواج إِلقِيلِي واحِد عَدِل [halʕamuːd biːh ʕawaːǰ ʔilgiːli waːħid ʕadil] • **5.** يَدَّة [yadda] يَدّات [yaddaːt] *pl:* Can you adjust the bows of my glasses? تِقدَر تعَدِّلِّي يَدّات مَنظَرتِي؟ [tiqdar tʕaddilli yaddaːt manðarti?]

bowl • **1.** مِنكاسَة [minčaːsa] مناكِيس [mnaːčiːs] *pl:* مَناكِيس [manaːkiːs, manaːčiːs] طاسَة [ṭaːsa] طاسات، طُوس [ṭaːsaːt, ṭuːs] *pl:* Put these apples into a bowl. حُطّ هالتُّفّاحات بِفَدّ مِنكاسَة [ħuṭṭ hattiffaːħaːt bfadd minčaːsa]

to bowl over • **1.** صِعَق [ṣiʕaq] اِنصِعَق [ʔinṣiʕaq] *p:* I was bowled over when I heard the news. اِنصِعَقِت مِن سِمِعت الخَبَر [ʔinṣiʕaqit min simiʕt ʔilxabar]

bowlegged • **1.** أَعوَج [ʔaʕwaǰ] عُوج [ʕuːǰ] *pl:* عَوجَة [ʕuːǰa] *Feminine:* مقَوَّس [mqawwas] He's bowlegged. رِجلَه عَوجَة [riǰlah ʕuːǰa] He's bowlegged. رِجلَه مقَوَّسَة [riǰlah mqawwsa]

bow tie • **1.** وَردَة [warda] وَردات، وُرُود، وَرِد [wardaːt, wuruːd, warid] *pl:* Teach me how to tie a bow tie. عَلِّمنِي شلُون أَشِدّ وَردَة [ʕallimni šluːn ʔašidd warda]

box • **1.** صَندُوق [ṣanduːg] صنادِيق [ṣnaːdiːg] *pl:* قُوطِيَّة [quːṭiyya] قواطِي [qwaːṭi] *pl:* Shall I put the shoes in a box? أَحُطّ القُندَرَة بقُوطِيَّة؟ [ʔaħuṭṭ ʔilqundara bquːṭiyya?] I have another box of cigars. عِندِي قُوطِيَّة لُخ جرُوت [ʕindi quːṭiyya lux čruːt] Would you drop this letter in the box for me? تِقدَر تذِبّلِي هَالمَكتُوب بصَندُوق البَرِيد؟ [tigdar dðibbli halmaktuːb biṣanduːg ʔilbariːd?] • **2.** لُوج [luːǰ] لُوجات [luːǰaːt] *pl:* لواج [lwaːǰ] مَقصُورَة [maqṣuːra] مَقصُورات [maqṣuːraːt] *pl:* All boxes are sold out for the play. كُلّ اللُّوجات مال الرِّوايَة مَبيُوعَة [kull ʔilluːǰaːt maːl ʔirruwaːya mabyuːʕa]

to box • **1.** لاكَم [laːkam] مُلاكَمَة [mulaːkama] *vn: sv* i. تلاكَم [tlaːkam] تَلاكُم [talaːkum] *vn: sv* a. Would you like to box? تحِبّ تِتلاكَم؟ [tħibb titlaːkam?]

boxer • **1.** مُلاكِم [mulaːkim] مُلاكمِين [mulaːkmiːn] *pl:* He has become a famous boxer. صار مُلاكِم شَهِير

[ṣaːr mulaːkim šahiːr] • **2.** كَلِب بُوكسَر [čalib buːksar] كلاب بُوكسَر [člaːb buːksar] *pl:* My brother brought back a boxer from England. أَخُويَا جاب ويّاه كَلِب بُوكسَر مِن إنكِلتَرا [ʔaxuːya ǰaːb wiyyaːh čalib buːksar min ʔingiltara]

box office • **1.** مَحَلّ بِطاقات [maħall biṭaːqaːt] مَحَلّات بِطاقات [maħallaːt biṭaːqaːt] *pl:* The box office is open from ten to four. مَحَلّ البِطاقات مَفتُوح مِن العَشرَة لِلأَربَعَة [maħall ʔilbiṭaːqaːt maftuːħ min ʔilʕašra lilʔarbaʕa]

boy • **1.** وَلَد [walad] وُلِد، ولِد، أولاد [wulid, wilid, ʔawlaːd] *pl:* This boy is Ali's son. هَالوَلَد إبِن عَلِي [halwalad ʔibin ʕali] • **2.** صانِع [ṣaːniʕ] صِنّاع [ṣinnaːʕ] *pl:* I'll have the boy deliver them. راح أَخَلّي الصّانِع يجِيب إلكُم إيّاهُم [raːħ ʔaxalli ʔiṣṣaːniʕ yǰiːb ʔilkum ʔiyyaːhum]

*** Boy, what a night!** • **1.** يا يابَة شلَون لَيلَة [yaː yaːba šlawn layla]

boycott • **1.** مُقاطَعَة [muqaːṭaʕa] مُقاطَعات [muqaːṭaʕaːt] *pl:* The boycott was lifted. اِنشالَت المُقاطَعَة [ʔinšaːlat ʔilmuqaːṭaʕa]

to boycott • **1.** قاطَع [qaːṭaʕ] مُقاطَعَة [muqaːṭaʕa] *vn:* تقاطَع [tqaːṭaʕ] *p:* We should boycott foreign products. لازِم نقاطِع المَصنُوعات الأَجنَبِيَّة [laːzim nqaːṭiʕ ʔilmaṣnuːʕaːt ʔilʔaǰnabiyya]

boy scout • **1.** كَشّاف [kaššaːf] كَشّافَة [kaššaːfa] *pl:* They have asked the Boy Scouts to take part in the parade. طِلبَوا مِن الكَشّافَة يِشتَركُون بالإستِعراض [ṭilbaw min ʔilkaššaafa yištarkuːn bilʔistiʕraːð̣]

boy's school • **1.** مَدرَسَة مال وِلِد [madrasa maːl wilid] مَدارِس مال وِلِد [madaːris maːl wilid] *pl:* That's a boy's school. هَذِيك مَدرَسَة مال وِلِد [haðiːč madrasa maːl wilid]

brace • **1.** مَشَدّ [mašadd] مَشَدّات [mašaddaːt] *pl:* He's still wearing a brace on his left leg. هُوَّ بَعدَه لابِس مَشَدّ عَلَى رِجلَه اليِسرَى [huwwa baʕdah laːbis mašadd ʕala rijlah ʔilyisra] • **2.** مَسنَد [masnad] مَسانِد [masaːnid] *pl:* This chair needs four braces to hold it firm. هَالكُرسِي يِنرادلَه أَربَع مَسانِد تلزِمَه [halkursi yinraːdlah ʔarbaʕ masaːnid tlizmah] • **3.** مزرَف [mazraf, mizraf] مزارُف [mazaːruf] *pl:* بَرِينَة [bariːna] بَرايِن [baraːyin] *pl:* Get a brace and bit and drill the holes in this board where I have marked. جِيب مِزرَف وَسَوِّي زرُوف بِهَاللَّوحَة بِالمَكانات اللِّي أَشَّرتها [ǰiːb mizaraf wsawwi zruːf bhallawħa bilmakaːnaːt ʔilli ʔaššartiha]

to brace • **1.** قَوَّى [qawwaː] تَقوِيَة [taqwiya] *vn:* *sv* i. Brace the corners with wooden cross-pieces. قَوِّي الزّاوِيَة بِخِشبات عُرضانِيَّة [qawwi ʔizzuwaːya bxišbaːt ʕurð̣aːniyya]

to brace oneself • **1.** تحضَّر [tħað̣ð̣ar] تَحَضُّر [taħað̣ð̣ur] *vn:* *sv* a. Brace yourself, here they come. تحَضَّر، تَرَة إجَوا [tħað̣ð̣ar, tara ʔiǰaw] • **2.** ذَبّ نَفِس [ðabb nafis-] ذَبّ نَفِس [ðabb nafis-] *vn:* اِنذَبّ [ʔinðabb nafis-] *p:* They both braced themselves against the door and didn't let anyone in. ثنَينهُم ذَبَّوا نَفِسهُم وَرا الباب وَما خَلَّوا أَحَّد يخُشّ. [θnaynhum ðabbaw nafishum wara ʔilbaːb wamaː xallaw ʔaħħad yxušš]

to brace oneself up • **1.** نَشنَش [našnaš] تنَشنَش [tnašnaš] *p:* I need a shot to brace me up. أَرِيدلِي فَدّ بِيك حَتَّى أنَشنِش [ʔariːdli fadd piːk ħatta ʔanašniš]

*** Brace up!** • **1.** شِدّ حَيلَك [šidd ħiːlak] / تشَجَّع [tšaǰǰaʕ]

to be braced • **1.** اِنسِنَد [ʔinsinad] *sv* i. The wall will need to be braced in two places. الحايِط يِنرادلَه يِنسِنِد بمُكانَين [ʔilħaːyiṭ yinraːdlah yinsinid bmukaːnayn]

bracelet • **1.** سوار [swaːr] سوارات [swaːraːt] *pl:* I've lost my bracelet. ضَيَّعت سوارِي [ð̣ayyaʕt swaːri]

bracket • **1.** عِكِس [ʕikis] عكُوس [ʕkuːs] *pl:* One of the brackets for the shelf has come loose. واحِد مِن عكُوس الرَّفّ مَشلُوع [waːħid min ʕkuːs ʔirraff mašluːʕ] • **2.** قَوس [qaws] أقواس [ʔaqwaːs] *pl:* Put the foreign words in brackets. حُطّ الكَلِمات الأَجنَبِيَّة بين قَوسَين [ħuṭṭ ʔilkalimaːt ʔilʔaǰnabiyya bayn qawsayn] • **3.** فِئَة [fiʔa] فِئات [fiʔaːt] *pl:* Mylast raise put me in a higher income-tax bracket. تَرفِيعِي الأَخِير حَطّنِي بِفِئَة مال ضَرِيبَة الدَّخَل أَعلَى [tarfiːʕi ʔilʔaxiːr ħaṭṭni bfiʔa maːl ð̣ariːbat ʔiddaxal ʔaʕla]

to brag • **1.** تبَجَّح [tbaǰǰaħ] تَبَجُّح [tabaǰǰuħ] *vn:* *sv* a. Does he always brag that way? هُوَّ دائِماً يِتبَجَّح هَالشِّكِل؟ [huwwa daːʔiman yitbaǰǰaħ haššikil?] • **2.** تباهَى [tbaːhaː] تَباهِي [tabaːhi] *vn:* *sv* a. Don't brag so much about your ancestors. لا تِتباهَى هَالقَدّ بأَجدادَك [laː titbaːhaː halgadd bʔaǰdaːdak]

braid • **1.** قِصِيبَة [giṣiːba] قِصايِب [giṣaːyib] *pl:* ضِفِيرَة [ð̣ifiːra] ضَفايِر [ð̣afaːyir] *pl:* I admire her thick braids. آنِي مُعجَب بِقِصايِبها المِتِينَة [ʔaːni muʕǰab bgiṣaːyibha ʔilmitiːna] • **2.** شَرِيط [šariːṭ] شَرايِط [šaraːyiṭ] *pl:* The doorman was wearing a uniform ornamented with gold braid, البَوّاب كان لابِس بَدلَة مزَركَشَة بِشَرايِط ذَهَب [ʔilbawwaːb čaːn laːbis badla mzarkaša bšaraːyiṭ ðahab]

to braid • **1.** ضُفَر [ð̣ufar] ضَفُر [ð̣afur] *vn:* اِنضُفَر [ʔinð̣ufar] *p:* Her mother braids her hair for her. أُمَّها تُضفُر إلها شَعَرها [ʔummaha tuð̣fur ʔilha šaʕarha]

brain • **1.** مُخّ [muxx] مخاخ، مخُوخَة [mxaːx, mxuːxa] *pl:* دَماغ [damaːɣ] أدمِغَة [ʔadmiɣa] *pl:* The bullet penetrated his brain. الرِّصاصَة خَشَّت بِدَماغَه [ʔirriṣaːṣa xaššat bdamaːɣah] He hasn't a brain in his head. ما عِندَه مُخّ [maː ʕindah muxx] He hasn't a brain in his head. هَذا مُخّ سِزّ [haːða muxx sizz]

to rack one's brain • **1.** شَغَّل فِكر [šaɣɣal fikr] تَشغِيل [tašɣiːl] *vn:* *sv* i. دَوَّخ راس [dawwax raːs]

تَدويخ [tadwi:x] *vn:* *sv* u. There's no use racking your brains over it. ما حاجَة تِشغِل فِكرَك هوايَة بِيها [ma: ħa:ja tišɣil fikrak hwa:ya bi:ha]

to brain • 1. كِسَر راس [kisar ra:s] كَسِر راس [kasir ra:s] *vn:* اِنكِسار راس [ʔinkisa:r ra:s] *p:* If you do that again I'll brain you. أَكسِر راسَك إذا تسَوِّيها مَرَّة لُخ [ʔaksir ra:sak ʔiða tsawwi:ha marra lux]

brake • 1. بريك [brayk] بريكات [brayka:t] *pl:* The brake doesn't work. البرَيك ما يِشتُغُل [ʔilbrayk ma: yištuɣul]

to put on the brakes • 1. لِزَم برَيك [lizam brayk] *sv* a. I tried to put on the brakes, but I didn't make it. آني حاوَلِت أَلزَم برَيك لَكِن ما لَحَّقِت [ʔa:ni ħa:walit ʔalzam brayk la:kin ma: laħħagit]

branch • 1. غُصِن [ɣuṣin] أَغصان، غُصُون [ʔaɣṣa:n, ɣuṣu:n] *pl:* The wind broke off several branches. الهَوا كِسَر كَم غُصِن [ʔilhawa kisar čam ɣuṣin] • **2.** فَرِع [fariʕ] فرُوع [fru:ʕ] *pl:* Our firm has a branch in Mosul. شَرِكَتنا عِدها فَرِع بِالمُوصِل [šarikatna ʕidha fariʕ bilmu:ṣil] The bank has two branches in town. البَنك عِندَه فَرعَين بِالوِلايَة [ʔilbank ʕindah farʕayn bilwila:ya]

to branch • 1. تفَرَّع [tfarraʕ] تَفَرُّع [tafarruʕ] *vn:* *sv* a. The road branches off here. الطَّرِيق يِتفَرَّع هنا [ʔiṭṭari:q yitfarraʕ hna]

brand • 1. مارکَة [ma:rka] مارکات [ma:rka:t] *pl:* What brand of cigarettes do you smoke? أَيّ ماركَة جِكايِر إنتَ تدَخِّن؟ [ʔayy ma:rkat jiga:yir ʔinta ddaxxin?] • **2.** نوع [nawʕ] أنواع [ʔanwa:ʕ] *pl:* صِنِف [ṣinif] أَصناف، صُنُوف [ʔaṣna:f, ṣunu:f] *pl:* We carry all the best brands of tea. عِدنا كُلّ الأَصناف الزَّينَة مِن الشاي [ʕidna kull ʔilʔaṣna:f ʔizzi:na min ʔičča:y] • **3.** دَمغَة [damɣa] دَمغات [damɣa:t] *pl:* طَمغَة [ṭamɣa] طَمغات [ṭamɣa:t] *pl:* We recognized our cattle from the brand mark. عِرَفنا بَقَرنا مِن الطَّمغَة [ʕirafna baqarna min ʔiṭṭamɣa]

to brand • 1. وُصَم [wuṣam] وَصُم [waṣum] *vn:* اِنوُصَم [ʔinwuṣam] *p:* *sv* i. He was branded as a traitor. اِنوُصَم بِالجّاسُوسِيَّة [ʔinwuṣam bijja:su:siyya] • **2.** دُمَغ [dumaɣ] دَمُغ [damuɣ] *vn:* نِدُمَغ [ʔindumaɣ] *p:* طُمَغ [ṭumaɣ] طَمُغ [ṭamuɣ] *vn:* اِنطُمَغ [ʔinṭumaɣ] *p:* Have they finished branding the new horses yet? خَلّصَوا يدَمغُون الحِصُونَة الجِّدِيدَة لَو بَعَد؟ [xallṣaw ydamɣu:n ʔilħṣu:na ʔijjidi:da law baʕad?]

brand-new • 1. كاغَد [ka:ɣad, qa:ɣad] It's still brand-new. بَعدَه بالكاغَد [baʕdah bilka:ɣad]

brandy • 1. براندي [brandi]

brass • 1. برِنج [prinǰ] (for castings) . The mortar is cast from brass. الهاوَن مَصبُوب مِن برِنج [ʔilha:wan maṣbu:b min prinǰ] • **2.** صِفِر [ṣifir] Some of our kitchen pans are of sheet brass. قِسِم مِن الجِّدُور بمُطبَخنا مِن صِفِر [qisim min ʔijjidu:r bmuṭbaxna min ṣifir] • **3.** ضابُط [ða:buṭ] ضُبّاط [ðubba:ṭ] *pl:* All the high brass were present. كافَّة كِبار الضُّبّاط كانَوا حاضرِين [ka:ffat kiba:r ʔiððubba:ṭ ča:naw ħa:ðri:n]

brassiere • 1. زخمَة [zaxma, zixma] زَخمات، زِخَم [zaxma:t, zixam] *pl:*

brat • 1. مَلعُون [malʕu:n] مَلاعِين [mala:ʕi:n] *pl:* He's a nasty brat. هَذا فَدّ مَلعُون زَفِر [ha:ða fadd malʕu:n zafir]

brave • 1. شُجاع [šuja:ʕ] شُجعان [šujʕa:n] *pl:* The brave die but one death. الشّجعان يمُوتُون موتَه وِحدَة [ʔiššjʕa:n ymu:tu:n mawtah wiħda]

bravery • 1. شَجاعَة [šaja:ʕa]

brawl • 1. عَرکَة [ʕarka] عَرکات [ʕarka:t] *pl:* Those two taxi-drivers started the brawl. هَالسُّواق التّاكسِي الثنَين بِدَوا العَركَة [hassuwwa:q ʔitta:ksi liθnayn bidaw ʔilʕarka]

to brawl • 1. تعارَك [tʕa:rak] عراك [ʕra:k] *vn:* *sv* a. Those people were always brawling and disturbing the whole neighborhood. هَذولَة كانَوا دائِماً يِتعاركُون وَيزعِجُون كُلّ المَحَلَّة [haðu:la ča:naw da:ʔiman yitʕa:rku:n wyizʕiju:n kull ʔilmaħalla] That man and his wife are always brawling with each other. هَالرِّجّال وَمَرتَه دائماً يِتعارکُون واحِد ويّا اللّاخ [harrijja:l wmartah da:ʔiman yitʕa:rku:n wa:ħid wiyya ʔilla:x]

bread • 1. خُبزَة [xubza] خُبزات [xubza:t] *pl:* خُبُز [xubuz] *Collective:* Our baker makes the best bread in town. خَبّازنا يسَوِّي أَحسَن خُبُز بالوِلايَة [xabba:zna ysawwi ʔaħsan xubuz bilwila:ya] • **2.** قُرصَة [gurṣa] قُرَص [guraṣ] *pl:* Give me six loaves of Arab flat bread. إنطِينِي سِتّ قُرَص [ʔinṭi:ni sitt guraṣ] • **3.** صَمُّونَة [ṣammu:na] صَمُّونات [ṣammu:na:t] *pl:* صَمُّون [ṣammu:n] *Collective:* May I have another half bread roll, please. أَرجُوك إنطِينِي نُصّ صَمُّونَة عوازَة [ʔarju:k ʔinṭi:ni nuṣṣ ṣammu:na ʕwa:za] Divide the bread into four pieces. قَسِّم الصَّمُّونَة إِلَى أَربَع وُصَل [qassim ʔiṣṣammu:na ʔila ʔarbaʕ wuṣal] You had better buy three extra bread rolls for dinner tonight. لازِم تِشتِرِي ثَلاث صَمُّونات لِلعَشا هاللَّيلَة [la:zim tištiri tlaθ ṣammu:na:t lilʕaša hallayla]

breadth • 1. عُرُض [ʕuruð] عُرُوض [ʕuru:ð] *pl:* اِتِّساع [ʔittisa:ʕ]

break • 1. كَسِر [kasir] كسُور [ksu:r] *pl:* They are trying to find the break in the water main. دَيحاوِلُون يلقُون الكَسِر بِالأَبِّي [dayħa:wlu:n yilgu:n ʔilkasir bilʔabbi] • **2.** اِنقِطاع [ʔinqiṭa:ʕ] A break in the relations between the two countries can no longer be avoided. اِنقِطاع العِلاقات بين البَلَدَين لابُدّ مِنَّه [ʔinqiṭa:ʕ ʔilʕila:qa:t bi:n ʔilbaladayn la:budd minnah]

• **3.** فطِر [faṭir] فطُور [fṭu:r] *pl:* Germs enter the body through a break in the skin. المِيكرُوبات تخُشّ بجِسمَك مِن فطِر بالجِلد [ʔilmi:kru:ba:t txušš bǰismak min faṭir biǰǰilid] • **4.** راحَة [ra:ħa] Take a short break before you start the next job. أُخذلَك فدّ راحَة قصَيّرَة قَبُل ما تباشِر بوَظِيفتَك الجِّدِيدَة [ʔuxuðlak fadd ra:ħa qṣayyra gabul ma: tba:šir bwaðḭ:ftak ʔiǰǰidi:da] Whenever they want a break, give it to them. كُلما يرِيدُون راحَة إنطِيهُم إيّاها [kullma: yri:du:n ra:ħa ʔinṭi:hum ʔiyya:ha] • **5.** فُرصَة [furṣa] فُرَص [furaṣ] *pl:* We have an hour break for lunch. عِدنا فُرصَة ساعَة وِحدَة لِلغدا [ʕidna furṣa sa:ʕa wiħda lilɣada] • **6.** حَظّ [ħaðð] حظُوظ [ħðu:ð] *pl:* He's had a lot of bad breaks in his life. صادَفَه هوايَة سُوء حَظّ بحَياتَه [ṣa:dafah hwa:ya su:ʔ ħaðð bħaya:tah]

*** That's a tough break!** • **1.** شلون حَظّ نَحِس [šlawn ħaðð naħis]

to give someone a break • **1.** إنطَى فُرصَة [ʔniṭa: furṣa] *sv* i. Give me a break. إنطِينِي فُرصَة [ʔinṭi:ni furṣa] • **2.** تساهَل ويّا [tsa:hal wiyya] *sv* a. I'll give you a break this time but don't do it again. هالمَرَّة راح أتساهَل ويّاك، لَكِن لا تسَوِّيها بَعَد [halmarra ra:ħ ʔatsa:hal wiyya:k, la:kin la: tsawwi:ha baʕad]

to break • **1.** كِسَر [kisar] كَسِر [kasir] *vn:* اِنكِسَر [ʔinkisar] *p:* I broke my leg. كِسَرِت رِجلِي [kisarit riǰli] My watch is broken. ساعتِي مكسُورَة [sa:ʕti maksu:ra] The boys broke the window pane. الوِلِد كِسرَوا الجّامَة مال الشّبّاك [ʔilwilid kisraw ʔiǰǰa:ma ma:l ʔiššibba:č] He won't break his word. هُوَّ ما يكسِر كِلمتَه [huwwa ma: yiksir čilimtah] • **2.** فُسَخ [fusax] فَصِخ [faṣix] *vn:* اِنفُصَخ [ʔinfuṣax] *p:* She broke her engagement. هِيَّ فُصخَت خُطبَتها [hiyya fuṣxat xuṭbatha] • **3.** نِطَى [niṭa:] *sv* i. We'll have to break the news to him gently. لازِم نِنطِيه الخَبَر بلُطُف [la:zim ninṭi:h ʔilxabar biluṭuf] • **4.** قِطَع [giṭaʕ] قَطِع [gaṭiʕ] *vn:* اِنقِطَع [ʔingiṭaʕ] *p:* He broke the string on the package. قِطَع خيط الرُّزمَة [giṭaʕ xi:ṭ ʔirruzma] He broke a string on his violin. قِطَع وَتَر بكَمَنجتَه [giṭaʕ watar bkamanǰtah] The wires are broken. الوايَرات مَقطُوعَة [ʔilwa:yara:t magṭu:ʕa] • **5.** اِنقِطَع [ʔingiṭaʕ] اِنقِطاع [ʔingiṭa:ʕ] *vn: sv* i. The string broke. الخَيط اِنقِطَع [ʔilxi:ṭ ʔingiṭaʕ] • **6.** خالَف [xa:laf] مُخالَفَة [muxa:lafa] *vn: sv* i. He has broken the law. هُوَّ خالَف القانُون [huwwa xa:laf ʔilqa:nu:n] • **7.** جَوَّز [ǰawwaz] تَجوِيز [taǰwi:z] *vn: sv* i. I'll break him of that habit. راح أجَوّزَه مِن هَالعادَة [ra:ħ ʔaǰawwzah min halʕa:da]

to break down • **1.** خِرَب [xirab] خَراب [xara:b] *vn: sv* a. The machine broke down this morning. المَكِينَة خُربَت هَاليُوم الصُّبُح [ʔilmaki:na xurbat halyu:m ʔiṣṣubuħ] • **2.** تَوَقَّف [twaqqaf] تَوَقُّف [tawaqquf] *vn: sv* a. تعَطَّل [tʕaṭṭal] تَعَطُّل [taʕaṭṭul] *vn: sv* a. The internal organization of the country broke down near the end of the war. التَّنظِيمات الدّاخلِيَّة لِلمَملَكَة توَقفَت قُرُب نِهايَة الحَرُب [ʔittanðḭ:ma:t ʔidda:xiliyya lilmamlaka twaqqfat qurub niha:yat ʔilħarub] • **3.** فُقَد [fuqad] فُقدان [fuqda:n] *vn: sv* u. He broke down when he heard the news. فِقَد السَّيطَرَة عَلَى عَواطفَه مِن سِمَع الخَبَر [fiqad ʔissayṭara ʕala ʕawa:ṭfah min simaʕ ʔilxabar]

to break in • **1.** دَرَّب [darrab] تَدرِيب [tadri:b] *vn: sv* u. I'll have to break in another beginner. آنِي راح أضطَرّ أدَرِّب واحِد لاخ جِدِيد عالشُّغُل [ʔa:ni ra:ħ ʔaðṭarr ʔadarrub wa:ħid la:x ǰidi:d ʕaššuɣul] • **2.** نِزَل عَلَى [nizal ʕala] نزُول [nuzu:l] *vn: sv* i. سِطَى عَلَى [siṭa: ʕala] سَطُو [saṭw] *vn:* اِنسِطَى [ʔinsiṭa:] *p:* Last night thieves broke in our neighbor's house. حَرامِيَّة نِزلَوا عَلَى بَيت الجِّيران البارحَة باللَّيل [ħara:miyya nizlaw ʕala bayt ʔiǰǰi:ra:n ʔilba:rħa billayl] • **3.** كِسَر [kisar] كَسِر [kasir] *vn: sv* i. They lost the key and had to break in the door. ضَيّعَوا المِفتاح وإضطَرَّوا يكِسرُون الباب [ðayyʕaw ʔilmifta:ħ w ʔiðṭarraw ykisru:n ʔilba:b]

to break off • **1.** قِطَع [giṭaʕ] قَطِع [gaṭiʕ] *vn:* اِنقِطَع [ʔingiṭaʕ] *p:* They have broken off relations with our country. قِطعَوا عَلاقاتهُم ويّا دَولَتنا [giṭʕaw ʕala:qa:thum wiyya dawlatna] • **2.** اِنكِسَر [ʔinkisar] اِنكِسار [ʔinkisa:r] *vn: sv* i. Then, the branch broke off. التّالِي، اِنكِسَر الغُصِن [ʔitta:li, ʔinkisar ʔilɣuṣin]

to break oneself • **1.** جاز [ǰa:z] جَوز [ǰawz] *vn: sv* u. I broke myself of that habit long ago. جِزت مِن هَالعادَة مِن زَمان [ǰizit min halʕa:da min zama:n]

to break out • **1.** اِنهِزَم [ʔinhizam] هَزِيمَة [hazi:ma] *vn: sv* i. He broke out of prison. اِنهِزَم مِن السِّجِن [ʔinhizam min ʔissiǰin] • **2.** ظِهَر [ðihar] ظهُور [ðuhu:r] *vn: sv* a. The plague has broken out in the south. مَرَض الطّاعُون ظِهَر بالجنُوب [marað ʔiṭṭa:ʕu:n ðihar biǰǰinu:b] • **3.** نِشَب [nišab] نشُوب [nušu:b] *vn: sv* i. بدا [bida:] اِبتِداء [ʔibtida:ʔ] *vn: sv* i. The fire broke out towards midnight. نِشَب الحَرِيق قَبُل نُصّ اللَّيل بشوَيَّة [nišab ʔilħari:q gabul nuṣṣ ʔillayl bšwayya] • **4.** حَصَّب [ħaṣṣab] تَحصِيب [taħṣi:b] *vn: sv* u. My oldest boy broke out with measles this morning. إبنِي الكِبِير حَصَّب هَاليُوم الصُّبُح [ʔibni ʔilčibi:r ħaṣṣab halyu:m ʔiṣṣubuħ] • **5.** جَدَّر [ǰaddar] تَجدِير [taǰdi:r] *vn: sv* i. If you have broken out with small pox when you were young, you won't do so again. إذا جَدَّرِت مِن كِنِت جاهِل، ما راح تجَدِّر بَعَد [ʔiða ǰaddarit min činit ǰa:hil, ma: ra:ħ dǰaddir baʕad]

to break up • **1.** فَرَّق [farraq, farrag] تَفرِيق، تفِرِّق [tafri:q, tfirriq] *vn: sv* i. فَضّ [faðð] فَضّ [faðð] *vn:* اِنفَضّ [ʔinfaðð] *p:* The police broke up the demonstration. الشُّرطَة فَرِّقوا المُظاهَرَة [ʔiššurṭa farriqaw ʔilmuða:hara] The party broke up early. الحَفلَة فَضَّت مِن وَقِت [ʔilħafla faððat min wakit] The police came and broke up the fight. الشُّرطَة إجَوا وَفَضّوا العَركَة [ʔiššurṭa ʔiǰaw wfaððaw ʔilʕarka] • **2.** تفَرَّق [tfarraq, tfarrag] *sv* a. We broke up about midnight. تفَرَّقنا حَوالِي نُصّ اللَّيل [tfarraqna ħawa:li nuṣṣ ʔilli:l to ayl] • **3.** اِنكِسَر [ʔinkisar] اِنكِسار [ʔinkisa:r] *vn: sv* i. The cold spell is about to break up. مَوجَة البَرِد راح تِنكِسِر [mawǰat ʔilbarid ra:ħ tinkisir]

B

*** Break it up! • 1.** بَسّ عاد [bass ʕa:d] / يَزِّي عاد [yazzi ʕa:d] / فُضُّوها [fuḍḍu:ha]

breakdown • 1. عَطَل [ʕaṭal] خَلَل [xalal] The breakdown happened about five miles outside of town. العَطَل صار حَوالِي خَمس أَميال خارِج البَلَد [ʔilʕaṭal ṣa:r ħawa:li xams ʔamya:l xa:rij ʔilbalad] **• 2.** إنقِطاع [ʔingiṭa:ʕ] إنقِطاعات [ʔingiṭa:ʕa:t] *pl:* فَشَل [fašal] We must avoid a breakdown in the negotiations at all costs. لازِم نِتحاشَى فَشَل المُفاوَضات بأيّ ثَمَن [la:zim nitħa:ša: fašal ʔilmufa:waḍa:t bʔayy θaman]

nervous breakdown • 1. إنهِيار عَصَبِي [ʔinhiya:r ʕaṣabi] She had a nervous breakdown. صار عِدها إنهِيار عَصَبِي [ṣa:r ʕidha ʔinhiya:r ʕaṣabi]

breakfast • 1. رِيُوق [riyu:g] فطُور [fṭu:r] I always have an egg for breakfast. آنِي دائِماً آكُلّي فَدّ بيضَة لِلرَّيُوق [ʔa:ni da:ʔiman ʔa:kulli fadd bayḍa lirrayu:g]

to give (someone his) breakfast • 1. رَيَّق [rayyag] *sv* i. His mother gave him his breakfast. أُمَّه رَيِّقَتَه [ʔummah rayyigatah]

to have breakfast • 1. تريَّق [trayyag] *sv* a. فُطَر [fuṭar] فُطُور [fuṭu:r] *vn: sv* u. Have you had your breakfast yet? تريَّقت لَو بَعَد؟ [trayyagit law baʕad?]

breast • 1. نَهِد [nahid] نهُود [nhu:d] *pl:* دِيس [di:s] ديُوس [dyu:s] *pl:* صَدِر [ṣadir] صدُور [ṣdu:r] *pl:*

breath • 1. نَفَس [nafas] نَفَسات، أنفاس [nafasa:t, ʔanfa:s] *pl:* Hold your breath. إقطَع نَفَسَك [ʔigṭaʕ nafasak]

to be out of breath • 1. نِهَق [nihag] *sv* a. I'm completely out of breath. دَأنهَق مِن التَّعَب [daʔanhag min ʔittaʕab]

to catch one's breath • 1. جَرّ نَفَس [ǰarr] *sv* u. أَخَذ نَفَس [ʔaxað nafas] *sv* u. I have to catch my breath first. خَلِّي شوَيَّة أَجُرّ نَفَسِي أَوَّل [xalli šwayya ʔaǰurr nafasi ʔawwal]

to breathe • 1. تنَفَّس [tnaffas] تَنَفُّس [tanaffus] *vn: sv* a. He's breathing regularly. دَيِتنَفَّس بِانتِظام [dayitnaffas bʔintiđa:m]

*** Don't breathe a word of this to anyone. • 1.** لا تطَلِّع هاي مِن حَلقَك [la: tṭalliʕ ha:y min ħalgak]

*** He is breathing his last. • 1.** دَيعالِج [dayʕa:liǰ] / دَيلفُظ أنفاسَه [dayilfuđ ʔanfa:sah]

*** I'll breathe again when I'm done with this job. • 1.** مِن أَخَلِّص هَالشَغلَة يِنزاح كابُوس عَن صَدرِي [min ʔaxalliṣ haššaɣla yinza:ħ ka:bu:s ʕan ṣadri]

to breed • 1. والَد [wa:lad] مُوالَدَة [muwa:lada] *vn: sv* i. My uncle breeds horses. عَمِّي يوالِد الخَيل [ʕammi ywa:lid ʔilxayl] **• 2.** توالَد [twa:lad] تَوالُد [tawa:lud] *vn: sv* a. Rabbits breed faster than many animals. الأرانِب تِتوالَد أَسرَع مِن هوايَة مِن الحَيوانات [ʔilʔara:nib titwa:lad ʔasraʕ min hwa:ya min ʔilħaywana:t]

breeze • 1. نَسمَة الهَوا [nasma ʔilhawa] نَسمات الهَوا [nasma:t ʔilhawa] *pl:* نِسمَة هَوا، هَوا طَيِّب [nismat hawa, hawa: ṭayyib] نِسمات هَوا [nisma:t hawa] *pl:* At night we got a cool breeze from the lake. باللَّيل هَبَّت عَلينا نَسمَة بَرِد مِن البُحَيرَة [billayl habbat ʕali:na nasma barid min ʔilbuħi:ra] There's not a breeze stirring. ماكُو وَلا نَسمَة هَوا تِتحَرَّك [ma:ku wala: nasmat hawa titħarrak] There's not a breeze stirring. الهَوا واقُف تَماماً [ʔilhawa wa:guf tama:man]

to brew • 1. خَمَّر [xammar] تَخمِير، تخُمُّر [taxmi:r, txummur] *vn:* تخَمَّر [txammar] *p:* We brew our own beer. إحنا نخَمُّر بيرَتنا بإيدنا [ʔiħna nxammur bi:ratna bʔi:dna]

brewery • 1. مَعمَل بيرَة [maʕmal bi:ra] مَعامِل بيرَة [maʕa:mil bi:ra] *pl:* Bavaria is known for its good breweries. بافاريا مَشهُورَة بِمَعامِل بيرَتها [bafa:rya mašhu:ra bmaʕa:mil bi:ratha]

bribe • 1. رَشوَة [rašwa] رَشوات، رَشاوِي [rašwa:t, raša:wi] *pl:* He was caught accepting a bribe. اِنلِزَم دَياخُذ رَشوَة [ʔinlizam daya:xuð rašwa]

to bribe • 1. رِشَى [riša:] رَشوَة [rašwa] *vn:* اِنرِشَى [ʔinriša:] *p:* You can't bribe him. ما تِقدَر تِرشِيه [ma: tigdar tirši:h]

brick • 1. طابُوقَة [ṭa:bu:ga] طابُوقات، طوابِيق [ṭa:bu:ga:t, ṭwa:bi:g] *pl:* طابُوق [ṭa:bu:g] *Collective:* Their house is built of yellow brick. بَيتهُم مَبنِي بطابُوق [baythum mabni bṭa:bu:g]

mud brick • 1. لِبنَة [libna] لِبنات [libna:t] *pl:* لِبِن [libin] *Collective:* The farmer and his sons are making mud bricks. الفَلّاح وَوِلدَه دَيسَوّوُن لِبِن [ʔilfalla:ħ wwildah daysawwu:n libin]

bricklayer • 1. بَنَّة [banna] بَنّايَة [banna:ya] *pl:* He's a bricklayer. هُوَّ بَنَّة [huwwa banna]

bride • 1. عَرُوس [ʕaru:s] عَرايِس [ʕara:yis] *pl:*

bridegroom • 1. عَرِّيس [ʕarri:s] عِرسان [ʕirsa:n] *pl:*

bridge • 1. جِسِر [ǰisir] جسُور [ǰsu:r] *pl:* There's a bridge across the river a mile from here. عَلَى بُعُد مِيل مِن هنا أكُو جِسِر عالنَّهَر [ʕala buʕud mi:l min hna ʔaku ǰisir ʕannahar] The dentist is making a new bridge for me. طَبِيب الأسنان دَيسَوِّيلِي جِسِر جِدِيد [ṭabi:b ʔilʔasna:n daysawwi:li ǰisir ǰidi:d] **• 2.** مَحَلّ قِيادَة [maħall qiya:da] غُرفَة قِيادَة [ɣurfat qiya:da] غُرَف قِيادَة [ɣuraf qiya:da] *pl:* Can you see the captain on the bridge? دَتشُوف الرُّبّان واقُف بغُرفَة القِيادَة؟ [datšu:f ʔirrubba:n wa:guf bɣurfat ʔilqiya:da?] **• 3.** بُرِج [buriǰ] برُوج، أبراج [buru:ǰ, ʔabra:ǰ] *pl:* Do you play bridge? إنتَ تِلعَب برِدج؟ [ʔinta tilʕab bridǰ?]

* **He burned his bridges behind him.**
• **1.** ما خَلّالَه خَطّ رَجعَة [ma: xalla:lah xaṭṭ rajʕa]
to bridge • **1.** بِنَى جِسِر [bina: ǰisir] *sv* i. There is some talk of bridging the river at a point near our village. أَكُو حَكِي راح يِبنُون جِسِر عَالشَّطّ يَمّ قَريَتنا [ʔaku ħači ra:ħ yibnu:n ǰisir ʕaššaṭṭ yamm qaryatna]

bridle • **1.** رِسَن [risan] أَرسان [ʔarsa:n] *pl:*

brief • **1.** قصَيِّر [gṣayyir] قصار [gṣa:r] *pl:* قصَيِّرَة [gṣayyira] *Feminine:* قصِير [gaṣi:r] He paid me a brief visit before he left. زارنِي زِيارَة قصِيرَة قَبُل ما سافَر [za:rni zya:ra qṣi:ra gabul ma: sa:far] • **2.** مُختَصَر [muxtaṣar] His speech was brief and helpful. خِطابَه كان مُختَصَر وَمُفِيد [xiṭa:bah ča:n muxtaṣar wmufi:d]
in brief • **1.** بِاختِصار [bixtiṣa:r] مُختَصَر مُفِيد [muxtaṣar mufi:d] In brief, our plan is this. مُختَصَر مُفِيد، هَذا مَنهَجنا [muxtaṣar mufi:d, ha:ða manhaǰna]
to brief • **1.** نَوَّر [nawwar] تَنوِير [tanwi:r] *vn: sv* u. زَوَّد [zawwad] تَزوِيد [tazwi:d] *vn:* تزَوَّد [tzawwad] *p:* Our leader briefed us on every detail of the operation. قائِدنا نَوَّرنا عَن كُلّ تَفاصِيل العَمَلِيَّة [qa:ʔidna nawwarna ʕan kull tafa:ṣi:l ʔilʕamaliyya] Tuesday you will be briefed with the final information. يوم الثَّلاثاء راح تِتزَوَّدُون بالمَعلُومات النِّهائِيَّة [yu:m ʔiθθala:θa:ʔ ra:ħ tidzawwdu:n bilmaʕlu:ma:t ʔinniha:ʔiyya]
to be brief • **1.** اِختِصَر [ʔixtiṣar] اِختِصار [ʔixtiṣa:r] *vn: sv* i. Please be brief. اِختِصِر، مِن فَضلَك [ʔixtiṣir, min faðlak]

brief case • **1.** جُنطَة مال كُتُب [ǰunṭat ma:l kutub] جُنطات مال كُتُب [ǰunṭa:t ma:l kutub] *pl:*

briefing • **1.** تَزوِيد بِالمَعلُومات [tazwi:d bilmaʕlu:ma:t] The briefing session lasted more than an hour. جَلسَة التَّزوِيد بالمَعلُومات اِستَمَرَّت أَكثَر مِن ساعَة [ǰalsat ʔittazwi:d bilmaʕlu:ma:t ʔistamarrat ʔakθar min sa:ʕa]

bright • **1.** وَهّاج [wahha:ǰ] I like a bright fire. تِعجِبنِي النّار الوَهّاجَة [tiʕǰibni ʔinna:r ʔilwahha:ǰa] • **2.** زاهِي [za:hi] She likes to wear bright colors. يعجِبها تِلبَس أَلوان زاهيَة [yiʕǰibha tilbas ʔalwa:n za:hya] • **3.** ذَكِي [ðaki] أَذكِياء [ʔaðkiya:ʔ] *pl:* He's a bright boy. هُوَّ وَلَد ذَكِي [huwwa walad ðaki] • **4.** حَصِيف [ħaṣi:f] That was a bright idea. هاي كانَت فِكرَة حَصِيفَة [ha:y ča:nat fikra ħaṣi:fa]
* **She's always bright and cheerful.**
• **1.** عَلَى طُول عَصافِيرها طايرَة وبَشُوشَة [ʕala ṭu:l ʕaṣa:fi:rha ṭa:yra wbašu:ša]
bright and early • **1.** غُبشَة [ɣubša] We're going to start out bright and early. راح نِطلَع مِن غُبشَة [ra:ħ niṭlaʕ min ɣubša] We're going to start out bright and early. راح نغَبُّش [ra:ħ nɣabbuš]

brilliant • **1.** صارِخ [ṣa:rix] You can tell his paintings by the brilliant colors. تِقدَر تُعرُف رسُومَه مِن الألوان الصّارخَة اللِّي يِستَعمِلها [tigdar tuʕruf rsu:mah min ʔilʔalwa:n ʔiṣṣa:rxa ʔilli yistaʕmilha] • **2.** بارِع [ba:riʕ] He's a brilliant speaker. هُوَّ فَدّ خَطِيب بارِع [huwwa fadd xaṭi:b ba:riʕ] • **3.** ذَكِي [ðaki] أَذكِياء [ʔaðkiya:ʔ] *pl:* He's the most brilliant man I know. هُوَّ أَذكَى واحِد أَعُرفَه [huwwa ʔaðka: wa:ħid ʔaʕurfah]

brim • **1.** راس [ra:s] رُؤُوس [ruʔu:s, ru:s] *pl:* The glass is filled to the brim. الكلاص مَترُوس لِلرّاس [ʔilgla:ṣ matru:s lirra:s] • **2.** حاشيَة [ħa:šya] حَواشِي [ħawa:ši] *pl:* The brim of your hat will protect your face and neck from the sun. حاشيَة شَفُقتَك راح تُحفُظ وِجهَك وَرُقُبتَك مِن الشَّمِس [ħa:šyat šafuqtak ra:ħ tuħfuð wiččak wrugubtak min ʔiššamis]

to bring • **1.** جاب [ǰa:b] جَيب [ǰayb] *vn:* اِنجاب [ʔinǰa:b] *p:* Bring me a glass of water. جِيبلِي فَدّ كلاص ماي [ǰi:bli fadd gla:ṣ ma:y] Won't you please bring me the other folder? ما تجِيبلِي المَلَفّ اللّاخ، مِن فَضلَك؟ [ma: dǰi:b li ʔilmalaff ʔilla:x, min faðlak?] He brought the children a present. جاب فَدّ هَدِيَّة لِلأطفال [ǰa:b fadd hadiyya lilʔaṭfa:l]
to bring about • **1.** أَنتَج [ʔantaǰ] إنتاج [ʔinta:ǰ] *vn: sv* i. سَبَّب [sabbab] تَسبِيب [tasbi:b] *vn: sv* i. The depression brought about a change in living standards. الكَساد أَنتَج تَبَدُّل بِمُستَوَى الحَياة [ʔilkasa:d ʔantaǰ tabaddul bmustawa ʔilħaya:t]
to bring along • **1.** جاب وِيّا [ǰa:b wiyya] *sv* i. Bring your children along. جِيب الجِّهّال وِيّاك [ǰi:b ʔiǰǰahha:l wiyya:k]
to bring back • **1.** رَجَّع [rajǰaʕ] ترِجِّع، تَرجِيع [triǰǰiʕ, tarǰi:ʕ] *vn:* ترَجَّع [traǰǰaʕ] *p:* Please bring the book back. أَرجُوك رَجِّع الكِتاب [ʔarǰu:k raǰǰiʕ ʔilkita:b]
to bring down • **1.** نَزَّل [nazzal] تنِزِّل، تَنزِيل [tnizzil, tanzi:l] *vn:* تنَزَّل [tnazzal] *p: sv* i. I also brought down the big box. هَمّ نَزَّلِت الصَّندُوق الكِبِير [hamm nazzalit ʔiṣṣandu:g ʔiččibi:r]
to bring in • **1.** جاب [ǰa:b] *sv* i. The dance brought in a hundred dollars. حَفلَة الرِّقِص جابَت مِيَّة دُولار [ħaflat ʔirrigiṣ ǰa:bat miyyat dula:r] • **2.** دَخَّل [daxxal] تَدخِيل [tadxi:l] *vn: sv* i. خَشَّش [xaššaš] تَخشِيش [taxši:š] *vn: sv* i. Bring the boxes in the house. خَشِّش الصَّنادِيق بِالبَيت [xaššiš ʔiṣṣana:di:g bilbayt]
to bring out • **1.** طَلَّع [ṭallaʕ] تَطلِيع [taṭli:ʕ] *vn: sv* i. Bring out the chairs and put them on the terrace. طَلِّع الكَراسِي وَحُطهُم بِالطَّرمَة [ṭalliʕ ʔilkara:si wħuṭṭhum biṭṭarma] They're bringing out a new edition of my book. راح يطَلّعُون طَبعَة جِدِيدَة مِن كتابِي [ra:ħ yṭallʕu:n ṭabʕah ǰidi:da min kta:bi] • **2.** عِرَض [ʕirað] عَرِض [ʕarið] *vn:* اِنعِرَض [ʔinʕirað] *p:* He brought out his point convincingly. هُوَّ عِرَض رأيَه بِطَرِيقَة مُقنِعَة [huwwa ʕirað raʔyah bṭari:qa muqniʕa]

B

to bring to • **1.** صَحَّى [ṣaħħa:] تَصحِيَة [taṣħiya] *vn: sv* i. Cold water will bring him to. الماي البارِد يصَحِّي [ʔilma:y ʔilba:rid yṣaħħi]

to bring to bear • **1.** اِستَعمَل [ʔistaʕmal] اِستِعمال [ʔistiʕma:l] *vn: sv* i. He brought all his influence to bear. اِستَعمَل كُلّ نُفُوذَه [ʔistaʕmal kull nufu:ðah]

to bring up • **1.** رَبَّى [rabba:] تَربِيَة [tarbiya] *vn: sv* i. Her aunt brought her up. عمَّتها رَبَّتها [ʕammatha rabbatha] • **2.** صَعَّد [ṣaʕʕad] تَصعِيد [taṣʕi:d] *vn: sv* i. Bring up my coat when you come. صَعِّد سِترتِي مِن تِصعَد [ṣaʕʕid sitirti min tiṣʕad] • **3.** ثار [θa:r] ثارات [θa:ra:t] *pl:* إثارَة [ʔiθa:ra] *vn: sv* i. I'll bring it up at the next meeting. راح أَثِير ها بِالجَّلسَة الجّايَّة [ra:ħ ʔaθi:rha bijjalsa ʔijja:yya]

brisk • **1.** * There is a brisk wind blowing today. الهَوا دَيلعَب اليُوم [ʔilhawa dayilʕab ʔilyu:m]

briskly • **1.** بنَشاط [bnaša:ṭ] He walks very briskly for such an old man. يِمشِي كُلِّش بنَشاط لواحِد شايِب مِثلَه [yimši kulliš bnaša:ṭ lwa:ħid ša:yib miθlah]

bristle • **1.** شَعرَة [šaʕra] شَعرات [šaʕra:t] *pl:* شَعَر [šaʕar] *Collective:* The bristles of this brush are beginning to fall out. شَعَر هَالفِرشَة بِدا يُوقَع [šaʕar halfirča bida: yu:gaʕ]

British • **1.** بَرِيطانِي [bari:ṭa:ni] بَرِيطانِيِّين [bari:ṭa:ni:yyi:n] *pl:*

brittle • **1.** هِشّ [hašš]

broad • **1.** عَرِيض [ʕari:ð̣] He has broad shoulders. كتافَه عَرِيضَة [čta:fah ʕari:ð̣a]

*** It happened in broad daylight.** • **1.** صارَت برابِعَة النَّهار [ṣa:rat bra:biʕt ʔinnaha:r]

*** That's as broad as it's long.** • **1.** كُلّها يَك حِساب [kullha yak ħisa:b] • **2.** منين مَا تجِيهَا سَوَى [mi:n ma: tji:ha sawa]

broadcast • **1.** إذاعَة [ʔiða:ʕa] Did you listen to the broadcast? سمَعت الإذاعَة؟ [smaʕt ʔilʔiða:ʕa?]

to broadcast • **1.** ذاع [ða:ʕ] إذاعَة [ʔiða:ʕa] *vn:* اِنذاع [ʔinða:ʕ] *p:* They will broadcast directly from London. راح يذِيعُون مِن لَندَن رأساً [ra:ħ yði:ʕu:n min landan raʔsan] If you tell her, she'll broadcast it all over the neighborhood. إذا تقُولها تَرَة تذِيعلَك إيّاه بكُلّ المَحَلَّة [ʔiða dgu:lilha tara dði:ʕlak ʔiyya:h bkull ʔilmaħalla] • **2.** نِشَر [nišar] نَشِر [našir] *vn:* اِنّشَر [ʔinnišar] *p:* I wouldn't broadcast it if I were you. ما أنشُرها، لَو بمَكانَك [ma: ʔanšurha, law bmaka:nak]

broadcloth • **1.** جَوخ [ču:x] جواخ [čwa:x] *pl:* I bought a good piece of broadcloth today. اِشتِرَيت قِطعَة جُوخ زينَة اليُوم [ʔištiri:t qiṭʕa ču:x zi:na ʔilyu:m]

broad-minded • **1.** صَدرَه رَحِب [ṣadrah raħib] She's a very broad-minded person. صَدِرها رَحِب هوايَة [ṣadirha raħib hwa:ya]

brochure • **1.** كُرّاسَة [kurra:sa] كُرّاسات [kurra:sa:t] *pl:* There is a very interesting brochure on that subject. أكُو كُرّاسَة مُمتِعَة عَن هَالمَوضُوع [ʔaku kurra:sa mumtiʕa ʕan halmawð̣u:ʕ]

to broil • **1.** شُوَى [šuwa:] شَوِي [šawy] *vn:* اِنشوَى [ʔinšwa:] *p:* Broil the chicken on a skewer. إشوِي الدِّجاجَة بشِيش [ʔišwi ʔiddija:ja bši:š]

broke • **1.** مِفلِس [miflis, muflis] مَفالِيس [mafa:li:s] *pl:* I was broke at that time and couldn't afford to buy it. كِنِت مِفلِس ذاك الوَقِت وَما قدَرت أشتِري [činit miflis ða:k ʔilwakit wama: gdarit ʔaštiri]

to go broke • **1.** فَلَّس [fallas] إفلاس [ʔifla:s] *vn: sv* i. أفلَس [ʔaflas] *sv* i. Ali went broke again. عَلِي هَمّ أفلَس [ʕali hamm ʔaflas] • **2.** اِنكِسَر [ʔinkisar] *sv* i. The merchant is about to go broke. التّاجِر عَلَى وَشَك يِنكِسِر [ʔitta:jir ʕala wašak yinkisir]

broker • **1.** دَلّال [dalla:l] If you want to sell your house quickly, get a broker. إذا ترِيد تبِيع بَيتَك بساع، شُوفلَك دَلّال [ʔiða tri:d tbi:ʕ baytak bsa:ʕ, šu:flak dalla:l]

customs broker • **1.** مطَلِّعجِي [mṭalliʕči] مطَلِّعجِيَّة [mṭalliʕči:yya] *pl:* Can you find me a customs broker to take on this job? تِقدَر تلقِيلِي مطَلِّعجِي ياخُذ هاي عَلَى عاتقَه؟ [tigdar tilgi:li mṭalliʕči ya:xuð ha:y ʕala ʕa:tqah?]

bronchitis • **1.** اِلتِهاب القَصَبات [ʔiltiha:b ʔilqaṣaba:t] Your boy has a bad case of bronchitis. إبنَك عِندَه اِلتِهاب قَصَبات شَدِيد [ʔibnak ʕindah ʔiltiha:b qaṣaba:t šadi:d]

bronze • **1.** برُونز [brunz]

brooch • **1.** برُوش [bru:š] برُوشات [bru:ša:t] *pl:* I'd like to buy a nice brooch for my wife. أرِيد أشتِرِي برُوش حِلو لِمَرتِي [ʔari:d ʔaštiri bru:š ħilw limarti]

brood • **1.** فَرخ [farix] فرُوخ [fru:x] *pl:* The hen and her brood come when you call her. الدِّجاجَة وَفرُوخها يجُون مِن تصِيحها [ʔiddija:ja wfru:xha yiju:n min tṣi:ħha]

to brood • **1.** اِنغَمّ [ʔinɣamm] غَمّ [ɣamm] *vn: sv* a. اِنهَمّ [ʔinhamm] هَمّ [hamm] *vn: sv* a. Don't brood about it; try and forget it. لا تِنغَمّ عَلَى مُود هَذا، حاوِل تِنسَى [la: tinɣamm ʕala mu:d ha:ða, ħa:wil tinsa:] • **2.** مَغمُوم، مَهمُوم [maɣmu:m, mahmu:m] What are you brooding about? لِيش مَغمُوم؟ [li:š maɣmu:m?] What are you brooding about? إنتَ لِيش مَهمُوم؟ [ʔinta li:š mahmu:m?]

brooder • **1.** مَكِينَة تَفرِيخ [maki:nat tafri:x] مَكايِن تَفرِيخ [maka:yin tafri:x] *pl:* If I can find a small brooder I'm going to hatch my own chickens. إذا أَلقي مَكِينَة تفرِيخ صغَيِّرَة راح أفَقِّس دِجاجِي بنَفسِي [ʔiða ʔalgi maki:nat tafri:x ṣɣayyra ra:ћ ʔafaggis dija:ji bnafsi]

brook • **1.** مَجرَى [majra] مَجارِي [maja:ri] *pl:* ساقيَة [sa:gya] سواقِي [swa:gi] *pl:* The brook dries up in the summer. يجِفّ المَجرَى بِالصَّيف [yjiff ʔilmajra: biṣṣi:f] The brook dries up in the summer. السّاقيَة تَيبَس بِالصَّيف [ʔissa:gya taybas biṣṣi:f]

broom • **1.** مَكنَسَة [maknasa] مكانِس [mka:nis] *pl:* مُكناسَة [mukna:sa] مُكناسات، مُكانِيس [mukna:sa:t, muka:ni:s] *pl:* Get the broom and sweep the floor. جِيب المُكناسَة وَإكنُس القاع [ji:b ʔilmukna:sa wʔiknus ʔilga:ʕ]

broth • **1.** ماي لَحَم [ma:y laћam] Drink a little of this chicken broth; it will do you good. إشرَب شوَيَّة مِن هَالمَيّ دِجاج، ينِفعَك [ʔišrab šwayya min halmayy dija:j, ynifʕak]

brothel • **1.** كَرخانَة [karxa:na] كَرخانات، كَرخايِن [karxa:na:t, karxa:yin] *pl:* كَلَّجِيَّة [kallačiyya] The club turned out to be nothing but a brothel. النّادِي طِلَع بِالحَقِيقَة كَرخانَة [ʔinna:di ṭilaʕ bilћaqi:qa karxa:na]

brother • **1.** أخ [ʔax] أُخوَة [ʔuxwa] *pl:* أُخوَة [ʔuxwa] أُخوان [ʔuxwa:n] *pl:* Have you a brother? عِندَك أخ؟ [ʕindak ʔax?] I bought it from Hasso Bros. إشتِرَيتَه مِن حَسُّو إخوان [ʔištiri:tah min ћassu: ʔixwa:n]

brotherhood • **1.** أُخُوَّة [ʔuxuwwa] His speech was all about brotherhood and pan-Arabism. خِطابَه كُلَّه كان عَن الأُخُوَّة وَالعُرُوبَة [xiṭa:bah kullah ča:n ʕann ʔilʔuxuwwa wilʕuru:ba]

brother-in-law • **1.** نسِيب [nisi:b] نِسبان، نِسابَة [nisba:n, nisa:ba] *pl:* رَجِل أُخُت [rajil ʔuxut] رياجِيل خَوات [riya:ji:l xawa:t] *pl:* • **2.** عَدِيل [ʕadi:l] عُدالاء، عِدلان [ʕuda:la:ʔ, ʕidla:n] *pl:* (wife's sister's husband)

brow • **1.** قُصَّة [guṣṣa] قُصَص [guṣaṣ] *pl:* He wiped the sweat off his brow. مِسَح العَرَق مِن قُصّتَه [misaћ ʔilʕarag min guṣṣṭah]

brown • **1.** بُنِّي [bunni] قَهوائِي [qahwa:ʔi] أسمَر [ʔasmar] سُمُر [sumur] *pl:* سَمرَة [samra] *Feminine:* Her hair and eyes are brown. لُون شَعَرها وَعيُونها بُنِّي [lu:n šaʕarha wʕyu:nha bunni]

to brown • **1.** إحمَرّ [ʔiћmarr] *sv* i. Leave the meat in the oven until it browns. خَلِّي اللَّحَم بِالفِرن إلَى أن يِحمَرّ [xalli ʔillaћam bilfirin ʔila ʔan yiћmarr] • **2.** حِمَس [ћimas] حَمِس [ћamis] *vn:* *sv* i. First brown the onions in a little fat. أوَّل إحمِس البُصَل بشوَيَّة دِهِن [ʔawwal ʔiћmis ʔilbuṣal bšwayya dihin]

to browse • **1.** تفَرَّج [tfarraj] تَفَرُّج [tafarruj] *vn:* *sv* a. I love to browse for books in a good book store. يعجِبنِي أتفَرَّج عالكُتُب بمَكتَبَة زينَة [yiʕjibni ʔatfarraj ʕalkutub bmaktaba zayna]

brucellosis • **1.** الحُمَّى المالطِيَّة [ʔilћumma ʔilma:lṭiyya]

bruise • **1.** رَضَّة [raðða] رَضّات [raðða:t] *pl:* He had a bruise on his left foot. كان عِندَه رَضَّة بِرِجلَه اليِسرَى [ča:n ʕindah raðða brijilah ʔilyisra]

to bruise • **1.** رَضّ [raðð] رَضّ [raðð] *vn:* إنرَضّ [ʔinraðð] *p:* The boy bruised his knee. الوَلَد رَضّ رُكُبتَه [ʔilwalad raðð rukubtah]

brunette • **1.** سَمرَة [samra] سُمُر [sumur] *pl:*

brunt • **1.** شِدَّة [šidda] The infantry bore the brunt of the attack. شِدَّة الهُجُوم وُقَع عالمُشاة [šiddat ʔilhuju:m wugaʕ ʕalmuša:t]

brush • **1.** فِرشَة [firča] فِرَش [firač] *pl:* برِشَة [pirča] بِرَش [pirač] *pl:* You can use this brush for your shoes. تِقدَر تِستَعمِل هَالفِرشَة لِقَنادرَك [tigdar tistaʕmil halfirča lqana:drak] Who left the brush in the paint? مِنُو تِرَك الفِرشَة بِالصُّبُغ؟ [minu tirak ʔilfirča biṣṣubuɣ?]

to brush • **1.** فَرَّش [farrač] تِفِرِّش [tfirrič] *vn:* تفَرَّش [tfarrač] *p:* I brush my hair every evening. آني أفَرِّش شَعرِي كُلّ لَيلَة [ʔa:ni ʔafarrič šaʕri kull layla] I have to brush my teeth. لازِم أفَرِّش سنُونِي [la:zim ʔafarrič snu:ni]

to brush aside • **1.** تجاهَل [tja:hal, dja:hal] تَجاهُل [taja:hul] *vn:* *sv* a. He brushed my protests aside. تجاهَل إحتِجاجاتِي [dja:hal ʔiћtija:ja:ti]

to brush up on • **1.** راجَع [ra:jaʕ] مُراجَعَة [mura:jaʕa] *vn:* *sv* i. I'm brushing up on German. دَأراجِع اللُّغَة الألمانِيَّة [daʔara:jiʕ ʔillu:ɣa ʔilʔalma:niyya]

brush off • **1.** دَفعَة [dafʕa] دَفعات [dafʕa:t] *pl:* She gave me the brush off. إنطَتنِي دَفعَة [ʔinṭatni dafʕa] She gave me the brush off. لِقَتلِي حِجَّة [ligatli ћijja]

to brush off • **1.** فَرَّك [farrač] تَفرِيك [tafri:č] *vn:* تفَرَّك [tfarrač] *p:* Brush off your overcoat. فَرِّك مِعطَفَك [farrič miʕṭafak] Brush off your overcoat. فَرِّك قَبُّوطَك [farrič qappu:ṭak]

brutal • **1.** وَحشِي [waћši] فَضّ [faðð] أفضاض [ʔafða:ð] *pl:* شَرِس [šaris] شَرِسِين [šarisi:n] *pl:*

brute • **1.** وَحِش [waћiš] وُحُوش [wuћu:š] *pl:* شَرِس [šaris] شَرِسِين [šarisi:n] *pl:* He's a brute. هُوَّ شَرِس [huwwa šaris]

brute strength • **1.** قُوَّة ذراع [quwwat ðra:ʕ] We raised the car by brute strength. طَلَّعنا السَّيّارَة بقُوَّة ذراعاتنا [ṭallaʕna ʔissayya:ra bquwwat ðra:ʕa:tna]

B

bubble • 1. بُقباقَة [buqba:qa] بُقباقات، بُقابِيق [buqba:qa:t, buqa:bi:q] *pl:* فُقّاعَة [fuqqa:ʕa] فُقّاعات [fuqqa:ʕa:t] *pl:* You can see the bubbles rise to the surface of the water. تِقدَر تشُوف البُقباقات دَتِطلَع فُوق الماي [tigdar tšu:f ʔilbuqba:qa:t datiṭlaʕ fu:g ʔilma:y]

to bubble • 1. بَقبَق [baqbaq] بَقبَقَة [baqbaqa] *vn: sv* u. The water is beginning to bubble. الماي بِدا يبَقبُق [ʔilma:y bida: ybaqbuq]

to buck • 1. قاوَم [qa:wam] مُقاوَمَة [muqa:wama] *vn: sv* u. We had to buck the current all the way. اِضطَرّينا نقاوُم التَّيّار طُول المَسافَة [ʔiḍṭarri:na nqa:wum ʔittayya:r ṭu:l ʔilmasa:fa]

bucket • 1. سَطلَة، سَطِل [saṭla, saṭil] سَطلات، سطُولَة [saṭla:t, sṭu:la] *pl:*

buckle • 1. بزِيم [bzi:m] بزيمات، بزايِم [bzi:ma:t, bza:yim] *pl:* I lost the buckle of my leather belt. ضَيَّعِت البزِيم مال حزامِي [ðayyaʕit ʔilbzi:m ma:l ħza:mi]

to buckle • 1. شَدّ [šadd] شَدّ [šadd] *vn:* اِنشَدّ [ʔinšadd] *p: sv* i. I can't buckle the strap. ما أَقدَر أَشِدّ السَّير [ma: ʔagdar ʔašidd ʔissayr] I can't buckle my belt. ما أَقدَر أَشِدّ حزامِي [ma: ʔagdar ʔašidd ħza:mi] • **2.** طَلَّع بَطِن [ṭallaʕ baṭin] *sv* i. The wall buckled. الحايِط طَلَّع بَطِن [ʔilħa:yiṭ ṭallaʕ baṭin] • **3.** تعَوَّج [tʕawwaǰ] تَعَوُّج [taʕawwuǰ] *vn: sv* a. The linoleum buckled from the heat. المشَمَّع تعَوَّج مِن الحَرّ [ʔilmšammaʕ tʕawwaǰ min ʔilħarr] • **4.** اِنعِوَج [ʔinʕiwaǰ] *sv* i. The beams buckled from the weight of roof. الشّيلمان اِنعُوَج مِن ثُقل السَّقُف [ʔišši:lma:n ʔinʕuwaǰ min θugl ʔissaguf]

*** It's about time we buckled down to work.**
• **1.** صار الوَقِت حَتَّى نشِدّ حَيلنا لِلشغُل [ṣa:r lwakit ħatta: nšidd ħi:lna liššyul] / صار الوَقِت حَتَّى نذِبّ نَفِسنا عالشُّغُل [ṣa:r ʔilwakit ħatta nðibb nafisna ʕaššuyul]

bud • 1. جُمبُدَة [ǰumbuda] جَنابِد [ǰana:bid] *pl:* جُمبُد [ǰumbud] *Collective:* The cold killed all the buds. البَرِد قِتَل كُلّ الجُمبُد [ʔilbarid kital kull ʔiǰǰumbud] • **2.** بُرعُم [burʕum] بَراعِم [bara:ʕim] *pl:* In spring, buds appear on the trees, بِالرَّبِيع البَراعُم تِطلَع بالأَشجار [birrabi:ʕ ʔilbara:ʕum tiṭlaʕ bilʔašǰa:r]

*** The uprising was nipped in the bud.**
• **1.** العِصيان اِنقِضَى عَلَيه وهُوَّ بِالمَهَد [ʔilʕiṣya:n ʔinqiða: ʕali:h whuwwa bilmahad]

to bud out • 1. طَقطَق [ṭagṭag] طَقطَقَة [ṭagṭaga] *vn: sv* i. The new cuttings are budding out. الأَقلام الجِّدِيدَة دَتطَقطِق [ʔilʔaqla:m ʔiǰǰidi:da daṭṭagṭig]

budding • 1. ناشِئ [na:šiʔ] ناشِئِين [na:šiʔi:n] *pl:* He's a budding author. هُوَّ فَدّ مُؤَلِّف ناشِئ [huwwa fadd muʔallif na:šiʔ]

to budge • 1. زَحزَح [zaħzaħ] زَحزَحَة [zaħzaħa] *vn: sv* i. I couldn't budge it. ما قِدَرِت أَزَحزِحها [ma: gidarit ʔazaħziħha]

budget • 1. مِيزانِيَّة [mi:za:niyya] مِيزانِيّات [mi:za:niyya:t] *pl:* Our budget doesn't allow that. مِيزانِيَّتنا ما تِتحَمَّل هَذاك [mi:za:niyyatna ma: titħammal haða:k] This is not in this year's budget. هَذا ما داخِل بمِيزانِيَّة هالسَّنَة [ha:ða ma: da:xil bmi:za:niyyat hassana]

to budget • 1. وازَن [wa:zan] مُوازَنَة [muwa:zana] *vn:* توازَن [twa:zan] *p:* You'll have to budget your expenses with your salary. إنتَ لازِم توازِن مَصرَفَك وِيّا راتبَك [ʔinta la:zim twa:zin maṣrafak wiyya ra:tbak]

to buff • 1. صِقَل [ṣiqal] صَقِل [ṣaqil] *vn: sv* u. They buff the trays to give them a high polish. يصِقلُون الصُّوانِي حَتَّى تصِير بيها لَمعَة [yṣiqlu:n ʔiṣṣuwa:ni ħatta tṣi:r bi:ha lamʕa]

buffalo • 1. جامُوس [ǰa:mu:s] جوامِيس، جِمَس [ǰwa:mi:s, ǰimas] *pl:*

buffet • 1. بُوفيَة [bu:fya] بُوفيَهات [bu:fyaha:t] *pl:* The dishes are in the buffet. المواعِين بالبُوفيَة [ʔilmwa:ʕi:n bilbu:fya]

bug • 1. حَشَرَة [ħašara] حَشَرات [ħašara:t] *pl:* This spray is good for all kinds of bugs. هَالدُّوا مُفِيد ضِدّ كُلّ الحَشَرات [hadduwa mufi:d ðidd kull ʔilħašara:t] • **2.** بَقّ [bagg] *Collective:* بَقّ [bagg] The leaves were covered with bugs. الأَوراق كانَت مغَطّايَة بِالبَقّ [ʔilʔawra:q ča:nat myaṭṭa:ya bilbagg] • **3.** قارِص [ga:riṣ] قارِصات [ga:riṣa:t] *pl:* بَقّ [bagg] I couldn't sleep because of bed bugs. ما قِدَرت أَنام بِسَبَب القارِص [ma: gidart ʔana:m bisabab ʔilga:riṣ] • **4.** بَرغَشَة [baryaša] بَرغَشات، بَراغِيش [baryaša:t, bara:yi:š] *pl:* بَرغَش [baryaš] *Collective:* At night on the river the flying bugs give you a lot of trouble. باللَّيل يَمّ الشَّطّ البَرغَش يضَوّج الواحِد [billayl yamm ʔiššaṭṭ ʔilbaryaš yðawwiǰ ʔilwa:ħid]

bugle • 1. بُوق [bu:q] أبواق [ʔabwa:q] *pl:*

to build • 1. بِنَى [bina:] بناء [binnaʔ] *vn:* اِنبِنَى [ʔinbina:] *p:* عَمَّر [ʕammar] تَعمِير [taʕmi:r] *vn:* تعَمَّر [tʕammar] *p:* Our neighbor is building a new house. جارنا دَيِبنِي بَيت جِدِيد [ǰa:rna dayibni bayt ǰidi:d] The company is going to build houses for its employees. الشَّرِكَة راح تعَمُّر بيُوت لِعُمّالها [ʔiššarika ra:ħ tʕammur byu:t liʕumma:lha]

to build in • 1. بِنَى بِالحَايِط [bina: bilħa:yiṭ] *sv* i. I'm going to build in bookcases here. راح أَبنِي هنا مَكتَبَة بِالحايِط [ra:ħ ʔabni hna maktaba bilħa:yiṭ]

to build on • 1. ضاف [ða:f] إضافَة [ʔiða:fa] *vn:* اِنضاف [ʔinða:f] *p:* We're going to build on a new wing to the hospital. راح نضِيف جَناح جِدِيد لِلمُستَشفَى [ra:ħ nði:f ǰana:ħ ǰidi:d lilmustašfa]

to build up • **1.** نَمَّى [namma:] تَنمِيَة [tanmiya] *vn:* تنَمَّى [tnamma:] *p:* كَبَّر [kabbar] تكبِير [takbi:r] *vn:* تكَبَّر [tkabbar] *p:* He built up the business. نَمَّى لِلشُّغُل [namma: liššuɣul] He built up the business. كَبَّر المَصلَحَة [kabbar ʔilmaṣlaħa]

building • **1.** بِنايَة [bina:ya] عِمارَة [ʕima:ra] عِمارات، عِمايِر [ʕima:ra:t, ʕima:yir] *pl:* Both offices are in one building. الدّائِرتَين بِفَدّ بِنايَة [ʔidda:ʔirtayn bfadd bina:ya] They're going to build a ten story building on this piece of ground. راح يِبنُون عِمارَة بِيها عَشِر طَوابِق عَلَى هالقِطعَة الأَرض [ra:ħ yibnu:n ʕima:ra bi:ha ʕašir ṭawa:biq ʕala halqiṭʕat ʔilʔarḍ]

bulb • **1.** كلُوب [glu:b] كلُوبات [glu:ba:t] *pl:* This bulb is burnt out. هالكلُوب مَحرُوق [halglu:b maħru:g] • **2.** بُصلَة [buṣla] بُصلات [buṣla:t] *pl:* بُصَل [buṣal] *Collective:* I have some Dutch bulbs in my garden. عِندِي أَبصال هَولَندِيَّة بحَدِيقتِي [ʕindi ʔabṣa:l hulandiyya bħadi:qti]

bulge • **1.** اِنتِفاخ [ʔintifa:x] اِنتِفاخات [ʔintifa:xa:t] *pl:* What's that bulge in your pocket? شِنُو هَالاِنتِفاخ بجَيبَك؟ [šinu: halʔintifa:x bǰi:bak?]

to bulge • **1.** طَلَّع بَطِن [ṭallaʕ baṭin] *sv* i. The wall is bulging dangerously. الحايِط مطَلِّع بَطِن بصُورَة مُخطِرَة [ʔilħa:yiṭ mṭalliʕ baṭin bṣu:ra muxṭira] • **2.** اِنتُفَخ [ʔintufax] اِنتِفاخ [ʔintifa:x] *vn: sv* u. Their stomachs were bulging with so much food. بَطِنهُم اِنتُفخَت مِن الأَكِل [baṭinhum ʔintufxat min ʔilʔakil]

bulging • **1.** مَنفُوخ [manfu:x] وَرَم [waram] أَورام [ʔawra:m] *pl:* His briefcase was bulging with papers. جُنطَتَه كانَت مَنفُوخَة بالأَوراق [ǰunṭatah ča:nat manfu:xa bilʔawra:q]

bulk • **1.** مُعظَم [muʕẓam] The bulk of my salary goes for rent and food. مُعظَم مَعاشِي يرُوح لِلإِيجار والأَكِل [muʕẓam maʕa:ši yiru:ħ lilʔi:ǰa:r wilʔakil] • **2.** وَزِن، بالوَزِن [wazin, bilwazin] أَوزان، [ʔawza:n, bilʔawza:n] *pl:* فَلَّة [falla] Buying bulk tea is cheaper than packaged tea. شِراء الشّاي بالوَزِن أَرخَص مِن شاي القَواطِي [šira:ʔ ʔičča:y bʔilwazin ʔarxaṣ min ča:y ʔilqwa:ṭi]

in bulk • **1.** بالجُملَة [bijǰumla] We buy dates in the bulk and package them ourselves. نِشتِرِي تَمُر بالجُملَة وَنعَلّبَه بنَفِسنا [ništiri tamur bijǰumla wnʕallbah bnafisna]

bulky • **1.** كِبِير [čibi:r] كبار [kba:r] *pl:* The sofa is too bulky to go through the door. القَنَفَة كُلِّش كِبِيرَة ما تفُوت مِن الباب [ʔilqanafa kulliš čibi:ra ma: tfu:t min ʔilba:b]

bull • **1.** ثُور [[θawr θu:r] ثِيران [θi:ra:n] *pl:*

to bulldoze (level) • **1.** سِحَق [siħag] سَحِق [saħig] *vn: sv* a. First of all, we have to bulldoze all this rock and gravel level. أَوَّلاً لازِم نِسحَق هَالصَّخَر والحَصو كُلَّه [ʔawwalan la:zim nisħag haṣṣaxar walħaṣw kullah] • **2.** وَخَّر بالبُلدُوزَر [waxxar bilbuldu:zar] *sv* i. Bulldoze them out of the way. وَخَّرهُم مِن الطَّرِيق بالبُلدَوزَر [waxxirhum min ʔiṭṭari:q bʔilbuldawzar]

bulldozer • **1.** بُلدَوزَر [buldawzar] بُلدَوزَرات [buldawzara:t] *pl:* The contractor is in the market for a new bulldozer. القُنطَرچِي دَيرِيد يِشتِرِي بُلدَوزَر جِدِيد [ʔilqunṭarči dayri:d yištiri buldawzar ǰidi:d]

bullet • **1.** رصاصَة [rṣa:ṣa] رصاصات [rṣa:ṣa:t] *pl:* رِصاص [riṣa:ṣ] *Collective:* The bullet lodged in his shoulder. الرِّصاصَة اِستَقَرَّت بچِتفَه [ʔirriṣa:ṣa ʔistaqarrat bčitfah]

bully • **1.** شَقِيّ [šaqiy] أَشقِياء [ʔašqiya:ʔ] *pl:* He is the bully of the school. هُوَّ شَقِيّ المَدرَسَة [huwwa šaqiy ʔilmadrasa]

to bully • **1.** باع شَقاوَة [ba:ʕ šaqa:wa] بَيع شَقاوَة [bayʕ šaqa:wa] *vn: sv* i. They are complaining about him bullying the smaller children. دَيِتشَكُّون مِنَّه لِأَنّ دَيبِيع شَقاوَة عَالجُّهال [dayitšakku:n minnah liʔann daybi:ʕ šaqa:wa ʕaǰǰaha:l]

bum • **1.** مهَتلَف [mhatlaf] مهَتلَفِين [mhatlafi:n] *pl:* عاطِل [ʕa:ṭil] عاطِلِين [ʕa:ṭili:n] *pl:*

bump • **1.** عِنجُرَّة [ʕinǰurra] عِنجُرّات، عَناجِير [ʕinǰurra:t, ʕana:ǰi:r] *pl:* Where did you get that bump on your head? منِين جَتَّك ذِيك العِنجُرَّة براسَك؟ [mni:n ǰattak ði:č ʔilʕinǰurra bra:sak?] • **2.** عُكرَة [ʕukra] عُكرات، عُكَر [ʕukra:t, ʕukar.] *pl:* طَسَّة [ṭassa] طَسّات [ṭassa:t] *pl:* The car went over a bump. السَّيّارَة طَسَّت بعُكرَة [ʔissayya:ra ṭassat bʕukra]

to bump (into) • **1.** عِثَر [ʕiθar] عُثُور [ʕuθu:r] *vn:* اِنعِثَر [ʔinʕiθar] *p:* He bumped into a chair in the dark. عِثَر بسكَملِي بالظَّلمَة [ʕiθar biskamli biððalma] • **2.** صادَف [ṣa:daf] مُصادَفَة [muṣa:dafa] *vn:* تصادَف [tṣa:daf] *p:* Guess who I bumped into yesterday. إحزِر إلمَن صادَفِت البارحَة [ʔiħzir ʔilman ṣa:dafit ʔilba:rħa]

bumper • **1.** دَعّامِيَّة [daʕʕa:miyya] دَعّامِيّات [daʕʕa:miyya:t] *pl:* He bent the bumper when he ran into me. عَوَج الدَّعّامِيَّة لَمّا دِعَمنِي [ʕuwaǰ ʔiddaʕʕa:miyya lamma diʕamni]

bumpy • **1.** بِيه طَسَّة [bi:h ṭassa] We drove for about an hour over a bumpy road. سِقنا حَوالِي ساعَة بدَرُب كُلَّه طَسّات [siqna ħawa:li sa:ʕa bdarub kullah ṭassa:t]

bunch • **1.** باقَة [ba:ga] باقات [ba:ga:t] *pl:* شَدَّة [šadda] شَدّات [šadda:t] *pl:* ضَبَّة [ḍabba] ضَبّات [ḍabba:t] *pl:* Let me have a bunch of radishes, please. بَالله إنطِينِي فَدّ باقَة فِجِل [balla ʔinṭi:ni fadd ba:ga fiǰil]

B

bundle • **1.** رَبطَة [rabṭa] رَبطات [rabṭa:t] *pl:* بُقجَة [buqča] بُقَج [buqač] *pl:* Is that bundle too heavy for you? هالبُقجَة ثِقِيلَة عَلِيك؟ [halbuqča θigi:la ʕali:k?] • **2.** ضَبَّة [ᵭabba] ضَبّات [ᵭabba:t] *pl:* I want two bundles of iron rods. أَرِيد ضَبّتَين شِيش [ʔari:d ᵭabbtayn ši:š] • **3.** شَدَّة [šadda] شَدّات [šadda:t] *pl:* لَفَّة [laffa] لَفّات [laffa:t] *pl:* I gave him a bundle of newspapers. إنطَيتَه شَدَّة جَرايِد [ʔinṭi:tah šaddat ǰara:yid]

to bungle • **1.** لاص [la:ṣ] لَوص [lu:ṣ] *vn: sv* u. It was a delicate job and he bungled it. كانَت فَدّ شَغلَة دَقِيقَة وَهُوَّ لاصها [ča:nat fadd šaɣla daqi:qa wahuwwa la:ṣha]

to bunk (with) • **1.** بات [ba:t] *sv* a. If you don't have a place to sleep, you can bunk with us. إذا ما عِندَك مَكان تنام بِيه، تِقدَر تبات عِدنا [ʔiða ma: ʕindak maka:n tna:m bi:h, tigdar tba:t ʕidna]

burden • **1.** ثُقُل [θugul] ثقال [θga:l] *pl:* I don't want to be a burden to you. ما أَرِيد أَصِير ثُقُل عَلِيك [ma: ʔari:d ʔaṣi:r θugul ʕali:k] • **2.** مَشَقَّة [mašaqqa] مَشَقّات [mašaqqa:t] *pl:* تَعَب [taʕab] Most of the burden of bringing up the children fell on the mother. أَكثَر مَشَقَّة تَربِيَة الأَطفال وُقعَت بِراس الأُمّ [ʔakθar mašaqqat tarbiyat ʔilʔaṭfa:l wuqʕat bra:s ʔilʔumm]

*** The burden of proof lies with the complainant.** • **1.** البَيِّنَة عَالمُدَّعِي [ʔilbayyina ʕalmuddaʕi] / المُدَّعِي لازِم يِثبِت [ʔilmuddaʕi la:zim yiθbit]

to burden • **1.** كَلَّف [kallaf] تَكلِيف [takli:f] *vn:* تكَلَّف [tkallaf] *p: sv* i. حَمَّل [ħammal] تَحمِيل [taħmi:l] *vn:* تحَمَّل [tħammal] *p: sv* i. I don't want to burden you with my troubles. آنِي ما أَرِيد أَكَلِّفَك بِمَشاكِلِي [ʔa:ni ma: ʔari:d ʔakallifak bmaša:kli] She is burdened with a lot of responsibilities. محَمَّلَة مَسؤُولِيّات هوايَة [mħammla masʔu:liyya:t hwa:ya]

bureau • **1.** دِيلاب [di:la:b] دَوالِيب [dawa:li:b] *pl:* كُنتُور [kuntu:r] كَناتِير [kana:ti:r] *pl:* The bottom drawer of the bureau is stuck. المجَرّ الجَّوّانِي مال دِيلاب الهدُوم عاصِي [ʔilmǰarr ʔiǰǰawwa:ni ma:l di:la:b ʔilhdu:m ʕa:ṣi] • **2.** دائِرَة [da:ʔira] دَوائِر [dawa:ʔir] *pl:* Bureau of Vital Statistics. دائِرَة الإحصاء [da:ʔirat ʔilʔiħṣa:ʔ]

burglar • **1.** حَرامِي [ħara:mi] حَرامِيَّة [ħara:miyya] *pl:* لِصّ [liṣṣ] لِصُوص [liṣu:ṣ] *pl:*

burglary • **1.** بُوقَة [bu:ga] بَوقات [bawga:t] *pl:* سَرِقَة [sariqa] سَرِقات [sariqa:t] *pl:* حَادِثَة سَطو [ħadiθat saṭw] حادِثَة سَطو [ħa:diθat saṭw] When was the burglary committed? شوَقِت صارَت البَوقَة؟ [šwakit ṣa:rat ʔilbu:qa?]

burial • **1.** دَفِن [dafin] دَفنَة [dafna] دَفنات [dafna:t] *pl:*

burn • **1.** حَرِق [ħarig] كَويَة [čawya] كَويات [čawya:t] *pl:* This is a serious burn. هٰذا حَرِق خَطِير [ha:ða ħarig xaṭi:r]

to burn • **1.** حِرَق [ħirag] حَرِق [ħarig] *vn:* اِنحِرَق [ʔinħirag] *p:* Have the boy burn the papers. خَلِّي الفَرّاش يِحرِق الأوراق [xalli ʔilfarra:š yiħrig ʔilʔawra:q] • **2.** اِحتِرَق [ʔiħtirag] اِحتِراق [ʔiħtira:g] *vn: sv* i. اِشتِعَل [ʔištiʕal] اِشتِعال [ʔištiʕa:l] *vn: sv* i. This wood burns well. هَالحَطَب يِحتِرِق زين [haʔilħaṭab yiħtirig zi:n] • **3.** كُوَى [čuwa:] كَوي [čawy] *vn:* اِنكوَى [ʔinčwa:] *p:* Don't touch the iron; it will burn your fingers. لا تطُخّ الأُوتِي؛ تَرَة يِكوِي أَصابعَك [la: ṭṭuxx ʔilʔu:ti; tara yičwi ʔaṣa:bʕak] • **4.** كَوَّى [čawwa:] تكَوِّي [tčwwi] *vn: sv* i. The sand is so hot it burns the feet. الرَّمُل هَالقَدّ حارّ يكَوِّي الرِّجِل [ʔirramul halgadd ħa:rr yčawwi ʔirriǰil]

*** I'm burning with curiosity.** • **1.** آنِي مَيِّت مِن الفُضُول [ʔa:ni mayyit min ʔilfuᵭu:l]

*** He's burnt his bridges behind him.** • **1.** قِطَع كُلّ أَمَل لِلرَّجعَة [giṭaʕ kull ʔamal lirraǰʕa] / ما خَلّالَه خَطّ رَجعَة [ma: xalla:lah xaṭṭ raǰʕa]

*** He has money to burn.** • **1.** عِندَه فلُوس مِثِل الزِبِل [ʕindah flu:s miθil ʔizzibil]

*** The building has burned down to the ground.** • **1.** البِنايَة دَمَّرها النار [ʔilbna:ya dammarha ʔinna:r]

to get burned • **1.** اِنكُوَى [ʔinčuwa:] *sv* i. I got burned on the iron. اِنكُوَيت بِالأُوتِي [ʔinčuwi:t bilʔu:ti]

to burn oneself • **1.** اِنكُوَى [ʔinčuwa:] *sv* i. I burned myself once already and I don't want to do it again. اِنكُوَيت مَرَّة وَما أَرِيد أَنكُوِي مَرَّة لُخ [ʔinčuwi:t marra wama: ʔari:d ʔančuwi marra lux]

to burn out • **1.** اِحتِرَق [ʔiħtirag] اِحتِراق [ʔiħtira:g] *vn: sv* i. This bulb burned out. هَالِقلُوب اِحتِرَق [halʔiglu:b ʔiħtirag]

to burn up • **1.** اِحتِرَق [ʔiħtirag] اِحتِراق [ʔiħtira:g] *vn: sv* i. His books burned up in the fire. كُتبَه اِحتِرقَت بِالحَرِيق [kutbah ʔiħtirgat bilħari:q]

to be burnt up • **1.** تقَرضَم [tgarᵭam] تقُرضُم [tgurᵭum] *vn: sv* a. He's burnt up because he can't come along. دَيتقَرضَم لِأَنّ ما يِقدَر يِجِي ويّانا [dayitgarᵭam liʔann ma: yigdar yiǰi wiyya:na]

burning hot • **1.** مِثِل النّار [miθl ʔinna:r] The soup is burning hot. الشّوربَة مِثِل النّار [ʔiššu:rba miθl ʔinna:r]

burr • **1.** شَوكَة [šawka] شَوكات [šawka:t] *pl:* شَوك [šawk, šu:k] *Collective:* The sheep's wool was filled with burrs. الغَنَم صُوفهُم كان مَليان شُوك [ʔilɣanam ṣu:fhum ča:n malya:n šu:k]

to burst • **1.** اِنفِجَر [ʔinfiǰar] اِنفِجار [ʔinfiǰa:r] *vn: sv* i. طَقّ [ṭagg] طَقّ [ṭagg] *vn:* اِنطَقّ [ʔinṭagg] *p:* اِنكِسَر [ʔinkisar] اِنكِسار [ʔinkisa:r] *vn: sv* i. The water pipe burst. بُورِي الماي اِنفِجَر [bu:ri ʔilma:y ʔinfiǰar] She's bursting with curiosity. راح تطُقّ مِن الفُضُول [ra:ħ ṭṭugg min ʔilfuᵭu:l] Last year the dam burst. السَّنَة اللِّي فاتَت اِنكِسَر السَّدّ [ʔissana ʔilli fa:tat ʔinkisar ʔissadd]

to burst into • **1.** كِفَت لِ [čifat li-] كِفِت لِ [čafit li-] *vn:* اِنكِفَت لِ [ʔinčifat li-] *p:* He burst into the room. كِفَت لِلقُبَّة [čifat lilgubba] • **2.** طَقّ [ṭagg] طَقّ [ṭagg] *vn:* اِنطَقّ [ʔinṭagg] *p:* She burst into tears. طَقَّت دمُوعها [ṭaggat dmuːʕha] • **3.** قام [gaːm] *sv* u. He burst into loud laughter. قام يقهقه [gaːm yqahqih] She burst into crying. قامَت تِبكِي [gaːmat tibči]

to burst out • **1.** طَقّ مِن [ṭagg min] طَقّ مِن [ṭagg min] *vn: sv* u. The rice is bursting out through the seams of the bag. التِّمَّن طَقّ مِن القُونِيَّة [ʔittimman ṭagg min ʔilguːniyya]

to bury • **1.** دِفَن [difan] دَفِن [dafin] *vn:* اِندِفَن [ʔindifan] *p:* We buried her yesterday. دِفَنّاها البارحَة [difannaːha ʔilbaːrħa] • **2.** طُمَر [ṭumar] طُمُر [ṭumur] *vn:* اِنطُمَر [ʔinṭumar] *p:* He buried my application under the rest of the papers on purpose. طُمَر عَرِيضتِي جَوَّة باقِي الأوراق عَمداً [ṭumar ʕariːðti ǰawwa baːqi ʔilʔawraːq ʕamdan]

bus • **1.** باص [paːṣ, baːṣ] باصات [paːṣaːt, baːṣaːt] *pl:* Would you rather go by bus? تفَضِّل ترُوح بِالباص؟ [tfaðððil truːħ bilpaːṣ?] There's a bus every ten minutes. يفُوت باص كُلّ عَشِر دَقايِق [yfuːt paːṣ kull ʕašir daqaːyiq]

bush • **1.** دَغلَة [daɣla] دَغلات [daɣlaːt] *pl:* دَغل [daɣl] *Collective:* He hid behind a bush. خِتَل وَرا الدَّغل [xital wara ʔiddaɣl] • **2.** زَرِع [zariʕ] He is hiding in the bushes. هُوّ خاتِل وَرا الزَّرِع [huww xaːtil wara ʔizzariʕ]

to beat around the bush • **1.** لَفّ ودار [laff wdaːr] Don't keep on beating around the bush. لا تظَلّ تلِفّ وَتدُور [laː tðall tliff widduːr]

business • **1.** تِجارَة [tiǰaːra] They're selling their business. دَيصَفُّون تِجارَتهُم [dayṣaffuːn tiǰaːrathum] • **2.** شُغُل [šuɣul] Business is flourishing. الشّغُل ماشِي [ʔiššuɣul maːši] Mind your own business. لا تِتداخَل [laː tiddaːxal] You have no business around here. إِنتَ ما إِلَك شُغُل هنا [ʔinta maː ʔilak šuɣul hna] What business is he in? شيِشتِغُل؟ [šyištiɣul?] What business is he in? شِنُو شُغلَه؟ [šinu šuɣlah?] That's none of your business. إِنتَ ما لَك دَخَل [ʔinta maː lak daxal] That's none of your business. هَذا ما يخُصَّك [haːða maː yxuṣṣak] That's none of your business. هَذا مُو شغلَك [haːða muː šuɣlak] Business is flourishing. السُّوق زين [ʔissuːg ziːn] Mind your own business. عَلِيك بِشُغلَك [ʕaliːk bšuɣlak] • **3.** شَغلَة [šaɣla] شَغلات [šaɣlaːt] *pl:* مَسأَلَة [masʔala] مَسائِل [masaːʔil] *pl:* قَضِيَّة [qaðiyya] قَضايا [qaðaːya] *pl:* Let's settle this business right away. خَلِّي نفُضّ هَالشَّغلَة حالاً [xalli nfuðð haššayla ħaːlan] • **4.** شَأن [šaʔn] شُؤُون [šuʔuːn] *pl:* Don't meddle in other people's business. لا تِتداخَل بِشؤُون غيرَك [laː tiddaːxal bšiʔuːn ɣiːrak]

* **What business is it of yours.** • **1.** إِنتَ ياهُو مالتَك [ʔinta yaːhu maːltak]

* **Business comes before pleasure.** • **1.** الجَدّ قبل اللِّعِب [ʔiǰǰadd qabl ʔilliʕib]

on business • **1.** بشُغُل [bšuɣul] I have to see him on business. لازِم أَشُوفه بِشُغُل [laːzim ʔašuwfah bšuɣul]

to go into business for oneself • **1.** اِشتِغَل عَلَى حسَاب [ʔištiɣal ʕala ħsaːb] *sv* u. They have gone into business for themselves. قامَوا يِشتَغلُون عَلَى حسابهُم [gaːmaw yištaɣluːn ʕala ħsaːbhum] Going into business for oneself requires a lot of capital. الشُّغُل عَلَى حساب الواحِد يِنرادلَه هوايَة راسمال [ʔiššuɣul ʕala ħsaːb ʔilwaːħid yinraːdlah hwaːya raːsmaːl]

businessman • **1.** رَجُل أَعمال [raǰul ʔaʕmaːl] رِجال أَعمال [riǰaːl ʔaʕmaːl] *pl:* He's a successful businessman. هُوَّ فَدّ رَجُل أَعمال ناجِح [huwwa fadd raǰul ʔaʕmaːl naːǰiħ]

bust • **1.** تِمثال نِصفِي [timθaːl niṣfi] تَماثِيل نِصفِيَّة [tamaːθiːl niṣfiyya] *pl:* The sculptor is doing a bust of Ahmad. النَّحّات دَيسَوِّي تِمثال نِصفِي لأحمَد [ʔinnaħħaːt daysawwi timθaːl niṣfi lʔaħmad] • **2.** صَدِر [ṣadir] صدُور [ṣduːr] *pl:* The blouse is a little too tight across the bust. هالبلُوز شوَيَّة ضَيِّق مِن يَمّ الصَّدِر [halbluːz šwayya ðayyig min yamm ʔiṣṣadir]

busy • **1.** مَشغُول [mašɣuːl] I'm even too busy to read the paper. ما أَقدَر أَقرا الجَّرِيدَة هَل قَدّ ما مَشغُول [maː ʔagdar ʔaqraː ʔiǰǰariːda hal gadd maː mašɣuːl] We're very busy at the office. بَالدّائِرَة إِحنا هوايَة مَشغُولِين [biddaːʔira ʔiħna hwaːya mašɣuːliːn] We're very busy at the office. ما نِقدَر نحُكّ راسنا بَالدّائِرَة مِن الشُّغُل [maː nigdar nħukk raːsna biddaːʔira min ʔiššuɣul] The line's busy. الخَطّ مَشغُول [ʔilxaṭṭ mašɣuːl] • **2.** بِيه حَرَكَة [biːh ħaraka] They live on a busy street. يسِكنُون بشارِع بِيه حَرَكَة وَشُغُل [ysiknuːn bšaːriʕ biːh ħaraka wšuɣul]

but • **1.** بَسّ [bass] لَكِن [laːkin] We can go with you, but we'll have to come back early. نِقدَر نرُوح ويّاك بَسّ لازِم نِرجَع مِن وَقِت [nigdar nruːħ wiyyaːk bass laːzim nirǰaʕ min wakit] But you'll admit she's pretty. بَسّ إِنتَ تِعترِف هِيَّ حِلوَة [bass ʔinta tiʕtirif hiyya ħilwa] But you know that I can't go. لَكِن إِنتَ تِدرِي آنِي ما أَقدَر أَرُوح [laːkin ʔinta tidri ʔaːni maː ʔagdar ʔaruːħ] I didn't mean you but your friend. آنِي ما عنَيتَك إِنتَ لَكِن عِنَيت صَدِيقَك [ʔaːni maː ʕniːtak ʔinta laːkin ʕiniːt ṣadiːqak] • **2.** غير [ɣayr, ɣiːr] Nobody was there but me. ما كان أَكُو أَحَّد هناك غيرِي [maː čaːn ʔaku ʔaħħad hnaːk ɣayri] • **3.** إِلّا [ʔilla] All but one escaped. الكُلّ خِلصَوا إِلّا واحِد [ʔilkull xilṣaw ʔilla waːħid] Nothing but lies! ماكُو إِلّا الكِذِب [maːku ʔilla ʔiččiðib] Now nothing but an operation can save him. هَسَّة ما تخَلّصَه إِلّا عَمَلِيَّة [hassa maː txallṣah ʔilla ʕamaliyya]

* **I was anything but pleased with it.** • **1.** آنِي وَلا راضِي بِيه أَبَداً [ʔaːni wala raːði biːh ʔabadan]

but then • **1.** لَكِن عاد [laːkin ʕaːd] The suit is expensive, but then it fits well. القاط غالِي، لَكِن عاد تُقعُد عَلَيّا زين [ʔilqaːṭ ɣaːli, laːkin ʕaːd tugʕud ʕalayya zayn]

B

butcher • **1.** قَصّاب [gaṣṣa:b] قَصّابين، قِصاصِيب [gaṣṣa:bi:n, giṣa:ṣi:b] *pl:* I always buy the meat at the same butcher's. آني دائماً أشتِري اللَّحَم مِن نَفس القَصّاب [ʔa:ni da:ʔiman ʔaštiri ʔillaħam min nafs ʔilgaṣṣa:b]

butcher shop • **1.** دُكّان قَصّاب [dukka:n gaṣṣa:b] دُكاكِين قصاصِيب [duka:ki:n gaṣa:ṣi:b] *pl:*

butt • **1.** مِقبَض [miqbað] مَقابِض [maqa:bið] *pl:* Take the gun by the butt. إلزَم البُندُقِيَّة مِن المِقبَض [ʔilzam ʔilbunduqiyya min ʔilmiqbað] • **2.** قُطُف [guṭuf] قطُوف [gṭu:f] *pl:* The ash tray is full of butts. النُّفّاضَة مَترُوسَة قطُوف [ʔinnuffa:ða matru:sa gṭu:f] • **3.** مَضحَكَة [maðħaka] Doesn't he realize that he's the butt of their jokes? هٰذا ما دَيحِسّ هُوَّ صايِر مَضحَكَة مالهُم؟ [ha:ða ma: dayħiss huwwa ṣa:yir maðħaka ma:lhum?]

to butt • **1.** نِطَح [niṭaħ] نَطِح [naṭiħ] *vn:* اِنّطَح [ʔinniṭaħ] *p:* The goat kept butting his head against the fence. الصَّخلَة ظَلَّت تِنطَح بالمحَجَّر [ʔiṣṣaxla ðallat tinṭaħ bilmħajjar]

to butt in • **1.** تدَخَّل [ddaxxal] تَدَخُّل [tadaxxul] *vn:* *sv* a. This is none of your business, so don't butt in! هٰذا مُو شُغلَك، فَلا تِتدَخَّل [ha:ða mu: šuɣlak, fala: tiddaxxal] • **2.** نَبّ عَلَى [nabb ʕala] نَبّ [nabb] *vn:* إنَّبّ [ʔinnaṭṭ] *p:* Every time we talk, her little brother butts in with a question. كُلَّما نِحكِي ينِبّ أخُوها الصّغَيِّر عَلينا بفَدّ سُؤال [kullma: niħči ynibb ʔaxu:ha ʔiṣṣɣayyir ʕali:na bfadd suʔa:l]

to butt together • **1.** راوَس [ra:was] مُراوَسَة [mura:wasa] *vn:* تراوَس [tra:was] *p:* Butt the two boards together. راوِس اللَّوحتَين [ra:wis ʔillawħtayn] • **2.** طَبَّق سُوَة [ṭubag suwa] طَبُق سُوَة [ṭabug suwa] *vn:* اِنطَبَق سُوَة [ʔinṭubag suwa] *p:* Butt the desks together this way. أطبُق المِيُوزَة سُوَة هِيكِي [ʔuṭbug ʔilmyu:za suwa hi:či]

butter • **1.** زِبِد [zibid] Let me have a pound of butter, please. إنطِينِي باوَن زِبِد مِن فَضلَك [ʔinṭi:ni pa:wan zibid min faðlak]

to butter • **1.** حَطّ زِبِد [ħaṭṭ zibid] *sv* u. Shall I butter your bread? ترِيد أحُطّلَك زِبِد عالخُبُز؟ [tri:d ʔaħuṭṭlak zibid ʕalxubuz?]

butterfly • **1.** فَراشَة [fara:ša] فَراشات [fara:ša:t] *pl:* فَراش [fara:š] *Collective*

button • **1.** دُقمَة [dugma] دُقَم، دِقَم [dugam, digam] *pl:* She sewed the button on for me. خَيّطَتلي الدُّقمَة [xayyṭatli ʔiddugma] • **2.** زِرّ [zirr] زرار، زرُور [zra:r, zru:r] *pl:* You have to press the button. لازِم تدُوس الزِّرّ [la:zim ddu:s ʔizzirr]

to button (up) • **1.** دَقَّم [daggam] تدُقُّم [tduggum] *vn:* تدَقَّم [tdaggam] *p:* Button up your overcoat. دَقَّم قَبُّوطَك [daggum qappu:ṭak]

buttonhole • **1.** بَيت دُقمَة [bayt dugma] بيُوت دُقَم [byu:t dugam] *pl:* زُرُوف دُقمَة [zuruf dugma] زرُوف دُقَم [zru:f dugam] *pl:* This buttonhole needs fixing. بَيت الدُّقمَة هَذا يِرّادلَه تَصلِيح [bayt ʔiddugma ha:ða yirra:dlah taṣli:ħ]

buy • **1.** شَروَة [šarwa] شَروات [šarwa:t] *pl:* That's a good buy. هٰذِي شَروَة تِسوَى [ha:ði šarwa tiswa:]

to buy • **1.** اِشتِرَى [ʔištira:] شِرَة [šira] *vn:* اِنشِرَى [ʔinšira:] *p:* What did you buy at Ali's shop? شِاشتِرَيت مِن دُكّان عَلِي؟ [šʔištiri:t min dukka:n ʕali?]

to buy a ticket • **1.** قَصّ بِطاقَة [gaṣṣ biṭa:qa] *sv* u. قِطَع بِطاقَة [giṭaʕ biṭa:qa] *sv* a. اِشتِرَى بِطاقَة [ʔištira: biṭa:qa] *sv* i. Buy me a ticket too. إلِي هَمّ قُصّلِي بِطاقَة [ʔili hamm guṣṣli biṭa:qa] Did you buy the theater tickets? قِطَعِت البِطاقات لِلرِّوايَة؟ [giṭaʕit ʔilbiṭa:qa:t lirriwa:ya?]

to buy into • **1.** اِشتِرَى أسهُم بِـ [ʔištira: ʔashum bi-] *sv* i. I'm thinking of buying into that company. دَأفَكِّر أشتِرِي أسهُم بِهَالشَّرِكَة [daʔafakkir ʔaštiri ʔashum bhaššarika]

to buy up • **1.** لَمّ [lamm] لَمّ [lamm] *vn:* اِنلَمّ [ʔinlamm] *p:* That monopolist bought up all the sugar in the market. هَالمُحتَكِر لَمّ كُلّ الشَّكَر اللِّي بالسُّوق [halmuħtakir lamm kull ʔiššakar ʔilli bissuwg]

buzz • **1.** طَنطَن [ṭanṭan] The buzz of the mosquito kept me awake. طَنِين البَقَّة ما خَلّانِي أنام [ṭani:n ʔilbagga ma: xalla:ni ʔana:m] • **2.** وَشوَشَة [wašwaša] A buzz of voices filled the courtroom. صارَت فَدّ وَشوَشَة بقاعَة المَحكَمَة [ṣa:rat fadd wašwaša bqa:ʕat ʔilmaħkama]

to buzz • **1.** طَنطَن [ṭanṭan] طَنطَنَة [ṭanṭana] *vn:* *sv* i. The bee buzzes. النَّحلَة تطَنطِن [ʔinnaħla ṭṭanṭin]

buzzer • **1.** جَرَس [jaras] أجراس [ʔajra:s] *pl:* Push the buzzer. دُقّ الجَّرَس [dugg ʔijjaras]

by • **1.** قَرِيب مِن [qari:b min] The house stands close by the river. البَيت مَبنِي قَرِيب مِن الشَّطّ [ʔilbayt mabni qari:b min ʔiššaṭṭ] • **2.** يَمّ [yamm] بجانِب [bja:nib] He went by me without saying a word. فات مِن يَمِّي بَلا ما يقُول وَلا كِلمَة [fa:t min yammi bala ma: yigu:l wala čilma] • **3.** بـ [b] The club has been closed by order of the police. اِنسَدّ النّادِي بأمُر مِن الشّرطَة [ʔinsadd ʔinna:di bʔamur min ʔiššrṭa] That horse won by a length. ذاك الحصان غِلَب بطُول واحِد [ða:k ʔilħṣa:n ɣilab bṭu:l wa:ħid] We came by car. جِينا بسَيّارَة [ji:na bsayya:ra] He'll be back by five o'clock. راح يرجَع بالخَمسَة [ra:ħ yirjaʕ bilxamsa] He'll be back by five o'clock. راح يرجَع ساعَة خَمسَة [ra:ħ yirjaʕ sa:ʕa xamsa] The table is four feet by six. المِيز كُبرَه أربَعَة فُوتات بسِتَّة [ʔilmi:z kubrah ʔarbaʕa fu:ta:t bsitta] • **4.** بـ [b] عَلَى [ʕala] She can't work by artificial light. ما تِقدَر تِشتُغُل بضُوَة اِصطِناعِي [ma: tigdar tištuɣul bðuwa ʔiṣṭina:ʕi] • **5.** بواسطَة [bwa:sṭa] بـ [b] I'll send it to you by mail. راح أدِزّ لَك إيّاها بواسطَة البَرِيد [ra:ħ ʔadizz lak ʔiyya:ha bwa:sṭat ʔilbari:d]

i, interjection; p, passive; pl, plural; sv, stem vowel; vn, verbal noun

*** This book was written by a Frenchman.** • **1.** هَذَا الِكتاب لِواحِد فرَنسِي [ha:ða ʔilkta:b liwa:ħid fransi]
*** Little by little he fought his way through the crowd.** • **1.** شوَيَّة شوَيَّة شَقلَه طَرِيق مِن بَين الناس [šwayya šwayya šaglah ṭari:q min bayn ʔinna:s]
*** I got the story out of him word by word.** • **1.** كِلمَة كِلمَة طَلَّعِت الحكايَة مِن حَلقَه [čilma čilma ṭallaʕit ʔiliħča:ya min ħalgah]
*** That's done by machine.** • **1.** هَذَا شُغُل مَكِينَة [ha:ða šuɣul maki:na]
by and by • **1.** بِالتَدرِيج [bittadri:ǰ] You'll get used to it by and by. راح تِتعَلَّم عَليها بِالتَّدرِيج [ra:ħ titʕallam ʕali:ha bittadri:ǰ] • **2.** بَعد شوَيَّة [baʕd šwayya] He told me he'd let me know by and by. قَال لِي ينطِينِي خَبَر بَعد شوَيَّة [ga:lliy yinṭi:ni xabar baʕd šwayya]
by and large • **1.** عَالعُمُوم [ʕalʕumu:m] By and large, the results were satifactory. عَالعُمُوم، النَّتايِج كانَت زينَة [ʕa:lʕumu:m, ʔinnata:yiǰ ča:nat zi:na]
by far • **1.** بهوايَة [bihwa:ya] This is by far the best hotel in town. هَذَا أحسَن أُوتِيل بِالوِلايَة بهوايَة [ha:ða ʔaħsan ʔuti:l bilwila:ya bhwa:ya]
by name • **1.** بِالإسِم [bilʔisim] I just know him by name. آنِي أعُرفَه بَسّ بالإسِم [ʔa:ni ʔaʕurfah bass bilʔisim]
by oneself • **1.** وَحَّد [waħħad] بِنَفِس [binafis] He did that by himself. هُوَّ سَوّاها وَحَدَه [huwwa sawwa:ha waħħdah] He did that by himself. سَوّاها بِنَفسَه [sawwa:ha bnafsah]
by sight • **1.** بِالشِكِل [biššikil] I know him only by sight. آنِي أعُرفَه بِالشَّكِل [ʔa:ni ʔaʕurfah biššikil]
by that • **1.** مِن هَذَا [min ha:ða] What do you understand by that? شتِفهِم مِن هَذَا؟ [štifhim min ha:ða?] • **2.** بهذا [bha:ða:] What do you mean by that? شتِعنِي بِهَذا؟ [štiʕni bha:ða?]
by the hour • **1.** بِالسّاعَة [bissa:ʕa] Do you know of a place where they rent boats by the hour? تُعرُف مَكان يأَجِّرُون بِيه بلام بِالسّاعَة؟ [tuʕruf maka:n yʔaǰǰiru:n bi:h bla:m bissa:ʕa?]
by the way • **1.** بِالمُناسَبَة [bilmuna:saba] By the way, I met a friend of your yesterday. بِالمُناسَبَة، صادَفِت واحِد مِن أصدِقائَك البارحَة [bilmuna:saba, ṣa:dafit wa:ħid min ʔaṣdiqa:ʔak ʔilba:rħa]
by way of • **1.** عَلَى طَرِيق [ʕala ṭari:q] Are you going to Europe by way of Beirut? إنتَ رايِح لأورُبّا عَلَى طَرِيق بَيرُوت؟ [ʔinta ra:yiħ lʔu:ruppa ʕala ṭari:q bayru:t?]
day by day • **1.** يَوم وَرَا يَوم [yawm wara yawm] يَوم عَلَى يَوم [yu:m ʕala yu:m] Day by day his condition improves. يوم وَرا يوم حالتَه دَتِتحَسَّن [yu:m wara yu:m ħa:ltah datitħassan]
one by one • **1.** واحِد وَرا واحِد [wa:ħid wara wa:ħid] واحِد وَرا اللاخ [wa:ħid wara ʔilla:x] واحِد واحِد [wa:ħid wa:ħid] One by one they left the room. واحِد وَرا اللّاخ طِلعَوا مِن الغُرفَة [wa:ħid wara ʔilla:x ṭilʕaw min ʔilɣurfa]

bylaw • **1.** نِظام [niḍa:m] أنظِمَة [ʔanḍima] *pl:* The bylaws of the society are available from the secretary. نِظام الجَمعِيَّة يِتحَصَّل مِن السِّكِرتَير [niḍa:m ʔiǰjamʕiyya yitħaṣṣal min ʔissikirti:r]

C

C

cab • **1.** تَكسِي [taksi] تَكسِيّات [taksiyya:t] *pl:* سَيّارَة أُجرَة [sayya:rat ʔujra] سَيّارات أُجرَة [sayya:ra:t ʔujra] *pl:*

cabbage • **1.** لَهانَة [laha:na] Cabbage is hard to digest. اللَّهانَة صَعُب تِنهُضُم [ʔilaha:na ṣaʕub tinhuḍum]

cabin • **1.** We have a cabin in the mountains. عِدنا كَبرَة بِالجِبَل [ʕidna kapra bijjibal] • **2.** قَمارَة [qama:ra] قَمارات [qama:ra:t] *pl:* كابِينَة [kabi:na] كابِينات [kabi:na:t] *pl:* Would you please tell me which deck my cabin is on? قُلِّي، مِن فَضلَك، بأي دَرَجَة القَمارَة مالتِي؟ [qulli, min faḍlak, bʔayy daraja ʔilqama:ra ma:lti?]

cabinet • **1.** مَواعِين [di:la:b] نَضَّم [dwa:li:b] *pl:* We keep our good dishes in a small cabinet. نَضُّم مَواعِين الزِّينَة بِدِيلاب صغَيِّر [nnaḍḍumm mawa:ʕi:n ʔizzi:na bdi:la:b ṣɣayyir] • **2.** وزارَة [wiza:ra] وِزارات [wiza:ra:t] *pl:* The cabinet met with the President of the Republic yesterday. البارحَة اِجتِمَع الوَزارَة ويّا رَئِيس الجّمهُورِيَّة [ʔilba:rħa ʔijtimaʕ ʔilwaza:ra wiyya raʔi:s ʔijjamhu:riyya]

cabinet maker • **1.** صانِع مَوبِيلِيات [ṣa:niʕ mubi:lya:t] صُنّاع مَوبِيلِيات [ṣunna:ʕ mubi:lya:t] *pl:*

cable • **1.** سِلك [silk] أَسلاك [ʔasla:k] *pl:* The cables support the bridge. الأسلاك لازمَتَه لِلجِّسِر [ʔilʔasla:k la:zimtah lijjisir] Can the cable be laid within ten days? مُمكِن تِنُّصُب الأسلاك بِخِلال عَشرَة أيّام؟ [mumkin tinnuṣub ʔilʔasla:k bxila:l ʕaširat ʔayya:m?] • **2.** بَرقِيَّة [barqiyya] لنُويُورك [barqiyya:t] *pl:* I want to send a cable to New York. أَرِيد أدِز بَرقِيَّة لنُويُورك [ʔari:d ʔadizz barqiyya linu: yu:rk]

to cable • **1.** أَبرَق [ʔabraq] إبراق [ʔibra:q] *vn: sv* i. Cable immediately when you arrive. إبرُق بَرقِيَّة أَوَّل ما تُوصَل [ʔibruq barqiyya ʔawwal ma: tu:ṣal]

cadet • **1.** تِلمِيذ حَربِي [tilmi:ð ħarbi] تَلامِيذ حَربِيِّين [tala:mi:ð ħarbiyyi:n] *pl:*

cafe • **1.** قَهوَة [gahwa] مَقهَى [maqha] مَقاهِي [maqa:hi] *pl:*

cage • **1.** قَفَص [qafaṣ] أَقفاص [ʔaqfa:ṣ] *pl:* The room is just like a cage. الغُرفَة عَبالَك قَفَص [ʔilɣurfa ʕaba:lak qafaṣ]

cake • **1.** كِيكَة [kayka] كَيكات [kayka:t] *pl:* كَيك [ki:k] *Collective:* I'd like cake with my coffee. أَرِيد كَيك وِيّا قَهوتِي [ʔari:d kayk wiyya gahwti] • **2.** قالَب [qa:lab] قَوالِب، قوالِب [qawa:lib, qwa:lib.] *pl:* Can you bring me a cake of soap and a towel? تِقدَر تجِيبلِي فَدّ قالَب صابُون وَخاولِي؟ [tigdar dji:bli fadd qa:lab ṣa:bu:n wxa:wli?]

calamity • **1.** نَكبَة [nakba] نَكبات [nakba:t] *pl:* كارِثَة [ka:riθa] كَوارِث [kawa:riθ] *pl:* فاجِعَة [fa:jiʕa] فَواجِع [fawa:jiʕ] *pl:*

calcium • **1.** كالسِيُوم [kalsyu:m]

to calculate • **1.** حِسَب [ħisab] حِساب [ħisa:b] *vn:* اِنحِسَب [ʔinħisab] *p:* It was difficult to calculate the costs. كان صَعُب الواحِد يِحسِب الكُلفَة [ča:n ṣaʕub ʔilwa:ħid yiħsib ʔilkulfa] • **2.** قَدَّر [qaddar] تَقدِير [taqdi:r] *vn:* تقَدَّر [tqaddar] *p:* Let's call in an expert to calculate the extent of the damage. خَلِّي نجِيب خَبِير حَتَّى يقَدِّر مَدَى الضَّرَر [xalli nji:b xabi:r ħatta yqaddir mada ʔiḍḍarar]

calculated • **1.** مَحسُوب [maħsu:b] This is a calculated risk. هَذِي مُجازَفَة مَحسُوب إلها حساب [ha:ði muja:zafa maħsu:b ʔilha ħsa:b]

calculating • **1.** نَفعِي [nafʕi] مَصلَحِي [maṣlaħi] She's a shrewd calculating woman. هاي فَدّ مَرَة داهيَة نَفعِيَّة [ha:y fadd mara da:hya nafʕiyya]

calculating machine • **1.** آلَة حاسِبَة [ʔa:la ħa:siba] آلات حاسِبَة [ʔa:la:t ħa:siba] *pl:*

calendar • **1.** تَقوِيم [taqwi:m] تَقاوِيم [taqa:wi:m] *pl:* رُزنامَة [ruzna:ma] رُزنامات [ruzna:ma:t] *pl:* I've noted it on my calendar. آنِي أَشَّرتها بِالتَّقوِيم مالِي [ʔa:ni ʔaššaritha bittaqwi:m ma:li] • **2.** مَنهَج [manhaj, minha:j] مَناهِج [mana:hij] *pl:* بَرنامَج [barna:maj] What events are on the calendar this month? شَكُو فَعالِيّات بالمَنهَج هَالشَّهَر؟ [šaku faʕa:liyya:t bilmanhaj haššahar?]

calf • **1.** عِجِل [ʕijil] عجُول، عِجُول [ʕju:l, ʕiju:l] *pl:* Cows and calves were grazing in the field. الهوايِش وَالعِجُول كانَوا دَيرعُون بالمَرعَى [ʔilhwa:yiš wʔiliʕju:l ča:naw dayirʕu:n bilmarʕa] That bag is made of genuine calf. هَالجَّنطَة مسَوّايَة مِن جِلد عِجِل أَصلِي [hajjanṭa msawwa:ya min jilid ʕijil ʔaṣli] • **2.** كِرشَة [kirša] كَرشات [karša:t] *pl:* The bullet struck him in the calf of his leg. الرِّصاصَة صابتَه بكَرشَة رِجلَه [ʔirriṣa:ṣa ṣa:batah bkaršat rijlah]

caliph • **1.** خَلِيفَة [xali:fa] خُلَفاء [xulafa:ʔ] *pl:*

caliphate • **1.** خِلافَة [xila:fa] خِلافات [xila:fa:t] *pl:*

call • **1.** نِداء [nida:ʔ] نِداءات [nida:ʔa:t] *pl:* مُخابَرَة [muxa:bara] مُخابَرات [muxa:bara:t] *pl:* Were there

i, interjection; p, passive; pl, plural; sv, stem vowel; vn, verbal noun

any calls for me? كان أكُو إلِي نِداءات؟ [čaːn ʔaku ʔili nidaːʔaːt?] How much was the call? شقَدّ كَلَّف النِّداء؟ [šgadd kallaf ʔinnidaːʔ?] • 2. دَعوَة [daʕwa] دَعوات، دَعاوِي [daʕwaːt, daʕaːwi] pl: He was the first to answer the call to arms. كان أوَّل مَن لَبَّى الدَّعوَة لِلجِهاد [čaːn ʔawwal man labbaː ʔiddaʕwa lijjihaːd]

*** I thought I heard a call for help.** • 1. أعتِقِد سِمَعِت واحِد يِستَنجِد [ʔaʕtiqid simaʕit waːhid yistanǰid]

to call • 1. صاح [ṣaːħ] صياح [ṣyaːħ] vn: اِنصاح [ʔinṣaːħ] p: نادَى [naːdaː] نِداء [nidaːʔ] vn: sv i. I called him but he didn't hear me. صِحِت عَليه لَكِن ما سِمَعنِي [ṣiħit ʕaliːh laːkin maː simaʕni] Shall I call you a cab? أصِيحلَك تَكسِي؟ [ʔaṣiːhlak taksi?] • 2. خابَر [xaːbar] مُخابَرَة [muxaːbara] vn: تخابَر [txaːbar] p: You can call me any time at my office. تِقدَر تخابُرنِي لِلدّائِرَة شوَقِت ما ترِيد [tigdar txaːburni liddaːʔira šwakit maː triːd] • 3. دَزّ عَلَى [dazz ʕala] دَزّ [dazz] vn: اِندَزّ [ʔindazz] p: sv i. Call a doctor! دِزّ عَلَى طَبِيب [dizz ʕala ṭabiːb] • 4. سَمَّى [sammaː] تَسمِيَة [tasmiya] vn: تسَمَّى [tsammaː] p: What do you call this in Arabic? شِتسَمِّي هَذا بِالعَرَبِي؟ [šitsammi haːða bilʕarabi?] Let's call him Ali. خَلِّي نسَمِّيه عَلِي [xalli nsammiːh ʕali]

to call attention to • 1. جِلَب اِنتِباه ل [ǰilab ʔintibaːh li-] جَلب اِنتِباه ل [ǰalb ʔintibaːh li-] vn: اِنجِلَب اِنتِباه لِ [ʔinǰilab] p: نَبَّه [nabbah] تَنبِيه عَلَى [tanbiːh ʕala] vn: تنَبَّه عَلَى [tnabbah ʕala] p: I called his attention to it. جِلَبت اِنتِباهَه إلها [ǰilabt ʔintibaːhah ʔilha] I called his attention to it. نَبَّهتَه عَليه [nabbahtah ʕaliːh]

to call down • 1. زَفّ [zaff] زَفّ [zaff] vn: اِنزَفّ [ʔinzaff] p: My boss called me down for being late. رَئِيسِي زَفنِي لِأنّ أتأخَّر [raʔiːsi zaffni liʔann ʔatʔaxxar]

to call for • 1. مَرّ عَلَى [marr ʕala] مُرُور [muruːr] vn: اِنمَرّ [ʔinmarr] p: جا عَلَى [ǰaː ʕala] مَجِيئ [maǰiːʔ] vn: sv i. Will you call for me at the hotel? تِقدَر تمُرّ عَلَيّا بالأوتيل؟ [tigdar tmurr ʕalayya bilʔutiːl?] • 2. راح عَلَى [raːħ ʕala] رَوح [ruːħ] vn: sv u I have to call for my laundry. لازِم أرُوح عَلَى هدُومِي عِند المَكوِي [laːzim ʔaruːħ ʕala hduːmi ʕind ʔilmakwi] • 3. اِستَدعَى [ʔistadʕaː] اِستِدعاء [ʔistidʕaːʔ] vn: sv i. هَذِي تِستَدعِي اِحتِفال [haːði tistadʕi ʔiħtifaːl] • 4. This calls for a celebration اِنراد ل [ʔinraːd l-] sv a. That calls for a drink. هَذا يِنرادلَه بِيك [haːða yinraːdlah piːk] • 5. طِلَب [ṭilab] طَلَب [ṭalab] vn: اِنطِلَب [ʔinṭilab] p: The president called for a vote on the matter. الرَّئِيس طِلَب التَّصوِيت عَالمَوضُوع [ʔirraʔiːs ṭilab ʔittaṣwiːt ʕalmawðuːʕ] • 6. قَرَّر [qarrar] تَقرِير [taqriːr] vn: تقَرَّر [tqarrar] p: The director has called for a rehearsal for four o'clock. المُخرِج قَرَّر يسَوِّي تَمرِين ساعَة أربَعَة [ʔilmuxriǰ qarrar ysawwi tamriːn saːʕa ʔarbaʕa] • 7. عَيَّن [ʕayyan] تَعيِين [taʕyiːn] vn: تعَيَّن [tʕayyan] p: He called the conference for Monday, the fourth. عَيَّن وَقِت المُؤتَمَر يوم الإثنَين أربَعَة بِالشَّهَر [ʕayyan wakit ʔilmuʔtamar yuːm ʔilʔiθnayn ʔarbaʕa biššahar]

to call in • 1. لَمّ [lamm] لَمّ [lamm] vn: اِنلَمّ [ʔinlamm] p: All old banknotes are being called in. كُلّ الأوراق النَّقدِيَّة العَتِيقَة دَتِنلَمّ [kull ʔilʔawraːq ʔinnaqdiyya ʔilʕatiːga datinlamm]

*** Call him in.** • 1. أُطلُبَه [ʔuṭlubah] / دِزّ عَليه [dizz ʕaliːh] / صِيِّحَه [ṣiːħah]

*** We had to call in a specialist.** • 1. اِضطَرّينا نِستَشِير اِختِصاصِي [ʔiðṭarriːna nistišiːr ʔixtiṣaːṣi]

to call off • 1. ألغَى [ʔalɣa] إلغاء [ʔilɣaːʔ] vn: اِنلِغَى [ʔinlaɣaː] p: Today's broadcast was called off for technical reasons. إذاعَة اليُوم اِنلِغَت لأسباب فَنِّيَّة [ʔiðaːʕat ʔilyuːm ʔinliɣat liʔasbaːb fanniyya]

to call on • 1. زار [zaːr] زارات [zaːraːt] pl: زِيارَة [zyaːra] vn: اِنزار [ʔinzaːr] p: جا [ǰaː] مَجِيئ [maǰiːʔ] vn: sv i. We'll call on you next Sunday. راح نزُورَك يوم الأحَّد الجّاي [raːħ nzuːrak yuːm ʔilʔaħħad ʔiǰǰaːy] We'll call on you next Sunday. راح نِجِيك يوم الأحَّد الجّاي [raːħ niǰiːk yuːm ʔilʔaħħad ʔiǰǰaːy] Our agent will call on you tomorrow. وَكِيلنا راح يِجِيك باكِر [wakiːlna raːħ yiǰiːk baːčir] • 2. اِستَنجَد [ʔistanǰad] اِستِنجاد [ʔistinǰaːd] vn: sv i. You can call on me for help in case of necessity. تِقدَر تِستَنجِد بِيّا عِند الضَّرُورَة [tigdar tistanǰid biyya ʕind ʔiððuruːra]

to call out • 1. طِلَب [ṭilab] طَلَب [ṭalab] vn: اِنطِلَب [ʔinṭilab] p: They had to call out the firemen to put out the fire. اِضطَرّوا يطُلبُون الإطفائِيَّة حَتَّى يطَفُّون النّار [ʔiðṭarraw yiṭulbuːn ʔilʔiṭfaːʔiyya ħatta yṭaffuːn ʔinnaːr] • 2. نادَى [naːdaː] نِداء [nidaːʔ] vn: تنادَى [tnaːdaː] p: The demonstrators began to call out his name with enthusiasm. المُتَظاهرِين قامَوا ينادُون إسمَه بحَماس [ʔilmutaðaːhriːn gaːmaw ynaːduːn ʔismah bħamaːs] • 3. عِلَن، أعلَن [ʕilan, ʔaʕlan] إعلان [ʔiʕlaːn] vn: اِنعِلَن [ʔinʕilan] p: The conductor calls out all the stops. الجّابِي يِعلِن إسِم كُلّ المَحَطّات [ʔiǰǰaːbi yiʕlin ʔisim kull ʔilmaħaṭṭaːt] • 4. صاح [ṣaːħ] صِياح [ṣiyaːħ] vn: اِنصاح [ʔinṣaːħ] p: They stopped in front of the door and called out my name. وُقفَوا قِدّام الباب وَصاحَوا إسمِي [wugfaw giddaːm ʔilbaːb wṣaːħaw ʔismi]

to call together • 1. لَمّ سِوَة [lamm siwa] لَمّ سِوَة [lamm siwa] vn: اِنلَمّ سِوَة [ʔinlamm siwa] p: جِمَع [ǰimaʕ] جَمِع [ǰamiʕ] vn: اِنجِمَع [ʔinǰimaʕ] p: sv a. He called all of us together in his office. لَمّنا كُلّنا سِوَى بغُرُفتَه [lammna kullna siwaː bɣuruftah]

to call (up) • 1. خابَر [xaːbar] مُخابَرَة [muxaːbara] vn: sv u. I'll call you up tomorrow. آنِي راح أخابرَك باكِر [ʔaːni raːħ ʔaxaːbrak baːčir] • 2. دِعَى [diʕaː] دَعوَة [daʕwa] vn: اِندِعَى [ʔindiʕaː] p: I heard they are calling up year group 1944 for duty. سِمَعِت راح يدعُون مَوالِيد ألِف وَتِسِع مِيَّة وأربَعَة وأربَعِين لخِدمَة العَلَم [simaʕit raːħ yidʕuːn mawaːliːd ʔalif wtisiʕ miyya wʔarbaʕa wʔarbaʕiːn lxidmat ʔilʕalam]

caller • 1. زاير [zaːyir, zaːʔir] زُوّار [zuwwaːr] pl: خُطّار [xuṭṭaːr] خطاطِير [xiṭaːṭiːr] pl: I'm expecting a gentleman caller this afternoon. دَأنتِظِر فَدّ رِجّال خُطّار اليُوم العَصِر [daʔantiðir fadd riǰǰaːl xuṭṭaːr ʔilyuːm ʔilʕaṣir]

• **2.** مُراجِع [mura:ǯiʕ] مُراجِعِين [mura:ǯiʕi:n] *pl:* Did I have any callers while I was out of the office? إجَوني مُراجِعين لِلمَكتَب مِن كِنِت طالِع؟ [ʔiǯu:ni mura:ǯiʕi:n lilmaktab min činit ṭa:liʕ?]

C

calling card • **1.** كارت شَخصِي [ka:rt šaxṣi] كارتات شَخصِيَّة [ka:rta:t šaxṣiyya] *pl:* بِطاقَة [biṭa:qa] بِطاقات، بِطايِق [biṭa:qa:t, biṭa:yiq] *pl:*

callus • **1.** بِسمار [bisma:r] بسامِير [bsa:mi:r] *pl:* I got calluses on my hand from digging. طِلَعلِي بِسمار بِيدِي مِن الحَفُر [ṭilaʕli bisma:r bi:di min ʔilħafur]

calm • **1.** ساكِن [sa:kin] هادِئ [ha:diʔ] The sea is calm again. البَحَر ساكِن مَرَّة لُخ [ʔilbaħar sa:kin marra lux] • **2.** هادِئ [ha:diʔ] He remained calm and in control of the situation. بُقَى هادِئ وَمسَيطِر عَالوَضِع [buqa: ha:diʔ wmṣayṭir ʕalwaðiʕ]

to keep calm • **1.** اِحتِفَظ بِهدُوء [ʔiħtifað bhidu:ʔ] اِحتِفاظ بِهدُوء [ʔiħtifa:ð bhidu:ʔ] *vn: sv* u. Keep calm, everybody. اِحتَفظُوا بهدُو كُم كُلّكُم [ʔiħtafðu: bhidu:ʔ kum kullkum]

to calm • **1.** هَدَّى [hadda:] تَهدِئَة [tahdiʔa] *vn:* تهَدَّى [thadda:] *p:* بَرَّد [barrad] تَبرِيد [tabri:d] *vn:* تبَرَّد [tbarrad] *p:* We tried to calm the frighten animals. حاوَلنا نهَدِّي الحَيوانات الجّافلَة [ħa:walna nhaddi ʔalħaywa:na:t ʔiǯǯa:fla]

to calm down • **1.** هَفَّت [haffat] تَهفِيت [tahfi:t] *vn:* تهَفَّت [thaffat] *p:* Try to calm him down. حاوُل تهَفّتَه [ħa:wul thafftah] • **2.** هِفَت [hifat] هَفِت [hafit] *vn: sv* i. هِدَأ [hidaʔ] هُدُوء [hudu:ʔ] *vn:* اِنهِدَأ [ʔinhidaʔ] *p:* It took her some time to calm down. ينراد إلها مُدَّة حَتَّى تِهفِت [yinra:d ʔilha mudda ħatta tihfit] The wind has calmed down. الهَوا هِفَت [ʔilhawa hifat] The wind has calmed down. الهَوا وُقَف [ʔilhawa wugaf] The wind has calmed down. هِدَأ الهَوا [hidaʔ ʔilhawa]

to calm oneself • **1.** طَوَّل بال [ṭawwal ba:l] تَطوِيل بال [taṭwi:l ba:l] *vn: sv* i. سَكَّن رُوح [sakkan ru:ħ] تَسكِين رُوح [taski:n ru:ħ] *vn: sv* i. بَرَّد نَفِس [barrad nafis] *sv* i. هَدَّى نَفِس [hadda: nafis] *sv* i. هِدَأ [hidaʔ] هُدُوء [hudu:ʔ] *vn: sv* a. Calm yourself! طَوُّل بالَك [ṭawwul ba:lak] Calm yourself! إهدَأ [ʔihdaʔ]

calmly • **1.** بِهدُوء [bihidu:ʔ] بِبرُود [biburu:d] She took the news calmly. أخذَت الخَبَر بهدُوء [ʔaxðat ʔilxabar bhidu:ʔ]

camel • **1.** جَمَل [ǯamal] جِمال [ǯima:l] *pl:* بِعِير [biʕi:r] بِعران، أباعِر [biʕra:n, ʔaba:ʕir] *pl:*

camel dung • **1.** بَعرَة [baʕra] بَعرات [baʕra:t] *pl:* بَعَر [baʕar] *Collective:* بَعرُورَة [baʕru:ra] بَعرُورات [baʕru:ra:t] *pl:* بَعرُور [baʕru:r] *Collective*

camel litter • **1.** هُودَج [hu:daǯ] هُوادِج [huwa:diǯ] *pl:*

camera • **1.** كامِيرَة [kami:ra] كامِيرات [kami:ra:t] *pl:* مَكِينَة رَسِم [maki:nat rasim] مَكايِن رَسِم [maka:yin rasim] *pl:*

camouflage • **1.** تَموِيه [tamwi:h]

to camouflage • **1.** مَوَّه [mawwah] تَموِيه [tamwi:h] *vn:* تمَوَّه [tmawwah] *p:*

camp • **1.** مُعَسكَر [muʕaskar] مُعَسكَرات [muʕaskara:t] *pl:* At what camp did you get your training? بيا مُعَسكَر تدَرَّبت؟ [bya: muʕaskar ddarrabit?] • **2.** مُخَيَّم [muxayyam] The boy scout camp is going to be in the north. الكَشّافَة راح يكُون مُخَيَّمهُم بِالشِّمال [ʔilkašša:fa ra:ħ yku:n muxayyamhum biššima:l]

to camp • **1.** خَيَّم [xayyam] تَخيِيم [taxyi:m] *vn: sv* i. We camped in the woods. خَيَّمنا بِالغابات [xayyamna bilɣa:ba:t] • **2.** عَسكَر [ʕaskar] عَساكِر [ʔas:kir] *pl:* تعِسكِر [tʕiskir] *vn: sv* i. The division camped a mile outside the city. الفِرقَة عَسكِرَت عَلَى بُعُد مِيل مِن الولايَة [ʔilfirqa ʕaskirat ʕala buʕud mi:l min ʔilwla:ya]

campaign • **1.** حَملَة [ħamla] حَملات [ħamla:t] *pl:* He took part in the African campaign. اِشتِرَك بالحَملَة الأفرِيقِيَّة [ʔištirak bilħamla ʔilʔafri:qiyya] His election campaign lasted three months. الحَملَة الانتِخابِيَّة مالتَه طَوِّلَت ثلَثّ أشهُر [ʔilħamla ʔilʔintixa:biyya ma:ltah ṭawwilat θlatt ʔašhur]

to campaign • **1.** قام بحَملَة [qa:m bħamla] *sv* u. He campaigned to get himself elected to the presidency. قام بِحَملَة لغَرض اِنتِخابَه لِلرِّياسَة [qa:m bħamla lɣarð ʔintixa:bah lirriya:sa]

camphor • **1.** كافُور [ka:fu:r]

can • **1.** قُوطِيَّة [qu:ṭiyya] قواطِي [qwa:ṭi] *pl:* عِلبَة [ʕilba] عِلَب [ʕilab] *pl:* Give me a can of green peas. إنطِينِي قُوطِيَّة بَزالِيَة خَضرَة [ʔinṭi:ni qu:ṭiyya baza:lya xaðra]

can • **1.** قِدَر [gidar] مَقدِرَة [maqdira] *vn:* اِنقِدَر [ʔingidar] *p:* تمَكَّن [tmakkan] تَمَكُّن [tamakkun] *vn: sv* a. أمكَن [ʔamkan] إمكان [ʔimka:n] *vn: sv* i. اِستَطاع [ʔistaṭa:ʕ] اِستِطاعَة [ʔistiṭa:ʕa] *vn: sv* i. Can you speak English? تِقدَر تِحكِي إنكِلِيزِي؟ [tigdar tiħči ʔingili:zi?] Can you speak English? بإمكانَك تِحكِي إنكِلِيزِي؟ [bʔimka:nak tiħči ʔingili:zi?] Could I look at it, please. أقدَر أشُوفَه مِن فَضلَك؟ [ʔagdar ʔašu:fah min faðlak?] She could be wrong. يمكِن غَلطانَة [yimkin ɣalṭa:na] Can't that be simplified? ما مُمكِن تَبسِيط هذا؟ [ma:mumkin tabsi:ṭ ha:ða?] Can't you delay this a few hours. ما مُمكِن تعَطِّل هَذا كَم ساعَة [ma: mumkin tʕaṭṭil ha:ða čam sa:ʕa] He did everything he could. سَوَّى كُلّ ما كان بإمكانَه [sawwa: kull ma: ča:n bʔimka:nah] He could have come. كان بإمكانَه يِجِي [ča:n bʔimka:nah yiǯi] If you can bring me the book tomorrow, I'll appreciate it. إذا تِتمَكَّن تجِيبلِي الكِتاب باكِر الصُّبح أكُون مَمنُون [ʔiða titmakkan dǯi:bli ʔilkita:b ba:čir ʔiṣṣubħ ʔaku:n mamnu:n] • **2.** جاز [ǰa:z] He could have said that. يجُوز قالَه لِهذا [yǰu:z ga:lah lha:ða]

*** I can't say yet whether I'll run for election or not.** • **1.** لهسَّة ما أعرُف بَعَد إذا راح أتقدَّم لِلانتِخاب لَو لا [lhassa ma: ʔaʕruf baʕad ʔiða ra:ħ ʔatqaddam lilʔintixa:b law la:]

to can • **1.** عَلَّب [ʕallab] تَعلِيب [taʕli:b] *vn:* تعَلَّب [tʕallab] *p:* This factory is set up to process and can all kinds of vegetables. هَالمَعمَل مُنشَأ لتَهيأة وتَعليب كُلّ أنواع المُخضَّرات [hallmaʕmal munšaʔ litahyiʔat wtaʕli:b ʔanwa:ʕ ʔilmuxaððara:t]

canal • **1.** قنال [qana:l] قَنالات [qana:la:t] *pl:* قناة [qana:t] قَنَوات [qanawa:t] *pl:* أقنِيَة [ʔaqniya] We came by way of the Suez Canal. جَينا عَلَى طَرِيق قَنال السُّوَيس [ǰayna ʕala tari:q qana:l ʔissuwi:s] • **2.** ساقيَة [sa:gya] سواقِي [swa:gi] *pl:* ساجيَة [sa:ǰya] سواجِي [swa:ǰi] *pl:* تُرعَة [turʕa] تُرَع [turaʕ] *pl:* We'll have to dig a canal here to drain the land. لازِم نُحفُر ساقيَة هنا لِبَزل الأرُض [la:zim nuħfur sa:ǰya hna lbazl ʔilʔaruð]

canary • **1.** كَنارِي [kana:ri] كَنارِيَّة [kana:riyya] *pl:*

to cancel • **1.** ألغَى [ʔalɣa:] إلغاء [ʔilɣa:ʔ] *vn:* اِنلِغَى [ʔinliɣa:] *p:* بَطَّل [battal] تَبطِيل، تبُطِّل [tabti:l, tbuttil] *vn:* تبَطَّل [tbattal] *p: sv* i. They have cancelled the order. ألغوا الأمُر [ʔalɣaw ʔilʔamur] I'd like to cancel my newspaper subscription. أحِبّ ألغِي اِشتِراكِي بِالجَّرِيدَة [ʔaħibb ʔalɣi ʔištira:ki biǰǰari:da] I had to cancel my doctor's appointment. اِضطَرَّيت ألغِي مَوعِدي ويّا الطَّبِيب [ʔiðtarri:t ʔalɣi mawʕidi wiyya ʔittabi:b] The meeting was canceled. الاجتِماع اِنلِغَى [ʔilʔiǰtima:ʕ ʔinliɣa:] • **2.** سَقَّط [saqqaṭ] تَسقِيط [tasqi:ṭ] *vn:* تسَقَّط [tsaqqaṭ] *p:* He cancelled the rest of my debt. سَقَّط الباقِي مِن دَينَه عَلَيّا [saqqaṭ ʔilba:qi min daynah ʕalayya] These postage stamps are canceled. هَالطَّوابِع البَرِيدِيَّة مسَقَّطَة [haṭṭawa:biʕ ʔilbari:diyya msaqqaṭa]

cancer • **1.** سَرَطان [saraṭa:n] سَرَطانات [saraṭa:na:t] *pl:* They discovered too late that he had cancer. لِقَوا عِندَه سَرَطان بَعَد ما فات الوَقِت [ligaw ʕindah saraṭa:n baʕad ma: fa:t ʔilwakit]

candid • **1.** صَرِيح [ṣari:ħ]

candidacy • **1.** تَرشِيح [tarši:ħ]

candidate • **1.** مُرَشَّح [muraššaħ] مُرَشَّحِين [muraššaħi:n] *pl:* Our party isn't putting up a candidate. حِزبنا ما راح يرَشِّح مُرَشَّح [ħizibna ma: ra:ħ yraššiħ muraššaħ] We have three candidates for the position. عِدنا ثلاث مُرَشَّحِين لِلوَظِيفَة [ʕidna tlaθ muraššaħi:n lilwaði:fa]

candle • **1.** شَمعَة [šamʕa] شَمعات، شمُوع [šamʕa:t, šmu:ʕ] *pl:* We had to light a candle. اِضطَرَّينا نِشعِل شَمعَة [ʔiðtarri:na nišʕil šamʕa]

candlestick • **1.** شَمعِدان [šamiʕda:n] شَمعِدانات [šamiʕda:na:t] *pl:*

candy • **1.** شَكَرايَة [šakara:ya] شَكَرايات [šakara:ya:t] *pl:* شَكَرات [šakara:t] *Collective*

chocolate candy • **1.** جِكلَيتايَة [čikli:ta:ya] جكلَيتايات [čikli:ta:ya:t] *pl:* جِكلَيت [čikli:t] *Collective*

to candy • **1.** شَكَّر [šakkar] تَشكِير [taški:r] *vn:* تشَكَّر [tšakkar] *p:* He brought us a box of candied fruits. جاب إلنا قُوطِيَّة فَواكِه مشَكَّرَة [ǰa:b ʔilna qu:ṭiyya fawa:kih mšakkira]

cane • **1.** قُصبَة [guṣba] قُصبات [guṣba:t] *pl:* قُصَب [guṣab] *Collective:* The marsh dwellers build their houses of cane. سُكّان الأهوار يبنُون بيُوتهُم مِن قُصَب [sukka:n ʔilʔahwa:r yibnu:n byu:thum min guṣab] • **2.** عُوجِيَّة [ʕu:čiyya] عُوجِيّات [ʕu:čiyya:t] *pl:* عُوجِيَّة [ʕu:čiyya] عَواجِي [ʕawa:či] *pl:* Ever since I broke my leg I have been walking with a cane. مِن وَقِت ما اِنكِسرَت رِجلِي قِمِت أمشِي عَالعُوجِيَّة [min wakit ma: ʔinkisrat riǰli gimit ʔamši ʕalʕu:čiyya] • **3.** باسطَون [ba:ṣṭu:n] باسطَونات [pa:ṣṭu:na:t] *pl:* He only carries the cane for show. هُوَّ شايِل الباسطَون لِلكَشخَة بَسّ [huwwa ša:yil ʔilba:ṣṭu:n lilkašxa bass] • **4.** عَصَى [ʕaṣa] عِصِي [ʕiṣi:] *pl:* The blind man feels his way with the cane. الأعمَى يِتحَسَّس طَرِيقَه بِالعَصا [ʔilʔaʕma yitħassas ṭari:qah bilʕaṣa]

canned goods • **1.** مُعَلَّب [muʕallab] Canned goods can be kept a long time. مُعَلَّبات الأطعِمَة تِنحُفُظ مُدَّة طَوِيلَة [muʕallaba:t ʔilʔaṭʕima tinħufuð mudda ṭawi:la]

cannibal • **1.** آكِل لَحَم البَشَر [ʔa:kil laħam ʔilbašar] أكِلات لَحَم البَشَر [ʔakila:t laħam ʔilbašar] *pl:*

cannon • **1.** مَدفَع [madfaʕ] مَدافِع [mada:fiʕ] *pl:* طَوب [ṭu:b] طواب [ṭwa:b] *pl:*

can opener • **1.** فَتّاحَة [fatta:ħa] فَتّاحات [fatta:ħa:t] *pl:*

cantaloupe • **1.** بَطِّيخَة [baṭṭi:xa] بَطِّيخات [baṭṭi:xa:t] *pl:* بَطِّيخ [baṭṭi:x] *Collective*

canteen • **1.** مَطّارَة [maṭṭa:ra] مَطّارات [maṭṭa:ra:t] *pl:* Did you fill your canteen? تِرَست المَطّارَة مالتَك؟ [tirast ʔilmaṭṭa:ra ma:ltak?] • **2.** كانتِين [ka:nti:n] كانتِينات [ka:nti:na:t] *pl:* The soldiers are waiting for the canteen to open. الجُنُود يِنتَظرُون الكانتِين يفَتِّح [ʔiǰǰunu:d yintaðrawn ʔilka:nti:n yfattiħ]

canvas • **1.** جنفاص [ǰinfa:ṣ, činfa:ṣ] جُنفاص [čunfa:ṣ] My gym shoes are made of canvas. قُندَرَة الرياضَة مالتِي مسَوّايَة مِن جُنفاص [qundarat ʔilriya:ða ma:lti msawwa:ya min čunfa:ṣ] • **2.** كِتّان [kitta:n] This picture is painted on canvas. هَالصُّورَة مَرسُومَة عَلَى كِتّان [haṣṣu:ra marsu:ma ʕala kitta:n]

C

to canvass • **1.** مَرّ عَلَى [marr ʕala] مُرُور [muru:r] *vn:* اِنمَرّ [ʔinmarr] *p:* They asked me to canvass the whole group to get their طِلبَوا مِنّي أَمُرّ عَلَى كُلّ الجَّماعَة وَأستَطلِع أرائهُم [ṭilbaw minni ʔamurr ʕala kull ʔijjama:ʕa wʔastaṭliʕ ʔara:ʔhum] opinions • **2.** جَسّ نَبُض [jass nabuð̣] جَسّ نَبُض [jass nabuð̣] *vn: sv* i. Before we change anything, let's canvass the group. قَبُل ما نغَيِّر شِي، خَلّي نجِسّ نَبض الجَّماعَة [gabul ma: nɣayyir ši, xalli njiss nabð̣ ʔijjama:ʕa]

cap • **1.** عَرَقچِين [ʕaraqči:n] عَرَقچِينات [ʕaraqči:na:t] *pl:* كلاو [kla:w] كلاوات [kla:wa:t] *pl:* He's wearing a small cap under his head cloth. لابِس عَرَقچِين جَوَّة غُترتَه [la:bis ʕaraqči:n jawwa ɣuṭurtah] • **2.** راس [ra:s] رُوس [ru:s] *pl:* I've lost the cap to my fountain pen. ضَيَّعِت الرّاس مال قَلَم الحِبِر مالي [ð̣ayyaʕit ʔirra:s ma:l qalam ʔilħibir ma:li] • **3.** غِطا [ɣiṭa] غُطايات [ɣuṭa:ya:t] *pl:* قَبَغ [qabaɣ] قَبَغات [qabaɣa:t] *pl:* Put the cap back on the bottle. رَجِّع قَبَغ البُوطِل بِمَكانَه [rajjiʕ qabaɣ ʔilbuṭul bmaka:nah] • **4.** تَلبِيسَة [talbi:sa] تَلبِيسات [talbi:sa:t] *pl:* The cap is cutting my gums. التَّلبِيسَة دَتِجرَح لَثّتي [ʔittalbi:sa datijrah laθθti] • **5.** كاب [ka:p] كابات [ka:pa:t] *pl:* The jockey's cap fell off during the race. وُقَع الكاب مال الجّاكِي أثناء السِّباق [wugaʕ ʔilka:b ma:l ʔijja:ki ʔaθna:ʔ ʔissiba:q]

to cap • **1.** لَبَّس [labbas] تَلبِيس [talbi:s] *vn:* تلَبَّس [tlabbas] *p:* This tooth needs capping. هالسِّن يِنرادلَه تَلبِيس [hassinn yinra:dlah talbi:s] • **2.** قَبَّغ [qabbaɣ] تقُبُّغ، تَقبِيغ [tqubbuɣ, taqbi:ɣ] *vn:* تقَبَّغ [tqabbaɣ] *p:* They cap the bottles with metal caps. يقَبُّغُون البطُولَة بِقَبَغات مَعدَن [yqabbuɣu:n ʔilbṭu:la bqabaɣa:t maʕdan]

capability • **1.** مَقدِرَة [maqdira]

capable • **1.** مُقتَدِر [muqtadir] قادِر [qa:dir] She's a very capable person. هِيَّ فَدّ وِحدَة كُلّش مِقتَدرَة [hiyya fadd wiħda kulliš miqtadra] He's capable of anything. هُوَّ قادِر عَلَى كُلّشِي [huwwa qa:dir ʕala kullši] He's capable of anything. يِطلَع مِن إيدَه كُلّشِي [yiṭlaʕ min ʔi:dah kullši]

capacity • **1.** سِعَة [siʕa] سِعات [siʕa:t] *pl:* The tank has a capacity of one hundred gallons. سِعَة التّانكي مِيَّة غَلِن [siʕat ʔitta:nki miyyat galin] • **2.** صِفَة [ṣifa] صِفات [ṣifa:t] *pl:* I am here in my capacity as guardian. آني هنا بِصِفَتي وَصِيّ [ʔa:ni hna bṣifati waṣiy] • **3.** طاقَة [ṭa:qa] طاقات [ṭa:qa:t] *pl:* It is already working up to full capacity. مِن هَسَّة دَتِشتُغُل كُلّ طاقَتها [min hassa datištuɣul kull ṭa:qatha]

* **The tank is full to capacity.** • **1.** التانكي مَليان لِلراس [ʔitta:nki malya:n lirra:s] / التّانكِي مَترُوس الأمانَة [ʔitta:nki matru:s ʔilʔama:na]

cape • **1.** راس [ra:s] رُؤُوس [ruʔu:s, ru:s] *pl:* The Cape of Good Hope. راس الرِّجاء الصّالِح [ra:s ʔirrija:ʔ ʔiṣṣa:liħ]

capital • **1.** عاصِمَة [ʕa:ṣima] عاصِمات، عَواصِم [ʕa:ṣima:t, ʕawa:ṣim] *pl:* Have you ever been in the capital? بعُمرَك رايِح لِلعاصِمَة؟ [bʕumrak ra:yiħ lilʕa:ṣima?] • **2.** رَاسمَال، رأسمال [ra:sma:l, raʔ sma:l] How much capital do you need to start your business? شقَدّ تِحتاج راسمال حَتّى تِبدِي شُغلَك؟ [šgadd tiħta:j ra:sma:l ħatta tibdi šuɣlak?] • **3.** مال [ma:l] أموال [ʔamwa:l] *pl:* His capital is invested abroad. أموالَه مُستَثمَرَة بالخارج [ʔamwa:lah mustaθmara bilxa:rij] • **4.** حَرُف كِبِير [ħaruf čibi:r] حُرُوف كِبِيرَة [ħuru:f čibi:ra] *pl:* When you write English, begin every sentence with a capital. مِن تِكتِب بالإنكلِيزِي إبدِي كُلّ جُملَة بِحَرُف كِبِير [min tiktib bilʔingili:zi ʔibdi kull jumla bħaruf čibi:r] • **5.** صُرمايَة [ṣurma:ya] Ahmed is going to provide me with a capital of 1,000 dinars to open a shop. أحمَد راح يِنطِينِي صَرمايَة ألف دِينار أفَتِّح بِيها دُكّان [ʔaħmad ra:ħ yinṭi:ni ṣarma:ya ʔalf dina:r ʔafattiħ bi:ha dukka:n]

capitalist • **1.** رَأسمالِي [raʔsma:li]

capitalism • **1.** رَأسمالِيَّة [raʔsma:liyya]

capitalistic • **1.** رَأسمالِي [raʔsma:li]

to capitalize • **1.** اِستَغَلّ [ʔistaɣall] اِستِغلال [ʔistiɣla:l] *vn: sv* i. We are planning to capitalize on the situation. بنِيَّتنا نِستِغِلّ الوَضِع [bniyyatna nistiɣill ʔilwað̣iʕ]

capital offense • **1.** جِنايَة [jina:ya] جِنايات [jina:ya:t] *pl:*

capital punishment • **1.** عُقُوبَة الإعدام [ʕuqu:bat ʔilʔiʕda:m]

capon • **1.** دِيك مَخصِي [di:č maxṣi] دْيُوك مَخصِيَّة [dyu:č maxṣiyya] *pl:*

capricious • **1.** هَوائِي [hawa:ʔi] سوَيعَتِي [swi:ʕati]

* **She is capricious.** • **1.** ساعاتها مُو سُوا [sa:ʕa:tha mu: suwa]

capsule • **1.** زِلّاجَة [zilla:ja] زِلّاجات [zilla:ja:t] *pl:* زِلّاج [zilla:j] *Collective:* قُلّاجَة [gulla:ja] قُلّاجات [gulla:ja:t] *pl:* قُلّاج [gulla:j] *Collective:* كَبسُولَة [kabsu:la] كَبسُولات [kabsu:la:t] *pl:*

captain • **1.** قُبطان [qubṭa:n] قُبطانِيَّة [qubṭa:niyya] *pl:* رَئِيس [raʔi:s] رُؤَساء [ruʔasa:, ruʔasa:ʔ] *pl:* The captain was the last to leave the sinking ship. القَبطان كان آخِر مَن تِرَك السِّفِينَة الغَرقانَة [ʔilqabṭa:n ča:n ʔa:xir man tirak ʔissifi:na ʔilɣarga:na] The captain was taken prisoner with his entire company. الرَّئِيس تأسَّر، هُوَّ وَالفَوج مالَه كُلَّه [ʔirraʔi:s tʔassar, huwwa walfawj ma:lah kullah] Who's the captain of the team? مِنُو رَئِيس الفَرِيق؟ [minu raʔi:s ʔilfari:q?]

to captivate • **1.** إِسَر (يأسَر أسِر) [ʔisar (yiʔsar ʔasir)] She captivated us all with her charm and good looks. إِسرَتنا كُلّنا بِفِتنَتها وَجَمالها [ʔisratna kullna bfitnatha wǰama:lha]

captive • **1.** أَسِير [ʔasi:r] أَسرَى [ʔasra] *pl:* The captives are arriving from the front in large numbers. الأَسرَى دَيُوصلُون مِن الجَبهَة بأَعداد كِبِيرَة [ʔilʔasra: dayu:ṣlu:n min ʔiǰǰabha bʔaʕda:d čibi:ra] The captive tiger hasn't eaten for two days. النِّمر الأَسِير صارلَه يومَين ما أَكَل [ʔinnimr ʔilʔasi:r ṣa:rlah yawmayn ma: ʔakal] • **2.** رَهِينَة [rahi:na] رَهائِن [raha:yin, raha:ʔin] *pl:* He was held captive by the band until his family paid the ransom. بُقَى رَهِينَة عِند العِصابَة إِلَى أَن عائِلتَه دِفعَوا الخاوَة [buqa: rahi:na ʕind ʔilʕiṣa:ba ʔila ʔan ʕa:ʔiltah difʕaw ʔilxa:wa] • **3.** مَسحُور [mashu:r] مَسحُورِين [mashu:ri:n] *pl:* He held his audience captive with his tales of adventure. تِرَك السّامعِين مَسحُورِين بِقِصَص مُغامَراتَه [tirak ʔissa:mʕi:n mashu:ri:n bqiṣaṣ muɣa:mara:tah]

captivity • **1.** أسِر [ʔasir]

to capture • **1.** أَسَّر [ʔassar] تاسِّر، تَأسِير [tʔissir, taʔsi:r] *vn:* تَأسَّر [tʔassar] *p:* They captured a general and his entire staff. أَسّرَوا جَنَرال وَكُلّ أَركان حَربَه [ʔassraw ǰanara:l wkull ʔarka:n ħarbah] • **2.** اِستَولَى [ʔistawla:] اِستِيلاء [ʔisti:la:ʔ] *vn: sv* i. Our armies have captured two cities. جَيشنا اِستَولَى عَلَى مَدِينتَين [ǰayšna ʔistawla: ʕala madi:nti:n] • **3.** أَخَذ مِن، أَخَذ عَلَى [ʔaxað min, ʔaxað ʕala] أَخِذ [ʔaxið] *vn:* اِنأَخَذ [ʔinʔaxað] *p:* We captured the town without a shot being fired. أَخَذنا المَدِينَة بِلا إطلاق نار [ʔaxaðna ʔilmadi:na bila ʔiṭla:q na:r]

car • **1.** سَيّارَة [sayya:ra] سَيّارات [sayya:ra:t] *pl:* Would you like to ride in my car? يِعجبَك تِركَب بسَيّارتي؟ [yiʕiǰbak tirkab bsayya:rti?] • **2.** فارقُون [fargu:n] فارقُونات، فَراقِين [fargu:na:t, fara:gi:n] *pl:* Two cars went off the track. فارقُونَين طِلعَت مِن السِّكَّة [fa:rgu:nayn ṭilʕat min ʔissičča]

carafe • **1.** سَراحِيَّة [sara:ħiyya] سَراحِيّات [sara:ħiyya:t] *pl:* Get the carafe of water out of the refrigerator. جِيب سَراحِيّة الماي مِن الثَّلاجَة [ǰi:b sara:ħiyyat ʔilma:y min ʔiθθilla:ǰa]

carat • **1.** قِيراط [qi:ra:ṭ] قِيراطات [qi:ra:ṭa:t] *pl:* حَبَّة [ħabba] حَبّات [ħabba:t] *pl:* These earrings are made of eighteen carat gold. هَالتَّراچِي ذَهَبها ثمُنطَعَش قِيراط [hattara:či ðahabha θmunṭaʕaš qi:ra:ṭ]

caravan • **1.** كَروان [karwa:n] كَراوِين [kara:wi:n] *pl:* قافِلَة [qa:fila] قَوافِل [qawa:fil] *pl:*

caravansary • **1.** خان [xa:n]

carbon • **1.** كاربُون [karbu:n]

carbon paper • **1.** وَرَق كاربون [waraq karbu:n] أوراق كاربون [ʔawra:q karbu:n] *pl:* I need some new carbon paper. أَحتاج شوَيَّة وَرَق كاربون جِدِيد [ʔaħta:ǰ šwayya waraq karbu:n ǰidi:d]

carburetor • **1.** كابرَيتَة [kabri:ta] كابرَيتات [ka:brita:t] *pl:*

card • **1.** وَرَقَة [waraqa] أوراق [ʔawra:q] *pl:* وَرَق [waraq] *Collective:* They played cards all evening. لِعبَوا وَرَق طُول اللَّيل [liʕbaw waraq ṭu:l ʔillayl] • **2.** بِطاقَة [biṭa:qa] بِطاقات، بِطايِق [biṭa:qa:t, biṭa:yiq] *pl:* They have a fine selection of greeting cards in that shop. عِدهُم مَجمُوعَة بَدِيعَة مِن بِطاقات التَّهانِي بذاك المَخزَن [ʕidhum maǰmu:ʕa badi:ʕa min biṭa:qa:t ʔittaha:ni bða:k ʔilmaxzan] He sent me a card from Beirut. أَرسَلّي بِطاقَة مِن بَيرُوت [ʔarsalli biṭa:qa min bayru:t] • **3.** كارت [ka:rt] كارتات [ka:rta:t] *pl:* He left me his card with his telephone number. تِرَكلِي كارتَه مَعَ رَقَم تِلِفُونَه [tirakli ka:rtah maʕa raqam tilifu:nah]

*** He's quite a card!** • **1.** هُوَّ فَدّ نِمرَة خاصَّة [huwwa fadd nimra xa:ṣṣa]

to card • **1.** مِشَط [mišaṭ] مَشِط [mašiṭ] *vn: sv* i. The women spent the whole day carding the wool. النِّساء قِضَوا كُلّ النَّهار يمِشطُون الصُّوف [ʔinnisa:ʔ giðaw kull ʔinnaha:r ymišṭu:n ʔiṣṣu:f] • **2.** نِدَف [nidaf] نَدِف [nadif] *vn:* اِنّدَف [ʔinnidaf] *p:* The cotton in this mattress needs carding. القُطِن مال هَذا الفراش يِنرادلَه نَدِف [ʔilguṭin ma:l ha:ða ʔilfra:š yinra:dlah nadif]

cardboard • **1.** مقَوّايَة [mqawwa:ya] مقَوّايات [mqawwa:ya:t] *pl:* مقَوَّى [mqawwa:] *Collective:* Put a piece of cardboard in between. حُطّ فَدّ مقَوّايَة بِالنُّص [ħuṭṭ fadd mqawwa:ya binnuṣṣ] Put them in a cardboard box. حُطّهُم بِصَندُوق مقَوَّى [ħuṭṭhum biṣandu:g mqawwa:]

cardomom • **1.** هَيل [hayl] Don't put too much cardomom in the tea. لا تحُطّ هَيل هوايَة بِالشّاي [la: tħuṭṭ hayl hwa:ya bičča:y]

care • **1.** مدارَة [mda:ra] Regular care of the teeth is important. مداراة السِّنُون بِانتِظام مُهِمّ جِدّاً [mda:ra:t ʔissnu:n bʔintiða:m muhimm ǰiddan] • **2.** عِنايَة [ʕina:ya] He's under the doctor's care. هُوَّ تَحَت عِنايَة الطَّبِيب [huwwa taħat ʕina:yat ʔiṭṭabi:b] • **3.** أَمانَة [ʔama:na] May I leave these documents in your care. أَقدَر أَخَلِّي هَالمُستَنَدات بِأَمانتَك؟ [ʔagdar ʔaxalli halmustanada:t bʔama:ntak?]

in care of • **1.** بواسطَة [bwa:sṭa] عَلَى عِنوان [ʕala ʕinwa:n] Send me the letter care of Ahmed Husayn. دِزّلِي المَكتُوب عَلَى عِنوان أَحمَد حسَين [dizzli ʔilmaktu:b ʕala ʕinwa:n ʔaħmad ħsayn]

to take care • **1.** اِهتَمّ [ʔihtamm] اِهتِمام [ʔihtima:m] *vn: sv* a. I took care to mention everything. اِهتَمَّيت أَذكُر كُلّشِي [ʔihtammi:t ʔaðkur kullši] • **2.** تحاشَى [tħa:ša:] تَحاشِي [taħa:ši] *vn: sv* a. I took care not to mention anything. تحاشَيت أَذكُر أَيّ شِي [tħa:ši:t ʔaðkur ʔayy ši]

C

career • **1.** مِهنَة [mihna] مِهَن [mihan] *pl:* Her career is more important for her than marriage. مِهنَتها أَهَمّ إلها مِن الزَّواج [mihnatha ʔahamm ʔilha min ʔizzawa:ǰ] He made medicine his career. اِتَّخَذ الطِّبّ مِهنَة إلَه [ʔittaxað ʔiṭṭibb mihna ʔilah] • **2.** سيرَة [si:ra] سِيَر [siyar] *pl:* I have been following his career with great interest. دَأتعَقَّب سيرتَه بإهتِمام شَدِيد [daʔatʕaqqab si:rtah bʔihtima:m šadi:d] • **3.** مَسلَك [maslak] مَسالِك [masa:lik] *pl:* He spent his life in this career. قِضَى عُمرَه بهَالمَسلَك [giḍa: ʕumrah bhalmaslak] • **4.** مَسلَكِي [maslaki] He is a career diplomat. هُوَّ دُبلوماسِي سِلِك [huwwa dublu:ma:si silik]

carefree • **1.** عَدَم مُبالاة [ʕadam muba:la:t] He leads a carefree life. يعِيش عِيشَة عَدَم مُبالاة [yiʕi:š ʕi:šat ʕadam muba:la:t]

careful • **1.** دَقِيق [daqi:q] He's a very careful person. هُوَّ شَخِص كُلِّش دَقِيق [huwwa šaxiṣ kulliš daqi:q] • **2.** حَذِر [ħaðir] مِتحَذِّر [mitħaððir] He is very careful about how he invests his money. هُوَّ كُلِّش حَذِر بإستِثمار فلوسَه [huwwa kulliš ħaðir bʔistiθma:r flu:sah]

to be careful • **1.** دار بال [da:r ba:l] دَيرَة بال [dayrat ba:l] *vn:* اِندار [ʔinda:r] *p:*. Be careful not to break this vase. دِير بالَك لا ترُوح تِكسِر هَالمَزهَرِيَّة [di:r ba:lak la: tru:ħ tiksir halmazhariyya] • **2.** كان حَرِيص [ča:n ħari:ṣ] I was careful not to mention anything. كُنت حَرِيص لا أجِيب ذِكِر فَدّ شي [kunit ħari:ṣ la: ʔaǰi:b ðikir fadd ši]

carefully • **1.** بعِنايَة [bʕina:ya] They lifted the stretcher carefully. شالَوا السَّدية بعِنايَة [ša:law ʔissadya bʕina:ya] • **2.** بدِقَّة [bdiqqa] Check the figures carefully. إفحَص الأرقام بدِقَّة [ʔifħaṣ ʔilʔarqa:m bdiqqa] • **3.** بحَذَر [bħaðar] He drives carefully. يسُوق السَّيّارَة بحَذَر [ysu:g ʔissayya:ra bħaðar]

careless • **1.** مُهمِل [muhmal] She's become careless lately. صايرَة مُهمِلَة بالأيّام الأخِيرَة [ṣa:yra muhmila bilʔayya:m ʔilʔaxi:ra]

*** He's careless with his money.** • **1.** ما يدِير بالَه عَلَى فلوسَه [ma: ydi:r ba:lah ʕala flu:sah]

cargo • **1.** حُمُولَة [ħumu:la] حُمُولات [ħumu:la:t] *pl:* شُحنَة [šuħna] شُحنات [šuħna:t] *pl:*

carnation • **1.** قرُنفلَة [qrunfila] قرُنفلات [qrunfila:t] *pl:* قرُنفل [qrunfil] *Collective*

carpenter • **1.** نَجّار [naǰǰa:r] نَجّارِين، نَجاجِير [naǰǰa:ri:n, naǰa:ǰi:r] *pl:*

carpet • **1.** زُولِيَّة [zu:liyya] زُولِيّات، زوالِي [zu:liyya:t, zwa:li] *pl:* سِجّادَة [sijǰa:da] سِجّادات، سجاجِيد [sijǰa:da:t, sǰa:ǰi:d] *pl:* This is a nice carpet. هَالزُّولِيَّة حِلوَة

to take care of • **1.** دار [da:r] دَير [dayr] *vn:* اِندار [ʔinda:r] *p:* The maids work is to take care of the children. الخادمَة شُغُلها دَير بالها عَالجَّهّال [ʔilxa:dma šuɣulha di:r ba:lha ʕaǰǰahha:l] Take care of my money for me. دِير بالَك عَلَى فلوسِي [di:r ba:lak ʕala flu:si] • **2.** سَوَّى [sawwa:] تَسوِيَة [taswiya] *vn:* تسَوَّى [tsawwa:] *p:* خَلَّص [xallaṣ] تَخلِيص [taxli:ṣ] *vn:* تخَلَّص [txallaṣ] *p:* I still have a few things to take care of. آنِي بَعَد عِندِي بَعض الأشياء لازِم أسَوِّيها [ʔa:ni baʕad ʕindi baʕð ʔilʔašya:ʔ la:zim ʔasawwi:ha] • **3.** اِعتِنَى ب [ʔiʕtina: b-] اِعتِناء [ʔiʕtina:ʔ] *vn: sv* i. حافَظ [ħa:fað] مُحافَظَة [muħa:faða] *vn:* تحافَظ [tħa:fað] *p:* He takes care of his clothes. يِعتِنِي بهدُومَه [yiʕtini bihdu:mah]

*** That takes care of that.** • **1.** خِلصَت والسَّلام [xilṣat wissala:m] / هَالمُشكِلَة اِنحَلَّت [halmuškila ʔinħallat] / هَذا اِنتِهَى أمرَه [ha:ða ʔintiha: ʔamrah] / شِي يسِدّ شِي [ši ysidd ši]

*** Good-bye, take care of yourself.** • **1.** فِي أمان الله، الله ويّاك [fi: ʔama:n ʔillah, ʔallah wiyya:k] فِي أمان إللّه، أمانَة الله عَلَى نَفسَك [fi: ʔama:n ʔilla:h, ʔama:nat ʔallah ʕala nafsak]

to care • **1.** مال [ma:l] مَيل [mayl] *vn: sv* i. I don't care much for movies. ما أمِيل هوايَة لِلسِّينَما [ma: ʔami:l hwa:ya lissinama] • **2.** دار بَال [da:r ba:l] دَير بَال [di:r ba:l, dayara:n ba:l] *vn:* اِندار بَال [ʔinda:r ba:l] *p:* Who cares? مِنُو يدِير بال؟ [minu ydi:r ba:l?]

*** What do I care?** • **1.** وانِي شَعلَيّا؟ [wa:ni šaʕlayya?]

*** I don't care what he thinks.** • **1.** ما يهِمّنِي هُوَّ شيفتِكِر [ma: yhimmni huwwa šiyiftikir]

*** For all I care, you can go wherever you like.** • **1.** وَلا يهِمّنِي، تِقدَر ترُوح وَين ما يعجبَك [wala: yhimmni, tigdar tru:ħ wi:n ma yʕiǰbak]

*** I don't care to go to the movies tonight.** • **1.** ما يعِجبنِي أرُوح لِلسِينَما هَاللَيلَة [ma: yiʕǰibni ʔaru:ħ lissinama hallayla]

to care for • **1.** اِعتِنَى ب [ʔiʕtina: bi-] اِعتِناء [ʔiʕtina:ʔ] *vn: sv* i. تِعَب عَلَى [tiʕab ʕala] تَعَب، تَعبان [taʕab, taʕba:n] *vn: sv* a. This garden is well cared for. هَالحَدِيقَة مِعتِنِين بِيها هوايَة [halħadi:qa miʕtini:n bi:ha hwa:ya] This garden is well cared for. هَالحَدِيقَة تَعبانِين عَلِيها هوايَة [halħadi:qa taʕba:ni:n ʕali:ha hwa:ya] • **2.** دار بَال [da:r ba:l] دَير بَال، دَيران بَال [di:r ba:l, dayara:n ba:l] *vn:* اِندار بَال [ʔinda:r] *p:* دارَى [da:ra:] مُداراة [muda:ra:(t)] *vn: sv* i. My sister is caring for the children today. أختِي دَتدِير بالها عالأطفال هَاليُوم [ʔuxti datdi:r ba:lha ʕalʔaṭfa:l halyu:m] • **3.** حَبّ [ħabb] حُبّ [ħubb] *vn: sv* i. Do you care for her? تحِبّها؟ [tħibbha?]

*** Would you care for gravy on the meat?** • **1.** يعِجبَك مَرَق عَلَى اللَّحَم؟ [yʕiǰbak marag ʕala ʔillaħam?]

to be cared for • **1.** كان مَتعُوب عَلَى [ča:n matʕu:b ʕala] اِندار بَال عَلَى [ʔinda:r ba:l ʕala] *sv* a. The children are well cared for. الأطفال هوايَة مَتعُوب عَلَيهُم [ʔilʔaṭfa:l hwa:ya matʕu:b ʕalayhum]

[hazzu:liyya ħilwa] This is a nice carpet. هَذِي خَوش سِجّادَة [ha:ði xu:š siǰǰa:da]

to have someone on the carpet • **1.** رَزَّل [razzal] رَزالَة [raza:la] *vn:* تَرَزَّل [trazzal] *p:* وَبَّخ [wabbax] تَوبِيخ [tawbi:x] *vn:* تَوَبَّخ [twabbax] *p:* The boss had him on the carpet again this morning. المُدِير رَزَّلَه اليُوم الصُّبُح مَرَّة لُخ [ʔilmudi:r razzalah ʔilyu:m ʔiṣṣubuħ marra lux]

to carpet • **1.** فُرَش بِالسَّجّاد [furaš bissaǰǰa:d] فَرِش بِالسَّجّاد [fariš bissaǰǰa:d] *vn:* اِنفُرَش بِالسَّجّاد [ʔinfuraš] *p:* غَطَّى بِالسَّجّاد [ɣaṭṭa: bissaǰǰa:d] تَغطِيَة بِالسَّجّاد [taɣṭiya bissaǰǰa:d] *vn:* تغَطَّى بِالسَّجّاد [tɣaṭṭa: bissaǰǰa:d] *p:* All the stairs were carpeted. كُلّ الدَّرجات كانَت مَفرُوشَة بِسِجّاد [kull ʔiddarǰa:t ča:nat mafru:ša bsiǰǰa:d]

carrot • **1.** جِزرَة [ǰizra] جِزرات [ǰizra:t] *pl:* جِزَر [ǰizar] *Collective*

to carry • **1.** شال [ša:l] شَيل [ši:l] *vn:* اِنشال [ʔinša:l] *p:* He'll carry your bags for you. هُوَّ راح يشِيل لَك الجُّنَط [huwwa ra:ħ yši:l lak ʔiǰǰunaṭ] • **2.** حِمَل [ħimal] حَمِل [ħamil] *vn:* اِنحِمَل [ʔinħimal] *p:* This truck carries five tons. هَاللُّورِي يحمِل خَمِس أَطنان [hallu:ri yiħmil xamis ʔaṭna:n] • **3.** باع [ba:ʕ] بَيع [bi:ʕ] *vn:* اِنباع [ʔinba:ʕ] *p:* Do you carry men's shirts? تبِيع ثياب مال رياجِيل؟ [tbi:ʕ θya:b ma:l riya:ǰi:l?] • **4.** نِقَل [niqal, nigal] نَقِل [naqil] *vn:* اِنَّقَل [ʔinniqal] *p:* Mosquitoes carry malaria. البَقّ ينقُل المَلاريا [ʔilbagg yinqul ʔilmala:rya] • **5.** فاز [fa:z] فَوز [fawz] *vn:* اِنفاز [ʔinfa:z] *p:* He carried the election with an overwhelming majority. فاز بِالإِنتِخابات بِأَكثَرِيَّة ساحِقَة [fa:z bilʔintixa:ba:t bʔakθariyya sa:ħiqa] • **6.** نِطَى [niṭa:] نَطِي [naṭy] *vn:* *sv* i. The grocer agreed to carry us until I get another job. البَقّال وافَق ينطِينا بِالدَّين حَتَّى أَلقِي شُغُل [ʔilbagga:l wa:faq yinṭi:na biddayn ħatta ʔalgi šuɣul] • **7.** قِبَل [qibal] قُبُول [qubu:l] *vn:* اِنقِبَل [ʔinqibal] *p:* The motion was carried. الاقتِراح اِنقِبَل [ʔilʔiqtira:ħ ʔinqibal]

*** This crime carries the death penalty.** • **1.** هَذِي الجَرِيمَة عَلَيها عُقُوبَة الإِعدام [ha:ði ʔiǰǰari:ma ʕali:ha ʕuqu:bat ʔilʔiʕda:m]

*** The captain carries himself well.** • **1.** الرَّئِيس شَمُرتَه حِلوَة [ʔirraʔi:s šamurtah ħilwa]

*** Isn't that carrying things a little too far?** • **1.** مُو ثِخنَت عاد؟ [mu: θixnat ʕa:d?]

to carry away • **1.** جِرَف [ǰiraf] جَرُف [ǰaruf] *vn:* اِنجِرَف [ʔinǰiraf] *p:* The flood carried the house away. الفَيَضان جِرَف البَيت [ʔilfayaḍa:n ǰiraf ʔilbayt] • **2.** أَطرَب [ʔaṭrab] طَرَب [ṭarab] *vn:* اِنطِرَب [ʔinṭurab] *p:* The music carried me away. المُوسِيقَى طِربَتنِي [ʔilmu:si:qa: ṭirbatni] • **3.** هَزّ [hazz] هَزّ [hazz] *vn:* اِنهَزّ [ʔinhazz] *p:* سِحَر [siħar] سَحِر [saħir] *vn:* اِنسِحَر [ʔinsiħar] *p:* The crowd was carried away by the eloquence of the speaker. الجُّمهُور اِنهَزَّت عَواطفَه بفَصاحَة الخَطِيب [ʔiǰǰamhu:r ʔinhazzat ʕawa:ṭfah bfaṣa:ħat ʔilxaṭi:b] • **4.** أَخَذ مِن، أَخَذ عَلَى [ʔaxað min, ʔaxað ʕala] أَخِذ [ʔaxið] *vn:* اِنأَخَذ [ʔinʔaxað] *p:* He was carried away by the idea. اِنأخَذ بِالفِكرَة [ʔinʔixað bilfikra]

to carry on • **1.** واصَل [wa:ṣal] مُواصَلَة [muwa:ṣala] *vn:* تواصَل [twa:ṣal] *p:* His son carries on his business. اِبنَه دَيواصِل تِجارتَه [ʔibnah daywa:ṣil tiǰa:rtah]

to carry out • **1.** نَفَّذ [naffað] تَنفِيذ [tanfi:ð] *vn:* تنَفَّذ [tnaffað] *p:* We'll try to carry out your plan. راح نحاوِل نِنَفِّذ الخُطَّة مالتَك [ra:ħ nħa:wil ninaffið ʔilxuṭṭa ma:ltak] • **2.** طَلَّع [ṭallaʕ] تَطلِيع، طَلِّع [taṭli:ʕ, ṭṭilliʕ] *vn:* تطَلَّع [ṭṭallaʕ] *p:* *sv* i. Carry out the garbage. طَلِّع الزِّبِل بَرَّة [ṭalliʕ ʔizzibil barra]

to carry weight • **1.** كان إِلَه وَزِن [ča:n ʔilah wazin] كان إِلَه أَهَمِّيَّة [ča:n ʔilah ʔahammiyya] His opinion carries great weight. رأيَه إِلَه وَزِن كِبِير [raʔyah ʔilah wazin čibi:r]

cart • **1.** عَرَبانَة [ʕaraba:na] عَرَباين [ʕaraba:yin] *pl:* The cart was so loaded that he could hardly push it. العَرَبانَة كانَت مَشحُونَة إِلَى دَرَجَة أَن كان بِالكاد يدفَعها [ʔilʕaraba:na ča:nat mašħu:na ʔila daraǰa ʔan ča:n bilka:d yidfaʕha]

to cart • **1.** حِمَل [ħimal] حَمِل [ħamil] *vn:* اِنحِمَل [ʔinħimal] *p:* The sand has to be carted away. الرَّمُل لازِم ينحِمِل مِن هنا [ʔirramul la:zim yinħimil min hna]

cartridge • **1.** فِشقَة [fišga] فِشقات، فِشَق [fišga:t, fišag] *pl:* طَلقَة [ṭalqa] طَلقات [ṭalqa:t] *pl:* Three shots remained in the revolver. بُقَت بِالمُسَدَّس ثلَث طَلقات [buqat bilmusaddas tlaθ ṭalqa:t] • **2.** إِقنَة [ʔigna] إِقنات [ʔigna:t] *pl:* I want to change the cartridge on my recordplayer. أَرِيد أَبَدِّل الإِقنَة مال فُونوغرافِي [ʔari:d ʔabaddil ʔilʔigna ma:l funuɣra:fi]

to carve • **1.** نِقَش [niqaš] نَقِش [naqiš] *vn:* اِنَّقَش [ʔinniqaš] *p:* This is the man who carved the teak doors of the mosque. هَذا الرَّجِل اللِّي نِقَش أَبواب الصّاج مال المَسجِد [ha:ða ʔirraǰil ʔilli niqaš ʔabwa:b ʔiṣṣa:ǰ ma:l ʔilmasǰid] • **2.** نِحَت [niħat] نَحِت [naħit] *vn:* اِنِّحَت [ʔinniħat] *p:* The Assyrians used to carve winged bulls from stone. الآشُورِيِّين اِعتادَوا ينحَتُون ثِيران مجَنَّحَة مِن الصَّخَر [ʔilʔašuriyyi:n ʔiʕta:daw yinħatu:n θi:ra:n mǰannaħa min ʔiṣṣaxar] • **3.** قَصقَص [gaṣgaṣ] تِقِصقِص [tigiṣgiṣ] *vn:* تقَصقَص [tgaṣgaṣ] *p:* *sv* i. Will you carve the turkey? تحِبّ تقَصقِص العَلِي شِيش؟ [tħibb tgaṣgiṣ ʔilʕališi:š?] • **4.** حُفَر [ħufar] حَفُر [ħafur] *vn:* اِنحُفَر [ʔinħufar] *p:* He carved his name on the trunk of the tree. حُفَر إِسمَه عَلَى جِذع الشَّجَرَة [ħufar ʔismah ʕala ǰiðʕ ʔiššaǰara]

case • **1.** صَندُوق [ṣandu:g] صَنادِيق [ṣna:di:g] *pl:* Leave the bottles in the case. خَلِّي البطُولَة بِالصَّندُوق [xalli ʔilbṭu:la biṣṣandu:g] • **2.** بَيت [bayt] بيُوت [biyu:t] *pl:* قُوطِيَّة [qu:ṭiyya] قواطِي [qwa:ṭi] *pl:* I need a new case for my glasses. أَحتاج بَيت جِدِيد لِلمَناظِر مالتِي [ʔaħta:ǰ bayt ǰidiːd lilmanaːđ̣ir maːlti] • **3.** إصابَة [ʔiṣaːba] إصابات [ʔiṣaːbaːt] *pl:* There were five new cases of malaria. كان أكُو خَمِس إصابات جِدِيدَة بِالمَلاريا [čaːn ʔaku xamis ʔiṣaːbaːt ǰidiːda bilmalaːrya] • **4.** قَضِيَّة [qađ̣iyya] قَضايا [qađ̣aːya] *pl:* حادِث [ħaːdiθ] حوادِث [ħwaːdiθ] *pl:* I read about the case in the newspaper. قرَيت عَن القَضِيَّة بِالجَرِيدَة [qrayt ʕan ʔilqađ̣iyya biǰǰariːda] He presented his case well. عِرَض قَضِيتَه عَرِض زين [ʕirađ̣ qađ̣iːtah ʕarið̣ ziːn] • **5.** دَعوَة [daʕwa] دَعوات، دَعاوِي [daʕwaːt, daʕaːwi] *pl:* He's lost his case. هُوَّ خِسَر دَعُوتَه [huwwa xiṣar daʕwtah] • **6.** حالَة [ħaːla] حالات [ħaːlaːt] *pl:* That being the case. . . طالَما الحالَة هِيكِي [ṭaːlamaː ʔilħaːla hiːči]

*** The doctor is out on a case.** • **1.** الطَبِيب راح يشُوف مَرِيض [ʔiṭṭabiːb raːħ yšuːf mariːđ̣]

in any case • **1.** عَلَى كُلّ حال [ʕala kull ħaːl] مَهما كان [mahma kaːn] I'll call in any case. آنِي أخابُر عَلَى كُلّ حال [ʔaːni ʔaxaːbur ʕala kull ħaːl]

in case • **1.** إذا [ʔiđa] Wait for me in case I'm late. إستَنظِرنِي إذا تأخَّرت [ʔistanđ̣irni ʔiđa tʔaxxarit]

in case of • **1.** بِحالَة [bħaːla] In case of fire, use the emergency exit. إستَعمِل باب الطَّوارِئ بِحالَة الحَرِيق [ʔistaʕmil baːb ʔiṭṭawaːri bħaːlat ʔilħariːq]

cash • **1.** نَقِد [naqid] I have no cash with me. ما عِندِي نَقِد ويّايا [maː ʕindi naqid wiyyaːya] I have no cash with me. ما شايِل فلُوس [maː šaːyil fluːs] • **2.** نَقدِي [naqdi] نَقداً [naqdan] I'll pay cash. راح أدفَع نَقدِي [raːħ ʔadfaʕ naqdi] We sell only for cash. إحنا ما نبِيع غير نَقدِي [ʔiħna maː nbiːʕ ɣiːr naqdi] We sell only for cash. نبِيع بَسّ بِالنَّقدِي [nbiːʕ bass binnaqdi]

to cash • **1.** صَرَّف [ṣarraf] تَصرِيف [taṣriːf] *vn:* تصَرَّف [tṣarraf] *p:* Can you cash a check for me? تِقدَر تصَرُّفلِي شَكّ؟ [tigdar tṣarrufli čakk?]

cashier • **1.** صَرّاف [ṣarraːf] صَرّافِين [ṣarraːfiːn] *pl:* أمِين صَندُوق [ʔamiːn ṣanduːq] أمَناء صَندُوق [ʔumanaːʔ ṣanduːq] *pl:*

cashmere • **1.** كَشمِير [kašmiːr] I bought my sister a cashmere sweater. إشتِرَيت لأُختِي بلُوز كَشمِير [ʔištiriːt lʔuxti bluːz kašmiːr]

casket • **1.** تابُوت [taːbuːt] تَوابِيت [tawaːbiːt] *pl:* Six of his best friends carried his casket. سِتَّة مِن أحسَن أصدِقائَه شالُوا تابُوتَه [sitta min ʔaħsan ʔaṣdiqaːʔah šaːlaw taːbuːtah]

cast • **1.** مَجمُوعَة [maǰmuːʕa] مَجمُوعات [maǰmuːʕaːt] *pl:* هَيئَة [hayʔa] هَيئات [hayʔaːt] *pl:* The new play has an excellent cast of actors. التَّمثِيلِيَّة الجِّدِيدَة بِيها خُوش مَجمُوعَة مُمَثِّلِين [ʔittamθiːliyya ʔiǰǰidiːda biːha xuːš maǰmuːʕat mumaθθiliːn] • **2.** قالَب [qaːlab] قوالِب [qwaːlib] *pl:* How long will you have to wear the cast? شقَدّ لازم تِلبَس القالَب؟ [šgadd laːzim tilbas ʔalqaːlab?]

to cast • **1.** صَبّ [ṣabb] صَبّ [ṣabb] *vn:* إنصَبّ [ʔinṣabb] *p:* The statue will be cast in bronze. التِّمثال راح ينصَبّ مِن برُونز [ʔittimθaːl raːħ yinṣabb min bruːnz] • **2.** نِطَى [niṭaː] نَطِي [naṭy] *vn:* *sv* i. I cast my vote for the majority party nominee. إنطَيت صُوتِي لِمُرَشَّح حِزب الأكثَرِيَّة [ʔinṭayt ṣuːti limuraššaħ ħizb ʔilʔakθariyya]

*** The die is cast.** • **1.** قُضِيَ الأمر [quđ̣iya ʔilʔamr]

to cast anchor • **1.** رِسَى [risaː] رَسُو [rasw] *vn:* إنرِسَى [ʔinrisaː] *p:* ذَبّ أنقَر [đabb ʔangar] ذَبّ [đabb] *vn:* إنذَبّ [ʔinđabb] *p:* *sv* i. We cast anchor at dawn. ذَبِّينا أنقَر ويّا الفَجِر [đabbiːna ʔangar wiyya ʔilfaǰir] The ship cast anchor. الباخِرَة رِسَت [ʔilbaːxira risat]

castle • **1.** قَلعَة [qalʕa] قِلاع [qilaːʕ] *pl:* Have you seen the old castle? شِفت القَلعَة القَدِيمَة؟ [šift ʔilqalʕa ʔilqadiːma?] I'm taking the pawn with the castle. راح أقتُل الجُّندِي بالقَلعَة [raːħ ʔaktul ʔiǰǰundi bilqalʕa]

castor oil • **1.** دِهِن الخَروَع [dihin ʔilxarwaʕ]

casual • **1.** عابِر [ʕaːbir] طارِئ [ṭaːriʔ] سَطحِي [saṭħi] عَرَضِي [ʕarađ̣i] It was nothing more than a casual remark. ما كانَت أزيَد مِن مُلاحَظَة عابرَة [maː čaːnat ʔazyad min mulaːħađ̣a ʕaːbira] He's only a casual acquaintance. أعُرفَه بَسّ مَعرِفَة سَطحِيَّة [ʔaʕurfah bass maʕrifa saṭħiyya]

to be casual about • **1.** ما إهتَمّ [maː ʔihtamm] *sv* a. ما أخَذ [maː ʔaxađ] *sv* u. I wish I could be as casual about it as he is. يا رَيت أقدَر أصِير مِثلَه وَما آخُذ لِلمَوضُوع هوايَة إعتِبار [yaː riːt ʔagdar ʔaṣiːr miθlah wmaː ʔaːxuđ lilmawđ̣uːʕ hwaːya ʔiʕtibaːr]

casually • **1.** عَرَضاً [ʕarađ̣an] صُدفَةً [ṣudfatan] He said it to me quite casually. قالِّي إيّاها عَرَضاً [gaːlli ʔiyyaːha ʕarađ̣an] • **2.** سَطحِياً [saṭħiyyan] بصُورَة سَطحِيَّة [bṣuːra saṭħiyya] I only know him casually. أعُرفَه بصُورَة سَطحِيَّة [ʔaʕurfah bṣuːra saṭħiyya]

casualties • **1.** إصابَة [ʔiṣaːba] إصابات [ʔiṣaːbaːt] *pl:* خَسارَة [xasaːra] خَسارات، خَساير [xasaːraː t, xasaːyir] *pl:* Our casualties in Africa were small. خَسائِرنا بِأفرِيقيا كانَت قَلِيلَة [xasaːʔirna bʔafriːqya čaːnat qaliːla]

cat • **1.** بَزُّون [bazzuːn] بِزازِين [bizaːziːn] *pl:* هِرّ [hirr] هرُورَة [hruːra] *pl:* Our cat had kittens yesterday. بَزُّونَتنا جابَت فرُوخ البارحَة [bazzuːnatna ǰaːbat fruːx ʔilbaːrħa] • **2.** قِطّ [qiṭṭ] قِطَط [qiṭaṭ] *pl:* When the cat's away, the mice will play. غاب القِطّ، إلعَب يا فار [ɣaːb ʔilqiṭṭ, ʔilʕab yaː faːr]

catalogue • **1.** كَتالُوج [kataːluːg] كَتالُوجات [kataːluːgaːt] *pl:* The sample clothes patterns in this catalogue are better. نَماذِج تَفصِيل المَلابِس بِهَالكَتالُوج أحسَن [namaːđiǰ tafṣiːl ʔilmalaːbis bhalkataːluːg ʔaħsan] Why don't you arrange your (card) catalogue alphabetically? لِيش ما ترَتِّبُون الكَتالَوج حَسَب الحُرُوف الأبجَدِيَّة؟ [liːš maː trattbuːn ʔilkataːluːg ħasab ʔilħuruːf ʔilʔabǰadiyya?]

catastrophe • **1.** كارِثَة [kaːriθa] كَوارِث [kawaːriθ] *pl:* نَكبَة [nakba] نَكبات [nakbaːt] *pl:*

catch • **1.** زُقفالَة [zuqfaːla] زُقفالات [zuqfaːlaːt] *pl:* قُفُل [quful] قفال، قفالَة [qfaːl, qfaːla] *pl:* The catch on the camera is broken. الزُّقفالَة مال الكامَيرَة مَكسُورَة [ʔizzuqfaːla maːl ʔilkamiraː maksuːra] • **2.** صِيدَة [ṣiːda] صِيدات [ṣiːdaːt] *pl:* The fish is a good catch. عَشِر سِمكات خُوش صِيدَة [ʕašir simčaːt xuːš ṣiːda] That girl is a good catch. هَالبِنيَّة خُوش صِيدَة [halbnayya xuːš ṣayda] • **3.** حِيلَة [ħiːla] حِيَل [ħiyal] *pl:* لِعبَة [liʕba] لِعبات، ألعاب، مَلاعِيب [liʕbaːt, ʔalʕaːb, malaːʕiːb] *pl:* There must be a catch to it. لازِم بِيها لِعبَة [laːzim biːha liʕba]

to catch • **1.** صاد [ṣaːd] صَيد [ṣayd] *vn:* اِنصاد [ʔinṣaːd] *p:* We caught a lot of fish. صِدنا سِمِك هوايَة [ṣidna simič hwaːya] • **2.** لِقَف [ligaf] لَقُف [laguf] *vn:* اِنلِقَف [ʔinligaf] *p:* Here, catch it! يَاللّه، اِلقُفها [yallah, ʔilgufha] • **3.** لَحَّق ب [laħħag b-] تَلحِيق [talħiːg] *vn:* تلَحَّق [tlaħħag] *p:* I have to catch a train at five o'clock. لازِم ألَحِّق بقِطار السّاعَة خَمسَة [laːzim ʔalaħħig bqiṭaːr ʔissaːʕa xamsa] • **4.** لِزَم [lizam] لَزِم [lazim] *vn:* اِنلِزَم [ʔinlizam] *p:* I caught him at it. آنِي لِزَمتَه بِيها [ʔaːni lzamtah biːha] They caught him red-handed. لِزمَوه مِتلَبِّس بالجَّرِيمَة [lizmawh mitlabbis bijǰariːma] They caught him before he could get over the border. لِزمَوه قَبُل ما يقدَر يُعبُر الحِدُود [lizmawh gabul maː yigdar yuʕbur ʔilħiduːd] • **5.** قُبَض عَلَى [qubaḍ ʕala] قَبُض [qabuḍ] *vn:* اِنقُبَض [ʔinqubaḍ] *p:* كُمَش [kumaš] كَمُش [kamuš] *vn:* اِنكُمَش [ʔinkumaš] *p:* The police caught the thief. الشُّرطَة قبضَوا عَلَى الحَرامِي [ʔiššurṭa qibḍaw ʕala ʔilħaraːmi] • **6.** أخَذ مِن، أخَذ عَلَى [ʔaxað min, ʔaxað ʕala] أخِذ [ʔaxið] *vn:* اِنأخَذ [ʔinʔaxað] *p:* The lock doesn't catch well. القِفِل ما دَياخُذ زين [ʔilqifil maː dayaːxuð ziːn] • **7.** سِمَع [simaʕ] سَمِع [samiʕ] *vn:* اِنسِمَع [ʔinsimaʕ] *p:* I didn't catch his name. ما سِمَعِت إسمَه زين [maː simaʕit ʔismah ziːn] • **8.** شَكَّل [šakkal] تَشكِيل [taškiːl] *vn:* تشَكَّل [tšakkal] *p:* My coat caught on a nail. سِترتِي شَكَّلَت بفَدّ بِسمار [sitirti šakklat bfadd bismaːr] • **9.** حِصَر [ħiṣar] حَصِر [ħaṣir] *vn: sv* i.

to catch cold • **1.** اِنّشَل [ʔinnišal] *sv* i. أخَذ بَرِد [ʔaxað barid] أخِذ بَرِد [ʔaxið barid] *vn: sv* u. You'll catch cold. إنتَ راح تِنّشِل [ʔinta raːħ tinnišil]

to catch fire • **1.** اِشتِعَل [ʔištiʕal] اِشتِعال [ʔištiʕaːl] *vn: sv* i. اِحتِرَق [ʔiħtirag] حَرِق [ħarig] *vn: sv* i. The wood is so dry that it will catch fire quickly. الخِشَب هَل قَدّ ما يابِس يِشتِعِل بِساع [ʔilxišab hal gadd maː yaːbis yištiʕil bsaːʕ] • **2.** اِعتِلَق [ʔiʕtilag] *sv* i. The wood didn't catch fire. الحَطَب ما اِعتِلَق [ʔilħaṭab maː ʔiʕtilag]

to catch hold • **1.** لِزَم [lizam] لَزِم [lazim] *vn:* اِنلِزَم [ʔinlizam] *p:* Catch hold of the other end. اِلزَم مِن صَفحَة اللُّخ [ʔilzam min ṣafħat ʔillux]

to catch on • **1.** دِرَج [diraǰ] دَرِج [dariǰ] *vn: sv* u. That song caught on very quickly. هَالأُغنِيَة دِرجَت بِالعَجَل [halʔuɣniya dirǰat bilʕaǰal] • **2.** لِقَف [ligaf] لَقُف [laguf] *vn:* اِنلِقَف [ʔinligaf] *p:* اِفتِهَم [ʔiftiham] اِفتِهام [ʔiftihaːm] *vn: sv* i. He catches on quickly. يِلقُفها بِالعَجَل [yilgufha bilʕaǰal] She immediately caught on to the idea. هِيَّ بِالعَجَل اِفتِهمَتها لِلفِكرَة [hiyya bilʕaǰal ʔiftihmatha lilfikra]

to catch the eye • **1.** لِفَت النَّظَر [lifat ʔinnaðar] لَفِت النَّظَر [lafit ʔinnaðar] *vn:* اِنلِفَت النَّظَر [ʔinlifat] *p:* جِلَب النَّظَر [ǰilab ʔinnaðar] جَلِب النَّظَر [ǰalib ʔinnaðar] *vn:* اِنجِلَب النَّظَر [ʔinǰilab ʔinnaðar] *p: sv* i. The neckties in the window caught my eye. الأربطَة بِالشِّبّاك لِفتَت نَظَري [ʔilʔarbiṭa biššibbaːč liftat naðari]

to catch the measles • **1.** حَصَّب [ħaṣṣab] تحِصِّب [tħiṣṣib] *vn:* تحَصَّب [tħaṣṣab] *p:* أخَذ الحَصبَة [ʔaxað ʔilħaṣba] أخِذ الحَصبَة [ʔaxið ʔilħaṣba] *vn:* اِنأخَذ الحَصبَة [ʔinʔaxað ʔilħaṣba] *p:* اِنصاب بِالحَصبَة [ʔinṣaːb bilħaṣba] *sv* a. I caught the measles from him. أخَذِت الحَصبَة مِنَّه [ʔaxaðit ʔilħaṣba minnah]

to catch up • **1.** لَحَّق [laħħag] تلِحِّق [tliħħig] *vn: sv* i. Try to catch up in your work. حاوِل تلَحِّق بشُغلَك [ħaːwil tlaħħig bišuɣlak] Go ahead, I'll catch up with you. رُوح، عُود آنِي ألَحِّق بِيك [ruːħ, ʕuːd ʔaːni ʔalaħħig biːk] • **2.** عَوَّض [ʕawwaḍ] تَعوِيض [taʕwiːḍ] *vn:* تعَوَّض [tʕawwaḍ] *p:* I have to catch up on my sleep. لازِم أعَوِّض عَن نَومِي [laːzim ʔaʕawwiḍ ʕan nawmi]

catching • **1.** مُعدِي [muʕdi] Measles are catching. الحَصبَة مُعدِيَة [ʔilħaṣba muʕdiya]

caterpillar • **1.** دُودَة قَزّ [duːdat qazz] دُودات قَزّ [duːdaːt qazz] *pl:* دُود قَزّ [duːd qazz] *Collective*

cathedral • **1.** كاتِدرائِيَّة [kaːtidraːʔiyya] كاتِدرائِيّات [kaːtidraːʔiyyaːt] *pl:*

cattle • **1.** ماشِيَة [maːšiya] مَواشِي [mawaːši] *pl:* هايشَة، هَوايِش [haːyša, hawaːyiš] بَقَر [baqar] They raise fine cattle in this part of the country. يرَبُّون خُوش مَواشِي بهالقِسِم مِن البَلَد [yrabbuːn xuːš mawaːši bhaːlqisim min ʔilbalad]

to get caught • **1.** وُقَف [wugaf] وَقُف، وُقُوف [waguf, wuguːf] *vn: sv* a. A fish bone got caught in his throat. عَظمَة سِمَك وُقفَت بلَهاتَه [ʕaḍmat simač wugfat blahaːtah] • **2.** اِنلِزَم [ʔinlizam] لَزِم [lazim] *vn: sv* i. I got caught in a shower on the way home. اِنلِزمِت بمَطرَة بطَرِيقِي لِلبَيت [ʔinlizamit bmaṭra bṭariːqi lilbayt] Don't get caught! لا تخَلِّي نَفسَك تِلزِم [laː txalli nafsak tillizim] Don't get caught! لا تخَلِّي نَفسَك تِنكُمُش [laː txalli nafsak tinkumuš]

cauliflower • **1.** قَرنَبِيط [qarnabiːṭ]

cause • **1.** سَبَب [sabab] أسباب [ʔasbaːb] *pl:* غايَة [ɣaːya] غايات [ɣaːyaːt] *pl:* What is the cause of the delay?

شِنُو سَبَب التّأخِير؟ [šinu sabab ʔittaʔxiːr?] He died for a good cause. هُوَّ مات بسَبِيل غايَة شَرِيفَة [huwwa maːt bsabiːl ɣaːya šariːfa]

to cause • **1.** سَبَّب [sabbab] تَسبِيب [tasbiːb] *vn:* تسَبَّب [tsabbab] *p:* What caused the accident? شسَبَّب الحادِث؟ [šsabbab ʔilħaːdiθ?] He causes her a lot of grief. هُوَّ يسَبِّب إلها هوايَة قَهَر [huwwa ysabbib ʔilha hwaːya qahar]

caution • **1.** حَذَر [ħaðar] تَحذِير [taħðiːr] اِحتِياط [ʔiħtiyaːṭ] اِحتِراس [ʔiħtiraːs] Caution in this work is just as important as speed. الحَذَر بهَذا الشُّغُل مُهِم مِثِل أهَمِّيَّة السُّرعَة [ʔilħaðar bhaːða ʔiššuɣul muhimm miθil ʔahammiyyat ʔissurʕa]

cautious • **1.** مِتحَذِّر [mitħaððir] مِحتِرِس [miħtiris] مِنتِبِه [mintibih] He's very cautious. هُوَّ كُلِّش مِتحَذِّر [huwwa kulliš mitħaððir]

cave • **1.** كَهَف [kahaf] كُهُوف [kuhuːf] *pl:* مَغارَة [maɣaːra] مَغارات [maɣaːraːt] *pl:* We hid in a cave. إحنا ختَلنا بِفَدّ كَهَف [ʔiħna xtalna bfadd kahaf]

to cave in • **1.** طُبَق [ṭubag, ṭabag] طباق [ṭbaːg] *pl:* طَبُق [ṭabug] *vn: sv* u. I'm afraid the house is going to cave in. دَأخاف البَيت راح يِطبُق [daʔaxaːf ʔilbayt raːħ yiṭbug]

cavity • **1.** حَفُر [ħafur] I have a cavity in this tooth. عِندِي حَفُر بِهَالسِّنّ [ʕindi ħafur bhassinn]

to cease • **1.** كَفّ [kaff] كَفّ [kaff] *vn:* اِنكَفّ [ʔinkaff] *p:* The company has decided to cease publication of its monthly magazine. الشَّرِكَة قَرَّرَت تكُفّ عَن نَشِر مَجَلّتها الشَّهرِيَّة [ʔiššarika qarrarat tkuff ʕan našir majallatha ʔiššahriyya]

cease-fire • **1.** وَقف إطلاق النار [waqf ʔiṭlaːq ʔinnaːr] A cease-fire is expected before midnight. وَقف إطلاق النّار مُنتَظَر قَبُل نُصّ اللَّيل [waqf ʔiṭlaːq ʔinnaːr muntaðar gabul nuṣṣ ʔillayl]

cedar • **1.** أرزَة [ʔarza] أرزات [ʔarzaːt] *pl:* أرِز [ʔariz] *Collective*

ceiling • **1.** سَقُف [saguf] سقُوف [sguːf] *pl:* The ceiling is painted white. السَّقُف مَصبُوغ بأبيَض [ʔissaguf maṣbuːɣ bʔabyað] • **2.** حَدّ أقصَى [ħadd ʔaqṣaː] We shouldn't exceed the ceiling the government has set. لازِم ما نِتجاوَز الحَدّ الأقصَى اللِّي عَيِّنَتَه الحُكُومَة [laːzim maː nidjaːwaz ʔilħadd ʔilʔaqṣaː ʔilli ʕayynatah ʔilħukuːma]

to celebrate • **1.** اِحتِفَل [ʔiħtifal] اِحتِفال [ʔiħtifaːl] *vn: sv* i. We're celebrating his birthday tomorrow. راح نِحتِفِل بعِيد مِيلادَه باكِر [raːħ niħtifil bʕiːd miːlaːdah baːčir]

celebration • **1.** اِحتِفال [ʔiħtifaːl] اِحتِفالات [ʔiħtifaːlaːt] *pl:* The celebration took place yesterday. الاحتِفال صار البارحَة [ʔilʔiħtifaːl ṣaːr ʔilbaːrħa]

cell • **1.** زِنزانَة [zinzaːna] زِنزانات [zinzaːnaːt] *pl:* Take the prisoner to his cell. وَدِّي المَحبُوس لِزِنزانتَه [waddi ʔilmaħbuːs lizinzaːntah] • **2.** خَلِيَّة [xaliyya] خَلايا [xalaːya] *pl:* حجَيرَة [ħǰayra] حجَيرات [ħǰayraːt] *pl:* We were able to observe the structure of the cells under the microscope. تمَكَّنّا نشُوف تَركِيب الخَلايا تَحت المِجهَر [tmakkanna nšuːf tarkiːb ʔilxalaːya taħt ʔilmiǰhar] The cell is the basic unit in the organization of the party. الخَلِيَّة هِيَّ الوُحدَة الأساسِيَّة المُنَضَّمَة الحِزِب [ʔilxaliyya hiyya ʔilwuħda ʔilʔasaːsiyya ʔilmunaḍḍamat ʔilħizib]

cellar • **1.** سِرداب [sirdaːb] سَرادِيب [saraːdiːb] *pl:*

cement • **1.** سمِنت، شمِنتُو، شبِنتُو [smint, šmintu, šbintu] كبِنتُو [čbintu] سمِنتُو [čmintu] Put more sand than cement in the mixture next time. حُطّ رَمُل أزيَد مِن السِّمَنت بالخَبطَة مَرَّة لُخ [ħuṭṭ ramul ʔazyad min ʔissimant bilxabṭa marra lux]

to cement • **1.** صَبّ بالشِّبِنتُو [ṣabb biččibintu] صَبّ بالشِّبِنتُو [ṣabb biččibintu] *vn:* اِنصَبّ بالشِّبِنتُو [ʔinṣabb biččibintu] *p:* بِنَى بالشِّبِنتُو [binaː biččibintu] بناء بالشِّبِنتُو [binaːʔ biččibintu] *vn:* اِنبِنَى بالشِّبِنتُو [ʔinbinaː biččibintu] *p:* Are you going to cement the basement floor or leave it dirt? راح تصُبّ قاع السِّرداب بالشِّبِنتُو لَو تخَلِّيها تراب؟ [raːħ tṣubb qaːʕ ʔissirdaːb bilčibintu law txalliːha traːb?] Are you going to cement it? راح تِبنِيها بالشِّبِنتُو؟ [raːħ tibniːha biččibintu?]

cemetery • **1.** مَقبَرَة [maqbara, magbara] مَقابِر [maqaːbir, magaːbur] *pl:*

censor • **1.** رَقِيب [raqiːb] رُقَباء [ruqabaːʔ] *pl:*

to censor • **1.** راقَب [raːqab] مُراقَبَة، رِقابَة [muraːqaba, riqaːba] *vn:* تراقَب [traːqab] *p:* During the state of emergency the government will censor all letters leaving the country. بِحالَة الطَّوارِئ الحُكُومَة راح تراقِب كُلّ المَكاتِيب المُرسَلَة خارِج البِلاد [bħaːlat ʔiṭṭawaːriʔ ʔilħukuːma raːħ traːqib kull ʔilmakaːtiːb ʔilmursala xaːriǰ ʔilbilaːd]

censorship • **1.** مُراقَبَة [muraːqaba] رَقابَة [raqaːba] The censorship has been lifted. اِنرِفعَت الرَّقابَة [ʔinrufiʕat ʔirriqaːba]

census • **1.** إحصاء [ʔiħṣaːʔ]

cent • **1.** سَنت [sant] There are a hundred cents in a dollar. الدُّولار بِيه مِيَّة سَنت [ʔiddulaːr biːh miyyat sant] • **2.** فِلِس [filis] فلاس، فِلسان [flaːs, filsaːn] *pl:* I haven't a cent in change. ما عِندِي وَلا فِلِس خُردَة

[maː ʕindi wala filis xurda] He doesn't have a cent. ما عِندَه فِلِس [maː ʕindah filis] He doesn't have a cent. هُوَّ مِفلِس [huwwa miflis] I wouldn't give a cent for it. ما أَشتِرِيها بِفلِس [maː ʔaštiriːha bfilis]

*** I'm almost down to my last cent. • 1.** آنِي تَقرِيباً فلَسِت [ʔaːni taqriːban flasit]

*** Do you have to put in your two cents worth?** • **1.** شِنُو هَاللَّغوَة الفارِغَة؟ [šinu hallaɣwa ʔilfaːrɣa?]

center • 1. نُصّ [nuṣṣ] نصاص [nṣaːṣ] *pl:* وَسَط [waṣaṭ] The table is standing in the center of the room. المِيز مَنصُوب بنُصّ الغُرفَة [ʔilmiːz manṣuːb bnuṣṣ ʔilɣurfa] He lives in the center of the town. يِسكُن بنُصّ الوِلايَة [yiskun bnuṣṣ ʔilwilaːya] • **2.** مَركَز [markaz] مَراكِز [maraːkiz] *pl:* She's the center of attention. هِيَّ مَركَز اِهتِمام الكُلّ [hiyya markaz ʔihtimaːm ʔilkull]

to center • 1. رَكَّز [rakkaz] تَركِيز، ترِكِّز [tarkiːz, trikkiz] *vn:* تَرَكَّز [trakkaz] *p:* Center the slide under the lens. رَكِّز السّلايد تَحت العَدَسَة [rakkiz ʔisslaːyd taħt ʔilʕadasa] All his thoughts were centered on her. كُلّ أفكارَه كانَت مِترَكّزَة عَليها [kull ʔafkaːrah čaːnat mitrakkza ʕaliːha]

centigrade • 1. مِئَوِي [miʔawi] The temperature today is 20 degrees centigrade. الحَرارَة اليُوم عِشرِين مِئَوِيَّة [ʔilħaraːra ʔilyuːm ʕišriːn miʔawiyya]

centimeter • 1. سَنتِيمَتِر [santiːmatir] سَنتِيمَترات [santiːmatraːt] *pl:*

centrally • 1. وَسَطِي [wasaṭi] مَركَزِي [markazi] بِالوَسَط [bilwasaṭ] The hotel is centrally located. الأوتَيل صايِر بِمَحَلّ وَسَطِي [ʔilʔutiːl ṣaːyir bimaħall wasaṭi]

century • 1. قَرِن [qarin] قُرُون [quruːn] *pl:*

ceremony • 1. اِحتِفال [ʔiħtifaːl] اِحتِفالات [ʔiħtifaːlaːt] *pl:* The ceremony will take place in the Embassy. الاحتِفال راح يِجرِي بِالسَّفارَة [ʔilʔiħtifaːl raːħ yiǰri bissafaːra]

certain • 1. مُحَقَّق [muħaqqaq] مُؤَكَّد [muʔakkad] He's certain to pass the exam. نَجاحَه بِالإمتِحان فَدّ شِي مُؤَكَّد [najaːħah bilʔimtiħaːn fadd ši muʔakkad] • **2.** مِتأَكِّد [mitʔakkid] I am certain that I signed the papers myself. آنِي مِتأَكِّد وَقَّعِت الأوراق بنَفسِي [ʔaːni mitʔakkid waqqaʕit ʔilʔawraːq bnafsi] • **3.** مُعَيَّن [muʕayyan] I mean certain people I'd rather not name. أعنِي أشخاص مُعَيَّنِين ما أَرِيد أجِيب أسماءهُم [ʔaʕni ʔašxaːṣ muʕayyaniːn maː ʔariːd ʔaǰiːb ʔasmaːʔhum] • **4.** بَعض [baʕaḏ, baʕḏ] There are certain things I want to discuss with you. أكُو بَعض الأشياء أرِيد أبحَثها ويّاك [ʔaku baʕḏ ʔilʔašyaːʔ ʔariːd ʔabħaθha wiyyaːk] • **5.** أكِيد [ʔakiːd] مقَرَّر [mqarrar] The date is certain but the time hasn't been set yet. المَوعِد أكِيد لَكِن السّاعَة ما تعَيَّنَت بَعَد [ʔilmawʕid ʔakiːd laːkin ʔissaːʕa maː tʕayyanat baʕad]

certainly • 1. تَأكِيد [taʔkiːd] تَأكِيدات [taʔkiːdaːt] *pl:* She's certainly right. هِيَّ بِالتَّأكِيد صحِيحَة [hiyya bittaʔakiːd ṣhiːħa] • **2.** مَعلُوم [maʕluːm] مَعلُومات [maʕluːmaːt] *pl:* طَبعاً [ṭabʕan] يَقِين، عَلَى يَقِين [yaqiːn, ʕala yaqiːn] Why, certainly! مَعلُوم [maʕluːm] He's certainly coming. يَقِين راح يِجِي [yaqiːn raːħ yiǰi]

certificate • 1. شَهادَة [šahaːda] شَهادات [šahaːdaːt] *pl:* تَقرِير [taqriːr] تَقارِير [taqaːriːr] *pl:* He needs a doctor's certificate. يِحتاج شَهادَة طِبِّيَّة [yiħtaːǰ šahaːda ṭibbiyya] Submit a copy of your birth certificate with the other papers. قَدِّم نُسخَة مِن شَهادَة وِلادتَك ويّا بَقِيَة الأوراق [qaddim nusxa min šahaːdat wilaːdtak wiyya baqiyat ʔilʔawraːq] Do you have a Certificate of Good Conduct? عِندَك شَهادَة حُسُن السّلُوك؟ [ʕindak šahaːdat ħusun ʔissiluːk?]

certified • 1. قانُونِي [qaːnuːni] He is a certified public accountant. هُوَّ مُحاسِب قانُونِي [huwwa muħaːsib qaːnuːni] • **2.** مُصَدَّق [muṣaddaq] This is a certified copy. هاي نُسخَة مُصَدَّقَة [haːy nusxa muṣaddaqa]

to certify • 1. شِهَد [šihad] شَهادَة [šahaːda] *vn:* اِنشِهَد [ʔinšihad] *p:* He says he will certify that they were all present at the time. يقُول راح يِشهَد بأن كُلّهُم كانَوا حاضرِين ذاك الوَقِت [yiguːl raːħ yišhad bʔan kullhum čaːnaw ħaːḍriːn ðaːk ʔilwakit] • **2.** صَدَّق عَلَى [ṣaddaq ʕala] تَصدِيق [taṣdiːq] *vn:* تصَدَّق [tsaddaq] *p:* A notary public has to certify the signature. كاتِب عَدِل لازِم يصَدِّق عالتَّوقِيع [kaːtib ʕadil laːzim yṣaddiq ʕattawqiːʕ]

chain • 1. مُعضَد [muʕḏad] مَعاضِد [maʕaːḏid] *pl:* She wears a golden chain. تِلبَس مِعضَد ذَهَب [tilbas miʕḏad ðahab] • **2.** زَنجِيل [zanǰiːl] زناجِيل [znaːǰiːl] *pl:* Do you have a chain I can use to tow the car? عِندَك زَنجِيل أقدَر أستَعمِلَه لسَحب السَّيّارَة؟ [ʕindak zanǰiːl ʔagdar ʔastaʕmilah lsaħb ʔissayyaːra?] • **3.** سِلسِلَة [silsila] سَلاسِل [salaːsil] *pl:* This firm operates a chain of food stores. هَالشَّرِكَة تدِير سِلسِلَة مَخازِن لِبَيع المَأكُولات [haššarika ddiːr silsilat maxaːzin libayʕ ʔilmaʔkuːlaːt]

to chain • 1. زَنجَل [zanǰal] زَنجَلَة [zanǰala] *vn:* تزَنجَل [tzanǰal] *p:* رُبَط بزَنجِيل [rubaṭ bizanǰiːl] رَبُط بزَنجِيل [rabuṭ bizanǰiːl] *vn:* اِنرُبَط [ʔinrubaṭ] *p:* They chained the prisoners together. زَنجِلَوا المَساجِين واحِد بِاللاخ [zanǰilaw ʔilmasaːǰiːn waːħid billaːx]

chair • 1. كُرسِي [kursi] كَراسِي [karaːsi] *pl:* سِكَملِي [sikamli, skamli] سِكَملِيّات [skamliyyaːt] *pl:* Please sit down in this chair. أرجُوك أقعُد عَلَى هَالكُرسِي [ʔarǰuːk ʔugʕud ʕala halkurṣi] • **2.** قُلتُغ [qultuɣ] قُلتُغات، قَلاتُغ [qultuɣaːt, qalaːtuɣ] *pl:* Sit in the upholstered chair. اقعُد عالقُلتُغ [ʔugʕud ʕalqultuɣ] Sit in the upholstered chair. أقعُد عالكُرسِي البَطِّيخَة [ʔugʕud ʕalkurṣi ʔilbaṭṭiːxa]

chalk • **1.** طَباشِير [ṭaba:ši:r, taba:ši:r] How many sticks of chalk are in the box? كَم قالَب طَباشِير أَكُو بِالقُوطِيَّة [čam qa:lab taba:ši:r ʔaku bilqu:ṭiyya]
 *** Chalk that up to experience.** • **1.** قَيِّدها خِبرَة لِلمُستَقبَل [qayyidha xibra lilmustaqbal]

C

challenge • **1.** تَحَدِّي [taħaddi] Our team accepted their challenge. فَرِيقنا قِبَل تَحَدِّيهُم [fari:qna qibal taħaddi:hum]
 to challenge • **1.** تَحَدَّى [tħadda:] تَحَدِّي [taħaddi] *vn: sv* a. I challenge the winner. آنِي أَتحَدَّى الغالُب [ʔa:ni ʔatħadda: ʔilɣa:lub]

chambermaid • **1.** خادمَة [xa:dma] خادمات [xa:dma:t] *pl:*

chamber of commerce • **1.** غُرفَة تِجارَة [ɣurfat tiǰa:ra] غُرَف تِجارَة [ɣuraf tiǰa:ra] *pl:*

chamber pot • **1.** قَعّادَة [qaʕʕa:da] قَعّادات [qaʕʕa:da:t] *pl:*

champagne • **1.** شَمبانيا [šampa:nya] شَمبانياهات [šampa:nya:ha:t] *pl:*

champion • **1.** بَطَل [baṭal] أَبطال [ʔabṭa:l] *pl:*

championship • **1.** بُطُولَة [buṭu:la] They're wrestling for the championship. دَيِتصارعُون عَلَى البُطُولَة [dayitṣa:rʕu:n ʕala ʔilbuṭu:la]

chance • **1.** فُرصَة [furṣa] فُرَص [furaṣ] *pl:* Give me a chance. إنطِينِي فَدّ فُرصَة [ʔinṭi:ni fadd furṣa] I had a chance to go to the ruins of Babel. صار عِندِي فَدّ فُرصَة أَرُوح لِخَرائِب بابِل [ṣa:r ʕindi fadd furṣa ʔaru:ħ lixaraaʔib ba:bil] • **2.** أَمَل [ʔamal] آمال [ʔa:ma:l] *pl:* Is there any chance of catching the train. أَكُو أَمَل نلَحِّق بِالقِطار؟ [ʔaku ʔamal nlaħħig bilqiṭa:r?] Not a chance. ما بِيها أَمَل [ma: bi:ha ʔamal] • **3.** يانَصِيب [yanaṣi:b] Won't you buy a chance? تِرِيد تِشتِرِي يا نَصِيب؟ [tri:d tištiri yanaṣi:b?]
 by chance • **1.** صِدفَةً [ṣidfatan] بالصِّدفَة، بالصُّدفَة [biṣṣidfa, biṣṣudfa] I met him by chance. لاقَيتَه بالصِّدفَة [la:gaytah biṣṣidfa]
 to take a chance • **1.** خاطَر [xa:ṭar] مُخاطَرَة [muxa:ṭara] *vn:* تخاطَر [txa:ṭar] *p:* جازَف [ǰa:zaf] مُجازَفَة [muǰa:zafa] *vn: sv* i. Let's take a chance on it. خَلِّي نخاطِر بِيها [xalli nxa:ṭir bi:ha]
 to chance • **1.** خاطَر [xa:ṭar] مُخاطَرَة [muxa:ṭara] *vn:* تخاطَر [txa:ṭar] *p:* جازَف [ǰa:zaf] مُجازَفَة [muǰa:zafa] *vn: sv* i. I'll chance it. راح أَخاطِر بِيه [ra:ħ ʔaxa:ṭir bi:h] I'll chance it. راح أَجَرُّب حَظِّي [ra:ħ ʔaǰarrub ħaðði]

chandelier • **1.** ثُرَيَّة [θurayya] ثُرَيّات [θurayya:t] *pl:*

change • **1.** تَغيِير [taɣyi:r] تَغيِيرات [taɣyi:ra:t] *pl:* تَبدِيل [tabdi:l] Have there been any changes in my absence? أَيّ تَغيِيرات صارَت أَثناء غِيابِي؟ [ʔayy taɣyi:ra:t ṣa:rat ʔaθna:? ɣiya:bi?] You need a change of air. يِنرادلَك شوَيَّة تَغيِير هَوا [yinra:dlak šwayya taɣyi:r hawa] I'm for a change in the present administration. آنِي مِن مُؤَيِّدِين تَغيِير النِّظام الحالِي [ʔa:ni min muʔayyidi:n taɣyi:r ʔinniða:m ʔilħa:li] • **2.** خُردَة [xurda] Have you any change? عِندَك خُردَة؟ [ʕindak xurda?]
 for a change • **1.** لِلتَبدِيل [littabdi:l] لِلتَغيِير [littagyi:r] For a change I'd like to go to the movies tonight. لِلتَّبدِيل يعجِبنِي أَرُوح لِلسِّينَما هاللَّيلَة [littabdi:l yiʕjibni ʔaru:ħ lissinama hallayla]
 to change • **1.** صَرَّف [ṣarraf] تَصرِيف [taṣri:f] *vn:* تصَرَّف [tṣarraf] *p:* Can you change a dinar for me? تِقدَر تصَرُّفلِي دِينار؟ [tigdar tṣarrufli dina:r?] • **2.** غَيَّر [ɣayyar] تَغيِير [taɣyi:r] *vn:* تغَيَّر [tɣayyar] *p:* We may have to change our plans. أَكُو احتِمال نِضطَرّ نغَيِّر مَنهَجنا [ʔaku ʔiħtima:l niðṭarr nɣayyir manhaǰna] • **3.** تغَيَّر [tɣayyar] تَغَيُّر [taɣayyur] *vn: sv* a. The weather is going to change. الطَّقس راح يِتغَيَّر [ʔiṭṭaqis ra:ħ yidɣayyar] You won't believe when you see him how much he has changed. ما تصَدِّق مِن تشُوفَه شقَدّ مِتغَيِّر [ma: tṣaddig min tšu:fah šgadd midɣayyir] Nothing has changed. – ما تغَيَّر شِي [ma: dɣayyar ši] • **4.** بَدَّل [baddal] تَبدِيل، تبِدِّل [tabdi:l, tbiddil] *vn:* Can you wait until I change my clothes? تِقدَر تِنتِظِر إِلَى أَن أَبَدِّل هدُومِي؟ [tigdar tintiðir ʔila ʔan ʔabaddil hdu:mi?] I haven't changed my mind. ما بَدَّلِت فِكرِي [ma: baddalit fikri] You'll have to change your tone if you want to talk to me. إِذا ترِيد تِحكِي وِيّايا لازِم تبَدِّل لَهجتَك [ʔiða tri:d tiħči wiyya:ya la:zim tbaddil lahiǰtak] We have to change trains at the next station. لازِم نبَدِّل القِطار بِالمَحَطَّة الجّايَة [la:zim nbaddil ʔilqiṭa:r bilmaħaṭṭa ʔiǰǰa:yya] We have to change trains at the next station. لازِم نغَيِّر القِطار بِالمَحَطَّة الجّايَة [la:zim nɣayyir ʔilqiṭa:r bilmaħaṭṭa ʔiǰǰa:yya] • **5.** تبَدَّل [tbaddal] تَبَدُّل [tabaddul] *vn: sv* a. The management of this hotel has changed hands a number of times. إدارَة هَالأُوتِيل تبَدّلَت كَم مَرَّة [ʔida:rat halʔuti:l tbaddlat čam marra] • **6.** حَوَّل [ħawwal] تَحوِيل، تَحَوُّل [taħwi:l, taħawwul] *vn:* تحَوَّل [tħawwal] *p:* Our plan is to change this hotel into a hospital. خُطَّتنا أَن نحَوِّل هَالأُوتِيل إِلَى مُستَشفَى [xuṭṭatna ʔan nħawwil halʔuti:l ʔila mustašfa:] • **7.** تحَوَّل [tħawwal] تَحوِيل، تَحَوُّل [taħwi:l, taħawwul] *vn: sv* i. This store has changed hands often. هَالدُّكّان تحَوَّل مِن إِيد لإيد [haddukka:n tħawwal min ʔi:d lʔi:d] • **8.** اِنقِلَب [ʔingilab] اِنقِلاب [ʔinqila:b] *vn: sv* i. She has changed from an ugly girl into a real beauty. اِنقُلبَت مِن بَشعَة إِلَى آيَة بِالجَّمال [ʔingulbat min bašʕa ʔila ʔa:ya biǰǰama:l]

changeable • **1.** مِتغَيِّر [mitɣayyir] The weather is very changeable at this time of year. الهَوا مِتغَيِّر هوايَة هَذا الوَقِت مِن السَّنَة [ʔilhawa midɣayyir hwa:ya ha:ða ʔilwakit min ʔissana] • **2.** مِتقَلِّب [mitqallib] She has a changeable disposition. عِدها طَبُع مِتقَلِّب [ʕidha ṭabuʕ mitqallib]

channel • **1.** مَجرَى [maǰra] مَجارِي [maǰa:ri] *pl:* قَناة [qana:t] قَنَوات [qanawa:t] *pl:* The two lakes are joined by a narrow channel. البُحَيرات الثِّنتَين مِتّصلَة بِمَجرى ضَيِّق [ʔilbuħayra:t ʔiθθintayn mittiṣla bmajra ḍayyig] The application will have to go through proper channels. العَرِيضَة لازِم تاخُذ مَجراها الأُصُولِي [ʔilʕari:ḍa la:zim ta:xuð majra:ha ʔalʔuṣu:li] • **2.** قَنال [qana:l] قَنالات [qana:la:t] *pl:* We crossed the English channel in the storm. عُبَرنا القَنال الإنكلِيزِي أثناء العاصِفَة [ʕubarna ʔilqana:l ʔilʔingli:zi ʔaθna:ʔ ʔilʕa:ṣifa] • **3.** مَحَطَّة [maħaṭṭa] How many channels can you get on your television set? كَم مَحَطَّة تِقدَر تحَصِّل بِتَلفِزيونَك؟ [čam maħaṭṭa tigdar tħaṣṣil btalfizyu:nak?]

to channel • **1.** وَجَّه [wajjah] تَوجِيه [tawji:h] *vn:* توَجَّه [twajjah] *p:* I'm trying to help him channel his efforts into useful activities. دَاحاوِل أساعدَه يوَجِّه جِهُودَه إلَى أعمال مُفِيدَة [daʔaħa:wil ʔasa:ʕdah ywajjih jihu:dah ʔila ʔaʕma:l mufi:da]

to chant • **1.** وَذَّن [waððan] تَوذِين [tawði:n] *vn:* توَذَّن [twaððan] *p:* أذَّن [ʔaððan] تَأذِين [taʔði:n] *vn:* تأَذَّن [tʔaððan] *p:* We hear the muezzin chanting from the minaret every morning. نِسمَع المُوَذِّن يوَذِّن مِن المَنارَة كُلّ يوم الصُّبُح [nismaʕ ʔilmuwaððin ywaððin min ʔilmana:ra kull yu:m ʔiṣṣubuħ] • **2.** جَوَّد [jawwad] تَجوِيد [tajwi:d] *vn:* تجَوَّد [tjawwad] *p:* We are learning to chant the Koran in religion class. دَنِتعَلَّم تَجوِيد القُرآن بدَرس الدِّين [danitʕallam tajwi:d ʔilqurʔa:n bdars ʔiddi:n] • **3.** رَتَّل [rattal] تَرتِيل [tarti:l] *vn:* ترَتَّل [trattal] *p:* He chants the passages from the Koran at the Friday service. يرَتِّل آيات القُرآن بصَلاة الجُمعَة [yrattil ʔa:ya:t ʔilqurʔa:n bṣala:t ʔijjumʕa]

chaos • **1.** فَوضَى [fawḍa:] هُوسَة [hu:sa] هَوسات [hu:sa:t] *pl:*

chaotic • **1.** فَوضَوِي [fawḍawi]

to chap • **1.** مَشَّق [maššag] تمِشِّق [tmiššig] *vn: sv* i. The wind chapped my face today. الهَوا مَشَّق وِجهِي اليُوم [ʔilhawa maššag wičči ʔilyu:m] • **2.** فَطَّر [faṭṭar] تَفطِير [tafṭi:r] *vn:* تفَطَّر [tfaṭṭar] *p:* My lips are chapped. شفافِي مفَطّرَة [šfa:fi mfaṭṭira]

chapter • **1.** فَصِل [faṣil] Did you read the last chapter of this book? قَرَيت الفَصل الأخِير مِن هَالكِتاب؟ [qrayt ʔilfaṣl ʔilʔaxi:r min halkita:b?] • **2.** جُزُء [juzuʔ] أجزاء [ʔajza:ʔ] *pl:* That's a closed chapter in my life. هَذا جُزُء مِنتِهِي مِن حَياتِي [ha:ða juzuʔ mintihi min ħaya:ti] • **3.** سُورَة [su:ra] سُوَر [suwar] *pl:* The Koran is divided into 114 chapters. القُرآن مقَسَّم إلَى مِيَّة وأربَطَعَش سُورَة [ʔilqurʔa:n mqassam ʔila miyya wʔarbaṭaʕaš su:ra]

character • **1.** خُلُق [xuluq] أخلاق [ʔaxla:q] *pl:* I've misjudged his character. أخطَأت بحُكمِي عَلَى أخلاقَه [ʔaxṭaʔit bħukmi ʕala ʔaxla:qah] Your son has character. إبنَك عِندَه خُلُق [ʔibnak ʕindah xuluq] • **2.** شَخصِيَّة [šaxṣiyya] شَخصِيّات [šaxṣiyya:t] *pl:* How many characters are there in the play? كَم شَخصِيَّة أكُو بِالرُّوايَة؟ [čam šaxṣiyya ʔaku birruwa:ya?] • **3.** صُورَة [ṣu:ra] صُوَر [ṣuwar] *pl:* This man is a familiar character here. هَالرِّجّال صُورَة مَألُوفَة هنا [harrijja:l ṣu:ra maʔlu:fa hna] • **4.** عَنتِيكَة، إنتِيكَة [ʕanti:ka, ʔinti:ka] عَنتِيكات [ʕanti:ka:t] *pl:* He's quite a character. هَذا صُدُق عَنتِيكَة [ha:ða ṣudug ʕanti:ka] • **5.** رَمِز [ramiz] رُمُوز [rumu:z] *pl:* He is trying to decipher the cuneiform characters on the stone. دَيحاوِل حَلّ الرُّمُوز المِسمارِيَّة عَلَى الصَّخَر [dayħa:wil ħall ʔirrumu:z ʔilmisma:riyya ʕala ʔiṣṣaxar]

characteristic • **1.** صِفَة [ṣifa] صِفات [ṣifa:t] *pl:* He has many good characteristics. عِندَه هوايَة صِفات زينَة [ʕindah hwa:ya ṣifa:t zi:na] • **2.** مِيزَة [mi:za] مِيزات [mi:za:t] *pl:* That's characteristic of our times. هَذِي مِيزَة هَالزَّمان [ha:ði mi:zat hazzama:n] • **3.** خاصِّيَّة [xa:ṣṣiyya] خَواصّ [xawa:ṣṣ] *pl:* One of the characteristics of salt is its solubility. إحدَى خَواصّ المِلِح قابلِيتَه لِلذَّوَبان [ʔiħda: xawa:ṣṣ ʔilmiliħ qa:bli:tah liððawaba:n]

charcoal • **1.** فَحمَة [faħma] فَحمات [faħma:t] *pl:* فَحَم [faħam] *Collective*

charge • **1.** كُلفَة [kulfa] كُلَف [kulaf] *pl:* أجرَة [ʔujra] أجُور [ʔuju:r] *pl:* What is the charge for shortening trousers? شقَدّ كُلفَة تقصِير البَنطَرُون؟ [šgadd kulfat tagṣi:r ʔilpanṭaru:n?] • **2.** تُهمَة [tuhma] تُهَم [tuham] *pl:* What are the charges against this man? شِنُو التُّهَم ضِدّ هَالرِّجّال؟ [šinu ʔittuham ḍidd harrijja:l?] • **3.** قُوَّة [quwwa, guwwa] قُوّات [quwwa:t] *pl:* The charge of dynamite is sufficient to destroy the whole building. قُوَّة الدِّنامَيت كافيَة لِهَدِم البِنايَة كُلّها [quwwat ʔiddina:mi:t ka:fya lihadim ʔilbina:ya kullha]

free of charge • **1.** بَلاش [bala:š] مَجّاناً [majja:nan] بِدُون رُسُوم [bidu:n rusu:m] We'll mail it to you free of charge. راح ندِزّلَك إيّاها بالبَرِيد مَجّاناً [ra:ħ ndizzlak ʔiyya:ha bilbari:d majja:nan]

in charge • **1.** مَسؤُول [masʔu:l] Who's in charge of this section? مِنُو مَسؤُول عَن هَالشُّعبَة؟ [minu masʔu:l ʕan haššuʕba?]

to take charge • **1.** توَلَّى [twalla:] تَوَلِّي [tawalli] *vn: sv* a. ترَأَّس [traʔʔas] تَرَأُّس [taraʔʔus] *vn: sv* a. He's taking charge of the new branch. راح يِتوَلَّى رِئاسَة الشُّعبَة الجِّدِيدَة [ra:ħ yitwalla: riʔa:sat ʔiššuʕba ʔijjidi:da]

to charge • **1.** سام [sa:m] سَوم [sawm] *vn:* اِنسام [ʔinsa:m] *p:* This merchant charges twice what the others do. هَالتّاجِر يسُوم ضِعف الباقِين [hatta:jir ysu:m ḍiʕf ʔilba:qi:n] • **2.** كَلَّف [kallaf] تَكلِيف [takli:f] *vn:* تكَلَّف [tkallaf] *p:* أخَذ مِن، أخَذ عَلَى [ʔaxað min, ʔaxað ʕala] أخِذ مِن، أخِذ عَلَى [ʔaxið min, ʔaxið ʕala] *vn: sv* u. عَلَى [ʕala] How much are you going to charge me for the stitching? شقَدّ راح تكَلّفنِي عَلَى الخِياطَة؟ [šgadd ra:ħ tkallifni ʕala ʔilxiya:ṭa?] • **3.** شِحَن [šiħan] شَحِن [šaħin] *vn:* اِنشِحَن [ʔinšiħan] *p:* We can charge your battery for you for a dirham. نِقدَر نِشحَنلَك الباتري بِدِرهَم [nigdar nišħanlak ʔilbaːtri bdirham] • **4.** هِجَم [hijam ʕala] هُجُوم عَلَى [hujuːm ʕala] *vn:* اِنهِجَم [ʔinhijam] *p:* The mounted police charged the crowd of demonstrators. الشُّرطَة الخَيّالَة هِجمَوا عالمُتَظاهِرين [ʔiššurṭa ʔilxayyaːla hijmaw ʕalmutaðaːhiriːn] • **5.** حِسَب عَلَى [ħisab ʕala] حساب عَلَى [ħsaːb ʕala] *vn:* [ʔinħisab] *p:* قَيَّد بِحسَاب [qayyad biħsaːb] تَقيِيد بِحسَاب [taqyiːd biħsaːb] *vn:* تقَيَّد [tqayyad] *p:* You have charged me for something I never got. حِسَبِت عَلَيّا سِعِر شِي ما ماخذَه [ħisabit ʕalayya siʕir ši maː maːxðah] I'd like to charge it, please. حُطَّه عَلَى الحساب، رَجاءاً [ħuṭṭah ʕala ʔilħsaːb, rajaːʔan] • **6.** اِتِّهَم [ʔittiham] اِتِّهام [ʔittihaːm] *vn: sv* i. تِهَم [tiham] تَهِم [tahim] *vn:* اِنتِهَم [ʔintiham] *p:* They charged him with theft. اِتِّهموُه بِالسَّرِقَة [ʔittihmuːh bissariqa]

charitable • **1.** خَيرِي [xayri] She is a member of several charitable organizations. هِيَّ عُضوَة بِجَمعِيّات خَيرِيَّة مُتَعَدِّدَة [hiyya ʕuðwa bjamʕiyyaːt xayriyya mutaʕaddida] • **2.** مُحسِن [muħsin] He is a charitable man; loves to do good. هُوَّ مُحسِن، مُحِبّ لِعَمَل الخير [huwwa muħsin, muħibb liʕamal ʔilxayr]

charity • **1.** خَير [xayr, xiːr] البَرّ والإحسان [ʔilbarr wilʔiħsaːn] He gives all his money to charity. يِنطِي فلُوسَه كُلّها لِلخَير [yinṭi fluːsah kullha lilxayr] • **2.** صَدَقَة [ṣadaqa] صَدَقات [ṣadaqaːt] *pl:* إحسان [ʔiħsaːn] She's too proud to accept charity. هاي تِستَنكِف تِقبَل صَدَقَة [haːy tistankif tiqbal ṣadaqa]
  *** Charity begins at home.** • **1.** الأَقرَبُون أَولَى بِالمَعرُوف [ʔilʔaqrabuːn ʔawlaː bilmaʕruːf]

charm • **1.** سِحِر [siħir] فِتنَة [fitna] She has a lot of charm. عِدها فَدّ سِحِر قَوِي [ʕidha fadd siħir qawi] • **2.** حِرِز [ħiriz] دِلّاعَة [dillaːʕa] دِلّاعات [dillaːʕaːt] *pl:* He always carries a charm against the evil eye. يشِيل حِرِز دائِماً ضِدّ العَين [yšiːl ħiriz daːʔiman ðidd ʔilʕayn]
  to charm • **1.** سِحَر [siħar] سِحِر [siħir] *vn:* اِنسِحَر [ʔinsiħar] *p:* فِتَن [fitan] فَتِن [fatin] *vn:* اِنفِتَن [ʔinfitan] *p:* She charmed us with her wit and pleasant personality. سِحرَتنا بظَرافتها وَشَخصِيَّتها اللَّطِيفَة [siħratna bðaraːfatha wšaxṣiyyatha ʔillaṭiːfa]

charming • **1.** ساحِر [saːħir] ساحِرين [saːħiriːn] *pl:* ساحِرَة [saːħira] *Feminine:* فَتّان [fattaːn] His sister is a very charming person. أُختَه كُلِّش فَتّانَة [ʔuxtah kulliš fattaːna]

charter • **1.** مِيثاق [miːθaːq] مَواثِيق [mawaːθiːq] *pl:* He took part in drawing up the United Nations' charter. اِشتِرَك بِوَضِع مِيثاق الأُمَم المُتَّحِدَة [ʔištirak bwaðiʕ miːθaːq ʔilʔumum ʔilmuttaħida]
  to charter • **1.** اِستَأجَر [ʔistaʔjar] اِستِئجار [ʔistiʔjaːr] *vn: sv* i. Our group is going to charter a bus for the trip. جَماعَتنا راح تِستَأجِر باص لِلسَّفرَة [jamaːʕatna raːħ tistaʔjir paːṣ lissafra]

chase • **1.** مُطارَدَة [muṭaːrada] مُطارَدات [muṭaːradaːt] *pl:* A wild chase began. فَدّ مُطارَدَة عَنِيفَة بِدَت [fadd muṭaːrada ʕaniːfa bidat] • **2.** تَعقِيب [taʕqiːb] اِقتِفاء [ʔiqtifaːʔ] The chase led them thru the market and down to the shore. التَّعقِيب قادهُم لِلسُّوق وَلِلسّاحِل [ʔittaʕqiːb qaːdhum lissuːq wlissaːħil]
  to chase • **1.** لِحَق [liħaq] لَحِق [laħiq] *vn:* اِنلِحَق [ʔinliħaq] *p:* Before he was married he used to chase the girls all the time. قَبِل ما يِتزَوَّج كان يِلحَق البَنات عَلَى طُول [gabil maː yidzawwaj čaːn yilħag ʔilbanaːt ʕala ṭuːl] • **2.** لَوحَق [luːħag] تلَوحِق [tluːħig] *vn: sv* i. Their dog is always chasing our cat. كَلِبهُم عَلَى طُول يلُوحِق بَزُّونَتنا [čalibhum ʕala ṭuːl yluːħig bazzuːnatna]
  to chase around • **1.** دار [daːr] دَور [dawr] *vn: sv* u. اِفتَرّ [ʔiftarr] اِفتِرار [ʔiftiraːr] *vn: sv* a. My son chases around with a pretty wild crowd. إبنِي دَيدُور وِيّا فَدّ جَماعَة وِكَّح [ʔibni dayduːr wiyya fadd jamaːʕa wikkaħ]
  to chase away • **1.** كَشّ [kašš] كَشّ [kašš] *vn:* اِنكَشّ [ʔinkašš] *p:* Chase the birds away from the tomato vines. كِشّ الطِّيُور مِن خُضرَة الطَّماطَة [kišš ʔiṭṭiyuːr min xuðrat ʔiṭṭamaːṭa]
  to chase down • **1.** تعَقَّب [tʕaqqab] تَعَقُّب [taʕaqqub] *vn: sv* a. I spent three days chasing down that reference. قِضَيت ثلَث أَيّام أَتعَقَّب هالمَرجَع [qiðiːt tlaθ ʔayyaːm ʔatʕaqqab halmarjaʕ]
  to chase out • **1.** طَرَّد [ṭarrad] تَطرِيد [taṭriːd] *vn:* تطَرَّد [ʔiṭṭarrad] *p:* I chased him out of the house. طَرَّدتَه مِن البَيت [ṭarradtah min ʔilbayt]

chassis • **1.** شاصِي [šaːṣi] شاصِيّات [šaːṣiyyaːt] *pl:*

chaste • **1.** عَفِيف [ʕafiːf] طاهِر [ṭaːhir]

chastity • **1.** عِفَّة [ʕiffa] طُهُر [ṭuhur]

chat • **1.** حَكِي [ħači] We had a nice chat. جِرَى بَينَنا حَكِي لَطِيف [jiraː baynna ħači laṭiːf]
  to chat • **1.** سُولَف [suːlaf] تسَولِف [tsawlif] *vn:* تسَولَف [tsawlaf] *p: sv* i. We spent a very pleasant hour chatting with each other. قِضَينا ساعَة لَطِيفَة نسُولِف [giðiːna saːʕa laṭiːfa nsawlif]

chatter • **1.** ثَرثَرَة [θarθara] لَغوَة [laywa] لَغوات، لَغاوِي [laywaːt, layaːwi] *pl:* Stop that foolish chatter. بَطِّل هالثَّرثَرَة [baṭṭil haθθarθara]
  to chatter • **1.** ثَرثَر [θarθar] ثَرثَرَة [θarθara] *vn: sv* i. لِغَى [liyaː] لَغوَة [laywa] *vn: sv* i. They chatter incessantly. يِلغُون عَلَى طُول [yilyuːn ʕala ṭuːl] • **2.** تصطَكّ [tiṣṭakk] *sv* a. طَقطَق [ṭagṭag] *sv* i. My teeth are chattering. سنُونِي دَتِصطَكّ [snuːni datiṣṭakk] My teeth are chattering. سنُونِي دَتطَقطِق [snuːni daṭṭagṭig]

chatterbox • **1.** ثَرثار [θarθaːr] ثَرثارين [θarθaːriːn] *pl:*

chauffeur • **1.** سايق [saːyiq] سُوّاق [suwwaːq] *pl:* دريول [draywil] دريوِلِيَّة [draywiliyya] *pl:*

cheap • **1.** رخِيص [rixiːṣ] Fruit is cheap this year. الفَواكِه رخِيصَة هالسَّنَة [ʔilfawaːkih rixiːṣa hassana] He offered it to me cheap. عِرَضها عَلَيّا بسِعِر رخِيص [ʕiraðha ʕalayya bsiʕir rixiːṣ] He offered it to me cheap. إنطانِي إيّاها رخِيص [ʔinṭaːniː ʔiyyaːha rixiːṣ] • **2.** ما يسوَى [maː yiswaː] That's cheap stuff. هَذا شِي ما يسوَى [haːða ši maː yiswaː] • **3.** واطِي [waːṭi] Her manners are cheap. أخلاقها واطيَة [ʔaxlaːqha waːṭya] • **4.** مُبتَذَل [mubtaðal] She looks cheap in those clothes. تبَيِّن عَبالَك مُبتَذَلَة بِهالهدُوم [tbayyin ʕabaːlak mubtaðala bhalhduːm] • **5.** دَنِيئ [daniːʔ] أدنِياء [ʔadniyaːʔ] *pl:* He played a cheap trick on me. سَوَّى بيّا حِيلَة دَنِيئَة [sawwaː biyya ħiːla daniːʔa] • **6.** وَضِيع [waðiːʕ] وَضِيعِين، وُضَعاء [waðiːʕiːn, wuðaʕaːʔ] *pl:* She is a cheap, vulgar woman. هاي فَدّ وِحدَة وَضِيعَة [haːy fadd wiħda waðiːʕa] • **7.** دُونِي [duːni] These goods are cheap quality. هَالبَضايِع دُونِيَّة [halbaðaːyiʕ duːniyya] He ruined his feet from wearing cheap shoes. عِدَم رِجلَه مِن لِبس القَنادِر الدُّونِيَّة [ʕidam rijlah min libis ʔilqanaːdir ʔidduːniyya]

* **His openhandedness made me feel cheap.** • **1.** كَرَمَه خَجَّلنِي [karamah xajjalni]

cheat • **1.** غشّاش [ɣaššaːš] غشّاشَة [ɣaššaːša] *pl:* They all know he's a cheat. كُلهُم يعرفُون هُوَّ فَدّ واحِد غشّاش [kullhum yʕurfuːn huwwa fadd waːħid ɣaššaːš]

to cheat • **1.** غَشّ [ɣašš] غِشّ [ɣišš] *vn:* اِنغَشّ [ʔinɣašš] *p:* Be careful you don't get cheated. دِير بالَك لا تِنغَشّ [diːr baːlak laː tinɣašš] He always cheats at cards. دائِماً يغُشّ بلِعِب الأوراق [daːʔiman yɣušš bliʕib ʔilʔawraːq] • **2.** سَوَّى قُوبِية [sawwa quːpya] [.] *vn:* *sv* i. He's always cheating at exams. دائِماً يسَوِّي قُوبيَة بالإمتِحانات [daːʔiman ysawwi quːpya bilʔimtiħaːnaːt] • **3.** خان [xaːn] خِيانَة [xiyaːna] *vn:* *sv* u. His wife is cheating on him. زَوجتَه دَتخُونَه [zuːjtah datxuːnah] • **4.** زاغَل ويّا [zaːɣal wiyya] زُغُل ويّا [zuɣul wiyya] *vn:* *sv* i. I know he's cheating me but I can't prove it. دَأعرُف دَيزاغِل ويّايا لَكِن ما أقدَر أثبِّتَه [daʔaʕruf dayzaːɣil wiyyaːya laːkin maː ʔagdar ʔaθabbtah] • **5.** قَشمَر [qašmar] قَشمَرَة [qašmara] *vn:* تقَشمَر [tqašmar] *p:* لَفلَف [laflaf] لَفلَفَة [laflafa] *vn:* *sv* i. He cheated him out of all his money. قَشمَرَه وَأخَذ كُلّ فلُوسَه [qašmarah waʔaxað kull fluːsah] He cheated him out of all his money. لَفلَف كُلّ فلُوسَه [laflaf kull fluːsah]

check • **1.** چَكّ [čakk] صَكّ [ṣakk] I'll send you a check tomorrow. عُود أدِزّلَك چَكّ باكِر [ʕuːd ʔadizzlak čakk baːčir] • **2.** وَصِل [waṣil] وُصُولات [wuṣuːlaːt] *pl:* Give your baggage check to the porter. إنطِي الوَصِل مال غَراضَك لِلحَمّال [ʔinṭi ʔilwaṣil maːl ɣaraːðak lilħammaːl] Here's your hat check, sir. سَيِّد، تفَضَّل وَصِل الشَّفقَة مالتَك [sayyid, tfaððal waṣl ʔiššafqa maːltak] • **3.** إشارَة [ʔišaːra] إشارات [ʔišaːraːt] *pl:* عَلامَة [ʕalaːma] عَلامات، عَلائِم [ʕalaːmaːt, ʕalaːʔim] *pl:* Put a check before the name of each one as he reports in. حُطّ إشارَة قِدّام إسِم كُلّ واحِد مِن يِجِي [ħuṭṭ ʔišaːra giddaːm ʔisim kull waːħid min yiji] • **4.** حساب [ħsaːb] Waiter, the check please. بُوي، الحساب مِن فَضلَك [buːy, ʔilħsaːb min faðlak]

in check • **1.** مَكشُوش [makšuːš] Your king is in check. المَلِك مالَك مَكشُوش [ʔilmalik maːlak makšuːš]

to keep in check • **1.** ضُبَط [ðubaṭ] ضَبُط [ðabuṭ] *vn:* اِنضُبَط [ʔinðubaṭ] *p:* I'm no longer able to keep him in check. ما أقدَر أضُبطَه بَعَد [maː ʔagdar ʔaðubṭah baʕad]

to check • **1.** أمَّن [ʔamman] تأمِين [taʔmiːn] *vn:* تأمَّن [tʔamman] *p:* وَدَّع [waddaʕ] تَودِيع [tawdiːʕ] *vn:* توَدَّع [twaddaʕ] *p:* Check your hat and coat here. أمِّن شَفُقتَك وَقَبُوطَك هنا [ʔammin šafuqtak wqappuːṭak hna] • **2.** أمَّن [ʔamman] تَأمِين [taʔmiːn] *vn:* تأمَّن [tʔamman] *p:* Can I check this suitcase at the station? أقدَر أئَمِّن هَالجُنطَة بِالمَحَطَّة؟ [ʔagdar ʔaʔammin hajjunṭa bilmaħaṭṭa?] • **3.** أشَّر [ʔaššar] تَأشِير [taʔšiːr] *vn:* تأشَّر [tʔaššar] *p:* Check the items you want. أشِّر الأشياء اللّي تريدها [ʔaššir ʔilʔašyaːʔ ʔilli triːdha] • **4.** شَيَّك [čayyak] تشيِيك [tačyiːk] *vn:* تشَيَّك [tčayyak] *p:* فُحَص [fuħaṣ] فَحِص [faħiṣ] *vn:* انفُحَص [ʔinfuħaṣ] *p:* Please check the oil. أرجُوك إفحَص الدِّهِن [ʔarjuːk ʔifħaṣ ʔiddihin] • **5.** فَتَّش [fattaš] تَفتِيش [taftiːš] *vn:* تفَتَّش [tfattaš] *p:* They will check your passports at the border. راح يفَتِّشُون باسبَورتاتكُم عالحدُود [raːħ yfattišuːn paːspuːrtaːtkum ʕalħiduːd] • **6.** دَقَّق [daqqaq] تَدقِيق [tadqiːq] *vn:* تدَقَّق [tdaqqaq] *p:* Will you please check the bill once more? أرجُوك ما تدَقِّق الحساب مَرَّة لُخ؟ [ʔarjuːk maː ddaqqiq ʔilħsaːb marra lux?] • **7.** راقَب [raːqab] مُراقَبَة [muraːqaba] *vn:* تراقَب [traːqab] *p:* We have been asked to check on the water table levels at all seasons of the year. اِنطِلَب مِن عِدنا نراقِب مُستوَى الماي بكُلّ فُصُول السَّنَة [ʔinṭilab min ʕidna nraːqib mustawaː ʔilmaːy bkull fuṣuːl ʔissana] We are required to check on each man's daily output. مَطلُوب مِنّا نراقِب شقَدّ كُلّ واحِد يطَلِّع بِاليُوم [maṭluːb minna nraːqib šgadd kull waːħid yṭalliʕ bilyuːm] • **8.** راجَع [raːjaʕ] مُراجَعَة [muraːjaʕa] *vn:* تراجَع [traːjaʕ] *p:* Check with me again before you go. راجِعنِي مَرَّة اللُّخ قَبُل ما ترُوح [raːjiʕni marrat ʔillux gabul maː truːħ] • **9.** كَشّ [kašš] كَشّ [kašš] *vn:* اِنكَشّ [ʔinkašš] *p:* *sv* i. You gave me a chance to check your king. إنطَيتنِي فُرصَة أكُشّ المَلِك مالَك [ʔinṭiːtni furṣa ʔakušš ʔilmalik maːlak]

to check in • **1.** سَجَّل [sajjal] تَسجِيل [tasjiːl] *vn:* تسَجَّل [tsajjal] *p:* They checked in at the hotel at 2 P. M. سَجّلوا بالأوتيل ساعَة بالثّنتَين [sajjlaw bilʔutiːl saːʕa biθθintayn] • **2.** حِضَر [ħiðar] حُضُور [ħuðuːr] *vn:* *sv* a. What time do we have to check in? شوَقِت لازِم نِحضَر؟ [šwakit laːzim niħðar?]

C

to check off • **1.** أَشَّر [ʔaššar] تَأشِير [taʔšiːr] *vn:* تأشَّر [tʔaššar] *p:* Check them off as you go. أشِّرهُم وإنتَ ماشِي [ʔašširhum wʔinta maːši]
to check out • **1.** غادَر [ɣaːdar] مُغادَرَة [muɣaːdara] *vn: sv* i. تِرَك [tirak] تَرِك [tarik] *vn: sv* u. What time did he check out of the hotel? شوَقِت غادَر الأوتيل؟ [šwakit ɣaːdar ʔilʔutiːl?]
to check over • **1.** فُحَص [fuħaṣ] فَحِص [faħiṣ] *vn:* اِنفُحَص [ʔinfuħaṣ] *p:* Check over the list and see if we can use any of the items. إفحَص القائمَة وشُوف إذا نِحتاج شِي مِن هالمَوادّ [ʔifħaṣ ʔilqaːʔima wšuːf ʔiða niħtaːǰ ši min halmawaːdd]
to check through • **1.** دَزّ ل [dazz l-] دَزّ [dazz] *vn:* اِندَزّ [ʔindazz] *p:* وَصَّل [waṣṣal] تَوصِيل [tawṣiːl] *vn:* توَصَّل [twaṣṣal] *p:* I want this baggage checked through Mosul. أرِيد هَالغَراض تِندَزّ لِلمُوصِل [ʔariːd halɣaraːð̣ tindazz lilmuːṣil]
to check up • **1.** دَقَّق [daqqaq] تَدقِيق [tadqiːq] *vn:* تدَقَّق [tdaqqaq] *p:* We had better check up on the accuracy of his accounts. الأحسَن ندَقِّق صِحَّة حِساباتَه [ʔilʔaħsan ndaqqiq ṣiħħat ħisaːbaːtah] • **2.** حَقَّق [ħaqqaq] تَحقِيق [taħqiːq] *vn:* تحَقَّق [tħaqqaq] *p:* اِستَعلَم [ʔistaʕlam] اِستِعلام [ʔistiʕlaːm] *vn: sv* i. Did you check up on him? حَقَّقت عَنَّه؟ [ħaqqaqit ʕannah?] Did you check up on him? سَوِّيت تَحقِيق عَنَّه [sawwiːt taħqiːq ʕannah] Did you check up on him? اِستَعلَمِت عَنَّه [ʔistaʕlamit ʕannah] • **3.** تحَقَّق [tħaqqaq] تَحَقُّق [taħaqquq] *vn: sv* a. We have to check up on his statements. لازم نِتحَقَّق مِن كَلامَه [laːzim nitħaqqaq min kalaːmah]
to check with • **1.** اِتِّفَق وِيّا، طَابَق [ʔittifaq wiyya, ṭaːbaq] اِتِّفاق، مُطَابَقَة [ʔittifaːq, muṭaːbaqa] *vn: sv* i. طابَق [ṭaːbaq] مُطابَقَة [muṭaːbaqa] *vn:* تطابَق [ʔittaːbaq] *p:* That checks with what he told me. هَذا يِتِّفِق وِيّا اللِّي قالِّي إيّاه [haːða yittifiq wiyya ʔilli galli ʔiyyaːh]

check book • **1.** دَفتَر شَكّات [daftar čakkaːt] دَفاتِر شَكّات [dafaːtir čakkaːt] *pl:*

check point • **1.** نُقطَة تَفتِيش [nuqṭat taftiːš] نُقَط تَفتِيش [nuqaṭ taftiːš] *pl:* مَركَز تَفتِيش [markaz taftiːš] مَراكِز تَفتِيش [maraːkiz taftiːš] *pl:*

check room • **1.** غُرفَة تَعلِيق الهِدُوم [ɣurfat taʕliːg ʔilihduːm] غُرَف تَعلِيق الهِدُوم [ɣuraf taʕliːq ʔilihduːm] *pl:*

check-up • **1.** فَحِص [faħiṣ] فُحُوص، فُحُوصات [fuħuːṣ, fuħuːṣaːt] *pl:* كَشِف [kašif] You should see your doctor for a general check-up once a year. لازِم ترُوح لِلطَّبِيب حَتَّى يسَوِّيلَك فَحِص عامّ مَرَّة بِالسَّنَة [laːzim truːħ littabiːb ħatta ysawwiːlak faħiṣ ʕaːmm marra bissana]

cheek • **1.** خَدّ [xadd] خدُود [xduːd] *pl:* My cheek is all swollen. خَدِّي كُلَّه موَرَّم [xaddi kullah mwarrum]

cheer • **1.** هِتاف [hitaːf] هِتافات [hitaːfaːt] *pl:* We heard the cheers from quite a distance. سمَعنا الهِتاف مِن مَسافَة بعِيدَة [simaʕna ʔilhitaːf min masaːfa bʕiːda] Three cheers for our team. ثلَث هِتافات لِفَرِيقنا [tlaθ hitaːfaːt lifariːqna]
* **They gave him a cheer.** • **1.** هِتفَولَه [hitfawla]
to cheer • **1.** هِتَف [hitaf] هِتاف [hitaːf] *vn:* اِنهِتَف [ʔinhitaf] *p:* The crowd cheered. الجَّماهِير هِتفَت [ʔiǰǰamaːhiːr hitfat] The crowd cheered the speaker. المُجتَمعِين هِتفَوا لِلخَطِيب [ʔilmuǰtamʕiːn hitfaw lilxaṭiːb]
to cheer up • **1.** فَرَّح [farraħ] تَفرِيح [tafriːħ] *vn:* تفَرَّح [tfarraħ] *p:* سَرّ [sarr] *sv* i. The news cheered her up. الأخبار فَرَّحَتها [ʔilʔaxbaːr farraħatha] • **2.** تشَجَّع [tšaǰǰaʕ] تَشَجُّع [tašaǰǰuʕ] *vn: sv* a. Cheer up, he'll be back soon. تشَجَّع، هُوَّ راح يِرجَع قَرِيباً [tšaǰǰaʕ, huwwa raːħ yirǰaʕ qariːban]

cheerful • **1.** فَرحان [farħaːn] فَرِح [fariħ] مِتوَنِّس [mitwannis] He's very cheerful today. هُوَّ كُلِّش فَرحان اليُوم [huwwa kulliš farħaːn ʔilyuːm] Isn't this a cheerful room. بالله مُو هَالقُبَّة كُلِّش فَرحَة [ballah muː halgubba kulliš farħa]

cheese • **1.** جِبِن [ǰibin] What kind of cheese do you have? يا نُوع جِبِن عِندَك؟ [yaː nuːʕ ǰibin ʕindak?]

chef • **1.** باش طَبّاخ [baːš ṭabbaːx] باش طَبّاخِين [baːš ṭabbaːxiːn] *pl:*

chemical • **1.** كِيمياوِي [kiːmyaːwi] He's working in a chemical laboratory. هُوَّ يِشتُغُل بِفَدّ مُختَبَر كِيمياوِي [huwwa yištuɣul bfadd muxtabar kiːmyaːwi]

chemist • **1.** كِيميائِي [kiːmyaːʔi] كِيميائِيِّين [kiːmyaʔiyyiːn] *pl:* كِيمياوِي [kiːmyaːwi] كِيمياوِيِّين [kiːmyawiyyiːn] *pl:*

cherry • **1.** كَرَزَة [karaza] كَرزات [karzaːt] *pl:* كَرَز [karaz] *Collective:* These are good cherries. هَذا خُوش كَرَز [haːða xuːš karaz]

chess • **1.** شِطرَنج [šiṭranǰ] Do you know how to play chess? تُعرُف تِلعَب شِطرَنج؟ [tuʕruf tilʕab šiṭranǰ?]

chess set • **1.** شِطرَنج [šiṭranǰ] شِطرَنجات [šiṭranǰaːt] *pl:* All the chess sets are in use. كُلّ الشِّطرَنجات دَتِلعَب [kull ʔiššiṭranǰaːt datilʕab]

chest • **1.** صَدِر [ṣadir] صدُور [ṣduːr] *pl:* He has a broad chest. عِندَه صَدِر عَرِيض [ʕindah ṣadir ʕariːð̣] That's a load off my chest. هَذا كان فَدّ حِمِل وِانزاح عَن صَدرِي [haːða čaːn fadd ħimil wnizaːħ ʕan ṣadri] • **2.** صَندُوق [ṣanduːg] صَنادِيق [ṣanaːdiːg] *pl:* Put the tools in the chest. حُطّ الأدوات بِالصَّندُوق [ħuṭṭ ʔilʔadawaːt biṣṣanduːg] • **3.** دِيلاب [diːlaːb] دوالِيب [dwaːliːb] *pl:* She bought a beautiful chest of drawers. اِشتِرَت دِيلاب أبُو مجَرّات حِلو [ʔištirat diːlaːb ʔabu mǰarraːt ħilw]

 i, interjection; p, passive; pl, plural; sv, stem vowel; vn, verbal noun

chestnut • **1.** كِستانايَة [kistana:ya] كَستَنايات [kastana:ya:t] *pl:* كِستانَة [kista:na] *Collective:* Let's buy some roasted chestnuts. خَلّي نِشتِري شوَيَّة كِستانَة محَمَّصَة [xalli ništiri šwayya kista:na mħammṣa] • **2.** كَستَنائِي [kastana:ʔi] Her hair is chestnut. شَعَرها كَستَنائِي [šaʕarha kastana:ʔi]

chestnut tree • **1.** شَجَرَة الكِستانَة [šaǰarat ʔilkista:na]

to chew • **1.** عِلَك [ʕilač] عَلِك [ʕalič] *vn:* اِنعِلَك [ʔinʕilač] *p:* عِلَس [ʕilas] عَلِس [ʕalis] *vn:* اِنعِلَس [ʔinʕilas] *p:* مُضَغ [muḏaɣ] مَضِغ [maḏiɣ] *vn:* اِنمُضَغ [ʔinmuḏaɣ] *p:* *sv* u. Chew your food well. إعلِس أكلَك زين [ʔiʕlis ʔaklak zi:n]

chewing gum • **1.** عِلِك [ʕilič] How many sticks of chewing gum are there in the package? كَم قِطعَة عِلِك أكُو بِالباكَيت؟ [čam qitʕat ʕilič ʔaku bilpa:kayt?]

chic • **1.** شِيك [ši:k] أنِيق [ʔani:q]

chicken • **1.** دِجاجَة [diǰa:ǰa] دِجاجات [diǰa:ǰa:t] *pl:* دِجاج [diǰa:ǰ] *Collective:* We're having chicken for dinner. عَشانا دِجاج [ʕaša:na diǰa:ǰ]

chicken pox • **1.** جِدرِي ماي [ǰidri ma:y]

chick peas • **1.** حُمُّص [ħummuṣ] لَبلَبِي [lablabi]

chief • **1.** رَئِيس [raʔi:s] رُؤَساء [ruʔasa:, ruʔasa:ʔ] *pl:* Who's the chief of the division? مِنُو رَئِيس القِسِم؟ [minu raʔi:s ʔilqisim?] • **2.** مُدِير [mudi:r] مُدَراء [mudara:ʔ] *pl:* Where's the office of the Chief of Police? وين دائِرَة مُدِير الشُّرطَة؟ [wi:n da:ʔirat mudi:r ʔiššurṭa?] • **3.** باش [ba:š] He has worked in our office as chief clerk for five years. صارلَه خَمس سنِين يِشتُغُل باش كاتِب بِدائِرَتنا [ṣa:rlah xams sni:n yištuɣul ba:š ka:tib bda:ʔiratna] • **4.** أَوَّل [ʔawwal] أَوائِل [ʔawa:ʔil] *pl:* أُولَى [ʔuwla] *Feminine:* He is chief legal advisor to the company. هُوَّ المُشاوِر القانُونِي الأَوَّل لِلشَّرِكَة [huwwa ʔilmuša:wir ʔilqa:nu:ni ʔilʔawwal liššarika] • **5.** رَئِيسِي [raʔi:si] These are the chief reasons why we should accept the plan. هاي الأسباب الرَّئِيسِيَّة اللّي تِجعَلنا نِقبَل الخُطَّة [ha:y ʔilʔasba:b ʔirraʔi:siyya ʔilli tiǰʕalna niqbal ʔilxuṭṭa] What are the chief exports of Iraq? شِنُو صادِرات العِراق الرَّئِيسِيَّة؟ [šinu ṣa:dira:t ʔilʕira:q ʔirraʔi:siyya?]

child • **1.** جاهِل [ǰa:hil] جَهال، جِهال [ǰaha:l, ǰiha:l] *pl:* طِفِل [tifil] أطفال [ʔaṭfa:l] *pl:* صغَيِّر [ṣɣayyir, zɣayyir] They took the child along on a trip. أخذَوا الجّاهِل وِيّاهُم بسَفرَة [ʔaxðaw ʔiǰǰa:hil wiyya:hum bsafra] Next year we have budgeted more money for child welfare. السَّنَة الجّايَّة خَصَّصنا فلُوس أزيَد لرِعايَة الأطفال [ʔissana ʔiǰǰa:yya xaṣṣaṣna flu:s ʔazyad liriʕa:yat ʔilʔaṭfa:l] I've been used to it ever since I was a child. هَذِي مِتعَلِّم عَليها مِن آني صغَيِّر [ha:ði mitʕallim ʕali:ha min ʔa:ni ṣɣayyir]

childhood • **1.** طُفُولَة [ṭufu:la] صُغُر [zuɣur] جُهُل [ǰuhul] I spent part of my childhood in the country. قضَيت قِسِم مِن طُفُولتِي بِالرِّيف [gðayt qisim min ṭufu:lti birri:f] In his childhood he didn't have much contact with other children. بِجُهلَه ما صار عِندَه هوايَة اِتِّصال بِبَقِيَّة الأطفال [bǰuhlah ma: ṣa:r ʕindah hwa:ya ʔittiṣa:l bibaqiyyat ʔilʔaṭfa:l]

childish • **1.** زَعطُوط [zaʕṭu:ṭ] زعاطِيط [zʕa:ṭi:ṭ] *pl:* He is very childish in his demands. هُوَّ كُلِّش زَعطُوط بِطَلَباتَه [huwwa kulliš zaʕṭu:ṭ bṭalaba:tah] • **2.** مَزعَطَة [mazʕaṭa] This is childish. هاي مَزعَطَة [ha:y mazʕaṭa] The whole thing was childish. المَسأَلَة كانَت مَزعَطَة [ʔilmasʔala ča:nat mazʕaṭa] • **3.** صِبيانِي [ṣibya:ni] What you did was childish. عَمَلَك كان صِبيانِي [ʕamalak ča:n ṣibya:ni]

to act childish • **1.** تزَعطَط [tzaʕṭaṭ] تزِعطِط [tziʕṭiṭ] *vn:* *sv* a. صار زَعطُوط [ṣa:r zaʕṭu:ṭ] Don't act so childish; you're old enough to know better. لا تصِير زَعطُوط هَالقَدّ؛ إنتَ كِبِير وتِفتِهِم [la: tṣi:r zaʕṭu:ṭ halgadd; ʔinta čibi:r wtiftihim]

chill • **1.** بَرِد [barid] I've got a chill. آنِي ماخِذ بَرِد [ʔa:ni ma:xið barid] • **2.** قَشعَرِيرَة [qašʕari:ra] Suddenly I felt a chill. عَلَى غَفلَة شِعَرِت بِقَشعَرِيرَة [ʕala ɣafla šiʕarit bqašʕari:ra]

to chill • **1.** بَرَّد [barrad] تَبرِيد [tabri:d] *vn:* تبَرَّد [tbarrad] *p:* Chill it before you serve it. بَرِّدها قَبُل ما تقَدِّمها [barridha gabul ma: tqaddimha]

*** I'm chilled to the bone.** • **1.** البَرِد يَبَّس عَظامِي [ʔilbarid yabbas ʕaða:mi]

chilly • **1.** بارِد [ba:rid] It's chilly outside. بارِدَة بَرَّة [ba:rda barra] They received us in a chilly manner. اِستَقبِلَونا اِستِقبال بارِد [ʔistaqbilu:na ʔistiqba:l ba:rid] • **2.** بَردان [barda:n] I'm chilly. آنِي بَردان [ʔa:ni barda:n]

chimney • **1.** مَدخَنَة [madxana] مداخِن [mda:xin] *pl:* They are repairing the chimney. دَيصَلّحَوها لِلمَدخَنَة [daysallħu:ha lilmadxana] • **2.** شِيشَة [ši:ša] شِيَش [šiyaš] *pl:* Where's the chimney for the lamp? وين الشِّيشَة مال الفانُوس؟ [wi:n ʔišši:ša ma:l ʔilfa:nu:s?]

chimpanzee • **1.** شِمبانزِي [šimba:nzi] شِمبانزِيات [šimba:nzya:t] *pl:*

chin • **1.** حِنِك [ħinič] حنُوك [ħnu:č] *pl:* ذِقِن [ðiqin] ذِقُون [ðiqu:n] *pl:* He has a protruding chin. عِندَه حِنِك بارِز [ʕindah ħinič ba:riz]

*** Chin up!** • **1.** تشَجَّع [tšaǰǰaʕ] / شِدّ حَيلَك [šidd ħaylak]

China • **1.** صِين [ṣi:n] He lived in China for a long time. عاش بالصِّين مُدَّة طوِيلَة [ʕa:š biṣṣi:n mudda ṭwi:la]

C

china • **1.** فَرفُورِي [farfu:ri] We got this set of china as a wedding present. هالطَّخم الفَرفُورِي جانا هَدِيَّة زَواج [haṭṭaxm ʔilfarfu:ri ǰa:na hadiyyat zawa:ǰ]

Chinese • **1.** صِينِي [ṣi:ni] The owner of this store is a Chinese. صاحِب هَالمَحَلّ صِينِي [ṣa:ħib halmaħall ṣi:ni] I got a Chinese vase. حَصَّلِت عَلَى مَزهَرِيَّة صِينِيَّة [ħaṣṣalit ʕala mazhariyya ṣi:niyya]

chip • **1.** ثِلمَة [θilma] ثِلمات، ثِلَم [θilma:t, θilam] *pl:* There is a chip out of the plate. أَكُو ثِلمَة طايرَة مِن الماعُون [ʔaku θilma ṭa:yra min ʔilma:ʕu:n] • **2.** شِقفَة [šigfa] شِقفات [šigfa:t] *pl:* Fill in the spaces between the stones with chips. إترِس الفَراغات بين الطّابُوق بِشُقَف [ʔitris ʔilfara:ɣa:t bi:n ʔiṭṭa:bu:g bšugaf] • **3.** فِيشَة [fi:ša] فِيشات، فِيَش [fi:ša:t, fiyaš] *pl:* When the game finished, I had three white chips left. مِن خِلَص اللِّعب كان بَعَد عِندِي ثلاث فِيَش بيضَة [min xilaṣ ʔilliʕib ča:n baʕad ʕindi tla:θ fiyaš bayð̣a] • **4.** نجارَة [nǰa:ra] The carpenter left the floor littered with chips. النَّجّار عاف القاع مَترُوسَة نجارَة [ʔinnaǰǰa:r ʕa:f ʔilga:ʕ matru:sa nǰa:ra] Where did this chip of wood come from? هَالشُّقفَة الخِشَب منِين جَتّي؟ [haššugfat ʔilxišab mni:n ǰatti?]

* **He always has a chip on his shoulder.**

• **1.** هٰذا يدَوُّر حِرشَة [ha:ða ydawwur ħirša]

to chip • **1.** ثِلَم [θilam] ثَلِم [θalim] *vn:* اِنثِلَم [ʔinθilam] *p:* قَشَّط [gaššaṭ] تَقشِيط [tagši:ṭ] *vn:* تقَشَّط [tgaššaṭ] *p:* Be careful you don't chip the dishes when you wash them. دِير بالَك لا تِثلِم المواعِين مِن تِغسِلها [di:r ba:lak la: tiθlim ʔilmwa:ʕi:n min tiɣsilha] The rim of this glass is chipped; bring me another. حاشيَة هالكلاص مَثلُومَة؛ جِيبلِي غَيرَه [ħa:šyat halgla:ṣ maθlu:ma; ǰi:bli ɣayrah] The edge of the table is chipped. حاشِيَة المِيز مَقشُوطَة [ħa:šiyat ʔilmi:z magšu:ṭa] • **2.** نِجَر [niǰar] نَجِر [naǰir] *vn:* اِنِّجَر [ʔinniǰar] *p:* This man can chip the bricks in any shape you want. هَالرَّجّال يِقدَر يِنجُر الطّابُوق بأيّ شِكِل تريدَه [harraǰǰa:l yigdar yinǰur ʔiṭṭa:bu:g bʔayy šikil tri:dah] • **3.** تقَشَّط [tgaššaṭ] تقِشِّط [tgiššiṭ] *vn: sv* a. The paint is beginning to chip. الصُّبُغ بِدا يِتقَشَّط [ʔiṣṣubuɣ bida: yitgaššaṭ]

to chirp • **1.** زَقزَق [zaqzaq] زَقزَقَة [zaqzaqa] *vn: sv* i. A little bird was chirping at the window and woke me up. طَير صغَيِّر كان يزَقزِق بالشِّبّاك وَقَعَّدنِي [ṭi:r ṣɣayyir ča:n yzaqziq biššibba:č wgaʕʕadni]

chisel • **1.** مِنقار [minqa:r, minga:r] مَناقِير [mana:qi:r] *pl:*

to chisel • **1.** حُفَر [ħufar] حَفُر [ħafur] *vn:* اِنحُفَر [ʔinħufar] *p:* Have them chisel the name on the stone in both languages. خَلِّيهُم يحُفرُون الإسم بالحَجَر بِاللُّغتَين [xalli:hum yħufru:n ʔilʔism bilħaǰar billuɣtayn]

chocolate • **1.** جُكلِيت [čukli:t] Is this chocolate bitter or sweet? هَالجُّكلِيت مُرّ لَو حِلو؟ [haččukli:t murr law ħilw?] I want to buy a box of chocolate. أَرِيد أَشتِرِي فَدّ قُوطِيَّة جُكلَيت [ʔari:d ʔaštiri fadd qu:ṭiyya čukli:t]

choice • **1.** اِختِيار [ʔixtiya:r] اِختِيارات [ʔixtiya:ra:t] *pl:* خِيار [xiya:r] I had no other choice. ما كان عِندِي غير اِختِيار [ma: ča:n ʕindi ɣi:r ʔixtiya:r] If I had a choice, I'd do it. لَو بِيدِي خِيار، سَوِّيتَه [law bi:di xiya:r, sawwi:tah] • **2.** تَشكِيلَة [taški:la] تَشكِيلات [taški:la:t] *pl:* They have a wide choice of colors to choose from. عِدهُم تَشكِيلَة كِبيرَة مِن الألوان تِختار مِنها [ʕidhum taški:la čibi:ra min ʔilʔalwa:n tixta:r minha] • **3.** مُمتاز [mumta:z] These are choice cuts of meat. هٰذِي وُصَل مُمتازَة مِن اللَّحَم [ha:ði wuṣal mumta:za min ʔillaħam] • **4.** مُختار [muxta:r] مخاتِير [mxa:ti:r] *pl:* مِستَنقَى [mistanga] He has a choice but small collection of books. عِندَه مَجمُوعَة مُختارَة وَلَو صغَيّرَة مِن الكُتُب [ʕindah maǰmu:ʕa muxta:ra walaw ṣɣayyra min ʔilkutub]

choir • **1.** كُورَس [kuwras] كُورَسات [kuwrasa:t] *pl:* He sings in a choir in the church. يغَنِّي بكُورَس بِالكَنِيسَة [yɣanni bku:ras bilkani:sa]

choke • **1.** چُوك [ču:k] The choke doesn't work. الچُوك ما دَيِشتُغُل [ʔiččuːk ma: dayuštuɣul]

to choke • **1.** خِنَق [xinag] خَنِق [xanig] *vn:* اِنخِنَق [ʔinxinag] *p:* I could choke you. مِن وِدِّي أَخُنقَك [min widdi ʔaxungak] The collar is choking me. الياخَة خانقَتنِي [ʔilya:xa xa:ngatni] • **2.** اِختِنَق [ʔixtinag] اِختِناق [ʔixtina:g] *vn: sv* i. I nearly choked ona fishbone. اِختِنَقِت بعَظم السِّمكَة إلّا شوَيَّة [ʔixtinagit bʕað̣um ʔissimča ʔilla šwayya]

to choke back • **1.** مِنَع [minaʕ] مَنع [maniʕ] *vn:* اِنمِنَع [ʔinminaʕ] *p:* حِصَر [ħiṣar] حَصِر [ħaṣir] *vn:* اِنحِصَر [ʔinħiṣar] *p:* ضُبَط [ð̣ubaṭ] ضَبُط [ð̣abuṭ] *vn:* اِنضُبَط [ʔinð̣ubaṭ] *p:* She choked back her tears. مِنعَت دمُوعها [minʕat dumu:ʕha]

to choke up • **1.** سَدّ [sadd] سَدّ [sadd] *vn:* اِنسَدّ [ʔinsadd] *p:* The stovepipe is choked up. بُورِي الدُّخّان مَسدُود [bu:ri ʔidduxxa:n masdu:d]

cholera • **1.** هَيضَة [hayð̣a] كُولِيرا [ku:li:ra]

to choose • **1.** اِنتِخَب [ʔintixab] اِنتِخاب [ʔintixa:b] *vn: sv* i. اِستَنقَى [ʔistanga:] *sv* i. اِختار [ʔixta:r] اِختِيار [ʔixtiya:r] *vn: sv* a. The editors chose the book of the month for their readers. المُحَرِّرِين اِختارَوا كِتاب الشَّهَر لِقُرّائهُم [ʔilmuħarriri:n ʔixta:raw kita:b ʔiššahar lqurra:ʔhum] Choose the oranges you want. اِستَنقِي البُرتُقالات اللِّي تريدها [ʔistangi l-purtiqa:la:t ʔilli tri:dha. -- They chose him as candidate for the party. اِنتِخبَوه مُرَشَّح عَن الحِزب [ʔintixbawh muraššaħ ʕann ʔilħizib]

choosy • **1.** دِقداقِي [diqda:qi] دِقداقِيَّة [diqda:qiyya] *pl:* There's no need to be so choosy. ماكُو حاجَة تصِير هَالقَدّ دِقداقِي [ma:ku ħa:ǰa tṣi:r halgadd diqda:qi]

to chop • **1.** فَشَّق [faššag] تَفشِيق، تفِشِّق [tafši:g, tfiššig] *vn:* تفَشَّق [tfaššag] *p:* كَسَّر [kassar] تكسِير [taksi:r] *vn:* تكَسَّر [tkassar] *p:* Did you chop some wood? فَشَّقِت شوَيَّة حَطَب؟ [faššagit šwayyat ħaṭab?]

to chop down • **1.** قَصّ [gaṣṣ] قَصّ [gaṣṣ] *vn:* اِنقَصّ [ʔingaṣṣ] *p:* They chopped the dead tree down. قَصُّوها لِلشَّجَرَة المَيْتَة [gaṣṣu:ha liššaǰara ʔilmayyta]

to chop off • **1.** قَصّ [gaṣṣ] قَصّ [gaṣṣ] *vn:* اِنقَصّ [ʔingaṣṣ] *p:* قِطَع [giṭaʕ] قَطِع [gaṭiʕ] *vn:* اِنقِطَع [ʔingiṭaʕ] *p:* Be careful you don't chop your finger off. دِير بالَك لا تقُصّ إصِبعَك [di:r ba:lak la: tguṣṣ ʔiṣibʕak]

to chop up • **1.** ثَرَّم، فَرَّم [θarram, farram] تثُرُّم، تفُرُّم [tθurrum, tfurrum] *vn:* تثَرَّم، تفَرَّم [tθarram, tfarram] *p:* *sv* i. ثِرَم، فِرَم [θiram, firam] ثَرُم، فَرُم [θarum, farum] *vn:* اِنثِرَم، اِنفِرَم [ʔinθiram, ʔinfiram] *p:* Chop the meat up fine. ثَرِّم اللَّحَم ناعِم [θarrim ʔillaħam na:ʕim] This dish calls for chopped meat. هَالطَّبخَة يِنرادِلها لَحَم مَثرُوم [haṭṭabxa yinra:dilha laħam maθru:m] • **2.** قَصقَص [gaṣgaṣ] تقِصقِص [tgiṣgiṣ] *vn:* تقَصقَص [tgaṣgaṣ] *p:* Have the butcher chop up the meat for you. خَلِّي القَصّاب يقَصقِصلَك اللَّحَم [xalli ʔilgaṣṣa:b ygaṣgiṣlak ʔillaħam]

chops • **1.** I'd like the lamb chops with vegetables and rice. يِعجِبنِي القُلباسطِي ويّا خُضرَة وتِمَّن [yiʕǰibni ʔilgulba:sṭi wiyya xuðra wtimman] • **2.** جاب [ča:p] Can you cut me some lamb chops? تِقدَر تقُصّلِي شوَيَّة جاب؟ [tigdar dguṣṣli šwayyat ča:b?] • **3.** بُوز [bu:z] بُوزات [bu:za:t] *pl:* The dog licked his chops. الكَلِب لِحَس بُوزَه [ʔiččalib liħas bu:zah]

to lick one's chops • **1.** مَطَّق [maṭṭag] تَمطِيق [tamṭi:g] *vn:* تمَطَّق [tmaṭṭag] *p:* The food he makes makes you lick your chops. الأكل اللِّي يسَوِّيه يخَلِّي الواحِد يمَطِّق [ʔilʔakl ʔilli ysawwi:h yxalli ʔilwa:ħid ymaṭṭig]

Christ • **1.** المَسِيح [ʔilmasi:ħ]

Christian • **1.** مَسِيحِي [masi:ħi] نَصرانِي [naṣra:ni] نَصارَى [naṣa:ra] *pl:* He's a member of the Young Men's Christian Association. هُوَّ عُضُو بجَمعِيَّة الشُّبّان المَسِيحِيِّين [huwwa ʕuðw bǰamʕiyyat ʔiššubba:n ʔilmasi:ħiyyi:n]

Christianity • **1.** مَسِيحِيَّة [masi:ħiyya]

Christmas • **1.** عِيد المِيلاد [ʕi:d ʔilmi:la:d] كرِيسمِس [kri:smis] Christmas comes on a Wednesday this year. عِيد المِيلاد هالسَّنَة راح يوَقع يوم أربَعَة [ʕi:d ʔilmi:la:d hassana ra:ħ yu:gaʕ yu:m ʔarbaʕa]

chromium • **1.** كرَوم [Krawm, kru:m]

chronic • **1.** مُزمِن [muzmin] He has a chronic disease. عِندَه مَرَض مُزمِن [ʕindah marað muzmin]

to chuckle • **1.** سَنتاوِي، ضِحَك وَحدَه [sanṭa:wi, ðiħak waħdah] He chuckles whenever he thinks of it. يِضحَك وَحدَه كُلّما تِجِي ببالَه [yiðħak waħdah kullma: tiǰi biba:lah]

church • **1.** كَنِيسَة [kani:sa, kini:sa] كَنايِس [kana:yis] *pl:* Is there a Catholic church here? أكُو كَنِيسَة كاثولِكِيَّة هنا؟ [ʔaku kani:sa ka:θu:likiyya hna?] • **2.** طائِفَة [ṭa:ʔifa] طائِفات، طَوائِف [ṭa:ʔifa:t, ṭawa:ʔif] *pl:* What church do you belong to? مِن أيّ طائِفَة إنتَ؟ [min ʔayy ṭa:ʔifa ʔinta?] What church do you belong to? شِنُو دِينَك؟ [šinu: di:nak?]

cider • **1.** عَصِير تِفّاح [ʕaṣi:r tiffa:ħ]

cigar • **1.** سِيجار [ǰi:ga:r] سِيجارات [ǰi:ga:ra:t] *pl:* كَرِد [čarid] كرُود [čru:d] *pl:*

cigarette • **1.** سِجارَة [ǰiga:ra] سِجايِر [ǰiga:yir] *pl:* Have a cigarette تفَضَّل فَدّ سِجارَة [tfaððal fadd ǰiga:ra]

cigarette case • **1.** قُوطِيَّة سِجايِر [qu:ṭiyyat ǰiga:yir] قواطِي سِجايِر [qwa:ṭi ǰiga:yir] *pl:* I've lost my cigarette case. آنِي ضَيَّعِت قُوطِيَّة السِّجايِر مالتِي [ʔa:ni ðayyaʕit qu:ṭiyyat ʔiǰǰiga:yir ma:lti]

cigarette lighter • **1.** قِدّاحَة [qidda:ħa, ǰidda:ħa] قِدّاحات [qidda:ħa:t, ǰidda:ħa:t] *pl:*

cinch • **1.** سَير [sayr] سيُور [syu:r] *pl:* The saddle is loose; tighten the cinch. السَّرِج راخِي؛ ضُبّ السَّير [ʔissariǰ ra:xi; ðubb ʔissayr] • **2.** مُؤَكَّدَة [muʔakkada] That's a cinch. هاي مُؤَكَّدَة [ha:y muʔakkada]

cinder • **1.** فَحمَة مَحرُوقَة [faħma maħru:ga] فَحمات مَحرُوقَة [faħma:t maħru:ga] *pl:* مَحرُوق [maħru:g] فَحَم [faħam] *Collective:* What are they doing with this big pile of cinders? شيسَوُّون بهالكَوم الكِبِير مِن الفَحَم المَحرُوق؟ [šysawwu:n bhalkawm ʔiččibi:r ʔilfaħam ʔilmaħru:g?] I've got a cinder in my eye. خَشَّت فَحمَة صغَيِّرَة بعَينِي [xaššat faħma ṣɣayyra bʕayni]

cinnamon • **1.** دارسِين [da:rsi:n]

circle • **1.** دائِرَة [da:ʔira] دَوائِر [dawa:ʔir] *pl:* Draw the circle with a compass. إرسِم الدّائِرَة بفُرجال [ʔirsim ʔidda:ʔira bfurǰa:l] • **2.** حَلقَة [ħalqa, ħalaqa] حَلَقات [ħalaqa:t] *pl:* He has a wide circle of friends. عِندَه فَدّ حَلَقَة كبِيرَة مِن الأصدِقاء [ʕindah fadd ħalaqa čbi:ra min ʔilʔaṣdiqa:ʔ?] • **3.** وَسَط [waṣaṭ] They are well-known in diplomatic circles. ذُولَة مَعرُوفِين زين بالأوساط الدِّبلَوماسِيَّة [ðu:la maʕru:fi:n zi:n bilʔawsa:ṭ ʔiddibluma:siyya]

to circle • **1.** اِفتَرّ [ʔiftarr] فَرّ [farr] *vn:* *sv* a. حام [ħa:m] حَوم [ħawm] *vn:* اِنحام [ʔinħa:m] *p:* *sv* u. The airplane is circling over the town. الطَّيّارَة دَتِفتَرّ فُوق الوِلايَة

[ʔiṭṭayya:ra datiftarr fu:g ʔilwila:ya] • **2.** دار [da:r] دَوَران [dawara:n] *vn:* اِندار [ʔinda:r] *p:* اِفتَرّ [ʔiftarr] فَرّ [farr] *vn: sv* a. The moon circles around the earth. القُمَر يدُور حَول الأرض [ʔilgumar ydu:r ħawl ʔilʔarð̣]

C

circular • **1.** دائِري [da:ʔiri] Apply the polish with a circular movement. أُضرُب البَولِش بحَرَكات دائِريَّة [ʔuð̣rub ʔilpu:liš bħaraka:t da:ʔiriyya] • **2.** مدَوَّر [mdawwar] A circular staircase leads to the top of the minaret. فَدّ دَرَج مدَوَّر يقُود لقِمَّة المَنارَة [fadd daraǰ mdawwar yqu:d lqummat ʔilmana:ra] • **3.** مَنشُور [manšu:r] We need some boys to distribute circulars. نِحتاج كَم وَلَد لِتَوزِيع المَناشِير [niħta:ǰ čam walad litawzi:ʕ ʔilmana:ši:r]

to circulate • **1.** دار [da:r] دَوَران [dawara:n] *vn:* اِندار [ʔinda:r] *p:* Cold water circulates through these pipes constantly. الماي البارِد يدُور بِهالبُورِيّات عَلَى طُول [ʔilma:y ʔilba:rid ydu:r bhalbu:riyya:t ʕala ṭu:l] There's a strange rumor circulating. أَكُو فَدّ إشاعَة غَرِيبَة دايرَة [ʔaku fadd ʔiša:ʕa ɣari:ba da:yra]

circulation • **1.** دَوَران [dawara:n] His blood circulation is not too good. دَوَران دَمَّه مُو كُلَّش زين [dawara:n dammah mu: kulliš zi:n] • **2.** تَوزِيع [tawzi:ʕ] اِنتِشار [ʔintiša:r] Our paper has a circulation of a hundred and fifty thousand. تَوزِيع الجَّرِيدَة مالَتنا يوَصِّل إِلَى مِيَّة وَخَمسِين أَلِف [tawzi:ʕ ʔiǰǰari:da ma:latna ywaṣṣil ʔila miyya wxamsi:n ʔalif] • **3.** تَداوُل [tada:wul] The government has put new bills into circulation. الحُكُومَة نَزلَت نواط جِدِيدَة بالتَّداوُل [ʔilħuku:ma nazlat nwa:ṭ ǰidi:da bittada:wul]

circumference • **1.** مُحِيط [muħi:ṭ] مُحِيطات [muħi:ṭa:t] *pl:* How do you get the circumference of the circle? شلُون تطَلِّع مُحِيط الدّائِرَة؟ [šlu:n ṭṭalliʕ muħi:ṭ ʔidda:ʔira?]

circumstances • **1.** ظَرُف [ð̣aruf] ظرُوف [ð̣ru:f] *pl:* Under these circumstances I can't blame her. تَحَت هَالظرُوف ما أَقدَر أَلُومها [taħat hað̣ð̣uru:f ma: ʔagdar ʔalu:mha] • **2.** حال [ħa:l] أَحوال [ʔaħwa:l] *pl:* أَمُر [ʔamur] أَوامِر [ʔawa:mir] *pl:* He's in very good circumstances. أَحوالَه زينَة [ʔaħwa:lah zi:na] He's in very good circumstances. أُمُورَه ماشيَة [ʔumu:rah ma:šya]

circus • **1.** سَركِيس [sarki:s] سَيركِيسات [sarki:sa:t] *pl:*

citation • **1.** اِستِشهاد [ʔistišha:d] His speech is full of citations from the Koran. خِطابَه حافِل بإستِشهادات مِن القُرآن [xiṭa:bah ħa:fil bʔistišha:da:t min ʔilqurʔa:n]

to cite • **1.** إستَشهَد ب [ʔistašhad b-] اِستِشهاد [ʔistišha:d] *vn: sv* i. Cite the passage exactly as the author wrote it. اِستَشهِد بالمَقطَع تَماماً مِثلما كِتَبَه المُؤَلِّف [ʔistašhid bilmaqṭaʕ tama:man miθilma: kitabah ʔilmuʔallif]

citizen • **1.** مُواطِن [muwa:ṭin] مُواطِنِين [muwa:ṭini:n] *pl:* Fellow citizens, choose your candidate carefully. أَيُّها المُواطِنِين، اِنتَخبُوا مُرَشَّحكُم بِدِقَّة [ʔayyuha ʔilmuwa:ṭini:n, ʔintaxbu: muraššaħkum bdiqqa]
 *** I am an Iraqi citizen.** • **1.** آنِي عِراقِي [ʔa:ni ʕira:qi]

citizenship • **1.** جِنسِيَّة [ǰinsiyya] جِنسيّات، جَناسِي [ǰinsiyya:t, ǰana:si:] *pl:* I have Iraqi citizenship. عِندِي جِنسِيَّة عِراقِيَّة [ʕindi ǰinsiyya ʕira:qiyya]

city • **1.** مَدِينَة [madi:na] مُدُن [mudun] *pl:* How far is the nearest city from here? شقَدّ تِبعِد أَقرَب مَدِينَة مِن هنا؟ [šgadd tibʕid ʔaqrab madi:na min hna?] • **2.** بَلَدِي [baladi] She is in the City Hospital. هِيَّ بِالمُستَشفى البَلَدِي [hiyya bilmustašfa ʔilbaladi]

city dweller • **1.** ساكِن مُدِن [sa:kin mudin] سُكّان مُدِن [sukka:n mudin] *pl:* حَضَرِي [ħað̣ari] He is a city dweller and doesn't know much about agriculture. هُوَّ مِن سُكّان المُدِن وَما يُعرُف هوايَة عَن الزِّراعَة [huwwa min sukka:n ʔilmudin wama: yuʕruf hwa:ya ʕann ʔizzira:ʕa] The bedouins and the city dwellers do not get on well together. البَدو والحَضَر ما يِتراهمُون [ʔilbadw walħað̣ar ma: yitra:hmu:n]

city hall • **1.** سَراي [sara:y]

city life • **1.** حَياة المَدِينَة [ħaya:t ʔilmadi:na] She is not accustomed to city life. ما مِتعَوّدَة عَلَى حَياة المَدِينَة [ma: mitʕawwda ʕala ħaya:t ʔilmadi:na]

civil • **1.** نازِك [na:zik] مُؤَدَّب [muʔaddab] At least he was civil to us. هَمّ زَين كان نازِك ويّانا [hamm zayn ča:n na:zik wiyya:na] • **2.** مَدَنِي [madani] This is the concern of the civil authorities. هَذِي مِن اِختِصاص السُّلطات المَدَنِيَّة [ha:ð̣i min ʔixtiṣa:ṣ ʔissulṭa:t ʔilmadaniyya] • **3.** أَهلِي [ʔahli] The difficulty almost led to civil war. المُشكِلَة تَقرِيباً أَدَّت إِلَى حَرُب أَهلِيَّة [ʔilmuškila taqri:ban ʔaddat ʔila ħarub ʔahliyya]

civil code • **1.** القانُون المَدَنِي [ʔilqa:nu:n ʔilmadani]

civilian • **1.** مَدَنِي [madani] There were civilians and soldiers in the crowd. كان أَكُو مَدَنِيِّين وَعَسكَرِيِّين بين الجَّمهُور [ča:n ʔaku madaniyyi:n wʕaskariyyi:n bayn ʔiǰǰamhu:r] Was he wearing civilian clothes? كان لابِس هِدُوم مَدَنِيَّة؟ [ča:n la:bis hidu:m madaniyya?] Was he wearing civilian clothes? كان لابِس سُوِيل؟ [ča:n la:bis suwi:l?] He used to work as a teacher in civilian life. كان يِشتُغُل مُعَلِّم أَثناء حَياتَه المَدَنِيَّة [ča:n yištuɣul muʕallim ʔaθna:ʔ ħaya:tah ʔilmadaniyya]

civilization • **1.** حَضارَة [ħað̣a:ra] حَضارات [ħað̣a:ra:t] *pl:* The Babylonians had an advanced civilization. البابِلِيِّين كان عِدهُم حَضارَة مِتقَدّمَة [ʔilba:biliyyi:n ča:n ʕidhum ħað̣a:ra mitqaddma]

to civilize • **1.** مَدَّن [maddan] تَمدِين [tamdi:n] *vn:* تمَدَّن [tmaddan] *p:* حَضَّر [ħaðður] تَحضِير [taħði:r] *vn:* تحَضَّر [tħaððar] *p:* They were unable to civilize them. They remain savages. ما قِدرَوا يمَدّنُوهُم بُقَوا مِتوَحّشِين [ma: gidraw ymaddinu:hum buqaw mitwaħħiši:n]

civilized • **1.** مِتمَدِّن [mitmaddin] مِتحَضّر [mitħaððir]

civil service • **1.** خِدمَة مَدَنِيَّة [xidma madaniyya]

claim • **1.** اِدِّعاء [ʔiddiʕa:ʔ] اِدِّعاءات [ʔiddiʕa:ʔa:t] *pl:* You must submit your claim within ten days. لازِم تقَدِّم اِدِّعائَك خِلال عَشرَة أيّام [la:zim tqaddim ʔiddiʕa:ʔak xila:l ʕašrat ʔayya:m] I don't believe his claim that he won the lottery. ما أصَدِّق اِدِّعائَه إنُّو رُبَح اليانَصِيب [ma: ʔaṣaddig ʔiddiʕa:ʔah ʔinnu rubaħ ʔilyanaṣi:b] • **2.** حَقّ [ħaqq, ħagg] I have no claim to that. ما عِندِي حَقّ بِيها [ma: ʕindi ħaqq bi:ha]

to claim • **1.** طالَب بـ [ṭa:lab bi-] مُطالَبَة بـ [muṭa:laba bi-] *vn:* تطالَب بـ [ʔitṭa:lab bi-] *p:* I claim my share. آني أطالِب بحُصّتِي [ʔa:ni ʔaṭa:lib bħuṣṣti] Where do I claim my baggage? وين أطالِب بِجنَطِي؟ [wi:n ʔaṭa:lib bijinaṭi?] • **2.** اِدَّعَى [ʔiddiʕa:] اِدِّعاء [ʔiddiʕa:ʔ] *vn: sv* i. She claims to know the man. هِيَّ تِدَّعِي تُعرفَه الرِّجّال [hiyya tiddiʕi tuʕurfah ʔirrijja:l]

to clap • **1.** صَفَّق [ṣaffag] تَصفِيق، تصُفُّق [taṣfi:g, tṣuffug] *vn: sv* u. He clapped to summon the waiter. صَفَّق حَتَّى يصِيح البُوي [ṣaffag ħatta yṣi:ħ ʔilbu:y]

to clarify • **1.** وَضَّح [waððaħ] توضِيح [tawði:ħ] *vn:* توَضَّح [twaððaħ] *p:* فَسَّر [fassar] تَفسِير [tafsi:r] *vn:* تفَسَّر [tfassar] *p:* We have asked you to come in and clarify a few points for us. طِلَبناك تِجِي حَتَّى توَضِّح إلنا كَم نُقطَة [ṭilabna:k tiji ħatta twaððiħ ʔilna čam nuqṭa]

clash • **1.** اِشتِباك [ʔištiba:k] اِشتِباكات [ʔištiba:ka:t] *pl:* He was wounded in a clash on the border. اِنجِرَح بإشتِباك عالحِدُود [ʔinjiraħ bʔištiba:k ʕalħidu:d] • **2.** تَصادُم [taṣa:dum] تَصادُمات [taṣa:duma:t] *pl:* مُصادَمَة [muṣa:dama] The real source of the trouble is a clash of personalities. السَّبَب الحَقِيقِي لِلمُشكِلَة هُوَّ التَّصادُم بالشَّخصِيّات [ʔissabab ʔilħaqi:qi lilmuškila huwwa ʔittaṣa:dum biššaxṣiyya:t]

to clash • **1.** تصادَم [tṣa:dam] تَصادُم [taṣa:dum] *vn: sv* a. Government troops clashed briefly with rebel forces yesterday. قُوّات الحُكُومَة تصادمَت البارحَة لِمُدَّة قَصِيرَة ويّا قُوّات الثُّوّار [quwwa:t ʔilħuku:ma tṣa:dmat ʔilba:rħa lmudda qaṣi:ra wiyya quwwa:t ʔiθθuwwa:r] • **2.** تضارَب [dða:rab] تَضارُب [taða:rub] *vn: sv* a. The interests of the two parties clashed over the question of government subsidies. مَصالِح الحِزبَين تضاربَت حَول المُساعَدات الحُكُومِيَّة [maṣa:liħ ʔilħizbayn dða:rbat ħawl ʔalmusa:ʕada:t ʔilħuku:miyya] These two colors clash with each other unpleasantly. هَاللُّونَين يتضاربُون واحِد ويّا اللاخ بصُورَة ما حِلوَة [hallu:nayn yidða:rbu:n wa:ħid wiyya ʔilla:x bṣu:ra ma: ħilwa]

clasp • **1.** قَبضَة [qabða] قَبضات [qabða:t] *pl:* He has a firm handclasp. عِندَه قَبضَة إيد قَوِيَّة [ʕindah qabðat ʔi:d qawwiyya] • **2.** طُبّاقَة [ṭubba:ga] طُبّاقات [ṭubba:ga:t] *pl:* Can you fix the clasp on my purse? تِقدَر تصَلّح الطُّبّاقَة مال جُنطتِي [tigdar tṣalliħ ʔiṭṭubba:ga ma:l junutti] • **3.** كِلّاب [čilla:b] كلالِيب [čla:li:b] *pl:* شِكّالَة [šikka:la] شِكّالات [šikka:la:t] *pl:* Hook the clasp on my necklace please. شَكِّل الكِلّاب مال قلادتِي رَجاءً [šakkil ʔiččilla:b ma:l gla:dti raja:ʔan]

to clasp • **1.** لِزَم [lizam] لَزِم [lazim] *vn:* اِنلِزَم [ʔinlizam] *p:* They walked down the street clasping hands. تمَشَّوا بالشّارِع لازمِين واحِد إيد اللاخ [tmaššaw bišša:riʕ la:zmi:n wa:ħid ʔi:d ʔilla:x]

class • **1.** صِنِف [ṣinif] أصناف، صُنُوف [ʔaṣna:f, ṣunu:f] *pl:* Arrange the items according to their classes. رَتِّب المَوادّ حَسَب أصنافها [rattib ʔilmawa:dd ħasab ʔaṣna:fha] • **2.** دَرِس [daris] درُوس [dru:s] *pl:* You're going to be late for class. راح تِتأَخَّر عَلَى الدَّرِس [ra:ħ titʔaxxar ʕala ʔiddaris] There are no classes on Friday. ماكُو درُوس يوم الجُمعَة [ma:ku dru:s yu:m ʔijjumʕa] • **3.** صَفّ [ṣaff] Our class is going on a field trip tomorrow. صَفّنا راح يِطلَع سَفرَة باكِر [ṣaffna ra:ħ yiṭlaʕ safra ba:čir] • **4.** طَبَقَة [ṭabaqa] طَبَقات [ṭabaqa:t] *pl:* He is popular with all classes of society. مَحبُوب مِن كُلّ الطَّبَقات الاجتِماعِيَّة [maħbu:b min kull ʔiṭṭabaqa:t ʔilʔijtima:ʕiyya] This word is not used by the educated classes. هَالكَلِمَة ما مُستَعمَلَة مِن قِبَل الطَّبَقات المُثَقَّفَة [halkalima ma: mustaʕmala min qibal ʔiṭṭabaqa:t ʔilmuθaqqafa] • **5.** وَجبَة [wajba] وَجبات [wajba:t] *pl:* دَفعَة [dafʕa] دَفعات [dafʕa:t] *pl:* We are all alumni of the class of 1934. كُلّنا مِن خِرِّيجِين وَجبَة ألِف وَتِسعمِيَّة وأربَع وثلاثِين [kullna min xirri:ji:n wajbat ʔalif wtisiʕmiyya wʔarbaʕ wtla:θi:n] • **6.** دَرَجَة [daraja] دَرَجات [daraja:t] *pl:* You'll find the first class coaches ahead just behind the engine. تِلقِي عَرَبات الدَّرَجَة الأُولَى لِقدّام مُباشَرَةً وَرا المَكِينَة [tilgi ʕaraba:t ʔiddaraja ʔilʔu:la ligidda:m muba:šaratan wara ʔilmaki:na] • **7.** طِراز [ṭira:z] أطرِزَة [ʔaṭriza] *pl:* He is a first class politician. هُوَّ سِياسِي مِن الطِّراز الأوَّل [huwwa siya:si min ʔiṭṭira:z ʔilʔawwal]

classical • **1.** كلاسِيكِي [klasi:ki] He prefers classical music to jazz. يفَضِّل المُوسِيقَى الكلاسِيكِيَّة عَلَى الجّاز [yfaððil ʔilmusi:qa ʔilklasi:kiyya ʕala ʔijja:z] • **2.** فَصِيح [faṣi:ħ] He is making good progress in his study of classical Arabic. دَيِتقَدَّم زين بدِراستَه لِلُّغَة العَرَبِيَّة الفَصِيحَة [dayitqaddam zi:n bdira:stah lilluγa ʔilʕarabiyya ʔilfaṣi:ħa] • **3.** تَقلِيدِي [taqli:di] This is a classical example of Eastern architecture. هَذا فَدّ مَثَل تَقلِيدِي لِلهَندَسَة الشَّرقِيَّة [ha:ða fadd maθal taqli:di lilhandasa ʔiššarqiyya]

classification • **1.** تَصنِيف [taṣni:f]

C

classified • **1.** مُبَوَّب [mubawwab] I found the car advertised in the classified ad section of the newspaper. لِقيت السَّيّارَة مَعلُون عَنها بِصَفحَة الإعلانات المُبَوَّبَة مِن الجَّريدَة [ligi:t ʔissayya:ra maʕlu:n ʕanha bṣafħat ʔilʔiʕla:na:t ʔilmubawwaba min ʔilǰari:da] • **2.** سِرِّي [sirri] These papers are all classified. هَالأَوراق كُلّها سِرِّيَّة [halʔawra:q kullha sirriyya]

to classify • **1.** صَنَّف [ṣannaf] تَصنيف [taṣni:f] *vn:* تصَنَّف [tṣannaf] *p:* بَوَّب [bawwab] تَبويب [tabwi:b] *vn:* تبَوَّب [tbawwab] *p:* The remaining items are hard to classify. المَوادّ الباقيَة يِصعَب تَصنيفها [ʔilmawa:dd ʔilba:qya yiṣʕab taṣni:fha]

classroom • **1.** صَفّ [ṣaff] صفُوف [ṣfu:f] *pl:* The teacher is still in the classroom. المُعَلِّم بَعدَه بِالصَّفّ [ʔilmuʕallim baʕdah biṣṣaff]

clatter • **1.** طَقطَقَة [ṭagṭaga] The clatter of dishes in the kitchen distrubs the guests. طَقطَقَة المواعين بالمَطبَخ تِزعِج الخُطّار [ṭagṭagat ʔilmwa:ʕi:n bilmaṭbax tizʕiǰ ʔilxuṭṭa:r] • **2.** طَرقَعَة [ṭargaʕa] We heard the clatter of the wagon wheels as he went through the alley. سِمَعنا طَرقَعَة جرُوخ العَرَبانَة مِن مَرّ بالعَقِد [simaʕna ṭargaʕat čru:x ʔilʕaraba:na min marr bilʕagid] • **3.** طَربَقَة [ṭarbaga] We awakened to the clatter of horses' hooves on the pavement. قِعَدنا عَلَى حِسّ طَربَقَة حَوافِر الخَيل بِالشّارِع [giʕadna ʕala ħiss ṭarbagat ħawa:fir ʔilxayl biššaːriʕ]

to clatter • **1.** طَرقَع [ṭargaʕ] طَرقَعَة [ṭargaʕa] *vn:* *sv* i. She clattered down the stairs in her clogs. نِزلَت الدَّرَج وَقُبقابها يطَرقِع [nizlat ʔiddaraǰ wqubqa:bha yṭargiʕ]

clause • **1.** بَند [band] بُنُود [bunu:d] *pl:* شَرط [šarṭ] شُرُوط [šuru:ṭ] *pl:* I won't sign the contract if it has that clause in it. ما أمضِي العَقِد إذا بِيه هالبَند [ma: ʔamḍi ʔilʕaqid ʔiða bi:h halband]

claw • **1.** مَخلَب [maxlab] مَخالِب [maxa:lib] *pl:* The hawk had a mouse in his claws. الصَّقَر لازِم جرَيدِي بمَخالبَه [ʔiṣṣigar la:zim ǰri:di bmaxa:lbah] • **2.** إظفُر [ʔiðfir] أظافِير، أظافِر [ʔaða:fi:r, ʔaða:fir] *pl:* The cat has sharp claws. البَزُّونَة عِدها أظافِر حادَّة [ʔilbazzu:na ʕidha ʔaða:fir ħa:dda]

clay • **1.** طِين [ṭi:n] Is this clay good for pottery? هالطِّين زين لِلكوازَة؟ [haṭṭi:n zi:n lilkwa:za?] The floor is made of clay pounded hard. القاعِيَّة مسَوّايَة مِن طِين مَدكُوك [ʔilga:ʕiyya msawwa:ya min ṭi:n madču:č]

clean • **1.** نَظِيف [naði:f] This plate is not clean. هَالماعُون مُو نَظِيف [halma:ʕu:n mu: naði:f] • **2.** بَسِيط [baṣi:ṭ] بَسِيطِين [baṣi:ṭi:n] *pl:* I like the clean lines of that building. يعجِبنِي التَّصمِيم البَسِيط مال ذِيك البِنايَة [yiʕǰibni ʔittaṣmi:m ʔilbasi:ṭ ma:l ði:č ʔilbina:ya]

*** Wipe the pane clean.** • **1.** نَظُّف الجّامَة زَين [naððuf ʔiǰǰa:ma zayn]

to clean • **1.** نَظَّف [naððaf] تَنظِيف [tanði:f] *vn:* تنَظَّف [tnaððaf] *p:* Has the maid cleaned the room yet? الخادمَة نَظّفَت الغُرفَة لَو بَعَد؟ [ʔilxa:dma naððfat ʔilɣurfa law baʕad?] Please clean the chicken for me. أرجُوك نَظّفلِي الدِّجاجَة [ʔarǰu:k naððufli ʔiddiǰa:ǰa] Where can I have my clothes cleaned? وين أقدَر أوَدِّي هدُومِي لِلتَّنظِيف؟ [wi:n ʔagdar ʔawaddi hdu:mi littanði:f?] We still have to clean the windows. بَعَد لازِم انَّظُّف الشَّبابِيك [baʕad la:zim ʔinnaððuf ʔiššiba:bi:č] • **2.** عَزَّل [ʕazzal] تَعزِيل [taʕzi:l] *vn:* تعَزَّل [tʕazzal] *p:* We gave the house a thorough cleaning today. عَزَّلنا البَيت تَعزِيلَة زينَة اليُوم [ʕazzalna ʔilbayt taʕzi:la zi:na ʔilyu:m]

*** He cleaned house in the poker game last night.** • **1.** البارحَة بِاللَيل شال كُلّ القاع بِالبَوكَر [ʔilba:rħa billayl ša:l kull ʔilga:ʕ bilpu:kar]

to clean out • **1.** فَرَّغ [farraɣ] تَفرِيغ [tafri:ɣ] *vn:* تفَرَّغ [tfarraɣ] *p:* This drawer has to be cleaned out. هَالمجَرّ لازِم يِتفَرَّغ [halmǰarr la:zim yitfarraɣ] • **2.** أخَذ الأكُو والماكُو مِن [ʔaxað ʔilʔaku: walma:ku min] They cleaned me out all right. أخذَوا مِنّي الأكُو والماكُو [ʔaxðaw minni ʔilʔaku walma:ku] They cleaned me out all right. ضِربَولِي جيُوبِي أُوتِي [ðirbawli ǰyu:bi ʔu:ti]

to clean up • **1.** غَسَّل [ɣassal, xassal] تَغسِيل [taɣsi:l] *vn:* تغَسَّل [tɣassal] *p:* I'd like to clean up before dinner. أرِيد أغَسِّل قَبِل العَشا [ʔari:d ʔiɣassil gabil ʔilʕaša] • **2.** نَظَّف [naððaf] تَنظِيف [tanði:f] *vn:* تنَظَّف [tnaððaf] *p:* *sv* u. When are you going to clean up this mess on your desk? شوَقِت راح تنَظُّف هالخَربَطَة مِن عَلَى مَيزَك؟ [šwakit ra:ħ tnaððuf halxarbaṭa min ʕala mayzak?]

cleaner • **1.** مُنَظِّف [munaððif] مُنَظِّفات [munaððifa:t] *pl:* This cleaner will remove all the spots. هالمُنَظِّف راح يرَوِّح كُلّ اللَّكّات [halmunaððif ra:ħ yrawwiħ kull ʔillakka:t] • **2.** مُكَوِّي [mukawwi] مَكوِي [makwi] مَكاوِي [maka:wi] *pl:* Do you know a good cleaner in this area? تُعرُف فَدّ مَكوِي زين بِهالمَنطقَة؟ [tuʕruf fadd makwi zi:n bhalmanṭaqa?]

cleaning • **1.** تَنظِيف [tanði:f] تَعزِيل [taʕzi:l] The house needs a good cleaning. البَيت يِنرادلَه تَنظِيف زين [ʔilbayt yinra:dlah tanði:f zi:n]

cleaning plant • **1.** مَحَلّ كَوِي [maħall kawy] مَحَلّات كَوِي [maħalla:t kawy] *pl:* They have their own cleaning plant. عِدهُم مَحَلّ كَوِي خاصّ بِيهُم [ʕidhum maħall kawy xa:ṣṣ bi:hum]

cleaning woman • **1.** صانعَة [ṣa:nʕa] صانعات [ṣa:nʕa:t] *pl:* Where can I find a good cleaning woman? وين أقدَر ألقِي فَدّ صانعَة؟ [wi:n ʔagdar ʔalgi fadd ṣa:nʕa?]

cleanser • **1.** مُنَظِّف [munaðöif] مُنَظِّفات [munaðöifa:t] *pl:* This cleanser cleans pans well. هالمُنَظِّف ينَظِّف الجِدُور تَنظِيف زين [halmunaðöif ynaðöif ʔilijdu:r tanði:f zi:n]

clear • **1.** صافِي [ṣa:fi] The water is deep and clear. الماي غَمِيج وَصافِي [ʔilma:y ɣami:j wṣa:fi] Try to keep a clear head. حاوِل تخَلِّي فِكرَك صافِي [ħa:wil txalli fikrak ṣa:fi] • **2.** واضِح [wa:ðiħ] His voice was very clear over the radio. صَوتَه كان كُلِّش واضِح بِالرّاديُو [ṣawtah ča:n kulliš wa:ðiħ birra:dyu] • **3.** صَحو [ṣaħw] مصَحِّي [mṣaħħi] We have had clear weather all week. كان الجَوّ عِدنا صَحو طُول الإسبُوع [ča:n ʔiǰǰaww ʕidna ṣaħw ṭu:l ʔilʔisbu:ʕ] • **4.** ظاهِر [ða:hir] It is clear from the letter that he isn't satisfied. ظاهِر مِن مَكتُوبَه إنُّو مُو راضِي [ða:hir min maktu:bah ʔinnu mu: ra:ði] • **5.** مَفتُوح [maftu:ħ] مَسلُوك [maslu:k] Is the road clear up ahead? الطَّرِيق قِدّام مَفتُوح؟ [ʔiṭṭari:q gidda:m maftu:ħ?] • **6.** مِرتاح [mirta:ħ] My conscious is clear. ضَمِيرِي مِرتاح [ðami:rah mirta:ħ] • **7.** بَرِيء [bari:ʔ, bari] بَرِيئِين، أبرِياء [bari:ʔi:n, ʔabriya:ʔ] *pl:* We're going to release you; you're in the clear. راح نهِدَّك، إنتَ بَرِيء [ra:ħ nhiddak, ʔinta bari:ʔ]

to clear • **1.** صِحَى [ṣiħa:] صَحُو [ṣaħw] *vn: sv* a. The sky is beginning to clear. السِّما بِدَت تِصحَى [ʔissima: bidat tiṣħa:] • **2.** نَظَّف [naððaf] تَنظِيف [tanði:f] *vn: sv* u. t-. We've finished eating; you may clear the table now. خَلَّصنا الأكِل هَسَّة تِقدَر تنَظُّف المِيز [xallaṣna ʔilʔakil hassa tigdar tnaððuf ʔilmi:z] • **3.** فَكّ [fakk] فَكّ [fakk] *vn:* اِنفَكّ [ʔinfakk] *p:* These drops will clear your head and sinuses. هالقَطرَة تفُكّ راسَك وَجيُوبَك الأنفِيَّة [halqaṭra tfukk ra:sak wiǰiyu:bak ʔalʔanfiyya] • **4.** عُبَر [ʕubar] عُبُور [ʕubu:r] *vn:* اِنعُبَر [ʔinʕubar] *p:* فات [fa:t] فَوت [fawt] *vn:* اِنفات [ʔinfa:t] *p:* The plane just barely cleared the tree tops as it took off. الطَّيّارَة بِالكاد عُبرَت فُوق رُوُوس الأشجار مِن طارَت [ʔiṭṭiyya:ra bilka:d ʕubrat fu:g ruʔu:s ʔilʔašǰa:r min ṭa:rat] • **5.** بَرَّى [barra:] تَبرِئَة [tabriʔap, tabriya] *vn:* تبَرَّى [tbarra:] *p:* The court cleared him of the charges against him. المَحكَمَة بَرَّتَه مِن التُّهَم اللِّي ضِدَّه [ʔilmaħkama barratah min ʔittuham ʔilli ðiddah] • **6.** خَلَّص [xallaṣ] تَخلِيص [taxli:ṣ] *vn:* تخَلَّص [txallaṣ] *p:* Look and see if I am going to clear that car. باوِعلِي وشُوف إذا أخَلِّص مِن هَالسَّيّارَة [ba:wiʕli wšu:f ʔiða ʔaxalliṣ min hassayya:ra] • **7.** أخلَى [ʔaxla:] إخلاء [ʔixla:ʔ] *vn: sv* i. Clear the court room. إخلُوا قاعَة المَحكَمَة [ʔixlu: qa:ʕat ʔilmaħkama] • **8.** طِلَع [ṭilaʕ] طُلُوع [ṭulu:ʕ] *vn: sv* a. Your residence permit will take a week or two to clear. إقامتَك راح تاخُذ إسبُوع لَو إسبُوعَين حَتَّى تِطلَع [ʔiqa:mtak ra:ħ ta:xuð ʔisbu:ʕ law ʔisbu:ʕayn ħatta tiṭlaʕ] • **9.** مَرّ [marr] مَرّ [marr] *vn:* اِنمَرّ [ʔinmarr] *p:* It took us an hour to clear customs. أخذَتنا ساعَة حَتَّى نمُرّ بِالجُمرُك [ʔaxðatna sa:ʕa ħatta nmurr bilgumruk]

to clear away • **1.** شال [ša:l] شَيل [šayl] *vn:* اِنشال [ʔinša:l] *p:* Tell her to clear away the dishes. قُل لها خَلِّي تشِيل المواعِين [gulilha xalli tši:li ʔilmwa:ʕi:n]

to clear off • **1.** شال مِن [ša:l min] شَيل مِن [šayl min] *vn:* اِنشال مِن [ʔinša:l min] *p:* Clear this stuff off your table. شِيل هَالأشياء مِن عَلَى مَيزَك [ši:l halʔašya:ʔ min ʕala mayzak]

to clear one's throat • **1.** اِتنَحنَح [ʔitnaħnaħ] نَحنَحَة [naħnaħa] *vn: sv* a. He cleared his throat before he entered the room. تنَحنَح قَبُل ما خَشّ لِلقُبَّة [tnaħnaħ gabul ma: xašš lilgubba]

to clear out • **1.** فَرَّغ [farraɣ] تَفرِيغ [tafri:ɣ] *vn:* تفَرَّغ [tfarraɣ] *p:* I'll clear out this closet so you can hang your clothes in it. راح أفَرِّغ هَالدِيلاب حَتَّى تِقدَر تعَلِّق هدُومَك بِيها [ra:ħ ʔafarriɣ haldi:la:b ħatta tigdar tʕallig hdu:mak bi:ha] • **2.** شِلَع [šilaʕ] شَلِع [šaliʕ] *vn: sv* a. He cleared out in the middle of the night. شِلَع بنُصّ اللَّيل [šilaʕ bnuṣṣ ʔillayl] He cleared out in the middle of the night. شَمَّع الخيط بنُصّ اللَّيل [šmmaʕ ʔilxayṭ bnuṣṣ ʔillayl]

to clear up • **1.** صَحَّى [ṣaħħa:] تَصحِيَّة [taṣħiya] *vn: sv* a. The weather has cleared up and the rain has stopped. صَحَّت الدِّنيا والمُطَر بَطَّل [ṣaħħat ʔiddinya wilmuṭar baṭṭal] • **2.** صِفَى [ṣifa:] صَفاء [ṣafa:ʔ] *vn: sv* a. The dust storm is over; the weather has cleared up. راحَت العَجَّة؛ صِفَى الجَوّ [ra:ħat ʔilʕaǰǰa; ṣifa: ʔiǰǰaww] • **3.** وَضَّح [waððaħ] تَوضِيح [tawði:ħ] *vn:* توَضَّح [twaððaħ] *p:* فَسَّر [fassar] تَفسِير [tafsi:r] *vn:* تفَسَّر [tfassar] *p:* Several points remain to be cleared up. عِدَّة نُقَط بَعَد يِنرادِلها تَوضِيح [ʕiddat nuqaṭ baʕad yinra:dilha tawði:ħ]

clearance • **1.** مَجال [maǰa:l] مَجالات [maǰa:la:t] *pl:* I don't think there is enough clearance here for the truck to turn around. ما أعتِقِد أكُو مَجال كافِي لِلُّورِي يدَيوُر هنا [ma: ʔaʕtiqid ʔaku maǰa:l ka:fi lillawri ydi:wur hna] • **2.** مُوافَقَة [muwa:faqa] مُصادَقَة [muṣa:dqa] Foreigners have to get clearance from the proper authorities to work in Iraq. الأجانِب لازِم ياخذُون مُوافَقَة السُّلطات المُختَصَّة لِلعَمَل بِالعِراق [ʔilʔaǰa:nib la:zim ya:xðu:n muwa:faqat ʔissulṭa:t ʔilmuxtaṣṣa lilʕamal bilʕira:q]

clearly • **1.** بوُضُوح [bwuðu:ħ] بصُورَة واضحَة [bṣu:ra wa:ðħa] Please speak more clearly. أرجُوك تكَلَّم بوُضُوح أكثَر [ʔarǰu:k tkallam bwuðu:ħ ʔakθar]

clergy • **1.** إكلِيرُس [ʔikli:rus]

clerical • **1.** كِتابِي [kita:bi] I am looking for a clerical job. دَأدَوِّرلِي فَدّ شَغلَة كِتابِيَّة [daʔadawwirli fadd šaɣla kita:biyya]

clerk • **1.** كاتِب [ka:tib] كُتّاب [kutta:b] *pl:* He's a clerk in a big office. هُوَّ كاتِب بدائِرَة كبِيرَة [huwwa ka:tib bda:ʔira čbi:ra]

clever • **1.** ذَكِي [ðaki] أذكِياء [ʔaðkiya:ʔ] *pl:* فَطِين [faṭi:n] He's a clever fellow. هُوَّ فَدّ واحِد ذَكِي [huwwa fadd wa:ħid ðaki] • **2.** ماهِر [ma:hir] حاذِق [ħa:ðiq] He's a very clever tailor. هُوَّ فَدّ خَيّاط كُلِّش ماهِر [huwwa fadd xayya:ṭ kulliš ma:hir] • **3.** لَبِق [labiq] He's a clever speaker. هُوَّ فَدّ خَطِيب لَبِق [huwwa fadd xaṭi:b labiq] • **4.** شاطِر [ša:ṭir] شُطّار، شُطَّر [šuṭṭar, šuṭṭa:r] *pl:* حاذِق [ħa:ðiq] فاهِم [fa:him] He's a clever business man. هُوَّ فَدّ رَجُل أعمال شاطِر [huwwa fadd rajul ʔaʕma:l ša:ṭir]

C

click • 1. طَقَّة [ṭagga] طَقّات [ṭagga:t] *pl:* I heard the click of the lock. سمَعِت طَقَّة الكَيلُون [smaʕit ṭaggat ʔilkaylu:n]

to click • 1. طَقّ [ṭagg] طَقّ [ṭagg] *vn:* اِنطَقّ [ʔinṭagg] *p:* He clicked his heels and saluted me. طَقّلي سَلام [ṭaggli sala:m] • **2.** طَقطَق [ṭagṭag] طَقطَقَ [ṭagṭaga] *vn: sv* i. I heard her heels clicking as she came toward me down the hall. سمَعِت كَعَب قُندَرَتها تطَقطِق مِن جَتّ مِتَّجهَة عَلَيّا بالمَمَرّ [smaʕit čaʕab qundaratha ṭṭagṭig min jatt mittajha ʕalayya bilmamarr] • **3.** نِجَح [nijaħ] نَجاح [naja:ħ] *vn: sv* a. The show clicked from the first night on. التَّمثِيلِيَّة نِجحَت مِن أوَّل لَيلَة [ʔittamθi:liyya nijħat min ʔawwal layla]

*** Everything clicked beautifully.**

• **1.** كُلّشِي مِشَى مِثل الساعَة [kullši miša: miθl ʔissa:ʕa]

client • 1. مَعمِيل [maʕmi:l, miʕmi:l] مَعامِيل [maʕa:mi:l] *pl:* مُراجِع [mura:jiʕ] مُراجِعِين [mura:jiʕi:n] *pl:*

cliff • 1. جُرُف [juruf] جرُوف [jru:f] *pl:*

climate • 1. مَناخ [mana:x] The climate here is not suitable for planting coconut. هنا المَناخ ما يلائِم زَرِع جُوز الهند [hna: ʔilmana:x ma: yla:ʔim zariʕ ju:z ʔilhind] • **2.** جَوّ [jaww] أجواء [ʔajwa:ʔ] *pl:* The political climate is favorable for his return to power. الجَوّ السِّياسِي يساعِد عَلَى رِجُوعَه لِلحُكُم [ʔijjaww ʔissiya:si ysa:ʕid ʕala riju:ʕah lilħukum]

climax • 1. ذَروَة [ðarwa] The climax of the excitement came when the president appeared on the balcony. ذَروَة الحَماس صار لَمّا الرَّئِيس ظِهَر بالبالكَون [ðarwat ʔilħama:s ṣa:r lamma ʔirraʔi:s ðihar bilbalku:n] • **2.** أوج [ʔawj] Islamic art reached a climax in the era of Haroun Al-Rashid. الفَنّ الإسلامِي وُصَل إلَى أوجَه بعَهَد هارُون الرَّشِيد [ʔilfann ʔilʔisla:mi wuṣal ʔila ʔawjah bʕahad ha:ru:n ʔirraši:d]

climb • 1. صَعدَة [ṣaʕda] You'll find the climb difficult. راح تشُوف الصَّعدَة صَعبَة [ra:ħ tšu:f ʔiṣṣaʕda ṣaʕba]

to climb • 1. صِعَد [ṣiʕad] صِعُود [ṣiʕu:d] *vn:* اِنصِعَد [ʔinṣiʕad] *p:* She can't climb the stairs anymore due to old age. ما تِقدَر تِصعَد الدَّرَب بَعَد مِن الكُبُر [ma: tigdar tiṣʕad ʔiddarab baʕad min ʔilkubur] They climb the date palms about five times a year. يِصعَدُون عَلَى النَّخَل حَوالِي خَمِس مَرّات بِالسَّنَة [yiṣʕadu:n ʕala ʔinnaxal ħawa:li xamis marra:t bissana] • **2.** تشَلبَه [tšalbah] تشِلبِه، شَلبَهَة [tšilbih, šalbaha] *vn: sv* a. The children enjoy climbing on the fence. الجِّهال يحِبُّون التِّشِلبِه عالمحَجَّر [ʔijjiha:l yħibbu:n ʔittišilbih ʕalmħajjar] • **3.** عَلَّى [ʕalla:] *sv* i. اِرتِفَع [ʔirtifaʕ] اِرتِفاع [ʔirtifa:ʕ] *vn: sv* i. The jet planes climb rapidly after take-off. الطَّيّارات الجَّتّ تعَلّي بسُرعَة بَعَد ما تطِير [ʔiṭṭiyya:ra:t ʔijjatt tʕalli bsurʕa baʕad ma: ṭṭi:r]

to climb down • 1. نِزَل [nizal] نِزُول [nizu:l] *vn:* اِنّزَل [ʔinnizal] *p:* The cat is afraid to climb down the tree. البَزُّونَة تخاف تِنزِل مِن الشَّجَرَة [ʔilbazzu:na txa:f tinzil min ʔiššajara]

to climb up • 1. صِعَد [ṣiʕad] صِعُود [ṣiʕu:d] *vn: sv* a. I climbed up on the rock first and then helped the rest of them up. صِعَدِت فُوق الصَّخرَة أوَّل وَساعَدِت الباقِين عالصَّعدَة [ṣiʕadit fu:g ʔiṣṣaxra ʔawwal wsa:ʕadit ʔilba:qi:n ʕaṣṣaʕda]

to cling • 1. كَلَّب [čallab] تَكلِيب [tačli:b] *vn: sv* i. The child is clinging to its mother. الجّاهِل مكَلِّب بأمَّه [ʔijja:hil mčallib bʔummah] • **2.** لِزَق [lizag] لَزِق [lazig] *vn:* اِنلِزَق [ʔinlizag] *p:* My shirt was clinging to my back with sweat. ثُوبِي كان لازِق عَلَى ظَهرِي مِن العَرَق [θawbi ča:n la:zig ʕala ðahri min ʔalʕarag]

clinic • 1. عِيادَة [ʕiya:da] عِيادات [ʕiya:da:t] *pl:* You can get a blood analysis at the clinic. تِقدَر تسَوِّي تَحلِيل دَمّ بالعِيادَة [tigdar tsawwi taħli:l damm bilʕiya:da] This hospital has an out-patient clinic. هَالمُستَشفَى بِيها عِيادَة خارِجِيَّة [halmustašfa bi:ha ʕiya:da xa:rijiyya]

clip • 1. دَنبُوس [danbu:s, dambu:s] دَنابِيس [dana:bi:s] *pl:* She put a golden clip on her dress. شَكّلَت دَنبُوس ذَهَب عَلَى نَفنُوفها [šakklat danbu:s ðahab ʕala nafnu:fha] • **2.** كلِبس [klips] كلِبسات [klipsa:t] *pl:* شِكّالَة [šikka:la] شِكّالات [šikka:la:t] *pl:* Please give me a box of paper clips. أَرجُوك إنطِينِي باكَيت كلِبس [ʔarju:k ʔinṭi:ni pa:ki:t klips] • **3.** مِشِط [mišiṭ] مشاط، مشُوطَة [mša:ṭ, mšu:ṭa] *pl:* Can you show me how to put the clip in the rifle? تِقدَر تراوِينِي شلُون أحُطّ المِشِط بِالبُندُقِيَّة؟ [tigdar tra:wi:ni šlu:n ʔaħuṭṭ ʔilmišiṭ bilbunduqiyya?]

to clip • 1. قَصّ [gaṣṣ] قَصّ [gaṣṣ] *vn:* اِنقَصّ [ʔingaṣṣ] *p:* Don't clip my hair too short. لا تقُصّ شَعَرِي كُلِّش قصَيِّر [la: tguṣṣ šaʕari kulliš gṣayyir] I clipped this article out of the magazine. قَصَّيت هالمَقالَة مِن المَجَلَّة [gaṣṣayt halmaqa:la min ʔilmajalla] • **2.** قَرطَف [garṭaf] قَرطَفَة [garṭafa] *vn:* تقَرطَف [tgarṭaf] *p:* The gardener clipped the hedges. البِستَنكِي قَرطَف السِّياج [ʔilbistanči garṭaf ʔissiya:j] • **3.** شَكَّل [šakkal] تَشكِيل [taški:l] *vn:* تشَكَّل [tšakkal] *p:* Clip these papers together. شَكِّل هَالأوراق سُوَة [šakkil halʔawra:q suwa]

clipping • 1. قصاصَة [gṣa:ṣa] He showed me some clippings from the local newspapers. راوانِي كَم قُصاصَة مِن الجَّرايِد المَحَلِّيَّة [ra:wa:ni čam quṣa:ṣa min ʔijjara:yid ʔilmaħaliyya]

cloak • 1. The sheikh's cloak is made of pure camel wool. العَبا مال الشَّيخ مِن وُبَر خالِص [ʔilʕaba: ma:l ʔiššsi:x min wubar xa:liṣ] • **2.** عَبايَة [ʕaba:ya] عَبايات [ʕaba:ya:t] *pl:* Only her face was visible in the cloak. بَسّ وُجهَها كان مبيَّن مِن العَبايَة [bass wuččha ča:n mbayyin min ʔilʕaba:ya]

to cloak • **1.** سِتَر [sitar] سَتِر [satir] *vn:* اِنسِتَر [ʔinsitar] *p:* He is using his social position to cloak his membership in the secret organization. دَيستِغِلّ مَركَزَه الاجتِماعِي حَتَّى يِستُر عُضويتَه بِالجَمعِيَّة السِّرِّيَّة [dayistiɣill markazah ʔilʔiǰtima:ʕi ħatta yistur ʕuðwi:tah biǰǰamʕiyya ʔissirriyya]

clock • **1.** ساعَة [sa:ʕa] ساعات [sa:ʕa:t] *pl:* We set our clock by the radio. نُضبُط ساعَتنا عَالرّاديُو [nuḍbuṭ sa:ʕatna ʕarra:dyu]

to clock • **1.** لِزَم وَقِت، وَقَّت [lizam wakit, waqqat] لَزِم وَقِت، تَوقِيت [lazim wakit, tawqi:t] *vn: sv* a. وَقَّت [waqqat] تَوقِيت [tawqi:t] *vn:* توَقَّت [twaqqat] *p:* Will you clock me for the hundred-meter run? تِلزَملِي وَقِت الرِّكض المِيَة مَتِر؟ [tilzamli wakit ʔirrikḍ ilmyat matir?] Clock the workers and see how much work they put out a day. وَقِّت هالعُمّال وشُوف شقَدّ يطَلّعُون شُغُل باليُوم [waqqit halʕumma:l wšu:f šgadd yṭalliʕu:n šuɣul bilyu:m]

to clog • **1.** سَدّ [sadd] سَدّ [sadd] *vn:* اِنسَدّ [ʔinsadd] *p:* The pipes are clogged. البواري مَسدُودَة [ʔilbwa:ri masdu:da] • **2.** سَدسَد [sadsad] تسِدسِد [tsidsid] *vn:* تسَدسَد [tsadsad] *p:* The holes in the strainer are clogged up. عُيُون المَصفِي مسَدسِدَة [ʕuyu:n ʔilmaṣfi msadsida]

clogs • **1.** قُبقاب [qubqa:b] قَباقِيب، قباقِب [qaba:qi:b, qba:qib] *pl:* She wears clogs instead of sandals. تِلبَس قُبقاب بَدَل النَّعال [tilbas qubqa:b badal ʔinnaʕa:l]

close • **1.** حَمِيم [ħami:m] حَمِيمِين [ħami:mi:n] *pl:* We are close friends. إحنا أَصدِقاء حَمِيمِين [ʔiħna ʔaṣdiqa:ʔ ħami:mi:n] • **2.** قِرِيب، قَرِيب [giri:b, qiri:b, gari:b, qari:b] قَرِيب [qari:b, gari:b] The hotel is close to the station. الأُوتَيل قَرِيب مِن المَحَطَّة [ʔalʔuti:l qari:b min ʔilmaħaṭṭa] This is close to what I had in mind. هَذا قَرِيب مِن الشِّي الكان بِبالِي [ha:ða qari:b min ʔišši ʔilča:n bba:li] He is one of my closest friends. هُوَّ مِن أَقرَب أَصدِقائِي [huwwa min ʔaqrab ʔaṣdiqa:ʔi] The car drove up very close. السَّيّارَة وُقفَت كُلِّش قَرِيب [ʔissayya:ra wugfat kulliš qari:b] • **3.** يَمّ [yamm] We sat close together. قِعَدنا واحِد يَمّ اللّاخ [giʕadna wa:ħid yamm ʔilla:x] • **4.** قُرُب [qurub, gurub] We use to live close to each other. كِنّا نِسكُن قُرُب بَعَضنا [činna niskun qurub baʕaðna] • **5.** مَحصُور [maħṣu:r] وَخِم [waxim] The air is very close in this room. الهَوا كُلِّش مَحصُور بِهالقُبَّة [ʔilhawa kulliš maħṣu:r bhalgubba] • **6.** زين [zi:n, zayn] Pay close attention. دِير بالَك زين [di:r ba:lak zi:n] • **7.** ضَئِيل [ða?i:l] He won the election by a close margin of the vote. رِبَح الانتِخاب بِفَرِق ضَئِيل بِالأَصوات [ribaħ ʔilʔintixa:b bfariq ðaʔi:l bilʔaṣwa:t] • **8.** دَقِيق [daqi:q] This problem needs close study. هَالمُشكِلَة تِحتاج دِراسَة دَقِيقَة [halmuškila tiħta:ǰ dira:sa daqi:qa] • **9.** ناعِم [na:ʕim] The barber gave me a close shave this morning. المِزَيِّن زَيَّنلِي وُجهِي ناعِم اليُوم الصُّبُح [ʔilmzayyin zayyanli wuččii na:ʕim ʔilyu:m ʔiṣṣubuħ]

* **He had a close call.** • **1.** خِلَص بِإعجُوبَة [xilaṣ biʕǰu:ba]

close by • **1.** بقُرُب [bqurub] Is there a restaurant close by? أَكُو مَطعَم بِهالقُرُب؟ [ʔaku maṭʕam bhalqurub?]

close • **1.** نِهايَة [niha:ya] نِهايات [niha:ya:t] *pl:* آخِر [ʔa:xir] أَواخِر [ʔawa:xir] *pl:* I'll see you at the close of the meeting. أَشُوفَك بِنِهايَة الاِجتِماع [ʔašu:fak bniha:yt ʔilʔiǰtima:ʕ]

to close • **1.** سَدّ [sadd] سَدّ [sadd] *vn:* اِنسَدّ [ʔinsadd] *p:* Please close the door. مِن فَضلَك، سِدّ الباب [min faðlak, sidd ʔilba:b] The museum is closed Sundays. المَتحَف يِنسَدّ أَيّام الأَحَّد [ʔilmatħaf yinsadd ʔayya:m ʔilʔaħħad] • **2.** غِلَق [ɣilaq, ɣilag] غَلِق [ɣalig] *vn:* اِنغِلَق [ʔinɣilag] *p: sv* u. سَدّ [sadd] سَدّ [sadd] *vn:* اِنسَدّ [ʔinsadd] *p:* The road is closed. الطَّرِيق مَغلُوق [ʔiṭṭari:q maɣlu:q] • **3.** عَزَّل [ʕazzal] تَعزِيل [taʕzi:l] *vn:* تعَزَّل [tʕazzal] *p:* They close at six. يعَزّلُون بالسِّتَّة [yʕazzlu:n bissitta] • **4.** خِتَم [xitam] خِتام [xita:m] *vn:* اِنخِتَم [ʔinxitam] *p:* They closed the program with the national anthem. خِتمَوا المَنهَج بالنَّشِيد الوَطَني [xitmaw ʔilmanhaǰ binnaši:d ʔilwaṭani] • **5.** غَمَّض [ɣammað] تغُمُّض [tɣummuð] *vn:* تغَمَّض [tɣammað] *p:* Close your eyes and go to sleep! غَمَّض عُيُونَك ونام [gammuð ʕuyu:nak wna:m]

to close one's eyes • **1.** تعامَى [tʕa:ma:] تَعامِي [taʕa:mi] *vn: sv* a. Don't close your eyes to the facts. لا تِتعامَى عَن الحَقايِق [la: titʕa:ma: ʕann ʔilħaqa:yiq]

closely • **1.** بدِقَّة [bdiqqa] Look at it closely. باوُعها بدِقَّة [ba:wuʕha bdiqqa]

closet • **1.** دِيلاب [di:la:b] دوالِيب [dwa:li:b] *pl:* خزانَة [xza:na] خزانات، خزايِن [xza:na:t, xza:yin] *pl:* Her closet is full of new clothes. دِيلابها مَترُوس هدُوم جِدِيدَة [di:la:bha matru:s hidu:m ǰidi:da]

close up • **1.** صُورَة مُقَرَّبَة [ṣu:ra muqarraba] صُوَر مُقَرَّبَة [ṣuwar muqarraba] *pl:* Have you seen the close-ups we took of the baby. شِفت الصُّوَر المُقَرَّبَة اللِّي أَخَذناها لِلجّاهِل [šift ʔiṣṣuwar ʔilmuqarraba ʔilli ʔaxaðna:ha liǰǰa:hil] • **2.** مِن قِرِيب [min giri:b] عَن قُرُب [ʕan qurub] From close up it looks different. مِن قَرِيب تبَيِّن غير شِكِل [min qari:b tbayyin ɣi:r šikil]

cloth • **1.** قماش [qma:š] قماشات، أَقمِشَة [qma:ša:t, ʔaqmiša] *pl:* In the cloth market you find cloth for dresses, shirts, and pajamas. بِسُوق القماشات تِلقِي قماش مال نَفانِيف، وثياب، وَبِيجامات [bsu:g ʔilqma:ša:t tilgi qma:š ma:l nafa:ni:f, wθya:b, wbiːǰaːmaːt] The book has a cloth binding. غلاف الكِتاب مِن قماش [ɣilaːf ʔilkitaːb min qmaːš] • **2.** خِرقَة [xirga] خِرَق [xirag] *pl:* Use a clean cloth for the dusting. إستَعمِل خِرقَة نظيفَة لِلتَّنظِيف [ʔistaʕmil xirga nđ̣iːfa littanđ̣iːf]

*** He made the story up out of whole cloth.** • **1.** خِلَق الحِكايَة مِن بَطنَه [xilaq ʔiliħčaːya min baṭnah] / خِلَق الحكايَة مِن جَوَّة القاع [xilaq ʔilħčaːya min ǰawwa ʔilgaːʕ]

to clothe • **1.** كِسَى [kisaː] إكساء [ʔiksaːʔ] *vn:* إنكِسَى [ʔinkisaː] *p:* The Red Crescent feeds and clothes the poor from its funds. الهِلال الأحمَر يطعِم وَيكسِي الفُقَراء مِن مَوارِدَه [ʔilhilaːl ʔilʔaħmar yiṭʕum wyiksi ʔilfuqaraːʔ min mawaːrdah]

clothes • **1.** هدُوم [hduːm] مَلابِس [malaːbis] I want these clothes cleaned and pressed. أرِيد هالهدُوم تِتنَظَّف وَتِنضُرُب أُوتي [ʔariːd halhduːm titnađ̣đ̣af wtinđ̣urub ʔuːti]

clothes hanger • **1.** تِعلاقَة [tiʕlaːga] تِعلاقات [tiʕlaːgaːt] *pl:*

clothes hook • **1.** عِلّاقَة [ʕillaːga] عِلّاقات، علالِيق [ʕillaːgaːt, ʕilaːliːg] *pl:* We need a few more clothes hooks to hang up the clothes. نِحتاج بَعَد فَدّ كَم عِلّاقَة لِتَعلِيق الهدُوم [niħtaːǰ baʕad fadd čam ʕillaːga litaʕliːg ʔilhduːm]

clothesline • **1.** حَبِل شَرّ الهدُوم [ħabil šarr ʔilhduːm] حبال شَرّ الهدُوم [ħbaːl šarr ʔilhduːm] *pl:*

clothespin • **1.** قِرّاصَة [qirraːṣa] قِرّاصات [qirraːṣaːt] *pl:* What has become of the clothespins? شصار مِن القِرّاصات؟ [šṣaːr min ʔilqirraːṣaːt?]

clothes rack • **1.** شِمّاعَة [šimmaːʕa] شِمّاعات [šimmaːʕaːt] *pl:* There's a clothes rack in the hall. أكُو شَمّاعَة بالمَمَرّ [ʔaku šammaːʕa bilmamarr]

clothing • **1.** مَلابِس [malaːbis] هدُوم [hduːm]

cloud • **1.** غيمَة [ɣayma, ɣiːma] غيُوم [ɣyuːm] *pl:* غيم [ɣaym] *Collective:* The sun has disappeared behind the clouds. الشَّمِس إختِفَت وَرا الغيم [ʔiššamis ʔixtifat wara ʔilɣiːm]

*** He always has his head in the clouds.** • **1.** هٰذا دالغَجِي، هٰذا دَلّاغ [haːđa daːlɣači, haːđa dallaːɣ]

to cloud up • **1.** غَيَّم [ɣayyam] تَغييم [taɣyiːm] *vn: sv* i. Just after we started the sky clouded up. بَعَد ما بدَينا بشوَيَّة غَيمَت الدِّنيا [baʕad maː bdiːna bšwayya ɣayymat ʔiddinya]

cloudy • **1.** مغَيِّم [mɣayyim]

clover • **1.** بَرسِيم [barsiːm]

club • **1.** دُونكي [duːnki] دُونكيّات [duːnkiyyaːt] *pl:* The policeman had to use his club. الشُّرطِي إنجُبَر يِستَعمِل دُونكِيَّة [ʔiššurṭi ʔinǰubar yistaʕmil duːnkiyya] • **2.** مُغوار [muɣwaːr] مغاوِير [mɣaːwiːr] *pl:* كلُنق [klung] كلُنقات [klungaːt] *pl:* They fought with clubs and sickles. تعارکوا بالمِغاوِير وَالمَناجِل [tʕaːrkaw bilmigaːwiːr wilmanaːǰil] • **3.** نادِي [naːdi] نَوادِي [nawaːdi] *pl:* Are you a member of the club? إنتَ عُضو بِالنّادِي؟ [ʔinta ʕuđ̣w binnaːdi?] • **4.** سِنَك [sinak] I played the ace of clubs. ذَبَّيت بِلّي السِّنَك [đabbiːt ʔissinak]

to club • **1.** ضِرَب بالمِغوار [đ̣irab] ضَرُب [đ̣irab bilmigwaːr] *vn:* إنضِرَب [ʔinđ̣irab] *p:* The man was clubbed. الرِّجّال إنضِرَب بالمِغوار [ʔirriǰǰaːl ʔinđ̣irab bilmigwaːr]

clue • **1.** إشارَة [ʔišaːra] إشارات [ʔišaːraːt] *pl:* Can you give me a clue? تِقدَر تنطِينِي فَدّ إشارَة؟ [tigdar tinṭiːni fadd ʔišaːra?] • **2.** دَلِيل [daliːl] أدِلَّة [ʔadilla] *pl:* The police found no clues. الشُّرطَة ما لِقَوا أيّ دَلِيل [ʔiššurṭa maː ligaw ʔayy daliːl]

clumsy • **1.** مخَربَط [mxarbaṭ] That's a clumsy sentence. هٰذِي جُملَة مخَربُطَة [haːđi ǰumla mxarbuṭa] • **2.** ثِقِيل [θigiːl] He's as clumsy as a bear. هُوَّ ثِقِيل مِثِل الدُّبّ [huwwa θigiːl miθil ʔiddubb]

clutch • **1.** كلَچ [klač] كلَچات [klačaːt] *pl:* Push in the clutch. دُوس عالكلَچ [duːs ʕalklač] • **2.** قَبضَة [qabđ̣a] قَبضات [qabđ̣aːt] *pl:* He fell into the clutches of some gangsters. وُقَع بقَبضَة كَم أشقِياء [wugaʕ bqabđ̣at čam ʔašqiyaːʔ]

*** He had him in his clutches.** • **1.** خَلّاه جَوَّة عباتَه [xallaːh ǰawwa ʕbaːṭah]

to clutch • **1.** عِصَر [ʕiṣar] عَصِر [ʕaṣir] *vn:* إنعِصَر [ʔinʕiṣar] *p: sv* i. كَلَّب ب [čallab b-] تكلِيب [tačliːb] *vn:* تكَلَّب [tčallab] *p: sv* i. The child clutched my hand. الطِّفِل عِصَر إيدِي [ʔiṭṭifil ʕiṣar ʔiːdi] • **2.** مَدّ [madd] مَدّ [madd] *vn:* إنمَدّ [ʔinmadd] *p:* He clutched at the rope but he wasn't able to get a hold of it. مَدّ إيدَه عالحَبِل لَكِن ما قِدَر يكُمشَه [madd ʔiːdah ʕalħabil laːkin maː gidar ykumšah]

coach • **1.** عَرَبانَة [ʕarabaːna] عَرَباين [ʕarabaːyin] *pl:* فَرقُون [farguːn] فَرقُونات، فَراقِين [farguːnaːt, faraːgiːn] *pl:* The train consists of the engine and four coaches. القِطار يتألَّف مِن مَكِينَة وأربَع فَرقُونات [ʔilqiṭaːr yitʔallaf min makiːna wʔarbaʕ farguːnaːt] • **2.** مُدَرِّب [mudarrib] He's the best coach in this school. هُوَّ أحسَن مُدَرِّب بهالمَدرَسَة [huwwa ʔaħsan mudarrib bhalmadrasa]

to coach • **1.** دَرَّب [darrab] تَدرِيب [tadriːb] *vn:* تدَرَّب [tdarrab] *p:* He coaches the soccer team. يدَرِّب فِرقَة كُرَة القَدَم [yidarrub firqat kurat ʔilqadam] • **2.** عَلَّم [ʕallam] تَعلِيم [taʕliːm] *vn:* تعَلَّم [tʕallam] *p:* Students in the back of the room began coaching him when he was asked a question. الطُّلّاب بأَخِر الغُرفَة بِدَوا يعَلّمُوه لَمّا اِنسِأل سُؤال [ʔiṭṭulla:b bʔa:xir ʔilɣurfa bidaw yʕallmu:h lamma ʔinsiʔil suʔa:l]

coal • **1.** فَحمَة [faħma] فَحمات [faħma:t] *pl:* فَحَم [faħam] *Collective:* We have to order coal. لازِم نُطلُب فَحَم [la:zim nuṭlub faħam]

coal bin • **1.** مَخزَن فَحَم [maxzan faħam] مَخازِن فَحَم [maxa:zin faħam] *pl:*

coarse • **1.** خَشِن [xašin] This material is very coarse. هَالقماش كُلِّش خَشِن [halqma:š kulliš xašin] He's a very coarse person. هُوَّ فَدّ واحِد كُلِّش خَشِن [huwwa fadd wa:ħid kulliš xašin]

coast • **1.** ساحِل [sa:ħil] سَواحِل [sawa:ħil] *pl:* We approached the coast at night. تقَرَّبنا مِن السّاحِل باللَّيل [tqarrabna min ʔissa:ħil billayl]

to coast • **1.** تدَهدَر [ddahdar] تدِهدِر [tdihdir] *vn: sv* a. We coasted for three hundred meters. تدَهدَرنا ثلاث مِيَّة مَتِر [ddahdarna tla:θ miyyat matir]

coast guard • **1.** خَفَر السَواحِل [xafar ʔissawa:ħil]

coat • **1.** قَبُّوط [qappu:ṭ, qabbu:ṭ] قَبُّوطات، قبابِيط [qappu:ṭa:t, qpa:pi:ṭ; qabbu:ṭa:t, qba:bi:ṭ] *pl:* مِعطَف [miʕṭaf] مَعاطِف [maʕa:ṭif] *pl:* You can't go out without a coat in this weather. ما تِقدَر تِطلَع بلَيّا قَبُّوط بهَالجَوّ [ma: tigdar tiṭlaʕ blayya qappu:ṭ bhalǰaww] • **2.** سِترَة [sitra] سِتَر [sitar] *pl:* The pants are fine but the coat's too tight. البَنطَرُون مَضبُوط لَكِن السِّترَة كُلِّش ضَيِّقَة [ʔilpanṭaru:n maðbu:ṭ la:kin ʔissitra kulliš ðayyga] • **3.** قاط [qa:ṭ] قُوط [qu:ṭ] *pl:* This house needs another coat of paint. هَالبَيت يِنرادلَه قاط صُبُغ ثانِي [halbayt yinra:dlah qa:ṭ ṣubuɣ θa:ni]

coated • **1.** مغَطَّى [mɣaṭṭa] The car was coated with mud. السَّيّارَة كانَت مغَطّايَة بالطِّين [ʔissayya:ra ča:nat mɣaṭṭa:ya biṭṭi:n]

coat hanger • **1.** تِعلاقَة [tiʕla:ga] تِعلاقات [tiʕla:ga:t] *pl:*

cobweb • **1.** عِشّ عَنكَبُوت [ʕišš ʕankabu:t] بَيت عَنكَبُوت [bayt ʕankabu:t] خيُوط عَنكَبُوت [xyu:ṭ ʕankabu:t]

cockroach • **1.** صُرصُر [ṣurṣur] صَراصِر [ṣara:ṣir] *pl:* بِنت مُردان [bint murda:n] بَنات مُردان [bana:t murda:n] *pl:*

cocktail • **1.** كُوكتِيل [ku:kti:l]

cocoa • **1.** كاكاو [ka:ka:w]

coconut • **1.** جَوز هِند [ǰawz hind] جَوزات هِند [ǰawzat hind] *pl:* جَوز هِند [ǰawz hind] *Collective*

code • **1.** رَمِز [ramiz] رُمُوز [rumu:z] *pl:* إشارَة [ʔiša:ra] إشارات [ʔiša:ra:t] *pl:* They sent the telegram in Morse code. دَزَّوا البَرقِيَّة بِرمُوز مُورس [dazzaw ʔilbarqiyya brumu:z mu:rs] • **2.** شَفرَة [šafra] شَفرات [šafra:t] *pl:* They tried to decipher the code. حاولَوا يفَسِّرُون الشَّفرَة [ħa:wlaw yfassiru:n ʔiššafra]

code of ethics • **1.** قَواعِد أَدَبِيَّة [qawa:ʕid ʔadabiyya]

code of Hammurabi • **1.** شَرِيعَة حَمُورابِي [šari:ʕat ħamu:ra:bi]

code of morals • **1.** قَواعِد أَخلاقِيَّة [qawa:ʕid ʔaxla:qiyya]

coffee • **1.** قَهوَة [gahwa] The coffee is freshly roasted. القَهوَة اِستَوها تحَمّصَت [ʔilgahwa ʔistawwha tħammṣat]

coffee pot • **1.** دَلَّة مال قَهوَة [dalla ma:l gahwa] دَلّات مال قَهوَة، دلال مال قَهوَة [dalla:t ma:l gahwa, dla:l ma:l gahwa] *pl:*

coffin • **1.** تابُوت [ta:bu:t] تَوابِيت [tawa:bi:t] *pl:*

cog • **1.** سِنّ [sinn] أسنان [ʔasna:n] *pl:* One of the cogs is broken off this gear. واحِد مِن سنُون هالدِّشلِي مَكسُور [wa:ħid min snu:n haddišli maksu:r]

cognac • **1.** كَونياك [ku:nya:k]

coil • **1.** لَفَّة [laffa] لَفّات [laffa:t] *pl:* You'll have to buy a coil of wire. لازِم تِشترِي لَفَّة وايَر [la:zim tištiri laffat wa:yar]

ignition coil • **1.** كُويل [ku:yil] كَويلات [ku:yla:t] *pl:*

to coil • **1.** اِلتَفّ [ʔiltaff] اِلتِفاف [ʔiltifa:f] *vn: sv* a. The snake coiled around the man's arm. الحَيَّة اِلتَفَّت حَول ذراع الرَّجّال [ʔilħayya ʔiltaffat ħawl ðra:ʕ ʔirraǰǰa:l]

to coil up • **1.** لَفّ [laff] لَفّ [laff] *vn:* اِنلَفّ [ʔinlaff] *p:* He coiled up the wire. لَفّ السِّيم [laff ʔissi:m]

coin • **1.** عُملَة [ʕumla] عُملات [ʕumla:t] *pl:* He collects old gold coins. يجَمِّع عُملَة ذَهَبِيَّة قَدِيمَة [yǰammiʕ ʕumla ðahabiyya qadi:ma]

to coin • **1.** ضِرَب [ðirab] ضَرُب [ðarub] *vn:* اِنضُرَب [ʔinðurab] *p:* This money was coined in Belgium. هالعُملَة اِنضُربَت بِبَلجِيكا [halʕumla ʔinðurbat bibalǰi:ka] • **2.** خِلَق [xilaq] خَلِق [xaliq] *vn:* اِنخِلَق [ʔinxilaq] *p:* Scientists are coining new words every day. العُلَماء دَيخِلقُون كَلِمات جِدِيدَة كُلّ يوم [ʔilʕulama:ʔ dayxilqu:n kalima:t ǰidi:da kull yu:m]

coincidence • **1.** صُدفَة [ṣudfa, ṣidfa] صُدَف [ṣudaf] *pl:* What a strange coincidence! شلُون صُدفَة غَرِيبَة [šlu:n ṣudfa ɣari:ba]

coke • **1.** فَحَم الكُوك [faħam ʔilku:k] We use coke for heating. نِستَعمِل فَحَم الكُوك لِلتَّدفِئَة [nistaʕmil faħam ʔilku:k littadfiʔa]

C

cold • **1.** بَرِد [barid] I can't stand this cold. ما أَقدَر أَتحَمَّل هَالبَرِد [maː ʔagdar ʔatħammal halbarid] • **2.** بَردان [bardaːn] I'm cold. آنِي بَردان [ʔaːni bardaːn] • **3.** بَرِد [barid] نَشلَة [našla] نَشلات [našlaːt] *pl:* زُكام [zukaːm] He has a bad cold. عِندَه نَشلَة قَوِيَّة [ʕindah našla qawiyya] • **4.** بارِد [baːrid] It was a cold night. كانَت لَيلَة بارِدَة [čaːnat layla baːrda]

*** The blow knocked him cold.** • **1.** الضَربَة أَفقِدَت شُعُورَه [ʔiððarba ʔafqidat šuʕuːrah]

to collaborate • **1.** تعاوَن [tʕaːwan] تَعاوُن [taʕaːwun] *vn: sv* a. She collaborated with the enemy. تعاونَت ويّا العَدُو [tʕaːwnat wiyya ʔilʕadu] • **2.** اِشتِرَك [ʔištirak] اِشتِراك [ʔištiraːk] *vn: sv* i. تعاوَن [tʕaːwan] تَعاوُن [taʕaːwun] *vn: sv* a. Two teams of scientists collaborated in the experiment. فِرقتَين مِن العُلَماء اِشتِرِكَت بعَمَل التَّجرُبَة [firiqtayn min ʔilʕulamaːʔ ʔištirkat bʕamal ʔittajruba]

to collapse • **1.** اِنهار [ʔinhaːr] اِنهيار [ʔinhiyaːr] *vn: sv* a. اِنهِدَم [ʔinhidam] اِنهِدام [ʔinhidaːm] *vn: sv* i. تدَهوَر [ddahwar] تَدَهوُر [tadahwur] *vn: sv* a. The bridge suddenly collapsed. الجِّسِر اِنهار عَلَى غَفلَة [ʔijjisir ʔinhaːr ʕala ɣafla] • **2.** وُقَع [wugaʕ] وقُوع [wquːʕ] *vn: sv* a. خِرَب [xirab] *sv* a. He collapsed in the middle of the street. وُقَع بِنُصّ الجّادَّة [wugaʕ bnuṣṣ ʔijjaːdda]

collar • **1.** ياخَة [yaːxa] ياخات [yaːxaːt] *pl:* Do you want your collars starched or not? تريد ياخاتَك مِنَشّايَة لَو لا؟ [triːd yaːxaːtak mnaššaːya law laː?]

collar bone • **1.** عَظم التَّرقُوَة [ʕaðm ʔitturquwa] عظام التَّرقُوَة [ʕðaːm ʔitturquwa] *pl:*

to collect • **1.** جِمَع [jimaʕ] جَمِع [jamiʕ] *vn:* اِنجِمَع [ʔinjimaʕ] *p:* جَمَّع [jammaʕ] تَجمِيع [tajmiːʕ] *vn:* تجَمَّع [tjammaʕ] *p:* لَمّ [lamm] لَمّ [lamm] *vn:* اِنلَمّ [ʔinlamm] *p:* I collect stamps. أَجَمِّع طَوابِع [ʔajammiʕ ṭawaːbiʕ] Give me a chance to collect my thoughts. إنطِينِي مَجال أَجمَع فِكرِي [ʔinṭiːni majaːl ʔajmaʕ fikri] • **2.** اِلتَمّ [ʔiltamm] اِلتِمام [ʔiltimaːm] *vn: sv* a. People collected in the square. النّاس اِلتَمّوا بِالسّاحَة [ʔinnaːs ʔiltammaw bissaːħa]

collected • **1.** ضابُط الأَعصاب [ðaːbuṭ ʔilʔaʕṣaːb] In spite of the danger, he remained calm and collected. بِرَغم الخَطَر، بُقَى هادِئ وَضابُط أَعصابَه [braɣm ʔilxaṭar, buqaː haːdiʔ wðaːbuṭ ʔaʕṣaːbah] • **2.** مَجمُوع [majmuːʕ] I bought the collected works of Taha Hussein. اِشتِرَيت المُؤَلَّفات المَجمُوعَة لِطَه حسَين [ʔištiriːt ʔilmuʔallafaːt ʔilmajmuːʕa liṭaha ħsiːn]

collection • **1.** مَجمُوعَة [majmuːʕa] مَجمُوعات [majmuːʕaːt] *pl:* مَجامِيع [majaːmiːʕ] The library has a famous collection of books on America. المَكتَبَة بِيها مَجمُوعَة مَشهُورَة مِن الكُتُب عَن أَمرِيكا [ʔilmaktaba biːha majmuːʕa mašhuːra min ʔilkutub ʕan ʔamriːka]

*** What time is the last mail collection?** • **1.** شوَقِت آخِر مَرَّة يِنلَمّ البَرِيد؟ [šwakit ʔaːxir marra yinlamm ʔilbariːd?]

*** They took up a collection for the beggar.** • **1.** جِمعَوا فلُوس لِلفَقِير [jimʕaw fluːs lilfaqiːr]

college • **1.** كُلِّيَّة [kulliyya] كُلِّيّات [kulliyyaːt] *pl:*

to collide • **1.** اِصطِدَم [ʔiṣṭidam] اِصطِدام [ʔiṣṭidaːm] *vn: sv* i. تصادَم [tṣaːdam] تَصادُم [taṣaːdum] *vn: sv* a. The cars collided at the intersection. السَّيّارات تصادمَت بِمَفرَق الطَّرِيق [ʔissayyaːraːt tṣaːdmat bmafraq ʔiṭṭariːq]

collision • **1.** تَصادُم [taṣaːdum] تَصادُمات [taṣaːdumaːt] *pl:* اِصطِدام [ʔiṣṭidaːm]

colloquial • **1.** عامِّي [ʕaːmmi] عَوامّ [ʕawaːmm] *pl:* جِلفِي [jilfi] How do I say this in the colloquial language? شلُون أَقُول هاي بِاللُّغَة العامِّيَّة؟ [šluːn ʔaguːl haːy billuɣa ʔilʕaːmmiyya?]

cologne • **1.** رِيحَة [riːħa] رَوائِح، رَوايِح، رِيَّح [rawaːʔiħ, rawaːyiħ, riyyaħ] *pl:* قَلُونيَة [qaluːnya]

colon • **1.** Use a comma instead of a colon. اِستَعمِل فارِزَة بَدَل نُقُطتَين [ʔistaʕmil faːriza badal nuqutiːn] • **2.** كُولُون [kuluːn] كُولُونات [kuluːnaːt] *pl:* Your colon is in an inflammed condition. الكُولُون مالَك مِلتِهِب [ʔilkuluːn maːlak miltihib]

colonel • **1.** عَقِيد [ʕaqiːd] عُقَداء [ʕuqadaːʔ] *pl:*

to colonize • **1.** اِستَعمَر [ʔistaʕmar] اِستِعمار [ʔistiʕmaːr] *vn: sv* i. They colonized the island. اِستَعمِرَوا الجَّزِيرَة [ʔistaʕmiraw ʔijjaziːra]

colony • **1.** مُستَعمَرَة [mustaʕmara] مُستَعمَرات [mustaʕmaraːt] *pl:* We were a colony until two years ago. كِنّا مُستَعمَرَة إِلَى قَبُل سَنتَين [činna mustaʕmara ʔila gabul santayn] There's a colony of ants in our back yard. أَكُو مُستَعمَرَة نَمِل بِحَدِيقَتنا [ʔaku mustaʕmarat namil bħadiːqatna] • **2.** جالِيَة [jaːliya] جالِيّات [jaːliyaːt] *pl:* The majority of the American colony lives in this district. أَكثَرِيَّة الجّالِيَة الأَمِيرِكِيَّة تُسكُن بِهالمَنطِقَة [ʔakθariyyat ʔijjaːliya ʔilʔamriːkiyya tuskun bhalmanṭiqa]

color • **1.** لَون [lawn, luːn] أَلوان [ʔalwaːn] *pl:* I don't like any of these colors. ما أَحِبّ أَيّ لُون مِن هَالأَلوان [maː ʔaħibb ʔayy luːn min halʔalwaːn] The team wore its school colors. الفَرِيق لِبَس لُون مَدرَستَه [ʔilfariːq libas luːn madrastah]

to color • **1.** لَوَّن [lawwan] تَلوِين [talwiːn] *vn:* تلَوَّن [tlawwan] *p:* She colored some pictures. لَوِّنَت كَم صُورَة [lawwinat čam ṣuːra]

colored • **1.** مْلَوَّن [mulawwan] Several colored families live near here. عِدَّة عَوائِل مِن المُلَوَّنِين تِعِيش قَرِيب مِن هنا [Ꜥiddat Ꜥawa:ʔil min ʔilmulawwini:n tꜤi:š qari:b min hna] Do you have any colored handkerchiefs? عِندَك أَيّ كفافِي مِلَوَّنَة؟ [Ꜥindak ʔayy čfa:fi mlawwna?] • **2.** مَصبُوغ [maṣbu:ɣ] مَصبُوغات [maṣbuwɣa:t] *pl:* His ideas are colored by Communism. آرائَه مَصبُوغَة بِالشُّيُوعِيَّة [ʔa:ra:ʔah maṣbu:ɣa biššuyu:Ꜥiyya]

color-blindness • **1.** عَمَى أَلوان [Ꜥama: ʔalwa:n]

colt • **1.** مُهُر [muhur] مهُور، مهار [mhu:r, mha:r] *pl:*

column • **1.** عَمُود [Ꜥamu:d] أَعمِدَة، عَوَامِيد [ʔaꜤmida, Ꜥawa:mi:d] *pl:* مغَبِّش [mɣabbiš] You can recognize the house by its white columns. تِقدَر تُعرُف البَيت مِن العَوامِيد البِيض اللِّي بِيه [tigdar tuꜤruf ʔilbayt min ʔilꜤawa:mi:d ʔilbi:ð ʔilli bi:h] Write your name in the right-hand column. إكتِب إسمَك بالعَمُود اللّي عاليِمنَى [ʔiktib ʔismak bilꜤamu:d ʔilli Ꜥalyimna] • **2.** طابُور [ṭa:bu:r] طوابِير [ṭwa:bi:r] *pl:* رَتِل [ratil] أَرتال [ʔarta:l] *pl:* Four columns of soldiers marched down the road. أَربَع أَرتال مِن الجِّنُود مِشَت بِالشّارِع [ʔarbaꜤ ʔarta:l min ʔijjinu:d mišat bišša:riꜤ] I believe she's a member of the fifth column. أَعتِقِد هِيَّ مِن الرَّتل الخامِس [ʔaꜤtiqid hiyya min ʔirratl ʔilxa:mis]

comb • **1.** مِشِط [mišiṭ] مشاط، مشُوطَة [mša:ṭ, mšu:ṭa] *pl:* Where can I buy a comb? منين أَقدَر أَشتِري مِشِط؟ [mni:n ʔagdar ʔaštiri mišiṭ?] • **2.** خَلِيَّة [xaliyya] خَلايا [xala:ya] *pl:* The comb is full of honey. الخَلِيَّة مَليانَة عَسَل [ʔilxaliyya malya:na Ꜥasal]

to comb • **1.** مَشَّط [maššaṭ] تَمشِيط، تمِشِّط [tamši:ṭ, tmiššiṭ] *vn:* تمَشَّط [tmaššaṭ] *p:* Did your mother comb your hair? أُمَّك مَشِّطَت شَعرَك؟ [ʔummak maššiṭat šaꜤrak?] The police combed the whole city. الشُّرطَة مَشّطُوها لِلوِلايَة كُلّها [ʔiššurṭa maššṭu:ha lilwila:ya kullha]

combination • **1.** جَمِع [jamiꜤ] How do you like the combination of red and gray? شلُون يِعجبَك الجَّمِع بين الأَحمَر وَالرَّمادِي؟ [šlu:n yiꜤijbak ʔijjamiꜤ bi:n ʔilʔaħmar wirrama:di?]

*** We are the only ones who know the combination to the safe.** • **1.** إحنا الوَحِيدِين اللِي نُعرُف تَرتِيب رُمُوز فَتح القاصَة [ʔiħna ʔilwaħi:di:n ʔilli nuꜤruf tarti:b rumu:z fatħ ʔilqa:ṣa]

to come • **1.** جا [ja:] مَجِيئ [maji:ʔ] *vn: sv* i. When does he come to town? شوَقِت يِجِي لِلوِلايَة؟ [šwakit yiji lilwila:ya?] Joking comes natural to him. التَّنكِيت يِجِي بِصُورَة طَبِيعِيَّة [ʔittanki:t yiji bṣu:ra ṭabi:Ꜥiyya] This cloth comes only in two colors. هَالقُماش ما يِجِي غير بِلُونَين [halquma:š ma: yiji ɣi:r blawnayn] • **2.** صادَف [ṣa:daf] مُصادَفَة [muṣa:dafa] *vn: sv* i. تصادَف [tṣa:daf] تَصادُف [taṣa:duf] *vn: sv* a. My birthday comes on a Monday this year. عِيد مِيلادِي يصادِف هالسَّنَة يوم الإثنين [Ꜥi:d mi:la:di yṣa:dif hassana yu:m ʔilʔiθnayn] • **3.** تَعال [taꜤa:l] Come here a minute, Nizar. تَعال فَدّ دَقِيقَة، نَزار [taꜤa:l fadd daqi:qa, naza:r] Hey boys, come over here! يا أَولاد، تَعالُوا [ya: ʔawla:d, taꜤa:lu:]

*** I don't know whether I'm coming or going.** • **1.** ما دَأعرُف شداَسَوِّي [ma: daʔaꜤruf šdaʔasawwi]

*** Come now, I'm not that foolish.** • **1.** بَسّ عاد، آني مُو لِهَالدَّرَجَة غَبِي [bass Ꜥa:d, ʔa:ni mu: lhaddaraja ɣabi]

to come about • **1.** جِرَى [jira:] مَجرَى [majra] *vn: sv* i. صار [ṣa:r] صَير [ṣi:r] *vn: sv* i. How did all this come about? شلُون جِرَى هَذا كُلَّه؟ [šlu:n jira: ha:ða kullah?]

to come across • **1.** عُبَر [Ꜥubar] عَبُر [Ꜥabur] *vn:* اِنعُبَر [ʔinꜤubar] *p:* He had to come across the bridge to visit us. اِضطَرّ يُعبُر الجِّسِر حَتَّى يزُورنا [ʔiðṭarr yuꜤbur ʔijjisir ħatta yzu:rna] • **2.** لِقَى [liga:] لِقي [lagi] *vn:* اِنلِقَى [ʔinliga:] *p:* I accidentally came across my friend's name in this book. لقَيت إسِم صَدِيقِي بِهَالِكتاب بِالصِّدفَة [lgi:t ʔisim ṣadi:qi bhalʔikta:b biṣṣidfa]

*** He's the wisest man I've ever come across.** • **1.** هُوَّ أَعقَل شَخِص شِفتَه [huwwa ʔaꜤqal šaxiṣ šiftah]

to come after (or for) • **1.** جا عَلَى [ja: Ꜥala] مَجِيئ [maji:ʔ] *vn: sv* i. I've come after my passport. جِيت عَلَى باسبَورتِي [ji:t Ꜥala pa:spu:rti]

to come along • **1.** مِشَى [miša:] مَشِي [mašy] *vn: sv* i. How's your work coming along? شلُون دَيِمشِي شُغلَك؟ [šlu:n dayimši šuɣlak?]

to come apart • **1.** تفَسَّخ [tfassax] تَفَسُّخ [tafassux] *vn: sv* a. تفَلَّش [tfallaš] تفِلِّش [tfilliš] *vn: sv* a. This chair is coming apart. هَالكُرسِي دَيِتفَسَّخ [halkursi dayitfassax]

to come around • **1.** عاوَد [Ꜥa:wad] مُعاوَدَة [muꜤa:wada] *vn: sv* i. The beggar comes around to us every Friday. المِجَدِّي يعاوِدنا كُلّ يوم جُمعَة [ʔilimgaddi yꜤa:widna kull yu:m jumꜤa]

to come back • **1.** رِجَع [rijaꜤ] رُجُوع [ruju:Ꜥ] *vn: sv* a. They're coming back tomorrow. يِرجَعُون باكِر [yirjaꜤu:n ba:čir]

to come by • **1.** مَرّ مِن [marr min] مُرُور مِن [muru:r min] *vn: sv* u. He's coming by here this afternoon. راح يمُرّ مِن هنَا اليُوم العَصِر [ra:ħ ymurr minna ʔilyu:m ʔilꜤaṣir] • **2.** دَبَّر [dabbar] تَدبِير [tadbi:r] *vn:* تدَبَّر [tdabbar] *p:* How did he come by all that money? شلُون دَبَّر كُلّ هَالفلُوس؟ [šlu:n dabbar kull halfilu:s?]

to come down • **1.** نِزَل [nizal] نُزُول [nuzu:l] *vn: sv* i. Can you come down a moment? تِقدَر تِنزِل فَدّ لَحظَة؟ [tigdar tinzil fadd laħða?] • **2.** خَفَّض [xaffað] تَخفِيض، تخُفُّض [taxfi:ð, txuffuð] *vn:* تخَفَّض [txaffað] *p:* نَزَّل [nazzal] تَنزِيل، تنِزِّل [tanzi:l, tnizzil] *vn:* تنَزَّل [tnazzal] *p:* We can't come down a bit on this price. ما نِقدَر نخَفُّض هَالسِّعِر وَلا فِلِس [ma: nigdar nxaffuð hassiꜤir wala filis] • **3.** اِنصاب [ʔinṣa:b] إصابَة [ʔiṣa:ba] *vn: sv* a. He came down with a bad cold. اِنصاب بِفَدّ نَشلَة قَوِيَّة [ʔinṣa:b bfadd našla qawiyya]

to come in • **1.** دِخَل [dixal] دُخُول [duxu:l] *vn: sv* u. خَشّ [xašš] خَشّ [xašš] *vn: sv* u. Please come in. أَرجُوك أُدخُل

[ʔarju:k ʔadxul] Please come in. رَجاءاً خُشّ [raja:ʔan xušš] • **2.** وُصَل [wuṣal] وُصُول [wuṣu:l] *vn: sv* a. What time does the train come in? شوَقِت يُوصَل القِطار؟ [šwakit yu:ṣal ʔilqiṭa:r?] • **3.** جا [ja:] مَجِيئ [maji:ʔ] *vn: sv* i. Requests for help are coming in daily. طَلَبات المُساعَدَة دَتِجِي يَومِيّاً [ṭalaba:t ʔilmusa:ʕada datiji yawmiyyan]

to come in handy • **1.** فاد [fa:d] فائِدَة [fa:ʔida] *vn: sv* i. نِفَع [nifaʕ] نَفع [nafiʕ] *vn: sv* a. It'll come in very handy to you later. راح تفِيدَك بَعدين [ra:ħ tfi:dak baʕdi:n]

to come off • **1.** اِنشِلَع [ʔinšilaʕ] *sv* i. One leg of the table has come off. وِحدَة مِن رِجلَين المِيز اِنشِلعَت [wiħda min rijlayn ʔilmi:z ʔinšilʕat] • **2.** اِنقِطَع [ʔinqiṭaʕ, ʔingiṭaʕ] اِنقِطاع [ʔinqiṭa:ʕ, ʔingiṭa:ʕ] *vn: sv* i. The button has come off. الدُّقمَة اِنقِطعَت [ʔiddugma ʔingiṭʕat] • **3.** قام [ga:m] قَوم [gu:m] *vn: sv* u. اِنحَكّ [ʔinħakk] *sv* a. The color comes off these gloves. الصُّبُغ دَيقُوم مِن هَالكِفُوف [ʔiṣṣubuɣ daygu:m min halčifu:f] • **4.** طِلَع [ṭilaʕ] The play came off real well. التَّمثِيلِيَّة طِلعَت زينَة [ʔittamθi:liyya ṭilʕat zi:na]

to come out • **1.** طِلَع [ṭilaʕ] طُلُوع [ṭulu:ʕ] *vn: sv* a. Are you going to come out to the farm with us? راح تِطلَع ويّانا لِلمَزرَعَة؟ [ra:ħ tiṭlaʕ wiyya:na lilmazraʕa?] The ink spot won't come out of this shirt. بُقعَة الحِبِر ما تِطلَع مِن هَالثُّوب [buqʕat ʔilħibir ma: tiṭlaʕ min haθθu:b] Who came out on top in the fight? مِنُو طِلَع غالُب بِالمُلاكَمَة؟ [minu ṭilaʕ ɣa:lub bilmula:kama?] Who came out on top in the fight? مِنُو غِلَب بِالمُلاكَمَة؟ [minu ɣilab bilmula:kama?] Who came out on top in the fight? مِنُو فاز بِالمُلاكَمَة؟ [minu fa:z bilmula:kama?] • **2.** ظِهَر [ðihar] ظُهُور [ðuhu:r] *vn: sv* a. إِجَى [ʔija:] مَجِيئ [maji:ʔ] *vn: sv* i. طِلَع [ṭilaʕ] طُلُوع [ṭulu:ʕ] *vn: sv* a. Their product came out on the market a month ago. مَنتُوجهُم ظِهَر بالسُّوق قَبُل شَهَر [mantu:jhum ðihar bissu:g gabul šahar] • **3.** بَيَّن [bayyan] تبِيِّن [tbiyyin] *vn:* تبَيَّن [tbayyan] *p:* The truth finally came out. الحَقِيقَة بَيِّنَت بالتّالي [ʔilħaqi:qa bayyinat bitta:li] • **4.** ظِهَر [ðihar] ظُهُور [ðuhu:r] *vn: sv* a. بَيَّن [bayyan] تبِيِّن [tbiyyin] *vn: sv* i. The president came out in favor of high taxes. الرَّئِيس ظِهَر يفَضِّل الضَّرائِب العالِيَة [ʔirraʔi:s ðihar yfaððil ʔiððara:ʔib ʔilʕa:lya]

to come over • **1.** إِجَى [ʔija:] مَجِيئ [maji:ʔ] *vn: sv* i. Some friends are coming over to see us this evening. بَعض الأَصدِقاء راح يجُون عِدنا هاللَّيلَة [baʕð ʔilʔaṣdiqa:ʔ ra:ħ yju:n ʕidna hallayla] • **2.** صِعَد [ṣiʕad] صُعُود [ṣuʕu:d] *vn: sv* a. فاض [fa:ð] فَيض [fayð] *vn: sv* i. The water's starting to come over the curb. المَيّ بدا يِصعَد عَلَى حافَّة الرَّصِيف [ʔilmayy bida: yiṣʕad ʕala ħa:ffat ʔirraṣi:f] • **3.** عُبَر [ʕubar] عَبُر [ʕabur] *vn:* اِنعُبَر [ʔinʕubar] *p:* They came over the bridge on their way to town. عُبرَوا الجِّسِر بطَرِيقهُم لِلمَدِينَة [ʕubraw ʔijjisir bṭari:qhum lilmadi:na]

*** I don't know what's come over him.**
• **1.** ما أَدري شبِيه [ma: ʔadri šbi:h]

to come through • **1.** مَرّ بِـ [marr bi-] مُرُور بِـ [muru:r bi-] *vn: sv* اِنمَرّ بِـ [ʔinmarr bi-] *p:* Did you come through the woods on your way here? مَرَّيت بالغابَة بطَرِيقَك لِهنا [marri:t bilɣa:ba bṭari:qak lihna] He came through the operation safely. مَرّ بالعَمَلِيَّة بسَلامَة [marr bilʕamaliyya bsala:ma] • **2.** خاض بِـ [xa:ð bi-] خَوض بِـ [xawð bi-] *vn:* اِنخاض بِـ [ʔinxa:ð bi-] *p:* مَرّ بِـ [marr b-] مُرُور [muru:r] *vn:* اِنمَرّ [ʔinmarr] *p:* He had to come through mud to get here. اِضطَرّ يخُوض بالطِّين حَتَّى يُوصَل لِهنا [ʔiðṭarr yxu:ð bitti:n ħatta yu:ṣal lihna]

to come to • **1.** وَصَّل [waṣṣal] توِصِّل [twiṣṣil] *vn: sv* i. The bill comes to two dollars. القائِمَة توَصِّل دُولارَين [ʔilqa:ʔima twaṣṣil dula:rayn] • **2.** صِحَى [ṣiħa:] صَحُو [ṣaħw] *vn: sv* i. After a few minutes she came to. صِحَت بَعَد فَدّ كَم دَقِيقَة [ṣiħat baʕad fadd čam daqi:qa] • **3.** صار [ṣa:r] صَير [ṣi:r] *vn: sv* i. Who knows what all this will come to? مِنُو يِدري شراح يصِير؟ [minu yidri šra:ħ yṣi:r?] • **4.** إِجَى [ʔija:] جا بِـ [ja: bi-] مَجِيئ بِـ [maji:ʔ bi-] *vn: sv* i. Her name doesn't come to me right now. إِسِمها ما يِجِي ببالِّي هَسَّة [ʔisimha ma: yiji bba:li hassa]

to come true • **1.** تحَقَّق [tħaqqaq] تَحَقُّق [taħaqquq] *vn: sv* a. Her dream came true. تحَقَّق حِلِمها [tħaqqaq ħilimha]

to come up • **1.** طِلَع [ṭilaʕ] طُلُوع [ṭulu:ʕ] *vn: sv* a. The diver came up after three minutes under water. الغَوّاص طِلَع لِفُوق بَعَد ما كان ثلَث دَقايِق تَحت المَيّ [ʔilɣawwa:ṣ ṭilaʕ lifu:g baʕad ma: ča:n tlaθ daqa:yiq taħt ʔilmayy] The wheat is beginning to come up. الحُنطَة بِدَت تِطلَع [ʔilħunṭa bidat tiṭlaʕ] • **2.** ظِهَر [ðihar] ظُهُور [ðuhu:r] *vn: sv* a. This problem comes up every day. هَالمُشكِلَة تِظهَر كُلّ يوم [halmuškila tiðhar kull yu:m] • **3.** صار [ṣa:r] صَير [ṣi:r] *vn: sv* i. A thunderstorm is coming up. راح تصِير عاصِفَة [ra:ħ tṣi:r ʕa:ṣifa] • **4.** صِعَد [ṣiʕad] صُعُود، صَعِد [ṣuʕu:d, ṣaʕid] *vn: sv* a. Can you come up for a minute? تِقدَر تِصعَد لِفَدّ دَقِيقَة؟ [tigdar tiṣʕad lfadd daqi:qa?] • **5.** جاب [ja:b] جَيب [ji:b] *vn:* اِنجاب [ʔinja:b] *p:* If you can come up with a better idea, go right ahead. إِذا تِقدَر تجِيب فِكرَة أَحسَن، تفَضَّل [ʔiða tigdar dji:b fikra ʔaħsan, tfaððal]

to come upon • **1.** توَصَّل لِـ [twaṣṣal li-] تَوَصُّل لِـ [tawaṣṣul li-] *vn: sv* a. I came upon the solution by accident. توَصَّلِت لِلحَلّ بِالصِّدفَة [twaṣṣalit lilħall biṣṣidfa] • **2.** إِجَا [ʔija:] جا عَلَى [ja: ʕala] مَجِيئ عَلَى [maji:ʔ ʕala] *vn: sv* i. We came upon a man lying in the street. جِينا عَلَى رِجّال واقِع بِالشّارِع [ji:na ʕala rijja:l wa:giʕ bišša:riʕ]

to come up to • **1.** طابَق [ṭa:baq] مُطابَقَة [muṭa:baqa] *vn: sv* i. اِنطُبَق عَلَ [ʔinṭubaq ʕala] اِنطِباق [ʔinṭiba:q] *vn: sv* u. The new bridge didn't come up to government specifications. الجِّسِر الجِّدِيد ما طابَق مُواصَفات الحُكُومَة [ʔijjisir ʔijjidi:d ma: ṭa:baq muwa:ṣafa:t ʔilħuku:ma]

comedy • **1.** رُوايَة هَزَلِيَّة [ruwa:ya hazaliyya] رُوايات هَزَلِيَّة [ruwa:ya:t hazaliyya] *pl:* Did you like the comedy? عِجبَتَك الرُّوايَة الهَزَلِيَّة؟ [ʕijbatak ʔirruwa:ya ʔilhazaliyya?]

comet • **1.** مُذَنَّب [muðannab] مُذَنَّبات [muðannaba:t] *pl:*

comfort • **1.** وَسِيلَة راحَة [wasi:lat ra:ħa] وَسائِل راحَة [wasa:ʔil ra:ħa] *pl:* This hotel has all the comforts you can ask for. هَالفُندُق بِيه جَمِيع وَسائِل الرّاحَة اللّي تُطلُبها [halfunduq bi:h ǰami:ʕ wasa:ʔil ʔirra:ħa ʔilli tuṭlubha]

to comfort • **1.** عَزَّى [ʕazza:] تَعزِيَة [taʕziya] *vn: sv* i. We went to comfort her after her son died. رِحنا نعَزِّيها بَعَد ما مات إبِنها [riħna nʕazzi:ha baʕad ma: ma:t ʔibinha]

comfortable • **1.** مُرِيح [muri:ħ] This chair is very comfortable. هَالكُرسِي كُلِّش مُرِيح [halkursi kulliš muri:ħ] • **2.** مِرتاح [mirta:ħ] I don't feel very comfortable. آنِي ما مِرتاح [ʔa:ni ma: mirta:ħ]

to make oneself comfortable • **1.** اِستَراح [ʔistara:ħ] اِستِراحَة [ʔistira:ħa] *vn: sv* i. Sit down and make yourself comfortable. أُقعُد وَاِستِرِيح [ʔugʕud wʔistiri:ħ] Sit down and make yourself comfortable. أُقعُد وأُخُذ راحتَك [ʔugʕud wʔuxuð ra:ħtak]

comical • **1.** هَزَلِي [hazali] فُكاهِي [fuka:hi] مُضحِك [muðħik] The movie was very comical. الفِلِم كان كُلِّش هَزَلِي [ʔilfilim ča:n kulliš hazali]

comma • **1.** فارِزَة [fa:riza] فَوارِز [fawa:riz] *pl:*

command • **1.** أَمُر [ʔamur] أَوامِر [ʔawa:mir] *pl:* Why wasn't my command carried out? لِيش ما تنَفَّذ أَمرِي؟ [li:š ma: tnaffað ʔamri?] • **2.** سَيطَرَة [sayṭara] He has an excellent command of English. عِندَه سَيطَرَة تامَّة عَاللُّغَة الإنكلِيزِيَّة [ʕindah sayṭara ta:mma ʕalluɣa ʔilʔingili:ziyya]

in command • **1.** آمِر [ʔa:mir] Who's in command of these soldiers? مِنُو آمِر هالجِنُود؟ [minu ʔa:mir halǰinu:d?]

to command • **1.** أُمَر [ʔumar] أَمُر [ʔamur] *vn: sv* u. He commanded the soldiers to return. أُمَر الجُنُود بِالرُّجُوع [ʔumar ʔiǰǰunu:d birruǰu:ʕ] • **2.** جِلَب [ǰilab] جَلِب [ǰalib] *vn:* اِنجِلَب [ʔinǰilab] *p:* He commands respect everywhere he goes. يِجلِب اِحتِرام وَين ما يرُوح [yiǰlib ʔiħtira:m wi:n ma: yiru:ħ] • **3.** قاد [qa:d, ga:d] قِيادَة [qiya:da] *vn:* اِنقاد [ʔinqa:d] My father commands the Fifth Army. أَبُويا يقُود الجَّيش الخامِس [ʔabu:ya yqu:d ʔiǰǰi:š ʔilxa:mis]

to command a view • **1.** طَلّ [ṭall] إطلال [ʔiṭla:l] *vn: sv* u. أَشرَف [ʔašraf] إشراف [ʔišra:f] *vn: sv* i. Our house commands a view of the entire lake. بَيتنا يطِلّ عالبُحَيرَة كُلّها [baytna yṭull ʕalbuħi:ra kullha]

commander • **1.** قائِد [qa:ʔid] قُوّاد [quwwa:d] *pl:* He's been appointed commander of the Fourteenth Army. هُوَّ تعَيَّن قائِد لِلجَّيش الرّابِع عَشِر [huwwa tʕayyan qa:ʔid liǰǰayš ʔirra:biʕ ʕašir]

to commend • **1.** مِدَح [midaħ] مَدِح [madiħ] *vn:* اِنمِدَح [ʔinmidaħ] *p:* حِمَد [ħimad] حَمِد [ħamid] *vn:* اِنحِمَد [ʔinħimad] *p:* He commended the soldiers for their bravery in the battle. مِدَح الجُّنُود لِبَسالَتهُم بِالمَعرَكَة [midaħ ʔiǰǰunu:d libasa:lathum bilmaʕraka] • **2.** سَلَّم [sallam] تَسلِيم [tasli:m] *vn:* تسَلَّم [tsallam] *p:* He commended his soul to God. سَلَّم رُوحَه لِلّٰه [sallam ru:ħa lʔallah]

comment • **1.** تَعلِيق [taʕli:q] مُلاحَظَة [mula:ħaḍa] مُلاحَظات [mula:ħaḍa:t] *pl:* Did he have any comments on the subject? كانَت عِندَه تَعلِيقات عَالمَوضُوع؟ [ča:nat ʕindah taʕli:qa:t ʕalmawḍu:ʕ?]

to comment • **1.** عَلَّق [ʕallaq] تَعلِيق [taʕli:q] *vn:* تعَلَّق [tʕallaq] *p:* The editor commented on the president's visit. المُحَرِّر عَلَّق عَلَى زِيارَة الرَّئِيس [ʔilmuħarrir ʕallaq ʕala ziya:rat ʔirraʔi:s]

commercial • **1.** تِجارِي [tiǰa:ri] He's well known in commercial circles. هُوَّ زين مَعرُوف بالأوساط التِّجارِيَّة [huwwa zi:n maʕru:f bilʔawsa:ṭ ʔittiǰa:riyya]

to commit • **1.** اِرتِكَب [ʔirtikab] اِرتِكاب [ʔirtika:b] *vn: sv* i. Who committed the crime? مِنُو اِرتِكَب الجَّرِيمَة؟ [minu ʔirtikab ʔiǰǰari:ma?] • **2.** دَخَّل [daxxal] تَدخِيل [tadxi:l] *vn: sv* i. They committed her to a mental hospital. دَخّلُوها بِمُستَشفَى الأمراض العَقلِيَّة [daxxlu:ha bmustašfa: ʔilʔamra:ḍ ʔilʕaqliyya]

to commit one's self • **1.** تعَهَّد [tʕahhad] تَعَهُّد [taʕahhud] *vn: sv* a. اِلتِزَم [ʔiltizam] اِلتِزام [ʔiltiza:m] *vn: sv* i. The president refused to commit himself. الرَّئِيس رُفَض يِتعَهَّد [ʔirraʔi:s rufaḍ yitʕahhad]

to commit suicide • **1.** اِنتِحَر [ʔintiħar] اِنتِحار [ʔintiħa:r] *vn: sv* i. He committed suicide last week. اِنتِحَر بالإسبُوع الماضِي [ʔintiħar bilʔisbu:ʕ ʔilma:ḍi]

committee • **1.** لُجنَة [luǰna] لِجان [liǰa:n, luǰa:n] *pl:*

common • **1.** شايِع [ša:yiʕ] Some French words are in common use in the Lebanese dialect. بَعَض الكِلمات الفرَنسِيَّة شايعَة الاستِعمال بِاللَّهجَة اللُّبنانِيَّة [baʕaḍ ʔiččilma:t ʔilfransiyya ša:yʕat ʔilʔistiʕma:l billahǰa ʔillubna:niyya] • **2.** مُشتَرَك [muštarak] We have common goals. عِدنا غايات مُشتَرَكَة [ʕidna ɣa:ya:t muštaraka] • **3.** عامِّي [ʕa:mmi] عَوامّ [ʕawa:mm] *pl:* The common people don't care about politics. العَوامّ ما يهتَمُّون بِالسِّياسَة [ʔilʕawa:mm ma: yihtammu:n bissiya:sa]

common knowledge • **1.** المَعرُوف عَن [ʔilmaʕru:f ʕan] It is common knowledge that he lies. المَعرُوف عَنَّه هُوَّ يِكذِب [ʔilmaʕru:f ʕannah huwwa yičðib]

common market • **1.** سُوق مُشتَرَك [su:q muštarak]

commotion • **1.** هَرَج ومَرَج [haraǰ wmaraǰ] There was a terrific commotion in the street. كان أَكُو هَرَج وَمَرَج بِالشّارِع [ča:n ʔaku haraǰ wmaraǰ biššari:ʕ]

C

to communicate • **1.** اِتِّصَل [ʔittiṣal] اِتِّصال [ʔittiṣaːl] *vn:* *sv* i. We communicate with them daily by radio. نِتِّصِل بِيهُم يَومِيّاً بِالرّاديُو [nittiṣil biːhum yawmiyyan birraːdyu] • **2.** تفاهَم [tfaːham] تَفاهُم [tafaːhum] *vn:* *sv* a. They have difficulty communicating because of a language problem. بِصُعُوبَة يِتفاهمُون بِسَبَب مُشكِلَة اللُّغَة [bṣuʕuːba yitfaːhmuːn bisabab muškilat ʔilluɣa]

communication • **1.** مُواصَلات [muwaːṣalaːt] He works in the communication branch. دَيِشتُغُل بِقِسم المُواصَلات [dayištuɣul bqism ʔilmuwaːṣalaːt] • **2.** مُراسَلَة [muraːsala] مُراسَلات [muraːsalaːt] *pl:* We received their communication a week ago. اِستِلَمنا مُراسَلاتهُم قَبِل إسبُوع [ʔistilamna muraːsalaːthum gabil ʔisbuːʕ]

Communism • **1.** الشِيُوعِيَّة [ʔiššiyuːʕiyya]

Communist • **1.** شِيُوعِي [šiyuːʕi]

community • **1.** He lives in a small community about four miles from Baghdad. يِعِيش بِولايَة صغَيّرَة حَوالِي أَربَع أَميال مِن بَغداد [yiʕiːš bwlaːya ṣɣayyra ħawaːli ʔarbaʕ ʔamyaːl min baɣdaːd]

compact • **1.** قُوطِيَّة بَودرَة [quːṭiyyat buːdra] قُوطِيّات بَودرَة [quːṭiyyaːt buːdra] *pl:* She bought a new compact. اِشتِرَيت قُوطِيَّة بُودرَة جِدِيدَة [ʔištiriːt quːṭiyyat puːdra ǰidiːda] • **2.** مَحشُوق [maħšuːg] مَرصُوص [marṣuːṣ] That's a very compact package. هَالرُّزمَة مَحشُوكَة حَشِك [harruzma maħšuːka ħašik]

company • **1.** فَوج [fawǰ] أَفواج [ʔafwaːǰ] *pl:* I served in his company. خِدَمِت بالفَوج مالَه [xidamit bilfawǰ maːlah] • **2.** شَرِكَة [šarika] شَرِكات [šarikaːt] *pl:* What company do you represent? أَيّ شَرِكَة تمَثِّلها؟ [ʔayy šarika tmaθθilha?] • **3.** خُطّار [xuṭṭaːr] خِطاطِير [xiṭaːṭiːr] *pl:* ضَيف [ðayf] ضِيُوف [ðiyuːf] *pl:* We are expecting company this evening. نِتوَقَّع خُطّار هاللَّيلَة [nitwaqqaʕ xiṭṭaːr halliːla] • **4.** جَماعَة [ǰamaːʕa] جَماعات [ǰamaːʕaːt] *pl:* أَصدِقاء [ʔaṣdiqaːʔ] A man is known by the company he keeps. الرَّجُل مَعرُوف مِن الجَّماعَة اللِّي يِمشِي وِيّاهُم [ʔirraǰul maʕruːf min ʔiǰǰamaːʕa ʔilli yimši wiyyaːhum] • **5.** رَفِيق [rafiːq] رُفَقاء [rufaqaːʔ] *pl:* رِفِيج [rifiːǰ] رِفجان [rifǰaːn] *pl:* I find him very good company. شِفتَه كُلِّش خُوش رَفِيق [šiftah kulliš xuːš rafiːq]

* **Keep me company for a while.** • **1.** أُبقَى وِيّايا فَدّ شوَيَّة [ʔubqaː wiyyaːya fadd šwayya]

comparatively • **1.** نِسبِيّاً [nisbiyyan] The test was comparatively easy. الاختِبار كان نِسبِيّاً سَهل [ʔilʔixtibaːr čaːn nisbiyyan sahil]

to compare • **1.** قارَن [qaːran] مُقارَنَة [muqaːrana] *vn:* تقارَن [tqaːran] *p:* We compared the two methods. قارَنّا بين الطَّرِيقتَين [qaːranna bayn ʔiṭṭariːqtayn]

comparison • **1.** مُقارَنَة [muqaːrana] مُقارَنات [muqaːranaːt] *pl:* Can you make another comparison between the two? تِقدَر تسَوِّي مُقارَنَة أُخرَى بين الإثنين؟ [tigdar tsawwi muqaːrana ʔuxra bayn ʔilʔiθnayn?]

* **There is no comparison between the two.** • **1.** هَذا وين وذاك وين؟ / وَين هَذا مِن ذاك [wayn haːða min ðaːk] / [haːða wiːn wðaːk wiːn?]

compartment • **1.** مَقصُورَة [maqṣuːra] مَقصُورات [maqṣuːraːt] *pl:* All compartments in this car are crowded with people. كُلّ المَقصُورات بِهالعَرَبَة مِزدَحمَة بِالنّاس [kull ʔilmaqṣuːraːt bhalʕaraba mizdaħma binnaːs] • **2.** خانَة [xaːna] خانات [xaːnaːt] *pl:* بَيت [bayt] بيُوت [biyuːt] *pl:* The drawer has compartments for knives, forks, and spoons. الجَّرار بِيه خانات لِلسَّكاكِين وَالجَّطَلات وَالخَواشِيق [ʔiǰǰaraːr biːh xaːnaːt lissičaːčiːn wiččaṭalaːt wilxawaːšiːg]

compass • **1.** بَوصلَة [buːṣala, buːṣla] بُوصَلات [buːṣalaːt, buːṣlaːt] *pl:* Without the compass we would have been lost. لَو ما البَوصلَة كان ضِعنا [law maː ʔilbuːṣla čaːn ðiʕna] • **2.** فِرجال [firǰaːl] فَراجِيل [faraːǰiːl] *pl:* I can draw a circle without a compass. أَقدَر أَرسِم دائِرَة بلَيّا فُرجال [ʔagdar ʔarsim daːʔira blayya furǰaːl]

to compel • **1.** جُبَر [ǰubar] جَبُر [ǰabur] *vn:* اِنجُبَر [ʔinǰubar] *p:* اِضطَرّ [ʔiðṭarr] اِضطِرار [ʔiðṭiraːr] *vn:* *sv* a. The accident compelled us to leave a day early. الحادِث جُبَرنا نِترُك يوم قَبُل [ʔilħaːdiθ ǰubarna nitruk yuːm gabul]

compensation • **1.** بِتَعوِيض [bitaʕwiːð] I demand full compensation. أطالُب بِتَعوِيض كامِل [ʔaṭaːlub btaʕwiːð kaːmil]

to compete • **1.** تنافَس [tnaːfas] تَنافُس [tanaːfus] *vn:* *sv* a. تسابَق [tsaːbaq] تَسابُق [tasaːbuq] *vn:* *sv* a. The two teams are competing for the silver cup. الفِرقتَين يِتنافسُون عالكَأس الفُضِّي [ʔilfiriqtayn yitnaːfsuːn ʕalkaːʔs ʔilfuðði] • **2.** نافَس [naːfas] مُنافَسَة [munaːfasa] *vn:* *sv* i. زاحَم [zaːħam] مُزاحَمَة [muzaːħama] *vn:* *sv* i. I won't ever be able to compete with him in the exams. ما راح أَقدَر أنافسَه بِالإمتِحانات [maː raːħ ʔagdar ʔanaːfsah bilʔimtiħaːnaːt]

competent • **1.** مُقتَدِر [muqtadir] كُفو [kufu, kafu]

competition • **1.** مُنافَسَة [munaːfasa] مُزاحَمَة [muzaːħama] مُزاحَمات [muzaːħamaːt] *pl:* Competition is necessary in business. المُنافَسَة ضَرُورِيَّة بِالحَياة التِّجارِيَّة [ʔilmunaːfasa ðaruːriyya bilħayaːt ʔittiǰaːriyya]

competitor • **1.** مُنافِس [munaːfis] مُنافِسِين [munaːfisiːn] *pl:* مُزاحِم [muzaːħim] مُزاحِمِين [muzaːħimiːn] *pl:* Our competitor's product is no good. إنتاج مُنافِسنا مُو زين [ʔintaːǰ munaːfisna muː zayn]

to compile • **1.** جَمَّع [ǰammaʕ] تجمِّع [tǰimmiʕ] *vn:* تجَمَّع [tǰammaʕ] *p:* He's compiling material for his new book. دَيجَمِّع مَوادّ لِكتابَه الجِّدِيد [dayǰammiʕ mawa:dd likta:bah ʔiǰǰidi:d]

to complain • **1.** اِشتِكَى [ʔištika:] تشِكِّي [tšikki] *vn: sv* i. تشَكَّى [tšakka:] تشِكِّي [tšikki] *vn: sv* a. She complains of severe pains. دَتِشتِكِي مِن وُجَع شَدِيد [datištiki min wuǰaʕ šadi:d] • **2.** تذَمَّر [dðammar] تَذَمُّر [taðammur] *vn: sv* a. He complains about his work. دَيِتذَمَّر مِن شُغلَه [dayiddammar min šuɣlah]

complaint • **1.** شَكوَى [šakwa] شَكاوِي [šaka:wi] *pl:* شِكايَة [šika:ya] شِكايات [šika:ya:t] *pl:* Do you have any complaints? عِندَك أيّ شَكوَى؟ [ʕindak ʔayy šakwa?] • **2.** دَعوَة [daʕwa] دَعوات، دَعاوِي [daʕwa:t, daʕa:wi] *pl:* I filed a complaint with the police after the assault took place. سَجَّلِت دَعوَة عِند الشُّرطَة بَعَد ما صار الاعتِداء [saǰǰalit daʕwa ʕind ʔiššurṭa baʕad ma: ṣa:r ʔiliʕtida:ʔ]

complete • **1.** كامِل [ka:mil] This volume makes my collection complete. هَالجُّزء يسَوِّي مَجمُوعَتِي كامِلَة [hаǰǰuzuʔ ysawwi maǰmu:ʕati ka:mla] • **2.** تَمام [tama:m] بِالمَرَّة [bilmarra] He's a complete fool. هُوَّ أَحمَق تَمام [huwwa ʔaħmaq tama:m]

to complete • **1.** كَمَّل [kammal] تكِمِّل [tkimmil] *vn:* تكَمَّل [tkammal] *p:* خَلَّص [xallaṣ] تخِلِّص [txilliṣ] *vn:* تخَلَّص [txallaṣ] *p:* تَمَّم [tammam] تُمِّم [ʕttimmim] *vn:* أنهَى [ʔanha:] إنهاء [ʔinha:ʔ] *vn:* We'll complete the arrangements for the trip tomorrow. راح نكَمِّل التَّرتِيبات لِلسَّفرَة باكِر [ra:ħ nkammil ʔittarti:ba:t lissafra ba:čir]

completely • **1.** تَماماً [tama:man] He convinced me completely. أقنَعنِي تَماماً [ʔaqnaʕni tama:man] • **2.** بِالمَرَّة [bilmarra] You're completely wrong. إنتَ غَلطان بِالمَرَّة [ʔinta ɣalṭa:n bilmarra]

complexion • **1.** بَشرَة [bašra] بَشرات [bašra:t] *pl:* He has a very dark complexion. البَشرَة مالتَه كُلِّش سَمرَة [ʔilbašra ma:ltah kulliš samra]

to complicate • **1.** عَقَّد [ʕaqqad] تَعقِيد [taʕqi:d] *vn: sv* i. Don't complicate matters any more than they are. لا تعَقِّد الأُمُور أكثَر مِمّا هِيَّ [la: tʕaqqid ʔilʔumu:r ʔakθar mimma hiyya]

complicated • **1.** مُعَقَّد [muʕaqqad]

compliment • **1.** مَدِح [madiħ] ثَناء [θana:ʔ] ثَناءات [θana:ʔa:t] *pl:* Thanks for the compliment. أشكُرَك عَلَى المَدِح [ʔaškurak ʕala ʔilmadiħ] • **2.** تَحِيَّة [taħiyya] تَحِيّات [taħiyya:t] *pl:* Please accept this gift with the compliments of the company. رَجاءاً تقَبَّل هالهَدِيَّة مَعَ تَحِيّات الشَّرِكَة [raǰa:ʔan tqabbal halhadiyya maʕa taħiyya:t ʔiššarika]

to compliment • **1.** مِدَح [midaħ] مَدِح [madiħ] *vn:* اِنمِدَح [ʔinmidaħ] *p:* أثنَى عَلَى [ʔaθna: ʕala] ثَناء [θana:ʔ] *vn:* اِنثِنَى عَلَى [ʔinθana: ʕala] *p:* He complimented me on my cooking. مِدَحنِي عَلَى طَبخِي [midaħni ʕala ṭabxi] He complimented me on my cooking. أثنَى عَلَيّا بِطَبخِي [ʔaθna: ʕalayya bṭabxi]

to comply • **1.** لَبَّى طَلَب [labba: talab] تَلبِيَة [talbiya] *vn:* تلَبَّى [tlabba:] *p:* We regret that we cannot comply with your request. آسفِين ما نِقدَر نلَبِّي طَلَبَك [ʔa:sfi:n ma: nigdar nlabbi ṭalabak] • **2.** تجاوَب [tǰa:wab, dǰa:wab] تَجاوُب [taǰa:wu:b] *vn: sv* a. طاع [ṭa:ʕ] إطاعَة [ʔiṭa:ʕa] *vn:* He refused to comply with the rules of the university. رُفَض يطِيع قَوانِين الجّامِعَة [rufað yṭi:ʕ qawa:ni:n ʔiǰǰa:miʕa] He refused to comply with the rules of the university. رُفَض يِتجاوَب ويّا قَوانِين الجّامِعَة [rufað yidǰa:wab wiyya qawa:ni:n ʔiǰǰa:miʕa]

to compose • **1.** ألَّف [ʔallaf] تَألِيف [taʔli:f] *vn:* تألَّف [tʔallaf] *p:* He composed a piece of music for the occasion. ألَّف قِطعَة مُوسِيقِيَّة لِلمُناسَبَة [ʔallaf qiṭʕa musi:qiyya lilmuna:saba] This sentence is composed of a subject and a predicate. هَالجُّملَة تِتألَّف مِن مُبتَدَأ وَخَبَر [halǰumla titʔllaf min mubtadaʔ wxabar] • **2.** ضُبَط [ðubaṭ] ضَبُط [ðabuṭ] *vn: sv* u. هَدَّى [haddaʔ] تهِدّأ، تَهدِئَة [thiddiʔ, tahdiʔa] *vn: sv* i. Just try to compose yourself a bit. حاوِل تُضبُط نَفسَك شوَيَّة [ħa:wil tuðbuṭ nafsak šwayya]

composed • **1.** ضابُط النَّفِس [ða:buṭ ʔinnafis] هادِئ [ha:diʔ] مسَيطِر عَلَى النَّفِس [msayṭir ʕala ʔinnafis] He remained composed during the whole trial. بُقَى ضابُط نَفسَه طُول المُحاكَمَة [buqa: ða:buṭ nafsah ṭu:l ʔilmuħa:kama] • **2.** مِتكَوِّن مِن [mitkawwin min] This fabric is composed of rayon and silk. هَالقُماش مِتكَوِّن مِن رِيُّون وَحَرِير [halquma:š mitkawwin min ri:yu:n wħari:r]

composition • **1.** تَألِيف [taʔli:f] تَآلِيف [taʔa:li:f] *pl:* The orchestra is going to play his compositions tonight. الفِرقَة المُوسِيقِيَّة راح تِعزِف تَآلِيفَه هاللَّيلَة [ʔilfirqa ʔilmu:si:qiyya ra:ħ tiʕzif taʔa:li:fah hallayla] • **2.** مُرَكَّب [murakkab] مُكَوَّن [mukawwan] The composition of this rock isn't known. مُرَكَّبات هالصَّخرَة مُو مَعرُوفَة [murakkaba:t haṣṣaxra mu: maʕru:fa] • **3.** إنشاء [ʔinša:ʔ] إنشاءات [ʔinša:ʔa:t] *pl:* Have you done your English composition? سَوَّيت إنشاءَك الإنكلِيزِي؟ [sawwi:t ʔinša:ʔak ʔilʔingli:zi?]

compress • **1.** ضَماد [ðama:d] ضَمادات [ðama:da:t] *pl:* كَمّادَة [kamma:da] كَمّادات [kamma:da:t] *pl:* A cold compress will relieve the pain. ضَمادَة بَرِد راح تخَفِّف الوُجَع [ðama:da barid ra:ħ txaffuf ʔilwuǰaʕ]

to compress • **1.** ضِغَط [ðiɣaṭ] ضَغِط [ðaɣiṭ] *vn:* اِنضِغَط [ʔinðiɣaṭ] *p:* It is difficult to compress water. مِن الصَّعُب تُضغُط المَيّ [min ʔiṣṣaʕub tuðɣuṭ ʔilmayy]

C

compromise • **1.** تَراضِي [tara:ði] The problem cannot be solved but by compromise. المَسألَة ما تِنحَلّ إلّا بالتَّراضِي [ʔilmasʔala ma: tinħall ʔilla bittara:ði]

to compromise • **1.** تراضَى [tra:ða:] تَراضِي [tara:ði] *vn: sv* i. تساهَل [tsa:hal] تَساهُل [tasa:hul] *vn: sv* a. ساوَى [sa:wa:] مُساواة [musa:wa:t] *vn: sv* i. They don't want to compromise. ما يِردُون يِتراضُون [ma: yirdu:n yitra:ðu:n] • **2.** عَرَّض [ʕarrað] تَعرِيض [taʕri:ð] *vn:* تعَرَّض [tʕarrað] *p:* You have compromised the security of our country. عَرَّضِت سَلامَة بَلَدنا لِلخَطَر [ʕarraðit sala:mat baladna lilxaṭar]

computer • **1.** كَمبيُوتَر [kambyuwtir] كَمبيُوتَرات [kambyuwtara:t] *Pl:*

comrade • **1.** رَفِيق [rafi:q] رُفَقاء [rufaqa:ʔ] *pl:* زَمِيل [zami:l] زُمَلاء [zumala:ʔ] *pl:*

to conceal • **1.** ضَمّ [ðamm] ضَمّ [ðamm] *vn:* اِنضَمّ [ʔinðamm] *p:* أخفَى [ʔaxfa:] إخفاء [ʔixfa:ʔ] *vn:* اِنخفَى [ʔinxafa:] *p:* He concealed himself behind a tree. ضَمّ نَفسَه وَرا فَدّ شِجَرَة [ðamm nafsah wara fadd šiǰara] He attempted to conceal the truth from the judge. حاوَل يِخفِي الحَقِيقَة عَن الحاكِم [ħa:wal yixfi ʔilħaqi:qa ʕan ʔilħa:kim]

conceited • **1.** مِتكَبُّر [mitkabbur] مَغرُور [maɣru:r] شايِف النَفِس [ša:yif ʔinnafis] Those girls are all very conceited. هَالبَنات كُلهِن مِتكَبُّرات [halbana:t kullhin mitkabbura:t]

conceivable • **1.** مُمكِن إدراك [mumkin ʔidra:k] A few years ago a trip to the moon wasn't even conceivable. قَبُل كَم سَنَة السَّفَر لِلقُمَر ما كان مُمكِن إدراكَه [gabul čam sana ʔissafar lilgumar ma: ča:n mumkin ʔidra:kah]

to conceive • **1.** تصَوَّر [tṣawwar] تَصَوُّر [taṣawwur] *vn: sv* a. I can't conceive of her doing such a thing. ما مُمكِن أتصَوَّرها تسَوِّي هِيكِي شِي [ma:mumkin ʔatṣawwarha tsawwi hi:či ši]

concentrate • **1.** مُرَكَّز [murakkaz] Mix one can of orange juice concentrate with three cans of water. إخلُط قُوطِيَّة عَصِير بُرتُقال مُرَكَّز ويّا ثلاث قَواطِي مَيّ [ʔixluṭ qu:ṭiyyat ʕaṣi:r purṭuqa:l murakkaz wiyya tlaθ qawa:ṭi mayy]

to concentrate • **1.** حَشَّد [ħaššad] تَحشِيد، تحِشِّد [taħši:d, tħiššid] *vn:* تحَشَّد [tħaššad] *p:* The commanders concentrated the armies at the base of the hill. القُوّاد حَشّدَوا الجُيُوش جَوَّة الجِّبَل [ʔilquwwa:d ħaššdaw ʔiǰǰuyu:š ǰawwa ʔiǰǰibal] • **2.** رَكَّز [rakkaz] تَركِيز [tarki:z] *vn:* ترَكَّز [trakkaz] *p:* We're going to concentrate on pronunciation today. راح نرَكِّز عالتَّلَفُّظ اليُوم [ra:ħ nrakkiz ʕattalaffuð ʔilyu:m] The textile industry is concentrated in the North. صِناعَة النَّسِيج مِترَكِّزَة بِالشِّمال [ṣina:ʕat ʔinnasi:ǰ mitrakkza biššima:l]

concern • **1.** شَرِكَة [šarika] شَرِكات [šarika:t] *pl:* How long have you been with this concern? شقَدّ صارلَك بهَالشَّرِكَة؟ [šgadd ṣa:rlak bhaššarika?] • **2.** دَعوَة [daʕwa] دَعوات، دَعاوِي [daʕwa:t, daʕa:wi] *pl:* شُغُل [šuɣul] أشغال [ʔašɣa:l] *pl:* She said it was no concern of mine. قالَت مالِي دَعوَة بِيها [ga:lat ma:li daʕwa bi:ha] • **3.** قَلَق [qalaq] There's no reason for concern. ماكُو داعِي لِلقَلَق [ma:ku da:ʕi lilqalaq]

to concern • **1.** خَصّ [xaṣṣ] *sv* u. هَمّ [hamm] هَمّ [hamm] *vn: sv* i. This bulletin concerns everyone in this office. هالمَنشُور يهِمّ كُلّ واحِد بِهَالدّايرَة [halmanšu:r yhimm kull wa:ħid bhadda:ʔira]

to be concerned • **1.** اِهتَمّ [ʔihtamm] اِهتِمام [ʔihtima:m] *vn: sv* i. قِلَق [qilaq] قَلِق [qaliq] *vn: sv* a. She gets very concerned over the smallest thing. دَتِهتَمّ هوايَة عَلَى أقَلّ شِي [datihtamm hwa:ya ʕala ʔaqall ši] The police are concerned with this increase in crime. الشُّرطَة مِهتَمَّة بِإزدِياد الجَّرائِم هَذِي [ʔiššurṭa mihtamma bʔizdiya:d ʔiǰǰara:ʔim ha:ði]

as far as one's concerned • **1.** بالنِسبَة إلَى [binnisba ʔila] مِن ناحِيَّة [min na:ħiyya] مِن يَمّ [min yamm] As far as I'm concerned you can do as you like. بِالنِّسبَة إلِي تِقدَر تسَوِّي شما ترِيد [binnisba ʔili tigdar tsawwi šma tri:d]

concerning • **1.** بخُصُوص [bxuṣu:ṣ] Nothing was said concerning the vacation. ما اِنقال شِي بِخُصُوص العُطلَة [ma: ʔinga:l ši bxuṣu:ṣ ʔilʕuṭla]

to conclude • **1.** أنهَى [ʔanha:] اِنهاء [ʔinha:ʔ] *vn: sv* i. خِتَم [xitam] خَتِم [xatim] *vn:* اِنخِتَم [ʔinxitam] *p:* فَضّ [faðð] فَضّ [faðð] *vn:* اِنفَضّ [ʔinfaðð] *p:* They concluded the meeting yesterday afternoon. أنهَوا الاجتِماع البارحَة العَصِر [ʔanhaw ʔilʔiǰtima:ʕ ʔilba:rħa ʔilʕaṣir] • **2.** عِقَد [ʕiqad] عَقِد [ʕaqid] *vn:* اِنعِقَد [ʔinʕiqad] *p:* أبرَم [ʔabram] إبرام [ʔibra:m] *vn:* اِنبُرَم [ʔinburam] *p:* The two countries concluded the trade agreement two days ago. البَلَدَين عِقدَوا الاتِّفاقِيَّة التِّجارِيَّة قَبُل يومَين [ʔilbaladayn ʕiqdaw ʔilʔittifa:qiyya ʔittiǰa:riyya gabul yawmayn] • **3.** اِستَنتَج [ʔistantaǰ] اِستِنتاج [ʔistinta:ǰ] *vn: sv* i. What do you conclude from his remark? شتِستَنتِج مِن مُلاحَظتَه؟ [štistantiǰ min mula:ħaðtah?]

conclusion • **1.** نَتِيجَة [nati:ǰa] نَتائِج [nata:ʔiǰ] *pl:* اِستِنتاج [ʔistinta:ǰ] اِستِنتاجات [ʔistinta:ǰa:t] *pl:* What conclusions did you draw from the debate? شِنُو النَّتائِج اللِّي اِستَلخَصِتها مِن المُناقَشَة؟ [šinu ʔinnata:ʔiǰ ʔilli ʔistalxaṣitha min ʔilmuna:qaša?] • **2.** خِتام [xita:m] In conclusion, I should like to state that. . . . وَبالخِتام، أحِبّ أن أبَيِّن إنُّو [wbilxita:m, ʔaħibb ʔan ʔabayyin ʔinnu...]

concrete • **1.** كونكريت [kuːnkiriːt] كَنكَري [kankari] The bridge is built of concrete. الجِّسِر مَبني بكَنكَري [ʔijjisir mabni bkankari] • **2.** مَضبُوط [maðbuːt] قَوي [qawi, guwi] أقوياء، قَويّين [ʔaqwiyaːʔ, qawiyyiːn] *pl:* Give me a concrete example. إنطِيني فَدّ مَثَل مَضبُوط [ʔintiːni fadd maθal maðbuːt]

to condemn • **1.** حِكَم [ħikam] حُكُم [ħukum] *vn:* اِنحِكَم [ʔinħikam] *p:* The judge condemned him to death. الحاكِم حِكَمَه بالإعدام [ʔilħaːkim ħikamah bilʔiʕdaːm] • **2.** ذَمّ [ðamm] ذَمّ [ðamm] *vn:* اِنذَمّ [ʔinðamm] *p:* They condemned him for his actions. ذَمّوا أعمالَه [ðammaw ʔaʕmaːlah] • **3.** أمَر [ʔumar] أمُر [ʔamur] *vn:* اِنأمَر [ʔinʔumar] *p:* The municipality condemned the old building. البَلَديَّة أمرَت بِهدم البِنايَة القَديمَة [ʔilbaladiyya ʔumrat bihadm ʔilbinaːya ʔilqadiːma]

condition • **1.** حالَة [ħaːla] حالات [ħaːlaːt] *pl:* أحوال [ʔaħwaːl] The house was in good condition. البَيت كان بحالَة زينَة [ʔilbayt čaːn bħaːla zayna] • **2.** شَرط [šarṭ] شُرُوط [šuruːṭ] *pl:* I'll accept the offer on one condition. راح أقبَل العَرِض بشَرط واحِد [raːħ ʔaqbal ʔilʕarið bšarṭ waːhid]

conduct • **1.** سُلُوك [suluːk, siluːk] سِيرَة [siːra] سِيَر [siyar] *pl:* Your conduct is disgraceful. سِلُوكَك شائِن [siluːkak šaːʔin]

to conduct • **1.** قاد [qaːd, gaːd] قِيادَة [qiyaːda] *vn:* اِنقاد [ʔinqaːd] *p:* Who's conducting the orchestra tonight? مِنُو دَيقُود الفِرقَة المُوسِيقِيَّة هاللَّيلَة؟ [minu dayquːd ʔilfirqa ʔalmuːsiːqiyya hallayla?] • **2.** دَوَّر [dawwar] تَدوير [tadwiːr] *vn:* *sv* i. فَرَّر [farrar] تَفرير، تفرِّر [tafriːr, tfirrir] *vn:* *sv* i. دَلَّى [dallaː] تدِلّي [tdilli] *vn:* *sv* i. The guide conducted us around the ruins. الدَّلِيل دَوَّرنا بين الآثار [ʔiddaliːl dawwarna bayn ʔilʔaθaːr] • **3.** وَصَّل [waṣṣal] تَوصِيل [tawṣiːl] *vn:* توَصَّل [twaṣṣal]. Metal conducts better than wood. المَعدَن يوَصِّل الحَرارَة أحسَن مِن الخِشَب [ʔilmaʕdan ywaṣṣil ʔilħaraːra ʔaħsan min ʔilxišab] • **4.** دار [daːr] إدارَة [ʔidaːra] *vn:* اِنْدار [ʔindaːr] *p:* He conducts his work very well. دَيدِير أشغالَه كُلِّش زين [daydiːr ʔašɣaːlah kulliš ziːn]

to conduct oneself • **1.** سِلَك [silak] سِلُوك [siluːk] *vn:* *sv* u. تصَرَّف [tṣarraf] تَصَرُّف [taṣarruf] *vn:* *sv* a. She conducts herself like a lady. تِسلُك سِلُوك السَّيِّدَة [tisluk siluːk ʔissayyida]

conductor • **1.** مُفَتِّش [mufattiš] تِيتي [tiːti] تِيتيّات [tiːtiyyaːt] *pl:* Did the conductor punch your ticket? المُفَتِّش قِرَض التِّكِت مالَك؟ [ʔilmufattiš girað ʔittikit maːlak?] • **2.** مُوصِل [muːṣil] Silver is a good conductor of electricity. الفُضَّة مُوصِلَة زينَة لِلكَهرَبائِيَّة [lfuðða muwṣila ziːna lilkahrabaːʔiyya] • **3.** قائِد [qaːʔid] قُوّاد [quwwaːd] *pl:* Who is the conductor of the orchestra? مِنُو قائِد الفِرقَة المُوسِيقِيَّة؟ [minu qaːʔid ʔilfirqa ʔilmuːsiːqiyya?]

cone • **1.** مَخرُوط [maxruːṭ] مَخارِيط [maxaːriːṭ] *pl:* pl. maxaariiṭ. The vase was made in the shape of a cone. المِزهَريَّة كانَت مَعمُولَة بشِكِل مَخرُوط [ʔilmizhariyya čaːnat maʕmuːla bšikil maxruːṭ]

conference • **1.** اِجتِماع [ʔijtimaːʕ] اِجتِماعات [ʔijtimaːʕaːt] *pl:* He had a conference with the doctor. كان عِندَه اِجتِماع وِيّا الطَّبِيب [čaːn ʕindah ʔijtimaːʕ wiyya ʔiṭṭabiːb] • **2.** مُؤتَمَر [muʔtamar] مُؤتَمَرات [muʔtamaraːt] *pl:* He wrote an article on the disarmament conference. كِتَب مَقال عَن مُؤتَمَر نَزع السِّلاح [kitab maqaːl ʕan muʔtamar nazʕ ʔissilaːħ] • **3.** مُداوَلَة [mudaːwala] مُداوَلات [mudaːwalaːt] *pl:* After a short conference with my wife, I agreed to buy the car. بَعَد مُداوَلَة قَصِيرَة وِيّا زَوجتي وافَقت أشتِري السَّيّارَة [baʕad mudaːwala qaṣiːra wiyya zawijti waːfaqit ʔaštiri ʔissayyaːra]

to confess • **1.** اِعتِرَف [ʔiʕtiraf] اِعتِراف [ʔiʕtiraːf] *vn:* *sv* i. قَرّ [qarr] قَرار [qaraːr] *vn:* The defendant confessed. المُتَّهَم اِعتِرَف [ʔilmuttaham ʔiʕtiraf]

confession • **1.** اِعتِراف [ʔiʕtiraːf] اِعتِرافات [ʕitiraːfaːt] *pl:* إقرار [ʔiqraːr] إقرارات [ʔiqraːraːt] *pl:* The criminal made a full confession. المُجرِم اِعتِرَف اِعتِراف كامِل [ʔilmujrim ʔiʕtiraf ʔiʕtiraːf kaːmil]

confidence • **1.** ثِقَة [θiqa] I have confidence in him. عِندي ثِقَة بِيه [ʕindi θiqa biːh]

confident • **1.** واثِق [waːθiq] مِتأكِّد [mitʔakkid] مِتيَقِّن [mityaqqin] I'm confident that everything will turn out all right. آني واثِق كُلشي راح يصِير حَسَب الأصُول [ʔaːni waːθiq kullši raːħ yṣiːr ħasab ʔilʔuṣuːl]

confidential • **1.** سِرِّي [sirri] This letter is confidential. هالمَكتُوب سِرِّي [halmaktuːb sirri]

confidentially • **1.** حَكي بَينات [ħači baynaːt-] بصُورَة سِرِّيَّة [bṣuːra sirriyya] Confidentially, I don't like that proposal. حَكي بَيناتنا ما يعجِبني هَالإقتِراح [ħačy baynaːtna maː yiʕjibni halʔiqtiraːħ]

to confirm • **1.** أيَّد [ʔayyad] تأيِيد، تايِّد [taʔyiːd, tʔiyyid] *vn:* تأيَّد [tʔayyad] *p:* أكَّد [ʔakkad] تأكِيد، تاكِّد [taʔkiːd, tʔikkid] *vn:* تأكَّد [tʔakkad] *p:* The president confirmed the news report. الرَّئِيس أيَّد نَشرَة الأخبار [ʔirraʔiːs ʔayyad našrat ʔilʔaxbaːr] You'll have to confirm the reservation tomorrow. لازم تأكِّد الحَجز الصُّبُح [laːzim tʔakkid ʔilħajiz ʔiṣṣubuħ] • **2.** ثَبَّت [θabbat] تَثبِيت، تثَبِّت [taθbiːt, taθibbit] *vn:* *sv* i. That confirms my faith in him. هَذا يثَبِّت إيماني بِيه [haːða yθabbit ʔiːmaːni biːh]

conflict • **1.** نِزاع [nizaːʕ] نِزاعات [nizaːʕaːt] *pl:* تَصادُم [taṣaːdum] تَصادُمات [taṣaːdumaːt] *pl:* عراك [ʕraːk] Four men were killed in the border conflict. أربَع رِياجِيل اِنقِتلَوا بنِزاع الحُدُود [ʔarbaʕ riyaːjiːl ʔinkitlaw bniza:ʕ ʔilħudu:d] • **2.** صِراع، صِراعات [ṣira:ʕ, ṣira:ʕa:t] نِزاع [niza:ʕ] نِزاعات [niza:ʕa:t] *pl:* It's the eternal conflict between good and evil. هُوَّ الصِّراع الأَبَدِي بين الخير وَالشَّرّ. [huwwa ʔiṣṣira:ʕ ʔilʔabadi bayn ʔilxayr wiššarr] • **3.** تَناقُض [tana:quð̣] تَناقُضات [tana:quð̣a:t] *pl:* تَعارُض [taʕa:ruð̣] Because of the conflict between the two reports another committee went to investigate the matter. بِسَبَب التَّناقُض بين التَّقرِيرَين لَجنَة لُخ راحَت تِتحَرَّى عَن القَضِيَّة [bsabab ʔittana:quð̣ bayn ʔittaqri:rayn lajna lux ra:ħat titħarra: ʕan ʔilqað̣iyya]

to conflict • **1.** تعارَض [tʕa:rað̣] تَعارُض [taʕa:ruð̣] *vn:* *sv* a. Will this appointment conflict with your schedule? هَالمَوعِد راح يِتعارَض ويّا مَنهَجَك؟ [halmawʕid ra:ħ yitʕa:rað̣ wiyya manhajak?] • **2.** تَعارُض [tʕa:rað̣] تعارَض [taʕa:ruð̣] *vn: sv* a. تناقَض [tna:qað̣] تَناقُض [tana:quð̣] *vn:* *sv* a. His philosophy conflicts with the basic tenets of Islam. فَلسَفتَه تِتعارَض ويّا مَبادِئ الإسلام الأَساسِيَّة [falsaftah titʕa:rað̣ wiyya maba:diʔ ʔilʔisla:m ʔilʔasa:siyya]

to confuse • **1.** خَربَط [xarbaṭ] تخُربُط [txurbuṭ] *vn:* تخَربَط [txarbaṭ] *p:* أَربَك [ʔarbak] إِرباك [ʔirba:k] *vn:* اِنربَك [ʔinrabak] *p:* حَيَّر [ħayyar] تحيِّر [tħiyyir] *vn:* تحَيَّر [tħayyar] *p:* The map confused me. الخَرِيطَة خَربُطَتنِي [ʔilxari:ṭa xarbuṭatni] The problem confused me. المُشكِلَة حَيِّرَتنِي [ʔilmuškila ħayyiratni] • **2.** اِشتِبَه ب [ʔištibah b-] اِشتِباه [ʔištiba:h] *vn: sv* i. He must have confused me with someone else. لازِم اِشتِبَه بِيّا بِشَخِص آخَر [la:zim ʔištibah biyya bšaxiṣ ʔa:xar]

confusion • **1.** اِرتِباك [ʔirtiba:k] That will cause a lot of confusion. هَذِي راح تسَبِّب اِرتِباك هوايَة [ha:ði ra:ħ tsabbib ʔirtiba:k hwa:ya] • **2.** خَبصَة [xabṣa] خَبصات [xabṣa:t] *pl:* هُوسَة [hu:sa] هَوسات [hawsa:t] *pl:* هَرجَة [harja] هَرجات [harja:t] *pl:* He escaped in the confusion. اِنهِزَم بالخَبصَة [ʔinhizam bilxabṣa]

to congratulate • **1.** هَنَّى [hanna:] تهنِّي، تَهنِئَة [thinni, tahniʔa] *vn:* تهَنَّى [thanna:] *p: sv* i. عالبَرَكَة [ba:rak] مُبارَكَة [muba:raka] *vn:* تبارَك [tba:rak] *p: sv* i. We congratulated him on his success. هَنِّيناه بنَجاحَه [hanni:na:h bnaja:ħah]

congratulations • **1.** تَهنِيَة، تَهنِئَة [tahniya, tahniʔa] تَهانِي [taha:ni] *pl:* مَبرُوك [mabru:k] عالبَرَكَة [ʕalbaraka] Congratulations on your appointment! تَهانِينا عَلَى تَعيِينَك [taha:ni:na ʕala taʕyi:nak]

congress • **1.** مَجلِس [majlis] مَجالِس [maja:lis] *pl:*

to connect • **1.** وَصَّل [waṣṣal] توصِّل، تَوصِيل [twiṣṣil, tawṣi:l] *vn:* توَصَّل [twaṣṣal] *p:* A short hallway connects our offices. مَمَرّ قَصِير يوَصِّل دَوائِرنا بَعَضها بِبَعَض [mamarr qaṣi:r ywaṣṣil dawa:ʔirna baʕað̣ha ʔibbaʕað̣] Have they connected the telephone for you yet? وَصّلولَك التِّلِفُون لَو بَعَد؟ [waṣṣlawlak ʔittilifu:n law baʕad?] • **2.** رُبَط [rubaṭ] رَبُط [rabuṭ] *vn:* اِنرُبَط [ʔinrubaṭ] *p:* Connect these wires to the battery. أُربُط هالوايَرات بالباتري [ʔurbuṭ halwa:yara:t bilpa:tri] • **3.** The police have connected the crime to two men who were seen in the area. الشُرطَة رُبطَت الجَّرِيمَة بِرجّالَين اِنشافَوا بالمَنطِقَة. [ʔiṣṣurṭa rubṭat ʔijjari:ma birijja:layn ʔinša:faw bilmanṭiqa]

connection • **1.** اِتِّصال [ʔittiṣa:l] اِتِّصالات [ʔittiṣa:la:t] *pl:* I can't hear you very well. There must be a bad connection. ما أَقدَر أَسِمعَك زين لازِم أَكُو اِتِّصال مُو زين [ma: ʔagdar ʔasimʕak zi:n la:zim ʔaku ʔittiṣa:l mu: zi:n] • **2.** عِلاقَة [ʕila:qa] عِلاقات [ʕila:qa:t] *pl:* He has very good connections with the government. عِندَه كُلِّش خُوش عِلاقات ويّا الحُكُومَة [ʕindah kulliš xu:š ʕila:qa:t wiyya ʔilħuku:ma] • **3.** مُناسَبَة [muna:saba] مُناسَبات [muna:saba:t] *pl:* عَلاقَة [ʕala:qa] عَلاقات [ʕala:qa:t] *pl:* In what connection did he mention it? بأَيّ مُناسَبَة ذِكَرها؟ [bʔayy muna:saba ðikarha?] • **4.** صِلَة [ṣila] صِلات [ṣila:t] *pl:* There's no connect between the two. ماكُو صِلَة بين الثّنَين [ma:ku ṣila bayn liθnayn]

to conquer • **1.** فِتَح [fitaħ] فَتِح [fatiħ] *vn:* اِنفِتَح [ʔinfitaħ] *p:* He wanted to conquer the whole world. راد يِفتَح العالَم كُلَّه [ra:d yiftaħ ʔilʕa:lam kullah] • **2.** قِهَر [qihar] قَهر [qahir] *vn:* اِنقِهَر [ʔinqihar] *p:* Scientists have conquered polio. العُلَماء قِهرَوا مَرَض شَلَل الأَطفال [ʔilʕulama:ʔ qihraw marað̣ šalal ʔilʔaṭfa:l]

conquest • **1.** فَتِح [fatiħ] فُتُوحات [ftu:ħa:t] *pl:*

conscience • **1.** ضَمِير [ð̣ami:r] ضَمائِر [ð̣ama:ʔir, ð̣ama:yir] *pl:* وُجدان [wujda:n] I have a clear conscience. ضَمِيرِي مِرتاح [ð̣ami:ri mirta:ħ]

conscientious • **1.** مُجِدّ [mujidd] He's a conscientious student. هُوَّ طالِب مُجِدّ [huwwa ṭa:lib mujidd]

conscious • **1.** حاسِس [ħa:sis] واعِي [wa:ʕi] صاحِي [ṣa:ħi] You can talk to him now. He's conscious. تِقدَر تحاكِيه هَسَّة هُوَّ حاسِس [tigdar tħa:či:h hassa huwwa ħa:sis]

consent • **1.** رِضا [rið̣a] مُوافَقَة [muwa:faqa] قُبُول [qubu:l] This was done without my consent. هَذِي صارَت بِدُون رِضايا [ha:ði ṣa:rat bidu:n rið̣a:ya]

to consent • **1.** وافَق [wa:faq] مُوافَقَة [muwa:faqa] *vn:* *sv* i. قِبَل [qibal] قُبُول [qubu:l] *vn: sv* a. رِضَى [rið̣a] رِضا [rið̣a] *vn: sv* a. He consented to stay. وافَق يِبقَى [wa:faq yibqa:]

consequence • **1.** عاقِبَة [ʕa:qiba] عَواقِب [ʕawa:qib] *pl:* نَتِيجَة [nati:ja] نَتائِج [nata:ʔij] *pl:* I'm afraid of the consequences. آنِي خايِف مِن العَواقِب [ʔa:ni xa:yif min ʔilʕawa:qib]

consequently • **1.** وَعَلَيه [waʕalayh] بِناءً عَلَى ذَلِك [bina:ʔan ʕala ða:lik] بِالنَّتِيجَة [binnati:ja]

conservative • **1.** مُحافِظ [muħa:fiḍ] He's a very conservative politician. هُوَّ سِياسِي مُحافِظ كُلِّش [huwwa siya:si muħa:fiḍ kulliš] • **2.** مِقتِصِد [miqtiṣid] You'll have to be more conservative with your allowance. لازِم تكُون مِقتِصِد أكثَر بمُخَصَّصاتَك [la:zim tku:n miqtiṣid ʔakθar bmuxaṣṣaṣa:tak]

to consider • **1.** اِعتُبَر [ʔiʕtubar] اِعتِبار [ʔiʕtiba:r] *vn: sv* u. حِسَب [ħisab] حساب [ħsa:b] *vn:* اِنحِسَب [ʔinħisab] *p:* I consider him an able chemist. أعتَبرَه كِيمياوِي قَدِير [ʔaʕtabrah ki:mya:wi qadi:r] • **2.** نِظَر ب [niḍar b-] نَظَر [naḍar] *vn:* اِنّظَر [ʔinniḍar] *p:* We're still considering your request. لهَسَّة دَنُنظُر بطَلَبَك [lhassa danunḍur bṭalabak]

considerable • **1.** ضَخُم [ḍaxum] مُحتَرَم [muħtaram] Building this house cost me a considerable sum of money. بناء هَالبَيت كَلَّفنِي مَبلَغ ضَخُم [bina:ʔ halbayt kallafni mablaɣ ḍaxum] Building this house cost me a considerable sum of money. بناء هَالبَيت كَلَّفنِي مَبلَغ لا بأس بِيه [bina:ʔ halbayt kallafni mablaɣ la: baʔs bi:h]

considerate • **1.** مُقَدِّر [muqaddir] مُنصِف [munṣif] مُنصِفِين [munṣifi:n] *pl:* My boss is very considerate. رَئِيسِي فَدّ واحِد مُقَدِّر [raʔi:si fadd wa:ħid muqaddir]

consideration • **1.** نَظَر [naḍar] أنظار [ʔanḍa:r] *pl:* We have three plans under consideration. عِدنا ثلاث مَشارِيع تَحت النَّظَر [ʕidna tla:θ maša:ri:ʕ taħt ʔinnaḍar] • **2.** اِعتِبار [ʔiʕtiba:r] He hasn't any consideration for anybody. ما عِندَه اِعتِبار لكُلّ أَحَّد [ma: ʕindah ʔiʕtiba:r lkull ʔaħħad]

consignment • **1.** وَدِيعَة [wadi:ʕa] أمانَة [ʔama:na] He took the goods on consignment. أخَذ البِضاعَة بالأمانَة [ʔaxað ʔilbiḍa:ʕa bilʔama:na]

to consist of • **1.** اِشتِمَل عَلَى [ʔištimal ʕala] اِشتِمال [ʔištima:l] *vn: sv* i. تَرَكَّب مِن [trakkab min] تَرَكُّب [tarakkub] *vn: sv* a. حُوَى عَلَى [ħuwa: ʕala] حَوِي [ħawy] *vn: sv* i. The meal consisted of fish, vegetables, and coffee. الوَجبَة اِشتِمِلَت عَلَى سِمَك وَخُضراوات وقَهوَة [ʔilwaǰba ʔištimlat ʕala simač wxuḍra:wa:t wgahwa]

consistent • **1.** مِتّفِق [mittifiq] مُلائِم [mula:ʔim] His ideas are consistent with those of his party. أفكارَه مُتَّفقَة مَعَ أفكار حِزبَه [ʔafka:rah muttafqa maʕa ʔafka:r ħizbah]

to consolidate • **1.** وَحَّد [waħħad] تَوحِيد، توحِّد [tawħi:d, twiħħid] *vn:* تَوَحَّد [twaħħad] *p:* The two presidents consolidated the two oil companies. الرَّئِيسَين وَحِّدَوا شَركتَين نَفُط [ʔirraʔi:sayn waħħidaw šariktayn nafuṭ]

conspiracy • **1.** مُؤامَرَة [muʔa:mara] مُؤامَرات [muʔa:mara:t] *pl:* تَآمُر [taʔa:mur]

constant • **1.** مِستِمِرّ [mistimirr] دائِمِي [da:ʔimi] This constant noise is making me nervous. هَالصَّوت المِستِمِرّ دَيسَوِّينِي عَصَبِي [haṣṣawt ʔilmistimirr daysawwi:ni ʕaṣabi] • **2.** مِتكَرِّر [mitkarrir] مِستِمِرّ [mistimirr] دائِمِي [da:ʔimi] These constant trips to the doctor are costing me money. هَالزِّيارات المِتكَرِّرَة لِلطَّبِيب دَتكَلِّفنِي فلُوس [hazziya:ra:t ʔilmitkarrira littabi:b datkallafni flu:s] • **3.** ثابِت [θa:bit] Wheat prices have remained constant for two months. أسعار الحُنطَة بُقَت ثابتَة شَهرَين [ʔasʕa:r ʔilħunṭa buqat θa:bta šahrayn] • **4.** نِسبَة ثابِتَة [nisba θa:bta] نِسَب ثابتَة [nisab θa:bta] *pl:* If you know the constant you can solve the problem. لَو تُعرُف النِّسبَة الثّابتَة تِقدَر تحِلّ المَسألَة [law tuʕruf ʔinnisba ʔaθθa:bta tigdar tħill ʔilmasʔala]

constantly • **1.** بإستِمرار [bʔistimra:r] عَلَى طُول [ʕala ṭu:l] دائِماً [da:ʔiman] The telephone rang constantly. التَّلِفُون دَقّ بإستِمرار [ʔittalifu:n dagg bʔistimra:r]

constellation • **1.** مَجمُوعَة النُّجُوم [maǰmu:ʕat ʔinnuǰu:m] مَجمُوعات النُّجُوم [maǰmu:ʕa:t ʔinnuǰu:m] *pl:*

constitution • **1.** دَستُور [dastu:r] دَساتِير [dasa:ti:r] *pl:* Our freedom is guaranteed by the constitution. حُرِّيَّتنا مَضمُونَة بالدَّستُور [ħurriyyatna maḍmu:na biddastu:r] • **2.** بُنيَة [bunya] He has a very strong constitution. عِندَه بُنيَة كُلِّش قَوِيَّة [ʕindah bunya kulliš qawiyya]

to construct • **1.** بِنَى [bina:] بناء [bina:ʔ] *vn:* اِنبِنَى [ʔinbina:] *p:* We're going to construct a new hotel here. راح نِبنِي فَدّ فِندُق جِدِيد هنا [ra:ħ nibni fadd finduq ǰidi:d hna]

construction • **1.** بناء [bina:ʔ] The construction of this dam will take five years. بناء هالسَّدّ راح يطَوِّل خَمس سنِين [bina:ʔ hassadd ra:ħ yṭawwil xams sni:n] My father works for a construction company. أبُويَا دَيِشتُغل إلَى شَرِكَة البِناء [ʔabu:ya dayištuɣl ʔila šarikat ʔilbina:ʔ]

consul • **1.** قُنصُل [qunṣul] قَناصِل [qana:ṣil] *pl:*

consulate • **1.** قُنصُلِيَّة [qunṣuliyya] قُنصُلِيّات [qunṣuliyya:t] *pl:* Were you at the American consulate? كِنِت بالقُنصُلِيَّة الأمرِيكِيَّة؟ [činit bilqunṣuliyya ʔilʔamri:kiyya?]

to consult • **1.** اِستَشار [ʔistaša:r] اِستِشارَة [ʔistiša:ra] *vn: sv* i. You should have consulted us. كان لازِم تِستِشِيرنا [ča:n la:zim tistiši:rna]

to consume • **1.** اِستَهلَك [ʔistahlak] اِستِهلاك [ʔistihla:k] *vn: sv* i. صِرَف [ṣiraf] صَرُف [ṣaruf] *vn:* اِنصِرَف [ʔinṣiraf] *p:* My car consumes a lot of gas. سَيّارتِي تِستَهلِك هوايَة بانزِين [sayya:rti tistahlik hwa:ya banzi:n]

consumption • **1.** إستِهلاك [ʔistihla:k] Consumption has gone up fifty per cent. الاستِهلاك زاد خَمسِين بِالمِيَّة [ʔilʔistihla:k za:d xamsi:n bilmiyya] • **2.** سِلّ [sill] He has consumption. عِندَه سِلّ [ʕindah sill]

C

contact • **1.** إتِّصال [ʔittiṣa:l] إتِّصالات [ʔittiṣa:la:t] *pl:* He's never had any contact with foreigners. أَبَد ما كان عِندَه أَيّ إتِّصال ويّا الأَجانِب [ʔabad ma: ča:n ʕindah ʔayy ʔittiṣa:l wiyya ʔilʔaǰa:nib] • **2.** عَلاقَة، عِلاقَة [ʕala:qa, ʕila:qa] عَلاقات، عِلاقات [ʕala:qa:t, ʕila:qa:t] *pl:* I've made several new contacts. سَوَّيت عِدَّة عِلاقات جِدِيدَة [sawwi:t ʕiddat ʕila:qa:t ǰidi:da]

to come into contact with • **1.** مَسّ [mass] مَسّ [mass] *vn:* إنمَسّ [ʔinmass] *p:* By accident, his hand came into contact with a bare electric wire. بِالصُّدفَة إيدَه مَسَّت سِلِك كَهرَبائِي عارِي [bisṣudfa ʔi:dah massat silik kahraba:ʔi ʕa:ri]

to contact • **1.** إتَّصَل ب [ʔittiṣal b-] إتِّصال [ʔittiṣa:l] *vn: sv* i. I'll contact you as soon as I arrive. راح أَتِّصِل بِيك أَوَّل ما أَوصَل [ra:ħ ʔattiṣil bi:k ʔawwal ma: ʔu:ṣal]

contagious • **1.** مُعدِي [muʕdi]

to contain • **1.** حُوَى [ħuwa:] حَوِي [ħawy] *vn: sv* i. إحتِوَى عَلَى [ʔiħtiwa: ʕala] إحتِواء [ʔiħtiwa:ʔ] *vn: sv* i. That trunk contains clothing. هَالصَّندُوق يِحوِي هدُوم [haṣṣandu:g yiħwi hdu:m] That trunk contains clothing. هَالصَّندُوق بِيه هدُوم [haṣṣandu:g bi:h hdu:m] • **2.** لِزَم [lizam] لَزِم [lazim] *vn: sv* a. ضُبَط [ḍubaṭ] ضَبُط [ḍabuṭ] *vn: sv* u. Don't get excited! Try to contain yourself. لا تِنخُبُص حاوِل تِلزَم نَفسَك [la: tinxubuṣ ħa:wil tilzam nafsak]

contempt • **1.** إستِخفاف [ʔistixfa:f] إزدِراء [ʔizdira:ʔ]

content • **1.** مِقدار [miqda:r] مَقادِير [maqa:di:r] *pl:* The alcoholic content is very low. مِقدار الكُحُول كُلِّش قَلِيل [miqda:r ʔilkuħu:l kulliš qali:l] • **2.** قانِع [qa:niʕ] راضِي [ra:ḍi] He was content with what we offered him. كان قانِع بِاللِّي عرَضنا عَلَيه [ča:n qa:niʕ billi ʕraḍna ʕali:h]

contents • **1.** مُحتَوَيات [muħtawaya:t] Dissolve the contents of this package in one glass of water. ذَوِّب مُحتَوَيات هَالباكِيت بِفَدّ كلاص ماي [ðawwib muħtawaya:t halpa:kayt bfadd gla:ṣ ma:y]

table of contents • **1.** فِهرَست، فَهرَس [fihrast, fahras] فَهارِس [faha:ris] *pl:*

contest • **1.** سِباق [siba:q] سِباقات [siba:qa:t] *pl:* مُسابَقَة [musa:baqa] مُسابَقات [musa:baqa:t] *pl:* مُنافَسَة [muna:fasa] مُنافَسات [muna:fasa:t] *pl:* Who won the contest? مِنُو فاز بالمُسابَقَة؟ [minu fa:z bilmusa:baqa?]

to contest • **1.** طِعَن [ṭiʕan] طَعِن [ṭaʕin] *vn:* إنطِعَن [ʔinṭiʕan] *p:* They're contesting the validity of the will. دَيطِعنُون بِصِحَّة الوَصِيَّة [dayṭiʕnu:n bṣiħħat ʔilwaṣiyya]

continent • **1.** قارَّة [qa:rra] قارّات [qa:rra:t] *pl:*

continual • **1.** مِستِمِرّ [mistimirr] مِتواصِل [mitwa:ṣil] This continual arguing is annoying me. هَالجِدال المِستِمِرّ دَيِزعِجنِي [hajǰida:l ʔilmistimirr dayizʕiǰni]

continually • **1.** دائِماً [da:ʔiman] بإستِمرار [bʔistimra:r] عَلَى طُول [ʕala ṭu:l] The line is continually busy. الخَطّ مَشغُول دائِماً [ʔilxaṭṭ mašɣu:l da:ʔiman]

to continue • **1.** إستَمَرّ ب [ʔistamarr b-] إستِمرار [ʔistimra:r] *vn: sv* i. داوَم [da:wam] دَوام، مُداوَمَة [dawa:m, muda:wama] *vn: sv* i. واصَل [wa:ṣal] مُواصَلَة [muwa:ṣala] *vn: sv* i. Let's continue with our work. خَلِّي نِستِمِرّ بِشُغُلنا [xalli nistimirr bšuɣulna] • **2.** واصَل [wa:ṣal] مُواصَلَة [muwa:ṣala] *vn: sv* i. We'll continue our discussion tomorrow. راح نواصِل مُناقَشَتنا باكِر [ra:ħ nwa:ṣil muna:qašatna ba:čir] • **3.** ظَلّ [ðall] ظَلّ [ðall] *vn: sv* u. His condition continued to be the same. حالتَه ظَلَّت عَلَى ما هِيَّ [ħa:ltah ðallat ʕala ma: hiyya]

continuously • **1.** بإستِمرار [biʔistimra:r] دائِماً [da:ʔiman] عَلَى طُول [ʕala ṭu:l] The phone has been ringing continuously. التَّلِفُون دَيدُقّ بإستِمرار [ʔittalifu:n daydugg biʔistimra:r]

contract • **1.** مُقاوَلَة [muqa:wala] مُقاوَلات [muqa:wala:t] *pl:* قُنطَرات [qunṭara:t] قُنطَراتات [qunṭara:ta:t] *pl:* عَقِد [ʕaqid] عُقُود [ʕuqu:d] *pl:* I refuse to sign that contract. أَرفُض أَوَقِّع هَالعَقِد [ʔarfuḍ ʔawaqqiʕ halʕaqid]

to contract • **1.** تقَلَّص [tqallaṣ] تَقَلُّص [taqalluṣ] *vn: sv* a. Which metal contracts the most? Iron or copper? أَيّ مَعدَن يِتقَلَّص أَكثَر؟ الحَدِيد لَو النُّحاس؟ [ʔayy maʕdan yitqallaṣ ʔakθar? ʔilħadi:d law ʔinnuħa:s?] • **2.** تقاوَل [tqa:wal] تَقاوُل [taqa:wul] *vn: sv* a. سَوَّى [sawwa:] تسِوِّي [tsiwwi] *vn: sv* i. They've contracted to build the building in five months. تقاولَوا يِبنُون العِمارَة بخَمسَة أَشهُر [tqa:wlaw yibnu:n ʔilʕima:ra bxamsat ʔašhur] • **3.** أَخَذ مِن، أَخَذ عَلَى [ʔaxað min, ʔaxað ʕala] أَخِذ [ʔaxið] *vn:* إنأَخَذ [ʔinʔaxað] *p:* I contracted pneumonia. أَخَذِت ذات الرِّئَة [ʔaxaðit ða:t ʔirriʔa]

contractor • **1.** مُقاوِل [muqa:wil] مُقاوِلِين [muqa:wili:n] *pl:*

to contradict • **1.** عارَض [ʕa:rað] مُعارَضَة [muʕa:raða] *vn: sv* i. ناقَض [na:qað] مُناقَضَة [muna:qaða] *vn: sv* i. Don't contradict me! لا تعارِضنِي [la: tʕa:riðni]

contradictory • **1.** مِتناقِض [mitna:qið] مِتخالِف [mitxa:lif] We heard the most contradictory reports on it. سِمَعنا عَنها تَقارِير كُلِّش مِتناقضَة [simaʕna ʕanha taqa:ri:r kulliš mitna:qða]

contrary • **1.** عنادِي [ʕnaːdi] She's very contrary. هِيَّ كُلِّش عنادِيَّة [hiyya kulliš ʕnaːdiyya] • **2.** بعَكِس [bʕakis] بخِلاف [bxilaːf] ضِدّ [ðidd] أضداد [ʔaððaːd] *pl:* Contrary to what we expected he passed the exam. بعَكِس ما توَقَّعنا نِجَح بالإمتِحان [bʕakis maː twaqqaʕna nijaħ bilʔimtiħaːn] • **3.** مُخالِف [muxaːlif] مُعاكِس [muʕaːkis] That's contrary to our agreement. هٰذا مُخالِف لإتِّفاقنا [haːða muxaːlif lʔittifaːqna]

on the contrary • **1.** بالعَكس [bilʕakis] On the contrary, nothing could be worse. بالعَكِس، ماكو أتعَس مِنَّه [bilʕakis, maːku ʔatʕas minnah]

contrast • **1.** إختِلاف [ʔixtilaːf] إختِلافات [ʔixtilaːfaːt] *pl:* تَبايُن [tabaːyun] There's a big contrast between the two brothers. أكُو إختِلاف كِبير بين الأخوَة الثّنين [ʔaku ʔixtilaːf čibiːr bayn ʔilʔuxwa liθnayn]

to contrast • **1.** بَيَّن [bayyan] تبيِّن [tbiyyin] *vn:* تبَيَّن [tbayyan] *p:* He contrasted the programs of the two parties. بَيَّن الاختِلاف بين مَناهِج الحِزبَين [bayyan ʔilixtilaːf bayn manaːhij ʔilħizbayn]

to contribute • **1.** تبَرَّع ب [tbarraʕ b-] تَبَرُّع [tabarruʕ] *vn:* *sv* a. I contributed five dinars to the Red Cross. تبَرَّعِت بخَمس دَنانِير لِلصَّلِيب الأحمَر [tbarraʕit bxams danaːniːr lissaliːb ʔilʔaħmar] • **2.** ساعَد [saːʕad] مُساعَدَة [musaːʕada] *vn:* *sv* i. The interference of the police just contributed to the confusion. تَدَخُّل الشُّرطَة بَسّ ساعَد عَالارتِباك [tadaxxul ʔiššurṭa bass saːʕad ʕalʔirtibaːk] • **3.** قَدَّم [qaddam] تقدِّم، تَقدِيم [tqiddim, taqdiːm] *vn:* تقَدَّم [tqaddam] *p:* He's continually contributing articles to the daily newspaper. دائِماً دَيقَدِّم مَقالات لِلجَّرِيدَة اليَومِيَّة [daːʔiman dayqaddim maqaːlaːt lijjariːda ʔilyawmiyya]

contribution • **1.** تَبَرُّع [tabarruʕ] تَبَرُّعات [tabarruʕaːt] *pl:* مُساعَدَة [musaːʕada] مُساعَدات [musaːʕadaːt] *pl:* We received your contribution yesterday. اِستِلَمنا تَبَرُّعَك البارحَة [ʔistilamna tabarruʕak ʔilbaːrħa]

control • **1.** سَيطَرَة [sayṭara] ضَبُط [ðabuṭ] He lost control of the car. فُقَد السَّيطَرَة عَلَى السَّيّارَة [fuqad ʔissayṭara ʕala ʔissayyaːra] • **2.** مُراقبَة [muraːqaba] The control tower is at the north end of the runway. بُرج المُراقبَة صايِر بالطَّرَف الشّمالِي مِن المَدرَج [burj ʔilmuraːqaba ṣaːyir bittaraf ʔiššimaːli min ʔilmadraj] • **3.** سُلطَة [sulṭa] سُلطات [sulṭaːt] *pl:* سَيطَرَة [sayṭara] The police have no control over diplomats. الشُّرطَة ما عِدها سُلطَة عالدِّبلُوماسِيِّين [ʔiššurṭa maː ʕidha sulṭa ʕaddibluːmaːsiyyiːn] • **4.** قِيادَة [qiyaːda] Let me take over control for a while. خَلِّينِي أستِلِم القِيادَة شوَيَّة [xalliːni ʔastilim ʔilqiyaːda šwayya]

to control • **1.** ضُبَط [ðubaṭ] ضَبُط [ðabuṭ] *vn:* اِنضُبَط [ʔinðubaṭ] *p:* سَيطَر [sayṭar] سَيطَرَة [sayṭara] *vn:* تسَيطَر [tsayṭar] *p:* The teacher couldn't control the class. المُعَلِّم ما قِدَر يُضبُط الصَّفّ [ʔilmuʕallim maː gidar yuðbuṭ ʔiṣṣaff]

convenience • **1.** وَسِيلَة راحَة [wasiːlat raːħa] وَسائِل راحَة [wasaːʔil raːħa] *pl:* Our apartment has every modern convenience. شُقَّتنا بِيها كُلّ وَسائِل الرّاحَة الحَدِيثَة [šuqqatna biːha kull wasaːʔil ʔirraːħa ʔilħadiːθa]

*** Call me at your earliest convenience.**
• **1.** خابُرنِي بأوَّل وَقِت يناسبَك [xaːburni bʔawwal wakit ynaːsbak]

convenient • **1.** مُناسِب [munaːsib] مُلائِم [mulaːʔim] مُرِيح [muriːħ] Will five o'clock be convenient for you? السّاعَة خَمسَة راح تكُون مُناسِبَة لَك؟ [ʔissaːʕa xamsa raːħ tkuːn munaːsiba lak?]

conveniently • **1.** بصُورَة مُلائِمَة [bṣuːra mulaːʔima] بصُورَة مُناسِبَة [bṣuːra munaːsiba] The telephone is conveniently located so everybody can reach it. التَّلَفُون مَحطُوط بصُورَة مُلائِمَة حَتَّى كُلّ واحِد يقدَر يوَصَلَّه [ʔittalifuːn maħṭuːṭ bṣuːra mulaːʔima ħatta kull waːħid yigdar yuːṣallah]

convent • **1.** دَير لِلراهِبات [dayr lirraːhibaːt] أديرَة لِلراهِبات [ʔadyira lirraːhibaːt] *pl:*

convention • **1.** مُؤتَمَر [muʔtamar] مُؤتَمَرات [muʔtamaraːt] *pl:* Were you at the convention last year? كِنِت بالمُؤتَمَر السَّنَة اللِّي فاتَت؟ [činit bilmuʔtamar ʔissana ʔilli faːtat?] • **2.** عُرُف [ʕuruf] عادَى [ʕaːda] Everything he does is according to convention. كُلّشِي يسَوِّيه حَسَب العُرف [kullši ysawwiːh ħasab ʔilʕurf]

conventional • **1.** مُتعارَف عَلَيه [mutʕaːraf ʕaliːh] مُعتاد عَلَيه [muʕtaːd ʕaliːh] I prefer the conventional methods. أفَضِّل الطُّرُق المُتعارَف عَليها [ʔafaððil ʔiṭṭuruq ʔilmutʕaːraf ʕaliːha]

conversation • **1.** مُكالَمَة [mukaːlama] مُكالَمات [mukaːlamaːt] *pl:* حَكِي [ħači] حَدِيث [ħadiːθ] Our telephone conversation lasted an hour. مُكالَمَتنا التَّلِفونِيَّة طَوِّلَت ساعَة [mukaːlamatna ʔittalifuːniyya ṭawwilat saːʕa]

convert • **1.** مِتنَصِّر [mitnaṣṣir] مِتنَصِّرِين [mitnaṣṣiriːn] *pl:* His wife became a Christian convert. زَوجتَه صارَت مِتنَصِّرَة [zawijtah ṣaːrat mitnaṣṣira] • **2.** مِستَسلِم [mistaslim] مِستَسلِمِين [mistaslimiːn] *pl:* There are many converts to Islam living here. أكُو مِستَسلِمِين هوايَة يعِيشُون هنا [ʔaku mistasilmiːn hwaːya yʕiːšuːn hna] • **3.** This man is a convert to Judaism. هَالرِّجّال مِتهَوِّد [harrijjaːl mithawwid]

to convert • **1.** بَدَّل [baddal] تبدِّل، تَبدِيل [tbiddil, tabdiːl] *vn:* حَوَّل [ħawwal] تَحوِيل، تحوِّل [taħwiːl, tħiwwil] *vn:* تحَوَّل [tħawwal] *p:* *sv* i. Where can I convert these dollars into dinars? وِين أقدَر أبَدِّل هَالدُّولارات إلَى دَنانِير؟ [wiːn ʔagdar ʔabaddil haddulaːraːt ʔila danaːniːr?] • **2.** حَوَّل [ħawwal] تَحوِيل، تحوِّل [taħwiːl, tħiwwil]

C

إنقِلَب [ʔingilab] قِلَب [galub] *vn:* This experiment converts starch into sugar. هَالتَّجرُبَة تحَوِّل النِّشا إلَى شَكَر [hattaǰruba tħawwil ʔinniša: ʔila šakar] He converted his house into a restaurant. حَوَّل بَيتَه إلَى مَطعَم [ħawwal baytah ʔila maṭʕam] • **3.** قِلَب [gilab] قَلُب [galub] *vn:* You cannot convert this atheist to any religion. ما تِقدَر تُقلُب هالمُلحِد لأي دِين [ma: tigdar tuglub halmulħid lʔayy di:n]

convict • **1.** مُدان [muda:n] مُدانِين [muda:ni:n] *pl:* مَحكُوم عَليه [maħku:m ʕali:h] Three convicts escaped. ثَلاث مَحكُوم عَلَيهُم هِربَوا [tlaθ maħku:m ʕali:hum hirbaw]

to convict • **1.** أدان [ʔada:n] إدانَة [ʔida:na] *vn: sv* i. The judge convicted him of murder. الحاكِم أدانَه بجَرِيمَة القَتِل [ʔilħa:kim ʔada:nah bǰari:mat ʔilqatil]

to convince • **1.** قَنَّع [qawwaʕ] تقِنِّع، تَقنِيع [tqinniʕ, taqni:ʕ] *vn:* تقَنَّع [ʔaqnaʕ] إقناع [ʔiqna:ʕ] *vn: sv* i. You can't convince me. ما تِقدَر تقَنِّعنِي [ma: tigdar tqanniʕni]

cook • **1.** طَبّاخ [ṭabba:x] طَبّاخِين [ṭabba:xi:n] *pl:* She a very good cook. هِيَّ طَبّاخَة كُلَّش زينَة [hiyya ṭabba:xa kulliš zi:na]

*** Too many cooks spoil the broth.** • **1.** السَفِينَة، إذا كِثرَوا ملالِيحها، تِغرَق [ʔissafi:na, ʔiða: kiθraw mla:li:ħha, tiɣrag]

to cook • **1.** طُبَخ [ṭubax, ṭibax] طَبُخ [ṭabux] *vn:* اِنطُبَخ [ʔinṭubax] *p:* We don't have time to cook tonight. ما عِدنا وَقِت نِطبُخ هاللَّيلَة [ma: ʕidna wakit niṭbux hallayla]

cookie • **1.** كليجايَة [kli:ča:ya] كليجايات [kli:ča:ya:t] *pl:* كلَيجَة [kli:ča] *Collective:* I brought you some cookies. جِبتلَك شوَيَّة كلَيجَة [ǰibitlak šwayya kli:ča]

cool • **1.** بارِد [ba:rid] The weather is cool here, especially at night. الدِّنيا بارِدَة هنا، خُصُوصاً باللَّيل [ʔiddinya ba:rda hna, xuṣu:ṣan billayl] Bring me some cool water. جِيبلِي شوَيَّة مَيّ بارِد [ǰi:bli šwayya mayy ba:rid] • **2.** هادِئ [ha:diʔ] بارِد [ba:rid] I tried to keep cool after the accident. حاوَلِت أبقَى هادِئ بَعد الحادِث [ħa:walit ʔabqa: ha:diʔ baʕd ʔilħa:diθ]

to cool • **1.** بُرَد [burad] بُرُود [buru:d] *vn: sv* a. Don't let the soup cool too long. لا تخَلِّي الشُّوربَة تُبرَد هوايَة [la: txalli ʔiššu:rba tubrad hwa:ya] • **2.** هِدَأ [hidaʔ] هُدُوء [hudu:ʔ] *vn: sv* a. بُرَد [burad] بُرُود [buru:d] *vn: sv* a. Leave him alone. He'll cool off after a while. خَلِّيه وَحدَه راح يِهدَأ بَعد شوَيَّة [xalli:h waħdah ra:ħ yihdaʔ baʕd šwayya] • **3.** بَرَّد [barrad] تبرِّد، تَبرِيد [tbirrid, tabri:d] *vn:* تبَرَّد [tbarrad] *p:* The air conditioner cools the entire house. المُكَيِّفَة تبَرِّد البَيت كُلَّه [ʔilmukayyifa tbarrid ʔilbayt kullah] • **4.** هَدَّى [haddaʔ] تَهدِئَة، تهِدِّئ [tahdiʔa, thiddiʔ] *vn:* تهَدَّأ [thaddaʔ] *p:* بَرَّد [barrad] تَبرِيد، تبرِّد [tabri:d, tbirrid] *vn:* تبَرَّد [tbarrad] *p:* Try to cool him down a bit. حاوِل تهَدِّئَه شوَيَّة [ħa:wil thaddiʔah šwayya]

coop • **1.** بَيت [bayt] بيُوت [biyu:t] *pl:* Clean out the chicken coop. نَظُّف بَيت الدِّجاج [naḍḍuf bayt ʔiddiǰa:ǰ]

to coop up • **1.** حِبَس [ħibas] حَبِس [ħabis] *vn:* اِنحِبَس [ʔinħibas] *p:* حِصَر [ħiṣar] حَصِر [ħaṣir] *vn:* اِنحِصَر [ʔinħiṣar] *p:* I cooped the children up in the house this morning for being naughty. حِبَسِت الجِّهال الصُّبُح بالبَيت لِأنّ كانَوا يأذُون [ħibasit ʔiǰǰaha:l ʔiṣṣubuħ bilbayt liʔann ča:naw yʔaððu:n]

to co-operate • **1.** تعاوَن [tʕa:wan] تَعاوُن [taʕa:wun] *vn: sv* a. I wish they would co-operate with us more. أتمَنَّى يتعاونُون ويّانا أكثَر [ʔatmanna: yitʕa:wnu:n wiyya:na ʔakθar]

co-operation • **1.** تَعاوُن [taʕa:wun] Can we count on your co-operation? نِقدَر نِعتِمِد عَلَى تَعاونَك؟ [nigdar niʕtimid ʕala taʕa:wnak?]

copper • **1.** صِفِر [ṣifir] صفارَة [ṣfa:ra] *pl:* نُحاس [nuħa:s]

Copt • **1.** قَبطِي [qabṭi] أقباط [ʔaqba:ṭ] *pl:*

copy • **1.** نُسخَة [nusxa] نُسَخ [nusax] *pl:* صُورَة [ṣu:ra] صُوَر [ṣuwar] *pl:* I made a copy of the letter. سَوَّيت نُسخَة مِن المَكتُوب [sawwayt nusxa min ʔilmaktu:b] • **2.** نُسخَة [nusxa] نُسَخ [nusax] *pl:* Do you have a copy of this morning's paper? عِندَك نُسخَة مِن الجَّرِيدَة الصَّباحِيَّة مال اليُوم [ʕindak nusxa min ʔiǰǰari:da ʔiṣṣaba:ħiyya ma:l ʔilyu:m]

to copy • **1.** نِقَل [niqal, nigal] نَقِل [naqil] *vn:* اِنّقَل [ʔinniqal] *p:* Copy these two sentences off the blackboard. اِنقِلُوا هَالجُّمَلتَين مِن السَّبُّورَة [ʔiniqlu: hajǰumaltayn min ʔissabbu:ra] • **2.** سَوَّى قُوبيَة [sawwa: qu:pya] The teacher gave him a zero in the examination because he copied. المُعَلِّم إنطاه صِفِر بالإمتِحان لِأنَّه سَوَّى قُوبيَة [ʔilmuʕallim ʔinṭa:h ṣifir bilʔimtiħa:n liʔannah sawwa: qu:pya] • **3.** قَلَّد [qallad] تقلِّد، تَقلِيد [tqillid, taqli:d] *vn:* تقَلَّد [tqallad] *p: sv* i. He copies his father in everything. يقَلِّد أبُوه بِكُلّشِي [yqallid ʔabu:h bikullši]

coral • **1.** مَرجان [marǰa:n, mirǰa:n] I'd like to buy a coral necklace. أرِيد أشتِري قلادَة مَرجان [ʔari:d ʔaštiri gla:da marǰa:n]

cord • **1.** خَيط [xayṭ] خيُوط [xyu:ṭ] *pl:* My son doesn't have enough cord to fly his kite. إبنِي ما عِندَه خيط كافِي يطَيِّر الطَّيّارَة بِيه [ʔibni ma: ʕindah xi:ṭ ka:fi yṭayyir ʔiṭṭiyya:ra bi:h] • **2.** وايَر [wa:yar] وايَرات [wa:yara:t] *pl:* We'll have to get a new cord for the iron. لازِم نجيب وايَر جِديد لِلأوتي [laːzim nǰiːb waːyar ǰidiːd lilʔuːti]

cordial • **1.** حارّ [ħaːrr] قَلبِي [qalbi] The host gave us a cordial welcome. المعزِّب اِستقبَلنا اِستِقبال حارّ [limʕazzib ʔistaqbalna ʔistiqbaːl ħaːrr]

cork • **1.** تَبَّدُور [tabbaduːr] فِلِّينَة [filliːna] فِلِّينات [filliːnaːt] *pl:* The cork fell into the bottle. التَّبَّدُور وُقَع بِالبُوطِل [ʔittabbaduːr wugaʕ bilbuṭul

to cork • **1.** سَدّ بِالتَّبَّدُور [sadd bittabbaduːr] سَدّ [sadd] *vn:* اِنسَدّ [ʔinsadd] *p:* Don't forget to cork the bottle. لا تِنسَى تسَدّ البُوطِل بِالتَّبَّدُور [laː tinsaː tsadd ʔilbuṭul bittabbaduːr]

corkscrew • **1.** بُرغِي [burɣi] بَراغِي [baraːgi] *pl:*

corn • **1.** ذِرَة، إذرَة [ðira, ʔiðra] He doesn't grow much corn. ما يِزرَع إذرَة هوايَة [maː yizraʕ ʔiðra hwaːya] • **2.** بِسمار [bismaːr] بسامِير [bsaːmiːr] *pl:* Doctor, this corn on my foot is bothering me. دِكتُور، هالبِسمار اللّي برِجلِي دَيُوجَعنِي [diktuːr, halbismaːr ʔilli brijli dayuːǰaʕni]

corn bread • **1.** خُبُز إذرَة [xubuz ʔiðra]

corner • **1.** رُكُن [rukun] أركان [ʔarkaːn] *pl:* The man stood by the corner of the building. الرَّجُل وُقَف يَمّ رُكن البِنايَة [ʔirrajul wugaf yamm rukn ʔilbinaːya] • **2.** زُوِيَّة [zuwiyya] زوايا [zwaːya] *pl:* Put the books in the corner. حُطّ الكُتُب بِالزُّوِيَّة [ħuṭṭ ʔilkutub bizzuwiyya]

to corner • **1.** حِصَر [ħiṣar] حَصِر [ħaṣir] *vn:* اِنحِصَر [ʔinħiṣar] *p:* I cornered him this morning and demanded my money. حِصَرتَه الصُّبُح وطلَبِت فلُوسِي [ħiṣartah ʔiṣṣubuħ wṭlabit fluːsi]

corn flour • **1.** طحِين إذرَة [ṭħiːn ʔiðra]

corporal • **1.** نايِب عَرِيف [naːyib ʕariːf] نُوّاب عُرَفاء [nuwwaːb ʕurafaːʔ] *pl:*

corpse • **1.** جِثَّة [ǰiθθa] جِثَث [ǰiθaθ] *pl:*

corral • **1.** زِرِيبَة [ziriːba] زَرايِب [zaraːyib] *pl:*

correct • **1.** صَحِيح [ṣaħiːħ] تَمام [tamaːm] مَضبُوط [maðbuːṭ] Is this the correct address? هَذا العِنوان الصَّحِيح [haːða ʔilʕinwaːn ʔiṣṣaħiːħ]

to correct • **1.** صَحَّح [ṣaħħaħ] تَصحِيح، تصِحِّح [taṣħiːħ, tṣiħħiħ] *vn:* تصَحَّح [ṣallaħ] تَصلِيح، تصِلِّح [taṣliːħ, tṣilliħ] *vn:* تصَلَّح [tṣallaħ] *p:* Please correct the mistakes in my French. أرجُوك صَحِّح أغلاطِي بِالفِرَنسِي [ʔarǰuːk ṣaħħiħ ʔaɣlaːṭi bilifiransi] • **2.** ضُبَط [ðubaṭ] ضَبُط [ðabuṭ] *vn:* اِنضُبَط [ʔinðubaṭ] *p:* عَدَّل [ʕaddal] تَعدِيل، تعِدِّل [taʕdiːl, tʕiddil] *vn:* تعَدَّل [tʕaddal] *p:* صَحَّح [ṣaħħaħ] تصَحَّح [tṣaħħaħ] *p:* صَلَّح [ṣallaħ] *sv* i These glasses will correct your vision. هالمَناظِر راح تُضبُط نَظَرَك [halmanaːðir raːħ tuðbuṭ naðarak]

correction • **1.** تَصحِيح [taṣħiːħ] تَصلِيح [taṣliːħ] تَعدِيل [taʕdiːl] تَعدِيلات [taʕdiːlaːt] *pl:* ضَبُط [ðabuṭ] Please make the necessary corrections. أرجُوك سَوِّي التَّصحِيحات اللازمَة [ʔarǰuːk sawwi ʔittaṣħiːħaːt ʔillaːzma]

to correspond • **1.** طابَق [ṭaːbaq] مُطابَقَة [muṭaːbaqa] *vn:* تطابَق [ʔittaːbaq] *p:* The translation does not correspond with the original. التَّرجُمَة ما تطابُق الأَصِل [ʔittarǰuma maː ṭṭaːbuq ʔilʔaṣil] • **2.** تراسَل [traːsal] تَراسُل [taraːsul] *vn:* *sv* a. تكاتَب [tkaːtab] تَكاتُب [takaːtub] *vn:* *sv* a. We've been corresponding for six years. صار إلنا سِتَّة سنِين نِتراسَل [ṣaːr ʔilna sitta sniːn nitraːsal]

correspondence • **1.** مُراسَلَة [muraːsala] مُراسَلات [muraːsalaːt] *pl:* مُكاتَبَة [mukaːtaba] مُكاتَبات [mukaːtabaːt] *pl:* My job is answering the correspondence. شُغلِي أجِيب عالمُراسَلات [šuɣli ʔaǰiːb ʕalmuraːsalaːt]

correspondent • **1.** مُراسِل [muraːsil] مُراسِلِين [muraːsiliːn] *pl:* He's a correspondent for the Times. هُوَّ مُراسِل جَرِيدَة التّايمز [huwwa muraːsil ǰariːdat ʔittaːymz]

corridor • **1.** مَمشَى [mamša] مَماشِي [mamaːši] *pl:* دِهلِيز [dihliːz] دَهالِيز [dahaːliːz] *pl:* مَمَرّ [mamarr] مَمَرّات [mamarraːt] *pl:* مجاز [mǰaːz] مجازات [mǰaːzaːt] *pl:*

corrugated • **1.** معَرَّج [mʕarraǰ]

cosmetic • **1.** مَسحُوق [masħuːq] مَساحِيق [masaːħiːq] *pl:* She uses a lot of cosmetics. دَتِستَعمِل مَساحِيق هوايَة [datistaʕmil masaːħiːq hwaːya]

cost • **1.** تَكلِيف [takliːf] تَكالِيف [takaːliːf] *pl:* كُلفَة [kulfa] كُلَف [kulaf] *pl:* He was forced to sell everything at less than cost. اِنجُبَر يبِيع كُلشِي بأقَلّ مِن التَّكلِيف [ʔinǰubar yibiːʕ kullši biʔaqall min ʔittakliːf] The cost of living is rising. كُلفَة المَعِيشَة دَتِرتِفِع [kulfat ʔilmaʕiːša datirtifiʕ] • **2.** قِيمَة [qiːma] قِيَم [qiyam] *pl:* سِعِر [siʕir] أسعار [ʔasʕaːr] *pl:* ثَمَن [θaman] أثمان [ʔaθmaːn] *pl:* تَكلِيف [takliːf] تَكالِيف [takaːliːf] *pl:* كُلفَة [kulfa] كُلَف [kulaf] *pl:* The cost of this item on the market is twenty dinars. قِيمَة هَالشِّي بالسُّوق عِشرِين دِينار [qiːmat hašši bissuːg ʕišriːn dinaːr]

at any cost • **1.** بأيّ ثَمَن [bʔayy θaman] مَهما يكُون الثَّمَن [mahma ykuːn ʔiθθaman] He wants it at any cost. يرِيدها بأيّ ثَمَن [yriːdha bʔayy θaman]

to cost • **1.** كَلَّف [kallaf] تَكلِيف [takliːf] *vn:* *sv* i. How much do these shoes cost? هَالقُندَرَة شقَدّ تكَلِّف؟

[halqundara šgadd tkallif?] The battle cost the enemy the loss of many lives. المَعرَكَة كَلَّفَت العَدُو خَسائِر هوايَة بالأرواح [ʔilmaʕraka kallifat ʔilʕadu xasaːʔir hwaːya bilʔarwaːħ]

C

costly • 1. غالِي [ɣaːli] She uses very costly perfume. دَتِستَعمِل رِيحَة غالِيَة هوايَة [datistaʕmil riːħa ɣaːlya hwaːya]

costume • 1. زَيّ [zayy] أَزياء [ʔazyaːʔ] *pl:* لِبِس [libis] أَزياء [ʔazyaːʔ] *pl:* The dancer wore a beautiful costume. الرّاقِصَة لِبسَت زَيّ حِلو [ʔirraːqiṣa libsat zayy ħilw]

cot • 1. جَربايَة سَفَرِيَّة [čarpaːya safariyya] جَربايات سَفَرِيَّة [čarpaːyaːt safariyya] *pl:* سِرِير سَفَري [siriːr safari] سَرايِر سَفَرِيَّة [saraːyir safariyya] *pl:*

cottage cheese • 1. لِبَن مَنَشَّف [liban mnaššaf] Give me a half kilo of cottage cheese. إنطِينِي نُصّ كِيلُو لِبَن مَنَشَّف [ʔinṭiːni nuṣṣ kiːlu liban mnaššaf]

cotton • 1. قُطِن، قُطُن [guṭin, guṭun] Bring me a piece of cotton. جِيبلِي فَدّ وُصلَة قُطِن [jiːbli fadd wuṣlat guṭin] I'd like to buy a pair of cotton socks. أَرِيد أَشتِري فَدّ زوج جواريب قُطِن [ʔariːd ʔaštiri fadd zuːǰ ǰwaːriːb guṭin]

couch • 1. قَنَفَة [qanafa] قَنَفات [qanafaːt] *pl:*

cough • 1. قَحَّة، كَحَّة [gaħħa] قَحّات، كَحّات [gaħħaːt] *pl:* Do you have something that's good for a cough? عِندَك شِي زين لِلقَحَّة؟ [ʕindak ši ziːn lilgaħħa?]

to cough • 1. قَحّ، كَحّ [gaħħ] قَحّ، كَحّ [gaħħ] *vn: sv* u. The baby coughed all night. الطِّفِل كَحّ طُول اللّيل [ʔiṭṭifil gaħħ ṭuːl ʔillayl]

council • 1. مَجلِس [maǰlis] مَجالِس [maǰaːlis] *pl:*

councilman • 1. عُضُو مَجلِس [ʕuðw maǰlis] أَعضاء مَجلِس [ʔaʕðaːʔ maǰlis] *pl:*

counsel • 1. نَصِيحَة [naṣiːħa] نَصايِح [naṣaːyiħ] *pl:* مَشورَة [mašuːra, mašwara] إستِشارَة [ʔistišaːra] إستِشارات [ʔistišaːraːt] *pl:* Let me give you some good counsel. خَلِّي أَنطِيك فَدّ نَصِيحَة زينَة [xalli ʔanṭiːk fadd naṣiːħa ziːna] **• 2.** مُحامِي [muħaːmi] مُحامِين [muħaːmiːn] *pl:* The counsel for the defense arrived late. مُحامِي الدِّفاع وُصَل مِتأَخِّر [muħaːmi ʔiddifaːʕ wuṣal mitʔaxxir]

count • 1. تِعداد [tiʕdaːd] تِعدادات [tiʕdaːdaːt] *pl:* عَدّ [ʕadd] حساب [ħsaːb] The count has not been taken yet. التِّعداد ما صار بَعَد [ʔittiʕdaːd maː ṣaːr baʕad] **• 2.** كَونت [kawnt] كَونتات [kawntaːt] *pl:* She married a count. تزَوّجَت كُونت [dzawwǰat kawnt]

to count • 1. حِسَب [ħisab] حساب [ħsaːb] *vn:* اِنحِسَب [ʔinħisab] *p:* عَدّ [ʕadd] تِعداد، عَدّ [tiʕdaːd, ʕadd] *vn:* اِنعَدّ [ʔinʕadd] *p:* Please count your change. أَرجُوك إحسِب الخُردَة مالتَك [ʔarǰuːk ʔiħsib ʔilxurda maːltak]

to count on • 1. اِعتِمَد عَلَى [ʔiʕtimad ʕala] اِعتِماد عَلَى [ʔiʕtimaːd ʕala] *vn: sv* i. وِثَق ب [wiθaq b-] ثِقَة [θiqa] *vn:* اِنوِثَق [ʔinwiθaq] *p:* You cannot count on him at all. ما تِقدَر تِعتِمِد عَليه بِالمَرَّة [maː tigdar tiʕtimid ʕaliːh bilmarra]

counter • 1. كاونتَر [kaːwintar] Your package is on the counter. الرُّزمَة مالتَك عالكاونتِر [ʔirruzma maːltak ʕalkaːwntir] **• 2.** ضِدّ [ðidd] أَضداد [ʔaðdaːd] *pl:* This is counter to our beliefs. هَذا ضِدّ مُعتَقَداتنا [haːða ðidd muʕtaqadaːtna]

counterfeit • 1. مُزَيَّف [muzayyaf] قَلِب [qalib] This money is counterfeit. هَالفِلُوس مزَيِّفَة [halfiluːs mzayyifa] **• 2.** مزَوَّر [mzawwar] This signature is counterfeit. هالتَّوقِيع مزَوَّر [hattawqiːʕ mzawwar]

to counterfeit • 1. زَيَّف [zayyaf] تَزيِيف، تزيِّف [tazyiːf, tziyyif] *vn:* تزَيَّف [tzayyaf] *p:* زَوَّر [zawwar] تَزوِير، تزوِّر [tazwiːr, tziwwir] *vn:* تزَوَّر [tzawwar] *p:* He counterfeited one thousand dinars. زَيَّف أَلف دِينار [zayyaf ʔalf dinaːr]

countess • 1. كَونتِيسَة [kuntiːsa] كَونتِيسات [kuntiːsaːt] *pl:*

country • 1. بَلَد [balad] بُلدان [buldaːn] *pl:* بلاد [blaːd] بُلدان [buldaːn] *pl:* قُطُر [quṭur] أَقطار [ʔaqṭaːr] *pl:* دَولَة [dawla] دَولات، دُوَل [dawlaːt, duwal] *pl:* I've seen many countries. شِفِت بُلدان هوايَة [šifit buldaːn hwaːya] **• 2.** رِيف [riːf] أَرياف [ʔaryaːf] *pl:* We spent our vacation in the country. قضَينا عُطلَتنا بِالرِّيف [gðiːna ʕuṭlatna birriːf] **• 3.** مَنطِقَة [manṭiqa, manṭaqa] مَناطِق [manaːṭiq, manaːṭig] *pl:* The country around Baghdad is agricultural. المَنطِقَة حَوالِي بَغداد زِراعِيَّة [ʔilmanṭiqa ħawaːli baɣdaːd ziraːʕiyya]

couple • 1. A young couple sat in front of us in the movie. فَدّ شابّ وَشابَّة قِعدَوا قِدّامنا بِالسِّينَما [fadd šaːbb wšaːbba giʕdaw giddaːmna bissinama] I'm living with an elderly couple. آنِي ساكِن وِيّا فَدّ شايِب وَعَجُوز [ʔaːni saːkin wiyya fadd šaːyib wʕaǰuːz]

a couple of • 1. فَدّ [fadd] I bought a couple of ties. اِشتِرَيت فَدّ رَبُطتَين [ʔištiriːt fadd rabuṭṭayn] Hand me a couple of nails. ناوُشنِي فَدّ بِسمارَين [naːwušni fadd bismaːrayn] He was here a couple of days ago. كان هنا قَبُل فَدّ يومَين [čaːn hna gabul fadd yawmayn]

to couple • 1. شَكَّل [šakkal] تَشكِيل، تشِكِّل [taškiːl, tšikkil] *vn: sv* i. They coupled the coach to the train. شَكّلَوا الفَرگون بِالقِطار [šakkilaw ʔilfarguːn bilqiṭaːr]

coupling • **1.** صَمُّونَة [ṣammuːna] صَمُّونات [ṣammuːnaːt] *pl:* They connected the two pipes with a rubber coupling. رُبطَوا البُوريِّين بِصَمُّونَة لاستِيك [rubṭaw ʔilbuːriyyayn bṣammuːna laːstiːk]

coupon • **1.** كَوبَون [kubuːn] كَوبَونات [kubuːnaːt] *pl:*

courage • **1.** شَجاعَة [šaǰaːʕa] جُرأة [ǰurʔa] Don't lose your courage. لا تُفقُد شَجاعتَك [laː tufqud šaǰaːʕtak]

course • **1.** اِتِّجاه [ʔittiǰaːh] اِتِّجاهات [ʔittiǰaːhaːt] *pl:* طَرِيق [ṭariːq] طُرُق [ṭuruq] *pl:* The plane is holding a straight course. الطَّيّارَة لازمَة اِتِّجاه عَدِل [ʔiṭṭiyyaːra laːzma ʔittiǰaːh ʕadil] • **2.** اِتِّجاه [ʔittiǰaːh] اِتِّجاهات [ʔittiǰaːhaːt] *pl:* مَجرَى [maǰra] مَجارِي [maǰaːri] *pl:* The river changed its course. النَّهَر غَيَّر اِتِّجاهَه [ʔinnahar γayyar tiǰaːhah] • **3.** دَرِس [daris] درُوس [druːs] *pl:* How many courses did you take? كَم دَرِس أخَذِت؟ [čam daris ʔaxaðit?] • **4.** طَرِيقَة [ṭariːqa] طُرُق [ṭuruq] *pl:* خُطَّة [xuṭṭa] خُطّات [xuṭṭaːt] *pl:* سَبِيل [sabiːl] سُبُل [subul] *pl:* Tell me the course of action you're going to follow. قُلّي طَرِيقَة العَمَل اللّي راح تِتبِعها [gulli ṭariːqat liʕamal ʔilli raːħ titbiʕha] • **5.** ساحَة [saːħa] ساحات [saːħaːt] *pl:* It takes almost a half hour to walk around the course. تطَوِّل حَوالِي نُصّ ساعَة مَشِي حَول السّاحَة [ṭṭawwil ħawaːli nuṣṣ saːʕa mašy ħawl ʔissaːħa] • **6.** دَفعَة [dafʕa] دَفعات [dafʕaːt] *pl:* They served the meal in three courses. قَدِّمَوا الأكِل عَلَى ثلاث دُفعات [qaddimaw ʔilʔakil ʕala tlaːθ dufʕaːt]

in due course • **1.** بوَقِتها [bwakitha] We will notify you in due course. راح نخَبّرَك بوَقِتها [raːħ nxabbrak bwakitha]

in the course • **1.** بخِلال [bxilaːl] أثناء [ʔaθnaːʔ] He got two promotions in the course of one year. حَصَّل عَلَى تَرفِيعَين بخِلال سَنَة وِحدَة [ħaṣṣal ʕala tarfiːʕayn bxilaːl sana wiħda]

of course • **1.** طَبعاً [ṭabʕan] بالطَّبُع [biṭṭabuʕ] Of course I know what you mean! طَبعاً، أعرُف شتُقصُد [ṭabʕan, ʔaʕruf štuqṣud]

court • **1.** مَحكَمَة [maħkama] مَحاكِم [maħaːkim] *pl:* I'll see you in court tomorrow. راح أشُوفَك بالمَحكَمَة باكِر [raːħ ʔašuːfak bilmaħkama baːčir] • **2.** ساحَة [saːħa] ساحات [saːħaːt] *pl:* The tennis court is still wet. ساحَة التَّنِس بَعَدها رَطبَة [saːħat ʔittanis baʕadha raṭba] • **3.** حُوش [ħuːš] حَواش [ħwaːš] *pl:* ساحَة [saːħa] ساحات [saːħaːt] *pl:* The maid is washing the clothes in the court. الخَدّامَة دَتِغسِل الهدُوم بالحُوش [ʔilxaddaːma datiγsil ʔilhduːm bilħuːš] • **4.** حاشِيَة [ħaːšiya] حَواشِي [ħawaːši] *pl:* The king attended the race with his court. المَلِك حِضَر السِّباق وِيّا حاشِيتَه [ʔilmalik ħiðar ʔissibaːq wiyya ħaːšiːtah]

to court • **1.** تقَرَّب إلَى، تحَبَّب إلَى [tqarrab ʔila, tħabbab ʔila] تَقَرُّب إلَى، تَحَبُّب إلَى [taqarrub ʔila, taħabbub ʔila] *vn: sv* a. تحَبَّب [tħabbab] تَحَبُّب [taħabbub] *vn: sv* a. He tried to court her several times. حاوَل يتقَرَّب إلها عِدَّة مَرّات [ħaːwal yitqarrab ʔilha ʕiddat marraːt]

courteous • **1.** مُجامِل [muǰaːmil] Try to be courteous while they're here. حاوِل تكُون مُجامِل لَمّا يكُونُون هنا [ħaːwil tkuːn muǰaːmil lamma ykuːnuːn hna]

courtesy • **1.** مُجامَلَة [muǰaːmala] مُجامَلات [muǰaːmalaːt] *pl:* You should learn some courtesy. لازِم تِتعَلَّم شوَيَّة مُجامَلَة [laːzim titʕallam šwayya muǰaːmala]

courtroom • **1.** قاعَة مَحكَمَة [qaːʕat maħkama] قاعات مَحكَمَة [qaːʕaːt maħkama] *pl:*

cousin • **1.** إبن/بِنت/وُلد عَمّ/عَمَّة [ʔibin/bint/wulid ʕamm/ʕamma] إبن/بِنت/وُلد خال/خالَة [ʔibin/bint/wulid xaːl/xaːla] father's brother's son, father's sister daugther, mother's brother's son, mother's sister's daughter etc. (8 terms in total) **وِلاد عَمّ** [wilaːd ʕamm] pl: (generic for cousins)

cover • **1.** غِطا [γiṭa] غطا [γaṭa] غَطايات [γaṭaːyaːt, γiṭaːyaːt] *pl:* شَرشَف [čarčaf] شَراشِف [čaraːčif] *pl:* The cover to this chair is dirty. غَطا هَالكُرسِي وَسِخ [γaṭa halkursi waṣix] • **2.** قَبَغ [qabaγ] قَبَغات [qabaγaːt] *pl:* غطا [γaṭaː] غَطايات [γaṭaːyaːt] *pl:* Where is the cover for this box? وين قَبَغ هَالقُوطِيَّة؟ [wiːn qabaγ halquːṭiyya?] • **3.** غِلاف [γilaːf] أغلِفَة [ʔaγlifa] *pl:* Who tore the cover off this book? مِنُو شَقَّق غلاف هَالكِتاب؟ [minu šaggag γlaːf halkitaːb?] • **4.** مَلجَأ [malǰaʔ] Deer don't have good cover in this area. الغِزلان ما عِدها مَلجَأ زين بهَالمَنطِقَة [ʔilγizlaːn maː ʕidha malǰaʔ ziːn bhalmanṭiqa] • **5.** لحاف [lħaːf] لِحِف، لِحفان [liħif, liħfaːn] *pl:* غِطا [γiṭa, γaṭa] Fatma, take the covers off the bed. فاطمَة، شِيلِي اللِّحِف مِن الفراش [faːṭma, šiːli ʔilliħif min ʔilfraːš]

to cover • **1.** غَطَّى [γaṭṭaː] تَغطِيَة، تغِطّي [taγṭiya, tγiṭṭi] *vn:* تغَطَّى [tγaṭṭaː] *p:* We covered the ground with a blanket. غَطَّينا القاع بِبَطّانِيَّة [γaṭṭiːna ʔilgaːʕ bibaṭṭaːniyya] • **2.** غَطَّى [γaṭṭaː] *sv* i. كَفَّى [kaffaː] تكِفّي [tkiffi] *vn:* تكَفَّى [tkaffaː] *p:* Will fifty dollars cover your expenses? خَمسِين دُولار تغَطّي مَصارِيفَك؟ [xamsiːn dulaːr tγaṭṭi maṣaːriːfak?] • **3.** غَطَّة [γaṭṭa] غَطّات [γaṭṭaːt] *pl: sv* i. ضَمضَم [ðamðam] تضُمضُم [tðumðum] *vn: sv* u. طَمطَم [ṭamṭam] طُمطُم [ṭṭumṭum] *vn: sv* u. She's always covering for her friend. هِيَّ دائِماً تغَطّي لِصَدِيقَتها [hiyya daːʔiman tγaṭṭi lṣadiːqatha] • **4.** شِمَل [šimal] شمُول [šumuːl] *vn:* اِنشِمَل [ʔinšimal] *p:* I believe that covers everything. أعتِقِد هَذا يشمِل كُلشي [ʔaʕtiqid haːða yišmil kullši] • **5.** قِطَع [qiṭaʕ] قَطِع [qaṭiʕ] *vn:* اِنقِطَع [ʔinqiṭaʕ] *p:* We covered the distance in four hours. قطَعنا المَسافَة بأربَع ساعات [qṭaʕna ʔilmasaːfa bʔarbaʕ saːʕaːt] • **6.** سَلَّط عَلَى [sallaṭ ʕala] تَسلِيط، تسِلِّط [tasliːṭ, tsilliṭ] *vn:* تسَلَّط [tsallaṭ] *p:* He covered us with a revolver. سَلَّط عَلينا المُسَدَّس [sallaṭ ʕaliːna ʔilmusaddas]

*** Is your house covered by insurance?** • **1.** بَيتَك مأمَّن عَلَيه؟ [baytak mʔamman ʕali:h?] / بَيتَك مصَوقَر؟ [baytak mṣawgar?]

C

cow • **1.** بَقَرَة [baqara] بَقَرات [baqara:t] *pl:* بَقَر [baqar] *Collective:* هايشَة [ha:yša] هوايِش [hwa:yiš] *pl:* هَوش [hu:š] *Collective:* The cows were milked this morning. الهوايِش اِنحِلبَوا هَالصُّبُح [ʔilhwa:yiš ʔinħilbaw haṣṣubuħ]

coward • **1.** جَبان [ǰaba:n] جُبَناء [ǰubana:ʔ] *pl:* خَوّاف [xawwa:f] Don't be such a coward! لا تصِير هَالشَّكِل جَبان [la: tṣi:r haššikil ǰaba:n]

cozy • **1.** مچَكنَم [mčaknam] I like this room because it's cozy. أحِبّ هَالغُرفَة لِأَنَّها مچَكنِمَة [ʔaħibb halɣurfa liʔannha mčaknima]

crab • **1.** أبُو الجِنِّيب [ʔabu ʔiǰǰinni:b] We saw four crabs at the seashore. شِفنا أربَع أبُو الجِنِّيب عَلَى ساحِل البَحَر [šifna ʔarbaʕ ʔabu ʔiǰǰinni:b ʕala sa:ħil ʔilbaħar] • **2.** نِقناقِي [niqna:qi] نِقناقِيِّين [niqna:qiyyi:n] *pl:* He's an old crab. هُوَّ فَدّ واحِد نِقناقِي [huwwa fadd wa:ħid niqna:qi]

crab lice • **1.** قَمُل شِعرَة [gamul šiʕra]

to crab • **1.** نَقنَق [naqnaq, nagnag] تِنِقنِق [tniqniq] *vn: sv* i. Stop crabbing. بَسّ عاد تنَقنِق [bass ʕa:d tnaqniq]

crack • **1.** فَطِر [faṭir] فطُور [fṭu:r] *pl:* فَلِع [faliʕ] فلُوع [flu:ʕ] *pl:* شَقّ [šagg] The crack in the dam is getting larger. الفَطِر اللِّي بالسَّدّ دَيكبَر [ʔilfaṭir ʔilli bissadd dayikbar] • **2.** طَقَّة [ṭagga] طَقّات [ṭagga:t] *pl:* I think I heard the crack of a rifle. أظُنّ سمَعِت طَقَّة مال بُندُقِيَّة [ʔaðunn smaʕit ṭagga ma:l bunduqiyya] • **3.** تَهَكُّم [tahakkum] تَهَكُّمات [tahakkuma:t] *pl:* That crack was very appropriate. هَالتَّهَكُّم كان كُلِّش بمَحَلَّه [hattahakkum ča:n kulliš bmaħallah] • **4.** ماهِر [ma:hir] He's a crack shot. هُوَّ رامِي ماهِر [huwwa ra:mi ma:hir]

*** We got up at the crack of dawn.** • **1.** قعَدنا ويّا طَرَّة الفَجِر [gʕadna wiyya ṭarrat ʔilfaǰir]

to crack • **1.** فُطَر [fuṭar] فَطِر [faṭir] *vn:* اِنفُطَر [ʔinfuṭar] *p:* I've cracked the crystal of my watch. فطَرت الجّامَة مال ساعتِي [fṭarit ʔiǰǰa:ma ma:l sa:ʕti] • **2.** كَسَّر [kassar] تكسِير، تكِسِّر [taksi:r, tkissir] *vn:* تكَسَّر [tkassar] *p:* Who's going to crack the nuts? مِنُو راح يكَسِّر الجُّوز؟ [minu ra:ħ ykassir ʔiǰǰu:z?] • **3.** حَلّ [ħall] حُلُول [ħulu:l] *pl:* حَلّ [ħall] *vn:* اِنحَلّ [ʔinħall] *p:* The police finally cracked the code. الشُّرطَة أخِيراً حَلَّت رُمُوز الشَّفرَة [ʔiššurṭa ʔaxi:ran ħallat rumu:z ʔiššafra] • **4.** طَقّ [ṭagg] طَقّ [ṭagg] *vn:* اِنطَقّ [ʔinṭagg] *p:* He cracked the whip several times. طَقّ القَمجِي عِدَّة مَرّات [ṭagg ʔilqamči ʕiddat marra:t] Crack another bottle of wine for the guests. طُقّ بُوطِل شَراب ثانِي لِلضِّيُوف [ṭugg buṭul šara:b θa:ni liððuyu:f] • **5.** طَقطَق [ṭagṭag] طقِطِق [ṭigṭig] *vn:* تطَقطَق [ʔiṭṭagṭag] p: He's always cracking his knuckles. هُوَّ دائِماً يطَقطِق أصابيعَه [huwwa da:ʔiman yṭagṭig ʔaṣa:bi:ʕah]

*** He didn't crack a smile.** • **1.** وَلا اِبتِسَم [wala ʔibtisam]

to crack jokes • **1.** نَكَّت [nakkat] تَنكِيت، تنِكِّت [tanki:t, tnikkit] *vn: sv* i. He's always cracking jokes. هُوَّ دائِماً ينَكِّت [huwwa da:ʔiman ynakkit]

to crack open • **1.** فِلَع [filaʕ] فَلِع [faliʕ] *vn:* اِنفِلَع [ʔinfilaʕ] *p:* He dropped the watermelon and cracked it open. وَقَّع الرَّقِّيَّة وَفِلَعها [waggaʕ ʔirraggiyya wfilaʕha]

to crack up • **1.** تخَبَّل [txabbal] تخُبُّل، خبال [txubbul, xba:l] *vn: sv* a. He cracked up under the strain. تخَبَّل مِن الإجهاد [txabbal min ʔilʔiǰha:d] • **2.** حَطَّم [ħaṭṭam] تحطِيم [taħṭi:m] *vn:* تحَطَّم [ʔitħaṭṭam] *p:* He cracked up his car three weeks ago. حَطَّم سَيّارتَه قَبُل ثلَث أسابيع [ħaṭṭam sayya:rtah gabul tlaθ ʔasa:bi:ʕ]

cradle • **1.** مَهَد [mahad] مهُود [mhu:d] *pl:* كارُوك [ka:ru:k] كوارِيك [kwa:ri:k] *pl:*

craft • **1.** مِهنَة [mihna] مِهَن [mihan] *pl:* شَغلَة [šaɣla] شَغلات [šaɣla:t] *pl:* صَنعَة [ṣanʕa] صَنعات [ṣanʕa:t] *pl:* Rugmaking is a difficult craft. عَمَل الزُّوالِي مِهنَة صَعبَة [ʕamal ʔizzuwa:li mihna ṣaʕba]

to cram • **1.** حِشَك [ħišag] حَشِك [ħašig] *vn:* حِشَر [ħišar] حَشِر [ħašir] *vn:* حِصَر [ʔħišar] حَصِر [ħaṣir] *vn:* اِنحِصَر [ʔinħiṣar] He crammed everything into one trunk. حِشَك كُلشِي بصَندُوق واحِد [ħišak kullši bṣandu:g wa:ħid] • **2.** حَشَّى [ħašša:] تَحشِيَة، تحِشِّي [taħšya, tħišši] *vn:* تحَشَّى [tħašša:] *p: sv* i. I started cramming the night before the exam. بدَيت أحَشِّي ذِهنِي باللَّيلَة اللِّي القَبل الامتِحان [bdayt ʔaħašši ðihni billayla ʔilli gabil ʔilʔimtiħa:n]

cramp • **1.** أبُو الشِّرقِيل [ʔabu ʔišširgi:l] أبُو الشِّرقِيط [ʔabu ʔišširgi:ṭ] تَشَنُّج الشِّرقِيل [tašannuǰ ʔišširgi:l] أبُو الشِّرقِيل [ʔabu ʔišširgi:l] *pl:* أبُو الشِّرقِيط [ʔabu ʔišširgi:ṭ] تَشَنُّج [tašannuǰ] I have a cramp in my leg. عِندِي أبُو الشِّرقِيل برِجلِي [ʕindi ʔabu ʔišširgi:l briǰli]

crane • **1.** We saw a flock of cranes in the marsh. شِفنا مَجمُوعَة مِن الغَرانِيق بالهُور [šifna maǰmu:ʕa min ʔilɣara:ni:q bilhu:r] • **2.** سلِنق [sling] سلِنقات [slinga:t] *pl:* They're using a crane to destroy the house. دَيستَعمِلُون سلِنق لِتَفلِيش البَيت [dayistaʕmilu:n sling litafli:š ʔilbayt]

crank • **1.** هِندِر [hindir] هِندِرات [hindira:t] *pl:* We have to use the crank to start the car. لازِم نِستَعمِل الهِندِر حَتَّى نشَغِّل السَّيّارَة [la:zim nistaʕmil ʔilhindir ħatta nšaɣɣil ʔissayya:ra] • **2.** يَدَّة [yadda] يَدّات [yadda:t] *pl:* The window crank is rusty and won't turn. يَدّة الشِّبّاك مزَنجِرَة وَما تِنفَر [yaddat ʔiššibba:č mzanǰira wma: tinfarr]

cranky • **1.** نِقناقِي [niqna:qi] نِقناقِيِّين [niqna:qiyyi:n] *pl:* Why are you so cranky this morning? إنتَ لِيش هِيكِي نِقناقِي هَالصُّبُح؟ [ʔinta li:š hi:či niqna:qi haṣṣubuħ?]

crash • **1.** اِصطِدام [ʔiṣṭida:m] تَصادُم [taṣa:dum] تَصادُمات [taṣa:duma:t] *pl:* صَدمَة [ṣadma] صَدمات [ṣadma:t] *pl:* Was anyone hurt in the crash? أَحَّد تأَذّى بالإصطِدام؟ [ʔaħħad tʔaððaː bilʔiṣṭida:m?] • **2.** صُوت [ṣu:t] أَصوات [ʔaṣwa:t] *pl:* حِسّ [ħiss] We heard a crash when the tree fell. سمَعنا حِسّ لَمّا الشِّجرَة وُقعَت [simaʕna ħiss lamma ʔiššiǰra wugʕat]

to crash • **1.** اِصطِدَم [ʔiṣṭidam] اِصطِدام [ʔiṣṭida:m] *vn: sv* i. صِدَم [ṣidam] صَدِم [ṣadim] *vn:* اِنصِدَم [ʔinṣidam] *p:* The car crashed into the wall. السَّيّارَة اِصطِدمَت بِالحايِط [ʔissayya:ra ʔiṣṭidmat bilħa:yiṭ]

crate • **1.** قُفَص [qufaṣ] I bought a crate of oranges. اِشتِرَيت قُفَص بُرتُقال [ʔištiri:t qufaṣ purtuqa:l]

to crawl • **1.** زِحَف [ziħaf] زَحِف [zaħif] *vn: sv* a. The dog crawled under the table. الكَلِب زِحَف جَوَّة الميز [ʔiččalib ziħaf ǰawwa ʔilmi:z] • **2.** حِبَى [ħiba:] حَبِي [ħaby] *vn: sv* i. زِحَف [ziħaf] زَحِف [zaħif] *vn: sv* a. Her child is beginning to crawl. طِفِلها بِدا يِحبِي [ṭifilha bida: yiħbi] • **3.** دِبَى [diba:] دَبِي [daby] *vn: sv* i. An ant was crawling on my hand. فَدّ نَملَة كانَت تِدبِي عَلَى إيدِي [fadd namla ča:nat tidbi ʕala ʔi:di]

crazy • **1.** مَجنُون [majnu:n] مخَبَّل [mxabbal] مخابِيل [mxa:bi:l] *pl:* They put him in the hospital because he was crazy. دَخّلَوه لِلمُستَشفى لِأَنّ كان مَجنُون [daxxilu:h lilmustašfa liʔann ča:n majnu:n] • **2.** متخَبُّل [mitxabbul] مَجنُون [majnu:n] He's crazy about that girl. هُوَّ مِتخَبُّل عَلَى ذِيك البنَيَّة [huwwa mitxabbul ʕala ði:č ʔilbnayya] • **3.** سَخِيف [saxi:f] That's a crazy idea. It'll never work. هاي فِكرَة سَخِيفَة ما تصِير أَبَداً [ha:y fikra saxi:fa ma: tṣi:r ʔabadan]

to creak • **1.** جَزجَز [ǰazǰaz] جُزجُز، جَزجَزَة [ǰuzǰuz, ǰazǰaza] *vn: sv* i. The wooden stairs are creaking. الدَّراج الخِشَب دَيجَزجِز [ʔiddara:ǰ ʔilxišab dayǰazǰiz]

cream • **1.** كرِيم [kri:m] You'll have to buy the cream canned. لازِم تِشتِرِي الكرِيم معَلَّب [la:zim tištiri ʔilkri:m mʕallab] • **2.** دِهِن [dihin] دُهُونات [duhu:na:t] *pl:* كرِيم [kri:m] This cream is good for the complexion. هَالدِّهِن زين لِلبَشَرَة [haddihin zayn lilbašara] • **3.** حَلِيبِي [ħali:bi] The color of the walls is cream. لُون الحَياطِين حَلِيبِي [lu:n ʔilħaya:ṭi:n ħali:bi]

* **These students are the cream of the crop.** • **1.** هَالطُّلّاب هُمَّ العَيِّنَة [haṭṭulla:b humma ʔilʕayyna]

Devonshire cream (clotted) • **1.** قَيمَر [gaymar]

crease • **1.** كَسرَة [kasra] كَسرات [kasra:t] *pl:* The rain took the crease out of my pants. المُطَر رَوَّح كَسرَة البَنطُرُون مالِي [ʔilmuṭar rawwaħ kasrat ʔilpanṭuru:n ma:li]

to create • **1.** خِلَق [xilaq] خَلِق [xaliq] *vn:* اِنخِلَق [ʔinxilaq] *p:* كَوَّن [kawwan] تَكوِين، تكِوِّن [takwi:n, tkiwwin] *vn:* God created the world. الله خِلَق العالَم [ʔallah xilaq ʔilʕa:lam] • **2.** أَحدَث [ʔaħdaθ] إحداث [ʔiħda:θ] *vn: sv* i. خِلَق [xilaq] خَلِق [xaliq] *vn:* اِنخِلَق [ʔinxilaq] *p:* أَوجَد [ʔawǰad] إيجاد [ʔi:ǰa:d] *vn:* اِنوجَد [ʔinwiǰad] *p:* We have to create a position for him. لازِم نِحدِثلَه وَظِيفَة [la:zim niħdiθlah waði:fa]

creature • **1.** مَخلُوق [maxlu:q] مَخلُوقات [maxlu:qa:t] *pl:* كائِن [ka:ʔin] كائِنات [ka:ʔina:t] *pl:* He wrote a story about the creatures in the forest. كِتَب قُصَّة عَن مَخلُوقات الغابَة [kitab quṣṣa ʕan maxlu:qa:t ʔilɣa:ba]

credentials • **1.** وَثِيقَة [waθi:qa] وَثايِق [waθa:yiq] *pl:* أَوراق الإعتِماد [ʔawra:q ʔiliʕtima:d] مُستَنَد، مُستَنَدات [mustanad, mustanada:t]

credible • **1.** صادِق [ṣa:diq, ṣa:dig] He's a credible witness. هُوَّ شاهِد صادِق [huwwa ša:hid ṣa:diq] • **2.** مصَدِّق [mṣaddig] His story wasn't credible. حكايتَه ما كانَت مصَدِّقَة [ħča:ytah ma: ča:nat mṣaddiga]

credit • **1.** دَين [dayn] ديُون [dyu:n] *pl:* حساب [ħsa:b] We can buy the furniture on credit. نِقدَر نِشتِرِي الأَثاث بِالدَّين [nigdar ništiri ʔilʔaθa:θ biddayn] • **2.** مَفخَرَة [mafxara] مَفاخِر [mafa:xir] *pl:* فَخَر [faxar] فَضِل [faðil] أَفضال [ʔafða:l] *pl:* The credit for his success goes to his teacher. بنَجاحَه يعُود الفَخَر لِلمُعَلِّم مالَه [bnaǰa:ħah yʕu:d ʔilfaxar lilmuʕallim ma:lah] He's a credit to his profession. هُوَّ فَدّ مَفخَرَة لِمِهنتَه [huwwa fadd mafxara limihintah] • **3.** إعتِماد [ʔiʕtima:d] They don't have enough credit to import this many cars. ما عِدهُم إعتِماد كافِي لِإستِيراد هَالقَدّ سَيّارات [ma: ʕidhum ʔiʕtima:d ka:fi liʔisti:ra:d halgadd sayya:ra:t]

to credit • **1.** أَضاف [ʔaða:f] إضافَة [ʔiða:fa] *vn:* اِنضاف [ʔinða:f] *p:* حِسَب [ħisab] حساب [ħsa:b] *vn:* اِنحِسَب [ʔinħisab] *p:* We're going to credit this amount to your account. راح نضِيف هَالمَبلَغ عَلَى حسابَك [ra:ħ nði:f halmablaɣ ʕala ħsa:bak] • **2.** نِطَى [niṭa:] نَطِي [naṭi] *vn:* اِنِّطَى [ʔinniṭa:] *p:* They credited him with saving her life. إنِّطَوه الفَضِل بِإنقاذ حَياتهَا [ʔinniṭu:h ʔilfaðil bʔinqa:ð ħaya:tha]

C

creditor • **1.** دايَن [da:yin] دَيّانَة [dayya:na] *Pl:*

to creep • **1.** زِحَف [ziħaf] زَحِف [zaħif] *vn: sv* a. My son is always creeping around the house. إبنِي دائِماً يِزحَف بِالبَيت [ʔibni da:ʔiman yizħaf bilbayt] • **2.** كَزبَر [kazbar] تكزبُر [tkizbur] *vn: sv* u. That movie made my skin creep. ذاك الفِلم خَلّى جِلدِي يكَزبُر [ða:k ʔilfilm xalla: ǰildi ykazbur]

crescent • **1.** هِلال [hila:l] The star and crescent is a symbol of Islam. النَّجمَة وَالهِلال رَمز الإسلام [ʔinnaǰma wilhila:l ramz ʔilʔisla:m]

the Fertile Crescent • **1.** الهِلال الخَصِيب [ʔilhila:l ʔilxaṣi:b]

the Red Crescent • **1.** الهِلال الأحمَر [ʔilhila:l ʔilʔaħmar]

crew • **1.** جَماعَة [ǰama:ʕa] جَماعات [ǰama:ʕa:t] *pl:* فِرقَة، فَرِيق [firqa, fari:q] فِرَق [firaq] *pl:* The entire crew drowned when the ship sank. جَماعَة البَحّارَة كُلّهُم غِرقوا لَمّا المَركَب غِرَق [ǰama:ʕat ʔilbaħħa:ra kullhum ɣirgaw lamma ʔilmarkab ɣirag] • **2.** مَلّاح [malla:ħ] The plane's crew consists of five persons. مَلّاحِين الطّائِرَة عَدَدهُم خَمسَة [malla:ħi:n ʔitta:ʔira ʕadadhum xamsa] • **3.** جَوقَة [ǰawga] The foreman divided his workmen into three crews with a special job for each. الأسطَة قَسَّم العَمّالَة إلَى ثَلاث جُوقات؛ كُلّ جَوقَة إلها شُغُل خاصّ [ʔilʔusṭa qassam ʔilʕamma:la ʔila tlaθ ǰu:ga:t; kull ǰu:ga ʔilha šuɣul xa:ṣṣ]

crib • **1.** مَعلَف [maʕlaf] معالِف [mʕa:lif] *pl:* Did you put hay in the crib? حَطّيت التِّبِن بِالمَعلَف؟ [ħaṭṭi:t ʔittibin bilmaʕlaf?] • **2.** كارُوك [ka:ru:k] كوارِيك [kwa:ri:k] *pl:* مَهَد [mahad] مهُود [mhu:d] *pl:* Don't take him out of the crib. لا تشِيلَه مِن الكارُوك [la: tši:lah min ʔilka:ru:k]

cricket • **1.** صُرصُر [ṣurṣur] صَراصِر [ṣara:ṣir] *pl:*

crime • **1.** جَرِيمَة [ǰari:ma] جَرايِم [ǰara:yim] *pl:* He committed several crimes. اِرتِكَب عِدَّة جَرائِم [ʔirtikab ʕiddat ǰara:ʔim]

criminal • **1.** مُجرِم [muǰrim] مُجرِمِين [muǰrimi:n] *pl:* He's a well-known criminal. هُوَّ فَدّ مُجرِم مَشهُور [huwwa fadd muǰrim mašhu:r] • **2.** جِنائِي [ǰina:ʔi] He's studying criminal law. هُوَّ دَيِدرُس القانُون الجِّنائِي [huwwa dayidrus ʔilqa:nu:n ʔiǰǰina:ʔi]

cripple • **1.** مُقعَد [muqʕad] مُقعَدِين [muqʕadi:n] *pl:* مقَرَّم [mgarram] سِقَط [sigaṭ] It is hard for cripples to get a job. المُقعَدِين صَعُب عَلَيهُم يحَصّلُون عَلَى شُغُل [ʔilmuqʕadi:n ṣaʕub ʕali:hum yħaṣṣlu:n ʕala šuɣul]

to cripple • **1.** قَرَّم [garram] تقُرُّم [tgurrum] *vn:* تقَرَّم [tgarram] *p:* سَقَّط [saggaṭ] تَسقِيط [tasgi:ṭ] *vn:* تسَقَّط [tsaggaṭ] *p:* He was crippled in an automobile accident. تسَقَّط بحادِث سَيّارَة [tsaggaṭ bħa:diθ sayya:ra]

crippled • **1.** They're going to open a school for crippled children. راح يِفتَحُون مَدرَسَة لِلأَطفال المُقعَدِين [ra:ħ yiftaħu:n madrasa lilʔaṭfa:l ʔilmuqʕadi:n]

crisis • **1.** أزمَة [ʔazma] أزمات [ʔazma:t] *pl:* The country is facing an economic crisis in the near future. البَلَد دَيجابِه أزمَة اِقتِصادِيَّة بالمُستَقبَل القَرِيب [ʔilbalad dayǰa:bih ʔazma ʔiqtiṣa:diyya bilmustaqbal ʔilqari:b] • **2.** شِدَّة [šidda] The patient passed the crisis safely. المَرِيض مَرّ بِالشِّدَّة بسَلامَة [ʔilmari:ð̣ marr biššidda bsala:ma]

crisp • **1.** مقَسِّب [mgassib] مقَسِّبِين [mgassibi:n] *pl:* مجَسِّب [mǰassib] مجَسِّبِين [mǰassibi:n] *pl:* The bread is fresh and crisp. الخُبُز تازَة ومقَسِّب [ʔilxubuz ta:za wimgassib] • **2.** هَشّ [hašš] This cucumber is crisp, not wilted. هالخيارَة هَشَّة، مُو ذابلَة [halxya:ra hašša, mu: ða:bla]

* **The air is a bit crisp tonight.** • **1.** الهَوا بِيه قَرصَة بَرِد اللَّيلَة [ʔilhawa bi:h garṣat barid ʔillayla]

critic • **1.** ناقِد [na:qid] نُقّاد [nuqqa:d] *pl:* Did you read the movie critic's article before you saw the film? قرَيت مَقال النّاقِد السِّينَمائِي قَبُل ما شِفت الفِلِم؟ [gri:t maqa:l ʔinna:qid ʔissi:nama:ʔi gabul ma: šift ʔilfilim?]

critical • **1.** مُنتَقِد [muntaqid] He is sharply critical of social conventions. هُوَّ مُنتَقِد لاذِع لِلأَوضاع الاجتِماعِيَّة [huwwa muntaqid la:ðiʕ lilʔawð̣a:ʕ ʔilʔiǰtima:ʕiyya] • **2.** خَطِير [xaṭi:r] خَطِر [xaṭir] His condition is critical. حالتَه خَطِرَة [ħa:ltah xaṭira]

criticism • **1.** اِنتِقاد [ʔintiqa:d] اِنتِقادات [ʔintiqa:da:t] *pl:* نَقِد [naqid] He can't stand criticism. هُوَّ ما يِتحَمَّل اِنتِقاد [huwwa ma: yitħammal ʔintiqa:d] She has nothing to offer but criticism. ما عِدها غير الانتِقاد [ma: ʕidha ɣayr ʔilʔintiqa:d]

to criticize • **1.** اِنتِقَد [ʔintiqad] اِنتِقاد [ʔintiqa:d] *vn: sv* i. عَيَّب [ʕayyab] تعِيِّب [tʕiyyib] *vn:* تعَيَّب [tʕayyab] *p:* They severely criticized him. اِنتِقدَوه اِنتِقاد مُرّ [ʔintiqdawh ʔintiqa:d murr] She criticizes the way I dress. هِيَّ تعَيِّب عَلَى لِبسِي [hiyya tʕayyib ʕala libsi]

to crochet • **1.** حاك [ħa:k, ħa:č] حِياكَة [ħiya:ka] *vn:* اِنحاك [ʔinħa:k] *p:* His mother crocheted a pair of slipper tops for him. أُمَّه حاكَتلَه زوج كلاش [ʔummah ħa:katlah zawǰ kla:š]

crock • **1.** بَستُوكَة [bastu:ga] بَستُوكات [bastu:ga:t] *pl:* When you go to the market buy a crock of pickles.

لَمّا تروح لِلسُّوق اِشتِري بَستُوكَة طُرشي [lamma tru:ħ lissu:g ʔištiri bastu:gat ṭurši]

crockery • **1.** فَخّار [faxxa:r] This is made of crockery. هَذا مَعمُول مِن الفَخّار [ha:ða maʕmu:l min ʔilfaxxa:r]

crocodile • **1.** تِمساح [timsa:ħ] تَماسِيح [tama:si:ħ] *pl:*

crocus • **1.** زَعفَران [zaʕfara:n, zuʕufra:n]

crook • **1.** عوجِيَّة [ʕu:čiyya] عَوجِيّات [ʕu:čiyya:t] *pl:* عَصايَة [ʕaṣa:ya] عَصايات [ʕaṣa:ya:t] *pl:* The shepherd struck the lamb with his crook. الرّاعِي ضِرَب الطِّلي بِالعُوجِيَّة [ʔirra:ʕi ḍirab ʔiṭṭili bilʕu:čiyya] • **2.** مقُرباز [mqurba:z] مقُربازِيِّين [mqurba:ziyyi:n, mqurba:ziyya] *pl:* مُحتال [muħta:l] مُحتالِين [muħta:li:n] *pl:* غَشّاش [ɣašša:š] غَشّاشَة [ɣašša:ša] *pl:* He's a crook. هُوَّ مقُرباز [huwwa mqurba:z]

crooked • **1.** أعوَج [ʔaʕwaǰ] عُوج [ʕu:ǰ] *pl:* عوجَة [ʕu:ǰa] *Feminine:* مَعوُوج [maʕwu:ǰ] معَوَّج [mʕawwaǰ] This pin is crooked. هَالدَّنبُوس مَعوُج [haddanbu:s maʕwu:ǰ] • **2.** All the merchants in this street are crooked. كُلّ التِّجّار بِهَالسُّوق مقُربازِيَّة [kull ʔittiǰǰa:r bhassu:g mqurba:ziyya]

crop • **1.** حاصِل [ħa:ṣil] حاصِلات [ħa:ṣila:t] *pl:* مَحصُول [maħṣu:l] مَحاصِيل [maħa:ṣi:l] *pl:* The farmers expect a good crop this year. الفَلاحِين يتوَقّعُون حاصِل زين هالسَّنَة [ʔilfala:ħi:n yitwaqqʕu:n ħa:ṣil zi:n hassana] • **2.** حُوصلَة [ħawṣla] حَوصلات، حَواصِل [ħawṣla:t, ħawa:ṣil] *pl:* The chickens are so full their crops are almost touching the ground. الدِّجاج شَبعان إلَى دَرَجَة حَواصلَه قَرِيباً تدُقّ القاع [ʔiddiǰa:ǰ šabʕa:n ʔila daraǰa ħawa:ṣlah qari:ban tdugg ʔilga:ʕ]

to crop up • **1.** ظِهَر [ḍihar] ظُهُور [ḍuhu:r] *vn: sv* a. Many new problems are sure to crop up. مَشاكِل جِدِيدَة هوايَة مِن المُوَكَّد تِظهَر [maša:kil ǰidi:da hwa:ya min ʔilmuʔakkad tiḍhar]

cross • **1.** صَلِيب [ṣali:b] صُلبان [ṣulba:n] *pl:* Do you see the church with the big cross on the steeple? تشُوف الكَنِيسَة اللِّي عَلَى بُرجها صَلِيب كِبِير؟ [tšu:f ʔilkani:sa ʔilli ʕala buruǰha ṣali:b čibi:r?] The central office of the International Red Cross is in Geneva. الدّائِرَة المَركَزِيَّة لِجَمعِيَّة الصَّلِيب الأحمَر العالَمِيَّة مَقَرّها بِجَنِيف [ʔidda:ʔira ʔilmarkaziyya liǰamʕiyyat ʔiṣṣali:b ʔilʔaħmar ʔilʕa:lamiyya maqarrha bǰani:f] • **2.** مضَرَّب [mḍarrab] The mule is a cross between a horse and a donkey. البَغَل مضَرَّب بين الحِصان وَالحِمار [ʔilbaɣal mḍarrab bi:n ʔilħiṣa:n wiliħma:r]

to cross • **1.** عُبَر [ʕubar] عُبُور [ʕubu:r] *vn:* Cross at the intersection of the street. أعبُر مِن راس الشّارِع [ʔuʕbur min ra:s ʔišša:riʕ] When do we cross the border? شوَقِت نُعبُر الحُدُود؟ [šwakit nuʕbur ʔilħudu:d?] • **2.** **تقاطَع ويّا** [tqa:ṭaʕ wiyya] تَقاطُع [taqa:ṭuʕ wiyya] *vn: sv* a. Rashid St. crosses Amin St. at Amin Square شارِع الرَّشِيد يتقاطَع ويّا شارِع الأمِين بساحَة الأمِين [ša:riʕ ʔirraši:d yitqa:ṭaʕ wiyya ša:riʕ ʔilʔami:n bsa:ħat ʔilʔami:n]

*** Cross your heart!** • **1.** توَجَّه عَالقِبلَة وإحلِف [twaǰǰah ʕalqibla wiħlif]

to cross out • **1.** شِطَب [šiṭab] شَطُب [šaṭub] *vn:* اِنشِطَب [ʔinšiṭab] *p:* كَزّ [čazz] كَزّ [čazz] *vn:* اِنكَزّ [ʔinčazz] *p:* Cross out the items you don't want. إشطُب المَوادّ اللِّي ما تِريدها [ʔišṭub ʔilmawa:dd ʔilli ma: tri:dha]

to crossbreed • **1.** ضَرَّب [ḍarrab] تَضرِيب [taḍri:b] *vn:* تضَرَّب [tḍarrab] *p:* On this farm they crossbreed varieties of sheep with each other. بِهَالمَزرَعَة يضَرّبُون أنواع الأغنام مَعَ بَعَضها [bhalmazraʕa yḍarrbu:n ʔanwa:ʕ ʔilʔaɣna:m maʕa baʕaḍha]

cross-eyed • **1.** أحوَل [ʔaħwal] حُول، حَولِين [ħu:l, ħawli:n] *pl:* حُولَة [ħu:la] *Feminine:* She's cross-eyed. هِيَّ حَولَة [hiyya ħawla]

crossing • **1.** مَفرَق [mafrag] مَفارِق [mafa:rig] *pl:* There's no traffic light at this crossing. ماكُو ضُوَا مال مُرُور بِهَالمَفرَق [ma:ku ḍuwa ma:l muru:r bhalmafraq] • **2.** عُبُور [ʕubu:r] How far are we from the crossing point. شقَدّ نبعِد عَن نُقطَة العُبُور؟ [šgadd nibʕid ʕan nugṭat ʔilʕubu:r?] • **3.** عَبرَة [ʕabra] عَبرات [ʕabra:t] *pl:* On the ferry they charge ten fils for each crossing. بِالعَبّارَة ياخذُون عَشِر فلُوس عَن كُلّ عَبرَة [bilʕabba:ra ya:xðu:n ʕašir flu:s ʕan kull ʕabra]

cross section • **1.** مَقطَع [maqṭaʕ] مَقاطِع [maqa:ṭiʕ] *pl:*

crosswise • **1.** بِالعُرُض [bilʕuruḍ] Cut this cucumber crosswise. قُصّ هالخيارَة بالعُرُض [guṣṣ halxya:ra bilʕuruḍ]

crossword puzzle • **1.** الكَلِمات المُتَقاطِعَة [ʔilkalima:t ʔilmutaqa:ṭiʕa]

to crouch • **1.** نَصَّى نَفسَه [naṣṣa: nafsah] تنِصِّي [tniṣṣi] *vn: sv* i. He crouched down behind the table so I couldn't see him. هُوَّ نَصَّى نَفسَه وَرا الميز حَتَّى ما أشُوفَه [huwwa naṣṣa: nafsah wara ʔilmi:z ħatta ma: ʔašu:fah]

crow • **1.** غراب [ɣra:b] زاغ [za:ɣ] زاغات، زِيغان [za:ɣa:t, zi:ɣa:n] *pl:* The black and white crows are bigger than the black crows. الغِربان أكبَر مِن الزّاغ [ʔilɣirba:n ʔakbar min ʔizza:ɣ]

to crow • **1.** عَوعَى [ʕawʕa:] تعَوعِي [tʕu:ʕi] *vn: sv* i. صاح [ṣa:ħ] صياح [ṣya:ħ] *vn: sv* i. I woke up when the rooster crowed. قِعَدت مِن النُّوم لَمّا الدِّيك عَوعَى [giʕadt min ʔinnu:m lamma ʔiddi:č ʕu:ʕa:]

C

crowbar • **1.** هيم [hi:m] هِيَم هيامَة [hiyam, hya:ma] *pl:*

crowd • **1.** اِزدِحام [ʔizdiħa:m] اِزدِحامات [ʔizdiħa:ma:t] *pl:* جَمهُور [ǰamhu:r] جَماهِير [ǰama:hi:r] *pl:* Have you seen the crowd in front of the theater? شِفت الازدِحام بِباب السِّينَما؟ [šift ʔilʔizdiħa:m biba:b ʔissi:nama?] There was a small crowd standing at the bus stop. كان أكُو جَمهُور صغَيِّر مَوجُود بمَوقِف الباص [ča:n ʔaku ǰamhu:r ṣɣayyir mawǰu:d bmawqif ʔilpa:ṣ] • **2.** جَماعَة [ǰama:ʕa] جَماعات [ǰama:ʕa:t] *pl:* He goes around with a bad crowd. يرُوح وِيّا جَماعَة مُو زينَة [yiru:ħ wiyya ǰama:ʕa mu: zi:na]

to crowd • **1.** اِزدِحَم [ʔizdiħam] اِزدِحام [ʔizdiħa:m] *vn:* *sv* i. اِندِحَس [ʔindiħas] اِندِحاس [ʔindiħa:s] *vn:* *sv* i. We all crowded into the bus. كُلّتنا اِزدِحَمنا بالباص [kullatna ʔizdiħamna bilpa:ṣ] • **2.** حِشَك [ħišak] حَشِك [ħašik] *vn:* حِشَر [ħišar] حَشِر [ħašir] *vn:* I don't think you can crowd another thing in there. ما أعتِقِد تِقدَر تِحشِك شِي لاخ هناك [ma: ʔaʕtiqid tigdar tiħšik ši la:x hna:k]

crowded • **1.** مِزدَحِم [mizdaħim] The bus was crowded, as usual. الباص كان مُزدَحِم كَالعادَة [ʔilpa:ṣ ča:n muzdaħim kalʕa:da]

crowded to capacity • **1.** مقبَّط [mqapput] The hall was crowded to capacity. القاعَة كانَت مقبَّطَة [ʔilqa:ʕa ča:nat mqappṭa]

crown • **1.** تاج [ta:ǰ] تيجان [ti:ǰa:n] *pl:* He wore a gold crown. لِبَس تاج ذَهَبِي [libas ta:ǰ ðahabi]

to crown • **1.** تَوَّج [tawwaǰ] تَتوِيج [tatwi:ǰ] *vn:* They crowned him king in 1925. تَوِّجُوه مَلِك سَنَة ألف وَتِسعمِيَّة وَخَمسَة وَعِشرِين [tawwiǰu:h malik sanat ʔalf wtisiʕmiyya wxamsa wʕišri:n]

crown prince • **1.** وَلِيّ عَهد [waliyy ʕahid] أولِياء عَهد [ʔawliya:ʔ ʕahid] *pl:*

to crucify • **1.** صِلَب [ṣilab] صَلُب [ṣalub] *vn:* اِنصِلَب [ʔinṣilab] *p:* The Romans used to crucify their prisoners. الرُّومانِيِّين كانَوا يصِلبُون مَساجِينهُم [ʔirru:ma:niyyi:n ča:naw yṣilbu:n masa:ǰi:nhum]

crude • **1.** خَشِن [xašin] فَضّ [faðð] He's a rather crude person. هُوَّ فَدّ واحِد خَشِن [huwwa fadd wa:ħid xašin] • **2.** خام [xa:m] These barrels contain crude oil. هَالبَرامِيل بِيها نَفُط خام [halbara:mi:l bi:ha nafuṭ xa:m]

cruel • **1.** قاسِي [qa:si] قُساة [qusa:t] *pl:* Why are you this cruel? إنتَ لُويش هِيكِي قاسِي؟ [ʔinta luwi:š hi:či qa:si?]

cruelty • **1.** قَساوَة [qasa:wa]

cruiser • **1.** طَرّاد [ṭarra:d] طَرّادات [ṭarra:da:t] *pl:* My brother is assigned to a cruiser. أخُويَا معَيَّن بطَرّاد [ʔaxu:ya mʕayyan bṭarra:d]

crumb • **1.** فتاتَة [fta:ta] فتات [fta:t] *pl:* فتات [fta:t] *Collective:* He left bread crumbs on the table. تِرَك فتات خُبُز عالميز [tirak fta:t xubuz ʕalmi:z]

to crumb • **1.** فَتَّت [fattat] تَفتِيت، تفِتِّت [tafti:t, tfittit] *vn:* Crumb the bread and mix it with the meat. فَتِّت الخُبُز وَخُبطَه وِيّا اللَّحَم [fattit ʔilxubuz wxubṭah wiyya ʔillaħam]

to crush • **1.** فُعَص [fuʕaṣ] فَعُص [faʕuṣ] *vn:* اِنفُعَص [ʔinfuʕaṣ] *p:* You're crushing my hat. إنتَ دَتُفعُص شَفُقتِي [ʔinta datufʕuṣ šafuqti] • **2.** سِحَق [siħag] سَحِق [saħig] *vn:* The army remained loyal and crushed the insurrection. الجَّيش بُقَى مُخلِص وَسِحَق التَّمَرُّد [ʔiǰǰayš buqa: muxliṣ wsiħag ʔittamarrud] He crushed out the cigarette with his foot. سِحَق السِجارَة برِجلَه [siħag ʔaǰǰiga:ra briǰlah] • **3.** جِرَش [ǰiraš] جَرِش [ǰariš] *vn:* اِنجِرَش [ʔinǰiraš] *p:* When are you going to crush the wheat? شوَقِت راح تِجرُش الحُنطَة؟ [šwakit ra:ħ tiǰruš ʔilħunṭa?] • **4.** كَسَّر [kassar] تَكسِير، تكِسِّر [taksi:r, tkissir] *vn:* This machine crushes the rocks. هَالمَكِينَة تكَسِّر الصُّخُور [halmaki:na tkassir ʔiṣṣuxu:r] • **5.** صِدَم [ṣidam] صَدِم [ṣadim] *vn:* اِنصِدَم [ʔinṣidam] *p:* The news crushed him. صِدَمَه الخَبَر [ṣidamah ʔilxabar]

crust • **1.** قِشرَة [gišra] I can't eat the crust. ما أقدَر آكُل القِشرَة [ma: ʔagdar ʔa:kul ʔilgišra] The thickness of the earth's crust is several miles. قِشرَة الأرُض سِمُكها عِدَّة أميال [gišrat ʔilʔaruḍ simukha ʕiddat ʔamya:l]

crutch • **1.** عِكّازَة [ʕikka:za] عِكّازات [ʕikka:za:t] *pl:* He has to walk on crutches. لازِم يِمشِي عَلَى عِكّازات [la:zim yimši ʕala ʕikka:za[t]

cry • **1.** صِيحَة [ṣi:ħa] صِيحات [ṣi:ħa:t] *pl:* عِيطَة [ʕi:ṭa] عِيطات [ʕi:ṭa:t] *pl:* صَرخَة [ṣarxa] صَرخات، صرِيخ، صراخ [ṣarxa:t, ṣri:x, ṣra:x] *pl:* We heard a loud cry and went to investigate. سِمَعنا صَيحَة عالِيَة وَرِحنا نِتحَرَّى [simaʕna ṣi:ħa ʕa:lya wriħna nitħarra:] • **2.** بَكيَة [bačya] بَكيات [bačya:t] *pl:* She'll feel better after a good cry. راح تِرتاح بَعَد فَدّ بَكيَة زينَة [ra:ħ tirta:ħ baʕad fadd bačya zi:na]

to cry • **1.** بِكَى [biča:] بَكِي [bačy] *vn:* *sv* i. The baby was crying for its mother. الطِّفِل كان يِبكِي عَلَى أُمَّه [ʔiṭṭifil ča:n yibči ʕala ʔummah] • **2.** صاح [ṣa:ħ] صياح [ṣya:ħ] *vn:* *sv* i. I heard an animal crying in the forest. سمَعِت حَيوان يصِيح بالغابَة [smaʕit ħaywa:n yṣi:ħ bilɣa:ba]

to cry out • **1.** صِرَخ [ṣirax] صراخ [ṣra:x] *vn:* *sv* a. عاط [ʕa:ṭ] عِياط [ʕya:ṭ] *vn:* *sv* i. صاح [ṣa:ħ] He cried out from the pain. صِرَخ مِن الألَم [ṣirax min ʔilʔalam]

to cry to oneself • **1.** ناح [na:ħ] نَوح [nawħ] *vn:* *sv* u. We saw her at her son's grave crying to herself. شِفناها عَلَى قَبُر إبنها تنُوح [šifna:ha ʕala gabur ʔibinha tnu:ħ]

crystal • **1.** بَلُّورَة [ballu:ra] بَلُّورات [ballu:ra:t] *pl:* بَلُّور [ballu:r] *Collective:* We studied salt crystals under the microscope. دِرَسنا بَلُّورات المِلِح تَحت المِكرِسكوب [dirasna ballu:ra:t ʔilmiliħ taħt ʔilmikrisku:b] I broke the last piece of crystal that I had. كِسَرِت آخِر قِطعَة مِن البَلُّور اللِّي عِندِي [kisarit ʔa:xir qitʕa min ʔilballu:r ʔilli ʕindi] They bought a crystal chandelier for the reception room. اِشتِرَوا ثُرَيَّة بَلُّور لغُرفَة الاستِقبال [ʔištiraw θurayya ballu:r lɣurfat ʔilistiqba:l] • **2.** جامَة [ǰa:ma] جامات [ǰa:ma:t] *pl:* I need a new crystal for my watch. أحتاج جامَة جِدِيدَة لِساعتِي [ʔaħta:ǰ ǰa:ma ǰidi:da lisa:ʕti]

cube • **1.** مُكَعَّب [mukaʕʕab] Draw a cube on the blackboard. إرسِم مُكَعَّب عَالسَّبُّورَة [ʔirsim mukaʕʕab ʕassabbu:ra]

cucumber • **1.** خيارَة [xya:ra] خيارات، خيار [xya:ra:t, xya:r] *pl:* خيار [xya:r] *Collective*

to cuddle • **1.** حِضَن [ħiđ̣an] حَضِن [ħađ̣in] *vn:* اِنحِضَن [ʔinħiđ̣an] *p:* The mother cuddled her children. الأمّ حِضنَت جَهّالها [ʔilʔumm ħiđ̣nat ǰahha:lha] • **2.** تلَفلَف [tlaflaf] تلِفلِف [tliflif] *vn: sv* a. The children cuddled up in their blankets. الأطفال تلَفلِفوا بِبَطّانِيّاتهُم [ʔilʔaṭfa:l tlaflifaw bibaṭṭa:niyya:thum]

cue • **1.** إشارَة [ʔiša:ra] إشارات [ʔiša:ra:t] *pl:* I'll give you the cue to start talking. رَح أنطِيك إشارَة الابتِداء بالكَلام [raħ ʔanṭi:k ʔiša:rat ʔilʔibtida:ʔ bilkala:m] • **2.** عَصَة [ʕaṣa] عِصِي [ʕiṣi] *pl:* He hit his friend on the head with a billiard cue. ضِرَب صَدِيقَه عَلَى راسَه بعَصَى بليارد [đ̣irab ṣadi:qah ʕala ra:sah bʕaṣa bilya:rd]

cuff • **1.** طَويَة [ṭawya] طَويات [ṭawya:t] *pl:* كَفَّة [kaffa] كَفّات [kaffa:t] *pl:* ثَنيَة [θanya] ثَنيات [θanya:t] *pl:* I tore my pants cuff. شَقَّيت طَويَة البَنطَرون مالِي [šaggi:t ṭawyat ʔilpanṭaru:n ma:li]

on the cuff • **1.** بالدَّين [biddayn] Can you put it on the cuff until tomorrow? تِقدَر تِحسِبها بالدَّين لباكِر؟ [tigdar tiħsibha biddayn lba:čir?]

cuff link • **1.** دُقمَة إردان [dugmat ʔirda:n] دِقَم الردان [digam ʔirda:n] *pl:* I lost one of my cuff links. ضَيَّعِت وِحدَة مِن دِقَم رداني [đ̣ayyaʕit wiħda min digam ʔirda:ni]

culprit • **1.** مُذنِب [muđnib] They found the culprit. لِقَوا المُذنِب [ligaw ʔilmuđnib]

cultural • **1.** ثَقافِي [θaqa:fi] He is Iraq's cultural attache. هُوَّ مُلحَق ثَقافِي مال العِراق [huwwa mulħaq θaqa:fi ma:l ʔilʕira:q]

culture • **1.** حَضارَة [ħađ̣a:ra] حَضارات [ħađ̣a:ra:t] *pl:* He's a specialist in ancient Greek culture. هُوَّ مُختَصّ بِحَضارَة اليُونان القَدِيم [huwwa muxtaṣṣ bħađ̣a:rat ʔilyu:na:n ʔilqadi:m] • **2.** ثَقافَة [θaqa:fa] He is a man of high culture. هُوَّ صاحِب ثَقافَة عالية [huwwa ṣa:ħib θaqa:fa ʕa:lya] • **3.** زَرع [zariʕ] He is studying microbe culture. دَيِدرُس زَرع المِكرَوبات [dayidrus zariʕ ʔilmikru:ba:t]

cultured • **1.** مهَذَّب [mhađđab] مُثَقَّف [muθaqqaf] She's a cultured woman. هِيَّ فَدّ وِحدَة مهَذّبَة [hiyya fadd wiħda mhađđba]

culvert • **1.** بُربُخ [burbux] بَرابِخ [bara:bix] *pl:*

cuneiform • **1.** مِسمارِي [misma:ri]

cunning • **1.** مُراوِغ [mura:wiɣ] حَيّال [ħayya:l] حَيّالِين [ħayya:li:n] *pl:* شَيطان [šayṭa:n] مَكّار [makka:r] The fox is a very cunning animal. الثَّعلَب فَدّ حَيوان مُراوِغ هوايَة [ʔiθθaʕlab fadd ħaywa:n mura:wiɣ hwa:ya]

cup • **1.** فِنجان [finǰa:n] فناجِين [fna:ǰi:n] *pl:* He drank three cups of coffee. شِرَب ثلَث فَناجِين قَهوَة [širab tlaθ fana:ǰi:n gahwa] • **2.** كُوب [ku:b] كواب، كوابَة [kwa:b, kwa:ba] *pl:* I asked our neighbors for a cup of sugar. طلَبِت مِن جيرانّا كُوب شَكَر [ṭlabit min ǰi:ra:nna ku:b šakar] • **3.** كَأس [kaʔs] كُؤوس [kuʔu:s] *pl:* Who won the cup? مِنُو حَصَّل عالكَأس؟ [minu ħaṣṣal ʕalkaʔs?]

cupboard • **1.** دِيلاب مواعِين [di:la:b mwa:ʕi:n] دوالِيب مواعِين [dwa:li:b mwa:ʕi:n] *pl:*

curb • **1.** رَصِيف [raṣi:f] أرصِفَة [ʔarṣifa] *pl:* I stood on the curb watching the parade. وقَفِت عَالرَّصِيف أتفَرَّج عالإستِعراض [wgafit ʕarraṣi:f ʔatfarraǰ ʕalʔistiʕra:đ̣] • **2.** تَقيِيد [taqyi:d] The government put a curb on emigration. الحُكومَة خَلَّت تَقيِيد عالهِجرَة [ʔilħuku:ma xallat taqyi:d ʕalhiǰra]

to curb • **1.** قَيَّد [qayyad, qayyid] تَقيِيد، تقَيِّد [taqyi:d, tqiyyid] *vn:* تقَيَّد [tqayyad] *p:* The government has begun curbing foreign imports. الحُكومَة بِدَت تقَيِّد الاستِيرادات الخارجِيَّة [ʔilħuku:ma bidat tqayyid ʔilʔistira:da:t ʔilxa:riǰiyya] • **2.** ضُبَط [đ̣ubaṭ] ضَبُط [đ̣abuṭ] *vn:* اِنضُبَط [ʔinđ̣ubaṭ] *p:* You have to try to curb your temper. لازِم تحاوِل تُضبُط أعصابَك [la:zim tħa:wil tuđ̣buṭ ʔaʕṣa:bak]

cure • **1.** دُوا [duwa] أدويَة [ʔadwiya] *pl:* عِلاج [ʕila:ǰ] عِلاجات [ʕila:ǰa:t] *pl:* There is no cure for cancer. ماكُو دُوا لِلسَّرَطان [ma:ku duwa lissaraṭa:n]

to cure • **1.** طَيَّب [ṭayyab] طَيِّب [ṭṭiyyib] *vn:* تطَيَّب [ṭṭayyab] *p:* شافَى [ša:fa:] شِفاء [šifa:ʔ] *vn:* تشافَى [tša:fa:] *p:* The doctors cured his deafness. الدَّكاتِرَة طَيِّبوا الطَّرَش مالَه [ʔiddaka:tra ṭayyibaw

ʔiṭṭaraš ma:lah] • **2.** خَمَّر [xammar] تَخمِير، تخُمُّر [taxmi:r, txummur] *vn:* تخَمَّر [txammar] They cure the tobacco in these warehouses. يخَمّرُون التِّتِن بِهَالمَخازِن [yxammru:n ʔittitin bhalmaxa:zin]

to curse • **1.** شَتَّم [šattam] تشِتِّم [tšittim] *vn:* سَبّ [sabb] سَبّ [sabb] *vn:* اِنسَبّ [ʔinsabb] *p:* شِتَم [šitam] He cursed him for his slow driving. شَتَّم عَليه لِسِّياقتَه البَطِيئَة [šattam ʕali:h lissiya:qatah ʔilbaṭi:ʔa] شَتِم [šatim] *vn:*

C

curfew • **1.** مَنع تَجَوُّل [maniʕ tajawwul]

curiosity • **1.** حُبّ اِستِطلاع [ħubb ʔistiṭla:ʕ] She aroused my curiosity. أثارَت حُبّ اِستِطلاعِي [ʔaθa:rat ħubb ʔistiṭla:ʕi] • **2.** غرِيب [ɣari:b] غُرَباء، غُربَة [ɣuraba:ʔ, ɣurba.] *pl:* He brought with him some curiosities from India. جاب وِيّاه غَرايِب مِن الهِند [ja:b wiyya:h ɣara:yib min ʔilhind]

curious • **1.** مُحِبّ لِلإستِطلاع [muħibb lilʔistiṭla:ʕ] Don't be so curious. لا تصِير هَالقَدّ مُحِبّ لِلإستِطلاع [la: tṣi:r halgadd muħibb lilʔistiṭla:ʕ] • **2.** غَرِيب [ɣari:b] غُرَباء، غُربَة [ɣuraba:ʔ, ɣurba.] *pl:* This is a very curious situation. هَذِي فَدّ وَضعِيَّة غَرِيبَة كُلَّش [ha:ði fadd waḍʕiyya ɣari:ba kulliš]

curl • **1.** تَجعِيد [tajʕi:d] تَجعِيدات [tajʕi:da:t] *pl:* كَعكُولَة [kaʕku:la] كَعكُولات [kaʕku:la:t] *pl:* Her hair is all curls. شَعَرها كُلّه تَجعِيدات [šaʕarha kullah tajʕi:da:t]

to curl • **1.** جَعَّد [jaʕʕad] تَجعِيد [tajʕi:d] *vn:* تجَعَّد [tjaʕʕad] *p:* كَعكَل [kaʕkal] تكِعكِل [tkiʕkil] *vn:* تكَعكَل [tkaʕkal] *p:* Fatma, who curled your hair? فاطمَة، مِنُو جَعَّد شَعَرِك؟ [fa:ṭma, minu jaʕʕad šaʕarič?]

to curl up • **1.** لَملَم نَفس [lamlam nafs] تِلمِليم نَفس [tlimli:m nafs] *vn: sv* i. تلَملَم [tlamlam] تِلمِلِم [tlimlim] *vn: sv* a. The dog curled up and went to sleep. الكَلِب تلَملَم ونام [ʔiččalib tlamlam wna:m]

currency • **1.** نَقِد [naqid] عُملَة [ʕumla] عُملات [ʕumla:t] *pl:* Their currency is made in this country. نُقُودهُم مَعمُولَة بهالبَلَد [nuqu:dhum maʕmu:la bhalbalad]

current • **1.** تَيّار [tayya:r] تَيّارات [tayya:ra:t] *pl:* The current is very swift here. التَّيّار كُلَّش سَرِيع هنا [ʔittayya:r kulliš sari:ʕ hna] The electric current has been turned off. اِنقِطَع التَّيّار الكَهرَبائِي [ʔinqiṭaʕ ʔittayya:r ʔilkahraba:ʔi] • **2.** جارِي [ja:ri] حالِي [ħa:li] The bill for the current month is attached. القائِمَة مال الشَّهر إلجارِي مُرفَقَة [ʔilqa:ʔima ma:l ʔiššahr ʔijja:ri murfaqa] • **3.** دارِج [da:rij] Wearing of the fez was current in Baghdad before the First World War. لِبس الفِينَة كان دارِج بِبَغداد قَبُل الحَرب العالَمِيَّة الأُولَى [libs ʔilfi:na ča:n da:rij bibayda:d gabul ʔilħarb ʔilʕa:lamiyya ʔilʔu:la]

curse • **1.** شَتُّومَة [šattu:ma] شَتُّومات، شتايِم [šattu:ma:t, šta:yim] *pl:* شَتمَة [šatma] شَتمات، شَتايِم [šatma:t, šata:yim] *pl:* لَعنَة [laʕna] نَعلَة [naʕla] نَعلات [naʕla:t] *pl:* شَتمَة [masabba] مَسَبّات [masabba:t] *pl:* I don't want to hear another curse out of you. ما أرِيد أسمَع شَتُّومَة لُخ مِنَّك [ma: ʔari:d ʔasmaʕ šattu:ma lux minnak]

curtain • **1.** بَردَة [parda] بَردات [parda:t] *pl:* سِتار [sita:r] سَتائِر [sata:ʔir] *pl:*

curtain rod • **1.** شِيش بَردَة [ši:š parda] شياش بَردَة [šya:š parda] *pl:*

curve • **1.** مُنعَطَف [munʕaṭaf] مُنعَطَفات [munʕaṭafa:t] *pl:* لَوفَة [law:fa] This road has a lot of curves. هَالطَّرِيق بِيه لُوفات هوايَة [haṭṭari:q bi:h lu:fa:t hwa:ya]

to curve • **1.** دار [da:r] دَوَران [dawara:n] *vn: sv* u. لاف [la:f] لَوف [lu:f] *vn: sv* u. اِنعِطَف [ʔinʕiṭaf] اِنعِطاف [ʔinʕiṭa:f] *vn: sv* u. The road curves to the right. الطَّرِيق يدُور لِليَمِين [ʔiṭṭari:q ydu:r lilyami:n]

cushion • **1.** كُشِن [kušin] كُشِنات، كُشنات [kušina:t, kušna:t] *pl:* مُخَدَّة [muxadda] مَخادِيد، مُخَدّات [maxa:di:d, muxadda:t] *pl:* مَندَر [mindar, mandar] مَنادِر [mana:dir.] *pl:* مَقعَد [maqʕad] مَقاعِد [maqa:ʕid] *pl:*

cuspidor • **1.** مِبصَقَة [mibṣaqa] مَباصِق [maba:ṣiq] *pl:*

custody • **1.** تَوقِيف [tawqi:f] حَجِز [ħajiz] They took him into custody. أخذُوه لِلتَّوقِيف [ʔaxðuwh littawqi:f]

custom • **1.** عادَة [ʕa:da] عادات [ʕa:da:t] *pl:* This is an old Iraqi custom. هَذِي عادَة عِراقِيَّة قَدِيمَة [ha:ði ʕa:da ʕira:qiyya qadi:ma] • **2.** تُوصاة [tu:ṣa:t] His cars are all custom-made. كُلّ سَيّاراتَه مَعمُولَة تُوصاة [kull sayya:ra:tah maʕmu:la tu:ṣa:t]

customary • **1.** حَسب العادَة [ħasb ʔilʕa:da] حَسب العُرُف [ħasb ʔilʕuruf] اِعتِيادِي [ʔiʕtiya:di]

customer • **1.** مَعمِيل [maʕmi:l, miʕmi:l] مَعامِيل [maʕa:mi:l] *pl:* زِبُون [zibu:n] زَبايِن [zaba:yin] *pl:* He's my best customer. هُوَّ أحسَن مَعمِيل عِندِي [huwwa ʔaħsan maʕmi:l ʕindi]

customs • **1.** جُمرُك [gumrug] جَمارِك [gama:rig] *pl:* Do we have to pay customs on this? لازِم ندفَع جُمرُك عَلَى هاي؟ [la:zim nidfaʕ gumrug ʕala ha:y?] • **2.** جُمرُكِي [gumrugi] We had to go through a customs inspection when we arrived. لَمّا وصَلنا كان لازِم نمُرّ بتَفتِيش جُمرُكِي [lamma wṣalna ča:n la:zim nmurr btafti:š gumrugi]

cut • **1.** جَرح [jariħ] جرُوح [jru:ħ] *pl:* The cut is nearly healed. الجَّرح اِندِمَل تَقرِيباً [ʔijjariħ ʔindimal taqri:ban] • **2.** تَخفِيض [taxfi:ð] تَخفِيضات [taxfi:ða:t] *pl:*

 i, interjection; p, passive; pl, plural; sv, stem vowel; vn, verbal noun

تنقيص [tanqi:ṣ] تَنزيل [tanzi:l] تَنزيلات [tanzi:la:t] pl: تَقليل [taqli:l] [tangi:ṣ] تَنقيصات [tangi:ṣa:t] pl: He had to take a cut in his salary. اِضطَرّ يِقبَل تَخفيض براتبَه [ʔiðṭarr yiqbal taxfi:ð bra:tbah] • 3. تفصال [tifṣa:l] تِفصالات [tifṣa:la:t] pl: تَفصيل [tafṣi:l] تَفصيلات [tafṣi:la:t] pl: I don't like the cut of this coat. ما يِعجِبني تِفصال هَالسِّترَة [ma: yiʕǰibni tifṣa:l hassitra] • 4. حُصَّة [ħuṣṣa, ħiṣṣa] حُصَص [ħuṣaṣ] pl: You'll get your cut after everything is sold. راح تاخُذ حُصّتَك بَعَد ما كُلشي ينباع [ra:ħ ta:xuð ħuṣṣtak baʕad ma: kullši yinba:ʕ] • 5. غِياب [ɣiya:b] اِنقِطاع [ʔinqiṭa:ʕ] اِنقِطاعات [ʔinqiṭa:ʕa:t] pl: He gave me a cut for being a quarter of an hour late for class. سَجَّل عَلَيّا غِياب لِأَنّ تأَخَّرِت رُبُع ساعَة عَن الدَّرِس [saǰǰal ʕalayya ɣiya:b liʔann tʔaxxarit rubuʕ sa:ʕa ʕan ʔiddaris] • 6. وُصلَة [wuṣla] وُصَل [wuṣal] pl: قِطعَة [qiṭʕa] قُطَع [qiṭaʕ] pl: Give me a good cut of beef. إنطِيني وُصلَة لَحَم هَوش زينَة [ʔinṭi:ni wuṣlat laħam hu:š zi:na]

cut rate • **1.** سِعِر مُخَفَّض [siʕir muxaffað] He bought it cut-rate. اِشتِراها بسِعِر مُخَفَّض [ʔištira:ha bsiʕir muxaffað]

to cut • **1.** قَصّ [gaṣṣ] قَصّ [gaṣṣ] vn: اِنقَصّ [ʔingaṣṣ] p: جِرَح [ǰiraħ] جَرِح [ǰariħ] vn: اِنجِرَح [ʔinǰirah] p: I cut my finger. جرَحِت إصبعِي [ǰraħit ʔiṣibʕi] That remark cut him a great deal. هَالمُلاحَظَة جِرحَتَه كثير [halmula:ħaða ǰirħatah kθi:r] • **2.** قَصّ [gaṣṣ] قَصّ [gaṣṣ] vn: اِنقَصّ [ʔingaṣṣ] p: Will you cut the watermelon please? بالله ما تقُصّ الرَّقِّيَّة رَجاءاً؟ [ballah ma: tguṣṣ ʔirraggiyya raǰa:ʔan?] Would you cut the cards please? بالله ما تقُصّ الوَرَق رَجاءاً؟ [ballah ma: tguṣṣ ʔilwaraq raǰa:ʔan?] • **3.** خَفَّض [xaffað] تَخفيض، تخُفُّض [taxfi:ð, txuffuð] vn: تخَفَّض [txaffað] p: نَزَّل [nazzal] تَنزيل، تنِزِّل [tanzi:l, tnizzil] vn: تنَزَّل [tnazzal] p: قَلَّل [qallal] تَقليل، تقِلِّل [taqli:l, tqillil] vn: تقَلَّل [tqallal] p: نَقَّص [naggaṣ, naqqaṣ] تَنقيص، تنِقِّص [tangi:ṣ, tniggiṣ] vn: تنَقَّص [tnaggaṣ] p: They've cut the prices on winter clothes. خَفِّضَوا الأَسعار لِلمَلابِس الشِّتَوِيَّة [xaffiðaw ʔilʔasʕa:r lilmala:bis ʔiššitwiyya] • **4.** غاب [ɣa:b] غِياب [ɣiya:b] vn: sv i. اِنقِطَع [ʔingiṭaʕ] He cut class three days in a row. غاب عَن الصَّفّ ثَلَث أَيّام مِتوالِيَة [ɣa:b ʕan ʔiṣṣaff tlaθ ʔayya:m mitwa:lya] • **5.** خَفَّف [xaffaf] تَخفيف، تخِفِّف [taxfi:f, txiffif] vn: تخَفَّف Cut the paint with a gallon of turpentine. خَفِّف الصُّبُغ بِغَلَن تَربَنتين [xaffif ʔiṣṣubuɣ bgalan tarpanti:n] • **6.** طَلَّع [ṭallaʕ] طَلِّع [ṭṭilliʕ] vn: Our son is beginning to cut his teeth. إبننا بِدَى يطَلِّع [ʔibinna bida: yṭalliʕ snu:n]

to cut across • **1.** قَصّ [gaṣṣ] قَصّ [gaṣṣ] vn: اِنقَصّ [ʔingaṣṣ] p: عُبَر [ʕubar] [ʕabur] vn: اِنعُبَر [ʔinʕubar] p: We cut across the orange grove on our way home. قَصّينا بِستان البُرتَقال بجَيَّتنا لِلبَيت [gaṣṣi:na bista:n ʔilpurtaqa:l bǰayyatna lilbayt]

to cut back • **1.** خَفَّض [xaffað] sv i. نَزَّل [nazzal] sv i. نَقَّص [naggaṣ, naqqaṣ] sv i. قَلَّل [qallal] sv i. They've cut back production fifty percent. خَفِّضَوا الإنتاج خَمسين بِالمِيَّة [xaffiðaw ʔilʔinta:ǰ xamsi:n bilmiyya]

to cut in • **1.** تدَخَّل [ddaxxal] تَدَخُّل [tadaxxul] vn: sv a. He's always cutting in when we're having a discussion. هُوَّ دائِماً يِتدَخَّل لَمّا تكُون عِدنا مُناقَشَة [huwwa da:ʔiman yiddaxxal lamma tku:n ʕidna muna:qaša]

to cut off • **1.** قِطَع [qiṭaʕ] قَطِع [qaṭiʕ] vn: اِنقِطَع [ʔinqiṭaʕ] They cut off his allowance. قِطعَوا مُخَصَّصاتَه [giṭʕaw muxaṣṣaṣa:tah] The police cut off the roads leading to town. الشُّرطَة قِطعَت الطُّرُق المُؤَدِّيَة لِلوِلايَة [ʔiššurṭa qiṭʕat ʔiṭṭuruq ʔilmuʔaddiya lilwila:ya] The company cut off the electricity. الشَّرِكَة قِطعَت الكَهرَباء [ʔiššarika qiṭʕat ʔilkahraba:ʔ] • **2.** بِتَر [bitar] بَتِر [batir] vn: اِنبِتَر [ʔinbitar] p: قَصّ [gaṣṣ] قَصّ [gaṣṣ] vn: اِنقَصّ [ʔingaṣṣ] p: He cut off the dog's tail. بِتَر ذَيل الكَلِب [bitar ðayl ʔiččalib]

to cut out • **1.** بَطَّل مِن [baṭṭal min] تَبطيل [tabṭi:l] vn: sv i. Cut out that running around the house. بَطِّلُوا مِن هَالرَّكُض بِالبَيت [baṭṭilu: min harrakuð bilbayt] • **2.** قَصّ [gaṣṣ] sv u. The censor cut two sentences out of the letter. الرَّقيب قَصّ جُملتَين مِن المَكتُوب [ʔirraqi:b qaṣṣ ǰumultayn min ʔilmaktu:b] • **3.** يَزي عاد [yazzi ʕa:d] بَسّ عاد [bass ʕa:d] Cut it out! Stop making that noise. يَزّي عاد بَطِّلُوا مِن هَاللَّغوَة [yazzi ʕa:d baṭṭilu: min hallaɣwa] *** He's not cut out to be a teacher.** • **1.** هُوَّ مُو مال مُعَلِّم [huwwa mu: ma:l muʕallim] / هُوَّ مُو وِجِه مُعَلِّم [huwwa mu: wiǰih muʕallim]

to cut up • **1.** قَصقَص [gaṣgaṣ] تقِصقِص [tgiṣgiṣ] vn: قَطَّع [gaṭṭaʕ] تقِطِّع [tgiṭṭiʕ] vn: Cut up the carrots in small pieces. قَصقِص الجِّزَر وُصَل صغار [gaṣgiṣ ʔiǰǰizar wuṣal ṣɣa:r]

cute • **1.** لَطيف [laṭi:f] لَطيفين [laṭi:fi:n] pl: حَبُّوب [ħabbu:b] She's a very cute girl. هِيَّ فَدّ بنَيَّة هوايَة حَبُّوبَة [hiyya fadd bnayya hwa:ya ħabbu:ba] He told a cute story. حِكَى قُصَّة لَطيفَة [ħiča: quṣṣa laṭi:fa]

cycle • **1.** دَورَة [dawra] دَورات [dawra:t] pl: This machine completes its cycle in five minutes. هَالمَكينَة تكَمِّل دَورَتها بخَمَس دَقايِق [halmaki:na tkammil dawratha bxamas daqa:yiq]

cylinder • **1.** سِلِندَر [silindar] سِلِندَرات [silindara:t] pl: This engine has six cylinders. هَالمَكينَة بيها سِتّ سِلِندَرات [halmaki:na bi:ha sitt silindara:t] • **2.** إسطُوانَة [ʔisṭuwa:na] إسطُوانات [ʔisṭuwa:na:t] pl: The volume of a cylinder is equal to multiplying the area of the base times its height. حَجم الإسطُوانَة يساوي ضَرب مَساحَة القاعِدَة بِالإرتِفاع [ħaǰm ʔilʔisṭuwa:na ysa:wi ðarb masa:ħat ʔilqa:ʕida bilʔirtifa:ʕ]

cymbal • **1.** طاس [ṭa:s] طُوس [ṭu:s] pl:

Cypriot • **1.** قُبرُصِي [qubruṣi] قُبرُصِيِّين [qubruṣiyyi:n] pl:

Cyprus • **1.** قُبرُص [qubruṣ]

czar • **1.** قَيصَر [qayṣar] قَياصِرَة [qaya:ṣira] pl:

D

dad • **1.** يابَة [ya:ba] ياب [ya:b] بابا [ba:ba] Dad, can I use the car? ياب، أقدَر أستَعمِل السَّيّارَة؟ [ya:b, ʔagdar ʔastaʕmil ʔissayya:ra?]

daddy • **1.** بابا [ba:ba] Is your daddy home? بابا بِالبَيت؟ [ba:bah bilbayt?]

daffodil • **1.** نَرجِسَة [narǰisa] نَرجِسات [narǰisa:t] *pl:* نَرجِس [narǰis] *Collective*

dagger • **1.** خَنجَر [xanǰar] خَناجِر [xana:ǰir] *pl:*

daily • **1.** بِاليَوم [bilyawm] كُلّ يَوم [kull yu:m] The mail is delivered twice daily. البَرِيد يِتوَزَّع مَرّتَين بِاليُوم [ʔilbari:d yitwazzaʕ marrtayn bilyu:m] • **2.** يَومِي [yawmi] The daily rate is three dollars. الأُجرَة اليَومِيَّة ثلاث دُولارات [ʔalʔuǰra ʔilyawmiyya tla:θ dulara:t]

dairy • **1.** مَعمَل ألبان [maʕmal ʔalba:n] مَعامِل ألبان [maʕa:mil ʔalba:n] *pl:* I bought the butter at the dairy. اِشتِرَيت الزِّبدَة مِن مَعمَل الألبان [ʔištiri:t ʔizzibda min maʕmal ʔilʔalba:n] • **2.** مزرَعَة ألبان [مزرَعَة ألبان] My uncle has a dairy farm. عَمِّي عِندَه مَزرَعَة ألبان [ʕammi ʕindah mazraʕat ʔalba:n]

dam • **1.** سَدّ [sadd] The dam is broken. السَّدّ مَكسُور [ʔissadd maksu:r]

damage • **1.** ضَرَر [ðarar] أضرار [ʔaðra:r] *pl:* تَلَف [talaf] How much damage took place? شقَدّ صار ضَرَر؟ [šgadd ṣa:r ðarar?]

to damage • **1.** تِلَف [tilaf] تَلِف [talif] *vn: sv* i. The storm damaged the roof. العاصِفَة تِلفَت السَطِح [ʔilʕa:ṣifa tilfat ʔiṣṣaṭiħ]

damages • **1.** تَعوِيض [taʕwi:ð] He had to pay damages. اِضطَر يِدفَع تَعوِيضات [ʔiðṭarr yidfaʕ taʕwi:ða:t]

Damascene • **1.** دِمِشقِي [dimišqi] دِمِشقِيِّين [dimišqiyyi:n] *pl:* شامِي [ša:mi] شامِيِّين [ša:miyyi:n] *pl:*

Damascus • **1.** دِمَشق [dimašq] الشام [ʔišša:m]

damn • **1.** مَلعُون [malʕu:n] Throw that damn cat out! طَلِّع هَالبَزُّونَة المَلعُونَة بَرَّة [ṭalliʕ halbazzu:na ʔilmalʕu:na barra]

* **I don't give a damn what he says.** • **1.** حكايتَه وقُندَرتِي [ħča:ytah wqundarti]

to damn • **1.** لِعَن [liʕan] لَعِن [laʕin] *vn:* اِنلِعَن [ʔinliʕan] *p: sv* a. Damn him! الله يِلعَنَه [ʔallah yilʕanah] • **2.** لِعَن [liʕan] لَعِن [laʕin] *vn:* اِنلِعَن [ʔinliʕan] *p:* نِعَل [niʕal] نَعِل [naʕil] *vn:* اِنِّعَل [ʔinniʕal] *p:* شِعَل [šiʕal] شَعِل [šaʕil] *vn:* اِنشِعَل [ʔinšiʕal] *p:* She damned me up and down for running over her cat. نِعلَت مَذهَبِي لِأنّ دِسِت بَزُّونَتها بسَيّارتِي [niʕlat maðhabi liʔann disit bazzu:natha bsayya:rti] I'll be damned if I'll do it! أنِّعِل إذا أسَوِّيها [ʔanniʕil ʔiða ʔasawwi:ha]

damned • **1.** مَلعُون [malʕu:n] مَنعُول [manʕu:l]

damp • **1.** رَطِب [raṭib] نادِي [na:di] نَوادِي [nawa:di] *pl:* Everything gets damp in the cellar. كُلّشِي يصِير رَطِب بِالسِّرداب [kullši yṣi:r raṭib bissirda:b]

dampness • **1.** رُطُوبَة [ruṭu:ba] نِدَة [nida]

dance • **1.** رِقصَة [rigṣa] رِقصات [rigṣa:t] *pl:* May I have the next dance? تِسمَحِيلِي بالرِّقصَة الجّايَّة؟ [tismaħi:li birrigṣa ʔiǰǰa:yya?] • **2.** حَفلَة رِقِص [ħaflat rigiṣ] حَفلات رِقِص [ħafla:t rigiṣ] *pl:* Are you going to the dance? راح ترُوح لِحَفلَة الرِّقِص؟ [ra:ħ tru:ħ liħaflat ʔirrigiṣ?]

to dance • **1.** رِقَص [rigaṣ] رِقِص [rigiṣ] *vn: sv* u. They danced until midnight. رِقصَوا إلَى نُصّ اللَّيل [rigṣaw ʔila nuṣṣ ʔillayl]

dancer • **1.** راقِصَة [ra:qiṣa] راقِصات [ra:qiṣa:t] *pl:* They have a good dancer at the Select Night Club. عِدهُم راقِصَة زينَة بِمَلهَى سَلَكت [ʕidhum ra:qiṣa zi:na bmalha salakt]

* **He's a good dancer.** • **1.** يِرقُص زَين [yirguṣ zayn]

danger • **1.** خَطَر [xaṭar] أخطار [ʔaxṭa:r] *pl:* The doctor says she is out of danger now. الطَّبِيب قال الخَطَر زال عَنها هَسَّة [ʔiṭṭabi:b ga:l ʔilxaṭar za:l ʕanha hassa] Caution! Danger! إنتِبِه لِلخَطَر [ʔintibih lilxaṭar]

in danger of • **1.** مُعَرَّض [muʕarrað] He's in danger of losing his job. هُوَّ مُعَرَّض لِفُقدان وَظِيفتَه [huwwa muʕarrað lifuqda:n waði:ftah]

dangerous • **1.** مُخطِر [muxṭir] Is swimming here dangerous? السِّبِح هنا مُخطِر؟ [ʔissibiħ hna: muxṭir?]

to dare • **1.** جِرَأ [ǰiraʔ] جُرأة [ǰurʔa] *vn: sv* a. جِسَر [ǰisar] جِسارَة [ǰisa:ra] *vn: sv* u. I didn't dare leave the baby alone. ما جرَأت أترُك الطِّفِل وَحدَه [ma: ǰraʔt ʔatruk ʔiṭṭifil waħdah] How dare you open my mail? شلُون تِجسُر تِفتَح بَرِيدِي؟ [šlu:n tiǰsur tiftaħ bari:di?]

dark • **1.** ظَلمَة [ðalma] The road is hard to find in the dark. الطَّرِيق صَعُب يِنلِقِي بِالظَلمَة [ʔiṭṭari:q ṣaʕub yinligi biððalma] • **2.** ظَلام [ðala:m] Don't keep me in the dark this way. لا تِترُكني بالظَّلام هِيكِي [la: titrukni biððala:m hi:či] • **3.** طوخ [ṭu:x] I want a darker color. أرِيد لُون أطوَخ [ʔari:d lu:n ʔaṭwax] • **4.** أسمَر [ʔasmar] سُمُر [sumur] *pl:* سَمرَة [samra] *Feminine:* She is quite dark. هِيَّ سَمرَة كُلِّش [hiyya samra kulliš]

to get dark • **1.** اِظلَمّ [ʔiðlamm] ظَلام [ðala:m] *vn: sv* a. In summer it gets dark late. بِالصَّيف تِظلَمّ فايت وَقِت [bissayf tiðlamm fa:yit wakit]

darling • **1.** مدَلَّل [mdallal] مدَلَّلِين [mdallali:n] *pl:* He's his mother's pampered darling. هُوَّ مدَلَّل مال أُمَّه [huwwa mdallal ma:l ʔummah] • **2.** حَبِيب [ħabi:b] أحِبَّة، أحباب [ʔaħibba, ʔaħba:b] *pl:* What's the matter, darling? شبِيك، حَبِيبي؟ [šbi:k, ħabi:bi?]

* **What a darling child!** • **1.** شلَون جاهِل يِنحَطّ بِالقَلب [šlu:n ǰa:hil yinħaṭṭ bilgalub]

to darn • **1.** خَيَّط [xayyaṭ] خياطَة [xya:ṭa] *vn: sv* i. Did you darn my socks? خَيَّطتِيلِي جوارِيبِي؟ [xayyaṭti:li ǰwa:ri:bi?]

* **I'll be darned if it isn't Jalil!**

• **1.** أقُصّ إيدِي إذا هَذا مُو جَلِيل [ʔaguṣṣ ʔi:di ʔiða: ha:ða mu: ǰali:l]

dash • **1.** خَطّ [xaṭṭ] خُطوط [xuṭu:ṭ] *pl:* شَخُط [šaxuṭ] شُخُوط [šuxu:ṭ] *pl:* Put a dash after the first word. حُطّ خَطّ بَعد الكَلِمَة الأولَى [ħuṭṭ xaṭṭ baʕd ʔilkalima ʔilʔu:la] • **2.** حَبَّة [ħabba] حَبّات [ħabba:t] *pl:* All it needs is a dash of salt. ما يِنرادلَه غير حَبَّة مِلِح [ma: yinra:dlah ɣi:r ħabbat miliħ] • **3.** رِكِض [rikið] Who won the hundred meter dash? مِنُو غِلَب بِركِض المِيَة مَتِر [minu ɣilab brikð ʔilmiyat matir]

to dash • **1.** رَشّ [rašš] رَشّ [rašš] *vn: sv* u. ذَبّ [ðabb] ذَبّ [ðabb] *vn: sv* i. He came to when I dashed some water in his face. رَدَّت رُوحَه لَمّا رَشَّيت شوَيَّة ماي عَلَى وُجَّه [raddat ru:ħah lamma raššayt šwayya ma:y ʕala wuččah] • **2.** طَفُر [ṭufar] طَفُر [ṭafur] *vn: sv* u. He grabbed his hat and made a dash for the door. لِقَف شَفُقتَه وَطُفَر طَفُر بِالباب [ligaf šafuqtah wṭufar ṭafur bilba:b]

to dash off • **1.** عَلَّق [ʕallag] تَعلِيق [taʕli:g] *vn: sv* i. He dashed off before I could answer. عَلَّق، قَبُل ما أجاوبَه [ʕallag, gabul ma: ʔaǰa:wbah]

dashboard • **1.** دَشبُول [dašbu:l] دَشبُولات [dašbu:la:t] *pl:*

date • **1.** تَمرَة [tamra] تَمرات [tamra:t] *pl:* تَمُر [tamur] *Collective:* How much is a kilo of dates? بيش كِيلُو التَّمُر [biyš ki:lu ʔittamur] • **2.** تارِيخ [ta:ri:x] تَوارِيخ [tawa:ri:x] *pl:* What's the date today? شِنُو تارِيخ اليُوم؟ [šinu: ta:ri:x ʔilyu:m?] What's the date today? اليُوم شقَدّ بِالشَّهَر؟ [ʔilyu:m šgadd biššahar?] • **3.** وَضِح [waðiħ] I have a date for lunch today. عِندِي مَوعِد لِلغَدا هَاليُوم [ʕindi mawʕid lilɣada: halyu:m] • **4.** يوم [yawm] أيّام [ʔayya:m] *pl:* You set the date. إنتَ عَيِّن اليُوم [ʔinta ʕayyin ʔilyu:m]

to date • **1.** هَسَّة [hassa] إلَى الآن [ʔila: ʔilʔa:n] We haven't heard from him to date. ما سمَعنا مِنَّه لهَسَّة [ma: simaʕna minnah lhassa]

to date • **1.** أرَّخ [ʔarrax] تَأرِيخ [taʔri:x] *vn:* تأَرَّخ [tʔarrax] *p:* The letter is dated June 6. المَكتُوب مأَرَّخ بسِتَّة حُزَيران [ʔilmaktu:b mʔarrax bsitta ħuzayra:n]

to date from • **1.** رِجَع التَّارِيخ إلَى [riǰaʕ ʔitta:ri:x ʔila] رُجُوع التَّارِيخ إلَى [ruǰu:ʕ ʔitta:ri:x ʔila] *vn: sv* a. The oldest house in town dates from the 17th century. أعتَق بَيت بِالمَدِينَة يِرجَع تارِيخَه إلَى القَرن السّابِع عَشِر [ʔaʕatag bayt bilmadi:na yirǰaʕ ta:ri:xah ʔila ʔilqarn ʔissa:biʕ ʕašir]

date palm • **1.** نَخِيل [naxi:l] نَخَل [naxal] *Collective*

daughter • **1.** بِتّ [bitt] بِنت [bint] بَنات [bana:t] *pl:*

daughter-in-law • **1.** كَنَّة [čanna] كنايِن [čna:yin] *pl:*

dawn • **1.** فَجِر [fajir] We had to get up at dawn. اِضطَرَّينا نُقعُد مِن الفَجِر [ʔiðṭarri:na nugʕud min ʔilfajir]

to dawn • **1.** صَبَّح [ṣabbaħ] تَصبِيح [taṣbi:ħ] *vn: sv* i. The day dawned, clear and sunny. صَبَّح النَّهار صاحِي وَمُشمِس [ṣabbaħ ʔinnaha:r ṣa:ħi wmušmis] • **2.** وُضَح ل [wuðaħ l-] وُضُوح [wuðu:ħ] *vn: sv* a. أدرَك [ʔadrak] إدراك [ʔidra:k] *vn: sv* i. It finally dawned on me what he meant. أخِيراً وُضَحلِي قَصدَه [ʔaxi:ran wuðaħli qaṣdah] It finally dawned on me what he meant. أخِيراً أدرَكِت شعنَى [ʔaxi:ran ʔadrakit šʕina:]

day • **1.** يوم [yawm, yu:m] أيّام [ʔayya:m] *pl:* I haven't seen him since that day. ما شِفتَه مِن ذاك اليُوم [ma: šiftah min ða:k ʔilyu:m] I'll drop by your house some day. راح أمُرّ لِبَيتكُم فَدّ يوم مِن الأيّام [ra:ħ ʔamurr lbaytkum fadd yu:m min ʔilʔayya:m] One of these days you'll be sorry. راح تِندَم فَدّ يوم [ra:ħ tindam fadd yu:m] • **2.** نَهار [naha:r] نَهارات [naha:ra:t] *pl:* He's been sleeping all day. صارلَه نايِم طُول النَّهار [ṣa:rlah na:yim ṭu:l ʔinnaha:r]

* **Let's call it a day!** • **1.** بايدَوس [pa:ydu:s]

a day • **1.** بِاليَوم [bilyawm] Take three pills a day. إبلَع ثلَث حَبّات بِاليُوم [ʔiblaʕ tlaθ ħabba:t bilyu:m]

by the day • **1.** يوم بَعَد يوم [yawm baʕad yawm] يوم عَلَى يوم [yawm ʕala yawm] It gets more difficult by the day. دَيصِير أصعَب يوم عَلَى يوم [dayṣi:r ʔaṣʕab yu:m ʕala yu:m] • **2.** عَلَى أساس الأيّام [ʕala ʔasa:s ʔilʔayya:m] كُلّ يوم بيُومَه [kull yu:m byu:mah] You can rent this room by the day. تِقدَر تأَجِّر هَالغُرفَة عَلَى أساس الأيّام [tigdar tʔaǰǰir halɣurfa ʕala ʔasa:s ʔilʔayya:m]

day after day • **1.** يَوم وَرا يَوم [yawm wara yawm] Day after day he tells us the same old story. يوم وَرا يوم يعِيد وَيصقُل بِنَفس القُصَّة [yu:m wara yu:m yʕi:d wyiṣqul bnafis ʔilquṣṣa]

day by day • **1.** يوم عَلَى يَوم [yu:m ʕala yu:m] يَوم بَعَد يَوم [yu:m baʕad yu:m] يَوم وَرا يَوم [yu:m wara yu:m] Day by day his condition is improving. يوم عَلَى يوم حالتَه دَتِتحَسَّن [yu:m ʕala yu:m ħa:ltah datitħassan]
day off • **1.** عُطلَة [ʕuṭla] عُطلات [ʕuṭla:t] *pl:* Tuesday is my day off. عُطِلتي يوم الثَّلاثاء [ʕuṭilti yu:m ʔiθθila:θa:ʔ]
every day • **1.** كُلّ يَوم [kull yawm] He works every day except Friday. يِشتُغُل كُلّ يوم ما عَدا يوم الجُمعَة [yištuɣul kull yu:m ma: ʕada: yu:m ʔiǰǰumʕa]

daybreak • **1.** فَجِر [faǰir] We're leaving at daybreak. راح نسافِر الفَجِر [ra:ħ nsa:fir ʔilfaǰir]

to daze • **1.** دَوَّخ [dawwax] *sv* u. سِطَر [siṭar] سَطِر [saṭir] *vn:* The explosion dazed him. الإنفِجار دَوَّخَه [ʔilʔinfiǰa:r dawwaxah]

dazed • **1.** دايِخ [da:yix] مَسطُور [masṭu:r] He seemed completely dazed. كان مبَيِّن عَليه دايِخ تَماماً [ča:n mbayyin ʕali:h da:yix tama:man]

dead • **1.** مَيِّت [mayyit] أموات, مَوتَى [ʔamwa:t, mawta] مَيِّتِين [mayyti:n] *pl:* They buried their dead. دِفنَوا مَوتاهُم [difnaw mawta:hum] The meeting was pretty dead. الجَّلسَة كانَت مَيِّتَة [ʔiǰǰalsa ča:nat mayyta] The meeting was pretty dead. الجَّلسَة ما كان بِيها حَياة [ʔiǰǰalsa ma: ča:n bi:ha ħaya:t] • **2.** تَماماً [tama:man] I'm dead tired. آنِي تَعبان تَماماً [ʔa:ni taʕba:n tama:man] I'm dead certain I put it there. آنِي مِتأكِّد تَماماً خَلّيتها هناك [ʔa:ni mitʔakkid tama:man xalli:tha hna:k]
*** The fire is dead.** • **1.** النار خُمدَت [ʔinna:r xumdat]

dead-end • **1.** ما بِيه طَلعَة [ma: bi:h ṭalʕa] ما يِطلَع [ma: yiṭlaʕ] This is a dead-end street. هَذا شارِع ما يِطلَع [ha:ða ša:riʕ ma: yiṭlaʕ]

deadly • **1.** قاتِل [qa:til] قاتِلِين، قَتَلَة [qa:tili:n, qatala] *pl:* قَتّال [katta:l] مُمِيت [mumi:t] This poison is deadly. هَالسَّمّ قاتِل [hassamm qa:til]

deaf • **1.** أطرَش [ʔaṭraš] طُرُش، طَرشِين [ṭuruš, ṭarši:n] *pl:* طَرشَة [ṭarša] *Feminine:* He's completely deaf. هُوَّ أطرَش تَماماً [huwwa ʔaṭraš tama:man]

to deafen • **1.** طَرَّش [ṭarraš] تَطرِيش [taṭri:š] *vn: sv* i. That noise is deafening. هَالصَّوت يطَرِّش [haṣṣawt yṭarriš]

deal • **1.** صَفقَة [ṣafqa] صَفقات [ṣafqa:t] *pl:* He made a lot of money on that deal. سَوَّى خُوش فلُوس بِهالصَّفقَة [sawwa: xu:š flu:s bhaṣṣafqa] • **2.** حُصَّة [ħuṣṣa] حُصَص [ħuṣaṣ] *pl:* All I want is a fair deal. كُلّ ما أرِيدَه هُوَّ حُصَّة عادلَة [kull ma: ʔari:dah huwwa ħuṣṣa ʕa:dla] • **3.** تَوزِيع [tawzi:ʕ] Whose deal is it now? دَور مَن هَسَّة بِالتَّوزِيع؟ [dawr man hassa bittawzi:ʕ?] Whose deal is it now? مِنُو يوَزِّع وَرَق؟ [minu ywazziʕ waraq?] • **4.** دَقَّة [dagga] دَقّات [dagga:t] *pl:* That's a good deal! هاي خُوش دَقَّة [ha:y xu:š dagga]
*** They gave him a raw deal.** • **1.** عاملَوه مُو خَوش [ʕa:mlu:h mu: xu:š] / خُمطَوا حَقَّه [xumṭaw ħaqqah]
a good deal • **1.** هوايَة [hwa:ya] There's a good deal to be done yet. أكُو بَعَد هوايَة يِرّادلَه مساواة [ʔaku baʕad hwa:ya yirra:dlah msa:wa:]
to deal • **1.** وَزَّع [wazzaʕ] تَوزِيع [tawzi:ʕ] *vn:* توَزَّع [twazzaʕ] *p:* قَسَّم [qassam] تَقسِيم [taqsi:m] *vn:* تقَسَّم [tqassam] *p:* فَرَّق [farrag] تَفرِيق [tafri:g] *vn:* تفَرَّق [tfarrag] Who dealt the cards? مِنُو وَزَّع الوَرَق؟ [minu wazzaʕ ʔilwaraq?]
to deal with • **1.** تعامَل مَعَ [tʕa:mal maʕa] تَعامُل مَعَ [taʕa:mul maʕa] *vn: sv* a. ويّا [wiyya] He dealt fairly with me. تعامَل ويّايا بعَدِل [tʕa:mal wiyya:ya bʕadil] He deals directly with the company. يِتعامَل مَعَ الشَّركَة رأساً [yitʕa:mal maʕa ʔiššarika raʔsan] • **2.** تعَلَّق ب [tʕallaq b-] تَعَلُّق [taʕalluq] *vn: sv* a. The book deals with labor problems. الكِتاب يِتعَلَّق بِمَشاكِل العُمّال [ʔilkita:b yitʕallaq bmaša:kil ʔilʕumma:l]
*** This problem has been dealt with.**
• **1.** هَالمُشكِلَة اِنبِحثَت وخِلصَت [halmuškila ʔinbiħθat wxilṣat]

dealer • **1.** تاجِر [ta:ǰir] تُجّار [tuǰǰa:r] *pl:* He's a dealer in Persian rugs. هُوَّ تاجِر بِالسِّجّاد العَجَمِي [huwwa ta:ǰir bissiǰǰa:d ʔilʕaǰmi] • **2.** بَيّاع [bayya:ʕ] بَيّاعَة [bayya:ʕa, bayya:ʕi:n] بَيّاعِين، *pl:* There's a used car dealer near our house. أكُو بَيّاع سَيّارات مُستَعمَلَة يَمّ بَيتنا [ʔaku bayya:ʕ sayya:ra:t mustaʕmila yamm baytna]

dear • **1.** عَزِيز [ʕazi:z] His sister is very dear to him. أختَه كُلَّش عَزِيزَة عَليه [ʔuxtah kulliš ʕazi:za ʕali:h] • **2.** غالِي [ɣa:li] Everything in the market is very dear these days. كُلْشِي بالسُّوق كُلَّش غالِي هَالأيّام [kullši bissu:g kulliš ɣa:li halʔayya:m]
oh dear • **1.** آخ يابَة [ʔa:x ya:ba] Oh dear, we'll be late again. آخ يابَة راح نكُون مِتأخّرِين مَرَّة لُخ [ʔa:x ya:ba ra:ħ nku:n mitʔaxxri:n marra lux]

dearly • **1.** غالِي [ɣa:li] He had to pay dearly for his mistake. اِضطَرّ يِدفَع غالِي عَلَى غَلطتَه [ʔiḍṭarr yidfaʕ ɣa:li ʕala ɣaliṭṭah]

death • **1.** موت [mawt, mu:t] وَفاة [wafa:, wafa:t] وَفايات، وَفيات [wafa:ya:t, wafiya:t] *pl:* وَفِيَّة [wafiyya] وَفِيّات [wafiyya:t] *pl:* His death was announced in the newspapers. موتَه اِنعِلَن بالجَّرايِد [mu:tah ʔinʕilan biǰǰara:yid] • **2.** إعدام [ʔiʕda:m] This crime carries the death penalty. هَالجَرِيمَة تِتضَمَّن عُقُوبَة الإعدام [halǰari:ma tidðamman ʕuqu:bat ʔilʔiʕda:m]
*** You'll catch your death of cold.**
• **1.** راح يصِيبَك بَرِد يمَوّتَك [ra:ħ yṣi:bak barid ymawwtak]

*** He'll be the death of me yet.** • **1.** راح يمَوِّتني وَالله [ra:ħ yimawwitni wallah]
*** Don't work yourself to death.** • **1.** لا تِهلِك نَفسَك مِن الشُغُل [la: tihlik nafsak min ʔiššuɣul]
*** He's in the throes of death.** • **1.** قِعَد ينازِع [giʕad yna:ziʕ]

debate • **1.** مُناقَشَة [muna:qaša] مُناقَشات [muna:qaša:t] *pl:* The debate lasted for hours. المُناقَشَة دامَت عِدَّة ساعات [ʔilmuna:qaša da:mat ʕiddat sa:ʕa:t]
to debate • **1.** ناقَش [na:qaš] مُناقَشَة [muna:qaša] *vn: sv* i. The students debated the subject among themselves. الطُلّاب ناقشَوا المَوضوع بَيناتهُم [ʔiṭṭulla:b na:qšaw ʔilmawðu:ʕ bayna:thum] The question was debated for a long time. السُؤال طَوّلَت مُناقَشتَه مُدَّة طويلَة [ʔissuʔa:l ṭawwlat muna:qaštah mudda ṭwi:la]
to debate with oneself • **1.** دانَش النَّفِس [da:naš ʔinnafis] مُدانَشَة النَّفِس [muda:našat ʔinnafis] *vn: sv* i. I debated with myself whether or not to go. دانَشِت نَفسِي أرُوح لَو لا [da:našit nafsi ʔaru:ħ law la:]

debt • **1.** دَين [dayn] دِيُون [dyu:n] *pl:* This payment settles your debt. هَالدَّفعَة تِنهي دَينَك [haddafʕa tinhi daynak]
in debt • **1.** مَديُون [madyu:n] Is he still in debt? هُوَّ بَعدَه مَديُون [huwwa baʕdah madyu:n] • **2.** بِالدَّين [biddayn] He's up to his ears in debt. هُوَّ طامُس بِالدَّين [huwwa ṭa:mus biddayn]

debtor • **1.** مَديُون [madyu:n]

decade • **1.** عَقِد [ʕaqid] عُقُود [ʕuqu:d] *pl:*

decay • **1.** اِنحِلال [ʔinħila:l] Some means must be found to prevent any further decay in our economic system. فَدّ وَسِيلَة لازِم تِنلِقِي لِمَنِع أَيّ اِنحِلال آخَر بِنِظامنا الاقتِصادِي [fadd wasi:la la:zim tinligi limaniʕ ʔayy ʔinħila:l ʔa:xar bniða:mna ʔilʔiqtiṣa:di]
to decay • **1.** خاس [xa:s] The vegetables decayed rapidly in the heat. الخُضرَوات خاسَت بِالعَجَل مِن حَرارَة الجَّوّ [ʔilxuðrawa:t xa:sat bilʕajal min ħara:rat ʔijjaww] • **2.** سَوَّس [sawwas] تَسوِيس [taswi:s] *vn:* تسَوَّس [tsawwas] The tooth decayed. السِّنّ سَوَّس [ʔissinn sawwas]

decayed • **1.** خايِس [xa:yis] Throw all the decayed vegetables into the garbage can. ذِب كُلّ الخُضرَوات الخايسَة بِتَنَكَة الزِّبِل [ðibb kull ʔilxuðrawa:t ʔilxa:ysa btanakat ʔizzibil] • **2.** مِتسَوِّس [mitsawwis] مسَوِّس [msawwis] The tooth is decayed and I'll have to pull it. السِّنّ مسَوِّس وَلازِم أشلَعَه [ʔissinn msawwis wla:zim ʔašlaʕah] • **3.** مِتفَسِّخ [mitfassix] The body was so decayed that it could not be identified. الجُثَّة هَل قَدّ ما مِتفَسّخَة ما مُمكِن التَّعَرُّف عَلَى هَوِيَّة صاحِبها [ʔijjuθθa hal gadd ma: mitfassxa ma: mumkin ʔittaʕarruf ʕala hawiyyat ṣa:ħibhah]

deceit • **1.** غِشّ [ɣišš] مُخاتَلَة [muxa:tala] خِداع [xida:ʕ] قَشمَرَة [qašmara]

deceitful • **1.** مُخادِع [muxa:diʕ] She is a lying, deceitful woman. هاي فَدّ مَرَة كَذّابَة وَمُخادِعَة [ha:y fadd mara čaðða:ba wmuxa:diʕa]

to deceive • **1.** غَشّ [ɣašš] غَشّ [ɣašš] *vn:* اِنغَشّ [ʔinɣašš] *p:* خِدَع [xidaʕ] خِداع [xida:ʕ] *vn:* اِنخِدَع [ʔinxidaʕ] *p:* قَشمَر [qašmar] قَشمَرَة [qašmara] *vn: sv* u. Appearances are deceiving. المَظاهِر تِخدَع [ʔilmaða:hir tixdaʕ] He deceived us. غَشّنا [ɣaššna] • **2.** خان [xa:n] خانات [xa:na:t] *pl:* خِيانَة [xiya:na] *vn: sv* u. خِدَع [xidaʕ] خِداع [xida:ʕ] *vn:* اِنخِدَع [ʔinxidaʕ] *p: sv* a. His wife is deceiving him. زَوجتَه دَتخُونَه [zawijtah datxu:nah]

December • **1.** كانُون الأوَّل [ka:nu:n ʔilʔawwal]

decency • **1.** أَدَب [ʔadab] آداب [ʔa:da:b] *pl:* لِياقَة [liya:qa] He didn't even have the decency to thank me. ما كان عِندَه حَتَّى أَدَب كافِي يِشكُرنِي [ma: ka:n ʕindah ħatta ʔadab ka:fi yiškurni]

decent • **1.** مُحتَرَم [muħtaram] مُؤَدَّب [muʔaddab] He's a decent fellow. هُوَّ فَدّ واحِد مُحتَرَم [huwwa fadd wa:ħid muħtaram] He lives a decent life. يِعِيش عِيشَة مُحتَرَمَة [yiʕi:š ʕi:ša muħtarama] • **2.** شَرِيف [šari:f] أشراف، شُرَفاء [ʔašra:f, šurafa:ʔ] *pl:* He did the decent thing and married her. سَوَّى شِي شَرِيف وَتزَوَّجها [sawwa: ši šari:f wdzawwajha] • **3.** زَين [zayn] I make a decent living from this job. هَالشَّغلَة توَفِّرلِي عِيشَة زينَة [haššaɣla twaffirli ʕi:ša zayna]

to decide • **1.** قَرَّر [qarrar] تَقرِير [taqri:r] *vn:* تقَرَّر [tqarrar] *p:* I decided to stay. قَرَّرِت أبقَى [qarrarit ʔabqa:] What did you decide on? شقَرَّرِت؟ [šqarrarit?]

decided • **1.** ثابِت [θa:bit] حَتماً [ħatman] His height gave him a decided advantage in the fight. طُولَه اِنطاه أفضَلِيَّة حَتماً بِالعَركَة [ṭu:lah ʔinṭa:h ʔafðaliyya ħatman bilʕarka]

decidedly • **1.** حَتماً [ħatman] أكِيد [ʔaki:d] He is decidedly worried about the examination. حَتماً هُوَّ قَلِق مِن الإمتِحان [ħatman huwwa qaliq min ʔilʔimtiħa:n]

decision • **1.** قَرار [qara:r] قَرارات [qara:ra:t] *pl:* At last he has come to a decision. وَأخِيراً وُصَل إلَى قَرار [wʔaxi:ran wuṣal ʔila qara:r] • **2.** حُكُم [ħukum] أحكام [ʔaħka:m] *pl:* The judge hasn't come to his decision yet. الحاكِم ما وُصَل إلَى حُكمَه بَعَد [ʔilħa:kim ma: wuṣal ʔila ħukmah baʕad]

deck • **1.** سَطِح باخِرَة [saṭiħ baːxira] سُطُوح باخِرَة [suṭuːħ baːxira] *pl:* Is he in his cabin or on the deck? هُوَّ بمَقصُورتَه لَو عَلَى سَطح الباخِرَة [huwwa bmaqṣuːrtah law ʕala saṭħ ʔilbaːxira] • **2.** دَستَة [dasta] دَستات [dastaːt] *pl:* شَدَّة [šadda] شَدّات [šaddaːt] *pl:* Let's take a new deck of cards. خَلّي ناخُذ دَستَة وَرَق جِدِيدَة [xalli naːxuð dastat waraq jidiːda]

to deck out • **1.** زَيَّن [zayyan] تَزيِين [tazyiːn] *vn:* *p:* زَروَق [zarwaq] زَروَقَة [zarwaqa] *vn:* The city was all decked out with lights. المَدِينَة كانَت مزَيّنَة بالأضوِيَة [ʔilmadiːna čaːnat mzayyna bilʔaðwiya]

declaration • **1.** تَصريح [taṣriːħ] تَصريحات، تَصاريح [taṣriːħaːt, taṣaːriːħ] *pl:* He presented his customs declaration to the customs inspector. قَدَّم تَصرِيحتَه الجُمرُجِيَّة لمُفَتِّش الجُمرُك [qaddam taṣriːħtah ʔalgumrugiyya lmufattiš ʔilgumrug] • **2.** إعلان [ʔiʕlaːn] إعلانات [ʔiʕlaːnaːt] *pl:* إشهار [ʔišhaːr] إشهارات [ʔišhaːraːt] *pl:* He broadcasted the declaration of war over the radio. ذاع إعلان الحَرُب بِالرّاديُو [ðaːʕ ʔiʕlaːn ʔilħarub birraːdyu]

to declare • **1.** أعلَن، عِلَن [ʔaʕlan, ʕilan] إعلان [ʔiʕlaːn] *vn:* *sv* i. They declared war on us. أَعلِنوا علينا حَرُب [ʔaʕlinaw ʕaliːna ħarub] • **2.** قَدَّم [qaddam] تَقدِيم [taqdiːm] *vn:* *sv* i. Do I have to declare the tobacco at the customs? لازِم أَقَدِّم تَصريح بالتِّبِغ بالجُمرُك؟ [laːzim ʔaqaddim taṣriːħ bittibiɣ bilgumrug?]

decline • **1.** تَناقُص [tanaːguṣ] The decline in new cases of cancer continued this month. التَّناقُص بالإصابات الجِّدِيدَة بِالسَّرَطان اِستَمَرّ هَالشَّهَر [ʔittanaːguṣ bilʔiṣaːbaːt ʔijjidiːda biṣṣaraṭaːn ʔistamarr haššahar] • **2.** تَدَهوُر [tadahwir] The empire's decline continued for several years. تَدَهوُر الإمبَراطورِيَّة اِستَمَرّ عِدَّة سنِين [tadahuːr ʔilimparaːṭuːriyya ʔistamarr ʕiddat sniːn]

to decline • **1.** اِنحَطّ [ʔinħaṭṭ] اِنحِطاط [ʔinħiṭaːṭ] *vn:* *sv* a. His health has declined over the past year. صِحّتَه اِنحَطَّت خِلال السَّنَة الماضِيَة [ṣiħħtah ʔinħaṭṭat xilaːl ʔissana ʔilmaːðiya] • **2.** تناقَص [tnaːgaṣ] تَناقُص [tanaːguṣ] *vn:* *sv* a. Club membership has declined recently. عُضوِيَّة النّادِي تناقصَت مُؤَخَّراً [ʕuðwiyyat ʔinnaːdi tnaːgṣat muʔaxxaran] • **3.** رُفَض [rufað] رَفُض [rafuð] *vn:* اِنرِفَض [ʔinrifað] *p:* They had to decline his invitation. اِضطَرَّوا يرُفضُون دَعوتَه [ʔiðṭarraw yirufðuːn daʕwtah]

to decorate • **1.** صَنَّع [ṣannaʕ] تَصنِيع [taṣniːʕ] *vn:* تصَنَّع [tṣannaʕ] *p:* The baker decorated the cake for our party. بايِع الكَيك صَنَّع الكَيكَة لِحَفلَتنا [baːyiʕ ʔilkayk ṣannaʕ ʔilkayka liħaflatna] • **2.** زَيَّن [zayyan] تَزيِين [tazyiːn] *vn:* تزَيَّن [tzayyan] *p:* They decorated the school for graduation. زَيَّنَوا المَدرَسَة لحَفلَة التَّخَرُّج [zayyinaw ʔilmadrasa lħaflat ʔittaxarruj] • **3.** زَخرَف [zaxraf] زَخرَفَة [zaxrafa] *vn:* تزَخرَف [tzaxraf] *p:* The walls of the mosque are decorated. حِيطان الجّامِع مزَخرَفَة [ħiːṭaːn ʔijjaːmiʕ mzaxrafa]

decoration • **1.** زِينَة [ziːna] زِينات [ziːnaːt] *pl:* The government is putting up decorations in the street for Republic Day. الحُكُومَة دَاِتحُطّ زِينَة بِالشَّوارِع لِعِيد الجَّمهُورِيَّة [ʔilħukuːma datħuṭṭ ziːna biššawaːriʕ liʕiːd ʔijjamhuriyya] • **2.** وِسام [wisaːm] أوسِمَة [ʔawsima] *pl:* What did they give him the decoration for? عَلَى وَيش إنطُوه الوِسام؟ [ʕala wiːš ʔinṭuːh ʔilwisaːm?]

decrease • **1.** اِنخِفاض [ʔinxifaːð̣] نُقصان [nuqṣaːn] Statistics show a decrease in the death rate in the last few years. الإحصائِيّات تبَيِّن اِنخِفاض بعَدَد الوَفِيّات بِالسِّنِين الأَخِيرَة [ʔalʔiħṣaːʔiyyaːt tbayyin ʔinxifaːð̣ bʕadad ʔilwafiyyaːt bissiniːn ʔilʔaxiːra]

decree • **1.** مَرسُوم [marsuːm] The decree goes into effect tomorrow. المَرسُوم يِتنَفَّذ مِن باكِر [ʔilmarsuːm yitnaffað min baːčir]

to decree • **1.** صَدَّر مَرسُوم بِـ [ṣaddar marsuːm bi-] تَصدِير مَرسُوم بِـ [taṣdiːr marsuːm bi-] *vn:* *sv* i. The government decreed a holiday. الحُكُومَة صَدِّرَت مَرسُوم بإحداث عُطلَة [ʔilħukuːma ṣaddirat marsuːm bʔiħdaːθ ʕuṭla]

to deduct • **1.** خِصَم [xiṣam] خَصُم [xaṣum] *vn:* *sv* u. اِستَقطَع [ʔistaqṭaʕ] اِستِقطاع [ʔistiqṭaːʕ] *vn:* *sv* i. Deduct ten per cent. إخصُم عَشرَة بِالمِيَّة [ʔixṣum ʕašra bilmiyya]

deed • **1.** حِجَّة [ħijja] حِجّات، حِجَج [ħijjaːt, ħijaj] *pl:* The deed to the house is at the lawyer's. حِجَّة البَيت عِند المُحامِي [ħijjat ʔilbayt ʕind ʔilmuħaːmi] • **2.** عَمَل [ʕamal] عَملَة [ʕamla] *Feminine:* There are good deeds and bad deeds. أكُو أعمال الخير وَأعمال الشَّرّ [ʔaku ʔaʕmaːl ʔilxayr wʔaʕmaːl ʔiššarr]

to deed • **1.** سَجَّل [sajjal] تَسجِيل [tasjiːl] *vn:* *sv* i. كِتَب [kitab] كِتابَة [kitaːba] *vn:* *sv* i. My father has deeded the house to me. أَبُويَا كِتَب البَيت بإسمِي [ʔabuːya kitab ʔilbayt bʔismi]

deep • **1.** عَمِيق [ʕamiːq] غَمِيق [ɣamiːg] This subject is too deep for me. هَالمَوضُوع كُلِّش عَمِيق بالنِّسبَة إلِي [halmawðuːʕ kulliš ʕamiːq binnisba ʔili]

*** The lake is ten feet deep.** • **1.** البُحَيرَة غُمُجها عَشِر أقدام [ʔilbuħayra ɣumujha ʕašir ʔaqdaːm]

deeply • **1.** كُلِّش [kulliš] هوايَة [hwaːya] He was deeply affected by their story. كان كُلِّش مِتأثِّر بقُصَّتهُم [čaːn kulliš mitʔaθθir bquṣṣathum]

defeat • **1.** هَزِيمَة [haziːma] هَزايِم [hazaːyim] *pl:* اِنكِسار [ʔinkisaːr] The enemy suffered a crushing defeat. العَدُو قاسَوا هَزِيمَة ساحِقَة [ʔilʕadu qaːsaw haziːma saːħiqa]

to defeat • **1.** غِلَب [ɣilab] غُلُب [ɣulub] *vn:* اِنغِلَب [ʔinɣilab] *p:* He defeated three candidates and got a seat in parliament. غِلَب ثلَث مُرَشَّحِين وَحَصَّل النِّيابَة [ɣilab tlaθ muraššaħi:n wħaṣṣal ʔinniya:ba] • **2.** رِفَض [rufaḍ] رَفُض [rafuḍ] *vn:* اِنرِفَض [ʔinrifaḍ] *p:* The motion was defeated. الاقتِراح اِنرُفَض [ʔilʔiqtira:ħ ʔinrufaḍ]

defect • **1.** عيب [ʕayb] عيُوب [ʕyu:b] *pl:* There's a natural defect in this cloth. أَكُو عِيب أَصلِي بِهالقماش [ʔaku ʕi:b ʔaṣli bhaliqma:š]

defective • **1.** بِيه عَيب [bi:h ʕi:b] بِيه خَلَل [bi:h xalal] The radio is defective; either exchange it or give me my money back. الرّاديُو بِيه عِيب؛ أَمّا تبَدّلَه لَو تِنطِينِي فلُوسِي [ʔirra:dyu bi:h ʕi:b; ʔamma tbaddlah law tinṭi:ni flu:si]

to defend • **1.** دافَع عَن [da:faʕ ʕan] دِفاع [difa:ʕ] *vn: sv* i. They decided not to defend the town. قَرِّرَوا أَن ما يدافعُون عَن المَدِينَة [qarriraw ʔan ma: yda:fʕu:n ʕan ʔilmadi:na] There's no need to defend yourself. ماكُو حاجَة تدافع عَن نَفسَك [ma:ku ħa:ja dda:faʕ ʕan nafsak] There's no need to defend yourself. ماكُو مَجال تِعتِذِر [ma:ku maja:l tiʕtiðir]

defense • **1.** دِفاع [difa:ʕ] The defense was weak. الدِّفاع كان ضَعِيف [ʔiddifa:ʕ ča:n ḍaʕi:f] He works for the Ministry of Defense. يِشتُغُل بوزارَة الدِّفاع [yištuɣul bwiza:rat ʔiddifa:ʕ]

to define • **1.** حَدَّد [ħaddad] تَحدِيد [taħdi:d] *vn:* تحَدَّد [tħaddad] *p:* عَرَّف [ʕarraf] تَعرِيف [taʕri:f] *vn:* تعَرَّف [tʕarraf] *p:* Can you define the word "democracy"? تِقدَر تحَدِّد مَعنى كَلِمَة "دِيمُقراطِيَّة"؟ [tigdar tħaddid maʕna: kalimat "dimuqra:ṭiyya"?] • **2.** عَيَّن [ʕayyan] تَعيِين [taʕyi:n] *vn:* تعَيَّن [tʕayyan] *p:* The boundaries were defined by the treaty. الحُدُود تعَيِّنَت بِالمُعاهَدَة [ʔilħudu:d tʕayyinat bilmuʕa:hada]

definite • **1.** مُحَدَّد [muħaddad] مُعَيَّن [muʕayyan] Do you have any definite plan? عِندَك أَيّ خُطَّة مُعَيَّنَة؟ [ʕindak ʔayy xuṭṭa muʕayyna?]

definitely • **1.** بِالتَّأكِيد [bittaʔki:d] أَكِيد [ʔaki:d] I'm definitely coming. آنِي جاي بِالتَّأكِيد [ʔa:ni ja:y bittaʔaki:d]

to defy • **1.** تحَدَّى [tħadda:] تَحَدِّي [taħaddi] *vn: sv* a. The opposition defied the government to find a solution to the problem. المُعارَضَة تحَدَّت الحُكُومَة أَن يِلقُون حَلّ لِلمُشكِلَة [ʔilmuʕa:raḍa tħaddat ʔilħuku:ma ʔan yilgu:n ħall lilmuškila]

degree • **1.** دَرَجَة [daraja] دَرَجات [daraja:t] *pl:* Last night the temperature dropped ten degrees. البارحَة بِاللَّيل اِنخُفضَت دَرَجَة الحَرارَة عَشِر دَرَجات [ʔilba:rħa billayl ʔinxufḍat darajat ʔilħara:ra ʕašir daraja:t] • **2.** شَهادَة [šaha:da] شَهادات [šaha:da:t] *pl:* I got my degree last year. أَخَذِت شَهادتِي بِالسَّنَة اللِّي فاتَت [ʔaxaðit šaha:dti bissana ʔilli fa:tat]

delay • **1.** تَأخِير [taʔxi:r] تَأخِيرات [taʔxi:ra:t] *pl:* What's causing the delay? شِنُو اللِّي مسَبِّب التَّأخِير؟ [šinu: ʔilli msabbib ʔittaʔxi:r?]

to delay • **1.** أَخَّر [ʔaxxar] تَأخِير [taʔxi:r] *vn:* تأَخَّر [tʔaxxar] *p:* عَطَّل [ʕaṭṭal] تَعطِيل [taʕṭi:l] *vn:* تعَطَّل [tʕaṭṭal] *p:* عَوَّق [ʕawwag] تَعوِيق [taʕwi:g] *vn:* تعَوَّق [tʕawwag] *p:* I was delayed on the way. آنِي تعَوَّقِت بِالطَّرِيق [ʔa:ni tʕawwagit biṭṭari:q] • **2.** أَجَّل [ʔajjal] تَأجِيل [taʔji:l] *vn:* تأَجَّل [tʔajjal] *p:* أَخَّر [ʔaxxar] تَأخِير [taʔxi:r] *vn:* تأَخَّر [tʔaxxar] *p:* We're going to delay the trip for a week. راح نأَجِّل السَّفرَة لِمُدَّة إِسبُوع [ra:ħ nʔajjil ʔissafra limuddat ʔisbu:ʕ]

delegate • **1.** مَندُوب [mandu:b] مَندُوبِين [mandu:bi:n] *pl:* The delegates will arrive tomorrow. المَندُوبِين راح يُوصلُون باكِر [ʔilmandu:bi:n ra:ħ yu:ṣlu:n ba:čir]

delegation • **1.** وَفِد [wafid] وُفُود [wufu:d] *pl:* بِعثَة [biʕθa] بِعثات [biʕθa:t] *pl:* The delegation arrived yesterday. الوَفِد وُصَل البارحَة [ʔilwafid wuṣal ʔilba:rħa]

deliberate • **1.** مِعتِمِد [miʕtimid] مَقصُود [maqṣu:d] That was a deliberate insult. هاي كانَت إِهانَة مَقصُودَة [ha:y ča:nat ʔiha:na maqṣu:da]

deliberately • **1.** عَن قَصِد [ʕan qaṣid] عَن عَمِد [ʕan ʕamid] قَصدَنِي [qaṣdani] I don't think he did it deliberately. ما أَعتِقِد سَوّاها عَن قَصِد [ma: ʔaʕtiqid sawwa:ha ʕan qaṣid]

delicate • **1.** ضَعِيف [ḍaʕi:f] نازِك [na:zik] Her health is very delicate. صِحَّتها كُلِّش ضَعِيفَة [ṣiħħatha kulliš ḍaʕi:fa] • **2.** مُحرِج [muħrij] That's a delicate question. هَذا سُؤال مُحرِج [ha:ða suʔa:l muħrij] • **3.** دَقِيق [daqi:q] Repairing watches is a delicate job. تَصلِيح السّاعات شَغلَة دَقِيقَة [taṣli:ħ ʔissa:ʕa:t šaɣla daqi:qa] • **4.** حَسّاس [ħassa:s] That's a delicate instrument. هاي آلَة حَسّاسَة [ha:y ʔa:la ħassa:sa]

delicious • **1.** لَذِيذ [laði:ð] This is delicious candy. هَذِي حَلَوِيّات لَذِيذَة [ha:ði ħalawiyya:t laði:ða]

delighted • **1.** مَسرُور [masru:r] فَرحان [farħa:n] مكَيِّف [mkayyif] I was delighted to see him. كِنِت فَرحان بِشَوفتَه [činit farħa:n bšawftah]

delightful • **1.** لَطِيف [laṭi:f] لَطِيفِين [laṭi:fi:n] *pl:* بَدِيع [badi:ʕ] رائِع [ra:ʔiʕ] It was a delightful evening. كانَت السَّهرَة لَطِيفَة [ča:nat ʔissahra laṭi:fa]

D

to deliver • **1.** سَلَّم [sallam] تَسلِيم [tasli:m] *vn:* تسَلَّم [tsallam] *p:* وَصَّل [waṣṣal] تَوصِيل [tawṣi:l] *vn:* توَصَّل [twaṣṣal] *p:* We'll deliver it to you tomorrow. راح نسَلِّمَك إيّاها باكِر [ra:ħ nsallmak ʔiyya:ha ba:čir] Please deliver these packages to my house. أرجُوك وَصِّل هَالرِّزَم لبَيتِي [ʔarǰu:k waṣṣil harrizam lbayti] • **2.** وَزَّع [wazzaʕ] تَوزِيع [tawzi:ʕ] *vn:* توَزَّع [twazzaʕ] *p:* How often is the mail delivered here? كَم مَرَّة يِتوَزَّع البَرِيد هنا؟ [čam marra yitwazzaʕ ʔilbari:d hna?] • **3.** وَلَّد [wallad] تَولِيد [tawli:d] *vn:* توَلَّد [twallad] *p:* The doctor only charged 5 dinars to deliver the baby. الطَّبِيب أخَذ خَمس دَنانِير بَسّ التَولِيد الطِّفِل [ʔiṭṭabi:b ʔaxað xams dana:ni:r bass ltawli:d ʔiṭṭifil]

delivery • **1.** تَسلِيم [tasli:m] تَسلِيمات [tasli:ma:t] *pl:* I'll pay you on delivery. أدفَعلَك عِند التَّسلِيم [ʔadfaʕlak ʕind ʔittasli:m] • **2.** تَوزِيع [tawzi:ʕ] There's no mail delivery today. ماكُو تَوزِيع بَرِيد اليُوم [ma:ku tawzi:ʕ bari:d ʔilyu:m]

demand • **1.** طَلَب [ṭalab] طَلَبات [ṭalaba:t] *pl:* There's a big demand for fresh fruit. أكُو هوايَة طَلَب عَلَى الفَواكِه التّازَة [ʔaku hwa:ya ṭalab ʕala ʔilfawa:kih ʔitta:za] The library can't supply the demand for books. المَكتَبَة ما تِقدَر تُوفِي الطَّلَب عالكُتُب [ʔilmaktaba ma: tigdar tu:fi ʔiṭṭalab ʕalkutub] Their demands never cease. طَلَباتهُم ما تِخلَص [ṭalaba:thum ma: tixlaṣ]

*** This job makes heavy demands on my time.** • **1.** هاي الشَغلَة ماخذَة وَقتِي كُلَّه [ha:y iššaɣla ma:xða waqti kullah]

in demand • **1.** مَطلُوب [maṭlu:b] عَلَيه طَلَب [ʕali:yh ṭalab] This model is very much in demand and is sold out. هَذا المُودِيل عَليه طَلَب هوايَة وَنِفَذ [ha:ða ʔilmu:di:l ʕali:h ṭalab hwa:ya wnifað]

to demand • **1.** طِلَب [ṭilab] طَلَب [ṭalab] *vn: sv* u. طالَب [ṭa:lab] مُطالَبَة [muṭa:laba] *vn: sv* u. He's demanding more money. دَيِطلُب فلُوس أكثَر [dayiṭlub flu:s ʔakθar]

democracy • **1.** دِيمُقراطِيَّة [dimuqra:ṭiyya]

democratic • **1.** دِيمُقراطِي [dimuqra:ṭi]

to demolish • **1.** هَدَّم [haddam] تَهدِيم [tahdi:m] *vn:* تهَدَّم [thaddam] *p:* The workers demolished the building. العُمّال هَدِّمَوا البِنايَة [ʔilʕumma:l haddimaw ʔilbina:ya]

demon • **1.** جِنِّي [ǰinni] جِن [ǰinn] *pl:* جِنّ [ǰinn] *Collective*

to demonstrate • **1.** راوَى [ra:wa:] ترَوِّي [truwwi] *vn: sv* i. بَيَّن [bayyan] تَبيِين [tabyi:n] *vn: sv* i. Now I'm going to demonstrate to you how the machine works. هَسَّة راح أراوِيكُم شلُون تِشتُغُل المَكِينَة [hassa ra:ħ ʔara:wi:kum šlu:n tištuɣul ʔilmaki:na] • **2.** تظاهَر [dða:har] تَظاهُر [taða:hur] *vn: sv* a. There is a group of students demonstrating in front of the embassy. أكُو جَماعَة مِن الطُّلّاب دَيِتظاهرُون قِدّام السَّفارَة [ʔaku ǰama:ʕa min ʔiṭṭulla:b dayitða:hru:n gidda:m ʔissafa:ra]

demonstration • **1.** مُظاهَرَة [muða:hara] مُظاهَرات [muða:hara:t] *pl:* There was a demonstration in the street yesterday. كان أكُو مُظاهَرَة بِالشّارِع البارحَة [ča:n ʔaku muða:hara bišša:riʕ ʔilba:rħa]

den • **1.** مَغارَة [maɣa:ra] مَغارات [maɣa:ra:t] *pl:* There's a fox den over there. أكُو مَغارَة مال ثَعلَب هناك [ʔaku maɣa:ra ma:l θaʕlab hna:k] • **2.** عَرِين [ʕari:n] عُرُن [ʕurun] *pl:* We found a lion's den, but the lion wasn't there. لِقَينا عَرِين أسَد، لَكِن الأسَد ما كان هناك [ligi:na ʕari:n ʔasad, la:kin ʔilʔasad ma: ča:n hna:k]

denial • **1.** إنكار [ʔinka:r] Nobody believed his denial of the charge. مَحَّد صَدَّق إنكارَه لِلتُّهمَة [maħħad ṣaddag ʔinka:rah littuhma]

dense • **1.** كَثِيف [kaθi:f] كثاف [kθa:f] *pl:* We drove through a dense fog. سِقنا بِضَباب كَثِيف [siqna bðaba:b kaθi:f] • **2.** بَلِيد [bali:d] بَلِيدِين، بُلَداء [bali:di:n, bulada:ʔ] *pl:* غَبِي [ɣabi] أغبِياء [ʔaɣbiya:ʔ] *pl:* Most of the time he's very dense. بأكثَر الحالات هُوَّ هوايَة بَلِيد [bʔakθar ʔilħa:la:t huwwa hwa:ya bali:d]

dent • **1.** طَعجَة [ṭaʕǰa] دَعمَة [daʕma] دَعمات [daʕma:t] *pl:* There's a new dent in the fender of my car. أكُو طَعجَة جِدِيدَة بِالجامُولُغ مال سَيّارتِي [ʔaku ṭaʕǰa ǰidi:da bilča:mu:lluɣ ma:l sayya:rti]

to dent • **1.** طِعَج [ṭiʕaǰ] طَعِج [ṭaʕiǰ] *vn:* اِنطِعَج [ʔinṭiʕaǰ] *p: sv* a. دِعَم [diʕam] دَعِم [daʕim] *vn: sv* a. The bumper was badly dented. الدَّعّامِيَّة كانَت مَطعُوجَة طَعجَة قَوِيَّة [ʔiddaʕʕa:miyya ča:nat maṭʕu:ǰa ṭaʕǰa qawwiyya]

dentist • **1.** طَبِيب أسنان [ṭabi:b ʔasna:n] أطِبّاء أسنان [ʔaṭibba:ʔ ʔasna:n] *pl:* Is there a good dentist around here? أكُو طَبِيب أسنان زين هنا؟ [ʔaku ṭabi:b ʔasna:n zi:n hna?]

to deny • **1.** نِكَر [nikar] إنكار [ʔinka:r] *vn: sv* u. He denies having been a member of that party. يِنكُر كَونَه عُضُو بِهالحِزِب [yinkur kawnah ʕuðw bhalħizib] • **2.** رِفَض [rifað] رَفُض [rafuð] *vn:* اِنرِفَض [ʔinrifað] *p:* I couldn't deny him such a small favor. ما قِدَرِت أرفُضلَه مَعرُوف صغَيِّر مِثِل هَذا [ma: gidarit ʔarfuðlah maʕru:f ṣɣayyir miθil ha:ða]

to depart from • **1.** خِرَج عَلَى [xiraǰ ʕala] خرُوج [xuru:ǰ] *vn: sv* u. You're not allowed to depart from standard procedure. ما مَسمُوحلَك تُخرُج عَلَى النِّظام المُتَّبَع [ma: masmu:ħlak tuxruǰ ʕala ʔinniða:m ʔilmuttabaʕ]

• **2.** غادَر [ɣaːdar] مُغادَرَة [muɣaːdara] *vn: sv* i. ترَك [tirak] تَرِك [tarik] *vn: sv* u. The train departed from the station at six o'clock. القِطار ترَك المَحَطَّة صار السّاعَة سِتَّة [ʔilqiṭaːr tirak ʔilmaħaṭṭa ṣaːr ʔ issaːʕa sitta]

department • **1.** قِسِم [qisim] أَقسام [ʔaqsaːm] *pl:* Which department does he work in. بأيّ قِسِم يِشتُغُل؟ [bʔayy qisim yištuɣul?] • **2.** وِزارَة [wizaːra] وِزارات [wizaːraːt] *pl:* This is a matter for the Department of State. هاي مَسأَلَة تخُصّ وِزارَة الخارِجِيَّة [haːy masʔala txuṣṣ wizaːrat ʔilxaːrijiyya]

departure • **1.** سَفَر [safar] The departure is scheduled for three o'clock. السَّفَر تقَرَّر السّاعَة ثلاثَة [ʔissafar tqarrar ʔissaːʕa tlaːθa]

to depend • **1.** اِعتِمَد [ʔiʕtimad] اِعتِماد [ʔiʕtimaːd] *vn: sv* i. Can I depend on him? أَقدَر أَعتِمِد عَليه؟ [ʔagdar ʔaʕtimid ʕaliːh?] • **2.** توَقَّف [twaqqaf] تَوَقُّف [tawaqquf] *vn: sv* a. That depends on the circumstances. هَذي تِتوَقَّف عالظُّروف [haːði titwaqqaf ʕaððuruːf]

dependent • **1.** مِتِّكِل [mittikil] مِعتِمِد [miʕtimid] I'm financially dependent on him. مالِيّاً آني مِتِّكِل عَليه [maːliyyan ʔaːni mittikil ʕaliːh]

*** How many dependents do you have?**
• **1.** كَم واحِد تِعيل؟ [čam waːħid tʕiːl?]

to deport • **1.** أَبعَد [ʔabʕad] إبعاد [ʔibʕaːd] *vn:* اِنبَعَد [ʔinbaʕad] *p:* سَفَّر [saffar] تَسفِير [tasfiːr] *vn: sv* i. They deported him. أَبعدُوه [ʔabʕiduːh]

to depose • **1.** خِلَع [xilaʕ] خَلِع [xaliʕ] *vn:* اِنخِلَع [ʔinxilaʕ] *p:* عِزَل عَن [ʕizal ʕan] عَزِل [ʕazil] *vn:* اِنعِزَل [ʔinʕizal] *p:* They want to depose the king. يِردُون يخِلعُون المَلِك [yirduːn yxilʕuːn ʔilmalik]

deposit • **1.** تَأمِين [taʔmiːn] عَرَبُون [ʕarabuːn] عَرابِين [ʕaraːbiːn] *pl:* We'll lay it aside for you, if you leave a deposit. نِحتُفُظلَك بيها إذا تحُطّ عَرَبُون [niħtufuðlak biːha ʔiða tħuṭṭ ʕarabuːn] I had to pay five fils deposit for the bottle. اِضطَرَّيت أَدفَع خَمس فلُوس تأمِينات عالبُطِل [ʔiðṭarriːt ʔadfaʕ xams fluːs taʔmiːnaːt ʕalbuṭul] • **2.** رَواسِب [rawaːsib] They've just discovered a rich deposit of iron in the north. هَسَّة اِكتِشفَوا رَواسِب غَنِيَّة مال الحَدِيد بِالشِّمال [hassa ʔiktišfaw rawaːsib ɣaniyya maːl ʔilħadiːd biššimaːl]

to deposit • **1.** وَدَّع [waddaʕ] تَودِيع [tawdiːʕ] *vn: sv* i. أَودَع [ʔawdaʕ] إيداع [ʔiːdaːʕ] *vn: sv* i. I'm going to deposit some money in the bank. راح أَوَدِّع شوَيَّة فلُوس بِالبَنك [raːħ ʔawaddiʕ šwayya fluːs bilbang]

to depress • **1.** قَبُض نَفِس حِزَن [qubað nafis] قَبُض نَفِس، حُزِن [qabuð nafis] *vn: sv* u. حِزَن [ħizan] حُزِن [ħuzin] *vn: sv* i. His letters always depress me. مَكاتِيبَه تُقبُض نَفسِي دائِماً [makaːtiːbah tuqbuð nafsi daːʔiman]

depressed • **1.** كَئِيب [kaʔiːb] حَزِين [ħaziːn] He's been very depressed lately. هُوَّ كُلِّش كَئِيب بِالأَيّام الأَخِيرَة [huwwa kulliš kaʔiːb bilʔayyaːm ʔilʔaxiːra]

depressing • **1.** مُقبِض النَّفِس [muqbið ʔinnafis]

depression • **1.** كَساد [kasaːd] We lost all our money in the depression. خسَرنا كُلّ فلُوسنا بِالكَساد [xsarna kull fluːsna bilkasaːd] • **2.** هَمّ [hamm] غَمّ [ɣamm] حِزِن [ħizin, ħuzun] No one can bring him out of his depression. مَحَّد يِقدَر يفَرِّج عَن هَمَّه [maħħad yigdar yfarrij ʕan hammah]

to deprive • **1.** حِرَم [ħiram] حِرمان [ħirmaːn] *vn:* اِنحِرَم [ʔinħiram] *p:* I wouldn't want to deprive you of your cigarettes. ما أَرِيد أَحَرمَك مِن جِكايرَك [maː ʔariːd ʔaħarmak min jigaːyrak] They were deprived of all their rights. اِنحِرمَوا مِن كُلّ حُقُوقهُم [ʔinħirmaw min kull ħuquːqhum]

depth • **1.** عُمُق [ʕumuq] أَعماق [ʔaʕmaːq] *pl:* غُمِق [ɣumij] غمُوق [ɣmuːj] *pl:* The depth of the lake has never been measured. عُمُق هالبُحَيرَة أَبَداً ما يِنقاس [ʕumuq halbuħayra ʔabadan maː yinqaːs]

deputy • **1.** نائِب [naːʔib] نُوّاب [nuwwaːb] *pl:* He's the deputy from our district. هُوَّ النّائِب مِن مَنطِقَتنا [huwwa ʔinnaːʔib min manṭiqatna]

chamber of deputies • **1.** مَجلِس نُوّاب [majlis nuwwaːb] مَجالِس نُوّاب [majaːlis nuwwaːb] *pl:*

to derail • **1.** أَخرَج عَن الخَطّ [ʔaxrajʕan ʔilxaṭṭ] إخراج [ʔixraːj] *vn:* The saboteurs derailed the train. المُخَرِّبِين أَخرِجَوا القِطار عَن الخَطّ [ʔilmuxarribiːn ʔaxrijaw ʔilqiṭaːr ʕan ʔilxaṭṭ]

derrick • **1.** بُرِج [burij] بُرُوج، أَبراج [buruːj, ʔabraːj] *pl:* They left the derrick up after they struck oil. ترِكَوا البُرِج بمَحَلَّه بَعَد ما خِرَج النُّفُط [tirkaw ʔilburij bmaħallah baʕad maː xiraj ʔinnafuṭ] • **2.** سلِنك [slink] سلِنكات [slinkaːt] *pl:* They set up a derrick on the dock to unload boat cargo. نُصبَوا سلِنك عالرَّصِيف حَتَّى يفَرِّغُون حمُولَة السَّفِينَة [nuṣbaw slink ʕarraṣiːf ħatta yfarriɣuːn ħumuːlat ʔissifiːna]

dervish • **1.** دَروِيش [darwiːš] دَراوِيش [daraːwiːš] *pl:*

to descend • **1.** نِزَل [nizal] نُزُول [nuzuːl] *vn: sv* i. هُبَط [hubaṭ] هُبُوط [hubuːṭ] *vn: sv* u. I'd never have thought she'd descend so low. أَبَداً ما تصَوَّرتها تِنزِل لِهالمُستَوَى [ʔabadan maː tṣawwaritha tinzil lhalmustawa] He's descended from a prominent family. هُوَّ مِنحِدِر مِن عائِلَة عَرِيقَة [huwwa minħidir min ʕaːʔila ʕariːqa] • **2.** نِزَل [nizal]

sv i. His relatives descended on him. قَرايبَه نِزلَوا عَليه [gara:ybah nizlaw ʕali:h]

descendent • 1. ذُرِّيَّة [ðurriyya] ذُرِّيّات [ðurriyya:t] *pl:* سَلِيل [sali:l] سُلالَة [sula:la] *pl:* This is a picture of Abu Khalil with all his descendents. هاي صُورَة أَبُو خَلِيل وِيّا كُلّ ذُرِّيتَه [ha:y ṣu:rat ʔabu xali:l wiyya kull ðurri:tah]

D

to describe • 1. وُصَف [wuṣaf] وَصُف [waṣuf] *vn: sv* u. He described it accurately. وصَفها بِضَبُط [wṣafha bðabuṭ]

description • 1. وَصُف [waṣuf] Can you give me a detailed description? تِقدَر تِنطِينِي وَصُف تَفصِيلِي؟ [tigdar tinṭi:ni waṣuf tafṣi:li?]

desert • 1. صَحراء [ṣaħra:ʔ] صَحارِي [ṣaħa:ri] *pl:* They crossed the desert in twenty days. قِطعَوا الصَّحراء بِعِشرِين يوم [giṭʕaw ʔiṣṣaħra:ʔ bʕišri:n yu:m]

to desert • 1. تِرَك [tirak] تَرِك [tarik] *vn: sv* u. Don't desert me now! لا تِترُكنِي هَسَّة [la: titrukni hassa] **• 2.** هِجَر [hijar] هَجِر، هِجران [hajir, hijra:n] *vn: sv* u. عاف [ʕa:f] عَوف [ʕawf] *vn: sv* u. He deserted his wife and children. هِجَر زَوجتَه وَأولادَه [hijar zawijtah wʔawla:dah] **• 3.** هِرَب [hirab] هَرَب، هُرُوب [harab, huru:b] *vn: sv* u. فَرّ [farr] فَرّ، فِرار [farr, fira:r] *vn: sv* u. The soldiers deserted in droves. الجُّنُود هِربَوا بأعداد [ʔijjunu:d hirbaw bʔaʕda:d]

deserted • 1. مَهجُور [mahju:r] After a long march they came to a deserted village. بَعَد مَشيَة طويلَة وُصلَوا إلَى قَريَة مَهجُورَة [baʕad mašya ṭwi:la wuṣlaw ʔila qarya mahju:ra]

to deserve • 1. اِستَحَقّ [ʔistaħaqq] اِستِحقاق [ʔistiħqa:q] *vn: sv* i. اِستاهَل [ʔista:hal] *sv* i. Such a good worker deserves higher pay. مِثلَه واحِد شاغُول يِستَحِقّ راتِب أعلَى [miθlah wa:ħid ša:ɣu:l yistaħiqq ra:tib ʔaʕla]

design • 1. تَصمِيم [taṣmi:m] تَخطِيط [taxṭi:ṭ] He is working on the design for a new house. دَيِشتُغُل بِتَصمِيم بَيت جِدِيد [dayištuɣul btaṣmi:m bayt jidi:d] **• 2.** نَقِش [naqiš] نُقُوش [nuqu:š] *pl:* رَسِم [rasim] The tablecloth has a simple design. النَّقِش اللِّي عَلَى غَطا المِيز بَسِيط [ʔinnaqiš ʔilli ʕala ɣaṭa: ʔilmi:z basi:ṭ]

to design • 1. صَمَّم [ṣammam] تَصمِيم [taṣmi:m] *vn: sv* i. فَصَّل [faṣṣal] تَفصِيل [tafṣi:l] *vn: sv* i. She designs her own clothes. هِيَّ تصَمِّم هدُومها بإيدَيها [hiyya tṣammim hdu:mha bʔi:dayha]

desirable • 1. مَرغُوب بِيه [marɣu:b bi:h] A change would be very desirable now. التَّغيِير فَدّ شِي كُلَّش مَرغُوب بِيه هَسَّة [ʔittaɣyi:r fadd ši kulliš marɣu:b bi:h hassa] **• 2.** مَرغُوب [marɣu:b] This is a very desirable neighborhood for a hotel. هاي مَنطِقَة مَرغُوبَة لِبناء فِندِق بِيها [ha:y manṭiqa marɣu:ba libina:ʔ findiq bi:ha]

desire • 1. رَغبَة [raɣba] رَغبات [raɣba:t] *pl:* My desires are easily satisfied. رَغباتِي مُمكِن تِتحَقَّق بسُهُولَة [raɣba:ti mumkin titħaqqaq bsuhu:la]

desk • 1. مَيز [mayz, mi:z] ميُوزَة [myu:za] *pl:* مِنضَدَة [minðada] مَناضِد [mana:ðid] *pl:* This desk is too small for me. هَالمِيز كُلَّش صغَيِّر عَلَيّا [halmi:z kulliš ṣɣayyir ʕalayya]

information desk • 1. مَكتَب اِستِعلامات [maktab ʔistiʕla:ma:t] مَكاتِب اِستِعلامات [maka:tib ʔistiʕla:ma:t] *pl:* Ask at the information desk over there. إسأل بِمَكتَب الاستِعلامات [ʔisʔal bmaktab ʔilʔistiʕla:ma:t]

desolate • 1. مُوحِش [mu:ħiš] This must be a desolate place in winter. هَذا لازِم يكُون مَكان مُوحِش بِالشِّتا [ha:ða la:zim yku:n maka:n mu:ħiš biššita]

despair • 1. يَأس [yaʔas, yaʔis] قُنُوط [qunu:ṭ] She was about to commit suicide in her despair. رادَت تِنتِحِر مِن يَأسها [ra:dat tintiħir min yaʔsha]

desperate • 1. يائِس [ya:ʔis] أَيِّس [ʔayyas] مَيؤُوس مِن [mayʔu:s min] مِستَقتِل [mistaqtil] بِلا أَمَل [bila: ʔamal] She's in a desperate situation. حالَتها يائسَة [ħa:latha ya:ʔsa] The situation's desperate. الوَضِع مَيؤُوس مِنَّه [ʔilwaðiʕ mayʔu:s minnah]

to despise • 1. اِحتِقَر [ʔiħtiqar] اِحتِقار [ʔiħtiqa:r] *vn: sv* i. I despise that man. آنِي أَحتِقِر هَذا الرِّجّال [ʔa:ni ʔaħtiqir ha:ða ʔirrijja:l]

dessert • 1. حَلا [ħala:] حَلَوِيّات [ħalawiyya:t] You forgot to bring the dessert. نِسِيت تجِيب الحَلَوِيّات [nisi:t dji:b ʔilħalawiyya:t]

destination • 1. حَدّ [ħadd] My destination is Baghdad. آنِي حَدِّي لِبَغداد [ʔa:ni ħaddi libayda:d]

destiny • 1. مَصِير [maṣi:r]

to destroy • 1. تِلَف [tilaf] تَلِف [talif] *vn:* اِنتِلَف [ʔintilaf] *p:* All my papers were destroyed in the fire. كُلّ أوراقِي اِنتِلفَت بِالحَرِيق [kull ʔawra:qi ʔintilfat bilħari:q] **• 2.** دَمَّر [dammar] تَدمِير [tadmi:r] *vn:* تدَمَّر [tdammar] *p:* خَرَّب [xarrab] تَخرِيب [taxri:b] *vn:* تخَرَّب [txarrab] *p:* The earthquake destroyed a third of the town. الزِّلزال دَمَّر ثِلث المَدِينَة [ʔizzilza:l dammar θilθ ʔilmadi:na]

destroyer • 1. مُدَمِّرَة [mudammira] مُدَمِّرات [mudammira:t] *pl:*

destruction • **1.** تَخريب [taxri:b] تَخريبات [taxri:ba:t] *pl:* دَمار [dama:r] دَمارات [dama:ra:t] *pl:* The fire caused a lot of destruction. النّار سَبِّبَت هوايَة دَمار [ʔinna:r sabbibat hwa:ya dama:r]

detail • **1.** تَفصِيل [tafṣi:l] تَفاصِيل، تَفصِيلات [tafa:ṣi:l, tafṣi:la:t] *pl:* تَفاصِيل [tafa:ṣi:l] تَفصِيلات [tafṣi:la:t] *pl:* Today's paper gives more details. جَرِيدَة اليُوم بِيها تَفاصِيل أكثَر [ǰari:dat ʔilyu:m bi:ha tafa:ṣi:l ʔakθar]

in detail • **1.** بالتَّفصِيل [bittafṣi:l] He described the incident in detail. وُصَف الحادِث بِالتَّفصِيل [wuṣaf ʔilħa:diθ bittafṣi:l]

detailed • **1.** مُفَصَّل [mufaṣṣal] He gave me a detailed report. قَدَّملِي تَقرِير مُفَصَّل [qaddamli taqri:r mufaṣṣal]

to detain • **1.** حِجَز [ħiǰaz] حَجِز [ħaǰiz] *vn:* اِنحِجَز [ʔinħiǰaz] *p:* The police detained him for questioning. الشُّرطَة حِجزَتَه لِلتَّحقِيق [ʔiššurṭa ħiǰzatah littaħqi:q] • **2.** أخَّر [ʔaxxar] تأخِير [taʔxi:r] *vn:* تأخَّر [tʔaxxar] *p:* Authorities detained the plane a half hour to look for a bomb. السُّلطات أخَّرَت الطِّيّارَة نُصّ ساعَة لِلبَحِث عَن القُنبُلَة [ʔissulṭa:t ʔaxxirat ʔiṭṭiyya:ra nuṣṣ sa:ʕa lilbaħiθ ʕan ʔilqumbula]

determination • **1.** تَصمِيم [taṣmi:m] عَزِم [ʕazim] He showed definite determination. هُوَّ بَيَّن عَزِم أكِيد [huwwa bayyan ʕazim ʔaki:d]

determined • **1.** مُصَمِّم [muṣammam] مُصِرّ [muṣirr] She's determined to have her way. هِيَّ مصَمِّمَة عَلَى أن تسَوِّي اللِّي ترِيدَه [hiyya mṣammima ʕala ʔan tsawwi ʔilli tri:dah] She's determined to have her way. هِيَّ مُصِرَّة عَلَى رَأيها [hiyya muṣirra ʕala raʔi:ha]

to detour • **1.** لاف [la:f] لَوف [lawf] *vn:* *sv* u. اِلتاف [ʔilta:f] اِلتِفاف [ʔiltifa:f] *vn:* *sv* a. اِلتَفّ [ʔiltaff] اِلتِفاف [ʔiltifa:f] *vn:* *sv* a. Rashid St. is closed at the Defence building and we had to detour by way of Waziria St. شارِع الرَّشِيد مَسدُود يَمّ الدِّفاع وإضطَرِّينا نلُوف عَلَى شارِع الوَزِيرِيَّة [ša:riʕ ʔirraši:d masdu:d yamm ʔiddifa:ʕ wiḍṭarri:na nlu:f ʕala ša:riʕ ʔilwazi:riyya]

deuce • **1.** ثنَين [θnayn] ثنَينات [θnayna:t] *pl:* أبُو ثنَين [ʔabu: θnayn] He held three deuces and two kings. كان عِندَه ثلاث ثنَينات وَشايبَين [ča:n ʕindah tla:θ θnayna:t wša:ybayn]

to develop • **1.** غِسَل [ɣisal, xisal] غَسِل [ɣasil] *vn:* اِنغِسَل [ʔinɣisal] *p:* Could you develop this film for me? مُمكِن تِغسِلِّي هَالفِلِم؟ [mumkin tiɣsilli halfilim?] • **2.** اتطَوَّر [ʔiṭṭawwar] تَطَوُّر [taṭawwur] *vn:* *sv* a. The situation's developed a lot in the last week. المُوقِف هوايَة تطَوَّر بِالإسبُوع الأخِير [ʔilmawgif hwa:ya ṭṭawwar bilʔisbu:ʕ ʔilʔaxi:r] • **3.** عَمَّر [ʕammar] تَعمِير [taʕmi:r] *vn:* تعَمَّر [tʕammar] *p:* حَسَّن [ħassan] تَحسِين [taħsi:n] *vn:* تحَسَّن [tħassan] *p:* The government is developing this area. الحُكُومَة دَاتعَمِّر هَالمَنطِقَة [ʔilħuku:ma daʔitʕammir halmanṭiqa]

development • **1.** تَطَوُّر [taṭawwur] تَطَوُّرات [taṭawwura:t] *pl:* Do you know anything about the latest developments? تُعرُف أيّ شِي عَن آخِر التَّطَوُّرات؟ [tuʕruf ʔayy ši ʕan ʔa:xir ʔittaṭawwura:t?] • **2.** إعمار [ʔiʕma:r] The development plan requires more money. خِطَّة الإعمار تِحتاج إلَى فلُوس أكثَر [xiṭṭat ʔilʔiʕma:r tiħta:ǰ ʔila flu:s ʔakθar]

device • **1.** تَدبِير [tadbi:r] تَدابِير [tada:bi:r] *pl:* خُطَّة [xuṭṭa] خُطَط [xuṭaṭ] *pl:* That's an ingenious device for getting his approval. هَذِي فَدّ تَدبِير بارِع لِإستِحصال مُوافَقتَه [ha:ði fadd tadbi:r ba:riʕ liʔistiħṣa:l muwa:faqtah] • **2.** جِهاز [ǰiha:z] أجهِزَة [ʔaǰhiza] *pl:* He invented a device to peel potatoes. اِختِرَع جِهاز لِتَقشِير البُتَيتَة [ʔixtiraʕ ǰiha:z ʔiltagši:r ʔilputayta]

devil • **1.** شَيطان [šayṭa:n] شَياطِين [šaya:ṭi:n] *pl:* إبلِيس [ʔibli:s] أبَالِيس [ʔaba:li:s] *pl:*

to devote • **1.** كَرَّس [karras] تكِرِّس، تَكرِيس [tkirris, takri:s] *vn:* *sv* i. خَصَّص [xaṣṣaṣ] تخِصِّص، تَخصِيص [txiṣṣiṣ, taxṣi:ṣ] *vn:* *sv* i. He devoted all his spare time to study. كَرَّس كُلّ وَقِت فَراغَه لِلدِّراسَة [karras kull wakit fara:ɣah liddira:sa] • **2.** وِهَب [wihab] وَهِب [wahib] *vn:* اِنوِهَب [ʔinwihab] *p:* He devoted his life to science. وِهَب حَياتَه لِلعِلِم [wihab ħaya:tah lilʕilim]

to be devoted • **1.** بَرّ [barr] بِرّ [birr] *vn:* *sv* u. He's very devoted to his mother. هُوَّ كُلِّش بارّ بأُمَّه [huwwa kulliš ba:rr bʔummah]

dew • **1.** نِدَة [nida]

diabetes • **1.** مَرَض السُّكَّر [marað̣ ʔissukkar]

diagonal • **1.** مُنحَرِف [munħarif] قِراج [qira:ǰ] Now draw a diagonal line. هَسَّة إرسِم خَطّ مُنحَرِف [hassa ʔirsim xaṭṭ munħarif]

diagonally • **1.** قِراج [qira:ǰ] You have to park diagonally here. لازِم تصُفّ السَّيّارَة قِراج هنا [la:zim tṣuff ʔissayya:ra qira:ǰ hna]

dial • **1.** قُرُص [quruṣ] أقراص [ʔaqra:ṣ] *pl:* The dial on the telephone is broken. قُرص التَّلِفُون مَكسُور [qurṣ ʔittalifu:n maksu:r] The dial on my watch is dirty. قُرص ساعتِي وَسِخ [qurṣ sa:ʕti waṣix]

to dial • **1.** فَرّ [farr] فَرّ [farr] *vn:* اِنفَرّ [ʔinfarr] *p:* دار [da:r] دَير [dayr] *vn:* اِندار [ʔinda:r] *p:* She dialed the wrong number. فَرَّت النِّمرَة الغَلَط [farrat ʔinnimra ʔilɣalaṭ]

dialect • **1.** لَهجَة [lahǰa] لَهجات [lahǰa:t] *pl:* Many dialects are spoken here. هوايَة لَهجات تِنحِكِي هنا [hwa:ya lahǰa:t tinħiči hna]

diameter • **1.** قُطُر دائِرَة [quṭur da:ʔira] أَقطار دَوائِر [ʔaqṭa:r dawa:ʔir] *pl:*

D

diamond • **1.** أَلماسَة [ʔalma:za] أَلماسات [ʔalma:za:t] *pl:* أَلماس [ʔalma:z] *Collective:* This ring has four diamonds. هَالمِحبَس بيه أَربَع أَلماسات [halmiħbas bi:h ʔarbaʕ ʔalma:sa:t] • **2.** مَعِين [maʕi:n] مَعِينات [maʕi:na:t] *pl:* The new traffic signs are diamond-shaped. إشارات المُرُور الجِّدِيدَة عَلَى شِكِل المَعِين [ʔiša:ra:t ʔilmuru:r ʔiǰǰidi:da ʕala šikil ʔilmaʕi:n] • **3.** دِيناري [dina:ri] I've got a diamond flush. عِندِي فلَوش دِينَارِي [ʕindi flu:š dina:ri]

diarrhea • **1.** إسهال [ʔisha:l]

to dictate • **1.** أَملَى [ʔamla:] إملاء [ʔimla:ʔ] *vn: sv* i. مَلَّى [malla:] إملاء [ʔimla:ʔ] *vn: sv* i. He's dictating a letter. هُوَّ دَيمِلِي مَكتُوب [huwwa dayimli maktu:b] He's dictating a letter to his secretary. دَيمَلِّي كِتاب عالسِّكِرتَيرَة مالتَه [daymalli kita:b ʕassikirti:ra ma:ltah] • **2.** تأَمَّر [tʔammar] تَأَمُّر [taʔammur] *vn: sv* a. I can't stand anyone dictating to me! آنِي ما أَقبَل واحِد يِتأَمَّر عَلَيّا [ʔa:ni ma: ʔaqbal wa:ħid yitʔammar ʕalayya]

dictation • **1.** إملاء [ʔimla:ʔ] I gave my class a dictation today. إنطَيت صَفِّي إملاء اليُوم [ʔinṭayt ṣaffi ʔimla:ʔ ʔilyu:m]

dictator • **1.** دِكتاتَور [diktatu:r] دِكتاتَورِيِّين [dikta:tu:riyyi:n] *pl:*

dictatorial • **1.** دِكتاتَورِي [diktatu:ri]

dictatorship • **1.** دِكتاتَورِيَّة [diktatu:riyya]

die • **1.** قالَب [qa:lab] قَوالِب، قوالِب [qawa:lib, qwa:lib.] *pl:* The die for that part is broken. قالَب هَالآلَة مَكسُور [qa:lab halʔa:la maksu:r] • **2.** زار [za:r] They play chuck-a-luck with three dice. يِلعَبُون لَقَو بتلَث زارات [yilʕabu:n lagaw btlaθ za:ra:t]

*** The die is cast.** • **1.** قِضَى الأَمر [giḍa: ʔilʔamr]

to die • **1.** مات [ma:t] مَوت [mawt] *vn: sv* u. توَفَّى [twaffa:] تَوَفِّي، وَفاة [tawiffi, wafa:t] *vn: sv* a. He died today at two o'clock. توَفَّى اليُوم ساعَة ثِنتَين [twaffa: ʔilyu:m sa:ʕa θintayn] • **2.** ذِبَل [ðibal] ذَبِل [ðabil] *vn: sv* a. The tree is dying. الشَّجَرَة دَتِذبَل [ʔiššaǰara datiðbal] • **3.** اِنطُفَى [ʔinṭufa:] اِنطِفاء [ʔinṭufa:ʔ] *vn: sv* i. طَفَّى [ṭaffa:] طَفِّي [ṭṭiffi] *vn:* تطَفَّى [iṭṭaffa:] *p:* The motor died. المَكِينَة اِنطُفَت [ʔilmaki:na ʔinṭufat]

*** I'm dying to find out what he said.** • **1.** مَحرُوق بَسّ أَرِيد أَعرُف هُوَّ شقال [maħru:g bass ʔari:d ʔaʕruf huwwa šga:l]

to die away • **1.** تلاشَى [tla:ša:] تَلاشِي [tala:ši] *vn: sv* a. The noise of the train died away in the distance. تلاشَى صُوت القِطار لَمَّن اِبتِعَد [tla:ša: ṣu:t ʔilqiṭa:r lamman ʔibtiʕad]

to die down • **1.** خِمَد [ximad] خَمُد [xamud] *vn: sv* i. اِنطُفَى [ʔinṭufa:] *sv* i. We let the fire die down. ترَكنا النّار تِخمِد [trakna ʔinna:r tixmid] We let the fire die down. ترَكنا النّار تِنطُفِي وَحِدها [trakna ʔinna:r tinṭufi waħidha] The excitement will die down in a few days. هَالهِياج راح يِخمِد بكَم يوم [halhiya:ǰ ra:ħ yixmid bkam yu:m]

to die laughing • **1.** طَقّ مِن الضِّحِك، مَات مِن الضِّحِك [ṭagg min ʔiððiħik, ma:t min ʔiððiħik] طَقّ مِن الضِّحِك، مَات مِن الضِّحِك [ṭagg min ʔiððiħik, ma:t min ʔiððiħik] *vn: sv* u. مات [ma:t] مَوت [mu:t] *vn: sv* u. I just about died laughing when I heard that. طَقَّيت مِن الضِّحِك مِن سمَعتها [ṭaggi:t min ʔiððiħik min smaʕitha]

to die off • **1.** اِضمَحَلّ [ʔiḍmaħall] اِضمِحلال [ʔiḍmiħla:l] *vn: sv* i. The older generation is dying off. الجِّيل القَدِيم قاعِد يضمَحِلّ [ʔiǰǰi:l ʔilqadi:m ga:ʕid yiḍmaħill]

diet • **1.** رَجِيم [raǰi:m] رَجِيمات [raǰi:ma:t] *pl:* I have to go on a diet. لازِم أَسَوِّي رَجِيم [la:zim ʔasawwi raǰi:m] • **2.** أَكِل [ʔakil] For weeks our diet consisted of nothing but fish. خِلال عِدَّة أَسابِيع أَكِلنا ما كان غير سِمَك [xila:l ʕiddat ʔasa:bi:ʕ ʔakilna ma: ča:n ɣayr simač]

to diet • **1.** سَوَّى رَجِيم [sawwa: raji:m] تَسوِيَّة رَجِيم [taswiyyat raji:m] *vn: sv* i. I've been dieting for a month, but I still haven't lost any weight. آنِي ما أَسَوِّي رَجِيم صارلِي شَهَر وَما فقَدِت شِي مِن وَزنِي [ʔa:ni ma: ʔasawwi raǰi:m ṣa:rli šahar wama: fqadit ši min wazni]

to differ • **1.** اِختِلَف [ʔixtilaf] اِختِلاف [ʔixtila:f] *vn: sv* i. They differ in every respect. يِختَلفُون بكُلّشِي [yixtalfu:n bkullši] I beg to differ with you. آنِي أَختِلِف ويّاك [ʔa:ni ʔaxtilif wiyya:k] I beg to differ with you. آنِي ما أَوافقَك [ʔa:ni ma: ʔawa:fqak] • **2.** تضارَب [tḍa:rab] تَضارُب [taḍa:rub] *vn: sv* a. Opinions differ on this topic. الآراء مِتضارِبَة بهَالمَوضُوع [ʔilʔa:ra:ʔ midḍa:rba bhalmawḍu:ʕ]

difference • **1.** اِختِلاف [ʔixtila:f] اِختِلافات [ʔixtila:fa:t] *pl:* فَرق [fariq] فُرُوق [furu:q] *pl:* Can you show me the difference? تِقدَر تبَيِّنلِي الفَرق؟ [tigdar tbayyinli ʔilfariq?] It makes no difference when you come. ماكُو فَرق شوَكِت ما تِجِي [ma:ku fariq šwakit ma: tiǰi] • **2.** خِلاف [xila:f] خِلافات [xila:fa:t] *pl:* They ironed out their differences. صَفَّوا خِلافاتهُم [ṣaffaw xila:fa:thum]

to make a difference • **1.** فِرَق [firaq] فَرِق [fariq] *vn: sv* u. Does it make any difference to you if I write in pencil? تِفرُقلَك إذا أكتِب بِقَلَم رِصاص؟ [tifruqlak ʔiða ʔaktib bqalam riṣa:ṣ?]

different • **1.** مُختَلِف [muxtalif] The brothers are very different. الأخوَة كُلِّش مِختَلفين [ʔilʔuxwa kulliš mixtalfi:n] • **2.** مِتضارُب [mitðạ:rub] مِتباين [mitba:yin] The two ideas are different. الفِكِرتَين مِتبايِنَة [ʔilfikirtayn mitba:yna] • **3.** غير [ɣayr] آخَر [ʔa:xar] أخَرين [ʔa:xari:n] *pl:* أخرَى [ʔuxra] *Feminine:* That's a different matter. هَذا غير مَوضُوع [ha:ða ɣi:r mawḍu:ʕ] That's a different matter. هاي مَسألَة تِختِلِف [ha:y masʔala tixtilif]

differently • **1.** غير شِكِل [ɣayr šikil] بشِكِل آخَر [bšikil ʔa:xar] بشِكِل مُختَلِف [bšikil muxtalif] I think differently about it. آني أنظُر لَه غير شِكِل [ʔa:ni ʔanḍur lah ɣi:r šikil]

difficult • **1.** صَعُب [ṣaʕub] It's difficult to understand what he means. صَعُب تِفهَم شيَعني [ṣaʕub tifham šyaʕni] That's a difficult assignment. هَذِي مُهِمَّة صَعبَة [ha:ði muhimma ṣaʕba] • **2.** مِتصَعُّب [mitṣaʕʕub] He's difficult (to deal with) . هُوَّ مِتصَعُّب [huwwa miṭṣaʕʕub]

difficulty • **1.** صُعُوبَة [ṣuʕu:ba] صُعُوبات، مَصاعُب [ṣuʕuba:t, maṣa:ʕub] *pl:* صِعاب [ṣiʕa:b] He overcame the difficulties. تغَلَّب عَلَى الصُّعُوبات [tɣallab ʕala ʔiṣṣuʕu:ba:t]

to dig • **1.** حُفَر [ħufar] حَفُر [ħafur] *vn:* اِنحُفَر [ʔinħufar] *p:* Dig the hole a little deeper. أحفُر الحُفرَة شوَيَّة أغمَج [ʔuħfur ʔilħufra šwayya ʔaɣmaǰ]
to dig up • **1.** نِبَش [nibaš] نَبِش [nabiš] *vn:* اِنّبَش [ʔinnibaš] *p:* the dog dug up a bone he had buried in the ground. الكَلِب نِبَش عَظُم كان دافنَه بِالقاع [ʔiččalib nibaš ʕaḍum ča:n da:fnah bilga:ʕ]
*** dig up the rose bush.** • **1.** أحفُر داير عِرق الوَرِد وطَلّعَه [ʔuħfur da:yir ʕirg ʔilwarid wṭallʕah]

to digest • **1.** هِضَم [hiḍam] هَضُم [haḍum] *vn:* اِنهِضَم [ʔinhiḍam] *p:* Nuts are hard for us to digest. الكَرَزات صَعُب عَلينا نِهضُمها [ʔiččaraza:t ṣaʕub ʕali:na nihḍumha]

digestion • **1.** هَضُم [haḍum]

dignified • **1.** وَقُور [waqu:r] His father was a dignified old gentlemen. أبُوه كان فَدّ شَيخ وَقُور [ʔabu:h ča:n fadd ši:x waqu:r]

dim • **1.** مِعتِم [miʕtimm] خافِت [xa:fit] ضَعِيف [ðạʕi:f] I couldn't see anything in the dim light. ما قِدَرِت أشُوف شِي بِالضُوَة المُعتِم [ma: gidarit ʔašu:f ši biḍḍuwa ʔilmuʕtimm]

to dim • **1.** خَفَّض [xaffað] تَخفِيض [taxfi:ð] *vn:* تخَفَّض [txaffað] *p:* Dim your lights! خَفِّض ضُواك [xaffið ḍuwa:k]

dimple • **1.** رَصعَة [raṣʕa] رَصعات [raṣʕa:t] *pl:* She has a nice dimple. عِدها رَصعَة حِلوَة [ʕidha raṣʕa ħilwa]

dinar • **1.** دِينار [dina:r] دَنانير [dana:ni:r] *pl:*

to dine • **1.** تعَشَّى [tʕašša:] تَعَشِّي [taʕašši] *vn: sv* a. They're dining with us tonight. دَيِتعَشُّون ويّانا هاللّيلَة [dayitʕaššu:n wiyya:na hallayla] We dine out occasionally. إحنا أحياناً نِتعَشَّى بَرَّة [ʔiħna ʔaħya:nan nitʕašša: barra]

dining room • **1.** غُرفَة أكِل [ɣurfat ʔakil] غُرَف أكِل [ɣuraf ʔakil] *pl:* غُرفَة طَعام [ɣurfat ṭaʕa:m] غُرَف طَعام [ɣuraf ṭaʕa:m] *pl:* Bring another chair into the dining room. جِيب كُرسِي لاخ لغُرفَة الأكِل [ǰi:b kursi la:x lɣurfat ʔilʔakil]

dinner • **1.** عَشا [ʕaša] عَشاوات [ʕašawa:t] *pl:* Dinner is ready. العَشا جاهِز [ʔilʕaša ǰa:hiz] • **2.** عَزِيمَة [ʕazi:ma] عَزايِم [ʕaza:yim] *pl:* We're giving a dinner in his honor. راح نسَوِّي عَزِيمَة عَلَى شَرَفَه [ra:ħ nsawwi ʕazi:ma ʕala šarafah]
to have dinner • **1.** تعَشَّى [tʕašša:] تَعَشِّي [taʕašši] *vn: sv* a. We have dinner at six o'clock every day. نِتعَشَّى السّاعَة سِتَّة يَومِيّاً [nitʕašša: ʔissa:ʕa sitta yawmiyyan]

dip • **1.** حَدرَة [ħadra] حَدرات [ħadra:t] *pl:* نَزلَة [nazla] نَزلات [nazla:t] *pl:* There's a dip in the road ahead of us. أكُو حَدرَة بِالطَّرِيق قِدّامنا [ʔaku ħadra bittari:q gidda:mna] • **2.** غَطسَة [ɣaṭṭ] غَطسَات [ɣaṭsa:t] *pl:* طَمسَة [ṭamsa] طَمسات [ṭamsa:t] *pl:* There's nothing like a dip in the river to refresh you on a hot day. ماكُو مِثِل الغَطسَة بِالشَّطّ تِنعِشَك بيُوم حارّ [ma:ku miθil ʔilɣaṭsa biššaṭṭ tiniʕšak byu:m ħa:rr]
to dip • **1.** طَمَّس [ṭammas] طُمُّس، تَطمِيس [ṭṭummus, taṭmi:s] *vn: sv* u. I dipped my finger into the water. طَمَّسِت إصبَعِي بِالماي [ṭammasit ʔiṣbaʕi bilma:y]

direct • **1.** مُباشِر [muba:šir] there is no direct route. ماكُو طَرِيق مُباشِر [ma:ku ṭari:q muba:šir] there is no direct route. ماكُو طَرِيق يِطلَع رأساً [ma:ku ṭari:q yiṭlaʕ raʔsan] • **2.** تَماماً [tama:man] It's the direct opposite of what we expected. هِيَّ عَكِس ما توَقَّعنا تَماماً [hiyya ʕakis ma: twaqqaʕna tama:man]
to direct • **1.** أمَر [ʔumar] أمُر [ʔamur] *vn: sv* u. He directed us to follow the old regulations. أمَرنا أن نِتبَع التَّعلِيمات القَدِيمَة [ʔumarna ʔan nitbaʕ ʔittaʕli:ma:t ʔilqadi:ma] • **2.** وَجَّه [wajjah] تَوجِيه [tawǰi:h] *vn: sv* i. A policeman is directing the traffic. شُرطِي دَيوَجِّه المُرُور [šurṭi daywaǰǰih ʔilmuru:r] • **3.** دَلَّى [dalla:] تدِلِّي [tdilli] *vn: sv* i. Can you direct me to the post office? تِقدَر تدَلِّينِي عَلَى مَركَز البَرِيد

[tigdar ddalli:ni ʕala markaz ʔilbari:d] • **4.** خَرَّج [xarraǰ] تَخريج [taxri:ǰ] *vn: sv* i. أَخرَج [ʔaxraǰ] إخراج [ʔixra:ǰ] *vn: sv* i. Who is directing the play? مِنُو دَيخرِج التَّمثِيلِيَّة؟ [minu dayixriǰ ʔittamθi:liyya?]

direct current • **1.** تَيّار مُباشِر [tayya:r muba:šir]

direction • **1.** جِهَة [ǰiha] جِهات [ǰiha:t] *pl:* اِتِّجاه [ʔittiǰa:h] اِتِّجاهات [ʔittiǰa:ha:t] *pl:* Which direction did he go? لِأَي جِهَة راح؟ [lʔayy ǰiha ra:ħ?] • **2.** إرشاد [ʔirša:d] إرشادات [ʔirša:da:t] *pl:* His directions are clear. إرشاداتَه واضحَة [ʔirša:da:tah wa:ðħa] • **3.** إدارَة [ʔida:ra] إشراف [ʔišra:f] They have made great progress under his direction. خِطَوا خَطوات واسِعَة تَحَت إشرافَه [xiṭaw xaṭwa:t wa:sʕa taħat ʔišra:fah] They have made great progress under his direction. حَقِّقَوا تَقَدُّم كِبير تَحَت إدارتَه [ħaqqiqaw taqaddum čabi:r taħat ʔida:rtah] • **4.** تَعليم [taʕli:m] تَعالِيم، تَعلِيمات [taʕa:li:m, taʕli:ma:t] *pl:* The government issued directions concerning the election. الحُكُومَة أَصدِرَت تَعلِيمات تِتعَلَّق بِالإنتِخابات [ʔilħuku:ma ʔaṣdirat taʕli:ma:t titʕallaq bilʔintixa:ba:t]

directly • **1.** مُباشَرَتاً [muba:šaratan] رَأساً [raʔsan] Let's go directly to the hotel. خَلِّي نرُوح لِلأُوتَيل رأساً [xalli nru:ħ lilʔuti:ti:l raʔsan] Our house is directly opposite the store. بَيتنا مُقابِل المَخزَن مُباشَرَةً [baytna muqa:bil ʔilmaxzan muba:šaratan]

dirham • **1.** دِرهِم [dirhim] دَراهِم [dara:him] *pl:*

dirt • **1.** تراب [tra:b] تُربان [turba:n] *pl:* How many trucks of dirt do we need to fill this in? كَم لوري تراب نِحتاج لِدَفِن هاي؟ [čam lu:ri tra:b niħta:ǰ lidafin ha:y?] • **2.** زمِيج [zimi:ǰ] The dirt in the flower pots should be replaced this year. الزِّمِيج بِسنادِين الوَرد لازم يِتبَدَّل هالسَّنَة [ʔizzimi:ǰ bisna:di:n ʔilwarid la:zim yitbaddal hassana] • **3.** وُسَخ [wusax] There is some dirt on your shirt. أَكُو شوَيَّة وُسَخ بثُوبَك [ʔaku šwayya wuṣax bθu:bak]

dirt-cheap • **1.** أَخُو البَلاش [ʔaxu ʔilbala:š] أُخت البَلاش [ʔuxt ʔilbala:š] I bought the car dirt-cheap. اِشتِرَيت السَّيّارَة أُخت البَلاش [ʔištiri:t ʔissayya:ra ʔuxt ʔalbala:š]

dirty • **1.** وَسِخ [wasix] The floor is dirty. القاع وَسخَة [ʔilga:ʕ wasxa] • **2.** بَذِيء [baði:ʔ] Most of his stories are pretty dirty. مُعظَم قُصَصَه بَذِيئَة [muʕðam quṣaṣah baði:ʔa] • **3.** دَنِيء [dani:ʔ] أَدنِياء [ʔadniya:ʔ] *pl:* حَقِير [ħaqi:r] حَقِيرِين، حُقَراء [ħaqi:ri:n, ħuqara:ʔ] *pl:* He played a dirty trick on us. سَوَّى بِينا نُكتَة دَنِيئَة [sawwa: bi:na nukta dani:ʔa]

He gave us a dirty look. • **1.** نِظَرنا بازدِراء [niðarna biʔizdira:ʔ] / باوَعنا باحتِقار [ba:waʕna bʔiħtiqa:r]

*** That is a dirty lie.** • **1.** هاي كِذبَة قَذرَة [ha:y čiðba qaðra]

to dirty • **1.** وَسَّخ [wassax] تَوسِيخ، توسِّخ [tawsi:x, twissix] *vn: sv* i. Don't dirty the carpet with your muddy shoes. لا توَسّخ الزُّولِيَّة بقُندَرتَك المطَيِّنَة [la: twassix ʔizzu:liyya bqundartak ʔilmṭayyna]

disability • **1.** عَجِز [ʕaǰiz] He can't play soccer because of a disability. ما يِقدَر يِلعَب كُرَة القَدَم بِسَبَب العَجِز [ma: yigdar yilʕab kurat ʔilqadam bisabab ʔilʕaǰiz]

to disable • **1.** سَوَّى عَجِز [sawwa: ʕaǰiz] *sv* i. The auto accident disabled him. حادِث السَّيّارَة سَوّاه عَجِز [ħa:diθ ʔissayya:ra sawwa:h ʕaǰiz]

to be disabled • **1.** اِنصاب بعَجِز [ʔinṣa:b bʕaǰiz] *sv* a. The soldier was permanently disabled. الجُندي اِنصاب بعَجِز دائِم [ʔiǰǰundi ʔinṣa:b bʕaǰiz da:ʔim]

disadvantage • **1.** مَضَرَّة [maðarra] مَضَرّات، مَضارّ [maðarra:t, maða:rr] *pl:* You'll have to weigh the advantages and disadvantages before you decide. لازِم توازِن بين المَضارّ وَالمَنافِع قَبُل ما تقَرِّر [la:zim twa:zin bi:n ʔilmaða:rr wilmana:fiʕ gabul ma: tqarrir]

to disagree • **1.** اِختِلَف [ʔixtilaf] اِختِلاف [ʔixtila:f] *vn: sv* i. I disagree with you. آنِي أَختِلِف وِيّاك [ʔa:ni ʔaxtilif wiyya:k] • **2.** خالَف [xa:laf] مُخالَفَة [muxa:lafa] *vn: sv* i. I disagree with the method. آنِي أَخالِف الطَّرِيقَة [ʔa:ni ʔaxa:lif ʔiṭṭari:qa] I disagree with the method. آنِي ما أَئيِّد هَالطَّرِيقَة [ʔa:ni ma: ʔaʔayyid haṭṭari:qa] • **3.** ما والَم [ma: wa:lam] مُوالَمَة [muwa:lama] *vn: sv* i. Melons disagree with me. البَطِّيخ ما يوالِمنِي [ʔilbaṭṭi:x ma: ywa:limni] Melons disagree with me. آنِي مُو صُحبَة وِيّا البَطِّيخ [ʔa:ni mu: ṣuħba wiyya ʔilbaṭṭi:x]

to disappear • **1.** اِختِفَى [ʔixtifa:] اِختِفاء [ʔixtifa:ʔ] *vn: sv* i. He disappeared in the crowd. اِختِفَى بالخَبصَة [ʔixtifa: bilxabṣa] • **2.** تلاشَى [tla:ša:] تَلاشِي [tala:ši] *vn: sv* a. the river disappears in the desert. النَّهَر يِتلاشَى بِالصَّحراء [ʔinnahar yitla:ša: biṣṣaħra:ʔ]

to disappoint • **1.** خاب أَمَل [xa:b ʔamal-] خَيَبان أَمَل، خَيبَة أَمَل [xayaba:n ʔamal, xaybat ʔamal] *vn: sv* i. I was very much disappointed. خاب أَمَلِي هوايَة [xa:b ʔamali hwa:ya]

disappointment • **1.** خَيبَة أَمَل [xi:bat ʔamal] خَيبات أَمَل [xayba:t ʔamal] *pl:* It was a great disappointment. كانَت خَيبَة أَمَل كِبيرَة [ča:nat xaybat ʔamal čibi:ra]

to disapprove • **1.** اِستَنكَر [ʔistankar] اِستِنكار [ʔistinka:r] *vn: sv* i. He disapproves of our plans. يِستَنكِر خُطَطنا [yistankir xuṭaṭna]

to disarm • **1.** جَرَّد [ǰarrad] تَجرِيد [taǰri:d] *vn:* تجَرَّد [tǰarrad] *p:* They disarmed the prisoners immediately. جَرِّدَوا الأَسرَى مِن السِّلاح بِالحال [ǰarridaw ʔilʔasra: min ʔissila:ħ bilħa:l]

disarmament • **1.** نَزع السِلاح [nazʕ ʔissila:ħ]

disaster • **1.** نَكبَة [nakba] نَكبات [nakba:t] *pl:* كارثَة [ka:riθa] كَوارِث [kawa:riθ] *pl:* مُصيبَة [muṣi:ba] مُصايِب [muṣa:yib] *pl:* The airplane crash was a great disaster. سُقُوط الطِّيّارَة كان كارثَة كِبيرَة [suqu:ṭ ʔiṭṭiyya:ra ča:n ka:riθa čibi:ra]

disastrous • **1.** مُروِّع [murwwiʕ] مُريع [muri:ʕ] The collision was disastrous. التَّصادُم كان كُلِّش مُروِع [ʔittaṣa:dum ča:n kulliš murwiʕ]

discharge • **1.** تَسريح [tasri:ħ] Your discharge is in November. تَسريحَك بِتِشرين الثّانِي [tasri:ħak btišri:n ʔiθθa:ni]

to discharge • **1.** فُصَل [fuṣal] فَصُل [faṣul] *vn:* اِنفُصَل [ʔinfuṣal] *p:* طِرَد [ṭirad] طَرِد [ṭarid] *vn:* اِنطِرَد [ʔinṭirad] *p:* The company discharged him for his carelessness. الشَّرِكَة فُصلَتَه لِإهمالَه [ʔiššarika fuṣlatah liʔihma:lah] • **2.** سَرَّح [sarrah] تَسريح [tasri:ħ] *vn:* تسَرَّح [tsarrah] *p:* You're going to be discharged when the war ends. راح تِتسَرَّحُون لَمّا تِنتِهِي الحَرُب [ra:ħ titsarraħu:n lamma tintihi ʔilħarub] • **3.** خَلَّص [xallaṣ] تَخلِيص [taxli:ṣ] *vn: sv* i. أَنهَى [ʔanha:] إنهاء [ʔinha:ʔ] *vn: sv* i. أَدَّى [ʔadda:] تادِّي [tʔiddi] *vn: sv* i. He discharges his responsibilities promptly. يخَلِّص واجباتَه بِسُرعَة [yxalliṣ wa:ǰiba:tah bsurʕa] • **4.** فَرَّغ [farraɣ] تَفريغ [tafri:ɣ] *vn:* تفَرَّغ [tfarraɣ] *p:* نَزَّل [nazzal] تَنزِيل [tanzi:l] *vn:* تنَزَّل [tnazzal] *p:* The ship discharged its cargo on the dock. السَّفِينَة فَرّغَت شُحنَتها عالرَّصِيف [ʔissafi:na farrɣat šuħnatha ʕarraṣi:f] • **5.** ضِعَف [ḍiʕaf] ضُعُف [ḍuʕuf] *vn: sv* a. Turn off the lights, don't discharge the battery. طَفِّي الأَضوِيَة، لا تضَعِّف الباترِي [ṭaffi ʔilʔaḍwiya, la: dḍaʕʕif ʔilpa:tri] • **6.** طِلَع [ṭilaʕ] طُلُوع [ṭulu:ʕ] *vn: sv* a. The hospital discharged him after 10 days. المُستَشفى طَلعَته بَعَد عَشرَة أَيّام [ʔilmustašfa ṭalʕatah baʕad ʕašrat ʔayya:m]

discipline • **1.** ضَبُط [ḍabuṭ] طاعَة [ṭa:ʕa] نِظام [niḍa:m] أَنظِمَة [ʔanḍima] *pl:* The teacher can't maintain discipline in class. الأُستاذ ما يِقدَر يحافُظ عالضَبُط بصَفَّه [ʔilʔusta:ð ma: yigdar yħa:fuḍ ʕaḍḍabuṭ bṣaffah]

to discipline • **1.** جازَى [ǰa:za:] مُجازاة [muǰa:za:(t)] *vn: sv* i. The lieutenant disciplined his troops for disobediance. المُلازِم جازَى الجُّنُود لِعَدَم طاعَتهُم [ʔilmula:zim ǰa:za: ʔiǰǰinu:d liʕadam ṭa:ʕathum]

to disclose • **1.** كِشَف عَن [kišaf ʕan] كَشِف [kašif] *vn: sv* i. أَظهَر [ʔaḍhar] إظهار [ʔiḍha:r] *vn: sv* i. The investigation disclosed new facts. التَّحقِيق كِشَف عَن حَقايِق جِدِيدَة [ʔittaħqi:q kišaf ʕan ħaqa:yiq ǰidi:da]

to disconnect • **1.** فُصَل [fuṣal] فَصِل [faṣil] *vn:* اِنفُصَل [ʔinfuṣal] *p:* If we disconnect these two wires the lights will go out. إذا فُصَلنا هَالوايرَين تِنطُفِي الأَضوِيَة [ʔiða fiṣalna halwa:yrayn tinṭufi ʔlʔaḍwiya]

discontented • **1.** ما راضِي [ma: ra:ḍi] He's discontented in his present job. هُوَّ ما راضِي بِشُغلَه الحالِيَّة [huwwa ma: ra:ḍi bšuɣlah ʔilħa:liyya]

to discontinue • **1.** بَطَّل [baṭṭal] *sv* i. وَقَّف [waggaf, wagguf] *sv* i. قِطَع [qiṭaʕ] قَطِع [qaṭiʕ] *vn:* اِنقِطَع [ʔinqiṭaʕ] *p: sv* a. We're going to discontinue mail service in this area. راح نبَطِّل خِدمَة البَرِيد بِهَالمَنطِقَة [ra:ħ nbaṭṭil xidmat ʔilbari:d bhalmanṭiqa]

discount • **1.** خَصُم [xaṣum] خُصُوم [xuṣu:m] *pl:* Can you get a discount on these books? تِقدَر تحَصِّل خَصُم عَلَى هَالكُتُب؟ [tigdar tħaṣṣil xaṣum ʕala halkutub?]

to discourage • **1.** ثَبَّط [θabbaṭ] تَثبِيط [taθbi:ṭ] *vn:* تثَبَّط [tθabbaṭ] *p:* He did his best to discourage me from going. حاوَل كُلّشِي حَتَّى يثَبِّط عَزِيمتِي وَما أَرُوح [ħa:wal kullši ħatta yθabbuṭ ʕazi:mti wama: ʔaru:ħ] He gets discouraged easily. يِتثَبَّط عَزِيمتَه بِسُهُولَة [yitθabbaṭ ʕazi:mtah bsuhu:la]

discouraging • **1.** مُثَبِّط لِلعَزِم [muθabbiṭ lilʕazim] غير مُشَجِّع [ɣayr mušaǰǰiʕ] The results are discouraging. النَّتائِج مُثَبِّطَة لِلعَزِم [ʔinnata:ʔiǰ muθabbiṭa lilʕazim]

to discover • **1.** اِكتِشَف [ʔiktišaf] اِكتِشاف [ʔiktiša:f] *vn: sv* i. Columbus discovered America. كُلُومبُس اِكتِشَف أَمرِيكا [kulu:mbus ʔiktišaf ʔamri:ka]

discovery • **1.** اِكتِشاف [ʔiktiša:f] اِكتِشافات [ʔiktiša:fa:t] *pl:* He made an important discovery in science. حَقَّق اِكتِشاف مُهِمّ بِالعِلِم [ħaqqaq ʔiktiša:f muhimm bilʕilim]

to discuss • **1.** ناقَش [na:qaš] مُناقَشَة [muna:qaša] *vn: sv* i. بِحَث [biħaθ] بَحِث [baħiθ] *vn: sv* a. They discussed the subject from all sides. ناقِشَوا المَوضُوع مِن كُلّ النَّواحِي [na:qišaw ʔilmawḍu:ʕ min kull ʔinnawa:ħi] Discuss the matter with him. إبحَث المَوضُوع وِيّاه [ʔibħaθ ʔilmawḍu:ʕ wiyya:h]

discussion • **1.** مُناقَشَة [muna:qaša] مُناقَشات [muna:qaša:t] *pl:* بَحِث [baħiθ] بُحُوث، أَبحاث [buħu:θ, ʔabħa:θ] *pl:*

disease • **1.** مَرَض [marað] أَمراض [ʔamra:ḍ] *pl:* This disease is contagious. هَذا المَرَض مُعدِي [ha:ða ʔilmarað muʕdi]

to disfigure • **1.** شَوَّه [šawwah] تَشوِيه [tašwi:h] *vn:* تشَوَّه [tšawwah] *p:* The injury disfigured his face. الجُّرح شَوَّه وُجَّه [ʔiǰǰariħ šawwah wuččah]

disgrace • **1.** عار [ʕa:r] خِزي [xizi] فَضِيحَة [faðiːħa] فَضايِح [faðaːyiħ] *pl:* He brought disgrace on his family. جاب الخِزي لِعائِلتَه [ǰa:b ʔilxizi lʕa:ʔiltah]

to disgrace • **1.** فُضَح [fuðah] فَضِيحَة [faðiːħa] *vn:* اِنفُضَح [ʔinfuðah] *p: sv* a. She disgraced her family. فُضحَت عائِلَتها [fuðħat ʕa:ʔilatha]

D

to disguise • **1.** نَكَّر [nakkar] تَنكِير، تَنكُّر [tankiːr, tnikkir] *vn:* تنكَّر [tnakkar] *p:* He disguised himself to avoid capture. تنكَّر حَتَّى يِتجَنَّب القَبُض عَليه [tnakkar ħatta yidǰannab ʔilqabuð ʕaliːh]

disguised • **1.** مِتنَكِّر [mitnakkir] Haroun al-Rashid had the habit of walking in the streets of Baghdad disguised as a merchant. هارُون الرَّشِيد كانَت عادتَه يِمشِي بِشَوارِع بَغداد مِتنَكِّر كَتاجِر [ha:ruːn ʔirrašiːd ča:nat ʕa:dtah yimši bšawa:riʕ baɣda:d mitnakkir kata:ǰir]

disgust • **1.** إشمِئزاز [ʔišmiʔza:z] تَقَزُّز [taqazzuz] He turned away in disgust. دار وُجَّه بإشمِئزاز [da:r wuččah bʔišmiʔza:z]

to disgust • **1.** قَزَّز [qazzaz] تَقزِيز [taqziːz] *vn:* تقَزَّز [tqazzaz] *p:* His conduct disgusts me. تَصَرُّفاتَه تقَزِّز نَفسِي [taṣarrufa:tah tqazziz nafsi]

to be disgusted • **1.** اِشمَئَزّ [ʔišmaʔazz] اِشمِئزاز [ʔišmiʔza:z] *vn: sv* i. تقَزَّز [tqazzaz] تَقَزُّز [taqazzuz] *vn: sv* a. I was disgusted by his conduct. اِشمَئزَّيت مِن تَصَرُّفاتَه [ʔišmaʔizziːt min taṣarrufa:tah]

*** I'm disgusted with everything.** • **1.** آنِي بَزعان مِن كُلْشِي [ʔa:ni bazʕa:n min kullši] / طافرَة رُوحِي مِن كُلْشِي [ṭa:fra ru:ħi min kullši]

dish • **1.** ماعُون [ma:ʕu:n] مواعِين [mwa:ʕi:n] *pl:* صَحِن [ṣaħin] صُحُون [ṣuħu:n] *pl:* He dropped the dish. وَقَّع الماعُون [waggaʕ ʔilma:ʕu:n] I'd like a dish of ice cream. أَرِيد ماعُون دوندِرمَة [ʔari:d ma:ʕu:n du:ndirma] • **2.** لَون أَكِل [lawn ʔakil] أَلوان أَكِل [ʔalwa:n ʔakil] *pl:* I have a recipe for a new dish. عِندِي وَصفَة لَون جِدِيد مِن الأَكِل [ʕindi waṣfat lawn ǰidi:d min ʔilʔakil]

dishonest • **1.** غَير شَرِيف [ɣayr šari:f] غَشّاش [ɣašša:š] غَشّاشَة [ɣašša:ša] *pl:* مُو شَرِيف [mu: šari:f]

to disinfect • **1.** عَقَّم [ʕaqqam] تَعقِيم [taʕqi:m] *vn:* تعَقَّم [tʕaqqam] *p:* طَهَّر [ṭahhar] تَطهِير [taṭhi:r] *vn:* تطَهَّر [ʔiṭṭahhar] p: Did you disinfect the wound? عَقَّمتَه لِلجَّرِح؟ [ʕaqqamtah lijǰariħ?]

disinfectant • **1.** مُطَهِّر [muṭahhir] مُطَهِّرات [muṭahhira:t] *pl:* مُعَقِّم [muʕaqqam] I need a disinfectant. أَحتاج مُطَهِّر [ʔaħta:ǰ muṭahhir]

to disinherit • **1.** حِرَم مِن الإرث [ħiram min ʔilʔirθ] حِرمان مِن الأَرث [ħirma:n min ʔilʔirθ] *vn: sv* a. His father threatened to disinherit him. أَبُوه هَدَّدَه بِحِرمانَه مِن الإرِث [ʔabu:h haddadah bħirma:nah min ʔilʔiriθ]

to disintegrate • **1.** تحَلَّل [tħallal] تَحَلُّل [taħallul] *vn: sv* a. The empire disintegrated. الإمبِراطُورِيَّة اِنحَلَّت [ʔilʔimbira:ṭu:riyya ʔinħallat]

dislike • **1.** نُفُور [nufu:r] كَراهَة [kara:ha] عَدَم مَحَبَّة [ʕadam maħabba] I couldn't conceal my dislike for him. ما قِدَرت أَكتِم نُفُورِي مِنَّه [ma: gidarit ʔaktim nufu:ri minnah]

to dislike • **1.** ما حَبّ [ma: ħabb] ما حَبّ [ma: ħabb] *vn: sv* i. نُفَر مِن [nufar min] نَفُر [nafur] *vn: sv* u. I dislike that fellow. ما أَحِبّ هَذا الرَّجّال [ma: ʔaħibb ha:ða ʔirrajǰa:l]

to dislocate • **1.** خِلَع [xilaʕ] خَلِع [xaliʕ] *vn:* اِنخِلَع [ʔinxilaʕ] *p: sv* a. He dislocated his shoulder. خِلَع كِتفَه [xilaʕ čitfah]

disloyal • **1.** غَير مُخلِص [ɣi:r muxliṣ] خائِن [xa:ʔin, xa:yin] خَوَنَة [xawana] *pl:*

dismal • **1.** كَئِيب [kaʔi:b] It's a dismal day today. هَاليُوم كَئِيب [halyu:m kaʔi:b] It's a dismal day today. هَاليُوم يُقبُض الصَّدِر [halyu:m yuqbuð ʔiṣṣadir]

to dismiss • **1.** طِرَد [ṭirad] طَرِد [ṭarid] *vn: sv* i. She was dismissed after two weeks. اِنطِرَدَت وَرا إسبُوعَين [ʔinṭiradat wara ʔisbu:ʕayn] • **2.** رُفَض [rufað] رَفُض [rafuð] *vn:* اِنرُفَض [ʔinrufað] *p:* The court dismissed the complaint. المَحكَمَة رُفضَت الشَّكوَى [ʔilmaħkama rufðat ʔiššakwa] • **3.** صِرَف [ṣiraf] صَرُف [ṣaruf] *vn:* اِنصِرَف [ʔinṣiraf] *p:* He dismissed the soldiers after an hour's drill. صِرَف الجِّنُود بَعَد تَدرِيب ساعَة [ṣiraf ʔijǰinu:d baʕad tadri:b sa:ʕa]

dispensary • **1.** مُستَوصَف [mustawṣaf] مُستَوصَفات [mustawṣafa:t] *pl:*

display • **1.** واجِهَة [wa:ǰiha] واجِهات [wa:ǰiha:t] *pl:* Have you seen the beautiful displays in the shops on Rashid St. ? شِفِت واجِهات المَخازِن الحِلوَة بشارِع الرَّشِيد؟ [šifit wa:ǰiha:t ʔilmaxa:zin ʔilħilwa bša:riʕ ʔirraši:d?]

on display • **1.** مَعرُوض [maʕru:ð] The statute is on display at the museum. التِّمثال مَعرُوض بالمَتحَف [ʔittimθa:l maʕru:ð bilmatħaf]

to display • **1.** راوَى [ra:wa:] مُراواة [mura:wa:t] *vn: sv* i. بَيَّن [bayyan] تَبيِين [tabyi:n] *vn: sv* i. أَظهَر [ʔaðhar] إظهار [ʔiðha:r] *vn: sv* i. He displayed great courage. بَيَّن شَجاعَة فائِقَة [bayyan šaja:ʕa fa:ʔiqa] There's no need to display your ignorance. ماكُو حاجَة تِظهِر جَهلَك [ma:ku ħa:ǰa tiðhir ǰahlak] • **2.** عِرَض [ʕirað] عَرِض [ʕarið] *vn:* اِنعِرَض [ʔinʕirað] *p:* You can't display your fruit on the side walks of a main street.

ما تِقدَر تُعرُض فَواكهَك عَالرَّصِيف بشارِع عامّ [maː tigdar tuʕruð̣ fawaːkhak ʕarraṣiːf bšaːriʕ ʕaːmm] • **3.** خَلّى [xallaː] تخلّي، تَخلِيَة [txilli, taxliya] *vn: sv* i. رُفَع [rufaʕ] رَفُع [rafuʕ] *vn: sv* a. All the houses displayed flags. كُلّ البيُوت خَلَّت أعلام [kull ʔilbyuːt xallat ʔaʕlaːm]

disposal • **1.** أمُر [ʔamur] أوامِر [ʔawaːmir] *pl:* I'm at your disposal. آني تَحَت أمرَك [ʔaːni taħat ʔamrak] • **2.** تَصريف [taṣriːf] There's no garbage disposal plant in this village. ماكُو مَحَلّ تَصريف المِياه القَذرَة بهالقَريَة [maːku maħall taṣriːf ʔilmiyaːh ʔilqaðra bhaːlqarya]

*** They agreed to put a car at my disposal.** • **1.** وافقوا يخَلُّون سَيّارَة جَوَّة إيدي [waːfqaw yxalluːn sayyaːra ǰawwa ʔiːdi]

to dispose • **1.** تخَلَّص [txallaṣ] تَخَلُّص [taxalluṣ] *vn: sv* a. They will leave as soon as they dispose of their furniture. راح يتُركُون أوَّل ما يتخَلّصُون مِن أثاثهُم [raːħ yturkuːn ʔawwal maː yitxallṣuːn min ʔaθaːθhum]

disposition • **1.** طَبُع [ṭabuʕ] He has a poor disposition. طَبعَه مُو زين [ṭabʕah muː ziːn]

to disregard • **1.** هِمَل [himal] إهمال [ʔihmaːl] *vn:* اِنهِمَل [ʔinhimal] *p:* If I were in your place, I'd disregard the letter. لَو بمَكانَك، أهمِلَه لِلمَكتُوب [law bmakaːnak, ʔahimlah lilmaktuːb] • **2.** تغاضى عَن [tɣaːð̣aː ʕan] تغاضِي عَن [tɣaːð̣i ʕan] *vn: sv* a. We can't disregard his objections. ما نِقدَر نِتغاضى عَن إعتِراضاتَه [maː nigdar nidɣaːð̣aː ʕan ʔiʕtiraːð̣aːtah]

to disrupt • **1.** قِطَع [giṭaʕ] قَطِع [gaṭiʕ] *vn:* اِنقِطَع [ʔingiṭaʕ] *p: sv* a. Communications were disrupted by the storm. المُواصَلات اِنقِطعَت مِن العاصِفَة [ʔilmuwaːṣalaːt ʔingiṭʕat min ʔilʕaːṣifa]

dissatisfied • **1.** مُو راضِي [muː raːð̣i] You look dissatisfied. يبَيِّن عَلِيك مُو راضِي [yibayyin ʕaliːk muː raːð̣i]

to dissipate • **1.** بَدَّد [baddad] تَبدِيد [tabdiːd] *vn:* تبَدَّد [tbaddad] *p:* He dissipated his entire fortune. بَدَّد كُلّ ثَرُوتَه [baddad kull θaruːtah] • **2.** اِنقِشَع [ʔingišaʕ] اِنقِشاع [ʔingišaːʕ] *vn: sv* i. We'd better wait until the fog dissipates a bit. أحسَن نِنتِظِر إلَى أن يِنقِشِع الضَّباب شوَيَّة [ʔaħsan nintið̣ir ʔila ʔan yinqišiʕ ʔið̣ð̣abaːb šwayya]

*** He leads a dissipated life.** • **1.** هُوَّ مُصرِف بِالمَلَذّات [huwwa muṣrif bilmalaððaːt]

to dissolve • **1.** ذاب [ðaːb] ذَوَبان [ðawabaːn] *vn: sv* u. تحَلَّل [tħallal] تَحَلُّل [taħallul] *vn: sv* a. Salt dissolves in water. المِلِح يذُوب بالماي [ʔilmiliħ yðuːb bilmaːy] • **2.** ذَوَّب [ðawwab] تَذويب [taðwiːb] *vn: sv* i. Dissolve the tablet in a glass of water. ذَوِّب القُرص بِگلاص ماي [ðawwib ʔilquruṣ biglaːṣ maːy]

distance • **1.** مَسافَة [masaːfa] مَسافات [masaːfaːt] *pl:* بُعُد [buʕud] أبعاد [ʔabʕaːd] *pl:* The distance between Baghdad and Najaf is about 180 kilometers. المَسافَة بين بَغداد وَالنَّجَف حَوالِي مِيَّة وَثمانين كِيلُومَتر [ʔilmasaːfa biːn baɣdaːd wʔinnaǰaf ħawaːli miyya wθmaːniːn kiːluːmatir] • **2.** مَسافَة [masaːfa] مَسافات [masaːfaːt] *pl:* بِعِيد [biʕiːd] You can see the tower from a distance. تِقدَر تشُوف البُرج مِن بِعِيد [tigdar tšuːf ʔilburiǰ min biʕiːd]

to keep one's distance • **1.** لِزَم حَدّ، ضِبَط حَدّ [lizam ħadd, ð̣ibaṭ ħadd] لَزِم حَدّ، ضَبُط حَدّ [lazim ħadd, ð̣abuṭ ħadd] *vn: sv* a. ضُبَط [ð̣ubaṭ] ضَبُط [ð̣abuṭ] *vn: sv* u. He knows how to keep his distance. يُعرُف وين يِلزَم حَدَّه [yuʕruf wiːn yilzam ħaddah]

distant • **1.** مِن بِعِيد [min biʕiːd] She's a distant relative of mine. هِيَّ قَرايبي مِن بِعِيد [hiyya garaːybi min biʕiːd]

distinct • **1.** واضِح [waːð̣iħ] مبَيِّن [mbayyin] ظاهِر [ð̣aːhir] There's a distinct difference between the two. أكُو اِختِلاف واضِح بين الإثنَين [ʔaku ʔixtilaːf waːð̣iħ bayn ʔilʔiθnayn]

distinctly • **1.** بوُضُوح [bwuð̣uːħ] I told him distinctly not to come. آني فَهَّمتَه بكُلّ وُضُوح أن ما يِجي [ʔaːni fahhamtah bkull wuð̣uːħ ʔan maː yiǰi]

to distinguish • **1.** فَرزَن [farzan] تفِرزِن [tfirzin] *vn: sv* i. مَيَّز [mayyaz] تَمييز [tamyiːz] *vn:* تمَيَّز [tmayyaz] *p:* I couldn't distinguish the features of his face in the dark. ما قِدَرت أفَرزِن مَلامِح وُچَّه بِالظَّلمَة [maː gidarit ʔafarzin malaːmiħ wuččah bið̣ð̣alma] I could hardly distinguish one from the other. بِصُعُوبَة قِدَرت أمَيِّز عَن بَعَضهُم [bṣuʕuːba gidarit ʔamayyiz ʕan baʕað̣hum] • **2.** مَيَّز [mayyaz] تَمييز [tamyiːz] *vn: sv* i. فَرَّق [farraq, farrag] تَفريق [tafriːq] *vn: sv* i. Can you distinguish between the two? تِقدَر تفَرِّق بين الإثنين؟ [tigdar tfarriq bayn ʔilʔiθnayn?] • **3.** أبرَز [ʔabraz] إبراز [ʔibraːz] *vn: sv* i. He distinguished himself by his courage. أبرَز نَفسَه بشَجاعتَه [ʔabraz nafsah bšaǰaːʕtah] He's a distinguished soldier and statesman. هُوَّ جُندي وَرَجُل دَولَة بارِز [huwwa ǰundi wraǰul dawla baːriz]

distress • **1.** شِدَّة [šidda] ضِيق [ð̣iːq] The Red Crescent did everything possible to relieve the distress. جَمعِيَّة الهِلال الأحمَر سَوَّت كُلّ ما مُمكِن لِلتَّخفِيف مِن الشِّدَّة [ǰamʕiyyat ʔilhilaːl ʔilʔaħmar sawwat kull maː mumkin littaxfiːf min ʔiššidda] The ship was in distress. الباخِرَة كانَت بضِيق [ʔilbaːxira čaːnat bð̣iːq] • **2.** غَمّ [ɣamm] He caused his mother much distress. سَبَّب لأمَّه هوايَة غَمّ [sabbab lʔummah hwaːya ɣamm]

to distribute • **1.** وَزَّع [wazzaʕ] تَوزيع [tawziːʕ] *vn:* توَزَّع [twazzaʕ] *p:* قَسَّم [qassam] تَقسِيم [taqsiːm] *vn:* تقَسَّم [tqassam] *p:* The profits were evenly distributed. الأرباح تقَسِّمَت بِالتَّساوي [ʔilʔarbaːħ tqassimat bittasaːwi]

district • **1.** مَنطِقَة [manṭiqa] مَناطِق [mana:ṭiq] *pl:* ناحِيَة [na:ħiya] نَواحِي [nawa:ħi] *pl:* This is a very poor district. هٰذِي مَنطِقَة كُلِّش فَقِيرَة [ha:ði manṭiqa kulliš faqi:ra] • **2.** قِسِم [qisim] أقسام [ʔaqsa:m] *pl:* مَنطِقَة [manṭiqa] مَناطِق [mana:ṭiq] *pl:* The city is divided into ten districts. المَدِينَة مقَسّمَة إلَى عَشِر أقسام [ʔilmadi:na mqassma ʔila ʕašir ʔaqsa:m]

D

to distrust • **1.** ما وِثَق [ma: wiθaq] *sv* i. I distrust him. آنِي ما أثِق بِيه [ʔa:ni ma: ʔaθiq bi:h]

to disturb • **1.** أزعَج [ʔazʕaǰ] إزعاج [ʔizʕa:ǰ] *vn: sv* i. شَوَّش [šawwaš] تَشوِيش [tašwi:š] *vn: sv* i. Don't disturb the others! لا تِزعِج الآخَرِين [la: tizʕiǰ ʔilʔa:xari:n] • **2.** قِلَق [qilaq] قَلِق [qaliq] *vn: sv* i. The news disturbed me. الأخبار قِلقَتنِي [ʔilʔaxba:r qilqatni] • **3.** خَربَط [xarbaṭ] تخُربُط [txurbuṭ] *vn: sv* u. Someone has disturbed my papers. واحِد خَربَط أوراقِي [wa:ħid xarbaṭ ʔawra:qi]

ditch • **1.** ساقيَة [sa:gya] سواقِي [swa:gi] *pl:* The car got stuck in the ditch. السَّيّارَة طُمسَت بِالسّاقيَة [ʔissayya:ra ṭumsat bissa:gya]

to dive • **1.** ذَبّ زَرِق [ðabb zarig] ذَبّ زَرِق [ðabb zarig] *vn: sv* i. Do you know how to dive? تُعرُف شلُون تذِبّ زَرِق؟ [tuʕruf šlu:n dðibb zarig?] • **2.** غاص [ɣa:ṣ] غَوص [ɣawṣ] *vn: sv* u. They dive for pearls in Kuwait. يغُوصُون مِن أجِل اللُّولُو بالكُوَيت [yɣu:ṣu:n min ʔaǰil ʔilluʔluʔ bilkuwi:t]

diver • **1.** غَوّاص [ɣawwa:ṣ] غَوّاصِين [ɣawwa:ṣi:n] *pl:* They hired a diver to inspect the wreck of the ship. اِستأجرَوا غَوّاص لفَحِص حِطام السَّفِينَة [ʔistaʔǰiraw ɣawwa:ṣ lifaħiṣ ħiṭa:m ʔissafi:na]
 *** He's a good diver.** • **1.** هُوَّ يذِبّ زَرِق زَين [huwwa yðibb zarig zayn]

to divide • **1.** قِسَم [qisam] قَسِم [qasim] *vn:* اِنقِسَم [ʔinqisam] *p:* قَسَّم [qassam] تَقسِيم [taqsi:m] *vn:* تقَسَّم [tqassam] *p:* Divide the total by four. إقسِم المَجمُوع عَلَى أربَعَة [ʔiqsim ʔilmaǰmu:ʕ ʕala ʔarbaʕa] The book is divided into two parts. الكِتاب مِنقِسِم إلَى قِسمَين [ʔilkita:b minqisim ʔila qismayn] Divide the group into two teams. قَسِّم الجَّماعَة إلَى فَرِيقَين [qassim ʔiǰǰama:ʕa ʔila fari:qayn] • **2.** تفَرَّع [tfarraʕ] تَفَرُّع [tafarruʕ] *vn: sv* a. تفَرَّق [tfarraq, tfarrag] تَفَرُّق [tafarruq] *vn: sv* a. The road divides at the end of the village. الطَّرِيق يِتفَرَّع بطَرَف القَريَة [ʔiṭṭari:q yitfarraʕ bṭaraf ʔilqarya] • **3.** قاسَم [qa:sam] مُقاسَمَة [muqa:sama] *vn: sv* i. I divide the profits between me and my partner. آنِي أقاسِم الأرباح بَينِي وَبَين شَرِيكِي [ʔa:ni ʔaqa:sim ʔilʔarba:ħ bayni wbayn šari:ki]

division • **1.** قِسِم [qisim] أقسام [ʔaqsa:m] *pl:* He works in another division. يِشتُغُل بقِسِم لاخ [yištuɣul bqisim la:x] • **2.** فِرقَة، فَرِيق [firqa, fari:q] فِرَق [firaq] *pl:* Ten divisions were destroyed. عَشِر فِرَق تدَمُّرَت [ʕašir firaq ddammurat] • **3.** قِسمَة [qisma] تَقسِيم [taqsi:m] تَقسِيمات، تَقاسِيم [taqsi:ma:t, taqa:si:m] *pl:* When are you going to learn division? شوَقِت راح تِتعَلَّم القِسمَة؟ [šwakit ra:ħ titʕallam ʔilqisma?]

divorce • **1.** طَلاق [ṭala:g] طَلاقات [ṭala:ga:t] *pl:* She's suing for divorce. قايمَة بدَعوَة طَلاق [ga:yma bdaʕwat ṭala:g]
 to divorce • **1.** طَلَّق [ṭallag, ṭallaq] تَطلِيق [taṭli:g] *vn:* تطَلَّق [ṭallag] *p:* It's been several years since he divorced his wife. صارلَه عِدَّة سَنَوات مِن طَلَّق مَرتَه [ṣa:rlah ʕiddat sanawa:t min ṭallag martah]

divorced • **1.** مطَلَّق [mṭallag] She's divorced. هِيَّ مطَلَّقَة [hiyya mṭalliga]
 *** He's divorced.** • **1.** هُوَّ كان مِتزَوِّج وطَلَّق [huwwa ča:n mitzawwaǰ wṭallag]

dizzy • **1.** دايخ [da:yix] I feel dizzy. آنِي دايخ [ʔa:ni da:yix] I feel dizzy. أشعُر بدُوخَة [ʔašʕur bdu:xa]

to do • **1.** سَوَّى [sawwa:] تَسوِيَة [taswiya] *vn: sv* i. عَمَل [ʕamal] عَملَة [ʕamla] *Feminine:* عَمَل [ʕamal] *vn: sv* i. Let him do it by himself. خَلِّي يسَوِّيها بنَفسَه [xalli ysawwi:ha bnafsah] What are we going to do now? شراح نسَوِّي هَسَّة؟ [šra:ħ nsawwi hassa?] Do it the way I do. سَوِّيها بالطَّرِيقَة اللِّي أسَوِّيها [sawwi:ha biṭṭari:qa ʔilli ʔasawwi:ha] I don't do things like that. آنِي ما أسَوِّي هِيكِي أشياء [ʔa:ni ma: ʔasawwi hi:či ʔašya:ʔ] • **2.** قام ب [qa:m b-] قِيام [qiya:m] *vn: sv* u. سَوَّى [sawwa:] *sv* i. He can't do this work because he has a hernia. ما يِقدَر يقُوم بهالشُّغُل لأنّ عِندَه فَتِق [ma: yigdar yqu:m bhaššuɣul liʔann ʕindah fatiq] Can I do anything for you? أقدَر أقُوملَك بأي خِدمَة؟ [ʔagdar ʔaqu:mlak bʔayy xidma?] • **3.** كَفَّى [kaffa:] كِفايَة [kifa:ya] *vn: sv* i. This meat will have to do for four people. هَاللَّحَم لازِم يكَفِّي لأربَع أشخاص [hallaħam la:zim ykaffi liʔarbaʕ ʔašxa:ṣ] That will do for now. هَذا يكَفِّي هَسَّة [ha:ða ykaffi hassa] • **4.** صِلَح [ṣilaħ] صَلاح [ṣala:ħ] *vn: sv* a. نِفَع [nifaʕ] نَفع [nafiʕ] *vn: sv* a. فاد [fa:d] فائِدَة [fa:ʔida] *vn: sv* i. This screwdriver won't do. هَالدَّرنَفِيس ما يِصلَح [haddarnafi:s ma: yiṣlaħ] • **5.** قِضَى [giða:] قَضِي [gaðy] *vn: sv* i. He did five years in jail. قِضَى خَمس سنِين بالسِّجِن [giða: xams sni:n bissiǰin] • **6.** خَصّ [xaṣṣ] *sv* u. That has nothing to do with the matter. هَذا ما يخُصّ المَوضُوع [ha:ða ma: yxuṣṣ ʔilmawðu:ʕ] That has nothing to do with the matter. هَذا ما إلَه عِلاقَة بالمَوضُوع [ha:ða ma: ʔilah ʕila:qa bilmawðu:ʕ] • **7.** طَلَّع [ṭallaʕ] تَطلِيع [taṭli:ʕ] *vn: sv* i. This car won't do more than forty miles per hour. هَالسَّيّارَة ما تطَلِّع غير أربَعِين مِيل بالسّاعَة [hassayya:ra ma: tṭaliʕ ɣayr ʔarbaʕi:n mi:l bissa:ʕa] • **8.** رَتَّب [rattab] تَرتِيب [tarti:b] *vn: sv* i. It takes her an hour to do her hair. يِنرادِلها ساعَة حَتَّى تِرَتِّب شَعَرها [yinra:dilha sa:ʕa ħatta trattib šaʕarha] • **9.** مِشَى [miša:] مَشِي [maši] *vn: sv* i. Your son is doing well in school this year. إبنَك ماشِي زين بِالمَدرَسَة هالسَّنَة [ʔibnak ma:ši zi:n bilmadrasa hassana] My tomato plants are doing well. الطَّماطَة مالتِي ماشيَة زين [ʔiṭṭama:ṭa ma:lti ma:šya zi:n]

*** He wears his hat just the way I do.** • **1.** يِلبَس شَفُقتَه تَماماً بِالشِكِل مِثِلما ألبَسها آني [yilbas šafuqtah tama:man biššikil miθilma: ʔalbasha ʔa:ni]

to do away with • **1.** تخَلَّص مِن [txallaṣ min] تخَلُّص [taxalluṣ] *vn: sv* a. They want to do away with most of the redtape. دَيرِيدُون يِتخَلّصُون مِن أكثَر الرُوتِينِيّات [dayri:du:n yitxallṣu:n min ʔakθar ʔilru:ti:niyya:t]

to do good • **1.** أحسَن [ʔaħsan] إحسان [ʔiħsa:n] *vn: sv* i. عَمَل [ʕamal] عَملَة [ʕamla] *Feminine:* عَمَل [ʕamal] *vn: sv* i. Our neighbor was well-known for his piety and doing good. جارنا كان مَشهُور بِالتَّقوَى وَالإحسان [ǰa:rna ča:n mašhu:r bittaqwa: wilʔiħsa:n] • **2.** فاد [fa:d] فائِدَة [fa:ʔida] *vn: sv* i. Complaining won't do you much good. الشَّكوَى ما راح إتفِيدَك هوايَة [ʔiššakwa: ma: ra:ħ tfi:dak hwa:ya] If you take a vacation, it will do you lots of good. لَو تاخُذ عُطلَة، تفِيدَك هوايَة [law ta:xuð ʕuṭla, tfi:dak hwa:ya]

to do harm • **1.** ضَرّ [ḍarr] Rerouting the traffic to the new street has done much harm to my business. تَغيِير المُرُور لِلشّارِع الجِّدِيد ضَرّ شُغلِي هوايَة [tayyi:r ʔilmuru:r lišša:riʕ ʔiǰǰidi:d ḍarr šuɣli hwa:ya] • **2.** أذَّى [ʔaðða:] إيذاء [ʔi:ða:ʔ] *vn: sv* i. His interference in our work has done us more harm than good. تَدَخُّلَه بِشُغُلنا أذانا أكثَر مِن ما فادنا [tadaxxulah bšuɣulna ʔaððа:na ʔakθar min ma: fa:dna]

to do in • **1.** قِتَل [kital] قَتِل [katil] *vn:* انقِتَل [ʔinkital] *p:* They did him in. قِتلَوه [kitlawh] Working in this heat has done me in. الشُّغُل بِهالحَرّ قِتَلنِي [ʔiššuɣul bhalħarr kitalni]

to do one's best • **1.** بِذَل جَهد [biðal ǰahid] بَذِل جَهد [baðil ǰahid] *vn: sv* i. I'll do my best to finish it on time. راح أبذِل جُهدِي حَتَّى أخَلّصها عالوَقِت [ra:ħ ʔabðil ǰuhdi ħatta ʔaxalliṣha ʕalwakit]

to do out of • **1.** سَوَّى ب [sawwa b-] *sv* i. He did me out of all my money. سَوّاها بِيّا وَأخَذ كُلّ فلُوسِي [sawwa:ha biyya wʔaxað kull flu:si]

to do without • **1.** إستَغنَى عَن [ʔistayna: ʕan] إستِغناء [ʔistiyna:ʔ] *vn: sv* i. Can you do without this pencil for a while? تِقدَر تِستَغنِي عَن هالقَلَم لِفَدّ فَترَة؟ [tigdar tistayni ʕan halqalam lfadd fatra?]

dock • **1.** رَصِيف مِيناء [raṣi:f mi:na:ʔ] أرصِفَة مِيناء [ʔarṣifat mi:na:ʔ] *pl:* I nearly fell off the dock. وُقَعِت مِن رَصِيف المِيناء إلّا شوَيَّة [wugaʕit min raṣi:f ʔilmi:na:ʔ ʔilla šwayya]

to dock • **1.** وَكَّى [wačča:] تُوكِّي، توكِيَة [tuwičči, tawčiya] *vn: sv* i. Where do most of the tugboats dock? وين توَجّي أكثَر الماطُورات بِبَغداد؟ [wi:n twačči ʔakθar ʔilma:ṭu:ra:t bibayda:d?] • **2.** رِسَى [risa:] رَسو [rasw] *vn:* إنرِسَى [ʔinrisa:] *p:* The ship will dock at Basra at seven o'clock. الباخِرَة راح تِرسِي بِالبَصرَة ساعَة سَبعَة [ʔilba:xira ra:ħ tirsi bilbaṣra sa:ʕa sabʕa] • **3.** إستَقطَع مِن [ʔistaqṭaʕ min] إستِقطاع [ʔistiqṭa:ʕ] *vn: sv* i. I was late 15 minutes, but they docked me an hour's wages. آني كِنِت مِتأخِّر بَسّ رُبُع ساعَة لَكِن إستَقطعَوا مِنّي أُجرَة ساعَة [ʔa:ni činit mitʔaxxir bass rubuʕ sa:ʕa la:kin ʔistaqṭiʕaw minni ʔuǰrat sa:ʕa]

doctor • **1.** طَبِيب [ṭabi:b] أطِبّاء [ʔaṭibba:ʔ] *pl:* دَكتُور [daktu:r, duktu:r] دَكاترَة [daka:tra] *pl:* Please send for a doctor. دِزّ عَلَى طَبِيب، مِن فَضلَك [dizz ʕala ṭabi:b, min faḍlak]

to doctor • **1.** طَبَّب [ṭabbab] تَطبِيب [taṭbi:b] *vn: sv* i. داوَى [da:wa:] مُداواة [muda:wa:t] *vn: sv* i. We doctored him ourselves. طَبَّبناه بنَفِسنا [ṭabbabna:h bnafisna]

doctorate • **1.** دِكتَورَة [diktu:ra] دِكتُورات [diktu:ra:t] *pl:* He has a doctorate. عِندَه دِكتُورَا [ʕindah diktu:ra]

document • **1.** وَثِيقَة [waθi:qa] وَثايِق [waθa:yiq] *pl:* مُستَنَد [mustanad] Do you have all the documents? عِندَك كُلّ الوَثايِق؟ [ʕindak kull ʔilwaθa:yiq?]

dodge • **1.** حِيلَة [ħi:la] حِيَل [ħiyal] *pl:* لِعبَة [liʕba] لِعبات، ألعاب، مَلاعِيب [liʕba:t, ʔalʕa:b, mala:ʕi:b] *pl:* What dodge has he thought of now? أيّ حِيلَة فَكَّر بِيها هَسَّة؟ [ʔayy ħi:la fakkar bi:ha hassa?]

to dodge • **1.** زاغ [za:ɣ] زاغات، زيغان [za:ɣa:t, zi:ɣa:n] *pl:* زَوغ [zawɣ] *vn: sv* u. تجَنَّب [dǰannab] تَجَنُّب، تجِنِّب [tajannub, tǰinnib] *vn: sv* a. If I hadn't dodged, he would have hit me. لَو ما أزُوغ مِنَّه، كان ضِرَبنِي [law ma: ʔazu:ɣ minnah, ča:n ḍirabni] • **2.** تمَلَّص [tmallaṣ] تَمَلُّص، تمِلِّص [tamalluṣ, tmilliṣ] *vn: sv* a. He tried to dodge the question. حاوَل يِتمَلَّص مِن السُّؤال [ħa:wal yitmallaṣ min ʔissuʔa:l]

dog • **1.** كَلِب [čalib, kalib] كلاب [čla:b, kla:b] *pl:* Take that dog out of here! وَخِّر هَالكَلِب مِن هنا [waxxir haččalib min hna]

*** He's going to the dogs.** • **1.** دَيدَمُّر نَفسَه بِيدَه [daydammur nafsah bi:dah]

dog-eared • **1.** مَثنِي [maθni] The pages are all dog-eared. الصَّفحات كُلّها مَثنِيَّة [ʔiṣṣafħa:t kullha maθniyya]

dogma • **1.** عَقِيدَة [ʕaqi:da] عَقائِد [ʕaqa:ʔid, ʕaqa:yid] *pl:*

dogmatic • **1.** مُتعَصُّب بِأفكارَه [mutʕaṣṣub biʔafka:rah] Our Arabic teacher is very dogmatic. مُدَرِّس العَرَبِي مالنَا مِتعَصِّب بِأفكارَه كُلِّش [mudarris ʔilʕarabi ma:lna mitʕaṣṣub bʔafka:rah kulliš]

doll • **1.** لَعّابَة [laʕʕa:ba] لَعّابات [laʕʕa:ba:t] *pl:* She likes to play with dolls. يعجِبها تِلعَب بِاللّعّابات [yiʕǰibha tilʕab bʔillaʕʕa:ba:t]

D

dollar • **1.** دُولار [dula:r] دُولارات [dulara:t] *pl:*

domestic • **1.** بَيتِي [bayti] She is studying to be a Domestic Science teacher. دَتِدرُس حَتَّى تكُون مُدَرِّسَة لِلفُنُون البَيتِيَّة [datidrus ħatta tku:n mudarrisa lilfunu:n ʔilbaytiyya] • **2.** مَحَلِّي [maħalli] وَطَنِي [waṭani] These are all domestic products. هَذِي كُلّها مُنتَجات وَطَنِيَّة [ha:ði kullha muntaǰa:t waṭaniyya] • **3.** بَيت [bayt] بيُوت [biyu:t] *pl:* It is hard to find domestic help these days. يِصعَب تِلقِي خَدّامِين بَيت هَالأَيّام [yiṣʕab tilgi xadda:mi:n bayt halʔayya:m]

domesticated • **1.** أَهلِي [ʔahli] داجِن [da:ǰin] دَواجِن [dawa:ǰin] *pl:* The chicken is a domesticated animal. الدِّجاج مِن الحَيوانات الأَهلِيَّة [ʔiddiǰa:ǰ min ʔilħaywa:na:t ʔilʔahliyya]

to donate • **1.** تبَرَّع ب [tbarraʕ bi-] تَبَرُّع [tabarruʕ] *vn: sv* a. I donated two dinars to the Red Crescent. تبَرَّعِت بدِينارَين لِلهِلال الأَحمَر [tbarraʕit bdina::rayn lilhila:l ʔilʔaħmar]

donation • **1.** تَبَرُّع [tabarruʕ] تَبَرُّعات [tabarruʕa:t] *pl:* Donations are welcome. باب التَّبَرُّعات مَفتُوح [ba:b ʔittabarruʕa:t maftu:ħ]

done • **1.** مسَوَّى [msawwa] مخَلِّص [mxalliṣ] خلصان [xalṣa:n] All my lessons are done. وَظايِفِي كُلّها مسَوّايَة [waðạ:yfi kullha msawwa:ya] • **2.** لاحِق [la:ħig] مِستُوِي [mistuwi] In ten minutes the meat will be done. بخِلال عَشِر دَقايِق اللَّحَم راح يكُون لاحِق [bxila:l ʕašir daqa:yiq ʔillaħam ra:ħ yku:n la:ħig]

done in • **1.** هَلكان [halka:n] مَنهُوك [manhu:k] I'm done in from working in this weather. آنِي هَلكان مِن الشُّغُل بهَالجَوّ [ʔa:ni halka:n min ʔiššuɣul bhalǰaww]

to be done for • **1.** اِنتِهَى أَمُر [ʔintiha: ʔamr-] اِنتِهاء أَمُر [ʔintiha:ʔ ʔamur] *vn: sv* i. If the boss finds this out I'm done for. إذا حَسّ بِيها الرَّئِيس، اِنتِهَى أَمرِي [ʔiða ħass bi:ha ʔirraʔi:s, ʔintiha: ʔamri] These tires are done for. هَالتّايرات مِنتِهِي أَمُرها [hatta:yira:t mintihi ʔamurha]

donkey • **1.** زمال [zma:l] زمايِل [zma:yil] *pl:* حمار [ħma:r] حمِير، حمايِر [ħami:r, ħma:yir] *pl:*

door • **1.** باب [ba:b] أَبواب، بِيبان [ʔabwa:b, bi:ba:n] *pl:* Please open the door. أَرجُوك فُكّ الباب [ʔarǰu:k fukk ʔilba:b]

doorbell • **1.** جَرَس باب [ǰaraṣ ba:b] أَجراس باب [ʔaǰra:ṣ ba:b] *pl:*

doorknob • **1.** يَدَّة باب [yadda ba:b] يَدّات باب [yadda:t ba:b] *pl:* قَبضَة باب [qabðạt ba:b] قَبضات باب [qabðạ:t ba:b] *pl:*

doorman • **1.** بَوّاب [bawwa:b] بَوّابِين [bawwa:bi:n] *pl:*

doorway • **1.** مَدخَل [madxal] مَداخِل [mada:xil] *pl:* Please don't stand in the doorway! رَجاءاً لا تُوقَف بالمَدخَل [raǰa:ʔan la: tu:gaf bilmadxal]

dope • **1.** مُخَدِّر [muxaddir] مُخَدِّرات [muxaddira:t] *pl:* He uses dope. يِستَعمِل مُخَدِّرات [yistaʕmil muxaddira:t]

dormitory • **1.** رَدهَة [radha] رَدهات [radha:t] *pl:*

dose • **1.** جُرعَة [ǰurʕa] جُرعات، جُرَع [ǰurʕa:t, ǰuraʕ] *pl:* That's too big a dose for a child. هَالجَّرعَة كُلّش كِبِيرَة لِلطِّفِل [haǰǰarʕa kulliš čibi:ra littifil] Take it in small doses. أُخُذها بجَرعات صغَيِّرَة [ʔuxuðha bǰarʕa:t ṣɣayyra]

dossier • **1.** ضبارَة [ðḅa:ra] ضبارات، أَضابِير [ðḅa:ra:t, ʔaðạ:bi:r] *pl:* مَلَفّ، مَلَفَّة [malaff, malaffa] مَلَفّات [malaffa:t] *pl:* فايِل [fa:yil] فايِلات [fa:yila:t] *pl:* Let me see Ali's dossier. خَلِّينِي أَشُوف اِضبارَة عَلِي [xalli:ni ʔašu:f ðba:rat ʕali]

dot • **1.** نُقطَة [nuqṭa] نُقَط [nuqaṭ] *pl:* Wear your dress with the blue dots. لِبسِي البَدلَة أُمّ النُّقَط الزَّرقَة [libsi ʔalbadla ʔumm ʔinnuqaṭ ʔizzarga] Add three dots. حُطّ ثلَث نُقَط [ħuṭṭ tlaθ nuqaṭ]

on the dot • **1.** بِالضَّبُط [biðḍðabuṭ] I'll see you at three on the dot. راح أَشُوفَك ساعَة ثلاثَة بِالضَّبُط [ra:ħ ʔašu:fak sa:ʕa tla:θa biðḍðabuṭ] • **2.** عَالمَوعِد [ʕalmawʕid] وَقِت [waqit, wakit] أَوقات [ʔawqa:t] *pl:* بالوَقِت [bilwakit] He came right on the dot. إجا عالوَقِت [ʔiǰa ʕalwakit]

double • **1.** دَبَل [dabal] ضُعُف [ðụʕuf] We got paid double today. اِستِلَمنا ضُعُف راتِب اليُوم [ʔistilamna ðụʕuf ra:tib ʔilyu:m] Bring me a double portion of ice cream. جِيبلِي دَبَل دوندرمَة [ǰi:bli dabal du:ndirma] It's double the size of mine. هَذِي ضُعُف الحَجم مالِي [ha:ði ðụʕuf ʔilħaǰim ma:li]

*** He could be your double.** • **1.** هُوَّ صُورَة طَبق الأَصِل مِنَّك [huwwa ṣu:ra ṭabq ʔilʔaṣil minnak]

to double • **1.** ضاعَف [ðạ:ʕaf] مُضاعَفَة [muðạ:ʕafa] *vn: sv* u. He doubled his capital in two years. ضاعَف راسماله بسَنتَين [ðạ:ʕaf ra:sma:lah bsantayn]

double-breasted • **1.** أَبُو سِراوَين [ʔabu: sirawayn] He wore a double-breasted suit. لِبَس قاط أَبُو سِراوَين [libas qa:ṭ ʔabu sirawayn]

doubles • **1.** زَوجِي [zawǰi] ثنَين ثنَين [θnayn θnayn] Let's play doubles. خَلِّي نِلعَب زَوجِي [xalli nilʕab zawǰi]

doubt • **1.** شَكّ [šakk] Do you have any doubts? عِندَك أَيّ شَكّ؟ [ʕindak ʔayy šakk?] Without a doubt he's the best man for the job. بدُون شَكّ هُوَّ أَحسَن واحِد لِلشَّغلَة [bidu:n šakk huwwa ʔaħsan wa:ħid liššaɣla]

in doubt • **1.** مَشكُوك ب [mašku:k b-] The result is still in doubt. النَّتِيجَة بَعَدها مَشكُوك بِيها [ʔinnati:ja baʕadha mašku:k bi:ha]

to doubt • **1.** شَكّ [šakk] شُكُوك [šuku:k] *pl:* شَكّ [šakk] *vn: sv* u. I doubt that the story is true. أشُكّ أن يكُون القُصَّة صَحِيحَة [ʔašukk ʔan yku:n ʔilquṣṣa ṣaḥi:ḥa] I don't doubt it in the least. آني أبَداً ما أشُكّ بِيها [ʔa:ni ʔabadan ma: ʔašukk bi:ha]

doubtful • **1.** مَشكُوك ب [mašku:k b-] It is doubtful if he'll get well. مَشكُوك بِيه أن يطِيب [mašku:k bi:h ʔan yṭi:b] • **2.** شاكِك بِـ [ša:kik bi-] I'm still doubtful about it. آني بَعَدنِي شاكِك بِيها [ʔa:ni baʕadni ša:kik bi:ha] I'm still doubtful about it. بَعَد عِندِي شَكّ بِيها [baʕad ʕindi šakk bi:ha]

dough • **1.** عَجِين [ʕaji:n] He put the dough in the oven. خَلَّى العَجِين بِالفِرِن [xalla: ʔilʕaji:n bilfirin]

down • **1.** رِيش ناعِم [ri:š na:ʕim] This pillow is filled with down. هالمِخَدَّة مَحَشّايَة رِيش ناعِم [halimxadda mḥašša:ya ri:š na:ʕim] • **2.** زَغَب [zaɣab] The chick is covered with down. فَرخ الدِّجاجَة مغَطَّى بِالزَّغَب [farx ʔiddija:ja mɣaṭṭa bizzaɣab] • **3.** جَوَّة [jawwa] Did you look down there? باوَعِت جَوَّة هناك؟ [ba:waʕit jawwa hna:k?]

*** Down with imperialism!** • **1.** يَسقُط الاِستِعمار [yasquṭ ʔilʔistiʕma:r]

to down • **1.** وَقَّع [waggaʕ] تَوقِيع [tawgi:ʕ] *vn:* توَقَّع [twaggaʕ] *p:* I downed the duck with one shot. وَقَّعِت البَطَّة بِفَدّ طَلقَة [waggaʕit ʔilbaṭṭa bfadd ṭalqa]

downgrade • **1.** اِنحِدار [ʔinḥida:r] The road has a steep downgrade. الطَّرِيق بِيه اِنحِدار شَدِيد [ʔiṭṭari:q bi:h ʔinḥida:r šadi:d]

downhearted • **1.** مَقهُور [maqhu:r] حَزِين [ḥazi:n] He looks downhearted. يبَيِّن عَليه مَقهُور [yibayyin ʕali:h maqhu:r]

downhill • **1.** مِنحِدِر [minḥadir, minḥidir] From here on the road is downhill all the way. مِن هِنا و هِيكِي الطَّرِيق مِنحِدِر عَلَى طُول [min hna whi:či ʔiṭṭari:q minḥidir ʕala ṭu:l]

down payment • **1.** مُقَدَّم [muqaddam] مُقَدَّمات [muqaddama:t] *pl:* عَرَبُون [ʕarabu:n] عَرابِين [ʕara:bi:n] *pl:* How much of a down payment can you make? شقَدّ تِقدَر تِدفَع مُقَدَّم؟ [šgadd tigdar tidfaʕ muqaddam?]

downpour • **1.** زَخّ [zaxx] We were caught in the downpour. لِزمَتنا الزَّخَّة [lizmatna ʔizzaxxa]

downstairs • **1.** جَوَّة [jawwa] I'll be waiting downstairs. راح أنتِظِر جَوَّة [ra:ḥ ʔantiðir jawwa]

*** He tripped and fell downstairs.** • **1.** عِثَر و وُقَع مِن الدَّرَج [ʕiθar wwugaʕ min ʔiddaraj]

downtown • **1.** *no equivalent* • * Let's go downtown. خَلِّي نِنزِل لِلوِلايَة [xalli: ninzil lilwila:ya] * Let's go downtown. خَلي نرُوح لِلسُّوق [xaly nru:ḥ lissu:g] * He's downtown right now. هُوَّ بالسُّوق هَسَّة [huwwa bissu:g hassa]

dowry • **1.** حَقّ [ḥagg] How much dowry did he pay her? شقَدّ دِفَع لَها حَقّ؟ [šgadd difaʕ lha ḥagg?]

to doze • **1.** أخَذ غَفوَة, أخَذ غَفيَة, أخَذ غَفَّة [ʔaxað ɣaffa, ʔaxað ɣafwa, ʔaxað ɣafya] غَفّات, غَفوات, غَفيات [ɣaffa:t, ɣafwa:t, ɣafya:t] *pl:* I've just been dozing. بَسّ كِنِت ماخِذ غَفوَة [bass činit ma:xið ɣafwa]

to doze off • **1.** غُفَى [ɣufa:] غَفِي [ɣafi] *vn: sv* i. He dozed off after supper. غُفَى وَرا العَشا [ɣufa: wara ʔilʕaša]

dozen • **1.** دَرزَن [darzan] دَرازِن [dara:zin] *pl:* Please give me a dozen eggs. بالله إنطِينِي دَرزَن بَيض [ballah ʔinṭi:ni darzan bayð]

draft • **1.** تَيّار هَوا [tayya:r hawa] تَيّارات هَوا [tayya:ra:t hawa] *pl:* I can't stand the draft in this room. ما أقدَر أتحَمَّل تَيّار الهَوا بهالغُرفَة [ma: ʔagdar ʔatḥammal tayya:r ʔilhawa bhalɣurfa] The fire went out because there wasn't enough draft. خُمدَت النّار لِأنّ ما كان أكُو تَيّار هَوا كافِي [xumdat ʔinna:r liʔann ma: ča:n ʔaku tayya:r hawa ka:fi] • **2.** مِفتاح هَوا [mifta:ḥ hawa] مَفاتِيح هَوا [mafa:ti:ḥ hawa] *pl:* Did you open the draft on the heater? فَكَّيت مِفتاح الهَوا بِالصُّوبَة؟ [fakki:t mifta:ḥ ʔilhawa bissu:ba?] • **3.** مِسوَدَّة [miswadda] مِسوَدّات [miswadda:t] *pl:* The first draft is ready. المِسوَدَّة الأُولَى حاضرَة [ʔilmiswadda ʔilʔu:la ḥa:ðra] • **4.** تَجنِيد [tajni:d] You have to report to the draft officer. لازِم تراجِع ضابُط التَّجنِيد [la:zim tra:jiʕ ða:buṭ ʔittajni:d]

to draft • **1.** أخَذ لِلجُندِيَّة [ʔaxað lijjundiyya] أخُذ لِالجُندِيَّة، [ʔaxuð lijjundiyya] *vn: sv* u. جَنَّد [jannad] تَجنِيد [tajni:d] *vn: sv* i. They drafted him last month. أخَذُوه لِلجُندِيَّة بِالشَّهر اللِّي فات [ʔaxðawh lijjundiyya biššahr ʔilli fa:t]

to drag • **1.** سِحَل [siḥal] سَحِل [saḥil] *vn:* اِنسِحَل [ʔinsiḥal] *p: sv* a. I had to drag the trunk into the house myself. اِضطَرِّيت أسحَل الصَّندُوق لِلبَيت بنَفسِي [ʔiðṭarri:t ʔasḥal ʔiṣṣandu:g lilbayt bnafsi] Your coat is dragging on the floor. قَبُّوطَك دَيِسحَل بِالقاع [qappu:ṭak dayisḥal bilga:ʕ] • **2.** مَرّ [marr] مَرّ [marr] *vn: sv* u. Time drags when you don't have anything to do. الوَقِت يمُرّ بِبُطُو مَن ما عِندَك شِي تسَوِّيه [ʔilwakit yumurr bbutuʔ lamman maː ʕindak ši tsawwiːh] • **3.** جَرّ [ǰarr] جَرّ [ǰarr] *vn: sv* u. He could hardly drag himself to work. بالمُوت يَالله يجُرّ نَفسَه لِلشُّغُل [bilmuːt yallah yǰurr nafsah liššuɣul]

to drag on • **1.** The meeting dragged on for three hours. الاجتِماع تمَطمَط ثلَث ساعات [ʔilʔiǰtimaːʕ ʔitmaṭmaṭ tlaθ saːʕaːt]

D

dragon • **1.** تِنّين [tinniːn] تَنانِين [tananiːn] *pl:*

drain • **1.** بَلُّوعَة [balluːʕa] بَلالِيع [balaːliːʕ] *pl:* The drain is stopped up again. البَلُّوعَة اِنسَدَّت مَرَّة لُخ [ʔilballuːʕa ʔinsaddat marra lux]

to drain • **1.** فَرَّغ [farraɣ] تَفرِيغ [tafriːɣ] *vn:* تفرَّغ [tfarraɣ] *p:* They drained the swimming pool only yesterday. بَسّ البارحَة فَرّغوا ماي المَسبَح [bass ʔilbaːrħa farrɣaw maːy ʔilmasbaħ]

to drain off • **1.** تصَرَّف [tṣarraf] تَصَرُّف [taṣarruf] *vn: sv* a. The water doesn't drain off quickly. المَيّ ما دَيِتصَرَّف بسُرعَة [ʔilmayy maː dayitṣarraf bsurʕa]

drastic • **1.** صارِم [ṣaːrim] شَدِيد [šadiːd] The government took drastic measures. الحُكُومَة اِتّخذَت إجراءات صارِمَة [ʔilħukuːma ʔittixðat ʔiǰraːʔaːt ṣaːrima]

to draw • **1.** رِسَم [risam] رَسِم [rasim] *vn:* اِنرِسَم [ʔinrisam] *p:* He likes to draw pictures of animals. يحِبّ يرسِم صُوَر حَيوانات [yħibb yirsim ṣuwar ħaywaːnaːt] • **2.** سِحَب [siħab] سَحِب [saħib] *vn:* اِنسِحَب [ʔinsiħab] *p: sv* a. He drew the winning number in the lottery. سِحَب الرَّقَم الرّابح باليانَصِيب [siħab ʔirraqam ʔirraːbiħ bilyanaṣiːb] • **3.** جِذَب [ǰiðab] جَذِب [ǰaðib] *vn:* اِنجِذَب [ʔinǰiðab] *p:* The concert is sure to draw a big crowd. أكِيد الحَفلَة المُوسِيقِيَّة راح تِجذِب جَمهُور كِبِير [ʔakiːd ʔilħafla ʔilmuwsiːqiyya raːħ tiǰðib ǰamhuːr čabiːr] • **4.** طَبّ [ṭabb] طَبّ [ṭabb] *vn: sv* u. The train is just drawing into the station. القِطار هَسَّة دَيطُبّ لِلمَحَطَّة [ʔilqiṭaːr hassa dayṭubb lilmaħaṭṭa] • **5.** جَرّ [ǰarr] جَرّ [ǰarr] *vn:* انجَرّ [ʔinǰarr] *p:* حِشَر [ħišar] حَشِر [ħašir] *vn:* اِنحِشَر [ʔinħišar] *p:* I was drawn into this argument against my will. اِنحِشَرت لِهالمُجادَلَة ضِدّ رَغُبتي [ʔinħišarit lihalmuǰaːdala ðidd raɣubti]

to draw conclusions • **1.** اِستَنتَج [ʔistantaǰ] اِستِنتاج [ʔistintaːǰ] *vn: sv* i. اِستَخلَص [ʔistaxlaṣ] اِستِخلاص [ʔistixlaːṣ] *vn: sv* i. Draw whatever conclusions you want to. اِستَنتِج شما ترِيد [ʔistantiǰ šmaː triːd]

to draw in • **1.** جَرّ [ǰarr] جَرّ [ǰarr] *vn:* اِنجَرّ [ʔinǰarr] *p:* Draw in your breath. جُرّ النَّفَس [ǰurr ʔinnafis] • **2.** قَلَّص [qallaṣ] تقَلُّص، تقلِيص [tqulluṣ, taqliːṣ] *vn: sv* i. Draw in your stomach. قَلِّص بَطنَك [qalliṣ baṭnak]

to draw out • **1.** سِحَب [siħab] سَحِب [saħib] *vn:* اِنسِحَب [ʔinsiħab] *p:* I'll have to draw out fifty dinars from the bank. لازِم أسحَب خَمسِين دِينار مِن البَنك [laːzim ʔasħab xamsiːn dinaːr min ʔilbank] • **2.** اِستَدرَج [ʔistadraǰ] اِستِدراج [ʔistidraːǰ] *vn: sv* i. See if you can draw him out. جَرُّب تِستَدرِجَه [ǰarrub tistadriǰah]

to draw up • **1.** وُضَع [wuðaʕ] وَضِع [waðiʕ] *vn:* انوُضَع [ʔinwuðaʕ] *p: sv* a. Who drew up the plan for your house? مِنُو وُضَع خُطَّة بَيتَك؟ [minu wuðaʕ xuṭṭat baytak?] I'm going to draw up the report. آنِي راح أوضَع التَّقرِير [ʔaːni raːħ ʔuːðaʕ ʔittaqriːr]

drawer • **1.** مجَرّ [mǰarr] مَجَرّات [maǰarraːt] *pl:* دُرُج [duruǰ] You'll find it in the top drawer. تِلقِيه بِالمَجَرّ الفَوقانِي [tilgiːh bilmaǰarr ʔilfugaːni]

drawn • **1.** مَنهُوك [manhuːk] His face looks drawn. يبَيِّن عَلَى وِجَّه مَنهُوك [yibayyin ʕala wiččah manhuːk]

dread • **1.** خَوف [xawf] خِشيَة [xišya] I have a dread of doctors. عِندِي خَوف مِن الأطِبّاء [ʕindi xawf min ʔilʔaṭibbaːʔ]

to dread • **1.** خاف [xaːf] خَوف [xawf] *vn: sv* a. خِشَى [xišaː] خَشِي [xašy] *vn: sv* a. I dread the dark. أخاف مِن الظُّلمَة [ʔaxaːf min ʔiððalma]

dreadful • **1.** فَظِيع [faðiːʕ] مُرِيع [muriːʕ] She wears dreadful clothes. تِلبَس هدُوم فَظِيعَة [tilbas hiduːm faðiːʕa] That was a dreadful accident. هَذِي كانَت حادِثَة مُرِيعَة [haːði čaːnat ħaːdiθa muriːʕa]

dream • **1.** حِلِم [ħilim] أحلام [ʔaħlaːm] *pl:* I had a strange dream last night. شِفِت حِلِم غَرِيب لَيلَة البارحَة [šifit ħilim ɣariːb laylat ʔilbaːrħa]

to dream • **1.** حِلَم [ħilam] حَلِم [ħalim] *vn: sv* a. Last night I dreamed that I was home. حِلَمِت آنِي كِنِت بِبَيتِي البارحَة بالليل [ħilamit ʔaːni činit bibayti ʔilbaːrħa billayl]

*** I wouldn't dream of doing it.**

• **1.** ما أتصَوَّر أقُوم بِيها حَتَّى بمَنامِي [maː ʔatṣawwar ʔaguːm biːha ħattaː bmanaːmi]

dreary • **1.** كَئِيب [kaʔiːb] It was an awfully dreary day. كان فَدّ نَهار كُلِّش كَئِيب [čaːn fadd nahaːr kulliš kaʔiːb]

dredge • **1.** حَفّارَة [ħaffaːra] حَفّارات [ħaffaːraːt] *pl:* The dredge is being repaired right now. الحَفّارَة دَتِتصَلَّح هَسَّة [ʔilħaffaːra datitṣallaħ hassa]

to dredge • **1.** كِرَى [kiraː] كَري [kary] *vn:* انكِرَى [ʔinkiraː] *p:* After the flood they had to dredge the river. بَعَد الفَيَضان اِضطَرّوا يكرُون النَّهَر [baʕad ʔilfayaðaːn ʔiðṭarraw yikruːn ʔinnahar]

dress • **1.** نَفنُوف [nafnuːf] نَفانِيف [nafaːniːf] *pl:* She wants to buy a new dress. ترِيد تِشتِري نَفنُوف جِدِيد [triːd tištiri nafnuːf ǰidiːd]

to dress • **1.** لِبَس [libas] لِبِس [libis] *vn:* اِنلِبَس [ʔinlibas] *p:* I'll dress quickly. راح ألبَس بِالعَجَل [raːħ ʔalbas bilʕaǰal] He's always well dressed. دائِماً لابِس زين [daːʔiman laːbis ziːn] He's always well dressed.

دائماً يِلبَس زين [da:ʔiman yilbas zi:n] • **2.** لَبَّس [labbas] تَلبيس [talbi:s] *vn: sv* i. Mother is dressing the baby. أُمِّي دَتلَبِّس الطِّفِل [ʔummi datlabbis ʔiṭṭifil] • **3.** ضَمَّد [ðammad] تَضميد [taðmi:d] *vn: sv* i. Did you dress the wound? ضَمَّدت الجَّرِح؟ [ðammadt ʔijjariħ?]

to dress up • **1.** كِشَخ [kišax] كَشِخ [kašix] *vn: sv* a. Look at him, all dressed up. شُوفَه شلُون كاشِخ [šu:fah šlu:n ka:šix]

dresser • **1.** دِيلاب [di:la:b] دُولاب [du:la:b] دواليب [dwa:li:b] *pl:* The handkerchiefs are in the dresser. الكِفافِي بالدِّيلاب [ʔiččifa:fi biddi:la:b] • **2.** مُضَمِّد [muðammid] مُضَمِّدين [muðammidi:n] *pl:* The doctor looked at my injuries and told the dresser to treat them. الطَّبيب كِشَف عالجُّرُوح مالتي وَخَلَّى المُضَمِّد يعالِجها [ʔiṭṭabi:b kišaf ʕajjuru:ħ ma:lti wxalla: ʔilmuðammid yʕa:lijha]

dressing • **1.** ضَماد [ðama:d] ضَمادات [ðama:da:t] *pl:* شَداد شداد [šada:d, šda:d] شدادات [šada:da:t, šda:da:t] *pl:* لَفّاف [laffa:f] لَفّافات [laffa:fa:t] *pl:* The nurse changes his dressings every morning. المُمَرِّضَة تبَدِّل ضَمّاداتَه كُلّ يوم الصُّبُح [ʔilmumarriða tbaddil ðamma:da:tah kull yu:m ʔiṣṣubuħ]

dressing gown • **1.** بُرنُص [burnuṣ] بَرانِص [bara:niṣ] *pl:* رُوب [ru:b] إرواب، روابَة [ʔirwa:b, rwa:ba] *pl:*

dressing table • **1.** مَيز توالَيت [mayz twa:li:t] ميُوزت توالَيت [myu:zit twa:li:t] *pl:*

dressmaker • **1.** خَيّاطَة [xayya:ṭa] خَيّاطات [xayya:ṭa:t] *pl:*

dried • **1.** يابِس [ya:bis] Buy me a kilo of dried beans. اِشتِرِيلِي كِيلُو فاصُولِيّا يابسَة [ʔištiri:li ki:lu fa:ṣu:liyya: ya:bsa]

to drift • **1.** سَيَّس [sayyas] تَسيِيس [tasyi:s] *vn: sv* i. They cut the motor and let the boat drift. وَقِّفوا المُحَرِّك وخَلّوا الماطُور يسَيِّس [waggifaw ʔilmuħarrik wxallaw ʔilma:ṭu:r ysayyis]

drill • **1.** مِزرَف [mizraf] مَزارُف [maza:ruf] *pl:* The mechanic needs another drill. المِيكانِيكي يِحتاج مِزرَف لاخ [ʔilmi:ka:ni:ki yiħta:j mizaraf la:x] I just bought a new set of drills. هَسَّة اِشترَيت طَخُم جِديد مَزارِف جِديد [hassa ʔištiri:t ṭaxum maza:rif jidi:d] • **2.** تَمرين [tamri:n] تَمرينات، تَمارين [tamri:na:t, tama:ri:n] *pl:* There are two drills on this rule on the fifth page. أكُو تَمارِين إثنَين عَلَى هَالقاعِدَة بالصَّفحَة الخامِسَة [ʔaku tama:ri:n ʔiθnayn ʕala halqa:ʕida biṣṣafħa ʔilxa:misa] • **3.** تَدرِيب [tadri:b] I was late for drill today and they gave me extra duty. تأَخَّرت عَن التَّدرِيب اليُوم وَإنطُونِي واجِب إضافِي [tʔaxxarit ʕan ʔittadri:b ʔilyu:m wʔinṭu:ni wa:jib ʔiða:fi]

to drill • **1.** زِرَف [ziraf] زَرُف [zaruf] *vn:* اِنزِرَف [ʔinziraf] *p:* سَوَّى [sawwa:] تَسوِيَة [taswiya] *vn: sv* i. Drill a hole in the beam. سَوِّي زُرُف بِالشِّيلمانَة [sawwi zuruf bišši:lma:na] • **2.** حُفَر [ħufar] حَفُر [ħafur] *vn:* اِنحُفَر [ʔinħufar] *p:* The dentist had to drill the tooth. طَبِيب الأَسنان اِضطَرّ يحفُر السِّنّ [ṭabi:b ʔilʔasna:n ʔiðṭarr yiħfur ʔissinn] • **3.** حَفَّظ [ħaffað] تَحفِيظ [taħfi:ð] *vn: sv* i. The teacher drilled us in the multiplication table. المُعَلِّم حَفَّظنا جَدوَل الضَّرُب [ʔilmuʕallim ħaffaðna jadwal ʔiððarub] • **4.** مَرَّن [marran] تَمرِين [tamri:n] *vn:* تمَرَّن [tmarran] *p:* دَرَّب [darrab] تَدرِيب [tadri:b] *vn:* تدَرَّب [tdarrab] *p:* The soldiers drill every day. الجِّنُود يِتمَرَّنُون كُلّ يوم [ʔijjinu:d yitmarranu:n kull yu:m]

drink • **1.** مَشرُوب [mašru:b] مَشارِيب [maša:ri:b] *pl:* Lemonade is a refreshing summer drink. اللَّيمُون مَشرُوب صَيفِي مُنعِش [ʔillaymu:n mašru:b ṣi:fi munʕiš] What kind of drinks have you got? يا نُوع مِن المَشرُوبات عِندَك؟ [ya: nu:ʕ min ʔilmašru:ba:t ʕindak?] • **2.** جُرعَة [jurʕa] جُرعات، جُرَع [jurʕa:t, juraʕ] *pl:* جِرَّع [jirraʕ] جُرعات [jurʕa:t] *pl:* قُمُع [gumuʕ] قمُوع [gmu:ʕ] *pl:* He's choking, give him a drink of water. دَيختِنِق، إنطِيه جُرعَة ماي [dayixtinig, ʔinṭi:h jurʕat ma:y] • **3.** شوَيَّة [šwayya] May I have a drink of water. تِسمَحلِي بشوَيَّة مَيّ [tismaħli bšwayyat mayy]

to drink • **1.** شِرَب [širab] شُرُب [šurub] *vn:* اِنشِرَب [ʔinširab] *p: sv* a. Drink plenty of water! إشرَب هوايَة مَيّ [ʔišrab hwa:ya mayy] Let's drink to your return. خَلِّي نِشرَب عَلَى شَرَف رُجُوعَك [xalli: nišrab ʕala šaraf ruju:ʕak]

to drip • **1.** نَقَّط [naggaṭ] نَقُوط [nagu:ṭ] *vn: sv* u. Let it drip dry. خَلِّيه يِنقُط لَمّا يِنشَف [xalli:h yinguṭ lamma yinšaf] • **2.** نَقَّط [naggaṭ] تنِقُّط [tniggut] *vn: sv* i. The faucet is dripping. الحَنَفِيَّة دَتنِقِّط [ʔilħanafiyya datnaggiṭ]

drive • **1.** حَملَة [ħamla] حَملات [ħamla:t] *pl:* We raised five thousand dinars in the last drive. جِمَعنا خَمسَة آلاف دِينار بالحَملَة الأَخِيرَة [jimaʕna xamsat ʔa:la:f dina:r bilħamla ʔilʔaxi:ra]

*** We took a drive.** • **1.** طلَعنا بالسَّيّارَة [ṭlaʕna bissayya:ra]

to drive • **1.** ساق [sa:q] سِياقَة [siya:qa] *vn:* اِنساق [ʔinsa:q] *p:* Can you drive a truck? تِقدَر تسُوق لوري؟ [tigdar tsu:q lawri?] • **2.** ساق [sa:g] سِياقَة [siya:ga] *vn:* اِنساق [ʔinsa:g] *p:* Drive the sheep to the pasture. سُوق الغَنَم لِلمَرعَى [su:g ʔilγanam lilmarʕa] • **3.** دِفَع [difaʕ] دَفِع [dafiʕ] *vn:* اِندِفَع [ʔindifaʕ] *p: sv* a. Hunger drove him to stealing. الجُّوع دِفَعَه لِلبُوق [ʔijju:ʕ difaʕah lilbu:g] • **4.** حَثّ [ħaθθ] حَثّ [ħaθθ] *vn: sv* i. The foreman drives his workers continually. رَئِيس العُمّال يحِثّ عُمّالَه عالعَمَل بِاستِمرار [raʔi:s ʔilʕumma:l yħiθθ ʕumma:lah ʕalʕamal biʔistimra:r] • **5.** دَقّ [dagg] دَقّ [dagg] *vn:* اِندَقّ [ʔindagg] *p:* Drive the nail into the wall. دُقّ البِسمار بِالحايِط [dugg ʔilbisma:r bilħa:yiṭ]

*** What are you driving at? • 1.** شتُقصُد؟ [štuqṣud?] / شتِعنِي؟ [štiʕni?]

to drive away • 1. طِرَد [ṭirad] طَرِد [ṭarid] *vn:* اِنطِرَد [ʔinṭirad] *p:* بِعَد [biʕad] بَعِد [baʕid] *vn:* اِنبِعَد [ʔinbiʕad] *p:* Drive the dog away. إبعِد الكَلِب [ʔibʕid ʔiččalib]

to drive crazy • 1. خَبَّل [xabbal] تخُبُّل [txubbul] *vn:* تخَبَّل [txabbal] *p:* You'll drive me crazy. راح تخَبُّلنِي [ra:ħ txabbulni]

to drive off • 1. حاد عَن [ħa:d ʕan] حَيد [ħayd] *vn:* اِنحاد [ʔinħa:d] *p:* The boat was driven off its course by the wind. المَركَب اِنحاد عَن اِتِّجاهَه بِسَبَب الرِّياح [ʔilmarkab ʔinħa:d ʕan ʔittija:hah bsabab ʔirriya:ħ]

driver • 1. سايِق [sa:yiq] سُوّاق [suwwa:q] *pl:* He's a good driver. هُوَّ خُوش سايِق [huwwa xu:š sa:yiq] **• 2.** عَرَبَنجِي [ʕarabanči] عَرَبَنجِيَّة [ʕarabančiyya] *pl:* The driver lost control of his horses. العَرَبَنجِي فُقَد السَّيطَرَة عَلَى خيُولَه [ʔilʕarabanči fuqad ʔissayṭara ʕala xyu:lah]

driving license • 1. إجازَة سِياقَة [ʔija:zat siya:qa] إجازات سِياقَة [ʔija:za:t siya:qa] *pl:* Let me see your driving license. خَلِّي أشُوف إجازَة سِياقتَك [xalli ʔašu:f ʔija:zat siya:qtak]

to drizzle • 1. نَثّ [naθθ] نَثّ [naθθ] *vn: sv* i. نَفّ [naff] نَفّ [naff] *vn: sv* i. It's been drizzling all day. صارِلها تنِثّ النَّهار كُلَّه [ṣa:rilha tniθθ ʔinnaha:r kullah]

to droop • 1. ذُوى [ðuwa:] ذَوِي [ðawy] vn: sv a. ذِبَل [ðibal] ذَبِل [ðabil] *vn: sv* a. The flowers are beginning to droop. الوَرِد بِدا يِذبَل [ʔilwarid bida: yiðbal] The flower is drooping. الوَرِد ذاوِي [ʔilwarid ða:wi]

drooping • 1. مهَدِّل [mhaddil] راخِي [ra:xi] He has drooping shoulders. كتافَه مهَدِّلَة [čta:fah mhaddila]

drop • 1. قَطرَة [qaṭra, gaṭra] قَطرات [qaṭra:t, gaṭra:t] *pl:* نُقطَة [nuqṭa] نُقَط [nuqaṭ] *pl:* Put three drops in a glass of water. حُطّ ثلَث قَطرات بِكلاص مَيّ [ħuṭṭ tlaθ qaṭra:t bigla:ṣ mayy]

to drop • 1. وُقَع [wugaʕ] وُقُوع [wugu:ʕ] *vn: sv* a. The box dropped out of the window. الصَّندُوق وُقعَت مِن الشِّبّاك [ʔiṣṣandu:g wugʕat min ʔiššibba:č] Some of them dropped from exhaustion. بَعَضهُم وُقعَوا مِن التَّعَب [baʕaðhum wugʕaw min ʔittaʕab] **• 2.** وَقَّع [waggaʕ] تَوقِيع [tawgi:ʕ] *vn:* توَقَّع [twaggaʕ] *p:* You dropped something. وَقَّعِت شِي [waggaʕit ši] **• 3.** نِزَل [nizal] نُزُول [nuzu:l] *vn: sv* i. اِنخُفَض [ʔinxufað] اِنخِفاض [ʔinxifa:ð] *vn: sv* u. The temperature dropped very rapidly. دَرَجَة الحَرارَة نِزلَت بِسُرعَة [darajat ʔilħara:ra nizlat bsurʕa] **• 4.** تِرَك [tirak] تَرِك [tarik] *vn:* اِنتِرَك [ʔintirak] *p:* هِمَل [himal] إهمال [ʔihma:l] *vn:* اِنهِمَل [ʔinhimal] *p:* Let's drop the subject. خَلِّي نِترُك المَوضُوع [xalli: nitruk ʔilmawðu:ʕ] **• 5.** نَزَّل [nazzal] تَنزِيل [tanzi:l] *vn:* تنَزَّل [tnazzal] *p:* Please drop me at the corner. رَجاءاً نَزِّلنِي بِاللَّوفَة [raja:ʔan nazzilni billawfa] **• 6.** طِرَد [ṭirad] طَرِد [ṭarid] *vn:* اِنطِرَد [ʔinṭirad] *p:* طِلَع [ṭilaʕ] طُلُوع [ṭulu:ʕ] *vn:* اِنطِلَع [ʔinṭilaʕ] *p: sv* a. I'll be dropped from the club. راح أنطِرِد مِن النّادِي [ra:ħ ʔanṭirid min ʔinna:di] **• 7.** ذَبّ [ðabb] ذَبّ [ðabb] *vn:* اِنذَبّ [ʔinðabb] *p:* Please drop this card in the mail box. رَجاءاً ذِبّ هَالكارت بِصَندُوق البَرِيد [raja:ʔan ðibb halka:rt biṣandu:g ʔilbari:d]

to drop a hint • 1. لَمَّح [lammaħ] تَلمِيح [talmi:ħ] *vn: sv* i. She dropped a hint to me that she wanted to go. لَمّحَتلِي هِيَّ ترِيد ترُوح [lammħatli hiyya tri:d tru:ħ]

to drop in • 1. مَرّ [marr] مَرّ [marr] *vn: sv* u. Drop in sometime. مُرّ فَدّ يوم [murr fadd yu:m]

drought • 1. جَفاف [jafa:f] The drought hurt the crop very much. الجَّفاف هوايَة أذَى الحاصِل [ʔijjafa:f hwa:ya ʔaðða: ʔilħa:ṣil]

drove • 1. قَطِيع [qaṭi:ʕ] قِطعان [qiṭʕa:n] *pl:* We waited for the drove of sheep to pass. اِنتِظَرنا حَتَّى يمُرّ قَطِيع الغَنَم [ʔintiðarna ħatta yumurr qaṭi:ʕ ʔilɣanam] **• 2.** جَماعَة [jama:ʕa] جَماعات [jama:ʕa:t] *pl:* People came in droves. النّاس إجَوا بِجَماعات [ʔinna:s ʔijaw bjama:ʕa:t]

to drown • 1. غِرَق [ɣirag] غَرِق [ɣarig] *vn: sv* a. He drowned in the river. غِرَق بِالشَّطّ [ɣirag biššaṭṭ] **• 2.** غَرَّق [ɣarrag] تَغرِيق [taɣri:g] *vn: sv* i. She had to drown the kittens. اِضطَرَّت تغَرِّق البَزازِين الصغار [ʔiðṭarrat tɣarrig ʔilbiza:zi:n ʔiṣṣiɣa:r]

to drown out • 1. طِغَى عَلَى [ṭiɣa: ʕala] طَغِي، طُغيان [ṭaɣy, ṭuɣya:n] *vn: sv* i. The noise drowned out his remarks. الهُوسَة طِغَى عَلَى صَوتَه [ʔilhu:sa ṭiɣat ʕala ṣawtah]

drowsy • 1. نَعسان [naʕsa:n] I feel drowsy. دَأحِسّ نَعسان [daʔaħiss naʕsa:n]

drug • 1. دُوا [duwa] أدوِيَة [ʔadwiya] *pl:* This drug is sold only on prescription. هَالدُّوا ما يِنباع إلّا بوَصفَه [hadduwa: ma: yinba:ʕ ʔilla bwaṣfa] **• 2.** مُخَدِّر [muxaddir] مُخَدِّرات [muxaddira:t] *pl:* He became addicted to drugs. صار مُدمِن عالمُخَدِّرات [ṣa:r mudmin ʕalmuxaddira:t]

drugstore • 1. صَيدَلِي [ṣaydali] صَيادِلَة [ṣaya:dila] *pl:* Where is the nearest drugstore? وِين أقرَب صَيدَلِيَّة؟ [wi:n ʔaqrab ṣaydaliyya?]

drum • 1. طَبُل [ṭabul] طبُول [ṭubu:l] *pl:* دُنبُك [dunbug; dumbug] دَنابُك [dana:bug] *pl:* Can you hear the sound of the drums? تِقدَر تِسمَع حِسّ الطُّبُول؟ [tigdar tismaʕ ħiss ʔiṭṭubu:l?] • **2.** بَرمِيل [barmi:l] بَرامِيل [bara:mi:l] *pl:* بِيب [pi:p] بياب [pya:p] *pl:* They unloaded six drums of kerosene. فَرّغوا سِتّ بَرامِيل نَفُط [farrɣaw sitt bara:mi:l nafuṭ]

to drum • **1.** دَقّ [dagg] دَقّ [dagg] *vn: sv* u. Please stop drumming on the table. باللّه بَسّ عاد تدُقّ عالميز [ballah bass ʕa:d tdugg ʕalmi:z]

drunk • **1.** سَكران [sakra:n] سكارَة [ska:ra] *pl:* Was that drunk annoying you? كان دَيزعجك هَالسَّكران؟ [ča:n dayizʕjič hassakra:n?] He's dead drunk; if you pull on him, he won't feel a thing. سَكران طِينَة؛ إذا تجُرَّه ما يحِسّ [sakra:n ṭi:na; ʔiða dǰurrah ma: yħiss]

to get drunk • **1.** سِكَر [sikar] سُكُر [sukur] *vn: sv* a. He got drunk at her birthday party. سِكَر بِحَفلَة عِيد مِيلادها [sikar bħaflat ʕi:d mi:la:dha]

dry • **1.** ناشِف [na:šif] يابِس [ya:bis] جافّ [ǰa:ff] Is the wash dry yet? الغَسِيل ناشِف لَو بَعَد؟ [ʔilɣasi:l na:šif law baʕad?] My throat is dry. زَردُومِي يابِس [zardu:mi ya:bis] My throat is dry. رِيقِي ناشِف [ri:gi na:šif] The well is dry. البِير ناشف [ʔilbi:r na:šf] • **2.** جافّ [ǰa:ff] It has been a dry summer. كان صَيف جافّ [ča:n ṣayf ǰa:ff] The lecture was so dry, I walked out. آنِي طلَعِت مِن وَقِت لِأَنّ المُحاضَرَة كانَت كُلِّش جافَّة [ʔa:ni ṭlaʕit min wakit liʔann ʔilmuħa:ðara ča:nat kulliš ǰa:ffa] • **3.** يابِس [ya:bis] Let's gather some dry wood. خَلِّي نِجمَع شوَيَّة حَطَب يابِس [xalli niǰmaʕ šwayya ħaṭab ya:bis]

to dry • **1.** يبَس [yibas] يباس [yiba:s] *vn: sv* a. نِشَف [nišaf] نَشِف [našif] *vn: sv* a. جَفّ [ǰaff] جَفاف [ǰafa:f] *vn: sv* i. The paint dries in five hours. الصُّبُغ يِنشَف بِخَمِس ساعات [ʔiṣṣubuɣ yinšaf bxamis sa:ʕa:t] • **2.** نَشَّف [naššaf] تَنشِيف [tanši:f] *vn: sv* i. Who's going to dry the dishes? مِنُو راح ينَشِّف المواعِين؟ [minu ra:ħ ynaššif ʔilmwa:ʕi:n?] Dry yourself well. نَشِّف نَفسَك زين [naššif nafsak zi:n]

to dry up • **1.** جَفّ [ǰaff] جَفاف [ǰafa:f] *vn: sv* i. يبَس [yibas] يباس [yiba:s] *vn: sv* a. نِشَف [nišaf] نَشِف [našif] *vn: sv* a. Every summer this stream dries up. كُلّ صَيف هَالمَجرَة يِنشَف [kull ṣayf halmaǰra yinšaf]

dry cleaner • **1.** مُكَوِّي [mukawwi] مُكَوِّيِّين [mukawwiyyi:n] *pl:* I sent your gray suit to the dry cleaner. دَزَّيت قاطَك الرَّمادِي لِلمُكَوِّي [dazzi:t qa:ṭak ʔirruma:di lilmukawwi]

dual • **1.** مُثَنَّى [muθanna] ثُنائِي [θuna:ʔi]

duck • **1.** بَطَّى [baṭṭa:] بَطّ [baṭṭ] *Collective:* We're having roast duck for dinner. عَشانا لَحَم بَطّ مَشوِي [ʕaša:na laħam baṭṭ mašwi]

to duck • **1.** نَصَّى [naṣṣa:] تنِصِّي، تَنصِيَة [tniṣṣi, tanṣiya] *vn: sv* i. حِنَى [ħina:] حَنِي [ħany] *vn:* اِنحِنَى [ʔinħina:] قِطَف [giṭaf] قَطُف [gaṭuf] *vn: sv* i. He ducked his head. نَصَّى راسَه [naṣṣa: ra:sah] • **2.** غِطَس [ɣiṭas] غَطِس [ɣaṭis] *vn: sv* u. غَطّ [ɣaṭṭ] غَطّ [ɣaṭṭ] *vn: sv* u. The duck ducked under the water. البَطَّة غِطسَت بِالمَيّ [ʔilbaṭṭa ɣiṭsat bilmayy] • **3.** غَطَّس [ɣaṭṭas] تغِطِّس، تَغطِيس [tɣiṭṭis, taɣṭi:s] *vn: sv* i. غَطَّط [ɣaṭṭaṭ] تغِطِّط [tɣiṭṭiṭ] *vn: sv* i. He ducked his brother's head under the water. غَطَّس راس أَخُوه بِالمَيّ [ɣaṭṭas ra:s ʔaxu:h bilmayy]

due • **1.** حَقّ [ħaqq, ħagg] حُقُوق [ħuqu:q, ħugu:g] *pl:* That's his due. هَذا حَقَّه [ha:ða ħaqqah]

*** He's due to arrive at ten.** • **1.** مُنتَظَر عَشرَة ساعَة عَشرَة [muntaðar wuṣu:lah sa:ʕa ʕašra]

due to • **1.** بسَبَب [bsabab] بنَتِيجَة [b nati:ǰa] Due to an oversight, she wasn't invited. ما اِنعِزمَت بِسَبَب سَهو [ma: ʔinʕizmat bisabab sahw] That was due to a mistake. صار بنَتِيجَة غَلطَة [ṣa:r bnati:ǰat ɣalṭa]

to be due • **1.** اِستَحَقّ [ʔistaħaqq] اِستِحقاق [ʔistiħqa:q] *vn: sv* i. The rent is due next Monday. الإيجار مِستِحِقّ الإثنَين الجّاي [ʔilʔi:ǰa:r mistiħiqq ʔilʔiθnayn ʔiǰǰa:y]

duel • **1.** صِراع [ṣira:ʕ] مُبارَزَة [muba:raza] مُبارَزات [muba:raza:t] *pl:*

dues • **1.** بَدَل [badal] I pay membership dues every month. آنِي أَدفَع بَدَلات الاشتِراك كُلّ شَهَر [ʔa:ni ʔadfaʕ badala:t ʔalʔištira:k kull šahar]

dull • **1.** أعمِي، أَعمَى [ʔaʕmi, ʔaʕma:] أَعمَى [ʔaʕma] عِمِي، عِميان، عِمِيِّن [ʕimi, ʕimya:n, ʕimiyyi:n] *pl:* عَمِيَة [ʕamya] *Feminine:* This knife is dull. هَالسِّكِّينَة عَمِيَة [hassičči:na ʕamya] • **2.** بَلِيد [bali:d] بَلِيدِين، بُلَداء [bali:di:n, bulada:ʔ] *pl:* He's terribly dull. هُوَّ كُلِّش بَلِيد [huwwa kulliš bali:d] • **3.** ثَقِيل [θagi:l] I feel a dull pain in my side. أَشعُر بوَجَع ثَقِيل بِصَفُحتِي [ʔašʕur bwaǰaʕ θaqi:l bṣafuħti] • **4.** شاحِب [ša:ħib] She likes dull colors. تعِجبها الألوان الشّاحبَة [tiʕǰibha ʔilʔalwa:n ʔišša:ħba]

dumb • **1.** أَخرَس [ʔaxras] خُرُس، خِرسان [xurus, xirsa:n] *pl:* خَرسَة [xarsa] *Feminine:* He's deaf and dumb. هُوَّ أَطرَش وَأَخرَس [huwwa ʔaṭraš wʔaxras] • **2.** غَبِي [ɣabi] أَغبِياء [ʔaɣbiya:ʔ] *pl:* بَلِيد [bali:d] بَلِيدِين، بُلَداء [bali:di:n, bulada:ʔ] *pl:* دَماغسِز [dama:ɣsizz] دَماغسِزِّيَّة [dama:ɣsizziyya] *pl:* He's too dumb to notice. هَالغَبِي ما يلاحِظ [halɣabi ma: yla:ħið]

to strike dumb • **1.** ذِهَل [ðihal] ذَهِل [ðahil] *vn:* اِنذِهَل [ʔinðihal] *p:* لِجَم [liǰam] لَجِم [laǰim] *vn:* اِنلِجَم [ʔinliǰam] *p:* We were struck dumb when we heard the news. نذِهَلنا لَمَّن سِمَعنا الخَبَر [nðihalna lamman simaʕna ʔilxabar]

dumbfounded • **1.** مَذهُول [maðhu:l] I was dumfounded when I heard it. صِرِت مَذهُول لَمَّن سِمَعِت بِيها [ṣirit maðhu:l lamman simaʕit bi:ha]

dump • **1.** مَزبَلَة [mazbala] مَزابِل [maza:bil] *pl:* Where's the dump? وِين المَزبَلَة؟ [wi:n ʔilmazbala?]

*** Their house is an awful dump.**
• **1.** بَيتهُم كُلَّش مخَربَط [baythum kulliš mxarbaṭ]

down in the dumps • **1.** مَقبُوض النَفِس [maqbu:ð̣ ʔinnafis] I've been down in the dumps all day. كِنِت مَقبُوض النَّفِس طُول النَّهار [činit maqbu:ð̣ ʔinnafis ṭu:l ʔinnaha:r] I've been down in the dumps all day. نَفسِي كانَت مَقبُوضَة طُول النَّهار [nafsi ča:nat maqbu:ð̣a ṭu:l ʔinnaha:r]

to dump • **1.** ذَبّ [ðabb] ذَبّ [ðabb] *vn:* اِنذَبّ [ʔinðabb] *p:* Don't dump the sand in front of the door. لا تذِبّ الرَّمُل قِدّام الباب [la: dðibb ʔirramul gidda:m ʔilba:b] Don't dump the coffee grounds in the sink. لا تذِبّ التِّلِف مال القَهوَة بِحَلق المَغسَل [la: dðibb ʔittilif ma:l ʔilgahwa bħalg ʔilmaɣsal]

dumpy • **1.** مدَحدَح [mdaħdaħ] She has a dumpy figure. عِدها جِسِم مدَحدَح [ʕidha ǰisim mdaħdaħ]

dune • **1.** كَثِيب [kaθi:b] كُثبان [kuθba:n] *pl:* The sand dunes extend for miles. كُثبان الرَّمُل تِمتَدّ لِبِعِد أميال [kuθba:n ʔirramul timtadd libiʕid ʔamya:l]

dung • **1.** دِمِن [dimin] Do you use chemical fertilizer or dung in your garden? تِستَعمِل سَماد كِيمياوِي لَو دِمِن بِحَدِيقتَك؟ [tistaʕmil sama:d ki:mya:wi law dimin bħadi:qtak?]

duplicate • **1.** نُسخَة [nusxa] نُسَخ [nusax] *pl:* You need a duplicate of your birth certificate. تِحتاج نُسخَة لِشَهادَة مِيلادَك [tiħta:ǰ nusxa liššaha:dat mi:la:dak]

to duplicate • **1.** اِستَنسَخ [ʔistansax] اِستِنساخ [ʔistinsa:x] *vn: sv* i. I'll have the secretary duplicate them for you. راح أخَلِّي السِّكِرتَيرَة تِستَنسِخهُم إلَك [ra:ħ ʔaxalli ʔissikirti:ra tistansixhum ʔilak]

duplication • **1.** اِزدِواج [ʔizdiwa:ǰ] اِزدِواجات [ʔizdiwa:ǰa:t] *pl:* We must avoid duplication in the work. لازِم نِتحاشَى الازدِواج بِالشُّغُل [la:zim nitħa:ša: ʔilʔizdiwa:ǰ biššuɣul]

to be durable • **1.** داوَم [da:wam] دَوام [dawa:m] *vn: sv* u. These tires are cheap but they are not durable. هَالتّايَرات رخِيصَة لَكِن ما تداوُم [hatta:yira:t rxi:ṣa la:kin ma: dda:wum]

during • **1.** أثناء [ʔaθna:ʔ] خِلال [xila:l] I met him during the war. عِرَفتَه خِلال الحَرُب [ʕiraftah xila:l ʔilħarub]

dust • **1.** غُبار [ɣuba:r] تراب [tra:b] تُربان [turba:n] *pl:* عَجاج [ʕaǰa:ǰ] There's a heavy layer of dust on the table. أكُو طَبَقَة ثِخِينَة مِن الغُبار عالميز [ʔaku ṭabaqa θixi:na min ʔilɣuba:r ʕalmayz]

to dust • **1.** نَفَّض مِن العَجاج [naffað̣ min ʔilʕaǰa:ǰ] تَنفِيض مِن العَجاج [tanfi:ð̣ min ʔilʕaǰa:ǰ] *vn: sv* u. Please dust my desk. أرجُوك نَفُّض مِيزِي مِن العَجاج [ʔarǰu:k naffuð̣ mayzi min ʔilʕaǰa:ǰ] • **2.** رَشّ [rašš] رَشّ [rašš] *vn: sv* u. They dusted a chemical substance on the cotton fields by plane. رَشّوا مَوادّ كِيمياوِيَّة عَلَى حُقُول القُطِن مِن الطَّيّارَة [raššaw mawa:dd ki:mya:wiyya ʕala ħuqu:l ʔilguṭin min ʔiṭṭayya:ra]

dust storm • **1.** عَجاج [ʕaǰa:ǰ]

Dutch • **1.** هَولَندِي [hulandi] هَولَندِيِّين [hulandiyyi:n] *pl:*

duty • **1.** واجِب [wa:ǰib] It was his duty to support his parents. أصبَح مِن واجبَه أن يعِيل أُمَّه وأبُوه [ʔaṣbaħ min wa:ǰbah ʔan yʕi:l ʔummah wʔabu:h] Answering the phone is one of my duties. الإجابَة عالتَّلِفُون مِن واجِباتِي [ʔilʔiǰa:ba ʕattalifu:n min wa:ǰiba:ti] I'm on duty all night. آنِي بِالواجِب طُول اللَّيل [ʔa:ni bilwa:ǰib ṭu:l ʔillayl] I'm on duty all night. آنِي خَفارَة طُول اللَّيل [ʔa:ni xafa:ra ṭu:l ʔillayl] • **2.** جُمرُك [gumrug] جَمارِك [gama:rig] *pl:* رسُوم جُمرُكِيَّة [rsu:m gumrugiyya] I paid 300 dinars duty on it. دِفَعِت ثلَث مِيَّة دِينار جُمرُك عَلِيه [difaʕit tlaθ miyyat dina:r gumrug ʕali:h]

to dwell • **1.** عاش [ʕa:š] عَيش [ʕayš] *vn:* اِنعاش [ʔinʕa:š] *p:* The Bedouins dwell in the desert most of the year. البَدو يعِيشُون بِالبَرّ مُعظَم السَّنَة [ʔilbadw yʕi:šu:n bilbarr muʕð̣am ʔissana] • **2.** اِستَمَرّ [ʔistamarr] اِستِمرار [ʔistimra:r] *vn: sv* i. There's no point in dwelling on this subject any longer. ماكُو داعِي نِستِمِرّ بِالمَوضُوع أكثَر [ma:ku da:ʕi nistimirr bilmawð̣u:ʕ ʔakθar]

dye • **1.** صُبُغ [ṣubuɣ] أصباغ [ʔaṣba:ɣ] *pl:*

to dye • **1.** صُبَغ [ṣubaɣ] صُبُغ [ṣubuɣ] *vn: sv* u. I dyed my blue dress with black dye. صبَغِت نَفنُوفِي الأزرَق بِصُبُغ أسوَد [ṣbaɣit nafnu:fi ʔilʔazrag bṣubuɣ ʔaswad]

dynamic • **1.** نَشِط [našiṭ] حَرِك [ħarik] He's a dynamic businessman. هُوَّ رَجُل أعمال نَشِط [huwwa raǰul ʔaʕma:l našiṭ]

dysentery • **1.** دِزَنتَرِي [dizantari]

E

each • **1.** كُلّ [kull] Each one of us received a pack of cigarettes. كُلّ واحِد مِن عِدنا أَخَذ باكَيت جِكايِر [kull waːħid min ʕidna ʔaxað paːkiːt ǰigaːyir] He comes here each week. يِجِي هنا كُلّ إسبُوع [yiǰi hnaː kull ʔisbuːʕ] Give one to each child. إنطِي وِحدَة لكُلّ جاهِل [ʔinṭi wiħda likull ǰaːhil] • **2.** واحِد [waːħid] وِحدَة [wiħda] *Feminine:* These apples are ten fils each. هَالتِّفّاح الوِحدَة بعَشِر فلُوس [hattiffaːħ ʔilwiħda bʕašr fl uːs]

each and every one • **1.** جَمِيع [ǰamiːʕ] You can count on each and every one of us. تِقدَر تِعتِمِد عَلَى جَمِيعنا [tigdar tiʕtimid ʕala ǰamiːʕna]

each other • **1.** واحِد إلّلاخ [waːħid ʔillaːx] بَعَضهُم بَعَض [baʕaðhum baʕað] They see each other every day. يشُوفُون واحِد اللّاخ كُلّ يوم [yšuːfuːn waːħid ʔillaːx kull yuːm] They have nothing to do with each other. ما إلهُم لِزُوم واحِد بِاللّاخ [maː ʔilhum lizuːm waːħid billaːx] • **2.** (sometimes expressed in sixth form of verb) They've been writing to each other for a year. كانَوا يِتراسلُون لِمُدَّة سَنَة [čaːnaw yitraːsluːn lmuddat sana] They're not talking to each other. ما يِتحاكُون [maː yitħaːčuːn]

eager • **1.** مِشتاق [mištaːq, mištaːg] مِتشَوِّق [mitšawwiq] I am eager to meet your friend. آنِي مِشتاق أتعَرَّف بِصَدِيقَك [ʔaːni mištaːq ʔatʕarraf bṣadiːqak]

eagle • **1.** نِسِر [nisir] نسُور [nsuːr] *pl:*

ear • **1.** إذِن [ʔiðin] إذان [ʔiðaːn] إذان، إذانات [ʔiðaːna t] *pl:* She's deaf in her right ear. إذِنها اليِمنَى طَرشَة [ʔiðinha ʔilyimnaː ṭarša] I have no ear for music. ما عِندِي إذِن مُوسِيقِيَّة [maː ʕindi ʔiðin musiːqiyya] • **2.** عَرنُوس [ʕarnuːs] عَرانِيس [ʕaraːniːs] *pl:* Make popcorn out of these ears of corn. سَوِّي شامِيَّة مِن عَرانِيس الإذرَة هَذِي [sawwi šaːmiyya min ʕaraːniːs ʔilʔiðra haːði] • **3.** سُنبُلَة [sunbula, sumbula] سَنابِل [sanaːbil] *pl:* This ear of wheat has fifty grains on it. سُنبُلَة الحُنطَة بِيها خَمسِين حَبَّة [sunbulat ʔilħunṭa biːha xamsiːn ħabba]

*** He's up to his ears in debt.** • **1.** طامُس بِالدَّين إلَى راسَه [ṭaːmus biddayn ʔilaː raːsah]

earlier • **1.** قَبُل [gabul, qabil] Come earlier than usual. تَعال قَبِل المُعتاد [taʕaːl gabil ʔilmuʕtaːd]

earliest • **1.** أَوَّل [ʔawwal] أوائِل [ʔawaːʔil] *pl:* The earliest immigrants came from Europe. أوائِل المُهاجِرِين إجَوا مِن أورُبّا [ʔawaːʔil ʔilmuhaːǰiriːn ʔiǰaw min ʔuːruppa] • **2.** أقدَم [ʔaqdam] He is one of the earliest advocates of this idea. هُوَّ مِن أقدَم دُعاة هَالفِكرَة [huwwa min ʔaqdam duʕaːt halfikra]

early • **1.** مِن وَقِت [min wakit] عَلَى وَقِت [ʕala wakit] Please wake me up early. أرجُوك قَعِّدنِي مِن وَقِت [ʔarǰuːk gaʕʕidni min wakit] • **2.** عاجِل [ʕaːǰil] سَرِيع [sariːʕ] We expect an early reply. نِتوَقَّع جَواب عاجِل [nitwaqqaʕ ǰawaːb ʕaːǰil] • **3.** مُبَكِّر [mubakkir] She got married at an early age. تزَوّجَت بعُمُر مُبَكِّر [dzawwǰat bʕumur mubakkir]

*** He will arrive early next month.**

• **1.** راح يَوصَل بأوائِل الشَّهر الجاي [raːħ yawṣal biʔawaːʔil ʔiššahr ʔiǰǰaːy]

to earmark • **1.** خَصَّص [xaṣṣaṣ] تَخصِيص [taxṣiːṣ] *vn:* تخَصَّص [txaṣṣaṣ] *p:* We earmarked two million dinars for the new bridge. خَصَّصنا مِليُونَين دِينار لِلجِّسِر الجِّدِيد [xaṣṣaṣna milyuːnayn dinaːr lijǰisir ʔiǰǰidiːd]

to earn • **1.** حَصَّل [ħaṣṣal] تَحصِيل [taħṣiːl] *vn:* تحَصَّل [tħaṣṣal] *p:* طَلَّع [ṭallaʕ] تَطلِيع [taṭliːʕ] *vn:* تطَلَّع [ʔiṭṭallaʕ] *p:* How much do you earn a week? شقَدّ تحَصِّل بالإسبُوع؟ [šgadd tħaṣṣil bilʔisbuːʕ?] She earns her living as a dressmaker. تطَلِّع عِيشَتها مِن الخِياطَة [tṭalliʕ ʕiːšatha min ʔilxyaːṭa] • **2.** اِكتِسَب [ʔiktisab] اِكتِساب [ʔiktisaːb] *vn: sv* i. He earned his reputation the hard way. اِكتِسَب شُهرتَه بشَقّ الأنفس [ʔiktisab šuhurtah bšaqq ʔilʔanfus] • **3.** كِسَب [kisab] كَسِب [kasib] *vn:* اِنكِسَب [ʔinkisab] *p:* His conduct earned him universal respect. تَصَرُّفاتَه كِسبَتلَه اِحتِرام الجَّمِيع [taṣarrufaːtah kisbatlah ʔiħtiraːm ʔiǰǰamiːʕ]

earnings • **1.** مَحصُول [maħṣuːl] مَحاصِيل [maħaːṣiːl] *pl:* مَكسَب [maksab] مَكاسِب [makaːsib] *pl:*

earrings • **1.** تِرجِيَّة [tirčiyya] تراجِي [taraːči] *pl:* She bought a new pair of earrings. اِشتِرَت زوج تَراجِي جِدِيدَة [ʔištirat zuːǰ taraːči ǰidiːda]

earth • **1.** دِنيا [dinya] عالَم [ʕaːlam] عِلّام، عُلَمَة [ʕillaːm, ʕulama] *pl:* أرض [ʔarð̣] أراضِي [ʔaraːð̣iː] *pl:* Nothing on earth can save him. ماكُو شِي بِالدِّنيا يخَلّصَه [maːku ši biddinya yxallṣah] • **2.** أرض [ʔarð̣] أراضِي [ʔaraːð̣iː] *pl:* The earth is a sphere. الأرض كُرَوِيَّة [ʔilʔarð̣ kurawiyya] • **3.** تراب [traːb] This ditch has to be filled with earth. هَالنُّقرَة لازِم تِندِفِن بتراب [hannugra laːzim tindifin bitraːb]

*** There is nothing like it on the face of the earth.**

• **1.** هَذا ماكُو مِنَّه عَلَى وَجه البَسِيطَة [haːða maːku minnah ʕala waǰh ʔilbasiːṭa]

*** He is very down to earth.** • **1.** هَذا كُلِّش واقِعِي [haːða kulliš waːqiʕi]

earthquake • **1.** زِلزال [zilzaːl] زَلازِل [zalaːzil] *pl:* The earthquake destroyed twenty houses. الزِّلزال دَمَّر عِشرِين بَيت [ʔizzilzaːl dammar ʕišriːn bayt]

ease • **1.** سُهُولَة [suhuːla] بَساطَة [basaːṭa] Did you notice the ease with which he does things? لاحَظِت شلُون يسَوِّي الأشياء بسُهُولَة؟ [laːħaðit šluːn ysawwi ʔilʔašyaːʔ bsuhuːla?]

at ease • **1.** مِرتاح [mirtaːħ] I never feel quite at ease when I'm with her. أَبَداً ما أشعُر مِرتاح مِن أكُون ويّاها [ʔabadan maː ʔašʕur mirtaːħ min ʔakuːn wiyyaːha]

*** At ease!** • **1.** اِستَرِيح [ʔistariːħ]

to ease • **1.** خَفَّف [xaffaf] تَخفِيف [taxfiːf] *vn:* تخَفَّف [txaffaf] *p:* This medicine will ease the pain. هَالدُّوا يخَفُّف الوُجَع [hadduwa yxaffuf ʔilwuǰaʕ] • **2.** هَوَّن [hawwan] تَهوِين [tahwiːn] *vn:* تهَوَّن [thawwan] *p:* Nothing will ease my grief. ماكُو شِي يهَوِّن قَهري [maːku ši yhawwin qahri]

*** We have to ease the box through the narrow door.** • **1.** لازِم نفَوِّت الصَّندُوق عَلَى كَيفنا مِن الباب الضَّيِّق [laːzim ʔinfawwit ʔiṣṣanduːg ʕala kiːfna min ʔilbaːb ʔiððayyig]

to ease up • **1.** خَفّ [xaff] خِفَّة [xiffa] *vn:* *sv* u. قَلّ [qall] قِلَّة [qilla] *vn:* *sv* i. The pressure is beginning to ease up. الضَّغِط بِدا يخُفّ [ʔiððagiṭ bidaː yxuff]

easily • **1.** بسُهُولَة [bishuːla] ببَساطَة [bibasaːṭa] He did it easily. سَوّاها بسُهُولَة [sawwaːha bsuhuːla] This can easily be believed. هاي تِتصَدَّق بسُهُولَة [haːy titṣaddag bsuhuːla]

east • **1.** شَرق [šarq] The arrow points east. السَّهم يأشِّر لِلشَّرق [ʔissahim yiʔaššir liššarq] • **2.** شَرقِي [šarqi,šargi,šarǰi] It's an east wind. الهَوا شَرقِي [ʔilhawa šargi]

the Far East • **1.** الشَرق الأقصَى [ʔiššarq ʔilʔaqṣa]

the Middle East • **1.** الشَرق الأوسَط [ʔiššarq ʔilʔawsaṭ]

the Near East • **1.** الشَرق الأدنَى [ʔiššarq ʔilʔadna]

Easter • **1.** عِيد القِيامَة [ʕiːd ʔilqiyaːma] عِيد الفُصِح [ʕiːd ʔilfuṣiħ] Easter comes early this year. عِيد القِيامَة يِجِي مِن وَقِت هالسَّنَة [ʕiːd ʔilqiyaːma yiǰi min wakit hassana]

eastern • **1.** شَرقِي [šarqi] I know the eastern part very well. أعرُف القِسم الشَّرقِي كُلِّش زين [ʔaʕruf ʔilqism ʔiššarqi kulliš ziːn]

easy • **1.** سَهل [sahil] بَسِيط [basiːṭ] بَسِيطِين [basiːṭiːn] *pl:* That was an easy question. ذاك كان سُؤال سَهل [ðaːk čaːn suʔaːl sahil]

*** Take it easy, don't get mad.** • **1.** عَلَى كَيفَك، لا تِزعَل [ʕala kiːfak, laː tizʕal] يَواش، لا تِزعَل [yawaːš, laː tizʕal]

easy-going • **1.** مِتساهِل [mitsaːhil] He's an easy-going fellow. هُوَّ فَدّ واحِد مِتساهِل [huwwa fadd waːħid mitsaːhil]

to eat • **1.** أكَل [ʔakal] أكِل [ʔakil] *vn:* إنأكَل [ʔinʔakal] *p:* I haven't eaten a thing in two days. صارلِي يومَين ما أكَلت شِي [ṣaːrli yawmayn maː ʔakalt ši] He walked in just as we sat down to eat. طَبّ مِن قِعَدنا ناكُل [ṭabb min giʕadna naːkul] • **2.** زِرَف [ziraf] زَرُف [zaruf] *vn:* *sv* u. The acid ate three holes in my pants. الحامُض زِرَف ثلَث زرُوف بِالبَنطَرُون مالِي [ʔilħaːmuð ziraf tlaθ zruːf bilpanṭaruːn maːli]

to eat out • **1.** أكَل، زِرَف [ʔakal, ʔakal barra, ziraf] *sv* u. زِرَف [ziraf] *sv* u. Rust ate out the bottom of the pan. الزِّنجار أكَل كَعب الجِّدِر [ʔizzinǰaːr ʔakal čaʕb ʔiǰǰidir] • **2.** أكَل [ʔakal] *sv* u. Why don't we eat out tonight? لِيش ما ناكُل بَرَّة هاللَّيلَة؟ [liːš maː naːkul barra hallayla?]

echo • **1.** صَدَى [ṣadaː] أصداء [ʔaṣdaːʔ] *pl:* If you listen you can hear the echo. إذا تِتصَنَّت تِقدَر تِسمَع الصَّدَى [ʔiða titṣannat tigdar tismaʕ ʔiṣṣada]

to echo • **1.** نِطَى [niṭaː] *sv* i. The sound of the shot echoed through the hills. صُوت الطَّلقَة نِطَى صَدَى بين التِّلال [ṣuːt ʔiṭṭalqa niṭaː ṣadaː bayn ʔittilaːl] • **2.** رَدَّد [raddad] تَردِيد [tardiːd] *vn:* *sv* i. Stop echoing every word he says. بَسّ عاد تِرَدِّد كُلّ كِلمَة يقُولها [bass ʕaːd traddid kull čilma yguːlha]

eclipse • **1.** خُسُوف [xusuːf, xisuːf] There will be a partial lunar eclipse tomorrow night. راح يصِير خُسُوف جُزئِي باكِر باللَّيل [raːħ yṣiːr xusuːf ǰuzʔi baːčir billayl] • **2.** كُسُوف [kusuːf] We watched the solar eclipse from the top of the building. شِفنا الكُسُوف مِن سَطِح البِنايَة [šifna ʔilkusuːf min saṭiħ ʔilbinaːya]

to eclipse • **1.** طِغَى عَلَى [ṭiɣaː ʕala] طُغيان [ṭuɣyaːn] *vn:* *sv* a. She eclipsed everybody else at the party. طِغَت عَلَى كُلّ الباقيات بِالحَفلَة [ṭiɣat ʕala kull ʔilbaːqyaːt bilħafla]

to be eclipsed • **1.** خِسَف [xisaf] خُسُوف [xusuːf] *vn:* *sv* i. The moon will be eclipsed tonight. القُمَر راح يخسِف هاللَّيلَة [ʔilgumar raːħ yixsif hallayla] • **2.** كِسَف [kisaf] كُسُوف [kusuːf] *vn:* *sv* i. Don't forget that the sun will be eclipsed this afternoon. لا تِنسَى الشَّمِس راح تِكسِف هَالعَصرِيَّة [laː tinsaː ʔiššamis raːħ tiksif halʕaṣriyya]

economic • **1.** اِقتِصادِي [ʔiqtiṣaːdi] Their economic situation is improving. حالَتهُم الاقتِصادِيَّة دَتِتحَسَّن [ħaːlathum ʔilʔiqtiṣaːdiyya datitħassan]

economical • **1.** مِقتِصِد [miqtiṣid] مدَبَّر [mdabbar] She's a very economical woman. هاي فَدّ مَرَة كُلِّش مِقتَصِدَة [haːy fadd mara kulliš miqtaṣida] • **2.** اِقتِصادِي [ʔiqtiṣaːdi] This car is very economical. هَالسَّيّارَة كُلِّش اِقتِصادِيَّة [hassayyaːra kulliš ʔiqtiṣaːdiyya]

economics • **1.** اِقتِصاد [ʔiqtiṣaːd] He's studying economics. دَيِدرُس اِقتِصاد [dayidrus ʔiqtiṣaːd]

to economize • **1.** اِقتِصَد [ʔiqtiṣad] اِقتِصاد [ʔiqtiṣa:d] *vn: sv* i. She economizes in household expenditures. هِيَّ تِقتِصِد بمَصارِيف البَيت [hiyya tiqtiṣid bmaṣa:ri:f ʔilbayt]

edge • **1.** طَرَف [ṭaraf] أَطراف [ʔaṭra:f] *pl:* He lives at the edge of town. يِسكُن بطَرَف الوِلايَة [yiskun bṭaraf ʔilwila:ya] • **2.** حاشِيَة [ħa:šiya] حَواشِي [ħawa:ši] *pl:* Don't put the glass real close to the edge. لا تحُطّ الكلاص كُلِّش قَرِيب لِلحاشيَة [la: tħuṭṭ ʔilgla:ṣ kulliš qari:b lilħa:šya] • **3.** حَدّ [ħadd] The knife's edge is dull. حَدّ السِّكِّينَة أَعمَى [ħadd ʔissičči:na ʔaʕma] • **4.** أَفضَلِيَّة [ʔafðaliyya] He has the edge on me. إِلَه الأفضَلِيَّة عَلَيّا [ʔilah ʔilʔafðaliyya ʕalayya]

on edge • **1.** مِحتَدّ [miħtadd] She's on edge today. هِيَّ مِحتَدَّة اليُوم [hiyya miħtadda ʔilyu:m]

edible • **1.** صالِح لِلأَكِل [ṣa:liħ lilʔakil] Is this edible? هَذا صالِح لِلأَكِل؟ [ha:ða ṣa:liħ lilʔakil?]

to edit • **1.** حَرَّر [ħarrar] تَحرِير [taħri:r] *vn:* تحَرَّر [tħarrar] *p:* He has been editing this magazine for several years. صارلَه عِدَّة سنِين يحَرِّر هالمَجَلَّة [ṣa:rlah ʕiddat sni:n yħarrir halmaǰalla]

edition • **1.** طَبعَة [ṭabʕa] طَبعات [ṭabʕa:t] *pl:* عَدَد [ʕadad] أَعداد [ʔaʕda:d] *pl:* Have you seen the new edition of his book? شِفت الطَّبعَة الجِّدِيدَة مِن كِتابَه؟ [šift ʔiṭṭabʕa ʔiǰǰidi:da min kita:bah?]

editor • **1.** مُحَرِّر [muħarrir] مُحَرِّرِين [muħarriri:n] *pl:* My brother has just become editor of our local newspaper. أَخُويَا هَستَوَّة صار مُحَرِّر جَرِيدَتنا المَحَلِّيَّة [ʔaxu:ya hastawwa ṣa:r muħarrir ǰari:datna ʔilmaħalliyya]

editorial • **1.** مَقال اِفتِتاحِي [maqa:l ʔiftita:ħi] مَقالات اِفتِتاحِيَّة [maqa:la:t ʔiftita:ħiyya] *pl:* Did you read the editorial? قرِيت المَقال الافتِتاحِي؟ [qiri:t ʔilmaqa:l ʔilʔiftita:ħi?]

editor-in-chief • **1.** رَئِيس التَّحرِير [raʔi:s ʔittaħri:r] رُؤَساء تَحرِير [ruʔasa:ʔ taħri:r] *pl:* You have to see the editor-in-chief about this. لازِم تراجِع رَئِيس التَّحرِير حَول هَذا [la:zim tra:ǰiʕ raʔi:s ʔittaħri:r ħawil ha:ða]

to educate • **1.** عَلَّم [ʕallam] تَعلِيم [taʕli:m] *vn:* تعَلَّم [tʕallam] *p:* We have to educate our children to tolerance. لازِم نعَلِّم أَطفالنا عالتَّسامُح [la:zim nʕallim ʔaṭfa:lna ʕattasa:muħ] • **2.** ثَقَّف [θaqqaf] تَثقِيف [taθqi:f] *vn:* تثَقَّف [tθaqqaf] عَلَّم [ʕallam] *sv* i.We need many more teachers to educate the masses. مِحتاجِين هوايَة بَعَد مُعَلِّمِين لِتَثقِيف أَبناء الشَّعب [miħta:ǰi:n hwa:ya baʕad muʕallimi:n litaθqi:f ʔabna:ʔ ʔiššaʕab]

educated • **1.** مُثَقَّف [muθaqqaf] مِتعَلِّم [mitʕallim] مِتعَلِّمِين [mitʕallimi:n] *pl:* He's an educated person. هَذا شَخِص مُثَقَّف [ha:ða šaxiṣ muθaqqaf]

education • **1.** ثَقافَة [θaqa:fa] تَعلِيم [taʕli:m] Her parents neglected her education. أَهَلها هِملَوا ثَقافَتها [ʔahalha himlaw θaqa:fatha] • **2.** دِراسَة [dira:sa] تَعلِيم [taʕli:m] تَحصِيل [taħṣi:l] تَحصِيلات [taħṣi:la:t] *pl:* I completed my education in England. كَمَّلِت دِراستِي بِإنكِلتَرا [kammalit dira:sti bʔingiltara] • **3.** تَربِيَة [tarbiya] He has an M. A. in education. عِندَه ماجِستِير بِالتَّربِيَة [ʕindah ma:ǰisti:r bittarbiya]

ministry of education • **1.** وِزارَة المَعارِف [wiza:rat ʔilmaʕa:rif]

educational • **1.** دِراسِي [dira:si] The new law provides many educational opportunities. القانُون الجِّدِيد يهَيِّئ فُرَص دِراسِيَّة هوايَة [ʔilqa:nu:n ʔiǰǰidi:d yhayyiʔ furaṣ dira:siyya hwa:ya]

effect • **1.** تَأثِير [taʔθi:r] His appeal produced the desired effect. اِستِغاثتَه أَنتِجَت التَّأثِير المَرغُوب [ʔistiɣa:θtah ʔantiǰat ʔittaʔθi:r ʔilmarɣu:b] • **2.** مَفعُول [mafʕu:l] مَفعُولات، مَفاعِيل [mafʕu:la:t, mafa:ʕi:l] *pl:* The effect of this medicine is not what I would like it to be. مَفعُول هَالدُّوا مُو مِثلما أَرِيدَه [mafʕu:l hadduwa: mu: miθilma ʔari:dah] • **3.** تَظاهُر [taða:hur] He does it for effect. يسَوِّيها لغَرَض التَّظاهُر [ysawwi:ha lɣarað ʔittaða:hur] • **4.** مُسَبِّب [musabbib] This is a cause, not an effect. هَذا سَبَب، مُو مُسَبِّب [ha:ða sabab, mu: musabbib]

to go into effect • **1.** سِرَى مَفعُول [sira: mafʕu:l] سَرَيان مَفعُول [saraya:n mafʕu:l] *vn: sv* i. This law will go into effect next month. هَالقانُون راح يِسرِي مَفعُولَه الشَّهر الجّاي [halqa:nu:n ra:ħ yisri mafʕu:lah ʔiššahr ʔiǰǰa:y]

to have an effect • **1.** أَثَّر [ʔaθθar] تَأثِير [taʔθi:r] *vn: sv* i. Scolding has no effect on him. التَّرذِيل ما يأَثِّر بِيه [ʔittarzi:l ma: yʔaθθir bi:h]

to take effect • **1.** سِرَى مَفعُول [sira: mafʕu:l] *sv* i. This injection is beginning to take effect. الأُبرَة بِدا يِسرِي مَفعُولها [ʔlʔubra bida: yisri mafʕu:lha]

to effect • **1.** سَوَّى [sawwa:] تَسوِيَة [taswiya] *vn:* تسَوَّى [tsawwa:] *p:* أَجرَى [ʔaǰra:] إِجراء [ʔiǰra:ʔ] *vn: sv* i. حَقَّق [ħaqqaq] تَحقِيق [taħqi:q] *vn:* تحَقَّق [tħaqqaq] *p:* He effected the change without difficulty. سَوَّى التَّغيِير بِلا صُعُوبَة [sawwa: ʔittaɣyi:r bila ṣuʕu:ba]

effective • **1.** مُؤَثِّر [muʔaθθir] They produced a very effective new weapon. أَنتِجَوا سِلاح جِدِيد كُلِّش مُؤَثِّر [ʔantiǰaw sila:ħ ǰidi:d kulliš muʔaθθir] • **2.** فَعّال [faʕʕa:l] The committee was very effective in handling the dispute. اللُّجنَة كانَت كُلِّش فَعّالَة بمُعالَجَة النِّزاع [ʔilluǰna ča:nat kulliš faʕʕa:la bmuʕa:laǰat ʔinniza:ʕ] • **3.** مَفعُول [mafʕu:l] مَفعُولات، مَفاعِيل [mafʕu:la:t, mafa:ʕi:l] *pl:* These pills have proved to be very effective. هالحُبُوب ثِبَت مَفعُولها قَوي [halħubu:b θibat mafʕu:lha qawi] • **4.** إعتِباراً مِن [ʔiʕtiba:ran min] Effective Monday, we'll go on summer time. إعتِباراً مِن يوم الإثنَين راح نِستَعمِل التَّوقِيت الصَّيفِي [ʔiʕtiba:ran min yawm ʔilʔiθnayn ra:ħ nistaʕmil ʔittawqi:t ʔiṣṣayfi]

efficiency • **1.** كَفاءَة [kafa:ʔa] اِقتِدار [ʔiqtida:r] We all admire his efficiency. كُلّنا نقَدِّر كَفاءتَه [kullna nqaddir kafa:ʔtah]

efficient • **1.** كَفُوء [kafu:ʔ] أكِفّاء [ʔakiffa:ʔ] *pl:* مُقتَدِر [muqtadir] He's very efficient. هَذا كُلِّش كَفُو [ha:ða kulliš kafwʔ]

effort • **1.** جُهُد [ǰuhud] مَجهُود [maǰhu:d] مَجهُودات [maǰhu:da:t] *pl:* All his efforts were in vain. كُلّ جُهُودَه راحَت عَبَث [kull ǰuhu:dah ra:ħat ʕabaθ] • **2.** مَسعَى [masʕa] مَساعِي [masa:ʕi] *pl:* I wouldn't have got the job without your efforts. ما كان حَصَّلت الوَظِيفَة بلَيّا مَساعِيك [ma: ča:n ħaṣṣalt ʔilwaði:fa blayya masa:ʕi:k] • **3.** تَعَب [taʕab] That isn't worth the effort. هَذا ما يِسوَى التَّعَب [ha:ða ma: yiswa: ʔittaʕab]

*** We spared no effort to make the program a success.** • **1.** بِذَلنا الغالِي والرِّخِيص حَتَّى نِجعَل المَشرُوع ناجِح [biðalna ʔilɣa:li wirrixi:ṣ ħatta niǰʕal ʔilmašru:ʕ na:ǰiħ]

to make an effort • **1.** سِعَة [siʕa] سَعِي [saʕy] *vn: sv* a. اِجتِهَد [ʔiǰtihad] اِجتِهاد [ʔiǰtiha:d] *vn: sv* i. بِذَل مَسعَى [biðal masʕa] I will make a real effort to get you the job. راح أسعَى مِن صُدُق حَتَّى أحَصِّلَلك الوَظِيفَة [ra:ħ ʔasʕa: min ṣudug ħatta ʔaħaṣṣillak ʔilwaði:fa]

egg • **1.** بَيضَة [bayḍa] بَيضات [bayḍa:t] *pl:* بَيض [bayḍ] *Collective:* How much is a dozen eggs? بيش دَرزَن البَيض؟ [biyš darzan ʔilbayð?]

*** Don't put all your eggs in one basket.** • **1.** لا تِكشِف كُلّ أوراقَك [la: tikšif kull ʔawra:qak] / دائِماً خَلِّيلَك خَطّ رَجعَة [da:ʔiman xalli:lak xaṭṭ raǰʕa]

eggplant • **1.** بَيتِنجانَة [baytinǰa:na] بَيتِنجانات [baytinǰa:na:t] *pl:* بَيتِنجان [baytinǰa:n] *Collective*

Egypt • **1.** مِصِر [miṣir, maṣir]

Egyptian • **1.** مِصرِي [miṣri, maṣri]

eight • **1.** ثمانيَة [θma:nya] It's eight o'clock. السّاعَة ثمانيَة [ʔissa:ʕa θma:nya] • **2.** ثمَن [θman] أثمان [ʔaθma:n] *pl:* He has eight children. عِندَه ثمَن أطفال [ʕindah θman ʔaṭfa:l]

eighteen • **1.** ثمُنطَعَش [θmunṭaʕaš]

eighteenth • **1.** الثّمُنطَعَش [ʔiθθmunṭaʕaš] That's the eighteenth time he hasn't come to work this month. هاي المَرَّة الثّمُنطَعَش ما إجا لِلشُّغُل هَالشَّهَر [ha:y ʔilmarra ʔiθθumunṭaʕaš ma: ʔiǰa: liššuɣul haššahar]

eighth • **1.** ثُمُن [θumun] أثمان [ʔaθma:n] *pl:* He could only get an eighth of a pound of butter. قِدَر ياخُذ ثُمُن باوَن زِبِد بَسّ [gidar ya:xuð θumun pa:wan zibid bass] • **2.** ثامِن [θa:min] This is his eighth book. هَذا كتابَه الثّامِن [ha:ða kta:bah ʔiθθa:min]

eightieth • **1.** الثّمانِين [ʔiθθima:ni:n] They celebrated his eightieth birthday. اِحتِفلَوا بِعِيد مِيلادَه الثّمانِين [ʔiħtiflaw biʕi:d mi:la:dah ʔiθθima:ni:n]

eighty • **1.** ثمانِين [θma:ni:n]

either • **1.** فَدّ واحِد مِن ثِنَين [fadd wa:ħid min θnayn] Does either of these roads lead to Baghdad? أكُو فَدّ طَرِيق مِن هَالثِّنِين يرُوح لِبَغداد [ʔaku fadd ṭari:q min haθθini:n yiru:ħ lbayda:d] • **2.** أي واحِد مِن ثِنَين [ʔayy wa:ħid min θinayn] Either (one) is correct. أيّ واحِد مِن الثِّنَين صَحِيح [ʔayy wa:ħid min ʔiθθinayn ṣaħi:ħ] • **3.** There are trees on either side of the road. أكُو أشجار عَلَى جيهتَين الشّارِع [ʔaku ʔašǰa:r ʕala ǰi:htayn ʔišša:riʕ] • **4.** أمّا [ʔamma] لَو [law] I leave either today or tomorrow morning. أسافِر أمّا اليُوم أو باكِر الصُّبُح [ʔasa:fir ʔamma ʔilyu:m ʔaw ba:čir ʔiṣṣubuħ] I leave either today or tomorrow morning. أسافِر لَو اليُوم لَو باكِر الصُّبُح [ʔasa:fir law ʔilyu:m law ba:čir ʔiṣṣubuħ] • **5.** هَمّ [hamm] He doesn't know it either. هُوَّ هَمّ ما يُعرُفها [huwwa hamm ma: yuʕrufha]

elaborate • **1.** مُفَصَّل [mufaṣṣal] He gave us an elaborate description of it. اِنطانا وَصُف مُفَصَّل عَنها [ʔinṭa:na waṣuf mufaṣṣal ʕanha]

to elaborate • **1.** فَصَّل [faṣṣal] تفِصِّل، تَفصِيل [tfiṣṣil, tafṣi:l] *vn: sv* i. وَضَّح [waððaħ] تَوضِيح [tawði:ħ] *vn: sv* i. Can you elaborate upon your decision? تِقدَر توَضِّح تَقرِيرَك أكثَر؟ [tigdar twaððiħ taqri:rak ʔakθar?]

elastic • **1.** لاستِيك [la:sti:g] Do you need any elastic for the blouse? تِحتاجِين أيّ لاستِيك لِلبلُوز؟ [tiħta:ǰi:n ʔayy la:sti:g lilblu:z?] • **2.** مَرِن [marin] This metal is very elastic. هَالمَعدَن كُلِّش مَرِن [halmaʕdan kulliš marin]

elbow • **1.** عِكِس [ʕikis] عكُوس [ʕku:s] *pl:* I banged my elbow. ضِرَبِت عِكسِي [ðirabit ʕiksi]

to elbow • **1.** شَقّ بعِكِس [šagg bʕikis]She elbowed her way through the crowd. شَقَّت طَرِيقها بعِكِسها بالخَبصَة [šaggat ṭari:qha bʕikisha bilxabṣa] • **2.** نَغّ [nayɣ] نَغّ

[nayɣ] *vn: sv* u. He shut up after she elbowed him in his ribs. سِكَت بَعَد ما نَغَّته بعِكِسها بِضلُوعَه [sikat baʕad maː nayɣatah bʕikisha biðluːʕah]

to elect • **1.** اِنتِخَب [ʔintixab] اِنتِخاب [ʔintixaːb] *vn: sv* i. Whom did they elect president? إلمَن اِنتِخبَوا رَئِيس؟ [ʔilman ʔintixbaw raʔiːs?]

election • **1.** اِنتِخاب [ʔintixaːb] اِنتِخابات [ʔintixaːbaːt] *pl:*

electric • **1.** كَهرَبائِي [kahrabaːʔi] Where can I plug in my electric razor? أكُو بلَك أشَكِّل بِيه مَكِينَة الزِّيان الكَهرَبائِيَّة مالتِي؟ [ʔaku plak ʔašakkil biːh makiːnat ʔizziyaːn ʔilkahrabaːʔiyya maːlti?]

electric bulb • **1.** كلَوب [gluːb] كلَوبات [gluːbaːt] *pl:*

electrician • **1.** أبُو الكَهرَباء [ʔabuː ʔilkahrabaːʔ] أهِل الكَهرَباء [ʔahil ʔilkahrabaːʔ] *pl:*

electricity • **1.** كَهرَباء [kahrabaːʔ] The electricity's been cut off! الكَهرَباء اِنقِطعَت [ʔilkahrabaːʔ ʔingiṭaʕat]

electron • **1.** إلكِترُون [ʔilkitruːn] إلكترُونات [ʔilkitruwnaːt] *pl:*

electronic • **1.** ألَكترُونِي [ʔalaktruːni]

elegant • **1.** أنِيق [ʔaniːq]

element • **1.** عُنصُر [ʕunṣur] عَناصِر [ʕanaːṣir] *pl:* What are the elements of water? شِنُو هِيَّ عَناصِر الماي؟ [šinuː hiyya ʕanaːṣir ʔilmaːy?] This group constitutes the important element of the population. هَالجَماعَة تكَوِّن العُنصُر المُهِمّ بالمَجمُوع [haljamaːʕa tkawwan ʔilʕunṣur ʔilmuhimm bilmajmuːʕ] • **2.** مُحِيط [muħiːṭ] مُحِيطات [muħiːṭaːt] *pl:* He's out of his element. هُوَّ مُو بِمُحِيطَه المُلائِم [huwwa muː bmuħiːṭah ʔilmulaːʔim]

elementary • **1.** أساسِي [ʔasaːsi] Practice is elementary to learning any language. التَّمرِين شِي أساسِي لِتَعَلُّم أيّ لُغَة [ʔittamriːn ši ʔasaːsi litaʕallum ʔayy luɣa] • **2.** أوَّلِي [ʔawwali] اِبتِدائِي [ʔibtidaːʔi] I studied in an elementary school in Baghdad. درَسِت بمَدرَسَة اِبتِدائِيَّة بِبَغداد [drasit bmadrasa ʔibtidaːʔiyya bibaɣdaːd]

elephant • **1.** فِيل [fiːl] فيال [fyaːl] *pl:*

elevation • **1.** اِرتِفاع [ʔirtifaːʕ] اِرتِفاعات [ʔirtifaːʕaːt] *pl:* The elevation of this village is six hundred meters above sea level. اِرتِفاع هالقَريَة عَن مُستَوَى البَحَر سِتّ مِيَّة مَتِر [ʔirtifaːʕ halqarya ʕan mustawaː ʔilbaħar sitt miyyat matir]

elevator • **1.** مَصعَد [maṣʕad] مَصاعِد [maṣaːʕid] *pl:* Let's take the elevator. خَلِّي ناخُذ المَصعَد [xalli naːxuð ʔilmaṣʕad] • **2.** مَخزَن [maxzan] مَخازِن [maxaːzin] *pl:* How much wheat does this elevator hold? شقَدّ هالمَخزَن يِلزَم مِن الحُنطَة؟ [šgadd halmaxzan yilzam min ʔilħunṭa?]

eleven • **1.** دَعَش [daʕaš] هَالدَّعَش [haddaʕaš] I had to fill out eleven forms. كان لازِم أملِي هدَعَش اِستِمارَة [čaːn laːzim ʔamli hdaʕaš ʔistimaːra]

eleventh • **1.** الدَّعَش [ʔiddaʕaš] لِهالدَعَش [lihdaʕaš] Take the tenth book and give me the eleventh. أخُذ الكِتاب العاشِر وَإنطِينِي الهدَعَش [ʔuxuð ʔilkitaːb ʔilʕaːšir wʔinṭiːni ʔilhdaʕaš]

to eliminate • **1.** زال [zaːl] إزالَة [ʔizaːla] *vn: sv* i. مِحَى [miħaː] مَحُو، مَحِي [maħw, maħy] *vn: sv* i. The robbers eliminated all traces of the crime. الحَرامِيَّة زالَوا كُلّ آثار الجَّرِيمَة [ʔilħaraːmiyya zaːlaw kull ʔaːθaːr ʔijjariːma] • **2.** سَقَّط [saqqaṭ] تسُقُّط، تَسقِيط [tsuqquṭ, tasqiːṭ] *vn:* تسَقَّط [tsaqqaṭ] *p:* They eliminated him in the third race. سَقَّطُوه بِثالِث مُسابَقَة [saqqṭawh bθaːliθ musaːbaqa] • **3.** حِذَف [ħiðaf] حَذِف [ħaðif] *vn:* اِنحِذَف [ʔinħiðaf] *p:* His name was eliminated from the candidate list. إسمَه اِنحِذَف مِن قائِمَة المُرَشَّحِين [ʔismah ʔinħiðaf min qaːʔimat ʔilmuraššaħiːn] • **4.** ألغَى [ʔalɣaː] إلغاء [ʔilɣaːʔ] *vn:* اِنلِغَى [ʔinliɣaː] *p:* They finally eliminated taxes. بالأخِير ألغَوا الضَّرايِب [bilʔaxiːr ʔalɣaw ʔiððaraːyib]

eloquence • **1.** بَلاغَة [balaːɣa]

else • **1.** بَعَد [baʕad] آخَر [ʔaːxar] أخَرِين [ʔaːxariːn] *pl:* أخرَى [ʔuxra] *Feminine:* What else can we do? شنِقدَر نسَوِّي بَعَد؟ [šnigdar nsawwi baʕad?] Do you want something else? ترِيد شِي آخَر؟ [triːd ši ʔaːxar?] • **2.** لاخ [laːx] باقِي [baːqi] I'll take everything else. راح آخُذ كُلْشِي لاخ [raːħ ʔaːxuð kullši laːx]

or else • **1.** تَرَة [tara] Hurry, or else we'll be late. بِالعَجَل، تَرَة راح نِتأخَّر [bilʕajal, tara raːħ nitʔaxxar]

elsewhere • **1.** مَحَلّ آخَر [maħall ʔaːxar] غَير مُكان [ɣayr mukaːn] If you don't like it here, we can go elsewhere. إذا ما يعِجبَك هَالمَحَلّ نِقدَر نرُوح لِمَحَلّ آخَر [ʔiða maː yʕijbak halmaħall nigdar nruːħ limaħall ʔaːxar]

embargo • **1.** مَنع [maniʕ] The government issued an embargo on all goods to that island. الحُكُومَة صَدِّرَت مَنع عَلَى جَمِيع البَضايِع اللِّي ترُوح لِهالجَّزِيرَة [ʔilħukuːma ṣaddirat maniʕ ʕala jamiːʕ ʔilbaðaːyiʕ ʔilli truːħ lihajjaziːra]

E

to embarrass • **1.** خَجَّل [xaǰǰal] تخجِّل، تَخجِيل [txiǰǰil, taxǰi:l] *vn:* تخَجَّل [txaǰǰal] *p:* فَشَّل [faššal] تَفشِيل [tafši:l] *vn:* تفَشَّل [tfaššal] *p:* That child is always embarrassing me in front of people. هَالطِّفِل دائِماً يخَجِّلنِي قِدّام النّاس [haṭṭifil da:ʔiman yxaǰǰilni gidda:m ʔinna:s]

embarrassed • **1.** خَجلان [xaǰla:n] فَشلان [fašla:n] I was terribly embarrassed. كِنِت خَجلان لِدَرَجَة مُزعِجَة [činit xaǰla:n lidaraǰa muzʕiǰa]

embarrassing • **1.** مُخجِل [muxǰil] مفَشِّل [mfaššil] It was an embarrassing situation. كانَت فَدّ وَضعِيَّة مُخجِلَة [ča:nat fadd waðʕiyya muxǰila]

embassy • **1.** سَفارَة [safa:ra] سَفارات [safa:ra:t] *pl:* Where is the American Embassy? وِين السَّفارَة الأمرِيكِيَّة؟ [wi:n ʔissafa:ra ʔilʔamri:kiyya?]

to embezzle • **1.** اِختِلَس [ʔixtilas] اِختِلاس [ʔixtila:s] *vn:* *sv* i. How much has he embezzled? شقَدّ اِختِلَس؟ [šgadd ʔixtilas?]

to embrace • **1.** حِضَن [ħiðan] حَضِن [ħaðin] *vn:* *sv* i. He embraced his mother tenderly. حِضَن أُمَّه بحَنان [ħiðan ʔummah bħana:n] • **2.** ضَمّ [ðamm] ضَمّ [ðamm] *vn:* اِنضَمّ [ʔinðamm] *p:* Islam embraces people from many various nationalities. الإسلام يضُمّ ناس مِن مُختَلَف الشُّعُوب [ʔilʔisla:m yðumm na:s min muxtalaf ʔiššuʕu:b]

emerald • **1.** زُمُرَّدَة [zumurrada] زمُرَّدات [zumurruda:t] *pl:* زُمُرُّد [zumurrud] *Collective*

to emerge • **1.** طِلَع [ṭilaʕ] طلُوع [ṭilu:ʕ] *vn:* *sv* a. خِرَج [xiraǰ] خُرُوج [xuru:ǰ] *vn:* *sv* u. He emerged from the meeting smiling. طِلَع مِن الإجتِماع وَوُجهَه يبتِسِم [ṭilaʕ min ʔiliǰtima:ʕ wwuččah yibtisim] • **2.** بِرَز [biraz] بُرُوز [buru:z] *vn:* *sv* i. He emerged as one of the leaders of the party. بِرَز كَأَحَّد زُعَماء الحِزِب [biraz kaʔaħħad zuʕama:ʔ ʔilħizib] • **3.** نِشَأ [niša?] نَشِئ [našy?] *vn:* *sv* i. ظِهَر [ðihar] ظُهُور [ðuhu:r] *vn:* *sv* a. These facts emerged from the study of the problem. هَالحَقايِق نِشأَت مِن دِراسَة المُشكِلَة [halħaqa:yiq niš?at min dira:sat ʔilmuškila] • **4.** بِزَغ [bizaɣ] بزُوغ [bizu:ɣ] *vn:* *sv* a. The sun emerged from behind the hills. بزِغَت الشَّمِس مِن وَرا الجِّبال [bizɣat ʔiššamis min wara ʔiǰǰiba:l]

emergency • **1.** طارِئ [ṭa:ri?] طَوارِي [ṭawa:ri] *pl:* A state of emergency was declared. حالَة الطَّوارِئ اِنعِلنَت [ħa:lat ʔiṭṭawa:ri? ʔinʕilnat] • **2.** اِضطِرارِي [ʔiðṭira:ri] مِستَعجِل [mistaʕǰil] This is an emergency case. هَذِي حالَة اِضطِرارِيَّة [ha:ði ħa:la ʔiðṭira:riyya] • **3.** ضَرُورَة [ðaru:ra] ضَرُورات [ðaru:ra:t] *pl:* In case of emergency call the doctor. عِند الضَّرُورَة خابُر الطَّبِيب [ʕind ʔiððaru:ra xa:bur ʔiṭṭabi:b]

emergency brake • **1.** هاندبرَيك [ha:ndbri:k] هاندبرَيكات [ha:ndbri:ka:t] *pl:*

emergency exit • **1.** باب طَوارِئ [ba:b ṭawa:ri?] أبواب طَوارِئ [ʔabwa:b ṭawa:ri?] *pl:*

emigrant • **1.** مُهاجِر [muha:ǰir] مُهاجِرِين [muha:ǰiri:n] *pl:* Lebanese emigrants have settled all over the world. المُهاجِرِين اللُّبنانِيِّين اِستَوطِنَوا بكُلّ مَكان بِالعالَم [ʔilmuha:ǰiri:n ʔillubna:niyyi:n ʔistawṭinaw bkull maka:n bilʕa:lam]

to emigrate • **1.** هاجَر [ha:ǰar] مُهاجَرَة [muha:ǰara] *vn:* *sv* i. In recent years many people have emigrated from Europe. بِالسِّنِين الأَخِيرَة هوايَة ناس هاجرَوا مِن أورُبّا [bissini:n ʔilʔaxi:ra hwa:ya na:s ha:ǰraw min ʔu:ruppa]

eminent • **1.** بارِز [ba:riz]

emir • **1.** أمِير [ʔami:r] أُمَراء [ʔumara:ʔ, ʔumara:] *pl:*

emotion • **1.** عاطِفَة [ʕa:ṭifa] عَواطِف [ʕawa:ṭif] *pl:* شُعُور [šuʕu:r] He couldn't hide his emotion. ما قِدَر يخفِي عاطِفتَه [ma: gidar yixfi ʕa:ṭiftah]

emperor • **1.** إمبراطُور [ʔimbraṭu:r] إمبراطُورِيَّة [ʔimbraṭu:riyya] *pl:*

emphasis • **1.** أهَمِّيَّة [ʔahammiyya] تَأكِيد [taʔki:d] تأكِيدات [taʔki:da:t] *pl:*

to emphasize • **1.** أكَّد [ʔakkad] تَأكِيد [taʔki:d] *vn:* تأَكَّد [tʔakkad] *p:* He emphasized the need for more teachers. أكَّد الحاجَة إلَى مُعَلِّمِين أكثَر [ʔakkad ʔilħa:ǰa ʔila muʕallimi:n ʔakθar]

emphatically • **1.** بشِدَّة [bšidda] بتأكِيد [btaʔki:d] تأكِيدات [taʔki:da:t] *pl:* I'll have to deny that emphatically. راح أضطَرّ أنفِي هَذاك بِشِدَّة [ra:ħ ʔaðṭarr ʔanfi haða:k bšidda]

empire • **1.** إمبرَاطُورِيَّة [ʔimbraṭu:riyya] إمبرَاطُورِيّات [ʔimbraṭu:riyya:t] *pl:*

to employ • **1.** اِستَخدَم [ʔistaxdam] اِستِخدام [ʔistixda:m] *vn:* *sv* i. شَغَّل [šaɣɣal] تشِغِّل، تَشغِيل [tšiɣɣil, tašɣi:l] *vn:* تشَغَّل [tšaɣɣal] *p:* This factory employs a thousand workers. هَالمَعمَل يِستَخدِم ألف عامِل [hallmaʕmal yistaxdim ʔalf ʕa:mil]
* **Where are you employed?** • **1.** إنتَ وَين تِشتُغُل؟ [ʔinta wi:n tištuɣul?]

employee • **1.** مُستَخدَم [mustaxdam] مُستَخدَمِين [mustaxdami:n] *pl:* مُوَظَّف [muwaððaf] مُوَظَّفِين [muwaððafi:n] *pl:*

employer • **1.** مُستَخدَم [mustaxdam]

employment • **1.** شُغُل [šuɣul] أشغال [ʔašɣa:l] *pl:* What kind of employment did you finally get? تالِيها شِنُو نُوع الشُّغُل اللِّي حَصَّلتَه؟ [ta:li:ha šinu nu:ʕ ʔiššuɣul ʔilli ħaṣṣaltah?] • **2.** اِستِخدام [ʔistixda:m] The employment of children is forbidden by law. اِستِخدام الصِّغار مَمنُوع قانُوناً [ʔistixda:m ʔiṣṣiɣa:r mamnu:ʕ qa:nu:nan]

empty • **1.** فارِغ [fa:riɣ] خالِي [xa:li] Do you have an empty box? عِندَك فَدّ صَندُوق فارِغ؟ [ʕindak fadd ṣandu:g fa:riɣ?] He made empty threats. هَدَّد تَهدِيدات فارغَة [haddad tahdi:da:t fa:rɣa]

to empty • **1.** فَرَّغ [farraɣ] تفُرُّغ، تَفرِيغ [tfurruɣ, tafri:ɣ] *vn:* تفَرَّغ [tfarraɣ] *p:* أخلَى [ʔaxla:] إخلاء [ʔixla:ʔ] *vn:* اِنخِلى [ʔinxila:] *p:* Please empty this tank. رَجاءاً فَرِّغ هالتّانكِي [raǰa:ʔan farriɣ hatta:nki] • **2.** أخلَى [ʔaxla:] إخلاء [ʔixla:ʔ] *vn: sv* i. The hall emptied in five minutes. القاعَة خِلَت بخَمِس دَقايِق [ʔilqa:ʕa xilat bxamis daqa:yiq] • **3.** صَبّ [ṣabb] صَبّ [ṣabb] *vn: sv* u. This river empties into the ocean. هَالنَّهَر يصُبّ بالمُحِيط [hannahar yṣubb bilmuħi:ṭ]

to enable • **1.** مَكَّن [makkan] تمِكِّن [tmikkin] *vn:* تمَكَّن [tmakkan] أهَّل [ʔahhal] تأهِّل [tʔihhil] *vn:* تأهَّل [tʔahhal] *p:* This experience will enable you to get a good position. هَالتَّجرُبَة لابُدّ تمَكِّنَك مِن الحُصُول عَلَى وَظِيفَة زينَة [hattaǰruba la:budd tmakkinak min ʔilħuṣu:l ʕala waðʕi:fa zi:na]

to enact • **1.** سَنّ [sann] سَنّ [sann] *vn:* اِنسَنّ [ʔinsann] *p:* This law was enacted in 1920. هَالقانُون اِنسَنّ بِسَنَة ألِف وَتِسعمِيَّة وَعِشرِين [halqa:nu:n ʔinsann bsanat ʔalif wtisiʕmiyya wʕišri:n]

to enclose • **1.** رِفَق [rifaq] إرفاق [ʔirfa:q] *vn:* اِنرِفَق [ʔinrifaq] *p:* I've enclosed herewith the newspaper clippings you wanted. رِفَقِت طَيّاً قُصاصات الجَّرايِد اللِّي رِدِتها [rifaqit ṭayyan quṣa:ṣa:t ʔiǰǰara:yid ʔilli riditha] The sum due you is enclosed herewith. المَبلَغ المَطلُوب بِيه إلَك مُرفَق طَيّاً [ʔilmablaɣ ʔilmaṭlu:b bi:h ʔilak murfaq ṭayyan]

to encourage • **1.** شَجَّع [šaǰǰaʕ] تَشجِيع [tašǰi:ʕ] *vn:* تشَجَّع [tšaǰǰaʕ] He encouraged me to stick it out. هُوَّ شَجَّعنِي عالإصرار عَلَيها [huwwa šaǰǰaʕni ʕalʔiṣra:r ʕalayha]

encouragement • **1.** تَشجِيع [tašǰi:ʕ]

to encroach • **1.** اِعتِدَى [ʔiʕtida:] اِعتِداء [ʔiʕtida:ʔ] *vn: sv* i. تجاوَز [tǰa:waz, dǰa:waz] تَجاوُز [taǰa:wuz] *vn: sv* a. That would be encroaching upon his rights. ذاك يكُون اِعتِداء عَلَى حُقُوقَه [ða:k yku:n ʔiʕtida:ʔ ʕala ħuqu:qah]

encyclopedia • **1.** دائِرَة مَعارِف [da:ʔirat maʕa:rif] دَوائِر مَعارِف [dawa:ʔir maʕa:rif] *pl:* إنسِكلَوبِيدِيَة [ʔinsiklupi:dya] إنسِكلَوبِيدِيات [ʔinsiklupidya:t] *pl:* مَوسُوعَة [mawsu:ʕa] مَوسُوعات [mawsu:ʕa:t] *pl:*

end • **1.** آخِر [ʔa:xir] أواخِر [ʔawa:xir] *pl:* نِهايَة [niha:ya] نِهايات [niha:ya:t] *pl:* I'll pay you the balance at the end of the month. راح أدفَعلَك الباقِي بآخِر الشَّهَر [ra:ħ ʔadfaʕlak ʔilba:qi bʔa:xir ʔiššahar] • **2.** نِهايَة [niha:ya] نِهايات [niha:ya:t] *pl:* Tie the two ends together. أربُط النِّهايَتَين سُوَة [ʔurbuṭ ʔinniha:yatayn suwa] That is the end of the program. هَذِي نِهايَة البَرنامِج [ha:ði niha:yat ʔilbarna:miǰ] • **3.** غايَة [ɣa:ya] غايات [ɣa:ya:t] *pl:* He believes that the end justifies the means. يعتِقِد إنّ الغايَة تبَرِّر الوَسِيلَة [yiʕtiqid ʔinn ʔilɣa:ya tbarrir ʔilwasi:la] • **4.** حَدّ [ħadd] Can't you put an end to these squabbles? ما تِقدَر تحُطّ حَدّ لِهَالنِّزاع؟ [ma: tigdar tħuṭṭ ħadd lihanniza:ʕ?]

He scolded a bit and that was the end of it. • **1.** رَبرَب شوَيَّة وانتِهَى المَوضُوع [rabrab šwayya wʔintiha: ʔilmawðu:ʕ]

*** Except for a few loose ends, everything is done.** • **1.** كُلشِي كِمَل ما عَدا بَعض الأشياء البَسِيطَة [kulši kimal ma: ʕada: baʕð ʔilʔašya:ʔ ʔilbasi:ṭa]

to end • **1.** أنهَى [ʔanha:] إنهاء [ʔinha:ʔ] *vn:* اِنّهَى [ʔinniha:] *p:* خَلَّص [xallaṣ] تخِلِّص [txilliṣ] *vn:* تخَلَّص [txallaṣ] *p:* He ended his speech with a quotation from the Koran. أنهَى مُحاضَرتَه بآيَة قُرآنِيَّة [ʔanha: muħa:ðartah bʔa:ya qurʔa:niyya] • **2.** خِلَص [xilaṣ] خَلاص [xala:ṣ] *vn: sv* a. اِنتِهَى [ʔintiha:] اِنتِهاء [ʔintiha:ʔ] *vn: sv* i. Won't this back-biting ever end? هَالقال وَقِيل ما راح يخلَص أبَد؟ [halqa:l wqi:l ma: ra:ħ yixlaṣ ʔabad?]

endeavor • **1.** مَسعَى [masʕa] مَساعِي [masa:ʕi] *pl:* He did not succeed in his endeavor. ما نِجَح بمَسعاه [ma: nijaħ bmasʕa:h]

to endorse • **1.** جَيَّر [ǰayyar] تَجيِير [taǰyi:r] *vn:* تجَيَّر [tǰayyar] *p:* ظَهَّر [ðahhar] تَظهِير [taðhi:r] *vn:* تظَهَّر [tðahhar] *p:* Endorse the check, please. جَيِّر الشِّيك رَجاءاً [ǰayyir ʔičči:k raǰa:ʔan] • **2.** أيَّد [ʔayyad] تأيِيد [taʔyi:d] *vn:* تأيَّد [tʔayyad] *p:* He endorsed my program. أيَّد بَرنامِجِي [ʔayyad barna:miǰi]

to endure • **1.** تحَمَّل [tħammal] تَحَمُّل [taħammul] *vn: sv* a. She endured the grief quietly. تحَمّلَت الفاجِعَة بكُلّ هُدُوء [tħammlat ʔilfa:ǰiʕa bkull hudu:ʔ]

enema • **1.** حُقنَة [ħuqna] حُقنات، حُقَن [ħuqna:t, ħuqan] *pl:*

enemy • **1.** عَدُو [ʕadu] أعداء، عُدوان [ʔaʕda:ʔ, ʕudwa:n] *pl:*

E

energy • **1.** حَيَوِيَّة [ħayawiyya] نَشاط [naša:ṭ] He's full of energy. هَذا مَليان حَيَوِيَّة [ha:ða malya:n ħayawiyya] He's full of energy. كُلّه حَيَوِيَّة [kullah ħayawiyya] • **2.** طاقَة [ṭa:qa] I read a book on atomic energy. قَرَيت كتاب عَن الطّاقَة الذَّرِّيَّة [qrayt kta:b ʕan ʔiṭṭa:qa ʔiððarriyya]

to enforce • **1.** طَبَّق [ṭabbaq] تَطبِيق [taṭbi:q] *vn:* تطَبَّق [ʔiṭṭabbaq] *p:* نَفَّذ [naffað] تَنفِيذ [tanfi:ð] *vn:* تنَفَّذ [tnaffað] *p:* This law has never been strictly enforced. هَالقانُون أَبَداً ما اِتطَبَّق بِالضَبُط [halqa:nu:n ʔabadan ma: ʔiṭṭabbaq biððabuṭ]

to engage • **1.** اِستَخدَم [ʔistaxdam] اِستِخدام [ʔistixda:m] *vn: sv* i. We've just engaged a new maid. هَستَّونا اِستَخدَمنا خادمَة جِدِيدَة [hastawwna ʔistaxdamna xa:dma ǰidi:da] • **2.** تعاقَد [tʕa:qad] تَعاقُد [taʕa:qud] *vn: sv* a. We engaged him for two concerts. تعاقَدنا وِيّاه بِحَفلتَين مُوسِيقِيَّة [tʕa:qadna wiyya:h bħafiltayn muwsi:qiyya] • **3.** تدَخَّل [ddaxxal] تَدَخُّل [tadaxxul] *vn: sv* a. I don't engage in politics. آنِي ما أَتدَخَّل بِالسِّياسَة [ʔa:ni ma: ʔaddaxxal bissiya:sa] • **4.** صادَم [ṣa:dam] مُصادَمَة [muṣa:dama] *vn: sv* i. They engaged the enemy on the hill. صادمَوا الأَعداء عَالتَّلّ [ṣa:dmaw ʔilʔaʕda:ʔ ʕattall]

engaged • **1.** مَخطُوب [maxṭu:b] How long have they been engaged? شقَدّ صارِلهُم مَخطُوبِين؟ [šgadd ṣa:rilhum maxṭu:bi:n?] • **2.** مَشغُول [mašɣu:l] I'm presently engaged in research. آنِي هَسَّة مَشغُول بِبَحِث [ʔa:ni hassa mašɣu:l bibaħiθ]

engagement • **1.** مَوعِد [mawʕid] مَواعِيد [mawa:ʕi:d] *pl:* I have an engagement this evening. عِندِي مَوعِد هالمِسَا [ʕindi mawʕid halmasa] • **2.** خُطبَة [xuṭba] خُطَب [xuṭab] *pl:* خَطَب [xaṭab] They announced her engagement. أَعلِنَوا خُطبَتها [ʔaʕlinaw xuṭbatha]

engine • **1.** مَكِينَة [maki:na] مَكايِن [maka:yin] *pl:* You left the engine running. إنتَ خَلِّيت المَكِينَة تِشتُغُل [ʔinta xalli:t ʔilmaki:na tištuɣul] This train has two engines. هَالقِطار بِيه مَكِينتَين [halqiṭa:r bi:h maki:ntayn] The factory is equipped with electric machines. المَعمَل مجَهَّز بِالمَكايِن الكَهرَبائِيَّة [ʔilmaʕmal mǰahhaz bilmaka:yin ʔilkahraba:ʔiyya]

engineer • **1.** مُهَندِس [muhandis] مُهَندِسِين [muhandisi:n] *pl:* I've asked the engineer to draw a new set of plans. طلَبِت مِن المُهَندِس أَن يِرسِم مَجمُوعَة جِدِيدَة مِن المُخَطَّطات [ṭlabit min ʔilmuhandis ʔan yirsim majmu:ʕa ǰidi:da min ʔilmuxaṭṭaṭa:t] • **2.** سايِق قِطار [sa:yiq qiṭa:r] سُوّاق قِطار [suwwa:q qiṭa:r] *pl:* The engineer stopped the train. سايِق القِطار وَقَّف القِطار [sa:yiq ʔilqiṭa:r waggaf ʔilqiṭa:r] • **3.** مَكِينَجِي [makina:či] مَكِينَجِين [makina:či:n] *pl:* The engineer says there'ssomething wrong with the boiler. المَكِينَجِي قال أَكُو فَدّ عَطَب بِالمَرجَل [ʔilmaki:nači ga:l ʔaku fadd ʕaṭub bilmarǰal]

to engineer • **1.** نَظَّم [naððam] تَنظِيم، تنُظُّم [tanði:m, tnuððum] *vn:* تنَظَّم [tnaððam] *p:* Who engineered this plan? مِنُو نَظَّم هالخُطَّة؟ [minu naððam halxuṭṭa?]

engineering • **1.** هَندَسَة [handasa]

English • **1.** إنكِلِيزِي [ʔingili:zi] He speaks English very well. يِحكِي إنكِلِيزِي كُلِّش زين [yiħči ʔingili:zi kulliš zayn] • **2.** إنكِلِيزِي [ʔingili:zi] إنكِلِيز [ʔingili:z] *pl:* إنكِلِيزِيَّة [ʔingili:ziyya] *Feminine:* That's an old English custom. هَذِي عادَة إنكِلِيزِيَّة قَدِيمَة [ha:ði ʕa:da ʔingili:ziyya qadi:ma] • **3.** إنكِلِيزِي [ʔingili:zi] إنكِلِيز [ʔingili:z] *pl:* The English fight well. الإنكلِيز يحارِبُون زين [ʔilʔingli:z yħa:rbu:n zayn]

to engrave • **1.** حُفَر [ħufar] حَفُر [ħafur] *vn:* اِنحُفَر [ʔinħufar] *p:* My name is engraved on my watch. إسمِي مَحفُور عَلَى ساعتِي [ʔismi maħfu:r ʕala sa:ʕti] • **2.** نَقَش [niqaš] نَقِش [naqiš] *vn:* اِنّقَش [ʔinniqaš] *p:* What is this design engraved on the sword? شِنُو هَالنَّقِش مَنقُوش عَلَى السَّيف؟ [šinu: hannaqaš manqu:š ʕala ʔissi:f?]

to enjoy • **1.** تمَتَّع ب [tmattaʕ b-] تَمَتُّع [tamattuʕ] *vn: sv* a. He's enjoying his life. هُوَّ مِتمَتِّع بِحَياتَه [huwwa mitmattiʕ bħaya:tah] He's enjoying excellent health. يِتمَتَّع بِصِحَّة مُمتازَة [yitmattaʕ bṣiħħa mumta:za]

to enjoy oneself • **1.** توَنَّس [twannas] تَوَنُّس [tawannus] *vn: sv* a. Did you enjoy yourself at the dance? توَنَّسِت بالرِّقُص؟ [twannasit birrigiṣ?]

enjoyment • **1.** تَمَتُّع [tamattuʕ] لَذَّة [laðða] لَذّات [laðða:t] *pl:*

to enlarge • **1.** كَبَّر [kabbar] تكُبُّر [tkubbur] *vn:* تكَبَّر [tkabbar] *p:* Do you enlarge pictures? إنتَ تكَبُّر صُوَر؟ [ʔinta tkabbur ṣuwar?] • **2.** وَسَّع [wassaʕ] تَوسِيع، توِسِّع [tawsi:ʕ, twissiʕ] *vn:* توَسَّع [wassaʕ] *p:* كَبَّر [kabbar] تكبِير [takbi:r] *vn:* تكَبَّر [tkabbar] *p:* We're going to have to enlarge this room. لازِم نوَسِّع هَالغُرفَة [la:zim nwassiʕ halɣurfa]

enlargement • **1.** صُورَة مُكَبَّرَة [ṣu:ra mukabbara] صُوَر مُكَبَّرَة [ṣuwar mukabbara] *pl:* How many enlargements do you want? كَم صُورَة مُكَبَّرَة ترِيد؟ [čam ṣu:ra mukabbara tri:d?]

to enlist • **1.** تطَوَّع [ṭṭawwaʕ] He enlisted in the navy two days ago. تطَوَّع بِسِلك البَحرِيَّة قَبُل يومَين [ṭṭawwaʕ bsilk ʔilbaħriyya gabul yawmayn]

enormous • **1.** ضَخُم [ðaxum] هائِل [ha:ʔil] جَسِيم [ǰasi:m] عَظِيم [ʕaði:m] عُظَماء [ʕuðama:ʔ] *pl:* That's an enormous

i, interjection; p, passive; pl, plural; sv, stem vowel; vn, verbal noun

project. هَذا فَدّ مَشرُوع ضَخُم [haːða fadd mašruːʕ ðaxum] He spent enormous amounts of money on this building. دِفَع مَبالِغ عَظِيمَة، بهالبِنايَة [difaʕ mabaːliɣ ʕaðiːma, bhalbinaːya]

enormously • **1.** بِدَرَجَة عَظِيمَة [bidaraǰa ʕaðiːma] بضَخامَة [bðaxaːma] بصُورَة كَبِيرَة [bṣuːra kabiːra] The need for raw materials has grown enormously. الحاجَة لِلمَوادّ الأَوَّلِيَّة إزدادَت بِدَرَجَة عَظِيمَة [ʔilħaːǰa lilmawaːdd ʔilʔawwaliyya ʔizdaːdat bdaraǰa ʕaðiːma]

enough • **1.** كِفايَة [kifaːya] كافِي [kaːfi] Have you had enough to eat? أَكَلِت كِفايَة؟ [ʔakalit kifaːya?] Do you have enough money? عِندَك فلُوس كافيَة؟ [ʕindak fluːs kaːfya?]
*** Would you be kind enough to open the window?** • **1.** تِسمَح تِفتَح الشِبّاك؟ [tismaħ tiftaħ ʔiššibbaːč?]
to be enough • **1.** كَفَّى [kaffaː] تكَفِّي [tkaffi] *vn: sv* i. Will that be enough? هَذا يكَفِّي؟ [haːða ykaffi?]
to have enough • **1.** شِبَع [šibaʕ] شِبع [šibiʕ] *vn: sv* a. تكَفَّى [tčaffaː] تكِفِّي [tkiffi] *vn: sv* a. I've had enough of that talk. شبَعِت مِن هَالحَكِي [šbaʕit min halħači]

to enroll • **1.** سَجَّل [sajjal] تَسجِيل [tasjiːl] *vn:* تسَجَّل [tsajjal] *p:* I'm going to enroll my son in first grade. آنِي راح أَسَجِّل إبنِي بِالصَّفّ الأَوَّل [ʔaːni raːħ ʔasajjil ʔibni bissaff ʔilʔawwal] • **2.** تسَجَّل [tsajjal] تَسَجُّل [tasajjul] *vn: sv* a. He's going to enroll in night school. راح يِتسَجَّل بمَدرَسَة مَسائيَّة [raːħ yitsajjal bmadrasa masaːʔiyya]

enslavement • **1.** إستِعباد [ʔistiʕbaːd]

to enter • **1.** خَشّ [xašš] خَشّ [xašš] *vn: sv* u. دِخَل [dixal] دُخُول [duxuːl] *vn: sv* u. طَبّ [ṭabb] طَبَّة [ṭabba] *vn: sv* u. Everyone rose when the guest of honor entered. كُلّ واحِد قام مِن خَشّ ضَيف الشَّرَف [kull waːħid gaːm min xašš ðayf ʔiššaraf] • **2.** دَخَّل [daxxal] تدِخِّل [tdixxil] *vn:* تدَخَّل [tdaxxal] *p:* Enter these names in the list. دَخِّل هالأسماء بِالقائِمَة [daxxil halʔasmaːʔ bilqaːʔima]

enterprise • **1.** مَشرُوع [mašruːʕ] The enterprise was successful. المَشرُوع نِجَح [ʔilmašruːʕ nijaħ]

enterprising • **1.** مُنتِج [muntij] He's the most enterprising one in the company. هُوَّ أَكثَر واحِد مُنتِج بِالشَّرِكَة [huwwa ʔakθar waːħid muntij biššarika]

to entertain • **1.** وَنَّس [wannas] توُنِّس [twunnis] *vn:* توَنَّس [twannas] *p:* He entertained the guests with his amusing stories. وَنَّس الخُطّار بقُصَصَه الجَذّابَة [wannas ʔilxuṭṭaːr bquṣaṣah ʔijjaððaːba]
*** They entertain a great deal.** • **1.** هُمَّ يسَوُّون هوايَة عَزايِم [humma ysawwuːn hwaːya ʕazaːyim]

entertainment • **1.** تَسلِيَة [tasliya] تَسلِيات [tasliyaːt] *pl:* Who's going to provide the program of entertainment? مِنُو راح يقَدِّم مَنهَج التَّسلِيَة؟ [minu raːħ yqaddim manhaǰ ʔittasliya?] • **2.** لَهُو [lahw] What do you do for entertainment around here? شَكُو وَسائِل لَهو بِهَالمَنطَقَة؟ [šaku wasaːʔil lahw bhalmanṭaqa?]

enthusiasm • **1.** حَماس [ħamaːs] He didn't show any enthusiasm. ما راوَى أَيّ حَماس [maː raːwaː ʔayy ħamaːs]

enthusiastic • **1.** مِتحَمِّس [mitħammis] I'm quite enthusiastic about it. آنِي كُلِّش مِتحَمِّس لهاي [ʔaːni kulliš mitħammis lhaːy]

entire • **1.** كُلّ [kull] كامِل [kaːmil] جَمِيع [ǰamiːʕ] The entire amount has to be paid in cash. كُلّ المَبلَغ لازِم يِندِفِع نَقداً [kull ʔilmablaɣ laːzim yindifiʕ naqdan]
*** The entire evening was wasted.**
• **1.** ضاعَت اللَّيلَة بكامِلها [ðaːʕat ʔillayla bkaːmilha]

entirely • **1.** تَماماً [tamaːman] You're entirely right. إنتَ مُحِقّ تَماماً [ʔinta muħiqq tamaːman] • **2.** كُلِّياً [kulliyyan] بِالكُلِّيَّة [bilkulliya] These two things are entirely different. هَالشَّيِّين مِختَلفِين كُلِّياً [haššiyyayn mixtalfiːn kulliyyan]

entrance • **1.** مَدخَل [madxal] مَداخِل [madaːxil] *pl:* باب [baːb] أبواب، بِيبان [ʔabwaːb, biːbaːn] *pl:*

entry • **1.** تَنزِيل [tanziːl] تَنزِيلات [tanziːlaːt] *pl:* The last entry in the account was five dinars. آخِر تَنزِيل بِالحِساب كان خَمس دَنانِير [ʔaːxir tanziːl biliħsaːb čaːn xams danaːniːr] • **2.** دُخُول [duxuːl] Entry into this room is not allowed. الدُّخُول لِهالغُرفَة مَمنُوع [ʔidduxuːl lihalɣurfa mamnuːʕ]

envelope • **1.** ظَرُف [ðaruf] ظرُوف [ðruːf] *pl:* I need an envelope for the letter. أَحتاج ظَرُف لِلمَكتُوب [ʔaħtaːǰ ðaruf lilmaktuːb]

environment • **1.** بِيئَة [biːʔa] بِيئات [biːʔaːt] *pl:* مُحِيط [muħiːṭ] مُحِيطات [muħiːṭaːt] *pl:* He was raised in a poor environment. تَرَبَّى بِبِيئَة مُو زينَة [trabbaː bibiːʔa muː ziːna]

envoy • **1.** مَندُوب [manduːb] مَندُوبِين [manduːbiːn] *pl:* مُمَثِّل دَولِي [mumaθθil dawli] مُمَثِّلِين دَولِيِّين [mumaθθiliːn dawliyyiːn] *pl:*

envy • **1.** غِيرَة [ɣiːra] حَسَد [ħasad] He was green with envy. دَيمُوت مِن غِيرتَه [daymuːt min ɣiːrtah]
• **2.** مَحسُود [maħsuːd] You'll be the envy of all your friends. راح تكُون مَحسُود مِن كُلّ أَصدِقائَك [raːħ tkuːn maħsuːd min kull ʔaṣdiqaːʔak]

to envy • **1.** حِسَد [ħisad] حَسَد [ħasad] *vn:* اِنحِسَد [ʔinħisad] *p:* غار مِن [ɣaːr min] غِيرَة [ɣiːra] *vn:* إنغار [ʔinɣaːr] *p:* I envy you! آني أحِسدَك [ʔaːni ʔaħisdak]

epidemic • **1.** وَباء [wabaːʔ] أوبِئَة [ʔawbiʔa] *pl:* An epidemic has broken out among the cattle. فَدّ وَباء اِنتِشَر بين الماشِيَة [fadd wabaːʔ ʔintišar bayn ʔilmaːšiya]

E

epilepsy • **1.** صَرَع [ṣaraʕ]

epoch • **1.** دَور [dawr, duːr] أدوار [ʔadwaːr] *pl:*

epsom salts • **1.** مِلح فرِنجي [milħ fringi]

equal • **1.** مِتساوي [mitsaːwiː] Cut this bread into three equal parts. قُصّ هَالصَّمُّونَة إلَى ثلَاث أقسام مِتساوِيَة [guṣṣ haṣṣammuːna ʔila tla θ ʔaqsaːm mitsaːwiya] • **2.** كَفُو [kafuʔ] أكِفّاء [ʔakiffaːʔ] *pl:* I don't think I'm equal to that job. ما أعتِقِد آني كَفُو لِهالعَمَل [maː ʔaʕtiqid ʔaːni kafuʔ lihalʕamal]

to equal • **1.** عادَل [ʕaːdal] مُعادَلَة [muʕaːdala] *vn:* *sv* i. تعادَل [tʕaːdal] تَعادُل [taʕaːdul] *vn:* *sv* a. It will be hard to equal him. مِن الصُّعُوبَة تِتعادَل وِيّاه [min ʔiṣṣuʕuːba titʕaːdal wiyyaːh] • **2.** ساوَى [saːwaː] مُساواة [musaːwat] *vn:* *sv* i. Five plus five equals ten. خَمسَة زائِداً خَمسَة يساوي عَشرَة [xamsa zaːʔidan xamsa ysaːwi ʕašara]

equality • **1.** مُساواة [musaːwaːt] I'm a believer in equality among men. آني مُؤمِن بِالمُساواة بين النّاس [ʔaːni muʔmin bilmusaːwaːt biːn ʔinnaːs]

equally • **1.** تَساوي [tasaːwi] The two books are equally important. الكتابَين مُهِمَّة بِالتَّساوي [ʔilktaːbayn muhimma bittasaːwi] • **2.** بقَدّ [bgadd] I liked his first play equally well. حَبَّيت تَمثِيلِيتَه الأولَى بقَدّ هاي [ħabbayt tamθiːliːtah ʔilʔuːla bgadd haːy]

equation • **1.** مُعادَلَة [muʕaːdala] مُعادَلات [muʕaːdalaːt] *pl:*

equator • **1.** خَطّ اِستِواء [xaṭṭ ʔistiwaːʔ] خطُوط اِستِوائِيَّة [xṭuːṭ ʔistiwaːʔiyya] *pl:*

equilibrium • **1.** تَوازُن [tawaːzun] مُوازَنَة [muwaːzana]

to equip • **1.** جَهَّز [ǰahhaz] تَجهيز [taǰhiːz] *vn:* تَجَهَّز [tǰahhaz] *p:* هَيَّأ [hayyaʔ] تَهَيُّؤ [tahayyuʔ] *vn:* تهَيَّأ [thayyaʔ] *p:* Our planes are equipped with the latest instruments. طَيّاراتنا مُجَهَّزَة بِأحدَث الوَسائِل [ṭayyaːraːtna muǰahhaza bʔaħdaθ ʔilwasaːʔil]

equipment • **1.** أداة [ʔadaːt] أدَوات [ʔadawaːt] *pl:* They make welding equipment. يسَوُّون أدَوات اللِّحِيم [ysawwuːn ʔadawaːt ʔilliħiːm] • **2.** لَوازِم [lawaːzim] غَرَض [ɣaraḍ] أغراض [ʔaɣraːḍ] *pl:* He put the hunting equipment in the trunk of the car. خَلَّى لَوازِم الصَّيد بِصَندُوق السَّيّارَة [xallaː lawaːzim ʔiṣṣiːd biṣanduːg ʔissayyaːra]

equivalent • **1.** مُعادِل [muʕaːdil] مُساوِي [musaːwiː] مُكافِئ [mukaːfiʔ]

era • **1.** عَصِر [ʕaṣir] عُصُور [ʕuṣuːr] *pl:*

to erase • **1.** مِسَح [misaħ] مَسِح [masiħ] *vn:* اِنمِسَح [ʔinmisaħ] *p:* مِحَى [miħaː] مَحِي [maħy] *vn:* اِنمِحَى [ʔinmiħaː] *p:* He erased the signature. مِسَح الإمضاء [misaħ ʔilʔimḍaːʔ] Will you please erase the board? أرجُوك إمسَح السَّبُّورَة؟ [ʔarǰuːk ʔimsaħ ʔissabbuːra?]

eraser • **1.** مِسّاحَة [missaːħa] مِسّاحات [missaːħaːt] *pl:* مَحّايَة [maħħaːya] مَحّايات [maħħaːyaːt] *pl:* I bought two pencils and an eraser. اِشتِرَيت قَلَمَين وَمِسّاحَة [ʔištiriːt qalamayn wmissaːħa] • **2.** مِسّاحَة [missaːħa] مِسّاحات [missaːħaːt] *pl:* We need some chalk and an eraser. نِحتاج شوَيَّة طَباشِير وفَدّ مَسّاحَة [niħtaːǰ šwayya tabaːšiːr wfadd massaːħa]

to erect • **1.** بِنَى [binaː] بِناء [binaːʔ] *vn:* اِنبِنَى [ʔinbinaː] *p:* Who erected this building? مِنُو بِنَى هَالبِنايَة؟ [minu binaː halbinaːya?]

erosion • **1.** تَآكُل [taʔaːkul]

to err • **1.** غِلَط [ɣilaṭ] غَلَط [ɣalaṭ] *vn:* *sv* a.

errand • **1.** شَغلَة [šaɣla] شَغلات [šaɣlaːt] *pl:* I have a few errands I want to do. عِندي كَم شَغلَة أرِيد أسَوِّيها [ʕindi čam šaɣla ʔariːd ʔasawwiːha]

erroneous • **1.** مَغلُوط [maɣluːṭ] The information he gave us was erroneous. المَعلُومات اللّي إنطانا إياها كانَت مَغلُوطَة [ʔilmaʕluːmaːt ʔilli ʔinṭaːna ʔiyyaːha čaːnat maɣluːṭa]

error • **1.** غَلطَة [ɣalṭa] غَلطات، أغلاط [ɣalṭaːt, ʔaɣlaːṭ] *pl:* I made four errors on the exam. غلَطِت أربَع غَلطات بِالإمتِحان [ɣlaṭit ʔarbaʕ ɣalṭaat bilʔimtiħaːn]

escape • **1.** هُرُوب [huruːb] هَزِيمَة [haziːma] هَزايِم [hazaːyim] *pl:* The prisoners' escape was cleverly planned. هُرُوب المَساجِين كان مدَبَّر بمَهارَة [huruːb ʔilmasaːǰiːn čaːn mdabbar bmahaːra] • **2.** تَخَلُّص [taxalluṣ] We had a narrow escape. تخَلُّصنا كان بإعجُوبَة [txalluṣna čaːn bʔiʕǰuːba]

to escape • **1.** هِرَب [hirab] هُرُوب [huru:b] *vn: sv* a. اِنهِزَم [ʔinhizam] اِنهِزام [ʔinhiza:m] *vn: sv* i. Two prisoners have escaped from the penitentiary. مَسجُونَين اِنهِزمَوا مِن السِّجِن [masǰu:nayn ʔinhizmaw min ʔissiǰin] • **2.** راح [ra:ħ] رَواح [rawa:ħ] *vn: sv* u. Her face is familiar but her name escapes me. وِجهَها مُو غَرِيب لَكِن إسِمها راح مِن بالِي [wiččha mu: ɣari:b la:kin ʔisimha ra:ħ min ba:li] • **3.** خِلَص [xilaṣ] خَلاص [xala:ṣ] *vn: sv* a. فات [fa:t] فَوت [fawt] *vn: sv* u. Nothing escapes her. ماكُو فَدّ شِي يِخلَص مِنها [ma:ku fadd ši yixlaṣ minha] Nothing escapes her. ما يفُوتها شِي [ma: yfu:tha ši] • **4.** تَخَلَّص مِن [txallaṣ min] تَخَلُّص [taxalluṣ] *vn: sv* a. خَلَّص مِن [xallaṣ min] تخِلِّص [txilliṣ] *vn: sv* i. That's the third time he's escaped punishment. هاي المَرَّة الثّالثَة تخَلَّص بِيها مِن العِقاب [ha:y ʔilmarra ʔiθθa:lθa txallaṣ bi:ha min ʔilʕiqa:b]

especially • **1.** لاسِيَّما [la:siyyama] بصُورَة خاصَّة [bṣu:ra xa:ṣṣa] خُصُوصاً [xuṣu:ṣan] She's been trying especially hard lately. دَتحاوِل جَهدها لا سِيَّما بِالمُدَّة الأَخِيرَة [datħa:wil ǰahidha la: siyyama: bilmudda ʔilʔaxi:ra] She's especially interested in sports. هِيَّ مِهتَمَّة بِالرِّياضَة بِصُورَة خاصَّة [hiyya mihtamma birriya:ḍa bṣu:ra xa:ṣṣa]

espionage • **1.** تَجَسُّس [taǰassus] جاسُوسِيَّة [ǰasu:siyya]

essay • **1.** مَقالَة [maqa:la] مَقالات [maqa:la:t] *pl:* إنشاء [ʔinša:ʔ] إنشاءات [ʔinša:ʔa:t] *pl:*

essence • **1.** جَوهَر [ǰawhar] جَواهِر [ǰawa:hir] *pl:* What was the essence of his lecture? شِنُو كان جَوهَر حَدِيثَه؟ [šinu: ča:n ǰawhar ħadi:θah?] • **2.** عِطِر [ʕiṭir] عُطُور [ʕuṭu:r] *pl:* رِيحَة [ri:ħa] رَوائِح، رَوايِح، رِيَح [rawa:ʔiħ, rawa:yiħ, riyaħ] *pl:* This contains essence of roses. هاي تِحتوِي عَطِر الوَرِد [ha:y tiħtiwi ʕaṭir ʔilwarid]

essential • **1.** أساسِي [ʔasa:si] ضَرُورِي [ḍaru:ri] جَوهَرِي [ǰawhari] Fresh vegetables are essential to good health. الخُضرَوات الطَّرِيَّة شِي أساسِي لِلصِّحَّة الزَّينَة [ʔilxuḍrawa:t ʔiṭṭariyya ši ʔasa:si liṣṣiħħa ʔizzayna]

essentials • **1.** أساس [ʔasa:s] أُسُس أَساسات [ʔasa:sa:t] *pl:* You can learn the essentials in an hour. تِقدَر تِتعَلَّم الأُسُس بساعَة وِحدَة [tigdar titʕallam ʔilʔusus bsa:ʕa wiħda]

to establish • **1.** أَسَّس [ʔassas] تَأسِيس [taʔsi:s] *vn:* تأَسَّس [tʔassas] *p:* أَنشَأ [ʔanšaʔ] إنشاء [ʔinša:ʔ] *vn:* إِنّشَأ [ʔinnišaʔ] *p:* This firm was established in 1905. هَالشَّرِكَة تأَسِّسَت بِسَنَة أَلِف وَتِسعِمِيَّة وخَمسَة [haššarika tʔassisat bsana ʔalif wtisiʕmiyya wxamsa] • **2.** ثِبَت [θibat] ثَبات [θaba:t] *vn:* إِنثِبَت [ʔinθibat] *p:* This is an established rule. هاي قاعِدَة ثابتَة [ha:y qa:ʕida θa:bta] • **3.** قَرَّر [qarrar] تَقرِير [taqri:r] *vn: sv* i. تقَرَّر [tqarrar] *p:* Contrary to regulations established in the law. خِلافاً لِلتَّعلِيمات المُقَرَّرَة بِالقانُون [xila:fan littaʕli:ma:t ʔilmuqarrara bilqa:nu:n] • **4.** ضِرَب [ḍirab] ضَرُب [ḍarub] *vn: sv* u. He established a new record. ضِرَب رَقَم قِياسِي جِدِيد [ḍirab raqam qiya:si ǰidi:d]

establishment • **1.** مُؤَسَّسَة [muʔassasa] مُؤَسَّسات [muʔassasa:t] *pl:* مُنشَأَة [munšaʔa] مُنشَآت [munšaʔa:t] *pl:*

estate • **1.** مُلُك [muluk] أَملاك [ʔamla:k] *pl:* His entire estate went to his eldest son. كُلّ مُلكَه راح لإبنَه الكِبِير [kull mulkah ra:ħ lʔibnah ʔiččibi:r]

real estate • **1.** عِقار [ʕiqa:r] عِقارات [ʕiqa:ra:t] *pl:*

esteem • **1.** اِحتِرام [ʔiħtira:m] اِحتِرامات [ʔiħtira:ma:t] *pl:*

estimate • **1.** تَقدِير [taqdi:r] تَقدِيرات [taqdi:ra:t] *pl:* My estimate was absolutely accurate. تَقدِيرِي كان مَضبُوط تَماماً [taqdi:ri ča:n maḍbu:ṭ tama:man] • **2.** سِعِر تَقدِيرِي [siʕir taqdi:ri] أَسعار تَقدِيرِيَّة [ʔasʕa:r taqdi:riyya] *pl:*

to estimate • **1.** قَدَّر [qaddar] تَقدِير [taqdi:r] *vn:* تقَدَّر [tqaddar] *p:* خَمَّن [xamman] تَخمِين [taxmi:n] *vn:* تخَمَّن [txamman] *p:* The flood damage was estimated at a million dinars. ضَرَر الفَيَضان تقَدَّر بمِليُون دِينار [ḍarar ʔilfayaḍa:n tqaddar bmilyu:n dina:r]

et cetera • **1.** إلَى آخِره [ʔila ʔa:xirihi]

eternal • **1.** أَزَلِي [ʔazali] أَبَدِي [ʔabadi] خالِد [xa:lid] The Imam spoke on eternal life. الإمام حِكَى عَن الحَياة الأَبَدِيَّة [ʔilʔima:m ħiča: ʕan ʔilħaya:t ʔilʔabadiyya]

ether • **1.** أَثِير [ʔaθi:r]

Ethiopia • **1.** الحَبَشَة [ʔilħabaša]

Ethiopian • **1.** حَبَشِي [ħabaši] حَبَشِيِّين، أَحباش [ħabašiyyi:n, ʔaħba:š] *pl:* Four Ethiopians visited our town today. أَربَع أَحباش زارَوا مَدِينَتنا اليُوم [ʔarbaʕ ʔaħba:š za:raw madi:natna ʔilyu:m] • **2.** حَبَشِي [ħabaši] I'd like to learn the Ethiopian language. يِعجِبنِي أَتعَلَّم اللُّغَة الحَبَشِيَّة [yiʕǰibni ʔatʕallam ʔilluɣa ʔilħabašiyya]

etiquette • **1.** أَصِل [ʔaṣil] أُصُول [ʔuṣu:l] *pl:* أَدَب [ʔadab] آداب [ʔa:da:b] *pl:*

Euphrates • **1.** الفُرات [ʔilfura:t]

Europe • **1.** أُورُبّا [ʔu:ruppa]

European • **1.** أُورُبِّي [ʔu:ruppi] أُورُبِّيِّين [ʔu:ruppi:yyi:n] *pl:*

E

to evacuate • **1.** أخلَى [ʔaxlaː] إخلاء [ʔixlaːʔ] *vn:* إنخِلَى [ʔinxilaː] *p:* We have to evacuate the town or else we'll be killed. لازِم نِخلِي المَدِينَة وَإلّا نِنقِتِل [laːzim nixli ʔilmadiːna waʔillaː ninkitil]

evacuation • **1.** إخلاء [ʔixlaːʔ]

to evade • **1.** تهَرَّب [tharrab] تَهَرُّب [taharrub] *vn: sv* a. تمَلَّص [tmallaṣ] تَمَلُّص [tamalluṣ] *vn: sv* a. She evaded the question. تهَرُّبَت مِن السُّؤال [tharrbat min ʔissuʔaːl]

to evaluate • **1.** عادَل [ʕaːdal] مُعادَلَة [muʕaːdala] *vn: sv* i. The college evaluated my diploma and accepted me. الكُلِّيَّة عادلَت شِهادتِي وَقِبلَتنِي [ʔilkulliyya ʕaːdlat šihaːdti wqiblatni]

to evaporate • **1.** تبَخَّر [tbaxxar] تَبَخُّر [tabaxxur] *vn: sv* a. طار [ṭaːr] طَيَران [ṭayaraːn] *vn: sv* i. The alcohol has all evaporated. الكُحُول كُلَّه تبَخَّر [ʔilkuħuːl kullah tbaxxar]

even • **1.** زَوجِي [zawǰi] Two, four, and six are even numbers. ثنَين وأربَعَة وَسِتَّة أرقام زَوجِيَّة [θnayn wʔarbaʕa wsitta ʔarqaːm zawǰiyya] • **2.** هادِئ [haːdiʔ] He has an even disposition. عِندَه طَبُع هادِئ [ʕindah ṭabuʕ haːdiʔ] • **3.** عَدِل [ʕadil] I have an even dozen left. بُقَى عِندِي دَرزَن عَدِل [buqaː ʕindi darzan ʕadil] • **4.** حَتَّى [ħatta] Even a layman can understand that. حَتَّى الشَّخص اللِّي ما مُختَصّ يِقدَر يِفتِهِمها لِهاي [ħatta ʔiššaxṣ ʔilli maː muxtaṣṣ yigdar yiftihimha lhaːy] Not even he knows the truth. حَتَّى هُوَّ ما يُعرُف الحَقِيقَة [ħatta huwwa maː yuʕruf ʔilħaqiːqa] That's even better. حَتَّى بَعَد أحسَن [ħatta baʕad ʔaħsan]

even now • **1.** حَتَّى هَسَّة [ħattaː hassa] Even now I can't convince him. حَتَّى هَسَّة ما أقدَر أقنِعَه [ħatta hassa maː ʔagdar ʔaqinʕah]

even so • **1.** مَعَ هٰذا [maʕa haːða] Even so I can't agree with you. مَعَ هٰذا آنِي ما أتِّفِق وِيّاك [maʕa haːða ʔaːni maː ʔattifiq wiyyaːk]

even though • **1.** وَلَو [walaw] Even though he succeeds in everything, he's not satisfied. وَلَو يِنجَح بِكُلِّشِي هُوَّ ما راضِي [walaw yinǰaħ bkullši huwwa maː raːḍi]

not even • **1.** حَتَّى ما [ħattaː maː] I couldn't even see him. آنِي حَتَّى ما قِدَرت أشُوفَه [ʔaːni ħatta maː gidart ʔašuːfah]

to be even • **1.** توافَى [twaːfaː] تَوافِي [tawaːfi] *vn: sv* a. تباوَك [tpaːwak] تَباوُك [tapaːwuk] *vn: sv* a. He took his money from me and we were even. أخَذ فلُوسَه مِنِّي وَتوافَينا [ʔaxað fluːsah minni wtwaːfayna]

to get even • **1.** تباوَك [tpaːwak] تَباوُك [tapaːwuk] *vn: sv* a. أخَذ مِن، أخَذ عَلَى [ʔaxað min, ʔaxað ʕala] *sv* u. Just you wait! I'll get even with you! أصبُرلِي شوَيَّة أتباوَك وِيّاك [ʔuṣburli šwayya ʔatpaːwak wiyyaːk] Just you wait! I'll get even with you! أصبُرلِي شوَيَّة راح آخُذ حَيفِي مِنَّك [ʔuṣburli šwayya raːħ ʔaːxuð ħayfi minnak]

to even up • **1.** عادَل [ʕaːdal] مُعادَلَة [muʕaːdala] *vn: sv* i. Your team is stronger than ours. Let's even them up before we play. فِرقَتكُم أقوَى مِن فِرقَتنا خَلِّي نعادِلهُم قَبُل ما نِلعَب [firqatkum ʔaqwaː min firqatna xalli nʕaːdilhum gabul maː nilʕab]

evening • **1.** مَسا، مَساء [masaː, masaːʔ] لَيلَة [laila, liːla] لَيلات، لَيالِي [laylaːt, layaːli] *pl:* The evenings here are cool. الأمسِيات هنا بارِدَة [ʔilʔumsiyaːt hnaː baːrda] Good evening! مَساء الخير [masaːʔ ʔilxiːr] We take a walk every evening. نِتمَشَّى كُلّ لَيلَة [nitmaššaː kull layla]

evenly • **1.** بِالتَّساوِي [bittasaːwi] تَعادُل [taʕaːdul] The paint isn't spread evenly. الصُّبُغ ما مِتوَزِّع بِالتَّساوِي [ʔiṣṣubuɣ maː mitwazziʕ bittasaːwi] Divide the apples evenly among you. إقسِمُوا التِّفّاح بَيناتكُم بِالتَّساوِي [ʔiqismuː ʔittiffaːħ baynaːtkum bittasaːwi]

event • **1.** حَدَث [ħadaθ] أحداث [ʔaħdaːθ] *pl:* حادِثَة [ħaːdiθa] حَوادِث [ħawaːdiθ] *pl:* It was the most important event of the year. كانَت أهَمّ حَدَث بِالسَّنَة [čaːnat ʔahamm ħadaθ bissana] • **2.** حال [ħaːl] I'll be there in any event. راح أكُون هناك عَلَى أيّ حال [raːħ ʔakuːn hnaːk ʕala ʔayy ħaːl] • **3.** حالَة [ħaːla] حالات [ħaːlaːt] *pl:* In the event of an accident, call the police. بِحالَة وُقُوع حادِثَة، خَبُّر الشُّرطَة [bħaːlat wuquːʕ ħaːdiθa, xabbur ʔiššurṭa]

eventually • **1.** أخِيراً [ʔaxiːran] أخِير [ʔaxiːr]

ever • **1.** أبَد [ʔabad] أبَداً [ʔabadan] (with negative) . Haven't you ever been in the United States? إنتَ أبَد ما رايِح لِلوِلايات المُتَّحِدَة؟ [ʔinta ʔabad maː raːyiħ lilwilaːyaːt ʔilmuttaħida?] Don't ever do this again. لا تسَوِّي هٰذا مَرَّة ثانيَة أبَداً [laː tsawwi haːða marra θaːniya ʔabadan]

*** Who ever heard of such a thing!** • **1.** مِنُو سامِع بهِيكِي شي [minu saːmiʕ bhiːči ši]

ever since • **1.** مِن [min] مِن وَكِت [min wakit] Ever since the accident I've had pains in my leg. مِن وَكِت الحادِث بُقَى عِندِي ألَم برِجلِي [min wakit ʔilħaːdiθ buqaː ʕindi ʔalam briǰli]

hardly ever • **1.** نادِراً [naːdiran] مِن النادِر [min ʔinnaːdir] I hardly ever have a headache. نادِراً يُوجَعنِي راسِي [naːdiran yuːǰaʕni raːsi]

every • **1.** كُلّ [kull] He comes here every week. هُوَّ يِجِي هنا كُلّ إسبُوع [huwwa yiǰi hna kull ʔisbuːʕ] Give every child one. إنطِي وِحدَة لِكُلّ طِفِل [ʔinṭi wiħda likull ṭifil] It rains every time we want to go out. كُلّ مَرَّة نرِيد نِطلَع تُمطُر الدِّنيا [kull marra nriːd niṭlaʕ tumṭur ʔiddinya]

every now and then • **1.** بَين كُلّ مُدَّة ومُدَّة [bayn kull mudda wmudda] He takes a drink every now and then. ياخُذلَه فَدّ بِيك بين كُلّ مُدَّة وَمُدَّة [yaːxuðlah fadd piːk bayn kull mudda wmudda]

every other • **1.** ... [و] بين [bayn ... [w] كُلّ [يوم] ين [kull [yi:m] -i:n] They have meat every other day. ياكلُون لَحَم بين يوم ويُوم [ya:klu:n laħam bi:n yu:m wyu:m] They have meat every other day. ياكلُون لَحَم كُلّ يومَين [ya:klu:n laħam kull yawmayn]

everybody • **1.** كُلّ واحِد [kull wa:ħid] كُلّ الناس [kull ʔinna:s] Everybody has to do his duty. كُلّ واحِد لازِم يقُوم بواجبَه [kull wa:ħid la:zim yqu:m bwa:ǰbah] I told it to everybody. قِلتها لكُلّ النّاس [gilitha likull ʔinna:s]

everybody else • **1.** كُلّ الآخَرين [kull ʔilʔa:xari:n] كُلّ الباقِين [kull ʔilba:qi:n] I have no objection if everybody else is agreed. آني ما عِندِي مانع إذا كُلّ الآخَرين موافقِين [ʔa:ni ma: ʕindi ma:niʕ ʔiða kull ʔilʔa:xari:n mwa:fqi:n]

everything • **1.** كُلّ شِي [kull ši] He's mixed up everything. خَربَط كُلّ شِي [xarbaṭ kull ši]

everywhere • **1.** بكُلّ مَكان [bkull maka:n] I've looked everywhere for that book. دَوَّرِت عَلَى ذاك الكِتاب بكُلّ مَكان [dawwarit ʕala ða:k ʔilkita:b bkull maka:n]

to evict • **1.** طَلَّع [ṭallaʕ] تَطلِيع [taṭli:ʕ] *vn:* تطَلَّع [ʔiṭṭallaʕ] *p:* The landlord evicted them from the house. صاحِب المُلك طَلَّعهُم مِن البَيت [ṣa:ħib ʔilmuluk ṭallaʕhum min ʔilbayt]

evidence • **1.** بَيِّنَة [bayyina] بَيِّنات [bayyina:t] *pl:* بُرهان [burha:n] بَراهِين [bara:hi:n] *pl:* حِجَّة [ħiǰǰa] حِجّات، حِجَج [ħiǰǰa:t, ħiǰaǰ] *pl:* دَلِيل [dali:l] أدِلَّة [ʔadilla] *pl:* He was convicted on the basis of false evidence. اِنحِكَم اِستِناداً عَلَى بَيِّنات كاذِبَة [ʔinħikam ʔistina:dan ʕala bayyina:t ka:ðiba]

evident • **1.** ظاهِر [ða:hir] واضِح [wa:ðiħ] It was evident that she was sick. كان واضِح هِيَّ مَرِيضَة [ča:n wa:ðiħ hiyya mari:ða]

evil • **1.** شَرّ [šarr] شِرِّير [širri:r] أشرار [ʔašra:r] *pl:* He chose the lesser of the two evils. اِختار أهوَن الشَّرَّين [ʔixta:r ʔahwan ʔiššarrayn] • **2.** سَيِّء [sayyiʔ] He has evil intention. عِندَه قَصِد سَيِّئ [ʕindah qaṣid sayyiʔ]

evolution • **1.** تَطَوُّر [taṭawwur] اِرتِقاء [ʔirtiqa:ʔ]

ewe • **1.** نَعجَة [naʕǰa] نَعجات، نعاج [naʕǰa:t, nʕa:ǰ] *pl:*

exact • **1.** طِبق الأَصِل [ṭibq ʔilʔaṣil] تَمام [tama:m] Is this an exact copy? هَذِي نُسخَة طَبق الأَصِل؟ [ha:ði nusxa ṭabq ʔilʔaṣil?]

*** Write down the exact amount.**

• **1.** إكتِب المَبلَغ بِالضَبُط [ʔiktib ʔilmablaɣ biððabuṭ]

exactly • **1.** تَماماً [tama:man] بِالضَبُط [biððabuṭ] مَضبُوط [maðbu:ṭ] That is exactly the same. هَذِي مِثلها بِالضَبُط [ha:ði miθilha biððabuṭ] That wasn't exactly nice of you. هَذِيك كانَت مُو حِلوَة تَماماً مِنَّك [haði:č ča:nat mu: ħilwa tama:man minnak]

to exaggerate • **1.** بالَغ [ba:laɣ] مُبالَغَة [muba:laɣa] *vn:* تبالَغ [tba:laɣ] *p:* هَوَّل [hawwal] تَهوِيل [tahwi:l] *vn:* تهَوَّل [thawwal] *p:* ضَخَّم [ðaxxam] تَضخِيم [taðxi:m] *vn:* تضَخَّم [tðaxxam] *p:* غالَى [ɣa:la:] مُغالاة [muɣa:la:] *vn:* تغالَى [tɣa:la:] *p:* You're exaggerating as usual. إنتَ دَتبالِغ حَسَب الأُصُول [ʔinta datba:liɣ ħasab ʔilʔuṣu:l]

exaggeration • **1.** تَهوِيل [tahwi:l] مُبالَغَة [muba:laɣa] مُبالَغات [muba:laɣa:t] *pl:* مُغالاة [muɣa:la:t] تَضخِيم [taðxi:m] There's no need for exaggeration. ماكُو حاجَة لِهَالتَّهوِيل [ma:ku ħa:ǰa lhattahwi:l]

exam • **1.** اِمتِحان [ʔimtiħa:n] اِمتِحانات [ʔimtiħa:na:t] *pl:*

examination • **1.** اِمتِحان [ʔimtiħa:n] اِمتِحانات [ʔimtiħa:na:t] *pl:* The examination was easy. الامتِحان كان سَهل [ʔilʔimtiħa:n ča:n sahil] • **2.** فَحِص [fahiṣ] فُحُوص، فُحُوصات [fuħu:ṣ, fuħu:ṣa:t] *pl:* What did the examination show? شطِلَع بالفَحِص؟ [šṭilaʕ bilfaħiṣ?] • **3.** اِستِجواب [ʔistiǰwa:b] اِستِجوابات [ʔistiǰwa:ba:t] *pl:* The examination of the witnesses lasted two hours. اِستِجواب الشُّهُود طَوَّل ساعتَين [ʔistiǰwa:b ʔiššuhu:d ṭawwal sa:ʕtayn]

to examine • **1.** فُحَص [fuħaṣ] فَحِص [faħiṣ] *vn:* اِنفُحَص [ʔinfuħaṣ] *p:* *sv* a. The doctor examined me thoroughly. الطَّبِيب فُحَصنِي فَحِص دَقِيق [ʔiṭṭabi:b fuħaṣni faħiṣ daqi:q] • **2.** اِستَجوَب [ʔistaǰwab] اِستِجواب [ʔistiǰwa:b] *vn:* *sv* i. The witnesses haven't been examined yet. لهَسَّة بَعَد ما إستَجوبَوا الشُّهُود [lhassa baʕad ma: ʔistaǰwibaw ʔiššuhu:d] • **3.** دَقَّق [daqqaq] تَدقِيق [tadqi:q] *vn:* *sv* i. I'm here to examine the books. آني هنا دَأَدَقِّق الدَّفاتِر [ʔa:ni hna: daʔadaqqiq ʔiddafa:tir] • **4.** اِمتِحَن [ʔimtiħan] اِمتِحان [ʔimtiħa:n] *vn:* *sv* i. اِختِبَر [ʔixtibar, ʔixtubar] اِختِبار [ʔixtiba:r] *vn:* *sv* i. He examined me in geography first. اِمتِحَنِّي بالجُغرافِيَة بِالأَوَّل [ʔimtiħanni biǰǰuɣra:fiya bilʔawwal]

example • **1.** مَثَل [maθal] أمثال [ʔamθa:l] *pl:* Give me an example. إنطِينِي مَثَل [ʔinṭi:ni maθal] • **2.** قُدوَة، قِدوَة [qudwa, qidwa] قُدوات [qudwa:t] *pl:* مِثال [miθa:l] أَمثِلَة [ʔamθila] *pl:* You should take him as an example in studying. لازم تِتَّخذَه قُدوَة بِالدِّراسَة [la:zim tittaxðah qudwa biddira:sa] • **3.** عِبرَة [ʕibra] عِبَر [ʕibar] *pl:* مِثال [miθa:l] أمثِلَة [ʔamθila] *pl:* The government punished him so he'd be an example to others. الحُكُومَة عاقبَتَه حَتَّى يكُون عِبرَة لغَيرَه [ʔilħuku:ma ʕa:qbatah ħatta yku:n ʕabra lɣayrah]

for example • **1.** مَثَلاً [maθalan] عَلَى سَبِيل المِثال [ʕala sabi:l ʔilmiθa:l] مَثَل [maθal] أمثال [ʔamθa:l] *pl:* Let's take Russia, for example. . . خَلِّي ناخُذ رُوسيَة مَثَلاً [xalli na:xuð ru:sya maθalan]

excavation • **1.** حَفُر [ħafur] When will the excavation for the new houses begin? شوَقِت راح يِبدِي حَفر الأَساسات لِلبيُوت الجِّدِيدَة؟ [šwakit ra:ħ yibdi ħafr ʔilʔasa:sa:t lilbyu:t ʔijjidi:da?] • **2.** جَزَع [jazaʕ] تَنقِيب [tanqi:b] تَنقِيبات [tanqi:ba:t] *pl:* Excavations in Iraq uncovered many relics of the past. الحَفريّات بِالعِراق كِشفَت عَن مُخَلَّفات أَثَريَّة كَثِيرَة عَن الماضِي [ʔilħafriyya:t bilʕira:q kišfat ʕan muxallafa:t ʔaθariyya kaθi:ra ʕan ʔilma:ði]

to exceed • **1.** زاد عَلَى [za:d ʕala] زِيادَة [ziya:da] *vn: sv* i. عَن [ʕan] The country's imports exceed the exports. الوارِدات بالبَلَد دَتزِيد عَن الصّادِرات [ʔilwa:rida:t bilbalad dadzi:d ʕan ʔiṣṣa:dira:t] • **2.** تجاوَز [tja:waz] تَجاوُز [taja:wuz] *vn: sv* a. They caught him exceeding the speed limit. لِزمَوه مِتجاوَز الحَدّ الأَقصَى لِلسُّرعَة [lizmawh midja:waz ʔilħadd ʔilʔaqṣa: lissurʕa] • **3.** فاق [fa:q] فَوق [fawq] *vn: sv* u. زاد عَلَى [za:d ʕala] زِيادَة [ziya:da] *vn: sv* i. The enemy's strength exceeded ours. قُوَّة العَدُو فاقت قُوَّتنا [quwwat ʔilʕadu fa:qat quwwatna]

exceedingly • **1.** كُلِّش [kulliš] She's exceedingly beautiful. هِيَّ حِلوَة كُلِّش [hiyya ħilwa kulliš]

to excel • **1.** فاق [fa:q] فَوق [fawq] *vn:* إنفاق [ʔinfa:q] *p:* تفَوَّق عَلَى [tfawwaq ʕala] تَفَوُّق [tafawwuq] *vn: sv* a. He excelled them all. فاقهُم كُلهُم [fa:qhum kullhum] • **2.** بِرَع ب [biraʕ b-] بَراعَة [bara:ʕa] *vn: sv* a. بِرَز [biraz] بُرُوز [buru:z] *vn: sv* i. He excelled in sports. بِرَع بِالرِّياضَة [biraʕ birriya:ða]

excellency • **1.** مَعالِي [maʕa:li] I'd like to present my brother to your excellency. أَحِبّ أَقَدِّم لِمَعالِيكُم أَخُويَا [ʔaħibb ʔaqaddim limaʕa:li:kum ʔaxu:ya]

excellent • **1.** مُمتاز [mumta:z] بارِع [ba:riʕ] فَلَّة [falla] فَلّات [falla:t] *pl:* He's an excellent tennis player. هُوَّ لاعِب تَنِس مُمتاز [huwwa la:ʕib tanis mumta:z]

except • **1.** ما عَدا [ma: ʕada:] إلّا [ʔilla] غير [ɣayr] بإستِثناء [bistiθna:ʔ] Everyone believed it except him. الكُلّ اِعتِقدَوا بِيها ما عَداه [ʔilkull ʔiʕtiqdaw bi:ha ma: ʕada:h] I like the book except for one chapter. أَحِبّ الكِتاب بِإستِثناء فَصِل واحِد [ʔaħibb ʔilkita:b biʔistiθna:ʔ faṣil wa:ħid]

exception • **1.** اِستِثناء [ʔistiθna:ʔ] اِستِثناءات [ʔistiθna:ʔa:t] *pl:* We make no exceptions. ما عِدنا اِستِثناءات [ma: ʕidna ʔistiθna:ʔa:t] We make no exceptions. ما نِستَثنِي أَحَّد [ma: nistaθni ʔaħħad]

excerpt • **1.** مَقطَع [maqṭaʕ] مَقاطِع [maqa:ṭiʕ] *pl:* He read me an excerpt from the new book. قِرالِي مَقطَع مِن الكِتاب الجّدِيد [qira:li maqṭaʕ min ʔilkta:b ʔijjdi:d]

excess • **1.** زايِد [za:yid] Pour off the excess fat. دِير الدِّهِن الزّايِد [di:r ʔiddihin ʔizza:yid]

to excess • **1.** بإفراط [bʔifra:ṭ] I drink sometimes, but not to excess. آنِي أَحياناً أَشرَب، لَكِن مُو بإفراط [ʔa:ni ʔaħya:nan ʔašrab, la:kin mu: bʔifra:ṭ]

excessive • **1.** فادِح [fa:diħ] باهِض [ba:hið] Their charges are excessive. أُجُورهُم فادِحَة [ʔuju:rhum fa:diħa] They've been making excessive profits. كانَوا دَيحَقّقُون أَرباح فادِحَة [ča:naw dayħaqqiqu:n ʔarba:ħ fa:diħa]

exchange • **1.** تَبادُل [taba:dul] We've arranged for an exchange of prisoners. تدَبَّرنا مَسأَلَة تَبادُل الأَسرَى [ddabbarna masʔalat taba:dul ʔilʔasra] • **2.** بَدّالَة [badda:la] بَدّالات [badda:la:t] *pl:* The rebels have captured the telephone exchange. الثُّوّار اِستَولَوا عَلَى بَدّالَة التِّلِفُون [ʔiθθuwwa:r ʔistawlaw ʕala badda:lat ʔittilifu:n]

rate of exchange • **1.** سِعِر العُملَة [siʕir ʔilʕumla] What's the rate of exchange today? شِنُو سِعِر العُملَة اليُوم؟ [šinu: siʕir ʔilʕumla ʔilyu:m?]

stock exchange • **1.** بُرصَة، بُورصَة [burṣa, bu:rṣa] بُورصات [bu:rṣa:t] *pl:* Where's the stock exchange? وين البُورصَة؟ [wi:n ʔilbu:rṣa?]

to exchange • **1.** بَدَّل [baddal] تَبدِيل [tabdi:l] *vn:* تبَدَّل [tbaddal] *p:* I want to exchange this book for another one. أَرِيد أَبَدِّل هَالكِتاب ويّا واحِد لاخ [ʔari:d ʔabaddil halkita:b wiyya wa:ħid la:x] • **2.** تبادَل [tba:dal] تَبادُل [taba:dul] *vn: sv* a. The ministers met to exchange views. الوُزَراء اِجتِمعَوا يِتبادَلُون وُجهات النَّظَر [lwuzara:ʔ ʔijtimʕaw yitba:dlu:n wujha:t ʔinnaðar]

to excite • **1.** هَيَّج [hayyaj] تَهيِيج [tahyi:j] *vn:* تهَيَّج [thayyaj] *p:* The way she walks excites me. طَرِيقَة مَشِيها تهَيِّجنِي [ṭari:qat maši:ha thayyijni] • **2.** حَمَّس [ħammas] حَماس [ħama:s] *vn:* تحَمَّس [tħammas] *p:* His speech excited the people. خِطابَه حَمَّس النّاس [xiṭa:bah ħammas ʔinna:s]

to get excited • **1.** حِمَق، اِنحُمَق [ħimaq, ʔinħumaq] حَماقَة [ħama:qa] *vn: sv* a. صار [ṣa:r] *sv* i. هاج [ha:j] هَيَجان [hayaja:n] *vn: sv* i. Don't get excited, I'll do it later on. لا تِحمَق، راح أَسَوِّيها بَعدين [la: tiħmaq, ra:ħ ʔasawwi:ha baʕdi:n] • **2.** تهَيَّج [thayyaj] تَهَيُّج [tahayyuj] *vn: sv* a. Don't get excited dear, we've got all night. لا تِتهَيَّج عَزِيزِي، اللَّيل كُلَّه إلنا [la: tithayyaj ʕazi:zi, ʔillayl kullah ʔilna] • **3.** اِضطِرَب [ʔiðṭirab] اِضطِراب [ʔiðṭira:b] *vn: sv* i. He got excited when he saw the enemy. اِضطِرَب مِن شاف العَدُو [ʔiðṭirab min ša:f ʔilʕadu] • **4.** تحَمَّس [tħammas] تَحَمُّس [taħammus] *vn: sv* a. The crowd got excited and stormed the embassy. الجَّماهِير تحَمّسَت وَهاجِمَت السَّفارَة [ʔijjama:hi:r thammisat wha:jimat ?issafa:ra] I'm so excited about the elections. آني كُلِّش مِتحَمِّس بالإنتخابات [?a:ni kulliš mithammis bil?intixa:ba:t]

exclamation mark • **1.** عَلامَة تَعَجُّب [ʕala:mat taʕajjub]

to exclude • **1.** اِستَثنَى [?istaθna:] اِستِثناء [?istiθna:?] *vn: sv* i. Our club rules exclude women. قَواعِد نادينا تِستَثني النِّسوان [qawa:ʕid na:di:na tistaθni ?inniswa:n]

exclusive • **1.** ما عَدا [ma: ʕada:] Your bill comes to 50 dinars exclusive of tax. قائِمتَك تسَوّي خَمسين دينار ما عَدا الضَريبَة [qa:?imtak tsawwi xamsi:n dina:r ma: ʕada: ðari:ba] • **2.** مُطلَق [mutlaq] We have exclusive rights to this invention. عِدنا حَقّ مُطلَق بهَالإختِراع [ʕidna haqq mutlaq bhal?ixtira:ʕ] • **3.** خاصّ [xa:ṣṣ] This is quite an exclusive club. هَذا نادي كُلِّش خاصّ [ha:ða na:di kulliš xa:ṣṣ]

excuse • **1.** عُذُر [ʕuður] أعذار [?aʕða:r] *pl:* That's no excuse! هَذا مُو عُذُر [ha:ða mu: ʕuður] • **2.** مُبَرِّر [mubarrir] مُبَرِّرات [mubarrira:t] *pl:* There's no excuse for this. ماكو مُبَرِّر لهاي [ma:ku mubarrir lha:y]

to excuse • **1.** سِمَح ل [simah l-] سَمِح [samih] *vn: sv* a. Excuse my broken Arabic. إسمَحلي بلُغَتي العَرَبيَّة المكَسِّرَة [?ismahli bluγati ?ilʕarabiyya ?ilmkassira] • **2.** عِفَى [ʕifa:] عَفي، إعفاء [ʕafy, ?iʕfa:?] *vn:* إنعِفَى [?inʕifa:] *p:* They excused him from military service. عِفوه مِن الخِدمَة العَسكَريَّة [ʕifu:h min ?ilxidma ?ilʕaskariyya]

to execute • **1.** عِدَم [ʕidam] إعدام [?iʕda:m] *vn:* اِنعِدَم [?inʕidam] *p:* The goverment executed the murderer at daybreak. الحُكومَة عِدمَت القاتِل الفَجِر [?ilhuku:ma ʕidmat ?ilka:til ?ilfajir] • **2.** نَفَّذ [naffað] تَنفيذ [tanfi:ð] *vn:* تنَفَّذ [tnaffað] *p:* They executed his orders promptly. نَفِّذوا أوامرَه حالاً [naffiðaw ?awa:mrah ha:lan]

execution • **1.** إعدام [?iʕda:m] إعدامات [?iʕda:ma:t] *pl:* When will his execution take place? شوَقت راح يِجري الإعدام بيه؟ [šwakit ra:h yijri ?il?iʕda:m bi:h?] • **2.** تَنفيذ [tanfi:ð] When do you expect to put the plan into execution? شوَقت تِتأمَّل تحُطّ الخُطَّة مَوضِع التَّنفيذ؟ [šwakit tit?ammal thuṭṭ ?ilxuṭṭa mawðiʕ ?ittanfi:ð?]

executive • **1.** إداري [?ida:ri] تَنفيذي [tanfi:ði] The executive branch has been given wide powers. السُّلطَة الإداريَّة اِنطَت سُلطات واسعَة [?issulṭa ?il?ida:riyya ?inniṭat sulṭa:t wa:sʕa]

to exempt • **1.** عِفَي [ʕifa:] عَفي [ʕafy] *vn:* اِنعِفَى [?inʕifa:] *p:* I've been exempted from the exam. إنعِفيت مِن الإمتِحان [?inʕifayt min ?il?imtiha:n] • **2.** اِستَثنَى [?istaθna:] اِستِثناء [?istiθna:?] *vn: sv* i. عِفَى [ʕifa:] *sv* i. The government exempted army officers from paying the new tax. الحُكومَة اِستَثنَت ضُبّاط الجَيش مِن دَفع الضَّرايِب الجِّديدَة [?ilhuku:ma ?istaθnat ðubba:ṭ ?ijji:š min dafiʕ ?iððara:yib ?ijjidi:da]

exercise • **1.** تَمرين [tamri:n] تَمارين [tama:ri:n] *pl:* The tenth exercise is difficult. التَّمرين العاشِر صَعُب [?ittamri:n ?ilʕa:šir ṣaʕub] • **2.** رياضَة [riya:ða] Walking is good exercise. المَشي خُوش رياضَة [?almašy xu:š riya:ða]

to exercise • **1.** رَيَّض [rayyað] تَرَيُّض [tarayyuð] *vn:* ترَيَّض [trayyað] *p:* I exercise the horse every day. أرَيِّض الحِصان كُلّ يوم [?arayyið ?ilhiṣa:n kull yu:m] • **2.** ترَيَّض [trayyað] تَرَيُّض [tarayyuð] *vn: sv* a. You have to exercise every morning. لازِم تِترَيَّض كُلّ يوم الصُّبُح [la:zim titrayyað kull yu:m ?iṣṣubuh] • **3.** مارَس [ma:ras] مُمارَسَة [muma:rasa] *vn: sv* i. تمارَس [tma:ris] *p:* He exercised his authority to end the strike. مارَس سُلطاتَه لإنهاء الإضراب [ma:ras sulṭa:tah li?inha:? ?il?iðra:b]

to exert • **1.** جِهَد [jihad] إجهاد، جُهُد [?ijha:d, juhud] *vn: sv* i. He never exerts himself. ما يِجهِد نَفسَه أبَداً [ma: yijhid nafsah ?abadan] • **2.** فُرَض [furað] فَرض [farið] *vn:* اِنفُرَض [?infurað] *p:* That group exerts considerable influence on the party's decisions. هَالجِّماعَة تُفرُض تَأثير كِبير عَلَى قَرارات الحِزب [hajjima:ʕa tufruð ta?θi:r čibi:r ʕala qara:ra:t ?ilhizib]

to exhaust • **1.** اِستَنفَذ [?istanfað] اِستِنفاذ [?istinfa:ð] *vn: sv* i. I've exhausted all possibilities. اِستَنفَذِت كُلّ الاحتِمالات [?istanfaðit kull ?il?ihtima:la:t] • **2.** خَلَّص [xallaṣ] تَخليص [taxli:ṣ] *vn:* تخَلَّص [txallaṣ] *p:* We've almost exhausted our ammunition. عَلَى وَشَك نخَلِّص عِتادنا [ʕala wašak nxalliṣ ʕita:dna] • **3.** اِستَنزَف [?istanzaf] اِستِنزاف [?istinza:f] *vn: sv* i. The oil reserves in this area are exhausted. اِحتِياط النَّفُط بهَالمَنطِقَة مُستَنزَف [?ihtiya:ṭ ?innafuṭ bhalmanṭiqa mustanzaf] • **4.** نِهَك [nihak] إنهاك [?inha:k] *vn: sv* i. اِنِّهَك [?innihak] *p:* Traveling eight hours by train is exhausting. سَفرَة ثمَن ساعات بالقِطار تِنهِك [safrat θman sa:ʕa:t bilqiṭa:r tinhik]

exhaustion • **1.** إعياء [?iʕya:?] The runner dropped from exhaustion. الرّاكُوض وُقَع مِن الإعياء [?irra:ku:ð wugaʕ min ?il?iʕya:?]

exhaust pipe • **1.** The exhaust pipe is broken. القَزوز مَكسُور [?ilgzu:z maksu:r]

exhibit • **1.** مَعرَض [maʕrað] مَعارِض [maʕa:rið] *pl:* Did you see the science exhibit? شِفت المَعرَض العِلمي؟ [šift ?ilmaʕrað ?ilʕilmi?]

to exhibit • **1.** راوَى [ra:wa:] مُراواة [mura:wa:t] *vn: sv* i. His wife loves to exhibit her jewelry. مَرتَه يعجِبها تراوي مُجوهَراتها [martah yiʕjibha tra:wi mujawhara:tha] • **2.** أظهَر [?aðhar] إظهار [?iðha:r] *vn: sv* i.

He exhibited great courage in the battle. شَجاعَة فائِقَة بِالمَعرَكَة [ʔaðhar šaǰa:ʕa fa:ʔiqa bilmaʕraka] • **3.** عِرَض [ʕirað] عَرِض [ʕarið] *vn:* اِنعِرَض [ʔinʕirað] *p:* The Russians exhibited their new farm machinery at the fair. الرُّوس عِرضَوا آلاتهُم الزِّراعِيَّة الجِّدِيدَة بِالمَعرَض [ʔirru:s ʕirðaw ʔa:la:thum ʔizzira:ʕiyya ʔiǰǰidi:da bilmaʕrað]

exhibition • **1.** مَعرَض [maʕrað] مَعارِض [maʕa:rið] *pl:*

exile • **1.** مَنفَى [manfa] مَنافِي [mana:fi] *pl:* He is in exile. هُوَّ بِالمَنفَى [huwwa bilmanfa] • **2.** مَنفِي [manfi] مَنفِيِّين [manfiyyi:n] *pl:* I met several exiles in Beirut. اِلتِقَيت وِيّا عِدَّة مَنفِيِّين بِبَيرُوت [ʔiltigi:t wiyya ʕiddat manfiyyi:n bbayru:t]

to exist • **1.** وُجَد [wuǰad] وِجُود [wiǰu:d] *vn:* اِنوِجَد [ʔinwiǰad] *p:* *sv* a. As far as I'm concerned, this issue doesn't exist. بِالنِّسبَة إِلِي هَلمُشكِلَة، غير مَوجُودَة [binnisba ʔili, halmuškila ɣi:r mawǰu:da] • **2.** عاش [ʕayš] عَيش [ʕayš] *vn:* *sv* i. How does he manage to exist on that amount of money? شلُون يِقدَر يعِيش عَلَى هَالمَبلَغ؟ [šlu:n yigdar yiʕi:š ʕala halmablaɣ?]

existence • **1.** عِيشَة [ʕi:ša] عِيشات [ʕi:ša:t] *pl:* He's leading a miserable existence. دَيعِيش عِيشَة تَعسَة [dayʕi:š ʕi:ṣa taʕsa] • **2.** وُجُود [wuǰu:d] He's not even aware of my existence. وَلا يِدرِي بِوُجُودِي [wala yidri bwuǰu:di] • **3.** بَقاء [baqa:ʔ] The professor explained the theory of the struggle for existence. الأُستاذ شِرَح نَظَرِيَّة الصِّراع مِن أَجل البَقاء [ʔilʔusta:ð širaħ naðariyyat ʔiṣṣira:ʕ min ʔaǰl ʔilbaqa:ʔ]

in existence • **1.** مَوجُود [mawǰu:d] This business has been in existence for fifty years. هَالشَّغلَة صارِلها مَوجُودَة خَمسِين سَنَة [haššaɣla ṣa:rilha mawǰu:da xamsi:n sana] • **2.** وُجُود [wuǰu:d] There is no such thing in existence. ماكُو هِيكِي شِي بالوُجُود [ma:ku hi:či ši bilwuǰu:d]

exit • **1.** باب طَلعَة [ba:b ṭalʕa] بِيبان طَلعَة [bi:ba:n ṭalʕa] *pl:* مَخرَج [maxraǰ] مَخارِج [maxa:riǰ] *pl:* I can't find the exit! ما أَقدَر أَلقِي باب الطَّلعَة [ma: ʔagdar ʔalgi ba:b ʔiṭṭalʕa]

to expand • **1.** وَسَّع [wassaʕ] تَوسِيع [tawsi:ʕ] *vn:* توَسَّع [twassaʕ] *p:* They're planning to expand the communications network. قاعِد يوضعُون خِطَّة لِتَوسِيع شَبَكَة المُواصَلات [ga:ʕid yu:ðaʕu:n xiṭṭa litawsi:ʕ šabakat ʔilmuwa:ṣala:t]

expansion • **1.** تَوَسُّع [tawassuʕ] Expansion of trade is beneficial to the country. تَوَسُّع التِّجارَة مُفِيد لِلبَلَد [tawassuʕ ʔittiǰa:ra mufi:d lilbaləd]

to expect • **1.** توَقَّع [twaqqaʕ] تَوَقُّع [tawaqquʕ] *vn:* *sv* a. تأَمَّل [tʔammal] تَأَمُّل [taʔammul] *vn:* *sv* a. I expect him at three o'clock. أَتوَقَّعَه ساعَة ثلاثَة [ʔatwaqqaʕah sa:ʕa tla:θa] Does he expect a tip? هَذا يِتأَمَّل بَخشِيش؟ [ha:ða yitʔammal baxši:š?] • **2.** اِنتِظَر [ʔintiðar] اِنتِظار [ʔintiða:r] *vn:* *sv* i. تأَمَّل [tʔammal] *sv* a. توَقَّع [twaqqaʕ] *sv* a. You can't expect that of him. ما مُمكِن تِنتِظِر هَذِي مِنَّه [ma: mumkin tintiðir ha:ði minnah]

expectation • **1.** تَوَقُّع [tawaqquʕ] Contrary to my expectations, the experiment succeeded. ضِدّ تَوَقُّعِي، التَّجرُبَة نِجحَت [ðidd tawaqquʕi, ʔittaǰruba niǰħat]

expedition • **1.** بِعثَة [biʕθa] بِعثات [biʕθa:t] *pl:* He's a member of the archaeological expedition. هُوَّ عُضو بالبِعثَة الأَثَرِيَّة [huwwa ʕuðw bilbiʕθa ʔilʔaθariyya]

to expel • **1.** طِرَد [ṭirad] طَرِد [ṭarid] *vn:* اِنطِرَد [ʔinṭirad] *p:* The boy was expelled from school. الوَلَد اِنطِرَد مِن المَدرَسَة [ʔilwalad ʔinṭirad min ʔilmadrasa]

expenditure • **1.** مَصرُوف [maṣru:f] مَصرُوفات، مَصارِيف [maṣru:fa:t, maṣa:ri:f] *pl:* مَصرَف [maṣraf] مَصارِيف [maṣa:ri:f] *pl:* Government expenditures will decrease this year. مَصرُوفات الحُكُومَة راح تقِلّ هالسَّنَة [maṣru:fa:t ʔilħuku:ma ra:ħ tqill hassana]

expense • **1.** مَصرَف [maṣraf] مَصارِيف [maṣa:ri:f] *pl:* نَفَقَة [nafaqa] نَفَقات [nafaqa:t] *pl:* I can't afford the expense. ما أَتحَمَّل هالمَصرَف [ma: ʔatħammal halmaṣraf]

at the expense of • **1.** عَلَى حساب [ʕala ħsa:b] عَلَى نَفَقَة [ʕala nafaqat] He made the trip at the expense of the company. قام بِالسَّفرَة عَلَى حساب الشَّرِكَة [ga:m bissafra ʕala ħsa:b ʔiššarika]

expensive • **1.** غالِي [ɣa:li] This house is very expensive. هَالبَيت كُلِّش غالِي [halbayt kulliš ɣa:li] • **2.** ثَمِين [θami:n] غالِي [ɣa:li] He was wearing a very expensive watch. كان لابِس ساعَة ثَمِينَة جِدّاً [ča:n la:bis sa:ʕa θami:na ǰiddan]

experience • **1.** خِبرَة [xibra] خِبرات، خِبَر [xibra:t, xibar] *pl:* Do you have any experience in these matters? عِندَك أَيّ خِبرَة بِهَالأُمُور؟ [ʕindak ʔayy xibra bhalʔumu:r?] • **2.** تَجرُبَة [taǰruba] تَجارُب [taǰa:rub] *pl:* I had a strange experience last night. مَرَّت عَلَيّا تَجرُبَة غَرِيبَة البارحَة باللَّيل [marrat ʕalayya taǰruba ɣari:ba ʔilba:rħa billayl]

to experience • **1.** مَرّ ب [marr b-] مَرّ [marr] *vn:* *sv* u. I never experienced anything like it before. ما مَرَّيت بشِي مِثِل هَذا قَبُل [ma: marrayt bši miθil ha:ða gabul]

experienced • **1.** مجَرَّب [mǰarrab] He's an experienced mechanic. هُوَّ مُجَرَّب مِيكانِيكِي [huwwa muǰarrab mikani:ki] • **2.** مُحَنَّك [muħannak] مُجَرِّب [muǰarrib] He's an experienced politician. هَذا سِياسِي مُحَنَّك [ha:ða siya:si muħannak]

experiment • **1.** تَجرُبَة [tajruba] تَجارُب [taja:rub] *pl:* The experiment was successful. التَّجرُبَة كانَت ناجحَة [ʔittajruba ča:nat na:jħa]

to experiment • **1.** سَوَّى تَجرُبَة [sawwa: tajruba] *sv* i. The scientist is experimenting with rabbits. العالِم دَيسَوِّي تَجارُب عالأَرانِب [ʔilʕa:lim daysawwi taja:rub ʕalʔara:nib] • **2.** جَرَّب [jarrab] تَجرِيب [tajri:b] *vn:* تجَرَّب [tjarrab] *p:* The artist experimented with a new technique. الفَنّان جَرَّب طَرِيقَة جِدِيدَة [ʔilfanna:n jarrab ṭari:qa jidi:da]

experimental • **1.** تَجرِيبِي [tajri:bi] This medicine is still in the experimental stage. هَالدُّوا بَعدَه بالطَّور التَّجرِيبِي [hadduwa: baʕdah bittawr ʔittajri:bi]

expert • **1.** خَبِير [xabi:r] خُبَراء [xubara:ʔ] *pl:* The experts declared the document a forgery. الخُبَراء صَرِّحوا إنُّو الوَثِيقَة مُزَوَّرَة [ʔilxubara:ʔ ṣarriħaw ʔinnu ʔilwaθi:qa muzawwara] • **2.** ماهِر [ma:hir] خَبِير [xabi:r] He's an expert salesman. هَذا بَيّاع ماهِر [ha:ða bayya:ʕ ma:hir]

to expire • **1.** خِلصَت مُدَّة [xilṣat muddat] اِنتِهَى [ʔintiha:] *sv* i. His visa expired last week. الفِيزَة مالتَه خِلصَت مُدَّتها الإسبُوع اللِّي فات [ʔilfi:za ma:ltah xilṣat muddatha ʔilʔisbu:ʕ ʔilli fa:t] His visa expired last week. الفِيزَة مالتَه اِنتِهَى مَفعُولها الإسبُوع اللِّي فات [ʔilfi:za ma:ltah ʔintiha: mafʕu:lha ʔilʔisbu:ʕ ʔilli fa:t]

to explain • **1.** فَسَّر [fassar] تَفسِير [tafsi:r] *vn:* تفَسَّر [tfassar] *p:* شِرَح [širaħ] شَرِح [šariħ] *vn:* اِنشِرَح [ʔinširaħ] *p:* I explained it to him. فَسَّرتلَه إيّاه [fassartlah ʔiyya:h]

explanation • **1.** تَفسِير [tafsi:r] شَرِح [šariħ] His explanation wasn't very clear. تَفسِيرَه ما كان كُلِّش واضِح [tafsi:rah ma: ča:n kulliš wa:ḍiħ]

explicit • **1.** واضِح [wa:ḍiħ] جَلِي [jali] We gave her explicit instructions. إنطَيناها تَعلِيمات واضحَة [ʔnṭi:na:ha taʕli:ma:t wa:ḍħa]

to explode • **1.** اِنفِجَر [ʔinfijar] اِنفِجار [ʔinfija:r] *vn: sv* i. A shell exploded near our house. فَدّ قُنبُلَة اِنفِجرَت يَمّ بَيتنا [fadd qunbula ʔinfijrat yamm baytna] • **2.** فَجَّر [fajjar] تَفجِير [tafji:r] *vn:* تفَجَّر [tfajjar] *p:* The government exploded an atomic bomb. الحُكُومَة فَجِّرَت قُنبُلَة ذَرِّيَّة [ʔilħuku:ma fajjirat qunbula ðarriyya]

exploit • **1.** مَأثَرَة [maʔθara] مَآثِر [maʔa:θir] *pl:* مَفخَرَة [mafxara] مَفاخِر [mafa:xir] *pl:* He never stops talking about his exploits. ما يِعجَز مِن الحَكِي عَن مَآثرَه [ma: yiʕjaz min ʔilħači ʕan maʔa:θrah] • **2.** شيطَنَة [šayṭana] He doesn't talk about his exploits with women. ما يِجِيب طارِي شَيطَنتَه وِيّا النِّسوان [ma: yji:b ṭa:ri šayṭantah wiyya ʔinniswa:n]

to exploit • **1.** اِستَغَلّ [ʔistaɣall] اِستِغلال [ʔistiɣla:l] *vn: sv* i. He exploits his workers. يِستِغِلّ عُمّالَه [yistiɣill ʕumma:lah] You've just begun to exploit the country's resources. تَوَّكُم بِدَيتُوا تِستِغِلُّون مَوارِد الدَّولَة [tawwkum bidaytu tistiɣillu:n mawa:rid ʔiddawla]

to explore • **1.** اِكتِشَف [ʔiktišaf] اِكتِشاف [ʔiktiša:f] *vn: sv* i. Sections of the Rub al Khali haven't been explored yet. بَعض أَجزاء الرُّبع الخالِي بَعدها ما مُكتَشَفَة [baʕḍ ʔajza:ʔ ʔirrubʕ ʔilxa:li baʕdha ma: muktašafa] • **2.** بِحَث [biħaθ] بَحِث [baħiθ] *vn:* اِنبِحَث [ʔinbiħaθ] *p:* We explored all the possibilities of understanding. بِحَثنا جَمِيع اِحتِمالات التَّفاهُم [biħaθna jami:ʕ ʔiħtima:la:t ʔittafa:hum]

explorer • **1.** مُكتَشِف [muktašif] مُكتَشِفِين [muktašifi:n] *pl:* رائِد [ra:ʔid] رُوّاد [ruwwa:d] *pl:*

explosion • **1.** اِنفِجار [ʔinfija:r] اِنفِجارات [ʔinfija:ra:t] *pl:* The explosion was heard for miles. الاِنفِجار كان يِنسِمِع عَلَى بُعد أَميال [ʔilʔinfija:r ča:n yinsimiʕ ʕala buʕd ʔamya:l]

export • **1.** تَصدِير [taṣdi:r] The government has stopped the export of wheat. الحُكُومَة وَقِّفَت تَصدِير الحُنطَة [ʔilħuku:ma waggfat taṣdi:r ʔilħunṭa]

exports • **1.** صادِر [ṣa:dir] صادِرات [ṣa:dira:t] *pl:* This year our exports exceeded our imports. هالسَّنَة صادِراتنا زادَت عَلَى اِستِيراداتنا [hassana ṣa:dira:tna za:dat ʕala ʔisti:ra:da:tna]

to export • **1.** صَدَّر [ṣaddar] تَصدِير [taṣdi:r] *vn:* تصَدَّر [tṣaddar] *p:* Germany exports lenses. أَلمانيَا تصَدِّر عَدَسات [ʔalma:nya: tṣaddir ʕadasa:t]

exporter • **1.** مُصَدِّر [muṣaddir] مُصَدِّرِين [muṣaddiri:n] *pl:*

to expose • **1.** عِرَض [ʕiraḍ] عَرِض [ʕariḍ] *vn:* اِنعِرَض [ʔinʕiraḍ] *p:* عَرَّض [ʕarraḍ] تَعرِيض [taʕri:ḍ] *vn:* تعَرَّض [tʕarraḍ] *p:* How long did you expose the shot? شقَدّ عَرَّضِت الصُّورَة لِلضُوَة؟ [šgadd ʕarraḍit ʔiṣṣu:ra liḍḍuwa?] He's constantly exposed to danger. هُوَّ مُعَرَّض لِلخَطَر دائِماً [huwwa muʕarraḍ lilxaṭar da:ʔiman] • **2.** فُضَح [fuḍaħ] فَضِح [faḍiħ] *vn:* اِنفُضَح [ʔinfuḍaħ] *p:* شِنَع [šinaʕ] شَنِع [šaniʕ] *vn:* اِنشِنَع [ʔinšinaʕ] *p:* He was exposed as a spy. اِنفُضَح كَجاسُوس [ʔinfuḍaħ kaja:su:s] • **3.** كِشَف [kišaf] كَشِف [kašif] *vn:* اِنكِشَف [ʔinkišaf] *p:* طَلَّع [ṭallaʕ] تَطلِيع [taṭli:ʕ] *vn: sv* i. She exposed her navel before the crowd. كِشفَت صُرَّتها قِدّام الجَّماهِير [kišfat ṣurratha gidda:m ʔijjama:hi:r]

E

exposure • **1.** تَعَرُّض [taʕarruð̣] He died from exposure to the sun. مات مِن التَّعَرُّض لِلشَّمِس [ma:t min ʔittaʕarruð̣ liššamis]

express • **1.** إكسِبرِس [ʔiksipris] I went to Basra by the express. رِحِت لِلبَصرَة بالإكسِبرَس [riħit lilbaṣra bilʔiksipras] • **2.** صَرِيح [ṣari:ħ] It was his express wish. هَذِي كانَت رَغُبتَه الصَّرِيحَة [ha:ði ča:nat rayubtah ʔiṣṣari:ħa] • **3.** مُعَيَّن [muʕayyan] The tool was bought for this express purpose. هَالألَة نشِرَت لِهالغَرَض المُعَيَّن [halʔa:la nširat lhalɣarað̣ ʔalmuʕayyan]

to express • **1.** عَبَّر عَن [ʕabbar ʕan] تَعبِير [taʕbi:r] *vn:* تعَبَّر [tʕabbar] *p:* أبدَى [ʔabda:] إبداء [ʔibda:ʔ] *vn: sv* i. He expressed his opinion freely. عَبَّر عَن رأيَه بِحُرِّيَّة [ʕabbar ʕan raʔyah bħurriyya] • **2.** أعرَب [ʔaʕrab] إعراب [ʔiʕra:b] *vn: sv* i. Did he express any wish? ما أعرَب عَن أيّ رَغبَة؟ [ma: ʔaʕrab ʕan ʔayy rayba?] • **3.** بَيَّن [bayyan] تَبيِين [tabyi:n] *vn:* تبَيَّن [tbayyan] *p:* He expressed his concern about the situation. بَيَّن قَلَقَه حَول الحالَة [bayyan qalaqah ħawl ʔilħa:la]

expression • **1.** تَعبِير [taʕbi:r] تَعابِير [taʕa:bi:r] *pl:* There's no better expression for it. ما إلها أحسَن مِن هالتَّعبِير [ma: ʔilha ʔaħsan min hattaʕbi:r] • **2.** مَلامِح [mala:miħ] تَعبِير [taʕbi:r] I can tell by the expression on your face that you don't like it. أقدَر أعرُف مِن مَلامِح وُجهَك إنُو ما يعجِبَك [ʔagdar ʔaʕruf min mala:miħ wuǰhak ʔinnu ma: yʕiǰbak]

expressive • **1.** مُعَبِّر [muʕabbir] She has very expressive eyes. عِدها عيُون كُلِّش مُعَبِّرَة [ʕidha ʕyu:n kulliš muʕabbira]

expressly • **1.** صَراحَةً [ṣara:ħatan] The law expressly says. . . القانُون ينُصّ صَراحَةً عَلَى [ʔilqa:nu:n ynuṣṣ ṣara:ħatan ʕala]

expulsion • **1.** طَرِد [ṭarid] We threatened him with expulsion from the party. هَدَّدناه بِالطَّرِد مِن الحِزب [haddadna:h biṭṭarid min ʔilħizib]

exquisite • **1.** رائع [ra:ʔiʕ] She has exquisite features. عِدها مَلامِح رائِعَة [ʕidha mala:miħ ra:ʔiʕa]

extemporaneous • **1.** اِرتِجالِي [ʔirtiǰa:li] مِرتِجِل [mirtiǰil] The minister gave an extemporaneous speech. الوَزِير ألقَى خِطاب اِرتِجالِي [ʔilwazi:r ʔalqa: xiṭa:b ʔirtiǰa:li]

to extend • **1.** اِمتَدّ [ʔimtadd] اِمتِداد [ʔimtida:d] *vn: sv* a. The dunes extend for miles. الرَّوابِي تِمتَدّ لِبُعُد أميال [ʔirrawa:bi timtadd lbuʕud ʔamya:l] • **2.** مَدّ [madd] مَدّ [madd] *vn:* اِنمَدّ [ʔinmadd] *p:* He extended a helping hand to me. مَدّلِي يَدّ المُساعَدَة [maddli yadd ʔilmusa:ʕada] • **3.** مَدَّد [maddad] تَمدِيد [tamdi:d] *vn:* تمَدَّد [tmaddad] *p:* I'd like to extend this visa. أحِبّ أمَدِّد هالفِّيزا [ʔaħibb ʔamaddid halfi:za] • **4.** قَدَّم [qaddam] تَقدِيم [taqdi:m] *vn:* تقَدَّم [tqaddam] *p:* We'd like to extend our sincere congratulations. نودّ أن نقَدِّم تَهانِينا القَلبِيَّة [nwidd ʔan nqaddim taha:ni:na ʔilqalbiyya]

extended • **1.** طُوِيل [ṭuwi:l] He remained in the hospital for an extended period. بُقَى بِالمُستَشفى مُدَّة طُوِيلَة [buqa: bilmustašfa mudda ṭuwi:la]

extension • **1.** تَمدِيد [tamdi:d] He gave me another week's extension. اِنطانِي تَمدِيد لِمُدَّة إسبُوع لاخ [ʔinṭa:ni tamdi:d limuddat ʔisbu:ʕ la:x] The extension of the new road to Mosul will be finished next year. تَمدِيد الطَّرِيق الجِّدِيد لِلمُوصِل راح يكمَل السَّنَة الجّايَّة [tamdi:d ʔiṭṭari:q ʔiǰǰidi:d lilmu:ṣil ra:ħ yikmal ʔissana ʔiǰǰa:yya] • **2.** فَرِع [fariʕ] فُرُوع [furu:ʕ] *pl:* We need two more extensions for our telephone. نِحتاج فَرعَين بَعَد لِلتِّلِفَون مالنَا [niħta:ǰ farʕayn baʕad littilifu:n ma:lna]

extension cord • **1.** وايَر سَيّارَة [wa:yar sayya:ra] وايَرات سَيّارَة [wa:yara:t sayya:ra] *pl:*

extensive • **1.** واسِع [wa:siʕ] He was given extensive powers. اِنِّطَى سُلطات واسِعَة [ʔinniṭa: sulṭa:t wa:sʕa]

extent • **1.** دَرَجَة [daraǰa] دَرَجات [daraǰa:t] *pl:* حَدّ [ħadd] To a certain extent, he's responsible for the disaster. إلَى دَرَجَة مُعَيَّنَة، هُوَّ مَسؤُول عَن الكارِثَة [ʔila daraǰa muʕayyana, huwwa masʔu:l ʕan ʔilka:riθa] • **2.** The extent of his influence is still not known. مَدَى نُفُوذَه بَعَد ما مَعرُوف [mada: nufu:ðah baʕad ma: maʕru:f]

*** He resembles his father to some extent.**
• **1.** يِشبَه أبُوه بَعض الشَّبَه [yišbah ʔabu:h baʕð̣ ʔiššabah]

exterior • **1.** خارِجِي [xa:riǰi] بَرّانِي [barra:ni] This is an exterior view of the house. هَذا مَنظَر خارِجِي لِلبَيت [ha:ða manð̣ar xa:riǰi lilbayt]

to exterminate • **1.** قِضَى عَلَى [qið̣a:, gið̣a: ʕala] قَضاء [qað̣a:ʔ] *vn:* اِنقِضَى [ʔinqið̣a:] *p:* اِستَأصَل [ʔistaʔṣal] اِستِئصال [ʔistiʔṣa:l] *vn: sv* i. We hired a man to exterminate the termites. شَغَّلنا رِجّال حَتَّى يِقضِي عالأرضَة [šayyalna riǰǰa:l ħatta yiqð̣i ʕalʔurð̣a]

external • **1.** خارِجِي [xa:riǰi] This medicine is for external use only. هَالدُّوا لِلإستِعمال الخارِجِي فَقَط [hadduwa: lilʔistiʕma:l ʔilxa:riǰi faqaṭ]

extinct • **1.** مُنقَرِض [munqarið̣] The dinosaur is an extinct animal. الدَّيناصُور حَيوان مُنقَرِض [ʔiddayna:ṣu:r ħaywa:n munqarið̣]

to extinguish • **1.** طَفَّى [ṭaffa:] تَطفِيَة [taṭfiya] *vn:* تطَفَّى [ʔiṭṭaffa:] *p:* The fire department extinguished the fire. دائرَة الإطفاء طَفَّت الحَريق [da:ʔirat ʔilʔiṭfa:ʔ ṭaffat ʔilħari:q]

extra • **1.** زايِد [za:yid] إضافِي [ʔiðˌa:fi] Do you have a few extra pencils? عِندَك كَم قَلَم زايِد؟ [ʕindak čam qalam za:yid?] • **2.** جِدّاً [ǰiddan] These are extra large eggs. هَالبَيض كبار جِدّاً [halbi:ð̣ kba:r ǰiddan]

extract • **1.** خُلاصَة [xula:ṣa] خُلاصات [xula:ṣa:t] *pl:* Give me a bottle of lemon extract. إنطِينِي شِيشَة مِن خُلاصَة اللَّيمُون [ʔinṭi:ni ši:ša min xula:ṣat ʔillimu:n]

to extract • **1.** شِلَع [šilaʕ] شَلِع [šaliʕ] *vn:* اِنشِلَع [ʔinšilaʕ] *p:* The dentist extracted two of my teeth. طَبِيب الأسنان شِلَع إثنَين مِن سنُونِي [ṭabi:b ʔilʔasna:n šilaʕ ʔiθnayn min snu:ni] • **2.** اِستَخلَص [ʔistaxlaṣ] اِستِخلاص [ʔistixla:ṣ] *vn: sv* i. He has a factory for extracting aluminum from its ore. عِندَه مَعمَل لِاستِخلاص الألَمنِيُوم مِن مادّتَه الخام [ʕindah maʕmal liʔistixla:ṣ ʔilʔalaminyu:m min ma:ddtah ʔilxa:m]

extradition • **1.** تَسلِيم المُجرِمِين [tasli:m ʔilmuǰrimi:n] We have extradition agreements with many countries. عِدنا مُعاهَدات تَسلِيم المُجرِمِين ويّا هوايَة دُوَل [ʕidna muʕa:hada:t tasli:m ʔilmuǰrimi:n wiyya hwa:ya duwal]

extraordinary • **1.** غَير اِعتِيادِي [ɣayr ʔiʕtiya:di] Only an extraordinary person could do that. بَسّ فَدّ شَخص غير اِعتِيادِي يِقدَر يسَوِّي هَذا [bass fadd šaxiṣ ɣi:r ʔiʕtiya:di yigdar ysawwi ha:ða] The president is given extraordinary powers in time of war. الرَّئِيس يِنْطِي سُلطات غير اِعتِيادِيَّة بوَقت الحَرُب [ʔirraʔi:s yinniṭi sulṭa:t ɣi:r ʔiʕtiya:diyya bwakit ʔilħarub] • **2.** فَوق العادَة [fu:g ʔilʕa:da] The cabinet will have an extraordinary session tomorrow. الوُزارَة راح تِعقُد اِجتِماع فُوق العادَة باكِر [ʔilwuza:ra ra:ħ tiʕqud ʔiǰtima:ʕ fu:g ʔilʕa:da ba:čir] • **3.** خارِق [xa:riq] That's something really extraordinary. هَذا فَدّ شِي صُدُق خارِق [ha:ða fadd ši ṣudug xa:riq]

extravagant • **1.** مُسرِف [musrif] مُبَذِّر [mubaððir] مُبَذِّرِين [mubaððiri:n] *pl:* She's very extravagant. هاي مُصرِفَة [ha:y kulliš muṣrifa]

extreme • **1.** شَدِيد [šadi:d] We had to resort to extreme measures. اِضطَرّينا نِلجَأ إلَى إجراءات شَدِيدَة [ʔiðṭarrayna nilǰaʔ ʔila ʔiǰra:ʔa:t šadi:da] • **2.** مُتَطَرِّف [mutaṭarrif] He is an extreme nationalist. هَذا وَطَنِي مِتطَرِّف [ha:ða waṭani miṭṭarrif]

extremely • **1.** غايَة [ɣa:ya] غايات [ɣa:ya:t] *pl:* جِدّاً [ǰiddan] هوايَة [hwa:ya] كُلِّش [kulliš] This news is extremely sad. هَالخَبَر مُحزِن لِلغايَة [halxabar muħzin lilɣa:ya] I am extremely surprised. آنِي مِندِهِش جِدّاً [ʔa:ni mindihiš ǰiddan]

eye • **1.** عين [ʕayn ʕi:n] عيُون [ʕyu:n] *pl:* On a clear day you can see the town from here with the naked eye. بِيُوم صَحو تِقدَر تشُوف المَدِينَة مِن هنَا بالعَين المُجَرَّدَة [byu:m ṣaħw tigdar tšu:f ʔilmadi:na min hna bilʕi:n ʔilmuǰarrada] I've had my eye on that for a long time. صارلِي مُدَّة طُويلَة حاطّ عينِي عَلَى هَذا [ṣa:rli mudda ṭuwi:la ħa:ṭṭ ʕi:ni ʕala ha:ða] Keep your eye on the children while I'm out. حُطّ عينَك عَالجُهّال مِن أطلَع [ħuṭṭ ʕaynak ʕaǰǰahha:l min ʔaṭlaʕ] • **2.** خُرُم [xurum] خرُوم [xru:m] *pl:* The eye of this needle is very small. خُرُم هالأبرَة كُلِّش صغَيِّر [xurum halʔubra kulliš ṣɣayyir] • **3.** نَظَر [naðar] أنظار [ʔanða:r] *pl:* I've been trying to catch your eye for a half hour. صارلِي نُصّ ساعَة دَاحاوِل أَلفِت نَظَرَك [ṣa:rli nuṣṣ sa:ʕa daʔaħa:wil ʔalfit naðarak] All are equal in the eyes of the law. الكُلّ مِتساوين بنَظَر القانُون [ʔilkull mitsa:wi:n bnaðar ʔilqa:nu:n]

*** He's lowered himself in her eyes.** • **1.** وُقَع مِن عَينها [wugaʕ min ʕaynha]

to eye • **1.** باوَع عَلَى [ba:waʕ ʕala] مباوَعَة [mba:waʕa] *vn: sv* i. He eyed the chocolate longingly. باوَع عالجُكلِيت بِشَهيَة [ba:waʕ ʕaččukli:t bšahya]

eyebrow • **1.** حاجِب [ħa:ǰib] حَواجِب [ħawa:ǰib] *pl:* He has thick eyebrows. عِندَه حواجِب ثِخِينَة [ʕindah ħwa:ǰib θixi:na]

eyedrops • **1.** قَطرَة [qaṭra, gaṭra] قَطرات [qaṭra:t, gaṭra:t] *pl:* Use these eyedrops three times a day. اِستَعمِل هالقَطرَة ثلَث مَرّات بِاليُوم [ʔistaʕmil halqaṭra tlaθ marra:t bilyu:m]

eyeglasses • **1.** مَنظَرَة [manðara] مَناظِر [mana:ðir] *pl:* عوَينات [ʕwayna:t] مَناظِر [mana:ðir] *pl:* Do you wear eyeglasses? تِلبَس مَناظِر؟ [tilbas mana:ðir?]

eyelash • **1.** رَمِش [ramiš] هِدِب، هَدَب [hidib, hadab] أهداب [ʔahda:b] *pl:* You have pretty black eyelashes. عِندِك رمُوش سُودَة حِلوَة [ʕindič rmu:š su:da ħilwa]

eyelid • **1.** جِفِن [ǰifin] جفُون [ǰfu:n] *pl:* She's wearing eyeshadow on her eyelids. هِيَّ خالَّة كُحُل عَلَى جفُونها [hiyya xa:lla kuħul ʕala ǰfu:nha]

eyesight • **1.** بَصَر [baṣar] نَظَر [naðar] أنظار [ʔanða:r] *pl:* You have weak eyesight. بَصَرَك ضَعِيف [baṣarak ðaʕi:f]

F

fabric • **1.** قماش [qmaːš] My wife bought some fabric to make a new jacket. مَرتِي اِشتِرَت قماش حَتَّى تخَيِّط سِترَة [marti ʔištirat qmaːš ħatta txayyiṭ sitra]

face • **1.** وُجِه [wuǰih] وجُوه [wǰuːh] *pl:* If I'd been in your place, I'd have told him to his face. لَو بِمَكانَك، كان قِتّلَه بوُجهَه [law bmakaːnak, čaːn gittlah bwuččah] She slammed the door in my face. سَدَّت الباب بوُجهِي [saddat ʔilbaːb bwuǰhi] • **2.** ظاهِر [ð̣aːhir] On the face of it, it looks like a good proposition. حَسَب الظّاهِر، يبَيِّن خُوش اِقتِراح [ħasab ʔiðð̣aːhir, yibayyin xuːš ʔiqtiraːħ]

at face value • **1.** بمَظاهِر خارِجِيَّة [bmaðaːhir xaːriǰiyya] She takes everything at face value. تاخُذ كُلّشِي بِمَظاهِره الخارِجِيَّة [taːxuð kullši bmaðaːhirha ʔilxaːriǰiyya]

to face • **1.** واجَه [waːǰah] مُواجَهَة [muwaːǰaha] *vn:* تَواجُه [twaːǰuh] *p:* Let's face the facts. خَلِّي نواجِه الحَقايِق [xalli nwaːǰih ʔilħaqaːyiq] I can't face him. ما أقدَر أَواجهَه [maː ʔagdar ʔawaːǰhah] Face the wall. واجِه الحايِط [waːǰih ʔilħaːyiṭ] • **2.** اِتِّجَه [ʔittiǰah] اِتِّجاه [ʔittiǰaːh] *vn: sv* i. واجَه [waːǰah] *sv* i. Our windows face south. شبابِيكنا تواجِه الجَّنُوب [šbaːbiːčna twaːǰih ʔiǰǰanuːb]

* **The building is faced with red brick.**

• **1.** واجهَة البِنايَة مَبنِيَّة بطابُوق أحمَر [waːǰhat ʔilibnaːya mabniyya bṭaːbuːg ʔaħmar]

facing • **1.** قبال [gbaːl] مواجِه [mwaːǰih] مُقابِل [muqaːbil] He lives in the house facing the theater. يِسكُن بِالبَيت اللّي قبال السِّينَما [yiskun bilbayt ʔilli gbaːl ʔissinama]

fact • **1.** حَقِيقَة [ħaqiːqa] حَقايِق، حَقائِق [ħaqaːyiq, ħaqaːʔiq] *pl:* واقِع [waːqiʕ] وَقائِع [waqaːyiʕ] *pl:* That's a well-known fact. هٰذِيك حَقِيقَة كُلِّش مَعرُوفَة [haðiːč ħaqiːqa kulliš maʕruːfa]

* **He has a matter-of-fact way about him.**

• **1.** هُوَّ رَجُل واقِعِي [huwwa raǰul waːqʕi]

factor • **1.** عامِل [ʕaːmil] عَوامِل [ʕawaːmil] *pl:* That's an important factor. هٰذا فَدّ عامِل مُهِمّ [haːða fadd ʕaːmil muhimm]

factory • **1.** مَعمَل [maʕmal] مَعامِل [maʕaːmil] *pl:* مَصنَع [maṣnaʕ] مَصانِع [maṣaːniʕ] *pl:* He's working in a factory. هُوَّ دَيِشتُغُل بمَعمَل [huwwa dayištuɣul ʔibmaʕmal]

factual • **1.** واقِعِي [waːqiʕi] His reports are always factual. تَقارِيرَه دائِماً واقِعِيَّة [taqaːriːrah daːʔiman waːqʕiyya]

to fade • **1.** كِشَف [kišaf] كَشِف [kašif] *vn: sv* i. My socks faded in the wash. جوارِيبِي كِشفَت بِالغَسِل [ǰwaːriːbi kišfat bilɣasil] The wallpaper is all faded. كُلّ أَوراق الحِياطِين لَونها كِشَف [kull ʔawraːq ʔilħiyaːṭiːn lawnha kišaf] • **2.** ذِبَل [ðibal] ذُبُول [ðubuːl] *vn: sv* i. These roses faded very quickly. هَالوَرِد ذِبَل كُلِّش بِالعَجَل [halwarid ðibal kulliš bilʕaǰal] • **3.** تلاشَى [tlaːšaː] تَلاشِي [talaːši] *vn: sv* a. The music faded in the distance. المُوسِيقَى تلاشَت مِن بِعِيد [ʔilmusiːqaː tlaːšat min biʕiːd]

to fail • **1.** فِشَل [fišal] فَشَل [fašal] *vn: sv* a. His experiment failed. تَجرُبتَه فِشلَت [taǰrubtah fišlat] All our efforts failed. كُلّ مُحاوَلاتنا فِشلَت [kull muħaːwalaːtna fišlat] • **2.** سِقَط ب [siqaṭ b-] سُقُوط [ṣuquːṭ] *vn: sv* u. رِسَب ب [risab b-] رُسُوب [rusuːb] *vn: sv* i. Five students failed in geometry. خَمِس تَلامِيذ سِقطَوا بالهَندَسَة [xamis talaːmiːð siqṭaw bilhandasa] • **3.** خان [xaːn] خانات [xaːnaːt] *pl:* خِيانَة [xiyaːna] *vn:* اِنخان [ʔinxaːn] *p:* If my eyes don't fail me, that's him. هٰذا هُوَّ إذا ما تخُونني عيني [haːða huwwa ʔiða maː txuːnni ʕiːni] • **4.** ضِعَف [ðiʕaf] ضُعُف [ðuʕuf] *vn: sv* a. His eyesight is failing. نَظَرَه دَيِضعَف [naðarah dayiðʕaf]

* **I won't fail you.** • **1.** ما راح أَخَيِّب ظَنَّك [maː raːħ ʔaxayyib ðannak]

don't fail ... • **1.** لا يكُون ما [laː ykuːn maː-] Don't fail to see that picture. لا يكُون ما تشُوف هَالفِلِم [laː ykuːn maː tšuːf halfilim]

without fail • **1.** مِن كُلّ بُدّ [min kull budd] حَتماً [ħatman] I'll be there without fail. آنِي راح أكُون هناك مِن كُلّ بُدّ [ʔaːni raːħ ʔakuːn hnaːk min kull budd]

failure • **1.** فَشَل [fašal] The failure of the experiment was due to carelessness. فَشَل التَّجرُبَة كان سَبَبَه الإهمال [fašal ʔittaǰruba čaːn sababah ʔilʔihmaːl] • **2.** فاشِل [faːšil] As a businessman he was a complete failure. كَرَجُل أعمال كان فاشِل تَماماً [karaǰul ʔaʕmaːl kaːn faːšil tamaːman] • **3.** سَكتَة [sakta] He died of heart failure. مات بِسَكتَة قَلبِيَّة [maːt bsakta qalbiyya]

faint • **1.** ضَعِيف [ðaʕiːf] خافِت [xaːfit] I heard a faint noise. سمَعِت حِسّ خافِت [smaʕit ħiss xaːfit] There's only a faint hope left. ما بُقَى غير أَمَل كُلِّش ضَعِيف [maː buqaː ɣiːr ʔamal kulliš ðaʕiːf] • **2.** دايخ [daːyix] I feel faint. أَحِسّ دايخ [ʔaħiss daːyix]

* **I haven't the faintest idea.** • **1.** ما عِندِي أَقَلّ فِكرَة [maː ʕindi ʔaqall fikra]

to faint • **1.** غابَت رُوح- [ɣaːbat ruːħ-] غِمَى عَلَى [ɣimaː ʕala] إغماء [ʔiɣmaːʔ] *vn: sv* i. She fainted with fright. غابَت رَوحها مِن الخَوف [ɣaːbat ruːħha min ʔilxawf] She fainted with fright. غِمَى عَليها مِن الخَوف [ɣimaː ʕaliːha min ʔilxawf]

fair • **1.** مَعرَض [maʕrað] مَعارِض [maʕaːrið] *pl:* Are you going to the Damasaus International Fair?

؟إنتَ رايح لِمَعرَض دِمَشق الدَّولي [ʔinta ra:yiħ lmaʕrað dimašq ʔiddawli?] • **2.** مِعتَدِل [miʕtadil] مُناسِب [muna:sib] That's a fair price. هَذا سِعِر مُعتَدِل [ha:ða siʕir muʕtadil] • **3.** صاحِي [ṣa:ħi] Tomorrow the weather will be fair and cool. باكِر الجَّوّ راح يكُون صاحِي وَشوَيَّة بَرِد [ba:čir ʔijjaww ra:ħ yku:n ṣa:ħi wšwayya barid] • **4.** أشقَر [ʔašgar] شُقُر [šugur] *pl:* شَقرَة [šagra] *Feminine:* She has blue eyes and fair hair. عِدها عيُون زُرُق وَشَعَر أَشقَر [ʕidha ʕyu:n zurug wšaʕar ʔašgar] • **5.** مُتَوَسِّط [mutawaṣṣiṭ, mitwaṣṣiṭ] The work is only fair. الشُّغُل مِتوَسِّط [ʔiššuɣul mitwassiṭ]

*** That wouldn't be fair!** • **1.** هَذاك ما يكُون إنصاف [haða:k ma: yku:n ʔinṣa:f]

fairy tale • **1.** قُصَّة خُرافِيَّة [quṣṣa xura:fiyya] قُصَص خُرافِيَّة [quṣaṣ xura:fiyya] *pl:*

faith • **1.** دِين [di:n] أَديان [ʔadya:n] *pl:* I don't know what his faith is. ما أعرُف دِينَه شِنُو [ma: ʔaʕruf di:nah šinu] • **2.** ثِقَة [θiqa] I lost faith in him. آنِي فقَدِت ثِقَتِي بِيه [ʔa:ni fqadit θiqati bi:h]

faithful • **1.** مُخلِص [muxliṣ] He's faithful to his wife. هُوَّ مُخلِص لِزَوجتَه [huwwa muxliṣ lzawijtah] She's very faithful in her work. هِيَّ كُلِّش مُخلِصَة بشُغُلها [hiyya kulliš muxliṣa bšuɣulha]

fake • **1.** مُقَلَّد [muqallad] مزَيَّف [mzayyaf] كاذِب [ka:ðib, ča:ðib] This picture is a fake. هَالصُّورَة مُقَلَّدَة [haṣṣu:ra muqallada] He's not a real doctor, he's a fake. هُوَّ مُو طَبِيب حَقِيقِي، هُوَّ مزَيَّف [huwwa mu: ṭabi:b ħaqi:qi, huwwa mzayyaf]

to fake • **1.** زَيَّف [zayyaf] تزِيِّف، تَزيِيف [tziyyif, tazyi:f] *vn:* تزَيَّف [tzayyaf] *p:* قَلَّد [qallad] تَقلِيد، تقِلِّد [taqli:d, tqillid] *vn:* تقَلَّد [tqallad] *p:* The documents are faked. الوَثايِق مزَيَّفَة [ʔalwaθa:yiq muzayyfa] • **2.** تظاهَر [tða:har] تَظاهُر [taða:hur] *vn: sv* a. He faked poverty. تظاهَر بالفُقُر [tða:har bilfuqur]

fall • **1.** وَقعَة [wagʕa] وَقعات [wagʕa:t] *pl:* He hasn't recovered from his fall yet. بَعَد لهَسَّة ما صِحَى مِن وَقِعتَه [baʕad lhassa ma: ṣiħa: min wagiʕtah] • **2.** سُقُوط [suqu:ṭ] What do you know about the fall of the Roman Empire? شتُعرُف عَن سُقُوط الدَّولَة الرُّومانِيَّة؟ [štuʕruf ʕan suqu:ṭ ʔiddawla ʔirru:ma:niyya?] • **3.** خَرِيف [xari:f] I'll be back next fall. آنِي راح أرجَع الخَرِيف الجّاي [ʔa:ni ra:ħ ʔarjaʕ ʔilxari:f ʔijja:y]

to fall • **1.** وُقَع [wugaʕ] وُقُوع [wugu:ʕ] *vn: sv* a. He fell from the ladder. هُوَّ وُقَع مِن الدَّرَج [huwwa wugaʕ min ʔiddaraj] • **2.** سِقَط [siqaṭ] سُقُوط [suqu:ṭ] *vn: sv* u. How did the Roman Empire fall? شلُون سِقطَت الدَّولَة الرُّومانِيَّة؟ [šlu:n siqṭat ʔiddawla ʔirru:ma:niyya?]

to fall apart • **1.** تكَسَّر [tkassar] تكِسِّر، تَكسِير [tkissir, taksi:r] *vn: sv* a. تفَصَّخ [tfaṣṣax] تفُصُّخ، تَفصِيخ [tfuṣṣux, tafṣi:x] *vn: sv* a. The chair is already falling apart. الكُرسِي مِن هَسَّة دَيتكَسَّر [ʔilkursi min hassa dayitkassar] • **2.** وُقَع [wugaʕ] وُقُوع [wugu:ʕ, wuqu:ʕ] *vn: sv* a. تفَلَّش [tfallaš] تفِلِّش [tfilliš] *vn: sv* a. That old house is falling apart. هَذاك البَيت العَتِيق دَيُوقَع [haða:k ʔilbayt ʔilʕati:g dayu:gaʕ]

to fall asleep • **1.** غُفَى [ɣufa:] غَفُو [ɣafw] *vn: sv* i. I fell asleep. آنِي غُفَيت [ʔa:ni ɣufayt]

to fall back on • **1.** لِجَا، لِجَأ ل [lija:, lijaʔ l] اِلتِجاء [ʔiltija:ʔ] *vn: sv* i. إنلِجَأ [ʔinlijaʔ] *p:* We can always fall back on what we've saved. إحنا دائماً نِقدَر نِلتِجِي لِلِّي وَفَّرنا [ʔiħna da:ʔiman nigdar niltiji lilli waffarna]

to fall behind • **1.** تأَخَّر [tʔaxxar] تَأَخُّر [taʔaxxur] *vn: sv* a. We fell behind in the rent. إحنا تأَخَّرنا عَن دَفِع الأَجار [ʔiħna tʔaxxarna ʕan dafiʕ ʔilʔaja:r]

to fall for • **1.** اِنخِدَع ب [ʔinxidaʕ b-] اِنخِداع [ʔinxida:ʕ] *vn: sv* i. I fell for his story. اِنخِدَعِت بحكايتَه [ʔinxidaʕit biħča:ytah]

to fall off • **1.** وُقَع [wugaʕ] وُقُوع [wugu:ʕ, wuqu:ʕ] *vn: sv* a. The lid fell off. القَبَغ وُقَع [ʔilqabaɣ wugaʕ] • **2.** نِزَل [nizal] نُزُول [nuzu:l] *vn: sv* i. Receipts have been falling off lately. الوارِد دَينزِل هَالأَيّام الأَخِيرَة [ʔilwa:rid dayinzil halʔayya:m ʔilʔaxi:ra]

to fall through • **1.** فِشَل [fišal] فَشَل [fašal] *vn: sv* a. The plans for the trip fell through. مَناهِج السَّفرَة فِشلَت [mana:hij ʔissafra fišlat]

false • **1.** غَلَط [ɣalaṭ] خَطَأ [xaṭaʔ] أخطاء [ʔaxṭa:ʔ] *pl:* كاذِب [ka:ðib] Is this true or false? هَذا صَحِيح لَو غَلَط؟ [ha:ða ṣaħi:ħ law ɣalaṭ?] • **2.** عارِي [ʕa:ri] مُستَعار [mustaʕa:r] Many people have false teeth. هوايَة ناس عِدهُم سنُون عارِيَّة [hwa:ya na:s ʕidhum snu:n ʕa:riyya]

familiar • **1.** مِتطَلِّع مِطَّلِع, [miṭṭiliʕ] I'm not familiar with that. آنِي ما مِتطَلِع عَلَى هاي [ʔa:ni ma: miṭṭiliʕ ʕala ha:y] • **2.** مَألُوف [maʔlu:f] Soldiers are a familiar sight these days. تشُوف جِنُود فَدّ شِي مألُوف هَالأَيّام [tšu:f ǰinu:d fadd ši maʔlu:f halʔayya:m] • **3.** مَعرُوف [maʕru:f] It's good to see a familiar person. زِين واحِد يشُوف فَدّ شَخِص مَعرُوف [zi:n wa:ħid yšu:f fadd šaxiṣ maʕru:f]

family • **1.** عائِلَة [ʕa:ʔila] عَوائِل [ʕawa:ʔil] *pl:* أَهَل [ʔahal] أهالِي [ʔaha:li] *pl:* أسرَة [ʔusra] أسَر [ʔusar] *pl:* Did you notify his family? أخبَرت عائِلتَه؟ [ʔaxbarit ʕa:ʔiltah?] • **2.** فَصِيلَة [faṣi:la] فَصائِل [faṣa:ʔil] *pl:* Is this animal of the cat family? هالحَيوان مِن فَصِيلَة القِطّ؟ [halħaywa:n min faṣi:lat ʔilqiṭṭ?]

famine • **1.** مَجاعَة [maǰa:ʕa] مَجاعات [maǰa:ʕa:t] *pl:* قَحَط [qaħaṭ] [.] *pl:* Many people died during the famine. هوايَة ناس ماتَوا أثناء المَجاعَة [hwa:ya na:s ma:taw ʔaθna:ʔ ʔilmaǰa:ʕa]

famous • **1.** مَشهُور [mašhu:r] مَعرُوف [maʕru:f] His book made him famous. كِتابَه سَوّاه مَشهُور [kita:bah sawwa:h mašhu:r]

to become famous • **1.** اِشتِهَر [ʔištihar] اِشتِهار [ʔištiha:r] *vn: sv* i. The restaurant became famous in a short time. المَطعَم اِشتِهَر بمُدَّة قَصِيرَة [ʔilmaṭʕam ʔištihar bmudda qaṣi:ra]
to make famous • **1.** شِهَر [šihar] شُهرَة [šuhra] *vn: sv* i. Her records made her famous. إسطِواناتها شِهرَتها [ʔisṭiwa:na:tha šihratha]

fan • **1.** بَنكَة [panka] بَنكات [panka:t] *pl:* مَروَحَة [marwaħa] Turn on the fan. شَغِّل البَنكَة [šaɣɣil ʔilpanka] • **2.** مهَفَّة [mhaffa] مهَفّات، مهافِيف [mhaffa:t, mha:fi:f] *pl:* Hand each one of the guests a fan. إنطِي مهَفَّة لكُلّ واحِد مِن الخُطّار [ʔinṭi mhaffa likull wa:ħid min ʔilxuṭṭa:r]

fancy • **1.** هَوا [hawa] مَيل [mayl] مِيُول [myu:l] *pl:* وَلَع [walaʕ] It's just a passing fancy with her. هَذا فَدّ هَوا وَقتِي جا براسها [ha:ða fadd hawa wakti ǰa: bra:sha] • **2.** فَخِم [faxim] أنِيق [ʔani:q] She doesn't like fancy clothes. ما تعجبها المَلابِس الفَخمَة [ma: tiʕǰibha ʔalmala:bis ʔilfaxma]
*** Don't you look fancy!** • **1.** أَمّا كاشِخ تَماماً [ʔamma ka:šix tama:man]

fantastic • **1.** خَيالِي [xaya:li] تَصَوُّرِي [taṣawwuri]

far • **1.** بِعِيد [biʕi:d] بعاد [biʕa:d] *pl:* People came from far and near. النّاس إجَوا مِن قَرِيب وَمِن بِعِيد [ʔinna:s ʔiǰaw min qari:b wamin biʕi:d] That's not far wrong. هَذا مُو بِعِيد عَن الحَقِيقَة [ha:ða mu: biʕi:d ʕan ʔilħaqi:qa] I'm far from satisfied with your work. آنِي بِعِيد عَن الرِّضَى عَن شُغُلَك [ʔa:ni biʕi:d ʕan ʔirriđa ʕan šuɣulak] • **2.** لِبعِيد [libʕi:d] Don't go far. لا ترُوح لِبعِيد [la: tru:ħ libʕi:d]
*** This joke has gone far enough.**
• **1.** هَالمَهزَلَة تعَدَّت حُدُودها [halmahzala tʕaddat ħudu:dha]
as far as • **1.** لِحَدّ، إلَى حَدّ [liħadd, ʔila ħadd] We walked together as far as the R. R. station. مِشَينا سُوَة لِحَدّ مَحَطَّة القِطار [miši:na suwa liħadd maħaṭṭat ʔilqiṭa:r] As far as it goes, your idea is good. إلَى حَدّ، فِكِرتَك زينَة [ʔila ħadd, fikirtak zi:na] • **2.** حَسَبما [ħasabma] As far as I can see, his papers are o. k. حَسَب ما أشُوف، أوراقَه زينَة [ħasab ma: ʔašu:f, ʔawra:qah zi:na]
by far • **1.** بهوايَة [bihwa:ya] This is the best book by far I have read this year. هَالكِتاب بهوايَة أحسَن كتاب قِرَيتَه هالسَّنَة [halkita:b bhwa:ya ʔaħsan kta:b qiraytah hassana]
so far • **1.** لِهَسَّة [lihassa] لهالحَدّ [lhalħadd] So far, you've been pretty lucky. لِهَسَّة، إنتَ كِنِت كُلِّش مَحظُوظ [lhassa, ʔinta činit kulliš maħđu:đ]

farce • **1.** مَهزَلَة [mahzala] مَهازِل [maha:zil] *pl:* The elections were a farce. الانتِخابات كانَت مَهزَلَة [ʔilʔintixa:ba:t ča:nat mahzala]

fare • **1.** أُجرَة [ʔuǰra] أُجُور [ʔuǰu:r] *pl:* How much is the fare? شقَدّ الأُجرَة؟ [šgadd ʔilʔuǰra?]

Far East • **1.** الشَّرق الأَقصَى [ʔiššarq ʔilʔaqṣa]

farewell • **1.** تَودِيع [tawdi:ʕ] وداع [wida:ʕ, wada:ʕ] They gave him a farewell party. سَوَّولَه حَفلَة تَودِيعِيَّة [sawwawlah ħafla tawdi:ʕiyya]

farm • **1.** مَزرَعَة [mazraʕa] مَزارِع [maza:riʕ] *pl:* The village is surrounded by farms. القَريَة مُحاطَة بالمَزارِع [ʔilqarya muħa:ṭa bilmaza:riʕ]
to farm • **1.** زِرَع [ziraʕ] زراعَة [zira:ʕa] *vn:* اِنزِرَع [ʔinziraʕ] *p:* My sons and I can farm the land by ourselves. آنِي وَوُلدِي نِقدَر نِزرَع هَالقاع وَحَدنا [ʔa:ni wwuldi nigdar nizraʕ halga:ʕ waħadna]

farmer • **1.** زَرّاع [zarra:ʕ] زَرّاعَة [zarra:ʕa] *pl:* مُزارِع [muza:riʕ] مُزارِعِين [muza:riʕi:n] *pl:* Most of the farmers have already harvested their crops. أكثَر الزُّرّاع حِصدَوا الحاصِل مالهُم [ʔakθar ʔizzurra:ʕ ħiṣdaw ʔilħa:ṣil ma:lhum]

farming • **1.** زِراعَة [zira:ʕa] There isn't much farming in this region. ماكُو زِراعَة هوايَة بهَالمَنطَقَة [ma:ku zira:ʕa hwa:ya bhalmanṭaqa]

farther • **1.** أبعَد [ʔabʕad] You'll have to walk a little farther. لازِم تِمشِي شوَيَّة أبعَد [la:zim timši šwayya ʔabʕad]

to fascinate • **1.** فِتَن [fitan] فَتِن [fatin] *vn:* اِنفِتَن [ʔinfitan] *p:* سِحَر [siħar] سَحِر [saħir] *vn:* اِنسِحَر [ʔinsiħar] *p:* جِذَب [ǰiðab] جَذِب [ǰaðib] *vn:* اِنجِذَب [ʔinǰiðab] *p:* The entire audience was fascinated by his story. كُلّ الحاضرِين اِنسِحرَوا بحكايتَه [kull ʔilħa:đri:n ʔinsiħraw biħča:ytah]

fascinating • **1.** جَذّاب [ǰaðða:b] فَتّان [fatta:n] مُسحِر [musħir] This is a fascinating book. هَذا كِتاب جَذّاب [ha:ða kita:b ǰaðða:b]

fashion • **1.** مُودَة [mu:da] مُودات [mu:da:t] *pl:* Is that the latest fashion? هَذا آخِر مُودَة؟ [ha:ða ʔa:xir mu:da?] • **2.** طَرِيقَة [ṭari:qa] طُرُق [ṭuruq] *pl:* طَرِز، طِراز [ṭariz, ṭira:z] شِكِل [šikil] أشكال، شكُول [ʔaška:l, šku:l] *pl:* نَمَط [namaṭ] أنماط [ʔanma:ṭ] *pl:* I want you to do it in this fashion. أحِبَّك تسَوِّيها عَلَى هَالطَّرِيقَة [ʔaħibbak tsawwi:ha ʕala haṭṭari:qa] • **3.** أُسلُوب [ʔuslu:b] أسالِيب [ʔasa:li:b] *pl:* He tries to write after the fashion of Manfaluti. يحاوِل يقَلِّد إسلُوب المَنفَلُوطِي [yħa:wil yqallid ʔislu:b ʔilmanfalu:ṭi]

fashionable • **1.** دارِج [da:riǰ] مُودَة [mu:da] مُودات [mu:da:t] *pl:* It is fashionable now for Iraqi women to wear western clothing. دارِج بهَالوَقت المرَيَّة العِراقِيَّة تِلبَس مَلابِس غَربِيَّة [da:riǰ bhalwakit ʔilmrayya ʔilʕira:qiyya tilbas mala:bis ɣarbiyya]

fast • **1.** صِيام [ṣiya:m] صَوم [ṣawm] Ramadan is the month of the fast. رَمَضان شَهَر الصِّيام [ramađa:n šahar ʔiṣṣiya:m] • **2.** بِالعَجَل [bilʕaǰal] بسُرعَة [surʕa] سَرِيع [sari:ʕ]

Don't talk so fast. لا تِحكِي هَالقَدّ بِالعَجَل [la: tiħči halgadd bilʕaǰal] • **3.** فاسِق [fa:siq] He travels in fast company. هُوَّ يِمشِي وِيّا جَماعَة فاسقِين [huwwa yimši wiyya ǰama:ʕa fa:sqi:n] • **4.** ثابِت [θa:bit] Are these colors fast? هَالألوان ثابتَة؟ [hal?alwa:n θa:bta?] In this case you can't make hard and fast rules. بِهالحالَة ما تِقدَر تحُطّ قَواعِد ثابتَة [bhalħa:la ma: tigdar tħutt qawa:ʕid θa:bta] • **5.** سابِق [sa:biq] راكِض [ra:kið] My watch is ten minutes fast. ساعتِي سابقَة عَشِر دَقايِق [sa:ʕti sa:bqa ʕašir daqa:yiq] • **6.** مُستَغرِق [mustaɣriq] I was fast asleep. آنِي كِنِت مِستَغرِق بنَومِي [?a:ni činit mistaɣriq bnawmi]

to fast • 1. صام [ṣa:m] صَوم [ṣawm] *vn: sv* u. I'm fasting. آنِي صايِم [?a:ni ṣa:yim]

to fasten • 1. شَدّ [šadd] شَدّ [šadd] *vn:* اِنشَدّ [?inšadd] *p:* رُبَط [rubaṭ] رَبُط [rabuṭ] *vn:* اِنرُبَط [?inrubaṭ] *p:* Where can I fasten the string? وِين أقدَر أشِدّ الخيط؟ [wi:n ?agdar ?ašidd ?ilxi:ṭ?]

fat • 1. شَحَم [šaħam] شُحُوم [šuħu:m] *pl:* This meat has very much fat on it. هَاللَّحَم بِيه كُلِّش هوايَة شَحَم [hallaħam bi:h kulliš hwa:ya šaħam] • **2.** دِهِين [dihi:n] The meat is too fat. اللَّحَم كُلِّش دِهِين [?illaħam kulliš dihi:n] • **3.** سِمِين [simi:n] He's gotten fat. هُوَّ صايِر سِمِين [huwwa ṣa:yir simi:n]

fatal • 1. قَتّال [qatta:l] مُمِيت [mumi:t] The blow was fatal. الضَّربَة كانَت قَتّالَة [?iððarba ča:nat qatta:la]

fate • 1. قَضاء وقَدَر [qaða:? wqadar] قِسمَة [qisma] بَخَت [baxat]

father • 1. أبُو [?abu] أب [?ab] آباء [?a:ba:?] *pl:* أبّ [?abb] أبَّهات [?a:ba:?, ?abbahaat] *pl:* He has no father. ما عِندَه أب [ma: ʕindah ?ab] The father was killed, but the mother is still alive. الأبّ اِنكِتَل لَكِن الأمّ بَعَدها طَيّبَة [?il?abb ?inkital la:kin ?il?umm baʕadha ṭayyba] How's your father? شلُون أبُوك؟ [šlu:n ?abu:k?]

father-in-law • 1. أبُو الزَّوج [?abu: ?izzawǰ] أبو الزَوجَة [?abu ?izzawǰa] His father-in-law is a merchant. أبُو زَوجتَه تاجِر [?abu zawiǰtah ta:ǰir]

faucet • 1. حَنَفِيَّة مزَمبِلَة [ħanafiyya mzambila] حَنَفِيّات مزَمبِلَة [ħanafiyya:t mzambila] *pl:* مزَمِّلَة [mzammila] مزَمِّلات [mzammila:t] *pl:* The faucet is dripping. الحَنَفِيَّة دَتنقِّط [?ilħanafiyya datnaggiṭ]

fault • 1. عَيب [ʕi:b] عيُوب [ʕyu:b] *pl:* We all have our faults. كُلّنا عِدنا عيُوب [kullna ʕidna ʕyu:b] • **2.** غَلطَة [ɣalṭa] غَلطات، أغلاط [ɣalṭa:t, ?aɣla:ṭ] *pl:* خَطَأ [xaṭa?] أخطاء [?axṭa:?] *pl:* It's not his fault. هِيَّ مُو غَلِطتَه [hiyya mu: ɣaliṭṭah]

to find fault • 1. اِنتِقَد [?intiqad] اِنتِقاد [?intiqa:d] *vn: sv* i. You're always finding fault. إنتَ عَلَى طُول تِنتِقِد [?inta ʕala ṭu:l tintiqid] You're always finding fault. إنتَ عَلَى طُول دَتطَلِّع مِن قَلبَك حَكِي [?inta ʕala ṭu:l daṭṭalliʕ min galbak ħači]

faulty • 1. خَطَأ [xaṭa?] أخطاء [?axṭa:?] *pl:* مُخطِئ [muxṭi?] مَغلُوط [maɣlu:ṭ] That's faulty thinking. هَذا تَفكِير خَطَأ [ha:ða tafki:r xaṭa?] • **2.** بِي عَيب [bi: ʕayb] This machine is faulty. هَالمَكِينَة بِيها عِيب [halmaki:na bi:ha ʕi:b]

favor • 1. جَمِيل [ǰami:l] جَمِيلات [ǰami:la:t] *pl:* إحسان [?iħsa:n] فَضِل [faðil] أفضال [?afða:l] *pl:* مَعرُوف [maʕru:f] مِنِّيَّة [minniyya] مِنِّيّات [minniyya:t] *pl:* I want you to do me a favor. أرِيدَك تسَوِّيلِي فَدّ جَمِيل [?ari:dak tsawwi:li fadd ǰami:l] • **2.** جانِب [ǰa:nib] جَوانِب [ǰawa:nib] *pl:* مَصلَحَة [maṣlaħa] مَصالِح [maṣa:liħ] *pl:* She spoke in my favor. حِكَت مِن جانبِي [ħičat min ǰa:nbi]

in favor of • 1. بجانِب [bǰa:nib] I'm in favor of immediate action. آنِي بِجانِب فِكرَة الابتِداء حالاً [?a:ni bǰa:nib fikrat ?il?ibtida:? ħa:lan]

to favor • 1. فَضَّل [faððal] تَفضِيل [tafði:l] *vn:* تفَضَّل [tfaððal] *p:* He favors the youngest child. هُوَّ يفَضِّل الإبن الأصغَر [huwwa yfaððil ?il?ibn ?il?aṣɣar]

favorable • 1. مُلائِم [mula:?im] مُناسِب [muna:sib] He bought the house on very favorable terms. اِشتِرَى البَيت بِشرُوط كُلِّش مُلائِمَة [?ištira: ?ilbayt bšuru:ṭ kulliš mula:?ima] • **2.** مُواتِي [muwa:ti] I' m only waiting for a favorable opportunity. آنِي بَسّ دَأنتِظِر الفُرصَة المواتِيَة [?a:ni bass da?antiðir ?ilfurṣa ?ilmwa:tiya]

favorite • 1. مُفَضَّل [mufaððal] مَحبُوب [maħbu:b] This is my favorite book. هَذا كتابِي المُفَضَّل [ha:ða kta:bi ?ilmufaððal] This book is a great favorite with children. هَالكِتاب هوايَة مَحبُوب مِن الأطفال [halkita:b hwa:ya maħbu:b min ?il?aṭfa:l]

fear • 1. خَوف [xawf, xu:f] مَخاوُف [maxa:wuf] *pl:* He doesn't know the meaning of fear. ما يُعرُف مَعنى الخَوف [ma: yuʕruf maʕna: ?ilxawf] Your fears are unfounded. مَخاوفَك ما إلها أساس [maxa:wfak ma: ?ilha ?asa:s]

for fear of • 1. خَوفاً مِن أن [xawfan min ?an] He took a taxi for fear of missing the train. أخَذ تاكسِي خَوفاً مِن أن يفُوتَه القِطار [?axað ta:ksi xawfan min ?an yfu:tah ?ilqiṭa:r]

to fear • 1. خاف مِن [xa:f min] خَوف [xawf] *vn:* اِنخاف [?inxa:f] *p:* He doesn't fear death. ما يخاف مِن المَوت [ma: yxa:f min ?ilmawt]

fearful • 1. خايِف [xa:yif] Mother is so fearful about my health. أمِّي كُلِّش خايفَة عَلَى صِحّتِي [?ummi kulliš xa:yfa ʕala ṣiħħti] • **2.** مُخِيف [muxi:f] يخَوُّف [yxawwuf] That's a fearful wound you have. هَذا الجَّرِح يخَوُّف عِندَك [ha:ða ?iǰǰariħ yxawwuf ʕindak]

feat • **1.** عَمَل عَظِيم [ʕamal ʕaðiːm] أعمال عَظِيمَة [ʔaʕmaːl ʕaðiːma] *pl:* That was quite a feat. ذاك كان فَدّ عَمَل عَظِيم [ðaːk čaːn fadd ʕamal ʕaðiːm]

feather • **1.** رِيشَة [riːša] رِيشات، رِيَش [riːšaːt, riyaš] *pl:* رِيش [riːš] *Collective:* The feathers are coming out of the pillow. الرِّيش دَيطلَع مِن المُخَدَّة [ʔirriːš dayiṭlaʕ min ʔilmuxadda] This hat is light as a feather. هَالشَّفقَة خَفِيفَة مِثل الرِّيشَة [haššafqa xafiːfa miθl ʔirriːša]

feature • **1.** ناحِيَة [naːħiya] نَواحِي [nawaːħi] *pl:* This plan has many good features. هَالمَشرُوع بِيه عِدَّة نَواحِي زينَة [halmašruːʕ biːh ʕiddat nawaːħi ziːna]

*** When does the main feature begin?**

• **1.** شوَقت يِبدِي الأساسِي؟ [šwakit yibdi ʔilʔasaːsi?]

features • **1.** تَقطِيعَة [taqtiːʕa] Her facial features are beautiful. تَقاطِيع وِجِهها حِلوَة [taqaːṭiːʕ wiččha ħilwa]

February • **1.** شباط [šbaːṭ]

fee • **1.** أُجرَة [ʔuǰra] أُجُور [ʔuǰuːr] *pl:* The doctor's fee was thirty dinars. أُجُور الطَّبِيب كانَت ثلاثِين دِينار [ʔuǰuːr ʔiṭṭabiːb čaːnat tlaːθiːn dinaːr]

feeble • **1.** ضَعِيف [ðaʕiːf] ضُعَفاء [ðuʕafaːʔ] *pl:* عاجِز [ʕaːǰiz] عاجِزين [ʕaːǰiziːn] *pl:* عاجِز [ʕaːǰiz] My grandmother is very feeble. جِدّتِي كُلِّش ضَعِيفَة [ǰiddti kulliš ðaʕiːfa]

feed • **1.** لُقُط [luguṭ] Did you tell them to bring the feed for the chickens? قِلتِلهُم يجِيبُون اللُّقُط لِلدِّجاج؟ [giltilhum yǰiːbuːn ʔilluguṭ liddiǰaːǰ?] • **2.** عَلَف [ʕalaf] Did you tell them to bring the feed for the cows? قِلتِلهُم يجِيبُون العَلَف لِلهَوايِش؟ [giltilhum yǰiːbuːn ʔilʕalaf lilhawaːyiš?]

to feed • **1.** طَعَّم [taʕʕam] تطُعُّم [tṭuʕʕum] *vn:* تطَعَّم [ʔiṭṭaʕʕam] *p:* وَكَّل [wakkal] توكِّل [twikkil] *vn: sv* i. She's feeding the chickens. هِيَّ دَتطَعِّم الدِّجاج [hiyya daṭṭaʕʕum ʔiddiǰaːǰ]

to be fed up with • **1.** ضاج مِن، ضَوَّج مِن [ðaːǰ min, ðawwaǰ min] ضَوج [ðawǰ] *vn: sv* u. بِزَع مِن [bizaʕ min] بَزَع [bazaʕ] *vn: sv* a. I'm fed up with this whole business. آنِي ضِجِت مِن هَالشَّغلَة كُلها [ʔaːni ðiǰit min haššaɣla kullha]

to feel • **1.** جَسّ [ǰass] جَسّ [ǰass] *vn:* اِنجَسّ [ʔinǰass] *p:* The doctor felt my pulse. الطَّبِيب جَسّ نَبضِي [ʔiṭṭabiːb ǰass nabði] • **2.** شِعَر [šiʕar] شُعُور [šuʕuːr] *vn: sv* u. حَسّ [ħass] حَسّ [ħass] *vn: sv* i. He doesn't feel well. هُوَّ ما دَيِشعُر زين [huwwa maː dayišʕur zayn] He feels very strongly against women drinking. كُلِّش يِشعُر ضِدّ شُرُب النِّسوان لِلمَشرُوبات [kulliš yišʕur ðidd šurub ʔinniswaːn lilmašruːbaːt] All of a sudden I felt a sharp pain in my back. عَلَى غَفلَة شِعَرِت بِأَلَم حادّ بظَهرِي [ʕala ɣafla šiʕarit bʔalam ħaːdd bðahri] • **3.** كَمكَش [kamkaš] تكُمكِش [tkumkiš] *vn: sv* i. تحَسَّس [tħassas] تحِسِّس [tħissis] *vn: sv* a. He felt his way to the window. هُوَّ كَمكَش طَرِيقَه لِلشُّبّاك [huwwa kamkaš ṭariːqah liššubbaːč]

to feel about • **1.** شِعَر [šiʕar] شُعُور [šuʕuːr] *vn: sv* u. How do you feel about this matter? إنتَ شتِشعُر بِهَالقَضِيَّة؟ [ʔinta štišʕur bhalqaðiyya?] How do you feel about this matter? شرَأيَك بِهَالمَوضُوع؟ [šraʔyak bhalmawðuːʕ?]

to feel for • **1.** تأَثَّر عَلَى [tʔaθθar ʕala] تَأَثُّر [taʔaθθur] *vn: sv* a. اِنكِسَر [ʔinkisar] اِنكِسار [ʔinkisaːr] *vn: sv* i. I really feel for you. آنِي صُدُق أتأثَّر عَلَى حالَك [ʔaːni ṣudug ʔatʔaθθar ʕala ħaːlak]

to feel out • **1.** تحَسَّس حالَة [tħassas ħaːla] تَحَسُّس حالَة [taħassus ħaːla] *vn: sv* a. I'll feel him out and let you know. آنِي راح أتحَسَّس حالتَه وأقُلَّك [ʔaːni raːħ ʔatħassas ħaːltah wʔagullak]

feeling • **1.** إحساس [ʔiħsaːs] I have no feeling in my right arm. إيدِي اليِمنَى ما بِيها كُلّ إحساس [ʔiːdi ʔilyimnaː maː biːha kull ʔiħsaːs] • **2.** شُعُور [šuʕuːr] I really didn't mean to hurt your feelings. ما كان قَصدِي أجرَح شُعُورَك أبَداً [maː čaːn qaṣdi ʔaǰraħ šuʕuːrak ʔabadan]

fellow • **1.** إنسان [ʔinsaːn] شَخِص [šaxiṣ] أشخاص [ʔašxaːṣ] *pl:* He's a nice fellow. هُوَّ فَدّ إنسان طَيِّب [huwwa fadd ʔinsaːn ṭayyib] How many fellows were there? كَم شَخِص كان أَكُو هناك؟ [čam šaxiṣ čaːn ʔaku hnaːk?]

*** Poor fellow!** • **1.** مِسكِين [miskiːn]

felt • **1.** جَوخ [čawx čuːx] جواخ [čwaːx] *pl:*

female • **1.** نِثيَة [niθya] نثايا [nθaːya] *pl:* Is this cat a male or a female? هَالبَزُّونَة فَحَل لَو نِثيَة؟ [halbazzuːna faħal law niθya?]

feminine • **1.** مُؤَنَّث [muʔannaθ] This word is feminine in Arabic. هَالكَلِمَة مُؤَنَّثَة بِالعَرَبِي [halkalima muʔannaθa bilʕarabi]

fence • **1.** سِياج [siyaːǰ] سِياجات [siyaːǰaːt] *pl:* حاجِز [ħaːǰiz] حَواجِز [ħawaːǰiz] *pl:* There's a hole in the fence. أَكُو زُرُف بِالسِّياج [ʔaku zuruf bissiyaːǰ]

to fence • **1.** تبارَز [tbaːraz] تَبارُز [tabaːruz] *vn: sv* a. لِعَب [liʕab] لِعِب [liʕib] *vn: sv* a. Do you know how to fence? تُعرُف شلُون تِتبارَز؟ [tuʕruf šluːn titbaːraz?]

to fence in • **1.** سَيَّج [sayyaǰ] تسِيِّج [tsiyyiǰ] *vn:* اِتسَيَّج [ʔitsayyaǰ] *p:* We fenced in the orchard. سَيَّجنا البِستان [sayyaǰna ʔilbistaːn]

to ferment • **1.** تخَمَّر [txammar] تَخمِير [taxmiːr] *vn: sv* a. The wine is fermenting. الشَّراب دَيِتخَمَّر [ʔiššaraːb dayitxammar]

fertile • **1.** خَصِب [xaṣib] The soil here is very fertile. التُّربَة هنا كُلِّش خَصبَة [ʔitturba hna kulliš xaṣba] He has a very fertile imagination. عِندَه خَيال خَصِب [ʕindah xayaːl xaṣib]

to fertilize • **1.** سَمَّد [sammad] تَسمِيد [tasmi:d] *vn:* تسَمَّد [tsammad] *p:* We fertilize the garden twice a year. نسَمِّد الحَدِيقَة مَرّتَين بالسَّنَة [nsammid ʔilħadi:qa marrtayn bissana] • **2.** لَقَّح [laqqaħ] تَلقِيح [talqi:ħ] *vn:* اِتلَقَّح [ʔitlaqqaħ] *p:* The female fish lays the eggs somewhere, and the male comes along and fertilizes them. السِّمكَة النِّثْيَة تخَلِّي البَيض بمُكان وَالفَحَل يِجِي يلَقِّحَه [ʔissimča ʔinniθya txalli ʔilbi:ð bmuka:n wilfaħal yiǰi ylaqqiħah]

fertilizer • **1.** سَماد [sama:d] أسمِدَة [ʔasmida] *pl:* I'd advise you to use a chemical fertilizer. أنصَحَك تِستَعمِل سَماد كِيمياوِي [ʔanṣaħak tistaʕmil sama:d ki:mya:wi] • **2.** دِمِن [dimin] سماد [sma:d] Your shoes are covered with fertilizer. قُندَرتَك كُلّها مغَطّايَة بِدِمِن [qundartak kullha myaṭṭa:ya bdimin]

to fester • **1.** تقَيَّح [tqayyaħ] تقِيِّح [tqiyyiħ] *vn: sv* a. Is the wound still festering? الجَّرِح بَعدَه مِتقَيِّح؟ [ʔiǰǰariħ baʕdah mitqayyiħ?]

festival • **1.** اِحتِفال [ʔiħtifa:l] اِحتِفالات [ʔiħtifa:la:t] *pl:* مَهرَجان [mahraǰa:n] مَهرَجانات [mahraǰa:na:t] *pl:* The festival was cancelled at the last minute. الاحتِفال اِنلِغَى بآخِر لَحظَة [ʔilʔiħtifa:l ʔinliɣa: bʔa:xir laħða]

festive • **1.** مُفرِح [mufriħ] مُبهِج [mubhiǰ]

festivity • **1.** اِحتِفال [ʔiħtifa:l] اِحتِفالات [ʔiħtifa:la:t] *pl:*

to fetch • **1.** جاب [ǰa:b] جَيبَ [ǰayba] *vn:* اِنجاب [ʔinǰa:b] *p:* Fetch me the newspaper. جِيبلِي الجَّرِيدَة [ǰi:bli ʔiǰǰari:da]

fever • **1.** سُخُونَة [suxu:na] حُمَّة [ħumma] حُمّايات [ħumma:ya:t] *pl:* Do you have any fever? عِندَك سُخُونَة؟ [ʕindak ṣuxu:na?] • **2.** حَرارَة [ħara:ra] They were all in a fever of excitement. كُلّهُم كانَوا بِحَرارَة الهَيَجان [kullhum ča:naw bħara:rat ʔilhayaǰa:n]

feverish • **1.** مسَخِّن [msaxxin] مَحمُوم [maħmu:m] He's feverish. جِسمَه مسَخِّن [ǰismah msaxxin]

*** Why all the feverish activity over there?** • **1.** لُوَيش كُلّ هَالاضطِرابات هناك؟ [luwi:š kull halʔiðṭira:ba:t hna:k?]

feverishly • **1.** بِحَرارَة [biħara:ra] بنَشاط [bnaša:ṭ] بِجِدّ [bǰidd] They're working feverishly on the new project. دَيِشتَغلُون بِحَرارَة بِالمَشرُوع الجِّدِيد [dayištaɣlu:n bħara:ra bilmašru:ʕ ʔiǰǰidi:d]

few • **1.** شوَيَّة [šwayya] قَلِيل [qali:l] Few people come to see us in the summer. شوَيَّة ناس يِجُون يزُورُونا بِالصَّيف [šwayya na:s yiǰu:n yzu:ru:na biṣṣayf] Good people are few and far between. الخُوش أوادِم قَلِيلِين وَصَعُب يِلتِقُون [ʔilxu:š ʔawa:dim qali:li:n wṣaʕub yiltigu:n] • **2.** كَم [čam] May I ask a few questions? مُمكِن أسأَل فَدّ كَم سُؤال؟ [mumkin ʔasʔal fadd čam suʔa:l?] May I ask a few questions? مُمكِن أسأَل شوَيَّة أسئِلَة؟ [mumkin ʔasʔal šwayyat ʔasʔila?] We go to see him every few days. إحنا نرُوح نشُوفَه كُلّ كَم يوم [ʔiħna nru:ħ nšu:fah kull čam yu:m]

quite a few • **1.** عَدَد لا بَأس بِيه [ʕadad la: baʔis bi:h] Quite a few people were present. عَدَد لا بَأس بِيه مِن النّاس كانَوا حاضرِين [ʕadad la: baʔs bi:h min ʔinna:s ča:naw ħa:ðri:n]

fiance • **1.** خَطِيب [xaṭi:b] خُطَباء [xuṭaba:] *pl:* Give my regards to your fiance. سَلِّمِيلِي عَلَى خَطِيبِك [sallimi:li ʕala xaṭi:bič]

fiancee • **1.** خَطِيبَة [xaṭi:ba] خَطِيبات [xaṭi:ba:t] *pl:* My fiancee writes me every day. خَطِيبتِي تِكتِبلِي كُلّ يوم [xaṭi:bti tiktibli kull yu:m]

fickle • **1.** هَوائِي [hawa:ʔi] مِتقَلِّب [mitqallib] She's a very fickle person. هِيَّ فَدّ وِحدَة كُلّش هَوائِيَّة [hiyya fadd wiħda kulliš hawa:ʔiyya]

fiddle • **1.** كَمَنجَة [kamanǰa] كَمَنجات [kamanǰa:t] *pl:* Quit scratching on that fiddle. بَسّ عاد توَصوُص بِهَالكَمَنجَة [bass ʕa:d twaṣwuṣ bhalkamanǰa]

*** He's not satisfied playing second fiddle to anyone.** • **1.** هُوَّ مَا يِرضَى يقُوم بعَمَل ثانَوِي [huwwa ma: yirða: yqu:m bʕamal θanawi]

to fiddle • **1.** لِعَب [liʕab] لِعب [liʕib] *vn: sv* a. Don't keep on fiddling with the radio! لا تظَلّ تِلعَب بِالرّادِيُو [la: tðall tilʕab birra:dyu]

to fiddle away • **1.** دَعفَس [daʕfas] تدِعفِس [tdiʕfis] *vn: sv* i. He fiddled away the whole day doing absolutely nothing. ظَلّ يدَعفِس طُول اليُوم وَكُلّشِي ما سَوَّى [ðall ydaʕfis ṭu:l ʔilyu:m wkullši ma: sawwa:]

field • **1.** حَقِل [ħaqil] حُقُول [ħuqu:l] *pl:* We walked across the fields. مِشَينا بالحُقُول [mišayna bilħuqu:l] • **2.** ساحَة [sa:ħa] ساحات [sa:ħa:t] *pl:* The teams are coming onto the field. الفِرَق راح تِنزِل لِلسّاحَة [ʔilfiraq ra:ħ tinzil lissa:ħa] • **3.** اِختِصاص [ʔixtiṣa:ṣ] He's the best man in his field. هُوَّ أحسَن واحِد بِاختِصاصَه [huwwa ʔaħsan wa:ħid bʔixtiṣa:ṣah]

fierce • **1.** حادّ [ħa:dd] He gave me a fierce look. نِظَرنِي فَدّ نَظرَة حادَّة [niðarni fadd naðra ħa:dda] • **2.** شَرِس [šaris] The lion is a fierce animal. الأسَد حَيَوان شَرِس [ʔilʔasad ħayawa:n šaris] • **3.** شَدِيد [šadi:d] The heat's fierce today. الحَرارَة شَدِيدَة هَاليُوم [ʔilħara:ra šadi:da halyu:m]

fiery • **1.** نارِي [na:ri] He made a fiery speech. ألقَى خِطاب نارِي [ʔalqa: xiṭa:b na:ri]

fifteen • **1.** خُمُسطَعَش [xumusṭaʕaš]

fifteenth • **1.** الخُمُسطَعَش [ʔilxumusṭaʕaš] This is my fifteenth car. هاي سَيّارتِي الخُمُسطَعَش [ha:y sayya:rti lxumusṭaʕaš]

fifth • **1.** خُمُس [xumus] أخماس [ʔaxma:s] *pl:* I got only a fifth of the money. أَخَذِت بَسّ خُمُس الفلُوس [ʔaxaðit bass xumus ʔilflu:s] • **2.** خامِس [xa:mis] This is my fifth car. هاي سَيّارتِي الخامِسَة [ha:y sayya:rti ʔilxa:misa]

fifties • **1.** خمسينات [xamsi:na:t] He's in his fifties. هُوَّ بِالخَمسِينات [huwwa bilxamsi:na:t]

fiftieth • **1.** خُمُسطَعَش [xumusṭaʕaš]

fifty • **1.** خَمسِين [xamsi:n] خَمسِينات [xamsi:na:t] *pl:* I gave him fifty dinars. إنطَيتَه خَمسِين دِينار [ʔinṭaytah xamsi:n dina:r]

fifty-fifty • **1.** خَمسِين بِالمِيَّة [xamsi:n bilmiyya] نُصّ ونُصّ [nuṣṣ wnuṣṣ] I'll go fifty-fifty with you on the expenses. راح أشارْكَك بخَمسِين بِالمِيَّة مِن المَصرُوفات [ra:ħ ʔaša:rkak bxamsi:n bilmiyya min ʔilmaṣru:fa:t]

fight • **1.** مُكافَحَة [muka:faħa] مُكافَحات [muka:faħa:t] *pl:* كِفاح [kifa:ħ] He played an important part in the fight against tuberculosis. هُوَّ لِعَب دَور مُهِمّ بمُكافَحَة السِّلّ [huwwa liʕab dawr muhimm bmuka:faħat ʔissill] • **2.** مَعرَكَة [maʕraka] مَعارِك [maʕa:rik] *pl:* It was a fight to the finish. كانَت فَدّ مَعرَكَة لِلمُوت [ča:nat fadd maʕraka lilmu:t] It was a fight to the finish. اِستَماتوا بالقِتال [ʔistama:taw bilqita:l] • **3.** عَركَة [ʕarka] عَركات [ʕarka:t] *pl:* مَعرَكَة [maʕraka] مَعارِك [maʕa:rik] *pl:* مباسَط [mba:saṭ] مَعارِك [maʕa:rik] *pl:* When the police arrived the fight was already over. مِن وُصلَوا الشُّرطَة العَركَة كانَت خَلصانَة [min wuṣlaw ʔiššurṭa ʔilʕarka ča:nat xalṣa:na] • **4.** مُلاكَمَة [mula:kama] Were you at the fight last night? كِنِت بِالمُلاكَمَة البارحَة باللَّيل؟ [činit bilmula:kama ʔilba:rħa billayl?] • **5.** مُقاوَمَة [muqa:wama] He hasn't any fight left in him. بَعَد ما بُقَى عِندَه أيّ مُقاوَمَة [baʕad ma: buqa: ʕindah ʔayy muqa:wama]

*** He had a fight with his wife.** • **1.** تعارَك ويّا مَرتَه [tʕa:rak wiyya martah]

to fight • **1.** حارَب [ħa:rab] مُحارَبَة [muħa:raba] *vn: sv* i. They fought bravely in World War II. حاربَوا بشَجاعَة بِالحَرُب العالَمِيَّة الثّانيَة [ħa:rbaw bšaǰa:ʕa bilħarub ʔilʕa:lamiyya ʔiθθa:nya] • **2.** قاوَم [qa:wam] مُقاوَمَة [muqa:wama] *vn:* تقاوَم [tqa:wam] *p:* You've got to fight that habit. إنتَ لازِم تقاوُم هَالعادَة [ʔinta la:zim tqa:wum halʕa:da] I'm going to fight this suit to the end. راح أقاوُم هَالدَّعوَة لِلآخِر [ra:ħ ʔaqa:wum haddaʕwa lilʔa:xir] • **3.** تعارَك [tʕa:rak] عَركَة [ʕarka] *vn: sv* a. Have you two been fighting again? هَم تعارَكتُوا مَرَّة لُخ؟ [hamm tʕa:raktu: marra lux?]

*** Let them fight it out by themselves.** • **1.** خَلِّيهُم يِنجازُون بِيها بنَفِسهُم [xalli:hum yinǰa:zu:n bi:ha bnafishum]

figure • **1.** رَقَم [raqam] أرقام [ʔarqa:m] *pl:* Add up these figures. إجمَع هَالأرقام [ʔiǰmaʕ halʔarqa:m] • **2.** كَسِم [kasim] أكسام [ʔaksa:m] *pl:* جِسِم [ǰisim] أجسام [ʔaǰsa:m] *pl:* She has a nice figure. عِدها كَسِم حِلو [ʕidha kasim ħilw] • **3.** شِكِل [šikil] أشكال، شكُول [ʔaška:l, šku:l] *pl:* Figure seven in the book shows you the parts of the locomotive engine. الشِّكِل رَقَم سَبعَة بِالكتاب يراوِيك أجزاء مَكِينَة القِطار [ʔiššikil raqam sabʕa bilkta:b yra:wi:k ʔaǰza:ʔ maki:nat ʔilqiṭa:r] • **4.** شَخصِيَّة [šaxṣiyya] شَخصِيّات [šaxṣiyya:t] *pl:* He's a mighty important figure in this town. هُوَّ فَدّ شَخصِيَّة كُلِّش مُهِمَّة بهالمَدِينَة [huwwa fadd šaxṣiyya kulliš muhimma bhalmadi:na]

*** Are you good at figures?** • **1.** إنتَ زَين بِالحِساب؟ [ʔinta zayn bilħsa:b?]

to figure • **1.** قَدَّر [qaddar] تَقدِير [taqdi:r] *vn:* تقَدَّر [tqaddar] *p:* I figure it's about five-thirty. أقَدِّر السّاعَة بِالخَمسَة وَنُصّ [ʔaqaddir ʔissa:ʕa bilxamsa wnuṣṣ]

*** The way I figure, it will cost about twenty dinars.** • **1.** بحِسابِي هِيَّ تكَلِّف حَوالِي عِشرِين دِينار [biħsa:bi hiyya tkallif ħawa:li ʕišri:n dina:r]

to figure on • **1.** حِسَب [ħisab] حساب [ħsa:b] *vn:* اِنحِسَب [ʔinħisab] *p:* We didn't figure on having company. ما حسَبنا حساب يِجِينا خُطّار [ma: ħsabna ħsa:b yiǰi:na xuṭṭa:r]

to figure out • **1.** حَلّ [ħall] حَلّ [ħall] *vn:* اِنحَلّ [ʔinħall] *p:* Can you figure out this problem? تِقدَر تحِلّ هَالمُشكِلَة؟ [tigdar tħill halmuškila?] • **2.** حِسَب [ħisab] حساب [ħsa:b] *vn:* اِنحِسَب [ʔinħisab] *p:* Figure out how much it will cost. إحسِب شقَدّ راح تكَلِّف [ʔiħsib šgadd ra:ħ tkallif] • **3.** فِهَم [fiham] فَهِم [fahim] *vn:* اِنفِهَم [ʔinfiham] *p:* اِفتِهَم [ʔiftiham] فَهِم [fahim] *vn: sv* i. Can you figure out what he means? تِقدَر تِفهَم شيُقصُد؟ [tigdar tifham šyuqṣud?] • **4.** حِزَر [ħizar] حَزِر [ħazir] *vn:* اِنحِزَر [ʔinħizar] *p:* I can't figure you out. ما أقدَر أحِزرَك [ma: ʔagdar ʔaħizrak]

to figure up • **1.** حِسَب [ħisab] حساب [ħsa:b] *vn:* اِنحِسَب [ʔinħisab] *p:* Figure up how much I owe you. إحسِب شقَدّ آنِي مَديُون إلَك [ʔiħsib šgadd ʔa:ni madyu:n ʔilak] Did you figure up the first column? حِسَبِت العَمُود الأوَّل؟ [ħisabit ʔilʕamu:d ʔilʔawwal?] • **2.** وَصَّل [waṣṣal] تَوصِيل [tawṣi:l] *vn: sv* i. The bill figures up to a hundred dollars. القائِمَة توَصِّل إلَى مِيَّة دُولار [ʔilqa:ʔima twaṣṣil ʔila miyyat dula:r]

file • **1.** مُبرَد [mubrad, mabrad] مَبارِد [maba:rid] *pl:* You need a finer file than that. تِحتاج مُبرَد أنعَم مِن هَذا [tiħta:ǰ mubrad ʔanʕam min ha:ða] • **2.** مَلَفَّة [malaffa] مَلَفّات [malaffa:t] *pl:* إضبارَة [ʔiḍba:ra] إضبارات، أضابِير [ʔiḍba:ra:t, ʔaḍa:bi:r] *pl:* فايَل [fa:yal] فايَلات [fa:yala:t] *pl:*

File the report in the Iraqi Oil Company file. إحفظ التَّقرير بِمَلَفَّات شَرِكَة النَّفط العِراقِيَّة [ʔiħfuð̣ ʔittaqri:r bimalaffa:t šarikat ʔinnafṭ ʔilʕira:qiyya] • **3.** مَحفَظَة [maħfað̣a] مَحافِظ [maħa:fið̣] *pl:* دُولاب [du:la:b] دواليب [dwa:li:b] *pl:* Isn't her address in the file? ما مَوجُود عِنوانها بِالمَحفَظَة؟ [ma: mawǰu:d ʕinwa:nha bilmaħfað̣a?] • **4.** سِرَة [sira] سِرايات، سِراوَات [sira:ya:t, sira:wa:t] *pl:* خَطّ [xaṭṭ] Line up in single file! إصطفّوا بسِرَة واحِد [ʔiṣṭaffu: bsira wa:ħid]

on file • **1.** مَحفُوظ [maħfu:ð̣] Do we have his application on file? عَرِيضتَه مَحفُوظَة عِدنا؟ [ʕari:ð̣tah maħfu:ð̣a ʕidna?]

to file • **1.** بُرَد [burad] بَرِد [barid] *vn:* اِنبُرَد [ʔinburad] *p:* I have to file this down first. لازم أبرُد هَذا أَوَّل [la:zim ʔabrud ha:ða ʔawwal] • **2.** حِفَظ [ħifað̣] حُفُظ [ħufuð̣] *vn:* اِنحُفَظ [ʔinħufað̣] *p:* The letters have not yet been filed. المَكاتِيب بَعَد لهَسَّة ما اِنحُفظَت [ʔilmaka:ti:b baʕad lhassa ma: ʔinħufð̣at] • **3.** قَدَّم [qaddam] تَقدِيم [taqdi:m] *vn:* اِتقَدَّم [ʔitqaddam] *p:* I filed my application today. قَدِّمِت طَلَبِي هاليُوم [qaddamit ṭalabi halyu:m]

filing cabinet • **1.** دُولاب [du:la:b] دواليب [dwa:li:b] *pl:*

fill • **1.** * I've had my fill of it, وُصلَت لِخَشمِي [wuṣlat lxašmi]

to fill • **1.** تِرَس [tiras] تَرِس [taris] *vn:* اِنتِرَس [ʔintiras] *p:* مِلَى [mila:] مَلِي [maly] *vn:* اِنمِلَى [ʔinmila:] *p:* Fill this bottle with water. إترُس هالبُطِل ماي [ʔitrus halbuṭul ma:y] The hall was filled to capacity. القاعَة كانَت مَترُوسَة تَماماً [ʔilqa:ʕa ča:nat matru:sa tama:man] • **2.** شِغَل [šiɣal] إشغال [ʔišɣa:l] *vn: sv* i. مِلَى [mila:] *sv* i. The position has been filled. الوَظِيفَة اِنشِغلَت [lwað̣i:fa ʔinšiɣlat] • **3.** أَخَذ مِن، أَخَذ عَلَى [ʔaxað min, ʔaxað ʕala] أَخِذ [ʔaxið] *vn:* اِناِخَذ [ʔinʔixað] *p:* تِرَس [tiras] تَرِس [taris] *vn:* اِنتِرس [ʔintiras] *p:* The sofa just about fills half the room. القَنَفَة تَقرِيباً تاخُذ نُصّ الغُرفَة [ʔilqanafa taqri:ban ta:xuð nuṣṣ ʔilɣurfa] • **4.** حَشَّى [ħašša:] تَحشِيَة [taħšiya] *vn:* تَحَشَّى [tħašša:] *p:* This tooth will have to be filled. هالسِّنّ لازم يِتحَشَّى [hassinn la:zim yitħašša:] • **5.** جَهَّز [ǰahhaz] تَجهِيز [taǰhi:z] *vn:* اِتجَهَّز [ʔidǰahhaz] *p:* The order hasn't been filled yet. الطَّلَبِيَّة بَعَدها ما تجَهّزَت [ʔiṭṭalabiyya baʕadha ma: dǰahhzat] • **6.** دِفَن [difan] دَفِن [dafin] *vn:* اِندِفَن [ʔindifan] *p:* We filled the ditch in an hour. دِفَنَّا النُّقرَة بساعَة [difanna: ʔinnugra bsa:ʕa]

to fill in • **1.** دِفَن [difan] دَفِن [dafin] *vn:* اِندِفَن [ʔindifan] *p:* The ditch has been filled in. اِندِفنَت النُّقرَة [ʔindifnat ʔinnugra] • **2.** مِلَى [mila:] مَلِي [maly] *vn:* اِنمِلَى [ʔinmila:] *p:* تِرَس [tiras] تَرِس [taris] *vn:* اِنتِرَس [ʔintiras] *p:* Fill in all the blanks. إملِي كُلّ الفَراغات [ʔimli: kull ʔilfara:ɣa:t]

*** Fill your name in here.** • **1.** إكتِب إسمَك هنا [ʔiktib ʔismak hna:]

*** I'm just filling in here temporarily.** • **1.** آنِي بَسّ دَأقُوم بِالعَمَل بصُورَة مُوَقَّتَة [ʔa:ni bass daʔaqu:m bilʕamal bṣu:ra muwaqqata]

to fill up • **1.** تِرَس [tiras] تَرِس [taris] *vn:* اِنتِرَس [ʔintiras] *p:* مِلَى [mila:] مَلِي [maly] *vn:* اِنمِلَى [ʔinmila:] *p:* He filled up the glasses. تِرَس الكلاصات [tiras ʔilgla:ṣa:t] Filler up! إترِسها [ʔitrisha] • **2.** اِنتِرَس [ʔintiras] *sv* i. اِنمِلَى [ʔinmila:] *sv* i. The theater was slowly filling up. السِّينَما كانَت دَتِنتِرِس شوَيَّة شوَيَّة [ʔissinama ča:nat datintiris šwayya šwayya]

filling • **1.** حَشوَة [ħašwa] حَشوات [ħašwa:t] *pl:* I've lost a filling from my tooth. وُقعَت الحَشوَة مال سِنِّي [wugʕat ʔilħašwa ma:l sinni] • **2.** حَشُو [ħašw] The cookie filling is walnuts and sugar. الحَشو مال الِكلَيجَة جُوز وَشَكَر [ʔilħašw ma:l ʔilkli:ča ǰu:z wšakar]

film • **1.** طَبَقَة [ṭabaqa] طَبَقات [ṭabaqa:t] *pl:* A thin film of oil formed on the water. طَبَقَة خَفِيفَة مِن الدِّهِن تكَوّنَت عَلَى المَي [ṭabaqa xafi:fa min ʔiddihin tkawwnat ʕala ʔilmayy] • **2.** فِلِم [filim] أفلام [ʔafla:m] *pl:* I don't like funny films. ما أَحِبّ الأفلام الهَزَلِيَّة [ma: ʔaħibb ʔilʔafla:m ʔilhazaliyya] I have to get another roll of film. لازم أشتِرِي فِلِم لاخ [la:zim ʔaštiri filim la:x]

to film • **1.** صَوَّر [ṣawwar] تَصوِير [taṣwi:r] *vn:* تصَوَّر [tṣawwar] *p:* أَخَذ رَسِم [ʔaxað rasim] أخِذ [ʔaxið] *vn:* اِنأَخَذ [ʔinʔaxað] *p:* They filmed the entire ceremony. صَوّرَوا كُلّ الاحتِفال [ṣawwraw kull ʔilʔiħtifa:l]

filter • **1.** مَصفِي [maṣfi] مَصافِي [maṣa:fi] *pl:* The water comes from the river and goes through the filter. المَيّ يِجِي مِن النَّهَر وَيِدخُل بِالمَصفِي [ʔilmayy yiǰi min ʔinnahar wyidxul bilmaṣfi] • **2.** أمّ قُطنَة [ʔumm guṭna] مزَبَّن [mzabban] I bought a pack of filter cigarettes. اِشتِرَيت باكَيت جِكايِر أمّ قُطنَة [ʔištiri:t pa:ki:t ǰiga:yir ʔumm guṭna]

to filter • **1.** صَفَّى [ṣaffa:] تَصفِيَة [taṣfiya] *vn:* تصَفَّى [tṣaffa:] *p:* The water will have to be filtered. الماي لازم يِتصَفَّى [ʔilma:y la:zim yitṣaffa:]

final • **1.** نِهائِي [niha:ʔi] How did you make out on your final exam? شلُون سَوَّيت بِالإمتِحان النِّهائِي؟ [šlu:n sawwi:t bilʔimtiħa:n ʔinniha:ʔi?] • **2.** قَطعِي [qaṭʕi] نِهائِي [niha:ʔi] Is this your final decision? هَذا قَرارَك النِّهائِي؟ [ha:ða qara:rak ʔinniha:ʔi?] • **3.** أخِير [ʔaxi:r] خِتامِي [xita:mi] This is the final lecture. هَذِي المُحاضَرَة الأخِيرَة [ha:ði ʔilmuħa:ð̣ara ʔilʔaxi:ra] • **4.** اِمتِحان نِهائِي [ʔimtiħa:n niha:ʔi] اِمتِحانات نِهائِيَّة [mtiħa:na:t niha:ʔiyya] *pl:* I passed the final. نِجَحت بِالإمتِحان النِّهائِي [niǰaħit bilʔimtiħa:n ʔinniha:ʔi] • **5.** سِباق نِهائِي [siba:q niha:ʔi] سِباقات نِهائِيَّة [siba:qa:t niha:ʔiyya] *pl:* لِعِب نِهائِي [liʕib niha:ʔi] ألعاب نِهائِيَّة [ʔalʕa:b niha:ʔiyya] *pl:* The finals are being played tomorrow. السِّباقات النِّهائِيَّة راح تصِير باكِر [ʔissiba:qa:t ʔinniha:ʔiyya ra:ħ tṣi:r ba:čir]

finally • **1.** أخيراً [ʔaxiːran] بالأخِير [bilʔaxiːr] He finally yielded. أخيراً أذعَن [ʔaxiːran ʔaðʕan] • **2.** تالِي ما تالِي [taːli maː taːli] تالِي [taːli] تُوالِي [tuwaːli] *pl:* So they finally got married. لَعَد تالِي ما تالِي تزَوّجَوا [laʕad taːliː maː taːli dzawwǰaw]

financial • **1.** مالِي [maːli] Our financial situation is improving. وَضِعنا المالِي دَيِتحَسَّن [waḏiʕna ʔilmaːli dayitħassan]

find • **1.** لِقيَة [ligya] لِقيات [ligyaːt] *pl:* This book is a real find. هَالكِتاب صُدُق لِقيَة [halkitaːb ṣudug ligya]

to find • **1.** لِقَى [ligaː] لَقِي [lagi] *vn:* اِنلِقَى [ʔinligaː] *p:* I found this pencil in the street. لِقيت هَالقَلَم بِالشّارِع [ligiːt halqalam biššaːriʕ] I can never find my way around here. آنِي مُستَحِيل ألقِي دَربِي هنا [ʔaːni mustaħiːl ʔalgi darbi hna] • **2.** وُجَد [wuǰad] وُجُود [wuǰuːd] *vn:* اِنوُجَد [ʔinwuǰad] *p:* I found him at home. وُجَدتَه بِالبَيت [wuǰadtah bilbayt]

to find out • **1.** شاف [šaːf] شَوف [šuːf] *vn: sv* u. Let's go out and find out what is going on. خَلِّي نِطلَع بَرَّة وَنشُوف شَكُو [xalli niṭlaʕ barra winšuːf šaku] • **2.** اِكتِشَف [ʔiktišaf] اِكتِشاف [ʔiktišaːf] *vn: sv* i. عِرَف [ʕiraf] مَعرِفَة [maʕrifa] *vn: sv* u. I found out he doesn't speak English. اِكتِشَفت إنُّو ما يِحكِي إنكِلِيزِي [ʔiktišfit ʔinnu maː yiħči ʔingiliːzi]

fine • **1.** غَرامَة [ɣaraːma] غَرامات [ɣaraːmaːt] *pl:* He had to pay a fine. اِضطَرّ يِدفَع غَرامَة [ʔiḏṭarr yidfaʕ ɣaraːma] • **2.** ناعِم [naːʕim] Strain it through a fine piece of cloth. صَفِّيه بوُصلَة قماش ناعمَة [ṣaffiːh bwuṣlat qmaːš naːʕma] • **3.** خُوش [xuːš] زَين [zayn] That's a fine car you've got. خُوش سَيّارَة عِندَك [xuːš sayyaːra ʕindak] That's a fine car you've got. سَيّارتَك زينَة [sayyaːrtak ziːna] • **4.** عال [ʕaːl] زَين [zayn] طَيِّب [ṭayyib] That's fine! عال [ʕaːl] • **5.** دَقِيق [daqiːq] That's too fine a distinction. هَذا تَفرِيق كُلِّش دَقِيق [haːða tafriːq kulliš daqiːq] • **6.** لُطُف [luṭuf] ألطاف [ʔalṭaːf] *pl:* That was mighty fine of him. هَذا كان لُطُف كِبِير مِنَّه [haːða čaːn luṭuf čibiːr minnah] • **7.** رِفِيع [rifiːʕ] I'd like a fountain pen with a fine point. أرِيد باندان سِلّايتَه رِفِيعَة [ʔariːd paːndaːn sillaːytah rifiːʕa] • **8.** زَين [zayn] Thanks, I'm feeling fine. شُكراً، آنِي زين [šukran, ʔaːni ziːn]

to fine • **1.** غَرَّم [ɣarram] تَغرِيم [taɣriːm] *vn:* تغَرَّم [tɣarram] *p:* جَزَّى [ǰazzaː] جَزاء [ǰazaːʔ] *vn:* تجَزَّى [tǰazzaː] *p:* The judge fined him half a dinar. الحاكِم غَرَّمَه نُصّ دِينار [ʔilħaːkim ɣarramah nuṣṣ dinaːr]

finger • **1.** إصبع [ʔiṣbiʕ] أصابع [ʔaṣaːbiʕ] *pl:* I cut my little finger. جِرَحت إصِبعِي الصّغَيِّر [ǰiraħit ʔiṣibʕi ʔiṣṣɣayyir]

*** He let the opportunity slip through his fingers.** • **1.** ضَيَّع الفُرصَة مِن إيدَه [ḍayyaʕ ʔilfurṣa min ʔiːdah]

*** Keep your fingers crossed.** • **1.** توَكَّل عَلَى الله [twakkal ʕalallah]

forefinger • **1.** سَبّابَة [sabbaːba]

little finger • **1.** خُنصُر [xunṣur] خَناصِر [xanaːṣir] *pl:*

middle finger • **1.** إصبع وُسط [ʔiṣbiʕ wuṣṭ] أصابع وُسط [ʔasaːbiʕ wuṣṭa] *pl:*

ring finger • **1.** بُنصُر [bunṣur] بَناصِر [banaːṣir] *pl:*

finger print • **1.** طَبعَة إصبع [ṭabʕat ʔiṣbiʕ] طَبعات أصابع [ṭabʕaːt ʔaṣaːbiʕ] *pl:* Have you taken his fingerprints? أخَذِت طَبعات أصابعَه؟ [ʔaxaðit ṭabʕaːt ʔaṣaːbʕah?]

finish • **1.** نِهايَة [nihaːya] نِهايات [nihaːyaːt] *pl:* أخِير [ʔaxiːr] I read the book from start to finish. قِريت الكِتاب مِن البِدايَة لِلنِّهايَة [qiriːt ʔilkitaːb min ʔilbidaːya linnihaːya] It was a fight to the finish. كانَت مَعرَكَة لِلأخِير [čaːnat maʕraka lilʔaxiːr] • **2.** صُبُغ [ṣubuɣ] You're rubbing off the finish of the car. دَتجَلِّغ صُبُغ السَّيّارَة [dadǰalliɣ ṣubuɣ ʔissayyaːra]

to finish • **1.** خَلَّص [xallaṣ] تَخلِيص [taxliːṣ] *vn: sv* i. كَمَّل [kammal] تَكمِيل [takmiːl] *vn: sv* i. Have you finished washing the car? خَلَّصِت غَسِل السَّيّارَة؟ [xallaṣit ɣasil ʔissayyaːra?] I couldn't even finish my coffee. حَتَّى ما قِدَرت أكَمِّل قَهوتِي [ħatta maː gidarit ʔakammil gahwti]

*** If he does it once more, he'll be finished.** • **1.** إذا سَوّاها مَرَّة لُخ يِنتِهِي أمرَه [ʔiða sawwaːha marra lux yintihi ʔamrah]

fire • **1.** نار [naːr] نِيران [niːraːn] *pl:* Has the fire gone out? النّار اِنطُفَت؟ [ʔinnaːr ʔinṭufat?] We were under fire all day. كِنّا تَحت النّار طُول اليُوم [činna taħt ʔinnaːr ṭuːl ʔilyuːm] • **2.** حَرِيق [ħariːq] حَرايِق [ħaraːyiq] *pl:* The fire damaged the building. الحَرِيق دَمَّر البِنايَة [ʔilħariːq dammar ʔilbinaːya]

to be on fire • **1.** اِحترَق [ʔiħtirag] اِحتِراق [ʔiħtiraːg] *vn: sv* i. اِشتِعَل [ʔištiʕal] اِشتِعال [ʔištiʕaːl] *vn: sv* i. The house is on fire. البَيت دَيِحترِق [ʔilbayt dayiħtirig]

to catch fire • **1.** أخَذ نار [ʔaxað naːr] أخِذ نار [ʔaxið naːr] *vn: sv* u. The hay caught fire. التِّبِن أخَذ نار [ʔittibin ʔaxað naːr]

to set on fire • **1.** حِرَق [ħirag] حَرِق [ħarig] *vn:* اِنحِرَق [ʔinħirag] *p:* He set the car on fire. حِرَق السَّيّارَة [ħirag ʔissayyaːra]

to fire • **1.** رِمَى [rimaː] رَمِي [ramy] *vn: sv* i. أطلَق [ʔaṭlaq] إطلاق [ʔiṭlaːq] *vn: sv* i. He fired two shots. رِمَى رَميتَين [rimaː ramytayn] He fired two shots. أطلَق نار مَرّتَين [ʔaṭlaq naːr marrtayn] • **2.** ضِرَب [ḍirab] ضَرُب [ḍarub] *vn: sv* u. He fired the gun twice. ضِرَب البُندُقِيَّة مَرّتَين [ḍirab ʔilbunduqiyya marrtayn] • **3.** طَلَّع [ṭallaʕ] تَطلِيع [taṭliːʕ] *vn:* تطَلَّع [ʔiṭṭallaʕ] *p:* طِرَد [ṭirad] طَرِد [ṭarid] *vn:* اِنطِرَد [ʔinṭirad] *p:* لَزَّم [lazzam] تَلزِيم [talziːm] *vn:* تلَزَّم [tlazzam] *p:* فُصَل [fuṣal] فَصِل [faṣil] *vn:* اِنفُصَل [ʔinfuṣal] *p:* I fired my driver when he wrecked the car. طَلَّعِت السّايِق مالِي مِن دِعَم السَّيّارَة [ṭallaʕit ʔissaːyiq maːli min diʕam ʔissayyaːra] I fired my driver when he wrecked the car. لَزَّمت السّايِق الباب مِن دِعَم السَّيّارَة

[lazzamit ʔissaːyiq ʔilbaːb min diʕam ʔissayyaːra] We are going to fire five workers. راح نُطرُد خَمِس عُمّال [raːħ nuṭrud xamis ʕummaːl]

fire department • **1.** دائِرَة الإِطفاء [daːʔirat ʔilʔiṭfaːʔ] إطفائِيَّة [ʔiṭfaːʔiyya] Call the fire department. خابُر دائِرَة الإِطفاء [xaːbur daːʔirat ʔilʔiṭfaːʔ]

fire extinguisher • **1.** آلَة الحَرِيق [ʔaːlat ʔilħariːq] آلَة الإِطفاء [ʔaːlat ʔilʔiṭfaːʔ] *pl:*

fireman • **1.** إطفائجِي [ʔiṭfaːʔčiː] إطفائجِيَّة [ʔiṭfaːʔčiyya] *pl:*

fireproof • **1.** ضِدّ النار [ðidd ʔinnaːr] The walls are fireproof. الحِيطان ضِدّ النّار [ʔilħiːṭaːn ðidd ʔinnaːr]

firm • **1.** شَرِكَة [šarika] شَرِكات [šarikaːt] *pl:* What firm do you represent? أَيّ شَرِكَة إنتَ تمَثِّل؟ [ʔayy šarika ʔinta tmaθθil?] • **2.** راسِخ [raːsix] وَطِيد [waṭiːd] ثابِت [θaːbit] I have a firm belief in God. عِندِي إيمان راسِخ بِالله [ʕindi ʔiːmaːn raːsix bʔallah] • **3.** صَلِب [ṣalib] قَوِي [qawi, guwi] قوّاي، أَقوِياء، قَوِيِّين [qwaːy, ʔaqwiyaːʔ, qawiyyiːn] *pl:* The ground is firm here. القاع صَلبَة هنا [ʔilgaːʕ ṣalba hna] • **4.** قاطِع [qaːṭiʕ] We have a firm agreement with your company to supply our paper needs. عِدنا اِتِّفاق قاطِع ويّا شَرِكَتكُم لِتَجهِيزنا بِكُلّ حاجاتنا مِن الوَرَق [ʕidna ʔittifaːq qaːṭiʕ wiyya šarikatkum litaǰhiːzna bkull ħaːǰaːtna min ʔilwaraq]

firmly • **1.** بصُورَة جازِمَة [bṣuːra ǰaːzima] I'm firmly convinced that she is innocent. آنِي مِقتِنِع بِصُورَة جازِمَة أنو هِيَّ بَرِيئَة [ʔaːni miqtiniʕ bṣuːura ǰaːzima ʔannu hiyya bariːʔa]

first • **1.** أَوَّل [ʔawwal] It's the first house on the left. هُوَّ أَوَّل بَيت عَاليِسرَة [huwwa ʔawwal bayt ʕalyisra] She's the first woman to become a minister. هِيَّ أَوَّل مَرَة صارَت وَزِيرَة [hiyya ʔawwal mara ṣaːrat waziːra] She's the first woman to become a minister. هِيَّ المَرَة الأُولَى اللّي صارَت وَزِيرَة [hiyya ʔilmara ʔilʔuːla ʔilli ṣaːrat waziːra] I get paid on the first of the month. آخُذ راتِب بِأَوَّل الشَّهَر [ʔaːxuð raːtib bʔawwal ʔiššahar] • **2.** قَبُل [gabul] أَوَّل [ʔawwal] The doctor will see the women first. الدِّكتُور راح يشُوف النِّساء قَبُل [ʔiddiktuːr raːħ yšuːf ʔinnisaːʔ gabul] • **3.** أَوَّلاً [ʔawwalan] First let me ask you a question. أَوَّلاً خَلِّي أَسأَلَك سُؤال [ʔawwalan xalli ʔasʔalak suʔaːl] • **4.** أَوَّلِي [ʔawwali] They gave him first aid. سَوّولَه إسعاف أَوَّلِي [sawwawlah ʔisʕaːf ʔawwali]

at first • **1.** بِالأَوَّل [bilʔawwal] I didn't believe it at first. ما صَدَّقتها بِالأَوَّل [maː ṣaddagitha bilʔawwal]

first of all • **1.** قَبُل كُلّشِي [gabul kullši] أَوَّلاً [ʔawwalan] First of all, you misunderstood me. قَبُل كُلّشِي، إنتَ ما إفتِهَمتنِي [gabul kullši, ʔinta maː ʔiftihamitni]

first-class • **1.** دَرَجَة أُولَى [daraǰa ʔuːla] I always travel first-class. آنِي دائِماً أَسافِر بِالدَّرَجَة الأُولَى [ʔaːni daːʔiman ʔasaːfir biddaraǰa ʔilʔuːla] • **2.** فاخِر [faːxir] مُمتاز [mumtaːz] It's a first-class job. هاي شَغلَة فاخرَة [haːy šaɣla faːxra]

fish • **1.** سِمكَة [simča] سِمكات [simčaːt] *pl:* سِمَك [simač] *Collective:* Do you like fish? تحِبّ السِّمَك؟ [tħibb ʔissimač?]

to fish • **1.** صاد سِمَك [ṣaːd simač] صَيد سِمَك [ṣayd simač] *vn: sv* i. Do you want to go fishing? ترِيد ترُوح تصِيد سِمَك؟ [triːd truːħ tṣiːd simač?] • **2.** دَوَّر [dawwar] تدُوُّر [tduwwur] *vn: sv* u. خَمّ [xamm] خَمّ [xamm] *vn: sv* u. He fished in his pocket for ten fils. دَوَّر بجِيبَه عَلَى عَشِر فلُوس [dawwar bǰiːbah ʕala ʕašir fluːs]

fishbone • **1.** عَظُم سِمَك [ʕaðum simač] عظام سِمَك [ʕðaːm simač] *pl:* A fishbone caught in his throat. عَظُم سِمَك وُقَف بزَردُومَه [ʕaðum simač wugaf bzarduːmah]

fisherman • **1.** سَمّاك [sammaːč] سَمّاكَة [sammaːča] *pl:* صَيّاد سِمَك [ṣayyaːd simač] صَيّادِين سِمَك [ṣayyaːdiːn simač] *pl:*

fish glue • **1.** غرا [ɣira, ɣara]

fist • **1.** قَبضَة إيد [qabðat ʔiːd] قَبضات إيد [qabðat ʔiːd] *pl:* He shook his fist at me. هَزّ قَبضَة إيدَه بوُجهِي [hazz qabðat ʔiːdah bwučči]

fit • **1.** نوبَة [nuːba] نوبات [nuːbaːt] *pl:* Every time I mention it, he has a fit of anger. كُلّما أَذكُرها تصِيبَه نُوبَة غَضَب [kullmaː ʔaðkurha tṣiːbah nuːbat ɣaðab]

* **This suit isn't a good fit.** • **1.** هَالقاط ما قاعِد زَين [halqaːṭ maː gaːʕid zayn]

to be fit • **1.** لاق [laːg] لِياقَة [liyaːga] *vn: sv* u. Is he fit for this kind of work? هُوَّ لايِق لِهَالنَّوع مِن الشُّغُل؟ [huwwa laːyig lihannawʕ min ʔiššuɣul?] • **2.** صِلَح [ṣilaħ] صَلاح [ṣalaːħ] *vn: sv* a. This meat isn't fit to eat. هَاللَّحَم مُو صالِح لِلأَكِل [hallaħam muː ṣaːliħ lilʔakil]

to fit • **1.** رِهَم [riham] رَهُم [rahum] *vn: sv* a. These shoes don't fit me. هالحِذاء ما يِرهَم عَلَيّا [halħiðaːʔ maː yirham ʕalayya] • **2.** رَهَّم [rahham] تَرهِيم [tarhiːm] *vn:* تَرَهَّم [trahham] *p:* Can you fit these rings to the pistons? تِقدَر ترَهمهُم هَالرِّنقات عَالبَساتِين؟ [tigdar trahhum harringaːt ʕalpasaːtiːn?]

to fit together • **1.** تطابَق [tṭaːbaq] مُطابَقَة [muṭaːbaqa] *vn: sv* a. These parts don't fit together. هَالقِطَع ما تِتطابَق [halqiṭaʕ maː tiṭṭaːbaq]

fitting • **1.** براوَة [praːwa] براوات [praːwaːt] *pl:* When will the suit be ready for a fitting? شوَقِت يكُون القاط حاضِر لِلبراوَة؟ [šwakit ykuːn ʔilqaːṭ ħaːðir lilpraːwa] • **2.** مناسِب [mnaːsib] Let's wait for a more fitting time. خَلِّي نِنتِظِر إلَى وَقِت مُناسِب أَكثَر [xalli nintiðir ʔila wakit munaːsib ʔakθar]

five • **1.** خَمِس [xamis] I bought it for five dinars. اِشتِرَيتَه بخَمس دَنانِير [ʔištiriːtah bxams danaːniːr] There are five starlings on the tree. أكُو خَمس زرازير عَالشِّجرَة [ʔaku xams zraːziːr ʕaššiǰra] • **2.** خَمسَة [xamsa] His salary is five thousand dinars a year. راتبَه خَمسَة آلاف دِينار بِالسَّنَة [raːtbah xamsat ʔaːlaːf dinaːr bissana] I spent five days on my uncle's farm. قضَيت خَمسَة أيّام بمَزرَعَة عَمِّي [gḍiːt xamsat ʔayyaːm bmazraʕat ʕammi] • **3.** خَمسَة [xamsa] Take five of them and leave the rest. أُخُذ خَمسَة مِنها وَخَلِّي الباقِي [ʔuxuð xamsa minha wxalli ʔilbaːqi] Take the five from here and add it to this number. أُخُذ الخمسَة مِن هِنَا وَضِيفها عَلَى هَالرَّقم [ʔuxuð ʔilxamsa min hna wḍiːfha ʕala harraqum]

F

fix • **1.** ورطَة [warṭa, wurṭa] ورطات [warṭaːt, wurṭaːt] *pl:* He's in a terrible fix. واقِع بوَرطَة كِبيرَة [waːqiʕ bwarṭa čibiːra]

to fix • **1.** حَدَّد [ħaddad] تَحدِيد [taħdiːd] *vn:* تحَدَّد [tħaddad] *p:* The price was fixed at ten dinars. السِّعِر تحَدَّد بعَشر دَنانِير [ʔissiʕir tħaddad bʕašr danaːniːr] • **2.** عَدَّل [ʕaddal] تَعدِيل [taʕdiːl] *vn:* تعَدَّل [tʕaddal] *p:* Fix your tie. عَدِّل بوينباغَك [ʕaddil buːyinbaːɣak] • **3.** صَلَّح [ṣallaħ] تَصلِيح [taṣliːħ] *vn:* تصَلَّح [tṣallaħ] *p:* Can you fix the typewriter for me? تِقدَر تصَلِّحلِي الآلَة الطّابِعَة [tigdar tṣalliħli ʔalʔaːla ʔiṭṭaːbiʕa] • **4.** سَوَّى [sawwaː] تَسوِيَة [taswiya] *vn:* تسَوَّى [tsawwaː] *p:* هَيَّأ [hayyaʔ] تَهيِئَة [tahyiʔa] *vn:* تهَيَّأ [thayyaʔ] *p:* I have to fix supper now. لازِم أسَوِّي العَشا هَسَّة [laːzim ʔasawwi ʔilʕaša hassa]

flag • **1.** عَلَم [ʕalam] أعلام [ʔaʕlaːm] *pl:* The colors of the American flag are red, white, and blue. ألوان العَلَم الأمِيركِي أحمَر، وأبيَض، وأزرَق [ʔalwaːn ʔilʕalam ʔilʔamriːki ʔaħmar, wʔabyaḍ, wʔazrag]

flake • **1.** ندفَة [nidfa] نِدَف [nidaf] *pl:* The snow is falling in big flakes. الثَّلج دَينزل بِندَف كبار [ʔiθθaliǰ dayinzil bnidaf kbaːr]

flames • **1.** شُعلَة [šuʕla] شُعلات [šuʕlaːt] *pl:* لَهَب [lahab, lahib] The whole house was in flames. البَيت كُلّه كان صايِر شُعلَة [ʔilbayt kullah čaːn ṣaːyir šuʕla]

flare • **1.** نُور كَشّاف [nuːr kaššaːf] أنوار كَشّافَة [ʔanwaːr kaššaːfa] *pl:* They fired flares so it would be known where they were. أطلِقوا أنوار كَشّافَة حَتَّى يِنعَرفُون وين [ʔaṭliqaw ʔanwaːr kaššaːfa ħatta yinʕarfuːn wiːn]

to flare up • **1.** اِضطِرَم [ʔiḍṭiram] اِضطِرام [ʔiḍṭiraːm] *vn:* *sv* i. The fire flared up when I poured some gasoline on it. النّار اِضطِرمَت مِن كَبَّيت عَليها شوَيَّة بانزين [ʔinnaːr ʔiḍṭirmat min čabbiːt ʕaliːha šwayya banziːn] • **2.** ثار [θaːr (u)] ثَورَة [θawra] *vn:* *sv* u. He flares up at the slightest provocation. هَذا يثُور مِن أقَلّ حِرشَة [haːða yθuːr min ʔaqall ħirša]

flash • **1.** لَمَعان [lamaʕaːn] Did you see the flash of lightning? شِفِت لَمَعان البَرِق؟ [šifit lamaʕaːn ʔilbariq?] • **2.** لَحظَة [laħða] لَحظات [laħðaːt] *pl:* It was all over in a flash. كُلّشِي خِلَص بلَحظَة [kullši xilaṣ blaħða] It was all over in a flash. كُلّشِي خِلَص مِثِل البَرق [kullši xilaṣ miθl ʔilbarq]

to flash • **1.** لِمَع [limaʕ] لَمَعان [lamaʕaːn] *vn:* *sv* a. His eyes flashed with anger. عيُونَه لِمعَت مِن الغَضَب [ʕyuːnah limʕat min ʔilɣaðab] • **2.** خِطَر [xiṭar] خُطران [xuṭraːn] *vn:* *sv* u. Many thoughts flashed through my mind. هوايَة أفكار خِطرَت عَلَى بالِي [hwaːya ʔafkaːr xiṭrat ʕala baːli] • **3.** شِعَل [šiʕal] شَعِل [šaʕil] *vn:* اِنشِعَل [ʔinšiʕal] *p:* He flashed the light in my face. شِعَل الضَّوَة بوُجهِي [šiʕal ʔiððuwa bwučči] • **4.** خِطَف [xiṭaf] خَطُف [xaṭuf] *vn:* *sv* u. The bird flashed by the window. الطِّير خِطَف مِن يَمّ الشِّبّاك [ʔiṭṭiːr xiṭaf min yamm ʔiššibbaːč]

flashlight • **1.** تُورج [tuːrč] تُورجَات [tuːrčaːt] *pl:* Can you lend me your flashlight? تِقدَر تعِيرنِي التَّورج مالَك؟ [tigdar tʕiːrni ʔittuːrč maːlak?]

flat • **1.** شُقَّة [šiqqa, šuqqa] شُقَق [šuqaq] *pl:* I just moved into a new flat. ستَوّنِي تحَوَّلت إلَى شُقَّة جِدِيدَة [stawwni tħawwalit ʔila šuqqa ǰidiːda] • **2.** بَنجَر [pančar] بَناجِر [panaːčir] *pl:* On the way back we had a flat. بطَرِيق رَجعَتنا صار عِدنا بَنجَر [bṭariːq raǰʕatna ṣaːr ʕidna pančar] • **3.** مِنبَسِط [minbasiṭ] مُستَوِي [mustawiː] The country around Baghdad is flat. الأراضِي حَول بَغداد مِنبَسطَة [ʔilʔaraːḍi ħawil baɣdaːd minbasṭa] • **4.** فاهِي [faːhi] بلا طَعَم [bilaː ṭaʕam] The soup is flat. الشّوربَة فاهيَة [ʔiššuːrba faːhya] • **5.** بات [baːt] قاطِع [qaːṭiʕ] His answer was a flat 'no'. جَوابَه كان نَفِي باتّ [ǰawaːbah čaːn nafy baːtt] • **6.** مفَلطَح [mfalṭaħ] He has a flat nose. عِندَه خَشِم مفَلطَح [ʕindah xašim mfalṭaħ]

flat feet • **1.** فلات فُوت [flaːt fuːt] He has flat feet. عِندَه فلات فُوت [ʕindah flaːt fuːt]

flat iron • **1.** أُوتي [ʔuːti] أُوتِيّات [ʔuːtiːyyaːt] *pl:*

to flatten • **1.** وَقَّع [waggaʕ] توقِّع [twiggiʕ] *vn:* *sv* i. He flattened him with one punch. وَقَّعَه ببُوكس واحِد [waggaʕah bibuːks waːħid] • **2.** طَبَّق [ṭabbag] تطُبِّق [tṭubbug] *vn:* تطَبَّق [tṭabbag] *p:* Flatten the cardboard boxes and stack them on the shelf. طَبُّق الصَّنادِيق المقَوَّى وَصَفُّطها عالرّازُونَة [ṭabbug ʔiṣṣanaːdiːg ʔilmqawwaː wṣaffuṭha ʕarrazuːna]

***** **He stepped on my hat and flattened it.** • **1.** داس عَلَى شَفُقتِي وسَوّاها ويّا القاع [daːs ʕala šafuqti wsawwaːha wiyya ʔilgaːʕ]

to flatter • **1.** تمَلَّق ل [tmallaq l-] تَمَلُّق [tamalluq] *vn:* *sv* a. He tried to flatter me. حاوَل يِتمَلَّقلِي [ħaːwal yitmallaqli]

to flatter oneself • **1.** تباهَى [tbaːhaː] تَباهِي [tabaːhi] *vn:* *sv* a. He flatters himself that he's a good judge of character. يِتباهَى بكَونَه يِقدَر يِحزِر أطباع النّاس [yitbaːhaː bkawnah yigdar yiħzir ʔaṭbaːʕ ʔinnaːs]

flattery • **1.** مَلَق [malaq] اتمَلَّق [ʔitmallaq] Flattery won't get you anywhere. المَلَق ما يفيدَك [ʔilmalaq maː yfiːdak]

flavor • **1.** طَعَم [ṭaʕam] The coffee has lost all its flavor. القَهوَة ما بُقَى بِيها طَعُم [ʔilgahwa maː buqaː biːha ṭaʕum]

flight • **1.** قاط [qaːṭ] قُوط [quːṭ] *pl:* طابِق [ṭaːbiq] طَوابِق [ṭawaːbiq] *pl:* How many more flights do we have to climb? كَم قاط بَعَد لازِم نِصعَد؟ [čam qaːṭ baʕad laːzim niṣʕad?] • **2.** طَيَران [ṭayaraːn] The flight to Rome took an hour. الطَّيَران إِلَى رُوما طَوَّل ساعَة [ʔiṭṭayaraːn ʔila ruːma ṭawwal saːʕa]

*** There are four flights a day to Mecca.**
• **1.** أَكُو أَربَع طَيّارات تطِير يَومِيّا إِلَى مَكَّة [ʔaku ʔarbaʕ ṭayyaːraːt yṭiːr yuːmiyya ʔilaː makka]

to fling • **1.** شُمَر [šumar] شَمُر [šamur] *vn:* اِنشُمَر [ʔinšumar] *p:* ذَبّ [ðabb] ذَبّ [ðabb] *vn:* اِنذَبّ [ʔinðabb] *p:* He flung his jacket on a chair and rushed to the telephone. شُمَر سِترتَه عَلَى السَّكَملِي وَرِكَض عَالتَّلَفون [šumar sitirtah ʕala ʔissakamli wrikaḍ ʕattalifuːn]

to flirt • **1.** غازَل [ɣaːzal] مُغازَلَة [muɣaːzala] *vn:* تغازَل [tɣaːzal] She flirts with every man she meets. هاي تغازِل أَيّ رِجّال تلاقِيه [haːy tɣaːzil ʔayy rijjaːl tlaːgiːh] She flirts with every man she meets. تِتغازَل وِيّا أَيّ رِجّال تلاقِيه [tidɣaːzal wiyya ʔayy rijjaːl tlaːgiːh]

*** I've been flirting with this idea for a long time.**
• **1.** هَالفِكرَة صارِلها مُدَّة تداعِب عَقلِي [halfikra ṣaːrilha mudda tdaːʕib ʕaqli]

float • **1.** عَوّامَة [ʕawwaːma] عَوّامات [ʕawwaːmaːt] *pl:* Let's swim to the float. خَلِّي نِسبَح لِلعَوّامَة [xalli nisbaħ lilʕawwaːma] • **2.** طَوّافَة [ṭawwaːfa] طَوّافات [ṭawwaːfaːt] *pl:* When the float starts bobbing around, you know there's a fish on the hook. مِن قامَت تِتحَرَّك الطَّوّافَة عرَفِت أَكُو سِمكَة بالشُّصّ [min gaːmat titħarrak ʔiṭṭawwaːfa ʕrafit ʔaku simča biššuṣṣ]

to float • **1.** طاف [ṭaːf] طَوف [ṭawf] *vn: sv* u. عام [ʕaːm] عَوم [ʕawm] *vn: sv* u. What is that floating on the water? شِنُو ذاك الطّايِف عَالمَيّ؟ [šinuː ðaːk ʔiṭṭaːyif ʕalmayy?] • **2.** سَيَّس [sayyas] تَسيِيس [tasyiːs] *vn: sv* i. They floated a raft loaded with watermelons down to Baghdad. سَيِّسَوا كَلَك محَمَّل رَقِّي إِلَى بَغداد [sayyisaw kalak mħammal raggi ʔila baɣdaːd] The logs were floated down the river. جِذُوع الأَشجار تسَيِّسَت بِالشَّطّ [jiðuːʕ ʔilʔašjaːr tsayyisat biššaṭṭ]

flock • **1.** قَطِيع [qaṭiːʕ] قِطعان [qiṭʕaːn] *pl:* They followed him like a flock of sheep. تِبعَوه مِثِل قَطِيع غَنَم [tibʕawh miθil qaṭiːʕ ɣanam] • **2.** سِرب [sirib] أَسراب [ʔasraːb] *pl:* We saw a flock of birds flying south. شِفنا سِرب طيُور طايِر لِلجَّنُوب [šifna sirib ṭyuːr ṭaːyir lijjanuːb]

to flock • **1.** تقاطَر [tgaːṭar] تَقاطُر [tagaːṭur] *vn: sv* a. The children flocked into the circus. الأَطفال تقاطرَوا عالسّيرك [ʔilʔaṭfaːl tgaːṭraw ʕassiːrk]

*** People came flocking to hear him.**
• **1.** الناس إِجَوا جَوقات جَوقات حَتَّى يِسمَعُوه [ʔinnaːs ʔijaw jawgaːt jawgaːt ħattaː yismaʕuːh]

flood • **1.** فَيَضان [fayaðaːn] فَيَضانات [fayaðaːnaːt] *pl:* Many perished in the flood. هوايَة ماتَوا بِالفَيَضان [hwaːya maːtaw bilfayaðaːn]

to flood • **1.** فاض [faːð] فَيَضان [fayaðaːn] *vn: sv* i. The river floods every year. الشَّطّ يفِيض كُلّ سَنَة [ʔiššaṭṭ yfiːð kull sana] • **2.** غِرَق [ɣirag] غَرَق [ɣarag] *vn: sv* a. The whole street was flooded. الشّارِع كُلَّه غِرَق [ʔiššaːriʕ kullah ɣirag] • **3.** غَرَّق [ɣarrag] تَغرِيق [taɣriːg] *vn: sv* i. The rain water flooded the basement. ماي المُطَر غَرَّق السِّرداب [maːy ʔilmuṭar ɣarrag ʔissirdaːb] They flooded the market with Egyptian cigarettes. غَرِّقَوا السُّوق بِجِكايِر مَصرِيَّة [ɣarrigaw ʔissuːg bjigaːyir maṣriyya]

floor • **1.** قاع [gaːʕ] قِيعان [giʕaːn] *pl:* My glasses fell on the floor. مَناظرِي وُقعَت بِالقاع [manaːðri wugʕat bilgaːʕ] • **2.** طابِق [ṭaːbiq] طَوابِق [ṭawaːbiq] *pl:* I live on the second floor. أَسكُن بِالطّابِق الثّانِي [ʔaskun biṭṭaːbiq ʔiθθaːni] • **3.** حَقّ الكَلام [ħaqq ʔilkalaːm] May I have the floor, Mr. Chairman? يا حَضرَة الرَّئِيس، أَقدَر آخُذ حَقّ الكَلام؟ [yaː ħaðrat ʔirraʔiːs, ʔagdar ʔaːxuð ħaqq ʔilkalaːm?]

flop • **1.** فاشِل [faːšil] فاشِلِين [faːšiliːn] *pl:* He's a flop as a singer. هَذا فاشِل كَمُغَنّي [haːða faːšil kamuɣanni]

to flop • **1.** ذَبّ نَفس [ðabb nafis] ذَبّ نَفِس [ðabb nafis] *vn: sv* i. She flopped into a chair. ذَبَّت نَفِسها عَلَى كُرسِي [ðabbat nafisha ʕala kursi] • **2.** فِشَل [fišal] فَشَل [fašal] *vn: sv* a. The play flopped. الرِّوايَة فِشلَت [ʔirruwaːya fišlat] • **3.** لُبَط [lubaṭ] لَبُط [labuṭ] *vn: sv* u. The fish flopped around on the bottom of the boat. السِّمكَة لُبطَت بِقاعِيَة البَلَم [ʔissimča lubṭat bgaːʕiyat ʔilbalam]

flour • **1.** طِحِين، طحِين [ṭiħiːn, ṭħiːn] I want a sack of flour. أَرِيد كِيس طِحِين [ʔariːd čiːs ṭiħiːn]

to flourish • **1.** اِزدِهَر [ʔizdihar] اِزدِهار [ʔizdihaːr] *vn: sv* i. A highly developed civilization flourished here 2, 000 years ago. فَدّ حَضارَة مِتقَدّمَة جِدّاً اِزدِهرَت هنا قَبُل أَلفَين سَنَة [fadd ħaðaːra mitqaddma jiddan ʔizdihrat hna gabul ʔalfayn sana]

flourishing • **1.** مُزدَهِر [muzdahir] We had a flourishing trade with Syria. كانَت عِدنا تِجارَة مُزدَهرَة وِيّا سُوريا [čaːnat ʕidna tijaːra muzdahra wiyya suːrya]

flow • **1.** وُرُود [wuruːd] The flow of food supplies was cut. اِنقِطَع وُرُود المَوادّ الغِذائِيَّة [ʔingiṭaʕ wuruːd ʔilmawaːdd ʔilɣiðaːʔiyya]

to flow • **1.** جِرَى [jiraː] جَرَيان [jarayaːn] *vn: sv* i. The Tigris flows from north to south. نَهَر دِجلَة يِجرِي مِن الشِّمال لِلجَّنُوب [nahar dijla yijri min ʔiššimaːl lijjanuːb] • **2.** صَبّ [ṣabb]

صَبّ [ṣabb] *vn: sv* u. The Shatt al-Arab flows into the Persian Gulf. شَطّ العَرَب يصُبّ بِالخَلِيج الفارِسِي [šaṭṭ ʔilʕarab yṣubb bilxali:ǰ ʔilfa:risi]

flower • 1. وَردَة [warda] وَردات، وُرُود، وَرِد [warda:t, wuru:d, warid] *pl:* وَرِد [warid] *Collective:* He took some flowers to a sick friend. وَدَّى شوَيَّة وَرِد لِفَدّ صَدِيق مَرِيض [wadda: šwayya warid lfadd ṣadi:q mari:ḍ]

flu • 1. فلاوَنزا [flawanza, ʔinflawanza] Our whole family had the flu. كُلّ عائِلَتنا صار بِيهُم إِنفلُونزا [kull ʕa:ʔilatna ṣa:r bi:hum ʔinfluwanza]

to fluctuate • 1. تقَلَّب [tqallab, tgallab] تَقَلُّب [taqallub] *vn: sv* a. Prices fluctuate. الأَسعار تِتقَلَّب [ʔilʔasʕa:r titqallab] **• 2.** تذَبذَب [dðabðab] تَذَبذُب، ذَبذَبَة [taðabðub, ðabðaba] *vn: sv* a. The gas gauge began to fluctuate. گَيج البَنزِين بِدا يِتذَبذَب [gayǰ ʔilbanzi:n bida: yiðabðab]

fluently • 1. بِطَلاقَة [bṭala:qa] He speaks Persian fluently. يِحكِي فارسِي بِطَلاقَة [yiħči fa:rsi bṭala:qa]

fluid • 1. سائِل [sa:ʔil] سائِلِين [sa:ʔili:n] *pl:* You should drink more water to replace your body fluids. لازِم تِشرَب مَيّ أَزيَد حَتَّى تعَوُّض سَوائِل جِسمَك [la:zim tišrab mayy ʔazyad ħatta tʕawwuḍ sawa:ʔil ǰismak] **• 2.** مايِع [ma:yiʕ] I watched them pour the fluid metal into the mold. راقَبِتهُم يدِيرُون المَعدَن المايِع بالقالَب [ra:qabithum ydi:ru:n ʔilmaʕdan ʔilma:yiʕ bilqa:lab]

flush • 1. He always beats me with a flush. عَلَى طُول دَيِغلُبنِي بِالفلَشّ [ʕala ṭu:l dayiɣlubni bilflašš] **• 2.** وِيّا [wiyya] The shelf is built flush with the wall. الرّازُونَة مَبنِيَة وِيّا الحايِط [ʔirra:zu:na mabniya wiyya ʔilħa:yiṭ]

to flush • 1. اِحمَرّ [ʔiħmarr] اِحمِرار [ʔiħmira:r] *vn: sv* a. His face flushed with anger. وِجهه اِحمَرّ مِن الغَضَب [wiččah ʔiħmarr min ʔilɣaḍab] **• 2.** شَيَّش [šayyaš] تَشيِيش [tašyi:š] *vn:* تشَيَّش [tšayyaš] *p:* We'll have to flush your radiator. لازِم نشَيِّش الرّادِيتَة مالَك [la:zim nšayyiš ʔirra:di:ta ma:lak]

*** Don't forget to flush the toilet. • 1.** لا تِنسَى تجُرّ السِيفُون [la: tinsa: tǰurr ʔissi:fu:n]

fly • 1. ذِبّانَة [ðibba:na] ذِبّانات [ðibba:na:t] *pl:* ذِبّان [ðibba:n] *Collective:* The flies around here are terrible. الذِّبّان هنا مُزعِج [ʔiððibba:n hna muzʕiǰ]

to fly • 1. طار [ṭa:r] طَيَران [ṭayara:n] *vn: sv* i. The birds are flying south. الطُّيُور دَيطِيرُون لِلجَنُوب [ʔiṭṭuyu:r dayṭi:ru:n liǰǰanu:b] We're flying to Paris tomorrow. راح نطِير لبارِيس باكِر [ra:ħ nṭi:r lpari:s ba:čir] **• 2.** طَيَّر [ṭayyar] تَطيِير [taṭyi:r] *vn:* تطَيَّر [ʕiṭṭayyar] *p:* Can you fly a plane? تِقدَر تطَيِّر طَيّارَة؟ [tigdar tṭayyir ṭiyya:ra?] **• 3.** أَخَذ [ʔaxað] *sv* u. وَدَّى [wadda:] *sv* i. The child was flown to a hospital. الطِّفِل اِنِّخَذ لِلمُستَشفَى بِطِيّارَة [ʔiṭṭifil ʔinnixað lilmustašfa: bṭiyya:ra] **• 4.** رُفَع [rufaʕ] رَفُع [rafuʕ] *vn:* اِنرُفَع [ʔinrufaʕ] *p:* The ship was flying the Indian flag. الباخِرَة كانَت رافعَة العَلَم الهِندِي [ʔilba:xira ča:nat ra:fʕa ʔilʕalam ʔilhindi]

flyer • 1. طَيّار [ṭayya:r] طَيّارِين [ṭayya:ri:n] *pl:* He's a famous flyer. هَذا فَدّ طَيّار مَشهُور [ha:ða fadd ṭayya:r mašhu:r]

foam • 1. وَغَف [waɣaf] There's more foam than beer. أَكُو وَغَف أَكثَر مِن البِيرَة [ʔaku waɣaf ʔakθar min ʔilbi:ra] **• 2.** زَبَد [zabad] The water below the falls was covered with foam. الماي جَوَّة الشَّلّال كان مغَطَّى بِالزَّبَد [ʔilma:y ǰawwa ʔiššalla:l ča:n mɣaṭṭa: bizzabad]

to foam • 1. زَبَّد [zabbad] تزِبِّد [tzibbid] *vn: sv* i. He was foaming at the mouth. حَلقَه كان يزَبِّد [ħalgah ča:n yzabbid]

to focus • 1. ضُبَط [ḍubaṭ] ضَبُط [ḍabuṭ] *vn:* اِنضِبَط [ʔinḍibaṭ] *p:* Focus the camera at 50 feet. إِضبُط الكامِيرَة عَلَى خَمسِين قَدَم [ʔiḍbuṭ ʔilkamira: ʕala xamsi:n qadam] **• 2.** رَكَّز [rakkaz] تَركِيز [tarki:z] *vn: sv* i. Try to focus your eyes on this dot. حاوِل ترَكِّز عيُونَك عَلَى هَالنُّقطَة [ħa:wil trakkiz ʕyu:nak ʕala hannuqṭa]

fog • 1. ضَباب [ḍaba:b] A dense fog shut out the view. ضَباب كَثِيف سَدّ المَنظَر [ḍaba:b kaθi:f sadd ʔilmanḍar]

fold • 1. ثَنيَة [θanya] ثَنيات [θanya:t] *pl:* The curtains are faded at the folds. البَردات كاشفَة مِن الثَّنيات [ʔilparda:t ka:šfa min ʔiθθanya:t] **• 2.** طَيَّة [ṭayya] طَيّات [ṭayya:t] *pl:* He hid the knife in the folds of his clothes. ضَمّ السِّكِّينَة بِطَيّات هدُومَه [ḍamm ʔissičči:na bṭayya:t hdu:mah]

to fold • 1. طَوَّى [ṭawwa:] تَطوِيَة [taṭwiya] *vn:* تطَوَّى [ʕiṭṭawwa:] *p:* طَبَّق [ṭabbag] تَطبِيق [taṭbi:g] *vn:* اِتطَبَّق [ʕiṭṭabbag] *p:* طِوَى [ṭiwa:] طَوِي [ṭawi:] *vn:* اِنطِوَى [ʔinṭiwa:] *p:* Help me fold the blanket. ساعِدنِي أَطَوِّي البَطّانِيَّة [sa:ʕidni ʔaṭawwi ʔilbaṭṭa:niyya]

to fold one's arms • 1. تكَتَّف [tčattaf, tkattaf] تَكَتُّف [tačattuf] *vn: sv* a. He folded his arms. تكَتَّف [tčattaf]

to fold up • 1. فِشَل [fišal] فَشَل [fašal] *vn: sv* a. His business folded up last year. شَغِلتَه فِشلَت السَّنَة اللِّي فاتَت [šaɣiltah fišlat ʔissana ʔilli fa:tat]

folder • 1. مَلَفّ [malaff] مَلَفّات [malaffa:t] *pl:* The copies are in the blue folder. النُّسَخ بِالمَلَف الأَزرَق [ʔinnusax bilmalaf ʔilʔazarg]

folks • 1. والِد [wa:lid] وَالِدَين [wa:lidayn] *pl:* How are your folks? شلُون والدَيك؟ [šlu:n wa:ldayk?] **• 2.** رَبُع [rabuʕ] جَماعَة [ǰama:ʕa] جَماعات [ǰama:ʕa:t] *pl:* Let's go, folks! خَلِّي نرُوح، يا رَبُع [xalli nru:ħ, ya: rabuʕ]

to follow • **1.** لِحَق [liħag] لَحِق [laħig] *vn:* اِنلِحَق [ʔinliħag] *p:* تِبَع [tibaʕ] تَبِع [tabiʕ] *vn: sv* a. You lead the way and we'll follow you. إِنتَ تقَدَّم وَإِحنا نِلحَقَك [ʔinta tqaddam wʔiħna nilħagak] • **2.** تعَقَّب [tʕaqqab] تَعَقُّب [taʕaqqub] *vn: sv* a. Somebody's following us. فَدّ واحِد دَيتِعَقَّبنا [fadd waːħid dayitʕaqqabna] • **3.** تِبَع [tibaʕ] اِنتِبَع [ʔintibaʕ] *p:* Follow these instructions exactly. إِتبَع هَالتَّعلِيمات بِدِقَّة [ʔitbaʕ hattaʕliːmaːt bdiqqa] He's following in his father's footsteps and becoming a doctor. دَيتِبَع خَطوات أَبُوه وَدَيصِير طَبِيب [dayitbaʕ xaṭawaːt ʔabuːh wadayṣiːr ṭabiːb] • **4.** عِقَب [ʕiqab] عَقِب [ʕaqib] *vn:* اِنعِقَب [ʔinʕiqab] *p:* تِبَع [tibaʕ] تَبع [tabiʕ] *vn:* اِنتِبَع [ʔintibaʕ] *p:* Rain followed the hot weather. الجَوّ الحارّ عِقَبَه مُطَر [ʔiǰǰaww ʔilħaːrr ʕiqabah muṭar] • **5.** اِتَّبَع [ʔittabbaʕ] تَتَبُّع [tatabbuʕ] *vn: sv* a. Have you been following the news lately? إِنتَ مِتَّبِّع الأَخبار هَالأَيّام؟ [ʔinta mittabbiʕ ʔilʔaxbaːr halʔayyaːm?] I couldn't follow his explanation. ما قِدَرِت أَتَّبَع التَّفسِير مالَه [maː gidarit ʔattabbaʕ ʔittafsiːr maːlah] I couldn't follow his explanation. ما قِدَرِت أَفهَم تَفسِيرَه [maː gidarit ʔafham tafsiːrah]

* **From this fact it follows that...** • **1.** يُبنَى عَلَى هَالحَقِيقَة أَنّو [yubna ʕala halħaqiːqa ʔannu ...]

as follows • **1.** كَما يَلِي [kamaː yaliː] The letter reads as follows. . . المَكتُوب يِقرا كَما يَلِي [ʔilmaktuːb yiqraː kama yali]

follower • **1.** تابِع [taːbiʕ] أَتباع [ʔatbaːʕ] *pl:* نَصِير [naṣiːr] أَنصار [ʔanṣaːr] *pl:* He's one of the party's most faithful followers. هَذا واحِد مِن أَخلَص أَتباع الحِزب [haːða waːħid min ʔaxlaṣ ʔatbaːʕ ʔilħizib]

following • **1.** تالِي [taːli] تُوالِي [tuwaːli] *pl:* The following day it rained. مُطرَت بِاليُوم التّالِي [muṭrat bilyuːm ʔittaːli] I need the following items. أَحتاج الأَشياء التّالِيَة [ʔaħtaːǰ ʔilʔašyaːʔ ʔittaːliya] • **2.** بَعَد [baʕad] Following the party we went to his house. بَعَد الحَفلَة رِحنا لبَيتَه [baʕad ʔilħafla riħna lbaytah]

* **He has a very large following.** • **1.** عِندَه أَتباع هوايَة [ʕindah ʔatbaːʕ hwaːya]

fond • **1.** مُولَع [muːlaʕ] We're fond of music. إِحنا مُولَعِين بِالمُوسِيقَى [ʔiħna muːlaʕiːn bilmusiːqa] We're fond of music. عِدنا وَلَع بِالمُوسِيقَى [ʕidna walaʕ bilmusiːqa] She's fond of children. هِيَّ مُولَعَة بِالأَطفال [hiyya muːlaʕa bilʔaṭfaːl] She's fond of children. هِيَّ تحِبّ الأَطفال [hiyya tħibb ʔilʔaṭfaːl] • **2.** مُتعَلِّق [mutʕalliq] مُتعَلقات [mutʕallqaːt] *pl:* Our boy is very fond of you. إِبنَنا هوايَة مِتعَلِّق بِيك [ʔibinna hwaːya mitʕalliq biːk]

to become fond of • **1.** تعَلَّق [tʕallaq] تَعَلُّق [taʕalluq] *vn: sv* a. The children became very fond of their teacher. الجِهّال تعَلّقَوا كُلِّش بِمُعَلِّمتَهُم [ʔiǰǰhhaːl tʕallqaw kulliš bmuʕallimathum]

food • **1.** أَكِل [ʔakil] The food is excellent in this restaurant. الأَكِل مُمتاز بِهَالمَطعَم [ʔilʔakil mumtaːz bihalmaṭʕam] • **2.** مَؤُونَة [maʔuːna] Food got scarcer day after day. المَؤُونَة قَلَّت يوم وَرا يوم [ʔilmaʔuːna qallat yuːm wara yuːm]

* **This will give you food for thought.** • **1.** هَذا يِنطِيك مادَّة لِلتَّفكِير [haːða yintiːk maːdda littafkiːr]

foodstuff • **1.** مَوادّ غِذائِيَّة [mawaːdd ɣiðaːʔiyya] We've got to increase our production of foodstuff. لازِم نزَيِّد اِنتاجنا مِن المَوادّ الغِذائِيَّة [laːzim nzayyid ʔintaːǰna min ʔilmawaːdd ʔilɣiðaːʔiyya]

fool • **1.** غَبِي [ɣabi] أَغبِياء [ʔaɣbiyaːʔ] *pl:* أَحمَق [ʔaħmaq] حُمُق، حَمقِين [ħumuq, ħamqiːn] *pl:* حَمقاء [ħamqaːʔ] *Feminine:* He's a fool if he believes that story. هُوَّ غَبِي إِذا يصَدِّق هَالحكايَة [huwwa ɣabi ʔiða yṣaddig halħčaːya]

* **He's nobody's fool.** • **1.** مَحَّد يِقدَر يضحَك عَلَيه [maħħad yigdar yiðħak ʕaliːh] / هَذا ما يِتقَشمَر [haːða maː yitqašmar]

to fool • **1.** تشاقَى [tšaːqaː] تَشاقِي [tašaːqi] *vn: sv* a. I was only fooling. كِنِت بَسّ دَأتشاقَى [činit bass daʔatšaːqaː] • **2.** قَشمَر [qašmar] قَشمَرَة [qašmara] *vn: sv* u. You can't fool me. ما تِقدَر تقَشمُرنِي [maː tigdar tqašmurni] • **3.** لِعَب [liʕab] لَعِب [laʕib] *vn:* اِنلِعَب [ʔinliʕab] *p:* Don't fool with the radio while I'm gone. لا تِلعَب بِالرّادِيُو مِن آنِي طالِع [laː tilʕab birraːdyu min ʔaːni ṭaːliʕ]

to fool around • **1.** t تَخَّم [taxxam] تَتخِيم [tatxiːm] *vn: sv* i. I just fooled around all afternoon. تَخَّمِت العَصرِيَّة كُلّها [taxxamit ʔilʕaṣriyya kullha]

foolish • **1.** سَخِيف [saxiːf] Don't be foolish! لا تصِير سَخِيف [laː tṣiːr saxiːf]

foot • **1.** رِجِل [riǰil] رِجلَين، [riǰlayn] *pl:* The shoe is tight on my foot. القُندَرَة ضَيقَة عَلَى رِجلِي [ʔilqundara ðayyga ʕala riǰli] • **2.** قَدَم [qadam] أَقدام [ʔaqdaːm] *pl:* فُوت [fuːt] فِيتات [fuːtaːt, fiːtaːt] *pl:* He's over six feet tall. طُولَه فُوق سِتّ أَقدام [ṭuːlah fuːg sitt ʔaqdaːm] • **3.** كَعَب [čaʕab] They camped at the foot of the mountain. خَيّمَوا بكَعب الجِّبَل [xayymaw bčaʕb ʔiǰǰibal]

* **It'll take a month to get back on our feet after the fire.** • **1.** يِنرادِلنا شَهَر حَتَّى نِستَعدِل بَعد الحَرِيق [yinraːdilna šahar ħatta nistaʕdil baʕd ʔilħariːq]

* **They'll keep on until you put your foot down.** • **1.** راح يضَلُّون يسَوُّوها إِلَى أَن تراوِيهُم عَين الحَمرَة [raːħ yðalluːn ysawwuːha ʔila ʔan traːwiːhum ʕayn ħamra]

* **I really put my foot in it that time!** • **1.** جِلَطتها خوش جَلطَة هَالنَوبَة [ǰilaṭitha xuːš ǰalṭa hannawba]

on foot • **1.** بِالرِّجِل [birriǰi] رِجلَين، رِجلِينات [riǰlayn, riǰliːnaːt] *pl:* مَشِي [mašy] We had to cover the rest of the distance on foot. اِضطَرَّينا نِقطَع باقِي المَسافَة بِالرِّجِل [ʔiðṭarrayna nigṭaʕ baːqi ʔilmasaːfa birriǰil]

on one's feet • **1.** واقُف عَلَى حَيل [waːguf ʕala ħayl] He's on his feet all day long. هَذا واقُف عَلَى حيلَه طُول النَّهار [haːða waːguf ʕala ħiːlah ṭuːl ʔinnahaːr]

footprint • **1.** أَثَر قَدَم [ʔaθar qadam] آثار أَقدام [ʔa:θa:r ʔaqda:m] *pl:* We followed the footprints. تبَعنا آثار الأَقدام [tbaʕna ʔa:θa:r ʔilʔaqda:m]

for • **1.** كَ [ka-] For an American, he speaks Arabic well. كَواحِد أَمريكاني، يحكِي عَرَبِي زين [kawa:ħid ʔamrika:ni, yiħči ʕarabi zi:n] What do you use for firewood? شتِستَعمِل كَحَطَب لِلنّار؟ [štistaʕmil kaħaṭab linna:r?] • **2.** لِ ، لَ [li-, la-] He married her for her money. تزَوَّجها لِفلُوسها [dzawwaǰha liflu:sha] Aspirin is good for headaches. الأَسبِرين زين لوُجَع الرّاس [ʔilʔaspiri:n zi:n liwuǰaʕ ʔirra:s] They continued talking about it for several days. ظَلَّوا يحكُون بيها لعِدَّة أَيّام [ðallaw yiħču:n bi:ha lʕiddat ʔayya:m] Take this fifty fils for some breakfast. أُخُذ هَالخَمسِين فِلِس لرِيُوقَك [ʔuxuð halxamsi:n filis liryu:gak] • **3.** ب [bi-] You can buy this table for a dinar. تِقدَر تِشترِي هَالميز بدِينار [tigdar tištiri halmi:z bdina:r] An eye for an eye, and a tooth for a tooth. العين بِالعَين، وَالسِّنّ بِالسِّنّ [ʔilʕayn bilʕayn, wissinn bissinn] • **4.** إِلَى [ʔila] I've got some letters for you. أَكُو إِلَك كَم مَكتُوب عِندِي [ʔaku ʔilak čam maktu:b ʕindi] • **5.** عَن [ʕan] عَلَى [ʕala] Did anyone ask for me? أَحَّد سِأَل عَنِّي؟ [ʔaħħad siʔal ʕanni?] • **6.** ل [li-] مِن [min] I haven't heard from him for a long time. ما سِمَعِت مِنَّه لِمُدَّة طوِيلَة [ma: simaʕit minnah lmudda ṭuwi:la] They laughed at him for his stupidity. ضِحكوا عَليه مِن سَخافتَه [ðiħkaw ʕali:h min saxa:ftah]

* **I've been wearing this coat for three years.**
• **1.** صارلي ثلَث سنين دألبَس هَالقَبُوط [ṣa:rli tlaθ sni:n daʔalbas halqappu:ṭ]

for heaven's sake • **1.** لِخاطِر الله، يا معَوَّد [lxa:ṭir ʔallah, ya: mʕawwad] For heaven's sake, stop! لخاطِر الله، بَسّ عاد [lxa:ṭir ʔallah, bass ʕa:d]

what ... for • **1.** لأَي شِي [lʔayy ši] What's that good for? لأَي شِي هَذا يِنفَع؟ [lʔayy ši ha:ða yinfaʕ?] • **2.** لَيش [layš] لُوَيش [luwi:š] What did you do that for? لِيش سَوَّيت هَذا؟ [li:š sawwayt ha:ða?]

force • **1.** قُوَّة [quwwa, guwwa] قُوّات [quwwa:t] *pl:* We had to use force. اِضطَرَّينا نِستَعمِل القُوَّة [ʔiðṭarrayna nistaʕmil ʔilquwwa] How large is the Baghdad police force? شقَدّ قُوّات الشُرطَة بِبَغداد [šgadd quwwa:t ʔiššurṭa bibayda:d] The land and sea forces are under the command of one commander. القُوّات البَرِّيَّة وِالقُوّات البَحرِيَّة تَحت إِمرَة قائِد واحِد [ʔilquwwa:t ʔilbarriyya wilquwwa:t ʔilbaħriyya taħat ʔimrat qa:ʔid wa:ħid] • **2.** شِدَّة [šidda] The storm hasn't reached its full force yet. العاصِفَة ما وُصلَت شِدَّتها بَعَد [ʔilʕa:ṣifa ma: wuṣlat šiddatha baʕad] • **3.** حُكُم [ħukum] She does it from force of habit. تسَوِّيها بحُكم العادَة [tsawwi:ha bħukm ʔilʕa:da]

in force • **1.** نافِذ [na:fið] جارِي المَفعُول [ǰa:ri ʔilmafʕu:l] Is that law still in force? هَالقانُون بَعدَه نافِذ؟ [halqa:nu:n baʕdah na:fið?]

in full force • **1.** بكامِل عَدَد [bka:mil ʕadad] The family turned out in full force. العائِلَة إِجَت بِكامِل عَدَدها [ʔilʕa:ʔila ʔiǰat bka:mil ʕadadha]

to force • **1.** جُبَر [ǰubar] إِجبار [ʔiǰba:r] *vn:* اِنجُبَر [ʔinǰubar] *p:* أَكرَه [ʔakrah] إِكراه [ʔikra:h] *vn: sv* i. رِغَم [riɣam] إِرغام [ʔirɣa:m] *vn: sv* u. اِضطَرّ [ʔiðṭarr] اِضطِرار [ʔiðṭira:r] *vn: sv* a. غِصَب [ɣiṣab] غَصُب [ɣaṣub] *vn: sv* u. You can't force me to sign. ما تِقدَر تِجبُرنِي أَمضِي [ma: tigdar tiǰburni ʔamði:] You can't force these things; we'll just have to wait. ما تِقدَر تسَوِّي هَالأَشياء غَصباً، لازِم نِنتِظِر [ma: tigdar tsawwi halʔašya:ʔ ɣaṣban, la:zim nintiðir] We'll have to force our way in. لازِم ندخُل بالإكراه [la:zim nidxul bilʔikra:h]

forced • **1.** اِضطِرارِي [ʔiðṭira:ri] The plane made a forced landing in the desert. الطَّيّارَة نِزلَت نزُول اِضطِرارِي [ʔiṭṭiyya:ra nizlat nizu:l ʔiðṭira:ri]

forecast • **1.** نُبُوءَة [nubu:ʔa] نُبُوءات [nubu:ʔa:t] *pl:* His forecast didn't turn out. نُبُوءتَه ما تحَقَّقَت [nubu:ʔtah ma: tħaqqiqat]

to forecast • **1.** تنَبَّأ ب [tnabbaʔ b-] تَنَبُّؤ [tanabbuʔ] *vn: sv* a. They forecast cooler weather. تنَبَّأوا بجَوّ أَبرَد [tnabbʔaw bǰaww ʔabrad]

forehead • **1.** قُصَّة [guṣṣa] قُصَص [guṣaṣ] *pl:* جَبهَة [ǰabha] جَبَهات [ǰabaha:t] *pl:*

foreign • **1.** أَجنَبِي [ʔaǰnabi] بلادِي [bla:di] مال بلاد [ma:l bla:d] That's a foreign make. هاي شُغُل أَجنَبِي [ha:y šuɣul ʔaǰnabi]

foreigner • **1.** أَجنَبِي [ʔaǰnabi] Before the war many foreigners came here. قَبِل الحَرب هوايَة أَجانِب إِجَوا هنا [gabil ʔilħarb hwa:ya ʔaǰa:nib ʔiǰaw hna]

forest • **1.** غابَة [ɣa:ba] غابات [ɣa:ba:t] *pl:*

forever • **1.** لِلأَبَد [lilʔabad] I'm afraid I'll be stuck in this place forever. أَخشَى راح أَضطَرّ أَبقَى بهَالمَكان لِلأَبَد [ʔaxša: ra:ħ ʔaðṭarr ʔabqa: bhalmaka:n lilʔabad]

to forget • **1.** نِسَى [nisa:] نَسِي، نِسيان [nasy, nisya:n] *vn:* اِنّسَى [ʔinnisa:] *p:* She has forgotten everything. هِيَّ نِسَت كُلّشِي [hiyya nisat kullši]

to forgive • **1.** سامَح [sa:maħ] مُسامَحَة [musa:maħa] *vn: sv* i. عِفَى عَن [ʕifa: ʕan] عَفي [ʕafy] *vn: sv* i. اِغتِفَر ل [ʔiɣtifar l-] اِغتِفار [ʔiɣtifa:r] *vn: sv* i. He'll never forgive you for that. أَبَداً ما يسامحَك عَلَى هَذا [ʔabadan ma: ysa:mħak ʕala ha:ða]

fork • **1.** جَطَل [čaṭal] جَطَلات [čaṭala:t] *pl:* Could you hand me a knife and fork? تِقدَر تِنطِينِي سِكِّينَة وَجَطَل؟ [tigdar tinṭi:ni sičči:na wčaṭal?] • **2.** مَفرَق [mafraq] مَفارِق [mafa:riq] *pl:* مُفتَرَق [muftaraq] When we get to the fork, you take the right road, and I'll take the road on the left. لَمّا نِجِي لِلمَفرَق، إِنتَ أُخُذ طَرِيق اليَمِين، وَآنِي آخُذ طَرِيق اليسار [lamma niǰi lilmafraq, ʔinta ʔuxuð ṭari:q ʔilyami:n, wʔa:ni ʔa:xuð ṭari:q ʔalyisa:r]

to fork • **1.** تشَعَّب [tšaʕʕab] تَشَعُّب [tašaʕʕub] *vn: sv* a. اِفتِرَق [ʔiftiraq] اِفتِراق [ʔiftira:q] *vn: sv* i. The road forks beyond the village. الطَّرِيق يِتشَعَّب مِن وَرا القَرِيَة [ʔiṭṭari:q yitšaʕʕab min wara ʔilqarya]

form • **1.** شِكِل [šikil] أشكال، شكُول [ʔaška:l, šku:l] *pl:* The sculptor uses many new forms. النَّحّات يِستَعمِل هوايَة أَشكال جِدِيدَة [ʔinnaħħa:t yistaʕmil hwa:ya ʔaška:l ǰidi:da] • **2.** صِيغَة [ṣi:ɣa] Can you put your question in a different form? تِقدَر تصِيغ سُؤالَك بغَير صِيغَة؟ [tigdar tṣi:ɣ suʔa:lak bɣayr ṣi:ɣa?] • **3.** قالَب [qa:lab] قوالِب [qwa:lib] *pl:* They built a form to pour the concrete into. سَوّوا قالَب حَتَّى يصُبُّون الشِمِنتُو بِيه [sawwa:w qa:lab ħatta yṣubbu:n ʔiččimintu: bi:h] • **4.** اِستِمارَة [ʔistima:ra] اِستِمارات [ʔistima:ra:t] *pl:* You'll have to fill out this form. لازِم تِملِي هَالاستِمارَة [la:zim timli: halʔistima:ra] • **5.** شِكلِي [šikli:] It's only a matter of form, but you'll have to do it. هَذا فَدّ شِي شِكلِي، بَسّ لازِم تسَوِّيه [ha:ða fadd ši šikli, bass la:zim tsawwi:h]

to form • **1.** شَكَّل [šakkal] تَشكِيل [taški:l] *vn:* تشَكَّل [tšakkal] *p:* أَلَّف [ʔallaf] تَألِيف [taʔli:f] *vn:* تأَلَّف [tʔallaf] *p:* He formed a new cabinet. شَكَّل وزارَة جِدِيدَة [šakkal wiza:ra ǰidi:da] • **2.** كَوَّن [kawwan] تَكوِين [takwi:n] *vn:* تكَوَّن [tkawwan] *p:* I haven't formed an opinion yet. بَعَد ما كَوَّنِت رَأي لهَسَّة [baʕad ma: kawwanit raʔy lhassa]

formal • **1.** رَسمِي [rasmi] you needn't be that formal. ماكُو حاجَة تصِير هَالقَدّ رَسمِي [ma:ku ħa:ǰa tṣi:r halgadd rasmi]

formalities • **1.** شَكلِيّات [šakliyya:t] رَسمِي [rasmi] She's very careful to observe the formalities. تدِير بالها حَتَّى ما تِطلَع عَن الشَّكلِيّات [ddi:r ba:lha ħatta ma: titlaʕ ʕan ʔiššakliyya:t]

former • **1.** سابِقاً [sa:biq] The former owner has retired. المالِك السّابِق تقاعَد [ʔilma:lik ʔissa:biq tqa:ʕad]

formerly • **1.** سابِقاً [sa:biqan] This was formerly the business section. سابِقاً هَذِي كانَت المَنطَقَة التِّجارِيَّة [sa:biqan ha:ði ča:nat ʔilmanṭaqa ʔittiǰa:riyya]

fort • **1.** حُصِن [ħuṣin, ħiṣin] حُصُون [ħuṣu:n] *pl:* There's an old fort on the hill. أَكُو فَدّ حُصِن قَدِيم عَالتَّلّ [ʔaku fadd ħuṣin qadi:m ʕattall]

fortieth • **1.** أَربَعِين [ʔarbaʕi:n] That's the fortieth day he's refused to eat meat. هَذا اليُوم الأَربَعِين اللّي مُضرِب بِيه عَن أَكِل اللَّحَم [ha:ða ʔilyu:m ʔilʔarbaʕi:n ʔilli muðrib bi:h ʕan ʔakil ʔillaħam]

to fortify • **1.** حَصَّن [ħaṣṣan] تَحصِين [taħṣi:n] *vn:* تحَصَّن [tħaṣṣan] *p:* The island was fortified. الجَّزِيرَة كانَت مُحَصَّنَة [ʔiǰǰazi:ra ča:nat muħaṣṣana]

fortress • **1.** قَلعَة [qalʕa] قِلاع [qila:ʕ] *pl:* حُصِن [ħuṣin, ħiṣin] حُصُون [ħuṣu:n] *pl:*

fortunate • **1.** سَعِيد [saʕi:d] سَعِيدِين، سُعَداء [saʕi:di:n, suʕada:ʔ] *pl:* That was a fortunate occurrence. هَذِي كانَت صِدفَة سَعِيدَة [ha:ði ča:nat ṣidfa saʕi:da] • **2.** مَحظُوظ [maħðu:ð] He was fortunate to get a bargain like that. كان مَحظُوظ لِلحُصُول عَلَى شَروَة مِثِل هاي [ča:n maħðu:ð lilħuṣu:l ʕala šarwa miθil ha:y]

fortunately • **1.** لِحُسن الحَظّ [lħusn ʔilħaðð] Fortunately, I got there in time. لِحُسُن الحَظّ، وُصَلِت هناك عالوَقِت [liħusun ʔilħaðð, wuṣalit hna:k ʕalwakit]

fortune • **1.** ثَروَة [θarwa] ثَروات [θarwa:t] *pl:* She inherited a large fortune. وُرثَت ثَروَة طائِلَة [wurθat θarwa ṭa:ʔila] • **2.** حَظّ [ħaðð] حظُوظ [ħðu:ð] *pl:* I had the good fortune to meet her the other day. كان حَظّ سَعِيد أَن أتعَرَّف عَليها ذاك اليُوم [ča:n ħaðð saʕi:d ʔan ʔatʕarraf ʕali:ha ða:k ʔilyu:m] • **3.** فال [fa:l] She told my fortune. فِتحَتلِي فال [fitħatli fa:l]

fortune teller • **1.** فَتّاح فال [fatta:ħ fa:l] فَتّاحِين فال [fatta:ħi:n fa:l] *pl:*

forty • **1.** أَربَعِين [ʔarbaʕi:n]

forward • **1.** إِلَى الأَمام [ʔila ʔilʔama:m] Forward, march! إِلَى الأَمام، سِرّ [ʔila ʔilʔama:m, sirr] • **2.** لِقِدّام [ligidda:m] They sent four men forward to investigate. دَزّوا أَربَع رياجِيل لِقِدّام يِتحَرّون [dazzaw ʔarbaʕ riya:ǰi:l ligidda:m yitħarru:n] • **3.** هُجُوم [huǰu:m] They have two good forwards on their soccer team. عِدهُم إِثنَين هجُوم مُمتازِين بفَرِيق كُرَة القَدَم مالهُم [ʕidhum ʔiθnayn hǰu:m mumta:zi:n bfari:q kurat ʔilqadam ma:lhum] • **4.** مِتجاسِر [mitǰa:sir] مِتجاسِرِين [mitǰa:siri:n] *pl:* They beat him up because he was so forward with girls. بُسطَوه لِأَنّ كان كُلِّش مِتجاسِر عَالبَنات [busṭawh liʔann ča:n kulliš midǰa:sir ʕalbana:t]

to forward • **1.** دَزّ [dazz] دَزّ [dazz] *vn:* اِندَزّ [ʔindazz] *p:* Your mail will be forwarded to your new address. بَرِيدَك راح يِندَزّ إِلَى عِنوانَك الجِّدِيد [bari:dak ra:ħ yindazz ʔila ʕinwa:nak ʔiǰǰidi:d]

foul • **1.** فاوُل [fa:wul] فاوُلات [fa:wula:t] *pl:* Touching the ball with your hand in soccer is a foul. طَخَّة الطُّوبَة بِالإِيد فاوُل بكُرَة القَدَم [ṭaxxat ʔiṭṭu:ba bilʔi:d fa:wul bkurat ʔilqadam] • **2.** غادِر [ɣa:dir] قَذِر [qaðir] That was a foul blow. هاي كانَت ضَربَة غادرَة [ha:y ča:nat ðarba ɣa:dra] • **3.** جايِف [ǰa:yif] Where does that foul smell come from? هَالرِّيحَة الجّايفَة منِين تِجِي؟ [harri:ħa ʔiǰǰa:yfa mni:n tiǰi?] • **4.** فشار [fša:r] He uses foul language a lot. يِحكِي كَلام فشار هوايَة [yiħči kala:m fša:r hwa:ya] He uses foul language a lot. يفَشِّر هوايَة [yfaššir hwa:ya]

to found • **1.** أَسَّس [ʔassas] تَأسِيس [taʔsiːs] *vn:* تأسَّس [tʔassas] *p:* When was the club founded? شوَكِت النّادِي تأسَّس؟ [šwakit ʔinnaːdi tʔassas?]

foundation • **1.** أساس [ʔasaːs] أساسات [ʔasaːsaːt] *pl:* The flood damaged the foundations of the building. الفَيَضان دَمَّر أساسات البِنايَة [ʔilfayaḍaːn dammar ʔasaːsaːt ʔilbinaːya] Your remarks are completely without foundation. تَعلِيقاتَك ما إلها أساس [taʕliːqaːtak maː ʔilha ʔasaːs] • **2.** مُؤَسَّسَة [muʔassasa] مُؤَسَّسات [muʔassasaːt] *pl:* They're setting up a charitable foundation. دَيأسِّسُون مُؤَسَّسَة خَيرِيَّة [dayʔassisuːn muʔassasa xayriyya]

fountain • **1.** شَدِروان [šadirwaːn] شَدِروانات [šadirwaːnaːt] *pl:* There's a fountain in the square. أكُو شَدِروان بِالسّاحَة [ʔaku šadirwaːn bissaːħa]

fountain pen • **1.** باندان [paːndaːn] باندانات [paːndaːnaːt] *pl:* قَلَم حِبِر [qalam ħibir] أقلام حِبِر [ʔaqlaːm ħibir] *pl:* I'll have to fill my pen. لازِم أترُس بانداني [laːzim ʔatrus paːndaːni]

four • **1.** أربَع [ʔarbaʕ] I bought it for four fils. اِشتِرَيتَه بأربَع فلُوس [ʔištiraytah bʔarbaʕ fluːs] We took four girls to the movie. أخَذنا أربَع بَنات لِلسِّينَما [ʔaxaðna ʔarbaʕ banaːt lissinama] • **2.** أربَعَة [ʔarbaʕa] Hold four of these in your hand. إلزَم أربَعَة مِنهُم بِيدَك [ʔilzam ʔarbaʕa minhum biːdak] Multiply this number by four. أضرُب هَالرَّقُم بِأربَعَة [ʔuḍrub harraqum bʔarbaʕa] • **3.** أربَعات [ʔarbaʕaːt] He has to take the medicine four times a day. لازِم يِشرَب الدُّوا أربَعَة أوقات بِاليُوم [laːzim yišrab ʔidduwaː ʔarbaʕat ʔawqaːt bilyuːm] He stayed with us four days. بُقَى عِدنا أربَعَة أيّام [buqaː ʕidna ʔarbaʕat ʔayyaːm]

fourteen • **1.** أربَطَعَش [ʔarbaṭaʕaš]

fourteenth • **1.** رابع عَشَر [raːbiʕ ʕašar] أربَطَعَش [ʔarbaṭaʕaš]

fourth • **1.** رُبُع [rubuʕ] أرباع [ʔarbaːʕ] *pl:* Only one fourth of the students were paying attention. بَسّ رُبُع الطُّلّاب كانَوا دايرِين بالهُم [bass rubuʕ ʔiṭṭullaːb čaːnaw daːyiriːn baːlhum] • **2.** رابع [raːbiʕ] He died on May fourth. مات بِالرّابع مِن أيّار [maːt birraːbiʕ min ʔayyaːr]

fox • **1.** ثَعلَب [θaʕlab] ثَعالِب [θaʕaːlib] *pl:* A fox is killing our chickens. فَدّ ثَعلَب دَيُقتُل دِجاجنا [fadd θaʕlab dayuktul dijaːjna]

fraction • **1.** كَسِر [kasir] كسُور [ksuːr] *pl:* Leave out the fractions and just give me the round numbers. أترُك الكسُور وَإنطِينِي بَسّ الأرقام الصَّحِيحَة [ʔutruk ʔilksuːr wʔinṭiːni bass ʔilʔarqaːm ʔiṣṣaħiːħa] • **2.** جُزُء [jʒuzuʔ] أجزاء [ʔajzaːʔ] *pl:* He got only a fraction of his father's fortune. حَصَّل عَلَى بَسّ جُزُء مِن ثَروَة أبُوه [ħaṣṣal ʕala bass juzuʔ min θarwat ʔabuːh]

fracture • **1.** كَسِر [kasir] كُسُور [kusuːr] *pl:* The fracture is healing slowly. الكَسِر دَيِلحَم بِبُطء [ʔilkasir dayilħam bibuṭʔ]

to fracture • **1.** كِسَر [kisar] كَسِر [kasir] *vn:* اِنكِسَر [ʔinkisar] *p:* He fell off the bicycle and fractured a bone. وُقَع مِن البايسِكِل وَكِسَر واحِد مِن عظامَه [wugaʕ min ʔilpaːysikil wkisar waːħid min ʕðaːmah]

frame • **1.** إطار [ʔiṭaːr] إطارات [ʔiṭaːraːt] *pl:* كَركُوبَة [čarčuːba] كَركُوبات، كَراكِيب [čarčuːbaːt, čaraːčiːb] *pl:* I'd like to have a frame for this picture. أرِيد إطار لِهَالصُّورَة [ʔariːd ʔiṭaːr lihaṣṣuːra] • **2.** هَيكَل [haykal] The frame of the hut is wood. الهَيكَل مال الكُوخ خِشَب [ʔilhaykal maːl ʔilkuːx xišab] • **3.** بُنيَة [bunya] He has a heavy frame. عِندَه بُنيَة خَشنَة [ʕindah buniya xašna] • **4.** حالَة [ħaːla] حالات [ħaːlaːt] *pl:* He's not in a very good frame of mind; better ask him later. هَسَّة هُوَّ مُو بخوش حالَة فِكرِيَّة؛ إسألَه بَعدين [hassa huwwa muː bxuːš ħaːla fikriyya; ʔisʔalah baʕdiːn]

to frame • **1.** كَركَب [čarčab] جَرجَبَة [čarčaba] *vn:* تجَرجَب [tčarčab] *p:* I'll have the picture framed. راح أجَرجِب الصُّورَة [raːħ ʔačarčib ʔiṣṣuːra]

*** They framed him.** • **1.** ذَبَّوا الصُّوج برُقُبتَه [ðabbaw ʔiṣṣuːč brugubtah]

France • **1.** فَرَنسا [faransa]

frank • **1.** صَرِيح [ṣariːħ] Be frank with me. كُون صَرِيح وِيّايا [kuːn ṣariːħ wiyyaːya]

frankly • **1.** بصَراحَة [bṣaraːħa] Frankly, I don't know. بصَراحَة، ما أعرُف [bṣaraːħa, maː ʔaʕruf]

frantic • **1.** جُنُوني [ǰunuːni] He made frantic efforts to free himself. سَوَّى مُحاوَلات جِنُونِيَّة حَتَّى يخَلِّص نَفسَه [sawwaː muħaːwalaːt ǰinuːniyya ħatta yxalliṣ nafsah]

freckles • **1.** نَمَش [namaš]

free • **1.** حُرّ [ħurr] أحرار [ʔaħraːr] *pl:* He's a free man again. هُوَّ حُرّ مِن جِدِيد [huwwa ħurr min ǰidiːd] You're free to go at any time. إنتَ حُرّ ترُوح شوَكِت ما ترِيد [ʔinta ħurr truːħ šwakit maː triːd] • **2.** فارِغ [faːriɣ] Will you be free tomorrow? راح تكُون فارِغ باكِر؟ [raːħ tkuːn faːriɣ baːčir?] • **3.** بَلاش [balaːš] مَجّاناً [maǰǰaːnan] I got it free. أخَذتها بَلاش [ʔaxaðitha balaːš] • **4.** مَجّانِي [maǰǰaːni] بَلاش [balaːš] The admission to the play is free tonight. الدُّخُول لِلرِّوايَة اللَّيلَة مَجّانِي [ʔidduxuːl lirriwaːya ʔillayla maǰǰaːni] • **5.** سَخِي [saxi] أسخِياء [ʔasxiyaːʔ] *pl:* He's free with his money. هُوَّ سَخِي بفلُوسَه [huwwa saxi bfluːsah]

*** He has a free and easy way about him.** • **1.** يحِيط نَفسَه بجَوّ ما بيه تَكَلُّف [yħiːṭ nafsah bǰaww maː biː takalluf]

to free • **1.** أطلَق سِراح [ʔaṭlaq siraːħ] إطلاق سِراح [ʔiṭlaːq siraːħ] *vn: sv* u. They freed the prisoners.

أَطلِقَوا سَراح المَساجِين [ʔaṭliqaw saraːħ ʔilmasaːjiːn] • **2.** حَرَّر [ħarrar] تَحرِير [taħriːr] *vn:* تحَرَّر [tħarrar] *p:* Our army freed the city from the invaders. جَيشنا حَرَّر المَدِينَة مِن الغُزاة [jayšna ħarrar ʔilmadiːna min ʔilɣuzaːt] • **3.** خَلَّص [xallaṣ] تخِلِّص [txilliṣ] *vn: sv* i. They tried for a half hour, but were unable to free the car from the mud. حاولَوا نُصّ ساعَة وما قِدرَوا يخَلّصُون السَّيّارَة مِن الطِّين [ħaːwlaw nuṣṣ saːʕa wmaː gidraw yxalliṣuːn ʔissayyaːra min ʔiṭṭiːn]

freedom • **1.** حُرِّيَّة [ħurriyya] حُرِّيّات [ħurriyyaːt] *pl:*

freely • **1.** بصَراحَة [bṣaraːħa] He admitted freely that he took it. اعتِرَف بصَراحَة إنُّو أَخَذها [ʔiʕtiraf bṣaraːħa ʔinnu ʔaxaðha] • **2.** بحُرِّيَّة [bħurriyya] حُرِّيّات [ħurriyyaːt] *pl:* You can speak freely. تِقدَر تِحكِي بحُرِّيتَك [tigdar tiħči bħurriːtak] • **3.** بسَخاء [bsaxaːʔ] He spends his money freely. يِصرُف فلُوسَه بسَخاء [yiṣruf fluːsah bsaxaːʔ]

to freeze • **1.** جِمَد [jimad] جَمِد [jamid] *vn:* اِنجِمَد [ʔinjimad] *p:* The water in the pitcher froze during the night. الماي جِمَد بالدُّولكَة أَثناء اللَّيل [ʔilmaːy jimad bidduːlka ʔaθnaːʔ ʔillayl] He froze to death. جِمَد مِن البَرِد وَمات [jimad min ʔilbarid wmaːt] • **2.** جَمَّد [jammad] تَجمِيد [tajmiːd] *vn:* تجَمَّد [tjammad] *p:* They're building a plant to freeze food. دَيبنُون مَعمَل لتَجمِيد الأَطعِمَة [dayibnuːn maʕmal ltajmiːd ʔilʔaṭʕima] The government has frozen all foreign accounts. الحُكُومَة جَمِّدَت كُلّ الحِسابات الأَجنَبِيَّة [ʔilħukuːma jammidat kull ʔilħisaːbaːt ʔilʔajnabiyya] • **3.** ثَلَّج [θallaj] تَثلِيج [taθliːj] *vn:* تثَلَّج [tθallaj] *p:* We'll freeze this winter if we don't get a better heater. راح نثَلِّج هَالشِّتا إذا ما نِشتِري صَوبَة أَحسَن [raːħ nθallij haššitaː ʔiða maː ništiri ṣuːba ʔaħsan] My feet are frozen. رِجلَيّا مثَلِّجَة [rijlayya mθallija]

freight • **1.** شَحِن [šaħin] Including freight and insurance the car will cost a thousand dinars. وِيّا الشَّحِن وَالتَّأمِين السَّيّارَة راح تكَلِّف أَلف دِينار [wiyya ʔiššaħin wittaʔmiːn ʔissayyaːra raːħ tkallif ʔalf dinaːr] • **2.** أُجرَة شَحِن [ʔujrat šaħin] How much is the freight on this trunk? شقَدّ أُجرَة الشَّحِن عَلَى هَالصَّندُوق؟ [šgadd ʔujrat ʔiššaħin ʕala haṣṣanduːg?] • **3.** حِمِل [ħimil] حمُول [ħmuːl] *pl:* He owns a freight company. يِملِك شَرِكَة حِمِل [yimlik šarikat ħimil]

freight car • **1.** عَرَبَة حِمِل [ʕarabat ħimil] عَرَبات حِمِل [ʕarabaːt ħimil] *pl:*

freighter • **1.** باخِرَة حِمِل [baːxirat ħimil] بَواخِر حِمِل [bawaːxir ħimil] *pl:*

French • **1.** فَرَنسِي [faransi] فَرَنساوِي [faransaːwi] He speaks very good French. يِتكَلَّم فَرَنسِي كُلِّش زين [yitkallam faransi kulliš ziːn] • **2.** فرَنسِي [fransi] Do you like French wines? يِعجبَك الشَّراب الفَرَنسِي؟ [yiʕjibak ʔiššaraːb ʔilfransi?]

Frenchman • **1.** فرَنسِي [fransi] فرَنسِيِّين [fransiyyin] *pl:* Our neighbor is a Frenchman. جارنا فرَنسِي [jaːrna fransi]

frequently • **1.** غالِباً [ɣaːliban] I see him frequently. أَشُوفَه غالِباً [ʔašuwfah ɣaːliban]

fresh • **1.** تازَة [taːza] Are these eggs fresh? هَالبَيض تازَة؟ [halbayð taːza?] • **2.** نَقِي [naqi] Let's go out for some fresh air. خَلّي نِطلَع نِشتَمّ هَوا نَقِي [xalli niṭlaʕ ništamm hawa naqi] • **3.** عَذِب [ʕaðib] The well water turned out to be fresh. طِلَع مَيّ البِير عَذِب [ṭilaʕ mayy ʔilbiːr ʕaðib] • **4.** وَقِح [wakiħ] I can't stand that fresh kid. ما أَقدَر أَتحَمَّل هَالوَلَد الوَقِح [maː ʔagdar ʔatħammal halwalad ʔilwaqiħ]

friction • **1.** اِحتِكاك [ʔiħtikaːk] Oiling the wheel would cut down the friction. تدهِين الچَرخ يقَلِّل الاحتِكاك [tadhiːn ʔilčarix yqallil ʔilʔiħtikaːk] • **2.** تَوَتُّر [tawattur] There's friction between the two countries. أَكُو تَوَتُّر بين الدَّولَتَين [ʔaku tawattur biːn ʔiddawultayn]

Friday • **1.** جُمعَة [jumʕa] جُمَع [jumaʕ] *pl:*

friend • **1.** صَدِيق [ṣadiːq, ṣadiːg] أَصدِقاء، صِدقان [ʔaṣdiqaːʔ, ṣidqaːn] *pl:* صاحِب [ṣaːħib] أَصحاب [ʔaṣħaːb] *pl:* Are we friends again? هَسَّة رجَعنا أَصدِقاء؟ [hassa rjaʕna ʔaṣdiqaːʔ?]

to make friends • **1.** تصادَق [tṣaːdaq, ʔitṣaːdag] تَصادُق [taṣaːduq] *vn: sv* a. He makes friends easily. هَذا يِصادِق بسُهُولَة [haːða yiṣaːdiq bsuhuːla]

friendly • **1.** وِدِّي [widdi] We came to a friendly agreement. وُصَلنا إلَى اِتِّفاق وِدِّي [wuṣalna ʔila ʔittifaːq widdi] The argument was settled in a friendly way. الخِلاف اِنحَلّ بطَرِيقَة وِدِّيَّة [ʔilxilaːf ʔinħall bṭariːqa widdiyya] The argument was settled in a friendly way. الخِلاف اِنحَلّ وِدِّياً [ʔilxilaːf ʔinħall widdiyyan]

friendship • **1.** صَداقَة [ṣadaːqa] صَداقات [ṣadaːqaːt] *pl:* صُحبَة [ṣuħba] صُحبات [ṣuħbaːt] *pl:* Our friendship lasted forty years. صَداقَتنا دامَت أَربَعِين سَنَة [ṣadaːqatna daːmat ʔarbaʕiːn sana]

fright • **1.** خَوف [xawf, xuːf] You gave me an awful fright. خَوَّفتِني خُوش خَوف [xawwafitni xuːš xuːf xawf]

to frighten • **1.** خَوَّف [xawwaf] تَخوِيف [taxwiːf] *vn:* تخَوَّف [txawwaf] *p:*

to be frightened • **1.** خاف [xaːf] خَوف [xuːf] *vn: sv* a. Don't be frightened. لا تخاف [laː txaːf]

frog • **1.** عُقرُقَّة [ʕugrugga] عُقرقّات [ʕuguggaːt] *pl:* عُقرُق [ʕugrug] *Collective*

from • **1.** مِن [min] He just received a check from his father. هُوَّ هَستَوَّة اِستِلَم صَكّ مِن أَبُوه [huwwa hastawwah ʔistilam ṣakk min ʔabu:h] • **2.** عَن [ʕan] مِن [min] I live ten miles from the city. أَسكُن بُعُد عَشِر أَميال عَن المَدِينَة [ʔaskun buʕud ʕašir ʔamya:l ʕan ʔilmadi:na]

from now on • **1.** مِن هنَا وهِيكِي [min hna whi:či] مِن هنَا وغادِي [min hna wɣa:di] From now on I'll be on time. مِنَّا وهِيكِي راح أَكُون عالوَقِت [min hna whi:či ra:ħ ʔaku:n ʕalwakit]

where ... from • **1.** منَين [mnayn, mni:n] Where are you from? منَين إنتَ؟ [mnayn ʔinta?] Where are you from? إِنتَ مِن أَيّ بَلَد؟ [ʔinta min ʔayy balad?]

front • **1.** واجِهَة [wa:ǰiha] واجِهات [wa:ǰiha:t] *pl:* The front of the house is painted white. واجِهَة البَيت مَصبُوغَة أَبيَض [wa:ǰihat ʔilbayt maṣbu:ɣa ʔabyað̣] • **2.** جَبهَة [ǰabha] جَبَهات [ǰabaha:t] *pl:* Were you at the front during the war? كِنِت بِالجَّبهَة أَثناء الحَرُب؟ [činit biǰǰabha ʔaθna:ʔ ʔilħarub?] • **3.** أَوَّل [ʔawwal] The table of contents is in the front of the book. جَدوَل المُحتَوَيّات بأَوَّل الكِتاب [ǰadwal ʔilmuħtawayya:t bʔawwal ʔilkita:b] • **4.** أَمامِي [ʔama:mi] We had seats in the front row. مَقاعِدنا كانَت بِالسِّرَة الأَمامِي [maqa:ʕidna ča:nat bissira ʔilʔama:mi]

in front • **1.** قِدّام [gidda:m] Let's meet in front of the post office. خَلِّي نِلتِقِي قِدّام دائِرَة البَرِيد [xalli niltigi gidda:m da:ʔirat ʔilbari:d] • **2.** لِقِدّام [ligidda:m] He always sits in front. هَذا دائِماً يُقعُد لِقِدّام [ha:ða da:ʔiman yugʕud ligidda:m] • **3.** أَمام [ʔama:m] قِدّام [gidda:m] The officer is marching in front of his men. الضّابُط يِمشِي أَمام جِنُودَه [ʔið̣ð̣a:buṭ yimši ʔama:m ǰinu:dah]

to frown • **1.** عَبَّس [ʕabbas] تَعبِيس [taʕbi:s] *vn:* تعَبَّس [tʕabbas] *p:* Why is he frowning? لِيش مِعَبِّس؟ [li:š mʕabbis?]

fruit • **1.** فاكِهَة [fa:kiha] فَواكِه [fawa:kih] *pl:* Do you have any fresh fruit? عِندَك فاكِهَة تازَة؟ [ʕindak fa:kiha ta:za?]

to bear fruit • **1.** أَثمَر [ʔaθmar] إِثمار [ʔiθma:r] *vn: sv* u. This tree doesn't bear fruit. هَالشَّجَرَة ما تِثمُر [haššaǰara ma: tiθmur]

to fry • **1.** قَلّى [galla:] تَقلِيَة [tagliya] *vn: sv* i. Shall I fry the fish? ترِيد أَقَلِّي السِّمَك؟ [tri:d ʔagalli ʔissimač?] • **2.** تقَلّى [tgalla:] تَقَلِّي [tagalli] *vn: sv* a. The meat is frying now. اللَّحَم دَيِتقَلّه [ʔillaħam dayitgallah]

fuel • **1.** وُقُود [wuqu:d] We use coal, wood, and oil as fuels here. نِستَعمِل الفَحَم والخِشَب والنَّفُط كَوُقُود هنا [nistaʕmil ʔilfaħam wilxišab winnafuṭ kawuqu:d hna] • **2.** بانزِين [banzi:n] Their fuel ran out over the desert. بانزِينهُم خِلَص فُوق بِالصَّحراء [banzi:nhum xilaṣ fu:g biṣṣaħra:ʔ]

to fulfill • **1.** حَقَّق [ħaqqaq] تَحقِيق [taħqi:q] *vn:* تحَقَّق [tħaqqaq] *p:* Her wishes were all fulfilled. رَغباتها كُلّها تحَقِّقَت [raɣba:tha kullha tħaqqiqat] • **2.** قام [qa:m] قِيام [qiya:m] *vn: sv* u. We couldn't fulfill the terms of the contract. ما قِدَرنا نقُوم بِشرُوط العَقِد [ma: gidarna nqu:m bšru:ṭ ʔilʕaqid]

full • **1.** مَليان [malya:n] مَترُوس [matru:s] Is the kettle full? الكِتلِي مَليان؟ [ʔilkitli malya:n?] The book is full of mistakes. الكِتاب مَترُوس أَغلاط [ʔilkita:b matru:s ʔaɣla:ṭ] • **2.** كامِل [ka:mil] I paid the full amount. دِفَعِت المَبلَغ كامِل [difaʕt ʔilmablaɣ ka:mil] Are you working full time now? دَتِشتُغُل دَوام كامِل هَسَّة؟ [datištuɣul dawa:m ka:mil hassa?] • **3.** شَبعان [šabʕa:n] I'm full. آنِي شَبعان [ʔa:ni šabʕa:n]

in full • **1.** بكامِل [bka:mil] I paid the bill in full. دفَعِت القائِمَة بكامِلها [dfaʕit ʔilqa:ʔima bka:milha]

fully • **1.** تَماماً [tama:man] Are you fully aware of what is going on? إِنتَ دَتُعرُف تَماماً شدَيصِير؟ [ʔinta datuʕruf tama:man šdayṣi:r?] • **2.** بصُورَة كامِلَة [bṣu:ra ka:mla] He described it fully. وُصَفها بِصُورَة كامِلَة [wuṣafha bṣu:ra ka:mla] • **3.** ما لا يَقِلّ عَن [ma: la: yaqill ʕan] There were fully 200 people at the reception. كان أَكُو ما لا يَقِلّ عَن المِيتَين شَخِص بِالحَفلَة [ča:n ʔaku ma: la: yaqill ʕan ʔilmi:tayn šaxiṣ bilħafla]

fume • **1.** غاز [ɣa:z] غازات [ɣa:za:t] *pl:* The escaping fumes were poisonous. الغازات الطّالعَة كانَت سامَّة [ʔilɣa:za:t ʔiṭṭa:lʕa ča:nat sa:mma]

fun • **1.** وَنسَة [wansa, winsa] Fishing is a lot of fun. صَيد السِّمَك كُلِّش ونسَة [ṣi:d ʔissimač kulliš winsa]

to make fun of • **1.** قَشمَر [qašmar] قَشمَرَة [qašmara] *vn:* تقَشمَر [tqašmar] *p:* ضِحَك عَلَى [ð̣iħak ʕala] ضِحِك [ð̣iħik] *vn:* اِنضِحَك [ʔinð̣iħak] *p:* Are you making fun of me? دَتقَشمُرنِي؟ [datqašmurni?]

function • **1.** شُغُل [šuɣul] أَشغال [ʔašɣa:l] *pl:* What's his function in the office? شِنُو شُغلَه بَالدّائِرَة؟ [šinu šuɣlah bidda:ʔira?] • **2.** مُناسَبَة [muna:saba] مُناسَبات [muna:saba:t] *pl:* I saw him at one of the functions at the embassy. شِفتَه بإِحدَى المُناسَبات بِالسَّفارَة [šiftah bʔiħda: ʔilmuna:saba:t bissafa:ra]

to function • **1.** اِشتِغَل [ʔištiɣal] اِشتِغال [ʔištiɣa:l] *vn: sv* u. The radio doesn't function properly. الرّاديُو ما دَيِشتُغُل زين [ʔirra:dyu ma: dayištuɣul zi:n]

fund • **1.** ذَخِيرَة [ðaxi:ra] ذَخاير [ðaxa:yir] *pl:* He has an inexhaustible fund of jokes. عِندَه ذَخِيرَة ما تِخلَص مِن النُّكَت [ʕindah ðaxi:ra ma: tixlaṣ min ʔinnukat] • **2.** اِعتِماد [ʔiʕtima:d] The government established a fund to care for the poor. الحُكُومَة فِتحَت اِعتِماد لِلصَّرُف عالفُقَراء؟ [ʔilħuku:ma fitħat ʔiʕtima:d liṣṣaruf ʕalfuqara:ʔ?]

funds • **1.** مال [ma:l] أَموال [ʔamwa:l] *pl:* He misappropriated public funds. أَساء اِستِعمال الأَموال العامَّة [ʔasa:ʔ ʔistiʕma:l ʔilʔamwa:l ʔilʕa:mma]

fundamental • **1.** جوهَري [ǰawhari] أساسِي [ʔasa:si] That's a fundamental difference. هَذا اِختِلاف جَوهَري [ha:ða ʔixtila:f ǰawhari]

funeral • **1.** جَنازَة [ǰana:za] جَنازات، جَنايِز [ǰana:za:t, ǰana:yiz] *pl:* I'm going to his funeral. راح أرُوح لِجَنازَتَه [ra:ħ ʔaru:ħ liǰana:ztah]

funnel • **1.** رَحَاتِي [raħa:ti], رَحَاتِيّات [raħa:tiyya:t] *pl:* مِحقان [miħga:n] مَحاقِن [maħa:gin] *pl:* The funnel is too big for the bottle. الرَّحاتِي كُلِّش كِبِير عالبُطُل [ʔirraħa:ti kulliš čibi:r ʕalbuṭul]

funny • **1.** مُضحِك [muðħik] That story is very funny. هَالقُصَّة كُلِّش مُضحِكَة [halquṣṣa kulliš muðħika] • **2.** هَزَلِي [hazali] He's a very funny actor. هَذا مُمَثِّل كُلِّش هَزَلِي [ha:ða mumaθθil kulliš hazali] • **3.** غَرِيب [ɣari:b] Funny, I can't find my pen. غَرِيب، ما دَأقدَر ألقِي باندانِي [ɣari:b, ma: daʔagdar ʔalgi pa:nda:ni]

funny bone • **1.** دَمار عِكِس [dama:r ʕikis] دَمارات عِكِس [dama:ra:t ʕikis] *pl:* He hit me on the funny bone. ضِرَبنِي عَلَى دَمار عِكسِي [ðirabni ʕala dama:r ʕiksi]

fur • **1.** فَرُو [farw] Most fur comes from Canada and Russia. أكثَر الفَرو يِجِي مِن كَنَدا وَرُوسيا [ʔakθar ʔilfarw yiǰi min kanada: wru:sya]

furious • **1.** ثايِر [θa:yir] هايِج [ha:yiǰ] My boss was furious when I arrived late. رَئِيسِي كان ثايِر مِن وُصَلِت مِتأخِّر [raʔi:si ča:n θa:yir min wuṣalit mitʔaxxir]

furnace • **1.** فِرِن [firin] أفران [ʔafra:n] *pl:*

to furnish • **1.** أثَّث [ʔaθθaθ] تَأثِيث [taʔθi:θ] *vn:* تَأثَّث [tʔaθθaθ] *p:* I rented a furnished house. أجَّرت بَيت مأثَّث [ʔaǰǰarit bayt mʔaθθaθ] • **2.** جَهَّز [ǰahhaz] تَجهِيز [taǰhi:z] *vn:* تَجَهَّز [tǰahhaz] *p:* The management will furnish you with everything you need. الإدارَة راح تجَهِّزَك بِكُلّما تِحتاج [ʔilʔida:ra ra:ħ dǰahhzak bkullma: tiħta:ǰ] • **3.** جاب [ǰa:b] جَيب [ǰi:b] *vn:* اِنجاب [ʔinǰa:b] *p:* قَدَّم [qaddam] تَقدِيم [taqdi:m] *vn:* تقَدَّم [tqaddam] *p:* Can you furnish proof? تِقدَر تجِيب دَلِيل؟ [tigdar dǰi:b dali:l?]

furniture • **1.** أثاث [ʔaθa:θ]

further • **1.** بَعَد [baʕad] أكثَر [ʔakθar] آخَر [ʔa:xar] Do you need any further information? تِحتاج مَعلُومات بَعَد؟ [tiħta:ǰ maʕlu:ma:t baʕad?] Do you need any further information? تِحتاج مَعلُومات أخرَى؟ [tiħta:ǰ maʕlu:ma:t ʔuxra?] • **2.** آخَر [ʔa:xar] I'm closing my store until further notice. راح أسِدّ المَخزَن مالِي إلَى إشعار آخَر [ra:ħ ʔasidd ʔilmaxzan ma:li ʔila ʔišʕa:r ʔa:xar] • **3.** أبعَد [ʔabʕad] He threw the rock further than me. ضِرَب الحجارَة أبعَد مِنِّي [ðirab ʔilħǰa:ra ʔabʕad minni]

furthermore • **1.** بالإضافَة إلَى هَذا [bilʔiða:fa ʔila ha:ða] Furthermore he's not a member. بِالإضافَة إلَى هَذا، هُوَّ مُو عُضُو [bilʔiða:fa ʔila ha:ða, huwwa mu: ʕuðw]

fuse • **1.** فيُوز [fyu:z] فيُوزات [fyu:za:t] *pl:* The fuse blew out. طَقّ الفيُوز [ṭagg ʔilfyu:z] • **2.** فِتِيلَة [fiti:la] فِتِيلات، فَتايِل [fiti:la:t, , fata:yil] *pl:* He lit the fuse and ran. شِعَل الفِتِيلَة وَركَض [šiʕal ʔilfiti:la wrikað]

fuss • **1.** ضَجَّة [ðaǰǰa] ضَجّات [ðaǰǰa:t] *pl:* Don't make such a fuss over him. لا تسَوِّي هِيكِي ضَجَّة حَولَه [la: tsawwi hi:či ðaǰǰa ħawlah]

to fuss • **1.** لِعَب [liʕab] لِعِب [liʕib] *vn:* اِنلِعَب [ʔinliʕab] *p:* He's always fussing with his tie. عَلَى طُول يِلعَب بِبُوينباغه [ʕala ṭu:l yilʕab bibuyinba:ɣah]

fussy • **1.** نَحِس [naħis] He's very fussy about his food. هُوَّ كُلِّش نَحِس بِالأكِل [huwwa kulliš naħis bilʔakil]

future • **1.** مُستَقبَل [mustaqbal] This job has no future. هَالشَّغلَة ما بِيها مُستَقبَل [haššaɣla ma: bi:ha mustaqbal] • **2.** He introduced his future son-in-law to us. قَدَّم إلنا نِسِيبَه المُقبِل [qaddam ʔilna nisi:bah ʔilmuqbil]

F

G

Gabriel • **1.** جُبرائِيل [ǰubraːʔiːl]

gag • **1.** كَمّامَة [kammaːma] كَمّامات [kammaːmaːt] *pl:* Take the gag out of his mouth. طَلِّع الكَمّامَة مِن حَلقَه [ṭalliʕ ʔilkammaːma min ħalgah] • **2.** نُكتَة [nukta] نُكَت [nukat] *pl:* There are a few good gags in the movie. أَكُو شوَيَّة خُوش نُكات بِالفِلِم [ʔaku šwayyat xuːš nukat bilfilim]

to gag • **1.** كَمَّم [kammam] تَكمِيم، تكِمِّم [takmiːm, tkimmim] *vn:* تكَمَّم [tkammam] *p: sv* i. They gagged him with a handkerchief. كَمّمُوه بكِفِّيَّة [kammimuːh bčiffiyya] • **2.** تهَوَّع [thawwaʕ] تهُوُّع [thuwwuʕ] *vn: sv* a. I got sick and began to gag. نَفسِي قامَت تِلعَب وَقُمت أَتهَوَّع [nafsi gaːmat tilʕab wgumt ʔathawwaʕ]

gain • **1.** رِبِح [ribiħ] أَرباح [ʔarbaːħ] *pl:* This table shows our net gain for the year. هَالجَدوَل يبَيِّن رِبِحنا الصّافِي لِلسَّنَة [haǰ ǰadwal yibayyin ribiħna ʔiṣṣaːfi lissana]

to gain • **1.** كِسَب [kisab] كَسِب [kasib] *vn:* اِنكِسَب [ʔinkisab] *p:* حَصَّل [ħaṣṣal] تحصِيل [taħṣiːl] *vn:* تحَصَّل [tħaṣṣal] *p:* اِكتِسَب [ʔiktisab] اِكتِساب [ʔiktisaːb] *vn: sv* i. What did he gain by that? شحَصَّل مِن هاي؟ [šħaṣṣal min haːy?] He gained my confidence. اِكتِسَب ثِقتِي [ʔiktisab θiqati] • **2.** رُبَح [rubaħ] رِبح [ribiħ] *vn:* اِنرُبَح [ʔinrubaħ] *p:* كِسَب [kisab] اِنكِسَب [ʔinkisab] *p:* حَصَّل [ħaṣṣal] تحَصَّل [tħaṣṣal] *p: sv* i. I gained ten dollars in the card game. رُبَحِت عَشِر دُولارات بِلِعب الوَرَق [rubaħit ʕašir dulaːraːt bliʕb ʔilwaraq] • **3.** زاد [zaːd] زِيادَة [ziyaːda] *vn: sv* i. I weighed myself and realized that I had gained four pounds. وِزَنِت نَفسِي وشِفِت آنِي زِدِت أَربَع باونات [wzanit nafsi wšifit ʔaːni zidit ʔarbaʕ paːwnaːt] • **4.** تقَدَّم [tqaddam] تقَدُّم [taqaddum] *vn: sv* a. تقَرَّب [tgarrab] تقَرُّب [tagarrub] *vn: sv* a. Can't you drive any faster? The car behind us is gaining on us. ما تِقدَر تسُوق أَسرَع؟ السَّيّارَة اللِّي وَرانا دَتِتقَدَّم مِنّا [maː tigdar tsuːg ʔasraʕ? ʔissayyaːra ʔilli waraːna datitqaddam minna] • **5.** ثَبَّت [θabbat] تَثبِيت، تثِبِّت [taθbiːt, tθibbit] *vn: sv* i. He tried to climb the hill, but he couldn't gain a footing. حاوَل يِصعَد التَّلّ لٰكِن ما قِدَر يثَبِّت قَدَمَه [ħaːwal yiṣʕad ʔittall laːkin maː gidar yθabbit qadamah]

galaxy • **1.** مَجَرَّة [maǰarra] مَجَرّات [maǰarraːt] *pl:*

gale • **1.** عاصِفَة [ʕaːṣifa] عَواصِف [ʕawaːṣif] *pl:* The gale caused great damage. العاصِفَة سَبِّبَت أَضرار بَلِيغَة [ʔilʕaːṣifa sabbibat ʔaðraːr baliːɣa]

gall • **1.** جَسارَة [ǰasaːra] He's got an awful lot of gall. عِندَه جَسارَة هوايَة [ʕindah ǰasaːra hwaːya]

gall bladder • **1.** مَرارَة [maraːra]

gallery • **1.** غَلَري، غالِيرِي [galari, galiːri] غَلَريّات، غالَرِيّات [galariyyaːt, galariyyaːt] *pl:* Our seats are in the back of the gallery. كَراسِينا بِآخِر الغَلَري [karaːsiːna bʔaːxir ʔilgalari]

gallon • **1.** غَلَن [galan, galin] غَلَنات [galanaːt] *pl:* The American gallon isn't exactly four liters. الغَلَن الأَمرِيكِي مُو أَربَع لَترات تَمام [ʔilgalan ʔilʔamriːki muː ʔarbaʕ latraːt tamaːm]

gallows • **1.** مَشنَقَة [mašnaqa] مَشانِق [mašaːniq] *pl:* صَلّابات [ṣallaːbaːt] *pl:* They erected a gallows in the center of town. نِصبَوا مَشنَقَة بنُصّ الوِلايَة [niṣbaw mašnaqa bnuṣṣ ʔilwilaːya]

galosh • **1.** جَزمَة [čazma] جِزَم [čizam] *pl:*

to galvanize • **1.** غَلوَن [ɣalwan] تغِلوِن، غَلوَنَة [tɣilwin, ɣalwana] *vn:* تغَلوَن [tɣalwan] *p: sv* i. This factory galvanizes metals. هَالمَعمَل يغَلوِن المَعادِن [hallmaʕmal yɣalwin ʔilmaʕaːdin] This pail is galvanized. هَالسَّطِل مغَلوَن [hassaṭil mɣalwan]

gamble • **1.** مُقامَرَة [muqaːmara] مُقامَرات [muqaːmaraːt] *pl:* It was a pure gamble, but we had to risk it. كانَت فَدّ مُقامَرَة أَكِيدَة لٰكِن اِضطَرَّينا نجازِف [čaːnat fadd muqaːmara ʔakiːda laːkin ʔiðṭarrayna nǰaːzif]

to gamble • **1.** لِعَب قمار، قامَر [liʕab qmaːr, qaːmar] لِعِب قمار، مُقامَرَة [liʕib ʔiqmaːr, muqaːmara] *vn: sv* a. They gambled all night. لِعبَوا قمار طُول اللَّيل [liʕbaw qmaːr ṭuːl ʔillayl] • **2.** جازَف [ǰaːzaf] مُجازَفَة [muǰaːzafa] *vn: sv* i. He was gambling with his life. كان دَيجازِف بحَياتَه [čaːn dayǰaːzif bħayaːtah]

to gamble away • **1.** خِسَر بِالقمار [xisar biliqmaːr] خَسارَة بِالقمار [xasaːra biliqmaːr] *vn: sv* a. He gambled his whole salary away. خِسَر راتبَه كُلَّه بِالقمار [xiṣar raːtbah kullah bilqmaːr]

gambling • **1.** قمار [qmaːr] He spends all his money gambling. يِصرُف كُلّ فلُوسَه بِالقمار [yiṣruf kull fluːsah bilqmaːr]

game • **1.** لِعبَة [liʕba] لِعبات، أَلعاب، مَلاعِيب [liʕbaːt, ʔalʕaːb, malaːʕiːb] *pl:* We bought a game for our son. اِشتِرَينا فَدّ لِعبَة لِإبنا [ʔištiriːna fadd liʕba lʔibinna] • **2.** لِعبَة [liʕba] لِعبات، أَلعاب [liʕbaːt, ʔalʕaːb] *pl:* داس [daːs] دُوس [duːs] *pl:* The children played a game of hopscotch. الجَّهال لِعبَوا لِعبَة تُوكِيَّة [ʔiǰǰahaːl liʕbaw liʕbat tuːkiyya] • **3.** لِعبَة [liʕba]

لِعبات، ألعاب، مَلاعِيب [liʕba:t, ʔalʕa:b, mala:ʕi:b] *pl:* لِعَب [liʕab] كَيم [gaym] كَيمات [gayma:t] *pl:* شَوط [šawṭ] أشواط [ʔašwa:ṭ] *pl:* The referee called the end of the game. الحَكَم عِلَن نِهايَة اللِّعبَة [ʔilħakam ʕilan niha:yat ʔilliʕba] • **4.** صيد [ṣayd] There's a lot of game in this area. أكُو صَيد هوايَة بِهَالمَنطَقَة [ʔaku ṣi:d hwa:ya bhalmanṭaqa] • **5.** وُجَع [wuǰaʕ, wiǰaʕ] I've got a game leg. عِندِي وُجَع رِجِل [ʕindi wuǰaʕ riǰil] • **6.** مِستِعِدّ [mistiʕidd] حاضِر [ħa:ðir] I'm game for anything. آنِي مِستِعِدّ لأيّ شِي [ʔa:ni mistiʕidd lʔayy ši]

*** I can see through his game. • 1.** عارُف كُلّ مَلاعِيبَه [ʕa:ruf kull mala:ʕi:bah]

gang • 1. عِصابَة [ʕiṣa:ba] عِصابات [ʕiṣa:ba:t] *pl:* The head of the gang was a notorious criminal. رَئِيس العِصابَة كان فَدّ مُجرِم مَعرُوف [raʔi:s ʔilʕiṣa:ba ča:n fadd muǰrim maʕru:f] • **2.** جَماعَة [ǰama:ʕa] جَماعات [ǰama:ʕa:t] *pl:* He runs around with a good gang. دَيمشِي ويّا خُوش جَماعَة [dayimši wiyya xu:š ǰama:ʕa] • **3.** جَماعَة [ǰama:ʕa] جَماعات [ǰama:ʕa:t] *pl:* زُمرَة [zumra] زُمَر [zumar] *pl:* He runs around with a bad gang. دَيمشِي ويّا زُمرَة مُو زينَة [dayimši wiyya zumra mu: zayna] • **4.** جَوقَة [ǰawga] جَوقات [ǰawga:t] *pl:* We saw a gang of workmen with shovels in the back of the truck. شِفنا جُوقَة عُمّال وِيّاهُم كَرَكات بآخِر اللُّورِي [šifna ǰawgat ʕumma:l wiyya:hum karaka:t biʔa:xir ʔillu:ri]

gangrene • 1. گَنگَرِين [gangari:n]

gap • 1. فَتحَة [fatħa] They're building a road through the mountain gap. دَيبنُون طَرِيق بالفَتحَة اللِّي بين الجِّبَلَين [dayibnu:n ṭari:q bilfatħa ʔilli bi:n ʔiǰǰibali:n] • **2.** ثَغرَة [θaɣra] ثَغرات [θaɣra:t] *pl:* Our infantry opened a wide gap in the enemy's lines. مُشاتنا فِتحَوا ثَغرَة واسِعَة بِخُطُوط العَدُو [muša:tna fitħaw θaɣra wa:sʕa bxuṭu:ṭ ʔilʕadu] • **3.** فَراغ [fara:ɣ] Your transfer will leave a gap in this office. نَقلَك راح يِترُك فَراغ بِهَالدّائِرَة [naqlak ra:ħ yitruk fara:ɣ bhadda:ʔira] • **4.** نَقص [naqiṣ, naquṣ] There's a large gap in his education. أكُو نَقص كِبِير بِثَقافتَه [ʔaku naqiṣ čabi:r bθaqa:ftah]

garage • 1. گَراج [gara:ǰ] گَراجات [gara:ǰa:t] *pl:*

garbage • 1. زِبِل [zibil] زبالَة [zba:la]

garden • 1. حَدِيقَة [ħadi:qa] حَدايِق [ħada:yiq] *pl:* These flowers are from our garden. هَالوَرِد مِن الحَدِيقَة مالتنا [halwarid min ʔilħadi:qa ma:latna] • **2.** جَنَّة [ǰanna] Garden of Eden. جَنَّة عَدَن [ǰannat ʕadan] Hanging Gardens of Babylon. جَنائِن بابِل المُعَلَّقَة [ǰana:ʔin ba:bil ʔilmuʕallaqa]

gargle • 1. غَرغَرَة [ɣarɣara] غَرغَرات [ɣarɣara:t] *pl:* Water and salt is a good gargle. المَيّ وَالمِلِح خُوش غَرغَرَة [ʔilmayy wilmiliħ xu:š ɣarɣara]

to gargle • 1. تغَرغَر [tɣarɣar] تغِرغِر [tɣirɣir] *vn: sv* a. You have to gargle three times a day. لازِم تغَرغَر ثلَث مَرّات باليُوم [la:zim tiɣarɣar tlaθ marra:t bilyu:m]

garlic • 1. ثُوم [θu:m]

garment • 1. هِدِم هدُوم [hidim, hdu:m] هدُوم [hdu:m] مَلابِس [mala:bis]

to garnish • 1. زَروَق [zarwaq] تزِروِق [tzirwiq] *vn:* تزَروَق [tzarwaq] *p: sv* i. The cook garnished the fish with parsley and lemon. الطَّبّاخ زَروَق السِّمكَة بِكرَفُس وَنُومِي حامُض [ʔiṭṭabba:x zarwag ʔissimča bkrafus wnu:mi ħa:muð]

garter • 1. آسقِي [ʔa:sqi] آسقِيّات [ʔa:sqiyya:t] *pl:*

gas • 1. غاز [ɣa:z] غازات [ɣa:za:t] *pl:* We use gas for cooking. نِستَعمِل الغاز لِلطَّبُخ [nistaʕmil ʔilɣa:z liṭṭabux] Cabbage always gives me gas. اللَّهانَة تَوَلِّد عِندِي غازات دائِماً [ʔillahha:na: twallid ʕindi ɣa:za:t da:ʔiman] The dentist uses an anesthetic gas. طَبِيب الأسنان يِستَعمِل غاز مُخَدِّر [ṭabi:b ʔilʔasna:n yistaʕmil ɣa:z muxaddir] • **2.** بانزِين [banzi:n] He had enough gas for ten miles. كان عِندَه بَنزِين يكَفِّي العَشِر أميال [ča:n ʕindah banzi:n ykaffi ʔilʕašir ʔamya:l]

to gas • 1. سَمَّم [sammam] تَسمِيم، تسِمِّم [tasmi:m, tsimmim] *vn:* تسَمَّم [tsammam] *p: sv* i. خِنَق [xinag] خَنِق [xanig] *vn:* اِنخِنَق [ʔinxinag] *p: sv* u. They gassed their prisoners during the war. سَمَّمَوا مَساجِينهُم بِالغاز خِلال الحَرُب [sammamaw masa:ǰi:nhum bilɣa:z xila:l ʔilħarub] • **2.** خَلَّى [xalla:] تخِلِّي [txilli] *vn:* تخَلَّى [txalla:] *p: sv* i. I gassed the car on my way to work. خَلَّيت بَنزِين بَالسَّيّارَة بطَرِيقِي لِلشُّغُل [xalli:t banzi:n bissayya:ra bṭari:qi liššɣul]

gasket • 1. كازگَيتَة [ga:zgi:ta] كازگَيتات [ga:zgi:ta:t] *pl:* كازگَيت [ga:zgi:t] *Collective*

gasoline • 1. بانزِين [banzi:n]

gasoline station • 1. مَحَطَّة بنزِين [maħaṭṭat banzi:n] مَحَطّات بنزِين [maħaṭṭa:t banzi:n] *pl:*

to gasp • 1. لِهَث [lihaθ] لَهِث [lahiθ] *vn: sv* a. We were gasping when we reached the top of the hill. كِنّا نِلهَث مِن وُصَلنا الرّاس التَّل [činna nilhaθ min wuṣalna ʔirra:s ʔittall]

gastric • 1. معِدِي [maʕidi, mʕidi]

gate • **1.** باب خارِجِي [ba:b xa:rijiy] بِيبان خارِجِيَّة [bi:ba:n xa:rijiyya] *pl:* باب بَرّانِي [ba:b barra:ni] بِيبان بَرّانِيَّة [bi:ba:n barra:niyya] *pl:* Who opened the gate? مِنُو فِتَح الباب الخارِجِيَّة؟ [minu fitaħ ʔilba:b ʔilxa:rijiyya?] • **2.** دَخَل [daxal] دُخُول [duxu:l] *pl:* The manager is counting the gate now. المُدِير دَيِحسِب الدَّخَل هَسَّة [ʔilmudi:r dayiħsib ʔiddaxal hassa]

to gather • **1.** جِمَع [jimaʕ] جَمِع [jamiʕ] *vn:* اِنجِمَع [ʔinjimaʕ] *p:* لَمّ [lamm] لَمّ [lamm] *vn:* اِنلَمّ [ʔinlamm] *p:* The children grathered firewood. الأطفال جِمعَوا حَطَب [ʔilʔaṭfa:l jimʕaw ħaṭab] • **2.** اِلتَمّ [ʔiltamm] اِلتِمام [ʔiltima:m] *vn: sv* a. تجَمَّع [tjammaʕ] تَجَمُّع [tajammuʕ] *vn: sv* a. Many people gathered in front of the platform. ناس هوايَة اِلتَمّوا قِدّام المَنَصَّة [na:s hwa:ya ʔiltammaw gidda:m ʔilmanaṣṣa] • **3.** اِستَنتَج [ʔistantaj] اِستِنتاج [ʔistinta:j] *vn: sv* i. فِهَم [fiham] فَهِم [fahim] *vn:* اِنفِهَم [ʔinfiham] *p:* From what you say, I gather that you don't like him. مِن اللِّي تقُولَه أستَنتِج إنتَ ما تحِبَّه [min ʔilli dgu:lah ʔastantij ʔinta ma: tħibbah] • **4.** اِستَجمَع [ʔistajmaʕ] اِستِجماع [ʔistijma:ʕ] *vn: sv* i. The patient gathered strength after the operation. المَرِيض اِستَجمَع قُواه بَعَد العَمَلِيَّة [ʔilmari:ð ʔistajmaʕ quwa:h baʕad ʔilʕamaliyya]

gauge • **1.** گَيج [gayj] گَيجات [gayja:t] *pl:* مِقياس [miqya:s] مَقايِيس [maqa:yi:s] *pl:* The gasoline gauge isn't working. الگَيج مال البانزِين ما دَيِشتُغُل [ʔilgayj ma:l ʔilbanzi:n ma: dayištuɣul] Bring me a gauge so I can measure these wires. جِيبلِي فَدّ مِقياس حَتَّى أقِيس هَالوايرات [ji:bli fadd miqya:s ħatta ʔaqi:s halwa:yara:t] • **2.** مِتِن [mitin] I want a roll of wire in this gauge. أرِيد لَفَّة وايَر بِهَالمِتِن [ʔari:d laffat wa:yar bhalmitin] • **3.** عِيار [ʕiya:r] He hunts with a twelve gauge shotgun. يِصِيد بِبُندُقِيَّة عِيار ثنَعَش [yiṣi:d bibunduqiyya ʕiya:r ʔiθnaʕaš]

to gauge • **1.** قاس [qa:s] قِياس [qiya:s] *vn:* اِنقاس [ʔinqa:s] *p:* This gauges the thickness. هَذا يقِيس السُّمُك [ha:ða yqi:s ʔissumuk] • **2.** قَدَّر [qaddar] تَقدِير [taqdi:r] *vn:* تقَدَّر [tqaddar] *p:* I would gauge the distance to be two hundred meters. أقَدِّر المَسافَة مِيتَين مَتِر [ʔaqaddir ʔilmasa:fa mitayn matir]

gauze • **1.** قَوز [gawz, gu:z]

gavel • **1.** مَطرَقَة [maṭraqa] مَطرَقات [maṭraqa:t] *pl:*

gay • **1.** مِبتِهِج [mibtihij] فَرحان [farħa:n] The children were gay. الجَّهال كانَوا مِبتِهجِين [ʔijjaha:l ča:naw mibtihiji:n]

gazelle • **1.** غَزالَة [ɣaza:la] غِزلان [ɣizla:n] *pl:* غَزال [ɣaza:l, ɣza:l] collective:

gear • **1.** دِشلِي [dišli] دِشلِيّات، دِشالِي [dišliyya:t, diša:li] *pl:* I broke a tooth of the gear. كِسَرت سِنّ مِن الدِّشلِي [kisarit sinn min ʔiddišli] • **2.** قِير [gi:r, ji:r] Shift into second gear. بَدِّل الگِير عَالثِّنَين [baddil ʔilgi:r ʕaθθinayn] • **3.** غَرَض [ɣarað] أغراض [ʔaɣra:ð] *pl:* We put the fishing gear in the trunk of my car. خَلِّينا غَراض صَيد السِّمَك بِصَندُوق سَيّارتِي [xalli:na ɣara:ð ṣayd ʔissimač biṣandu:g sayya:rti] • **4.** آلَة [ʔa:la] آلات [ʔa:la:t] *pl:* Fix the steering gear. صَلِّح آلات السُّكّان [ṣalliħ ʔa:la:t ʔissukka:n]

gelatin • **1.** جَلاتِين [jala:ti:n]

to geld • **1.** خِصَى [xiṣa:] خَصِي [xaṣi] *vn:* اِنخِصَى [ʔinxiṣa:] *p:* The army gelds all its horses. الجَّيش يِخصِي كُلّ الخَيل مالَه [ʔijjayš yixṣi kull ʔilxayl ma:lah]

gem • **1.** جَوهَرَة [jawhara] جَواهِر [jawa:hir] *pl:* These gems are invaluable. هَالجَواهِر ما تِتثَمَّن [hajjawa:hir ma: titθamman]

general • **1.** عامّ [ʕa:mm] Have you heard anything about the general elections? سمَعِت أيّ شِي عَن الانتِخابات العامَّة؟ [smaʕit ʔayy ši ʕan ʔilʔintixa:ba:t ʔilʕa:mma?] • **2.** عُمُومِي [ʕumu:mi] They gave him a general anesthetic. إنطُوه بَنج عُمُومِي [ʔinṭu:h banj ʕumu:mi] • **3.** جِنِرال [jinira:l] جِنِرالات [jinira:la:t] *pl:* (not applied to Arab officer of that rank) . They nominated the general to the presidency of the republic. رَشِّحَوا الجِّنِرال لِرئاسَة الجَّمهُورِيَّة [raššiħaw ʔijjinira:l liriʔa:sat ʔijjamhu:riyya] • **4.** عَمِيد [ʕami:d] عُمَداء [ʕumada:ʔ] *pl:* He was promoted general. رَفّعُوه عَمِيد [raffiʕu:h ʕami:d]

in general • **1.** بصُورَة عامَّة [bṣu:ra ʕa:mma] عَالعُمُوم [ʕalʕumu:m] In general, things are all right. بِصُورَة عامَّة، الأحوال زينَة [bṣu:ra ʕa:mma, ʔilʔaħwa:l zayna]

brigadier general • **1.** زَعِيم [zaʕi:m] زُعَماء [zuʕama:ʔ] *pl:*

lieutenant general • **1.** فَرِيق [fari:q] فُرَقاء [furaqa:ʔ] *pl:*

major general • **1.** أمِير لِواء [ʔami:r liwa:ʔ] أمَراء ألوِيَة [ʔumara:ʔ ʔalwiya] *pl:*

general delivery • **1.** شِبّاك البَرِيد [šibba:č ʔilbari:d] Send the letter to me in care of general delivery. دِزّلِي المَكتُوب بِواسطَة شِبّاك البَرِيد [dizzli ʔilmaktu:b bwa:sṭat šibba:č ʔilbari:d]

generally • **1.** بصُورَة عامَّة [bṣu:ra ʕa:mma] عَلعُمُوم [ʕalʕumu:m] He's generally here before eight. هُوَّ عَالعُمُوم هنا قَبل الثَّمانيَة [huwwa ʕa:lʕumu:m hna: qabl ʔiθθima:nya]

generation • **1.** جِيل [ji:l] أجيال [ʔajya:l] *pl:* His family has been in America for four generations. عائلَته صارلها أربَع أجيال بأمرِيكا [ʕa:ʔiltah ṣa:rilha ʔarbaʕ ʔajya:l bʔamri:ka]

generous • **1.** كَرِيم [kari:m] كُرَماء [kurama:ʔ] *pl:* سَخِي [saxy] أَسخِياء [ʔasxiya:ʔ] *pl:* بَرمَكِي [barmaki] بَرمَكِيَّة [barmakiyya] *pl:* Don't be so generous! لا تكُون هَالقَدّ بَرمَكِي [la: tku:n halgadd barmaki]

genius • **1.** نُبُوغ [nubu:ɣ] عَبقَرِيَّة [ʕabqariyya] That man has genius. ذاك الرِّجّال عِندَه عَبقَرِيَّة [ða:k ʔirrijja:l ʕindah ʕabqariyya] • **2.** genius in mathematics. هُوَّ نابِغَة بِالرِّياضِيّات [huwwa na:biɣa birriya:ðiyya:t]

gentle • **1.** لَطِيف [laṭi:f] A gentle breeze was coming from the sea. نَسِيم لَطِيف كان دَيجِي مِن البَحَر [nasi:m laṭi:f ča:n dayiji min ʔilbaħar] • **2.** وَدِيع [wadi:ʕ] هادِئ [ha:diʔ] This horse is very gentle. هَالحِصان كُلِّش وَدِيع [halħiṣa:n kulliš wadi:ʕ]

gentleman • **1.** سَيِّد [sayyid] سادَة [sa:da] *pl:* Will you see what this gentleman wants, please? بالله ما تشُوف هَالسَّيِّد شِيرِيد؟ [ballah ma: tšu:f hassayyid šiyri:d?] Ladies and gentlemen. سَيِّداتِي وسادَتِي [sayyida:ti wsa:dati] • **2.** رِجّال [rijja:l] رِياجِيل [riya:ji:l] *pl:* There are two gentlemen outside waiting for you. أَكُو رِجّالَين دَينتَظرُوك بَرَّة [ʔaku rijja:layn dayintaðru:k barra]

gently • **1.** يَواش [yawa:š] عَلَى كَيف [ʕala ki:f] He knocked gently on the door. دَقّ الباب عَلَى كيفه [dagg ʔilba:b ʕala ki:fah] • **2.** يَواش [yawa:š] عَلَى كَيف [ʕala kayf] لُطُف [luṭuf] أَلطاف [ʔalṭa:f] *pl:* You'll have to treat him gently. لازِم تعامِلَه بِلُطُف [la:zim tʕa:mlah biluṭuf]

genuine • **1.** أَصلِي [ʔaṣli] This suitcase is genuine leather. هَالجُّنطَة جِلِد أَصلِي [hajjunṭa jilid ʔaṣli]

geography • **1.** جُغرافِيَة [juɣra:fya]

geometry • **1.** هَندَسَة [handasa]

germ • **1.** جَرثُوم [jarθu:m] جَراثِيم [jara:θi:m] *pl:* Don't eat that! It's full of germs. لا تاكُل هاي كُلّها جَراثِيم [la: ta:kul ha:y kullha jara:θi:m]

German • **1.** أَلمانِي [ʔalma:ni] أَلمانِيِّين، أَلمان [ʔalma:niyyi:n, ʔalma:n] *pl:* Are there many Germans here? أَكُو هوايَة أَلمان هنا؟ [ʔaku hwa:ya ʔalma:n hna?] • **2.** أَلمانِي [ʔalma:ni] He speaks German. يِتكَلَّم أَلمانِي [yitkallam ʔalma:ni] • **3.** أَلمانِي [ʔalma:ni] I bought a German watch. اِشتِرَيت ساعَة أَلمانِيَّة [ʔištirayt sa:ʕa ʔalma:niyya]

Germany • **1.**

gesture • **1.** إشارَة [ʔiša:ra] إشارات [ʔiša:ra:t] *pl:* His gestures are very expressive. إشاراتَه كُلِّش مُعَبِّرَة [ʔiša:ra:tah kulliš muʕabbira]

to get • **1.** اِستِلَم [ʔistilam] اِستِلام [ʔistila:m] *vn: sv* i. When did you get my letter? شوَقِت اِستِلَمِت مَكتُوبِي؟ [šwakit ʔistilamit maktu:bi?] • **2.** حَصَّل [ħaṣṣal] تحِصِّل، حُصُول [tħiṣṣil, ħuṣu:l] *vn:* تحَصَّل [tħaṣṣal] *p:* We can get apples cheaper here. نِقدَر نحَصِّل التِّفّاح بِأَرخَص هنا [nigdar nħaṣṣil ʔittiffa:ħ bʔarxaṣ hna] Try to get him on the telephone. حاوِل تحَصِّلَه بِالتَّلِفُون [ħa:wil tħaṣṣilah bittalifu:n] • **3.** دَبَّر [dabbar] تَدبِير، تدُبُّر [tadbi:r, tdubbur] *vn:* تدَبَّر [tdabbar] *p:* حَصَّل [ħaṣṣal] تحَصَّل [tħaṣṣal] *p:* Can you get me another copy? تِقدَر تدَبُّرلِي نُسخَة لُخ؟ [tigdar ddabburli nusxa lux?] • **4.** أَخَذ مِن، أَخَذ عَلَى [ʔaxað min, ʔaxað ʕala] أَخِذ [ʔaxið] *vn:* اِنأخَذ [ʔinʔixað] *p:* حَصَّل [ħaṣṣal] تحَصَّل [tħaṣṣal] *p:* He got the highest grade in the class. أَخَذ أَعلَى دَرَجَة بِالصَّفّ [ʔaxað ʔaʕla daraja biṣṣaff] • **5.** خَلَّى [xalla:] تخِلِّي [txilli] *vn: sv* i. Can you get him to go there? تِقدَر تخَلِّيه يرُوح لِهناك؟ [tigdar txalli:h yiru:ħ lihna:k?] Get him to do it for you. خَلِّيه يسَوِّيلَك إيّاها [xalli:h ysawwi:lak ʔiyya:ha] • **6.** جاب [ja:b] جَيبَة [jayba] *vn:* اِنجاب [ʔinja:b] *p:* Go get my hat. رُوح جِيب شَفُقتِي [ru:ħ ji:b šafuqti] • **7.** وَصَّل [waṣṣal] توصِّل [twiṣṣil] *vn: sv* i. Can you get this message to him? تِقدَر توَصِّلَّه هَالخَبَر؟ [tigdar twaṣṣillah halxabar?] • **8.** وُصَل [wuṣal] وُصُول [wuṣu:l] *vn: sv* a. جا [ja:] مَجِيء [maji:ʔ] *vn: sv* i. We got to Baghdad the next day. وُصَلنا لِبَغداد ثانِي يوم [wuṣalna libayda:d θa:ni yu:m] • **9.** صار [ṣa:r] *sv* i. Do you think he'll get well again? تِعتِقِد راح يصِير زين مَرَّة لُخ؟ [tiʕtiqid ra:ħ yṣi:r zayn marra lux?]

* **Do you get the idea?** • **1.** تشُوف شلَون؟ [tšu:f šlu:n?]
* **He got sentenced to a year in jail.** • **1.** اِنحِكَم سَنَة حَبِس [ʔinħikam sana ħabis]
* **He got hit in the mouth.** • **1.** اِنضِرَب بِحَلقَه [ʔinðirab biħalga]
* **He got hurt in the accident.** • **1.** تعَوَّر بِالحادِث [tʕawwar bilħa:diθ]
* **He is getting treated at the hospital.** • **1.** دَيتعالَج بِالمُستَشفَى [dayitʕa:laj bilmustašfa]
* **His face got real red.** • **1.** وِجَّه اِحمَرّ كُلِّش [wiččah ʔiħmarr kulliš]
* **The grass is getting green.** • **1.** الحَشِيش دَيِخضَرّ [ʔilħaši:š dayixðarr]
* **He got drunk.** • **1.** سِكَر [sikar]
* **He went to get a drink of water.** • **1.** راح يِشرَب جُرعَة مَيّ [ra:ħ yišrab jurʕat mayy]
* **I got four hours sleep.** • **1.** نِمِت أَربَع ساعات [nimit ʔarbaʕ sa:ʕa:t]
* **His lying really gets me. I hate it.** • **1.** كِذبَه يخَبُّلنِي أَمُوت مِنَّه [čiðbah yxabbulni ʔamu:t minnah]
* **I got to bed early, but I couldn't sleep.** • **1.** اِنطِرَحِت بِالفراش مِن وَقِت لَكِن ما قدَرت أنام [ʔintiraħit bilifra:š min wakit la:kin ma: gdart ʔana:m]
* **We get twenty miles to the gallon in our new car.** • **1.** نطَلِّع عِشرِين مِيل بِالغَلَن بسَيّارَتنا الجِّدِيدَة [nṭalliʕ ʕišri:n mi:l bilgalan bsayya:ratna ʔijjidi:da]
* **Get lost!** • **1.** وَلِّي [walli]

G

*** You beat me three games in a row, but I'll get even tomorrow night.** • **1.** غِلَبِتنِي ثلَث لِعبات وِحدَة وَرا اللُّخ، راح أنتِقِم مِنَّه عَلَى مَوتَة أخُويَة [ɣilabitni tlaθ liʕba:t wiħda wara ʔillux, ra:ħ ʔatpa:wak wiyya:k ba:čir billayl]

*** I'll get even with him for the death of my brother.** • **1.** راح أنتِقِم مِنَّه عَلَى مَوتَة أخُويا [ra:ħ ʔantiqim minnah ʕala mawtat ʔaxuwya]

to get about • **1.** دار ب [da:r b-] دَور [dawr] *vn: sv* u. اِفتَرّ ب [ʔiftarr b-] فَرّ [farr] *vn: sv* a. He gets about the house in a wheelchair. يدُور بالبَيت بكُرسِي أبُو جرُوخ [ydu:r bilbayt bkursi ʔabu čru:x] A rumor got about that he was going to resign. فَدّ إشاعَة دارَت بأنَّه راح يستِقِيل [fadd ʔiša:ʕa da:rat biʔannah ra:ħ yistiqi:l]

to get across • **1.** فَهَّم [fahham] تَفهِيم [tafhi:m] *vn:* تفَهَّم [tfahham] *p:* I wasn't able to get the idea across to him. ما قِدَرت أفَهِّمَه الفِكرَة [ma: gidart ʔafahhimah ʔilfikra] • **2.** عُبَر [ʕubar] عَبُر [ʕabur] *vn:* اِنعُبَر [ʔinʕubar] *p:* I got across the river in a boat. عبَرت الشَّطّ بِبَلَم [ʕbarit ʔiššaṭṭ bibalam]

to get ahead • **1.** تقَدَّم [tqaddam] تَقَدُّم [taqaddum] *vn: sv* a. He'll never get ahead in business with that attitude. وَلا راح يِتقَدَّم بالتِّجارَة بهَالوَضِع [wala ra:ħ yitqaddam bittija:ra bhalwaðiʕ]

to get a glimpse of • **1.** لِمَح [limaħ] لَمِح [lamiħ] *vn:* اِنلِمَح [ʔinlimaħ] *p:* I got a glimpse of a man wearing a red shirt. لِمَحِت رِجّال لابِس ثُوب أحمَر [limaħit rijja:l la:bis θu:b ʔaħmar]

to get along • **1.** دَبَّر أمُر [dabbar ʔamur] تَدبِير أمُر [tadbi:r ʔamur] *vn: sv* u. We get along on very little money. ندَبُّر أمُرنا بشوَيَّة فلُوس [ndabbur ʔamurna bšwayya flu:s] • **2.** توالَم [twa:lam] تَوالُم [tawa:lum] *vn: sv* a. تلائَم [tla:ʔam] تَلائُم [tala:ʔum] *vn: sv* a. We get along well with each other. نِتوالَم زين واحِد ويّا اللاخ [nitwa:lam zi:n wa:ħid wiyya ʔilla:x] • **3.** مِشَى [miša:] مَشِي [mašy] *vn: sv* i. راح [ra:ħ] رَواح [rawa:ħ] *vn: sv* u. I'll have to be getting along now. لازم أمشِي هَسَّة [la:zim ʔamši hassa] • **4.** تقَدَّم [tqaddam] تَقَدُّم [taqaddum] *vn: sv* a. He's getting along in years. دَيِتقَدَّم بالعُمُر [dayitqaddam bilʕumur]

*** How are you getting along?** • **1.** شلَون أحوالَك؟ [šlawn ʔaħwa:lak?] / شلُون دَتِمشِي؟ [šlu:n datimši?]

to get around • **1.** اِحتال [ʔiħta:l] اِحتِيال [ʔiħtiya:l] *vn: sv* a. اِتمَلَّص [ʔitmallaṣ] تَمَلُّص [tamalluṣ] *vn: sv* a. They tried to get around the tax regulations. حاوَلوا يِحتالُون عَلَى نِظام الضَّرايِب [ħa:wilaw yiħta:lu:n ʕala niða:m ʔiððara:yib] • **2.** تجَوَّل [djawwal] تَجَوُّل [tajawwul] *vn: sv* a. جال [ja:l] تِجوال [tijwa:l] *vn: sv* u. As president, naturally he gets around a lot. بصِيفتَه رَئِيس، طَبعاً يِتجَوَّل هوايَة [bṣi:ftah raʔi:s, ṭabʕan yidjawwal hwa:ya] • **3.** اِنتِشَر [ʔintišar] اِنتِشار [ʔintiša:r] *vn: sv* i. The story got around quickly. الحكايَة اِنتِشرَت بالعَجَل [ʔilħča:ya ʔintišrat bilʕajal] • **4.** اِفتَرّ [ʔiftarr] فَرّ [farr] *vn: sv* a. دار [da:r] دَور [dawr] *vn: sv* u. She can't get around the house very easily. ما تِقدَر تدُور بالبَيت بسُهُولَة [ma: tigdar ddu:r bilbayt bisuhu:la]

to get at • **1.** حَصَّل [ħaṣṣal] تَحصِيل [taħṣi:l] *vn:* تحَصَّل [tħaṣṣal] *p:* توَصَّل [twaṣṣal] تَوَصُّل [tawaṣṣul] *vn: sv* a. His family won't let him get at the money that's in his name in the bank. أهلَه ما يخَلُّوه يحَصِّل الفلُوس اللِّي بإسمَه بالبَنك [ʔahlah ma: yxallu:h yħaṣṣil ʔilflu:s ʔilli bʔismah bilbang] We didn't get at the real reason. ما توَصَّلنا لِلسَّبَب الحَقِيقِي [ma: twaṣṣalna lissabab ʔilħaqi:qi] • **2.** ناش [na:š] نَوش [nawš] *vn:* اِناش [ʔinna:š] *p:* I can't get at the bolt from here. ما أقدَر أنُوش البُرغِي مِن هنا [ma: ʔagdar ʔanu:š ʔilburɣi minhna]

to get away • **1.** تمَلَّص [ʔitmallaṣ] تَمَلُّص [tamalluṣ] *vn: sv* a. I'm sorry but I couldn't get away. آسِف بَسّ ما قِدَرت أتمَلَّص [ʔa:sif bass ma: gidarit ʔitmallaṣ] • **2.** اِنهِزَم [ʔinhizam] هَزِيمَة، اِنهِزام [hazi:ma, ʔinhiza:m] *vn: sv* i. هِرَب [hirab] هَرَب [harab] *vn: sv* u. فِلَت [filat] فَلِت [falit] *vn: sv* i. The criminal got away. المُجرِم اِنهِزَم [ʔilmujrim ʔinhizam] • **3.** وَخَّر [waxxar] تَوخِير، توخِّر [tawxi:r, twixxir] *vn:* توَخَّر [twaxxar] *p:* Get the children away from the stove. وَخِّر الجُّهّال مِن الطَّبّاخ [waxxir ʔijjahha:l min ʔiṭṭabba:x] • **4.** تِرَك [tirak] تَرِك [tarik] *vn:* اِنتِرَك [ʔintirak] *p:* I want to get away from town for a few days. أرِيد أترُك الوِلايَة فَدّ كَم يوم [ʔari:d ʔatruk ʔilwila:ya fadd čam yu:m]

*** You won't get away with it.** • **1.** هاي ما تفُوتلَك [ha:y ma: tfu:tlak]

to get back • **1.** رِجَع [rijaʕ] رُجُوع [ruju:ʕ] *vn: sv* a. When did you get back? شوَقِت رِجَعِت؟ [šwakit rijaʕit?] I have to get these books back before noon. لازم أرَجِّع هَالكُتُب قَبِل الظُّهُر [la:zim ʔarajjiʕ halkutub gabil ʔiððuhur] • **2.** اِسترجَع [ʔistarjaʕ] اِسترِجاع [ʔistirja:ʕ] *vn: sv* i. رَجَّع [rajjaʕ] تَرجِيع، ترجِّع [tarji:ʕ, trijjiʕ] *vn: sv* i. I want to get my money back. أرِيد أسترجِع فلُوسِي [ʔari:d ʔastarjiʕ flu:si] • **3.** اِنتِقَم مِن [ʔintiqam min] اِنتِقام [ʔintiqa:m] *vn: sv* i. He got me back for fighting with his brother. اِنتِقَم مِنِّي لِعراكِي ويّا أخُوه [ʔintiqam minni liʕra:ki wiyya ʔaxu:h]

to get behind • **1.** سانَد [sa:nad] مُسانَدَة [musa:nada] *vn: sv* i. The industrialists are getting behind him for the presidencey. رِجّال الصِّناعَة دَيساندُوه لِلرِّئاسَة [rijja:l ʔiṣṣina:ʕa daysa:ndu:h lirriʔa:sa] • **2.** تأخَّر [tʔaxxar] تَأخُّر [taʔaxxur] *vn: sv* a. We've started to get behind in our work. بدَينا نِتأخَّر بشُغُلنا [bdayna nitʔaxxar bšugulna]

to get by • **1.** دَبَّر نَفِس [dabbar nafis] تَدبِير نَفِس [tadbi:r nafis] *vn: sv* u. I get by on thirty dinars a month. أدَبُّر نَفسِي بثلاثِين دِينار بالشَّهَر [ʔadabbur nafsi bitlaθi:n dina:r biššahar] • **2.** خَلَّص [xallaṣ] تَخلِيص، تخِلِّص [taxli:ṣ, txilliṣ] *vn: sv* i. How did you get by the guard? شلُون خَلَّصِت مِن الحارِس؟ [šlu:n xallaṣit min ʔilħa:ris?]

to get in • **1.** دِخَل [dixal] دُخُول [duxu:l] *vn:* اِندِخَل [ʔindixal] *p:* خَشّ [xašš] خَشّ [xašš] *vn:* اِنخَشّ [ʔinxašš] *p:* How did you get in the house? شلُون دِخَلِت بِالبَيت؟ [šlu:n dixalit bilbayt?] • **2.** وُصَل [wuṣal] وُصُول [wuṣu:l] *vn: sv* a. طَبّ [ṭabb] طَبَّة [ṭabba] *vn: sv* u. What time did the train get in? شوَكِت طَبّ القِطار؟ [šwakit ṭabb ʔilqiṭa:r?] • **3.** خَشَّش [xaššaš] تَخشِيش [taxši:š] *vn:* تخَشَّش [txaššaš] *p:* فَوَّت [fawwat] تَفوِيت [tafwi:t] *vn:* تفَوَّت [tfawwat] *p:* دَخَّل [daxxal] تَدخِيل [tadxi:l] *vn:* تدَخَّل [ddaxxal] *p:* Get the clothes in before it rains. خَشِّش الهدُوم قَبُل ما تُمطُر [xaššiš ʔilhdu:m gabul ma: tumṭur]

*** I'd like to get in a game of tennis before it rains.** • **1.** أَرِيد أَلعَب فَدّ لِعبَة تَنِس قَبُل ما تُمطُر [ʔari:d ʔalʕab fadd liʕbat tanis gabul ma: tumṭur]

to get off • **1.** نِزَل مِن [nizal min] نُزُول [nuzu:l] *vn: sv* i. I'll get off the train at the next station. راح أَنزِل مِن القِطار بِالمَحَطَّة الجّايَّة [ra:ħ ʔanzil min ʔilqiṭa:r bilmaħaṭṭa ʔijja:yya] • **2.** ذَبّ [ðabb] ذَبّ [ðabb] *vn:* اِنذَبّ [ʔinðabb] *p:* He got off a couple of funny jokes. ذَبّ نُكُتَّين مُضحِكَة [ðabb nukuttayn muðħika] He got off a couple of funny jokes. ذَبّلَه نُكُتَّين مُضحِكَة [ðabblah nukuttayn muðħika] • **3.** شال عَن [ša:l ʕan] شَيل [šayl] *vn:* اِنشال [ʔinša:l] *p: sv* i.
Get your elbows off the table. شِيل عكُوسَك عَن المِيز [ši:l ʕku:sak ʕann ʔilmi:z] • **4.** نِزَع [nizaʕ] نَزِع [naziʕ] *vn:* اِنّزَع [ʔinnizaʕ] *p: sv* a. Get your clothes off and take a bath. إِنزَع هدُومَك وأُخُذ حَمّام [ʔinzaʕ hdu:mak wʔuxuð ħamma:m] • **5.** خِلَص [xilaṣ] خَلاص [xala:ṣ] *vn: sv* a. He got off with a light sentence. خِلَص بِعُقُوبَة بَسِيطَة [xilaṣ biʕuqu:ba basi:ṭa]

*** The team got off to a bad start.** • **1.** الفَرِيق بِدا بِدايَة مُو زَينَة [ʔilfari:q bida: bida:ya mu: zi:na]

*** He told the boss where to get off and left.** • **1.** فَرَّغ سِمَّه بِالمُدِير وطِلَع [farraɣ simmah bilmudi:r wṭilaʕ]

to get on • **1.** صِعَد [ṣiʕad] صُعُود [ṣuʕu:d] *vn:* اِنصِعَد [ʔinṣiʕad] *p:* رِكَب [rikab] رُكُوب [ruku:b] *vn:* اِنرِكَب [ʔinrikab] *p:* These passengers got on in Kirkuk. هَالرُّكّاب صِعَدَوا بكَركُوك [harrukka:b ṣiʕadaw bkarku:k] • **2.** لِبَس [libas] لِبِس [libis] *vn:* اِنلِبَس [ʔinlibas] *p:* Help me get my coat on. ساعِدنِي أَلبَس قَبُوطِي [sa:ʕidni ʔalbas qappu:ṭi] • **3.** اِستَمَرّ [ʔistamarr] اِستِمرار [ʔistimra:r] *vn: sv* i. Get on with your work. Don't mind me. اِستِمِرّ بِشُغلَك لا تدِيرلِي بال [ʔistimirr bišuɣlak la: ddi:rli ba:l]

to get out • **1.** طِلَع [ṭilaʕ] طُلُوع [ṭulu:ʕ] *vn:* اِنطِلَع [ʔinṭilaʕ] *p:* I got out of the office at five. طِلَعِت مِن الدّائِرَة بِالخَمسَة [ṭilaʕit min ʔidda:ʔira bilxamsa] We must not let this news get out. ما لازِم نخَلِّي هَالخَبَر يِطلَع [ma: la:zim nxalli halxabar yiṭlaʕ] • **2.** طَلَّع [ṭallaʕ] تَطلِيع [taṭli:ʕ] *vn:* تطَلَّع [ʔiṭṭallaʕ] *p:* Get this beggar out of the store. طَلِّع هَالمجَدِّي مِن الدُّكّان [ṭalliʕ halmjaddi min ʔiddukka:n] • **3.** خِلَص [xilaṣ] خَلاص [xala:ṣ] *vn: sv* a. خَلَّص [xallaṣ] تَخلِيص، تخَلَّص [taxli:ṣ, txallaṣ] *vn: sv* i. He got out of it by paying a fine. خِلَص مِنها بدَفِع غَرامَة [xilaṣ minha bdafiʕ ɣara:ma] • **4.** وَخَّر [waxxar] تَوخِير [tawxi:r] *vn: sv* i. اتوَخَّر [ʔitwaxxar] تَوَخُّر [tawaxxur] *vn: sv* a. Get out of my way! وَخِّر مِن دَربِي [waxxir min darbi] • **5.** حَصَّل [ħaṣṣal] تَحصِيل [taħṣi:l] *vn:* تحَصَّل [tħaṣṣal] *p:* You can't get much out of him. ما تِقدَر تحَصِّل مِنَّه شِي [ma: tigdar tħaṣṣil minnah ši] • **6.** حَصَّل [ħaṣṣal] تَحصِيل [taħṣi:l] *vn:* تحَصَّل [tħaṣṣal] *p:* رُبَح [rubaħ] رِبِح [ribiħ] *vn:* اِنرُبَح [ʔinrubaħ] *p:* How much did you get out of this deal? شقَدّ حَصَّلِت بهالصَّفقَة [šgadd ħaṣṣalit bhaṣṣafqa] • **7.** نِزَل [nizal] نِزُول [nizu:l] *vn: sv* i. I'll have to get out at the next stop. لازِم أَنزِل بالمَوقِف الجّاي [la:zim ʔanzil bilmawqif ʔijja:y]

*** How much can I get out of this camera?** • **1.** هَالكامِرَة شقَدّ راح تجِيبلِي؟ [halkamira: šgadd ra:ħ tji:bli?]

to get over • **1.** تخَلَّص مِن [txallaṣ min] تَخَلُّص مِن [taxalluṣ min] *vn: sv* a. I had a cold, but I'm getting over it now. كانَت عِندِي نَشلَة لَكِن دَاتخَلَّص مِنها هَسَّة [ča:nat ʕindi našla la:kin daʔatxallaṣ minha hassa] • **2.** تخَلَّص مِن [txallaṣ min] تَخلِيص مِن [taxli:ṣ min] *vn: sv* i. He still hasn't gotten over his wife's death. بَعدَه ما طَلَّع موت مَرتَه مِن فِكرَه [baʕdah ma: ṭallaʕ mawt martah min fikrah] • **3.** تنَحَّى [tnaħħa:] تَنَحِّي [tanaħħi] *vn: sv* a. توَخَّر [twaxxar] تَوَخُّر [tawaxxur] *vn: sv* a. Get over a little. Let me sit down. تنَحَّى شوَيَّة، خَلِّي أَقعُد [tnaħħa: šwayya, xalli ʔagʕud]

to get rid of • **1.** تخَلَّص مِن [txallaṣ min] تَخَلُّص مِن [taxalluṣ min] *vn: sv* a. How can I get rid of him? شلُون أَقدَر أَتخَلَّص مِنَّه؟ [šlu:n ʔagdar ʔatxallaṣ minnah?]

to get through • **1.** اِنتِهَى [ʔintiha:] انتِهاء [ʔintiha:ʔ] *vn: sv* i. خَلَّص [xallaṣ] تخِلِّص [txilliṣ] *vn: sv* i. Can you get through in two hours? تِقدَر تخَلِّص بساعتَين؟ [tigdar txalliṣ bsa:ʕtayn?] • **2.** فات [fa:t] فَوت [fawt] *vn: sv* u. مَرّ مِن [marr min] مَرّ، مُرُور [marr, muru:r] *vn: sv* u. You can't get through here. ما تِقدَر تفُوت مِن هنا [ma: tigdar tfu:t min hna]

to get together • **1.** تلاقَى [tla:ga:] تَلاقِي [tala:gi] *vn: sv* a. اِجتِمَع [ʔijtimaʕ] اِجتِماع [ʔijtima:ʕ] *vn: sv* i. Let's get together during lunch. خَلِّي نِتلاقَى وَقِت الغَدا [xalli: nitla:ga: wakit ʔilɣada] • **2.** اِتَّفَق [ʔittifaq] اِتِّفاق [ʔittifa:q] *vn: sv* i. We weren't able to get together on a good solution. ما قِدَرنا نِتِّفِق عَلَى حَلّ زين [ma: gidarna nittifiq ʕala ħall zi:n]

to get up • **1.** قام [ga:m] قَوم [gawm] *vn: sv* u. قِعَد [giʕad] قَعدَة [gaʕda] *vn: sv* u. I get up at six every morning. آني أَقعُد يَومِيّاً السّاعَة سِتَّة الصُّبُح [ʔa:ni ʔagʕud yawmiyyan ʔissa:ʕa sitta ʔiṣṣubuħ] • **2.** قَعَّد [gaʕʕad] تقِعِّد [tgiʕʕid] *vn:* تقَعَّد [tgaʕʕad] *p:* فَزَّز [fazzaz] تفِزِّز [tfizziz] *vn:* تفَزَّز [tfazzaz] *p: sv* i. Would you get me up in the morning, please? باللّه ما تقَعِّدني الصُّبُح رَجاءاً؟ [ballah maː tgaʕʕidni ʔiṣṣubuħ rajaːʔan?] • **3.** صِعَد [ṣiʕad] صَعِد [ṣaʕid] *vn:* اِنصِعَد [ʔinṣiʕad] *p:* We had a hard time getting up the hill. لاقينا صُعُوبَة بِصَعدَة الجِّبَل [laːqiːna ṣuʕuːba bṣaʕdat ʔijjibal]

ghost • **1.** رُوح [ruːħ] أرواح [ʔarwaːħ] *pl:* شَبَح [šabaħ] أشباح [ʔašbaːħ] *pl:* I don't believe in ghosts. ما أعتِقِد بالأرواح [maː ʔaʕtiqid bilʔarwaːħ] He read a story about the Holy Ghost. قِرا قُصَّة عَن الرُّوح القُدُس [qiraː quṣṣa ʕan ʔirruːħ ʔilqudus] He hasn't a ghost of a chance in this matter. ما إلَه وَلا شَبَح أمَل بهَالقَضِيَّة [maː ʔilah wala šabaħ ʔamal bhalqaðiyya]

G

ghoul • **1.** غُول [ɣuːl] غِيلان [ɣiːlaːn] *pl:*

giant • **1.** عِملاق [ʕimlaːq] عَمالِقَة [ʕamaːliqa] *pl:* Compared to me, he's a giant. بِالنِّسبَة إلِي، هُوَّ عِملاق [binnisba ʔili, huwwa ʕimlaːq]

Gibraltar • **1.** جَبَل طارِق [jabal ṭaːriq]

gift • **1.** هَدِيَّة [hadiyya] هَدَايا [hadaːya] *pl:* Thank you for your nice gift. أشكُرَك عَلَى هَدِيّتَك اللَّطِيفَة [ʔaškurak ʕala hadiyytak ʔillaṭiːfa] • **2.** مَوهِبَة [mawhiba] مَواهِب [mawaːhib] *pl:* He has a gift for drawing. عِندَه مَوهِبَة بِالرَّسِم [ʕindah mawhiba birrasim]

gifted • **1.** مَوهُوب [mawhuːb] مُلهَم [mulham] He's a gifted boy. هُوَّ وَلَد مَوهُوب [huwwa walad mawhuːb]

to giggle • **1.** كَركَر [karkar] تكِركِر [tkirkir] *vn: sv* i. The girls kept on giggling. البَنات ظَلَّوا يكَركِرُون [ʔilbanaːt ðallaw ykarkiruːn]

ginger • **1.** سكَنجَبِيل [skanjabiːl]

giraffe • **1.** زَرافَة [zaraːfa] زَرافات [zaraːfaːt] *pl:*

girder • **1.** شَيلمانَة [šiːlmaːna] شَيلمانات [šiːlmanaːt] *pl:* شَيلمان [šiːlmaːn] *Collective:* They reinforced the roof with girders. قَوّوا السَّقُف بِشَيلمان [qawwaw ʔissaguf bšiːlmaːn]

girdle • **1.** كُورسَي [kursay] كُورسَيهات [kursayhaːt] *pl:* She went in to buy a girdle. دِخلَت تِشتِري كُورسَي [dixlat tištiri kuːrsay]

girl • **1.** بِنت [bint] بَنات [banaːt] *pl:* بنَيَّة [bnayya] بنَيّات [bnayyaːt] *pl:* That girl is nice. هالبِنت لَطِيفَة [halbint laṭiːfa]

girlfriend • **1.** صَدِيقَة [ṣadiːqa] صَدِيقات [ṣadiːqaːt] *pl:* She went to the movie with her girlfriends. راحَت لِلسِّينَما ويّا صَدِيقاتها [raːħat lissinama wiyya ṣadiːqaːtha]

to give • **1.** نِطَى [niṭaː] نَطِي [naṭy] *vn:* اِنِّطَى [ʔinniṭaː] *p:* Please give me the letter. أرجُوك إنطِينِي المَكتُوب [ʔarjuːk ʔinṭiːni ʔilmaktuːb] I'll give you five dollars for it. رَح أنطِيك بِيها خَمِس دُولارات [raħ ʔanṭiːk biːha xamis dulaːraːt] • **2.** وِهَب [wihab] وَهِب [wahib] *vn:* اِنوِهَب [ʔinwihab] *p:* The king gave a car to the foreign minister in recognition of his service. المَلِك وِهَب سَيّارَة لِوَزِير الخارِجِيَّة كَاعتِراف بِخَدَماتَه [ʔilmalik wihab sayyaːra liwaziːr ʔilxaːrijiyya kaʔiʕtiraːf bxadamaːtah] • **3.** تبَرَّع ب [tbarraʕ b-] تَبَرُّع [tabarruʕ] *vn: sv* a. We gave money to the poor. إنطَينا فلُوس لِلفُقرَة [ʔinṭayna fluːs lilfuqra] • **4.** بَلَّغ [ballaɣ] تَبلِيغ، إبلاغ [tabliːɣ, ʔiblaːɣ] *vn:* تبَلَّغ [tballaɣ] *p:* Give him my regards. بَلّغَه تَحِيّاتِي [balliɣah taħiyyaːti] • **5.** سَبَّب ل [sabbab l-] تَسبِيب، تسِبِّب [tasbiːb, tsibbib] *vn: sv* i. This noise gives me a headache. هَالصَّوت يسَبِّبلِي وُجَع راس [haṣṣawt ysabbibli wujaʕ raːs] This fellow gives me a lot of trouble. هَالشَّخِص دَيسَبِّبلِي هوايَة مَشاكِل [haššaxiṣ daysabbibli hwaːya mašaːkil] • **6.** ألقَى [ʔalqaː] إلقاء [ʔilqaːʔ] *vn:* اِنلَقَى [ʔinlaqaː] *p:* قَدَّم [qaddam] تَقدِيم [taqdiːm] *vn:* تقَدَّم [tqaddam] *p:* Who's giving the speech this evening? مِنُو راح يلقِي الخِطاب هالمِسَا؟ [minu raːħ yilqi ʔilxiṭaːb halmasa?] • **7.** تحَلحَل [tħalħal] تَحَلحُل [taħalħul] *vn: sv* a. The window's stuck; it won't give. الشُّبّاك مشَكَّل، ما يِتحَلحَل [ʔiššubbaːč mšakkil, maː yitħalħal]

to give away • **1.** فِشَى [fišaː] إفشاء [ʔifšaːʔ] *vn:* اِنفِشَى [ʔinfišaː] *p:* باح ب [baːħ b-] بَوح [buːħ] *vn:* إنباح [ʔinbaːħ] *p:* Don't give away my secret! لا تِفشِي سِرِّي [laː tifši sirri]

to give back • **1.** رَجَّع ل [rajjaʕ l-] تَرجِيع [tarjiːʕ] *vn:* ترَجَّع [trajjaʕ] *p:* رَدّ ل [radd l-] رُدُود [ruduːd] *pl:* رَدّ [radd] *vn:* اِنرَدّ [ʔinradd] *p:* Please give me back my pen. رَجِّعلِي قَلَم الحِبِر مالِي مِن فَضلَك [rajjiʕli qalam ʔilħibir maːli min faðlak]

to give in • **1.** أذعَن [ʔaðʕan] إذعان [ʔiðʕaːn] *vn: sv* a. Don't give in to your son every time he asks for something. لا تِذعَن لإبنَك كُلّ وَقِت يُطلُب مِنَّك شِي [laː tiðʕan lʔibnak kull wakit yuṭlub minnak ši]

to give off • **1.** نِطَى [niṭaː] نَطِي [naṭy] *vn:* اِنِّطَى [ʔinniṭaː] *p: sv* i. بِعَث [biʕaθ] بَعِث [baʕiθ] *vn:* اِنبِعَث [ʔinbiʕaθ] *p: sv* a. This flower gives off a strange odor. هَالوَرد دَينطِي رِيحَة غَرِيبَة [halwarid dayinṭi riːħa ɣariːba]

to give out • **1.** وَزَّع [ʔiwazzaʕ] تَوزِيع، تَوَزِّع [tawziːʕ, twazziʕ] *vn:* توَزَّع [twazzaʕ] *p:* Who's giving out the candy? مِنُو دَيوَزِّع الحَلَوِيّات؟ [minu daywazziʕ ʔilħalawiyyaːt?] • **2.** خِلَص [xilaṣ] خَلاص [xalaːṣ] *vn: sv* a. My supply of ink is giving out. الحِبِر المَوجُود عِندِي دَيخلَص [ʔilħibir ʔilmawjuːd ʕindi dayixlaṣ]

to give up • **1.** بَطَّل [baṭṭal] تبَطِّل [tbaṭṭil] *vn: sv* i. تِرَك [tirak] تَرِك [tarik] *vn:* اِنتِرَك [ʔintirak] *p:* I'm going to give up smoking. راح أبَطِّل التَّدخِين [raːħ ʔabaṭṭil ʔittadxiːn] • **2.** سَلَّم [sallam] تَسلِيم، تسِلِّم [tasliːm, tsillim] *vn: sv* i. The police gave him twenty-four hours to give up. الشُّرطَة إنطُوه مُهلَة أربَعَة وَعِشرِين ساعَة حَتَّى يسَلِّم

[ʔiššurṭa ʔinṭu:h muhlat ʔarbaʕa wʕišri:n sa:ʕa ħatta ysallim] • **3.** أَيَّس [ʔayyas] تِيَّس [tʔiyyis] *vn: sv* i. After ten days searching for him, we gave up. بَعَد عَشرَة أَيّام ندَوِّر عَليه، أَيَّسنا [baʕad ʕašrat ʔayya:m ndawwir ʕali:h, ʔayyasna]

to give way • **1.** اِنخِسَف [ʔinxisaf] اِنخِساف [ʔinxisa:f] *vn: sv* i. خِسَف [xisaf] خَسِف [xasif] *vn: sv* i. While he was walking the ground gave way, and he fell in a big hole. لَمّا كان يمشي اِنخِسفت بيه القاع وَوُقع بنُقرَة كبيرَة [lamma ča:n yimši ʔinxisfat bi:h ʔilga:ʕ wwugaʕ bnugra čbi:ra]

given • **1.** مُعَيَّن [muʕayyan] مُحَدَّد [muħaddad] I have to finish it in a given time. لازِم أَخَلِّصها بخِلال وَقِت مُعَيَّن [la:zim ʔaxallişha bxila:l wakit muʕayyan]

gizzard • **1.** حُوصلَة [ħu:şla] حَوصلات، حَواصِل [ħu:şla:t, ħawa:şil] *pl:* Faisal likes to eat chicken gizzards. فَيصَل يحِبّ ياكُل حَواصِل دِجاج [fayşal yħibb ya:kul ħawa:şil diǰa:ǰ]

glad • **1.** فَرحان [farħa:n] فَرحانين [farħa:ni:n] *pl:* The children were glad to see us. الأَطفال كانَوا فَرحانين يشُوفُونا [ʔilʔaṭfa:l ča:naw farħa:ni:n yšu:fu:na] • **2.** مِن سُرُور [min suru:r] سَرّ [sarr] I'll be glad to help you. مِن سُرُورِي أَساعدَك [min suru:ri ʔasa:ʕdak]

gladly • **1.** بكُلّ سُرُور [bkull suru:r] بمَمنُونيَّة [bimamnu:niyya] Would you do me a favor? Gladly! أَكَلِّفَك بفَدّ شِي تسَوِّيه؟ بكُلّ سُرُور [ʔakallfak bfadd ši tsawwi:h? bkull suru:r]

glance • **1.** نَظرَة [naḍ̣ra] نَظرات [naḍ̣ra:t] *pl:* At a glance I knew something was wrong. بنَظرَة وِحدَة عرَفِت كان أَكُو فَدّ شِي مُو تَمام [bnaḍ̣ra wiħda ʕrafit ča:n ʔaku fadd ši mu: tama:m]

to glance • **1.** باوَع [ba:waʕ] مُباوَعَة [muba:waʕa] *vn: sv* i. I glanced at my watch. باوَعِت بساعتِي [ba:waʕit bsa:ʕti]

to glance off • **1.** اِنحِرَف [ʔinħiraf] اِنحِراف [ʔinħira:f] *vn: sv* i. The bullet hit a rock and glanced off. الطَّلقَة ضُربَت الصَّخرَة وَاِنحِرفَت [ʔiṭṭalqa ḍ̣urbat ʔişşaxra wʔinħirfat]

gland • **1.** غُدَّة [ɣudda] غُدَد [ɣudad] *pl:*

glare • **1.** لَمَعان [lamaʕa:n] بَرِيق [bari:q] The glare hurts my eyes. اللَّمَعان يأَذّي عيُونِي [ʔillamaʕa:n yʔaḍ̣ḍi ʕyu:ni] • **2.** خَزرَة [xazra] خَزرات [xazra:t] *pl:* He gave me a glare when I entered. خِزَرنِي خَزرَة لَمّا دخَلِت [xizarni xazra lamma dxalit]

to glare • **1.** سِطَع [siṭaʕ] سَطِع [saṭiʕ] *vn: sv* a. لِمَع [limaʕ] لَمَعان [lamaʕa:n] *vn: sv* a. The sunlight glared off the surface of the water. ضُوَا الشَّمِس سِطَع مِن وِجه المَيّ [ḍ̣uwa ʔiššamis siṭaʕ min wiǰh ʔilmayy] • **2.** خَنزَر [xanzar] تخِنزِر [txinzir] *vn: sv* i. خِزَر [xizar] خَزِر [xazir] *vn: sv* i. Why are you glaring at me like that? لُويش دَتخَنزِر عَلَيّا هَالشِّكِل؟ [luwi:š datxanzir ʕalayya haššikil?]

glaring • **1.** لَمّاع [lamma:ʕ] ساطِع [sa:ṭiʕ] How can you work in that glaring light? شلُون تِقدَر تِشتُغُل بهَالضُّوَة الساطِع؟ [šlu:n tigdar tištuɣul bhaḍ̣ḍ̣uwa ʔişşa:ṭiʕ?]

glass • **1.** قزِيز [gzi:z] زُجاج [zuǰa:ǰ] This pitcher is made of glass. هَالدُّولكَة مِن قزِيز [haddu:lka min gzi:z] • **2.** گلاص [gla:ş] گلاصات [gla:şa:t] *pl:* Bring me a glass of water. جِيبلِي فَدّ گلاص مَيّ [ǰi:bli fadd gla:ş mayy] • **3.** زُجاجِي [zuǰa:ǰi] Some acids must be kept in glass containers. بَعَض الحَوامِض لازِم تِنحُفُظ بأَوعِيَة زُجاجِيَّة [baʕaḍ̣ ʔilħawa:miḍ̣ la:zim tinħufuḍ̣ biʔawʕiya zuǰa:ǰiyya]

glasses • **1.** مَنظَرَة [manḍ̣ara] مَناظِر [mana:ḍ̣ir] *pl:* I can't read without glasses. ما أَقدَر أَقرا بِلا مَناظِر [ma: ʔagdar ʔaqra: bila mana:ḍ̣ir]

gleam • **1.** بَرِيق [bari:q] لَمَعان [lamaʕa:n] There was a gleam in his eye. كان أَكُو بَرِيق بعَينَه [ča:n ʔaku bari:q bʕaynah]

to gleam • **1.** لِمَع [limaʕ] لَمَعان [lamaʕa:n] *vn: sv* a. بِرَق [biraq] بَرِق، بَرِيق [bariq, bari:q] *vn: sv* i. The floor was gleaming. القاع كانَت دَتبرِق [ʔilga:ʕ ča:nat datibrig]

glider • **1.** طَيّارَة شِراعِيَّة [ṭayya:ra šira:ʕiyya] طَيّارات شِراعِيَّة [ṭayya:ra:t šira:ʕiyya] *pl:*

glisten • **1.** تَلالَى [tlaʔlaʔ] تَلالُو [talaʔluʔ] *vn: sv* a. تألَّق [tʔallaq] تَألُّق [taʔalluq] *vn: sv* a. لِمَع [limaʕ] لَمَعان [lamaʕa:n] *vn: sv* a. شَعّ [šaʕʕ] شُعاع [šuʕa:ʕ] *vn: sv* i. The stars were glistening in the sky. النِّجُوم كانَت تِتلالَى بالسِّما [ʔinniǰu:m ča:nat titlaʔla bissima]

globe • **1.** كُرَة أَرضِيَّة [kura ʔarḍ̣iyya] كُرات أَرضِيَّة [kura:t ʔarḍ̣iyya] *pl:* The teacher brought a globe to class for our geography lesson. المُعَلِّم جاب كُرَة أَرضِيَّة لِدَرس الجُغرافِيَة مالنا [ʔilmuʕallim ǰa:b kura ʔarḍ̣iyya lidars ʔiǰǰuɣra:fiya ma:lna]

gloomy • **1.** مدَلهِم [mdalhim] Yesterday was a gloomy day. البارحَة كانَت الدِّنيا مدَلهِمَة [ʔilba:rħa ča:nat ʔiddinya mdalhima] • **2.** مدَلهِم [mdalhim] كَئِيب [kaʔi:b] He's always gloomy. هُوَّ دائِماً مدَلهِم [huwwa dyudda[ɣudɣudda:ʔiman mdalhim] He's always gloomy. هُوَّ دائِماً قالُب وِجَّه [huwwa da:ʔiman ga:lub wiččah]

glorious • **1.** رائِع [ra:ʔiʕ] بَدِيع [badi:ʕ] فاخِر [fa:xir] لَطِيف [laṭi:f] We spent a glorious day at the fair.

قضَينا يوم رائِع بِالمَعرَض [gðiːna yuːm raːʔiʕ bilmaʕrað] • **2.** مَجِيد [majiːd] Yesterday was a glorious day in the history of the country. البارحَة كان يوم مَجِيد بتاريخ البَلَد [ʔilbaːrħa čaːn yuːm majiːd btaːriːx ʔilbalad]

glory • **1.** مَجد [majd] عَظَمَة [ʕaðama] He spoke on the glory of our ancestors. حِكَى عَن مَجد أجدادنا [ħičaː ʕan majd ʔajdaːdna]

glove • **1.** كَفّ [čaff] كفُوف [čfuːf] *pl:* I bought a pair of gloves yesterday. اِشتِرَيت زوج كفُوف البارحَة [ʔištiriːt zuːj čfuːf ʔilbaːrħa]

*** This suit fits him like a glove.**

• **1.** هَالبَدلَة راهمَة عَلَيه مِثل المِحبَس [halbadla raːhma ʕaliːh miθl ʔilmiħbas]

glove compartment • **1.** جَكمَجَة [čakmača] جَكمَجات [čakmačaːt] *pl:*

glue • **1.** صَمُغ [ṣamuɣ] صُمُوغ [ṣumuːɣ] *pl:* شريس [šriːs, šriːṣ] I bought a bottle of glue. اِشتِرَيت شِيشَة صَمُغ [ʔištiriːt šiːšat ṣamuɣ]

to glue • **1.** لِزَق [lizag] لَزِق [lazig] *vn:* اِنلِزَق [ʔinlizag] *p:* صَمَّغ [ṣammaɣ] تصُمُّغ [tṣummuɣ] *vn:* تصَمَّغ [tṣammaɣ] *p:* He glued the two boards together. لِزَق اللّوحتَين سُوَة [lizag ʔilluːħtayn suwa]

*** She stood glued to the spot.** • **1.** وُقفَت مبَسمرَة [wugfat mbasumra]

glutton • **1.** شَرِه [šarih] نَهِم [nahim] نَهِمِين [nahimiːn] *pl:* Don't be such a glutton. لا تكُون هَالقَدّ شَرِه [laː tkuːn halgadd šarih]

*** He's a glutton for punishment.**

• **1.** هُوَّ مِثل الكَلِب الِّي يِحِبّ دامغَه [huwwa miθl ʔiččalib ʔilli yiħibb daːmɣah]

to gnash • **1.** قَزقَز [gazgaz] تقِزقِز [tgizgiz] *vn:* *sv* i. He gnashed his teeth. قَزقَز سنُونَه [gazgaz snuːnah]

to gnaw • **1.** قِرَض ب [girað b-] قَرِض [garið] *vn:* اِنقِرَض [ʔingirað] *p:* A mouse was gnawing at the rope. فَدّ فارَة كانَت تِقرُض بالحَبِل [fadd faːra čaːnat tigruð bilħabil] • **2.** قَرمَط ب [garmaṭ b-] تقُرمُط [tgurmuṭ] *vn:* تقَرمَط [tgarmaṭ] *p:* The dog gnawed the bone. الكَلِب قَرمَط العَظُم [ʔiččalib garmaṭ ʔilʕaðum]

to go • **1.** راح [raːħ] رَوحَة [rawħa] *vn:* اِنراح [ʔinraːħ] *p:* I go to the movies once a week. أَرُوح لِلسِّينَما مَرَّة بِالإِسبُوع [ʔaruːħ lissinama marra bilʔisbuːʕ] • **2.** مِشَى [mišaː] مَشِي [mašy] *vn:* اِنمِشَى [ʔinmišaː] *p:* *sv* i. This train goes to Baghdad. هَالقِطار يرُوح لِبَغداد [halqiṭaːr yiruːħ lbaɣdaːd] • **3.** مِشَى [mišaː] انمِشَى [ʔinmišaː] *p:* *sv* i. The car goes sixty miles an hour. السَّيّارَة تِمشِي سِتِّين مِيل بِالسّاعَة [ʔissayyaːra timši sittiːn miːl bissaːʕa] Red doesn't go with yellow. الأحمَر ما يِمشِي ويّا الأَصفَر [ʔilʔaħmar maː yimši wiyya ʔilʔaṣfar] • **4.** اِشتِغَل [ʔištiɣal] اِشتِغال [ʔištiɣaːl] *vn:* *sv* u.

مِشَى [mišaː] *sv* i. This engine won't go on poor gas. هَالمَكِينَة ما تِشتُغُل بِبانزين دُوني [halmakiːna maː tištuɣul bibanziːn duːni] • **5.** مِشَى [mišaː] *sv* i. إِجَى [ʔijaː] مَجِيء [majiːʔ] *vn:* *sv* i. The first line of the poem goes this way. أَوَّل بَيت مِن القَصِيدَة يِمشِي هَالشِّكِل [ʔawwal bayt min ʔilqaṣiːda yimši haššikil] • **6.** جِرَى [jiraː] جَرَيان [jarayaːn] *vn:* *sv* i. مِشَى [mišaː] *sv* i. صار [ṣaːr] صَيرَة [ṣayra] *vn:* *sv* i. Whatever he says goes. اللِّي يقُولَه يِجرِي [ʔilli yguːlah yijri] • **7.** بُقَى [buqaː] بَقاء [baqaːʔ] *vn:* *sv* a. They went without food for three days. بُقَوا بلَيّا أَكِل ثلَث أَيّام [buqaw blayya ʔakil tlaθ ʔayyaːm]

to go ahead • **1.** تفَضَّل [tfaððal] *sv* a. Go ahead and eat. تفَضَّل أُكُل [tfaððal ʔukul] • **2.** اِستَمَرّ [ʔistamarr] اِستِمرار [ʔistimraːr] *vn:* *sv* i. راح [raːħ] *sv* u. I'll just go ahead with what I'm doing. آنِي راح أَستَمِرّ بِالشَّي اللِّي دَأَسَوِّيه [ʔaːni raːħ ʔastamirr bišši ʔilli daʔasawwiːh] I'll just go ahed with what I'm doing. آنِي راح أَرُوح بِفالِي بِالشَّي اللِّي دَأَسَوِّيه [ʔaːni raːħ ʔaruːħ bfaːli bišši ʔilli daʔasawwi]

to go at • **1.** جا [jaː] مَجِيء [majiːʔ] *vn:* *sv* i. You're not going at it the right way. إِنتَ ما دَتِجِيها مِن الطَّرِيق الصَّحِيح [ʔinta maː datijiːha min ʔiṭṭariːq ʔiṣṣaħiːħ] • **2.** راح عَلَى [raːħ ʕala] رَوحَة [rawħa] *vn:* *sv* u. هِجَم عَلَى [hijam ʕala] هُجُوم [hujuːm] *vn:* *sv* i. He went at the man with a knife. هِجَم عَالرِّجّال بِسِكِّينَة [hijam ʕarrijjaːl bisiččiːna]

to go back • **1.** رِجَع [rijaʕ] رُجُوع [rujuːʕ] *vn:* *sv* a. She went back to the house. رِجعَت لِلبَيت [rijʕat lilbayt] This style of architecture in Spain goes back to the time of the Arabs in Andalusia. هَالطِّراز مال البِناء بِإسبانيا يِرجَع لِزَمان العَرَب بالأَندَلُس [haṭṭiraːz maːl ʔilbinaːʔ biʔispaːnya yirjaʕ lizamaːn ʔilʕarab bilʔandalus]

to go back on • **1.** تراجَع عَن [traːjaʕ ʕan] تَراجُع عَن [taraːjuʕ ʕan] *vn:* *sv* a. I never go back on my word. ما أَتراجَع عَن كِلمتِي [maː ʔatraːjaʕ ʕan kilimti]

to go by • **1.** مَرّ [marr] مُرُور [muruːr] *vn:* اِنمَرّ [ʔinmarr] *p:* فات [faːt] فَوتَة [fawta] *vn:* اِنفات [ʔinfaːt] *p:* Are you going by the grocer's on your way to work? راح تمُرّ عالبَقّال بطَرِيقَك لِلشُّغُل؟ [raːħ tmurr ʕalbaggaːl btariːqak liššuɣul?] • **2.** مِشَى عَلَى [mišaː ʕala] مَشِي عَلَى [mašy ʕala] *vn:* اِنمِشَى عَلَى [ʔinmišaː ʕala] *p:* *sv* i. تِبَع [tibaʕ] تَبِع [tabiʕ] *vn:* اِنتِبَع [ʔintibaʕ] *p:* *sv* a. Don't go by this map. لا تِمشِي عَلَى هَالخَرِيطَة [laː timši ʕala halxariːṭa] • **3.** اِستَعمَل [ʔistaʕmal] اِستِعمال [ʔistiʕmaːl] *vn:* *sv* i. He goes by an assumed name. يِستَعمِل إِسِم مُستَعار [yistaʕmil ʔisim mustaʕaːr]

to go down • **1.** نِزَل [nizal] نُزُول [nuzuːl] *vn:* *sv* i. Prices are going down. الأَسعار دَتِنزِل [ʔilʔasʕaːr datinzil] • **2.** غاب [ɣaːb] غَيبَة [ɣayba] *vn:* *sv* i. The sun is going down. الشَّمِس دَتغِيب [ʔiššamis datɣiːb]

to go in • **1.** دِخَل [dixal] دُخُول [duxu:l] *vn:* اِندِخَل [ʔindixal] *p:* خَشّ [xašš] خَشّ [xašš] *vn:* اِنخَشّ [ʔinxašš] *p:* They went in at four o'clock. دِخلَوا السّاعَة أربَعَة [dixlaw ʔissa:ʕa ʔarbaʕa] • **2.** اِشتِرَك [ʔištirak] اِشتِراك [ʔištira:k] *vn: sv* i. تشارَك [tša:rak] تَشارُك، مُشارَكَة [taša:ruk, muša:raka] *vn: sv* a. Would you like to go in with me on this transaction? يِعجبَك تِشتِرِك وِيّايا بِهالصَّفقَة؟ [yiʕijbak tištirik wiyya:ya bhaṣṣafqa?]

to go in for • **1.** اِهتَمّ ب [ʔihtamm b-] اِهتِمام [ʔihtima:m] *vn: sv* a. عِندَه رَغبَة [ʕindah raɣba] I don't go in for sports. ما عِندِي رَغبَة بِالرِّياضَة [ma: ʕindi raɣba birriya:ða]

to go into • **1.** دِخَل ب [dixal b-] دُخُول [duxu:l] *vn:* اِندِخَل [ʔindixal] *p:* خَشّ ب [xašš b-] خَشّ [xašš] *vn:* اِنخَشّ [ʔinxašš] *p:* He went into politics. دِخَل بِالسِّياسَة [dixal bissiya:sa]

to go off • **1.** ثار [θa:r] ثَورَة [θawra] *vn: sv* u. The bomb went off. القُمبُلَة ثارَت [ʔilqumbula θa:rat] • **2.** خِتَم [xitam] خِتام [xita:m] *vn:* اِنخِتَم [ʔinxitam] *p:* We go off the air at ten in the evening. نِختِم الإذاعَة السّاعَة عَشرَة مَساءاً [nixtim ʔilʔiða:ʕa ʔissa:ʕa ʕašra masa:ʔan]

to go on • **1.** اِستَمَرّ [ʔistamarr] اِستِمرار [ʔistimra:r] *vn: sv* i. This can't go on any longer. هاي ما مُمكِن تِستِمِرّ بَعَد أكثَر [ha:y ma: mumkin tistimirr baʕad ʔakθar] • **2.** اِنعِلَق [ʔinʕilag] اِنعِلاق [ʔinʕila:g] *vn: sv* i. The light went on. الضَّوَة اِنعِلَق [ʔiððuwa ʔinʕilag]

* **Go on! I don't believe that.** • **1.** يَزِي عاد ماصَدِّق هَذا [yazi ʕa:d ma: ṣaddig ha:ða]

to go out • **1.** اِنطِفَى [ʔinṭufa:] اِنطِفاء [ʔinṭifa:ʔ] *vn: sv* i. The candle just went out. هَسَّة اِنطُفَت الشَّمعَة [hassa ʔinṭufat ʔiššamʕa] • **2.** طِلَع [ṭilaʕ] طَلعَة [ṭalʕa] *vn: sv* a. He just went out. هَستَوَّة طِلَع [hastawwa ṭilaʕ] • **3.** زال [za:l] زَوال [zawa:l] *vn: sv* u. The use of the horse and buggy went out with the advent of the automobile. اِستِعمال الحِصان والعَربانَة زال بمَجِيئ السَّيّارَة [ʔistiʕma:l ʔilħiṣa:n wilʕaraba:na za:l bmaji:ʔ ʔissayya:ra]

to go over • **1.** راجَع [ra:jaʕ] مُراجَعَة [mura:jaʕa] *vn:* تراجَع [tra:jaʕ] *p:* Let's go over the details once more. خَلِّي نراجِع التَّفاصِيل مَرَّة لُخ [xalli nra:jiʕ ʔittafa:ṣi:l marra lux] • **2.** مِشَى [miša:] مَشِي [mašy] *vn: sv* i. It was a good product, but it didn't go over. كانَت خُوش بِضاعَة لَكِن ما مِشَت [ča:nat xu:š biða:ʕa la:kin ma: mišat] • **3.** عُبَر [ʕubar] عَبُر [ʕabur] *vn:* اِنعُبَر [ʔinʕubar] *p:* We didn't go over the bridge. ما عُبَرنا الجِّسِر [ma: ʕubarna ʔijjisir]

to go through • **1.** عُبَر [ʕubar] عَبُر، عُبُور [ʕabur, ʕubu:r] *vn:* اِنعُبَر [ʔinʕubar] *p:* He went through the red light. عُبَر الضُّوَة الأحمَر [ʕubar ʔiððuwa ʔilʔaħmar] • **2.** مَرّ ب [marr b-] مُرُور [muru:r] *vn: sv* u. That poor woman has gone through a lot of hardships. هالمَرَة المَسكِينَة مَرَّت بمَصايِب هوايَة [halmara ʔilmaski:na marrat bmaṣa:yib hwa:ya]

to go through with • **1.** سَوَّى [sawwa:] تِسوِّي [tsiwwi] *vn:* تسَوَّى [tsawwa:] *p: sv* i نَفَّذ [naffað] تَنفِيذ، تنِفِّذ [tanfi:ð, tniffið] *vn:* اِتنَفَّذ [ʔitnaffað] *p:* Did you go through with your plan? نَفَّذِت خُطَّتَك؟ [naffaðit xuṭṭtak?]

to go under • **1.** غاص [ɣa:ṣ] غَوص [ɣawṣ] *vn:* اِنغاص [ʔinɣa:ṣ] *p:* He went under and drowned. غاص وَغِرَق [ɣa:ṣ waɣirag]

to go up • **1.** صِعَد [ṣiʕad] صَعِد [ṣaʕid] *vn:* اِنصِعَد [ʔinṣiʕad] *p: sv* a. We watched him going up the mountain. باوَعنا عَلَيه يِصعَد الجِّبَل [ba:waʕna ʕali:h yiṣʕad ʔijjibal] • **2.** صِعَد [ṣiʕad] *sv* a. اِرتِفَع [ʔirtifaʕ] اِرتِفاع [ʔirtifa:ʕ] *vn: sv* i. The price of meat is going up. سِعِر اللَّحَم دَيِرتِفِع [siʕir ʔillaħam dayirtifiʕ]

to go with • **1.** رِهَم وِيَّا، مِشَى وِيَّا [riham wiyya, miša wiyya] رَهُم، تَرهِيم [rahum, tarhi:m] *vn: sv* a. مِشَى [miša:] مَشِي [mašy] *vn: sv* i. This tie doesn't go with the suit. هالرِّباط ما يِرهَم وِيَّا القاط [harriba:ṭ ma: yirham wiyya ʔilqa:ṭ] • **2.** تِبَع [tibaʕ] تَبِع، اِتِّباع [tabiʕ, ʔittiba:ʕ] *vn: sv* a. The trip and all that went with it cost me a hundred dinars. السَّفرَة وما يِتبَعها كَلَّفَتنِي مِيَّة دِينار [ʔissafra wma: yitbaʕha kallfatni miyyat dina:r]

goal • **1.** هَدَف [hadaf] أهداف [ʔahda:f] *pl:* غَرَض [ɣarað] أغراض [ʔaɣra:ð] *pl:* مَقصَد [maqṣad] مَقاصِد [maqa:ṣid] *pl:* He has set himself a very high goal. حَطّ قِدّامَه فَدّ هَدَف عالِي [ħaṭṭ gidda:mah fadd hadaf ʕa:li] • **2.** كَول [gu:l] كوال [gwa:l] *pl:* هَدَف [hadaf] أهداف [ʔahda:f] *pl:* Our team made three goals in the first half. فَرِيقنا سَوَّى ثلَث كوال بِالشُّوط الأوَّل [fari:qna sawwa: tlaθ gwa:l biššu:ṭ ʔilʔawwal]

goat • **1.** صَخَل [ṣaxal] صخُول [ṣxu:l] *pl:* عَنز [ʕanz] He raises goats. يرَبِّي صخُول [yrabbi ṣxu:l] • **2.** ضَحِيَّة [ðaħiyya] ضَحايا [ðaħa:ya] *pl:* He's always the goat. هُوَّ دائِماً الضَّحِيَّة [huwwa da:ʔiman ʔiððaħiyya]

* **Don't let him get your goat.** • **1.** لا تخَلِّيه يغُثَّك [la: txalli:h yɣuθθak]

goatee • **1.** لِحيَة كُوسَة [liħya ku:sa] لِحَى كُوسَة [liħa ku:sa] *pl:* He has a goatee. عِندَه لِحيَة كُوسَة [ʕindah liħya ku:sa]

God • **1.** الله [ʔalla:h, ʔallah] إلاه [ʔila:h] آلِهَة [ʔa:liha] *pl:* God forbid. لا سامَح الله [la: sa:maħ ʔalla:h] In the name of God, the Merciful, the Compassionate. بِسمِ اللهِ الرَّحمَنِ الرَّحِيم [bisim ʔallah ʔirraħma:n ʔirraħi:m] God willing. إن شاء الله [ʔin ša:ʔa ʔallah]

god • **1.** إلاه [ʔila:h] آلِهَة [ʔa:liha] *pl:* They worship false gods. يِعبدُون الآلِهَة [yʕibdu:n ʔilʔa:liha]

goggles • **1.** مَناظِر [mana:ðir] مَنظَرَة [manðara] مَناظِر [mana:ðir] *pl:*

G

going • **1.** دارِج [da:rij] ماشِي [ma:ši] جَارِي [ǰa:ri] The going rate on the dinar is two dollars and eighty cents. السِّعِر الدّارِج لِلدِّينار هُوَّ دُولارَين وثمانِين سَنت [ʔissiʕir ʔidda:rij liddina:r huwwa dula:rayn wʔiθma:ni:n sant] • **2.** ماشِ [ma:ši] They have a going concern. عِدهُم شَرِكَة ماشيَة [ʕidhum šarika ma:šya]

going to • **1.** راح [ra:ħ] I'm going to bake a cake. آنِي راح أَطبُخ كَيك [ʔa:ni ra:ħ ʔaṭbux kayk]

goiter • **1.** تَضَخُّم الغُدَّة الدَّرَقِيَّة [taðaxxum ʔilɣudda ʔiddaraqiyya]

G

gold • **1.** ذَهَب [ðahab] Is that real gold? هَذا ذَهَب حَقِيقِي؟ [ha:ða ðahab ħaqi:qi?] • **2.** ذَهَبِي [ðahabi] They awarded him a gold medal. هِدَولَه مَدالِيَة ذَهَبِيَّة [hidu:lah mada:liyya ðahabiyya]

goldsmith • **1.** صايِغ [ṣa:yiɣ] صِيَّاغ [ṣiyya:g] *pl:*

golf • **1.** غُولف [gu:lf]

gonorrhea • **1.** سَيَلان [sayala:n]

good • **1.** فائِدَة [fa:ʔida] فَوائِد [fawa:ʔid] *pl:* مَصلَحَة [maṣlaħa] مَصالِح [maṣa:liħ] *pl:* I did that for your own good. سَوَّيت هَذا لمَصلَحتَك [sawwi:t ha:ða lmaṣlaħtak] • **2.** خَير [xayr] He doesn't know the difference between good and evil. ما يُعرُف الفَرِق بين الخير وَالشَّرّ [ma: yuʕruf ʔilfariq bayn ʔilxayr wʔiššarr] • **3.** زَين [zi:n] مِشَى [miša:] This coupon is good for ten days. هالكُوبَون زين لِمُدَّة عَشرَة أَيّام [halku:pu:n zi:n lmuddat ʕašra ʔayya:m] This coupon is good for ten days. هالكُوبَون يِمشِي لِمُدَّة عَشرَة أَيّام [halku:pu:n yimši limuddat ʕašra ʔayya:m] • **4.** زَين [zayn] خُوش [xu:š] He does good work. يسَوِّي خُوش شُغُل [ysawwi xu:š šuɣul] He does good work. يسَوِّي شُغُل زين [ysawwi šuɣul zi:n] • **5.** خُوش [xu:š] زَين [zi:n] طَيِّب [ṭayyib] The weather isn't good today. الجَوّ مُو طَيِّب اليُوم [ʔiǰǰaww mu: ṭayyib ʔilyu:m] He did me a good turn yesterday. سَوّالِي فَدّ خُوش دَقَّة البارحَة [sawwa:li fadd xu:š dagga ʔilba:rħa] He's from a good family. هُوَّ مِن عائِلَة طَيِّبَة [huwwa min ʕa:ʔila ṭayyba] • **6.** صالِح [ṣa:liħ] He's a good Moslem. هُوَّ مُسلِم صالِح [huwwa muslim ṣa:liħ] • **7.** بِالقَلِيل [bilqali:l] There's a good dozen eggs in the refrigerator. أَكُو بالقَلِيل دَرزَن بَيض بالثَّلاجَة [ʔaku bilqali:l darzan bayð biθθala:ǰa] • **8.** عاقِل [ʕa:qil] زَين [zi:n] زَينِين [zi:ni:n] *pl:* The children were good all day. الأَطفال كانُوا عُقّال طُول اليُوم [ʔilʔaṭfa:l ča:naw ʕuqqa:l ṭu:l ʔilyu:m]

* **One good turn deserves another.** • **1.** زَينِيَّة بزَينِيَّة [zayniyya bzayniyya]

* **If you ask him to do something, it's as good as done.** • **1.** إذا تُطلُب مِنَّه يسَوِّي شِي، اِحسِبَه صار [ʔiða tuṭlub minnah ysawwi ši. ʔiħisbah ṣa:r]

a good deal • **1.** هوايَة [hwa:ya] He spent a good deal of time in Baghdad. قِضى وَقِت هوايَة بِبَغداد [giða: wakit hwa:ya bibaɣda:d]

a good many • **1.** خُوش عَدَد مِن [xu:š ʕadad min] عَدَد زَين مِن [ʕadad zi:n min] There are a good many foreigners in the hotel. أَكُو خُوش عَدَد مِن الأَجانِب بِالأُتِيل [ʔaku xu:š ʕadad min ʔilʔaǰa:nib bilʔuti:l]

a good while • **1.** مُدَّة طوِيلَة [mudda ṭwi:la] I haven't seen him for a good while. ما شِفتَه مِن مُدَّة طوِيلَة [ma: šiftah min mudda ṭwi:la]

for good • **1.** نِهائِيّاً [niha:ʔiyyan] بِالمَرَّة [bilmarra] I've given up smoking for good. قِطَعِت التَّدخِين نِهائِيّاً [qiṭaʕit ʔittadxi:n niha:ʔiyyan]

good and • **1.** كُلِّش [kulliš] Make the tea good and strong. سَوِّي الشاي كُلِّش طُوخ [sawwi ʔičča:y kulliš ṭu:x]

Good Friday • **1.** الجُمعَة العَظِيمَة [ʔiǰǰumʕa ʔilʕaði:ma] الجُمعَة الحَزِينَة [ʔiǰǰumʕa ʔilħazi:na]

not good enough for • **1.** مُو مال [mu: ma:l] These shoes aren't good enough for school. هالحِذاء مُو مال مَدرَسَة [halħiða:ʔ mu: ma:l madrasa] • **2.** مُو مال [mu: ma:l] مُو قَدّ [mu: gadd] This girl's not good enough for him. هالبِنت مُو قَدَّه [halbint mu: gaddah]

to be good • **1.** عِقَل [ʕiqal, ʕigal] *sv* a. Both of you be good when the guests arrive. إنتُو الثنَين عِقلُوا مِن يِجُون الخُطّار [ʔintu liθnayn ʕiqlu: min yiǰu:n ʔilxuṭṭa:r] • **2.** صِلَح [ṣilaħ] صَلاح [ṣala:ħ] *vn: sv* a. This clay is good for making bricks. هالطِّين يِصلَح لِعَمَل الطّابُوق [haṭṭi:n yiṣlaħ liʕamal ʔiṭṭa:bu:g]

to do good • **1.** فاد [fa:d] فائِدَة [fa:ʔida] *vn: sv* i. The vacation did him good. العُطلَة فادَتَه [ʔilʕuṭla fa:datah]

to make good • **1.** سَوَّى زَين [sawwa: zayn] تَسوِّي، تَسوِيَّة [tasiwwi, taswiyya] *vn: sv* i. I'm sure he'll make good in the city. آنِي مِتأَكِّد راح يسَوِّي زين بِالمَدِينَة [ʔa:ni mitʔakkid ra:ħ ysawwi zi:n bilmadi:na] • **2.** وَفَّى [waffa:, wuffa:] *sv* i. وُفَى [wufa:] وَفِي [wafy] *vn: sv* i. He made good his promise. وَفَّى بوَعدَه [waffa: bwaʕdah]

good-bye • **1.** مَعَ السَّلامَة [maʕa ʔissala:ma] فِي أَمان الله [fi: ʔama:n ʔilla:h]

to say good-bye • **1.** وَدَّع [waddaʕ] تَودِيع [tawdi:ʕ] *vn: sv* i. We said good-bye to him at the airport. وَدَّعناه بِالمَطار [waddaʕna:h bilmaṭa:r]

good-for-nothing • **1.** تَلَف [talaf] ما يِسوَى شِي [ma: yiswa: ši] Your brother is a good-for-nothing! أَخُوك ما يِسوَى شِي [ʔaxu:č ma: yiswa: ši]

good-looking • **1.** جَذّاب [ǰaðða:b] حِلو [ħilw] She's a good-looking girl. هِيَّ بنَيَّة حِلوَة [hiyya bnayya ħilwa]

good-natured • **1.** حَبُّوب [ħabbu:b] أَخلاقَه لَطِيفَة [ʔaxla:qah laṭi:fa] خَوش طَبُع [xawš ṭabuʕ] He's good-natured. هُوَّ عِندَه خُوش طَبُع [huwwa ʕindah xu:š ṭabuʕ]

goodness • **1.** خَير [xayr] طِيب [ṭiːb] زينِيَّة [ziːniyya] زينِيّات [ziːniyyaːt] *pl:* She's full of goodness. كُلها طِيب [kulha ṭiːb]

goods • **1.** بِضاعَة [biðaːʕa] بَضايِع [baðaːyiʕ] *pl:* We import many goods from abroad. نِستَورِد بَضايِع هوايَة مِن الخارِج [nistawrid baðaːyiʕ hwaːya min ʔilxaːrij]

goose • **1.** وَزَّة [wazza] وَزّات [wazzaːt] *pl:* وَزّ [wazz] *Collective:* We ate a goose for dinner. أَكَلنا وَزَّة بِالعَشا [ʔakalna wazza bilʕaša]

*** The police are going to cook his goose.**
• **1.** الشُرطَة راح تشُوف شُغُلها ويّاه [ʔiššurṭa raːħ tšuːf šuɣulha wiyyaːh]

gorgeous • **1.** بَدِيع [badiːʕ] زاهي [zaːhi] رائع [raːʔiʕ] It was a gorgeous day. كان فَدّ نَهار بَدِيع [čaːn fadd nahaːr badiːʕ]

gorilla • **1.** غورِيلا [ɣuriːla] غورِيلات [ɣuriːlaːt] *pl:*

gospel • **1.** إِنجِيل [ʔinǰiːl] أَناجِيل [ʔanaːǰiːl] *pl:* He memorized the four gospels. حُفَظ الأَناجِيل الأَربَعَة [ħufaðˌ ʔilʔanaːǰiːl ʔilʔarbaʕa]

gossip • **1.** حَكِي عَالناس [ħači ʕannaːs] حَكِي وَرا الناس [ħači wara ʔinnaːs] She likes to hear gossip. يعِجِبها تِسمَع الحَكِي عالنّاس [yiʕǰibha tismaʕ ʔilħači ʕannaːs]

to gossip • **1.** حِكَى وَرَا النّاس، قِشَب [ħičaː wara ʔinnaːs, qišab] حَكِي وَرَا النّاس، قَشِب [ħači wara ʔinnaːs, qašib] *vn:* *sv* i. قَشَب [qišab] قَشِب، قِشبَة [qašib, qišba] *vn:* *sv* i. She's always gossiping. هِيَّ دائِماً تِحكِي وَرا النّاس [hiyya daːʔiman tiħči wara ʔinnaːs]

got • **1.** عِند [ʕind-] He's got a nice house. عِندَه خُوش بَيت [ʕindah xuːš bayt]

got to • **1.** لازِم [laːzim] I've got to leave now. لازِم أَرُوح هَسَّة [laːzim ʔaruːħ hassa]

gourd • **1.** قَرعَة [qarʕa] قَرعات [qarʕaːt] *pl:* قَرَع [qaraʕ] *Collective:* The colocynth is a variety of gourd. الحَنظَل نُوع مِن القَرَع [ʔilħanðal nuːʕ min ʔilqaraʕ]

to govern • **1.** حِكَم [ħikam] حُكُم [ħukum] *vn:* اِنحِكَم [ʔinħikam] *p:* He governed the country well. هُوَّ حِكَم البَلَد زين [huwwa ħikam ʔilbalad ziːn] • **2.** ضُبَط [ðubaṭ] ضَبُط [ðabuṭ] *vn:* اِنضُبَط [ʔinðubaṭ] *p:* This invention governs the heat of the room. هالإختِراع يُضبُط حَرارَة الغُرفَة [halʔixtiraːʕ yuðbuṭ ħaraːrat ʔilɣurfa]

government • **1.** حُكُومَة [ħukuːma] حُكُومات [ħukuːmaːt] *pl:* Who heads the new government? مِنُو يِرأَس الحُكُومَة الجِّدِيدَة؟ [minu yirʔas ʔilħukuːma ʔiǰǰidiːda?]

governor • **1.** حاكِم [ħaːkim] حُكّام [ħukkaːm] *pl:* I read an article on the governor of New York State. قِريت مَقال عَن حاكِم وِلايَة نيُو يَورك [qiriːt maqaːl ʕan ħaːkim wilaːyat nyuː yuːrk] • **2.** مُتَصَرِّف [mutaṣarrif] مُتَصَرِّفِين [mutaṣarrifiːn] *pl:* The governor of Basra province visited Syria. مُتصَرِّف لِواء البَّصرَة زار سُوريا [mutṣarrif liwaːʔ ʔibbaṣra zaːr suːrya]

gown • **1.** دِشداشَة [dišdaːša] دِشادِيش [dišaːdiːš] *pl:* The boy put the tail of his gown in his mouth and ran. الوَلَد خَلَّى ذيال دِشداشتَه بحَلقَه وَركَض [ʔilwalad xallaː ðyaːl dišdaːštah bħalgah wrikað] • **2.** رُوب [ruːb] إرواب، روابَة [ʔirwaːb, rwaːba] *pl:* The students wore black gowns for graduation. الطُّلّاب لِبسَوا روابَة سُودَة لحَفلَة التَّخَرُّج [ʔiṭṭullaːb libsaw rwaːba suːda lħaflat ʔittaxarruǰ]

evening gown • **1.** سواري [swaːriː] سواريهات [swaːriyhaːt] *pl:*

to grab • **1.** لِزَم [lizam] لَزِم [lazim] *vn:* اِنلِزَم [ʔinlizam] *p:* لِقَف [ligaf] لَقُف [laguf] *vn:* اِنلِقَف [ʔinligaf] *p:* The police grabbed the thief in the market. الشُرطَة لِزمَت الحَرامي بالسُّوق [ʔiššurṭa lizmat ʔilħaraːmi bissuːg] • **2.** تناوَش [tnaːwaš] تَناوُش [tanaːwuš] *vn:* *sv* a. لِقَف [ligaf] لَقُف [laguf] *vn:* اِنلِقَف [ʔinligaf] *p:* *sv* u. He grabbed a bottle off the shelf. تناوَش فَدّ بُوطِل مِن الرَّفّ [tnaːwaš fadd buṭul min ʔirraff] • **3.** هِمَش [himaš] هَمِش [hamiš] *vn:* اِنهِمَش [ʔinhimaš] *p:* *sv* i. Don't grab. You'll get your share. لا تِهمِش راح تاخُذ حُصّتَك [laː tihmiš raːħ taːxuð ħuṣṣṭak]

grace • **1.** رَشاقَة [rašaːqa] خِفَّة [xiffa] She walks with grace. تِمشِي بِرَشاقَة [timši brašaːqa] • **2.** وِدّ [widd] He wants to get into her good graces. يرِيد يِكسِب وِدّها [yriːd yiksib widdha]

to say grace • **1.** سَمَّى [sammaː] تَسمِيَة [tasmiya] *vn:* *sv* i. Say grace before you eat! سَمِّي قَبُل ما تاكُل [sammi gabul maː taːkul]

grade • **1.** دَرَجَة [daraǰa] دَرَجات [daraǰaːt] *pl:* He received the highest grades in the class. حَصَّل عَلَى أَعلَى دَرَجات بِالصَّفّ [ħaṣṣal ʕala ʔaʕla daraǰaːt biṣṣaff] • **2.** صَفّ [ṣaff] صفُوف [ṣfuːf] *pl:* What grade is your son in? بيا صَفّ إبنَك؟ [biyaː ṣaff ʔibnak?] • **3.** صِنِف [ṣinif] Do you have a better grade of wool than this? عِندَك صِنِف صُوف أَحسَن مِن هَذا؟ [ʕindak ṣinif ṣuːf ʔaħsan min haːða?] • **4.** اِنحِدار [ʔinħidaːr] اِنحِدارات [ʔinħidaːraːt] *pl:* عَلوَة [ʕalwa] عَلاوي [ʕalaːwi] *pl:* The truck couldn't climb the grade. اللُّوري ما قِدَر يِصعَد الانحِدار [ʔilluːri maː gidar yiṣʕad ʔilʔinħidaːr]

*** He'll never make the grade.** • **1.** مُستَحِيل يِقدَر يدَبُّرها [mustaħiːl yigdar ydabburha]

to grade • **1.** صَنَّف [ṣannaf] تصِنِّف، تَصنِيف [tṣinnif, taṣniːf] *vn:* تصَنَّف [tṣannaf] *p:* *sv* i. We grade potatoes according to size. نصَنِّف البُتَيتَة حَسَب الكُبُر [nṣannif ʔilputayta ħasab ʔilkubur] • **2.** عَدَّل [ʕaddal] تعِدِّل، تَعدِيل [tʕiddil, taʕdiːl] *vn:* تعَدَّل [tʕaddal] *p:* They're grading the road. يعَدِّلُون الطَّرِيق [yʕaddiluːn ʔiṭṭariːq]

gradual • **1.** تَدرِيجِي [tadriːǰi] I noticed a gradual improvement. لاحَظِت تَقَدُّم تَدرِيجِي [laːħaðit taqaddum tadriːǰi]

gradually • **1.** بِالتَدرِيج [bittadriːǰ] He's gradually getting better. دَيتحَسَّن بِالتَّدرِيج [dayitħassan bittadriːǰ]

graduate • **1.** خِرِّيج [xirriːǰ] مِتخَرِّج [mitxarriǰ] Most of the graduates of our university have good positions. أكثَر الخِرِّيجِين مِن جامِعَتنا عِدهُم وَظايِف زينَة [ʔakθar ʔilxirriːǰiːn min ǰaːmiʕatna ʕidhum waðaːyif ziːna] • **2.** عالِي [ʕaːli] He is doing graduate study in America. دَيدرُس دِراسَة عالِيَة بأمِيركا [dayidrus diraːsa ʕaːlya bʔamriːka]

to graduate • **1.** خَرَّج [xarraǰ] تَخرِيج، تخِرِّج [taxriːǰ, txirriǰ] *vn:* تخَرَّج [txarraǰ] *p:* Our university graduates four hundred students per years. جامِعَتنا تخَرِّج أربَع مِيَّة طالِب بِالسَّنَة [ǰaːmiʕatna txarriǰ ʔarbaʕ miyyat ṭaːlib bissana]

to be graduated • **1.** تدَرَّج [ddarraǰ] تَدَرُّج [tadarruǰ] *vn: sv* a. Taxes are graduated according to income. الضَّرايِب تِتدَرَّج حَسَب الدَّخَل [ʔiððaraːyib tiddarraǰ ħasab ʔiddaxal]

grain • **1.** حَبَّة [ħabba] حَبّات [ħabbaːt] *pl:* A few grains of salt were on the table. شوَيَّة حَبابِي مِلح كانَت عالميز [šwayyat ħabaːbi miliħ čaːnat ʕalmiːz] • **2.** حَبّ [ħabb] Canada exports meat and grain. كَنَدا تصَدِّر اللُّحُوم والحُبُوب [kanadaː tṣaddir ʔilluħuːm wilħubuːb] • **3.** طَبُع [ṭabuʕ] That goes against my grain. هَذا ضِدّ طَبعِي [haːða ðidd ṭabʕi] • **4.** ذَرَّة [ðarra] There isn't a grain of truth in the story. ماكُو ذَرَّة مِن حَقِيقَة بهَالقُصَّة [maːku ðarra min ħaqiːqa bhalquṣṣa] • **5.** عُرُوق الخِشَب [ʕuruːg ʔilxišab] Don't plane against the grain. لا ترَندِج ضِدّ عرُوق الخِشَب [laː trandiǰ ðidd ʕruːg ʔilxišab]

gram • **1.** غرام [ɣraːm] غرامات [ɣraːmaːt] *pl:* Give me four grams of saffron. إنطِينِي أربَع غرامات زُعفران [ʔinṭiːni ʔarbaʕ ɣraːmaːt zuʕufraːn]

grammar • **1.** قواعِد [qawaːʕid] نَحو [naħw] I never studied Arabic grammar. آنِي أبَد ما درَسِت قواعِد اللُّغَة العَرَبِيَّة [ʔaːni ʔabad maː drasit qawaːʕid ʔilluɣa ʔilʕarabiyya] • **2.** كتاب قواعِد [ktaːb qawaːʕid] كُتُب قواعِد [kutub qawaːʕid] *pl:* Do you have a good grammar for beginners? عِندَك كتاب قَواعِد زين لِلمُبتَدِئِين؟ [ʕindak ktaːb qawaːʕid ziːn lilmubtadiʔiːn?]

grand • **1.** كبِير [čibiːr] The dance will take place in the grand ballroom. حَفلَة الرِّقص راح تصِير بِالقاعَة الكِبِيرَة [ħaflat ʔirriqiṣ raːħ tṣiːr bilqaːʕa ʔiččibiːra] • **2.** كُلِّي [kulli] عامّ [ʕaːmm] The grand total comes to three hundred and seventeen. المَجمُوع الكُلِّي يوَصِّل ثلَث مِيَّة وِسبَعتَعَش [ʔilmaǰmuːʕ ʔilkulli ywaṣṣil tlaθ miyya wisbaʕtaʕaš] • **3.** عَظِيم [ʕaðiːm] عُظَماء [ʕuðamaːʔ] *pl:* مُمتاز [mumtaːz] We saw grand scenery on our way to Europe. شِفنا مَناظِر عَظِيمَة بطَرِيقنا لِأورُبّا [šifna manaːðir ʕaðiːma bṭariːqna liʔuːruppa] That's a grand idea. هَذِي فِكرَة عَظِيمَة [haːði fikra ʕaðiːma]

granddaughter • **1.** حَفِيدَة [ħafiːda] حَفِيدات [ħafiːdaːt] *pl:*

grandfather • **1.** جِدّ [ǰidd] جدُود، أجداد [ǰduːd, ʔaǰdaːd] *pl:*

grandmother • **1.** جِدِّيَّة [ǰiddiyya] جِدِّيّات [ǰiddiyyaːt] *pl:* بِيبِي [biːbi] بِيبِيّات [biːbiyyaːt] *pl:*

grandson • **1.** حَفِيد [ħafiːd] أحفاد [ʔaħfaːd] *pl:*

grant • **1.** مِنحَة [minħa] مِنَح [minaħ] *pl:* He received a grant for further study from the government. اِستِلَم مِن الحُكُومَة مِنحَة لِلإستِمرار بِالدِّراسَة [ʔistilam min ʔilħukuːma minħa lilistimraːr biddiraːsa]

to grant • **1.** مِنَح [minaħ] مَنِح [maniħ] *vn:* اِنمِنَح [ʔinminaħ] *p:* They granted us the entire amount. مِنحَونا المَبلَغ بكامله [minħuːna ʔilmablaɣ bkaːmlah] • **2.** اِعتِرَف [ʔiʕtiraf] اِعتِراف [ʔiʕtiraːf] *vn: sv* i. سَلَّم [sallam] تسِلِّم، تَسلِيم [tsillim, tasliːm] *vn: sv* i. I grant that I was wrong. آنِي أعتِرِف بأنِّي كِنِت غَلطان [ʔaːni ʔaʕtirif bʔanni činit ɣalṭaːn]

granted • **1.** مَمنُوح [mamnuːħ] The money which was orginally granted has been spent. الفلُوس اللِّي كانَت بالأصِل مَمنُوحَة اِنصُرفَت [ʔilfluːs ʔilli čaːnat bilʔaṣil mamnuːħa ʔinṣurfat] • **2.** مِن المَقبُول [min ʔilmaqbuːl] مِن المُسَلَّم [min ʔilmusallam] Granted that your philosophy is correct, but its application is difficult. مِن المَقبُول أن فَلسَفتَك صَحِيحَة، لَكِن تَطبِيقها صَعُب [min ʔilmaqbuːl ʔan falsaftak ṣaħiːħa, laːkin taṭbiːqha ṣaʕub]

to take for granted • **1.** اِفتِرَض [ʔiftirað] اِفتِراض [ʔiftiraːð] *vn: sv* i. حِسَب [ħisab] حَسِب [ħasib] *vn: sv* i. I took it for granted that he'd be there. اِفتِرَضِت راح يكُون هناك [ʔiftiraðit raːħ ykuːn hnaːk] • **2.** اِستَغَلّ [ʔistaɣall] اِستِغلال [ʔistiɣlaːl] *vn: sv* i. We were friends until he started taking me for granted. كِنّا أصدِقاء إلَى أن بِدا يِستِغِلنِي [činna ʔaṣdiqaːʔ ʔila ʔan bidaː yistiɣillni]

grape • **1.** عِنبَة [ʕinba] عِنبات [ʕinbaːt] *pl:* عِنَب [ʕinab] *Collective*

grapefruit • **1.** سِندِيَّة [sindiyya] سِندِيّات [sindiyyaːt] *pl:* سِندِي [sindi] *Collective*

graph • **1.** رَسِم بَيانِي [rasim baya:ni] رُسُوم بَيانِيَّة [rusu:m baya:niyya] *pl:* خَطّ بَيانِي [xaṭṭ baya:ni] خُطُوط بَيانِيَّة [xuṭu:ṭ baya:niyya] *pl:*

to grasp • **1.** كَلَّب [čallab] تِكلِّب، تَكلِيب [tčillib, tačli:b] *vn:* تكَلَّب [tčallab] *p:* لِزَم [lizam] لَزِم [lazim] *vn:* اِنلِزَم [ʔinlizam] *p:* كُمَش [kumaš] كَمُش [kamuš] *vn:* اِنكُمَش [ʔinkumaš] *p:* لِقَف [ligaf] لَقُف [laguf] *vn:* اِنلِقَف [ʔinligaf] *p:* She grasped the rope with both hands. كَلّبَت بالحَبِل بإيدَينها الثّنتَين [čallbat bilħabil bʔidaynha ʔiθθintayn] • **2.** فِطَن [fiṭan] فَطِن [faṭin] *vn:* اِنفِطَن [ʔinfiṭan] *p:* فِهَم [fiham] فَهِم [fahim] *vn:* اِنفِهَم [ʔinfiham] *p:* Do you grasp what I mean? دَتُفطُن عَاللّي دَأقُولَه؟ [datufṭun ʕalli daʔagu:lah?]

grass • **1.** ثَيِّل [θayyil] Did you cut the grass? قَصَّيت الثَّيِّل؟ [gaṣṣi:t ʔiθθayyil?] • **2.** حَشِيش [ħaši:š] The farmer cut some grass and gave it to the cow. الفَلّاح قَصّ حَشِيش وإنطاه للِهايشَة [ʔilfalla:ħ gaṣṣ ħaši:š wʔinṭa:h lilha:yša] • **3.** عِشِب [ʕišib] The sheep are grazing on grass in the desert. الغَنَم دَتِرعَى العِشِب بالبَرّ [ʔilɣanam datirʕa: ʔilʕišib bilbarr]

grasshopper • **1.** جَرادَة [ǰara:da] جَرادات [ǰara:da:t] *pl:* جَراد [ǰara:d] *Collective*

grate • **1.** شِبكَة [šibča] شِبكات [šibča:t] *pl:* The easiest way to cook the meat is to put a grate on three stones. أسهَل طَرِيقَة لِطَبخ اللَّحَم هِيَّ أنّ تخَلِّي الشِّبكَة عَلَى ثلاث حجارات [ʔashal ṭari:qa liṭabx ʔillaħam hiyya ʔann txalli ʔiššibča ʕala tla:θ ħǰa:ra:t]

to grate • **1.** حَكّ بِرَندَة [ħakk biranda] حَكّ [ħakk] *vn:* *sv* u. Grate the carrots when you have time. حُكِّي الجِّزَر بالرَّندَة لَمّا يكُون عِندِك وَقِت [ħukki ʔiǰǰizar birranda lamma yku:n ʕindič wakit] • **2.** كَزبَر [kazbar] تكَزبُر [tkuzbur] *vn:* *sv* u. The scratching of chalk on a blackboard grates on me. شَخطَة الطَّباشِير عالسَّبُّورَة تكَزبُر جِلدِي [šaxṭat ʔiṭṭaba:ši:r ʕassabbu:ra tkazbur ǰildi]

grateful • **1.** مِمتَنّ [mimtann] شاكِر [ša:kir] مِتشَكِّر [mitšakkir] I'm grateful to you for your help. آني مِمتَنّ إلَك عَلَى مُساعَدتَك [ʔa:ni mimtann ʔilak ʕala musa:ʕadtak]

to gratify • **1.** رَضَّى [raðða:] تَرضِيَة، ترضِّي [tarðiya, triðði] *vn:* *sv* i. شَبَّع [šabbaʕ] تَشبِيع، تشِبِّع [tašbi:ʕ, tšibbiʕ] *vn:* *sv* i. He gratified her every wish. شَبَّع كُلّ رَغبَة مِن رَغباتها [šabbaʕ kull raɣba min raɣba:tha]

gratifying • **1.** مُرضِي [murði] Your grades this semester are very gratifying. دَرَجاتَك هالفَصِل كُلِّش مُرضِيَة [daraǰa:tak halfaṣil kulliš murðiya]

gratitude • **1.** اِمتِنان [ʔimtina:n] شُكُر [šukur] اِعتِراف بالجَّمِيل [ʔiʕtira:f biǰǰami:l] I don't know how to express my gratitude. ما دَأعرُف شلُون أعبُّر عَن اِمتِنانِي [ma: daʔaʕruf šlu:n ʔaʕbbur ʕan ʔimtina:ni]

grave • **1.** قَبُر [gabur] قبُور [gbu:r] *pl:* The coffin was lowered into the grave. التّابُوت اِتنَزَّل بالقَبُر [ʔitta:bu:t ʔitnazzal bilgabur] • **2.** سَيِّء [sayyiʔ] His condition is grave. حالتَه سَيِّئَة [ħa:ltah sayyiʔa] • **3.** فَظِيع [faði:ʕ] That's a grave mistake. ذِيك فَدّ غَلطَة فَظِيعَة [ði:č fadd ɣalṭa faði:ʕa] • **4.** وَخِيم [waxi:m] Children's playing with matches brings grave consequences. لِعِب الأطفال بالشَّخّاط يجِيب عَواقِب وَخِيمَة [liʕib ʔilʔaṭfa:l biššixxa:ṭ yǰi:b ʕawa:qib waxi:ma]

gravel • **1.** حَصُو [ħaṣw] The path is covered with gravel. الطَّرِيق مغَطَّى بالحَصو [ʔiṭṭari:q mɣaṭṭa: bilħaṣw]

gravestone • **1.** مَرمَرَة [marmara] مَرمَرات [marmara:t] *pl:*

graveyard • **1.** مَقبَرَة [maqbara] مَقابُر [maqa:bur] *pl:*

gravity • **1.** جاذِبِيَّة [ǰa:ðibiyya]

gravy • **1.** مَرقَة [marga] مَرقات [marga:t] *pl:* مَرَق [marag] Do you want only gravy on the rice? ترِيد مَرقَة خالِيَة فُوق التِّمَّن؟ [tri:d marga xa:lya fu:g ʔittimman?]

gray • **1.** رِصاصِي [riṣa:ṣi] رُمادِي [ruma:di] Gray and red go together well. الرُّمادِي والأحمَر يِتلاومُون زين [ʔirruma:di wilʔamar yitwa:lmu:n zi:n] • **2.** رِصاصِي [riṣa:ṣi] رُمادِي [ruma:di] He always wears gray suits. دائماً يِلبَس بَدلات رُمادِيَّة [da:ʔiman yilbas badla:t ruma:diyya]

to graze • **1.** رِعَى [riʕa:] رَعِي [raʕy] *vn:* *sv* a. The sheep grazed in the fields. الغَنَم رِعَى بالحُقُول [ʔilɣanam riʕa: bilħuqu:l] • **2.** قِشَط [gišaṭ] قَشِط [gašiṭ] *vn:* اِنقِشَط [ʔingišaṭ] *p:* خِدَش [xidaš] خَدِش [xadiš] *vn:* اِنخِدَش [ʔinxidaš] *p:* The bullet grazed his shoulder. الرِّصاصَة قِشطَت كِتفَه [ʔirriṣa:ṣa gišṭat čitfah]

grease • **1.** دِهِن [dihin] دُهُون [duhu:n] *pl:* شَحمَة [šaħma] شَحمات [šaħama:t] *pl:* دَسَم [dasam] دُسُومات [dusu:ma:t] *pl:* Don't leave the grease in the pan. لا تِترُك الدِّهِن بالطّاوَة [la: titruk ʔiddihin bitṭa:wa] • **2.** قرِيز [gri:z] Do you need any grease for your car? تِحتاج أيّ قرِيز لِسَيّارتَك؟ [tiħta:ǰ ʔayy gri:z lisayya:rtak?]

to grease • **1.** دَهَّن [dahhan] تدِهِّن، تَدهِين [tdihhin, tadhi:n] *vn:* اَتدَهَّن [ʔiddahhan] *p:* Grease the pan before you put the meat in. دَهِّن الطّاوَة قَبُل ما تخَلِّي اللَّحَم [dahhin ʔiṭṭa:wa gabul ma: txalli ʔillaħam] • **2.** شَحَّم [šaħħam] تَشحِيم، تشِحِّم [tašħi:m, tšiħħim] *vn:* تشَحَّم [tšaħħam] *p:* *sv* i. Our best mechanic greased your car. أحسَن المِيكانِيكِيِّين مالنَا شَحَّم سَيّارتَك [ʔaħsan ʔalmikani:kiyyi:n ma:lna šaħħam sayya:rtak]

greasy • **1.** مدَهَّن [mdahhan] دَسِم [dasim] The dishes are still greasy. المَواعِين بَعدها مدَهَنَة [ʔimawa:ʕi:n baʕadha mdahhna] • **2.** دِهِين [dihi:n] دَسِم [dasim] You eat a lot of greasy foods. تاكُل هوايَة أكِل دِهِين [ta:kul hwa:ya ʔakil dihi:n]

great • **1.** عَظِيم [ʕaði:m] عُظَماء [ʕuðama:ʔ] *pl:* كِبِير [čibi:r, kibi:r] كبار [kba:r] *pl:* He's one of the greats of contemporary poetry. هُوَّ مِن عُظَماء الشِّعر المُعاصِر [huwwa min ʕuðama:ʔ ʔiššiʕir ʔilmuʕa:ṣir] • **2.** عَظِيم [ʕaði:m] عُظَماء [ʕuðama:ʔ] *pl:* كَبِير [kabi:r] She's a great singer. هِيَّ مُغَنِّيَة عَظِيمَة [hiyya muɣanniya ʕaði:ma] That's a great idea. هَذِي فِكرَة عَظِيمَة [ha:ði fikra ʕaði:ma] • **3.** كَبِير [kabi:r] عَظِيم [ʕaði:m] عُظَماء [ʕuðama:ʔ] *pl:* بَلِيغ [bali:ɣ] جَسِيم [ǰasi:m] The war did great damage. الحَرب أحدَثَت أضرار كَبِيرَة [ʔilħarb ʔaħdaθat ʔaḍra:r kabi:ra] • **4.** جَسِيم [ǰasi:m] كَبِير [kabi:r] عَظِيم [ʕaði:m] عُظَماء [ʕuðama:ʔ] *pl:* He's in great danger. هُوَّ بخَطَر جَسِيم [huwwa bxaṭar ǰasi:m] • **5.** بَلِيغ [bali:ɣ] كَبِير [kabi:r] His father's death left a great mark on him. وَفاة أَبُوه تِركَت أَثَر بَلِيغ بِيه [wafa:t ʔabu:h tirkat ʔaθar bali:ɣ bi:h] • **6.** كَبِير [kabi:r] هوايَة [hwa:ya] He was in great pain. كان عِندَه ألَم هوايَة [ča:n ʕindah ʔalam hwa:ya] • **7.** هوايَة [hwa:ya] كُلِّش [kulliš] They live in a great big house. يسِكنُون بِبَيت كُلِّش كِبِير [ysiknu:n bibayt kulliš čibi:r]

Great Britain • **1.** بريطانيا العُظمَى [briṭa:nya ʔilʕuðma]

greatly • **1.** بصُورَة كَبِيرَة [bṣu:ra kabi:ra] بصُورَة عَظِيمَة [bṣu:ra ʕaði:ma] She exaggerated greatly. بالغَت بصُورَة كَبِيرَة [ba:lɣat bṣu:ra kabi:ra]

Greece • **1.** اليُونان [ʔilyuna:n]

greedy • **1.** نَهِم [nahim] نَهِمِين [nahimi:n] *pl:* شَرِه [šarih] شَرِهِين [šarihi:n] *pl:* He's very greedy when we sit down to eat. هُوَّ كُلِّش نَهِم لَمّا نُقعُد ناكُل [huwwa kulliš nahim lamma nugʕud na:kul] • **2.** طَمّاع [ṭamma:ʕ] جَشِع [ǰašiʕ] He's a greedy merchant. هُوَّ تاجِر طَمّاع [huwwa ta:ǰir ṭamma:ʕ]

Greek • **1.** يُونانِي [yuna:ni] يُونانِيِّين [yuna:niyyi:n] *pl:* His father is a Greek. أَبُوه يُونانِي [ʔabu:h yuna:ni] • **2.** يُونانِي [yuna:ni] He speaks Greek. يِحكِي يُونانِي [yiħči yuna:ni] • **3.** يُونانِي [yuna:ni] Do you like Greek wines? يِعجبَك شَراب يُونانِي؟ [yiʕiǰbak šara:b yuna:ni?]

green • **1.** أخضَر [ʔaxðar] خُضُر [xuður] *pl:* خَضرَة [xaðra] *Feminine*

to turn green • **1.** اِخضَرّ [ʔixðarr] اِخضِرار [ʔixðira:r] *vn: sv* a. The grass turns green in the spring. العِشِب يِخضَرّ بالرَّبِيع [ʔilʕišib yixðarr birrabi:ʕ]

*** He's still green at this work.** • **1.** بَعدَه لِحِيمِي بهالشُّغُل [baʕdah lhi:mi bhaššuɣul]

greens • **1.** خُضرَة [xuðra] You should eat some greens everyday. لازِم تاكُل شوَيَّة خُضرَة كُلّ يوم [la:zim ta:kul šwayya xuðra kull yu:m]

to greet • **1.** سَلَّم عَلَى [sallam ʕala] تَسلِيم، تسِلِّم [tasli:m, tsillim] *vn: sv* i. حَيّا [ħayya:] تَحِيَّة [taħiyya] *vn: sv* i. He greeted him with a wave of the hand. سَلَّم عَليه بِيدَه [sallam ʕali:h bi:dah] • **2.** اِستَقبَل [ʔistaqbal] اِستِقبال [ʔistiqba:l] *vn: sv* i. They greeted him with applause. اِستَقبِلُوه بالتَّصفِيق [ʔistaqbilu:h bittaṣfi:g]

greeting • **1.** تَحِيَّة [taħiyya] تَحِيّات [taħiyya:t] *pl:* اِستِقبال [ʔistiqba:l] اِستِقبالات [ʔistiqba:la:t] *pl:* سَلام [sala:m] We never expected such a warm greeting. أَبَداً ما توَقَّعنا هِيك تَحِيَّة حارَّة [ʔabadan ma: twaqqaʕna hi:č taħiyya ħa:rra]

grenade • **1.** قُمبُلَة يَدَوِيَّة [qumbula yadawiyya, qunbula yadawiyya] قَنابِل يَدَوِيَّة [qana:bil yadawiyya] *pl:*

grief • **1.** حِزن [ħizin, ħuzun] غَمّ [ɣamm] حَسرَة [ħasra] She couldn't conceal her grief. ما قِدرَت تِخفِي حُزنها [ma: gidrat tixfi ħuzunha]

grill • **1.** شِبكَة [šibča] شِبكات [šibča:t] *pl:* I don't like the grill on your new car. ما أحِبّ شِبكَة سَيّارتَك الجِّدِيدَة [ma: ʔaħibb šibčat sayya:rtak ʔiǰǰidi:da] Take the meat off the grill as soon as it's done. شِيل اللَّحَم مِن الشِّبكَة بَس ما يِستِوِي [ši:l ʔillaħam min ʔiššibča bas ma: yistiwi]

to grill • **1.** شَوَى [šuwa:] شَوِي [šawy] *vn:* اِنشُوَى [ʔinšuwa:] *p: sv* i. They grilled the meat in the garden. شُوَوا اللَّحَم عالشِّبكَة بالحَدِيقَة [šuwaw ʔillaħam ʕaššibča bilħadi:qa] • **2.** طَوَّل [ṭawwal] تَطوِيل [taṭwi:l] *vn: sv* i. The police grilled the prisoner for hours. الشُّرطَة طَوِّلَت بأَسئِلَتها لِلمَحبُوس لعِدَّة ساعات [ʔiššurṭa ṭawwilat bʔasʔilatha lilmaħbu:s lʕiddat sa:ʕa:t]

grim • **1.** معَبِّس [mʕabbis] His face was grim. كان وِجَّه معَبِّس [ča:n wiččah mʕabbis]

grin • **1.** اِبتِسامَة واضحَة [ʔibtisa:ma wa:ðħa] There was a grin on his face. كان أكُو اِبتِسامَة واضحَة عَلَى وُجَّه [ča:n ʔaku ʔibtisa:ma wa:ðħa ʕala wuččah]

to grin • **1.** كَشَّر [kaššar] تكِشِّر [tkiššir] *vn: sv* i. He grinned at me. كَشَّر عَلَيّا [kaššar ʕalayya]

grind • **1.** طَحِن [ṭaħin] طَحنات [ṭaħna:t] *pl:* I bought a medium grind of coffee. اِشتِرَيت قَهوَة مَطحُونَة طَحِن وَسَط [ʔištiri:t gahwa maṭħu:na ṭaħin wasaṭ] • **2.** شِدَّة [šidda] شِدّات، شَدائِد [šidda:t, šada:ʔid] *pl:* It was a long grind, but we made it. كانَت فَدّ شِدَّة طوِيلَة لَكِن دَبَّرناها [ča:nat fadd šidda ṭwi:la la:kin dabbarna:ha]

to grind • **1.** طِحَن [ṭiħan] طَحِن [ṭaħin] *vn:* اِنطِحَن [ʔinṭiħan] *p: sv* a. جِرَش [ǰiraš] جَرِش [ǰariš] *vn:* اِنجِرَش

[ʔinǰiraš] *p: sv* i. We saw the miller grinding flour. شِفنا الطَّحّان يِطحَن الطَّحِين [šifna ʔiṭṭaħħaːn yiṭħan ʔiṭṭaħiːn] • **2.** جِرَخ [čirax] جَرِخ [čarix] *vn:* اِنجِرَخ [ʔinčirax] *p: sv* a. He ground the meat for hamburger. جِرَخ اللَّحَم لِلكَباب [čirax ʔillaħam lilkabaːb] How much does he charge to grind knives? شقَدّ ياخُذ عَلَى جَرخ السِّكاكِين؟ [šgadd yaːxuð ʕala čarx ʔissičaːčiːn?] He keeps on grinding out one novel after the other. ظَلّ يِجرَخ بِهالرُّوايات وِحدَة وَرا اللُّخ [ðall yičrax bharruwaːyaːt wiħda wara ʔillux] • **3.** قِرَط ب [giraṭ b-] قَرِط [gariṭ] *vn: sv* u. He grinds his teeth in his sleep. يِقرُط بِسنُونَه بِنَومَه [yigruṭ bsnuːnah bnawmah]

grip • **1.** لَزمَة [lazma] لَزمات [lazmaːt] *pl:* قَبضَة [qabða] قَبضات [qabðaːt] *pl:* مَسكَة [maska] He has a strong grip. عِندَه فَدّ قَبضَة قَوِيَّة [ʕindah fadd qabða qawiyya] • **2.** يَدَّة [yadda] يَدّات [yaddaːt] *pl:* I can't carry it. It doesn't have a grip. ما أَقدَر أَشِيلها ما بِيها يَدَّة [maː ʔagdar ʔašiːlha maː biːha yadda] • **3.** جُنطَة [ǰunṭa] جُنَط، جَنطات [ǰunaṭ, ǰanṭaːt] *pl:* Where can I check my grip? وين أَقدَر أَئمِّن جُنطِتي؟ [wiːn ʔagdar ʔaʔammin ǰuniṭti?] • **4.** لَزمَة [lazma] لَزمات [lazmaːt] *pl:* I can carry the trunk if I can get a grip. أَقدَر أَشِيل الصَّندُوق إذا بِيه لَزمَة [ʔagdar ʔašiːl ʔiṣṣanduːg ʔiða biːh lazma]

to grip • **1.** لِزَم [lizam] لَزِم [lazim] *vn:* اِنلِزَم [ʔinlizam] *p:* كُمَش [kumaš] كَمِش [kamiš] *vn:* اِنكُمَش [ʔinkumaš] *p:* He gripped her arm tightly. كُمَش إيدها بِقُوَة [kumaš ʔiːdha bquwa]

gripe • **1.** تَشِكِّي [tšikki] تَشِكِّيات [tišikkiyyaːt] *pl:* Don't tell me your gripes. لا تقُلّي بِتشِكّياتَك [laː tgulli bitšikkiyyaːtak]

to gripe • **1.** تشَكَّى [tšakkaː] تَشَكِّي، تشِكِّي [tašakki, tšikki] *vn: sv* a. He gripes about everything. يِتشَكَّى مِن كُلِّشي [yitšakkaː min kullši]

gripping • **1.** مُؤَثِّر [muʔaθθir] It was a very gripping film. كان فِلِم مُؤَثِّر كُلِّش [čaːn filim muʔaθθir kulliš]

grit • **1.** حَصُو [ħaṣw] Chicken gizzards are full of grit. حَواصِل الدِّجاج مَترُوسَة حَصو [ħawaːṣil ʔiddiǰaːǰ matruːsa ħaṣw] • **2.** عَزِم [ʕazim] عَزائِم [ʕazaːʔim] *pl:* That boy has grit. هَالوَلَد عِندَه عَزِم [halwalad ʕindah ʕazim]

to grit • **1.** قَزقَز ب [gazgaz b-] تقِزقِز، قَزقَزَة [tgizgiz, gazgaza] *vn: sv* i. He gritted his teeth and set to work. قَزقَز بِسنُونَه وبِدا يِشتُغُل [gazgaz bsnuːnah wbidaː yištuɣul]

groan • **1.** ونِين [winiːn] تَأَوُّه [taʔawwuh] تَأَوُّهات [taʔawwuhaːt] *pl:* We heard his groans all night. سِمَعنا وِنِينَه طُول اللَّيل [simaʕna winiːnah ṭuːl ʔillayl]

to groan • **1.** وَنّ [wann] ونِين [wniːn] *vn: sv* i. تَأَوَّه [tʔawwah] تَأَوُّه [taʔawwuh] *vn: sv* a. The sick man was groaning. المَرِيض كان يوِنّ [ʔilmariːð čaːn ywinn]

grocer • **1.** بَقّال [baggaːl] بَقّالِين، بقاقِيل [baggaːliːn, bgaːgiːl] *pl:* Our grocer sells nice apples. بَقّالنا يبِيع خُوش تُفّاح [baggaːlna yibiːʕ xuːš tuffaːħ]

groceries • **1.** مِسواق [miswaːg] Would you deliver these groceries to our house? ما توَدّي هالمِسواق لِبَيتنا؟ [maː twaddi halmiswaːg lbaytna?]

grocery store • **1.** دُكّان بقالَة [dukkaːn bgaːla] دكاكِين بقالَة [dkaːkiːn bgaːla] *pl:*

groom • **1.** عِرِّيس [ʕirriːs] عَرارِيس [ʕaraːriːs] *pl:* That man's the father of the groom. هَالرِّجّال أَبُو العِرِّيس [harriǰǰaːl ʔabu ʔilʕirriːs] • **2.** سايِس [saːyis] سِيّاس [siyyaːs] *pl:* The groom is walking the horse. السّايِس دَيمَشّي الحصان [ʔissaːyis daymašši ʔilħṣaːn]

to groom • **1.** هَندَم [handam] هَندَمَة [handama] *vn:* تهَندَم [thandam] *p:* He grooms himself nicely. يهَندِم نَفسَه زين [yhandim nafsah ziːn] Her children are always well-groomed. أَطفالها دائِماً مهَندِمِين [ʔaṭfaːlha daːʔiman mhandimiːn]

groove • **1.** حَزّ [ħazz] We watched the carpenter chisel a groove in the board. تفَرَّجنا عالنَّجّار يِحفُر حَزّ بالخِشبَة [tfarraǰna ʕannaǰǰaːr yiħfur ħazz bilxišba]

to grope • **1.** تلَمَّس [tlammas] تلِمِّس [tlimmis] *vn: sv* a. تحَسَّس [tħassas] تحِسِّس [tħissis] *vn: sv* a. He groped for the switch in the dark. تلَمَّس السُّوِيچ بالظِّلمَة [tlammas ʔissuwiːč biððilma]

gross • **1.** كلُوص [gluːṣ] كلُوصات [gluːṣaːt] *pl:* These are sold in grosses only. هاي تِنباع بالكلُوصات بَسّ [haːy tinbaːʕ bilgluːṣaːt bass] • **2.** فَظِيع [faðiːʕ] That was a gross mistake. ذِيك كانَت فَدّ غَلطَة فَظِيعَة [ðiːč čaːnat fadd ɣalṭa faðiːʕa] • **3.** خَلِيع [xaliːʕ] He told us a gross story. حِكَى إلنا قُصَّة خَلِيعَة [ħičaː ʔilna quṣṣa xaliːʕa] • **4.** مَجمُوع عامّ [maǰmuːʕ ʕaːmm] How much was your gross income? شقَدّ كان مَجمُوع الدَّخَل العامّ مالَك؟ [šgadd čaːn maǰmuːʕ ʔiddaxal ʔilʕaːmm maːlak?]

grouchy • **1.** مَقلُوب الوِجِه [magluːb ʔilwiǰih] مغَيِّم [mɣayyim] He's always grouchy. هُوَّ دائِماً مَقلُوب الوِجِه [huwwa daːʔiman magluːb ʔilwiǰih]

ground • **1.** قاع [gaːʕ] قِيعان [giːʕaːn] *pl:* أَرض [ʔarð] أَراضِي [ʔaraːði] *pl:* Leave it on the ground. خَلِّيهَا عالقاع [xalliːha ʕalgaːʕ] The ground in this area is not fit for agriculture. القاع هنا مُو صالحَة لِلزِّراعَة [ʔilgaːʕ hna muː ṣaːlħa lizziraːʕa] • **2.** ساحَة [saːħa] ساحات [saːħaːt] *pl:* This palace has beautiful grounds. هالقَصِر بِيه ساحات جَمِيلَة [halqaṣir biːh saːħaːt ǰamiːla] • **3.** مَكان [makaːn, mukaːn] مُكانات، أَماكِن، أَمكِنَة [mukaːnaːt, ʔamaːkin, ʔamkina] *pl:*

مَحَل [mahall] مَحَلّات [mahalla:t] *pl:* Are there any good fishing grounds near here? أكُو أماكِن لِصَيد السِّمَك قَرِيب مِن هنا؟ [ʔaku ʔama:kin liṣayd ʔissimač qari:b min hna?] • **4.** أرضِي [ʔarđi] أرضِيَّة [ʔarđiyya] *pl:* Connect the ground to the radio. شِدّ الأرضِي بِالرّادِيُو [šidd ʔilʔarđi birra:dyu] • **5.** أساس [ʔasa:s] أساسات [ʔasa:sa:t] *pl:* On what grounds did you jail him? عَلَى أيّ أساس سِجَنتُوه؟ [ʕala ʔayy ʔasa:s sijantu:h?] • **6.** تِلِف [tilif, tifil] Don't put the coffee grounds down the drain. لا تخَلّي التِّلِف مال القَهوَة بالبَلُّوعَة [la: txalli ʔittilif ma:l ʔilgahwa bilballu:ʕa] • **7.** أرضِي [ʔarđi] The dining room is on the ground floor. قاعَة الطَّعام بِالطّابِق الأرضِي [qa:ʕat ʔiṭṭaʕa:m biṭṭa:biq ʔilʔarđi]

to ground • **1.** شَكَّل [šakkal] تَشكِيل، تشِكِّل [taški:l, tšikkil] *vn:* تشَكَّل [tšakkal] *p:* *sv* i. You have to ground the battery before you use it. لازِم تشَكِّل أرضِي الباترِي قَبُل ما تِستَعمِلَه [la:zim tšakkil ʔarđi ʔilpa:tri gabul ma: tistaʕmilah] • **2.** مِنَع [minaʕ] مَنع [maniʕ] *vn:* انِمنَع [ʔinminaʕ] *p:* *sv* a. The Aviation Commission grounded four pilots this month. لُجنَة الطَّيَران مِنعَت أربَع طَيّارِين مِن الطَّيَران هَالشَّهَر [lujnat ʔiṭṭayara:n minʕat ʔarbaʕ ṭayya:ri:n min ʔiṭṭayara:n haššahar]

to ground out • **1.** سَرَّب [sarrab] تَسرِيب، تَسَرُّب [tasri:b, tasarrub] *vn:* تسَرَّب [tsarrab] *p:* He grounded out the circuit with a screwdriver. سَرَّب الكَهرَباء مِن الإتِّصال بِدَرنَفِيس [sarrab ʔilkahraba:ʔ min ʔilittiṣa:l bidarnafi:s]

group • **1.** جَماعَة [jama:ʕa] جَماعات [jama:ʕa:t] *pl:* جَوقَة [jawga] جَوقات [jawga:t] *pl:* The class was divided into three groups. الصَّفّ كان مقَسَّم إلَى تلَث جَماعات [ʔiṣṣaff ča:n mqassam ʔila tlaθ jama:ʕa:t]

to group • **1.** قَسَّم [qassam] تَقسِيم [taqsi:m] *vn:* تقَسَّم [tqassam] *p:* *sv* i. Group the children according to age. قَسِّم الأطفال إلَى جَماعات حَسَب العُمُر [qassim ʔilʔaṭfa:l ʔila jama:ʕa:t ħasab ʔilʕumur] • **2.** تجَمَّع [tjammaʕ] تَجَمُّع [tajammuʕ] *vn:* *sv* a. اِلتَمّ [ʔiltamm] اِلتِمام [ʔiltima:m] *vn:* *sv* a. The students grouped around the teacher to see the experiment. الطُّلّاب تجَمّعوا حَول المُعَلِّم حَتَّى يشُوفُون التَّجرُبَة [ʔiṭṭulla:b djammiʕaw ħawl ʔilmuʕallim ħatta yšu:fu:n ʔittajruba]

grove • **1.** بِستان [bista:n] بساتِين [bsa:ti:n] *pl:* He's working in an orange grove. يِشتُغل بِبِستان بُرتُقال [yištuɣl bibista:n purtuqa:l]

to grow • **1.** نِمَى [nima:] نُمُوّ [numuww] *vn:* *sv* i. Cactus grows in the desert. الصُّبِّير يِنمُو بِالبَرّ [ʔiṣṣubbayr yinmu: bilbarr] • **2.** نِمَي [nima:] نُمُوّ [numuw] *vn:* *sv* i. كُبَر [kubar] كُبُر [kubur] *vn:* *sv* a. Your boy has certainly grown a lot. إبنَك بِلا شَكّ كُبَر هوايَة [ʔibnak bila šakk kubar hwa:ya] • **3.** صار [ṣa:r] صَير [ṣi:r] *vn:* *sv* i. His financial condition grew worse. حالتَه المالِيَّة صارَت أتعَس [ħa:ltah ʔilma:liyya ṣa:rat ʔatʕas] • **4.** زِرَع [ziraʕ] زَرِع [zariʕ] *vn:* اِنزِرَع [ʔinziraʕ] *p:* He grows flowers in the garden. يزرَع وَرد بِالحَدِيقَة [yizraʕ warid bilħadi:qa]

to grow up • **1.** رُبَى [ruba:] تَربِيَة [tarbiya] *vn:* *sv* a. My friend grew up in Najef. صَدِيقِي رُبَى بِالنَّجَف [ṣadi:qi ruba: binnajaf]

growl • **1.** هَمهَمَة [hamhama] هَمهَمات [hamhama:t] *pl:* The dog's growl scared the children. هَمهَمَة الكَلب خَوَّفَت الجَّهّال [hamhamat ʔiččalib xawwafat ʔijjahha:l]

to growl • **1.** هَمهَم [hamham] تهمهم [thimhim] *vn:* *sv* i. The dog began growling before it barked. الكَلب بِدا يهَمهِم قَبُل ما نِبَح [ʔiččalib bida: yhamhim gabul ma: nibaħ]

grown-up • **1.** كِبِير [čibi:r] كَبِير [kabi:r] كبار [kba:r] *pl:* The admission price for grown-ups is fifty fils. أجرَة الدُّخُول لِلكِبار خَمسِين فِلِس [ʔujrat ʔidduxu:l lilikba:r xamsi:n filis] • **2.** كَبران [kabra:n] كِبِير [čibi:r] She has a grown up daughter. عِدها بنَيَّة كَبرانَة [ʕidha bnayya kabra:na]

growth • **1.** نُمُوّ [numuww] He spoke on economic growth. تكَلَّم عَن النُّمُوّ الاقتِصادِي [tkallam ʕan ʔinnumuww ʔilʔiqtiṣa:di] They say smoking stunts the growth. يقُولُون التَّدخِين يأخِّر النُّمُوّ [ygu:lu:n ʔittadxi:n yʔaxxir ʔinnumuww]

*** He has two day's growth.** • **1.** لِحِيتَه مال يَومَين [liħi:tah ma:l yawmayn]

grudge • **1.** حِقِد [ħiqid] أحقاد [ʔaħqa:d] *pl:* ضَغِينَة [đaɣi:na] ضَغائِن [đaɣa:ʔin] *pl:* Forget your grudges and be friends. اِنسُوا الأحقاد وصِيرُوا أصدِقاء [ʔinsu: ʔilʔaħqa:d wṣi:ru: ʔaṣdiqa:ʔ]

grudgingly • **1.** بِإمتِعاض [bʔimtiʕa:đ] He gave in grudgingly. اِستَسلَم بِإمتِعاض [ʔistaslam bʔimtiʕa:đ]

gruesome • **1.** فَظِيع [fađi:ʕ] The scene of the automobile accident was a gruesome sight. مَنظَر حادِث السَّيّارَة كان مَنظَر تَقشَعِرّ مِنَّه الأبدان [manđar ħa:diθ ʔissayya:ra ča:n manđar taqšaʕirr minnah ʔilʔabda:n]

gruff • **1.** خَشِن [xašin] غَلِيظ [ɣali:đ] فَضّ [fađđ] He has a gruff voice. عِندَه صُوت خَشِن [ʕindah ṣu:t xašin]

to grumble • **1.** دَمدَم [damdam] تدِمدِم [tdimdim] *vn:* *sv* i. He grumbles everytime we ask him for help. يدَمدِم كُلّما نُطلُب مِنَّه مُساعَدَة [ydamdim kullma nuṭlub minnah musa:ʕada]

guarantee • **1.** ضَمان [đama:n] ضَمانات [đama:na:t] *pl:* صَوقَرتَة [ṣu:garta] تَأمِين [taʔmi:n] This watch has a five year guarantee. هَالسّاعَة بِيها خَمس سنِين ضَمان [hassa:ʕa bi:ha xamis sni:n đama:n] • **2.** ضَمان [đama:n] ضَمانات

[ðamaːnaːt] *pl:* What guarantee do I have that he'll pay me? شِنُو الضَّمان هُوَّ راح يِدفَعلِي [šinu ʔiððamaːn huwwa raːħ yidfaʕli]

to guarantee • 1. ضَمَن [ðuman] ضَمان [ðamaːn] *vn:* اِنضُمَن [ʔinðuman] *p:* كِفَل [kifal] كَفالَة [kafaːla] *vn:* اِنكِفَل [ʔinkifal] *p:* We guarantee our product for a year. اِنضُمَن إنتاجنا لسَنَة وِحدَة [ʔinðuman ʔintaːjna lsana wiħda] **• 2.** ضُمَن [ðuman] صُوقَر [ṣawgar] تصَوكِر [tṣawgir] *vn:* تصَوكَر [tṣawgar] *p:* I can't guarantee that he'll be here tomorrow. ما أقدَر أصُوكِر راح يكُون هنا باكِر [maː ʔagdar ʔaṣawgir raːħ ykuːn hna baːčir]

guard • 1. حارِس [ħaːris] حُرّاس [ħurraːs] *pl:* The guard didn't let me enter. الحارِس ما خَلّانِي أخُشّ [ʔilħaːris maː xallaːni ʔaxušš] **• 2.** مُرافِق [muraːfiq] مُرافِقِين [muraːfiqiːn] *pl:* The king got off the plane with his personal guards. المَلِك نِزَل مِن الطَّيّارَة مَعَ مُرافِقِينَه الخاصِّين [ʔilmalik nizal min ʔiṭṭayyaːra maʕa muraːfiqiːnah ʔilxaːṣṣiːn] **• 3.** حامِي [ħaːmi] The army is the country's guard against enemy attack. الجَّيش حامِي الوَطَن مِن هِجُوم الأعداء [ʔijjiːš ħaːmi ʔilwaṭan min hijuːm ʔilʔaʕdaːʔ]

to guard • 1. حِرَس [ħiras] حِراسَة [ħiraːsa] *vn:* اِنحِرَس [ʔinħiras] *p:* حِمَى [ħimaː] حَمِي [ħamy] *vn:* اِنحِمَى [ʔinħimaː] *p:* The army is guarding the town. الجَّيش دَيِحرِس البَلَد [ʔijjiːš dayiħris ʔilbalad] **• 2.** حِمَى [ħimaː] This toothpaste guards the teeth against decay. هالمَعجُون يِحمِي الأسنان مِن التَّآكُل [halmaʕjuːn yiħmi ʔilʔasnaːn min ʔittaʔaːkul]

to be on one's guard • 1. اِحتِرَس [ʔiħtiras] اِحتِراس [ʔiħtiraːs] *vn:* sv i. You have to be on your guard with her. لازِم تِحتِرِس مِنها [laːzim tiħtiris minha]

guardian • 1. وَصِيّ [waṣiyy] أوصِياء [ʔawṣiyyaːʔ] *pl:* He was appointed guardian of his brother's son. كان مِتعَيِّن وَصِيّ عَلَى إبن أخُوه [čaːn mitʕayyin waṣiyy ʕala ʔibin ʔaxuːh]

guess • 1. تَخمِين [taxmiːn] تَخمِينات [taxmiːnaːt] *pl:* تَقدِير [taqdiːr] تَقدِيرات [taqdiːraːt] *pl:* حَزِر [ħazir] That wasn't right, but it's a good guess. هَذا ما كان صَحِيح، لَكِن خُوش تَخمِين [haːða maː čaːn ṣaħiːħ, laːkin xuːš taxmiːn]

to guess • 1. حِزَر [ħizar] حَزِر [ħazir] *vn:* اِنحِزَر [ʔinħizar] *p:* خَمَّن [xamman] تَخمِين [taxmiːn] *vn:* تخَمَّن [txamman] *p:* قَدَّر [qaddar] تَقدِير [taqdiːr] *vn:* تقَدَّر [tqaddar] *p:* Guess how much money I've got in my pocket. اِحزِر شقَدّ عِندِي فلُوس بجِيبِي [ʔiħzir šgadd ʕindi fluːs bjiːbi] **• 2.** ظَنّ [ðann] ظَنّ [ðann] *vn:* اِنظَنّ [ʔinðann] *p:* I guess he's sick. أظُنّ هُوَّ مَرِيض [ʔaðunn huwwa mariːð]

guest • 1. خُطّار [xuṭṭaːr] خطاطِير [xṭaːṭiːr] *pl:* [.] *Collective:* ضَيف [ðayf] ضيُوف [ðiyuːf] *pl:* خُطّار [xuṭṭaːr] *Collective:* Our guests ate all our food. خُطّارنا أكلَوا كُلّ أكِلنا [xuṭṭaːrna ʔaklaw kull ʔakilna]

guide • 1. دَلِيل [daliːl] أدِلّاء، دَلِيلات [ʔadillaːʔ, daliːlaːt] *pl:* Our guide showed us the things in the museum. الدَّلِيل مالنا فَرَّجنا عالأشياء المَوجُودَة بالمَتحَف [ʔiddaliːl maːlna farrajna ʕalʔašyaːʔ ʔilmawjuːda bilmatħaf] **• 2.** دَلِيل [daliːl] دَلِيلات [daliːlaːt] *pl:* All the theatres are listed in the guide. كُلّ السِّينَمات مسَجّلَة بالدَّلِيل [kull ʔissinamawaːt msajjla bilddaliːl]

to guide • 1. دَلّى [dallaː] دَلّات تدِلّي، دلال [tdilli] *vn:* تدَلَّى [tdallaː] *p:* sv i. أرشَد [ʔaršad] إرشاد [ʔiršaːd] *vn:* sv i. Mister can you direct us to this address? سَيِّدِي، تِقدَر تدَلِّينا عَلَى هالعِنوان؟ [sayyid, tigdar ddalliːna ʕala halʕinwaːn?] **• 2.** دَوَّر [dawwar] تَدوِير [tadwiːr] *vn:* تدَوَّر [tdawwar] *p:* فَرَّر [farrar] تَفرِير، تفِرِّر [tafriːr, tfirrir] *vn:* تفُرُّر [tfurrur] *p:* sv i. She guided us around the ruins. دَوَّرَتنا بين الآثار [dawwaratna biːn ʔilʔaaθaːr]

guilt • 1. ذَنِب [ðanib] ذنُوب [ðnuːb] *pl:* جُرُم [jurum] أجرام [ʔajraːm] *pl:* He admitted his guilt. اِعتِرَف بذَنبَه [ʔiʕtiraf bðanbah]

guilty • 1. مُذنِب [muðnib] The judge found him not guilty. الحاكِم وُجَدَه غير مُذنِب [ʔilħaːkim wujadah ɣayr muðnib]

guitar • 1. قِيثارَة [qiːθaːra] قِيثارات [qiːθaːraːt] *pl:*

gulf • 1. خَلِيج [xaliːj] خِلجان [xiljaːn] *pl:* We swam in the Persian Gulf. سبَحنا بالخَلِيج الفارِسِي [sbaħna bilxaliːj ʔilfaːrisi] **• 2.** هُوَّة عَمِيقَة [huwwa ʕamiːqa] There's a gulf between us. أكُو هُوَّ عَمِيقَة بَيناتنا [ʔaku huwwa ʕamiːqa baynaːtna]

gull • 1. [nʕiːja] (a small ewe) نعِيجات [nʕiːjaːt] *pl:* نعِيج [nʕiːj] Collective: The sea gulls followed our ship. نعِيج المَيّ تِبَع مَركَبنا [nʕiːj ʔilmayy tibaʕ markabna]

gum • 1. لَثَّة [laθθa] لَثّات [laθθaːt] *pl:* This toothpaste is good for the gums. هالمَعجُون خَوش لِلَّثَّة [halmaʕjuːn xuːš lillaθθa] **• 2.** عِلِك [ʕilič] علُوك [ʕluːč] *pl:* Do you have some gum? عِندَك شوَيَّة عِلِك؟ [ʕindak šwayyat ʕilič?] **• 3.** صَمُغ [ṣamuɣ] We import gum Arabic from the Sudan. نِستَورِد الصَّمُغ العَرَبِي مِن السُّودان [nistawrid ʔiṣṣamuɣ ʔilʕarabi min ʔissuːdaːn]

to gum • 1. لِزَق [lizag] لَزِق [lazig] *vn:* اِنلِزَق [ʔinlizag] *p:* sv i. صَمَّغ [ṣammaɣ] تصُمُّغ [tṣummuɣ] *vn:* تصَمَّغ [tṣammaɣ] *p:* sv u. Did you gum the labels? لِزَقِت البِطاقات؟ [lizagit ʔilbiṭaːqaːt?]

gun • 1. بُندُقِيَّة [bunduqiyya] بُندُقِيّات [bunduqiyyaːt] بَنادِق [banaːdiq] *pl:* بَنادِق [banaːdiq] *Collective:* تُفقَة [tufga] تُفَق، تُفقات [tufag, tufgat] *pl:* بَنادِق [banaːdiq] *Collective:* The soldiers were carrying their guns in the parade.

G

الجِّنُود كانَوا شايلِين بَنادِقهُم بالإستِعراض [ʔiǰǰinu:d ča:naw ša:yli:n bana:diqhum bilʔistiʕra:ð] • **2.** طَلْقَة [ṭalqa] طَلَقات [ṭalqa:t] *pl:* They fired a twenty-one gun salute for the visiting king. ضِربَوا واحِد وَعِشرِين طَلْقَة تَحِيَّة لِلمَلِك الزّائِر [ðirbaw wa:ħid wʕišri:n ṭalqa taħiyya lilmalik ʔizza:ʔir]
 *** Don't jump the gun! • 1.** لا تِتسَرَّع بِالأُمُور [la: titsarraʕ bilʔumu:r]
 *** They gunned him down. • 1.** وَقّعَوه بِالبَنادِق [waggʕawh bilbana:diq]

gunpowder • 1. بارُود [ba:ru:d]

gust • 1. حَبَّة [ħabba] حَبّات [ħabba:t] *pl:* A gust of wind blew the boy's cap off. حَبَّة هَوا وَقّعَت عَرَقجِين الوَلَد [ħabbat hawa waggʕat ʕaraqči:n ʔilwalad]

gutter • 1. ساقيَة [sa:gya] سواقِي [swa:gi] *pl:* مَجرَى [majra] مَجارِي [maja:ri] *pl:* My cigarettes fell in the gutter. جيكارتِي وُقعَت بالمَجرَى [ǰiga:rti wugʕat bilmajra]
 *** His mind's in the gutter. • 1.** يِحكِي فَساد [yiħči fasa:d]

guy • 1. وَلَد [walad] وِلِد [wilid] *pl:* He's a good guy. هُوَّ خُوش وَلَد [huwwa xu:š walad]

gym • 1. قاعَة الرِياضَة [qa:ʕat ʔirriya:ða] قاعات الرِياضَة [qa:ʕat ʔirriya:ða] *pl:* The party will be in the gym. الحَفلَة راح تكُون بِقاعَة الرِّياضَة [ʔilħafla ra:ħ tku:n bqa:ʕat ʔirriya:ða] • **2.** رِياضَة [riya:ða] We have gym three times a week. عِدنا رِياضَة ثلَاث مَرّات بِالإسبُوع [ʕidna riya:ða tla:θ marra:t bilʔisbu:ʕ]

to gyp • 1. غَشّ [ɣašš] غِشّ [ɣišš] *vn:* اِنغَشّ [ʔinɣašš] *p:* غِلَب [ɣilab] غَلُب [ɣalub] *vn:* اِنغِلَب [ʔinɣilab] *p:* He gypped me. غَشّنِي [ɣaššni]

gypsy • 1. كاولِي [ka:wli] ،كاولِيَّة [ka:wli:yya] *pl:* غَجَرِي [ɣajari] غَجَر [ɣajar] *pl:* That woman is a gypsy. هَالمَرَة كاولِيَّة [halmara ka:wliyya]

H

habit • **1.** عادَة [ʕaːdaː] That's a bad habit. هَذِي عادَة مُو زينَة [haːði ʕaːda muː ziːna] • **2.** هدُوم [hduːm] Have you seen my riding habit? شِفِت هِدُوم الرُّكُوب مالتِي؟ [šifit hiduːm ʔirrukuːb maːlti?]

to get into the habit of • **1.** تعَوَّد عَلَى [tʕawwad ʕala] تَعوِيد [taʕwiːd] *vn: sv* a. I got into the habit of smoking at college. تعَوَّدِت عالتَّدخِين مِن كِنِت بِالكُلِّيَّة [tʕawwadit ʕattadxiːn min činit bilkulliyya]

haggard • **1.** مَمصُوص [mamṣuːṣ] He looks very haggard. يبَيِّن عَليه مَمصُوص كُلِّش [yibayyin ʕaliːh mamṣuːṣ kulliš]

hail • **1.** حَالُوبَة [ħaːluːba] حالُوبات، [ħaːluːbaːt] *pl:* حالُوب [ħaːluːb] *Collective:* That's hail, not rain. هَذا حالُوب، مُو مُطَر [haːða ħaluːb, muː muṭar]

to hail • **1.** ذَبّ حَالُوب [ðabb ħaːluːb] ذَبّ حَالُوب [ðabb ħaːluːb] *vn: sv* i. It's hailing, not raining. دَتذِبّ حالُوب، ما دَتُمطُر [dadðibb ħaluːb, maː datumṭur] • **2.** صاح [ṣaːħ] صِيح، صِياح [ṣayħ, ṣiyaːħ] *vn:* اِنصاح [ʔinṣaːħ] *p:* The doorman hailed a passing cab. البَوّاب صاح تاكسِي فايِت [ʔilbawwaːb ṣaːħ taːksi faːyit] • **3.** رَحَّب ب [raħħab b-] تَرحِيب، ترُحُّب [tarħiːb, truħħub] *vn:* ترَحَّب [traħħab] *p:* The critics hailed it as the best play of the year. النُّقّاد رَحِّبَوا بِيها بِإعتِبار ها أحسَن تَمثِيلِيَّة هالسَّنَة [ʔinnuqqaːd raħħibaw biːha biʕtibaːrha ʔaħsan tamθiːliyya hassana] • **4.** حَيّا [ħayyaː] تحِيِّي [tħiyyi] *vn:* تحَيَّى [tħayyaː] *p:* The crowd hailed him as he entered the city. الجُمُوع حَيّاوُه مِن دِخَل المَدِينَة [ʔijjumuːʕ ħayyaːwh min dixal ʔilmadiːna]

hair • **1.** شَعرَة [šaʕra] شَعرات [šaʕraːt] *pl:* شَعَر [šaʕar] *Collective:* What color is her hair? شِنُو لُون شَعَرها؟ [šinu luːn šaʕarha?]

*** He's always getting into people's hair.**
• **1.** دائماً يِتداخَل بشُؤُون الآخَرين [daːʔiman yitdaːxal bšuʔuːn ʔilʔaːxariːn]

haircut • **1.** زيان [zyaːn] زيانات [zyaːnaːt] *pl:* زيان راس [ziyaːn raːs] زِيانات رُوس [ziyaːnaːt ruːs] *pl:* Where'd you get that funny haircut? وين زَيَّنِت هالزِّيان المُضحِك؟ [wiːn ʔizayyanit haziyyaːn ʔilmuðħik?]

to get a haircut • **1.** زَيَّن [zayyan] تزِيِّن [tziyyin] *vn:* تزَيَّن [tzayyan] *p:* I have to get a haircut. لازِم أزَيِّن شَعرِي [laːzim ʔazayyin šaʕri]

hair-dresser • **1.** حَلّاق تَجمِيل [ħallaːq tajmiːl] حَلّاقِين تَجمِيل [ħallaːqiːn tajmiːl] *pl:*

half • **1.** نُصّ [nuṣṣ] نصاص [nṣaːṣ] *pl:* I'll give him half of my share. راح أنطِيه نُصّ حُصّتِي [raːħ ʔanṭiːh nuṣṣ ħuṣṣti] I got it for half price at a sale. اِشتِرَيتها بنُصّ قِيمَة بالتَّنزِيلات [ʔištiraytha bnuṣṣ qiːma bittanziːlaːt] We'll be there at half past eight. نكُون هناك السّاعَة ثمانيَة وَنُصّ [nkuːn hnaːk ʔissaːʕa θmaːnya wnuṣṣ]

halfway • **1.** مُو كامِل [muː kaːmil] Halfway measures will not suffice. إجراءات مُو كامِلَة مُو كافيَة [ʔijraːʔaːt muː kaːmla muː kaːfya] • **2.** بنُصّ الطَّرِيق [bnuṣṣ ʔiṭṭariːq] We ran out of gas halfway to town. خِلَص البَنزِين بِنُصّ الطَّرِيق لِلمَدِينَة [xilaṣ ʔilbanziːn bnuṣṣ ʔiṭṭariːq lilmadiːna]

*** I'm willing to meet him halfway.**
• **1.** آنِي مُستَعِدّ أتساهَل وِيّاه [ʔaːni mustaʕidd ʔatsaːhal wiyyaːh]

hall • **1.** مَمَرّ [mamarr] مَمَرّات [mamarraːt] *pl:* Mr. Ani lives at that end of the hall. السَّيِّد عانِي يِسكُن بذِيك الجِّهَة مِن المَمَرّ [ʔissayyid ʕaːni yiskun bðiːč ʔijjiha min ʔilmamarr] • **2.** مَجاز [majaːz] مَجازات [majaːzaːt] *pl:* We need a new rug for our hall. نِحتاج زُولِيَّة جِدِيدَة لِلمَجاز [niħtaːj zuːliyya jidiːda lilmajaːz] • **3.** قاعَة [qaːʕa] قاعات [qaːʕaːt] *pl:* He gave his speech in a large hall. ألقَى خِطابَه بِقاعَة كبِيرَة [ʔalqaː xiṭaːbah bqaːʕa čbiːra]

halt • **1.** تَوَقُّف [tawaqquf] There's been a halt in steel production. صار تَوَقُّف بإنتاج الحَدِيد [ṣaːr tawaqquf bʔintaːj ʔilħadiːd]

to halt • **1.** وُقَف [wugaf] وُقُوف [wuguːf] *vn: sv* a. Halt! Who's there? أُوقَف، مِنُو هناك؟ [ʔuːgaf, minu hnaːk?] • **2.** وَقَّف [waggaf] توُقُّف [twugguf] *vn:* توَقَّف [twaggaf] *p:* He halted the soldiers in front of the barracks. وَقَّف الجِّنُود أمام الثَّكنَة [waggaf ʔijjinuːd ʔamaːm ʔiθθakana]

halting • **1.** مِترَدِّد [mitraddid] He spoke in a halting voice. حِكَى بصُوت مِترَدِّد [ħičaː bṣuːt mitraddid]

ham • **1.** لَحَم خَنزِير [laħam xanziːr] Would you like some ham for breakfast? ترِيد شوَيَّة لَحَم خَنزِير لِلرَّيُوق؟ [triːd šwayya laħam xanziːr lirrayuːg?]

hammer • **1.** جاكُوج [čaːkuːč] جواكِيج [čwaːkiːč] *pl:* Please hand me the hammer. مِن فَضلَك، ناوِشنِي الجاكُوك [min faðlak, naːwišni ʔilčaːkuːč] • **2.** مِطرَقَة [miṭraqa] مَطارِق [maṭaːriq] *pl:* The students were carrying a flag with a picture of a hammer and sickle on it. الطُّلّاب كانَوا شايلِين عَلَم بِيه صُورَة مِطرَقَة وَمِنجَل [ʔiṭṭullaːb čaːnaw šaːyliːn ʕalam biːh ṣuːrat miṭraqa wminjal]

to hammer • **1.** دَقّ [dagg] دَقّ [dagg] *vn: sv* u. دَقدَق [dagdag] تدِقدِق [ddigdig] *vn: sv* i. Our neighbor has been hammering all day long. جارنا طُول النَّهار كان دَيدِقّ [jaːrna ṭuːl ʔinnahaːr čaːn daydigg] Hammer this nail in please. دُقّ هالبِسمار رَجاءاً [dugg halbismaːr rajaːʔan] • **2.** رَسَّخ [rassax] تَرسِيخ [tarsiːx] *vn: sv* i. He hammered the rules into me. رَسَّخ التَّعلِيمات عِندِي [rassax ʔittaʕliːmaːt ʕindi]

hand • **1.** إيد [ʔiːd] إيدَين، إيدِينات [ʔiːdayn, ʔiːdiːnaːt] *pl:* Where can I wash my hands? وين أقدَر أغسِل إيدِي؟ [wiːn ʔagdar ʔaɣsil ʔiːdi?] My hand was very strong. I had three queens. إيدِي كانَت قَوِيَّة كان عِندِي ثَلاث قِزَز [ʔiːdi čaːnat qawiyya čaːn ʕindi tlaːθ qizaz] He asked for her hand from her father. طِلَب إيدها مِن أبُوها [ṭilab ʔiːdha min ʔabuːha] The matter is not in my hands. القَضِيَّة مُو بِيدِي [ʔilqaḍiyya muː biːdi] Just keep your hands off that! وَخِّر إيدَك مِن هاي [waxxir ʔiːdak min haːy] This job has to be done by hand. هالشُّغُل لازِم يصِير بالإيد [haššuɣul laːzim yṣiːr bilʔiːd] • **2.** يَدّ [yadd] إيد [ʔiːd] إيدَين، إيدِينات [ʔiːdiːn, ʔiːdiːnaːt] *pl:* He must have had a hand in that. لازِم كان إلَه يَد بِيها [laːzim čaːn ʔilah yad biːha] • **3.** مِيل [miːl] أميال، ميال [ʔamyaːl, myaːl] *pl:* مِيل، عَقرَب [miːl, ʕaqrab] ميالَة، عَقارِب [myaːla, ʕaqaːrub] *pl:* The minute hand doesn't work. مِيل الدَّقائِق ما يِشتُغُل [miːl ʔiddaqaːʔiq maː yištuɣul] • **4.** جِهَة [jiha] جِهات [jihaːt] *pl:* On the other hand, he wants it finished. وَمِن جِهَة لُخ، يرِيدها تِخلَص [wamin jiha lux, yriːdha tixlaṣ] • **5.** يَدَوِي [yadawi] He wanted to blow up the factory with a hand grenade. راد ينسِف المَعمَل بقُمبُلَة يَدَوِيَّة [raːd yinsif ʔilmaʕmal bqumbula yadawiyya]

*** I can't lay my hands on it right now.**
• **1.** ما أقدَر أحَصِّلها هَسَّة [maː ʔagdar ʔaħaṣṣilha hassa]

on hand • **1.** جَوَّة الإيد [jawwa ʔilʔiːd] حاضِر [ħaːḍir] مَوجُود [mawjuːd] We haven't that size on hand. ما عِدنا هالحَجِم جَوَّة الإيد [maː ʕidna halħajim jawwa ʔilʔiːd]

to hand • **1.** نِطَى [niṭaː] نَطِي [naṭi] *vn:* اِنِّطَى [ʔinniṭaː] *p:* ناوَش [naːwaš] مُناوَشَة [munaːwaša] *vn:* تناوَش [tnaːwaš] *p:* Please hand me that pencil. باللّه إنطِينِي هَالقَلَم [ballah ʔinṭiːni halqalam]

to hand in • **1.** سَلَّم [sallam] تِسلِيم [tsilliːm] *vn:* تسَلَّم [tsallam] *p:* I'm going to hand in my application tomorrow. راح أرُوح باكِر أسَلِّم عَرِيضتِي [raːħ ʔaruːħ baːčir ʔasallim ʕariːḍti]

to hand out • **1.** وَزَّع [wazzaʕ] تَوزِيع [tawziːʕ] *vn:* توَزَّع [twazzaʕ] *p:* فَرَّق [farrag] تَفرِيق [tafriːg] *vn:* تفَرَّق [tfarrag] *p:* Hand these tickets out! وَزِّع هالبِطاقات [wazziʕ halbiṭaːqaːt]

handbag • **1.** جُنطَة إيد [junṭat ʔiːd] جَنطات إيد، جُنَط إيد [janṭaːt ʔiːd, junaṭ ʔiːd] *pl:*

hand brake • **1.** هَندِبرَيك [handibriːk] هَندِبرَيكات [handibriːkaːt] *pl:*

handcuff • **1.** كَلَبشَة [kalabča] كَلَبشات [kalabčaːt] *pl:* Here every policeman carries a pair of handcuffs. كُلّ شُرطِي هنا يشِيل كَلَبجَة وِيّاه [kull šurṭi hna yšiːl kalabča wiyyaːh]

to handcuff • **1.** كَلبَش [kalbač] تكِلبِج [tkilbič] *vn:* تكَلبَج [tkalbač] *p:* They handcuffed the prisoners. كَلبِجَوا المَساجِين [kalbičaw ʔilmasaːjiːn]

hand drill • **1.** مِزرَف يَدَوِي [mizraf yadawi] مَزارُف يَدَوِيَّة [mazaːruf yadawiyya] *pl:*

handful • **1.** كَفّ [čaff] كفُوف [čfuːf] *pl:* He took a handful of nuts. أخَذ فَدّ كَفّ كَرَزات [ʔaxað fadd čaff čarazaːt]

handkerchief • **1.** كَفِّيَّة [čaffiyya] كفافِي، كَفِّيّات [čfaːfi, čaffiyyaːt] *pl:*

handle • **1.** يَدَّة [yadda] يَدّات [yaddaːt] *pl:* My suitcase needs a new handle. ينراد لجَنطَتِي يَدَّة جِدِيدَة [yinraːd ljaniṭṭi yadda jidiːda] • **2.** عُروَة [ʕurwa] عراوِي [ʕraːwi] *pl:* The handle of this teapot is broken. هالقُورِي عُروتَه مَكسُورَة [halquːri ʕurwtah maksuːra]

*** At the slightest occasion he flies off the handle.**
• **1.** يثُور مِن أدنَى شِي [yθuːr min ʔadnaː ši]

to handle • **1.** عامَل [ʕaːmal] مُعامَلَة [muʕaːmala] *vn: sv* i. He knows how to handle people. يُعرُف شلُون يعامِل النّاس [yuʕruf šluːn yiʕaːmil ʔinnaːs] • **2.** لِزَم [lizam] لَزِم [lazim] *vn:* اِنلِزَم [ʔinlizam] *p:* Look at it all you want, but don't handle it. باوِع عَلِيها شقَدّ ما ترِيد، بَسّ لا تِلزَمها [baːwiʕ ʕaliːha šgadd maː triːd, bass laː tilzamha] • **3.** تعاطَى ب [tʕaːṭaː b-] تَعاطِي [taʕaːṭi] *vn: sv* a. We don't handle that commodity. ما نِتعاطَى بهالسِّلعَة [maː nitʕaːṭaː bhassilʕa] • **4.** ضُبَط [ḍubaṭ] ضَبُط [ḍabuṭ] *vn:* اِنضُبَط [ʔinḍubaṭ] *p:* I can't handle him anymore. بَعَد ما أقدَر أضُبطَه [baʕad maː ʔagdar ʔaḍubṭah] • **5.** دَبَّر [dabbar] تَدبِير [tadbiːr] *vn:* تدَبَّر [tdabbar] *p:* I simply can't handle all the work by myself. مِن الواضِح آنِي ما أقدَر أدَبُّر كُلّ الشُّغُل وَحدِي [min ʔilwaːḍiħ ʔaːni maː ʔagdar ʔadabbur kull ʔiššuɣul waħdi] • **6.** اِستَعمَل [ʔistaʕmal] اِستِعمال [ʔistiʕmaːl] *vn: sv* i. Do you know how to handle a revolver? تُعرُف شلُون تِستَعمِل مُسَدَّس؟ [tuʕruf šluːn tistaʕmil musaddas?]

*** Handle that glass with care.** • **1.** دِير بالَك عَلَى هالجّامَة [diːr baːlak ʕala hajjaːma]

handmade • **1.** شُغُل إيد [šuɣul ʔiːd] That's all handmade. هَذا كُلَّه شُغُل إيد [haːða kullah šuɣul ʔiːd]

handsome • **1.** وَسِيم [wasiːm] He's a handsome man. هُوَّ رَجُل وَسِيم [huwwa rajul wasiːm]

*** That's a handsome sum of money.**
• **1.** هَذا خَوش مَبلَغ مِن المال [haːða xuːš mablaɣ min ʔilmaːl]

handwriting • **1.** كِتابَة [kitaːba] كِتابات [kitaːbaːt] *pl:* خَطّ إيد [xaṭṭ ʔiːd] His handwriting is illegible. كِتابتَه ما تِنقِرِي [kitaːbtah maː tinqiri]

handy • **1.** مُفِيد [mufi:d] This potato peeler is very handy. هالقَشّارَة مال البُتَيتَة مُفِيدَة [halgaššaːra maːl ʔilputayta mufiːda] • **2.** ماهِر [maːhir] He's a very handy fellow in everything. هُوَّ واحِد ماهِر بكُلْشِي [huwwa waːħid maːhir bkullši] • **3.** جَوَّة إيد [ǰawwa ʔiːd] Have you got a pencil handy? جَوَّة إيدَك قَلَم؟ [ǰawwa ʔiːdak qalam?]

to come in handy • **1.** فاد [faːd] فائِدَة [faːʔida] *vn: sv* i. A knowledge of typing will come in handy to you some day. تَعَلّم الطّابِعَة يفِيدَك فَدّ يوم [taʕallum ʔiṭṭaːbiʕa yfiːdak fadd yuːm]

*** The extra money comes in very handy.** • **1.** الفلُوس الإضافِيَّة إلها مَكان مُفِيد مِن تِجِي [ʔilifluːs ʔilʔiḍaːfiyya ʔilha makaːn mufiːd min tiǰi]

to hang • **1.** شِنَق [šinaq] شَنِق [šaniq] *vn:* اِنشِنَق [ʔinšinaq] *p:* صِلَب [ṣilab] صَلُب [ṣalub] *vn:* اِنصِلَب [ʔinṣilab] *p:* He was hanged yesterday. البارحَة اِنشِنَق [ʔilbaːrħa ʔinšinaq] • **2.** عَلَّق [ʕallag] تَعلِيق [taʕliːg] *vn:* تعَلَّق [tʕallag] *p:* Can't you hang the picture a little higher? ما تِقدَر تعَلِّق الصُّورَة شوَيَّة أعلَى؟ [maː tigdar tʕallig ʔiṣṣuːra šwayya ʔaʕla?] Where can I hang my coat? وين أعَلِّق سِترتِي؟ [wiːn ʔaʕallig sitirti?] • **3.** تعَلَّق [tʕallag] تَعَلُّق [taʕallug] *vn: sv* a. He hung from the limb and started swinging. تعَلَّق بالغُصُن وَقام يتمَرجَح [tʕallag bilɣuṣun wgaːm yitmarǰaħ] • **4.** دَندَل [dandal] تدِندِل [tdindil] *vn: sv* i. Why are you hanging your head? لِيش مدَندِل راسَك؟ [liːš mdandil raːsak?]

*** His life hung by a thread.** • **1.** حَياتَه كانَت واقفَة عَلَى شَعرَة [ħayaːtah čaːnat waːgfa ʕala šaʕra]

to hang around • **1.** رابَط [raːbaṭ] مُرابَطَة [muraːbaṭa] *vn: sv* u. He's always hanging around the tavern. عَلَى طُول مرابُط بالمَيخانَة [ʕala ṭuːl mraːbuṭ bilmayxaːna]

to hang on • **1.** لِزَم [lizam] لَزِم [lazim] *vn:* اِنلِزَم [ʔinlizam] *p:* I hung on with all my strength. آنِي لِزَمِت بكُلّ قُوتِي [ʔaːni lizamit bkull quːti]

to hang onto • **1.** لِزَم [lizam] اِنلِزَم [ʔinlizam] *p:* كَلَّب [čallab] تكِلِّب [tčillib] *vn:* تكَلَّب [tčallab] *p:* I hung onto the dog as long as I could. لِزَمِت الكَلِب طُول ما قِدَرِت [lizamit ʔiččalib ṭuːl maː gidarit] • **2.** بَقَّى [baqqaː] تبِقِّي [tbiqqi] *vn:* تبَقَّى [tbaqqaː] *p:* I'll hang on to the stock until its price goes up again. راح أبَقِّي الأسهُم إلَى أن يِرتِفِع سِعِرها [raːħ ʔabaqqi ʔilʔashum ʔila ʔan yirtifiʕ siʕirha] • **3.** خَلَّى [xallaː] تخِلِّي [txilli] *vn:* تخَلَّى [txallaː] *p:* Hang onto this money for me. خَلِّيلِي هَالفلُوس عِندَك [xalliːli halfiluːs ʕindak]

to hang out • **1.** شَرّ [šarr] شَرّ [šarr] *vn:* اِنِّشَر [ʔinnišar] *p:* عَلَّق [ʕallag] تَعلِيق [taʕliːg] *vn:* تعَلَّق [tʕallag] *p:* Did you hang the wash out? شَرَّيتِي الهِدُوم بَرَّة؟ [šarriːti ʔilhduːm barra?] • **2.** دَندَل [dandal] تدِندِل [tdindil] *vn:* تدَندَل [tdandal] *p:* The rope is hanging out the window. الحَبِل مدَندَل مِن الشِّبّاك [ʔilħabil mdandal min ʔiššibbaːč]

to hang up • **1.** عَلَّق [ʕallag] تَعلِيق [taʕliːg] *vn:* تعَلَّق [tʕallag] *p:* Hang up your hat and coat. عَلِّق شَفُقتَك وَسِترتَك [ʕallig šafuqtak wsitirtak]

*** He got angry and hung up on me.** • **1.** زِعَل عَلَيَّ وسَدّ التِلِفُون بوجهِي [ziʕal ʕalayya wsadd ʔittilifuːn bwučči]

hangar • **1.** گَراج طَيّارات [garaːǰ ṭayyaːraːt] گَراجات الطّيّارات [garaːǰaːt ṭayyaːraːt] *pl:*

hanger • **1.** تِعلاقَة [tiʕlaːga] تِعلاقات [tiʕlaːgaːt] *pl:* Put your coat on a hangar. خَلِّي سِتِرتَك عالتّعلاقَة [xalli sitirtak ʕattiʕlaːga]

hangover • **1.** خمارِيَّة [xmaːriyya] خمارِيّات [xmaːriyyaːt] *pl:* Take yourself a shot to get rid of the hangover. أخُذلَك فَدّ بِيك حَتَّى تِكسِر الخمارِيَّة [ʔuxuðlak fadd piːk ħatta tiksir ʔilxmaːriyya]

to happen • **1.** حِدَث [ħidaθ] حُدُوث [ħuduːθ] *vn: sv* i. صار [ṣaːr] صَير [ṣiːr] *vn: sv* i. وُقَع [wugaʕ] وُقُوع [wuquːʕ] *vn: sv* a. When did that happen? شوَقِت حِدثَت؟ [šwakit ħidθat?] What happened to the typewriter? Did someone use it? شصايِر بالطّابِعَة؟ أحَّد اِستَعمَلها؟ [šṣaːyir biṭṭaːbiʕa? ʔaħħad ʔistaʕmalha?] • **2.** صادَف [ṣaːdaf] تَصادُف، مُصادَفَة [taṣaːduf, muṣaːdafa] *vn: sv* i. I don't happen to agree with you this time. صادَف أن ما أتِّفِق ويّاك هَالمَرَّة [ṣaːdaf ʔan maː ʔattifaq wiyyaːk halmarra] He doesn't happen to be here. صادَف أن ما يكُون هنا [ṣaːdaf ʔan maː ykuːn hna]

*** Everything happens to me.** • **1.** كُلّ البَلاء دَيِنزِل عَلَى راسِي [kull ʔilbalaʔ dayinzil ʕala raːsi]

happily • **1.** بسَعادَة [bsaʕaːda] They are spending their married life happily. دَيِقضُون حَياتهُم الزَّوجِيَّة بسَعادَة [dayigḍuːn ħayaːthum ʔizzawǰiyya bsaʕaːda] • **2.** بسُرُور [bsuruːr] بفَرَح [bfaraħ] She does her work happily. تسَوِّي شُغُلها بسُرُور [tsawwi šuɣulha bsuruːr]

happiness • **1.** سَعادَة [saʕaːda] سُرُور [suruːr] فَرَح [faraħ]

happy • **1.** سَعِيد [saʕiːd] فَرحان [farħaːn] مَسرُور [masruːr] I'm very happy you won. آنِي سَعِيد لأنَّك ربَحِت [ʔaːni saʕiːd liʔannak rbaħit]

*** Happy New Year!** • **1.** كُلّ عام وَأنتُم بخَير [kull ʕaːm wʔintum bxayr]

*** Happy birthday!** • **1.** عِيد مِيلاد سَعِيد [ʕiːd miːlaːd saʕiːd]

harbor • **1.** مِيناء [miːnaːʔ, miːna] مَوانِئ [mawaːniʔ] *pl:* مَرفَأ [marfaʔ] مَرافِئ [maraːfiʔ] *pl:*

hard • **1.** قَوِي [qawi, guwi] قوَاي، أقوِياء، قَوِيِّين [qwaːy, ʔaqwiyaːʔ, qawiyyiːn] *pl:* I can't sleep on a hard mattress. ما أقدَر أنام عَلَى فراش قَوِي [maː ʔagdar ʔanaːm ʕala fraːš qawi] His death was a hard blow to us. وَفاتَه كانَت صَدمَة قَوِيَّة عَلينا [wafaːtah čaːnat ṣadma qawiyya ʕaliːna] • **2.** يابِس [yaːbis] The bread is hard

H

as a rock. الخُبُز يابِس مِثِل الحجارَة [ʔilxubuz ya:bis miθl ʔilħja:ra] • **3.** مُجِدّ [mujidd] He's a hard worker. هُوَّ عامِل مُجِدّ [huwwa ʕa:mil mujidd] • **4.** صَعُب [ṣaʕub] It's hard for me to climb stairs. صَعُب عَلَيّا أصعَد الدَّرَج [ṣaʕub ʕalayya ʔaṣʕad ʔiddaraj] Those were hard times. كانَت أوقات صَعبَة [ča:nat ʔawqa:t ṣaʕba] He's a hard man to get along with. هُوَّ رَجُل صَعُب تِتفاهَم ويّاه [huwwa rajul ṣaʕub titfa:ham wiyya:h] • **5.** بجِدّ [bjidd] He worked hard all day. اِشتِغَل بجِدّ طُول اليُوم [ʔištiɣal bjidd ṭu:l ʔilyu:m] • **6.** بقُوَّة [bquwwa] حَيل [ħayl, ħi:l] It was raining hard when he left. كانَت تُمطُر بقُوَّة لَمَّن طِلَع [ča:nat tumṭur bquwwa lamman ṭilaʕ] He hit him on the head hard. ضِرَبَه عَلَى راسَه حيل [ðirabah ʕala ra:sah ħi:l] • **7.** جامِد [ja:mid] قَوي [qawi, guwi] This ice cream is extremely hard. It can't be cut even with a knife. هالدُّوندِرمَة جامدَة كُلِّش، ما تِنقَصّ حَتَّى بِالسِّكِّينَة [haddu:ndirma ja:mda kulliš, ma: tingaṣṣ ħatta bissičči:na]

hard and fast • **1.** ثابِت [θa:bit] In this case you can't make hard and fast rules. بِهالحالَة ما تِقدَر تحُطّ قَواعِد ثابتَة [bhalħa:la ma: tigdar tħuṭṭ qawa:ʕid θa:bta]

hard of hearing • **1.** سَمِع ثِقِيل [samiʕ θigi:l] He's hard of hearing. سَمعَه ثِقِيل [samʕah θigi:l]

to be hard up for • **1.** اِحتاج [ʔiħta:j] اِحتِياج [ʔiħtiya:j] *vn: sv* a. He's always hard up for money. هُوَّ عَلَى طُول يِحتاج فلُوس [huwwa ʕala ṭu:l yiħta:j flu:s]

to try hard • **1.** حاوَل [ħa:wal] مُحاوَلَة [muħa:wala] *vn:* تحاوَل [tħa:wal] *p:* اِجتِهَد [ʔijtihad] اِجتِهاد [ʔijtiha:d] *vn: sv* i. He tried hard to do it right. حاوَل كُلّ جَهدَه حَتَّى يسَوِّيها زين [ħa:wal kull jahdah ħatta ysawwi:ha zi:n]

to harden • **1.** تصَلَّب [tṣallab] تَصَلُّب [taṣallub] *vn: sv* a. جِمَد [jimad] جَمِد، جُمُود [jamid, jumu:d] *vn: sv* a. سَكّ [sakk] سَكّ [sakk] *vn: sv* u. How long will it take the cement to harden? شقَدّ يِنراد لِلشِّبِنتُو حَتَّى يِتصَلَّب؟ [šgadd yinra:d liššibintu: ħatta yitṣallab?]

hardly • **1.** بصُعُوبَة [bṣuʕu:ba] مِن الصَعُب [min ʔiṣṣaʕub] I hardly believe that. بِصُعُوبَة أصَدِّقها [bṣuʕu:ba ʔaṣaddigha] • **2.** بالكاد [bilka:d] He had hardly begun to speak when. . . بِالكاد بِدا يِحكِي لَمَّن [bilka:d bida: yiħči lamman. . .]

*** You can hardly expect me to believe that.** • **1.** لا تِتصَوَّر راح أصَدِّق ذاك بسُهُولَة [la: titṣawwar ra:ħ ʔaṣaddig ða:k bsuhu:la]

hardly ever • **1.** مِن النّادِر [min ʔinna:dir] نادِراً [na:diran] I hardly ever go out. مِن النّادِر أطلَع بَرَّة [min ʔinna:dir ʔaṭlaʕ barra]

harm • **1.** ضَرَر [ðarar] أذِيَّة [ʔaðiyya] أذِيّات [ʔaðiyya:t] *pl:* You can never undo the harm you've done. ما تِقدَر تزِيل الضَّرَر اللّي سَوَّيتَه [ma: tigdar dzi:l ʔiððarar ʔilli sawwi:tah] No harm done! ما حِدَث أيّ ضَرَر [ma: ħidaθ ʔayy ðarar]

to harm • **1.** ضَرّ [ðarr] ضَرَر [ðarar] *vn:* اِنضَرّ [ʔinðarr] *p:* أذَّى [ʔaðða:] تاذِّي [tʔiðði] *vn:* تأذَّى [tʔaðða:] *p:* A vacation wouldn't harm you. العُطلَة ما راح تضُرَّك [ʔilʕuṭla ma: ra:ħ dðurrak] This dry weather has harmed the crops a lot. هَالجَوّ الجّافّ أذَّى الزَّرِع هوايَة [hajjaww ʔijja:ff ʔaðða: ʔizzariʕ hwa:ya]

harmful • **1.** مُضِرّ [muðirr] مُؤذِي [muʔði] This drought is harmful for the crops. هالجَفاف مُضِرّ لِلزَّرِع [hajjafa:f muðirr lizziriʕ]

harmonica • **1.** هارمَونِيكا [harmuni:ka] هارمَونِيكات [harmuni:ka:t] *pl:*

harmony • **1.** اِنسِجام [ʔinsija:m] There was perfect harmony between the two. كان أكُو انسِجام كامِل بين الإثنَين [ča:n ʔaku ʔinsija:m ka:mil bayn ʔilʔiθnayn] This song has beautiful harmony. هالأغنِيَة بِيها اِنسِجام لَطِيف [halʔuɣniya bi:ha ʔinsija:m laṭi:f] • **2.** مِتناسِق [mitna:siq] مِتَّفِق [mittifiq] مِتلائِم [mitla:ʔim] His plans are in complete harmony with mine. مَشارِيعَه كُلِّش مِتناسقَة ويّا مالتِي [maša:ri:ʕah kulliš mitna:sqa wiyya ma:lti]

harness • **1.** عِدَّة [ʕidda] I just bought a new harness for my horse. هَستَوّنِي اِشتِرَيت عِدَّة لِحصانِي [hastawwni ʔištiri:t ʕidda lħṣa:ni]

to harness • **1.** سَرَّج [sarraj] تسِرِّج [tsirrij] *vn:* تسَرَّج [tsarraj] *p: sv* i. Has he harnessed the horses? سَرَّج الخَيل؟ [sarraj ʔilxayl?] • **2.** اِستَخدَم [ʔistaxdam] اِستِخدام [ʔistixda:m] *vn: sv* i. Man is attempting to harness atomic energy. الإنسان دَيحاوِل يِستَخدِم الطّاقَة الذَّرِّيَّة [ʔilʔinsa:n dayħa:wil yistaxdim ʔiṭṭa:qa ʔiððarriyya]

harp • **1.** قِيثارَة [qiθa:ra] قِيثارات [qiθa:ra:t] *pl:*

to harp • **1.** دَقّ [dagg] دَقّ [dagg] *vn:* اِندَقّ [ʔindagg] *p: sv* u. Stop harping on the same subject. بَسّ عاد تدُقّ عَلَى نَفس المَوضُوع [bass ʕa:d tdugg ʕala nafs ʔilmawðu:ʕ]

harsh • **1.** قاسِي [qa:si] قُساة [qusa:t] *pl:* Those are harsh terms. هاي شُرُوط قاسيَة [ha:y šuru:ṭ qa:sya] • **2.** مُخَدِّش [muxaddiš] This soap contains no harsh ingredients. ماكُو عَناصِر مُخَدِّشَة بِهالصّابُون [ma:ku ʕana:ṣir muxaddiša bhaṣṣa:bu:n]

to harvest • **1.** حِصَد [ħiṣad] حَصِد [ħaṣid] *vn:* اِنحِصَد [ʔinħiṣad] *p: sv* i. When you harvest the wheat around here? شوَقت تحِصدُون الحُنطَة بِهالمَنطَقَة؟ [šwakit tħiṣdu:n ʔilħunṭa bhalmanṭaqa?]

haste • **1.** عَجَلَة [ʕajala] سُرعَة [surʕa]

*** Haste makes waste.** • **1.** العَجَلَة مِن الشَيطان [ʔilʕajala min ʔiššayṭa:n]

hastily • **1.** بعَجَلَة [bʕajala] بسُرعَة [bsurʕa] They took leave hastily. طِلعَوا بالعَجَل [ṭilʕaw bilʕajal]

hasty • **1.** بسُرعَة [bsurʕa] مِتسَرِّع [mitsarriʕ] You mustn't make hasty decisions. ما لازم تِتَّخِذ قَرارات بسُرعَة [ma: la:zim tittixið qara:ra:t bsurʕa]

*** I wouldn't be hasty about it, if I were you.** • **1.** لَو بمَكانَك ما أَستَعجِل بيها [law: bmaka:nak ma: ʔastaʕjil bi:ha]

hat • **1.** شَفقَة [šafqa] شَفقات [šafqa:t] *pl:* برنَيطَة، كَاسكيتَة [birni:ṭa, ka:ski:ta] برنَيطات، كَاسكيتات [birni:ṭa:t, ka:ski:ta:t] *pl:*

to hatch • **1.** فَقَّس [faggas] تَفقِيس [tafgi:s] *vn: sv* i. The hen sits on the eggs until they hatch. الدِّجاجَة تقُف عالبَيض حَتَّى يفقِّس [ʔiddija:ja tguff ʕalbayð ħatta yfaggis]

hatchet • **1.** بَلطَة [balṭa] بَلطات [balṭa:t] *pl:*

hate • **1.** كُرُه [kuruh] بُغُض [buɣuð] His dislike gradually turned into hate. بِالتَّدرِيج عَدَم مَحَبّتَه تحَوّلَت إلَى كُرُه [bittadri:j ʕadam maħabbtah tħawwlat ʔila kuruh]

to hate • **1.** كِرَه [kirah] كُرُه [kuruh] *vn:* انكِرَه [ʔinkirah] *p:* I hate people who are selfish. أكرَه النّاس الأنانِيِّين [ʔakrah ʔinna:s ʔilʔana:niyyi:n]

hatred • **1.** كَراهَة [kara:ha] بُغُض [buɣuð] كَراهِيَّة [kara:hiyya] كَراهِيّات [kara:hiyya:t] *pl:*

haul • **1.** صَيد [ṣayd] The fishermen had a good haul today. صَيّادِين السِّمَك طَلّعَوا خُوش صَيد هَاليُوم [ṣayya:di:n ʔissimač ṭalliʕaw xu:š ṣayd halyu:m] • **2.** حِمِل [ħimil] حمُول [ħmu:l] *pl:* This haul is too big for the truck. هالحِمِل كُلِّش كِبِير عاللُّوري [halħimil kulliš čibi:r ʕallu:ri]

*** It's a long haul from here to Bagdad.** • **1.** مَسافَة طَوِيلَة مِن هِنَا لبَغداد [masa:fa ṭawi:la min hna lbayda:d]

to haul • **1.** جَرّ [jarr] جَرّ [jarr] *vn:* انجَرّ [ʔinjarr] *p:* سِحَب [siħab] سَحِب [saħib] *vn:* انسِحَب [ʔinsiħab] *p:* The horses were unable to haul the heavy load. الخيل ما قِدرَت تجُرّ الحِمِل الثِّقِيل [ʔilxayl ma: gidrat djurr ʔilħimil ʔiθθigi:l] They hauled me out of bed at six this morning. جَرّوني مِن الفراش ساعَة سِتَّة اليُوم الصُّبُح [jarrawni min ʔilfra:š sa:ʕa sitta ʔilyu:m ʔiṣṣubuħ]

*** He hauled off as if he meant to hit me.** • **1.** تراجَع وتحَفّز عَبالَك كان يرِيد يضرُبنِي [tra:jaʕ witħaffaz ʕaba:lak ča:n yri:d yiðrubni]

to haul down • **1.** نَزَّل [nazzal] تَنزِيل [tanzi:l] *vn:* تنَزَّل [tnazzal] *p:* Has the flag been hauled down yet? العَلَم تنَزَّل لَو بَعَد؟ [ʔilʕalam tnazzal law baʕad?]

to have • **1.** عِند [ʕind] ويّا [wiyya] I have two tickets for the theater. عِندِي بِطاقتَين لِلتَّمثِيلِيَّة [ʕindi biṭa:qtayn littamθi:liyya] Do you have a pencil you can lend me? عِندَك قَلَم تِقدَر تعِيرنِي؟ [ʕindak qalam tigdar tʕi:rni?] Who had the book last? مِنُو آخِر واحِد كان عِندَه الكِتاب؟ [minu ʔa:xir wa:ħid ča:n ʕindah ʔilkita:b?] He has a heart disease. عِندَه مَرَض القَلب [ʕindah marað ʔilqalb] I have a headache. ويّايا وُجَع راس [wiyya:ya wujaʕ ra:s] Do you have the key? ويّاك المِفتاح؟ [wiyya:k ʔilmifta:ħ?] • **2.** ب [b] The room has three windows. القُبَّة إلها ثلاث شبابِيك [ʔilgubba ʔilha tla:θ šba:bi:č] The argument has no end. المُجادَلَة ما بِيها نِهايَة [ʔilmuja:dala ma: bi:ha niha:ya] The streets have no sidewalks. الشَّوارِع ما بِيها أَرصِفَة [ʔiššawa:riʕ ma: bi:ha ʔarṣifa] • **3.** عِند [ʕind] ال [ʔil] He has a very uncouth uncle. إلَه عَمّ كُلِّش أَدَبسِزّ [ʔilah ʕamm kulliš ʔadabsizz] She has beautiful eyes. عِدها عيُون حِلوَة [ʕidha ʕyu:n ħilwa] You have a talent for music. إلَك مَوهِبَة بِالمُوسِيقى [ʔilak mawhiba bilmusi:qa] • **4.** خَلَّى [xalla:] تخِلِّي [txilli] *vn: sv* i. Have him wash my car. خَلِّيه يغسِل سَيّارتي [xalli:h yiɣsil sayya:rti]

*** Have you had a haircut today?** • **1.** زَيَّنِت هَاليَوم؟ [zayyanit halyawm?]

*** Has he done his job well?** • **1.** سَوَّى شُغلَه زَين؟ [sawwa: šuɣla zayn?]

*** How long have you been in Baghdad?** • **1.** شقَدّ صارلَك ببَغداد؟ [šgadd ṣa:rlak bibayda:d?]

*** How long have you been waiting for me?** • **1.** شقَدّ صارلَك تِنتِظِرنِي؟ [šgadd ṣa:rlak tintiðirni?]

*** I've been standing here for two hours.** • **1.** صارلِي واقُف هنا ساعتَين [ṣa:rli wa:guf hna sa:ʕtayn]

*** I'm having my teeth treated.** • **1.** دا أداوِي أسنانِي [da: ʔada:wi ʔasna:ni]

*** We're having a house built.** • **1.** دَنِبنِي بَيت [danibni bayt]

*** I'll have to have my appendix out.** • **1.** لازِم أسَوِّي عَمَلِيَّة المُصران الأعوَر [la:zim ʔasawwi ʕamaliyyat ʔilmuṣra:n ʔilʔaʕwar]

*** Good stockings are simply not to be had.** • **1.** الجُوارِيب الزَينَة مُستَحِيل تِنلِقِي عِند أحَّد [ʔijjuwa:ri:b ʔizzayna mustaħi:l tinligi ʕind ʔaħħad]

*** Please have a seat.** • **1.** تفَضَّل، إستَرِيح [tfaððal, ʔistari:ħ]

*** He has it in for you.** • **1.** هُوَّ ضَمّها إلَك [huwwa ðammha ʔilak]

*** Let's have the knife!** • **1.** إنطِينِي السِّكِّين [ʔinṭi:ni ʔissičči:n]

*** What did she have on?** • **1.** شكانَت لابسَة؟ [šča:nat la:bsa?]

*** Wouldn't it be better to have it out with him right now?** • **1.** مُو أحسَن لَو تخَلّصها ويّاه هَسَّة؟ [mu: ʔaħsan law txallaṣha wiyya:h hassa?]

I had better, you had better, etc. • **1.** أحسَنلِي [ʔaħsanli] أحسَنلَك [ʔaħsanlak] etc. You'd better do it right away. أحسَنلَك سَوِّيها هَسَّة [ʔaħsanlak sawwi:ha hassa]

to have to • **1.** لازِم [la:zim] عَلَى [ʕala -] واجِب عَل [wa:jib ʕal-] I have to go get my wife. لازِم أرُوح أجِيب زَوجتِي [la:zim ʔaru:ħ ʔaji:b zawijti] We'll have to throw a party for these people. لازِم نسَوِّي حَفلَة لِهَالجَّماعَة [la:zim nsawwi ħafla lihajjama:ʕa] • **2.** اِضطَرّ [ʔiðṭarr] اِضطِرار [ʔiðṭira:r] *vn: sv* a. اِنجُبَر [ʔinjubar] اِنجِبار [ʔinjiba:r] *vn: sv* i. I had to leave early. اِضطَرَّيت أرُوح مِن وَقِت [ʔiðṭarrayt ʔaru:ħ min wakit] They had to fire him. اِضطَرّوا يفُصلُوه [ʔiðṭarraw yufuṣlu:h]

* **You have to have new shoes.** • **1.** لازمَك قُندَرَة جِديدَة [la:zmak qundara ǰidi:da]

not to have to • **1.** ماكُو حاجَة [ma:ku ħa:ǰa] مُو ضَرُوري [mu: ḏaru:ri] ماكُو لزُوم [ma:ku lzu:m] ما لازِم [ma: la:zim] You don't have to go. ماكُو حاجَة تَرُوح [ma:ku ħa:ǰa tru:ħ] You won't have to sign again. ماكُو لزُوم تِمضِي مَرَّة لُخ [ma:ku lzu:m timḏi marra lux] You didn't have to shout like that. ما كان لازِم تصَيِّح هِيكِي [ma: ča:n la:zim tṣayyiħ hi:či]

hawk • **1.** صَقُر [ṣagur] صُقُور [ṣugu:r] *pl:*

hay • **1.** تِبِن [tibin] The hay isn't dry yet. التِّبِن بَعدَه ما يابِس لهَسَّة [ʔittibin baʕdah ma: ya:bis lhassa]

* **It's time to hit the hay.** • **1.** صار وَقت النَوم [ṣa:r wakt ʔinnawm]

* **Let's make hay while the sun shines.**
• **1.** خَلِّي نِستِغِلّ الفُرصَة قَبُل ما تفُوت [xalli nistiɣill ʔilfurṣa gabul ma: tfu:t]

hay fever • **1.** حُمَّى القَشّ [ħumma: ʔilqašš]

haystack • **1.** بَيدَر تِبِن [baydar tibin] بَيادِر تِبِن [baya:dir tibin] *pl:*

hazard • **1.** خَطَر [xaṭar] أخطار [ʔaxṭa:r] *pl:* مُخاطَرَة [muxa:ṭara] مُخاطَرات [muxa:ṭara:t] *pl:* Factory workers are exposed to hazards very much. عُمّال المَعامِل مُعَرَّضِين لِلأخطار كَثِيرَة [ʕumma:l ʔalmaʕa:mil muʕarraḏi:n lilʔaxṭa:r kaθi:ra]

hazelnut • **1.** فِندِقَة [findiqa] فِندِقات [findiqa:t] *pl:* فِندِق [findiq] *Collective:* بُندُقَة [bunduqa] بُندُقات، بَنادِق [bunduqa:t, bana:diq] *pl:* بُندُق [bunduq] *Collective*

hazy • **1.** مغَوَّش [mɣawwaš] It's rather hazy today. عَالأكثَر الدِّنيا مغَوّشَة اليُوم [ʕalʔakθar ʔiddinya mɣawwša ʔilyu:m] • **2.** مُبهَم [mubham] Your ideas are hazy. أفكارَك مُبهَمَة [ʔafka:rak mubhama]

he • **1.** هُوَّ [huwwa] He's very glad. هُوَّ كُلِّش مَسرُور [huwwa kulliš masru:r] He came yesterday. (هُوَّ) جا البارحَة [(huwwa) ǰa: ʔilba:rħa]

head • **1.** راس [ra:s] رُؤُوس [ruʔu:s, ru:s] *pl:* My head hurts. راسِي يَوجَعنِي [ra:si yu:ǰaʕni] Lettuce is ten fils a head. راس الخَسّ بعَشر فلُوس [ra:s ʔilxass bʕašr flu:s] I need nails with larger heads. أحتاج بسامِير راسها أكبَر [ʔaħta:ǰ bsa:mi:r ra:sha ʔakbar] I can't make head nor tail of the story. ما دَأقدَر ألقِي لِهالقُصَّة لا راس وَلا أساس [ma: daʔagdar ʔalgi lihalquṣṣa la: ra:s wala ʔasa:s] He sold five head of cattle. باع خَمِس رُؤُوس هَوش [ba:ʕ xamis ruʔu:s hu:š] Begin at the head of the page. إبدِي مِن راس الصَّفحَة [ʔibdi min ra:s ʔiṣṣfħa] The mayor rode at the head of the procession. رَئِيس البَلَدِيَّة مِشَى عَلَى راس المَوكِب [raʔi:s ʔilbaladiyya miša: ʕala ra:s ʔilmawkib] • **2.** عَقِل [ʕaqil] He has a good head for arithmetic. عِندَه خُوش عَقِل بالحِسابات [ʕindah xu:š ʕaqil bilħisa:ba:t] • **3.** رَئِيس [raʔi:s] رُؤَساء [ruʔasa:, ruʔasa:ʔ] *pl:* He's the head of the gang. هُوَّ رَئِيس العِصابَة [huwwa raʔi:s ʔilʕiṣa:ba] • **4.** رَبّ [rabb] أرباب، ربُوب [ʔarba:b, rbu:b] *pl:* He's the head of the family. هُوَّ رَبّ العائِلَة [huwwa rabb ʔilʕa:ʔila] • **5.** صَدِر [ṣadir] We were sitting at the head of the table. كِنّا قاعدِين بصَدر المِيز [činna ga:ʕdi:n bṣadr ʔilmayz]

* **That's over my head.** • **1.** آني أطرَش بالزَفَّة [ʔa:ni ʔaṭraš bizzaffa]

* **You hit the nail on the head.** • **1.** إنتَ لقَفِتها [ʔinta lgafitha]

* **My friend is head over heels in love.**
• **1.** صَدِيقِي واقِع بِالغَرام [ṣadi:qi wa:giʕ bilɣara:m]

* **That may cost him his head.** • **1.** هَذِي مُمكِن تكَلّفَه حَياتَه [ha:ði mumkin tkallfah ħaya:tah]

* **Heads or tails?** • **1.** طُرَّة لَو كِتبَة؟ [ṭurra lu: kitbaʔ] / شِير لَو خَطّ؟ [ši:r law xaṭṭʔ]

* **I can't keep everything in my head.**
• **1.** ما أقدَر أتذَكَّر كُلّ شِي [ma: ʔagdar ʔatðakkar kull ši]

* **The man is positively out of his head.**
• **1.** هَالرِجّال عَقلَه مُو براسَه [harrijja:l ʕaqlah mu: bra:sah]

* **I don't want to go over his head.**
• **1.** ما أرِيد أرُوح لِلّي أعلَى مِنَّه [ma: ʔari:d ʔaru:ħ lilli ʔaʕla minnah]

* **Things had to come to a head sooner or later.** • **1.** الأشياء لازِم فَدّ يَوم تَوصَل حَدّها [ʔilʔašya:ʔ la:zim fadd yu:m tu:ṣal ħaddha]

* **Everyone kept his head.** • **1.** كُلّ واحِد حافَظ عَلَى إتِّزانَه [kull wa:ħid ħa:faḏ ʕala ʔittiza:nah]

to head • **1.** رأس [riʔas] رئاسَة [riʔa:sa] *vn: sv* a. He hopes to head the department some day. يِتأمَّل يِرأس القِسِم فَدّ يوم [yitʔammal yirʔas ʔilqisim fadd yu:m] • **2.** وَجَّه [wajǰah] تَوجِيه [tawǰi:h] *vn:* توَجَّه [twaǰǰah] *p:* He headed the car at me to murder me. وَجَّه السَّيّارَة عَلَيّا حَتَّى يمَوّتنِي [wajǰah ʔissayya:ra ʕalayya ħatta ymawwitni] • **3.** تفَوَّق عَلَى [tfawwaq ʕala] تَفَوُّق [tafawwuq] *vn: sv* a. My boy heads his class at school. إبنِي مِتفَوِّق عَلَى طُلّاب صَفَّه بِالمَدرَسَة [ʔibni mitfawwiq ʕala ṭulla:b ṣaffah bilmadrasa] • **4.** اِتِّجَه [ʔittiǰah] اِتِّجاه [ʔittiǰa:h] *vn: sv* i. راح [ra:ħ] *sv* u. They're heading for Bagdad. هُمَّ مِتَّجهِين إلَى بَغداد [humma mittaǰhi:n ʔila baɣda:d] Where are you headed? لوَين مِتجِه؟ [lwi:n mittiǰihʔ] Where are you headed? لوَين رايِح؟ [lwi:n ra:yiħʔ]

* **You're heading in the wrong direction.**
• **1.** إنتَ ماخِذ اِتِّجاه غَلَط [ʔinta ma:xið ʔittiǰa:h ɣalaṭ]

* **His name heads the list of candidates.**
• **1.** إسمَه براس قائِمَة المُرَشَّحِين [ʔismah bra:s qa:ʔimat ʔilmuraššaħi:n]

headache • **1.** وُجَع راس [wuǰaʕ ra:s] أوجاع راس [ʔawǰa:ʕ ra:s] *pl:* صُداع [ṣuda:ʕ] I've a bad headache. عِندِي وِجَع راس شَدِيد [ʕindi wiǰaʕ raːs šadiːd] This problem is really a headache. هَالمُشكِلَة حَقِيقَةً وِجَع راس [halmuškila ħaqiːqatan wiǰaʕ raːs]

*** The noise gives me a headache. • 1.** اللَّغوَة دَتوَجِّع راسِي [ʔillaɣwa datwaǰǰiʕ raːsi]

headdress • 1. لِباس راس [libaːs raːs]

heading • 1. اِتِّجاه [ʔittiǰaːh] اِتِّجاهات [ʔittiǰaːhaːt] *pl:* The plane took a new heading. الطَّيّارَة أَخذَت اِتِّجاه جِدِيد [ʔiṭṭayyaːra ʔaxðat ʔittiǰaːh ǰidiːd]

headlight • 1. لايت [laːyt] لايتات [laːytaːt] *pl:*

headline • 1. عِنوان [ʕinwaːn] عَناوِين [ʕanaːwiːn] *pl:* What are the headlines in today's paper? شِنُو العَناوِين مال جَرِيدَة اليُوم؟ [šinu ʔilʕanaːwiːn maːl ǰariːdat ʔilyuːm?]

headlong • 1. عَلَى راس [ʕala raːs] He plunged headlong into the river. كَيَّت بِالشَّطّ عَلَى راسَه [čayyat biššaṭṭ ʕala raːsah]

headquarters • 1. مَركَز قِيادَة [markaz qiyaːda] مَراكِز قِيادَة [maraːkiz qiyaːda] *pl:* مَقَرّ قِيادَة [maqarr qiyaːda] مَقَرّات قِيادَة [maqarraːt qiyaːda] *pl:* This officer was attached to headquarters. هَالضابُط كان مِرتِبُط بمَركَز القِيادَة [haððaːbuṭ čaːn mirtibuṭ bmarkaz ʔilqiyaːda] **• 2.** مَركَز عامّ [markaz ʕaːmm] مَراكِز عامَّة [maraːkiz ʕaːmma] *pl:* مَقَرّ عامّ [maqarr ʕaːmm] مَقَرّات عامَّة [maqarraːt ʕaːmma] *pl:* For further information, apply to party headquarters. لِلحُصُول عَلَى مَعلُومات أَكثَر قَدِّم طَلَب لِلمَقَرّ العامّ لِلحِزب [lilħuṣuːl ʕala maʕluːmaːt ʔakθar qaddim ṭalab lilmaqarr ʔilʕaːmm lilħizib]

headwaiter • 1. رَئِيس بُويَات [raʔiːs buːyaːt] رُؤَساء بُويَات [ruʔasaːʔ buːyaːt] *pl:*

to make headway • 1. تقَدَّم [tqaddam] تَقَدُّم [taqaddum] *vn:* *sv* a. We made headway slowly in the sand. تقَدَّمنا بِبُطء بالرَّمُل [tqaddamna bibuṭuʔ birramul]

head wind • 1. رِيح معاكِس [riːħ mʕaːkis] رِياح معاكسَة [riyaːħ mʕaːksa] *pl:* We had strong head winds all the way. صادفَتنا رِياح معاكسَة قَوِيَّة طُول الطَّرِيق [ṣaːdfatna riyaːħ mʕaːksa qawiyya ṭuːl ʔiṭṭariːq]

to heal • 1. لِحَم [liħam] لَحِم [laħim] *vn:* اِنلِحَم [ʔinliħam] *p:* The treatment is healing the wound successfully. المُعالَجَة دَتِلحَم الجَرِح كُلِّش زين [ʔalmuʕaːlaǰa datilħam ʔiǰǰariħ kulliš ziːn] **• 2.** اِنلِحَم [ʔinliħam] The wound isn't healing properly. الجَرِح ما دَيِنلِحِم زين [ʔiǰǰariħ maː dayinliħim ziːn]

health • 1. صِحَّة [ṣiħħa] How's his health? شلُون صِحّتَه؟ [šluːn ṣiħħtah?] **• 2.** صِحِّي [ṣiħħi] He's working on a new health project. دَيِشتُغُل بِمَشرُوع صِحِّي جدِيد [dayištuɣul bmašruːʕ ṣiħħi ǰdiːd]

healthy • 1. صِحِّي [ṣiħħi] This isn't a healthy climate. هَالجَوّ مُو صِحِّي [haǰǰaww muː ṣiħħi]

*** She looks very healthy. • 1.** مبَيّنَة عَلَيها الصِحَّة [mbayyna ʕaliːha ʔiṣṣiħħa]

heap • 1. كَومَة [kawma] كَومات [kawmaːt] *pl:* What's this heap of sand for? لُويش هالكَومَة مال الرَّمُل؟ [luwiːš halkuːma maːl ʔirramul?]

to heap • 1. كَوَّم [kawwam] تكُوُّم [tkuwwum] *vn:* تكَوَّم [tkawwam] *p:* كَدَّس [kaddas] تَكدِيس [takdiːs] *vn:* تكَدَّس [tkaddas] *p:* The table was heaped with all kinds of food. أَلوان الأَكِل كانَت مكَوَّمَة عالميز [ʔalwaːn ʔilʔakil čaːnat mkawwma ʕalmiːz]

to hear • 1. سِمَع [simaʕ] سَمِع [samiʕ] *vn:* اِنسِمَع [ʔinsimaʕ] *p:* I didn't hear anything. ما سِمَعِت أَيّ شِي [maː simaʕit ʔayy ši] I won't hear of it! ما أَرِيد أَسمَعها [maː ʔariːd ʔasmaʕha] Well then, I'll expect to hear from you. زين إِذَن، أَتوَقَّع أَسمَع مِنَّك [zayn ʔiðan, ʔatwaqqaʕ ʔasmaʕ minnak]

*** You can't hear yourself in this noise.**
• 1. مِن هَاللَّغوَة ما يِنسِمِع شِي [min hallaɣwa maː yinsimiʕ ši]

hearing • 1. مُرافَعَة [muraːfaʕa] مُرافَعات [muraːfaʕaːt] *pl:* The hearing was set for June sixth. تعَيَّن يوم المُرافَعَة سِتَّة حُزَيران [tʕayyan yuːm ʔalmuraːfaʕa sitta ħuzayraːn] **• 2.** سَمِع [samiʕ] His hearing is very poor. سَمعَه كُلِّش ضَعِيف [samʕah kulliš ðaʕiːf]

to lose one's hearing • 1. طِرَشّ [ṭirašš] طَرَش [ṭaraš] *vn:* *sv* a. When did he lose his hearing? شوَقِت طرَشّ؟ [šwakit ṭirašš?]

hearse • 1. عَرَبانَة جنازَة [ʕarabaːnat ǰnaːza] عَرَباين جنازَة [ʕarabaːyin ǰnaːza] *pl:* سَيّارَة جنازَة [sayyaːrat ǰnaːza] سَيّارات جنازَة [sayyaːrataːt ǰnaːza] *pl:*

heart • 1. قَلب [galub] قلُوب [gluːb] *pl:* His heart is weak. قَلبَه ضَعِيف [galbah ðaʕiːf] It breaks my heart to let him go. شِي يِفَطِّر القَلب أَن أَخَلِّيه يرُوح [ši yifaṭṭir ʔilgalub ʔan ʔaxalliːh yiruːħ] I didn't have the heart to tell him. قَلبِي ما نطانِي أَقُلَّه [galbi maː nṭaːni ʔagullah] **• 2.** غَيب [ɣayb, ɣiːb] I learned the poem by heart. حُفَظِت القَصِيدَة عالغَيب [ħufaðit ʔilqaṣiːda ʕalɣayb] **• 3.** حَقِيقَة [ħaqiːqa] أَساس [ʔasaːs] حَقايِق، حَقائِق [ħaqaːyiq, ħaqaːʔiq] *pl:* أَساسات [ʔasaːsaːt] *pl:* I want to get to the heart of this matter. أَرِيد أَتوَصَّل إِلَى حَقِيقَة هَالمَوضُوع [ʔariːd ʔatwaṣṣal ʔila ħaqiːqat halmawðuːʕ]

*** I haven't got the heart to do it. • 1.** قَلبِي ما يِنطِينِي أَسَوِّيها [galbi maː yinṭiːni ʔasawwiːha]

*** Cross my heart! I didn't do it!**
• 1. أَقسِم بِاللّه العَظِيم، ما سَوَّيتها [ʔaqsim billaːh ʔilʕaðiːm, maː sawwiːtha]

* **He's a man after my own heart.**
• **1.** هُوَّ فَدّ واحِد مَيَّه مِثِل مَيِّي [huwwa fadd waːħid mayyah miθil mayyi]
* **Don't lose heart!** • **1.** لا تِفقِد شَجاعتَك [laː tifqid šajaːʕtak]
* **At heart he's really a good fellow.** • **1.** جَوهَرَه زَين [ǰawharah zayn]
hearts • **1.** كُوبَة [kuːpa] Hearts are highest. الكُوبَة أَعلَى شِي [ʔilkuːpa ʔaʕla ši]
to take to heart • **1.** أَخَذ مِن، أَخَذ عَلَى [ʔaxað min, ʔaxað ʕala] أَخِذ [ʔaxið] *vn:* اِنأَخَذ [ʔinʔaxað] *p:* He's taking it very much to heart. هُوَّ ماخِذها كُلِّش بجِدّ [huwwa maːxiðha kulliš bǰidd]

heart attack • **1.** سَكتَة قَلبِيَّة [sakta qalbiyya] سَكتات قَلبِيَّة [saktaːt qalbiyya] *pl:*

H

heartily • **1.** بشَهِيَّة [bšahiyya] برَغبَة [braɣba] We ate heartily. أَكَلنا بشَهِيَّة [ʔakalna bšahiyya] • **2.** مِن كُلّ قَلب [min kull galub] We laughed heartily. ضحَكنا مِن كُلّ قَلبنا [ḍ̄ħakna min kull galubna]

hearty • **1.** دَسِم [dasim] We had a hearty meal. أَكَلنا أَكلَة دَسمَة [ʔakalna ʔakla dasma] We had a hearty meal. أَكَلنا بشَهِيَّة [ʔakalna bšahiyya]
* **He's hale and hearty in spite of his age.**
• **1.** مَترُوس صِحَّة برَغُم سِنَّه [matruːs ṣiħħa braɣum sinnah] / كُلَّه صِحَّة بِرَغُم سِنَّه [kullah ṣiħħa braɣum sinnah]

heat • **1.** حَرارَة [ħaraːra] سُخُونَة [suxuːna] I can't stand the heat. ما أَقدَر أَتحَمَّل الحَرارَة [maː ʔagdar ʔatħammal ʔilħaraːra] The stove doesn't give enough heat. الصُّوبَة ما تِنطِي حَرارَة كافيَة [ʔiṣṣuːpa maː tinṭi ħaraːra kaːfya] • **2.** شَوط [šawṭ] My horse won the first heat. حصانِي غِلَب بِالشُّوط الأَوَّل [ħṣaːni ɣilab biššuːṭ ʔilʔawwal]
* **It happened in the heat of the battle.**
• **1.** صارَت مِن كانَت المَعرَكَة حامية [ṣaːrat min čaːnat ʔilmaʕraka ħaːmya]
in heat • **1.** متهَيِّجَة [mithayyiǰa] Our cat's in heat. بَزُّونَتنا متهَيِّجَة [bazzuːnatna mithayyiǰa]
to heat • **1.** دَفَّى [daffaː] *vn:* اتدَفَّى [ʔiddaffaː] *p:* The room is well heated. الغُرفَة مدَفَّايَة زين [ʔilɣurfa mdaffaːya ziːn] • **2.** حِمَى [ħimaː] حَمِي [ħamy] *vn: sv* a. The living-room radiator doesn't heat up. صَوبَة غُرفَة القَعدَة ما دَتِحمَى [ṣuːpat ɣurfat ʔilgaʕda maː datiħmaː] It'll be five minutes before the iron heats up. الأُوتِي ينرادلَه خَمِس دَقايِق حَتَّى يِحمَى [ʔilʔuːti yinraːdlah xamis daqaːyiq ħatta yiħmaː] • **3.** حِمَى [ħimaː] اِنحِمَى [ʔinħimaː] *p:* سَخَّن [saxxan] تَسخِين [tasxiːn] *vn:* تسَخَّن [tsaxxan] *p:* I'll have to heat up some water first. أَوَّل لازِم أَحمِي شوَيَّة ماي [ʔawwal laːzim ʔaħmi šwayya maːy]

heater • **1.** صَوبَة [ṣuːpa] صَوبات [ṣuːpaːt] *pl:* مَدفَأَة [madfaʔa] مَدفَآت، مَدافِئ [madfaʔaːt, madaːfiʔ] *pl:*

heat-resistant • **1.** مُقاوُم لِلحَرارَة [muqaːwum lilħaraːra] Is that glass heat-resistant? هَالزُّجاج مُقاوُم لِلحَرارَة؟ [hazzuǰaːǰ muqaːwum lilħaraːra?]

heaven • **1.** جَنَّة [ǰanna] When the good man dies he goes to heaven. الرَّجُل الصَّالِح مِن يمُوت يرُوح لِلجَنَّة [ʔirraǰul ʔiṣṣaːliħ min ymuːt yiruːħ liǰǰanna]
* **She was in seventh heaven.** • **1.** كانَت فِي أَوج السَعادَة [čaːnat fi ʔawǰ ʔissaʕaːda]
* **For heaven's sake, stop that noise!**
• **1.** دَخِيل الله بَطِّل هَالحِسّ [daxiːl ʔallah baṭṭil halħiss] / يا معَوَّد، بَطِّل هَاللَّغوَة [yaː mʕawwad, baṭṭil hallaɣwa]
* **Only heaven knows how often I've tried.**
• **1.** بَسّ الله يِدرِي كَم مَرَّة حاوَلِت [bass ʔallah yidri čam marra ħaːwalit]

heavy • **1.** ثِقِيل [θigiːl] Is that box too heavy for you? هَالصَّندُوق كُلِّش ثِقِيل عَلِيك؟ [haṣṣanduːg kulliš θigiːl ʕaliːk?] I can't take heavy food. ما أَقدَر آكُل شِي ثِقِيل [maː ʔagdar ʔaːkul ši θigiːl] • **2.** كبِير [čbiːr] كَبِير [kabiːr] كبار [kbaːr] *pl:* He had to pay a heavy fine. اِضطَرّ يِدفَع غَرامَة كبِيرَة [ʔiḍ̄ṭarr yidfaʕ ɣaraːma čibiːra] • **3.** قَوِي [qawi, guwi] قوَاي، أَقوِياء، قَوِيِّين [qwaːy, ʔaqwiyaːʔ, qawiyyiːn] *pl:* شَدِيد [šadiːd] We can't leave in that heavy rain. ما نِقدَر نرُوح بهالمُطَر القَوِي [maː nigdar nruːħ bhaːlmuṭar ʔilqawi]
* **He's a heavy drinker.** • **1.** هُوَّ سِكِّير [huwwa sikkiːr]

Hebrew • **1.** عِبرِي [ʕibri] عِبرانِي [ʕibraːni] Do you know the Hebrew alphabet? تُعرُف الحُرُوف العِبرِيَّة؟ [tuʕruf ʔilħuruːf ʔilʕibriyya?] • **2.** عِبرِيَّة [ʕibriyya] عِبرِيّات [ʕibriyyaːt] *pl:* عِبرِي [ʕibri] عِبرِيَّة [ʕibriːyya] *pl:* Do you speak Hebrew? تِتكَلَّم بالعِبرِيَّة؟ [titkallam bilʕibriyya?]

hedge • **1.** سِياج ياس [siyaːǰ yaːs] سِياجات ياس [siyaːǰaːt yaːs] *pl:*

heel • **1.** كَعَب [čaʕab] كعُوب [čʕuːb] *pl:* I have a blister on my heel of my foot. عِندِي بُطباطَة بكَعَب رِجلِي [ʕindi buṭbaːṭa bčaʕab riǰli] These shoes need new heels. هَالقُندَرَة تِحتاج كَعَب جِدِيد [halqundara tiħtaːǰ čaʕab ǰidiːd]

hegira • **1.** هِجرَة [hiǰra] هِجرات [hiǰraːt] *pl:*

height • **1.** اِرتِفاع [ʔirtifaːʕ] اِرتِفاعات [ʔirtifaːʕaːt] *pl:* How do you determine the height of a triangle? شلُون تعَيِّن اِرتِفاع المُثَلَّث؟ [šluːn tʕayyin ʔirtifaːʕ ʔilmuθallaθ?] • **2.** أَوج [ʔawǰ] He was then at the height of his power. بذاك الوَقِت كان بأَوج قُوَّتَه [bðaːk ʔilwakit čaːn biʔawǰ quwwtah] • **3.** غايَة [ɣaːya] غايات [ɣaːyaːt] *pl:* That's the height of stupidity. هَذِي غايَة الغَباء [haːði ɣaːyat ʔilɣabaːʔ]

heir • **1.** وارِث [wariːθ] وَرَثَة [waraθa] *pl:* He's the sole heir. هُوَّ الوارِث الوَحِيد [huwwa ʔilwaːriθ ʔilwaħiːd]

hell • **1.** جِهَنَّم [ǰihannam] جَحِيم [ǰaħiːm] He died and went to hell. مات وَراح لِجهَنَّم [maːt wraːħ liǰhannam]

hello • **1.** هَلُو [halaw] Hello, operator! You've cut me off. هَلو، مَأمُورَة البَدّالَة، قِطَعتِي الخَطّ عَنِّي [halaw, maʔamuːrat ʔilbaddaːla, qiṭaʕti ʔilxaṭṭ ʕanni]

helmet • **1.** خُوذَة [xuːða] خُوَذ [xuwað] *pl:*

help • **1.** مُساعَدَة [musaːʕada] مُساعَدات [musaːʕadaːt] *pl:* مُعاوَنَة [muʕaːwana] مَعُونَة [maʕuːna] Do you need any help? تِحتاج أَيّ مُساعَدَة؟ [tiħtaːǰ ʔayy musaːʕada?]
*** It's difficult to get help these days.**
• **1.** صَعُب تِلقِي أَحَّد يعاوِنَك هَالأَيّام [ṣaʕub tilgi ʔaħħad yʕaːwinak halʔayyaːm]
*** Help!** • **1.** يا أَهل الرَّحَم [yaː ʔahl ʔirraħam]
to help • **1.** ساعَد [saːʕad] مُساعَدَة [musaːʕada] *vn:* تساعَد [tsaːʕad] *p:* عاوَن [ʕaːwan] مُعاوَنَة [muʕaːwana] *vn:* تعاوَن [tʕaːwan] *p:* عان [ʕaːn] عَون [ʕuːn] *vn:* *sv* i. Please help me. مِن فَضلَك ساعِدنِي [min faðlak saːʕidni] • **2.** ساعَد [saːʕad] مُساعَدَة [musaːʕada] *vn:* تساعَد [tsaːʕad] *p:* She helps us out on Sunday. هِيَّ تساعِدنا بالشّغُل يوم الأَحَّد [hiyya tsaːʕidna biššɣul yuːm ʔilʔaħħad]
*** I can't help it, but that's my opinion.** • **1.** شَسَوِّي [šasawwi] / لا تلُومنِي، هَذا رَأيِي [laː tluːmni, haːða raʔyi]
*** I couldn't help but see it.** • **1.** ما قدَرِت إلّا أَشُوفها [maː gdarit ʔilla ʔašuːfha]
*** Sorry, that can't be helped.** • **1.** مِتأَسِّف، ما مُمكِن تِتغَيَّر [mitʔassif, maː mumkin titɣayyar]
to help oneself • **1.** تفَضَّل [tfaððal] تَفَضُّل [tafaððul] *vn:* *sv* a. Please help yourself! تفَضَّل [tfaððal]

helper • **1.** صانِع [ṣaːniʕ] صِنّاع [ṣinnaːʕ] *pl:* He has two helpers. عِندَه صانعَين [ʕindah ṣaːnʕayn]

helpful • **1.** خَدُوم [xaduːm] She's always very helpful. هِيَّ دائِماً كُلّش خَدُومَة [hiyya daːʔiman kulliš xaduːma]
• **2.** مُفِيد [mufiːd] You've given me a very helpful hint. إنطِيتنِي فَدّ إشارَة كُلّش مُفِيدَة [ʔinṭiːtni fadd ʔišaːra kulliš mufiːda]

helping • **1.** تَرِس ماعُون [taris maːʕuːn] I had two helpings. أَكَلِت تَرِس ماعُونَين [ʔakalit taris maːʕuːniːn]

helpless • **1.** عاجِز [ʕaːǰiz] عاجِزِين [ʕaːǰiziːn] *pl:* عَجَزَة [ʕaǰaza] عاجِزِين [ʕaːǰiziːn] *pl:* A baby is helpless. الطِّفِل عاجِز عَن كُلّشِي [ʔiṭṭifil ʕaːǰiz ʕan kullši]

hem • **1.** حاشِيَة [ħaːšiya] حَواشِي [ħawaːši] *pl:* I want to let out the hem. أَرِيد أَفُكّ الحاشِيَة [ʔariːd ʔafukk ʔilħaːšya]
to hem • **1.** كَفّ [kaff] كَفّ [kaff] *vn:* اِنكَفّ [ʔinkaff] *p:* Mother, hem this skirt for me. يوم كُفِّيلِي التَّنُّورَة [yuːm kuffiːli ʔittannuːra]
to hem in • **1.** حِصَر [ħiṣar] حَصِر [ħaṣir] *vn:* اِنحِصَر [ʔinħiṣar] *p:* أحاط [ʔaħaːṭ] حَوط [ħawṭ] *vn:* اِنحاط [ʔinħaːṭ] *p:* The house is hemmed between two tall buildings. البَيت مَحصُور بين بنايتَين عالية [ʔilbayt maħṣuːr bayn binaːytayn ʕaːlya]

hen • **1.** دِجاجَة [diǰaːǰa] دِجاجات [diǰaːǰaːt] *pl:* دِجاج [diǰaːǰ] *Collective*

her • **1.** ها [ha] I saw her last week. شِفِتها بالإسبُوع الماضِي [šifitha bilʔisbuːʕ ʔilmaːði] That was very nice of her. هَذِي كانَت كُلِّش حِلوَة مِنها [haːði čaːnat kulliš ħilwa minha] This is her house. هَذا بَيتها [haːða baytha]

herb • **1.** عِشِب [ʕišib] In Iraq they still use herbs as remedies. بالعِراق بَعَدهُم يِستَعمِلُون الأَعشاب كَأَدوِيَة [bilʕiraːq baʕadhum yistaʕmiluːn ʔilʔaʕšaːb kaʔadwiya]

herd • **1.** قَطِيع [qaṭiːʕ] قِطعان [qiṭʕaːn] *pl:* Who owns this herd? مِنُو صاحِب هالقَطِيع؟ [minu ṣaːħib halqaṭiːʕ?]
to herd • **1.** حِشَر [ħišar] حَشِر [ħašir] *vn:* اِنحِشَر [ʔinħišar] *p:* جِمَع [ǰimaʕ] جَمِع [ǰamiʕ] *vn:* اِنجِمَع [ʔinǰimaʕ] *p:* They herded us all into a small room. حِشرَونا كُلّنا بِفَدّ غُرفَة صغَيِّرَة [ħišrawna kullna bfadd ɣurfa ṣɣayyra]

here • **1.** هنا [hna] هنايَة [hnaːya] We can't stay here. ما نِقدَر نِبقى هنا [maː nigdar nibqaː hna] Let's cross the street (from) here. خَلّي نُعبُر الشّارِع مِن هنا [xalliː nuʕbur ʔiššaːriʕ min hna] The papers here say nothing about the accident. الجَّرايِد هنا ما تِكتِب أَيّ شِي عَن الحادِثَة [ʔiǰǰaraːyid hnaː maː tiktib ʔayy ši ʕan ʔilħaːdiθa]
*** Here's the book.** • **1.** هَذا الِكتاب [haːða ʔiliktaːb] / هاك الِكتاب [haːk ʔilkitaːb]
*** Here's to you!** • **1.** لصِحّتَك [lṣiħħtak] / لِنَخبَك [lnaxbak]

hereafter • **1.** مِسَّة غادِي، مِن هَنا وغادِي [missa ɣaːdi, min hna wɣaːdi] بَعدَين [baʕdayn] Hereafter I'll be more alert. مِسَّة غادِي أَكُون مِنتِبِه أَزيَد [missa ɣaːdi ʔakuːn mintibih ʔazyad] • **2.** الآخرَة [ʔilʔaːxra] Some people believe in the hereafter. بَعَض النّاس يِعتِقدُون بالآخرَة [baʕað ʔinnaːs yiʕtiqduːn bilʔaːxra]

hernia • **1.** فَتِق رِيح [fatig riːħ] فتُوق رِيح [ftuːg riːħ] *pl:*

hero • **1.** بَطَل [baṭal] أبطال [ʔabṭaːl] *pl:*

heroic • **1.** بُطُولِي [buṭuːli] مالها [maːlha] مالِتها [maːlitha]

hers • **1.** مال [maːl-] مالها [maːlha] مالِتها [maːlitha] My hat is bigger than hers. شَفُقتِي أَكبَر مِن مالَتها [šafuqti ʔakbar min maːlatha]
*** A friend of hers told me.** • **1.** صَدِيق مِن أَصدِقائها قالِّي [ṣadiːq min ʔaṣdiqaːʔha gaːlli]

H

herself • **1.** نَفِس [nafis] نُفُوس، أَنفُس [nufuːs, ʔanfus] *pl:* رُوح [ruːħ] أَرواح [ʔarwaːħ] *pl:* She fell on the stairs and hurt herself. وُقعَت عَالدَّرَج وَأَذَّت نَفِسها [wugʕat ʕaddarağ wʔaððat nafisha] She fell on the stairs and hurt herself. وُقعَت عَالدَّرَج وَتأَذَّت [wugʕat ʕaddarağ wtʔaððat] She did it by herself. هِيَّ سَوَّتَها بنَفِسها [hiyya sawwatha bnafsha]

*** She's not herself today.** • **1.** هِيَّ مُو عَلَى بَعَضها هَاليَوم [hiyya muː ʕala baʕaðha halyawm]

to hesitate • **1.** تَرَدَّد [traddad] تَرَدُّد [taraddud] *vn: sv* a. He hesitated a moment before he answered. تَرَدَّد فَدّ لَحظَة قَبُل ما جاوِب [traddad fadd laħða gabul maː ǧaːwab] Don't hesitate to call if you need me. لا تِتَرَدَّد تخابُرنِي إذا تِحتاجنِي [laː titraddad txaːburni ʔiða tiħtaːǧni]

hesitation • **1.** تَرَدُّد [taraddud] He answered without hesitation. جاوُب بِدُون تَرَدُّد [ǧaːwab biduːn taraddud]

hiccup • **1.** شِهَّيقَة [šihhiːga] شِهَّيقات [šihhiːgaːt] *pl:* شَهقَة [šahga] شَهقات [šahgaːt] *pl:* I have the hiccups again. هَمّ جَتنِي الشِّهَّيقَة [hamm ǧatni ʔiššihhiːga]

hide • **1.** جِلِد [ǧilid] جُلُود [ǧuluːd] *pl:* These hides still have to be tanned. هالجِّلُود لازِم بَعَد تِندُبُغ [haǧǧiluːd laːzim baʕad tindubuɣ]

to hide • **1.** ضَمّ [ðamm] ضَمّ [ðamm] *vn:* اِنضَمّ [ʔinðamm] *p:* خِفَى [xifaː] خَفِي [xafy] *vn:* اِنخِفَى [ʔinxifaː] *p:* خَفَّى [xaffaː] تخِفِّي [txiffi] *vn:* تخَفَّى [txaffaː] *p:* He hid the money in the drawer. ضَمّ الفلُوس بِالمَجَرّ [ðamm ʔilfluːs bilmaǧarr] • **2.** خِفَى [xifaː] خَفِي [xafi] *vn:* اِنخِفَي [ʔinxifaː] *p:* The trees hide the view. الأشجار تِخفِي المَنظَر [ʔilʔašǧaːr tixfi ʔilmanðar] • **3.** خِتَل [xital] خَتِل [xatil] *vn: sv* i. Let's hide in the garage. خَلِّي نِختِل بِالكَراج [xalli nixtil bilgaraːǧ]

hideous • **1.** بَشِع [bašiʕ] That's a hideous face you have! شلُون وِجِه بَشِع عِندَك [šluːn wiǧih bašiʕ ʕindak] • **2.** قَبِيح [qabiːħ] Where did you buy that hideous hat? منِين إشتِرَيتِي هَالشَّفقَة القَبِيحَة؟ [mniːn ʔištiriːti haššafqa ʔilqabiːħa?]

hieroglyphics • **1.** الهِيرُوغلِيفِيَّة [ʔilhiːruːɣliːfiyya]

high • **1.** مُستَوَي (مِن الإرتِفاع) [mustawa (min ʔilʔirtifaːʕ)] Prices have reached a new high. الأسعار وُصلَت إلَى مُستَوَى جِدِيد مِن الإرتِفاع [ʔilʔasʕaːr wuṣlat ʔila mustawa ǧidiːd min ʔilirtifaːʕ] • **2.** عالِي [ʕaːli] I have a high opinion of him. رَأيِي بِيه كُلِّش عالِي [raʔyi biːh kulliš ʕaːli] The airplane is too high to see. الطَّيّارَة كُلِّش عالِيَة ما تِنشاف [ʔiṭṭayyaːra kulliš ʕaːlya maː tinšaːf] • **3.** طاب [ṭaːb] Now shift into high gear. هَسَّة حُطها عَلَى طاب قِير [hassa ħuṭṭha ʕala ṭaːb giːr]

*** That building is eight stories high.** • **1.** هَالبِناية اِرتِفاعها ثمَن طَوابِق [halbinaːya ʔirtifaːʕha θman ṭawaːbiq]

highlight • **1.** أَهَمّ مُناسَبَة [ʔahamm munaːsaba] أَهَمّ مُناسَبات [ʔahamm munaːsabaːt] *pl:* Our party was the highlight of the season. حَفلَتنا كانَت أَهَمّ مُناسَبَة بِالسَّنَة [ħaflatna čaːnat ʔahamm munaːsaba bissana]

highly • **1.** كُلِّش [kulliš] She seemed highly pleased. ظِهرَت كُلِّش مَمنُونَة [ðiharat kulliš mamnuːna] • **2.** بكُلّ خَير [bkull xiːr] He spoke very highly of him. جاب ذِكرَه بِكُلّ خير [ǧaːb ðikrah bkull xiːr]

high school • **1.** مَدرَسَة ثانَوِيَّة [madrasa θanawiyya] مَدارِس ثانَوِيَّة [madaːris θanawiyya] *pl:*

high tide • **1.** مَدّ [madd] Let's wait till high tide. خَلِّي نِنتِظِر لَمَّن يصِير المَدّ [xalli nintiðir lamman yṣiːr ʔilmadd]

highway • **1.** طَرِيق [ṭariːq] طُرُق [ṭuruq] *pl:* The highway between Baghdad and Najef is completely paved. الطَّرِيق بين بَغداد وَالنَّجَف كُلَّه مبَلَّط [ʔiṭṭariːq bayn baɣdaːd wʔinnaǧaf kullah mballaṭ]

hike • **1.** سَفرَة مَشِي [safra mašy] سَفرات مَشِي [safraːt mašy] *pl:* Let's go on a hike! خَلِّي نِطلَع سَفرَة مَشِي [xalli niṭlaʕ safra mašy] Let's go on a hike! خَلِّي نسَوِّي مَشيَة [xalli nsawwi mašya] **2.** مَشيَة [mašya]

to hike • **1.** مِشَى [mišaː] مَشِي [maši] *vn: sv* i. We hiked five miles. مِشَينا خَمس أَميال [mišayna xams ʔamyaːl]

hill • **1.** تَلّ [tall] تلال، تلُول [tlaːl, tluːl] *pl:* What's on the other side of the hill? شَكُو بالجِّهَة الثّانيَة مِن التَّلّ؟ [šaku biǧǧiha ʔiθθaːnya min ʔittall?]

him • **1.** ه [h] I've seen him. شِفتَه [šiftah]

himself • **1.** نَفسَه [nafsah] نُفُوس، أَنفُس [nufuːs, ʔanfus] *pl:* رُوحَه [ruːħah] رُوح أَرواح [ʔarwaːħ] *pl:* He hurt himself badly. أَذَّى نَفسَه كُلِّش [ʔaððaː nafsah kulliš] He hurt himself badly. تأَذَّى كُلِّش [tʔaððaː kulliš] Did he do it by himself? هُوَّ بِنَفسَه سَوّاها؟ [huwwa bnafsah sawwaːha?]

*** He's quite beside himself.** • **1.** ما يِدرِي بنَفسَه [maː yidri bnafsah]

*** He's himself again.** • **1.** رِجَع لحالتَه الطَّبِيعِيَّة [riǧaʕ lħaːltah ʔiṭṭabiːʕiyya]

*** He's not himself today.** • **1.** هَذا مُو عَلَى بَعضَه اليَوم [haːða muː ʕala baʕðah ʔilyuːm]

to hinder • **1.** عَوَّق [ʕawwag] تَعوِيق [taʕwiːq] *vn:* تعَوَّق [tʕawwaq] *p:* You're hindering me in my work. إنتَ تعَوُّقنِي بِشغلِي [ʔinta tʕawwugni bšɣli]

hinge • **1.** نُرمادَة [nurmaːda] نُرمادات [nurmaːdaːt] *pl:* One of the hinges of the door is broken. وِحدَة مِن نُرمادات الباب مَكسُورَة [wiħda min nurmaːdaːt ʔilbaːb maksuːra]

to hinge • **1.** توَقَّف [twaqqaf] تَوَقُّف [tawaqquf] *vn: sv* a. Everything hinges on his decisions. كُلْشِي يِتوَقَّف عَلَى قَرارَه [kullši yitwaqqaf ʕala qaraːrah]

hint • **1.** إشارَة [ʔišaːra] إشارات [ʔišaːraːt] *pl:* تَلمِيحَة [talmiːħa] تَلمِيحات [talmiːħaːt] *pl:* تَنوِيهَة [tanwiːha] تَنوِيهات [tanwiːhaːt] *pl:* Can't you give me a hint? ما تِقدَر تِنطِينِي فَدّ إشارَة؟ [maː tigdar tinṭiːni fadd ʔišaːra?]

*** There's just a hint of mint in this drink.**

• **1.** أكُو رِيحَة نِعناع بِالمَشرُوب [ʔaku riːħat niʕnaːʕ bilmašruːb]

to hint • **1.** أشَّر [ʔaššar] تاشِّر [tʔiššir] *vn:* تأشَّر [tʔaššar] *p:* لَمَّح [lammaħ] تلِمِّح، تَلمِيح [tlimmiħ, talmiːħ] *vn:* تلَمَّح [tlammaħ] *p: sv* i. نَوَّه [nawwah] تَنوِيه [tanwiːh] *vn:* تنَوَّه [tnawwah] *p: sv* i. He hinted that something was up. أشَّر بِأن أكُو فَدّ شِي [ʔaššar bʔan ʔaku fadd ši]

hip • **1.** ورِك [wirik] ورُوك [wruːk] *pl:*

hire • **1.** أُجرَة [ʔuǰra] أُجُور [ʔuǰuːr] *pl:* كَري [kary] We have boats for hire. عِدنا بلام لِلأُجرَة [ʕidna blaːm lilʔuǰra]

to hire • **1.** أجَّر [ʔaǰǰar] تاجِّر، تَأجِير [tʔiǰǰir, taʔǰiːr] *vn:* تأجَّر [tʔaǰǰar] *p:* كِرَى [kiraː] كَري [kary] *vn:* اِنكِرَى [ʔinkiraː] *p:* We hired the boat for the whole day. أجَّرنا البَلَم لِليوم كُلَّه [ʔaǰǰarna ʔilbalam lilyuːm kullah] • **2.** أجَّر [ʔaǰǰar] تاجِّر، تَأجِير [tʔiǰǰir, taʔǰiːr] *vn:* تأجَّر [tʔaǰǰar] *p:* شَغَّل [šaɣɣal] تَشغِيل [tašɣiːl] *vn:* تشَغَّل [tšaɣɣal] *p:* اِستَخدَم [ʔistaxdam] اِستِخدام [ʔistixdaːm] *vn: sv* i. We have to hire some people. لازِم نأجِّر بَعَض النّاس [laːzim nʔaǰǰir baʕaḍ ʔinnaːs]

his • **1.** ه [h] Have you got his address? عِندَك عِنوانَه؟ [ʕindak ʕinwaːnah?] This car is his. هَذِي السَّيّارَة مالتَه [haːði ʔissayyaːra maːltah]

*** I met a friend of his.** • **1.** قابَلِت واحِد مِن أصدِقائَه [qaːbalit waːħid min ʔaṣdiqaːʔah]

hiss • **1.** فَحِيح [faħiːħ] نَفخَة [nafxa] نَفخات [nafxaːt] *pl:* I heard the hiss of a snake. سِمَعِت فَحِيح حَيَّة [simaʕit faħiːħ ħayya]

to hiss • **1.** نِفَخ [nifax] نَفُخ [nafux] *vn: sv* u. فَحّ [faħħ] فِحِيح [fiħiːħ] *vn: sv* i. Snakes hiss. الحَيّات تِنفُخ [ʔilħayyaːt tinfux]

historian • **1.** مُؤَرِّخ [muʔarrix] مُؤَرِّخِين [muʔarrix iːn] *pl:*

historic • **1.** تارِيخِي [taːriːxi]

history • **1.** تارِيخ [taːriːx] Have you studied European history? دِرَسِت تارِيخ أورُبِّي؟ [dirasit taːriːx ʔuːruppi?] That picture has quite a history. هَالصُّورَة إلها تارِيخ [haṣṣuːra ʔilha taːriːx]

hit • **1.** إصابَة [ʔiṣaːba] إصابات [ʔiṣaːbaːt] *pl:* ضَربَة [ḍarba] ضَربات [ḍarbaːt] *pl:* There are two hits in the bull's-eye. أكُو إصابتَين بمَركَز الهَدَف [ʔaku ʔiṣaːbtayn bmarkaz ʔilhadaf]

*** His song became a hit over night.**

• **1.** غِنُوتَه اِنشِهرَت بيَوم ولَيلَة [ɣinuːtah ʔinšiharat byawm wlayla]

to hit • **1.** ضِرَب [ḍirab] ضَرُب [ḍarub] *vn:* اِنضِرَب [ʔinḍirab] *p:* The ball hit the door. الكُرَة ضُربَت الباب [ʔilkura ḍurbat ʔilbaːb] Who hit you? مِنُو ضِرَبَك؟ [minu ḍirabak?] • **2.** صِدَم [ṣidam] صَدِم [ṣadim] *vn:* اِنصِدَم [ʔinṣidam] *p:* The news hit me hard. الأخبار صِدمَتنِي صَدمَة عَنِيفَة [ʔilʔaxbaːr ṣidmatni ṣadma ʕaniːfa] • **3.** صِدَم [ṣidam] *sv* i. ضِرَب [ḍirab] *sv* u. The car hit him and broke his leg. السَّيّارَة صِدمَتَه وكِسرَت رِجلَه [ʔissayyaːra ṣidmatah wkisrat riǰlah] • **4.** طَخّ [ṭaxx] طَخّ [ṭaxx] *vn:* اِنطَخّ [ʔinṭaxx] *p:* I hit my knee against the door. طَخَّيت رُكُبتِي بِالباب [ṭaxxiːt rukubti bilbaːb]

to hit it off • **1.** تلائَم [tlaːʔam] تَلائُم [talaːʔum] *vn: sv* a. They hit it off pretty well after they met. تلائمُوا كُلِّش زين بَعَد ما اِلتِقَوا [tlaːʔmaw kulliš ziːn baʕad maː ʔiltiqaw]

*** How did you hit on the right answer?**

• **1.** شلُون جا الجَواب؟ [šluːn ǰaː ʔiǰǰawaːb?]

hitch • **1.** تَعقِيد [taʕqiːd] تَعقِيدات [taʕqiːdaːt] *pl:* Everything came off without a hitch. كُلْشِي كان بِدُون تَعقِيد [kullši čaːn biduːn taʕqiːd] That's where the hitch comes in! هنا مَصدَر التَّعقِيد [hna maṣdar ʔittaʕqiːd]

*** I'm sure there's a hitch somewhere.**

• **1.** آنِي مِتأكِّد أكُو فَدّ لِعبَة بهَالشِّي [ʔaːni mitʔakkid aku fadd liʕba bhašši]

to hitch • **1.** رُبَط [rubaṭ] رَبُط [rabuṭ] *vn:* اِنرُبَط [ʔinrubaṭ] *p:* Hitch your horse to the post. أربُط حصانَك بالعَمُود [ʔurbuṭ ħṣaːnak bilʕamuːd] • **2.** شَكَّل [šakkal] تشِكِّل [tšikkil] *vn: sv* i. كَلَّب [čallab] تكِلِّب [tčillib] *vn: sv* i. Did you hitch the horses to the wagon yet? شَكَّلِت الخَيل بِالعَرَبانَة لَو بَعَد؟ [šakkalit ʔilxayl bilʕarabaːna law baʕad?]

hive • **1.** خَلِيَّة [xaliyya] خَلِيّات [xaliyyaːt] *pl:* We have six hives of honey bees. عِدنا سِتّ خَلِيّات مال نَحَل العَسَل [ʕidna sitt xaliyyaːt maːl naħal ʔilʕasal]

hives • **1.** شِرَى [širaː] شَرَع [šaraʕ] I've got hives. عِندِي شِرَة [ʕindi šira]

to hoard • **1.** خِزَن [xizan] خَزِن [xazin] *vn:* اِنخِزَن [ʔinxizan] *p:* They're hoarding sugar. دَيخِزنُون شَكَر [dayxiznuːn šakar]

hoarse • **1.** مَبحُوح [mabħuːħ] He's hoarse today. صَوتَه مَبحُوح اليُوم [ṣuːtah mabħuːħ ʔilyuːm]

H

hobby • **1.** هِوايَة [hiwaːya] هِوايات [hiwaːyaːt] *pl:* وَلَع [walaʕ] His latest hobby is collecting stamps. هِوايتَه الأَخِيرَة جَمع الطَّوابِع [hiwaːytah ʔilʔaxiːra ǰamʕ ʔiṭṭawaːbiʕ]

hog • **1.** خَنزِير [xanziːr, xinziːr] خَنازِير [xanaːziːr] *pl:* He raises hogs. هُوَّ يرَبِّي خَنازِير [huwwa yrabbi xanaːziːr]
*** Don't be such a hog!** • **1.** لا تكُون شَرِه [laː tkuːn šarih]

to hold • **1.** شال [šaːl] شَيل [šayl] *vn:* اِنشال [ʔinšaːl] *p:* She's holding the baby in her arms. شايلَة الجّاهِل بِيدها [šaːyla ʔiǰǰaːhil biːdha] • **2.** لِزَم [lizam] لَزِم [lazim] *vn:* اِنلِزَم [ʔinlizam] *p:* That knot will hold. هَالعُقدَة تِلزَم [halʕugda tilzam] Hold your tongue! اِلزَم لِسانَك [ʔilzam lisaːnak] Hold your tongue! سِدّ حَلقَك [sidd ħalgak] The room holds twenty people. الغُرفَة تِلزَم عِشرِين شَخِص [ʔilɣurfa tilzam ʕišriːn šaxiṣ] • **3.** كُمَش [kumaš] كَمِش [kamiš] *vn:* اِنكُمَش [ʔinkumaš] *p:* لِزَم [lizam] *sv* a. Hold him! أُكُمشَه [ʔukumšah] • **4.** سَوَّى [sawwaː] تسُوِّي [tsuwwi] *vn:* تسَوَّى [tsawwaː] *p:* قام [qaːm] قِيام [qiyaːm] *vn:* اِنقام [ʔinqaːm] *p:* *sv* u. When shall we hold the election? شوَقِت نسَوِّي الانتِخاب؟ [šwakit nsawwi ʔilʔintixaːb?] • **5.** عِند [ʕind] He holds a high position. عِندَه مَركَز عالِي [ʕindah markaz ʕaːli] • **6.** عِقَد [ʕiqad] عَقِد [ʕaqid] *vn:* اِنعِقَد [ʔinʕiqad] *p:* The meetings are held once a week. الاجتِماعات تِنعِقِد مَرَّة بالإسبُوع [ʔilʔiǰtimaːʕaːt tinʕiqid marra bilʔisbuːʕ] • **7.** تطَبَّق [tṭabbaq] تطُبُّق [tṭubbuq] *vn:* *sv* a. This rule doesn't hold in every case. هَالأَمُر ما يِتطَبَّق عَلَى كُلّ حالَة [halʔamur maː yiṭṭabbaq ʕala kull ħaːla] • **8.** جِذَب [ǰiðab] جَذِب [ǰaðib] *vn:* اِنجِذَب [ʔinǰiðab] *p:* That speaker knows how to hold his audience. هالخَطِيب يُعرُف شلُون يِجذِب المُستَمِعِين [halxaṭiːb yuʕruf šluːn yiǰðib ʔilmustamiʕiːn]
to hold back • **1.** مِنَع [minaʕ] مَنِع [maniʕ] *vn:* اِنمِنَع [ʔinminaʕ] *p:* لِزَم [lizam] لَزِم [lazim] *vn:* اِنلِزَم [ʔinlizam] *p:* I wanted to go, but he held me back. آنِي رِدِت أرُوح، بَسّ هُوَّ مِنَعنِي [ʔaːni ridit ʔaruːħ, bass huwwa minaʕni]
to hold on • **1.** اِنتِظَر [ʔintiđar] اِنتِظار [ʔintiđaːr] *vn:* *sv* i. Can you hold on for a minute? تِقدَر تِنتِظِر فَدّ دَقِيقَة؟ [tigdar tintiđir fadd daqiːqa?]
to hold on to • **1.** كَلَّب [čallab] تكلِيب، تكِلِّب [tačliːb, tčillib] *vn:* تكَلَّب [tčallab] *p:* ب [b] لِزَم [lizam] لَزِم [lazim] *vn:* اِنلِزَم [ʔinlizam] *p:* كُمَش [kumaš] كَمِش [kamiš] *vn:* اِنكُمَش [ʔinkumaš] *p:* Hold on to me. كَلِّب بِيّا [čallib biyya] • **2.** حافَظ [ħaːfađ] مُحافَظَة [muħaːfađa] *vn:* تحافَظ [tħaːfađ] *p:* عَلَى [ʕala] اِحتِفَظ ب [ʔiħtifađ b-] اِحتِفاظ [ʔiħtifaːđ] *vn:* *sv* u. Can you hold on to that job just a little longer? تِقدَر تحافُظ عَلَى ذِيك الشَّغلَة لِمُدَّة شوَيَّة أطوَل؟ [tigdar tħaːfuđ ʕala điːč ʔiššaɣla lmudda šwayya ʔaṭwal?]
to hold out • **1.** قاوَم [qaːwam] مُقاوَمَة [muqaːwama] *vn:* *sv* u. We would have held out for months if we had had enough food. لَو كان عِدنا أكِل كافِي كان قاوَمنا أشهُر [law čaːn ʕidna ʔakil kaːfi čaːn qaːwamna ʔašhur]

to hold over • **1.** مَدَّد [maddad] تمِدِّد، تَمدِيد [tmiddid, tamdiːd] *vn:* تمَدَّد [tmaddad] *p:* The movie was held over for another week. تمَدَّد عَرض الفِلِم إلَى إسبُوع لاخ [tmaddad ʕarđ ʔilfilim ʔila ʔisbuːʕ laːx]
to hold up • **1.** عَطَّل [ʕaṭṭal] تعطِّل، تَعطِيل [tʕiṭṭil, taʕṭiːl] *vn:* تعَطَّل [tʕaṭṭal] *p:* أخَّر [ʔaxxar] تأخِّر، تَأخِير [tʔaxxir, taʔxiːr] *vn:* تأخَّر [tʔaxxar] *p:* You're holding me up. إنتَ دَتعَطِّلنِي [ʔinta datʕaṭṭilni] • **2.** قاوَم [qaːwam] مُقاوَمَة [muqaːwama] *vn:* تقاوَم [tqaːwam] *p:* Will these shoes hold up? هالقَنادِر تقاوُم؟ [halqanaːdir tqaːwum?] • **3.** سِلَب [silab] سَلِب [salib] *vn:* اِنسِلَب [ʔinsilab] *p:* Two men held me up yesterday. سَلبُونِي ثنَين البارحَة [salbuːni θnayn ʔilbaːrħa]
to get hold of • **1.** لِقَى [ligaː] لَقِي [lagy] *vn:* اِنلِقَى [ʔinligaː] *p:* Where can I get hold of him? وين أقدَر ألقِيه؟ [wiːn ʔagdar ʔalgiːh?] • **2.** لِزَم [lizam] لَزِم [lazim] *vn:* *sv* a. Stop crying. Get hold of yourself. بَطِّل البَكِي اِلزَم نَفسَك [baṭṭil ʔilbači ʔilzam nafsak]

holdup • **1.** تَسلِيب [tasliːb] تَسلِيبات [tasliːbaːt] *pl:* He had nothing to do with the holdup. ما إلَه دَخَل بالتَّسلِيب [maː ʔilah daxal bittasliːb]
*** What's the holdup?** • **1.** شِنُو اللِّي معَطِّلنا؟ [šinu ʔilli mʕaṭṭilna?]

hole • **1.** زُرُف [zuruf] زرُوف [zruːf] *pl:* There is a hole in his pants. أكُو زُرُف بِبَنطَرُونَه [ʔaku zuruf bipanṭruːnah] • **2.** حُفرَة [ħufra] حُفَر، حُفرِيّات [ħufar, ħufriyyaːt] *pl:* Who dug that hole? مِنُو حُفَر ذِيك الحُفرَة؟ [minu ħufar điːč ʔilħufra?]
*** He lives in a dingy hole.** • **1.** يِسكُن بمَكان رَزِيل [yiskun ibmakaːn raziːl]
*** I'm five dinars in the hole.** • **1.** عِندِي خَمس دنانِير عَجِز [ʕindi xams dnaːniːr ʕaǰiz]

holiday • **1.** عُطلَة [ʕuṭla] عُطلات [ʕuṭlaːt] *pl:*

Holland • **1.** هَولَندا [huːlanda]

hollow • **1.** مُجَوَّف [muǰawwaf] These walls seem to be hollow. هَالحياطِين تبَيِّن مجَوَّفَة [halħyaːṭiːn tbayyin mǰawwfa] • **2.** مَمصُوص [mamṣuːṣ] Her cheeks are hollow. خدُودها مَمصُوصَة [xduːdha mamṣuːṣa]

holy • **1.** مُقَدَّس [muqaddas]

home • **1.** بَيت [bayt,biːt] بيُوت [byuːt] *pl:* My home is in Baghdad. بَيتنا بِبَغداد [baytna bibagdaːd] We're building a new home. دَنِبنِي بَيت جِدِيد [danibni bayt ǰidiːd] Make yourself at home. البَيت بَيتَك [ʔilbayt baytak] Make yourself at home. اِعتُبُر هَذا بَيتَك [ʔiʕtubur haːđa baytak] • **2.** بَلَد [balad] بُلدان، بِلاد، وَطَن [buldaːn, bilaːd, waṭan] *pl:* Where's your home? (country) وين بَلَدَك؟ [wiːn baladak?] • **3.** داخِل [daːxil] At home and abroad. . . بِالدّاخِل والخارِج [biddaːxil wilxaːriǰ]

homeless • **1.** بدُون مَأوَى [bdu:n maʔwa] Thousands of people were made homeless by the flood. آلاف النّاس صاروا بدُون مَأوَى مِن الفَيَضان [ʔa:la:f ʔinna:s ṣa:raw bidu:n maʔwa: min ʔilfayaḏa:n]

homemade • **1.** شُغُل بَيت [šuɣul bayt] This is homemade jelly. هَذِي مرَبَّى شُغُل بَيت [ha:ði mrabba šuɣul bayt]

to be homesick • **1.** حَنّ [ħann] حَنين [ħani:n] *vn: sv* i. I'm homesick for my country. آنِي دَأحِنّ لوَطَنِي [ʔa:ni daʔaħinn lwaṭani]

home town • **1.** بَلدَة [balda] بَلدات [balda:t] *pl:* مَدِينَة [madi:na] مُدُن [mudun] *pl:* He's from my home town. هُوَّ مِن بَلِدتِي [huwwa min balidti]

homework • **1.** واجِب بَيتِي [wa:ǰib bayti] واجبات بَيتِيَّة [wa:ǰiba:t baytiyya] *pl:* Have you done all your homework? سَوِّيت كُلّ واجباتَك البَيتِيَّة؟ [sawwi:t kull wa:ǰiba:tak ʔilbaytiyya?]

honest • **1.** مُستَقِيم [mustaqi:m] أمِين [ʔami:n] Do you think he's honest? تِفتكِر هُوَّ مُستَقِيم؟ [tiftikir huwwa mustaqi:m?] He has an honest face. يبَيِّن عَلَى وِجهَه أمِين [yibayyin ʕala wuččah ʔami:n]

*** An honest man is as good as his word.**
• **1.** الرَّجُل الشَّرِيف قَول وفِعِل [ʔirrajul ʔiššari:f gawl wfiʕil]

honestly • **1.** صُدُق [ṣudug] بشَرَفِي [bšarafi:] فِي الحَقِيقَة [filħaqi:qa] حَقِيقَةً [ħaqi:qatan] I was honestly surprised. صُدُق آنِي كِنِت مِتعَجِّب [ṣudug ʔa:ni činit mitʕajjib] • **2.** بصَراحَة [bṣara:ħa] Honestly, I don't know what to do with you. بصَراحَة ما أدرِي شراح أسَوِّي ويّاك [bṣara:ħa ma: ʔadri šra:ħ ʔasawwi wiyya:k]

honesty • **1.** اِستِقامَة [ʔistiqa:ma] أمانَة [ʔama:na] There's no question about his honesty. ماكُو شَكّ بإستِقامتَه [ma:ku šakk biʔistiqa:mtah] Honesty is the best policy. الأمانَة أحسَن طَرِيق [ʔalʔama:na ʔaħsan ṭari:q]

to honk • **1.** طَوَّط [ṭawwaṭ] تطُوُّط [tṭuwwuṭ] *vn: sv* u. دَقّ [dagg] دَقّ [dagg] *vn:* اِندَقّ [ʔindagg] *p:* Honk three times, and I'll come down. طَوُّط ثلَث مَرّات وَآنِي أنزِل [ṭawwuṭ tlaθ marra:t wʔa:ni ʔanzil]

honor • **1.** شَرَف [šaraf] It's an honor to be elected. مِن الشَّرَف واحِد يُنتَخَب [min ʔiššaraf wa:ħid yuntaxab] On my honor! بشَرَفِي [bišarafi] We gave a banquet in his honor. سَوَّينا دَعوَة عَلَى شَرَفَه [sawwayna daʕwa ʕala šarafah] We gave a barquet in his honor. سَوَّينا دَعوَة تَكرِيماً إلَه [sawwi:na daʕwa takri:man ʔilah]

to honor • **1.** شَرَّف [šarraf] تشرُّف [tširruf] *vn:* تشَرَّف [tšarraf] *p:* كَرَّم [karram] تَكرِيم [takri:m] *vn:* تكَرَّم [tkarram] *p:* I feel very much honored. آنِي أشعُر كُلِّش مُكَرَّم [ʔa:ni ʔašʕur kulliš mukarram] • **2.** قِبَل [qibal] قَبُول [qabu:l] *vn:* اِنقِبَل [ʔinqibal] *p:* We can't honor this check. ما نِقدَر نِقبَل هَالشِّيك [ma: nigdar niqbal hačči:k]

hood • **1.** غِطَة رَاس، رَاس [ɣiṭa ra:s] غِطايات رَاس، غِطاوات رَاس [ɣiṭa:ya:t ra:s, ɣiṭa:wa:t ra:s] *pl:* This raincoat has a hood attached to it. هَالمشَمَّع مشَكَّل بيه غِطا راس [halmšammaʕ mšakkal bi:h ɣiṭa ra:s] • **2.** بَنِد [banid] Lift up the hood and check the car's oil. شِيل البَنِيد وَإفحَص دِهِن السَّيّارَة [ši:l ʔilbani:d wʔifħas dihin ʔilsayya:ra]

hoof • **1.** حافِر [ħa:fir] حَوافِر [ħawa:fir] *pl:* There's a nail in our horse's hoof. أكُو بِسمار بحافِر حصانَه [ʔaku bisma:r bħa:fir ħṣa:nah]

*** We had to hoof it.** • **1.** اضطَرَّينا ندُقها مَشِي [ʔiḍṭarri:na nduggha mašy]

cloven hoof • **1.** ضِلِف [ðilif] أضلاف [ʔaðla:f] *pl:*

hook • **1.** تِعلاقَة [tiʕla:ga] تِعلاقات [tiʕla:ga:t] *pl:* Hang your coat on the hook. عَلِّق سِترتَك بالتِّعلاقَة [ʕallig sitirtak bittiʕla:ga] • **2.** كِلّاب [čilla:b] كلاليب [čla:li:b] *pl:* شِنقال [činga:l] شَناقِيل [čana:gi:l] *pl:* We need a new hook for the crane. نرِيد كِلّاب جِدِيد لِلسِّلنك [nri:d čilla:b ǰidi:d lissilink] • **3.** شُصّ [šuṣṣ] شصُوص [šṣu:ṣ] *pl:* What kind of hook are you using to fish? يا نُوع شُصّ دَتِستَعمِل بصَيد السِّمَك؟ [ya: nu:ʕ šuṣṣ datistaʕmil bṣayd ʔissimač?]

*** He intends to get rich, by hook or by crook.**
• **1.** يرِيد يصِير زَنقِين بأيّ وَسِيلَة [yri:d yṣi:r zangi:n bʔayy wasi:la]

to hook • **1.** صاد [ṣa:d] صَيد [ṣayd] *vn:* اِنصاد [ʔinṣa:d] *p:* How many fish did you hook? كَم سِمكَة صِدِت؟ [čam simča ṣidit?] • **2.** شَنكَل [čangal] تشِنكِل [tčingil] *vn: sv* i. شَكَّل [šakkal] تشِكِّل [tšikkil] *vn: sv* i. كَلَّب [čallab] تكِلِّب [tčillib] *vn: sv* i. Help me hook this chain. ساعِدنِي أشَنكِل هَالزَّنجِيل [sa:ʕidni ʔačangil hazzanǰi:l] • **3.** لِقَف [ligaf] لَقُف [laguf] *vn:* اِنلِقَف [ʔinligaf] *p: sv* u. She finally hooked him. أخِيراً هِيَّ لُقفَتَه [ʔaxi:ran hiyya lugfatah]

to hook up • **1.** شَكَّل [šakkal] تشِكِّل [tšikkil] *vn:* تشَكَّل [tšakkal] *p:* I haven't hooked up the new radio yet. لهَسَّة بَعَد ما شَكَّلت الرّادِيُو [lhassa baʕad ma: šakkalit ʔirra:dyu]

hop • **1.** طَفرَة [ṭafra] طَفرات [ṭafra:t] *pl:* قَمزَة [gamza] قَمزات [gamza:t] *pl:* It's just a short hop by plane. بالطَّيّارَة كُلها طَفرَة [biṭṭayya:ra kullha ṭafra]

to hop • **1.** قُمَز [gumaz] قَمُز [gamuz] *vn: sv* u. طُفَر [ṭufar] طَفُر [ṭafur] *vn: sv* u. She hooped with joy. قُمزَت مِن الفَرَح [gumzat min ʔilfaraħ]

to hop around • **1.** قَمَّز [gammaz] تقُمُّز [tgummuz] *vn: sv* u. طَفَّر [ṭaffar] تطُفُّر [tṭuffur] *vn: sv* u. He was hopping around on one leg. كان دَيقَمُّز عَلَى فَدّ رِجِل [ča:n daygammuz ʕala fadd riǰil]

hope • **1.** أَمَل [ʔamal] آمال [ʔaːmaːl] *pl:* Don't give up hope. لا تِقطَع الأَمَل [laː tigtaʕ ʔilʔamal]

to hope • **1.** تَمَنَّى [tmannaː] تَمَنِّي [tamanni] *vn: sv* a. تأَمَّل [tʔammal] تَأَمُّل [taʔammul] *vn: sv* a. She had hoped to see you. كانَت تِتمَنَّى تشُوفَك [čaːnat titmannaː tšuːfak]

*** I hope you didn't catch cold.** • **1.** إنشاء الله ما أَخَذِت بَرِد [ʔinšaːllah maː ʔaxaðit barid]

hopeful • **1.** عِند أَمَل [ʕind- ʔamal] مِتأَمِّل [mitʔammil] I am hopeful. عِندِي أَمَل [ʕindi ʔamal]

hopeless • **1.** مَيؤُوس مِن [mayʔuːs min-] The situation is completely hopeless. الحالَة كُلِّش مَيؤُوس مِنها [ʔilħaːla kulliš mayʔuːs minha]

horizon • **1.** أُفُق [ʔufuq] آفاق [ʔaːfaːq]

horizontal • **1.** أُفُقِي [ʔufuqi]

horn • **1.** قِرِن [girin] قرُون [gruːn] *pl:* That cow's horn is broken. قِرِن ذِيك الهايشَة مَكسُور [girin ðiːč ʔiːlhaːyša maksuːr] • **2.** هُورَن [huːran] هَورنات [huːrinaːt] *pl:* Blow your horn next time! دُقّ الهَورِن مالَك المَرَّة الجّايَّة [dugg ʔilhuːrin maːlak ʔilmarra ʔijjaːyya] • **3.** بُوق [buːq] بواق [bwaːq] *pl:* Can you play this horn? تِقدَر تدُقّ هَالبُوق؟ [tigdar tdugg halbuːq?]

hornet • **1.** زَنبُور [zanbuːr] زنابِير [znaːbiːr] *pl:*

horrible • **1.** فَظِيع [faðiːʕ] It was a horrible sight. كان مَنظَر فَظِيع [čaːn manðar faðiːʕ]

horrid • **1.** مُزعِج [muzʕij] كَرِيه [kariːh]

horrors • **1.** فَظاعَة [faðaːʕa] فَظاعات [faðaːʕaːt] *pl:* The horrors of war are indescribable. فَظاعَة الحَرب ما تِنوُصُف [faðaːʕat ʔilħarb maː tinwuṣuf]

horse • **1.** حصان [ħṣaːn] حُصُن [ħuṣun] *pl:* خَيل [xayl] *Collective*

*** A team of wild horses couldn't drag me there.** • **1.** مَا أَرُوح هناك لَو تجُرّنِي بعَرَبانَة [maː ʔaruːħ hnaːk law tjurrni bʕarabaːna]

*** You shouldn't look a gift horse in the mouth.** • **1.** الهَدِيَّة مُو بثَمَنها [ʔilhadiyya muː bθamanha]

horse race • **1.** سِباق الخَيل [sibaːq ʔilxayl] رَيسِز [raysiz]

hose • **1.** بُورِي لاستِيق [buːri laːstiːg] بواري لاستِيق [bwaːri laːstiːg] *pl:* صُوندَة [ṣuːnda] صُوندات [ṣuːndaːt] *pl:* The hose is still in the garden. بُورِي اللّاستِيك بَعدَه بِالحَدِيقَة [buːri ʔillaːstiːk baʕdah bilħadiːqa] • **2.** جوراب [ǰuːraːb] جوارِيب [ǰwaːriːb] *pl:* We just got a new shipment of women's hose. هَستَوّنا اِستِلَمنا شُحنَة جوارِيب نِسائِيَّة جِدِيدَة [hastawwna ʔistilamna šuħnat ǰwaːriːb nisaːʔiyya ǰidiːda]

hospital • **1.** مُستَشفَى [mustašfa] مُستَشفَيات [mustašfayaːt] *pl:* خَستَخانَة [xastaxaːna] خَستَخانات، خَستَخاين [xastaxaːyin, xastaxaːnaːt] *pl:*

hospitality • **1.** كَرَم [karam] حُسُن ضِيافَة [ħusun ḍiyaːfa]

host • **1.** مُضَيِّف [muḍayyif] مُضَيِّفِين [muḍayyifiːn] *pl:* صاحِب الدَعوَة [ṣaːħib ʔiddaʕwa] أَصحاب الدَعوَة [ʔaṣħaːb ʔiddaʕwa] *pl:* He's a wonderful host. هُوَّ كُلِّش خُوش مُضَيِّف [huwwa kulliš xuːš muḍayyif]

hostess • **1.** مُضَيِّفَة [muḍayyifa] مُضَيِّفات [muḍayyifaːt] *pl:* She's a charming hostess. هِيَّ مُضَيِّفَة كُلِّش لَطِيفَة [hiyya muḍayyifa kulliš laṭiːfa] She works as a hostess with Iraqi Airlines. تِشتُغُل مُضَيِّفَة بِالخُطُوط الجَّوِّيَّة العِراقِيَّة [tištuɣul muḍayyifa bilxuṭuːṭ ʔiǰǰawwiyya ʔilʕiraːqiyya]

hot • **1.** حارّ [ħaːrr] Do you have hot water? عِندَك ماي حارّ؟ [ʕindak maːy ħaːrr?] This mustard sure is hot. هَالخَردَل صُدُق حارّ [halxardal ṣudug ħaːrr] • **2.** حادّ [ħaːdd] He has a hot temper. عِندَه طَبُع حادّ [ʕindah ṭabuʕ ħaːdd] • **3.** قَوِي [qawi, guwi] أَقوِياء، قَوِيِّين [ʔaqwiyaːʔ, qawiyyiːn] *pl:* The scent is still hot. رِيحَة الصَّيد لا تَزال قَوِيَّة [riːħat ʔiṣṣayd laː tazaːl qawiyya]

*** I made it hot for him.** • **1.** نطَيتَه دَرِس ما يِنساه [nṭaytah daris maː yinsaːh]

*** I haven't had a hot meal in three days.** • **1.** صارلِي ثلَث إيّام ما ماكِل طَبُخ [ṣaːrli tlaθ ʔiyyaːm maː maːkil ṭabux]

*** We were hot on his trail.** • **1.** كِنّا دَنتبِعَه بلَيَّة كَلَل [činna danitbʕah blayya kalal]

hotel • **1.** بالأُتِيل [ʔutiːl] أُوتَيلات [ʔutiːlaːt] *pl:* فِندِق [findiq] فَنادِق [fanaːdiq] *pl:*

hour • **1.** ساعَة [saːʕa] ساعات [saːʕaːt] *pl:* I'll be back in an hour. راح أَرجَع بَعَد ساعَة [raːħ ʔarjaʕ baʕad saːʕa] I'm taking nine hours a week in night school. آنِي ماخِذ تِسِع ساعات بِالإسبُوع بِالمَدرَسَة المَسائِيَّة [ʔaːni maːxið tisiʕ saːʕaːt bilʔisbuːʕ bilmadrasa ʔalmasaʔiyya] • **2.** دَوام [dawaːm] See me after hours. شُوفنِي وَرا الدَّوام [šuːfni wara ʔiddawaːm] My hours are from nine to five. دَوامِي مِن السّاعَة تِسعَة لِسّاعَة خَمسَة [dawaːmi min ʔissaːʕa tisʕa lissaːʕa xamsa]

at all hours • **1.** بأَيّ وَقِت [bʔayy wakit] كُلّ وَقِت [kull wakit] I can be reached at all hours. بِالإمكان الاتِّصال بِيّا بأَي وَقِت [bilʔimkaːn ʔilʔittiṣaːl biyya bʔayy wakit]

hour hand • **1.** مِيل [miːl] ميالَة [myaːla] *pl:* عَقرَب [ʕagrab] عَقارُب [ʕagaːrub] *pl:*

house • **1.** بَيت [bayt] بيُوت [byuːt] *pl:* دار [daːr] دُور [duːr] *pl:* I want to rent a house. أَرِيد أأَجِّر بَيت [ʔariːd ʔaʔajjir bayt]

• **2.** مَجلِس [majlis] مَجالِس [maja:lis] *pl:* Both houses will meet in joint session tomorrow. المَجلِسَين راح يِجتَمعُون بِجَلسَة مُشتَرَكَة باكِر [ʔilmajlisi:n ra:ħ yijtamʕu:n bjalsa muštaraka ba:čir]

*** The house was sold out.** • **1.** كُل التِكِتات اِنباعَت [kull ʔittikita:t ʔinba:ʕat]

to house • **1.** نَزَّل [nazzal] تنزِّل [tnizzil] *vn:* تنَزَّل [tnazzal] *p:* سَكَّن [sakkan] تسِكِّن، تسكِين [tsikkin, taski:n] *vn:* تسَكَّن [tsakkan] *p:* Where are we going to house the visitors? وين راح أنَزِّل الزُّوّار؟ [wi:n ra:ħ ʔanazzil ʔizzuwwa:r?]

household • **1.** أهل البَيت [ʔahl ʔilbayt] We have something for the whole household. عِدنا أشياء لكُلّ أهل البَيت [ʕidna ʔašya:ʔ lkull ʔahl ʔilbayt]

housemaid • **1.** خادمَة [xa:dma] خادمات [xa:dma:t] *pl:* صانعَة [ṣa:nʕa] صانعات [ṣa:nʕa:t] *pl:*

housework • **1.** شُغُل [šuɣul] أشغال [ʔašɣa:l] *pl:*

how • **1.** شلُون [šlu:n] كَيف [kayf] How shall I do it? شلُون أسَوّيها؟ [šlu:n ʔasawwi:ha?] He'll show you how. راح يراويك شلُون [ra:ħ yra:wi:k šlu:n] How do you do? شلُونَك؟ [šlu:nak?] How do you do? شلُون أحوالَك؟ [šlu:n ʔaħwa:lak?]

*** My name's Ahmad - How do you do?** • **1.** إسمِي أحمَد تشَرَّفنا [ʔismi ʔaħmad tšarrafna]

*** That's a fine how-do-you-do!** • **1.** يا فَتّاح، يا رَزّاق [ya: fatta:ħ, ya: razza:q]

how come • **1.** شلَون [šlawn] شِنُو السَبَب [šinu ʔissabab] لُويش [luwi:š] How come you're still here? شلُون إنتَ بَعدَك هنا؟ [šlu:n ʔinta baʕdak hna?]

how many • **1.** كَم [čam] شقَدّ [šgadd] How many oranges shall I take? كَم بُرتقالَة آخُذ؟ [čam purtaqa:la ʔa:xuð?] How many oranges shall I take? شقَدّ بُرتُقال آخُذ؟ [šgadd purtuqa:l ʔa:xuð?]

how much • **1.** شقَدّ [šgadd] How much did he pay? شقَدّ دِفَع؟ [šgadd difaʕ?] • **2.** بَيش [bayš, bi:š] شقَدّ [šgadd] How much is this? هاي بيش؟ [ha:y bi:š?]

however • **1.** لَكِن مَعَ ذَلِك [la:kin maʕa ða:lik] بَسّ [bass] I'd like to do it, however I have no time. يعجِبنِي أسَوِّيها، لَكِن مَعَ ذَلِك ما عِندِي وَقت [yiʕjibni ʔasawwi:ha, la:kin maʕa ða:lik ma: ʕindi wakit]

howl • **1.** عَوِي [ʕawi] I thought I heard the howl of a wolf. عَبالَك سِمَعِت عَوِي ذِيب [ʕaba:lak simaʕit ʕawi ði:b]

to howl • **1.** عَوَّى [ʕawwa:] تعُوِّي، عواء [tʕuwwi, ʕawa:ʔ] *vn: sv* i. The dog has been howling all night. الكَلِب صارلَه دَيعَوِّي طُول اللَّيل [ʔiččalib ṣa:rlah dayʕawwi ṭu:l ʔillayl] • **2.** طَق [ṭagg] طَقّ [ṭagg] *vn: sv* u. The audience howled with laughter. المُتفَرّجِين طَقّوا مِن الضِّحِك [ʔilmutfarrjin ṭaggaw min ʔiððiħik]

to huddle • **1.** اِلتَمّ [ʔiltamm] اِلتِمام [ʔiltima:m] *vn: sv* a. تزاحَم [dza:ħam] تَزاحُم [taza:ħum] *vn: sv* a. They huddled in a corner. اِلتَمّوا بفَدّ زوِيَّة [ʔiltammaw bfadd zwiyya] The sheep huddled close together. الغَنَم اِلتَمّوا واحِد يَمّ اللاخ [ʔilɣanam ʔiltammaw wa:ħid yamm ʔilla:x]

hug • **1.** حَضنَة [ħaðna] حَضنات [ħaðna:t] *pl:* She gave him a big hug. حِضنَتَه فَدّ حَضنَة زينَة [ħiðnatah fadd ħaðna zi:na]

to hug • **1.** حِضَن [ħiðan] حَضِن [ħaðin] *vn: sv* i. She hugged her mother tightly. حِضنَت أُمّها بقُوَّة [ħiðnat ʔummaha bquwwa] • **2.** لازَم [la:zam] مُلازَمَة [mula:zama] *vn: sv* i. Our boat hugged the coastline all the way. مَركَبنا لازَم السّاحِل طُول الطَّرِيق [markabna la:zam ʔissa:ħil ṭu:l ʔiṭṭari:q]

huge • **1.** ضَخُم [ðaxum] ضخام [ðxa:m] The elephant is a huge animal. الفِيل حَيَوان ضَخُم [ʔilfi:l ħayawa:n ðaxum]

hum • **1.** طَنِين [ṭani:n] What's that strange hum? شِنُو هَالطَّنِين الغَرِيب؟ [šinu haṭṭani:n ʔilɣari:b?]

to hum • **1.** هَمهَم [hamham] تهِمهِم [thimhim] *vn: sv* i. What's that tune you're humming? يا لَحِن دَتهَمهِم؟ [ya: laħin dathamhim?] • **2.** وَنّ [wann] وَنِين [wani:n] *vn: sv* i. وَنوَن [wanwan] تونوِن [twinwin] *vn: sv* i. This top won't hum. هَالمُصرَع ما دَيوِنّ [halmuṣraʕ ma: daywinn] • **3.** طَنّ [ṭann] أطنان [ʔaṭna:n] *pl:* طَنِين [ṭani:n] *vn: sv* i. طَنطَن [ṭanṭan] تطِنطِن [tṭinṭin] *vn: sv* i. My ears are humming. إذنِي دَتطِنّ [ʔiðni daṭṭinn]

*** Things are always humming at this corner.** • **1.** هَالزُّوِيَّة دائِماً بِيها حَرَكَة [hazzuwiyya da:ʔiman bi:ha ħaraka]

human • **1.** بَشَرِي [bašari] Is this a human eye? هاي عَين بَشَرِيَّة؟ [ha:y ʕayn bašariyya?] • **2.** بَشَر [bašar] بَشَرِين [bašari:n] *pl:* بَنِي آدَم [bani ʔa:dam] I'm only human. آنِي بَسّ بَشَر [ʔa:ni bass bašar]

humble • **1.** مِتواضِع [mitwa:ðiʕ] Abraham Lincoln grew up in humble circumstances. براهام لِنكولِن نِشَأ بظرُوف مِتواضعَة [ʔabraha:m linkun nišaʔ bðuru:f mitwa:ðʕa] In the beginning he acted very humble. أوَّل مَرَّة كان مُتَواضِع بتَصَرُّفَه [ʔawwal marra ča:n mutawa:ðiʕ btaṣarrufah]

humidity • **1.** رُطُوبَة [ruṭu:ba]

to humiliate • **1.** ذَلّ [ðall] ذَلّ [ðall] *vn:* اِنذَلّ [ʔinðall] *p:* حَقَّر [ħaqqar] تَحقِير [taħqi:r] *vn:* تحَقَّر [tħaqqar] *p:* Poverty humiliated me in front of a lot of people. الفَقُر ذَلّنِي قِدّام ناس هوايَة [ʔilfuqur ðallni gidda:m na:s hwa:ya]

humor • **1.** مَزاج [maza:j] كَيف [kayf, ki:f] Are you in a good humor today? مَزاجَك زين هَاليُوم؟ [maza:jak zi:n halyu:m?] • **2.** تَنكِيت [tanki:t] فُكاهَة [fuka:ha] فُكاهات [fuka:ha:t] *pl:* The humor in this magazine is very biting. التَّنكِيت بهالمَجَلَّة كُلَّش لاذِع [ʔittanki:t bhalmajalla kulliš la:ðiʕ]

humorous • 1. مُضحِك [muḏħik] He told a very humorous joke. حِكَى نُكتَة كُلِّش مُضحِكَة. [ħiča: nukta kulliš muḏħika] • **2.** فَكِه [fakih] هَزَلِي [hazali] He's a very humorous man. هَذا فَدّ رِجّال كُلِّش فَكِه [ha:ða fadd rijja:l kulliš fakih]

hunch • 1. شُعُور داخِلِي [šuʕu:r da:xili] I have a hunch that something is wrong there. عِندِي فَدّ شُعُور داخِلِي أَكُو شِي مُو تَمام هناك [ʕindi fadd šuʕu:r da:xili ʔaku ši mu: tama:m hna:k]

hunchback • 1. حِدبَة [ħidba] حِدبات، حِدَب [ħidba:t, ħidab] *pl:* One has a hunchback. واحِد عِندَه حِدبَة [wa:ħid ʕindah ħidba] • **2.** أَحدَب [ʔaħdab] حِدِب، حَدبِين [ħidib, ħadbi:n] *pl:* حَدبَة [ħadba] *Feminine:* She's a hunchback. هِيَّ حَدبَة [hiyya ħadba]

hunched up • 1. محَودِب [mħawdib] محَدِّب [mħaddib] Your back hurts because you're sitting all hunched up. ظَهرَك دَيوجعَك لِأَنّ إنتَ محَودِب بقَعِدتَك [ḏahrak dayu:jʕak liʔann ʔinta mħawdib bgaʕidtak]

hundred • 1. مِيَّة [miyya] About a hundred people were present. حَوالِي مِيَّة واحِد كانَوا حاضرِين [ħawa:li miyyat wa:ħid ča:naw ħa:ḏri:n] • **2.** مِيَّة [miyya] مِيّات [miyya:t] *pl:* Hundreds of people were present. مِئات النّاس كانَوا حاضرِين [miʔa:t ʔinna:s ča:naw ħa:ḏri:n]

Hungarian • 1. مَجَرِي [majari] He owns a Hungarian ship. يِملُك باخِرَة مَجَرِيَّة [yimluk ba:xira majariyya] • **2.** مَجَرِي [majari] مَجَرِيِّين [majariyyi:n] *pl:* The Hungarians left at twelve. المَجَرِيِّين راحَوا السّاعَة ثنَعَش [ʔilmajariyyi:n ra:ħaw ʔissa:ʕa θnaʕaš] • **3.** مَجَرِي [majari] He speaks Hungarian very well. يِحكِي مَجَرِي كُلِّش زين [yiħči majari kulliš zi:n]

Hungary • 1. المَجَر [ʔilmajar]

hunger • 1. جُوع [ju:ʕ] I nearly died of hunger. مِتِت مِن الجُوع إلّا شوَيَّة [mitit min ʔilju:ʕ ʔilla šwayya]

hungry • 1. جُوعان [ju:ʕa:n] جُوعانِين، جواعَة [ju:ʕa:ni:n, jwa:ʕa] *pl:* He has to feed ten hungry stomachs. لازِم يطَعِّم عَشِر بطُون جُوعانَة [la:zim ytaʕʕim ʕašir bṭu:n ju:ʕa:na] We didn't go hungry. ما ضَلَّينا جواعَى [ma: ḏalli:na jwa:ʕa]

to hunt • 1. صاد [ṣa:d] صَيد [ṣayd] *vn: sv* i. تصَيَّد [tṣayyad] تَصَيُّد [taṣayyud] *vn: sv* a. They're hunting rabbits. دَيصِيدُون أَرانِب [dayṣi:du:n ʔara:nib] We're going hunting tomorrow. باكِر راح نِتصَيَّد [ba:čir ra:ħ nitṣayyad]

to hunt for • 1. دَوَّر عَلَى [dawwar ʕala] تدَوُّر [tduwwur] *vn:* تدَوَّر [tdawwar] *p:* We were hunting for an apartment. كِنّا دَندَوُّر عَلَى شِقَّة [činna dandawwur ʕala šiqqa] Help me hunt for my shoes. ساعِدنِي أَدَوُّر عَلَى قُندَرتِي [sa:ʕidni ʔadawwur ʕala qundarti]

to hunt up • 1. لِقَف [ligaf] لَقُف [laguf] *vn:* انلِقَف [ʔinligaf] *p:* لِقَى [liga:] لَقِي [lagy] *vn:* انِلقَى [ʔinliga:] *p:* How many did you hunt up? كَم واحِد لِقَفِت؟ [čam wa:ħid ligafit?]

hunter • 1. صَيّاد [ṣayya:d] صَيّادِين [ṣayya:di:n] *pl:*

hunting license • 1. إجازَة صَيد [ʔija:zat ṣayd] إجازات صَيد [ʔija:zata:t ṣayd] *pl:*

hurry • 1. عَجَلَة [ʕajala] There's no hurry. ماكُو عَجَلَة [ma:ku ʕajala]

in a hurry • 1. مِستَعجِل [mistaʕjil] I'm in a big hurry. آنِي كُلِّش مِستَعجِل [ʔa:ni kulliš mistaʕjil]

to hurry • 1. اِستَعجَل [ʔistaʕjal] اِستِعجال [ʔistiʕja:l] *vn: sv* i. Don't hurry! لا تِستَعجِل [la: tistaʕjil] Hurry up! اِسرَع [ʔisraʕ] Hurry up! اِستَعجِل [ʔistaʕjil] • **2.** عَجَّل [ʕajjal] تَعجِيل [taʕji:l] *vn: sv* i. Don't hurry me! لا تعَجِّلنِي [la: tʕajjilni] Don't hurry me! لا تخَلِّينِي أَستَعجِل [la: txalli:ni ʔastaʕjil]

to hurt • 1. وُجَع [wujaʕ, wajaʕ, wijaʕ] أَوجاع [ʔawja:ʕ] *pl:* وُجَع [wujaʕ] *vn: sv* a. أَلَّم [ʔallam] أَلَم [ʔalam] *vn: sv* i. أَذَّى [ʔaðða:] تأَذِّي، أَذِيَّة [tʔiðði, ʔaðiyya] *vn: sv* i. My arm hurts. إيدِي تُوجَعنِي [ʔi:di tu:jaʕni] • **2.** عَوَّر [ʕawwar] تعُوُّر [tʕuwwur] *vn:* تعَوَّر [tʕawwar] *p:* جِرَح [jirah] جَرِح [jariħ] *vn:* اِنجِرَح [ʔinjirah] *p:* Where are you hurt? وين مِتعَوِّر؟ [wi:n mitʕawwir?] I didn't mean to hurt your feelings. ما رِدِت أَجرَح شُعُورَك [ma: ridit ʔajrah šuʕu:rak] • **3.** أَلَّم [ʔallam] أَلَم [ʔalam] *vn:* أَذَّى [ʔaðða:] أَذَى [ʔaða:] *vn:* تأَذَّى [tʔaðða:] *p: sv* i. She's easily hurt. هِيَّ تِتأَلَّم مِن أَقَلّ شِي [hiyya titʔallam min ʔaqall ši] • **4.** أَذَّى [ʔaðða:] تأَذِّي [tʔiðði] *vn:* تأَذَّى [tʔaðða:] *p: sv* i. ضَرّ [ḏarr] ضَرّ [ḏarr] *vn:* اِنضَرّ [ʔinḏarr] *p:* This will hurt business. هاي راح تأَذِّي السُّوق [ha:y ra:ħ tʔaðði ʔissu:g]

*** Will it hurt if I'm late? • 1.** راح يصِير ضَرَر إذا آنِي أَتأَخَّر؟ [ra:ħ yṣi:r ḏarar ʔiða: ʔa:ni ʔatʔaxxar?]

husband • 1. زَوج [zawj, zu:j] زواج، أَزواج [ʔazwa:j, zwa:j] *pl:* رَجِل [rajil] رجُولَة، رِياجِيل [rju:la, riya:ji:l] *pl:*

to hush up • 1. طَمطَم [ṭamṭam] تطُمطُم [tṭumṭum] *vn:* تطَمطَم [tṭamṭam] *p:* The scandal was quickly hushed up. الفَضِيحَة بِالعَجَل تطَمطُمَت [ʔilfaḏi:ħa bilʕajal tṭamṭumat] • **2.** سَكَّت [sakkat] تسِكِّت [tsikkit] *vn:* تسَكَّت [tsakkat] *p:* Try to hush up the child. حاوِلِي تسَكِّتِي الجّاهِل [ħa:wli tsakkiti ʔijja:hil]

husky • 1. جِثِيث [jiθi:θ] جِثِيثِين، جثاث [jiθi:θi:n, jθa:θ.] *pl:* He's quite husky. هُوَّ كُلِّش جَثِيث [huwwa kulliš jaθi:θ] • **2.** خَشِن [xašin] His voice is husky. صَوتَه خَشِن [ṣawtah xašin]

hut • 1. كُوخ، جَرداغ [ku:x, čarda:ɣ] أَكواخ، كواخَة، جَرادِغ [kwa:x, kwa:xa, čara:diɣ] *pl:*

hyena • 1. ضَبُع [ḏabuʕ] ضباع [ḏba:ʕ] *pl:*

I

I • **1.** آنِي [ʔaːni] I'm cold. آنِي بَردان [ʔaːni bardaːn] If I ask him, he'll do it. إذا آنِي أقُلَّه، يسَوِّيها [ʔiða ʔaːni ʔagullah, ysawwiːha]

ice • **1.** ثَلِج [θaliǰ] ثُلُوج [θuluːǰ] *pl:* Put some ice in the glasses. خَلّي ثَلِج بِالكلاصات [xalli θaliǰ bilglaːṣaːt]

ice box • **1.** صَندُوق ثَلِج [ṣanduːg θaliǰ] صَنادِيق ثَلِج [ṣanaːdiːg θaliǰ] *pl:* ثَلّاجَة [θallaːǰa] ثَلّاجات [θallaːǰaːt] *pl:*

ice cream • **1.** دوندِرمَة [duːndirma] دوندِرمات [duːndirmaːt] *pl:* A dish of ice cream, please. بالله، فَدّ ماعُون دوندِرمَة [ballah, fadd maːʕuːn duːndirma]

iced • **1.** مثَلَّج [mθallaǰ] Do you serve iced tea here? عِدكُم شاي مثَلَّج هنا؟ [ʕidkum čaːy mθallaǰ hna?]

icy • **1.** بارِد مِثل الثَّلِج [baːrid miθl ʔiθθaliǰ] كُلِّش بارِد [kulliš baːrid] The water is icy cold. الماي بارِد مِثل الثَّلِج [ʔilmaːy baːrid miθl ʔiθθaliǰ]

idea • **1.** فِكرَة [fikra] فِكرات، فِكِر، أفكار [fikraːt, fikir, ʔafkaːr.] *pl:* That's a good idea! هاي خُوش فِكرَة [haːy xuːš fikra] I haven't the faintest idea what he wants. ما عِندي أيّ فِكرَة عَن الشِّي اللّي يرِيدَه [maː ʕindi ʔayy fikra ʕan ʔišši ʔilli yriːdah]

*** What gives you that idea?** • **1.** شدَيخَلّيك تفكِّر هَالشِكِل؟ [šdayxalliːk tfakkir haššikil?]

*** Who gave you the bright idea?** • **1.** هَذا مِنُو اللي نطاك هَالعَقِل؟ [haːða minu ʔilli nṭaːk halʕaqil?]

*** I couldn't get used to the idea.** • **1.** ما قدَرِت أعَوِّد نَفسِي عَلَى هَالشّي [maː gdarit ʔaʕawwid nafsi ʕala hašši]

*** Of all the ideas!** • **1.** مِن دُون كُلّ الأَشياء [min duːn kull ʔilʔašyaːʔ]

*** She has big ideas.** • **1.** هِيَّ طَمُوحَة [hiyya ṭamuːḥa]

*** That's the idea!** • **1.** هَسَّة تَمام [hassa tamaːm]

*** The idea!** • **1.** هِيكِي [hiːči]

ideal • **1.** المَثَل الأَعلَى [ʔilmaθal ʔilʔaʕla] Our ideal is freedom and independence for all people. مَثَلنا الأعلَى الحُرِّيَّة وَالإستِقلال لكُلّ الشُّعُوب [maθalna ʔilʔaʕla ʔilḥurriyya wʔilʔistiqlaːl lkull ʔiššuʕuːb] • **2.** قُدوَة، قِدوَة [qudwa, qidwa] قُدوات [qudwaːt] *pl:* He's my ideal. هُوَّ قُدُوتي [huwwa quduwti] • **3.** مِثالِي [miθaːli] This is an ideal place for swimming. هَذا مَكان مِثالِي لِلسِّبح [haːða makaːn miθaːli lissibiḥ]

idealism • **1.** مِثالِيَّة [miθaːliyya]

idealist • **1.** مِثالِي [miθaːli] مِثالِيِّين [miθaːliyyiːn] *pl:*

idealistic • **1.** مِثالِي [miθaːli]

identical • **1.** فَدّ شِكِل [fadd šikil] مِتشابِه [mitšaːbih] The two copies are identical. هَالنُّسُختَين فَدّ شِكِل تَماماً [hannusuxtayn fadd šikil tamaːman] The two girls are wearing identical dresses. البِنتَين لابسات نَفانِيف فَدّ شِكِل تَماماً [ʔilbintayn laːbsaːt nafaːniːf fadd šikil tamaːman]

identification card • **1.** هَوِيَّة [hawiyya] هَوِيّات [hawiyyaːt] *pl:*

to identify • **1.** عِرَف [ʕiraf] عَرُف [ʕaruf] *vn:* اِنعِرَف [ʔinʕiraf] *p:* The police identified him by his fingerprints. الشُّرطَة عُرفُوه مِن طَبعَة أصابعَه [ʔiššurṭa ʕurfuːh min ṭabʕat ʔaṣaːbʕah] • **2.** عَرَّف [ʕarraf] *sv* u. Everyone must stand up and identify himself. كُلّ واحِد لازِم يوقَف وَيعَرُّف نَفسَه [kull waːḥid laːzim yuːgaf wayʕarruf nafsah]

*** I don't want to identify myself with them.**

• **1.** ما أرِيد يِنقِرِن إسمِي وِيّاهُم [maː ʔariːd yinqirin ʔismi wiyyaːhum]

identity • **1.** هَوِيَّة [hawiyya] هَوِيّات [hawiyyaːt] *pl:* The police don't know the identity of the dead man. الشُّرطَة ما يعُرفُون هَوِيَّة المَيِّت [ʔiššurṭa maː yʕurfuːn hawiyyat ʔilmayyit]

*** The police still do not know the identity of the thief.**

• **1.** الشُّرطَة لِهَسَّة بَعَد ما يعُرفُون مِنُو الحَرامِي [ʔiššurṭa lihassa baʕad maː yʕurfuːn minu ʔilḥaraːmi]

ideology • **1.** مَذهَب [maðhab] مَذاهِب [maðaːhib] *pl:* He won't support their political ideology. ما يأيِّد مَذهَبهُم السِّياسِي [maː yʔayyid maðhabhum ʔissiyaːsi]

idiot • **1.** هِبِل [hibil] أبلَه [ʔablah]

idle • **1.** عاطِل [ʕaːṭil] He is an idle fellow. هُوَّ فَدّ واحِد عاطِل [huwwa fadd waːḥid ʕaːṭil] • **2.** فارِغ [faːriɣ] That's just idle talk. هَذا حَكِي فارِغ [haːða ḥači faːriɣ] • **3.** بَطّال [baṭṭaːl] عاطِل [ʕaːṭil] He's been idle for some time. صارلَه مُدَّة بَطّال [ṣaːrlah mudda baṭṭaːl]

*** The factory's been idle for years.**

• **1.** المَعمَل ما دَيِشتُغُل صارلَه سنِين [ʔilmaʕmal maː dayištuɣul ṣaːrlah sniːn]

*** This machine is idle, we can use it.**

• **1.** هَالمَكِينَة مَحَّد دَيشَغِّلها، نِقدَر نِستَعمِلها [halmakiːna maḥḥad daySaɣɣilha, nigdar nistaʕmilha]

*** Her tongue is never idle.** • **1.** لسانها لا يكِلّ وَلا يِتعَب [lsaːnha laː yčill wala yitʕab]

*** Let the motor idle.** • **1.** خَلّي المَكِينَة تِشتُغُل [xalli ʔilmakiːna tištuɣul] / لا تطَفّي المَكِينَة [laː tṭaffi ʔilmakiːna]

idol • **1.** صَنَم [ṣanam] أصنام [ʔaṣnaːm] *pl:* Worshipping idols is forbidden. عِبادَة الأصنام حَرام [ʕibaːdat ʔilʔaṣnaːm ħaraːm]

if • **1.** إذا [ʔiða] لَو [luː] If anyone asks for me, say I'll be right back. إذا أَحَّد سِأَل عَلَيّا، قُلّه هَسَّة يِرجَع [ʔiða ʔaħħad siʔal ʕalayya, gullah hassa yirǰaʕ] I don't know if he'll come or not. ما أَدري إذا راح يِجِي لَو لا [maː ʔadri ʔiða raːħ yiǰi law laː] I'll go even if it rains. أَرُوح حَتَّى لَو تُمطُر [ʔaruːħ ħatta law tumṭur] He talks as if he had been there. يِحكِي عَبالَك لَو هُوَّ كان هناك [yiħči ʕabaːlak law huwwa čaːn hnaːk]

ignorance • **1.** غَباوَة [ɣabaːwa] غَباء [ɣabaːʔ] جَهَل، جَهِل [ǰahal, ǰahil] I've never seen such ignorance. بَعَد بعُمري ما شايِف هِيكِي غَباوَة [baʕad bʕumri maː šaːyif hiːči ɣabaːwa] • **2.** جَهَل، جَهِل [ǰahal, ǰahil] Ignorance of the law is no excuse. الجَّهَل بِالقانُون مُو عُذُر [ʔiǰǰahal bilqaːnuːn muː ʕuður]

ignorant • **1.** غَبِي [ɣabi] أغبِياء [ʔaɣbiyaːʔ] *pl:* جاهِل [ǰaːhil] جُهَلاء [ǰuhalaːʔ] *pl:* She's such an ignorant person. هِيَّ فَدّ مَرَة غَبِيَّة [hiyya fadd mara ɣabiyya]

to ignore • **1.** تجاهَل [tǰaːhal] تَجاهُل [taǰaːhul] *vn: sv* a. I would ignore his remark if I were you. لَو بِمَكانَك أَتجاهَل حكايتَه [law bmakaːnak ʔadǰaːhal ħčaːytah] I ignored him. تجاهَلتَه [dǰaːhaltah] I ignored him. ما دِرِتلَه بال [maː diritlah baːl]

ill • **1.** مَرِيض [mariːð̣] He was very ill. كان كُلِّش مَرِيض [čaːn kulliš mariːð̣]

*** He can ill afford to quit his job now.**

• **1.** ما يحَمِّل وَضعَه يبَطِّل مِن شَغلَه هَسَّة [maː yħammal wað̣ʕah ybaṭṭil min šaɣlah hassa]

*** He's ill at ease in such company.**

• **1.** هُوَّ ما يِرتاح وِيّا هِيكِي جَماعَة [huwwa maː yirtaːħ wiyya hiːči ǰamaːʕa]

illegal • **1.** غَير قانُونِي [ɣayr qaːnuːni] مُو قانُونِي [muː qaːnuːni] This illegal action will be opposed by all responsible governments. هَذا العَمَل غير القانُونِي تعارضَه كُلّ الحُكُومات المَسؤولَة [haːða ʔilʕamal ɣiːr ʔilqaːnuːni tʕaːrð̣ah kull ʔilħukuːmaːt ʔilmasʔuːla]

illegitimate • **1.** غَير شَرعِي [ɣayr šarʕi] He's an illegitimate child. هُوَّ وَلَد غير شَرعِي [huwwa walad ɣiːr šarʕi]

illiteracy • **1.** أُمِّيَّة [ʔummiyya] The illiteracy rate is high here. مُستَوَى الأُمِّيَّة عالِي هنا [mustawa lʔummiyya ʕaːli hna]

illiterate • **1.** أُمِّي [ʔummi] The people of this village are all illiterate. أَهِل هالقَريَة كُلهُم أُمِّيِّين [ʔahil halqarya kullhum ʔummiyyiːn]

illness • **1.** مَرَض [marað̣] أمراض [ʔamraːð̣] *pl:*

to illustrate • **1.** وَضَّح [wað̣ð̣aħ] تَوضِيح [tawð̣iːħ] *vn: sv* i. The book is illustrated. الكِتاب موَضَّح بِصُوَر [ʔilkitaːb mwað̣ð̣aħ biṣuwar] • **2.** شِرَح [širaħ] شَرِح [šariħ] *vn:* اِنشِرَح [ʔinširaħ] *p:* وَضَّح [wað̣ð̣aħ] *sv* i. I can illustrate this best by an example. أَقدَر أَشرَح هَذا أَحسَن بِفَدّ مِثال [ʔagdar ʔašraħ haːða ʔaħsan bfadd miθaːl]

illustration • **1.** صُورَة [ṣuːra] صُوَر [ṣuwar] *pl:* The catalogue has many illustrations. الكَتالُوج بِيه صُوَر هوايَة [ʔilkataːluːg biːh ṣuwar hwaːya] • **2.** شِكِل [šikil] أشكال، شكُول [ʔaškaːl, škuːl] *pl:* Look at illustration no. 10, on page 115. شُوف الشِّكِل رَقَم عَشرَة، صَفحَة مِيَّة وخمُسطَعَش [šuːf ʔiššikil raqam ʕašra, ṣafħa miyya wixmusṭaʕaš]

ill will • **1.** كُرُه [kuruh] His insults caused a lot of ill will. إهاناتَه سَبَّبَت كُرُه النّاس إلَه [ʔihaːnaːtah sabbabat kuruh ʔinnaːs ʔilah]

image • **1.** صُورَة [ṣuːra] صُوَر [ṣuwar] *pl:* The image I have of him is that of an old man. صُورتَه المَطبُوعَة بفِكري مال واحِد شايِب [ṣuːrtah ʔilmaṭbuːʕa bfikri maːl waːħid šaːyib] She's the image of her mother. هِيَّ صُورَة مِن أُمَّها [hiyya ṣuːra min ʔummaha] • **2.** شِكِل [šikil] أشكال، شكُول [ʔaškaːl, škuːl] شكُولات [škuːlaːt] *pl:* She examined her image in the mirror. باوعَت شِكِلها بالمِرايَة [baːwʕat šikilha bilmraːya]

imaginable • **1.** مُمكِن تَصَوُّر [mumkin taṣawwur] He tried everything imaginable. حاوَل كُلشِي مُمكِن تِتصَوَّرَه [ħaːwal kullši mumkin titṣawwarah] That's hardly imaginable! هَذا شِي ما مُمكِن تِتصَوَّرَه [haːða ši maː mumkin titṣawwarah] That's hardly imaginable! هَذا شِي ما يخُشّ بِالعَقِل [haːða ši maː yxušš bilʕaqil]

imaginary • **1.** خَيالِي [xayaːli] Juha is an imaginary character. جُحّا فَدّ شَخصِيَّة خَيالِيَّة [ǰuħħaː fadd šaxṣiyya xayaːliyya]

*** Children sometimes live in an imaginary world.**

• **1.** الجَّهال دُورات يعِيشُون بدُنيا الخَيال [ʔiǰǰahhaːl duːraːt yʕiːšuːn bdunya ʔilxayaːl]

imagination • **1.** خَيال [xayaːl] That's pure imagination! هَذا خَيال صِرف [haːða xayaːl ṣirf] She has a fertile imagination. عِدها خَيال خَصِب [ʕidha xayaːl xaṣib]

to imagine • **1.** تصَوَّر [tṣawwar] تَصَوُّر [taṣawwur] *vn: sv* a. I can't imagine what you mean. ما أَقدَر أَتصَوَّر شدَتُقصُد [maː ʔaqdar ʔatṣawwar šdatuqṣud] I imagine so. أَتصَوَّر هَالشِّكِل [ʔatṣawwar haššikil] I imagine so. أَظِنّ [ʔað̣inn] • **2.** تخَيَّل [txayyal] تَخَيُّل [taxayyul] *vn: sv* a. You're only imagining things. إنتَ بَسّ دَتِتخَيَّل أَشياء ما مَوجُودَة [ʔinta bass datitxayyal ʔašyaːʔ maː mawǰuːda]

to imitate • **1.** قَلَّد [qallad] تَقْلِيد [taqli:d] *vn:* تقَلَّد [tqallad] *p:* He can imitate my voice. يِقدَر يقَلِّد صُوتِي [yigdar yqallid şu:ti]

imitation • **1.** تَقْلِيد [taqli:d] تَقالِيد [taqa:li:d] *pl:* The Japanese put out a poor imitation of this lighter. اليابانِيِّين طَلعَوا فَدّ تَقلِيد مُو زين لِهَل قِدّاحَة [ʔilyabaniyyi:n ṭalʕaw fadd taqli:d mu: zi:n lihal qidda:ħa] • **2.** اِصطِناعِي [ʔiṣṭina:ʕi] إكذُوبَة [ʔikðu:ba] أكاذِيب، إكذُوبات [ʔaka:ði:b, ʔikðu:ba:t] *pl:* This pocketbook is made of imitation leather. هَالجَّنطَة مَعمُولَة مِن جِلِد اِصطِناعِي [hajjanṭa maʕmu:la min jilid ʔiṣṭina:ʕi] This necklace is made of imitation pearls. هَالقلادَة مسَوّايَة مِن لِيلُو كَذّابِي [halgla:da msawwa:ya min li:lu čaðða:bi]

immature • **1.** مُو ناضِج [mu: na:ðij] His actions are immature for his age. تَصَرُّفاتَه مُو ناضجَة بِالنِّسبَة لعُمرَه [taṣarrufa:tah mu: na:ðja binnisba lʕumrah]

immediate • **1.** مُباشِر [muba:šir] Ahmad is my immediate superior. أحمَد رَئِيسِي المُباشِر [ʔaħmad raʔi:si ʔilmuba:šir]

*** There's no school in the immediate neighborhood.** • **1.** ماكُو مَدرَسَة يَمّنا مُباشَرَةً [ma:ku madrasa yammna muba:šaratan]

*** This amount will take care of your immediate needs.** • **1.** هَالمَبلَغ يكَفِّي اِحتياجَك هَسَّة [halmablaɣ ykaffi ʔiħtya:jak hassa]

immediately • **1.** مُباشَرَتاً [muba:šaratan] حالاً [ħa:lan] Immediately afterwards I heard a scream. مُباشَرَةً وَراها سمَعِت فَدّ عَيطَة [muba:šaratan wara:ha smaʕit fadd ʕayṭa] I'll go there immediately. راح أرُوح هناك حالاً [ra:ħ ʔaru:ħ hna:k ħa:lan]

immense • **1.** ضَخُم [ðaxum] هائِل [ha:ʔil] They have an immense living room. عِدهُم صالُون ضَخُم [ʕidhum ṣa:lu:n ðaxum] They stored immense quantities of meat. خِزنَوا كَمِّيّات هائِلَة مِن اللَّحَم [xiznaw kammiyya:t ha:ʔila min ʔillaħam]

immigrant • **1.** مُهاجِر [muha:jir] مُهاجِرين [muha:jiri:n] *pl:* About one thousand immigrants enter the country every year. حَوالِي ألف مُهاجِر يدُخلُون البَلَد كُلّ سَنَة [ħawa:li ʔalf muha:jir yduxlu:n ʔilbalad kull sana]

immigration • **1.** هِجرَة [hijra] هِجرات [hijra:t] *pl:* The Immigration Office is in that building. دائِرَة الهُجرَة بهالبِناية [da:ʔirat ʔilhujra bhalbina:ya]

immoral • **1.** دُونِي [du:ni] That is an immoral act. هَذا عَمَل دُونِي [ha:ða ʕamal du:ni] • **2.** مُنحَطّ [munħaṭṭ, minħaṭṭ] دُونِي [du:ni] This man is immoral. هَالرِّجّال مُنحَطّ [harrijja:l munħaṭṭ] This man is immoral. هَالرِّجّال ما عِندَه قِيَم أخلاقِيَّة [harrijja:l ma: ʕindah qiyam ʔaxla:qiyya]

immortal • **1.** خالِد [xa:lid] Mutanabbi is an immortal Arab poet. المُتَنَبِّي فَدّ شاعِر عَرَبِي خالِد [ʔilmutanabbi fadd ša:ʕir ʕarabi xa:lid]

immunity • **1.** مَناعَة [mana:ʕa] Do you have immunity to smallpox? عِندَك مَناعَة ضِدّ الجِّدرِي؟ [ʕindak mana:ʕa ðidd ʔijjidri?] • **2.** حَصانَة [ħaṣa:na] All ambassadors have diplomatic immunity. كُلّ السُّفَراء عِدهُم حَصانَة دِبلُوماسِيَّة [kull ʔissufara:ʔ ʕidhum ħaṣa:na dibluma:siyya]

impartial • **1.** مُنصِف [munṣif] عادِل [ʕa:dil] حَقّانِي [ħaqqa:ni] حَقّانِيَّة، حَقّانِيِّين [ħaqqa:niyya, ħaqqa:niyyi:n] *pl:* I'll try to be impartial. راح أحاوِل أكُون مُنصِف [ra:ħ ʔaħa:wil ʔaku:n munṣif]

impatient • **1.** ما عِند صَبُر [ma: ʕind- ṣabur] Don't be so impatient! لا تكُون هَالقَدّ ما عِندَك صَبُر [la: tku:n halgadd ma: ʕindak ṣabur]

imperative • **1.** فِعِل أمُر [fiʕil ʔamur] 'Iktib' is the imperative of 'kitab'. "إكتِب هِيَّ فِعِل الأمُر مال "كِتَب" ['ʔiktib' hiyya fiʕil ʔilʔamur ma:l 'kitab'] • **2.** إجبارِي [ʔijba:ri] It is imperative for all students to attend the meeting. الحُضُور بالاِجتِماع إجبارِي عَلَى كُلّ التَّلامِيذ [ʔilħuðu:r bilʔijtima:ʕ ʔijba:ri ʕala kull ʔittala:mi:ð]

imperialism • **1.** اِستِعمار [ʔistiʕma:r] Imperialism is on the decline. الاستِعمار بطَرِيقه لِلزَّوال [ʔilʔistiʕma:r bṭari:qah lizzawa:l]

impersonal • **1.** غَير شَخصِي [ɣayr šaxṣi] I always keep my relations with the staff impersonal. دائِماً أخَلِّي عِلاقاتِي ويّا المُوَظَّفِين غير شَخصِيَّة [da:ʔiman ʔaxalli ʕila:qa:ti wiyya ʔilmuwaððafi:n ɣi:r šaxṣiyya]

to imply • **1.** تضَمَّن [tðamman] *sv* a. His statement implied he was in favor of the plan. كَلامَه تضَمَّن موافقتَه عالخِطَّة [kala:mah dðamman mwa:faqtah ʕalxiṭṭa]

impolite • **1.** مُو مهَذَّب [mu: mhaððab] She is very impolite. هِيَّ كُلِّش مُو مهَذَّبَة [hiyya kulliš mu: mhaððaba] Why are you so impolite? لِيش هِيكِي إنتَ مُو مهَذَّب؟ [li:š hi:či ʔinta mu: mhaððab?] • **2.** خَشِن [xašin] That was very impolite of him. هاي كانَت كُلِّش خَشنَة مِنَّه [ha:y ča:nat kulliš xašna minnah]

import • **1.** اِستِيراد [ʔisti:ra:d] اِستِيرادات [ʔisti:ra:da:t] *pl:* The government encourages the import of raw materials. الحُكُومَة تشَجِّع اِستِيراد المَوادّ الخام [ʔilħuku:ma tšajjiʕ ʔisti:ra:d ʔilmawa:dd ʔilxa:m]

I

to import • **1.** اِستَورَد [ʔistawrad] اِستِيراد [ʔistiːraːd] *vn: sv* i. Iraq imports a lot of Australian cheese. العِراق يِستَورِد هوايَة جِبِن أُستُرالِي [ʔilʕiraːq yistawrid hwaːya ǰibin ʔusturaːli]

importance • **1.** أَهَمِّيَّة [ʔahammiyya] You attach too much importance to the problem. إِنتَ هوايَة تخَلِّي أَهَمِّيَّة لِلمَسأَلَة [ʔinta hwaːya txalli ʔahammiyya lilmasʔala] That's of no importance. هَذا ما إِلَه أَهَمِّيَّة [haːða maː ʔilah ʔahammiyya]

important • **1.** مُهِمّ [muhimm] I want to see you about an important matter. أَرِيد أَشُوفَك بقَضِيَّة مُهِمَّة [ʔariːd ʔašuːfak bqaðiyya muhimma] He was the most important man in town. هُوَّ كان أَهَمّ رَجُل بِالمَدِينَة [huwwa čaːn ʔahamm rajul bilmadiːna]

imports • **1.** وارِد، وَارِدَات [waːrid, waːridaːt] مُستَورَد، مُستَورَدات [mustawrad, mustawradaːt] Our imports still exceed our exports. وارِداتنا بَعَدها تزِيد عَلَى صادِراتنا [waːridaːtna baʕadha dziːd ʕala ṣaːdiraːtna]

to impose on • **1.** اِستَغَلّ [ʔistaɣall] اِستِغلال [ʔistiɣlaːl] *vn: sv* i. He's imposing on your good nature. هُوَّ يِستِغِلّ طِيبَة أَخلاقَك [huwwa yistiɣill ṭiːbat ʔaxlaːqak] • **2.** فُرَض [furað] فَرِض [farið] *vn: sv* u. Don't let them impose their will on you. لا تخَلِّيهُم يفُرضُون عَلِيك مِثِلما يرِدُون [laː txalliːhum yfurðuːn ʕaliːk miθilma yirduːn]

imposing • **1.** رائِي [raːʔi] That's certainly an imposing building. هَذِي حَقِيقَة بِنايَة رائيَة [haːði ħaqiːqa binaːya raːʔya]

imposition • **1.** زَحمَة [zaħma] زَحمات [zaħmaːt] *pl:* تَكلِيف [takliːf] تَكلِيفات [takliːfaːt] *pl:* If it's not an imposition, could you give me a ride? إِذا ماكُو زَحمَة عَلِيك مُمكِن توَصِّلنِي؟ [ʔiða maːku zaħma ʕaliːk mumkin twaṣṣilni?]

impossible • **1.** مُستَحِيل [mustaħiːl] Why is it impossible? لُويش هَذا مُستَحِيل؟ [luwiːš haːða mustaħiːl?]

 * **That man is absolutely impossible!**
 • **1.** هَالشَّخِص أَبَداً ما ينِحمِل [haššaxiṣ ʔabadan maː yinħimil]

to impress • **1.** أَثَّر [ʔaθθar] تَأثِير [taʔθiːr] *vn:* تأَثَّر [tʔaθθar] *p:* That doesn't impress me. هَذِي ما تأَثِّرنِي [haːði maː tʔaθθirni]

impression • **1.** تَأثِير [taʔθiːr] He made a good impression on me. كان تَأثِيرَه عَلَيَّا زين [čaːn taʔθiːrah ʕalayya ziːn] • **2.** نَظرَة [naðra] نَظرات [naðraːt] *pl:* اِنطِباع [ʔintibaːʕ] I got a bad impression of him. أَخَذِت عَنَّه نَظرَة مُو زينَة [ʔaxaðit ʕannah naðra muː ziːna] He tries to give the impression that he's a good fellow. يحاوِل يِنطِي الانطِباع إِنُّو خُوش رِجال [yħaːwil yinṭi ʔilʔintibaːʕ ʔinnu xuːš rijaːl]

 under the impression • **1.** عَبال [ʕabaːl-] I was under the impression that he wanted to go. عَبالِي راد يرُوح [ʕabaːli raːd yiruːħ]

impressionism • **1.** إِنطِباعِيَّة [ʔintibaːʕiyya]

to imprison • **1.** حَبَس [ħibas] حَبِس [ħabis] *vn:* اِنحِبَس [ʔinħibas] *p:* سِجَن [sijan] سَجِن [sajin] *vn:* اِنسِجَن [ʔinsijan] *p:* The men were imprisoned for two months. الرِّياجِيل كانَوا مَحبُوسِين لمُدَّة شَهرَين [ʔirriyaːjiːl čaːnaw maħbuːsiːn lmuddat šahrayn]

to improve • **1.** حَسَّن [ħassan] تَحسِين [taħsiːn] *vn:* تحَسَّن [tħassan] *p:* I don't know how we can improve our product. ما أَدرِي شلُون مُمكِن نحَسِّن إِنتاجنا [maː ʔadri šluːn mumkin nħassin ʔintaːjna] • **2.** تحَسَّن [tħassan] تَحَسُّن [taħassun] *vn: sv* a. His condition has improved. صِحّتَه تحَسّنَت [ṣiħħtah tħassnat] Ahmad is improving in school. أَحمَد دَيِتحَسَّن بِالمَدرَسَة [ʔaħmad dayitħassan bilmadrasa]

improvement • **1.** تَحَسُّن [taħassun] تَحَسُّنات [taħassunaːt] *pl:* I don't see any improvement in her condition. ما دَأشُوف أَيّ تَحَسُّن بحالَتها [maː daʔašuːf ʔayy taħassun bħaːlatha] • **2.** تَحسِين [taħsiːn] تَحسِينات [taħsiːnaːt] *pl:* We're making some improvements in the house. دَنسَوِّي بَعض التَّحسِينات بالبَيت [dansawwi baʕð ʔittaħsiːnaːt bilbayt]

 * **That's no improvement over our former method.**
 • **1.** ما جاب أَي شِي جدِيد عَن طَرِيقَتنا السّابقَة [maː jaːb ʔayy šiː jdiːd ʕan ṭariːqatna ʔissaːbiqa]

impudence • **1.** صَلافَة [ṣalaːfa] وَقاحَة [waqaːħa] Such impudence! هِيكِي صَلافَة [hiːči ṣalaːfa] Such impudence! أَمّا وَقاحَة [ʔamma waqaːħa]

impulse • **1.** اِندِفاع [ʔindifaːʕ] You've got to control your impulses. لازِم تُضبُط اِندِفاعَك [laːzim tuðbuṭ ʔindifaːʕak] • **2.** دافِع [daːfiʕ] دَوافِع [dawaːfiʕ] *pl:* باعِث [baːʕiθ] I had an impulse to give the beggar a dinar. حَسِّيت بفَدّ دافِع أَنطِي دِينار لِلفَقِير [ħassiːt bfadd daːfiʕ ʔanṭi dinaːr lilfaqiːr]

impulsive • **1.** مِندَفِع [mindafiʕ] She is a very impulsive person. هِيَّ كُلَّش مِندَفعَة [hiyya kulliš mindafʕa]

in • **1.** ب [b] There's no heater in my room. ماكُو صُوبَة بغُرُفتِي [maːku ṣuːpa byurufti] He's in Najaf now. هَسَّة هُوَّ بِالنَّجَف [hassa huwwa binnajaf] He's the smartest student in the entire class. هُوَّ أَذكَى طالِب بِالصَّفّ كُلَّه [huwwa ʔaðka ṭaːlib biṣṣaff kullah] Say it in English. قُولها بالإِنكِلِيزِي [guːlha bilʔingiliːzi] That in itself isn't important. هِيَّ بحَدّ ذاتها مُو مُهِمَّة [hiyya bħadd ðaːtah muː muhimma] If I were in your place, I would've gone. لَو كِنِت بمَحَلَّك، كان رِحِت [law činit bimaħallak, čaːn riħit] Did it happen in the daytime or at night? حِدثَت بِالنَّهار لَو باللَّيل؟ [ħidθat binnahaːr law billayl?] I can finish it in a week. أَقدَر أَخَلّصها بإِسبُوع [ʔagdar ʔaxalliṣha bʔisbuːʕ] Write in ink. إِكتِب بِالحِبر

[ʔiktib bilħibir] • **2.** بَعَد [baʕad] I'll be back in three days. راح أَرجَع بَعَد ثلَث أَيّام [raːħ ʔarǰaʕ baʕad tlaθ ʔayyaːm] I'll pay you in two weeks. راح أدفَعلَك بَعَد إِسبُوعَين [raːħ ʔadfaʕlak baʕad ʔisbuːʕayn] • **3.** مَوجُود [mawǰuːd] He's not in. هُوَّ مُو مَوجُود [huwwa muː mawǰuːd] • **4.** واسطَة [waːsṭa] وَسائِط، وَسايِط [waṣaːʔiṭ, waṣaːyiṭ] *pl:* He has an in at the Ministry of the Interior. عِندَه واسطَة بوِزارَة الدّاخِلِيَّة [ʕindah waːsṭa bwizaːrat ʔiddaːxiliyya]

*** He was the only one at the party in tails.** • **1.** هُوَّ كان الوَحِيد بِالحَفلَة لابِس فراك [huwwa čaːn ʔilwaħiːd bilħafla laːbis fraːk]

*** Sift the flour before you put the water in.** • **1.** أنخُل الطَحِين قَبُل ما تخَلِّيلَه مَيّ [ʔunxul ʔiṭṭaħiːn gabul maː txalliːlah mayy]

*** Padded shoulders aren't in any more.** • **1.** السِتَر بكَتّافِيّات مُو مَودَة هالوَقِت [ʔissitar bčattaːfiyyaːt muː muːdat halwakit] / السِّتَر بِكَتّافِيّات اِضمَحَلَّت [ʔissitar bičattaːfiyyaːt ʔiðmaħallat]

*** Are you in on it with them, too?** • **1.** إِنتَ هَمّ مِشتِرِك وِيّاهُم؟ [ʔinta hamm mištirik wiyyaːhum?]

*** He has it in for you.** • **1.** هُوَّ ضامِلَك إِيّاها [huwwa ðaːmlak ʔiyyaːha]

*** He knows all the ins and outs.** • **1.** يُعرُف الأَكُو والماكُو [yuʕruf ʔilʔaku wilmaːku] / يُعرُف خَتلاتها [yuʕruf xatlaːtha]

*** He's in good with the boss.** • **1.** عِلاقتَه زَينَة بِالمُدِير [ʕilaːqtah zayna bilmudiːr]

*** Now we're in for it!** • **1.** أَكَلناها [ʔakalnaːha]

all in • **1.** تَعبان كُلِّش [taʕbaːn kulliš] هوايَة تَعبان [hwaːya taʕbaːn] مَيِّت مِن التَعَب [mayyit min ʔittaʕab] I'm all in. آنِي تَعبان كُلِّش [ʔaːni taʕbaːn kulliš]

inauguration • **1.** حَفل تَنصِيب [ħafl tanṣiːb] اِحتِفال تَنصِيب [ʔiħtifaːl tanṣiːb] The inauguration of the President will be next January. الاحتِفال بِتَنصِيب الرَّئِيس راح يكُون بِكانُون الثّانِي الجّاي [ʔilʔiħtifaːl bitanṣiːb ʔirraʔiːs raːħ ykuːn bikaːnuːn ʔiθθaːni ʔiǰǰaːy]

incense • **1.** بُخُور [buxuːr] بخُورات [bxuːraːt]

incentive • **1.** حافِز [ħaːfiz] حَوافِز [ħawaːfiz] *pl:* It's hard to work without an incentive. صَعُب تِشتُغُل بدُون وُجُود حافِز [ṣaʕub tištuɣul biduːn wuǰuːd ħaːfiz]

inch • **1.** إِنج [ʔinǰ] إِنجات [ʔinǰaːt] *pl:* Bring me a three-inch nail. جِيبِلِي بِسمار طُولَه ثلاث إِنجات [ǰiːbli bismaːr ṭuːlah tlaθ ʔinǰaːt]

*** He came within an inch of being run over.** • **1.** هُوَّ تَقرِيباً راد يِنسِحِق [huwwa taqriːban raːd yinsiħig]

*** He's every inch a soldier.** • **1.** هُوَّ جُندِي بمَعنَى الكَلِمَة [huwwa ǰundi bmaʕnaː ʔilkalima]

incident • **1.** حادِث [ħaːdiθ] حَوادِث [ħawaːdiθ] *pl:* There've been several border incidents lately. صارَت عِدَّة حَوادِث عالحُدُود بِالمُدَّة الأَخِيرَة [ṣaːrat ʕiddat ħawaːdiθ ʕalħuduːd bilmudda ʔilʔaxiːra] They crossed the river without incident. عُبرَوا النَّهَر بَلا ما يصِير حادِث [ʕubraw ʔinnahar bala maː yṣiːr ħaːdiθ]

incidentally • **1.** عَرَضاً [ʕaradan] He just said it incidentally. قالها عَرَضاً [gaːlha ʕarað̣an] • **2.** بِالمُناسَبَة [bilmunaːsaba] Incidentally, I saw our friend Ali the other day. بِالمُناسَبَة، شِفِت صاحِبنا عَلِي ذاك اليُوم [bilmunaːsaba, šifit ṣaːħibna ʕali ðaːk ʔilyuːm]

incinerator • **1.** مِحرَقَة [miħraqa] مَحارِق [maħaːriq] *pl:*

incline • **1.** مُنحَدَر [munħadar] I climbed the incline. صعَدِت المُنحَدَر [ṣʕadit ʔilmunħadar]

to incline • **1.** مال [maːl] مَيِل [mayil] *vn: sv* i. The minaret inclines to the right. المَنارَة مايلَة لِليِمنَى [ʔilmanaːra maːyla lilyimna]

inclined • **1.** مَيّال [mayyaːl] I'm inclined to believe him. آنِي مَيّال إِلَى تَصدِيقَه [ʔaːni mayyaːl ʔila taṣdiːqah] • **2.** مايِل [maːyil] Water naturally flows down an inclined surface. الماي عادَةً يِنحِدِر عالأَرض المايلَة [ʔilmaːy ʕaːdatan yinħidir ʕalʔarð̣ ʔilmaːyla]

to include • **1.** اِحتِوَى عَلَى [ʔiħtiwaː ʕala] *sv* i. The dictionary doesn't include technical expressions. القامُوس ما يِحتِوِي عَلَى اِصطِلاحات فَنِّيَّة [ʔilqaːmuːs maː yiħtiwi ʕala ʔiṣṭilaːħaːt fanniyya] • **2.** دَخَّل [daxxal] تَدخِيل [tadxiːl] *vn:* اتدَخَّل [ʔiddaxxal] *p:* Include this in my bill. دَخِّل هَذِي ضِمِن حسابِي [daxxil haːði ð̣imin ħsaːbi]

included • **1.** وِيّا [wiyya] The room is five dinars, service included. إِيجار الغُرفَة خَمس دَنانِير وِيّا الخِدمَة [ʔiːǰaːr ʔilɣurfa xams danaːniːr wiyya ʔilxidma] • **2.** بضِمِن [bð̣imin] Were you included in the group that was promoted? كِنِت بِضِمِن الجَّماعَة اللِّي تَرَفّعَوا؟ [činit bið̣imin ʔiǰǰamaːʕa ʔilli traffʕaw?]

including • **1.** بضِمِن [bð̣imin] وِيّا [wiyya] He earns thirty dollars, including tips. هُوَّ يطَلِّع ثلاثِين دُولار، بِضِمِنها البَخشِيش [huwwa yṭalliʕ tlaːθiːn dulaːr, bið̣iminha ʔilbaxšiːš]

income • **1.** وارِد [waːrid] وارِدات [waːridaːt] *pl:* How much of an income does he have? شقَدّ الوارِد مالَه؟ [šgadd ʔilwaːrid maːlah?]

incompetent • **1.** مُو كَفُو [muː kafu] The ambassador is incompetent. السَّفِير مُو كَفُو [ʔissafiːr muː kafu]

incomplete • **1.** مُو كامِل [muː kaːmil] ناقِص [naːgiṣ] The details of the report are incomplete. تَفاصِيل التَّقرِير مُو كامِلَة [tafaːṣiːl ʔittaqriːr muː kaːmla]

I

inconceivable • **1.** مُو مَعقُول [mu: maʕqu:l] ما يشِيلَه العَقِل [ma: yši:lah ʔilʕaqil] It's inconceivable that he'd do anything like that. مُو مَعقُول يسَوِّي هِيكِي شِي [mu: maʕqu:l ysawwi hi:či ši]

inconclusive • **1.** مُو مُقنِع [mu: muqniʕ] مُو قاطِع [mu: qa:ṭiʕ] The evidence so far is inconclusive. الأدِلَّة لهَسَّة مُو مُقنِعَة [ʔilʔadilla lhassa mu: muqniʕa]

inconvenience • **1.** إزعاج [ʔizʕa:ǰ] The trip caused us a lot of inconvenience. السَّفرَة سَبِّبَت إلنا هوايَة إزعاج [ʔissafra sabbibat ʔilna hwa:ya ʔizʕa:ǰ]

to inconvenience • **1.** ثَقَّل عَلَى [θaggal, θaqqal ʕala] تَثقِيل [taθqi:l] *vn: sv* i. أزعَج [ʔazʕaǰ] إزعاج [ʔizʕa:ǰ] *vn: sv* i. I don't want to inconvenience you. ما أرِيد أثَقِّل عَلِيك [ma: ʔari:d ʔaθaqqil ʕali:k]

inconvenient • **1.** مُو مُلائِم [mu: mula:ʔim] He visited us at a very inconvenient time. زارنا بفَدّ وَقِت أبَد مُو مُلائِم [za:rna bfadd wakit ʔabad mu: mula:ʔim] It will be inconvenient to go to the market today. اليُوم مُو هَالقَدّ مُلائِم لِلرُّوحَة لِلسُّوق [ʔilyu:m mu: halgadd mula:ʔim lirru:ħa lissu:g]

incorrect • **1.** مُو صَحِيح [mu: ṣaħi:ħ] غَلَط [ɣalaṭ] Some of what he said was incorrect. بَعَض اللّي قالَه مُو صَحِيح [baʕaḍ ʔilli ga:lah mu: ṣaħi:ħ]

increase • **1.** زِيادَة [ziya:da] اِرتِفاع [ʔirtifa:ʕ] اِرتِفاعات [ʔirtifa:ʕa:t] *pl:* Statistics show a considerable increase in population. الإحصاءات تبَيِّن زِيادَة كَبِيرَة بِالنُّفُوس [ʔilʔiħṣa:ʔa:t tbayyin ziya:da kabi:ra binnufu:s]

on the increase • **1.** اِرتِفاع [ʔirtifa:ʕ] اِرتِفاعات [ʔirtifa:ʕa:t] *pl:* The birth rate is on the increase. نِسبَة الوِلادَة بِارتِفاع [nisbat ʔilwila:da bʔirtifa:ʕ]

to increase • **1.** زَيَّد [zayyad] تَزيِيد [tazyi:d] *vn:* تزَيَّد [tzayyad] *p:* كَثَّر [kaθθar, čaθθar] تَكثِير [takθi:r] *vn:* تكَثَّر [tkaθθar] *p:* You have to increase your output. لازِم تزَيِّد الإنتاج [la:zim dzayyid ʔilʔinta:ǰ] • **2.** زاد [za:d] زِيادَة [ziya:da] *vn:* اِنزاد [ʔinza:d] *p:* The population increased tremendously. زادَت النُّفُوس بِنِسبَة كَبِيرَة [za:dat ʔinnufu:s binisba kabi:ra]

incredible • **1.** * She told an incredible story. حِكَت حكايَة ما يشِيلها العَقِل [ħičat ħča:ya ma: yši:lha ʔilʕaqil]

indecent • **1.** بَذِيء [baði:ʔ] His language is indecent. لُغَتَه بَذِيئَة [luɣatah baði:ʔa]

indeed • **1.** حَقِيقَةً [ħaqi:qatan] That's very good indeed! هاي حَقِيقَةً كُلِّش زينَة [ha:y ħaqi:qatan kulliš zi:na] • **2.** صِدُق [ṣidug] Indeed? صُدُق؟ [ṣudug?]

indefinite • **1.** ما معَيَّن [ma: mʕayyan] ما مَحدُود [ma: maħdu:d] We'll be staying for an indefinite period. راح نِبقَى إلَى مُدَّة ما مُعَيَّنَة [ra:ħ nibqa: ʔila mudda ma: muʕayyna]

independence • **1.** اِستِقلال [ʔistiqla:l] In these days, all African people want independence. بهَالأيّام، كُلّ الشُّعُوب الأفرِيقِيَّة ترِيد اِستِقلال [bhalʔayya:m, kull ʔiššuʕu:b ʔilʔafri:qiyya tri:d ʔistiqla:l]

* **He insists on complete independence in his work.** • **1.** يُصِرّ عَلَى أن مَحَّد أبَد يِتدَخَّل بشُغلَه [yuṣirr ʕala ʔan maħħad ʔabad yiddaxxal bšuɣlah]

independent • **1.** مُستَقِلّ [mustaqill] Lebanon is an independent state. لُبنان بَلَد مُستَقِلّ [lubna:n balad mustaqill] • **2.** ما مِرتِبُط [ma: mirtibuṭ] She's independent of her family. هِيَّ ما مِرتَبطَه بعائِلَتها [hiyya ma: mirtabṭah biʕa:ʔilatha] • **3.** مِعتِمِد عَلَ نَفس [miʕtimid ʕala nafs-] He's been independent every since he was sixteen. كان مِعتِمِد عَلَى نَفسَه مِن عُمرَه سِطَّعَش سَنَة [ča:n miʕtimid ʕala nafsah min ʕumrah siṭṭaʕaš sana]

index • **1.** فِهرَست [fihrast] فَهارِس [faha:ris] *pl:* Look for the name in the index. دَوُّر الإسِم بالفِهرَست [dawwur ʔilʔisim bilfihrast]

index finger • **1.** سَبّابَة [sabba:ba] سَبّابات [sabba:ba:t] *pl:*

India • **1.** الهِند [ʔilhind]

Indian • **1.** هِندِي [hindi] هنُود [hinu:d, hunu:d] *pl:* Not all Indians are Hindus. مُو كُلّ الهنُود هِندَوس [mu: kull ʔilhinu:d hindu:s] • **2.** هِندِي أحمَر [hindi ʔaħmar] هنُود حُمُر [hnu:d ħumur] *pl:* The original inhabitants of America were the Indians. سُكّان أمرِيكا الأصلِيِّين هُمَّ الهنُود الحُمُر [sukka:n ʔamri:ka ʔilʔaṣliyyi:n humma ʔilhnu:d ʔilħumur] • **3.** هِندِي [hindi] The Indian delegation arrived yesterday. الوَفد الهِندِي وُصَل البارحَة [ʔilwafd ʔilhindi wuṣal ʔilba:rħa]

Indian Ocean • **1.** المُحِيط الهِندِي [ʔilmuħi:ṭ ʔilhindi]

to indicate • **1.** دَلّ عَلَى [dall ʕala] دَلّ [dall] *vn:* اِندَلّ [ʔindall] *p:* بَيَّن [bayyan] تَبيِين [tabyi:n] *vn:* تبَيَّن [tbayyan] *p:* His statement indicates that he's serious about the decision. حكايتَه تدُلّ عَلَى إنُّو جِدِّي بِهَالقَرار [ħča:ytah ddull ʕala ʔinnu ǰiddi bihalqara:r]

indication • **1.** دَلِيل [dali:l] دَلائِل [dala:ʔil] *pl:* Did she give you any indication that she liked you? بَيَّنَتلَك أيّ دَلِيل عَلَى حُبّها؟ [bayynatlak ʔayy dali:l ʕala ħubbha?]

Indies • **1.** جُزُر الهِند، جَزائِر الهِند [ǰuzur ʔilhind, ǰaza:ʔir ʔilhind]

indifference • **1.** عَدَم اِهتِمام [ʕadam ʔihtimaːm] He showed complete indifference in the matter. بَيَّن فَدّ عَدَم اِهتِمام كُلِّي بِهَالمَوضُوع [bayyan fadd ʕadam ʔihtimaːm kulli bhalmawd̩uːʕ]

indifferent • **1.** لا أُبالِي [laː ʔubaːli] Don't be so indifferent. لا تكُون هَالقَدّ لا أُبالِي [laː tkuːn halgadd laː ʔubaːli]

*** Why are you so indifferent to her?**
• **1.** لَيش هَالقَدّ ما تدِيرلها بال؟ [liːš halgadd maː tdiːrilha baːl?] / لِيش ما تِهتَمّ بِيها؟ [liːš maː tihtamm biːha?]

indigestion • **1.** سُوء هَضُم [suːʔ had̩um] I have indigestion. عِندِي سُوء هَضُم [ʕindi suːʔ had̩um]

indignant • **1.** ساخِط [saːxiṭ] He was indignant at the unfair treatment. كان ساخِط عالمُعامَلَة السَّيِّئَة [čaːn saːxiṭ ʕalmuʕaːmala ʔissayyiʔa]

indiscreet • **1.** ما مِتحَفُّظ [maː mitħaffuð̩] Your remark was very indiscreet. إنتَ ما كِنِت مِتحَفُّظ بذِيك الحكايَة [ʔinta maː činit mitħaffuð̩ bðiːč ʔilħčaːya] • **2.** ما مِتبَصِّر [maː mitbaṣṣir] We feel you were indiscreet in your decision. إحنا نِعتِقِد إنتَ ما كِنِت مِتبَصِّر بِقَرارَك [ʔiħna niʕtiqid ʔinta maː činit mitbaṣṣir biqaraːrak]

individual • **1.** شَخِص [šaxiṣ] أشخاص [ʔašxaːṣ] *pl:* واحِد [waːħid] وِحدَة [wiħda] *Feminine:* He's a peculiar individual. هُوَّ فَدّ شَخِص أعمالَه غَرِيبَة [huwwa fadd šaxiṣ ʔaʕmaːlah ɣariːba] • **2.** فَرِد [farid] The communists don't respect the rights of the individual. الشُّيُوعِيِّين ما يهتَمُّون بحُقُوق الفَرِد [ʔiššuyuːʕiyyiːn maː yihtammuːn bħuquːq ʔilfarid] • **3.** خاصّ [xaːṣṣ] We each have our individual taste. كُلّ واحِد مِنّا إلَه ذَوقَه الخاصّ بِيه [kull waːħid minna ʔilah ðawqah ʔilxaːṣṣ biːh]

*** The individual can do nothing.** • **1.** إِيد وِحدَة مَا تصَفُّق [ʔiːd wiħda maː tṣaffug]

individually • **1.** واحِد واحِد [waːħid waːħid] I wish to speak to the students individually. أرِيد أحكِي وِيّا كُلّ تِلمِيذ واحِد واحِد [ʔariːd ʔaħči wiyya kull tilmiːð waːħid waːħid] • **2.** كُلّ واحِد وَ وَحدَه [kull waːħid waħda] They came individually to the station. إجَوا لِلمَحَطَّة كُلّ واحِد وَحدَه [ʔijaw lilmaħaṭṭa kull waːħid waħdah]

Indonesia • **1.** أندَونِيسيا [ʔanduniːsya]

Indonesian • **1.** أندَونِيسِي [ʔanduːniːsiː] أندَونِيسِيِّين [ʔanduniːsiyyiːn] *pl:* He's an Indonesian. هُوَّ أندُونِيسِي [huwwa ʔanduniːsi]

indoors • **1.** جَوَّة [jawwa] داخِل [daːxil] You'd better stay indoors today. أحسَن لَو تِبقَى جَوَّة اليُوم [ʔaħsan law tibqaː jawwa ʔilyuːm] If it rains the concert will be held indoors. الحَفلَة المُوسِيقِيَّة تصِير بداخِل القاعَة إذا تُمطُر الدِّنيا [ʔilħafla ʔalmuːsiːqiyya tṣiːr bdaːxil ʔilqaːʕa ʔiða tumṭur ʔiddinya]

industrial • **1.** صِناعِي [ṣinaːʕi] They are setting up industrial centers all over the UAR. هُمَّ قاعدِين يبنُون مَراكِز صِناعِيَّة بكُلّ أنحاء الجَمهُورِيَّة العَرَبِيَّة المُتَّحِدَة [humma gaːʕdiːn yibnuːn maraːkiz ṣinaːʕiyya bkull ʔanħaːʔ ʔijjamhuːriyya ʔilʕarabiyya ʔilmuttaħida]

industrialist • **1.** صِناعِي [ṣinaːʕi] He's a famous industrialist. هُوَّ صِناعِي مَشهُور [huwwa ṣinaːʕi mašhuːr]

industrialization • **1.** تَصنِيع [taṣniːʕ] The industrialization of Egypt is making considerable progress. التَّصنِيع بِمَصِر قاعِد يِتقَدَّم بسُرعَة [ʔittaṣniːʕ bimaṣir gaːʕid yitqaddam bsurʕa]

industry • **1.** صِناعَة [ṣinaːʕa] صِناعات [ṣinaːʕaːt] *pl:* Many industries were developed after the war. هوايَة صِناعات تطَوّرَت بَعد الحَرب [hwaːya ṣinaːʕaːt ṭṭawwrat baʕad ʔilħarb]

inevitable • **1.** حَتمِي [ħatmi] لا بُدّ مِنُّه [laː budd minnu] ما مُمكِن تَفادِيه [maː mumkin tafaːdiːh] This was an inevitable result. هاي كانَت نَتِيجَة حَتمِيَّة [haːy čaːnat natiːja ħatmiyya] An argument with him is inevitable now. التَّلاغِي وِيّاه ما مُمكِن تَفادِيه هَسَّة [ʔittalaːɣi wiyyaːh maː mumkin tafaːdiːh hassa]

inexpensive • **1.** رِخِيص [rixiːṣ] مُو غالِي [muː ɣaːli] I bought an inexpensive watch. اِشتِرَيت ساعَة رخِيصَة [ʔištirayt saːʕa rxiːṣa]

infant • **1.** رَضِيع [rad̩iːʕ] رُضَعاء، رُضَّع [rud̩aʕaːʔ, rud̩d̩aʕ] *pl:*

infantile • **1.** مال جهال [maːl jihaːl] صِبيانِي [ṣibyaːni] His actions are quite infantile. تَصَرُّفاتَه بَعَدها مال جهال [taṣarrufaːtah baʕadha maːl jihaːl]

infantile paralysis • **1.** شَلَل [šalal] He has infantile paralysis. هُوَّ مُصاب بالشَّلَل [huwwa muṣaːb biššalal]

infantry • **1.** ماشِي [maːši] مُشات [mušaːt] *pl:*

to infect • **1.** حَمَّل [ħammal] تَحمِيل [taħmiːl] *vn: sv* i. The dirt will infect that wound. الوَساخَة تحَمِّل الجَّرِح [ʔilwaṣaːxa tħammil ʔijjariħ]

to be infected • **1.** حَمَّل [ħammal] *sv* i. اِلتِهَب [ʔiltihab] اِلتِهاب [ʔiltihaːb] *vn: sv* i. The wound is infected. الجَّرِح مِحَمِّل [ʔijjariħ mħammil]

infection • **1.** مَرَض [marad̩] أمراض [ʔamraːd̩] *pl:* عَدوَى [ʕadwa] Is there any way to keep that infection from spreading to the rest of the people? هَل أكُو طَرِيقَة تخَلِّي هَذا المَرَض ما يِنتِشِر إلَى باقِي النّاس؟ [hal ʔaku ṭariːqa txalli haːða ʔilmarad̩ maː yintišir ʔila baːqi

ʔinna:sʔ] • **2.** اِلتِهاب [ʔiltiha:b] اِلتِهابات [ʔiltiha:ba:t] *pl:* This medicine will get rid of the infection. هَذا الدُّوا راح يِقضِي عالإلتِهاب [ha:ða ʔidduwa ra:ħ yiqḍi ʕalʔiltiha:b]

infectious • **1.** مُعدِي [muʕdi] He has a very infectious disease. مَرَضَه كُلِّش مُعدِي [maraḍah kulliš muʕdi]

inferior • **1.** واطِي [wa:ṭi] How can you tell that it's an inferior quality? شلُون تُعرُف هَذا مِن نُوع واطِي؟ [šlu:n tuʕruf ha:ða min nu:ʕ wa:ṭiʔ] • **2.** أَقَلّ نَوعِيَّة [ʔaqall nawʕiyya] This material is inferior to that. هَذِي المادَّة أَقَلّ نَوعِيَّة مِن اللُّخ [ha:ði ʔilma:dda ʔaqall nawʕiyya min ʔillux]

* **He is doing inferior work.** • **1.** شُغلَه مُو زَين [šuɣlah mu: zayn]

inferiority complex • **1.** مُرَكَّب نَقِس [murakkab naqis] She has an inferiority complex. عِدها مُرَكَّب نَقِص [ʕidha murakkab naqiṣ]

I

infidel • **1.** كافِر [ka:fir] كَفَرَة، كُفّار [kafara, kuffa:r] *pl:*

infidelity • **1.** خِيانَة [xiya:na] Marital infidelity is a sin. الخِيانَة الزَّوجِيَّة حَرام [ʔilxiya:na ʔizzawǰiyya ħara:m]

* **He suspects his wife of infidelity.**
• **1.** هُوَّ يظُنّ إِنُّو زَوجتَه خائِنَة [huwwa yḍunn ʔinnuw zawiǰta xa:ʔina]

infinite • **1.** ما لَه نِهايَة [ma: lah niha:ya] ما إِلَه حَدّ [ma: ʔilah ħadd] She has infinite patience. عِدها خُلُق ما إِلَه نِهايَة [ʕidha xulug ma: ʔilah niha:ya]

to be inflamed • **1.** اِلتِهَب [ʔiltihab] اِلتِهاب [ʔiltiha:b] *vn: sv* i. My eye is inflamed. عينِي مِلتَهبَة [ʕayni miltahba]

inflammable • **1.** قابِل لِلالتِهاب [qa:bil lilʔiltiha:b] Don't smoke here. The gas is inflammable. لا تدَخِّن هنا البانزين قابِل لِلإلتِهاب [la: ddaxxin hna ʔilbanzi:n qa:bil lilʔiltiha:b]

inflammation • **1.** اِلتِهاب [ʔiltiha:b] The inflammation is going down. الالتِهاب دَيقِلّ [ʔilʔiltiha:b dayqill]

influence • **1.** تَأثِير [taʔθi:r] نُفُوذ [nufu:ð] He has no influence whatsoever. ما عِندَه أَيّ تَأثِير [ma: ʕindah ʔayy taʔθi:r] • **2.** نُفُوذ [nufu:ð] The people resist outside influence in the country. الشَّعَب يقاوُم النُّفُوذ الأَجنَبِي بِبَلَدَه [ʔiššaʕab yqa:wum ʔinnufu:ð ʔilʔaǰnabi bibaladah]

* **He was driving under the influence.**
• **1.** كان يسُوق وهُوَّ سَكران [ča:n ysu:q whuwwa sakra:n]

to influence • **1.** أَثَّر عَلَى [ʔaθθar ʕala] تَأثِير [taʔθi:r] *vn: sv* i. I'm not trying to influence you. ما دَأحاوِل أَثِّر عَلِيك [ma: daʔaħa:wil ʔaʔaθθir ʕali:k] He is trying to influence her in his favor يحاوِل التَّأثِير عَليها لِصالحَه [yħa:wil ʔittaʔθi:r ʕali:ha lṣa:lħah]

influential • **1.** * He's an influential man. هُوَّ عِندَه تَأثِير كِبِير هُوَّ صاحِب نُفُوذ واسِع [huwwa ʕindah taʔθi:r čibi:r huwwa ṣa:ħib nufu:ð wa:siʕ]

influenza • **1.** فلاوَنزا [flawanza, ʔinflawanza]

to inform • **1.** خَبَّر [xabbar] تَخبِير [taxbi:r] *vn:* تخَبَّر [txabbar] *p:* قال [ga:l] قَول [gawl] *vn:* اِنقال [ʔinga:l] *p:* Keep me informed of your decisions. خَبُّرنِي بِكُلّ قَرار تِتَّخذُوا [xabburni bkull qara:r tittaxðu:h]

* **He's unusually well informed.** • **1.** عِندَه عِلِم بكُلّ الأَخبار [ʕindah ʕilim bkull ʔilʔaxba:r] / عِندَه إِطِّلاع واسِع [ʕindah ʔiṭṭila:ʕ wa:siʕ]

informant • **1.** مُخبِر [muxbir] We got the news from a reliable informant. حَصَّلنا عالأَخبار مِن مُخبِر مَوثُوق بِيه [ħaṣṣalna ʕalʔaxba:r min muxbir mawθu:q bi:h]

information • **1.** مَعلُومات [maʕlu:ma:t] خَبَر [xabar] أَخبار [ʔaxba:r] *pl:* I can't give you any information about this case. ما أَقدَر أَنطِيك أَيّ مَعلُومات تِتعَلَّق بِالقَضِيَّة [ma: ʔagdar ʔanṭi:k ʔayy maʕlu:ma:t titʕallaq bilqaḍiyya] • **2.** اِستِعلام [ʔistiʕla:m] اِستِعلامات [ʔstiʕlama:t] *pl:* Where's the information desk, please? مِن فَضلَك، وين مَكتَب الاستِعلامات؟ [min faḍlak, wi:n maktab ʔilʔistiʕla:ma:tʔ]

infraction • **1.** مُخالَفَة [muxa:lafa] مُخالَفات [muxa:lafa:ṭ] *pl:* We'll charge a fine for any infraction of the rules. راح نَضَع غَرامَة عَلَى كُلّ مُخالَفَة لِلتَّعلِمات [ra:ħ naḍaʕ ɣara:ma ʕala kull muxa:lafa littaʕlima:t]

ingenious • **1.** بارِع [ba:riʕ] Your idea is very ingenious. فِكِرتَك بارِعَة [fikirtak ba:riʕa]

to inhabit • **1.** سِكَن [sikan] سَكَن [sakan] *vn: sv* u. The Rualla tribe inhabits the northern portion of the Arabian Peninsula. قَبِيلَة رَولَة سِكنَت القِسم الشَّمالِي مِن الجَّزِيرَة العَرَبِيَّة [qabi:lat rwala siknat ʔilqism ʔiššama:li min ʔiǰǰazi:ra ʔilʕarabiyya] This area was not inhabited until two years ago. هَالمَنطِقَة ما كانَت مَسكُونَة إِلّا قَبِل سَنتَين [halmanṭiqa ma: ča:nat masku:na ʔilla qabil santayn]

inhabitant • **1.** ساكِن [sa:kin] سُكّان [sukka:n] *pl:* All the inhabitants of the island are fishermen. سُكّان الجَّزِيرَة كُلّهُم صَيّادِين سِمَك [sukka:n ʔiǰǰazi:ra kullhum ṣayya:di:n simač] In 1960 Baghdad had a million inhabitants. بِسَنَة أَلِف وَتِسِع مِيَّة وسِتِّين سُكّان بَغداد كانَوا مِليَون [bsanat ʔalif wtisiʕ miyya wsitti:n sukka:n bayda:d ča:naw milyu:n]

to inhale • **1.** أَخَذ نَفَس [ʔaxað nafas] *sv* u. The doctor told me to inhale. الطَّبِيب قَلِّي أُخُذ نَفَس [ʔiṭṭabi:b galli ʔuxuð nafas] • **2.** بِلَع [bilaʕ] بَلِع [baliʕ] *vn: sv* a. She's just learning to smoke, but she doesn't inhale. هَستَوّها تعلَّمَت تِشرَب جِكايِر بَسّ ما تِبلَع الدُّخّان [hastawwha tʕallmat tišrab ǰiga:yir bass ma: tiblaʕ ʔidduxxa:n]

to inherit • **1.** إستارَث [ʔista:raθ] إستِيراث [ʔisti:ra:θ] *vn: sv* i. وُرَث [wuraθ] وَرِث [wariθ] *vn:* اِنوُرَث [ʔinwuraθ] *p:* I inherited the ring from my mother. اِستارَثِت المِحبَس مِن أُمّي [ʔista:raθit ʔilmiħbas min ʔummi]

inheritance • **1.** وِرِث [wiriθ] مِيراث [mi:ra:θ] مَوارِيث [mawa:ri:θ] *pl:* My uncle left me a small inheritance. عَمّي خَلَّفلي فَدّ شوَيَّة وُرِث [ʕammi xallafli fadd šwayya wuriθ]

inhuman • **1.** وَحشِي [waħši] The terrorists used inhuman methods against the populace. الإرهابِيّين استَعمَلَوا أَسالِيب وَحشِيَّة ضِدّ السُّكّان [ʔalʔirha:biyyi:n ʔistaʕmalaw ʔasa:li:b waħšiyya ḍidd ʔissukka:n]

initial • **1.** أَوَّلي [ʔawwali] بدائي [bida:ʔi] The project is still in its initial stages. المَشرُوع بَعدَه بمَراحلَه الأَوَّلِيَّة [ʔilmašru:ʕ baʕdah bimara:ħlah ʔilʔawwaliyya]

initially • **1.** مَبدَئِيّاً [mabdaʔiyyan] أَوَّلاً [ʔawwalan] بِالأَوَّل [bilʔawwal] Initially, the government is going to appropriate one million dinars. مَبدَئِيّاً، الحُكُومَة راح تخَصِّص مِليَون دِينار [mabdaʔiyyan, ʔilħuku:ma ra:ħ txaṣṣiṣ milyu:n dina:r]

initiative • **1.** هِمَّة [himma] That engineer doesn't have much initiative. هالمُهَندِس ما عِندَه هَالقَدّ هِمَّة [halmuhandis ma: ʕindah halgadd himma]

*** Someone has to take the initiative so the others will follow.** • **1.** فَدّ أَحَّد لازِم يِبدِي حَتَّى الباقِين يِتبَعُوه [fadd ʔaħħad la:zim yibdi ħatta ʔilba:qi:n yitbʕu:h]

to inject • **1.** بِعَث [biʕaθ] بَعِث [baʕiθ] *vn:* اِنبِعَث [ʔinbiʕaθ] *p:* The change injected new life into the project. التَّغيِير بِعَث حَياة جِدِيدَة بِالمَشرُوع [ʔittaɣyi:r biʕaθ ħaya:t ǰidi:da bilmašru:ʕ] • **2.** ضُرَب، ضِرَب [ḍurab, ḍirab] ضَرُب [ḍarub] *vn: sv* u. They injected penicillin in his hip. ضُربَوه أُبرَة بَنسِلِين بِورِكَه [ḍurbawh ʔubrat pansili:n biwirkah]

injection • **1.** أُبرَة [ʔubra] أُبَر [ʔubar] *pl:* Are you getting injections for diabetes? دَتاخُذ أُبَر مال سُكَّر؟ [data:xuð ʔubar ma:l sukkar?]

to injure • **1.** جِرَح [ǰirah] جَرِح [ǰariħ] *vn:* اِنجِرَح [ʔinǰirah] *p:* How many people were injured in the accident? شقَدّ ناس اِنجِرحَوا بِالحادِثَة؟ [šgadd na:s ʔinǰirħaw bilħa:diθa?]

injury • **1.** جَرِح [ǰariħ] جرُوح [ǰru:ħ] *pl:* His injuries were not serious. جرُوحَه ما كانَت خَطرَة [ǰru:ħah ma: ča:nat xaṭra]

ink • **1.** حِبِر [ħibir] I need ink for my fountain pen. أَحتاج حِبِر لِقَلَم الباندان مالِي [ʔaħta:ǰ ħibir lqalam ʔilpa:nda:n ma:li]

to ink • **1.** خَلَّى حِبِر عَلَى [xalla: ħibir ʕala] *sv* i. Don't ink the pad too heavily. لا تخَلّي هوايَة حِبِر عالإسطَمبَة [la: txalli hwa:ya ħibir ʕalʔisṭampa]

inlaid • **1.** مطَعَّم [mṭaʕʕam] That box has a cover inlaid with ivory. قَبَغ القُوطِيَّة مطَعَّم بعاج [qabaɣ ʔilqu:ṭiyya mṭaʕʕam biʕa:ǰ]

inner • **1.** داخلِي [da:xili] جَوّانِي [ǰawwa:ni] The inner door is locked. الباب الدّاخلِي مَقفُول [ʔilba:b ʔidda:xli maqfu:l]

innocence • **1.** بَراءَة [bara:ʔa] How did he prove his innocence? شلُون ثِبَت بَراءتَه؟ [šlu:n θibat bara:ʔtah?]

innocent • **1.** بَرِيء [bari:ʔ] أَبرِياء [ʔabriya:ʔ] *pl:* He's innocent of this charge. هُوَّ بَرِيء مِن هَالتُّهمَة [huwwa bari:ʔ min hattuhma] • **2.** بَسِيط [baṣi:ṭ] بَسِيطِين [baṣi:ṭi:n] *pl:* He's as innocent as a new-born babe. هُوَّ بَسِيط مِثل الطِّفِل [huwwa basi:ṭ miθl ʔiṭṭifil] • **3.** بحُسن نِيَّة [bħusin niyya] It was just an innocent remark. كانَت مُلاحَظَة بحُسُن نِيَّة [ča:nat mula:ħaḍa bħusun niyya]

innovation • **1.** اِبتِكار [ʔibtika:r] اِبتِكارات [ʔibtika:ra:t] *pl:* The minister introduced many innovations in his department. الوَزِير قَدَّم عِدَّة اِبتِكارات لِتَطبِيقها بدائِرتَه [ʔilwazi:r qaddam ʕiddat ʔibtika:ra:t litaṭbi:qha bda:ʔirtah]

to inoculate • **1.** طَعَّم [ṭaʕʕam] تَطعِيم [taṭʕi:m] *vn:* تطَعَّم [tṭaʕʕam] *p:* I haven't been inoculated against yellow fever yet. ما تطَعَّمِت بَعَد ضِدّ الحِمَّى الصَّفراء [ma: ṭṭaʕʕamit baʕad ḍidd ʔilħimma ʔiṣṣafra:ʔ]

inoculation • **1.** تَطَعُّم [taṭaʕʕum] تَطَعُّمات [taṭaʕʕuma:t] *pl:*

to inquire • **1.** اِستَعلَم [ʔistaʕlam] اِستِعلام [ʔistiʕla:m] *vn: sv* i. اِستَفسَر [ʔistafsar] اِستِفسار [ʔistifsa:r] *vn: sv* i. I'll inquire about it. راح أَستَعلِم عَنها [ra:ħ ʔastaʕlim ʕanha]

inquiry • **1.** تَحقِيق [taħqi:q] تَحقِيقات [taħqi:qa:t] *pl:* An inquiry revealed that. . . التَّحقِيق بَيَّن عَلَى إنُّو [ʔittaħqi:q bayyan ʕala ʔinnu...] • **2.** اِستِفسار [ʔistifsa:r] اِستِفسارات [ʔistifsa:ra:t] *pl:* اِستِعلام [ʔistiʕla:m] اِستِعلامات [ʔstiʕlama:t] *pl:* We had a lot of inquiries about this subject. عِدنا هوايَة اِستِفسارات عَن هَذا المَوضُوع [ʕidna hwa:ya ʔistifsa:ra:t ʕan ha:ða ʔilmawḍu:ʕ]

insane • **1.** مَجنُون [majnu:n] مَجانِين [maǰa:ni:n] *pl:* مخَبَّل [mxabbal] مخابِيل [mxa:bi:l] *pl:* That man is insane. هَذا الرَّجُل مَجنُون [ha:ða ʔirrajul majnu:n]

I

insane asylum • **1.** مُستَشفَى المجانِين [mustašfa ʔilmja̰ːniːn] When did they release him from the insane asylum? يَمتَى فَكُّوه مِن مُستَشفى المَجانِين؟ [yamta fakkuːh min mustašfa ʔilmaja̰ːniːn?]

inscription • **1.** كِتابَة مَحفُورَة [kitaːba maħfuːra] كِتابَة مَنقُوشَة [kitaːba manquːša] Can you read this inscription? تِقدَر تِقرا هَالكِتابَة المَحفُورَة؟ [tigdar tiqraː halkitaːba ʔilmaħfuːra?]

insect • **1.** حَشَرَة [ħašara] حَشَرات [ħašaraːt] *pl:* Insects are a problem here. الحَشَرات فَدّ مُشكِلَة هنا [ʔilħašaraːt fadd muškila hna]

insecticide • **1.** قاتِل حَشَرات [qaːtil ħašaraːt]

to insert • **1.** دِمَج [dimaǰ] دَمِج [damiǰ] *vn: sv* i. Insert this sentence in the beginning of your report. إدمِج هَالجُملَة بِبِدايَة تَقرِيرَك [ʔidmiǰ halǰumla bibidaːyat taqriːrak]

inside • **1.** داخِل [daːxil] May I see the inside of the house? أَقدَر أَشُوف داخِل البَيت؟ [ʔagdar ʔašuːf daːxil ʔilbayt?] • **2.** بِالداخِل [biddaːxil] He left it inside. تِرَكها بِالدّاخِل [tirakha biddaːxil] • **3.** بخِلال [bxilaːl] بضِمِن [bðimin] Inside of five minutes the theater was empty. بخِلال خَمِس دَقايِق صارَت السِّينَما فارغَة [bxilaːl xamis daqaːyiq ṣaːrat ʔissinama faːrɣa] • **4.** داخِلِي [daːxili] Could you please give us an inside room? مُمكِن مِن فَضلَك تِنطِينا غُرفَة داخِلِيَّة؟ [mumkin min faðlak tintiːna ɣurfa daːxiliyya?]

inside out • **1.** بِالقُفا [bilgufa] مَقلُوب [magluːb] He has his sweater on inside out. لابِس بلُوزَه بالقُفَا [laːbis bluːzah bilgufa] • **2.** شِبِر شِبِر [šibir šibir] تَماماً [tamaːman] He knows the town inside out. يُعرُف المَدِينَة شِبِر شِبِر [yuʕruf ʔilmadiːna šibir šibir] He knows his business inside out. خاتِم مَصلَحتَه تَماماً [xaːtim maṣlaħtah tamaːman]

to come (or go) inside • **1.** دِخَل [dixal] دُخُول [duxuːl] *vn: sv* u. خَشّ [xašš] Why don't you come inside? لِيش ما تِدخُل؟ [liːš maː tidxul?]

insight • **1.** إدراك [ʔidraːk] فَهِم [fahim, fihim] أَفهام [ʔafhaːm] *pl:* He showed great insight in handling economic problems. بَيَّن إدراك واسِع بمُعالَجَة المَشاكِل الاقتِصادِيَّة [bayyan ʔidraːk waːsiʕ bmuʕaːlaǰat ʔilmašaːkil ʔilʔiqtiṣaːdiyya]

insignia • **1.** عَلامَة [ʕalaːma] عَلامات، عَلائِم [ʕalaːmaːt, ʕalaːʔim] *pl:* إشارَة [ʔišaːra] إشارات [ʔišaːraːt] *pl:* The cavalry's insignia is crossed rifles. عَلامَة الخَيّالَة بُندُقِيتَين مِتقاطعَة [ʕalaːmat ʔilxayyaːla bunduqiːtayn mitqaːṭʕa]

insignificant • **1.** طَفِيف [ṭafiːf] تافِه [taːfih] مُو مُهِمّ [muː muhimm] The difference is insignificant. الاختِلاف طَفِيف [ʔilʔixtilaːf ṭafiːf]

to insinuate • **1.** لَمَّح [lammaħ] تَلمِيح [talmiːħ] *vn:* تلَمَّح [tlammaħ] *p:* He insinuated that the prime minister was taking bribes. لَمَّح عَلَى أَنُّو رَئِيس الوُزَراء كان ياخُذ رَشوَة [lammaħ ʕala ʔannu raʔiːs ʔilwuzaraːʔ čaːn yaːxuð rašwa]

insinuation • **1.** تَصجِيم [taṣčiːm] تَلمِيح [talmiːħ] تَلمِيحات [talmiːħaːt] *pl:* Those insinuations are out of place. هَالتَّصجِيم أَبَد مُو بِمَحَلَّه [hattaṣčiːm ʔabad muː bimaħallah]

to insist • **1.** n صَرّ [ṣarr] إصرار [ʔiṣraːr] *vn: sv* i. Why do you insist on going? لُويش تصِرّ عالرَّوحَة؟ [luwiːš tṣirr ʕarrawħa?] • **2.** لَحّ [laħħ] إلحاح، لَحّ [ʔilħaːħ, laħħ] *vn: sv* i. Don't insist if she doesn't want to go. لا تلِحّ إذا هِيَّ ما ترِيد ترُوح [laː tliħħ ʔiða hiyya maː triːd truːħ]

insistent • **1.** لَحُوح [lahuːħ] This beggar is very insistent. هَالمِقَدّي كُلِّش لَحُوح [halimgaddi kulliš lahuːħ]

insolence • **1.** صَلافَة [ṣalaːfa] Children, I don't want any more insolence from you. وِلِد، بَسّ عاد صَلافَة [wilid, bass ʕaːd ṣalaːfa]

insolent • **1.** صَلِف [ṣalif] صَلِفِين [ṣalifiːn] *pl:* He's an insolent fellow. هُوَّ فَدّ واحِد كُلِّش صَلِف [huwwa fadd waːħid kulliš ṣalif]

insomnia • **1.** أَرَق [ʔaraq] I have insomnia these days. دَيصِير عِندِي أَرَق هَالأَيّام [dayṣiːr ʕindi ʔaraq halʔayyaːm]

to inspect • **1.** فَتَّش [fattaš] تَفتِيش [taftiːš] *vn:* تفَتَّش [tfattaš] *p:* They inspected the baggage carefully. فَتّشَوا الجُنَط كُلِّش زين [fattšaw ʔiǰǰunaṭ kulliš ziːn]

inspection • **1.** تَفتِيش [taftiːš] Our baggage is ready for inspection. جِنَطنا حاضرَة لِلتَّفتِيش [ǰinaṭna ħaːðra littaftiːš]

inspector • **1.** مُفَتِّش [mufattiš] مُفَتِّشِين [mufattišiːn] *pl:*

inspiration • **1.** وَحِي [waħy] إلهام [ʔilhaːm] A good poet can't write without inspiration. الشّاعِر الزّين ما يِقدَر يُنظُم بَلا ما يِجِيه الوَحِي [ʔiššaːʕir ʔizziːn maː yigdar yunðum bala maː yiǰiːh ʔilwaħi]

to inspire • **1.** أَوحَى [ʔawħaː] وُحَى [wuħaː] إيحاء [ʔiːħaːʔ] *vn:* اِنوُحَى [ʔinwuħaː] *p:* His calm manner inspires confidence. هُدُوئَه يُوحِي بِالثِّقَة [huduːʔah yuːħi biθθiqa]

to install • **1.** نِصَب [niṣab] نَصُب [naṣub] *vn:* اِنِّصَب [ʔinniṣab] *p:* A telephone will be installed tomorrow. باكِر راح يِنُّصُب تِلِفُون [baːčir raːħ yinnuṣub tilifuːn]

installation • **1.** نَصُب [naṣub] Telephone installation costs 15 pounds. نَصُب تِلِفُون يكَلِّف خمُسطَعَش دِينار [naṣub tilifuːn ykallif xmustaʕaš dina:r] • **2.** مُنشَأَة [munša?a] مُنشَآت [munša?a:t] *pl:* مُؤَسَّسَة [mu?assasa] مُؤَسَّسات [mu?assasa:t] *pl:* He was collecting intelligence on military and industrial installations. كان دَيجمَع مَعلُومات عَن المُنشَآت الصِّناعِيَّة وِالعَسكَرِيَّة [ča:n dayijmaʕ maʕlu:ma:t ʕan ?ilmunša?a:t ?iṣṣina:ʕiyya wilʕaskariyya]

installment • **1.** قِسِم مِتسَلسِل [qisim mitsalsil] أَقسام مِتسَلسِلَة [?aqsa:m mitsalsila] *pl:* The novel is appearing in installments. الرُّوايَة دَتِطلَع عَلَى أَقسام مِتسَلسِلَة [?irruwa:ya datiṭlaʕ ʕala ?aqsa:m mitsalsila] • **2.** قُسُط [qusuṭ, qisiṭ] أَقساط [?aqsa:ṭ] *pl:* You can pay it in five installments. تِقدَر تِدفَعها بِخَمس أَقساط [tigdar tidfaʕha bxams ?aqsa:ṭ]

on installments • **1.** بِالتَّقسِيط [bittaqsi:ṭ] قُسُط [qusuṭ, qisiṭ] أَقساط [?aqsa:ṭ] *pl:* We bought the furniture on installments. اِشتِرَينا الأَثاث بِالتَّقسِيط [?ištirayna ?il?aθa:θ bittaqsi:ṭ]

to pay in installments • **1.** قَسَّط [qassaṭ] تَقسِيط [taqsi:ṭ] *vn: sv* i. I'll pay you the amount in installments. عُود أَقَسِّطلَك المَبلَغ [ʕu:d ?aqassiṭlak ?ilmablaɣ]

instance • **1.** مَثَل [maθal] أَمثال [?amθa:l] *pl:* This is another instance of his carelessness. هَذا مَثَل لاخ عَلَى عَدَم اِهتِمامَه [ha:ða maθal la:x ʕala ʕadam ?ihtima:mah] • **2.** حالَة [ħa:la] حالات [ħa:la:t] *pl:* مَرَّة [marra] مَرّات [marra:t] *pl:* In this instance you're wrong. بِهالحالَة إِنتَ غَلطان [bhalħa:la ?inta ɣalṭa:n]

for instance • **1.** مَثَلاً [maθalan] There are quite a few possibilities, for instance. . . أَكُو عِدَّة اِحتِمالات، مَثَلاً [?aku ʕiddat ?iħtima:la:t, maθalan...]

instant • **1.** لَحظَة [laħđa] لَحظات [laħđa:t] *pl:* Let me know the instant he arrives. خَبُرني بِاللَّحظَة اللِّي يُوصَل بيها [xaburni billaħđa ?illi yu:ṣal bi:ha] He was gone in an instant. اِختِفَى بلَحظَة وِحدَة [?ixtifa: blaħđa wiħda]

instantly • **1.** حالاً [ħa:lan] فَوراً [fawran] He came instantly when I called. جا حالاً مِن صِحِّتَه [ǰa: ħa:lan min ṣiħħtah]

instead • **1.** بِدال، بَدَل [bida:l, badal] بَدَلاً مِن [badalan min] مَكان [maka:n, muka:n] مُكانات، أَماكِن، أَمكِنَة [muka:na:t, ?ama:kin, ?amkina] *pl:* عِوَضاً عَن [ʕiwađan ʕan] What do you want instead of it? شتِرِيد بَدالَه؟ [šitri:d bada:lah?] He gave me tangerines instead of oranges. اِنطانِي لالِنكِي بِدال البُرتَقال [?inṭa:ni la:lingi bida:l ?ilpurtaqa:l] Why don't you do something instead of complaining all the time? لُويش ما تسَوِّي شِي بَدَلاً مِن أَن تِتشَكَّى عَلَى طُول؟ [luwi:š ma: tsawwi ši badalan min ?an titšakka: ʕala ṭu:l?] Can you go instead of me? تِقدَر ترُوح عِوَضاً عَنِّي؟ [tigdar tru:ħ ʕiwađan ʕanni?]

to instigate • **1.** حَرَّض [ħarrađ] تَحرِيض [taħri:đ] *vn: sv* i. He instigated the strike. هُوَّ اللِّي حَرَّض عالإِضراب [huwwa ?illi ħarrađ ʕal?iđra:b]

instigator • **1.** مُحَرِّض [muħarriđ] مُحَرِّضِين [muħarriđi:n] *pl:*

instinct • **1.** فِطرَة [fiṭra] غَرِيزَة [ɣari:za] غَرائِز [ɣara:?iz] *pl:* Women love children by instinct. النِّسوان يحِبُّون الأَطفال بالفِطرَة [?inniswa:n yħibbu:n ?il?aṭfa:l bilfiṭra]

institute • **1.** مَعهَد [maʕhad] مَعاهِد [maʕa:hid] *pl:* I'm studying at the Scientific Institute. آنِي أَدرُس بِالمَعهَد العِلمِي [?a:ni ?adrus bilmaʕhad ?ilʕilmi]

institution • **1.** مَعهَد [maʕhad] مَعاهِد [maʕa:hid] *pl:* It's a state institution. هَذا مَعهَد حُكُومِي [ha:ða maʕhad ħuku:mi]

instruction • **1.** مُحاضَرَة [muħa:đara] مُحاضَرات [muħa:đara:t] *pl:* Professor Ahmed will give instruction in Arabic. الأُستاذ أَحمَد راح يِلقِي مُحاضَرات بِاللُّغَة العَرَبِيَّة [?il?usta:ð ?aħmad ra:ħ yilqi muħa:đara:t billuɣa ?ilʕarabiyya]

instructions • **1.** تَعلِيمات [taʕli:ma:t] The head nurse will give you instructions. رَئِيسَة المُمَرِّضات راح تِنطِيك التَّعلِيمات [ra?i:sat ?ilmumarriđa:t ra:ħ tinṭi:k ?ittaʕli:ma:t]

instructive • **1.** تَوجِيهِي [tawǰi:hi] The lecture was very instructive. المُحاضَرَة كانَت كُلِّش تَوجِيهِيَّة [?ilmuħa:đara ča:nat kulliš tawǰi:hiyya]

instrument • **1.** آلَة [?a:la] آلات [?a:la:t] *pl:* Lay out the instruments for the operation. حَضِّرِي الآلات لِلعَمَلِيَّة [ħađđiri ?il?a:la:t lilʕamaliyya] Do you play a musical instrument? تِقدَر تدُقّ عَلَى آلَة مُوسِيقِيَّة؟ [tigdar tdugg ʕala ?a:la musi:qiyya?]

to insulate • **1.** عِزَل [ʕizal] عَزِل [ʕazil] *vn:* اِنعِزَل [?inʕizal] *p:* Wrap the tape around the wire to insulate it. لِفّ التَّيب عالواير حَتَّى تعزلَه [liff ?ittayb ʕalwa:yir ħatta tʕizlah] We'll have to insulate the heating pipes. لازِم نِعزِل بوارِي الحَرارَة [la:zim niʕzil bwa:ri ?ilħara:ra]

insulated • **1.** مَعزُول [maʕzu:l] A well insulated wire won't give you a shock. الواير المَعزُول زين ما يِنتِل [?ilwa:yar ?ilmaʕzu:l zi:n ma: yintil]

insulator • **1.** عازِل [ʕa:zil] مادَّة عازِلَة [ma:dda ʕa:zila] مَوادّ عازِلَة [mawa:dd ʕa:zila] *pl:*

insult • **1.** إِهانَة [?iha:na] إِهانات [?iha:na:t] *pl:* I consider that an insult. أَعتُبُرها إِهانَة [?aʕtuburha ?iha:na]

to insult • **1.** أَهان [?aha:n] إِهانَة [?iha:na] *vn:* إِنهان [?inha:n] *p:* You've insulated him. إِنتَ أَهَنتَه [?inta ?ahantah]

I

insurance • **1.** تَأمِين [taʔmiːn] You can sign the insurance policy tomorrow. تِقدَر توَقِّع عَقد التَّأمِين باكِر [tigdar twaqqiʕ ʕaqd ʔittaʔmiːn baːčir]

to insure • **1.** أَمَّن عَلَى [ʔamman ʕala] تَأمِين [taʔmiːn] *vn:* تأَمَّن [tʔamman] *p:* I have insured my house for 5,000 dinars. أَمَّنِت عَلَى بَيتِي بِمَبلَغ خَمسَة آلاف دِينار [ʔammanit ʕala bayti bimablaɣ xamsat ʔaːlaːf dinaːr]

intellectual • **1.** مُثَقَّف [muθaqqaf] عاقِل [ʕaːqil] عُقَلاء [ʕuqalaːʔ] *pl:* Many intellectuals read this magazine. هوايَة مُثَقَّفِين يِقرُون هَذِي المَجَلَّة [hwaːya muθaqqafiːn yiqruːn haːði ʔilmaǰalla] • **2.** فِكرِي [fikri] ذِهنِي [ðihni] عَقلِي [ʕaqli] There's an intellectual bond between them. أَكُو بينهُم اِرتِباط فِكرِي [ʔaku baynhum ʔirtibaːṭ fikri] She's not interested in intellectual matters. هِيَّ ما عِدها رَغبَة بالأُمُور الفِكرِيَّة [hiyya maː ʕidha raɣba bilʔumuːr ʔilfikriyya]

I

intelligence • **1.** مَجهُود فِكرِي [maǰhuːd fikri] مَجهُود عَقلِي [maǰhuːd ʕaqli] The exam requires a lot of intelligence. الامتِحان يِرّادلَه هوايَة مَجهُود فِكرِي [ʔilʔimtiħaːn yirraːdlah hwaːya maǰhuːd fikri] • **2.** اِستِخبار [ʔistixbaːr] اِستِخبارات [ʔistixbaːraːt] *pl:* He works in the intelligence service. هُوَّ يِشتُغُل بِدائِرَة الاستِخبارات [huwwa yištuɣul bidaːʔirat ʔilʔistixbaːraːt]

intelligent • **1.** ذَكِي [ðaki] أَذكِياء [ʔaðkiyaːʔ] *pl:* She's very intelligent. هِيَّ كُلِّش ذَكِيَّة [hiyya kulliš ðakiyya]

to intend • **1.** نَوَى [nuwaː] نَوِي، نِيَّة [nawy, niyya] *vn: sv* i. What do you intend to do? شتِنوِي تسَوِّي؟ [štinwi tsawwi?] What do you intend to do? شِنُو نِيَّتَك؟ [šinu niyytak?] I intend to go to Basra in April. ناوِي أَرُوح لِلبَصرَة بنِيسان [naːwi ʔaruːħ lilbaṣra bniːsaːn]

intended • **1.** مَقصُود [maqṣuːd] That remark was intended for him. هاي المُلاحَظَة كانَت مَقصُودَة إلَه [haːy ʔilmulaːħaða čaːnat maqṣuːda ʔilah] * This merchandise is intended for Spain. هاي البِضاعَة مَقصُود بِيها ترُوح لإسبانيا [haːy ʔilbiðaːʕa maqṣuːd biːha truːħ lʔispaːnya] * This merchandise is intended for Spain. هالبِضاعَة مَنوِي إرسالها لإسبانيا [halbiðaːʕa manwi ʔirsaːlha lʔispaːnya]

intense • **1.** قَوِي [qawi, guwi] شَدِيد [šadiːd] I couldn't stand the intense heat. ما قِدَرت أَتحَمَّل الحَرارَة القَوِيَّة [maː gidarit ʔatħammal ʔilħaraːra ʔilqawiyya]

intensity • **1.** شِدَّة [šidda] قُوَّة [quwwa, guwwa] قُوّات [quwwaːt] *pl:* I was amazed at the intensity of her anger. تعَجَّبت مِن شِدَّة غَضَبها [tʕaǰǰabit min šiddat ɣaðabha]

intensive • **1.** قَوِي [qawi, guwi] شَدِيد [šadiːd] The government is conducting an intensive campaign to stamp out prostitution. الحُكُومَة دَتسَوِّي حَملَة قَوِيَّة حَتَّى تِقضِي عالبَغاء [ʔilħukuːma datsawwi ħamla qawiyya ħatta tiqði ʕalbaɣaːʔ] • **2.** كَثِيف [kaθiːf] They're using intensive cultivation to increase their crops. قاعِد يِستَعمِلُون الزِّراعَة الكَثِيفَة حَتَّى يزِيدُون مَحاصِيلهُم [gaːʕid yistaʕmiluːn ʔizziraːʕa ʔilkaθiːfa ħatta yziːduːn maħaːṣiːlhum]

intention • **1.** نِيَّة [niyya] نِيّات [niyyaːt] *pl:* قَصِد [qaṣid] Was that really your intention? صُدُق هَذِي كانَت نِيَّتَك؟ [ṣudug haːði čaːnat niyytak?]

intentional • **1.** عَمدِي [ʕamdi] That was an intentional killing. ذاك كان قَتِل عَمدِي [ðaːk čaːn qatil ʕamdi]

intentionally • **1.** عَمداً [ʕamdan] I did it intentionally. سَوِّيتها عَمداً [sawwiːtha ʕamdan]

intently • **1.** اِنتِباه [ʔintibaːh] They were listening intently. كانَوا دَيسِمعُون بانتِباه [čaːnaw daysimʕuːn bʔintibaːh]

to intercept • **1.** اِلتِقَط [ʔiltiqaṭ] اِلتِقاط [ʔiltiqaːṭ] *vn: sv* i. We intercepted a message from the enemy's headquarters. لِقَطنا رِسالَة مِن مَركَز الأعداء [ligaṭna risaːla min markaz ʔilʔaʕdaːʔ]

intercourse • **1.** اِتِّصال جِنسِي [ʔittiṣaːl ǰinsi] جِماع [ǰimaːʕ] Have you had intercourse with her? صار عِندَك اِتِّصال جِنسِي ويّاها؟ [ṣaːr ʕindak ʔittiṣaːl ǰinsi wiyyaːha?] • **2.** We never had any social intercourse with that family. أَبَد ما صار عِدنا عِلاقات اِجتِماعِيَّة ويّا ذِيك العائِلَة [ʔabad maː ṣaːr ʕidna ʕilaːqaːt ʔiǰtimaːʕiyya wiyya ðiːč ʔilʕaːʔila]

to have intercourse • **1.** جامَع [ǰaːmaʕ] جِماع [ǰimaːʕ] *vn: sv* i. The doctor forbade him to have intercourse. الدُّكتُور مِنَعَه مِن الجِّماع [ʔidduktuːr minaʕah min ʔiǰǰimaːʕ]

interest • **1.** اِهتِمام [ʔihtimaːm] He shows a special interest in it. يِبدِي اِهتِمام خاصّ بِيها [yibdi ʔihtimaːm xaːṣṣ biːha] • **2.** مَصلَحَة [maṣlaħa] مَصالِح [maṣaːliħ] *pl:* This is in your own interest. هاي لِمَصلَحتَك [haːy limaṣlaħtak] • **3.** هَوايَة [huwaːya] هُوايات [huwaːyaːt] *pl:* He has many interests. عِندَه هوايَة هُوايات [ʕindah hwaːya huwaːyaːt] • **4.** وَلَع [walaʕ] He has a great interest in stamp collecting. عِندَه هوايَة وَلَع بِجَمع الطَّوابِع [ʕindah hwaːya walaʕ bijamʕ ʔiṭṭawaːbiʕ] • **5.** فائِدَة [faːʔida] فايِز [faːyiz] How much interest does the bank pay? شقَدّ فائِدَة يِنطِي البَنك؟ [šgadd faːʔida yinṭi ʔilbang?] • **6.** حُصَّة [ħuṣṣa] Do you have an interest in the business? عِندَك حُصَّة بِالشُّغُل؟ [ʕindak ħuṣṣa biššuɣul?]

to interest • **1.** جِذَب [ǰiðab] جَذِب [ǰaðib] *vn: sv* i. She doesn't interest me at all. هِيَّ ما تِجذِبنِي أَبَد [hiyya maː tijðibni ʔabad] • **2.** رَغَّب [rayyab] تَرغِيب [taryiːb] *vn: sv* u. Can't you interest him in that? ما تِقدَر تَرَغّبَه بِيها؟ [maː tigdar trayybah biːha?]

interested • **1.** مُولَع [muːlaʕ] عِندَه رَغبَة [ʕindah rayba] I'm interested in sports. آنِي مُولَع بِالألعاب الرِّياضِيَّة [ʔaːni muːlaʕ bilʔalʕaːb ʔirriyaːðiyya] • **2.** مِهتَمّ [mihtamm] عِندَه رَغبَة [ʕindah rayba] I'm interested in these studies. آنِي مِهتَمّ بهِيكِي الدِّراسات [ʔaːni mihtamm bhiːči diraːsaːt] He's more interested in science than art. مِهتَمّ بالعِلُوم أكثَر مِن الفِنُون [mihtamm bilʕiluːm ʔakθar min ʔilfinuːn] • **3.** عِندَه واهِس [ʕindah waːhis] I'm not interested in going. ما عِندِي واهِس أرُوح [maː ʕindi waːhis ʔaruːħ] • **4.** عِندَه غايَة [ʕindah yaːya] He's only interested in her money. ما عِندَه غايَة غير فلُوسها [maː ʕindah yaːya yayr fluːsha]

interesting • **1.** مُمتِع [mumtiʕ] That's an interesting article. هَذِي مَقالَة مُمتِعَة [haːði maqaːla mumtiʕa]
*** What are the most interesting places to visit in Baghdad?**
• **1.** شِنُو هِيَّ ألطَف المَحَلّات اللّي يُمكِن واحِد يزُورها بِبَغداد؟ [šinu hiyya ʔalṭaf ʔilmaħallaːt ʔilli yumkin waːħid yzuːrha bibaydaːd?]

to interfere • **1.** عاق [ʕaːq] إعاقَة [ʔiʕaːqa] *vn: sv* i. He'll leave on Sunday if nothing interferes. يسافِر الأحَّد إذا ما يعِيقَه فَدّ شِي [ysaːfir ʔilʔaħħad ʔiða maː yʕiːqah fadd ši] • **2.** تَدَخَّل [tdaxxal] تَدَخُّل [tadaxxul] *vn: sv* a. Don't interfere in other people's affairs! لا تِتدَخَّل بِشُغُل غيرَك [laː tiddaxxal bišuyul yayrak] You're interfering with my work. إنتَ دَتِتدَخَّل بشُغلِي [ʔinta datiddaxxal bšuyli]

interference • **1.** وَشوَشَة [wašwaša] تَدَخُّل [tadaxxul] We can't hear that station because there's so much interference in the air. ما نِقدَر نِسمَع هالمَحَطَّة لِأنّ أكُو هوايَة وَشوَشَة بِالجَوّ [maː nigdar nismaʕ halmaħaṭṭa liʔann ʔaku hwaːya wašwaša bijǰaww]

interior • **1.** داخِل [daːxil] جَوَّة [ǰawwa] The interior of their house is very beautiful. داخِل بَيتهُم كُلِّش حِلو [daːxil baythum kulliš ħilw] The interior of their house is very beautiful. بَيتهُم مِن جَوَّة كُلِّش حِلو [baythum min ǰawwa kulliš ħilw] • **2.** داخِلِي [daːxili] جَوّانِي [ǰawwaːni] The interior walls are covered with cracks. الحِياطِين الدّاخِلِيَّة كُلّها مفَطّرَة [ʔilħiyaːṭiːn ʔiddaːxiliyya kullha mfaṭṭra] • **3.** داخِلِيَّة [daːxiliyya] The Ministry of the Interior is on the river. وِزارَة الدّاخِلِيَّة عالشَّطّ [wizaːrat ʔiddaːxiliyya ʕaššaṭṭ]

intermission • **1.** فَترَة [fatra] فَترات [fatraːt] *pl:* I was in the foyer during the intermission. أثناء الفَترَة كِنِت بِالصّالُون [ʔaθnaːʔ ʔilfatra činit biṣṣaːluːn]

internal • **1.** داخِلِي [daːxili] The internal affairs of the country are in bad shape. أحوال البَلَد الدّاخِلِيَّة مُو زينَة [ʔaħwaːl ʔilbalad ʔiddaːxiliyya muː ziːna] • **2.** داخِلِي [daːxili] باطِنِي [baːṭini] He died of internal injuries. مات نَتِيجَة جُرُوح داخِلِيَّة [maːt natiːǰat ǰuruːħ daːxiliyya]

international • **1.** دَولِي [dawli] Do you think the International Bank will underwrite this loan? تِتصَوَّر إنُّو البَنك الدَّولِي راح يُضمُن هالقَرض؟ [titṣawwar ʔinnu ʔilbang ʔiddawli raːħ yuðmun halqarið?]

to interpret • **1.** فَسَّر [fassar] تَفسِير [tafsiːr] *vn:* تفَسَّر [tfassar] *p:* You can interpret it this way, too. مُمكِن تفَسِّرها بِهالطَّرِيقَة هَمّ [mumkin tfassirha bhaṭṭariːqa hamm] • **2.** تَرجَم [tarǰam] تَرجَمَة [tarǰama] *vn: sv* i. When the ambassador spoke with the king, he interpreted. مِن كان السَّفِير يِحكِي وِيّا المَلِك هُوَّ كان يتَرجِم [min čaːn ʔissafiːr yiħči wiyya ʔilmalik huwwa čaːn ytarǰim]

interpreter • **1.** مُتَرجِم [mutarǰim] مُتَرجِمِين [mutarǰimiːn] *pl:* تُرجُمان [turǰumaːn] تُرجُمانِيَّة [turǰumaːniyya] *pl:* I acted as interpreter. قُمت بعَمَل مُتَرجِم [qumt bʕamal mutarǰim]

to interrupt • **1.** قاطَع [qaːṭaʕ] مُقاطَعَة [muqaːṭaʕa] *vn: sv* i. Don't interrupt me all the time. لا تقاطِعنِي دائِماً [laː tqaːṭiʕni daːʔiman] • **2.** سَبَّب [sabbab] *sv* i. Am I interrupting? آنِي دَأسَبِّب تَعطِيل؟ [ʔaːni daʔasabbib taʕṭiːl?]

interruption • **1.** مُضايَقَة [muðaːyaqa] مُضايَقات [muðaːyaqaːt] *pl:* مُقاطَعَة [muqaːṭaʕa] مُقاطَعات [muqaːṭaʕaːt] *pl:* I can't concentrate on my work with all these interruptions. ما أقدَر أرَكِّز عَلَى شُغلِي مِن كُثرَة المُضايَقات [maː ʔagdar ʔarakkiz ʕala šuyli min kuθrat ʔilmuðaːyaqaːt]

intersection • **1.** تَقاطُع [taqaːṭuʕ] تَقاطُعات [taqaːṭuʕaːt] *pl:* The accident occurred at the intersection. الحادِث حِصَل عِند تَقاطُع الطُّرُق [ʔilħaːdiθ ħiṣal ʕind taqaːṭuʕ ʔiṭṭuruq]

interval • **1.** اِستِراحَة [ʔistiraːħa] تَوَقُّف [tawaqquf] After a short interval we continued on our trip. بَعَد اِستِراحَة قَصِيرَة كَمَّلنا سَفرَتنا [baʕad ʔistiraːħa qaṣiːra kammalna safratna] • **2.** مَسافَة [masaːfa] مَسافات [masaːfaːt] *pl:* The trees are set at close intervals. الأشجار مَزرُوعَة عَلَى مَسافات مِتقاربَة [ʔilʔašǰaːr mazruːʕa ʕala masaːfaːt mitqaːrba] • **3.** فَترَة [fatra] فَترات [fatraːt] *pl:* The bombs are set to go off at five-minute intervals. القَنابِل موَقَّتَة تِنفِجِر بِفَترَة خَمِس دَقايِق [ʔilqanaːbil mwaqqata tinfiǰir bifatrat xamis daqaːyiq]

to intervene • **1.** تدَخَّل [tdaxxal] تَدَخُّل [tadaxxul] *vn: sv* i. توَسَّط [twaṣṣaṭ] تَوَسُّط [tawassuṭ] *vn: sv* i. It won't do any

I

good to intervene in their quarrel. ماكو فايدَة مِن تَدَخُّلَك بَيناتهُم [ma:ku fa:yda min tadaxxulak bayna:thum]

intervention • 1. تَدَخُّل [tadaxxul] تَوَسُّط [tawassuṭ] Both sides would welcome U. N. intervention in the dispute. الطَّرَفَين يرَحِّبُون بِتَدَخُّل هَيئَة الأُمَم المُتَّحِدَة بِالنِّزاع [ʔiṭṭarafayn yraħħibu:n bitadaxxul hayʔat ʔilʔumam ʔilmuttaħida binniza:ʕ]

interview • 1. مُقابَلَة [muqa:bala] مُقابَلات [muqa:bala:t] *pl:* The reporter asked for an interview with the minister. المُراسِل طِلَب مُقابَلَة الوَزِير [ʔilmura:sil ṭilab muqa:balat ʔilwazi:r]

to interview • 1. قابَل [qa:bal, ga:bal] مُقابَلَة [muqa:bala] *vn: sv* i. The reporter interviewed the minister. المُراسِل قابَل الوَزِير [ʔilmura:sil qa:bal ʔilwazi:r]

I

intestines • 1. أمعاء [ʔamʕa:ʔ] The doctor removed a part of his intestines. الدِّكتُور شال وُصلَة مِن أمعائَه [ʔiddiktu:r ša:l wuṣla min ʔamʕa:ʔah]

intimate • 1. صَمِيمِي [ṣami:mi] We're intimate friends. إحنا أصدِقاء صَمِيمِيِّين [ʔiħna ʔaṣdiqa:ʔ ṣami:miyyi:n] We're intimate friends. إحنا أصدِقاء كُلِّش [ʔiħna ʔaṣdiqa:ʔ kulliš]

into • 1. ب [b] Put it into the box. خَلِّيهَا بِالصَّندُوق [xalli:ha biṣṣandu:q] Get into the car. إدخُل بَالسَّيّارَة [ʔidxul bissayya:ra] We have to take that into account, too. هاي هَمّ لازِم نحُطّها بِالحِساب [ha:y hamm la:zim nħuṭṭha biliħsa:b] **• 2.** ل [li-] Can you translate this into English? تِقدَر تتَرجُم هاي لِلإنكلِيزِي؟ [tigdar ʔittarǰum ha:y lilʔingli:zi?]

*** Can these boards be made into something useful? • 1.** هَالَوحات يِمكِن يِتسَوَّى مِنها شِي يفِيد؟ [hallawħa:t yimkin yitsawwa: minha ši: yfi:d?] هَاللَّوحات يِمكِن تِتحَوَّل إلَى شِي مُفِيد؟ [hallu:ħa:t yimkin titħawwal ʔila ši mufi:d?]

*** Those kids are always into everything.**
• 1. هَالجِهال يشَعبِثُون بكُلَّشِي [hajǰihha:l yšaʕbiθu:n bkullši]

intolerance • 1. عَدَم التَّسامُح [ʕadam ʔittasa:muħ]

intolerant • 1. مِتعَصُّب [mitʕaṣṣub] That man is very intolerant. هَذا الرِّجّال مِتعَصُّب كُلِّش [ha:ða ʔirrijǰa:l mitʕaṣṣub kulliš]

intoxicant • 1. مُسَكِّر [musakkir] مُسَكِّرات [musakkira:t] *pl:* The sale of intoxicants to minors is prohibited. بَيع المُسَكِّرات لِغَير البالغِين مَمنُوع [bayʕ ʔilmusakkira:t lɣayr ʔilba:lɣi:n mamnu:ʕ]

intoxicated • 1. خَدران [xadra:n] سَكران [sakra:n] I'm a little intoxicated tonight. آنِي شوَيَّة خَدران اللَّيلَة [ʔa:ni šwayya xadra:n ʔillayla]

intoxicating • 1. مُسَكِّر [musakkir] This wine is very intoxicating. هَالشَّراب كُلِّش مُسَكِّر [haššara:b kulliš musakkir]

to introduce • 1. عَرَّف [ʕarraf] تَعرِيف [taʕri:f] *vn:* تعَرَّف [tʕarraf] *p:* قَدَّم [qaddam] تَقدِيم [taqdi:m] *vn:* تقَدَّم [tqaddam] *p:* I'd like to introduce you to my father. أحِبّ أعَرّفَك عَلَى أبُويَا [ʔaħibb ʔaʕarrfak ʕala ʔabu:ya] **• 2.** أدخَل [ʔadxal] إدخال [ʔidxa:l] *vn: sv* i. دَخَّل [daxxal] تَدخِيل [tadxi:l] *vn:* تدَخَّل [tdaxxal] *p:* He introduced a number of changes in his government's policy. هُوَّ أدخَل بَعض التَّعدِيلات عَلَى سِياسَة الحُكُومَة [huwwa ʔadxal baʕð ʔittaʕdi:la:t ʕala siya:sat ʔilħuku:ma] **• 3.** قَدَّم [qaddam] تَقدِيم [taqdi:m] *vn:* تقَدَّم [tqaddam] *p:* They introduced new proposals in the legislature. قَدِّمَوا اقتِراحات جِدِيدَة لِلبَرلَمان [qaddimaw ʔiqtira:ħa:t ǰidi:da lilbarlama:n]

introduction • 1. مُقَدِّمَة [muqaddima] مُقَدِّمات [muqaddima:t] *pl:* It's mentioned in the introduction. مَذكُورَة بِالمُقَدِّمَة [maðku:ra bilmuqaddima]

intrusion • 1. تَطَفُّل [taṭafful] Sorry for the intrusion, sir, but we've just been invaded. إعذرُونِي مِن التَّطَفُّل، أُستاذ، لَكِن هَسَّة اِنهِجَم عَلينا [ʔiʕðru:ni min ʔittaṭafful, ʔusta:ð, la:kin hassa ʔinhijam ʕali:na]

intuition • 1. بَدِيهَة [badi:ha] بَداهَة [bada:ha] You'll just have to use your intuition. ما عَلَيك إلّا أن تِستَعمِل بَداهتَك [ma: ʕali:k ʔilla ʔan tistaʕmil bada:htak]

to invade • 1. غِزا [ɣiza:] غَزُو [ɣazw] *vn:* اِنغِزَى [ʔinɣiza:] *p:* Napoleon tried to invade England. نابلِيُون حاوَل يِغزِي إنكِلترا [na:pilyu:n ħa:wal yiɣzi ʔingiltara]

invalid • 1. عاجِز [ʕa:ǰiz] عاجِزِين [ʕa:ǰizi:n] *pl:* For many years my grandmother has been an invalid. جِدِّيتِي صارِلها عِدَّة سَنَوات عاجِزَة [ǰiddi:ti ṣa:rilha ʕiddat sanawa:t ʕa:ǰiza] **• 2.** باطِل [ba:ṭil] غَير شَرعِي [ɣayr šarʕi] A will without a signature is invalid. الوَصِيَّة باطلَة بِدُون تَوقِيع [ʔilwaṣiyya ba:ṭla bidu:n tawqi:ʕ]

invasion • 1. غَزوَة [ɣazwa] غَزوات [ɣazwa:t] *pl:* The invasion has failed. الغَزوَة فِشلَت [ʔilɣazwa fišlat]

to invent • 1. اِختِرَع [ʔixtiraʕ] اِختِراع [ʔixtira:ʕ] *vn: sv* i. Every day they invent something new. كُلّ يوم يِختَرعُون شِي جدِيد [kull yu:m yixtarʕu:n ši ǰdi:d] **• 2.** اِختِلَق [ʔixtilaq] اِختِلاق [ʔixtila:q] *vn: sv* i. Did you invent that story? إنتَ اِختِلَقِت هَالقُصَّة؟ [ʔinta ʔixtilaqit halquṣṣa?]

invention • 1. اِختِراع [ʔixtira:ʕ] اِختِراعات [ʔixtira:ʕa:t] *pl:*

inventor • **1.** مُختَرِع [muxtariʕ] مُختَرِعِين [muxtariʕi:n] *pl:*

inventory • **1.** جَرِد [ǰarid] Our shop takes inventory each year. إحنا نسَوِّي جَرِد كُلّ سَنَة [ʔiħna nsawwi ǰarid kull sana]

to invest • **1.** اِستَثمَر [ʔistaθmar] اِستِثمار [ʔistiθma:r] *vn: sv* a. شَغَّل [šaɣɣal] تَشغِيل [tašɣi:l] *vn: sv* i. He invested his money in real estate. هُوَّ اِستَثمَر فلُوسَه بِالعِقار [huwwa ʔistaθmar flu:sah bilʕiqa:r]

to investigate • **1.** حَقَّق [ħaqqaq] تَحقِيق [taħqi:q] *vn:* تحَقَّق [tħaqqaq] *p:* They're investigating the case. دَيحَقِّقُون بِالقَضِيَّة [dayħaqqiqu:n bilqaðiyya]

investigation • **1.** تَحقِيق [taħqi:q] تَحقِيقات [taħqi:qa:t] *pl:* An investigation has been ordered by the court. المَحكَمَة أُمرَت بإجراء تَحقِيق [ʔilmaħkama ʔumrat bʔiǰra:ʔ taħqi:q]

investment • **1.** مَكان اِستِثمار [maka:n ʔistiθma:r] What is the best financial investment nowadays? شِنُو أَحسَن مَكان لِاستِثمار الفلُوس هَالأَيّام؟ [šinu ʔaħsan maka:n lʔistiθma:r ʔilflu:s halʔayya:m?]

investor • **1.** مُستَثمِر [mustaθmir] مُستَثمِرِين [mustaθmiri:n] *pl:* We need more investors. يِنراد إلنا مُستَثمِرِين بَعَد [yinra:d ʔilna mustaθmiri:n baʕad]

invisible • **1.** غَير مَنظُور [ɣayr manðu:r] Carbon monoxide is an invisible gas. أَوَّل أوكسِيد الكاربُون غاز غير مَنظُور [ʔawwal ʔuksi:d ʔilka:rbu:n ɣa:z ɣi:r manðu:r]

invitation • **1.** دَعوَة [daʕwa] دَعوات، دَعاوِي [daʕwa:t, daʕa:wi] *pl:* عَزِيمَة [ʕazi:ma] عَزايِم [ʕaza:yim] *pl:* Many thanks for your kind invitation. أَشكُرَك عَلَى دَعوتَك [ʔaškurak ʕala daʕwtak]

to invite • **1.** عِزَم [ʕizam] عَزِيمَة [ʕazi:ma] *vn:* اِنعِزَم [ʔinʕizam] *p:* دِعَى [diʕa:] دَعوَة [daʕwa] *vn:* اِندِعَى [ʔindiʕa:] *p:* Who did you invite to the party? إلمَن عزَمِت لِلحَفلَة؟ [ʔilman ʕzamit lilħafla?] He invited me to lunch. عِزَمنِي عَالغدا [ʕizamni ʕalɣada]

inviting • **1.** مُشَهِّي [mušahhi] مُشَهِّيّات [mušahhiyya:t] *pl:* The food looks very inviting. الأَكِل مَنظَرَه مُشَهِّي [ʔilʔakil manðarah mušahhi] • **2.** مُغرِي [muɣri] This low price is very inviting. هَالسِّعِر الرَّخِيص كُلِّش مُغرِي [hassiʕir ʔirraxi:ṣ kulliš muɣri]

*** The sea looks inviting today.**
• **1.** البَحَر يِغرِي عَالسِبِح هَاليَوم [ʔilbaħar yiɣri ʕassibiħ halyu:m]

to involve • **1.** أَشرَك [ʔašrak] إشراك [ʔišra:k] *vn: sv* i. He involved me in the crime, and I wasn't even there! أَشرَكنِي بِالجَّرِيمَة، وَآنِي حَتَّى ما كِنِت هناك [ʔašrakni bijǰari:ma, wʔa:ni ħatta ma: činit hna:k] • **2.** تطَلَّب [tṭallab] تَطَلُّب [taṭallub] *vn: sv* a. The trip involved a lot of expense. السَّفرَة تطَلِّبَت هوايَة مَصارِيف [ʔissafra tṭallibat hwa:ya maṣa:ri:f]

*** The work involves a certain amount of risk.**
• **1.** الشَّغلَة بِيها خَطُورَة [ʔiššaɣla bi:ha xaṭu:ra]

involved • **1.** معَقَّد [mʕaqqad] That's a very involved process. هَذا إجراء كُلِّش معَقَّد [ha:ða ʔiǰra:ʔ kulliš mʕaqqad]
to get involved • **1.** حَطّ نَفسَه [ħaṭṭ nafsah] حَطّ نَفسَه [ħaṭṭ nafsah] *vn: sv* u. I don't want to get involved in this. ما أَرِيد أَحُطّ نَفسِي بِهاي [ma: ʔari:d ʔaħuṭṭ nafsi bha:y]

iodine • **1.** يَود [yawd, yu:d] We studied iodine in class today. دِرَسنا اليُود بصَفّنا اليُوم [dirasna ʔilyu:d bṣaffna ʔilyu:m] • **2.** تَنتَريُوك [tantaryu:k] يَود [yawd] Put a little iodine on the wound so it doesn't swell up. خَلِّي شوَيَّة تَنتَريُوك عَالجَرِح حَتَّى ما يَورَم [xalli šwayyat tantaryu:k ʕaǰǰariħ ħatta ma: yawram]

Iran • **1.** إيران [ʔira:n]

Iranian • **1.** إيرانِي [ʔi:ra:ni] عَجَمِي [ʕaǰami] عَجَمِيَّة [ʕaǰamiyya] *pl:* فارسِي [fa:risi] فارسِيِّين [fa:risi:yyi:n] *pl:* عَجمِي [ʕaǰmi] عَجَم [ʕaǰam] *pl:* She's an Iranian. هِيَّ إيرانِيَّة [hiyya ʔira:niyya]

Iraq • **1.** العِراق [ʔilʕira:q] Baghdad is the capital of Iraq. بَغداد هِيَّ عاصِمَة العِراق [baɣda:d hiyya ʕa:ṣimat ʔilʕira:q]

Iraqi • **1.** عِراقِي [ʕira:qi] عِراقِيِّين [ʕira:qiyyi:n] *pl:* Are there many Iraqis here? أَكُو هوايَة عِراقِيِّين هنا؟ [ʔaku hwa:ya ʕira:qiyyi:n hna?] • **2.** عِراقِي [ʕira:qi] Iraqi industry is advancing. الصِّناعَة العِراقِيَّة دَتِتقَدَّم [ʔiṣṣina:ʕa ʔilʕira:qiyya datitqaddam]

irksome • **1.** مُزعِج [muzʕiǰ] He still has to cope with many irksome problems. بَعَد عِندَه هوايَة مَشاكِل مُزعِجَة [baʕad ʕindah hwa:ya maša:kil muzʕiǰa]

iron • **1.** حَدِيد [ħadi:d] You have to be made of iron to stand all that. لازِم تكُون مِن حَدِيد حَتَّى تِقدَر تِتحَمَّل كُلّ هَذا [la:zim tku:n min ħadi:d ħatta tigdar titħammal kull ha:ða] They're putting an iron gate up at the entrance way. دَيحُطُّون باب حَدِيد لِباب الحَدِيقَة [dayħuṭṭu:n ba:b ħadi:d lba:b ʔilħadi:qa] • **2.** أُوتِي [ʔu:ti] أُوتِيّات [ʔu:ti:yya:t] *pl:* Is the iron still hot? الأُوتِي بَعدَه حارّ؟ [ʔilʔu:ti baʕdah ħa:rr?] • **3.** قَوِي [qawi, guwi] He has an iron will. عِندَه إرادَة قَوِيَّة [ʕindah ʔira:da qawiyya]

cast iron • **1.** آهين [ʔa:hi:n] This drainpipe is made of cast iron. هَالبُوري مِن آهين [halbu:ri min ʔa:hi:n]

to iron • **1.** كُوَى [kuwa:] كَوِي [kawy] *vn:* اِنكُوَى [ʔinkuwa:] *p:* ضِرَب [ðirab] ضَرُب [ðarub] *vn:* اِنضِرَب [ʔinðirab] *p:* Did you iron my shirt? كوَيتي ثُوبِي؟ [kwi:ti θu:bi?]

to iron out • **1.** تساوَى [tsa:wa:] تَساوِي [tasa:wi] *vn: sv* a. تصَفَّى [tṣaffa:] تَصَفِّي [taṣaffi] *vn: sv* a. There are still a few things to be ironed out. بَعد أكُو بَعض الأشياء لازم تِتساوَى [baʕd ʔaku baʕð ʔilʔašya:ʔ la:zim titsa:wa:]

Iron Curtain • **1.** السِّتار الحَدِيدِي [ʔissita:r ʔilħadi:di]

ironical • **1.** مِن مَهزَلَة الأقدار [min mahzalat ʔilaqda:r] This turn of events is ironical. مِن مَهزَلَة الأقدار أن يصِير هِيكِي شِي [min mahzalat ʔilʔaqda:r ʔan yṣi:r hi:či ši]

ironing board • **1.** مَيز أُوتِي [mayz ʔu:ti] ميُوزَة مال أُوتِي [myu:za ma:l ʔu:ti] *pl:*

irony • **1.** عُنُف [ʕunuf] صَرامَة [ṣara:ma] He's prone to using irony. هُوَّ مَيّال إلَى اِستِعمال العُنُف [huwwa mayya:l ʔila ʔistiʕma:l ʔalʕunuf]

irrational • **1.** غير مِتّزِن [ɣayr mittizin] His statements are irrational. كَلامَه غير مِتّزِن [kala:mah ɣayr mittizin]

irregular • **1.** غير مُنتَظَم [ɣayr muntaðam] غير مُنَظَّم [ɣayr munaððam] The awarding of contracts was irregular. أحكام العُقُود كانَت غير مُنتَظمَة [ʔaħka:m ʔilʕuqu:d ča:nat ɣayr muntaðma] • **2.** غير نِظامِي [ɣayr niða:mi] We were attacked by irregular forces. هاجمَتنا قُوّات غير نِظامِيَّة [ha:ǰmatna quwwa:t ɣayr niða:miyya]

irregularity • **1.** تَلاعُب [tala:ʕub] تَلاعُبات [tala:ʕuba:t] *pl:* Some irregularities were discovered in his accounts. اِنلِقَى تَلاعُب بحساباتَه [ʔinliga: tala:ʕub bħsa:ba:tah]

irrelevant • **1.** ما إلَه عِلاقَة [ma: ʔilah ʕila:qa] This question is irrelevant to the case. هَذا سُؤال ما إلَه عِلاقَة بِالقَضِيَّة [ha:ða suʔa:l ma: ʔilah ʕila:qa bilqaðiyya]

irresponsible • **1.** ما عِندَه مَسؤُولِيَّة [ma: ʕindah masʔu:liyya] That child is irresponsible. هَالطِّفِل ما عِندَه مَسؤُولِيَّة [haṭṭifil ma: ʕindah masʔu:liyya]

to irrigate • **1.** رُوَى [ruwa:] رَوِي [rawy] *vn:* اِنرُوَى [ʔinruwa:] *p:* سِقَى [siga:] سَقِي [sagy] *vn:* اِنسِقَى [ʔinsiga:] *p:* We're going to irrigate this field next year. راح نِروِي هَذا الحَقِل السَّنَة القادِمَة [ra:ħ nirwi ha:ða ʔilħaqil ʔissana ʔilqa:dima]

irrigation • **1.** سَقِي [sagy] رَوِي [rawi:] We couldn't raise anything on this land without irrigation. ما نِقدَر ننَمِّي شِي عَلَى هَالقاع بِلا سَقِي [ma: nigdar nnammi ši ʕala halga:ʕ bila sagy]

irritable • **1.** مِنفِعِل [minfiʕil] عَصَبِي [ʕaṣabi] He was very irritable this morning. كان كُلِّش مِنفِعِل اليُوم الصُّبُح [ča:n kulliš minfiʕil ʔilyu:m ʔiṣṣubuħ]

to irritate • **1.** أثار [ʔaθa:r] إثارَة [ʔiθa:ra] *vn: sv* i. أزعَج [ʔazʕaǰ] إزعاج [ʔizʕa:ǰ] *vn: sv* i. His remark irritated me. عِبارتَه أثارَتنِي [ʕiba:rtah ʔaθa:ratni] • **2.** هَيَّج [hayyaǰ] تَهيِيج [tahyi:ǰ] *vn:* تهَيَّج [thayyaǰ] *p:* This soap doesn't irritate the skin. هاي الصّابُونَة ما تهَيِّج الجِّلِد [ha:y ʔiṣṣa:bu:na ma: thayyiǰ ʔiǰǰilid]

Islam • **1.** إسلام [ʔisla:m]

Islamic • **1.** إسلامِي [ʔisla:mi] We're studying Islamic history. إحنا نِدرُس التّارِيخ الإسلامِي [ʔiħna nidrus ʔitta:ri:x ʔilʔisla:mi]

island • **1.** جَزِيرَة [ǰazi:ra] جَزائِر، جُزُر [ǰaza:ʔir, ǰuzur] *pl:* I just came from the island of Cyprus. هَسَّة جِيت مِن جَزِيرَة قُبرُص [hassa ǰi:t min ǰazi:rat qubruṣ]

to isolate • **1.** عِزَل [ʕizal] عَزِل [ʕazil] *vn:* اِنعِزَل [ʔinʕizal] *p:* The sick children were isolated. الأطفال المَرضَى كانَوا مَعزُولِين [ʔilʔaṭfa:l ʔilmarða: ča:naw maʕzu:li:n]

isolated • **1.** مَفصُول [mafṣu:l] مَعزُول [maʕzu:l] They live in a house isolated from the village. هُمَّ يعِيشُون بِبَيت مَفصُول عَن القَريَة [humma yʕi:šu:n bibayt mafṣu:l ʕan ʔilqarya]

Israel • **1.** إسرائِيل [ʔisraʔi:l]

Israeli • **1.** إسرائِيلِي [ʔisraʔi:li]

issue • **1.** عَدَد [ʕadad] أعداد [ʔaʕda:d] *pl:* I haven't read the last issue. ما قرَيت العَدَد الأخِير [ma: qrayt ʔilʕadad ʔilʔaxi:r] • **2.** مَوضُوع [mawðu:ʕ] مَواضِيع [mawa:ði:ʕ] *pl:* This question will be an important issue in the coming elections. هَالسُّؤال راح يكُون مَوضُوع مُهِمّ بِالإنتِخابات الجّايَة [hassuʔa:l ra:ħ yku:n mawðu:ʕ muhimm bilʔintixa:ba:t ʔiǰǰa:ya] I don't want to make an issue of it. ما أرِيد أسَوِّيها مَوضُوع بَحِث [ma: ʔari:d ʔasawwi:ha mawðu:ʕ bahiθ]

to issue • **1.** صَدَّر [ṣaddar] تَصدِير [taṣdi:r] *vn:* تصَدَّر [tṣaddar] *p: sv* i. Where did they issue the passports? وِين صَدّرَوا جَوازات السَّفَر؟ [wi:n ṣaddraw ǰawa:za:t ʔissafar?]

it • **1.** هُوَّ [huwwa] (or) هِيَّ [hiyya] (respectively) . Which is my book? Oh, that's it. ياهُو كتابِي؟ هَذاك هُوَّ

[ya:hu kta:bi? haða:k huwwa] Where is my hat? Here it is! وين شَفُقتي؟ هِيّاتها [wi:n šafuqti? hiyya:tha] • **2.** (or) هَا [ha] (respectively) . I can't do it. ما أقدَر أسَوِّيها [ma: ʔagdar ʔasawwi:ha] I knew it! عِرَفِتها [ʕirafitha] I can't give you the money today. I forgot it. ما أقدَر أنطِيك الفلُوس اليُوم نِسيتها [ma: ʔagdar ʔanṭi:k ʔilflu:s ʔilyu:m nisi:tha]

*** Who's it? Ali's it. Run before he tags you!** • **1.** بِي مَن؟ بعَلِي أركُض قبُل ما يجِيسَك [bi: man? bʕali: ʔirkuḍ gabul ma ygi:sak]

*** It's cold outside.** • **1.** بَرَّة بارِدَة [barra ba:rda]

*** It's raining.** • **1.** قاعِد تُمطُر [ga:ʕid tumṭur]

*** It's lovely today.** • **1.** اليَوم كُلِّش بَدِيع [ʔilyawm kulliš badi:ʕ]

*** It doesn't matter.** • **1.** ما يهِمّ [ma: yhimm]

*** It doesn't make any difference.** • **1.** ما تِفرُق [ma: tifruq]

*** He's had it!** • **1.** وُصَل حَدَّه [wuṣal ħaddah]

itch • **1.** حَكَّة [ħakka] حَكّات [ħakka:t] *pl:* I've got an itch. عِندِي حَكَّة [ʕindi ħakka]

to itch • **1.** حَكّ [ħakk] حَكّ [ħakk] *vn:* اِنحَكّ [ʔinħakk] *p:* The wound itches. الجُرِح دَيحُكّنِي [ʔiǰǰariħ dayħukkni] I itch all over. كُلّ جِسمِي دَيحُكّنِي [kull ǰismi dayħukkni]

*** I'm itching to get started.** • **1.** آنِي كُلِّش مُشتاق أبدِي [ʔa:ni kulliš mušta:q ʔabdi]

item • **1.** شِي [ši] أشياء [ʔašya:ʔ] *pl:* We don't carry that item. ما عِدنا هَالشِّي [ma: ʕidna hašši] • **2.** مَوضُوع [mawḍu:ʕ] مَواضِيع [mawa:ḍi:ʕ] *pl:* Did you see the item in the paper? شِفت المَوضُوع بِالجَّرِيدَة؟ [šift ʔilmawḍu:ʕ biǰǰari:da?] • **3.** فَقرَة [faqara] فَقَرات [faqara:t] *pl:* How many items are on that bill? كَم فقرَة بِهَالقائِمَة؟ [čam faqara bihalqa:ʔima?]

to itemize • **1.** صَنَّف [ṣannaf] تَصنِيف [taṣni:f] *vn:* تصَنَّف [tṣannaf] *p:* Itemize all your expenses. صَنِّف كُلّ مَصارِيفَك [ṣannif kull maṣa:ri:fak]

itself • **1.** نَفِس [nafis-] The child hurt itself. الجّاهِل عَوَّر نَفسَه [ʔiǰǰa:hil ʕawwar nafsah] The car itself isn't damaged, but the driver was injured. السَّيّارَة نَفِسها ما تأذَّت، لَكِن السّايِق اِنجِرَح [ʔissayya:ra nafisha ma: tʔaððat, la:kin ʔissa:yiq ʔinǰirah] • **2.** وَحِد [waħid-] The house itself is worth that. البَيت وَحدَه يِسوَى هَالقَدّ [ʔilbayt waħdah yiswa: halgadd]

*** That speaks for itself.** • **1.** هاي ما يِنرادِلها حَكِي [ha:y ma: yinra:dilha ħači]

by itself • **1.** مِن كَيف [min kayf-] This door closes by itself. هالباب يِنسَدّ مِن كيفَه [halba:b yinsadd min kayfah]

in itself • **1.** بحَدّ ذات [bħadd ða:t-] The plan in itself is good. المَشرُوع بحَدّ ذاتَه زين [ʔilmašru:ʕ bħadd ða:tah zi:n]

ivory • **1.** عاج [ʕa:ǰ] The knife handle is ivory. إيد السِّكِّينَة مِن عاج [ʔi:d ʔissičči:na min ʕa:ǰ]

I

J

to jab • **1.** نَغّ [naɣɣ] نَغّ [naɣɣ] *vn:* اِنْغَّ [ʔinnaɣɣ] *p:* He jabbed me with the pencil. نَغّني بالقَلَم [naɣɣni bilqalam]

jack • **1.** جَكّ [ǰagg] جَكّات [ǰagga:t] *pl:* I left the jack in the garage. تَرَكِت الجَّكّ بِالكَراج [trakit ʔiǰǰagg bilgara:ǰ] • **2.** وَلَد [walad] وُلِد [wulid] *pl:* بَجَغ [bajaɣ] بَجَغات [bajaɣa:t] *pl:* I've got three jacks. عِندي ثَلاث وِلِد [ʕindi tlaθ wilid]

*** You look as if you had hit the jackpot.**
• **1.** يبَيِّن جايَة الدِنيا وِيّاك [ybayyin ǰa:ya ʔiddinya wiyya:k]

to jack up • **1.** شال [ša:l] شَيل [šayl] *vn: sv* i. You'll have to jack up the car. لازِم تشيل السَّيّارَة بِجَكّ [la:zim tši:l ʔissayya:ra biǰagg] • **2.** رِفَع [rifaʕ] رَفُع [rafuʕ] *vn:* اِنرِفَع [ʔinrifaʕ] *p:* زَيَّد [zayyad] تَزيِيد [tazyi:d] *vn:* تزَيَّد [tzayyad] *p:* They've jacked up the price again. رِفعَوا السِّعِر مَرَّة ثانيَة [rifʕaw ʔissiʕir marra θa:nya]

jackal • **1.** واوِي [wa:wi] واويَّة [wa:wiyya] *pl:*

jackass • **1.** زمال [zma:l] زمايِل [zma:yil] *pl:* حمار [ħma:r] حَمِير [ħami:r] *pl:*

jacket • **1.** سِترَة [sitra] سِتَر [sitar] *pl:* جاكِيت [ǰa:ki:t] You can wear that jacket with flannel slacks. تِقدَر تِلبَس هَالسِّترَة عَلَى بَنطَرُون فانيلَة [tigdar tilbas hassitra ʕala panṭaru:n fani:la] • **2.** قِشِر [gišir] قشُور [gšu:r] *pl:* I boiled the potatoes in their jackets. سلَقِت البُتَيتَة بِقشُورها [slagit ʔilputayta bigšu:rha] • **3.** The jacket of the book is all torn. الغِلاف مال الكِتاب كُلّه مشَقَّق [ʔilɣila:f ma:l ʔilkita:b kullah mšaggag]

jackknife • **1.** سِكّينَة [sičči:na] سِكاكِين [siča:či:n] *pl:*

jail • **1.** سِجِن [siǰin] سِجُون [siǰu:n] *pl:* حَبِس [ħabis] He was sentenced to six months in jail. اِنحِكَم سِتّ أَشهُر بِالسِّجِن [ʔinħikam sitt ʔašhur bissiǰin]

to jail • **1.** حِبَس [ħibas] حَبِس [ħabis] *vn:* اِنحِبَس [ʔinħibas] *p:* سِجَن [siǰan] سِجِن [siǰin] *vn:* اِنسِجَن [ʔinsiǰan] *p:* He was jailed for theft. اِنحِبَس لِأَنّ باق [ʔinħibas liʔann ba:g]

jalopy • **1.** سَيّارَة بَلَشقَة [sayya:ra palašqa] سَيّارات بَلَشقَة [sayya:ra:t palašqa] *pl:* He bought an old jalopy. اِشتِراله سَيّارَة بَلَشقَة [ʔištira:lah sayya:ra palašqa]

jam • **1.** مرَبَّى [mrabba] مرَبّات، مرَبّايات [mrabba:t, mrabba:ya:t] *pl:* I prefer homemade jam. أَفَضِّل مرَبَّى مال بَيت [ʔafaððil mrabba ma:l bayt] • **2.** ضِيق [ði:q] I'm in an awful jam. آني بِضِيق شَدِيد [ʔa:ni biði:q šadi:d]

traffic jam • **1.** مُشكِلَة إزدِحام [muškilat ʔizdiħa:m] The police untangled the traffic jam. شُرطَة المُرُور حَلَّوا مُشكِلَة الازدِحام [šurṭat ʔilmuru:r ħallaw muškilat ʔilʔizdiħa:m]

to jam • **1.** شَوَّش عَلَى [šawwaš ʕala] تَشويش [tašwi:š] *vn: sv* i. Somebody is jamming our broadcast. واحِد دَيشَوِّش عَلَى إذاعَتنا [wa:ħid dayšawwiš ʕala ʔiða:ʕatna] • **2.** حِصَر [ħiṣar] حَصِر [ħaṣir] *vn:* اِنحِصَر [ʔinħiṣar] *p:* He jammed his finger in the door. حِصَر إصبِعَه بِالباب [ħiṣar ʔiṣibʕah bilba:b] • **3.** عِصَى [ʕiṣa:] *sv* i. The drawer jammed when I tried to open it. المجَرّ عِصَى لَمّا رِدِت أَفتَحَه [ʔilmǰarr ʕiṣa: lamma ridit ʔafitħah] • **4.** جَيَّم [ǰayyam] تَجيِيم [taǰyi:m] *vn:* تجَيَّم [tǰayyam] *p:* شَكَّل [šakkal] تَشكِيل [taški:l] *vn:* تشَكَّل [tšakkal] *p:* The gears are jammed. الكَير مجَيِّم [ʔilgi:r mǰayyim] • **5.** اِزدِحَم [ʔizdiħam] اِزدِحام [ʔizdiħa:m] *vn:* The elevator was jammed with people. المَصعَد كان مُزدَحِم بِالنّاس [ʔilmaṣʕad ča:n muzdaħim binna:s]

janitor • **1.** فَرّاش [farra:š] فَرّاشِين، فراريش [farra:ši:n, fra:ri:š] *pl:* بَوّاب [bawwa:b] بَوّابِين [bawwa:bi:n] *pl:* The janitor cleaned the windows last night. الفَرّاش نَظَّف الشِبابِيك البارحَة بِاللَّيل [ʔilfarra:š naððaf ʔilšiba:bi:k ʔilba:rħa billayl]

January • **1.** كانُون الثاني [ka:nu:n ʔiθθa:ni]

Japan • **1.** اليابان [ʔilyaba:n]

Japanese • **1.** يابانِي [yaba:ni] يابانِيِّين [yaba:niyyi:n] *pl:* He's a Japanese. هُوَّ يابانِي [huwwa yaba:ni]
• **2.** يابانِي [yaba:ni] I bought a beautiful Japanese radio. اِشتِرَيت رادِيُو يابانِي حِلو [ʔištirayt ra:dyu yaba:ni ħilw]

jar • **1.** شِيشَة [ši:ša] شِيَش [šiyaš] *pl:* شِياش [šiyaš] [šiya:š] *pl:* I want a jar of jam. أَرِيد شِيشَة مرَبَّى [ʔari:d ši:šat mrabba]

to jar • **1.** هَزّ [hazz] هَزّ [hazz] *vn:* اِنهَزّ [ʔinhazz] *p:* خَضّ [xaðð] خَضّ [xaðð] *vn:* اِنخَضّ [ʔinxaðð] *p:* Don't jar the table when you sit down. لا تهِزّ الميز مِن تِقعُد [la: thizz ʔilmi:z min tigʕud]

jasmine • **1.** ياسمِين [ya:smi:n] The jasmine is a common flower in Iraq. الياسمِين وَرِد شايِع بِالعِراق [ʔilya:smi:n warid ša:yiʕ bilʕira:q]

jaundice • **1.** مَرَض الصُفار [marð ʔiṣṣufa:r] أَبُو صُفرَة [ʔabu ṣufra] اِصفَرّ [ʔiṣfarr]

jaw • **1.** فَكّ [fačč] فكُوك [fču:č] *pl:* He broke his jaw. كِسَر فَكّه [kisar faččah]

jawbone • **1.** عَظُم فَكّ [ʕaðum fačč] عُظام فَكّ [ʕuða:m fačč] *pl:* Samson killed a whole lot of guys with an ass's jawbone. شَمشُون قِتَل ناس هوايَة بعَظُم فَكّ مال حمار [šamšu:n kital na:s hwa:ya biʕaðum fačč ma:l ħma:r]

jealous • **1.** غَيّار [ɣayya:r] She's jealous because you have a new coat. هِيَّ غَيّارَة لِأنّ عِندِك قَبُّوط جِدِيد [hiyya ɣayya:ra liʔann ʕindič qappu:ṭ ǰidi:d]

to be jealous • **1.** غار [ɣa:r] *sv* a. He became jealous of me because I've got a car. غار مِنّي لِأنّ عِندِي سَيّارَة [ɣa:r minni liʔann ʕindi sayya:ra]

jealousy • **1.** غِيرَة [ɣi:ra] I'm dying of jealousy since he got the new position. الغِيرَة قاعدَة تمَوّتنِي، مِن أخَذ وَظِيفتَه الجِّدِيدَة [ʔilɣi:ra ga:ʕid tmawwitni, min ʔaxað waði:ftah ʔiǰǰidi:da]

jeep • **1.** سَيّارَة جِيب [sayya:ra ǰi:b] سَيّارات جِيب [sayya:ra:t ǰi:b] *pl:*

to jeer • **1.** سِخَر [sixar] سُخرِيَّة [suxriyya] *vn:* *sv* a. The audience jeered at the singer. المُتَفَرِّجِين سِخرَوا مِن المُغَنِّي [ʔilmutafarriǰi:n sixraw min ʔilmuɣanni]

jelly • **1.** مرَبَّى [mrabba] مرَبّات، مرَبّايات [mrabba:t, mrabba:ya:t] *pl:* I want rolls and jelly. أرِيد صَمُّون ومرَبَّى [ʔari:d ṣammu:n wmrabba]

to jeopardize • **1.** عَرَّض لِلخَطَر [ʕarrað lilxaṭar] تَعرِيض لِلخَطَر [taʕri:ð lilxaṭar] *vn:* تعَرَّض لِلخَطَر [tʕarrað lilxaṭar] *p:* The incident jeopardized his future. الحادِث عَرَّض مُستَقبَلَه لِلخَطَر [ʔilħa:diθ ʕarrað mustaqbalah lilxaṭar]

jeopardy • **1.** خَطَر [xaṭar] He put his own life in jeopardy. عَرَّض حَياتَه لِلخَطَر [ʕarrað ħaya:tah lilxaṭar]

jerboa • **1.** جَربُوع [ǰarbu:ʕ] جَرابِيع [ǰara:bi:ʕ] *pl:*

Jericho • **1.** أرِيحا [ʔari:ħa]

jerk • **1.** رَجَّى [raǰǰa:] The train stopped with a jerk. القِطار وُقَف برَجَّة [ʔilqiṭa:r wugaf braǰǰa]

to jerk • **1.** عَتّ [ʕatt] عَتّ [ʕatt] *vn:* اِنعَتّ [ʔinʕatt] *p:* نَتَش [nitaš] نَتِش [natiš] *vn:* اِنّتَش [ʔinnitaš] *p:* She jerked the book out of his hand. عَتَّت الكِتاب مِن إيدَه [ʕattat ʔilkita:b min ʔi:dah]

jerry-built • **1.** بِناء شَلّالِي [bina:ʔ šalla:li] Those houses are jerry-built. هاي البِيُوت بِناءها شَلّالِي [ha:y ʔilbiyu:t bina:ʔha šalla:li]

Jerusalem • **1.** القُدُس [ʔilqudus]

Jesus • **1.** عِيسَى [ʕi:sa]

jet • **1.** طَيّارَة نَفّاثَة [ṭayya:ra naffa:θa] We took a jet plane from Paris to Beirut. أخَذنا طَيّارَة نَفّاثَة مِن بارِيس إلَى بَيرُوت [ʔaxaðna ṭiyya:ra naffa:θa min pa:ri:s ʔila bayru:t]

jet-black • **1.** أسوَد مِثل الفَحَم [ʔaswad miθl ʔilfaħam] أسوَد طوخ [ʔaswad ṭu:x] Her hair is jet-black. شَعَرها مِثل الفَحَم [šaʕarha miθl ʔilfaħam]

Jew • **1.** يَهُودِي [yahu:di] يَهُودِيِّين، يَهُود [yahu:diyyi:n, yahu:d] *pl:* She is a Jew. هِيَّ يَهُودِيَّة [hiyya yahu:diyya]

jewel • **1.** جَوهَرَة [ǰawhara] جَواهِر [ǰawa:hir] *pl:* جَواهِر [ǰawa:hir] جَوهَرات [ǰawhara:t] *pl:* جَوهَر [ǰawhar] *Collective:* The dancer had a jewel in her navel. الرّاقِصَة حاطَّة جَوهَرَة بصُرَّتها [ʔirra:qiṣa ħa:ṭṭa ǰawhara biṣurratha] • **2.** حَجرَة [ħaǰra] حَجَرات [ħaǰara:t] *pl:* حِجار [ħiǰa:r] حَجَر [ħaǰar] *Collective:* My watch has seventeen jewels. ساعَتِي بِيها سباطَعَش حَجَر [sa:ʕati bi:ha sba:ṭaʕaš ħaǰar]

jewels • **1.** جَواهِر [ǰawa:hir] مُجَوهَرات [muǰawhara:t] She pawned her jewels. رِهنَت جَواهِرها [rihnat ǰawa:hirha]

jeweler • **1.** صايِغ [ṣa:yiɣ] صِيّاغ [ṣiyya:ɣ] *pl:* جَوهَرجِي [ǰawharči] جَوهَرجِيَّة [ǰawharči:yya] *pl:* I'm looking for a jeweler to fix my ring. دَأدَوُّرلِي فَدّ صايِغ يصَلِّح المِحبَس مالِي [daʔadawwurli fadd ṣa:yiɣ yṣalliħ ʔilmiħbas ma:li]

jewelry • **1.** مُجَوهَرات [muǰawhara:t] Did you see her jewelry? شِفِت مُجَوهَراتها؟ [šifit muǰawhara:tha?]

Jewish • **1.** يَهُودِي [yahu:di] يَهُودِيِّين، يَهُود [yahu:diyyi:n, yahu:d] *pl:* يَهُودِيَّة [yahu:diyya] *Feminine*

to jibe • **1.** اِنطُبَق [ʔinṭubaq] اِنطِباق [ʔinṭiba:q] *vn:* *sv* u. This doesn't jibe with what I saw. هاي ما تِنطُبُق عَلَى اللّي شِفتَه آنِي [ha:y ma: tinṭubuq ʕala ʔilli šiftah ʔa:ni]

Jidda • **1.** جِدَّة [ǰidda]

jiffy • **1.** لَحظَة [laħða] لَحظات [laħða:t] *pl:* It'll only take a jiffy. ما تاخُذ غير فَدّ لَحظَة [ma: ta:xuð ɣayr fadd laħða]

to jiggle • **1.** أخَذ مِن، أخَذ عَلَى [ʔaxað min, ʔaxað ʕala] أخِذ [ʔaxið] *vn:* اِنإخَذ [ʔinʔixað] *p:* حَزّ [ħazz] حَزّ [ħazz] *vn:* اِنحَزّ [ʔinħazz] *p:* Stop jiggling the table. بَسّ عاد تخُضّ الميز [bass ʕa:d txuðð ʔilmi:z]

to jilt • **1.** خِدَع [xidaʕ] خَدِع [xadiʕ] *vn:* اِنخِدَع [ʔinxidaʕ] *p:* His fiancee jilted him. خَطِيبتَه خِدعَتَه [xaṭi:btah xidʕatah]

jitters • **1.** هَوَس [hawas] هُوسَة [hu:sa] هَوسات [hu:sa:t] *pl:* هواس [hwa:s] He's got the jitters. عِندَه هَوَس [ʕindah hawas]

job • **1.** شَغلَة [šaɣla] شَغلات [šaɣla:t] *pl:* شُغُل، عَمَل [šuɣul, ʕamal] *Collective:* I'm looking for a job. دَأدَوُّر عَلَى شُغُل [daʔadawwur ʕala šuɣul] It wasn't an easy job to persuade her. إقناعها ما كان فَدّ عَمَل سَهِل [ʔiqna:ʕha ma: ča:n fadd ʕamal sahil] I've got several jobs to do today. عِندِي عِدَّة شَغلات أسَوِّيها اليُوم [ʕindi ʕiddat šaɣla:t ʔasawwi:ha ʔilyu:m] It isn't my job to tell him that. آنِي مُو شُغلِي أقُلَّه هاي [ʔa:ni mu: šuɣli ʔagullah ha:y]

jockey • **1.** جاكِي [ǰa:ki] جاكِيَّة [ǰa:kiyya] *pl:*

to join • **1.** اِنضَمّ ل [ʔinḍamm l-] اِنضِمام [ʔinḍima:m] *vn: sv* a. اِنتِمَى ل [ʔintima: l-] اِنتِماء [ʔintima:ʔ] *vn: sv* i. اِشتِرَك ب [ʔištirak b-] اِشتِراك [ʔištira:k] *vn: sv* i. When did he join the party? شوَقِت اِنضَمّ لِلحِزِب؟ [šwakit ʔinḍamm lilħizib?] • **2.** اِنضَمّ [ʔinḍamm] *sv* i. اِنتِمَى [ʔintima:] *sv* i. اِلتِحَق [ʔiltiħaq] اِلتِحاق [ʔiltiħa:q] *vn: sv* i. I'm joining the Army. راح أنضَمّ لِلجَّيش [ra:ħ ʔanḍamm lijǰi:š] • **3.** شَكَّل [šakkal] تَشكِيل [taški:l] *vn:* تشَكَّل [tšakkal] *p:* Would you like to join us? ترِيد تشَكِّل وِيّانا؟ [tri:d tšakkil wiyya:na?] • **4.** رَكَّب [rakkab] تَركِيب [tarki:b] *vn:* ترَكَّب [trakkab] *p:* شَكَّل [šakkal] *sv* i. How do you join these two parts? شلُون ترَكُّب هَذُول القِسمَين؟ [šlu:n trakkub haðu:l ʔilqismayn?] • **5.** اِتِّصَل [ʔittiṣal] اِتِّصال [ʔittiṣa:l] *vn: sv* u. Where does this road join the main road? وين هَذا الطَّرِيق يِتَّصِل بِالطَّرِيق الرَّئِيسِي؟ [wi:n ha:ða ʔiṭṭari:q yittiṣil biṭṭari:q ʔirraʔi:si?] • **6.** شارَك [ša:rak] مُشارَكَة [muša:raka] *vn: sv* i. اِشتِرَك [ʔištirak] اِشتِراك [ʔištira:k] *vn: sv* i. Everybody joined in the singing. الكُلّ شارکوا بالغِناء [ʔilkull ša:rkaw bilɣina:ʔ] • **7.** وَحَّد [waħħad] تَوحِيد [tawħi:d] *vn:* توَحَّد [twaħħad] *p:* Let's join forces. خَلِّي نوَحِّد جُهُودنا [xalli nwaħħid ǰuhu:dna]

joint • **1.** مَفصَل [mafṣal] مَفاصِل [mafa:ṣil] *pl:* All my joints ache. كُلّ مَفاصِلي تُوجَعنِي [kull mafa:ṣli tu:ǰaʕni] • **2.** مُشتَرَك [muštarak] The land is their joint property. الأراضِي مُشتَرَكَة بَيناتهُم [ʔilʔara:ḍi muštaraka bayna:thum]

out of joint • **1.** مَفسُوخ [mafsu:x] مَخلُوع [maxlu:ʕ] My knee's out of joint. رُكُبتِي مَفصُوخَة [rukubti mafṣu:xa]

to throw out of joint • **1.** خِلَع [xilaʕ] خَلِع [xaliʕ] *vn:* اِنخِلَع [ʔinxilaʕ] *p:* فُسَخ [fusax] فَسِخ [fasix] *vn: sv* i. I threw my shoulder out of joint. خِلَعِت كِتفِي [xilaʕit čitfi]

joke • **1.** نُكتَة [nukta] نُكَت [nukat] *pl:* I've heard that joke before. آنِي سمَعِت هَالنُّكتَة قَبُل [ʔa:ni smaʕit hannukta gabul] I played a joke on him. سَوَّيت بِيه نُكتَة [sawwi:t bi:h nukta] I played a joke on him. قَشمَرت عَليه [qašmarit ʕali:h] He tried to make a joke of the whole thing. حاوَل يُقلُب المَوضُوع إلَى نُكتَة [ħa:wal yuglub ʔilmawḍu:ʕ ʔila nukta] • **2.** شَقَا [šaqa] That's carrying the joke too far. طَوَّختها بِالشَّقَة [ṭawwaxtha biššaqa] That's carrying the joke too far. رِحِت بالشَّقا زايِد [riħit biššaqa za:yid] He can't take a joke. ما يِتحَمَّل شَقَا [ma: yitħammal šaqa]

to joke • **1.** تشاقَى [tša:qa:] شَقَة [šaqa] *vn: sv* a. This time I'm not joking. هَالمَرَّة ما دَأتشاقا [halmarra ma: daʔatša:qa] All joking aside, are you really going? إترُك الشَّقا هَسَّة، صُدُق إنتَ رايِح؟ [ʔitruk ʔiššaqa hassa, ṣudug ʔinta ra:yiħ?]

to tell jokes • **1.** نَكَّت [nakkat] تَنكِيت [tanki:t] *vn: sv* i. He's always telling jokes. هُوَّ ينَكِّت عَلَى طُول [huwwa ynakkit ʕala ṭu:l]

jolly • **1.** مَرِح [mariħ] مَرحِين [marħi:n] *pl:* بَشُوش [bašu:š] He's always jolly. هُوَّ دائِماً مَرِح [huwwa da:ʔiman mariħ]

jolt • **1.** رَجَّة [rajǰa] رَجّات [rajǰa:t] *pl:* The car stopped with a sudden jolt. السَّيّارَة وُقفَت بِرَجَّة مُفاجِئَة [ʔissayya:ra wugfat brajǰa mufa:ǰʔa]

to jolt • **1.** رَجّ [rajǰ] رَجّ [rajǰ] *vn:* اِنرَجّ [ʔinrajǰ] *p:* The explosion jolted the whole house. الإنفِجار رَجّ البَيت كُلَّه [ʔilʔinfiǰa:r rajǰ ʔilbayt kullah] • **2.** هَزّ [hazz] هَزّ [hazz] *vn:* اِنهَزّ [ʔinhazz] *p:* The news jolted us. الأخبار هَزَّتنا [ʔilʔaxba:r hazzatna]

Jordan • **1.** الأُردُن [ʔilʔurdun] I'm going to Jordan tomorrow. آنِي رايِح لِلأُردُن باكِر [ʔa:ni ra:yiħ lilʔurdun ba:čir]

Jordanian • **1.** أُردُنِي [ʔurduni] أُردُنِيِّين [ʔurduniyyi:n] *pl:* Many Jordanians live in Kuwait. هوايَة أُردُنِيِّين يعِيشُون بالكُوَيت [hwa:ya ʔurduniyyi:n yʕi:šu:n bilkuwi:t] • **2.** أُردُنِي [ʔurduni] The Jordanian embassy was bombed last night. السِّفارَة الأُردُنِيَّة اِنِّسفَت البارحَة باللَّيل [ʔassifa:ra ʔilʔurduniyya ʔinnisfat ʔilba:rħa billayl]

to jostle • **1.** دِفَع [difaʕ] دَفِع [dafiʕ] *vn:* اِندِفَع [ʔindifaʕ] *p:* He jostled me as he went by. هُوَّ دِفَعنِي مِن مَرّ مِن يَمِّي [huwwa difaʕni min marr min yammi]

to jot down • **1.** قَيَّد [qayyad] تَقيِيد [taqyi:d] *vn:* تقَيَّد [tqayyad] *p:* I jotted her telephone number down. قَيَّدِت رَقَم التِّلِفُون مالها [qayyadit raqam ʔittilifu:n ma:lha]

journalist • **1.** صُحُفِي [ṣuħufi] صُحُفِيِّين [ṣuħufiyyi:n] *pl:*

journey • **1.** رِحلَة [riħla] رِحلات [riħla:t] *pl:* سَفرَة [safra] سَفرات [safra:t] *pl:*

jovial • **1.** مَرِح [mariħ] بَشُوش [bašu:š] There is a jovial fellow! هُوَّ كُلِّش مَرِح [huwwa kulliš mariħ]

i, interjection; p, passive; pl, plural; sv, stem vowel; vn, verbal noun

joy • **1.** فَرَح [farah] Her eyes were beaming with joy. عيُونها كانَت تِلمَع مِن الفَرَح [ʕyu:nha ča:nat tilmaʕ min ʔilfarah]

joyful • **1.** سارّ [sa:rr] مُفرِح [mufrih] It was a joyful occasion. كانَت مُناسَبَة سارَّة [ča:nat muna:saba sa:rra]

Judaism • **1.** الدِيانَة اليَهُودِيَّة [ʔiddiya:na lyahu:diyya]

judge • **1.** حاكِم [ħa:kim] حُكّام [ħukka:m] *pl:* قاضِي [qa:ði] قُضاة [quða:(t)] *pl:* When is the judge going to pass sentence? شوَقِت الحاكِم راح يِنطُق بِالحُكُم [šwakit ʔilħa:kim ra:ħ yintuq bilħukum] The judge ruled that the divorce was valid. القاضِي اِعتُبَر الطَّلاق صَحِيح [ʔilqa:ði ʔiʕtubar ʔittala:q sahi:ħ] • **2.** حَكَم [ħakam] حُكّام، حَكَمِيَّة [ħukka:m, ħakamiyya] *pl:* حاكِم [ħa:kim] حُكّام [ħukka:m] *pl:* The judges awarded his picture the first prize. الحُكّام إنطُوه الجّائِزَة الأولَى عَلَى صُورتَه [ʔilħukka:m ʔintu:h ʔijja:ʔiza ʔilʔu:la ʕala su:rtah] The judge said the ball fell outside. الحَكَم قال الطُّوبَة طِلعَت خارِج [ʔilħakam ga:l ʔittu:ba tilʕat xa:rij]

*** You be the judge of that!** • **1.** إنتَ قَرِّر [ʔinta qarrir]

*** He's as sober as a judge.** • **1.** هُوَّ كُلِّش صاحِي [huwwa kulliš sa:ħi]

*** She's not a good judge of human nature.** • **1.** ما تِقدَر تُحكُم عَلَى طَبِيعَة الناس [ma: tigdar tuħkum ʕala tabi:ʕat ʔinna:s]

to judge • **1.** حِكَم [ħikam] حُكُم [ħukum] *vn:* اِنحِكَم [ʔinħikam] *p:* Don't judge him too harshly. لا تُحكُم عَلِيه بِالمُوزَين [la: tuħkum ʕali:h bil mu: zayn] • **2.** قاس [qa:s] قِياس [qiya:s] *vn: sv* i. حِكَم [ħikam] Never judge others by yourself. لا تقِيس النّاس عَلَى نَفسَك [la: tqi:s ʔinna:s ʕala nafsak] Never judge others by yourself. لا تُحكُم عالنّاس حَسَب اِعتِقادَك بَسّ [la: tuħkum ʕanna:s ħasab ʔiʕtiqa:dak bass]

*** To judge by his face he isn't very enthusiastic.** • **1.** مِن وُچَّه مبَيِّن ما مِتحَمِّس [min wuččah mbayyin ma: mitħammis]

judgment • **1.** تَقدِير [taqdi:r] You can rely on his judgment. تِقدَر تِعتِمِد عَلَى تَقدِيرَه [tigdar tiʕtimid ʕala taqdi:rah] The president of the court will hand down his judgment today. رَئِيس المَحكَمَة راح يِصدُر حُكمَه اليُوم [raʔi:s ʔilmaħkama ra:ħ yisdur ħukmah ʔilyu:m] Don't make snap judgments. لا تُصدِر أحكام سَرِيعَة [la: tusdir ʔaħka:m sari:ʕa] He showed good judgment. كان قَرارَه حَكِيم [ka:n qara:rah ħaki:m] • **2.** رَأي [raʔy] آراء [ʔa:ra:ʔ] *pl:* In my judgment you're doing the wrong thing. بِرَأيِي إنتَ قاعِد تسَوِّي غَلَط [braʔyi ʔinta ga:ʕid tsawwi ɣalat]

judicial • **1.** قانُونِي [qa:nu:ni] Judicial procedures are very involved. الإجراءات القانُونِيَّة كُلِّش مُعَقَّدَة [ʔilʔijra:ʔa:t ʔilqa:nu:niyya kulliš muʕaqqada]

judicious • **1.** مُوَفَّق [muwaffaq] He made a judicious selection. كان اِختِيارَه مُوَفَّق [ča:n ʔixtiya:rah muwaffaq]

jug • **1.** The women carried water jugs on their heads. النِّسوان شالَوا جَرّات المَيّ عَلَى رُوسهُم [ʔinniswa:n ša:law jarra:t ʔilmayy ʕala ru:shum]

juice • **1.** عَصِير [ʕasi:r] I'd like a glass of orange juice, please. أرِيد كلاص عَصِير بُرتُقال، مِن فَضلَك [ʔari:d gla:s ʕasi:r purtuqa:l, min faðlak]

juicy • **1.** رَيّان [rayya:n] مَليان مَيّ [malya:n mayy] These oranges are very juicy. هَالبُرتُقالات كُلِّش رَيّانَة [halpurtuqa:la:t kulliš rayya:na]

July • **1.** تَمُّوز [tammu:z]

jump • **1.** قَفزَة [qafza] قَفزات [qafza:t] *pl.* طَفرَة [tafra] طَفرات [tafra:t] *pl:* His jump broke the national record. قَفزتَه كِسرَت الرَّقَم الوَطَني [qafiztah kisrat ʔirraqam ʔilwatani] • **2.** قَمزَة [gamza] قَمزات [gamza:t] *pl:* With one jump he was over the wall. بقَمزَة وِحدَة عُبَر الحايِط [bgamza wiħda ʕubar ʔilħa:yit]

*** You don't want him to get the jump on you, do you?** • **1.** ما ترِيدَه يسبِقَك، تَمام؟ [ma: tri:dah ysibqak, tama:m?]

to jump • **1.** طُفَر [tufar] طَفُر [tafur] *vn: sv* u. قُمَز [gumaz] قَمُز [gamuz] *vn: sv* u. How high can you jump? شقَدّ عِلو تِقدَر تُطفُر؟ [šgadd ʕilw tigdar tutfur?] He jumped off the bus before it stopped. قُمَز مِن الباص قَبُل ما يوقَف [gumaz min ʔilpa:s gabul ma: yu:gaf] • **2.** قِلَب [gilab] قَلُب [galub] *vn: sv* u. عُبَر [ʕubar] عَبُر [ʕabur] *vn: sv* u. We jumped pages seven to twelve. قلَبنا مِن صَفحَة سَبعَة إلَى ثنَعَش [glabna min safħa sabʕa ʔila θnaʕaš] • **3.** فَزّ [fazz] تَفزِيز [tafzi:z] *vn: sv* i. He jumped when he heard the noise. فَزّ مِن سِمَع الصَّوت [fazz min simaʕ ʔissawt]

*** He jumped at the offer.** • **1.** قِبَل العَرِض رَأساً [qibal ʔilʕarið raʔsan] / قِبَل العَرِض بِلَهفَة [qibal ʔilʕarið bilahfa]

*** Don't jump to conclusions about things.** • **1.** لا تُحكُم بسُرعَة عَالأشياء [la: tuħkum bsurʕa ʕalʔašya:ʔ]

*** The train jumped the track.** • **1.** القِطار طِلَع مِن الخَطّ [ʔilqita:r tilaʕ min ʔilxatt]

*** He can go jump in the lake!** • **1.** خَلِّي يذِبّ نَفسَه بِالشَطّ [xalli yðibb nafsah biššatt]

to jump around • **1.** قَمَّز [gammaz] تقُمُّز، تَقمِيز [tgummuz, tagmi:z] *vn: sv* u. Stop jumping around. يِكفِي عاد تقَمُّز [yikfi ʕa:d tgummuz]

junction • **1.** تَقاطُع الخُطُوط [taqa:tuʕ ʔilxutu:t]

June • **1.** حُزَيران [ħuzayra:n]

jungle • **1.** غابَة [ɣa:ba] غابات [ɣa:ba:t] *pl:* He was lost in the African jungle. ضاع بِغابات أفرِيقيا [ða:ʕ biɣa:ba:t ʔafri:qiya]

J

junior • **1.** * She's a junior in college. هِيَّ طالِبَة بصَفّ ثالِث بِالكُلِّيَّة [hiyya ṭaːliba bṣaff θaːliθ bilkulliyya]

junk • **1.** قَلاقِيل [qalaːqiːl] We'll have to clean the junk out of the storeroom. لازِم اِنَّظُّف القَلاقِيل مِن المَخزَن [laːzim ʔinnaðˌðuf ʔilqalaːqiːl min ʔilmaxzan] • **2.** غَراض [ɣaraːð̣] Where did you get that junk? منين جِبِت هاي الغَراض؟ [mniːn jibit haːy ʔilɣaraːð̣?]

to junk • **1.** وَدّى لِلسّكراب [waddaː lisskraːb] تودِّي لِلسّكراب [twiddi lisskraːb] *vn: sv* i. I'm afraid I'll just have to junk that car. آني خايِف أضطَرّ أوَدّي السَّيّارَة لِلسِّكراب [ʔaːni xaːyif ʔaḍṭarr ʔawaddi ʔissayyaːra lissikraːb]

jurisdiction • **1.** اِختِصاص [ʔixtiṣaːṣ] The matter's outside my jurisdiction. القَضِيَّة خارِج اِختِصاصِي [ʔilqaḍiyya xaːrij ʔixtiṣaːṣi]

jurist • **1.** فَقِيه [faqiːh] فُقَهاء [fuqahaːʔ] *pl:*

jury • **1.** مُحَلِّفِين [muħallifiːn]

just • **1.** عادِل [ʕaːdil] That's a just punishment. هَذي عُقُوبَة عادِلَة [haːði ʕuquːba ʕaːdila] • **2.** مُستَقِيم [mustaqiːm] عادِل [ʕaːdil] He is a just man. هُوَّ رَجُل مُستَقِيم [huwwa rajul mustaqiːm] • **3.** هَسَّة [hassa] هَستَوّ [hastaww-] I just arrived. هَسَّة وُصَلِت [hassa wuṣalit] I just arrived. هَستَوّنِي وُصَلِت [hastawwni wuṣalit] • **4.** بِالضَبُط [biððabuṭ] تَماماً [tamaːman] That's just the word I meant. هاي هِيَّ الكَلِمَة اللّي أرِيدها بِالضَبُط [haːy hiyya ʔilkalima ʔilli ʔariːdha biððabuṭ] That's just what I wanted. هَذا تَماماً مِثلما رِدِت [haːða tamaːman miθilmaː ridit] That's just what I wanted. هَذا اللّي رِدتَه [haːða ʔilli ridtah] He's just like his father. هُوَّ بِالضَبُط مِثِل أبُوه [huwwa biððabuṭ miθil ʔabuːh] He is just as his brother. هُوَّ مِثل أخُوه بِالضَبُط [huwwa miθl ʔaxuːh biððabuṭ] It was just the other way around. هِيَّ كانَت تَماماً بِالعَكِس [hiyya čaːnat tamaːman bilʕakis] That takes just as long. هاي تاخُذ نَفس الوَقِت بِالضَبُط [haːy taːxuð nafs ʔilwakit biððabuṭ] Just what do you mean? شتِعنِي بِالضَبُط؟ [štiʕni biððabuṭ?] • **5.** تَماماً [tamaːman] The table was just covered with dust. المِيز كان مغَطّى بِالتّراب تَماماً [ʔilmiːz čaːn mɣaṭṭa bittiraːb tamaːman] • **6.** مُجَرَّد [mujarrad] بَس [bass] He's just a little boy. هُوَّ مُجَرَّد طِفِل [huwwa mujarrad ṭifil] I just said one word, and he got mad. قِلِت كِلمَة وِحدَة بَس وَزعَل [gilit čilma wiħda bass waziʕal] I just want one glass of water. أرِيد كلاص واحِد مَيّ بَس [ʔariːd glaːṣ waːħid mayy bass] • **7.** دُوب [duːb] You just made it to class on time. دُوب وُصَلِت لِلصَّفّ عالوَقِت [duːb wuṣalit liṣṣaff ʕalwakit] • **8.** عَلى الحافَّة [ʕalħaːffa] دُوب [duːb] You just passed the exam. إنتَ نِجَحِت بِالإمتِحان عالحافَّة [ʔinta nijaħit bilʔimtiħaːn ʕalħaːffa]

*** That's just the way it is!** • **1.** الأمُور هِيكِي ماشيَة [ʔilʔumuːr hiːči maːšya]

*** There's just nothing you can do about it.** • **1.** كُلّشِي ما تِقدَر تسَوّي [kullši maː tigdar tsawwi]

*** Just a minute!** • **1.** فَدّ دَقِيقَة [fadd daqiːqa]

*** Just what did you mean by that crack?** • **1.** شتُقصُد بهاي المُلاحَظَة؟ [štuqṣud bhaːy lmulaːħaða?]

*** Just for that I won't do it.** • **1.** لِهالسَبَب آني ما أسَوِّيها [lhassabab ʔaːni maː ʔasawwiːha]

just right • **1.** عَلَى المَرام [ʕalmaraːm] The water is just right. الماي عالمَرام [ʔilmaːy ʕalmaraːm] My coffee's just right. قَهوتي عالمَرام [gahwti ʕalmaraːm]

justice • **1.** إنصاف [ʔinṣaːf] عَدالَة [ʕadaːla] Don't expect justice from him. لا تِتوَقَّع أيّ اِنصاف مِنَّه [laː titwaqqaʕ ʔayy ʔinṣaːf minnah]

to do justice • **1.** نِصَف [niṣaf] نَصِف [naṣif] *vn:* اِنّصَف [ʔinniṣaf] *p:* عِدَل [ʕidal] عَدِل [ʕadil] *vn:* اِنعِدَل [ʔinʕidal] *p:* You're not doing him justice. إنتَ ما دَتِنصِف وِيّاه [ʔinta maː datinṣif wiyyaːh]

*** The picture doesn't do you justice.** • **1.** الصُّورَة ما تِشبَهَك تَماماً [ʔiṣṣuːra maː tišbahak tamaːman] / الصُّورَة مُو حِلوَة مِثلَك [ʔiṣṣuːra muː ħilwa miθlak]

justifiable • **1.** إلَه مُبَرِّر [ʔilah mubarrir] I think this expenditure is justifiable. أعتِقِد هَالمَصرُوف إلَه مُبَرِّر [ʔaʕtiqid halmaṣruːf ʔilah mubarrir]

justified • **1.** مُحِق [muħiqq] I think you were perfectly justified in doing that. أظُنّ إنَّك كِنت كُلِّش مُحِقّ بعَمَلَك [ʔaðunn ʔinnak čint kulliš muħiqq bʕamalak] You were perfectly justified in asking for more pay. كِنِت تَماماً مُحِقّ بطَلَبَك بزِيادَة راتبَك [činit tamaːman muħiqq bṭalabak bziyaːdat raːtbak]

to justify • **1.** بَرَّر [barrar] تَبرِير [tabriːr] *vn:* تبَرَّر [tbarrar] *p:* She tried to justify her actions. حاوِلَت تبَرِّر أعمالها [ħaːwlat tbarrir ʔaʕmaːlha]

i, interjection; p, passive; pl, plural; sv, stem vowel; vn, verbal noun

K

Kaaba • **1.** الكَعبَة [ʔilkaʕba]

kangaroo • **1.** كَنغَر [kanɣar]

keen • **1.** حادّ [ħaːdd] He has a keen mind. هُوَّ حادّ الذَّكاء [huwwa ħaːdd ʔiððakaːʔ] His sense of smell is keen. حاسَّة الشَّمّ مالتَه حادَّة [ħaːssat ʔiššamm maːltah ħaːdda] This knife has a keen edge. حاشيَة هَالسِّكّينَة حادَّة [ħaːšyat hassiččiːna ħaːdda] • **2.** مِتحَمِّس [mitħammis] I'm not so keen on that. آنِي مُو كُلِّش مِتحَمِّس إلها [ʔaːni muː kulliš mitħammis ʔilha] I'm not so keen on that. ما عِندي وَلَع بيه [maː ʕindi walaʕ biːh]

to keep • **1.** اِحتِفَظ ب [ʔiħtifað b-] اِحتِفاظ [ʔiħtifaːð] *vn: sv* u. May I keep this picture? أَقدَر أَحتُفُظ بهاي الصُّورَة؟ [ʔagdar ʔaħtufuð bhaːy ʔiṣṣuːra?] If the team wins three times in a row, they get to keep the cup. الفِرقَة إذا تُغلُب ثلَث مَرّات مُتَتالِيَة تِقدَر تِحتُفُظ بِالكأس [ʔilfirqa ʔiða tuɣlub tlaθ marraːt mutataːlya tigdar tiħtufuð bilkʔas] He keeps the company's books. هُوَّ يِحتِفِظ بسِجِلّات الشَّرِكَة [huwwa yiħtifið bisijjilaːt ʔiššarika] • **2.** رَبَّى [rabbaː] تَربِيَة [tarbiya] *vn: sv* i. We've been keeping chickens for the last three years. صار إلنا نرَبّي دِجاج لِمُدَّة ثلَث سنين [ṣaːr ʔilna nrabbi dijaːj lmuddat tlaθ sniːn] • **3.** دار [daːr] دُور [duːr] *pl:* إدارَة [ʔidaːra] *vn: sv* i. She keeps house for her uncle. هِيَّ تدير أُمُور بَيت عَمّها [hiyya ddiːr ʔumuːr bayt ʕammha] • **4.** بُقَى [buqaː] بَقِي، بَقاء [baqiy, baqaːʔ] *vn: sv* a. ظَلّ [ðall] ظَلّ [ðall] *vn: sv* i. The policeman asked us to keep moving. الشُّرطِي طِلَب مِن عِدنا أَن نِبقى ماشِين [ʔiššurṭi ṭilab min ʕidna ʔan nibqaː maːšiːn] He kept talking all the time. ظَلّ يِحكِي الوَقِت كُلّه [ðall yiħči ʔilwakit kullah] Keep calm! إبقُوا هادئِين [ʔibquː haːdʔiːn] Keep clam! إهدَوا [ʔihdaːw] Can't you keep quiet? ما تِقدَر تظَلّ ساكِت؟ [maː tigdar tðill saːkit?] Can't you keep quiet? ما تِقدَر تُسكُت؟ [maː tigdar tuskut?] He's keeping me company. هُوَّ يِبقَى وِيّايا [huwwa yibqaː wiyyaːya] This milk won't keep till tomorrow. هَالحَليب ما يِتحَمَّل يِبقَى لباكِر [halħaliːb maː yitħammal yibqaː lbaːčir] • **5.** خَلَّى [xallaː] تَخلِيَة، تخِلّي [taxliya, txilli] *vn: sv* i. Sorry to have kept you waiting. مِتأَسِّف لِأَنّ خَلَّيتَك تِنتِظِر [mitʔassif liʔann xalliːtak tintiðir] Keep to the right. خَلّيك عاليمنَى [xalliːk ʕalyimna] Keep to the right. إبقَى عاليمنَى [ʔibqaː ʕalyimna] Keep me posted. خَلّيني عَلَى عِلِم عَلَى طُول [xalliːni ʕala ʕilim ʕala ṭuːl] Keep that in mind! خَلّيها بفِكرَك [xalliːha bfikrak] • **6.** ضَمّ [ðamm] ضَمّ [ðamm] *vn:* اِنضَمّ [ʔinðamm] *p:* اِحتِفَظ ب [ʔiħtifað b-] اِحتِفاظ [ʔiħtifaːð] *vn: sv* i. حُفَظ [ħufað] حَفُظ [ħafuð] *vn: sv* u. Please keep this for me. مِن فَضلَك ضُمّلي إيّاها [min faðlak ðummli ʔiyyaːha] Please keep this for me. رَجاءاً اِحتِفِظلي بِيها [rajaːʔan ʔiħtifiðli biːha] • **7.** عَطَّل [ʕaṭṭal] تَعطِيل [taʕṭiːl] *vn:* تعَطَّل [tʕaṭṭal] *p:* I won't keep you very long. ما راح أَعَطّلَك هوايَة [maː raːħ ʔaʕaṭṭlak hwaːya] • **8.** ضَمّ [ðamm] *sv* u. كِتَم [kitam] كَتِم، كِتمان [katim, kitmaːn] *vn: sv* i. خَبَّى [xabbaː] تَخبِيَة، تخِبّي [taxbiya, txibbi] *vn: sv* i. Can you keep a secret? تِقدَر تضُمّ سِرّ؟ [tigdar dðumm sirr?] He kept his real intentions from me for quite a while. خَبَّى قَصدَه الحَقِيقِي مُدَّة طُوِيلَة عَنّي [xabbaː qaṣdah ʔilħaqiːqi mudda ṭuwiːla ʕanni] • **9.** بَقَّى [baqqaː] تَبقِيَة [tabqiya] *vn:* تبَقَّى [tbaqqaː] *p:* اِحتِفَظ [ʔiħtifað] اِحتِفاظ [ʔiħtifaːð] *vn: sv* i. خَلَّى [xallaː] تخِلّي [txilli] *vn: sv* i. Shall I keep your dinner warm? تريدِني أبَقّي أَكلَك حارّ؟ [triːdni ʔabaqqi ʔaklak ħaːrr?] • **10.** ضِبَط [ðibaṭ] ضَبُط [ðabuṭ] *vn: sv* u. Does your watch keep good time? ساعتَك تُضبُط الوَقِت زَين؟ [saːʕtak tuðbuṭ ʔilwakit zayn?] Keep your temper! أُضبُط أَعصابَك [ʔuðbuṭ ʔaʕṣaːbak] Keep your temper! هَدّي نَفسَك [haddi nafsak] • **11.** وُفَى [wufaː] وَفاء، وُفا [wafaːʔ, wufa] *vn: sv* i. I rely on you to keep your word. آنِي أَعتِمِد عَلِيك أَن تُوفي بوَعدَك [ʔaːni ʔaʕtimid ʕaliːk ʔan tuːfi bwaʕdak]

*** Everytime we kick him out, he keeps coming back.** • **1.** كُلّ ما نطُردَه يرجَع [kull maː nṭurdah yirjaʕ]

*** His wife just found out he's been keeping a mistress.** • **1.** مَرتَه هَسَّة عُرفَت عِندَه عَشِيقَة [martah hassa ʕurfat ʕindah ʕašiːqa]

to keep away • **1.** اِبتِعَد [ʔibtiʕad] اِبتِعاد [ʔibtiʕaːd] *vn: sv* i. Keep away from that radio! اِبتِعِد عَن هَذا الرّاديُو [ʔibtiʕid ʕan haːða ʔirraːdyu] • **2.** بِعَد [biʕad] إبعاد [ʔibʕaːd] *vn: sv* i. Keep the children away from the fire. إبعِد الجِّهال عَن النّار [ʔibʕid ʔijjahaːl ʕan ʔinnaːr]

to keep from • **1.** مِنَع مِن [minaʕ min] مَنِع [maniʕ] *vn:* اِنمِنَع [ʔinminaʕ] *p:* Nobody can keep you from going there. مَحَّد يِقدَر يِمنَعَك مِن أَن ترُوح هناك [maħħad yigdar yimnaʕak min ʔan truːħ hnaːk] • **2.** بَطَّل مِن [baṭṭal min] تَبطِيل [tabṭiːl] *vn: sv* i. اِبتِعَد عَن [ʔibtiʕad ʕan] اِبتِعاد [ʔibtiʕaːd] *vn: sv* i. He can't keep from drinking. ما يِقدَر يبَطِّل مِن الشُّرُب [maː yigdar ybaṭṭil min ʔiššurub]

to keep off • **1.** اِبتِعَد عَن [ʔibtiʕad ʕan] اِبتِعاد عَن [ʔibtiʕaːd ʕan] *vn: sv* i. وَخَّر مِن [waxxar min] تَوخِير [tawxiːr] *vn: sv* i. Keep off the grass! اِبتِعِد عَن الثَّيِّل [ʔibtiʕid ʕan ʔilθayyal] Keep your hands off that car! وَخِّر إيدَك مِن هَالسَّيّارَة [waxxir ʔiːdak min hassayyaːra] Keep your hands off that car! لا تخَلّي إيدَك عَلَى هَالسَّيّارَة [laː txalli ʔiːdak ʕala hassayyaːra]

to keep on • **1.** ظَلّ [ðall] ظَلّ [ðall] *vn: sv* i. بُقَى [buqaː] بَقاء [baqaːʔ] *vn: sv* a. اِستَمَرّ [ʔistamarr] اِستِمرار [ʔistimraːr] *vn: sv* i. We kept on walking. ظَلَّينا نِمشِي [ðallayna nimši] Keep on trying. اِستَمِرّ بِالمُحاوَلَة

[ʔistamirr bilmuħa:wala] Keep right on talking. اِستَمِرّ بالكَلام [ʔistamirr bilkala:m]
to keep out • 1. مِنَع [minaʕ] مَنِع [maniʕ] *vn: sv* a. Ordinary glass keeps out utraviolet rays. الزُّجاج العادِي يِمنَع الأشَعَّة ما وَرا البَنَفسَجِيَّة [ʔizzuǰa:ǰ ʔilʕa:di yimnaʕ ʔilʔašaʕʕa ma: wara ʔilbanafsaǰiyya] This isn't a beautiful raincoat, but in any event, it keeps out the rain. هَذا مُو قَبُّوط مُطَر لَطِيف، لَكِن عَلَى كُلّ حال، يِمنَع المُطَر [ha:ða mu: qappu:ṭ muṭar laṭi:f, la:kin ʕala kull ħa:l, yimnaʕ ʔilmuṭar] **• 2.** اِبتِعَد عَن [ʔibtiʕad ʕan] اِبتِعاد [ʔibtiʕa:d] *vn: sv* i. Keep out of my garden! اِبتِعِد عَن حَدِيقتِي [ʔibtiʕid ʕan ħadi:qti] It's his affair. You'd better keep out of it! هَذا شُغلَه أحسَنلَك اِبتِعِد عَنَّه [ha:ða šuɣlah ʔaħsanlak ʔibtiʕid ʕannah] **• 3.** بِعَد [biʕad] إبعاد [ʔibʕa:d] *vn: sv* i. I'll try to keep him out of trouble. راح أحاوِل أبعِدَه عَن المَشاكِل [ra:ħ ʔaħa:wil ʔabiʕdah ʕan ʔilmaša:kil] Keep him out of my way! إبعِدَه عَن طَرِيقِي [ʔibiʕdah ʕan ṭari:qi]
to keep up • 1. اِستِمَرّ عَلَى [ʔistimarr ʕala] اِستِمرار عَلَى [ʔistimra:r ʕala] *vn: sv* i. Keep it up and see where it gets you! اِستَمِرّ عَلِيها وشُوف شلُون راح تِتأذَّى [ʔistamirr ʕali:ha wšu:f šlu:n ra:ħ titʔaððа:] **• 2.** حافَظ عَلَى [ħa:fað ʕala] مُحافَظَة عَلَى [muħa:fuða ʕala] *vn: sv* u. How much does it cost you per month to keep up your car? شقَدّ يكَلِّفَك بالشَّهَر حَتَّى تحافُظ عَلَى سَيّارتَك؟ [šgadd ykallifak biššahar ħatta tħa:fuð ʕala sayya:rtak?] **• 3.** بِقَى عَلَى [biqa: ʕala] بَقاء عَلَى [baqa:ʔ ʕala] *vn: sv* a. Keep up the good work. إبقَى عَلَى شُغلَك الزّين [ʔibqa: ʕala šuɣlak ʔizzi:n] **• 4.** لَحَّق ب [laħħag b-] تَلحِيق، اِلتِحاق [talħi:g, ʔiltiħa:q] *vn:* تلَحَّق [tlaħħag] *p:* I can't keep up with you when you dictate so fast. ما أقدَر ألَحِّق بِيك مِن تِملِي عَلَيّا بسُرعَة [ma: ʔagdar ʔalaħħig bi:k min timli: ʕalayya bsurʕa] It's hard for me to keep up with the others in the class. يِصعَب عَلَيّا ألَحِّق بالآخَرِين بالصَّفّ [yiṣʕab ʕalayya ʔalaħħig bilʔa:xari:n biṣṣaff] I can't keep up with my work. ما دَأقدَر ألَحِّق أخَلِّص شُغلِي [ma: daʔagdar ʔalaħħig ʔaxalliṣ šuɣli]

keepsake • 1. تِذكار [tiðka:r] تِذكارات [tiðka:ra:t] *pl:* She gave him her ring as a keepsake. اِنطَاتَه مِحبَسها كَتِذكار [ʔinṭa:tah miħbasha katiðka:r]

kernel • 1. حَبّايَة [ħabba:ya] حَبّايات [ħabba:ya:t] *pl:* حَبّ [ħabb] *Collective*

kerosene • 1. نَفُط أبيَض [nafuṭ ʔabyað]

kettle • 1. قُورِي [qu:ri] قُورِيّات، قواري [qu:ri:yya:t, qwa:ri] *pl:* كِتلِي [kitli] كِتلِيّات، كتالِي [kitliyya:t, kta:li] *pl:* The water in the kettle is boiling. الماي دَيغلِي بالقُورِي [ʔilma:y dayiɣli bilqu:ri]
*** That's a pretty kettle of fish! • 1.** هَذا مَوقِف مُزعِج [ha:ða mawqif muzʕiǰ] / هِيَّ لِيصَة [hiyya li:ṣa] / صايرَة خَبِيصَة [ṣa:yra xabi:ṣa]

K

key • 1. مِفتاح [mifta:ħ] مَفاتِيح [mafa:ti:ħ] *pl:* I've lost the key to my room. ضَيَّعِت مِفتاح غُرُفتِي [ðayyaʕit mifta:ħ ɣurufti] That was the key to the mystery. هَذا كان مِفتاح اللُّغز [ha:ða ča:n mifta:ħ ʔilluɣuz] **• 2.** حَرُف [ħaruf] حُرُوف [ħuru:f] *pl:* One of the keys on my typewriter gets stuck. واحِد مِن حُرُوف الطّابِعَة مالتِي يشَكِّل [wa:ħid min ħuru:f ʔiṭṭa:biʕa ma:lti yšakkil] **• 3.** مُهِمّ [muhimm] He holds a key position in the government. هُوَّ عِندَه مَركَز مُهِمّ بالحُكُومَة [huwwa ʕindah markaz muhimm bilħuku:ma] **• 4.** دَلِيل [dali:l] أدِلَّة [ʔadilla] *pl:* إيضاح [ʔi:ða:ħ] The key to the map is in the right-hand corner. دَلِيل الخَرِيطَة بالزُّوِيَّة اليِمنَى [dali:l ʔilxari:ṭa bizzuwiyya ʔilyimna]
off key • 1. نَشاز [naša:z] Who's singing off key? مِنُو دَيغَنِّي نَشاز؟ [minu dayɣanni naša:z?]

keyhole • 1. بَيت مِفتاح [bayt mifta:ħ] بيُوت مِفتاح [byu:t mifta:ħ] *pl:*

khaki • 1. خاكِي [xa:ki] This merchant doesn't sell anything but khaki. هَالتّاجِر ما يبِيع غير خاكِي [hatta:ǰir ma: ybi:ʕ ɣi:r xa:ki]

Khartoum • 1. خَرطُوم [xarṭu:m]

kick • 1. جِلّاق [čilla:q] جلالِيق [čla:li:q] *pl:* دَفرَة [dafra] دَفرات [dafra:t] *pl:* I felt like giving him a good hard kick. عِجَبنِي أضُربَه جِلّاق قَوِي [ʕiǰabni ʔaðurbah čilla:q qawi] **• 2.** رَفسَة [rafsa] رَفسات [rafsa:t] *pl:* زَقطَة [zagṭa] زَقطات [zagṭa:t] *pl:* The horse's kick broke his leg. رَفسَة الحصان كِسرَت رِجلَه [rafsat ʔilħṣa:n kisrat riǰlah] **• 3.** رَدَّة [radda] رَدّات [radda:t] *pl:* The kick of a rifle can break your collar bone. رَدَّت البُندُقِيَّة يِمكِن تِكسِر عَظم التُّرقُوَة مالَك [raddat ʔilbunduqiyya yimkin tiksir ʕaðm ʔitturquwa ma:lak] **• 4.** وَلَع [walaʕ] واهِس [wa:his] He gets a big kick out of sports. عِندَه وَلَع بالرِّياضَة [ʕindah walaʕ birriya:ða]
to kick • 1. ضِرَب [ðirab] ضَرِب [ðarib] *vn:* اِنضِرَب [ʔinðirab] *p:* Kick the ball! أضرُب الطُّوبَة [ʔuðrub ʔiṭṭu:ba] **• 2.** رُفَس [rufas] رَفُس [rafus] *vn:* اِنرِفَس [ʔinrifas] *p:* I hope this horse doesn't kick. إن شاء الله هَذا الحصان ما يرفُس [ʔinša:llah ha:ða ʔilħṣa:n ma: yirfus] **• 3.** تشَكَّى [tšakka:] تَشَكِّي [tašakki] *vn: sv* a. He kicks about everything. يِتشَكَّى مِن كُلّشِي [yitšakka: min kullši]
*** I can't kick. • 1.** عَلَى الله [ʕala ʔallah]
to kick out • 1. طِرَد [ṭirad] طَرِد [ṭarid] *vn:* اِنطِرَد [ʔinṭirad] *p:* I nearly kicked him out of the house. تَقرِيباً طِرَدتَه مِن البَيت [taqri:ban ṭiradtah min ʔilbayt]

kicks • 1. وَنسَة [wansa] What do you do for kicks around here? شِتسَوِّي لِلوَنسَة بِهالمَنطَقَة؟ [šitsawwi lilwansa bhalmanṭaqa?]

kid • **1.** جَدي [ǰady] جِديان [ǰidya:n] *pl:* The goat had two kids. المَعزَة عِدها جَديَين [ʔilmaʕza ʕidha ǰadyayn] • **2.** وَلَد [walad] وُلِد، وِلِد، أولاد [wulid, wilid, ʔawla:d] *pl:* طِفِل [ṭifil] أطفال [ʔaṭfa:l] *pl:* جاهِل [ǰa:hil] جَهَلَة [ǰahala] *pl:* We'll feed the kids first. نطَعُّم الوِلِد قَبُل [nṭaʕʕum ʔilwilid gabul] Don't act like a kid! لا تِتصَرَّف مِثل الأطفال [la: titṣarraf miθl ʔilʔaṭfa:l] • **3.** جِلِد مَعَز [ǰilid maʕaz] I bought some kid gloves. اِشتِرَيت كفُوف جِلِد مَعَز [ʔištiraytčfu:f ǰilid maʕaz]

*** You have to handle her with kid gloves.**

• **1.** لازِم تعامِلها برِقَّة [la:zim tʕa:milha briqqa]

to kid • **1.** تشاقَى [tša:qa:] تَشاقِي [taša:qi] *vn: sv* a. مِزَح [mizaħ] مَزِح [maziħ] *vn: sv* a. تمازَح [tma:zaħ] مَزِح [maziħ] *vn: sv* a. I'm only kidding. آنِي دَأتشاقَى [ʔa:ni daʔatša:qa:]

to kidnap • **1.** خِطَف [xiṭaf] خَطُف [xaṭuf] *vn:* اِنخِطَف [ʔinxiṭaf] *p:* He kidnapped his sweetheart from her family. خِطَف حَبِيبتَه مِن أهِلها [xiṭaf ħabi:btah min ʔahilha]

kidney • **1.** كِليَة [kilya] كِليات [kilya:t] *pl:* He's having trouble with his kidneys. كِلياتَه توَجعَه [kilya:tah tu:ǰʕah] • **2.** كِلوَة [čilwa] كِلوات، كَلاوِي [čilwa:t, čala:wi] *pl:* We have kidneys for supper. عِدنا كَلاوِي لِلعَشا اليُوم [ʕidna čala:wi lilʕaša ʔilyu:m]

kill • **1.** قَتِل [qatil] The wolves closed in on the sheep for the kill. الذِّياب طُبقَوا عالخَرُوف لقَتلَه [ʔiððiya:b ṭubgaw ʕalxaru:f liqatlah] • **2.** فَرِيسَة [fari:sa] فَرِيسات، فَرايِس [fari:sa:t, fara:yis] *pl:* The lion returned to its kill the next day. الأسَد رِجَع لِفَرِيستَه بِاليُوم الثّانِي [ʔilʔasad rijaʕ lifari:stah bilyu:m ʔiθθa:ni]

to kill • **1.** قِتَل [kital, qital] قَتِل [katil, qatil] *vn:* اِنقِتَل [ʔinkital, ʔinqital] *p:* Be careful with that car, or you'll kill some-body. دِير بالَك مِن هَالسَّيّارَة، لا ترُوح تُقتُل أحَّد [di:r ba:lak min hassayya:ra, la: tru:ħ tuktul ʔaħħad] Her son was killed in action. اِبِنها اِنقِتَل بِالمَعرَكَة [ʔibinha ʔinkital bilmaʕraka] • **2.** طَفَّى [ṭaffa:] تَطفِيَة [taṭfiya] *vn: sv* i. Be careful, or you'll kill the engine. دِير بالَك، لا ترُوح تطَفِّي المَكِينَة [di:r ba:lak, la: tru:ħ ṭṭaffi ʔilmaki:na] • **3.** قِضَى عَلَى [qiđa: ʕala] قَضِي عَلَى [qađy ʕala] *vn:* اِنقِضَى عَلَى [ʔinqiđa: ʕala] *p:* I'll give you something to kill the pain. أنطِيك دُوا حَتَّى يِقضِي عالألَم [ʔanṭi:k duwa ħatta yiqđi ʕalʔalam] • **4.** قِتَل [kital] قَتِل [katil] *vn: sv* i. ضَيَّع [đayyaʕ] تضِيِّع [tđiyyiʕ] *vn: sv* i. We played cards to kill time. لِعَبنا وَرَق حَتَّى نُقتُل وَقِت [lʕabna waraq ħatta nuktu wakit]

*** I killed two birds with one stone.**

• **1.** ضرَبِت عَصفُورَين بحَجَر واحِد [đrabit ʕaṣfu:rayn bħaǰar wa:ħid]

killer • **1.** قاتِل [qa:til] قَتَلَة [qatala] قاتِلِين [qa:tili:n] *pl:* The killer escaped. القاتِل هِرَب [ʔilqa:til hirab]

killing • **1.** قَتِل [qatil] We're trying to stop this useless killing. نحاوِل نوَقُّف هَذا القَتِل اللِّي ما بِيه نَتِيجَة [nħa:wil nwagguf ha:ða ʔilqatil ʔilli ma: bi:h nati:ǰa]

kilogram • **1.** كِيلُو [ki:lu] كِيلُوات [ki:luwa:t] *pl:* Give me three kilograms of sugar, please. إنطِينِي ثلاث كِيلُوات شَكَر، مِن فَضلَك [ʔinṭi:ni tlaθ kiluwa:t šakar, min fađlak]

kilometer • **1.** كِيلُو مَتِر [ki:lu matir] كِيلُو مَترات [ki:lu: matra:t] *pl:* Our car does more than a hundred kilometers an hour. سَيّارَتنا تطَلِّع أكثَر مِن مِيَّة كِيلُومَتِر بِالسّاعَة [sayya:ratna ṭṭalliʕ ʔakθar min miyyat ki:lumatir bissa:ʕa]

kind • **1.** نوع [nawʕ, nu:ʕ] أنواع [ʔanwa:ʕ] *pl:* جِنِس [ǰinis] أجناس [ʔaǰna:s] *pl:* This building is the only one of its kind. هاي البِنايَة هِيَّ الوَحِيدَة مِن نَوعها [ha:y ʔilbina:ya hiyya ʔilwaħi:da min nuwʕha] We have only two kinds of coffee. عِدنا نَوعَين بَسّ مِن القَهوَة [ʕidna nawʕayn bass min ʔilgahwa] What kind of car is that? شِنُو نُوع هَالسَّيّارَة؟ [šinu nu:ʕ hassayya:ra?] • **2.** لَطِيف [laṭi:f] لَطِيفِين [laṭi:fi:n] *pl:* She is a very kind person. هِيَّ شَخصِيَّة لَطِيفَة [hiyya šaxṣiyya laṭi:fa] That was a kind thing to do. هَذا كان شِي لَطِيف أن تسَوِّي [ha:ða ča:n ši laṭi:f ʔan tsawwi]

*** Would you be so kind as to mail this letter for me?**

• **1.** إذا تِسمَح تدِزّ هَذا المَكتُوب بِالبَرِيد [ʔiða: tismaħ tdizz ha:ða ʔilmaktu:b bilbari:d]

kind of • **1.** بنَوع مِن [bnawʕ min] I felt kind of sorry for him. شِعَرِت بنَوع مِن الأسَف اِتِّجاهَه [šiʕarit bnawʕ min ʔilʔasaf ʔittiǰa:hah]

kindergarten • **1.** رَوضَة أطفال [rawđat ʔaṭfa:l]

to kindle • **1.** شِعَل [šiʕal] شَعِل [šaʕil] *vn:* اِنشِعَل [ʔinšiʕal] *p:* Were you able to kindle a fire? قِدَرت تِشعِل النّار؟ [gidarit tišʕil ʔinna:r?]

kindling • **1.** عُودَة [ʕu:da] عُودات، عُوَد [ʕu:da:t, ʕuwad] *pl:* We could not find kindling to start a fire. ما قِدَرنا نِلقِي عُوَد نِشعِل بِيها نار [ma: gidarna nilgi ʕuwad nišʕil bi:ha na:r]

kindly • **1.** شَفُوق [šufu:q] Her grandmother is a kindly old lady. جِدِّيتها مرَيَّة شَفُوقَة [ǰiddiyatha mrayya šafu:qa] • **2.** بلُطُف [bluṭuf] She received us kindly. اِستَقبِلَتنا بِلُطُف [ʔistaqbilatna biluṭuf] • **3.** رَجاءاً [raǰa:ʔan] مِن فَضلَك [min fađlak] Kindly stop when your time is up. رَجاءاً أُوقَف مِن يِنتِهِي الوَقِت [raǰa:ʔan ʔu:gaf min yintihi ʔilwakit] Kindly mind your own business! مِن فَضلَك، لا تِتدَخَّل [min fađlak, la: tiddaxxal]

kindness • **1.** فَضِل [fađil] أفضال [ʔafđa:l] *pl:* لُطُف [luṭuf] ألطاف [ʔalṭa:f] *pl:* I appreciate your kindness. أقَدِّر فَضلَك [ʔaqaddir fađlak]

king • **1.** مَلِك [malik] مُلُوك [mulu:k] *pl:* مَلِكَة، مَلِكات [malika, malika:t] *Feminine:* Their king died two weeks ago. مَلِكهُم مات مِن مُدَّة إسبُوعَين [malikhum ma:t min

K

muddat ʔisbuːʕayn] • **2.** شايِب [šaːyib] شِيّاب [šiyyaːb] *pl:* I've got three kings. عِندِي ثلاث شِيّاب [ʕindi tlaθ šiyyaːb]

kingdom • **1.** مَملَكَة [mamlaka] مَمالِك [mamaːlik] *pl:* The kingdom of Jordan was created after the First World War. مَملَكَة الأردُن تأسِّسَت بَعَد الحَرب العالَمِيَّة الأولَى [mamlakat ʔilʔurdun tʔassisat baʕad ʔilħarb ʔilʕaːlamiyya ʔilʔuːla]

kinship • **1.** قَرابَة [qaraːba, garaːba] Kinship ties are very important among the Arabs. صِلَة القَرابَة مُهِمَّة جِدّاً عِند العَرَب [ṣilat ʔilqaraːba muhimma ǰiddan ʕind ʔilʕarab]

Kirkuk • **1.** كَركُوك [karkuːk]

kiss • **1.** بَوسَة [bawsa] بَوسات [bawsaːt] *pl:* قُبلَة [qubla] قُبلات [qublaːt] *pl:* Give me a kiss. إنطِينِي بُوسَة [ʔinṭiːni buːsa]

to kiss • **1.** باس [baːs] بَوس [baws] *vn:* اِنباس [ʔinbaːs] *p:* He kissed him on both checks. باسَه مِن خدُودَه [baːsah min xduːdah]

kitchen • **1.** مَطبَخ [maṭbax, muṭbax] مَطابِخ [maṭaːbix] *pl:* Do you mind if we eat in the kitchen? عِندَك مانِع إذا ناكُل بالمَطبَخ؟ [ʕindak maːniʕ ʔiða naːkul bilmaṭbax?]

kitchenware • **1.** أدَوات طَبُخ [ʔadawaːt ṭabux] This store sells kitchenware. هَذا المَخزَن يبِيع أدَوات طَبُخ [haːða ʔilmaxzan yibiːʕ ʔadawaːt ṭabux]

kite • **1.** طَيّارَة [ṭiyyaːra] طَيّارات [ṭiyyaːraːt] *pl:* The boys are out flying kites. الوِلِد دَيطَيِّرُون طَيّارات [ʔilwilid dayṭayyiruːn ṭayyaːraːt]

*** Aw, go fly a kite!** • **1.** رُوح دَوُّرلَك شَغلَة [ruːħ dawwurlak šaɣla]

kitten • **1.** فَرِخ بَزُّونَة [farix bazzuːna] فرُوخ بَزُّونَة [fruːx bazzuːna] *pl:* Our cat has some little kittens. بَزُّونَتنا عِدها فرُوخ صغار [bazzuːnatna ʕidha fruːx ṣɣaːr]

knack • **1.** مَهارَة [mahaːra] He has a knack for photography. عِندَه مَهارَة أخذ التَّصاوِير [ʕindah mahaːra ʔaxð ʔittaṣaːwiːr] • **2.** سِرّ [sirr] أسرار [ʔasraːr] *pl:*

knapsack • **1.** حَقِيبَة [ħaqiːba] حَقائِب [ħaqaːʔib] *pl:* The boy scouts carried their food in knapsacks. الكَشّافَة حِملَوا أكِلهُم بِحَقائِب عَلَى ظَهَرهُم [ʔilkaššaːfa ħimlaw ʔakilhum biħaqaːʔib ʕala ðaharhum]

to knead • **1.** عِجَن [ʕiǰan] عَجِن [ʕaǰin] *vn:* اِنعِجَن [ʔinʕiǰan] *p:* You have to knead the dough thoroughly. لازِم تِعجِن العَجِين زين [laːzim tiʕǰin ʔilʕaǰiːn ziːn]

knee • **1.** رُكبات [rukbaːt] رُكبات [rukbaːt] رُكَب [rukab, rikab] *pl:* رِكَب [rikab] My knee hurts. رُكُبتِي تُوجَعنِي [rukubti tuːǰaʕni]

kneecap • **1.** صابُونَة رِجِل [ṣaːbuːna riǰil] صابُونات رِجِل [ṣaːbuːnaːt riǰil] *pl:*

kneel • **1.** بُرَك [burak] بَرُك [baruk] *vn:* *sv* u. The camel knelt while they tied the load on. الجِّمَل بُرَك لَمّا كانَوا يشِدُّون الحِمِل عَليه [ʔiǰǰimal burak lamma čaːnaw yšidduːn ʔilħimil ʕaliːh] • **2.** ثِنَى رُكبَة [θinaː rukba] ثَنِي [θany] *vn:* *sv* i. The soldiers knelt and fired. الجِّنُود ثِنَوا رُكباتهُم وَأطلَقوا النّار [ʔiǰǰinuːd θinaw rukbaːthum waʔaṭlaqaw ʔinnaːr]

knife • **1.** سِكِّين [siččiːn] سِكاكِين [sičaːčiːn] *pl:* He cut himself with a knife. جِرَح نَفسَه بِالسِّكِّين [ǰirah nafsah bissiččiːn]

knight • **1.** فَرَس [faras] أفراس، فرُوسَة [ʔafraːs, fruːsap] *pl:* I'll take the pawn with the knight. راح آخُذ الجُّندِي بِالفَرَس [raːħ ʔaːxuð ʔiǰǰundi bilfaras]

to knit • **1.** حاك [ħaːk, ħaːč] حَوك، حِياكَة [ħuːk, ħiyaːka] *vn:* إنحاك [ʔinħaːk] *p:* Did you knit these gloves. Mary? حِكتِي الكفُوف، مَريَم؟ [ħikti ʔiččifuːf, maryam?] • **2.** ثِنَى رُكبَة [liħam] اِلتِحام [ʔiltiħaːm] *vn:* *sv* a. اِلتِحَم [ʔiltiħam] اِلتِحام [ʔiltiħaːm] *vn:* *sv* i. It took a long time for the bone to knit. العَظُم أخَذ وَقِت هوايَة حَتَّى لِحَم [ʔilʕaðum ʔaxað wakit hwaːya ħatta liħam]

knitting • **1.** حِياكَة [ħiyaːka] Did you notice where she left her knitting? شِفِت وِين خَلَّت حياكَتها؟ [šifit wiːn xallat ħyaːkatha?]

knob • **1.** زِرّ [zirr] زرار، زرُور [zraːr, zruːr] *pl:* دُقمَة [dugma] دُقَم، دِقَم [dugam, digam] *pl:* The maid broke one of the knobs off the radio. الخادمَة كِسرَت واحِد مِن زرار الرّادِيُو [ʔilxaːdma kisrat waːħid min zraːr ʔirraːdyu] • **2.** يَدَّة [yadda] يَدّات [yaddaː *pl:* The door knob still has to be polished. يَدَّة الباب يِنرادِلها تَلمِيع [yaddat ʔilbaːb yinraːdilha talmiːʕ]

knock • **1.** دَقّ [dagg] Did you hear the knock at the door? سِمَعِت الدَّقّ عَالباب؟ [simaʕit ʔiddagg ʕalbaːb?]

*** Can you find the knock in the engine?** • **1.** تِقدَر تشُوف لَيش المَكِينَة تدُقّ؟ [tigdar tšuːf liːš ʔilmakiːna tdugg?]

to knock • **1.** دَقّ [dagg] دَقّ [dagg] *vn:* *sv* u. Someone's knocking at the door. واحِد دَيدُقّ عَالباب [waːħid daydugg ʕalbaːb] Please knock before you come in. مِن فَضلَك، دُقّ الباب قَبُل ما تِدخُل [min faðlak, dugg ʔilbaːb gabul maː tidxul] When I drive uphill the engine knocks. مِن أصعَد عَالتَّل، المَكِينَة تدُقّ [min ʔaṣʕad ʕattall, ʔilmakiːna ddugg] • **2.** اِنتِقَد [ʔintiqad] اِنتِقاد

[ʔintiqa:d] *vn: sv* i. حَكِي عَلَى [ħiča: ʕala] حِكَى عَلَى [ħači ʕala] *vn: sv* i. He's always knocking American capitalism. هَذا دائِماً يِنتقِد الرّاسمالِيَّة الأَمَيرِكِيَّة [ha:ða da:ʔiman yintiqid ʔirra:sma:liyya ʔilʔamri:kiyya] • **3.** وَقَّع [waggaʕ] تَوقِيع [tawgi:ʕ] *vn:* توَقَّع [twaggaʕ] *p:* I knocked the knife out of his hand. وَقَّعِت السِّكِّينَة مِن إِيدَه [waggaʕit ʔissičči:na min ʔi:dah]

to knock around • **1.** دار [da:r] دَوَران [dawara:n] *vn: sv* u. He's knocked around all over the world. هُوَّ دايِر الدِّنيا كُلّها [huwwa da:yir ʔiddinya kullha]

*** She's been knocked around a lot.**
• **1.** شافَت صُعُوبات هوايَة بحَياتها [ša:fat ṣuʕu:ba:t hwa:ya bħaya:tha]

to knock down • **1.** وَقَّع [waggaʕ] تَوقِيع [tawgi:ʕ] *vn:* اِتدَمَّر [twaggaʕ] *p:* He knocked him down with his fist. وَقَّعَه بِضَربَة جَمعَة [waggaʕah bðarbat ǰamʕa] Be careful not to knock anything down. دِير بالَك لا توَقِّع شِي [di:r ba:lak la: twaggiʕ ši]

to knock off • **1.** وَقَّع [waggaʕ] تَوقِيع [tawgi:ʕ] *vn:* توَقَّع [twaggaʕ] *p:* طَيَّر [ṭayyar] تَطيِير [taṭyi:r] *vn:* تطَيَّر [tṭayyar] *p:* He nearly knocked my hat off of my head. تَقرِيباً وَقَّع الشَّفقَة مِن راسِي [taqri:ban waggaʕ ʔiššafqa min ra:si] • **2.** خِصَم [xiṣam] خَصُم [xaṣum] *vn: sv* i. نَزَّل [nazzal] تَنزِيل [tanzi:l] *vn: sv* i. He knocked off ten dinars from the bill. خِصَم عَشِر دَنانِير مِن القائِمَة [xiṣam ʕašir dana:ni:r min ʔilqa:ʔima] • **3.** خَلَّص [xallaṣ] تَخلِيص [taxli:ṣ] *vn:* تخَلَّص [txallaṣ] *p:* We knocked off work at 6 o'clock. خَلَّصنا الشُّغُل ساعَة سِتَّة [xallaṣna ʔiššuɣul sa:ʕa sitta]

*** I'll knock your block off!** • **1.** أَضُربَك ضَربَة تِكسِر راسَك [ʔaðurbak ðarba tiksir ra:sak]

*** All right, knock it off!** • **1.** زَين هَسَّة، بَطّلُوا [zayn hassa, baṭṭlu:] زِين هَسَّة، بَسّ عاد [zi:n hassa, bass ʕa:d]

to knock out • **1.** دَمَّر [dammar] تَدمِير [tadmi:r] *vn:* اِتدَمَّر [ʔiddammar] *p:* The bomb knocked out the radio station. القُمبُلَة دَمُّرَت مَحَطَّة الإِذاعَة [ʔilqumbula dammurat maħaṭṭat ʔalʔiða:ʕa] • **2.** قِضَى عَلَى [qiða:, giða: ʕala] *sv* i. He hit him hard and knocked him out. ضِرَبَه ضَربَة قَوِيَّة وَقِضَى عَليه [ðirabah ðarba qawiyya wqiða: ʕali:h]

to knock over • **1.** قِلَب [gilab] قَلُب [galub] *vn:* اِنقِلَب [ʔingilab] *p:* Who knocked the pail over? مِنُو قِلَب السَّطِل؟ [minu gilab ʔissaṭil?] • **2.** وَقَّع [waggaʕ] تَوقِيع [tawgi:ʕ] *vn:* توَقَّع [twaggaʕ] *p:* You almost knocked me over. تَقرِيباً وَقَّعِتنِي [taqri:ban waggaʕitni]

knocker • **1.** دَقّاقَة [dagga:ga] دَقّاقات [dagga:ga:t] *pl:* The knocker on our door needs fixing. دَقّاقَة بابنا يِنرادِلها تَصلِيح [dagga:gat ba:bna yinra:dilha taṣli:ħ]

knot • **1.** عُقدَة [ʕugda] عُقَد [ʕugad] *pl:* Can you untie this knot? تِقدَر تفُكّ هاي العُقدَة؟ [tigdar tfukk ha:y ʔilʕugda?] The board is full of knots. اللَّوحَة مَليانَة عُقَد [ʔillawħa malya:na ʕugad] • **2.** بَوصَة [bawsa, bu:ṣa] بَوصات [bawṣa:t] *pl:* The ship's speed is fifteen knots. السَّفِينَة سُرعَتها خُمسطَعَش عُقدَة [ʔissafi:na surʕatha xumusṭaʕaš ʕuqda]

to knot • **1.** عِقَد [ʕigad] عَقِد [ʕagid] *vn:* اِنعِقَد [ʔinʕigad] *p:* Shall I knot the string? ترِيد أَعقُد الخيط؟ [tri:d ʔaʕgud ʔilxi:ṭ?] • **2.** شَدّ [šadd] شَدّ [šadd] *vn:* اِنشَدّ [ʔinšadd] *p:* عِقَد [ʕiqad] عَقِد [ʕaqid] *vn:* اِنعِقَد [ʔinʕiqad] *p:* You have to knot the two ends together. لازِم تشِدّ الطَّرَفَين سُوَة [la:zim tšidd ʔiṭṭarafayn suwa]

knotted • **1.** معَقَّد [mʕaggad] The string is all knotted. الخَيط كُلّه معَقَّد [ʔilxayṭ kullah mʕaggad] The string is all knotted. الخَيط كُلّه عُقَد [ʔilxi:ṭ kullah ʕugad] • **2.** مشَنَّج [mšannaǰ] The calf muscle in my leg is all knotted up. باجَة رِجلِي مشَنِّجَة [pa:čat rijli mšanniǰa]

knotty • **1.** صَعُب [ṣaʕub] عَوِيص [ʕawi:ṣ] That's a knotty problem. هَذِي مُشكِلَة صَعبَة [ha:ði muškila ṣaʕba]

to know • **1.** عِرَف [ʕiraf] مَعرِفَة [maʕrifa] *vn:* اِنعِرَف [ʔinʕiraf] *p:* Do you know his address? تُعرُف عِنوانَه؟ [tuʕruf ʕinwa:nah?] Do you know Arabic? تُعرُف عَرَبِي؟ [tuʕruf ʕarabi?] I don't know how to drive a car. ما أَعرُف أَسُوق سَيّارَة [ma: ʔaʕruf ʔasu:q sayya:ra] Do you know anything about farming? تُعرُف شِي عَن الزِّراعَة؟ [tuʕruf ši ʕan ʔizzira:ʕa?] • **2.** دِرَى [dira:] دَرِي، درايَة [dary, dra:ya] *vn:* اِندِرَى [ʔindira:] *p:* عِرَف [ʕiraf] عَرِف [ʕarif] *vn:* اِنعِرَف [ʔinʕiraf] *p:* I know he's ill. أَدرِي هُوَّ مَرِيض [ʔadri huwwa mari:ð]

to let someone know • **1.** خَبَّر [xabbar] إِخبار [ʔixba:r] *vn: sv* u. I'll let you know tomorrow. أَخَبّرَك باكِر [ʔaxabbrak ba:čir]

well-known • **1.** مَشهُور [mašhu:r] مَعرُوف [maʕru:f] He's a well-known author. هُوَّ مُؤَلِّف مَشهُور [huwwa muʔallif mašhu:r]

know-how • **1.** مَعرِفَة [maʕrifa] مَعارِف [maʕa:rif] *pl:* خِبرَة [xibra] خِبرات، خِبَر [xibra:t, xibar] *pl:* He hasn't the kind of know-how that would qualify him for this job. ما عِندَه المَعرِفَة الكافيَة حَتَّى تأَهِّلَه لِهاي الشَّغلَة [ma: ʕindah ʔilmaʕrifa ʔilka:fiya ħatta tʔahhilah lha:y ʔiššaɣla]

knowingly • **1.** عَن قَصِد [ʕan qaṣid] He wouldn't knowingly cheat us. ما يِخدَعنا عَن قَصِد [ma: yixdaʕna ʕan qaṣid]

*** She looked at him knowingly.**
• **1.** نِظرَتلَه نَظرَة بِيها مَعنَى [niðratlah naðra bi:ha maʕna]

knowledge • **1.** مَعرِفَة [maʕrifa] مَعارِف [maʕa:rif] *pl:* عِلِم [ʕilim] His knowledge of Arabic is poor. مَعرِفتَه بِالعَرَبِي قَلِيلَة [maʕriftah bilʕarabi qali:la] To my knowledge he's not there. حَسَب عِلمِي هُوَّ مُو هناك [ħasab ʕilmi huwwa mu: hna:k]

*** He likes to display his knowledge.**
• **1.** يحِبّ يراوِي نَفسَه فاهِم [yħibb yraːwi nafsah faːhim]
*** Answer to the best of your knowledge.**
• **1.** جاوُب شقَدّ ما تُعرُف [ǰaːwub šgadd maː tuʕruf]

knowledgeable • **1.** • He's quite knowledgeable on Iraqi history. مَعرِفتَه واسِعَة بِتارِيخ العِراق [maʕriftah waːsʕa bitaːriːx ʔilʕiraːq]

known • **1.** مَعرُوف [maʕruːf] That's a known fact. هاي حَقِيقَة مَعرُوفَة [haːy ħaqiːqa maʕruːfa]

knuckle • **1.** مَفصَل [mafṣal] مَفاصِل [mafaːṣil] *pl:* I skinned the knuckles of my right hand. جِلَخِت مَفصَل إيدِي اليِمنَى [ǰilaxit mafṣal ʔiːdi ʔilyimna]

*** He sat in the coffee shop cracking his knuckles.** • **1.** قِعَد بِالقَهوَة يطِقّ بِأَصابعَه [giʕad bilgahwa yṭigg biʔaṣaːbʕah]
*** You'd better knuckle down and work.**
• **1.** أَحسَنلَك لَو تِبدِي تِشتُغُل [ʔaħsanlak law tibdi tištuɣul]

kohl • **1.** كُحُل [kuħul]

Kurd • **1.** كُردِي [kurdi] أكراد [ʔakraːd] *pl:* Most of the Kurds are Muslims. مُعظَم الأكراد مُسلِمِين [muʕðam ʔilʔakraːd muslimiːn]

Kuwait • **1.** الكُويت [ʔilkuwayt, ʔilkuwiːt]

K

L

label • **1.** عَلامَة [ʕala:ma] عَلامات، عَلائِم [ʕala:ma:t, ʕala:ʔim] *pl:* مارگة [ma:rka] ماركات [ma:rka:t] *pl:* لَيبِل [laybil] ليبِلات [laybila:t] *pl:* There's no label on this bottle. ماكُو عَلامَة عَلَى هالبُطِل [ma:ku ʕala:ma ʕala halbuṭul]

to label • **1.** عَلَّم [ʕallam] تعلِّم [tʕillim] *vn: sv* i. Please label those jars for me. مِن فَضلَك عَلِّملِي هَالشِّيَش [min faðlak ʕallimli haššiyaš]

labor • **1.** شُغُل [šuɣul] أشغال [ʔašɣa:l] *pl:* عَمَل [ʕamal] عَملَة [ʕamla] *Feminine:* Labor alone will cost three hundred dinars. الشُّغُل وَحدَه يكَلِّف ثلث مِيَّة دِينار [ʔiššuɣul waḥdah ykallif tlaθ miyyat dina:r] He was sentenced to five years at hard labor. اِنحِكَم عَليه خَمِس سَنَوات بِالأَشغال الشّاقَة [ʔinḥikam ʕali:h xamis sanawa:t bilʔašɣa:l ʔišša:qa] • **2.** كَدّ [kadd] مَجهُود [majhu:d] مَجهُودات [majhu:da:t] *pl:* This task involves a great deal of labor and perseverance. هَالشَّغلَة تِحتاج إِلَى كَدّ وَمُثابَرَة [haššaɣla tiḥta:j ʔila kadd wamuθa:bara] All our labor has been in vain. كُلّ مَجهُودنا ضاع [kull majhu:dna ða:ʕ] • **3.** عامِل [ʕa:mil] عَوامِل، عُمّال [ʕawa:mil, ʕumma:l] *pl:* Labor will never agree to that proposal. العُمّال أَبَداً ما يوافقُون عَلَى هَالإِقتِراح [ʔilʕumma:l ʔabadan ma: ywa:fqu:n ʕala halʔiqtira:ḥ]

to be in labor • **1.** طِلَق [ṭilag] طَلِق [ṭalig] *vn: sv* a. She was in labor nine hours. ظَلَّت تِطلَق تِسِع ساعات [ðallat tiṭlag tisiʕ sa:ʕa:t]

laboratory • **1.** مُختَبَر [muxtabar] مُختَبَرات [muxtabara:t] *pl:*

laborer • **1.** عامِل [ʕa:mil] عَوامِل، عُمّال [ʕawa:mil, ʕumma:l] *pl:*

lace • **1.** دانتَيل [danti:l] I'd like five meters of that lace. أَرِيد خَمِس أَمتار مِن هَالدّانتَيل [ʔari:d xamis ʔamta:r min haddanti:l] • **2.** قِيطان [qi:ṭa:n] قياطِين [qya:ṭi:n] *pl:* I need a pair of shoe laces. أَحتاج زوج قِيطان لقُندَرتِي [ʔaḥta:j zu:j qi:ṭa:n lqundarti]

to lace • **1.** رَكَّب قِياطِين [rakkab qiya:ṭi:n] *sv* u. Wait till I lace my shoes. اِنتِظِر إِلَى أَن أَرَكُّب القِياطِين مال قُندَرتِي [ʔintiðir ʔila ʔan ʔarakkub ʔilqiya:ṭi:n ma:l qundarti]

lack • **1.** نَقِص [naqiṣ] There's a lack of experts. أَكُو نَقِص بِالخُبَراء [ʔaku naqiṣ bilxubara:ʔ] • **2.** عَدَم [ʕadam] He was acquitted for lack of evidence. فِرجَوا عَنَّه لعَدَم وُجُود أَدِلَّة [firjaw ʕannah lʕadam wuju:d ʔadilla] He was acquitted for lack of evidence. أَطلِقَوا سَراحَه لعَدَم الأَدِلَّة [ʔaṭliqaw sara:ḥah lʕadam ʔilʔadilla] For lack of anything else to do I went to the movies. رِحِت لِلسِّينَما لعَدَم وُجُود أَيّ شِي لاخ أَسَوِّيه [riḥit lissinama lʕadam wuju:d ʔayy ši la:x ʔasawwi:h]

to lack • **1.** نِقَص [nigaṣ, niqaṣ] نُقصان [nuqṣa:n] *vn: sv* u. عاز [ʕa:z] عَوز [ʕawz] *vn: sv* u. Many conveniences are lacking in this hotel. هَالفِندِق تِنُقصَه هوايَة وَسائِل راحَة [halfindiq tinuqṣah hwa:ya wasa:ʔil ra:ḥa] I didn't lack anything there. ما عازنِي شِي هناك [ma: ʕa:zni ši hna:k]

lad • **1.** وَلَد [walad] وُلِد، وِلِد، أَولاد [wulid, wilid, ʔawla:d] *pl:* صَبِيّ [ṣabiyy, ṣabi] صِبيان [ṣibya:n] *pl:*

ladder • **1.** دَرَج [daraj] دَرَجات [daraja:t] *pl:*

ladle • **1.** جَمچَة [čamča] جَمچات [čamča:t] *pl:*

lady • **1.** مرَيَّة [mrayya] مرَيّات [mrayya:t] *pl:* مَرَة [mara] حُرمَة [ḥurma] Is that lady his mother? هَالمرَيَّة أُمَّه؟ [halimrayya ʔummah?] • **2.** سَيِّدَة [sayyida] سَيِّدات [sayyida:t] *pl:* Ladies and Gentlemen! سَيِّداتِي وسادَتِي [sayyida:ti wsa:dati] Where's the ladies' room? وِين غُرفَة السَّيِّدات؟ [wi:n ɣurfat ʔissayyida:t?]

*** We've never had a lady president.**

• **1.** مَصارَت عِدنا رَئِيسَة أَبَداً [maṣa:rat ʕidna raʔi:sa ʔabadan]

to lag • **1.** تأَخَّر [tʔaxxar] تَأَخُّر [taʔaxxur] *vn: sv* a. تخَلَّف [txallaf] تَخَلُّف [taxalluf] *vn: sv* a. He's always lagging behind the others. دائِماً مِتأَخِّر عَن البَقِيَّة [da:ʔiman mitʔaxxir ʕan ʔilbaqiyya]

lake • **1.** بُحَيرَة [buḥayra] بُحَيرات [buḥayra:t] *pl:* We went bathing in the lake. رِحنا نِسبَح بالبُحَيرَة [riḥna nisbaḥ bilbuḥayra]

lamb • **1.** طِلِي [ṭili] طِليان [ṭilya:n] *pl:* Our ewe gave birth to a lamb yesterday. نَعجَتنا جابَت طِلِي البارحَة [naʕjatna ja:bat ṭili ʔilba:rḥa] • **2.** لَحَم غَنَم [laḥam ɣanam] Beef is cheaper than lamb. لَحم الهُوش أَرخَص مِن لَحم الغَنَم [laḥm ʔilhu:š ʔarxaṣ min laḥm ʔilɣanam] • **3.** قُوزِي [qu:zi] قوازِي [qwa:zi] *pl:* Bring me a dish of lamb and rice. جِيبلِي ماعُون قُوزِي عَلَى تِمَّن [ji:bli ma:ʕu:n qu:zi ʕala timman]

lame • **1.** أَعرَج [ʔaʕraj] عِرِج، عَرجِين [ʕirij, ʕarji:n] *pl:* عَرجَة [ʕarja] *Feminine:* He seems to be lame. يبَيِّن أَعرَج [yibayyin ʔaʕraj] He has a lame leg. عِندَه رِجِل عَرجَة [ʕindah rijil ʕarja] • **2.** واهِي [wa:hi] That's a lame excuse. هاي حِجَّة واهيَة [ha:y ḥijja wa:hya]

lamp • **1.** لَمبَة [lamba] لَمبات [lamba:t] *pl:*

L

lamp shade • **1.** شَمسِيَّة [šamsiyya] شَمسِيّات [šamsiyya:t] *pl:*

lance • **1.** رُمُح [rumuħ] رماح [rma:ħ] *pl:* His lance broke when he was fighting with it. اِنكِسَر الرُّمُح مِن كان يحارِب بِيه [ʔinkisar ʔirrumuħ min ča:n yħa:rib bi:h]

to lance • **1.** فِجَر [fiǰar] فَجِر [faǰir] *vn: sv* i. ضِرَب [ðirab] ضَرُب [ðarub] *vn: sv* u. The doctor lanced the boil. الطَّبِيب فِجَر الحَبّايَة [ʔiṭṭabi:b fiǰar ʔilħabba:ya]

land • **1.** أَرض [ʔarð] أَراضِي [ʔara:ði] *pl:* قاع [ga:ʕ] قِيعان [giʕa:n] *pl:* بَرّ [barr] We were glad to see land again. فِرَحنا بِشَوفَة الأَرض مَرَّة لُخ [firaħna bšawfat ʔilʔarð marra lux] • **2.** قاع [ga:ʕ] The land here is very fertile. الأَرض هنا كُلِّش خَصبَة [ʔilʔarð hna: kulliš xaṣba] • **3.** I have a lot of land near Baghdad. عِندِي أَراضِي هوايَة يَمّ بَغداد [ʕindi ʔara:ði hwa:ya yamm bayda:d]

to land • **1.** نَزَّل [nazzal] تَنزِيل [tanzi:l] *vn:* تنَزَّل [tnazzal] *p:* He had to land his plane in the desert. اِضطَرّ ينَزِّل طِيّارتَه بِالصَّحراء [ʔiðṭarr ynazzil ṭiyya:rtah biṣṣaħra:ʔ] • **2.** نِزَل [nizal] نِزُول [nizu:l] *vn: sv* i. The plane landed without trouble. الطِّيّارَة نِزلَت بِلا مَشاكِل [ʔiṭṭiyya:ra nizlat bila maša:kil] • **3.** طَلَّع [ṭallaʕ] تطِلِّع [tṭilliʕ] *vn: sv* i. I spent a quarter of an hour before I could land the fish. صرَفِت رُبع ساعَة حَتَّى قِدَرِت أَطَلِّع السِّمَك مِن المَيّ [ṣrafit rubuʕ sa:ʕa ħatta gidarit ʔaṭalliʕ ʔissimač min ʔilmayy] • **4.** اِنذَبّ [ʔinðabb] *sv* a. He landed in jail for fighting. اِنذَبّ بِالسِّجِن لِأَنّ كان يِتعارَك [ʔinðabb bissiǰin liʔann ča:n yitʕa:rak] We nearly landed in jail. رِحنا لِلحَبِس إِلّا شوَيَّة [riħna lilħabis ʔilla šwayya] • **5.** حَصَّل عَلَى [ħaṣṣal ʕala] حُصُول عَلَى [ħuṣu:l ʕala] *vn: sv* i. I landed a job after a week of interviews. حَصَّلِت عَلَى شُغُل بَعَد مُقابَلات مُدَّة إِسبُوع [ħaṣṣalit ʕala šuyul baʕad muqa:bala:t muddat ʔisbu:ʕ]

landing • **1.** نُزُول [nuzu:l] They lowered the plane's wheels preparing for the landing. نَزّلَوا چُرُوخ الطِّيّارَة اِستِعداداً لِلنُّزُول [nazzlaw čuru:x ʔiṭṭayya:ra ʔistiʕda:dan linnizu:l] • **2.** إِنزال [ʔinza:l] إِنزالات [ʔinza:la:t] *pl:* The landing took place at dawn. الإِنزال جِرَى وَقِت الفَجِر [ʔilʔinza:l ǰira: wakit ʔilfaǰir]

landlord • **1.** صاحِب مُلُك [ṣa:ħib muluk] أَصحاب مُلُك [ʔaṣħa:b muluk] *pl:*

landmark • **1.** عَلامَة مُمَيِّزَة [ʕala:ma mumayyiza] * The monument is a landmark in this area. النُّصُب فَدّ عَلامَة مُمَيِّزَة بِهَالمَنطَقَة [ʔinnaṣub fadd ʕala:ma mumayyiza bhalmanṭaqa]

landowner • **1.** صاحِب مُلُك [ṣa:ħib muluk] أَصحاب أَملاك [ʔaṣħa:b ʔamla:k] *pl:* The big landowners are usually conservatives. كِبار أَصحاب الأَملاك عادَةً مُحافِظِين [kiba:r ʔaṣħa:b ʔilʔamla:k ʕa:datan muħa:fiði:n]

landslide • **1.** إِنهِيار [ʔinhiya:r] إِنهِيارات [ʔinhiya:ra:t] *pl:* The road through the mountains was blocked by a landslide. طَرِيق الجِّبَل كان مَسدُود بِسَبَب اِنهِيار [ṭari:q ʔiǰǰibal ča:n masdu:d bisabab ʔinhiya:r] • **2.** أَغلَبِيَّة ساحِقَة [ʔaylabiyya sa:ħiqa] He won the election by a landslide. فاز بالإِنتِخاب بِأَغلَبِيَّة ساحِقَة [fa:z bilʔintixa:b biʔaylabiyya sa:ħiqa]

lane • **1.** دَرُب [darub] درُوب [dru:b] *pl:* Follow this lane to the main road. إِتبَع هَالدَّرُب إِلَى الطَّرِيق الرَّئِيسِي [ʔitbaʕ haddarub ʔila ʔiṭṭari:q ʔirraʔi:si]

language • **1.** لُغَة [luya] لُغات [luya:t] *pl:* He knows several languages. يُعرُف عِدَّة لُغات [yuʕruf ʕiddat luya:t] • **2.** لَهجَة [lahǰa] He used strong language in dealing with them. اِستَعمَل لَهجَة شَدِيدَة بمُعامَلتَه وِيّاهُم [ʔistaʕmal lahǰa šadi:da bmuʕa:maltah wiyya:hum]

lantern • **1.** فانُوس [fa:nu:s] فوانِيس [fwa:ni:s] *pl:* Walk in front of me with the lantern so I can see the path. إِمشِي بِالفانُوس قِدّامِي حَتَّى أَشُوف الطَّرِيق [ʔimši bilfa:nu:s gidda:mi ħatta ʔašu:f ʔiṭṭari:q] • **2.** لُوكس [lu:ks] I need a new mantle for my coleman lantern. أَحتاج فَتِيلَة جِدِيدَة لِلُّوكس مالِي [ʔaħta:ǰ fati:la ǰidi:da lillu:ks ma:li]

lap • **1.** حُضُن [ħuðun] أَحضان [ʔaħða:n] *pl:* حِجِر [ħiǰir] She put the baby in her lap. حَطَّت الطِّفِل بِحُضِنها [ħaṭṭat ʔiṭṭifil biħuðinha] • **2.** دَورَة [dawra] دَورات [dawra:t] *pl:* فَرَّة [farra] فَرّات [farra:t] *pl:* He was in the lead by five yards in the first lap. كان بِالمُقَدِّمَة خَمس أَمتار بِالدَّورَة الأُولَى [ča:n bilmuqaddima xams ʔamta:r biddawra ʔilʔu:la]

to lap • **1.** طَبَّق سُوَة [ṭubag suwa] طَبُق [ṭabug] *vn:* اِنطُبَق [ʔinṭubag] *p:* Lap the boards one over the other so the roof won't leak. أُطبُق اللَّوحات وِحدَة عالّلُخ حَتَّى السَّقُف ما يخُرّ [ʔuṭbug ʔillawħa:t wiħda ʕallux ħatta ʔissaguf ma: yxurr]

to lap up • **1.** لِطَع [liṭaʕ] لَطِع [laṭiʕ] *vn: sv* a. The cats lapped up the milk. البَزازِين لِطعَت الحَلِيب [ʔilbaza:zi:n liṭʕat ʔilħali:b]

lapel • **1.** قَلبَة [galba] ياخَة سِترَة [ya:xat sitra] ياخات سِتَر [ya:xa:t sitar] *pl:*

to lapse • **1.** بُطَل [buṭal] بُطلان [buṭla:n] *vn: sv* a. خِلَص [xilaṣ] خَلِص، خَلاص [xaliṣ, xala:ṣ] *vn: sv* a. اِنتِهَى [ʔintiha:] اِنتِهاء [ʔintiha:ʔ] *vn: sv* i. If I don't pay this premium my insurance policy will lapse. إِذا ما أَدفَع هَالقِسِط تَأمِينِي يِبطَل [ʔiða ma: ʔadfaʕ halqisiṭ taʔmi:ni yibṭal]

lard • **1.** شَحَم خَنزِير [šaħam xanzi:r]

large • **1.** چِبِير [čibi:r] كَبِير [kabi:r] واسِع [wa:siʕ] This room isn't large enough. هَالغُرفَة مُو كبِيرَة كافِي

[halɣurfa muː čbiːra kaːfi] This room isn't large enough. هَالغُرفَة كُبُرها مُو كافِي [halɣurfa kuburha muː kaːfi] The mouth of this jar is large enough for me to put my hand in. حَلِق هَالتُّنقَة ما واسِع بِحَيث أَقدَر أَفَوِّت إِيدِي بِيه [ħalig hattunga maː waːsiʕ biħayθ ʔagdar ʔafawwit ʔiːdi biːh] • **2.** كبِير [čbiːr] كَبِير [kabiːr] That's the largest table in the house. هَذا أَكبَر مَيز بالبَيت [haːða ʔakbar mayz bilbayt] He's a large importer from the Middle East. هُوَّ مُستَورِد كِبِير مِن الشَّرق الأَوسَط [huwwa mustawrid čabiːr min ʔiššarq ʔilʔawsaṭ]

at large • **1.** حُرّ [ħurr] أَحرار [ʔaħraːr] *pl:* The thief is still at large. الحَرامِي بَعدَه حُرّ [ʔilħaraːmi baʕdah ħurr]

largely • **1.** بالأَكثَر [bilʔakθar] Our company is made up largely of volunteers. فِرقَتنا مِتكَوِّنَة بِالأَكثَر مِن مُتَطَوِّعِين [firqatna mitkawwina bilʔakθar min mutaṭawwiʕiːn]

large-scale • **1.** نِطاق واسِع [niṭaːq waːsiʕ] The city is studying a large-scale building program. البَلَدِيَّة دَتِدرُس مَنهَج إِنشاء أَبنِيَة عَلَى نِطاق واسِع [ʔilbaladiyya datidrus manhaǰ ʔinšaːʔ ʔabniya ʕala niṭaːq waːsiʕ]

lark • **1.** قُمبُرَة [qumbura] قُمبُرات [qumburaːt] *pl:*

laryngitis • **1.** اِلتِهاب لِحُنجَرَة [ʔiltihaːb ʔilħunǰara]

lash • **1.** قَمجِي [qamči] قماجِي [qmaːči] *pl:* جَلدَة [ǰalda] جَلدات [ǰaldaːt] *pl:* زَوبَة [zawba, zuːba] زَوبات [zawbaːt] *pl:* They gave him forty lashes for stealing a loaf of bread. ضُربَوه أَربَعِين قَمجِي لِأَنّ باق قُرصَة خُبُز [ðurbawh ʔarbaʕiːn qamči liʔann baːg gurṣat xubuz]

last • **1.** آخِر [ʔaːxir] أَواخِر [ʔawaːxir] *pl:* She spent her last cent on that dress. صُرفَت آخِر فِلِس عِدها عَلَى هَالنَّفنُوف [ṣurfat ʔaːxir filis ʕidha ʕala hannafnuːf] She was the last to leave. هِيَّ آخِر وِحدَة تِركَت [hiyya ʔaːxir wiħda tirkat] • **2.** أَخِير [ʔaxiːr] ماضِي [maːði] Last year I was in Europe. السَّنَة الماضِيَة كِنِت بأُورُبّا [ʔissana ʔilmaːðya činit bʔuːruppa] Last year I was in Europe. العام كِنِت بأُورُبّا [ʔilʕaːm činit bʔuːruppa] • **3.** أَخِير [ʔaxiːr] The last thing he said was that he didn't want to come. أَخِير شِي قالَه كان ما يرِيد يِجِي [ʔaxiːr ši gaːlah čaːn maː yriːd yiǰi] He came in last in the race. كان الأَخِير بِالسِّباق [čaːn ʔilʔaxiːr bissibaːq] • **4.** بِالأَخِير [bilʔaxiːr] He came last. جا بِالأَخِير [ǰaː bilʔaxiːr] He came last. جا آخِر واحِد [ǰaː ʔaːxir waːħid]

at last • **1.** أَخِيراً [ʔaxiːran] Here we are at last! وُصَلنا أَخِيراً [wuṣalna ʔaxiːran]

last night • **1.** البارحَة بِاللَّيل [ʔilbaːrħa billayl] Did you sleep well last night? نِمِت زين البارحَة باللَّيل؟ [nimit ziːn ʔilbaːrħa billayl?]

last year • **1.** العامّ [ʔilʕaːmm] Last year I spent the summer in Lebanon. العام قِضَيت الصَّيف بلُبنان [ʔilʕaːm giðiːt ʔiṣṣiːf blubnaːn]

to last • **1.** دام [daːm] دَوام [dawaːm] *vn: sv* u. طَوَّل [ṭawwal] تطُوُّل، تَطوِيل [tṭuwwul, taṭwiːl] *vn: sv* i. The war lasted six years. الحَرب دامَت سِتّ سنِين [ʔilħarb daːmat sitt sniːn] I'm afraid this good weather won't last long. خايِف أَن هَالجَوّ الحِلو ما يطَوِّل هوايَة [xaːyif ʔan halǰaww ʔilħilw maː yṭawwil hwaːya] • **2.** قاوَم [qaːwam] مُقاوَمَة [muqaːwama] *vn: sv* u. This suit didn't last at all. هَالبَدلَة ما قاومَت أَبَداً [halbadla maː qaːwmat ʔabadan] Do you think you can last another mile? تِعتِقِد تِقدَر تقاوُم مِيل لاخ؟ [tiʕtiqid tigdar tqaːwum miːl laːx?] • **3.** كَفَّى [kaffaː] تكَفِّي [tkiffi] *vn: sv* i. I don't think my money will last till the end of the month. ما أَتصَوَّر فلُوسِي تكَفِّي لآخِر الشَّهَر [maː ʔatṣawwar fluːsi tkaffi lʔaːxir ʔiššahar]

lasting • **1.** دائِم [daːʔim] Let's hope for a lasting peace. خَلِّينا نِأمَل بسَلام دائِم [xalliːna niʔmal bsalaːm daːʔim]

Latakia • **1.** اللاذِقِيَّة [ʔillaːðiqiyya]

latch • **1.** سِقّاطَة [siqqaːṭa] سِقّاطات [siqqaːṭaːt] *pl:* زِلقاطَة [zilgaːṭa] زِلقاطات [zilgaːṭaːt] *pl:* مِزلاج [mizlaːǰ] مَزالِج [mazaːliǰ] *pl:*

late • **1.** أَخِير [ʔaxiːr] The late news is broadcast at ten o'clock. الأَخبار الأَخِيرَة تِنذاع السّاعَة عَشرَة [ʔilʔaxbaːr ʔilʔaxiːra tinðaːʕ ʔissaːʕa ʕašara] • **2.** مَرحُوم [marħuːm] Your late father was a friend of mine. المَرحُوم أَبُوك كان صَدِيقِي [ʔilmarħuːm ʔabuːk čaːn ṣadiːqi] • **3.** سابِق [saːbiq] The late government encouraged exporting. الحُكُومَة السّابِقَة شَجِّعَت التَّصدِير [ʔilħukuːma ʔissaːbiqa šaǰǰiʕat ʔittaṣdiːr] • **4.** مِتأَخِّر [mitʔaxxir] You're late again! إِنتَ مِتأَخِّر مَرَّة لُخ [ʔinta mitʔaxxir marra lux] This installment is four days late. هَالقُسِط مِتأَخِّر أَربَعَة أَيّام [halqusiṭ mitʔaxxir ʔarbaʕat ʔayyaːm]

*** He is in his late fifties.** • **1.** عُمرَه قَرِيب مِن الخَمسِينات [ʕumrah qariːb min ʔilxamsiːnaːt]

late afternoon • **1.** العَصِر [ʔilʕaṣir] I'll be home late in the afternoon. راح أَكُون بِالبَيت العَصِر [raːħ ʔakuːn bilbayt ʔilʕaṣir]

late morning • **1.** الضَحَى العالِي [ðððaħaː ʔilʕaːli] He comes to work late in the morning. الضَحَى يا الله يِجِي لِلشُّغُل [ððaħa: ʔilʕaːli yaː ʔallah yiǰi liššuɣul]

lately • **1.** بِالمُدَّة الأَخِيرَة [bilmudda ʔilʔaxiːra] I haven't been feeling so well lately. ما دَأشعُر زين بِالمُدَّة الأَخِيرَة [maː daʔašʕur ziːn bilmudda ʔilʔaxiːra]

later • **1.** بَعدِين [baʕdiːn] You'll find out later. راح تُعرُف بَعدين [raːħ tuʕruf baʕdiːn] • **2.** بَعَد [baʕad] One day later a letter came. وَبَعَد يوم جا مَكتُوب [wabaʕad yuːm ǰaː maktuːb]

L

latest • **1.** آخِر [ʔaːxir] What's the latest news? شِنُو آخِر الأخبار؟ [šinu ʔaːxir ʔilʔaxbaːr?] That's the latest style. هاي آخِر مُودَة [haːy ʔaːxir muːda]

lathe • **1.** جَرِخ [čarix] جرُوخ [čruːx] *pl:* مِخرَطَة [mixraṭa] مَخارِط [maxaːriṭ] *pl:*

lather • **1.** وَغفَة [wayfa] وَغفات [wayfaːt] *pl:* وَغَف [wayaf] *Collective:* رَغوَة [raywa] رَغوات [raywaːt] *pl*: Put a little soap lather on so you can shave well. خَلِّي شوَيَّة وَغَف صابُون حَتَّى تِحلِق زين [xalli šwayya wayaf ṣaːbuːn ħatta tiħliq ziːn]

to lather • **1.** رِغَى [riyaː] رَغوَة [raywa] *vn: sv* u. وَغَّف [wayyaf] توُغُّف [twuyyuf] *vn: sv* u. This soap doesn't lather well. هَالصّابُون ما يِرغُو زين [haṣṣaːbuːn maː yiryuː ziːn]

Latin • **1.** لاتِينِي [latiːni] The language of the Latin American countries is either Spanish or Portugese. دُوَل أَميركا اللّاتِينِيَّة لُغَتها إمّا إسبانِيَّة أَو بُرتُغالِيَّة [duwal ʔamriːka ʔillaːtiniyya luyatha ʔimma ʔispaːniyya ʔaw purtuyaːliyya] • **2.** اللاتِينِيَّة [ʔillaːtiniyya] Latin is a dead language. اللّاتِينِيَّة لُغَة مَيتَة [ʔillaːtiniyya luya mayyta]

L

latitude • **1.** خَطّ عَرِض [xaṭṭ ʕariđ] خُطُوط عَرِض [xuṭuːṭ ʕariđ] *pl:* It's position is at 40 degrees north latitude. هاي مَوقِعهَا عَلَى خَطّ عَرِض أَربَعِين شِمالاً [haːy mawqiʕhaː ʕala xaṭṭ ʕariđ ʔarbaʕiːn šimaːlan]

lattice • **1.** خِشَب مشَبَّك [xišab mšabbač] The balcony is hidden by a lattice. البَلكُون مَستُور بخِشَب مشَبَّك [ʔilbalkuːn mastuːr bxišab mšabbač]

laugh • **1.** ضِحكَة [điħka] ضِحكات [điħkaːt] *pl:* He has an unusual laugh. عِندَه ضِحكَة غير عادِيَّة [ʕindah điħka yiːr ʕaːdiyya]

to laugh • **1.** ضِحَك [điħak] ضَحِك [đaħik] *vn: sv* a. Everybody laughed at him. الكُلّ ضِحكَوا عَليه [ʔilkull điħkaw ʕaliːh] We laughed up our sleeves at his pronunciation. ضِحَكنا بعِبّنا عَلَى تَلَفُّظَه [điħakna biʕibbna ʕala talaffuđah]

*** That's no laughing matter.** • **1.** هَذا مُو شَقَة [haːđa muː šaqa]

laughingstock • **1.** مَضحَكَة [mađħaka] مَسخَرَة [masxara] مَساخِر [masaːxir] *pl:* His gullibility made him a laughingstock in front of everybody. تَصدِيقَه بكُلّشِي سَوّاه مَضحَكَة قِدّام النّاس [taṣdiːgah bikullši sawwaːh mađħaka giddaːm ʔinnaːs]

laughter • **1.** ضِحِك [điħik] We heard loud laughter behind us. سِمَعنا ضِحِك عالِي وَرانا [simaʕna điħik ʕaːli waraːna]

launch • **1.** ماطَور [maːṭuːr] ماطَورات [maːṭuːraːt] *pl:* We went down the river in his launch. اِنحِدَرنا بالنَّهَر بماطَورَه [ʔinħidarna binnahar bimaːṭuːrah]

to launch • **1.** نِزَل لِلمَاي [nizal lilmaːy] نُزُول لِلمَاي [nuzuːl lilmaːy] *vn:* اِنّزَل لِلمَاي [ʔinnizal lilmaːy] *p:* Another ship was launched on Monday. سَفِينَة لُخ نِزلَت لِلماي يوم الإثنين [safiːna lux nizlat lilmaːy yuːm ʔilʔiθnayn] • **2.** أَطلَق [ʔaṭlaq] إطلاق [ʔiṭlaːq] *vn: sv* i. I hear they launched a new satellite. سِمَعِت أَطلِقَوا كَوكَب اِصطِناعِي جِدِيد [simaʕit ʔaṭliqaw kawkab ʔiṣṭinaːʕi ǰidiːd] • **3.** شَنّ [šann] شَنّ [šann] *vn:* اِنشَنّ [ʔinšann] *p:* The press launched a fierce attack against the Prime Minister. الصَّحافَة شَنَّت هِجُوم عَنِيف عَلَى رَئِيس الوُزَراء [ʔiṣṣaħaːfa šannat hiǰuːm ʕaniːf ʕala raʔiːs ʔilwuzaraːʔ] • **4.** اِفتِتَح [ʔiftitaħ] اِفتِتاح [ʔiftitaːħ] *vn: sv* i. They launched the program for fighting illiteracy by holding a convention in Baghdad. اِفتِتحَوا مَشرُوع مُكافَحَة الأُمِّيَّة بعَقِد مُؤتَمَر بِبَغداد [ʔiftitħaw mašruːʕ mukaːfaħat ʔilʔummiyya biʕaqid muʔtamar bibaydaːd]

to launder • **1.** غِسَل [yisal, xisal] غَسِل [yasil, xasil] *vn:* اِنغِسَل [ʔinyisal, ʔinxisal] *p:* My landlady launders my clothes for me. أُمّ البَيت تِغسِلّي هدُومِي [ʔumm ʔilbayt tiysilli hduːmi]

laundress • **1.** غَسّالَة [yassaːla, xassaːla] غَسّالات [yassaːlaːt] *pl:* We have a laundress who comes to the house. عِدنا غَسّالَة تِجِينا لِلبَيت [ʕidna yassaːla tiǰiːna lilbayt]

laundry • **1.** مَكوِي [makwi] مَكاوِي [makaːwi] *pl:* Where's the nearest laundry? وِين أَقرَب مَكوِي؟ [wiːn ʔaqrab makwi?] • **2.** غَسِيل [yasiːl] My laundry just came back. غَسِيلِي هَسَّة جا [yasiːli hassa ǰaː]

laurel • **1.** غار [yaːr] This soap has laurel oil in it. هَالصّابُون بِيه زَيت الغار [haṣṣaːbuːn biːh ziːt ʔilyaːr]

lavatory • **1.** مِرحاض [mirħaːđ] مَراحِيض [maraːħiːđ] *pl:* خَلوَة [xalwa] خَلاوِي [xalaːwi] *pl:* أَدَبخانَة [ʔadabxaːna] أَدَبخانات [ʔadabxaːnaːt] *pl:* بَيت مَيّ [bayt mayy] بيُوت مَيّ [byuːt mayy] *pl:*

lavish • **1.** بإفراط [biʔifraːṭ] They gave him lavish praise. مِدحُوه بإفراط [midħuːh bʔifraːṭ]

law • **1.** قانُون [qaːnuːn] قَوانِين [qawaːniːn] *pl:* That's against the law. هاي ضِدّ القانُون [haːy điddʔilqaːnuːn] He's studying law. دَيِدرُس قانُون [dayidrus qaːnuːn] According to the law of nature, the strong devour the weak. حَسَب قانُون الطَّبِيعَة القَوِي ياكُل الضَّعِيف [ħasab qaːnuːn ʔiṭṭabiːʕa ʔilqawi yaːkul ʔiđđaʕiːf] Those people are very law abiding. هَذُول النّاس يِلتَزمُون بِالقانُون [hađuːl ʔinnaːs yiltazmuːn bilqaːnuːn] • **2.** حُكُم [ħukum] أَحكام

[ʔaħka:m] *pl:* The government is going to do away with martial law. الحُكومَة راح تشيل الحُكم العُرفي [ʔilħuku:ma ra:ħ tši:l ʔilħukm ʔilʕurfi]

by law • 1. قانُوناً [qa:nu:nan] بحُكم القانُون [bħukm ʔilqa:nu:n] That's prohibited by law! هَذا مَمنُوع قانُوناً [ha:ða mamnu:ʕ qa:nu:nan]

canon law • 1. الشَّريعَة [ʔiššari:ʕa] Islamic law provides that a woman's inheritance is half that of a man. الشَّريعَة الإسلامِيَّة تنُصّ عَلَى أن حَقّ المَرأة بالإرث نُص حَقّ الرَّجُل [ʔiššari:ʕa ʔilʔisla:miyya tnuṣṣ ʕala ʔan ħaqq ʔilmarʔa bilʔiriθ nuṣṣ ħaqq ʔirrajul]

lawn • 1. ثَيِّل [θayyil] The lawn still has to be sprinkled. الثَّيِّل بَعدَه لازم يِنرَشّ [ʔiθθayyal baʕdah la:zim yinrašš]

law school • 1. كُلِّيَّة الحُقُوق [kulliyya ʔilħuqu:q] كُلِّيَّات الحُقُوق [kulliyya:t ʔilħuqu:q] *pl:*

lawsuit • 1. دَعوَة [daʕwa] دَعوات، دَعاوي [daʕwa:t, daʕa:wi] *pl:* Did Adnan win the lawsuit? عَدنان رُبَح الدَّعوَة؟ [ʕadna:n rubaħ ʔiddaʕwa?]

lawyer • 1. مُحامِي [muħa:mi] مُحامِين [muħa:mi:n] *pl:*

lax • 1. مِتماهِل [mitma:hil] مِتهاوِن [mitha:win] He's rather lax in his work. هُوَّ شوَيَّة مِتماهِل بشُغلَه [huwwa šwayya mitma:hil bšuɣlah] **• 2.** لَيِّن [layyin] مِتساهِل [mitsa:hil] مِتماهِل [mitma:hil] مِتهاوِن [mitha:win] She's always been much too lax with her children. دائماً لَيِّنَة ويّا أطفالها [da:ʔiman layyna wiyya ʔaṭfa:lha]

laxative • 1. مُسهِل، مُسَهِّل [mushil, musahhil] مُسهِلات، مُسَهِّلات [mushila:t, musahhila:t] *pl:*

laxity • 1. تَهاوُن [taha:wun] He was accused of laxity in his work. اِتِّهمُوه بِتَهاوُنَه بشُغلَه [ʔittihmu:h bitaha:wunah bšuɣlah]

to lay • 1. خَلَّى [xalla:] تخِلِّي [txilli] *vn:* تخَلَّى [txalla:] *p:* حَطّ [ħaṭṭ] حَطّ [ħaṭṭ] *vn:* اِنحَطّ [ʔinħaṭṭ] *p:* Lay the book on the table. خَلِّي الكِتاب عالميز [xalli ʔilkita:b ʕalmi:z] He laid aside 50 dinars for emergencies. خَلَّى خَمسِين دِينار عَلَى صَفحَة لِلإحتِياط [xalla: xamsi:n dina:r ʕala ṣafħa lilʔiħtiya:ṭ] **• 2.** بِنَى [bina:] بناء [bina:ʔ] *vn: sv* i. The workmen were laying tile on the ground floor. العُمّال كانَوا يبنُون كاشِي عَالطّابِق الأَوَّل [ʔilʕumma:l ča:naw yibnu:n ka:ši ʕaṭṭa:biq ʔilʔawwal] The workmen were laying tile on the ground floor. العُمّال كانَوا يطَبُّقُون الطّابِق الأَوَّل بكاشِي [ʔilʕumma:l ča:naw yṭabbuqu:n ʔiṭṭa:biq ʔilʔawwal bka:ši] **• 3.** ذَبّ [ðabb] ذَبّ [ðabb] *vn:* اِنذَبّ [ʔinðabb] *p:*. خَلَّى [xalla:] *sv* i. حَطّ [ħaṭṭ] *sv* u. Don't lay the blame on me. لا تذِبّ اللَّوم عَلَيّا [la: dðibb ʔillawm ʕalayya] **• 4.** باض [ba:ð̣] *sv* i. The hen laid four eggs. الدِّجاجَة باضَت أربَعَة بَيضات [ʔiddija:ja ba:ð̣at ʔarbaʕa bayða:t] **• 5.** بَيَّض [bayyað̣] تَبيِيض، تِبيِّض [tabyi:ð̣, tbiyyið̣] *vn:* Our hens are laying well. دِجاجنا زين دَيبَيِّض [dija:jna zi:n daybayyið̣] **• 6.** تَراهَن [tra:han] تَراهُن [tara:hun] *vn: sv* a. I'll lay ten to one that he does it. تَراهَنِت عَشرَة عَلَى واحِد هُوَّ راح يسَوِّيها [tra:hanit ʕašra ʕala wa:ħid huwwa ra:ħ ysawwi:ha] **• 7.** نَيَّم [nayyam] تنِيِّم [tniyyim] *vn:* تنَيَّم [tnayyam] *p:* طِرَح [ṭirah] طَرِح [ṭariħ] *vn:* اِنطِرَح [ʔinṭirah] *p:* Lay the barrel on its side. نَيِّم البَرمِيل عَلَى صَفحتَه [nayyim ʔilbarmi:l ʕala ṣafuħtah]

*** He's certainly laying it on thick! • 1.** هوايَة دَيثَخِّنها [hwa:ya dayθaxxinha]

to lay claim to • 1. اِدَّعَى بِ [ʔiddiʕa: bi-] اِدِّعاء بِ [ʔiddiʕa:ʔ bi-] *vn: sv* i. A distant relative laid claim to the estate. فَدّ واحِد إلَه قَرابَة بِعِيدَة اِدَّعَى حَقَّه بالمُلُك [fadd wa:ħid ʔilah qara:ba biʕi:da ʔiddʕa: ħaqqah bilmuluk]

to lay down • 1. جِطَل [jiṭal] جَطِل [jaṭil] *vn:* اِنجِطَل [ʔinjiṭal] *p:* Lay him down gently. جِطلَه عَلَى كَيفَك [jiṭlah ʕala kayfak] **• 2.** تِرَك [tirak] تَرِك [tarik] *vn:* اِنتِرَك [ʔintirak] *p:* ذَبّ [ðabb] ذَبّ [ðabb] *vn:* اِنذَبّ [ʔinðabb] *p:* They were ready to lay down their arms. كانَوا مُستَعِدِّين يتركُون سلاحهُم [ča:naw mustaʕiddi:n yitruku:n sla:ħhum] **• 3.** وُضَع [wuð̣aʕ] وَضِع [wað̣iʕ] *vn:* اِنوُضَع [ʔinwuð̣aʕ] *p:* Let me lay down the rules for the game. خَلِّي آنِي أُوضَع قَواعِد اللِّعبَة [xalli ʔa:ni ʔu:ð̣aʕ qawa:ʕid ʔilliʕba]

to lay for • 1. خِتَل ل [xital l-] خَتِل [xatil] *vn: sv* i. تَرَصَّد ل [traṣṣad l-] تَرَصُّد [taraṣṣud] *vn: sv* a. They laid for him at the corner. خِتلُولَه بالزُّوِيَّة [xitlu:lah bizzuwiyya]

to lay off • 1. اِستَغنَى عَن [ʔistaɣna ʕan] اِستِغناء عَن [ʔistigna:ʔ ʕan] *vn: sv* i. بَطَّل [baṭṭal] تَبطِيل [tabṭi:l] *vn: sv* i. We have to lay off some workers. لازم نِستَغنِي عَن بَعض العُمّال [la:zim nistaɣni ʕan baʕð̣ ʔilʕumma:l] You're going to have to lay off the drinking for awhile! لازم تبَطِّل مِن الشُّرُب فَدّ مُدَّة [la:zim tbaṭṭil min ʔiššurub fadd mudda]

to lay out • 1. صِرَف [ṣiraf] صَرِف [ṣarif] *vn: sv* u. How much did you lay out for the party? شقَدّ صِرَفِت لِلحَفلَة؟ [šgadd ṣirafit lilħafla?] **• 2.** حَدَّد [ħaddad] تَحدِيد [taħdi:d] *vn: sv* i. خَطَّط [xaṭṭaṭ] تَخطِيط [taxṭi:ṭ] *vn: sv* i. Lay out the dimensions before you start digging. حَدِّد الأَبعاد قَبِل ما تِبدِي تُحفُر [ħaddad ʔilʔabʕa:d qabil ma: tibdi tuħfur] **• 3.** عِرَض [ʕirað̣] عَرِض [ʕarið̣] *vn:* اِنعِرَض [ʔinʕirað̣] *p:* The chairman laid out his plans for the future. مُدِير المَجلِس عِرَض خِطَّتَه لِلمُستَقبَل [mudi:r ʔilmajlis ʕirað̣ xiṭṭatah lilmustaqbal]

to lay waste • 1. دُمَر [dumar] دَمُر [damur] *vn:* اِندُمَر [ʔindumar] *p:* The whole region was laid waste by the storm. المَنطِقَة كُلها اِندُمرَت بالعاصِفَة [ʔilmanṭiqa kullha ʔindumrat bilʕa:ṣifa]

L

layer • **1.** طَبَقَة [ṭabaqa] طَبَقات [ṭabaqa:t] *pl:* Everything was covered with a thick layer of sand. كُلْشِي كان مغطّى بِطَبَقَة ثخِينَة مِن الرَّمُل [kullši ča:n myaṭṭa: biṭabaqa θxi:na min ʔirramul]

layman • **1.** شَخِص عادِي [šaxiṣ ʕa:di] أشخاص عادِيِّين [ʔašxa:ṣ ʕa:diyyi:n] *pl:* The layman wouldn't be interested in this book. الشَّخص العادِي ما يِهتَمّ بهالكتاب [ʔiššaxṣ ʔilʕa:di ma: yihtamm bhalkta:b]

lazier • **1.** أكسَل [ʔaksal] They say he's lazier than me. يقُولُون هُوَّ أكسَل مِنِّي [ygu:lu:n huwwa ʔaksal minni]

laziness • **1.** كَسَل [kasal]

lazy • **1.** كَسلان [kasla:n] كَسلانِين، كَسالَة [kasla:ni:n, kasa:la] *pl:* Don't be so lazy! لا تصِير هَالقَدّ كَسلان [la: tṣi:r halgadd kasla:n]

lead • **1.** رصاص [rṣa:ṣ] Is this made of lead? هذِي مَصنُوعَة مِن رِصاص؟ [hði maṣnu:ʕa min riṣa:ṣ?] Do you have some lead for my pencil? عِندَك رِصاص لِلقَلَم مالِي؟ [ʕindak riṣa:ṣ lilqalam ma:li?]

lead • **1.** دَور رَئِيسِي [dawr raʔi:si] أدوار رَئِيسِيَّة [ʔadwa:r raʔi:siyya] *pl:* Who's playing the lead? مِنُو دَيقُوم بِالدَّور الرَّئِيسِي؟ [minu dayqu:m biddawr ʔirraʔi:si?] • **2.** دَلِيل [dali:l] أدِلَّة [ʔadilla] *pl:* The police had a number of leads on the case. كان عِند الشُّرطَة بَعض الأدِلَّة مُتَعَلِّقَة بِالقَضِيَّة [ča:n ʕind ʔiššurṭa baʕð ʔilʔadilla mutaʕallqa bilqaðiyya] • **3.** مُقَدِّمَة [muqaddima] He was in the lead by five yards in the first lap. كان بِالمُقَدِّمَة بخَمِس ياردات بِالفَرَّة الأُولَى [ča:n bilmuqaddima bxamis ya:rda:t bilfarra ʔilʔu:la] When the army entered the town the tanks were in the lead. لَمّا الجَّيش دِخَل المَدِينَة كانَت الدَّبّابات بِالمُقَدِّمَة [lamma ʔijji:š dixal ʔilmadi:na ča:nat ʔiddabba:ba:t bilmuqaddima] The first hour he had a five-mile lead on us. بِالسّاعَة الأُولَى كان غالبنا خَمس أميال [bissa:ʕa ʔilʔu:la ča:n ɣa:lubna xams ʔamya:l]

to lead • **1.** قاد [qa:d, ga:d] قِيادَة [qiya:da] *vn: sv* u. The lieutenant led his men to the top of the hill. المُلازِم قادّ جنُودَه إلَى فُوق التَّلّ [ʔilmula:zim qa:dd ǰunu:dah ʔila fu:g ʔittall] • **2.** تفَوَّق عَلَى [tfawwaq ʕala] تَفَوُّق عَلَى [tafawwuq ʕala] *vn: sv* a. تقَدَّم عَلَى [tqaddam ʕala] تَقَدُّم [taqaddum] *vn: sv* a. Ahmed leads his class in arithmetic. أحمَد مِتفَوِّق عَلَى طُلّاب صَفّه بِالحِساب [ʔaħmad mitfawwuq ʕala ṭulla:b ṣaffah bilħisa:b] • **3.** قاد [qa:d, ga:d] قَود [gawd] *vn:* اِنقاد [ʔinga:d] *p:* He led the child across the street. قاد الجّاهِل وعَبَّرَه الشّارِع [ga:d ʔiǰǰa:hil wʕabbarah ʔišša:riʕ] • **4.** تقَدَّم عَلَى [tqaddam ʕala] تَقَدُّم [taqaddum] *vn: sv* a. Iraq leads all countries in the production of dates. العِراق يِتقَدَّم عَلَى جَمِيع الدُّوَل بِإنتاج التَّمُر [ʔilʕira:q yitqaddam ʕala ǰami:ʕ ʔidduwal biʔinta:ǰ ʔittamur]

to lead the way • **1.** تقَدَّم [tqaddam] تَقَدُّم [taqaddum] *vn: sv* a. I'll lead the way and you follow. آنِي راح أتقَدَّم وَإنت إتبَعنِي [ʔa:ni ra:ħ ʔatqaddam waʔint ʔitbaʕni]

to lead to • **1.** أدَّى [ʔadda:] *sv* i. Where will all this lead to? هَذا وِين راح يأدِّي؟ [ha:ða wi:n ra:ħ yʔaddi?] Where does this road lead to? وين يأدِّي هَالطَّرِيق؟ [wi:n yʔaddi haṭṭari:q?] • **2.** سَبَّب [sabbab] تَسبِيب [tasbi:b] *vn: sv* i. أدَّى [ʔadda:] *sv* i. Drink led to his downfall. الشُّرُب سَبَّب خَرابَه [ʔiššurub sabbab xara:bah] The information you gave us led to his arrest. المَعلُومات اللّي نطَيتنا إيّاها أدَّت إلَى تَوقِيفَه [ʔilmaʕlu:ma:t ʔilli nṭi:tna ʔiyya:ha ʔaddat ʔila tawqi:fah]

to led up to • **1.** قِصَد [qiṣad] قَصِد [qaṣid] *vn: sv* u. What do you think he was leading up to? لِأي شِي تِعتِقِد كان قاصِد؟ [lʔayy ši tiʕtiqid ča:n qa:ṣid?] That's just what I was leading up to. هَذا اللّي كِنِت أقصدَه بِالضَبُط [ha:ða ʔilli činit ʔaquṣdah biððabuṭ]

leader • **1.** زَعِيم [zaʕi:m] زُعَماء [zuʕama:ʔ] *pl:* The leaders of all parties were present. زُعَماء كُلّ الأحزاب كانَوا حاضرِين [zuʕama:ʔ kull ʔilʔaħza:b ča:naw ħa:ðri:n] • **2.** رَئِيس [raʔi:s] رُؤَساء [ruʔasa:, ruʔasa:ʔ] *pl:* Who is the leader of the group? مِنُو رَئِيس الجَّمعِيَّة؟ [minu raʔi:s ʔiǰǰamʕiyya?] I know the band leader. أعرُف رَئِيس الفِرقَة المُوسِيقِيَّة [ʔaʕruf raʔi:s ʔilfirqa ʔilmusi:qiyya]

leading • **1.** بارِز [ba:riz] كَبِير [kabi:r] He's one of the leading scientists in his field. هَذا واحِد مِن أبرَز العُلَماء بِفَرعَه [ha:ða wa:ħid min ʔabraz ʔilʕulama:ʔ bifarʕah] This is the leading newspaper in Baghdad. هَذِي أكبَر جَرِيدَة بِبَغداد [ha:ði ʔakbar ǰari:da bibaɣda:d]

leaf • **1.** وَرقَة [warga] وَرَق [warag] *pl:* In the fall the leaves turn brown. بِالخَرِيف الوَرَق يِنقُلِب لونَه قَهوائِي [bilxari:f ʔilwarag yingulub lu:nah qahwa:ʔi] If you add an additional leaf to the spring it'll bear a heavier weight. إذا تخَلِّي وَرقَة لُخ عالسِّبرنك يِتحَمَّل وَزِن أكثَر [ʔiða txalli warga lux ʕassipring yitħammal wazin ʔakθar] • **2.** صَحِيفَة [ṣaħi:fa] صَحايِف، صُحُف [ṣaħa:yif, ṣuħuf] *pl:* He promised to turn over a new leaf. وُعَد يِفتَح صَحِيفَة جِدِيدَة بِحَياتَه [wuʕad yiftaħ ṣaħi:fa ǰidi:da biħaya:tah]

to leaf through • **1.** قَلَّب بِ [gallab bi-] تَقلِيب بِ [tagli:b bi-] *vn:* تقَلَّب بِ [tgallab bi-] *p:* I am only leafing through the book. بَسّ دَأقَلِّب بِالكتاب [bass daʔagallub bilkta:b]

leaflet • **1.** مَنشُور [manšu:r] مَناشِير [mana:ši:r] *pl:*

league • **1.** جامِعَة [ǰa:miʕa] جامِعات [ǰa:miʕa:t] *pl:* The Arab Leage has its headquarters in Cairo.

الجّامِعَة العَرَبِيَّة مَركَزها بالقاهِرَة [ʔijja:miʕa ʔilʕarabiyya markazha blqa:hira] • **2.** اِتِّحاد [ʔittiħa:d] اِتِّحادات [ʔittiħa:da:t] *pl:* The soccer league's having a dinner today. اِتِّحاد كُرَة القَدَم مسَوِّي دَعوَة عَشا اليُوم [ʔittiħa:d kurat ʔilqadam msawwi daʕwat ʕaša ʔilyu:m]

leak • **1.** طَلِع مَيّ [ṭalliʕ mayy] * There's a leak in the boat. أَكُو مُكان بالبَلَم يطَلِّع مَيّ [ʔaku muka:n bilbalam yṭalliʕ mayy]

to leak • **1.** طَلَّع [ṭallaʕma:y] تطِلِّع [tṭilliʕ] *vn: sv* i. نَدَّى [nadda:] تنِدِّي [tniddi] *vn: sv* i. The boat is leaking. البَلَم دَيطَلِّع مَيّ [ʔilbalam dayṭalliʕ mayy] • **2.** خَرّ [xarr] خَرّ [xarr] *vn: sv* u. This pot leaks. هَالجِدِر يخُرّ [hajjidir yxurr] The faucet is leaking. الحَنَفِيَّة دَتخُرّ [ʔilħanafiyya datxurr] • **3.** تسَرَّب [tsarrab] تَسَرُّب [tasarrub] *vn: sv* a. The story leaked out somehow. القُصَّة تسَرُّبَت بِصُورَة مِن الصُّوَر [ʔilquṣṣa tsarrubat bṣu:ra min ʔiṣṣuwar] All the water is leaking out. المَيّ كُلَّه دَيِتسَرَّب لِبَرَّة [ʔilmayy kullah dayitsarrab libarra]

lean • **1.** شِرِح [širiħ] Do you want lean meat or some with fat on it? ترِيد لَحَم شِرِح لَو بِيه شَحَم؟ [tri:d laħam širiħ law bi:h šaħam?] • **2.** مَحَل [maħal] قَحَط [qaħaṭ] It was a lean year for farmers. كانَت سَنَة مَحَل لِلفَلّاحِين [ča:nat sanat maħal lilfalla:ħi:n] • **3.** نَحِيف [naħi:f] هَزِيل [hazi:l] He's a lean man. هُوَّ رَجُل نَحِيف [huwwa rajul naħi:f]

to lean • **1.** مال [ma:l] مَيل، مَيَلان [mayl, mayala:n] *vn: sv* i. دَنَّق [dannag, dannaj] تدِنِّق [ddinnig] *vn: sv* i. Don't lean out of the window. لا تمِيل مِن الشِّبّاك [la: tmi:l min ʔiššibba:k] • **2.** مال [ma:l] *sv* i. He leans toward the right in polities. يمِيل نَحو اليَمِين بِالسِّياسَة [ymi:l naħw ʔilyami:n bissiya:sa] • **3.** مال [ma:l] *sv* i. مَيَّل [mayyal] تَمييل [tamyi:l] *vn: sv* i. She leaned over the balcony and looked to see who was knocking. مالَت مِن البالكُون حَتَّى تشُوف مِنُو كان يدُقّ الباب [ma:lat min ʔilbalku:n ħatta tšu:f minu ča:n ydugg ʔilba:b] • **4.** تَكَّى [tačča:] تتِكِّي [titičči] *vn: sv* i. رِكَى [riča:] رَكِي [rači] *vn:* اِنرِكَى [ʔinriča:] *p:* سِنَد [sinad] سَنِد [sanid] *vn:* اِنسِنَد [ʔinsinad] *p:* Don't lean your chair against the wall. لا ترَكِّي كُرسِيَّك عَالحايِط [la: trači kursiyyak ʕalħa:yiṭ] • **5.** اِستِنَد [ʔistinad] اِستِناد [ʔistina:d] *vn: sv* i. اِنتِكَى [ʔintiča:] *sv* i. There's nothing to lean against. ماكُو شِي تِستِنِد عَلِيه [ma:ku ši tistinid ʕali:h] May I lean on your arm? أَقدَر أَستِنِد عَلَى ذراعَك؟ [ʔagdar ʔastinid ʕala ðra:ʕak?] She leaned on the railing. اِنتِكَت عالمحَجَّر [ʔintičat ʕa:lmħajjar] • **6.** اِنحِنَى [ʔinħina:] اِنحِناء [ʔinħina:ʔ] *vn: sv* i. مال [ma:l] *sv* i. If you lean forward you can see him. إذا اِنحِنَيت لِقِدّام تِقدَر تشُوفَه [ʔiða ʔinħini:t ligidda:m tigdar tšu:fah]

leap • **1.** طَفرَة [ṭafra] طَفرات [ṭafra:t] *pl:* قَمزَة [gamza] قَمزات [gamza:t] *pl:* He cleared the ditch with one leap. عُبَر السّاقيَة بِطَفرَة وِحدَة [ʕubar ʔissa:gya biṭafra wiħda]

to leap • **1.** قُمَز [gumaz] قَمُز [gamuz] *vn: sv* u. He leaped out of bed at the noise. قُمَز مِن فراشَه مِن سِمَع الصَّوت [gumaz min fra:šah min simaʕ ʔiṣṣawt]

leap year • **1.** سَنَة كَبِيسَة [sana kabi:sa]

to learn • **1.** تعَلَّم [tʕallam] تَعَلُّم [taʕallum] *vn: sv* i. He hasn't learned a thing. ما تعَلَّم شِي [ma: tʕallam ši] • **2.** عِرَف [ʕiraf] مَعرِفَة [maʕrifa] *vn: sv* u. He learned the truth too late. عِرَف الحَقِيقَة بَعَد فَوات الوَقِت [ʕiraf ʔilħaqi:qa baʕad fawa:t ʔilwakit]

to learn by heart • **1.** حِفَظ عَلَى قَلُب [ħifað ʕala: galub] حُفُظ [ħufuð] *vn: sv* u. She learned the poem by heart. حُفظَت القَصِيدَة عَلَى قَلُبها [ħufðat ʔilqaṣi:da ʕala galubha]

lease • **1.** عَقِد إيجار [ʕaqid ʔi:ja:r] عُقُود إيجار [ʕuqu:d ʔi:ja:r] *pl:* We had to sign a lease for one year. اِضطَرَّينا نوَقِّع عَقِد إيجار لِمُدَّة سَنَة [ʔiðṭarrayna nwaqqiʕ ʕaqid ʔi:ja:r lmuddat sana]

to lease • **1.** اِستَأجَر [ʔistaʔjar] اِستِئجار [ʔistiʔja:r] *vn: sv* i. Did you lease an apartment yet? اِستَأجَرت شِقَّة لَو بَعَد؟ [ʔistaʔajarit šiqqa law baʕad?] • **2.** أَجَّر [ʔajjar] تَأجِير [taʔji:r] *vn:* تأَجَّر [tʔajjar] *p:* The landlord doesn't want to lease the apartment. صاحِب المُلك ما يرِيد يأَجِّر الشِّقَّة [ṣa:ħib ʔilmuluk ma: yri:d yʔajjir ʔiššuqqa]

least • **1.** أَقَلّ [ʔaqall] That's the least of my worries. هاي أَقَلّ مَشاكلِي [ha:y ʔaqall maša:kli] She deserves it least of all. هِيَّ تِستاهِلها أَقَلّ الكُلّ [hiyya tista:hilha ʔaqall ʔilkull] That's the least you could do for him. هَذا أَقَلّ ما مُمكِن تسَوِّي تِجاهَه [ha:ða ʔaqall ma: mumkin tsawwi tija:hah]

at least • **1.** عَالأَقَلّ [ʕalʔaqall] These shoes cost at least two dinars. هَالأَحذِيَة كَلفَت عَالأَقَلّ دِينارَين [halʔaħðiya kallfat ʕalʔaqall dina:rayn] At least you might have written to me. عالأَقَلّ كان كِتَبِتلِي [ʕalʔaqall ča:n kitabitli]

not in the least • **1.** ما أَبَداً [ma: ʔabadan] ما أَبَد [ma: ʔabad] It doesn't bother me in the least. ما تهِمنِي أَبَداً [ma: tihimni ʔabadan] It wouldn't surprise me in the least if. . . ما أَستَغرُب أَبَد إذا [ma: ʔastaɣrub ʔabad ʔiða]

leather • **1.** جِلِد [jilid] جُلُود [julu:d] *pl:* The meat is tough as leather. اللَّحَم قَوِي مِثل الجِّلِد [ʔillaħam qawi miθl ʔijjilid]

leave • **1.** إجازَة [ʔija:za] إجازات [ʔija:za:t] *pl:* He's taken a three months' leave. أَخَذ إجازَة ثلَث أَشهُر [ʔaxað ʔija:za tlaθ ʔašhur]

to leave • **1.** تِرَك [tirak] تَرك [tarik] *vn:* اِنتِرَك [ʔintirak] *p:* راح [ra:ħ] *sv* u. عاف [ʕa:f] عوف [ʕawf] *vn:* اِنعاف [ʔinʕa:f] *p:* مِشَى [miša:] مَشِي [mašy] *vn: sv* i. I have to leave now. لازم أَترُك هَسَّة

[la:zim ʔatruk hassa] I have to leave now. لازِم أَعُوفكُم هَسَّة [la:zim ʔaʕu:fkum hassa] I'm leaving for good. راح أَترُك نِهائِيّاً [ra:ħ ʔatruk niha:ʔiyyan] The train leaves at two-thirty. القِطار بِترُك السّاعَة تِنتَين وَنُص [ʔilqiṭa:r yitruk ʔissa:ʕa θintayn wnuṣṣ] • 2. سافَر [sa:far] سَفَر [safar] *vn: sv* i. تِرَك [tirak] مِشَى [miša:] راح [ra:ħ] My father left yesterday for Europe. أَبُويا سافَر لأُورُبّا البارحَة [ʔabu:ya sa:far lʔu:ruppa: ʔilba:rħa] • 3. خَلَّى [xalla:] تخِلّي [txilli] *vn:* تخَلَّى [txalla:] *p:* تِرَك [tirak] *sv* u. He left his food on the plate. خَلَّى أَكلَه بِالماعُون [xalla: ʔaklah bilma:ʕu:n] Where did you leave your suitcase? وَين خَلَّيت جِنُطتَك؟ [wi:n xallayt ǰinuṭṭak?] My brother got all the money, and left me out in the cold. أَخُويا أَخَذ كُلّ الفلُوس وَخَلّانِي أَصَفِّق إيد بإيد [ʔaxu:ya ʔaxað kull ʔilflu:s wxalla:ni ʔaṣaffug ʔi:d bʔi:d] Leave it to me! خَلِّيها عَلَيّا [xalli:ha ʕalayya] When he died he left eight grand-children. مِن مات تِرَك ثمَن أَحفاد [min ma:t tirak θman ʔaħfa:d] He left word that he would be back soon. خَلَّى خَبَر إنُّو راح يِرجَع بَعد شوَيَّة [xalla: xabar ʔinnu ra:ħ yirǰaʕ baʕd šwayya]

*** Are there any tickets left for tonight's performance? • 1.** بُقَت أَيّ بِطاقات لِحَفلَة اللَّيلَة؟ [buqat ʔayy biṭa:qa:t liħaflat ʔillayla?]

*** Eight from fifteen leaves seven.**
• **1.** ثمانيَة مِن خُمُسطَعَش يِبقَى سَبعَة [θma:nyap min xumusṭaʕaš yibqa: sabʕa]

*** Where does that leave me?**
• **1.** آني شراح يكُون مَصِيرِي؟ [ʔa:ni šraħ yku:n maṣi:ri?]

to leave out • 1. فَوَّت [fawwat] تَفوِيت، تفُوُّت [tafwi:t, tfuwwut] *vn:* تفَوَّت [tfawwat] *p:* حِذَف [ħiðaf] حَذِف [ħaðif] *vn:* اِنحِذَف [ʔinħiðaf] *p:* When you copy it, don't leave anything out. مِن تُنقُلها، لا تفَوِّت شِي [min tunqulha, la: tfawwit ši]

Lebanese • 1. لُبنانِي [lubna:ni] لُبنانِيِّين [lubna:niyyi:n] *pl:* Most of the Lebanese know how to speak French. أَكثَر اللُّبنانِيِّين يعُرفُون يِحكُون فرَنسِي [ʔakθar ʔillubna:niyyi:n yʕurfu:n yiħču:n fransi] • **2.** لُبنانِي [lubna:ni] I visited the Lebanese capital twice last summer. رت العاصِمَة اللُّبنانِيَّة مَرّتَين بِالصَّيف الماضِي [zirit ʔilʕa:ṣima ʔillubna:niyya marrtayn biṣṣayf ʔilma:ḍi]

Lebanon • 1. لُبنان [lubna:n]

lecture • 1. مُحاضَرَة [muħa:ḍara] مُحاضَرات [muħa:ḍara:t] *pl:* It was an interesting lecture. كانَت مُحاضَرَة لَطِيفَة [ča:nat muħa:ḍara laṭi:fa]

to lecture • 1. أَلقَى مُحاضَرَة، حاضَر [ʔalqa: muħa:ḍara, ħa:ðar] إلقاء مُحاضَرَة [ʔilqa:ʔ muħa:ḍara] *vn: sv* i. حاضَر [ħa:ḍar] He's lecturing on international trade. دَيِلقِي مُحاضَرَة عَن التِّجارَة الدَّولِيَّة [dayilqi muħa:ḍara ʕan ʔittiǰa:ra ʔiddawliyya] He lectures on zoology at the university. يحاضِر بِعِلم الحَيوان بِالجّامِعَة [yħa:ḍir biʕilm ʔilħaywa:n biǰǰa:miʕa] He always lectures us when we're late. دائِماً يِلقِي عَلينا مُحاضَرَة مِن نكُون مِتأَخّرِين [da:ʔiman yilqi ʕali:na muħa:ḍara min nku:n mitʔaxxri:n] Don't lecture me! لا تِلقِي براسِي مُحاضَرَة [la: tilqi bra:si muħa:ḍara]

lecturer • 1. مُحاضِر [muħa:ḍir] مُحاضِرِين [muħa:ḍiri:n] *pl:*

ledge • 1. حاشيَة [ħa:šiya] حَواشِي [ħawa:ši] *pl:* The bird hopped onto the ledge of the window. الطَّير قُمَز لِحاشيَة الشِّبّاك [ʔiṭṭayr gumaz liħa:šyat ʔiššibba:č]

ledger • 1. دَفتَر حِساب [daftar ħisa:b] دَفاتِر حِساب [dafa:tir ħisa:b] *pl:*

leek • 1. كُرّاث [kurra:θ]

left • 1. يَسار [yasa:r] أَيسَر [ʔaysar] Take the other bag in your left hand. شِيل الجُنطَة اللُّخ بإيدَك اليِسرَة [ši:l ʔiǰǰunṭa ʔillux bi:dak ʔilyisra] We had seats at the left of the stage. مَقاعِدنا كانَت عَلَى يَسار المَسرَح [maqa:ʕidna ča:nat ʕala yasa:r ʔilmasraħ] I sat on the speaker's left. قعَدِت عَلَى يَسار الخَطِيب [gʕadit ʕala yasa:r ʔilxaṭi:b] Turn left at the next corner. لُوف عَاليِسرَة بِالشّارِع الجّاي [lu:f ʕalyisra biššaːriʕ ʔiǰǰa:y]

left-handed • 1. يِسراوِي [yisra:wi] يِسراوِيِّين [yisrawiyyi:n] *pl:* He's left-handed. هُوَّ يِسراوِي [huwwa yisra:wi]

leftist • 1. يِسارِي [yisa:ri] He always was a leftist. دائِماً كان يِسارِي [da:ʔiman ča:n yisa:ri]

leg • 1. رِجل [riǰil] رِجلَين، رِجلينات [riǰlayn, riǰli:na:t] *pl:* I have a pain in my right leg. عِندِي أَلَم برِجلِي اليِمنَى [ʕindi ʔalam briǰli ʔilyimna] The table leg's broken. رِجل المِيز مَكسُورَة [riǰl ʔilmi:z maksu:ra] The left pant leg is torn. رِجل بَنطَرُون اليِسرَة مَمزُوقَة [riǰil panṭaru:n ʔilyisra mamzu:ga] • **2.** مَرحَلَة [marħala] مَراحِل [mara:ħil] *pl:* We're now on the last leg of our trip. إحنا هَسَّة بآخِر مَرحَلَة مِن سَفرَتنا [ʔiħna hassa bʔa:xir marħala min safratna] • **3.** فُخُذ [fuxuð] أَفخاذ [ʔafxa:ð] *pl:* Give me a small leg of lamb. إنطِينِي فُخُذ غَنَم صغَيِّر [ʔinṭi:ni fuxuð ɣanam ṣɣayyir] They say he's on his last legs. يقُولُون أَمرَه تَقرِيباً مِنتِهِي [ygu:lu:n ʔamrah taqri:ban mintihi]

*** Stop pulling my leg. • 1.** بَسّ عاد تِتشاقَى [bass ʕa:d titša:qa:]

legal • 1. قانُونِي [qa:nu:ni] That's perfectly legal. هَذا تَماماً قانُونِي [ha:ða tama:man qa:nu:ni] He's our legal adviser. هُوَّ مُستَشارنا القانُونِي [huwwa mustaša:rna ʔilqa:nu:ni]

legality • **1.** القانُونِيَّة [ʔilqa:nu:niyya]

legation • **1.** مُفَوَّضِيَّة [mufawwaðiyya] مُفَوَّضِيّات [mufawwaðiyya:t] *pl:* Where is the Swiss legation? وين المُفَوَّضِيَّة السُّويسرِيَّة؟ [wi:n ʔilmufawwaðiyya ʔissuwi:sriyya?]

legend • **1.** إسطُورَة [ʔisṭu:ra] أَساطِير [ʔasa:ṭi:r] *pl:* The origin of the legend is unknown. مَنشَأ الأسطُورَة غير مَعلُوم [manšaʔ ʔilʔusṭu:ra ɣayr maʕlu:m]

legible • **1.** واضِح [wa:ðiħ] His handwriting is hardly legible. كِتابتَه مُو واضحَة [kita:btah mu: wa:ðħa] His handwriting is hardly legible. كِتابتَه ما تِنقِري بِسُهُولَة [kita:btah ma: tinqiri bsuhu:la]

legion • **1.** فِرقَة، فَرِيق [firqa, fari:q] فِرَق [firaq] *pl:* The Foreign Legion's mostly mercenaries. الفِرقَة الأَجنَبِيَّة مُعظَمها يِتكَوَّن مِن مُرتَزَقَة [ʔilfirqa ʔilʔaǰnabiyya muʕðamha yitkawwan min murtazaqa] • **2.** فَيلَق [faylaq] فَيالِق [faya:liq] *pl:* جَيش [ǰayš, ǰi:š] جِيُوش [ǰiyu:š] *pl:* The Arab Legion's conducting exercises near the border of occupied Palestine. الفَيلَق العَرَبِي دَيقُوم بِتَمارِين عَلَى حِدُود فِلِسطِين المُحتَلَّة [ʔilfaylaq ʔilʕarabi dayqu:m bitama:ri:n ʕala ħidu:d filisṭi:n ʔilmuħtalla]

legislation • **1.** تَشرِيع [tašri:ʕ]

legislator • **1.** مُشَرِّع [mušarriʕ] مُشَرِّعِين [mušarriʕi:n] *pl:*

legislature • **1.** مُشَرِّعِين [mušarriʕi:n] سُلطَة تَشرِيعِيَّة [sulṭa tašri:ʕiyya]

legitimate • **1.** شَرعِي [šarʕi] He is the legitimate heir. هُوَّ الوَرِيث الشَّرعِي [huwwa ʔilwari:θ ʔiššarʕi] Are all her children legitimate? كُلّ وِلِدها شَرعِيِّين؟ [kull wilidha šarʕiyyi:n?] • **2.** صَحِيح [ṣaħi:ħ] those conclusions are not legitimate. هاي الاستِنتاجات مُو صَحِيحَة [ha:y ʔilʔistinta:ǰa:t mu: ṣaħi:ħa]

leisure • **1.** فَراغ [fara:ɣ] فَراغات [fara:ɣa:t] *pl:* This job doesn't leave me much leisure. هَالشَّغلَة ما تِترُكلِي فَراغ كافِي [haššaɣla ma: titrukli fara:ɣ ka:fi] Do it at your leisure. سَوِّيها بِفَراغَك [sawwi:ha bifara:ɣak]

lemon • **1.** نُومِيَّة حامُض [nu:miyya ħa:muð] نُومِيّات حامضَة [nu:miyya:t ħa:mða] *pl:* نُومِي حامُض [nu:mi ħa:muð] *Collective:* Go buy some lemons. رُوح اِشتِري شوَيَّة نُومِي حامُض [ru:ħ ʔištiri šwayya nu:mi ħa:muð]

lemonade • **1.** شَربَت نُومِي حامُض [šarbat nu:mi ħa:muð]

lemon juice • **1.** عَصِير نُومِي حامُض [ʕaṣi:r nu:mi ħa:muð]

lemon tea • **1.** شاي حامُض [ča:y ħa:muð] حامُض [ħa:muð] شاي نُومِي بَصرَة [ča:y nu:mi baṣra]

to lend • **1.** عار [ʕa:r] إعارَة [ʔiʕa:ra] *vn: sv* i. Can you lend me this book? تِقدَر تعِيرنِي هَالكِتاب؟ [tigdar tʕi:rni halkita:b?] • **2.** دايَن [da:yan] مِدايَن [mida:yan] *vn:* اِتدايَن [ʔidda:yan] *p:* Would you lend me ten dinars? تِقدَر تدايِنِّي عَشِر دَنانِير؟ [tigdar dda:yinni ʕašir dana:ni:r?]

* **Lend me a hand, will you?** • **1.** ساعِدنِي شوَيَّة؟ [sa:ʕidni šwayya?] / بالله إيدَك شوَيَّة؟ [ballah ʔi:dak šwayya?]

length • **1.** طُول [ṭu:l] Let's measure the length of the room. خَلِّي نقِيس طُول الغُرفَة [xalli nqi:s ṭu:l ʔilɣurfa] He stretched full length on the bed. تمَدَّد بِطُولَه عالتَّخِت [tmaddad biṭu:lah ʕattaxit] • **2.** فَترَة [fatra] فَترات [fatra:t] *pl:* مُدَّة [mudda] مُدَد [mudad] *pl:* He can do a lot of work in a short length of time. يِقدَر يسَوِّي أَشياء هوايَة بفَترَة وَقِت قَصِيرَة [yigdar ysawwi ʔašya:ʔ hwa:ya bfatrat wakit qaṣi:ra] • **3.** وُصلَة [wuṣla] وُصَل [wuṣal] *pl:* We need a short length of pipe so the faucet will reach. يرّاد إلنا وُصلَة بُورِي صغَيرَة حَتَّى الحَنَفِيَّة توَصِّل [yirra:d ʔilna wuṣlat bu:ri ṣɣayyra ħatta ʔilħanafiyya twaṣṣil]

* **I went to great lengths to get a passport for you.** • **1.** تعبِت هوايَة حَتَّى خَلَّصتلَك الباسبَورت [tʕabit hwa:ya ħatta: xallaṣtlak ʔilpa:spu:rt]

at length • **1.** بِالتَّفصِيل [bittafṣi:l] They discussed the plan at length. بِحثَوا الخُطَّة بِالتَّفصِيل [biħθaw ʔilxuṭṭa bittafṣi:l]

to lengthen • **1.** طَوَّل [ṭawwal] تَطوِيل [taṭwi:l] *vn:* تطَوَّل [tṭawwal] *p:* These trousers have to be lengthened. هَالبَنطَرُون لازِم يِطَّوَّل [halpanṭaru:n la:zim yiṭṭawwal]

lengthwise • **1.** طُول [ṭu:l] Cut the material lengthwise. قُصّ القماش بِالطُّول [guṣṣ ʔilqma:š biṭṭu:l]

lengthy • **1.** مُطَوَّل [muṭawwal] He made a lengthy speech. خِطَب خُطبَة مُطَوَّلَة [xiṭab xuṭba muṭawwala]

lenient • **1.** لَيِّن [layyin] مِتساهِل [mitsa:hil] You're too lenient with him. إنتَ كُلَش لَيِّن ويّاه [ʔinta kulliš layyin wiyya:h]

lens • **1.** عَدَسَة [ʕadasa] عَدَسات [ʕadasa:t] *pl:* Your camera has a good lens. الكامِيرَة مالتَك بِيها خُوش عَدَسَة [ʔilkamira: ma:ltak bi:ha xu:š ʕadasa]

lentil • **1.** عَدَسَة [ʕadasa] عَدَسات [ʕadasa:t] *pl:* عَدَس [ʕadas] *Collective:* Add some lentils to the soup. ضِيف شوَيَّة عَدَس بِالشُّوربَة [ði:f šwayya ʕadas biššu:rba]

L

leopard • **1.** نِمِر منَقَّط [nimir mnaqqaṭ] نمُور منَقَّطَة [nmu:r mnaqqaṭa] *pl:* فَهَد [fahad] فُهُود [fuhu:d] *pl:*

leper • **1.** مَجذُوم [majðu:m] مَجذُومِين [majðu:mi:n] *pl:*

leprosy • **1.** مَرض الجُذام [marḍ ʔijjuða:m]

lesbian • **1.** سُحاقِيَّة [suħaqiyya] سُحاقِيّات [suħa:qiyya:t] *pl:*

less • **1.** أَقَلّ [ʔaqall] I have less money with me than I thought. عِندِي فلُوس أَقَلّ مِن ما اِعتِقَدِت [ʕindi flu:s ʔaqall min ma: ʔiʕtiqadit] • **2.** ناقِص [na:qiṣ] ناقِصِين، نُواقِيص [na:qiṣi:n, nuwa:qi:ṣ] *pl:* The price is 10 dinars, less the discount. السِّعِر، عَشِر دَنانِير ناقِص الخَصُم [ʔissiʕir, ʕašir dana:ni:r na:qiṣ ʔilxaṣum] Five less three leaves two. خَمسَة ناقِص ثلاثَة يِبقَى ثنَين [xamsa na:qiṣ tla:θa yibqa: θnayn]

lesson • **1.** دَرِس [daris] درُوس [dru:s] *pl:* Translate lesson five for tomorrow. تَرجُم الدَّرس الخامِس لِباكِر [tarjum ʔiddars ʔilxa:mis lba:čir] I'll have to do my lessons first. لازِم أَسَوِّي درُوسِي أَوَّل [la:zim ʔasawwi dru:si ʔawwal] She gives Spanish lessons. تِنطِي درُوس بالإسبانِي [tinṭi dru:s bilʔispa:ni] • **2.** عِبرَة [ʕibra] عِبَر [ʕibar] *pl:* Let that be a lesson to you. خَلِّي هَذا يكُون عِبرَة إِلَك [xalli ha:ða yku:n ʕabra ʔilak] I hope you've learned a good lesson from that. إِن شاء الله أَخَذِت خُوش دَرِس مِن هاي [ʔinša:llah ʔaxaðit xu:š daris min ha:y]

let • **1.** نَتّ [natt] شَبَكَة [šabaka] That serve was let. Take two more serves. هَالضَربَة كانَت نَتّ أُخُذلَك بَعَد ضَرُبتَين [haððarba ča:nat natt ʔuxuðlak baʕad ḍarubtayn]

let alone • **1.** بِغَضّ النَظَر عَن [biɣaḍḍ ʔinnaḍar ʕan] He can't even read Arabic, let alone speak it. ما يُعرُف يِقرَأ عَرَبِي، بغَضّ النَّظَر عَن الحَكِي [ma: yuʕruf yiqraʔ ʕarabi, bɣaḍḍ ʔinnaḍar ʕan ʔilħači]

let's • **1.** خَلِّي [xalli] يا الله [yallah] Let's go home. خَلِّي نرُوح لِلبَيت [xalli nru:ħ lilbayt] Let's not leave the party until twelve o'clock. خَلِي ما نِترُك الحَفلَة حَتَّى السّاعَة ثنَعَش [xalli ma: nitruk ʔilħafla ħatta ʔissa:ʕa θnaʕaš]

to let • **1.** خَلَّى [xalla:] تخِلِّي [txilli] *vn:* تخَلَّى [txalla:] *p:* سِمَح ل [simaħ l-] سَمِح [samiħ] *vn:* اِنسِمَح ل [ʔinsimaħ l-] *p:* He wouldn't let me do it. ما خَلانِي أَسَوِّيها [ma: xalla:ni ʔasawwi:ha] Please let me have the menu. إِنطِينِي قائِمَة الأَكِل رَجاءاً [ʔinṭi:ni qa:ʔimat ʔilʔakil raja:ʔan] Please let me have the menu. إِسمَحلِي بِقائِمَة الأَكِل [ʔismaħli biqa:ʔimat ʔilʔakil] I can't let his statement stand. ما أَخَلِّي كَلامَه يرُوح بِفالَه [ma: ʔaxalli kala:mah yiru:ħ bifa:lah] Will the customs officials let us pass? عَجَباً مُوَظَفِين الجُمرُك راح يِسمَحُوا إِلنا بِالمُرُور؟ [ʕajaban muwaḍafi:n ʔilgumrug ra:ħ yismaħu:lna bilmuru:r?] He wouldn't let me out. ما خَلانِي أَطلَع [ma: xalla:ni ʔaṭlaʕ] Don't let anybody in. لا تخَلِّي أَحَّد يفُوت [la: txalli ʔaħħad yfu:t] This time I'll let it go. هَالمَرَّة راح أَسمَحلَك [halmarra ra:ħ ʔasmaħlak] This time I'll let it go. هَالمَرَّة راح أَخَلِّيها تفُوت [halmarra ra:ħ ʔaxalli:ha tfu:t] Can you let me have five dinars until I get paid? تِقدَر تِسمَحلِي بخَمس دَنانِير إِلَى أَن آخُذ راتبِي؟ [tigdar tismaħli bxams dana:ni:r ʔila ʔan ʔa:xuð ra:tbi?] • **2.** تِرَك [tirak] تَرِك [tarik] *vn:* *sv* u. خَلَّى [xalla:] تخِلِّي [txilli] *vn:* *sv* i. Can't you let me alone for five minutes? ما تِقدَر تِترُكنِي وَحدِي خَمِس دَقايِق؟ [ma: tigdar titrukni waħdi xamis daqa:yiq?]

*** Have you rooms to let?** • **1.** عِندَك غُرَف لِلأيجار؟ [ʕindak ɣuraf lilʔi:ja:r?]

*** I really let him have it!** • **1.** نطَيتَه حَقَّه بإيدَه [nṭi:tah ħagga bʔi:dah]

to let down • **1.** نَزَّل [nazzal] تَنزِيل [tanzi:l] *vn:* تنَزَّل [tnazzal] *p:* Please let down the store front. بالله ما تنَزِّل الكَبَنكات [ballah ma: tnazzil ʔilkabanga:t] • **2.** خَيَّب [xayyab] تخِيِّب [txiyyib] *vn:* *sv* i. His son has let him down badly. إبنَه خَيَّب أَمَلَه كُلِّش [ʔibnah xayyab ʔamalah kulliš] He let me down when I needed him. خَيَّبنِي مِن اِحتِجِت إِلَه [xayyabni min ʔiħtijit ʔilah] He let me down when I needed him. عافنِي مِن اِحتِجِت إِلَه [ʕa:fni min ʔiħtijit ʔilah] • **3.** تماهَل [tma:hal] تَماهُل [tama:hul] *vn:* *sv* a. He's beginning to let down in his work. بِدا يِتماهَل بشُغلَه [bida: yitma:hal bšuɣlah]

to let go of • **1.** هَدّ [hadd] هَدّ [hadd] *vn:* اِنهَدّ [ʔinhadd] *p:* حَلّ [ħall] حُلُول [ħulu:l] *pl:* حَلّ [ħall] *vn:* اِنحَلّ [ʔinħall] *p:* Don't let go of the rope. لا تهِدّ الحَبِل [la: thidd ʔilħabil]

to let in on • **1.** فِشَى [fiša:] فَشِي [faši] *vn:* *sv* i. Did you let him in on the secret, too? فِشَيتلَه السِّرّ هَمِّينَة؟ [fiši:tlah ʔissirr hammi:na?]

to let off • **1.** نَزَّل [nazzal] Please let me off at the next stop. نَزِّلنِي بِالمَحَطَّة [nazzilni bilmaħaṭṭa] • **2.** سامَح [sa:maħ] مُسامَحَة [musa:maħa] *vn:* تسامَح [tsa:maħ] *p:* I'll let you off easy this time. راح أَسامحَك هَالمَرَّة [ra:ħ ʔasa:mħak halmarra]

to let on • **1.** بَيَّن عَلَى نَفس [bayyan ʕala nafs] تَبيِين عَلَى نَفس [tabyi:n ʕala nafs] *vn:* *sv* i. خَلَّى [xalla:] [.] *vn:* *sv* i. He didn't let on that he knew anything about it. ما بَيَّن عَلَى نَفسَه إِنُّو يعرُف شِي عَنها [ma: bayyan ʕala nafsah ʔinnu yuʕruf ši ʕanha]

to let out • **1.** فَرَّغ [farraɣ] تَفرِيغ [tafri:ɣ] *vn:* تفَرَّغ [tfarraɣ] *p:* Let the water out of the sink. فَرِّغ المَيّ مِن المَغسَلَة [farriɣ ʔilmayy min ʔilmaɣsala] • **2.** عَرَّض [ʕarraḍ] تَعرِيض [taʕri:ḍ] *vn:* تعَرَّض [tʕarraḍ] *p:* I told the tailor to let out the waist. قِتلَه الخَيّاط يعَرِّض الخَصِر [gittlah ʔilxayya:ṭ yʕarriḍ ʔilxaṣir]

to let up • **1.** خَفّ [xaff] خَفّ [xaff] *vn:* *sv* u. The storm has let up. العاصِفَة خَفَّت [ʔilʕa:ṣifa xaffat]

letdown • **1.** خَيبَة أَمَل [xaybat ʔamal] خَيبات أَمَل [xayba:t ʔamal] *pl:* The failure of our plan was a big letdown. فَشَل مَشرُوعنا كان خَيبَة أَمَل كبِيرَة [fašal mašru:ʕna ča:n xaybat ʔamal čbi:ra]

letter • **1.** مَكتُوب [maktu:b] مَكاتِيب [maka:ti:b] *pl:* رِسالَة [risa:la] رَسائِل [rasa:ʔil] *pl:* Are there any letters for me? أَكُو أَيّ مَكاتِيب إِلِي؟ [ʔaku ʔayy maka:ti:b ʔili?] I want to send an airmail letter. أَرِيد أَبعَث رِسالَة بِالبَرِيد الجَوِّي [ʔari:d ʔabʕaθ risa:la bilbari:d ʔiǰǰawwi] • **2.** حَرُف [ħaruf] حُرُوف [ħuru:f] *pl:* The word has five letters. الكَلِمَة بِيها خَمس حرُوف [ʔilkalima bi:ha xams ħru:f] • **3.** نَصّ [naṣṣ] He sticks to the letter of the law. يِتقَيَّد بِنصُوص القانُون [yitqayyad biniṣu:ṣ ʔilqa:nu:n]

letter carrier • **1.** أَبُو البَرِيد [ʔabu ʔilbari:d] ساعِي البَرِيد [sa:ʕi ʔilbari:d] سُعاة البَرِيد [suʕa:t ʔilbari:d] *pl:*

lettuce • **1.** خَسّ [xass]

letup • **1.** اِنقِطاع [ʔinqiṭa:ʕ] فَكَّة [fakka] فَكّات [fakka:t] *pl:* It's been raining without any letup all day. صارِلها تُمطُر بِدُون اِنقِطاع اليُوم كُلَّه [ṣa:rilha tumṭur bidu:n ʔinqiṭa:ʕ ʔilyu:m kullah]

level • **1.** مُستَوَى [mustawa] His work isn't up to the usual level. شُغلَه مُو بِالمُستَوَى الاعتِيادِي [šɣlah mu: bilmustawa ʔilʔiʕtiya:di] The Dead Sea is below sea level. البَحَر المَيِّت تَحِت مُستَوَى البَحَر [ʔilbaħar ʔilmayyit taħit mustawa ʔilbaħar] The bookcase is level with the table. المَكتَبَة بِمُستَوَى المِيز [ʔilmaktaba bmustawa ʔilmi:z] The water level this year is very low. مُستَوَى الماي هالسَّنَة كُلِّش واطِي [mustawa ʔilma:y hassana kulliš wa:ṭi] • **2.** صِنِف [ṣinif] أَصناف، صُنُوف [ʔaṣna:f, ṣunu:f] *pl:* دَرَجَة [daraǰa] دَرَجات [daraǰa:t] *pl:* There are five salary levels in our office. أَكُو خَمِس أَصناف لِلرَّواتِب بِدائِرَتنا [ʔaku xamis ʔaṣna:f lirrawa:tib bda:ʔiratna] • **3.** قُبّان [gubba:n] قُبابِين [guba:bi:n] *pl:* Have you a level handy to check the tiles? أَكُو جَوَّة إِيدَك قُبّان حَتَّى نُضبُط الكاشِي؟ [ʔaku ǰawwa ʔi:dak gubba:n ħatta nuðbuṭ ʔilka:ši?] • **4.** مُستَوِي [mustawi] عَدِل [ʕadil] Is the country level or hilly? المَنطِقَة مُستَوِيَة لَو جَبَلِيَّة؟ [ʔilmanṭiqa mustawiya law ǰabaliyya?]

* **He did his level best.** • **1.** سَوَّى اللِّي يِقدَر عَلَيه [sawwa: ʔilli yigdar ʕali:h]

* **He always keeps a level head.** • **1.** دائِماً ضابُط أَعصابَه [da:ʔiman ða:buṭ ʔaʕṣa:bah]

* **Is he on the level?** • **1.** هُوَّ صادِق؟ [huwwa ṣa:diq?]

to level • **1.** سَوَّى [sawwa:] تَسوِيَة [taswiya] *vn:* تسَوَّى [tsawwa:] *p:* عَدَّل [ʕaddal] تَعدِيل [taʕdi:l] *vn:* تعَدَّل [tʕaddal] *p:* The ground has to be leveled. القاع يِنرادِلها تَسوِيَة [ʔilga:ʕ yinra:dilha taswiya] The artillery fire leveled the town to the ground. ضَرُب المَدفَعِيَّة سَوَّى المَدِينَة وِيّا القاع [ðarub ʔilmadfaʕiyya sawwa: ʔilmadi:na wiyya ʔilga:ʕ] • **2.** وَجَّه [waǰǰah] تَوجِيه [tawǰi:h] *vn: sv* i. He leveled a number of insults at the president. وَجَّه عِدَّة شتايِم لِلرَّئِيس [waǰǰah ʕiddat šta:yim lirraʔi:s] He leveled the gun at me and threatened to fire. وَجَّه البُندُقِيَّة عَلَيّا وَهَدَّدنِي بِإِطلاق النّار [waǰǰah ʔilbunduqiyya ʕalayya whaddadni bʔiṭla:q ʔinna:r]

to level off • **1.** اِستَعدَل [ʔistaʕdal] اِستِعدال [ʔistiʕda:l] *vn: sv* i. اِعتِدَل [ʔiʕtidal] اِعتِدال [ʔiʕtida:l] *vn: sv* i. The plane leveled off at 10, 000 feet. الطَّيّارَة اِستَعدِلَت عَلَى إِرتِفاع عَشرَة آلاف قَدَم [ʔiṭṭiyya:ra ʔistaʕdilat ʕala ʔirtifa:ʕ ʕašrat ʔa:la:f qadam]

lever • **1.** عَتَلَة [ʕatala] عَتَلات [ʕatala:t] *pl:*

to levy • **1.** فِرَض [firaḍ] فَرُض [faruḍ] *vn:* اِنفِرَض [ʔinfiraḍ] *p:* خَلَّى [xalla:] تَخلِيَة [taxliya] *vn:* تخَلَّى [txalla:] *p:* The government will levy a tax on gasoline. الحُكُومَة راح تِفرُض ضَرِيبَة عَلَى البانزِين [ʔilħuku:ma ra:ħ tifruḍ ḍari:ba ʕala ʔilbanzi:n]

lewd • **1.** خِلاعِي [xila:ʕi] She did a lewd dance. قامَت بِرَقصَة خِلاعِيَّة [ga:mat braqṣa xila:ʕiyya]

liable • **1.** مَسؤُول [masʔu:l] You will be liable for any damages. راح تكُون مَسؤُول عَن كُلّ ضَرَر [ra:ħ tku:n masʔu:l ʕan kull ðarar] • **2.** مُحتَمَل [muħtamal] You're liable to catch cold if you're not careful. مُحتَمَل تاخُذ بَرِد إِذا ما تدِير بالَك [muħtamal ta:xuð barid ʔiða ma: ddi:r ba:lak]

* **He's liable to forget!** • **1.** مُحتَمَل يِنسَى [muħtamal yinsa:]

liability • **1.** دَين [dayn] دْيُون [dyu:n] *pl:* His liabilities exceed his assets. دْيُونَه أَكثَر مِن ما يِملُك [dyu:nah ʔakθar min ma: yimluk]

liaison officer • **1.** ضابُط اِتِّصال [ða:buṭ ʔittiṣa:l] ضُبّاط اِتِّصال [ðubba:ṭ ʔittiṣa:l] *pl:*

liar • **1.** كَذّاب [čaðða:b, kaðða:b] كَذّابِين [čaðða:bi:n, kaðða:bi:n] *pl:*

libel • **1.** تَشهِير [tašhi:r] طَعِن [ṭaʕin] This report is pure libel. هذا التَّقرِير كُلَّه تَشهِير [ha:ða ʔittaqri:r kullah tašhi:r]

liberal • **1.** مِتحَرِّر [mitħarrir] He has liberal views. عِندَه آراء مِتحَرِّرَة [ʕindah ʔa:ra:ʔ mitħarrira] He's a liberal. هُوَّ مِتحَرِّر [huwwa mitħarrir] • **2.** سَخِي [saxi] كَرِيم [kari:m] كُرَماء [kurama:ʔ] *pl:* She's very liberal with her money. هِيَّ كُلِّش سَخِيَّة بِفلُوسها [hiyya kulliš saxiyya biflu:sha]

to liberate • **1.** حَرَّر [ħarrar] تَحرِير [taħri:r] *vn:* تحَرَّر [tħarrar] *p:* عِتَق [ʕitaq] عَتِق [ʕatiq] *vn:* اِنعِتَق [ʔinʕitaq] *p:* He liberated his slaves. حَرَّر عَبِيدَه [ħarrar ʕabi:dah]

L

liberty • **1.** حُرِّيَّة [ħurriyya] حُرِّيّات [ħurriyya:t] *pl:* We are all fighting for liberty. كُلْنا ندافِع بسَبِيل الحُرِّيَّة [kullna nda:fiʕ bsabi:l ʔalħurriyya]

*** He takes too many liberties for his position.** • **1.** يِتعَدَّي حِدُود وَظِيفتَه [yitʕadda: ħidu:d waðiːftah]

at liberty • **1.** حُرّ [ħurr] You're at liberty to say what you wish. إنتَ حُرّ، تِقدَر تِقُول شما تريد [ʔinta ħurr, tigdar tigu:l šma tri:d]

librarian • **1.** أَمِين مَكتَبَة [ʔami:n maktaba] أُمَناء مَكتَبَة [ʔumana:ʔ maktaba] *pl:*

library • **1.** مَكتَبَة [maktaba] مَكتَبات [maktaba:t] *pl:*

Libya • **1.** لِيبيا [li:bya]

Libyan • **1.** لِيبِي [li:bi] لِيبِيِّين [li:biyyi:n] *pl:* There are three Libyans in my office. أَكُو ثلاث لِيبِيِّين بدائِرتِي [ʔaku tla:θ li:biyyi:n bda:ʔirti] • **2.** لِيبِي [li:bi] Where can I buy a Libyan newspaper? وين أَقدَر أَشتِري جَرِيدَة لِيبِيَّة؟ [wi:n ʔagdar ʔaštiri ǰari:da li:biyya?]

license • **1.** إجازَة [ʔiǰa:za] إجازات [ʔiǰa:za:t] *pl:* You need a license to open a restaurant. تِحتاج إجازَة حَتَّى تِفتَح مَطعَم [tiħta:ǰ ʔiǰa:za ħatta tiftaħ matʕam] You cannot drive without a license. ما تِقدَر تسُوق بِلا إجازَة [ma: tigdar tsu:g bila ʔiǰa:za]

to license • **1.** أَجاز [ʔaǰa:z] إجازَة [ʔiǰa:za] *vn: sv* i. They licensed him to practice medicine in Iraq. أجازَوا لِمُمارَسَة الطِّبّ بِالعِراق [ʔaǰa:zawh limuma:rasat ʔittibb bilʕira:q]

licensed • **1.** مُجاز [muǰa:z] He's a licensed pharmacist. هُوَّ صَيدَلِي مُجاز [huwwa ṣaydali muǰa:z]

license plate • **1.** قُطعَة [qutʕa] قُطَع [qutaʕ] *pl:* My car's license plates are dirty. قُطَع سَيّارتِي وَسخَة [qutaʕ sayya:rti wasxa]

lick • **1.** لَطعَة [latʕa] لَطعات [latʕa:t] *pl:* Let him have a lick of your ice cream. خَلِّي ياخُذ لَطعَة مِن الدَّوندِرمَة مالتَك [xalli ya:xuð latʕa min ʔiddu:ndirma ma:ltak]

to lick • **1.** لِحَس [liħas] لَحِس [laħis] *vn:* اِنلِحَس [ʔinliħas] *p:* لِطَع [litaʕ] لَطِع [latiʕ] *vn:* اِنلِطَع [ʔinlitaʕ] *p:* Just look at the cat licking her kitten. شُوف البَزُّونَة دَتلِحَس وِلِدها [šu:f ʔilbazzu:na datilħas wilidha] • **2.** ضِرَب [ðirab] ضَرُب [ðarub] *vn:* اِنضِرَب [ʔinðirab] *p:* بُسَط [busat] بَسُط [basut] *vn:* اِنبُسَط [ʔinbusat] *p:* I'm going to lick you if you don't stop. تَرَة راح أَضُربَك إذا ما تبَطِّل [tara ra:ħ ʔaðurbak ʔiða ma: tbattil] • **3.** وَرَّم [warram] تَورِيم [tawri:m] *vn:* توَرَّم [twarram] *p:* غِلَب [ɣilab] غَلُب [ɣalub] *vn:* اِنغِلَب [ʔinɣilab] *p:* I can still lick you! بَعَدنِي أَقدَر أَوَرِّمَك [baʕadni ʔagdar ʔawarrmak] All right, I'm licked. أَعتِرِف آنِي اِنغِلَبِت [ʔaʕtirif ʔa:ni ʔinɣilabit]

licking • **1.** بَسطَة [basta] بَسطات [basta:t] *pl:* What you need is a good licking. اللِّي تِحتاجَه بَسطَة ناشفَة [ʔilli tiħta:ǰah basta na:šfa]

licorice • **1.** عِرق السُّوس [ʕirg ʔissu:s]

lid • **1.** غِطَة [ɣita] أَغطِيَة [ʔaɣtiya] *pl:* غِطيات [ɣitya:t] Put the lid back on the pot. رَجِّع الغِطا عالجِدِر [raǰǰiʕ ʔilɣita ʕaǰǰidir]

lie • **1.** كِذبَة [čiðba, kiðba] كِذبات، أَكاذِيب [čiðba:t, kiðba:t, ʔaka:ði:b] *pl:* كِذِب [čiðib] *Collective*

to lie • **1.** كِذَب [čiðab, kiðab] كِذِب [kiðib] *vn: sv* i. There's no doubt that he's lying. ماكُو شَكّ هُوَّ دَيكِذِب [ma:ku šakk huwwa dayikðib] • **2.** تمَدَّد [tmaddad] تَمَدُّد [tamaddud] *vn: sv* a. He is lying on the couch. هُوَّ مِتمَدِّد عالقَنَفَة [huwwa mitmaddid ʕa:lqanafa] • **3.** Most of the town lies on the right side of the river. مُعظَم المَدِينَة واقِع عَالجِّهَة اليِمنَى مِن النَّهَر [muʕðam ʔilmadi:na wa:qiʕ ʕaǰǰiha ʔilyimna min ʔinnahar]

*** The book is lying on the table.** • **1.** الِكتاب عَالمَيز [ʔilikta:b ʕalmayz]

to lie down • **1.** تمَدَّد [tmaddad] تَمَدُّد [tamaddud] *vn: sv* a. اِنجِطَل [ʔinǰital] اِنجِطال [ʔinǰita:l] *vn: sv* i. I want to lie down for a few minutes. أَرِيد أَتمَدَّد كَم دَقِيقَة [ʔari:d ʔatmaddad čam daqi:qa]

*** He's lying down on the job.** • **1.** مَا ذابّ نَفسَه عَالشُّغُل [ma: ða:bb nafsah ʕaššuɣul]

lieutenant • **1.** مُلازِم [mula:zim] مُلازِمِين [mula:zimi:n] *pl:*

lieutenant colonel • **1.** مُقَدَّم [muqaddam] مُقَدَّمِين [muqaddami:n] *pl:*

life • **1.** حَياة [ħaya:t] It was a matter of life or death. كانَت مَسأَلَة حَياة أَو موت [ča:nat masʔalat ħaya:t ʔaw mawt] The night life in this town is dull. الحَياة اللَّيلِيَّة بهالبَلَد جامدَة [ʔilħaya:t ʔillayliyya bha:lbalad ǰa:mda] He lost his life in an accident. فُقَد حَياتَه بحادِث [fuqad ħaya:tah bħa:diθ] Such a life! الحَياة هِيكِي [ʔilħaya:t hi:či] Such a life! هاي هِيَّ الحَياة [ha:y hiyya ʔilħaya:t] Such a life! هاي هِيَّ الدِّنيا [ha:y hiyya ʔiddinya] • **2.** قُصَّة حَياة [quṣṣat ħaya:t] قُصَص حَياة [quṣaṣ ħaya:t] *pl:* He's writing a life of the President. دَيكِتِب قُصَّة حَياة الرَّئِيس [dayiktib quṣṣat ħaya:t ʔirraʔi:s] • **3.** حَيَوِيَّة [ħayawiyya] She's full of life. كُلّها حَيَوِيَّة [kullha ħayawiyya] • **4.** رُوح [ru:ħ] أَرواح [ʔarwa:ħ] *pl:* He was the life of the party. هُوَّ كان رُوح الحَفلَة [huwwa ča:n ru:ħ ʔilħafla] I can't for the life of me remember where I put it. لَو تاخُذ رُوحِي ما أَقدَر أَتذَكَّر وِين حَطَّيتها [law ta:xuð ru:ħi ma: ʔagdar ʔadðakkar wi:n ħatti:tha]

I can't for the life of me remember where I put it. وَالله راح أتخَبَّل ما أقدَر أتذَكَّر وين حَطّيتها [w?allah ra:ħ ?atxabbal ma: ?agdar ?adðakkar wi:n ħaṭṭi:tha]
• **5.** أحياء [?aħya:?] We visited an exhibition of marine life. زرنا مَعرَض الأحياء المائيَّة [zirna maʕrað ?il?aħya:? ?ilma:?iyya] • **6.** مُؤَبَّد [mu?abbad] He was sentenced to life imprisonment. اِنحِكَم عَليه بِالسِّجِن المُؤَبَّد [?inħikam ʕali:h bissiǰin ?ilmu?abbad]

*** This bulb has a life of six hundred hours.** • **1.** هَالِكلوب يدُوم سِتّ مِيَّة ساعَة [haliglu:b ydu:m sitt miyat sa:ʕa]

*** There he stood as big as life.**
• **1.** وُقَف هناك واضِح مِثِل الشَّمِس [wugaf hna:k wa:ðiħ miθil ?iššamis]

*** You can bet your life on that.** • **1.** أكِيد [?aki:d] / بِالتَّأكِيد [bitta?aki:d]

life belt • **1.** حزام نَجاة [ħza:m naǰa:t] حزامات نَجاة [ħza:ma:t naǰa:t] *pl:* أحزِمَة نَجاة [?aħzimat naǰa:t] *pl:*

lifeboat • **1.** زَورَق نَجاة [zawraq naǰa:t] زَوارِق نَجاة [zawa:riq naǰa:t] *pl:* قارِب نَجاة [qa:rib naǰa:t] قَوارِب نَجاة [qawa:rib naǰa:t] *pl:*

life insurance • **1.** تَأمِين عَالحَياة [ta?mi:n ʕalħaya:t]

lifetime • **1.** عُمُر [ʕumur] أعمار [?aʕma:r] *pl:* A thing like that happens only once in a lifetime. مِثِل هَالشِّي يصِير مَرَّة بِالعُمُر بَسّ [miθil hašši yṣi:r marra bilʕumur bass]

lift • **1.** مَصعَد [maṣʕad] مَصاعِد [maṣa:ʕid] *pl:* Let's take the lift to the fifth floor. خَلّي ناخُذ المَصعَد لِلطّابِق الخامِس [xalli na:xuð ?ilmaṣʕad litṭa:biq ?ilxa:mis]

*** A glass of tea in the afternoon gives me a lift.**
• **1.** اِستِكان شاي العَصِر ينعِشني [?istika:n ča:y ?ilʕaṣir yinʕišni] / اِستِكان شاي العَصِر يقَعِّد راسِي [?istika:n ča:y ?ilʕaṣir ygaʕʕid ra:si]

*** Can I give you a lift?** • **1.** أقدَر أوَصّلَك؟ [?agdar ?awaṣṣlak?]

to lift • **1.** شال [ša:l] شَيل [šayl] *vn:* اِنشال [?inša:l] *p:* He lifted the baby out of the cradle. شال الطِّفِل مِن الكارُوك [ša:l ?iṭṭifil min ?ilka:ru:k] • **2.** رِفَع [rifaʕ] رَفُع [rafuʕ] *vn: sv* a. The good news lifted our spirits. الأخبار الزِّينَة رِفعَت مَعنَوِيّاتنا [?il?axba:r ?izzayna rifʕat maʕnawiyya:tna]
• **3.** رِفَع [rifaʕ] رَفُع [rafuʕ] *vn:* اِنرِفَع [?inrifaʕ] *p:* شال [ša:l] شَيل [šayl] *vn:* اِنشال [?inša:l] *p:* After two weeks the ban was lifted. بَعَد إسبُوعَين المَنع انرُفَع [baʕad ?isbu:ʕayn ?ilmaniʕ ?inrufaʕ] • **4.** زال [za:l] زَوال [zawa:l] *vn: sv* u. Toward noon the fog lifted. زال الضُّباب حَوالِي الظُّهُر [za:l ?iððuba:b ħawa:li ?iððuhur]

*** I won't lift a finger for him no matter what.**
• **1.** وَالله ما أساعدَه لَو شِيصِير [w?allah ma: ?asa:ʕdah law šiyṣi:r]

light • **1.** ضُوَة، ضُوَا [ðuwa] أضوِيَة، ضُوايات [ðuwa:ya:t, ?aðwiya] *pl:* The light is too glaring. الضُوا كُلِّش ساطِع [?iððuwa kulliš sa:ṭiʕ] The lights of the town came on one by one. أضوِيَة المَدِينَة اِشتِعلَت واحِد بَعد اللّاخ [?aðwiyat ?ilmadi:na ?ištiʕlat wa:ħid baʕd ?illa:x] Don't cross until the light changes to green. لا تُعبُر قَبُل ما يِتبَدَّل الضُوَة إلَى أخضَر [la: tuʕbur gabul ma: yitbaddal ?iððuwa ?ila ?axðar]
• **2.** شِخّاطَة [šixxa:ṭa] شِخّاطات [šixxa:ṭa:t] *pl:* نار [na:r] نِيران [ni:ra:n] *pl:* Do you have a light? عِندَك شِخّاطَة؟ [ʕindak šixxa:ṭa?] • **3.** ضاوِي [ða:wi] It's staying light much longer. الدِّنيا تِبقَى ضاوِيَة مُدَّة أطوَل [?iddinya tibqa: ða:wya mudda ?aṭwal] • **4.** أبيَض [?abyað] بِيض [bi:ð] *pl:* بَيضَة [bayða] *Feminine:* كاشِف [ka:šif] She has a light complexion. لُون وِجهَها أبيَض [lu:n wiččha ?abyað] • **5.** فاتِح [fa:tiħ] كاشِف [ka:šif] She prefers light colors. تفَضِّل الألوان الفاتحَة [tfaððil ?il?alwa:n ?ilfa:tħa] I want a light blue hat. أرِيد شَفقَة ماوِيَّة فاتحَة [?ari:d šafqa ma:wiyya fa:tiħa] • **6.** خَفِيف [xafi:f] خفاف [xfa:f] *pl:* Why don't you take your light coat? لِيش ما تاخُذ بالطُّوك الخَفِيف؟ [li:š ma: ta:xuð pa:ltuwwak ?ilxafi:f?] There was a light rain today. صارَت مَطرَة خَفِيفَة اليُوم [ṣa:rat maṭra xafi:fa ?ilyu:m] I had a light breakfast today. رِيُوقِي كان خَفِيف اليُوم [ryu:gi ča:n xafi:f ?ilyu:m]

*** He's very light-fingered.** • **1.** إيدَه طُويلَة [?i:dah ṭuwi:la]

*** He's at last seen the light.** • **1.** وأخِيراً اِكتِشَف الحَقِيقَة [w?axi:ran ?iktišaf ?ilħaqi:qa]

to bring to light • **1.** أظهَر [?aðhar] إظهار [?iðha:r] *vn: sv* i. The investigation brought many new facts to light. التَّحقِيق أظهَر حَقايِق جِدِيدَة [?ittaħqi:q ?aðhar ħaqa:?iq ǰidi:da]

to come to light • **1.** ظِهَر [ðihar] ظهُور [ðhu:r] *vn: sv* a. A number of problems came to light during our research. بَعض المَشاكِل ظِهرَت أثناء بَحِثنا [baʕð ?ilmaša:kil ðihrat ?aθna:? bahiθna]

to light • **1.** شِعَل [šiʕal] شَعِل [šaʕil] *vn:* اِنشِعَل [?inšiʕal] *p:* Wait till I light the fire. اِنتِظِر حَتَّى أشعِل النّار [?intiðir ħatta ?ašʕil ?inna:r] Light a match. إشعِل شِخّاطَة [?išʕil šixxa:ṭa] • **2.** وَرَّث [warraθ] تورِيث [tawri:θ] *vn:* توَرَّث [twarraθ] *p:* شِعَل [šiʕal] شَعِل [šaʕil] *vn:* اِنشِعَل [?inšiʕal] *p:* I want to light my pipe first. أرِيد أوَرِّث البايب مالِي أوَّل [?ari:d ?awarriθ ?ilpa:yip ma:li ?awwal] Is your cigarette still lit? جِكارتَك بَعَدها موَرّثَة؟ [ǰiga:rtak baʕadha mwarrθa?] • **3.** ضَوَّى [ðawwa:] تَضوِيَة [taðwiya] *vn:* تضَوَّى [tðawwa:] *p:* The hall was brightly lighted. القاعَة كانَت مضَوّايَة زين [?ilqa:ʕa ča:nat mðawwa:ya zi:n] The street is poorly lighted. الشّارِع تَضوِيتَه مُو زينَة [?išša:riʕ taðwi:tah mu: zi:na]

to light up • **1.** لِمَع [limaʕ] لَمِع [lamiʕ] *vn: sv* a. The children's eyes lit up. عيُون الأطفال لِمعَت [ʕyu:n ?il?aṭfa:l limʕat]

L

lightbulb • **1.** كلوب [gluːb] كلوبات [gluːbaːt] *pl:*

to lighten • **1.** بَرَق [biraq] بَرِق [bariq] *vn: sv* i. وُمَض [wumaǒ] وَميض [wamiːǒ] *vn: sv* a. It's thundering and lightening. دَتِرعِد وَتبرِق [datirʕid wtibriq] • **2.** خَفَّف [xaffaf] تَخفِيف [taxfiːf] *vn: sv* i. كِشَف [kišaf] كَشِف [kašif] *vn: sv* i. Add a little white paint to lighten the color. خَلّي شوَيَّة بُويَة بيضة حَتّى تخَفِّف اللّون [xalli šwayya buːya biːǒa ħatta txaffif ʔilluːn] • **3.** خَفَّف [xaffaf] *sv* i. نَزَّل [nazzal] تَنزِيل [tanziːl] *vn: sv* i. If you don't lighten the weight, the tires will blow out. إذا ما تخَفِّف الوَزِن تَرَة التّايرات تدُق [ʔiǒa maː txaffif ʔilwazin tara ʔittaːyiraːt tdugg]

lighthouse • **1.** فَنار [fanaːr] فَنارات [fanaːraːt] *pl:* مَنارَة [manaːra] مَنايِر [manaːyir] *pl:*

lighting • **1.** إضاءَة [ʔiḍaːʔa] تَضوِيَة [taǒwiya] The lighting is bad here. الإضاءَة مُو زينَة هنا [ʔilʔiḍaːʔa muː ziːna hna]

lightning • **1.** صاعِقَة [ṣaːʕiqa] صَواعِق [ṣawaːʕiq] *pl:* Lightning struck the church steeple. الصّاعِقَة نِزلَت عَلَى بُرج الكَنِيسَة [ʔiṣṣaːʕiqa nizlat ʕala burǰ ʔilkaniːsa] • **2.** بَرق [barq] بُرُوق [buruːq] *pl:* There's thunder and lightning. أكُو بَرق وَرَعَد [ʔaku barq wraʕad]

like • **1.** مِثِل [miθil] You're just like my sister. إنتِي بِالضَبُط مِثِل أُختِي [ʔinti biǒǒabuṭ miθil ʔuxti] He ran like mad. ركَض مِثل المَجنُون [rikaǒ miθl ʔilmajnuːn] There's nothing like traveling! ماكُو شِي مِثِل السَّفَر [maːku ši miθil ʔissafar] • **2.** مِثِل ما [miθil maː] She's just like I pictured her. هِيَّ بِالضَبُط مِثِلما تصَوَّرتها [hiyya biǒǒabuṭ miθilma tṣawwaritha]

* **That's more like it!** • **1.** هَذا أقرَب إلَى [haːǒa ʔaqrab ʔila] / هَسَّة أحسَن [hassa ʔaħsan]

* **That's just like him.** • **1.** هاي دَقّاتَه [haːy daggaːtah] / هاي عَمايلَه [haːy ʕamaːylah]

* **Did you ever see the likes of it?** • **1.** شايِف شَبِيه إلَه؟ [šaːyif šabiːh ʔilah?] What's the weather like today? شلُون الجَّوّ اليُوم؟ [šluːn ʔiǰǰaww ʔilyuːm?]

* **Like father, like son.** • **1.** إبن الوَزّ عَوّام [ʔibn ʔilwazz ʕawwaːm]

* **I don't feel like dancing.** • **1.** ما عِندِي رَغبَة لِلرقُص [maː ʕindi rayba lirriguṣ]

* **It looks like rain.** • **1.** تبَيِّن راح تُمطُر [tbayyin raːħ tumṭur]

like this, like that • **1.** هِيكِي [hiːči] It's not like that at all. مُو هِيكِي أبَداً [muː hiːči ʔabadan] Ordinarily, we do it like this. عادَةً هِيكِي نسَوِّيها [ʕaːdatan hiːči nsawwiːha] • **2.** مِثِل هَذا [miθil haːǒa] I want something like this. أرِيد شِي مِثِل هَذا [ʔariːd ši miθil haːǒa]

to like • **1.** حَبّ [ħabb] حُبّ [ħubb] *vn:* اِنحَبّ [ʔinħabb] *p:* I don't like cats. ما أحِبّ البزازِين [maː ʔaħibb ʔilbzaːziːn] I don't like cats. ما تِعجِبنِي البزازِين [maː tiʕǰibni ʔilbizaːziːn] He never liked to do it. أبَداً ما حَبّ يسَوِّيها [ʔabadan maː ħabb ysawwiːha] He never liked to do it. ما يعجبَه يسَوِّيها [maː yʕiǰbah ysawwiːha] Would you like another cup of coffee? تحِبّ فِنجان قَهوَة لاخ؟ [tħibb finǰaːn gahwa laːx?] Would you like another cup of coffee? يِعجبَك فِنجان قَهوَة لاخ؟ [yiʕiǰbak finǰaːn gahwa laːx?] • **2.** شاف [šaːf] *sv* u. How do you like this town? شتشُوف هالمَدِينَة؟ [šitšuːf halmadiːna?]

likelihood • **1.** اِحتِمال [ʔiħtimaːl] There is a great likelihood that he'll come. أكُو اِحتِمال كِبِير هُوَّ راح يجِي [ʔaku ʔiħtimaːl čibiːr huwwa raːħ yiǰi]

in all likelihood • **1.** عَلَى الأرجَح [ʕala ʔilʔarǰaħ] In all likelihood he'll get the job. عَلَى الأرجَح هُوَّ راح ياخُذ الشّغلَة [ʕala ʔiʔarǰaħ huwwa raːħ yaːxuǒ ʔiššayla]

likely • **1.** مُحتَمَل [muħtamal] That's more likely. هَذا مُحتَمَل أكثَر [haːǒa muħtamal ʔakθar]

lilac • **1.** لَيلَكِي [laylaki] She bought a lilac blouse. اِشتِرَت بلُوز لَيلَكِي [ʔištirat bluːz laylaki]

lily • **1.** زَنبَقَة [zanbaqa] زَنابِق [zanaːbiq] *pl:* زَنبَق [zanbaq] *Collective*

lily-of-the-valley • **1.** سَوسَنَة [sawsana] سَوسَنات [sawsanaːt] *pl:* سَوسَن [sawsan] *Collective*

limb • **1.** فَرِع [fariʕ] فرُوع [fruːʕ] *pl:* He sawed off a limb from the tree. قَصّ فَرِع مِن الشَّجَرَة [gaṣṣ fariʕ min ʔiššaǰara]

lime • **1.** كِلس [kils] The soil doesn't contain enough lime. التُّربَة ما بِيها كِلِس كافِي [ʔitturba maː biːha kilis kaːfi]

limestone • **1.** حَجَر الكِلِس [ħaǰar ʔilkilis] حَجَر جِيرِ [ħaǰar ǰiːri]

limit • **1.** حَدّ [ħadd] حُدُود [ħuduːd] *pl:* There's a limit to everything. أكُو حَدّ لِكُلّشِي [ʔaku ħadd likullši] * I've reached the limit of my patience. نِفَذ صَبرِي [nifaǒ ṣabri]

* **The speed limit is thirty-five miles an hour.** • **1.** السُرعَة المَسمُوحَة خَمسَة وثلاثِين مِيل بِالساعَة [ʔissurʕa ʔilmasmuːħa xamsa wtlaːθiːn miːl bissaːʕa]

to limit • **1.** حَدَّد [ħaddad] تَحدِيد [taħdiːd] *vn:* اِتحَدَّد [ʕitħaddad] *p:* حِصَر [ħiṣar] حَصِر [ħaṣir] *vn:* اِنحِصَر [ʔinħiṣar] *p:* Please limit your talk to three minutes. مِن فَضلَك حَدِّد كَلامَك لِثلَث دَقايِق [min faǒlak ħaddid kalaːmak litlaθ daqaːyiq]

limited • **1.** مَحدُود [maħduːd] Our time is limited. وَقِتنا مَحدُود [wakitna maħduːd]

limp • **1.** راخي [raːxi] رَخي [raxi] He has a limp handshake. إيدَه راخيَة مِن يصافحُ [ʔiːdah raːxya min yṣaːfuħ] • **2.** عَرَج [ʕaraǰ] He has a slight limp when he walks. بيه شوَيَّة عَرَج مِن يِمشِي [biːh šwayya ʕaraǰ min yimši] * His arm hung limp. إيدَه هَدَّلَت [ʔiːdah haddilat]

to limp • **1.** عِرَج [ʕiraǰ] عَرَج [ʕaraǰ] *vn: sv* i. قِزَل [gizal] قَزِل [gazil] *vn: sv* i. He limps noticeably. هُوَّ دَيِعرِج بِصُورَة مبَيّنَة [huwwa dayiʕriǰ bṣuːra mbayyna]

linden • **1.** زَيزَفُون [ziːzafuːn]

line • **1.** خَطّ [xaṭṭ] خُطُوط [xuṭuːṭ] *pl:* Draw a line between these two points. إرسِم خَطّ بين هَالنُّقُطتَين [ʔirsim xaṭṭ bayn hannuquṭṭayn] There's heavy traffic on that line. أكُو اِزدِحام عَلَى هالخَط [ʔaku ʔizdiħaːm ʕala halxaṭṭ] There's a new airlines company serving Baghdad. أكُو شَرِكَة خُطُوط جَوِّيَّة جِدِيدَة تمُرّ بِبَغداد [ʔaku šarikat xuṭuːṭ ǰawwiyya ǰidiːda tmurr bibaɣdaːd] • **2.** صَفّ [ṣaff] صفُوف [ṣfuːf] *pl:* خَطّ [xaṭṭ] خُطُوط [xuṭuːṭ] *pl:* سِرَة [sira] سِراوات [siraːwaːt] *pl:* There's a long line of cars ahead of us. أكُو صَفّ طويل مِن السَّيّارات قِدّامنا [ʔaku ṣaff ṭwiːl min ʔissayyaːraːt giddaːmna] Keep in line! إبقَى بِالسِّرَة [ʔibqaː bissira] • **3.** سَطِر [saṭir] سطُور [sṭuːr] *pl:* I still have a few lines to write. بَعَدلِي كَم سَطِر لازم أكتِبها [baʕadli čam saṭir laːzim ʔaktibha] • **4.** خَطّ [xaṭṭ] خُطُوط [xuṭuːṭ] *pl:* تَجعِيد [taǰʕiːd] تَجعِيدات [taǰʕiːdaːt] *pl:* تَجاعِيد [taǰaːʕiːd] There are deep lines in his face. أكُو خُطُوط عَمِيقَة بوُجهَه [ʔaku xuṭuːṭ ʕamiːqa bwuččah] • **5.** صِنِف [ṣinif] أصناف [ʔaṣnaːf] *pl:* نوع [nawʕ] أنواع [ʔanwaːʕ] *pl:* He handles three lines of shirts. هُوَّ يبِيع ثلَث أصناف مِن القُمصان [huwwa yibiːʕ tlaθ ʔaṣnaːf min ʔilqumṣaːn] • **6.** حَبِل [ħabil] The wash is still hung out on the line. الهِدُوم بَعَدها مَشرُورَة عَالحَبِل [ʔilhduːm baʕadha mašruːra ʕalħabil]

*** Boy, does he have a smooth line!** • **1.** أمّا عِندَه طَرِيقَة بَلِف عَجِيبَة [ʔamma ʕindah ṭariːqat balif ʕaǰiːba]

*** It's along the line of what we discussed.** • **1.** تِتماشَى وِيّا المَوضُوع الِّي بِحَثناه [titmaːšaː wiyya ʔilmawḍuːʕ ʔilli biħaθnaːh]

*** Drop me a line.** • **1.** إكتِبلِي كَم كَلِمَة [ʔiktibli čam kilma] / عَلَى الأقَلّ إكتِبلِي سَلام [ʕala ʔilʔaqall ʔiktibli salaːm]

*** He was killed in the line of duty.** • **1.** اِنكِتَل مِن كان يأدِّي واجبَه [ʔinkital min čaːn yʔaddi waːǰbah]

*** What line is he in?** • **1.** شِنُو شُغلَه؟ [šinu šuɣlah?]

*** That's not in my line.** • **1.** هاي مُو شَغِلتِي [haːy muː šaɣilti] / هَذا مُو اِختِصاصِي [haːða muː ʔixtiṣaːṣi]

to keep in line • **1.** ضِبَط [ḍ̣ibaṭ] ضَبُط [ḍ̣abuṭ] *vn:* اِنضِبَط [ʔinḍ̣ibaṭ] *p:* I can't keep the soldiers in line any more. بَعَد ما أقدَر أضبُط الجِّنُود [baʕad maː ʔagdar ʔaḍ̣buṭ ʔiǰǰinuːd]

to line • **1.** بَطَّن [baṭṭan] تَبطِين [tabṭiːn] *vn:* تبَطَّن [tbaṭṭan] *p:* The jacket is lined with nylon. السِّترَة مبَطَّنَة بنايلُون [ʔissitra mbaṭṭina bnayluːn]

to line up • **1.** اِصطَفّ [ʔiṣṭaff] اِصطِفاف [ʔiṣṭifaːf] *vn: sv* a. Have the boys line up in the hall. خَلِّي الوِلِد يِصطَفُّون بِالقاعَة [xalli ʔilwilid yiṣṭaffuːn bilqaːʕa] People lined up all along the streets to watch the parade. النّاس اِصطَفَّوا عَلَى طُول الشَّوارِع حَتَّى يتفَرّجُون عالإستِعراض [ʔinnaːs ʔiṣṭaffaw ʕala ṭuːl ʔiššawaːriʕ ħatta yitfarriǰuːn ʕalʔistiʕraːḍ̣]

linen • **1.** كِتّان [kittaːn] This tablecloth is made of linen. غِطا الميز مَصنُوع مِن كِتّان [ɣiṭa ʔilmiːz maṣnuːʕ min kittaːn] • **2.** شَراشِف [čaraːčif] The linen is changed every week. الشَراشِف تِتبَدَّل كُلّ إسبُوع [ʔiččaraːčif titbaddal kull ʔisbuːʕ]

liner • **1.** باخِرَة [baːxira] بَواخِر [bawaːxir] *pl:* We took a liner to Europe. أخَذنا باخِرَة إلَى أورُبّا [ʔaxaðna baːxira ʔila ʔuːruppa]

to linger • **1.** بُقَى [buqaː] بَقاء [baqaːʔ] *vn: sv* i. We'd better not linger around here. أحسَن ما نِبقَى هنا [ʔaħsan maː nibqaː hna]

linguist • **1.** لُغَوي [luɣawi]

linguistic • **1.** لُغَوي [luɣawi]

linguistics • **1.** اللُّغَوِيّات [ʔilluɣawiyyaːt]

lining • **1.** بطانَة [bṭaːna] بطانات [bṭaːnaːt] *pl:* My coat needs a new lining. سِترتِي تِحتاج بطانَة جِدِيدَة [sitirti tiħtaːǰ bṭaːna ǰidiːda]

link • **1.** حَلقَة [ħalaqa] حَلقات [ħalaqaːt] *pl:* One link of my watch chain is broken. فَدّ حَلقَة مِن زَنجِيل ساعَتِي مَكسُورَة [fadd ħalaqa min zanǰiːl saːʕati maksuːra]

to link • **1.** رُبَط [rubaṭ] رَبُط [rabuṭ] *vn:* اِنرُبَط [ʔinrubaṭ] *p:* You have to link the two ends of the chain. لازم تُربُط الزَّنجِيل مِن الطَّرَفَين [laːzim turbuṭ ʔizzanǰiːl min ʔiṭṭarafayn] How can you link me with the crime? شلُون تُربُطنِي بِالجَّرِيمَة؟ [šluːn turbuṭni biǰǰariːma?]

lint • **1.** نِفايَة [nifaːya] نِفايات [nifaːyaːt] *pl:* Lint from the fabrics collects under the furniture. نِفايَة القماش دَتِتجَمَّع جَوَّة الأثاث [nifaːyat ʔilqmaːš datidǰammaʕ ǰawwa ʔilʔaθaːθ]

lion • **1.** أسَد [ʔasad] أسُود [ʔusuːd] *pl:* سَبِع [sabiʕ] سباع [sbaːʕ] *pl:*

lion cub • **1.** شِبِل [šibil] أشبال [ʔašbaːl] *pl:*

lioness • **1.** لَبوَة [labwa] لَبوات [labwaːt] *pl:*

L

lip • **1.** شِفَّة [šiffa] شِفّات، شفايِف [šiffa:t, šfa:yif] *pl:* I bit my lip. عَضّيت شِفّتي [ʕaðði:t šiffti] • **2.** جَسارَة [ǰasa:ra] I don't want anymore lip from you! ما أرِيد مِنَّك جَسارَة بَعَد [ma: ʔari:d minnak ǰasa:ra baʕad]

lipstick • **1.** حُمرَة شَفايِف [ħumrat šafa:yif]

liquid • **1.** سائِل [sa:ʔil] سَوائِل [sawa:ʔil] *pl:* He's only allowed to drink liquids. بَسّ مَسمُوحلَه يِشرَب سَوائِل [bass masmu:ħlah yišrab sawa:ʔil] Do you have liquid soap? عِندَك صابُون سائِل؟ [ʕindak ṣa:bu:n sa:ʔil?]

to liquidate • **1.** صَفّى [ṣaffa:] تَصفِيَة [taṣfiya] *vn:* تصَفّى [tṣaffa:] *p:* The company had to be liquidated to pay off its debts. الشَّرِكَة تصَفَّت حَتّى تِدفَع ديُونها [ʔiššarika tṣaffat ħatta tidfaʕ dyu:nha]

*** His political opponents had him liquidated.**
• **1.** خُصُومَه السِياسِيِّين تخَلِّصَوا مِنَّه [xuṣu:mah ʔissiya:siyyi:n txalliṣaw minnah]

liquor • **1.** مَشرُوب [mašru:b] مَشارِيب [maša:ri:b] *pl:* He doesn't touch liquor. ما يِشرَب مَشرُوب [ma: yišrab mašru:b]

lira • **1.** لِيرَة [li:ra] لَيرات [li:ra:t] *pl:*

lisp • **1.** لَثغَة [laθɣa] She speaks with a lisp. هِيَّ تِحكِي بِلَثغَة [hiyya tiħči bilaθɣa]

to lisp • **1.** لِثَغ [liθaɣ] لَثِغ [laθiɣ] *vn: sv* i. Her youngest son lisps when he talks. إبِنها الصِّغَيِّر يِلثِغ مِن يِحكِي [ʔibinha ʔiṣṣiɣayyir yilθiɣ min yiħči]

list • **1.** قائِمَة [qa:ʔima] قَوائِم [qawa:ʔim] *pl:* His name is not on the list. إسمَه مُو بِالقائِمَة [ʔismah mu: bilqa:ʔima]

to list • **1.** سَجَّل [sajjal] تَسجِيل [tasji:l] *vn:* تسَجَّل [tsajjal] *p:* This item isn't listed. هاي الفَقرَة ما مسَجِّلَة [ha:y ʔilfaqara ma: msajjila] • **2.** مال [ma:l] مَيل [mayl] *vn: sv* i. The ship is listing to port. السَّفِينَة مايلَة عَلَى جانِبها الأيسَر [ʔissafi:na ma:yla ʕala ǰa:nibha ʔilʔaysar]

to listen • **1.** صِغى [ʔaṣɣa:] إستِمَع [ʔistimaʕ] They listened intently. أصغوا بإهتِمام [ʔaṣɣaw bʔihtima:m] She'll listen to reason. تِصغِي لِلحَكِي المَعقُول [tiṣɣi lilħači ʔilmaʕqu:l] • **2.** سِمَع [simaʕ] سَمِع [samiʕ] *vn:* اِنسِمَع [ʔinsimaʕ] *p:* Now listen! إسمَع [ʔismaʕ] Listen! Somebody's coming. إسمَع، واحِد دَيِجي [ʔismaʕ, wa:ħid dayiǰi]

to listen in • **1.** تصَنَّت [tṣannat] تصَنُّت [taṣannuṭ] *vn: sv* a. Somebody must be listening in. واحِد لازِم يكُون دَيِتصَنت [wa:ħid la:zim yku:n dayitṣannat]

to listen to • **1.** سِمَع [simaʕ] سَمِع [samiʕ] *vn:* اِنسِمَع [ʔinsimaʕ] *p:* اِستِمَع ل [ʔistimaʕ l-] اِستِماع [ʔistima:ʕ] *vn: sv* i. I like to listen to classical music. أحِبّ أسمَع مُوسِيقى كلاسِيكِيَّة [ʔaħibb ʔasmaʕ musi:qa kla:si:kiyya] Why didn't you listen to me? لِيش ما سِمَعِت كَلامِي؟ [li:š ma: simaʕit kala:mi?]

listener • **1.** مُستَمِع [mustamiʕ] مُستَمِعِين [mustamiʕi:n] *pl:*

liter • **1.** لتِر [latir, litir] Olive oil is sold by the liter, sir. زَيت الزَّيتُون يِنباع بِاللِّترات أُستاذ [zayt ʔizzaytu:n yinba:ʕ billitra:t ʔusta:ð]

literal • **1.** حَرفِي [ħarfi] This is a literal translation. هاي تَرجُمَة حَرفِيَّة [ha:y tarǰuma ħarfiyya]

literally • **1.** حَرفِيّاً [ħarfiyyan] Please translate this literally. أرجُوك، تَرجُمها حَرفِيّاً [ʔarǰu:k, tarǰumha ħarfiyyan] They took the order literally. طَبُّقَوا الأمُر حَرفِيّاً [ṭabbuqaw ʔilʔamur ħarfiyyan]

literature • **1.** أدَب [ʔadab] آداب [ʔa:da:b] *pl:* Have you read a great deal of Arabic literature? قِرِيت هوايَة مِن الأدَب العَرَبِي [qiri:t hwa:ya min ʔilʔadab ʔilʕarabi] • **2.** مُؤَلَّفات [muʔallafa:t] The ministry has sent out a lot of literature on the topic. الوِزارَة أصدِرَت هوايَة مُؤَلَّفات بِالمَوضُوع [ʔilwiza:ra ʔaṣdirat hwa:ya muʔallafa:t bilmawðu:ʕ]

litter • **1.** وُسَخ [wusax] قَذارَة [qaða:ra] The alley is full of litter. الدَّربُونَة مَليانَة وُسَخ [ʔiddarbu:na malya:na wuṣax] • **2.** نَقّالَة [naqqa:la] سَديَة [sadya] سَديات [sadya:t] *pl:* They carried him out on a litter. شالَوه بِالنَّقّالَة [ša:lu:h binnaqqa:la] • **3.** دَفعَة [dafʕa] دَفعات [dafʕa:t] *pl:*

to litter • **1.** وَسَّخ [wassax] تَوسِيخ [tawsi:x] *vn:* توَسَّخ [twassax] *p:* Don't litter the road with trash. لا توَسِّخ الطَّرِيق بِالزِبالَة [la: twassix ʔiṭṭari:q bilizba:la]

little • **1.** صغَيِّر [ṣɣayyir, zɣayyir] She has a little girl. عِدها بنَيَّة صغَيّرَة [ʕidha bnayya ṣɣayyra] We need a little table in this room. نِحتاج مَيز صغَيِّر بِهَالقُبَّة [niħta:ǰ mayz ṣɣayyir bihalgubba] • **2.** شوَيَّة [šwayya] I have a little money. عِندِي شوَيَّة فلُوس [ʕindi šwayya flu:s] I can speak a little French. أقدَر أحكِي شوَيَّة فرَنسِي [ʔagdar ʔaħči šwayya fransi] • **3.** قَلِيل [qali:l] ضَئِيل [ðaʔi:l] It's of little importance. أهَمِّيَّتها قَلِيلَة [ʔahammiyyatha qali:la]

*** He's little better than a thief.** • **1.** هُوَّ ثلاثَة أرباع حَرامِي [huwwa tla:θa ʔarba:ʕ ħara:mi]

*** That's of little value to me.** • **1.** ما إلَه قِيمَة بِالنِسبَة إلِي [ma:ʔilah qi:ma binnisba ʔili]

in a little while • **1.** بَعد شوَيَّة [baʕd šwayya] I'll come back in a little while. راح أرجَع بَعد شوَيَّة [ra:ħ ʔarǰaʕ baʕd šwayya]

little by little • **1.** تَدرِيجِيّاً [tadri:ǰiyyan] Little by little he calmed down. هِدَأ تَدرِيجِيّاً [hida tadri:ǰiyyan]

live • **1.** * I bought some live fish. اِشتِرَيت سِمَك بَعدَه يِلبُط [ʔištirayt simač baʕdah yilbuṭ]

* Careful, that's a live wire. دِير بالَك، هالوايَر يِنتِل [di:r ba:lak, halwa:yar yintil]

to live • **1.** عاش [ʕa:š] عَيش [ʕayš] *vn: sv* i. He lived a happy life. عاش حَياة سَعِيدَة [ʕa:š ħaya:t saʕi:da] Before the war I lived in France. قَبِل الحَرب عِشِت بفرَنسا [gabil ʔilħarb ʕišit bifransa:] Live and learn! عِيش وشُوف [ʕi:š wšu:f] The people on this island live on nothing but fish. سُكّان هَالجَزِيرَة يعِيشُون بَسّ عالسِّمَك [sukka:n hajjazi:ra yʕi:šu:n bass ʕassimač] I couldn't live on so little. ما أقدَر أعِيش بِهَالمُقدار [ma: ʔagdar ʔaʕi:š bhalmuqda:r] • **2.** سِكَن [sikan] سُكنَة، سَكِن [sukna, sakin] *vn: sv* u. Does anyone live in this house? أكُو أحَّد يِسكُن بِهَالبَيت؟ [ʔaku ʔaħħad yiskun bihalbayt?]

* **He has barely enough to live on.** • **1.** هُوَّ دُوب يكَفِّي عِيشتَه [huwwa du:b ykaffi ʕi:štah] / هُوَّ بِالكاد يسِدّ عِيشتَه [huwwa bilka:d ysidd ʕi:štah]

* **He always worked hard and never really lived.** • **1.** بُقَي يكِدّ طُول حَياتَه لَكِن ما تهَنَّى بعِيشتَه [buqa: ykidd ṭu:l ħaya:tah la:kin ma: thanna: biʕi:štah]

* **She won't live out the winter.** • **1.** ما راح يطَوِّل الرَّبِيع [ma: ra:ħ yiṭṭawwil ʔirrabi:ʕ]

to live up to • **1.** تمَسَّك ب [tmassak b-] تَمَسُّك [tamassuk] *vn: sv* a. They didn't live up to the terms of the contract. ما تمَسّكَوا بشُرُوط العَقِد [ma: tmassikaw bšuru:ṭ ʔilʕaqid]

* **He didn't live up to my expectation.** • **1.** ما صار مِثِل ما توَقَّعِت [ma: ṣa:r miθil ma: twaqqaʕit]

live coal • **1.** جَمرَة [ǰamra] جَمرات [ǰamra:t] *pl:* جَمُر [ǰamur] *Collective:* There are still live coals in the brazier. أكُو بَعَد جَمُر بِالمَنقَلَة [ʔaku baʕad ǰamur bilmanqala]

lively • **1.** نَشِط [našiṭ] He's a lively boy. هُوَّ وَلَد نَشِط [huwwa walad našiṭ] • **2.** شَيِّق [šayyiq] We had a lively conversation. صار بَيناتنا مُناقَشَة شَيِّقَة [ṣa:r bayna:tna muna:qaša šayyiqa]

* **Step lively!** • **1.** حَرِّك نَفسَك [ħarrik nafsak]

liver • **1.** كَبدَة، كِبدَة [kabda, kibda] كَبِد [kabid] *pl:* Do you care for liver? يِعجبَك الكَبِد [yiʕijbak ʔilkabid]

livestock • **1.** ماشِيَة [ma:šiya] مَواشِي [mawa:ši] *pl:* We can't get feed for our livestock. ما نِقدَر ندَبُّر عَلَف لِلماشِيَة مالتنا [ma: nigdar ndabbur ʕalaf lilma:šiya ma:latna]

living • **1.** عِيشَة [ʕi:ša] مَعِيشَة [maʕi:ša] مَعِيشات [maʕi:ša:t] *pl:* Living is awfully expensive here. العِيشَة كُلّش غالية هنا [ʔilʕi:ša kulliš ɣa:lya hna] Living conditions are very bad. ظرُوف المَعِيشَة كُلّش مُو زينَة [ðru:f ʔilmaʕi:ša kulliš mu: zi:na] He'll have to earn his own living. لازِم يدَبُّر مَعِيشتَه بنَفسَه [la:zim ydabbur maʕi:štah bnafsah] • **2.** حَيّ [ħayy] أحياء [ʔaħya:ʔ] *pl:* Arabic is a living language. اللُّغَة العَرَبِيَّة لُغَة حَيَّة [ʔilluɣa ʔilʕarabiyya luɣa ħayya] • **3.** طِبق الأَصِل [ṭibq ʔilʔaṣil] He's the living image of his father. هُوَّ صُورَة طِبق الأَصِل مِن أبُوه [huwwa ṣu:ra ṭibq ʔilʔaṣil min ʔabu:h] • **4.** طَيِّب [ṭayyib] عايِش [ʕa:yiš] I don't know whether he's still living. ما أدرِي إذا كان بَعدَه طَيِّب [ma: ʔadri ʔiða ča:n baʕdah ṭayyib] Is your grandmother still living? جِدِّيتَك بَعدها عايشَة؟ [ǰiddi:tak baʕdha ʕa:yša?]

living room • **1.** غُرفَة قَعدَة [ɣurfat gaʕda] غُرَف قَعدَة [ɣuraf gaʕda] *pl:*

lizard • **1.** برَيعصِي [bri:ʕṣi] برَيعصِيَّة [bri:ʕṣiyya] *pl:* أبُو برَيص [ʔabu bri:ṣ] برَيعصِيَّة [bri:ʕṣiyya] *pl:*

load • **1.** حِمِل [ħimil] حمُول [ħmu:l] *pl:* The load is too heavy for him. الحِمِل كُلّش ثقِيل عَلَيه [ʔilħimil kulliš θgi:l ʕali:h] I ordered a load of sand. وَصَّيت عَلَى حِمِل رَمُل [waṣṣi:t ʕala ħimil ramul] It took a load off my mind. انزاح حِمل كِبِير عَن كِتفِي [ʔinza:ħ ħiml čibi:r ʕan čitfi]

* **He has loads of money.** • **1.** عِندَه فلُوس بِالكَوم [ʕindah flu:s bilkawm]

to load • **1.** حَمَّل [ħammal] تَحمِيل [taħmi:l] *vn:* تحَمَّل [tħammal] *p:* Load the cases on the truck. حَمِّل الصَّنادِيق بِاللُّورِي [ħammil ʔiṣṣana:di:g billu:ri] The cargo is just being loaded. البِضاعَة هَسَّة دَتِتحَمَّل [ʔilbiða:ʕa hassa datitħammal] • **2.** حَشَّى [ħašša:] تَحشِيَة [taħšiya] *vn:* تحَشَّى [tħašša:] *p:* عَبَّى [ʕabba:] تعِبِّي [tʕibbi] *vn:* تعَبَّى [tʕabba:] *p:* He loaded the gun. حَشَّى البُندُقِيَّة [ħašša: ʔilbunduqiyya] • **3.** رَكَّب [rakkab] تَركِيب [tarki:b] *vn:* ترَكَّب [trakkab] *p:* Do you know how to load film in a camera? تُعرُف شلُون ترَكُّب فِلِم بِالكامِرَة؟ [tuʕruf šlu:n trakkub filim bilkamira:?] • **4.** كَوَّم [kawwam] تَكوِيم [takwi:m] *vn:* تكَوُّم [tkuwwum] *p:* We're loaded with work. الشُّغُل مكَوَّم عَلينا [ʔiššuɣul mkawwam ʕali:na]

loaf • **1.** صَمُّونَة لُوف [ṣammu:na lu:f] صَمُّونات لُوف [ṣammu:na:t lu:f] *pl:* Please give me three loaves of bread. بالله إنطِينِي ثلاث صَمُّونات خُبُز لُوف [ballah ʔinṭi:ni tlaθ ṣammu:na:t xubuz lu:f]

to loaf • **1.** تكاسَل [tka:sal] تَكاسُل [taka:sul] *vn: sv* a. He was loafing on the job. كان يِتكاسَل بشُغلَه [ča:n yitka:sal bšuɣlah]

loafer • **1.** كَتَة [čata] كَتَوات [čatawa:t] *pl:* He's a loafer. هُوَّ كَتَة [huwwa čata] • **2.** حِذاء قَبَغلِي [ħiða:ʔ qabaɣli] Have you seen my other loafer? شِفِت تَكّ حِذائِي القَبَغلِي اللّاخ؟ [šifit takk ħiða:ʔi ʔilqabaɣli ʔilla:x?]

loam • **1.** غَرَين [ɣaryan]

loan • **1.** سُلفَة [sulfa] سُلفات [sulfa:t] *pl:* سُلَف [sulaf] *Collective:* قَرِض [qarið] قرُوض [qru:ð] *pl:* *Collective:*

L

I'd like to get a loan from the bank. أَرِيد آخُذ سُلفَة مِن البَنك [ʔariːd ʔaːxuð sulfa min ʔilbank]

to loan • 1. دايَن [daːyan] مُدايَنَة [mudaːyana] *vn: sv* i. دَيَّن [dayyan] تدِيِّن [tdiyyin] *vn: sv* i. She loaned him 250 fils. دايِنتَه مِيتَين وَخَمسِين فِلِس [daːynatah mitayn wxamsiːn filis] • **2.** عار [ʕaːr] إعارَة [ʔiʕaːra] *vn: sv* i. He loaned me an interesting book. عارنِي كِتاب لَطِيف [ʕaːrni kitaːb laṭiːf]

loan shark • 1. مُرابِي [muraːbi] مُرابِين [muraːbiːn] *pl:*

lobby • 1. مَدخَل [madxal] مَداخِل [madaːxil] *pl:* I'll meet you in the lobby after the movie. أَشُوفَك بالمَدخَل بَعد الفِلِم [ʔašuːfak bilmadxal baʕd ʔilfilim]

local • 1. مَحَلِّي [maħalli] The local papers say nothing about the accident. الصُّحُف المَحَلِّيَّة ما تِذكُر شِي عَن الحادِث [ʔiṣṣuħuf ʔilmaħaliyya maː tiðkur ši ʕan ʔilħaːdiθ] He wasn't familiar with local conditions. ما كان عِندَه مَعرِفَة بِالظُرُوف المَحَلِّيَّة [maː čaːn ʕindah maʕrifa biððuruːf ʔilmaħaliyya] • **2.** داخِلِي [daːxili] How much is a local call? شقَدّ تكَلِّف المُكالَمَة الدّاخِلِيَّة؟ [šgadd tkallif ʔilmukaːlama ʔiddaːxiliyya?] • **3.** مَوضِعِي [mawðiʕi] A local anesthetic will do. بَنج مَوضِعِي يِكفِي [banǰ mawðiʕi yikfi]

to locate • 1. عَيَّن [ʕayyan] تَعيِين [taʕyiːn] *vn:* تعَيَّن [tʕayyan] *p:* I couldn't locate him. ما قِدَرِت أَعَيِّن مَوقِعَه [maː gidarit ʔaʕayyin mawqiʕah] • **2.** حَدَّد [ħaddad] تَحدِيد [taħdiːd] *vn:* تحَدَّد [tħaddad] *p:* I can't locate the trouble. ما أقدَر أَحَدِّد مَحَلّ الخَلَل [maː ʔagdar ʔaħaddid maħall ʔilxalal]

located • 1. واقِع [waːqiʕ] Where is your new store located? وِين واقِع مَخزَنَك الجِدِيد؟ [wiːn waːqiʕ maxzanak ʔaǰǰidiːd?]

location • 1. مَوقِع [mawqiʕ] مَواقِع [mawaːqiʕ] *pl:* The location of the hotel is ideal. مَوقِع الفِندِق مُمتاز [mawqiʕ ʔilfindiq mumtaːz]

lock • 1. قُفُل [quful] قفال، قفالَة [qfaːl, qfaːla] *pl:* The lock needs oiling. القُفُل يِحتاج تَدهِين [ʔilquful yiħtaːǰ tadhiːn]

to lock • 1. قَفَل [qufal] قَفُل [qaful] *vn:* اِنقُفَل [ʔinqufal] *p:* Don't forget to lock the door when you leave. لا تِنسَى تُقفُل الباب مِن تِطلَع [laː tinsaː tuqful ʔilbaːb min tiṭlaʕ] I'm locked out. اِنقُفَل الباب عَلَيّا [ʔinqufal ʔilbaːb ʕalayya] • **2.** شَكَّل [šakkal] تَشكِيل [taškiːl] *vn:* تشَكَّل [tšakkal] *p:* The bumpers of the two cars were locked together. دَعّامِيّات السَّيّارتَين شَكِّلَت بِبَعَضها [daʕʕaːmiyyaːt ʔissayyaːrtayn šakkilat bibaʕaðha]

to lock up • 1. حِبَس [ħibas] حَبِس [ħabis] *vn:* اِنحِبَس [ʔinħibas] *p:* He was locked up. هُوَّ كان مَحبُوس [huwwa čaːn maħbuːs]

locker • 1. صَندُوق [ṣanduːg] صنادِيق [ṣnaːdiːg] *pl:* I left my racquet in the locker. تِرَكِت الرِّكِت مالِي بِالصَّندُوق [tirakit ʔirrikit maːli biṣṣanduːg]

lockjaw • 1. كزّاز [gazzaːz, guzzaːz]

locksmith • 1. أَبُو قفال [ʔabu qfaːl] Do you know of a good locksmith near here? تُعرُف أبُو قَفال زين قَرِيب مِن هنا؟ [tuʕruf ʔabu ʔaqfaːl ziːn qariːb minhna?]

locomotive • 1. مَكِينَة قِطار [makiːnat qiṭaːr]

locust • 1. جَرادَة [ǰaraːda] جَرادات [ǰaraːdaːt] *pl:* جَرّاد [ǰarraːd] *Collective*

lodge • 1. كَبرَة [kapra] كَبرات [kapraːt] *pl:* كُوخ، جَرداغ [kuːx, čardaːɣ] أكواخ، كواخَة، جَرادِغ [kwaːx, kwaːxa, čaraːdiɣ] *pl:* We have a hunting lodge in the north. عِدنا كَبرَة صَيد بالشِّمال [ʕidna kaprat ṣayd biššimaːl] • **2.** مَحفَل [maħfal] مَحافِل [maħaːfil] *pl:* Is there a Masonic lodge in Baghdaad? أَكُو مَحفَل ماسَونِي بِبَغداد؟ [ʔaku maħfal maːsuːni bibaɣdaːd?]

to lodge • 1. حِشَك [ħišag] حَشِق [ħašig] *vn:* اِنحِشَق [ʔinħišag] *p:* A piece of wood is lodged in the machine. أَكُو وُصلَة خِشَب مَحشُوقَة، مَحشُوكَة بِالمَكِينَة [ʔaku wuṣlat xišab maħšuːga bilmakiːna] • **2.** قَدَّم [qaddam] تَقدِيم [taqdiːm] *vn:* تقَدَّم [tqaddam] *p:* He lodged a complaint with the police. قَدَّم شَكوَى لِلشُّرطَة [qaddam šakwa liššurṭa]

log • 1. جِذع شَجَرَة [ǰiðiʕ šaǰara] جذُوع شَجَرَة [ǰðuːʕ šaǰara] *pl:* The people put a log across the road to stop traffic. النّاس خَلّوا جِذع الشَّجَرَة بِالشّارِع حَتَّى يوَقِّفُون السَّيّارات [ʔinnaːs xallaw ǰiðiʕ ʔiššaǰara biššaːriʕ ħatta ywaggfuːn ʔissayyaːraːt]

*** He sat there like a bump on a log.**
• **1.** قِعَد هناك مِثل الصَّنَم [giʕad hnaːk miθl ʔiṣṣanam] / قِعَد هناك مِثل الأَطرَش بِالزَّفَّة [giʕad hnaːk miθl ʔilʔaṭraš bizzaffa]

*** I slept like a log.** • **1.** نِمت مِثِل الحجارَة [nimit miθil ʔiliħǰaːra] / نِمت مِثِل اللَّوح [nimit miθl ʔilluːħ] / نِمت مِثِل المَيِّت [nimit miθil ʔilmayyit]

logic • 1. مَنطِق [manṭiq] Your logic is faulty. مَنطِقَك غير مَعقُول [manṭiqak ɣiːr maʕquːl]

logical • 1. مَنطِقِي [manṭiqi]

logically • 1. مَنطِقِيّاً [manṭiqiyyan]

lone • 1. وَحِيد [waħi:d] He was the lone surviver. كان الوَحِيد اللّي نِجَح [ča:n ʔilwaħi:d ʔilli nijaħ]

lonely • 1. مُوحِش [mu:ħiš] This place is quite lonely in winter. هَالمَحَلّ كُلِّش مُوحِش بِالشِّتا [halmaħall kulliš mu:ħiš biššita]

lonesome • 1. بِوحدة [bwiħdah] She feels very lonesome. تِشعُر بِوحدَة [tišʕur biwiħda]

to be lonesome for • 1. شِعَر بوحشَة إلَى [šiʕar bwiħša ʔila] شُعُور بوحشَة إلَى [šuʕu:r bwiħša ʔila] *vn: sv* u. I'm very lonesome for you. أَشعُر بِوَحشَة إِلَك [ʔašʕur bwaħša ʔilak]

long • 1. طُويل [ṭuwi:l] We had to make a long detour. اِضطَرَّينا نسَوّي فَرَّة طويلَة [ʔiðṭarrayna nsawwi farra ṭwi:la] It's a long way to the top of the mountain. الطَّرِيق طُويل إلَى قُمَّة الجِّبَل [ʔiṭṭari:q ṭuwi:l ʔila qummat ʔijjibal] He got there a long time after we did. وُصَل بَعَد ما جَينا بمُدَّة طويلَة [wuṣal baʕad ma: ji:na bmudda ṭwi:la] **• 2.** هوايَة [hwa:ya] Did you stay long at the party? بُقيت هوايَة بِالحَفلَة؟ [buqi:t hwa:ya bilħafla?]

*** The room is twenty feet long.**
• 1. الغُرفَة طُولهَا عِشرِين قَدَم [ʔilɣurfa ṭu:lha ʕišri:n qadam]
*** How long is it? • 1.** شقَدّ طُولَه؟ [šgadd ṭu:lah?]
*** The child cried all night long.**
• 1. الطِّفِل بِكَى طُول اللَيل [ʔiṭṭifil biča: ṭu:l ʔillayl]
*** How long will it take? • 1.** شقَدّ يِطَوِّل؟ [šgadd yiṭawwil?] / شقَدّ تاخُذ وَقِت؟ [šgadd ta:xuð wakit?]
*** So long! • 1.** مَع السَّلامَة [maʕa ʔissala:ma]
*** Everything will work out in the long run. • 1.** بالمَدَى البَعِيد الأمُور رَح تِتحَسَّن [bilmada: ʕilbaʕi:d ʕilʔumu:r raħ titħassan]

long ago • 1. مِن زَمان [min zama:n] مِن مُدَّة طويلَة [min mudda ṭwi:la] I knew that long ago. عِرَفتها مِن زَمان [ʕirafitha min zama:n]

as long as • 1. شقَدّ ما [šgadd ma:] You can keep it as long as you wish. تِقدَر تخَلّيها عِندَك شقَدّ ما ترِيد [tigdar txalli:ha ʕindak šgadd ma: tri:d] **• 2.** مَا دام [ma: da:m] It doesn't bother me as long as the work gets done. ما يهِمّني ما دام الشُّغُل دَيمشي [ma: yhimmni ma: da:m ʔiššuɣul dayimši] As long as you're here, you might as well have dinner with us. ما دام إنتَ هنا، ظَلّ تعَشّى وِيّانا [ma: da:m ʔinta hna, ðall tʕašša: wiyya:na]

to long • 1. اِشتاق [ʔišta:q, ʔišta:g] اِشتِياق [ʔištiya:q] *vn: sv* a. حَنّ [ħann] حَنِين [ħani:n] *vn: sv* i. I'm longing to see my mother and father again. مِشتاق أَشُوف أمِّي وَأَبُويَة مَرَّة لُخ [mišta:q ʔašu:f ʔummi wʔabu:ya marra lux] She's longing for a man. تِشتاق الرِّجّال [tišta:q ʔirrijja:l] He's longing for home. دَيحِنّ لأَهلَه [dayħinn lʔahlah]

long-distance call • 1. مُخابَرَة خارِجِيَّة [muxa:bara xa:rijiyya] مُخابَرات خارِجِيَّة [muxa:bara:t xa:rijiyya] *pl:* Please, I'd like to make a long-distance call. مِن فَضلِك، أَرِيد أَسَوّي مُخابَرَة خارِجِيَّة [min faðlič, ʔari:d ʔasawwi muxa:bara xa:rijiyya]

longer • 1. أَطوَل [ʔaṭwal] This table is longer than that one. هَالميز أَطوَل مِن ذاكَه [halmi:z ʔaṭwal min ða:kah] **• 2.** أكثَر [ʔakθar] مُدَّة أَطوَل [mudda ʔaṭwal] He wanted to stay longer, but I was sleepy. راد يبقَى أكثَر، بَسّ آني كِنِت نَعسان [ra:d yibqa: ʔakθar, bass ʔa:ni činit naʕsa:n] **• 3.** أكثَر [ʔakθar] أَزيَد [ʔazyad] I can't stand it any longer. ما أَقدَر أتحَمَّلها أكثَر [ma: ʔagdar ʔatħammalha ʔakθar]

longshoreman • 1. عامِل شَحِن [ʕa:mil šaħin] عُمّال شَحِن [ʕumma:l šaħin] *pl:*

look • 1. نَظرَة [naðra] نَظرات [naðra:t] *pl:* You can see with one look that the town is dirty. بنَظرَة وِحدَة تِقدَر تُعرُف المَدِينَة وَسخَة [bnaðra wiħda tigdar tuʕruf ʔilmadi:na wasxa]

*** He gave her an angry look. • 1.** باوَع عَلَيها بزَعَل [ba:waʕ ʕali:ha bzaʕal]
*** Take a good look! • 1.** لَك، باوِع زَين [lak, ba:wiʕ zayn]

to look • 1. تفَرَّج [tfarraj] تَفَرُّج [tafarruj] *vn: sv* a. I enjoy looking at pictures. أَحِبّ أتفَرَّج عالصُّوَر [ʔaħibb ʔatfarraj ʕaṣṣuwar] **• 2.** باوَع [ba:waʕ] مُباوَعَة [muba:waʕa] *vn: sv* i. She looked at me when I came into the room. باوعَت عَلَيّا مِن فِتِت لِلغُرفَة [ba:wʕat ʕalayya min fitit lilɣurfa] Don't look now but the president just came in. لا تباوِع، الرَّئِيس هَسَّة دِخَل [la: tba:wiʕ, ʔirraʔi:s hassa dixal] She didn't so much as look at me. حَتَّى مباوَعَة ما باوَعَتني [ħatta mba:waʕa ma: ba:waʕatni] **• 3.** باوَع [ba:waʕ] مُباوَعَة [muba:waʕa] *vn: sv* i. شاف [ša:f] شَوف [šawf] *vn: sv* u. Look, a falling star! باوِع أكُو نَجمَة دَتوقَع [ba:wiʕ ʔaku najma datu:gaʕ] May I look at Ahmad's file? أَقدَر أَشُوف مَلَفّات أحمَد [ʔagdar ʔašu:f malaffat ʔaħmad] **• 4.** بَيَّن [bayyan] تَبيِين [tabyi:n] *vn: sv* i. You look well. مبَيِّن عَلِيك صِحّتَك زينَة [mbayyin ʕali:k ṣiħħtak zi:na] It looks like rain. تبَيِّن راح تُمطُر [tbayyin ra:ħ tumṭur]

to look after • 1. دار بَال مِن [da:r ba:l min] دَيرَة بَال مِن [dawrat ba:l min] *vn: sv* i. Do you have someone to look after the child? عِندَك أَحَّد يدِير بالَه عَالطِّفِل؟ [ʕindak ʔaħħad ydi:r ba:lah ʕaṭṭifil?] Looking after this kid is no picnic. دَيرَة البال عَلَى هَالجّاهِل مُو شَقَا [di:rat ʔilba:l ʕala hajja:hil mu: šaqa]

to look down on • 1. اِحتِقَر [ʔiħtiqar] اِحتِقار [ʔiħtiqa:r] *vn: sv* i. You mustn't look down on people just because they're poor. ما لازِم تِحتِقِر النّاس لِأَنّهُم فُقَراء [ma: la:zim tiħtiqir ʔinna:s liʔannhum fuqara:ʔ]

*** She looks down her nose at everyone. • 1.** شايفَة نَفسها [ša:yfa nafisha] / شايلَة خَشِمها عالنّاس [ša:yla xašimha ʕanna:s]

to look for • 1. دَوَّر عَلَى [dawwar ʕala] تَدوِير عَلَى [tadwi:r ʕala] *vn: sv* u. We're looking for rooms.

L

دَنْدَوُّر عَلَى غُرَف [dandawwur ʕala ɣuraf] He's always looking for trouble. هُوَّ دائِماً يدَوُّر عَلَى مَشاكِل [huwwa daːʔiman ydawwur ʕala mašaːkil]

to look forward to • 1. اِنتِظَر [ʔintiðar] اِنتِظار [ʔintiðaːr] *vn: sv* i. We're looking forward to our vacation impatiently. دَنِنتِظِر عُطلَتنا يوم يوم [danintiðir ʕuṭlatna yuːm yuːm] We're looking forward to the nineteenth of May when you're going to get married. دَنِنتِظِر يوم تِساطَعَش مايس اللّي راح تِتزَوَّج بيه [danintiðir yuːm tisaːṭaʕaš maːyis ʔilli raːħ tidzawwaǰ biːh] **• 2.** اِشتاق [ʔištaːq, ʔištaːg] اِشتِياق [ʔištiyaːq] *vn: sv* a. I'm looking forward to seeing you. آنِي مِشتاق أَشُوفَك [ʔaːni mištaːq ʔašuːfak]

to look into • 1. بِحَث [biħaθ] بَحِث [baħiθ] *vn:* انبِحَث [ʔinbiħaθ] *p:* We'll have to look into the matter. لازِم نِبحَث المَوضُوع [laːzim nibħaθ ʔilmawḍuːʕ]

to look on • 1. باوَع [baːwaʕ] مُباوَعَة [mubaːwaʕa] *vn: sv* i. تفَرَّج [tfarraǰ] تَفَرُّج [tafarruǰ] *vn: sv* a. I was just looking on. كِنِت بَسّ دَأَباوِع [činit bass daʔabaːwiʕ] **• 2.** اِعتِبَر [ʔiʕtibar] اِعتِبار [ʔiʕtibaːr] *vn: sv* u. They looked on her as a stranger. أعتِبرَوها غَرِيبَة عَنهُم [ʔiʕtibruːha ɣariːba ʕanhum]

to look out • 1. دار بال مِن [daːr baːl min] Look out! دِير بالَك [diːr baːlak] **• 2.** أَشرَف [ʔašraf] إشراف [ʔišraːf] *vn: sv* i. طَلّ [ṭall] طَلّ [ṭall] *vn: sv* i. The big window looks out on the garden. الشِّبّاك الكِبير يِشرِف عَلَى الحَدِيقَة [ʔiššibbaːk ʔiččibiːr yišrif ʕala ʔilħadiːqa]

to look over • 1. شاف [šaːf] شَوف [šawf] *vn: sv* u. Will you look over these papers? تِسمَح تشُوف هَالأَوراق؟ [tismaħ tšuːf halʔawraːq?]

to look up • 1. شال راسَه [šaːl raːsah] شَيل راس [šayl raːs] *vn: sv* i. He didn't even look up when I called him. حَتَّى راسَه ما شالَه مِن صِحِتلَه [ħatta raːsah maː šaːlah min ṣiħitlah] **• 2.** نِظَر [niðar] نَظَر [naðar] *vn: sv* u. She looks up to him. تُنظُرلَه بإحتِرام [tunðurlah bʔiħtiraːm] **• 3.** دَوَّر عَلَى [dawwar ʕala] تَدوير [tadwiːr] *vn:* تدَوَّر [tdawwar] *p:* I have to look up this word in a dictionary. لازِم أَدَوُّر عَلَى هَالكَلِمَة بالقامُوس [laːzim ʔadawwur ʕala halkalima bilqaːmuːs] **• 4.** تحَسَّن [tħassan] تَحَسُّن [taħassun] *vn: sv* a. Things are beginning to look up. الأُمُور بِدَت تِتحَسَّن [ʔilʔumuːr bidat titħassan]

*** Look me up some time, won't you? • 1.** زُورنِي فَدّ يوم [zuːrni fadd yawm]

lookout • 1. رَقِيب [raqiːb] رُقَباء [ruqabaːʔ] *pl:* A lookout was placed on every hill. حَطّوا رَقِيب عَلَى راس كُلّ تَلّ [ħaṭṭaw raqiːb ʕala raːs kull tall] **• 2.** مَسؤُولِيَّة [masʔuːliyya] مَسؤُولِيّات [masʔuːliyyaːt] *pl:* شَغلَة [šaɣla] It's your lookout now. هاي مَسؤُولِيتَك [haːy masʔuːliːtak]

to be on the lookout for • 1. خَلَّى عِينَه عَلَى [xallaː ʕiːnah ʕala] *sv* i. Be on the lookout for a black '59 Cadillac license number 354. خَلِّي عينَك عَلَى سَيّارَة كادِيلاك سُودَة، مُودَيل تِسعَة وَخَمسِين، رَقَم قِطعَتها ثلَث مِيَّة وأَربَعَة وَخَمسِين [xalli ʕaynak ʕala sayyaːra kadilaːk suːda, muːdiːl tisʕa wxamsiːn, raqam qitʕatha tlaθ miyya wʔarbaʕa wxamsiːn]

looks • 1. مَظهَر [maðhar] مَظاهِر [maðaːhir] *pl:* To judge by his looks, he's a criminal. مِن مَظهَرَه، يبَيِّن عَليه مُجرِم [min maðharah, yibayyin ʕaliːh muǰrim]

*** From the looks of things it may take much longer than we thought. • 1.** عَلَى ما يِظهَر، المَسأَلَة راح تاخُذ أَكثَر مِن ما ظَنَّينا [ʕala maː yiðhar, ʔilmasʔala raːħ taːxuð ʔakθar min maː ðannayna]

loom • 1. نُول [nuːnawl] أَنوال [ʔanwaːl] *pl:*

loop • 1. حَلَقَة [ħalaqa] حَلَقات [ħalaqaːt] *pl:* Run the rope through this loop. فَوِّت الحَبِل مِن هَالحَلَقَة [fawwit ʔilħabil min halħalaqa]

to loop • 1. لَفّ [laff] لَفّ [laff] *vn: sv* i. He looped the rope over the post. لَفّ الحَبِل عالعَمُود [laff ʔilħabil ʕalʕamuːd]

loophole • 1. مَجال لِلتَّمَلُّص [maǰaːl littamalluṣ] مَجالات لِلتَّمَلُّص [maǰaːlaːt littamalluṣ] *pl:* Many loopholes have been left in this law. أَكُو هوايَة مَجالات لِلتَّمَلُّص بهالقانُون [ʔaku hwaːya maǰaːlaːt littamalluṣ bhaːlqaːnuːn]

loose • 1. راخِي [raːxi] The button is loose. الدُّقمَة راخيَة [ʔiddugma raːxya] **• 2.** مَهدُود [mahduːd] مَحلُول [maħluːl] Do you ever let the dog loose? تخَلُّون الكَلِب مَهدُود؟ [txalluːn ʔiččalib mahduːd?] **• 3.** فاسِد [faːsid] فَسّاد [fassaːd] *pl:* She has loose morals. أخلاقها فاسدَة [ʔaxlaːqha faːsda]

*** He must have a screw loose! • 1.** لازِم يكُون مَشخُوط [laːzim ykuːn mašxuːṭ] / لازِم عِندَه خيط [laːzim ʕindah xiːṭ]

*** She has a loose tongue. • 1.** ما تضُمّ حكايَة [maː ṭðumm ħčaːya]

to turn loose • 1. هَدّ [hadd] هَدّ [hadd] *vn:* اِنهَدّ [ʔinhadd] *p:* Don't turn the dog loose! لا تهِدّ الكَلِب [laː thidd ʔiččalib]

to loosen • 1. رَخَّى [raxxaː] تَرخِيَة [tarxiya] *vn:* ترَخَّى [traxxaː] *p:* Can you loosen this screw? تِقدَر ترَخّي هَالبُرغِي؟ [tigdar traxxi halburɣi?] I want to loosen my shoelaces. أَرِيد أَرَخّي قِيطان قُندَرتِي [ʔariːd ʔaraxxi qiːṭaːn qundarti]

loot • 1. غَنِيمَة [ɣaniːma] غَنايِم [ɣanaːyim, ganaːʔim] *pl:* بُوقَة [buːga] بَوقات [buːgaːt] *pl:* The thieves hid the loot in a tree. الحَرامِيَّة ضَمّوا الغَنِيمَة بِالشَّجَرَة [ʔilħaraːmiyya ðammaw ʔilɣaniːma biššaǰara]

to loot • 1. نِهَب [nihab] نَهِب [nahib] *vn:* اِنّهَب [ʔinnihab] *p:* سِلَب [silab] The enemy looted the town. العَدُو نِهَب المَدِينَة [ʔilʕadu nihab ʔilmadiːna]

lopsided • **1.** عوجَة [ʕawǰa, ʕuːǰa] The picture's lopsided. الصُّورَة عَوجَة [ʔiṣṣuːra ʕuːǰa]

to lose • **1.** ضَيَّع [ðayyaʕ] تَضييع [taðyiːʕ] *vn:* تضَيَّع [tðayyaʕ] *p:* فِقَد [fiqad] فَقِد [faqid] *vn:* اِنفِقَد [ʔinfiqad] *p:* I lost my pencil again. ضَيَّعت قَلَمِي مَرَّة لُخ [ðayyaʕit qalami marra lux] I lost track of them after the war. ضَيَّعت أَثَرهُم بَعَد الحَرب [ðayyaʕit ʔaθarhum baʕad ʔilħarb] I've lost all my strength, since I got sick. ضَيَّعت كُلّ قُوتِي مِن تمَرَّضِت [ðayyaʕit kull quwwti min tmarraðit] Don't lose your way! لا تضَيِّع طَريقَك [laː dðayyiʕ ṭariːqak] • **2.** خِسَر [xisar] خَسارَة [xasaːra] *vn:* اِنخِسَر [ʔinxisar] *p:* فِقَد [fiqad] فَقِد [faqid] *vn:* اِنفِقَد [ʔinfiqad] *p:* He lost his entire fortune during the war. خِسَر كُلّ ثَرُوتَه أثناء الحَرب [xisar kull θaruwtah ʔaθnaːʔ ʔilħarb] I'm afraid he'll lose the game. خايِف يكُون يِخسَر اللِّعبَة [xaːyif ykuːn yixsar ʔilliʕba] • **3.** فِقَد [fiqad] فَقِد [faqid] *vn:* اِنفِقَد [ʔinfiqad] *p:* After a few steps he lost his balance. كَم خُطوَة وفِقَد تَوازنَه [čam xuṭwa wfiqad tawaːznah] He lost his life in the fire. فُقَد حَياتَه بِالحَرِيق [fuqad ħayaːtah bilħariːq] He loses his temper easily. يِفقُد أعصابَه بِالعَجَل [yifqud ʔaʕṣaːbah bilʕaǰal] They lost their son in the war. فِقدَوا إِبِنهُم بِالحَرُب [fiqdaw ʔibinhum bilħarub] • **4.** قَصَّر [qaṣṣar, gaṣṣar] تَقصِير [taqṣiːr] *vn:* *sv* i. أَخَّر [ʔaxxar] تَأخِير [taʔxiːr] *vn:* *sv* i. My watch loses three minutes a day. ساعتِي تقَصِّر ثلَث دَقايِق بِاليُوم [saːʕti tqaṣṣir tlaθ daqaːyiq bilyuːm] • **5.** تِلَف [tilaf] تَلِف [talif] *vn:* اِنتِلَف [ʔintilaf] *p:* My things were lost in the fire. غَراضِي اِنتِلفَت بِالحَرِيق [ɣaraːði ʔintilfat bilħariːq] My things were lost in the fire. غَراضِي راحَت بِالحَرِيق [ɣaraːði raːħat bilħariːq]

*** I lost a part of what he said.** • **1.** فاتنِي بَعض اللِّي قالَه [faːtni baʕð ʔilli gaːlah]

*** I'm losing my hair.** • **1.** شَعرِي دَيوقَع [šaʕri dayuːgaʕ]

to lose face • **1.** صَخَّم وجهَه، سَوَّد وجهَه [ṣaxxam wiččah, sawwad wiččah] تَصخِيم وِجه، تَسوِيد وِجه [taṣxiːm wičč, taswiːd wičč] *vn:* *sv* i. He lost face when he couldn't come through on his promise. سَخَّم وِجهه مِن ما قِدَر يُوفِي بوَعدَه [ṣaxxam wiččah min maː gidar yuːfi bwaʕdah]

loser • **1.** خَسران [xasraːn] He was the loser. هُوَّ كان الخَسران [huwwa čaːn ʔilxasraːn]

*** He's a real loser.** • **1.** حاسِبتَه واقفَة [ħaːsibtah waːgfa]

losing • **1.** خاسِر [xaːsir] They are fighting a losing battle. داخلِين مَعرَكَة خاسرَة [daːxliːn maʕraka xaːsra]

loss • **1.** خَسارَة [xasaːra] خَسارات، خَسايِر [xasaːraː t, xasaːyir] *pl:* They suffered heavy losses. تكَبِّدَوا خَسائِر جَسِيمَة [tkabbidaw xasaːʔir ǰasiːma] I sold the house at a loss. بِعت البَيت بِخَسارَة [biʕt ʔilbayt bixasaːra] • **2.** فَقِد [faqid] فُقدان [fuqdaːn] She is griefstricken at the loss of her husband. هِيَّ حَزِينَة عَلَى فَقِد زَوُجها [hiyya ħaziːna ʕala faqid zawuǰha]

*** He's never at a loss for an excuse.**

• **1.** ما يِصعَب عَلَيه عُذُر [maː yiṣʕab ʕaliːh ʕuður] / عُذرَه براس لسانَه [ʕuðrah braːs lsaːnah]

*** She's never at a loss for an answer.**

• **1.** ما يِعصَى عَلَيها جَواب [maː yiʕṣaː ʕaliːha ǰawaːb]

*** I'm at a loss to explain his absence.**

• **1.** عِصَى عَلَيَّ أعرُف غِيابَه [ʕiṣaː ʕalayya ʔaʕruf ɣiyaːbah]

lost • **1.** مَفقُود [mafquːd] مَفقُودات [mafquːdaːt] *pl:* ضايِع [ðaːyiʕ] I'm going to run an ad about my lost watch. راح أنشُر إعلان عَن ساعَتِي المَفقُودَة [raːħ ʔanšur ʔiʕlaːn ʕan saːʕati ʔilmafquːda]

to be lost • **1.** ضاع [ðaːʕ] ضِياع [ðiyaːʕ] *vn:* *sv* i. My shirt was lost in the laundry. ثَوبِي ضاع عِند المُكَوِّي [θuːbi ðaːʕ ʕind ʔilmukawwi] I hope nothing is lost in the moving. إن شاء الله ما يضِيع شِي بِالتَّحوِيل [ʔinšaːllah maː yðiːʕ ši bittaħwiːl]

*** Since his wife's death he's completely lost.** • **1.** تخَربَط مِن ماتَت زَوُجتَه [txarbaṭ min maːtat zawuǰtah]

*** He was lost in thought.** • **1.** كان ضارُب دالغَة [čaːn ðaːrub daːlɣa]

*** I'm lost when it comes to mathematics.**

• **1.** يضِيع عَلَيَّ الحساب مِن تِجِي يَمّ الرِياضِيّات [yðiːʕ ʕalayya ʔiliħsaːb min tiǰi yamm ʔirriyaːðiyyaːt]

lot • **1.** قَطعَة أرض [qatʕat ʔarð] قُطَع أراضِي [qutaʕ ʔarð] *pl:* How big is your lot? شقَدّ كُبُر قُطعَة الأرض مالتَك [šgadd kubur qutʕat ʔilʔarið maːltak] • **2.** مَكتُوب [maktuːb] مَكاتِيب [makaːtiːb] *pl:* I don't envy his lot. ما أحِسدَه عالمَكتُوب لَه [maː ʔaħisdah ʕalmaktuːblah] • **3.** دَفعَة [dafʕa] دَفعات [dafʕaːt] *pl:* I'll send the books in three separate lots. راح أدِزّ الكُتُب عَلَى ثَلاث دُفعات [raːħ ʔadizz ʔilkutub ʕala tlaθ dufʕaːt] • **4.** قُرعَة [qurʕa] قُرَع [quraʕ] *pl:* Let's draw lots. خَلِّي نسَوِّي قُرعَة [xalli nsawwi qurʕa]

*** He's a bad lot.** • **1.** هُوَّ دُونِي [huwwa duːni] / هُوَّ مُو خُوش وَلَد [huwwa muː xuːš walad]

a lot • **1.** هوايَة [hwaːya] كِثِير [kiθiːr, čiθiːr] I ate a lot. أكَلِت هوايَة [ʔakalit hwaːya] We like him a lot. نحِبَّه هوايَة [nħibbah hwaːya] I still have a lot of work. بَعَد عِندِي هوايَة شُغُل [baʕad ʕindi hwaːya šuɣul] She's a lot better than people think. هِيَّ هوايَة أحسَن مِن ما النّاس يظِنُّون [hiyya hwaːya ʔaħsan min maː ʔinnaːs yðinnuːn]

lots of • **1.** هوايَة [hwaːya] كثِير [kθiːr] She has lots of money. عِدها هوايَة فلُوس [ʕidha hwaːya fluːs] We had lots of fun at the dance. هوايَة توَنَّسنا بِالرِّقص [hwaːya twannasna birrigiṣ]

loud • **1.** عالِي [ʕaːli] She has a loud, unpleasant voice. عِدها صُوت عالِي مُزعِج [ʕidha ṣuːt ʕaːli muzʕiǰ] • **2.** بَرّاق

L

[barra:q] I don't like loud colors. ما أَحِبّ الأَلوان البَرّاقَة [ma: ʔaħibb ʔilʔalwa:n ʔilbarra:qa]

loud-speaker • 1. سِمّاعَة [simma:ʕa] سِمّاعات [simma:ʕa:t] *pl:* مُكَبِّر صَوت [mukabbir ṣawt] مُكَبِّر صَوت [mukabbira:t ṣawt] *pl:*

lounge • 1. غُرفَة إِستِراحَة [ɣurfat ʔistira:ħa] غُرَف إِستِراحَة [ɣuraf ʔistira:ħa] *pl:* We had coffee in the lounge. شرَبنا قَهوَة بغُرفَة الاستِراحَة [šrabna gahwa bɣurfat ʔilʔistira:ħa]

to lounge around • 1. تفَتَّل [tfattal] تَفَتُّل [tafattul] *vn: sv* a. I like to lounge around the house on holidays. أَحِبّ أَتفَتَّل بالبَيت بِالعُطلَة [ʔaħibb ʔatfattal bilbayt bilʕuṭla]

louse • 1. قَملَة [gamla] قَملات [gamla:t] *pl:* قَمُل [gamul] *Collective*

love • 1. حُبّ [ħubb] Love is blind. الحُبّ أَعمى [ʔalħubb ʔaʕma] He must be in love. لازِم يكُون واقِع بالحُبّ [la:zim yku:n wa:giʕ bilħubb] He must be in love. لازِم دَيحِبّ [la:zim dayħibb]

*** You can't get it for love or money.**

• 1. ما مُمكِن تِتحَصَّل مَهما كان [ma: mumkin titħaṣṣal mahma ka:n]

to love • 1. حَبّ [ħabb] حُبّ [ħubb] *vn:* اِنحَبّ [ʔinħabb] *p:* He loves her very much. هُوَّ يحِبّها هوايَة [huwwa yħibbha hwa:ya] I love apples. أَحِبّ التِّفّاح [ʔaħibb ʔittiffa:ħ] I love to dance. أَحِبّ أَرقُص [ʔaħibb ʔarguṣ]

*** Would you like a cup of coffee? - I'd love one! • 1.** يعجِبَك فِنجان قَهوَة؟ إِي، وَالله بمَكانَه [yʕijbak finja:n gahwa? ʔi:, wʔallah bmaka:nah]

lovely • 1. بَدِيع [badi:ʕ] لَطِيف [laṭi:f] They have a lovely home. عِدهُم بَيت بَدِيع [ʕidhum bayt badi:ʕ]

loving • 1. مُحِبّ [muħibb] This is my loving wife. هاي زَوجتِي المُحِبَّة [ha:y zawijti ʔilmuħibba]

low • 1. ناصِي [na:ṣi] واطِي [wa:ṭi] Do you want shoes with high or low heels? ترِيدِين حِذاء كَعَب عالِي لَو ناصِي؟ [tri:di:n ħiða:ʔ čaʕab ʕa:li law na:ṣi?] That plane is flying too low. هَالطَّيّارَة دَتطِير كُلِّش ناصِي [haṭṭayya:ra daṭṭi:r kulliš na:ṣi] **• 2.** واطِي [wa:ṭi] ضَعِيف [ðaʕi:f] نازِل [na:zil] He always gets low marks. دائِماً يحَصِّل عَلَى دَرَجات واطيَة [da:ʔiman yħaṣṣil ʕala daraja:t wa:ṭya] His pulse is low. نَبضَه واطِي [nabðah wa:ṭi] She spoke in a low voice. تكَلّمَت بِصَوت واطِي [tkallimat bṣawt wa:ṭi] You have very low blood pressure. ضَغطَك كُلِّش واطِي [ðaɣṭak kulliš wa:ṭi] **• 3.** مَعقُوج [maʕqu:č] I feel very low today. آنِي شوَيَّة مَعقُوج اليُوم [ʔa:ni šwayya maʕqu:č ʔilyu:m] **• 4.** واحِد [wa:ħid] وِحدَة [wiħda] *Feminine:* Put the car in low. خَلِّي السَّيّارَة عالواحِد [xalli ʔissayya:ra ʕalwa:ħid] **• 5.** حَقارَة [ħaqa:ra] دَناءَة [dana:ʔa] That was low of him. كانَت حَقارَة مِنَّه [ča:nat ħaqa:ra minnah]

*** He made a low bow. • 1.** اِنحِنَي هوايَة [ʔinħina: hwa:ya]

*** The sun is quite low already.**

• 1. الشَّمِس تَقرِيباً راح تغِيب [ʔiššamis taqri:ban ra:ħ tɣi:b]

*** I have a low opinion of him. • 1.** رَأي مُو زَين بِيه [raʔy mu: zayn bi:h]

*** Our funds are getting low. • 1.** رَصِيدنا دَيِنخُفُض [raṣi:dna dayinxufuð]

lower • 1. أَنصَى [ʔanṣa] أَوطا [ʔawṭa] This chair is lower than that one. هَالكُرسِي أَنصَى مِن اللّاخ [halkursi ʔanṣa: min ʔilla:x] **• 2.** جَوّانِي [jawwa:ni] Put it on the lower shelf. حُطّها بِالرَّفّ الجَّوّانِي [ħuṭṭha birraff ʔijjawwa:ni]

to lower • 1. نَزَّل [nazzal] تَنزِيل [tanzi:l] *vn:* تنَزَّل [tnazzal] *p:* Lower the lifeboats. نَزِّل زَوارِق النَّجاة [nazzil zawa:riq ʔinnaja:t] He lowered himself in their eyes. نَزَّل نَفسَه بعَينهُم [nazzal nafsah biʕaynhum] They will lower the price some day. راح ينزِّلُون السِّعِر فَدّ يوم [ra:ħ ynizzlu:n ʔissiʕir fadd yu:m] **• 2.** نَصَّى [naṣṣa:] تَنصِيَة [tanṣiya] *vn:* تنَصَّى [tnaṣṣa:] *p:* وَطَّى [waṭṭa:] تَوطِيَة [tawṭiya] *vn:* توَطَّى [twaṭṭa:] *p:* He lowered his voice when he saw her come in. نَصَّى صَوتَه مِن شافها تِدخُل [naṣṣa: ṣawtah min ša:fha tidxul]

loyal • 1. مُخلِص [muxliṣ] مُخلِصِين [muxliṣi:n] *pl:* He has always been loyal to the government. دائِماً كان مُخلِص لِلحُكُومَة [da:ʔiman ča:n muxliṣ lilħuku:ma] **• 2.** وَفِي [wafi] أَوفِياء [ʔawfiya:ʔ] *pl:* مُخلِص [muxliṣ] مُخلِصِين [muxliṣi:n] *pl:* You couldn't have a more loyal friend. ما تِلقِي صَدِيق أَوفَى مِنَّه [ma: tilgi ṣadi:q ʔawfa minnah] I've always been a loyal friend, haven't I? دائِماً كِنِتلَك صَدِيق وَفِي، مُو؟ [da:ʔiman činitlak ṣadi:q wafi, mu:ʔ]

loyalty • 1. إِخلاص [ʔixla:ṣ] Nobody questioned his loyalty to the government. مَحَّد شَكّ بإخلاصَه لِلحُكُومَة [maħħad šakk bʔixla:ṣah lilħuku:ma] You can depend on his loyalty. تِقدَر تِعتِمِد عَلَى إِخلاصَه [tigdar tiʕtimid ʕala ʔixla:ṣah]

lubricant • 1. دِهِن تَشحِيم [dihin tašħi:m]

to lubricate • 1. شَحَّم [šaħħam] تَشحِيم [tašħi:m] *vn:* تشَحَّم [tšaħħam] *p:* Please lubricate the car. مِن فَضلَك شَحِّم السَّيّارَة [min faðlak šaħħim ʔissayya:ra]

lubrication • 1. تَشحِيم [tašħi:m]

luck • 1. حَظّ [ħaðð] حظُوظ [ħðu:ð] *pl:* My luck has changed. حَظّي اِستَعدَل [ħaðði ʔistaʕdal] **• 2.** تَوفِيق [tawfi:q] حَظّ [ħaðð] I wish you all the luck in the world. أَتمَنّالَك كُلّ التَّوفِيق [ʔatmanna:lak kull ʔittawfi:q] Now you try your luck! هَسَّة إِنتَ جَرُّب حَظَّك [hassa ʔinta jarrub ħaððak]

* **Good luck!** • **1.** مُوَفَّق إن شاءَ الله [muwaffaq ʔin šaːʔa ʔallaːh] / حَظّ سَعِيد [ħaðð saʕiːd]

luckily • **1.** مِن حُسن الحَظّ [min ħusn ʔilħaðð] Luckily, he doesn't bite. مِن حُسُن الحَظّ ما يعَضّ [min ħusun ʔilħaðð maː yʕaðð]

lucky • **1.** سَعِيد [saʕiːd] سَعِيدِين، سُعَداء [saʕiːdiːn, suʕadaːʔ] *pl:* It was a lucky coincidence. كانَت صِدفَة سَعِيدَة [čaːnat ṣidfa saʕiːda] • **2.** مَحظُوظ [maħðuːð] You can consider yourself lucky. تِقدَر تِعتِبُر نَفسَك مَحظُوظ [tigdar tiʕtibur nafsak maħðuːð] You're a lucky fellow. إنتَ واحِد مَحظُوظ [ʔinta waːħid maħðuːð]

luggage • **1.** جُنَط [ǰunaṭ] We stowed our luggage on the back seat of the car. خَلِّينا جُنَطنا بالمَقعَد الخَلفِي بِالسَّيّارَة [xalliːna ǰunaṭna bilmaqʕad ʔilxalfi bissayyaːra]

lukewarm • **1.** دافِي [daːfi] فاتِر [faːtir] Take a lukewarm bath. أُخُذ حَمّام دافِي [ʔuxuð ħammaːm daːfi] • **2.** ما مِهتَمّ [maː mihtamm] He's very lukewarm about your plan. هُوَّ ما مِهتَمّ لِمَشرُوعَك [huwwa maː mihtamm limašruːʕak]

lull • **1.** * We went out during the lull in the storm. طلَعنا مِن خَفَّت العاصِفَة [ṭlaʕna min xaffat ʔilʕaːṣifa]

to lull to sleep • **1.** نَوَّم [nawwam] تَنوِيم [tanwiːm] *vn:* تنَوَّم [tnawwam] *p:* Her singing lulled the boy to sleep. غِناها نَوَّم الطِّفِل [ɣinaːha nawwam ʔiṭṭifil]

lullaby • **1.** لَيلُوَّة [layluwwa] لَيلُوّات [layluwwaːt] *pl:*

lumber • **1.** خِشَب [xišab] How much lumber will be needed for the book shelves? شقَدّ خِشَب تِحتاج لِرفُوف الكُتُب [šgadd xišab tiħtaːǰ lirfuːf ʔilkutub]

luminous • **1.** فِسفُورِي [fisfuːri] Has your watch got a luminous dial? ساعتَك بِيها ميال فِسفُورِيَّة؟ [saːʕtak biːha myaːl fisfuːriyya?]

lump • **1.** كُتلَة [kutla] كُتَل [kutal] *pl:* What are you going to do with that lump of clay? شراح تسَوِّي بِكُتلَة الطِّين هاي؟ [šraːħ tsawwi bkutlat ʔiṭṭiːn haːy?] • **2.** وَرَم [waram] أورام [ʔawraːm] *pl:* He has a big lump on his forehead. أكُو وَرَم بِقُصّتَه [ʔaku waram biguṣṣṭah] • **3.** قالَب [qaːlab] قوالِب، قوالِب [qawaːlib, qwaːlib.] *pl:* فُصّ [fuṣṣ] فصُوص [fṣuːṣ] *pl:* I take only one lump (of sugar) in my coffee. آني آخُذ قالَب واحِد لِقَهُوتِي [ʔaːni ʔaːxuð qaːlab waːħid ligahwti]

lump sugar • **1.** قَند [qand]

lumpy • **1.** مفَصَّص [mfaṣṣaṣ] The sugar is lumpy. الشَّكَر مفَصَّص [ʔiššakar mfaṣṣaṣ] • **2.** معَقَّد [mʕaggad] This pillow is very lumpy. هالمِخَدَّة معَقَّدَة [halimxadda mʕaggida]

lunar • **1.** قَمَرِي [qamari] The Moslem holidays follow the lunar calendar. العُطَل الإسلامِيَّة تِتبَع التَّقوِيم القَمَرِي [ʔilʕuṭal ʔilʔislaːmiyya titbaʕ ʔittaqwiːm ʔalqamari]

lunatic • **1.** مخَبَّل [mxabbal] مَخابِيل [maxaːbiːl] *pl:* مَجنُون [majnuːn] He's acting like a lunatic. دَيِتصَرَّف مِثل المخَبَّل [dayitṣarraf miθl ʔilmxabbal]

lunch • **1.** غَدا [ɣada] غَدايات، غِديات [ɣadaːyaːt, ɣidyaːt] *pl:* It's time for lunch. صار وَقِت الغَدا [ṣaːr wakit ʔilɣada]

to lunch • **1.** تغَدَّى [tɣaddaː] Will you lunch with me? تِتغَدَّى وِيّايا؟ [tidɣaddaː wiyyaːya?]

lung • **1.** رِئَة [riʔa] رِئات [riʔaːt] *pl:* His left lung is infected. رِئتَه اليسرَى مُصابَة [riʔatah ʔilyisra muṣaːba]

* **The boy yelled at the top of his lungs.** • **1.** الوَلَد عاط بعِلُو حِسَّه [ʔilwalad ʕaːṭ bʕilu ħissah]

to lurk • **1.** خِتَل [xital] خَتِل [xatil] *vn: sv* i. We found him lurking in an alley. شِفناه خاتِل بِالدَّربُونَة [šifnaːh xaːtil biddarbuːna]

lute • **1.** عُود [ʕuːd] أعواد [ʔaʕwaːd] *pl:* The lute is out of tune. العُود ما مَنصُوب [ʔilʕuːd maː manṣuːb]

luxury • **1.** تَرَف [taraf] They lived in unbelievable luxury. عاشَوا بِتَرَف فَظِيع [ʕaːšaw btaraf faðiːʕ] • **2.** فَخِم [faxim] They're building a luxury hotel. دَيِبنُون فِندِق فَخِم [dayibnuːn findiq faxim]

luxuries • **1.** كَمالِيّات [kamaːliyyaːt] They're raising the tax on luxuries. دَيزَيّدُون الضَّرِيبَة عالكَمالِيّات [dayzayyduːn ʔiððariːba ʕalkamaːliyyaːt]

lying • **1.** كِذِب [čiðib, kiðib] Lying won't get you anywhere. الكِذِب ما يفِيدَك [ʔilkiðib maː yfiːdak]

lyre • **1.** قِيثارَة [qiθaːra] قِيثارات [qiθaːraːt] *pl:*

L

M

machine • **1.** مَكِينَة [maki:na] مَكايِن [maka:yin] *pl:* آلَة [ʔa:la] آلات [ʔa:la:t] *pl:* The machine is working again. المَكِينَة قامَت تِشتُغل مَرَّة لُخ [ʔilmaki:na ga:mat tištuɣul marra lux]

machine gun • **1.** رَشّاشَة [rašša:ša] رَشّاشات [rašša:ša:t] *pl:* رَشّاش [rašša:š] رَشّاشات [rašša:ša:t] *pl:* مَطرِلّوز [maṭrillu:z] مَطرِلّوزات [maṭrillu:za:t] *pl:*

machinery • **1.** مَكايِن [maka:yin] آلات [ʔa:la:t]

mad • **1.** مَجنُون [majnu:n] مخَبَّل [mxabbal] مخابِيل [mxa:bi:l] *pl:* He is a little mad and unpredictable. هَذا شوَيَّة مَجنُون وَما تِقدَر تُعرُف شيِطلَع مِنَّه [ha:ða šwayya majnu:n wama: tigdar tuʕruf šyiṭlaʕ minnah] He drove like mad. ساق مِثل المخَبَّل [sa:q miθl ʔilmxabbal] • **2.** مَكلُوب [mačlu:b] He was bitten by a mad dog. عَضَّة كَلِب مَكلُوب [ʕaððа čalib mačlu:b] • **3.** زَعلان [zaʕla:n] زَعلانِين، زعالَة [zaʕla:ni:n, zʕa:la] *pl:* غَضبان [ɣaðba:n] What are you mad about? عَلَى وَيش زَعلان؟ [ʕala wi:š zaʕla:n?] What are you mad about? شِمزَعَّلَك؟ [šimzaʕʕlak?] What are you mad about? إيش بيك زَعلان؟ [ʔišbi:k zaʕla:n?]

to drive mad • **1.** جَنَّن [jannan] تجِنِّن [tjinnin] *vn:* تجَنَّن [tjannan] *p:* خَبَّل [xabbal] تخُبُّل [txubbul] *vn:* تخَبَّل [txabbal] *p:* The heat is driving me mad. الحَرّ راح يجَنِّنِني [ʔilħarr ra:ħ yjanninni]

to be mad about • **1.** تخَبَّل عَلَى [txabbal ʕala] تخُبُّل عَلَى [txubbul ʕala] *vn:* *sv* a. She's mad about him. هِيَّ مِتخَبّلَة عَليه [hiyya mitxabbla ʕali:h] My boy is mad about ice cream. إبنِي يِتخَبَّل عالدُّوندِرمَة [ʔibni yitxabbal ʕaddu:ndirma]

to be mad at • **1.** زِعَل عَلَى [ziʕal ʕala] زَعَل عَلَى [zaʕal ʕala] *vn:* اِنزِعَل عَلَى [ʔinziʕal ʕala] *p:* مِن [min] She's mad at me again. زِعلَت عَلَيّا مَرَّة لُخ [ziʕlat ʕalayya marra lux] She's mad at me again. هِيَّ هَمّ زَعلانَة عَلَيّا [hiyya hamm zaʕla:na ʕalayya]

madam • **1.** خاتُون [xatu:n] خواتِين [xwa:ti:n] *pl:* سَيِّدَة [sayyida] سَيِّدات [sayyida:t] *pl:* Is somebody waiting on you, Madam? خاتُون، أَحَّد فَضّ شُغلِك؟ [xa:tu:n, ʔaħħad faðð šuɣlič?]

madman • **1.** مَجنُون [majnu:n] مَجانِين [maja:ni:n] *pl:* مخَبَّل [mxabbal] مخابِيل [mxa:bi:l] *pl:*

magazine • **1.** مَجَلَّة [majalla] مَجَلّات [majalla:t] *pl:* Where can I buy the magazine? منين أَقدَر أَشتِرِي المَجَلَّة؟ [mni:n ʔagdar ʔaštiri ʔilmajalla?]

magnificent • **1.** فاخِر [fa:xir] نَفِيس [nafi:s] نَفائِس [nafa:ʔis] *pl:* مُمتاز [mumta:z]

to magnify • **1.** كَبَّر [kabbar] تَكُبُّر [takubbur] *vn:* تكَبَّر [tkabbar] *p:* This lens magnifies six times. هَالعَدَسَة تكَبُّر سِتّ مَرّات [halʕadasa tkabbur sitt marra:t]

magnifying glass • **1.** مُكَبِّرَة [mukabbira] مُكَبِّرات [mukabbira:t] *pl:* You can only see it with a magnifying glass. ما تِقدَر تشُوفها إلّا بِمُكَبِّرَة [ma: tigdar tšu:fha ʔilla bmukabbira]

maid • **1.** خَدّامَة [xadda:ma] خَدّامات [xadda:ma:t] *pl:* خادمَة [xa:dma] خادمات [xa:dma:t] *pl:* We let our maid go. بَطَّلنا خَدّامَتنا [baṭṭalna xadda:matna]

old maid • **1.** عانِس [ʕa:nis] عَوانِس [ʕawa:nis] *pl:* عَزبَة [ʕazba] عَزبات [ʕazba:t] *pl:* She acts like an old maid. تِتصَرَّف عَبالَك فَدّ وِحدَة عانِس [titṣarraf ʕaba:lak fadd wiħda ʕa:nis] She died an old maid. ماتَت بنَيَّة [ma:tat bnayya]

mail • **1.** بَرِيد [bari:d] مَكتُوب [maktu:b] مَكاتِيب [maka:ti:b] *pl:* The mail is delivered at four o'clock. البَرِيد يِتوَزَّع ساعَة أَربَعَة [ʔilbari:d yitwazzaʕ sa:ʕa ʔarbaʕa] Is there any mail for me? أَكُو مَكاتِيب إلِي؟ [ʔaku maka:ti:b ʔili?]

mails • **1.** بَرِيد [bari:d] مُواصَلات بَرِيدِيَّة [muwa:ṣala:t bari:diyya] The storm held up the mails. العاصِفَة عَطِّلَت المُواصَلات البَرِيدِيَّة [ʔilʕa:ṣifa ʕaṭṭilat ʔilmuwa:ṣala:t ʔilbari:diyya]

to mail • **1.** دَزّ بالبَرِيد [dazz bilbari:d] اِندَزّ بالبَرِيد [ʔindazz bilbari:d] *p:* Did you mail the package? إنتَ دَزَّيت الرُّزمَة بالبَرِيد؟ [ʔinta dazzayt ʔirruzma bilbari:d?] Please mail the letter for me. أَرجُوك دِزّلِي المَكتُوب بالبَرِيد [ʔarju:k dizzli ʔilmaktu:b bilbari:d] Please mail the letter for me. أَرجُوك ذِبّلِي المَكتُوب بالبَرِيد [ʔarju:k ðibbli ʔilmaktu:b bilbari:d]

mailbox • **1.** صَندُوق بَرِيد [ṣandu:g bari:d] صَنادِيق بَرِيد [ṣana:di:g bari:d] *pl:*

mailman • **1.** مُوَزِّع بَرِيد [muwazziʕ bari:d] مُوَزِّعِين بَرِيد [muwazziʕi:n bari:d] *pl:*

main • **1.** أَبّي [ʔabbi] أَبِّيّات [ʔabbiyya:t] *pl:* The main has burst. الأَبِّي طَقّ [ʔilʔabbi ṭagg] • **2.** أَساسِي [ʔasa:si] رَئِيسِي [raʔi:si] That's one of our main problems. هَذِيك وِحدَة مِن مَشاكِلنا الأَساسِيَّة [haði:č wiħda min maša:kilna ʔilʔasa:siyya] Did you inquire at the main office? سِأَلِت بالدّائِرَة الرَّئِيسِيَّة؟ [siʔalt bidda:ʔira ʔirraʔi:siyya?]

You've forgotten the main thing. نسَيت الشّي الأساسِي [nsayt ʔišši ʔalʔasa:si]

in the main • **1.** عَلَى العُمُوم [ʕala ʔilʕumu:m] بالعُمُوم [bilʕumu:m] غالِباً [ɣa:liban] The discussion revolved in the main around two questions. المُناقَشَة دارَت عَلَى العُمُوم حَوُل مَسألتَين [ʔilmuna:qaša da:rat ʕala ʔalʕumu:m ħawul masʔaltayn] I agree with him in the main. آنِي غالِباً أَتّفِق ويّاه [ʔa:ni ɣa:liban ʔattifiq wiyya:h]

mainly • **1.** عَلَى الأكثَر [ʕala ʔilʔakθar] He comes mainly on Tuesdays. عَلَى الأكثَر يِجِي أيّام الثّلاثاء [ʕala ʔilʔakθar yiǰi ʔayya:m ʔiθθla:θa]

to maintain • **1.** صَرّ عَلَى [ṣarr ʕala] إصرار [ʔiṣra:r] *vn:* اِنصَرّ [ʔinṣarr] *p:* He maintains that he was there. هُوَّ يصِرّ عَلَى إنّو كان هناك [huwwa yṣirr ʕala ʔinnu ča:n hna:k] • **2.** اِحتِفَظ ب [ʔiħtifað̣ b-] اِحتِفاظ [ʔiħtifa:ð̣] *vn:* *sv* u. They have moved to Karrada, but they have decided to maintain their house in Fadhil. اِنتِقلوا لِلكَرّادَة لَكِن قَرِّروا يحتفظُون ببَيتهُم العَتِيق بالفَضِل [ʔintiqlaw lilkarra:da la:kin qarriraw yiħtafð̣u:n bibaythum ʔilʕati:g bilfað̣il]

maintenance • **1.** صِيانَة [ṣiya:na]

major • **1.** رَئِيس أوَّل [raʔi:s awwal] رُؤساء أوَّلِين [ruʔasa:ʔ awwali:n] *pl:* Has anyone seen the major? أَحَّد شاف الرَّئِيس الأوَّل؟ [ʔaħħad ša:f ʔirraʔi:s ʔilʔawwal?] • **2.** مَوضُوع رَئِيسِي [mawð̣u:ʕ raʔi:si] مَواضِيع رَئِيسِيَّة [mawa:ð̣i:ʕ raʔi:siyya] *pl:* What's your major? شِنُو مَوضُوعَك الرَّئِيسِي؟ [šinu mawð̣u:ʕak ʔirraʔi:si?] • **3.** أكثَر [ʔakθar] أكبَر [ʔakbar] أعظَم [ʔaʕð̣am] The major part of my income goes for rent. القِسم الأكبَر مِن دَخلِي يرُوح لِلإيجار [ʔilqism ʔilʔakbar min daxli yiru:ħ lilʔi:ǰa:r]

majority • **1.** أكثَرِيَّة [ʔakθariyya] أغلَبِيَّة [ʔaɣlabiyya] The majority was against it. الأكثَرِيَّة عارضَت المَوضُوع [ʔilʔakθariyya ʕa:rð̣at ʔilmawð̣u:ʕ] The majority of the students were sick. أغلَبِيَّة التَّلامِيذ كانَوا وَجعانِين [ʔaɣlabiyyat ʔittala:mi:ð ča:naw waǰʕa:ni:n]

make • **1.** مارگَة [ma:rka] ماركات [ma:rka:t] *pl:* نوع [nawʕ] أنواع [ʔanwa:ʕ] *pl:* What make is your radio? الرّاديُو مالَك يا مارگَة؟ [ʔirra:dyu ma:lak ya: ma:rka?] What make is your radio? الرّاديُو مالَك شُغُل مَن؟ [ʔirra:dyu ma:lak šuɣul man?]

to make • **1.** سَوَّى [sawwa:] تسِوِّي [tsiwwi] *vn:* تسَوَّى [tsawwa:] *p:* عِمَل [ʕimal] عَمَل [ʕamal] *vn:* اِنعِمَل [ʔinʕimal] *p:* He made a big mistake. سَوَّى غَلطَة كبِيرَة [sawwa: ɣalṭa čbi:ra] • **2.** صِنَع [ṣinaʕ] صَنع [ṣaniʕ] *vn:* اِنصِنَع [ʔinṣinaʕ] *p:* This factory makes bottles. هَالمَعمَل دَيِصنَع بطالَة [hallmaʕmal dayiṣnaʕ bṭa:la] • **3.** سَوَّى [sawwa:] They made him president. سَوَّوَه رَئِيس [sawwawah raʔi:s] How much do you make a week? شقَدّ تسَوِّي بالإسبُوع؟ [šgadd tsawwi bilʔisbu:ʕ?] You'll have to make a few changes. لازِم تسَوِّي شوَيَّة تَبدِيلات [la:zim tsawwi šwayya tabdi:la:t] • **4.** خَلَّى [xalla:] تخِلِّي [txilli] *vn:* تخَلَّى [txalla:] *p:* Onions make my eyes water. البُصَل يخَلِّي عيُونِي تِدمَع [ʔilbuṣal yxalli ʕyu:ni tidmaʕ] • **5.** صار [ṣa:r] صَيرَة [ṣi:ra] *vn:* *sv* i. He'd really make a good king. هُوَّ حَقِيقَةً يصِير خُوش مَلِك [huwwa ħaqi:qatan yṣi:r xu:š malik] • **6.** لَحَّق ب [laħħag b-] تلِحِّق ب [tliħħig b-] *vn:* *sv* i. Do you think we'll make the train? تِعتِقِد راح نلَحِّق بالقِطار؟ [tiʕtiqid ra:ħ nlaħħig bilqiṭa:r?] • **7.** دَبَّر [dabbar] تَدبِير، تدُبُّر [tadbi:r, ddubbur] *vn:* *sv* u. How does he make his living? شلُون يدَبُّر عِيشتَه؟ [šlu:n ydabbur ʕi:štah?]

*** He made a fool of himself in front of the people.** • **1.** اِرتِكَب حَماقَة قِدّام الناس [ʔirtikab ħama:qa gidda:m ʔinna:s]

to make a choice • **1.** اِختار [ʔixta:r] اِختِيار [ʔixtiya:r] *vn:* *sv* a. You have to make a choice. لازِم تِختار [la:zim tixta:r]

to make off with • **1.** باق [ba:g] بَوق [bu:g] *vn:* اِنباق [ʔinba:g] *p:* They made off with our car. باقَوا سَيّارَتنا [ba:gaw sayya:ratna]

to make out • **1.** فَرزَن [farzan] تفِرزِن [tfirzin] *vn:* تفَرزَن [tfarzan] *p:* Can you make out the date on the postmark? تِقدَر تفَرزِن التّارِيخ عَلَى طَمغَة البَرِيد؟ [tigdar tfarzin ʔitta:ri:x ʕala ṭamgat ʔilbari:d?] • **2.** مِلَى [mila:] مَلِي [maly] *vn:* اِنمِلَى [ʔinmila:] *p:* Have you made out the application blank? ملَيت العَرِيضَة؟ [mli:t ʔilʕari:ð̣a?] • **3.** سَوَّى [sawwa:] تسِوِّي [tsiwwi] *vn:* *sv* i. How did you make out in the exam yesterday? شلُون سَوِّيت بالإمتِحان البارحَة؟ [šlu:n sawwi:t bilʔimtiħa:n ʔilba:rħa?]

to make time • **1.** سِرَع [siraʕ] إسراع [ʔisra:ʕ] *vn:* *sv* i. We can make time if we take the other road. نِقدَر نِسرِع إذا أخَذنا الطَّرِيق الثّانِي [nigdar nisriʕ ʔiða ʔaxaðna ʔittari:q ʔiθθa:ni]

to make up • **1.** سَوَّى [sawwa:] تسِوِّي [tsiwwi] *vn:* تسَوَّى [tsawwa:] *p:* Make up a list of all the things you need. سَوِّي قائِمَة بكُلّ الأشياء اللِّي تِحتاجها [sawwi qa:ʔima bkull ʔilʔašya:ʔ ʔilli tiħta:ǰha] • **2.** خِلَق [xilaq] خَلِق [xaliq] *vn:* اِنخِلَق [ʔinxilaq] *p:* He made up a story about his absence. خِلَق قُصَّة عَن غِيابَه [xilaq quṣṣa ʕan ɣiya:bah] • **3.** تصالَح [tṣa:laħ] تَصالُح [taṣa:luħ] *vn:* *sv* a. They've made up again. تصالَحَوا مَرَّة لُخ [tṣa:laħaw marra lux] • **4.** عَوَّض [ʕawwað̣] تَعوِيض، تعُوُّض [taʕwi:ð̣, tʕuwwuð̣] *vn:* *sv* u. You can make up the hours you didn't work yesterday, today.

M

تِقدَر تعوُّض السّاعات اللّي ما إشتغلِتها البارحَة، اليُوم [tigdar tʕawwuḍ ʔissaːʕaːt ʔilli maː ʔištaɣlitha ʔilbaːrħa, ʔilyuːm]

makeshift • 1. إرتجالي [ʔirtiǰaːli] This is just a makeshift arrangement. هَذا فَدّ تَرتِيب إرتِجالِي [haːða fadd tartiːb ʔirtiǰaːli]

make-up • 1. زواقَة [zwaːga] Shall I put a little more make-up on? أحُطّ زواقة شوَيَّة أزيَد؟ [ʔaħuṭṭ zwaːga šwayya ʔazyad?]

*** She uses an awful lot of make-up.**

• **1.** تِتزَوَّق أكثَر مِن اللازِم [titzawwag ʔakθar min ʔillaːzim]

makings • 1. قابلِيَّة [qaːbliyya] قابلِيّات [qaːbliyyaːt] *pl:* The boy has the makings of an actor. الوَلَد عِندَه قابلِيَّة يصير مُمَثِّل [ʔilwalad ʕindah qaːbliyya yṣiːr mumaθθil]

male • 1. ذَكَر [ðakar] ذُكُور [ðukuːr] *pl:* فَحَل [faħal] فحُول [fħuːl] *pl:* Is that dog a male or female? هَالكَلب فَحَل لَو نِثيَة؟ [haččalib faħal law niθya?]

male nurse • 1. مُضَمِّد [muḍammid] مُضَمِّدِين [muḍammidiːn] *pl:*

malicious • 1. حَقُود [ħaquːd] خَبِيث [xabiːθ] خُبَثاء [xubaθaːʔ] *pl:* مَسمُوم [masmuːm] That was a malicious remark. هَذِيك كانَت فَدّ حكايَة مَسمُومَة [haðiːč čaːnat fadd ħčaːya masmuːma]

malt • 1. شِعِير منَقَّع [šiʕiːr mnaggaʕ]

Malta • 1. مالطا [maːlṭa]

man • 1. رِجّال [riǰǰaːl] رياجِيل [riyaːǰiːl] *pl:* رَجُل [raǰul] رِجال [riǰaːl] *pl:* زِلمَة [zilma, zlima] زِلِم [zilim] *pl:* Who's that man? مِنُو هَالرِّجّال؟ [minu harriǰǰaːl?] He's not the man for it. هَذا مُو زِلمَتها [haːða muː zlimatha] He's not the man for it. ما يِطلَع مِن حَقها [maː yiṭlaʕ min ħaggha] What does the man in the street say about it? شَيقُول عَنها رَجُل الشّارِع؟ [šayguːl ʕanha raǰul ʔiššaːriʕ?] Tell the men to unload the furniture from the truck. قُول لِلرِّياجِيل خَلّي يفَرّغُون الأثاث مِن اللّوري [guːl lirriyaːǰiːl xalli yfarryuːn ʔilʔaθaːθ min ʔillawri] • **2.** إنسان [ʔinsaːn] Man used to live in caves. الإنسان كان يِعِيش بِالكُهُوف [ʔilʔinsaːn čaːn yiʕiːš bilkuhuːf]

*** One officer and four men volunteered.**

• **1.** ضابُط واحِد وأربَع جُنُود تطَوّعَوا [ḍaːbuṭ waːħid wʔarbaʕ ǰunuːd ṭṭawwʕaw]

to manage • 1. دار [daːr] دَوَران [dawaraːn] *vn:* اِندار [ʔindaːr] *p:* Who manages the estate? مِنُو يدِير المُقاطَعَة؟ [minu ydiːr ʔilmuqaːṭaʕa?] He managed the store for six years. دار المَخزَن سِتّ سنِين [daːr ʔilmaxzan sitt sniːn] • **2.** دَبَّر [dabbar] تَدبِير، تدُبُّر [tadbiːr, tdubbur] *vn:* تدَبَّر [tdabbar] *p:* How did you manage to get the tickets? شلُون دَبَّرت البِطاقات؟ [šluːn dabbarit ʔilbiṭaːqaːt?] Can you manage on your salary? تِقدَر تعِيش عَلَى مَعاشَك؟ [tigdar tʕiːš ʕala maʕaːšak?] We have to manage very carefully on our small salary. لازِم ندَبُّر أُمُورنا زين حَتَّى نعِيش عَلَى راتِبنا القَلِيل [laːzim ndabbur ʔumuːrna ziːn ħatta nʕiːš ʕala raːtibna ʔilqaliːl] • **3.** ضَبَط [ḍubaṭ] ضَبُط [ḍabuṭ] *vn:* اِنضُبَط [ʔinḍubaṭ] *p:* I can't manage the children. ما أقدَر أضبُط الجِّهال [maː ʔagdar ʔaḍbuṭ ʔiǰǰihaːl] • **4.** دَستَر [dastar] دَستَرَة [dastara] *vn:* تدَستَر [tdastar] *p:* رَتَّب [rattab] تَرتِيب [tartiːb] *vn:* ترَتَّب [trattab] *p:* Wasn't that cleverly managed? ما كانَت ذِيك مدَستَرَة بمَهارَة؟ [maː čaːnat ðiːč mdastara bmahaːra?]

management • 1. إدارَة [ʔidaːra] Complain to the management! اِشتِكِي عِند الإدارَة! [ʔištiki ʕind ʔilʔidaːra]

manager • 1. مُدِير [mudiːr] مُدَراء [mudaraːʔ] *pl:* Where is the manager? وين المُدِير؟ [wiːn ʔilmudiːr?] • **2.** مُدَبِّر [mudabbir] His wife is a good manager. مَرتَه مُدَبِّرَة تَماماً [martah mudabbira tamaːman]

mankind • 1. الجِّنس البَشَري [ʔiǰǰins ʔilbašari] بَشَر [bašar] بَشَرِين [bašariːn] *pl:* إنسان [ʔinsaːn]

manner • 1. طَرِيقَة [ṭariːqa] طُرُق [ṭuruq] *pl:* إسلُوب [ʔisluːb] أساليب [ʔasaːliːb] *pl:* I liked the manner in which he went about the job. عِجبَتنِي طَرِيقتَه بِالشُّغُل [ʕiǰbatni ṭariːqtah biššuɣul]

manners • 1. أدَب [ʔadab] آداب [ʔaːdaːb] *pl:* أخلاق [ʔaxlaːq] She has no manners. ما عِدها أدَب [maː ʕidha ʔadab]

to manufacture • 1. صِنَع [ṣinaʕ] صُنُع [ṣunuʕ] *vn:* اِنصِنَع [ʔinṣinaʕ] *p:* عِمَل [ʕimal] عَمَل [ʕamal] *vn:* اِنعِمَل [ʔinʕimal] *p:* What do they manufacture here? شِيصِنعُون هنا؟ [šiyiṣniʕuːn hna?]

manufacturer • 1. صاحِب مَصنَع [ṣaːħib maṣnaʕ] أصحاب مَصانِع [ʔaṣħaːb maṣaːniʕ] *pl:* مُنتِج مَصنَع [muntiǰ maṣnaʕ] مُنتِجِين مَصنَع [muntiǰiːn maṣnaʕ] *pl:*

manure • 1. سَماد [samaːd] أسمِدَة [ʔasmida] *pl:*

many • 1. هوايَة [hwaːya] مِتعَدِّد [mitʕaddid] عَدِيد [ʕadiːd] كِثِير [kiθiːr, čiθiːr] I have many reasons. عِندِي هوايَة أسباب [ʕindi hwaːya ʔasbaːb] Many a person has been fooled by that. هوايَة ناس تقَشمُرَوا بيه [hwaːya naːs tqašmuraw biːh]

how many • 1. شقَدّ [šgadd] كَم [čam] How many tickets do you want? شقَدّ ترِيد بطاقات؟ [šgadd triːd biṭaːqaːt?]

map • **1.** خَرِيطَة [xari:ṭa] خَرايِط [xara:yiṭ] *pl:* I want a map of Asia. أَرِيد خَرِيطَة مال آسيا [ʔari:d xari:ṭa ma:l ʔa:sya] Is it possible to get a road map of Iraq? هَل مِن المُمكِن الحُصُول عَلَى خَرِيطَة لِطُرُق العِراق؟ [hal min ʔilmumkin ʔilħuṣu:l ʕala xari:ṭa lṭuruq ʔilʕira:q?]

to map • **1.** خَطَّط [xaṭṭaṭ] تَخطِيط [taxṭi:ṭ] *vn:* تخَطَّط [txaṭṭaṭ] *p:* The mapping of this area will be finished in a week. تَخطِيط هَالمَنطِقَة يِخلَص بَعد إِسبُوع [taxṭi:ṭ halmanṭiqa yixlaṣ baʕd ʔisbu:ʕ]

to map out • **1.** عَيَّن [ʕayyan] تَعيين [taʕyi:n] *vn:* تعَيَّن [tʕayyan] *p:* Have you mapped out your route yet? عَيَّنِت طَرِيق سَفَرَك لَو بَعَد؟ [ʕayyanit ṭari:q safarak law baʕad?]

maple • **1.** سفَندِيان [sfandiya:n]

marble • **1.** مَرمَر [marmar] رُخام [ruxa:m] The statue is made of marble. التِّمثال مسَوَّى مِن مَرمَر [ʔittimθa:l msawwa min marmar] • **2.** دُعبُلَّة [duʕbulla] دُعبُلات، دَعابُل [duʕbulla:t, daʕa:bul] *pl:* I used to play marbles, too. آنِي هَمّ كِنِت أَلعَب دُعبُل [ʔa:ni hamm činit ʔalʕab duʕbul]

March • **1.** آذار [ʔa:ða:r] I plan to stay here until March. نِيَّتِي أَبقَى هنا إِلَى آذار [niyyti ʔabqa: hna ʔila ʔa:ða:r]

march • **1.** مَشيَة [mašya] مَشيات [mašya:t] *pl:* مَسِيرَة [masi:ra] مَسِيرات [masi:ra:t] *pl:* We still have a long march ahead of us. بَعَد قِدّامنا مَشيَة طوِيلَة [baʕad gidda:mna mašya ṭwi:la] • **2.** مارش [ma:rš] مارشات [ma:rša:t] *pl:* مُوسِيقَى مَسِير [musi:qa masi:r] مارشات مَسِير [ma:rša:t masi:r] *pl:* The band began with a march. الجَوق بِدا بمارش [ʔijǰawq bida: bma:rš]

to march • **1.** مِشَى [miša:] مِشِي [mišy] *vn:* اِنمِشَى [ʔinmiša:] *p:* زِحَف [ziħaf] زَحِف [zaħif] *vn:* اِنزِحَف [ʔinziħaf] *p:* Did you see the soldiers marching? شِفت الجِّنُود دَيِمشُون؟ [šift ʔijǰinu:d dayimšu:n?]

mare • **1.** فَرَس [faras] أَفراس، فرُوسَة [ʔafra:s, fru:sa] *pl:*

margin • **1.** هامِش [ha:miš] هَوامِش [hawa:miš] *pl:* حاشِيَة [ħa:šiya] حَواشِي [ħawa:ši] *pl:* Leave a wide margin on the left side. إِترُك هامِش عَرِيض بِالجِّهَة اليِسرَى [ʔitruk ha:miš ʕari:ḍ bijǰiha ʔilyisra] • **2.** حَدّ [ħadd] We're operating on a very small margin of profit. دَنِشتُغُل عَلَى حَدّ ضَئِيل مِن الرِّبِح [daništuɣul ʕala ħadd ḍaʔi:l min ʔirribiħ] • **3.** اِحتِياطِي [ʔiħtiya:ṭi] I'm allowing a margin for incidental expenses. آنِي حاطّ اِحتِياطِي لِلنَّثرِيّات [ʔa:ni ħa:ṭṭ ʔiħtiya:ṭi linnaθriyya:t] • **4.** فَرِق [fariq] فُرُوق [furu:q] *pl:* We won by a narrow margin. غِلَبنا بِفَرِق قَلِيل [ɣilabna bifariq qali:l]

mark • **1.** عَلامَة [ʕala:ma] عَلامات، عَلائِم [ʕala:ma:t, ʕala:ʔim] *pl:* Make a mark next to the names of those present. حُطّ عَلامَة يَمّ أَسماء الأَشخاص الحاضرِين [ħuṭṭ ʕala:ma yamm ʔasma:ʔ ʔilʔašxa:ṣ ʔilħa:ḍri:n] • **2.** دَرَجَة [daraǰa] دَرَجات [daraǰa:t] *pl:* He always gets good marks in mathematics. هُوَّ دائِماً ياخُذ دَرَجات زينَة بِالحِساب [huwwa da:ʔiman ya:xuð daraǰa:t zi:na bilħisa:b] • **3.** أَثَر [ʔaθar] آثار [ʔa:θa:r] *pl:* He left his mark in the world. تِرَكلَه أَثَر بِالدِّنيا [tiraklah ʔaθar biddinya]

*** You hit the mark that time.**

• **1.** إِنتَ صِبت الهَدَف ذِيك المَرَّة [ʔinta ṣibt ʔilhadaf ði:č ʔilmarra] / حكايتَك كانَت عالجَرِح [ħča:ytak ča:nat ʕalǰariħ]

*** I don't feel quite up to the mark today.**

• **1.** آنِي مُو عَلَى بَعضِي هَاليَوم [ʔa:ni mu: ʕala baʕḍi halyu:m]

*** Where did you get those black and blue marks?** • **1.** منَين جَتَّك هَالكَدمات والرَّضّات؟ [mnayn ǰattak halkadma:t wirraḍḍa:t?]

to mark • **1.** أَشَّر [ʔaššar] تَأشِير [taʔši:r] *vn:* تأَشَّر [tʔaššar] *p:* I've marked the important parts of the article. أَشَّرِت الأَقسام المُهِمَّة مِن المَقالَة [ʔaššarit ʔalʔaqsa:m ʔilmuhimma min ʔalmaqa:la] I marked the date red on the calendar. أَشَّرِت عاليَوم بِقَلَم أَحمَر بِالتَّقوِيم [ʔaššarit ʕalyu:m bqalam ʔaħmar bittaqwi:m] • **2.** عَلَّم [ʕallam] تَعلِيم [taʕli:m] *vn:* تعَلَّم [tʕallam] *p:* The road is well marked. الطَّرِيق زين معَلَّم [ʔiṭṭari:q zi:n mʕallam] • **3.** حَطّ بالبَال [ħaṭṭ bilba:l] *sv* u. Mark my word. حُطّ حكايتِي بِبالَك [ħuṭṭ ħča:yti bba:lak]

• **4.** حَطّ إِسم عَلَى [ħaṭṭ ʔism ʕala] *sv* u. Have you marked your laundry? حَطَّيت إِسمَك عَلَى هدُومَك اللِّي تِنغِسِل؟ [ħaṭṭi:t ʔismak ʕala hdu:mak ʔilli tinɣisil?]

• **5.** صَلَّح [ṣallaħ] تَصلِيح [taṣli:ħ] *vn:* تصَلَّح [tṣallaħ] *p:* When will you mark our examination papers? شوَقِت تصَلِّح أَوراق الامتِحان مالَتنا؟ [šwakit tṣalliħ ʔawra:q ʔilʔimtiħa:n ma:latna?]

to mark down • **1.** سَجَّل [saǰǰal] تَسجِيل [tasǰi:l] *vn:* تسَجَّل [tsaǰǰal] *p:* قَيِّد [qayyid] تَقيِيد [taqyi:d] *vn:* تقَيَّد [tqayyad] *p:* I've marked down the things I want. سَجَّلت الأَشياء اللِّي أَرِيدها [saǰǰalt ʔilʔašya:ʔ ʔilli ʔari:dha] Mark down my address. قَيِّد عِنوانِي [qayyid ʕinwa:ni]

• **2.** رَخَّص [raxxaṣ] ترِخِّص [trixxiṣ] *vn:* ترَخَّص [traxxaṣ] *p:* They have marked the coats down from 20 to 15 dinars. رَخّصَوا المَعاطِف مِن عِشرِين إِلَى خمُسطَعَش دِينار [raxxṣaw ʔalmaʕa:ṭif min ʕišri:n ʔila xmusṭaʕaš dina:r]

market • **1.** سُوق [su:g] أَسواق [ʔaswa:q] *pl:* Everything is cheaper at the market. كُلشِي أَرخَص بالسُّوق [kullši ʔarxaṣ bissu:g] A new market is being built here. سُوق جِدِيد دَيِنبِنِي هنا [su:g ǰidi:d dayinbini hna] They bought it on the black market. اِشتِرَوها بِالسُّوق السَّوداء [ʔištiru:ha bissu:q ʔissawda]

*** There is no market here for cars.**

• **1.** السَّيّارات ما عَلَيها رَغبَة هنا [ʔissayya:ra:t ma: ʕali:ha raɣba hna]

to be in the market for • **1.** دَوَّر عَلَى [dawwar ʕala] تَدوِير [tadwi:r] *vn:* *sv* u. راد يِشتِري [ra:d yištiri] *sv* i. Are you in the market for a good car? دَترِيد تِشتِري سَيّارَة زينَة؟ [datri:d tištiri sayya:ra zi:na?] She's still in the market (for a husband). بَعَدها دَتدَوُّر عَلَى رِجّال

[baʕadha daddawwur ʕala rijja:l] She's still in the market (for a fiance). بَعَدها دَتِنتِظِر خَطِيب [baʕadha datintiðir xaṭi:b]

to market • 1. نَزَّل [nazzal] تَنزِيل [tanzi:l] *vn:* تنَزَّل [tnazzal] *p:* عِرَض [ʕirað] عَرِض [ʕarið] *vn:* اِنعِرَض [ʔinʕirað] *p:* باع [ba:ʕ] بَيع [bayʕ] *vn:* اِنباع [ʔinba:ʕ] *p:* The farmers market their produce in town. الفَلاحِين ينَزّلُون مَنتُوجاتهُم لِلبيع بِالوِلايَة [ʔilfalla:ħi:n ynazzlu:n mantu:ja:thum lilbi:ʕ bilwila:ya]

to do marketing • 1. تسَوَّق [tsawwag] مِسواق [miswa:g] *vn: sv* a. She does her marketing in the morning. هِيَّ تِتسَوَّق الصُّبُح [hiyya titsawwag ʔiṣṣubuħ]

marriage • 1. زَواج [zawa:j] She has a daughter from her first marriage. عِدها بنَيَّة مِن زَواجها الأَوَّل [ʕidha bnayya min zawa:jha ʔilʔawwal] Before her marriage she worked in an office. قَبُل زَواجها كانَت تِشتُغُل بدائِرَة [gabul zawa:jha ča:nat tištuɣul bda:ʔira]

married • 1. مِتزَوِّج [mitzawwij] مِتزَوِّجَة [mitzawwija] *Feminine*

to marry • 1. زَوَّج [zawwaj] تَزوِيج [tazwi:j] *vn:* تزَوَّج [tzawwaj] *p:* They married their daughter to her first cousin. زَوّجَوا بِنِتهُم لِإبن عَمّها [zawwjaw binithum lʔibin ʕammha] **• 2.** تزَوَّج [dzawwaj] Is she going to marry him? راح تِتزَوَّجَه؟ [ra:ħ tidzawwajah?] Were you married in the courthouse or at home? إنتَ تزَوَّجِت بِالمَحكَمَة لَو بِالبَيت؟ [ʔinta dzawwajit bilmaħkama law bilbayt?] **• 3.** عِقَد [ʕiqad] *sv* i. Who married you? مِنُو عِقَد زَواجكُم؟ [minu ʕiqad zawa:jkum?]

marvelous • 1. بَدِيع [badi:ʕ] عال [ʕa:l] عَجِيب [ʕaji:b]

marsh • 1. مُستَنقَع [mustanqaʕ] مُستَنقَعات [mustanqaʕa:t] *pl:* هُور [hu:r] أهوار [ʔahwa:r] *pl:*

marshal • 1. مارشال [ma:rša:l] مارشالِيَّة [ma:rša:liyya] *pl:* مُشِير [muši:r] مُشِيرِين [muši:ri:n] *pl:*

masculine • 1. مُذَكَّر [muðakkar] "Window" is a masculine noun while "door" is feminine. الشُّبّاك إسِم مُذَكَّر بَينما الباب إسِم مُؤَنَّث [ʔiššubba:č ʔisim muðakkar baynama ʔilba:b ʔisim muʔannaθ]

to mash • 1. هِرَس [hiras] هَرِس [haris] *vn:* اِنهِرَس [ʔinhiras] *p:* I want to mash the potatoes. أرِيد أهرِس البُتَيتَة [ʔari:d ʔahris ʔilputayta]

mass • 1. جَمهُور [jamhu:r] جَماهِير [jama:hi:r] *pl:* He has the masses with him. عِندَه الجَّماهِير وِيّاه [ʕindah ʔijjama:hi:r wiyya:h] **• 2.** كَمِّيَّة [kammiyya] كَمِّيّات [kammiyya:t] *pl:* He's collected a mass of material about it. جِمَع كَمِّيَّة كِبِيرَة عَن المَوضُوع [jimaʕ kammiyya čibi:ra ʕan ʔilmawðu:ʕ]

mass production • 1. إنتاج بِالجُملَة [ʔinta:j bijjumla] We're not geared to mass production. إحنا ما مِتهَيّئِين لِلإنتاج بِالجُملَة [ʔiħna ma: mithayyʔi:n lilʔinta:j bijjumla]

master • 1. سَيِّد [sayyid] سادَة [sa:da] *pl:* No man can serve two masters. ماكُو أحَّد يِقدَر يِخدِم سادَة ثنَين [ma:ku ʔaħħad yigdar yixdim sa:da θnayn] He is master of the situation. هُوَّ سَيِّد المَوقِف [huwwa sayyid ʔilmawqif] He is master of the situation. هُوَّ مسَيطِر عالمَوقِف [huwwa msayṭir ʕalmawqif]

to master • 1. تِقَن [tiqan] إتقان [ʔitqa:n] *vn: sv* i. He mastered English in a relatively short time. اِتِّقَن الإنكلِيزِي بمُدَّة قَصِيرَة نِسبِيّاً [ʔittiqan ʔalʔingli:zi bmudda qaṣi:ra nisbiyyan]

masterpiece • 1. فَرِيدَة [fari:da] فَرائِد [fara:ʔid] *pl:* His poem is one of the masterpieces of Arabic literature. قَصِيدته مِن فَرائِد الأدَب العَرَبِي [qaṣi:dtah min fara:ʔid ʔilʔadab ʔilʕarabi] **• 2.** تُحفَة [tuħfa] تُحَف، تُحَفِيات [tuħaf, tuħafiya:t] *pl:* The Iraqi Museum contains a number of masterpieces of Sumerian art. المَتحَف العِراقِي بِيه عِدَّة تُحَف مِن الفَنّ السَومَرِي [ʔilmatħaf ʔilʕira:qi bi:h ʕiddat tuħaf min ʔilfann ʔissu:mari]

match • 1. عُودَة شِخّاط [ʕu:dat šixxa:ṭ] شِخّاطَة [šixxa:ṭa] شِخّاطات [šixxa:ṭa:t] *pl:* Give me a box of matches, please. رَجاءاً إنطِينِي قُوطِيَّة مال شِخّاط [raja:ʔan ʔinṭi:ni qu:ṭiyya ma:l šixxa:ṭ] **• 2.** مُسابَقَة [musa:baqa] مُسابَقات [musa:baqa:t] *pl:* Who won the match? مِنُو غِلَب المُسابَقَة؟ [minu ɣilab ʔilmusa:baqa?] **• 3.** نِدّ [nidd] He's a match for anybody. هُوَّ نِدّ لأَي واحِد [huwwa nidd lʔayy wa:ħid] I'm no match for him. آنِي مُو نِدّ إلَه [ʔa:ni mu: nidd ʔilah] I'm no match for him. آنِي مُو مِن وَزنَه [ʔa:ni mu: min waznah] I'm no match for him. ما عِندِي قابلِيتَه [ma: ʕindi qa:bli:tah]

to be a match • 1. تراهَم [tra:ham] تَراهُم [tara:hum] *vn: sv* a. توالَم [twa:lam] تَوالُم [tawa:lum] *vn: sv* a. These colors aren't a good match. هَالألوان ما تِتراهَم [halʔalwa:n ma: titra:ham]

to match • 1. طابَق [ṭa:baq] مُطابَقَة [muṭa:baqa] *vn: sv* u. This rug matches the other one in size exactly. هَالزُّولِيَّة تطابِق اللَّخ بِالكُبُر تَماماً [hazzu:liyya tṭa:baq ʔillux bilkubur tama:man] **• 2.** زاحَم [za:ħam] مُزاحَمَة [muza:ħama] *vn: sv* i. No one can match our prices. مَحَّد يِقدَر يزاحِمنا بأسعارنا [maħħad yigdar yza:ħimna bʔasʕa:rna] **• 3.** واشَق [wa:šag] مُواشَقَة [muwa:šaga] *vn:* تواشَق [twa:šag] *p:* You'll never be able to match this color. ما راح تِقدَر تواشِق هَاللَّون أبَداً [ma: ra:ħ tigdar twa:šig hallu:n ʔabadan]

*** I'll match you for the coffee.**
• 1. خَلِّي نسَوِّي طُرَّة كِتبَة عَالقَهوَة [xalli nsawwi ṭurra kitba ʕalgahwa]

M

material • **1.** مادَّة [maːdda] مَوادّ [mawaːdd] *pl:* We use only the best materials. إحنا بَسّ نِستَعمِل أحسَن المَوادّ [ʔiħna bass nistaʕmil ʔaħsan ʔilmawaːdd] • **2.** مَعلُومات [maʕluːmaːt] He's collecting material for a book. هُوَّ دَيِجمَع مَعلُومات لِفَدّ كتاب [huwwa dayiǰmaʕ maʕluːmaːt lfadd ktaːb] • **3.** قماش [qmaːš] قماشات، أقمِشَة [qmaːšaːt, ʔaqmiša] *pl:* Can you wash this material? هَالقُماش يِنغِسِل؟ [halqumaːš yinɣisil?] • **4.** مادِّي [maːddi] She's only interested in material things. هِيَّ بَسّ مِهتَمَّة بالأشياء المادِّيَّة [hiyya bass mihtamma bilʔašyaːʔ ʔilmaːddiyya] • **5.** جَوهَري [ǰawhari] There is no material difference between the two. ماكُو اِختِلاف جَوهَرِي بين لثنَين [maːku ʔixtilaːf ǰawhari bayn liθnayn]

matter • **1.** قَضِيَّة [qaðiyya] قَضايا [qaðaːya] *pl:* مَوضُوع [mawðuːʕ] مَواضِيع [mawaːðiːʕ] *pl:* I'll look into the matter. آني راح أنظُر بِالقَضِيَّة [ʔaːni raːħ ʔanður bilqaðiyya] This is no laughing matter. هاي مُو قَضِيَّة شَقَا [haːy muː qaðiyyat šaqa] What's the matter? شِنُو القَضِيَّة؟ [šinuː ʔilqaðiyya?] • **2.** مَسألَة [masʔala] مَسائِل [masaːʔil] *pl:* It's a matter of life and death. هاي مَسألَة حَياة ومُوت [haːy masʔalat ħayaːt wmuːt] It's not a matter of price. مُو مَسألَة سِعِر [muː masʔalat siʕir]

*** Something's the matter with his lungs.** • **1.** رِئتَه بِيها شِي [riʔtah biːha ši]

*** What's the matter with you?** • **1.** شبِيك؟ [šbiːk?]

*** That doesn't matter.** • **1.** ما يخالِف [maː yxaːlif] / ما يهِمّ [maː yhimm]

as a matter of course • **1.** بطَبِيعَة الحال [bṭabiːʕat ʔilħaːl] We did it as a matter of course. سَوَّينا بطَبِيعَة الحال [sawwiːna bṭabiːʕt ʔilħaːl]

as a matter of fact • **1.** حَقِيقَة [ħaqiːqa] حَقايِق، حَقائِق [ħaqaːyiq, ħaqaːʔiq] *pl:* بالواقِع [bilwaːqiʕ] As a matter of fact I wasn't there. بِالحَقِيقَة آنِي ما كِنِت هناك [bilħaqiːqa ʔaːni maː činit hnaːk]

for that matter • **1.** بِالنِسبَة لهَالمَوضُوع [binnisba lhalmawðuːʕ] For that matter he can stay where he is. بِالنِّسبَة لهالمَوضُوع يِقدَر يِبقَى بمَحَلَّه [binnisba lhalmawðuːʕ yigdar yibqaː bmaħallah]

matter-of-fact • **1.** واقِعِي [waːqiʕi] عَمَلِي [ʕamali] He's a very matter-of-fact person. هُوَّ فَدّ شَخِص كُلِّش واقِعِي [huwwa fadd šaxiṣ kulliš waːqiʕi]

no matter how • **1.** شلَون ما [šluːn maː] No matter how we distribute them, there won't be enough for everyone. شلُون ما نقَسِّمهُم، ما راح يكُون أكُو كافِي لكُلّ واحِد [šluːn maː nqassimhum, maː raːħ ykuːn ʔaku kaːfi likull waːħid]

no matter how much • **1.** شقَدّ ما [šgadd maː] No matter how much you rush me, it won't get done any sooner. شقَدّ ما تخَلِّينِي أستَعجِل، ما راح تِخلَص بِساع [šgadd maː txalliːni ʔastaʕǰil, maː raːħ tixlaṣ bsaːʕ]

no matter what • **1.** لَو شما [law šma] شما [šma] لَو كُلّما [lawkullma] ما يخالِف [mayxaːlif] We're going no matter what you say. لَو شما تقُول إنتَ، إحنا راح نرُوح [law šma dguːl ʔinta, ʔiħna raːħ nruːħ] • **2.** شما [šma] No matter what I do, it doesn't please him. شما أسَوِّي، ما يعجبَه [šmaː ʔasawwi, maː yʕiǰbah]

matters • **1.** أُمُور [ʔumuːr] You're only making matters worse. إنتَ بَسّ دَتعَقِّد الأُمُور [ʔinta bass datʕaqqid ʔilʔumuːr] • **2.** أشياء [ʔašyaːʔ] You take matters too seriously. إنتَ تاخُذ الأشياء بجِدّ أكثَر مِن اللّازِم [ʔinta taːxuð ʔilʔašyaːʔ bǰidd ʔakθar min ʔillaːzim]

matting • **1.** حَصِير [ħaṣiːr] We're going to cover the floor with matting for the summer. راح نفرُش القاع بِحِصران عَالصَّيف [raːħ nufruš ʔilgaːʕ biħiṣraːn ʕaṣṣayf] • **2.** بارية [baːrya] بوارِي [bwaːri] *pl:* We need some matting to make a partition here. يِرّاد إلنا كَم بارِيَّة حَتَّى نسَوِّي حاجِز هنا [yirraːd ʔilna čam baːriyya ħatta nsawwi ħaːǰiz hna]

mattress • **1.** دَوشَك [duːšag] دواشِك [dwaːšig] *pl:*

mature • **1.** ناضِج [naːðiǰ] The boy is very mature for his age. الوَلَد كُلِّش ناضِج بِالنِّسبَة لعُمرَه [ʔilwalad kulliš naːðiǰ binnisba lʕumrah]

maximum • **1.** الحَدّ الأعلَى ل [ʔilħadd ʔilʔaʕla l-] أقصَى [ʔaqṣa] The maximum salary for this position is eighty dinars a month. الحَدّ الأعلَى راتِب هَالوَظِيفَة ثمانِين دِينار بِالشَّهَر [ʔilħadd ʔilʔaʕla raːtib halwaðiːfa θmaːniːn dinaːr biššahar] The maximum penalty for this crime is ten years in prison. أقصى عُقُوبَة لهَالجَرِيمَة هِيَّ عَشِر سنِين حَبِس [ʔaqṣa ʕuquːba lhalǰariːma hiyya ʕašir sniːn ħabis]

*** I'm willing to pay twenty dinars, but that's the maximum.** • **1.** آنِي مِستِعِدّ أدفَع عِشرِين دِينار، لَكِن هَذا أزيَد شِي [ʔaːni mistiʕidd ʔadfaʕ ʕišriːn dinaːr, laːkin haːða ʔazyad ši]

May • **1.** مايِس [maːyis] أيّار [ʔayyaːr]

may • **1.** مُمكِن [mumkin] May I keep this pencil? مُمكِن أحتُفُظ بهالقَلَم؟ [mumkin ʔaħtufuð bhaːlqalam?] May I keep this pencil? تِسمَحلِي أحتُفُظ بهالقَلَم [tismaħli ʔaħtufuð bhaːlqalam] May I have the next game? مُمكِن ألعَب اللِّعبَة الجّايَّة؟ [mumkin ʔalʕab ʔilliʕba ʔiǰǰaːyya?] May I meet with you at five o'clock? مُمكِن أجِي أواجهَك ساعَة خَمسَة؟ [mumkin ʔaǰi ʔawaːǰhak saːʕa xamsa?] May I offer you a cup of coffee? أقدَر أقَدِّملَك فَدّ فِنجان قَهوَة؟ [ʔagdar ʔaqaddimlak fadd finǰaːn gahwa?] • **2.** مُمكِن [mumkin] يِمكِن [yimkin] يجُوز [yǰuːz] That may be so. يِمكِن هِيكِي [yimkin hiːči] I may be able to come. آنِي يِمكِن أقدَر أجِي [ʔaːni yimkin ʔagdar ʔaǰi] • **3.** رُبَّما [rubbama] مُحتَمَل [muħtamal] يِمكِن [yimkin] مُمكِن [mumkin] I may have said it. رُبَّما آنِي قِلتها [rubbamaː ʔaːni gilitha]

*** Be that as it may ...** • **1.** وَلَو هَذا هِيكِي [wa law haːða hiːčiy]

M

maybe • **1.** يمكِن [yimkin] مُمكِن [mumkin] مُحتَمَل [muħtamal] رُبَّما [rubbama] Maybe he's not at home. يمكِن مُو بِالبَيت [yimkin muː bilbayt]

meadow • **1.** مَرعَى [marʕa] مَراعِي [maraːʕi] *pl:* I want to rent some meadow land for my horse. أَرِيد أَئجِّر قِطعَة قِصِيل لحصانِي [ʔariːd ʔaʔaǰǰir qitʕat giṣiːl lħṣaːni]

meager • **1.** قَلِيل [qaliːl] ضَئِيل [ðaʔiːl] طَفِيف [ṭafiːf] The results were meager. النَّتائِج كانَت قَلِيلَة [ʔinnataːʔiǰ čaːnat qaliːla]

meal • **1.** أَكلَة [ʔakla] أَكلات [ʔaklaːt] *pl:* وَجبَة [waǰba] وَجبات [waǰbaːt] *pl:* Three meals a day aren't enough for him. ما تكَفِّي ثلاث أَكلات بِاليُوم [maː tkaffiːhtlaːθ ʔaklaːt bilyuːm] I haven't eaten a decent meal in weeks. صارلِي كَم إسبُوع ما ماكِل وَجبَة بِيها خير [ṣaːrli čam ʔisbuːʕ maː maːkil waǰba biːha xiːr]

mean • **1.** خِسَّة [xissa] It was mean of him to treat you like that. كانَت خِسَّة مِنَّه يعاملَك هَالشِّكِل [čaːnat xissa minnah yʕaːmlak haššikil] • **2.** خَسِيس [xasiːs] لَئِيم [laʔiːm] لَئِيمِين، لُؤَماء [laʔiːmiːn, luʔamaːʔ] *pl:* That's a mean trick. هَذِيك فَدّ حِيلَة خَسِيسَة [haðiːč fadd ħiːla xasiːsa] • **3.** وَضِيع [waðiːʕ] وَضِيعِين، وُضعاء [waðiːʕiːn, wuðaʕaːʔ] *pl:* He says very mean things to me. يقُلِّي أَشياء كُلِّش وَضِيعَة [ygulli ʔašyaːʔ kulliš waðiːʕa] • **4.** مُوذِي [muːði] مُوذِيَّة [muːðiyya] *pl:* وَقِيح [wakiːħ] وُقَّح [wukkaħ] *pl:* Those mean boys in the street are teasing me. هالوِلد المُوذِيَّة بِالدَّرُب دَيضَوّجُونِي [halwulid ʔilmuːðiyya biddarub dayðawwǰuːni] • **5.** شَرِس [šaris] Our neighbors have a mean dog. جِيرانّا عِدهُم كَلِب شَرِس [ǰiːraːnna ʕidhum čalib šaris]

* **He plays mean.** • **1.** يبِيع نَذالَة [ybiːʕ naðaːla]

to mean • **1.** عِنَى [ʕinaː] مَعنَى [maʕna] *vn:* اِنعِنَى [ʔinʕinaː] *p:* قِصَد [qiṣad] قَصِد [qaṣid] *vn:* اِنقِصد [ʔinqiṣd] *p:* نَوَى [nawaː] نِيَّة [niyya] *vn:* اِنّوَى [ʔinnuwaː] *p:* What do you mean by that? شتِعنِي بِهاي؟ [štiʕni bhaːy?] You mean to say you saw everything? يَعنِي إنتَ شِفِت كُلّشِي؟ [yaʕni ʔinta šifit kullši?] I didn't mean any harm. آنِي ما قِصَدِت أَيّ أَذِيَّة [ʔaːni maː qṣadit ʔayy ʔaðiyya] What do you mean to do? شتِنوِي تسَوِّي؟ [štinwi tsawwi?] • **2.** هَمّ [hamm] هُمُوم [humuːm] *pl:* *sv* i. It means a lot to me to see him tonight. يهِمّنِي كُلِّش أَشُوفَه هاللَّيلَة [yhimmni kulliš ʔašuːfah hallayla] • **3.** كان قَصِد [čaːn qaṣid-] I meant to call, but I forgot. كان قَصدِي أَخابُر لٰكِن نِسِيت [čaːn qaṣdi ʔaxaːbur laːkin nisiːt]

* **His friendship means a lot to me.**
• **1.** صَداقتَه عَزِيزَة عَلَيّا [ṣadaːqtah ʕaziːza ʕalayya]

* **That remark was meant for you.**
• **1.** هَالمُلاحَظات إِنتَ اِنعِنَيت بِيهَا [halmulaːħaðaːt ʔinta ʔinʕiniːt biːha]

* **Is the book meant for me?**
• **1.** المَقصُود بهَالكِتاب أَن آخذَه آنِي؟ [lmaqṣuːd bhalikta:b ʔan ʔaːxðah ʔaːni?] / يَعنِي هَذا الكِتاب إِلِي؟ [yaʕni haːða ʔilkitaːb ʔili?]

meaning • **1.** مَعنَى [maʕna] مَعانِي [maʕaːni] *pl:* This word has several meanings. هَالكِلمَة إِلها عِدَّة مَعانِي [halkilma ʔilha ʕiddat maʕaːni] What's the meaning of this? شِنُو مَعنى هاي؟ [šinuː maʕna haːy?]

means • **1.** وَسِيلَة [wasiːla] وَسائِل [wasaːʔil] *pl:* It was just a means to an end. ما كانَت غير وَسِيلَة لفَدّ غايَة [maː čaːnat ɣiːr wasiːla lfadd ɣaːya] He doesn't have the means to do it. ما عِندَه الوَسائِل حَتَّى يسَوِّيها [maː ʕindah ʔilwasaːʔil ħatta ysawwiːha] • **2.** قابلِيَّة [qaːbliyya] قابلِيّات [qaːbliyyaːt] *pl:* He lives beyond his means. يُصرُف أَكثَر مِن قابليتَه [yuṣruf ʔakθar min qaːbliːtah]

* **She married a man of means.**
• **1.** تزَوّجَت رِجّال الله مفَضِّل عَلَيه [tzawwǰat riǰǰaːl ʔallah mfaððil ʕaliːh]

by all means • **1.** مِن كُلّ لابُدّ [min kull laː budd] By all means take the job. مِن كُلّ لابُدّ، اِقبَل هَالوَظِيفَة [min kull laːbudd, ʔiqbal halwaðiːfa] • **2.** مَعلُوم [maʕluːm] Could I have the book now? By all means! تِسمَحلِي بِالكتاب هَسَّة؟ مَعلُوم [tismaħli bilktaːb hassa? maʕluːm]

by means of • **1.** بواسطَة [bwaːsṭa] You can regulate it by means of a screw. تِقدَر تنَظُّمها بواسطَة بُرغِي [tigdar tnaððimha bwaːsṭat burɣi]

by no means • **1.** أَبَداً مُو [ʔabadan muː] مُطلَقاً مُو [muṭlaqan muː] He's by no means stupid. هُوَّ أَبَداً مُو غَبِي [huwwa ʔabadan muː ɣabi]

meanwhile • **1.** بهَالأَثناء [bhalʔaθnaːʔ] خِلال هَالفَترَة [xilaːl halfatra]

measles • **1.** حَصبَة [ħaṣba, ħuṣba]

measly • **1.** مشَحَّط [mšaħħaṭ] He can't get along on his measly salary. ما يِقدَر يدَبُّر أَمرَه بهَالمَعاش المشَحَّط [maː yigdar ydabbur ʔamrah bhalmaʕaːš ʔilmšaħħaṭ]

measure • **1.** مِقياس [miqyaːs] مَقايِيس [maqaːyiːs] *pl:* A table of weights and measures. جَدوَل بِالأَوزان والمَقايِيس [ǰadwal bilʔawzaːn wilmaqaːyiːs] • **2.** قِياس [qiyaːs] قِياسات [qiyaːsaːt] *pl:* What is his waist measure? شِنُو قِياس خِصرَه؟ [šinu qiyaːs xiṣrah?] • **3.** كَيلَة [čiːla] كَيلات [čiːlaːt] *pl:* How much is popcorn by the measure? بيش كَيلَة الشّامِيَّة؟ [biyš čiːlat ʔiššaːmiyya?] • **4.** إجراء [ʔiǰraːʔ] إجراءات [ʔiǰraːʔat] *pl:* We'll have to take strong measures. لازِم نِتِّخِذ إجراءات حازمَة [laːzim nittixið ʔiǰraːʔaːt ħaːzima] • **5.** وَزِن، بِالوَزِن [wazin, bilwazin] أَوزان، بِالأَوزان [ʔawzaːn, bilʔawzaːn] *pl:* This word is on the measure "faʕlaan". هَالكَلِمَة عَلَى وَزِن ‹فَعلان› [halkalima ʕala wazin "faʕlaːn"]

to measure • **1.** قاس [qa:s] قِياس [qiya:s] *vn:* اِنقاس [ʔinqa:s] *p:* Measure the height of the window exactly. قِيس اِرتِفاع الشِّبّاك بِالضَبُط [qi:s ʔirtifa:ʕ ʔiššibba:č biððabuṭ] We'll have to measure the room before we buy the rug. لازِم نقِيس الغُرفَة قَبُل ما نِشتِري السِّجّادَة [la:zim nqi:s ʔilɣurfa gabul ma: ništiri ʔissijja:da] • **2.** كال [ča:l] كَيل [čayl] *vn:* اِنكال [ʔinča:l] *p:* He measured out two measures of watermelon seeds and put them in a bag. كال كَيلتَين حَبّ رَقِّي وَحَطّهُم بكِيس [ča:l či:ltayn ħabb raggi wħaṭṭahum bči:s]

measurement • **1.** قِياس [qiya:s] قِياسات [qiya:sa:t] *pl:* Are these measurements correct? هَالقِياسات صَحِيحَة؟ [halqiya:sa:t ṣaħi:ħa?] Did the tailor take your measuremens? الخَيّاط أَخَذ قِياساتَك؟ [ʔilxayya:ṭ ʔaxað qiya:sa:tak?]

meat • **1.** لَحَم [laħam] لُحُوم [luħu:m.] *pl:* Do you have any meat today? عِندَك لَحَم هَاليُوم؟ [ʕindak laħam halyu:m?]

mechanic • **1.** مِيكانِيكِي [mikani:ki] مِيكانِيكِيِّين [mi:ka:ni:kiyyi:n] *pl:* فِيتَرجِي [fi:tarči] فِيتَرجِيَّة [fi:tarčiyya] *pl:*

mechanical • **1.** مِيكانِيكِي [mikani:ki]

medal • **1.** وِسام [wisa:m] أَوسِمَة [ʔawsima] *pl:* مَدالِيَة [mada:liyya] مَدالِيات [madaliyya:t] *pl:*

to meddle • **1.** تدَخَّل [ddaxxal] تَدَخُّل [tadaxxul] *vn: sv* a. تداخَل [dda:xal] تَداخُل [tada:xul] *vn: sv* a. He likes to meddle in other people's business. هُوَّ يعجبَه يِتدَخَّل بِشُؤُون النّاس [huwwa yʕijbah yiddaxxal bišuʔu:n ʔinna:s]

medical • **1.** طِبِّي [ṭibbi] I'm under medical treatment. آنِي تَحت العِلاج الطِّبِّي [ʔa:ni taħt ʔilʕila:j ʔiṭṭibbi] I'm under medical treatment. آنِي تَحت التَّداوِي [ʔa:ni taħt ʔittada:wi] Look it up in the medical dictionary. طَلِّعها بالقامُوس الطِّبِّي [ṭalliʕha bilqa:mu:s ʔiṭṭibbi]

medicine • **1.** دُوا [duwa] دُويات، أَدوِيَة [duwya:t, ʔadwiya] *pl:* This medicine tastes bitter. هَالدُّوا طَعمَه مُرّ [hadduwa ṭaʕmah murr] Have you taken your medicine yet? أَخَذِت الدُّوا مالَك لَو بَعَد [ʔaxaðit ʔidduwa ma:lak law baʕad] • **2.** طِبّ [ṭibb] My daughter is studying medicine. بِنتِي دَتِدرُس طِبّ [binti datidrus ṭibb]

Mediterranean sea • **1.** البَحر الأَبيَض المُتَوَسِّط [ʔilbaħr ʔilʔabyað ʔilmutawassiṭ] البَحر المُتَوَسِّط [ʔilbaħr ʔilmutawassiṭ]

medium • **1.** مِتوَسِّط [mitwassiṭ] مِعتَدِل [miʕtadil] He's of medium height. طُولَه مِتوَسِّط [ṭu:lah mitwassiṭ] • **2.** نُصّ [nuṣṣ] نصاص [nṣa:ṣ] *pl:* I like my steak medium-broiled. أَرِيد السِتَيك مالِي مَشوِي عَالنُّصّ [ʔari:d ʔisstayk ma:li mašwi ʕannuṣṣ]

*** It's hard to find a happy medium.**
• **1.** مِن الصَعُب تِلقِي حَلّ وَسَط [min ʔiṣṣaʕub tilgi ħall wasaṭ]

medium-sized • **1.** مِتوَسِّط [mitwassiṭ] It's a medium-sized task. هِيَّ فَدّ شَغلَة مِتوَسّطَة [hiyya fadd šaɣla mitwaṣṣṭa]

to meet • **1.** اِجتِمَع [ʔijtimaʕ] اِجتِماع [ʔijtima:ʕ] *vn: sv* i. The committee is going to meet at Ahmad's house. اللَّجنَة راح تِجتِمِع بِبَيت أَحمَد [ʔillujna ra:ħ tijtimiʕ bibayt ʔaħmad] • **2.** حَقَّق [ħaqqaq] تَحقِيق [taħqi:q] *vn:* تحَقَّق [tħaqqaq] *p:* My demands are easily met. تَحقِيق طَلَباتِي مُو صَعُب [taħqi:q ṭalaba:ti mu: ṣaʕub] • **3.** تلاقَى [tla:ga:] تَلاقِي [tala:qi] *vn: sv* i. اِلتِقَى [ʔiltiqa:] اِلتِقاء [ʔiltiqa:ʔ] *vn: sv* i. Let's meet at the coffee shop at six o'clock. خَلِّي نِتلاقَى بِالقَهوَة ساعَة سِتَّة [xalli nitla:qa: bilqahwa sa:ʕa sitta] • **4.** واجَه [wa:jah] مُواجَهَة [muwa:jaha] *vn:* تواجَه [twa:jah] *p:* صادَف [ṣa:daf] مُصادَفَة [muṣa:dafa] *vn:* تصادَف [tṣa:daf] *p:* لاقَى [la:ga:] مُلاقاة [mula:ga: (t)] *vn:* تلاقَى [tla:ga:] *p:* Did you meet him on the street? واجَهتَه بِالشّارِع؟ [wa:jahtah bišša:riʕ?] • **5.** قابَل [qa:bal, ga:bal] مُقابَلَة [muqa:bala] *vn:* تقابَل [tqa:bal] *p:* تلَقَّى [tlaqqa:] تَلَقِّي [talaqqi] *vn: sv* a. اِستَقبَل [ʔistaqbal] اِستِقبال [ʔistiqba:l] *vn: sv* i. He met us with a smile. قابَلنا بِإبتِسامَة [qa:balna biʔibtisa:ma] Will you please meet them at the train station? بالله ما ترُوح تِتلَقّاهُم بمَحَطَّة القِطار؟ [ballah ma: tru:ħ titlagga:hum bmaħaṭṭat ʔilqiṭa:r?] • **6.** تعَرَّف ب [tʕarraf b-] تَعَرُّف [taʕarruf] *vn: sv* a. I met him at a party last night. تعَرَّفِت بِيه بحَفلَة البارحَة باللَّيل [tʕarrafit bi:h biħaflat ʔilba:rħa billayl] I'm interested in meeting some artists. يعجبنِي أَتعَرَّف عَلَى بَعض الفَنّانِين [yiʕjibni ʔatʕarraf ʕala baʕð ʔilfanna:ni:n] • **7.** توَصَّل [twaṣṣal] *sv* a. The two ends of the wire don't meet. نِهايتَين التِّيل ما يِتوَصَّلُون [niha:ytayn ʔitti:l ma: yitwaṣṣalu:n] • **8.** اِتَّفَق [ʔittifaq] اِتِّفاق [ʔittifa:q] *vn: sv* i. We hope these pipes will meet with your specifications. نِتأَمَّل هَالبُورِيّات تِتَّفِق ويّا مُواصَفاتكُم [nitʔammal halbu:riyya:t tittifiq wiyya muwa:ṣafa:tkum] • **9.** وَفَّى ب [waffa:, wuffa: b-] تَوفِيَة [tawfiya] *vn: sv* i. They couldn't meet their obligations. ما قِدرَوا يوَفُّون بِالتِزاماتهُم [ma: gidraw ywaffu:n biʔiltiza:ma:thum] • **10.** سَدّ [sadd] سُدُود [sudu:d] *pl:* سَدّ [sadd] *vn: sv* i. I can barely meet my expenses. بالكاد أَقدَر أَسِدّ مَصارِيفِي [bilka:d ʔagdar ʔasidd maṣa:ri:fi]

*** I'll be glad to meet you halfway.**
• **1.** ما عِندِي مانِع نسَوِي تَسوِيَة بَيناتنا [ma: ʕindi ma:niʕ nsawi taswiya bayna:tna]

*** Pleased to meet you.** • **1.** أَتشَرَّف [ʔatšarraf] / تشَرَّفنا [tšarrafna]

to meet with • **1.** حِصَل عَلَى [ħiṣal ʕala] حُصُول [ħuṣu:l] *vn: sv* a. I think this will meet with your approval. أَعتِقِد هَذا الشِّي راح يِحصَل عَلَى رِضائَك [ʔaʕtiqid ha:ða ʔišši ra:ħ yiħṣal ʕala riða:ʔak]

meeting • **1.** اِجتِماع [ʔijtima:ʕ] اِجتِماعات [ʔijtima:ʕa:t] *pl:* جَلسَة [jalsa] جَلسات [jalsa:t] *pl:* There were five hundred people at the meeting. كان أَكُو خَمِس مِيَّة شَخِص بالاِجتِماع [ča:n ʔaku xamis miyyat šaxiṣ bilʔijtima:ʕ] The committee meeting lasted two hours. جَلسَة اللَّجنَة اِستَمَرَّت ساعتين [jalsat ʔillajna ʔistamarrat sa:ʕtayn] • **2.** مُقابَلَة [muqa:bala] مُقابَلات [muqa:bala:t] *pl:* I arranged for a meeting of the two رَتَّبِت فَدّ مُقابَلَة بَينَاتهُم [rattabit fadd muqa:bala bayna:thum]

melody • **1.** نَغمَة [naɣma] نَغمات [naɣma:t] *pl:* لَحِن [laħin] أَلحان [ʔalħa:n] *pl:*

to melt • **1.** ذاب [ða:b] ذَوَبان [ðawaba:n] *vn: sv* u. ماع [ma:ʕ] مَوَعان [mawaʕa:n] *vn: sv* u. The ice is all melted. الثَّلِج كُلَّه ذاب [ʔiθθalij kullah ða:b] • **2.** مَوَّع [mawwaʕ] تَمويع [tamwi:ʕ] *vn:* تمَوَّع [tmawwaʕ] *p:* Melt the butter. مَوِّع الزِّبِد [mawwiʕ ʔizzibid]

member • **1.** عُضُو [ʕuðw] أَعضاء [ʔaʕða:ʔ] *pl:* Are you a member of this club? إِنتَ عُضُو بِهالنّادِي؟ [ʔinta ʕuðw bihanna:di?] We'll have to amputate the injured member. لازِم نِقطَع العُضُو المُصاب [la:zim nigtaʕ ʔilʕuðw ʔilmuṣa:b]

membership • **1.** عُضوِيَّة [ʕuðwiyya] عُضوِيّات [ʕuðwiyya:t] *pl:* Our membership is down to less than one hundred. العُضوِيَّة عِدنا نِزلَت إِلَى أَقَلّ مِن مِيَّة [ʔilʕuðwiyya ʕidna nizlat ʔila ʔaqall min miyya]

memory • **1.** ذاكِرَة [ða:kira] My memory is not what it used to be. ذاكِرتي مُو مِثلما كانَت [ða:kirti mu: miθilma: ča:nat] • **2.** ذِكرَى [ðikra] ذِكرَيات [ðikraya:t] *pl:* I have pleasant memories of this town. عِندي ذِكرَيات حِلوَة بهالمَدِينَة [ʕindi ðikraya:t ħilwa bhalmadi:na]

menace • **1.** خَطَر [xaṭar] أَخطار [ʔaxṭa:r] *pl:* He's a menace to society. هُوَّ خَطَر عَالمُجتَمَع [huwwa xaṭar ʕalmujtamaʕ] The menace of atomic war occupies everyone's mind. خَطَر الحَرب الذَّرِّيَّة شاغِل بال كُلّ النّاس [xaṭar ʔilħarb ʔiððarriyya ša:ɣil ba:l kull ʔinna:s]

to mend • **1.** راف [ra:f] رواف [rwa:f] *vn:* انراف [ʔinra:f] *p:* خَيَّط [xayyaṭ] خياط، تخيِّط [xya:ṭ, txiyyiṭ] *vn:* تخَيَّط [txayyaṭ] *p:* When will you mend my jacket? يَمتَى راح ترُوف سِترتي؟ [yamta ra:ħ tru:f sitirti?] • **2.** لِحَم [liħam] لَحِم [laħim] *vn:* اِنلِحَم [ʔinliħam] *p:* Have the tinsmith mend the crack in this pan. خَلِّي التَّنَكچِي يِلحَم الفَطِر بِالجِّدِر [xalli ʔittanakči yilħam ʔilfaṭir bjjidir] the broken bone will take some time to mend. العَظُم المَكسُور يريدلَه مُدَّة حَتَّى يِلحَم [ʔilʕaðum ʔilmaksu:r yri:dlah mudda ħatta yilħam] • **3.** حَسَّن [ħassan] تَحسِين [taħsi:n] *vn:* تحَسَّن [tħassan] *p:* You'll have to mend your ways. لازِم تحَسِّن أَخلاقَك [la:zim tħassin ʔaxla:qak] You'll have to mend your ways. لازِم تِعقَل [la:zim tiʕqal]

to mention • **1.** ذِكَر [ðikar] ذِكِر [ðikir] *vn:* اِنذِكَر [ʔinðikar] *p:* He didn't mention the price. ما ذِكَر السِّعِر [ma: ðikar ʔissiʕir] he didn't mention the price. ما جاب طارِي السِّعِر [ma: ja:b ṭa:ri ʔissiʕir] I heard his name mentioned. سمَعِت إسمَه انذِكَر [smaʕit ʔismah ʔinðikar] I would also like to mention. . . هَمّ أَحِبّ أَذكُر أَن [hamm ʔaħibb ʔaðkur ʔan...]

*** Thank you very much. Don't mention it.**
• **1.** أَشكُرَك جِدّاً مَمنُون [ʔaškurak jiddan mamnu:n] / العَفو [ʔilʕafw]
*** That's not worth mentioning.** • **1.** ما تِستِحِقّ الذِكِر [ma: tistiħiqq ʔiððikir] / هَذا مُو شِي [ha:ða mu: ši]

menu • **1.** قائِمَة أَكِل [qa:ʔimat ʔakil] قَوائِم أَكِل [qawa:ʔim ʔakil] *pl:*

merchandise • **1.** بِضاعَة [biða:ʕa] بَضايِع [baða:yiʕ] *pl:* سِلعَة [silʕa] سِلَع [silaʕ] *pl:* The merchandise arrived in good order. البِضاعَة وُصلَت بحالَة زينَة [ʔilbiða:ʕa wuṣlat bħa:la zi:na]

merchant • **1.** تاجِر [ta:jir] تُجّار [tujja:r] *pl:*

merchant marine • **1.** إِسطَول تِجارِي [ʔisṭu:l tija:ri]

mercury • **1.** زَيبَق، سليمَانِي [zaybag (quicksilver) slima:ni (mercuric chloride)] • **2.** عُطارِد [ʕuṭa:rid (planet)]

mercy • **1.** رَحمَة [raħma] رَأفَة [raʔfa] رَأفات [raʔfa:t] *pl:* He pleaded for mercy. طِلَب الرَّحمَة [ṭilab ʔirraħma] He has no mercy. ما عِندَه رَحمَة [ma: ʕindah raħma]

mere • **1.** بَسّ [bass] مُجَرَّد [mujarrad] The mere thought of it disturbs me. مُجَرَّد التَّفكِير بِيها يزعِجنِي [mujarrad ʔittafki:r bi:ha yizʕijni] She's a mere child; too young to get married. هِيَّ مُجَرَّد طِفلَة، مُو بِسِنّ الزَّواج [hiyya mujarrad ṭifla, mu: bisinn ʔizzawa:j]

merely • **1.** فَقَط [faqaṭ] لا غير [la: ɣayr] I was merely joking. كان قَصدِي النُّكتَة، لا غير [ča:n qaṣdi ʔinnukta, la: ɣi:r]

merit • **1.** قِيمَة [qi:ma] قِيَم [qiyam] *pl:* There is little of merit in his book. أَكُو قِيمَة قَلِيلَة لِكتابَه [ʔaku qi:ma qali:la likita:bah]
to merit • **1.** اِستاهَل [ʔista:hal] *sv* i. اِستَحَقّ [ʔistaħaqq] اِستِحقاق [ʔistiħqa:q] *vn: sv* i. اِستَوجَب [ʔistawjab] *sv* i. I think he merits a raise. أَعتِقِد يِستاهِل تَرفِيع [ʔaʕtiqid yista:hil tarfi:ʕ]

merry • **1.** مَرِح [mariħ]

mess • **1.** خَربَطَة [xarbaṭa] خَرابِيط، خَربَطات [xara:bi:ṭ, xarbaṭa:t] *pl:* هَوسَة [hawsa] هَوسات [hawsa:t] *pl:*

 i, interjection; p, passive; pl, plural; sv, stem vowel; vn, verbal noun

Did you see the mess the painters left? شِفت الخَربَطَة اللّي خَلّوها الصَّبّاغِين وَراهُم [šift ʔilxarbaṭa ʔilli xalluːha ʔiṣṣabbaːɣiːn waraːhum] I can't find anything in this mess. ما أقدَر ألقِي أيّ شِي بهالهَوسَة [maː ʔagdar ʔalgi ʔayy ši bihalhawsa] • **2.** ورطَة [warṭa, wurṭa] ورطات [warṭaːt, wurṭaːt] *pl:* You certainly got yourself into a nice mess! لَكِن إنتَ صُدُق مَوَقِّع نَفسَك بفَدّ وُرطَة ملَبلبَة [laːkin ʔinta ṣudug mwaggiʕ nafsak bfadd wurṭa mlablba] • **3.** قاعَة طَعام [qaːʕat ṭaʕaːm] قاعات طَعام [qaːʕaːt ṭaʕaːm] *pl:* I'm invited to dinner at the officer's mess. آني مَدعُو لِلأكِل بقاعَة طَعام الضُّبّاط [ʔaːni madʕuː lilʔakil bqaːʕat ṭaʕaːm ʔiððubbaːṭ]

*** The house is an awful mess.** • **1.** البَيت واقُف طُول [ʔilbayt waːguf ṭuːl] / البَيت كُلِّش مخَربَط [ʔilbayt kulliš mxarbaṭ]

to mess • **1.** اِشتِرَك بالأكِل [ʔištirak bilʔakil] اِشتِراك بالأكِل [ʔištiraːk bilʔakil] *vn: sv* i. You will mess with the officers during your tour of duty here. راح أشترِك ويّا الضُّبّاط بالأكِل مُدَّة اِلتِحاقَك هنا [raːħ ʔaštirik wiyya ʔiððubbaːṭ bilʔakil muddat ʔiltiħaːqak hna] • **2.** لِعَب [liʕab] لِعِب [liʕib] *vn:* اِنلِعَب [ʔinliʕab] *p:* Don't mess with the radio! لا تِلعَب بالرّاديُو [laː tilʕab birraːdyu]

to mess up • **1.** وَسَّخ [wassax] توسِّخ [twissix] *vn:* توَسَّخ [twassax] *p:* Don't mess up the floor with your wet feet. لا توَسِّخ القاع برِجلَك المبَلّلَة [laː twassix ʔilgaːʕ brijlak ʔilmballila] • **2.** خَربَط [xarbaṭ] خَربَطَة [xarbaṭa] *vn:* تخَربَط [txarbaṭ] *p:* Who messed up the papers on my desk? مِنُو خَربَط الأوراق عَلَى مَيزي؟ [minu xarbaṭ ʔilʔawraːq ʕala mayzi?]

message • **1.** خَبَر [xabar] أخبار [ʔaxbaːr] *pl:* رِسالَة [risaːla] رَسائِل [rasaːʔil] *pl:* مَكتُوب [maktuːb] مَكاتِيب [makaːtiːb] *pl:* Did anyone leave a message for me? أحَّد تِرَكلِي خَبَر؟ [ʔaħħad tirakli xabar?] Could you take a message for him? أقدَر أحُطلَه خَبَر عِندَك؟ [ʔagdar ʔaħuṭṭlah xabar ʕindak?] Did you give him the message? بَلّغتَه الرِّسالَة؟ [ballaɣtah ʔirrisaːla?]

messenger • **1.** مُوَزِّع بَرق [muwazziʕ barq] مُوَزّعِين بَرق [muwazziʕiːn barq] *pl:* The telegraph office employs ten messengers. دائِرَة البَرق تِستَخدِم عَشِر مُوَزّعِين [daːʔirat ʔilbarq tistaxdim ʕašir muwazziʕiːn] • **2.** فَرّاش [farraːš] The messenger from the Director's office wants to speak to you. فَرّاش المُدِير يرِيد يكَلّمَك [farraːš ʔilmudiːr yriːd ykallmak] • **3.** طارِش [ṭaːriš] طوارِش، طراريش [ṭwaːriš, ṭraːriːš] *pl:* A messenger came from the village to invite us to the wedding. جانا طارِش مِن القَريَة حَتّى يعِزمنا عالعِرس [ǰaːna ṭaːriš min ʔilqarya ħatta yiʕzimna ʕalʕiris]

metal • **1.** مَعدَن [maʕdan] مَعادِن [maʕaːdin] *pl:*

method • **1.** طَرِيقَة [ṭariːqa] طُرُق [ṭuruq] *pl:* إسلُوب [ʔisluːb] أساليِب [ʔasaːliːb] *pl:* He's discovered a new method. اِكتِشَف طَرِيقَة جِدِيدَة [ʔiktišaf ṭariːqa ǰidiːda]

middle • **1.** نُصّ [nuṣṣ] نصاص [nṣaːṣ] *pl:* I'm leaving the middle of next week. آني رايِح بنُصّ الإسبُوع الجّاي [ʔaːni raːyiħ bnuṣṣ ʔilʔisbuːʕ ʔiǰǰaːy] • **2.** مِتوَسِّط [mitwassiṭ] He's a man of middle height. هُوَّ فَدّ رِجّال مِتوَسِّط الطُّول [huwwa fadd riǰǰaːl mitwassiṭ ʔiṭṭuːl] • **3.** وَسَط [waṣaṭ] He was standing in the middle of the room. كان واقُف بوَسَط الغُرفَة [čaːn waːquf biwasaṭ ʔilɣurfa] The man fell in the middle of the street. الرِّجّال وُقَع بنُصّ الشّارِع [ʔirriǰǰal wugaʕ bnuṣṣ ʔiššaːriʕ] • **4.** وَسطانِي [wasṭaːni] Open the middle window. فُكّ الشِّبّاك الوَسطانِي [fukk ʔiššibbaːč ʔilwasṭaːni] • **5.** أثناء [ʔaθnaːʔ] He got up in the middle of the session and walked out. قام بأثناء الجَّلسَة وَطِلَع بَرَّة [gaːm bʔaθnaːʔ ʔiǰǰalsa wṭilaʕ barra]

*** I'm in the middle of packing.** • **1.** آني مَخبُوص دَألِمّ غَراضِي [ʔaːni maxbuːṣ daʔalimm ɣaraːði]

*** He's in his middle forties.** • **1.** عُمرَه بَين الأربَعِين والخَمسِين [ʕumrah bayn ʔilʔarbaʕiːn wilxamsiːn]

middle-aged • **1.** مُتوَسِّط بالعُمُر [mutwassiṭ bilʕumur] She's a middle aged woman. هِيَّ فَدّ وِحدَة مُتوَسطَة بالعُمُر [hiyya fadd wiħda mutwassiṭa bilʕumur]

Middle Ages • **1.** القُرُون الوُسطَى [ʔilquruːn ʔilwusṭa]

Middle East • **1.** الشَرق الأوسَط [ʔiššarħ ʔilʔawṣaṭ]

midnight • **1.** نُصّ اللَيل [nuṣṣ ʔillayl] It was past midnight when we fell asleep. كانَت بَعَد نُصّ اللَّيل لَمَّن غفَينا [čaːnat baʕad nuṣṣ ʔillayl lamman ɣfayna]

might • **1.** قُوَّة [quwwa, guwwa] قُوّات [quwwaːt] *pl:* Might makes right, as they say. الحَقّ لِلقُوَّة، مِثلما يقُولُون [ʔilħaqq lilquwwa, miθilmaː yguːluːn] • **2.** عَظَمَة [ʕaðama] The might of the Babylonian kings will never he forgotten. عَظَمَة المِلُوك البابلِيِّين أبَداً ما تِنّسِي [ʕaðamat ʔilmiluːk ʔilbabiliyyiːn ʔabadan maː tinnisi]

mighty • **1.** عَظِيم [ʕaðiːm] عُظَماء [ʕuðamaːʔ] *pl:* هائِل [haːʔil] He got together a mighty force and stormed the city. جِمَع قُوَّة عَظِيمَة وَإنقَضّ عالمَدِينَة [ǰimaʕ quwwa ʕaðiːma waʔinqaðð ʕalmadiːna] • **2.** قَوِي [qawi, guwi] شَدِيد [šadiːd] A mighty wind destroyed their crops. فَدّ رِيح قَوِيَّة دَمّرَت حاصلاتهُم [fadd riːħ qawwiyya dammurat ħaːṣlaːthum] • **3.** كُلِّش [kulliš] He's done mighty little work today. هُوَّ طَلَّع كُلِّش شوَيَّة شُغُل هاليُوم [huwwa ṭallaʕ kulliš šwayya šuɣul halyuːm]

mild • **1.** مُعتَدِل [muʕtadil] This is a mild climate. هَذا جَوّ مُعتَدِل [haːða ǰaww muʕtadil] • **2.** لَطِيف [laṭiːf] The sun is mild today. الشَّمِس لَطِيفَة اليُوم [ʔiššamis laṭiːfa ʔilyuːm] • **3.** بارِد [baːrid] Do you have a mild tobacco.

M

عِندَك تِتِن بارِد [ʕindak titin ba:rid] • **4.** ضَعِيف [ðaʕi:f] خَفِيف [xafi:f] خفاف [xfa:f] *pl:* He suffered a mild heart attack last winter. صارَت عِندَه نَوبَة قَلبِيَّة ضَعِيفَة الشِّتا الفات [ṣa:rat ʕindah nawba qalbiyya ðaʕi:fa ʔiššita ʔilfa:t]

mile • 1. مِيل [mi:l] أَميال، ميال [ʔamya:l, mya:l] *pl:* It's three miles from here. هِيَّ بِبُعُد تْلَث أَميال مِن هِنَا [hiyya bibuʕud tlaθ ʔamya:l minhna]

military • 1. عَسكَرِي [ʕaskari] They have military discipline. عِدهُم ضَبُط عَسكَرِي [ʕidhum ðabuṭ ʕaskari]

milk • 1. حَلِيب [ħali:b] The milk has turned sour. الحَلِيب حَمَّض [ʔilħali:b ħammað]

*** There's no use crying over spilt milk.**

• 1. اللِّي فَات مات [ʔilli fa:t ma:t]

to milk • 1. حِلَب [ħilab] حَلِب [ħalib] *vn:* اِنحِلَب [ʔinħilab] *p:* Do you know how to milk a cow? تُعرُف شلُون تِحلِب بَقَرَة؟ [tuʕruf šlu:n tiħlib baqara?] They tried to milk him of his money. حاولَوا يِحلِبُون كُلّ فلُوسَه مِنَّه [ħa:wlaw yħilbu:n kull flu:sah minnah]

mill • 1. طاحُونَة، طاحُونَة هَوَائِيَّة [ṭa:ħu:na, ṭa:ħu:na hawa:ʔiyya] طَواحِين [ṭawa:ħi:n] *pl:* مَعمَل [maʕmal] مَعامِل [maʕa:mil] *pl:* When are you going to take the grain to the mill? شوَقِت راح تاخُذ الحُبُوب لِلطَّاحُونَة؟ [šwakit ra:ħ ta:xuð ʔilħubu:b litta:ħu:na?] • **2.** مَعمَل [maʕmal] مَعامِل [maʕa:mil] *pl:* We ordered the paper straight from the mill. طلَبنا الوَرَق رأساً مِن المَعمَل [ṭlabna ʔilwaraq raʔsan min ʔilmaʕmal]

miller • 1. طَحَّان [ṭaħħa:n] طَحَّانَة [ṭaħħa:na] *pl:*

million • 1. مِليُون [milyu:n] مَلايِين [mala:yi:n] *pl:* New York has seven and half million inhabitants. نيُويُورك بِيها سَبع مَلايِين وَنُصّ مِن السُّكَّان [nyu:yu:rk bi:ha sabiʕ mala:yi:n wnuṣṣ min ʔissukka:n] I've got a million things to do before dinner. لازِم أسَوِّي مِليُون شِي قَبل العَشا [la:zim ʔasawwi milyu:n ši gabil ʔilʕaša]

mind • 1. فِكِر [fikir] He had a very keen mind. كان عِندَه فِكِر كُلِّش حادّ [ča:n ʕindah fikir kulliš ħa:dd] He doesn't know his own mind. ما يِستَقِرّ عَلَى فِكِر [ma: yistiqirr ʕala fikir] I have something else in mind. عِندِي غير شِي بفِكرِي [ʕindi ɣi:r ši bfikri] • **2.** بال [ba:l] Keep your mind on your work. دِير بالَك عَلَى شُغلَك [di:r ba:lak ʕala šuɣlak] Keep your mind on your work. إحصِر فِكرَك بِشُغلَك [ʔiħṣir fikrak bišuɣlak] What's on your mind? شَكُو عَلَى بالَك؟ [šaku ʕala ba:lak?] What's on your mind? شدَتفَكَّر؟ [šdatfakkir?] • **3.** ذِهِن [ðihin] أذهان [ʔaðha:n] *pl:* The thought went through my mind that I had seen him before. الفِكرَة مَرَّت بذِهنِي آنِي شِفتَه قَبُل [ʔilfikra marrat bðihni ʔa:ni šiftah gabul] • **4.** عَقلِيَّة [ʕaqliyya] He has a good mind. عَقلِيتَه زينَة [ʕaqli:tah zi:na] • **5.** رَأي [raʔy] آراء [ʔa:ra:ʔ] *pl:* To my mind she's the right person for the job. برَأيِي آنِي هِيَّ الشَّخص المُلائِم لِلشَّغلَة [braʔyi ʔa:ni hiyya ʔiššaxiṣ ʔilmula:ʔim liššaɣla]

*** You can't be in your right mind.**

• 1. هَذا حَكِي مال واحِد عاقِل [ha:ða ħači ma:l wa:ħid ʕa:qil] / إنتَ خَرفان؟ [ʔinta xarfa:n?]

*** My mind is not clear on what happend.**

• 1. ما أعرُف بِالضَبُط شصار [ma: ʔaʕruf biððabuṭ šṣa:r]

*** I have a good mind to tell him so. • 1.** عَقلِي يِقطَع أقُلَّه [ʕaqli yigṭaʕ ʔagullah]

to call to mind • 1. ذَكَّر ب [ðakkar b-] تَذكِير، تِذكِّر [taðki:r, tðikkir] *vn:* تذَكَّر [tðakkar] *p:* That calls to mind a story I know. هاي تذَكِّر بِفَدّ قُصَّة أعرُفها [ha:y dðakkir bfadd quṣṣa ʔaʕrufha]

to make up one's mind • 1. اِستَقَرّ عَلَى قَرار [ʔistaqarr ʕala qara:r] اِستِقرار عَلَى قَرار [ʔistiqra:r ʕala qara:r] *vn: sv* i. We'll have to make up our minds shortly. لازِم نِستَقِرّ عَلَى قَرار بَعَد فَترَة قَصِيرَة [la:zim nistaqirr ʕala qara:r baʕad fatra qaṣi:ra]

to set one's mind on • 1. صَمَّم [ṣammam] تَصمِيم [taṣmi:m] *vn: sv* i. She has her mind set on going shopping today. هِيَّ صَمِّمَت ترُوح تِتسَوَّق اليُوم [hiyya ṣammimat tru:ħ titsawwag ʔilyu:m]

to mind • 1. دار بال [da:r ba:l] دَيَران بال [dayara:n ba:l] *vn: sv* i. Don't mind what he says. لا تدِير بالَك لِلِّي يقُولَه [la: ddi:r ba:lak lilli ygu:lah] Who's going to mind the baby? مِنُو راح يدِير بالَه عَالجَّاهِل؟ [minu ra:ħ ydi:r ba:lah ʕajja:hil?] My son doesn't mind me anymore. إبنِي بَعَد ما يدِيرلِي بال [ʔibni baʕad ma: ydi:rli ba:l] Mind your own business. دِير بالَك عَلَى شُغلَك [di:r ba:lak ʕala šuɣlak] Mind your own business. ما عَلَيك مِن شُغُل غيرَك [ma: ʕali:k min šuɣul ɣi:rak]

*** I hope you don't mind me leaving now.**

• 1. آنِي أتأمَّل ما عِندَك مانِع إذا أرُوح هَسَّة [ʔa:ni ʔatʔammal ma: ʕindak ma:niʕ ʔiða ʔaru:ħ hassa]

*** I don't mind going alone. • 1.** ما عِندِي مانِع أرُوح وَحدِي [ma: ʕindi ma:niʕ ʔaru:ħ waħdi]

*** I don't mind the hot weather anymore.**

• 1. تعَلَّمِت عَالجَوّ الحارّ [tʕallamit ʕajjaww ʔilħa:rr]

mine • 1. مَنجَم [manjam] مَناجِم [mana:jim] *pl:* Who owns this mine? مِنُو يِملِك هَالمَنجَم؟ [minu yimlik halmanjam?] • **2.** لَغَم [laɣam, luɣum] ألغام [ʔalɣa:m] *pl:* Their ship ran into a mine. باخِرَتهُم اِصطِدمَت بِلُغُم [ba:xirathum ʔiṣṭidmat biluɣum]

to mine • 1. طَلَّع [ṭallaʕ] تَطلِيع [taṭli:ʕ] *vn:* تطَلَّع [tṭallaʕ] *p:* How much coal did they mine in May? شقَدّ فَحَم طَلّعَوا مِن المَنجَم خِلال مايِس؟ [šgadd faħam ṭallʕaw min ʔilmanjam xila:l ma:yis?] • **2.** لِغَم [liɣam] لَغُم [laɣum] *vn:* اِنلِغَم [ʔinliɣam] *p:* The roads are mined. الطُّرُق مَلغُومَة [ʔiṭṭuruq malɣu:ma]

miner • 1. عامِل مَنجَم [ʕa:mil manjam] عُمّال مَنجَم [ʕumma:l manjam] *pl:* The miners live near the mine. عُمّال المَنجَم يِسكنُون يَمَّه [ʕumma:l ʔilmanjam ysiknu:n yamma]

M

mine sweeper • **1.** كاسِحَة ألغام [ka:siħat ʔalɣa:m] كاسِحات ألغام [ka:siħa:t ʔalɣa:m] *pl:*

minimum • **1.** أقَلّ [ʔaqall] حَدّ أدنَى [ħadd ʔadna] What's the minimum? شِنُو أقَلّ شي [šinu ʔaqall ši] The minimum wage is three dinars a week. أقَلّ أجرَة ثلَث دَنانِير بالإسبُوع [ʔaqall ʔuǰra tlaθ dana:ni:r bilʔisbu:ʕ]

minister • **1.** قَسّ [qass] قَسَسَة [qasasa] *pl:* Our church has a new minister. كَنِيسَتنا بِيها قَسّ جِدِيد [kani:satna bi:ha qass ǰidi:d] • **2.** وَزِير [wazi:r] وُزَراء [wuzara:ʔ] *pl:* Three ministers have resigned. ثلاث وُزَراء إستَقالَوا [tlaθ wuzara:ʔ ʔistaqa:law] He was appointed minister to Portugal. تعَيَّن وَزِير مُفَوَّض بالبُرتُغال [tʕayyan wazi:r mufawwaḍ bilpurtuɣa:l]

minor • **1.** بَسِيط [baṣi:ṭ] بَسِيطِين [baṣi:ṭi:n] *pl:* طَفِيف [ṭafi:f] تافِه [ta:fih] I made only minor changes. بَسّ سَوَّيت تَبدِيلات بَسِيطَة [bass sawwi:t tabdi:la:t basi:ṭa] That's a minor matter. هَذا فَدّ شي تافِه [ha:ða fadd ši ta:fih] • **2.** قاصِر [qa:ṣir] قاصِرِين، قُصَّر [qa:ṣiri:n, quṣṣar] *pl:* As long as the boy is a minor, his uncle will be his guardian. ما دام الوَلَد قاصِر، عَمَّه راح يبقَى وَصِي عَلَيه [ma: da:m ʔilwalad qa:ṣir, ʕammah ra:ħ yibqa: waṣiyy ʕali:h]

minority • **1.** أقَلِّيَّة [ʔaqalliyya] أقَلِّيّات [ʔaqalliyya:t] *pl:* We were in the miniority. كِنّا مِن الأقَلِّيَّة [činna min ʔilʔaqalliyya]

minute • **1.** دَقِيق [daqi:q] صغَيِّر [ṣɣayyir, zɣayyir] It was so minute it could hardly be seen. هَل قَدّ ما صغَيِّرَة بالكاد تِنشاف [hal gadd ma: ṣɣayyra bilka:d tinša:f] I have checked the most minute detail. راجَعِت حَتَّى أدَقّ التَّفاصِيل [ra:ǰaʕit ħatta ʔadaqq ʔittafa:ṣi:l]

minute • **1.** دَقِيقَة [daqi:qa] دَقايِق [daqa:yiq] *pl:* I'll be back in five minutes. راح أرجَع خِلال خَمِس دَقايِق [ra:ħ ʔarǰaʕ xila:l xamis daqa:yiq] I'll drop in for a minute. راح أمُرّ فَدّ دَقِيقَة [ra:ħ ʔamurr fadd daqi:qa] • **2.** لَحظَة [laħḍa] لَحظات [laħḍa:t] *pl:* Just a minute, please. فَدّ لَحظَة، مِن فَضلَك [fadd laħḍa, min faḍlak]

  *** I'll call you the minute I know.**

  • **1.** راح أخابرَك أوَّل ما يصِير عِندي خَبَر [raħ ʔaxa:brak ʔawwal ma: yṣi:r ʕindi xabar]

minutes • **1.** مَحضَر [maħḍar] مَحاضِر [maħa:ðir] *pl:* The secretary will read the minutes of the last meeting. السِّكِرتَير راح يِقرا مَحضَر الجَّلسَة السّابقَة [ʔissikirti:r ra:ħ yiqra: maħḍar ʔiǰǰalsa ʔissa:biqa]

miracle • **1.** مُعجِزَة [muʕǰiza] مُعجِزات [muʕǰiza:t] *pl:*

mirror • **1.** مرايَة [mra:ya] مرايات [mra:ya:t] *pl:* Look at yourself in the mirror. شُوف نَفسَك بالمرايَة [šu:f nafsak bilmra:ya]

miscarriage • **1.** إجهاض [ʔiǰha:ḍ] طَرح [ṭariħ] She had a miscarriage. صار عِدها إجهاض [ṣa:r ʕidha ʔiǰha:ḍ] She had a miscarriage. هِيَّ طِرحَت [hiyya ṭirħat]

mischief • **1.** أذِيَّة [ʔaðiyya] أذِيّات [ʔaðiyya:t] *pl:* That boy is always up to some mischief. هَالوَلَد دائِماً وَرا الأذِيَّة [halwalad da:ʔiman wara ʔilʔaðiyya]

miser • **1.** شَحِيح [šaħi:ħ] شَحِيحِين [šaħi:ħi:n] *pl:* بَخِيل [baxi:l] بُخَلاء [buxala:ʔ] *pl:*

miserable • **1.** تَعِيس [taʕi:s] تُعَساء [tuʕasa:ʔ] *pl:* بائِس [ba:ʔis] مِسكِين [miski:n] مَساكِين [masa:ki:n] *pl:* I feel miserable today. أشعُر تَعِيس هَاليُوم [ʔašʕur taʕi:s halyu:m] I feel miserable today. تَلفان هَاليُوم [talfa:n halyu:m] I feel miserable today. نَفسِي مَقبُوضَة [nafsi maqbuḍa] She makes life miserable for him. دَتسَوِّي حَياتَه تَعِيسَة [datsawwi ħaya:tah taʕi:sa] She makes life miserable for him. دَتنَغِّص عِيشتَه [datnaɣɣiṣ ʕi:štah] She makes life miserable for him. دَتمَرمُر حَياتَه [datmarmur ħaya:tah] • **2.** مهَلهَل [mhalhal] They live in a miserable shack. يسِكنُون بفَدّ كُوخ مهَلهَل [ysiknu:n bfadd ku:x mhalhal] They live in a miserable shack. ساكنِين ببَيت مِثل الخَرابَة [sa:kni:n bibayt miθl ʔilxara:ba] • **3.** كَسِيف [kasi:f] What miserable weather! شلُون جَوّ كَسِيف [šlu:n ǰaww kasi:f]

misery • **1.** تَعاسَة [taʕa:sa] شَقاء [šaqa] بُؤس [buʔs] ضَنَك [ḍanak] They lived in utter misery. عاشَوا بتَعاسَة [ʕa:šaw bitaʕa:sa]

misfortune • **1.** مُصِيبَة [muṣi:ba] مُصايِب [muṣa:yib] *pl:* نَكبَة [nakba] نَكبات [nakba:t] *pl:* It won't be a great misfortune if you don't get it. يَعني ما راح تصِير فَدّ مُصِيبَة إذا ما تِقدَر تحَصّلَه [yaʕni ma: ra:ħ tṣi:r fadd muṣi:ba ʔiða ma: tigdar tħaṣṣlah]

to misjudge • **1.** خِطَأ [xiṭaʔ] خَطأ [xaṭaʔ] *vn:* إنخِطأ [ʔinxitaʔ] *p:* We mustn't misjudge the seriousness of the situation. ما لازِم نِخطِئ بالحُكُم عَلَى خُطُورَة الحالَة [ma: la:zim nixṭiʔ bilħukum ʕala xuṭu:rat ʔilħa:la] You misjudge him. إنتَ خِطأت بالحُكُم عَلَيه [ʔinta xiṭaʔit bilħukum ʕali:h]

to mislead • **1.** خِدَع [xidaʕ] خُداع [xuda:ʕ] *vn:* إنخِدَع [ʔinxidaʕ] *p:* This advertisement misleads the reader. هَالإعلان يِخدَع القارِئ [halʔiʕla:n yixdaʕ ʔilqa:riʔ]

misleading • **1.** خَدّاع [xadda:ʕ] The description is misleading. الوَصُف خَدّاع [ʔilwaṣuf xadda:ʕ]

misprint • **1.** غَلَط مَطبَعِي [ɣalaṭ maṭbaʕi] أغلاط مَطبَعِيَّة [ʔaɣla:ṭ maṭbaʕiyya] *pl:* غَلطَة مَطبَعِيَّة [ɣalṭa maṭbaʕiyya] غَلطات مَطبَعِيَّة [ɣalṭa:t maṭbaʕiyya] *pl:*

miss • **1.** آنِسَة [ʔaːnisa] آنِسات، أوانِس [ʔaːnisaːt, ʔawaːnis] *pl:* How do you do, Miss Suad? شلُون كَيفِك، آنِسَة سُعاد؟ [šluːn kiːfič, ʔaːnisa suʕaːd?] • **2.** خَطيَة [xaṭya] خَطيات [xaṭyaːt] *pl:* You have two hits and three misses. عِندَك إصابتَين وثلَث خَطيات [ʕindak ʔiṣaːbtayn wtlaθ xaṭyaːt]

*** A miss is as good as a mile.** • **1.** الغَلطَةغَلطَة ولَو بقَدّ الشَعرَة [ʔilɣalṭa ɣalṭa wlaw bgadd ʔiššaʕra]

to miss • **1.** خِطَى [xiṭaː] خَطِي [xaṭiy] *vn:* اِنخِطَى [ʔinxiṭaː] *p:* You missed the target. خِطَيت الهَدَف [xiṭayt ʔilhadaf] Our house is so easy to find you can't miss it. بَيتنا يِنلِقِي بسُهُولَة، ما تِقدَر تِخطِيه [baytna yinligi bsuhuːla, maː tigdar tixṭiːh] He missed hitting me by a hair. ضَرُبتَه خِطَتنِي بشَعرَة [ðarubtah xiṭatni bišaʕra] • **2.** تفاوَت [tfaːwat] تَفاوُت [tafaːwut] *vn: sv* a. I missed him at the station. تفاوَتِت ويّاه بالمَحَطّة [tfaːwatit wiyyaːh bilmaħaṭṭa] • **3.** اِستَوحَش ل [ʔistawħaš l-] اِستِوحاش [ʔistiwħaːš] *vn: sv* i. I'll miss you terribly. راح أستَوحِشلَك كُلَّش هوايَة [raːħ ʔastawħišlak kulliš hwaːya] I'll miss you terribly. مَكانَك راح يبَيِّن [makaːnak raːħ ybayyin]

*** Don't miss this picture.** • **1.** لا يفُوتَك هَالفِلِم [laː yfuːtak halfilim]

*** Do you think I'll miss my train?** • **1.** تِعتِقِد راح يفُوتنِي القِطار؟ [tiʕtiqid raːħ yfuːtni ʔilqiṭaːr?]

*** You haven't missed a thing.** • **1.** ما فاتَك فَدّ شِي مُهِمّ [maː faːtak fadd ši muhimm]

*** You missed the point of my story.** • **1.** فاتَك مَغزَى حكايتِي [faːtak maɣza ħčaːyti]

missing • **1.** ضايِع [ðaːyiʕ] The child has been missing for three days. الطِّفِل صارلَه ثلَث أيّام ضايِع [ʔiṭṭifil ṣaːrlah tlaθ ʔayyaːm ðaːyiʕ]

mist • **1.** ضُباب خَفِيف [ðubaːb xafiːf]

mistake • **1.** غَلَط [ɣalaṭ] أغلاط [ʔaɣlaːṭ] *pl:* غَلطَة [ɣalṭa] غَلطات [ɣalṭaːt] *pl:* How did you make such a mistake? شلُون غِلَطتِي هِيكِي غَلطَة [šluːn ɣilaṭti hiːči ɣalṭa] Sorry, I took it by mistake. آسِف أخَذتها بالغَلَط [ʔaːsif ʔaxaðitha bilɣalaṭ] There must be some mistake. لازِم أكُو فَدّ شِي غَلَط [laːzim ʔaku fadd ši ɣalaṭ] • **2.** صُوچ [ṣuːč] Sorry, my mistake. مِتأسِّف، صُوچِي [mitʔassif, ṣuːči] Sorry, my mistake. آسِف، هاي غِلطتِي [ʔaːsif, haːy ɣaliṭti]

to make a mistake • **1.** اِشتِبَه [ʔištibah] اِشتِباه [ʔištibaːh] *vn: sv* i. Make no mistake, this is a serious matter. لا تِشتِبِه، المَوضُوع جِدِّي [laː tištibih, ʔilmawðuːʕ ǰiddi]

to mistake • **1.** فِهَم غَلَط [fiham ɣalaṭ] فهم [fahim] *vn:* sv a.) أساء فِهِم إساءَة [ʔasaːʔ fihim] [ʔisaːʔa] *vn: sv* i. I mistook his intention. فِهِمِت نيتَه غَلَط [fihamit niːtah ɣalaṭ] Please don't mistake me. أرجُوك لا تسِيئ فهمِي [ʔarǰuːk laː tsiːʔ fihmi] • **2.** اِشتِبَه [ʔištibah] اِشتِباه [ʔištibaːh] *vn: sv* i. Sorry, I mistook you for someone else. آسِف، اِشتِبَهِت بِيك بشَخِص آخَر [ʔaːsif, ʔištibahit biːk bišaxiṣ ʔaːxar]

mistaken • **1.** غَلطان [ɣalṭaːn] خاطِئ [xaːṭiʔ] That's a mistaken belief. هَذا اِعتِقاد غَلطان [haːða ʔiʕtiqaːd ɣalṭaːn] There you're mistaken. إنتَ غَلطان بذِيكِي [ʔinta ɣalṭaːn biðiːči] • **2.** خَطَأ ب [xaṭaʔ b-] It was a case of mistaken identity. كانَت قَضِيَّة خَطَأ بالتَّشرِيف [čaːnat qaðiyyat xaṭaʔ bittašriːf]

to mistreat • **1.** أساء مُعامَلَة [ʔasaːʔ muʕaːmala] إساءَة مُعامَلَة [ʔisaːʔat muʕaːmala] *vn:* [.] *p:* The servant mistreated the children. الخادِم أساء مُعامَلَة الجُّهال [ʔilxaːdim ʔasaːʔ muʕaːmalat ʔiǰǰahaːl]

mistress • **1.** صاحبَة [ṣaːħba] صاحبات [ṣaːħbaːt] *pl:* سَيِّدَة [sayyida] سَيِّدات [sayyidaːt] *pl:* The dog didn't recognize his mistress. الكَلِب ما عِرَف صاحِبتَه [ʔiččalib maː ʕiraf ṣaːħibtah] • **2.** عَشِيقَة [ʕašiːqa] عَشِيقات [ʕašiːqaːt] *pl:* رفِيقَة [rfiːǰa] رفِيقات [rfiːǰaːt] *pl:* She's his mistress. هِيَّ رفِيقتَه [hiyya rfiːǰtah]

to mix • **1.** خُبَط [xubaṭ] خَبُط [xabuṭ] *vn:* اِنخُبَط [ʔinxubaṭ] *p:* I mixed yellow and red. خبَطِت أصفَر وأحمَر [xbaṭit ʔaṣfar wʔaħmar] Mix the paint well before you use it. أخبُط الصُّبُغ زين قَبُل ما تِستَعمِلَه [ʔuxbuṭ ʔiṣṣubuɣ ziːn gabul maː tistaʕmilah] • **2.** تراهَم [traːham] تَراهُم [taraːhum] *vn: sv* a. Pickles and milk don't mix. الطُّرشِي والحَلِيب ما يِتراهمُون [ʔiṭṭurši wilħaliːb maː yitraːhmuːn] • **3.** تخالَط [txaːlaṭ] تَخالُط [taxaːluṭ] *vn: sv* a. اِختِلَط [ʔixtilaṭ] خَلط، اِختِلاط [xlaṭ, ʔixtilaːt] *vn: sv* i. We don't mix much with our neighbors. إحنا ما نِتخالَط هوايَة ويّا جوارِينا [ʔiħna maː nitxaːlaṭ hwaːya wiyya ǰwaːriːna] • **4.** دَخَّل [daxxal] تَدخِيل، تدِخِّل [tadxiːl, tdixxil] *vn: sv* i. She likes to mix in other people's business. هِيَّ يعجِبها تدَخِّل نَفِسها بشُغُل النّاس [hiyya yiʕǰibha ddaxxil nafisha bišuɣul ʔinnaːs]

to mix in • **1.** اِتداخَل [ʔiddaːxal] تَداخُل [tadaːxul] *vn: sv* a. اِتدَخَّل [ʔiddaxxal] تَدَخُّل [tadaxxul] *vn: sv* a. Don't mix in, this is none of your business. لا تِتداخَل، هَذا مُو شُغلَك [laː tiddaːxal, haːða muː šuɣlak]

to mix up • **1.** خَربَط [xarbaṭ] خَربَطَة، تخُربُط [xarbaṭa, txurbuṭ] *vn:* تخَربَط [txarbaṭ] *p:* Don't mix up the cards. لا تخَربُط البِطاقات [laː txarbuṭ ʔilbiṭaːqaːt] • **2.** شَوَّش [šawwaš] تَشوِيش [tašwiːš] *vn:* تشَوَّش [tšawwaš] *p:* أربَك [ʔarbak] إرباك [ʔirbaːk] *vn:* اِنربَك [ʔinribak] *p:* Don't mix me up. لا تشَوّشنِي [laː tšawwišni] • **3.** دَخَّل [daxxal] تَدخِيل، تدِخِّل [tadxiːl, tdixxil] *vn:* Don't mix me up in your argument. لا تدَخِّلنِي بجَدَلكُم [laː ddaxxilni biǰadalkum]

mixed up • **1.** هُوسَة [hawsa] هَوسات [hawsaːt] *pl:* Your work is all mixed up. شُغلَك هُوسَة [šuɣlak huːsa] • **2.** مِتخَربُط [mitxarbuṭ] مِرتِبِك [mirtibik] I'm so mixed up I don't know what I'm doing. آنِي هَل قَدّ ما مِتخَربُط ما داعرُف شداسَوِّي [ʔaːni hal gadd maː mitxarbuṭ maː daʔaʕruf šdaʔasawwi]

mixture • **1.** مَزِيج [maziːǰ] مَزِيجات [maziːǰaːt] *pl:* خَلِيط [xaliːṭ] خَلِيطات [xaliːṭaːt] *pl:*

mix-up • **1.** خَربَطَة [xarbaṭa] خَرابِيط، خَربَطات [xaraːbiːṭ, xarbaṭaːt] *pl:* There was an awful mix-up. صارَت فَدّ خَربَطَة فَظِيعَة [ṣaːrat fadd xarbaṭa faðiːʕa]

to moan • **1.** وَنّ [wann] وَنّ [wann] *vn: sv* i. I could hear him moaning in the next room. قِدَرِت أَسِمعَه يونّ بغُرفَة اللُّخ [gidarit ʔasimʕah ywinn bɣurfat ʔillux]

mob • **1.** غَوغاء [ɣawɣaːʔ] The mob almost lynched him. الغَوغاء تَقرِيباً عَلِّقُوه [ʔilɣawɣaːʔ taqriːban ʕalliquːh] • **2.** جَماعَة [ǰamaːʕa] جَماعات [ǰamaːʕaːt] *pl:* There's a mob of people waiting for you. أَكُو فَدّ جَماعَة بِإنتِظارَك [ʔaku fadd ǰamaːʕa biʔintiðaːrak]

to mob • **1.** هِجَم [hiǰam.] هُجُوم عَلَى [huǰuːm ʕala] *vn: sv* i. The girls mobbed him for his autograph. البَنات هِجمَوا عَليه بطَلَب تَوقِيعَه [ʔilbanaːt hiǰmaw ʕaliːh bṭalab tawqiːʕah] • **2.** تكَدَّس عَلَى [tkaddas ʕala] تَكَدُّس [takaddus] *vn: sv* a. People mob the stores before the holiday. المَخازِن يِتكَدَّس عَليها النّاس قَبِل العِيد [ʔilmaxaːzin titkaddas ʕaliːha ʔinnaːs gabil ʔilʕiːd]

model • **1.** نَمُوذَج [namuːðaǰ] نَماذِج [namaːðiǰ] *pl:* He's working on the model of a bridge. هُوَّ دَيسَوِّي نَمُوذَج لِفَدّ جِسِر [huwwa daysawwi namuːðaǰ lfadd ǰisir] • **2.** مُودِيل [mudiːl] مُوديلات [mudiːlaːt] *pl:* This is the latest model. هَذِي آخِر مُودَيل [haːði ʔaːxir mudiːl] • **3.** عارِضَة [ʕaːriḍa] عارِضات [ʕaːriḍaːt] *pl:* She is a clothes model in a fashionable dress shop. هِيَّ عارِضَة أَزياء بمَخزَن عَصري [hiyya ʕaːriḍat ʔazyaːʔ bimaxzan ʕaṣri] • **4.** مِثال [miθaːl] أَمثِلَة [ʔamθila] *pl:* قُدوَة، قِدوَة [qudwa, qidwa] قُدوات [qudwaːt] *pl:* They took him as a model. اِتّخذُوه كَقِدوَة [ʔittixðawh kaqidwa] • **5.** مِثالِي [miθaːli] نَمُوذَجِي [namuːðaǰi] She's a model wife. هِيَّ زَوجَة مِثالِيَّة [hiyya zawǰa miθaːliyya]

to model • **1.** عِرَض [ʕiraḍ] عَرِض [ʕariḍ] *vn:* اِنعِرَض [ʔinʕiraḍ] *p:* She models women's clothing. تِعرُض أَزياء نِسائِيَّة [tiʕruḍ ʔazyaːʔ nisaːʔiyya] • **2.** تشَكَّل [tšakkal] *sv* i. The boy has begun to model himself after his hero. الوَلَد بِدا يِتشَكَّل بشِكِل بَطَلَه [ʔilwalad bidaː yitšakkal bišikil baṭalah]

moderate • **1.** مِعتَدِل [miʕtadil] مُتَوَسِّط [mutwaṣṣiṭ] He has moderate political views. أَفكارَه السِّياسِيَّة مُعتَدلَة [ʔafkaːrah ʔissiyaːsiyya muʕtadla]

modern • **1.** حَدِيث [ħadiːθ] عَصري [ʕaṣri] مُودَة [muːda] She has a modern kitchen. عِدها فَدّ مَطبَخ عَصري [ʕidha fadd maṭbax ʕaṣri]

modest • **1.** مُحتَشِم [muħtašim] مِتواضِع [mitwaːðiʕ] She's a very modest person. هِيَّ فَدّ وِحدَة كُلِّش مُحتَشمَة [hiyya fadd wiħda kulliš muħtašma] The king is modest. المَلِك مِتواضِع [ʔilmalik mitwaːðiʕ]

moist • **1.** رَطِب [raṭib] نَدِي [nadi] مبَلَّل [mballal]

to moisten • **1.** بَلّل [ballal] تَبلِيل، تبِلِّل [tabliːl, tbillil] *vn:* تبَلَّل [tballal] *p:* Moisten the stamp. بَلِّل الطّابِع [ballil ʔiṭṭaːbiʕ]

moisture • **1.** رُطُوبَة [ruṭuːba] نِدَى [nida]

mold • **1.** عُفُونَة [ʕufuːna] There was a layer of mold on the cheese. كان أَكُو طَبَقَة مِن العُفُونَة عالجِّبِن [čaːn ʔaku ṭabaqa min ʔilʕufuːna ʕaǰǰibin] • **2.** قالَب [qaːlab] قَوالِب، قوالِب [qawaːlib, qwaːlib.] *pl:* You can use this mold for the pudding. تِقدَر تِستَعمِل هَالقالَب لِلبُدنِك [tigdar tistaʕmil halqaːlab lilpuding]

to mold • **1.** عَفَّن [ʕaffan] تَعفِين [taʕfiːn] *vn:* تعَفَّن [tʕaffan] *p:* If you leave the cheese here it will mold. إذا تِترُك الجِّبِن هنا يعَفِّن [ʔiða titruk ʔiǰǰibin hnaː yʕaffin] • **2.** كَيَّف [kayyaf] تَكيِيف [takyiːf] *vn:* تكَيَّف [tkayyaf] *p:* شَكَّل [šakkal] تَشكِيل [taškiːl] *vn:* تشَكَّل [tšakkal] *p:* Mold the clay with your hands. كَيِّف الطِّين بِيدَك [kayyif ʔiṭṭiːn biːdak]

moldy • **1.** معَفِّن [mʕaffin] مِتعَفِّن [mitʕaffin] The bread is moldy. الخُبُز معَفِّن [ʔilxubuz mʕaffin]

mole • **1.** خُلد [xuld] حَيوانات خُلد [ħaywaːnaːt xuld] *pl:* We've a mole in our gaden. عِدنا فَدّ خُلد بحَدِيقَتنا [ʕidna fadd xuld bħadiːqatna] • **2.** شامَة [šaːma] شامات [šaːmaːt] *pl:* He has a large mole on his cheek. عِندَه شامَة كبِيرَة عَلَى خَدَّه [ʕindah šaːma čibiːra ʕala xaddah]

molecule • **1.** جُزَيئَة [ǰuzayʔa] جُزَيئات [ǰuzayʔaːt] *pl:*

moment • **1.** لَحظَة [lahða] لَحظات [lahðaːt] *pl:* Wait a moment. اِنتِظِر لَحظَة [ʔintiðir lahða]

at a moment's notice • **1.** بأَي لَحظَة [bʔayy lahða] Be ready to leave at a moment's notice. كُون حاضِر تغادِر بأَي لَحظَة [kuːn ħaːðir tɣaːdir bʔayy lahða]

at the moment • **1.** بهَالوَقِت، بهاللَّحظَة [bhalwakit, bhallahða] اِنلِحَس [ʔinlihas] At the moment I can't give you any further information. بِهَالوَكِت ما أَقدَر أَنطِيك أَيّ مَعلُومات أَكثَر [bihalwakit maː ʔagdar ʔanṭiːk ʔayy maʕluːmaːt ʔakθar]

in a moment • **1.** بخِلال لَحظَة [bxilaːl lahða] بَعَد لَحظَة [baʕad lahða] I'll give you your change in a moment. أَنطِيك بَقِيَّة فلُوسَك بخِلال لَحظَة [ʔanṭiːk baqiyyat fluːsak bxilaːl lahða]

monastery • **1.** دَير [diːr] أَديِرَة [ʔadyira] *pl:*

Monday • **1.** يَوم الاِثنَين [yuːm ʔiθθiniːn]

M

money • **1.** فلُوس [flu:s] Do you take American money? تِقبَل فلُوس أمرِيكِيَّة؟ [tiqbal flu:s ʔamri:kiyya?]

*** He has money to burn.** • **1.** عِندَه فلُوس مِثِل الزِبَل [ʕindah flu:s miθl ʔizzibal]

*** You can't get that for love or money.** • **1.** قُوَّة مرُوَّة ما تِتحَصَّل [guwwa mruwwa ma: titħaṣṣal]

money order • **1.** حَوالَة مالِيَّة [ħawa:la ma:liyya] حَوالات مالِيَّة [ħawa:la:t ma:liyya] *pl:*

monk • **1.** راهِب [ra:hib] رُهبان [ruhba:n] *pl:*

monkey • **1.** شادِي [ša:di] شوادِي [šwa:di] *pl:* قِرد [qird] قُرُود [quru:d] *pl:*

monopoly • **1.** إحتِكار [ʔiħtika:r]

monotonous • **1.** * The work here is monotonous but the salary is good. الشُغُل هنا يِمشِي عَلَى فَدّ نَمَط لَكِن الرّاتِب زين [ʔiššuɣul hna: yimši ʕala fadd namaṭ la:kin ʔirra:tib zi:n]

monster • **1.** غُول [ɣu:l] غِيلان [ɣi:la:n] *pl:* سِعلُوَّة [siʕluwwa] سِعلُوّات [siʕluwwa:t] *pl:*

month • **1.** شَهَر [šahar] أشهُر [ʔašhur] *pl:* He came last month. إجا بِالشَهَر اللّي فات [ʔiǰa biššahar ʔilli fa:t]

monthly • **1.** شَهرِي [šahri] He writes for a monthly magazine. هُوَّ يِكتِب بمَجَلَّة شَهرِيَّة [huwwa yiktib bmaǰalla šahriyya] You can pay the amount in monthly installments. تِقدَر تِدفَع المَبلَغ بأقساط شَهرِيَّة [tigdar tidfaʕ ʔilmablaɣ bʔaqsa:ṭ šahriyya] • **2.** شَهرِيّاً [šahriyyan] He comes to Baghdad monthly. يِجِي لِبَغداد شَهرِيّاً [yiǰi libaɣda:d šahriyyan]

*** You can make a monthly payment of five dinars.** • **1.** تِقدَر تِدفَع خَمس دنانِير بِالشَهَر [tigdar tidfaʕ xams dna:ni:r biššahar]

monument • **1.** نَصُب تِذكارِي [naṣub tiðka:ri] أنصِبَة تِذكارِيَّة [ʔanṣiba tiðka:riyya] *pl:*

mood • **1.** مِزاج [miza:ǰ] أمزِجَة [ʔamziǰa] *pl:* He is in a good mood today. مِزاجَه زين اليُوم [miza:ǰah zi:n ʔilyu:m] • **2.** وَهَس [wahas] خُلُق [xuluq] أخلاق [ʔaxla:q] *pl:* I'm not in the mood for that. آنِي ما عِندِي وَهَس لِهاي [ʔa:ni ma: ʕindi wahas lha:y]

moody • **1.** مَقهُور [maqhu:r]

moon • **1.** قُمَر [gumar] أقمار، قمارَة [gma:ra, ʔaqma:r] *pl:* There's a ring around the moon tonight. أكُو حَلقَة دايِر مَدايِر القُمَر هاللَّيلَة [ʔaku ħalqa da:yir mada:yir ʔilgumar hallayla]

full moon • **1.** بَدِر [badir] Is there a full moon tonight? القُمَر بَدِر هاللَّيلَة؟ [ʔilgumar badir hallayla?]

mop • **1.** مَمسَحَة [mamsaħa] مَمسَحات [mamsaħa:t] *pl:* Take a wet mop. أخُذ فَدّ مَمسَحَة مبَلَّلَة [ʔuxuð fadd mamsaħa mballila]

to mop • **1.** مِسَح [misaħ] مَسِح [masiħ] *vn:* اِنمِسَح [ʔinmisaħ] *p:* Did you mop the floor? مِسَحِت القاع؟ [misaħit ʔilga:ʕ?] He mopped his forehead. مِسَح قُصّتَه [misaħ guṣṣtah]

to mop up • **1.** قِضَى عَلَى [qiða:, giða: ʕala] قَضاء [qaða:ʔ] *vn:* اِنقِضَى [ʔinqiða:] *p:* The government forces mopped up the remnant of the rebels. الحُكُومَة قِضَت عَلَى آخِر بَقايا الثُّوّار [ʔilħuku:ma qiðat ʕala ʔa:xir baqa:ya ʔiθθuwwa:r]

moral • **1.** مَغزَى [maɣza] مَغازِي [maɣa:zi] *pl:* حِكمَة [ħikma] حِكَم [ħikam] *pl:* And the moral of the story is. . . وَمَغزَى القُصَّة هُوَّ [wamaɣza ʔilquṣṣa huwwa..] • **2.** أدَبِي أخلاقِي [ʔadabi ʔaxla:qi] Children have a moral obligation to support their parents. الأبناء عَلَيهُم مَسؤُولِيَّة أدَبِيَّة يعِيلُون الوالِدَين [ʔilʔabna:ʔ ʕali:hum masʔu:liyya ʔadabiyya yʕi:lu:n ʔilwa:lidi:n]

morals • **1.** أخلاق [ʔaxla:q] He has no morals at all. ما عِندَه أخلاق أبَداً [ma: ʕindah ʔaxla:q ʔabadan] He has no morals at all. هُوَّ أخلاق سِزّ [huwwa ʔaxla:q sizz] She's a woman of low morals. هِيَّ مَرَة أخلاقها واطيَة [hiyya mara ʔaxla:qha wa:ṭya]

morale • **1.** الرُوح المَعنَوِيَّة [ʔirru:ħ ʔilmaʕnawiyya] إمعان [ʔimʕa:n] The morale of the troops was excellent. مَعنَوِيّات الجِّنُود كانَت مُمتازَة [maʕnawiyya:t ʔiǰǰinu:d ča:nat mumta:za]

morality • **1.** نَزاهَة [naza:ha] We do not question the morality of his actions. ما نشُكّ بِنَزاهَة أعمالَه [ma: nšukk binaza:hat ʔaʕma:lah]

more • **1.** أكثَر [ʔakθar] أزيَد [ʔazyad] He is asking for more money. دَيرِيد فلُوس أكثَر [dayri:d flu:s ʔakθar] He is asking for more money. دَيرِيد فلُوس بَعَد [dayri:d flu:s baʕad] He has more money than he needs. عِندَه أكثَر فلُوس مِن ما يِحتاج [ʕindah ʔakθar flu:s min ma: yiħta:ǰ] That's more likely. هَذِيك مُحتَمَلَة أكثَر [haði:č muħtamala ʔakθar] He got more and more involved in the matter. توَرَّط بِالمَوضُوع أكثَر فَأكثَر [twarraṭ bilmawðu:ʕ ʔakθar faʔakθar] The price will be a little more. راح يصِير السِّعر شوَيَّة أزيَد [ra:ħ yṣi:r ʔissiʕr šwayya ʔazyad]

*** What's more? I don't believe him.** • **1.** والأكثَر مِن هَذا، آنِي ما أصَدِّق بِيه [wilʔakθar min ha:ða, ʔa:ni ma: ʔaṣaddig bi:h]

more or less • **1.** شِي عَلَى شِي [ši ʕala ši] نَوعاً ما [nawʕan ma:] I believe that report is more or less true. أعتِقِد هَالتَّقرِير شِي عَلَى شِي صَحِيح [ʔaʕtiqid hattaqri:r ši ʕala ši ṣaħi:ħ]

once more • **1.** مَرَّة لُخ [marra lux] Try once more. جَرُّب مَرَّة لُخ [ǰarrub marra lux]

some more • **1.** بَعَد [baʕad] Won't you have some more soup? ما تريد بَعَد شُوربَة؟ [maː triːd baʕad šuːrba?]

the more ... the more • **1.** كُلّما كُلّما [kullma...kullma] The more money they get, the more they want. كُلّما يحَصّلُون عَلَى فلُوس كُلّما يِردُون بَعَد [kullma yħaṣṣluːn ʕala fluːs kullma yirduːn baʕad] The more I see him, the more I like him. كُلّما أَشُوفه، كُلّما أَحِبَّه أَزيَد [kullmaː ʔašuːfah, kullma ʔaħibbah ʔazyad]

*** The more I give him, the more he wants.**

• **1.** شقَدّ ما أنطِيه يرِيد بَعَد أزيَد [šgadd maː ʔanṭiːh yriːd baʕad ʔazyad] / عَينَه ما تِشبَع [ʕaynah maː tišbaʕ]

moreover • **1.** و عَلاوَةً عَلَى ذلِك [wʕalaːwatan ʕala ðaːlik]

morning • **1.** صُبُح [ṣubuħ] أصباح [ʔaṣbaːħ] *pl:* صَباح [ṣabaːħ] He works from morning till night. يِشتُغُل مِن الصُّبُح لِلّيل [yištuɣul min ʔiṣṣubuħ lillayl]

in the morning • **1.** الصُبُح [ʔiṣṣubuħ] She's only here in the morning. هِيَّ هنا بَسّ الصُّبُح [hiyya hna bass ʔiṣṣubuħ] We stayed up till one in the morning. سِهَرنا لِسّاعَة وِحدَة الصُّبُح [siharna lissaːʕa wiħda ʔiṣṣubuħ]

this morning • **1.** اليَوم الصُبُح [ʔilyawm ʔiṣṣubuħ] There was a lot to do this morning. كان أكُو هوايَة شُغُل اليُوم الصُّبُح [čaːn ʔaku hwaːya šuɣul ʔilyuːm ʔiṣṣubuħ]

mortal • **1.** زائِل [zaːʔil] زائِلِين [zaːʔiliːn] *pl:* We are mortal and God is immortal. إحنا زائِلِين وَالله دائِم [ʔiħna zaːʔiliːn wʔallah daːʔim] • **2.** بَشَرِي [bašari] بَشَر [bašar] *Collective:* That isn't for ordinary mortals. هَذا فَوق مُستَوَى البَشَر [haːða fawq mustawa ʔilbašar]

mortality • **1.** وَفِيّات [wafiyyaːt] Infant mortality here is still a serious problem. وَفِيّات الأطفال هنا لهَسَّة مُشكِلَة كِبِيرَة [wafiyyaːt ʔilʔaṭfaːl hna lhassa muškila čibiːra] • **2.** فَناء [fanaːʔ] It is difficult for human beings to accept the idea of their mortality. البَشَر يِصعَب عَلَيهُم قُبُول فِكرَة فَناءهُم [ʔilbašar yiṣʕab ʕaliːhum qubuːl fikrat fanaːʔhum]

mortar • **1.** مُونَة [muːna] Mortar is made from sand and slaked lime. المُونَة مسَوّايَة مِن الرَّمُل وِالجُّصّ [ʔilmuːna msawwaːya min ʔirramul wiǰǰuṣṣ] • **2.** هاوَن [haːwan] هاوَنات [haːwanaːt] *pl:* Pound the coffee beans in a mortar. دُقّ البُنّ بِهاوَن [dugg ʔilbunn bihaːwan]

mortgage • **1.** رَهَن [rahan] رُهُون [ruhuːn] *pl:* The interest on the mortgage is due. الفايِز عالرَّهِن اِستَحَقّ [lfaːyiz ʕarrahin ʔistaħaqq]

to mortgage • **1.** رِهَن [rihan] رَهَن [rahan] *vn:* اِنرِهَن [ʔinrihan] *p:* He had to mortgage his house. اِضطَرّ يِرهِن بَيتَه [ʔiðṭarr yirhin baytah]

Moslem • **1.** مُسلِم [muslim] مُسلِمِين [muslimiːn] *pl:*

mosquito • **1.** بَقَّة [bagga] بَقّات [baggaːt] *pl:* بَق [bagg] *Collective:* We were all bitten up by the mosquitos. أكَلنا البَقّ كُلّتنا [ʔakalna ʔilbagg kullatna]

moss • **1.** طُحلُب [ṭuħlub] طَحالِب [ṭaħaːlib] *pl:*

most • **1.** أكثَر ما [ʔakθar maː] أقصَى ما [ʔaqṣaː ma] That's the most I can pay. هَذا أكثَر ما أقدَر أدفَعَه [haːða ʔakθar maː ʔagdar ʔadfaʕah] • **2.** مُعظَم [muʕðam] أكثَر [ʔakθar] Most of the day I'm at the office. آنِي بَالدّائِرَة مُعظَم النَّهار [ʔaːni biddaːʔira muʕðam ʔinnahaːr] Most people went home early. أكثَر النّاس راحَوا لِلبَيت مِن وَقِت [ʔakθar ʔinnaːs raːħaw lilbayt min wakit] He's on the road most of the time. هُوَّ مسافِر أكثَر الأوقات [huwwa msaːfir ʔakθar ʔilʔawqaːt] Who did most of the work? مِنُو طَلَّع أكثَر الشُّغُل؟ [minu ṭallaʕ ʔakθar ʔiššuɣul?] • **3.** كُلِّش [kulliš] The talk was most interesting. الحَدِيث كان كُلِّش مُمتِع [ʔilħadiːθ čaːn kulliš mumtiʕ]

*** We'd better make the most of our time.**

• **1.** أحسَنِلنا نحاوِل نِستِفِيد وَقِتنا أكثَر ما يِمكِن [ʔaħsanilna nħaːwil nistifiːd wakitna ʔakθar maː yimkin]

at the most • **1.** عَالأكثَر [ʕalʔakθar] At the most it's worth ten dinars. عَالأكثَر يِسوَى عَشِر دَنانِير [ʕalʔakθar yiswaː ʕašir danaːniːr]

mostly • **1.** عَلَى الأغلَب [ʕala ʔilʔaɣlab] عَلَى الأكثَر [ʕala ʔilʔakθar] He's mostly right. هُوَّ صَحِيح عالأغلَب [huwwa ṣaħiːħ ʕalʔaɣlab] The audience consisted mostly of women. الحاضرِين كانَوا عَلَى الأكثَر نِسوان [ʔilħaːðriːn čaːnaw ʕala ʔilʔakθar niswaːn]

moth • **1.** عِثّة [ʕiθθa] عِثّات [ʕiθθaːt] *pl:* عِث [ʕiθθ] *Collective*

moth ball • **1.** دُعبُلَّة نَفتالِين [duʕbulla naftaliːn] دُعبُلّات نَفتالِين [duʕbullaːt naftaliːn] *pl:*

moth-eaten • **1.** مَعثُوث [maʕθuːθ]

mother • **1.** أُمّ [ʔumm] أُمَّهات [ʔummahaːt] *pl:* والِدَة [waːlida] والِدات [waːlidaːt] *pl:* She takes care of us like a mother. تدِير بالها عَلينا عَبالَك أمّنا [ddiːr baːlha ʕaliːna ʕabaːlak ʔummna]

to mother • **1.** دارَى مِثل الأمّ [daːraː miθl ʔilʔumm] مداراة مِثل الأمّ [mdaːraːt miθl ʔilʔumm] *vn:* تدارَى مِثل الأمّ [tdaːraː miθl ʔilʔumm] *p:* She mothers him all the time. تدارِيه مِثِل الأمّ عَلَى طُول [ddaːriːh miθil ʔilʔumm ʕala ṭuːl]

mother-in-law • **1.** حَماة [ħamaː] حَمَوات [ħamawaːt] *pl:* My mother-in law is living with us. حَماتِي ساكنَة وِيّانا [ħamaːti saːkna wiyyaːna] • **2.** مَرة عَمّ [mart ʕamm] نِسوان العَمّ [niswaːn ʔilʕamm] *pl:* The bride and her mother-in-law never get along. العَرُوسَة وَمَرة العَمّ ما يِتراهمُون [ʔilʕaruːsa wamarat ʔilʕamm maː yitraːhmuːn]

M

mother tongue • **1.** لُغَة أَصلِيَّة [luɣa ʔaṣliyya] لُغات أَصلِيَّة [luɣa:t ʔaṣliyya] *pl:* What is your mother tongue? شِنُو لُغَتَك الأَصلِيَّة؟ [šinu: luɣatak ʔilʔaṣliyya?]

motion • **1.** حَرَكَة [ħaraka] All of her motions are graceful. كُلّ حَرَكاتها رَشِيقَة [kull ħaraka:tha: raši:qa] • **2.** اِقتِراح [ʔiqtira:ħ] اِقتِراحات [ʔiqtira:ħa:t] *pl:* I'd like to make a motion. أَرِيد أَقَدِّم اِقتِراح [ʔari:d ʔaqaddim ʔiqtira:ħ]

to motion • **1.** أَشَّر [ʔaššar] تَأشِير [taʔši:r] *vn: sv* i. أَومَى [ʔu:ma:] أَوماء، إِيماء [ʔu:ma:ʔ, ʔi:ma:ʔ] *vn: sv* i. He motioned the taxi to stop. أَشَّر لِلتّاكسِي حَتَّى يوقَف [ʔaššar litta:ksi ħatta yu:gaf] He motioned me to come. أَومالِي أَجِي [ʔawma:li ʔaǰi]

motionless • **1.** بَلا حَرَكَة [bala: ħaraka] The patient slept motionless all night. المَرِيض نام بِلا حَرَكَة طُول اللَّيل [ʔilmari:ð̣ na:m bila ħaraka ṭu:l ʔillayl] • **2.** جامِد [ǰa:mid] I stayed in my place motionless with fear until it was clear there was no snake. بقِيت جامِد بِمَكانِي مِن الخَوف إِلَى أَن تبَيَّنلِي ما كان أَكُو حَيَّة [biqi:t ǰa:mid bimaka:ni min ʔilxawf ʔila ʔan tbayyanli ma: ča:n ʔaku ħayya] • **3.** راكِد [ra:kid] The surface of the water was motionless. سَطِح الماي كان راكِد [saṭiħ ʔilma:y ča:n ra:kid] • **4.** واقِف [wa:gif] The air is motionless. الهَوا واقُف [ʔilhawa wa:quf]

motion picture • **1.** فِلِم [filim] أَفلام [ʔafla:m] *pl:*

to motivate • **1.** حَثّ [ħaθθ] حَثّ [ħaθθ] *vn:* اِنحَثّ [ʔinħaθθ] *p: sv* i. We are trying to find some way to motivate our son to study. دَندَوِّر عَلَى طَرِيقَة نحِثّ بِيها إِبنَنا عَلَى الدِّراسَة [dandawwir ʕala ṭari:qa nħiθθ bi:ha ʔibinna ʕala ʔiddira:sa]

motivation • **1.** حَثّ [ħaθθ] The motivation of the employees in their work is a part of the duties of the Personnel Section. حَثّ المُستَخدَمِين عَالشّغُل مِن واجبات شُعبَة الذّاتِيَّة [ħaθθ ʔilmustaxdami:n ʕaššɣul min wa:ǰiba:t šuʕbat ʔiðða:tiyya]

motive • **1.** دافِع [da:fiʕ] دَوافِع [dawa:fiʕ] *pl:* باعِث [ba:ʕiθ] What is the motive behind the crime? شِنُو الدّافِع لِلجَّرِيمَة؟ [šinu: ʔidda:fiʕ liǰǰari:ma?]

motor • **1.** ماطَور [ma:ṭu:r] ماطَورات [ma:ṭu:ra:t] *pl:* مَكِينَة [maki:na] مَكايِن [maka:yin] *pl:* I let the motor run. خَلَّيت الماطُور يِشتُغُل [xalli:t ʔilma:ṭu:r yištuɣul]

motorcycle • **1.** ماطُورسِكِل [ma:ṭu:rsikil] ماطُورسِكِلات [ma:ṭu:rsikila:t] *pl:*

to mount • **1.** رِكَب [rikab] رُكُوب [ruku:b] *vn:* اِنرِكَب [ʔinrikab] *p:* He mounted his horse and rode off. رِكَب حصانَه وَراح [rikab ħṣa:nah wra:ħ] • **2.** صِعَد [ṣiʕad] صُعُود [ṣuʕu:d] *vn:* اِنصِعَد [ʔinṣiʕad] *p:* طِلَع [ṭilaʕ] طُلُوع [ṭulu:ʕ] *vn:* اِنطِلَع [ʔinṭilaʕ] *p:* They mounted the steps slowly. صِعدَوا الدَّرَج يَواش يَواش [ṣiʕdaw ʔiddaraǰ yawa:š yawa:š] • **3.** نِصَب [niṣab] نَصُب [naṣub] *vn:* اِنّصَب [ʔinniṣab] *p:* رَكَّب [rakkab] تَركِيب [tarki:b] *vn:* ترَكَّب [trakkab] *p:* The machine will be mounted on concrete blocks. المَكِينَة راح تِنُّصُب عَلَى قَوالِب كُنكرِيت [ʔilmaki:na ra:ħ tinnuṣub ʕala qawa:lib kunkiri:t] I'd like to have this picture mounted and framed. أَرِيد هَالصُّورَة تِترَكَّب وَتِتكَركَب [ʔari:d haṣṣu:ra titrakkab wtitčarčab] Can you mount this stone in a ring for me? تِقدَر ترَكُّب هَالحَجَر بِمَحبَس إِلِيّا؟ [tigdar trakkub halħaǰar bimaħbas ʔilayya?]

mountain • **1.** جِبَل [ǰibal] جبال [ǰiba:l] *pl:* How high is the mountain? شقَدّ عُلو ذاك الجِّبَل؟ [šgadd ʕulw ða:k ʔiǰǰibal?] We're going to spend a month in the mountains. راح نِقضِي شَهَر بِالجبال [ra:ħ nigð̣i šahar biǰǰiba:l]

*** Don't make a mountain out of a molehill.**

• **1.** لا تسَوِّي من الحَبَّة قُبَّة [la: tsawwi min ʔilħabba gubba]

mountainous • **1.** جَبَلِي [ǰabali]

mounted police • **1.** شُرطِي خَيّال [šurṭi xayya:l] شُرطَة خَيّالَة [šurṭa xayya:la] *pl:* He's a member of the mounted police corps. هُوَّ بسِلك الشُّرطَة الخَيّالَة [huwwa bsilk ʔiššurṭa ʔilxayya:la]

to mourn • **1.** بِكَى عَلَي [biča: ʕala] بَكِي [bačy] *vn: sv* i. The widow is still mourning the death of her husband ten years ago. الأَرمَلَة بَعَدها تِبكِي عَلَى زوجها اللِّي مات قَبِل عَشِر سنِين [ʔilʔarmala baʕadha tibči ʕala zu:ǰha ʔilma:t gabul ʕašir sni:n]

mourning • **1.** عزا [ʕaza] عَزايات، عِزيات [ʕaza:ya:t, ʕizya:t] *pl:* The mourning period is seven days. مُدَّة عزا سَبعَة أَيّام [muddat ʔilʕaza sabʕa ʔayya:m]

in mourning • **1.** مِتعَزِّي [mitʕazzi] مِتعَزِّين [mitʕazzi:n] *pl:* مِتعَزّايَة [mitʕazza:ya] *Feminine:* She's in mourning because of her brother's death. هِيَّ مِتعَزّايَة بِسَبَب موت أَخُوها [hiyya mitʕazza:ya bsabab mu:t ʔaxu:ha]

mouse • **1.** فارَة [fa:ra] فارات، فِيران [fa:ra:t, fi:ra:n] *pl:* فار [fa:r] *Collective*

mouth • **1.** حَلِق [ħalig] حلُوق [ħlu:g] *pl:* I've got a bad taste in my mouth. حَلقِي طَعمَه مُو طَيِّب [ħalgi ṭaʕmah mu: ṭayyib] The story passed from mouth to mouth. الحكايَة اِنتِقلَت مِن حَلِق لِحَلِق [ʔilħča:ya ʔintiqlat min ħalig liħalig] • **2.** مَصَبّ [maṣabb] مَصَبّات [maṣabba:t] *pl:* Qurna is at the mouth of the Shatt al-Arab. القُرنَة صايرَة عَلَى مَصَبّ شَطّ العَرَب [ʔilqurna ṣa:yra ʕala maṣabb šaṭṭ ʔilʕarab] • **3.** مَدخَل [madxal] مَداخِل [mada:xil] *pl:* باب [ba:b] أَبواب، بِيبان [ʔabwa:b, bi:ba:n] *pl:* The dog stopped at the mouth of the cave. الكَلب وُقَف بِباب الكَهف [ʔiččalib wugaf biba:b ʔilkahif]

*** They live from hand to mouth.**
• **1.** دُوب يقدرُون يسِدُّون رَمَقهُم [du:b ygidru:n ysiddu:n ramaqhum]

*** Don't look a gift horse in the mouth.**
• **1.** لَا تِعتِرِض عالهَدِيَّة شمَا كان نَوُعها [la: tiʕtirið ʕalhadiyya šma ča:n nawuʕha] / الهَدِيَّة مُو بثَمِنها [ʔilhadiyya mu: bθaminha]

mouth wash • **1.** غَسِيل حَلِق [ɣasi:l ħalig]

move • **1.** حَرَكَة [ħaraka] Every move I make hurts. كُلّ حَرَكَة أسَوِّيها تأذِّيني [kull ħaraka ʔasawwi:ha tʔaðði:ni] • **2.** دَور [dawr, du:r] أدوار [ʔadwa:r] *pl:* It's your move. هَسَّة دُورَك [hassa du:rak] It's your move. إلَك اللِّعَب [ʔilak ʔilliʕab] • **3.** خَطوَة [xaṭwa] خَطوات [xaṭwa:t] *pl:* He can't make a move without asking his wife. ما يِقدَر يخطِي خَطوَة بلَيّا ما يقُول لمَرتَه [ma: yigdar yixṭi xaṭwa blayya ma: ygu:l lmartah]

to be on the move • **1.** رِحَل [riħal] رَحِيل [raħi:l] *vn: sv* a. The Bedouins are always on the move. البَدو دائماً يِرحلُون [ʔilbadw da:ʔiman yirħalu:n] • **2.** تنَقَّل [tnaqqal] تَنَقُّل [tanaqqul] *vn: sv* a. He never lives in one town for long; he's always on the move. ما يِثبِت فَدّ ولايَة، عَلَى طُول يِتنَقَّل [ma: yiθbit fadd wla:ya, ʕala ṭu:l yitnaqqal]

*** My boy can't sit still; he's always on the move.**
• **1.** إبني ما يُقعُد راحَة عَبالَك ماكُوك [ʔibni ma: yugʕud raːħa ʕaba:lak ma:ku:k]

to move • **1.** حَرَّك [ħarrak] تَحرِيك، تحِرِّك [taħri:k, tħirrik] *vn:* تحَرَّك [tħarrak] *p:* She can't move her foot. ما تِقدَر تحَرِّك رِجِلها [ma: tigdar tħarrik riǰilha] You'll have to move your car. لازِم تحَرِّك سَيّارتَك [la:zim tħarrik sayya:rtak] • **2.** تحَرَّك [tħarrak] تَحَرُّك [taħarruk] *vn: sv* a. I can't move. ما أقدَر أتحَرَّك [ma: ʔagdar ʔatħarrak] Don't move, or I'll shoot. لا تِتحَرَّك، تَرَة أرمِيك [la: titħarrak, tara ʔarmi:k] • **3.** اِنتِقَل [ʔintiqal] اِنتِقال [ʔintiqa:l] *vn: sv* i. تحَوَّل [tħawwal] تَحَوُّل [taħawwul] *vn: sv* a. Do you know where they are moving to? تُعرُف لوَين دَيِنتَقلُون؟ [tuʕruf lwi:n dayintaqlu:n?] • **4.** اِقتِرَح [ʔiqtiraħ] اِقتِراح [ʔiqtira:ħ] *vn: sv* i. I move we adjourn the session. آني أقتِرِح نأجِّل الجَّلسَة [ʔa:ni ʔaqtiriħ nʔaǰǰil ʔiǰǰalsa] • **5.** أثار [ʔaθa:r] إثارَة [ʔiθa:ra] *vn: sv* i. She moved me with her tears. أثارَت حَناني بِدمُوعها [ʔaθa:rat ħana:ni bidimu:ʕha] • **6.** لِعَب [liʕab] لَعِب [laʕib] *vn: sv* a. It's your play. I just moved. هَذا دُورَك آني هَسَّة لِعَبِت [ha:ða du:rak ʔa:ni hassa liʕabit] • **7.** قِلَب [gilab] قَلُب [galub] *vn:* اِنقِلَب [ʔingilab] *p:* We moved heaven and earth to get it. قلَبنا الدِّنيا حَتَّى قِدَرنا نحَصِّلها [glabna ʔiddinya ħatta gidarna nħaṣṣilha]

*** They move in the best circles.**
• **1.** مِتَّصلِين بأحسَن جَماعات [mittaṣli:n bʔaħsan ǰama:ʕa:t]

*** I was moved to tears.** • **1.** بِكَيت مِن التَأثُّر [biči:t min ʔittaʔaθθur]

to move along • **1.** مِشَى [miša:] مَشِي [maši] *vn: sv* i. تحَرَّك [tħarrak] تَحَرُّك [taħarruk] *vn: sv* a. Things are finally moving along now. الأمُور أخِيراً بِدَت تِمشِي شوَيَّة [ʔilʔumu:r ʔaxi:ran bidat timši šwayya]

to move away • **1.** اِنتِقَل [ʔintiqal] اِنتِقال [ʔintiqa:l] *vn: sv* i. تحَوَّل [tħawwal] تَحَوُّل [taħawwul] *vn: sv* a. They moved away a long time ago. صارِلهُم هوايَة مِن اِنتِقلَوا مِن هنا [ṣa:rilhum hwa:ya min ʔintiqlaw minhna] They moved away a long time ago. تحَوّلَوا مِن زَمان [tħawwlaw min zama:n] • **2.** وَخَّر [waxxar] توَخِّر [twixxir] *vn:* توَخَّر [twaxxar] *p:* Move the table away, please. وَخِّر الميز، مِن فَضلَك [waxxir ʔilmi:z, min faðlak]

to move on • **1.** مِشَى [miša:] مَشِي [mašy] *vn: sv* i. تحَرَّك [tħarrak] *sv* a. Move on! يَالله، اِمشِي [yallah, ʔimši]

to be moved • **1.** تأثَّر [tʔaθθar] تَأثُّر [taʔθθur] *vn: sv* a. I was deeply moved. تأثَّرت كُلِّش [tʔaθθarit kulliš] I was deeply moved. اِنكِسَر خاطري كُلِّش [ʔinkisar xa:ṭri kulliš]

movement • **1.** حَرَكَة [ħaraka] They watched his movements closely. راقبَوا حَرَكاتَه بدِقَّة [ra:qbaw ħaraka:tah bdiqqa] He never belonged to any political movement. ما انتِمَى بأي حَرَكَة سِياسِيَّة [ma: ʔintima:bʔayy ħaraka siya:siyya] • **2.** فَصِل [faṣil] That theme is from the second movement of the Fifth Symphony. هَاللَّحِن مِن الفَصِل الثّاني مِن السِّمفُونِيَّة الخامسَة [hallaħin min ʔillfaṣil ʔiθθa:ni min ʔissimfu:niyya ʔilxa:misa] • **3.** مَكِينَة [maki:na] مَكايِن [maka:yin] *pl:* I checked your watch; the movement is dirty. فُحَصِت ساعتَك؛ المَكِينَة وَسخَة [fuħaṣit sa:ʕtak; ʔilmaki:na wasxa]

movie • **1.** فِلِم [filim] أفلام [ʔafla:m] *pl:* Is there a good movie playing tonight? أكُو فِلِم زين دَيِشتُغُل هاللّيلَة؟ [ʔaku filim zi:n dayištuɣul hallayla?]

movies • **1.** سِينَما [sinama] سِينَمات [sinama:ha:t] *pl:* We rarely go to the movies. إحنا نادِراً نرُوح لِلسِّينَما [ʔiħna na:diran nru:ħ lissinama]

to mow • **1.** قَصّ [gaṣṣ] قَصّ [gaṣṣ] *vn:* اِنقَصّ [ʔingaṣṣ] *p:* I'm mowing the lawn. دَأقُصّ الثَّيِّل [daʔaguṣṣ ʔiθθayyil]

Mr. • **1.** سَيِّد [sayyid] سادَة [sa:da] *pl:* Could I speak to Mr. Mounir? أقدَر أكَلِّم السَّيِّد مُنير؟ [ʔagdar ʔakallim ʔissayyid muni:r?]

Mrs. • **1.** سَيِّدَة [sayyida] سَيِّدات [sayyida:t] *pl:* Address the letter to Mrs. Ali Sheesh. عَنوِن الرِّسالَة إلَى السَّيِّدَة عَلِي شِيش [ʕanwin ʔirrisa:la ʔila ʔissayyida ʕali ši:š]

much • **1.** هوايَة [hwa:ya] كِثِير [kiθi:r, čiθi:r] I haven't much time. ما عِندِي هوايَة وَقت [ma: ʕindi hwa:ya wakit] I feel much better today. أشعُر هوايَة أحسَن هَاليُوم [ʔašʕur hwa:ya ʔaħsan halyu:m]

M

how much • **1.** شقَدّ [šgadd] How much will it cost me? شقَدّ راح تكَلّفني؟ [šgadd ra:ħ tkallifni?] How much will it cost me? بيش راح تصير عَلَيّا؟ [biyš ra:ħ tṣi:r ʕalayya?]

that much • **1.** هَالمِقدار [halmiqda:r] I think that much will be enough for you. أعتِقِد هالمِقدار يكَفّيك [ʔaʕtiqid halmiqda:r ykaffi:k] • **2.** هَالقَدّ [halgadd] I didn't know you liked it that much. ما كِنِت أدري تحَبّه هَالقَدّ [ma: činit ʔadri tħabbah halgadd] I can tell you that much. أقدَر أقُلّك هَالقَدّ [ʔagdar ʔagullak halgadd]

very much • **1.** كُلِّش هوايَة [kulliš hwa:ya] جِدّاً [ǰiddan] جَزيل [ǰazi:l] We didn't like it very much. ما عِجبَتنا كُلِّش هوايَة [ma: ʕiǰbatna kulliš hwa:ya] Thank you very much. شُكراً جَزيلاً [šukran ǰazi:lan] Thank you very much. أشكُرَك جِدّاً [ʔaškurak ǰiddan]

mucus • **1.** مخاط [mxa:ṭ] • **2.** بَلغَم [balɣam]

mucus membrane • **1.** غِشاء مُخاطي [ɣiša:ʔ muxa:ṭi] أغشِيَة مُخاطِيَّة [ʔaɣšiya muxa:ṭiyya] *pl:*

mud • **1.** طين [ṭi:n] وَحَل [waħal] وُحول، أوحال [wuħu:l, ʔawħa:l] *pl:* The car got stuck in the mud. السَّيّارَة عِصَت بِالطّين [ʔissayya:ra ʕiṣat bitṭi:n]

M

muddy • **1.** مطَيِّن [mṭayyin] موَحَّل [mwaħħal] Your shoes are muddy. قُندَرتَك مطَيّنَة [qundartak mṭayyna] • **2.** خابُط [xa:buṭ] This water is muddy. هالماي خابُط [halma:y xa:buṭ]

muggy • **1.** وَخِم [waxim] It's awfully muggy today. الدِّنيا كُلِّش وَخمَة اليُوم [ʔiddinya kulliš waxma ʔilyu:m]

mule • **1.** بَغَل [baɣal] بغال، بغُولَة [bɣa:l, bɣu:la] *pl:*

multiplication table • **1.** جَدوَل الضَرب [ǰadwal ʔiḍḍarb] جَداوِل الضَرب [ǰada:wil ʔiḍḍarb] *pl:*

to multiply • **1.** ضِرَب [ḍirab] ضَرُب [ḍarub] *vn:* اِنضِرَب [ʔinḍirab] *p:* Multiply three by four! أضرُب ثلاثَة بأربَعَة [ʔuḍrub tla:θa biʔarbaʕa] • **2.** تكاثَر [tka:θar] تَكاثُر [taka:θur] *vn: sv* a. Rabbits multiply quickly. الأرانِب تِتكاثَر بِسُرعَة [ʔilʔara:nib titka:θar bsurʕa]

to mumble • **1.** تَمتَم [tamtam] تِّمتِم، تَمتَمَة [ttimtim, tamtama] *vn: sv* i. He is always mumbling. هُوَّ عَلَى طُول دَيتَمتِم [huwwa ʕala ṭu:l daytamtim]

mumps • **1.** نُكاف [nuka:f]

municipal • **1.** بَلَدي [baladi]

municipality • **1.** بَلَدِيَّة [baladiyya]

murder • **1.** حادِث قَتِل [ħa:diθ qatil] حَوادِث قَتِل [ħawa:diθ qatil] *pl:* The murder was not discovered until a few days later. حادِث القَتِل ما اِنكِشَف إلّا بَعَد مُرُور عِدَّة أيّام [ħa:diθ ʔilqatil ma: ʔinkišaf ʔilla baʕad muru:r ʕiddat ʔayya:m]

to murder • **1.** قِتَل [kital] قَتِل [katil] *vn:* اِنقِتَل [ʔinkital] *p:* He was accused of having murdered his wife. هُوَّ اِنتِهَم بِقَتِل مَرتَه [huwwa ʔintiham bikatil martah] • **2.** لاص [la:ṣ] لَوص [lawṣ] *vn:* اِنلاص [ʔinla:ṣ] *p:* She murdered that song. لاصَت هَالغِنيَّة [la:ṣat halɣiniyya]

murderer • **1.** قاتِل [qa:til] قاتِلين، قَتَلَة [qa:tili:n, qatala] *pl:*

muscle • **1.** عَضَلَة [ʕaḍala] عَضَلات [ʕaḍala:t] *pl:* All my muscles hurt. عَضَلاتي كُلّها تُوجَعني [ʕaḍala:ti kullha tu:ǰaʕni]

museum • **1.** مَتحَف [matħaf] مَتاحِف [mata:ħif] *pl:* I've seen the museum. آني شايفَه لِلمَتحَف [ʔa:ni ša:yfah lilmatħaf]

mushroom • **1.** فطِرَّة [fṭirra] فطِرّات [fṭirra:t] *pl:* فطِرّ [fṭirr] *Collective:* Are these mushrooms poisonous? هَالفطِرّ سامّ؟ [halʔifṭirr sa:mm?]

music • **1.** مَوسيقَى [musi:qa] Where's the music coming from? منين دَتجي هَالمُوسيقَى؟ [mni:n datiǰi halmusi:qa?] • **2.** نَوطَة [nu:ṭa] نَوطات [nu:ṭa:t] *pl:* I didn't bring my music with me. ما جِبِت النَّوطَة مالتي ويّايا [ma: ǰibit ʔinnu:ṭa ma:lti wiyya:ya]

musical • **1.** مَوسيقي [musi:qi]

musical instrument • **1.** آلَة مَوسيقِيَّة [ʔa:la musi:qiyya] آلات مَوسيقِيَّة [ʔa:la:t musi:qiyya] *pl:* Do you play any musical instrument? إنتَ تدُقّ فَدّ آلَة مَوسيقِيَّة؟ [ʔinta ddugg fadd ʔa:la musi:qiyya?]

musician • **1.** مُوسيقار [musiqa:r] مُوسيقارِيَّة [musiqa:riyya] *pl:*

must • **1.** لُزُوم [luzu:m, lizu:m] There is no such thing as must. ماكُو فَدّ شي إسمَه لِزُوم [ma:ku fadd ši ʔismah lizu:m] • **2.** لازِم [la:zim] He must be sick. هُوَّ لازِم مَريض [huwwa la:zim mari:ḍ] You must never forget that. لازِم أبَد ما تِنسَى [la:zim ʔabad ma: tinsa:] You must never forget that. ما لازِم تِنسَى هَذا أبَداً [ma: la:zim tinsa: ha:ða ʔabadan] • **3.** واجِب عَلَى [wa:ǰib ʕala] You must pray five times a day. واجِب عَلَيك تصَلّي خَمِس مَرّات بِاليُوم [wa:ǰib ʕali:k tṣalli xamis marra:t bilyu:m]

mustache • **1.** شارِب [ša:rib] شوارُب [šwa:rub] *pl:*

mustard • **1.** خَردَل [xardal]

to mutilate • **1.** شَوَّه [šawwah] تَشوِيه [tašwi:h] *vn:* تشَوَّه [tšawwah] *p:* The machine mutilated his hand. المَكِينَة شَوّهَت إيدَه [ʔilmaki:na šawwhat ʔi:dah] The police found the body badly mutilated. الشُرطَة لِقَوا الجُثَّة مُشَوَّهَة كُلِّش [ʔiššurṭa ligaw ʔijjuθθa mušawwaha kulliš]

mutiny • **1.** عِصيان [ʕiṣya:n] عِصيانات [ʕiṣya:na:t] *pl:*

to mutter • **1.** تَمتَم [tamtam] تِّمتِم، تَمتَمَة [ttimtim, tamtama] *vn: sv* i. He muttered something to himself. تَمتَم بِفَدّ شِي بَينَه وَبَين نَفسَه [tamtam bfadd ši baynah wbayn nafsah]

mutton • **1.** لَحَم غَنَم [laħam ɣanam]

mutual • **1.** مُتَبادَل [mutaba:dal] This treaty provides for mutual aid in case of war. هَالمُعاهَدَة تنُصّ عَلَى فَدّ تَعاوُن مُتَبادَل بحالَة الحَرب [halmuʕa:hada tnuṣṣ ʕala fadd taʕa:wun mutaba:dal bħa:lat ʔilħarb] • **2.** مُشتَرَك [muštarak] The two prime ministers issued a mutual statement. رَئِيسَيّ الوُزَراء طَلّعَوا بَيان مُشتَرَك [raʔi:say ʔilwuzara:ʔ ṭallʕaw baya:n muštarak]

*** He's a mutual friend of ours.** • **1.** هُوَّ صَدِيق الطَرَفَين [huwwa ṣadi:q ʔiṭṭarafayn] / هُوَّ صَدِيقنا ثنينّا [huwwa ṣadi:qna θnaynna]

muzzle • **1.** كَمّامَة [kamma:ma] كَمّامات [kamma:ma:t] *pl:* Dogs are not allowed on the street without muzzles. مَمنُوع تَرك الكِلاب بِالشّارِع بِلا كَمّامات [mamnu:ʕ tark ʔiččila:b bišša:riʕ bila kamma:ma:t] • **2.** فوهَة [fawha] فوهات [fawha:t] *pl:* Don't point the muzzle of the gun at anyone. لا تنَيشِن فوهَة البُندُقِيَّة عَلَى أَحَّد [la: tni:šin fawhat ʔilbunduqiyya ʕala ʔaħħad]

to muzzle • **1.** كَمَّم [kammam] تَكمِيم [takmi:m] *vn:* تكَمَّم [tkammam] *p:* That dog ought to be muzzled. هَالكَلِب لازِم يتكَمَّم [haččalib la:zim yitkammam] The press is muzzled. أَفواه الصُحُف مكَمِّمَة [ʔafwa:h ʔiṣṣuħuf mkammima]

mysterious • **1.** غامِض [ɣa:miḍ] مُبهَم [mubham]

mystery • **1.** لُغُز [luɣuz] أَلغاز [ʔalɣa:z] *pl:* How they stole it is still a mystery. شلُون باقُوه لهَسَّة لُغُز [šlu:n ba:gu:h lhassa luɣiz] • **2.** غُمُوض [ɣumu:ḍ] The meeting is surrounded with mystery. الاجتِماع مُحاط بِالغُمُوض [ʔilʔijtima:ʕ muħa:ṭ bilɣumu:ḍ]

mystery story • **1.** قُصَّة بَولِيسِيَّة [quṣṣa bu:li:siyya] قُصَص بَولِيسِيَّة [quṣaṣ bu:li:siyya] *pl:* I like to read mystery stories. يعجِبنِي أَقرا قُصَص بُولِيسِيَّة [yiʕjibni ʔaqra: quṣaṣ pu:li:siyya]

M

N

nag • **1.** كِدِيش [kidi:š] كِدَّش، كِدشان [kiddaš, kidša:n] *pl:* He put all his money on that nag. خَلّى كُلّ فلوسَه بِهالكِدِيش [xalla: kull flu:sah bihalkidi:š] • **2.** نِقناقِيَّة [niqna:qiyya] نِقناقِيّات [niqna:qiyya:t] *pl:* His wife's a real nag. مَرتَه نِقناقِيَّة تَمام [martah niqna:qiyya tama:m]

to nag • **1.** نَقنَق [naqnaq, nagnag] تِنقنِق [tniqniq] *vn: sv* i. Her husband got sick of her nagging. زَوجها ضاج مِن تِنِقنِيقها [zawiǰha ḍa:ǰ min tniqni:qha]

nail • **1.** بِسمار [bisma:r] بسامِير [bsa:mi:r] *pl:* Don't hammer the nail in too far. لا تدُقّ البِسمار كُلِّش زايد [la: ddugg ʔilbisma:r kulliš za:yid] • **2.** إظفُر [ʔiðfur] أظافِير، أظافِر [ʔaða:fi:r, ʔaða:fir] *pl:* She painted her nails red. صُبغَت أظافِرها بأحمَر [ṣubɣat ʔaða:firha bʔaħmar]

*** You hit the nail on the head.** • **1.** جِبتها بمُكانها [ǰibitha bmuka:nha]

to nail • **1.** بَسمَر [basmar] تبِسمِر [tbismir] *vn:* تبَسمَر [tbasmar] *p:* Please nail the board to the wall. مِن فَضلَك بَسمِر الخِشبَة بِالحايِط [min faðlak basmir ʔilxišba bilħa:yiṭ]

*** It's difficult to nail him down to anything.** • **1.** ما يِنطِي لَزمَة [ma: yinṭi lazma]

naked • **1.** مسَلَّخ [msallax] مسالِيخ [msa:li:x] *pl:* عَريان [ʕarya:n] عَريانِين، عرايا [ʕarya:ni:n, ʕra:ya] *pl:* They took a picture of their son naked. أخذوا صُورَة طِفلهُم مسَلَّخ [ʔaxðaw ṣu:rat ṭifilhum msallax] • **2.** مُجَرَّد [muǰarrad] You can see the satellite with the naked eye. تِقدَر تشُوف القَمَر الاصطِناعِي بِالعَين المُجَرَّدَة [tigdar tšu:f ʔilqamar ʔilʔiṣṭina:ʕi bilʕayn ʔilmuǰarrada]

name • **1.** إسِم [ʔisim] أسامِي، أسماء [ʔasa:mi, ʔasma:ʔ] *pl:* I've heard of his name before. آنِي سامِع بإسمَه قَبُل [ʔa:ni sa:miʕ bʔismah gabul] Please give me your full name; your first name, your father's first name and your family name. أرجُوك إنطِينِي إسمَك الكامِل، إسمَك، إسم أبُوك، وَلَقَبَك [ʔarǰu:k ʔinṭi:ni ʔismak ʔilka:mil, ʔismak, ʔism ʔabu:k, walaqabak] • **2.** شُهرَة [šuhra] إسِم [ʔisim] أسماء [ʔasma:ʔ] *pl:* أسامِي [ʔasa:mi] سُمعَة [sumʕa] He made a good name for himself in industry. سَوّالَه خُوش إسِم بِالصِّناعَة [sawwa:lah xu:š ʔisim bišṣina:ʕa]

to name • **1.** سَمَّى [samma:] تَسمِيَة، تسِمِّي [tasmiya, tsimmi] *vn:* تسَمَّى [tsamma:] *p:* They named their son Ali Sheesh. سَمَّوا إبنهُم عَلِي شِيش [sammaw ʔibinhum ʕali ši:š] • **2.** عَدّ [ʕadd] عَدّ [ʕadd] *vn:* اِنعَدّ [ʔinʕadd] *p:* Can you name all the planets? تِقدَر تعِدّ كُلّ الكَواكِب السَّيّارَة؟ [tigdar tʕidd kull ʔilkawa:kib ʔissayya:ra?] • **3.** عَيَّن [ʕayyan] تَعيِين [taʕyi:n] *vn:* تعَيَّن [tʕayyan] *p:* The president named his ministry yesterday. الرَّئِيس عَيَّن وِزارتَه البارحَة [ʔirraʔi:s ʕayyan wiza:rtah ʔilba:rħa]

namely • **1.** وهُوَّ [whuwwa] وهِيَّ [whiyya] يَعنِي [yaʕni] I have only one wish, namely, that we leave soon. عِندِي رَغبَة وِحدَة، وهِيَّ نرُوح قَرِيباً [ʕindi raɣba wiħda, whiyya nru:ħ qari:ban]

nap • **1.** غَفوَة [ɣafwa] غَفوات [ɣafwa:t, ɣaffa] *pl:* I took a short nap after lunch. أخَذِت غَفوَة صغَيّرَة بَعَد الغدا [ʔaxaðit ɣafwa ṣɣayyra baʕad ʔilɣada] • **2.** خَملَة [xamla] The nap's all worn off this rug. الخَملَة كُلها مَحكُوكَة مِن هَالزُّولِيَّة [ʔilxamla kullha maħku:ka min hazzu:liyya]

to nap • **1.** غُفَى [ɣufa:] غَفُو [ɣafw] *vn: sv* i. The baby napped all afternoon. الطِّفِل غُفَى طُول العَصِر [ʔiṭṭifil ɣufa: ṭu:l ʔilʕaṣir]

*** The inspectors caught us napping.** • **1.** المُفَتِّشِين لِزمَونا عَلَى غَفلَة [ʔilmufattiši:n lizmu:na ʕala ɣafla]

napkin • **1.** كَفِّيَّة [čaffiyya] كفافِي [čfa:fi] *pl:*

narcotics • **1.** مُخَدِّرات [muxaddira:t]

narghile • **1.** أركِيلَة، نَركِيلَة [ʔargi:la, nargi:la] أركِيلات، أراكِيل نَركِيلات، نَراكِيل [ʔargi:la:t, ʔara:gi:l, nargi:la:t, nara:gi:l] *pl:* غَرشَة [ɣarša] غَرشات، غراش [ɣarša:t, ɣra:š] *pl:*

narrow • **1.** ضَيِّق [ðayyig] This is a narrow street. هَذا شارِع ضَيِّق [ha:ða ša:riʕ ðayyig] His opinions on education are very narrow. آرائَه بِالتَّعلِيم كُلِّش ضَيقَة [ʔa:ra:ʔah bittaʕli:m kulliš ðayyga] • **2.** ضَيِّق [ðayyig] قَلِيل [qali:l] Our company's margin of profit is very narrow. مَجال رِبح شَرِكتنا كُلِّش ضَيِّق [maǰa:l ribiħ šarikatna kulliš ðayyiq]

*** I had a narrow escape.** • **1.** نجَيت بقِيد شَعرَة مِنها [nǰi:t bqi:d šaʕra minha] / خلَصِت بإعجُوبَة [xlaṣit bʔiʕǰu:ba]

narrows • **1.** مَضِيق [maði:q] مَضايِق [maða:yiq] *pl:* We watched the ship pass through the narrows. شِفنا الباخِرَة تمُرّ بِالمَضِيق [šifna ʔilba:xira tmurr bilmaði:q]

to narrow • **1.** ضاق [ða:g] ضِيق [ði:q] *vn: sv* i. The road narrows a mile from here. الطَّرِيق يضِيق مَسافَة مِيل مِن هنا [ʔiṭṭari:q yði:q masa:fat mi:l min hna] • **2.** ضَيَّق [ðayyaq] تَضيِيق، تضِيِّق [taðyi:q, tðiyyiq] *vn:* تضَيَّق [tðayyaq] *p:* The government is narrowing the road instead of widening it. الحُكُومَة دَتضَيِّق الطَّرِيق بَدَل تَوَسِّعَه [ʔilħuku:ma dadðayyiq ʔiṭṭari:q badalma: twassiʕah]

to narrow down • **1.** حِصَر [ħiṣar] حَصِر [ħaṣir] *vn:* اِنحِصَر [ʔinħiṣar] *p:* We narrowed down the suspicion to three men. حصَرنا التُّهمَة بثلَث رياجيل [ħṣarna ʔittuhma btlaθ riyaːǰiːl]

nasty • **1.** قَبِيح [qabiːħ] Spitting on the floor is a nasty habit. التِّفِل عَالقاع عادَة قبِيحَة [ʔittafil ʕalgaːʕ ʕaːda qabiːħa] • **2.** مَلعُون [malʕuːn] قَبِيح [qabiːħ] Don't be so nasty! لا تصِير هَالقَدّ مَلعُون [laː tṣiːr halgadd malʕuːn] • **3.** كَسِيف [kasiːf] London has nasty weather. لَندَن بيها جَوّ كَسِيف [landan biːha ǰaww kasiːf]

nation • **1.** بَلَد [balad] بِلاد [bilaːd] *pl:* أُمَّة [ʔumma] أُمَم [ʔumam] *pl:* The entire nation mourned his death. البَلَد كُلّه حِزنَوا عَلَى موتَه [ʔilbalad kullah ħiznaw ʕala mawtah]

national • **1.** وَطَنِي [waṭani] Can you sing the national anthem? تِقدَر تِقرا النَّشِيد الوَطَنِي؟ [tigdar tiqraː ʔinnašiːd ʔilwaṭani?] • **2.** مُواطِن [muwaːṭin] مُواطِنِين [muwaːṭiniːn] *pl:* We hired four Egyptian nationals. شَغَّلنا أَربَع مُواطِنِين مَصرِيِّين [šaɣɣalna ʔarbaʕ muwaːṭiniːn maṣriyyiːn]

nationalism • **1.** قَومِيَّة [qawmiyya] He gave a speech on Arab nationalism. أَلقَى خِطاب عَن القَومِيَّة العَرَبِيَّة [ʔalqaː xiṭaːb ʕan ʔilqawmiyya ʔilʕarabiyya] • **2.** وَطَنِيَّة [waṭaniyya] He's one of the advocates of Iraqi nationalism. هُوَّ واحِد مِن المُناصِرِين لِلوَطَنِيَّة العِراقِيَّة [huwwa waːħid min ʔilmunaːṣiriːn lilwaṭaniyya ʔilʕiraːqiyya]

nationality • **1.** جِنسِيَّة [ǰinsiyya] جِنسِيّات، [ǰinsiyyaːt] *pl:*

native • **1.** أَهَل [ʔahal] أَهالِي [ʔahaːli] *pl:* The natives of the island were very nice. أَهالِي الجَّزِيرَة كانَوا كُلِّش طَيّبِين [ʔahaːli ʔiǰǰaziːra čaːnaw kulliš ṭayybiːn] He's a native of Najaf. هُوَّ مِن أَهل النَّجَف [huwwa min ʔahl ʔinnaǰaf] He's a native of Najaf. هُوَّ نَجَفِي [huwwa naǰafi] • **2.** أَصلِي [ʔaṣli] His native language is Arabic. لُغتَه الأَصلِيَّة عَرَبِيَّة [luɣatah ʔilʔaṣliyya ʕarabiyya] • **3.** وَطَنِي [waṭani] They attended the festival in their native costumes. حِضرَوا المَهرَجان بِمَلابِسهُم الوَطَنِيَّة [ħiðraw ʔilmahraǰaːn bimalaːbishum ʔilwaṭaniyya]

* **Potatoes are native to America.**

• **1.** البُتَيتَة أَصلها مِن أَمِيركا [ʔlputiːta ʔaṣilha min ʔamriːka]

natural • **1.** طَبِيعِي [ṭabiːʕi] We visited a natural cave south of the town. زرنا فَدّ كَهَف طَبِيعِي جَنُوب البَلدَة [zirna fadd kahaf ṭabiːʕi ǰanuːb ʔilbalda] The fruit in this picture looks natural. الفاكِهَة بِهالصُّورَة تبَيِّن طَبِيعِيَّة [ʔilfaːkiha bihaṣṣuːra tbayyin ṭabiːʕiyya] The use of natural rubber is declining. اِستِعمال المَطّاط الطَّبِيعِي دَيقِلّ [ʔistiʕmaːl ʔilmaṭṭaːṭ ʔiṭṭabiːʕi dayqill]

naturally • **1.** طَبعاً [ṭabʕan] بِالطَّبُع [biṭṭabuʕ] Naturally she's a little afraid. طَبعاً هِيَّ خايفَة شوَيَّة [ṭabʕan hiyya xaːyfa šwayya]

nature • **1.** طَبِيعَة [ṭabiːʕa] طَبايِع [ṭabaːyiʕ] *pl:* My girl friend enjoys the beauty of nature. صَدِيقتِي تِتمَتَّع بجَمال الطَّبِيعَة [ṣadiːqti titmattaʕ bǰamaːl ʔiṭṭabiːʕa] I can't tell you anything about the nature of my work. ما أَقدَر أَقُلَّك أَيّ شِي عَن طَبِيعَة شُغلِي [maː ʔagdar ʔagullak ʔayy ši ʕan ṭabiːʕat šuɣli] • **2.** طَبُع [ṭabuʕ] خُلُق [xulug] طَبِيعَة [ṭabiːʕa] طَبايِع [ṭabaːyiʕ] *pl:* He has a very good nature. عِندَه خُوش طَبُع [ʕindah xuːš ṭabuʕ] • **3.** فِطرَة [fiṭra] He's an artist by nature. هُوَّ فَنّان بالفِطرَة [huwwa fannaːn bilfiṭra] • **4.** قَبِيل [qabiːl] I enjoy doing things of this nature. أَرتاح مِن عَمَل أَشياء مِن هالقَبِيل [ʔartaːħ min ʕamal ʔašyaːʔ min halqabiːl]

nature lover • **1.** عاشِق الطَّبِيعَة [ʕaːšiq ʔiṭṭabiːʕa] عُشّاق الطَّبِيعَة [ʕuššaːq ʔiṭṭabiːʕa] *pl:*

naughty • **1.** وَكِح وَقِح [wakiːħ waqiːħ] وَكِيح وَقِيح [wakiħ waqiħ] You've been very naughty today. كِنِت كُلِّش وَقِيح اليُوم [činit kulliš wakiːħ ʔilyuːm]

nauseated • **1.** *no equivalent* • * I feel nauseated. أَشعُر نَفسِي دَتِلعَب [ʔašʕur nafsi datilʕab]

naval • **1.** بَحرِي [baħri] He studied at the naval academy. دِرَس بِالكُلِّيَّة البَحرِيَّة [diras bilkulliyya ʔilbaħriyya]

navel • **1.** صُرَّة [ṣurra] صُرّات، صُرَر [ṣurraːt, ṣurar] *pl:*

navy blue • **1.** أَزرَق طُوخ [ʔazrag ṭuːx] I bought a navy blue suit. اِشتِرَيت قاط أَزرَق طُوخ [ʔištirayt qaːṭ ʔazrag ṭuːx]

near • **1.** قَرِيب مِن [giriːb min] قَرِيب مِن [qariːb min] بقُرُب [bqurub] The ball landed near us. الطَّوبَة وُقعَت قَرِيب مِنّا [ʔiṭṭuːba wugʕat qariːb minna] That's a little nearer to the truth. هَذا شوَيَّة أَقرَب لِلصِّدُق [haːða šwayya ʔaqrab liṣṣidug]

to near • **1.** قِرَب مِن [qirab, girab min] قُرُب [gurub] *vn:* *sv* a. The semester is nearing its end. الفَصل الدِّراسِي يِقرَب مِن اِنتِهائَه [ʔilfaṣl ʔiddiraːsi yigrab min ʔintihaːʔah] We neared the city about five o'clock. قِرَبنا مِن المَدِينَة حَوالِي السّاعَة خَمسَة [girabna min ʔilmadiːna ħawaːli ʔissaːʕa xamsa]

nearby • **1.** عَن قُرُب [ʕan qurub] The children stood nearby watching the fire. الأَطفال وُقفوا عَن قُرُب يِتفَرِّجُون عالحَرِيق [ʔilʔaṭfaːl wugfaw ʕan qurub yitfarriǰuːn ʕalħariːq]

Near East • **1.** الشَّرق الأَدنَى [ʔiššarq ʔilʔadna]

nearly • **1.** عَلَى وَشَك [ʕala wašak] بِالتَّقرِيب [bittaqriːb] تَقرِيباً [taqriːban] She's nearly twenty years old.

N

عُمرها عَلَى وَشَك تكُون عِشرين سَنَة [ʕumurha ʕala wašak tku:n ʕišri:n sana]

neat • 1. أنِيق [ʔani:q] مهَندَم [mhandam] She always looks very neat. هِيَّ دائِماً تِظهَر كُلَّش أنِيقَة [hiyya da:ʔiman tiðhar kulliš ʔani:qa] **• 2.** نَظِيف [naði:f] He turns out neat work. دَيطَلِّع شُغُل نَظِيف [dayṭalliʕ šuɣul naði:f] **• 3.** مرَتَّب [mrattab] His desk is always neat. مَيزَه دائِماً مرَتَّب [mayzah da:ʔiman mrattab]

necessary • 1. لازِم [la:zim] لُزُوم [luzu:m, lizu:m] He eats more than is necessary. ياكُل أكثَر مِن اللُّزُوم [ya:kul ʔakθar min ʔilluzu:m] **• 2.** ضَرُورِي [ðaru:ri] لازِم [la:zim] I'll stay if it's absolutely necessary. راح أبقَى إذا كُلَّش ضَرُورِي [ra:ħ ʔabqa: ʔiða kulliš ðaru:ri]

necessity • 1. ضَرُورَة [ðaru:ra] ضَرُورات [ðaru:ra:t] *pl:* حاجَة [ħa:ǰa] حاجات، حَوايِج [ħa:ǰa:t, ħawa:yiǰ] *pl:* لُزُوم [luzu:m] There's no necessity for it. ماكُو ضَرُورَة إلها [ma:ku ðaru:ra ʔilha] Necessity is the mother of invention. الحاجَة أمّ الاختِراع [ʔilħa:ǰa ʔumm ʔilʔixtira:ʕ] **• 2.** اِحتِياج [ʔiħtiya:ǰ] اِحتِياجات [ʔiħtiya:ǰa:t] *pl:* My necessities are few. اِحتِياجاتِي قَلِيلَة [ʔiħtiya:ǰa:ti qali:la]

neck • 1. رُقبَة [rugba] رُقَب، رقاب [rugab, rga:b] *pl:* Wrap the scarf around your neck. لِفّ اللَّفّاف عَلَى رُقُبتَك [liff ʔillaffa:f ʕala rugubtak] The bottle has a very narrow neck. البُطِل رُقُبتَه كُلَّش ضَيِّقَة [ʔilbuṭul rugubtah kulliš ðayyga]

necklace • 1. قلادَة [gla:da] قلادات، قلايِد [gla:da:t, gla:yid] *pl:*

neckline • 1. فَتحَة الصَدِر [fatħat ʔiṣṣadir]

necktie • 1. بَوينباغ [bu:yinba:ɣ] بَوينباغات [bu:yinba:ɣa:t] *pl:* بَينباغ [bayinba:ɣ] بَينباغات [bayinba:ɣa:t] *pl:* رِباط [riba:ṭ] أربِطَة [ʔarbiṭa] *pl:*

nectarine • 1. خَوخَة مرَكَّبَة [xawxa mrakkaba] خَوخات مرَكّبَة [xu:xa:t mrakkuba] *pl:* خَوخ مرَكَّب [xawx mrakkab] *Collective*

need • 1. حاجَة [ħa:ǰa] حاجات، حَوايِج [ħa:ǰa:t, ħawa:yiǰ] *pl:* اِحتِياج [ʔiħtiya:ǰ] اِحتِياجات [ʔiħtiya:ǰa:t] *pl:* There is a need for a better hospital here. أكُو حاجَة إلَى مُستَشفى أحسَن هنا [ʔaku ħa:ǰa ʔila mustašfa: ʔaħsan hna] **• 2.** ضِيق [ði:q] You're certainly a friend in need. إنتَ حَقِيقَةً صَدِيق عِند الضِّيق [ʔinta ħaqi:qatan ṣadi:q ʕind ʔiðði:q]

needs • 1. مُتَطَلَّبات [mutaṭallaba:t] حاجَة [ħa:ǰa] حاجات، حَوايِج [ħa:ǰa:t, ħawa:yiǰ] *pl:* اِحتِياج [ʔiħtiya:ǰ] My salary just covers our needs. راتبِي يكَفِّي مُتَطَلَّباتنا بَسّ [ra:tbi ykaffi mutaṭalliba:tna bass]

if need be • 1. إذا اِقتِضَت الحاجَة [ʔiða: ʔiqtiðat ʔilħa:ǰa] عِند الحاجَة [ʕind ʔillizu:m] عِند اللِزُوم [ʕind ʔilħa:ǰa] إن لِزَم الحال [ʔin lizam ʔilħa:l] I'll go myself if need be. أرُوح بنَفسِي إذا اِقتِضَت الحاجَة [ʔaru:ħ bnafsi ʔiða ʔiqtiðat ʔilħa:ǰa]

in need of • 1. بحاجَة إلَى [bħa:ǰa ʔila] he's badly in need of a vacation. هُوَّ كُلَّش بحاجَة إلَى عُطلَة [huwwa kulliš bħa:ǰa ʔila ʕuṭla]

to need • 1. اِحتاج [ʔiħta:ǰ] اِحتِياج [ʔiħtiya:ǰ] *vn: sv* a. I need a new coat. أحتاج سِترَة جِدِيدَة [ʔaħta:ǰ sitra ǰidi:da]

*** I need to leave at five o'clock. • 1.** لازِم أرُوح الساعَة خَمسَة [la:zim ʔaru:ħ ʔissa:ʕa xamsa]

needle • 1. أبرَة [ʔubra] أبَر [ʔubar] *pl:* Bring me a needle so I can sew on this button. جِيبلِي فَدّ أبرَة حَتَّى أخَيِّط هَالدُّقمَة [ǰi:bli fadd ʔubra ħatta ʔaxayyiṭ haddugma] The phonograph needle is worn out. أبرَة الفُنُغراف سايفَة [ʔubrat ʔilfunnuɣra:f sa:yfa] **• 2.** مُخيَط [muxyaṭ, mixyaṭ] مَخايِط [maxa:yiṭ] *pl:* The upholsterer uses a curved needle in his work. الدُّوشَمچِي يِستَعمِل مُخيَط مَعوُج بشُغلَه [ʔiddu:šamči yistaʕmil muxyaṭ maʕwu:ǰ bšuɣlah]

needy • 1. مِحتاج [miħta:ǰ] مِحتاجِين [miħta:ǰi:n] *pl:* فَقِير [faqi:r] فُقَراء، فُقرَة [fuqara:ʔ, fuqra] *pl:* He donated money to the needy. تبَرَّع بفلُوس لِلمُحتاجِين [tbarraʕ bflu:s lilmuħta:ǰi:n]

negative • 1. جامَة [ǰa:ma] جامات [ǰa:ma:t] *pl:* Make four prints from this negative. إطبَع أربَع صُوَر عَلَى هَالجّامَة [ʔiṭbaʕ ʔarbaʕ ṣuwar ʕala hajǰa:ma] **• 2.** سالِب [sa:lib] سوَالِب [sawa:lib] *pl:* Hook this wire to the negative terminal of the battery. أربُط هالوايَر بالقُطب السّالِب مال الباترِي [ʔurbuṭ halwa:yar bilquṭb ʔissa:lib ma:l ʔilpa:tri] **• 3.** نَفِي [nafy] Put this sentence in the negative. حَوِّل هَالجُّملَة إلَى النَّفِي [ħawwil hajǰumla ʔila ʔinnafy]

neglect • 1. إهمال [ʔihma:l] They fired him due to his neglect. فِصلوه عَلَى إهمالَه [fiṣlawh ʕala ʔihma:lah]

to neglect • 1. هِمَل [himal] إهمال [ʔihma:l] *vn: sv* i. Don't neglect to water the plants. لا تِهمِل تِسقِي الزَّرِع [la: tihmil tisgi ʔizzariʕ]

to negotiate • 1. تفاوَض عَلَى [tfa:wað ʕala] تَفاوُض [tafa:wuð] *vn: sv* a. They're negotiating the peace treaty. دَيتفاوضُون عَلَى اِتِّفاقِيَّة السَّلام [dayitfa:wðu:n ʕala ʔittifa:qiyyat ʔissala:m]

negotiation • 1. The negotiations lasted a week. المُفاوَضات طَوَّلَت إسبُوع [ʔilmufa:waða:t ṭawwlat ʔisbu:ʕ]

negress • 1. عَبدَة [ʕabda] عَبدات [ʕabda:t] *pl:*

Negro • 1. عَبِد [ʕabid] عَبِيد [ʕabi:d] *pl:*

neighbor • **1.** جار [ǰaːr] جيران [ǰiːraːn] جِيارين، جُوارين [ǰiyaːriːn, ǰuwaːriːn] *pl:* My neighbor visited me this morning. جيرانِي زارنِي الصُّبُح [ǰiːraːni zaːrni ʔiṣṣubuħ]

neighborhood • **1.** جيران [ǰiːraːn] جار [ǰaːr] جيران، جِيارين، جُوارين [ǰiːraːn, ǰiyaːriːn, ǰuwaːriːn] *pl:* The whole neighborhood was there. كُلّ الجِّيران كانَوا هناك [kull ʔiǰǰiːraːn čaːnaw hnaːk] • **2.** طَرَف [ṭaraf] أطراف [ʔaṭraːf] *pl:* مَحَلَّة [maħalla] مَحَلّات [maħallaːt] *pl:* We live in a good neighborhood. نِسكُن بمَحَلَّة زينَة [niskun bmaħalla zayna] We talked for an hour in the neighborhood coffee shop. حِكَينا ساعَة بِقهوَة الطَّرَف [ħičiːna saːʕa bigahwat ʔiṭṭaraf]

in the neighborhood of • **1.** بحُدُود [bħuduːd] Your bill will run in the neighborhood of five hundred dinars. القائمَة مالتَك راح توَصِّل بِحِدُود الخَمِس مِيَّة دِينار [ʔilqaːʔima maːltak raːħ twaṣṣil bħiduːd ʔilxamis miyyat dinaːr]

neighboring • **1.** مُجاوِر [muǰaːwir] The neighboring village was flooded. القَريَة المُجاورَة كانَت غَرقانَة [ʔilqariya ʔilmuǰaːwra čaːnat ɣargaːna]

neither • **1.** وَلا [wala] Neither one of the two was there. وَلا واحِد مِن الإثنَين كان هناك [wala waːħid min ʔilʔiθnayn čaːn hnaːk]

neither ... nor • **1.** لا وَلا [laː. . . wala] This word is neither Turkish nor Persian. هَالكِلمَة لا تُركِيَّة وَلا فارسِيَّة [halčilma laː turkiyya wala faːrsiyya]

nephew • **1.** إبِن أخ [ʔibin ʔax] وُلِد أخ [wulid ʔax] *pl:* • **2.** إبِن أخت [ʔibin ʔuxt] وُلِد أخت [wulid ʔuxt] *pl:*

nerve • **1.** عَصَب [ʕaṣab] أعصاب [ʔaʕṣaːb] *pl:* That noise is getting on my nerves. هَالصَّوت دَيدُق بأعصابِي [haṣṣawt daydugg biʔaʕṣaːbi] Instead of removing the tooth, he deadened the nerves around it. بَدَل ما يِشلَع السِّنّ، قِتَل الأعصاب اللِّي حَولَه [badalma yišlaʕ ʔissinn, kital ʔilʔaʕṣaːb ʔilli ħawlah] • **2.** جَسارَة [ǰasaːra] عين [ʕiːn] عيُون [ʕyuːn] *pl:* You mean you've got the nerve to ask such a question? أمّا عِندَك جَسارَة تِسألنِي هِيك سُؤال [ʔamma ʕindak ǰasaːra tisʔalni hiːč suʔaːl]

nervous • **1.** عَصَبِي [ʕaṣabi] The last few days I've been very nervous. الأيّام الأخِيرَة كِنِت كُلِّش عَصَبِي [ʔilʔayyaːm ʔilʔaxiːra činit kulliš ʕaṣabi] His mother had a nervous breakdown last year. أُمَّها صار عِدها اِنهِيار عَصَبِي السَّنَة اللِّي فاتَت [ʔummaha ṣaːr ʕidha ʔinhiyaːr ʕaṣabi ʔissana ʔilli faːtat]

nest • **1.** عِشّ [ʕišš] عشُوش [ʕšuːš] *pl:*

net • **1.** شِبكَة [šibča] شِبكات [šibčaːt] *pl:* He caught a lot of fish in his net. صاد سِمَك هوايَة بِشِبكتَه [ṣaːd simač hwaːya bišibičtah] He jumped over the tennis net. طُفَر فُوق شَبكَة التَّنِس [ṭufar fuːg šibčat ʔittanis] • **2.** صافِي [ṣaːfi] The net weight is a kilo and a half. الوَزن الصّافِي كِيلُو وَنُصّ [ʔilwazn ʔiṣṣaːfi kiːlu wnuṣṣ]

mosquito net • **1.** كُلَّة [kulla] كُلّات، كُلَل [kullaːt, kulal] *pl:*

to net • **1.** رُبَح [rubaħ] ربح [ribiħ] *vn: sv* a. We netted four hundred dollars. ربَحنا أربَع مِيَّة دُولار [rbaħna ʔarbaʕ miyyat dulaːr]

The Netherlands • **1.** الأراضِي المُنخَفِضَة [ʔilʔaraːði ʔilmunxafiða]

neutral • **1.** مُحايِد [muħaːyid] مُحايِدِين [muħaːyidiːn] *pl:* He prefers to remain a neutral. يفَضِّل يُبقَى مُحايِد [yfaððil yubqaː muħaːyid] • **2.** بَوش [bawš, buːš] He left the car in neutral. خَلَّى السَّيّارَة عالبُوش [xallaː ʔissayyaːra ʕalbuːš] • **3.** حِيادِي [ħiyaːdi] مُحايِد [muħaːyid] He fled to a neutral country. اِنهِزَم إلَى بَلَد حِيادِي [ʔinhizam ʔila balad ħiyaːdi] • **4.** مُتعادِل [mutʕaːdil] He changed the acid into a neutral solution. غَيَّر الحامُض إلَى مَحلُول مُتعادِل [ɣayyar ʔilħaːmuð ʔila maħluːl mutʕaːdil]

neutrality • **1.** حِياد [ħiyaːd] What's your opinion on neutrality? شِنُو هِيَّ فِكرتَك عَن الحِياد؟ [šinu hiyya fikirtak ʕan ʔilħiyaːd?]

never • **1.** أبَداً [ʔabadan] I've never seen Najef. ما شايِف النَّجَف أبَداً [maː šaːyif ʔinnaǰaf ʔabadan] • **2.** أبَداً [ʔabadan] قَطعاً [qaṭʕan] Never do that again. لا تسَوِّي هِيكِي شِي مَرَّة لُخ أبَداً [laː tsawwi hiːči ši marra lux ʔabadan]

*** Never mind, I'll buy you another.** • **1.** لا تدِير بال، راح أشتِرِيلَك واحِد لاخ [laː tdiːr baːl, raːħ ʔaštiriːlak waːħid laːx]

*** Never mind, let it go for now.** • **1.** عِيفها، خَلِّيها هَسَّة [ʕiːfha, xalliːha hassa]

*** Never mind, I'll do it myself.** • **1.** ما يخالِف، أسَوِّيها بنَفسِي [maː yxaːlif, ʔasawwiːha bnafsi]

nevertheless • **1.** مَعَ ذَلِك [maʕa ðaːlik] بِالرَغُم مِن ذَلِك [birraɣum min ðaːlik] Nevertheless, I still can't believe it. مَعَ ذَلِك، آنِي ما مُمكِن أصَدِّق بِيها [maʕa ðaːlik, ʔaːni maː mumkin ʔaṣaddig biːha]

new • **1.** جدِيد [ǰidiːd] Are these shoes new? هالقَنادِر جِدِيدَة؟ [halqanaːdir ǰidiːda?] What's new today? شَكُو شِي جِدِيد اليُوم؟ [šaku ši ǰidiːd ʔilyuːm?] • **2.** تازَة [taːza] جِدِيد [ǰidiːd] Is there any new news about it? أكُو أخبار تازَة عَنها اليُوم؟ [ʔaku ʔaxbaːr taːza ʕanha ʔilyuːm?]

*** I feel like a new man.** • **1.** دَأشعُر عَبالَك مَخلُوق مِن جِدِيد [daʔašʕur ʕabaːlak maxluːq min ǰidiːd]

new moon • **1.** هلال [hlaːl] أهِلَّة [ʔahilla] *pl:* The new moon will be visible either tomorrow or the day after. الهِلال راح يهِلّ لَو باكِر لَو عُقبَة [ʔilhlaːl raːħ yhill law baːčir law ʕugba]

news • **1.** خَبَر [xabar] أَخبار [ʔaxba:r] *pl:* نَبأ [nabaʔ] أَنباء [ʔanba:ʔ] *pl:* Did you hear the news on the radio this morning? سمَعِت الأَخبار بِالرّاديُو اليُوم الصَّبُح؟ [smaʕit ʔilʔaxba:r birra:dyu ʔilyu:m ʔiṣṣubħ?] We'll have to break the news to him gently. لازِم نقُلَّه الخَبَر بِلُطُف [la:zim ngullah ʔilxabar biluṭuf] That isn't news to me. هَذا مُو خَبَر جِدِيد عَلَيّا [ha:ða mu: xabar ǰidi:d ʕalayya]

newspaper • **1.** جَرِيدَة [ǰari:da] جَرايِد [ǰara:yid] *pl:*

newsreel • **1.** أَخبار سِينَمائِيَّة [ʔaxba:r sinama:ʔiyya] I missed the newsreel last night. ما لحَقِت الأَخبار السِّينَمائِيَّة البارحَة باللَّيل [ma: lħagit ʔilʔaxba:r ʔissinama:ʔiyya ʔilba:rħa billayl]

new year • **1.** راس السَّنَة [ra:s ʔissana]

next • **1.** جاي [ǰa:y] تالِي [ta:li] تُوالِي [tuwa:li] *pl:* We're coming to Baghdad next month. جايِّين لِبَغداد الشَّهَر الجّاي [ǰa:yyi:n lbaɣda:d ʔiššahar ʔiǰǰa:y] Next time do it right! المَرَّة الجّايَّة سَوِّيها زين [ʔilmarra ʔiǰǰa:yya sawwi:ha zi:n] It's your turn next. الجّايَة نُوبتَك [ʔiǰǰa:ya nu:btak] • **2.** وَرا [wara] بَعَد [baʕad] I'm next after you. آنِي وَراك [ʔa:ni wara:k] • **3.** بَعدَين [baʕdayn] What shall I do next? بَعدين شراح أَسَوِّي؟ [baʕdi:n šra:ħ ʔasawwi?] • **4.** ثانِي [θa:ni] The next day he got sick. اليُوم الثّانِي تمَرَّض [ʔilyu:m ʔiθθa:ni tmarraḍ] The next day he got sick. اليُوم اللِّي بَعدَه تمَرَّض [ʔilyu:m ʔilli baʕdah tmarraḍ]

next door to • **1.** صَفّ [ṣaff] صفُوف [ṣfu:f] *pl:* The tailor lives next door to us. الخَيّاط يِسكُن بصَفّنا [ʔilxayya:ṭ yiskun bṣaffna] We live next door to the school. نِسكُن بصَفّ المَدرَسَة [niskun bṣaff ʔilmadrasa]

next to • **1.** يَمّ [yamm] بصَفّ [bṣaff] Sit down next to me. أُقعُد يَمِّي [ʔugʕud yammi]

nib • **1.** سِلّايَة [silla:ya] سِلّايات [silla:ya:t] *pl:* رِيشَة [ri:ša] رِيشات، رِيَش [ri:ša:t, riyaš] *pl:*

to nibble • **1.** قَرمَط [garmaṭ] تقُرمُط [tgurmuṭ] *vn:* تقَرمَط [tgarmaṭ] *p:* Some mouse has been nibbling on this cheese. فَدّ فارَة كانَت تقَرمُط بهَالجِّبِن [fadd fa:ra ča:nat dgarmuṭ bihaǰǰibin]

nice • **1.** لَطِيف [laṭi:f] زين [zi:n, zayn] خُوش [xu:š] حِلُو [ħilw] She had on a nice dress. كانَت لابسَة فِستان لَطِيف [ča:nat la:bsah fista:n laṭi:f] Our doctor has a nice way with his patients. طَبِيبنا مُعامَلتَه زينَة وِيّا المَرضَى [ṭabi:bna muʕa:maltah zi:na wiyya ʔilmarða] He's a nice polite little boy. هُوَّ فَدّ وَلَد لَطِيف وَمُؤَدَّب [huwwa fadd walad laṭi:f wamuʔaddab] That wasn't very nice of him to say that. ما كانَت حِلوَة مِنَّه يقُولها [ma: ča:nat ħilwa minnah ygu:lha] Did you have a nice time? قضَيت خُوش وَقِت؟ [gði:t xu:š wakit?] Did you have a nice time? توَنَّسِت؟ [twannasit?] The room is nice and warm. هَالغُرفَة زينَة ودافيَة [halɣurfa zi:na wda:fya]

nicely • **1.** تَمام [tama:m] زين [zi:n] خَوش [xu:š] Our daughter has learned to sew nicely. بِتّنا تعَلّمَت تخَيِّط زين [bittna tʕallimat txayyiṭ zi:n]

* **This will do nicely.** • **1.** هَذا يؤَدِّي الغَرَض [ha:ða yʔaddi ʔilɣarað]

nickname • **1.** لَقَب [laqab] أَلقاب [ʔalqa:b] *pl:*

niece • **1.** بِنت أَخ [bint, ʔax] بَنات أَخ [bana:t ʔax] *pl:* • **2.** بِنت أُخت [bint ʔuxt] بَنات أُخت [bana:t ʔuxt] *pl:*

night • **1.** لَيلَة [layla li:la] لَيلات، لَيالِي [layla:t, laya:li] *pl:* He only stayed with us one night. بُقَى وِيّانا فَدّ لَيلَة وِحدَة [buqa: wiyya:na fadd layla wiħda]

* **Good night!** • **1.** تِصبَح عَلَى خَير [tiṣbaħ ʕala xi:r]

night club • **1.** مَلهَى [malha] مَلاهِي [mala:hi] *pl:* She sings in the night clubs. هِيَّ تغَنِّي بِالمَلاهِي [hiyya tɣanni bilmala:hi]

nightgown • **1.** دِشداشَة نَوم [dišda:šat nawm] دِشادِيش نَوم [diša:di:š nawm] *pl:* My father prefers a nightgown to pajamas. أَبُويا يفَضِّل الدِّشداشَة عالبِجامَة [ʔabu:ya yfaððil ʔiddišda:ša ʕalbiǰa:ma] • **2.** ثَوب نَوم [θawb nawm] ثياب نَوم [θya:b nawm] *pl:* I bought my wife a nylon nightgown. إشتِرَيت لزَوجتِي ثُوب نُوم نايلُون [ʔištiri:t lzawiǰti θu:b nu:m naylu:n]

nightingale • **1.** بلبِل [bilbil] بَلابِل [bala:bil] *pl:*

night watchman • **1.** حارِس لَيلِي [ħa:ris layli] حُرّاس لَيلِيِّين [ħurra:s layliyyi:n] *pl:* ناطُور [na:ṭu:r] نواطِير [nwa:ṭi:r] *pl:* جَرخَجِي [čarxači] جَرخَجِيَّة [čarxačiyya] *pl:* بِيصوان [pi:ṣwa:n] بِيصوانِيَّة [pi:ṣwa:niyya] *pl:*

nine • **1.** تِسعَة [tisʕa] تِسعات [tisʕa:t] *pl:* The train leaves at nine o'clock. القِطار يطلَع ساعَة تِسعَة [ʔilqiṭa:r yiṭlaʕ sa:ʕa tisʕa] • **2.** تِسعَة [tisʕa] تِسعات [tisʕa:t] *pl:* I lived there for nine months. سِكَنِت هناك تِسعَة أَشهُر [sikanit hna:k tisʕat ʔašhur] • **3.** تِسِع [tisiʕ] The atmosphere will be full of radio-activity in another nine years. الجَّوّ راح يكُون بِيه إشعاع ذَرِّي بَعَد تِسع سنِين [ʔiǰǰaww ra:ħ yku:n bi:h ʔišʕa:ʕ ðarri baʕad tisʕ sni:n]

nineteen • **1.** تساطَعَش [tsa:ṭaʕaš]

nineteenth • **1.** التساطَعَش [ʔittsa:ṭaʕaš] This is the nineteenth of the month. هَذا اليُوم التِساطَعَش مِن الشَّهَر [ha:ða ʔilyu:m ʔaltisa:ṭaʕaš min ʔiššahar]

ninetieth • **1.** التِّسعِين [ʔittisʕi:n]

ninety • **1.** تِسعِين [tisʕi:n]

ninth • **1.** تاسِع [taːsiʕ] This is the ninth of the month. هَذا اليُوم التّاسِع مِن الشَّهَر [haːða ʔilyuːm ʔattaːsiʕ min ʔiššahar] • **2.** تُسُع [tusuʕ] أتساع [ʔatsaːʕ] *pl:* Subtract two ninths from five ninths. إطرَح تِسعَين مِن خَمس أتساع [ʔiṭraħ tisʕayn min xams ʔatsaːʕ]

nip • **1.** عَضّة [ʕaððа] عَضّات [ʕaððaːt] *pl:* The dog took a good nip of my leg. الكَلِب أخَذ خُوش عَضّة مِن رِجلي [ʔiččalib ʔaxað xuːš ʕaðða min riǰli] • **2.** مَصّة [maṣṣa] مَصّات [maṣṣaːt] *pl:* He took himself a good nip out of the bottle. أخَذلَه خُوش مَصّة مِن البُطِل [ʔaxaðlah xuːš maṣṣa min ʔalbuṭul]

nippy • **1.** بيه قَرصَة بَرِد [biːh garṣat barid] The air is nippy this morning. الهَوا بيه قَرصَة بَرِد هَالصُّبُح [ʔilhawa biːh garṣat barid haṣṣubuħ] • **2.** حادّ [ħaːdd] This is a nippy cheese. هَالجِّبن طَعمَه حادّ [hajǰibin ṭaʕmah ħaːdd]

nitrogen • **1.** نيتروجين [niːtruǰiːn]

no • **1.** لا [laː] Answer me, yes or no. جاوُبني، إي لَو لا [ǰaːwubni, ʔi law laː] Do you always have to say no? ما تقُول غير لا؟ [maː tguːl ɣiːr laː?] • **2.** مُو [muː] This pen is no good. هَالقَلَم مُو زين [halqalam muː ziːn]

*** This screwdriver is no good for this job.** • **1.** هَالدَرنَفيس ما يفيد لِهَالشُغُل [haddarnafiːs maː yfiːd lhaššuɣul]

*** This bicycle is no good anymore.** • **1.** هَالبايسِكِل ما بيه فائِدَة بَعَد [halpaːysikil maː biːh faːʔida baʕad]

*** He has no money.** • **1.** ما عِندَه فلُوس [maː ʕindah fluːs]

*** No smoking!** • **1.** التدخين مَمنُوع [ʔittadxiːn mamnuːʕ]

*** There are no more seats.** • **1.** ماكُو مَقاعِد بَعَد [maːkuː maqaːʕid baʕad]

*** No sooner did we arrive than the telephone rang.** • **1.** ويّا ما وصَلنا دَقّ التَلِفون [wiyya maː wṣalna dagg ʔittilifuːn]

*** I have no doubt of it whatsoever.** • **1.** ماعِندي كُلّ شَكّ بيها أبَداً [maː ʕindi kull šakk biːha ʔabadan]

noble • **1.** نَبيل [nabiːl] That was very noble of you. هَذا كان عَمَل نَبيل مِنَّك [haːða čaːn ʕamal nabiːl minnak]

nobleman • **1.** نَبيل [nabiːl] نُبَلاء [nubalaːʔ] *pl:* شَريف [šariːf] أشراف، شُرَفاء [ʔašraːf, šurafaːʔ] *pl:*

nobody • **1.** لَحَد [laħħad] وَلا واحِد [walaː waːħid] Nobody may leave this room. لا حَدّ يطلَع مِن الغُرفَة [laː ħadd yiṭlaʕ min ʔilɣurfa] • **2.** مَحَّد [maħħad] وَلا واحِد [wala waːħid] Nobody saw us, I'm sure. مَحَّد شافنا، آني مِتأكِّد [maħħad šaːfna, ʔaːni mitʔakkid] Nobody came to the party at all. وَلا واحِد جا لِلحَفلَة أبَداً [wala waːħid ǰaː lilħafla ʔabadan]

nod • **1.** هَزّة راس [hazzat raːs] هَزّات راس [hazzaːt raːs] *pl:* He greeted us with a nod. سَلَّم عَلينا بِهَزّة راس [sallam ʕaliːna bihazzat raːs]

to nod • **1.** هَزّ [hazz] هَزّ [hazz] *vn:* اِنهَزّ [ʔinhazz] *p:* She nodded her head yes. هَزّت راسها قابلَة [hazzat raːsha qaːbla] • **2.** غَفّى [ɣaffaː] تغفّي [tɣiffi] *vn: sv* i. He began to nod over his book. قام يغفّي عَلَى كتابَه [gaːm yɣaffi ʕala ktaːbah]

to nod to • **1.** أشَّر [ʔaššar] تأشير، تأشِّر [taʔsiːr, tʔiššir] *vn: sv* i. The teacher nodded to me to go on reading. المُعَلِّم أشَّرلي براسَه أستِمِرّ بالقِراءَة [ʔilmuʕallim ʔaššarli braːsah ʔastimirr bilqiraːʔa] • **2.** سَلَّم بِالرّاس [sallam birraːs] سَلام بِالرّاس [salaːm birraːs] *vn: sv* i. She nodded to me as she passed. سَلِّمَت عَلَيّا براسها لَمّا مَرَّت [sallimat ʕalayya braːsha lamma marrat]

noise • **1.** ضَجيج [ðaǰiːǰ] صُوت [ṣawt] أصوات [ʔaṣwaːt] *pl:* The noise of the traffic keeps me awake at night. ضَجيج المُرُور يخَلّيني قاعِد طُول اللَّيل [ðaǰiːǰ ʔilmuruːr yxalliːni gaːʕid ṭuːl ʔillayl] • **2.** حِسّ [ħiss] I heard a noise downstairs, and I went down to investigate. سمَعِت فَدّ حِسّ جَوَّة وَنِزَلِت الدَّرَج أشُوف شَكُو [smaʕit fadd ħiss ǰawwa wanizalit ʔiddaraǰ ʔašuːf šaku] • **3.** لَغوَة [laɣwa] لَغوات، لَغاوي [laɣwaːt, laɣaːwi] *pl:* ضَوضاء [ðawðaːʔ] لَغوات [laɣwaːt] *pl:* The noise of the crowd at the auction gave me a headache. لَغوَة النّاس بِالمَزاد دُوّخَت راسي [laɣwat ʔinnaːs bilmazaːd duwwxat raːsi]

to nominate • **1.** رَشَّح [raššaħ] تَرشيح [taršiːħ] *vn:* تَرَشَّح [traššaħ] *p:* He's going to nominate himself for the member from the third district in Baghdad. راح يرَشِّح نَفسَه نائِب عَن المَنطَقَة الثّالثَة بِبَغداد [raːħ yraššiħ nafsah naːʔib ʕan ʔilmanṭaqa ʔaθθaːliθa bibaɣdaːd]

noncommissioned officer • **1.** ضابُط صَفّ [ðaːbuṭ ṣaff] ضُبّاط صَفّ [ðubbaːṭ ṣaff] *pl:*

none • **1.** مَحَّد [maħħad] وَلا واحِد [wala waːħid] None of my friends could help me. مَحَّد مِن أصدِقائي قِدَر يساعِدني [maħħad min ʔaṣdiqaːʔi gidar ysaːʕidni] None of the women know anything about it. وَلا وِحدَة مِن النِّسوان تُعرُف شي عَنَّه [wala wiħda min ʔanniswaːn tuʕruf ši ʕannah]

*** That's none of your business!** • **1.** هَذا مُو شُغلَك [haːða muː šuɣlak]

nonsense • **1.** كَلام فارِغ [kalaːm faːriɣ] حَكِي خَرُط [ħači xaruṭ] Now you're talking nonsense. هَسَّة دَتِحكِي كَلام فارِغ [hassa datiħči kalaːm faːriɣ] Now you're talking nonsense. هَسَّة حَكيَك خَرُط [hassa ħačyak xaruṭ]

N

noodles • **1.** شَعرِيَّة [šaʕriyya]

noon • **1.** ظُهُر [ðuhur] ظَهارِي [ðaha:ri] *pl:* It wasn't as hot at noon today as it was yesterday noon. ما كانَت حارَّة اليُوم الظُّهُر مِثْلما كانَت البارحَة الظُّهُر [ma: ča:nat ħa:rra ʔilyu:m ʔiððuhur miθilma ča:nat ʔilba:rħa ʔiððuhur]

nor • **1.** وَلا [wala] I haven't seen it nor do I want to see it. ما شِفتَه وَلا أَرِيد أَشُوفَه [ma: šiftah wala ʔari:d ʔašu:fah]

normal • **1.** اِعتِيادِي [ʔiʕtiya:di] His temperature is normal. دَرَجَة حَرارتَه اِعتِيادِيَّة [darajat ħara:rtah ʔiʕtiya:diyya]

normally • **1.** اِعتِيادِيّاً [ʔiʕtiya:diyyan] حَسَب العادَة [ħasab ʔilʕa:da]

north • **1.** شِمال [šima:l] The wind is coming from the north. الهَوا جاي مِن الشِّمال [ʔilhawa ja:y min ʔiššima:l] Mosul is north of Baghdad. المَوصِل بِشِمال بَغداد [ʔilmu:ṣil bišima:l bayda:d]

northern • **1.** شِمالِي [šima:li] You can find snow in the northern part of Iraq. تِقدَر تِلقِي ثِلُوج بِالقِسم الشِّمالِي مِن العِراق [tigdar tilgi θilu:j bilqism ʔiššima:li min ʔilʕira:q]

Norway • **1.** النَرويج [ʔinnarwi:j]

Norwegian • **1.** نَروِيجِي [narwi:ji] نَروِيجِيِّين [narwi:jiyyi:n] *pl:*

nose • **1.** خَشِم [xašim] خشُوم [xšu:m] *pl:* He can't breathe through his nose because of the operation. ما يِقدَر يِتنَفَّس مِن خَشمَه بِسَبَب العَمَلِيَّة [ma: yigdar yitnaffas min xašmah bsabab ʔilʕamaliyya] • **2.** مُقَدَّمَة [muqaddama] مُقَدَّمات [muqaddama:t] *pl:* There was a fire in the nose of the aircraft. كان أَكُو حَرِيق بِمُقَدِّمَة الطَّيّارَة [ča:n ʔaku ħari:q bimuqaddamat ʔiṭṭayya:ra]

*** He sticks his nose into everything.** • **1.** يدَخِّل نَفسَه بكُلشِي [ydaxxil nafsah bkullši]

nostril • **1.** مَنخَر [manxar] مَناخِر [mana:xir] *pl:*

not • **1.** مُو [mu:] He is not a man. هُوَّ مُو رِجّال [huwwa mu: rijja:l] • **2.** ما [ma:] He did not come. هُوَّ ما إجا [huwwa ma: ʔija:] • **3.** لا [la:] Do not go. لا ترُوح [la: tru:ħ]

not at all • **1.** مُو كُلِّش [mu: kulliš] I'm not at all sure. آنِي مُو كُلِّش مِتأَكِّد [ʔa:ni mu: kulliš mitʔakkid] • **2.** مَا أَبَداً [ma: ʔabadan] مُو أَبَداً [mu: ʔabadan] They're not at all happy in their new home. هُمَّ مُو فَرحانِين بِبَيتهُم الجِّدِيد أَبَداً [humma mu: farħa:ni:n bibaythum ʔijjidi:d ʔabadan] • **3.** عَفُو [ʕafw] Thank you very much. Not at all. أَشكُرَك هوايَة العَفو [ʔaškurak hwa:ya ʔilʕafw]

to notarize • **1.** صَدَّق [ṣaddaq] تَصدِيق [taṣdi:q] *vn:* تصَدَّق [tṣaddaq] *p:* I have a friend that can notarize this document. عِندِي صَدِيق يِقدَر يصَدِّق هالوَرَقَة [ʕindi ṣadi:q yigdar yṣaddiq halwaraqa]

notary public • **1.** كاتِب عَدِل [ka:tib ʕadil] كُتّاب عَدِل [kutta:b ʕadil] *pl:* كُتّاب عُدُول [kutta:b ʕudu:l] كُتّاب [kutta:b] *pl:*

notch • **1.** ثَلمَة [θalma] ثَلمات [θalma:t] *pl:* There's a notch on the edge of the table. أَكُو ثَلمَة عَلَى حافَّة المِيز [ʔaku θalma ʕala ħa:ffat ʔilmi:z]

to notch • **1.** ثِلَم [θilam] ثَلِم [θalim] *vn:* اِنثِلَم [ʔinθilam] *p:* He notched the ruler with his knife. ثِلَم المَسطَرَة بِسِكِّينتَه [θilam ʔilmasṭara bisičči:ntah]

note • **1.** وَرَقَة [waraqa] وَرَقات [waraqa:t] *pl:* He left a note on the table and went out. تِرَك وَرَقَة عالمِيز وَطِلَع [tirak waraqa ʕalmi:z wṭilaʕ] • **2.** نَوطَة [nu:ṭa] نَوطات [nu:ṭa:t] *pl:* Try to sing this note. حاوِل تغَنِّي هَالنُّوطَة [ħa:wil tɣanni hannu:ṭa] • **3.** مُلاحَظَة [mula:ħaða] مُلاحَظات [mula:ħaða:t] *pl:* The teacher wrote several notes on the margin of my paper. المُعَلِّم كِتَب عِدَّة مُلاحَظات عَلَى هامِش وَرَقتِي [ʔilmuʕallim kitab ʕiddat mula:ħaða:t ʕala ha:miš waraqti] • **4.** عَلامَة [ʕala:ma] عَلامات، عَلائِم [ʕala:ma:t, ʕala:ʔim] *pl:* أَثَر [ʔaθar] آثار [ʔa:θa:r] *pl:* There was a note of fear in his voice. كان أَكُو أَثَر خَوف بِصُوتَه [ča:n ʔaku ʔaθar xawf bișu:tah] • **5.** كُمبِيالَة [kumbya:la, kumpya:la] كُمبِيالات [kumbya:la:t, kumpya:la:t] *pl:* He gave me a note for the balance. اِنطانِي كُمبِيالَة عَلَى بَقِيَّة الفلُوس [ʔinṭa:ni kumpiya:la ʕala baqiyyat ʔilflu:s]

notes • **1.** رُؤُوس أَقلام [ruʔu:s ʔaqla:m] I didn't take notes in class today. ما أَخَذِت رُؤُوس أَقلام بِالصَّفّ اليُوم [ma: ʔaxaðit ruʔu:s ʔaqla:m biṣṣaff ʔilyu:m]

of note • **1.** مَعرُوف [maʕru:f] مَلحُوظ [malħu:ð] He's written three books of note. كِتَب ثلَث كُتُب مَعرُوفَة [kitab tlaθ kutub maʕru:fa]

to note • **1.** ذِكَر [ðikar] ذِكِر [ðikir] *vn:* اِنذِكَر [ʔinðikar] *p:* نَوَّه [nawwah] تَنوِيه [tanwi:h] *vn:* تنَوَّه [tnawwah] *p:* He noted our assistance in a letter to the manager. ذِكَر مُساعَدَتنا بِكِتاب لِلمُدِير [ðikar musa:ʕadatna bikita:b lilmudi:r] • **2.** لاحَظ [la:ħað] مُلاحَظَة [mula:ħaða] *vn:* تلاحَظ [tla:ħað] *p:* Note the beautiful carving. لاحِظ النَّقش الجِّمِيل [la:ħið ʔannaqš ʔijjami:l]

notebook • **1.** دَفتَر [daftar] دَفاتِر [dafa:tir] *pl:*

nothing • **1.** ماكُو [ma:ku] لا شِي [la: ši] Something is better than nothing. شِي أَحسَن مِن لا شِي [ši ʔaħsan min la: ši] • **2.** ما شِي [ma: ... ši] We did nothing all afternoon. ما سَوَّينا شِي طُول العَصِر [ma: sawwi:na ši ṭu:l ʔilʕaṣir]

for nothing • **1.** بِبَلاش [bibala:š] مَجّاناً [majja:nan] He gave me this shirt for nothing. اِنطانِي هَالثُّوب ببَلاش [ʔinṭa:ni haθθu:b bibla:š]

notice • **1.** إعلان [ʔiʕla:n] إعلانات [ʔiʕla:na:t] *pl:* Did you read the notice on the bulletin board? قريت الإعلان عاللّوحَة؟ [qrayt ʔilʔiʕla:n ʕallawħa?] • **2.** إشعار [ʔišʕa:r] إشعارات [ʔišʕa:ra:t] *pl:* They fired him without notice. طَلّعُوه مِن الشُّغُل بِدُون إشعار [ṭallʕu:h min ʔiššuɣul bidu:n ʔišʕa:r] • **3.** خَبَر [xabar] You'll have to give notice a month before you move. لازِم تِنطِي خَبَر قَبُل شَهَر مِن وَقِت ما تِتحَوَّل [la:zim tinṭi xabar gabul šahar min wakit ma: titħawwal]

*** I don't know how it escaped my notice.**

• **1.** ما أدري شلَون فاتَت عَلَيّا [ma: ʔadri šlu:n fa:tat ʕalayya]

to notice • **1.** لاحَظ [la:ħaḏ̣] مُلاحَظَة [mula:ħaḏ̣a] *vn:* تلاحَظ [tla:ħaḏ̣] *p:* اِنتِبَه [ʔintibah] اِنتِباه [ʔintiba:h] *vn: sv* i. Did you notice if he was in his office or not? لاحَظِت إذا كان بِدائِرتَه لَو لا؟ [la:ħaḏ̣it ʔiða ka:n bida:ʔirtah law la:?] • **2.** لاحَظ [la:ħaḏ̣] مُلاحَظَة [mula:ħaḏ̣a] *vn:* تلاحَظ [tla:ħaḏ̣] *p:* Everybody noticed his tie. كُلّ واحِد لاحَظ رباطَه [kull wa:ħid la:ħaḏ̣ rba:ṭah]

to notify • **1.** بَلَّغ [ballaɣ] تَبلِيغ، تبلِّغ [tabli:ɣ, tbilliɣ] *vn:* تبَلَّغ [tballaɣ] *p:* خَبَّر [xabbar] تخُبُّر [txubbur] *vn:* تخَبَّر [txabbar] *p:* أعلَم [ʔaʕlam] إعلام [ʔiʕla:m] *vn:* انعِلَم [ʔiʕilam] *p:* Notify me when you arrive. خَبُّرنِي لَمّا تُوصَل [xabburni lamma tu:ṣal]

notion • **1.** مَيل [mayl, mi:l] مِيُول [miyu:l] *pl:* I had a notion to stay home today. كان عِندِي مَيل أبقَى بِالبَيت اليُوم [ča:n ʕindi mayl ʔabqa: bilbayt ʔilyu:m] • **2.** فِكرَة [fikra] فِكرات، فِكِر، أفكار [fikra:t, fikir, ʔafka:r.] *pl:* I haven't any notion of what he wants. ما عِندِي أيّ فِكرَة شيرِيد [ma: ʕindi ʔayy fikra šiyri:d]

notorious • **1.** مَشهُور [mašhu:r] He's a notorious criminal. هُوَّ مُجرِم مَشهُور [huwwa mujrim mašhu:r]

noun • **1.** إسِم [ʔisim] أسامِي، أسماء [ʔasa:mi, ʔasma:ʔ] *pl:*

nourishing • **1.** مُغَذِّي [muɣaðði] We ate a nourishing breakfast. أكَلنا رِيُوق مُغَذِّي [ʔakalna riyu:g muɣaðði]

nourishment • **1.** غِذاء [ɣiða:ʔ] قُوت [qu:t] تَغذِيَة [taɣðiya] He needs more nourishment. يرِيدلَه غِذاء أكثَر [yri:dlah ɣiða:ʔ ʔakθar]

novel • **1.** رُوايَة [ruwa:ya, riwa:ya] رُوايات [ruwa:ya:t] *pl:* قُصَّة [quṣṣa] قُصَص [quṣaṣ] *pl:* I read a good novel last night. قريت خُوش رُوايَة البارحَة باللَّيل [qrayt xu:š ruwa:ya ʔilba:rħa billayl] • **2.** جِدِيد [jidi:d] That's a novel idea. هَذِي فِكرَة جِدِيدَة [ha:ði fikra jidi:da]

November • **1.** تِشرِين الثانِي [tišri:n ʔiθθa:ni]

now • **1.** هَسَّة [hassa] الآن [ʔilʔa:n] I have to go now. لازِم أرُوح هَسَّة [la:zim ʔaru:ħ hassa]

by now • **1.** هَسَّة [hassa] الآن [ʔilʔa:n] He should have been here by now. لازِم يكُون هَسَّة هنا [la:zim yku:n hassa hna]

from now on • **1.** مِن هَسَّة وجاي [min hassa wja:y] مِن هنا وهِيك [min hna wra:yiħ] مِن هنا ورايح [min hna whi:č] From now on I'll keep quiet. مِنّا وهِيك راح أسكُت [min hna whi:č ra:ħ ʔaskut]

just now • **1.** هَستَوّا [hastawwa] هَسَّة [hassa] الآن [ʔilʔa:n] I talked to him just now. هَستَوّنِي حكَيت وِيّاه [hastawwni ħči:t wiyya:h]

now and then • **1.** بَين حَين وآخَر [bayn ħi:n wʔa:xar] بَين مُدَّة ومُدَّة [bayn mudda wmudda] بَين فَترَة وفَترَة [bi:n fatra wfatra] أحياناً [ʔaħya:nan] I hear from him now and then. أسمَع مِنَّه بين حِين وآخَر [ʔasmaʕ minnah bayn ħi:n wʔa:xar]

up to now • **1.** لحَدّ الآن [lħadd ʔilʔa:n] لِهَسَّة [lihassa] I haven't been sick up to now. ما تمَرَّضِت لِحَدّ الآن [ma: tmarraḏ̣it liħadd ʔilʔaan]

nowadays • **1.** هَالأيّام [halʔayya:m] Nowadays, every house has television. هَالأيّام كُلّ بَيت بِيه تَلَفزِيُون [halʔayya:m kull bayt bi:h talafizyu:n]

nowhere • **1.** ما بأيّ مُكان [ma: bʔayy muka:n] He's nowhere to be seen. ما يِنشاف بأيّ مُكان [ma: yinša:f bʔayy muka:n]

nozzle • **1.** راس [ra:s] رُؤُوس [ruʔu:s, ru:s] *pl:* The hose needs a new nozzle. الصُّوندَة يرِيدلها راس جِدِيد [ʔaṣṣu:nda yri:dilha ra:s jidi:d]

nuclear energy • **1.** الطاقَة النَوَوِيَّة [ʔiṭṭa:qa ʔinnawawiyya]

nucleus • **1.** نَواة [nawa: (t)] نُوايات [nuwa:ya:t] *pl:* نُوَى [nuwa] *Collective*

nude • **1.** مسَلَّخ [msallax] مسَلَّخِين، مسالِيخ [msallaxi:n, msa:li:x] *pl:* عَريان [ʕarya:n] عَريانِين، عَرايا [ʕarya:ni:n, ʕra:ya] *pl:*

nudge • **1.** نَغَّة [naɣɣa] نَغّات [naɣɣa:t] *pl:* He gave me a nudge when she walked by. اِنطانِي نَغَّة لَمّا مَرَّت [ʔinṭa:ni naɣɣa lamma marrat]

to nudge • **1.** نَغّ [naɣɣ] نَغّ [naɣɣ] *vn:* اِنَّغّ [ʔinnaɣɣ] *p:* Don't nudge me! لا تنُغّنِي [la: tnuɣɣni]

nuisance • **1.** ضَوَجان [ḏ̣awaja:n] Neckties are a nuisance. الأربِطَة ضَوَجان [ʔilʔarbiṭa ḏ̣awaja:n]

numb • **1.** خَدران [xadra:n] My fingers are numb from the cold. أصابعِي خَدرانَة مِن البَرِد [ʔaṣa:bʕi xadra:na min ʔilbarid] • **2.** مِتخَدِّر [mitxaddir] خَدران [xadra:n] I feel completely numb. أشعُر كُلّ جِسمِي مِتخَدِّر [ʔašʕur kull jismi mitxaddir]

N

to numb • **1.** خَدَّر [xaddar] تَخدِير [taxdi:r] *vn:* تخَدَّر [txaddar] *p:* The blow numbed my shoulder. الضَّربَة خَدَّرَت كِتفِي [ʔiððarba xaddrat čitfi]

number • **1.** رَقَم [raqam] أرقام [ʔarqa:m] *pl:* What's your house number? شقَدّ رَقَم بَيتكُم؟ [šgadd raqam baytkum?] Did you write down the number? كتَبِت الرَّقَم؟ [ktabit ʔirraqam?] • **2.** عَدَد [ʕadad] أعداد [ʔaʕda:d] *pl:* A number of cars are still available at reduced prices. عَدَد مِن السَّيّارات بَعدَه مَوجُود بأسعار مُخَفَّضَة [ʕadad min ʔissayya:ra:t baʕdah mawǰu:d bʔasʕa:r muxaffaða] • **3.** عِدَّة [ʕidda] He's been imprisoned a number of times. اِنسِجَن عِدَّة مَرّات [ʔinsiǰan ʕiddat marra:t]

*** I've got his number.** • **1.** أعرُف دُواه [ʔaʕruf duwa:h]

to number • **1.** رَقَّم [raqqam] ترُقُّم، تَرقِيم [truqqum, tarqi:m] *vn:* *sv* u. نَمَّر [nammar] نُمَر [numar] *pl:* تنُمُّر [tnummur] *vn:* تنَمَّر [tnammar] *p:* Number the boxes from one to ten. رَقُّم العِلَب مِن واحِد إلَى عَشرَة [raqqum ʔalʕilab min wa:ħid ʔila ʕašra]

*** His days are numbered.** • **1.** أيّامَه مَعدُودَة [ʔayya:mah maʕdu:da]

numeral • **1.** رَقَم [raqam] أرقام [ʔarqa:m] *pl:*

nun • **1.** راهِبَة [ra:hiba] راهِبات [ra:hiba:t] *pl:*

nurse • **1.** مُمَرِّض [mumarrið] مُمَرِّضات، مُمَرِّضِين [mumarriða:t, mumarriði:n] *pl:* مُمَرِّضَة [mumarriða] *Feminine:* The patient needs a nurse. المَرِيض يِحتاج مُمَرِّضَة [ʔilmari:ð yiħta:ǰ mumarriða] • **2.** مُرَبِّيَة [murabbiya] مُرَبِّيات [murabbiya:t] *pl:* The children are out in the park with their nurse. الجِّهال بَرَّة بِالحَدِيقَة وِيّا مُرَبِّيَتهُم [ʔiǰǰaha:l barra bilħadi:qa wiyya murabbiyathum]

wet nurse • **1.** دايَة [da:ya] دايات [da:ya:t] *pl:*

to nurse • **1.** رِضَع [riðaʕ] رَضِع [raðiʕ] *vn:* اِنرِضَع [ʔinriðaʕ] *p:* They brought a woman to nurse the baby. جابَوا مَرَة ترَضِّع الجّاهِل [ǰa:baw mara traððiʕ ʔiǰǰa:hil] • **2.** اِعتِنَى ب [ʔiʕtina: b-] اِعتِناء [ʔiʕtina:ʔ] *vn:* *sv* i. He's nursing his broken leg. دَيِعتِنِي بِرِجلَه المَكسُورَة [dayiʕtini briǰlah ʔalmaksu:ra]

nursery • **1.** رَوضَة [rawða] رَوضات [rawða:t] *pl:* I take my child to the nursery at eight o'clock every day. آخُذ اِبنِي لِلرَّوضَة السّاعَة ثمانيَة كُلّ يوم [ʔa:xuð ʔibni lirrawða ʔissa:ʕa θma:nya kull yu:m] • **2.** مَشتَل [maštal] مَشاتِل [maša:til] *pl:* I bought these flowers at the nursery. اِشتِرَيت هَالوَرِد مِن المَشتَل [ʔištiri:t halwarid min ʔalmaštal]

nut • **1.** كَرَزَة [karaza] كَرزات [karza:t] *pl:* كَرَز [čaraz] *Collective:* This shop sells all kinds of nuts. هَالبَقّال يبِيع جَمِيع أنواع الكَرَزات [halbagga:l yibi:ʕ ǰami:ʕ ʔanwa:ʕ ʔiččaraza:t] • **2.** صَمُّونَة [ṣammu:na] صَمُّونات [ṣammu:na:t] *pl:* This nut doesn't fit the bolt. هَالصَّمُّونَة ما ترهَم عَالبُرغِي [haṣṣammu:na ma: tirham ʕalburɣi] • **3.** مخَبَّل [mxabbal] مخابِيل [mxa:bi:l] *pl:* He's a real nut. هُوَّ مخَبَّل تَمام [huwwa mxabbal tama:m]

nut cracker • **1.** كَسّارَة جَوز [kassa:rat ǰawz] كَسّارات جَوز [kassa:ra:t ǰawz] *pl:*

nutmeg • **1.** جَوز بَوَّة [ǰawz bawwa]

nylon • **1.** نايلَون [nay أيّامَه lu:n] He bought nylon socks. اِشتِرَى جوارِيب نايلَون [ʔištira: ǰwa:ri:b naylu:n]

N

O

oak • **1.** بَلُّوط [ballu:ṭ]

oar • **1.** مِجداف [mijda:f] مَجادِيف [maja:di:f] *pl:* The oars are in the boat. المَجادِيف بالبَلَم [ʔalmaja:di:f bilbalam]

oasis • **1.** واحَة [wa:ħa] واحات [wa:ħa:t] *pl:*

oats • **1.** هُرطُمان [hurṭuma:n, huruṭma:n] They plant a lot of oats here. هوايَة يزرعُون هُرطُمان هنا [hwa:ya yzirʕu:n hurṭuma:n hna]

obedience • **1.** طاعَة [ṭa:ʕa]

obedient • **1.** طايِع [ṭa:yiʕ] مُطِيع [muṭi:ʕ]

to obey • **1.** طاع [ṭa:ʕ] طاعَة [ṭa:ʕa] *vn:* اِنطاع [ʔinṭa:ʕ] *p:* خِضَع [xiđaʕ] خَضِع [xađiʕ] *vn:* اِنخِضَع [ʔinxiđaʕ] *p:* He doesn't obey me. هُوَّ ما يطِيعنِي [huwwa ma: yṭi:ʕni] I can't obey that order. ما أقدَر أطِيع هَالأمُر [ma: ʔagdar ʔaṭi:ʕ halʔamur]

object • **1.** شِي [ši] أشياء [ʔašya:ʔ] *pl:* حاجَة [ħa:ja] حاجات، حَوايِج [ħa:ja:t, ħawa:yij] *pl:* He was struck on the head with a heavy object. اِنضِرَب عَلَى راسَه بشِي ثِقِيل [ʔinđirab ʕala ra:sah bši θigi:l] • **2.** قَصِد [qaṣid] مَقصَد [maqṣad] مَقاصِد [maqa:ṣid] *pl:* What is the object of that? شِنُو القَصِد مِن ذاك؟ [šinu ʔalqaṣid min ða:k?]

to object • **1.** اِعتِرَض [ʔiʕtirađ] اِعتِراض [ʔiʕtira:đ] *vn: sv* i. مانَع [ma:naʕ] مُمانَعَة [muma:naʕa] *vn: sv* i. I don't know why you object to it. ما أعرُف لِيش دَتِعتِرِض عَلِيها [ma: ʔaʕruf li:š datiʕtiriđ ʕali:ha] I hope you don't object to my smoking. أتأمَّل ما عِندَك مانِع إذا أدَخِّن [ʔatʔammal ma: ʕindak ma:niʕ ʔiða ʔadaxxin]

objection • **1.** اِعتِراض [ʔiʕtira:đ] مانِع [ma:niʕ] مَوانِع [mawa:niʕ] *pl:* He didn't raise any objection. ما أثار أيّ اِعتِراض [ma: ʔaθa:r ʔayy ʔiʕtira:đ] Is there any objection? أكُو أيّ مانِع؟ [ʔaku ʔayy ma:niʕ?]

objectionable • **1.** ما مَقبُول [ma: maqbu:l]

objective • **1.** هَدَف [hadaf] أهداف [ʔahda:f] *pl:* We reached our objective. وُصَلنا هَدَفنا [wuṣalna hadafna]

obligated • **1.** مَمنُون [mamnu:n] مُمتَنّ [mumtann] We're very much obligated to you. إحنا مَمنُونِين هوايَة مِنَّك [ʔiħna mamnu:ni:n hwa:ya minnak]

obligation • **1.** واجِب [wa:jib] اِلتِزام [ʔiltiza:m] اِرتِباط [ʔirtiba:ṭ] اِرتِباطات [ʔirtiba:ṭa:t] *pl:* He can't meet his obligations. ما يِقدَر يوَفِّي اِلتِزاماتَه [ma: yigdar ywaffi ʔiltiza:ma:tah]

*** We're under no obligation to him.**
• **1.** إحنا مُو مَربُوطِين بِيه [ʔiħna mu: marbu:ṭi:n bi:h]

obligatory • **1.** إجبارِي [ʔijba:ri] Military service is obligatory. الخِدمَة بِالجَيش إجبارِيَّة [ʔilxidma bijjayš ʔijba:riyya]

to oblige • **1.** جُبَر [jubar] إجبار [ʔijba:r] *vn: sv* u. His illness obliged him to leave school for a year. مَرَضتَه جُبرَتَه يترُك المَدرَسَة لسَنَة وِحدَة [marađṭah jubratah yitruk ʔilmadrasa lsana wiħda]

to be obliged • **1.** اِضطَرّ [ʔiđṭarr] اِضطِرار [ʔiđṭira:r] *vn: sv* a. اِنجُبَر [ʔinjubar] اِنجِبار [ʔinjiba:r] *vn: sv* u. I was obliged to take shelter in a cave. اِضطَرَّيت ألتِجِي بِالكَهَف [ʔiđṭarri:t ʔaltiji bilkahaf]

obscene • **1.** بَذِيء [baði:ʔ]

observance • **1.** اِحتِفال [ʔiħtifa:l] اِحتِفالات [ʔiħtifa:la:t] *pl:* اِحتِرام [ʔiħtira:m] اِحتِرامات [ʔiħtira:ma:t] *pl:* The parade is a part of the observance of Army Day. الاستِعراض قِسِم مِن الإحتِفال بِيُوم الجَّيش [ʔalʔistiʕra:đ qisim min ʔalʔiħtifa:l byu:m ʔijji:š]

observant • **1.** مُلاحِظ [mula:ħiđ] مُلاحِظِين [mula:ħiđi:n] *pl:* He is observant and has a good mind. هُوَّ فَدّ واحِد مُلاحِظ وعاقِل [huwwa fadd wa:ħid mula:ħiđ wʕa:qil]

observation • **1.** مُعايَنَة [muʕa:yana] مُعايَنات [muʕa:yana:t] *pl:* He entered the hospital for observation. دِخَل المُستَشفَى لِلمُعايَنَة [dixal ʔilmustašfa lilmuʕa:yana] • **2.** مُلاحَظَة [mula:ħađa] مُلاحَظات [mula:ħađa:t] *pl:* In his speech he made a number of acute observations on the political situation. بخِطابَه سَوَّى عِدَّة مُلاحَظات حادَّة عَن الحالَة السِّياسِيَّة [bxiṭa:bah sawwa: ʕiddat mula:ħađa:t ħa:dda ʕan ʔilħa:la ʔissiya:siyya]

observatory • **1.** مَرصَد جَوِّي [marṣad jawwi] مَراصِد جَوِّيَّة [mara:ṣid jawwiyya] *pl:*

to observe • **1.** لاحَظ [la:ħađ] مُلاحَظَة [mula:ħađa] *vn: sv* i. Did you observe the reaction she had? لاحَظِت رَدّ الفِعِل اللِّي صار عِدها؟ [la:ħađit radd ʔilfiʕil ʔilli ṣa:r ʕidha?] • **2.** راعَى [ra:ʕa:] مُراعاة [mura:ʕa:t] *vn: sv* i. Which holidays do you observe in Iraq? يا عُطَل تراعُون بِالعِراق؟ [ya: ʕuṭal tra:ʕu:n bilʕira:q?] All employees here are expected to observe the regulations. كُلّ المُستَخدَمِين هنا مَفرُوض بِيهُم يراعُون التَّعلِيمات [kull ʔilmustaxdami:n hna mafru:đ bi:hum yra:ʕu:n ʔittaʕli:ma:t]

O

obstacle • **1.** عَقَبَة [ʕaqaba] عَقَبات [ʕaqaba:t] *pl:* مانع [ma:niʕ] مَوانِع [mawa:niʕ] *pl:* He had to overcome many obstacles before he was successful. اِضطَرّ يِتغَلَّب عَلَى هوايَة عَقَبات قبُل ما يِتوَفَّق [ʔiđṭarr yidɣallab ʕala hwa:ya ʕaqaba:t gabul ma: yitwaffaq]

obstinate • **1.** عَنِيد [ʕani:d] عَنُود [ʕanu:d] It won't do you any good to be obstinate about it. ما يِفِيدَك تصِير عَنِيد بِهَالخُصُوص [ma: yfi:dak tṣi:r ʕani:d bihalxuṣu:ṣ]

to obtain • **1.** حَصَّل [ħaṣṣal] تَحصِيل [taħṣi:l] *vn:* تحَصَّل [tħaṣṣal] *p:* He obtained all of his education abroad. حَصَّل كُلّ تَعلِيمَه العالِي بالخارِج [ħaṣṣal kull taʕli:mah ʔilʕa:li bilxa:rij]

obvious • **1.** واضِح [wa:điħ] ظاهِر [đa:hir] مبَيِّن [mbayyin] It's obvious that he doesn't want to do it. مِن الواضِح إنُّو ما يرِيد يسَوِّيها [min ʔilwa:điħ ʔinnu ma: yri:d ysawwi:ha] His annoyance is obvious from his voice. اِنزِعاجَه مبَيِّن مِن صَوتَه [ʔinziʕa:jah mbayyin min ṣawtah]

obviously • **1.** مِن الواضِح [min ʔilwa:điħ] مِن الظّاهِر [min ʔiđđa:hir] She was obviously wrong. مِن الواضِح كانَت غَلطانَة [min ʔilwa:điħ ča:nat ɣalṭa:na]

occasion • **1.** مُناسَبَة [muna:saba] مُناسَبات [muna:saba:t] *pl:* A dress like this can be worn for any occasion. فِستان مِثِل هَذا يِنلِبِس بكُلّ مُناسَبَة [fista:n miθil ha:đa yinlibis bkull muna:saba] What's the occasion? شِنُو المُناسَبَة؟ [šinu ʔilmuna:saba?]

occasionally • **1.** أحياناً [ʔaħya:nan] Except for a trip to Basra occasionally, I never leave Baghdad. ما عَدا سَفرَة لِلبَصرَة أحياناً، أبَد ما أطلَع مِن بَغداد [ma: ʕada: safra lilbaṣra ʔaħya:nan, ʔabad ma: ʔaṭlaʕ min baɣda:d]

occupation • **1.** شُغُل [šuɣul] أشغال [ʔašɣa:l] *pl:* مِهنَة [mihna] مِهَن [mihan] *pl:* What's your occupation? شِنُو شُغلَك؟ [šinu šuɣlak?] • **2.** اِحتِلال [ʔiħtila:l] Where were you during the occupation? وين كِنِت بزَمَن الاحتِلال؟ [wi:n činit bzaman ʔalʔiħtila:l?]

occupied • **1.** مُحتَلّ [muħtall] He is a refugee from occupied Palestine. هَذا لاجِئ مِن فِلِسطِين المُحتَلَّة [ha:đa la:ji? min filisṭi:n ʔilmuħtalla]

to occupy • **1.** اِحتَلّ [ʔiħtall] اِحتِلال [ʔiħtila:l] *vn: sv* a. The Turks occupied the town first. الأتراك اِحتَلّوا المَدِينَة بالأوَّل [ʔalʔatra:k ʔiħtallaw ʔilmadi:na bilʔawwal] • **2.** سِكَن [sikan] سُكنَة [sukna] *vn:* اِنسِكَن [ʔinsikan] *p:* The house hasn't been occupied for years. البَيت ما اِنسِكَن مِن سنِين [ʔilbayt ma: ʔinsikan min sni:n] • **3.** شِغَل [šiɣal] إشغال [ʔišɣa:l] *vn:* اِنشِغَل [ʔinšiɣal] *p:* Studying occupies all my time. الدِّراسَة دَتِشغِل كُلّ وَقتِي [ʔiddira:sa datišɣil kull waqti] The boss is occupied at the moment. الرَّئِيس مَشغُول هَسَّة [ʔirraʔi:s mašɣu:l hassa]

to occur • **1.** صار [ṣa:r] *sv* i. حِدَث [ħidaθ] حُدُوث [ħudu:θ] *vn: sv* i. وُقَع [wugaʕ] وَقِع [wagiʕ] *vn: sv* a. When did the accident occur? شوَقِت صار الحادِث؟ [šwakit ṣa:r ʔilħa:diθ?] • **2.** إجَى [ʔija:] *sv* i. The name occurred twice in the same chapter. إجا الإسِم مَرّتَين بنَفِس الفَصِل [ʔija ʔalʔisim marrtayn bnafis ʔilfaṣil] • **3.** خِطَر [xiṭar] خُطُور [xuṭu:r] *vn: sv* u. That would never have occurred to me. ذاك وَلا كان يُخطُر عَلَى بالِي [đa:k wala ča:n yuxṭur ʕala ba:li] • **4.** تبادَر [tba:dar] تَبادُر [taba:dur] *vn: sv* a. Suddenly it occurred to me that I forgot to lock the door. فُجأةً تبادَرلِي آنِي نِسِيت أقفُل الباب [fujʔatan tba:darli ʔa:ni nisi:t ʔaqful ʔilba:b]

ocean • **1.** مُحِيط [muħi:ṭ] مُحِيطات [muħi:ṭa:t] *pl:* The U. S. A. lies between two oceans. الوِلايات المُتَّحِدَة واقعَة بين مُحِيطَين [ʔilwila:ya:t ʔilmuttaħida wa:qʕa bi:n muħi:ṭayn]

o'clock • **1.** ساعَة [sa:ʕa] ساعات [sa:ʕa:t] *pl:* The train leaves at seven o'clock. القِطار يِترُك ساعَة سَبعَة [ʔilqiṭa:r yitruk sa:ʕa sabʕa]

October • **1.** تِشرِين الأوَّل [tišri:n ʔilʔawwal]

oculist • **1.** طَبِيب عيُون [ṭabi:b ʕyu:n] أطِبّاء عيُون [ʔaṭibba:ʔ ʕyu:n] *pl:*

odd • **1.** شاذّ [ša:đđ] شَواذ [šawa:đđ] *pl:* غَرِيب [ɣari:b] غُرَباء، غُربَة [ɣuraba:ʔ, ɣurba.] *pl:* He's a very odd person. هُوَّ فَدّ واحِد شاذّ [huwwa fadd wa:ħid ša:đđ] • **2.** تَكّ [takk] Haven't you seen an odd glove anywhere? ما شِفِت تَكّ كَفّ بفَدّ مَكان؟ [ma: šifit takk čaff bfadd maka:n?] • **3.** فَردِي [fardi] Pick an odd number. اِختار رَقَم فَردِي [ʔixta:r raqam fardi] • **4.** كَسِر [kasir] كسُور [ksu:r] *pl:* It cost me thirty-odd dinars. كَلّفَتنِي ثلاثِين دِينار وكسُور [kallifatni tla:θi:n dina:r wksu:r] • **5.** مِتفَرِّغ [mitfarriɣ] He does all the odd jobs around the house. هُوَّ يسَوِّي كُلّ الأشغال المِتفَرّغَة بالبَيت [huwwa ysawwi kull ʔalʔašɣa:l ʔalmitfarrɣa bilbayt] • **6.** مُخالِف [muxa:lif] We only have a few odd pairs left. عِدنا بَسّ فَدّ كَم زوج مخالفَة بُقَت [ʕidna bass fadd čam zawj mxa:lfa buqat]

odor • **1.** رِيحَة [ri:ħa] رَوايِح [rawa:yiħ] *pl:* What is that bad odor I smell? شِنُو هَالرِّيحَة الجّايفَة اللّي قاعِد أشتَمها [šinu harri:ħa ʔijja:yfa ʔilli qa:ʕid ʔaštammha]

of • **1.** مِن [min] I have a complete edition of his works. عِندِي نُسخَة كامِلَة مِن مُؤَلَّفاتَه [ʕindi nusxa ka:mla min muʔallafa:tah] The watch is of gold. السّاعَة مِن ذَهَب

[ʔissaːʕa min ðahab] • **2.** مال [maːl] The roof of our house is very high. السَّطِح مال بَيتنا كُلِّش عالي [ʔassaṭiħ maːl baytna kulliš ʕaːli]

*** Could I have a glass of water, please?** • **1.** أقدَر آخُذ كلاص ماي رَجاءاً [ʔagdar ʔaːxuð glaːṣ maːy rajaːʔan]

*** He's a manager of a big store.** • **1.** هُوَّ مُدير مَخزَن كِبير [huwwa mudiːr maxzan čibiːr]

off • **1.** مِن [min] This thing has been off the market for a year. هَالشِّي مِختِفي مِن السُّوق مِن سَنَة [hašši mixtifi min ʔissuːg min sana] This thing has been off the market for a year. هَالشِّي صارلَه سَنَة مِختِفي مِن السُّوق [hašši ṣaːrlah sana mixtifi min ʔissuːg] There's a button off your jacket. أكُو دُقمَة واقِعَة مِن سِترتَك [ʔaku dugma waːgiʕa min sitirtak]

*** The post office isn't far off.** • **1.** دائِرَة البَريد مُو كُلِّش بعِيدَة [daːʔirat ʔilbariːd muː kulliš biʕiːda]

*** Our maid is off today.** • **1.** خادمَتنا عِدها عُطلَة اليَوم [xaːdmatna ʕidha ʕuṭla ʔilyuːm] / خادمَتنا ما دَتِشتُغُل اليُوم [xaːdmatna maː datištuɣul ʔilyuːm]

*** He's a little off.** • **1.** هُوَّ شوَيَّة عِندَه خيُوط [huwwa šwayya ʕindah xyuːṭ] / شوَيَّة عَقلَه لاعِب [šwayya ʕaqlah laːʕib]

*** He was off in a flash.** • **1.** غاب مِثِل البَرق [ɣaːb miθil ʔilbarq]

*** They aren't so badly off.** • **1.** هُمَّة مُو كُلِّش مِحتاجِين [humma muː kulliš miħtaːjiːn]

*** They are very well off.** • **1.** هُمَّة كُلِّش زناكِين [humma kullis znaːgiːn]

*** The ship anchored three miles off shore.** • **1.** الباخِرَة ذَبَّت أنقَر ثَلث أميال عَن الساحِل [ʔilbaːxira ðabbat ʔangar tlaθ ʔamyaːl ʕan ʔissaːħil]

*** June is still three months off.** • **1.** بَعَد ثَلث أشهُر لحُزَيران [baʕad tlaθ ʔašhur lħuzayraːn] / حُزَيران بَعَدلَه ثلَث أشهُر يَاللّه يِجي [ħuzayraːn baʕadlah tlaθ ʔašhur yallah yiji]

*** His figures are way off.** • **1.** حساباتَه كُلّها غَلَط [ħsaːbaːtah kullha ɣalaṭ]

*** This is an off year for wheat.** • **1.** هاي مُو خَوش سَنَة لِلحُنطَة [haːy muː xuːš sana lilħunṭa]

*** I'm going to take a week off soon.** • **1.** راح آخُذ إسبُوع عُطلَة قَريباً [raːħ ʔaːxuð ʔisbuːʕ ʕuṭla qariːban]

*** This thing has been off the market for a year.** • **1.** هَالشِّي مِختِفي مِن السُوق مِن سَنَة [hašši mixtifi min ʔissuːg min sana] / هَالشِّي صارلَه سَنَة مِختِفي مِن السُّوق [hašši ṣaːrlah sana mixtifi min ʔissuːg]

*** There's a button off your jacket.** • **1.** أكُو دُقمَة واقِعَة مِن سِترتَك [ʔakuː dugma waːgiʕa min sitirtak]

*** Hands off!** • **1.** وَخِّر إيدَك مِن هاي [waxxir ʔidak min haːy]

*** They've broken off relations.** • **1.** قِطعَوا عَلاقاتهُم [qiṭʕaw ʕalaːqaːthum]

*** The branch broke off.** • **1.** اِنكِسَر الغُصِن [ʔinkisar ʔilɣuṣin]

*** One leg of the table has come off.** • **1.** اِنشِلعَت رِجِل مِن المَيز [ʔinšilʕat rijil min ʔilmiːz]

*** Ladies are requested to take their hats off.** • **1.** مَطلُوب مِن النِسوان يشِيلُون شَفقاتهُم [maṭluːb min ʔinniswaːn yšiːluːn šafaqaːthum]

*** When does the plane take off?** • **1.** شوَقِت تطِير الطَيّارَة؟ [šwakit tṭiːr ʔiṭṭayyaːra?]

off and on • **1.** أحياناً [ʔaħyaːnan] مَرَّة [marra] مَرّات [marraːt] *pl:* She works off and on. هِيَّ تِشتُغُل أحياناً [hiyya tištuɣul ʔaħyaːnan]

to offend • **1.** أساء إلَى [ʔasaːʔ ʔila] إساءَة إلَى [ʔisaːʔa ʔila] *vn: sv* i. I hope I didn't offend you. إن شاء الله ما أسَاءت إلَك [ʔinšaːllah maːʔasaːʔit ʔilak]

offense • **1.** إساءَة [ʔisaːʔa] إساءات [ʔisaːʔaːt] *pl:* I didn't mean any offense. ما قِصَدِت أيّ إساءَة [maː qṣadit ʔayy ʔisaːʔa] • **2.** مُخالَفَة [muxaːlafa] مُخالَفات [muxaːlafaːt] *pl:* Is this your first offense? هَذِي أوَّل مُخالَفَة إلَك؟ [haːði ʔawwal muxaːlafa ʔilak?]

to take offense • **1.** اِستاء [ʔistaːʔ] اِستِياء [ʔistiyaːʔ] *vn: sv* a. تكَدَّر [tkaddar] تكَدُّر [takaddur] *vn: sv* a. He took offense at my remark. اِستاء مِن مُلاحَظتِي [ʔistaːʔ min mulaːħaḍti]

offensive • **1.** مُسِيء [musiːʔ] His behavior was offensive to the local people. تَصَرُّفَه كان مُسِيئ لِلسُّكّان المَحَلِّيِّين [taṣarrufah čaːn musiːʔ lissukkaːn ʔalmaħalliyyiːn] • **2.** مَكرُوه [makruːh] كَريه [kariːh] It has an offensive odor. بِيها رِيحَة كَرِيهَة [biːha riːħa kariːha]

offer • **1.** عَرِض [ʕariðˌ] عُرُوض [ʕuruːð̣] *pl:* He made me a good offer. سَوّالِي خُوش عَرِض [sawwaːli xuːš ʕarið̣]

to offer • **1.** قَدَّم [qaddam] تَقدِيم [taqdiːm] *vn:* تقَدَّم [tqaddam] *p:* May I offer you a cup of coffee? أقدَر أقَدِّملَك فِنجان قَهوَة؟ [ʔagdar ʔaqaddimlak finjaːn gahwa?] • **2.** عِرَض [ʕirað̣] عَرِض [ʕarið̣] *vn:* اِنعِرَض [ʔinʕirað̣] *p:* He offered me a hundred dinars for it. عِرَض عَلَيّا مِيَّة دِينار بِيها [ʕirað̣ ʕalayya miyyat dinaːr biːha] • **3.** تبَرَّع [tbarraʕ] تَبَرُّع [tabarruʕ] *vn: sv* a. عِرَض [ʕirað̣] عَرض [ʕarið̣] *vn: sv* i. My brother-in-law offered to help me paint the house. نِسِيبِي تبَرَّع يعاوِنّي بِصُبغ البَيت [nisiːbi tbarraʕ yʕaːwinni bišubɣ ʔilbayt] • **4.** بَيَّن [bayyan] تَبيِين [tabyiːn] *vn:* تبَيَّن [tbayyan] *p:* Didn't they offer any resistance? ما بَيَّنوا أيّ مُقاوَمَة؟ [maː bayynaw ʔayy muqaːwama?]

offhand • **1.** بصُورَة مُرتَجَلَة [bṣuːra murtajala] I can't tell you offhand. ما أقدَر أقُلَّك بصُورَة مُرتَجَلَة [maː ʔagdar ʔagullak bṣuːra murtajala]

*** He treated me in an offhand manner.** • **1.** ما قَدَّرني [maː qaddarni] / عامَلنِي بِبُرُود [ʕaːmalni biburuːd]

office • **1.** مَكتَب [maktab] مَكاتِب [maka:tib] *pl:* دائِرَة [da:ʔira] دَوائِر [dawa:ʔir] *pl:* You can see me in my office. تِقدَر تشُوفنِي بِمَكتَبِي [tigdar tšu:fni bimaktabi] The offices close at five o'clock. الدَّوائِر تِنسَدّ السّاعَة خَمسَة [ʔaddawa:ʔir tinsadd ʔissa:ʕa xamsa] • **2.** مَركَز [markaz] مَراكِز [mara:kiz] *pl:* مَنصِب [manṣab] مَناصِب [mana:ṣib] *pl:* He has a high office in the government. عِندَه مَركَز عالِي بالحُكُومَة [ʕindah markaz ʕa:li bilħuku:ma]

*** The whole office was invited.**

• **1.** كُلّ المُوَظَّفِين كانَوا مَدعُوِّين [kull ʔilmuwaðð̣afi:n ča:naw madʕuwwi:n]

officer • **1.** ضابُط [ð̣a:buṭ] ضُبّاط [ð̣ubba:ṭ] *pl:* He was an officer during the last war. كان ضابُط بِالحَرُب الأَخِيرَة [ča:n ð̣a:buṭ bilħarub ʔilʔaxi:ra] • **2.** شُرطِي [šurṭi] شُرطِيِّين، شُرطَة [šurṭi:yyi:n, šurṭa] *pl:* Ask the officer how we get to the station. إسأَل الشُّرطِي شلُون نُوصَل لِلمَحَطَّة [ʔisʔal ʔiššurṭi šlu:n nu:ṣal lilmaħaṭṭa] • **3.** عُضُو إدارَة [ʕuð̣w ʔida:ra] أَعضاء إدارَة [ʔaʕð̣a:ʔ ʔida:ra] *pl:* Are you an officer of this club? إنتَ مِن أَعضاء إدارَة النّادِي؟ [ʔinta min ʔaʕð̣a:ʔ ʔida:rat ʔinna:di?]

official • **1.** مَأمُور [maʔmu:r] مأمُورِين [maʔmu:ri:n] *pl:* The customs official who examined my bags was very thorough. مَأمُور الجُمرُك اللِّي فُحَص جُنَطِي كان كُلِّش دَقِيق [maʔmu:r ʔilgumrug ʔilli fuħaṣ ǰunaṭi ča:n kulliš daqi:q] • **2.** مُوَظَّف [muwaðð̣af] مُوَظَّفِين [muwaðð̣afi:n] *pl:* He's a State Department official. هُوَّ مُوَظَّف مِن وِزارَة الخارِجِيَّة [huwwa muwaðð̣af min wiza:rat ʔilxa:riǰiyya] • **3.** رَسمِي [rasmi] He is here on official business. هُوَّ هنا بِشُغُل رَسمِي [huwwa hna bšuɣul rasmi]

officially • **1.** رَسمِيّاً [rasmiyyan] It was announced officially. اِنعِلنَت رَسمِيّاً [ʔinʕilnat rasmiyyan]

often • **1.** هوايَة [hwa:ya] كَثِير [kaθi:r] Do you see him often? تشُوفَه هوايَة؟ [tšu:fah hwa:ya?] He is absent often. هَذا يغِيب كَثِير [ha:ða yɣi:b kaθi:r] • **2.** غالِباً [ɣa:liban] غالِباً ما [ɣa:liban ma:] He often spends his afternoons with us. غالِباً ما يِقضِي عَصرِيّاتَه وِيّانا [ɣa:liban ma: yigð̣i ʕaṣriyya:tah wiyya:na]

how often • **1.** كَم مَرَّة [čam marra] How often do you go to the movies in a month? كَم مَرَّة ترُوح لِلسِّينَما بِالشَّهَر؟ [čam marra tru:ħ lissinama biššahar?] • **2.** يا ما [ya:ma] How often I have wished that I had gone to college. ياما أَتمَنَّى لَو داخِل كُلِّيَّة [ya:ma ʔatmanna: law da:xil kulliyya]

to ogle • **1.** بَصبَص ل [baṣbaṣ l-] بَصبَصَة [baṣbaṣa] *vn:* تبَصبَص [tbaṣbaṣ] *p:* The boys stand in front of the school and ogle the girls as they come out. الوِلِد يُوقفُون قِدّام المَدرَسَة ويبَصبِصُون لِلبَنات مِن يطلعُون [ʔilwulid yu:gfu:n gidda:m ʔilmadrasa wybaṣbiṣu:n lilbana:t min yṭilʕu:n]

oil • **1.** نَفُط [nafuṭ] زَيت [zayt, zi:t] زيُوت [zyu:t] *pl:* Oil is the most important export in Iraq. النَّفُط أَهَمّ صادِرات العِراق [ʔinnafuṭ ʔahamm ṣa:dira:t ʔilʕira:q] We need some oil for the stove. نِحتاج نَفُط لِلطَّبّاخ [niħta:ǰ nafuṭ liṭṭabba:x] • **2.** دِهِن [dihin] Vegetable oil is often used for cooking. الدِّهن النَّباتِي هوايَة مُستَعمَل لِلطَّبُخ [ʔaddihn ʔinnaba:ti hwa:ya mustaʕmal liṭṭabux] • **3.** زَيت [zayt zi:t] زيُوت [zyu:t] *pl:* I really prefer olive oil on the salad. آنِي بِالحَقِيقَة أَفَضِّل زَيت الزَّيتُون عالزَّلاطَة [ʔa:ni bilħaqi:qa ʔafað̣ð̣il zi:t ʔizzaytu:n ʕazzala:ṭa]

to oil • **1.** دَهَّن [dahhan] تدهِين [tadhi:n] *vn:* تدَهَّن [tdahhan] *p:* The sewing machine needs to be oiled. مَكِينَة الخِياطَة يِراد إلها تِتدَهَّن [maki:nat ʔilxiya:ṭa yira:d ʔilha tiddahhan]

oilcake • **1.** كِسبَة [kisba] Our water buffalo lives on oilcakes. جامُوسنا يعِيش عالكِسبَة [ǰa:mu:sna yiʕi:š ʕalkisba]

oilcan • **1.** ياغدان [ya:ɣda:n] ياغدانات [ya:ɣda:na:t] *pl:*

oilcloth • **1.** قماش مشَمَّع [qma:š mšammaʕ] أَقمِشَة مشَمّعَة [ʔaqmiša mšammʕa] *pl:*

ointment • **1.** مَلحَم [malħam] دِهِن [dihin]

O.K. • **1.** مُوافَقَة [muwa:faqa] مُصادَقَة [muṣa:daqa] قُبُول [qubu:l] I need his O. K. أَحتاج مُوافَقتَه [ʔaħta:ǰ muwa:faqtah] • **2.** زَين [zayn] Everything is O. K. now. هَسَّة كُلِّشِي زين [hassa kullši zi:n]

*** I'll go along, if it's O.K. with you.**

• **1.** أَرُوح وِيّاك، إذا ما عِندَك مانِع [ʔaru:ħ wiyya:k, ʔiða: ma: ʕindak ma:niʕ]

to O.K. • **1.** وافَق [wa:faq] مُوافَقَة [muwa:faqa] *vn: sv* u. صادَق [ṣa:daq, ṣa:dag] مُصادَقَة [muṣa:daqa] *vn: sv* i. He has to O. K. it first. لازِم يوافُق عَليها أَوَّل [la:zim ywa:fuq ʕali:ha ʔawwal]

old • **1.** عَتِيق [ʕati:g] عِتَّق [ʕittag] *pl:* قَدِيم [qadi:m] قُدَماء [qudama:ʔ] *pl:* I gave all my old clothes to the poor. إنطَيت كُلّ هدُومِي العَتِيقَة لِلفُقَراء [ʔinṭi:t kull hdu:mi ʔilʕati:ga lilfuqara:ʔ] Is this an old model? هاي نَوعها قَدِيمَة؟ [ha:y nawʕha qadi:ma?] • **2.** كِبِير [čibi:r] كبار [kba:r] *pl:* He's pretty old. هُوَّ كُلِّش كِبِير [huwwa kulliš čibi:r]

*** How old are you?** • **1.** شقَدّ عُمرَك؟ [šgadd ʕumrak?]

old man • **1.** شايِب [ša:yib] شِيّاب [šiyya:b] *pl:* My uncle is an old man, but he is still very active. عَمِّي شايِب لَكِن لا يَزال كُلِّش نَشِيط [ʕammi ša:yib la:kin la: yaza:l kulliš naši:ṭ]

old woman • **1.** عَجُوز [ʕaǰu:z] عَجَزَة [ʕaǰaza] *pl:* عَجُوزَة [ʕaǰu:za] عَجُوزات، عَجايِز [ʕaǰu:za:t, ʕaǰa:yiz] *pl:* She's an old woman now. هَسَّة هِيَّ عَجُوز [hassa hiyya ʕaǰu:z]

old-fashioned • **1.** رَجعِي [rajʕi] مِتعَصُّب [mitʕaṣṣub] She's very old-fashioned in her ideas. هِيَّ كُلِّش رَجعِيَّة بِأَفكارها

O

[hiyya kulliš rajʕiyya biʔafka:rha] • **2.** مِن طِراز قَدِيم [min ṭira:z qadi:m] His clothes are old-fashioned, but of good quality. مَلابسَه مِن طِراز قَدِيم لَكِن مِن نَوعِيَّة زينَة [mala:bsah min ṭira:z qadi:m la:kin min nawʕiyya zi:na]

to omit • **1.** حِذَف [ḥiðaf] حَذِف [ḥaðif] *vn:* اِنحِذَف [ʔinḥiðaf] *p:* Omit that word. إحذِف هَالكِلمَة [ʔiḥðif haččilma]

on • **1.** عَلَى [ʕala] He sat on the speaker's left. قِعَد عَلَى يَسار الخَطِيب [giʕad ʕala yasa:r ʔilxaṭi:b] The drinks are on the house. الشُّرُب عَلَى حساب المَحَل [ʔiššurub ʕala ḥsa:b ʔilmaḥall] • **2.** عَلَى [ʕala] فوق [fu:g, fu:q] Put it on the table. خَلِّيهَا عالميز [xalli:ha ʕalmi:z] • **3.** ب [b] On what day? بأَي يوم؟ [bʔayy yu:m?] Do you sell on credit? تبيع بأَقساط؟ [tbi:ʕ bʔaqsa:ṭ?] I live on Rashid St. أَسكُن بشارِع الرَّشِيد [ʔaskun bša:riʕ ʔirraši:d] Who's on the team? مِنُو بالفِرقَة؟ [minu bilfirqa?] What's on the radio today? شَكُو بالرّاديُو اليُوم؟ [šaku birra:dyu ʔilyu:m?] • **4.** عَن [ʕan] His lecture was on Arab solidarity. مُحاضَرتَه كانَت عَن التَّضامُن العَرَبِي [muḥa:ḍartah ča:nat ʕan ʔattaḍa:mun ʔilʕarabi]

* **Are you open on Friday?** • **1.** تفَتِّح الجُمعَة؟ [tfattiḥ ʔijjumʕa?]

* **Is the gas on?** • **1.** الغاز مَشغُول؟ [ʔilɣa:z mašʕu:l?]

and so on • **1.** و إلَى آخِرِه [w ʔila ʔa:xirih] I need paper, ink, and so on. أَحتاج وَرَق، حِبِر وَإلَى آخِرِه [ʔaḥta:j waraq, ḥibir waʔila ʔa:xirih]

once • **1.** مَرَّة وِحدَة [marra wiḥda] فَدّ مَرَّة [fadd marra] مَرَّة [marra] مَرّات [marra:t] *pl:* I've seen him only once. شِفتَه مَرَّة وِحدَة بَس [šiftah marra wiḥda bass] He feeds the dog once a day. يطَعُّم الكَلِب مَرَّة باليُوم [yṭaʕʕum ʔiččalib marra bilyu:m] • **2.** فَدّ يوم [fadd yu:m] This was once the business section. فَدّ يوم هَذا كان المَركَز التِّجارِي [fadd yu:m ha:ða ča:n ʔalmarkaz ʔattija:ri]

at once • **1.** سُوَة، سُوا [suwa] مَرَّة وِحدَة [marra wiḥda] فَدّ مَرَّة [fadd marra] Everything came at once. كُلشِي إجا مَرَّة وِحدَة [kullši ʔija marra wiḥda] • **2.** حالاً [ḥa:lan] بساع [bsa:ʕ] سَرِيعاً [sari:ʕan] Come at once. بساع تَعال [bsa:ʕ taʕa:l]

once in a while • **1.** بَعض الأَحيان [baʕð ʔilʔaḥya:n] أَحياناً [ʔaḥya:nan] دَورات [dawra:t] Once in a while I like a good glass of cold buttermilk. بَعض الأَحيان أَحِبّ فَدّ كلاص لِبَن بارِد [baʕð ʔilʔaḥya:n ʔaḥibb fadd gla:ṣ liban ba:rid]

one • **1.** واحِد [wa:ḥid] وِحدَة [wiḥda] *Feminine:* Count from one to a hundred. عِدّ مِن الواحِد لِلمِيَّة [ʕidd min ʔilwa:ḥid lilmiyya] One or two will be enough. واحِد أَو إثنَين كافِي [wa:ḥid ʔaw ʔiθnayn ka:fi] It's almost one o'clock. السّاعَة حَوالِي الوِحدَة [ʔissa:ʕa ḥawa:li ʔalwiḥda] One never knows. الواحِد شمَدرِيه [ʔilwa:ḥid šmadri:h] One of us can buy the tickets. واحِد مِنّا يِقدَر يِشتِرِي البِطاقات [wa:ḥid minna yigdar yištiri ʔalbiṭa:qa:t] • **2.** فَدّ [fadd] واحِد [wa:ḥid] وِحدَة [wiḥda] *Feminine:* I have one question I want to ask. عِندِي فَدّ سُؤال أَرِيد أَسأَلَه [ʕindi fadd suʔa:l ʔari:d ʔasʔalah] • **3.** أَبُو [ʔabu] The one with the cover is the best box for our purpose. أَبُو الغِطا أَحسَن صَندُوق لِغَرَضنا [ʔabu ʔalɣiṭa: ʔaḥsan ṣandu:g liɣaraḍna] The one with the cover is the best box for our purpose. اللِّي بالغِطا أَحسَن صَندُوق لِغَرَضنا [ʔilli bilɣiṭa ʔaḥsan ṣandu:g liɣaraḍna] The one with the top down is my car. أُمّ التَّنتَة النّازلَة السَّيّارَة مالتِي [ʔumm tanta ʔanna:zla ʔissayya:ra ma:lti]

* **I prefer the more expensive one.** • **1.** أَفَضِّل الأَغلَى [ʔafaḍḍil ʔilʔaɣla]

* **Take that one.** • **1.** أُخُذ هَذاك [ʔuxuð haða:k]

* **One of these days, I'll be back.** • **1.** فَدّ يوم مِن الأَيّام أَرجَع [fadd yu:m min ʔilʔayya:m ʔarjaʕ]

* **On the one hand he wants it finished, on the other hand he doesn't give us the material.** • **1.** مِن جِهَة يرِيدها تِخلَص ومِن جِهَة ما دَينطِينا المَوادّ [min jiha yri:dha tixlaṣ wmin jiha ma: dayinṭi:na ʔilmawa:dd]

one another • **1.** واحِد اللاخ [wa:ḥid ʔilla:x] They like one another. يحِبُّون واحِد اللّاخ [yḥibbu:n wa:ḥid ʔilla:x]

one at a time • **1.** واحِد واحِد [wa:ḥid wa:ḥid] Let them in one at a time. خَشِّشهُم واحِد واحِد [xaššišhum wa:ḥid wa:ḥid]

onion • **1.** بُصلَة [buṣla] بُصلات [buṣla:t] *pl:* بُصَل [buṣal] *Collective*

only • **1.** بَسّ [bass] I was going to buy it, only he told me not to. كان إشتِرَيتها بَسّ هُوَّ قَلِّي لا [ča:n ʔištiri:tha bass huwwa galli la:] This is only for you. هَذِي بَسّ إلَك [ha:ði bass ʔilak] • **2.** وَحِيد [waḥi:d] He's our only child. هُوَّ إبننا الوَحِيد [huwwa ʔibinna ʔilwaḥi:d]

open • **1.** مَفتُوح [maftu:ḥ] مَفكُوك [mafku:k] He may have come in through an open window. يجُوز دِخَل مِن شِبّاك مَفتُوح [yju:z dixal min šibba:č maftu:ḥ] The dining room is not open yet. غُرفَة الأَكِل ما مَفتُوحَة لهَسَّة [ɣurfat ʔilʔakil ma: maftu:ḥa lhassa] • **2.** شاغِر [ša:ɣir] Is the job still open? الوَظِيفَة بَعَدها شاغرَة؟ [lwaḍi:fa baʕadha ša:ɣra?] • **3.** مَفتُوق [maftu:g] The shoulder seam of your jacket is open. خياط كِتِف سِترتَك مَفتُوق [xya:ṭ čitif sitirtak maftu:g] • **4.** طَلِق [ṭaliq] He's in the open air all day long. هُوَّ بالهَوا الطَّلِق طُول اليُوم [huwwa bilhawa ʔaṭṭaliq ṭu:l ʔilyu:m]

to open • **1.** فِتَح [fitaḥ] فَتِح [fatiḥ] *vn:* اِنفِتَح [ʔinfitaḥ] *p:* فَكّ [fakk] فَكّ [fakk] *vn:* اِنفَكّ [ʔinfakk] *p:* Open the door please. إفتَح الباب، مِن فَضلَك [ʔiftaḥ ʔilba:b, min faḍlak] They opened an account at the bank. فِتحَوا حِساب بالبَنك [fitḥaw ḥisa:b bilbang] • **2.** فَتَّح [fattaḥ] تَفتِيح [tafti:ḥ] *vn: sv* i. We open every day at 9 A. M. نفَتِّح ساعَة تِسعَة الصُّبُح كُلّ يوم [nfattiḥ sa:ʕa tisʕa ʔiṣṣubuḥ kull yu:m] • **3.** شَقّ [šaqq] شَقّ [šaqq] *vn:* اِنشَقّ [ʔinšaqq] *p:* The government is going to open a new highway through the mountains.

الحُكُومَة راح تشُقّ طَرِيق جِدِيد يِختِرِق الجِّبال [ʔilħuku:ma ra:ħ tšuqq ṭari:q ǰidi:d yixtiriq ʔiǰǰiba:l] The police opened a way through the crowd for us. الشُّرطَة شَقُّوا إلنا طَرِيق بين الجّماهِير [ʔiššurṭa šaggaw ʔilna ṭari:q bayn ʔiǰǰama:hi:r] • **4.** بدا [bida:] بِدايَة [bida:ya] *vn:* اِنبِدا [ʔinbida:] *p:* When does hunting season open? شوَقِت يِبدِي مَوسِم الصَّيد؟ [šwakit yibdi mawsim ʔiṣṣayd?] • **5.** اِنفِتَح [ʔinfitaħ] اِنفِتاح [ʔinfita:ħ] *vn: sv* i. The door opens easily now. الباب هَسَّة دَينفِتِح بسُهُولَة [ʔilba:b hassa dayinfitiħ bsuhu:la]

*** He's always open to reasonable suggestions.**
• **1.** هُوَّ دائِماً يِقبَل اِقتِراحات مَعقُولَة [huwwa da:ʔiman yiqbal ʔiqtira:ħa:t maʕqu:la]

to open onto • **1.** طِلَع عَلَى [ṭilaʕ ʕala] طَلِع [ṭaliʕ] *vn: sv* a. Our room opens onto a balcony. غُرفَتنا تِطلَع عَلَى بالكُون [ɣurfatna tiṭlaʕ ʕala balku:n]

to open up • **1.** فَكّ [fakk] فَكّ [fakk] *vn:* اِنفَكّ [ʔinfakk] *p:* فِتَح [fitaħ] فَتِح [fatiħ] *vn:* اِنفِتَح [ʔinfitaħ] *p:* Open up the package. فُكّ الرُّزمَة [fukk ʔirruzma] Can you open up the safe? تِقدَر تفُكّ القاصَة؟ [tigdar tfukk ʔilqa:ṣa?]

opening • **1.** فَتحَة [fatħa] The opening isn't big enough. الفَتحَة مُو كِبِيرَة كِفايَة [ʔilfatħa mu: čibi:ra kifa:ya] • **2.** بِدايَة [bida:ya] بِدايات [bida:ya:t] *pl:* We missed the opening of his speech. ما لَحَّقنا عَلَى بدايَة خِطابَه [ma: laħħagna ʕala bda:yat xiṭa:bah] • **3.** اِفتِتاح [ʔiftita:ħ] Were you at the opening of the exhibition? كِنِت بِافتِتاح المَعرَض؟ [činit biʔiftita:ħ ʔilmaʕrað?] • **4.** شاغِر [ša:ɣir] We'll call you as soon as we have an opening. نخابرَك أوَّل ما يصِير عِدنا شاغِر [nxa:brak ʔawwal ma: yṣi:r ʕidna ša:ɣir]

opera • **1.** أوبرا [ʔu:pra] أوبرات [ʔu:pra:t] *pl:*

opera house • **1.** دار أوبرا [da:r ʔu:pra] دُور أوبرا [du:r ʔu:pra] *pl:*

to operate • **1.** شَغَّل [šaɣɣal] تَشغِيل [tašɣi:l] *vn:* تشَغَّل [tšaɣɣal] *p:* How do you operate this machine? شلُون تشَغِّل هَالمَكِينَة؟ [šlu:n tšaɣɣil halmaki:na?] • **2.** اِشتِغَل [ʔištiɣal] اِشتِغال [ʔištiɣa:l] *vn: sv* u. This machine operates on electricity. هَالمَكِينَة تِشتُغُل بالكَهرَباء [halmaki:na tištuɣul bilkahraba:ʔ] • **3.** سَوَّى [sawwa:] تَسوِيَة [taswiya] *vn: sv* i. The doctor says he'll have to operate on her. الدّكتور قال لازِم يسَوِّيلها العَمَلِيَّة [ʔiddiktu:r ga:l la:zim ysawwi:lha ʔilʕamaliyya]

operation • **1.** عَمَلِيَّة [ʕamaliyya] عَمَلِيّات [ʕamaliyya:t] *pl:* This is her third operation. هاي ثالِث عَمَلِيَّة إلها [ha:y θa:liθ ʕamaliyya ʔilha] • **2.** حَرَكَة [ħaraka] One machine does the whole process in a single operation. مَكِينَة وِحدَة تقُوم بكُلّ العَمَلِيَّة بحَرَكَة وحدَة [maki:na wiħda tqu:m bkull ʔilʕamaliyya biħaraka wiħda] • **3.** اِستِعمال [ʔistiʕma:l] They just put this line into operation. هَسَّة خَلّوا هالخَطّ بالإستِعمال [hassa xallaw halxaṭṭ bilʔistiʕma:l]

opinion • **1.** رَأي [raʔy] آراء [ʔa:ra:ʔ] *pl:* فِكِر [fikir] I have a very high opinion of him. فِكِرتِي عَنَّه كُلِّش زينَة [fikirti ʕannah kulliš zi:na] What's your opinion? شِنُو رَأيَك؟ [šinu: raʔayak?] We'll have to get the opinion of an expert. لازِم ناخُذ رَأي خَبِير [la:zim na:xuð raʔy xabi:r]

opponent • **1.** مُعارِض [muʕa:rið] مُنافِس [muna:fis] مُنافِسِين [muna:fisi:n] *pl:* خَصُم [xaṣum] خُصُوم [xuṣu:m] *pl:* He's a dangerous opponent. هُوَّ مُنافِس خَطِر [huwwa muna:fis xaṭir]

opportunity • **1.** فُرصَة [furṣa] فُرَص [furaṣ] *pl:* When will you have an opportunity to see him? شوَقِت يصِير عِندَك فُرصَة تشُوفَه؟ [šwakit yṣi:r ʕindak furṣa tšu:fah?] This is a big opportunity for you. هاي فُرصَة كبِيرَة إلَك [ha:y furṣa čibi:ra ʔilak]

to oppose • **1.** عارَض [ʕa:rað] مُعارَضَة [muʕa:raḍa] *vn: sv* i. He's the one who opposed your admission to the club. هُوَّ اللّي عارَض اِنتِمائَك لِلنّادِي [huwwa ʔilli ʕa:rað ʔintima:ʔak linna:di] • **2.** نافَس [na:fas] مُنافَسَة [muna:fasa] *vn: sv* i. He opposed me in the last election. نافَسنِي بالإنتِخابات الأخِيرَة [na:fasni bilʔintixa:ba:t ʔilʔaxi:ra]

opposite • **1.** مُقابِل [muqa:bil] قبال [gba:l] We live opposite the library. نِسكُن قبال المَكتَبَة [niskun gba:l ʔilmaktaba] • **2.** مُعاكِس [muʕa:kis] مُخالِف [muxa:lif] عَكِس [ʕakis] He came from the opposite direction. إجا مِن الجِّهَة المُعاكِسَة [ʔiǰa min ʔaǰǰiha ʔalmuʕa:ksa] This is just the opposite of what I meant. هَذا تَماماً مُخالِف لِما عنَيتَه [ha:ða tama:man muxa:lif lima ʕnaytah] This is just the opposite of what I meant. هَذا تَماماً عَكِس اللّي عِنَيتَه [ha:ða tama:man ʕakis ʔilli ʕnaytah]

opposition • **1.** مُعارَضَة [muʕa:raḍa] The proposal met with unexpected opposition. الاقتِراح واجَه مُعارَضَة غير مُتَوَقَّعَة [ʔilʔiqtira:ħ wa:ǰah muʕa:raḍa ɣi:r mutawaqqaʕa]

to oppress • **1.** طِغَى عَلَى [ṭiɣa: ʕala] طُغيان [ṭuɣya:n] *vn:* اِنطِغَى [ʔinṭiɣa:] *p:* They oppressed the poor and the weak. طِغَوا عَلَى الفُقَراء والضُعَفاء [ṭiɣaw ʕala ʔilfuqara:ʔ wiḍḍuʕafa:ʔ]

oppressive • **1.** مضايِق [mḍa:yiq] مِستِبِدّ [mistibidd] The heat's oppressive today. الحَرّ اليُوم مضايِق [ʔilħarr ʔilyu:m mḍa:yiq]

optician • **1.** نَظّاراتِي [naḍḍa:ra:ti] نَظّاراتِيَّة [naḍḍa:ra:tiyya] *pl:* صاحِب نَظّارات [ṣa:ħib naḍḍa:ra:t] أصحاب نَظّارات [ʔaṣħa:b naḍḍa:ra:t] *pl:*

optimism • **1.** تَفاؤُل [tafa:ʔul]

O

optimist • **1.** مِتفائِل [mitfa:ʔil]

optimistic • **1.** مِتفائِل [mitfa:ʔil] Don't be so optimistic. لا تكُون هَالقَدّ مِتفائِل [la: tku:n halgadd mitfa:ʔil]

or • **1.** لَو [law] أَو [law] He's coming today or tomorrow. هُوَّ جاي اليُوم لَو باكِر [huwwa ǰa:y ʔilyu:m law ba:čir]

oral • **1.** شَفَهِي [šafahi] شَفَوِي [šafawi] She passed the oral examination. نِجحَت بِالإمتِحان الشَّفَهِي [niǰħat bilʔimtiħa:n ʔaššafahi]

orally • **1.** شَفَهِيّاً [šafahiyyan] شَفَوِيّاً [šafawiyyan]

orange • **1.** بُرتُقالَة [purtuqa:la] بُرتُقالات [purtuqa:la:t] *pl:* بُرتَقال [purtaqa:l] *Collective:* How much are the oranges? بيش البُرتَقال؟ [biyš ʔilpurtaqa:l?] • **2.** بُرتُقالِي [purtuqa:li] Her dress was orange and white. نَفنُوفها كان بُرتُقالِي وأَبيَض [nafnu:fha ča:n purtuqa:li wʔabyað̣]

orange juice • **1.** شَربَت بُرتَقال [šarbat purtaqa:l] عَصِير بُرتَقال [ʕaṣi:r purtaqa:l]

orchard • **1.** بِستان [bista:n] بساتِين [bsa:ti:n] *pl:*

orchestra • **1.** فِرقَة مَوسِيقِيَّة [firqa mu:siqiyya] فِرَق موسِيقِيَّة [firaq mawsi:qiyya] *pl:* جَوق مَوسِيقِي [ǰu:q mawsi:qi] أَجواق مَوسِيقِيَّة [ʔaǰwa:q mawsi:qiyya] *pl:*

order • **1.** أَمُر [ʔamur] أَوامِر [ʔawa:mir] *pl:* I'm just obeying orders. آنِي بَسّ دَاطِيع الأَوامِر [ʔa:ni bass daʔaṭi:ʕ ʔilʔawa:mir] • **2.** طَلَب [ṭalab] طَلَبات [ṭalaba:t] *pl:* Waiter, I'd like to change my order. بُوي، أَرِيد أَبَدِّل الطَّلَب مالِي [bu:y, ʔari:d ʔabaddil ʔiṭṭalab ma:li] • **3.** تَرتِيب [tarti:b] Please put these cards in order. مِن فَضلَك خَلِّي هالبِطاقات حَسَب التَّرتِيب [min fað̣lak xalli halbiṭa:qa:t ħasab ʔattarti:b] • **4.** نِظام [nið̣a:m] أَنظِمَة [ʔanð̣ima] *pl:* The police restored order quickly. الشُّرطَة اِستَعادَت النِّظام بِسُرعَة [ʔiššurṭa ʔistaʕa:dat ʔinnið̣a:m bsurʕa]

*** I disposed of it in short order.** • **1.** دَبَّرتها بِالعَجَل [dabbaritha bilʕaǰal]

in order • **1.** بمَحَلّ [bmaħall] Your remark is quite in order. مُلاحَظتَك بمَحَلّها تَماماً [mula:ħað̣tak bmaħallha tama:man] • **2.** مرَتَّب [mrattab] منَظَّم [mnað̣ð̣am] I'd like to see your room in order just once. بوُدّي أَشُوف غُرفَتَك مرَتَّبَة وَلَو مَرَّة [biwuddi ʔašu:f ɣuraftak mrattaba walaw marra] • **3.** كامِل [ka:mil] His papers are in order. أَوراقَه كامِلَة [ʔawra:qah ka:mla] • **4.** حَسَب [ħasab] Line up in order of height. اِصطَفُّوا حَسَب الطُّول [ʔiṣṭaffu: ħasab ʔiṭṭu:l]

in order to • **1.** حَتَّى [ħatta] I've come from Amara in order to see you. جاي مِن العمارَة حَتَّى أَشُوفَك [ǰa:y min ʔalʕma:ra ħatta ʔašu:fak]

made to order • **1.** تِفصال [tifṣa:l] تُوصاة [tu:ṣa:] All his suits are made to order. كُلّ قُوطَه تُفصال [kull qu:ṭah tufṣa:l] • **2.** تُوصاة [tu:ṣa:] Did you buy your furniture ready-made or is it made to order? اِشتِرَيت أَثاثَك حاضرَة لَو تُوصاة؟ [ʔištiri:t ʔaθa:θak ħa:ð̣ra law tu:ṣa:?]

out of order • **1.** خَربان [xarba:n] The fan is out of order. البَنكَة خَربانَة [ʔalpanka xarba:na]

to order • **1.** أَمَر ب [ʔumar b-] أَمُر [ʔamur] *vn:* اِنأَمَر [ʔinʔumar] *p:* He ordered their arrest. أَمَر بتَوقِيفهُم [ʔumar bitawqi:fhum] • **2.** طِلَب [ṭilab] طَلِب [ṭalib] *vn:* اِنطِلَب [ʔinṭilab] *p:* Order the taxi for six o'clock. أُطلُبَه لِلتَّكسِي يِجِي ساعَة سِتَّة [ʔuṭulbah littaksi yiǰi saːʕa sitta] • **3.** وَصَّى [waṣṣa:] تَوصِيَة [tawṣiya] *vn: sv* i. I ordered a new set of tires for the car. وَصَّيت عَلَى طَخُم تايَرات جِدِيد لِلسَّيّارَة [waṣṣi:t ʕala ṭaxum ta:yira:t ǰidi:d lissayya:ra]

to order around • **1.** تأَمَّر عَلَى [tʔammar ʕala] تَأَمُّر [taʔammur] *vn: sv* a. Don't order me around! لا تِتأَمَّر عَلَيّا [la: titʔammar ʕalayya]

ordinary • **1.** اِعتِيادِي [ʔiʕtiya:di] عادِي [ʕa:di] He's just an ordinary mechanic. هُوَّ مِيكانِيكِي اِعتِيادِي [huwwa mikani:ki ʔiʕtiya:di]

ore • **1.** * He brought in a piece of copper ore for analysis. جاب قِطعَة مِن نُحاس خام لِلتَّحلِيل [ǰa:b qiṭʕa min nuħa:s xa:m littaħli:l]

organ • **1.** عُضُو [ʕuð̣w] أَعضاء [ʔaʕð̣a:ʔ] *pl:* Our lesson in Health today was on the genital organs. دَرِسنا بِعِلم الصِّحَّة اليُوم كان عَن الأَعضاء التَّناسُلِيَّة [darisna biʕilm ʔiṣṣiħħa ʔilyu:m ča:n ʕann ʔilʔaʕð̣a:ʔ ʔattana:suliyya]

organization • **1.** تَنظِيم [tanð̣i:m] تَرتِيب [tarti:b] The material is good, but the organization is poor. المادَّة زينَة لَكِن التَّنظِيم مُو زين [ʔilma:dda zi:na la:kin ʔattanð̣i:m mu: zi:n] • **2.** مُنَظَّمَة [munað̣ð̣ama] مُنَظَّمات [munað̣ð̣ama:t] *pl:* He is a member of our organization. هُوَّ عُضُو بمُنَظَّمَتنا [huwwa ʕuð̣w bmunað̣ð̣amatna]

to organize • **1.** نَظَّم [nað̣ð̣am] تَنظِيم [tanð̣i:m] *vn:* اِتنَظَّم [ʔitnað̣ð̣am] *p:* رَتَّب [rattab] تَرتِيب [tarti:b] *vn:* ترَتَّب [trattab] *p:* They have asked me to organize the election campaign for them. طُلبَوا مِنِّي أَنظِّملهُم حَملَة الانتِخابات [ṭulbaw minni ʔanað̣ð̣imilhum ħamlat ʔilintixa:ba:t] We'll call you up as soon as we get ourselves organized. نخابرَك أَوَّل ما نرَتِّب أُمُورنا [nxa:brak ʔawwal ma: nrattib ʔumu:rna]

*** All the employees in our plant are organized.** • **1.** كُلّ العُمّال بمَصنَعنا مِنظَمِّين لِلنَقابَة [kull ʔilʕumma:l bmaṣnaʕna minð̣ammi:n linnaqa:ba]

Orient • **1.** الشَّرق [ʔiššarq]

O

oriental • **1.** شَرقِي [šarqi]

origin • **1.** أَصِل [ʔaṣil] أُصُول [ʔuṣu:l] *pl:* Darwin named his book "The Origin of the Species." دارون سَمَّى كتابَه "أصل الأنواع" [da:rwin samma: kta:bah "ʔaṣl ʔalʔanwa:ʕ"] • **2.** أساس [ʔasa:s] أساسات [ʔasa:sa:t] *pl:* I'm trying to get at the origin of the trouble between them. أحاوِل أتوَصَّل إلَى أساس المُشكِلَة بينهُم [ʔaħa:wil ʔatwaṣṣal ʔila ʔasa:s ʔalmuškila baynhum] • **3.** تَحَرُّك [taħarruk] تَحَرُّكات [taħarruka:t] *pl:* We will pay your way back to your point of origin. راح نِدفَعلَك نَفَقات الرُّجُوع حَتَّى نُقطَة تَحَرُّكَك [ra:ħ nidfaʕlak nafaqa:t ʔirruǰu:ʕ ħatta nuqṭat taħarrukak] • **4.** مَنشَأ [manšaʔ] مَناشِئ [mana:šiʔ] *pl:* All importers must submit a certificate of origin for their goods. كُلّ المِستورِدِين لازِم يبِرزُون شَهادات مَنشَأ لِبَضائِعهُم [kull ʔilmistawridi:n la:zim ybirzu:n šaha:da:t manšaʔ libaða:ʔiʕhum] • **5.** مَصدَر [maṣdar] مَصادِر [maṣa:dir] *pl:* What is the origin of this information? هالأخبار مَصدَرها منين؟ [halʔaxba:r maṣdarha mni:n?]

original • **1.** أَصلِي [ʔaṣli] The original plan was altogether different. المَشرُوع الأَصلِي كان مِختِلِف تَماماً عَن هاي [ʔilmašru:ʕ ʔilʔaṣli ča:n mixtilif tama:man ʕan ha:y] • **2.** مُبتَكِر [mubtakir] مُبتَدِئ [mubtadiʔ] مُبتَدِئِين [mubtadiʔi:n] *pl:* This architect has original ideas. هالمُهَندِس النّاشِئ عِندَه أفكار مُبتَكِرَة [halmuhandis ʔanna:šiʔ ʕindah ʔafka:r mubtakira]

originally • **1.** أوَّلاً [ʔawwalan] أصلاً [ʔaṣlan] بالأَصِل [bilʔaṣil] Originally he wanted to be a doctor. بِالأَوَّل راد يصِير طَبِيب [bilʔawwal ra:d yṣi:r ṭabi:b]

to originate • **1.** صِدَر [ṣidar] صُدُور [ṣudu:r] *vn: sv* u. نِشَأ [nišaʔ] نِشُوء [nišu:ʔ] *vn: sv* a. Where did this rumor originate? هَالإشاعَة منين صِدرَت؟ [halʔiša:ʕa mni:n ṣidrat?] • **2.** تحَرَّك [tħarrak] تَحَرُّك [taħarruk] *vn: sv* a. Where does this train originate? هَالقِطار منين يِتحَرَّك؟ [halqiṭa:r mni:n yitħarrak?]

orphan • **1.** يَتِيم [yati:m] يتامَة، أيتام [yta:ma, ʔayta:m] *pl:*

orphanage • **1.** مَيتَم [maytam] مَياتِم [maya:tim] *pl:* دار أيتام [da:r ʔayta:m] دُور أيتام [du:r ʔayta:m] *pl:* مَعهَد أيتام [maʕhad ʔayta:m] مَعاهِد أيتام [maʕa:hid ʔayta:m] *pl:*

ostrich • **1.** نَعام [naʕa:m] *Collective*

other • **1.** آخَر [ʔa:xar] أخَرين [ʔa:xari:n] *pl:* أُخرَى [ʔuxra] *Feminine:* ثانِي [θa:ni] All the others got a raise but me. كُلّ الآخَرين تَرفَعَوا إلّا آنِي [kull ʔilʔa:xari:n traffʕaw ʔilla ʔa:ni] • **2.** لاخ [la:x] ثانِي [θa:ni] Take the other car, I'm going to wash this one. أُخُذ السَّيّارَة اللُّخ، راح أغسِلها لِهاي [ʔuxuð ʔissayya:ra ʔillux, ra:ħ ʔaɣsilha lha:y] I can't tell one from another. ما دَأعرُف واحِد مِن اللّاخ [ma: daʔaʕruf wa:ħid min ʔilla:x] • **3.** باقِي [ba:qi] Put six on the shelf and leave the others in the box. حُطّ سِتَّة عَالرَّفّ وَإترُك الباقِين بِالصَّندُوق [ħuṭṭ sitta ʕarraff wʔitruk ʔilba:qi:n biṣṣandu:g]

*** I saw your friend the other day.**
• **1.** ذاك اليَوم شِفِت صَدِيقَك [ða:k ʔilyu:m šifit ṣadi:qak]

*** Send me someone or other, it doesn't matter who.**
• **1.** دِزّلِي ياهُو اِللّي كَان، ما يهِمّ [dizzli ya:hu ʔilliča:n, ma: yhimm]

*** We have to get it done on time somehow or other.**
• **1.** لازم نخَلّصَه عَالوَقِت بطَرِيقَة ما [la:zim nxallṣah ʕalwakit bṭari:qa ma:]

every other • **1.** بين وبين [bayn. . .. wbayn] Our poker group meets every other week. جَماعَة البَوكَر مالّتنا تِجتِمِع بين إسبُوع وإسبُوع [ǰama:ʕat ʔilpu:kar ma:latna tiǰtimiʕ bayn ʔisbu:ʕ wʔisbu:ʕ]

otherwise • **1.** ما عَدا [ma: ʕada:] Otherwise, I'm satisfied with him. ما عَدا هاي، آنِي راضِي وِيّاه [ma: ʕada: ha:y, ʔa:ni ra:ði wiyya:h] • **2.** لَعَد [laʕad] What would you do otherwise? لَعَد شِي تسَوِّي؟ [laʕad ši tsawwi?] • **3.** وَإلّا [waʔilla] I have to return the book today, otherwise I'll have to pay a fine. لازِم أرَجِّع الكِتاب اليُوم وَإلّا لازم أدفَع غَرامَة [la:zim ʔaraǰǰiʕ ʔilkita:b ʔilyu:m waʔilla la:zim ʔadfaʕ ɣara:ma]

ought • **1.** يِنبِغِي [yinbiɣi] I ought to tell him but it's hard to. يِنبِغِي أقُلّه لَكِن يِصعَب عَلَيّا [yinbiɣi ʔagullah la:kin yiṣʕab ʕalayya]

ounce • **1.** أونص [ʔu:nṣ] أونصات [ʔu:nṣa:t] *pl:*

our • **1.** نَ، نَا [-na] (with preceding definite noun). Their house is larger than our house. بَيتهُم أكبَر مِن بَيتنا [baythum ʔakbar min baytna]

ours • **1.** مالنا [ma:lna] مالّتنا [ma:latna] *Feminine:* This book is ours. هَالكِتاب مالنَا [halkita:b ma:lna]

ourselves • **1.** نَفِسنا [nafisna] أنفُسنا [ʔanfusna] We're just hurting ourselves. إحنا دَنأذِي نَفِسنا بَسّ [ʔiħna danʔaðði nafisna bass]

to oust • **1.** أقصَى [ʔaqṣa] إقصاء [ʔiqṣa:ʔ] *vn: sv i* Their main purpose is to oust the prime minister from his office. غَرَضهُم الرَّئِيسِي يقصُون رَئِيس الوُزَراء مِن وَظِيفتَه [ɣaraðhum ʔirraʔi:si yiqṣu:n raʔi:s ʔilwuzara:ʔ min waði:ftah]

out • **1.** بَرَّة [barra] They were out when we called them. كانَوا بَرَّة مِن خابَرناهُم [ča:naw barra min xa:barna:hum]

*** The lights are out.** • **1.** الضُوَة مَطفِي [ʔiððuwa maṭfi]

*** Straw hats are out of fashion.**
• **1.** شَفقات الخُوص رايحَة مُودَتها [šafqa:t ʔilxu:ṣṣ ra:yħa mu:datha]

out of • **1.** مِن [min] He did it out of spite. سَوّاها مِن حِقِد [sawwa:ha min ħiqid] • **2.** بَلا [bala] بلَيّا [blayya] She's out of work. هِيَّ بلَيّا شُغُل [hiyya blayya šuɣul] • **3.** خارِج [xa:rij] I'm from out of town. آنِي مِن خارِج المَدِينَة [ʔa:ni min xa:rij ʔilmadi:na]

*** That's out of the question.** • **1.** هَذا ما مُمكِن [ha:ða ma: mumkin]

*** We're out of bread.** • **1.** الخُبِز خَلصان [ʔilxubiz xalṣa:n]

*** I have been out of work for two months.** • **1.** صارلِي شَهرَين بَطّال [ṣa:rli šahrayn baṭṭa:l]

*** You're out of step.** • **1.** مَشيَك ما مُنتَظَم [mašyak ma: muntaðam]

outbreak • **1.** نُشُوب [nušu:b] اِندِلاع [ʔindila:ʕ] We left Europe a little before the outbreak of the war. تركنا أورُبّا شوَيَّة قَبُل نُشُوب الحَرُب [trakna ʔu:ruppa šwayya gabul nušu:b ʔilħarub] • **2.** ظُهُور [ðuhu:r] There's an outbreak of cholera in that district. أَكُو ظُهُور مَرَض الكُولَيرا بهَالمَنطَقَة [ʔaku ðuhu:r marað ʔalku:li:ra bhalmanṭaqa]

outfit • **1.** لَوازِم [lawa:zim] We bought our son a complete Scout outfit for his birthday. اِشتِرَينا لَوازِم كَشّافَة كامِلَة لإبنّا لِيُوم عِيد مِيلادَه [ʔištirayna lawa:zim kašša:fa ka:mla lʔibinna lyu:m ʕi:d mi:la:dah] • **2.** مَلابِس [mala:bis] She bought her wedding outfit in Paris. اِشتِرَت مَلابِس عِرِسها بباريس [ʔištirat mala:bis ʕirisha bipa:ri:s] • **3.** وِحدَة [wiħda] Corporal Muhammad was transferred to another outfit. نائِب العَرِيف مَحَمَّد اِنّقَل لِغَير وِحدَة [na:ʔib ʔilʕari:f mħammad ʔinniqal lɣayr wiħda] • **4.** جَماعَة [ǰama:ʕa] جَماعات [ǰama:ʕa:t] *pl:* I wouldn't work for such an outfit. ما أَشتُغُل لِهِيكِي جَماعَة [ma: ʔaštuɣul lhi:či ǰama:ʕa]

to outfit • **1.** جَهَّز [ǰahhaz] تَجهِيز [tajhi:z] *vn:* تجَهَّز [tǰahhaz] *p:* You'll be able to outfit your expedition in Mosul. بإمكانكُم تجَهّزُون بعثَتكُم مِن المُوصِل [biʔimka:nkum dǰahhizu:n biʕθatkum min ʔalmu:ṣil]

to outgrow • **1.** كُبَر عَلَى [kubar ʕala] كُبُر [kabur] *vn: sv* a. The children have outgrown their clothes. الجُّهال كُبرَوا عَلَى هدُومهُم [ʔiǰǰaha:l kubraw ʕala hdu:mhum]

outlet • **1.** مَنفَذ [manfað] مَنافِذ [mana:fið] *pl:* مَخرَج [maxraǰ] مَخارِج [maxa:rij] *pl:* The lake has two outlets. البُحَيرَة بِيها مَنفَذَين [ʔilbuħayra bi:ha manfaðayn] Our company is looking for new outlets. شَرِكَتنا تدَوُّر مَنافِذ تَصرِيف جِدِيدَة [šarikatna ddawwur mana:fið taṣri:f ǰidi:da] Children have to have an outlet for their energy. الجُّهال لازِم يكُون عِدهُم مَنفَذ لِنَشاطهُم [ʔiǰǰaha:l la:zim yku:n ʕidhum manfað linnaša:ṭhum] • **2.** نُقطَة [nuqṭa] نُقَط [nuqaṭ] *pl:* We need another electrical outlet in this room. نِحتاج نُقطَة كَهرَبائِيَّة ثانيَة بهَالغُرفَة [niħta:ǰ nuqṭa kahraba:ʔiyya θa:nya bhalɣurfa]

outline • **1.** مَلمَح [malmaħ] مَلامِح [mala:miħ] *pl:* We learned to recognize the planes from their outlines. تعَلَّمنا نمَيِّز الطَّيّارات مِن مَلامِحها [tʕallamna nmayyiz ʔaṭṭayya:ra:t min mala:miħha] • **2.** رُوس أقلام [ru:s aqla:m] Did you make an outline of what you're going to say yet? سَوَّيت رُؤُوس أقلام لِلّي تقُولَه، لَو بَعَد؟ [sawwi:t ruʔu:s ʔaqla:m lilli dgu:lah, law baʕad?]

outlook • **1.** طَباشِير [taba:ši:r] The outlook for the future isn't very bright. طَباشِير المُستَقبَل ما تبَيِّن زِينَة [taba:ši:r ʔilmustaqbal ma: tbayyin zi:na] • **2.** نَظرَة [naðra] نَظرات [naðra:t] *pl:* His outlook on life is narrow. نَظِرتَه لِلحَياة ضَيقَة [naðirtah lilħaya:t ðayyqa]

to outnumber • **1.** فاق بالعَدَد [fa:q bilʕadad] *sv* u. In that class the girls outnumber the boys. بذاك الصَّفّ البَنات يفُوقُون الوِلِد بالعَدَد [bða:k ʔiṣṣaff ʔilbana:t yfu:qu:n ʔilwilid bilʕadad]

out-of-the-way • **1.** مِنعِزِل [minʕizil] مِنعَزلِين [minʕizil, minʕizli:n] *pl:* Our house is on an out-of-the-way street. بَيتنا عَلَى شارِع مِنعِزِل [baytna ʕala ša:riʕ minʕizil]

outpost • **1.** مَركَز أمامِي [markaz ʔama:mi] مَراكِز أمامِيَّة [mara:kiz ʔama:miyya] *pl:* نُقطَة أمامِيَّة [nuqṭa ʔama:miyya] نُقَط أمامِيَّة [nuqaṭ ʔama:miyya] *pl:*

outrage • **1.** إساءَة [ʔisa:ʔa] إساءات [ʔisa:ʔa:t] *pl:* This is an outrage to my personal dignity. هَذِي إساءَة لِكَرامتِي الشَّخصِيَّة [ha:ði ʔisa:ʔa likara:mti ʔššaxṣiyya]

to outrage • **1.** أساء ل [ʔasa:ʔ l-] إساءَة [ʔisa:ʔa] *vn: sv* i. His behavior outraged the whole community. تَصَرُّفَه أساء لِلمُجتَمَع كُلَّه [taṣarrufah ʔasa:ʔ lilmujtamaʕ kullah]

outrageous • **1.** مُهَوِّل [muhawwil] Don't buy anything there; he charges outrageous prices. لا تِشتِرِي أيّ شِي هناك؛ هَذا يُطلُب أسعار مَهَوِّلَة [la: tištiri ʔayy ši hna:k; ha:ða yuṭlub ʔasʕa:r mahawwila]

outright • **1.** مُطبَق، مُطَبَّق [muṭbaq, muṭabbaq] That's an outright lie. هَذا كِذب مُطبَق [ha:ða čiðib muṭbaq]

outside • **1.** بَرَّة [barra] خارِج [xa:rij] He's outside. هُوَّ بَرَّة [huwwa barra] He lives outside the city. يِسكُن خارِج المَدِينَة [yiskun xa:rij ʔilmadi:na] • **2.** بَرّانِي [barra:ni] You left the outside door open. خَلَّيت الباب البَرّانِي مَفتُوح [xalli:t ʔilba:b ʔalbarra:ni maftu:ħ]

outsider • **1.** خارِجِي [xa:riǰi] بَرّانِي [barra:ni] We don't permit outsiders to attend our meetings. ما نِسمَح لِلخارِجِيِّين يحضَرُون اِجتِماعاتنا [ma: nismaħ lilxa:riǰiyyi:n yiħðaru:n ʔiǰtima:ʕa:tna]

O

outskirts • **1.** أطراف [ʔaṭra:f] Many people have orchards on the outskirts of the city. ناس هوايَة عِدهُم بَساتِين بأطراف المَدِينَة [na:s hwa:ya ʕidhum basa:ti:n biʔaṭra:f ʔilmadi:na]

outstanding • **1.** بارِز [ba:riz] He's an outstanding scholar. هُوَّ عالِم بارِز [huwwa ʕa:lim ba:riz] • **2.** مُبدِع [mubdiʕ] He's an outstanding performer on the lute. هَذا عازِف مُبدِع عَلعُود [ha:ða ʕa:zif mubdiʕ ʕalʕu:d] • **3.** مَوقُوف [mawqu:f] We still have a number of outstanding bills to collect. عِدنا بَعَد عَدَد مِن القَوائِم المَوقُوفَة [ʕidna baʕad ʕadad min ʔilqawa:ʔim ʔalmawqu:fa]

oven • **1.** تَنُّور [tannu:r] تنانِير [tna:ni:r] *pl:* Our neighbor's wife has an oven, and she sells the bread she bakes. مَرَة جارنَا عِدها تَنُّور وَتبِيع الخُبُز اللّي تخُبزَه [marat ǰa:rna ʕidha tannu:r wtbi:ʕ ʔilxubuz ʔilli txubzah] • **2.** فِرِن [firin] أفران [ʔafra:n] *pl:* Baking the fish at home is a lot of bother; let's send it to the neighborhood oven. طَبخ السِّمَك بِالبَيت دُوخَة؛ خَلّي ندِزَّه لِلفِرن مال الطَّرَف [ṭabx ʔissimač bilbayt du:xa; xalli ndizzah lilfirin ma:l ʔiṭṭaraf]

over • **1.** فَوق [fu:g] My room is over the kitchen. غُرُفتِي فُوق المَطبَخ [ɣurufti fu:g ʔilmaṭbax] I don't know exactly, but over a hundred at least. ما أعرُف بِالضَبط، لَكِن عَالأَقَلّ فُوق المِيَّة [ma: ʔaʕruf biððabuṭ, la:kin ʕalʔaqall fu:g ʔalmiyya] • **2.** عَلَى [ʕala] Don't pull the cover over your head. لا تجُرّ الغِطا عَلَى راسَك [la: dǰurr ʔilɣiṭa ʕala ra:sak] • **3.** أكثَر مِن [ʔakθar min] That village is over a mile away. ذِيك القَريَة تِبعِد أكثَر مِن مِيل واحِد [ði:č ʔilqarya tibʕid ʔakθar min mi:l wa:ħid]

*** The water is over your head there.**

• **1.** ما راح تقَيِّش هناك [ma: ra:ħ tgayyiš hna:k]

*** Let's go over the details once more.**

• **1.** خَلّي نراجِع التَفصِيلات مَرَّة ثانيَة [xalli nra:ǰiʕ ʔittafṣi:la:t marra θa:nya]

all over • **1.** بكُلّ مَكان [bkull maka:n] I've looked all over, but I can't find it. دَوَّرت بكُلّ مُكان لَكِن ما دَأقدَر ألقاها [dawwarit bkull muka:n la:kin ma: daʔagdar ʔalga:ha]

over again • **1.** مَرَّة ثانيَة [marra θa:nya] Do it over again. سَوِّيها مَرَّة ثانيَة [sawwi:ha marra θa:nya] Do it over again. عِيدها [ʕi:dha]

over and over again • **1.** عِدَّة مَرّات [ʕiddat marra:t] He asked the same question over and over again. سِأل نَفس السُّؤال عِدَّة مَرّات [siʔal nafs ʔissuʔa:l ʕiddat marra:t]

over there • **1.** هناك [hna:k] What's that over there? شِنُو ذاك هناك [šinu ða:k hna:k]

to get over • **1.** خَلَّص [xallaṣ] تَخلِيص [taxli:ṣ] *vn:* تخَلَّص [txallaṣ] *p:* I got over my cold in a week. خَلَّصِت مِن النَّشلَة بإسبُوع [xallaṣit min ʔinnašla bʔisbu:ʕ]

overcoat • **1.** قَبُوط [qappu:ṭ, qabbu:ṭ] قَبُوطات، قبابِيط [qappu:ṭa:t, qpa:pi:ṭ; qabbu:ṭa:t, qba:bi:ṭ] *pl:*

to overcome • **1.** تغَلَّب عَلَى [tɣallab ʕala] تَغَلُّب [taɣallub] *vn: sv* a. She had many difficulties to overcome. كان عِدها هوايَة صُعُوبات تِتغَلَّب عَليها [ča:n ʕidha hwa:ya ṣuʕu:ba:t tidɣallab ʕali:ha] She was overcome with grief. كان مِتغَلِّب عَليها الحُزُن [ča:n midɣallib ʕali:ha ʔalħuzun] • **2.** قِضَى عَلَى [qiða:, giða: ʕala] قَضاء [qaða:ʔ] *vn: sv* i. The gas almost overcame me. كان قِضَى عَلَيَّا الغاز [ča:n giða: ʕalayya ʔalɣa:z]

to overdo • **1.** لَحّ [laħħ] لَحّ [laħħ] *vn: sv* i. It doesn't hurt to eat fatty meat, but don't overdo it. ما يخالِف تاكُل أكِل دَسِم، بَسّ لا تلِحّ [ma: yxa:lif ta:kul ʔakil dasim, bass la: tliħħ] • **2.** كَثَّر [kaθθar, čaθθar] تَكثِير [takθi:r] *vn: sv* i. I like spices, but our cook overdoes it. تِعجِبنِي البهارات لَكِن طَبّاخنا دَيكَثِّر مِنها [tiʕǰibni ʔalbha:ra:t la:kin ṭabba:xna daykaθθir minha]

to overflow • **1.** طُفَح [ṭufaħ] طَفُح [ṭafuħ] *vn: sv* a. فاض [fa:ð] فَيض [fayð] *vn: sv* i. Don't put so much water in the glass; it will overflow. لا تخَلِّي مَيّ هوايَة بالكلاص وَإلّا يطفَح [la: txalli mayy hwa:ya bilgla:ṣ waʔilla: yiṭfaħ]

overfull • **1.** طافِح [ṭa:fiħ]

to overlook • **1.** غُفَل عَن [ɣufal ʕan] غَفُل [ɣaful] *vn: sv* u. I must have overlooked it. لازِم آنِي غِفلِت عَنها [la:zim ʔa:ni ɣifalit ʕanha] • **2.** تغاضَى [tɣa:ða:] تَغاضِي [taɣa:ði] *vn: sv* a. I'll overlook your mistakes this time, but don't do it again. راح أتغاضَى عَن أغلاطَك هَالمَرَّة لَكِن لا تعِيدها مَرَّة ثانيَة [ra:ħ ʔadɣa:ða: ʕan ʔaɣla:ṭak halmarra la:kin la: tʕi:dha marra θa:nya] • **3.** أشرَف [ʔašraf] إشراف [ʔišra:f] *vn: sv* i. طَلّ [ṭall] إطلال [ʔiṭla:l] *vn: sv* i. سَيطَر [sayṭar] سَيطَرَة [sayṭara] *vn: sv* i. My window overlooks the garden. شِبّاك غُرُفتِي يشرِف عالحَدِيقَة [šibba:č ɣurufti yišrif ʕalħadi:qa]

overnight • **1.** لَيلَة [laila, li:la] لَيلات، لَيالِي [layla:t, laya:li] *pl:* He got rich overnight. صار زَنكِين بِاللَّيلَة [ṣa:r zangi:n billayla]

to stay overnight • **1.** بات [ba:t] بَيتُوتَة [baytu:ta] *vn: sv* a. I'm going to stay overnight in Najaf. راح أبات بِالنَّجَف [ra:ħ ʔaba:t binnaǰaf]

oversight • **1.** سَهُو [sahw] غَفلَة [ɣafla] That must have been an oversight. لازِم هَذا سَهو [la:zim ha:ða sahw]

to oversleep • **1.** *no equivalent* * I overslept this morning. أخَذنِي النَّوم اليُوم الصُّبُح [ʔaxaðni ʔinnawm ʔilyu:m ʔiṣṣubuħ]

overthrow • **1.** إنقِلاب [ʔinqila:b] إنقِلابات [ʔinqila:ba:t] *pl:* The foreign correspondents predicted the overthrow a month ago. المُراسِلِين الأجانِب تنَبَّأوا بالإنقِلاب قَبُل شَهَر [ʔalmura:sili:n ʔilʔaǰa:nib tnabbiʔaw bilʔinqila:b gabul šahar]

to overthrow • **1.** قِلَب [gilab] قَلُب [galub] *vn:* اِنقِلَب [ʔingilab] *p:* They overthrew the government. قِلبَوا نِظام الحُكُم [gilbaw niðaːm ʔilħukum]

overtime • **1.** إضافِي [ʔiðaːfi] I had to work 2 hrs. overtime last night. اِضطَرَّيت أشتُغُل ساعتِين إضافِيَّة البارحَة باللَّيل [ʔiðṭarrayt ʔaštuɣul saːʕtayn ʔiðaːfiyya ʔilbaːrħa billayl] Beginning next month our office will be on an overtime basis. اِعتِباراً مِن الشَّهر القادِم دائِرَتنا راح تقُوم بأعمال إضافِيَّة [ʔiʕtibaːran min ʔiššahr ʔilqaːdim daːʔiratna raːħ tquːm bʔaʕmaːl ʔiðaːfiyya]

to owe • **1.** * How much do I owe you? شقَدّ تُطلُبنِي؟ [šgadd tuṭlubni?] * How much do I owe you? شقَدّ آنِي مَديُون إلَك؟ [šgadd ʔaːni madyuːn ʔilak?] * How much do I owe you? شقَدّ آنِي مَطلُوبلَك؟ [šgadd ʔaːni maṭluːblak?] * How much do I owe you? شقَدّ إلَك عَلَيّا؟ [šgadd ʔilak ʕalayya?] * You still owe me 20 dinars. إنتَ لا زِلت مَطلُوبلِي عِشرِين دِينار [ʔinta laː zilit maṭluːbli ʕišriːn dinaːr] * You still owe me 20 dinars. إنتَ لا زِلت مَديُونلِي عِشرِين دِينار [ʔinta laː zilit madyuːnli ʕišriːn dinaːr] * I owe a lot of money. آنِي مِندان فلُوس هوايَة [ʔaːni mindaːn fluːs hwaːya]

owl • **1.** بُومَة [buːma] بُومات، بُوَم [buːmaːt, buwam] *pl:*

own • **1.** عُهدَة [ʕuhda] مَسؤُولِيَّة [masʔuːliyya] مَسؤُولِيّات [masʔuːliyyaːt] *pl:* From here on, you are on your own. مِن هِنا وهِيكِي، إنتَ عَلَى عُهُدتَك [min hna whiːči, ʔinta ʕala ʕuhudtak] From here on, your on your own. مِن هنا وفايِت، إنتَ ونَفسَك [min hna wfaːyit, ʔinta wnafsak] As soon as you are familiar with the filing system here, you'll be on your own. حالما تلِمّ بِنظام الفايلات هنا، راح تكُون عَلَى مَسؤُولِيتَك [ħaːlmaː tlimm bniðaːm ʔilfaːylaːt hna, raːħ tkuːn ʕala masʔuːliːtak] He's been on his own ever since he was sixteen. مِن كان عُمرَه سِطَّعَش سَنَة صار مَسؤُول عَن نَفسَه [min čaːn ʕumrah siṭṭaʕaš sana ṣaːr masʔuːl ʕan nafsah]

* **I have my own room.** • **1.** عِندِي غُرفَة إلِي وَحدِي [ʕindi ɣurfa ʔili waħdi]

* **Are these your own things?** • **1.** هاي أشياء مُلكَك إنتَ؟ [haːy ʔašyaːʔ mulkak ʔinta?]

to own • **1.** مِلَك [milak] مُلُك [muluk] *vn:* انمِلَك [ʔinmilak] *p:* He owns a house. هُوَّ يِملُك فَدّ بَيت [huwwa yimluk fadd bayt]

owner • **1.** صاحِب [ṣaːħib] أصحاب [ʔaṣħaːb] *pl:* مالِك [maːlik] مُلّاك [mullaːk] *pl:* Who is the owner of the store? مِنُو صاحِب هَالدُّكّان؟ [minu ṣaːħib haddukkaːn?]

ownership • **1.** مِلكِيَّة [milkiyya] مِلكِيّات [milkiyyaːt] *pl:* You'll have to pay me in full before I transfer the ownership into your name. لازِم تِدفَعلِي كُلّ المَبلَغ قَبُل ما أنقُل المِلكِيَّة بإسمَك [laːzim tidfaʕli kull ʔilmablaɣ gabul maː ʔanqul ʔalmilkiyya bismak]

ox • **1.** ثُور [θuːr θawr] ثِيران [θiːraːn] *pl:*

oxygen • **1.** أوكسِجِين [ʔuksijiːn]

oyster • **1.** مَحّارَة [maħħaːra] مَحّارات [maħħaːraːt] *pl:* مَحّار [maħħaːr] *Collective*

O

P

pace • **1.** خَطوَة [xaṭwa] خَطوات [xaṭwa:t] *pl:* Take a pace forward. تقَدَّم خَطوَة لِقِدّام [tqaddam xaṭwa ligidda:m] • **2.** سُرعَة [surʕa] This worker sets the pace for the others on the job. هَالعامِل يحَدِّد سُرعَة الشُّغُل لِلآخَرِين [halʕa:mil yħaddid surʕat ʔiššuɣul lilʔa:xari:n]

to keep pace with • **1.** جارَى [ǰa:ra:] مُجارات [muǰa:ra:t] *vn: sv* i. I can't keep pace with him at work. ما أقدَر أجارِيه بِالشُّغُل [ma: ʔagdar ʔaǰa:ri:h biššuɣul]

to pace off • **1.** قاس [qa:s] قِيس [qays] *vn:* اِنقاس [ʔinqa:s] *p:* Pace off a hundred feet. قِيس بِالخَطوات مِيَّة قَدَم [qi:s bilxaṭwa:t miyyat qadam]

to pace up and down • **1.** تخَطَّى [txaṭṭa:] تَخَطِّي [taxaṭṭi] *vn: sv* a. تمَشَّى [tmašša:] تَمَشِّي [tamašši] *vn: sv* a. He paced up and down the room. ظَلّ يِتخَطَّى بالغُرفَة [ðall yitxaṭṭa: bilɣurfa]

Pacific Ocean • **1.** المُحِيط الهادِي [ʔilmuħi:ṭ ʔilha:di]

pack • **1.** قَطِيع [qaṭi:ʕ] قِطعان [qiṭʕa:n] *pl:* They went at the food like a pack of hungry wolves. نِزلَوا عَالأكِل مِثِل قَطِيع مِن الذّياب الجُوعانَة [nizlaw ʕalʔakil miθil qaṭi:ʕ min ʔaððiya:b ʔiǰǰu:ʕa:na] • **2.** حِمِل [ħimil] حمُول [ħmu:l] *pl:* The donkeys were loaded with heavy packs. الزُّمايِل كانَت مَحَمَّلَة حمُول ثقال [ʔizzuma:yil ča:nat mħammila ħmu:l θga:l] • **3.** دَستَة [dasta] دَستات [dasta:t] *pl:* Where is that new pack of cards? وِين دَستَة الوَرَق الجِّدِيدَة؟ [wi:n dastat ʔilwaraq ʔiǰǰidi:da?]

* **That's a pack of lies!** • **1.** هَذا كِذب بكِذِب [ha:ða čiðb bčiðib] / هَذا كُلَّه شِيلمان [ha:ða kullah ši:lma:n]

to pack • **1.** لَمّ [lamm] لَمّ [lamm] *vn: sv* i. Have you packed your stuff yet? لَمَّيت غَراضَك لَو بَعَد؟ [lammi:t ɣara:ðak law baʕad?] Have you packed your stuff yet? حَضَّرت الجُّنطَة مالتَك؟ [ħaððart ʔiǰǰunṭa ma:ltak?] • **2.** حِشَك [ħišak] حَشِك [ħašik] *vn:* اِنحِشَك [ʔinħišak] *p:* They packed more people into that little room. حِشكَوا بَعَد ناس بذِيك الغُرفَة الصِّغَيِّرَة [ħiškaw baʕad na:s bði:č ʔilɣurfa ʔiṣṣiɣayyra] • **3.** دِحَس [diħas] دَحِس [daħis] *vn:* اِندِحَس [ʔindiħas] *p:* The doctor packed cotton in my ear. الطَّبِيب دِحَس قُطِن بإذني [ʔiṭṭabi:b diħas guṭin biʔiðni] • **4.** دَكّ [dačč] دَكّ [dačč] *vn:* اِندَكّ [ʔindačč] *p:* Don't pack the clothes into the suitcase tightly. لا تدِكّ الهِدُوم بِالجُنطَة دَكّ [la: ddičč ʔilhdu:m biǰǰunṭa dačč]

to pack up • **1.** لَمّ [lamm] لَمّ [lamm] *vn:* اِنلَمّ [ʔinlamm] *p:* He packed up his things and left. لَمّ كُلّ غَراضَه وَراح [lamm kull ɣara:ðah wra:ħ]

package • **1.** رُزمَة [ruzma] رُزَم [ruzam] *pl:* The mailman brought a package for you. مُوَزِّع البَرِيد جابلَك رُزمَة [muwazziʕ ʔilbari:d ǰa:blak ruzma] • **2.** باكِيت [pa:ki:t] Do you sell the coffee in the bulk or in packages? تبِيع القَهوَة فراطَة لَو بباكَيتات؟ [tbi:ʕ ʔilgahwa fra:ṭa law bipa:kayta:t?]

packed • **1.** مقَبُّط [mqabbuṭ] مَترُوس [matru:s] The bus was packed this morning. الباص كان مقَبُّط الصُّبُح [ʔilpa:ṣ ča:n mqabbuṭ ʔiṣṣubuħ] • **2.** مَليان [malya:n] مَترُوس [matru:s] The store was packed with people. المَخزَن كان مَليان ناس [ʔilmaxzan ča:n malya:n na:s] • **3.** مُعَلَّب [muʕallab] This fish is packed in Norway. هَالسِّمَك معَلَّب بِالنَّروِيج [hassimač mʕallab binnarwi:ǰ]

* **My things are all packed.** • **1.** غَراضِي حاضرَة بِالجُّنطَة [ɣara:ði ħa:ðra biǰǰunṭa]

* **Are these sardines packed in olive oil?** • **1.** هَالسارِدِين بزَيت الزَّيتُون؟ [hassardi:n bzayt ʔizzaytu:n?]

pack-horse • **1.** كِدِيش [kidi:š] كِدَّش، كِدشان [kiddaš, kidša:n] *pl:*

pack-saddle • **1.** جلال [ǰla:l] جلالات [ǰla:la:t] *pl:*

pact • **1.** مِيثاق [mi:θa:q] مَواثِيق [mawa:θi:q] *pl:*

pad • **1.** كِبنَة [čibna] كِبنات، كِبَن [čibna:t, čiban] *pl:* I need a pad to put my typewriter on. أحتاج كِبنَة أحُطّ عَليها الطّابِعَة مالتِي [ʔaħta:ǰ čibna ʔaħuṭṭ ʕali:ha ʔaṭṭa:biʕa ma:lti] • **2.** مِندَر [mindar] مَنادِر [mana:dir] *pl:* Who took my chair pad? مِنُو أخَذ مِندَر الكُرسِي مالِي؟ [minu ʔaxað mindar ʔilkursi ma:li?] • **3.** سطَمبَة [sṭampa] سطَمبات [sṭampa:t] *pl:* I have the stamp, but I can't find the pad. الخَتَم هِيّاتَه، لَكِن ما دَألقِي الإسطَمبَة [ʔalxatam hiyya:tah, la:kin ma: daʔalgi ʔalʔisṭampa] • **4.** دَفتَر [daftar] دَفاتِر [dafa:tir] *pl:* Bring me one or two pads of note paper. جِيبلِي دَفتَر أو دَفتَرَين وَرَق مِسوَدَّة [ǰi:bli daftar ʔaw daftarayn waraq miswadda] • **5.** كَتّافِيَّة [čatta:fiyya] كَتّافِيّات [čatta:fiyya:t] *pl:* I had the tailor take the pads out of the shoulders of this jacket. خَلّيت الخَيّاط يطَلِّع الكَتّافِيّات مِن كتافات هَالسِّترَة [xalli:t ʔilxayya:ṭ yṭalliʕ ʔalkatta:fiyya:t min čta:fa:t hassitra]

to pad • **1.** حَشَّى [ħašša:] تحِشِّي [tħišši] *vn:* تحَشَّى [tħašša:] *p:* I want the shoulders padded. أرِيد الكتافات تِتحَشَّى [ʔari:d ʔilčta:fa:t titħašša:]

padding • **1.** حَشوَة [ħašwa] حَشوات [ħašwa:t] *pl:*

padlock • **1.** قُفُل [quful] قفال، قفالَة [qfa:l, qfa:la] *pl:*

page • **1.** صَفحَة [ṣafħa] صَفحات [ṣafħa:t] *pl:* صَحِيفَة [ṣaħi:fa] صَحايِف، صُحُف [ṣaħa:yif, ṣuħuf] *pl:* The book is two hundred pages long. الكِتاب بِيه مِيتَين صَفحَة [ʔilkita:b bi:h mitayn ṣafħa]

P

pail • **1.** سَطِل [saṭil] سَطَلات، سطُولَة [saṭalaːt, sṭuːla] *pl:* سَطلَة [saṭla] سَطلات [saṭlaːt] *pl:* Get a pail of water! جِيب سَطِل ماي [ǰiːb saṭil maːy]

pain • **1.** أَلَم [ʔalam] آلام [ʔaːlaːm] *pl:* وُجَع [wuǰaʕ, waǰaʕ, wiǰaʕ] أَوجاع [ʔawǰaːʕ] *pl:* I feel a sharp pain in my back. دَأحِسّ فَدّ وُجَع شَدِيد بظَهري [daʔaħiss fadd wuǰaʕ šadiːd bðahri]

to take pains • **1.** أَجهَد نَفسَه [ʔaǰhad nafsah] إجهاد نَفِس [ʔiǰhaːd nafis] *vn: sv* i. دَقَّق [daqqaq] تَدقِيق [tadqiːq] *vn:* تَدَقَّق [tdaqqaq] *p:* She takes great pains with her work. تِجهِد نَفِسها كُلِّش بشُغُلها [tiǰhid nafisha kulliš bšuɣulha]

to pain • **1.** أَلَّم [ʔallam] تَألِيم [taʔliːm] *vn:* It pains me to have to say this but. . . يُؤلِمنِي إنّو لازِم أَقُول هَذا لَكِن [yuʔlimni ʔinnu laːzim ʔaguːl haːða laːkin]

painful • **1.** أَلِيم [ʔaliːm] مُؤلِم [muʔlim] That was a painful experience. هاي كانَت فَدّ تَجرُبَة أَلِيمَة [haːy čaːnat fadd taǰruba ʔaliːma] • **2.** مُزعِجَة [muzʕiǰa] فَظِيعَة [faðiːʕa] Our progress was painfully slow. تَقَدُّمنا كان بَطِيئ إِلَى دَرَجَة مُزعِجَة [taqaddumna čaːn baṭiːʔ ʔila daraǰa muzʕiǰa]

*** It is painful to watch him.** • **1.** مَنظَرَه يِكسِر القَلب [manðarah yiksir ʔilgalub]

*** Was the extraction of the tooth painful?** • **1.** شَلع السِنّ أَذّاك؟ / شَلع السِّنّ وُجَعَك؟ [šalʕ ʔissinn ʔaððaːk?] [šalʕ ʔissinn wuǰaʕak?]

paint • **1.** صُبُغ [ṣubuɣ] أَصباغ [ʔaṣbaːɣ] *pl:* بَويَة [bawya] بَويات [bawyaːt] *pl:* The paint isn't dry yet. الصُّبُغ بَعدَه ما يابِس [ʔiṣṣubuɣ baʕdah maː yaːbis]

to paint • **1.** صُبَغ [ṣubaɣ] صُبُغ [ṣubuɣ] *vn:* اِنصُبَغ [ʔinṣubaɣ] *p:* What color are you going to paint the house? يا لُون راح تُصبُغ البَيت؟ [yaː luːn raːħ tuṣbuɣ ʔilbayt?] • **2.** رِسَم [risam] رَسِم [rasim] *vn:* اِنرِسَم [ʔinrisam] *p:* She paints in oils. تِرسِم بِالزَّيت [tirsim bizzayt]

paint brush • **1.** فِرگَة [firča] فِرَك [firač] *pl:*

painter • **1.** صَبّاغ [ṣabbaːɣ] صَبّاغِين، صبابِيغ [ṣabbaːɣiːn, ṣbaːbiːɣ] *pl:* The painters will finish the kitchen tomorrow. الصَّبّاغِين راح يخَلّصُون المَطبَخ باكِر [ʔiṣṣabbaːɣiːn raːħ yxallṣuːn ʔilmaṭbax baːčir] • **2.** رَسّام [rassaːm] رَسّامِين [rassaːmiːn] *pl:* He is a famous painter. هَذا رَسّام مَشهُور [haːða rassaːm mašhuːr]

painting • **1.** لَوحَة [lawħa] لَوحات [lawħaːt] *pl:* صُورَة [ṣuːra] صُوَر [ṣuwar] *pl:* This is a beautiful painting. هَذِي لَوحَة بَدِيعَة [haːði lawħa badiːʕa] • **2.** رَسِم [rasim] I'm especially interested in Persian painting. آنِي مِهتَمّ بِصُورَة خاصَّة بِفَنّ الرَّسِم الإيرانِي [ʔaːni mihtamm bṣuːra xaːṣṣa bifann ʔirrasim ʔalʔiːraːni] • **3.** صُبُغ [ṣubuɣ] Painting the house was hard. صُبُغ البَيت كان صَعُب [ṣubuɣ ʔilbayt čaːn ṣaʕub]

pair • **1.** زَوج [zawǰ] زَواج، أَزواج [zwaːǰ, ʔazwaːǰ] *pl:* I bought myself a pair of gloves. اِشتِرَيتلِي زوج كفُوف [ʔištirayli zuːǰ čfuːf]

*** I bought a new pair of scissors.**
• **1.** إشتِرَيت مقَصّ جِدِيدَة [ʔʔištirayt magaṣṣ ǰidiːd]

pajamas • **1.** بَيجامَة [biːǰaːma] بَيجامات [biːǰaːmaːt] *pl:*

pal • **1.** رَفِيق [rafiːq] رُفَقاء [rufaqaːʔ] *pl:* صاحِب [ṣaːħib] أَصحاب [ʔaṣħaːb] *pl:* You're a real pal. إنتَ حَقِيقَةً خُوش رَفِيق [ʔinta ħaqiːqatan xuːš rafiːq]

to pal around • **1.** تصاحَب [tṣaːħab] تَصاحُب [taṣaːħub] *vn: sv* a. تعاشَر [tʕaːšar] تَعاشُر [taʕaːšur] *vn: sv* a. They've palled around for years. تصاحبَوا مُدَّة سنِين [tṣaːħbaw muddat sniːn] They've palled around for years. صارِلهُم مِتعاشرِين مُدَّة سنِين [ṣaːrilhum mitʕaːšriːn muddat sniːn]

palace • **1.** قَصِر [qaṣir] قصُور [qṣuːr] *pl:*

palate • **1.** سَقُف حَلِق [saguf ħalig] سقُوف حلُوق [sguːf ħluːg] *pl:*

pale • **1.** أَصفَر [ʔaṣfar] صُفُر، [ṣufur] *pl:* صَفرَة [ṣafra] *Feminine:* شاحِب [šaːħib] Why are you so pale? شبِيك هِيكِي أَصفَر؟ [šbiːk hiːči ʔaṣfar?] • **2.** فاتِح [faːtiħ] آچُغ [ʔaːčuɣ] She had on a pale blue dress. كانَت لابسَة نَفنُوف أَزرَق فاتِح [čaːnat laːbsah nafnuːf ʔazrag faːtiħ]

to turn pale • **1.** اِصفَرّ [ʔiṣfarr] *sv* a. شِحَب [šiħab] شُحُوب [šuħuːb] *vn: sv* a. When he heard that, he turned pale. مِن سِمَعها، اِصفَرّ لونَه [min simaʕha, ʔiṣfarr luːnah]

Palestine • **1.** فَلَسطِين [falasṭiːn]

Palestinian • **1.** فَلَسطِينِي [falasṭiːni]

palm • **1.** كَفّ [čaff] كفُوف [čfuːf] *pl:* My palm is all calloused. كَفِّي كُلَّه مبَسمِر [čaffi kullah mbasmir] • **2.** نَخلَة [naxla] نَخلات [naxlaːt] *pl:* نَخَل [naxal] *Collective:* We have four palm trees in our garden. عِدنا أَربَع نَخلات بِحَدِيقَتنا [ʕidna ʔarbaʕ naxlaːt bħadiːqatna] • **3.** شَجَرَة جوز هِند [šaǰarat ǰawz hind] شَجَرات جَوز هِند [šaǰaraːt ǰawz hind] *pl:* شَجَر جَوز هِند [šaǰar ǰawz hind] *Collective:* We don't grow any coconut palms here. ما نِزرَع شَجَر جُوز هِند هنا [maː nizraʕ šaǰar ǰawz hind hna]

Palm shoot • **1.** فِسِيلَة [fisiːla] فِسِيلات، فِسايِل [fisiːlaːt, fisaːyil] *pl:*

P

palpitation • **1.** خَفَقان [xafaqa:n]

pamphlet • **1.** كُرّاسَة [kurra:sa] كُرّاسات [kurra:sa:t] *pl:*

pan • **1.** جِدِر [ǰidir] جدُور، جدُورَة [ǰdu:r, ǰdu:ra] *pl:* I need a bigger pan for the rice. أحتاج جِدِر أكبَر لِلتِّمَّن [ʔaħta:ǰ ǰidir ʔakbar littimman] • **2.** طاوَة [ṭa:wa] طاوات [ṭa:wa:t] *pl:* Use this pan for the eggs. اِستَعمِل هَالطّاوَة لِلبَيض [ʔistaʕmil haṭṭa:wa lilbayð̣]
to pan out badly • **1.** فِشَل [fišal] فَشَل [fašal] *vn: sv* a. خاب [xa:b] خَيبَة [xayba] *vn: sv* i. My scheme panned out badly. خُطَّتِي فِشلَت [xuṭṭti fišlat]
to pan out well • **1.** نِجَح [nijaħ] نَجاح [naja:ħ] *vn: sv* a. My scheme panned out well. خُطَّتِي نِجحَت [xuṭṭti nijħat]

pane • **1.** جامَة [ǰa:ma] جامات [ǰa:ma:t] *pl:* جام [ǰa:m] *Collective:* The storm blew in several panes. العاصِفَة كِسرَت عِدَّة جامات [ʔilʕa:ṣifa kisrat ʕiddat ǰa:ma:t]

panel • **1.** حَلَقَة [ħalaqa] حَلَقات [ħalaqa:t] *pl:* A panel of well-known educators discussed the problem on TV. حَلَقَة مِن مَشاهِير المُرَبِّين بِحثَوا المُشكِلَة بِالتَّلَفِزيَون [ħalaqa min maša:hi:r ʔalmurabbi:n biħθaw ʔilmuškila bittalafizyu:n] • **2.** هَيئَة [hayʔa] هَيئات [hayʔa:t] *pl:* A panel of three experts will study this problem. هَيئَة مِن ثلَث خُبَراء راح تُدرُس المُشكِلَة [hayʔa min tlaθ xubara:ʔ ra:ħ tudrus ʔilmuškila]

panic • **1.** ذُعُر [ðuʕur] رُعُب [ruʕub]

to pant • **1.** لِهَث [lihaθ] لَهِث [lahiθ] *vn: sv* a. He came panting up the stairs. صِعَد الدَّرَج دَيلهَث [ṣiʕad ʔiddaraǰ dayilhaθ]

pants • **1.** بَنطَرُون [panṭaru:n] بَنطَرُونات [panṭaru:na:t] *pl:* بَناطِير [pana:ṭi:r] *pl:* My pants have to be pressed. لازِم بَنطَرُونِي يِنضُرُب أُوتِي [la:zim panṭaru:ni yinð̣urub ʔu:ti] • **2.** شِروال [širwa:l] شِروالات، شِراوِيل [širwa:la:t, šira:wi:l] *pl:* You can tell he's a Kurd from his (baggy) pants. تِقدَر تعُرفَه كُردِي مِن شِروالَه [tigdar tʕurfah kurdi min širwa:lah]

paper • **1.** وَرَقَة [waraqa] وَرَقات [waraqa:t] *pl:* أوراق [ʔawra:q] وَرَق [waraq] *pl:* كاغَدَة [ka:ɣada] كاغَدات، كواغِد [ka:ɣada:t, kwa:ɣid] *pl:* كاغَد [ka:ɣad, qa:ɣad] كَواغِد [kawa:ɣid] *pl:* Do you have a sheet of paper?
عِندَك فَدّ طَبقَة وَرَق؟ [ʕindak fadd ṭabqa waraq?] Some important papers are missing. بَعض الأوراق المُهِمَّة ضايعَة [baʕð̣ ʔilʔawra:q ʔilmuhimma ð̣a:yʕa] • **2.** جَرِيدَة [ǰari:da] جَرايِد [jara:yid] *pl:* Where is today's paper? وين جَرِيدَة اليُوم؟ [wi:n ǰari:dat ʔilyu:m?]

paper weight • **1.** ثِقّالَة [θigga:la] ثِقّالات [θigga:la:t] *pl:*

parachute • **1.** بَرَشُوت [parašu:t] بَرَشُوتات [parašu:ta:t] *pl:* مَظَلَّة [mað̣alla] مَظَلّات [mað̣alla:t] *pl:*

parade • **1.** اِستِعراض [ʔistiʕra:ð̣] اِستِعراضات [ʔistiʕra:ð̣a:t] *pl:* Did you see the parade yesterday? شِفت الاستِعراض البارحَة؟ [šift ʔilʔistiʕra:ð̣ ʔilba:rħa?]

paradise • **1.** جَنَّة [ǰanna] فِردَوس [firdaws]

paragraph • **1.** فَقَرَة [faqara] فَقَرات [faqara:t] *pl:* This is the beginning of a new paragraph. هَذِي بدايَة فَقَرَة جِدِيدَة [ha:ði bda:yat faqara ǰidi:da]

parallel • **1.** مُوازِي [muwa:zi] مُحاذِي [muħa:ði] Draw a parallel to this line. إرسِم مُوازِي لِهَالخَطّ [ʔirsim muwa:zi lihalxaṭṭ] The road runs parallel to the river. الطَّرِيق مُحاذِي لِلنَّهَر [ʔiṭṭari:q muħa:ði linnahar]

paralysis • **1.** شَلَل [šalal] فالَج [fa:laǰ, fa:liǰ]

to paralyze • **1.** شَلّ [šall] شَلَل [šalal] *vn:* اِنشَلّ [ʔinšall] *p:* This disease sometimes paralyses the victim's legs. هَالمَرَض أحياناً يشِلّ رِجلَين المُصاب [halmarað̣ ʔaħya:nan yšill rijlayn ʔilmuṣa:b]

paralyzed • **1.** مَشلُول [mašlu:l] مَشلُولِين [mašlu:li:n] *pl:* مِنشَلّ [minšall] مِنشَلِّين [minšalli:n] *pl:* He is completely paralyzed. هَذا مَشلُول تَماماً [ha:ða mašlu:l tama:man] She has been paralyzed ever since she had that stroke. هِيَّ مِنشَلَّة مِن صابَتها ذِيك الصَّدمَة [hiyya minšalla min ṣa:batha ðiːč ʔiṣṣadma] • **2.** أعضَب [ʔaʕð̣ab] عُضُب، عَضبِين [ʕuð̣ub, ʕað̣bi:n] *pl:* عَضبَة [ʕað̣ba] *Feminine:* He has a paralyzed hand. عِندَه إيد عَضبَة [ʕindah ʔi:d ʕað̣ba] • **3.** مقَرَّم [mgarram] He can't walk because he is paralyzed. ما يِقدَر يِمشِي لِأنّ مقَرَّم [ma: yigdar yimši liʔann mgarram] • **4.** معَطِّل [mʕaṭṭil] Communications were completely paralyzed. المُواصَلات كانَت معَطَّلَة تَماماً [ʔalmuwa:ṣala:t ča:nat mʕaṭṭla tama:man]

paramount • **1.** عَظِيم [ʕað̣i:m] عُظَماء [ʕuð̣ama:ʔ] *pl:* كَبِير [kabi:r] That's of paramount importance. هَذا عَظِيم الأهَمِّيَّة [ha:ða ʕað̣i:m ʔilʔahammiyya]

parapet • **1.** سُور [su:r] أسوار [ʔaswa:r] *pl:* Stay behind the parapet or you'll get killed. إبقَى وَرا السُّور وَإلّا تِنقِتِل [ʔibqa: wara ʔassu:r waʔilla tinqitil]

parasite • **1.** طُفَيلِي [ṭufayli] طُفَيلِيِّين [ṭufayliyyi:n] *pl:*

parasitical • **1.** مِتطَفِّل [mitṭaffil]

parasol • **1.** شَمسِيَّة [šamsiyya] شَمسِيّات [šamsiyya:t] *pl:*

parcel • **1.** رُزمَة [ruzma] رُزَم [ruzam] *pl:* لَفَّة [laffa] لَفّات [laffa:t] *pl:* You forgot your parcels. إنتَ نِسِيت رُزَمَك [?inta nisi:t ruzamak]

*** I'll send it by parcel post.** • **1.** راح أدِزّها رُزمَة بالبَرِيد [ra:ħ ?adizzha ruzma bilbari:d]

*** Where is the parcel post window?** • **1.** وَين شِبّاك الرُّزَم؟ [wi:n šibba:k ?irruzam?]

pardon • **1.** مَرحَمَة [marħama] مَراحِم [mara:ħim] *pl:* His pardon was refused. اِنرُفضَت مَرحَمتَه [?inrufðat marħamtah]

*** I beg your pardon, I did'nt mean to step on your foot.** • **1.** العَفو، ما قصَدِت أدُوس عَلَى رِجلَك [?ilʕafw, ma: qṣadit ?adu:s ʕala rijlak]

to pardon • **1.** عِفَى عَن [ʕifa: ʕan] عَفو [ʕafw] *vn:* اِنعِفَى [?inʕifa:] *p:* He pardoned me this time. عِفَى عَنِّي هَالمَرَّة [ʕifa: ʕanni halmarra] • **2.** غُفَر [ɣufar] اِنغُفَر [?inɣufar] *p:* God will pardon my sins. الله راح يُغفُر ذنُوبِي [?allah ra:ħ yuɣfur ðnu:bi]

*** Pardon me, I didn't hear what you said.** • **1.** عَفواً، ما سمَعِت شقِلِت [ʕafwan, ma: smaʕit šgilit]

*** Pardon me, when does the movie begin?** • **1.** إسمَحلِي، شوَقِت يِبدِي الفِلِم؟ [?ismaħli, šwakit yibdi ?ilfilim?]

to pare • **1.** قَشَّر [gaššar] تَقشِير، تقِشِّر [tagši:r, tgiššir] *vn:* تقَشَّر [tgaššar] *p:* Pare the potatoes and put them in a pan of cold water. قَشّرِي البُتَيتَة وَحُطِّيها بجِدِر ماي بارِد [gaššri ?ilputi:ta wħuṭṭi:ha bjidir ma:y ba:rid] • **2.** قَصّ [gaṣṣ] قَصّ [gaṣṣ] *vn:* اِنقَصّ [?ingaṣṣ] *p:* You should be more careful when you pare your nails. لازِم تدِير بالَك أزيَد مِن تقُصّ أظافرَك [la:zim ddi:r ba:lak ?azyad min dguṣṣ ?aða:frak] • **3.** قَلَّل [qallal] تَقلِيل [taqli:l] *vn:* تقَلَّل [tqallal] *p:* You'll have to pare down your estimates, or else they'll turn down the budget. لازِم تقَلِّل تَخمِيناتَك وَلّا يرُفضُون المِيزانِيَّة [la:zim tqallil taxmi:na:tak walla yirufðu:n ?ilmi:za:niyya]

parentage • **1.** أَصِل [?aṣil] أُصُول [?uṣu:l] *pl:* She is of good parentage. هَذِي أصِلها زين [ha:ði ?aṣilha zi:n]

parenthesis • **1.** قَوس [qaws] أقواس [?aqwa:s] *pl:* Put the word between parentheses. حُطّ الكِلمَة بين قَوسَين [ħuṭṭ ?iččilma bayn qawsayn]

parents • **1.** والِدين [wa:lidayn] أَبَوَين [?abawayn] Respect for one's parents is a virtue. اِحتِرام الوالِدَين فَضِيلَة [?iħtira:m ?ilwa:lidayn faði:la] May God keep your parents! الله يخَلِّي والدَيك [?allah yxalli wa:ldayk]

*** Both my parents are still living.** • **1.** أمِّي وأَبُويَا ثنَينهُم بَعَدهُم طَيِّبِين [?ummi w?abu:ya θnaynhum baʕadhum ṭayybi:n]

parish • **1.** أبرَشِيَّة [?abrašiyya] أبرَشِيّات [?abrašiyya:t] *pl:*

park • **1.** حَدِيقَة [ħadi:qa] حَدايِق [ħada:yiq] *pl:* There is a beautiful public park in the center of the city. أكُو حَدِيقَة عامَّة لَطِيفَة بنُص الوِلايَة [?aku ħadi:qa ʕa:mma laṭi:fa bnuṣṣ ?ilwila:ya]

to park • **1.** وَقَّف [waggaf, wagguf] تَوقِيف [tawgi:f] *vn: sv* u. بَرَّك [parrak] تبِرِّك [tpirrik] *vn: sv* i. You can park your car here. تِقدَر توَقُّف سَيّارتَك هنا [tigdar twagguf sayya:rtak hna]

parking • **1.** وُقُوف [wugu:f] Car parking is prohibited here. وُقُوف السَّيّارات مَمنُوع هنا [wugu:f ?issayya:ra:t mamnu:ʕ hna]

parking place • **1.** مَوقِف [mawqif] مَواقِف [mawa:qif] *pl:* There's a parking place for cars behind the building. أكُو مَوقِف لِلسَّيّارات وَرا البِنايَة [?aku mawqif lissayya:ra:t wara ?ilbina:ya]

Parliament • **1.** بَرلَمان [barlama:n] بَرلَمانات [barlama:na:t] *pl:* مَجلِس أُمَّة [majlis ?umma] مَجالِس أُمَّة [maja:lis ?umma] *pl:*

parlor • **1.** غُرفَة خُطّار [ɣurfat xuṭṭa:r] غُرُف خُطّار [ɣuruf xuṭṭa:r] *pl:* غُرفَة اِستِقبال [ɣurfat ?istiqba:l] غُرُف اِستِقبال [ɣuruf ?istiqba:l] *pl:*

to parole • **1.** * He was paroled. اِنفَكّ وَتخَلَّى تَحت المُراقَبَة [?infakk wtxalla: taħt ?ilmura:qaba]

parrot • **1.** بِيبِمَتُّو [bi:bimattu] بِيبِمَتُّوات [bi:bimattuwa:t] *pl:* بَبَغاء [babaɣa:?] بَبَغاءات [babaɣa:?a:t] *pl:*

parsley • **1.** كرَفُس [krafus] مَعدَنُوس [maʕdanu:s] جَعفَرِي [jaʕfari]

part • **1.** جُزُء [juzu?] أجزاء [?ajza:?] *pl:* قِسِم [qisim] أقسام [?aqsa:m] *pl:* That part of the work isn't finished yet. هَالجُزُء مِن الشُّغُل بَعَد ما خِلَص [hajjuzu? min ?iššuɣul baʕad ma: xilaṣ] This little screw is a very important part of the machine. هَالبُرغِي الصّغَيِّر فَدّ جُزُء كُلِّش مُهِمّ مِن المَكِينَة [halburɣi ?iṣṣɣayyir fadd juzu? kulliš muhimm min ?almaki:na] Can you get spare parts for your bicycle? تِقدَر تِلقِي أجزاء اِحتِياطِيَّة لِلبايسِكل مالَك؟ [tigdar tilgi ?ajza:? ?iħtiya:ṭiyya lilpa:ysikil ma:lak??] The fence is part wood and part stone. الحاجِز قِسِم خِشَب وقِسِم حَجَر [?alħa:jiz qisim xišab wqisim ħajar] • **2.** دَور [dawr] أدوار [?adwa:r] *pl:* He played the part of a king in the play. مَثَّل دُور مَلِك بِالتَّمثِيلِيَّة [maθθal dawr malik bittamθi:liyya] • **3.** مَنطِقَة [manṭiqa] مَناطِق [mana:ṭiq] *pl:* ناحِيَة [na:ħiya] نَواحِي [nawa:ħi] *pl:* طَرَف [ṭaraf] أطراف [?aṭra:f] *pl:* What part of the city are you from? إنتَ مِن يا مَنطِقَة مِن الوِلايَة؟ [?inta min ya: manṭiqa min ?alwla:ya] I haven't traveled much in these parts. آنِي ما مسافِر هوايَة بهَالمَنطَقَة [?a:ni ma: msa:fir hwa:ya bhalmanṭaqa]

*** For my part I have no objection.** • 1. مِن جهتي، ما عِندي مانِع [min ǰihti, maː ʕindi maːniʕ]
for the most part • 1. عَالأكثَر [ʕalʔakθar] عَالأغلَب [ʕalʔaɣlab] His company is made up, for the most part, of volunteers. حَضِيرتَه مِتكَوّنَة عَالأكثَر مِن مِطّوّعِين [ħaðiːrtah mitkawwna ʕalʔakθar min miṭṭawwʕiːn] For the most part, the weather has been nice this summer. عَالأغلَب الطّقس كان لَطِيف هَالصّيف [ʕalʔaɣlab ʔiṭṭaqis čaːn laṭiːf haṣṣayf]
in part • 1. نَوعاً ما [nawʕan maː] بِبَعض [bibaʕð] بقِسِم مِن [bqisim min] I agree with you in part. آني أتّفِق وِيّاك نَوعاً ما [ʔaːni ʔattifiq wiyyaːk nawʕan maː]
on the part of • 1. مِن جانِب [min ǰaːnib] مِن قِبَل [min qibal] We regret any discrimination against a minority on the part of a government official. نِأسَف لأي تَفرقَة ضِدّ الأقَلّيَّة مِن جانِب أيّ مُوَظَّف حُكُومِي [niʔsaf lʔayy tafriqa ðidd ʔilʔaqalliyya min ǰaːnib ʔayy muwaððaf ħukuːmi]
to take part in • 1. اِشتِرَك ب [ʔištirak b-] اِشتِراك [ʔištiraːk] *vn: sv* i. ساهَم [saːham] مُساهَمَة [musaːhama] *vn: sv* i. Are you going to take part in the discussion? راح تِشتِرِك بالمُناقَشَة؟ [raːħ tištirik bilmunaːqaša?]
to take the part of • 1. لِزَم جَانِب [lizam jaːnib] لَزِم جَانِب [lazim jaːnib] *vn:* اِنلِزَم جَانِب [ʔinlizam jaːnib] *p:* He always takes his brother's part. دائِماً يِلزَم جانِب أخُوه [daːʔiman yilzam ǰaːnib ʔaxuːh]
to part • 1. اِفتِرَق [ʔiftiraq] اِفتِراق [ʔiftiraːq] *vn: sv* i. They parted as friends. اِفتِرقَوا كَأصدِقاء [ʔiftirqaw kaʔaṣdiqaːʔ] • 2. تفارَق [tfaːrag] تَفارُق [tafaːrug] *vn: sv* a. Let's part here. خَلّي نِتفارَق هنا [xalli nitfaːrag hna] • 3. وَخَّر [waxxar] توُخُّر، توخِير [twuxxur, tawxiːr] *vn:* She parted the curtains and looked out. وَخّرَت البَردات وَباوعَت لِبَرّة [waxxirat ʔilpardaːt wbaːwʕat libarra] • 4. فُرَق [furag] فَرِق [farig] *vn:* اِنفُرَق [ʔinfurag] *p:* He parts his hair on the left side. يُفرُق شَعرَه عَاليِسرَة [yufrug šaʕrah ʕalyisra]
to part with • 1. تخَلّى عَن [txallaː ʕan] تخَلّي عَن [txalli ʕan] *vn: sv* a. I wouldn't part with that book for any price. ما أتخَلّى عَن ذاك الكِتاب بأي ثَمَن [maː ʔatxallaː ʕan ðaːk ʔilkitaːb bʔayy θaman]

partial • 1. مِتحَيِّز [mitħayyiz] مُغرِض [muɣrið] He tries not to be partial. يحاوِل أن ما يكُون مِتحَيِّز [yħaːwil ʔan maː ykuːn mitħayyiz] • 2. جُزئِي [ǰuzʔi] This is only a partial solution. هَذا فَدّ حَل جُزئِي بَسّ [haːða fadd ħall ǰuzʔi bass]
to be partial to • 1. حابَى [ħabaː] مُحاباة [muħaːbaː(t)] *vn: sv* i. He's always been partial to his youngest daughter. دائِماً يحابِي بِنتَه الصّغَيّرَة [daːʔiman yiħaːbi bintah ʔiṣṣiɣayyra] • 2. فَضَّل [faððal] تَفضِيل [tafðiːl] *vn:* تفضَّل [tfaððal] *p:* He's partial to blondes. يفَضِّل الشُّقُر [yfaððil ʔiššugur]

partiality • 1. مُحاباة، مُحابات [muħaːbaːt] The other employees resent the partiality in his recommendations for advancements. بَقيَة المُستَخدَمِين اِستَنكِرَوا المُحابات بتَوصِياتَه لِلتّرفِيع [baqiyat ʔilmustaxdamiːn ʔistankiraw ʔilmuħaːbaːt bitawṣiyaːtah littarfiːʕ]

partially • 1. نَوعاً ما [nawʕan maː] جُزئِيّاً [ǰuzʔiyyan] You are partially right. إنتَ صَحِيح نَوعاً ما [ʔinta ṣaħiːħ nawʕan maː] It's partially finished. خَلصانَة جُزئِيّاً [xalṣaːna ǰuzʔiyyan]

to participate • 1. اِشتِرَك [ʔištirak] اِشتِراك [ʔištiraːk] *vn: sv* i. شارَك [šaːrak] مُشارَكَة [mušaːraka] *vn: sv* i. ساهَم [saːham] مُساهَمَة [musaːhama] *vn: sv* i. They have invited us to participate in the project. دِعَونا نِشتِرِك بالمَشرُوع [diʕuːna ništirik bilmašruːʕ]

participation • 1. اِشتِراك [ʔištiraːk] مُشارَكَة [mušaːraka] مُساهَمَة [musaːhama]

participle • 1. إسِم فاعِل [ʔisim faːʕil] (active) إسِم مَفعُول [ʔisim mafʕuːl] (passive)

particle • 1. ذَرَّة [ðarra] ذَرّات [ðarraːt] *pl:* حَبّة [ħabba] حَبّات [ħabbaːt] *pl:* There isn't a particle of truth in that story. ماكُو ذَرَّة مِن الحَقِيقَة بهالقُصَّة [maːku ðarra min ʔilħaqiːqa bhalquṣṣa] The inflammation is from a particle of dirt on the eyeball. الالتِهاب مِن ذَرَّة وُسَخ عَلَى كُرَة العَين [ʔilʔiltihaːb min ðarrat wuṣax ʕala kurat ʔilʕayn]

particular • 1. بالتَّفصِيل [bittafṣiːl] تَفاصِيل [tafaːṣiːl] *pl:* For further particulars write to the publishers. لِلحُصُول عَلى تَفاصِيل أكثَر، إكتِب لِلنَّشِر [lilħuṣuːl ʕala tafaːṣiːl ʔakθar, ʔiktib linnašir] My wife will give you all the particulars. مَرتِي تِنطِيك كُلّ التَّفاصِيل [marti tinṭiːk kull ʔittafaːṣiːl] • 2. خاصّ [xaːṣṣ] Our city has its own particular problems. مَدِينَتنا عِدها مَشاكِلها الخاصَّة بِيها [madiːnatna ʕidha mašaːkilha ʔilxaːṣṣa biːha] • 3. مُعَيَّن [muʕayyan] For no particular reason, he stopped visiting us. بَطَّل يزُورنا بدُون سَبَب مُعَيَّن [baṭṭal yzuːrna bduːn sabab muʕayyan] • 4. مُقَرَّب [muqarrab] مُقَرَّبِين [muqarrabiːn] *pl:* He is no particular friend of mine. هَذا مُو فَدّ صَدِيق مُقَرَّب إلِي [haːða muː fadd ṣadiːq muqarrab ʔili] • 5. دِقداقِي [diqdaːqi] دِقداقِيَّة [diqdaːqiyya] *pl:* My husband is very particular about his food. زَوجِي كُلِّش دِقداقِي بأكلَه [zawǰi kulliš diqdaːqi bʔaklah] • 6. بالذّات [biððaːt] This particular dress costs more. هَالبَدلَة بِالذّات تكَلِّف أكثَر [halbadla biððaːt tkallif ʔakθar]
in particular • 1. بصُورَة خاصَّة [bṣuːra xaːṣṣa] عَلَى الخُصُوص [ʕala ʔilxuṣuːṣ] I remember one man in particular. أتذَكَّر فَدّ رِجّال بصُورَة خاصَّة [ʔadðakkar fadd rijjaːl bṣuːra xaːṣṣa] • 2. عَلَى وَجه التَّعيِين [ʕala wajh ʔittaʕyiːn] Are you looking for anything in particular? دَتدَوُّر عَلَى فَدّ شِي عَلَى وَجه التَّعيِين؟ [daddawwur ʕala fadd ši ʕala wajh ʔittaʕyiːn?]

P

particularly • **1.** بصُورَة خاصَّة [bṣu:ra xa:ṣṣa] He is particularly interested in science. هُوَّ مِهتَمّ بِصُورَة خاصَّة بالعِلُوم [huwwa mihtamm bṣu:ra xa:ṣṣa bilʕilu:m]

partition • **1.** حاجِز [ħa:ǰiz] حَواجِز [ħawa:ǰiz] *pl:* We are going to put in a partition here. راح نحُطّ حاجِز هنا [ra:ħ nħuṭṭ ħa:ǰiz hna] • **2.** تَقسِيم [taqsi:m] تَقسِيمات، تَقاسِيم [taqsi:ma:t, taqa:si:m] *pl:* The partition of Palestine took place as a result of a decision taken by the United Nations. تَقسِيم فِلِسطِين جِرَى عَلَى أَثَر قَرار اِتّخذَته الأُمَم المُتَّحِدَة [taqsi:m filisṭi:n ǰira: ʕala ʔaθar qara:r ʔittixðatah ʔilʔumam ʔilmuttaħida] • **3.** اِنقِسام [ʔinqisa:m] The disagreement caused the partition of the party. الخِلاف سَبَّب اِنقِسام الحِزب [ʔilxila:f sabbab ʔinqisa:m ʔilħizib]

partly • **1.** جُزئِيّاً [ǰuzʔiyyan] بَعضاً [baʕðan] The book is only partly finished as yet. الكِتاب خَلصان جُزئِيّاً بَسّ لِحَدّ الآن [ʔilkita:b xalṣa:n ǰuzʔiyyan bass liħadd ʔilʔaan]

partner • **1.** شَرِيك [šari:k] شُركاء، شُركان [suraka:ʔ, šurka:n] *pl:* My business partner is coming back tomorrow. شَرِيكِي بِالشُّغُل راجِع باكِر [šari:ki biššuɣul ra:ǰiʕ ba:čir] • **2.** صاحِب [ṣa:ħib] أصحاب [ʔaṣħa:b] *pl:* My partner and I have been winning every game. آنِي وصاحِبِي دَنِربَح كُلّ لِعبَة [ʔa:ni wṣa:ħbi danirbaħ kull liʕba]

partridge • **1.** قَبَك [qabač] I bought a pair of partridges. اِشتِرَيت زوج طيُور قَبَك [ʔištirayt zawǰ ṭyu:r qabač]

part-time • **1.** نُصّ دَوام [nuṣṣ dawa:m] Do you have any part-time work in this office? أَكُو وَظِيفَة نُصّ دَوام بِهالمَكتَب؟ [ʔaku waði:fa nuṣṣ dawa:m bihalmaktab?]

party • **1.** حِزب [ħizib] أحزاب [ʔaħza:b] *pl:* What political party do you belong to? إنتَ لِيا حِزب سِياسِي مِنتِمِي؟ [ʔinta liya: ħizib siya:si mintimi?] • **2.** طَرَف [ṭaraf] أطراف [ʔaṭra:f] *pl:* جانِب [ǰa:nib] جَوانِب [ǰawa:nib] *pl:* Neither of the two parties appeared at the trial. الطَّرَفَين ما حِضرَوا بِالمُحاكَمَة [ʔiṭṭarafayn ma: ħiðraw bilmuħa:kama] Both parties agreed to the terms. الجّانِبَين وافقَوا عَالشُّرُوط [ʔiǰǰa:nibayn wa:fqaw ʕaššuru:ṭ] • **3.** حَفلَة [ħafla] حَفلات [ħafla:t] *pl:* She likes to give big parties. يعجِبها تقِيم حَفلات فَخمَة [yiʕǰibha tqi:m ħafla:t faxma] • **4.** عَزِيمَة [ʕazi:ma] عَزايِم [ʕaza:yim] *pl:* Good-night; it was a lovely dinner party. تِصبَحُون عَلَى خَير؛ عَزِيمَتكُم كانَت مُمتازَة [tiṣbaħu:n ʕala xayr; ʕazi:matkum ča:nat mumta:za]

*** I won't be a party to that.** • **1.** آنِي ماحُطّ نَفسِي بهاي [ʔa:ni ma: ħuṭṭ nafsi bha:y]

party line • **1.** خَطّ مُشتَرَك [xaṭṭ muštarak] خُطُوط مُشتَرَكَة [xuṭu:ṭ muštaraka] *pl:* Our telephone is on a party line. تَلِفُونّا عَلَى خَطّ مُشتَرَك [talifu:nna ʕala xaṭṭ muštarak] • **2.** مَنهَج حِزب [manhaǰ ħizib] The party leader called upon all members to hold to the party line. رَئِيس الحِزب دِعَى كُلّ الأعضاء لِلتَّمَسُّك بِمَنهَج الحِزب [raʔi:s ʔilħizib diʕa: kull ʔilʔaʕða:ʔ littamassuk ʔibmanhaǰ ʔilħizib]

pass • **1.** مَمَرّ [mamarr] مَمَرّات [mamarra:t] *pl:* The pass is covered with snow in winter. المَمَرّ يِنطُمُر بِالثَّلِج بِالشِّتا [lmamarr yinṭumur biθθaliǰ biššita] • **2.** بِطاقَة مُرُور [biṭa:qat muru:r] بِطاقات مُرُور [biṭa:qa:t muru:r] *pl:* You'll need a pass to get through the gate. تِحتاج بِطاقَة مُرُور يَاللّه تِقدَر تفُوت مِن المَدخَل [tiħta:ǰ biṭa:qat muru:r yallah tigdar tfu:t min ʔilmadxal] • **3.** مَأذُونِيَّة [maʔðu:niyya] مَأذُونِيّات [maʔðu:niyya:t] *pl:* He has a weekend pass. عِندَه مَأذُونِيَّة بنِهايَة هَالإسبُوع [ʕindah maʔðu:niyya bniha:yat halʔisbu:ʕ]

to pass • **1.** مَرّ ب [marr b-] مُرُور [muru:r] *vn:* *sv* u. I pass this bank building every day. أمُرّ بِبِنايَة هَالبَنك كُلّ يوم [ʔamurr bibina:yat halbang kull yu:m] The play finally passed the censor. التَّمثِيلِيَّة أخِيراً مَرَّت بِالرَّقِيب [ʔittamθi:liyya ʔaxi:ran marrat birraqi:b] • **2.** مَشَّى [mašša:] تَمشِيَة [tamšiya] *vn:* تمَشَّى [tmašša:] *p:* The censor refused to pass the film. الرَّقِيب رُفَض يمَشِّي الفِلِم [ʔirraqi:b rufað ymašši ʔilfilim] • **3.** ناوَش [na:waš] مُناوَشَة [muna:waša] *vn:* *sv* u. Will you please pass me the bread? ما تناوُشنِي الخُبُز مِن فَضلَك؟ [ma: tna:wušni ʔilxubuz min faðlak?] • **4.** صَدَّق [ṣaddaq] تَصدِيق [taṣdi:q] *vn:* تصَدَّق [tṣaddaq] *p:* The House of Representatives passed the bill unanimously. مَجلِس النُّوّاب صَدَّق اللّائِحَة بِالإجماع [maǰlis ʔinnuwwa:b ṣaddaq ʔilla:ʔiħa bilʔiǰma:ʕ] • **5.** صاح بَاص [ṣa:ħ ba:ṣ] It's your turn; I passed. هَسَّة دُورَك؛ آنِي صِحِت باص [hassa du:rak; ʔa:ni ṣiħit pa:ṣ] • **6.** مَرَّر [marrar] تَمرِير [tamri:r] *vn:* تمَرَّر [tmarrar] *p:* عَبَّر [ʕabbar] تَعبِير [taʕbi:r] *vn:* تعَبَّر [tʕabbar] *p:* They passed the buckets from hand to hand. مَرِّرَوا السُّطُول مِن إيد الإيد [marriraw ʔissuṭu:l min ʔi:d ʔilʔi:d] • **7.** فات مِن [fa:t min] فَوت [fawt] *vn:* اِنفات [ʔinfa:t] *p:* The train passes here at three o'clock. القِطار يفُوت مِن هنا السّاعَة ثلاثَة [ʔilqiṭa:r yfu:t min hna ʔissa:ʕa tla:θa] • **8.** طِلَع [ṭilaʕ] طُلُوع [ṭulu:ʕ] *vn:* اِنطِلَع [ʔinṭilaʕ] *p:* غِلَب [ɣilab] غُلُب [ɣulub] *vn:* اِنغِلَب [ʔinɣilab] *p:* Pass that car! إطلَع ذِيك السَّيّارَة [ʔiṭlaʕ ði:č ʔissayya:ra] • **9.** قَضَّى [gaðða:] تَغضِيَة [taqðiya] *vn:* تقَضَّى [tgaðða:] *p:* He passed most of the time reading. قَضَّى أكثَر الوَقت بِالقِراءَة [qaðða: ʔakθar ʔilwakit bilqira:ʔa] • **10.** مُضَى [muða:] مُضِي [muðiy] *vn:* *sv* i. The days pass quickly when you're busy. الأيّام تِمضِي بِسُرعَة مِن واحِد يكُون مَشغُول [ʔilʔayya:m timði bsurʕa min wa:ħid yku:n mašɣu:l] • **11.** نِجَح ب [niǰaħ b-] نَجاح [naǰa:ħ] *vn:* *sv* a. عُبَر [ʕubar] عُبُور [ʕubu:r] *vn:* *sv* u. Did you pass the examination? نِجَحِت بِالإمتِحان؟ [niǰaħit bilʔimtiħa:n?] • **12.** عَبَر [ʕubar] عَبُر [ʕabur] *vn:* *sv* u. مَرّ ب [marr b-] مُرُور [muru:r] *vn:* *sv* u. You passed through a red light.

P

عبرت ضُوَا أحمَر [ʕbarit ðuwa ʔaħmar] • **13.** اِنتِقَل [ʔintiqal] اِنتِقال [ʔintiqaːl] *vn: sv* i. The farm passes from father to son. المَزرَعَة تِنتِقِل مِن الأب لِلإبِن [ʔilmazraʕa tintiqil min ʔalʔab lilʔibin]

to pass around • **1.** دَوَّر [dawwar] تَدوِير [tadwiːr] *vn:* تدَوَّر [tdawwar] *p:* فَرَّر [farrar] تَفرِير [tafriːr] *vn:* تفَرَّر [tfarrar] *p:* They passed around cookies. دَوِّرَوا الكِلَيجَة عالكُلّ [dawwiraw ʔalkliːča ʕalkull] • **2.** طَشّ [ṭašš] طَشّ [ṭašš] *vn:* اِنطَشّ [ʔinṭašš] *p:* نِشَر [nišar] نَشِر [našir] *vn:* اِنِّشَر [ʔinnišar] *p:* Pass the word around so that everyone hears. طُشّ الحكايَة حَتَّى الكُلّ يسِمعُون [ṭušš ʔilħčaːya ħatta ʔilkull ysimʕuːn]

* **We passed around the hat to help him pay his hospital bill.** • **1.** جِمَعنالَه فلُوس حَتَّى نساعدَه يدفَع مَصاريف المُستَشفَى [ǰimaʕnaːlah fluːs ħatta nsaːʕdah yidfaʕ maṣaːriːf ʔilmustašfa]

to pass away • **1.** توَفَّى [twaffaː] *sv* a. مات [maːt] مَوت [mawt] *vn: sv* u. Her mother passed away last week. أُمَّها توَفَّت إسبُوع اللِّي فات [ʔummaha twaffat ʔisbuːʕ ʔilli faːt]

to pass by • **1.** مَرّ مِن يَمّ [marr min yamm] مُرُور مِن يَمّ [muruːr min yamm] *vn: sv* u. مَرّ بـ [marr bi-] He passed right by me without seeing me. مَرّ مِن يَمِّي تَماماً وَما شافنِي [marr min yammi tamaːman wma šaːfni]

to pass judgment on • **1.** حِكَم [ħikam] حُكُم [ħukum] *vn:* اِنحِكَم [ʔinħikam] *p:* Don't pass judgment on him too quickly. لا تُحكُم عَليه كُلِّش بِالعَجَل [laː tuħkum ʕaliːh kulliš bilʕaǰal]

to pass off • **1.** فَوَّت [fawwat] تَفوِيت [tafwiːt] *vn:* تفَوَّت [tfawwat] *p:* مَرَّر [marrar] تَمرِير [tamriːr] *vn:* تمَرَّر [tmarrar] *p:* He tried to pass off an imitation as the original. حاوَل يفَوُّت شِي مزَيِّف كَشِي حَقِيقِي [ħaːwal yfawwut ši mzayyif kaši ħaqiːqi] • **2.** عَبَّر [ʕabbar] تَعبِير [taʕbiːr] *vn: sv* u. He tried to pass himself off as an officer. حاوَل يعَبُّر نَفسَه كَضابُط [ħaːwal yʕabbur nafsah kaðaːbuṭ]

to pass on • **1.** وَصَّل [waṣṣal] تَوصِيل [tawṣiːl] *vn: sv* i. فِشَى [fišaː] إفشاء [ʔifšaːʔ] *vn: sv* i. Don't pass this on to anyone. لا توَصِّل هاي لِأَحَّد [laː twaṣṣil haːy lʔaħħad]

to pass out • **1.** * Several people passed out from the heat. عِدَّة أشخاص غابَت رُوحهُم مِن الحَرّ [ʕiddat ʔašxaːṣ ɣaːbat ruːħhum min ʔilħarr]

* **They passed out from drinking too much.** • **1.** فُقدَوا وَعِيهُم مِن كُثرَة الشُّرُب [fuqdaw waʕyhum min kuθrat ʔiššurub]

to pass sentence • **1.** أصدَر حُكُم [ʔaṣdar ħukum] إصدار حُكُم [ʔiṣdaːr ħukum] *vn: sv* u. The court will pass sentence today. المَحكَمَة راح تُصدُر حُكُم اليُوم [ʔilmaħkama raːħ tuṣdur ħukum ʔilyuːm]

to pass through • **1.** مَرّ مِن [marr min] مُرُور [muruːr] *vn: sv* u. فات مِن [faːt min] فَوت [fawt] *vn: sv* u. You can't pass through there. ما تِقدَر تمُرّ مِن هناك [maː tigdar tmurr minhnak] • **2.** فَوِّت [fawwit] تَفوِيت [tafwiːt] *vn:* تفَوَّت [tfawwat] *p:* Pass the rope through here. فَوِّت الحَبل مِن هنا [fawwit ʔilħabil min hna]

to pass up • **1.** فَوَّت [fawwat] تَفوِيت [tafwiːt] *vn: sv* i. ضَيَّع [ðayyaʕ] تَضيِيع [taðyiːʕ] *vn: sv* i. You ought not to pass up an opportunity like that. ما لازم تفَوِّت هِيكِي فُرصَة [maː laːzim tfawwit hiːči furṣa] • **2.** ناوَش [naːwaš] مُناوَشَة [munaː waša] *vn:* تناوَش [tnaːwaš] *p:* Pass your papers up to the front row. ناوشُوا أوراقكُم لِلسِّرَة الأمامِي [naːwšuː ʔawraːqkum lissira ʔilʔamaːmi]

passable • **1.** مَقبُول [maqbuːl] The work is passable. الشُّغُل مَقبُول [ʔiššuɣul maqbuːl]

passage • **1.** مَمَرّ [mamarr] مَمَرّات [mamarraːt] *pl:* We had to go through a dark passage. اِضطَرَّينا نِسلُك مَمَرّ مُظلِم [ʔiðṭarriːna nisluk mamarr muðlim] • **2.** مَقطَع [maqṭaʕ] مَقاطِع [maqaːṭiʕ] *pl:* He read us several passages from his book. قِرالنا عِدَّة مَقاطِع مِن كِتابَه [qiraːlna ʕiddat maqaːṭiʕ min kitaːbah] • **3.** عَبرَة [ʕabra] The passage across the river by boat takes a half hour. عَبرَة النَّهَر بالبَلَم تاخُذ نُصّ ساعَة [ʕabrat ʔinnahar bilbalam taːxuð nuṣṣ saːʕa]

passenger • **1.** راكِب [raːkib] رُكّاب [rukkaːb] *pl:* عِبرِي [ʕibri] The bus holds thirty passengers. الباص يلِزَم ثلاثِين راكِب بَسّ [ʔilpaːṣ yilzam tlaːθiːn raːkib bass] • **2.** مُسافِر [musaːfir] مُسافِرِين [musaːfiriːn] *pl:* The passengers must go through customs. المُسافِرِين لازم يمُرُّون بالجُمرُك [ʔalmusaːfiriːn laːzim ymurruːn bilgumrug]

passer-by • **1.** عابِر سَبِيل [ʕaːbir sabiːl] عابرِين سَبِيل [ʕaːbiriːn sabiːl] *pl:* مارّ [maːrr] مارَّة [maːrra] *pl:* Some passer-by must have picked it up. لازِم أخَذها فَدّ عابِر سَبِيل [laːzim ʔaxaðha fadd ʕaːbir sabiːl]

passing • **1.** وَفاة [wafaːt] موت [mawt, muːt] The whole nation mourned his passing. الأُمَّة كُلّها حِزنَت عَلَى وَفاتَه [ʔalʔumma kullha ħiznat ʕala wafaːtah] • **2.** عابِر [ʕaːbir] زائِل [zaːʔil] وَقتِي [waqti] It's just a passing fancy. هَذا فَدّ وَلَع عابِر [haːða fadd walaʕ ʕaːbir] • **3.** نَجاح [naǰaːħ] I got passing grades in all my subjects. حَصَّلِت دَرَجات نَجاح بكُلّ درُوسِي [ħaṣṣalit daraǰaːt naǰaːħ bkull druːsi] • **4.** مُرُور [muruːr] طُلُوع [ṭuluːʕ] Passing on the right is dangerous. المُرُور عاليَمِين خَطَر [ʔilmuruːr ʕalyamiːn xaṭar] • **5.** عُبُور [ʕubuːr] After passing through the sand, you'll hit a hard surface. بَعد العُبُور مِن الرَّمُل، راح تصادِف قاع قَوِيَّة [baʕd ʔilʕubuːr min ʔarramul, raːħ tṣaːdif gaːʕ qawiyya]

passion • **1.** وَلَع، وَهَس [walaʕ, wahas] He has a passion for music. عِندَه وَلَع بِالمُوسِيقى [ʕindah walaʕ bilmusiːqa] • **2.** عاطِفَة [ʕaːṭifa] عَواطِف [ʕawaːṭif] *pl:* You should try to control your passions better. لازِم تحاوِل تسَيطِر عَلَى عَواطفَك أكثَر [laːzim tħaːwil tsayṭir ʕala ʕawaːṭfak ʔakθar]

P

passionate • **1.** عاطِفِي [ʕaːṭifi] She has a very passionate nature. هِيَّ عاطِفِيَّة [hiyya ʕaːṭifiyya]

passive • **1.** مَجهُول [majhuːl] Change this sentence to the passive voice. حَوِّل هالجُملَة إِلَى صِيغَة المَجهُول [ħawwil haljumla ʔila ṣiːɣat ʔilmajhuːl] • **2.** سَلبِي [salbi] Passive resistance is a peaceful but effective weapon. المُقاوَمَة السَّلبِيَّة طَرِيقَة سِلمِيَّة وَلَكِنَّها سِلاح نَفّاذ [ʔilmuqaːwama ʔassalbiyya ṭariːqa silmiyya wlaːkinnaha silaːħ naffaːð]

*** He is a passive spectator.** • **1.** هَذا مِتفَرِّج ما إِلَه دَخَل [haːða mitfarrij maː ʔilah daxal]

Passover • **1.** عِيد الفُصح [ʕiːd ʔilfuṣħ]

past • **1.** ماضِي [maːḍi] The police uncovered some suspicious activities in his past. الشُّرطَة إِكتِشفَت أَعمال مَشبُوهَة بِماضِيه [ʔiššurṭa ʔiktišfat ʔaʕmaːl mašbuːha bimaːḍiːh] That's a thing of the past. هَذا فَدّ شِي بِالماضِي [haːða fadd ši bilmaːḍi] That's a thing of the past. هَذا صار تارِيخ [haːða ṣaːr taːriːx] • **2.** فايِت [faːyit] Where were you this past week? وِين كِنِت بِالإِسبُوع الفايِت؟ [wiːn činit bilʔisbuːʕ ʔilfaːyit?] • **3.** مِتجاوِز [mitjaːwiz] I am past that stage. آنِي مِتجاوِز هالمَرحَلَة [ʔaːniː midjaːwiz halmarħala]

*** It's five minutes past twelve.** • **1.** الساعَة ثنَعَش وخَمسَة [ʔissaːʕa θnaʕaš wxamsa]

*** It's way past my bedtime.** • **1.** فات وَقِت نَومِي بِهوايَة [faːt wakit nuːmi bihwaːya]

*** The worst part of the trip is past.** • **1.** أَسوَء قِسِم مِن السَفرَة فات [ʔaswaʔ qisim min ʔissafra faːt]

*** He walked past me.** • **1.** فات مِن يَمِّي [faːt min yammi]

in the past • **1.** قَبُل [gabul, qabil] ماضِي [maːḍi] سابِق [saːbiq] That has often happened in the past. هاي حِدثَت هوايَة قَبُل [haːy ħidθat hwaːya gabul]

paste • **1.** صَمُغ [ṣamuɣ] صُمُوغ [ṣumuːɣ] *pl:* شرِيس [šriːs, šriːṣ] Where did you put the paste jar? وِين حَطَّيت شِيشَة الصَّمُغ؟ [wiːn ħaṭṭiːt šiːšat ʔiṣṣamuɣ?]

to paste • **1.** لِزَق [lizag] لَزِق [lazig] *vn:* اِنلِزَق [ʔinlizag] *p:* لَزَّق [lazzag] تَلزِيق [talziːg] *vn:* تلَزَّق [tlazzag] *p:* Paste these labels on the boxes. إِلزِق هَالعَلامات عالصَّنادِيق [ʔilzig halʕalaːmaːt ʕaṣṣanaːdiːg]

pastime • **1.** تَسلِيَة [tasliya] لَهُو [lahw] What is your favorite pastime? شِنُو هِيَّ تَسلِيتَك المَحبُوبَة؟ [šinuː hiyya tasliːtak ʔalmaħbuːba?]

pastry • **1.** حَلَوِيّات [ħalawiyyaːt]

pastry shop • **1.** مَحَل حَلَوِيّات [maħall ħalawiyyaːt] مَحَلّات حَلَوِيّات [maħallaːt ħalawiyyaːt] *pl:*

pasture • **1.** مَرعَى [marʕa] مَراعِي [maraːʕi] *pl:* Are the cows still in the pasture? البَقَرات بَعَدهُم بالمَرعَى؟ [ʔalbaqaraːt baʕadhum bilmarʕa?]

pat • **1.** طَبطَبَة [ṭabṭaba] طَبطَبات [ṭabṭabaːt] *pl:* I got a congratulatory pat on the shoulder. حَصَّلِت طَبطَبَة عَفارِم عَلَى كِتفِي [ħaṣṣalit ṭabṭubat ʕafaːrim ʕala čitfi]

to pat • **1.** طَبطَب [ṭabṭab] طَبطَبَة [ṭabṭaba] *vn:* تطَبطَب [tṭabṭab] *p:* He patted him encouragingly on the shoulder. طَبطَب عَلَى كِتفَه بِتَشجِيع [ṭabṭab ʕala čitfah btašjiːʕ] He patted the dog. طَبطَبلَه لِلكَلِب [ṭabṭablah liččalib]

patch • **1.** رُقعَة [rugʕa] رُقَع [rugaʕ] *pl:* I'll have to put a patch on it. لازِم أَحُطّ رُقعَة [laːzim ʔaħuṭṭ rugʕa] • **2.** قِطعَة [qiṭʕa] قِطَع [qiṭaʕ] *pl:* وُصلَة [wuṣla] وُصَل [wuṣal] *pl:* He raises alfalfa and rents out patches of it to people who have horses. يِزرَع جَتّ ويأَجِّر قُطَع مِنَّه لِلنّاس اللِّي عِدهُم خَيل [yizraʕ jatt wʔajjir quṭaʕ minnah linnaːs ʔilli ʕidhum xayl] • **3.** لَزقَة [lazga] لَزقات [lazgaːt] *pl:* He had a patch over his eye for days. حَطّ لَزقَة عَلَى عَينَه أَيّام [ħaṭṭ lazga ʕala ʕaynah ʔayyaːm]

to patch • **1.** رَقَّع [raggaʕ] تَرقِيع [targiːʕ] *vn:* *sv* i. Mother had to patch my trousers. أُمِّي اِضطَرَّت تَرَقِّع بَنطَرُونِي [ʔummi ʔiḍṭarrat traggiʕ panṭaruːni]

to patch up • **1.** فَضّ [faḍḍ] فَضّ [faḍḍ] *vn:* اِنفَضّ [ʔinfaḍḍ] *p:* Have they patched up their quarrel yet? فَضَّوا الخِلاف بَيناتهُم لَو بَعَد؟ [faḍḍaw ʔilxilaːf baynaːthum law baʕad?]

patchwork • **1.** تَلزِيق [talziːg] تَلطِيش [talṭiːš]

patent • **1.** بَراءَة [baraːʔa] I have applied for a patent to protect my rights on my new invention. قَدَّمِت طَلَب عَلَى بَراءَة لِلمُحافُظَة عَلَى حُقُوقِي بِالإِختِراع مالِي [qaddamit ṭalab ʕala baraːʔa lilmuħaːfuḍa ʕala ħuquːqi bilʔixtiraːʕ maːli]

to patent • **1.** سَجَّل [sajjal] تَسجِيل [tasjiːl] *vn:* تسَجَّل [tsajjal] *p:* You ought to patent your process. لازِم تسَجِّل طَرِيقتَك [laːzim tsajjil ṭariːqtak]

path • **1.** دَرُب [darub] درُوب [druːb] *pl:* A narrow path leads to the river. فَدّ دَرُب ضَيِّق يأَدِّي إِلَى النَّهَر [fadd darub ḍayyiq yʔaddi ʔila ʔinnahar] • **2.** سَبِيل [sabiːl] سُبُل [subul] *pl:* He put many obstacles in my path. حَطّ هوايَة عَقَبات بِسَبِيلِي [ħaṭṭ hwaːya ʕaqabaːt bisabiːli]

patience • **1.** صَبُر [ṣabur] I lost my patience. نِفَذ صَبرِي [nifað ṣabri]

patient • **1.** مَرِيض [mariːḍ] مُرضَة [murḍa] *pl:* وَجعان [wajʕaːn] وَجعانِين، وجاعَة [wajʕaːniːn, wjaːʕa] *pl:* How's the patient today? شلُون المَرِيض اليُوم؟ [šluːn ʔilmariːḍ ʔilyuːm?] • **2.** صَبُور [ṣabuːr] طَوِيل [ṭuwiːl] He is a very patient man. هُوَّ كُلِّش صَبُور [huwwa kulliš ṣabuːr] This is a very patient man. هَذا كُلِّش صَبُور [haːða kulliš ṣabuːr]

patriarch • **1.** بَطرِيق [baṭriːq] بَطارِقَة [baṭaːriqa] *pl:*

P

patriot • **1.** وَطَنِي [waṭani] وَطَنِيِّين [waṭaniyyi:n] *pl:*

patriotism • **1.** وَطَنِيَّة [waṭaniyya]

patrol • **1.** دَورِيَّة [dawriyya] دَورِيّات [dawriyya:t] *pl:* We sent a patrol out to reconnoiter. دَزَّينا دَورِيَّة لِلإِستِطلاع [dazzi:na dawriyya lilʔistiṭla:ʕ] Ali went out on patrol. عَلِي طِلَع دَورِيَّة [ʕali ṭilaʕ dawriyya]

to patrol • **1.** طاف [ṭa:f] طَوَفان [ṭawafa:n] *vn: sv* u. An armored police car patrols the streets all night. سَيّارَة شُرطَة مُسَلَّحَة تطُوف الشَّوارِع طُول اللَّيل [sayya:rat šurṭa musallaħa ṭṭu:f ʔiššawa:riʕ ṭu:l ʔillayl]

pattern • **1.** نَقِش [naqiš] نُقُوش [nuqu:š] *pl:* This rug has a nice pattern. هَالزُّولِيَّة نَقِشها لَطِيف [hazzu:liyya naqišha laṭi:f] • **2.** فَصال [faṣa:l] فَصالات [faṣa:la:t] *pl:* Where did you get the pattern for your new dress? وِين لِقَيتِي الفَصال لِبَدلتِك الجِّدِيدَة؟ [wi:n ligi:ti ʔilfaṣa:l libadaltič ʔijjidi:da?] • **3.** شاكِلَة [ša:kila] شاكِلات [ša:kila:t] *pl:* طِراز [ṭira:z] طِرازات [ṭira:za:t] *pl:* All his thefts are on this pattern. كُلّ سَرِقاتَه عَلَى هَالطِّراز [kull sariqa:tah ʕala haṭṭira:z]

pause • **1.** وَقفَة [wagfa, waqfa] وَقفات [wagfa:t, waqfa:t] *pl:* سَكتَة [sakta] تَوَقُّف [tawaqquf] تَوَقُّفات [tawaqqufa:t] *pl:* After a short pause the speaker continued. الخَطِيب اِستِمَرّ بَعَد وَقفَة قَصِيرَة [ʔalxaṭi:b ʔistimarr baʕad waqfa qaṣi:ra]

to pause • **1.** توَقَّف [twaqqaf] توُقُّف [twugguf] *vn: sv* a. He paused in his work to greet us as we entered. توَقَّف عَن شُغلَه حَتَّى يسَلِّم عَلينا مِن دِخَلنا [twaqqaf ʕan šuɣlah ħatta ysallim ʕali:na min dixalna]

P

to pave • **1.** بَلَّط [ballaṭ] تَبلِيط [tabli:ṭ] *vn: sv* i. They are paving this street. دَيبَلِّطُون هَالشّارِع [dayballiṭu:n haššа:riʕ] • **2.** مَهَّد [mahhad] تَمهِيد [tamhi:d] *vn:* تمَهَّد [tmahhad] *p:* Their efforts paved the way for independence. مَجهُودهُم مَهَّد الطَّرِيق لِلإِستِقلال [majhu:dhum mahhad ʔiṭṭari:q lilʔistiqla:l]

pavement • **1.** تَبلِيط [tabli:ṭ] تَمهِيد [tamhi:d] تَمهِيدات [tamhi:da:t] *pl:* أَرضِيَّة [ʔarđiyya] أَرضِيّات [ʔarđiyya:t] *pl:* The pavement is very narrow here. التَّبلِيط هنا كُلَّش ضَيِّق [ʔattabli:ṭ hna kulliš đayyig]

paw • **1.** إيد [ʔi:d] إيدَين، إيدِينات [ʔi:dayn, ʔi:dayna:t] *pl:* رِجِل [rijil] رِجلَين، رِجلِينات [rijlayn, rijli:na:t] *pl:* The dog has hurt his paw. الكَلِب عَوَّر إيدَه [ʔiččalib ʕawwar ʔi:dah]

pawn • **1.** لِعبَة [liʕba] لِعبات، أَلعاب، مَلاعِيب [liʕba:t, ʔalʕa:b, mala:ʕi:b] *pl:* لِعَب [liʕab] لِعبات [liʕba:t] *pl:* We are tired of being nothing but a pawn in their political schemes. عِجَزنا إحنا بَسّ لِعبَة بِخُطَطهُم السِّياسِيَّة [ʕijazna ʔiħna bass liʕba bxuṭaṭhum ʔissiya:siyya] • **2.** جُندِي [jundi] جُنُود [jinu:d] *pl:* You have lost another pawn. خسَرت جُندِي لاخ [xsarit jundi la:x]

to pawn • **1.** رِهَن [rihan] رَهَن [rahan] *vn:* اِنرِهَن [ʔinrihan] *p:* I had to pawn my watch. اِضطَرَّيت أَرهَن ساعتِي [ʔiđṭarrayt ʔarhan sa:ʕti]

pawnshop • **1.** مَحَل رُهُونات [maħall ruhu:na:t] مَحَلّات رُهُونات [maħalla:t ruhu:na:t] *pl:*

pawn ticket • **1.** وَصِل رَهَن [waṣil rahan] وُصُولات رَهَن [wuṣu:la:t rahan] *pl:*

pay • **1.** راتِب [ra:tib] رَواتِب [rawa:tib] *pl:* مَعاش [maʕa:š] How is the pay on your new job? شلُون الرّاتِب بِشُغلَك الجِّدِيد؟ [šlu:n ʔirra:tib bišuɣlak ʔijjidi:d?]

to pay • **1.** دِفَع [difaʕ] دَفِع [dafiʕ] *vn:* اِندِفَع [ʔindifaʕ] *p:* How much did you pay for your car? شقَدّ دِفَعت بِسَيّارتَك؟ [šgadd difaʕit bsayya:rtak?] I would like to pay my bill. أَرِيد أَدفَع قائمتِي [ʔari:d ʔadfaʕ qa:ʔimti] • **2.** قام ب [ga:m b-] قِيام [qiya:m] *vn: sv* u. He paid all the expenses. قام بِكُلّ المَصارِيف [ga:m bkull ʔalmaṣa:ri:f]

*** That doesn't pay.** • **1.** ما مِن وَراهَا فايدَة [ma: min wara:ha fa:yda] / الشَّغلَة ما تِسوَى [ʔiššaɣla ma: tiswa:] / هاي ما تطَعُّم خُبُز [ha:y ma: ṭṭaʕʕum xubuz]

*** You couldn't pay me to do that.** • **1.** لَو تِنطِينِي فلُوس الدنيا ما سَوِّيها [law tinṭi:ni flu:s ʔiddinya: ma: sawwi:ha]

to pay attention • **1.** دار بَل، اِنتِبَه [da:r ba:l] [ʔintibah] اِنتِباه [ʔintiba:h] The pupils didn't pay attention today at all. التَّلامِيذ ما دارَوا بالهُم اليُوم أَبَد [ʔittala:mi:ð ma: da:raw ba:lhum ʔilyu:m ʔabad] Pay no attention to him. لا تدِيرلَه بال [la: ddi:rlah ba:l] Pay no attention to him. ما عَلَيك مِنَّه [ma: ʕli:k minnah]

to pay a visit • **1.** زار [za:r] زِيارَة [zya:ra] زِيارات [zya:ra:t] *pl:* راح خُطّار عَلَى [ra:ħ xuṭṭa:r ʕala] رَوح [rawħ] *vn: sv* u. I must pay him a visit. لازِم أَزُورَه [la:zim ʔazu:rah] Let's pay our new neighbors a visit. خَلِّي نرُوح خُطّار عَلَى جِيرانّا الجِّدَد [xalli nru:ħ xuṭṭa:r ʕala ji:ra:nna ʔajjidad]

to pay back • **1.** وَفَّى [waffa:, wuffa:] تَوفِيَة [tawfiya] *vn: sv* i. I'll pay you back the dinar on Monday. أَوَفِّيلَك الدِّينار يوم الإِثنَين [ʔawaffi:lak ʔaddina:r yu:m ʔilʔiθnayn] • **2.** رَجَّع [rajjaʕ] تَرجِيع [tarji:ʕ] *vn:* ترَجَّع [trajjaʕ] *p:* When are you going to pay me back what you owe me? شوَقِت راح ترَجِّعلي دَينِي؟ [šwakit ra:ħ trajjiʕli dayni?]

to pay down • **1.** دِفَع عَرَبُون [difaʕ ʕarabu:n] دَفع عَرَبُون [dafiʕ ʕarabu:n] *vn: sv* a. They require you to pay one-third down and the rest in monthly installments. يرِيدُوك تِدفَع ثُلث المَبلَغ عَربُون والباقِي بِأَقساط شَهرِيَّة

[yriːduːk tidfaʕ θulθ ʔilmablaɣ ʕarabuːn wilbaːqi biʔaqsaːṭ šahriyya]
to pay for • **1.** دِفَع ب [difaʕ b-] دَفِع [dafiʕ] *vn:* اِندِفَع [ʔindifaʕ] *p:* دِفَع عَلَى [difaʕ ʕala] How much did you pay for the car? شقَدّ دِفَعِت بَالسَّيّارَة؟ [šgadd difaʕit bissayyaːra?] He said he would pay for the rest of us. قال راح يِدفَع عَلينا كُلّنا [qaːl raːħ yidfaʕ ʕaliːna kullna]
*** I paid dearly for my mistake** • **1.** غَلِطتِي كَلَّفَتني غالِي [ɣaliṭṭi kallfatni ɣaːli]
to pay for itself • **1.** طَلَّع فلُوس [ṭallaʕfluːs] تَطلِيع [taṭliːʕ] *vn:* This machine will pay for itself in five months. هَالمَكِينَة راح تطَلِّع فلُوسها بخَمِسَة أَشهُر [halmakiːna raːħ ʔiṭṭalliʕ fluːsha bxamisat ʔašhur]
to pay off • **1.** وَفَّى [waffaː, wuffaː] تَوفِيَة [tawfiya] *vn: sv* i. سَدَّد حساب [saddad ħsaːb] تَسدِيد حساب [tasdiːd ħsaːb] *vn: sv* i. He paid off his debts. وَفَّى كُلّ ديُونَه [waffaː kull dyuːnah] • **2.** سَدّ [sadd] سَدّ [sadd] *vn:* اِنسَدّ [ʔinsadd] *p:* He sold the farm and paid off the help. باع المَزرَعَة وسَدّ حِساب العُمّال [baːʕ ʔalmazraʕa wsadd ħisaːb ʔilʕummaːl]
to pay out • **1.** صِرَف [ṣiraf] صَرُف [ṣaruf] *vn:* اِنصِرَف [ʔinṣiraf] *p:* We paid out more than we took in today. اليُوم صِرَفنا أَكثَر مِن دِخَلنا [ʔilyuːm ṣirafna ʔakθar min dixalna] • **2.** رَخَّى [raxxaː] تَرخِيَة [tarxiya] *vn:* تَرَخَّى [traxxaː] *p:* Pay out the rope slowly. رَخِّي الحَبِل عَلَى كَيفَك [raxxi ʔilħabil ʕala kayfak]
to pay up • **1.** وَفَّى [waffaː, wuffaː] تَوفِيَة [tawfiya] *vn:* توَفَّى [twaffaː] *p:* سَدَّد [saddad] تَسدِيد [tasdiːd] *vn:* تسَدَّد [tsaddad] *p:* In a month I'll have it all paid up. بخِلال شَهَر راح أَوَفِّيها كُلّها [bxilaːl šahar raːħ ʔawaffiːha kullha] • **2.** أَدَّى [ʔaddaː] تَأدِيَة [taʔdiya] *vn:* تأَدَّى [tʔaddaː] *p:* I paid up all my debts on payday. أَدَّيت كُلّ ديُونِي يوم المَعاش [ʔaddiːt kull dyuːni yuːm ʔilmaʕaːš]

payment • **1.** دَفِع [dafiʕ] Prompt payment is requested. الرَّجاء الدَّفِع بِسُرعَة [ʔarrajaːʔ ʔiddafiʕ bsurʕa] • **2.** قُسُط [qusuṭ, qisiṭ] أَقساط [ʔaqsaːṭ] *pl:* دَفعَة [dafʕa] دَفعات [dafʕaːt] *pl:* I have two more payments on my car. بُقالِي قِسطَين عَلَى سَيّارتِي [buqaːli qisṭayn ʕala sayyaːrti] I paid up the debt in three payments. سَوِّيت الدَّين ثلَث دُفعات [sawwiːt ʔiddayn tlaθ dufʕaːt]

pea • **1.** بَزالِيايَة [bazaːlyaːya] بَزالِيايات [bazaːlyaːyaːt] *pl:* بَزاليا [bazaːlya] *Collective*

peace • **1.** سَلام [salaːm] سِلِم [silim] The whole world wants peace. كُلّ الدِّنيا ترِيد السَّلام [kull ʔiddinya triːd ʔissalaːm] • **2.** أَمِن [ʔamin] The police are doing all they can to maintain peace. الشُّرطَة دَيسَوّوُن كُلّما يِقدَرُون لِلمُحافَظَة عَلَى الأَمِن [ʔiššurṭa daysawwuːn kullma yigdaruːn lilmuħaːfaða ʕala ʔalʔamin] • **3.** هُدُوء [huduːʔ, hiduːʔ] If only I could work in peace! لَو بَسّ أَقدَر أَشتِغُل بهُدُوء [law bass ʔagdar ʔaštiɣul bhiduːʔ]
*** He doesn't give me any peace.** • **1.** ما يخَلِّي بالِي يِرتاح [maː yxalli baːli yirtaːħ]
*** I'm doing it just to keep the peace.** • **1.** آنِي داسَوِّيها كِفيان شَرّ [ʔaːni daʔasawwiːha čifyaːn šarr]
*** Leave me in peace!** • **1.** فُكّ ياخَة مِنِّي [fukk yaːxa minni] / جُوز عَنِّي [ǰuːz ʕanni] / عُوفنِي [ʕuːfni]
to make peace • **1.** صالَح [ṣaːlaħ] مُصالَحَة [muṣaːlaħa] *vn:* تصالَح [tṣaːlaħ] *p:* He tried to make peace between them. حاوَل يصالِح بينهُم [ħaːwal yṣaːliħ baynhum]

peaceful • **1.** هادِئ [haːdiʔ] Everything is so peaceful around here. كُلّشِي شقَدّ هادِئ هنا [kullši šgadd haːdiʔ hna] • **2.** مُسالِم [musaːlim] He is very peaceful. هَذا كُلّش مُسالِم [haːða kulliš musaːlim] • **3.** سِلمِي [silmi] There is no peaceful solution to this problem. ماكُو حَلّ سِلمِي لِهَالمُشكِلَة [maːku ħall silmi lihalmuškila]

peach • **1.** خُوخَة [xawxa] خَوخات [xawxaːt] *pl:* خوخ [xawx] *Collective:* These peaches are very juicy. هَالخَوخ كُلّش رَيّان [halxawx kulliš rayyaːn]

peacock • **1.** طاوُوس [ṭaːwus] طواوِيس [ṭwaːwiːs] *pl:*

peak • **1.** قِمَّة [qimma, qumma] قِمَم [qimam, qumam] *pl:* We climbed to the peak of the mountains. تسَلَّقنا لقِمَّة الجِّبَل [tsallaqna lqimmat ʔiǰǰibal] • **2.** أَوج [ʔawǰ] ذَروَة [ðarwa] He was then at the peak of his power. كان بأَوج قُوَّتَه بذاك الوَقِت [kaːn ʔibʔawǰ quwwtah bðaːk ʔilwakit]

peanut • **1.** فِستِقَة عَبِيد [fistiqat ʕabiːd] فِستِقات عَبِيد [fistiqaːt ʕabiːd] *pl:* فِستِق [fistiq] *Collective*

pear • **1.** عَرمُوطَة [ʕarmuːṭa] عَرمُوطات [ʕarmuːṭaːt] *pl:* عَرمُوط [ʕarmuːṭ] *Collective:* How much is a kilo of pears? بيش كِيلُو العَرمُوط؟ [biyš kiːlu ʔilʕarmuːṭ?]

pearl • **1.** لِيلُوَّة [liːluwwa] لِيلُوّات [liːluwwaːt] *pl:* لِيلُو [liːlu] *Collective*

peasant • **1.** فَلّاح [fallaːħ] فَلّاحِين، فلالِيح [fallaːħiːn, flaːliːħ] *pl:* The peasant took some tomatoes to market. الفَلّاح نَزَّل طَماطَة لِلسُّوق [ʔilfallaːħ nazzal ṭamaːṭa lissuːq] • **2.** معِيدِي [mʕiːdi] مِعدان [miʕdaːn] *pl:* You peasant, why don't you learn some manners? إِي معَيدِي، لِيش ما تِتعَلَّم شوَيَّة أُصُول؟ [ʔayy mʕiːdi, liːš maː titʕallam šwayya ʔuṣuːl?]

pebble • **1.** حَصوَة [ħaṣwa] حَصوات [ħaṣwaːt] *pl:* حَصُو [ħaṣw] *Collective:* The path is covered with pebbles. المَمَرّ مغَطَّى بِالحَصو [lmamarr mɣaṭṭaː bilħaṣw]

peck • **1.** نَقرَة [nagra] نَقرات [nagraːt] *pl:* Give me another peach, some bird took a peck out of this one. إنطِينِي غير خَوخَة، هاي فَدّ طَير ماخِذلَه نَقرَة مِنها [ʔinṭiːni ɣayr xawxa, haːy fadd ṭiːr maːxiðlah nagra minha]

to peck • **1.** نِقَر [nigar] نَقِر [nagir] *vn:* اِنْقَر [ʔinnigar] *p:* نَقَّر [naggar] تَنقِير [tangi:r] *vn:* تنَقَّر [tnaggar] *p:* The birds are pecking at the fruit again; chase them away. الطَّيُور هَمّ دَينَقّرُون بِالفاكِهَة؛ رُوح كِشّهُم [ʔiṭṭyu:r hamm daynaggiru:n bilfa:kiha; ru:ħ kiššhum]

peculiar • **1.** غَرِيب [ɣari:b] غُرَباء، غُربَة [ɣuraba:ʔ, ɣurba.] *pl:* شاذّ [ša:ðð] شَواذ [šawa:ðð] *pl:* He's a peculiar fellow. هُوَّ فَدّ واحِد غَرِيب [huwwa fadd wa:ħid ɣari:b] The incident was hushed up under peculiar circumstances. الحادِثَة تلَغمُطَت بظُرُوف شاذَّة [ʔilħa:diθa tlaɣmuṭat bðuru:f ša:ðða] • **2.** خاصّ [xa:ṣṣ] This style turban is peculiar to the people in the north. هَالشِّكِل لَفَّة خاصَّة بِأَهل الشِّمال [haššikil laffa xa:ṣṣa biʔahl ʔiššima:l]

peculiarity • **1.** خاصِّيَّة [xa:ṣṣiyya] خاصِّيّات، خَواصّ [xa:ṣṣiyya:t, xawa:ṣṣ] *pl:* خاصِّيَة [xa:ṣṣiyya] خَصائِص [xaṣa:ʔiṣ] *pl:* They are easy to identify from certain peculiarities in their speech. مِن السِّهُولَة تُعرُفهُم مِن خَواصّ مُعَيَّنَة بِحَكِيهُم [min ʔassihu:la tuʕrufhum min xawa:ṣṣ muʕayyana bħačyhum]

pedal • **1.** بايدار [pa:yda:r] بايدارات [pa:yda:ra:t] *pl:* One of the pedals on this bicycle is longer than the other. واحِد مِن البايدَرات بِهَالبايسِكِل أَطوَل مِن اللّاخ [wa:ħid min ʔalpa:ydara:t ʔibhalpa:ysikil ʔaṭwal min ʔilla:x] • **2.** رِجِل [rijil] رِجلَين، رِجلِينات [rijlayn, rijli:na:t] *pl:* Does your sewing machine have a pedal or do you operate by hand? مَكِينَة الخِياطَة مالتِك مال رِجِل لَو مال إيد؟ [maki:nat ʔilxiya:ṭa ma:ltič ma:l rijil law ma:l ʔi:d?] • **3.** دَوسَة [dawsa] دَوسات [dawsa:t] *pl:* My foot slipped off the pedal. رِجلِي زِلقَت مِن الدُّوسَة [rijli zilgat min ʔaddawsa]

to pedal • **1.** ضِرَب بَايدَار [ðirab pa:yda:r] ضَرُب بَايدَار [ðarub pa:yda:r] *vn: sv* u. His legs are still too short to pedal a bicycle. رِجلَيه بَعَدها كُلِّش قصَيِّرَة لِضَرب البايدَر [rijlayh baʕadha kulliš gṣayyra liðarb ʔalpa:ydar]

to peddle • **1.** دَوَّر ب [dawwar b-] تدُوُّر [tduwwur] *vn: sv* u. The farmer sent his son to peddle tomatoes in this neighborhood. الفَلّاح دَزّ إبنَه يدَوُّر بِالطَّماطَة بِهالمَحَلَّة [ʔilfalla:ħ dazz ʔibnah ydawwur biṭṭama:ṭa bhalmaħalla]

peddler • **1.** دَوّار [dawwa:r] دَوّارِين، دَوّارَة [dawwa:ri:n, dawwa:ra] *pl:*

pedestrian • **1.** مارّ [ma:rr] مارَّة [ma:rra] *pl:* ماشِي [ma:ši] مُشَات [muša:t] *pl:* Drivers must watch out for pedestrians crossing the street. السُّوّاق لازِم ينتِبهُون عالمارِّين اللِّي دَيعبرُون الشّارِع [ʔissuwwa:q la:zim yintibhu:n ʕalma:rri:n ʔilli dayiʕburu:n ʔišša:riʕ]

pediatrician • **1.** طَبِيب أَطفال [ṭabi:b ʔaṭfa:l] أَطِبّاء أَطفال [ʔaṭibba:ʔ ʔaṭfa:l] *pl:*

pedigree • **1.** أَصِل [ʔaṣil] أُصُول [ʔuṣu:l] *pl:* نَسَب [nasab] أنساب [ʔansa:b] *pl:* This horse's pedigree goes back for fifty years. هَالحِصان أَصلَه يِرجَع الخَمسِين سَنَة [halħiṣa:n ʔaṣlah yirjaʕ lxamsi:n sana]

pedigreed • **1.** أَصِيل [ʔaṣi:l]

peel • **1.** قِشِر [gišir] قشُور [gšu:r] *pl:* These oranges have a thick peel. هَالبُرتقال بِيه قِشِر ثِخِين [halpurtaqa:l bi:h gišir θixi:n]

to peel • **1.** قَشَّر [gaššar] تقِشِّر [tgiššir] *vn:* تقَشَّر [tgaššar] *p:* I have to peel the potatoes. لازِم أَقَشِّر البُتيتَة [la:zim ʔagaššir ʔilputayta] My skin is peeling. جِلدِي دَيقَشِّر [jildi daygaššir]

to peel off • **1.** تقَشَّط [tgaššaṭ] *sv* a. The whitewash is peeling off the ceiling. البَياض دَيتقَشَّط مِن السَّقُف [ʔilbaya:ð dayitgaššaṭ min ʔissaguf]

peep • **1.** وَصوَصَة [waṣwaṣa] وَصوَصات [waṣwaṣa:t] *pl:* The peeps of the baby chicks made their mother run over to them. وَصوَصات فرُوخ الدِّجاج خَلَّت أمَّهُم تُركُض عَلَيهُم [waṣwaṣa:t fru:x ʔiddija:j xallat ʔummhum turkuð ʕali:hum] • **2.** طَقَّة [ṭagga] طَقّات [ṭagga:t] *pl:* I don't want to hear another peep out of you. ما أَرِيد أَسمَع وَلا طَقَّة بَعَد [ma: ʔari:d ʔasmaʕ wala ṭagga baʕad] • **3.** نَظرَة [naðra] نَظرات [naðra:t] *pl:* Take a peep into the room. إلقِي نَظرَة بالغُرفَة [ʔilqi naðra bilɣurfa]

to peep • **1.** وَصوَص [waṣwaṣ] وَصوَصَة [waṣwaṣa] *vn: sv* u. The baby chicks are peeping because their mother left them. فرُوخ الدِّجاج دَيوَصوُصُون لِأَنّ أَمَّهُم قامَت مِن عَلَيهُم [fru:x ʔiddija:j daywaṣwuṣu:n liʔann ʔummhum ga:mat min ʕali:hum] • **2.** باوَع [ba:waʕ] مباوَعَة [mba:waʕa] *vn: sv* u. دَحَّق [daħħag] تَدحِيق [tadħi:g] *vn: sv* i. He peeped through the hole in the fence. باوَع مِن زُرف السِّياج [ba:waʕ min zurf ʔissiya:j]

peeved • **1.** زَعلان [zaʕla:n] She was peeved about the remark you made. كانَت زَعلانَة عالحكايَة اللِّي حِكَيتها [ča:nat zaʕla:na ʕalħča:ya ʔilli ħiči:tha]

peg • **1.** وَتَد [watad] أَوتاد [ʔawta:d] *pl:* He tripped over a tent peg and fell. عِثَر بوَتَد شادِر وَوُقَع [ʕiθar ʔibwatad ča:dir wawugaʕ] • **2.** عُودَة [ʕu:da] عُودات، عُوَد [ʕu:da:t, ʕuwad] *pl:* خِشبَة [xišba] خِشبات، خِشَب [xišba:t, xišab] *pl:* There are some pegs on the wall to hang your clothes on. أَكُو عُوَد بِالحايِط خاطِر تعَلِّق هدُومَك بِيها [ʔaku ʕuwad bilħa:yiṭ xa:ṭir tʕallig hdu:mak bi:ha]

pelican • **1.** أَبُو جراب، بَجعَة [ʔabu jra:b, bajʕa] طيُور أَبُو جراب، بَجعَات [ṭyu:r ʔabu jra:b, bajʕa:t] *pl:* بَجَع [bajaʕ] *Collective*

pelvis • **1.** حَوض [ħu:ð] أَحواض [ʔaħwa:ð] *pl:*

P

i, interjection; p, passive; pl, plural; sv, stem vowel; vn, verbal noun

pen • **1.** سِلّايَة [silla:ya] سِلّايات [silla:ya:t] *pl:* This pen scratches. هَالسِّلّايَة دَتشَخِّط [hassilla:ya datšaxxiṭ] • **2.** باندان [pa:nda:n] باندانات [pa:nda:na:t] *pl:* قَلَم حِبِر [qalam ħibir] أقلام حِبِر [ʔaqla:m ħibir] *pl:* This is an expensive fountain pen. هَذا باندان غالِي [ha:ða pa:nda:n ɣa:li] • **3.** زَرِيبَة [zari:ba] زَرايِب [zara:yib] *pl:* We'll have to build a pen for the sheep. لازِم نِبنِي زَرِيبَة لِلغَنَم [la:zim nibni zari:ba lilɣanam]

penal code • **1.** قانُون العُقُوبات [qa:nu:n ʔilʕuqu:ba:t]

penalty • **1.** عُقُوبَة [ʕuqu:ba] عُقُوبات [ʕuqu:ba:t] *pl:* جَزاء [ǰaza:ʔ] جَزاءات [ǰaza:ʔa:t] *pl:* The penalty is ten years' imprisonment. العُقُوبَة عَشِر سنِين حَبِس [ʔilʕuqu:ba ʕašir sni:n ħabis]

pencil • **1.** قَلَم [qalam] أقلام [ʔaqla:m] *pl:* Give me that pencil, please. إنطِينِي ذاك القَلَم، مِن فَضلَك [ʔinṭi:ni ða:k ʔilqalam, min faðlak]

pending • **1.** رَهِن [rahin] They have cancelled all permits, pending further investigation. لِغَوا كُلّ الإجازات، رَهن التَّحقِيقات الإضافِيَّة [liɣaw kull ʔilʔiǰa:za:t, rahn ʔittaħqi:qa:t ʔilʔiḍa:fiyya] • **2.** مُعَلَّق [muʕallaq] The matter is still pending. هَالقَضِيَّة بَعَدها مُعَلَّقَة [halqaḍiyya baʕadha muʕallaqa] The matter is still pending. هَالقَضِيَّة بَعَد ما مَبتُوت بِيها [halqaḍiyya baʕad ma: mabtu:t bi:ha]

pendulum • **1.** رَقّاص [raggaṣ, raqqa:ṣ] رَقّاصَة [raqqa:ṣa, ragga:ṣa] *pl:*

to penetrate • **1.** اِختِرَق [ʔixtiraq] اِختِراق [ʔixtira:q] *vn: sv* i. The enemy tanks penetrated our lines. دَبّابات العَدُو اِختِرقَت خُطُوطنا [dabba:ba:t ʔilʕadu ʔixtirqat xuṭu:ṭna] • **2.** تغلغَل [tɣalɣal] تَغَلغُل [taɣalɣul] *vn: sv* a. The Locust Control Expedition penetrated deep into the desert. فِرقَة مُكافَحَة الجَّراد تغَلغِلَت بِالصَّحراء [firqat muka:faħat ʔaǰǰara:d tɣalɣilat biṣṣaħra:ʔ]

peninsula • **1.** شِبه جَزِيرَة [šibih ǰazi:ra] أشباه جُزُر [ʔašba:h ǰuzur] *pl:*

penitentiary • **1.** سِجِن [siǰin] سِجُون [siǰu:n] *pl:*

penknife • **1.** جاكُوج، سِكِّينَة، سِكِّينَة جِيب [ča:ku:č, sičči:na, sičči:nat ǰi:b] جَواكِيج، سِكِّينات، سَكاكِين جَيب [čawa:ki:č, sičči:na, sača:či:n ǰi:b] *pl:*

penname • **1.** إسِم مُستَعار [ʔisim mustaʕa:r] أسماء مُستَعارَة [ʔasma:ʔ mustaʕa:ra] *pl:* أسامِي مُستَعارَة [ʔasa:mi mustaʕa:ra] أسماء مُستَعارَة [ʔasma:ʔ mustaʕa:ra] *pl:*

penny • **1.** بَيزَة [bayza] فِلِس [filis] فلاس، فِلسان [fla:s, filsa:n] *pl:* I'm broke, I haven't got a penny. آنِي مِفلِس؛ ما عِندِي بَيزَة [ʔa:ni miflis; ma: ʕindi bayza]

pension • **1.** تَقاعُد [taqa:ʕud] He gets a pension from the government. ياخُذ تَقاعُد مِن الحُكُومَة [ya:xuð taqa:ʕud min ʔilħuku:ma]

to pension • **1.** حال [ħa:l] إحالَة [ʔiħa:la] *vn:* اِنحال [ʔinħa:l] *p:* He was pensioned last year. اِنحال عالتَّقاعُد السَّنَة اللِّي فاتَت [ʔinħa:l ʕattaqa:ʕud ʔissana ʔilli fa:tat]

people • **1.** ناس [na:s] What will people say? شراح يقُولُون النّاس؟ [šra:ħ ygu:lu:n ʔinna:s?] • **2.** شَعَب [šaʕab] شُعُوب [šuʕu:b] *pl:* The government always sounds out the opinion of the people in serious matters. الحُكُومَة دائِماً تِتحَسَّس رَأي الشَّعَب حَول الأمُور الخَطِيرَة [ʔilħuku:ma da:ʔiman titħassas raʔy ʔiššaʕab ħawl ʔilʔumu:r ʔilxaṭi:ra] • **3.** قَوم [gawm] The Babylonians were a people who built up a powerful kingdom in ancient times. البابلِيِّين قَوم بِنَوا مَملَكَة قَوِيَّة بِالعُصُور القَدِيمَة [ʔilba:biliyyi:n qawm binaw mamlaka qawwiyya bilʕuṣu:r ʔilqadi:ma] • **4.** عالَم [ʕa:lam] Were there many people at the meeting? كان أكُو عالَم هوايَة بالاِجتِماع؟ [ča:n ʔaku ʕa:lam hwa:ya bilʔiǰtima:ʕ?] • **5.** أهَل [ʔahal] أهالِي [ʔaha:li] *pl:* I want you to meet my people. أرِيدَك تِتعَرَّف عَلَى أهلِي [ʔari:dak titʕarraf ʕala ʔahli] • **6.** شَخِص [šaxiṣ] أشخاص [ʔašxa:ṣ] *pl:* I only knew a few people at the party. عِرَفِت كَم شَخِص بَسّ بِالحَفلَة [ʕirafit čam šaxiṣ bass bilħafla]

pep • **1.** حَيَوِيَّة [ħayawiyya] نَشاط [naša:ṭ] Where do you get your pep? مِنَين جَتَّك هَالحَيَوِيَّة؟ [minni:n ǰattak halħayawiyya?] He's full of pep today. هُوَّ اليُوم مَترُوس نَشاط [huwwa ʔilyu:m matru:s naša:ṭ]

to pep up • **1.** نَشَّط [naššaṭ] تَنشِيط [tanši:ṭ] *vn:* تنَشَّط [tnaššaṭ] *p:* I need something to pep me up. أحتاج فَدّ شِي ينَشِّطنِي [ʔaħta:ǰ fadd ši ynaššiṭni]

pepper • **1.** فِلفِل، فِلفِلَة [filfil, filfila] Pass me the pepper, please. ناوُشنِي الفِلفِل، مِن فَضلَك [na:wušni ʔalfilfil, min faðlak] • **2.** فِلفِل [filfil] *Collective:* See if you can find some nice peppers in the market. شُوف إذا تِقدَر تِلقِي كَم فِلفِل زين بالسُّوق [šu:f ʔiða tigdar tilgi čam filfil zi:n bissu:g]

peppermint • **1.** نِعناع [niʕna:ʕ]

per • **1.** ب [b] How much do you sell the oranges for per dozen? شلُون تبِيع البُرتِقال بِالدَّرزَن؟ [šlu:n tbi:ʕ ʔalpurtiqa:l biddarzan?] He makes sixty dinars per month. يطَلِّع سِتِّين دِينار بِالشَّهَر [yṭalliʕ sitti:n dina:r biššahar] • **2.** عَلَى [ʕala] عَن [ʕan] They charge two dinars per person. ياخذُون دِينارَين عَلَى كُلّ نفَر [ya:xðu:n dina:rayn ʕala kull nafar]

*** We paid fifty cents per person.**
• **1.** دفَعنا خَمسِين فِلِس كُلّ واحِد [dfaʕna xamsiːn filis kull waːħid]

per cent • **1.** بِالمِيَّة [bilmiyya] The cost of living has risen ten per cent. كُلفَة المَعِيشَة اِرتِفعَت عَشرَة بِالمِيَّة [kulfat ʔilmaʕiːša ʔirtifʕat ʕašra bilmiyya] Our bank pays two percent interest. البَنك مالنَا يِدفَع فائِدَة ثنَين بِالمِيَّة [ʔilbank maːlna yidfaʕ faːʔida θnayn bilmiyya] We'll each share fifty percent of the profits. راح نِتقاسَم الأرباح كُلّ مَن بِالمِيَّة خَمسِين [raːħ nitqaːsam ʔilʔarbaːħ kull man bilmiyya xamsiːn]

percentage • **1.** نِسبَة مِئَوِيَّة [nisba miʔawiyya] نِسَب مِئَوِيَّة [nisab miʔawiyya] *pl:*

perennial • **1.** حايِل [ħaːyil] These plants are perennial. هَالنَّباتات حايلَة [hannabaːtaːt ħaːyla] These plants are perennial. هَالنَّباتات تِحِيل [hannabaːtaːt tħiːl] • **2.** مُزمِن [muzmin] He is a perennial candidate for the House of Representatives. هَذا فَدّ مُرَشَّح مُزمِن لِلنِّيابَة [haːða fadd muraššaħ muzmin linniyaːba]

perfect • **1.** كامِل [kaːmil] Nothing is perfect. ماكُو شِي كامِل [maːku ši kaːmil] • **2.** تَمام [tamaːm] This is perfect nonsense. هاي لَغوَة تَمام [haːy laɣwa tamaːm] • **3.** مَضبُوط [maðbuːṭ] تَمام [tamaːm] He speaks perfect French. يِحكِي فرَنسِي مَضبُوط [yiħči fransi maðbuːṭ] • **4.** مُحكَم [muħkam] مَضبُوط [maðbuːṭ] مُتقَن [mutqan] Their plan was perfect. خِطِّتهُم كانَت مُحكَمَة [xiṭṭathum čaːnat muħkama] This process is not perfect yet. هَالطَّرِيقَة بَعَدها مُو مُتقَنَة [haṭṭariːqa baʕadha muː mutqana]
to perfect • **1.** * The method hasn't been perfected yet. الطَّرِيقَة بَعَد لهَسَّة ما وُصلَت دَرَجَة الكَمال [ʔiṭṭariːqa baʕad lhassa maː wuṣlat darajat ʔalkamaːl]

perfection • **1.** كَمال [kamaːl]

perfectly • **1.** تَماماً [tamaːman] He was perfectly satisfied. كان راضِي تَماماً [čaːn raːði tamaːman] • **2.** بِالضَبُط [biððabuṭ] بإتقان [bʔitqaːn] عَالمَضبُوط [ʕalmaðbuːṭ] He did it perfectly the first time. أَوَّل مَرَّة سَوّاها بِالضَبُط [ʔawwal marra sawwaːha biððabuṭ] • **3.** كُلِّش [kulliš] I know him perfectly well. أعُرفَه كُلِّش زين [ʔaʕurfah kulliš ziːn]

to perform • **1.** سَوَّى [sawwaː] تَسوِيَة [taswiya] *vn:* تسَوَّى [tsawwaː] *p:* قام ب [qaːm b-] قِيام [qiyaːm] *vn:* *sv* u. Who performed the operation? مِنُو سَوَّى العَمَلِيَّة؟ [minu sawwaː ʔilʕamaliyya?] The acrobats performed the most difficult feats. البَهلَوانِيَّة قامَوا بِأخطَر الحَرَكات [ʔalpahlawaːniyya gaːmaw biʔaxṭar ʔalħarakaːt] • **2.** أَدَّى [ʔaddaː] تَأدِيَة [taʔdiya] *vn:* تأَدَّى [tʔaddaː] *p:* He performed his duty. أَدَّى واجبَه [ʔaddaː waːjbah] • **3.** مَثَّل [maθθal] تَمثِيل [tamθiːl] *vn: sv* i. This group of players has been performing this play for two years. هَالجَماعَة المُمَثِّلِين يمَثِّلُون هَالرُّوايَة مُدَّة سَنتَين [halǰamaːʕa ʔilmumaθθiliːn ymaθθiluːn harruwaːya muddat santayn]

performance • **1.** عَرِض [ʕariḍ] Did you like the performance of the dancing troupe? عِجَبَك عَرِض هالفِرقَة الرّاقِصَة؟ [ʕiǰabak ʕariḍ halfirqa ʔarraːqiṣa?] • **2.** تَمثِيلِيَّة [tamθiːliyya] تَمثِيلِيّات [tamθiːliyyaːt] *pl:* What time does the performance begin? شوَقِت تِبدِي التَّمثِيلِيَّة؟ [šwakit tibdi ʔittamθiːliyya?]

perfume • **1.** رِيحَة [riːħa] رَوائِح، رَوايِح، رِيَّح [rawaːʔiħ, rawaːyiħ, riyyaħ] *pl:*
to perfume • **1.** عَطَّر [ʕaṭṭar] تَعطِير [taʕṭiːr] *vn:* تعَطَّر [tʕaṭṭar] *p:* She perfumes her handkerchiefs. تعَطِّر كفافِيها [tʕaṭṭir čfaːfiːha]

perhaps • **1.** رُبَّما [rubbama] يِمكِن [yimkin] Perhaps I'll come to the meeting. رُبَّما أجِي لِلإجتِماع [rubbama ʔaǰi lilʔiǰtimaːʕ] • **2.** بَلكِي [balki] يِمكِن [yimkin] يجُوز [yǰuːz] Perhaps he is sick. بَلكِي مَرِيض [balki mariːḍ]

period • **1.** مُدَّة [mudda] مُدَد [mudad] *pl:* He worked here for a short period. اِشتِغَل هنا مُدَّة قَصِيرَة [ʔištiɣal hna mudda qaṣiːra] • **2.** فَترَة [fatra] فَترات [fatraːt] *pl:* This is an important period in our history. هاي فَترَة مُهِمَّة بتارِيخنا [haːy fatra muhimma btaːriːxna] • **3.** نُقطَة [nuqṭa] نُقَط [nuqaṭ] *pl:* You forgot to put a period here. نِسِيت تحُطّ نُقطَة هنا [nisiːt tħuṭṭ nuqṭa hna] • **4.** دَرِس [daris] درُوس [druːs] *pl:* I have the third period free. عِندِي فَراغ بِالدَّرِس الثّالِث [ʕindi faraːɣ biddars ʔiθθaːliθ] • **5.** عادَة [ʕaːda] Doctor, my period is late this month. دِكتُور، عادتِي تأَخرَت هَالشَّهَر [diktuːr, ʕaːdti tʔaxxrat haššahar]
period of grace • **1.** مُهلَة [muhla] مُهلات [muhlaːt] *pl:* The period of grace expires on the tenth. المُهلَة تِخلَص يوم عَشرَة بِالشَّهَر [ʔalmuhla tixlaṣ yuːm ʕašra biššahar]

periodical • **1.** دَورِي [dawri] He suffered periodical setbacks. عانَى نَكسات دَورِيَّة [ʕaːnaː naksaːt dawriyya] I subscribe to a number of periodical magazines. آنِي مِشتِرِك بعَدَد مِن المَجَلّات الدَّورِيَّة [ʔaːni mištirik bʕadad min ʔalmaǰallaːt ʔiddawriyya]

perjury • **1.** شَهادَة زُور [šahaːdat zuːr]

permanent • **1.** بَرمَنانت [parmanant] I need a permanent. شَعرِي يِرّادلَه بَرمَنَنت [šaʕri yirraːdlah parmanant] • **2.** دائِمِي [daːʔimi] ثابِت [θaːbit] I have no permanent address. ما عِندِي عِنوان ثابِت [maː ʕindi ʕinwaːn θaːbit] This is a permanent job. هَذا شُغُل دائِمِي [haːða šuɣul daːʔimi]

permission • **1.** رُخصَة [ruxṣa] إذِن [ʔiðin] Did you get his permission? أَخَذِت رُخصَة مِنَّه؟ [ʔaxaðit ruxṣa minnah?]

to ask permission • **1.** اِستَرخَص [ʔistarxaṣ] اِستِرخاص [ʔistirxa:ṣ] *vn: sv* i. He asked permission of his supervisor to leave an hour early. اِستَرخَص مِن المُلاحِظ مالَه يِطلَع ساعَة قَبِل الدَّوام [ʔistarxaṣ min ʔilmula:ħiḍ ma:lah yiṭlaʕ sa:ʕa gabil ʔiddawa:m]

permit • **1.** إجازَة [ʔiǰa:za] إجازات [ʔiǰa:za:t] *pl:* You need a permit before you can start building. تِحتاج إجازَة قَبُل ما تبَلِّش بالبِناء [tiħta:ǰ ʔiǰa:za gabul ma: tballiš bilbina:ʔ]

to permit • **1.** سِمَح ل [simaħ l-] سَماح [sama:ħ] *vn:* اِنسِمَح [ʔinsimaħ] *p:* نِطَى [niṭa:] *sv* i. I can't permit that. ما أسمَح لِهيكِي شِي [ma: ʔasmaħ lhiči ši] • **2.** رَخَّص [raxxaṣ] تَرخِيص [tarxi:ṣ] *vn:* ترَخَّص [traxxaṣ] *p:* My supervisor permitted me to leave early. المُلاحِظ مالِي رَخَّصنِي أطلَع عَلَى وَقِت [ʔilmula:ħiḍ ma:li raxxaṣni ʔaṭlaʕ ʕala wakit]

permitted • **1.** مَسمُوح ل [masmu:ħ l-] مُرَخَّص [muraxxaṣ] No one is permitted to enter this building. مَحَّد مَسمُوحلَه يِدخُل هالبِنايَة [maħħad masmu:ħlah yidxul halbina:ya] Is smoking permitted? مَسمُوح التَّدخِين؟ [masmu:ħ ʔittadxi:n?]

perpendicular • **1.** عَمُودِي [ʕamu:di]

to perpetuate • **1.** خَلَّد [xallad] تَخلِيد [taxli:d] *vn:* تخَلَّد [txallad] *p:* This deed will perpetuate his name in history. هَالعَمَل راح يخَلِّد إسمَه بالتّارِيخ [halʕamal ra:ħ yxallid ʔismah bitta:ri:x]

to perplex • **1.** حَيَّر [ħayyar] تَحيير [taħyi:r] *vn:* تحَيَّر [tħayyar] *p:* His lack of interest in his studies perplexes me. قِلَّة اِهتِمامَه بِدرُوسَه تحَيِّرنِي [qillat ʔihtima:mah bidru:sah tħayyirni]

perplexing • **1.** مَحَيِّر [mħayyar] This is a very perplexing problem. هاي فَدّ مُشكِلَة كُلِّش مَحَيِّرَة [ha:y fadd muškila kulliš mħayyira]

perplexity • **1.** حِيرَة [ħi:ra] I was in such a state of perplexity I didn't know what to do. كِنِت بِفَدّ شِكِل حِيرَة ما عرَفِت شأسَوِّي [činit bfadd šikil ħi:ra ma: ʕrafit šʔasawwi]

perse • **1.** بحَدّ ذات [bħadd ða:t] It's not worth much per se, but it has sentimental value. ما تِسوَى شِي بِحَد ذاتَه لَكِن الأسباب عاطِفِيَّة [ma: tiswa: ši biħadd ða:tah la:kin ʔilʔasba:b ʕa:ṭifiyya]

to persecute • **1.** اِضطِهَد [ʔiḍṭihad] اِضطِهاد [ʔiḍṭiha:d] *vn: sv* i. He imagines people are persecuting him. يِتصَوَّر النّاس دَيِضطَهدُوه [yitṣawwar ʔinna:s dayiḍṭahdu:h]

persecution • **1.** اِضطِهاد [ʔiḍṭiha:d] He suffers from a persecution complex. مِبتِلِي بعُقدَة اِضطِهاد [mibtili biʕuqdat ʔiḍṭiha:d]

to persevere • **1.** واظَب [wa:ḍab] مُواظَبَة [muwa:ḍaba] *vn: sv* i. داوَم [da:wam] تَدوِيم [tadwi:m] *vn: sv* i. If you persevere in your efforts, you might get the promotion. إذا تواظُب عَلَى جُهُودَك يمكِن تحَصِّل التَّرفِيع [ʔiða twa:ḍub ʕala ǰuhu:dak yimkin tħaṣṣil ʔitttarfi:ʕ]

Persia • **1.** إيران [ʔi:ra:n] بِلاد الفُرس [bila:d ʔilfurs]

Persian • **1.** فارسِي [fa:rsi] فُرس [furs] *pl:* عَجَمِي [ʕaǰami] عَجَمِيَّة [ʕaǰamiyya] *pl:* إيرانِي [ʔi:ra:ni] He's a Persian. هُوَّ فارسِي [huwwa fa:rsi] • **2.** فارسِي [fa:rsi] Translate that into Persian. تَرجَم هَذِي لِلفارسِي [tarǰam ha:ði lilfa:rsi]

to persist • **1.** لَحّ [laħħ] إلحاح، لَحّ [ʔilħa:ħ, laħħ] *vn:* اِنلَحّ [ʔinlaħħ] *p:* لَجّ [laǰǰ] لَجّ [laǰǰ] *vn:* اِنلَجّ [ʔinlaǰǰ] *p:* The boy persisted with his questions until the old man got angry. الوَلَد لَحّ بأسئِلتَه إلَى أن الرِّجّال الشّايِب غِضَب [ʔilwalad laħħ bʔasʔiltah ʔila ʔan ʔirriǰǰa:l ʔišša:yib ɣiḍab] • **2.** دام [da:m] دَوام [dawa:m] *vn: sv* u. طَوَّل [ṭawwal] تَطوِيل [taṭwi:l] *vn: sv* i. The effects of the disease persisted a long time. نَتائِج المَرَض دامَت مُدَّة طُويلَة [nata:ʔiǰ ʔilmaraḍ da:mat mudda ṭuwi:la] • **3.** تمادَى [tma:da:] تَمادِي [tama:di] *vn: sv* a. He persisted in lying. تمادَى بالكِذِب [tma:da: bilkiðib]

persistent • **1.** مُصِرّ [muṣirr] He is persistent in his efforts to obtain a highter education. مُصِرّ عَلَى جُهُودَه لِلحُصُول عَلَى ثَقافَة عالِيَة [muṣirr ʕala ǰuhu:dah lilħuṣu:l ʕala θaqa:fa ʕa:lya] • **2.** مُثابِر [muθa:bir] Your son doesn't learn quickly, but he is very persistent. إبنَك ما يِتعَلَّم بسُرعَة، لَكِن هُوَّ كُلِّش مُثابِر [ʔibnak ma: yitʕallam bsurʕa, la:kin huwwa kulliš muθa:bir]

person • **1.** شَخِص [šaxiṣ] أشخاص [ʔašxa:ṣ] *pl:* He is the same person. هُوَّ نَفس الشَّخِص [huwwa nafs ʔiššaxiṣ] • **2.** آدَمِي [ʔa:dami] أوادِم [ʔawa:dim] *pl:* إنسان [ʔinsa:n] He is a nice person. هَذا خُوش آدَمِي [ha:ða xu:š ʔa:dami] He is a nice person. هُوَّ إنسان طَيِّب [huwwa ʔinsa:n ṭayyib] • **3.** نَفَر [nafar] أنفار [ʔanfa:r] *pl:* We have place for two more persons. عِدنا مَكان لنَفَرَين بَعَد [ʕidna maka:n lnafarayn baʕad] • **4.** واحِد [wa:ħid] وِحدَة [wiħda] *Feminine:* She's a nice person. هِيَّ فَدّ وِحدَة لَطِيفَة [hiyya fadd wiħda laṭi:fa]

*** What sort of a person is he?** • **1.** هُوَّ شِنُو مِن شِي؟ [huwwa šinu min ši?]

in person • **1.** بالذّات [biðða:t] شَخصِيّاً [šaxṣiyyan] بنَفس [bnafs] Please deliver this to him in person. أرجُوك سَلِّملَه هاي بالذّات [ʔarǰu:k sallimlah ha:y biðða:t]

P

personal • 1. شَخصِي [šaxṣi] He asks too many personal questions. يِسأَل هوايَة أَسئِلَة شَخصِيَّة [yisʔal hwaːya ʔasʔila šaxṣiyya] He would like to discuss a personal matter with you. دَيرِيد يِحكِي وِيّاك عَلَى فَدّ مَوضُوع شَخصِي [dayriːd yiħči wiyyaːk ʕala fadd mawðuːʕ šaxṣi] **• 2.** خاصّ [xaːṣṣ] خُصُوصِي [xuṣuːṣi] These are my personal belongings. هاي غَراضِي الخاصَّة [haːy ɣaraːði ʔilxaːṣṣa]

personality • 1. شَخصِيَّة [šaxṣiyya] شَخصِيّات [šaxṣiyyaːt] *pl:* She has a loveable personality. عِدها شَخصِيَّة مَحبُوبَة [ʕidha šaxṣiyya maħbuːba]

personally • 1. شَخصِيّاً [šaxṣiyyan] I'd like to speak to him personally. أَرِيد أَحكِي وِيّاه شَخصِيّاً [ʔariːd ʔaħči wiyyaːh šaxṣiyyan] Personally I don't like him. شَخصِيّاً آنِي ما أَمِيل إِلَه [šaxṣiyyan ʔaːni maː ʔamiːl ʔilah]

personnel • 1. مُوَظَّف [muwaððaf] مُوَظَّفِين [muwaððafiːn] *pl:* مُستَخدَم [mustaxdam] We don't have enough personnel. ما عِدنا مُوَظَّفِين كافِين [maː ʕidna muwaððafiːn kaːfiːn] **• 2.** ذاتِيَّة [ðaːtiyya] He's the director of the personnel section. هَذا مُدِير قِسِم الذّاتِيَّة [haːða mudiːr qisim ʔiððaːtiyya]

perspiration • 1. عَرَق [ʕarag]

to perspire • 1. عِرَق [ʕirag] عَرَق [ʕarag] *vn: sv* a. I perspire a lot at night. أَعرَق هوايَة باللَّيل [ʔaʕrag hwaːya billayl]

to persuade • 1. قَنَّع [qannaʕ] تَقنِيع [taqniːʕ] *vn: sv* i. أَقنَع [ʔaqnaʕ] إِقناع [ʔiqnaːʕ] *vn: sv* i. He persuaded me to go. قَنَّعنِي أَرُوح [qannaʕni ʔaruːħ]

P

persuasion • 1. تَقنِيع [taqniːʕ] إِقناع [ʔiqnaːʕ] We had to use persuasion to get him to agree. اِستَعمَلنا الإِقناع حَتَّى نخَلِّيه يوافُق [ʔistaʕmalna ʔalʔiqnaːʕ ħatta nxalliːh ywaːfuq]

pertinent • 1. عائِد [ʕaːʔid] I don't think these facts are pertinent to the case. ما أَظُنّ هَالوَقائِع عائِدَة لِلقَضِيَّة [maː ʔaðunn halwaqaːʔiʕ ʕaːʔida lilqaðiyya]

perversion • 1. اِنحِراف [ʔinħiraːf] Sexual perversion can be treated. الانحِراف الجِّنسِي يِمكِن يِتعالَج [ʔalʔinħiraːf ʔaǰǰinsi yimkin yitʕaːlaǰ]

pervert • 1. مِنحِرِف [minħirif] مِنحَرِفِين [minħarifiːn] *pl:* A sexual pervert approached me on the street. اِندَقّ بِيّا فَدّ واحِد مِنحَرِف جِنسِيّاً بِالشّارِع [ʔindagg biyya fadd waːħid minħarif ǰinsiyyan biššaːriʕ]

to pervert • 1. أَفسَد [ʔafsad] إِفساد [ʔifsaːd] *vn: sv* i. He was accused of perverting the youth. اِنتِهَم بِإِفساد الشَّباب [ʔintiham biʔifsaːd ʔaššabaːb]

pessimism • 1. تَشاؤُم [tašaːʔum]

pessimist • 1. مِتشائِم [mitšaːʔim]

to be pessimistic • 1. تشائَم [tšaːʔam] تَشاؤُم [tašaːʔum] *vn: sv* a. Don't be pessimistic. لا تِتشائَم [laː titšaːʔam]

pest • 1. بَلاء [balaːʔ] The sparrows have become a pest in the orchard. العَصافِير صايرَة بَلاء بِالحَدِيقَة [ʔilʕaṣaːfiːr ṣaːyra balaːʔ bilħadiːqa] **• 2.** حَشَرَة [ħašara] حَشَرات [ħašaraːt] *pl:* The government has begun a campaign against insect pests. الحُكُومَة شانَّة حَملَة عالحَشَرات [ʔilħikuːma šaːnna ħamla ʕalħašaraːt]

to pester • 1. بَزَّع [bazzaʕ] تبزِّع [tbizziʕ] *vn:* تبَزَّع [tbazzaʕ] *p:* He pestered me to death with his questions. بَزَّعنِي بِأَسئِلتَه [bazzaʕni bʔasʔiltah]

pestle • 1. إِيد هاوَن [ʔiːd haːwan] إِيدَين هاوَن [ʔiːdiːn haːwan] *pl:*

pet • 1. حَيوان أَلِيف [ħaywaːn ʔaliːf] حَيوانات أَلِيفَة [ħaywaːnaːt ʔaliːfa] *pl:* We're not allowed to keep pets in our apartments. ما مَسمُوح نرَبِّي حَيوانات أَلِيفَة بِبِنايَتنا [maː masmuːħ nrabbi ħaywaːnaːt ʔaliːfa bibnaːyatna] **• 2.** وَلَد مدَلَّل [walad mdallal] وُلِد مدَلَّلِين [wulid mdallaliːn] *pl:* بِتّ، بنَيَّة مدَلَّلَة [bitt, bnayya mdallala] *Feminine:* بَنات مدَلَّلات [banaːt mdallalaːt] *Feminine pl:* She's her mother's pet. هِيَّ البنَيَّة المدَلَّلَة عِد أُمَّها [hiyya ʔilbnayya ʔilmdallila ʕid ʔummaha]

to pet • 1. مَسَّد ل [massad l-] تَمسِيد [tamsiːd] *vn:* تمَسَّد [tmassad] *p:* Don't pet the dog! لا تمَسِّدلَه لِلكَلِب [laː tmassidlah liččalib]

petition • 1. عَرِيضَة [ʕariːða] عَرايِض [ʕaraːyið] *pl:* عَرضَحال [ʕarðaħaːl] عَرضَحالات [ʕarðaħaːlaːt] *pl:* مَضبَطَة [maðbaṭa] مَضابُط [maðaːbuṭ] *pl:* Why don't you get up a petition? لِيش ما تقَدِّم عَرِيضَة؟ [liːš maː tqaddim ʕariːða?]

to petition • 1. قَدَّم عَرِيضَة [qaddam ʕariːða] تَقدِيم عَرِيضَة [taqdiːm ʕariːða] *vn: sv* i. The villagers petitioned the central government for a new school building. أَهل القُرَى قَدّمَوا عَرِيضَة لِلحُكُومَة المَركَزِيَّة لِأَجِل بِنايَة جَدِيدَة لِلمَدرَسَة [ʔahl ʔilquraː qaddimaw ʕariːða lilħukuːma ʔilmarkaziyya liʔaǰil binaːya ǰadiːda lilmadrasa]

petitioner • 1. مُستَدعِي [mustadʕi] مُستَدعِين [mustadʕiːn] *pl:*

petroleum • 1. نَفُط [nafuṭ]

petty • 1. طَفِيف [ṭafiːf] زَهِيد [zahiːd] This is a petty sum. هَذا مَبلَغ طَفِيف [haːða mablaɣ ṭafiːf] **• 2.** تافِه [taːfih] I'm tired of these petty objections. يِكفِي هَالإِعتِراضات التّافهَة [yikfi halʔiʕtiraːðaːt ʔittaːfha]

petty expenses • 1. نَثرِي، نَثرِيّات [naθri, naθriyyaːt]

pharaoh • **1.** فِرعَون [firʕu:n] فَراعِين [fara:ʕi:n] *pl:*

pharmacist • **1.** صَيدَلِي [ṣaydali] صَيادِلَة [ṣaya:dila] *pl:*

pharmacy • **1.** صَيدَلِيَّة [ṣaydaliyya] صَيدَلِيّات [ṣaydaliyya:t] *pl:*

phase • **1.** مَرحَلَة [marħala] مَراحِل [mara:ħil] *pl:* طَور [ṭawr] The second phase of the project will begin next month. المَرحَلَة الثّانيَة مِن المَشرُوع راح تِبدِي الشَّهر الجّاي [ʔilmarħala ʔiθθa:nya min ʔilmašru:ʕ ra:ħ tibdi ʔiššahr ʔijja:y]

Ph. D. • **1.** دِكتُوراه [diktu:ra:h] He has a Ph. D. in economics. عِندَه دِكتُوراه بالاِقتِصاد [ʕindah diktu:ra bilʔiqtiṣa:d]

phenomenon • **1.** ظاهِرَة [ða:hira] ظَواهِر [ðawa:hir] *pl:* This is a strange phenomenon. هاي ظاهِرَة غَرِيبَة [ha:y ða:hira ɣari:ba]

phenomenal • **1.** خارِق [xa:riq] He has a phenomenal memory. عِندَه ذاكِرَة خارِقَة [ʕindah ða:kira xa:riqa]

philanthropic • **1.** خَيرِي [xayri] بِرِّي [birri] Philanthropic societies provide the schools for orphans with food and clothing. الجَّمعِيّات الخَيرِيَّة تزَوِّد مَدارِس الأيتام بِالأكِل وَالهِدُوم [ʔijjamʕiyya:t ʔalxayriyya dzawwid mada:ris ʔilʔayta:m bilʔakil wilhidu:m] • **2.** إنسانِي [ʔinsa:ni] That's not a very philanthropic idea. هَالفِكرَة مُو فِكرَة إنسانِيَّة كُلِّش [halfikra mu: fikra ʔinsa:niyya kulliš]

philanthropist • **1.** رَجُل مُحسِن [rajul muħsin] رِجال مُحسِنِين [rija:l muħsini:n] رِياجِيل مُحسِنِين [riya:ji:l muħsini:n] *pl:*

philanthropy • **1.** حُبّ الإنسانِيَّة [ħubb ʔilʔinsa:niyya] عَمَل إحسان، عَمَل خير [ʕamal ʔiħsa:n, ʕamal xi:r] أعمال إحسان، أعمال خير [ʔaʕma:l ʔiħsa:n, ʔaʕma:l xi:r] *pl:*

philologist • **1.** لُغَوِي [luɣawi]

philology • **1.** عِلم اللُّغات [ʕilm ʔilluɣa:t]

philosopher • **1.** فَيلَسُوف [faylasu:f] فَلاسِفَة [fala:sifa] *pl:*

philosophic • **1.** فَلسَفِي [falsafi]

philosophy • **1.** فَلسَفَة [falsafa]

phone • **1.** تَلِيفُون [talifu:n] You're wanted on the phone. دَيرِيدُوك عَالتَّلَفُون [dayri:du:k ʕattalifu:n]

to phone • **1.** تَلفَن [talfan] تَلفَنَة [talfana] *vn: sv* i. خابَر [xa:bar] مُخابَرَة [muxa:bara] *vn: sv* i. I'll phone you after lunch. راح أتَلفِنلَك بَعد الغَدا [ra:ħ ʔatalfinlak baʕd ʔilɣada]

phonograph • **1.** غرَمُفُون [ɣramufu:n] غرَمُفُونات [ɣramufu:na:t] *pl:* فُنُغراف [funuɣra:f] فُنُغرافات [funuɣra:fa:t] *pl:*

phony • **1.** مُلَفَّق [mulaffaq] That story is phony. هالقِصَّة ملَفَّقَة [halqiṣṣa mlaffaqa] • **2.** دَعِي [daʕi] مُدَّعِي [muddaʕi] The guy is a phony. هَذا واحِد مُدَّعِي [ha:ða wa:ħid muddaʕi]

phosphorus • **1.** فُسفُور [fusfu:r]

photograph • **1.** رَسِم [rasim] صُورَة [ṣu:ra] صُوَر [ṣuwar] *pl:* تَصوِير [taṣwi:r] Where can I have a passport photograph taken? وين أقدَر آخُذ رَسِم مال باسبُورت [wi:n ʔagdar ʔa:xuð rasim ma:l pa:ṣpu:rt]

to photograph • **1.** أخَذ صُورَة [ʔaxað ṣu:ra] أخِذ صُورَة [ʔaxið ṣu:ra] *vn: sv* u. Have you photographed the statue? أخَذِت صُورَة التِّمثال؟ [ʔaxaðit ṣu:rat ʔittimθa:l?]

photographer • **1.** مُصَوِّر [muṣawwir] مُصَوِّرِين [muṣawwiri:n] *pl:* رَسّام [rassa:m] رَسّامِين [rassa:mi:n] *pl:*

phrase • **1.** عِبارَة [ʕiba:ra] عِبارات [ʕiba:ra:t] *pl:* قَول [gawl] أقوال [ʔaqwa:l] *pl:* This phrase is not a complete sentence. هالعِبارَة مُو جُملَة كامِلَة [halʕiba:ra mu: jumla ka:mla]

to phrase • **1.** عَبَّر عَن [ʕabbar ʕan] تَعبِير عَن [taʕbi:r ʕan] *vn: sv* i. Can you phrase it in a better way? تِقدَر تعَبُّر عَنها بطَرِيقَة أحسَن؟ [tigdar tʕabbur ʕanha bṭari:qa ʔaħsan?] • **2.** صاغ [ṣa:ɣ] صِياغَة [ṣiya:ɣa] *vn:* اِنصاغ [ʔinṣa:ɣ] *p:* He phrased his speech so as to appeal to the masses. صاغ خِطابَه بِصُورَة تأثِّر بِالجَّماهِير [ṣa:ɣ xiṭa:bah bṣu:ra tʔaθθir biljama:hi:r]

physical • **1.** جِسمِي [jismi] بَدَنِي [badani] جِسمانِي [jisma:ni] Avoid every form of physical exertion. تحاشَى أيّ إرهاق جِسمِي [tħa:ša: ʔayy ʔirha:q jismi] • **2.** طَبِيعِي [ṭabi:ʕi] This contradicts all physical laws. هَذا يناقِض كُلّ القَوانِين الطَّبِيعِيَّة [ha:ða yina:qið kull ʔilqawa:ni:n ʔiṭṭabi:ʕiyya]

physical education • **1.** رِياضَة [riya:ða] الرِياضَة البَدَنِيَّة [ʔirriya:ða ʔilbadaniyya]

physical exercise • **1.** رِياضَة [riya:ða] تَمرِين بَدَنِي [tamri:n badani] تَمرِينات بَدَنِيَّة [tamri:nat badaniyya] تمارِين بَدَنِيَّة [tama:ri:n badaniyya] *pl:*

physician • **1.** دَكتُور [daktu:r] دَكاترَة [daka:tra] *pl:* طَبِيب [ṭabi:b] أطِبّاء [ʔaṭibba:ʔ] *pl:*

physicist • **1.** فِيزيائِي [fi:zya:ʔi] فِيزيائِيِّين [fi:zya:ʔiyyi:n] *pl:*

physics • **1.** فِيزياء [fi:zya:ʔ] He is studying physics. دَيِدرُس فِيزيَاء [dayidrus fi:zya]

P

physiology • **1.** فَسلَجَة [faslaǰa]

physique • **1.** بُنيَة [bunya] قَلافَة [qala:fa] قَلافات [qala:fa:t] *pl:* He has a nice physique. عِندَه خُوش بُنيَة [ʕindah xu:š buniya]

pianist • **1.** عازِف بِيانُو [ʕa:zif piya:nu] عازِفِين بِيانُو [ʕa:zifi:n piya:nu] *pl:*

piano • **1.** بيانُو [pya:nu] بيانوات [pya:nuwa:t] *pl:*

pick • **1.** قَزمَة [qazma] قَزمات [qazma:t] *pl:* The men were carrying picks and shovels. العُمّال كانَوا شايلِين قَزمات وَكَرَكات [ʔilʕumma:l ča:naw ša:yli:n qazma:t wkaraka:t] • **2.** رِيشَة [ri:ša] رِيشات، رِيَش [ri:ša:t, riyaš] *pl:* رِيش [ri:š] *Collective:* The pick for my lute broke. الرِّيشَة مال عُودِي اِنكِسرَت [ʔirri:ša ma:l ʕu:di ʔinkisrat] • **3.** خِيرَة [xi:ra] خِيرات [xi:ra:t] *pl:* This is the pick of the lot. هَذا خِيرَة المَوجُود [ha:ða xi:rat ʔilmawǰu:d] • **4.** خِيار [xiya:r] I have three apples; take your pick. عِندِي ثلَث تِفّاحات؛ اِلَك الخِيار [ʕindi tlaθ tiffa:ħa:t; ʔilak ʔilxiya:r] • **5.** نُخبَة [nuxba] نُخَب [nuxab] *pl:* زُبدَة [zubda] زُبدات، زُبَد [zubda:t, zubad] *pl:* These men are the pick of the army. هَالجِنُود نُخبَة الجَّيش [halǰinu:d nuxbat ʔiǰǰayš]

to pick • **1.** حُوَى [ħuwa:] حَوِي [ħawy] *vn:* اِنحُوَى [ʔinħuwa:] *p:* *sv* i. When are you going to pick the fruit? شوَكِت راح تَحوِي المَيوَة؟ [šwakit ra:ħ taħwi ʔilmi:wa?] • **2.** اِختار [ʔixta:r] اِختِيار [ʔixtiya:r] *vn:* *sv* a. اِستَنقَى [ʔistanga:] اِستِنقاء [ʔistinga:ʔ] *vn:* *sv* i. You certainly picked a nice time for an argument. بِلا شَكّ إنتَ اِخبرت الوَقِت المُناسِب لِلمُجادَلَة [bila šakk ʔinta ʔixtarit ʔilwakit ʔilmuna:sib lilmuǰa:dala] • **3.** نَقنَق ب [nagnag b-] تِنقِنِق [tnignig] *vn:* *sv* i. Don't pick at your food! لا تنَقنِق بأكلَك [la: tnagnig bʔaklak] • **4.** نَغبَش ب [naɣbaš b-] نَغبَشَة [naɣbaša] *vn:* *sv* u. Don't pick your teeth! لا تنَغبُش بإسنُونَك [la: tnaɣbuš bʔisnu:nak] • **5.** نَقبَر [nagbar] تنُقبُر [tnugbur] *vn:* *sv* u. Don't pick your nose! لا تنَقبُر بخَشمَك [la: tnagbur bxašmak] • **6.** فَشّ [fašš] فَشّ [fašš] *vn:* اِنفَشّ [ʔinfašš] *p:* Someone must have picked this lock. فَدّ أَحَّد لازِم فَشّ هَالقُفُل [fadd ʔaħħad la:zim fašš halquful]

*** They picked him to pieces.** • **1.** شَرَّوه عَالحَبِل [šarrawh ʕalħabil] / تناوشُوه [tna:wšu:h]

*** I have a bone to pick with you.** • **1.** عِندِي حساب أَرِيد أصَفِّيه ويّاك [ʕindi ħsa:b ʔari:d ʔaṣaffi:h wiyya:k]

*** Are you trying to pick a quarrel with me?** • **1.** إنتَ دَتدَوُّرلَك حِرش ويّايا؟ [ʔinta datdawwurlak ħirš wiyya:ya?]

to pick on • **1.** شَدّ دُوب ويّا [šadd du:b wiyya] He's been picking on me all day. شادّ دُوبَه ويّايا النَّهار كُلَّه [ša:dd du:bah wiyya:ya ʔinnaha:r kullah]

to pick out • **1.** اِختار [ʔixta:r] اِختِيار [ʔixtiya:r] *vn:* *sv* a. اِستَنقَى [ʔistanga:] اِستِنقاء [ʔistinga:ʔ] *vn:* *sv* i. He picked out a very nice gift for his wife. اِختار هَدِيَّة كُلِّش حِلوَة لِزَوجتَه [ʔixta:r hadiyya kulliš ħilwa lizawiǰtah]

to pick up • **1.** شال [ša:l] شَيل [šayl] *vn:* اِنشال [ʔinša:l] *p:* Please pick up the paper from the floor. بالله ما تشِيل الجَّرِيدَة مِن القاع [ballah ma: tši:l ʔiǰǰari:da min ʔilga:ʕ] The bus stopped here to pick up passengers. الباص وُقَف هنا حَتَّى يشِيل رُكّاب [ʔilpa:ṣ wugaf hna: ħatta yši:l rukka:b] • **2.** لِقَط [ligaṭ] لَقِط [lagiṭ] *vn:* اِنلِقَط [ʔinligaṭ] *p:* I picked up quite a bit of Italian on my trip. لِقَطِت مِقدار لا بَأس بِيه مِن الحَكِي الإيطالِي بسَفرتِي [ligaṭit miqda:r la: baʔas bi:h min ʔilħači ʔilʔi:ṭa:li bsafurti] • **3.** لِزَم [lizam] لَزِم [lazim] *vn:* اِنلِزَم [ʔinlizam] *p:* كُمَش [kumaš] كَمُش [kamuš] *vn:* اِنكُمَش [ʔinkumaš] *p:* The police picked up several suspects. الشُّرطَة لِزمَوا بَعض المُشتَبِه بِيهُم [ʔiššurṭa lizmaw baʕð̣ ʔilmuštabih bi:hum] • **4.** اِكتِسَب [ʔiktisab] اِكتِساب [ʔiktisa:b] *vn:* *sv* a. The train gradually picked up speed. القِطار اِكتِسَب سُرعَة تَدرِيجِيّاً [ʔilqiṭa:r ʔiktisab surʕa tadri:ǰiyyan]

pickle • **1.** طُرشِيَّة [ṭuršiyya] طُرشِيّات، طَراشِي [ṭuršiyya:t, ṭara:ši] *pl:* طُرشِي [ṭurši] *Collective:* Do you have any pickles? عِندَك طُرشِي؟ [ʕindak ṭurši?]

*** He's in a pretty pickle now.** • **1.** هُوَّ مِتوَرِّط هَسَّة [huwwa mitwarriṭ hassa] / هُوَّ واقِع بمَأزَق هَسَّة [huwwa wa:giʕ bmaʔzaq hassa]

to pickle • **1.** كِبَس [čibas] كَبِس [čabis] *vn:* *sv* i. كَمَّخ [kammax] تكُمُّخ [tkummux] *vn:* *sv* u. Did you pickle the turnips I brought you? كِبَستِي الشَّلغَم اللِّي جِبتَه إلِك؟ [čibasti ʔiššalɣam ʔilli ǰibtah ʔilič?]

pickled • **1.** مخَلَّل [mxallal] Buy a bowl of pickled beets. اِشتِرِيلِي كاسَة شُوندَر مخَلَّل [ʔištiri:li ka:sa šuwandar mxallal]

pick pocket • **1.** نَشّال [našša:l] نَشّالِين [našša:li:n] *pl:* ضَرّاب جَيب [ð̣arra:bǰayb] ضَرّابِين جَيب [ð̣arra:bi:n ǰayb] *pl:*

picnic • **1.** نُزهَة [nuzha] نُزهات [nuzha:t] *pl:*

picture • **1.** صُورَة [ṣu:ra] صُوَر [ṣuwar] *pl:* رَسِم [rasim] They have some beautiful pictures for sale. عِدهُم بَعض الصُّوَر البَدِيعَة لِلبيع [ʕidhum baʕð̣ ʔiṣṣuwar ʔilbadi:ʕa lilbayʕ] This is my picture when I was in the army. هَذا رَسمِي مِن كِنِت بالجَيش [ha:ða rasmi min činit biǰǰayš] • **2.** فِلِم [filim] أفلام [ʔafla:m] *pl:* Was the picture good? الفِلِم كان زين؟ [ʔilfilim ča:n zi:n?] • **3.** فِكرَة [fikra] فِكرات، فِكِر، أفكار [fikra:t, fikir, ʔafka:r.] *pl:* I have to get a clear picture of it first. لازِم يصِير عِندِي فِكرَة واضحَة عَنَّه أوَّل [la:zim yṣi:r ʕindi fikra wa:ð̣ħa ʕannah ʔawwal]

to give a picture of • **1.** صَوَّر [ṣawwar] تَصوِير [taṣwi:r] *vn:* *sv* u. He gave you a false picture of it. صَوَّر لَك إيّاها غَلَط [ṣawwar lak ʔiyya:ha ɣalaṭ]

to picture • **1.** صَوَّر [ṣawwar] طَصوِير [ṭaṣwi:r] *vn:* تصَوَّر [tṣawwar] *p:* This novel pictures life a thousand

P

years ago. هَالرُّوايَة تصَوُّر الحَياة قَبُل أَلف سَنَة [harruwa:ya tṣawwur ʔilħaya:t gabul ʔalf sana] • **2.** تصَوَّر [tṣawwar] تَصَوُّر [taṣawwur] *vn: sv* a. I pictured it differently. تصَوَّرتها غير شِكِل [tṣawwaritha ɣayr šikil]

pictures • **1.** سِينَما [sinama] سِينَمات [si:nama:t] *pl:* فِلِم [filim] أَفلام [ʔafla:m] *pl:* She has been in pictures since she was a child. تِطلَع بِالسِّينَما مِن هِيَّ بَعَدها طِفلَة [tiṭlaʕ bissi:nama min hiyya baʕadha ṭifla]

piece • **1.** وُصلَة [wuṣla] وُصَل [wuṣal] *pl:* May I take a piece of the watermelon. أَقدَر آخُذ وُصلَة مِن الرَّقِّي؟ [ʔagdar ʔa:xuð wuṣla min ʔirraggi?] Sew these two pieces together. خَيِّطِي هَالوُصلَتَين سُوَة [xayyṭi halwuṣiltayn suwa] • **2.** قِطعَة [qiṭʕa] قِطَع [qiṭaʕ] *pl:* Get a piece of wire and fasten them together. جِيب قِطعَة مِن السِّلك وَأربُطهُم سُوَة [ǰi:b qiṭʕa min ʔissilk wʔurbuṭhum suwa] • **3.** مَقطُوعَة [maqṭu:ʕa] مَقاطِيع [maqa:ṭi:ʕ] *pl:* What is the name of the piece the orchestra is playing? شاِسم هَالمَقطُوعَة اللِّي دَتِعزِفها الفِرقَة؟ [šʔism halmaqṭu:ʕa ʔilli datiʕzifha ʔilfirqa?]

*** I gave him a good piece of my mind!** • **1.** زَفَّيتَه [zaffaytah] / وَبَّختَه زين [wabbaxtah zi:n]

to fall to pieces • **1.** تفَسَّخ [tfassax] تَفَسُّخ [tafassux] *vn: sv* a. The book is falling to pieces. الكِتاب تفَسَّخ [ʔilkita:b tfassax] The book is falling to pieces. الكِتاب صار وُصلَة وُصلَة [ʔilkita:b ṣa:r wuṣla wuṣla]

to go to pieces • **1.** اِنهار [ʔinha:r] اِنهيار [ʔinhiya:r] *vn: sv* a. She went completely to pieces. اِنهارَت تَماماً [ʔinha:rat tama:man] • **2.** تفَلَّش [tfallaš] تَفَلُّش [tafalluš] *vn: sv* a. Sooner or later their business is bound to go to pieces. أَوَّل وتالِي تِجارَتهُم لازم تِتفَلَّش [ʔawwal wta:li tiǰa:rathum la:zim titfallaš]

to tear to pieces • **1.** شَقَّق [šaggag] تشِقِّق [tšiggig] *vn: sv* i. مَلَّخ [mallax] تمِلِّخ [tmillix] *vn: sv* i. The dog tore my shoe to pieces. الكَلِب مَلَّخ قُندَرتِي [ʔiččalib mallax qundarti]

piece work • **1.** بِالقِطعَة [bilqiṭʕa] بِالوِحدَة [bilwiħda] They work piece work. يِشتُغلُون بِالقِطعَة [yištuɣlu:n bilqiṭʕa]

pier • **1.** دِنگَة [dinga] دِنگات، دِنَك [dinga:t, dinag] *pl:* The bridge rests on four piers. الجِّسِر مُرَكَّب عَلَى أَربَع دِنَك [ʔiǰǰisir murakkab ʕala ʔarbaʕ dinag] • **2.** رَصِيف [raṣi:f] أَرصِفَة [ʔarṣifa] *pl:* We were standing on the harbor's pier waiting for the boat. كِنّا واقفِين عَلَى رَصِيف المِيناء دَنِنتِظِر المَركَب [činna wa:gfi:n ʕala raṣi:f ʔilmi:na:ʔ danintiðir ʔilmarkab]

to pierce • **1.** نِقَب [nigab] نَقُب [nagub] *vn:* اِنِّقَب [ʔinnigab] *p:* زِرَف [ziraf] زَرُف [zaruf] *vn:* اِنزِرَف [ʔinziraf] *p:* Bullets cannot pierce this armored plate. الرِّصاص ما يِقدَر يِنقُب هَالحَدِيد المُدَرَّع [ʔirriṣa:ṣ ma: yigdar yingub halħadi:d ʔilmudarraʕ]

pig • **1.** خَنزِير [xanzi:r] خَنازِير [xana:zi:r] *pl:*

pigeon • **1.** حَمامَة [ħama:ma] حَمامات [ħama:ma:t] *pl:* حَمام [ħama:m] *Collective*

wild pigeon • **1.** طوارني [ṭwa:rni] طوارنِيَّة [ṭwa:rniyya] *pl:*

pigeonhole • **1.** خانَة [xa:na] خانات [xa:na:t] *pl:* You'll find it in one of the pigeon holes of the desk. تِلقِيها بوَحدَة مِن خانات المِيز [tilgi:ha bwaħda min xa:na:t ʔilmi:z]

to pigeonhole • **1.** نَيَّم [nayyam] تنِيِّم [tniyyim] *vn: sv* i. Apparently they have pigeonholed our request. يِظهَر نَيِّمَوا الطَّلَب مالنا [yiðhar nayyimawh ʔiṭṭalab ma:lna]

pigeon house • **1.** بُرِج [burij] بُرُوج، أَبراج [buru:ǰ, ʔabra:ǰ] *pl:*

pigheaded • **1.** عنادِي [ʕna:di] عَنُود [ʕanu:d] He is so pigheaded that he won't even listen to my explanation. هَذا هَالقَدّ عنادِي حَتَّى ما يِسمَع الشَّرِح مالِي [ha:ða halgadd ʕna:di ħatta ma: yismaʕ ʔiššariħ ma:li]

pile • **1.** كُوم [ku:m] كُوام [kuwam] *pl:* كَومَة [kawma] كوام [kwa:m] *pl:* Leave space between the piles of sand and gravel. خَلِّي مَسافَة بين كوام الرَّمُل والحَصو [xalli masa:fa bayn kwa:m ʔirramul walħaṣw] This pile of letters needs to be answered. هاي كَومَة مِن المَكاتِيب يِنرادِلها جَواب [ha:y kawma min ʔilmaka:ti:b yinra:dilha ǰawa:b] • **2.** ثَروَة [θarwa] ثَروات [θarwa:t] *pl:* He made his pile during the war. جِمَع ثَروتَه بِالحَرُب [ǰimaʕ θarwtah bilħarub]

to pile • **1.** كَوَّم [kawwam] تَكوِيم [takwi:m] *vn:* تكَوَّم [tkawwam] *p:* كَدَّس [kaddas] تَكدِيس [takdi:s] *vn:* تكَدَّس [tkaddas] *p:* Pile the bricks next to the wall. كَوُّم الطّابُوق يَمّ الحايِط [kawwum ʔiṭṭa:bu:g yamm ʔilħa:yiṭ] • **2.** دِحَس [diħas] دَحِس [daħis] *vn:* اِندِحَس [ʔindiħas] *p:* We piled all the suitcases into the trunk of the car. دِحَسنا كُلّ الجُّنَط بِصَندُوق السَّيّارَة [diħasna kull ʔiǰǰunaṭ bişandu:g ʔissayya:ra] • **3.** اِندِحَس [ʔindiħas] اِندِحاس [ʔindiħa:s] *vn: sv* i. We all piled into one car. كُلّنا اندِحَسنا بِفَدّ سَيّارَة [kullna ʔindiħasna bfadd sayya:ra]

to pile up • **1.** تراكَم [tra:kam] تَراكُم [tara:kum] *vn: sv* a. My debts are piling up. دِيُونِي دَتِتراكَم [dyu:ni datitra:kam]

piles • **1.** بُواسِير [buwa:si:r] He was operated on in the hospital for piles. سَوّولَه عَمَلِيَّة بَواسِير بِالمُستَشفى [sawwawlah ʕamaliyyat bawa:si:r bilmustašfa]

pilgrim • **1.** حَجِّي [ħaǰǰi] حِجّاج [ħiǰǰa:ǰ] *pl:*

pilgrimage • **1.** حَجّ [ħaǰǰ]

pill • **1.** حَبَّة [ħabba] حَبّات [ħabba:t] *pl:* حُبُوب [ħubu:b] *Collective*

P

pillar • **1.** عَمُود [ʕamuːd] أعمِدَة [ʔaʕmida] *pl:* عَوامِيد [ʕawaːmiːd] A large pillar blocked my view of the stage. فَدّ عَمُود كِبِير سَدّ مَنظَر المَسرَح مِن قِدّامِي [fadd ʕamuːd čibiːr sadd manðar ʕilmasrah min giddaːmi]

pillow • **1.** مُخَدَّة [muxadda] مَخادِيد، مُخَدّات [maxaːdiːd, muxaddaːt] *pl:*

pillowcase • **1.** بَيت مَخَدَّة [bayt mxadda] بيُوت مخادِيد [byuːt mxaːdiːd] *pl:*

pilot • **1.** رُبّان [rubbaːn] رَبابِنَة [rabaːbina] *pl:* قبطان [qabṭaːn] قبطانِيَّة [qabṭaːniyya] *pl:* The ship is waiting for the pilot. الباخِرَة دَتِنتِظِر الرُّبّان [ʔilbaːxira datintiðir ʔirrubbaːn] • **2.** طَيّار [ṭayyaːr] طَيّارِين [ṭayyaːriːn] *pl:* He is an Air Force pilot. هُوَّ طَيّار بالقُوَّة الجَوِّيَّة [huwwa ṭayyaːr bilquwwa ʔiǰǰawwiyya]

pimple • **1.** زُنكُطَة [zunguṭa] زَناكِط [zanaːgiṭ] *pl:* Her face is full of pimples. وِجهَها مطَلَّع زَناكِط [wiččha mṭallaʕ zanaːgiṭ] • **2.** حَبَّة [ħabba] حَبّات [ħabbaːt] *pl:* حَبّ [ħabb] *Collective:* When he grew up he got rid of his adolescent pimples. مِن كُبَر خَلَّص مِن حَبّ الشَّباب [min kubar xallaṣ min ħabb ʔiššabaːb]

pin • **1.** دَنبُوس [danbuːs] دَنابِيس [danaːbiːs] *pl:* She stuck herself with a pin. شَكَّت نَفِسها بدَنبُوس [čakkat nafisha bdanbuːs] She wore a silver pin. لِبسَت دَنبُوس فُضَّة [libsat danbuːs fuðða]

*** I was on pins and needles.** • **1.** كِنِت عَلَى أَحَرّ مِن الجَمُر [činit ʕala ʔaħarr min ʔiǰǰamur] / كِنِت قاعِد عَلَى نار [činit gaːʕid ʕala naːr]

hairpin • **1.** فُركِيتَة [furkiːta] فُركِيتات [furkiːtaːt] *pl:*

to pin • **1.** دَنبَس [danbas, dambas] تدِمبِس [tdimbis] *vn: sv* i. Pin your hankerchief to your coat. دَمبِس الكَفِّيَّة بسِترتَك [dambis ʔiččiffiyya bsitirtak] • **2.** عِصَى [ʕiṣaː] عَصِي [ʕaṣy] *vn: sv* a. The two men were pinned under the car. الرِّجّالَين عِصَوا جَوَّة [ʔirriǰǰaːlayn ʕiṣaw ǰawwa]

to pin down • **1.** لِزَم [lizam] لَزِم [lazim] *vn: sv* a. We couldn't pin him down to anything definite. ما قِدَرنا نِلزَمَه بشِي أكِيد [maː gidarna nilzamah bši ʔakiːd]

to pin on • **1.** شَكَّل [šakkal] تشِكِّل [tšikkil] *vn: sv* i. عَلَّق [ʕallag] تعِلِّق [tʕillig] *vn: sv* i. I'll pin it on for you. آني أشَكِّلَك إيّاها [ʔaːni ʔašakkil lak ʔiyyaːha] She pinned a flower on her dress. شَكِّلَت وَردَة عَلَى بَدلَتها [šakkilat warda ʕala badlatha] • **2.** ثَبَّت [θabbat] تَثبِيت [taθbiːt] *vn:* تثَبَّت [tθabbat] *p:* The police pinned the crime on him. الشُّرطَة ثَبِّتَت الجَرِيمَة عَلَيه [ʔiššurṭa θabbitat ʔiǰǰariːma ʕaliːh]

to pin up • **1.** شَكَّل [šakkal] تشِكِّل [tšikkil] *vn: sv* i. عَلَّق [ʕallag] تعِلِّق [tʕillig] *vn: sv* i. Let me pin up the hem first. خَلِّي أوَّل أشَكِّل الحاشيَة لِفُوق [xalli ʔawwal ʔašakkil ʔilhaːšya lifuːg] • **2.** فَركَت [farkat] تفُركِت [tfurkit] *vn:* تفَركَت [tfarkat] *p:* She pinned up her hair. فَركِتَت شَعَرها [farkitat šaʕarha] She pinned up her hair. حاطَّة فُركِيتَة بشَعَرها [ħaːṭṭa furkiːta bšaʕarha]

pinch • **1.** نِتفَة [nitfa] نِتفات [nitfaːt] *pl:* رَشَّة [rašša] Add a pinch of salt to the soup. ضِيف فَدّ نِتفَة مِلح عالشُّوربَة [ðiːf fadd nitfa miliħ ʕaššuːrba] • **2.** قَرصَة [garṣa] قَرصات [garṣaːt] *pl:* The boy gave his little sister a good pinch. الوَلَد قِرَص أُختَه الصِّغَيِّرَة قَرصَة قَوِيَّة [ʔilwalad giraṣ ʔuxtah ʔiṣṣiɣayyra garṣa qawiyya]

in a pinch • **1.** عِند الضَرُورَة [ʕind ʔiððaruːra] بوَقت الضِيق [bwakt ʔiððiːq] In a pinch it will do. عِند الضُّرُورَة هاي تسِدّ الحاجَة [ʕind ʔiððuruːra haːy tsidd ʔilhaːǰa] You can always count on him in a pinch. بإمكانَك دائماً تِقدَر تِعتِمِد عَليه بوَقت الضِّيق [bʔimkaːnak daːʔiman tigdar tiʕtimid ʕaliːh bwakit ʔiððiːq]

to pinch • **1.** قِرَص [giraṣ] قَرِص [gariṣ] *vn:* اِنقِرَص [ʔingiraṣ] *p:* قَرَّص [garraṣ] تَقرِيص [tagriːṣ] *vn:* تقَرَّص [tgarraṣ] *p:* Don't pinch! لا تِقرُص [laː tigruṣ] The door pinched my finger. الباب قِرصَت إصِبعِي [ʔilbaːb girṣat ʔiṣibʕi] • **2.** ضَيَّق عَلَى [ðayyaq ʕala] تَضيِيق [taðyiːg] *vn:* تضَيَّق [tðayyag] *p:* أذَى [ʔaððaː] أذِيَّة [ʔaðiyya] *vn:* تأذَّى [tʔaððaː] *p:* Where does the shoe pinch your foot? منِين القُندَرَة دَتضَيِّق عَلَى رِجلَك [miniːn ʔilqundara dadðayyig ʕala rijlak]

pine • **1.** صِنُوبرَة [ṣinuːbra] صنُوبَرات [ṣnuːbaraːt] *pl:* صنَوبَر [ṣnawbar] *Collective:* These pine trees are almost fifty years old. أشجار الصنَوبَر هاي عُمُرها حوالِي خَمسِين سَنَة [ʔašǰaːr ʔiṣṣnawbar haːy ʕumurha ħwaːli xamsiːn sana]

pineapple • **1.** أناناس [ʔananaːs]

pine wood • **1.** خِشَب كام [xišab čaːm]

pink • **1.** وَردِي [wardi] She was wearing a pink dress. كانَت لابسَة نَفنُوف وَردِي [čaːnat laːbsah nafnuːf wardi] • **2.** قرَنفِلَة وَردِي [qranfila wardi] قرَنفِلات وَردِيَّة [qranfilaːt wardiyya] *pl:* قرِنفِل [qrinfil] *Collective:* We had pinks in this place last year. كان عِدنا بهَالمَحَلّ قرَنفِل وَردِي السَّنَة الماضيَة [čaːn ʕidna bhalmaħall qranfil wardi ʔissana ʔilmaːðiya]

pious • **1.** مِتدَيِّن [middayyin] تَقِي [taqi] أتقِياء [ʔatqiyaːʔ] *pl:* صالِح [ṣaːliħ] He is a very pious man. هُوَّ رِجّال مِتدَيِّن هوايَة [huwwa riǰǰaːl middayyin hwaːya]

pipe • **1.** بُورِي [buːri] بُورِيّات، بُوارِي [buːriːyyaːt, bwaːri] *pl:* إنبُوب [ʔinbuːb] أنابِيب [ʔanaːbiːb] *pl:* The pipe has burst. البُورِي طَقّ [ʔilbuːri ṭagg] The oil pipe line runs from Kirkuk to Tripoli. أنابِيب النَّفُط تِمتَدّ مِن كَركُوك إلَى طَرابلُس [ʔanaːbiːb ʔinnafuṭ timtadd min karkuːk ʔila ṭaraːblus] • **2.** بايب [paːyp] بايبات [paːypaːt] *pl:* He smokes a pipe. يدَخِّن بايب [ydaxxin paːyp]

to pipe • **1.** * We pipe our water from a spring. ناخُذ الماي بِالبُواري مِن العَين [naːxuð ʔilmaːy bilbuwaːri min ʔilʕayn]

piracy • **1.** قَرصَنَة [qarṣana]

pirate • **1.** قُرصان [qurṣaːn] قَراصِنَة [qaraːṣina] *pl:*

pistachio • **1.** فِستِقَة [fistiqa, fistiqaːya] فِستِقايات [fistiqaːyaːt] *pl:* فِستِق [fistiq] *Collective*

pistol • **1.** مُسَدَّس [musaddas] مُسَدَّسات [musaddasaːt] *pl:* وَروَر [warwar] وَراوِر [waraːwir] *pl:*

piston • **1.** بِستِن [pistin] بِستِنات، بَساتِن [pistinaːt, pasaːtin] *pl:*

pit • **1.** مَنجَم [manǰam] مَناجِم [manaːǰim] *pl:* No one was in the pit when the explosion occurred. مَحَّد كان بِالمَنجَم مِن صار الإنفِجار [maħħad čaːn bilmanǰam min ṣaːr ʔilʔinfiǰaːr] • **2.** نواية [nwaːya] نوايات [nwaːyaːt] *pl:* نوَة [niwa] *Collective:* The boy swallowed an olive pit. الوَلَد بِلَع نُوايَة زَيتُون [ʔilwalad bilaʕ nuwaːyat zaytuːn]

pitch • **1.** زِفت [zifit] What's the difference between pitch and tar? شِنُو الفَرِق بين الزِّفت وَالقِير؟ [šinu ʔilfarig bayn ʔizzifit wilgiːr?] • **2.** ضَربَة [ḍarba] ضَربات [ḍarbaːt] *pl:* شَمرَة [šamra] شَمرات [šamraːt] *pl:* That was a good pitch. هَذي كانَت خُوش ضَربَة [haːði čaːnat xuːš ḍarba] • **3.** حالِك [ħaːlik] دامِس [daːmis] It was pitch dark when we came home. كان ظَلام دامِس لَمَّن جَينا لِلبَيت [čaːn ḍalaːm daːmis lamman ǰiːna lilbayt]

to pitch • **1.** نِصَب [niṣab] نَصُب [naṣub] *vn:* اِنُّصَب [ʔinnuṣab] *p:* Where shall we pitch the tent? وين نِنصُب الخَيمَة؟ [wiːn ninṣub ʔilxiːma?] • **2.** شُمَر [šumar] شَمُر [šamur] *vn:* اِنشُمَر [ʔinšumar] *p:* Pitch it out of the window. إشمُرها مِن الشِّبّاك [ʔišmurha min ʔiššibbaːk]

to pitch in • **1.** تشَلَّه [tšallah] تَشَلُّه [tašalluh] *vn: sv* a. شَمَّر [šammar] تَشمِير [tašmiːr] *vn: sv* u. We pitched in and helped him. تشَلَّهنا وَنِزَلنا نعاونَه [tšallahna wnizalna nʕaːwnah]

pitcher • **1.** دُولكَة [duːlka, duːlča] دُولكات [duːlkaːt, duːlčaːt] *pl:* Please get me a pitcher of water. بالله جِيبلِي دُولكَة ماي [ballah ǰiːbli duːlka maːy]

pitiable • **1.** مُرثِي [murθi] He is in a pitiable condition. حالتَه مُرثِيَة [ħaːltah murθiya] He is in a pitiable condition. حالتَه يِنرِثِي لَها [ħaːltah yinriθi laha]

pitiful • **1.** مُؤلِم [muʔlim] أَلِيم [ʔaliːm]

pity • **1.** شَفَقَة [šafaqa] I don't want your pity. ما أَرِيد شَفَقتَك [maː ʔariːd šafaqtak] • **2.** حَسافَة [ħasaːfa] It's a pity you can't come. حَسافَة ما تِقدَر تِجي [ħasaːfa maː tigdar tiǰi] • **3.** حَيف [ħayf] It's a pity he is only seventeen, otherwise I could have employed him. يا حَيف عُمرَه سباطَعَش، وَإلّا كان شَغَّلتَه [yaː ħayf ʕumrah sbaːṭaʕaš, waʔilla čaːn šaɣɣaltah]

* **She took pity on him.** • **1.** قَلُبها اِنكِسَر عَلَيه [galubha ʔinkisar ʕaliːh]

to pity • **1.** شِفَق عَلَى [šifaq ʕala] شَفَقَة [šafaqa] *vn:* اِنشِفَق [ʔinšifaq] *p:* رِثَى ل [riθaː l-] رَثاء [raθaːʔ] *vn:* اِنرِثَى [ʔinriθaː] *p:* She doesn't want anyone to pity her. ما تريد أَحَّد يِشفِق عَليها [maː triːd ʔaħħad yišfiq ʕaliːha] I pity them. أَرثِي لِحالهُم [ʔarθi lħaːlhum]

place • **1.** مَحَلّ [maħall] مَحَلّات [maħallaːt] *pl:* مَكان [makaːn] مَكانات [makaːnaːt] *pl:* Please put it back in the same place. أَرجُوك رَجِّعها بِنَفس المَحَلّ [ʔarǰuːk raǰǰiʕha bnafis ʔilmaħall] If I were in his place I wouldn't have done it. لَو بِمَكانَه، ما كان سَوَّيتها [law bmakaːnah, maː čaːn sawwiːtha] Do you know a good place to eat? تُعرُف فَدّ مَكان زين واحِد ياكُل بِيه؟ [tuʕruf fadd makaːn ziːn waːħid yaːkul biːh?] Do you know the place where we stopped reading? تُعرُف المَحَلّ اللّي وُصَلناه بِالقِرايَة؟ [tuʕruf ʔilmaħall ʔilli wuṣalnaːh bilqiraːya?] What is the name of this place? شاِسِم هَالمَحَلّ؟ [šʔisim halmaħall?] How many places did you set at the table? كَم مَحَلّ حَضَّرت عالميز؟ [kam maħall ħaḍḍarit ʕalmiːz?]

* **Somebody ought to put him in his place.** • **1.** فَدّ أَحَّد لازِم يوَقّفَه عِند حَدَّه [fadd ʔaħħad laːzim ywaggfah ʕind ħaddah]

* **His heart is in the right place.** • **1.** خوش آدمِي [xuːš ʔaːdmi] / آدمِي طَيِّب [ʔaːdmi ṭayyib] / قَلبَه نَظِيف [qalbah naḍiːf]

in place of • **1.** بَدال [badaːl] عِوَض [ʕiwaḍ] May I have another book in place of this one? تِسمَح تِنطِيني كِتاب لاخ بَدال هَذا؟ [tismaħ tinṭiːni kitaːb laːx badaːl haːða?]

in the first place • **1.** أَوَّلاً [ʔawwalan] قَبُل كُلشِي [gabul kullši] In the first place, we can't leave until tomorrow. قَبُل كُلشِي، إحنا ما نِقدَر نِطلَع إلّا باكِر [gabul kullši, ʔiħna maː nigdar niṭlaʕ ʔilla baːčir]

to place • **1.** حَطّ [ħaṭṭ] حَطّ [ħaṭṭ] *vn:* اِنحَطّ [ʔinħaṭṭ] *p:* وُضَع [wuḍaʕ] وَضِع [waḍiʕ] *vn:* اِنوُضَع [ʔinwuḍaʕ] *p:* خَلَّى [xallaː] تخَلِّي [txilli] *vn:* تخَلَّى [txallaː] *p:* Place the table next to the window. حُطّ المَيز بصَفّ الشِّبّاك [ħuṭṭ ʔilmiːz bṣaff ʔiššibbaːk] • **2.** خَلَّى [xallaː] تخَلَّى [txallaː] *p:* Place the guest of honor next to the host. خَلّي ضيف الشَّرَف يَمّ أَبُو الدَّعوَة [xalli ḍiːf ʔiššaraf yamm ʔabu ʔiddaʕwa] • **3.** عَيَّن [ʕayyan] تَعيين [taʕyiːn] *vn:* تعَيَّن [tʕayyan] *p:* We have placed all of our graduates. عَيَّنّا كُلّ المِتخَرّجين مِن عدنا [ʕayyanna kull ʔilmitxarrǰiːn min ʕidna] We have placed all of our graduates. لِقينا لِكُلّ المِتخَرّجين شُغُل [ligiːna likull ʔilmitxarrǰiːn šuɣul] • **4.** وَجَّه [wajjah] تَوجِيه [tawǰiːh] *vn:* توَجَّه [twaǰǰah] *p:* A charge was placed against him. فَدّ تُهمَة توَجّهَت ضِدَّه [fadd tuhma

P

twaǰǰihat ḍiddah] • **5.** أَلقَى [ʔalqaː] إلقاء [ʔilqaːʔ] *vn: sv* i. He placed the responsibility for the damage on the proper man. أَلقَى مَسؤُولِيَّة التَّلَف عَلَى الفاعِل الحَقِيقِي [ʔalqaː masʔuːliyyat ʔittalaf ʕala ʔilfaːʕil ʔilħaqiːqi] • **6.** تذَكَّر [dðakkar] تَذَكُّر [taðakkur] *vn: sv* a. I've met him before, but I can't place him. آنِي ملاقِيه قَبُل، بَسّ ما أتذَكَّر مِنُو هُوَّ [ʔaːni mlaːgiːh gabul, bass maː ʔadðakkar minu huwwa]

plague • **1.** طاعُون [ṭaːʕuːn] طَواعِين [ṭawaːʕiːn] *pl:*

plain • **1.** سَهِل [sahil] There is a wide plain between the two mountain ranges. أَكُو سَهِل واسِع بين سِلسِلتَين الجِّبال [ʔaku sahil waːsiʕ bayn silsiltayn ʔiǰǰibaːl] • **2.** بَسِيط [basiːṭ] بَسِيطِين [basiːṭiːn] *pl:* They are plain people. هُمَّة ناس بُسَطاء [humma naːs busaṭaːʔ] We have a plain home. عِدنا بَيت بَسِيط [ʕidna bayt basiːṭ] • **3.** اِعتِيادِي [ʔiʕtiyaːdi] She is a plain-looking woman, but very intelligent. هاي وِحدَة مَلامِحها اِعتِيادِيَّة، لَكِن كُلِّش ذَكِيَّة [haːy wiħda malaːmiħha ʔiʕtiyaːdiyya, laːkin kulliš ðakiyya] • **4.** واضِح ظاهِر [waːḍiħ ḍaːhir]

*** It is as plain as the nose on your face.**

• **1.** واضحَ مِثِل عَين الشَّمِس [waːḍħa miθil ʕiːn ʔiššamis]

*** The ship now is in plain view.** • **1.** الباخِرَة هَسَّة مبَيَّنَة [ʔilbaːxira hassa mbayyna]

*** I told him the plain truth.** • **1.** قِتلَه الحَقِيقَة مِثِلما هِيَّ [gitlah ʔilħaqiːqa miθilmaː hiyya]

plan • **1.** خَرِيطَة [xariːṭa] خَرايِط [xaraːyiṭ] *pl:* مُخَطَّط [muxaṭṭaṭ] مُخَطَّطات [muxaṭṭaṭaːt] *pl:* تَصمِيم [taṣmiːm] The plan for the new house is ready. الخَرِيطَة مال البَيت الجِّدِيد حاضرَة [ʔilxariːṭa maːl ʔilbayt ʔiǰǰidiːd ħaːḍra] • **2.** خُطَّة [xuṭṭa] خُطَط [xuṭaṭ] *pl:* تَدبِير [tadbiːr] تَدابِير [tadaːbiːr] *pl:* Have you made any plans yet for the future? فَكَّرت بأَيّ خُطَط لِلمُستَقبَل لَو بَعَد؟ [fakkarit bʔayy xuṭaṭ lilmustaqbal law baʕad?] This is an excellent plan. هَذا فَدّ تَدبِير مُمتاز [haðaː fadd tadbiːr mumtaːz] • **3.** مَشرُوع [mašruːʕ] They have great plans for beautifying the city. عِدهُم مَشارِيع عَظِيمَة لتَجمِيل المَدِينَة [ʕidhum mašaːriːʕ ʕaḍiːma ltaǰmiːl ʔilmadiːna] • **4.** مَنهَج [manhaǰ] مَناهِج [manaːhiǰ] *pl:* What are your plans for tomorrow? شِنُو مَنهَجَك باكِر؟ [šinu manhaǰak baːčir?]

to plan • **1.** رَتَّب [rattab] تَرتِيب [tartiːb] *vn:* ترَتَّب [trattab] *p:* دَبَّر [dabbar] تَدبِير [tadbiːr] *vn:* تدَبَّر [tdabbar] *p:* Our trip was carefully planned. سَفرَتنا كانَت كُلِّش زينَة مرَتّبَة [safratna čaːnat kulliš ziːna mrattba] • **2.** نَظَّم [naḍḍam] تَنظِيم [tanḍiːm] *vn:* تنَظَّم [tnaḍḍam] *p:* He doesn't know how to plan his time. ما يُعرُف شلُون ينَظِّم وَقتَه [maː yuʕruf šluːn ynaḍḍum waktah] • **3.** سَوَّى [sawwaː] *sv* i. Who planned your house? مِنُو سَوَّى الخَرِيطَة مال بَيتَك؟ [minu sawwaː ʔilxariːṭa maːl baytak?] • **4.** صَمَّم [ṣammam] تَصمِيم [taṣmiːm] *vn:* تصَمَّم [tṣammam] *p:* Who planned your garden for you? مِنُو صَمَّملَك الحَدِيقَة مالتَك؟ [minu ṣammamlak ʔilħadiːqa maːltak?] • **5.** نَوَى [nuwaː] نِيَّة [niyya] *vn:* اِنُّوَى [ʔinnuwaː] *p:* Where do you plan to spend the summer? وين تِنوِي تِقضِي الصَّيف؟ [wiːn tinwi tigḍi ʔiṣṣayf?] • **6.** حِسَب حسَاب [ħisab ħsaːb] حساب [ħsaːb] *vn:* اِنحِسَب حسَاب [ʔinħisab ħsaːb] *p:* دَبَّر أَمر [dabbar ʔamr] تَدبِير أَمر [tadbiːr ʔamr] *vn:* تدَبَّر [tdabbar] *p:* On the salary I get, I have to plan very carefully. بِالرّاتِب اللّي أَستِلمَه، آنِي مُضطَرّ أَحسِب حسابِي بِدِقَّة [birraːtib ʔilli ʔastilmah, ʔaːni muḍṭarr ʔaħsib ħsaːbi bdigga]

to plan on • **1.** اِعتِمَد عَلَى [ʔiʕtimad ʕala] اِعتِماد [ʔiʕtimaːd] *vn: sv* i. You'd better not plan on it. أَحسَنلَك لا تِعتِمِد عَلَيه [ʔaħsanlak laː tiʕtimid ʕaliːh]

plane • **1.** مُستَوَى [mustawa] The discussion was not on a very high plane. المُناقَشَة ما كانَت عَلَى مُستَوَى كُلِّش عالِي [ʔilmunaːqaša maː čaːnat ʕala mustawaː kulliš ʕaːli] • **2.** رَندَج [randaǰ] I borrowed a plane from the carpenter. طلَبِت رَندَج مِن النَّجّار [ṭlabit randaǰ min ʔinnaǰǰaːr] • **3.** طِيّارَة [ṭiyyaːra] طِيّارات [ṭiyyaːraːt] *pl:* What sort of plane is this? هَالطِّيّارَة مِن أَيّ نُوع؟ [haṭṭiyyaːra min ʔayy nawʕ?] • **4.** مُستَوِي [mustawi] I studied plane geometry for two years. درَسِت الهَندَسَة المُستَوِيَة سَنتَين [drasit ʔilhandasa ʔilmustawya santayn]

to plane • **1.** صَفَّى [ṣaffaː] تصفِّي [tṣiffi] *vn:* تصَفَّى [tṣaffaː] *p:* ضِرَب رَندَج [ḍirab randaǰ] ضَرب رَندَج [ḍarib randaǰ] *vn:* اِنضِرَب [ʔinḍ irab] *p:* ساوَى [saːwaː] تَسوِيَة [taswiya] *vn:* تساوَى [tsaːwaː] *p:* These boards have to be planed. هَاللَّوحات لازِم تِتصَفَّى [hallawħaːt laːzim titṣaffaː]

to plane down • **1.** رَندَج [randaǰ] رَنادِج [ranaːdiǰ] *pl:* ترَندِج [trindiǰ] *vn:* ترَندَج [trandaǰ] *p:* ساوَى [saːwaː] مُساوات [musaːwaːt] *vn:* تساوَى [tsaːwaː] *p:* We'll have to plane the door down. لازِم شوَيَّة نرَندِج الباب [laːzim šwayya nrandiǰ ʔilbaːb]

planet • **1.** كَوكَب سَيّار [kawkab sayyaːr] كَواكِب سَيّارَة [kawaːkib sayyaːra] *pl:*

planned • **1.** مَرسُوم [marsuːm] We'll carry out the project as planned. راح نِنَفِّذ الخُطَّة مِثِلما مَرسُومَة [raːħ ninaffið ʔilxuṭṭa miθilma marsuːma]

plant • **1.** نَبات [nabaːt] زَرِع [zariʕ] What kind of plants are they? هُمَّ مِن أَيّ نُوع مِن النَّباتات؟ [humma min ʔayy nawʕ min ʔinnabaːtaːt] I water the plants every day. أَسقِي الزَّرِع كُلّ يوم [ʔasgi ʔizzariʕ kull yuːm] • **2.** مَعمَل [maʕmal] مَعامِل [maʕaːmil] *pl:* مَصنَع [maṣnaʕ] مَصانِع [maṣaːniʕ] *pl:* The manager showed me around the plant. المُدِير فَرَّجنِي عالمَعمَل [ʔilmudiːr farraǰni ʕalmaʕmal]

to plant • **1.** زِرَع [ziraʕ] زَرِع [zariʕ] *vn:* اِنزِرَع [ʔinziraʕ] *p:* We planted flowers in our garden. زرَعنا وَرِد بحَدِيقَتنا [zraʕna warid bħadiːqatna] • **2.** شِكَخ [šičax] شَكِخ [šačix] *vn:* اِنشِكَخ

[ʔinšičax] *p:* رَكَّز [rakkaz] تَركِيز [tarki:z] *vn:* تَرَكَّز [trakkaz] *p:* The boy scouts planted the flag in the sand and put up their tents around it. الكَشّافَة شِكخَوا العَلَم بِالرَّمُل وَنُصبَوا خيامهُم داير دايرَة [ʔilkašša:fa šičxaw ʔilʕalam birramul wnuṣbaw xaya:mhum da:yir da:yra] • **3.** خَشَّش [xaššaš] تَخشِيش [taxši:š] *vn:* تخَشَّش [txaššaš] *p:* دَخَّل [daxxal] تدخِيل، إدخال [tadxi:l, ʔidxa:l] *vn:* تدَخَّل [tdaxxal] *p:* The teacher planted bad ideas in the students' minds. المُعَلِّم خَشَّش بِعُقُول الطُّلّاب آراء مُو زينَة [ʔilmuʕallim xaššaš bʕuqu:l ʔiṭṭulla:b ʔa:ra:ʔ mu: zi:na]
*** They planted mines in the road to protect their retreat.** • **1.** ألغمَوا الطَرِيق حَتَّى يِحمُون تَراجِعهُم [ʔalɣimaw ʔiṭṭari:q ħatta yiħmu:n tara:ǰiʕhum]

plaster • **1.** بَياض [baya:ḍ] جُصّ [ǰuṣṣ] The plaster on the wall is all cracked. البَياض عَالحايِط كُلَّه مفَطَّر [ʔilbaya:ḍ ʕalħa:yiṭ kullah mfaṭṭar] • **2.** لَزقَة [lazga] لَزقات [lazga:t] *pl:* The nurse applied a mustard plaster to my back. المُمَرِّضَة حَطَّت لَزقَة خَردَل عَلَى ظَهرِي [ʔilmumarriḍa ħaṭṭat lazgat xardal ʕala ḍahri] • **3.** جبس [ǰibs] Her arm is still in a plaster cast. إيدها بَعَدها بقالَب جِبس [ʔi:dha baʕadha bqa:lab ǰibs] This figure is made of plaster of Paris. هَالتِّمثال مسَوَّى مِن جِبس [hattimθa:l msawwa: min ǰips]
to plaster • **1.** بَيَّض [bayyaḍ] تِبياض [tibya:ḍ] *vn:* تبَيَّض [tbayyaḍ] *p:* Have they finished plastering the walls yet? خَلّصَوا تِبياض الحِياطِين لَو بَعَد [xallṣaw tibya:ḍ ʔilħiya:ṭi:n law baʕad]

plastic • **1.** بلاستِك [pla:stik]

plastic surgery • **1.** جِراحَة التَجمِيل [ǰira:ħat ʔittaǰmi:l]

plate • **1.** ماعُون [ma:ʕu:n] مواعِين [mwa:ʕi:n] *pl:* There's a crack in the plate. أكُو فَطِر بِالماعُون [ʔaku faṭir bilma:ʕu:n] • **2.** شِكِل [šikil] أشكال، شكُول [ʔaška:l, šku:l] *pl:* The illustration is on Plate Three. التَّوضِيح عَلَى شِكِل رَقَم ثلاثَة [ʔittawḍi:ħ ʕala šikil raqam tla:θa] • **3.** لَوحَة [lawħa] لَوحات [lu:ħa:t] *pl:* It's very difficult to get plates for this camera. كُلِّش صَعُب تِنلِقِي لَوحات لِهَالكَامِيرا [kulliš ṣaʕub tinligi lawħa:t lihalkamira] • **4.** طَخُم [ṭaxum] طخُومَة [ṭxu:ma] *pl:* I didn't know she wore a plate. ما كِنِت أدري تِلبَس طَخُم [ma: činit ʔadri tilbas ṭaxum] • **5.** بلَيتَة [pli:ta] بلَيتات [pli:ta:t] *pl:* The floor of the tank is one single plate. قاع تانكِي الماي بلَيتَة وِحدَة [ga:ʕ ta:nki ʔilma:y pli:ta wiħda]
to plate • **1.** لَبَّس [labbas] تَلبِيس [talbi:s] *vn:* تلَبَّس [tlabbas] *p:* They make these knives of steel and then plate them with silver. يسَوُّون هَالسِّكاكِين مِن فُولاذ وَبَعدين يلَبّسُوها بالفُضَّة [ysawwu:n hassiča:či:n min fu:la:ð wbaʕdiyn ylabbisu:ha bilfuḍḍa]

platform • **1.** رَصِيف [raṣi:f] أرصِفَة [ʔarṣifa] *pl:* Let's meet on the railway platform. خَلِّي نِتلاقَى عَلَى رَصِيف المَحَطَّة [xalli: nitla:ga: ʕala raṣi:f ʔilmaħaṭṭa] • **2.** دَكَّة [dačča] دَكّات، دِكَك [dačča:t, dičač] *pl:* Back up the truck to the loading platform. رَجِّع التِّرَك مالَك لدَكَّة الحِمِل [rajjiʕ ʔittirak ma:lak ldaččat ʔilħimil] • **3.** مَنَصَّة [manaṣṣa] مَنَصّات [manaṣṣa:t] *pl:* There is a platform for the speaker in the front part of the room. أكُو مَنَصَّة لِلخَطِيب بِالجِّهَة الأمامِيَّة بالغُرفَة [ʔaku manaṣṣa lilxaṭi:b biǰǰiha ʔilʔama:miyya bilɣurfa] • **4.** مَسرَح [masraħ] مَسارِح [masa:riħ] *pl:* مَرسَح [marsaħ] The speakers were all seated on the platform. الخُطَباء كانَوا قاعدِين عَالمَسرَح [ʔilxuṭaba:ʔ ča:naw qa:ʕdi:n ʕalmasraħ]

platoon • **1.** فَصِيل [faṣi:l] فَصائِل [faṣa:ʔil] *pl:*

platter • **1.** بَلَم [balam] بلام [bla:m] *pl:* The platter won't hold the whole melon. البَلَم ما يِلزَم كُلّ الرَّقِّيَّة [ʔilbalam ma: yilzam kull ʔirraggiyya]

plausible • **1.** مَعقُول [maʕqu:l] His explanation is plausible but I don't agree with him. إيضاحاتَه مَعقُولَة بَسّ ما أتِّفِق وِيّاه [ʔi:ḍa:ħa:tah maʕqu:la bass ma: ʔattifiq wiyya:h]

play • **1.** لِعِب [liʕib] ألعاب [ʔalʕa:b] *pl:* The children are completely absorbed in their play. الأطفال مِلتِهِين بِاللِّعِب تَماماً [ʔilʔaṭfa:l miltihi:n billiʕib tama:man] • **2.** تَمثِيلِيَّة [tamθi:liyya] تَمثِيلِيّات [tamθi:liyya:t] *pl:* I heard an amusing play on the radio in spoken Iraqi. سمَعِت تَمثِيلِيَّة مُضحِكَة بِالرّادِيُو بِحَكِي عِراقِي [smaʕit tamθi:liyya muḍħika birra:dyu bħači ʕira:qi] • **3.** مَسرَحِيَّة [masraħiyya] مَسرَحِيّات [masraħiyya:t] *pl:* That company is going to perform three plays of Shakespeare this week. هالفِرقَة راح تقُوم بِتَمثِيل ثلَث مَسرَحِيّات شَكسبِير هَالإسبُوع [halfirqa ra:ħ tqu:m btamθi:l tlaθ masraħiyya:t šakspi:r halʔisbu:ʕ] • **4.** رُوايَة [ruwa:ya, riwa:ya] رُوايات [ruwa:ya:t] *pl:* We don't often get to see plays by professional actors here. ما دَيصادِف نشُوف رِوايات مِن قِبَل مُمَثِّلِين مُحتَرِفِين هنا [ma: dayṣa:dif nšu:f riwa:ya:t min qibal mumaθθili:n muħtarifi:n hna] • **5.** مَلعَب [malʕab] مَلاعِب [mala:ʕib] *pl:* The steering wheel has too much play. السُّكّان بِيه هوايَة مَلعَب [ʔissukka:n bi:h hwa:ya malʕab]
to play • **1.** لِعَب [liʕab] لَعِب [laʕib] *vn:* اِنلِعَب [ʔinliʕab] *p:* The children are playing in the garden. الجِّهال دَيلِعبُون بِالحَدِيقَة [ʔiǰǰiha:l dayliʕbu:n bilħadi:qa] We played for money. لِعَبنا عَلَى فلُوس [liʕabna ʕala flu:s] • **2.** دَقّ [dagg] دَقّ [dagg] *vn:* اِندَقّ [ʔindagg] *p:* عِزَف [ʕizaf] عَزِف [ʕazif] *vn:* اِنعِزَف [ʔinʕizaf] *p:* He plays the violin very well. يدُقّ كَمَنجَة كُلِّش زين [ydugg kamanǰa kulliš zi:n] • **3.** قام بِالدَّور [qa:m biddawr] قِيام [qiya:m] *vn: sv* u. مَثَّل [maθθal] تَمثِيل [tamθi:l] *vn:* تمَثَّل [tmaθθal] *p:* Who is playing the lead? مِنُو دَيقُوم بِدَور البَطَل؟ [minu dayqu:m bdawr ʔalbaṭal?] • **4.** اِشتِغَل [ʔištiɣal] شُغُل [šuɣul] *vn: sv* u. اِنعِرَض [ʔinʕiraḍ] عَرِض [ʕariḍ] *vn: sv* i. What film is playing tonight? يا فِلِم دَيِشتِغِل هاللَّيلَة؟ [ya: filim dayištiɣul

hallayla?] • **5.** ذَبّ [ðabb] ذَبّ [ðabb] *vn:* اِنذَبّ [ʔinðabb] *p:* He played his highest card. ذَبّ أعلَى وَرَقَة بِيدَه [ðabb ʔaʕla waraqa biːdah] • **6.** سَوَّى [sawwaː] تَسوِيَة [taswiya] *vn: sv* i. He played a joke on me. سَوَّى بِيّا نُكتَة [sawwaː biyya nukta]

to play a role • **1.** مَثَّل [maθθal] تَمثِيل [tamθiːl] *vn:* تمَثَّل [tmaθθal] *p:* They asked me to play the role of the Juliet in the play طِلبَوا مِنّي أَمَثِّل جُوليات بِالمَسرَحِيَّة [ṭilbaw minni ʔamaθθil juːlyaːt bilmasraħiyya] • **2.** لِعَب [liʕab] لِعِب [liʕib] *vn: sv* a. He played an important role in the negotiations. لِعَب دَور مُهِمّ بالمُفاوَضات [liʕab dawr muhimm bilmufaːwaðaːt]

to play around • **1.** ضَيَّع وَقِت [ðayyaʕ wakit] تَضيِيع وَقِت [taðyiːʕ wakit] *vn: sv* i. You've been playing around long enough. يِكفِي بَعَد تضَيِّع وَقتَك [yikfi baʕad dðayyiʕ waktak] • **2.** عِبَث [ʕibaθ] عَبِث [ʕabiθ] *vn: sv* a. لِعَب [liʕab] لِعِب [liʕib] *vn: sv* a. Stop playing around with the radio. بَسّ عاد، لا تِعبَث بِالرّاديُو [bass ʕaːd, laː tiʕbaθ birraːdyu]

to play fair • **1.** أنصَف [ʔanṣaf] إنصاف [ʔinṣaːf] *vn: sv* i. He didn't play fair with me. ما أنصَف وِيّايا [maː ʔanṣaf wiyyaːya]

to play up • **1.** أظهَر [ʔaðhar] اِظهار [ʔiðhaːr] *vn: sv* i. He played up her good qualities. أظهَر صِفاتها الزَّينَة [ʔaðhar ṣifaːtha ʔizzayna]

player • **1.** لَعُوب [laʕuːb] لُواعِيب [luwaːʕiːb] *pl:* One of the players got hurt during the game. واحِد مِن اللُّواعِيب تأذَّى أثناء اللِّعِب [waːħid min ʔilluwaːʕiːb tʔaððaː ʔaθnaːʔ ʔilliʕib] • **2.** مُمَثِّل [mumaθθil] مُمَثِّلِين [mumaθθiliːn] *pl:* There was a party for the players after the play. كانَت حَفلَة لِلمُمَثِّلِين بَعد التَّمثِيل [čaːnat ħafla lilmumaθθiliːn baʕd ʔittamθiːl]

playground • **1.** مَلعَب [malʕab] مَلاعِب [malaːʕib] *pl:*

playing card • **1.** وَرَقَة [warqa] وَرقات [warqaːt] *pl:*

plea • **1.** اِلتِماس [ʔiltimaːs] اِلتِماسات [ʔiltimaːsaːt] *pl:* رَجاء [rajaːʔ] رَجاءات [rajaːʔaːt] *pl:* He ignored my plea. ما دار بال لإلتِماسِي [maː daːr baːl lʔiltimaːsi] • **2.** تَوَسُّل [tawassul] تَوَسُّلات [tawassulaːt] *pl:* All my pleas were in vain. كُلّ تَوَسُّلاتِي راحَت عَبَث [kull tawassulaːti raːħat ʕabaθ]

to plead • **1.** توَسَّل [twassal] تَوَسُّل [tawassul] *vn: sv* a. اِلتِمَس [ʔiltimas] اِلتِماس [ʔiltimaːs] *vn: sv* i. رِجَى [rijaː] رَجاء [rajaːʔ] *vn: sv* u. She pleaded with him to stay. توَسَّلَت بِيه يبقَى [twassalat biːh yibqaː] • **2.** ترافَع [traːfaʕ] تَرافُع [taraːfuʕ] *vn: sv* a. I have retained the best lawyer in town to plead my case. لِزَمِت أحسَن مُحامِي بِالوِلايَة حَتَّى يترافَع بدَعوتِي [lizamit ʔaħsan muħaːmi bilwilaːya ħatta yitraːfaʕ bdaʕwti]

* **Do you plead guilty?** • **1.** إنتَ مُذنِب أم لا؟ [ʔinta muðnib ʔam laː?]

pleasant • **1.** لَطِيف [laṭiːf] لَطِيفِين، لُطَفاء [laṭiːfiːn, luṭafaːʔ] *pl:* She's a pleasant person. هِيَّ فَدّ وِحدَة لَطِيفَة [hiyya fadd wiħda laṭiːfa] • **2.** مُبهِج [mubhij] We spent a rather pleasant evening there. قضَينا هناك فَدّ لَيلَة مُبهِجَة نوعاً ما [gðiːna hnaːk fadd layla mubhija nawʕan maː] • **3.** سَعِيد [saʕiːd] سَعِيدِين، سُعَداء [saʕiːdiːn, suʕadaːʔ] *pl:* Good-bye! Have a pleasant trip! مَعَ السَّلامَة أتمَنّالَك سَفرَة سَعِيدَة [maʕa ʔissalaːma ʔatmannaːlak safra saʕiːda] • **4.** سارّ [saːrr] What a pleasant surprise! هاي شلُون مُفاجَأة سارَّة [haːy šluːn mufaːjaʔa saːrra]

* **It isn't pleasant for me to have to do this.** • **1.** يُؤسِفنِي أن أضطَرّ أسَوِّيها [yuʔsifni ʔan ʔaðṭarr ʔasawwiːha] / ما يهُون عَلَيّا أسَوِّيها [maː yhuːn ʕalayya ʔasawwiːha]

please • **1.** رَجاءاً [rajaːʔan] بَلَّه [ballah] لُطفاً [luṭfan] مِن فَضلَك [min faðlak] أرجُوك [ʔarjuːk] Please shut the door. رَجاءاً سِدّ الباب [rajaːʔan sidd ʔilbaːb]

to please • **1.** عِجَب [ʕijab] إعجاب [ʔiʕjaːb] *vn:* اِنعِجَب [ʔinʕijab] *p:* How does this hat please you? شلُون تِعجبَك هَالشَّفقَة؟ [šluːn tiʕijbak haššafqa?] Do as you please. سَوِّي اللِّي يِعجبَك [sawwiː ʔilli yiʕijbak] Do as you please. بكَيفَك [bkayfak] • **2.** أرضَى [ʔarðaː] إرضاء [ʔirðaːʔ] *vn: sv* i. He's hard to please. هُوَّ فَدّ واحِد صَعُب إرضاءه [huwwa fadd waːħid ṣaʕub ʔirðaːʔah] • **3.** رَضَّى [raððaː] تَرضِيَة، ترضِّي [tarðiya, triððī] *vn:* ترَضَّى [traððaː] *p:* You can't please the whole world. ما تِقدَر ترَضِّي كُلّ العالَم [maː tigdar traððī kull ʔilʕaːlam] • **4.** سَرّ [sarr] سُرُور [suruːr] *vn:* اِنسَرّ [ʔinsarr] *p:* Your letter pleased me very much. مَكتُوبَك سَرّنِي هوايَة [maktuːbak sarrni hwaːya]

to be pleased • **1.** كَيَّف [kayyaf] تكَيِّف [tkiyyif] *vn: sv* i. اِنسَرّ [ʔinsarr] اِنسِرار [ʔinsiraːr] *vn: sv* a. He was pleased with it. كَيَّف بِيها [kayyaf biːha]

pleasing • **1.** لَطِيف [laṭiːf] لَطِيفِين [laṭiːfiːn] *pl:* He has a pleasing personality. عِندَه شَخصِيَّة لَطِيفَة [ʕindah šaxṣiyya laṭiːfa] • **2.** حِلو [ħilw] She has a pleasing voice. عِدها صَوت حِلو [ʕidha ṣawt ħilw]

pleasure • **1.** لَذَّة [laðða] لَذّات [laððaːt] *pl:* I get a lot of pleasure out of the work. أشعُر بلَذَّة بِالشُّغُل [ʔašʕur blaðða biššuɣul] I get a lot of pleasure out of the work. أتلَذَّذ بِالشُّغُل [ʔatlaððað biššuɣul] • **2.** مِتعَة [mitʕa] مِتَع [mitaʕ] *pl:* Watching him swim was a real pleasure. شُوفتَه يِسبَح كانَت مِتعَة لِلعَين [šawftah yisbaħ čaːnat mitʕa lilʕayn] • **3.** لَهو [lahw] هَزَل [hazal] Business before pleasure. الشُّغُل قَبِل اللَّهو [ʔiššuɣul gabil ʔillahw] • **4.** سُرُور [suruːr] We accepted their invitation to dinner with great pleasure. قِبَلنا عَزِيمَتهُم عالعَشا بكُلّ سُرُور [qibalna ʕaziːmathum ʕalʕaša bkull suruːr]

* **The pleasure is all mine.** • **1.** آنِي المَمنُون [ʔaːni ʔilmamnuːn]

pleat • **1.** كَسرَة [kasra] كَسرات [kasra:t] *pl:* ثَنيَة [θanya] ثَنيَات [θanya:t] *pl:* Do you want the dress with or without pleats? تريدين البَدلَة بيها كَسرات لَو لا؟ [tri:di:n ʔilbadla bi:ha kasra:t law la:?]

to pleat • **1.** كَسَّر [kassar] تكِسِّر [tkissir] *vn:* تكَسَّر [tkassar] *p:* ثَنّى [θanna:] تثِنّي [tθinni] *vn:* تثَنّى [tθanna:] *p:* Are you going to pleat the skirt or leave it straight? إنتي رايحَة تثَنِّين التَّنّورَة لَو تخَلّيها عَدلَة [ʔinti ra:yħa tθanni:n ʔittannu:ra law txalli:ha ʕadla]

plebiscite • **1.** اِستِفتاء [ʔistifta:ʔ] اِستِفتاءات [ʔistifta:ʔa:t] *pl:*

pledge • **1.** عَهَد [ʕahad] He didn't keep his pledge. ما وُفى بعَهدَه [ma: wufa: bʕahdah]

to pledge • **1.** أخَذ عَهَد مِن [ʔaxað ʕahad min] أخِذ عَهَد مِن [ʔaxið ʕahad min] *vn: sv* u. He pledged me to secrecy. أخَذ عَهَد مِنّي بالكُتمان [ʔaxað ʕahad minni bilkutma:n] • **2.** تعَهَّد [tʕahhad] تَعَهُّد [taʕahhud] *vn: sv* a. I pledged to vote for him in the election. تعَهَّدِت أنطيه صَوتي بالإنتِخاب [tʕahhadit ʔanṭi:h ṣawti bilʔintixa:b]

plentiful • **1.** وافِر [wa:fir] غَزير [ɣazi:r] مَبذُول [mabðu:l]

plenty • **1.** هوايَة [hwa:ya] كثير [kθi:r] You have plenty of time. عِندَك هوايَة وَقِت [ʕindak hwa:ya wakit] You have to get plenty of sleep. لازِم تنام كثير [la:zim tna:m kθi:r] • **2.** مِتوَفِّر [mitwaffir] هوايَة [hwa:ya] كثير [kθi:r] There is plenty of rice in the market. التِّمَّن مِتوَفِّر بالسُّوق [ʔittimman mitwaffir bissu:g]

pleurisy • **1.** ذات الجَّنب [ða:t ʔiǰǰanb]

pliable • **1.** لَيِّن [layyin]

pliers • **1.** كِلّابتَين [čilla:btayn] كِلّابتَينات [čilla:bti:na:t] *pl:* بلايِس [pla:yis] بلايِسات [pla:yisa:t] *pl:*

plight • **1.** وَضِع [waḍiʕ] أوضاع [ʔawḍa:ʕ] *pl:* We are aware of their plight and will do everything we can to help them. إحنا نِدري وَضِعهُم وَراح نسَوّي كُلّ ما نِقدَر عَليه حَتّى نعاونهُم [ʔiħna nidri waḍiʕhum wra:ħ nsawwi kull ma: nigdar ʕali:h ħatta nʕa:winhum]

plot • **1.** مُؤامَرَة [muʔa:mara] مُؤامَرات [muʔa:mara:t] *pl:* دَسيسَة [dasi:sa] دَسائِس [dasa:ʔis] *pl:* The plot was discovered in time. المُؤامَرَة اِنكِشفَت بالوَقت المُناسِب [ʔilmuʔa:mara ʔinkišfat bilwaqt ʔilmuna:sib] • **2.** قِطعَة [qiṭʕa] قِطَع [qiṭaʕ] *pl:* وُصلَة [wuṣla] وُصَل [wuṣal] *pl:* We bought a plot of land near the river. اِشتِرَينا قِطعَة قاع عالنَّهَر [ʔištiri:na qiṭʕat ga:ʕ ʕannahar] • **3.** سِلسِلَة [silsila] سَلاسِل [sala:sil] *pl:* The story has an interesting plot. القُصَّة سِلسِلَة حَوادِثها مُمتِعَة [ʔilquṣṣa silsilat ħawa:diθha mumtiʕa]

plot of land (leased) • **1.** عَرَصَة [ʕaraṣa] عَرَصات [ʕaraṣa:t] *pl:*

to plot • **1.** تآمَر [tʔa:mar] تَآمُر [taʔa:mur] *vn: sv* a. They plotted against the government. تآمرَوا ضِدّ الحُكُومَة [tʔa:mraw ḍidd ʔilħuku:ma]

plow • **1.** مِحراث [miħra:θ] مَحاريث [maħa:ri:θ] *pl:* You need a heavier plow. تِحتاج مِحراث أثقَل [tiħta:ǰ miħra:θ ʔaθgal]

to plow • **1.** حِرَث [ħiraθ] حَرِث [ħariθ] *vn:* اِنحِرَث [ʔinħiraθ] *p:* كِرَب [kirab] كَرُب، كَراب [karub, kara:b] *vn:* اِنكِرَب [ʔinkirab] *p:* I'll need all day to plow this field. أحتاج طُول النَّهار حَتّى أحرِث هالحَقِل [ʔaħta:ǰ ṭu:l ʔinnaha:r ħatta ʔaħriθ halħaqil]

to pluck • **1.** نِتَف [nitaf] نَتِف [natif] *vn:* اِنّتَف [ʔinnitaf] *p:* Did you pluck the chicken yet? نِتَفتها لِلدِّجاجَة لَو بَعَد؟ [nitafitha liddiǰa:ǰa law baʕad?]

plug • **1.** قَبَغ [qabaɣ] قَبَغات [qabaɣa:t] *pl:* سَدّاد [sadda:d] سَدّادات [sadda:da:t] *pl:* The sink needs a new plug. المَسلَخ يِرّادلَه قَبَغ جِديد [ʔilmaslax yirra:dlah qabaɣ ǰidi:d] • **2.** بلَك [plakk] بلَكّات [plakka:t] *pl:* Your car needs a new set of plugs. سَيّارتَك يِنرادِلها طَخُم بلَكّات جِديد [sayya:rtak yinra:dilha ṭaxum plakka:t ǰidi:d]

to plug • **1.** سَدّ [sadd] سَدّ [sadd] *vn:* اِنسَدّ [ʔinsadd] *p:* Plug the hole. سِدّ الزِّرُف [sidd ʔizziruf] The pipe is plugged. البُوري مَسدُود [ʔilbu:ri masdu:d]

to plug in • **1.** شَكَّل بلَك [šakkal plakk] تَشكِيل، تشِكِّل [taški:l tšikkil] *vn: sv* i. Plug in the fan. شَكِّل البلَك مال المَهَفَّة [šakkil ʔilplakk ma:l ʔilmhaffa]

plum • **1.** عِنجاصَة [ʕinǰa:ṣa] عِنجاصات [ʕinǰa:ṣa:t] *pl:* عِنجاص [ʕinǰa:ṣ] *Collective*

plumber • **1.** أبُو بُوريّات [ʔabu bu:riyya:t] أهَل بُوريّات [ʔahal bu:riyya:t] *pl:*

plump • **1.** مَترُوس [matru:s] ثِخِين [θixi:n] ثخان [θxa:n] *pl:* She is a little on the plump side. هاي شوَيَّة مَترُوسَة [ha:y šwayya matru:sa]

to plunge • **1.** غَطّ [ɣaṭṭ] غَطّ [ɣaṭṭ] *vn: sv* u. غِطَس [ɣiṭas] غَطِس [ɣaṭis] *vn: sv* u. He plunged into the water. غَطّ بالماي [ɣaṭṭ bilma:y] When he heard the boy shouting in the river, he plunged in after him and pulled him out. مِن سِمَع الوَلَد دَيصَيِّح بالنَّهَر، غِطَس عَليه وَجَرَّه [min simaʕ ʔilwalad dayṣayyiħ binnahar, ɣiṭas ʕali:h wǰarrah] • **2.** كَيَّت [čayyat] تكَيِّت [tčiyyit] *vn: sv* i. He plunged into the burning house. كَيَّت بالبَيت اللّي دَيحتِرِق [čayyat bilbayt ʔilli dayiħtirig] • **3.** غَطَّس [ɣaṭṭas] تغِطِّس [tɣiṭṭis] *vn: sv* i. He plunged his hand into the cold water. غَطَّس إيدَه بالماي البارِد [ɣaṭṭas ʔi:dah bilma:y ʔilba:rid]

P

plural • **1.** جَمع [ǰamiʕ] جُمُوع [ǰumu:ʕ] *pl:* What is the plural of "bayt"? شِنُو جَمِع "بَيت"؟ [šinu ǰamiʕ "bayt"?]

broken plural • **1.** جَمِع تَكسِير [ǰamiʕ taksi:r]

sound plural • **1.** جَمِع سالِم [ǰamiʕ sa:lim]

plus • **1.** زايِد [za:yid] وَ [w-] Four plus three is seven. أربَعَة زايِد ثلاثَة يسَوِّي سَبعَة [ʔarbaʕa za:yid tla:θa ysawwi sabʕa]

plywood • **1.** خِشَب معاكَس [xišab mʕa:kas]

pneumonia • **1.** ذات الرِئَة [ða:t ʔirriʔa]

pocket • **1.** جيب [ǰayb] Put this in your pocket. حُطّ هاي بجَيبَك [ħuṭṭ ha:y bǰaybak]

to pocket • **1.** ضِرَب [ḍirab] ضَرب [ḍarib] *vn: sv* u. لَفّ [laff] لَفّ [laff] *vn: sv* i. His partner pocketed all the profits. شَريكَه ضِرَب عَليه كُلّ الأرباح [šari:kah ḍirab ʕali:h kull ʔilʔarba:ħ]

pocketbook • **1.** جَنطَة إيد [ǰanṭat ʔi:d] جُنَط إيد [ǰunaṭ ʔi:d] *pl:* The thief stole the pocketbook from the woman and ran away. الحَرامِي باق جَنطَة الإيد مِن المِريَّة وَانهِزَم [ʔilħara:mi ba:g ǰanṭat ʔilʔi:d min ʔilimrayya wʔinhizam] • **2.** جِزدان [ǰizda:n] جِزدانات، جَزادِين [ǰizda:na:t, ǰaza:di:n] *pl:* He took out his pocketbook and gave me some change. طَلَّع جِزدانَه وَإنطانِي خُردَة [ṭallaʕ ǰizda:nah wʔinṭa:ni xurda]

pocketknife • **1.** جاكُوجَة [ča:ku:ča] جَواكِيج [čawa:ki:č] *pl:* May I borrow your pocketknife? أقدَر أطلُب الجّاكُوجَة مالتَك؟ [ʔagdar ʔaṭlub ʔičča:ku:ča ma:ltak?]

P

podium • **1.** مَنَصَّة [manaṣṣa] مَنَصّات [manaṣṣa:t] *pl:* The conductor stepped up onto the podium. رَئِيس الفِرقَة المُوسِيقِيَّة صِعَد عالمَنَصَّة [raʔi:s ʔilfirqa ʔilmusi:qiyya ṣiʕad ʕalmanaṣṣa]

poem • **1.** قَصِيدَة [qaṣi:da] قَصائِد [qasa:ʔid] *pl:* This book contains all his poems. هَالكِتاب يِحوِي كُلّ قَصايدَه [halkita:b yiħwi kull qaṣa:ydah]

poet • **1.** شاعِر [ša:ʕir] شُعَراء [šuʕara:ʔ] *pl:*

poetry • **1.** شِعِر [šiʕir] أشعار [ʔašʕa:r] *pl:* My brother writes beautiful poetry. أخُويَا يِنظُم شِعِر بَدِيع [ʔaxu:ya yinḍum šiʕir badi:ʕ]

point • **1.** نَبُّولَة [nabbu:la] نَبُّولات [nabbu:la:t] *pl:* I broke the point of my pencil. كِسَرِت نَبُّولَة القَلَم مالِي [kisarit nabbu:lat ʔilqalam ma:li] • **2.** راس [ra:s] رُوس [ru:s] *pl:* طَرَف [ṭaraf] أطراف [ʔaṭra:f] *pl:* I broke the point of my knife. كِسَرِت راس السِّكِّينَة مالتِي [kisarit ra:s ʔissiččì:na ma:lti] • **3.** نُقطَة [nuqṭa] نُقَط [nuqaṭ] *pl:* Our team scored 23 points. فَرِيقنا سَجَّل ثلاثَة وَعِشرِين نُقطَة [fari:qna saǰǰal tla:θa wʕišri:n nuqṭa] We have gone over the contract point by point. دِرَسنا العَقِد نُقطَة نُقطَة [dirasna ʔilʕaqid nuqṭa nuqṭa] Women are his weak point. النِّساء نُقطَة الضُّعُف عِندَه [ʔinnisa:ʔ nuqṭat ʔiḍḍuʕuf ʕindah] • **4.** مَقصُود [maqṣu:d] بَيت القَصِيد [bayt ʔilqaṣi:d] قَصِد [qaṣid] You missed the point. فاتَك المَقصُود [fa:tak ʔilmaqṣu:d] You missed the point. فاتَك بَيت القَصِيد [fa:tak bayt ʔalqaṣi:d] • **5.** مَوضُوع [mawḍu:ʕ] مَواضِيع [mawa:ḍi:ʕ] *pl:* That is beside the point. هَذا خارِج المَوضُوع [ha:ða xa:riǰ ʔilmawḍu:ʕ] • **6.** حَدّ [ħadd] حدُود [ħdu:d] *pl:* I can understand it up to a certain point. أقدَر أفتِهِمها إلَى حَدّ مُعَيَّن [ʔagdar ʔaftihimha ʔila ħadd muʕayyan] • **7.** ناحِيَة [na:ħiya] نَواحِي [nawa:ħi] *pl:* مَزِيَّة [maziyya] مَزايا [maza:ya] *pl:* He has good points, too. عِندَه نَواحِي [ʕindah nawa:ħi] He has good points, too. بِيه مَزايا [bi:h maza:ya] • **8.** مُوجِب [mu:ǰib] There is no point in getting there before they open the doors. ماكُو مُوجِب نكُون هناك قَبُل ما يِفتَحُون الباب [ma:ku mu:ǰib nku:n hna:k gabul ma: yiftaħu:n ʔilba:b] • **9.** مَركَز [markaz] مَراكِز [mara:kiz] *pl:* The police set up their strong point at the entrance to the city. الشُّرطَة حَطُّوا مَركَز قُوَّتهُم بمَدخَل المَدِينَة [ʔiššurṭa ħaṭṭaw markaz quwwathum bmadxal ʔilmadi:na]

*** Come to the point and stop beating about the bush.** • **1.** قُول الحَقِيقَة ولا تظَلّ تِتهَزَّم [gu:l ʔilħaqi:qa wla: tḍull tithazzam]

on the point of • **1.** عَلَى وَشَك [ʕala wašak] We were on the point of leaving when company arrived. كِنّا عَلَى وَشَك دَنِطلَع مِن جُونا خُطّار [činna ʕala wašak daniṭlaʕ min ǰu:na xuṭṭa:r]

point of view • **1.** وُجهَة نَظَر [wuǰhat naḍar] وَجهات نَظَر [waǰha:t naḍar] *pl:* Our points of view differ. وَجهات نَظَرنا تِختِلِف [waǰha:t naḍarna tixtilif] • **2.** جِهَة [ǰiha] جِهات [ǰiha:t] *pl:* ناحِيَة [na:ħiya] نَواحِي [nawa:ħi] *pl:* From this point of view he's right. مِن هَالجِهَة هُوَّ مُحِقّ [min haǰǰiha huwwa muħiqq]

to the point • **1.** بِالصَّمِيم [bişṣami:m] مُصِيب [muṣi:b] His comments are always to the point. تَعلِيقاتَه دائِماً بِالصَّمِيم [taʕli:qa:tah da:ʔiman bişṣami:m]

to make a point of • **1.** حَطّ عالبَال [ħaṭṭ ʕalba:l] Make a point to be on time. حُطّ عَلَى بالَك تكُون عالوَقِت [ħuṭṭ ʕala ba:lak tku:n ʕalwakit]

to point • **1.** شار [ša:r] إشارَة [ʔiša:ra] *vn:* اِنشار [ʔinša:r] *p:* أشَّر [ʔaššar] تَأشِير [taʔši:r] *vn:* تأشَّر [tʔaššar] *p:* The arrow points north. السَّهِم يشِير لِلشِّمال [ʔissahim yši:r liššima:l] Point to the man you mean. أشِّر عالرِّجّال اللّي تِعنِيه [ʔaššir ʕarriǰǰa:l ʔilli tiʕni:h] Point out the place you told me about. أشِّر عالمَكان اللّي قِتلِي عَنَّه [ʔaššir ʕalmaka:n ʔilli gitli ʕannah] • **2.** دَلّ [dall] تدِلِّي [tdilli] *vn:* اِندَلّ [ʔindall] *p:* دَلَّى [dalla:] تدِلِّي [tdilli] *vn:* تدَلَّى [tdalla:] *p:* All the signs point towards a cold winter. كُلّ المَظاهِر تدِلّ عَلَى شِتا بارِد [kull ʔilmaḍa:hir ddill ʕala šita ba:rid] • **3.** وَجَّه [waǰǰah] تَوجِيه [tawǰi:h] *vn:* توَجَّه [twaǰǰah] *p:* Don't point the gun at me! لا توَجِّه البُندُقِيَّة عَلَيّا [la: twaǰǰih ʔilbunduqiyya ʕalayya]

pointed • **1.** مِنَبَّل [mnabbal] حادّ [ħa:dd] Be careful with that pointed stick. دير بالَك مِن هَالعَصايَة المَنَبْلَة [di:r ba:lak min halʕaṣa:ya ʔilmnabbla] • **2.** حادّ [ħa:dd] She's always making pointed remarks. هِيَّ دائماً تعَلِّق تَعليقات حادَّة [hiyya da:ʔiman tʕalliq taʕli:qa:t ħa:dda]

poise • **1.** رَزانَة [raza:na] اِتِّزان [ʔittiza:n] She never loses her poise. أَبَداً ما تِفقُد رَزانَتها [ʔabadan ma: tifqud raza:natha]

poised • **1.** رَزينَة [razi:na] She is very poised for her age. كُلِّش رَزينَة بِالنِّسبَة لعُمُرها [kulliš razi:na binnisba lʕumurha]

poison • **1.** سِمّ [simm] سَمّ [samm] Don't touch it, it's a poison. لا تطُخَّه، هَذا سَمّ [la: ṭṭuxxah, ha:ða samm] • **2.** سامّ [sa:mm] They're using poison gases in their war against the royalists. يِستَعمِلُون غازات سامَّة بِحَربهُم ضِدّ المَلَكِيِّين [yistaʕmilu:n ɣa:za:t sa:mma bħarubhum ðidd ʔilmalakiyyi:n]

to poison • **1.** سَمّ [samm] سَمّ [samm] *vn:* اِنسَمّ [ʔinsamm] *p:* Our dog has been poisoned. كَلبنا اِنسَمّ [čalibna ʔinsamm] • **2.** سَمَّم [sammam] تَسمِيم [tasmi:m] *vn:* تسَمَّم [tsammam] *p:* Our dog got poisoned from eating rotten meat. كَلِبنا تسَمَّم مِن أَكَل لَحَم جايِف [čalibna tsammam min ʔakal laħam ǰa:yif]

poisonous • **1.** سامّ [sa:mm] مُسِمّ [musimm]

to poke • **1.** نَغّ [naɣɣ] نَغّ [naɣɣ] *vn:* اِنَّغّ [ʔinnaɣɣ] *p:* He'll wake up if you poke him. يِقعُد إذا تنُغَّه [yigʕud ʔiða tnuɣɣah]

poker • **1.** بوكَر [pu:kar] Do you know how to play poker? تُعرُف تِلعَب بُوكَر؟ [tuʕruf tilʕab pu:kar?]

polar • **1.** قُطبِي [quṭbi] This is a polar bear. هَذا دِبّ قُطبِي [ha:ða dibb quṭbi]

pole • **1.** The water was so shallow they had to use the pole to push the boat. الماي كان كُلِّش ضَحِل اِضطَرّوا يِستَعمِلُون المَردِي الدَفع البَلَم [ʔilma:y ča:n kulliš ðaħil ʔiðṭarraw yistaʕmilu:n ʔilmardi lidafʕ ʔilbalam] • **2.** عَمُود [ʕamu:d] عَوامِيد، أَعمِدَة [ʕawa:mi:d, ʔaʕmida] *pl:* The car hit a telephone pole. السَّيّارَة ضُربَت عَمُود تِلِفُون [ʔissayya:ra ðurbat ʕamu:d tilifu:n] • **3.** زانَة [za:na] زانات [za:na:t] *pl:* The pole broke just as he went over the bar. اِنكِسرَت الزّانَة مِن دَيُقمُز فُوق العارِضَة [ʔinkisrat ʔizza:na min dayugmuz fu:g ʔilʕa:riða] • **4.** قُطُب [quṭub] أَقطاب [ʔaqṭa:b] *pl:* How cold does it get at the poles? شقَدّ تصِير بارِدَة بِالقُطبَين؟ [šgadd tṣi:r ba:rda bilquṭbayn?]

to pole • **1.** مَشّى بِالمَردِي [mašša: bilmardi] تمِشِّي بِالمَردِي [tmišši] *vn:* *sv* i. In the marshes they pole the boats from one place to another. بِالأَهوار يمَشُّون المَشاحِيف بِالمَردِي مِن مُكان لمَكان [bilʔahwa:r ymaššu:n ʔilmaša:ħi:f bilmardi min muka:n lmuka:n]

police • **1.** شُرطَة [šurṭa]

to police • **1.** خُفَر [xufar] خَفَر [xafar] *vn:* اِنخُفَر [ʔinxufar] *p:* The streets are well - policed. الشَّوارِع زين مَخفُورَة [ʔiššawa:riʕ zi:n maxfu:ra]

police blotter • **1.** سِجِل وَقائِع الشُرطَة [siǰil waqa:ʔiʕ ʔiššurṭa]

policeman • **1.** شُرطِي [šurṭi] شُرطِيِّين، شُرطَة [šurṭi:yyi:n, šurṭa] *pl:*

police station • **1.** مَركَز شُرطَة [markaz šurṭa] مَراكِز شُرطَة [mara:kiz šurṭa] *pl:* Where is the nearest police station? وين أَقرَب مَركَز شُرطَة؟ [wi:n ʔaqrab markaz šurṭa?] • **2.** مَخفَر [maxfar] مَخافِر شُرطَة [maxa:fir šurṭa] *pl:* There is a police station halfway between the two villages. أَكُو مَخفَر الشُّرطَة بنُصّ الطَّرِيق اللِّي بين القَريتَين [ʔaku maxfar ʔiššurṭa bnuṣṣ ʔiṭṭari:q ʔilli bayn ʔilqaryatayn]

policy • **1.** سِياسَة [siya:sa] سِياسات [siya:sa:t] *pl:* I make it a policy to be on time. مِن سِياستِي أَن أَكُون عالوَقت [min siya:sti ʔan ʔaku:n ʕalwakit] We can't support his policy. ما نِقدَر نأَيِّد سِياستَه [ma: nigdar nʔayyid siya:stah] • **2.** عَقِد [ʕaqid] عُقُود [ʕuqu:d] *pl:* Don't let your life-insurance police lapse. لا تخَلِّي عَقد التَّأمِين مالَك تفُوت مُدَّتَه [la: txalli ʕaqd ʔittaʔmi:n ma:lak tfu:t muddatah]

polish • **1.** صُبُغ [ṣubuɣ] أَصباغ [ʔaṣba:ɣ] *pl:* I need some brown polish for my new shoes. أَحتاج شوَيَّة صُبُغ قَهوائِي لحِذائِي الجِّدِيد [ʔaħta:ǰ šwayya ṣubuɣ qahwa:ʔi lħiða:ʔi ʔijǰidi:d] • **2.** صَقِل [ṣaqil] تَهذِيب [tahði:b] He needs a little more polish. يِحتاج شوَيَّة صَقِل بَعَد [yiħta:ǰ šwayya ṣaqil baʕad]

to polish • **1.** لَمَّع [lammaʕ] تَلمِيع [talmi:ʕ] *vn:* تلَمَّع [tlammaʕ] *p:* صِقَل [ṣiqal] صَقِل [ṣaqil] *vn:* اِنصِقَل [ʔinṣiqal] *p:* I haven't polished the furniture yet. بَعَد ما لَمَّعِت الأَثاث [baʕad ma: lammaʕit ʔilʔaθa:θ] The silver needs polishing. الفُضِّيّات تِحتاج تَلمِيع [ʔilfuððiyya:t tiħta:ǰ talmi:ʕ] • **2.** صَبَغ [ṣubaɣ] صَبُغ [ṣabuɣ] *vn:* اِنصُبَغ [ʔinṣubaɣ] *p:* I didn't have time to polish my shoes. ما صار عِندِي وَقت أَصبُغ قُندَرتِي [ma: ṣa:r ʕindi wakit ʔaṣbuɣ qundarti]

polite • **1.** مُجامِل [muǰa:mil] مُؤَدَّب [muʔaddab] He's not very polite. هُوَّ مُو مُجامِل كُلِّش [huwwa mu: muǰa:mil kulliš]

political • **1.** سِياسِي [siya:si] Do you belong to any political party? إنتَ مِنتِمِي لأَيّ حِزِب سِياسِي؟ [ʔinta mintimi lʔayy ħizib siya:si?]

P

politician • **1.** سِياسِي [siya:si] سِياسِيِّين [siya:siyyi:n] *pl:*

politics • **1.** سِياسَة [siya:sa] سِياسات [siya:sa:t] *pl:* I'm not interested in politics. السِّياسَة مُو شُغلِي [ʔissiya:sa mu: šuɣli] I'm not interested in politics. السِّياسَة ما تهِمّني [ʔissiya:s ma: thimmni]

pollen • **1.** طَلِيع [ṭali:ʕ]

to pollinate • **1.** لَقَّح [laqqaħ] تَلقِيح [talqi:ħ] *vn:* تلَقَّح [tlaqqaħ] *p:* Date palms are pollinated by hand. النَّخَل يِتلَقَّح بالإيد [ʔinnaxal yitlaggaħ bilʔi:d]

polls • **1.** مَركَز اِنتِخابِي [markaz ʔintixa:bi] مَراكِز اِنتِخابِيَّة [mara:kiz ʔintixa:biyya] *pl:*

to pollute • **1.** لَوَّث [lawwaθ] تَلوِيث [talwi:θ] *vn:* تلَوَّث [tlawwaθ] *p:* نَجَّس [naǰǰas, naggas] تَنجِيس [tangi:s] *vn:* تنَجَّس [tnaggas] *p:* First we must find what is polluting the water in the well. أَوَّلاً لازِم نشُوف شِنُو اللِّي دَيلَوِّث الماي بالبِير [ʔawwalan la:zim nšu:f šinu ʔilli daylawwiθ ʔilma:y bilbi:r]

polygamy • **1.** تَعَدُّد الزَوجات [taʕaddud ʔizzawǰa:t]

pomegranate • **1.** رُمّانَة [rumma:na] رُمّانات [rumma:na:t] *pl:* رُمّان [rumma:n] *Collective*

pond • **1.** بُركَة [burka] بُرَك [burak] *pl:* بُحَيرَة صِغِيرَة [buħayra ṣiɣi:ra] بُحَيرات صِغار [buħayra:t ṣiɣa:r] *pl:* بُحَيرَة صغَيِّرَة [buħayra ṣɣayyra] بُحَيرات صغَيِّرَة [buħayra:t ṣɣayyra] *pl:*

pool • **1.** بُركَة [burka] بُرَك [burak] *pl:* The police found him lying in a pool of blood. الشُّرطَة لِقاتَه مَجطُول بِبُركَة دَمّ [ʔiššurṭa liga:tah maǰṭu:l bburkat damm] • **2.** حَوض [ħawð̣] أَحواض [ʔaħwa:ð̣] *pl:* The new pool has improved the appearance of our garden. الحَوض الجِّدِيد حَسَّن مَنظَر حَدِيقَتنا [ʔilħawð̣ ʔiǰǰidi:d ħassan manð̣ar ħadi:qatna] • **3.** بُول [pu:l] بوالَة [pwa:la] *pl:* بِليارد [bilya:rd] Do you play pool? تِلعَب بُول؟ [tilʕab pu:l?]

swimming pool • **1.** حَوض سِباحَة [ħawð̣ siba:ħa] أَحواض سِباحَة [ʔaħwa:ð̣ siba:ħa] *pl:* مَسبَح [masbaħ] مَسابِح [masa:biħ] *pl:* They have a very large swimming pool. عِدهُم حَوض سِباحَة كبِير [ʕidhum ħu:ð̣ siba:ħa čbi:r]

poor • **1.** فَقِير [faqi:r] فُقَراء، فُقرَة [fuqara:ʔ, fuqra] *pl:* He is well known for his generosity to the poor. هُوَّ كُلِّش مَعرُوف بكَرَمَه عالفُقَراء [huwwa kulliš maʕru:f bkaramah ʕalfuqara:ʔ] Many poor people live in this neighborhood. هوايَة ناس فُقرَة يِعِيشُون بهالمَنطِقَة [hwa:ya na:s fuqra yʕi:šu:n bhalmanṭiqa] • **2.** مِسكِين [miski:n] مَساكِين [masa:ki:n] *pl:* The poor fellow is blind. المِسكِين أَعمى [ʔilmiski:n ʔaʕma] • **3.** دُونِي [du:ni] This is poor soil for raising wheat. هَذِي تُربَة دُونِيَّة لِزِراعَة الحُنطَة [ha:ði turba du:niyya lzira:ʕat ʔilħunṭa] • **4.** ضَعِيف [ð̣aʕi:f] He's very poor in arithmetic. هُوَّ كُلِّش ضَعِيف بِالحِساب [huwwa kulliš ð̣aʕi:f bilħisa:b] • **5.** رَكِيك [raki:k] ركاك [rka:k] *pl:* That was a poor article in today's paper. ذِيك كانَت فَدّ مَقالَة رَكِيكَة بجَرِيدَة اليُوم [ði:č ča:nat fadd maqa:la raki:ka bǰari:dat ʔilyu:m]

poorly • **1.** * She was poorly dressed. لِبِسها مبَهذَل [libisha mbahðal] The book is poorly written. الكِتاب رَكِيك [ʔilkita:b raki:k] His business was doing so poorly he has decided to sell out. شُغلَه كان مُو زين إلَى دَرَجَة قَرَّر يصَفِّيه [šuɣlah ča:n mu: zi:n ʔila daraǰa qarrar yṣaffi:h]

to do poorly • **1.** تدَهوَر [ddahwar] تدَهوُر [tduhwur] *vn: sv* a. He's doing poorly after the operation. صِحّتَه تدَهوُرَت وَرا العَمَلِيَّة [ṣiħħtah ddahwurat wara ʔilʕamaliyya]

to pop • **1.** طَقّ [ṭagg] طَقّ [ṭagg] *vn: sv* u. The balloon popped. النُّفّاخَة طَقَّت [ʔinnuffa:xa ṭaggat] • **2.** طَقطَق [ṭagṭag] طَقطَقَة [ṭagṭaga] *vn: sv* i. Come listen; the corn's popping! تَعال إسمَع؛ الإذرَة دَتطَقطِق [taʕa:l ʔismaʕ; ʔilʔiðra daṭṭagṭig]

Pope • **1.** البابَّة [ʔilba:bba] بابا [pa:ppa]

poppy • **1.** خِشخاشَة [xišxa:ša] خِشخاشات [xišxa:ša:t] *pl:* خِشخاش [xišxa:š] *Collective*

popular • **1.** شَعبِي [šaʕbi] They played only popular songs. قَدّمَوا أَغانِي شَعبِيَّة بَسّ [qaddimaw ʔaɣa:ni šaʕbiyya bass] • **2.** مَحبُوب [maħbu:b] He's very popular with the masses. هُوَّ كُلِّش مَحبُوب مِن الجَّماهِير [huwwa kulliš maħbu:b min ʔiǰǰama:hi:r] • **3.** شايِع [ša:yiʕ] دارِج [da:riǰ] That's a popular notion, but it's wrong. هَذا فَدّ رَأي شايِع لَكِن غَلَط [ha:ða fadd raʔi ša:yiʕ la:kin ɣalaṭ]

*** It's a very popular restaurant.**

• **1.** هَذا فَدّ مَطعَم عَلَيه هوايَة رِجِل [ha:ða fadd maṭʕam ʕali:h hwa:ya rijil]

populated • **1.** آهِل [ʔa:hil] مَأهُول [maʔhu:l] مَسكُون [masku:n] This area is not populated. هَالمَنطِقَة ما مَأهُولَة [halmanṭiqa ma: maʔhu:la]

population • **1.** سُكّان [sukka:n] نُفُوس [nufu:s] The population has doubled in the last twenty years. تضاعَف عَدَد السُّكّان بِالعِشرِين سَنَة الأَخِيرَة [dð̣a:ʕaf ʕadad ʔissukka:n bilʕišri:n sana ʔilʔaxi:ra]

porcelain • **1.** صِينِي [ṣi:ni] We gave her a tea set of fine porcelain. إنطِيناها طَخُم مال شاي مِن الصِّينِي الفاخِر [ʔinṭi:na:ha ṭaxum ma:l ča:y min ʔiṣṣi:ni ʔilfa:xir]

i, interjection; p, passive; pl, plural; sv, stem vowel; vn, verbal noun

porch • **1.** طَارمَة [ṭarma] طَرامِي، طَرمات [ṭara:mi ṭarma:t] *pl:*

porcupine • **1.** قُنفُذ [qunfuð, gunfuð] قَنافِذ [qana:fuð, gana:fuð] *pl:*

pore • **1.** مَسامَة [masa:ma] مَسامات، مَسام [masa:ma:t, masa:m] *pl:* The dust got into the pores and caused inflammation. العَجاج خَشّ بِالمَسامات وَسَبَّب اِلتِهاب [ʔilʕaǰa:ǰ xašš bilmasa:ma:t wsabbab ʔiltiha:b]

pork • **1.** لَحَم خَنزِير [laħam xanzi:r]

port • **1.** مِيناء [mi:na:ʔ, mi:na] مَوانِئ [mawa:niʔ] *pl:* The ship is at anchor in the port. الباخِرَة ذابَّه أَنقَر بالمِيناء [ʔilba:xira ða:bba ʔangar bilmi:na:ʔ]

portable • **1.** سَفَرِي [safari] I want to buy a portable typewriter. أَرِيد أَشتِرِي آلَة طابِعَة سَفَرِيَّة [ʔari:d ʔaštiri ʔa:la ṭa:biʕa safariyya]

porter • **1.** حَمّال [ħamma:l] حَمّالِين، حمامِيل [ħamma:li:n, ħma:mi:l] *pl:* Can I call you a porter? أَقدَر أَصِيحلَك حَمّال؟ [ʔagdar ʔaṣi:ħlak ħamma:l?]

portion • **1.** قِسِم [qisim] أَقسام [ʔaqsa:m] *pl:* جُزء [ǰuzuʔ] أَجزاء [ʔaǰza:ʔ] *pl:* A large portion of the city was destroyed by fire. قِسِم كِبِير مِن المَدِينَة تدَمَّر بِالنّار [qisim čibi:r min ʔilmadi:na ddammar binna:r] • **2.** وُصلَة [wuṣla] وُصَل [wuṣal] *pl:* قِطعَة [qitʕa] قِطَع [qiṭaʕ] *pl:* Just give me a small portion of meat and a vegetable. بَسّ إنطِينِي وُصلَة صغَيِّرَة مِن اللَّحَم وفَدّ خُضرَة [bass ʔinṭi:ni wuṣla ṣγayyra min ʔillaħam wfadd xuðra]

Portugal • **1.** بُرتُغال [purtuγa:l burtuγa:l]

Portugese • **1.** بُرتُغالِي [burtuγa:li] بُرتُغالِيِّين [purtuγa:liyyi:n] *pl:*

pose • **1.** وَضعِيَّة [waðʕiyya] وَضعِيّات [waðʕiyya:t] *pl:* Let's try another pose to make sure we have a good picture. خَلِّي نجَرُّب وَضعِيَّة لُخ حَتَّى نِتأَكَّد الصُّورَة زينَة [xalli nǰarrub waðʕiyya lux ħatta nitʔakkad ʔiṣṣu:ra zi:na]

to pose • **1.** أَخَذ وَضعِيَّة [ʔaxað waðʕiyya] أَخِذ وَضعِيَّة [ʔaxið waðʕiyya] *vn: sv* u. They posed for the photographer in front of the fountain. أَخذَوا وَضعِيَّة لِلمُصَوِّر قِدّام النافُورَة [ʔaxðaw waðʕiyya lilmuṣawwir gidda:m ʔilna:fu:ra] The photographer posed me like this. المُصَوِّر خَلّانِي آخُذ هِيك وَضعِيَّة [ʔilmuṣawwir xalla:ni ʔa:xuð hi:č waðʕiyya]

to pose a question • **1.** أَثار سُؤال [ʔaθa:r suʔa:l] إثارَة سُؤال [ʔiθa:rat suʔa:l] *vn: sv* i. I'll pose the questions, and you answer them. آنِي أَثِير الأَسئِلَة وَإنتَ جاوُبها [ʔa:ni ʔaθi:r ʔilʔasʔila wʔinta ǰa:wubha]

position • **1.** وَضِع [waðiʕ] أَوضَاع [ʔawða:ʕ] *pl:* وَضعِيَّة [waðʕiyya] وَضعِيّات [waðʕiyya:t] *pl:* I'm not in a position to pay right now. آنِي مُو بوَضِع أَقدَر أَدفَع هَسَّة [ʔa:ni mu: bwaðiʕ ʔagdar ʔadfaʕ hassa] • **2.** مَوقِف [mawqif] مَواقِف [mawa:qif] *pl:* This places me in a very difficult position. هاي تحُطنِي بِمَوقِف حَرِج [ha:y tħuṭṭni bmawqif ħariǰ] What is your position on this subject? شِنُو مَوقِفَك بِهالمَوضُوع؟ [šinu mawqifak bhalmawðu:ʕ?] • **3.** مَركَز [markaz] مَراكِز [mara:kiz] *pl:* مَقام [maqa:m] مَقامات [maqa:ma:t] *pl:* A man in your position has to be careful of his appearance. رَجُل بِمَقامَك لازِم يِهتَمّ هواية بِمَظهَره [rajul bmaqa:mak la:zim yihtamm hwa:ya bmaðharah] He was accused of using his position as director for his own personal interests. اِنتِهَم بِاستِغلال مَركَزَه كَمُدِير لمُصلَحتَه الخاصَّة [ʔintiham bʔistiγla:l markazah kamudi:r ʔilmuṣlaħtah ʔilxa:ṣṣa] Our army has abandoned the forward positions. جَيشنا تخَلَّى عَن المَراكِز الأَمامِيَّة [ǰayšna txalla: ʕan ʔilmara:kiz ʔilʔama:miyya] • **4.** وَظِيفَة [waði:fa] وَظايِف [waða:yif] *pl:* مَنصِب [manṣab] مَناصِب [mana:ṣib] *pl:* He has a good position with a wholesale house. عِندَه وَظِيفَة كُلِّش زينَة بِمَحَلّ بَيع بِالجُملَة [ʕindah waði:fa kulliš zi:na bmaħall bayʕ biǰǰumla]

positive • **1.** مِتأَكِّد [mitʔakkid] I'm positive that he was there. آنِي مِتأَكِّد هُوَّ كان هناك [ʔa:ni mitʔakkid huwwa ča:n hna:k] • **2.** إيجابِي [ʔi:ǰa:bi] The Arab policy is one of positive neutrality in world affairs. سِياسَة العَرَب هِيَّ الحِياد الإيجابِي بِالشُّؤُون العالَمِيَّة [siya:sat ʔilʕarab hiyya ʔilħiya:d ʔilʔi:ǰa:bi biššuʔu:n ʔilʕa:lamiyya] • **3.** بالإيجاب [bilʔi:ǰa:b] I expect a positive answer. أَتوَقَّع جَواب بالإيجاب [ʔatwaqqaʕ ǰawa:b bilʔi:ǰa:b]

positively • **1.** بِالتَّأكِيد [bittaʔki:d] Do you know it positively? تُعرُفَه بِالتَّأكِيد؟ [tuʕrufah bittaʔki:d?] • **2.** حَقِيقَةً [ħaqi:qatan] This is positively awful. هاي حَقِيقَةً فَظِيعَة [ha:y ħaqi:qatan faði:ʕa] The way she talks is positively vulgar. أَمّا حَقِيقَةً تِحكِي بِأَدَبسِزّ لُغِيَّة [ʔamma ħaqi:qatan tiħči bʔadabsizz luγiyya]

to possess • **1.** مِلَك [milak] مُلُك [muluk] *vn:* اِنمِلَك [ʔinmilak] *p:* اِمتِلَك [ʔimtilak] اِمتِلاك [ʔimtila:k] *vn: sv* i. That's all I possess. هَذا كُلّ ما أَملُك [ha:ða kull ma: ʔamluk]

*** What possessed you to do that?** • **1.** شجاك وسَوَّيت هاي؟ [šǰa:k wsawwi:t ha:y?]

possession • **1.** حِيازَة [ħiya:za] مُلكِيَّة [mulkiyya] How long has that been in your possession? شقَدّ صارلها بِحِيازتَك؟ [šgadd ṣa:rilha bħiya:ztak?]

*** They lost all their possessions.** • **1.** فُقدَوا كُلّما يِملكُون [fuqdaw kullma yimilku:n] / فُقدَوا كُلّ اللِّي كان عِدهُم [fuqdaw kull ʔilli ča:n ʕidhum] / خِسرَوا الأَكُو والماكُو [xiṣraw ʔilʔaku walma:ku]

P

to take possession • **1.** اِستِلَم [ʔistilam] اِستِلام [ʔistila:m] *vn: sv* i. أَخَذ مِن، أَخَذ عَلَى [ʔaxað min, ʔaxað ʕala] أَخِذ [ʔaxið] *vn: sv* u. The new owner hasn't taken possession of the house yet. المالِك الجِّدِيد بَعَد ما اِستِلَم البَيت [ʔilma:lik ʔijjidi:d baʕad ma: ʔistilam ʔilbayt]

possibility • **1.** اِحتِمال [ʔiħtima:l] I see no other posibility. ما شُوف أَكُو أَيّ اِحتِمال آخَر [ma: šu:f ʔaku ʔayy ʔiħtima:l ʔa:xar]

possible • **1.** مُمكِن [mumkin] Call me, if possible. خابُرنِي، إذا مُمكِن [xa:burni, ʔiða mumkin] Call me, if possible. خابُرنِي، إذا بإمكانَك [xa:burni, ʔiða bʔimka:nak]

possibly • **1.** مُمكِن [mumkin] مِن المُمكِن [min ʔilmumkin] Could you possibly call me? مُمكِن تخابُرنِي؟ [mumkin txa:burni?]

post • **1.** عَمُود [ʕamu:d] عَوامِيد [ʕawa:mi:d] *pl:* أَعمِدَة [ʔaʕmida] عَوامِيد [ʕawa:mi:d] *pl:* We need new posts for our fence. نِحتاج عَوامِيد جِدِيدَة لِلمحَجَّر مالنَا [niħta:j ʕawa:mi:d jidi:da lilimħajjar ma:lna] • **2.** مَوقِع [mawqiʕ] مَواقِع [mawa:qiʕ] *pl:* مَوضِع [mawđiʕ] مَواضِع [mawa:điʕ] *pl:* A good soldier never deserts his post. الجُّندِي الزَّين مُستَحِيل يِترُك مَوضِعَه [ʔijjundi ʔizzi:n mustaħi:l yitruk mawđiʕah] • **3.** مُكان [muka:n] مُكانات، أَماكِن [muka:na:t, ʔama:kin] *pl:* This ambassador has served in numerous posts. هَالسَّفِير خِدَم بِأَماكِن مُتَعَدِّدَة [hassafi:r xidam bʔama:kin mutaʕaddida]

to post • **1.** وَقَّف [waggaf, wagguf] تَوُقُّف [twugguf] *vn:* تَوَقَّف [twaggaf] *p:* حَطّ [ħaṭṭ] حَطّ [ħaṭṭ] *vn:* اِنحَطّ [ʔinħaṭṭ] *p:* Post two men at each exit. وَقِّف رِجّالَين بِكُلّ مَحَلّ خُرُوج [wagguf rijja:layn bkull maħall xuru:j] • **2.** عَلَّق [ʕallag] تَعلِيق [taʕli:g] *vn:* تعَلَّق [tʕallag] *p:* Post the sign on the wall. عَلِّق الإعلان عَالحايِط [ʕallig ʔilʔiʕla:n ʕalħa:yiṭ] The order has been posted since yesterday. القَرار صارلَه معَلَّق مِن البارحَة [ʔilqara:r ṣa:rlah mʕallag min ʔilba:rħa]

postage • **1.** أُجرَة بَرِيد [ʔujrat bari:d] أُجُور بَرِيد [ʔuju:r bari:d] *pl:* How much is the postage on a registered letter? شقَدّ أُجرَة البَرِيد عَلَى مَكتُوب مُسَجَّل؟ [šgadd ʔujrat ʔilbari:d ʕala maktu:b musajjal?] There is postage due on this letter. هَالمَكتُوب أُجرتَه ناقصَة [halmaktu:b ʔujurtah na:qṣa] • **2.** طابَع [ṭa:biʕ] طَوابِع [ṭawa:biʕ] *pl:* The letter didn't have enough postage. المَكتُوب ما كان عَليه طَوابِع كافيَة [ʔilmaktu:b ma: ča:n ʕali:h ṭawa:biʕ ka:fya]

postal rate • **1.** أُجرَة بَرِيد [ʔujrat bari:d] أُجُور بَرِيد [ʔuju:r bari:d] *pl:*

post card • **1.** بَوست كارت [pu:st ka:rt] بَوست كارتات [pu:st ka:rta:t] *pl:* بِطاقَة [biṭa:qa] بِطاقات، بِطايِق [biṭa:qa:t, biṭa:yiq] *pl:* كارت [ka:rt] كارتات [ka:rta:t] *pl:* Did you get my post card? اِستِلَمت البِطاقَة مالتِي؟ [ʔistilamt ʔilbiṭa:qa ma:lti?]

to be posted • **1.** اِطِّلَع [ʔiṭṭilaʕ] اِطِّلاع [ʔiṭṭila:ʕ] *vn: sv* i. He's pretty well posted. هُوَّ مُطَّلِع زِين [huwwa muṭṭaliʕ zi:n] Keep me posted! خَلِّينِي عَلَى اِطِّلاع [xalli:ni ʕala ʔiṭṭila:ʕ] Keep me posted! خَلِّينِي عَلَى اِطِّلاع مُستَمِرّ [xalli:ni ʕala ʔiṭṭila:ʕ mustamirr] Keep me posted! خَلِّينِي عَلَى عِلِم [xalli:ni ʕala ʕilim]

poster • **1.** إعلان دِعايَة [ʔiʕla:n diʕa:ya] إعلانات دِعايَة [ʔiʕla:na:t diʕa:ya] *pl:*

postman • **1.** بَوسطَچِي، مُوَزِّع البَرِيد [bu:sṭači, muwazziʕ bari:d] بَوسطَچِيَّة، مُوَزِّعِين البَرِيد [bu:sṭačiyya, muwazziʕi:n bari:d] *pl:*

postmark • **1.** خَتِم [xatim] أَختام [ʔaxta:m] *pl:* The postmark is illegible. خَتم البَرِيد ما يِنقِرِي [xatim ʔilbari:d ma: yinqiri]

to postmark • **1.** خِتَم [xitam] خَتِم [xatim] *vn:* اِنخِتَم [ʔinxitam] *p:* طُمَغ [ṭumaɣ] طَمُغ [ṭamuɣ] *vn:* اِنطُمَغ [ʔinṭumaɣ] *p:* سَقَّط [saqqaṭ] تَسقِيط [tasqi:ṭ] *vn:* تسَقَّط [tsaqqaṭ] *p:* The letter was post-marked May fifteenth. المَكتُوب مَختُوم خُمُسطَعَش مايس [ʔilmaktu:b maxtu:m xumusṭaʕaš ma:yis]

post office • **1.** دائرَة بَرِيد [da:ʔirat bari:d] دَوائِر بَرِيد [dawa:ʔir bari:d] *pl:* بُوسطَة [pu:sṭa] بُوسطات [pu:sṭa:t] *pl:* We have five post offices. عِدنا خَمِس دَوائِر بَرِيد [ʕidna xamis dawa:ʔir bari:d] The post office is open from nine to six. البَوسطَة مَفتُوحَة مِن التِّسعَة لِلسِّتَّة [ʔilpu:sṭa maftu:ħa min ʔittisʕa lissitta]

post-office box • **1.** صَندُوق بَرِيد [ṣandu:q bari:d] صَنادِيق بَرِيد [ṣana:di:q bari:d] *pl:*

to postpone • **1.** أَجَّل [ʔajjal] تَأجِيل [taʔji:l] *vn:* تأَجَّل [tʔajjal] *p:* أَخَّر [ʔaxxar] تَأخِير [taʔxi:r] *vn:* تأَخَّر [tʔaxxar] *p:* عَوَّق [ʕawwag] تَعوِيق [taʕwi:g] *vn:* تعَوَّق [tʕawwag] *p:* I can't postpone the appointment. ما أَقدَر أَأجِّل المَوعِد [ma: ʔagdar ʔaʔajjil ʔilmawʕid]

posture • **1.** وَقفَة [wagfa, waqfa] وَقفات [wagfa:t, waqfa:t] *pl:* She has poor posture. وَقفَتها مُو حِلوَة [wagfatha ma: ħilwa]

pot • **1.** جِدِر، قِدِر [jidir] جدُور، جدُورَة [jdu:r, jdu:ra] *pl:* There is a pot of soup on the stove. أَكُو جِدِر شُوربَة عَالطَّبّاخ [ʔaku jidir šu:rba ʕaṭṭabba:x]

potato • **1.** بُتَيتايَة [putayta:ya] بُتَيتايات [putayta:ya:t] *pl:* بُتَيتَة [putayta] *Collective*

potential • **1.** مُحتَمَل [muħtamal] We must consider him a potential enemy. لازم نِعتَبرَه عَدُو مُحتَمَل [la:zim niʕtabrah ʕadu muħtamal] • **2.** قُدرَة الإنتاج [qudrat ʔilʔinta:ǰ] The industrial potential of our country is enormous. قُدرَة الإنتاج الصِّناعِيَّة لِدَولَتنا هائلَة [qudrat ʔilʔinta:ǰ ʔiṣṣina:ʕiyya ldawlatna ha:ʔila] • **3.** كامِن [ka:min] Water has great potential power. الماي بِيه قُوَّة كامِنَة هائلَة [ʔilma:y bi:h quwwa ka:mina ha:ʔla] • **4.** اِستِعداد [ʔistiʕda:d] قابلِيَّة [qa:bliyya] قابلِيّات [qa:bliyya:t] *pl:* He has the potential to become a good engineer. عِندَه قابلِيَّة أن يِصبَح مُهَندِس مُمتاز [ʕindah qa:bliyya ʔan yiṣbaħ muhandis mumta:z]

potentiality • **1.** إمكانِيَّة [ʔimka:niyya] إمكانِيّات [ʔimka:niyya:t] *pl:*

potter • **1.** فَخّار [faxxa:r] فَخّارين [faxxa:ri:n] *pl:* كَوّاز [kawwa:z] كَوّازين، كوازَة [kwa:za, kawwa:zi:n] *pl:*

pottery • **1.** خَزَف [xazaf]

poultry • **1.** طِيُور داجِنَة [ṭiyu:r da:ǰina]

pound • **1.** باوَن [pa:wan] باوَنات [pa:wana:t] *pl:* The metric pound is a bit more than the American pound. الباوَن المَتري شوَيَّة أزيَد مِن الباوَن الأمرِيكِي [ʔilpa:wan ʔilmatri šwayya ʔazyad min ʔilpa:wan ʔilʔamri:ki] How much is the English pound in American money? شقَدّ يِسوَى الباوَن الإنكلِيزي بِالفلُوس الأمرِيكِيَّة؟ [šgadd yiswa: ʔilpa:wan ʔalʔingili:zi bilfilu:s ʔilʔamri:kiyya?]

*** An ounce of prevention is worth a pound of cure.** • **1.** دِرهَم وِقايَة خَيرٌ مِن قِنطار عِلاج [dirham wiqa:ya xayrun min qinṭa:r ʕila:ǰ]

to pound • **1.** دَقّ [dagg] دَقّ [dagg] *vn:* اِندَقّ [ʔindagg] *p:* We pounded on the door for five minutes before they heard us. دَقّينا عَالباب مُدَّة خَمِس دَقايِق قَبُل ما سَمعُونا [daggi:na ʕalba:b muddat xamis daqa:yiq gabul ma: samʕu:na] I wish our upstairs neighbors wouldn't pound kubba at seven in the morning. أتمَنّى لَو ذُولَة القاعِدِين فَوقانا ما يدُقُّون كُبَّة ساعَة سَبعَة الصُّبُح [ʔatmanna: law ðu:la ʔilga:ʕdi:n fu:ga:na ma: yduggu:n kubba sa:ʕa sabʕa ʔiṣṣubuħ] • **2.** خُفَق [xufag] خَفَقان [xafaqa:n] *vn: sv* u. دَقّ [dagg] دَقّ [dagg] *vn: sv* u. His heart was pounding with anxiety. قَلبَه كان دَيُخفُق مِن القَلَق [galbah ča:n dayuxfuq min ʔilqalaq]

to pour • **1.** صَبّ [ṣabb] صَبّ [ṣabb] *vn:* اِنصَبّ [ʔinṣabb] *p:* دار [da:r] دَير [di:r] *vn: sv* i. Please pour me a cup of coffee. أرجُوك صُبّلِي فَدّ كُوب قَهوَة [ʔarǰu:k ṣubbli fadd ku:b gahwa] • **2.** تَدَفَّق [ddaffaq] تَدَفُّق [tadaffuq] *vn: sv* a. The water was pouring out of the faucet. الماي كان دَيتدَفَّق مِن البُوري [ʔilma:y ča:n dayiddaffaq min ʔilbu:ri] • **3.** زَخّ [zaxx] زَخّ [zaxx] *vn: sv* u. It is pouring out. دَتزُخّ بَرَّة [datzuxx barra]

*** The crowd was just then pouring out of the theater.** • **1.** الجَّماهِير كانَوا دَيطلِعُون مِن السِّينَما فَدّ طَلعَة [ʔiǰǰama:hi:r ča:naw dayiṭlʕu:n min ʔissinama fadd ṭalʕa]

to pour off • **1.** كَبّ مِن [čabb, kabb min] كَبّ [čabb] *vn:* اِنكَبّ [ʔinčabb] *p:* Pour the water off of the rice. كِبّ الماي مِن التِّمَّن [čibb ʔilma:y min ʔittimman]

to pour out • **1.** كَبّ [čabb, kabb] كَبّ [čabb] *vn:* اِنكَبّ [ʔinčabb] *p:* Pour out the water and fill the glass with milk. كِبّ الماي وإترُس الكلاص بالحَلِيب [čibb ʔilma:y wʔitrus ʔilgla:ṣ bilħali:b] • **2.** شِكَى [šika:] شَكوَة [šakwa] *vn: sv* i. She poured out her troubles to me. شِكَتلِي همُومها [šikatli hmu:mha]

poverty • **1.** فَقُر [fuqur] عَوز [ʕawz] He is living in great poverty. دَيعِيش بِفقُر مُدقِع [dayʕi:š bfuqur mudqaʕ]

poverty-stricken • **1.** فَقِير [faqi:r] فُقَراء، فقارَة [fuqara:ʔ, fqa:ra, fuqra] *pl:*

powder • **1.** بودرَة [pu:dra] You've got too much powder on your nose. أكُو هوايَة بُودرَة عَلَى خَشمِك [ʔaku hwa:ya pu:dra ʕala xašmič] • **2.** مَسحُوق [masħu:q] مَساحِيق [masa:ħi:q] *pl:* What is that white powder in this bag? شِنُو هالمَسحُوق الأبيَض بِهالكِيس؟ [šinu halmasħu:q ʔilʔabyað bhačči:s?] • **3.** بارُود [ba:ru:d] There is enough powder here to blow up the whole town. أكُو هنا بارُود كافِي لِنَسف المَدِينَة بكامِلها [ʔaku hna ba:ru:d ka:fi lnasf ʔilmadi:na bka:milha]

to powder • **1.** سِحَن [siħan] سَحِن [saħin] *vn:* اِنسِحَن [ʔinsiħan] *p:* The pharmacist powdered some tablets and put the powder in capsules. الصَّيدَلِي سِحَن كَم حَبّايَة وَخَلّى المَسحُوق بِالكَبسُولات [ʔiṣṣaydali siħan čam ħabba:ya wxalla: ʔilmasħu:q bilkapsu:la:t] • **2.** حَطّ [ħaṭṭ] حَطّ [ħaṭṭ] *vn:* اِنحَطّ [ʔinħaṭṭ] *p:* She powdered her nose. حَطَّت بَودرَة عَلَى خَشِمها [ħaṭṭat pu:dra ʕala xašimha]

power • **1.** قُوَّة [quwwa, guwwa] قُوّات [quwwa:t] *pl:* طاقَة [ṭa:qa] طاقات [ṭa:qa:t] *pl:* The machine is operated by electrical power. المَكِينَة تِشتُغُل بالقُوَّة الكَهرَبائيَّة [ʔilmaki:na tištuɣul bilquwwa ʔilkahrabaʔiyya] The power has been turned off. القُوَّة اِنقِطعَت [ʔilquwwa ʔingiṭʕat] The purchasing power is improving. القُوَّة الشِّرائيَّة دَتِتحَسَّن [ʔilquwwa ʔiššira:ʔiyya datitħassan] • **2.** اِستِطاعَة [ʔistiṭa:ʕa] إمكان [ʔimka:n] قُوَّة [quwwa, guwwa] قُوّات [quwwa:t] *pl:* طاقَة [ṭa:qa] I will do everything in my power. راح أسَوِّي كُلّما بِاستِطاعتِي [ra:ħ ʔasawwi kullma biʔistiṭa:ʕti] I will do everything in my power. راح أسَوِّي كُلّ ما يِطلَع مِن إيدِي [ra:ħ ʔasawwi kull ma: yiṭlaʕ min ʔi:di] • **3.** صَلاحِيَّة [ṣala:ħiyya] Parliament has complete power in this matter. البَرلَمان عِندَه صَلاحِيَّة تامَّة بِهالمَوضُوع [ʔilbarlama:n ʕindah ṣala:ħiyya ta:mma bhalmawðu:ʕ] • **4.** حُكُم [ħukum] أحكام [ʔaħka:m] *pl:* How long has this party been in power? هَالحِزِب شقَدّ صارلَه بِالحُكُم؟ [halħizib šgadd ṣa:rlah bilħukum?] • **5.** سَيطَرَة [sayṭara] He lost all power on his followers. فُقَد كُلّ سَيطَرَة عَلَى أتباعَه [fuqad kull sayṭara ʕala ʔatba:ʕah] • **6.** سُلطَة [sulṭa]

P

سُلطات [sulṭaːt] *pl:* نُفُوذ [nufuːð] He wields a lot of power. عِندَه نُفُوذ كِبير [ʕindah nufuːð čibiːr]

to come into power • 1. إجا لِلحُكُم [ʔiǰaː lilħukum] مَجِيئ لِلحُكُم [maǰiːʔ lilħukum] *vn: sv* i. When did the Republicans come into power? الجُمهُوريِّين شوَقِت إجَوا لِلحُكُم؟ [ʔiǰǰumhuːriyyiːn šwakit ʔiǰaw lilħukum?]

powerful • 1. قَوِي [qawi, guwi] قوَاي، أقوِياء، قَوِيِّين [qwaːy, ʔaqwiyaːʔ, qawiyyiːn] *pl:* He has a powerful voice. عِندَه صَوت قَوِي [ʕindah ṣawt qawi]

powerless • 1. * I'm sorry, but I'm powerless in this matter. مِتأسِّف لَكِن ما بِيدِي شِي بهالقَضِيَّة [mitʔassif laːkin maː biːdi ši bhalqaðiyya]

practical • 1. عَمَلِي [ʕamali] That isn't very practical. هاي مُو كُلِّش عَمَلِيّ [haːy muː kulliš ʕamaliyy]

practically • 1. بصُورَة عَمَلِيَّة [bṣuːra ʕamaliyya] عَمَلِيّاً [ʕamaliyyan] You have to look at things practically. لازم تِنظُر لِلأمُور بِصُورَة عَمَلِيَّة [laːzim tinður lilʔumuːr bṣuːra ʕamaliyya] **• 2.** تَقرِيباً [taqriːban] We're practically there. تَقرِيباً وُصَلنا [taqriːban wuṣalna]

practice • 1. تَمرِين [tamriːn] تَمرِينات، تَمارِين [tamriːnaːt, tamaːriːn] *pl:* I need more practice. أحتاج تَمرِين بَعَد [ʔaħtaːǰ tamriːn baʕad] Practice makes perfect. التَّمرِين يوَصِّل لِلأتقان [ʔittamriːn ywaṣṣil lilʔitqaːn] **• 2.** عادَة [ʕaːda] I've made it a practice to get to work on time. صارَت عادَة عِندِي أرُوح لِلدّائرَة عالوَقِت [ṣaːrat ʕaːda ʕindi ʔaruːħ liddaːʔira ʕalwakit] **• 3.** تَصَرُّف [taṣarruf] تَصَرُّفات [taṣarrufaːt] *pl:* They complained of his dictatorial practices. اِشتِكَوا مِن تَصَرُّفاتَه الدِّكتاتورِيَّة [ʔištikaw min taṣarrufaːtah ʔiddiktatuːriyya]

*** Dr. Ali has a wide practice.**

• 1. الدِكتَور عَلِي عِندَه مُراجِعِين هوايَة [ʔiddiktuːr ʕali ʕindah muraːǰiʕiːn hwaːya]

in practice • 1. عَمَلِيّاً [ʕamaliyyan] عَمَل [ʕamal] عَملَة [ʕamla] *Feminine:* تَطبِيق [taṭbiːq] It is easy in theory, but difficult in practice. هِيَّ سَهلَة نَظَرِيّاً لَكِن صَعبَة عَمَلِيّاً [hiyya sahla naðariyyan laːkin ṣaʕba ʕamaliyyan] He put his theory into practice. وُضَع نَظَريتَه موضَع التَّطبِيق [wuðaʕ naðariːtah mawðaʕ ʔittaṭbiːq]

to practice • 1. تدَرَّب [ddarrab] تَدَرُّب [tadarrub] *vn: sv* a. تمَرَّن [tmarran] تَمَرُّن [tamarrun] *vn: sv* a. He's practicing on the piano. دَيتدَرَّب عالبِيانُو [dayiddarrab ʕalpyaːnu] **• 2.** مارَس [maːras] مُمارَسَة [mumaːrasa] *vn: sv* i. زاوَد [zaːwad] مُزاوَدَة [muzaːwada] *vn: sv* i. How long has he been practicing medicine? شقَدّ صارلَه يمارِس الطِّبّ؟ [šgadd ṣaːrlah ymaːris ʔiṭṭibb?] **• 3.** طَبَّق [ṭabbaq] تَطبِيق [taṭbiːq] *vn: sv* i. I wish he would practice what he preaches. يا رَيت يطَبُّق اللِّي يقُولَه [yaː rayt yṭabbuq ʔilli yguːlah]

praise • 1. مَدِح [madiħ] ثَناء [θanaːʔ] The praise went to his head. المَدِح كَبَّر راسَه [ʔilmadiħ kabbar raːsah]

to praise • 1. مِدَح [midaħ] مَدِح [madiħ] *vn: sv* a. أثنَى عَلَى [ʔaθna: ʕala] ثَناء [θanaːʔ] *vn: sv* i. Everybody praises his work. الجَّمِيع يِثنُون عَلَى شُغلَه [ʔiǰǰamiːʕ yiθnuːn ʕala šuɣlah] **• 2.** حِمَد ب [ħimad b-] حَمِد [ħamid] *vn:* اِنحِمَد [ʔinħimad] *p:* I don't want to praise myself, but. . . ما أرِيد أحمِد بنَفسِي، لَكِن [maː ʔariːd ʔaħmid bnafsi, laːkin]

*** He praised her to the skies. • 1.** صَعَّدها لِلسَماوات [ṣaʕʕadha lissamaːwaːt]

prank • 1. نُكتَة [nukta] نُكَت [nukat] *pl:* حِيلَة [ħiːla] حِيَل [ħiyal] *pl:* That's a silly prank. هاي نُكتَة سَخِيفَة [haːy nukta saxiːfa] They played a prank on me. سَوَّوا بِيّا نُكتَة [sawwaːw biyya nukta]

to pray • 1. صَلَّى [ṣallaː] صَلاة [ṣalaː t] *vn: sv* i. Moslems are expected to pray five times a day. مَفرُوض بِالمُسلِمِين يصَلُّون خمس أوقات بِاليُوم [mafruːð bilmuslimiːn yṣalluːn xams ʔawqaːt bilyuːm] **• 2.** دِعَى [diʕaː] دُعاء [duʕaːʔ] *vn:* اِندِعَى [ʔindiʕaː] *p:* I'll pray for you. راح أدعِيلَك [raːħ ʔadʕiːlak]

prayer • 1. صَلاة [ṣala] صَلَوات [ṣalawaːt] *pl:* دَعوَة [daʕwa] دَعوات، دَعاوِي [daʕwaːt, daʕaːwi] *pl:* دُعاء [duʕaːʔ] أدعِيَة [ʔadʕiya] *pl:*

to preach • 1. وُعَظ [wuʕað] وَعِض [waʕið] *vn:* اِنوُعَض [ʔinwuʕað] *p:* I heard him preach at the mosque in the month of Ramadhan. سِمَعتَه يُوعَظ بِالجّامِع بشَهَر رَمَضان [simaʕtah yuːʕað biǰǰaːmiʕ bšahar ramaðaːn] **• 2.** بَشَّر ب [baššar b-] تَبشِير [tabšiːr] *vn:* تبَشَّر [tbaššar] *p:* The Prophet first preached the Islamic religion to the people of Mecca. الرَّسُول بَشَّر بِالدِّيانَة الإسلامِيَّة لأهِل مَكَّة بِالأوَّل [ʔirrasuːl baššar biddiyaːna ʔilʔislaːmiyya lʔahil makka bilʔawwal]

preacher • 1. واعِظ [waːʕið] واعِظِين، وُعّاظ [waːʕiðiːn, wuʕʕaːð] *pl:* خَطِيب [xaṭiːb] خُطَباء [xuṭabaː] *pl:*

precaution • 1. اِحتِياط [ʔiħtiyaːṭ] You should take better precautions against fire. لازِم تِتَّخِذ اِحتِياطات أحسَن ضِدّ النّار [laːzim tittixið ʔiħtiyaːṭaːt ʔaħsan ðidd ʔinnaːr]

to precede • 1. سِبَق [sibaq] سَبِق [sabiq] *vn:* اِنسِبَق [ʔinsibaq] *p:* A strange silence preceded the storm. هُدُوء غَرِيب سِبَق العاصِفَة [huduːʔ ɣariːb sibaq ʔilʕaːṣifa]

to give precedence • 1. بَدَّى [baddaː] تبِدِّي [tbiddi] *vn:* تبَدَّى [tbaddaː] *p:* قَدَّم [qaddam] تَقدِيم [taqdiːm] *vn:* تقَدَّم [tqaddam] *p:* I gave him precedence over myself. بَدَّيتَه عَلَى نَفسِي [baddiːtah ʕala nafsi]

P

precedent • **1.** سابِقَة [saːbiqa] سَوابِق [sawaːbiq] *pl:* This will constitute a dangerous precedent. هَذا يشَكِّل سابِقَة خَطرَة [haːða yšakkil saːbiqa xaṭra]

precepts • **1.** فَرض [fariḍ] فُرُوض [furuːḍ] *pl:* تَعالِيم [taʕaːliːm] He follows the precepts of Islam implicitly. يتِّبِع فُرُوض الإسلام بِحَذافِيرها [yittibiʕ furuːḍ ʔilʔislaːm bħaðaːfiːrha]

precious • **1.** ثَمِين [θamiːn] نَفِيس [nafiːs] He gave me a very precious gift. اِنطانِي هَدِيَّة كُلِّش ثَمِينَة [ʔinṭaːni hadiyya kulliš θamiːna] • **2.** غالِي [ɣaːli] عَزِيز [ʕaziːz] Your friendship is precious to me. صَداقتَك غالِيَة عِندِي [ṣadaːqtak ɣaːlya ʕindi] • **3.** كَرِيم [kariːm] كُرَماء [kuramaːʔ] *pl:* Emeralds are precious stones. الزُمُرُّد حَجَر كَرِيم [ʔizzumurrud ħajar kariːm]

precipitation • **1.** سُقُوط المُطَر [suquːṭ ʔilmuṭar] What's the average annual precipitation in this area? شقَدّ مُعَدَّل سُقُوط المُطَر السَّنَوِي بِهَالمَنطَقَة؟ [šgadd muʕaddal suquːṭ ʔilmuṭar ʔissanawi bhalmanṭaqa?] • **2.** راسِب [raːsib] What's this white precipitation in this bottle? شِنُو هَالرّاسِب الأَبيَض بِهالبُطُل؟ [šinu harraːsib ʔilʔabyaḍ bhalbuṭul?] • **3.** ترَسَّب [trassab] When precipitation is over take it off the fire. بَعَد ما يِكمَل التَّرَسُّب شِيلَه مِن النّار [baʕad maː yikmal ʔittarassub šiːlah min ʔinnaːr]

precise • **1.** دَقِيق [daqiːq] He is very precise in his work. هُوَّ كُلِّش دَقِيق بشُغلَه [huwwa kulliš daqiːq bšuɣlah] • **2.** بِالضَبُط [biḍḍabuṭ] Those were his precise words. هاي كانَت كَلِماتَه بِالضَبُط [haːy čaːnat kalimaːtah biḍḍabuṭ]

precisely • **1.** بصُورَة دَقِيقَة [bṣuːra daqiːqa] Translate this precisely. تَرجُم هَذا بِصُورَة دَقِيقَة [tarjum haːða bṣuːra daqiːqa] • **2.** بِالضَبُط [biḍḍabuṭ] That is precisely what I had in mind. هَذا بِالضَبُط نَفس الشِّي اللِّي كان عَلَى بالِي [haːða biḍḍabuṭ nafs ʔišši lli čaːn ʕala baːli]

precision • **1.** دِقَّة [diqqa] ضَبُط [ḍabuṭ] The measurements must be taken with precision. القِياسات لازِم تِنِّخِذ بِدِقَّة [ʔilqiyaːsaːt laːzim tinnixið bdiqqa] • **2.** دَقِيق [daqiːq] This company specializes in the manufacturing of precision instruments. هَالشَّرِكَة مِتخَصِّصَة بِصُنع الآلات الدَّقِيقَة [haššarika mitxaṣṣiṣa bṣunʕ ʔilʔaːlaːt ʔiddaqiːqa]

predecessor • **1.** سَلَف [salaf]

predestination • **1.** قَضاء وقَدَر [qaðaːʔ wqadar]

to predict • **1.** تنَبَّأ ب [tnabbaʔ b-] تَنَبُّؤ [tanabbuʔ] *vn: sv* a. تكَهَّن ب [tkahhan b-] تَكَهُّن [takahhun] *vn: sv* a. He predicted this. تنَبَّأ بهَذا [tnabbaʔ bhaːða]

prediction • **1.** نُبُوءَة [nubuːʔa] نُبُوءات [nubuːʔaːt] *pl:*

predominant • **1.** غالِب [ɣaːlib] Red is the predominant color for cars this year. الأحمَر هُوَّ اللَّون الغالِب بسَيّارات هالسَّنَة [ʔilʔaħmar huwwa ʔilluːn ʔilɣaːlib bsayyaːraːt hassana]

preface • **1.** مُقَدِّمَة [muqaddima] مُقَدِّمات [muqaddimaːt] *pl:*

to prefer • **1.** فَضَّل [faḍḍal] تَفضِيل [tafḍiːl] *vn:* تفَضَّل [tfaḍḍal] *p:* I prefer the brand I've been using. أَفَضِّل النَّوع اللِّي دَأستَعمِلَه [ʔafaḍḍil ʔinnawʕ ʔilli daʔastaʕmilah] I prefer brunettes to blondes. أَفَضِّل السُّمُر عالشُّقُر [ʔafaḍḍil ʔissumur ʕaššuqur]

preference • **1.** أفضَلِيَّة [ʔafḍaliyya] أقدَمِيَّة [ʔaqdamiyya] I don't give preference to anyone. ما أنطِي أفضَلِيَّة لأَحَّد [maː ʔanṭi ʔafḍaliyya lʔaħħad]

*** I have no preference.** • **1.** ماكُو فَرِق [maːku fariq] / كُلَّه سِوَى [kullah siwa] / ما تُفرُق عِندِي [maː tufruq ʕindi]

pregnancy • **1.** حَبَل [ħabal] How many pregnancies have you had? كَم حبالَة صارَت عِندِك؟ [čam ħbaːla ṣaːrat ʕindič?] How many pregnancies have you had? كَم بَطِن جِبتِي؟ [čam baṭin jibti?]

pregnant • **1.** حِبلَة [ħibla] حِبلات [ħiblaːt] *pl:* حامِل [ħaːmil] حَوامِل [ħawaːmil] *pl:*

to become pregnant • **1.** حِبَل [ħibal] حَبِل [ħabil] *vn: sv* a. She became pregnant a year after we were married. حِبلَت بَعَد سَنَة مِن تزَوَّجنا [ħiblat baʕad sana min dzawwajna]

prejudice • **1.** تَحَيُّز [taħayyuz] تَحَزُّب [taħazzub] So far as I can see he hasn't any prejudices at all. حَسَب ما أشُوف ما عِندَه أَيّ تَحَيُّزات أَبَداً [ħasab maː ʔašuːf maː ʕindah ʔayy taħayyuzaːt ʔabadan] • **2.** تَعَصُّب [taʕaṣṣub] Prejudice and ignorance are hard to combat. التَّعَصُّب وَالجَّهل صَعُب تحارُبهُم [ʔittaʕaṣṣub wijjahil ṣaʕub tħaːrubhum]

prejudiced • **1.** مِتحَيِّز [mitħayyiz] مِتحَيِّزِين [mitħayyiziːn] *pl:* مِتحَزِّب [mitħazzib] مِتحَزِّبِين [mitħazzibiːn] *pl:* The judge is obviously prejudiced in the case. القاضِي مِن الواضِح مِتحَيِّز بِالدَّعوَة [ʔilqaːḍi min ʔilwaːḍiħ mitħayyiz biddaʕwa] • **2.** مِتعَصِّب [mitʕaṣṣub] He is prejudiced against the new ways. هُوَّ مِتعَصِّب ضِدّ التَّقالِيد الحَدِيثَة [huwwa mitʕaṣṣib ḍidd ʔittaqaːliːd ʔilħadiːθa]

preliminary • **1.** تَمهِيدِي [tamhiːdi] اِبتِدائِي [ʔibtidaːʔi] This is just a preliminary investigation. هَذا بَسّ تَحقِيق تَمهِيدِي [haːða bass taħqiːq tamhiːdi]

premature • **1.** قَبُل أَوان [gabul ʔawaːn] I am afraid that step was premature. أَخشَى هالخَطوَة كانَت قَبُل أَوانها [ʔaxšaː halxaṭwa čaːnat gabul ʔawaːnha]

premier • **1.** رَئِيس وُزَراء [raʔiːs wuzaraːʔ] رُؤَساء وُزَراء [ruʔasaːʔ wuzaraːʔ] *pl:* The Premier is scheduled to speak to Parliament tomorrow. المُقَرَّر يُخطُب رَئِيس الوُزَراء بالبَرلَمان باكِر [ʔilmuqarrar yuxṭub raʔiːs ʔilwuzaraːʔ bilbarlamaːn baːčir] • **2.** حَفلَة اِفتِتاحِيَّة [ħafla ʔiftitaːħiyya] حَفلات اِفتِتاحِيَّة [ħaflaːt ʔiftitaːħiyya] *pl:* We attended the premier of the film in a body. حِضَرنا الحَفلَة الافتِتاحِيَّة لِلفِلِم بلَمَّتنا [ħiḍarna ʔilħafla ʔilʔiftitaːħiyya lilfilim blammatna]

premium • **1.** قِسِط [qisiṭ] أَقساط [ʔaqsaːṭ] *pl:* I have to pay the premium on the insurance policy. لازِم أَدفَع القِسِط مال عَقد التَّأمِين [laːzim ʔadfaʕ ʔilqisiṭ maːl ʕaqd ʔittaʔmiːn]

preparation • **1.** تَحضِير [taħḍiːr] اِستِعداد [ʔistiʕdaːd] The preparations for the trip took us a week. الاستِعدادات لِلسَّفرَة طَوِّلَت عِدنا إسبُوع [ʔilʔistiʕdaːdaːt lissafra ṭawwilat ʕidna ʔisbuːʕ] The plans are still in a state of preparation. الخِطَط بَعَدها بدَور التَّحضِير [ʔilxiṭaṭ baʕadha bdawr ʔittaħḍiːr] • **2.** تَهَيُّؤ [tahayyuʔ] تَأَهَّب [taʔahhab] تَحضِير [taħḍiːr] اِستِعداد [ʔistiʕdaːd] War preparation consumes a large part of the budget. التَّهَيُّؤ لِلحَرُب يِستَهلِك قِسِم كِبِير مِن المِيزانِيَّة [ʔittahayyuʔ lilħarub yistahlik qisim čabiːr min ʔilmiːzaːniyya]

to prepare • **1.** حَضَّر [ħaḍḍar] تَحضِير [taħḍiːr] *vn:* تحَضَّر [tħaḍḍar] *p:* اِستَعَدّ [ʔistaʕadd] اِستِعداد [ʔistiʕdaːd] *vn: sv* i. Did you prepare for tomorrow's exam? اِستَعَدَّيت لِلإمتِحان مال باكِر [ʔistaʕaddayt lilʔimtiħaːn maːl baːčir] • **2.** هَيَّأ [hayyaʔ] تَهيِّأ [tahiyyiʔ] *vn: sv* i. Have the nurse prepare the patient for the operation. خَلِّي المُمَرِّضَة تهَيِّئ المَرِيض لِلعَمَلِيَّة [xalli ʔilmumarriḍa thayyiʔ ʔilmariːḍ lilʕamaliyya] You had better prepare him for the shock first. قَبُل كُلّشِي أَحسَنلَك تهَيِّئَه لِلصَّدمَة [gabul kullši ʔaħsanlak thayyiʔah liṣṣadma] Prepare for the worst. هَيِّئ نَفسَك لأَسوَأ الاحتِمالات [hayyiʔ nafsak lʔaswaʔ ʔilʔiħtimaːlaːt]

prepared • **1.** حاضِر [ħaːḍir] مِستِعِدّ [mistiʕidd] We are prepared to do whatever you suggest. إحنا حاضرِين نسَوِّي اللِّي تِقتَرحَه [ʔiħna ħaːḍriːn nsawwi ʔilli tiqtarħah] • **2.** جاهِز [ǰaːhiz] حاضِر [ħaːḍir] The papers are all prepared except for the signature. الأَوراق كُلّها جاهزَة ما عَدا التَّوقِيع [ʔilʔawraːq kullha ǰaːhza maː ʕadaː ʔittawqiːʕ]

preposition • **1.** حَرُف جَرّ [ħaruf ǰarr] حُرُوف جَرّ [ħuruːf ǰarr] *pl:*

to prescribe • **1.** وُصَف [wuṣaf] وَصُف [waṣuf] *vn:* اِنوُصَف [ʔinwuṣaf] *p:* The doctor prescribed these pills for me. الطَّبِيب وُصَفلِي هالحُبُوب [ʔiṭṭabiːb wuṣafli halħubuːb]

prescription • **1.** وَصفَة [waṣfa] وَصفات [waṣfaːt] *pl:* راچِيتَة [raːčiːta] راچِيتات [raːčiːtaːt] *pl:*

presence • **1.** حُضُور [ħuḍuːr] The document has to be signed in your presence. الوَثِيقَة لازِم تِتوَقَّع بحُضُورَك [ʔilwaθiːqa laːzim titwaqqaʕ bħuḍuːrak] • **2.** وُجُود [wuǰuːd] They resented the presence of the foreign army strongly. عارضَوا وُجُود الجَّيش الأَجنَبِي بشِدَّة [ʕaːrḍaw wuǰuːd ʔiǰǰayš ʔilʔaǰnabi bšidda]

presence of mind • **1.** سُرعَة خاطِر [surʕat xaːṭir-] I admire your presence of mind. تِعجِبنِي سُرعَة خاطرَك [tiʕǰibni surʕat xaːṭrak]

present • **1.** هَدِيَّة [hadiyya] هَدايَة [hadaːya] *pl:* Did you give him a present for his birthday? إنطَيتَه هَدِيَّة بمُناسَبَة عِيد مِيلادَه [ʔinṭiːtah hadiyya bimunaːsabat ʕiːd miːlaːdah] • **2.** حاضِر [ħaːḍir] We live in the present, not in the past. إحنا نعِيش بالحاضِر مُو بالماضِي [ʔiħna nʕiːš bilħaːḍir muː bilmaːḍi] • **3.** مَوجُود [mawǰuːd] All of his friends were present. كُلّ أَصدِقائَه كانَوا مَوجُودِين [kull ʔaṣdiqaːʔah čaːnaw mawǰuːdiːn] • **4.** حالِي [ħaːli] In my present position I can't do anything else. بوَضعِي الحالِي ما أَقدَر أَسَوِّي أَيّ شِي آخَر [bwaḍʕi ʔilħaːli maː ʔagdar ʔasawwi ʔayy ši ʔaːxar]

at present • **1.** حالِيّاً [ħaːliyyan] بالوَقت الحالِي [bilwaqt ʔilħaːli] They aren't working at present. ما يِشتَغلُون حالِيّاً [maː yištaɣluːn ħaːliyyan]

for the present • **1.** هَسَّة [hassa] الآن [ʔilʔaːn] مُوَقَّتاً [muwaqqatan] That will be enough for the present. هاي تِكفِي لِهَسَّة [haːy tikfi lhassa] We are out of pencils for the present. الأَقلام خَلصانَة مُؤَقَّتاً [ʔilʔaqlaːm xalṣaːna muʔaqqatan]

to present • **1.** قَدَّم [qaddam] تَقدِيم [taqdiːm] *vn:* تقَدَّم [tqaddam] *p:* The ambassador is going to present his credentials tomorrow. السَّفِير راح يقَدِّم أَوراق اِعتِمادَه باكِر [ʔissafiːr raːħ yqaddim ʔawraːq ʔiʕtimaːdah baːčir] • **2.** طَلَّع [ṭallaʕ] تَطلِيع [taṭliːʕ] *vn: sv* i. خِلَق [xilaq] خَلِق [xaliq] *vn: sv* u. Each case presents new difficulties. كُلّ قَضِيَّة عَلَى حِدَة تطَلِّع مَشاكِل جِدِيدَة [kull qaḍiyya ʕala ħida ṭṭalliʕ mašaːkil ǰidiːda] • **3.** عِرَض [ʕirаḍ] عَرِض [ʕariḍ] *vn:* اِنعِرَض [ʔinʕiraḍ] *p:* Why don't you present the facts as they are? لِيش ما تِعرُض الحَقايِق مِثلما هِيَّ [liːš maː tiʕruḍ ʔilħaqaːyiq miθilmaː hiyya]

to present with • **1.** هِدَى [hidaː] إهداء [ʔihdaːʔ] *vn:* اِنهِدَى [ʔinhidaː] *p:* The company presented him with a gold watch. الشَّرِكَة هِداتَه ساعَة ذَهَب [ʔiššarika hidaːtah saːʕa ðahab]

to preserve • **1.** حافَظ [ħaːfaḍ] مُحافَظَة [muħaːfaḍa] *vn: sv* i. صان [ṣaːn] صِيانَة [ṣiyaːna] *vn:* اِنصان [ʔinṣaːn] *p:* I did this in order to preserve my dignity. سَوِّيت هَذا حَتَّى أَحافُظ عَلَى كَرامتِي [sawwiːt haːða ħatta ʔaħaːfuḍ ʕala karaːmti] • **2.** أَبقَى [ʔabqaː] إبقاء [ʔibqaːʔ] *vn: sv* i.

P

i, interjection; p, passive; pl, plural; sv, stem vowel; vn, verbal noun

We are trying to preserve what is left. دَنحاوِل الإبقاء عالبَقِيَّة الباقِيَة [danħa:wil ʔilʔibqa:ʔ ʕalbaqiyya ʔilba:qya] • **3.** حُفَظ [ħufaỏ] حَفُظ [ħafuỏ] *vn:* اِنحُفَظ [ʔinħufaỏ] *p:* The refrigerator will preserve the meat until we can use it. الثَّلّاجَة تُحفُظ اللَّحَم إلَى أَن نِقدَر نِستعمِلَه [ʔiθθalla:ǰa tuħfuỏ ʔillaħam ʔila ʔan nigdar nistaʕmilah]

preserved • **1.** مَحفُوظ [maħfu:ỏ] The specimens are preserved in formaldehyde solution in the laboratory. النَّماذِج مَحفُوظَة بِمَحلُول الفُرمَلدَهايد بالمُختَبَر [ʔinnama:ỏiǰ maħfu:ỏa bmaħlu:l ʔilfurmaldahayd bilmuxtabar] • **2.** محافَظ عَلَى [mħa:fuỏ ʕala] The house is well-preserved. البَيت محافَظ عَليه زين [ʔilbayt mħa:fuỏ ʕali:h zi:n]

preserves • **1.** مرَبَّى [mrabba:]

to preside • **1.** تَرَأَّس [traʔʔas] تَرَأُّس [taraʔʔus] *vn: sv* a. Ali presided over the meeting. عَلِي تَرَأَّس الجَّلسَة [ʕali traʔʔas ʔiǰǰalsa]

president • **1.** رَئِيس [raʔi:s] رُؤَساء [ruʔasa:, ruʔasa:ʔ] *pl:* He has been appointed president of the board of directors. تعَيَّن رَئِيس لمَجلِس الإدارَة [tʕayyan raʔi:s lmaǰlis ʔilʔida:ra] The President of the Republic announced the formation of a new cabinet. رَئِيس الجُمهُورِيَّة أَعلَن تَشكِيل وُزارَة جِدِيدَة [raʔi:s ʔiǰǰumhu:riyya ʔaʕlan taški:l wuza:ra ǰidi:da] • **2.** مُحافِظ [muħa:fiỏ] He was president of the Central Bank. كان مُحافِظ البَنك المَركَزِي [ča:n muħa:fiỏ ʔilbang ʔilmarkazi]

press • **1.** صَحافَة [ṣaħa:fa] Will the press be admitted to the conference? راح يُسمَح لِلصَّحافَة تِحضَر المُؤتَمَر؟ [ra:ħ yusmaħ liṣṣaħa:fa tiħỏar ʔilmuʔtamar?] • **2.** مَطبَعَة [maṭbaʕa] مَطابِع [maṭa:biʕ] *pl:* The manuscript is ready to go to press. المِبيَضَّة جاهزَة ترُوح لِلمَطبَعَة [ʔilmibyaỏỏa ǰa:hza tru:ħ lilmaṭbaʕa] • **3.** مَكبَس [makbas, mačbas] مَكابِس [mača:bis, maka:bis] *pl:* Can you operate a date press? تِقدَر تشَغِّل مَكبَس تُمُور؟ [tigdar tšaɣɣil makbas tumu:r?] • **4.** مِعصارَة [miʕṣa:ra] مِعصارات [miʕṣa:ra:t] *pl:* I operate this fruit-juicing press. آنِي أَشَغِّل هَالمِعصارَة مال فَواكِه [ʔa:ni ʔašaɣɣil halmiʕṣa:ra ma:l fawa:kih]

*** The film had a good press.** • **1.** الفِلِم اِنمِدَح بِالجَرايِد [lfilim ʔinmidaħ biǰǰara:yid]

in the press • **1.** تَحت الطَّبُع [taħt ʔiṭṭabuʕ] The book is still in the press. الكِتاب بَعدَه تَحت الطَّبُع [ʔilkita:b baʕdah taħt ʔiṭṭabuʕ]

to press • **1.** ضُرَب [ỏurab] ضَرُب [ỏarub] *vn:* اِنضُرَب [ʔinỏurab] *p:* They pressed my suit nicely. ضِرَب القاط مالِي خُوش أُوتِي [ỏirab ʔilqa:ṭ ma:li xu:š ʔu:ti] • **2.** داس [da:s] دُوس [du:s] *pl:* دَوس [daws] *vn:* اِنداس [ʔinda:s] *p:* Press the button. دُوس الزِّر [du:s ʔizzirr] • **3.** عَصَّر [ʕaṣṣar] تَعصِير [taʕṣi:r] *vn:* تعَصَّر [tʕaṣṣar] *p:* They pressed the grapes and fermented them. عَصِّرَوا العِنَب وَخَمِّرَوه [ʕaṣṣiraw ʔilʕinab wxammiru:h] • **4.** كِبَس [kibas, čibas] كَبِس [kabis] *vn:* اِنكِبَس [ʔinkibas] *p:* This is where the cured dates are pressed and packaged. هَذا المَكان اللِّي يكِبسُون بِيه التَّمُر وَيحُطُّوا بِالباكَيتات [ha:ỏa ʔilmaka:n ʔilli ykibsu:n bi:h ʔittamur wyħuṭṭu: bilpa:kayta:t] • **5.** ضَيَّق عَلَى [ỏayyaq ʕala] تَضيِيق [taỏyi:q] *vn: sv* i. His creditors are pressing him. الدَّيّانَة دَيضَيِّقُون عَليه [ʔiddayya:na dayỏayyiqu:n ʕali:h] • **6.** لَحّ ب [laħħ b-] إلحاح [ʔilħa:ħ] *vn: sv* i. I wouldn't press the matter any further, if I were you. لَو بمَكانَك ما أَلِحّ بِالمَوضُوع بَعَد [law bmaka:nak ma: ʔaliħħ bilmawỏu:ʕ baʕad] • **7.** ضِغَط [ỏiɣaṭ] ضَغِط [ỏaɣiṭ] *vn: sv* u. The party is pressing the President to appoint him to the Commission. الحِزب دَيضغُط عَلَى الرَّئِيس حَتَّى يعَيِّنَه بِالهَيئَة [ʔilħizib dayuỏɣuṭ ʕala ʔirraʔi:s ħatta yʕayyinah bilhayʔa]

to press together • **1.** داس [da:s] دَوس [daws] *vn:* انداس [ʔinda:s] *p:* رَصّ [raṣṣ] رَصّ [raṣṣ] *vn:* اِنرَصّ [ʔinraṣṣ] *p:* Press the peppers together tightly so you can get them all in the pot. دُوس الفِلفِل بقُوَّة حَتَّى تِقدَر تدَخِّل كُلّهُم بِالجَرَّة [du:s ʔilfilfil bquwwa ħatta tigdar ddaxxil kullhum biǰǰarra]

presser • **1.** أُوتَجِي [ʔu:tači] أُوتَجِيَّة [ʔu:tačiyya] *pl:* I worked as a presser for five years. اِشتِغَلِت أُوتَجِي لِمُدَّة خَمس سنِين [ʔištiɣalit ʔu:tači limuddat xams sni:n]

pressing • **1.** مُستَعجَل [mustaʕǰal] I have a pressing engagement. عِندِي مَوعِد مُستَعجَل [ʕindi mawʕid mustaʕǰal]

pressure • **1.** ضَغِط [ỏaɣiṭ] We work under constant pressure. نِشتُغُل تَحَت ضَغِط مُستَمِرّ [ništuɣul taħat ỏaɣiṭ mustamirr]

to put pressure on • **1.** ضِغَط [ỏiɣaṭ] ضَغِط [ỏaɣiṭ] *vn:* اِنضِغَط [ʔinỏiɣaṭ] *p:* لَحّ [laħħ] إلحاح [ʔilħa:ħ] *vn: sv* i. We'll have to put pressure on him. لازِم نلِحّ عَليه [la:zim nliħħ ʕali:h]

prestige • **1.** مَقام [maqa:m] مَقامات [maqa:ma:t] *pl:* هَيبَة [hayba] مَكانَة [maka:na] مَكانات [maka:na:t] *pl:* He has great prestige. عِندَه مَقام عالِي [ʕindah maqa:m ʕa:li]

to presume • **1.** تصَوَّر [tṣawwar] تَصَوُّر [taṣawwur] *vn: sv* a. ظَنّ [ỏann] ظُنُون [ỏunu:n] *pl:* ظَنّ [ỏann] *vn: sv* u. I presume he is at home. أَتصَوَّر هُوَّ بِالبَيت [ʔatṣawwar huwwa bilbayt]

to pretend • **1.** اِدِّعَى [ʔiddiʕa:] اِدِّعاء [ʔiddiʕa:ʔ] *vn: sv* i. زِعَم [ziʕam] زَعِم [zaʕim] *vn: sv* i. He pretended that he was a doctor. اِدّعَى إنُّو طَبِيب [ʔiddʕa: ʔinnu ṭabi:b] • **2.** تظاهَر [tỏa:har] تَظاهُر [taỏa:hur] *vn: sv* a. He's just pretending! هَذا دَيتظاهَر [ha:ỏa dayidỏa:har]

*** He pretended not to know a thing about it.** • **1.** سَوَّى نَفسَه ما يُعرُف أَي شِي عَنها [sawwa: nafsah ma: yuʕruf ʔayy ši ʕanha]

P

pretense • **1.** اِدِّعاء [ʔiddiʕaːʔ] اِدِّعاءات [ʔiddiʕaːʔaːt] *pl:* His pretense fooled no one. اِدِّعائَه ما خِدَع أَحَّد [ʔiddiʕaːʔah maː xidaʕ ʔaħħad] • **2.** حِيلَة [ħiːla] حِيَل [ħiyal] *pl:* تَظاهُر [taðaːhur] تَظاهُرات [taðaːhuraːt] *pl:* His illness is only a pretense. مَرَضَه ما هُوَّ إِلّا حِيلَة [maraðah maː huwwa ʔilla ħiːla]

pretext • **1.** عُذُر [ʕuður] أَعذار [ʔaʕðaːr] *pl:* حِجَّة [ħijja] حِجّات، حِجَج [ħijjaːt, ħijaj] *pl:* He's just looking for a pretext. هُوَّ دَيدَوُّرلَه فَدّ عُذُر [huwwa daydawwurlah fadd ʕuður]

pretty • **1.** حِلو [ħilw] She's a very pretty girl. هِيَّ فَدّ بنَيَّة كُلِّش حِلوَة [hiyya fadd bnayya kulliš ħilwa] • **2.** خُوش [xuːš] That's a pretty mess! أَمّا هاي خُوش خَربَطَة [ʔamma haːy xuːš xarbaṭa] • **3.** لا بَئِس ب [laː baʔis b-] It tastes pretty good. طَعَمها لا بأس بِيه [ṭaʕamha laː baʔs biːh]

*** He's sitting pretty.** • **1.** هذا مايَه بِالصَدِر [haːða maːyah biṣṣadir]

pretty much • **1.** تَقرِيباً [taqriːban] He eats pretty much everything. ياكُل كُلشِي تَقرِيباً [yaːkul kullši taqriːban] It's pretty much the same. هِيَّ نَفس الشِّي تَقرِيباً [hiyya nafs ʔišši taqriːban]

to prevail • **1.** جِرَى [jiraː] جَري [jary] *vn: sv* i. مِشَى [mišaː] مَشِي [mašy] *vn: sv* i. This custom still prevails. هَالعادَة بَعَدها ماشيَة [halʕaːda baʕadha maːšya] • **2.** ساد [saːd] سِيادَة [siyaːda] *vn: sv* u. This opinion prevails at the moment. هَالرَّأي يسُود بالوَقت الحاضِر [harraʔi ysuːd bilwaqt ʔilħaːðir]

to prevail over • **1.** تغَلَّب عَلَى [tɣallab ʕala] تَغَلُّب [taɣallub] *vn: sv* a. The opinion of the majority prevailed over the desires of the minority. رَأي الأَكثَرِيَّة تغَلَّب عَلَى رَغبات الأَقَلِّيَّة [raʔi ʔilʔakθariyya tɣallab ʕala raɣbaːt ʔilʔaqalliyya]

to prevail upon • **1.** قَنَّع [qannaʕ] تَقنِيع [taqniːʕ] *vn:* تقَنَّع [tqannaʕ] *p:* Can't we prevail upon you to come along? ما راح نِقدَر نقَنّعَك تِجِي وِيّانا؟ [maː raːħ nigdar nqanniʕak tiji wiyyaːna?]

to prevent • **1.** مِنَع [minaʕ] مَنع [maniʕ] *vn:* اِنمِنَع [ʔinminaʕ] *p:* The police prevented the crowd from entering. الشُّرطَة مِنعَوا النّاس مِن الدِّخُول [ʔiššurṭa minʕaw ʔinnaːs min ʔiddixuːl]

preventive • **1.** وِقائِي [wiqaːʔi] My son has decided to specialize in preventive medicine. إِبنِي قَرَّر يِتخَصَّص بِالطِّبّ الوِقائِي [ʔibni qarrar yitxaṣṣaṣ biṭṭibb ʔilwiqaːʔi]

previous • **1.** سابِق [saːbiq] ماضِي [maːði] I met him on a previous visit. تعَرَّفِت بِيه بزِيارَة سابقَة [tʕarrafit biːh bziyaːra saːbqa] He has no previous experience in that field. ما عِندَه خِبرَة سابِقَة بهَالمِيدان [maː ʕindah xibra saːbiqa bhalmiːdaːn]

previously • **1.** سابِقاً [saːbiqan] مِن قَبُل [min gabul]

prey • **1.** غَنِيمَة [ɣaniːma] غَنايِم [ɣanaːyim, ganaːʔim] *pl:* He is an easy prey for dishonest schemers. هَذا غَنِيمَة باردَة بايد الحَيّالِين [haːða ɣaniːma baːrda bʔiːd ʔilħayyaːliːn]

price • **1.** سِعِر [siʕir] أَسعار [ʔasʕaːr] *pl:* The prices are very high here. الأَسعار كُلِّش مِرتَفعَة هنا [ʔilʔasʕaːr kulliš mirtafʕa hna] • **2.** ثَمَن [θaman] أَثمان [ʔaθmaːn] *pl:* I wouldn't do that for any price. ما أَسَوِّي هَذا مَهما كان الثَّمَن [maː ʔasawwi haːða mahma kaːn ʔiθθaman]

*** I want it regardless of price.** • **1.** أَرِيدَه مَهما كَلَّف [ʔariːdah mahma kallaf]

to price • **1.** سَعَّر [saʕʕar] تَسعِير [tasʕiːr] *vn:* تسَعَّر [tsaʕʕar] *p:* سام [saːm] سَوم [sawm] *vn:* اِنسام [ʔinsaːm] *p:* This merchant prices his goods too high for me. هَالتّاجِر يسَعِّر بَضايعَه كُلِّش غالِي عَلَيّا [hattaːjir ysaʕʕir baðaːyʕah kulliš ɣaːli ʕalayya] • **2.** عامَل عَلَى [ʕaːmal ʕala] مُعامَلَة [muʕaːmala] *vn: sv* i. I priced this radio in several stores. عامَلِت عَلَى هَالرّاديُو بعِدَّة مَحَلّات [ʕaːmalit ʕala harraːdyu bʕiddat maħallaːt]

to prick • **1.** شَكّ [čakk] شَكّ [čakk] *vn:* اِنشَكّ [ʔinčakk] *p:* نِغَز [niɣaz] نَغِز [naɣiz] *vn:* اِنّغَز [ʔinniɣaz] *p:* pricked my finger with a pin. شَكَّيت إِصبِعِي بدَنبُوس [čakkiːt ʔiṣibʕi bdanbuːs]

to prick up • **1.** شَنتَر [šantar] شَنتَرَة [šantara] *vn: sv* i. The horse pricked up his ears. الحصان شَنتَر إِيذانَه [ʔilħṣaːn šantar ʔiːðaːnah]

prickly heat • **1.** حَصَف [ħaṣaf]

pride • **1.** عِزَّة [ʕizza] Don't you have any pride in your self? ما عِندَك أَيّ عِزَّة نَفِس؟ [maː ʕindak ʔayy ʕizzat nafis?] It is a matter of national pride. هاي مَسأَلَة عِزَّة قَومِيَّة [haːy masʔalat ʕizza qawmiyya] • **2.** فَخَر [faxar] He is the pride of his school. هَذا فَخَر مَدرَستَه [haːða faxar madrastah] • **3.** أَنَفَة [ʔanafa] كِبرِياء [kibriyaːʔ] His pride is unbearable. كِبرِيائَه ما تِنحِمِل [kibriyaːʔah maː tinħimil]

to take pride • **1.** اِفتِخَر [ʔiftixar] اِفتِخار [ʔiftixaːr] *vn: sv* i. اِعتَزّ [ʔiʕtazz] اِعتِزاز [ʔiʕtizaːz] *vn: sv* a. He takes great pride in his work. هُوَّ هوايَة يِعتَزّ بشُغلَه [huwwa hwaːya yiʕtazz bšuɣlah]

to pride oneself on • **1.** تباهَى ب [tbaːhaː b-] تَباهِي [tabaːhi] *vn: sv* a. She prides herself on her good cooking. تِتباهَى بطَبِيخها الزَّين [titbaːhaː bṭabixha ʔizziːn]

priest • **1.** قِسِّيس [qissiːs] قِسِّيسِين قَساوسَة قِسّان [qissiːsiːn, qasaːwsa, qissaːn] *pl:* خُورِي [xuːri] خُورِيَّة، خَوارنَة [xuːriyya, xawaːrna] *pl:*

i, interjection; p, passive; pl, plural; sv, stem vowel; vn, verbal noun

priesthood • **1.** كَهَنُوت [kahanu:t] He is going to enter the priesthood. راح يِدخُل الكَهَنُوت [ra:ħ yidxul ʔilkahanu:t]

primarily • **1.** بِالأَصِل [bilʔaṣil] بِالدَرَجَة الأُولَى [biddaraǰa ʔilʔu:la] أَوَّلاً أَصلِيّاً [ʔawwalan ʔaṣliyyan] I am primarily a clerk, but I work as a driver. آنِي بالأَصِل كاتِب وَلكِن أَشتُغُل كَسايِق [ʔa:ni bilʔaṣil ka:tib wlakin ʔaštuɣul kasa:yiq] This is primarily a matter for the court. هاي بِالدَّرَجَة الأُولَى شَغلَة المَحكَمَة [ha:y biddaraǰa ʔilʔu:la šaɣlat ʔilmaħkama]

primary • **1.** رَئِيسِي [raʔi:si] أَساسِي [ʔasa:si] His primary objective is profit. هَدَفَه الرَّئِيسِي هُوَّ الرِّبح [hadafah ʔirraʔi:si huwwa ʔirribiħ] • **2.** أَوَّلِي [ʔawwali] The primary elections will be held next month. الانتِخابات الأَوَّلِيَّة راح تصِير الشَّهر الجّاي [ʔilʔintixa:ba:t ʔilʔawwaliyya ra:ħ tṣi:r ʔiššahr ʔiǰǰa:y] • **3.** اِبتِدائِي [ʔibtida:ʔi] He hasn't even completed primary school. هُوَّ ما كَمَّل حَتَّى المَدرَسَة الأَبتِدائِيَّة [huwwa ma: kammal ħatta ʔilmadrasa ʔilʔibtida:ʔiyya]

prime • **1.** مُمتاز [mumta:z] فاخِر [fa:xir] خُوش [xu:š] This butcher sells only prime meat. هَالقَصّاب يبِيع لَحَم مُمتاز بَسّ [halgaṣṣa:b yibi:ʕ laħam mumta:z bass] • **2.** عِزّ [ʕizz] زَهرَة [zahra] He died in the prime of life. مات بزَهرَة العُمُر [ma:t bzahrat ʔilʕumur]

prime minister • **1.** رَئِيس وُزَراء [raʔi:s wuzara:ʔ] رُؤَساء وُزَراء [ruʔasa:ʔ wuzara:ʔ] *pl:*

primitive • **1.** بِدائِي [bida:ʔi] Primitive societies lived on hunting. المُجتَمَعات البِّدائِيَّة عاشَت عَالصَّيد [ʔilmuǰtamaʕa:t ʔilbida:ʔiyya ʕa:šat ʕaṣṣi:d] The gufa is a primitive type of water transportation. القُفَّة نَوع بِدائِي مِن المُواصَلات المائِيَّة [ʔilguffa nawʕ bida:ʔi min ʔilmuwa:ṣala:t ʔilma:ʔiyya]

primus stove • **1.** برِيمِز [bri:miz] برَيمِزات [bri:miza:t] *pl:*

prince • **1.** أَمِير [ʔami:r] أُمَراء [ʔumara:ʔ, ʔumara:] *pl:*

princess • **1.** أَمِيرَة [ʔami:ra] أَمِيرات [ʔami:ra:t] *pl:*

principal • **1.** مُدِير [mudi:r] مُدَراء [mudara:ʔ] *pl:* The principal called the teachers into his office. المُدِير جِمَع المُعَلِّمِين بغُرُفتَه [ʔilmudi:r ǰimaʕ ʔilmuʕallimi:n bɣuruftah] • **2.** مَبلَغ أَصلِي [mablaɣ ʔaṣli] مَبالِغ أَصلِيَّة [maba:liɣ ʔaṣliyya] *pl:* Have you paid anything on the principal? دفَعِت شِي مِن المَبلَغ الأَصلِي [dfaʕit ši min ʔilmablaɣ ʔilʔaṣli] • **3.** أَساسِي [ʔasa:si] رَئِيسِي [raʔi:si] The principal cause of the delay is lack of money. السَّبَب الرَّئِيسِي لِلتَّأخِير هُوَّ عَدَم وُجُود الفلُوس [ʔissabab ʔirraʔi:si littaʔxi:r huwwa ʕadam wuǰu:d ʔilflu:s]

principality • **1.** إمارَة [ʔima:ra] إمارات [ʔima:ra:t] *pl:* We have a branch office in the principality of Bahrein. عِدنا دائِرَة فَرعِيَّة بِإمارَة البَحرَين [ʕidna da:ʔira farʕiyya bʔima:rat ʔilbaħrayn]

principle • **1.** قاعِدَة [qa:ʕida] قَواعِد [qawa:ʕid] *pl:* I make it a principle to save some money every month. سَوَّيتها قاعِدَة أَوَفُّر فَدّ مَبلَغ كُلّ شَهَر [sawwi:tha qa:ʕida ʔawaffur fadd mablaɣ kull šahar] • **2.** مَبدَأ [mabdaʔ] مَبادِئ [maba:diʔ] *pl:* He is a man of principles. هَذا واحِد صاحِب مَبدَأ [ha:ða wa:ħid ṣa:ħib mabdaʔ]

a matter of principle • **1.** مَبدَأ [mabdaʔ] مَبادِئ [maba:diʔ] *pl:* قاعِدَة [qa:ʕida] قَواعِد [qawa:ʕid] *pl:* I don't do such things as a matter of principle. كَمَبدَأ، ما أَسَوِّي هِيكِي أَشياء [kamabdaʔ, ma: ʔasawwi hi:či ʔašya:ʔ]

print • **1.** طَبُع [ṭabuʕ] The print in this book is too small. الطَّبُع بهالكتاب كُلِّش ناعِم [ʔiṭṭabuʕ bha:lkta:b kulliš na:ʕim] • **2.** بَصمَة [baṣma] بَصمات [baṣma:t] *pl:* طَبعَة [ṭabʕa] طَبعات [ṭabʕa:t] *pl:* The prints left by his fingers were found on the doorknob. بَصمات أَصابعَه اِنلِقَت عَلَى يَدَّة الباب [baṣma:t ʔaṣa:bʕah ʔinligat ʕala yaddat ʔilba:b] • **3.** أَثَر [ʔaθar] آثار [ʔa:θa:r] *pl:* It was easy to follow his footprints in the sand. كان مِن السُّهُولَة تَعَقُّب آثار أَقدامَه عالرَّمُل [ča:n min ʔissuhu:la taʕaqqub ʔa:θa:r ʔaqda:mah ʕarramul] • **4.** نُسخَة [nusxa] نُسَخ [nusax] *pl:* How many prints shall I make of each picture? كَم نُسخَة أَطَلِّع مِن كُلّ صُورَة [kam nusxa ʔaṭalliʕ min kull ṣu:ra] • **5.** رَسِم مَطبُوع [rasim maṭbu:ʕ] رُسُوم مَطبُوعَة [rusu:m maṭbu:ʕa] *pl:* The museum has a fine collection of prints. المَتحَف بِيه خُوش مَجمُوعَة مِن الرُّسُوم المَطبُوعَة [ʔilmatħaf bi:h xu:š maǰmu:ʕa min ʔirrusu:m ʔilmaṭbu:ʕa] • **6.** منَقَّش [mnaqqaš] You always look good in a print. إنتِي دائِماً تِطلَعِين حِلوَة بِنَفنُوف منَقَّش [ʔinti da:ʔiman tiṭlaʕi:n ħilwa bnafnu:f mnaqqaš]

to print • **1.** طَبَع [ṭubaʕ] طَبُع [ṭabuʕ] *vn:* اِنطِبَع [ʔinṭibaʕ] *p:* We can print them for you for twenty fils per page. نِقدَر نِطبَعلَك إيّاهُم بِعِشرِين فِلِس الصَّحِيفَة [nigdar niṭbaʕlak ʔiyya:hum bʕišri:n filis ʔiṣṣaħi:fa] The letter was printed in yesterday's paper. المَكتُوب اِنطُبَع بجَرِيدَة البارحَة [ʔilmaktu:b ʔinṭubaʕ bǰari:dat ʔilba:rħa]

*** Print your name.** • **1.** إكتِب إسمَك بحُرُوف مِنفَصلَة [ʔiktib ʔismak bħuru:f minfaṣla]

printed matter • **1.** مَطبُوعات [maṭbu:ʕa:t] What are the postage rates for printed matter? شقَدّ الأُجرَة البَرِيدِيَّة عالمَطبُوعات [šgadd ʔilʔuǰra ʔilbari:diyya ʕalmaṭbu:ʕa:t]

printer • **1.** طَبّاع [ṭabba:ʕ] طَبّاعِين [ṭabba:ʕi:n] *pl:*

print shop • **1.** مَطبَعَة [maṭbaʕa] مَطابِع [maṭa:biʕ] *pl:*

prior • **1.** قَبُل [gabul, qabil] Prior to the war the cost of living was much lower. قَبِل الحَرُب تَكالِيف المَعِيشَة كانَت هوايَة أَقَلّ [gabil ʔilħarub taka:li:f ʔilmaʕi:ša ča:nat hwa:ya ʔaqall] • **2.** سابِق [sa:biq] Have you had any prior experience in this type of work? عِندَك خِبرَة سابقَة بهَالنَّوع مِن الشُّغُل [ʕindak xibra sa:bqa bhannu:ʕ min ʔiššuɣul]

P

priority • **1.** أَسبَقِيَّة [ʔasbaqiyya] أَفضَلِيَّة [ʔafðaliyya] This job has priority over the others. هَالشَّغلَة إِلها أَسبَقِيَّة عالباقِي [haššaɣla ʔilha ʔasbaqiyya ʕalba:qi] • **2.** تَوجِيب [tawǰi:b] It is our policy to give priority to regular customers. تَوجِيب المَعامِيل العِتَّق مِن سِياسَتنا [tawǰi:b ʔilmaʕa:mi:l ʔilʕittag min siya:satna]

prism • **1.** مَنشُور [manšu:r] مَناشِير [mana:ši:r] *pl:*

prison • **1.** سِجِن [siǰin] سِجُون [siǰu:n] *pl:* The prison is heavily guarded. السِّجِن عَليه حِراسَة قَوِيَّة [ʔissiǰin ʕali:h ħira:sa qawiyya] • **2.** حَبِس [ħabis] The court sentenced him to five years in prison. المَحكَمَة حُكمَت عَليه بِالحَبِس خَمس سنِين [ʔilmaħkama ħukmat ʕali:h bilħabis xams sni:n]

prisoner • **1.** سَجِين [saǰi:n] سُجَناء [suǰana:ʔ] *pl:* مَسجُون [masǰu:n] مَحبُوس [maħbu:s] A prisoner has just escaped. فَدّ سَجِين هَستَوَّة اِنهِزَم [fadd saǰi:n hastawwah ʔinhizam]

prisoner of war • **1.** أَسِير حَرب [ʔasi:r ħarb] أَسرَى حَرب [ʔasra ħarb] *pl:*

to take prisoner • **1.** أَسَّر [ʔassar] تَأسِير [taʔsi:r] *vn:* تَأَسَّر [tʔassar] *p:* We took the wounded soldier prisoner. أَسَّرنا الجُندِي المَجرُوح [ʔassarna ʔiǰǰundi ʔilmaǰru:ħ]

private • **1.** جُندِي [ǰundi] جنُود [ǰinu:d] *pl:* I was a private in the second world war. كِنِت جُندِي بِالحَرُب العالَمِيَّة الثّانيَة [činit ǰundi bilħarub ʔilʕa:lamiyya ʔiθθa:nya] • **2.** خاصّ [xa:ṣṣ] This is my private property. هَذا مُلكِي الخاصّ [ha:ða mulki ʔilxa:ṣṣ] • **3.** خُصُوصِي [xuṣu:ṣi] خاصّ [xa:ṣṣ] Do you have a single room with a private bath? عِندَك غُرفَة بِيها حَمّام خُصُوصِي؟ [ʕindak ɣurfa bi:ha ħamma:m xuṣu:ṣi?]

in private • **1.** عَلَى اِنفِراد [ʕala ʔinfira:d] I'd like to talk to you in private. أَرِيد أَحكِي وِيّاك عَلَى اِنفِراد [ʔari:d ʔaħči wiyya:k ʕala ʔinfira:d]

privates • **1.** عَورَة [ʕawra] عَورات [ʕawra:t] *pl:* Do not expose your privates under any circumstances. لا تِكشِف عَورتَك بِأَي حال مِن الأَحوال [la: tikšif ʕawurtak bʔayy ħa:l min ʔalʔaħwa:l]

privation • **1.** حِرمان [ħirma:n]

privilege • **1.** اِمتِياز [ʔimtiya:z] اِمتِيازات [ʔimtiya:za:t] *pl:* He was deprived of all privileges. اِنحِرَم مِن كُلّ الامتِيازات [ʔinħiram min kull ʔilʔimtiya:za:t] • **2.** حَقّ [ħaqq, ħagg] حُقُوق [ħuqu:q, ħugu:g] *pl:* If you want to leave, it's your privilege. إِذا تَرِيد تَرُوح، هَذا حَقَّك [ʔiða tri:d tru:ħ, ha:ða ħaqqak]

*** It would be a privilege to do this for you.** • **1.** أَكُون مَمنُون أَقُوملَك بهَالخِدمَة [ʔaku:n mamnu:n ʔaqu:mlak bhalxidma] / يسُرّنِي أَسَوِّيلَك هَذا [ysurrni ʔasawwi:lak ha:ða]

prize • **1.** Who won the first prize? مِنُو رِبَح الجّائِزَة الأُولَى؟ [minu ribaħ ʔiǰǰa:ʔiza ʔilʔu:la?]

probability • **1.** اِحتِمال [ʔiħtima:l] That is well within the bounds of probability. هَذا جِدّاً ضِمِن نِطاق الاحتِمال [ha:ða ǰiddan ðimin niṭa:q ʔalʔiħtima:l]

probable • **1.** مُحتَمَل [muħtamal] It might be possible, but it is not very probable. هاي مُمكِنَة بَسّ مُو كُلِّش مُحتَمَلَة [ha:y mumkina bass mu: kulliš muħtamala]

probably • **1.** مِن المُحتَمَل [mn ʔilmuħtamal] You'll probably meet him on the train. مِن المُحتَمَل راح تلاقِيه بِالقِطار [min ʔilmuħtamal ra:ħ tla:gi:h bilqiṭa:r]

most probably • **1.** أَغلَب الظَّنّ [ʔaɣlab ʔiððann] Most probably he is the one that should be blamed for it. أَغلَب الظَّنّ هُوَّ اللِّي لازِم يِنلام عَليها [ʔaɣlab ʔiððann huwwa ʔilli la:zim yinla:m ʕali:ha]

probation • **1.** تَجرُبَة [taǰruba] تَجارُب [taǰa:rub] *pl:* He is still on probation. بَعدَه تَحت التَّجرُبَة [baʕdah taħt ʔittaǰruba]

problem • **1.** مُشكِلَة [muškila] مَشاكِل [maša:kil] *pl:* We all have our problems. كُلَّتنا عِدنا مَشاكِلنا [kullatna ʕidna maša:kilna] That's your problem. هَذِي مُشكِلَة تخُصَّك إِنتَ [ha:ði muškila txuṣṣak ʔinta] • **2.** مَسأَلَة [masʔala] مَسائِل [masa:ʔil] *pl:* I couldn't solve the second problem. ما قِدَرت أَحِلّ المَسأَلَة الثّانيَة [ma: gidart ʔaħill ʔilmasʔala ʔiθθa:nya]

problematical • **1.** مُشكِل [muškil]

procedure • **1.** أُصُول [ʔuṣu:l] What is the usual procedure? شِنُو الأُصُول المُتَّبَعَة؟ [šinu: ʔilʔuṣu:l ʔilmuttabaʕa?] • **2.** إِجراء [ʔiǰra:ʔ] إِجراءات [ʔiǰra:ʔat] *pl:* The procedures for terminating the services of an employee are in this directive. الإِجراءات لِإِنهاء خَدَمات مُوَظَّف مَوجُودَة بِهَالنِّظام [ʔilʔiǰra:ʔa:t liʔinha:ʔ xadama:t muwaððaf mawǰu:da bhanniða:m]

to proceed • **1.** اِستَمَرّ [ʔistamarr] اِستِمرار [ʔistimra:r] *vn:* *sv* i. مِشَى [miša:] مَشِي [mašy] *vn:* *sv* i. They have decided to proceed according to the original plan. صَمِّمَوا عَلَى أَن يِستِمِرُّون حَسَب الخُطَّة المَرسُومَة [ṣammimaw ʕala ʔan yistimirru:n ħasab ʔilxuṭṭa ʔilmarsu:ma] Then he proceeded to talk about the differences in the two dialects. بَعَد ذَلِك اِستَمَرّ يِحكِي عَن الخِلاف بِاللَّهجتَين [baʕad ða:lik ʔistamarr yiħči ʕan ʔilxila:f billahiǰtayn] • **2.** داوَم [da:wam] دَوام [dawa:m] *vn:* *sv* i. We stopped the car to look at the view and then proceeded on our way. وَقَّفنا السَّيّارَة لِمُشاهَدَة المَنظَر وبَعدين داوَمنا بسَيرنا [waggafna ʔissayya:ra limuša:hadat ʔilmanðar wbaʕdi:n da:wamna bsayrna] • **3.** كَمَّل [kammal] تَكمِيل [takmi:l] *vn:* تكَمَّل [tkammal] *p:* Let's proceed with the class. خَلِّي نكَمِّل الدَّرس [xalli nkammil ʔiddaris]

P

proceeding • **1.** إجراء [ʔijra:ʔ] إجراءات [ʔijra:ʔat] *pl:* I watched the proceedings with great interest. لاحَظِت سَير الإجراءات بِشَوق عَظِيم [la:ħaðit sayr ʔilʔijra:ʔa:t bšawq ʕaði:m]

proceeds • **1.** واردات [wa:rida:t] إيراد [ʔi:ra:d] إيرادات [ʔi:ra:da:t] *pl:* The proceeds will go to charity. الوارِدات ترُوح للأعمال الخَيريَّة [ʔilwa:rida:t tru:ħ lilʔaʕma:l ʔilxayriyya]

process • **1.** طَرِيقَة [ṭari:qa] طُرُق [ṭuruq] *pl:* Our engineers have developed a new process. مُهَندِسِينّا طَلّعوا طَرِيقَة جِدِيدَة [muhandisi:nna: ṭallʕaw ṭari:qa ǰidi:da] • **2.** عَمَلِيَّة [ʕamaliyya] عَمَلِيّات [ʕamaliyya:t] *pl:* مُعامَلَة [muʕa:mala] That will be a long drawn-out process. هاي راح تكُون عَمَلِيَّة طُويلَة [ha:y ra:ħ tku:n ʕamaliyya ṭuwi:la]

to process • **1.** صَفَّى [ṣaffa:] تَصفِيَة [taṣfiya] *vn:* تصَفَّى [tṣaffa:] *p:* This refinery can process enough oil to cover our internal gasoline needs. هَالمَصفَى يِستَطِيع يصَفِّي كَمِّيَّة نَفُط تسِدّ حاجَتنا الدّاخِلِيَّة مِن البَنزِين [halmaṣfa: yistaṭi:ʕ yṣaffi kammiyyat nafuṭ tsidd ħa:ǰatna ʔidda:xiliyya min ʔilbanzi:n]

*** The consulate is going to process your visa.** • **1.** القُنصُلِيَّة راح تِجري مُعامَلَة الفِيزَة مالتَك [ʔilqunṣuliyya ra:ħ tiǰri muʕa:malat ʔilvi:za ma:ltak]

procession • **1.** مَوكِب [mawkib] مَواكِب [mawa:kib] *pl:* The procession of the President and his official guest will pass through this street. مَوكِب الرَّئِيس وضَيفَه الرَّسمِي راح يمُرّ مِن هَالشّارِع [mawkib ʔirraʔi:s wḍi:fah ʔirrasmi ra:ħ ymurr min haššа:riʕ] • **2.** زَفَّة [zaffa] زَفّات [zaffa:t] *pl:* The wedding procession will leave from the restaurant at seven o'clock. الزَّفَّة راح تِطلَع مِن المَطعَم ساعَة سَبعَة [ʔizzaffa ra:ħ tiṭlaʕ min ʔilmaṭʕam sa:ʕa sabʕa] • **3.** جَنازَة [ǰana:za] جَنازات، جَنايِز [ǰana:za:t, ǰana:yiz] *pl:* All of his old friends walked in his funeral procession. كُلّ أصدِقائَه العِتّق مِشَوا بجَنازتَه [kull ʔaṣdiqa:ʔah ʔilʕittag mišaw bǰana:ztah]

to proclaim • **1.** أعلَن [ʔaʕlan] إعلان [ʔiʕla:n] *vn: sv* i. They proclaimed the 14th of July a holiday. أعلِنَوا يوم أربَطَعَش تمُوز عُطلَة [ʔaʕlinaw yu:m ʔarbaṭaʕaš tammu:z ʕuṭla]

proclamation • **1.** إعلان [ʔiʕla:n] إعلانات [ʔiʕla:na:t] *pl:* بَلاغ [bala:ɣ] بَلاغات [bala:ɣa:t] *pl:*

to procure • **1.** حَصَّل [ħaṣṣal] تَحصِيل [taħṣi:l] *vn:* تحَصَّل [tħaṣṣal] *p:* They hired me to procure fresh vegetables and meat for them from local sources. اِستَخدِموني حَتَّى أحَصِّللهُم خُضرَوات ولَحَم تازَة مِن المَصادِر المَحَلِّيَّة [ʔistaxdimu:ni ħatta ʔaħaṣṣililhum xuðrawa:t wlaħam ta:za min ʔilmaṣa:dir ʔilmaħaliyya]

produce • **1.** مَحصُول [maħṣu:l] مَحاصِيل [maħa:ṣi:l] *pl:* The farmers sell their produce on market day. الفَلّاحِين يبِيعُون مَحاصِيلهُم بيُوم القَعدَة [ʔilfalla:ħi:n ybi:ʕu:n maħa:ṣi:lhum byu:m ʔilgaʕda]

to produce • **1.** أنتَج [ʔantaǰ] إنتاج [ʔinta:ǰ] *vn: sv* i. We don't produce enough grain to cover our need. ما نِنتِج حُبُوب كافيَة تسِدّ حاجَتنا [ma: nintiǰ ħubu:b ka:fya tsidd ħa:ǰatna] • **2.** طَلَّع [ṭallaʕ] تَطلِيع [taṭli:ʕ] *vn:* تطَلَّع [tṭallaʕ] *p:* How many cars do they produce a month? كَم سَيّارَة يطَلّعُون بالشَّهَر [čam sayya:ra yṭallʕu:n biššahar] • **3.** أبرَز [ʔabraz] إبراز [ʔibra:z] *vn: sv* i. Can you produce any written proof? تِقدَر تبرِز فَدّ دَلِيل خَطِّي؟ [tigdar tibriz fadd dali:l xaṭṭi?]

product • **1.** مَنتُوج [mantu:ǰ] مَنتُوجات [mantu:ǰa:t] *pl:* This company is getting ready to put a new product on the market. هَالشَّرِكَة دَتِستَعِدّ لِتَنزِيل مَنتُوج جِدِيد لِلسُّوق [haššarika datistiʕidd litanzi:l mantu:ǰ ǰidi:d lissu:g]

production • **1.** إنتاج [ʔinta:ǰ]

productive • **1.** مُنتِج [muntiǰ] مُثمِر [muθmir] He's a very productive writer. هُوَّ فَدّ كاتِب كُلِّش مُنتِج [huwwa fadd ka:tib kulliš muntiǰ]

profession • **1.** مِهنَة [mihna] مِهَن [mihan] *pl:* حِرفَة [ħirfa] My son is preparing himself for the legal profession. إبنِي دَيهَيِّئ نَفسَه لمِهنَة المُحاماة [ʔibni dayhayyiʔ nafsah lmihnat ʔilmuħa:ma:t] • **2.** سِلك [silk] أسلاك [ʔasla:k] *pl:* He is in the teaching profession. هُوَّ بسِلك التَّعلِيم [huwwa bsilk ʔittaʕli:m]

professional • **1.** مُحتَرِف [muħtarif] مُمتَهِن [mumtahin] مُمتَهِنِين [mumtahini:n] *pl:* He's a professional gambler. هُوَّ فَدّ قُمارجِي مُحتَرِف [huwwa fadd quma:rči muħtarif] • **2.** صاحِب مِهنَة [ṣa:ħib mihna] أصحاب مِهَن [ʔaṣħa:b mihan] *pl:* All of our friends are professional people. كُلّ أصدِقاءنا مِن أصحاب المِهَن [kull ʔaṣdiqa:ʔna min ʔaṣħa:b ʔilmihan]

professor • **1.** أُستاذ [ʔusta:ð] أساتِذَة [ʔasa:tiða] *pl:* برُوفِيسَور [pru:fisu:r] برُوفِيسورِيَّة [pru:fisu:riyya] *pl:*

proficiency • **1.** When I applied for the job, they gave me a proficiency test in typing. لَمّا قَدَّمِت عالوَظِيفَة، إنطَوني اِمتِحان كَفاءَة بالطِّباعَة [lamma qaddamit ʕalwaði:fa, ʔinṭu:ni ʔimtiħa:n kafa:ʔa biṭṭiba:ʕa]

proficient • **1.** بارِع [ba:riʕ] How long did it take you to become proficient in English? شقَدّ أخَذَك إلَى أن صِرت بارِع بالإنكلِيزِي؟ [šgadd ʔaxaðak ʔila ʔan ṣirit ba:riʕ bilʔingili:zi?]

to become proficient • **1.** بِرَع [biraʕ] بَراعَة [bara:ʕa] *vn: sv* a. You can't expect to become proficient in typing and shorthand in a month.

لا تِنتِظِر تِبرَع بالطِّباعَة وَالإختِزال خِلال شَهَر [laː tintiðir tibraʕ bittibaːʕa wilʔixtizaːl xilaːl šahar]

profit • **1.** رِبِح [ribiħ] أَرباح [ʔarbaːħ] *pl:* I sold it at a profit. بِعتها بِربِح [biʕitha bribiħ] • **2.** فائِدَة [faːʔida] فَوائِد [fawaːʔid] *pl:* مَكسَب [maksab] مَكاسِب [makaːsib] *pl:* I don't expect to get any profit out of that. ما أَتوَقَّع أَيّ فائِدَة مِن وَراها [maː ʔatwaqqaʕ ʔayy faːʔida min waraːha]

to make a profit • **1.** رُبَح [rubaħ] رِبِح [ribiħ] *vn: sv* a. He makes a profit of at least 10% on every item. يِربَح عَلَى الأَقَلّ عَشرَة بِالمِيَّة عَلَى كُلّ سِلعَة [yirbaħ ʕala ʔilʔaqall ʕašra bilmiyya ʕala kull silʕa]

to profit • **1.** اِنتِفَع [ʔintifaʕ] اِنتِفاع [ʔintifaːʕ] *vn: sv* i. اِستَفاد [ʔistafaːd] اِستِفادَة [ʔistifaːda] *vn: sv* i. Did you profit much from the lecture? اِستَفادَيت هوايَة مِن المُحاضَرَة؟ [ʔistafaːdiːt hwaːya min ʔilmuħaːðara?]

*** One profits from his mistakes.**

• **1.** الواحِد يِتعَلَّم مِن أَغلاطَه [ʔilwaːħid yitʕallam min ʔaɣlaːṭah]

profitable • **1.** مُربِح [murbiħ] مُفِيد [mufiːd] نافِع [naːfiʕ] Is it a profitable business? هَالشَّغلَة مُربِحَة؟ [haššaɣla murbiħa?]

profound • **1.** عَمِيق [ʕamiːq] He had a profound influence on me. كان إلَه تَأثِير عَمِيق عَلَيّا [čaːn ʔilah taʔθiːr ʕamiːq ʕalayya]

profusion • **1.** كُثرَة [kuθra, kaθra] There is a profusion of roses blooming in the garden. أَكُو كُثرَة بوَرد الجُورِي مفَتَّح بِالحَدِيقَة [ʔaku kuθra bward ʔijjuːri mfattaħ bilħadiːqa]

program • **1.** مَنهَج [manhaj] مَناهِج [manaːhij] *pl:* The program sells for a dirham. المَنهَج دَينباع بدِرهَم [lmanhaj dayinbaːʕ bdirham] What's on our program tonight? شِنُو مَنهَجنا هاللَّيلَة؟ [šinu manhajna hallayla?] • **2.** بَرنامِج [barnaːmij] بَرامِج [baraːmij] *pl:* How did you like the program? شلُون عِجَبَك البَرنامِج؟ [šluːn ʕijabak ʔilbarnaːmij?]

progress • **1.** تَقَدُّم [taqaddum] The students are making good progress. التَّلامِيذ دَيصِير عِدهُم تَقَدُّم مَحسُوس [ʔittalaːmiːð dayṣiːr ʕidhum taqaddum maħsuːs] Are you making any progress with your book? دَيصِير عِندَك أَيّ تَقَدُّم بكِتابَك؟ [dayṣiːr ʕindak ʔayy taqaddum biktaːbak?]

to progress • **1.** تحَسَّن [tħassan] تَحَسُّن [taħassun] *vn: sv* a. You've progressed a lot in the six weeks I've been away. إنتَ هوايَة تحَسَّنِت خِلال الأَسابِيع السِّتَّة اللّي غِبِت بِيها [ʔinta hwaːya tħassanit xilaːl ʔilʔasaːbiːʕ ʔissitta ʔilli ɣibit biːha] • **2.** تقَدَّم [tqaddam] تَقَدُّم [taqaddum] *vn: sv* a. ترَقَّى [traqqaː] ترَقِّي [triqqi] *vn: sv* a. Our country has progressed fast during the past few years. بَلَدنا تقَدَّم بسُرعَة خِلال السَّنَوات الأَخِيرَة [baladna tqaddam sariːʕ xilaːl ʔissanawaːt ʔilʔaxiːra] • **3.** تقَدَّم [tqaddam] تَقَدُّم [taqaddum] *vn: sv* a. We progressed slowly toward the enemy. تقَدَّمنا بِبُطء عَلَى الأَعداء [tqaddamna bibuṭuʔ ʕala ʔilʔaʕdaːʔ]

progressive • **1.** مِتجَدِّد [mitjaddid] مِتقَدِّم [mitqaddim] مِتدَرِّج [mitdarrij] مِتدَرِّجِين [mitdarrijiːn] *pl:* He's a progressive teacher. هُوَّ مُعَلِّم مِتجَدِّد [huwwa muʕallim midjaddid]

progressively • **1.** بِالتَدرِيج [bittadriːj] The war grew progressively worse. الحَرُب ساءَت بِالتَّدرِيج [ʔilħarub saːʔat bittadriːj]

to prohibit • **1.** مِنَع [minaʕ] مَنِع [maniʕ] *vn:* اِنمِنَع [ʔinminaʕ] *p:* The law prohibits smoking here. القانُون يِمنَع التَّدخِين هنا [ʔilqaːnuːn yimnaʕ ʔittadxiːn hna] • **2.** حَرَّم [ħarram] تَحرِيم [taħriːm] *vn:* تحَرَّم [tħarram] *p:* The Moslem religion prohibits alcoholic drinks. الدِّيانَة الإسلامِيَّة حَرَّمَت شُرُب الخَمُر [ʔilʔislaːmiyya ħarramat šurub ʔilxamur]

project • **1.** مَشرُوع [mašruːʕ] We're working on a project together. دَنِشتُغُل سُوَة بفَدّ مَشرُوع [daništuɣul suwa bfadd mašruːʕ]

to project • **1.** عِرَض [ʕirað] عَرُض [ʕaruð] *vn:* اِنعِرَض [ʔinʕirað] *p:* The film was projected on the wall. الفِلِم اِنعِرَض عَالحايِط [ʔilfilim ʔinʕirað ʕalħaːyiṭ] • **2.** طِلَع [ṭilaʕ] طُلُوع [ṭuluːʕ] *vn: sv* a. بِرَز [biraz] بَرِز، بُرُوز [bariz, buruːz] *vn: sv* i. The rear end of our new car projects one foot out of our garage. مُؤَخَّر سَيّارَتنا الجِّدِيدَة يِطلَع قَدَم واحِد مِن الكَراج [muʔaxxar sayyaːratna ʔijjidiːda yiṭlaʕ qadam waːħid min ʔilgaraːj]

projector • **1.** برُوجَكتَر [prujaktar] برُوجَكتَرات [prujaktaraːt] *pl:*

to prolong • **1.** طَوَّل [ṭawwal] تَطوِيل [taṭwiːl] *vn:* تطَوَّل [tṭawwal] *p:* You are only prolonging the agony. إنتَ بَسّ دَتطَوِّل العَذاب [ʔinta bass daṭṭawwil ʔilʕaðaːb]

prominent • **1.** بارِز [baːriz] مُعتَبَر [muʕtabar] He's a prominent artist. هُوَّ فَنّان بارِز [huwwa fannaːn baːriz] He has a prominent chin. عِندَه فَدّ حِنِك بارِز [ʕindah fadd ħinič baːriz]

promise • **1.** وَعَد [waʕad] وُعُود [wuʕuːd] *pl:* You didn't keep your promise. ما وُفِّيت بوَعدَك [maː wuffiːt bwaʕdak] • **2.** أَمَل [ʔamal] آمال [ʔaːmaːl] *pl:* تَباشِير [tabaːšiːr] There is some promise of change. أَكُو أَمَل بِالتَّغيِير [ʔaku ʔamal bittaɣyiːr]

to promise • **1.** وُعَد [wuʕad] وَعَد [waʕad] *vn: sv* a. نِطَى [niṭaː] نَطِي [naṭy] *vn:* اِنطَى [ʔinniṭaː] *p:* We

P

promised him a present. وُعَدنا بهَدِيَّة [wuʕadna bhadiyya] Promise me that you won't do it again. أُوعِدنِي أن ما تسَوِّيها مَرَّة لُخ [ʔuːʕidni ʔan maː tsawwiːha marra lux]

promising • **1.** مُبَشِّر بالخَير [mubašširbilxayr] The horse lost the race after a promising start. الحصان خِسَر السِّباق بَعَد بِدايَة مبَشّرَة بِالخير [ʔilħşaːn xişar ʔissibaːq baʕad bidaːya mbaššra bilxiːr]

promissory note • **1.** كُمبيالَة [kumpyaːla] كُمبيالات [kumpyaːlaːt] *pl:*

to promote • **1.** رَفَّع [raffaʕ] تَرفِيع [tarfiːʕ] *vn:* ترَفَّع [traffaʕ] *p:* He was promoted to captain. ترَفَّع إِلَى رَئِيس [traffaʕ ʔila raʔiːs] • **2.** شَجَّع [šajjaʕ] تشجِّع [tšijjiʕ] *vn:* تشَجَّع [tšajjaʕ] *p:* Most countries promote their foreign trade. أكثَر الدُّوَل تشَجِّع تِجارَتها الخارجِيَّة [ʔakθar ʔidduwal tšajjiʕ tijaːratha ʔilxaːrijiyya]

promotion • **1.** تَرفِيع [tarfiːʕ] تَرفِيعات [tarfiːʕaːt] *pl:* My promotion is overdue. تَرفِيعِي تأخَّر [tarfiːʕi tʔaxxar]

prompt • **1.** سَرِيع [sariːʕ] عاجِل [ʕaːjil] I expect a prompt reply. أتوَقَّع جَواب سَرِيع [ʔatwaqqaʕ jawaːb sariːʕ] • **2.** بِالوَقِت [bilwakit] He's prompt in paying his debts. يِدفَع دَينَه بالوَقِت [yidfaʕ daynah bilwakit]

to prompt • **1.** حَفَّز [ħaffaz] تحِفِّز [tħiffiz] *vn:* تحَفَّز [tħaffaz] *p:* What prompted you to say that? شِنُو اللِّي حَفَّزَك تِقُول هاي؟ [šinu ʔilli ħaffazak tiguːl haːy?]

promptly • **1.** بِالضَبُط [biððabuṭ] We start promptly at five. نِبدِي ساعَة خَمسَة بِالضَبُط [nibdi saːʕa xamsa biððabuṭ] • **2.** حالاً [ħaːlan] عَالفور [ʕalfawr] The police arrived promptly. الشُّرطَة وُصلَت حالاً [ʔiššurṭa wuṣlat ħaːlan]

pronoun • **1.** ضَمِير [ðamiːr] ضَمائِر [ðamaːʔir, ðamaːyir] *pl:*

to pronounce • **1.** لُفَظ [lufað] لَفُظ [lafuð] *vn:* اِنلُفَظ [ʔinlufað] *p:* Am I pronouncing the word correctly? دَألفُظ الكَلِمَة صَحِيحَة؟ [daʔalfuð ʔilkalima ṣaħiːħa?] • **2.** نِطَق ب [niṭaq b-] نُطُق [nuṭuq] *vn:* اِنِّطَق [ʔinniṭaq] *p:* The judge will pronounce the sentence tomorrow. الحاكِم راح يِنطُق بِالحُكُم بِالعُقُوبَة باكِر [ʔilħaːkim raːħ yinṭuq bilħukum bilʕuquːba baːčir]

pronounciation • **1.** لَفُظ [lafuð] ألفاظ [ʔalfaːð] *pl:* That's not correct pronunciation. هَاللَّفُظ مُو صَحِيح [hallafuð muː ṣaħiːħ]

proof • **1.** بُرهان [burhaːn] بَراهِين [baraːhiːn] *pl:* دَلِيل [daliːl] أدِلَّة [ʔadilla] *pl:* What proof do you have of that? شِنُو بُرهانَك عَلَى هاي؟ [šinu burhaːnak ʕala haːy?] • **2.** إثبات [ʔiθbaːt] إثباتات [ʔiθbaːtaːt] *pl:* There's definite proof that he killed her. أكُو إثبات أكِيد إنُّو هُوَّ اللِّي قِتَلها [ʔaku ʔiθbaːt ʔakiːd ʔinnu huwwa ʔilli qitalha] • **3.** مِسوَدَّة [miswadda] مِسوَدّات [miswaddaːt] *pl:* I've just finished reading proof on my new article. هَستَوّنِي خَلَّصِت قرايَة المِسوَدَّة لِمَقالتِي الجِّدِيدَة [hastawwni xallaṣit qraːyat ʔilmiswadda limaqaːlti ʔijjidiːda]

propaganda • **1.** دِعايَة [diʕaːya]

to propagate • **1.** كَثَّر [kaθθar, čaθθar] تَكثِير [takθiːr] *vn:* *sv* i. There are many ways of propagating this plant. أكُو طُرُق مُتَعَدِّدَة لِتكثِير هَالأشجار [ʔaku ṭuruq mutaʕaddida litakθiːr halʔašjaːr] • **2.** نِشَر [nišar] نَشِر [našir] *vn:* اِنِّشَر [ʔinnišar] *p:* The first four caliphs propagated the Islamic religion. الخُلَفاء الرّاشِدِين نِشرَوا الإسلام [ʔilxulafaːʔ ʔirraːšidiːn nišraw ʔilʔislaːm]

propeller • **1.** پَروانَة [parawaːna] پَروانات [parawaːnaːt] *pl:*

proper • **1.** صَحِيح [ṣaħiːħ] لايِق [laːyig, laːyiq] That isn't the proper way to handle people. هَذِي مُو الطَّرِيقَة الصَّحِيحَة المُعامَلَة النّاس [haːði muː ʔiṭṭariːqa ʔiṣṣaħiːħa limuʕaːmalat ʔinnaːs] • **2.** مُناسِب [munaːsib] مُلائِم [mulaːʔim] This isn't the proper time to ask questions. هَذا مُو الوَقت المُلائِم السُؤال أسئِلَة [haːða muː ʔilwakt ʔilmulaːʔim lisuʔaːl ʔasʔila] • **3.** أصلِي [ʔaṣli] In 1937 the Japanese invaded China proper. سَنَة ألِف وَتِسِع مِيَّة وَسَبعَة وَثلاثِين اليابانِيِّين غِزَوا أرض الصِّين الأصلِيَّة [sana ʔalif wtisiʕ miyya wsabʕa wtlaːθiːn ʔilyabaːniyyiːn ɣizaw ʔarð ʔiṣṣiːn ʔilʔaṣliyya] • **4.** مِختَصّ [mixtaṣṣ] You have to talk to the proper person. لازِم تِحكِي وِيّا الشَّخص المُختَصّ [laːzim tiħči wiyya ʔiššaxṣ ʔilmuxtaṣṣ]

properly • **1.** كَما يَجِب [kama yajib] حَسب الأُصُول [ħasb ʔilʔuṣuːl] I'll show you how to do it properly. راح أراوِيك شلَون تسَوِّيها كَما يَجِب [raːħ ʔaraːwiːk šluːn tsawwiːha kama yajib] • **2.** لِياقَة [liyaːqa] Can't you behave properly? ما تِقدَر تِتصَرَّف بلِياقَة؟ [maː tigdar titṣarraf bliyaːqa?]

property • **1.** مُلك [muluk] أملاك [ʔamlaːk] *pl:* All the furniture is my property. كُلّ الأثاث مُلكِي [kull ʔilʔaθaːθ mulki] He has a mortgage on his property. مسَوِّي رَهان عَلَى مُلكَه [msawwi rahaːn ʕala mulkah] • **2.** خاصِّيَّة [xaːṣṣiyya] خَواصّ [xawaːṣṣ] *pl:* خاصِّيَة [xaːṣṣiyya] خَصائِص [xaṣaːʔiṣ] *pl:* one of the properties of copper is its reddish color. وِحدَة مِن خَواصّ الصِّفِر لونَه الأحمَر [wiħda min xawaːṣṣ ʔiṣṣifir luːnah ʔilʔaħmar]

prophecy • **1.** نُبُوءَة [nubuːʔa] نُبُوءات [nubuːʔaːt] *pl:*

to prophesy • **1.** تنَبَّأ [tnabbaʔ] تَنَبُّؤ [tanabbuʔ] *vn:* *sv* a. He prophesied that the world would come to an end

P

this coming year. تنَبّأ العالَم راح ينتِهِي السَّنَة الجّايَّة [tnabbaʔ ʔilʕaːlam raːħ yintihi ʔissana ʔiǰǰaːyya]

prophet • **1.** نَبِي [nabi] أنبِياء [ʔanbiyaːʔ] *pl:*

proportion • **1.** تَناسُب [tanaːsub] That picture is all out of proportion. التّناسُب بِهالصُّورَة كُلّه غَلَط [ʔittanaːsub bhaṣṣuːra kullah ɣalaṭ] • **2.** نِسبَة [nisba] نِسَب [nisab] *pl:* Everybody is paid in proportion to what he does. كُلّ واحِد ياخُذ بِالنِّسبَة لِشُغلَه [kull waːħid yaːxuð binnisba liššuɣlah] • **3.** فِئَة [fiʔa] فِئات [fiʔaːt] *pl:* قِسِم [qisim] أقسام [ʔaqsaːm] *pl:* A small proportion of the people approved. فِئَة قَلِيلَة مِن النّاس وافقوا [fiʔa qaliːla min ʔinnaːs waːfqaw]

*** His expenses are entirely out of proportion to his income.** • **1.** مَصرُوفاته ما تِتناسَب ويّا وارِداته أبَداً [maṣruːfaːtah maː titnaːsab wiyya waːridaːtah ʔabadan]

proportional • **1.** نِسبِي [nisbi] These figures show the proportional distribution of population. هَالأرقام تبَيِّن التَّوزِيع النِّسبِي لِلسُّكّان [halʔarqaːm tbayyin ʔittawziːʕ ʔinnisbi lissukkaːn] • **2.** مِتناسِب [mitnaːsib] Your wages will be proportional to your education. أُجُورَك راح تكُون مِتناسبَة ويّا دِراستَك [ʔuǰuːrak raːħ tkuːn mitnaːsba wiyya diraːstak]

proportioned • **1.** مِتناسِق [mitnaːsiq] مِتناسِب [mitnaːsib] Her figure is well-proportioned. جِسِمها حِلو مِتناسِق [ǰisimha ħilw mitnaːsiq]

proposal • **1.** عَرِض [ʕarið] عُرُوض [ʕuruːð] *pl:* He made me an interesting proposal. قَدَّملِي عَرِض مُغرِي [qaddamli ʕarið muɣri] • **2.** اِقتِراح [ʔiqtiraːħ] اِقتِراحات [ʔiqtiraːħaːt] *pl:* Your proposal met with the approval of all members. اِقتِراحَك نال مُوافَقَة كُلّ الأعضاء [ʔiqtiraːħak naːl muwaːfaqat kull ʔilʔaʕðaːʔ] • **3.** خُطبَة [xuṭba] خُطَب [xuṭab] *pl:* Our daughter had two proposals at the same time. بِنِتنا جَتّها خُطبَتَين بِنَفِس الوَقِت [binitna ǰattha xuṭubtayn bnafis ʔilwakit]

to propose • **1.** اِقتِرَح [ʔiqtiraħ] اِقتِراح [ʔiqtiraːħ] *vn:* *sv* i. I propose we go to the movies. أقتِرِح نرُوح لِلسِّينَما [ʔaqtiriħ nruːħ lissinama]

to propose to • **1.** خِطَب [xiṭab] خُطبَة [xuṭba] *vn:* اِنخِطَب [ʔinxiṭab] *p:* طِلَب إيد [ṭilabʔiːd] طَلَب [ṭalab] *vn:* اِنطِلَب [ʔinṭilab] *p:* He proposed to her. خِطَبها [xiṭabha] He proposed to her. طِلَب إيدها [ṭilab ʔiːdha]

proposition • **1.** عَرِض [ʕarið] عِرَض [ʕirað] He made me an excellent proposition. عِرَض عَلَيّا عَرِض مُمتاز [ʕirað ʕalayya ʕarið mumtaːz] • **2.** شَغلَة [šaɣla] شَغلات [šaɣlaːt] *pl:* It is a paying proposition. هاي شَغلَة مُربِحَة [haːy šaɣla murbiħa] • **3.** اِقتِراح [ʔiqtiraːħ] اِقتِراحات [ʔiqtiraːħaːt] *pl:* Your proposition is very sound. اِقتِراحَك كُلِّش مَعقُول [ʔiqtiraːħak kulliš maʕquːl]

proprietor • **1.** مالِك [maːlik] مُلّاك [mullaːk] *pl:* صاحِب [ṣaːħib] أصحاب [ʔaṣħaːb] *pl:*

pros and cons • **1.** مَحاسِن ومَساوِئ [maħaːsin wmasaːwiʔ]

prose • **1.** نَثِر [naθir]

rhymed prose • **1.** سَجِع [saǰiʕ]

to prosecute • **1.** قام [qaːm] n أقام [ʔaqaːm] إقامَة [ʔiqaːma] *vn:* *sv* i. Do you think the government will prosecute him? تِفتِكِر الحُكُومَة راح تقِيم دَعوَة عَليه؟ [tiftikir ʔilħukuːma raːħ tqiːm daʕwa ʕaliːh?]

prosecutor • **1.** مِشتِكِي [mištiki] مُدَّعِي [muddaʕi] مُدَّعِين [muddaʕiːn] *pl:*

prospect • **1.** أمَل [ʔamal] آمال [ʔaːmaːl] *pl:* What are his prospects of getting a job? شقَدّ عِندَه أمَل بِالحُصُول عَالوَظِيفَة؟ [šgadd ʕindah ʔamal bilħuṣuːl ʕalwaðiːfa?] • **2.** فِكرَة [fikra] فِكرات، فِكِر، أفكار [fikraːt, fikir, ʔafkaːr.] *pl:* I don't like the prospect of having to work with him. فِكرَة الشُّغُل ويّاه ما تِعجِبنِي [fikrat ʔiššuɣul wiyyaːh maː tiʕǰibni]

*** This boy has good prospects.** • **1.** هَالوَلَد عِندَه مُستَقبَل زَين [halwalad ʕindah mustaqbal zayn]

prospective • **1.** مُنتَظَر [muntaðar] مَأمُول [maʔmuːl] He is my prospective son-in-law. هُوَّ نِسِيبِي المُنتَظَر [huwwa nisiːbi ʔilmuntaðar]

prostitute • **1.** قَحبَة [gaħba] قحاب [għaːb] *pl:* مُومِس [muːmis] مُومِسات [muːmisaːt] *pl:* عاهِرَة [ʕaːhra] عاهِرات [ʕaːhraːt] *pl:*

prostitution • **1.** دَعارَة [daʕaːra] بَغاء [baɣaːʔ]

to protect • **1.** حِمَى [ħimaː] حَمِي [ħami] *vn:* انحِمَى [ʔinħimaː] *p:* I wear these glasses to protect my eyes. آنِي ألبَس هالمَناظِر أحمِي عيُونِي [ʔaːni ʔalbas halmanaːðir ʔaħmi ʕyuːni] • **2.** حافَظ عَلَى [ħaːfað ʕala] مُحافَظَة [muħaːfaða] *vn:* تحافَظ [tħaːfað] *p:* I will protect your interests. آنِي راح أحافُظ عَلَى مَصلَحتَك [ʔaːni raːħ ʔaħaːfuð ʕala maṣlaħtak] • **3.** دافَع عَن [daːfaʕ ʕan] دِفاع [difaːʕ] *vn:* *sv* i. Everyone must protect his own property. كُلّ واحِد لازِم يدافِع عَن مُلكَه [kull waːħid laːzim yidaːfiʕ ʕan mulkah] • **4.** وُقَى [wuqaː] وُقايَة [wuqaːya] *vn:* اِنوُقَى [ʔinwuqaː] *p:* This medicine protects the eyes from disease. هَالدُّوا يوَقِي العين مِن الأمراض [hadduwa yuːqi ʔilʕiːn min ʔilʔamraːð]

protection • **1.** حِمايَة [ħimaːya] There is no protection against that. ماكُو حِمايَة ضِدّ هاي [maːku ħimaːya ðidd haːy]

protectorate • **1.** مَحمِيَّة [maħmiyya] مَحمِيّات [maħmiyya:t] *pl:*

to protest • **1.** اِحتَجّ [ʔiħtaǰǰ] اِحتِجاج [ʔiħtiǰa:ǰ] *vn: sv* a. I protest! آنِي أَحتَجّ [ʔa:ni ʔaħtaǰǰ] • **2.** أَصَرّ عَلَى [ʔaṣarr ʕala] إِصرار [ʔiṣra:r] *vn: sv* i. He protested his innocence throughout the trial. أَصَرّ عَلَى بَرائتَه طُول المُحاكَمَة [ʔaṣarr ʕala bara:ʔtah ṭu:l ʔilmuħa:kama]

Protestant • **1.** برَوتِستانِي [prutista:ni] برَوتِستانِيِّين [prutista:niyyi:n] *pl:*

protestantism • **1.** برَوتِستانِيَّة [prutista:niyya]

protocol • **1.** برَوتَوكَول [prutuku:l]

proton • **1.** برَوتَون [prutu:n] برَوتَونات [prutu:na:t] *pl:*

proud • **1.** فَخُور [faxu:r] I am proud of you. آنِي فَخُور بِيك [ʔa:ni faxu:r bi:k] I am proud of you. آنِي أَفتِخِر بِيك [ʔa:ni ʔaftixir bi:k] • **2.** أَنُوف [ʔa:nu:f] She is too proud, to ask for someone's help. هاي أَأنَف مِن أَن تِستَنجِد بأَحَّد [ha:y ʔaʔnaf min ʔan tistanǰid bʔaħħad]

to prove • **1.** أَثبَت [ʔaθbat] إِثبات [ʔiθba:t] *vn: sv* i. بَرهَن [barhan] تبُرهِن [tburhin] *vn:* تبَرهَن [tbarhan] *p:* I can prove I didn't do it. أَقدَر أَثبِت بأَنني ما سَوَّيتها [ʔagdar ʔaθbit bʔanni ma: sawwi:tha]

to prove to be • **1.** طِلَع [ṭilaʕ] طُلُوع [ṭulu:ʕ] *vn: sv* a. The rumor proved to be lies. هَالحَكِي طِلَع كِذِب [halħači ṭilʕat čiðib]

proverb • **1.** مَثَل [maθal] أَمثال [ʔamθa:l] *pl:* قَول مَأثُور [qawl maʔθu:r] أَقوال مَأثُورَة [ʔaqwa:l maʔθu:ra] *pl:*

to provide • **1.** جَهَّز [ǰahhaz] تَجهِيز، تجهِّز [taǰhi:z, tǰihhiz] *vn:* تجَهَّز [tǰahhaz] *p:* زَوَّد [zawwad] تَزوِيد [tazwi:d] *vn:* تزَوَّد [tzawwad] *p:* The university is going to provide the laboratory with modern equipment. الجّامِعَة راح تجَهِّز المُختَبَر بلَوازِم حَدِيثَة [ʔiǰǰa:miʕa ra:ħ dǰahhiz ʔilmuxtabar blawa:zim ħadi:θa] • **2.** هَيَّأ [hayyaʔ] تهَيِّئ [thiyyiʔ] *vn:* تهَيَّأ [thayyaʔ] *p:* We will provide the place for the meeting. راح نهَيِّئ مَكان لِلإِجتِماع [ra:ħ nhayyiʔ maka:n lilʔiǰtima:ʕ] • **3.** وَفَّر [waffar] تَوفِير [tawfi:r] *vn:* توَفَّر [twaffar] *p:* We provided all means of comfort. وَفَّرنا كُلّ أَسباب الرّاحَة [waffarna kull ʔasba:b ʔirra:ħa]

to provide for • **1.** عال [ʕa:l] إِعالَة [ʔiʕa:la] *vn: sv* i. He has to provide for the whole family. لازِم يعِيل العائِلَة كُلّها [la:zim yʕi:l ʔilʕa:ʔila kullha] • **2.** حِسَب [ħisab] حساب [ħsa:b] *vn:* اِنحِسَب [ʔinħisab] *p:* The law provides for such special cases. القانُون يِحسِب حِساب مِثِل هَالقَضايا الخاصَّة [ʔilqa:nu:n yiħsib ħisa:b miθil halqaða:ya: ʔilxa:ṣṣa] • **3.** اِحتاط [ʔiħta:ṭ] اِحتِياط [ʔiħtiya:ṭ] *vn: sv* a. We will provide for a long winter. راح نِحتاط إِلَى شِتا طَوِيل [ra:ħ niħta:ṭ ʔila šita ṭawi:l]

provided, providing • **1.** بشَرط [bšarṭ] عَلَى شَرط [ʕala šarṭ] I'll go, provided you come with me. أَرُوح بشَرط تِجِي وِيّايا [ʔaru:ħ bšarṭ tiǰi wiyya:ya]

province • **1.** لِواء [liwa:ʔ] أَلوِيَة [ʔalwiya] *pl:* Iraq is divided into fourteen provinces. العِراق مِنقِسِم إِلَى أَربَاطَعَش لِواء [ʔilʕira:q minqisim ʔila ʔarba:ṭaʕaš liwa:ʔ]

provision • **1.** نَصّ [naṣṣ] نصُوص [nṣu:ṣ] *pl:* There is no provision made for this in the law. ماكُو نَصّ عَلَى هَذا بِالقانُون [ma:ku naṣṣ ʕala ha:ða bilqa:nu:n]

provisions • **1.** تَجهِيزات [taǰhi:za:t] مَؤُونَة [maʔu:na] Our provisions are running low. تَجهِيزاتنا دَتقِلّ [taǰhi:za:tna datqill]

to provoke • **1.** أَثار [ʔaθa:r] إِثارَة [ʔiθa:ra] *vn: sv* i. His remark provoked a roar of laughter. مُلاحَظتَه أَثارَت عاصِفَة مِن الضِّحِك [mula:ħaðtah ʔaθa:rat ʕa:ṣifa min ʔiððiħik] • **2.** اِستَفَزّ [ʔistafazz] اِستِفزاز [ʔistifza:z] *vn: sv* i. Don't provoke him. لا تِستَفِزَّه [la: tistafizzah] His behavior is provoking. تَصَرُّفَه يِستَفِزّ الواحِد [taṣarrufah yistafizz ʔilwa:ħid]

*** He's provoked about it.** • **1.** هُوَّ مِغتاض عَنها [huwwa miɣta:ð ʕanha]

prune • **1.** عِنجاصَة مِيَبَّسَة [ʕinǰa:ṣa myabbasa] عِنجاصات مِيَبِّسَة [ʕinǰa:ṣa:t myabbisa] *pl:* عِنجاص مِيَبَّس [ʕinǰa:ṣ myabbas] *Collective*

to prune • **1.** قَلَّم [qallam] تَقلِيم [taqli:m] *vn:* تقَلَّم [tqallam] *p:* The rose bushes need to be pruned. عرُوق الوَرِد يِنرادِلها تِتقَلَّم [ʕru:g ʔilwarid yinra:dilha titqallam]

psychiatrist • **1.** طَبِيب نَفسانِي [ṭabi:b nafsa:ni] أَطِبّاء نَفسانِيِّين [ʔaṭibba:ʔ nafsa:niyyi:n] *pl:*

psychology • **1.** عِلم النَّفس [ʕilm ʔinnafs]

public • **1.** عُمُوم [ʕumu:m] ناس [na:s] Is this park open to the public? هَالحَدِيقَة مَفتُوحَة لِلعُمُوم؟ [halħadi:qa maftu:ħa lilʕumu:m?] • **2.** عامّ [ʕa:mm] Public opinion is against him. الرَّأي العامّ ضِدَّه [ʔirraʔy ʔilʕa:mm ðiddah] Public health requires these measures. الصِّحَّة العامَّة تِتطَلَّب هَالإِجراءات [ʔiṣṣiħħa ʔilʕa:mma tiṭṭallab halʔiǰra:ʔa:t] • **3.** عُمُومِي [ʕumu:mi] Is there a public telephone here? أَكُو تِلِفُون عُمُومِي هنا؟ [ʔaku tilifu:n ʕumu:mi hna?] • **4.** عَلَنِي [ʕalani]

P

عُمُومِي [ʕumuːmi] I bought this rug at a public auction. اِشْتِرَيت هَالسِّجَّادَة بِمَزاد عَلَنِي [ʔištiriːt hassijjaːda bmazaːd ʕalani]

*** He embezzled public funds. • 1.** اِختِلَس أَموال الدَّولَة [ʔixtilas ʔamwaːl ʔiddawla]

*** Such books will always find a public.**
• 1. هِيكِي كُتُب تشُوفِلها قُرّاء دائِماً [hiːči kutub tšuːfilha qurraːʔ daːʔiman]

in public • 1. قِدّام النّاس [giddaːm ʔinnaːs] You shouldn't behave like this in public. ما لازِم تِتصَرَّف هِيكِي قِدّام النّاس [maː laːzim titṣarraf hiːči giddaːm ʔinnaːs]

publication • 1. نَشِر [našir] What is the date of publication? شوَقت تارِيخ النَّشِر؟ [šwakit taːriːx ʔinnašir?] **• 2.** نَشرَة [našra] نَشرات [našraːt] *pl:* This is a useful publication. هاي نَشرَة مُفِيدَة [haːy našra mufiːda]

publicity • 1. دِعايَة [diʕaːya] That's what I call clever publicity. هَذا اللِّي أَسَمِّيه دِعايَة ماهرَة [haːða ʔilli ʔasammiːh diʕaːya maːhra]

to publish • 1. نِشَر [nišar] نَشِر [našir] *vn:* اِنِّشَر [ʔinnišar] *p:* He hopes to publish his new book very soon. يِتأَمَّل يِنشُر كِتابَه الجِّدِيد قَرِيباً [yitʔammal yinšur kitaːbah ʔijjidiːd qariːban]

publisher • 1. ناشِر [naːšir] ناشِرِين [naːširiːn] *pl:*

publishing house • 1. دار نَشِر [daːr našir]

puddle • 1. نُقرَة [nugra] نُقَر [nugar] *pl:* بُركَة [burka] بُرَك [burak] *pl:* Careful, don't step into the puddle! دِير بالَك، لا تِخطِي بِالنُّقرَة [diːr baːlak, laː tixṭi binnugra]

puff • 1. نَفَس [nafas] أنفاس [ʔanfaːs] *pl:* I got sick after only one puff. نَفسِي لِعبَت بَعَد نَفَس واحِد [nafsi liʕbat baʕad nafas waːħid]

pull • 1. One more pull and we'll have it open. جَرَّة لُخ بَعَد راح تِنفَكّ [jarra lux baʕad raːħ tinfakk] **• 2.** واسطَة [waːsṭa] وَسائِط، وَسايِط [waṣaːʔiṭ, waṣaːyiṭ] *pl:* خاطرانَة [xaːṭraːna] ظِهَر [ðihar] ظُهُور، ظهُورَة [ðuhuːr, ðhuːra] *pl:* You need a lot of pull to get a job here. تِحتاج هوايَة واسطات يَاللّٰه تِقدَر تحَصِّل شُغُل هنا [tiħtaːj hwaːya waːsṭaːt yallah tigdar tħaṣṣil šuɣul hna]

to pull • 1. جَرّ [jarr] جَرّ [jarr] *vn:* اِنجَرّ [ʔinjarr] *p:* Don't pull so hard! لا تجُرّ هَالقَدّ حيل [laː djurr halgadd ħiːl] **• 2.** شِلَع [šilaʕ] شَلِع [šaliʕ] *vn:* اِنشِلَع [ʔinšilaʕ] *p:* This tooth must be pulled. هَالسِّنّ لازِم يِنشِلِع [hassinn laːzim yinšiliʕ]

*** Don't pull any funny stuff! • 1.** لا تبِيع شَطارَة براسِي [laː tbiːʕ šaṭaːra braːsi]

*** Don't try to pull the wool over my eyes!**
• 1. لَ تحاوِل تعَبُّر عَلَيّا قِرِش قَلب [laː tħaːwil tʕabbur ʕalayya qiriš qalb] / لا تحاوِل تلَفلِفنِي [laː tħaːwil tlaflifni]

*** He pulled a fast one on me. • 1.** دَولَبنِي [dawlabni] / ضِرَبنِي كَلَك [ðirabni kalak]

*** I pulled a big boner. • 1.** سَوَّيت مِن نَفسِي مَضحَكَة [sawwiːt min nafsi maðħaka]

*** Pull over to the side! • 1.** أوقَف عَلَى صَفحَة [ʔuːgaf ʕala ṣafħa] / أُطبُق [ʔuṭbug]

to pull apart • 1. فاكَك [faːkak] تفاكُك [tfaːkuk] *vn:* تفاكَك [tfaːkak] *p:* It took three men to pull them apart. ثلاث رِياجِيل يَاللّٰه قِدرَوا يفاكِكُوهُم [tlaθ riyaːjiːl yallah gidraw yfaːkikuːhum] **• 2.** فَسَّخ [fassax] تَفسِيخ [tafsiːx] *vn:* تفَسَّخ [tfassax] *p:* I had to pull the radio apart in order to find what was wrong. اِضطَرَّيت أَفَسِّخ الرّادِيُو حَتَّى أَلقِي العَيب [ʔiðṭarriːt ʔafassix ʔirraːdyu ħatta ʔalgi ʔilʕawb]

to pull down • 1. نَزَّل [nazzal] تَنزِيل [tanziːl] *vn:* تنَزَّل [tnazzal] *p:* Shall I pull down the shades? أَنَزِّل البَردات؟ [ʔanazzil ʔilpardaːt?] **• 2.** هِدَم [hidam] هَدِم [hadim] *vn:* اِنهِدَم [ʔinhidam] *p:* They're going to pull down all the old houses. راح يهِدمُون كُلّ البيُوت العَتِيقَة [raːħ yhidmuːn kull ʔilbyuːt ʔilʕatiːga]

to pull in • 1. طَبّ [ṭabb] طَبّ [ṭabb] *vn: sv* u. وُصَل [wuṣal] وُصُول [wuṣuːl] *vn: sv* a. When did your train pull in? قِطارَك شوَقِت طَبّ؟ [qiṭaːrak šwakit ṭabb?]

to pull oneself together • 1. شَدّ [šadd] شَدّ [šadd] *vn:* اِنشَدّ [ʔinšadd] *p:* Pull yourself together! شِدّ حَيلَك [šidd ħiːlak]

to pull out • 1. شِلَع [šilaʕ] شَلِع [šaliʕ] *vn:* اِنشِلَع [ʔinšilaʕ] *p:* The childdren pulled out all the weeds. الأَطفال شِلعَوا كُلّ الحَشِيش [ʔilʔaṭfaːl šilʕaw kull ʔilħašiːš] **• 2.** طِلَع [ṭilaʕ] طُلُوع [ṭuluːʕ] *vn: sv* a. The train will pull out any minute. القِطار راح يِطلَع بِأَي لَحظَة [ʔilqiṭaːr raːħ yiṭlaʕ bʔayy laħða]

to pull through • 1. دَبَّر [dabbar] تَدبِير [tadbiːr] *vn:* تدَبَّر [tdabbar] *p:* عُبَر [ʕubar] عَبَر [ʕabar] *vn: sv* u. We were afraid she might not pull through it. كِنّا خايفِين ما راح تدَبُّرها [činna xaːyfiːn maː raːħ ddabburha]

to pull up • 1. طُبَق سُوَة [ṭubag suwa] طَبُق [ṭabug] *vn: sv* u. The car pulled up in front of the house. السَّيّارَة طُبقَت قِدّام البَيت [ʔissayyaːra ṭubgat giddaːm ʔilbayt] **• 2.** جَرّ [jarr] جَرّ [jarr] *vn:* اِنجَرّ [ʔinjarr] *p:* Pull up a chair! جُرّلَك فَدّ كُرسِي [jurrlak fadd kursi]

pulley • 1. بَكرَة [bakra] بَكرات، بَكَر [bakraːt, bakar.] *pl:*

pulse • 1. نَبُض [nabuð] The nurse took my pulse. المُمَرِّضَة أَخذَت نَبضِي [ʔilmumarriða ʔaxðat nabði]

pump • 1. مَضَخَّة [maðaxxa] مَضَخّات [maðaxxaːt] *pl:* We have a pump in our country house. عِدنا مَضَخَّة بِبَيتنا الرِّيفِي [ʕidna maðaxxa bibaytna ʔirriːfi] **• 2.** بَمب [pamp] بَمبات [pampaːt] *pl:* I need a new pump for the bicycle. أَحتاج بَمب جِدِيد لِلبايسِكل [ʔaħtaːj pamb jidiːd lilpaːysikil]

to pump • 1. ضَخّ [ðaxx] ضَخّ [ðaxx] *vn:* اِنضَخّ [ʔinðaxx] *p:* Shall I pump some water? أَضُخّ شوَيَّة ماي؟ [ʔaðuxx šwayya maːy?] • **2.** اِستَدرَج [ʔistadraǰ] اِستِدراج [ʔistidraːǰ] *vn: sv* i. Don't let him pump you. لا تخَلّيه يِستَدرِجَك [laː txalliːh yistadriǰak]

to pump up • **1.** ضَخّ [ðaxx] ضَخّ [ðaxx] *vn:* اِنضَخّ [ʔinðaxx] *p:* Our water is pumped up from the spring. الماي مالنا يِنضَخّ مِن العَين [ʔilmaːy maːlna yinðaxx min ʔilʕayn] • **2.** نُفَخ [nufax] نَفُخ [nafux] *vn:* اِنُّفَخ [ʔinnufax] *p:* Will you please pump up the front tires? باللّه ما تِنفُخ التّايِرات القِدّامِيَّة؟ [ballah maː tinfux ʔittaːyiraːt ʔilgiddaːmiyya?]

pumping station • **1.** مَحَطّة ضَخّ [maħaṭṭat ðaxx] مَحَطّات ضَخّ [maħaṭṭaːt ðaxx] *pl:*

pumpkin • **1.** شِجرَة أسكَلَة [šiǰrat ʔaskala] شِجرات أسكَلَة [šiǰraːt ʔaskala] *pl:* شِجَر أسكَلَة [šiǰar ʔaskala] *Collective*

punch • **1.** ضَربَة جِمع [ðarbat ǰimiʕ] ضَربات جِمع [ðarbaːt ǰimiʕ] *pl:* لَكمَة [lakma] لَكمات [lakmaːt] *pl:* بوكس [buːks] بوكسات [buːksaːt] *pl:* The punch knocked him down. ضَربَة الجِّمع وَقّعَتَه [ðarbat ʔiǰǰimiʕ waggʕatah] • **2.** قُوَّة [quwwa, guwwa] قُوّات [quwwaːt] *pl:* His speech lacked punch. حَدِيثَه كان يِنقُصّه القُوَّة [ħadiːθah čaːn yinquṣṣah ʔilquwwa] • **3.** شَربَت [šarbat] شَرابِت [šaraːbit] *pl:* Would you like some more punch? تحِبّ تِشرَب بَعَد شَربَت؟ [tħibb tišrab baʕad šarbat?]

to punch • **1.** زِرَف [ziraf] زَرُف [zaruf] *vn:* اِنزِرَف [ʔinziraf] *p:* قِرَض [girað] قَرُض [garuð] *vn:* اِنقِرَض [ʔingirað] *p:* The conductor punched our tickets. مُفَتِّش الباص زِرَف تِكتاتنا [mufattiš ʔilpaːṣ ziraf tiktaːtna] • **2.** ضِرَب [ðirab] ضَرُب [ðarub] *vn:* اِنضِرَب [ʔinðirab] *p:* Shut up, or I will punch you in the nose. إنكَبّ، تَرَة أضُربَك بِالخَشم [ʔinčabb, tara ʔaðurbak bilxašm]

puncture • **1.** زُرُف [zuruf] زرُوف [zruːf] *pl:* ثُقُب [θ ugub] ثُقُوب [θuguːb] *pl:* بَنجَر [pančar] Is there a puncture in the tire? أكُو زُرُف بِالتّايَر؟ [ʔaku zuruf bittaːyir?]

to puncture • **1.** زِرَف [ziraf] زَرُف [zaruf] *vn:* اِنزِرَف [ʔinziraf] *p:* نِقَب [nigab] نَقُب [nagub] *vn:* اِنِّقَب [ʔinnigab] *p:* He has a punctured eardrum. طَبلَة إذنَه مَزرُوفَة [ṭablat ʔiðnah mazruːfa]

to punish • **1.** عاقَب عَلَى [ʕaːqab ʕala] مُعاقَبَة [muʕaːqaba] *vn:* تعاقَب [tʕaːqab] *p:* Violations will be severely punished. المُخالَفات يِتعاقَب عَليها بشِدَّة [ʔilmuxaːlafaːt yitʕaːqab ʕaliːha bšidda] • **2.** نِطَى [niṭaː] نَطِي [naṭy] *vn:* اِنِّطَى [ʔinniṭaː] *p:* I think he's been punished enough. أعتِقِد اِنِّطَى قَصاص كافي [ʔaʕtiqid ʔinniṭaː qaṣaːṣ kaːfi]

punishment • **1.** عُقُوبَة [ʕuquːba] عُقُوبات [ʕuquːbaːt] *pl:* قَصاص [qaṣaːṣ] The punishment was too severe. العُقُوبَة كانَت كُلِّش قاسيَة [ʔilʕuquːba čaːnat kulliš qaːsya]

*** Our car has taken a lot of punishment.** • **1.** سَيّارَتنا اِشتِغَل دِينها [sayyaːratna ʔištiʕal diːnha]

punitive • **1.** تَأدِيبِي [taʔdiːbi] We have to send a punitive expedition to the strike area. لازم ندِزّ حَملَة تَأدِيبِيَّة لِمَنطِقَة الإضطِراب [laːzim ndizz ħamla taʔdiːbiyya lmanṭiqat ʔilʔiðṭiraːb]

pupil • **1.** تِلمِيذ [tilmiːð] تَلامِيذ [talaːmiːð] *pl:* طالِب [ṭaːlib] طُلّاب [ṭullaːb] *pl:* She has twenty pupils in her class. عِدها عِشرِين تِلمِيذ بِصَفّها [ʕidha ʕišriːn tilmiːð bṣaffha] • **2.** بُؤبُؤ [buʔbuʔ] pl. baʔaabiʔ. The pupil of the left eye is dilated. البُؤبُؤ مال العَين اليِسرَة توَسَّع [ʔilbuʔbuʔ maːl ʔilʕayn ʔilyisra twassaʕ]

puppy • **1.** جِرو [ǰirw] جراوَة [ǰraːwa] *pl:* بُوجِي [buːǰi] أبواج [ʔabwaːǰ] *pl:*

purchase • **1.** شَروَة [šarwa] شَروات [šarwaːt] *pl:* This boat was a wonderful purchase. هَالبَلَم كان خُوش شَروَة [halbalam čaːn xuːš šarwa]

to purchase • **1.** اِشتِرَى [ʔištiraː] شرايَة، شَروَة [šraːya, šarwa] *vn: sv* i. We're going to purchase a new home this fall. راح نِشتِري بَيت جِدِيد هَالخَرِيف [raːħ ništri bayt ǰidiːd halxariːf]

pure • **1.** خالِص [xaːliṣ] The necktie is pure silk. الرِّباط حَرِير خالِص [ʔirribaːṭ ħariːr xaːliṣ] • **2.** نَقِي [naqi] Do you have pure alcohol? عِندَك كُحُول نَقِيَّة؟ [ʕindak kuħuːl naqiyya?] • **3.** صِرف [ṣirf] بَحت [baħt] That's pure nonsense. هَذِي لَغوَة صِرفَة [haːði laɣwa ṣirfa]

purely • **1.** بَحت [baħt] صِرف [ṣirf] This is a purely political matter. هَذا مَوضُوع سِياسِي بَحت [haːða mawðuːʕ siyaːsi baħt]

purge • **1.** تَطهِير [taṭhiːr] تَطهِيرات [taṭhiːraːt] *pl:* This government needs a purge of all corruption. هَالحُكُومَة تِحتاج إلَى تَطهِير الفَساد [halħukuːma tiħtaːǰ ʔila taṭhiːr ʔilfasaːd]

to purge • **1.** طَهَّر [ṭahhar] تَطهِير [taṭhiːr] *vn:* تطَهَّر [tṭahhar] *p:* The government is planning to purge its police department. الحُكُومَة ناوِيَه تطَهِّر سِلك الشُّرطَة [ʔilħukuːma naːwiyah tṭahhir silk ʔiššurṭa]

to purify • **1.** صَفَّى [ṣaffaː] تَصفِيَة [taṣfiya] *vn:* تصَفَّى [tṣaffaː] *p:* This water needs to be purified. هالماي لازم يِتصَفَّى [halmaːy laːzim yitṣaffaː]

purple • **1.** شَرابِي، بَنَفسَجِي [šaraːbi, banafsaǰi]

purpose • **1.** غَرَض [ɣarað] أغراض [ʔaɣraːð] *pl:* مُراد [muraːd] مَبغَة [mabɣa] مَباغِي [mabaːɣi] *pl:* قَصِد [qaṣid] غايَة [ɣaːya] غايات [ɣaːyaːt] *pl:* What's the purpose of all this?

P

شِنُو الغَرَض مِن كُلّ هَذا؟ [šinu ʔilɣarað min kull haːða?] He left without achieving his purpose. تِرَك بَلا ما ينال غَرَضَه [tirak bala maː ynaːl ɣaraðah] What purpose did he have in doing that? شِنُو كان غَرَضَه مِن السوايات هاي؟ [šinu čaːn ɣaraðah min ʔiswaːyaːt haːy?] You can use this tool for many purposes. تِقدَر تِستَعمِل هَالأَلَة لعِدَّة غايات [tigdar tistaʕmil halʔaːla lʕiddat ɣaːyaːt]

on purpose • **1.** عَن قَصِد [ʕan qaṣid] عَمداً [ʕamdan] قَصداً [qaṣdan] قَصطَنِي [qaṣṭani] I left my coat home on purpose. آني تَرَكِت قَبُّوطِي بِالبَيت عَن قَصِد [ʔaːni trakit qappuːṭi bilbayt ʕan qaṣid]

purse • **1.** جُنطَة [ǰunṭa] جُنَط، جَنطات [ǰunaṭ, ǰanṭaːt] *pl:* This purse doesn't go well with my new dress. هَالجُنطَة ما تِرهَم زين وِيّا بَدِلتِي الجِّدِيدَة [haǰǰunṭa maː tirham ziːn wiyya badilti ʔiǰǰidiːda] • **2.** جائِزَة [ǰaːʔiza] جَوائِز [ǰawaːʔiz] *pl:* The purse was divided among the winners. الجّائِزَة تقَسّمَت بين الرّابِحِين [ʔiǰǰaːʔiza tqassmat bayn ʔirraːbħiːn]

to pursue • **1.** تابَع [taːbaʕ] مُتابَعَة [mutaːbaʕa] *vn:* تتابَع [ttaːbaʕ] *p:* I don't want to pursue the subject any further. ما أَرِيد أتابِع هَالمَوضُوع بَعَد أَزيَد [maː ʔariːd ʔataːbiʕ halmawðuːʕ baʕad ʔazyad] • **2.** عَقَّب [ʕaqqab] تعِقِّب [tʕiqqib] *vn:* تعَقَّب [tʕaqqab] *p:* تعَقَّب [tʕaqqab] تعِقِّب [tʕiqqib] *vn: sv* a. The police are pursuing the smugglers. الشُّرطَة دَتعَقَّب المُهَرِّبِين [ʔiššurṭa datʕaqqab ʔilmuharribiːn] • **3.** تِبَع [tibaʕ] تَبِع [tabiʕ] *vn:* اِنتِبَع [ʔintibaʕ] *p:* We all pursue the policies of our party. كُلّنا نِتبَع سِياسَة حِزبنا [kullna nitbaʕ siyaːsat ħizibna]

pursuit plane • **1.** طِيّارَة مُطارِدَة [ṭiyyaːra muṭaːrida] طِيّارات مُطارِدَة [ṭiyyaːraːt muṭaːrida] *pl:*

pus • **1.** قَيح [qayħ, qiːħ] جَراحَة [ǰaraːħa]

push • **1.** دَفعَة [dafʕa] دَفعات [dafʕaːt] *pl:* He gave me such a push that I nearly fell over. اِنطانِي فَدّ شِكِل دَفعَة خَلّتنِي أوقَع تَقرِيباً [ʔinṭaːni fadd šikil dafʕa xallatni ʔuːgaʕ taqriːban]

to push • **1.** دِفَع [difaʕ] دَفِع [dafiʕ] *vn:* اِندِفَع [ʔindifaʕ] *p:* Push the table over by the window. إدفَع الميز لِيَمّ الشِّبّاك [ʔidfaʕ ʔilmiːz lyamm ʔiššibbaːč] He was pushed way back. اِندِفَع لِلأَخِير [ʔindifaʕ lilʔaxiːr] • **2.** دِفَع [difaʕ] دَفِع [dafiʕ] *vn:* اِندِفَع [ʔindifaʕ] *p:* دَفَّع [daffaʕ] تَدفِيع [tadfiːʕ] *vn:* تدَفَّع [tdaffaʕ] *p:* Don't push! لا تِدفَع [laː tidfaʕ] • **3.** كِفَت [čifat] كَفِت [čafit] *vn: sv* i. The people pushed into the elevator النّاس كِفتَوا لِلمَصعَد [ʔinnaːs čiftawh lilmaṣʕad] • **4.** داس [daːs] دَوس [daws] *vn:* اِنداس [ʔindaːs] *p:* Did you push the button? دِست الزِّرّ؟ [dist ʔizzirr?] • **5.** ذَبّ [ðabb] ذَبّ [ðabb] *vn:* اِنذَبّ [ʔinðabb] *p:* He tried to push the blame on me. حاوَل يِذِبّ اللَّوم عَلَيّا [ħaːwal yðibb ʔillawm ʕalayya] • **6.** خَلَّى [xallaː] تخِلِّي [txilli] *vn:* تخَلَّى [txallaː] *p:* What pushed you to do it? شخَلّاك تسَوِّيها؟ [šxallaːk tsawwiːha?]

* **I tried to push my way through the crowd.** • **1.** حاوَلِت أَشُقّ طَرِيقِي بَين الجَماهِير [ħaːwalit ʔašuqq ṭariːqi bayn ʔiǰǰamaːhiːr]

to push off • **1.** طِلَع [ṭilaʕ] طُلُوع، طِلُوع [ṭuluːʕ, ṭiluːʕ] *vn: sv* a. Right after we pushed off, the boat capsized. بَعَد ما طِلَعنا بشوَيَّة اِنقِلَب البَلَم [baʕad maː ṭilaʕna bšwayya ʔingilab ʔilbalam]

to put • **1.** حَطّ [ħaṭṭ] حَطّ [ħaṭṭ] *vn:* اِنحَطّ [ʔinħaṭṭ] *p:* خَلَّى [xallaː] تخِلِّي [txilli] *vn:* تخَلَّى [txallaː] *p:* Put the table over there. حُطّ المِيز هناك [ħuṭṭ ʔilmiːz hnaːk] Put an ad in the paper. حُطّ إعلان بِالجَّرِيدَة [ħuṭṭ ʔiʕlaːn biǰǰariːda] Put an ad in the paper. أُنشُر [ʔunšur] • **2.** وُضَع [wuðaʕ] وَضِع [waðiʕ] *vn:* اِنوُضَع [ʔinwuðaʕ] *p:* That puts me in an embarrassing position. هَذا يوضَعنِي بوَضِع حَرِج [haːða yuːðaʕni bwaðiʕ ħarij] I'll have to put an end to this situation. راح أوضَع حَدّ لهَالحالَة [raːħ ʔuːðaʕ ħadd lhalħaːla]

* **I wouldn't put any faith in that story.** • **1.** هَالحِكايَة ما عَلَيها اِعتِماد [haliħčaːya maː ʕaliːha ʔiʕtimaːd]

* **Why don't you put it straight to him?** • **1.** لَيش ما تقُلّه إيّاها بصَراحَة؟ [liːš maː tgullah ʔiyyaːha bṣaraːħa?]

* **Put it this way; we don't like each other.** • **1.** بكَلِمَة أُخرَى إحنا واحِد ما يحِبّ اللاخ [bkalima ʔuxraː ʔiħna waːħid maː yħibb ʔillaːx]

to put across • **1.** فَهَّم [fahham] تَفهِيم [tafhiːm] *vn: sv* i. I don't know how to put it across to him that. . . ما دَأدري شلُون أفَهمَه إنُّو [maː daʔadri šluːn ʔafahhmah ʔinnu] • **2.** أَنهَى [ʔanhaː] إنهاء [ʔinhaːʔ] *vn: sv* i. خَلَّص [xallaṣ] تَخلِيص [taxliːṣ] *vn: sv* i. Did you put the deal across? أنهَيت الصَّفقَة؟ [ʔanhiːt ʔiṣṣafqa?]

to put aside • **1.** خَلَّى [xallaː] تخِلِّي [txilli] *vn:* تخَلَّى [txallaː] *p:* She's been putting aside a little money each month. دَتخَلِّي شوَيَّة فلُوس عَلَى صَفحَة كُلّ شَهَر [datxalli šwayya fluːs ʕala ṣafħa kull šahar] • **2.** ذَبّ [ðabb] ذَبّ [ðabb] *vn:* اِنذَبّ [ʔinðabb] *p:* Put that newspaper aside and let us finish this. ذِبّ الجَّرِيدَة عَلَى صَفحَة وَخَلِّي نخَلِّص هاي [ðibb ʔiǰǰariːda ʕala ṣafħa wxalli nxalliṣ haːy]

to put away • **1.** ضَمّ [ðamm] ضَمّ [ðamm] *vn:* اِنضَمّ [ʔinðamm] *p:* Put your jewelry away in a safe place. ضُمّ مُجَوهَراتَك بمَكان أَمِين [ðumm muǰawharaːtak bmakaːn ʔamiːn] Put your summer clothes away. ضُمّ هدُومَك الصَّيفِيَّة [ðumm hduːmak ʔiṣṣayfiyya]

to put back • **1.** رَجَّع [rajjaʕ] تَرجِيع [tarjiːʕ] *vn:* ترَجَّع [trajjaʕ] *p:* رَدّ [radd] رُدُود [ruduːd] *pl:* رَدّ [radd] *vn:* اِنرَدّ [ʔinradd] *p:* Put the book back where you got it. رَجِّع الكِتاب مِنَين ما أَخَذتَه [rajjiʕ ʔilkitaːb miniːn maː ʔaxaðtah]

to put to bed • **1.** نَيَّم [nayyam] تنيِيم [tanyiːm] *vn: sv* i. نَوَّم [nawwam] تَنوِيم [tanwiːm] *vn: sv* u. I have to put the kids to bed. لازِم أنَيِّم الأَطفال [laːzim ʔanayyim ʔilʔaṭfaːl]

P

to put down • **1.** نَزَّل [nazzal] تنزِّل، تَنزِيل [tnizzil, tanzi:l] *vn:* تنَزَّل [tnazzal] *p:* حَطّ [ħaṭṭ] حَطّ [ħaṭṭ] *vn:* اِنحَطّ [ʔinħaṭṭ] *p:* Put the box down here. نَزِّل الصَّندُوق هنا [nazzil ʔiṣṣandu:g hna] • **2.** كِتَب [kitab] كِتابَة [kita:ba] *vn:* اِنكِتَب [ʔinkitab] *p: sv* i. Put down your name and address. إكتِب إسمَك وعنوانَك [ʔiktib ʔismak wʕinwa:nak] • **3.** قُمَع [gumaʕ] قَمِع [qamiʕ] *vn:* اِنقِمَع [ʔinqimaʕ] *p:* أخمَد [ʔaxmad] إخماد [ʔixma:d] *vn:* اِنخُمَد [ʔinxumad] *p:* The army put down the revolution. الجَّيش قِمَع الثَّورَة [ʔiǰǰi:š qimaʕ ʔiθθawra]

to put in • **1.** صِرَف [ṣiraf] صَرُف [ṣaruf] *vn:* اِنصِرَف [ʔinṣiraf] *p:* They put in a lot of time on that job. صِرفَوا هوايَة وَقِت عَلَى هالشُّغُل [ṣirfaw hwa:ya wakit ʕala haššuɣul] • **2.** رَكَّب [rakkab] تَركِيب [tarki:b] *vn:* تَرَكَّب [trakkab] *p:* Did they put in a new windowpane? رَكّبَوا جامَة جِدِيدَة لِلشُّبّاك؟ [rakkbaw ǰa:ma ǰidi:da liššubba:č?]

to put in a word for • **1.** حِكَى ل [ħiča: l-] حَكِي [ħači] *vn: sv* i. تشَفَّع [tšaffaʕ] تشِفُّع [tšiffiʕ] *vn: sv* a. I want you to put in a word for me with the director. أَرِيدَك تِحكِيلِي وِيّا المُدِير [ʔari:dak tiħči:li wiyya ʔilmudi:r]

to put in order • **1.** رَتَّب [rattab] تِرتِّب، تَرتِيب [trittib, tarti:b] *vn:* تَرَتَّب [trattab] *p:* نَظَّم [naðõam] تنِظِّم، تَنظِيم [tniðõim, tanði:m] *vn:* تنَظَّم [tnaðõam] *p:* He is putting his affairs in order. دَيرَتِّب أُمُورَه [dayrattib ʔumu:rah]

to put into words • **1.** عَبَّر عَن [ʕabbar ʕan] تَعبِير [taʕbi:r] *vn:* تعَبَّر [tʕabbar] *p:* This is something hard to put into words. هَذا فَدّ شِي صَعُب التَّعبِير عَنَّه [ha:ða fadd ši ṣaʕub ʔittaʕbi:r ʕannah]

to put off • **1.** نَيَّم [nayyam] تَنيِيم [tanyi:m] *vn: sv* i. I can't put the matter off any longer. ما أَقدَر أنَيِّم القَضِيَّة بَعَد [ma: ʔagdar ʔanayyim ʔilqaðiyya baʕad] • **2.** عَطَّل [ʕaṭṭal] تَعطِيل، تعِطِّل [taʕṭi:l, tʕiṭṭil] *vn:* تعَطَّل [tʕaṭṭal] *p:* عَوَّق [ʕawwag] تَعوِيق [taʕwi:g] *vn:* تعَوَّق [tʕawwag] *p:* Let's put off the decision until tomorrow. خَلِّي نعَطِّل القَرار لِباكِر [xalli nʕaṭṭil ʔilqara:r liba:čir] • **3.** أَجَّل [ʔaǰǰal] تاجِّل، تَأجِيل [tʔiǰǰil, taʔǰi:l] *vn:* تأَجَّل [tʔaǰǰal] *p:* I can't put off the appointment. ما أَقدَر أَأَجِّل المَوعِد [ma: ʔagdar ʔaʔaǰǰil ʔilmawʕid] • **4.** ماطَل [ma:ṭal] مُماطَلَة [muma:ṭala] *vn:* تماطَل [tma:ṭal] *p:* Can't you put him off for a while? ما تِقدَر تماطلَه مُدَّة؟ [ma: tigdar tma:ṭlah mudda?]

to put on • **1.** لِبَس [libas] لِبِس [libis] *vn:* اِنلِبَس [ʔinlibas] *p:* Put your hat on! اِلبَس شَفِقتَك [ʔilbas šafiqtak] Which dress shall I put on? أَيّ بَدلَة أَلبَس؟ [ʔayy badla ʔalbas?] • **2.** شِعَل [šiʕal] شَعِل [šaʕil] *vn:* اِنشِعَل [ʔinšiʕal] *p:* عِلَق [ʕilag] عَلِق [ʕalig] *vn:* اِنعِلَق [ʔinʕilag] *p:* فِتَح [fitaħ] فَتِح [fatiħ] *vn:* اِنفِتَح [ʔinfitaħ] *p:* فَكّ [fakk] فَكّ [fakk] *vn:* اِنفَكّ [ʔinfakk] *p:* Put on the light, please. بالله إشعِل الضُّوَة [ballah ʔišʕil ʔiðõuwa]

*** I've put on three pounds.** • **1.** زاد وَزنِي ثلَث باونات [za:d wazni tlaθ pa:wna:t]

*** Don't you think her accent is put on?** • **1.** ما تِعتِقِد لَهجَتها متصَنّعَة؟ [ma: tiʕtiqid lahǰatha mitṣannʕa?]

to put oneself out • **1.** تكَلَّف [tkallaf] تَكَلُّف [takalluf] *vn: sv* a. غَثّ [ɣaθθ] غَثّ [ɣaθθ] *vn:* اِنغَثّ [ʔinɣaθθ] *p:* Don't put yourself out on my account. لا تِتكَلَّف عَلَى مُودِي [la: titkallaf ʕala mu:di]

to put out • **1.** طَفَّى [ṭaffa:] تطُفِّي، تَطفِيَة [ṭṭuffi, taṭfiya] *vn:* تطَفَّى [ṭṭaffa:] *p:* The fire was put out quickly. الحَرِيق تطَفَّى بِالعَجَل [ʔilħari:g ṭṭaffa: bilʕaǰal] Put out the light before you leave. طَفِّي الضُّوا قَبُل ما تروح [ṭaffi ʔiðõuwa gabul ma: tru:ħ] • **2.** طَلَّع [ṭallaʕ] طَلِّع، تَطلِيع [ṭṭilliʕ, taṭli:ʕ] *vn:* تطَلَّع [ṭṭallaʕ] *p:* Put him out if he makes too much noise. طَلّعَه بَرَّة إذا يسَوِّي لَغوَة هوايَة [ṭallʕah barra ʔiða ysawwi laɣwa hwa:ya] • **3.** نِشَر [nišar] نَشِر [našir] *vn:* اِنَّشَر [ʔinnišar] *p:* Who's putting out your book? مِنُو دَينشُر كتابَك؟ [minu dayinšur kta:bak?]

to put over on • **1.** عَبَّر عَلَى [ʕabbar ʕala] تَعبِير [taʕbi:r] *vn:* تعَبَّر [tʕabbar] *p:* You can't put anything over on him. ما تِقدَر تعَبُّر عَلَيه شِي [ma: tigdar tʕabbur ʕali:h ši]

to put through • **1.** نَفَّذ [naffað] تَنفِيذ [tanfi:ð] *vn:* تنَفَّذ [tnaffað] *p:* He put his own plan through. نَفَّذ مَشرُوعَه الخاصّ [naffað mašru:ʕah ʔilxa:ṣṣ]

to put to death • **1.** عِدَم [ʕidam] إعدام [ʔiʕda:m] *vn:* اِنعِدَم [ʔinʕidam] *p:* The criminal was put to death this morning. المُجرِم اِنعِدَم هاليُوم الصُّبُح [ʔilmuǰrim ʔinʕidam halyu:m ʔiṣṣubuħ]

to put together • **1.** حَطّ سُوَة ، حَطّ سُوَى [ħaṭṭ] حَطّ [ħaṭṭsuwa] *vn:* اِنحَطّ [ʔinħaṭṭ] *p:* Don't put the dog and the cat together, they will fight. ما تحُطّ الكَلِب وَالبَزّون سُوَة تَرَة يِتعارِكُون [ma: tħuṭṭ ʔiččalib wilbazzu:n suwa tara yitʕa:rku:n] • **2.** رَكَّب [rakkab] تَركِيب [tarki:b] *vn:* تَرَكَّب [trakkab] *p:* We must put the pieces together. لازِم نرَكُّب الوُصَل سُوَة [la:zim nrakkub ʔilwuṣal suwa]

to put up • **1.** نِصَب [niṣab] نَصُب [naṣub] *vn:* اِنَّصَب [ʔinniṣab] *p:* New telephone poles are being put up. ينُّصبُون عَوامِيد تِلِفُون جِدِيدَة [yinnuṣbu:n ʕawa:mi:d tilifu:n ǰidi:da] • **2.** عِرَض [ʕirað] عَرِض [ʕarið] *vn:* اِنعِرَض [ʔinʕirað] *p:* نَزَّل [nazzal] تَنزِيل [tanzi:l] *vn:* تنَزَّل [tnazzal] *p:* The farm will be put up for sale this week. المَزرَعَة راح تِنعِرِض لِلبيع هَالإسبُوع [ʔilmazraʕa ra:ħ tinʕirið lilbayʕ halʔisbu:ʕ] • **3.** عَمَّر [ʕammar] تَعمِير [taʕmi:r] *vn:* تعَمَّر [tʕammar] *p:* بِنَى [bina:] بِناء، بَنِي [bina:ʔ, bani] *vn:* اِنبِنَى [ʔinbina:] *p:* This building was put up in six months. هالبِنايَة تعَمّرَت بِستّ أَشهُر [halbina:ya tʕammrat bsitt ʔašhur] • **4.** حَطّ [ħaṭṭ] حَطّ [ħaṭṭ] *vn:* اِنحَطّ [ʔinħaṭṭ] *p:* We put up a fence around the house. حَطّينا سِياج دايِر ما دايِر البَيت [ħaṭṭayna siya:ǰ da:yir ma: da:yir ʔilbayt] • **5.** خَلَّى [xalla:] تخَلِّي [txilli] *vn:* تخَلَّى [txalla:] *p:* Each of them

P

put up a thousand dollars. كُلّ واحِد مِنهُم خَلَّى أَلف دُولار [kull wa:ħid minhum xalla: ʔalf ħaṭṭayna:r] • **6. n** أَبدَى [ʔabda:] *sv* i.

*** Who'll put up the bail for him? • 1.** مِنُو راح يِتكَلَّفَه؟ [minu ra:ħ yitkallafah?]

*** Can you put us up for the night? • 1.** تِقدَر تبَيِّتنا؟ [tigdar tbayyitna?]

to put up to • 1. دَلَّة [dalla] دلال، دَلّات [dla:l, dalla:t] *pl:* تدِلِّي [tdilli] *vn:* تدَلَّى [tdalla:] *p:* His friends put him up to it. أَصدِقائَه دَلُّوه عَليها [ʔaṣdiqa:ʔah dallu:h ʕali:ha]

to put up with • 1. تحَمَّل [tħammal] تحِمِّل [tħimmil] *vn: sv* a. I don't know why you put up with it. ما دَأدري لوَيش تِتحَمَّلها [ma: daʔadri lwi:š titħammalha]

puzzle • 1. حَزُّورَة [ħazzu:ra] حَزُّورات [ħazzu:ra:t] حَزازِير [ħaza:zi:r] *pl:* Can you solve the puzzle? تِقدَر تحِلّ هَالحَزُّورَة؟ [tigdar tħill halħazzu:ra?] • **2.** لُغُز [luɣuz] أَلغاز [ʔalɣa:z] *pl:* That is a puzzle to me. هَذِي لُغُز بِالنِّسبَة إِلِي [ha:ði luɣiz binnisba ʔili]

to puzzle • 1. حَيَّر [ħayyar] تحِيِّر [tħiyyir] *vn:* تحَيَّر [tħayyar] *p:* His letter had us puzzled. مَكتُوبَه حَيَّرنا [maktu:bah ħayyarna]

to puzzle out • 1. حِزَر [ħizar] حَزِر [ħazir] *vn:* اِنحِزَر [ʔinħizar] *p:* حَلّ [ħall] حَزازِير حَلّ [ħhaza:zi:rħall] *vn:* اِنحَلّ [ʔinħall] *p:* I can't puzzle it out. ما أَقدَر أَحزِرها [ma: ʔagdar ʔaħzirha]

pyramid • 1. هَرَم [haram] أَهرام [ʔahra:m] *pl:*

P

Q

quack • **1.** دَجّال [dajja:l] مُشَعوِذ [mušaʕwið] مُشَعوِذين [mušaʕwiði:n] *pl:* The Ministry of Health has been able to track down a great many quacks and prevent them from practicing medicine. وِزارَة الصِّحَّة توَفَّقَت بِالعُثُور عَلَى الدَّجّالِين هوايَة وَمنِعَتهُم مِن مُمارَسَة الطِّبّ [wiza:rat ʔiṣṣiħħa twaffqat bilʕuθu:r ʕala ʔiddajja:li:n hwa:ya wminʕathum min muma:rasat ʔiṭṭibb]

quadrangle • **1.** شِكِل رُباعِي [šikil ruba:ʕi] أشكال رُباعِيَّة [ʔaška:l ruba:ʕiyya] *pl:*

quake • **1.** زِلزال [zilza:l] زَلازِل [zala:zil] *pl:* هَزَّة أَرضِيَّة [hazza ʔarðiyya] هَزّات أرضِيَّة [hazza:t ʔarðiyya] *pl:*

qualification • **1.** مُؤَهِّلات [muʔahhila:t] Do you think she has the necessary qualifications for the job? تِعتِقِد عِدها المُؤَهِّلات اللّازِمَة لِلوَظِيفَة [tiʕtiqid ʕidha ʔilmuʔahhila:t ʔilla:zima lilwaði:fa] • **2.** تَحَفُّظ [taħaffuð] I agree to it with some qualification. أوافِق عَليه مَعَ بَعض التَّحَفُّظ [ʔawa:fiq ʕali:h maʕa baʕð ʔittaħaffuð]

qualified • **1.** أَهَل [ʔahal] أهالِي [ʔaha:li] *pl:* صالِح [ṣa:liħ] لايِق [la:yiq] He is well-qualified for the position. هَذا أَهِل جِدّاً لِلوَظِيفَة [ha:ða ʔahil jiddan lilwaði:fa] He is not qualified to marry into such a rich and famous family. هَذا مُو أَهِل يِتزَوَّج مِن عائِلَة مَشهُورَة غَنِيَّة مِثِل هاي [ha:ða mu: ʔahil yidzawwaj min ʕa:ʔila mašhu:ra ɣaniyya miθil ha:y]

to qualify • **1.** حَدَّد [ħaddad] تَحدِيد [taħdi:d] *vn:* تحَدَّد [tħaddad] *p:* I want to qualify my previous statement. أُرِيد أحَدِّد مَعنى كَلامِي السّابِق [ʔari:d ʔaħaddid maʕna kala:mi ʔassa:biq] • **2.** أَهَّل [ʔahhal] تَأهِيل [taʔhi:l] *vn:* تأَهَّل [tʔahhal] *p:* That does not qualify you for this kind of job. هَذا ما يأَهِّلَك لِهَالنَّوع مِن الشُّغُل [ha:ða ma: yʔahhlak lihannawʕ min ʔiššuɣul] • **3.** صِلَح [ṣilaħ] صَلاح [ṣala:ħ] *vn: sv* a. لاق [la:g] لِياق [liya:q] *vn: sv* i. You don't qualify for the job. ما تِصلَح لِلوَظِيفَة [ma: tiṣlaħ lilwaði:fa]

quality • **1.** خِصلَة [xiṣla] خِصلات، خِصال، خُصَل، خِصَل [xiṣla:t, xiṣa:l, xuṣal, xiṣal] *pl:* صِفَة [ṣifa] صِفات [ṣifa:t] *pl:* He has many good qualities. عِندَه هوايَة خِصَل زينَة [ʕindah hwa:ya xiṣal zi:na] • **2.** مِيزَة [mi:za] مِيزات [mi:za:t] *pl:* This machine has special qualities. هَالمَكِينَة بِيها مِيزات خاصَّة [halmaki:na bi:ha mi:za:t xa:ṣṣa] • **3.** نَوعِيَّة [nawʕiyya] نَوعِيّات [nawʕiyya:t] *pl:* It is a matter of quality, not quantity. المَسأَلَة مَسأَلَة نَوعِيَّة مُو كَمِّيَّة [ʔilmasʔala masʔalat nawʕiyya mu: kammiyya]

quandary • **1.** حِيرَة [ħi:ra]

quantity • **1.** كَمِّيَّة [kammiyya] كَمِّيّات [kammiyya:t] *pl:* مِقدار [miqda:r] مَقادِير [maqa:di:r] *pl:* We have a sufficient quantity on hand for the present. عِدنا كَمِّيَّة كافيَة مَوجُودَة بالوَقِت الحاضِر [ʕidna kammiyya ka:fya mawju:da bilwakt ʔilħa:ðir] This item is available in quantity. هَالمادَّة مِتوَفِّرَة بِكَمِّيّات كِبِيرَة [halma:dda mitwaffra bkammiyya:t čibi:ra]

quarantine • **1.** حَجِر صِحِّي [ħajir ṣiħħi] عَزِل [ʕazil] You will have to spend three days in quarantine. لازِم تِبقَى ثْلَث أيّام بِالحَجِر الصِّحِّي [la:zim tibqa: tlaθ ʔayya:m bilħajir ʔiṣṣiħħi]

to quarantine • **1.** حِجَر [ħijar] حَجِر [ħajir] *vn:* اِنحِجَر [ʔinħijar] *p:* They quarantined all the passengers on the plane. حِجرَوا كُلّ رُكّاب الطَّيّارَة [ħijraw kull rukka:b ʔiṭṭiyya:ra]

quarrel • **1.** عَركَة [ʕarka] عَركات [ʕarka:t] *pl:* The policeman broke up the quarrel in the street. الشُّرطِي فَضّ العَركَة بِالشّارِع [ʔiššurṭi faðð ʔilʕarka biššа:riʕ] • **2.** خِصام [xiṣa:m] خِصامات [xiṣa:ma:t] *pl:* The quarrel between the two politicians has become serious. الخِصام بين السِّياسِيِّين صار جِدِّي [ʔilxiṣa:m bayn ʔissiya:siyyayn ṣa:r jiddi] • **3.** نِزاع [niza:ʕ] نِزاعات [niza:ʕa:t] *pl:* The farmers took their quarrel over water rights to the Bureau of Irrigation. الفَلاحِين وَصَّلَوا نِزاعهُم عَلَى حُقُوق السَّقِي لِدائِرَة الرَّيّ [ʔilfala:ħi:n waṣṣlaw niza:ʕhum ʕala ħuqu:q ʔissagi lda:ʔirat ʔirrayy]

to quarrel • **1.** تعارَك [tʕa:rak] عَركَة [ʕarka] *vn: sv* a. This man quarels with everyone. هَذا يِتعارَك وِيّا الكُلّ [ha:ða yitʕa:rak wiyya ʔilkull] • **2.** تخاصَم [txa:ṣam] تَخاصُم [taxa:ṣum] *vn: sv* a. تجادَل [dja:dal] تَجادُل [taja:dul] *vn: sv* a. The committee members quarreled over financial matters. أعضاء اللَّجنَة تخاصمَوا حَول الشُّؤُون المالِيَّة [ʔaʕða:ʔ ʔillajna txa:ṣmaw ħawl ʔiššuʔu:n ʔilma:liyya] • **3.** تنازَع [tna:zaʕ] تَنازُع [tana:zuʕ] *vn: sv* a. The sons of the deceased quarreled over his estate the day after he died. وِلد المَرحُوم تنازعَوا عَلَى تَركَتَه أوَّل يوم بَعَد وَفاتَه [wild ʔilmarħu:m tna:zʕaw ʕala taraktah ʔawwal yu:m baʕad wafa:tah]

quarrelsome • **1.** جَدَلِي [jadali] جَدَلِيِّين [jadaliyyi:n] *pl:* He is so quarrelsome nobody likes him. هَذا فَدّ واحِد جَدَلِي مَحَّد يحِبَّه [ha:ða fadd wa:ħid jadali maħħad yħibbah] • **2.** قَرَج [qarač] قَرايِج [qara:yic] *pl:* She is the most quarrelsome woman in the whole neighborhood. هاي أكثَر وِحدَة قَرَج بِالمَحَلَّة [ha:y ʔakθar wiħda qarač

Q

bilmaħalla] • **3.** وَكِيح [waki:ħ] وَكِح [wakiħ] He is a quarrelsome boy, always picking fights with the other children. هَذا وَلَد وَكِح كُلّ وَقِت يدَوِّر عَركات ويّا الوُلِد الباقِين [ha:ða walad wakiħ kull wakit ydawwir ʕarka:t wiyya ʔilwulid ʔilba:qi:n]

quarry • **1.** مَقلَع [maqlaʕ] مَقالِع [maqa:liʕ] *pl:* مَحجَر [maħǰar] مَحاجِر [maħa:ǰir] *pl:* All the stone is from a local quarry. كُلّ الصَّخَر مِن مَقلَع مَحَلّي [kull ʔiṣṣaxar min maqlaʕ maħalli]

quarter • **1.** رُبُع [rubuʕ] أَرباع [ʔarba:ʕ] *pl:* كارَك [ča:rak] كوارِيك [čwa:ri:k] *pl:* It's a quarter to seven. ساعَة سَبعَة إِلّا رُبُع [sa:ʕa sabʕa ʔilla rubuʕ] • **2.** رُبُع [rubuʕ] أَرباع [ʔarba:ʕ] *pl:* Three quarters of the harvest was damaged. ثلاث أَرباع المَحصُول تِلَف [tlatt ʔarba:ʕ ʔilmaħṣu:l tilaf] • **3.** حَيّ [ħayy] أَحياء [ʔaħya:ʔ] *pl:* These are the old quarters of the city. هاي الأَحياء القَدِيمَة مِن المَدِينَة [ha:y ʔilʔaħya:ʔ ʔilqadi:ma min ʔilmadi:na] • **4.** مَسكَن [maskan] مَساكِن [masa:kin] *pl:* The officers' quarters are at the far end of the camp. مَساكِن الضُّبّاط بِنِهايَة المُعَسكَر [masa:kin ʔiđđubba:ṭ bniha:yat ʔilmuʕaskar] • **5.** وَسَط [waṣaṭ] It is maintained in some quarters that the plan will not work. يقُولُون بِبَعض الأَوساط أَنّ الخُطَّة ما راح تِنجَح [yguːlu:n bbaʕđ ʔilʔawsa:ṭ ʔann ʔilxuṭṭa ma: ra:ħ tinǰaħ]

to quarter • **1.** سَكَّن [sakkan] تَسكِين [taski:n] *vn:* تسَكَّن [tsakkan] *p:* They quartered the troops in the schoolhouse during the emergency. سَكّنَوا الجِّنُود بِبِنايَة المَدرَسَة أَثناء حالَة الطَّوارِئ [sakknaw ʔiǰǰinu:d bibina:yat ʔilmadrasa ʔaθna:ʔ ħa:lat ʔiṭṭawa:riʔ]

quarterly • **1.** مَجَلَّة فَصلِيَّة [maǰalla faṣliyya] مَجَلّات فَصلِيَّة [maǰalla:t faṣliyya] *pl:* This article appeared in the quarterly published by the society. هالمَقال اِنّشَر بِالمَجَلَّة الفَصلِيَّة اللّي تُصدُرها الجَّمعِيَّة [halmaqa:l ʔinnišar bilmaǰalla ʔilfaṣliyya ʔilli tuṣdurha ʔiǰǰamʕiyya] • **2.** كُلّ ثَلاث شهُور [kull tla:θ šhu:r] أَربَع مَرّات بِالسَّنَة [ʔarbaʕ marra:t bissana] We pay the interest on the loan quarterly. نِدفَع الفايز عَلَى الدَّين كُلّ ثَلاث أَشهُر [nidfaʕ ʔalfa:yiz ʕala ʔiddayn kull tla:θ ʔašhur]

quarter-master • **1.** ضابُط إِعاشَة [đa:buṭ ʔiʕa:ša] ضُبّاط إِعاشَة [đubba:ṭ ʔiʕa:ša] *pl:*

quarters • **1.** مَسكَن [maskan] مَساكِن [masa:kin] *pl:* Did you find decent quarters? لِقَيتلَك فَدّ مَسكَن مُحتَرَم؟ [ligaytlak fadd maskan muħtaram?]

at close quarters • **1.** مِتلازِم [mitla:zim] مَخبُوص [maxbu:ṣ] They fought at close quarters. تعارگوا مِتلازمِين [tʕa:rkaw mitla:zmi:n]

quartz • **1.** كوارتس [kwa:rits]

quaver • **1.** رَعشَة [raʕša] رَعشات [raʕša:t] *pl:* رَجفَة [raǰfa] رَجفات [raǰfa:t] *pl:* There was a quaver in her voice as she asked the question. كان أَكُو رَعشَة بِحِسّها مِن سِألَت السُّؤال [ka:n ʔaku raʕša bħissha min siʔlat ʔissuʔa:l]

to quaver • **1.** رِعَش [riʕaš] رَعِش [raʕiš] *vn: sv* i. رِجَف [riǰaf] رَجِف [raǰif] *vn: sv* i. The old man is feeble, and his voice quavers when he talks. الشّايب ضَعِيف وحِسَّه يرعِش مِن يحكِي [ʔašša:yib đaʕi:f wħissah yirʕiš min yiħči]

quay • **1.** رَصِيف [raṣi:f] أَرصِفَة [ʔarṣifa] *pl:*

queasy • **1.** * I feel queasy from all the rich food. نَفسِي دَتِلعَب مِن كُلّ الأَكِل الدَّسِم [nafsi datilʕab min kull ʔilʔakil ʔiddasim]

queen مَلِكَة [malika] مَلِكات [malika:t] *pl:* • **1.** Her majesty, the Queen, has come! صاحِبَة الجَّلالَة، المَلِكَة، جَتّي [ṣa:ħibat ʔiǰǰala:la, ʔilmalika, ǰatti] • **2.** وَزِير [wazi:r] وُزَراء [wuzara:ʔ] *pl:* I am going to take your queen with the knight. راح آخُذ وَزِيرَك بِالحصان [ra:ħ ʔa:xuð wazi:rak bilħṣa:n] • **3.** بنَيَّة [bnayya] بنَيّات [bnayya:t] *pl:* قِزَّة [qizza] قِزّات، قِزَز [qizza:t, qizaz] *pl:* I have two jacks and three queens in my hand. عِندِي وَلَدَين وِثلَث بَنات بِيدِي [ʕindi waladayn wtlaθ bana:t bi:di]

queer • **1.** نَمُّونَة [nammu:na] عَنتِيكَة، إِنتِيكَة [ʕanti:ka, ʔinti:ka] عَنتِيكات [ʕanti:ka:t] *pl:* He is a queer bird. هَذا فَدّ واحِد نَمُّونَة [ha:ða fadd wa:ħid nammu:na] • **2.** شاذّ [ša:ðð] What a queer idea! شلُون فِكرَة شاذَّة [šlu:n fikra ša:ðða]

to quell • **1.** قِمَع [qimaʕ] قَمِع [qamiʕ] *vn:* اِنقِمَع [ʔinqimaʕ] *p:* أَخمَد [ʔaxmad] إِخماد [ʔixma:d] *vn:* اِنخُمَد [ʔinxumad] *p:* Troops were quickly dispatched to quell the uprising. الجِّيُوش اِندَزَّت بِسُرعَة حَتَّى تِقمَع الثَّورَة [ʔiǰǰiyu:š ʔindazzat bsurʕa ħatta tiqmaʕ ʔiθθawra]

to quench • **1.** رُوَى [ruwa:] رَوِي [rawy] *vn:* اِنرُوَى [ʔinruwa:] *p:* This won't quench my thirst. هَذا ما يِروِي عَطَشِي [ha:ða ma: yirwi ʕaṭaši]

querulous • **1.** نَحِس [naħis] She has become a querulous old lady. صايرَة فَدّ عَجُوز نَحسَة [ṣa:yra fadd ʕaǰu:z naħsa]

query • **1.** اِستِفهام [ʔistifha:m] اِستِعلام [ʔistiʕla:m] اِستِعلامات [ʔistiʕla:ma:t] *pl:* This pamphlet should answer any queries there might be. هالكُرّاسَة لازِم تجاوُب عَلَى كُلّ الاستِفهامات [halkurra:sa la:zim dǰa:wub ʕala kull ʔilʔistifha:ma:t]

quest • **1.** بَحِث [baħiθ] بُحُوث، أَبحاث [buħu:θ, ʔabħa:θ] *pl:* The quest for happiness continues all our life. البَحث عَن السَّعادَة يِستَمِرّ طُول عُمُرنا [ʔilbaħθ ʕan ʔissaʕa:da yistamirr ṭu:l ʕumurna]

question • **1.** سُؤال [suʔaːl] أَسئِلَة [ʔasʔila] *pl:* Have you any further questions. عِندَك أَسئِلَة لُخ؟ [ʕindak ʔasʔila lux?] • **2.** قَضِيَّة [qaðiyya] قَضايا [qaðaːya] *pl:* It was a question of saving a human life. كانَت قَضِيَّة إِنقاذ حَياة بَشَرِيَّة [čaːnat qaðiyyat ʔinqaːð ħayaːt bašariyya] • **3.** مَسأَلَة [masʔala] مَسائِل [masaːʔil] *pl:* It's still an open question. بَعَدها مَسأَلَة بِيها أَخِذ وَرَدّ [baʕadha masʔala biːha ʔaxið wradd]

*** That's completely out of the question.**
• **1.** هاي لا تسَولِفها / هَذا مُستَحِيل [haːða mustaħiːl / haːy laː tsaylifha] / هاي تِطَلّعها مِن الحساب [haːy ttalliʕha min ʔilħsaːb]

beyond question • **1.** ما بِيه سُؤال [maː biːh suʔaːl] ما مَشكُوك بِيه [maː maškuːk biːh] فَوق الشُّبهات [fuːg ʔiššubhaːt] His honesty is beyond question. نَزاهتَه ما بِيها سُؤال [nazaːhtah maː biːha suʔaːl]

in question • **1.** مَقصُود [maqṣuːd] مَعنِي [maʕni] The gentleman in question was not there. الرِّجّال المَقصُود ما كان هناك [ʔirrijjaːl ʔilmaqṣuːd maː čaːn hnaːk]

to ask a question • **1.** سِأَل [siʔal] سُؤال [suʔaːl] *vn:* اِنسِأَل [ʔinsiʔal] *p:* They asked a lot of questions. سِأَلُوه هوايَة أَسئِلَة [siʔluwh hwaːya ʔasʔila]

to question • **1.** اِستَجوَب [ʔistajwab] اِستِجواب [ʔistijwaːb] *vn: sv* i. The police questioned him all night long. الشُّرطَة اِستَجوبُوه طُول اللَّيل [ʔiššurṭa ʔistajwibuːh ṭuːl ʔillayl] • **2.** شَكّ ب [šakk b-] شُكُوك [šukuːk] *pl:* شَكّ [šakk] *vn:* اِنشَكّ [ʔinšakk] *p:* I question his sincerity. أَشُكّ بإخلاصَه [ʔašukk bʔixlaːṣah]

question mark • **1.** عَلامَة سُؤال [ʕalaːmat suʔaːl] عَلامات أَسئِلَة [ʕalaːmataːt ʔasʔila] عَلامَة اِستِفهام [ʕalaːmat ʔistifhaːm] عَلامَة اِستِفهام [ʕalaːmat ʔistifhaːm] عَلامات اِستِفهام [ʕalaːmat ʔistifhaːm] *pl:*

queue • **1.** سِرَة [sira] سِراوات [siraːwaːt] *pl:* The queue in front of the ticket window was so long I didn't want to wait. السِّرَة قِدّام شِبّاك البِطاقات كان هَالقَدّ طُويل ما رِدِت أَنتِظِر [ʔissira qiddaːm šibbaːk ʔilbiṭaːqaːt čaːn halgadd ṭuwiːl maː ridit ʔantiðir]

to queue up • **1.** لِزَم سِرَة [lizam sira] اِنلِزَم سِرَة [ʔinlizam sira] *p:* People usually queue up for the buses at rush hours. النّاس عادَةً يِلزَمُون سِرَة عالباص وَقِت الازدِحام [ʔinnaːs ʕaːdatan yilzamuːn sira ʕalpaːṣ wakit ʔilʔizdiħaːm]

quick • **1.** سَرِيع [sariːʕ] عاجِل [ʕaːjil] That was a quick decision. هَذا كان قَرار سَرِيع [haːða čaːn qaraːr sariːʕ] All his movements are quick. كُلّ حَرَكاتَه سَرِيعَة [kull ħarakaːtah sariːʕa] • **2.** لَحَم حَيّ [laħam ħayy] I cut my fingernail to the quick. قَصَّيت إِظِفري لِلَّحَم الحَيّ [gaṣṣiːt ʔiðifri lillaħam ʔilħayy]

*** His remark touched the quick.**
• **1.** حِكايتَه وُصلَت لِلَحَم الحَيّ [ħičaːytah wuṣlat lilaħam ʔilħayy] / حِكايتَه دَقَّت العَظُم [ħičaːytah daggat ʔilʕaðum]

to be quick • **1.** اِستَعجَل [ʔistaʕjal] اِستِعجال [ʔistiʕjaːl] *vn: sv* i. Be quick about it. اِستَعجِل بِيها [ʔistaʕjil biːha]

to quicken • **1.** عَجَّل ب [ʕajjal b-] تعجِّل [tʕijjil] *vn:* تعَجَّل [tʕajjal] *p:* سَرَّع [sarraʕ] تَسرِيع [tasriːʕ] *vn:* تسَرَّع [tsarraʕ] *p:* He quickened his steps. عَجَّل بِخَطواتَه [ʕajjal bxaṭwaːtah]

quickly • **1.** بسُرعَة [bsurʕa] بِالعَجَل [bilʕajal] He does things quickly. يسَوِّي كُلّشِي بِسُرعَة [ysawwi kullši bsurʕa]

quicksilver • **1.** زَيبَق [zaybag] سلَيمانِي [slimaːni]

quick-tempered • **1.** حادّ الطَّبُع [ħaːdd ʔiṭṭabuʕ] She is very quick-tempered. هِيَّ كُلِّش حادَّة الطَّبُع [hiyya kulliš ħaːddat ʔiṭṭabuʕ] She is very quick-tempered. راسها حارّ [raːsha ħaːrr]

quiet • **1.** هادِئ [haːdiʔ] I live in a quiet neighborhood. أَسكُن بطَرَف هادِئ [ʔaskun bṭaraf haːdiʔ] • **2.** صَنتَة [ṣanta] هادِئ [haːdiʔ] It is very quiet here. كُلِّش صَنتَة هنا [kulliš ṣanta hna] • **3.** ساكِت [saːkit] صَنتَة [ṣanta] Why are you so quiet? لِيش ساكِت؟ [liːš saːkit?] Why are you so quiet? شبِيك هَالقَدّ صَنتَة؟ [šbiːk halgadd ṣanta?] • **4.** سُكُوت [sukuːt] صَنتَة [ṣanta] Quiet, please! سُكُوت، رَجاءاً [sukuːt, rajaːʔan] Quiet, please! صَنتَة، رَجاءاً [ṣanta, rajaːʔan]

to keep quiet • **1.** بُقَى ساكِت، سِكَت [buqaː saːkit, sikat] بَقاء ساكِت [baqaːʔ saːkit] *vn: sv* a. سِكَت [sikat] سُكُوت [sukuːt] *vn: sv* u. Why didn't you keep quiet? لوَيش ما بُقِيت ساكِت؟ [lwiːš maː buqiːt saːkit?]

to quiet • **1.** هَدَّأ، هَدَّى [haddaʔ, haddaː] تَهدِيَة، تهدِّي [tahdiya, thiddi] *vn:* تهَدَّى [thaddaː] *p:* سَكَّت [sakkat] تَسكِيت [taskiːt] *vn:* تسَكَّت [tsakkat] *p:* Samira, go see if you can quiet the baby. سَمِيرَة، رُوحِي شُوفِي إِذا تِقدرِين تهَدِّين الجّاهِل [samiːra, ruːħi šuːfi ʔiða tgidriːn thaddiːn ʔijjaːhil] • **2.** هِدَأ [hidaʔ] هُدُوء [huduːʔ] *vn: sv* a. Let's wait until the excitement quiets down a bit. خَلِّي نِنتِظِر إِلَى أَن يِهدَأ الحَماس [xalli nintiðir ʔila ʔan yihdaʔ ʔilħamaːs] She quieted down after a while. هِدأَت بَعَد فَدّ فَترَة [hidʔat baʕad fadd fatra]

quilt • **1.** لحاف [lħaːf] لِحِف، لِحفان [liħif, liħfaːn] *pl:*

quince • **1.** سفَرجَلَة [sfarjala] سفَرجَلات [sfarjalaːt] *pl:* سفَرجَل [sfarjal] *Collective*

quinine • **1.** كِنِين [kiniːn] قَنقِينَة [qanaqiːna]

to quit • **1.** بَطَّل مِن [baṭṭal min] تبُطُّل [tbuṭṭul] *vn:* تبَطَّل [tbaṭṭal] *p:* He quit his job yesterday. بَطَّل مِن شُغلَه البارحَة [baṭṭal min šuɣlah ʔilbaːrħa] Quit it! بَطِّل [baṭṭil] Quit it! بَسّ عاد [bass ʕaːd] Quit it!

Q

جُوز [ǰu:z] Let's call it quits! خَلِّي نبَطِّل [xalli nbaṭṭil] • **2.** جاز [ǰa:z] جَوز [ǰu:z] *vn:* اِنجاز [ʔinǰa:z] *p:* I told him a thousand times to quit and he didn't. قِلتلَه ألف مَرَّة يجُوز لَكِن ما جاز [gilitlah ʔalf marra yǰu:z la:kin ma: ǰa:z]

*** It's time to quit. • 1.** صار وَقت التَبطِيلَة [ṣa:r wakt ʔittabṭi:la] / صار وَقِت الحَلَّة [ṣa:r wakit ʔilħalla] / بايدُوس [pa:ydu:s]

quite • 1. هوايَة [hwa:ya] كُلِّش [kulliš] That's quite possible. هاي كُلِّش جائِز [ha:y kulliš ǰa:ʔiz] It turned quite cold during the night. بُردَت كُلِّش هوايَة بالليل [burdat kulliš hwa:ya billayl] • **2.** صُدُق [ṣudug] That was quite an experience. هاي صُدُق كانَت تَجرُبَة [ha:y ṣudug ča:nat taǰruba] • **3.** تَماماً [tama:man] ضَبُط [ðabuṭ] كُلِّش [kulliš] Are you quite sure that you can't go? إنتَ مِتأكِّد تَماماً ما تِقدَر ترُوح؟ [ʔinta mitʔakkid tama:man ma: tigdar tru:ħ?]

quiz • 1. اِختِبار [ʔixtiba:r] The teacher gives us a short quiz everyday. المُعَلِّم ينطِينا اِختِبار قَصِير كُلّ يوم [ʔilmuʕallim yinṭi:na ʔixtiba:r qaṣi:r kull yu:m]

quorum • 1. نِصاب [niṣa:b] We couldn't vote on the bill because we didn't have a quorum. ما قِدَرنا نصَوِّت عَاللائِحَة لِأنّ ما حِصَل النِّصاب [ma: gidarna nṣawwit ʕalla:ʔiħa liʔann ma: ħiṣal ʔinniṣa:b]

quota • 1. كَوتا [ku:ta:] حُصَّة [ħuṣṣa, ħiṣṣa] حُصَص [ħuṣaṣ] *pl:* تَخصِيص [taxṣi:ṣ] تَخصِيصات [taxṣi:ṣa:t] *pl:* There is some talk of increasing the quota for foreign cars next year. أكُو حَكِي حَول زِيادَة الكَوتَة لِلسَّيّارات الأجنَبِيَّة السَّنَة الجّايَة [ʔaku ħači ħawl ziya:dat ʔilku:ta lissayya:ra:t ʔilʔaǰnabiyya ʔissana ʔiǰǰa:ya]

quotation • 1. اِستِشهاد [ʔistišha:d] اِستِشهادات [ʔistišha:da:t] *pl:* His speech was full of quotations. حَدِيثَه كان مَليان بِالاِستِشهادات [ħadi:θah ča:n malya:n bilʔistišha:da:t] • **2.** سِعِر [siʕir] أسعار [ʔasʕa:r] *pl:* This newspaper publishes the stock market quotations. هَالجَرِيدَة تِنشُر أسعار البُورصَة [halǰari:da tinšur ʔasʕa:r ʔilbu:rṣa]

quotation mark • 1. عَلامَة حَصِر [ʕala:mat ħaṣir] عَلامات حَصِر [ʕala:ma:t ħaṣir] *pl:*

to quote • 1. اِستَشهَد ب [ʔistašhad b-] اِستِشهاد [ʔistišha:d] *vn: sv* i. That's quoted on page ten. هاي مُستَشهَد بِيها بِصَفحَة عَشرَة [ha:y mustašhad bi:ha bṣafħa ʕašra] • **2.** عِرَض [ʕirað] عَرِض [ʕarið] *vn:* اِنعِرَض [ʔinʕirað] *p:* نِطَى [niṭa:] اِنِّطَى [ʔinniṭa:] *p:* What price did he quote you? شِنُو السِّعِر اللّي عِرَضلَك إيّاه؟ [šinu ʔissiʕir ʔilli ʕiraðlak ʔiyya:h?]

*** Don't quote me. • 1.** لا تِنقُلها عَنّ لساني [la: tinqulha ʕann lsa:ni]

quotient • 1. حاصِل القِسمَة [ħa:ṣil ʔilqisma] If you divide fifteen by five the quotient is three. إذا تقَسِّم خمُسطَعَش عَلَى خَمسَة حاصِل القِسمَة ثلاثَة [ʔiða tqassim xmusṭaʕaš ʕala xamsa ħa:ṣil ʔilqisma tla:θa]

Q

R

rabbit • **1.** أَرنَب [ʔarnab] أَرانِب [ʔara:nib] *pl:*

race • **1.** سِباق [siba:q] سِباقات [siba:qa:t] *pl:* When does the race start? شوَقت يِبدِي السِّباق؟ [šwakit yibdi ʔissiba:q?] • **2.** جِنس [jinis] أَجناس [ʔajna:s] *pl:* The yellow race is found in eastern Asia. الجِّنس الأَصفَر مَوجُود بشَرق آسيا [ʔijjins ʔilʔaṣfar mawju:d bšarq ʔa:sya]

to race • **1.** تسابَق [tsa:baq] مُسابَقَة [musa:baqa] *vn: sv* a. تغالَب [tɣa:lab] تَغالُب، مُغالَبَة [taɣa:lub, muɣa:laba] *vn: sv* a. Let's race. خَلّي نِتسابَق [xalli nitsa:baq]

* **Don't race the engine.** • **1.** لا تِجهِد المَكِينَة [la: tijhid ʔilmaki:na]

* **The car raced through the streets.** • **1.** السَيّارَة كانَت طايرَة بِالشَوارِع [ʔissayya:ra ča:nat ṭa:yra biššawa:riʕ]

rack • **1.** رَفّ [raff] Put the books back on the rack. رَجِّع الكُتُب عالرَّفّ [rajjiʕ ʔilkutub ʕarraff] Put your baggage up on the rack. حُطّ جُنَطَك عَالرَّفّ [ħuṭṭ junaṭak ʕarraff] • **2.** تِعلاقَة [tiʕla:ga] تِعلاقات [tiʕla:ga:t] *pl:* I hung my coat on the rack. عَلَّقِت سِترتِي عَالتِّعلاقَة [ʕallaqit sitirti ʕattiʕla:ga] • **3.** مِشجَب [mišjab] مَشاجِب [maša:jib] *pl:* The soldiers put the guns on the rack. الجُنُود حَطّوا البَنادِق بِالمِشجَب [ʔijjunu:d ħaṭṭaw ʔilbana:diq bilmišjab]

* **Don't rack your brains over it.** • **1.** لا تدَوُّخ راسَك بِيها [la: tdawwux ra:sak bi:ha]

racket • **1.** هُوسَة [hu:sa] هُوسات [hu:sa:t] *pl:* The children are making an awful racket. الأَطفال دَيسَوّوُن غير هُوسَة [ʔilʔaṭfa:l daysawwu:n ɣi:r hu:sa] • **2.** لِعبَة [liʕba] لِعبات، ألعاب، مَلاعِيب [liʕba:t, ʔalʕa:b, mala:ʕi:b] *pl:* This whole business is nothing but a racket. هَالشَّغلَة لِعبَة مِن الأَساس [haššaɣla liʕba min ʔalʔasa:s] • **3.** رَكِيت [raki; t] رَكِتات [rakita:t] *pl:* مَضرَب [maḍrab] مَضارِب [maḍa:rib] *pl:* Her racket is much too heavy for you. الرَّكِت مالها كُلِّش ثقِيل عَلَيك [ʔirrakit ma:lha kulliš θigi:l ʕali:č]

radiator • **1.** راديتَة [radi:ta] راديتات [radi:ta:t] *pl:* Something is wrong with the radiator of my car. أكُو شِي بِالرّادَيتَة مال سَيّارتِي [ʔaku ši birradi:ta ma:l sayya:rti]

radical • **1.** مِتطَرِّف [mittarrif] مِتطَرِّفين [mittarrifi:n] *pl:* I consider him a radical. آنِي أَعتَبرَه مِتطَرِّف [ʔa:ni ʔaʕtabrah mittarrif] He has very radical views. عِندَه وَجهات نَظَر كُلِّش مِتطَرِّفَة [ʕindah wajha:t naḍar kulliš mittarrafa] • **2.** أَساسِي [ʔasa:si] He wants to make some radical changes. يرِيد يسَوِّي بَعض التَّغيِيرات الأَساسِيَّة [yri:d ysawwi baʕḍ ʔittaɣyi:ra:t ʔilʔasa:siyya]

radio • **1.** راديُو [ra:dyu] راديُوّات [ra:dyuwwa:t] *pl:* Was it announced over the radio? اِنذاعَت بِالرّاديُو؟ [ʔinða:ʕat birra:dyu?]

to radio • **1.** ذاع [ða:ʕ] إذاعَة [ʔiða:ʕa] *vn:* اِنذاع [ʔinða:ʕ] *p:* They radioed from the plane that they were in trouble. ذاعَوا مِن الطَّيّارَة بأَن عِدهُم مُشكِلَة [ða:ʕaw min ʔiṭṭayya:ra bʔan ʕidhum muškila]

radio station • **1.** مَحَطَّة إذاعَة [maħaṭṭat ʔiða:ʕa] مَحَطّات إذاعَة [maħaṭṭa:t ʔiða:ʕa] *pl:*

radish • **1.** فِجلايَة [fijla:ya] فِجلايات [fijla:ya:t] *pl:* فِجِل [fijil] *Collective:* Shall I slice up the radishes? أَقَصقِص الفِجِل؟ [ʔagaṣgiṣ ʔilfijil?]

raft • **1.** كَلَك [kalak, čalač] كَلَكات [kalaka:t] *pl:*

rag • **1.** خِرقَة [xirga] خِرَق [xirag] *pl:* وُصلَة [wuṣla] وُصَل [wuṣal] *pl:* Do you have a rag to dust the table? عِندِك فَدّ وُصلَة لمَسح الميز؟ [ʕindič fadd wuṣla lmasħ ʔilmi:z?]

to rage • **1.** هاج [ha:j] هَياج، هَيَجان [haya:j, hayaja:n] *vn: sv* i. اِحتَدّ [ʔiħtadd] حِدَّة [ħidda] *vn: sv* a. ثار [θa:r] ثَورَة [θawra] *vn: sv* u. He raged like a bull. هاج مِثل الثَّور [ha:j miθl ʔiθθawr] • **2.** قَبّ [gabb] قَبّ [gabb] *vn: sv* u. The storm raged all night long. العاصِفَة ظَلَّت قابَّة طُول اللَّيل [ʔilʕa:ṣifa ḍallat ga:bba ṭu:l ʔillayl]

ragged • **1.** مخَلقَن [mxalgan] They were wearing ragged clothes. كانَوا لابسِين هِدُوم مخَلقِنَة [ča:naw la:bsi:n hidu:m mxalgina]

rail • **1.** سِكَّة [sikka, sičča] سِكَك [sičač] *pl:* A loose rail caused the accident. فَدّ قِسِم راخِي مِن السِّكَّة سَبَّب الحادِث [fadd qisim ra:xi min ʔissičča sabbab ʔilħa:diθ]

railing • **1.** محَجَّر [mħajjar] محَجَّرات [mħajjara:t] *pl:* Hold on to the railing. إلزَم المحَجَّر [ʔilzam ʔilmħajjar]

railroad • **1.** قِطار [qiṭa:r] قِطارات [qiṭa:ra:t] *pl:* سِكَّة حَدِيد [sikka ħadi:d] سِكَك حَدِيدِيَّة [sikak ħadi:diyya] *pl:* I prefer to go by railroad. أَفَضِّل أَرُوح بِالقِطار [ʔafaḍḍil ʔaru:ħ bilqiṭa:r] Our house is near the railroad. بَيتنا يَمّ السِّكَّة [baytna yamm ʔissičča]

railroad station • **1.** مَحَطَّة قِطار [maħaṭṭat qiṭa:r] مَحَطّات قِطار [maħaṭṭa:t qiṭa:r] *pl:*

R

rain • 1. مُطَر [muṭar] We stayed home because of the rain. بقَينا بالبَيت بِسَبَب المُطَر [bqayna bilbayt bisabab ʔilmuṭar]

to rain • 1. مُطَر [muṭar] أمطار [ʔamṭa:r] *pl:* مُطَر [muṭar] *vn: sv* u. It rained hard all morning. مُطرَت بقُوَّة طُول الصُّبُح [muṭrat bquwwa ṭu:l ʔiṣṣubuħ]

rainbow • 1. قوس قَزَح، قوز قَدَح [qu:s qazaħ, gu:z gadaħ]

raincoat • 1. مشَمَّع [mšammaʕ]

rainy • 1. مُمطِر [mumṭir]

raise • 1. زِيادَة [ziya:da] تَرفِيع [tarfi:ʕ] تَرفيعات [tarfi:ʕa:t] *pl:* They gave me a raise. إنطَونِي زِيادَة [ʔinṭu:ni ziya:da]

to raise • 1. شال [ša:l] شَيل [šayl] *vn:* اِنشال [ʔinša:l] *p:* Use the jack to raise the car. اِستَعمِل الجَّكّ لشَيل السَّيّارَة [ʔistaʕmil ʔiǰǰagg lšayl ʔissayya:ra] They didn't even raise their heads from their work as we passed. وَلا شالَوا رُوسهُم مِن شُغُلهُم مِن مَرَّينا [wala ša:law ru:shum min šuɣulhum min marri:na] **• 2.** دَبَّر [dabbar] تدبير [tadbi:r] *vn:* تدَبَّر [tdabbar] *p:* I couldn't raise the money. ما قِدَرت أدَبُّر الفلُوس [ma: gidarit ʔadabbur ʔilflu:s] **• 3.** جِمَع [ǰimaʕ] جَمِع [ǰamiʕ] *vn:* اِنجِمَع [ʔinǰimaʕ] *p:* Our club is raising money to aid the flood victims. نادِينا دَيجمَع فلُوس لإغاثَة مَنكُوبِي الفَيَضان [na:di:na dayiǰmaʕ flu:s lʔiɣa:θat manku:bi:n ʔilfayaḍa:n] **• 4.** رُفَع [rufaʕ] رَفُع [rafuʕ] *vn:* اِنرُفَع [ʔinrufaʕ] *p:* All those in favor, raise your hands. كُلّ المُؤَيِّدِين، إرفَعُوا إيدَيكُم [kull ʔilmuʔayyidi:n, ʔirfaʕu: ʔi:di:kum] They raised the siege and withdrew. رِفعَوا الحِصار وَانسِحبَوا [rifʕaw ʔilħiṣa:r wʔinsiħbaw] **• 5.** اِرتِفَع [ʔirtifaʕ] اِرتِفاع [ʔirtifa:ʕ] *vn: sv* i. The bread won't raise without yeast. العَجِين ما يِرتِفِع بَلا خُمرَة [ʔilʕaǰi:n ma: yirtifiʕ bala xumra] **• 6.** عَلَّى [ʕalla:] تَعلِيَة [taʕliya] *vn:* تعَلَّى [tʕalla:] *p:* Raise the picture a little; it's not all on the screen. عَلِّي الصُّورَة شوَيَّة، مُو كُلّها عالبَردَة [ʕalli ʔiṣṣu:ra šwayya, mu: kullha ʕalparda] Raise the volume a little on the radio. عَلِّي حِسّ الرّاديُو شوَيَّة [ʕalli ħiss ʔirra:dyu šwayya] **• 7.** صَعَّد [ṣaʕʕad] تَصعِيد [taṣʕi:d] *vn:* تصَعَّد [tṣaʕʕad] *p:* He showed us how they raise and lower the irrigation gates. راوانا شلُون يصَعِّدُون وَينَزِّلُون أبواب السَّقِي [ra:wa:na šlu:n yṣaʕʕidu:n wynazzilu:n ʔabwa:b ʔissagi] **• 8.** زَيَّد [zayyad] تَزيِيد، زِيادَة [tazyi:d, ziya:da] *vn:* تزَيَّد [tzayyad] *p:* The rent will be raised on October first. الإيجار راح يِتزَيَّد بأوَّل تِشرِين الأوَّل [ʔilʔi:ǰa:r ra:ħ yidzayyad bʔawwal tišri:n ʔalʔawwal] The company has promised to raise our salaries all across the board. الشَّرِكَة وُعدَت تزَيِّد رَواتِبنا جَمِيعاً [ʔiššarika wuʕdat dzayyid rawa:tibna ǰami:ʕan] **• 9.** رَقَّى [raqqa:] تَرقِيَة [tarqiya] *vn:* ترَقَّى [traqqa:] *p:* They raised him from clerk to supervisor. رَقُّوه مِن كاتِب إلَى مُدِير [raqqawh min ka:tib ʔila mudi:r] **• 10.** زِرَع [ziraʕ] زَرِع [zariʕ] *vn:* اِنزِرَع [ʔinziraʕ] *p:* They raise a lot of wheat here. يزرعُون هوايَة حُنطَة هنا [yzirʕu:n hwa:ya ħunṭa hna] **• 11.** رَبَّى [rabba:] تَربِيَة [tarbiya] *vn:* ترَبَّى [trabba:] *p:* She has raised nine children. رَبَّت تِسِع أطفال [rabbat tisiʕ ʔaṭfa:l] Most farmers here raise sheep. أكثَر الزُّرّاع هنا يربُّون غَنَم [ʔakθar ʔizzurra:ʕ hna: yrabbu:n ɣanam]

* **The kids are raising the roof again.**

• 1. الجِهال دَيقَلبُون الدِنيا مَرَّة لُخ [ʔiǰǰiha:l daygulbu:n ʔiddinya marra lux]

to raise a question • 1. أثار مَوضُوع [ʔaθa:r mawḍu:ʕ] إثارَة مَوضُوع [ʔiθa:rat mawḍu:ʕ] *vn: sv* i. Who raised the question? مِنُو أثار المَوضُوع؟ [minu ʔaθa:r ʔilmawḍu:ʕ?]

range • 1. طَبّاخ [ṭabba:x] طَبّاخِين [ṭabba:xi:n] *pl:* We just bought a new range. هَستَوّنا اِشتِرَينا طَبّاخ جِدِيد [hastawwna ʔištiri:na ṭabba:x ǰidi:d] **• 2.** مَرعَى [marʕa] مَراعِي [mara:ʕi] *pl:* In the spring the sheep go out on the range. بالرَّبِيع الغَنَم يرُوحُون لِلمَرعَى [birrabi:ʕ ʔilɣanam yru:ħu:n lilmarʕa] **• 3.** ساحَة [sa:ħa] ساحات [sa:ħa:t] *pl:* مَيدان [mayda:n] مَيادِين [maya:di:n] *pl:* The new recruits spent their first day on the firing range today. المُجَنَّدِين الجِّدِد قِضَوا يومهُم الأوَّل بساحَة الرَّمِي هاليُوم [ʔilmuǰannadi:n ʔaǰǰidid giḍaw yu:mhum ʔilʔawwal bsa:ħat ʔirramy halyu:m] **• 4.** مَدَى [mada] مَرمَى [marma] مَرامِي [mara:mi] *pl:* نِطاق [niṭa:q] نِطاقات، أنطِقَة [niṭa:qa:t, ʔanṭiqa] *pl:* The tanks were out of range of our guns. الدَّبّابات كانَت خارِج نِطاق مَدافِعنا [ʔiddabba:ba:t ča:nat xa:riǰ niṭa:q mada:fiʕna]

to range • 1. تراوَح [tra:wah] تَراوُح [tara:wuħ] *vn: sv* a. The prices range from one to five dinars. الأسعار تِتراوَح مِن دِينار إلَى خَمِس دَنانِير [ʔilʔasʕa:r titra:wah min dina:r ʔila xamis dana:ni:r] **• 2.** تجَوَّل [dǰawwal] تَجَوُّل [taǰawwul] *vn: sv* a. The bedouin range the western desert with their flocks. البَدو يِتجَوَّلُون بِالصَّحراء الغَربِيَّة وِيّا قِطعانهُم [ʔilbadw yidǰawwalu:n biṣṣaħra:ʔ ʔalɣarbiyya wiyya qiṭʕa:nhum]

rank • 1. رُتبَة [rutba] رُتَب [rutab] *pl:* What's the officer's rank? شِنُو رُتبَة هَالضابُط؟ [šinu: rutbat haḍḍa:buṭ?] **• 2.** كَثّ [kaθθ] His face was covered by a rank growth of beard. وُجّه كان مغَطَّى بِلحيَة كَثَّة [wuččah ča:n mɣaṭṭa: bliħya kaθθa]

rapid • 1. سَرِيع [sari:ʕ]

rare • 1. نادِر [na:dir] That's a rare flower. هَذِي وَردَة نادرَة [ha:ði warda na:dra] **• 2.** عَالنُّصّ [ʕannuṣṣ] I'd like my steak broiled rare. أرِيد اللَّحَم مالِي مَشوِي عَالنُّصّ [ʔari:d ʔillaħam ma:li mašwi ʕannuṣṣ]

R

rarely • 1. نادِراً [na:diran] مِن النادِر [min ʔinna:dir] That rarely happens. هَذا نادِراً يِحدُث [ha:ða na:diran yiħduθ]

rascal • 1. شيطان [šayṭa:n] شياطِين [šya:ṭi:n] *pl:*

rash • 1. حَصَف [ħaṣaf] There is a rash on his face. أكُو حَصَف بوُجَّه [ʔaku ħaṣaf bwuččah] **• 2.** موجَة [mawǰa, mu:ǰa] مَوجات [mawǰa:t, mu:ǰa:t] *pl:* Last month there was a rash of robberies. الشَّهر اللّي فات كان أكُو مَوجَة بَوق [ʔiššahr ʔilli fa:t ča:n ʔaku mu:ǰat bawg] **• 3.** مِتسَرِّع [mitsarriʕ] بَلا تَرَوِّي [bala tarawwi] بَلا إمعان [bala ʔimʕa:n] Don't make any rash promises. لا تِنطِي وُعُود بَلا تَرَوِّي [la: tinṭi wuʕu:d bala tarawwi]

rat • 1. جرَيدِي [ǰri:di] جرَيدِيَّة [ǰri:di:yya] *pl:*

rate • 1. سِعِر [siʕir] أسعار [ʔasʕa:r] *pl:* أُجرَة [ʔuǰra] أُجُور [ʔuǰu:r] *pl:* أجِر [ʔaǰir] What are the rates for single rooms? شقَدّ سِعِر الغُرفَة أمّ سَرِير واحِد؟ [šgadd siʕir ʔilɣurfa ʔumm sari:r wa:ħid?] What are the new rates for airmail? شِنُو الأُجُور الجِّدِيدَة لِلبَرِيد الجَّوِّي؟ [šinu ʔalʔuǰu:r ʔiǰǰidi:da lilbari:d ʔiǰǰawwi?] The rate of interest is four per cent. سِعِر الفائِدَة أربَعَة بالمِيَّة [siʕir ʔilfa:ʔida ʔarbaʕa bilmiyya] **• 2.** مُعَدَّل [muʕaddal] مُعَدَّلات [muʕaddala:t] *pl:* At this rate we'll never get done. عَلَى هَالمُعَدَّل وَلا راح نخَلِّص [ʕala halmuʕaddal wala ra:ħ nxalliṣ]

at any rate • 1. عَلَى كُلّ حال [ʕala kull ħa:l] At any rate, I'd like to see you. عَلَى كُلّ حال، آنِي دَأرِيد أشُوفَك [ʕala kull ħa:l, ʔa:ni daʔari:d ʔašu:fak]

first-rate • 1. دَرَجَة أولَى [daraǰa ʔu:la] صِنِف أوَّل [ṣinif ʔawwal] مُمتاز [mumta:z] It's definitely a first-rate hotel. هَذا بِلا شَكّ أُتيل دَرَجَة أولَى [ha:ða bila šakk ʔuti:l daraǰa ʔu:la]

rather • 1. شوَيَّة [šwayya] نوعاً ما [nawʕan ma:] The play was rather long. الرُّوايَة كانَت نوعاً ما طوِيلَة [ʔirruwa:ya ča:nat nawʕan ma: ṭwi:la]

* **I would rather wait. • 1.** آنِي أفَضِّل أنتِظِر [ʔa:ni ʔafaððil ʔantiðir]

* **I'd rather die than give in. • 1.** آنِي أفَضِّل المَوت عَالتَسلِيم [ʔa:ni ʔafaððil ʔilmawt ʕattasli:m]

ration • 1. قُصعَة [guṣʕa] قُصَع [guṣaʕ] *pl:* تَعيِين [taʕyi:n] Our rations consisted of bread and soup. قُصعَتنا كانَت خُبُز وَشَوربَة [quṣʕatna ča:nat xubuz wšu:rba]

to ration • 1. وَزَّع بِالبِطاقات، حَدَّد التَّوزِيع [wazzaʕ bilbiṭa:qa:t, ħaddad ʔattawzi:ʕ] تَحدِيد التَوزِيع [taħdi:d ʔattawzi:ʕ] *vn: sv* i. حَدَّد [ħaddad] تَحدِيد [taħdi:d] *vn:* تحَدَّد [tħaddad] *p:* Sugar was rationed. الشَّكَر توَزَّع بِالبِطاقات [ʔiššakar twazzaʕ bilbiṭa:qa:t] They rationed the meats. حَدِّدوا تَوزِيع اللَّحَم [ħaddidaw tawzi:ʕ ʔillaħam]

rattle • 1. خِرخاشَة [xirxa:ša] خِرخاشات [xirxa:ša:t] *pl:* They bought the baby a rattle. اِشتِرَوا خِرخاشَة لِلطِّفِل [ʔištiraw xirxa:ša liṭṭifil]

to rattle • 1. طَربَق [ṭarbag] طَربَقَة [ṭarbaga] *vn: sv* i. خَشخَش [xašxaš] خَشخَشَة، تخِشخِش [xašxaša, txišxiš] *vn: sv* i. Do you have to rattle the dishes that way? أكُو مُوجِب تطَربِق هِيكِي بِالمّاعِين؟ [ʔaku mu:ǰib ṭṭarbig hi:či bilimma:ʕi:n?] There is a kind of snake that rattles. أكُو نُوع مِن الحَيّات تخَشخِش [ʔaku nu:ʕ min ʔilħayya:t txašxiš] **• 2.** شَوَّش [šawwaš] تَشوِيش [tašwi:š] *vn:* تشَوَّش [tšawwaš] *p:* خَربَط [xarbaṭ] خَربَطَة [xarbaṭa] *vn:* تخَربَط [txarbaṭ] *p:* Don't rattle me. لا تشَوِّشنِي [la: tšawwišni]

to rattle on • 1. ثَرثَر [θarθar] ثَرثَرَة [θarθara] *vn: sv* i. لِغَى [liɣa:] لَغوَة [laɣwa] *vn: sv* i. She can rattle on like that for hours. تِقدَر تثَرثِر هَالشِّكِل لِمُدَّة ساعات [tigdar tθarθir haššikil lmuddat saʕa:t]

to rave • 1. هِذَى [hiða:] هَذَيان [haðaya:n] *vn: sv* i. He raved like a madman. هِذَى مِثل المَجنُون [hiða: miθl ʔilmaǰnu:n]

raw • 1. نِيّ [niyy] The meat is almost raw. اللَّحَم نِيّ تَقرِيباً [ʔillaħam niyy taqri:ban] **• 2.** مِلتِهِب [miltihib] My throat is raw. زَردُومِي مِلتِهِب [zardu:mi miltihib]

* **He got a raw deal. • 1.** صابَه غُبُن [ṣa:bah ɣubun]

ray • 1. شُعاع [šuʕa:ʕ] أشِعَّة [ʔašiʕʕa] *pl:* Ordinary panes of glass keep out ultraviolet rays. الجّام العادِي يِمنَع الأشَعَّة فَوق البَنَفسَجِيَّة [ʔiǰǰa:m ʔilʕa:di yimnaʕ ʔilʔašaʕʕa fu:q ʔilbanafsaǰiyya] **• 2.** بَصِيص [baṣi:ṣ] There's still a ray of hope. لهَسَّة أكُو فَدّ بَصِيص مِن الأمَل [lhassa ʔaku fadd baṣi:ṣ min ʔilʔamal]

rayon • 1. رايُون [rayu:n]

razor • 1. مُوس [mu:s] مواس، مواسَة [mwa:s, mwa:sa] *pl:* I have to stop my razor. لازِم أحِدّ المُوس مالِي [la:zim ʔaħidd ʔilmu:s ma:li]

safety razor • 1. مَكِينَة زيان [maki:nat ziya:n] مَكاين زِيان [maka:yin ziya:n] *pl:* I can't find my safety razor. ما دَأقدَر ألقِي مَكِينَة الزِّيان مالتِي [ma: daʔagdar ʔalgi maki:nat ʔizziya:n ma:lti]

razor blade • 1. مُوس [mu:s] مواس، مواسَة [mwa:s, mwa:sa] *pl:* Please buy me a dozen razor blades. أرجُوك اِشترِيلِي دَرزَن مواسَة [ʔarǰu:k ʔišti:ri:li darzan mwa:sa]

to reach • 1. مَدّ إيد [madd ʔi:d] مَدّ إيد [madd ʔi:d] *vn: sv* i. The little fellow reaches for everything he sees. هَالزَّعطُوط يمِدّ إيدَه عَلَى كُلشِي يشُوفَه [hazzaʕṭu:ṭ ymidd ʔi:dah

R

ʕala kullši yšu:fah] He reached into his pocket. مَدّ إيدَه بجَيبَه [madd ʔi:dah bǰi:bah] • **2.** اِمتَدّ [ʔimtadd] اِمتِداد [ʔimtida:d] *vn: sv* a. The garden reaches all the way to the river. الحَدِيقَة تِمتَدّ لِلشَّطّ [ʔilħadi:qa timtadd liššaṭṭ] • **3.** وُصَل [wuṣal] وُصُول [wuṣu:l] *vn: sv* a. The rumor even reached us. الإشاعَة وُصلَت حَتَّى إلنا [ʔilʔiša:ʕa wuṣlat ħatta ʔilna] The radio reaches millions of people. الرّاديُو يُوصَل إلَى مَلايِين مِن النّاس [ʔirra:dyu yu:ṣal ʔila mala:yi:n min ʔanna:s] We reached the city at daybreak. وُصَلنا الوِلايَة وُجِه الصُّبُح [wuṣalna ʔilwila:ya wučč ʔiṣṣubuħ] • **4.** اِتِّصَل [ʔittiṣal] اِتِّصال [ʔittiṣa:l] *vn: sv* i. There was no way of reaching him. ما كان أكُو فَدّ طَرِيقَة نِتَّصِل بيه [ma: ča:n ʔaku fadd ṭari:qa nittiṣil bi:h] • **5.** ناش [na:š] نَوش [nawš] *vn:* اِنناش [ʔinna:š] *p:* Can you reach that shelf? تِقدَر تنُوش ذاك الرَّفّ؟ [tigdar tnu:š ða:k ʔirraff?] • **6.** ناوَش [na:waš] مناوَشَة [mna:waša] *vn: sv* u. Reach me the hammer. ناوُشنِي الجاكُوك [na:wušni ʔilča:ku:č]

reaction • 1. رَدّ فِعِل [radd fiʕil] What was his reaction? شكان رَدّ الفِعِل عِندَه؟ [šča:n radd ʔilfiʕil ʕindah?] • **2.** تَفاعُل [tafa:ʕul] You can speed up the reaction if you beat the mixture. تِقدَر تسَرِّع التَّفاعُل إذا تسَخِّن المَزِيج [tigdar tsarriʕ ʔittafa:ʕul ʔiða tsaxxin ʔilmazi:ǰ]

reactionary • 1. رَجعِي [rajʕi]

to read • 1. قِرا [qira:] قرايَة [qra:ya] *vn:* اِنقرَى [ʔinqira:] *p:* You should read this book. لازِم تِقرا هَالكِتاب [la:zim tiqra: halkita:b] The text reads differently. المَتِن يِقرا غير شِكِل [ʔilmatin yiqra: ɣi:r šikil] Please read it to me. أرجُوك إقرا لِي إيّاها [ʔarǰu:k ʔiqra: li ʔiyya:ha] • **2.** أشَّر عَلَى [ʔaššar ʕala] تَأشِير [taʔši:r] *vn:* تأشَّر [tʔaššar] *p:* The thermometer reads 35 degrees. المِحرار يأشِّر عَلَى خَمسَة وثلاثِين دَرَجَة [ʔilmiħra:r yiʔaššir ʕala xamsa wtla:θi:n daraǰa]

reader • 1. قارِئ [qa:riʔ] قُرّاء [qurra:ʔ] *pl:* This newspaper has more than a million readers. هَالجَرِيدَة إلها أزيَد مِن مِليَون قارِئ [halǰari:da ʔilha ʔazyad min milyu:n qa:riʔ] • **2.** كتاب مُطالَعَة [kta:b muṭa:laʕa] كُتُب مُطالَعَة [kutub muṭa:laʕa] *pl:* Do you have my English reader? عِندَك كتاب المُطالَعَة الإنكلِيزِي مالِي؟ [ʕindak kta:b ʔilmuṭa:laʕa ʔilʔingli:zi ma:li?]

readily • 1. بلا تَرَدُّد [bila taraddud] بسُرعَة [bsurʕa] بِالعَجَل [bilʕaǰal] He admitted it readily. اِعتِرَف بِيها بلا تَرَدُّد [ʔiʕtiraf bi:ha bila taraddud] She consented readily. قِبلَت بسُرعَة [qiblat bsurʕa]

reading • 1. قِراءَة [qira:ʔa] He got excellent in reading. أخَذ جَيِّد جِدّاً بالقِراءَة [ʔaxað ǰayyid ǰiddan bilqira:ʔa]

ready • 1. حاضِر [ħa:ðir] When will dinner be ready? شوَقِت يكُون العَشا حاضِر؟ [šwakit yku:n ʔilʕaša ħa:ðir?] • **2.** مِستِعِدّ [mistiʕidd] حاضِر [ħa:ðir] I'm ready for anything. آني مِستِعِدّ لِكُلّشِي [ʔa:ni mistiʕidd likullši] • **3.** جاهِز [ǰa:hiz] The house is ready for occupancy. البَيت جاهِز لِلسَّكَن [ʔilbayt ǰa:hiz lissakan] • **4.** جَوَّة الإيد [ǰawwa ʔilʔi:d] I don't have any ready cash just now. ماكُو فلُوس جَوَّة إيدِي هَسَّة [ma:ku flu:s ǰawwa ʔi:di hassa]

to get ready • 1. اِستَعَدّ [ʔistaʕadd] اِستِعداد [ʔistiʕda:d] *vn: sv* i. تحَضَّر [tħaððar] تَحَضُّر [taħaðður] *vn: sv* a. Get ready, go! اِستَعِدُّوا، إبدَء [ʔistaʕiddu: ʔibdaʔ] My brother is getting ready to go out. أخُويَا دَيِتحَضَّر لِلطَّلعَة [ʔaxu:ya dayitħaððar littalʕa] • **2.** حَضَّر [ħaððar] تَحضِير [taħði:r] *vn:* تحَضَّر [tħaððar] *p:* My wife is getting the food ready. مَرتِي دَتحَضِّر الأكِل [marti datħaððir ʔilʔakil]

ready-made • 1. جاهِز [ǰa:hiz] حاضِر [ħa:ðir] Do you buy your clothes ready-made? تِشتِرِي هدُومَك جاهزَة؟ [tištiri hdu:mak ǰa:hza?]

real • 1. حَقِيقِي [ħaqi:qi] That's not his real name. هَذا مُو إسمَه الحَقِيقِي [ha:ða mu: ʔismah ʔilħaqi:qi] • **2.** أصلِي [ʔaṣli] Is this real silk? هَذا حَرِير أصلِي؟ [ha:ða ħari:r ʔaṣli?] • **3.** مِن صِدُق [min ṣidug] That's what I call a real friend. هَذا اللِّي أسَمِّيه صَدِيق مِن صُدُق [ha:ða ʔilli ʔasammi:h ṣadi:q min ṣudug] • **4.** واقِع [wa:qiʕ] That never happens in real life. هَذا أبَد ما يِحدُث بِالواقِع [ha:ða ʔabad ma: yiħduθ bilwa:qiʕ]

real estate • 1. مُلك [muluk] أملاك [ʔamla:k] *pl:*

reality • 1. حَقِيقَة [ħaqi:qa] حَقايِق، حَقائِق [ħaqa:yiq, ħaqa:ʔiq] *pl:* واقِع [wa:qiʕ]

to realize • 1. حَقَّق [ħaqqaq] تَحقِيق [taħqi:q] *vn:* تحَقَّق [tħaqqaq] *p:* He never realized his ambition to become a doctor. أبَداً ما حَقَّق طُمُوحَه بأن يصِير طَبِيب [ʔabadan ma: ħaqqaq ṭumu:ħah bʔan yṣi:r ṭabi:b] • **2.** طَلَّع [ṭallaʕ] تَطلِيع [taṭli:ʕ] *vn:* تطَلَّع [tṭallaʕ] *p:* He realized quite a profit on that deal. طَلَّع خُوش رِبِح بذِيك الشَّغلَة [ṭallaʕ xu:š ribiħ bði:č ʔiššaɣla] • **3.** تصَوَّر [tṣawwar] تَصَوُّر [taṣawwur] *vn: sv* a. I simply can't realize he's dead. ما دَأقدَر أتصَوَّر إنُّو مَيِّت [ma: daʔagdar ʔatṣawwar ʔinnu mayyit] I didn't realize it was so late. ما تصَوَّرت هَالقَدّ الوَقت مِتأخِّر [ma: tṣawwarit halgadd ʔilwakit mitʔaxxir] • **4.** أدرَك [ʔadrak] إدراك [ʔidra:k] *vn: sv* u. Does he realize how sick he is? دَيِدرُك شقَدّ مَرِيض هُوَّ؟ [dayidruk šgadd mari:ð huwwa?] • **5.** قَدَّر [qaddar] تَقدِير [taqdi:r] *vn:* تقَدَّر [tqaddar] *p:* He doesn't realize how much work is involved. ما دَيقَدِّر شقَدّ بِيها شُغُل [ma: dayqaddir šgadd bi:ha šuɣul] I never realized the danger. ما قَدَّرت الخَطَر أبَداً [ma: qaddart ʔilxaṭar ʔabadan]

really • 1. حَقِيقَةً [ħaqi:qatan] صُدُق [ṣudug] Do you really mean it? إنتَ حَقِيقَةً تِعنِيها [ʔinta ħaqi:qatan tiʕni:ha]

R

I really wanted to stay at home. الصُدُق آني رِدِت أبقَى بالبَيت [ʔiṣṣudug ʔaːni ridit ʔabqaː bilbayt] • **2.** بالحَقِيقَة [bilħaqiːqa] He is really younger than he looks. هُوَّ بالحَقِيقَة أصغَر مِن ما يبَيِّن عَليه [huwwa bilħaqiːqa ʔaṣɣar min maː yibayyin ʕaliːh]

* **I really don't know.** • **1.** وَالله ما أدري [wallah maː ʔadri]

rear • **1.** ظَهَر [ðihar] ظهُور، ظهُورَة [ðuhuːr, ðhuːra] *pl:* The rear of the house is being painted. ظَهر البَيت دَينصُبُغ [ðahir ʔilbayt dayinṣubuɣ] • **2.** مَقعَد [maqʕad] مَقاعِد [maqaːʕid] *pl:* She fell on her rear. وُقعَت عَلَى مَقعَدها [wugʕat ʕala maqʕadha] • **3.** خَلفِي [xalfi] The rear row is empty. السِّرَة الخَلفِي فارِغ [ʔissira ʔilxalfi faːriɣ] • **4.** وَرّانِي [warraːni] The rear windows haven't been cleaned yet. الشِّبابِيك الوَرّانِيَّة بَعَد ما تنَظّفَت [ʔiššibaːbiːč ʔilwarraːniyya baʕad maː tnaððfat]

in the rear • **1.** بالخَلف [bilxalf] لِوَرا [liwara] The emergency exit is in the rear. باب الطَّوارِئ بالخَلف [baːb ʔiṭṭawaːriʔ bilxalf]

to rearrange • **1.** أعاد تَرتِيب، أعاد تَنظِيم [ʔaʕaːd tartiːb, ʔaʕaːd tanðiːm] إعادَة تَرتِيب، إعادَة تَنظِيم [ʔiʕaːdat tartiːb, ʔiʕaːdat tanðiːm] *vn: sv* i. You ought to rearrange the furniture. لازِم تعِيد تَرتِيب الأثاث [laːzim tʕiːd tartiːb ʔilʔaθaːθ]

reason • **1.** داعِي [daːʕi] دَواعِي [dawaːʕi] *pl:* She really has no reason for acting like that. حَقِيقَةً ماكُو داعِي هِيَّ تِتصَرَّف هَالشَّكِل [ħaqiːqatan maːku daːʕi hiyya titṣarraf haššikil] • **2.** باعِث [baːʕiθ] I see no reason for complaint. ما شُوف باعِث لِلشَّكوَى [maː šuːf baːʕiθ liššakwa] • **3.** سَبَب [sabab] أسباب [ʔasbaːb] *pl:* عِلَّة [ʕilla] عِلات [ʕillaːt] *pl:* Is that the reason you didn't go? هَذا سَبَب عَدَم رُوحتَك؟ [haːða sabab ʕadam rawħtak?] • **4.** عَقِل [ʕaqil] صَواب [ṣawaːb] Please use your reason. رَجاءاً حَكُّم عَقلَك [rajaːʔan ħakkum ʕaqlak] If this keeps up, I'll lose my reason. إذا هاي راح تِستِمِرّ آني راح أفقُد صَوابِي [ʔiða haːy raːħ tistimirr ʔaːni raːħ ʔafqud ṣawaːbi]

to reason • **1.** تحاجَج [tħaːjaj] تَحاجُج [taħaːjuj] *vn: sv* a. تفاهَم [tfaːham] تَفاهُم [tafaːhum] *vn: sv* a. You can't reason with him. ما تِقدَر تِتحاجَج وِيّاه [maː tigdar titħaːjaj wiyyaːh]

reasonable • **1.** مَعقُول [maʕquːl] She's a very reasonable person. هِيَّ فَدّ وِحدَة كُلِّش مَعقُولَة [hiyya fadd wiħda kulliš maʕquːla] • **2.** مُناسِب [munaːsib] They sell their books at reasonable prices. يبِيعُون كُتُبهُم بأسعار مُناسبَة [ybiːʕuːn kutubhum bʔasʕaːr munaːsba]

reasonably • **1.** بعَقِل [bʕaqil] He acted reasonably. تصَرَّف بِعَقِل [tṣarraf bʕaqil]

to rebel • **1.** عِصَى [ʕiṣaː] عِصيان [ʕiṣyaːn] *vn: sv* a. The troops rebelled against their commander. الجُنُود عِصَوا عَلَى قائِدهُم [ʔijjunuːd ʕiṣaw ʕala qaːʔidhum]

* **My stomach simply rebelled.** • **1.** نَفسِي ما قِبلَت [nafsi maː qiblat]

to recall • **1.** تذَكَّر [dðakkar] تَذَكُّر [taðakkur] *vn: sv* a. Do you recall whether he was there or not? تِتذَكَّر إذا هُوَّ كان هناك لَو لا؟ [tidðakkar ʔiða huwwa čaːn hnaːk law laː?] • **2.** اِستَدعَى [ʔistadʕaː] اِستِدعاء [ʔistidʕaːʔ] *vn: sv* i. I read in the paper that your government has recalled its ambassador. قِريت بالجَّرِيدَة حُكُومَتكُم اِستَدعَت سَفِيرها [qiriːt bijjariːda ħukuːmatkum ʔistadʕat safiːrha]

receipt • **1.** وَصِل [waṣil] وُصُولات [wuṣuːlaːt] *pl:* Please give me a receipt. رَجاءاً إنطِينِي وَصِل [rajaːʔan ʔinṭiːni waṣil] • **2.** دَخَل [daxal] دُخُول [duxuːl] *pl:* The receipts were low today. الدَّخَل كان قَلِيل هَاليُوم [ʔiddaxal čaːn qaliːl halyuːm] • **3.** وُصُول [wuṣuːl] Please acknowledge receipt of this letter. رَجاءاً أعلِمُونا بوُصُول هَالمَكتُوب [rajaːʔan ʔaʕlimuːna bwuṣuːl halmaktuːb]

to receipt • **1.** * Please receipt this bill. أرجُوك أشِّر هالقائِمَة إعترافاً بالوُصُول [ʔarjuːk ʔaššir halqaːʔima ʔiʕtiraːfan bilwuṣuːl]

to receive • **1.** اِستِلَم [ʔistilam] اِستِلام [ʔistilaːm] *vn: sv* i. Did you receive my telegram? اِستِلَمِت بَرقِيتِي؟ [ʔistilamit barqiːti?] • **2.** قُبَض [qubað] قَبُض [qabuð] *vn:* اِنقُبَض [ʔinqubað] *p:* You'll receive your salary in case on the first of the month. راح تِقبُض راتبَك بأوَّل الشَّهَر [raːħ tiqbuð raːtbak bʔawwal ʔiššahar] • **3.** اِستَقبَل [ʔistaqbal] اِستِقبال [ʔistiqbaːl] *vn: sv* i. They received us cordially. اِستَقبِلُونا بتَرحِيب [ʔistaqbiluːna btarħiːb]

receiver • **1.** سِمّاعَة [simmaːʕa] سِمّاعات [simmaːʕaːt] *pl:* You didn't put the receiver back on the hook. ما رَجَّعت السَّمّاعَة بمَكانها [maː rajjaʕt ʔissimmaːʕa bmakaːnha] • **2.** مُستَلِم [mustalim] مُستَلِمِين [mustalimiːn] *pl:* Write the receiver's name legibly. إكتِب إسم المُستَلِم بوُضُوح [ʔiktib ʔism ʔilmustalim bwuðuːħ]

recent • **1.** حَدِيث [ħadiːθ] Television is a comparatively recent invention. التَّلَفِزيُون فَدّ اِختِراع حَدِيث نِسبِيّاً [ʔittalafizyuːn fadd ʔixtiraːʕ ħadiːθ nisbiyyan] • **2.** جِدِيد [jidiːd] Don't you have any recent issues? ما عِندَك أيّ أعداد جِدِيدَة؟ [maː ʕindak ʔayy ʔaʕdaːd jidiːda?] • **3.** أخِير [ʔaxiːr] Did you hear of the recent revolution in the north? سِمَعِت عَن الثَّورَة الأخِيرَة بالشِّمال؟ [simaʕit ʕan ʔiθθawra ʔilʔaxiːra biššimaːl?]

recently • **1.** أخِيراً [ʔaxiːran] حَدِيثاً [ħadiːθan] I heard it recently. سمَعِتها أخِيراً [smaʕitha ʔaxiːran]

R

reception • **1.** اِستِقبال [ʔistiqbaːl] اِستِقبالات [ʔistiqbaːlaːt] *pl:* He gave us a warm reception. اِستَقبَلنا اِستِقبال حارّ [ʔistaqbalna ʔistiqbaːl ħarr] • **2.** اِلتِقاط [ʔiltiqaːṭ] Reception is poor today on the radio. الاِلتِقاط مُو زين هَاليُوم بِالرّاديُو [ʔilʔiltiqaːṭ muː ziːn halyuːm birraːdyu] • **3.** حَفلَة اِستِقبال [ħaflat ʔistiqbaːl] حَفلات اِستِقبال [ħaflaːt ʔistiqbaːl] *pl:* Have you been invited to the reception? اِنعِزَمِت لِحَفلَة الاستِقبال؟ [ʔinʕizamit liħaflat ʔilʔistiqbaːl?]

recess • **1.** فُرصَة [furṣa] فُرَص [furaṣ] *pl:* فَترَة [fatra] فَترات [fatraːt] *pl:* We have a short recess at ten in the morning. ناخُذ فُرصَة قصَيرَة ساعَة عَشرَة الصُّبُح [naːxuð furṣa gṣayyra saːʕa ʕašra ʔiṣṣubuħ] • **2.** لِيوان [liːwaːn] لُواوين [luwaːwiːn] *pl:* The recesses of the mosque are cool. لَواوين المَسجِد باردَة [lawaːwiːn ʔilmasǰid baːrda]

recipe • **1.** وَصفَة [waṣfa] وَصفات [waṣfaːt] *pl:* Do you have a simple recipe for a cake? عِندِك فَدّ وَصفَة بَسِيطَة مال كَيك؟ [ʕindič fadd waṣfah basiːṭa maːl kayk?]

reckless • **1.** أهوَج [ʔahwaǰ] هُوج، هَوجين [huːǰ, hawǰiːn] *pl:* هُوجَة [huːǰa] *Feminine:* He's reckless driver. هُوَّ فَدّ سايِق أهوَج [huwwa fadd saːyiq ʔahwaǰ]

recognition • **1.** تَقدِير [taqdiːr] تَقدِيرات [taqdiːraːt] *pl:* اِعتِراف [ʔiʕtiraːf] اِعتِرافات [ʔiʕtiraːfaːt] *pl:* He didn't get the recognition he deserved. ما حَصَّل عَلَى التَّقدِير اللِّي يِستِحِقَّه [maː ħaṣṣal ʕala ʔittaqdiːr ʔilli yistiħiqqah]

to recognize • **1.** عِرَف [ʕiraf] مَعرِفَة [maʕrifa] *vn:* اِنعِرَف [ʔinʕiraf] *p:* At first I didn't recognize you. بِالأَوَّل ما عرَفتَك [bilʔawwal maː ʕraftak] • **2.** اِعتِرَف [ʔiʕtiraf] اِعتِراف [ʔiʕtiraːf] *vn: sv* i. The United States does not recognize that country. الوِلايات المُتَّحِدَة ما تِعتِرِف بِهَالدَّولَة [ʔilwilaːyaːt ʔilmuttaħida maː tiʕtirif bhaddawla]

to recommend • **1.** وَصَّى [waṣṣaː] تَوصِيَة [tawṣiya] *vn: sv* i. I recommended her highly to him. وَصّيتَه كُلِّش بِيها [waṣṣiːtah kulliš biːha] I recommended her highly to him. إنطَيتَه بِيها تَوصِيَة قَوِّيَّة [ʔinṭiːtah biːha tawṣiya qawwiyya]

recommendation • **1.** تَوصِيَة [tawṣiya] تَوصِيات [tawṣiyaːt] *pl:* I did it on your recommendation. سَوَّيتها حَسَب تَوصِيتَك [sawwiːtha ħasab tawṣiːtak]

record • **1.** قَيد [qiːd] قُيُود [qiyuːd] *pl:* I can't find any record of that bill. ما دَأقدَر ألقِي أيّ قَيد بِهَالقائِمَة [maː daʔagdar ʔalgi ʔayy qayd bhalqaːʔima] • **2.** سِجِل [siǰil] سِجِلّات [siǰillaːt] *pl:* He has a criminal record. عِندَه سِجِلّ سَوابِق [ʕindah siǰill sawaːbiq] • **3.** تارِيخ [taːriːx] تَوارِيخ [tawaːriːx] *pl:* That was the worst earthquake on record. هَذا كان أسوَء زِلزال بِالتّارِيخ [haːða čaːn ʔaswaʔ zilzaːl bittaːriːx] That was the worst earthquake on record. هَذا كان أسوَء زِلزال مسَجَّل [haːða čaːn ʔaswaʔ zilzaːl msaǰǰal] • **4.** إسطِوانَة [ʔisṭiwaːna] إسطِوانات [ʔisṭiwaːnaːt] *pl:* قَوانَة [qawaːna] قَوانات [qawaːnaːt] *pl:* They have a good selection of classical records. عِدهُم خُوش مَجمُوعَة مِن الإسطِوانات الكلاسِيكِيَّة [ʕidhum xuːš maǰmuːʕa min ʔilʔisṭiwaːnaːt ʔilklaːsikiyya] • **5.** رَقَم قِياسِي [raqam qiyaːsi] أرقام قِياسِيَّة [ʔarqaːm qiyaːsiyya] *pl:* He broke all records in free style swimming. كِسَر كُلّ الأرقام القِياسِيَّة بِالسِّباحَة الحُرَّة [kisar kull ʔilʔarqaːm ʔilqiyaːsiyya bissibaːħa ʔilħurra] We had a record crop this year. صار عِدنا مَحصُول قِياسِي هالسَّنَة [ṣaːr ʕidna maħṣuːl qiyaːsi hassana]

to record • **1.** سَجَّل [saǰǰal] تَسجِيل [tasǰiːl] *vn:* تسَجَّل [tsaǰǰal] *p:* Have you recorded everything he said? سَجَّلِت كُلّشِي قالَه؟ [saǰǰalit kullši gaːlah?] Can I use your tape recorder to record something? أقدَر أستَعمِل المُسَجِّل مالَك حَتَّى أسَجِّل شِي؟ [ʔagdar ʔastaʕmil ʔilmusaǰǰil maːlak ħatta ʔasaǰǰil ši?] • **2.** قَيَّد [qayyad, qayyid] تَقيِيد [taqyiːd] *vn:* تقَيَّد [tqayyad] *p:* Record all payments in this book. قَيِّد كُلّ المَدفُوعات بِهَالسِّجِلّ [qayyid kull ʔilmadfuːʕaːt bhassiǰill]

to recover • **1.** تشافَى [tšaːfaː] تَشافِي [tašaːfi] *vn: sv* a. تعافَى [tʕaːfaː] تَعافِي [taʕaːfi] *vn: sv* a. He recovered from his illness quickly. بِالعَجَل تشافَى مِن مَرَضَه [bilʕaǰal tšaːfaː min maraðah] • **2.** اِستَرجَع [ʔistarǰaʕ] اِستِرجاع [ʔistirǰaːʕ] *vn: sv* i. Did you finally recover your watch? تالِيها اِستَرجَعِت ساعتَك؟ [taːliːha ʔistarǰaʕit saːʕtak?] • **3.** اِستَرَدّ [ʔistaradd] اِستِرداد [ʔistirdaːd] *vn: sv* i. اِستَعاد [ʔistaʕaːd] اِستِعادَة [ʔistiʕaːda] *vn: sv* i. He recovered his balance immediately. اِستَرَدّ مُوازَنتَه بِالعَجَل [ʔistaradd muwaːzantah bilʕaǰal]

recovery • **1.** شَفاء [šafaːʔ] He's on the road to recovery. هُوَّ بِطَرِيقَه لِلشِّفاء [huwwa bṭariːqah liššifaːʔ]

red • **1.** أحمَر [ʔaħmar] حُمُر [ħumur] *pl:* حَمرَة [ħamra] *Feminine:* I want to buy a red hat. أرِيد أشتِري شَفقَة حَمرَة [ʔariːd ʔaštiri šafqa ħamra] • **2.** أحمَر [ʔaħmar] Red is not becoming to her. الأحمَر ما يلُوق إلها [ʔilʔaħmar maː yluːg ʔilha]

* **I'd rather be dead than Red.** • **1.** أفَضِّل المَوت عَالشُّيُوعِيَّة [ʔafaððil ʔilmawt ʕaššuyuːʕiyya]

* **I saw red when I heard that.** • **1.** فار دَمِّي مِن سمَعِتها [faːr dammi min smaʕitha]

Red Crescent • **1.** الهِلال الأحمَر [ʔilhilaːl ʔilʔaħmar]

Red Cross • **1.** الصَّلِيب الأحمَر [ʔiṣṣaliːb ʔilʔaħmar]

to reduce • **1.** خَفَّض [xaffað] تَخفِيض [taxfiːð] *vn:* تخَفَّض [txaffað] *p:* نَزَّل [nazzal] تَنزِيل [tanziːl] *vn:* تنَزَّل [tnazzal] *p:* We reduced the prices ten per cent.

i, interjection; p, passive; pl, plural; sv, stem vowel; vn, verbal noun

خففضنا الأسعار عَشرَة بالمِيَّة [xaffaðna ʔilʔasʕaːr ʕašra bilmiyya] • **2.** قَلّل [qallal] تَقلِيل [taqliːl] *vn:* تقَلّل [tqallal] *p:* نَقَّص [naggaṣ, naqqaṣ] تَنقِيص [tangiːṣ] *vn:* تنقَّص [tnaggaṣ] *p:* We have to reduce our expenses. لازِم نقَلّل مَصارِيفنا [laːzim nqallil maṣaːriːfna] • **3.** ضَعَّف [ðaʕʕaf] تَضعِيف [taðʕiːf] *vn: sv* i. نَزَّل [nazzal] تَنزِيل [tanziːl] *vn: sv* i. He can reduce his weight whenever he wants to. يِقدَر ينَزِّل وَزنَه شوَقِت ما يرِيد [yigdar ynazzil waznah šwakit maː yriːd]

to refer • **1.** حَوَّل [ħawwal] تَحوِيل [taħwiːl] *vn:* تحَوَّل [tħawwal] *p:* حال [ħaːl] أحوال [ʔaħwaːl] *pl:* إحالَة [ʔiħaːla] *vn:* اِنحال [ʔinħaːl] *p:* They referred me to the manager. حَوّلوني عَالمُدِير [ħawwluːni ʕalmudiːr] • **2.** شار [šaːr] إشارَة [ʔišaːra] *vn:* اِنشار [ʔinšaːr] *p:* She referred to it in her book. أشارَت إلها بكتابها [ʔašaːrat ʔilha biktaːbha]

reference • **1.** مَرجِع [marǰiʕ] مَراجِع [maraːǰiʕ] *pl:* You may give my name as a reference. تِقدَر تِنطِي إسمِي كَمَرجِع [tigdar tinṭi ʔismi kamarǰiʕ] • **2.** كتاب تَوصِيَة [ktaːb tawṣiya] كُتُب تَوصِيَة [kutub tawṣiya] *pl:* May I see your references? أقدَر أشُوف كُتُب التَّوصِيَة مالتَك؟ [ʔagdar ʔašuːf kutub ʔittawṣiya maːltak?]

to reflect • **1.** عِكَس [ʕikas] عَكِس [ʕakis] *vn:* اِنعِكَس [ʔinʕikas] *p:* The mirror reflects the light. المرايَة تِعكِس الضُّوَة [ʔilmraːya tiʕkis ʔiððuwa] • **2.** فَكَّر [fakkar] تَفكِير [tafkiːr] *vn: sv* i. I need time to reflect on it. أرِيد وَقِت أفَكِّر بِيها [ʔariːd wakit ʔafakkir biːha]

reflection • **1.** خَيال [xayaːl] You can see your reflection in the water. تِقدَر تشُوف خَيالَك بالماي [tigdar tšuːf xayaːlak bilmaːy] • **2.** تَعرِيض [taʕriːð]

reform • **1.** إصلاح [ʔiṣlaːħ] إصلاحات [ʔiṣlaːħaːt] *pl:* He introduced many reforms. أدخَل إصلاحات هوايَة [ʔadxal ʔiṣlaːħaːt hwaːya]

to reform • **1.** أصلَح [ʔaṣlaħ] إصلاح [ʔiṣlaːħ] *vn: sv* i. He's always trying to reform the world. دائماً يرِيد يصلِح الدِّنيا [daːʔiman yriːd yiṣliħ ʔiddinya] • **2.** اِنصلَح [ʔinṣilaħ] *sv* i. I'm sure he'll reform. آنِي مِتأكِّد راح ينصلِح [ʔaːni mitʔakkid raːħ yinṣiliħ]

refreshing • **1.** مُنعِش [munʕiš] On the banks of the Tigris the breeze is always refreshing. عَلَى ضِفاف دِجلَة الهَوا دائماً مُنعِش [ʕala ðifaːf dijla ʔilhawa daːʔiman munʕiš]

refreshments • **1.** مُرَطِّبات [murattibaːt] Refreshments were served during the intermission. توَزّعَت المُرَطِّبات أثناء الفَترَة [twazzʕat ʔilmurattibaːt ʔaθnaːʔ ʔilfatra]

refrigerator • **1.** ثَلّاجَة [θallaːǰa] ثَلّاجات [θallaːǰaːt] *pl:*

refugee • **1.** لاجِئ [laːǰiʔ]

refund • **1.** إرجاع [ʔirǰaːʕ] إرجاعات [ʔirǰaːʕaːt] *pl:* تَرجِيع [tarǰiːʕ] No refunds without a receipt. إرجاع المَبالغ ما يكُون إلّا بوَصِل [ʔirǰaːʕ ʔilmabaːliɣ maː ykuːn ʔilla bwaṣil]

to refund • **1.** رَجَّع [rajjaʕ] تَرجِيع [tarǰiːʕ] *vn:* ترَجَّع [trajjaʕ] *p:* أعاد [ʔaʕaːd] إعادَة [ʔiʕaːda] *vn:* اِنعاد [ʔinʕaːd] *p:* I'll refund your expenses. عُود أرَجِّعلَك مَصارِيفَك [ʕuːd ʔarajjiʕlak maṣaːriːfak]

refusal • **1.** رَفُض [rafuð] I didn't expect a refusal from him. ما توَقَّعِت مِنَّه الرَّفُض [maː twaqqaʕit minnah ʔirrafuð]

refuse • **1.** أوساخ [ʔawsaːx] You'll find a refuse box outside. تِلقِي صَندُوق أوساخ بَرَّة [tilqi ṣanduːg ʔawsaːx barra]

to refuse • **1.** رُفَض [rufað] رَفُض [rafuð] *vn:* اِنرُفَض [ʔinrufað] *p:* He doesn't refuse me anything. ما يِرفُضلِي أيّ طَلَب [maː yirfuðli ʔayy ṭalab]

regard • **1.** خُصُوص [xuṣuːṣ] شَأن [šaʔn] شُؤُون [šuʔuːn] *pl:* In that regard, I agree with you. بِهالخُصُوص أتِّفِق ويّاك [bhalxuṣuːṣ ʔattifiq wiyyaːk] • **2.** اِعتِبار [ʔiʕtibaːr] He has no regard at all for others. ما عِندَه أيّ اِعتِبار لِلآخَرِين [maː ʕindah ʔayy ʔiʕtibaːr lilʔaːxariːn] • **3.** اِحتِرام [ʔiħtiraːm] اِحتِرامات [ʔiħtiraːmaːt] *pl:* Give my regards to your wife. قَدِّم اِحتِراماتِي لِزَوجتَك [qaddim ʔiħtiraːmaːti lzawǰtak]

to regard • **1.** اِعتِبَر [ʔiʕtibar] اِعتِبار [ʔiʕtibaːr] *vn: sv* u. We regard him as an authority on law. نِعتَبُرَه حُجَّة بِالقانُون [niʕtaburah ħujja bilqaːnuːn] • **2.** قَدَّر [qaddar] تَقدِير [taqdiːr] *vn: sv* i. I regard him highly. آنِي أقَدّرَه هوايَة [ʔaːni ʔaqaddrah hwaːya]

region • **1.** مَنطِقَة [manṭiqa] مَناطِق [manaːṭiq] *pl:* إقلِيم [ʔiqliːm] أقالِيم [ʔaqaːliːm] *pl:*

register • **1.** سِجِلّ [sijill] سِجِلّات [sijillaːt] *pl:* قَيد [qayd] قيُود [qyuːd] *pl:* Did you sign the register? وَقَّعِت السِّجِلّ؟ [waqqaʕit ʔissijill?]

to register • **1.** سَجَّل [sajjal] تَسجِيل [tasǰiːl] *vn:* تسَجَّل [tsajjal] *p:* He's not registered at this hotel. هُوَّ ما مِتسَجِّل بهالأوتيل [huwwa maː mitsajjil bhalʔutiːl] I couldn't vote because I forgot to register. ما قِدرِت أصَوُّت لِأنّ نِسِيت أسَجِّل [maː gidarit ʔaṣawwut liʔann nisiːt ʔasajjil] Where can I register this letter? وِين أقدَر أسَجِّل هَالمَكتُوب [wiːn ʔagdar ʔasajjil halmaktuːb]

registered • **1.** مُسَجَّل [musajjal] I got a registered letter today. اِستِلَمِت مَكتُوب مُسَجَّل هَاليُوم [ʔistilamit maktuːb musajjal halyuːm]

regret • **1.** أسَف [ʔasaf] I had to decline the invitation with regret. اِضطَرِّيت أعتِذِر عَن الدَّعوَة مَعَ الأسَف

R

[ʔiðṭarri:t ʔaʕtiðir ʕan ʔiddaʕwa maʕa ʔilʔasaf] • **2.** اِعتِذار [ʔiʕtiða:r] Mr. and Mrs. Doe send their regrets. السَيِّد وَالسَيِّدَة فلان يقَدِّمُون اِعتِذارهُم [sayyid wissayyida fla:n yqaddimu:n ʔiʕtiða:rhum]

* **I'd rather wait than have regrets later.**
• **1.** آني أَفَضِّل أَنتِظِر عَلَى أَن أكُون مِتنَدِّم بَعدَين [ʔa:ni ʔafaðððil ʔantiðir ʕala ʔan ʔaku:n mitnaddim baʕdayn]

to regret • **1.** تأَسَّف [tʔassaf] تَأَسُّف [taʔassuf] *vn: sv* a. إسَف [ʔisaf] أَسَف [ʔasaf] *vn: sv* a. I've always regretted not having traveled much. تأَسَّفت دائِماً بأَنِّي ما سافَرت هوايَة [tʔassafit da:ʔiman biʔanni ma: sa:farit hwa:ya] • **2.** نِدَم [nidam] نَدَم [nadam] *vn: sv* a. He regretted having said it. نِدَم عَلَى قَولَتها [nidam ʕala gu:latha]

regrettable • **1.** مُؤسِف [muʔsif] This is a regrettable mistake. هَذِي غَلطَة مُؤسِفَة [ha:ði ɣalṭa muʔsifa]

regular • **1.** اِعتِيادِي [ʔiʕtiya:di] عادِي [ʕa:di] The regular price is 5 dinars. السِّعر الاعتِيادِي خَمس دَنانِير [ʔissiʕr ʔilʔiʕtiya:di xams dana:ni:r] • **2.** مِنتِظِم [mintiðim] His pulse is regular. نَبضَه مُنتَظَم [nabðah muntaðam] • **3.** منَضَّم [mnaððam] He lives a very regular life. يعِيش حَياة مِنَظَّمَة كُلِّش [yiʕi:š ħaya:t minaððma kulliš]

regularly • **1.** بانتِظام [biʔintiða:m] He pays regularly. هُوَّ يِدفَع بانتِظام [huwwa yidfaʕ bʔintiða:m]

to regulate • **1.** نَظَّم [naððam] تَنظِيم [tanði:m] *vn:* تنَظَّم [tnaððam] *p:* I can't regulate the temperature. ما دَأَقدَر أَنَظِّم الحَرارَة [ma: daʔagdar ʔanaððim ʔilħara:ra] • **2.** ضُبَط [ðubaṭ] ضَبُط [ðabuṭ] *vn:* اِنضُبَط [ʔinðubaṭ] *p:* Can you regulate the carburetor? تِقدَر تُضبُط الكَبرِيتَر؟ [tigdar tuðbuṭ ʔilkabri:ta?]

regulation • **1.** نِظام [niða:m] أَنظِمَة [ʔanðima] *pl:* That's against police regulations. هَذِي مُخالَفَة لأَنظِمَة الشُّرطَة [ha:ði muxa:lifa lʔanðimat ʔiššurṭa]

rein • **1.** رَشمَة [rašma] رَشمات [rašma:t] *pl:*

to reject • **1.** رُفَض [rufað] رَفُض [rafuð] *vn:* اِنرُفَض [ʔinrufað] *p:* My application was rejected. عَرِيضتِي اِنرُفضَت [ʕari:ðti ʔinrufðat]

related • **1.** مِتعَلِّق [mitʕalliq] I want all the information related to this matter. أَرِيد كُلّ المَعلُومات المِتعَلِّقَة بهَالأَمُر [ʔari:d kull ʔilmaʕlu:ma:t ʔilmitʕalliqa bhalʔamur]

* **We're related on my mother's side.**
• **1.** عِدنا قَرابَة مِن جِهَة أُمِّي [ʕidna qara:ba min ǰihat ʔummi]
* **That's a related matter.** • **1.** هَذا مَوضُوع إلَه عَلاقَة [ha:ða mawðu:ʕ ʔilah ʕala:qa]

relation • **1.** عَلاقَة [ʕala:qa] عَلاقات [ʕala:qa:t] *pl:* The relations between the two countries are strained. العَلاقات بين البَلَدَين توَتّرَت [ʔilʕala:qa:t bayn ʔilbaladayn twattrat] • **2.** صِلَة [ṣila] صِلات [ṣila:t] *pl:* عَلاقَة [ʕala:qa] عَلاقات [ʕala:qa:t] *pl:* Why don't you talk to him, you have better relations with him. لِيش ما إنتَ تِحكِي وِيّاه، صِلتَك بِيه أَحسَن [li:š ma: ʔinta tiħči wiyya:h, ṣiltak bi:h ʔaħsan] • **3.** قَرِيب [qari:b, gari:b] Are they all your relation? هَذولَة كُلّهُم قَرايبَك؟ [haðu:la kullhum qara:ybak?]

relationship • **1.** عَلاقَة [ʕala:qa] What's the relationship between those two? شِنُو العَلاقَة بين هَالثنَين؟ [šinu: ʔilʕala:qa bi:n haθθnayn?]

relative • **1.** قَرِيب [qari:b, gari:b] قَرايِب [gara:yib] He is a relative of mine. هَذا قَرِيبِي [ha:ða qari:bi] He is a relative of mine. هَذا قَرايِبِي [ha:ða gara:ybi] • **2.** نِسبِي [nisbi] He said everything in life is relative. قال كُلّشِي نِسبِي بالحَياة [ga:l kullši nisbi bilħaya:t]

to relax • **1.** رَخَّى [raxxa:] تَرخِيَة [tarxiya] *vn:* ترَخَّى [traxxa:] *p:* Relax your muscles. رَخِّي عَضَلاتَك [raxxi ʕaðala:tak] • **2.** اِرتاح [ʔirta:ħ] راحَة [ra:ħa] *vn: sv* a. I can't relax until it's finished. ما أَقدَر أَرتاح إلَى أَن تِخلَص [ma: ʔagdar ʔarta:ħ ʔila ʔan tixlaṣ] • **3.** هِدَأ [hidaʔ] هُدُوء [hudu:ʔ] *vn: sv* a. Relax! Nobody's going to hurt you. إهدَأ، مَحَّد راح يأَذِّيك [ʔihdaʔ, maħħad ra:ħ yʔaðði:k]

release • **1.** إفراج عَن [ʔifra:ǰʕan-] إفراجات عَن [ʔifra:ǰa:t ʕan-] *pl:* إطلاق سِراح [ʔiṭla:q sira:ħ] The lawyer has applied for her release. المُحامِي قَدَّم طَلَب لِلإفراج عَنها [ʔilmuħa:mi qaddam ṭalab lilʔifra:ǰ ʕanha]

to release • **1.** أَفرَج [ʔafraǰ] إفراج [ʔifra:ǰ] *vn:* اِنفَرَج [ʔinfaraǰ] *p:* أَطلَق [ʔaṭlaq] إطلاق [ʔiṭla:q] *vn:* اِنطِلَق [ʔinṭilaq] *p:* The police released him right away. الشُّرطَة أَفرَجوا عَنَّه حالاً [ʔiššurṭa ʔafraǰaw ʕannah ħa:lan] • **2.** فَكّ [fakk] فَكّ [fakk] *vn:* اِنفَكّ [ʔinfakk] *p:* Release the safety catch. فُكّ مِفتاح الأَمان [fukk mifta:ħ ʔilʔama:n]

reliable • **1.** عَلَيه اِعتِماد [ʕali:h ʔiʕtima:d] He is a reliable person. هُوَّ فَدّ شَخِص عَليه اِعتِماد [huwwa fadd šaxiṣ ʕali:h ʔiʕtima:d] This is a reliable firm. هَذِي فَدّ شَرِكَة تِعتِمِد عَليها [ha:ði fadd šarika tiʕtimid ʕali:ha] • **2.** مَوثُوق ب [mawθu:q b-] I got it from a reliable source. حَصَّلتها مِن مَصدَر مَوثُوق بِيه [ħaṣṣalitha min maṣdar mawθu:q bi:h]

relief • **1.** فَرَج [faraǰ] There is no hope of immediate relief from the heat. ماكُو أَمَل فَرَج قَرِيب مِن الحَرّ [ma:ku ʔamal faraǰ qari:b min ʔilħarr] • **2.** إعانَة [ʔiʕa:na] إعانات [ʔiʕa:na:t] *pl:* They want to organize a relief committee. يرِيدُون يشَكّلُون لَجنَة لِلإعانَة [yri:du:n yšakklu:n laǰna lilʔiʕa:na]

R

i, interjection; p, passive; pl, plural; sv, stem vowel; vn, verbal noun

to give relief • **1.** رَيَّح [rayyaħ] تَرييح [taryi:ħ] *vn:* تَرَيَّح [trayyaħ] *p:* Did the medicine give you any relief? الدُّوا رَيَّحَك شوَيَّة؟ [ʔidduwa rayyaħak šwayya?]

to relieve • **1.** خَفَّف [xaffaf] تَخفِيف [taxfi:f] *vn:* تخَفَّف [txaffaf] *p:* This will relieve your headache. هاي راح تخَفِّف وُجَع راسَك [ha:y ra:ħ txaffuf wujaʕ ra:sak] • **2.** راح [ra:ħ] إراحَة [ʔira:ħa] *vn: sv* i. Why don't you tell me the story and relieve me of my anxiety. لِيش ما تِحكِيلِي القُصَّة وَترَيِّحنِي مِن قَلَقِي [li:š ma: tiħči:li ʔilquṣṣa wtrayyiħni min qalaqi] • **3.** خَلَّص [xallaṣ] تَخلِيص [taxli:s] *vn:* تخَلَّص [txallaṣ] *p:* We're trying to find a servant to relieve my wife of the cleaning. دَنحاوِل نِلقِي خَدّامَة حَتَّى نخَلِّص مَرتِي مِن التَّنظِيف [danħa:wil nilqi xadda:ma ħatta nxalliṣ marti min ʔittanði:f]

* **We relieve one another.** • **1.** إحنا نحِلّ واحِد مَحَلّ اللاخ [ʔiħna nħill wa:ħid maħall ʔilla:x]

religion • **1.** دِين [di:n] أديان [ʔadya:n] *pl:*

religious • **1.** مِتدَيِّن [mitdayyin] مِتدَيِّنِين [mitdayyini:n] *pl:* تَقِي [taqi] تَقِيِّين، أتقِيّاء [taqiyyi:n, ʔatqiya:ʔ] *pl:* He's very religious. هُوَّ كُلِّش مِتدَيِّن [huwwa kulliš middayyin] • **2.** دِينِي [di:ni] He belongs to a religious order. هُوَّ مِن أتباع طَرِيقَة دِينِيَّة [huwwa min ʔatba:ʕ ṭari:qa di:niyya]

to rely on • **1.** اِعتِمَد عَلَى [ʔiʕtimad ʕala] اِعتِماد [ʔiʕtima:d] *vn: sv* i. You can't rely on him. ما تِقدَر تِعتِمِد عَلِيه [ma: tigdar tiʕtimid ʕali:h]

to remain • **1.** ظَلّ [ọall] *sv* a. بُقَى [buqa:] بَقاء [baqa:ʔ] *vn: sv* a. He remained silent. ظَلّ ساكِت [ọall sa:kit] There remains nothing else for us to do but wait. ما يِبقَى إلنا شِي نسَوِّيه غير نِنتِظِر [ma: yibqa: ʔilna ši nsawwi:h ɣi:r nintiọir]

* **That remains to be seen.** • **1.** هَذِي راح تبَيِّن بَعدَين [ha:ði ra:ħ tbayyin baʕdi:n]

remaining • **1.** باقِي [ba:qi] What did you do with the remaining cards? شسَوِّيت بِالبِطاقات الباقية؟ [ššawwi:t bilbiṭa:qa:t ʔilba:qya?]

remains • **1.** آثار [ʔa:θa:r] I'm anxious to see the historical remains. آنِي مِشتاق أشُوف الآثار التّارِيخِيَّة [ʔa:ni mišta:q ʔašu:f ʔilʔa:θa:r ʔitta:ri:xiyya] • **2.** مَيِّت [mayyit] مَيِّتِين [mayyti:n] *pl:* The remains were taken to Najaf for burial. المَيِّت اِنإخَذ لِلنَّجَف لِلدَّفِن [ʔilmayyit ʔinʔixað linnajaf liddafin]

remark • **1.** مُلاحَظَة [mula:ħaọa] مُلاحَظات [mula:ħaọa:t] *pl:* That remark wasn't called for. هَالمُلاحَظَة ما إلها داعِي [halmula:ħaọa ma: ʔilha da:ʕi]

remarkable • **1.** فوق العادَة [fu:q ʔilʕa:da] خارِق [xa:riq] What's so remarkable about it. شِنُو اللّي الفَوق العادَة بِيها؟ [šinu ʔilli fawq ʔilʕa:da bi:ha?]

remedy • **1.** عِلاج [ʕila:j] عِلاجات [ʕila:ja:t] *pl:* دَوَى [duwa] That's a good remedy for colds. هَذا خُوش عِلاج لِلنَّشلَة [ha:ða xu:š ʕila:j linnašla]

to remedy • **1.** عالَج [ʕa:laj] مُعالَجَة [muʕa:laja] *vn:* تعالَج [tʕa:laj] *p:* داوَى [da:wa:] مُداواة [muda:wa:t] *vn:* تداوَى [tda:wa:] *p:* I don't know how that can be remedied. ما أَدري هاي شلُون تِتعالَج [ma: ʔadri ha:y šlu:n titʕa:laj]

to remember • **1.** تذَكَّر [dðakkar] تَذَكُّر [taðakkur] *vn: sv* a. تفَطَّن [tfaṭṭan] تَفَطُّن [tafaṭṭun] *vn: sv* a. It was in May, as far as I remember. كانَت بِمايِس، حَسَب ما أتذَكَّر [ča:nat bma:yis, ħasab ma: ʔadðakkar]

* **I simply can't remember his name.** • **1.** إسمَه أبَد ما دَيجِي عَلَى بالِي [ʔismah ʔabad ma: dayiji ʕala ba:li]

* **He always remembers us at Christmas.** • **1.** دائِماً نُخطُر عَلَى بالَه بعِيد المِيلاد [da:ʔiman nuxṭur ʕala ba:lah bʕi:d ʔilmi:la:d]

* **Remember to turn out the light.** • **1.** لا تِنسَى طَفِّي الضُّوَة [la: tinsa: ṭaffi ʔiọọuwa]

* **Remember me to your father.** • **1.** سَلِّملِي عَلَى أبُوك [sallimli ʕala ʔabu:k]

to remind • **1.** ذَكَّر [ðakkar] تَذكِير [taðki:r] *vn: sv* i. He reminded me of my promise. ذَكَّرنِي بِالوَعَد مالِي [ðakkarni bilwaʕad ma:li] He reminds me of his father. يذَكِّرنِي بأبُوه [yðakkirni bʔabu:h] • **2.** جاب ببالِّي [ja:b bba:li] *sv* i. ذَكَّر [ðakkar] تَذكِير [taðki:r] *vn: sv* i. Remind me about it later. جِيبها ببالِّي بَعدين [ji:bha bba:li baʕdi:n]

reminder • **1.** تأكِيد [taʔki:d] تأكِيدات [taʔki:da:t] *pl:* I'll send him a reminder, if he doesn't pay by tomorrow. أدِزلَه تأكِيد إذا ما يِدفَع باكِر [ʔadizzlah tʔaki:d ʔiða ma: yidfaʕ ba:čir]

remnant • **1.** بَقِيَّة [baqiyya] بَقايا [baqa:ya] فَضلَة [faọla] فَضلات [faọla:t] *pl:* How much do you want for those three remnants? هَالثِّلث بَقايا مال القماش بيش تبِيعهُم؟ [halitlaθ baqa:ya: ma:l ʔilqma:š biyš tbi:ʕhum?]

remote • **1.** كُلِّش بعِيد [kulliš biʕi:d] There's a remote possibility that it will succeed. أكُو اِحتِمال كُلِّش بعِيد راح يِنجَح [ʔaku ʔiħtima:l kulliš biʕi:d ra:ħ yinjaħ]

to remove • **1.** نِزَع [nizaʕ] نَزِع [naziʕ] *vn:* اِنّزَع [ʔinnizaʕ] *p:* شال [ša:l] شَيِل [ši:l] *vn:* اِنشال [ʔinša:l] *p:* Please remove your hat. أرجُوك إنزَع شَفقتَك [ʔarju:k ʔinzaʕ šafugtak] • **2.** زال [za:l] إزالَة [ʔiza:la] *vn: sv* i.

R

شال [šaːl] *sv* i. This should remove all doubt. هاي لازِم تزِيل كُلّ شَكّ [haːy laːzim dziːl kull šakk] • **3.** رَوَّح [rawwaħ] تَروِيح [tarwiːħ] *vn:* تَروَّح [trawwaħ] *p:* زال [zaːl] *sv* i. شال [šaːl] *sv* i. That cleaner will remove all stains. هَالمادَّة المُنَظِّفَة تَروِّح كُلّ اللَّكّات [halmaːdda ʔilmunaððifa trawwiħ kull ʔillakkaːt] • **4.** عِزَل [ʕizal] عَزِل [ʕazil] *vn:* اِنعِزَل [ʔinʕizal] *p:* He was removed from office. اِنعِزَل مِن الوَظِيفَة [ʔinʕizal min ʔilwaðiːfa] • **5.** نِقَل [niqal, nigal] نَقِل [naqil] *vn:* اِنِّقَل [ʔinniqal] *p:* The phone was removed from here. التَّلِفُون اِنِّقَل مِن هِنا [ʔittalifuːn ʔinniqal minhna]

to renew • **1.** جَدَّد [ǰaddad] تَجدِيد [tajdiːd] *vn:* تجَدَّد [tǰaddad] *p:* I went to the police to renew my license. رِحِت لِلشُّرطَة أَجَدِّد إجازتِي [riħit liššurṭa ʔaǰaddid ʔiǰaːzti]

rent • **1.** إيجار [ʔiːǰaːr] How much rent do you pay for your house? شقَدّ تِدفَع إيجار بِبَيتَك؟ [šgadd tidfaʕ ʔiːǰaːr bbaytak?]

to rent • **1.** أَجَّر [ʔaǰǰar] تَأجِير [taʔǰiːr] *vn:* تأَجَّر [tʔaǰǰar] *p:* اِستَأجَر [ʔistaʔǰar] اِستِئجار [ʔistiʔǰaːr] *vn: sv* i. I rented a room for three months. أَجَّرِت غُرفَة لِتلَث أَشهُر [ʔaǰǰarit ɣurfa litlaθ ʔašhur] They rented a garage. اِستَأجِرَوا كَراج [ʔistaʔǰiraw garaːǰ] • **2.** أَجَّر [ʔaǰǰar] تَأجِير [taʔǰiːr] *vn: sv* i. He rented me the room for one month. أَجَّرلِي الغُرفَة شَهَر واحِد [ʔaǰǰarli ʔilɣurfa šahar waːħid]

repair • **1.** تَصلِيح [taṣliːħ] تَصلِيحات [taṣliːħaːt] *pl:* The car needs only minor repairs. السَّيّارَة تِحتاج تَصلِيحات بَسِيطَة بَسّ [ʔissayyaːra tiħtaːǰ taṣliːħaːt basiːṭa bass] • **2.** تَعمِير [taʕmiːr] تَرمِيم [tarmiːm] تَرمِيمات [tarmiːmaːt] *pl:* تَصلِيح [taṣliːħ] تَصلِيحات [taṣliːħaːt] *pl:* This house needs a lot of repairs. هَالبَيت يِرّادلَه هوايَة تَعمِير [halbayt yirraːdlah hwaːya taʕmiːr]

to repair • **1.** صَلَّح [ṣallaħ] تَصلِيح [taṣliːħ] *vn:* تصَلَّح [tṣallaħ] *p:* He repaired the radio for me. صَلَّحلِي الرّادِيُو [ṣallaħli ʔirraːdyu] • **2.** رَمَّم [rammam] تَرمِيم [tarmiːm] *vn:* ترَمَّم [trammam] *p:* عَمَّر [ʕammar] تَعمِير [taʕmiːr] *vn:* تعَمَّر [tʕammar] *p:* When are you going to repair this house? شوَقِت راح ترَمِّم هَالبَيت؟ [šwakit raːħ trammim halbayt?]

to repeat • **1.** عاد [ʕaːd] إعادَة [ʔiʕaːda] *vn:* اِنعاد [ʔinʕaːd] *p:* كَرَّر [karrar] تَكرِير [takriːr] *vn:* تكَرَّر [tkarrar] *p:* Repeat what I just said. عِيد اللِّي قِلتَه هَسَّة [ʕiːd ʔilli giltah hassa] They repeat everything they hear. يكَرِّرُون كُلّشِي اللِّي يِسمَعُوه [ykarriruːn kullši ʔilli yismaʕuːh]

to replace • **1.** حَلّ مَحَلّ [ħall maħall] حَلّ [ħall] *vn: sv* i. أَخَذ مُكان [ʔaxað mukaːn] أَخِذ [ʔaxið] *vn: sv* u. We haven't been able to get anyone to replace her. ما دَنِقدَر نِلقِي أَحَّد يحِلّ مَحَلّها [maː danigdar nilgi ʔaħħad yħill maħallha] • **2.** بَدَّل [baddal] تَبدِيل [tabdiːl] *vn:* They replaced some tubes and made other repairs in the T.V. set. بَدِّلَوا بَعَض اللَّمبات وسَوَّوا تَصلِيحات أُخرَى بِجهاز التَّلِفِزيُون [baddilaw baʕað ʔillambaːt wsawwaw taṣliːħaːt ʔuxra bǰihaːz ʔittalifizyuːn] • **3.** اِستَبدَل [ʔistabdal] اِستِبدال [ʔistibdaːl] *vn: sv* i. The prime minister is going to replace two members of his cabinet. رَئِيس الوُزَراء راح يِستَبدِل عُضوَين مِن أَعضاء وِزارتَه [raʔiːs ʔilwuzaraːʔ raːħ yistabdil ʕuðwayn min ʔaʕðaːʔ wizaːrtah]

reply • **1.** جَواب [ǰawaːb] أَجوِبَة [ʔaǰwiba] *pl:* رَدّ [radd] رُدُود [ruduːd] *pl:* I never received a reply to my letter. أَبَد ما اِستِلَمِت جَواب لمَكتُوبِي [ʔabad maː ʔistilamit ǰawaːb lmaktuːbi]

to reply • **1.** جاوَب [ǰaːwab] إجابَة [ʔiǰaːba] *vn: sv* u. رَدّ [radd] رَدّ [radd] *vn: sv* i. He replied to my letter immediately. جاوَب عَلَى مَكتُوبِي حالاً [ǰaːwab ʕala maktuːbi ħaːlan]

report • **1.** تَقرِير [taqriːr] تَقارِير [taqaːriːr] *pl:* I've already read the report. آنِي قرَيتَه لِلتَّقرِير [ʔaːni qriːtah littaqriːr]

to report • **1.** رُوَى [ruwaː] رَوِي [rawi] *vn:* اِنرُوَى [ʔinruwaː] *p:* The newspapers reported the accident in detail. الجَّرايِد رُوَت الحادِث بِالتَّفصِيل [ʔiǰǰaraːyid ruwat ʔilħaːdiθ bittafṣiːl] • **2.** بَلَّغ [ballaɣ] تَبلِيغ [tabliːɣ] *vn: sv* i. Somebody must have reported him to the police فَدّ أَحَّد لازِم بَلَّغ الشُّرطَة عَنَّه [fadd ʔaħħad laːzim ballaɣ ʔiššurṭa ʕannah]

to report to • **1.** راجَع [raːǰaʕ] مُراجَعَة [muraːǰaʕa] *vn: sv* i. Tomorrow report to the director for your work. باكِر راجِع المُدِير عَن شُغلَك [baːčir raːǰiʕ ʔilmudiːr ʕan šuɣlak]

* **To whom do I report?** • **1.** مِنُو المَرجَع مالِي؟ [minu ʔilmarǰaʕ maːli?]

report card • **1.** وَثِيقَة دَرَجات [waθiːqat daraǰaːt] وَثايِق دَرَجات [waθaːyiq daraǰaːt] *pl:* She always comes home with good report cards in her hand. دائماً تِجِي لِلبَيت وَبِايدها وَثايِق دَرَجات مُمتازَة [daːʔiman tiǰi lilbayt wbʔiːdha waθaːyiq daraǰaːt mumtaːza]

reporter • **1.** صُحُفِي [ṣuħufi] صُحُفِيِّين [ṣuħufiyyiːn] *pl:*

to represent • **1.** مَثَّل [maθθal] تَمثِيل [tamθiːl] *vn:* تمَثَّل [tmaθθal] *p:* Who is representing the defendant? مِنُو دَيمَثِّل المُدَّعَى عَلِيه؟ [minu daymaθθil ʔilmuddaʕaː ʕaliːh?] What does this symbol represent? هَالرَّمِز شيمَثِّل؟ [harramiz šymaθθil?]

representative • **1.** مُمَثِّل [mumaθθil] مُمَثِّلِين [mumaθθiliːn] *pl:* He is the European representative of a big concern. هَذا المُمَثِّل الأُورُبِّي لِشَرِكَة كبِيرَة [haːða ʔilmumaθθil ʔilʔuːruppi lšarika čibiːra]

R

• **2.** نائِب [na:ʔib] نُوّاب [nuwwa:b] *pl:* Who's the representative from your district? مِنُو النّائِب مِن مَنطِقتَك [minu ʔinna:ʔib min manṭiqtak]

reproach • **1.** تَعنِيف [taʕni:f] مُؤاخَذَة [muʔa:xaða] I didn't mean that as a reproach. ما قِصَدِت المُآخَذَة [ma: qṣadit ʔilmuʔa:xaða]

to reproach • **1.** واخَذ [wa:xað] مُواخَذَة [muwa:xaða] *vn:* تواخَذ [twa:xað] *p:* زِجَر [zijar] زَجِر [zajir] *vn:* اِنزِجَر [ʔinzijar] *p:* My mother is always reproaching me for my extravagance. أُمِّي دائِماً تواخِذنِي عَلَى إسرافِي [ʔummi da:ʔiman twa:xiðni ʕala ʔisra:fi]

reputation • **1.** سُمعَة [sumʕa] شُهرَة [šuhra] صِيت [ṣi:t] He has a good reputation. عِندَه سُمعَة طَيِّبَة [ʕindah sumʕa ṭayyba] • **2.** مَعرُوف عَن [maʕru:f ʕan] He has a reputation for being a good worker. مَعرُوف عَنَّه بأَنَّه شاغُول [maʕru:f ʕannah bʔannah ša:ɣu:l]

request • **1.** طَلَب [ṭalab] طَلَبات [ṭalaba:t] *pl:* رَجاء [raja:ʔ] رَجاءات [raja:ʔa:t] *pl:* They granted the request. وافقوا عَالطَّلَب [wa:fqaw ʕaṭṭalab] I am writing you at the request of a friend. آنِي دَأكتِبلَك بِناءاً عَلَى رَجاء صَدِيق [ʔa:ni daʔaktiblak bina:ʔan ʕala raja:ʔ ṣadi:q]

to request • **1.** ترَجَّى مِن [trajja: min] تَرَجِّي [tarajji] *vn: sv* a. I must request you to leave this place. آنِي مُضطَرّ أَترَجَّى مِنَّك تِترُك هَالمَحَلّ [ʔa:ni muðṭarr ʔatrajja: minnak titruk halmaħall]

to require • **1.** اِستَلزَم [ʔistalzam] اِستِلزام [ʔistilza:m] *vn: sv* i. A thing like that requires careful study. فَدّ شِي مِثِل هَذا يِستَلزِم دِراسَة دَقِيقَة [fadd ši miθil ha:ða yistalzim dira:sa daqi:qa] • **2.** اِحتاج [ʔiħta:j] اِحتِياج [ʔiħtiya:j] *vn: sv* a. اِنراد ل [ʔinra:d l-] *sv* a. تطَلَّب [ṭṭallab] تَطَلُّب [taṭallub] *vn: sv* a. That requires no proof. هَذا ما يِحتاج أَيّ إثبات [ha:ða ma: yiħta:j ʔayy ʔiθba:t] How much time will that require? هاي شقَدّ يِنرادِلها وَقِت؟ [ha:y šgadd yinra:dilha wakit?] How much money does that require? شقَدّ فلُوس هاي تِتطَلَّب؟ [šgadd flu:s ha:y tiṭṭallab?] • **3.** طِلَب [ṭilab] Do you require a deposit? تِطلُبُون تأمِينات؟ [tiṭlubu:n taʔmi:na:t?] • **4.** اِستَدعَى [ʔistadʕa:] اِستِدعاء [ʔistidʕa:ʔ] *vn: sv* i. اِقتِضَى [ʔiqtiða:] اِقتِضاء [ʔiqtiða:ʔ] *vn: sv* i. The situation requires firm measures. الحالَة تِستَدعِي إجراءات صارمَة [ʔilħa:la tistadʕi ʔijra:ʔa:t ṣa:rima]

requirement • **1.** مُتَطَلَّبات [mutaṭallaba:t] The requirements for graduation are numerous. مُتَطَلبات التَّخَرُّج كَثِيرَة [mutaṭalba:t ʔittaxarruj kaθi:ra] • **2.** اِحتِياج [ʔiħtiya:j] اِحتِياجات [ʔiħtiya:ja:t] *pl:* حاجَة [ħa:ja] حاجات، حَوايِج [ħa:ja:t, ħawa:yij] *pl:* He asked us to estimate what our manpower requirements in the crafts will be. طِلَب مِن عِدنا نقَدِّر شقَدّ راح تكُون حاجَتنا مِن العُمّال الماهرِين [ṭilab min ʕidna nqaddir šgadd ra:ħ tku:n ħa:jatna min ʔilʕumma:l ʔilma:hri:n] • **3.** شَرط مَطلُوب [šarṭ maṭlu:b] شُرُوط مَطلُوبَة [šuru:ṭ maṭlu:ba] *pl:* Does he meet our requirements? تِتوَفَّر بِيه الشُّرُوط المَطلُوبَة؟ [titwaffar bi:h ʔiššuru:ṭ ʔilmaṭlu:ba?]

to resemble • **1.** شِبَه [šibah] شِبِه [šibih] *vn: sv* a. طِلَع عَلَى [ṭilaʕ ʕala] طُلُوع [ṭulu:ʕ] *vn: sv* a. Don't you think he resembles his mother? ما تِعتِقِد يِشبَه أُمَّه؟ [ma: tiʕtiqid yišbah ʔummah?] Don't you think he resembles his mother? ما تِعتِقِد طالع عَلَى أُمَّه؟ [ma: tiʕtiqid ṭa:liʕ ʕala ʔummah?]

reservation • **1.** حَجِز [ħajiz] I want to cancel my reservation. أَرِيد أَلغِي الحَجِز مالِي [ʔari:d ʔalɣi ʔilħajiz ma:li] • **2.** تَحَفُّظ [taħaffuð] تَحَفُّظات [taħaffuða:t] *pl:* He said it with some reservation. قالها مَعَ بَعض التَّحَفُّظ [qa:lha maʕa baʕð ʔittaħaffuð]

reserve • **1.** اِحتِياطِي [ʔiħtiya:ṭi] I'm afraid we'll have to dig into our reserves. أَعتِقِد راح نِضطَرّ نِستَعمِل الاحتياطي مالنا [ʔaʕtiqid ra:ħ niðṭarr nistaʕmil ʔilʔiħtiya:ṭi ma:lna] One-fifth of the world's oil reserves are in Kuwait. خُمِس اِحتِياطِي العالَم مِن النَّفُط بالكُوَيت [xumis ʔiħtiya:ṭi ʔilʕa:lam min ʔinnafuṭ bilkuwayt] • **2.** اِحتِياط [ʔiħtiya:ṭ] He is a reserve officer. هَذا ضابُط اِحتِياط [ha:ða ða:buṭ ʔiħtiya:ṭ]

to reserve • **1.** حِجَز [ħijaz] حَجِز [ħajiz] *vn:* اِنحِجَز [ʔinħijaz] *p:* Can you reserve a place for me? تِقدَر تِحجِزلِي مَحَلّ؟ [tigdar tiħjizli maħall?] • **2.** حُفَظ [ħufað] حُفُظ [ħufuð] *vn:* اِنحُفَظ [ʔinħufað] *p:* He reserved the right of using the car for himself. حُفَظ حَقّ اِستِعمال السَّيّارَة لنَفسَه [ħufað ħaqq ʔistiʕma:l ʔissayya:ra lnafsah]

reserved • **1.** هادِئ [ha:diʔ] هادِئِين [ha:diʔi:n] *pl:* I found him very reserved. شِفتَه كُلِّش هادِئ [šiftah kulliš ha:diʔ] • **2.** مَحجُوز [maħju:z] All seats are reserved. كُلّ المَحَلّات مَحجُوزَة [kull ʔilmaħalla:t maħju:za]

to resign • **1.** اِستَقال [ʔistaqa:l] اِستِقالَة [ʔistiqa:la] *vn: sv* i. He resigned as chairman of the committee. اِستَقال مِن رِئاسَة اللَّجنَة [ʔistaqa:l min riʔa:sat ʔillajna]

resignation • **1.** اِستِقالَة [ʔistiqa:la] اِستِقالات [ʔistiqa:la:t] *pl:* He handed in his resignation today. قَدَّم اِستِقالتَه اليُوم [qaddam ʔistiqa:ltah ʔilyu:m] • **2.** اِستِسلام [ʔistisla:m] إِذعان [ʔiðʕa:n] He received the news with resignation. تقَبَّل الأَخبار بِاستِسلام [tqabbal ʔilʔaxba:r bʔistisla:m] • **3.** تَسلِيم [tasli:m] We have nothing left but resignation to the will of God. ما عِدنا غير التَّسلِيم لإرادَة الله [ma: ʕidna ɣi:r ʔittasli:m lʔira:dat ʔallah]

resigned to • **1.** راضِي ب [ra:ði b-] She's resigned to her fate of remaining an old maid for the rest of her life.

R

راضيَة بِقِسمَتها تِبقَى بنَيَّة طُول عُمُرها [ra:ðya bqismatha tibqa: bnayya ṭu:l ʕumurha]

to resist • **1.** قاوَم [qa:wam] مُقاوَمَة [muqa:wama] *vn:* تقاوَم [tqa:wam] *p:* He tried to resist, but the police arrested him. حاوَل يقاوُم لَكِن الشُّرطَة ألقَت القَبُض عَليه [ħa:wal yqa:wum la:kin ʔiššurṭa ʔalqat ʔilqabuð ʕali:h] I couldn't resist the temptation. ما قِدَرت أقاوُم الإغراء [ma: gidart ʔaqa:wum ʔilʔiɣra:ʔ]

resistance • **1.** مُقاوَمَة [muqa:wama] He didn't put up any resistance. ما بَيَّن أيّ مُقاوَمَة [ma: bayyan ʔayy muqa:wama]

to resole • **1.** حَطّ نَعَل [ħaṭṭ naʕal] حَطّ [ħaṭṭ] *vn:* اِنحَطّ [ʔinħaṭṭ] *p:* I'm having my shoes resoled. دَأحُطّ نَعَل لقُندَرتي [daʔaħuṭṭ lqundarti]

resolution • **1.** قَرار [qara:r] قَرارات [qara:ra:t] *pl:* The resolution was adopted unanimously. القَرار تصَدَّق بالإجماع [ʔilqara:r tṣaddaq bilʔiǰma:ʕ]

resort • **1.** مَلجَأ [malǰaʔ] مَلاجِئ [mala:ǰiʔ] *pl:* As a last resort I can turn to him. كَآخِر مَلجَأ أقدَر أرجَع إلَه [kaʔa:xir malǰaʔ ʔagdar ʔarǰaʕ ʔilah]

health resort • **1.** مَصَحّ [maṣaħħ] مَصَحّات [maṣaħħa:t] *pl:* She's not going to a health resort this year. ما راح ترُوح لِلمَصَحّ هالسَّنَة [ma: ra:ħ tru:ħ lilmaṣaħħ hassana]

summer resort • **1.** مَصِيف [maṣi:f] مَصايِف [maṣa:yif] *pl:* Do you know a nice summer resort? تُعرُف فَدّ مَصِيف لَطِيف؟ [tuʕruf fadd maṣi:f laṭi:f?]

to resort • **1.** اِلتِجَأ [ʔiltiǰaʔ] اِلتِجاء [ʔiltiǰa:ʔ] *vn: sv* i. I don't want to resort to force. ما أرِيد ألتِجأ لِلقُوَّة [ma: ʔari:d ʔaltiǰiʔ lilquwwa]

resource • **1.** وَسِيلَة [wasi:la] وَسائِل [wasa:ʔil] *pl:* I have exhausted all resources. اِستَنفَذِت كُلّ الوَسائِل [ʔistanfaðit kull ʔilwasa:ʔil] • **2.** مَورِد [mawrid] مَوارِد [mawa:rid] *pl:* Oil is one of our important resources. النَّفُط أحَد مَوارِدنا المُهِمَّة [ʔinnafuṭ ʔaħad mawa:ridna ʔilmuhimma]

respect • **1.** اِحتِرام [ʔiħtira:m] اِحتِرامات [ʔiħtira:ma:t] *pl:* He has won the respect of everyone. اِكتِسَب اِحتِرام الجَّمِيع [ʔiktisab ʔiħtira:m ʔiǰǰami:ʕ] • **2.** جِهَة [ǰiha] جِهات [ǰiha:t] *pl:* ناحِيَة [na:ħiya] نَواحِي [nawa:ħi] *pl:* We were satisfied in every respect. كِنّا راضِين مِن كُلّ الجِّهات [činna ra:ði:n min kull ʔiǰǰiha:t]

to respect • **1.** اِحتِرَم [ʔiħtiram] اِحتِرام [ʔiħtira:m] *vn: sv* u. I respect your opinion. آني أحتِرُم رَأيَك [ʔa:ni ʔaħturum raʔyak] You must respect your elders. لازِم تِحتِرُم اللّي أكبَر مِنَّك [la:zim tiħturum ʔilli ʔakbar minnak]

respectable • **1.** مُحتَرَم [muħtaram] مُعتَبَر [muʕtabar] Respectable people don't go in a place like that. النّاس المُحتَرَمِين ما يطُبُّون هِيكِي مَكان [ʔinna:s ʔilmuħtarami:n ma: yṭubbu:n hi:či maka:n]

respected • **1.** مُحتَرَم [muħtaram] مُعتَبَر [muʕtabar] He is a respected business man in this city. هُوَّ فَدّ رَجُل أعمال مُحتَرَم بِهالوِلايَة [huwwa fadd raǰul ʔaʕma:l muħtaram bhalwila:ya]

responsibility • **1.** مَسؤُولِيَّة [masʔu:liyya] مَسؤُولِيّات [masʔu:liyya:t] *pl:* I'll take the responsibility. آني راح أتحَمَّل المَسؤُلِيَّة [ʔa:ni ra:ħ ʔatħammal ʔilmasʔuliyya]

responsible • **1.** مَسؤُول [masʔu:l] They held him responsible for the damage. اِعتِبرُوه مَسؤُول عَن الضَّرَر [ʔiʕtibru:h masʔu:l ʕann ʔiððarar]

rest • **1.** باقِي [ba:qi] بَقِيَّة [baqiyya] Eat some now and save the rest. أكُل قِسِم هَسَّة وَضُمّ الباقِي [ʔukul qisim hassa wðumm ʔilba:qi] You raise the money, and I'll do the rest. إنتَ دَبُّر الفلُوس وَآني عَلَيّا الباقِي [ʔinta dabbur ʔilflu:s wʔa:ni ʕalayya ʔilba:qi] Where are the rest of the boys? وين بَقِيَّة الوِلد؟ [wi:n baqiyyat ʔilwilid?] • **2.** راحَة [ra:ħa] I went to the mountains for a rest. رِحِت لِلجِّبال لطَلَب الرّاحَة [riħit liǰǰiba:l lṭalab ʔirra:ħa] • **3.** اِستِراحَة [ʔistira:ħa] اِستِراحات [ʔistira:ħa:t] *pl:* Let's take a short rest. خَلّي ناخُذ فَدّ اِستِراحَة قصَيِّرَة [xalli na:xuð fadd ʔistira:ħa gṣayyra]

at rest • **1.** راكِد [ra:kid] واقُف [wa:guf] Wait until the pointer is at rest. اِنتِظِر إلَى أن يكُون المُؤَشِّر راكِد [ʔintiðir ʔila ʔan yku:n ʔilmuʔaššir ra:kid]

* **This will put your mind at rest.** • **1.** هاي راح ترَيِّح فِكرَك [ha:y ra:ħ trayyiħ fikrak]

to take a rest • **1.** اِستَراح [ʔistara:ħ] اِستِراحَة [ʔistira:ħa] *vn: sv* i. اِرتاح [ʔirta:ħ] راحَة [ra:ħa] *vn: sv* a. Let's take a little rest. خَلّي نِرتاح شوَيَّة [xalli nirta:ħ šwayya]

to rest • **1.** اِرتاح [ʔirta:ħ] راحَة [ra:ħa] *vn: sv* a. اِستَراح [ʔistara:ħ] اِستِراحَة [ʔistira:ħa] *vn: sv* a. Rest awhile. اِرتاح شوَيَّة [ʔirta:ħ šwayya] • **2.** رَيَّح [rayyaħ] ترِييح [taryi:ħ] *vn: sv* a. أراح [ʔara:ħ] راحَة [ra:ħa] *vn: sv* i. Try to rest your eyes. حاوِل ترَيِّح عينَك [ħa:wil trayyiħ ʕaynak] • **3.** وُقَع [wugaʕ] وُقُوع [wugu:ʕ] *vn: sv* a. The whole responsibility rests on him. كُلّ المَسؤُلِيَّة توقَع عَليه [kull ʔilmasʔuliyya tu:gaʕ ʕali:h] • **4.** اِتَّكَى [ʔittačča:] تَتكِيَة، تتكّي [tatčiya, ttičči] *vn:* The ladder was resting against the wall. الدَّرَج كان مِتَّكَى عَالحايِط [ʔiddaraǰ ča:n mittačča: ʕalħa:yiṭ]

* **The decision rests with you.** • **1.** القَرار بِيدَك [ʔilqara:r bi:dak]

to rest assured • **1.** اِطمَأنّ [ʔiṭmaʔann] اِطمِئنان [ʔiṭmiʔna:n] *vn: sv* i. Rest assured that I'll do what

R

you want. إطمَئِنّ راح أسَوّي اللّي تريدَه [ʔiṭmaʔinn raːħ ʔasawwi ʔilli triːdah]

restaurant • **1.** مَطعَم [maṭʕam] مَطاعِم [maṭaːʕim] *pl:* Is there a good restaurant around here? أكُو مَطعَم زين بِهالمَنطِقَة؟ [ʔaku maṭʕam ziːn bhalmanṭiqa?]

restless • **1.** قَلِق [qaliq] قَلِقين [qaliqiːn] *pl:* I'm very restless today. آني كُلّش قَلِق اليُوم [ʔaːni kulliš qaliq ʔilyuːm]

to restore • **1.** اِستَعاد [ʔistaʕaːd] اِستِعادَة [ʔistiʕaːda] *vn: sv* i. The police restored order. الشُّرطَة اِستَعادوا النِّظام [ʔiššurṭa ʔistaʕaːdaw ʔinniðaːm] • **2.** رَجَّع [rajjaʕ] تَرجِيع [tarjiːʕ] *vn:* تَرَجَّع [trajjaʕ] *p:* All the stolen goods were restored. كُلّ المَسرُوقات تَرَجِّعَت [kull ʔilmasruːqaːt trajjiʕat] • **3.** جَدَّد [jaddad] تَجدِيد [tajdiːd] *vn:* تجَدَّد [tjaddad] *p:* The government is going to restore this old mosque. الحُكُومَة راح تجَدِّد هَالجّامِع العَتِيق [ʔilħukuːma raːħ djaddid hajjaːmiʕ ʔilʕatiːg]

to restrain • **1.** سَيطَر عَلى [sayṭar ʕala] سَيطَرَة [sayṭara] *vn: sv* i. She couldn't restrain her curiosity. ما قِدرَت تسَيطِر عَلَى فُضُولها [maː gidrat tsayṭir ʕala fuðuːlha] • **2.** ضُبَط [ðubaṭ] ضَبُط [ðabuṭ] *vn:* اِنضُبَط [ʔinðubaṭ] *p:* Can't you restrain your children? ما تِقدَر تُضبُط جهالَك؟ [maː tigdar tuðbuṭ jhaːlak?]

rest room • **1.** مِرحاض [mirħaːð] مَراحِيض [maraːħiːð] *pl:* أدَبخانَة [ʔadabxaːna] أدَبخانات [ʔadabxaːnaːt] *pl:* خَلوَة [xalwa] خَلاوِي [xalaːwi] *pl:* بَيت ماي [bayt maːy] بيُوت ماي [byuːt maːy] *pl:*

result • **1.** نَتِيجَة [natiːja] نَتائِج [nataːʔij] *pl:* The results were very satisfactory. النَّتائِج كانَت كُلّش مُرضِيَة [ʔinnataːʔij kaːnat kulliš murðiya]

retail • **1.** بَاع بِالمُفرَد [bilmufrad] He sells wholesale and retail. يبِيع بِالجُملَة وَبِالمُفرَد [yibiːʕ bijjumla wbilmufrad]

to retail • **1.** بَاع بِالمُفرَد [baːʕ] بَيع [biːʕ] *vn:* اِنباع [ʔinbaːʕ] *p:* This coat retails at about thirty dinars. هالقَبُّوط ينباع بالمُفرَد بحَوالِي ثلاثِين دِينار [halqappuːṭ yinbaːʕ bilmufrad bħawaːli tlaːθiːn dinaːr]

to retire • **1.** اِنسِحَب [ʔinsiħab] اِنسِحاب [ʔinsiħaːb] *vn: sv* i. He has retired from public life. اِنسِحَب مِن الحَياة العامَّة [ʔinsiħab min ʔilħayaːt ʔilʕaːmma] • **2.** تقاعَد [tqaːʕad] تَقاعُد [taqaːʕud] *vn: sv* a. He'll be able to retire next year. يكُون بإمكانَه يِتقاعَد السَّنَة الجّايَّة [ykuːn bʔimkaːnah yitqaːʕad ʔissana ʔijjaːyya]

retreat • **1.** تَراجُع [taraːjuʕ] تَراجُعات [taraːjuʕaːt] *pl:* تَقَهقُر [taqahqur] تَقَهقُرات [taqahquraːt] *pl:* اِنسِحاب [ʔinsiħaːb] اِنسِحابات [ʔinsiħaːbaːt] *pl:* The retreat was orderly. التَّراجُع كان مُنتَظَم [ʔittaraːjuʕ čaːn muntaðam]

to retreat • **1.** تراجَع [traːjaʕ] تَراجُع [taraːjuʕ] *vn: sv* a. تقَهقَر [tqahqar] تَقَهقُر [taqahqur] *vn: sv* a. اِنسِحَب [ʔinsiħab] اِنسِحاب [ʔinsiħaːb] *vn: sv* i. They were forced to retreat after two day's fighting. اِضطَرّوا يِتراجعُون بَعَد قِتال يومَين [ʔiðṭarraw yitraːjʕuːn baʕad qitaːl yawmayn]

return • **1.** وارِد [waːrid] وارِدات [waːridaːt] *pl:* How much of a return did you get on your investment? شقَدّ وارِد إجاك مِن تَشغِيل فلُوسَك؟ [šgadd waːrid ʔijaːk min tašɣiːl fluːsak?] • **2.** رَجعَة [rajʕa] رَجعات [rajʕaːt] *pl:* عَودَة [ʕawda] I found many things changed on my return. بِرَجعتِي شِفت هوايَة أشياء مِتبَدّلَة [brajiʕti šift hwaːya ʔašyaːʔ mitbaddla] • **3.** مُرَجَّع [murajjaʕ] I didn't use my return ticket. ما إستَعمَلت بِطاقتِي المُرَجَّع [maː ʔistaʕmalit biṭaːqati ʔilmurajjaʕ]

to return • **1.** رِجَع [rijaʕ] رُجُوع [rujuːʕ] *vn: sv* a. When did you return? شوَكِت رِجَعِت؟ [šwakit rijaʕit?] I've returned to my original idea. رجَعِت إلَى رَأيي العَتِيق [rjaʕit ʔila raʔyi ʔilʕatiːg] • **2.** رَجَّع [rajjaʕ] تَرجِيع [tarjiːʕ] *vn:* تَرَجَّع [trajjaʕ] *p:* She didn't return my visit. ما رَجّعَتلِي الزِّيارَة [maː rajjʕatli ʔizziyaːra] • **3.** عاد [ʕaːd] إعادَة [ʔiʕaːda] *vn: sv* i. رَجَّع [rajjaʕ] تَرجِيع [tarjiːʕ] *vn: sv* i. Don't forget to return the book. لا تِنسَى تعِيد الكِتاب [laː tinsaː tʕiːd ʔilkitaːb]

returns • **1.** نَتِيجَة [natiːja] نَتائِج [nataːʔij] *pl:* Have the election returns come in yet? نَتائِج الانتِخابات وُصلَت لَو بَعَد؟ [nataːʔij ʔilintixaːbaːt wuṣlat law baʕad?]

* **Many happy returns!** • **1.** الله يعِيدَه عَلَيك بِالسُّرُور [ʔallah yʕiːdah ʕaliːk bissuruːr]

revenge • **1.** ثار [θaːr] اِنتِقام [ʔintiqaːm]

to revenge • **1.** ثَأَر [θiʔar] ثار [θaːr] *vn: sv* a. اِنتِقَم [ʔintiqam] اِنتِقام [ʔintiqaːm] *vn: sv* i. He revenged the death of his father. ثِأَر قَتِل أَبُوه [θiʔr qatil ʔabuːh] He revenged the death of his father. أخَذ ثار أَبُوه [ʔaxað θaːr ʔabuːh]

reverse • **1.** قُفَا [gufaː] ثانِي [θaːni] Don't forget to fill in the reverse side of the card. لا تِنسَى تِترُس قُفَا الكارت [laː tinsaː titrus gufaː ʔilkaːrt] Don't forget to fill in the reverse side of the card. لا تِنسَى تِترُس الوُجه الثّانِي مِن الكارت [laː tinsaː titrus ʔilwujħ ʔiθθaːni min ʔilkaːrt] • **2.** بَقّ [bagg] Put the transmission in reverse. خَلِّي القِير عالبَقّ [xalli ʔilgiːr ʕalbagg]

to reverse • **1.** رِجَع لِلوَرَا [rijaʕ lilwara] رُجُوع لِلوَرَا [rujuːʕ lilwara] *vn: sv* a. Tell him to reverse. قُلَّه يرجَع لوَرا [gullah yirjaʕ lwara] • **2.** عِكَس [ʕikas] عَكِس [ʕakis] *vn:* اِنعِكَس [ʔinʕikas] *p:* In order to put it together, reverse the procedure. حَتَّى تَركّبها، إعكِس العَمَلِيَّة [ħatta trakkibha, ʔiʕkis ʔilʕamaliyya]

R

review • **1.** مُراجَعَة [mura:ǰaʕa] مُراجَعات [mura:ǰaʕa:t] *pl:* He publishes book reviews in this magazine. يِنشُر مُراجَعات بِالكُتُب بهالمَجَلَّة [yinšur mura:ǰaʕa:t bilkutub bhalmaǰalla]

to review • **1.** نِقَد [niqad] نَقِد [naqid] *vn:* اِنِّقَد [ʔinniqad] *p:* Who's going to review the play? مِنُو راح يِنقُد التَّمثِيلِيَّة؟ [minu ra:ħ yinqud ʔittamθi:liyya?]

review lesson • **1.** دَرِس مُراجَعَة [daris mura:ǰaʕa] درُوس مُراجَعَة [dru:s mura:ǰaʕa] *pl:*

to revolt • **1.** ثار [θa:r] ثَورَة [θawra] *vn: sv* u. Why did they revolt? لَيش ثارَوا؟ [li:š θa:raw?]

revolution • **1.** ثَورَة [θawra] ثَورات [θawra:t] *pl:* He was the hero of the revolution and was later killed. كان بَطَل الثَّورَة وَبَعدين اِنكِتَل [ča:n baṭal ʔiθθawra wbaʕdayn ʔinkital] • **2.** فَرَّة [farra] فَرّات [farra:t] *pl:* How many revolutions does this motor make per minute? كَم فَرَّة تِفتَرّ هَالمَكِينَة بِالدَّقِيقَة؟ [čam farra tiftarr halmaki:na biddaqi:qa?]

to revolve • **1.** دار [da:r] دَوَران [dawara:n] *vn: sv* u. The moon revolves around the earth. القُمَر يدُور حَول الأَرض [ʔilgumar ydu:r ħawl ʔilʔarḍ] • **2.** اِفتَرّ [ʔiftarr] *sv* a. The wheel revolves on its axle. الچَرِخ يِفتَرّ حَوِل مَحوَرَه [ʔilčarix yiftarr ħawil maħwarah]

reward • **1.** مُكافَأَة [muka:faʔa] مُكافَآت [muka:faʔa:t] *pl:* He was promised a substantial reward. اِنوِعَد بِجائِزَة ثَمِينَة [ʔinwiʕad bǰa:ʔiza θami:na]

to reward • **1.** جازَى [ǰa:za:] مُجازات [muǰa:za:t] *vn:* تجازَى [tǰa:za:] *p:* كافَأ [ka:faʔ] مُكافَأَة [muka:faʔa] *vn:* تكافَأ [tka:faʔ] *p:* He was well rewarded for his diligence. زين تكافَأ عَلَى اِجتِهادَه [zi:n tka:faʔ ʕala ʔiǰtiha:dah]

rhyme • **1.** قافِيَة [qa:fiya] قَوافِي [qawa:fi] *pl:* This word doesn't fit the rhyme. هَالكِلمَة ما تِجِي عالقافِيَة [halčilma ma: tiǰi ʕalqa:fiya]

rhymed prose • **1.** سَجِع [saǰiʕ]

rib • **1.** ضِلِع [ðiliʕ] ضلُوع، أَضلاع [ðlu:ʕ, ʔaðla:ʕ] *pl:* He's so thin you can see his ribs. هُوَّ ضِعِيف إِلَى دَرَجَة تشُوف ضلُوعَه [huwwa ðiʕi:f ʔila daraǰa tšu:f ðlu:ʕah] Two ribs of my boat were broken. اِنكِسرَت ضِلعَين مِن ضلُوع البَلَم مالِي [ʔinkisrat ðilʕayn min ðlu:ʕ ʔilbalam ma:li] • **2.** سِيم [si:m] سيامَة [sya:ma] *pl:* The wind broke one of the ribs of my umbrella. الهَوا كِسَر سِيم مِن سيام شَمسِيتِي [ʔilhawa kisar si:m min sya:m šamsi:ti]

ribbon • **1.** قُردِيلَة [qurdi:la] قُردِيلات [qurdi:la:t] *pl:* She was wearing a blue ribbon in her hair. كانَت لابسَة قِردَيلَة زَرقَة بشَعَرها [ča:nat la:bsah qirdi:la zarga bšaʕarha] • **2.** شَرِيط [šari:ṭ] أَشرِطَة، شَرائِط [ʔašriṭa, šara:yiṭ] *pl:* I need a new ribbon for my typewriter. أَحتاج شَرِيط جِدِيد لِلآلَة الطّابِعَة مالتِي [ʔaħta:ǰ šari:ṭ ǰidi:d liʔa:lat ʔiṭṭa:biʕa ma:lti]

rice • **1.** تِمَّن [timman] I'd like a pound of rice. أَرِيد باوَن تِمَّن [ʔari:d pa:wan timman] • **2.** شِلِب [šilib] تِمَّن [timman] This man is one of the biggest rice merchants in Iraq. هَذا مِن أَكبَر تُجّار الشِّلِب بِالعِراق [ha:ða min ʔakbar tuǰǰa:r ʔiššilib bilʕira:q]

rich • **1.** زَنكِين [zangi:n] زَناكِين [zana:gi:n] *pl:* غَنِي [ɣani] أَغنِياء [ʔaɣniya:ʔ] *pl:* He is a rich man. هَذا واحِد زَنكِين [ha:ða wa:ħid zangi:n] • **2.** ثَرِي [θari] أَثرِياء [ʔaθriya:ʔ] *pl:* He comes from a rich family. هُوَّ مِن عائِلَة ثَرِيَّة [huwwa min ʕa:ʔila θariyya] • **3.** دَسِم [dasim] The food is too rich. الأَكِل كُلِّش دَسِم [ʔilʔakil kulliš dasim] • **4.** خَصِب [xaṣib] It's rich soil. هِيَّ تُربَة خَصبَة [hiyya turba xaṣba]

rickets • **1.** كُساح [kusa:ħ]

riddle • **1.** لُغُز [luɣuz] أَلغاز [ʔalɣa:z] *pl:* حَزُّورَة [ħazzu:ra] حَزُّورات [ħazzu:ra:t] *pl:*

ride • **1.** رَكبَة [rakba] رَكبات [rakba:t] *pl:* It's only a short ride by bus. هِيَّ مُو أَزيَد مِن رُكبَت باص قَصِيرَة [hiyya mu: ʔazyad min rukbat pa:ṣ qaṣi:ra] • **2.** فَرَّة [farra] فَرّات [farra:t] *pl:* Let's take a ride in the car. خَلِّي نسَوِّي إِلنا فَدّ فَرَّة بَالسَّيّارَة [xalli nsawwi: ʔilna fadd farra bissayya:ra] Let's take a ride in the car. خَلِّي نِطلَع بَالسَّيّارَة [xalli niṭlaʕ bissayya:ra]

* **He gave me a ride all the way.** • **1.** وَصَّلنِي بسَيّارتَه كُلّ الطَّرِيق [waṣṣalni bsayya:rtah kull ʔiṭṭari:q]

to ride • **1.** رِكَب [rikab] رُكُوب [ruku:b] *vn:* اِنرِكَب [ʔinrikab] *p:* Do you know how to ride a motorcycle? تُعرُف تِركَب ماطورسِكِل؟ [tuʕruf tirkab maṭu:rsikil?] We rode in a beautiful car. رِكَبنا بسَيّارَة حِلوَة [rikabna bsayya:ra ħilwa] • **2.** مِشَى [miša:] مَشِي [mašy] *vn: sv* i. This car rides smoothly. هَالسَّيّارَة تِمشِي مِثل الدِّهِن [hassayya:ra timši miθl ʔiddihin]

* **Stop riding me!** • **1.** بَسّ عادِ تِلِحّ [bass ʕa:d tliħħ] / ما تفُكّ ياخَة عاد [ma: tfukk ya:xa ʕa:d]

ridiculous • **1.** سَخِيف [saxi:f] سَخافَة [saxa:fa] سَخافات [saxa:fa:t] *pl:* Don't be ridiculous! لا تصِير سَخِيف [la: tṣi:r saxi:f] That's ridiculous. هاي سَخافَة [ha:y saxa:fa] That's ridiculous. هَذا شِي سَخِيف [ha:ða ši saxi:f]

rid of • **1.** خَلصان مِن [xalṣa:n min] I'm glad I'm rid of it. آنِي فَرحان خَلصان مِنَّه [ʔa:ni farħa:n xalṣa:n minnah]

R

to get rid of • **1.** خِلَص مِن [xilaṣ] خَلاص [xala:ṣ] *vn: sv* a. تخَلَّص [txallaṣ] تَخَلُّص [taxalluṣ] *vn: sv* a. I got rid of her at last. أَخِيراً خلَصِت مِنها [ʔaxi:ran xlaṣit minha]

rifle • **1.** بُندُقِيَّة [bunduqiyya] بَنادِق [bana:diq] *pl:* تُفقَة [tufga] تُفَق، تُفقات [tufag, tufga:t] *pl:*

right • **1.** حَقّ [ħaqq, ħagg] I insist on my rights. آنِي أَصِرّ عَلَى حُقُوقِي [ʔa:ni ʔaṣirr ʕala ħuqu:qi] You have no right to say that. ما إِلَك حَقّ تِقُول هاي [ma: ʔilak ħaqq tigu:l ha:y] He's right. الحَقّ وِيّاه [ʔilħaqq wiyya:h] • **2.** يَمِين [yami:n] I've lost the glove for my right hand. ضَيَّعِت الكَفّ مال إِيدي اليِمنَى [ðayyaʕit ʔiččaff ma:l ʔi:di ʔilyimna] • **3.** قائِم [qa:ʔim] A right angle has ninety degrees. الزّاوِيَة القائِمَة بِيها تِسعِين دَرَجَة [ʔizza:wiya ʔilqa:ʔima bi:ha tisʕi:n daraǰa] • **4.** مُناسِب [muna:sib] He came just at the right time. إِجا بالوَقِت المُناسِب تَماماً [ʔiǰa bilwakt ʔilmuna:sib tama:man] • **5.** صَحِيح [ṣaħi:ħ] Are we going the right way? إِحنا دَنِمشِي عالطَّرِيق الصَّحِيح؟ [ʔiħna danimši ʕaṭṭari:q ʔiṣṣaħi:ħ?] • **6.** رَأساً [raʔsan] فَدّ راس [fadd ra:s] عَدِل [ʕadil] I'm coming right home from the office. راح أَجِي مِن الشُّغُل لِلبَيت رَأساً [ra:ħ ʔaǰi min ʔiššuɣul lilbayt raʔsan] • **7.** تَماماً [tama:man] The house is right next to the church. البَيت يَمّ الكَنِيسَة تَماماً [ʔilbayt yamm ʔilkani:sa tama:man] • **8.** زين [zi:n, zayn] We'll leave tomorow if the weather is right. نِطلَع باكِر إِذا الجَوّ زين [niṭlaʕ ba:čir ʔiða ʔiǰǰaww zi:n]

* **You can't be in your right mind.** • **1.** إِنتَ لازِم مُو بكامِل عَقلَك [ʔinta la:zim mu: bka:mil ʕaqlak]

* **It serves him right!** • **1.** يِستاهِل [yista:hil] / يِستَحِقّ [yistaħiqq]

* **Go right ahead.** • **1.** فُوت بفالَك [fu:t bfa:lak] توَكَّل عَلَى الله [twakkal ʕala ʔallah]

* **He's right here next to me.** • **1.** هِيّاتَه هنا بصَفّي [hiyya:tah hna bṣaffi]

right away • **1.** حالاً [ħa:lan] رَأساً [raʔsan] فَوراً [fawran] Let's go right away or we'll be late. خَلِّي نرُوح حالاً وَإِلّا نِتأَخَّر [xalli nru:ħ ħa:lan waʔilla: nitʔaxxar] Tell him to come to see me right away. قُلَّه يِجِي يواجِهنِي فَوراً [gullah yiǰi ywa:ǰihni fawran]

right now • **1.** هَسَّة [hassa] I'm busy right now. آنِي مَشغُول هَسَّة [ʔa:ni mašɣu:l hassa]

right off • **1.** فَوراً [fawran] I can't answer that right off. ما أَقدَر أَجاوُب عَلَى هاي فَوراً [ma: ʔagdar ʔaǰa:wub ʕala ha:y fawran]

rightful • **1.** شَرعِي [šarʕi] He is the rightful owner of the house. هُوَّ المالِك الشَّرعِي لِلبَيت [huwwa ʔilma:lik ʔiššarʕi lilbayt]

right-hand • **1.** يَمِين [yami:n] يِمنَى [yimna] Feminine. The school is on the right-hand side of the street. المَدرَسَة عالجِّهَة اليِمنَى مِن الشّارِع [ʔilmadrasa ʕaǰǰiha ʔilyimna: min ʔišša:riʕ]

* **He's the boss's right-hand man.** • **1.** هُوَّ الإِيد اليِمنَى لِلرَّئِيس [huwwa ʔilʔi:d ʔilyimna lirraʔi:s]

rim • **1.** إطار [ʔiṭa:r] إطارات [ʔiṭa:ra:t] *pl:* The rim of my glasses is broken. إطار مَناظرِي مَكسُور [ʔiṭa:r mana:ðri maksu:r]

ring • **1.** مِحبَس [miħbas] محابِس [mħa:bis] *pl:* خاتَم [xa:tam] خَواتِم [xawa:tim] *pl:* She wears a ring on her right hand. تِلبَس مِحبَس بِيدها اليِمنَى [tilbas miħbas bi:dha ʔilyimna] • **2.** حَلقَة [ħalqa, ħalaqa] حَلَقات [ħalaqa:t] *pl:* Tie the rope to the iron ring. شِدّ الحَبِل بِحَلقَة الحَدِيد [šidd ʔilħabil bħalqat ʔilħadi:d] • **3.** دَقَّة [dagga] دَقّات [dagga:t] *pl:* رَنَّة [ranna] That bell has a peculiar ring. هالجَّرَس إِلَه رَنَّة غَرِيبَة [haǰǰaras ʔilah ranna ɣari:ba] • **4.** رِنق [ring] رِنقات [ringa:t] *pl:* I had the mechanic put in a new set of rings. خَلَّيت الفِيتَرجِي يحُطِّلِي طَخُم رِنقات جِدِيدَة [xalli:t ʔilfi:tarči yħuṭṭli ṭaxum ringa:t ǰidi:da]

to give a ring • **1.** دَقّ تَلَفُون [dagg talifu:n] *sv* u. Give me a ring tomorrow. دُقلِي تِلِفُون باكِر [duggli tilifu:n ba:čir]

to ring • **1.** رَنّ [rann] رَنّ [rann] *vn: sv* i. The noise is still ringing in my ears. اللَّغوَة بَعَدها دَترِنّ بإِذنِي [ʔillaɣwa baʕadha datrinn bʔiðni] • **2.** دَقّ [dagg] دَقّ [dagg] *vn: sv* u. The phone rang. دَقّ التِّلِفُون [dagg ʔittilifu:n] Did you ring the bell? دَقَّيت الجَّرَس؟ [daggayt ʔiǰǰaras?]

* **Somehow it doesn't ring true.** • **1.** أَشُو ما تبَيِّن صُدُق [ʔašu ma: tbayyin ṣudug]

rinse • **1.** خَضَّة [xaðða] خَضّات [xaðða:t] *pl:* Two rinses will be enough. خَضّتَين تكَفِّي [xaððtayn tkaffi]

to rinse • **1.** خَضّ [xaðð] خَضّ [xaðð] *vn:* اِنخَضّ [ʔinxaðð] *p:* I rinse my wash twice. آنِي أَخُضّ الغَسِيل مالِي مَرّتَين [ʔa:ni ʔaxuðð ʔilɣasi:l ma:li marrtayn] Rinse the glasses under the faucet. خُضّ الكلاصات جَوَّة البُورِي [xuðð ʔilgla:ṣa:t ǰawwa ʔilbu:ri] • **2.** مَضمَض [maðmað] مَضمَضَة [maðmaða] *vn:* تمَضمَض [tmaðmað] *p:* Rinse out your mouth with water and a little salt. مَضمُض حَلقَك بماي وَشوَيَّة مِلِح [maðmuð ħalgak bma:y wšwayya miliħ]

riot • **1.** هَياج [haya:ǰ] عَربَدَة [ʕarbada] شَغَب [šaɣab] Two people were killed in the riot. شَخصَين اِنقِتلَوا أَثناء الهَياج [šaxṣayn ʔinkitlaw ʔaθna:ʔ ʔilhaya:ǰ] The riot was caused by several drunkards. العَربَدَة سَبَبها كَم سَكران [ʔilʕarbada sababha čam sakra:n]

* **He's a riot.** • **1.** هَذا فَدّ مصَنِّفجِي [ha:ða fadd mṣannifči]

to riot • **1.** شاغَب [ša:ɣab] مُشاغَبَة [muša:ɣaba] *vn: sv* i. They ignored the presence of the police and kept on rioting all night. أَهمِلَوا وُجُود الشُّرطَة وَظَلّوا يشاغبُون طُول اللَّيل [ʔahmilaw wuǰu:d ʔiššurṭa wðallaw yša:ɣbu:n ṭu:l ʔillayl]

R

rip • **1.** شَقّ [šagg] شقُوق [šgu:g] *pl:* مَزِق [mazig] مزُوق [mzu:g] *pl:* Do you know you have a rip in your jacket? تِدري أَكُو مَزِق بسِترتَك؟ [tidri ʔaku mazig bsitirtak?] • **2.** فتِق [fatig] فتُوق [ftu:g] *pl:* There is a rip in the seam of your shirt under the arm. أَكُو فتِق بثُوبَك جَوَّة أبطَك [ʔaku fatig bθu:bak ǰawwa ʔubṭak]

to rip • **1.** مِزَق [mizaq] مَزِق [mazig] *vn:* اِنمزَق [ʔinmizag] *p:* شَقّ [šagg] شَقّ [šagg] *vn:* اِنشَقّ [ʔinšagg] *p:* I ripped my pants climbing the fence. شَقّيت بَنطُروني أَثناء ما كِنِت أَتشَلبَه عَالسِّياج [šaggi:t panṭuru:ni ʔaθna:ʔ ma: činit ʔatšalbah ʕassiya:ǰ] • **2.** فِتَق [fitag] فتِق [fatig] *vn:* اِنفتَق [ʔinfitag] *p:* I have to rip out the seams. لازِم أفتِق الكواكَة [la:zim ʔaftig ʔilkwa:ka]

ripe • **1.** لاحِق [la:ħig] ناضِج [na:ðiǰ] The apples aren't ripe yet. التِّفّاح بَعدَه ما لاحِق [ʔittiffa:ħ baʕdah ma: la:ħig] • **2.** متهَيِّأ [mithayyiʔ] The situation is ripe for trouble. الوَضع مِتهَيِّأ لِلمَشاكِل [ʔilwaðiʕ mithayyiʔ lilmaša:kil]

* **He lived to a ripe old age.** • **1.** عَمَّر هوايَة [ʕammar hwa:ya]

to rise • **1.** طِلَع [ṭilaʕ] طُلُوع [ṭulu:ʕ] *vn:* *sv* i. أَشرَق [ʔašraq] شُرُوق [šuru:q] *vn:* *sv* i. The sun rises early. الشَّمِس تِطلَع مِن وَقِت [ʔiššamis tiṭlaʕ min wakit] • **2.** صِعَد [ṣiʕad] صُعُود [ṣuʕu:d] *vn:* *sv* a. Over there the road rises again. هناك الطَّرِيق يِصعَد مَرَّة لُخ [hna:k ʔiṭṭari:q yiṣʕad marra lux] • **3.** اِرتِفَع [ʔirtifaʕ] اِرتِفاع [ʔirtifa:ʕ] *vn:* *sv* i. صِعَد [ṣiʕad] صُعُود [ṣuʕu:d] *vn:* *sv* i. The river is rising rapidly. النَّهَر دَيِرتِفِع بِالعَجَل [ʔinnahar dayirtifiʕ bilʕaǰal] Prices are still rising. الأسعار بَعدها دَتِرتِفِع [ʔilʔasʕa:r baʕadha datirtifiʕ] • **4.** قام [ga:m] قِيام [qiya:m] *vn:* *sv* u. All rose from their seats. كُلّهُم قامَوا مِن مَكاناتهُم [kullhum ga:maw min maka:na:thum] • **5.** اِنُّفَخ [ʔinnufax] *sv* u. The cake is rising. الكَيكَة دَتِنُّفُخ [ʔilkayka datinnufux]

* **He rose from the ranks.** • **1.** هَذا مَسلَكِي [ha:ða maslaki]

risk • **1.** مُخاطَرَة [muxa:ṭara] مُخاطَرات [muxa:ṭara:t] *pl:* مُجازَفَة [muǰa:zafa] مُجازَفات [muǰa:zafa:t] *pl:* I can't take such a risk. ما أَقدَر أَسَوِّي هِيكِي مُجازَفَة [ma: ʔagdar ʔasawwi hi:či muǰa:zafa]

to risk • **1.** خاطَر ب [xa:ṭar b-] مُخاطَرَة [muxa:ṭara] *vn:* *sv* i. جازَف ب [ǰa:zaf b-] مُجازَفَة [muǰa:zafa] *vn:* *sv* i. He risked his life to save her. خاطَر بِحَياتَه حَتَّى يُنقُذها [xa:ṭar bħaya:tah ħatta yunguðha] He's risked his entire fortune. جازَف بِكُلّ ثَروتَه [ǰa:zaf bkull θarwtah]

* **He risked his life.** • **1.** حَطّ حَياتَه عَلَى كَفَّه [ħaṭṭ ħaya:tah ʕala čaffah]

rival • **1.** مُنافِس [muna:fis] مُنافِسِين [muna:fisi:n] *pl:* مُزاحِم [muza:ħim] مُزاحِمِين [muza:ħimi:n] *pl:* They were rivals for many years. كانَوا مُنافسِين لِبَعَضهُم لِمُدَّة سنِين هوايَة [ča:naw muna:fsi:n libaʕaðhum lmuddat sni:n hwa:ya] He works for a rival company. يِشتُغُل بِفَدّ شَرِكَة مُزاحِمَة [yištuɣul bfadd šarika muza:ħima]

river • **1.** نَهَر [nahar] أَنهار [ʔanha:r] *pl:* شَطّ [šaṭṭ] شطُوط [šṭu:ṭ] *pl:* What's the name of this river? هَالنَّهَر شِسمَه؟ [hannahar šismah?]

road • **1.** طَرِيق [ṭari:q] طُرُق [ṭuruq] *pl:* دَرُب [darub] درُوب [dru:b] *pl:* Where does this road go to? هَالطَّرِيق لِوَين يوَصِّل؟ [haṭṭari:q lwi:n ywaṣṣil?] He's on the road to recovery. هُوَّ بطَرِيقَه لِلشِفاء [huwwa bṭari:qah liššifa:ʔ]

to go on the road • **1.** طِلَع يِفتَرّ [ṭilaʕ yiftarr] *sv* a. Our salesman is going on the road next week. الدَّوّار مالنَا راح يِطلَع يِفتَرّ إِسبُوع الجّاي [ʔiddawwa:r ma:lna ra:ħ yiṭlaʕ yiftarr ʔisbu:ʕ ʔiǰǰa:y] • **2.** سَوَّى [sawwa:] *sv* i. قام [qa:m] *sv* u. Next month our team is going on the road for two weeks. الشَّهر الجّاي فَرِيقنا راح يسَوِّي جَولَة لِمُدَّة إِسبُوعَين [ʔiššahr ʔiǰǰa:y fari:qna ra:ħ ysawwi ǰawla limuddat ʔisbu:ʕayn]

roar • **1.** هَدِير [hadi:r] We can hear the roar of the waterfall from here. نِقدَر نِسمَع هَدِير الشَّلّال مِن هنَا [nigdar nismaʕ hadi:r ʔiššalla:l min hna] • **2.** زَئِير [zaʔi:r] It sounded like the roar of a lion. كان عَبالَك زَئِير مال أَسَد [ča:n ʕaba:lak zaʔi:r ma:l ʔasad]

to roar • **1.** زِئَر [ziʔar] زَئِير [zaʔi:r] *vn:* *sv* a. When he's angry he roars like a lion. عِندَما يِغضَب يِزأر مِثل الأسَد [ʕindama yiɣðab yizʔar miθl ʔilʔasad] • **2.** قَهقَه [qahqah] قَهقَهَة [qahqaha] *vn:* *sv* i. They roared with laughter. قَهقِهَوا مِن الضِّحِك [qahqihaw min ʔiððaħik]

to roast • **1.** شُوَى [šuwa:] شَوِي [šawy] *vn:* اِنشُوَى [ʔinšuwa:] *p:* You didn't roast the meat long enough. ما شُوَيت اللَّحَم مُدَّة كافيَة [ma: šuwi:t ʔillaħam mudda ka:fya] There's leg of lamb roasted in the oven for dinner. أَكُو رِجِل قُوزِي مَشوِي لِلعَشا [ʔaku riǰil qu:zi mašwi lilʕaša]

to rob • **1.** باق [ba:g] بَوق [bu:g] *vn:* اِنباق [ʔinba:g] *p:* I've been robbed. اِنباقِيت [ʔinba:gi:t] • **2.** سَلَّب [sallab] تَسلِيب [tasli:b] *vn:* تسَلَّب [tsallab] *p:* نِهَب [nihab] نَهِب [nahib] *vn:* اِنّهَب [ʔinnihab] *p:* They'll rob you of your last cent. راح يسَلّبُون آخِر فِلِس عِندَك [ra:ħ ysallibu:n ʔa:xir filis ʕindak]

robbery • **1.** بُوقَة [bu:ga] بَوقات [bawga:t] *pl:* سَرِقَة [sariqa] سَرِقات [sariqa:t] *pl:* When was the robbery committed? شوَقِت صارَت البَوقَة؟ [šwakit ṣa:rat ʔilbu:ga?] • **2.** تَسلِيب [tasli:b] نَهِب [nahib] بَوق [bawg] That's highway robbery! هَذا تَسلِيب [ha:ða tasli:b]

robe • **1.** رُوب، رَوابَة [ru:b, rwa:ba] رُوبات [ru:ba:t] *pl:* Please get me my robe and my slippers.

R

 i, interjection; p, passive; pl, plural; sv, stem vowel; vn, verbal noun

أرجوك جيبلي الرُوب وَالنَّعَل مالِي [ʔarǰuːk ǰiːbli ʔirruːb winnaʕal maːli] • **2.** زبُون [zibuːn] زبُونات [zbuːnaːt] *pl:* عَبايَة [ʕabaːya] عِبِي [ʕibi] عَبايات [ʕabaːyaːt] *pl:* The chiefs who come from their tribes wear inner and outer robes. الشِّيُوخ اللّي يِجُون مِن عَشايِّرهُم يِلبِسُون زبُونات وَعِبِي [ʔiššiyuːx ʔilli yiǰuːn min ʕašaːyirhum ylibsuːn zbuːnaːt wʕibi]

rock • **1.** صَخرَة [ṣaxra] صَخرات [ṣaxraːt] *pl:* They had to blast the rock. اِضطَرَّوا ينِسفُون الصَّخرَة [ʔiðṭarraw ynisfuːn ʔiṣṣaxra] • **2.** حجارَة [ħǰaːra] حجارات، حِجار [ħǰaːraːt, ħijaːr] *pl:* He was throwing rocks. كان دَيشَمُّر حجار [čaːn dayšammur ħǰaːr]

to rock • **1.** اِهتَزّ [ʔihtazz] اِهتِزاز [ʔihtizaːz] *vn: sv* a. The floor rocked under our feet. القاع اِهتَزَّت جَوَّة رِجلَينا [ʔilgaːʕ ʔihtazzat ǰawwa rijlayna] The boat's rocking. البَلَم دَيِهتَزّ [ʔilbalam dayihtazz] • **2.** هَزّ [hazz] هَزّ [hazz] *vn:* اِنهَزّ [ʔinhazz] *p:* She rocked the cradle until the baby fell asleep. هَزَّت الكارُوك إلَى أن نام الجّاهِل [hazzat ʔilkaːruːk ʔila ʔan naːm ʔiǰǰaːhil] • **3.** خَضّ [xaðð] خَضّ [xaðð] *vn:* اِنخَضّ [ʔinxaðð] *p:* She showed us how to rock the churn to make butter. شَوّفَتنا شلُون نخُضّ الشَّكوَة حَتَّى نسَوّي زِبِد [šawwfatna šluːn nxuðð ʔiššičwaː ħatta nsawwi zibid]

rocky • **1.** صَخرِي [ṣaxri] This soil is too rocky for farming. هَالأَرض كُلِّش صَخرِيَّة، ما تِصلَح لِلزِّراعَة [halʔarð kulliš ṣaxriyya, maː tiṣlaħ lizziraːʕa]

rod • **1.** شِيش [šiːš] شياش [šyaːš] *pl:* The parts are connected by an iron rod. الوُصَل مِتِّصلَة وِحدَة بِاللَّخ بشِيش [ʔilwuṣal mittiṣla wiħda billux bšiːš]

lightning rod • **1.** مانِعَة الصَواعِق [maːniʕat ʔiṣṣawaːʕiq] مانِعات الصَواعِق [maːniʕaːt ʔiṣṣawaːʕiq] *pl:* Most large buildings have lightning rods. أكثَر العِمارات بِيها مانِعات صَواعِق [ʔakθar ʔilʕimaːraːt biːha maːniʕaːt ṣawaːʕiq]

role • **1.** دَور [dawr, duːr] أدوار [ʔadwaːr] *pl:* He played an important role. لِعَب دَور مُهِمّ [liʕab dawr muhimm]

roll • **1.** لَفَّة [laffa] لَفّات [laffaːt] *pl:* He used up a whole roll of wrapping paper. اِستَعمَل لَفَّة كامِلَة مِن وَرَق التَّغلِيف [ʔistaʕmal laffa kaːmla min waraq ʔittaɣliːf] • **2.** صَمُّونَة [ṣammuːna] صَمُّونات [ṣammuːnaːt] *pl:* صَمُّون [ṣammuːn] *Collective:* Shall I get bread or rolls? شَآخُذ خُبُز لَو صَمُّون؟ [šʔaːxuð xubuz law ṣammuːn?]

roll of film • **1.** فِلِم [filim] أفلام [ʔaflaːm] *pl:* I'd like two rolls of 120 film. أرِيد فِلمَين حَجَم مِيَّة وَعِشرِين [ʔariːd filmayn ħaǰam miyya wʕišriːn]

to roll • **1.** دَعبَل [daʕbal] تدِعبِل [tdiʕbil] *vn:* تدَعبَل [tdaʕbal] *p:* دَحرَج [daħraǰ] دَحرَجَة، تدِحرِج [daħraǰa, tdiħriǰ] *vn:* تدَحرَج [tdaħraǰ] *p:* Don't roll the barrel. لا تدَعبِل البَرمِيل [laː ddaʕbil ʔilbarmiːl] • **2.** تدَعبَل [ddaʕbal] تَدَعبُل [tadaʕbul] *vn: sv* a. تدَحرَج [ddaħraǰ] تَدَحرُج [tadaħruǰ] *vn: sv* a. The ball rolled under the table. الطُّوبَة تدَعبِلَت جَوَّة المِيز [ʔiṭṭuːba ddaʕbilat ǰawwa ʔilmiːz] • **3.** تمايَل [tmaːyal] *sv* a. The ship was rolling heavily. الباخِرَة كانَت دَتِتمايَل بشِدَّة [ʔilbaːxira čaːnat datitmaːyal bšidda] • **4.** دَكّ [dačč] اِندَكّ [ʔindačč] *p:* The tennis court must be rolled. ساحَة التَّنِس لازِم تِندَكّ بِالرَّولَة [saːħat ʔittanis laːzim tindačč birrawla] The tennis court must be rolled. ساحَة التَّنِس يراد إلها دَوس بِالرَّولَة [saːħat ʔittanis yiraːd ʔilha duːs birrawla] • **5.** لَفّ [laff] لَفّ [laff] *vn:* اِنلَفّ [ʔinlaff] *p:* I roll my own cigarettes. آنِي ألِفّ جِكايِري [ʔaːni ʔaliff ǰigaːyri]

to roll around • **1.** تمَرغَل [tmarɣal] تمُرغُل [tmurɣul] *vn: sv* a. The buffalo rolled around in the mud. الجّامُوسَة تمَرغِلَت بِالطِّين [ʔiǰǰaːmuːsa tmarɣilat bittiːn] • **2.** تدَعبَل [ddaʕbal] تدِعبِل [tdiʕbil] *vn: sv* a. The marbles rolled around in the box. الدُّعبُل تدَعبَل بِالصَّندُوق [ʔidduʕbul ddaʕbal bissanduːg]

to roll out • **1.** فُرَش [furaš] فَرِش [fariš] *vn:* اِنفُرَش [ʔinfuraš] *p:* The servant rolled out the mattress on the bedstead. الخادِم فُرَش الدُّوشَك عالسَّرِير [ʔilxaːdim furaš ʔidduːšag ʕassariːr] • **2.** فَكّ [fakk] فَكّ [fakk] *vn:* اِنفَكّ [ʔinfakk] *p:* Roll the dough out thin. فُكّي العَجِين خَفِيف [fukki ʔilʕaǰiːn xafiːf]

to roll over • **1.** قِلَب [gilab] قَلُب [galub] *vn:* اِنقِلَب [ʔingilab] *p:* The nurse rolled the patient over. المُمَرِّضَة قُلبَت المَرِيض [ʔilmumarriða gulbat ʔilmariːð] The horse rolled over on the grass. الحصان اِنقِلَب عَلَى صَفحَة اللُّخ عالحَشِيش [ʔilħṣaːn ʔingilab ʕala ṣafħat ʔillux ʕalħašiːš] • **2.** تقَلَّب [tgallab] تقُلُّب [tgullub] *vn: sv* a. I rolled over in bed. تقَلَّبِت بِالفراش [tgallabit bilfraːš]

to roll up • **1.** لَفّ [laff] لَفّ [laff] *vn:* اِنلَفّ [ʔinlaff] *p:* We rolled up the rug. لَفَّينا الزُّولِيَّة [laffiːna ʔizzuːliyya]

rollcall • **1.** تِعداد [tiʕdaːd] تِعدادات [tiʕdaːdaːt] *pl:* Did the sergeant take a roll call? العَرِيف سَوَّى تِعداد [ʔilʕariːf sawwaː tiʕdaːd]

Roman • **1.** رُومانِي [rumaːni] Use Roman numerals. اِستَعمِل أرقام رُومانِيَّة [ʔistaʕmil ʔarqaːm ruːmaniyya]

Rome • **1.** رُوما [ruːma]

roof • **1.** سَطِح [saṭiħ] سطُوح [sṭuːħ] *pl:* In Iraq people sleep on the roof in the summer. بِالعِراق النّاس ينامُون بِالسَّطِح بِالصَّيف [bilʕiraːq ʔinnaːs ynaːmuːn bissaṭiħ bissayf] • **2.** سَقُف [saguf] سقُوف [sguːf] *pl:* I burned the roof of my mouth. حرَقِت سَقُف حَلقِي [ħragit saguf ħalgi]

room • **1.** غُرفَة [ɣurfa] غُرَف [ɣuraf] *pl:* قُبَّة [gubba] قُبَب [gubab] *pl:* Where can I get a furnished room? وين ألقِي غُرفَة مأثَّثَة؟ [wiːn ʔalgi ɣurfa mʔaθθiθa?] • **2.** مُكان

R

[muka:n] مُكانات [muka:na:t] *pl:* Is there any room left for my baggage? بُقَى مُكان لجُنطِي؟ [buqa: muka:n lijunṭti?] • **3.** مَنام [mana:m] سَكَن [sakan] What do they charge for room and board? شقَدّ ياخذُون عَلَى الأكِل وَالمَنام؟ [šgadd ya:xðu:n ʕala ʔilʔakil wʔilmana:m?]

roomy • 1. واسِع [wa:siʕ] رَحِب [raħib] We have a roomy apartment. عِدنا فَدّ شُقَّة واسِعَة [ʕidna fadd šuqqa wa:sʕa]

rooster • 1. دِيك [di:č] ديُوكَة [dyu:ča] *pl:*

root • 1. عِرِق [ʕirig] عُرُوق [ʕuru:g] *pl:* جَذِر [ǰaðir] جذُور [ǰðu:r] *pl:* The roots of this tree are very deep. عرُوق هَالشَّجَر كُلِّش غَمِيقَة [ʕru:g haššaǰar kulliš ɣami:ǰa] The root of the tooth is decayed. عِرق السِّنّ خايِس [ʕirg ʔissinn xa:yis]

to take root • 1. طَلَّع عُرُوق [ṭallaʕ ʕuru:g] تَطلِيع عُرُوق [taṭli:ʕ ʕuru:g] *vn: sv* i. How can you tell whether the cutting has taken root? شلُون تُعرُف إذا القَلَم طَلَّع عُرُوق؟ [šlu:n tuʕruf ʔiða ʔilqalam ṭallaʕ ʕuru:g?] • **2.** دِرَج [diraǰ] دُرُوج [duru:ǰ] *vn: sv* u. The custom never really took root. العادَة بِالحَقِيقَة أَبَد ما دِرجَت [ʔilʕa:da bilħaqi:qa ʔabad ma: dirǰat]

to root out • 1. اِستَأصَل [ʔistaʔṣal] اِستِئصال [ʔistiʔṣa:l] *vn: sv* i. We must root out crime. لازِم نِستَأصِل الإجرام [la:zim nistaʔṣil ʔilʔiǰra:m]

* **He stood there as if rooted to the spot.** • **1.** وُقَف هناك عَبالَك مِتبَسمُر بمُكانَه [wugaf hna:k ʕaba:lak mitbasmur bmuka:nah]

rope • 1. حَبِل [ħabil] He was leading the calf by a rope. كان قايِد العِجِل بحَبِل [ča:n ga:yid ʔilʕiǰil bħabil]

* **Give him enough rope and he'll hang himself.** • **1.** رَخِّيلَه الحَبِل شوَيَّة وشُوف شلُون يِدمُر نَفسَه [raxxi:lah ʔilħabil šwayya wšu:f šlu:n yidmur nafsah]

* **I'm at the end of my rope.** • **1.** آنِي اِستَنفَذِت كُلّ ما بطاقتِي [ʔa:ni ʔistanfaðit kull ma: bṭa:qti]

* **He knows all the ropes.** • **1.** يُعرُف كُلّ الدِّرُوب [yuʕruf kull ʔiddiru:b]

to rope off • 1. قِطَع بِحَبِل [giṭaʕbħabil] قَطِع [gaṭiʕ] *vn: sv* a. They roped off the street for the parade. قِطعَوا الشّارِع بحَبِل لِلإستِعراض [giṭʕaw ʔišša:riʕ bħabil lilʔistiʕra:ð̣]

rose • 1. وَردَة جُورِي [wardat ǰu:ri] وَردات جُورِي [warda:t ǰu:ri] *pl:* جُورِي [ǰu:ri] وَردات جُورِي [warda:t ǰu:ri] *pl:* وَرِد جُورِي [warid ǰu:ri] *Collective:* He brings me roses everyday. يجِيبلِي وَرِد جُورِي يَومِيّاً [yǰi:bli warid ǰu:ri yawmiyyan]

rosebush • 1. هِرَش وَرِد جُورِي [hiraš warid ǰu:ri] هرُوش وَرِد جُورِي [hru:š warid ǰu:ri] *pl:*

to rot • 1. خاس [xa:s] خَيَسان [xayasa:n] *vn: sv* i. The fruit is rotting on the trees. الفَواكِه دَتخِيس عالأشجار [ʔilfawa:kih datxi:s ʕalʔašǰa:r]

rotten • 1. خايِس [xa:yis] The peaches are rotten. الخَوخ خايِس [ʔilxawx xa:yis] • **2.** قَذِر [qaðir] They played a rotten trick on us. لِعبَوا عَلينا فَدّ لِعبَة قَذرَة [liʕbaw ʕali:na fadd liʕba qaðra]

rough • 1. خَشِن [xašin] Why are your hands so rough? لِيش إيدَك هِيكِي خَشنَة؟ [li:š ʔi:dak hi:či xašna?] He has a rough voice. عِندَه حِسّ خَشِن [ʕindah ħiss xašin] The bench is made of rough planks. المَسطَبَة مسَوّايَة مِن لَوح خَشِن [ʔilmaṣṭaba msawwa:ya min lawħ xašin] She isn't used to such rough work. ما مِتعَلِّمَة عَلَى هِيكِي شُغُل خَشِن [ma: mitʕallma ʕala hi:či šuɣul xašin] • **2.** وَعِر [waʕir] This road is very rough. هَالطَّرِيق كُلِّش وَعِر [haṭṭari:q kulliš waʕir] • **3.** تَقرِيبِي [taqri:bi] This will give you a rough idea. هَذا يِنطِيك فِكرَة تَقرِيبِيَّة [ha:ða yinṭi:k fikra taqri:biyya]

roughly • 1. بقَسوَة [bqaswa] You've got to treat him roughly. لازِم تعامله بقَسوَة [la:zim tʕa:mlah bqaswa] You've got to treat him roughly. لازِم تِقسِي وِيّاه [la:zim tiqsi wiyya:h] • **2.** تَقرِيباً [taqri:ban] Can you tell me roughly how much it will be? تِقدَر تقُلّي تَقرِيباً شقَدّ راح تكُون؟ [tigdar dgulli taqri:ban šgadd ra:ħ tku:n?]

roughneck • 1. قاسِي [qa:si] قُساة [qusa:t] *pl:*

round • 1. جَولَة [ǰawla] جَولات [ǰawla:t] *pl:* He was knocked out in the first round. اِنضِرَب نوك آوت بِأَوَّل جَولَة [ʔinð̣irab nu:k ʔa:wt bʔawwal ǰawla] • **2.** دُورَة [du:ra] دُورات [du:ra:t] *pl:* Let's have another round of coffee. خَلِّي نِشرَب دورَة ثانيَة قَهوَة [xalli nišrab du:ra θa:nya gahwa] The watchman made his last round and went to bed. النّاطُور دار دَورتَه الأخِيرَة وَراح ينام [ʔinna:ṭu:r da:r dawrtah ʔilʔaxi:ra wra:ħ yna:m] • **3.** مدَوَّر [mdawwar] دائِرِي [da:ʔiri] I bought a round copper tray. اِشتِرَيت صِينِيَّة صِفِر مدَوَّرَة [ʔištiri:t ṣi:niyya ṣifir mdawwura]

to round off • 1. قَرَّب [qarrab] تَقرِيب [taqri:b] *vn:* تقَرَّب [tqarrab] *p:* Round off your answer to the nearest ten. قَرُّب جَوابَك لأقرَب عَشرَة [qarrub ǰawa:bak lʔaqrab ʕašara] • **2.** كَوَّر [kawwar] تَكوِير [takwi:r] *vn:* تكَوَّر [tkawwar] *p:* I'm not interested in details, round off the result and give me it. ما عَلَيّا بِالتَّفاصِيل؛ كَوُّرلِي النَّتِيجَة وَإنطِينِي إيّاها [ma: ʕalayya bittafa:ṣi:l; kawwurli ʔinnati:ǰa wʔinṭini ʔiyya:ha] • **3.** عَدَّل [ʕaddal] تَعدِيل [taʕdi:l] *vn:* تعَدَّل [tʕaddal] *p:* Round off the edges a little. عَدِّل الحَواشِي شوَيَّة [ʕaddil ʔilħawa:ši šwayya]

to round out • 1. كَمَّل [kammal] إكمال [ʔikma:l] *vn:* تكَمَّل [tkammal] *p:* I need this to round out my

R

i, interjection; p, passive; pl, plural; sv, stem vowel; vn, verbal noun

collection. آني أحتاج هاي حَتَّى أكَمِّل مَجموعتِي [ʔa:ni ʔaħta:ǰ ha:y ħatta ʔakammil majmu:ʕti]

round trip • **1.** رَوحَة وجَيَّة [ru:ħa wǰayya] رَواح ومَجِيء [rawa:ħ wmaǰi:ʔ] How much is the round trip? شقَدّ تكَلّف الرّوحَة وَالجَيَّة؟ [šgadd tkallif ʔirrawħa wiǰǰayya?]

round-trip ticket • **1.** بِطاقَة مُرَجَّع [biṭa:qa muraǰǰaʕ] بِطاقات مُرَجَّع [biṭa:qa:t muraǰǰaʕ] *pl:* He bought a round-trip ticket. اِشتِرَى بِطاقَة مُرَجَّع [ʔištira: biṭa:qa muraǰǰaʕ]

rout • **1.** هَزيمَة [hazi:ma] هَزايِم [haza:yim] *pl:* The demonstration ended with the complete rout of the students. المُظاهَرَة اِنتِهَت بِهَزيمَة كامِلَة مِن قِبَل الطُّلاب [ʔilmuḍa:hara ʔintihat bhazi:ma ka:mla min qibal ʔiṭṭulla:b]

route • **1.** طَريق [ṭari:q] طُرُق [ṭuruq] *pl:* Which route did you take? أيّ طَريق أخَذِت [ʔayy ṭari:q ʔaxaðit]

row • **1.** هُوسَة [hu:sa] هَوسات [hawsa:t] *pl:* لَغوَة [laɣwa] لَغوات، لَغاوِي [laɣwa:t, laɣa:wi] *pl:* My neighbor made a terrible row last night. جِيرانِي سَوَّى هُوسَة فَظِيعَة البارحَة باللّيل [ǰi:ra:ni sawwa: hu:sa faḍi:ʕa ʔilba:rħa billayl] I had a row with him. صار عِندِي لَغوَة وِيّاه [ṣa:r ʕindi laɣwa wiyya:h]

row • **1.** سِرَة [sira] سِرايات، سِراوات [sira:ya:t, sira:wa:t] *pl:* We had seats in the first row. كان عِدنا مَقاعِد بِالسِّرَة الأوَّل [ča:n ʕidna maqa:ʕid bissira ʔilʔawwal]

in a row • **1.** مَرَّة وَرَا اللُّخ [marra wara ʔillux] مَرَّة عَلَى مَرَّة [marra ʕala marra] He won three times in a row. رِبَح ثلَث مَرّات مَرَّة عَلَى مَرَّة [ribaħ tlaθ marra:t marra ʕala marra]

to row • **1.** جِذَف [ǰidaf] جَدِف [ǰadif] *vn:* اِنجِدَف [ʔinǰidaf] *p:* We rowed across the lake. جِدَفنا لصَفحَة اللُّخ مِن البُحَيرَة [ǰidafna lṣafħat ʔillux min ʔilbuħayra]

rowboat • **1.** بَلَم [balam] بلام [bla:m] *pl:*

royal • **1.** مَلَكِي [malaki]

rub • **1.** فَركَة [farka] فَركات [farka:t] *pl:* One rub with this material will remove the spot. فَركَة وِحدَة بِهالمادَّة ترَوِّح اللَّكَّة [farka wiħda bhalma:dda trawwiħ ʔillakka]

to rub • **1.** جَلَّخ [ǰallax] تَجليخ [tajli:x] *vn:* تجَلَّخ [tǰallax] *p:* My shoes rub at the heel. قُندَرتِي دَتجَلِّخ رِجلِي مِن الكَعَب [qundarti dadǰalliɣ riǰli min ʔiččaʕab] • **2.** مِسَح [misaħ] مَسِح [masiħ] *vn:* اِنمِسَح [ʔinmisaħ] *p:* Keep rubbing it until it shines. ظَلّ إمسَح بِيها إلَى أن تقُوم تِلمَع [ðall ʔimsaħ bi:ha ʔila ʔan tgu:m tilmaʕ] • **3.** فُرَك [furak] فَرِك [farik] *vn:* اِنفُرَك [ʔinfurak] *p:* He rubbed his hands together to get warm. فُرَك إيد بإيد حَتَّى يِحمَى [furak ʔi:d bʔi:d ħatta yiħma:] Rub his back with alcohol. أفرُك ظَهرَه بكُحُول [ʔufruk ḍahrah kuħu:l]

to rub against • **1.** حَكّ ب [ħakk b-] حَكّ [ħakk] *vn:* اِنحَكّ [ʔinħakk] *p:* تمَسَّح ب [tmassaħ b-] تمِسِّح [tmissiħ] *vn: sv* a. The cat rubbed against my leg. البَزّونَة حَكَّت نَفِسها برِجلِي [ʔilbazzu:na ħakkat nafisha briǰli]

to rub down • **1.** دَلَّك [dallak] تَدلِيك [tadli:k] *vn: sv* i. The public baths employ men to rub down their customers. الحَمّامات الشَّعبِيَّة تشَغِّل كَم رِجّال يدَلّكُون المَعامِيل [ʔilħamma:ma:t ʔiššaʕbiyya tšaɣɣil čam riǰǰa:l ydalliku:n ʔilmaʕa:mi:l]

to rub in • **1.** فُرَك ب [furak b-] فَرِك [farik] *vn:* اِنفُرَك [ʔinfurak] *p:* Rub the salve in well. أفرُك زايِد بِالدِّهِن [ʔufruk za:yid biddihin]

* **I know I'm wrong, but you don't have to rub it in.** • **1.** أدرِي آنِي غَلطان بَسّ ماكُو حاجَة تعِيد وتصَقُّل [ʔadri ʔa:ni ɣalṭa:n bass ma:ku ħa:ǰa tʕi:d wtiṣqul]

to rub out • **1.** مِسَح [misaħ] مَسِح [masiħ] *vn:* اِنمِسَح [ʔinmisaħ] *p:* You forgot to rub out the price. نِسِيت تِمسَح السِّعِر [nisi:t timsaħ ʔissiʕir]

rubber • **1.** مَطّاط [maṭṭa:ṭ] لاستِيك [lasti:k] لاستِيكات [lasti:ka:t] *pl:* These tires are made of synthetic rubber. هَالتّايَرات مَصنُوعَة مِن مَطّاط اِصطِناعِي [hatta:yira:t maṣnu:ʕa min maṭṭa:ṭ ʔiṣṭina:ʕi] • **2.** كالُوش [ka:lu:š] كالُوشات، كوالِيش [ka:lu:ša:t, kwa:li:š] *pl:* I lost one of my rubbers yesterday. ضَيَّعِت فَردَة مِن كالُوشِي البارحَة [ḍayyaʕit farda min ka:lu:ši ʔilba:rħa]

rubbish • **1.** زِبِل [zibil] Don't mix the rubbish in with the garbage. لا تُخبُط الزِّبِل وِيّا بَقايا الأكِل [la: tuxbuṭ ʔizzibil wiyya baqa:ya ʔilʔakil] • **2.** خَرِط [xariṭ, xaruṭ] Don't talk such rubbish! لا تِحكِي هِيكِي خَرُط [la: tiħči hi:či xaruṭ]

rude • **1.** جِلِف [ǰilif] أجلاف [ʔaǰla:f] *pl:* Don't be so rude! لا تصِير هَالقَدّ جِلِف [la: tṣi:r halgadd ǰilif]

rudeness • **1.** جَلافَة [ǰala:fa] His rudeness is inexcusable. جَلافتَه ما يِنصُفُح عَنها [ǰala:ftah ma: yinṣufuħ ʕanha]

rug • **1.** سِجّادَة [siǰǰa:da] سِجّادات، سجاجِيد [siǰǰa:da:t, sǰa:ǰi:d] *pl:* زُولِيَّة [zu:liyya] زُولِيّات، زوالِي [zu:liyya:t, zwa:li] *pl:*

ruin • **1.** خَراب [xara:b] دَمار [dama:r] دَمارات [dama:ra:t] *pl:* هَلاك [hala:k] You'll be the ruin of me. راح تكُون سَبَب دَمارِي [ra:ħ tku:n sabab dama:ri]

to ruin • **1.** تِلَف [tilaf] إتلاف [ʔitla:f] *vn: sv* i. دُمَر [dumar] دَمُر [damur] *vn: sv* u. The rain will ruin the crop. المُطَر راح يِتلِف المَحصُول [ʔilmuṭar ra:ħ yitlif ʔilmaħṣu:l] • **2.** خَرَّب [xarrab] تَخرِيب [taxri:b] *vn:*

R

تخَرَّب [txarrab] The volcano ruined the city. البُركان خَرَّب الوِلايَة [ʔilburka:n xarrab ʔilwila:ya] • **3.** هِلَك [hilak] هَلاك [hala:k] *vn: sv* i. The war ruined them. الحَرُب هِلكَتهُم [ʔilħarub hilkathum] • **4.** دُمَر [dumar] دَمُر [damur] *vn:* اِندُمَر [ʔindumar] *p:* دَمَّر [dammar] تَدمِير [tadmi:r] *vn:* تدَمَّر [tdammar] *p:* His new suit is completely ruined. بَدِلتَه الجِّدِيدَة اِندُمرَت تَماماً [badiltah ʔijǰidi:da ʔindumrat tama:man]

ruins • **1.** خَرابَة [xara:ba] خَرابات، خَرايِب [xara:ba:t, xara:yib] *pl:* The city is in ruins. المَدِينَة صايرَة خَرايِب [ʔilmadi:na ṣa:yra xara:yib] • **2.** أطلال [ʔaṭla:l] آثار [ʔa:θa:r] They discovered the ruins of an old temple. اِكتِشفَوا أطلال مَعبَد قَدِيم [ʔiktišfaw ʔaṭla:l maʕbad qadi:m]

rule • **1.** حُكُم [ħukum] أحكام [ʔaħka:m] *pl:* In old times Spain was under Arab rule. بِالزَّمان القَدِيم إسبانيا كانَت تَحَت حُكُم العَرَب [bizzama:n ʔilqadi:m ʔispa:nya ča:nat taħat ħukum ʔilʕarab] • **2.** نِظام [niḍa:m] أنظِمَة [ʔanḍima] *pl:* That's against the rules. هَذا مُخالِف لِلأنظِمَة [ha:ða muxa:lif lilʔanḍima] • **3.** أُصُول [ʔuṣu:l] I'm sticking to the rules. آنِي مِتقَيِّد بِالأُصُول [ʔa:ni mitqayyid bilʔuṣu:l] • **4.** قاعِدَة [qa:ʕida] قَواعِد [qawa:ʕid] *pl:* This rule doesn't apply here. هَالقاعِدَة ما تِنطُبُق هنا [halqa:ʕida ma: tinṭubuq hna]

as a rule • **1.** اِعتِيادِيّاً [ʔiʕtiya:diyyan] As a rule, I don't smoke. اِعتِيادِيّاً آنِي ما أَدَخِّن [ʔiʕtiya:diyyan ʔa:ni ma: ʔadaxxin]

to rule • **1.** حِكَم [ħikam] حُكُم [ħukum] *vn:* اِنحِكَم [ʔinħikam] *p:* They wanted to rule the entire world. رادَوا يحُكمُون الدِّنيا كُلّها [ra:daw yħukmu:n ʔiddinya kullha]

to rule out • **1.** نِفَى [nifa:] نَفِي [nafy] *vn:* اِنِّفَى [ʔinnifa:] *p:* This doesn't rule out the other possibility. هَذا ما يِنفِي الاحتِمال اللّاخ [ha:ða ma: yinfi ʔilʔiħtima:l ʔilla:x]

R

ruler • **1.** حاكِم [ħa:kim] حُكّام [ħukka:m] *pl:* He was an absolute ruler. كان حاكِم مُطلَق [ča:n ħa:kim muṭlaq] • **2.** مَسطَرَة [masṭara] مَساطِر [masa:ṭir] *pl:* The ruler is too short. المَسطَرَة كُلِّش قصَيِّرَة [ʔilmasṭara kulliš qṣayyra]

to rumble • **1.** طَرقَع [ṭargaʕ] طَرقَعَة [ṭargaʕa] *vn: sv* i. We heard trucks rumbling over the bridge. سمَعنا لُورِيات دَتطَرقِع عَالجِّسِر [simaʕna lu:riyya:t daṭṭargiʕ ʕaǰǰisir] • **2.** قَرقَر [qarqar] قَرقَرَة [qarqara] *vn: sv* i. My stomach is rumbling. بَطنِي دَتقَرقِر [baṭni datqarqir]

rumor • **1.** إشاعَة [ʔiša:ʕa] The rumor spread like wildfire. الإشاعَة اِنتِشرَت مِثل البَرق [ʔilʔiša:ʕa ʔintišrat miθl ʔilbarq]

run • **1.** دَرُب [darub] درُوب [dru:b] *pl:* The city bus makes ten runs to Kufa every day. باص الأمانَة يرُوح عَشرَة درُوب لِلكُوفَة كُلّ يوم [pa:ṣ ʔilʔama:na yiru:ħ ʕašra dru:b lilku:fa kull yu:m] • **2.** سَلِت [salit] You've got a run in your stocking. جوارِيبك بِيها سَلِت [ǰwa:ri:bič bi:ha salit] You've got a run in your stocking. جوارِيبك اِنسِلَت مِنها خيط [ǰwa:ri:bič ʔinsilat minha xi:ṭ]

in the long run • **1.** بِالمُدَّة [bilmudda] عَلَى مُرُور الزَّمَن [ʕala muru:r ʔizzaman] ويّا الوَقِت [wiyya ʔilwakit] In the long run you'll get tired of that. بِالمُدَّة راح تِعجَز مِنها [bilmudda ra:ħ tiʕǰaz minha]

to run • **1.** رِكَض [rikaḍ] رِكِض [rikiḍ] *vn: sv* u. Don't run so fast. لا تِركُض هِيكِي سَرِيع [la: tirkuḍ hi:či sari:ʕ] • **2.** وُصَل [wuṣal] وُصُول [wuṣu:l] *vn: sv* a. بِلَغ [bilaɣ] بُلُوغ [bulu:ɣ] *vn: sv* i. The casualties ran into thousands. الإصابات وُصلَت إلَى آلاف [ʔilʔiṣa:ba:t wuṣlat ʔila ʔa:la:f] • **3.** فَوَّت [fawwat] تَفوِيت [tafwi:t] *vn:* تفَوَّت [tfawwat] *p:* Run the rope through this loop. فَوِّت الحَبِل مِن هَالحَلقَة [fawwit ʔilħabil min halħalqa] • **4.** تخَلَّل [txallal] تَخَلُّل [taxallul] *vn: sv* a. The theme runs through the novel from beginning to end. الفِكرَة تِتخَلَّل القُصَّة مِن البِدايَة لِلنِّهايَة [ʔilfikra titxallal ʔilquṣṣa min ʔilbida:ya linniha:ya] • **5.** مِشَى [miša:] مَشِي [mašy] *vn: sv* i. My car runs smoothly. سَيّارتِي تِمشِي مِثل الدِّهِن [sayya:rti timši miθl ʔiddihin] • **6.** اِشتِغَل [ʔištiɣal] شُغُل [šuɣul] *vn: sv* u. Why do you keep the motor running? لِيش دَتخَلِّي المَكِينَة تِشتُغُل؟ [li:š datxalli ʔilmaki:na tištuɣul?] How many weeks has this movie been running? هَالفِلِم كَم إسبُوع صارلَه دَيِشتُغُل؟ [halfilim čam ʔisbu:ʕ ṣa:rlah dayištuɣul?] How many weeks has this movie been running? هَالفِلِم شقَدّ صارلَه مَعرُوض؟ [halfilim šgadd ṣa:rlah maʕru:ḍ?] • **7.** شَغَّل [šaɣɣal] تَشغِيل [tašɣi:l] *vn:* تشَغَّل [tšaɣɣal] *p:* Can you run a washing machine? تِقدَر تشَغِّل مَكِينَة مال غَسِل هِدُوم؟ [tigdar tšaɣɣil maki:na ma:l ɣasil hidu:m?] • **8.** كِشَف [kišaf] كَشِف [kašif] *vn: sv* i. The color runs. اللَّون يِكشِف [ʔillu:n yikšif] • **9.** فات [fa:t] فَوت [fu:t] *vn: sv* u. How often does this bus run? كُلّ شقَدّ هالباص يفُوت؟ [kull šgadd halpa:ṣ yfu:t?] • **10.** جِرَى [ǰira:] جَرَيان [ǰaraya:n] *vn: sv* i. The irrigation ditch has water running through it. السّاقيَة دَيجرِي بِيها ماي [ʔissa:gya dayiǰri bi:ha ma:y] Does that run in the family? هَذا يِجرِي بدَمّ العائلَة؟ [ha:ða yiǰri bdamm ʔilʕa:ʔila?] • **11.** دار [da:r] إدارَة [ʔida:ra] *vn:* اِنِدار [ʔinda:r] *p:* He's been running the business for three years. صارلَه ثلاث سنِين دَيدِير الشُّغُل [ṣa:rlah tlaθ sni:n daydi:r ʔiššuɣul] • **12.** مَرّ [marr] مَرّ [marr] *vn: sv* u. The road runs right in front of my house. الشّارِع يمُرّ قِدّام بَيتِي [ʔišša:riʕ yumurr gidda:m bayti]

to run across • **1.** صادَف [ṣa:daf] مُصادَفَة [muṣa:dafa] *vn:* تصادَف [tṣa:daf] *p:* Maybe I'll run across him someday. يِمكِن أصادفَه فَدّ يوم [yimkin ʔaṣa:dfah fadd yu:m]

to run aground • **1.** قَيَّش [gayyaš] تَقيِيش [tagyi:š] *vn: sv* i. My boat ran aground. بَلَمِي قَيَّش [balami gayyaš]

to run around • **1.** خَوَّر [xawwar] تَخوِير [taxwi:r] *vn:* Where have you been running around? وين كِنِت دَتخَوُّر؟ [wi:n činit datxawwur?] • **2.** مِشَى [miša:] مَشِي [mašy] *vn: sv* i. صاحَب [ṣa:ħab] مُصاحَبَة [muṣa:ħaba] *vn: sv* i. He's running around with a bad crowd. مصاحِبلَه مُو خُوش جَماعَة [mṣa:ħiblah mu: xu:š ǰama:ʕa]
to run away • **1.** هِرَب [hirab] هُرُوب، هَرَب [huru:b, harab] *vn: sv* u. فَرّ [farr] فِرار [fira:r] *vn: sv* u. His wife has run away. مَرتَه هُربَت [martah hurbat] The thief ran away before the police arrived. الحَرامِي فَرّ قَبُل ما تِجِي الشُّرطَة [ʔilħara:mi farr gabul ma: tiǰi ʔiššurṭa] • **2.** اِنهِزَم [ʔinhizam] هَزِيمَة [hazi:ma] *vn: sv* i. عَلَّق [ʕallag] تَعلِيق [taʕli:g] *vn: sv* i. When he saw us, he ran away. مِن شافنا اِنهِزَم [min ša:fna ʔinhizam] When he saw us, he ran away. مِن شافنا شَمَّع الخيط [min ša:fna šammaʕ ʔilxi:ṭ]
to run down • **1.** تقَصَّى [tqaṣṣa:] تَقَصِّي [taqaṣṣi] *vn: sv* a. We ran down all the clues. تقَصَّينا كُلّ الأدِلَّة [tqaṣṣi:na kull ʔilʔadilla] • **2.** سِحَق [siħag] سَحِق [saħig] *vn:* اِنسِحَق [ʔinsiħag] *p:* He was run down by a truck. اِنسِحَق بسَيّارَة لوري [ʔinsiħag bsayya:rat lu:ri] • **3.** حِكَى عَلَى [ħiča: ʕala] حَكِي [ħači] *vn: sv* i. She's always running her friends down behind their backs. هاي دائماً تِحكِي عَلَى أصدِقاءها وَراهُم [ha:y da:ʔiman tiħči ʕala ʔaṣdiqa:ʔha wara:hum] • **4.** خِلَص نَصُب [xilaṣnaṣub] خَلاص [xala:ṣ] *vn: sv* a. The clock has run down. السّاعَة خِلَص نَصُبها [ʔissa:ʕa xilaṣ naṣubha]
to run dry • **1.** نِشَف [nišaf] نَشِف [našif] *vn: sv* a. يِبَس [yibas] يَبِس [yabis] *vn: sv* a. The well ran dry last summer. البِير نِشَف السَّنَة اللِّي فاتَت [ʔilbi:r nišaf ʔissana ʔilli fa:tat]
to run errands • **1.** تصَخَّر [tṣaxxar] تَصَخُّر [taṣaxxur] *vn: sv* a. I don't have time to run errands for you. ما عِندِي وَقِت أتصَخَّرلَك [ma: ʕindi wakit ʔatṣaxxarlak]
to run for • **1.** رَشَّح ل [raššaħ l-] تَرشِيح [tarši:ħ] *vn:* ترَشَّح [traššaħ] *p:* Who's running for the lower house from this district? مِنُو مرَشَّح لِلنِّيابَة مِن هَالمَنطِقَة؟ [minu mraššiħ linniya:ba min halmanṭiqa?]
to run into • **1.** دِعَم ب [diʕam b-] دَعِم [daʕim] *vn: sv* a. He ran the car into a tree. دِعَم السَّيّارَة بشَجَرَة [diʕam ʔissayya:ra bšaǰara] • **2.** صادَف [ṣa:daf] مُصادَفَة [muṣa:dafa] *vn: sv* i. We ran into them in Paris last summer. صادَفناهُم بباريس الصَّيف الماضِي [ṣa:dafna:hum bpa:ri:s ʔiṣṣayf ʔilma:ḍi]
* **He's running into debt.** • **1.** دَيوَقِّع نَفسَه بِالدَّين [daywaggiʕ nafsah biddayn]
to run low • **1.** شَحّ [šaħħ] شَحّ [šaħħ] *vn: sv* i. My money is running low. فلُوسِي دَتشِحّ [flu:si datšiħħ]
to run off • **1.** عَلَّق [ʕallag] تَعلِيق [taʕli:g] *vn: sv* i. هِرَب [hirab] هُرُوب [huru:b] *vn: sv* a. اِنهِزَم [ʔinhizam] اِنهِزام [ʔinhiza:m] *vn: sv* i. He ran off with the club's funds. أخَذ فلُوس النّادِي وعَلَّق [ʔaxað flu:s ʔinna:di wʕallag] • **2.** طُفَح [ṭufaħ] طَفُح [ṭafuħ] *vn: sv* a. The water ran off the fields. الماي طُفَح مِن الحُقُول [ʔilma:y ṭufaħ min ʔilħuqu:l]

to run out • **1.** خِلَص [xilaṣ] خَلاص [xala:ṣ] *vn: sv* a. نِفَذ [nifað] نَفاذ [nafa:ð] *vn: sv* a. Our supply of sugar has run out. خِلَص مَوجُودنا مِن الشَّكَر [xilaṣ mawǰu:dna min ʔiššakar] All their supplies ran out. نِفذَت كُلّ مَؤُونَتهُم [nifðat kull maʔu:nathum] • **2.** هَجَّج مِن [haǰǰaǰ min] They ran him out of town. هَجِّجُوه مِن البَلَد [haǰǰiǰu:h min ʔilbalad]
to run over • **1.** طُفَح [ṭufaħ] طَفُح [ṭafuħ] *vn: sv* a. Watch out that the bathtub doesn't run over. دِير بالَك لا تخَلِّي البانيُو يِطفَح [di:r ba:lak la: txalli ʔalba:nyu yiṭfaħ] • **2.** سِحَق [siħag] سَحِق [saħig] *vn:* اِنسِحَق [ʔinsiħag] *p:* Watch out you don't run over the children. دِير بالَك لا تِسحَق الجِّهال [di:r ba:lak la: tisħag ʔiǰǰaha:l] • **3.** راجَع [ra:ǰaʕ] مُراجَعَة [mura:ǰaʕa] *vn: sv* i. Run over your part before the rehearsal. راجِع دُورَك قَبِل التَّدرِيب [ra:ǰiʕ du:rak gabil ʔittadri:b]
to run the risk • **1.** تحَمَّل خَطَر، خاطَر، جازَف [tħammal xaṭar, xa:ṭa:r, ja:zaf] تَحَمُّل خَطَر، مُخاطَرَة، مُجازَفَة [taħammul xaṭar, muxa:ṭara, muǰa:zafa] *vn: sv* a. He ran the risk of losing all his money. تحَمَّل خَطَر خَسارَة كُلّ فلُوسَه [tħammal xaṭar xasa:rat kull flu:sah]

rundown • **1.** بُختَة [puxta] خَرابَة [xara:ba] خَرابات، خَرايِب [xara:ba:t, xara:yib] *pl:* The house is rundown. البَيت صايِر بُختَة [ʔilbayt ṣa:yir puxta] The house is rundown. البَيت غادِي خَرابَه [ʔilbayt ɣa:di xara:bah] • **2.** مِنهار [minha:r] مُنحَطّ [munħaṭṭ, minħaṭṭ] تَلفان [talfa:n] His health is run-down; he needs a tonic. صِحّتَه مِنحَطَّة، يرِيدلَه مُقَوِّيات [ṣiħħtah minħaṭṭa, yri:dlah muqawwiyya:t] • **3.** مِنهَدّ [minhadd] She looks terribly rundown. يبَيِّن عَليها مِنهَدَّة تَماماً [yibayyin ʕali:ha minhadda tama:man] She looks terribly rundown. يبَيِّن عَليها صايرَة بَرباذَة [yibayyin ʕali:ha ṣa:yra barba:da] • **4.** مُلَخَّص [mulaxxaṣ] مُلَخَّصات [mulaxxaṣa:t] *pl:* They gave us a rundown on the news. إنطُونا مُلَخَّص الأخبار [ʔinṭu:na mulaxxaṣ ʔilʔaxba:r]

rung • **1.** دَرجَة [darǰa] دَرجات [darǰa:t] *pl:* The top rung of the ladder is broken. الدَّرجَة الفُوقانِيَّة مال الدَّرَج مَكسُورَة [ʔiddarǰa ʔalfu:ga:niyya ma:l ʔiddaraǰ maksu:ra]

runner • **1.** راكُوض [ra:ku:ḍ] He's a famous runner. هَذا فَدّ راكُوض مَشهُور [ha:ða fadd ra:ku:ḍ mašhu:r]

rupture • **1.** فَتِق [fatiq] فُتُوق [futu:q] *pl:* He has a rupture. عِندَه فَتِق [ʕindah fatiq]

ruse • **1.** حِيلَة [ħi:la] حِيَل [ħiyal] *pl:* خُدعَة [xudʕa] خُدَع [xudaʕ] *pl:* We had to resort to a ruse. اِضطَرَّينا نِلتِجِي إلَى خُدعَة [ʔiḍṭarri:na niltiǰi ʔila xudʕa]

rush • **1.** بَردِيَّة [bardiyya] بَردِيّات [bardiyya:t] *pl:* بَردِي [bardi] *Collective:* This mat is made of rushes.

R

هالحَصِير مِن بَرِدِي [halħaṣi:r min bardi] • **2.** عَجَلَة [ʕaǰala] What's the rush for? عَلَى وَيش هَالعَجَلَة؟ [ʕala wi:š halʕaǰala?] • **3.** اِزدِحام [ʔizdiħa:m] Let's wait till the rush is over. خَلِّي ننتِظِر إِلَى أَن يِخلَص الازدِحام [xalli nintiðir ʔila ʔan yixlaṣ ʔilʔizdiħa:m]

to rush • **1.** خُبَص [xubaṣ] خبصَة [xabṣa] *vn:* اِنخُبَص [ʔinxubaṣ] *p:* Don't rush me, I'm going to do it. لا تُخبُصني آني راح أَسَوِّيها [la: tuxbuṣni ʔa:ni ra:ħ ʔasawwi:ha] • **2.** اِستَعجَل [ʔistaʕǰal] اِستِعجال [ʔistiʕǰa:l] *vn: sv* i. Don't rush, we have lots of time. لا تِستَعجِل، عِدنا هوايَة وَقِت [la: tistaʕǰil, ʕidna hwa:ya wakit] She rushed through her work and was done by noon. اِستَعجِلَت بشُغُلها وَخَلّصَت الظُّهُر [ʔistaʕǰilat bšuɣulha wxallṣat ʔiððuhur] • **3.** مَشَّى [mašša:] تَمشِيَة [tamšiya] *vn:* تَمَشَّى [tmašša:] *p:* They rushed the bill through. مَشّوا اللائِحَة بِالعَجَل [maššaw ʔilla:ʔiħa bilʕaǰal] • **4.** وَدَّى [wadda:] تَودِيَة [tawdiya] *vn: sv* i. They rushed him to the hospital. وَدّوه لِلمُستَشفَى بالعَجَل [waddu:h lilmustašfa bilʕaǰal] • **5.** هِجَم [hiǰam] هُجُوم [huǰu:m] *vn: sv* i. The blood rushed to his head. الدَّم هِجَم إِلَى راسَه [ʔiddamm hiǰam ʔila ra:sah]

Russia • **1.** رُوسيا [ru:sya]

Russian • **1.** رُوسِي [ru:si] رُوس [ru:s] *pl:* Those technicians are Russians. هَالفَنِّيِّين روس [halfanniyyi:n ru:s] • **2.** رُوسِي [ru:si] They have a class in Russian I want to join. عِدهُم دَرِس بِالرُّوسِي أَرِيد أَشتِرِك بِيه [ʕidhum daris birru:si ʔari:d ʔaštirik bi:h]

rust • **1.** زِنجار [zinǰa:r] صَدَأ [ṣadaʔ] Before you paint the fence, scrape off the rust. حُكّ الزِّنجار قَبُل ما تُصبُغ السِّياج [ħukk ʔizzinǰa:r gabul ma: tuṣbuɣ ʔissiya:ǰ]

to rust • **1.** زَنجَر [zanǰar] زِنجار [zinǰa:r] *vn:* تزَنجَر [tzanǰar] *p:* صَدَّى [ṣadda:] *sv* i. Oil the machine or it will rust. دَهِّن المَكِينَة وَإِلّا تزَنجِر [dahhin ʔilmaki:na waʔilla dzanǰir]

to rustle • **1.** خَشخَش [xašxaš] خَشخَشَة [xašxaša] *vn: sv* i. I thought I heard something rustle. أَظِنّ سمَعِت شِي يخَشخِش [ʔaðinn smaʕit ši yxašxiš]

rusty • **1.** مزَنجِر [mzanǰir] مصَدِّي [mṣaddi] He scratched his hand on a rusty nail. جِلَغ إِيدَه بِبِسمار مزَنجِر [ǰilaɣ ʔi:dah bibisma:r mzanǰir] The knife is rusty. السِّكِّينَة مصَدّيَة [ʔissičči:na mṣaddya]

* **I'm afraid my French is a little rusty.** • **1.** أَخشَى الفِرَنسِي مالِي يِنرادلَه صَقِل [ʔaxša: ʔilifransi ma:li yinra:dlah ṣaqil]

rut • **1.** نُقرَة [nugra] Keep out of the ruts made by the cars ahead of us. وَخِّر مِن النُقرَة اللّي سَوَّتها السَّيّارات اللّي قَبُلنا [waxxir min ʔilnugra ʔilli sawwatha ʔissayya:ra:t ʔilli gabulna]

in rut • **1.** حامِي [ħa:mi] مِتهَيِّج [mithayyiǰ] Don't let the dog out; she's in rut. لا تخَلّي الكَلبَة تِطلَع؛ تَرَة حامية [la: txalli ʔiččalba titlaʕ; tara ħa:mya]

R

S

sack • **1.** كِيس [či:s] كياس [čya:s] *pl:* I want a sack of rice. أَرِيد كِيس تِمَّن [ʔari:d či:s timman]

sacred • **1.** مُقَدَّس [muqaddas] The mosque is a sacred place. الجّامِع مَكان مُقَدَّس [ʔijja:miʕ maka:n muqaddas]
*** Nothing is sacred to him.** • **1.** ما يُعرُف الحَرام [ma: yuʕruf ʔilħara:m]

sacrifice • **1.** تَضحِيَة [taðħiya] They made many sacrifices for their children. هواية قَدِّمَوا تَضحِيات لِولِدهُم [hwa:ya qaddimaw taðħiya:t liwilidhum] • **2.** خَسارَة [xasa:ra] خَسارات، خَساير [xasa:ra: t, xasa:yir] *pl:* I sold my car at a big sacrifice. بِعِت سَيّارتِي بِخَسارَة كبِيرَة [biʕit sayya:rti bxaṣa:ra čbi:ra]
to sacrifice • **1.** ضَحَّى [ðaħħa:] تَضحِيَة [taðħiya] *vn:* تضَحَّى [tðaħħa:] *p:* She sacrificed her life to him. ضَحَّت حَياتها مِن أجلَه [ðaħħat ħaya:tha min ʔajlah]

sad • **1.** حَزِين [ħazi:n] Why is he so sad? لِيش هُوَّ هَالقَدّ حَزِين؟ [li:š huwwa halgadd ħazi:n?]

saddle • **1.** سَرِج [sarij] سرُوج [sru:j] *pl:* Can you ride without a saddle? تِقدَر تِركَب بِلا سَرِج؟ [tigdar tirkab bila sarij?]
to saddle • **1.** سَرَّج [sarraj] تَسرِيج [tasri:j] *vn:* تسَرَّج [tsarraj] *p:* Do you know how to saddle a horse? تُعرُف شلُون تسَرِّج الحصان؟ [tuʕruf šlu:n tsarrij ʔilħṣa:n?]
*** He saddled me with all his troubles.**
• **1.** ذَبّ كُلّ مَصايبَه براسِي [ðabb kull maṣa:ybah bra:si] / ذَبّ كُلّ همُومَه عَلَيّا [ðabb kull hmu:mah ʕalayya]

safe • **1.** قاصَة [qa:ṣa] قاصات [qa:ṣa:t] *pl:* خزانَة [xza:na] خزانات، خزاين [xza:na:t, xza:yin] *pl:* We keep our safe in the office. إحنا نحُطّ قاصَتنا بَالدّائرَة [ʔiħna nħuṭṭ qa:ṣatna bidda:ʔira] • **2.** بأمان [bʔama:n] You are safe now. إنتَ هَسَّة بأمان [ʔinta hassa bʔama:n] • **3.** أَمِين [ʔami:n] مَأمُون [maʔmu:n] This neighborhood isn't quite safe. هَالمَنطِقَة مُو هَالقَدّ أَمِينَة [halmanṭiqa mu: halgadd ʔami:na] • **4.** سَلِيم [sali:m] That's a safe guess. هَذا تَخمِين سَلِيم [ha:ða taxmi:n sali:m]
*** Is the bridge safe for cars?** • **1.** الجِسِر يِتحَمَّل سَيّارات؟ [ʔijjisir yitħammal sayya:ra:t?]
*** To be on the safe side, let's ask him again.**
• **1.** حَتَّى نكُون مِتأكِّدِين، خَلِّي نسِألَه مَرَّة لُخ [ħatta: nku:n mitʔakkidi:n, xalli: nsiʔlah marra lux]

safe and sound. • **1.** صاغ سَلِيم [ṣa:ɣ sali:m] He's back safe and sound. رِجَع صاغ سَلِيم [rijaʕ ṣa:ɣ sali:m]

safely • **1.** بِسَلامَة [bsala:ma] They arrived safely. وُصلَوا بِسَلامَة [wuṣlaw bsala:ma]

safety • **1.** سَلامَة [sala:ma] This is for your personal safety. هَذِي لِسَلامتَك الشَّخصِيَّة [ha:ði lsala:mtak ʔiššaxṣiyya]
*** First the children were brought to safety.**
• **1.** أخذَوا الأَطفال بالأوَّل إلَى مَكان أمِين [ʔaxðaw ʔilʔaṭfa:l bilʔawwal ʔila: maka:n ʔami:n]

safety razor • **1.** مَكِينَة حِلاقَة [maki:nat ħila:qa] مَكايِن حِلاقَة [maka:yin ħila:qa] *pl:*

to sag • **1.** هُبَط [hubaṭ] هَبُط [habuṭ] *vn:* *sv* u. اِرتِخَى [ʔirtixa:] إرتِخاء [ʔirtixa:ʔ] *vn:* *sv* i. The bookshelf sags in the middle. رَفّ الكُتُب هابُط مِن النُّصّ [raff ʔilkutub ha:buṭ min ʔinnuṣṣ] • **2.** خِسَف [xisaf] خَسِف [xasif] *vn:* *sv* u. The mattress sags in the middle. الفراش خاسِف مِن النُّصّ [ʔilfra:š xa:sif min ʔinnuṣṣ]

Sahara Desert • **1.** الصَّحراء الكُبرَى [ʔiṣṣaħra:ʔ ʔilkubra]

sail • **1.** شراع [šra:ʕ] شراعات، أَشرِعَة [šra:ʕa:t, ʔašriʕa] *pl:* The wind tore the sail. الهَوا شَقّ الشِّراع [ʔilhawa šagg ʔiššra:ʕ]
to sail • **1.** تِرَك [tirak] تَرِك [tarik] *vn:* *sv* u. طِلَع [ṭilaʕ] طلُوع [ṭlu:ʕ] *vn:* *sv* a. The boat sails at five. السَّفِينَة تِترُك ساعَة خَمسَة [ʔissafi:na titruk sa:ʕa xamsa]
*** We go sailing every week.**
• **1.** كُلّ إسبُوع نِطلَع بِالبَلَم أبُو شراع [kull ʔisbu:ʕ niṭlaʕ bilbalam ʔabu: šra:ʕi?]
*** Do you know how to sail a boat?**
• **1.** تُعرُف شلُون تقُود بَلَم شِراعِي؟ [tuʕruf šlu:n tqu:d balam šira:ʕi:?]

sailboat • **1.** بَلَم شِراعِي [balam šira:ʕi] أبلام شِراعِيَّة [ʔabla:m šira:ʕiyya] *pl:*

sailor • **1.** بَحّار [baħħa:r] بَحّارَة [baħħa:ra] *pl:* How many sailors are on the boat? كَم بَحّار أكُو عالسَّفِينَة؟ [čam baħħa:r ʔaku ʕassafi:na?]

sake • **1.** خاطِر [xa:ṭir] مُود [mu:d] أجِل [ʔajil] I did it for your sake. سَوَّيتها عَلَى مُودَك [sawwi:tha ʕala mu:dak] He gave his life for his country's sake. ضَحَّى بِنَفسَه مِن أجِل بِلادَه [ðaħħa: bnafsah min ʔajil bila:dah] At least do it for your son's sake! عالأَقَلّ سَوِّيها لخاطِر إبنَك [ʕalʔaqall sawwi:ha lxa:ṭir ʔibnak]
*** For the sake of argument, let's say he did go.**
• **1.** خَلِّي نِفتِرِض إنّو راح [xalli: niftiriḍ ʔinnu: ra:ħ]

S

salad • **1.** سَلاطَة [zala:ṭa] سَلاطات، سَلَطات [zala:ṭa:t, zalaṭa:t] *pl:*

salary • **1.** راتِب [ra:tib] رَواتِب [rawa:tib] *pl:* مَعاش [maʕa:š] مَعاشات [maʕa:ša:t] *pl:* How can you manage on that salary? شلُون تدَبُّر أمرَك بِهالرّاتِب؟ [šlu:n ddabbur ʔamrak bharra:tib?]

sale • **1.** بَيع [bayʕ, bi:ʕ] The sale of alcoholic drinks to minors is prohibited. بَيع المَشرُوبات لِلصِّغار مَمنُوع [bayʕ ʔalmašru:ba:t liṣṣiɣa:r mamnu:ʕ] Our neighbor's house is for sale. بَيت جَارنا لِلبيع [bayt ǰa:rna lilbayʕ] Sales of cotton goods have doubled this year. بَيع المَنتُوجات القُطنِيَّة تضاعَف هالسَّنَة [bayʕ ʔilmantu:ǰa:t ʔilquṭniyya dḍa:ʕaf hassana] • **2.** تَنزِيل [tanzi:l] تَنزِيلات [tanzi:la:t] *pl:* I bought this coat at a sale. اِشتِرَيت هالقَبُّوط مِن مَحَلّ عِندَه تَنزِيلات [ʔištiri:t halqappu:ṭ min maħall ʕindah tanzi:la:t]

sales clerk • **1.** بَيّاع [bayya:ʕ] بَيّاعِين، بَيّاعَة [bayya:ʕa, bayya:ʕi:n] *pl:* He's a sales clerk in a department store. هُوَّ بَيّاع بِمَحَلّ تِجارِي [huwwa bayya:ʕ bimaħall tiǰa:ri]

salesman • **1.** بَيّاع [bayya:ʕ] بَيّاعِين [bayya:ʕi:n] بَيّاعَة [bayya:ʕa] *pl:* One of our salesmen will call on you tomorrow. واحِد مِن بَيّاعِينّا راح يزُورَك باكِر [wa:ħid min bayya:ʕi:nna: ra:ħ yzu:rak ba:čir]

salt • **1.** مِلِح [miliħ] Pass me the salt, please. ناوُشنِي المِلِح رَجاءاً [na:wušni ʔilmiliħ raǰa:ʔan] • **2.** ممَلَّح [mmallaħ] Do you have salt cheese? عِندَك جِبِن ممَلَّح؟ [ʕindak ǰibin mmallaħ?]

to salt • **1.** مَلَّح [mallaħ] تَملِيح [tamli:ħ] *vn:* تمَلَّح [tmalliħ] *p:* Did you salt the soup? مَلَّحتِي الشّورِبَة؟ [mallaħti ʔiššu:rba?]

to salt away • **1.** خَزَّن [xazzan] تَخزِين [taxzi:n] *vn:* تخَزَّن [txazzan] *p:* صَمَّد [ṣammad] تَصمِيد [taṣmi:d] *vn:* تصَمَّد [tṣammad] *p:* He salted away a tidy sum of money. هذا خَزَّن خُوش كَمِّيَّة مِن الفلُوس [ha:ða xazzan xu:š kammiyya min ʔiliflu:s]

S

salt flat • **1.** صَبخَة [ṣabxa] صَبخات [ṣabxa:t] *pl:*

salt shaker • **1.** مَملَحَة [mamlaħa] مَمالِح [mama:liħ] *pl:*

salt works • **1.** مَملَحَة [mamlaħa] مَملَحات، مَمالِح [mamlaħa:t, mama:liħ] *pl:* We visited the salt works near Basra. زِرنا المُملَحَة قُرب البَصرَة [zirna ʔilmamlaħa qurb ʔilbaṣra]

salty • **1.** مالِح [ma:liħ] The fish is awfully salty. السِّمَك كُلِّش مالح [ʔissimač kulliš ma:liħ]

same • **1.** نَفِس [nafis] نُفُوس، أنفُس [nufu:s, ʔanfus] *pl:* I can be back on the same day. أقدَر أرجَع بِنَفِس اليُوم [ʔagdar ʔarǰaʕ bnafis ʔilyu:m] We're the same age. إحنا بِنَفِس العُمُر [ʔiħna bnafis ʔilʕumur] We're the same age. إحنا عُمُرنا سُوَة [ʔiħna ʕumurna suwa] Thanks, the same to you! شُكراً، أتمَنّالَك نَفس الشّي [šukran, ʔatmanna:lak nafs ʔišši] Thanks, the same to you! إنتَ هَمِّين [ʔinta hammi:n] • **2.** سُوَة، سُوا [suwa] That's all the same to me. كُلّها سُوَة عِندِي [kullha suwa ʕindi] That's all the same to me. هاي كُلّها فَدّ شِي بِالنِّسبَة إلِي [ha:y kullha fadd ši binnisba ʔili]

all the same • **1.** مَعَ ذلِك [maʕa ða:lik] All the same, I want to see it. مَعَ ذَلِك، أرِيد أشُوفها [maʕa ða:lik, ʔari:d ʔašu:fha]

sample • **1.** نَمُوذَج [namu:ðaǰ] نَماذِج [nama:ðiǰ] *pl:* نَمُونَة [namu:na] نمايِن، نَمايِم [nama:yin, nama:yim] *pl:* Do you have a sample of the material with you? عِندَك نَمُوذَج مِن القماش جايبَة ويّاك؟ [ʕindak namu:ðaǰ min ʔalqma:š ǰa:yba wiyya:k?]

sand • **1.** رَمُل [ramul]

sandal • **1.** نَعَل [naʕal] نعلات [naʕla:t] *pl:* نعال [naʕa:l] نعالات، نِعِل، نِعلان، نعُولَة [nʕa:la:t, niʕil, niʕla:n, nʕu:la] *pl:*

sandwich • **1.** سَندويشَة [sandwi:ča] سَندويشات [sandwi:ča:t] *pl:* Take a few sandwiches along. أُخُذ وِيّاك كَم سَندوِيشَة [ʔuxuð wiyya:k čam sandwi:ča]

to sandwich in • **1.** حِصَر [ħiṣar] حَصِر [ħaṣir] *vn:* اِنحِصَر [ʔinħiṣar] *p:* He was sandwiched in between two stout women. اِنحِصَر بين نِسوان إثنَين سمان [ʔinħiṣar bayn niswa:n ʔiθnayn sma:n]

sanitary • **1.** صِحِّي [ṣiħħi] Your kitchen is not sanitary enough. مَطبَخَك مُو صِحِّي كِفايَة [maṭbaxak mu: ṣiħħi kifa:ya]

sarcastic • **1.** مِتهَكِّم [mithakkim] مِتهَكِّمِين [mithakkimi:n] *pl:*

sardine • **1.** سَردِينَة [sardi:na] سَردِينات [sardi:na:t] *pl:* سَردِين [sardi:n] *Collective*

satisfaction • **1.** اِرتِياح [ʔirtiya:ħ] إرضاء [ʔirḍa:ʔ] It gives me great satisfaction to hear that. أشعُر بِارتِياح كِبِير مِن أسمَعها [ʔašʕur bʔirtiya:ħ čibi:r min ʔasmaʕha]

*** Was everything settled to your satisfaction?** • **1.** اِنتِهَت المَسألَة مِثلما ترِيد؟ [ʔintihat ʔilmasʔala miθilma tri:d?] / كُلّشِي كان صايِر عَلَى كَيفَك؟ [kullši ča:n ṣa:yir ʕala kayfak?]

satisfactory • **1.** مُرضِي [murḍi] His condition is satisfactory. حالتَه مُرضِيَة [ħa:ltah murḍiyya]

to be satisfactory • **1.** وُفا بِالمَرام [wufa: bilmara:m] This room is quite satisfactory. هَالغُرفَة تُوفِي بالمَرام تَماماً [halɣurfa tu:fi bilmara:m tama:man]

to satisfy • **1.** أرضى [ʔarða] إرضاء [ʔirða:ʔ] *vn:* انرضى [ʔinraða:] *p:* تَرضِيَة [tarðiya] *vn:* تَرضّى [traððaː] *p:* Your answer doesn't satisfy me. جَوابَك ما يرضيني [ǰawa:bak ma: yirði:ni] I'm not satisfied with my new apartment. آني ما راضي عَلَى شُقّتي الجِّدِيدَة [ʔa:ni ma: ra:ði ʕala šuqqti ʔiǰǰidi:da] You can't satisfy everybody. ما تِقدَر تَرضّي كُلّ واحِد [ma: tigdar traððí kull wa:ħid] • **2.** قِنَع [qinaʕ] قَناعَة [qana:ʕa] *vn:* اِنقِنَع [ʔinqinaʕ] *p:* We'll have to be satisfied with less. لازِم نِقنَع بأَقَلّ [la:zim niqnaʕ bʔaqall]

Saturday • **1.** السَّبِت [ʔissabit] يَوم السَّبِت [yawm ʔissabit]

sauce • **1.** مَرقَة [marga, murga] مَرقات [marga:t, murga:t] *pl:* مَرَق [marag] *Collective:* How do you make the sauce for this dish? شلُون تسَوّي المَرقَة مال هَالأَكلَة؟ [šlu:n tsawwi ʔalmarga ma:l halʔakla?] • **2.** صَوص [ṣu:ṣ] صَوصات [ṣu:ṣa:t] *pl:* صاص [ṣa:ṣ] صاصات [ṣa:ṣa:t] *pl:* Put some sauce on your kabob. خَلّي شوَيَّة صَوص عَلَى الكَباب [xalli šwayya ṣu:ṣ ʕala ʔilkaba:b]

saucepan • **1.** جِدِر، قِدِر [ǰidir] جدُور، جدُورَة [ǰdu:r, ǰdu:ra] *pl:*

saucer • **1.** ماعُون [ma:ʕu:n] مواعِين [mwa:ʕi:n] *pl:* صَحِن [ṣaħin] صُحُون [ṣuħu:n] *pl:*

Saudi • **1.** سُعُودِي [suʕu:di] I met a Saudi yesterday. لاقَيت فَدّ سُعُودِي البارحَة [la:gi:t fadd suʕu:di ʔilba:rħa]

Saudi Arabia • **1.** المَملَكَة العَرَبِيَّة السُعُودِيَّة [ʔilmamlaka ʔilʕarabiyya ʔissuʕu:diyya]

savage • **1.** وَحشِي [waħši] وَحِش [waħiš] وُحُوش [wuħu:š] *pl:* هَمَجِي [hamaǰi:] هَمَجِيِّين، هَمَج [hamaǰiyyi:n, hamaǰ] *pl:* You're behaving like a savage. إنتَ تِتصَرَّف مِثل الوُحُوش [ʔinta titṣarraf miθl ʔilwuħu:š] • **2.** قاسِي [qa:si] قُساة [qusa:t] *pl:* He started a savage attack on the government. بدا هِجُوم قاسِي عَالحُكُومَة [bida: hiǰu:m qa:si ʕalħuku:ma]

to save • **1.** أنقَذ [ʔanqað] إنقاذ [ʔinqa:ð] *vn:* اِنّقَذ [ʔinniqað] *p:* He saved her life. أنقَذ حَياتهَا [ʔanqað ħaya:tha] • **2.** ضَمّ [ðamm] ضَمّ [ðamm] *vn:* اِنضَمّ [ʔinðamm] *p:* اِحتِفَظ ب [ʔiħtifað b-] اِحتِفاظ [ʔiħtifa:ð] *vn:* *sv* u. Could you save this for me until tomorrow? تِقدَر تضمّلي هاي إلَى باكِر؟ [tigdar dðummli ha:y ʔila ba:čir?] Why do you save these old papers? لوَيش تِحتِفظ بِهَالأَوراق العَتِيقَة؟ [lwi:š tiħtifuð bihalʔawra:q ʔilʕati:ga?] • **3.** حِجَز [ħiǰaz] حَجِز [ħaǰiz] *vn:* اِنحِجَز [ʔinħiǰaz] *p:* Is this seat being saved for anyone? هَالمَكان مَحجُوز الأَحَّد؟ [halmaka:n maħǰu:z ʔilʔaħħad?] • **4.** جِمَع [ǰimaʕ] جَمِع [ǰamiʕ] *vn:* اِنجِمَع [ʔinǰimaʕ] *p:* جَمَّع [ǰammaʕ] تَجمِيع [tajmi:ʕ] *vn:* تجَمَّع [tǰammaʕ] *p:* he saves stamps. يِجمَع طَوابِع [yiǰmaʕ ṭawa:biʕ] • **5.** وَفَّر [waffar] تَوفِير [tawfi:r] *vn:* توَفَّر [twaffar] *p:* اِدَّخَر [ʔiddixar] اِدِّخار [ʔiddixa:r] *vn:* *sv* a. Have you saved any money? وَفَّرت أيّ فلُوس؟ [waffarit ʔayy flu:s?] • **6.** خَلَّص [xallaṣ] تَخلِيص [taxli:ṣ] *vn:* تخَلَّص [txallaṣ] *p:* جَنَّب مِن [ǰannab min] تَجنِيب [taǰni:b] *vn:* تجَنَّب [tǰannab] *p:* You could have saved yourself the trouble. كان خَلَّصِت نَفسَك مِن هَالدَّوخَة [ča:n xallaṣit nafsak min haddawxa]

*** Save your breath. He's not listening.**
• **1.** لا تتَعَّب نَفسَك، هُوَّ مَا دايِرلَك بال [la: ttaʕʕib nafsak, huwwa ma: da:yirlak ba:l]

savings • **1.** مُدَّخَرات [muddaxara:t] He's used up all his savings. صِرَف كُلّ مُدَّخَراتَه [ṣiraf kull muddaxara:tah]

saw • **1.** مِنشار [minša:r] مناشِير [mna:ši:r] *pl:* Could I borrow a saw from you? أقدَر أطلُب مِنشار مِنَّك؟ [ʔagdar ʔaṭlub minša:r minnak?]
to saw • **1.** قَصّ [gaṣṣ] قَصّ [gaṣṣ] *vn:* اِنقَصّ [ʔingaṣṣ] *p:* He's been sawing wood all morning. صارلَه مِن الصُّبُح يقُصّ خِشَب [ṣa:rlah min ʔiṣṣubuħ yguṣṣ xišab]

to say • **1.** قال [ga:l] قَول [gawl] *vn:* اِنقال [ʔinga:l] *p:* What did you say? شقِلِت؟ [šgilit?] The paper says rain. الجَّرِيدَة تقُول راح تُمطُر [ʔiǰǰari:da dgu:l ra:ħ tumṭur] What does the sign say? شِتقُول هاي الإشارَة؟ [šitgu:l ha:y ʔilʔiša:ra?] I'll meet you, say, in an hour. أشُوفَك، خَلّي نقُول بَعَد ساعَة [ʔašu:fak, xalli ngu:l baʕad sa:ʕa] They say he speaks several languages. يقُولُون هُوَّ يتكَلَّم عِدَّة لُغات [ygu:lu:n huwwa yitkallam ʕiddat luɣa:t] • **2.** كِتَب [kitab] كِتابَة [kita:ba] *vn:* اِنكِتَب [ʔinkitab] *p:* ذِكَر [ðikar] ذِكرَى [ðikra] *vn:* اِنذِكَر [ðikra] *p:* اِنقال [ʔinga:l] *p:* The papers didn't say a thing about it. الجَّرايِد ما كِتبَت أيّ شِي عَنها [ʔiǰǰara:yid ma: kitbat ʔayy ši ʕanha]
*** There's much to be said for his suggestion.**
• **1.** اِقتِراحَ يِستِحِقّ الإهتِمام [ʔiqtira:ħa yistiħiqq ʔilʔihtima:m]
to say good-bye • **1.** وَدَّع [waddaʕ] تَودِيع [tawdi:ʕ] *vn:* توَدَّع [twaddaʕ] *p:* I said good-bye to him yesterday. وَدَّعتَه البارحَة [waddaʕtah ʔilba:rħa]
to say nothing of • **1.** مِن عَدَى [min ʕada:] It takes a lot of time, to say nothing of the expense. تاخُذ هوايَة وَقِت هاي مِن عَدا المَصارِيف [ta:xuð hwa:ya wakit ha:y min ʕada: ʔilmaṣa:ri:f]

saying • **1.** قَول [gawl] أقوال [ʔaqwa:l] *pl:* مَثَل [maθal] أمثال [ʔamθa:l] *pl:* That's a very common saying. هَذا قَول كُلِّش شايع [ha:ða qawl kulliš ša:yiʕ]
*** That goes without saying.** • **1.** هَذا ما بِيه مُناقَشَة [ha:ða ma: bi:h muna:qaša]

scaffold • **1.** سكَلَّة [skalla] سكَلّات [skalla:t] *pl:* أسكَلَة [ʔaskala] أسكَلات [ʔaskala:t] *pl:* He fell from the scaffold. وُقَع مِن عالسكَلَّة [wugaʕ min ʕalskalla]

S

scale • **1.** مِقياس [miqya:s] مَقايِيس [maqa:yi:s] *pl:* I bought myself a new scale. اِشتِرَيتلِي فَدّ مِقياس جِديد [ʔištiri:tli fadd miqya:s ǰidi:d] The scale is one to one thousand. مِقياس الرَّسِم واحِد عَلَى أَلف [miqya:s ʔirrasim wa:ħid ʕala ʔalf] • **2.** سُلَّم [sullam] سَلالِم [sala:lim] *pl:* She practices musical scales all day. تِتدَرَّب عَلَى السُّلَّم المَوسِيقِي طُول النَّهار [tiddarrab ʕala ʔissullam ʔilmusi:qi ṭu:l ʔinnaha:r] • **3.** قِشِر [gišir] قشُور [gšu:r] *pl:* فِلِس [filis] فلُوس [flu:s] *pl:* The fish has big scales. السِّمكَة عِدها قشُور كبار [ʔissimča ʕidha qšu:r kba:r] • **4.** مِيزان [mi:za:n] مِيازِين، مَوازِين [miya:zi:n, mawa:zi:n] *pl:* Put the meat on the scales. خَلِّي اللَّحَم بالمِيزان [xalli ʔillaħam bilmi:za:n]

to scale • **1.** صِعَد عَلَى [ṣiʕad ʕala] صَعُود [ṣaʕu:d] *vn:* اِنصِعَد [ʔinṣiʕad] *p:* تسَلَّق [tsallaq] تَسَلُّق [tasalluq] *vn: sv* a. Ten of us scaled the wall. عَشرَة مِنّا صِعدَوا عَالحايِط [ʕašra minna ṣiʕdaw ʕalħa:yiṭ] • **2.** قَشَّر [gaššar] تَقشِير [tagši:r] *vn:* تقَشَّر [tgaššar] *p:* The fish hasn't been scaled yet. السِّمكَة ما تقَشِّرَت بَعَد [ʔissimča ma: tgašširat baʕad]

scandal • **1.** فَضِيحَة [faḏi:ħa] فَضايِح [faḏa:yiħ] *pl:*

scar • **1.** أَثَر جَرِح [ʔaθar ǰariħ] آثار جُرُوح [ʔa:θa:r ǰuru:ħ] *pl:* أُخُت [ʔuxut] He has a scar on his right cheek. عِندَه أَثَر جَرِح عَلَى خَدَّه الأَيمَن [ʕindah ʔaθar ǰariħ ʕala xaddah ʔilʔayman]

scarce • **1.** نادِر [na:dir] Gold coins have become scarce. العُملَة الذَّهَبِيَّة صايرَة نادرَة جِدّاً [ʔilʕumla ʔiððahabiyya ṣa:yra na:dra ǰiddan]

*** Eggs are scarce at this time of year.**

• **1.** البَيض يقِلّ بهَالوَقِت مِن السَنَة [ʔilbayð yqill bhalwakit min ʔissana]

scarcely • **1.** بِالكاد [bilka:d] I scarcely know him. آنِي بِالكاد أَعُرفَه [ʔa:ni bilka:d ʔaʕurfah]

scare • **1.** فَزَع [fazaʕ] فَزَّة [fazza] You gave me an awful scare. فَزَّعتنِي فَزَع فَظِيع [fazzaʕitni fazaʕ faḏi:ʕ] You gave me an awful scare. خَوَّفتنِي هوايَة [xawwafitni hwa:ya]

to scare • **1.** خَوَّف [xawwaf] تَخوِيف [taxwi:f] *vn:* تخَوَّف [txawwaf] *p:* The dog scared me to death. الكَلِب خَوَّفنِي هوايَة [ʔiččalib xawwafni hwa:ya]

• **2.** خاف [xa:f] خَوف [xawf] *vn:* اِنخاف [ʔinxa:f] *p: sv* a. I scare easily. آنِي أَخاف بِالعَجَل [ʔa:ni ʔaxa:f bilʕaǰal]

*** We were scared stiff.** • **1.** جِمَدنا مِن الخُوف [ǰimadna min ʔilxawf]

*** Where did he scare up the money?**

• **1.** مَنَين جاب الفلُوس؟ [mnayn ǰa:b ʔilflu:s?] / مِنِين دَبَّر الفلُوس؟ [mni:n dabbar ʔilflu:s?]

scarf • **1.** لَفّاف [laðða:f] لَفّافات [laffa:fa:t] *pl:*

scarlet • **1.** قِرمِزِي [qirmizi]

to scatter • **1.** تفَرَّق [tfarraq, tfarrag] تَفَرُّق [tafarruq] *vn: sv* a. طَشَّر [ṭaššar] تَطشِير [taṭši:r] *vn:* تطَشَّر [tṭaššar] *p:* The crowd scattered when the police arrived. الجُمهُور تفَرَّق مِن وُصلَت الشُّرطَة [ʔiǰǰamhu:r tfarraq min wuṣlat ʔiššurṭa] The books were scattered all over the floor. الكُتُب كانَت مطَشَّرَة بكُلّ صَفحَة عَالقاع [ʔilkutub ča:nat mṭaššara bkull ṣafħa ʕalga:ʕ]

scene • **1.** مَشهَد [mašhad] مَشاهِد [maša:hid] *pl:* مَنظَر [manḏar] مَناظِر [mana:ḏir] *pl:* That's in the third scene of the second act. هَذا بِالمَشهَد الثّالِث مِن الفَصِل الثّانِي [ha:ða bilmašhad ʔiθθa:liθ min ʔilfaṣil ʔiθθa:ni] • **2.** فُرجَة [furǰa] Don't make a scene. لا تسَوِّينا فُرجَة [la: tsawwi:na furǰa]

behind the scenes • **1.** جَوَّة العَبا [ǰawwa ʔilʕaba:] وَرَة السِتار [wara ʔissita:r] Nobody knows what's going on behind the scenes. مَحَّد يِدرِي شدَيصِير جَوَّة العَبا [maħħad yidri šdayṣi:r ǰawwa ʔilʕaba:]

scenery • **1.** مَشاهِد [maša:hid] مَناظِر [mana:ḏir] Who designed the scenery? مِنُو صَمَّم المَشاهِد؟ [minu ṣammam ʔilmaša:hid?] • **2.** مَناظِر [mana:ḏir] We didn't have time to look at the scenery. ما صار عِدنا وَقِت نشُوف المَناظِر [ma: ṣa:r ʕidna wakit nšu:f ʔilmana:ḏir]

scent • **1.** رِيحَة [ri:ħa] رِيحات، رَوايِح، رِيَّح [ri:ħa:t, rawa:yiħ, riyyaħ] *pl:* The dogs have got the scent. الكِلاب شَمُّوا الرِّيحَة [ʔiččila:b šammaw ʔirri:ħa] • **2.** حاسَّة الشَّمّ [ħassat ʔiššamm] Our dog has a keen scent. كَلبنا عِندَه حاسَّة الشَّمّ حادَّة [čalibna ʕindah ħa:ssat ʔiššamm ħa:dda]

to scent • **1.** اِشتَمّ رِيحَة [ʔištamm ri:ħa] شَمّ اِشتِمام [ʔištima:m, šamm] *vn: sv* a. The dogs have scented the fox. الكِلاب اِشتَمُّوا رِيحَة الثَّعلَب [ʔilčila:b ʔištammaw ri:ħat ʔiθθaʕlab] • **2.** عَطَّر [ʕaṭṭar] تَعطِير [taʕṭi:r] *vn:* تعَطَّر [tʕaṭṭar] *p:* She scented the clothes. عَطِّرَت الهدُوم [ʕaṭṭirat ʔilhdu:m]

schedule • **1.** جَدوَل [ǰadwal] جَداوِل [ǰada:wil] *pl:* We'll have to work out a schedule if we want to finish on time. لازِم نسَوِّي جَدوَل إذا رِدنا نخَلِّص عالوَقِت [la:zim nsawwi ǰadwal ʔiða ridna nxalliṣ ʕalwakit]

on schedule • **1.** عَالوَقِت [ʕalwakit] The train arrived on schedule. القِطار وُصَل عالوَقِت [ʔilqiṭa:r wuṣal ʕalwakit]

to schedule • **1.** حَدَّد [ħaddad] تَحدِيد [taħdi:d] *vn:* تحَدَّد [tħaddad] *p:* عَيَّن [ʕayyan] تَعيِين [taʕyi:n] *vn: sv* i. The meeting's scheduled for tomorrow. الاجتِماع تحَدَّد وَقتَه باكِر [ʔilʔiǰtima:ʕ tħaddad waktah ba:čir]

scheme • **1.** خُطَّة [xuṭṭa] خُطّات [xuṭṭa:t] *pl:* مَشرُوع [mašru:ʕ] مَشارِيع [maša:ri:ʕ] *pl:* مَنهَج [manhaǰ]

مَناهِج [mana:hij] *pl:* Has he thought up a new scheme? هَذا فَكَّر بِخُطَّة جِدِيدَة؟ [ha:ða fakkar bxuṭṭa ǰidi:da?] • **2.** تَرتِيب [tarti:b] تَرتِيبات [tarti:ba:t] *pl:* We've changed the color scheme. غَيَّرنا تَرتِيب الأَلوان [ɣayyarna tarti:b ʔilʔalwa:n]

to scheme • **1.** دَبَّر مُؤامَرَة [dabbar muʔa:mara] تَدبِير [tadbi:r] *vn:* تدَبَّر [tdabbar] *p:* مُؤامَرَة [muʔa:mara] مُؤامَرات [muʔa:mara:t] *pl:* They're always scheming. هُمَّ عَلَى طُول يدَبّرُون مُؤامَرات [humma ʕala ṭu:l ydabbru:n muʔa:mara:t]

scholar • **1.** عالِم [ʕa:lim] عُلَماء [ʕulama:ʔ] *pl:* طالِب عِلِم [ṭa:lib ʕilim] طُلّاب عِلِم [ṭulla:b ʕilim] *pl:* He's a great scholar. هُوَّ عالِم كِبِير [huwwa ʕa:lim čibi:r]

school • **1.** مَدرَسَة [madrasa] مَدارِس [mada:ris] *pl:* Do you go to school? إِنتَ ترُوح لِلمَدرَسَة؟ [ʔinta tru:ħ lilmadrasa?]

science • **1.** عِلِم [ʕilim] He's more interested in science than art. عِندَه رَغبَة بِالعِلِم أَكثَر مِن الفَنّ [ʕindah rayba bilʕilim ʔakθar min ʔilfann]

scientific • **1.** عِلمِي [ʕilmi]

scientist • **1.** عالِم [ʕa:lim] عُلَماء [ʕulama:ʔ] *pl:*

scissors • **1.** مُقَص، مقَصّ، مقاصَة [mugaṣ, mugaṣṣ] مُقَصّات، مقاصِيص [mugaṣṣa:t, mga:ṣi:ṣ] *pl:* The scissors are dull. المُقَص أعمى [ʔilmugaṣ ʔaʕma]

to scold • **1.** زَفّ [zaff] زَفّ [zaff] *vn:* اِنزَفّ [ʔinzaff] *p:* تَرَزَّل (تَرَذَّل) [razzal] (تَرذِيل) تَرزِيل [tarzi:l] *vn:* رَزَّل (رَذَّل) [trazzal] *p:* My mother scolded me. أُمِّي زَفَّتنِي [ʔummi zaffatni]

to scorch • **1.** حِرَق [ħirag] حَرِق [ħarig] *vn:* اِنحِرَق [ʔinħirag] *p:* I nearly scorched my dress. حرَقِت بَدِلتِي إِلّا شوَيَّة [ħragit badilti ʔilla šwayya]

* **The sun is scorching hot.** • **1.** الشَّمِس دَتِلفَح [ʔiššamis datilfaħ]

scorcher • **1.** * It's a scorcher today. هَاليُوم حارّ [halyu:m ħa:rr]

score • **1.** مَجمُوع [majmu:ʕ] What's the score? شقَدّ المَجمُوع؟ [šgadd ʔilmajmu:ʕ?] What's the score? شقَدّ صارَت النُّقاط؟ [šgadd ṣa:rat ʔinnuqa:ṭ?] • **2.** ثار [θa:r] I have a score to settle with him. عِندِي ثار وِيّاه لازِم أَنهِيه [ʕindi θa:r wiyya:h la:zim ʔanhi:h]

* **Scores of people died in the epidemic.**
• **1.** عَدَد كِبِير مات مِن الوَباء [ʕadad čibi:r ma:t min ʔilwaba:ʔ]

to score • **1.** سَجَّل [sajjal] تَسجِيل [tasji:l] *vn:* تسَجَّل [tsajjal] *p:* We scored five points in the second half. سَجَّلنا خَمِس نُقاط بِالنُّصّ الثّانِي [sajjalna xamis nuqa:ṭ binnuṣṣ ʔiθθa:ni]

scorpion • **1.** عَقرَب [ʕagrab] عَقارُب [ʕaga:rub] *pl:*

scoundrel • **1.** سافِل [sa:fil] سَفَلَة [safala] *pl:* مِنحَطّ [minħaṭṭ] مِنحَطِّين [minħaṭṭi:n] *pl:*

to scour • **1.** جِلَف [ǰilaf] She scoured the kettle. جِلفَت القُورِي [ǰilfat ʔilqu:ri]

scouring pad • **1.** سُمّاطَة [summa:ṭa] سُمّاطات [summa:ṭa:t] *pl:* جَلّافَة [ǰalla:fa] جَلّافات [ǰalla:fa:t] *pl:*

scrambled eggs • **1.** بَيض مَطرُوق [bayð maṭru:g]

scrap • **1.** وُصلَة [wuṣla] وُصَل [wuṣal] *pl:* That's only a scrap of paper. هَذِي مُجَرَّد وُصلَة وَرَق [ha:ði mujarrad wuṣlat waraq] • **2.** عَركَة [ʕarka] عَركات [ʕarka:t] *pl:* They had an awful scrap last night. كانَت بَيناتهُم عَركَة ثِخِينَة البارحَة باللَّيل [ča:nat bayna:thum ʕarka θixi:na ʔilba:rħa billayl]

to scrape • **1.** قِشَط [gišaṭ] قَشِط [gašiṭ] *vn:* اِنقِشَط [ʔingišaṭ] *p:* He scraped his hand on the rock. قِشَط إِيدَه بِالصَّخرَة [gišaṭ ʔi:dah biṣṣaxra]

to scrape off • **1.** حَكّ [ħakk] حَكّ [ħakk] *vn:* اِنحَكّ [ʔinħakk] *p:* Scrape the paint off before you paint. حُكّ الصُّبُغ قَبُل ما تُصبُغ [ħukk ʔiṣṣubuɣ gabul ma: tuṣbuɣ]

to scrape together • **1.** لَمّ [lamm] لَمّ [lamm] *vn:* اِنلَمّ [ʔinlamm] *p:* جِمَع [ǰimaʕ] جَمِع [ǰamiʕ] *vn:* اِنجِمَع [ʔinǰimaʕ] *p:* I couldn't scrape the money together. ما قِدَرِت أَلِمّ الفلُوس [ma: gidarit ʔalimm ʔilflu:s]

scrap metal • **1.** سِكراب [sikra:b] He deals in scrap metal. يِشتُغُل بِالسِّكراب [yištuɣul bissikra:b]

scratch • **1.** خَدِش [xadiš] خُدُوش [xudu:š] *pl:* تخِرمُش [txirmuš] تخِرمُشات [txirmuša:t] *pl:* What's that scratch on your cheek? شِنُو هَالخَدِش بِخَدَّك؟ [šinu: halxadiš bxaddak?] • **2.** شُخُط [šuxuṭ] شخُوط [šxu:ṭ] *pl:* How'd that scratch get on the table? مِنِين جا هَالشُّخُط عالميز؟ [mni:n ǰa: haššuxuṭ ʕalmi:z?]

* **We escaped without a scratch.**
• **1.** اِنهِزَمنا مِن دُون أَي أَذَى [ʔinhizamna min du:n ʔayy ʔaða]

* **After the fire he had to start from scratch.**
• **1.** بَعد الحَرِيق اِضطَرّ يِبدِي مِن الأَوَّل [baʕd ʔilħari:q ʔiðṭarr yibdi: min ʔilʔawwal]

to scratch • **1.** خَدَّش [xaddaš] تَخدِيش [taxdi:š] *vn:* تخَدَّش [txaddaš] *p:* خِدَش [xidaš] خَدِش [xadiš] *vn:*

S

اِنخِدَش [ʔinxidaš] *p:* Be careful not to scratch the furniture. دِير بالَك لا تخَدِّش الأَثاث [di:r ba:lak la: txaddiš ʔilʔaθa:θ] • **2.** شِخَط [šixaṭ] شَخُط [šaxuṭ] *vn:* اِنشِخَط [ʔinšixaṭ] *p:* This pen scratches. هَالقَلَم يِشخُط [halqalam yišxuṭ]

to scratch out • **1.** شِطَب [šiṭab] شَطُب [šaṭub] *vn:* اِنشِطَب [ʔinšiṭab] *p:* شِخَط [šixaṭ] شَخُط [šaxuṭ] *vn:* اِنشِخَط [ʔinšixaṭ] *p:* Scratch out the last sentence. إشطُب الجُملَة الأَخِيرَة [ʔišṭub ʔijjumla ʔilʔaxi:ra]

scream • **1.** صَرخَة [ṣarxa] صَرخات، صريخ، صراخ [ṣarxa:t, ṣri:x, ṣra:x] *pl:* صِيحَة [ṣi:ħa] صِيحات [ṣi:ħa:t] *pl:* صِياح [ṣiya:ħ] I thought what I heard was a scream. ظَنَّيت اللِّي سمَعِتها صَرخَة [ðanni:t ʔilli smaʕitha ṣarxa]

*** He's a scream!** • **1.** هُوَّ كُلِّش مُضحِك [huwwa kulliš muðħik]

to scream • **1.** صِرَخ [ṣirax] صراخ [ṣra:x] *vn: sv* u. The child screamed with fright. الطِّفِل صِرَخ مِن الخُوف [ʔiṭṭifil ṣirax min ʔilxu:f]

screen • **1.** سِتار [sita:r] سَتائِر [sata:ʔir] *pl:* حاجِز [ħa:jiz] حَواجِز [ħawa:jiz] *pl:* Change behind the screen. بَدِّل وَرا السِّتار [baddil wara ʔissita:r] • **2.** شاشَة [ša:ša] شاشات [ša:ša:t] *pl:* He looks older on the screen. يِبَيِّن أَكبَر مِن عُمرَه عالشّاشَة [yibayyin ʔakbar min ʕumrah ʕašša:ša] • **3.** تِيل [ti:l] تيُولَة [tyu:la] *pl:* We need a new screen on that window. نِحتاج تَيل جِدِيد عَلَى هَذا الشِّبّاك [niħta:j ti:l jidi:d ʕala ha:ða ʔiššibba:k]

screw • **1.** بُرغِي [burɣi] بَراغِي [bara:ɣi] *pl:* These screws need tightening. هَالبَراغِي تِحتاج تَقوِيَة [halbara:ɣi tiħta:j taqwiya]

to screw • **1.** بُرَم [buram] بَرُم [barum] *vn:* اِنبُرَم [ʔinburam] *p:* He screwed the nut on the bolt. بُرَم الجُوزَة عَالبُرغِي [buram ʔijju:za ʕalburɣi]

*** Screw the cap on tight.** • **1.** شِدّ القَبَغ زَين [šidd ʔilqabaɣ zi:n]

*** Things are all screwed up at work.** • **1.** كُلّ المَسائِل مخَربُطَة بِالشُّغُل [kull ʔilmasa:ʔil mxarbuṭa biššuɣul]

*** If I can screw up enough courage, I'll ask for a raise.** • **1.** إذا أقدَر أَشِدّ حَيلِي، راح أَطلُب زِيادَة راتِب [ʔiða: ʔagdar ʔašidd ħi:li, ra:ħ ʔaṭlub ziya:dat ra:tib]

screw driver • **1.** دَرنَفِيس [darnafi:s] دَرنَفِيسات [darnafi:sa:t] *pl:* مَفَلّ [mafall] مَفَلّات [mafalla:t] *pl:*

to scrub • **1.** فُرَك [furak] فَرِك [farik] *vn:* اِنفُرَك [ʔinfurak] *p:* We've got to scrub the floor. لازِم نِفرُك القاع [la:zim nifruk ʔilga:ʕ]

sculptor • **1.** نَحّات [naħħa:t] نَحّاتَة، نَحّاتِين [naħħa:ta, naħħa:ti:n] *pl:* مَثّال [maθθa:l] مَثّالِين [maθθa:li:n] *pl:*

scythe • **1.** مِنجَل [minjal] مَناجِل [mana:jil] *pl:*

sea • **1.** بَحَر [baħar] أَبحُر، بِحار، بُحُور [ʔabħur, bħa:r, bħu:r] *pl:* How far are we from the sea? شقَدّ نِبعِد مِن البَحَر؟ [šgadd nibʕid min ʔilbaħar?] The Nile empties into the Mediterranean Sea. النِّيل يصُبّ بالبَحر الأَبيَض المُتَوَسِّط [ʔinni:l yṣubb bilbaħr ʔilʔabyað ʔilmutawaṣṣiṭ]

seal • **1.** فَقمَة [faqma] فَقمات [faqma:t] *pl:* We watched them feed the seals. تفَرَّجنا عَلَيهُم يطَعّمُون الفَقمات [tfarrajna ʕali:hum ytaʕʕmu:n ʔilfaqma:t] • **2.** طَمغَة [ṭamɣa] طَمغات [ṭamɣa:t] *pl:* خَتِم [xatim] أختام [ʔaxta:m] *pl:* The papers bore the official seal. الأَوراق حامِلَة الطَّمغَة الرَّسمِيَّة [ʔilʔawra:q ħa:mla ʔiṭṭamɣa ʔirrasmiyya] • **3.** خَتِم [xatim] أَختام [ʔaxta:m] *pl:* Somebody must have broken the seal. واحِد لازِم كاسِر الخَتِم [wa:ħid la:zim ka:sir ʔilxatim]

to seal • **1.** سَدّ [sadd] سَدّ [sadd] *vn:* اِنسَدّ [ʔinsadd] *p:* لِزَق [lizag] لَزِق [lazig] *vn:* اِنلِزَق [ʔinlizag] *p:* Have you sealed the letter yet? سَدَّيت المَكتُوب لَو بَعَد؟ [saddi:t ʔilmaktu:b law baʕad?]

seam • **1.** خياط [xya:ṭ] Rip open the seam. إفتِق الخياط [ʔiftig ʔilxya:ṭ]

search • **1.** بَحِث [baħiθ] بُحُوث، أَبحاث [buħu:θ, ʔabħa:θ] *pl:* تَفتِيش [tafti:š] The police made a thorough search. الشُّرطَة قامَت بِبَحِث شامِل [ʔiššurṭa ga:mat bibaħiθ ša:mil]

to search • **1.** فَتَّش [fattaš] تَفتِيش [tafti:š] *vn:* تفَتَّش [tfattaš] *p:* We'll have to search you. لازِم نفَتِّشَك [la:zim nfattišak] • **2.** دَوَّر [dawwar] تَدوِير [tadwi:r] *vn:* تدَوَّر [tdawwar] *p:* I've searched the whole house. دَوَّرِت البَيت كُلَّه [dawwarit ʔilbayt kullah] • **3.** بِحَث [biħaθ] بَحِث [baħiθ] *vn:* اِنبِحَث [ʔinbiħaθ] *p:* دَوَّر [dawwar] *sv* i. فَتَّش [fattaš] *sv* i. We searched for him everywhere. بِحَثنا عليه بِكُلّ مَكان [biħaθna ʕali:h bkull maka:n]

seasick • **1.** * I was terribly seasick on my last trip. صابنِي دُوار بَحَر كُلِّش قَوِي بِالسَّفرَة اللِّي فاتَت [ṣa:bni duwa:r baħar kulliš qawi bissafra ʔilli fa:tat]

seasickness • **1.** دُوار بَحَر [duwa:r baħar]

season • **1.** فَصِل [faṣil] فُصُول [fuṣu:l] *pl:* Which season do you like best, winter or summer? يا فَصِل تحِبّ أَكثَر، الشِّتا لَو الصَّيف؟ [ya: faṣil tħibb ʔakθar, ʔiššita law ʔiṣṣayf?] • **2.** مَوسِم [mawsim] مَواسِم [mawa:sim] *pl:* This is the best season for swimming. هَذا أَحسَن مَوسِم لِلسِّبِح [ha:ða ʔaħsan mawsim lissibiħ]

to season • **1.** حَطّ بَهارات عَلَى [ħaṭṭ bahara:t ʕala] *sv* u. What did you season the meat with? شحَطِّيت عاللَّحَم؟ [šħaṭṭi:t ʕallaħam?]

S

i, interjection; p, passive; pl, plural; sv, stem vowel; vn, verbal noun

seasoned • **1.** مجَرَّب [mǰarrab] They were seasoned troops. كانوا جنُود مجَرُّبِين [čaːnaw ǰnuːd mǰarrubiːn]

seat • **1.** مَقعَد [maqʕad] مَقاعِد [maqaːʕid] *pl:* This seat needs fixing. هَالمَقعَد يِحتاج تَصلِيح [halmaqʕad yiħtaːǰ taşliːħ] The pants are tight in the seat. البَنطُرون ضَيِّق مِن المَقعَد [ʔilpanţuruːn ðayyig min ʔilmaqʕad]

to have a seat • **1.** قِعَد [giʕad] قُعُود [guʕuːd] *vn:* اِنقِعَد [ʔingiʕad] *p:* Please have a seat. تفَضَّل، أقعُد [tfaððal, ʔugʕud]

to seat • **1.** قَعَّد [gaʕʕad] تَقعِيد [tagʕiːd] *vn:* تقَعَّد [tgaʕʕad] *p:* Seat the children in the front row. قَعِّد الأَطفال بِالصَّفّ الأَمامِي [gaʕʕid ʔilʔaţfaːl bişşaff ʔilʔamaːmi] • **2.** لِزَم [lizam] لَزِم [lazim] *vn:* اِنلِزَم [ʔinlizam] *p:* كَفَّى [kaffaː] تَكفِيَة [takfiya] *vn:* تكَفَّى [tkaffaː] *p:* The theater seats five hundred people. السِّينَما تِلزَم خَمِس مِيَّة شَخِص [ʔissiːnamaː tilzam xamis miyyat šaxiş]

second • **1.** ثانِيَة [θaːniya] ثَوانِي [θawaːni] *pl:* He ran a hundred yards in ten seconds. رِكَض مِيَّة يارِدَة بعَشِر ثَوانِي [rikað miyyat yaːrda bʕašir θawaːni] • **2.** لَحظَة [laħða] لَحظات [laħðaːt] *pl:* Wait a second. اِنتِظِر لَحظَة [ʔintiðir laħða] • **3.** ثانِي [θaːni] Will you please give me the second book from the left? بالله ما تِنطِينِي الكِتاب الثّانِي اللِّي عَالِيسرَة؟ [ballah maː tinţiːni ʔilkitaːb ʔiθθaːni ʔilli ʕalyisra?] Give me a second class ticket to Basra, please. رَجاءاً إنطِينِي تَذكَرَة دَرَجَة ثانيَة لِلبَصرَة [raǰaːʔan ʔinţiːni taðkara daraǰa θaːnya lilbaşra]

in the second place • **1.** ثانِياً [θaːniyan] In the first place I have no time, and in the second place I don't want to go anyway. أوَّلاً ما عِندِي وَقِت، وَثانِياً آنِي ما أرِيد أرُوح عَلَى كُلّ حال [ʔawwalan maː ʕindi wakit, wθaːnyan ʔaːni maː ʔariːd ʔaruːħ ʕala kull ħaːl]

to second • **1.** ثَنَّى عَلَى [θannaːʕala] تَثنِيَة [taθniya] *vn:* تثَنَّى [tθannaː] *p:* عَلَى [ʕala] I second the motion. أثَنِّي عالإقتِراح [ʔaθanni ʕaːlʔiqtiraːħ]

second-hand • **1.** مُستَعمَل [mustaʕmal] He bought the book second-hand. اِشتِرَى الكِتاب مُستَعمَل [ʔištiraː ʔilkitaːb mustaʕmal] • **2.** مِن مَصدَر ثانَوِي [min maşdar θanawi] I only know that story secondhand. أعرُف هَالقُصَّة مِن مَصدَر ثانَوِي بَسّ [ʔaʕruf halquşşa min maşdar θanawi bass]

secondly • **1.** ثَنَّى عَلى [θaːnyan] Secondly, I don't want to go anyway. ثانِياً ما أرِيد أرُوح عَلَى كُلّ حال [θaːnyan maː ʔariːd ʔaruːħ ʕala kull ħaːl]

second-rate • **1.** دَرَجَة ثانِيَة [daraǰa θaːnya] It's definitely a second-rate hotel. بِالتَّأكِيد هَذا فِندِق دَرَجَة ثانِيَة [bittaʔakiːd haːða findiq daraǰa θaːnya]

secret • **1.** سِرّ [sirr] أسرار [ʔasraːr] *pl:* Let me in on the secret. خَبُّرنِي عَن السِّرّ [xabburni ʕan ʔissirr] • **2.** سِرِّي [sirri] They have a secret plan. عِدهُم خُطَّة سِرِّيَّة [ʕidhum xuţţa sirriyya]

secretary • **1.** سِكرِتير [sikirtiːr] سِكرِتيرِيَّة [sikirtiːriyya] *pl:* She's my secretary. هِيَّ السِّكرِتَيرَة مالتِي [hiyya ʔissikirtiːra maːlti] I talked to the second secretary at the embassy. حكَيت وِيّا السِّكرِتَير الثّانِي بِالسَّفارَة [ħčiːt wiyya ʔissikirtiːr ʔiθθaːni bissafaːra]

secretly • **1.** سِرّ [sirr] أسرار [ʔasraːr] *pl:* سِرّاً [sirran] خِفيَة [xifya] They met secretly. اِجتِمعَوا بِالسِّرّ [ʔiǰtimʕaw bissirr]

sect • **1.** مَذهَب [maðhab] مَذاهِب [maðaːhib] *pl:* طائِفَة [ţaːʔifa] طائِفات، طَوائِف [ţaːʔifaːt, ţawaːʔif] *pl:*

section • **1.** جُزء [ǰuzuʔ] أجزاء [ʔaǰzaːʔ] *pl:* You'll find it in section three of chapter one. تشُوفه بِالجُّزء الثّالِث مِن الفَصل الأوَّل [tšuːfah biǰǰuzʔ ʔiθθaːliθ min ʔilfaşil ʔilʔawwal] • **2.** قِسِم [qisim] أقسام [ʔaqsaːm] *pl:* مَنطِقَة [manţiqa] مَناطِق [manaːţiq] *pl:* I was brought up in this section of Baghdad. آنِي ربَيت بِهَالقِسم مِن بَغداد [ʔaːni rbiːt bhalqism min baɣdaːd]

secure • **1.** مصوقَر [mşuːgar] مَضمُون [maðmuːn] It's a secure investment. هِيَّ شَغلَة مصُوقرَة [hiyya šaɣla mşuːgra] • **2.** أمان [ʔamaːn] Nobody feels secure these days. مَحَّد يِشعُر بِالأمان هَالأيّام [maħħad yišʕur bilʔamaːn halʔayyaːm] • **3.** مَشدُود [mašduːd] Is the load secure? الحِمِل مَشدُود زين؟ [ʔilħimil mašduːd ziːn?]

to secure • **1.** ضُمَن [ðuman] ضَمان [ðamaːn] *vn:* اِنضِمَن [ʔinðiman] *p:* His future is secured. مُستَقبَلَه مَضمُون [mustaqbalah maðmuːn]

security • **1.** طَمَأنِينَة [ţamaʔniːna] We feel a sense of security if we lock our door at night. نِشعُر بِطَمَأنِينَة إذا قفَلنا بابنا باللَّيل [nišʕur bţamaʔniːna ʔiða qfalna baːbna billayl] • **2.** ضَمان [ðamaːn] What security can you give me? أيّ ضَمان تِقدَر تِنطِينِي؟ [ʔayy ðamaːn tigdar tinţiːni?] • **3.** رَهِن [rahin] I had to leave my watch as security. اِضطَرَّيت أحُطّ ساعتِي كَرَهِن [ʔiðţarriːt ʔaħuţţ saːʕati karahin] • **4.** أمِن [ʔamin] The meeting of the security council lasted an hour. اِجتِماع مَجلِس الأمِن طَوَّل ساعَة [ʔiǰtimaːʕ maǰlis ʔilʔamin ţawwal saːʕa]

securities • **1.** أسهُم و سَنَدات [ʔashum w sanadaːt] He's invested most of his money in securities. شَغَّل مُعظَم أموالَه بالأسهُم والسَّنَدات [šaɣɣal muʕðam ʔamwaːlah bilʔashum wʔissanadaːt]

to see • **1.** شاف [šaːf] شَوف [šawf] *vn:* اِنشاف [ʔinšaːf] *p:* May I see your passport? أقدَر أشُوف جَواز سَفَرَك؟ [ʔagdar ʔašuːf ǰawaːz safarak?] • **2.** تصَوَّر [tşawwar] تَصَوُّر [taşawwur] *vn:* *sv* a. شاف [šaːf] I don't see it that way. ما أتصَوَّرها هِيكِي [maː ʔatşawwarha hiːči]

S

• **3.** اِلتِقَى [ʔiltiqa:, ʔiltiga:] اِلتِقاء [ʔiltiqa:ʔ] *vn: sv* i. I'd like to see more of you. أَحِبّ اَلتِقِي وِيّاك أَكثَر [ʔaħibb ʔaltigi wiyya:č ʔakθar]

*** Anybody can see through him.**

• **1.** أَي واحِد يِقدَر يُعرُف شَكُو بِقَلبَه [ʔayy wa:ħid yigdar yuʕruf šaku bgalbah]

*** I'll see you through this year.**

• **1.** راح أَبقَى ساعدَك إِلَى نِهايَة هاي السَنَة [ra:ħ ʔabqa: ʔasa:ʕdak ʔila niha:yat ha:y ʔissana]

*** Please see to it that this letter is mailed today.**

• **1.** رَجاءاً تأَكَّد بِأَن هَالمَكتُوب يرُوح بِالبَرِيد اليَوم [raǰa:ʔan tʔakkad biʔan halmaktu:b yru:ħ bilbari:d ʔilyawm]

*** See to it that you are on time.**

• **1.** تأَكَّد مِن أَن تِجي عَالوَقِت [tʔakkad min ʔan tiǰi ʕalwakit]

to see one home • **1.** وَصَّل للبَيت [waṣṣal lilbayt] تَوصِيل [tawṣi:l] *vn:* توَصَّل [twaṣṣal] *p:* May I see you home? تِسمَحِيلي أَوَصّلِك لِلبَيت؟ [tismaħi:li ʔawaṣṣlič lilbayt?]

seed • **1.** بَزرَة [bazra] بَزرات، بزُور [bazra:t, bzu:r] *pl:* بَزِر [bazir] *Collective:* حَبَّة [ħabba] حَبّات [ħabba:t] *pl:* حُبُوب [ħubuwb] *Collective:* Did you buy any seeds? اِشتِرَيت بَزِر؟ [ʔištiri:t bazir?] Some types of oranges have no seeds. بَعَض أَنواع البُرتقال ما بِيها حَبّ [baʕaḍ ʔanwa:ʕ ʔilpurtaqa:l ma: bi:ha ħabb]

to seed • **1.** بِذَر [biðar] بَذِر [baðir] *vn:* اِنبِذَر [ʔinbiðar] *p:* طَشّ [ṭašš] طَشّ [ṭašš] *vn:* اِنطَشّ [ʔinṭašš] *p:* When did you seed this field? شوَقِت بِذَرت هالحَقِل؟ [šwakit biðarit halħaqil?]

to seem • **1.** بَيَّن [bayyan] تَبيِين [tabyi:n] *vn:* تبَيَّن [tbayyan] *p:* I seem to be interrupting. يبَيِّن آني دَأَقاطِع [yibayyin ʔa:ni daʔaqa:ṭiʕ] • **2.** بِدَى [bida:] بَدُو [badw] *vn: sv* u. It seems to me he wanted to go last week. يِبدُولِي كان يرِيد يرُوح ذاك الإسبُوع [yibdu:li ča:n yri:d yiru:ħ ða:k ʔilʔisbu:ʕ] It seems to me he wanted to go last week. عَلَى ما أَعتِقِد راد يرُوح ذاك الإسبُوع [ʕala ma: ʔaʕtiqid ra:d yiru:ħ ða:k ʔilʔisbu:ʕ]

to seize • **1.** كُمَش [kumaš] كَمُش [kamuš] *vn:* اِنكُمَش [ʔinkumaš] *p:* لِزَم [lizam] لَزِم [lazim] *vn:* اِنلِزَم [ʔinlizam] *p:* He seized the rope with both hands. كُمَش الحَبِل بِيدَه [kumaš ʔilħabil bi:dah] • **2.** مِلَك [milak] مَلِك [malik] *vn:* اِنمِلَك [ʔinmilak] *p: sv* i. لِزَم [lizam] اِنلِزَم [ʔinlizam] *p:* Fear seized him. مِلَكَه الخَوف [milakah ʔilxawf] • **3.** سَيطَر [sayṭar] سَيطَرَة [sayṭara] *vn:* تسَيطَر [tsayṭar] *p:* لِزَم [lizam] اِنلِزَم [ʔinlizam] *p:* The police seized his papers. الشُّرطَة سَيطَرَت عَلَى أَوراقَه [ʔiššurṭa sayṭarat ʕala ʔawra:qah] • **4.** اِغتِنَم [ʔiɣtinam] اِغتِنام [ʔiɣtina:m] *vn:* اِنتِهَز [ʔintihaz] اِنتِهاز [ʔintiha:z] *vn:* If I don't seize this opportunity, it may be too late. مُحتَمَل يرُوح عَلَيّا كُلّشِي إِذا ما أَغتِنِم هالفُرصَة [muħtamal yiru:ħ ʕalayya kullši ʔiða ma: ʔaɣtinim halfurṣa]

seldom • **1.** نادِراً [na:diran] نادِراً ما [na:diran ma:] I seldom see him in the coffee shop. نادِراً ما أَشُوفَه بِالقَهوَة [na:diran ma: ʔašu:fah bilgahwa]

to select • **1.** اِنتِخَب [ʔintixab] اِنتِخاب [ʔintixa:b] *vn: sv* i. اِختار [ʔixta:r] اِختِيار [ʔixtiya:r] *vn: sv* a. Have you selected anything yet? اِنتِخَبت شِي لَو بَعَد؟ [ʔintixabit ši law baʕad?]

selection • **1.** مَجمُوعَة الأَشكال [maǰmu:ʕat ʔilʔaška:l] We have a big selection of shirts. عِدنا مَجمُوعَة مشكَلَة الأَشكال مِن الثِّياب [ʕidna maǰmu:ʕat ʔilʔaška:l min ʔiθθiyya:b]

selfish • **1.** أَناني [ʔana:ni] How can anyone be so selfish? شلُون واحِد يِقدَر يكُون هَالقَدّ أَناني؟ [šlu:n wa:ħid yigdar yku:n halgadd ʔana:ni?]

to sell • **1.** باع [ba:ʕ] بَيع [bayʕ] *vn:* اِنباع [ʔinba:ʕ] *p:* Did you sell your old car? بِعِت سَيّارتَك القَدِيمَة؟ [biʕit sayya:rtak ʔilqadi:ma?] Sorry the tickets are all sold out. مَعَ الأَسَف، التَّذاكِر اِنباعَت كُلّها [maʕa ʔilʔasaf, ʔittaða:kir ʔinba:ʕat kullha] • **2.** اِنباع [ʔinba:ʕ] *sv* a: How are the glasses selling? شلُون دَتِنباع الكلاصات؟ [šlu:n datinba:ʕ ʔilgla:ṣa:t?]

*** He sold us out to the enemy.** • **1.** خانّا ويّا الأَعداء [xa:nna wiyya ʔilʔaʕda:ʔ] / هُوَّ وِشَى بِينا لِلأَعداء [huwwa wiša: bi:na lilʔaʕda:ʔ]

Semite • **1.** سامِي [sa:mi] سامِيِّين [sa:miyyi:n] *pl:* The Semites established the first civilization in Iraq. السّامِيِّين أَنشَأُوا أَوَّل حَضارَة بِالعِراق [ʔissa:miyyi:n ʔanšaʔaw ʔawwal ħaḍa:ra bilʕira:q]

Semitic • **1.** سامِي [sa:mi] Arabic is a Semitic language. اللُّغَة العَرَبِيَّة هِيَّ لُغَة سامِيَّة [ʔilluɣa ʔilʕarabiyya hiyya luɣa sa:miyya]

to send • **1.** دَزّ [dazz] دَزّ [dazz] *vn:* اِندَزّ [ʔindazz] *p:* أَرسَل [ʔarsal] إِرسال [ʔirsa:l] *vn:* اِنرِسَل [ʔinrisal] *p:* بِعَث [biʕaθ] بَعِث [baʕiθ] *vn:* اِنبِعَث [ʔinbiʕaθ] *p:* Send it by mail. دِزّها بالبَرِيد [dizzha bilbari:d]

to send for • **1.** اِستَدعَى [ʔistadʕa:] اِستِدعاء [ʔistidʕa:ʔ] *vn: sv* i. Have you sent for the doctor? اِستَدعِيت طَبِيب؟ [ʔistadʕi:t ṭabi:b?]

to send in • **1.** دَخَّل [daxxal] تَدخِيل [tadxi:l] *vn:* تدَخَّل [tdaxxal] *p:* Send him in. دَخّلَه [daxxlah] Send him in. خَلِّيه يِدخُل [xalli:h yidxul]

to send out for • **1.** دَزّ عَلَى [dazz ʕala] دَزّ [dazz] *vn:* اِندَزّ [ʔindazz] *p:* Shall I send out for ice cream? ترِيد أَدِزّ عَلَى دوندِرمَة؟ [tri:d ʔadizz ʕala du:ndirma?]

senior • **1.** أَقدَم [ʔaqdam] أَسبَق [ʔasbaq] He's the senior man in the office. هُوَّ أَقدَم واحِد بِالمَكتَب [huwwa ʔaqdam wa:ħid bilmaktab]

sensation • **1.** ضَجَّة [ðajja] ضَجّات [ðajja:t] *pl:* حَماس [ħama:s] His speech created a sensation. حَدِيثَه أثار ضَجَّة كِبِيرَة [ħadi:θah ʔaθa:r ðajja čibi:ra] • **2.** شُعُور [šuʕu:r] It's a very pleasant sensation. هُوَّ فَدّ شُعُور لَطِيف [huwwa fadd šuʕu:r laṭi:f]

sense • **1.** حاسَّة [ħa:ssa] حَواسّ [ħawa:ss] *pl:* My dog has a keen sense of smell. كَلبِي عِندَه حاسَّة شَمّ قَوِيَّة [čalbi ʕindah ħa:ssat šamm qawiyya] • **2.** إدراك [ʔidra:k] عَقِل [ʕaqil] I hope he has sense enough to take a taxi. آمَل أن يكُون عِندَه إدراك كافِي حَتَّى ياخُذ تاكسِي [ʔa:mal ʔan yku:n ʕindah ʔidra:k ka:fi ħatta ya:xuð ta:ksi] • **3.** شُعُور [šuʕu:r] It gives us a sense of security. تِنطِينا شُعُور بالإطمِئنان [tinṭi:na šuʕu:r bilʔiṭmiʔna:n]

*** There's no sense in doing that.** • **1.** ما إلها مَعنَى تسَوِّيها [ma: ʔilha maʕna tsawwi:ha]

in a sense • **1.** مِن ناحِيَة [min na:ħiya] مِن جِهَة [min jiha] That's true, in a sense. مِن ناحِيَة هَذا صَحِيح [min na:ħiya ha:ða ṣaħi:ħ]

to sense • **1.** حَسّ [ħass] حِسّ [ħiss] *vn:* اِنحَسّ [ʔinħass] *p:* أدرَك [ʔadrak] إدراك [ʔidra:k] *vn:* اِندرَك [ʔindrak] *p:* I sensed right away that something was wrong. حَسَّيت رأساً أكُو فَدّ شِي غَلَط [ħassi:t raʔsan ʔaku fadd ši ɣalaṭ]

senseless • **1.** ما بِيها عَقِل [ma: bi:ha ʕaqil] It would be senseless to go out in this rain. ما بِيها عَقِل إذا تِطلَع بَرَّة بهالمُطَر [ma: bi:ha ʕaqil ʔiða tiṭlaʕ barra bha:lmuṭar]

sensible • **1.** عاقِل [ʕa:qil] مُدرِك [mudrik] Be sensible! كُون عاقِل [ku:n ʕa:qil]

sensitive • **1.** حَسّاس [ħassa:s] I'm sensitive to cold. آنِي حَسّاس لِلبَرِد [ʔa:ni ħassa:s lilbarid]

sentence • **1.** جُملَة [jumla] جُمَل [jumal] *pl:* I didn't understand the last sentence. ما إفتِهَمت الجُملَة الأخِيرَة [ma: ʔiftihamt ʔijjumla ʔilʔaxi:ra] • **2.** حُكُم [ħukum] أحكام [ʔaħka:m] *pl:* The judge has just pronounced sentence. الحاكِم هَسَّة أصدَر الحُكُم [ʔilħa:kim hassa ʔaṣdar ʔilħukum]

to sentence • **1.** حِكَم [ħikam] حُكُم [ħukum] *vn:* اِنحِكَم [ʔinħikam] *p:* He was sentenced to five years. اِنحِكَم خَمس سنِين [ʔinħikam xams sni:n]

sentry • **1.** حارِس [ħa:ris] حُرّاس [ħurra:s] *pl:* The sentry didn't let me pass. الحارِس ما خَلّانِي أفُوت [ʔilħa:ris ma: xalla:ni ʔafu:t]

separate • **1.** مِنفِصِل [minfiṣil] Could we have separate rooms? نِقدَر ناخُذ غُرَف مِنفَصلَه؟ [nigdar na:xuð ɣuraf minfaṣlah?]

to separate • **1.** فَرَّق [farraq, farrag] تَفرِيق [tafri:q] *vn:* تفَرَّق [tfarraq] *p:* I could hardly separate those two. بِصُعُوبَة قِدَرت أفَرِّق هالثّنَين [bṣuʕu:ba gidarit ʔafarriq haθθini:n] • **2.** قَسَّم [qassam] تَقسِيم [taqsi:m] *vn:* تقَسَّم [tqassam] *p:* Separate the group into five sections. قَسِّم الجَماعَة إلَى خَمِس أقسام [qassim ʔijjama:ʕa ʔila xamis ʔaqsa:m]

separately • **1.** عَلَى حِدَة [ʕala ħida] Can you buy each volume separately? تِقدَر تِشتِرِي كُلّ جُزُء عَلَى حِدَة؟ [tigdar tištiri kull juzuʔ ʕala ħida?]

September • **1.** أيلُول [ʔaylu:l]

sergeant • **1.** عَرِيف [ʕari:f] عُرَفاء [ʕurafa:ʔ] *pl:*

series • **1.** سِلسِلَة [silsila] سَلاسِل [sala:sil] *pl:* He's written a series of articles about it. كِتَب سِلسِلَة مَقالات عَنها [kitab silsilat maqa:la:t ʕanha]

serious • **1.** جِدِّي [jiddi] Why are you so serious? لِيش إنتَ هالقَدّ جِدِّي؟ [li:š ʔinta halgadd jiddi?] • **2.** مُهِمّ [muhimm] It isn't serious. مُو شِي مُهِمّ [mu: ši muhimm] • **3.** خَطَر [xaṭar] خَطِير [xaṭi:r] That's a serious mistake. هَذا غَلط خَطِر [ha:ða ɣalṭ xaṭir]

*** Are you serious?** • **1.** دَتِحكِي صُدُق؟ [datiħči ṣudug?]

seriously • **1.** جِدِّيَّة [jiddiyya] جِدِّيّات [jiddiyya:t] *pl:* عَن جِدّ [ʕan jidd] Don't take it so seriously. لا تاخُذها جِدِّيّات [la: ta:xuðha jiddiyya:t] I'm seriously considering getting married. آنِي جِدِّيّات دَأفَكِّر بِالزَّواج [ʔa:ni jiddiyya:t daʔafakkir bizzawa:j]

sermon • **1.** خُطبَة [xuṭba] خُطَب [xuṭab] *pl:* The Imam gave a good sermon Friday. الإمام خُطَب خُطبَة زينَة يوم الجُمعَة [ʔilʔima:m xuṭab xuṭba zi:na yu:m ʔijjumʕa]

servant • **1.** خادِم، خادِمَة [xa:dim, xa:dima] خُدّام، خَدَم [xudda:m, xadam] *pl:* I'm not your servant. آنِي مُو خادِم مالَك [ʔa:ni mu: xa:dim ma:lak]

serve • **1.** سِيرف [si:rv] Whose serve is it? بإيد من السِّيرف [bʔi:d man ʔissi:rv?]

to serve • **1.** قَدَّم [qaddam] تَقدِيم [taqdi:m] *vn:* تقَدَّم [tqaddam] *p:* *sv* i. Shall I serve the drinks now? أقَدِّم المَشرُوبات هَسَّة؟ [ʔaqaddim ʔalmašru:ba:t hassa?] • **2.** خِدَم [xidam] خَدِم [xadim] *vn:* *sv* i. He served in the Navy. خِدَم بِالبَحرِيَّة [xidam bilbaħriyya]

*** This will serve as a substitute.** • **1.** هاي راح تقُوم مَقامها [ha:y ra:ħ tqu:m maqa:mha]

*** Dinner is served!** • **1.** العَشا حاضِر [ʔilʕaša ħa:ðir] / العَشا جاهِز [ʔilʕaša ja:hiz] * That serves you right! تِستاهِلها [tista:hilha]

service • **1.** خِدمَة [xidma] خِدمات، خِدَم، خَدَمات [xidma:t, xidam, xadama:t] *pl:* The service is bad in this restaurant. الخِدمَة مُو زينَة بِهالمَطعَم [ʔilxidma mu: zi:na bhalmaṭʕam]

S

This is a civil service regulation. هَذا قانُون الخِدمَة المَدَنِيَّة [haːða qaːnuːn ʔilxidma ʔilmadaniyya] • **2.** جَيش [ǰayš, ǰiːš] جِيُوش [ǰiyuːš] *pl:* How long have you been in the service? شقَدّ صارلَك بِالجَّيش؟ [šgadd ṣaːrlak biǰǰayš?]

service station • **1.** مَحَطَّة بانزين [maħaṭṭat banziːn] مَحَطّات بانزين [maħaṭṭaːt banziːn] *pl:* بانزين خانَة [banziːn xaːna] بانزين خانات [banziːn xaːnaːt] *pl:* Let's stop at the next service station. خَلِّي نُوقف بمَحَطَّة البانزين الجّايَة [xalli nuːgaf bmaħaṭṭat ʔilbanziːn ʔiǰǰaːya]

set • **1.** طَخُم [ṭaxum] طخُوم [ṭxuːm] *pl:* مَجمُوعَة [maǰmuːʕa] مَجمُوعات [maǰmuːʕaːt] *pl:* We have a whole set of these ash trays. عِدنا طَخُم كامِل مِن هَالطَّبلات مال سِجايِر [ʕidna ṭaxum kaːmil min haṭṭablaːt maːl ǰigaːyir]

all set • **1.** حاضِر [ħaːðir] Everything all set? كُلّشِي حاضِر؟ [kullši ħaːðir?]

to set • **1.** حَطّ [ħaṭṭ] حَطّ [ħaṭṭ] *vn: sv* u. خَلَّى [xallaː] *sv* i. Set it on the desk. حُطّها عالميز [ħuṭṭha ʕalmiːz] • **2.** حَضَّر [ħaðđar] تَحضِير [taħðiːr] *vn:* تحَضَّر [tħaðđar] *p:* Quick, set the table! حَضّري الميز بالعَجَل [ħaðđiri ʔilmiːz bilʕaǰal] • **3.** نِصَب [niṣab] نَصُب [naṣub] *vn:* اِنّصَب [ʔinniṣab] *p:* I set my watch by the station clock. نِصَبِت ساعَتي عَلَى ساعَة المَحَطَّة [niṣabit saːʕati ʕala saːʕat ʔalmaħaṭṭa] • **4.** عَيَّن [ʕayyan] تَعيين [taʕyiːn] *vn:* تعَيَّن [tʕayyan] *p:* حَدَّد [ħaddad] تَحدِيد [taħdiːd] *vn:* تحَدَّد [tħaddad] *p:* Why don't you set the time? لِيش ما تعَيِّن الوَقت؟ [liːš maː tʕayyin ʔilwakit?] • **5.** كَرَّك [karrak] تَكرِيك [takriːk] *vn:* تكَرَّك [tkarrak] *p:* Is the hen setting on the eggs? الدِّجاجَة مكَرِّكَة عالبَيض؟ [ʔiddiǰaːǰa mkarrika ʕalbayð?] • **6.** جَبَّر [ǰabbar] تَجبِير [tajbiːr] *vn:* تجَبَّر [tǰabbar] *p:* The doctor will have to set your arm. الطَّبِيب لازِم يجَبُّر إيدَك [ʔiṭṭabiːb laːzim yǰabbur ʔiːdak] • **7.** رَكَّب [rakkab] تَركِيب [tarkiːb] *vn:* ترَكَّب [trakkab] *p: sv* i. He set the stone in a ring for me. رَكّبلِي الحَجَر عَالمِحبَس [rakkabli ʔilħaǰar ʕalmiħbas] • **8.** غُرَب [ɣurab] غَرُب [ɣarub] *vn:* اِنغُرَب [ʔinɣurab] *p:* The sun has already set. الشَّمِس غُربَت [ʔiššamis ɣurbat] • **9.** صَفَّف [ṣaffaf] تَصفِيف [taṣfiːf] *vn:* تصَفَّف [tṣaffaf] *p:* I want my hair washed and set. أرِيد شَعرِي ينغِسِل وَيتصَفَّف [ʔariːd šaʕri yinɣisil wyiṭṣaffaf] • **10.** بِدَى [bidaː] بِدايَة [bidaːya] *vn: sv* i. He set to work immediately. بِدا بِالعَمَل حالاً [bidaː bilʕamal ħaːlan]

*** You've got to set a good example.**

• **1.** لازِم تِجعَل مِن نَفسَك مَثَل لِغَيرَك [laːzim tiǰʕal min nafsak maθal liɣayrak]

to set ahead • **1.** قَدَّم [qaddam] تَقدِيم [taqdiːm] *vn:* تقَدَّم [tqaddam] *p:* I set my watch five minutes ahead. قَدَّمِت ساعَتِي خَمس دَقايِق [qaddamit saːʕti xams daqaːyiq]

to set at • **1.** حَدَّد [ħaddad] تَحدِيد [taħdiːd] *vn:* تحَدَّد [tħaddad] *p:* He set the price at fifty dinars. حَدَّد السِّعِر بِخَمسِين دِينار [ħaddad ʔissiʕir bxamsiːn dinaːr]

to set down • **1.** نَزَّل [nazzil] تَنزِيل [tanziːl] *vn:* تنَزَّل [tnazzal] *p:* Set the box down gently. نَزِّل الصَّندُوق عَلَى كَيفَك [nazzil ʔiṣṣanduːg ʕala kayfak]

to set free • **1.** أَطلَق سَراح [ʔaṭlaq saraːħ] إطلاق سَراح [ʔiṭlaːq saraːħ] *vn: sv* i. The prisoners were set free. المَسجُونِين أَطلِقَوا سَراحهُم [ʔilmasǰuːniːn ʔaṭliqaw saraːħhum]

to set off • **1.** فَجَّر [faǰǰar] تَفجِير [tafǰiːr] *vn:* تفَجَّر [tfaǰǰar] *p:* They didn't have time to set off the explosives. ما كان عِدهُم وَقِت يفَجّرُون المُتَفَجِّرات [maː čaːn ʕidhum wakit yfaǰǰruːn ʔilmutafaǰǰiraːt]

to set on • **1.** شَيَّش عَلَى [šayyaš ʕala] تَشيِيش [tašyiːš] *vn:* تشَيَّش [tšayyaš] *p:* عَلَى [ʕala] He set the dogs on me. شَيَّش الكِلاب عَلَيّا [šayyaš ʔiččilaːb ʕalayya]

to set out • **1.** توَجَّه [twaǰǰah] تَوَجُّه [tawaǰǰuh] *vn: sv* a. سافَر [saːfar] سَفَر [safar] *vn: sv* i. He set out for home on Monday. توَجَّه لبَيتَه يوم الإثنَين [twaǰǰah lbaytah yuːm ʔilʔiθnayn]

to set straight • **1.** عَدَّل [ʕaddal] تَعدِيل [taʕdiːl] *vn:* تعَدَّل [tʕaddal] *p:* Can you set me straight on this? تِقدَر تعَدِّلنِي بهاي؟ [tigdar tʕaddilni bhaːy?]

to set up • **1.** نِصَب [niṣab] نَصُب [naṣub] *vn:* اِنّصَب [ʔinniṣab] *p:* The new machines have just been set up. المَكايِن الجِّدِيدَة هَسَّة اِنّصبَت [ʔilmakaːyin ʔiǰǰidiːda hassa ʔinnuṣbat] • **2.** أَسَّس [ʔassas] تَأسِيس [taʔsiːs] *vn:* تأسَّس [tʔassas] *p:* Are you going to set up housekeeping? راح تأسِّس بَيت؟ [raːħ tʔassis bayt?] His father set him up in business. أَبُوه أَسَّسلَه شُغُل [ʔabuːh ʔassaslah šuɣul]

to settle • **1.** صَفَّى [ṣaffaː] تَصفِيَة [taṣfiya] *vn:* تصَفَّى [tṣaffaː] *p:* He settled his bill with his creditors. صَفَّى حسابَه مَعَ الدَّيّانَة [ṣaffaː ħsaːbah maʕa ʔiddayyaːna] • **2.** حَلّ [ħall] حَلّ [ħall] *vn:* اِنحَلّ [ʔinħall] *p:* You must settle the misundertanding between yourselves. لازِم تِحِلُّون الخِلاف بَيناتكُم [laːzim tħilluːn ʔilxilaːf baynaːtkum] • **3.** اِستَوطَن [ʔistawṭan] اِستِيطان [ʔistiːṭaːn] *vn: sv* i. The Americans settled their country gradually. الأمرِيكان اِستَوطِنَوا بَلَدهُم بِالتَّدرِيج [ʔilʔamriːkaːn ʔistawṭinaw baladhum bittadriːǰ] • **4.** سَكَّن [sakkan] تَسكِين [taskiːn] *vn:* تسَكَّن [tsakkan] *p:* The government is going to settle farmers on the newly developed land. الحُكُومَة راح تسَكِّن الفَلّاحِين بِالأراضِي المُستَثمَرَة حَدِيثاً [ʔilħukuːma raːħ tsakkin ʔilfallaːħiːn bilʔaraːði ʔilmustaθmara ħadiːθan] • **5.** اِستَقَرّ [ʔistaqarr] اِستِقرار [ʔistiqraːr] *vn:* The Bedouin don't want to settle anywhere. البَدو ما يرِيدُون يِستِقِرُّون بأَي مُكان [ʔilbadw maː yriːduːn yistiqirruːn bʔayy mukaːn] • **6.** The wall has settled a little. الحَيط طاخ شوَيَّة [ʔilħayiṭ ṭaːx šwayya] • **7.** ترَسَّب [trassab] تَرَسُّب [tarassub] *vn: sv* a. Wait until the coffee grounds have settled. اِنتِظِر إلَى أَن يترَسَّب التِّلِف مال القَهوَة [ʔintiðir ʔila ʔan yitrassab ʔittilif maːl ʔilgahwa] • **8.** نِهَى [nihaː] نَهي [nahy] *vn:* اِنّهَى [ʔinihaː] *p:* That settles the matter. هَذا ينهِي المَسأَلَة [haːða yinhi ʔilmasʔala]

S

settled people • **1.** حَضَر [ħaðar] There is a great difference in the lives of nomad and settled peoples. أكُو فرق كِبِير بِحَياة البَدو والحَضَر [ʔaku fariq čibiːr bħayaːt ʔilbadw walħaðar]

settlement • **1.** اِتِّفاق [ʔittifaːq] اِتِّفاقات [ʔittifaːqaːt] *pl:* They couldn't reach a settlement. ما قِدرَوا يوصلُون إلَى اِتِّفاق [maː gidraw yuːṣluːn ʔila ʔittifaːq] • **2.** مَأوَى [maʔwa] مَآوِي [maʔaːwi] *pl:* مُستَقَرّ [mustaqarr] مُستَقَرّات [mustaqarraːt] *pl:* We uncovered the remains of an ancient settlement. اِكتِشَفنا آثار مَأوَى قَدِيم [ʔiktišafna ʔaːθaːr maʔwaː qadiːm]

seven • **1.** سَبِع [sabiʕ] He's seven years old. عُمرَه سَبِع سِنِين [ʕumrah sabiʕ siniːn] • **2.** سَبعَة [sabʕa] I was there seven days. بُقيت هناك سَبعَة أيّام [buqiːt hnaːk sabʕa ʔayyaːm] • **3.** سَبعَة [sabʕa] سَبعات، سِبَع [sabʕaːt, sibaʕ] *pl:* These numbers are all sevens. هَالأرقام كُلّها سَبعات [halʔarraqaːm kullha sabʕaːt]

seventeen • **1.** سباطَعَش [sbaːṭaʕaš]

seventeenth • **1.** السَّبَاطَعَش [ʔissbaːṭaʕaš]

seventh • **1.** سابِع [saːbiʕ]

seventieth • **1.** السَّبعين [ʔissabʕiːn]

seventy • **1.** سَبعِين [sabʕiːn]

several • **1.** عِدَّة [ʕidda] I'd like to stay here for several days. أرِيد أبقَى هنا عِدَّة أيّام [ʔariːd ʔabqaː hnaː ʕiddat ʔayyaːm]

severe • **1.** قاسِي [qaːsi] قُساة [qusaːt] *pl:* It was a very severe winter. كان الشِّتا قاسِي [čaːn ʔiššitaː qaːsi] • **2.** شَدِيد [šadiːd] حادّ [ħaːdd] She complains of severe pains. هِيَّ تِشكِي مِن آلام شَدِيدَة [hiyya tiški min ʔaːlaːm šadiːda]

to sew • **1.** خَيَّط [xayyaṭ] تَخيِيط [taxyiːṭ] *vn:* تخَيَّط [txayyaṭ] *p:* She sews her own clothes. تخَيِّط هدُومها بنَفِسها [txayyiṭ hduːmha bnafisha] Please sew the buttons on for me. رَجاءاً خَيِّطلِي الدِّقَم [rajaːʔan xayyiṭli ʔiddigam]

sewer • **1.** بُربُخ [burbux] بَرابِخ [baraːbix] *pl:* The sewer is clogged. البُربُخ مَسدُود [ʔilburbux masduːd]

sex • **1.** جِنِس [ǰinis] In your application, state your age and sex. بطَلَبَك إذكُر العُمُر وَالجِنِس [bṭalabak ʔiðkur ʔilʕumur wiǰǰinis] • **2.** جِنسِي [ǰinsi] She's got a lot of sex appeal. عِدها هوايَة جاذِبِيَّة جِنسِيَّة [ʕidha hwaːya ǰaːðibiyya ǰinsiyya]

sexual • **1.** جِنسِي [ǰinsi] He has sexual relations with her. عِندَه عِلاقَة جِنسِيَّة وِيّاها [ʕindah ʕilaːqa ǰinsiyya wiyyaːha]

sexy • **1.** مُهَيِّج [muhayyiǰ] She's a very sexy girl. هِيَّ فَدّ بِنت كُلِّش تهَيِّج [hiyya fadd bint kulliš thayyiǰ]

shabby • **1.** مشَقَّق [mšaggag] His suit looks shabby. بَدِلتَه تبَيِّن مشَقَّقَة [badiltah tbayyin mšaggiga] • **2.** خَسِيس [xasiːs] دَنِيئ [daniːʔ] أدنِياء [ʔadniyaːʔ] *pl:* That was very shabby of him. هاي كانَت كُلِّش خِسَّة مِنَّه [haːy čaːnat kulliš xissa minnah]

shade • **1.** ظِلّ [ðill] أظلال، ظِلال [ʔaðlaːl, ðilaːl] *pl:* فَيّ [fayy] • **2.** بَردَة [parda] بَردات [pardaːt] *pl:* Pull down the shades. نَزِّل البَردات [nazzil ʔilpardaːt] • **3.** لَون [lawn] ألوان [ʔalwaːn] *pl:* This red is too dark a shade. هَذا اللَّون الأحمَر شوَيَّة طُوخ [haːða ʔilluːn ʔilʔaħmar šwayya ṭuːx]

shadow • **1.** خَيال [xayaːl] خَيالات [xayaːlaːt] *pl:* The trees cast long shadows. الأشجار تسَوِّي خَيالات طوِيلَة [ʔilʔašǰaːr tsawwi xayaːlaːt ṭwiːla]

*** There is not a shadow of doubt about it.** • **1.** ما بِيها شَكّ أبَداً [maː biːha šakk ʔabadan]

to shadow • **1.** راقَب [raːqab] مُراقَبَة [muraːqaba] *vn:* تراقَب [traːqab] *p:* They assigned a detective to shadow him. عَيّنَوا شُرطِي سِرِّي حَتَّى يراقبَه [ʕayynaw šurṭi sirri ħatta yraːqbah]

shady • **1.** That's a shady business. هاي شَغلَة مَشبُوهَة [haːy šaɣla mašbuːha] * It's shady over here. بِيها فَيّ هنا [biːha fayy hna]

shaft • **1.** شَفت [šaft] شَفتات [šaftaːt] *pl:* The shaft on this machine is bent. شَفت هَالمَكِينَة مَعوُج [šaft halmakiːna maʕwuːǰ]

to shake • **1.** هَزّ [hazz] هَزّ [hazz] *vn:* اِنهَزّ [ʔinhazz] *p:* He shook his head. هَزّ راسَه [hazz raːsah] • **2.** خَضّ [xaðð] خَضّ [xaðð] *vn:* اِنخَضّ [ʔinxaðð] *p:* Shake it well before using it. خُضّها زين قَبُل ما تِستَعمِلها [xuððha ziːn gabul maː tistaʕmilha] • **3.** رَجّ [rajj] رَجّ [rajj] *vn:* اِنرَجّ [ʔinrajj] *p:* The earthquake shook everything in the city. الزَّلزِلَة رَجَّت كُلشِي بالمَدِينَة [ʔizzalzila rajjat kullši bilmadiːna]

*** Come on, shake a leg!** • **1.** يا الله، إستَعجِل [yalla, ʔistaʕjil]

to shake hands • **1.** تصافَح [tṣaːfaħ] تَصافُح [taṣaːfuħ] *vn: sv* a. They shook hands. تصافحَوا [tṣaːfħaw]

shaky • **1.** مِرتِعِش [mirtiʕiš] I'm still shaky. آنِي بَعَدنِي مِرتِعِش [ʔaːni baʕadni mirtiʕiš] • **2.** مقَلقَل [mgalgal] The table's shaky. الميز مقَلقَل [ʔilmiːz mgalgal]

shall • **1.** راح [raːħ] عُود [ʕuːd] أعواد [ʔaʕwaːd] *pl:* We shall see who's right. راح نشُوف مِنُو مَضبُوط [raːħ nšuːf minu maðbuːṭ]

S

*** I'll never go there.** • **1.** أبَد ما رُوح هناك [ʔabad maː ruːħ hnaːk]

*** Shall I wait?** • **1.** ترِيد أنتِظِر؟ [triːd ʔantiðir?]

shallow • **1.** ضَحِل [ðaħil] The lake is very shallow in this area. البُحَيرَة كُلِّش ضَحلَة بِهَالمَنطِقَة [ʔilbuħayra kulliš ðaħla bhalmantiga] He's a very shallow person. هُوَّ فَدّ واحِد كُلِّش ضَحِل [huwwa fadd waːħid kulliš ðaħil] • **2.** مُو غَمِيق [muː ɣamiːǰ] Put it in a shallow bowl. حُطّها بمِنكاسَة مُو غَمِيقَة [ħuṭṭha bminčaːsa muː ɣamiːǰa]

shame • **1.** خَجَل [xaǰal] Haven't you any shame? ما عِندَك أيّ خَجَل؟ [maː ʕindak ʔayy xaǰal?] Haven't you any shame? ما تِستِحِي أبَد؟ [maː tistiħi ʔabad?] • **2.** عيب [ʕayb, ʕiːb] عيُوب [ʕyuːb] *pl:* Shame on you! عِيب عَلِيك [ʕiːb ʕaliːk]

*** What a shame you can't come!** • **1.** مَعَ الأسَف مَا تِقدَر تِجِي [maʕa ʔilʔasaf maː tigdar tiǰi]

shape • **1.** شِكِل [šikil] أشكال، شكُول [ʔaškaːl, škuːl] *pl:* What shape is the table? شلُون شِكلَه لِلمَيز [šluːn šiklah lilmayz] • **2.** حالَة [ħaːla] حالات [ħaːlaːt] *pl:* What shape is the car in? شلُون حالَة السَّيّارَة؟ [šluːn ħaːlat ʔissayyaːra?] • **3.** وَضعِيَّة [waðʕiyya] وَضعِيّات [waðʕiyyaːt] *pl:* حالَة [ħaːla] حالات [ħaːlaːt] *pl:* I'm in bad shape. وَضعِيّتِي مُو زينَة [waðʕiːti muː ziːna]

in shape • **1.** حاضِر [ħaːðir] Is everything in shape? كُلشِي حاضِر؟ [kullši ħaːðir?]

out of shape • **1.** مُعَقَّج، مَعقُوش [muʕaqqač, mʕaqqač] مَعقُوج [maʕquːč] The hat's all out of shape. الشَّفقَة كُلها معَقَّجَة [ʔiššafqa kullha mʕaqqača]

to shape up • **1.** تحَسَّن [tħassan] تَحَسُّن [taħassun] *vn: sv* i. Things are gradually shaping up. الأشياء تَدرِيجِياً دَتِتحَسَّن [ʔilʔašyaːʔ tadriːǰiyyan datitħassan]

share • **1.** حُصَّة [ħuṣṣa] حُصَص [ħuṣaṣ] *pl:* سَهَم [saham] أسهُم [ʔashum] *pl:* Everybody has to pay his share. كُلّ واحِد لازِم يِدفَع حُصّتَه [kull waːħid laːzim yidfaʕ ħuṣṣtah] • **2.** سَهِم [sahim] أسهُم [ʔashum] *pl:* How many shares did you buy? كَم سَهِم اِشتِرَيت؟ [čam sahim ʔištiriːt?]

to share • **1.** تشارَك ب [tšaːrak b-] تَشارُك [tašaːruk] *vn: sv* i. Let's share the cake. خَلِّي نِتشارَك بِالكَيكَة [xalli nitšaːrak bilkayka]

to share with • **1.** شارَك ب [šaːrak b-] مُشارَكَة [mušaːraka] *vn: sv* i. Will you share my lunch with me? تِقدَر تشارِكنِي بِالغَدا؟ [tigdar tšaːrikni bilɣadaː?]

shareholder • **1.** مُساهِم [musaːhim] مُساهِمِين [musaːhimiːn] *pl:*

shark • **1.** كَوسَج [kuːsaǰ] كَواسِج، كواسِج [kawaːsiǰ, kwaːsiǰ] *pl:*

loan shark • **1.** مُرابِي [muraːbi] مُرابِين [muraːbiːn] *pl:*

sharp • **1.** حادّ [ħaːdd] Do you have a sharp knife? عِندَك سِچِّينَة حادَّة؟ [ʕindak siččiːna ħaːdda?] • **2.** لاذِع [laːðiʕ] سَلِيط [saliːt] She has a sharp tongue. عِدها لسان لاذِع [ʕidha lsaːn laːðiʕ] • **3.** بِالضَبُط [biððabuṭ] تَماماً [tamaːman] We have to be there at five o'clock sharp. لازِم نكُون هناك ساعَة خَمسَة بِالضبُط [laːzim nkuːn hnaːk saːʕa xamsa biððabuṭ]

*** Keep a sharp eye on him.** • **1.** راقبَه زَين [raːqbah zayn]

to sharpen • **1.** حَدّ [ħadd] حَدّ [bary] *vn:* اِنحَدّ [ʔinħadd] *p:* This knife needs sharpening. هَالسِّچِّينَة تِحتاج حَدّ [hassiččiːna tiħtaːǰ ħadd] • **2.** قَطّ [qaṭṭ] قَطّ [qaṭṭ] *vn:* اِنقَطّ [ʔinqaṭṭ] *p:* برَى [biraː] بَرِي [bariː] *vn:* اِنبرَى [ʔinbiraː] *p:* Sharpen the pencil for me, please. قُطّلِي القَلَم مِن فَضلَك [quṭṭli ʔilqalam min faðlak]

shave • **1.** حِلاقَة [ħilaːqa] حِلاقات [ħilaːqaːt] *pl:* زيان [ziyaːn] زِيانات [ziyaːnaːt] *pl:* I want a shave and a haircut. أرِيد حِلاقَة وُجهِي وزيان شَعَري [ʔariːd ħilaːqat wučči wziyaːn šaʕari]

to shave • **1.** زَيَّن [zayyan] زيان [ziyaːn] *vn:* تزَيَّن [tzayyan] *p:* حِلَق [ħilaq] حِلاقَة [ħilaːqa] *vn:* اِنحِلَق [ʔinħilaq] *p:* Who shaved you? مِنُو زَيَّنَك؟ [minu zayyanak?] Who shaved you? مِنُو حِلَق وِجهَك؟ [minu ħilaq wiččak?]

she • **1.** هِيَّ [hiyya] هَذِي [haːði] هاي [haːy] She is a capable woman. هِيَّ مرَيَّة مُقتَدرَة [hiyya mrayya muqtadra]

*** She was in town last night.** • **1.** كانَت بِالبَلَد البارحَة بِاللَيل [čaːnat bilbalad ʔilbaːrħa billayl]

shed • **1.** عَنبار [ʕambaːr] عَنابِير [ʕanaːbiːr] *pl:* مَخزَن [maxzan] مَخازِن [maxaːzin] *pl:* Put the tools back in the shed. رَجِّع الأدَوات لِلعَنبَر [raǰǰiʕ ʔilʔadawaːt lilʕambar]

to shed • **1.** ألقَى [ʔalqaː] إلقاء [ʔilqaːʔ] *vn:* اِنلَقى [ʔinlqaː] *p:* That sheds some light on the matter. هَذا يِلقِي ضَوء عَالمَوضُوع [haːða yilqi ðawʔ ʕalmawðuːʕ] • **2.** نِزَع [nizaʕ] نَزِع [naziʕ] *vn: sv* a. ذَبّ [ðabb] ذَبّ [ðabb] *vn:* اِنذَبّ [ʔinðabb] *p:* As soon as I got into my room I shed all my clothes. أوَّل ما وُصَلِت لغُرُفتِي نِزَعِت كُلّ هدُومِي [ʔawwal maː wuṣalit ʔilɣurufti nizaʕit kull hduːmi] • **3.** ذِرَف [ðiraf] ذَرِف [ðarif] *vn:* اِنذِرَف [ʔinðiraf] *p:* She shed bitter tears. ذِرفَت دمُوع حارَّة [ðirfat dumuːʕ ħaːrra] • **4.** ذَبّ [ðabb] ذَبّ [ðabb] *vn: sv* i. My dog's shedding his hair. كَلبِي دَيذِبّ شَعرَه [čalbi dayðibb šaʕrah] • **5.** مِنَع [minaʕ] مَنِع [maniʕ] *vn: sv* a. This overcoat doesn't shed water at all. هالقَبُّوط ما يِمنَع المُطَر بِالمَرَّة [halqappuːṭ maː yimnaʕ ʔilmuṭar bilmarra]

sheep • **1.** خَرُوف [xaruːf] خِرفان [xirfaːn] *pl:* غَنَم [ɣanam] أغنام [ʔaɣnaːm] *pl:* غَنَم [ɣanam] *Collective*

sheer • **1.** صِرف [ṣirf] That's sheer nonsense. هَذِي سَخافَة صِرف [haːði saxaːfa ṣirf] • **2.** شَفّاف [šaffaːf]

S

I'd like some sheer material like voile. أريد قماش شَفّاف مِثل الوايل [ʔari:d qma:š šaffa:f miθl ʔilwa:yil]

sheet • **1.** شَرشَف [čarčaf] شَراشِف [čara:čif] *pl:* Shall I change the sheets? تريد أغَيِّر الشَراشِف؟ [tri:d ʔaɣayyir ʔiččara:čif?] • **2.** قُطعَة [qutʕa] قُطعات [qutʕa:t] *pl:* Please give me a sheet of paper. رَجاءاً إنطِيني فَدّ قُطعَة وَرَق [raǰa:ʔan ʔinṭi:ni fadd qutʕat waraq] • **3.** طَبقَة [ṭabqa] طَبقات [ṭabqa:t] *pl:* لَوحَة [lawħa] لَوحات [lawħa:t] *pl:* We bought a sheet of plywood. اِشتِرَينا طَبقَة خِشَب مُعاكِس [ʔištiri:na ṭabqat xišab muʕa:kis]

*** She turned as white as a sheet.**
• **1.** وُجِهها صار أصفر مِثل الكُركُم [wuǰihhaA ṣa:r ʔaṣfar miθl ʔilkurkum]

sheik • **1.** شَيخ [šayx] شيُوخ [šyu:x] *pl:*

shelf • **1.** رَفّ [raff] رفُوف [rfu:f] *pl:* The shelves are empty. الرُّفُوف خالِيَة [ʔirrufu:f xa:lya]

shell • **1.** قِشِر [gišir] قشُور [gšu:r] *pl:* The hazelnut shell is hard. قِشِر البُندُق قَوي [gišir ʔilbunduq qawi] • **2.** قُنبُلَة [qunbula] قَنابِل [qana:bil] *pl:* A shell exploded near our house. فَدّ قُنبُلَة اِنفِجرَت يَمّ بَيتنا [fadd qunbula ʔinfiǰrat yamm baytna] • **3.** صَدفَة [ṣadfa] صَدفات [ṣadfa:t] *pl:* صَدَف [ṣadaf] *Collective:* What'll I do with the shells of the snails? شَأسَوّي بِصِدَف الحَلَزُون هاي؟ [šʔasawwi bṣidaf ʔilħalazu:n ha:y?]

to shell • **1.** قَشَّر [gaššar] تَقشِير [tagši:r] *vn:* تقَشَّر [tgaššar] *p:* Do you want to shell the nuts? تريد تقَشِّر الجُوز؟ [tri:d tgaššir ʔiǰǰu:z?] • **2.** فَلَّس [fallas] تَفلِيس [tafli:s] *vn:* تفَلَّس [tfallas] *p:* قَشَّر [gaššar] تَقشِير [tagši:r] *vn:* تقَشَّر [tgaššar] *p:* The peas have to be shelled. البَزالِيَة لازِم تِتفَلَّس [ʔilbaza:lya la:zim titfallas] • **3.** ضِرَب بالقَنابِل [ðirab bilqana:bul] ضَرِب [ðarib] *vn:* اِنضِرَب [ʔinðirab] *p:* The army shelled the town. الجَّيش ضِربَوا المَدِينَة بالقَنابُل [ʔiǰǰayš ðirbaw ʔilmadi:na bilqana:bul]

shelter • **1.** مَلجَأ [malǰaʔ] مَلاجِئ [mala:ǰiʔ] *pl:* مَأوَى [maʔwa] مَآوِي [maʔa:wi] *pl:* We found shelter in a hut during the storm. اِتِّخَذنا الكُوخ مَلجَأ أثناء العاصِفَة [ʔittixaðna ʔilku:x malǰaʔ ʔaθna:ʔ ʔilʕa:ṣifa]

to shelter • **1.** آوَى [ʔa:wa:] They sheltered and fed us. آوُونا وَطَعّمَونا [ʔa:wu:na wtaʕʕmu:na]

shepherd • **1.** راعِي [ra:ʕi] رِعيان [riʕya:n] *pl:*

shield • **1.** دِرع [diriʕ] درُوع [dru:ʕ] *pl:* He has a collection of shields and swords. عِندَه مَجمُوعَة مِن الدُّرُوع وَالسِّيُوف [ʕindah maǰmu:ʕa min ʔidduru:ʕ wissiyu:f]

to shield • **1.** حِمَى [ħima:] حِمايَة [ħima:ya] *vn:* اِنحِمَى [ʔinħima:] *p:* حِفَظ [ħifað] حَفُظ [ħafuð] *vn:* اِنحِفَظ [ʔinħifað] *p:* You ought to shield your eyes against the sun. لازِم تِحمِي عينَك مِن الشَّمِس [la:zim tiħmi ʕaynak min ʔiššamis] • **2.** تسَتَّر عَلَى [tsattar ʕala] تَسَتُّر [tasattur] *vn:* *sv* a. حِمَى [ħima:] حِمايَة [ħima:ya] *vn:* اِنحِمَى [ʔinħima] *p:* *sv* i. He must be shielding someone. لازِم دَيِتسَتَّر عَلَى فَدّ أحَّد [la:zim dayitsattar ʕala fadd ʔaħħad]

shift • **1.** دَفعَة [dafʕa] دَفعات [dafʕa:t] *pl:* وَجبَة [waǰba] وَجبات [waǰba:t] *pl:* Our workers work in two shifts. عُمّالنا يِشتَغلُون عَلَى دُفِعتَين [ʕumma:lna yištaɣlu:n ʕala dufiʕtayn]

to shift • **1.** بَدَّل [baddal] تَبدِيل [tabdi:l] *vn:* تبَدَّل [tbaddal] *p:* You ought to shift into second. لازِم تبَدِّل كَير عَالثَّنَين [la:zim tbaddil gi:r ʕaθθinayn] • **2.** غَيَّر [ɣayyar] تَغيِير [taɣyi:r] *vn:* تغَيَّر [tɣayyar] *p:* بَدَّل [baddal] تَبدِيل [tabdi:l] *vn:* تبَدَّل [tbaddal] *p:* We have to shift the meeting to Tuesday. لازِم نغَيِّر الاِجتِماع إلَى الثَّلاثاء [la:zim nɣayyir ʔilʔiǰtima:ʕ ʔila ʔiθθila:θa:ʔ] • **3.** تغَيَّر [tɣayyar] تَغَيُّر [taɣayyur] *vn:* *sv* a. The direction of the wind has shifted. الهَوا تغَيَّر اتِّجاهَه [ʔilhawa tɣayyar ʔittiǰa:hah]

*** I've always had to shift for myself.**
• **1.** آني كِنِت مِضطَرّ دائِماً أدَبُّر أمُوري بنَفسِي [ʔa:ni: činit miðṭarr da:ʔiman ʔadabbur ʔumu:ri: bnafsi]

shin • **1.** ساق [sa:q] سِيقان [si:qa:n] *pl:* I got kicked in the shinbone. أكَلِت ضَربَة عَلَى عَظمَة ساقِي [ʔakalit ðarba ʕala ʕaðmat sa:qi]

shine • **1.** لَمعَة [lamʕa] لَمعات [lamʕa:t] *pl:* See if you can take the shine out of these pants. شُوف إذا تِقدَر توَخِّر اللَّمعَة مِن هَالبَنطَرُون [šu:f ʔiða tigdar twaxxir ʔillamʕa min halpanṭaru:n]

to shine • **1.** شَعّ [šaʕʕ] شَعّ [šaʕʕ] *vn:* اِنشَعّ [ʔinšaʕʕ] *p:* *sv* i. لِمَع [limaʕ] لِمِع [lamiʕ] *vn:* اِنلِمَع [ʔinlimaʕ] *p:* Her eyes were shining with joy. عيُونها كانَت دَتشِعّ مِن الفَرَح [ʕyu:nha ča:nat datšiʕʕ min ʔilfaraħ] • **2.** بَدَّع [baddaʕ] تَبدِيع [tabdi:ʕ] *vn:* تبَدَّع [tbaddaʕ] *p:* He's good in all his subjects, but mathematics is where he shines. هَذا زين بِكُلّ درُوسَه بَسّ يبَدِّع عَلَى الأخَصّ بِالرِّياضِيّات [ha:ða zi:n bkull dru:sah bass ybaddiʕ ʕala ʔilʔaxaṣṣ birriya:ðiyya:t] • **3.** صُبَغ [ṣubaɣ] صَبُغ [ṣabuɣ] *vn:* اِنصُبَغ [ʔinṣubaɣ] *p:* I have to shine my shoes. لازِم أصبُغ قُندَرتِي [la:zim ʔaṣbuɣ qundarti]

*** The sun isn't shining today.** • **1.** الشَّمِس ما طالعَة اليَوم [ʔiššamis ma: ṭa:lʕa ʔilyawm]

ship • **1.** باخِرَة [ba:xira] بَواخِر [bawa:xir] *pl:* When does the ship leave? شوَقِت تغادِر الباخِرَة؟ [šwakit tɣa:dir ʔilba:xira?]

to ship • **1.** شِحَن [šiħan] شَحِن [šaħin] *vn:* اِنشِحَن [ʔinšiħan] *p:* دَزّ [dazz] دَزّ [dazz] *vn:* اِندَزّ [ʔindazz] *p:* Has the case been shipped yet? الصَّندُوق اِنشِحَن لَو بَعَد؟ [ʔiṣṣandu:g ʔinšiħan law baʕad?]

S

shipment • **1.** شَحنَة [šaħna] شَحنات [šaħna:t] *pl:* إرساليَّة [ʔirsa:liyya] إرساليّات [ʔirsa:liyya:t] *pl:* We've just received a new shipment of shoes. هَسَّة اِستِلَمنا شَحنَة جِديدَة مِن الأَحذِيَة [hassa ʔistilamna šaħna ǰidi:da min ʔalʔaħðiya]

shipwreck • **1.** حُطام سَفينَة [ħuṭa:m safi:na]

shirt • **1.** ثُوب [θu:b] ثِياب [θya:b] *pl:* قَمِيص [qami:ṣ] قُمصان [qumṣa:n] *pl:* Are my shirts back from the laundry? ثيابِي رِجعَت مِن المَكوي؟ [θya:bi riǰʕat min ʔilmakwi?]

*** He'd give you the shirt off his back.** • **1.** إيدَه مُو إلَه [ʔi:dah mu: ʔilah] / هُوَّ كُلِّش بَرمَكِي [huwwa kulliš barmaki]

*** Keep your shirt on, I'll be right there.** • **1.** لا تَخبُصنِي، آنِي جاي [la: taxbuṣni, ʔa:ni ǰa:y]

shish kebab • **1.** تِكَّة [tikka]

to shiver • **1.** رِجَف [riǰaf] رَجِف [raǰif] *vn:* اِنرِجَف [ʔinriǰaf] *p:* رِعَش [riʕaš] رَعِش [raʕiš] *vn:* اِنرِعَش [ʔinriʕaš] *p:* The child shivered with cold. الطِّفِل رِجَف مِن البَرِد [ʔiṭṭifil riǰaf min ʔilbarid]

shock • **1.** صَدمَة [ṣadma] صَدمات [ṣadma:t] *pl:* His death was a great shock to us all. مُوتَه كانَت صَدمَة عَنِيفَة عَلينا كُلّنا [mu:tah ča:nat ṣadma ʕani:fa ʕali:na kullna] He's still suffering from shock. بَعَد يقاسِي مِن الصَّدمَة [baʕad yqa:si min ʔiṣṣadma] • **2.** نَتِل [natil] You can get a bad shock from this machine. مُمكِن تاكُل نَتِل قَوِي مِن هالمَكِينَة [mumkin ta:kul natil qawi min halmaki:na] • **3.** كُوم [ku:m] كُوام [kuwam] *pl:* They stacked up the wheat in shocks. كَدِّسَوا الحُنطَة عَلَى شِكِل قوان [kaddisaw ʔilħunṭa ʕala šikil qwa:n]

to get a shock • **1.** اِنِّتَل [ʔinnital] *sv* i. I got a shock from the lamp. اِنِّتَلت مِن الضُّوَّة [ʔinnitalit min ʔiððuwwa]

to shock • **1.** صِعَق [ṣiʕaq] صَعِق [ṣaʕiq] *vn:* اِنصِعَق [ʔinṣiʕaq] *p:* صِدَم [ṣidam] صَدِم [ṣadim] *vn:* اِنصِدَم [ʔinṣidam] *p:* I was shocked by the death of his father. اِنصِعَقِت بخَبَر موت أبُوه [ʔinṣiʕaqit bxabar mawt ʔabu:h]

shockproof • **1.** ضِدّ الكَسَر [ðidd ʔilkasar] This watch isn't shockproof. هَالسّاعَة مُو ضِدّ الكَسَر [hassa:ʕa mu: ðidd ʔilkasar]

shoe • **1.** قُندَرَة [qundara] قَنادِر [qana:dir] *pl:* حِذاء [ħiða:ʔ] أَحذِيَة [ʔaħðiya] *pl:* I'd like a pair of shoes. أَرِيد زَوج قَنادِر [ʔari:d zawǰ qana:dir] • **2.** نَعَل [naʕal] نَعلات [naʕla:t] *pl:* The horse lost one shoe. الحصان وَقَّع نَعَل مِن نعالاتَه [ʔilħṣa:n waggaʕ naʕal min nʕa:la:tah]

to shoe • **1.** نَعَّل [naʕʕal] تَنعِيل [tanʕi:l] *vn:* *sv* i. The horse needs shoeing. الحصان يِرّادلَه تَنعِيل [ʔilħṣa:n yirra:dlah tanʕi:l]

shoehorn • **1.** كَرَتَة [karata] كَرَتات [karata:t] *pl:*

shoelace • **1.** قِيطان [qi:ṭa:n] قياطِين [qya:ṭi:n] *pl:* I want a pair of shoelaces. أَرِيد زوج قياطِين [ʔari:d zawǰ qya:ṭi:n]

shoemaker • **1.** قُندَرجِي [qundarči] قُندَرجِيَّة [qundarčiyya] *pl:* Is there a shoemaker nearby? أَكُو قُندَرجِي قَرِيب مِن هنا؟ [ʔaku qundarči qari:b min hna?]

shoe polish • **1.** صُبُغ قَنادِر [ṣubuɣ qana:dir]

shoeshine • **1.** صُبُغ قُندَرَة [ṣubuɣ qundara] I need a shoeshine. أَحتاج صُبُغ قُندَرَة [ʔaħta:ǰ ṣubuɣ qundara]

to shoot • **1.** رِمَى [rima:] رَمِي [ramy] *vn:* *sv* i. أَطلَق [ʔaṭlaq] إطلاق [ʔiṭla:q] *vn:* *sv* i. He shot the gun four times. رِمَى البُندُقِيَّة أَربَع مَرّات [rima: ʔilbunduqiyya ʔarbaʕ marra:t] • **2.** ضُرَب [ðurab] ضَرُب [ðarub] *vn:* *sv* u. He shot him in the back and killed him. ضِرَبَه رِصاصَه بظَهرَه وَمَوَّتَه [ðirabah riṣa:ṣa bðahrah wmawwatah] • **3.** خِطَف [xiṭaf] خَطُف [xaṭuf] *vn:* اِنخِطَف [ʔinxiṭaf] *p:* The car shot past us. السَّيّارَة خُطفَت مِن يَمّنا [ʔissayya:ra xuṭfat min yammna] • **4.** مَدَّد [maddad] تَمدِيد [tamdi:d] *vn:* *sv* i. طَلَّع [ṭallaʕ] تَطلِيع [taṭli:ʕ] *vn:* *sv* i. The seed, when it starts growing, shoots out roots. الحَبَّة مِن تِنبِت تمَدِّد جذُور [ʔilħabba min tinbit tmaddid ǰdu:r] • **5.** أَخَذ مِن، أَخَذ عَلَى [ʔaxað min, ʔaxað ʕala] أَخِذ [ʔaxið] *vn:* اِنأَخَذ [ʔinʔaxað] *p:* I shot eight pictures today. أَخَذِت ثَمَن صُوَر اليُوم [ʔaxaðit θaman ṣuwar ʔilyu:m]

*** You ought to be shot for that.** • **1.** يِنرادلَك تَعلِيق عَلَيها [yinra:dlak taʕli:g ʕali:ha]

to shoot down • **1.** وَقَّع [waggaʕ] تَوقِيع [tawgi:ʕ] *vn:* توَقَّع [twaggaʕ] *p:* They shot down one of our planes. وَقَّعوا وِحدَة مِن طِيّاراتنا [waggaʕaw wiħda min ṭiyya:ra:tna]

shop • **1.** دُكّان [dukka:n] دِكاكِين [dika:ki:n] *pl:* مَحَلّ [maħall] مَحَلّات [maħalla:t] *pl:* There are many shops on this street. أَكُو هوايَة دَكاكِين بِهالشّارِع [ʔaku hwa:ya daka:ki:n bhašša:riʕ]

to shop • **1.** تسَوَّق [tsawwag] تسُوُّق [tsuwwug] *vn:* *sv* a. We shop at the market. إحنا نِتسَوَّق مِن السُّوق [ʔiħna nitsawwag min ʔissu:g]

*** I want to shop around before I buy the present.** • **1.** أَرِيد أَدُور شوَيَّة واخُذ فِكرَة قَبُلما أَشتِرِي الهَديَّة [ʔari:d adu:r šwayya waxuð fikra gabulma ʔaštiri: ʔilhadiyya]

shopping • **1.** مِسواق [miswa:g] I still have a lot of shopping to do. بَعَد عِندِي هوايَة مِسواق [baʕad ʕindi hwa:ya miswa:g]

shore • **1.** ساحِل [sa:ħil] سَواحِل [sawa:ħil] *pl:* How far is it to the shore? شقَدّ يِبعِد السّاحِل؟ [šgadd yibʕid ʔissa:ħil?]

S

short • **1.** شوط [šu:ṭ] There was a short in your radio. صار شوط بوايَرات الرّاديُو مالَك [ṣa:r šu:ṭ bwa:yara:t ʔirra:dyu ma:lak] • **2.** قصَيِّر [gṣayyir] قصار [gṣa:r] *pl.* قصَيِّرَة [gṣayyira] *Feminine:* He's rather short. هُوَّ قصَيِّر [huwwa gṣayyir] She wears short dresses. تِلبَس مَلابِس قصَيِّرَة [tilbas mala:bis gṣayyra] Cut my hair short. قُصّ شَعري قصَيِّر [guṣṣ šaʕri gṣayyir] • **3.** ناقِص [na:qiṣ] His books are short today. حسابَه ناقِص هَاليُوم [ħsa:bah na:qiṣ halyu:m]

in short • **1.** مُختَصَر الكِلام [muxtaṣar ʔilkila:m] خَصم الحَكِي [xaṣm ʔilħači] In short, I can't come. مُختَصَر الكِلام، ما أقدَر أجِي [muxtaṣar ʔilkila:m, ma: ʔagdar ʔaǰi]

to cut short • **1.** قَصَّر [qaṣṣar, gaṣṣar] تقصِير [tagṣi:r] *vn:* تقَصَّر [tgaṣṣar] *p:* They had to cut their trip short. اِضطَرَّوا يقَصّرُون سَفرَتهُم [ʔiðṭarraw ygaṣṣru:n safrathum]

to run short • **1.** نِقَص [niqaṣ] نَقُص [naquṣ] *vn: sv* u. Our ammunition is running short. ذَخِيرَتنا دَتِنقُص [ðaxi:ratna datinguṣ]

shortage • **1.** نَقِص [naqiṣ] قِلَّة [qilla] The shortage of materials is reducing our production. نَقص المَوادّ الأوَّلِيَّة دَيخَفُّض اِنتاجنا [naqṣ ʔilmawa:dd ʔilʔawwaliyya dayxaffuð ʔinta:ǰna] • **2.** عَجِز [ʕaǰiz] أعجاز [ʔaʕǰa:z] *pl:* نَقِص [naqiṣ] The auditors discovered a shortage in his accounts. المُدَقِّقِين اِكتِشفَوا عَجِز بحساباتَه [ʔilmudaqqiqi:n ʔiktišfaw ʕaǰiz bħsa:ba:tah]

shortcoming • **1.** عَيب [ʕayb, ʕi:b] عِيُوب [ʕiyu:b] *pl:* The house has many shortcomings. البَيت بِيه عِدَّة عِيُوب [ʔilbayt bi:h ʕiddat ʕiyu:b]

short cut • **1.** طَرِيق مُختَصَر [ṭari:q muxtaṣar] طُرُق مُختَصَرَة [ṭuruq muxtaṣara] *pl:* He knows a short cut to the beach. يُعرُف طَرِيق مُختَصَر لِلشَّطّ [yuʕruf ṭari:q muxtaṣar liššaṭṭ]

to shorten • **1.** قَصَّر [gaṣṣar] Shorten the pants for me, please. قَصِّرلِي البَنطَرُون رَجاءاً [gaṣṣirli ʔilpanṭaru:n raǰa:ʔan]

shorter • **1.** أقصَر [ʔagṣar] These pants are shorter than mine. هاي البَنطَرُونات أقصَر مِن مالتِي [ha:y ʔilpanṭaru:na:t ʔaqṣar min ma:lti]

shortly • **1.** بَعد شوَيَّة [baʕd šwayya] He'll be here shortly. راح يكُون هنا بَعد شوَيَّة [ra:ħ yku:n hna baʕd šwayya]

shorts • **1.** لِباس، لِبسَان [liba:s, libsa:n] لِباسات [liba:sa:t] *pl:* He ordered six pairs of shorts. وَصَّى عَلَى سِتّ لِبسان [waṣṣa: ʕala sitt libsa:n] • **2.** بَنطَرُون قصَيِّر [panṭaru:n gṣayyir] بَناطِير قصَيِّرَة [pana:ṭi:r gṣayyra] *pl:* The girls all wore shorts and sweaters. كُلّ البَنات لِبسَوا بَنطَرُونات قصَيِّرَة وَبلُوزات صُوف [kull ʔilbana:t libsaw panṭaru:na:t gṣayyra wblu:za:t ṣu:f]

short wave • **1.** مَوجَة قَصِيرَة [mawǰa qaṣi:ra] You can get short wave too, on this radio. تِقدَر تحَصِّل عَلَى مَوجَة قَصِيرَة هَمّ بهَالرّاديُو [tigdar tħaṣṣil ʕala mawǰa qaṣi:ra hamm bharra:dyu]

shot • **1.** طَلَقَة [ṭalqa] طَلَقات [ṭalqa:t] *pl:* Did you hear a shot? سمَعِت طَلقَة؟ [smaʕit ṭalqa?] • **2.** نِيشانجِي [niša:nči] نِيشانجِيَّة [niša:nčiyya] *pl:* He is a good shot. هُوَّ خُوش نِيشانجِي [huwwa xu:š niša:nči] • **3.** لَقطَة [laqṭa] لَقطات [laqṭa:t] *pl:* صُورَة [ṣu:ra] صُوَر [ṣuwar] *pl:* We got good shots of the prime minister. أخَذنا خُوش لَقطات لِرَئِيس الوُزَراء [ʔaxaðna xu:š laqṭa:t liraʔi:s ʔilwuzara:ʔ] • **4.** أبرَة [ʔubra] أبَر [ʔubar] *pl:* Are you getting shots? دَتاخُذ أبَر؟ [data:xuð ʔubar?] • **5.** مِتوَتِّر [mitwattir] His nerves are all shot. أعصابَه مِتوَتّرَة [ʔaʕṣa:bah mitwattra] • **6.** مُستَهلِك [mustahlik] مُستَهلِكِين [mustahliki:n] *pl:* That machine's all shot. هاي المَكِينَة مِستَهلكَة [ha:y ʔilmaki:na mistahlika]

* **He thinks he's a big shot.** • **1.** يِتصَوَّر نَفسَه فَدّ شَخصِيَّة [yitṣawwar nafsah fadd šaxṣiyya]

to take a shot • **1.** أطلَق رِصاص [ʔaṭlaq riṣa:ṣ] إطلاق رِصاص [ʔiṭla:q riṣa:ṣ] *vn: sv* i. Somebody took a shot at him. فَدّ واحِد أطلَق عَليه رِصاص [fadd wa:ħid ʔaṭlaq ʕali:h riṣa:ṣ]

shoulder • **1.** كِتِف [čitif, kitif] كتاف، كتافات [čta:f, čta:fa:t; kta:f, kta:fa:t] *pl:* كتافات [čta:fa:t] كتاف [čta:f] *pl:* His shoulders are broad. كتافَه عَرِيضَة [čta:fah ʕari:ða]

* **I gave it to him straight from the shoulder.** • **1.** كَلَّمتَه بصَراحَة [kallamtah bṣara:ħa]

* **We'll have to put our shoulders to the wheel.** • **1.** لازم نِبذِل أقصَى جُهُدنا [la:zim nibðil ʔaqṣa: ǰuhudna]

to give the cold shoulder • **1.** تجاهَل [tǰa:hal, dǰa:hal] تَجاهُل [taǰa:hul] *vn: sv* i. عامَل ببرُود [ʕa:mal bibru:d] مُعامَلَة [muʕa:mala] *vn: sv* i. Why'd you give him the cold shoulder? لِيش تجاهَلتَه؟ [li:š dǰa:haltah?]

to shoulder • **1.** خَلَّى عَلَى كِتِف [xalla: ʕala čitif] He shouldered the sack of wheat and walked home. خَلَّى كِيس الحُنطَة عَلَى كِتفَه ومِشَى لِلبَيت [xalla: či:s ʔilħunṭa ʕala čitfah wmiša: lilbayt] • **2.** أخَذ [ʔaxað] *sv* u. تحَمَّل [tħammal] تَحَمُّل [taħammul] *vn: sv* a. He shouldered the responsibility. أخَذ المَسؤُلِيَّة عَلَى عاتقَه [ʔaxað ʔilmasʔuliyya ʕala ʕa:tqah] Why should I shoulder the blame for it? لِيش آنِي لازم أتحَمَّل اللَّوم؟ [li:š ʔa:ni la:zim ʔatħammal ʔillawm?] • **3.** تنَكَّب [tnakkab] تَنَكُّب [tanakkub] *vn: sv* a. The soldiers shouldered their rifles and marched off. الجِّنُود نَكّبَوا بَنادُقهُم وَمِشَوا [ʔiǰǰinu:d nakkbaw bana:duqhum wmišaw]

to shout • **1.** صَيَّح [ṣayyaħ] صِياح [ṣiya:ħ] *vn:* تصَيَّح [tṣayyaħ] *p:* صاح [ṣa:ħ] صياح [ṣya:ħ] *vn:* اِنصاح

[ʔinṣaːħ] *p:* You don't have to shout! ماكُو حاجَة تصَيِّح [maːku ħaːǰa tṣayyiħ]

*** The speaker was shouted down by the crowd.** • **1.** صياح الجَماهِير خَلّى الخَطِيب يِسكُت [ṣyaːħ ʔiǰǰamaːhiːr xallaː ʔilxaṭiːb yiskut]

shouting • **1.** صياح [ṣyaːħ] Your shouting is getting on my nerves. صياحكُم دَيسَوِّينِي عَصَبِي [ṣyaːħkum daysawwiːni ʕaṣabi]

shove • **1.** دَفعَة [dafʕa] دَفعات [dafʕaːt] *pl:* He gave me a shove that knocked me over. دِفعَنِي دَفعَة وَقَّعَتنِي [difaʕni dafʕa waggaʕatni]

to shove • **1.** دَفَّع [daffaʕ] تَدفيع [tadfiːʕ] *vn:* تدَفَّع [tdaffaʕ] *p:* دَعَّك [daʕʕač] تَدعِيك [tadʕiːč] *vn:* تدَعَّك [tdaʕʕač] *p:* Don't shove! لا تدَفِّع [laː ddaffiʕ] • **2.** دِفَع [difaʕ] دَفِع [dafiʕ] *vn:* اِندِفَع [ʔindifaʕ] *p:* They shoved him in front of a bus. دِفعَوه قِدّام الباص [difʕuːh giddaːm ʔilpaːṣ]

to shove around • **1.** جاوَز عَلَى [ǰaːwaz ʕala] تَجاوُز عَلَى [taǰaːwuz ʕala] *vn:* *sv* a. People keep shoving him around. النّاس يجاوزُون عَليه [ʔinnaːs yǰaːwzuːn ʕaliːh]

shovel • **1.** كَرَك [karak] كَرَكات [karakaːt] *pl:* مِجرَف [miǰraf] مِجرَفات [miǰrafaːt] *pl:* You'll need a pickax and shovel. راح تِحتاج قَزمَة وكَرَك [raːħ tiħtaːǰ qazma wkarak]

to shovel • **1.** كِرَف [kiraf] كَرُف [karuf] *vn:* *sv* u. Shovel this sand into the truck. أكرُف الرَّمُل وذِبَّه بِاللّوري [ʔukruf ʔirramul wđibbah billuːri]

show • **1.** عَرِض [ʕariđ] عُرُوض [ʕuruːđ] *pl:* Other than that, how did you like the show? ما عَدا هَذا، شلُون عِجَبَك العَرِض؟ [maː ʕadaː haːđa, šluːn ʕiǰabak ʔilʕariđ?] • **2.** دَور [dawr, duːr] أدوار [ʔadwaːr] *pl:* عَرِض [ʕariđ] عُرُوض [ʕuruːđ] *pl:* When does the first show start? السّاعَة بيش يِبدِي الدُّور الأوَّل؟ [ʔissaːʕa biyš yibdi ʔidduːr ʔilʔawwal?]

to show • **1.** راوَى [raːwaː] مراواة [mraːwaːt] *vn:* تراوَى [traːwaː] *p:* بَيَّن [bayyan] تَبيِين [tabyiːn] *vn:* تبَيَّن [tbayyan] *p:* Show me how you do it. راوِينِي شلُون تسَوِّيها [raːwiːni šluːn tsawwiːha] • **2.** بَيَّن [bayyan] تَبيِين [tabyiːn] *vn:* تبَيَّن [tbayyan] *p:* *sv* i. Only his head showed above water. بَسّ راسَه بَيَّن مِن فُوق الماي [bass raːsah bayyan min fuːg ʔilmaːy] • **3.** دَلَّى [dallaː] دلال، دَلّات [dlaːl, dallaːt] *pl:* تدِلِّي [tdilliː] *vn:* Could you show me the way? تِقدَر تدِلِّينِي الطَّرِيق؟ [tigdar ddilliːni ʔiṭṭariːq?] • **4.** عِرَض [ʕirađ] عَرِض [ʕariđ] *vn:* اِنعِرَض [ʔinʕirađ] *p:* What are they showing at the theater this evening? شراح يِعرضُون بِالسِّينَما هاللَّيلَة؟ [šraːħ yʕirđuːn bissinama hallayla?] • **5.** أَظهَر [ʔađhar] إظهار [ʔiđhaːr] *vn:* اِنظَهَر [ʔinđahar] *p:* The investigation didn't show a thing. التَّحقِيقات ما أظهَرَت شِي [ʔittaħqiːqaːt maː ʔađharat ši] • **6.** ظِهَر [đihar] إظهار [ʔiđhaːr] *vn:* *sv* i. I'm going to show you for what you are. راح أظهِرَك عَلَى حَقِيقتَك [raːħ ʔađihrak ʕala ħaqiːqtak]

*** This picture shows a new automobile.** • **1.** هَالصُورَة تِظهِر سَيّارَة جدِيدَة [haṣṣuːra tiđhir sayyaːra ǰdiːda]

to show around • **1.** فَرَّج عَلَى [farraǰ ʕala] تَفرِيج [tafriːǰ] *vn:* تفَرَّج [tfarraǰ] *p:* She's showing her guests around the town. دَتفَرِّج ضيُوفها عالمَدِينَة [datfarriǰ đyuːfha ʕalmadiːna]

to show off • **1.** تباهَى [tbaːhaː] تَباهِي [tabaːhi] *vn:* *sv* i. راوَى [raːwaː] مُراواة [muraːwaːt] *vn:* *sv* i. He's just showing off. هُوَّ بَسّ دَيتباها [huwwa bass dayitbaːha] He likes to show his children off. يعِجبَه يِتباهَى بأولادَه [yʕiǰbah yitbaːhaː bʔawlaːdah]

to show up • **1.** جا [ǰaː] جَيَّة [ǰayya] *vn:* *sv* i. بَيَّن [bayyan] تَبيِين [tabyiːn] *vn:* تبَيَّن [tbayyan] *p:* Nobody showed up. مَحَّد جا [maħħad ǰaː] • **2.** ظِهَر [đihar] ظُهُور [đuhuːr] *vn:* *sv* a. Yellow shows up well against a black background. الأصفَر يِظهَر زين عَلَى قاعِيَّة سُودَة [ʔilʔaṣfar yiđhar ziːn ʕala gaːʕiyya suːda]

showcase • **1.** جامخانَة [ǰaːmxaːna] جامخانات [ǰaːmxaːnaːt] *pl:* Let me see that ring in the showcase. راوِينِي المِحبَس اللّي بِالجّامخانَة [raːwiːni ʔilmiħbas ʔilli biǰǰaːmxaːna]

shower • **1.** زَخَّة [zaxxa] زَخّات [zaxxaːt] *pl:* We were caught in a heavy shower. لِزمَتنا زَخَّة قَوِيَّة [lizmatna zaxxa qawiyya] • **2.** دُوش [duːš] Does your new apartment have a shower? الشِّقَّة الجِّدِيدَة مالتَك بِيها دُوش؟ [ʔaššiqqa ʔiǰǰidiːda maːltak biːha duːš?]

to shower • **1.** غَرَّق [ɣarrag] تغِرِّق [tɣirrig] *vn:* تغَرَّق [tɣarrag] *p:* Their friends showered them with presents. أصدِقائهُم غَرّقوهُم بِالهَدايَا [ʔaṣdiqaːʔhum ɣarrguːhum bilhadaːya]

show-off • **1.** مباهِيچِي [mbaːhiːči] مباهِيچِيَّة [mbaːhičiyya] *pl:* He's a big show-off. هُوَّ مباهِيچِي كِبِير [huwwa mbaːhiːčičibiːr]

shrewd • **1.** مِقتدِر [miqtidir] حاذِق [ħaːdiq] He's a shrewd businessman. هُوَّ فَدّ رَجُل أعمال مِقتدِر [huwwa fadd raǰul ʔaʕmaːl miqtidir]

shrill • **1.** رفِيع [rifiːʕ] She has a shrill voice. عِدها حِسّ رَفِيع [ʕidha ħiss rafiːʕ]

shrimp • **1.** رُبيان [rubyaːn] We're having shrimp for dinner. راح يكُون عِدنا رُبيان بِالعَشا [raːħ ykuːn ʕidna rubyaːn bilʕaša] • **2.** قِزِم [qizim] أقزام [ʔaqzaːm] *pl:* He's a little shrimp. هُوَّ قِزِم [huwwa qizim] He's a little shrimp. هَذا نُصّ نِيكَة [haːđa nuṣṣ niːča]

to shrink • **1.** خَشّ [xašš] خَشّ [xašš] *vn:* اِنخَشّ [ʔinxašš] *p:* Does this material shrink when washed?

S

هَالقُماش يخُشّ بِالغَسِل؟ [halquma:š yxušš bilγasil?] • **2.** اِنكُمَش [ʔinkumaš] اِنكِماش [ʔinkima:š] *vn: sv* i. The meat shrank when we cooked it. اللَّحَم اِنكُمَش مِن طُبَخناه [ʔillaħam ʔinkumaš min ṭubaxna:h] • **3.** تجبجَب [dǰabǰab] تَجَبجُب [taǰabǰub] *vn: sv* a. He shrinks from responsibility. هَذا يِتجَبجَب مِن المَسؤُولِيَّة [ha:ða yidǰabǰab min ʔilmasʔu:liyya]

shrub • **1.** شُجَيرَة [šuǰayra] شُجَيرات [šuǰayra:t] *pl:*

to shrug • **1.** هَزّ [hazz] هَزّ [hazz] *vn:* اِنهَزّ [ʔinhazz] *p:* He shrugged his shoulders. هَزّ كتافَه [hazz čta:fah]

to shuffle • **1.** خَربَط [xarbaṭ] تخُربُط [txurbuṭ] *vn:* تخَربَط [txarbaṭ] *p:* خِلَط [xilaṭ] خَلِط [xaliṭ] *vn:* اِنخِلَط [ʔinxilaṭ] *p:* Have the cards been shuffled? الوَرَق تخَربَط؟ [ʔilwaraq txarbaṭ?] • **2.** شَحَّط ب [šaħħaṭ bi-] تَشحِيط [tašħi:ṭ] *vn: sv* i. Stop shuffling your feet; you're ruining your shoes! بَسّ عاد تشَحِّط برِجلَك، مُو عِدَمِت قُندَرتَك [bass ʕa:d tšaħħiṭ briǰlak, mu: ʕidamit qundartak]

to shut • **1.** سَدّ [sadd] سَدّ [sadd] *vn:* اِنسَدّ [ʔinsadd] *p:* Please shut the door! سِدّ الباب رَجاءاً [sidd ʔilba:b raǰa:ʔan] • **2.** حِبَس [ħibas] Who shut the dog in the garage? مِنُو حِبَس الكَلِب بِالكَراج؟ [minu ħibas ʔiččalib bilgara:ǰ?]

to shut down • **1.** عَزَّل [ʕazzal] تعِزِّل [tʕizzil] *vn: sv* i. Why did the factory shut down? لِيش المَعمَل عَزَّل [li:š ʔilmaʕmal ʕazzal]

to shut off • **1.** قِطَع [giṭaʕ] قَطِع [gaṭiʕ] *vn:* اِنقِطَع [ʔingiṭaʕ] *p:* قَصّ [gaṣṣ] قَصّ [gaṣṣ] *vn:* اِنقَصّ [ʔingaṣṣ] *p:* The workers shut off our water for two days. العُمّال قِطعَوا الماي عَنَّه لمُدَّة يومَين [ʔilʕumma:l giṭʕaw ʔilma:y ʕannah lmuddat yawmayn] • **2.** سَدّ [sadd] سَدّ [sadd] *vn:* اِنسَدّ [ʔinsadd] *p:* Shut off the water. سِدّ الماي [sidd ʔilma:y]

to shut up • **1.** سِكَت [sikat] سُكُوت [suku:t] *vn:* اِنسِكَت [ʔinsikat] *p:* Shut up! إِسكُت [ʔiskut] Shut up! اِنكَبّ [ʔinčabb]

shutter • **1.** أَبَجور [ʔabaǰu:r] أَبَجورات [ʔabaǰu:ra:t] *pl:* Open the shutters, please. فُكّ الأَبَجورات، مِن فَضلَك [fukk ʔilʔabaǰu:ra:t, min faðlak] • **2.** حاجِز [ħa:jiz] حَواجِز [ħawa:jiz] *pl:* حاجِب [ħa:ǰib] حَواجِب [ħawa:ǰib] *pl:* The lens shutter in my camera is stuck. حاجِز العَدَسَة مال كامَرتِي مشَكَّل [ħa:jiz ʔilʕadasa ma:l kamira:ti mšakkal] • **3.** كَبَنك [kabang, kabank] كَبَنكات [kabanka:t] *pl:* The storekeeper shut the door and rolled down the shutter. صاحِب المَحَلّ سَدّ الباب وَنَزَّل الكَبَنك [ṣa:ħib ʔilmaħall sadd ʔilba:b wnazzal ʔilkabang]

shy • **1.** خَجُول [xaǰu:l] خَجُولِين [xaǰu:li:n] *pl:* Don't be so shy! لا تكُون هَالقَدّ خَجُول [la: tku:n halgadd xaǰu:l] Don't be so shy! لا تِستِحِي [la: tistiħi]

to shy • **1.** جِفَل [ǰifal] جَفِل [ǰafil] *vn: sv* i. The horse shied at the car. الحصان جِفَل مِن السَّيّارَة [ʔilħṣa:n ǰifal min ʔissayya:ra]

to shy away from • **1.** تجَنَّب [tǰannab] تَجَنُّب [taǰannub] *vn: sv* a. He shies away from hard work. يِتجَنَّب الشُّغُل الشّاق [yidǰannab ʔiššuγul ʔišša:q]

sick • **1.** مَرِيض [mari:ð] مُرضَة [murða] *pl:* He's sick in bed. هُوَّ مَرِيض بِالفراش [huwwa mari:ð bilfra:š] The sick are given the best of care. المَرضَى يدارُوهُم زين [ʔilmarða yda:ru:hum zi:n]

*** I get sick when I fly.** • **1.** نَفسِي تِلعَب مِن أَطِير [nafsi: tilʕab min ʔaṭi:r]

*** I'm getting sick and tired of this job.** • **1.** مَلِّيت مِن الشَّغلَة [malli:t min ʔiššaγlah] / بِزعَت نَفسِي مِن الشَّغلَة [bizʕat nafsi min ʔiššaγla]

to be taken sick • **1.** تمَرَّض [tmarrað] *p:*تمُرُّض [tmurruð] *vn: sv* a. He was suddenly taken sick. عَلَى غَفلَة تمَرَّض [ʕala γafla tmarrað]

sickle • **1.** مِنجَل [minǰal] مَناجِل [mana:ǰil] *pl:*

sickness • **1.** مَرَض [marað] أمراض [ʔamra:ð] *pl:*

side • **1.** جِهَة [ǰiha] جِهات [ǰiha:t] *pl:* صوب [ṣu:b] جانِب [ǰa:nib] جَوانِب [ǰawa:nib] *pl:* On this side of the street there are only a few houses. مِن هَالجِهَة مِن الشّارِع أَكُو شوَيَّة أحواش بَسّ [min halǰiha min ʔišša:riʕ ʔaku šwayya ħwa:š bass] I saw him on the other side of the city. شِفتَه بِالصُّوب الثّانِي مِن المَدِينَة [šiftah bišṣu:b ʔiθθa:ni min ʔilmadi:na] • **2.** جانِب [ǰa:nib] جَوانِب [ǰawa:nib] *pl:* He is on our side. هُوَّ مِن جانِبنا [huwwa min ǰa:nibna] • **3.** جانِبِي [ǰanibi] Please use the side door. رَجاءاً إِستَعمِل الباب الجّانِبِيَّة [raǰa:ʔan ʔistaʕmil ʔilba:b ʔiǰǰa:nibiyya] • **4.** خاصرَة [xa:ṣra] خَواصِر [xawa:ṣir] *pl:* She's a thorn in his side. واقفَة سِچِّينَة بخاصِرتَه [wa:gfa siččiːna bxa:ṣirtah]

*** To be on the safe side, I asked him again.** • **1.** سِأَلتَه مَرَّة الُّخ حَتَّى أَتأَكَّد [siʔaltah marra ʔillux ħatta: ʔatʔakkad]

side by side • **1.** سُوَة، سُوا [suwa] They walked along silently side by side. مِشَوا بِهدُوء سُوَة [mišaw bhidu:ʔ suwa]

to take sides • **1.** اِنحاز إِلَى جِهَة، أَيَّد جِهَة [ʔinħa:z ʔila ǰiha, ʔayyad ǰiha] اِنحِياز تَأيِيد [ʔinħiya:z, taʔyi:d] *vn: sv* a. أَيَّد [ʔayyad] تَأيِيد [taʔyi:d] *vn:* تأَيَّد [tʔayyad] *p:* It's difficult to take sides on this question. صَعُب واحِد يِنحاز إِلَى جِهَة بهَالقَضِيَّة [ṣaʕub wa:ħid yinħa:z ʔila ǰiha bhalqaðiyya]

to side with • **1.** اِنحاز لِ [ʔinħa:z li-] اِنحِياز [ʔinħiya:z] *vn: sv* a. أَيَّد ل [ʔayyad l-] تَأيِيد [taʔyi:d] *vn:* تأَيَّد [tʔayyad] *p:* You always side with him! إِنتَ دائِماً تِنحازلَه [ʔinta da:ʔiman tinħa:zlah]

sidewalk • **1.** رَصِيف [raṣi:f] أَرصِفَة [ʔarṣifa] *pl:*

siege • **1.** حِصار [ħiṣaːr] حِصارات [ħiṣaːraːt] *pl:*

sieve • **1.** مُنخُل [munxul] مَناخِل [manaːxil] *pl:*

to sift • **1.** نِخَل [nixal] نَخِل [naxil] *vn:* اِنّخَل [ʔinnixal] *p:* The flour has to be sifted first. الطَّحِين لازِم يِنُّخُل بِالأوَّل [ʔiṭṭaħiːn laːzim yinnuxul bilʔawwal]

to sigh • **1.** تحَسَّر [tħassar] تَحَصُّر [taħaṣṣur] *vn: sv* a. تنَهَّد [tnahhad] تَنَهُّد [tanahhud] *vn: sv* a. What are you sighing about? لِيش دَتِتحَصَّر؟ [liːš datitħaṣṣar?]

sight • **1.** نَظَر [naðar] أنظار [ʔanðaːr] *pl:* بَصَر [baṣar] He lost his sight in the accident. فُقَد نَظَرَه بِالحادِث [fuqad naðarah bilħaːdiθ] • **2.** مَنظَر [manðar] مَناظِر [manaːðir] *pl:* That's a beautiful sight! هَذا مَنظَر جَمِيل وَالله [haːða manðar ǰamiːl wallah]

*** I recognized you at first sight.** • **1.** أوَّل ما شِفتَك عِرَفتَك [ʔawwal maː šiftak ʕiraftak]

*** Don't lose sight of him.** • **1.** لا تخَلِّيه يغِيب عَن نَظَرَك [laː txalliːh yɣiːb ʕan naðarak]

*** They had orders to shoot him on sight.** • **1.** كان عِدهُم أوَامِر يِطلِقُون النّار أوَّل ما يشُوفُوه [čaːn ʕidhum ʔawaːmir yiṭliquːn nnaːr ʔawwal ma yšuːfuːh]

sights • **1.** مَعالِم [maʕaːlim] Have you seen the sights of the town? شِفِت مَعالِم المَدِينَة؟ [šifit maʕaːlim ʔilmadiːna?]

by sight • **1.** بِالوُجِه [bilwuǰih] I know him only by sight. أعُرفَه بَسّ بِالوُجِه [ʔaʕurfah bass bilwuǰih]

in sight • **1.** مبَيِّن [mbayyin] ضاهِر [ðaːhir] The end is not yet in sight. النِّهايَة بَعَدها ما مبَيّنَة [ʔinnihaːya baʕadha maː mbayyna]

to catch sight of • **1.** لِمَح [limaħ] لَمِح [lamiħ] *vn: sv* a. As soon as he caught sight of you, he vanished. أوَّل ما لِمَحَك، اِختِفَى [ʔawwal maː limaħak, ʔixtifaː]

S

sign • **1.** قُطعَة [quṭʕa] قُطَع [quṭaʕ] *pl:* إشارَة [ʔišaːra] إشارات [ʔišaːraːt] *pl:* عَلامَة [ʕalaːma] عَلامات، عَلائِم [ʕalaːmaːt, ʕalaːʔim] *pl:* What does that sign say? شمَكتُوب عالقُطعَة؟ [šmaktuːb ʕalquṭʕa?] • **2.** بادِرَة [baːdira] بَوادِر [bawaːdir] *pl:* Is that a good sign? هاي بادِرَة طَيِّبَة؟ [haːy baːdira ṭayyba?] • **3.** إشارَة [ʔišaːra] إشارات [ʔišaːraːt] *pl:* He gave us a sign to follow him. اِنطانا إشارَة نتبِعَه [ʔinṭaːna ʔišaːra ntibʕah] • **4.** دَلِيل [daliːl] دَلائِل [dalaːʔil] *pl:* All signs point to an early winter. كُلّ الدَّلائِل تشِير عَلَى إنُّو الشِّتا راح يِجِي مُبَكِّر [kull ʔiddalaːʔil tšiːr ʕala ʔinnu ʔiššita raːħ yiǰi mubakkir]

to sign • **1.** وَقَّع [waqqaʕ] تَوقِيع [tawqiːʕ] *vn:* توَقَّع [twaqqaʕ] *p:* مُضَى [muðaː] إمضاء [ʔimðaːʔ] *vn:* اِنمُضَى [ʔinmuðaː] *p: sv* i. He forgot to sign the letter. نِسَى يوَقِّع الرِّسالَة [nisaː ywaqqiʕ ʔirrisaːla] Don't forget to sign in. لا تِنسَى تِمضِي مِن تِجِي [laː tinsaː timði min tiǰi]

to sign up • **1.** سَجَّل [saǰǰal] تَسجِيل [tasǰiːl] *vn: sv* i. I signed up for three courses. سَجَّلِت بِثلَث مَواضِيع [saǰǰalit bitlaθ mawaːðiːʕ]

to sign over • **1.** سَلَّم [sallam] تسِلِّم [tsillim] *vn: sv* i. He signed over the business to his son. سَلَّم شُغلَه لإبنَه [sallam šuɣlah lʔibnah]

signal • **1.** إشارَة [ʔišaːra] إشارات [ʔišaːraːt] *pl:* We agreed on a signal. اِتَّفَقنا عَلَى إشارَة [ʔittifaqna ʕala ʔišaːra] We're getting a strong signal from him. دَنِتلَقَّى إشارَة قَوِيَّة مِنَّه [danitlaqqaː ʔišaːra qawiyya minnah]

to signal • **1.** أشَّر [ʔaššar] تَأشِير [taʔšiːr] *vn:* تأشَّر [tʔaššar] *p:* Will you signal the waiter, please? ما تأشِّر لِلبُوي، بالله؟ [maː tʔaššir lilbuːy, ballah?]

signalman • **1.** مَأمُور سَير [maʔmuːr sayr] مَأمُورِين سَير [maʔmuːriːn sayr] *pl:* The signalman stopped the train in time. مَأمُور السَّير وَقَّف القِطار بالوَقِت المُناسِب [maʔmuːr ʔissayr waggaf ʔilqiṭaːr bilwakt ʔilmunaːsib]

signature • **1.** تَوقِيع [tawqiːʕ] تَواقِيع [tawaːqiːʕ] *pl:* The letter has no signature. المَكتُوب ما عَلَيه تَوقِيع [ʔilmaktuːb maː ʕaliːh tawqiːʕ]

signet ring • **1.** مُهُر [muhur] مهُور، مهار [mhuːr, mhaːr] *pl:* He signs documents with his signet ring. يُمهُر الوَثايِق بِالمُهُر مالَه [yumhur ʔilwaθaːyiq bilmuhur maːlah]

silence • **1.** سُكُون [sukuːn] سُكُوت [sukuːt] There was complete silence in the room. كان أكُو سُكُون شامِل بالغُرفَة [čaːn ʔaku sukuːn šaːmil bilɣurfa] • **2.** هُدُوء [huduːʔ, hiduːʔ] They listened in silence. اِنتِبهَوا بهُدُوء [ʔintibhaw bhiduːʔ]

to silence • **1.** سَكَّت [sakkat] تَسكِيت [taskiːt] *vn:* تسَكَّت [tsakkat] *p:* I couldn't silence him. ما قِدَرت أسَكّتَه [maː gidart ʔasakktah]

silent • **1.** ساكِت [saːkit] Why are you so silent? لِيش إنتَ هَالقَدّ ساكِت؟ [liːš ʔinta halgadd saːkit?] • **2.** صامِت [ṣaːmit] She used to play in silent pictures. كانَت تمَثِّل بِالأفلام الصّامِتَة [čaːnat tmaθθil bilʔaflaːm ʔiṣṣaːmita]

silk • **1.** حَرِير [ħariːr] How much is this silk? بيش هَالحَرِير؟ [biyš halħariːr?]

silly • **1.** أحمَق [ʔaħmaq] That's a silly thing to do. هَذا عَمَل أحمَق [haːða ʕamal ʔaħmaq] • **2.** سَخِيف [saxiːf] فُطِير [fuṭiːr] That was a silly thing to say. كَلامَك سَخِيف [kalaːmak saxiːf] Don't be so silly! لا تصِير هَالقَدّ سَخِيف [laː tṣiːr halgadd saxiːf] • **3.** أبلَه [ʔablah] He's not so silly as he looks. هُوَّ مُو هَالقَدّ أبلَه مِثلما دَيبَيِّن عَلِيه [huwwa muː halgadd ʔablah miθilma daybayyin ʕaliːh]

silver • **1.** فُضَّة [fuð̣ð̣a] I gave her a lighter made of silver. نطَيتها قِدّاحَة مِن فُضَّة [nṭiːtha qiddaːħa min fuð̣ð̣a] • **2.** فُضّي [fuð̣ð̣i] She's wearing a silver ring. لابسَة مِحبَس فُضّي [laːbsah miħbas fuð̣ð̣i]

similar • **1.** مُشابِه [mušaːbih] شَبِيه [šabiːh] أشباه [ʔašbaːh] *pl:* مُماثِل [mumaːθil] I know of a similar case. أعرُف قَضِيَّة مُشابِهَة [ʔaʕruf qað̣iyya mušaːbiha]

simple • **1.** بَسِيط [basiːṭ] بَسِيطِين [basiːṭiːn] *pl:* سَهل [sahil] That's quite a simple matter. هَذا فَدّ مَوضُوع كُلِّش بَسِيط [haːða fadd mawð̣uːʕ kulliš basiːṭ] • **2.** ساذِج [saːðij] سُذَّج [suððaj] *pl:* بَسِيط [basiːṭ] بَسِيطِين [basiːṭiːn] *pl:* I may sound simple to you, but I don't understand it. مُمكِن تِتصَوَّرنِي ساذِج، لَكِن ما دَأفتِهِمها [mumkin titṣawwarni saːðij, laːkin maː daʔaftihimha]

simplicity • **1.** تَبسِيط [tabsiːṭ] For the sake of simplicity let's say that. . . مِن أجِل تَبسِيط المَوضُوع خَلّي نقُول [min ʔajil tabsiːṭ ʔilmawð̣uːʕ xalli nguːl] • **2.** بَساطَة [basaːṭa] All his designs are characterized by simplicity. كُلّ تَصامِيمَه تِغلِب عَلِيها البَساطَة [kull taṣaːmiːmah tiɣlib ʕaliːha ʔilbaṣaːṭa]

simply • **1.** قَطعاً [qaṭʕan] That's simply impossible! هَذِي مُستَحِيلَة قَطعاً [haːði mustaħiːla qaṭʕan] • **2.** بِبَساطَة [bibaṣaːṭa] He explained it to the children simply. شِرَحها لِلأطفال بِبَساطَة [širaħha lilʔaṭfaːl bbaṣaːṭa]

sin • **1.** ذَنِب [ðanib] ذنُوب [ðnuːb] *pl:* مَعصِيَة [maʕṣiya] مَعاصِي [maʕaːṣiː] *pl:* He's committed a lot of sins. اِرتِكَب عِدَّة ذِنُوب [ʔirtikab ʕiddat ðinuːb]

to sin • **1.** أذنَب [ʔaðnab] إذناب [ʔiðnaːb] *vn: sv* i. He sins more than he does good. يِذنِب أكثَر مِن ما يسَوِّي خير [yiðnib ʔakθar min maː ysawwi xiːr]

Sinai Peninsula • **1.** شبُه جَزِيرَة سِينا [šubuh jaziːrat siːna]

since • **1.** مِن [min] He hasn't been here since Monday. ما كان هنا مِن يوم الإثنين [maː čaːn hna min yuːm ʔilʔiθnayn] • **2.** مِن وَكِت ما [min wakit maː] مِن [min] I haven't seen anyone since I got back. ما شِفِت أحَّد مِن وَكِت ما رِجَعِت [maː šifit ʔaħħad min wakit maː rijaʕit] • **3.** لِأن [liʔan] Since I didn't have the money I couldn't go. آني ما قِدَرِت أرُوح لِأنّ ما كان عِندِي فلُوس [ʔaːni maː gidarit ʔaruːħ liʔann maː čaːn ʕindi fluːs]

ever since • **1.** مِن ذاك الوَكِت [min ðaːk ʔilwakit] I haven't spoken with him ever since. ما حكَيت وِيّاه مِن ذاك الوَكِت [maː ħčiːt wiyyaːh min ðaːk ʔilwakit]

sincere • **1.** مُخلِص [muxliṣ] He's a sincere person. هُوَّ فَدّ واحِد مُخلِص [huwwa fadd waːħid muxliṣ]

sincerely • **1.** مِن كُلّ عَقِل [min kull ʕaqil] مِن صُدُق [min ṣudug] مِن كُلّ قَلُب [min kull galub] You sincerely believe it? مِن كُلّ عَقلَك تِعتِقِد بِيها؟ [min kull ʕaqlak tiʕtiqid biːha?]

to sing • **1.** غَنَّى [ɣannaː] غِنَى [ɣinaː] *vn:* تغَنَّى [tɣannaː] *p:* I don't sing very well. ما أغَنّي زين [maː ʔaɣanni ziːn]

to singe • **1.** حِرَق [ħirag] حَرِق [ħarig] *vn:* اِنحِرَق [ʔinħirag] *p:* I singed my eyebrows when I got too close to the fire. حرَقِت حَواجبِي مِن تقَرَّبِت لِلنّار [ħragit ħawaːjbi min tqarrabit linnaːr] • **2.** لَهَّب [lahhab] تلِهِّب [tlihhib] *vn: sv* i. After you pluck the chicken's feathers, singe it. بَعَد ما تِنتِف رِيش الدِّجاجَة، لَهِّبها [baʕad maː tintif riːš ʔiddijaːja, lahhibha]

singer • **1.** مُغَنّي [muɣanni] مُغَنِّين [muɣanniːn] *pl:* He's a well-known singer. هُوَّ مُغَنّي مَعرُوف [huwwa muɣanni maʕruːf]

single • **1.** أعزَب [ʔaʕzab] عُزّاب [ʕuzzaːb] *pl:* Are you married or single? إنتَ مِتزَوِّج لَو أعزَب؟ [ʔinta midzawwij law ʔaʕzab?] • **2.** واحِد [waːħid] He made just a single mistake. سَوَّى فَدّ غَلطَة وِحدَة بَسّ [sawwaː fadd ɣalṭa wiħda bass]

*** He didn't make a single mistake.** • **1.** ما سَوَّى وَلا غَلطَة [maː sawwaː wala ɣalṭa]

to single out • **1.** اِختار [ʔixtaːr] اِختِيار [ʔixtiyaːr] *vn: sv* a. اِنتِخَب [ʔintixab] اِنتِخاب [ʔintixaːb] *vn: sv* i. Why did they single you out? لِيش بَسّ إلَك اِختارَوك؟ [liːš bass ʔilak ʔixtaːrawk?]

singular • **1.** مُفرَد [mufrad] مُفرَدات [mufradaːt] *pl:* 'Boy' is the singular of 'boys'. وَلَد مُفرَد أولاد ['walad' mufrad 'ʔawlaːd']

sink • **1.** مَغسَلَة [maɣsala] مَغسَل [maɣsal] مَغاسِل [maɣaːsil] *pl:* The dishes are still in the sink. المَواعِين بَعَدها بِالمَغسَلَة [ʔilmwaːʕiːn baʕadha bilmaɣsala]

to sink • **1.** غِرَق [ɣirag] غَرَق [ɣarag] *vn:* اِنغَرَق [ʔinɣarag] *p:* The ship sank in 10 minutes. السَّفِينَة غِرقَت بعَشِر دَقايِق [ʔissafiːna ɣirgat bʕašir daqaːyiq] • **2.** غَرَّق [ɣarrag] تغِرِّق [tɣirrig] *vn:* تغَرَّق [tɣarrag] *p:* They sank three enemy ships. غَرِّقوا تلَث بَواخِر لِلعَدُو [ɣarrigaw tlaθ bawaːxir lilʕadu] • **3.** طُمَس [ṭumas] طَمُس [ṭamus] *vn: sv* u. The car sank into the mud. السَّيّارَة طُمسَت بِالطِّين [ʔissayyaːra ṭumsat bittiːn] • **4.** هُبَط [hubaṭ] هبُوط [hubuːṭ] *vn:* اِنهِبَط [ʔinhibaṭ] *p:* The house has sunk ten inches. البَيت هِبَط عَشِر إنجات [ʔilbayt hibaṭ ʕašir ʔinjaːt] • **5.** تدَهوَر [tdahwar] تَدَهوُر [tadahwur] *vn: sv* a. His health is sinking rapidly. صِحّتَه قاعِد تِتدَهوَر بسُرعَة [ṣiħħtah gaːʕid tiddahwar bsurʕa]

sip • **1.** شَفطَة [šafṭa] شَفطات [šafṭaːt] *pl:* مَصَّة [maṣṣa] مَصّات [maṣṣaːt] *pl:* I only had a sip of my coffee. أخَذِت شَفطَة وِحدَة مِن القَهوَة [ʔaxaðit šafṭa wiħda min ʔilgahwa]

S

to sip • **1.** رِشَف [rišaf] رَشِف [rašif] *vn:* اِنرِشَف [ʔinrišaf] *p:* شُفَط [šufaṭ] شَفُط [šafuṭ] *vn:* اِنشِفَط [ʔinšifaṭ] *p:* He sipped the hot coffee. رِشَف القَهوَة الحارَّة [rišaf ʔilgahwa ʔilħaːrra]

sir • **1.** سَيِّد [sayyid] سادَة [saːda] *pl:* Sir, the colonel is here. سَيِّدِي، العَقِيد هنا [sayyidi, ʔilʕaqiːd hna] • **2.** أُستاذ [ʔustaːð] أَساتِذَة [ʔasaːtiða] *pl:* Yes sir, I'll call him now. نَعَم أُستاذ، راح أَخابرَه هَسَّة [naʕam ʔustaːð, raːħ ʔaxaːbrah hassa] • **3.** عَمّ [ʕamm] No sir, I didn't break the vase. لا عَمِّي، ما كسَرت المَزهَرِيَّة [laː ʕammi, maː ksart ʔalmazhariyya] No sir, I didn't break the vase. لا عَمُّو، ما كسَرت المَزهَرِيَّة [laː ʕammu, maː ksart ʔalmazhariyya]

sister • **1.** أُخُت [ʔuxut] أخوات [(ʔa) xwaːt] *pl:* Do you have any sisters? أخوات؟ [ʕindak ʔaxawaːt?]

sister-in-law • **1.** أُخُت مَرَة [ʔuxut mara] خَوات مَرَة [xawaːt mara] *pl:* مَرت أَخُو [mart ʔaxu] مرَيّات أَخُو [mrayyaːt ʔaxu] *pl:* She's my sister-in-law. هِيَّ أُخُت مَرتي [hiyya ʔuxut marti]

to sit • **1.** قِعَد [giʕad] قَعِد [gaʕid] *vn: sv* u. جِلَس [jilas] جِلُوس [jiluːs] *vn: sv* i. We sat in the front row. قعَدنا بِالصَّفّ الأمامِي [gʕadna biṣṣaff ʔilʔamaːmi]
  to sit in on • **1.** حِضَر [ħiðar] حُضُور [ħuðuːr] *vn: sv* a. I sat in on all the conferences. حِضَرِت كُلّ المُؤتَمَرات [ħiðarit kull ʔilmuʔtamaraːt]
  to sit up • **1.** سِهَر [sihar] سَهَر [sahar] *vn: sv* a. We sat up all night waiting for him. سِهَرنا طُول اللَّيل نِنتَظرَه [siharna ṭuːl ʔillayl nintaðrah]

sitting • **1.** قَعدَة [gaʕda] He finished the food in one sitting. خَلَّص الأَكِل بقَعدَة وِحدَة [xallaṣ ʔilʔakil bgaʕda wiħda] • **2.** قُعُود [guʕuːd] قِعَد [giʕad] Sitting at home alone makes her nervous. قُعُودها وَحَّدها بالبَيت يسَوِّيها عَصَبِيَّة [guʕuːdha waħħadha bilbayt ysawwiːha ʕaṣabiyya]

S

situation • **1.** مَوقِف [mawqif] مَواقِف [mawaːqif] *pl:* She saved the situation. هِيَّ أَنقِذَت المَوقِف [hiyya ʔanqiðat ʔilmawqif]

six • **1.** سِتَّة [sitta] Will six be enough? سِتَّة تكَفِّي؟ [sitta tkaffi?] • **2.** سِتّ [sitt] They were here six days ago. كانَوا هنا قَبُل سِتّ أَيّام [čaːnaw hna gabul sitt ʔayyaːm]

sixteen • **1.** سِطَّعَش [siṭṭaʕaš]

sixteenth • **1.** السِطَّعَش [ʔiṣṣiṭṭaʕaš]

sixth • **1.** سادِس [saːdis]

sixtieth • **1.** السِتِّين [ʔissittiːn]

sixty • **1.** سِتِّين [sittiːn]

size • **1.** قِياس [qiyaːs] قِياسات [qiyaːsaːt] *pl:* What size shoe do you wear? أَيّ قِياس قُندَرَة تِلبَس؟ [ʔayy qiyaːs qundara tilbas?] • **2.** حَجِم [ħajim] حُجُوم، أَحجام [ħujuːm, ʔaħjaːm] *pl:* What size refrigerator are you going to buy? أَيّ حَجِم ثَلّاجَة راح تِشتِرِي؟ [ʔayy ħajim θallaːja raːħ tištiri?]
  to size up • **1.** قَدَّر [qaddar] تقدِّير [tqiddiːr] *vn:* تقَدَّر [tqaddar] *p:* How do you size up the situation? شلُون تقَدِّر الوَضِع؟ [šluːn tqaddir ʔilwaðiʕ?]

skate • **1.** سكَيت [skayt] سكَيتات [skaytaːt] *pl:* A wheel came off my skate. الچَرِخ وُقَع مِن السكَيت مالِي [ʔilčarix wugaʕ min ʔisskayt maːli]
  to skate • **1.** تزَلَّج [tzallaj] تَزَلُّج [tazalluj] *vn: sv* a. We Baghdadis don't skate. إحنا البَغدادِيِّين ما نتزَلَّج [ʔiħna ʔilbaɣdaːdiyyiːn maː ntidzallaj]

skeleton • **1.** هَيكَل [haykal] هَياكِل [hayaːkil] *pl:*

skeptical • **1.** شَكّاك [šakkaːk] Don't be so skeptical! لا تكُون هَالقَدّ شَكّاك [laː tkuːn halgadd šakkaːk]

sketch • **1.** مُخَطَّط [muxaṭṭaṭ] مُخَطَّطات [muxaṭṭaṭaːt] *pl:*

to ski • **1.** تزَحلَق [dzaħlag] تَزَحلُق [tazaħlug] *vn: sv* a. I never learned how to ski on snow. أَبَد ما تعَلَّمِت شلُون أَتزَحلَق عالثَّلِج [ʔabad maː tʕallamit šluːn ʔadzaħlag ʕaθθalij]

to skid • **1.** تزَحلَق [tzaħlag] تَزَحلُق [tazaħlug] *vn: sv* a. The car started to skid. السَّيّارَة قامَت تِتزَحلَق [ʔissayyaːra gaːmat tidzaħlag]

skill • **1.** مَهارَة [mahaːra] بَراعَة [baraːʕa] That requires a lot of skill. ذِيك تِتطَلَّب هوايَة مَهارَة [ðiːč tiṭṭallab hwaːya mahaːra]

skilled • **1.** ماهِر [maːhir] He is a skilled cabinetmaker. هُوَّ نَجّار مُوبِليات ماهِر [huwwa najjaːr muːbilyaːt maːhir]

skillfully • **1.** بمَهارَة [bmahaːra] بَراعَة [bibaraːʕa] You got yourself out of that problem very skillfully. خَلَّصِت نَفسَك مِن المُشكِلَة بمَهارَة [xallaṣit nafsak min ʔilmuškila bmahaːra]

to skim • **1.** شال القِشوَة [šaːl ʔilgišwa] شِيالَة [šiyaːla] *vn:* إنشال [ʔinšaːl] *p:* I skimmed the milk. شِلت القِشوَة مِن الحَلِيب [šilt ʔilgišwa min ʔilħaliːb]
  to skim through • **1.** تصَفَّح [tṣaffaħ] تَصَفُّح [taṣaffuħ] *vn: sv* a. I just skimmed through the book. تصَفَّحِت الكِتاب بَسّ [tṣaffaħit ʔilkitaːb bass]

skin • **1.** جِلِد [jilid] جلُود [jluːd] *pl:* She had very sensitive skin. عِدها جِلِد كُلِّش حَسّاس [ʕidha jilid kulliš ħassaːs]

• **2.** فَروَة [farwa] فَروات، فراوي [farwa:t, fra:wi] *pl:* How many skins will you need for the coat? كَم فَروَة تِحتاج لِلسِّترَة؟ [čam farwa tiħta:ǰ lissitra?] • **3.** قِشِر [gišir] قشُور [gšu:r] *pl:* These apples have a thick skin. هَالتِّفّاح قِشرَتَه ثِخِين [hattiffa:ħ gišratah θixi:n] • **4.** جِلدِي [ǰildi] He's got a skin disease. عِندَه مَرَض جِلدِي [ʕindah marað ǰildi]

*** I got a passing grade by the skin of my teeth.**
• **1.** حَصَّلِت عَلَى دَرَجَة النَّجاح عَالحافَّة [ħaṣṣalit ʕala daraǰt ʔinnaǰa:ħ ʕalħa:ffa]

to skin • **1.** سِلَخ [silax] سَلِخ [salix] *vn: sv* a. After you slaughter the calf, skin it. بَعَد ما تِذبَح العِجِل إصلَخَه [baʕad ma: tiðbaħ ʔilʕiǰil ʔiṣlaxah] • **2.** جِلَخ [ǰilax] جَلِخ [ǰalix] *vn: sv* a. When he fell he skinned his knee. مِن وُقَع جِلَخ رُكُبتَه [min wugaʕ ǰilax rukubtah]

to skip • **1.** طُفَر [ṭufar] طَفُر [ṭafur] *vn:* اِنطُفَر [ʔinṭufar] *p:* Skip a few lines. أُطفُر كَم سَطِر [ʔuṭfur čam saṭir] Can you skip rope? تُعرُف تُطفُر عَالحَبِل؟ [tuʕruf tuṭfur ʕalħabil?] • **2.** عُبَر [ʕubar] عَبُر، عُبُور [ʕabur, ʕubu:r] *vn:* اِنعُبَر [ʔinʕubar] *p:* I skipped second grade. عُبَرِت الصَّفّ الثّانِي [ʕubarit ʔiṣṣaff ʔiθθa:ni] • **3.** قِلَب [gilab] قَلُب [galub] *vn:* اِنقِلَب [ʔingilab] *p:* Skip a few pages. أُقلُب عِدَّة صَفحات [ʔuglub ʕiddat ṣafħa:t] • **4.** تِرَك [tirak] تَرِك [tarik] *vn: sv* u. Skip the hard words. إترُك الكَلِمات الصَّعبَة [ʔitruk ʔilkalima:t ʔiṣṣaʕba] • **5.** اِنهِزَم مِن [ʔinhizam min] اِنهِزام [ʔinhiza:m] *vn: sv* i. He skipped town. اِنهِزَم مِن المَدِينَة [ʔinhizam min ʔilmadi:na]

skirt • **1.** تَنُّورَة [tannu:ra] تَنُّورات [tannu:ra:t] *pl:* تنانِير [tna:ni:r] تَنُّورات [tannu:ra:t] *pl:* Her skirt is too long. تَنُّورَتها طوِيلَة [tannu:ratha ṭwi:la]

skull • **1.** جُمجُمَة [ǰumǰuma] جماجُم [ǰma:ǰum] *pl:* He fractured his skull. اِنكِسرَت جُمجُمتَه [ʔinkisrat ǰumǰumtah]

skullcap • **1.** عَرَقچِين [ʕaraqči:n] عَرَقچِينات [ʕaraqči:na:t] *pl:* They wear skullcaps under their headcloths. يِلبَسُون عَرَقچِين جَوَّة اليِشماغ [yilbasu:n ʕaraqči:n ǰawwa ʔilyišma:ɣ]

sky • **1.** سمَا [sima] سِمات [samawa:t] *pl:* How does the sky look today? شلُون السِّما اليُوم؟ [šlu:n ʔissima: ʔilyu:m?]

*** The news came out of a clear blue sky.**
• **1.** الأخبار نِزلَت مِثل الصاعِقَة [ʔilʔaxba:r nizlat miθl iṣṣa:ʕiqa]

*** He praised her to the skies.** • **1.** مِدَحها هوايَة [midaħha hwa:ya]

slack • **1.** واقُف [wa:guf] كَساد [kasa:d] Business is slack. الشّغُل واقُف [ʔiššyul wa:guf] • **2.** بَطِيئ [baṭi:ʔ] His work has become very slack. شُغلَه صايِر كُلِّش بَطِيئ [šuɣlah sa:yir kulliš baṭi:ʔ] • **3.** رَخِي [raxi] Your tentropes are too slack. حبال خَيمتَك رَخِيَّة [ħba:l xaymtak raxiyya]

slacks • **1.** بَنطَرُون [panṭaru:n] بَنطَرُونات [panṭaru:na:t] *pl:*

to slap • **1.** لِطَم [liṭam] لَطُم [laṭum] *vn:* اِنلِطَم [ʔinliṭam] *p:* She slapped him when he tried to kiss her. لِطمَتَه مِن حاوَل يبُوسها [liṭmatah min ħa:wal ybu:sha]

slaughter • **1.** مَجزَرَة [maǰzara] مَجازِر [maǰa:zir] *pl:* مَذبَحَة [maðbaħa] مَذابِح [maða:biħ] *pl:* The slaughter was terrific. المَجزَرَة كانَت فَظِيعَة [ʔilmaǰzara ča:nat faði:ʕa]

to slaughter • **1.** ذِبَح [ðibaħ] ذَبِح [ðabiħ] *vn:* اِنذِبَح [ʔinðibaħ] *p:* We usually slaughter sheep on holidays. عادَةً نِذبَح خَرُوف بأيّام العِيد [ʕa:datan niðbaħ xaru:f bʔayya:m ʔilʕi:d]

slave • **1.** عَبِد [ʕabid] عَبِيد [ʕabi:d] *pl:* He treats them like slaves. يعامِلهُم عَبالَك عَبِيد [yʕa:milhum ʕaba:lak ʕabi:d]

*** I've really slaved today.** • **1.** إشتِغَلِت مِثل الحمار اليَوم [ʔiššta:ɣalit miθl ʔilħma:r ʔilyu:m]

sleep • **1.** نُوم [nu:m, nawm] Sleep is important. النُّوم مُهِمّ [ʔinnu:m muhimm]

to get sleep • **1.** نام [na:m] نَوم [nawm] *vn: sv* a. I didn't get enough sleep last night. ما نِمِت كِفايَة البارحَة باللَّيل [ma: nimit kifa:ya ʔilba:rħa billayl]

to sleep • **1.** نام [na:m] نَوم [nu:m] *vn: sv* a. Did you sleep well? نِمِت زين؟ [nimit zi:n?]

*** Sleep on it before you decide.**
• **1.** فَكِّر بِيها هَاللَّيلَة قَبُل ما تقرِّر [fakkar bi:ha hallayla gabul ma: tqarrir]

sleepy • **1.** نَعسان [naʕsa:n] منَعِّس [mnaʕʕis] I'm still sleepy. بَعَدنِي نَعسان [baʕadni naʕsa:n]

to make sleepy • **1.** نَعَّس [naʕʕas] تَنعِيس [tanʕi:s] *vn:* إتنَعَّس [tnaʕʕas] *p:* The heat's making me sleepy. الحَرارَة تنَعِّسنِي [ʔilħara:ra tnaʕʕisni]

sleeve • **1.** ردِن [ridin] ردانات [rda:na:t] *pl:* ردان [rda:n] The sleeves are too short. الرِّدانات كُلِّش قصار [ʔirrida:na:t kulliš gṣa:r]

*** He laughed up his sleeve.** • **1.** ضِحَك بعِبَّه [ðiħak bʕibbah]

slender • **1.** رَشِيق [raši:q] She's gotten very slender. صايرَة كُلِّش رَشِيقَة [ṣa:yra kulliš raši:ga]

slice • **1.** قُطعَة [quṭʕa] قُطَع [quṭaʕ] *pl:* وُصلَة [wuṣla] وُصَل [wuṣal] *pl:* How many slices of bread shall I cut? كَم قُطعَة خُبُز أَقُصّ؟ [čam quṭʕat xubuz ʔaguṣṣ?] • **2.** شِيف [ši:f] شياف [šya:f] *pl:* Have another slice of watermelon. أُخُذ شِيف لاخ رَقِّي [ʔuxuð ši:f la:x raggi]

to slice • **1.** شَرَّح [šarrah] تشرِّح [tširrih] *vn:* تشَرَّح [tšarrah] *p:* Do you want to slice the roast?

تريد تشَرِّح اللَّحَم؟ [tri:d tšarriħ ʔillaħam?] • **2.** شَيَّف [šayyaf] تَشْيِيف [tašyi:f] *vn: sv* i. Slice up the cucumbers. شَيِّفي الخيارَة [šayyifi ʔilxya:ra]

slide • **1.** سلايدَة [sla:yda] سلايدات [sla:yda:t] *pl:* He gave a lecture with slides. نِطَى مُحاضَرَة بِالسّلايدات [niṭa: muħa:ðara bissla:yda:t] • **2.** زِحلَيقَة [ziħlayga] زِحليقات [ziħli:ga:t] *pl:* The city put a new slide in the playground. البَلَدِيَّة حَطّت زِحلاقَة جِدِيدَة بِالمَلعَب [ʔilbaladiyya ħaṭṭat ziħla:ga ǰidi:da bilmalʕab]

to slide • **1.** زَحلَق [zaħlag] تزحلِق [tziħlig] *vn: sv* i. Pick the desk up; don't slide it on the floor. شِيل الميز، لا تزَحلِقَه عَالقاع [ši:l ʔilmi:z, la: dzaħilgah (ʕalga:ʕ)]

slight • **1.** بَسِيط [baṣi:ṭ] بَسِيطِين [baṣi:ṭi:n] *pl:* طَفِيف [ṭafi:f] قَلِيل [qali:l] There's a slight difference. أَكُو اِختِلاف بَسِيط [ʔaku ʔixtila:f basi:ṭ] • **2.** خَفِيف [xafi:f] He has a slight cold. عِندَه نَشلَة خَفِيفَة [ʕindah našla xafi:fa] • **3.** نَحِيف [naħi:f] she's very slight. هِيَّ كُلِّش نَحِيفَة [hiyya kulliš naħi:fa]

slightest • **1.** أَقَلّ [ʔaqall] I haven't the slightest doubt. ما عِندِي أَقَلّ شَكّ [ma: ʕindi ʔaqall šakk]

slim • **1.** نَحِيف [naħi:f] ضَعِيف [ðaʕi:f] She's gotten very slim. صارَت كُلِّش نَحِيفَة [ṣa:rat kulliš naħi:fa] • **2.** ضَعِيف [ðaʕi:f] His chances are very slim. أَمَلَه كُلِّش ضِعِيف [ʔamalah kulliš ðiʕi:f]

sling • **1.** مِعكال [miʕča:l] مَعاكِيل [maʕa:či:l] *pl:* مِعجان [miʕǰa:n] مَعاجِين [maʕa:ǰi:n] *pl:* David killed Goliath with a sling. داوُود قِتَل جالُوت بِالمِعكال [da:wud kital ǰa:lu:t bilmiʕča:l] • **2.** عِلّاقَة [ʕilla:ga] عِلّاقات، علالِيق [ʕilla:ga:t, ʕila:li:g] *pl:* They put his broken arm in a sling. عَلّقَوا إِيدَه بِعِلّاقَة [ʕalligaw ʔi:dah bʕilla:ga]

slingshot • **1.** مُصيادَة [muṣya:da] مُصيادات [muṣya:da:t] *pl:* I'm looking for some rubber to make a slingshot. دَأدَوِّر عَلَى وُصلَة لاستِيك حَتَّى أَسَوِّي مُصيادَة [daʔadawwir ʕala wuṣlat la:sti:g ħatta ʔasawwi muṣya:da]

slip • **1.** بَيت [bayt] بيُوت [byu:t] *pl:* Our pillows need new slips. مخادِيدنا ينرادِلها بيُوت جِدِيدَة [mxa:di:dna yinra:dilha byu:t ǰidi:da] • **2.** أَتَق [ʔatag] أَتَقات [ʔataga:t] *pl:* Your slip is showing. أَتَقِك دَيبَيِّن [ʔatagič daybayyin] • **3.** زَلَّة [zalla] زَلّات [zalla:t] *pl:* زَلقَة [zalga] زَلقات [zalga:t] *pl:* It was just a slip of the tongue. كانَت بَسّ زَلَّة لِسان [ča:nat bass zallat lisa:n] • **4.** وُصلَة [wuṣla] وُصَل [wuṣal] *pl:* He wrote it on a slip of paper. كِتَبها عَلَى وُصلَة وَرَق [kitabha ʕala wuṣlat waraq]

to give someone the slip • **1.** مِلَص مِن [milaṣ min] مَلِص [maluṣ] *vn: sv* a. فِلَت مِن [filat min] فَلِت [falit] *vn: sv* i. He's given us the slip again. مُلَص مِن عِدنا مَرَّة لُخ [mulaṣ min ʕidna marra lux]

to slip • **1.** زِلَق [zilaq] زَلِق [zaliq] *vn: sv* a. تزَحلَق [tzaħlag] تزِحلِق [tziħlig] *vn: sv* a. I slipped on the ice. زَلَقِت عالثَّلِج [zalagit ʕaθθaliǰ] • **2.** طِلَع [ṭilaʕ] طُلُوع [ṭulu:ʕ] *vn: sv* a. It slipped my mind completely. طلَع مِن بالِي تَماماً [ṭlaʕ min ba:li tama:man]
*** He slipped the policeman some money.**
• **1.** عَبَّر الفلُوس لِلشُرطِي [ʕabbar ʔilflu:s liššurṭi]
*** Wait until I slip into a coat.** • **1.** إِنتِظِر إِلَى أَن أَلبَس سِترَة [ʔintiðir ʔila ʔan ʔalbas sitra]
to slip away • **1.** شِلَع [šilaʕ] شَلِع [šaliʕ] *vn: sv* a. نَسّ [nass] نَسّ [nass] *vn: sv* i. Let's slip away, before he sees us. خَلِّي نِشلَع قَبُل ما يشُوفنا [xalli nišlaʕ gabul ma: yšu:fna]
to slip by • **1.** فات [fa:t] فَوت [fawt] *vn: sv* u. I let the chance slip by me. خَلَّيت الفُرصَة تفُوتنِي [xalli:t ʔilfurṣa tfu:tni]
to slip out • **1.** فِلَت مِن [filat min] فَلِت [falit] *vn: sv* i. I really didn't want to tell him, but it just slipped out. بِالحَقِيقَة ما رِدِت أَقُلَّه، بَسّ فِلتَت مِن لِسانِي [bilħaqi:qa ma: ridit ʔagullah, bass filtat min lisa:ni] The bird slipped out of my hand. العَصفُور فِلَت مِن إِيدِي [ʔilʕaṣfu:r filat min ʔi:di] • **2.** زُبَق [zubag] زَبُق [zabug] *vn: sv* u. The fish slipped out of my hand. زُبقَت السِّمكَة مِن إِيدِي [zubgat ʔissimča min ʔi:di]
to slip up • **1.** خَربَط [xarbaṭ] تخُربُط [txurbuṭ] *vn: sv* u. I slipped up badly on the next question. خَربَطِت هوايَة بالسّوال الثّانِي [xarbaṭit hwa:ya bissuʔa:l ʔiθθa:ni] • **2.** توَهدَن [twahdan] توهدِن [twihdin] *vn: sv* a. I don't know how I could have slipped up on that job. ما أَدرِي شلُون توَهدَنِت بِهَالشَّغلَة [ma: ʔadri šlu:n twahdanit bhaššaɣla]

slipper • **1.** نَعال [naʕa:l] نِعِل ،نعالات [nʕa:la:t, niʕil] *pl:* I can't find my slippers. ما دَأقدَر أَلقِي نَعالِي [ma: daʔagdar ʔalgi naʕa:li] • **2.** بابُوج [ba:bu:ǰ] بوابِيج [bwa:bi:ǰ] *pl:* My wife lost her slippers. زَوجتِي ضَيّعَت بابُوجها [zawiǰti ðayyʕat ba:bu:ǰha]

slippery • **1.** زَلَق [zalag] The streets are very slippery. الشَّوارِع كُلِّش زَلَق [ʔiššawa:riʕ kulliš zalag] • **2.** مِتقَلِّب [mitqallib] مِتقَلّبِين [mitqallibi:n] *pl:* He's a slippery character. هُوَّ واحِد مِتقَلِّب [huwwa wa:ħid mitqallib]

slit • **1.** فَتحَة [fatħa] شَقّ [šagg] شقُوق [šgu:g] *pl:* Make the slit a bit longer. سَوِّي الفَتحَة شوَيَّة أَطوَل [sawwi ʔilfatħa šwayya ʔaṭwal]
to slit • **1.** قَصّ [gaṣṣ] قَصّ [gaṣṣ] *vn: sv* u. The criminals slit his throat. المُجرِمِين قَصُّوا جُوزتَه [ʔilmuǰrimi:n gaṣṣaw ǰu:ztah]

slogan • **1.** شِعار [šiʕa:r] شِعارات [šiʕa:ra:t] *pl:* The students wrote slogans on the walls. الطُّلّاب كِتبَوا شِعارات عالحِيطان [ʔiṭṭulla:b kitbaw šiʕa:ra:t ʕalħi:ṭa:n] • **2.** هِتاف [hita:f] هِتافات [hita:fa:t] *pl:* I didn't hear their slogans. ما سِمَعِت هِتافاتهُم [ma: simaʕit hita:fa:thum]

S

slope • **1.** مُنحَدَر [munħadar] مُنحَدَرات [munħadara:t] *pl:* اِنحِدار [ʔinħida:r] اِنحِدارات [ʔinħida:ra:t] *pl:* دِهدِوانَة [dihidwa:na] دِهدِوانات [dihidwa:na:t] *pl:* Is the slope very steep? المُنحَدَر قَوي؟ [ʔilmunħadar qawi?]

to slope • **1.** اِنحِدَر [ʔinħidar] اِنحِدار [ʔinħida:r] *vn: sv* i. The floor slopes. القاع مِنحَدرَة [ʔilga:ʕ minħadra]

sloppy • **1.** مبَهدَل [mbahðal] Don't be so sloppy! لا تكُون هَالقَدّ مبَهدَل. [la: tku:n halgadd mbahðal] • **2.** مخَربَط [mxarbaṭ] They always do sloppy work. دائِماً يسَوُّون شُغُل مخَربَط [da:ʔiman ysawwu:n šuɣul mxarbaṭ]

slot • **1.** فَتحَة [fatħa] Put ten fils in the slot when you want to call from a public phone. حُطّ عَشِر فلُوس بالفَتحَة مِن ترِيد تخابُر مِن تِلِفُون عُمُومِي [ħuṭṭ ʕašir flu:s bilfatħa min tri:d txa:bur min tilifu:n ʕumu:mi]

slow • **1.** بَطِيء [baṭi:ʔ] He's very slow in his work. هُوَّ كُلِّش بَطِيئ بشُغلَه [huwwa kulliš baṭi:ʔ bšuɣlah] • **2.** مأخِّرَة [mʔaxxira] مُقصِّرَة [mqaṣṣira] Your watch is slow. ساعتَك مأخِّرَة [sa:ʕtak mʔaxxira] • **3.** هادِي [ha:di] خَفِيف [xafi:f] Cook the soup over a slow fire. أُطبُخ الشُّوربَة عَلَى نار هادِيَة [ʔuṭbux ʔiššu:rba ʕala na:r ha:diya]

to slow down • **1.** خَفَّف [xaffaf] تَخفِيف [taxfi:f] *vn:* تخَفَّف [txaffaf] *p:* تمَهَّل [tmahhal] تَمَهُّل [tamahhul] *vn: sv* a. Slow down when you come to an intersection. خَفُّف مِن تُوصَل لِلتَّقاطُع [xaffuf min tu:ṣal littaqa:ṭuʕ] Slow down; I can't keep up with you. خَفُّف مَشيَك؛ ما أَقدَر أَلحَّق بِيك [xaffuf mašyak; ma: ʔagdar ʔalaħħig bi:k] • **2.** تماهَل [tma:hal] تَماهُل [tama:hul] *vn: sv* a. He's slowing down in his work. دَيِتماهَل بشُغلَه [dayitma:hal bšuɣlah]

slowly • **1.** يَواش [yawa:š] بُطُء [buṭuʔ] Drive slowly. سُوق يَواش [su:q yawa:š] Drive slowly. سُوق عَلَى كَيفَك [su:q ʕala kayfak]

sly • **1.** مَكّار [makka:r] ماكِر [ma:kir]

small • **1.** صغَيِّر [ṣɣayyir] صغار [ṣɣa:r] *pl:* The room is rather small. الغُرفَة شوَيَّة صغَيّرَة [ʔilɣurfa šwayya ṣɣayyra] • **2.** بَسِيط [baṣi:ṭ] بَسِيطِين [baṣi:ṭi:n] *pl:* قَلِيل [qali:l] The difference is very small. الاختِلاف كُلِّش بَسِيط [ʔilʔixtila:f kulliš basi:ṭ] • **3.** وَضِيع [waḏi:ʕ] That was an awfully small thing to do. هَذا عَمَل وَضِيع [ha:ða ʕamal waḏi:ʕ]

smaller • **1.** أَصغَر [ʔaṣɣar, ʔazɣar] I haven't anything smaller. ما عِندِي شِي أَصغَر [ma: ʕindi ši ʔaṣɣar]

smallpox • **1.** جِدرِي [ǰidri] We have all been vaccinated against smallpox. كُلّتنا تطَعَّمنا ضِدّ الجِّدرِي [kullatna ʔiṭṭaʕʕamna ḏidd ʔiǰǰidri]

smart • **1.** لَطِيف [laṭi:f] أَنِيق [ʔani:q] That's a smart dress. هَذِي بَدلَة لَطِيفَة [ha:ði badla laṭi:fa] • **2.** ذَكِي [ðaki] أَذكِياء [ʔaðkiya:] *pl:* He's a smart boy. هَذا وَلَد ذَكِي [ha:ða walad ðaki]

to smart • **1.** حِرَق [ħirag] حَرِق [ħarig] *vn: sv* i. The wound smarts. الجُّرِح يِحرِق [ʔiǰǰariħ yiħrig]

to smash • **1.** كَسَّر [kassar] تكِسِّر [tkissir] *vn:* تكَسَّر [tkassar] *p:* حَطَّم [ħaṭṭam] تحُطُّم [tħuṭṭum] *vn:* تحَطَّم [tħaṭṭam] *p:* The boys smashed the window. الوِلِد كَسِّرَوا الشِّبّاك [ʔilwilid kassiraw ʔiššibba:č]

smell • **1.** رِيحَة [ri:ħa] رِيحات، [ri:ħa:t, riyyaħ] *pl:* What's that smell? شِنُو هَالرِّيحَة؟ [šinu: harri:ħa?] • **2.** شَمّ [šamm] His sense of smell is keen. حاسَّة الشَّمّ مالتَه حادَّة [ħa:ssat ʔiššamm ma:ltah ħadda]

to smell • **1.** اِشتَمّ [ʔištamm] اِشتِمام [ʔištima:m] *vn: sv* a. Do you smell gasoline? تِشتَمّ رِيحَة البَنزِين؟ [tištamm ri:ħat ʔilbanzi:n?] • **2.** نِطَى رِيحَة [ri:ħa] *sv* i. It smells like a cooked lamb. تِنطِي رِيحَة لَحَم الغَنَم المَشوِي [tinṭi ri:ħat laħam ʔilɣanam ʔilmašwi]

smile • **1.** اِبتِسامَة [ʔibtisa:ma] اِبتِسامات [ʔibtisa:ma:t] *pl:* She has a charming smile. عِدها فَدّ اِبتِسامَة جَذّابَة [ʕidha fadd ʔibtisa:ma ǰaððaba]

*** She was all smiles.** • **1.** وُجِهّا كان ضَحُوك [wuččha ča:n ḏaħu:k]

to smile • **1.** اِبتِسَم [ʔibtisam] اِبتِسام [ʔibtisa:m] *vn: sv* i. Did I see you smile? شِفتَك تِبتِسِم؟ [šiftak tibtisim?]

smoke • **1.** دُخان [duxxa:n] Where's that smoke coming from? منِين دَيِجِي هَالدُّخّان؟ [mni:n dayiǰi hadduxxa:n?]

to smoke • **1.** دَخَّن [daxxan] تَدخِين، تدِخِّن [tadxi:n, tdixxin] *vn:* تدَخَّن [tdaxxan] *p:* Do you smoke? إِنتَ تدَخِّن؟ [ʔinta ddaxxin?] The stove is smoking again. الطَّبّاخ دَيدَخِّن مَرَّة لُخ [ʔiṭṭabba:x daydaxxin marra lux]

smoking • **1.** تَدخِين [tadxi:n] Smoking is forbidden here. التَّدخِين مَمنُوع هنا [ʔattadxi:n mamnu:ʕ hna]

smooth • **1.** ناعِم [na:ʕim] أَملَس [ʔamlas] مِلِس، مَلسِين [milis, malsi:n] *pl:* مَلسَة [malsa] *Feminine:* Her skin is very smooth. جِلدها كُلِّش ناعِم [ǰilidha kulliš na:ʕim] • **2.** هادِئ [ha:diʔ] The sea was very smooth. البَحَر كان كُلِّش هادِئ [ʔilbaħar ča:n kulliš ha:diʔ]

*** I can't get a smooth shave with this blade.** • **1.** هَالمُوس ما ينَعِّم زَين [halmu:s ma: ynaʕʕim zayn]

to smooth down • **1.** نَوَّم [nawwam] تَنوِيم [tanwi:m] *vn:* تنَوَّم [tnawwam] *p:* صَفَّف [ṣaffaf] تَصفِيف [taṣfi:f] *vn:* تصَفَّف [tṣaffaf] *p:* Smooth down your hair نَوُّم شَعرَك [nawwum šaʕrak]

to smooth out • **1.** عَدَّل [ʕaddal] تَعدِيل [taʕdi:l] *vn:* تعَدَّل [tʕaddal] *p:* رَتَّب [rattab] تَرتِيب [tarti:b] *vn:* ترَتَّب [trattab] *p:* Smooth out the tablecloth. عَدِّل غطا المِيز [ʕaddil ɣaṭa ʔilmayz]

S

smoothly • **1.** بهُدوء [bhudu:ʔ] سَلام [sala:m] Everything went smoothly. كُلّشِي مِشَى بهُدوء [kullši miša: bhidu:ʔ]

to smother • **1.** خِنَق [xinag] خَنِق [xanig] *vn:* اِنخِنَق [ʔinxinag] *p:* He smothered the child with the pillow. خِنَق الطِّفِل بِالمَخَدَّة [xinag ʔiṭṭifil bilʔimxadda] • **2.** اِختِنَق [ʔixtinag] اِختِناق [ʔixtina:g] *vn: sv* i. We nearly smothered. اِختِنَقنا إلّا شوَيَّة [ʔixtinagna ʔilla šwayya]

to smuggle • **1.** هَرَّب [harrab] تَهريب [tahri:b] *vn:* تهَرَّب [tharrab] *p:* They smuggled in arms. هَرِّبَوا سلاح لِلدّاخِل [harribaw sla:ħ lidda:xil]

snail • **1.** حَلَزُونَة [ħalazu:na] حَلَزُونات [ħalazu:na:t] *pl:* حَلَزُون [ħalazu:n] *Collective*

snake • **1.** حَيَّة [ħayya] حَيّات [ħayya:t] *pl:*

snap • **1.** طُبّاقَة [ṭubba:ga] طُبّاقات [ṭubba:ga:t] *pl:* I have to sew snaps on my dress. لازِم أخَيِّط طُبّاقات عَلَى نَفنُوفِي [la:zim ʔaxayyiṭ ṭubba:ga:t ʕala nafnu:fi] • **2.** حَرَكَة [ħaraka] رُوح [ru:ħ] Put some snap in your marching. خَلّوا شوَيَّة حَرَكَة بمَشيكُم [xallu: šwayya ħaraka bmašykum] • **3.** سَرِيع [sari:ʕ] Don't make snap judgments. لا تِنطِي أحكام سَرِيعَة [la: tinṭi ʔaħka:m sari:ʕa]

* **The exam was a snap.** • **1.** الامتِحان كان بَسِيط [ʔilʔintiħa:n ča:n basi:ṭ] / الامتِحان كان زَلاطَة [ʔilʔimtiħa:n ča:n zala:ṭa]

to snap • **1.** طَقّ [ṭagg] طَقّ [ṭagg] *vn: sv* u. If the cucumber's fresh and crisp, just bend it and it snaps. الخيارَة، إذا هَشَّة، بَسّ تِثنِيها تطُقّ [ʔilxya:ra, ʔiða hašša, bass tiθni:ha ʔiṭṭugg] • **2.** دَقّ [dagg] دَقّ [dagg] *vn: sv* u. He snaps two fingers when he sings. مِن يغَنِّي يدُقّ إصبِعتين [min yɣanni ydugg ʔiṣbiʕtayn] • **3.** نَتَر [nitar] نَتِر [natir] *vn:* اِنَّتَر [ʔinnitar] *p:* I don't know why he snapped at me that way. ما أدري لِيش نِتَر بِيّا هِيكِي [ma: ʔadri li:š nitar biyya hi:či]

* **Snap out of it!** • **1.** أترُكها [ʔutrukha]

* **The dog snapped at me.** • **1.** الكَلِب حاوَل يعَضِّنِي [ʔiččalib ħa:wal yʕaðḍni]

to snap up • **1.** فَلّ [fall] فَلّ [fall] *vn: sv* i. Snap it up! The train leaves in half an hour. فِلها القِطار راح يِتحَرَّك بَعَد نُصّ ساعَة [fillha ʔilqiṭa:r ra:ħ yitħarrak baʕad nuṣṣ sa:ʕa]

snappy • **1.** أنِيق [ʔani:q] He's a snappy dresser. هُوَّ أنِيق بِاللِّبِس [huwwa ʔani:q billibis]

* **Come on, make it snappy.** • **1.** يا الله، بِالعَجَل [yalla, bilʕajal]

snapshot • **1.** صُورَة [ṣu:ra] صُوَر [ṣuwar] *pl:* Where did you take these snapshots? وين أخَذِت هَالصُّوَر؟ [wi:n ʔaxaðit haṣṣuwar?]

to sneak • **1.** دِخَل بِلبَسكُوت [dixal bilbasku:t] He must have sneaked into the house. لازِم دِخَل البَيت بالبَسكُوت [la:zim dixal ʔilbayt bilbasku:t]

sneaky • **1.** سَختَجِي [saxtači] سَختَجِيَّة [saxtači:yya] *pl:* He's pretty sneaky. هُوَّ سَختَجِي [huwwa saxtači]

sneeze • **1.** عَطسَة [ʕaṭsa] عَطسات [ʕaṭsa:t] *pl:* That sure was a loud sneeze. حَقِيقَةً كانَت عَطسَة قَوِيَّة [ħaqi:qatan ča:nat ʕaṭsa qawiyya]

to sneeze • **1.** عِطَس [ʕiṭas] عَطِس [ʕaṭis] *vn: sv* i. I sneezed from the dust. عِطَسِت مِن العَجاج [ʕiṭasit min ʔilʕaja:j] • **2.** عَطَّس [ʕaṭṭas] تعِطِّس [tʕiṭṭis] *vn:* تعَطَّس [tʕaṭṭas] *p:* He's been sneezing all morning. صارلَه دَيعَطِّس مِن الصُّبُح [ṣa:rlah dayʕaṭṭis min ʔiṣṣubuħ]

to sniff • **1.** اِشتَمّ [ʔištamm] شَمّ [šamm] *vn: sv* a. شَمشَم [šamšam] تشِمشِم [tšimšim] *vn: sv* i. He sniffed the food. اِشتَمّ رِيحَة الأكِل [ʔištamm ri:ħat ʔilʔakil]

to snore • **1.** شِخَر [šixar] شَخِير [šaxi:r] *vn: sv* u. He snored all night long. كان يِشخُر اللَّيل كُلَّه [ča:n yišxur ʔillayl kullah]

snow • **1.** ثَلِج [θalij] ثُلوج [θulu:j] *pl:* How deep is the snow? شقَدّ عُمق الثَّلِج؟ [šgadd ɣumuj ʔiθθalij?]

to snow • **1.** ثِلَج [θilaj] ثَلِج [θalij] *vn: sv* i. It snowed all night. بُقَت تِثلِج اللَّيل كُلَّه [buqat tiθlij ʔillayl kullah]

* **We're snowed under with work.** • **1.** غِرَقنا بِالشُّغُل [ɣiragna biššuɣul]

so • **1.** هِيكِي [hi:či] صُدُق [ṣudug] صَحِيح [ṣaħi:ħ] تَمام [tama:m] Isn't that so? مُو هِيكِي؟ [mu: hi:či?] • **2.** لَعَد [laʕad] إذَن [ʔiðan] يَعنِي [yaʕni] So you think it's a good idea. لَعَد تِعتِقِد هاي خُوش فِكرَة [laʕad tiʕtiqid ha:y xu:š fikra] So you don't want to go. يَعنِي ما تريد ترُوح [yaʕni ma: tri:d tru:ħ] So what? شِنُو، يَعنِي؟ [šinu, yaʕni?] • **3.** هَمّ [hamm] هَمّ، هَمِّين، هَمِّينَة [hamm, hammi:n, hammi:na] If I can do it, so can you. إذا آنِي أقدَر أسَوِّيها، إنتَ هَمّ تِقدَر [ʔiða ʔa:ni ʔagdar ʔasawwi:ha, ʔinta hamm tigdar] • **4.** هَلقَدّ [halgadd] Why are you so lazy? إنتَ لِيش هَالقَدّ كَسلان؟ [ʔinta li:š halgadd kasla:n?] • **5.** إلَى دَرَجَة [ʔila: daraja] I'm so tired, I can't work. آنِي تَعبان إلَى دَرَجَة ما أقدَر أشتُغُل [ʔa:ni taʕba:n ʔila daraja ma: ʔagdar ʔaštuɣul] • **6.** كُلِّش [kulliš] You look so tired! مبَيِّن عَلِيك كُلِّش تَعبان [mbayyin ʕali:k kulliš taʕba:n]

* **So long!** • **1.** في امان الله [fiʔama:nʔilla:h] مَعَ السَّلامَة [maʕa ʔissala:ma]

* **I need five dinars or so.** • **1.** أحتاج حَوالِي خَمس دنانير [ʔaħta:j ħawa:li xams dana:ni:r]

so as to • **1.** حَتَّى [ħatta] I did some of the work so as to make things easier for you. سَوِّيت قِسِم مِن الشُّغُل حَتَّى أخَفِّف عَلِيك [sawwi:t qisim min ʔišuɣul ħatta ʔaxaffif ʕali:k]

S

so far • **1.** لِهَسَّة [lihassa] لحَدّ ِلآن [lħadd ilʔa:n] لحَدّ هَسَّة [lħadd hassa] I haven't had any news so far. لهَسَّة ما عِندِي أيّ أخبار [lhassa ma: ʕindi ʔayy ʔaxba:r] How are things? So far, so good. شلُون الأحوال؟ لهَسَّة، كُلّشِي زين [šlu:n ʔilʔaħwa:l? lhassa, kullši zi:n]

so far as • **1.** حَسَب ما [ħasab ma:] So far as I know, he's still in Austrila. حَسَب ما أعرُف هُوَّ بَعدَه بأسترالِيَا [ħasab ma: ʔaʕruf huwwa baʕdah bʔustra:lya]

so much • **1.** هَلقَدّ [halgadd] Not so much rice please. مُو هَالقَدّ تِمَّن، مِن فَضلَك [mu: halgadd timman, min faðlak] • **2.** جِدّاً [ǰiddan] هوايَة [hwa:ya] Thanks ever so much. أشكُرَك كُلّش هوايَة [ʔaškurak kulliš hwa:ya]

so on • **1.** إلَى آخِره [ʔila ʔa:xirihi] He went to the market and bought potatoes, tomatoes, and so on. راح لِلسُّوق وإشتِرَى بُتَيتَة، طَماطَة، وَإلَى آخِره [ra:ħ lissu:g wʔištira: puti:ta, ṭama:ṭa, waʔila ʔa:xirih]

so so • **1.** نُصّ ونُصّ [nuṣṣ wnuṣṣ] يَعنِي [yaʕni] How are you? So so. شلَونَك؟ نُصّ وَنُصّ [šlu:nak? nuṣṣ wnuṣṣ]

so that • **1.** حَتَّى [ħatta] I'm telling you so that you'll know آنِي دَأقُلَّك حَتَّى تُعرُف [ʔa:ni daʔagullak ħatta tuʕruf]

to soak • **1.** نِقَع [nigaʕ] نَقِع [nagiʕ] *vn:* اِنّقَع [ʔinnigaʕ] *p:* Leave the beans to soak. خَلّي الباقِلّا بالماي حَتَّى تِنقَع [xalli ʔilbagilla bilma:y ħatta tingaʕ] • **2.** نَقَّع [naggaʕ] تَنقِيع، تِنقِّع [tangi:ʕ, tniggiʕ] *vn:* تنَقَّع [tnaggaʕ] *p:* We soaked the laundry overnight. نَقَّعنا الهِدُوم طُول اللَّيل [naggaʕna ʔilhdu:m ṭu:l ʔillayl] • **3.** شَرَّب [šarrab] تشَرُّب، تَشرِيب [tšurrub, tašri:b] *vn:* تشَرَّب [tšarrab] *p:* Soak the bread in the gravy. شَرِّب الخُبُز بالمَرقَة [šarrib ʔilxubuz bilmarga]

to soak up • **1.** اِمتَصّ [ʔimtaṣṣ] اِمتِصاص [ʔimtiṣa:ṣ] *vn: sv* a. مَصّ [maṣṣ] مَصّ [maṣṣ] *vn: sv* u. The sponge will soak the water. الإسفَنجَة تِمتَصّ الماي [ʔilʔisfanǰa timtaṣṣ ʔilma:y]

soaked • **1.** منَقَّع [mnaggaʕ] منَقَّعِين [mnaggaʕi:n] *pl:* مبَلَّل [mballal] مبَلَّلِين [mballali:n] *pl:* We came home soaked. وُصَلنا لِلبَيت منَقَّعِين [wuṣalna lilbayt mnaggaʕi:n]

to get soaked • **1.** تنَقَّع [tnaggaʕ] تَنَقُّع [tanagguʕ] *vn: sv* a. تبَلَّل [tballal] تَبَلُّل [taballul] *vn: sv* a. I got soaked because I didn't have an umbrella. تنَقَّعِت لِأنّ ما كانَت عِندِي شَمسِيَّة [tnaggaʕit liʔann ma: ča:nat ʕindi šamsiyya]

soap • **1.** صابُونَة [ṣa:bu:na] صابُونات [ṣa:bu:na:t] *pl:* صابُون [ṣa:bu:n] *Collective:* I want a cake of soap. أرِيد قالَب صابُون [ʔari:d qa:lab ṣa:bu:n]

to soap • **1.** صَوبَن [ṣawban] تصَوبِن [tṣawbin] *vn: sv* i. Dad is soaping his face. أبُويَا دَيصَوبِن وُجّه [ʔabu:ya dayṣawbin wuččah]

*** Soap your face well before shaving.**

• **1.** خَلِّي الصابُون زَين قبل الحِلاقَة [xalli ʔiṣṣa:bu:n zi:n gabl ʔilħila:qa]

sob • **1.** شَهقَة بَكِي [šahgat bačy] شَهقات بَكِي [šahga:t] *pl:* We heard sobs in the next room. سمَعنا شَهقات بَكِي بالغُرفَة المُقابِلَة [simaʕna šahga:t bačy bilɣurfa ʔilmuqa:bila]

to sob • **1.** شِهَق مِن البَكِي [šihag min ʔilbačy] شَهِق مِن البَكِي [šahig min ʔilbačy] *vn: sv* a. The child sobbed bitterly. الطِّفِل شِهَق مِن البَكِي حيل [ʔiṭṭifil šihag min ʔilbačy ħi:l]

sober • **1.** صاحِي [ṣa:ħi] صاحِين [ṣa:ħi:n] *pl:* You never find him real sober. أبَد ما تِلقِيه صاحِي تَماماً [ʔabad ma: tilgi:h ṣa:ħi tama:man]

to sober up • **1.** صِحَى [ṣiħa:] صَحِي [ṣaħy] *vn: sv* a. He sobered up quickly. صِحَى بِالعَجَل [ṣiħa: bilʕaǰal]

soccer • **1.** كُرَة القَدَم [kurat ʔilqadam] Soccer is a very popular sport in Iraq. كُرَة القَدَم فَدّ لِعبَة كُلّش مَحبُوبَة بِالعِراق [kurat ʔilqadam fadd liʕba kulliš maħbu:ba bilʕira:q]

social • **1.** اِجتِماعِي [ʔiǰtima:ʕi] Social conditions have changed tremendously. الأحوال الاجتماعِيَّة تغَيِّرَت كُلّش هوايَة [ʔilʔaħwa:l ʔilʔiǰtima:ʕiyya tɣayyirat kulliš hwa:ya]

socialism • **1.** اِشتِراكِيَّة [ʔištira:kiyya]

socialist • **1.** اِشتِراكِي [ʔištira:ki] اِشتِراكِيِّين [ʔištira:kiyyi:n] *pl:*

socialistic • **1.** اِشتِراكِي [ʔištira:ki]

society • **1.** مُجتَمَع [muǰtamaʕ] مُجتَمَعات [muǰtamaʕa:t] *pl:* He doesn't feel at ease in society. ما ياخُذ حُرِّيتَه مِن هُوَّ بمُجتَمَع [ma: ya:xuð ħurri:tah min huwwa bmuǰtamaʕ] • **2.** جَمعِيَّة [ǰamʕiyya] جَمعِيّات [ǰamʕiyya:t] *pl:* The society was founded ten years ago. الجَّمعِيَّة تأسّسَت قَبُل عَشِر سنِين [ʔiǰǰamʕiyya tʔassisat gabul ʕašir sni:n]

sociological • **1.** اِجتِماعِي [ʔiǰtima:ʕi] I subscribed to a sociological journal. اِشترَكِت بمَجَلَّة اِجتِماعِيَّة [ʔištirakit bmaǰalla ʔiǰtima:ʕiyya]

sociologist • **1.** عالِم اِجتِماعِي [ʕa:lim ʔiǰtima:ʕi] عُلَماء اِجتِماعِيِّين [ʕulama:ʔ ʔiǰtima:ʕiyyi:n] *pl:*

sociology • **1.** عِلم الاجتِماع [ʕilm ʔilʔiǰtima:ʕ]

sock • **1.** لَكمَة [lakma] لَكمات [lakma:t] *pl:* بَوكس [bu:ks] بَوكسات [bu:ksa:t] *pl:* I'd give him a sock on the jaw if I were you. لَو بمَكانَك، أنطِيه لَكمَة عَلَى فَكَّه [law bmaka:nak, ʔanṭi:h lakma ʕala faččah] • **2.** تَكّ [takk] فَردَة جوارِيب [farda ǰwa:ri:b] جوارِيب [ǰwa:ri:b] *pl:* I want three pairs of socks. أرِيد ثلَث أزواج جوارِيب [ʔari:d tlaθ ʔ azwa:ǰ ǰwa:ri:b]

soda • **1.** صُودَة [ṣu:da] Bring me a bottle of soda water. جِيبلِي بُوطِل صُودَا [ǰi:bli buṭul ṣu:da]

S

soft • **1.** رَخُو [raxw] The ground's too soft to drive on. القاع رَخوَة؛ ما تِقدَر تسُوق عَليها [ʔilgaːʕ raxwa; maː tigdar tsuːq ʕaliːha] • **2.** لَيِّن [layyin] The bread is soft. الخُبُز لَيِّن [ʔilxubuz layyin] He's too soft with the prisoners. هُوَّ كُلِّش لَيِّن وِيّا المَساجِين [huwwa kulliš layyin wiyya ʔilmasaːjiːn] • **3.** ضَعِيف [ðaʕiːf] He's soft from lack of exercise. هُوَّ ضَعِيف بِسَبَب عَدَم لِعِب رِياضَة [huwwa ðaʕiːf bisabab ʕadam liʕib riyaːða] • **4.** رَقِيق [raqiːq] عَذِب [ʕaðib] ناعِم [naːʕim] Her voice is soft. صَوتها رَقِيق [ṣawtha raqiːq] • **5.** خَفِيف [xafiːf] A soft light would be better. تكُون أحسَن لَو الضُوا خَفِيف [tkuːn ʔaħsan law ʔiðuwa xafiːf] • **6.** سَهِل [sahil] He's got a soft job. شَغِلتَه سَهلَة [šagiltah sahla]

soft drinks • **1.** مُرَطِّبات [muraṭṭibaːt] Only soft drinks are served here. هنا عِدنا بَسّ مُرَطِّبات [hna ʕidna bass muraṭṭabaːt]

soil • **1.** تُربَة [turba] تراب [traːb] The soil here is very fertile. التُّربَة هنا كُلِّش خَصبَة [ʔitturba hna kulliš xaṣba]

to soil • **1.** وَسَّخ [wassax] توسِيخ، توُسُّخ [tawsiːx, twussux] *vn:* توَسَّخ [twassax] *p:* You soiled your suit. إنتَ وَسَّخِت قاطَك [ʔinta wassaxit qaːṭak]

soiled • **1.** موَسَّخ [mwassax] وَسِخ [wasix] Everything is soiled. كُلشِي موَسَّخ [kullši mwassax]

soldier • **1.** جُندِي [jundi] جنُود [jinuːd] *pl:*

sole • **1.** كَفّ رِجِل [čaff rijil] كفُوف رِجلَينات [čfuːf rijliːnaːt] *pl:* I have a cut on my sole. عِندِي جَرح بكَفّ رِجلِي [ʕindi jariħ bčaff rijli] • **2.** نَعَل [naʕal] نَعلات [naʕlaːt] *pl:* The soles of the brown shoes are worn. نَعَل القُندَرَة الجَّوزِي قايِم [naʕal ʔilqundara ʔijjawzi gaːyim] • **3.** وَحِيد [waħiːd] وَحِيدِين [waħiːdiːn] *pl:* He was the sole survivor. هُوَّ كان الوَحِيد اللِّي نِجا [huwwa čaːn ʔilwaħiːd ʔilli nijaː]

to sole • **1.** حَطّ نَعَل [ħaṭṭ naʕal] حَطّ نَعَل [ħaṭṭ naʕal] *vn: sv* u. I have to have my shoes half-soled. لازِم أحُطّ نُصّ نَعَل لقُندَرتِي [laːzim ʔaħuṭṭ nuṣṣ naʕal lqundarti]

solely • **1.** وَحِد [waħd-] I'm solely responsible. آنِي وَحدِي المَسؤُول [ʔaːni waħdi ʔilmasʔuːl]

solid • **1.** صَلِب [ṣalib] جامِد [jaːmid] Is the ice solid? الثَّلِج صار صَلِب؟ [ʔiθθalij ṣaːr ṣalib?] • **2.** كامِل [kaːmil] We waited a solid hour for him. اِنتِظَرنا لِمُدَّة ساعَة كامِلَة [ʔintiðarna limuddat saːʕa kaːmla] • **3.** قَوِي [qawi, guwi] تُكمَة [tukma] تُكمات، تُكَم [tukamaːt, tukam] *pl:* This chair doesn't seem very solid to me. ما أشُوف هَالسكَملِي كُلِّش قَوِي [maː ʔašuːf halskamli kulliš qawi] • **4.** خالِص [xaːliṣ] This ring is made of solid gold. هالمِحبَس مَعمُول مِن ذَهَب خالِص [halmiħbas maʕmuːl min ðahab xaːliṣ] • **5.** جامِد [jaːmid] جَوامِد [jawaːmid] *pl:* All liquids turn into solids by cooling. جَمِيع السَّوائِل تِتحَوَّل إلَى جَوامِد بالبُرُودَة [jamiːʕ ʔissawaːʔil titħawwal ʔila jawaːmid bilburuːda]

solution • **1.** مَحلُول [maħluːl] مَحالِيل [maħaːliːl] *pl:* You need a stronger solution. تِحتاج مَحلُول أقوَى [tiħtaːj maħluːl ʔaqwa] • **2.** حَلّ [ħall] حُلُول [ħuluːl] *pl:* We'll find some solution for it. راح نشُوف إلها حَلّ [raːħ nšuːf ʔilha ħall]

to solve • **1.** حَلّ [ħall] حَلّ [ħall] *vn:* اِنحَلّ [ʔinħall] *p: sv* i. I can't solve the riddle. ما أقدَر أحِلّ اللُّغُز [maː ʔaqdar ʔaħill ʔilluɣuz]

some • **1.** شوَيَّة [šwayya] He lent me some money. دايَنِّي شوَيَّة فلُوس [daːyanni šwayya fluːs] • **2.** بَعَض، بَعض [baʕað, baʕð] Some people can't stand noise. بَعض النّاس ما يِقدرُون يِتحَمَّلُون الضَّجَّة [baʕð ʔinnaːs maː ygidruːn yitħammaluːn ʔiððajja] • **3.** قِسِم [qisim] Some of us are going by train and some by car. قِسِم مِن عِدنا راح يرُوحُون بالقِطار وقِسِم بالسَّيّارَة [qisim min ʕidna raːħ yruːħuːn bilqiṭaːr wqisim bissayyaːra] • **4.** حَوالِي [ħawaːli] We stayed some two or three hours. بْقَينا حَوالِي ساعَتَين أو ثلاثَة [buqiːna ħawaːli saːʕatayn ʔaw tlaːθa] • **5.** فَدّ [fadd] You'll regret that some day. فَدّ يوم راح تِندَم عَليها [fadd yuːm raːħ tindam ʕaliːha]

somebody • **1.** فَدّ شَخِص [fadd šaxiṣ] واحِد [waːħid] Somebody asked for you. فَدّ شَخِص سأل عَنَّك [fadd šaxiṣ siʔal ʕannak]

somehow • **1.** بشِكِل مِن الأشكال [bšikil min ʔilʔaškaːl] We'll do it somehow. عُود نسَوِّيها بشِكِل مِن الأشكال [ʕuːd nsawwiːha bšikil min ʔilʔaškaːl] • **2.** بِصُورَة مِن الصُوَر [bṣuːra min ʔiṣṣuwar] The letter got lost somehow. المَكتُوب ضاع بِصُورَة مِن الصُّوَر [ʔilmaktuːb ðaːʕ bṣuːra min ʔiṣṣuwar]

someone • **1.** فَدّ أحَّد [fadd ʔaħħad] فَدّ واحِد [fadd waːħid] Is there someone here who can play the lute? أكُو فَدّ أحَّد هنا يُعرُف يدُقّ عُود؟ [ʔaku fadd ʔaħħad hnaː yuʕruf ydugg ʕuːd?]

something • **1.** شِي [ši] فَدّ شِي [fadd ši] Is something the matter? أكُو شِي؟ [ʔaku ši?] That's something to think about. هَذا فَدّ شِي يِسوَى التَّفكِير [haːða fadd ši yiswaː ʔattafkiːr] Something or other reminded me of home. فَدّ شِي ذَكَّرنِي بأهلِي [fadd ši ðakkarni bʔahli]

sometime • **1.** فَدّ يَوم [fadd yuːm] فَدّ وَكِت [fadd wakit] Why don't you visit us sometime? لِيش ما تزُورنا فَدّ يوم [liːš maː dzuːrna fadd yuːm]

sometimes • **1.** أحياناً [ʔaħyaːnan] بَعض الأحيان [baʕð ʔilʔaħyaːn] دَورات [dawraːt] مَرّات [marraːt] نوبَة

[nawba] نوبات [nawba:t] *pl:* Sometimes it gets very hot here. أحياناً تصير كُلِّش حارَّة هنا [ʔaħya:nan tṣi:r kulliš ħa:rra hna]

somewhat • **1.** شوَيَّة [šwayya] نَوعاً ما [nawʕan ma:] I feel somewhat tired. دَأَشعُر شوَيَّة تَعبان [daʔašʕur šwayya taʕba:n]

somewhere • **1.** بفَدّ مَكان [bfadd maka:n] بفَدّ مَحَلّ [bfadd maħall] I saw it somewhere, but I don't remember where. شِفِتها بفَدّ مَكان بَسّ ما أتذَكَّر وين [šifitha bfadd maka:n bass ma: ʔadðakkar wi:n]

son • **1.** وَلَد [walad] وُلِد [wulid] *pl:* إبِن [ʔibin] أبنَاء [ʔabna:ʔ] *pl:* Has he any sons? أكُو عِندَه وِلِد؟ [ʔaku ʕindah wilid?] Is this your son? هَذا إبنَك؟ [ha:ða ʔibnak?]

song • **1.** غُنُوَّة [ɣunnuwwa] غُنُوّات [ɣunnuwwa:t] *pl:* أغنِية [ʔuɣniya] أغنِيات، أغانِي [ʔuɣniya:t, ʔaɣa:ni] *pl:* غَنِّيَة [ɣanniyya] غَنِّيات [ɣanniyya:t] *pl:* Do you know the song? تُعرُف الغُنُوَّة؟ [tuʕruf ʔilɣunnuwwa?]

*** He always gives me the same song and dance.** • **1.** دائِماً يعِيد عَلَيّا نَفس الفَتلَبِيج [da:ʔiman yʕi:d ʕalayya: nafs ʔilfatlapi:č]

*** We bought the chair for a song.** • **1.** اِشتِرَينا السكَملِي بأخُو البَلاش [ʔištirayna ʔisskamli bʔaxu ʔilbala:š]

son-in-law • **1.** زَوج بِنت [zawǰ bint-] أزواج بَنات [ʔazwa:ǰ bana:t] *pl:* رَجِل بِنت [rajil bint] رجُولَة بَنات [rǰu:la bana:t] *pl:* My son-in-law is no good. زوج بِنتِي ما يِسوَى فِلِس [zawǰ binti ma: yiswa: filis]

soon • **1.** قَرِيباً [qaryiban] بَعد شوَيَّة [baʕd šwayya] He's coming back soon. راح يِرجَع قَرِيباً [ra:ħ yirǰaʕ qari:ban]

*** It's too soon to tell what's the matter with him.** • **1.** بَعَد لِهَسَّة ما نِقدَر نِعرُف شَكُو بِيه [baʕad lihassa ma: nigdar niʕruf šaku: bi:h]

*** I'd just as soon not go.** • **1.** أفَضِّل ما أرُوح [ʔafaðððil ma: ʔaru:ħ] / أحسَنلِي ما أرُوح [ʔaħsanli ma: ʔaru:ħ]

as soon as • **1.** أوَّل ما [ʔawwal ma:] Let me know as soon as you get here. قُلِّي أوَّل ما تُوصَل لِهنا [gulli ʔawwal ma: tu:ṣal lihna]

sooner • **1.** أسرَع [ʔasraʕ] The sooner you come, the better. شقَدّ ما تِجِي أسرَع، بَعَد أحسَن [šgadd ma: tiǰi ʔasraʕ, baʕad ʔaħsan]

*** No sooner said than done.** • **1.** أخَلِّصلَك إيّاها بلَحضَتها [ʔaxalliṣlak ʔiyya:ha blaħðatha]

sooner or later • **1.** عاجِلاً أو آجِلاً [ʕa:ǰilan ʔaw ʔa:ǰilan] أوَّل وتالِي [ʔawwal wta:li] Sooner or later we'll have to make up our minds. عاجِلاً أو آجِلاً لازِم نقَرِّر [ʕa:ǰilan ʔaw ʔa:ǰilan la:zim nqarrir]

to soothe • **1.** سَكَّن [sakkan] تَسكِين [taski:n] *vn:* تسَكَّن [tsakkan] *p:* هَدَّى [hadda?] تَهدِئَة [tahdiʔa] *vn:* تهَدَّى [thaddaʔ] *p:* This salve will soothe the pain. هَالدِّهِن راح يسَكِّن الوَجَع [haddihin ra:ħ ysakkin ʔilwaǰaʕ]

sore • **1.** جَرِح [ǰariħ] جرُوح [ǰru:ħ] *pl:* The sore is pretty well healed up. الجُّرِح تَقرِيباً لِحَم [ʔiǰǰariħ taqri:ban liħam] • **2.** حَبّ [ħabb] حَبابِي [ħaba:bi] *pl:* His leg was covered with sores. رِجلَه كانَت مغَطّايَة بِالحَبابِي [riǰlah ča:nat mɣaṭṭa:ya bilħaba:bi] • **3.** حَسّاس [ħassa:s] That's a sore point with him. هاي مَسألَة حَسّاسَة بِالنِّسبَة إلَه [ha:y masʔala ħassa:sa binnisba ʔilah] • **4.** زَعلان [zaʕla:n] زَعلانِين [zaʕla:ni:n] *pl:* Are you sore at me? إنتَ زَعلان عَلَيّا؟ [ʔinta zaʕla:n ʕalayya?]

*** I have a sore toe.** • **1.** عِندِي إصبِع برِجلِي دَيوجَعنِي [ʕindi ʔiṣbiʕ briǰli dayu:ǰaʕni]

*** Where's the sore spot?** • **1.** وَين مَنطِقَة الوَجَع؟ [wi:n manṭiqt ʔilwaǰaʕ?]

to get sore • **1.** زِعَل [ziʕal] زَعَل [zaʕal] *vn:* اِنزِعَل [ʔinziʕal] *p:* You needn't get sore so quickly. ماكُو حاجَة تِزعَل بِالعَجَل [ma:ku ħa:ǰa tizʕal bilʕaǰal]

sorrow • **1.** حِزِن [ħizin, ħuzun] She can't get over her sorrow. ما دَتِقدَر تِنسَى قَهَرها [ma: datigdar tinsa: qaharha]

sorry • **1.** مِتأسِّف [mitʔassif] آسِف [ʔa:sif] I'm really sorry. آنِي حَقِيقَةً مِتأسِّف [ʔa:ni ħaqi:qatan mitʔassif] I'm sorry to say it can't be done. آسِف أن أقُول ما مُمكِن تصِير [ʔa:sif ʔan ʔagu:l ma: mumkin tṣi:r] • **2.** العَفو [ʔilʕafw] آسِف [ʔa:sif] مِتأسِّف [mitʔassif] Sorry! Did I hurt you? العَفو، أذَّيتَك؟ [ʔilʕafw, ʔaðði:tak?]

*** I'm sorry for her.** • **1.** أشعُر بأسَف اِتِّجاهَا [ʔašʕur bʔasaf ʔittiǰa:hha]

sort • **1.** نوع [nawʕ, nu:ʕ] أنواع [ʔanwa:ʕ] *pl:* شِكِل [šikil] أشكال [ʔaška:l] *pl:* صِنِف [ṣinif] أصناف [ʔaṣna:f] *pl:* I can't get along with that sort of person. ما أقدَر أتِّفِق ويّا شَخِص مِن هَالنَّوع [ma: ʔagdar ʔattifiq wiyya šaxiṣ min hannu:ʕ]

*** What sort of person is he?** • **1.** هُوَّ شِنُو مِن شِي؟ [huwwa šinu min ši?]

sort of • **1.** نَوعاً ما [nawʕan ma:] فَدّ نَوع [fadd nawʕ] She's sort of nice. هِيَّ لَطِيفَة نَوعاً ما [hiyya laṭi:fa nawʕan ma:] • **2.** تَقرِيباً [taqri:ban] I sort of knew it was going to happen. تَقرِيباً عِرَفِت هَذا كان راح يصِير [taqri:ban ʕirafit ha:ða ča:n ra:ħ yṣi:r]

to sort • **1.** صَنَّف [ṣannaf] تَصنِيف [taṣni:f] *vn:* تصَنَّف [tṣannaf] *p:* عِزَل [ʕizal] عَزِل [ʕazil] *vn:* اِنعِزَل [ʔinʕizal] *p:* Have the stockings been sorted? الجّوارِيب تصَنِّفَت؟ [ʔiǰǰwa:ri:b tṣannifat?]

soul • **1.** رُوح [ru:ħ] رواح [rwa:ħ] *pl:* If someone dies, his soul will go to heaven. إذا الواحِد يمُوت، ترُوح رُوحَه لِلسِّما [ʔiða ʔilwa:ħid ymu:t, tru:ħ ru:ħah lissima]

S

• **2.** أَحَّد [ʔaħħad] إنسان [ʔinsaːn] نَفِس [nafis] نُفُوس، أنفُس [nufuːs, ʔanfus] *pl:* There wasn't a soul to be seen. ما كان أَحَّد مَوجُود [maː čaːn ʔaħħad mawǰuːd]

*** He's with us heart and soul. • 1.** هُوَّ وِيّانا تَماماً [huwwa wiyyaːna tamaːman]

sound • 1. صُوت [ṣuːt] أصوات [ʔaṣwaːt] *pl:* Light travels faster than sound. الضُوا يِنتِقِل أَسرَع مِن الصُّوت [ʔiððuwa yintiqil ʔasraʕ min ʔiṣṣuːt] • **2.** حِسّ [ħiss] حسُوس [ħsuːs] *pl:* What was that sound? شكان ذاك الحِسّ؟ [ščaːn ðaːk ʔilħiss?] • **3.** نَغمَة [naɣma] رَنَّة [ranna] I recognized her by the sound of her voice. عِرَفتها مِن نَغمَة حِسّها [ʕirafitha min naɣmat ħissha] • **4.** سَلِيم [saliːm] مِتِين [mitiːn] قَوِي [qawi, guwi] He has a sound constitution. عِندَه بُنيَة سَلِيمَة [ʕindah buniya saliːma]

*** That's a sound bit of advice. • 1.** هاي خُوش نَصِيحَة [haːy xuːš naṣiːħa]

*** He's sound asleep. • 1.** هُوَّ غاطّ بنَومَه [huwwa ɣaːṭṭ binnuːmah]

safe and sound • 1. صاغ سَلِيم [ṣaːɣ saliːm] He's back, safe and sound. رِجَع صاغ سَلِيم [rijaʕ ṣaːɣ saliːm]

to sound • 1. بَيَّن [bayyan] تَبيِين [tabyiːn] *vn:* تبَيَّن [tbayyan] *p:* The report sounds good. التَّقرِير يبَيِّن زين [ʔittaqriːr yibayyin ziːn]

to sound out • 1. جَسّ نَبَض [ǰass nabaḍ] جَسّ نَبَض [ǰass nabaḍ] *vn: sv* i. I'll have to sound him out first. لازِم أَوَّل أَجِسّ نَبضَه [laːzim ʔawwal ʔaǰiss nabḍah]

soup • 1. شورِبَة [šuːrba] شَوربات [šuːrbaːt] *pl:* Bring us the soup. جِيب إلنا الشُّورِبَة [ǰiːb ʔilna ʔiššuːrba]

sour • 1. حامُض [ħaːmuḍ] محَمُّض [mħammuḍ] The milk has turned sour. الحَلِيب صار حامُض [ʔilħaliːb ṣaːr ħaːmuḍ]

*** Don't make such a sour face. • 1.** لا تصِير هِيكِي معَبِّس [laː tṣiːr hiːči mʕabbis]

source • 1. مَصدَر [maṣdar] مَصادِر [maṣaːdir] *pl:* I have it from a reliable source. حَصَّلت عَليها مِن فَدّ مَصدَر مَوثُوق بِيه [ħaṣṣalit ʕaliːha min fadd maṣdar mawθuːq biːh] • **2.** أساس [ʔasaːs] أساسات [ʔasaːsaːt] *pl:* أُسُس [ʔusus] *pl:* Have you found the source of the trouble? عِرَفِت أساس المُشكِلَة؟ [ʕirafit ʔasaːs ʔilmuškila?] • **3.** نَبع [nabiʕ] The source of the river is north of here. مَنبَع النَّهَر مِن الشِّمال [manbaʕ ʔinnahar min ʔiššimaːl]

south • 1. جنُوب [ǰinuːb, ǰanuːb] The wind is coming from the south. الرِّياح جايَة مِن الجِنُوب [ʔirriyaːħ ǰaːya min ʔilǰinuːb] The arrow points south. السَّهِم يأَشِّر عالجِّنُوب [ʔissahim yiʔaššir ʕaǰǰinuːb]

southern • 1. جِنُوبِي [ǰinuːbi] This plant is found only in southern regions. هَالنَّبات يِنلِقِي بالمَناطِق الجِّنُوبِيَّة بَسّ [hannabaːt yinligi bilmanaːṭiq ʔiǰǰinuːbiyya bass]

souvenir • 1. تِذكار [tiðkaːr] تِذكارات [tiðkaːraːt] *pl:* I want to buy some souvenirs here. أَرِيد أَشتِرِيلِي كَم تِذكار مِن هنا [ʔariːd ʔaštiriːli čam tiðkaːr min hna]

sovereign • 1. ذات سِيادَة [ðaːt siyaːda] Iraq is a soverign state. العِراق دَولَة ذات سِيادَة [ʔilʕiraːq dawla ðaːt siyaːda]

Soviet • 1. سُوفياتِي [sufyaːti] They're in the Soviet sphere of influence. هُمَّ بمَنطِقَة النُّفُوذ السُّوفيَتِي [humma bmanṭiqat ʔinnufuːð ʔissufyaːti]

Soviet Russia • 1. رُوسيا السَوفياتِيَّة [ruːsyaː ʔissufyaːtiyya]

sow • 1. خَنزِيرَة [xanziːra, xinziːra] خَنزِيرات [xinziːraːt] *pl:*

to sow • 1. بِذَر [biðar] بَذِر [baðir] *vn:* اِنبِذَر [ʔinbiðar] *p: sv* i. He's sowing the field with wheat. دَيبِذِر حُنطَة بالحَقِل [dayibðir ħunṭa bilħaqil]

space • 1. فَضاء [faḍaːʔ] They've just fired another rocket into space. هَسَّة أَطلِقَوا صارُوخ لاخ لِلفَضاء [hassa ʔaṭliqaw ṣaːruːx laːx lilfaḍaːʔ] • **2.** مَكان [makaːn] The desk takes up too much space. المِيز ياخُذ مَكان كُلِّش كِبِير [ʔilmiːz yaːxuð makaːn kulliš čibiːr] • **3.** مَجال [maǰaːl] مَجالات [maǰaːlaːt] *pl:* There's a large space between the two houses. أَكُو مَجال واسِع بين البَيتَين [ʔaku maǰaːl waːsiʕ bayn ʔilbaytayn] • **4.** فَضوَة [faḍwa] فَضوات [faḍwaːt] *pl:* ساحَة [saːħa] ساحات [saːħaːt] *pl:* There's an open space behind the house. أَكُو فَضوَة وَرا البَيت [ʔaku faḍwa wara ʔilbayt] • **5.** خِلال [xilaːl] مُدَّة [mudda] فَترَة [fatra] He did the work in the space of two weeks. سَوَّى الشُّغُل بخِلال إسبُوعَين [sawwaː ʔiššuɣul bxilaːl ʔisbuːʕayn]

*** He was staring out into space. • 1.** كان صافُن [čaːn ṣaːfun] / كان ضارُب دالغَة [čaːn ḍaːrub daːlɣa]

to space • 1. باعَد [baːʕad] مُباعَدَة [mubaːʕada] *vn:* تباعَد [tbaːʕad] *p:* The posts are spaced a foot apart. العَوامِيد مِتباعِدَة عَن بَعَضها مَسافَة قَدَم [ʔilʕawaːmiːd mitbaːʕida ʕan baʕaḍha masaːfa qadam]

spade • 1. مِسحَة [misħa] مَساحِي [masaːħi] *pl:* Grab a spade and dig. أُخُذلَك مِسحا وَاُحفُر [ʔuxuðlak misħaː wʔuħfur]

*** Why don't you call a spade a spade? • 1.** لَيش ماتِحكِي الحَقِيقَة؟ [liːš maː tiħči ʔilħaqiːqa?]

spare • 1. فَراغ [faraːɣ] What do you do in your spare time? شِتسَوِّي بوَقِت فَراغَك؟ [šitsawwi bwakit faraːɣak?] • **2.** اِحتِياطِي [ʔiħtiyaːṭi] Can you find spare parts for your radio? تِقدَر تحَصِّل عَلَى أَدَوات اِحتِياطِيَّة لراديُوَك؟ [tigdar tħaṣṣil ʕala ʔadawaːt ʔiħtiyaːṭiyya lraːdyuwwak?] • **3.** زايِد [zaːyid] Is there any spare room in that car?

أكو مَكان زايِد بِهالسَّيّارَة؟ [ʔaku maka:n za:yid bhassayya:ra?] • **4.** إضافِي [ʔiđa:fi] سبَير [spayr] سبَيرات [spayra:t] *pl:* We never travel without a spare tire. أبَداً ما نسافِر بِلا تايَر سبَير [ʔabadan ma: nsa:fir bila ta:yir spayr]

to spare • **1.** وَفَّر عَن [waffar ʕan] تَوفِير [tawfi:r] *vn:* توَفَّر [twaffar] *p:* You can spare yourself the trouble. تِقدَر توَفُّر عَن نَفسَك الإزعاج [tigdar twaffur ʕan nafsak ʔilʔizʕa:ǰ] • **2.** خَلَّى مِن [xalla: min] *sv* i. Spare me the details. خَلِّينِي مِن التَّفاصِيل [xalli:ni min ʔittafa:ṣi:l] • **3.** اِستَغنَى عَن [ʔistaɣna: ʕan] اِستِغناء [ʔistiɣna:ʔ] *vn:* *sv* i. Can you spare the pencil? تِقدَر تِستَغنِي عَن القَلَم؟ [tigdar tistaɣni ʕan ʔilqalam?] • **4.** سِمَح ب [simaħ b-] سَمِح [samiħ] *vn:* *sv* a. Can you spare me a minute of your time? تِسمَحلِي بدَقِيقَة مِن وَقتَك؟ [tismaħli bdaqi:qa min waqtak?] • **5.** أبقَى عَلَى [ʔabqa:] إبقاء [ʔibqa:ʔ] *vn:* *sv* i. The commander spared the captives'! lives by putting them in a prison outside the city. القائِد أبقَى عَلَى حَياة الأسرَى بِوَضِعهُم بِسِجِن خارِج المَدِينَة [ʔilqa:ʔid ʔabqa: ʕala ħaya:t ʔilʔasra bwađiʕhum bsiǰin xa:riǰ ʔilmadi:na]

* **He spared no expense.** • **1.** ما بُخَل بشِي [ma: buxal bši]

sparingly • **1.** بِاقتِصاد [bʔiqtiṣa:d] بِتدَبِير [btadbi:r] Use it sparingly. اِستَعمِلها بِاقتِصاد [ʔistaʕmilha biqtiṣa:d]

spark • **1.** شَرارَة [šara:ra] شَرارات [šara:ra:t] *pl:* The fire was started by a spark. الحَرِيق بِدَى بِفَدّ شَرارَة [ʔilħari:q bida: bfadd šara:ra]

to sparkle • **1.** تلألأ [tlaʔlaʔ] تلِألِأ [tliʔliʔ] *vn:* *sv* a. The moonlight is sparkling on the water. ضُوَا القُمَر قاعِد يِتلألأ عالماي [đuwa ʔilgumar ga:ʕid yitlaʔlaʔ ʕalma:y]

spark plug • **1.** بلَك [plakk] بلَكّات [plakka:t] *pl:* I need new spark plugs for my car. أحتاج بلَكّات جِدِيدَة لسَيّارتِي [ʔaħta:ǰ plakka:t ǰidi:da lsayya:rti]

sparrow • **1.** عَصفُور [ʕaṣfu:r] عَصافِير [ʕaṣa:fi:r] *pl:*

to speak • **1.** حِچَى [ħiča:] حَچِي [ħači:] *vn:* اِنحِچَى [ʔinħiča:] *p:* تكَلَّم [tkallam] تَكَلُّم [takallum] *vn:* *sv* a. Am I speaking clearly enough? دَأحچِي بُوضُوح؟ [daʔaħči bwuđu:ħ?] May I speak to you? أقدَر أحچِي وِيّاك؟ [ʔagdar ʔaħči wiyya:k?]

* **It's nothing to speak of.** • **1.** مُو فَدّ شِي يِسوَى الذِكِر [mu: fadd ši yiswa: ʔiððikir] / ما بِيها شِي مُهِمّ [ma: bi:ha ši muhimm]

to speak to • **1.** كَلَّم [kallam] تكَلَّم [tkallam] *vn:* *sv* i. He spoke to me for half an hour. كَلَّمنِي لِمُدَّة نُصّ ساعَة [kallamni limuddat nuṣṣ sa:ʕa]

to speak up for • **1.** دافَع [da:faʕ] دِفاع [difa:ʕ] *vn:* *sv* a. Nobody spoke up for him. مَحَّد دافَع عَنَّه [maħħad da:faʕ ʕannah]

speaker • **1.** مُحَدِّث [muħaddiθ] مُحَدِّثِين [muħaddiθi:n] *pl:* مُتكَلِّم [mutkallim] مُتكَلِّمِين [mutkallimi:n] *pl:* He's an excellent speaker. هُوَّ مُتحَدِّث مُمتاز [huwwa mutħaddiθ mumta:z]

speaking • **1.** كَلام [kala:m] حَچِي [ħači] I prefer speaking to writing. أفَضِّل الكَلام عَالكِتابَة [ʔafađđil ʔilkala:m ʕalkita:ba]

* **We're not on speaking terms.** • **1.** إحنا ما نِتحاچَى [ʔiħna: ma: nitħa:ča]

spear • **1.** رُمُح [rumuħ] رِماح [rima:ħ] *pl:*

special • **1.** خاصّ [xa:ṣṣ] خُصُوصِي [xuṣu:ṣi] I'm saving it for a special occasion. آنِي ضامُنها لِمُناسَبَة خاصَّة [ʔa:ni đa:munha limuna:saba xa:ṣṣa]

specialty • **1.** اِختِصاص [ʔixtiṣa:ṣ] Children's diseases are his specialty. أمراض الأطفال اِختِصاصَه [ʔamra:đ ʔilʔaṭfa:l ʔixtiṣa:ṣah]

specific • **1.** مُعَيَّن [muʕayyan] He proposed specific means to remedy the situation. قَدَّم اِقتِراحات مُعَيَّنَة لِمُعالَجَة الوَضِع [qaddam ʔiqtira:ħa:t muʕayyana lmuʕa:lajat ʔilwađiʕ]

specifications • **1.** مُواصَفات [muwa:ṣafa:t] We can build it to your specifications. نِقدَر نِبنِيها حَسَب مُواصَفاتكُم [nigdar nibni:ha ħasab muwa:ṣafa:tkum]

spectator • **1.** مِتفَرِّج [mitfarriǰ] مِتفَرِّجِين [mitfarriǰi:n] *pl:*

speech • **1.** نُطُق [nuṭuq] he lost his speech after the accident. فُقَد نُطقَه بَعد الحادِث [fuqad nuṭqah baʕd ʔilħa:diθ] • **2.** خُطبَة [xuṭba] خُطَب [xuṭab] *pl:* That was a very good speech. هاي كانَت كُلِّش خُوش خُطبَة [ha:y ča:nat kulliš xu:š xuṭba]

speed • **1.** سُرعَة [surʕa] Let's put on a little speed. خَلِّي نزَيِّد السُّرعَة شوَيَّة [xalli nzayyid ʔissurʕa šwayya]

to speed • **1.** عَدَّى السُّرعَة [ʕadda: ʔissurʕa] تَعدِيَة [taʕdiyap] *vn:* تعَدَّى [tʕadda:] *p:* فات السُّرعَة [fa:t ʔissurʕa] فَوت [fawt] *vn:* اِنفات [ʔinfa:t] *p:* أسرَع [ʔasraʕ] إسراع [ʔisra:ʕ] *vn:* *sv* i. You're speeding now. إنتَ مِتعَدِّي السُّرعَة هَسَّة [ʔinta mitʕaddi ʔissurʕa hassa]

to speed up • **1.** عَجَّل [ʕaǰǰal] تَعجِيل [taʕǰi:l] *vn:* تعَجَّل [tʕaǰǰal] *p:* اِستَعجَل [ʔistaʕǰal] اِستِعجال [ʔistiʕǰa:l] *vn:* *sv* i. Can you speed things up a little? تِقدَر تعَجِّل شوَيَّة؟ [tigdar tʕaǰǰil šwayya?]

speed limit • **1.** سُرعَة مَحدُودَة [surʕa maħdu:da] The speed limit is thirty-five miles an hour. السُّرعَة المَحدُودَة خَمسَة وثلاثِين مِيل بالسّاعَة [ʔissurʕa ʔilmaħdu:da xamsa wtla:θi:n mi:l bissa:ʕa]

spell • **1.** سِحِر [siħir] She's completely under his spell. مأخُوذَة بِسِحرَه تَماماً [maʔxu:ða bsiħrah tama:man] She's completely under his spell. هِيَّ مَسحُورَة بِيه [hiyya masħu:ra bi:h] • **2.** نوبَة [nawba] نوبات [nawba:t] *pl:* Does she often get spells like that? هِيَّ دائماً تِجيها هِيكِي نُوبات؟ [hiyya da:ʔiman tiǰi:ha hi:či nu:ba:t?]

to spell • **1.** تهَجَّى [thaǰǰa:] تهجّي [thiǰǰi:] *vn: sv* a. Please spell your name. أرجُوك تهَجَّى إسمَك [ʔarǰu:k thaǰǰa: ʔismak] • **2.** ناب عَن [na:b ʕan] نِيابَة [niya:ba] *vn:* اِنّاب [ʔinna:b] *p:* Let me spell you awhile. خَلّينِي أنُوب عَنَّك شوَيَّة [xalli:ni ʔanu:b ʕannak šwayya]

to spend • **1.** صِرَف [ṣiraf] صَرُف [ṣaruf] *vn:* اِنصِرَف [ʔinṣiraf] *p:* We spent a lot of money. صرَفنا هوايَة فلُوس [ṣrafna hwa:ya flu:s] • **2.** قِضَى [giđa:] قَضِي [gađy] *vn:* اِنقِضَى [ʔingiđa:] *p:* I'd like to spend my vacation here. يعجِبنِي أقضِي إجازتِي هنا [yiʕǰibni ʔagđi ʔiǰa:zti hna]

sperm • **1.** مَنِي [maniy]

sphere • **1.** كُرَة [kura] كُرات [kura:t] *pl:* How do you find the capacity of a sphere? شلُون تحَصِّل عَلَى سِعَة الكُرَة؟ [šlu:n tħaṣṣil ʕala siʕat ʔilkura?] • **2.** مَنطِقَة [manṭiqa] مَناطِق [mana:ṭiq] *pl:* They're in the Russian sphere of influence. هُمَّ بمَنطِقَة النُّفُوذ الرُّوسِيَّة [humma bmanṭiqat ʔinnufu:đ ʔirru:siyya]

spice • **1.** بهار [bha:r] بهارات [bha:ra:t] *pl:* Do you use spices much in your cooking? تِستَعمِلِين هوايَة بهارات بالطَّبُخ؟ [tistaʕmili:n hwa:ya bha:ra:t biṭṭabux?]

to spice • **1.** خَلَّى بَهارات [xalla baha:ra:t] *sv* i. She spiced the food too much. خَلَّت هوايَة بهارات بالأكِل [xallat hwa:ya bha:ra:t bilʔakil]

* **The meat is highly spiced.** • **1.** اللَّحَم بِيه هوايَة بهارات [ʔillaħam bi:h hwa:ya bha:ra:t]

spider • **1.** عَنكَبُوت [ʕankabu:t] عَنكَبُوتات [ʕankabu:ta:t] *pl:* عَناكِب [ʕana:kib] [.] *pl:*

to spill • **1.** كَبّ [čabb, kabb] كَبّ [čabb] *vn:* اِنكَبّ [ʔinčabb] *p:* Who spilled the milk? مِنُو كَبّ الحَلِيب؟ [minu čabb ʔilħali:b?]

spin • **1.** فَرَّة [farra] فَرّات [farra:t] *pl:* We took a spin in his car. أخَذنا فَرَّة بسَيّارتَه [ʔaxađna farra bsayya:rtah]

to spin • **1.** فَرّ [farr] فَرّ [farr] *vn:* إنفَرّ [ʔinfarr] *p:* He spun the top. فَرّ المُصرَع [farr ʔilmuṣraʕ] • **2.** اِفتَرّ [ʔiftarr] My head is spinning. راسِي دَيِفتَرّ [ra:si dayiftarr] My head is spinning. راسِي دايخ [ra:si da:yix] • **3.** غِزَل [ɣizal] غَزِل [ɣazil] *vn:* اِنغِزَل [ʔinɣizal] *p:* فِتَل [fital] فَتِل [fatil] *vn:* اِنفِتَل [ʔinfital] *p:* The thread isn't spun evenly. الخَيط ما مَغزُول بالتَّساوِي [ʔilxi:ṭ ma: maɣzu:l bittasa:wi]

to spin around • **1.** اِلتاف [ʔilta:f] اِلتِفاف [ʔiltifa:f] *vn: sv* a. اِنِدار [ʔinda:r] *sv* a. He spun around and fired. اِلتاف وأطلَق رِصاصَة [ʔilta:f wʔaṭlaq riṣa:ṣa]

spinach • **1.** سبَيناغ [sbi:na:ɣ]

spine • **1.** شوكَة [šawka] شوكات [šawka:t] *pl:* I've got a spine from the cactus in my hand. أكُو شوكَة صُبَّير بِيدِي [ʔaku šawkat ṣubbi:r bi:di] • **2.** عَمُود فَقَرِي [ʕamu:d faqari] عَوامِيد فَقَرِيَّة [ʕawa:mi:d faqariyya] He broke his spine in the accident. كِسَر العَمُود الفَقَرِي مالَه بالحادِث [kisar ʔilʕamu:d ʔilfaqari ma:lah bilħa:diθ]

spiral • **1.** مَلوِي [malwi] لَولَبِي حَلَزُونِي [lawlabi ħalazu:ni] The minaret has a spiral staircase. المَنارَة بِيها دَرَج مَلوِي [ʔilmana:ra bi:ha daraǰ malwi]

spirit • **1.** رُوح [ru:ħ] أرواح [ʔarwa:ħ] *pl:* جِنِّي [ǰinni] جِنّ [ǰinn] *pl:* The natives believe in evil spirits. السُّكّان يِعتِقدُون بالأرواح الشِّرِّيرَة [ʔissukka:n yiʕtiqdu:n bilʔarwa:ħ ʔišširri:ra] • **2.** رَوح [ru:ħ] أرواح [ʔarwa:ħ] *pl:* I assume his spirit went to heaven when he died. أفتِرِض رُوحَه راحَت لِلجَنَّة مِن مات [ʔaftiriđ ru:ħa ra:ħat liǰǰanna min ma:t] • **3.** هِمَّة [himma] That's the proper spirit! هاي الهِمَّة الصَّحِيحَة [ha:y ʔilhimma ʔiṣṣaħi:ħa]

in good spirits • **1.** مِرتاح [mirta:ħ] I hope you're in good spirits. إن شاء الله تكُون مِرتاح [ʔinša:llah tku:n mirta:ħ]

in low spirits • **1.** مَهمُوم [mahmu:m] He seemed to be in low spirits. يبَيِّن عَليه مَهمُوم [yibayyin ʕali:h mahmu:m]

spiritual • **1.** رُوحِي [ru:ħi] There's a spiritual bond between them. أكُو فَدّ رابطَة رُوحِيَّة بَيناتهُم [ʔaku fadd ra:biṭa ru:ħiyya bayna:thum]

spit • **1.** سِيخ [si:x] سياخ [sya:x] *pl:* شِيش [ši:š] شِياش [šiya:š] *pl:* They're roasting a sheep on a spit. قاعِد يحَمِّصُون الخَرُوف بسِيخ [ga:ʕid yħammiṣu:n ʔilxaru:f bsi:x] • **2.** تَفلَة [tafla] تَفلات, تفال [tafla:t tfa:l] *pl:* His spit is yellow because he uses snuff. التَّفلَة مالتَه صَفرَة لِأنّ يِستَعمِل بَرنُوطِي [ʔittafla ma:ltah ṣafra liʔann yistaʕmil barnu:ṭi]

to spit • **1.** تِفَل [tifal] تفال [tfa:l] *vn: sv* i. بِصَق [bişaq] بصاق [bişa:q] *vn: sv* u. He spat on the ground. تِفَل عَالقاع [tifal ʕalga:ʕ]

spite • **1.** نِكايَة [nika:ya] He did it just for spite. سَوّاها بَسّ لِلنِّكايَة [sawwa:ha bass linnika:ya]

in spite of • **1.** بالرَّغُم مِن [b̈ʔirraɣum min] برَغُم [braɣum] I went in spite of the rain. رِحِت برَغُم المُطَر [riħit braɣum ʔilmuṭar]

to spite • **1.** غاض [ɣa:đ] إغاضَة [ʔiɣa:đa] *vn:* اِنغاض [ʔinɣa:đ] *p:* Are you doing that just to spite me? إنتَ دَتسَوِّيها حَتَّى تغِيضنِي بَسّ؟ [ʔinta datsawwi:ha ħatta tɣi:đni bass?]

S

to splash • **1.** طَفَّر [ṭaffar] تَطفِير [taṭfi:r] *vn:* تطَفَّر [ṭṭaffar] *p:* The car splashed water on me. السَّيّارَة طَفِّرَت عَلَيّا ماي [ʔissayya:ra ṭaffirat ʕalayya ma:y] • **2.** تطَفَّر [ṭṭaffar] تَطَفُّر [taṭaffur] *vn: sv* a. The water splashes in all directions. الماي دَيِتطَفَّر لكُلّ جِهَة [ʔilma:y dayiṭṭaffar lkull ǰiha] • **3.** طَبَّش [ṭabbaš] تَطبِيش، تطُبُّش [taṭbi:š, ṭṭubbuš] *vn:* تطَبَّش [ṭṭabbaš] *p:* The boy splashed through the shallow water. الوَلَد طَبَّش بِالكَيش [ʔilwalad ṭabbaš bilgi:š]

splendid • **1.** رائع [ra:ʔiʕ] فاخِر [fa:xir] مُمتاز [mumta:z] That was a splendid idea! ذِيك كانَت فَدّ فِكرَة رائِعَة [ði:č ča:nat fadd fikra ra:ʔiʕa]

splint • **1.** جِبِيرَة [ǰibi:ra] His arm has to be put in splints. إيدَه لازِم تِنحَطّ بِالجِبِيرَة [ʔi:dah la:zim tinħaṭṭ biǰǰabi:ra]

splinter • **1.** سِلّايَة [silla:ya] سِلّايات [silla:ya:t] *pl:* لِيطَة [li:ṭa] لِيطات [li:ṭa:t] *pl:* I've got a splinter under my nail. أَكُو سِلّايَة جَوَّة إظفِري [ʔaku silla:ya ǰawwa ʔiðifri]

split • **1.** اِنشِقاق [ʔinšiqa:q] اِنشِقاقات [ʔinšiqa:qa:t] *pl:* خِلاف [xila:f] خِلافات [xila:fa:t] *pl:* There was a split in the party. كان أَكُو اِنشِقاق بالحِزِب [ča:n ʔaku ʔinšiqa:q bilħizib] • **2.** فَطِر [faṭir] فطُور [fṭu:r] *pl:* شَقّ [šagg] شقُوق [šgu:g] *pl:* There's a split in that board. أَكُو فَطِر بِهَاللَّوحَة [ʔaku faṭir bhallawħa]

to split • **1.** فِلَق [filaq] فَلِق [faliq] *vn:* اِنفِلَق [ʔinfilaq] *p:* شَقّ [šagg] شَقّ [šagg] *vn:* اِنشَقّ [ʔinšagg] *p:* فِلَع [filaʕ] فَلِع [faliʕ] *vn:* اِنفِلَع [ʔinfilaʕ] *p:* The lightning split the tree from top to bottom. الصّاعِقَة فِلقَت الشَّجَرَة مِن فُوق لِجَوَّة [ʔiṣṣa:ʕiqa filqat ʔiššaǰara min fu:g liǰawwa] • **2.** اِنشَقّ [ʔinšaqq] اِنشِقاق [ʔinšiqa:q] *vn: sv* i. The party has split into three groups. الحِزِب اِنشَقّ إلَى ثَلاث أَقسام [ʔilħizib ʔinšaqq ʔila tlaθ ʔaqsa:m] • **3.** تقاسَم [tqa:sam] تَقاسُم [taga:sum] *vn: sv* a. They split the profits with the workers. تقاسمَوا الأَرباح ويّا العُمّال [tga:smaw ʔilʔarba:ħ wiyya ʔilʕumma:l] • **4.** قَسَّم [qassam] تَقسِيم [taqsi:m] *vn:* تقَسَّم [tqassam] *p:* The directors split the profits between the workers and investors. المُدَراء قَسّمَوا الأَرباح بين العُمّال وَالمُستَثمِرين [ʔilmudara:ʔ qassmaw ʔilʔarba:ħ bi:n ʔilʕumma:l wilmustaθmiri:n] • **5.** فِتَق [fitag] فَتِق [fatig] *vn:* اِنفِتَق [ʔinfitag] *p:* Your pants have split in the seat. بَنطَرُونَك اِنفِتَق بالمَقعَد [panṭaru:nak ʔinfitag bilmaqʕad]

*** I nearly split my sides laughing.**

• **1.** رِدت أَمُوت مِن الضِحِك [ridt ʔamu:t min ʔiððiħik] / طَقَّت بَطنِي مِن الضِّحِك [ṭaggat baṭni min ʔiððiħik]

to split hairs • **1.** دَقدَق [daqdaq] تدِقدِق [tdiqdiq] *vn: sv* i. Don't split hairs, please. بالله لا تدَقدِق [ballah la: ddaqdiq]

to spoil • **1.** خاس [xa:s] خَيس [xays] *vn: sv* i. جاف [ǰa:f] جَيف [ǰayf] *vn: sv* i. The apples are beginning to spoil. التَّفّاح دَيِبدِي يخِيس [ʔittiffa:ħ dayibdi yxi:s] • **2.** جاف [ǰa:f] جَيف [ǰi:f] *vn: sv* i. The meat will spoil in this heat. اللَّحَم راح يجِيف بِهَالحَرارَة [ʔillaħam ra:ħ yǰi:f bhalħara:ra] • **3.** فِسَد [fisad] فَسِد [fasid] *vn: sv* i. خِرَب [xirab] خَربان [xarba:n] *vn: sv* a. The eggs have spoiled. البَيض فِسَد [ʔilbayð fisad] • **4.** دَلَّل [dallal] تَدلِيل [tadli:l] *vn:* تدَلَّل [tdallal] *p:* You're spoiling him. إنتِي دَتدَلِّلِيه [ʔinti datdallili:h]

spoke • **1.** سِيم [si:m] سيامَة [sya:ma] *pl:* I broke two spokes in the front wheel. كِسَرِت سِيمَين بِالجَّرخ القِدّامِي [kisarit si:mayn biččarx ʔilgidda:mi]

sponge • **1.** إسفَنجَة [ʔisfanǰa] إسفَنجات [ʔisfanǰa:t] *pl:* سفَنج [sfanǰ] *Collective:* Where'd you buy that sponge? منِين اِشتِرَيت هاي الإسفَنجَة؟ [mni:n ʔištiri:t ha:y ʔilʔissfanǰa?] • **2.** طُفَيلِي [ṭufayli] طُفَيلِيَّة [ṭufayliyya] *pl:* He's an awful sponge. هُوَّ طُفَيلِي [huwwa ṭufayli]

to sponge off • **1.** مِسَح بِالإسفَنجَة [misaħ bilʔisfanǰa] مَسِح بِالإسفَنجَة [masiħ bilʔisfanǰa] *vn: sv* a. She sponged off the water. مِسحَت الماي بِالإسفَنجَة [misħat ʔilma:y bilʔisfanǰa] • **2.** تطَفَّل عَلَى [ṭṭaffal ʕala] تَطَفُّل [taṭafful] *vn: sv* a. He's always sponging off his friends. دائِماً يِتطَفَّل عَلَى أَصدِقاءه [da:ʔiman yiṭṭaffal ʕala ʔaṣdiqa:h]

spoon • **1.** خاشُوقَة [xa:šu:ga] خواشِيق [xwa:ši:g] *pl:* A spoon fell off the table. فَدّ خاشُوقَة وُقعَت مِن المَيز [fadd xa:šu:ga wugʕat min ʔalmi:z]

sport • **1.** لِعبَة رياضِيَّة [liʕbat riya:ðiyya] لِعبات رياضِيَّة [liʕba:t riya:ðiyya] *pl:* Soccer is a good sport. كُرَة القَدَم خُوش لِعبَة رياضِيَّة [kurat ʔilqadam xu:š liʕba riya:ðiyya]

sports • **1.** رياضَة [riya:ða] Do you go in for sports? تحِبّ الرِّياضَة؟ [tħibb ʔirriya:ða?]

spot • **1.** بُقعَة [buqʕa] بُقَع [buqaʕ] *pl:* لَطخَة [laṭxa] لَطخات [laṭxa:t] *pl:* لَكَّة [lakka] لَكّات [lakka:t] *pl:* You have a spot on your tie. أَكُو بُقعَة عَلَى رِباطَك [ʔaku buqʕa ʕala riba:ṭak] • **2.** مُكان [muka:n] أَماكِن [ʔama:kin] مُكانات [muka:na:t] *pl:* I stood in the same spot for a whole hour. بُقِيت بِنَفس المَكان لِمُدَّة ساعَة كامِلَة [buqi:t bnafis ʔilmaka:n lmuddat sa:ʕa ka:mila] A cup of coffee would just hit the spot. فَدّ فِنجان قَهوَة هَسَّة يكُون بِمُكانَه تَمام [fadd finǰa:n gahwa hassa yku:n bimuka:nah tama:m] • **3.** نُقطَة [nuqṭa] نُقَط [nuqaṭ] *pl:* You've touched a sore spot. إنتَ تطَرَّقِت إلَى نُقطَة حَسّاسَة [ʔinta ṭṭarraqit ʔila nuqṭa ħassa:sa] • **4.** مَنطِقَة [manṭiqa] مَناطِق [mana:ṭiq] *pl:* مُكان [muka:n] مُكانات [muka:na:t] *pl:* نُقطَة [nuqṭa] نُقَط [nuqaṭ] *pl:* Where is the sore spot? وين مَنطِقَة الأَلَم؟ [wi:n manṭiqat ʔilʔalam?]

on the spot • **1.** بلَحظَة [blaħða] لَحظات [laħða:t] *pl:* They fired him on the spot. طِردوه بِلَحضَتها

S

[ṭirdawh blaħðatha] • **2.** بنَفِس المَكان [bnafis ʔilmaka:n] I was right on the spot when the accident happened. مِن صار الحادِث، كِنِت بنَفِس المَكان [min ṣa:r ʔilħa:diθ, činit bnafis ʔalmaka:n] • **3.** بوَضِع حَرِج [bwaðiʕ ħarij] You put me on the spot. إنتَ خَلّيتني بوَضِع حَرِج [ʔinta xalli:tni bwaðiʕ ħarij] You put me on the spot. أحرَجِت مَوقِفي [ʔaħrajit mawqifi]

to spot • **1.** لِمَح [limaħ] لَمِح [lamiħ] *vn:* اِنلِمَح [ʔinlimaħ] *p:* I spotted him in the crowd. لِمَحتَه بالخَبصَة [limaħtah bilxabṣa] • **2.** مَيِّز [mayyaz] تَمييز [tamyi:z] *vn:* تمَيِّز [tmayyaz] *p:* I could spot him anywhere. أقدَر أمَيِّزَه وَين ما كان [ʔagdar ʔamayyzah wi:n ma: ča:n]

sprain • **1.** فَسِخ [fasix] فسُوخ [fsu:x] *pl:* You've got a bad sprain there. عِندَك فَسِخ قَوي [ʕindak fasix qawi]

to sprain • **1.** فُسَخ [fusax] فَصِخ [faṣix] *vn:* اِنفُصَخ [ʔinfuṣax] *p:* She sprained her ankle. فُصخَت مَرفَق رِجِلها [fuṣxat marfaq rijilha]

to spray • **1.** رَشّ [rašš] رَشّ [rašš] *vn:* اِنرَشّ [ʔinrašš] *p:* We have to spray the peach trees. لازِم نرُشّ أشجار الخُوخ [la:zim nrušš ʔašja:r ʔilxawx]

spread • **1.** اِنتِشار [ʔintiša:r] تَوَسُّع [tawassuʕ] They tried to check the spread of the disease. حاولَوا يوَقّفون اِنتِشار المَرَض [ħa:wlaw ywaggfu:n ʔintiša:r ʔilmarað] • **2.** شَرشَف [čarčaf] شَراشِف [čara:čif] *pl:* They put new spreads on the beds. حَطّوا شَراشِف جِديدَة عالجُرباپات [ħaṭṭaw čara:čif jidi:da ʕaččurpa:ya:t]

to spread • **1.** نِشَر [nišar] نَشِر [našir] *vn:* اِنّشَر [ʔinnišar] *p:* The gardener is spreading manure on the lawn. البُستَنجي دَينشُر السماد عالثَّيِّل [ʔilbustanči dayinšur ʔilsma:d ʕaθθayyal] • **2.** اِمتَدّ [ʔimtadd] اِمتِداد [ʔimtida:d] *vn: sv* a. اِنتِشَر [ʔintišar] اِنتِشار [ʔintiša:r] *vn: sv* a. The fire's spreading rapidly. النّار دَتِمتَدّ بسُرعَة [ʔinna:r datimtadd bsurʕa] The news spread quickly. الأخبار اِنتِشرَت بالعَجَل [ʔilʔaxba:r ʔintišrat bilʕajal] • **3.** وَزَّع [wazzaʕ] تَوزيع [tawzi:ʕ] *vn:* توَزَّع [twazzaʕ] *p:* The payments were spread over several years. الدَّفعات توَزّعَت عَلَى عِدَّة سنين [ʔiddafʕa:t twazzʕat ʕala ʕiddat sni:n]

to spread out • **1.** فُرَش [furaš] فَرِش [fariš] *vn:* اِنفُرَش [ʔinfuraš] *p:* مَدّ [madd] مَدّ [madd] *vn:* اِنمَدّ [ʔinmadd] *p:* Spread the map out. أفرُش الخَريطَة [ʔufruš ʔilxari:ṭa] • **2.** اِمتَدّ [ʔimtadd] اِمتِداد [ʔimtida:d] *vn: sv* a. We saw the whole valley spread out below us. شِفنا الوادي كُلَّه مِمتَدّ جَوّانا [šifna ʔilwa:di kullah mimtadd jawwa:na]

spring • **1.** رَبيع [rabi:ʕ] We arrived in spring. وُصَلنا بالرَّبيع [wuṣalna birrabi:ʕ] • **2.** عين [ʕayn ʕi:n] عيُون [ʕyu:n] *pl:* يَنبُوع، نَبع [yanbu:ʕ, nabiʕ] يَنابيع [yana:bi:ʕ] *pl:* There's a spring behind our house. أكو عَين وَرا بَيتنا [ʔaku ʕi:n wara baytna] • **3.** زُنبَلَق [zunbalag] زُنبَلَقات [zunbalaga:t] *pl:* The spring in my watch is broken. الزُّنبَلَك مال ساعتي مَكسُور [ʔizzunbalag ma:l sa:ʕti maksu:r] • **4.** سِبرِنك [sibring] سِبرِنكات [sibringa:t] *pl:* We broke a spring on the car on our trip. كسَرنا سِبرِنك السَّيّارَة بِسَفرَتنا [ksarna sipring ʔissayya:ra bsafratna]

to spring • **1.** قُمَز [gumaz] قَمُز [gamuz] *vn:* اِنقُمَز [ʔingumaz] *p:* He sprang from his seat. قُمَز مِن كُرسِيَّه [gumaz min kursiyyah] • **2.** طِلَع [ṭilaʕ] طُلُوع [ṭulu:ʕ] *vn: sv* a. All the rumors spring from the same source. كُلّ الإشاعات تِطلَع مِن نَفس المَصدَر [kull ʔilʔiša:ʕa:t tiṭlaʕ min nafs ʔilmaṣdar] • **3.** نِبَع [nibaʕ] نَبِع [nabiʕ] *vn: sv* a. The plant sprang up overnight. الزَّرِع نِبَع عَلَى غَفلَة [ʔizzariʕ nibaʕ ʕala ɣafla]

to sprinkle • **1.** رَشّ [rašš] رَشّ [rašš] *vn:* اِنرَشّ [ʔinrašš] *p:* طَشّ [ṭašš] طَشّ [ṭašš] *vn:* اِنطَشّ [ʔinṭašš] *p:* Have the streets been sprinkled yet? الشّوارِع اِنرَشَّت لَو بَعَد؟ [ʔiššawa:riʕ ʔinraššat law baʕad?]

spy • **1.** جاسُوس [ja:su:s] جواسِيس [jwa:si:s] *pl:* We're going to send a team of spies to Saudi Arabia. راح ندِزّ جَماعَة جَواسِيس لِلمَملَكَة العَرَبِيَّة السَّعُودِيَّة [ra:ħ ndizz jama:ʕat jawa:si:s lilmamlaka ʔilʕarabiyya ʔissaʕu:diyya]

to spy • **1.** تجَسَّس [djassas] تَجَسُّس [tajassus] *vn: sv* a. They caught him spying on a military installation. لِزمَوه دَيتجَسَّس بمُؤَسَّسَة عَسكَرِيَّة [lizmawh dayidjassas bmuʔassasa ʕaskariyya]

squad • **1.** حَضيرَة [ħaði:ra] حَضايِر [ħaða:yir] *pl:* An eight man squad was guarding the intersection. حَضيرَة مِن ثمَن رجال كانَوا يحِرسُون التَّقاطُع [ħaði:ra min θman rja:l ča:naw yħirsu:n ʔittaqa:ṭuʕ]

square • **1.** ساحَة [sa:ħa] ساحات [sa:ħa:t] *pl:* Our windows look out on a large square. شبابِيكنا تِشرِف عَلَى ساحَة كبيرَة [šba:bi:čna tišrif ʕala sa:ħa čbi:ra] • **2.** مُرَبَّع [murabbaʕ] That's not a square, that's a rectangle. هَذا مُو مُرَبَّع، هَذا مُستَطِيل [ha:ða mu: murabbaʕ, ha:ða mustaṭi:l] • **3.** عَدِل [ʕadil] He's a pretty square fellow. هُوَّ فَدّ واحِد عَدِل [huwwa fadd wa:ħid ʕadil]

*** I haven't eaten a square meal in days.** • **1.** صار هوايَة ما ماكِل أكلَة دَسمَة [ṣa:r hwa:ya ma: ma:kil ʔakla dasma]

*** Our back yard is twenty feet square.** • **1.** الساحَة الوَرّانِيَّة مالّتنا عَلَى شِكِل مُرَبَّع طُولَه وضِلعَه عِشرين قَدَم [ʔissa:ħa ʔilwarra:niyya ma:latna ʕala šikil murabbaʕ ṭu:lah wðilʕah ʕišri:n qadam]

*** This squares our account.** • **1.** هَذا يسَدِّد حسابنا [ha:ða ysaddid ħsa:bna]

squash • **1.** شِجرَة [šijra, šajra] شِجرات، أشجار، شَجَرات [šijra:t, ʔašja:r, šajara:t] *pl:* شِجَر [šijar] *Collective:* Buy some squash while you're at the market. اِشتِري شوَيَّة شِجَر مِن تكُون بالسُّوق [ʔištiri šwayya šijar min tku:n bissu:q]

S

to squash • **1.** جعَص [ǰiʕaṣ] جَعِص [ǰaʕiṣ] *vn:* اِنجِعَص [ʔinǰiʕaṣ] *p:* عِقَج [ʕiqač] عَقِك [ʕaqič] *vn:* اِنعِقَك [ʔinʕiqač] *p:* I squashed my hat when I sat down. جعَصِت شَفُقتِي مِن قِعَدِت [ǰiʕaṣit šafuqti min giʕadit] • **2.** حِصَر [ħiṣar] حَصِر [ħaṣir] *vn:* اِنحِصَر [ʔinħiṣar] *p:* I squashed my finger in the door. حصَرِت إصِبعِي بِالباب [ħṣarit ʔiṣibʕi bilba:b]

to squeal • **1.** صِرَخ [ṣirax] صراخ [ṣra:x] *vn: sv* u. عاط [ʕa:ṭ] عياط [ʕya:ṭ] *vn: sv* i. The child squealed with joy, الجّاهِل صِرَخ مِن الفَرَح [ʔiǰǰa:hil ṣirax min ʔilfaraħ] • **2.** وُشَى [wuša:] وُشايَة [wuša:ya] *vn:* اِنوِشَى [ʔinwiša:] *p:* Somebody must have squealed on us to the police. واحِد لازِم يكُون وِشَى بِينا لِلشُّرطَة [wa:ħid la:zim yku:n wiša: bi:na liššurṭa]

to squeeze • **1.** عِصَر [ʕiṣar] عَصِر [ʕaṣir] *vn:* اِنعِصَر [ʔinʕiṣar] *p:* Don't squeeze my hand so hard. لا تِعصِر إيدِي هَالقَدّ حيل [la: tiʕṣir ʔi:di halgadd ħi:l] I'll squeeze the oranges. راح أعصِر البُرتَقال [ra:ħ ʔaʕṣir ʔilpurtaqa:l] • **2.** دِحَس [diħas] دَحِس [daħis] *vn:* اِندِحَس [ʔindiħas] *p:* I can't squeeze another thing into my suitcase. ما أقدَر أدحَس أيّ شِي لاخ بِجنُطتِي [ma: ʔagdar ʔadħas ʔayy ši la:x bǰinuṭṭi]

squirrel • **1.** سِنجاب [sinǰa:b] سناجِيب، سَناجِب [sna:ǰi:b, sana:ǰib] *pl:*

to squirt • **1.** رَشّ [rašš] رَشّ [rašš] *vn:* اِنرَشّ [ʔinrašš] *p:* The elephant squirted water on the spectators. الفِيل رَشّ الماي عالمُتفَرِّجِين [ʔilfi:l rašš ʔilma:y ʕalmutafarriǰi:n]

to stab • **1.** طِعَن [ṭiʕan] طَعِن [ṭaʕin] *vn:* اِنطِعَن [ʔinṭiʕan] *p:* He was stabbed in the brawl. اِنطِعَن بِالعَركَة [ʔinṭiʕan bilʕarka] He's just waiting for a chance to stab me in the back. دَينتِهِز فُرصَة حَتَّى يطعَنِّي مِن الخَلف [dayintihiz furṣa ħatta yiṭʕanni min ʔilxalf]

stable • **1.** إسطَبِل [ʔisṭabil] إسطَبلات [ʔisṭabila:t] *pl:* Where are the stables? وين الإسطَبلات؟ [wi:n ʔilʔisṭabla:t?] • **2.** مُستَقِرّ [mustaqirr] They haven't had a stable government for years. ما صار عِدهُم حُكُومَة مُستَقِرَّة مِن مُدَّة طوِيلَة [ma: ṣa:r ʕidhum ħuku:ma mustaqirra min mudda ṭwi:la] • **3.** ثابِت [θa:bit] A stable currency is absolutely necessary. وُجود عُملَة ثابِتَة ضَرُورِي جِدّاً [wuǰu:d ʕumla θa:bita ðaru:ri ǰiddan]

stack • **1.** تَكَدُّس [takaddus] كُوم [ku:m] كُوام [kuwam] *pl:* I had to go through a whole stack of newspapers to find it. كان لازِم أدَوُّر أكداس مِن الجَّرايِد حَتَّى ألقاها [ča:n la:zim ʔadawwur ʔakda:s min ʔiǰǰara:yid ħatta ʔalga:ha]

to stack • **1.** كَدَّس [kaddas] تكدِيس [takdi:s] *vn:* تكَدَّس [tkaddas] *p:* كَوَّم [kawwam] تكوِيم [takwi:m] *vn:* تكَوَّم [tkawwam] *p:* Stack the books in the corner. كَدِّس الكُتُب بِالزُّوِيَّة [kaddis ʔilkutub bizzuwiyya]

staff • **1.** مُوَظَّفِين [muwaððafi:n] He dismissed part of his staff. طِرَد قِسِم مِن مُوَظَّفِيه [ṭirad qisim min muwaððafi:h]

general staff • **1.** قِيادَة الأركان [qiya:da ʔilʔarka:n] That officer has been attached to the general staff. هَذا الضّابُط اِلتَحَق بِقِيادَة الأركان [ha:ða ʔiððа:buṭ ʔiltaħaq bqiya:dat ʔilʔarka:n]

stage • **1.** مَسرَح [masraħ] مَسارِح [masa:riħ] *pl:* That hall has a nice stage. هاي القاعَة بِيها مَسرَح حِلو [ha:y ʔilqa:ʕa bi:ha masraħ ħilw] • **2.** مَرحَلَة [marħala] مَراحِل [mara:ħil] *pl:* It depends on what stage it's in. تِعتِمِد عَلَى المَرحَلَة اللّي هِيَّ بِيها [tiʕtimid ʕala ʔilmarħala ʔilli hiyya bi:ha]

to stage • **1.** قام ب [qa:m b-] قِيام [qiya:m] *vn:* اِنقام [ʔinqa:m] *p:* They staged the robbery in broad daylight. قامَوا بِالسَّرِقَة بِوَاضَح النَّهار [ga:maw bissariqa bwa:ðaħ ʔinnaha:r]

to stagger • **1.** تطَوطَح [tṭawṭaħ] تَطَوطُح [taṭawṭuħ] *vn: sv* a. ترَنَّح [trannaħ] تَرَنُّح [tarannuħ] *vn: sv* a. I saw him stagger out of a bar. شِفتَه طالِع مِن البار يِتطَوطَح [šiftah ṭa:liʕ min ʔilba:r yiṭṭu:ṭaħ] The blow staggered him. الضَّربَة خَلّاتَه يِتطُوطَح [ʔiððarba xalla:tah yiṭṭu:ṭaħ]

staggering • **1.** مُذهِل [muðhil] خَيالِي [xaya:li] فَضِيع [faði:ʕ] The prices are staggering. الأسعار صايرَة مُذهِلَة [ʔilʔasʕa:r ṣa:yra muðhila] Expenditures have reached staggering proportions. المَصرُوفات وُصلَت إلَى حَدّ فَظِيع [ʔalmaṣru:fa:t wuṣlat ʔila ħadd faði:ʕ] Expenditures have reached staggering proportions. المَصرُوفات تجاوزَت المَعقُول [ʔalmaṣru:fa:t dǰa:wzat ʔilmaʕqu:l]

stagnant • **1.** خايِس [xa:yis] جايِف [ǰa:yif] The water is stagnant. الماي خايِس [ʔilma:y xa:yis]

stain • **1.** بُقعَة [buqʕa] بُقَع [buqaʕ] *pl:* لَطخَة [laṭxa] لَطخات [laṭxa:t] *pl:* I can't get the stains out of my shirt. ما أقدَر أشِيل البُقَع مِن ثَوبِي [ma: ʔagdar ʔaši:l ʔilbuqaʕ min θu:bi]

to stain • **1.** لَوَّخ [lawwax] تَلوِيخ [talwi:x] *vn:* تلَوَّخ [tlawwax] *p:* You've stained your shirt. لَوَّخِت ثوبَك [lawwaxit θu:bak]

stairs • **1.** دَرَج [daraǰ] دَرَجات [daraǰa:t] *pl:* Take the stairs to your right. أخُذ الدَّرَج اللّي عَلَى يَمِينَك [ʔuxuð ʔiddaraǰ ʔilli ʕala yami:nak]

stake • **1.** عَمُود [ʕamu:d] أعمِدَة [ʔaʕmida] *pl:* You get the stakes for the fence. إنتَ جِيب الأعمِدَة مال السِّياج [ʔinta ǰi:b ʔilʔaʕmida ma:l ʔissiya:ǰ] • **2.** ثبات [θba:t] ثباتات [θba:ta:t] *pl:* وَتَد [watad] أوتاد [ʔawta:d] *pl:* He drove in a stake to tie up the cow to. دَقّ ثبات حَتَّى يشِدّ الهايشَة بِيه [dagg θba:t ħatta yšidd ʔilha:yša bi:h]

S

*** There's too much at stake.** • **1.** بِيها هوايَة مُخاطَرَة [biːha hwaːya muxaːṭara]
*** His life is at stake.** • **1.** حَياتَه مُهَدَّدَة بِالخَطَر [ħayaːtah muhaddada bilxaṭar] / دَيراهِن عَلَى حَياتَه [dayraːhin ʕala ħayaːtah]
*** My money's at stake.** • **1.** جازِفِت بأموالِي [ǰaːzafit bʔamwaːli]

stakes • **1.** رِهان [rihaːn] رَهِن [rahin] They doubled the stakes. ضاعفوا الرِّهان [ðaːʕfaw ʔirrihaːn]

to stall • **1.** طِفَى [ṭufaː] طَفِي [ṭafiy] *vn:* اِنطِفَى [ʔinṭufaː] *p:* The motor's stalled again. المُحَرِّك اِنطِفَى مَرَّة لُخ [ʔilmuħarrik ʔinṭufaː marra lux] • **2.** ماطَل [maːṭal] مُماطَلَة [mumaːṭala] *vn: sv* i. Quit stalling! لا تماطِل، عاد [laː tmaːṭil, ʕaːd] Quit stalling! يَزّي مُماطَلَة [yazzi mumaːṭala]

to stammer • **1.** تلَعثَم [tlaʕθam] تلِعثِم [tliʕθim] *vn: sv* a. He stammers when he talks. هُوَّ يِتلَعثَم بِكَلامَه [huwwa yitlaʕθam bkalaːmah]

stamp • **1.** طابِع [ṭaːbiʕ] طَوابِع [ṭawaːbiʕ] *pl:* Give me five ten-fils stamps, please. إنطِيني خَمِس طَوابِع أُمّ عَشِر فلُوس رَجاءاً [ʔinṭiːni xamis ṭawaːbiʕ ʔumm ʕašir fluːs raǰaːʔan] • **2.** طَمغَة [ṭamɣa] طَمغات [ṭamɣaːt] *pl:* خَتِم [xatim] أختام [ʔaxtaːm] *pl:* Where's the "Air Mail" stamp? وين طَمغَة البَرِيد الجَّوِّي؟ [wiːn ṭamɣat ʔilbariːd ʔiǰǰawwi?]
to stamp • **1.** طُمَغ [ṭumaɣ] طَمُغ [ṭamuɣ] *vn:* اِنطِمَغ [ʔinṭumaɣ] *p:* I stamped all the papers. طُمَغِت كُلّ الأوراق [ṭumaɣit kull ʔilʔawraːq] • **2.** دَقّ [dagg] دَقّ [dagg] *vn: sv* u. She stamped her foot. دَقَّت رِجِلها [daggat riǰilha]
to stamp out • **1.** أخمَد [ʔaxmad] خِمِد، خُمُود [xamid, xumuːd] *vn:* اِنخَمَد [ʔinxamad] *p:* He stamped out the fire. أخمَد النّار برِجلَه [ʔaxmad ʔinnaːr briǰlah]
• **2.** قِضَى عَلَى [qiðaː, giðaː ʕala] قَضِي [qaðiː] *vn:* اِنقِضَى [ʔinqiðaː] *p:* All opposition was ruthlessly stamped out. كُلّ المُعارَضَة اِنقِضَت عَليها [kull ʔilmuʕaːraða ʔinqiðat ʕaliːha]

S

stand • **1.** مَوقِف [mawqif] مَواقِف [mawaːqif] *pl:* He's changed his stand on this matter several times. غَيَّر مَوقِفَه بِالنِّسبَة لِهالمَوضُوع عِدَّة مَرّات [ɣayyar mawqifah binnisba ʔilhamawðuːʕ ʕiddat marraːt]
*** The witness will take the stand!** • **1.** الشاهِد ياخُذ مَكانَه [ʔiššaːhid yaːxuð makaːnah]
to stand • **1.** وُقَف [wugaf] وُقُوف [wuguːf] *vn: sv* a. He's standing in the rain. هُوَّ واقُف بالمُطَر [huwwa waːguf bilmuṭar] • **2.** صِمَد [ṣimad, ṣumad] صُمُود [ṣumuːd] *vn: sv* i. ثِبَت [θibat] ثُبُوت، ثَبات [θubuːt, θabaːt] *vn: sv* i. The soldiers stood their ground. الجِّنُود صِمدَوا بِمَراكِزهُم [ʔiǰǰinuːd ṣimdaw bmaraːkizhum] • **3.** بُقَى [buqaː] بَقاء [baqaːʔ] *vn: sv* a. He stood his ground. بُقَى ثابِت عَلَى مَوقِفَه [buqaː θaːbit ʕala mawqifah] • **4.** قاوَم [qaːwam] مُقاوَمَة [muqaːwama] *vn: sv* u. The city's defenders stood for three days. المُدافِعِين عَن المَدِينَة قاوُمَوا ثلَث أيّام [ʔilmudaːfiʕiːn ʕan ʔilmadiːna qaːwumaw tlaθ ʔayyaːm] • **5.** وَقَّف [waggaf] تَوقِيف [tawgiːf] *vn:* توَقَّف [twaggaf] *p:* Stand the ladder in the corner. وَقُف الدَّرَج بالزُّوِيَّة [wagguf ʔiddaraǰ bizzuwiyya]
• **6.** تحَمَّل [tħammal] تَحَمُّل [taħammul] *vn: sv* a. I can't stand it any longer there. ما أقدَر أتحَمَّل أكثَر هناك [maː ʔagdar ʔatħammal ʔakθar hnaːk] • **7.** واجَه [waːǰah] مُواجَهَة [muwaːǰaha] *vn: sv* i. جابَه [ǰaːbah] مُجابَهَة [muǰaːbaha] *vn: sv* i. You'll have to stand trial if they catch you. لازِم تواجِه مُحاكَمَة إذا لِزمُوك [laːzim twaːǰih muħaːkama ʔiða lizmuːk]
*** You don't stand a chance of getting accepted.** • **1.** ماكُو أمَل تِنقِبِل [maːku ʔamal tinqibil]
*** What I said the other day still stands.** • **1.** اللي قِلتَه البارحَة بَعدَه ماشِي [ʔilli giltah ʔilbaːrħa baʕda maːši] / اللّي قِلتَه البارحَة بَعدَه ما تغَيَّر [ʔilli giltah ʔilbaːrħa baʕdah maː tɣayyar]
*** You can have it as it stands for 50 dinars.** • **1.** تِقدَر تاخُذها مِثِل ما هِيَّ بخَمسِين دِينار [tigdar taːxuðha miθil maː hiyya bxamsiːn dinaːr]
to stand by • **1.** طُبَق [ṭubag] طَبُق [ṭabug] *vn: sv* u. He always stands by his friends. دائماً يِطبُق ويّا أصحابَه [daːʔiman yiṭbug wiyya ʔaṣħaːbah] • **2.** بِقَى [biqaː] إبقاء [ʔibiqaːʔ] *vn: sv* a. I'm standing by my decision. آني باقِي عَلَى قَرارِي [ʔaːni baːqi ʕala qaraːri]
*** Stand by, I may need you later.** • **1.** كُون حاضِر، يِمكِن أحتاجَك بَعدَين [kuːn ħaːðir, yimkin ʔaħtaːǰak baʕdiːn]
*** He stood by, doing nothing.** • **1.** وُقَف مِثِل اللّوح [wugaf miθl ʔilluːħ]
to stand for • **1.** أيَّد [ʔayyad] تَأيِيد [taʔyiːd] *vn:* تأيَّد [tʔayyad] *p:* He stands for greater cooperation with neighboring states. يأيِّد زِيادَة التَّعاوُن مَعَ الأقطار المُجاوِرَة [yʔayyid ziyaːdat ʔittaʕaːwun maʕa ʔilʔaqṭaːr ʔilmuǰaːwira] • **2.** مَثَّل [maθθal] تَمثِيل [tamθiːl] *vn: sv* i. The olive branch stands for peace. غُصن الزَّيتُون يمَثِّل السَّلام [ɣuṣn ʔizzaytuːn ymaθθil ʔissalaːm] • **3.** قِبَل [qibal] قُبُول [qubuːl] *vn:* اِنقِبَل [ʔinqibal] *p:* I won't stand for that sort of treatment. ما أقبَل هِيكِي مُعامَلَة [maː ʔaqbal hiːči muʕaːmala]
*** He stands for equality.** • **1.** هُوَّ مِن دُعاة المُساواة [huwwa min duʕaːt ʔilmusaːwaːt]
to stand on • **1.** اِعتِمَد عَلَى [ʔiʕtimad ʕala] *sv* i. I'll stand on my record. أعتِمِد عَلَى الماضِي مالِي [ʔaʕtimid ʕala ʔalmaːði maːli]
to stand out • **1.** بِرَز [biraz] بُرُوز [buruːz] *vn: sv* i. ظِهَر [ðihar] ظُهُور [ðuhuːr] *vn: sv* u. She stands out in a crowd. هِيَّ ظاهرَة بين المَجمُوعَة [hiyya ðaːhra bayn ʔilmaǰmuːʕa] He stands out in physics. هُوَّ كُلِّش بارِز بِالفِيزيا [huwwa kulliš baːriz bilfiːzya]
to stand up • **1.** وُقَف [wugaf] وُقُوف [wuguːf] *vn: sv* a. Don't bother standing up. لا تِزحِّم نَفسَك وَتُوقَف

[la: dzaħħim nafsak wtu:gaf] • **2.** قاوَم [qa:wam] مُقاوَمَة [muqa:wama] *vn: sv* u. صَمَخ [ṣumax] صَمُخ [ṣamux] *vn: sv* u. كَدّ [kadd] كَدّ [kadd] *vn: sv* u. The car has stood up well. السَّيّارَة صُمخَت زين [ʔissayya:ra ṣumxat zi:n]

*** She stood me up at the last minute.**
• **1.** اِعتِذرَت بآخِر لَحظَة [ʔiʕtiðrat bʔa:xir laħða]

to stand up for • **1.** دافَع [sa:ʕad, da:faʕ] مُساعَدَة، دِفاع [musa:ʕada, difa:ʕ] *vn: sv* i. دافع [da:faʕ] دِفاع [difa:ʕ] *vn: sv* i. If we don't stand up for him, no one else will. إذا ما نساعَدَه، مَحَّد راح يساعدَه [ʔiða ma: nsa:ʕadah, maħħad ra:ħ ysa:ʕdah]

standard • **1.** مِقياس [miqya:s] مَقاييس [maqa:yi:s] *pl:* You can't judge him by ordinary standards. ما تِقدَر تُحكُم عَليه بِالمَقاييس العادِيَّة [ma: tigdar tuħkum ʕali:h bilmaqa:yi:s ʔilʕa:diyya] • **2.** مِعيار [miʕya:r] مَعايير [maʕa:yi:r] *pl:* Their standards are high. مَعاييرهُم عالية [maʕa:yi:rhum ʕa:lya] • **3.** مُستَوَى [mustawa] Their standard of living is lower than ours. مُستَوَى مَعيشَتهُم أَقَلّ مِن عِدنا [mustawa: maʕi:šathum ʔaqall min ʕidna] • **4.** اِعتِيادِي [ʔiʕtiya:di] We carry all the standard sizes. عِدنا كُلّ الأَحجام الاعتِيادِيَّة [ʕidna kull ʔilʔaħja:m ʔilʔiʕtiya:diyya]

stand-by • **1.** حالَة إنذار [ħa:lat ʔinða:r] I'm on stand-by this week. آني بِحالَة إنذار هَالإسبُوع [ʔa:ni bħa:lat ʔinða:r halʔisbu:ʕ]

standing • **1.** مَقام [maqa:m] مَركَز [markaz] He has a high standing in the community. مَقامَه عالِي بِالمُجتَمَع [maqa:mah ʕa:li bilmujtamaʕ] • **2.** ساكِن [sa:kin] راكِد [ra:kid] It's standing water. هَذا الماي ساكِن [ha:ða ʔilma:y sa:kin] • **3.** وُقوف [wugu:f] There's standing room only. أَكُو مَحَلّ لِلوُقُوف بَسّ [ʔaku maħall lilwuqu:f bass]

*** They're friends of long-standing.**
• **1.** هُمَّ أَصدِقاء صارلهُم زَمان [humma ʔaṣdiqa:ʔ ṣa:rilhum zama:n]

star • **1.** نَجمَة [najma] نَجمات [najma:t] *pl:* نَجم [najim] نُجُوم [nuju:m] *pl:* The sky's full of stars. السَّماء مَليانَة نجُوم [ʔissama:ʔ malya:na nju:m] • **2.** بَطَل [baṭal] أَبطال [ʔabṭa:l] *pl:* Who was the star in that picture? مِنُو كانَت البَطَلَة بذاك الفِلم؟ [minu ča:nat ʔilbaṭala bða:k ʔilfilim?]

*** He's my star pupil.** • **1.** هَذا أَحسَن طالِب عِندِي [ha:ða ʔaħsan ṭa:lib ʕindi]

starch • **1.** نِشا [niša] Put some starch in the shirts. خَلّي شوَيَّة نِشا لِلثِّياب [xalli šwayya niša liθθiya:b]

to starch • **1.** نَشّى [nišša:] تَنشِيَة [tanšiya] *vn: sv* i. Did you starch the shirts? نَشّيت الثِّياب؟ [naššiːt ʔiθθiya:b?]

to stare • **1.** بَحلَق [baħlaq] بَحلَقَة [baħlaqa] *vn: sv* i. He just stared into space. بَحلَق بِالسِّما [baħlaq bissima]

start • **1.** بِدايَة [bida:ya] بِدايات [bida:ya:t] *pl:* It was all wrong from the start. كان مُخطِئ مِن البِدايَة [ča:n muxṭiʔ min ʔilbida:ya]

*** You gave me quite a start.** • **1.** فَزّزتنِي [fazzazitni] / جَفّلتِنِي [jaffalitni]

to start • **1.** بِدا [bida:] بِدايَة [bida:ya] *vn:* اِنبِدا [ʔinbida:] *p:* The movie has just started. الفِلِم هَسَّة بِدا [ʔilfilim hassa bida:] How did the fire start? شلُون بِدا الحَريق؟ [šlu:n bida: ʔilħari:q?] • **2.** بِدا [bida:] بِدايَة [bida:ya] *vn:* اِنبِدا [ʔinbida:] *p:* Who started this rumor? مِنُو بِدا بهَالإشاعَة؟ [minu bida: bhalʔiša:ʕa?] • **3.** شَغَّل [šayɣal] تَشغِيل [tašɣi:l] *vn:* تشَغَّل [tšayɣal] *p:* حَرَّك [ħarrak] تَحرِيك [taħri:k] *vn: sv* i. Start the motor. شَغِّل المُحَرِّك [šayɣil ʔilmuħarrik] • **4.** شِعَل [šiʕal] شَعِل [šaʕil] *vn:* اِنشِعَل [ʔinšiʕal] *p:* Let's start a fire and get warm. خَلّي نِشعِل نار وَنِتدَفّى [xalli nišʕil na:r wniddaffa:] • **5.** تحَرَّك [tħarrak] تَحَرُّك [taħarruk] *vn: sv* i. The train started slowly. القِطار تحَرَّك بِبُطء [ʔilqiṭa:r tħarrak bibuṭʔ]

starting • **1.** اِبتِداءً مِن [ʔibtida:ʔan min] Starting today the bus will stop here. اِبتِداءً مِن اليَوم الباص راح يُوقَف هنا [ʔibtida:ʔan min ʔilyu:m ʔilpa:ṣ ra:ħ yu:gaf hna]

to startle • **1.** جَفَّل [jaffal] تَجفِيل [tajfi:l] *vn:* تجَفَّل [tjaffal] *p:* فَزَّز [fazzaz] تفزِيز [tafzi:z] *vn:* تفَزَّز [tfazzaz] *p:* The noise startled me. الصَّوت جَفّلنِي [ʔiṣṣawt jaffalni]

to be startled • **1.** جِفَل [jifal] جَفِل [jafil] *vn: sv* i. I was startled by the shot. جِفَلِت مِن الطَّلقَة [jifalit min ʔiṭṭalqa]

to starve • **1.** جاع [ja:ʕ] جُوع [ju:ʕ] *vn: sv* u. Thousands of people starved. آلاف مِن النّاس جاعَوا [ʔa:la:f min ʔanna:s ja:ʕaw] • **2.** جَوَّع [jawwaʕ] تَجوِيع [tajwi:ʕ] *vn:* تجَوَّع [tjawwaʕ] *p:* We can't attack them, we'll have to starve them out first. ما نِقدَر نهاجِمهُم هَسَّة، خَلّي نجَوِّعهُم أَوَّل [ma: nigdar nha:jimhum hassa, xalli njawwiʕhum ʔawwal]

*** They almost starved to death.** • **1.** تَقريباً ماتَوا مِن الجُوع [taqri:ban ma:taw min ʔijju:ʕ]

S

state • **1.** وِلايَة [wila:ya] وِلايات [wila:ya:t] *pl:* What's the largest state in the U. S. ? شِنُو هِيَّ أَكبَر وِلايَة بِالوِلايات المُتَّحِدَة [šinu hiyya ʔakbar wila:ya bilwila:ya:t ʔilmuttaħida] • **2.** دَولَة [dawla] دَولات، دُوَل [dawla:t, duwal] *pl:* حُكُومَة [ħuku:ma] حُكُومات [ħuku:ma:t] *pl:* The railroads are owned by the state. السِّكَك الحَدِيدِيَّة تِملِكها الدَّولَة [ʔissikak ʔilħadi:diyya timlikha ʔiddawla] • **3.** حالَة [ħa:la] حالات [ħa:la:t] *pl:* وَضعِيَّة [waðʕiyya] وَضعِيّات [waðʕiyya:t] *pl:* حال [ħa:l] أحوال [ʔaħwa:l] *pl:* وَضِع [waðiʕ] أَوضاع [ʔawða:ʕ] *pl:* His affairs are in a bad state. أُمُورَه بِحالَة مخَربُطَة [ʔumu:rah biħa:la mxarbuṭa] Don't speak to her when she's in this state. لا تكَلّمها وهِيَّ بِهَالوَضعِيَّة [la: tkallimha whiyya bhalwaðʕiyya] • **4.** حُكُومِي [ħuku:mi] It's a state hospital. هَذا مُستَشفى حُكُومِي [ha:ða mustašfa ħuku:mi] • **5.** خارِجِيَّة [xa:rijiyya] He works for the state department. يِشتُغُل بِوِزارَة الخارِجِيَّة [yištuɣul bwiza:rat ʔilxa:rijiyya]

to state • **1.** قال [ga:l] قول [gu:l] *vn:* إنقال [ʔinga:l] *p: sv* u. You just stated that you were not there. هَسَّة قِلت ما كِنِت هناك [hassa gilit ma: činit hna:k] • **2.** وَضَّح [waððah] تَوضِيح [tawði:ħ] *vn:* توَضَّح [twaððah] *p: sv* i. بَيَّن [bayyan] تَبيين [tabyi:n] *vn:* تبَيَّن [tbayyan] *p: sv* i. The terms are stated in the contract. الشُّرُوط موَضَّحَة بِالعَقِد [ʔiššuru:ṭ mwaððaħa bilʕaqid] I thought he stated his case well. أَعتقِد بَيَّن قَضِيتَه زين [ʔaʕtiqid bayyan qaði:tah zi:n]

statement • **1.** بَيان [baya:n] بَيانات [baya:na:t] *pl:* The prime minister issued his policy statement to parliament. رَئِيس الوُزَراء قَدَّم بَيان سِياستَه لِلمَجلِس [raʔi:s ʔilwuzara:ʔ qaddam baya:n siya:stah lilmajlis] • **2.** كَشِف حِساب [kašif ħisa:b] كشُوف حِساب [kšu:f ħisa:b] *pl:* My bank sends me a statement each month. البَنك يدِزّلِي كَشف الحِساب كُلّ شَهَر [ʔilbank ydizzli kašf ʔilħisa:b kull šahar]

static • **1.** وَشوَشَة [wašwaša] خَشخَشَة [xašxaša] خَشخَشات [xašxaša:t] *pl:* There's so much static I can't get the station. هوايَة أَكُو وَشوَشَة بِالرّاديُو ؛ ما دَأقدَر أَطَلّع المَحَطَّة [hwa:ya ʔaku wašwaša birra:dyu; ma: daʔagdar ʔaṭalliʕ ʔilmaħaṭṭa]

station • **1.** مَحَطَّة [maħaṭṭa] مَحَطّات [maħaṭṭa:t] *pl:* Get off at the next station. إنزِل بِالمَحَطَّة الجّايَّة [ʔinzil bilmaħaṭṭa ʔijja:yya] We're going to visit a radio station. راح نزُور مَحَطَّة الإذاعَة [ra:ħ nzu:r maħaṭṭat ʔilʔiða:ʕa]

to station • **1.** خَلَّى [xalla:] تخلِّي [txilli:] *vn:* تخَلَّى [txalla:] *p: sv* i. The police stationed a man at the door. الشُّرطَة خَلَّت حارِس عَالباب [ʔiššurṭa xallat ħa:ris ʕalba:b]

*** Where are you stationed?** • **1.** وَين مَركَزَك؟ [wi:n markazak?]

stationery • **1.** قِرطاسِيَّة [qirṭa:siyya] I need some stationery. أَحتاج شوَيَّة قِرطاسِيَّة [ʔaħta:j šwayya qirṭa:siyya]

statue • **1.** تِمثال [timθa:l] تَماثِيل [tama:θi:l] *pl:*

stay • **1.** بَقاء [baqa:ʔ] Our stay in the mountains during the summer was very pleasant. بَقاءنا بِالجِبَل بِالصَّيف كان كُلِّش لَطِيف [baqa:ʔna bijjibal biṣṣi:f ča:n kulliš laṭi:f]

to stay • **1.** بُقَى [buqa:] بَقاء [baqa:ʔ] *vn: sv* a. How long will you stay? شقَدّ راح تُبقَى؟ [šgadd ra:ħ tubqa:?] Are you staying with friends? باقِي وِيّا أَصدِقائَك؟ [ba:qi wiyya ʔaṣdiqa:ʔak?] You've stayed away a long time. بُقيت بِعِيد مُدَّة طَوِيلَة [buqi:t biʕi:d mudda ṭuwi:la]

to stay up • **1.** سِهَر [sihar] سَهَر [sahar] *vn: sv* a. Our children stay up until nine o'clock. وِلِدنا يِسهَرُون لِسّاعَة تِسعَة [wilidna yisharu:n lissa:ʕa tisʕa]

steady • **1.** ثابِت [θa:bit] This needs a steady hand. هاي تِحتاج إلها إيد ثابتَة [ha:y tiħta:j ʔilha ʔi:d θa:bta] We kept a good steady pace. حافَظنا عَلَى سُرعَة ثابتَة [ħa:faðna ʕala surʕa θa:bta] • **2.** مِستِمِرّ [mistimirr] He's made steady progress. حَصَّل عَلَى تَقَدُّم مُستَمِرّ [ħaṣṣal ʕala taqaddum mustamirr] • **3.** دائِمِي [da:ʔimi] مُستَمِرّ [mustamirr] He's one of our steady customers. هُوَّ مِن مَعامِيلنا الدّائِمِيِّين [huwwa min maʕa:mi:lna ʔidda:ʔimiyyi:n]

to steal • **1.** باق [ba:g] بَوق [bu:g] *vn:* اِنباق [ʔinba:g] *p: sv* u. سِرَق [siraq] سَرِق [sariq] *vn:* اِنسِرَق [ʔinsiraq] *p: sv* u. He stole all my money. باق كُلّ فلُوسِي [ba:g kull flu:si]

to steal away • **1.** نَسّ [nass] نَسّ [nass] *vn: sv* i. We had to steal away. اِضطَرَّينا اِننِسّ [ʔiðṭarri:na ʔinniss]

steam • **1.** بُخار [buxa:r] There's steam coming from the teapot. أَكُو بُخار دَيِطلَع مِن القُورِي [ʔaku buxa:r dayiṭlaʕ min ʔilqu:ri] • **2.** بُخارِي [buxa:ri] He showed us a model of a steam engine. راوانا نِمُوذَج مَكِينَة بُخارِيَّة [ra:wa:na nimu:ðaj maki:na buxa:riyya]

*** You'll have to get up some steam if you want to get done on time.** • **1.** يِنرادلَك هِمَّة إذا كِنِت تريد تخَلِّص بِالوَقِت [yinra:dlak himma ʔiða: činit itri:d itxalliṣ bilwakit]

to steam • **1.** بَخَّر [baxxar] تَبخِير [tabxi:r] *vn:* اِتبَخَّر [ʔitbaxxar] *p: sv* i. The rice is still steaming. التِّمَّن بَعدَه يبَخِّر [ʔittimman baʕdah ybaxxir]

steamer • **1.** باخِرَة [ba:xira] بَواخِر [bawa:xir] *pl:* The steamer sails at 10 o'clock. الباخِرَة تِبحِر السّاعَة عَشرَة [ʔilba:xira tibħ ir ʔissa:ʕa ʕašra]

steel • **1.** فُولاذ [fu:la:ð] The bridge is built entirely of steel. الجِّسِر مِبنِي كُلَّه مِن فُولاذ [ʔijjisir mibni kullah min fu:la:ð]

steep • **1.** مِنحِدِر بشِدَّة [minħidir bšidda] كُلِّش مِنحِدِر [kulliš minħidir] Be careful, the stairs are steep. دِير بالَك، الدَّرَج مِنحَدِر بشِدَّة [di:r ba:lak, ʔiddaraj minħadr bšidda] • **2.** عالِي [ʕa:li] The price is too steep. السِّعِر كُلِّش عالِي [ʔissiʕir kulliš ʕa:li]

to steep • **1.** خِدَر [xidar] خَدِر [xadir] *vn:* تخَدَّر [txiddar] *p: sv* a. Let the tea steep a little longer. خَلِّي الشاي يِخدَر أَكثَر [xalli ʔičča:y yixdar ʔakθar]

to steer • **1.** وَجَّه [wajjah] تَوجِيه [tawji:h] *vn:* توَجَّه [twajjah] *p: sv* i. Steer the launch in to shore. وَجِّه الماطُور عالجُّرُف [wajjih ʔilma:ṭu:r ʕajjuruf] Steer the car to the right of that policeman. وَجِّه السَّيّارَة بِجِهَة اليَمِين مِن هَالشُّرطِي [wajjih ʔissayya:ra bjihat ʔilyami:n min haššurṭi] • **2.** دَيوَر [di:war] تدَيوُر [tdi:wur] *vn: sv* u. Okay, you steer and I'll push. زين، إنتَ تدَيوُر وَآنِي أدفَع [zi:n, ʔinta ddi:wur wʔa:ni ʔadfaʕ] • **3.** دَزّ [dazz] دَزّ [dazz] *vn:* اِندَزّ [ʔindazz] *p: sv* i. He's steered a lot of customers my way. دَزّلِي مَعامِيل هوايَة [dazzli maʕa:mi:l hwa:ya]

*** Better steer clear of him.** • **1.** تكَفَّى شَرَّه [tčaffa: šarrah]

to steer away • **1.** وَخَّر [waxxar] توخِّر [twixxir] *vn:* توَخَّر [twaxxar] *p: sv* i. بَعَّد [baʕʕad] تَبعِيد [tabʕi:d] *vn:*

تبَعَّد [tbaʕʕad] *p:* Steer away from those kids. وَخِّر السَّيّارَة مِن هالجُّهال [waxxir ʔissayya:ra min hajjiha:l]

steering wheel • **1.** سُكّان [sukka:n]

stem • **1.** ساق [sa:g] Don't cut the stems too short. لا تقُصّ السّيقان قصار [la: tguṣṣ ʔissi:ga:n gṣa:r]

step • **1.** دَرَجَة [daraja] دَرَجات [daraja:t] *pl:* The steps are carpeted. الدَّرَجات مَفرُوشَة بِالسِّجّاد [ʔiddaraja:t mafru:ša bissijja:d] • **2.** خَطوَة [xaṭwa] خَطوات [xaṭwa:t] *pl:* He took one step forward. تقَدَّم خُطوَة لِقِدّام [tqaddam xuṭwa ligidda:m] We built up our business step by step. بنَينا شُغُلنا خُطوَة خُطوَة [bini:na šuɣulna xuṭwa xuṭwa] • **3.** إجراء [ʔijra:ʔ] إجراءات [ʔijra:ʔat] *pl:* The goverment is taking steps to wipe out crime. الحُكُومَة قاعِد تِتّخِذ الإجراءات لِلقَضاء عَلَى الجَّرائِم [ʔilħuku:ma ga:ʕid tittixið ʔilʔijra:ʔa:t lilqaḍa:ʔ ʕala ʔijjara:ʔim]

*** Watch your step.** • **1.** لاحِظ مِن تِمشِي [la:ħið min timši:]

to step • **1.** وُقَف [wugaf] وُقُوف [wugu:f] *vn: sv* a. Perhaps if you step on a chair you can reach it. يمكِن تنُوشها إذا وُقفِت عَلَى كُرسِي [yimkin tnu:šha ʔiða wugafit ʕala kursi] • **2.** داس [da:s] دَوس [du:s] *vn: sv* u. I stepped into the mud. دِست عَالطِّين [disit ʕaṭṭi:n]

*** Step lively!** • **1.** خُفّ رِجلَك [xuff rijlak]

to step aside • **1.** تنَحَّى [tnaħħa:] تنَحِّي [tanaħħi] *vn: sv* a. وَخَّر [waxxar] توخِّر [twixxir] *vn:* توَخَّر [twaxxar] *p:* I stepped aside to let him by. تنَحَّيت وَخَلّيته يمُرّ [tnaħħi:t wxalli:tah yumurr]

to step in • **1.** دِخَل [dixal] دُخُول [duxu:l] *vn: sv* u. I saw him step into the store. شِفته يدخُل بالمَخزَن [šiftah yidxul bilmaxzan] • **2.** تدَخَّل [tdaxxal] تَدَخُّل [tadaxxul] *vn: sv* a. The president himself may have to step in. الرَّئِيس نَفسَه مُحتَمَل يِتدَخَّل [ʔirraʔi:s nafsah muħtamal yiddaxxal]

to step off • **1.** نِزَل [nizal] نِزُول [nizu:l] *vn: sv* i. He just stepped off the train. هَسَّة نِزَل مِن القِطار [hassa nizal min ʔilqiṭa:r]

to step out • **1.** طِلَع [ṭilaʕ] طُلُوع [ṭulu:ʕ] *vn: sv* a. He just stepped out for a minute. طِلَع دَقِيقَة ويرجَع [ṭilaʕ daqi:qa wyirjaʕ]

to step up • **1.** زَيَّد [zayyad] تَزيِيد [tazyi:d] *vn:* تزَيَّد [tzayyad] *p:* We'll have to step up the pace. لازِم نزَيِّد السُّرعَة [la:zim nzayyid ʔissurʕa] • **2.** شَدَّد [šaddad] تشدِيد [tašdi:d] *vn:* تشَدَّد [tšaddad] *p:* The government stepped up its campaign against VD. الحُكُومَة شَدِّدَت حَملَتها ضِدّ الأمراض الزُّهرِيَّة [ʔilħuku:ma šaddidat ħamlatha ḍidd ʔilʔamra:ḍ ʔizzuhriyya] • **3.** جا يَمّ [ja: yamm] A strange man stepped up to me on the street. شَخِص غَرِيب جا يَمّي بِالشّارِع [šaxiṣ ɣari:b ja: yammi bišša:riʕ]

sterile • **1.** مُعَقَّم [muʕaqqam] Get me a sterile dressing. جِيبلِي قوز مُعَقَّم [ji:bli gu:z muʕaqqam] • **2.** عَقِيم [ʕaqi:m] عاقِر [ʕa:qir] I think my wife is sterile. أظِنّ زَوجتِي عَقِيمَة [ʔaðinn zawijti ʕaqi:ma]

to sterilize • **1.** عَقَّم [ʕaqqam] تَعقِيم [taʕqi:m] *vn:* تعَقَّم [tʕaqqam] *p:* Sterilize the needle before you use it. عَقِّم الأُبرَة قَبُل ما تِستَعمِلها [ʕaqqim ʔilʔubra gabul ma: tistaʕmilha]

sterling • **1.** أصلِي [ʔaṣli] That's sterling silver. هاي فُضَّة أصلِيَّة [ha:y fuḍḍa ʔaṣliyya]

stern • **1.** مُؤَخِّرَة [muʔaxxira] مُؤَخِّرات [muʔaxxira:t] *pl:* Sit in the stern of the boat and I'll row. أُقعُد بمُؤَخِّرَة البَلَم وَآني أجذِف [ʔugʕud bmuʔaxxirat ʔilbalam wʔa:ni ʔajðif] • **2.** جاف [ja:f] مِعَبِّس [mʕabbis] He's a stern man. هُوَّ جاف [huwwa ja:f]

stew • **1.** مَرقَة [marga] مَرقات [marga:t] *pl:* مَرَق [marag] *Collective:* We had okra stew and rice. أكَلنا مَرقَة بامية وتِمَّن [ʔakalna margat ba:mya wtimman]

*** He's in a stew again.** • **1.** هُوَّ مِتهَيِّج مَرَّة لُخ [huwwa mithayyij marra lux]

to stew • **1.** طُبَخ [ṭubax] طَبُخ [ṭabux] *vn:* اِنطُبَخ [ʔinṭubax] *p:* Shall I stew the chicken or roast it? ترِيدنِي أطبُخ الدِّجاج أو أحَمُّصَه؟ [tri:dni ʔaṭbux ʔiddija:j ʔaw ʔaħammuṣah?]

stick • **1.** عُودَة [ʕu:da] عُودات، عُوَد [ʕu:da:t, ʕuwad] *pl:* عَصَة [ʕaṣa] عِصِي [ʕiṣi] *pl:* He hit me with a stick. ضِرَبنِي بالعُودَة [ðirabni bilʕu:da]

to stick • **1.** نَغَّز [nayyaz] تَنغِيز [tanyi:z] *vn:* اِنَغَّز [ʔinnayyaz] *p:* شَكشَك [čakčak] تشِكشِك [tčikčik] *vn:* تشَكشَك [tčakčak] *p:* Something is sticking me. فَدّ شِي دَينَغِّزنِي [fadd ši daynayyizni] • **2.** شَكّ [čakk] شَكّ [čakk] *vn:* اِنشَكّ [ʔinčakk] *p:* I stuck my finger. شَكّيت أُصبَعِي [čakki:t ʔuṣbaʕi] • **3.** لِزَق [lizag] لَزِق [lazig] *vn:* اِنلِزَق [ʔinlizag] *p:* This stamp doesn't stick. هَذا الطّابِع ما يِلزَق [ha:ða ʔiṭṭa:biʕ ma: yilzag] • **4.** كَلَّب [čallab] تَكلِيب، تِكِلِّب [tačli:b, tčillib] *vn: sv* i. The door always sticks in damp weather. الباب دائِماً يكَلِّب بِالرِّطُوبَة [ʔilba:b da:ʔiman yčallib birriṭu:ba] • **5.** بُقَى [buqa:] بَقاء [baqa:ʔ] *vn:* اِنبُقَى [ʔinbuqa:] *p:* Nothing sticks in his mind. ما يِبقَى شِي بِدَماغَه [ma: yibqa: ši bdama:ɣah] • **6.** خَلَّى [xalla:] تخِلِّي [txilli] *vn:* تخَلَّى [txalla:] *p:* Just stick it in your pocket. بَسّ خَلِّيها بجَيبَك [bass xalli:ha bji:bak] • **7.** دَخَّل [daxxal] تَدخِيل [tadxi:l] *vn:* تدَخَّل [tdaxxal] *p:* حَطّ [ħaṭṭ] حَطّ [ħaṭṭ] *vn: sv* u. He sticks his nose into everything. يدَخِّل نَفسَه بِكُلّشِي [ydaxxil nafsah bikullši] He sticks his nose into everything. حُمُّص بِالجِّدِر يِنبُص [ħummuṣ bjjidir yinbuṣ]

to stick out • **1.** تحَمَّل [tħammal] تَحَمُّل [taħammul] *vn: sv* a. Try and stick it out a little longer. حاوِل تِتحَمَّلها شوَيَّة أكثَر [ħa:wil titħammalha šwayya ʔakθar]

to stick to • **1.** تمَسَّك [tmassak] تَمَسُّك [tamassuk] *vn: sv* a. I'm sticking to my opinion. آني مِتمَسِّك بِرأيِي [ʔa:ni mitmassik braʔyi] I'm sticking to my opinion. آني مُصِرّ عَلَى رَأيِي [ʔa:ni muṣirr ʕala raʔyi] • **2.** لِزَق عَلَى

S

[lizag ʕala] لَزَق [lazig] *vn:* اِنلِزَق [ʔinlizag] *p:* That won't stick to a smooth surface. هَذا ما يِلزَق عَلَى سَطِح أَملَس [haːða maː yilzag ʕala satiħ ʔamlas]

to stick up • **1.** دافَع [daːfaʕ] دِفاع [difaːʕ] *vn:* تدافَع [tdaːfaʕ] *p:* He stuck up for me. دافَع عَنّي [daːfaʕ ʕanni]

sticky • **1.** مدَبُّق [mdabbug] My fingers are all sticky with honey. أَصابعِي مدَبَّقَة مِن العَسَل [ʔaṣaːbʕi mdabbga min ʔilʕasal] • **2.** رَطِب [raṭib] It's awfully sticky today. كُلِّش رَطبَة اليُوم [kulliš raṭba ʔilyuːm]

* **He's got sticky fingers.** • **1.** إيدَه طويلَة [ʔiːdah ṭwiːla]

stiff • **1.** يابِس [yaːbis] His collars are always stiff. ياختَه عَلَى طُول يابسَة [yaːxtah ʕala ṭuːl yaːbsa] • **2.** قَوي [qawi, guwi] قَواي، أَقوِياء، قَوِيِّين [qwaːy, ʔaqwiyaːʔ, qawiyyiːn] *pl:* The steering is awful stiff! السَتِيرِن كُلِّش قَوي [ʔalstiːrin kulliš qawi] • **3.** مِتشَنِّج [mitšannij] My legs are stiff. رِجلَيّا مِتشَنِّجَة [rijlayya mitšannija] • **4.** ناشِف [naːšif] Don't be so stiff! لا تكُون كُلِّش ناشِف [laː tkuːn kulliš naːšif] • **5.** صَعُب [ṣaʕub] Was it a stiff examination? كان الامتِحان صَعُب؟ [čaːn ʔilʔimtiħaːn ṣaʕub?] • **6.** كِبِير [čibiːr] He paid a stiff fine. دِفَع غَرامَة كبِيرَة [difaʕ ɣaraːma čbiːra]

to be stiff • **1.** تصَلَّب [tṣallab] تَصَلُّب [taṣallub] *vn:* *sv* a. Relax and don't be stiff when you're swimming. رَخّي نَفسَك؛ لا تِتصَلَّب مِن تِسبَح [raxxi nafsak; laː titṣallab min tisbaħ]

still • **1.** هادِئ [haːdiʔ] ساكِن [saːkin] The night was still. اللَّيل كان هادِئ [ʔillayl čaːn haːdiʔ] • **2.** واقُف [waːguf] The wheels of industry were still. عَجَلات الصِّناعَة كانَت واقفَة [ʕajalaːt ʔiṣṣinaːʕa čaːnat waːgfa] • **3.** بَعَد [baʕad] لا زال [laː zaːl] *sv* a. I'm still of the same opinion. آني بَعَدني بنَفس الرَّأي [ʔaːni baʕadni bnafis ʔirraʔi] This box is big, but that box is still bigger. هَالصَّندُوق كبِير، لَكِن ذاك الصَّندُوق بَعدَه أَكبَر [haṣṣanduːg čabiːr, laːkin ðaːk ʔiṣṣanduːg baʕdah ʔakbar] It's still raining. لا تزال تُمطُر [laː dzaːl tumṭur] I'm still eating. لا أَزال آكُل [laː ʔazaːl ʔaːkul] They were still playing. كانَوا لا يزالُون يِلعَبُون [čaːnaw laː yzaːluːn yilʕabuːn]

to hold still • **1.** وُقَف [wugaf] وُقُوف [woguːf] *vn:* *sv* a. Hold still a minute! أُوقَف دَقِيقَة [ʔuːgaf daqiːqa] Hold still a minute! لا تِتحَرَّك [laː titħarrak]

to keep still • **1.** سِكَت [sikat] سُكُوت [sukuːt] *vn:* *sv* u. Why don't you keep still? لِيش ما تِسكُت؟ [liːš maː tiskut?]

to stimulate • **1.** نَبَّه [nabbah] تَنبِيه [tanbiːh] *vn:* تنَبَّه [tnabbah] *p:* Coffee stimulates the nerves. القَهوَة تنَبِّه الأَعصاب [ʔilgahwa tnabbih ʔilʔaʕṣaːb] We stimulated the muscle with an electric current. نَبَّهنا العَضَلَة بِالتَّيّار الكَهرَبائِي [nabbahna ʔilʕaðala bittayyaːr ʔilkahrabaːʔi] • **2.** شَجَّع [šajjaʕ] تَشجِيع [tašjiːʕ] *vn:* تشَجَّع [tšajjaʕ] *p:* We must stimulate foreign trade. لازِم نشَجِّع التِّجارَة الخارِجِيَّة [laːzim nšajjiʕ ʔittijaːra ʔilxaːrijiyya]

* **Running fast stimulates the breathing.** • **1.** رِكِض سَرِيع يزَيِّد سُرعَة التَّنَفُّس [rrikiḍ issariːʕ yzayyid surʕat ʔittanaffus]

stingy • **1.** بَخِيل [baxiːl] بُخَلاء [buxalaːʔ] *pl:* Don't be stingy! لا تصِير بَخِيل [laː tṣiːr baxiːl]

stir • **1.** هَرجَة [harja] هَرجات [harjaːt] *pl:* There was a stir in the crowd when he got up to speak. صارَت هَرجَة بِالنّاس مِن قام دَيِحكِي [ṣaːrat harja binnaːs min gaːm dayiħči] • **2.** حَرَكَة [ħaraka] خَرخَشَة [xarxaša] خَرخَشات [xarxašaːt] *pl:* I heard a stir in the bush. سِمَعِت حَرَكَة بِالدَّغَل [simaʕit ħaraka biddaɣal]

to stir • **1.** خاط [xaːṭ] خُوط [xuːṭ] *vn:* *sv* u. She forgot to stir the soup. نِسَت تخُوط الشَّوربَة [nisat txuːṭ ʔiššuːrba] • **2.** حَرَّك [ħarrak] تَحرِيك [taħriːk] *vn:* تحَرَّك [tħarrak] *p:* هَزّ [hazz] هَزّ [hazz] *vn:* اِنهَزّ [ʔinhazz] *p:* The wind stirred the branches. الهَوية حَرَّكَت الغُصُون [ʔilhawya ħarrkat ʔilɣuṣuːn] • **3.** تحَرَّك [tħarrak] تَحَرُّك [taħarruk] *vn:* *sv* a. He's stirring. دَيِتحَرَّك [dayitħarrak]

stirring • **1.** مُثِير [muθiːr] مُهَيِّج [muhayyij] He made a stirring speech. خِطَب خِطاب مُثِير [xiṭab xiṭaːb muθiːr]

stitch • **1.** نُفذَة [nufða] نُفذات [nufðaːt] *pl:* The injury needed four stitches. الجِّرِح ينرادلَه أَربَع نِفذات [ʔijjariħ ynraːdlah ʔarbaʕ nifðat]

* **When is the doctor going to take out the stitches?** • **1.** يَمتَى الطَّبِيب راح يجُرّ الخَيط؟ [yamtaː ʔiṭṭabiːb raːħ yjurr ʔilxiːṭ?]

* **I haven't done a stitch of work today.** • **1.** ما اِشتِغَلِت وَلا حَبايَة اليُوم [maː ʔištiɣalit wala ħabbaːya ʔilyuːm] / ما سَوَّيت وَلا نِتفَة شُغُل هَاليُوم [maː sawwiːt wala nitfat šuɣul halyuːm]

* **Don't take big stitches.** • **1.** لا تخَيِّط خَشِن [laː txayyiṭ xašin]

to stitch • **1.** خَيَّط [xayyaṭ] تَخيِيط [taxyiːṭ] *vn:* تخَيَّط [txayyaṭ] *p:* Did you stitch the hem yet? خَيَّطِت الحاشيَة لَو بَعَد؟ [xayyaṭit ʔilħaːšya law baʕad?]

stock • **1.** مَجمُوعَة [majmuːʕa] مَجمُوعات [majmuːʕaːt] *pl:* He has a large stock of shirts. عِندَه مَجمُوعَة كبِيرَة مِن القُمصان [ʕindah majmuːʕa čbiːra min ʔilqumṣaːn] • **2.** سَهَم [saham] أَسهُم [ʔashum] *pl:* I advise you not to buy these stocks. أَنصَحَك لا تِشتِري هَالأَسهُم [ʔanṣaħak laː tištiri halʔashum] • **3.** أَخمَص [ʔaxmaṣ] The stock of a rifle is usually made of wood. أَخمَص البُندُقِيَّة عادَةً مَعمُول مِن الخِشَب [ʔaxmaṣ ʔilbunduqiyya ʕaːdatan maʕmuːl min ʔilxišab]

* **I don't put much stock in what he says.** • **1.** ما خَلِّي وَزِن لِحَكيَه [maː xalli wazin liħačyah] / ما أَعتِمِد عَلَى حَكيَه [maː ʔaʕtimid ʕala ħačyah]

in stock • **1.** مَخزُون [maxzuːn] What colors do you have in stock? أَيّ أَلوان مَخزُونَة عِندَك؟ [ʔayy ʔalwaːn maxzuːna ʕindak?]

S

out of stock • **1.** خَلصان [xalṣa:n] Sorry, that color is out of stock. مِتأَسِّف ذاك النَّوع خَلصان [mitʔassif ða:k ʔinnu:ʕ xalṣa:n]

to take stock • **1.** جِرَد [jirad] جَرِد [jarid] *vn:* اِنجِرَد [ʔinjirad] *p:* Next week we're going to take stock. الإسبُوع الجّاي راح نِجرُد [ʔilʔisbu:ʕ ʔijja:y ra:ħ nijrud] • **2.** راجَع [ra:jaʕ] مُراجَعَة [mura:jaʕa] *vn: sv* i. Let's take stock of what we've done. خَلِّي نراجِع اللّي سَوَّينا [xalli nra:jiʕ ʔilli sawwi:na]

to stock • **1.** خِزَن [xizan] خَزِن [xazin] *vn:* اِنخِزَن [ʔinxizan] *p:* We don't stock that brand. ما نِخزِن هَالمارکَة [ma: nixzin halma:rka] We don't stock that brand. ما عِدنا هَالمارکَة [ma: ʕidna halma:rka]

stocked • **1.** مُجَهَّز [mujahhaz] Our store is stocked with everything. مَخزَنّا مجَهَّز بکُلْشي [maxzanna mjahhaz bkullši] • **2.** مَخزُون [maxzu:n] Sorry that color isn't stocked by us. مِتأَسِّف هَاللَّون مُو مَخزُون عِدنا [mitʔassif hallu:n mu: maxzu:n ʕidna]

stock exchange • **1.** بَورصَة [bu:rṣa] بَورصات [bu:rṣa:t] *pl:*

stockholder • **1.** مُساهِم [musa:him] مُساهِمِين [musa:himi:n] *pl:* I'm a stockholder in that company. آنِي مُساهِم بذِيك الشَّرِكَة [ʔa:ni musa:him bði:č ʔiššarika]

stocking • **1.** جوراب [ju:ra:b] جواريب [jwa:ri:b] *pl:* I'd like three paris of stockings. أَحِبّ ثْلَث أَزوَاج جُوارِيب [ʔaħibb tlaθ ʔ azwa:j juwa:ri:b]

stomach • **1.** مِعدَة [miʕda] مِعدات، مِعَد [miʕda:t, miʕad] *pl:* He has an upset stomach. مِعِدتَه مخَربَطَة [miʕidtah mxarbaṭa] • **2.** بَطِن [baṭin] بطُون [bṭu:n] *pl:* Don't lie on your stomach. لا تِنبُطِح عَلَى بَطنَك [la: tinbuṭiħ ʕala baṭnak]

*** I'm sick to my stomach.** • **1.** نَفسِي دَتِلعَب [nafsi datilʕab]

to stomach • **1.** تحَمَّل [tħammal] تَحَمُّل [taħammul] *vn: sv* a. I can't stomach that fellow. ما أَقدَر أَتحَمَّل هَالشَّخِص [ma: ʔagdar ʔatħammal haššaxiṣ]

stone • **1.** حجارَة [ħja:ra] حجارات، حِجار [ħja:ra:t, ħija:r] *pl:* He killed two birds with one stone. قِتَل عَصفُورَين بحجارَة [kital ʕaṣfu:rayn bħja:ra] • **2.** نُوايَة [nuwa:ya] نُوايات [nuwa:ya:t] *pl:* نُوَا [nuwa:] *Collective:* Swallowing peach stones is dangerous. بَلِع نُوا الخَوخ خَطَر [baliʕ nuwa ʔilxawx xaṭar] • **3.** مِن حجار [min ħja:r] حَجَري [ħajari] We sat on a stone bench. قِعَدنا عَلَى مَقعَد مِن حجار [giʕadna ʕala maqʕad min ħja:r] We noticed a stone statue. لاحَظنا تِمثال حَجَري [la:ħaðna timθa:l ħajari]

*** He left no stone unturned.** • **1.** ما خَلَّى زوِيَّة مَا دَوَّرها [ma: xalla: zwiyya ma: dawwarha]

stool • **1.** تَختَة [taxta] تَختات [taxta:t] *pl:* When he milks the cow, he sits on a stool. مِن يِحلِب الهايشَة يِقعُد عَلَى تَختَة [min yiħlib ʔi:lha:yša yigʕud ʕala taxta] • **2.** خُرُوج [xuru:j] We have to make three tests, for the blood, the urine, and the stool. لازم نسَوِّي ثْلَث تَحلِيلات لِلدَّم، لِلبُول وَلِلخُرُوج [la:zim nsawwi tlaθ taħli:la:t liddamm, lilbu:l wlilxuru:j]

stoop • **1.** حَنيَة [ħanya] حَنيات [ħanya:t] *pl:* He has a slight stoop. عِندَه حَنيَة شوَيَّة [ʕindah ħanya šwayya]

to stoop • **1.** اِنحِنَى [ʔinħina:] اِنحِناء [ʔinħina:ʔ] *vn: sv* i. نَصَّة [naṣṣa] نَصّات [naṣṣa:t] *pl:* تنَصِّي [tnaṣṣi] *vn: sv* i. He stooped to pick up the newspaper. نَصَّى حَتَّى يِتناوَش الجَّرِيدَة [naṣṣa: ħatta yitna:waš ʔijjari:da]

to stoop to • **1.** تنازَل [tna:zal] تَنازُل [tana:zul] *vn: sv* a. نِزَل [nizal] نُزُول [nuzu:l] *vn: sv* i. I don't think she'd stoop to such a thing. ما أَظِنّها تِتنازَل لِهِيكِي شِي [ma: ʔaðinnha titna:zal lhi:či ši]

stop • **1.** مَوقِف [mawqif] مَواقِف [mawa:qif] *pl:* You have to get off at the next stop. لازِم تِنزِل بالمَوقِف الجّاي [la:zim tinzil bilmawqif ʔijja:y] • **2.** وَقفَة [waqfa] وَقفات [waqfa:t] *pl:* We have a ten-minute stop in Basra. عِدنا وَقفَة عَشِر دَقايِق بِالبَصرَة [ʕidna waqfat ʕašir daqa:yiq bilbaṣra] • **3.** حَدّ [ħadd] We'll have to put a stop to that practice. لازِم نُوضَع حَدّ لِهالعادَة [la:zim nu:ðaʕ ħadd lihalʕa:da] We'll have to put a stop to that practice. لازِم نبَطِّل هَالعادَة [la:zim nbaṭṭil halʕa:da]

to stop • **1.** وُقَف [wugaf] وُقُوف [wugu:f] *vn:* اِنوُقَف [ʔinwuqaf] *p:* The bus stops on the other side of the street. الباص يوقَف بِالصَفحَة اللُّخ مِن الشّارِع [ʔilpa:ṣ yu:gaf bṣṣafħat ʔillux min ʔišša:riʕ] My watch stopped. ساعتِي وُقفَت [sa:ʕti wugfat] I stopped for a drink of water on the way. وُقَفِت بِالطَّرِيق حَتَّى أَشرَب ماي [wugafit biṭṭari:q ħatta ʔašrab ma:y] • **2.** وَقَّف [waggaf] توقِيف [tawgi:f] *vn:* توَقَّف [twaggaf] *p:* Stop the car at the next street. وَقِّف السَّيّارَة بِالشّارِع الجّاي [wagguf ʔissayya:ra bišša:riʕ ʔijja:y] • **3.** بَطَّل [baṭṭal] تَبطِيل [tabṭi:l] *vn:* تبَطَّل [tbaṭṭal] *p: sv* i. Please stop that noise. أَرجُوك بَطِّل هَالحِسّ [ʔarju:k baṭṭil halħiss] Stop it! بَطِّل [baṭṭil] Stop it! بَسّ عاد [bass ʕa:d]

to stop over • **1.** وُقَف [wugaf] وُقُوف [wugu:f] *vn: sv* a. بِقَى [biqa:] بَقاء [baqa:ʔ] *vn: sv* a. Why don't you stop over at my house on the way? لِيش ما تُوقَف بِبَيتِي عَلَى طَرِيقَك؟ [li:š ma: tu:gaf bibayti ʕala ṭari:qak?]

to stop overnight • **1.** بات [ba:t] بَيتُوتَة [baytu:ta] *vn: sv* a. We'll stop in Hilla overnight. راح نبات بِالحِلَّة [ra:ħ nba:t bilħilla]

to stop short • **1.** سَكَّت [sakkat] تَسكِيت [taski:t] *vn:* تسَكَّت [tsakkat] *p:* I stopped him short before he could say much. سَكَّتَه بِسُرعَة قَبُل ما يِحكِي هوايَة [sakkattah bsurʕa gabul ma: yiħči hwa:ya]

to stop up • **1.** سَدّ [sadd] سَدّ [sadd] *vn:* اِنسَدّ [ʔinsadd] *p:* You're going to stop up the drain. راح تسِدّ البَلُّوعَة [ra:ħ tsidd ʔilballu:ʕa]

stopper • **1.** سَدّاد [sadda:d] سَدّادات [sadda:da:t] *pl:* Put the stopper in the kettle. خَلِّي السَّدّاد بِالبُوطِل [xalli ʔissadda:d bilbu:ṭil]

S

store • **1.** مَخزَن [maxzan] مَخازِن [maxa:zin] *pl:* مَحَلّ [maħall] مَحَلّات [maħalla:t] *pl:* دُكّان [dukka:n] دِكاكِين [dika:ki:n] *pl:* I know a store where you can buy a good suit. أعرُف فَدّ مَخزَن تِقدَر تِشتِري مِنَّه بَدلَة زينَة [ʔaʕruf fadd maxzan tigdar tištiri minnah badla zi:na] • **2.** ذَخِيرَة [ðaxi:ra] ذَخايِر [ðaxa:yir] *pl:* مُونَة [mu:na] We have a sufficient store of food in the basement. عِدنا ذَخِيرَة كافيَة مِن الأكِل بِالسِّرداب [ʕidna ðaxi:ra ka:fya min ʔilʔakil bissirda:b] The army has a large store of rifles in the city. الجَّيش عِندَه ذَخِيرَة كِبِيرَة مِن التُّفَق بِالمَدِينَة [ʔijǰayš ʕindah ðaxi:ra čibi:ra min ʔittufag bilmadi:na]

*** Who knows what the future has in store for us?** • **1.** مِنُو يُعرُف شضامنِنّا المُستَقبَل؟ [minu yuʕruf šḍa:mninna ʔilmustaqbal?]

to store • **1.** خِزَن [xizan] خَزِن [xazin] *vn:* اِنخِزَن [ʔinxizan] *p:* ضَمّ [ḍamm] ضَمّ [ḍamm] *vn:* اِنضَمّ [ʔinḍamm] *p:* حِرَز [ħiraz] حَرِز [ħariz] *vn: sv* i. Where shall I store the potatoes? وِين أخزِن البُتَيتَة؟ [wi:n ʔaxzin ʔilputayta?]

*** I stored up a lot of energy during my vacation.** • **1.** تنَشَّطِت هوايَة بِعُطُلتِي [tnaššaṭit hwa:ya bʕuṭulti]

storm • **1.** عاصِفَة [ʕa:ṣifa] عَواصِف [ʕawa:ṣif] *pl:* There was a big storm last night. جَتّ عاصِفَة كِبِيرَة البارحَة باللَّيل [ǰatt ʕa:ṣifa čibi:ra ʔilba:rħa billay]

to storm • **1.** صارَت عاصِفَة [ṣa:rat ʕa:ṣifa] *sv* i. It's going to storm tonight. راح تصِير عاصِفَة هاللَّيلَة [ra:ħ tṣi:r ʕa:ṣifa hallayla]

stormy • **1.** عاصِف [ʕa:ṣif]

story • **1.** سَالُوفَة سَالُوفات، سُوالِيف [sa:lu:fa -- sa:lu:fa:t, suwa:li:f] قُصَّة [quṣṣa] قُصَص [quṣaṣ] *pl:* حكايَة [ħča:ya] حكايات [ħča:ya:t] *pl:* Do you want me to tell you a story? ترِيدنِي أحكِيلَك سالُوفَة؟ [tri:dni ʔaħči:lak sa:lu:fa?] It's always the same old story. دائماً نفس الحكايَة [da:ʔiman nafs ʔilħča:ya] It's always the same old story. دائماً نَفس القُصَّة العَتِيقَة [da:ʔiman nafs ʔilquṣṣa ʔilʕati:ga] • **2.** طابِق [ṭa:biq] طَوابِق [ṭawa:biq] *pl:* The building has five stories. البِنايَة بِيها خَمِس طَوابِق [ʔilbina:ya bi:ha xamis ṭawa:biq]

stout • **1.** سِمِين [simi:n] He's a stout man. هُوَّ رِجّال سِمِين [huwwa rijǰa:l simi:n] سمَان [sma:n] *pl:*

to get stout • **1.** سِمَن [siman] سِمِن [simin] *vn: sv* a. He's gotten very stout lately. سِمَن هوايَة بهالأيّام [siman hwa:ya bhalʔayya:m]

stove • **1.** طَبّاخ [ṭabba:x] طَبّاخات [ṭabba:xa:t] *pl:* أوجاغ [ʔu:ǰa:ɣ] أوجاغات [ʔu:ǰa:ɣa:t] *pl:* Put the meat on the stove. خَلِّي اللَّحَم عالطَّبّاخ [xalli ʔillaħam ʕaṭṭabba:x] • **2.** صُوبَة [ṣu:pa] صُوبات [ṣu:pa:t] *pl:* I need a stove in my bedroom. أحتاج صَوبَة بغُرفَة نَومِي [ʔaħta:ǰ ṣu:ba bɣurfat nawmi]

straight • **1.** عَدِل [ʕadil] Draw a straight line. إرسِم خَطّ عَدِل [ʔirsim xaṭṭ ʕadil] He gave me a straight answer. جاوَبنِي جَواب عَدِل [ǰa:wabni ǰawa:b ʕadil] She's always straight with me. هِيَّ دائماً عَدلَة ويَايا [hiyya da:ʔiman ʕadla wiyya:ya] Is my hat on straight? شَفُقتِي عَدلَة؟ [šafuqti ʕadla?] She stands very straight. تُوقَف كُلِّش عَدِل [tu:gaf kulliš ʕadil] He worked for fifteen hours straight. اِشتِغَل خُمُسطَعَش ساعَة عَدِل [ʔištiɣal xumusṭaʕaš sa:ʕa ʕadil] • **2.** عَدِل [ʕadil] رَاساً [raʔsan] Go straight home. رُوح عَدِل لِلبَيت [ru:ħ ʕadil lilbayt] • **3.** سادَة [sa:da] I take my arrack straight. آخُذ العَرَق مالِي سادَة [ʔa:xuð ʔilʕarag ma:li sa:da] • **4.** تَمام [tama:m] تَماماً [tama:man] Try to get the story straight. حاوِل تِفهَم القُصَّة تَمام [ħa:wil tifham ʔilquṣṣa tama:m] You didn't get me straight. ما فِهَمِتنِي تَمام [ma: fhamitni tama:m] Our house is straight across from the church. بَيتنا تَماماً قُبال الكَنِيسَة [baytna tama:man guba:l ʔilkani:sa]

*** He can't think straight.** • **1.** فِكرَه مشَوَّش [fikrah mšawwaš]

*** Now let's get this straight! I'm the boss here!** • **1.** فُكّ عَينَك آنِي الرَّئِيس هنا [fukk ʕaynak ʔa:ni ʔirraʔi:s hna]

straight ahead • **1.** قُبَل [gubal] Walk straight ahead. إمشِي قُبَل [ʔimši gubal]

to straighten • **1.** عَدَّل [ʕaddal] تَعدِيل [taʕdi:l] *vn:* تعَدَّل [tʕaddal] *p:* Can you straighten the rod? تِقدَر تعَدِّل الشِّيش؟ [tigdar tʕaddil ʔišši:š?] Straighten the tablecloth. عَدِّل شَرشَف المِيز [ʕaddil čarčaf ʔilmi:z]

to straighten out • **1.** عَدَّل [ʕaddal] تَعدِيل [taʕdi:l] *vn:* تعَدَّل [tʕaddal] *p:* Have you straightened out your financial affairs? عَدَّلِت أمُورَك المالِيَّة؟ [ʕaddalit ʔumu:rak ʔilma:liyya?] • **2.** صالَح [ṣa:lah] مُصالَحَة [muṣa:laħa] *vn: sv* i. Have you straightened out everything between them? صالَحِت بينهُم [ṣa:lahit baynhum] Have you straightened out everything between them? صالَحِتهُم؟ [ṣa:lahithum?] • **3.** عِدَل [ʕidal] عَدِل [ʕadil] *vn: sv* a. تعَدَّل [tʕaddal] تَعَدُّل [taʕaddul] *vn: sv* a. Tomorrow everything will straighten out. باكِر كُلِّشِي يِعدَل [ba:čir kullši yiʕdal]

to straighten up • **1.** عَدَّل [ʕaddal] تَعدِيل [taʕdi:l] *vn:* تعَدَّل [tʕaddal] *p:* رَتَّب [rattab] تَرتِيب [tarti:b] *vn:* ترَتَّب [trattab] *p:* Will you please straighten up the room? أرجُوك عَدِّل الغُرفَة [ʔarǰu:k ʕaddil ʔilɣurfa]

strain • **1.** مَتاعِب [mata:ʕib] He can't stand the strain of modern living. ما يِقدَر يِتحَمَّل مَتاعِب الحَياة الحَدِيثَة [ma: yigdar yitħammal mata:ʕib ʔilħaya:t ʔilħadi:θa] • **2.** شِلعان قَلب [šilʕa:n galub] Reading this small print is a strain. قرايَة هَالكِتابَة النّاعِمَة شِلعان قَلب [qra:yat halkita:ba ʔinna:ʕima šilʕa:n galub] • **3.** تَوَتُّر [tawattur] What caused the strain in relations between the two countries? شسَبَّب تَوَتُّر العِلاقات بين الدَّولَتَين؟ [šsabbab tawattur ʔilʕila:qa:t bayn ʔiddawiltayn?]

*** I don't think the rope will stand the strain.** • **1.** ما أظُن الحَبِل راح يِتحَمَّل [ma: ʔaḍunn ʔilħabil ra:ħ yitħammal]

S

to strain • **1.** شَلَع [šilaʕ] شَلَع، شِلعان [šaliʕ, šilʕa:n] *vn:* اِنشِلَع [ʔinšilaʕ] *p:* تَعَّب [taʕʕab] تَتعِيب [tatʕi:b] *vn:* تتَعَّب [ttaʕʕab] *p:* That last effort strained me. هَالمَجهُود الأخِير شِلَع قَلبِي [halmajhu:d ʔilʔaxi:r šilaʕ galbi] Reading this small print strained my eyes. قرايَة هَالكِتابَة النّاعِمَة تَعَّبِت عينِي [qra:yat halkita:ba ʔinna:ʕima taʕʕabit ʕi:ni] Don't strain yourself. لا تِشلَع قَلبَك [la: tišlaʕ galbak] Don't strain yourself. لا تتَعَّب نَفسَك [la: ʔittaʕʕib nafsak] • **2.** وَتَّر [wattar] تَوتِير [tawti:r] *vn:* توَتَّر [twattar] *p:* The blockade strained relations between the two countries. الحِصار وَتَّر العِلاقات بين الدَّولتَين [ʔilħiṣa:r wattar ʔilʕila:qa:t bayn ʔiddawiltayn] • **3.** صَفَّى [ṣaffa:] تَصفِيَة [taṣfiya] *vn:* تصَفَّى [tṣaffa:] *p:* She strained the rice. صَفَّت التِّمَّن [ṣaffat ʔittimman]

strained • **1.** مِتوَتِّر [mitwattir] Relations between the two countries are strained. العَلاقات بين الدَّولتَين مِتوَتّرَة [ʔilʕala:qa:t bayn ʔiddawiltayn mitwattra] • **2.** مصَفَّى [mṣaffa] I prefer strained honey. أَفَضِّل عَسَل مصَفَّى [ʔafaððil ʕasal mṣaffa]

strainer • **1.** مَصفِي [maṣfi] مَصافِي [maṣa:fi:] *pl:*

strait • **1.** مَضِيق [maði:q] مَضايِق [maða:yiq] *pl:*

Straits of Gibraltar • **1.** مَضِيق جِبَل طارِق [maði:q jibal ṭa:riq]

strange • **1.** غَرِيب [ɣari:b] عَجِيب [ʕaji:b] All this is strange to me. كُلّ هَذا غَرِيب عَلَيّا [kull ha:ða ɣari:b ʕalayya] What a strange question! شلُون سُؤال غَرِيب [šlu:n suʔa:l ɣari:b]

stranger • **1.** غَرِيب [ɣari:b] غُرَباء [ɣuraba:ʔ] *pl:* The stranger gave me a book. الغَرِيب اِنطانِي كِتاب [ʔilɣari:b ʔinṭa:ni kita:b]

strap • **1.** سَير [sayr] سيُور [syu:r] سَيرات [sayra:t] *pl:* The man beat his horse with a leather strap. الرِّجّال ضِرَب حصانَه بسَير جِلِد [ʔirrijja:l ðirab ħṣa:nah bsi:r jilid]

straw • **1.** تِبِن [tibin] We feed our horse straw. نِنطِي الحصان مالنَا تِبِن [ninṭi ʔilħṣa:n ma:lna tibin] • **2.** مُصّاصَة [muṣṣa:ṣa] مُصّاصات [muṣṣa:ṣa:t] *pl:* قُصبَة [guṣba] قُصبات [guṣba:t] *pl:* Please bring me a drinking straw. أَرجُوك جِيبِلي مُصّاصَة [ʔarju:k ji:bli muṣṣa:ṣa]

*** That's the last straw!** • **1.** وُصلَت حَدّها [wuṣlat ħaddha]

strawberry • **1.** شِلكَة [čilka] شِلكات [čilka:t] *pl:* شِلَك [čilak] *Collective*

stray • **1.** تايِه [ta:yih] He was hit by a stray bullet. اِنضِرَب بِرصاصَة تايهَة [ʔinðirab briṣa:ṣa ta:yha] Have you found the stray lamb? لِقِيت الطِّلِي التّايِه؟ [ligi:t ʔiṭṭili ʔitta:yih?] • **2.** سايِب [sa:yib] Stray dogs are becoming a problem. الكِلاب السّايبَة دَتصِير مُشكِلَة [ʔiččila:b ʔissa:yba datṣi:r muškila]

to stray • **1.** تاه [ta:h] تَيه [tayh] *vn:* *sv* i. The lamb strayed from the flock. الطِّلِي تاه مِن القَطِيع [ʔiṭṭili ta:h min ʔilqaṭi:ʕ]

stream • **1.** شَطّ [šaṭṭ] شطُوط [šṭu:ṭ] *pl:* نَهَر [nahar] أنهار [ʔanha:r] *pl:* أَنهُر [ʔanhur] *pl:* Where can we ford the stream? وين نِقدَر نِعبُر الشَّطّ خياضَة؟ [wi:n nigdar niʕbur ʔiššaṭṭ xya:ða?] • **2.** ساقيَة [sa:gya, sa:jya] سواقِي [swa:gi, swa:ji] *pl:* A little stream flows through our farm. فَدّ ساقيَة صغَيّرَة تِجرِي بمَزرَعَتنا [fadd sa:gya ṣɣayyra tijri bmazraʕatna] • **3.** سَيل [sayl] سيُول [syu:l] *pl:* A stream of refugees left the city. سَيل مِن اللّاجِئِين تِرَك الوِلايَة [sayl min ʔalla:jiʔi:n tirak ʔilwila:ya] • **4.** مَجرَى [majra] مَجارِي [maja:ri] *pl:* You interrupted my stream of thought. قِطَعِت مَجرَى أفكارِي [giṭaʕit majra ʔafka:ri]

to stream • **1.** جِرَى [jira:] جَرَيان [jaraya:n] *vn:* *sv* i. Tears streamed down her cheeks. الدُّمُوع جِرَت عَلَى خدُودها [ʔiddumu:ʕ jirat ʕala xdu:dha]

street • **1.** شارِع [ša:riʕ] شَوارِع [šawa:riʕ] *pl:* جادَّة [ja:dda] جادّات [ja:dda:t] *pl:* دَرُب [darub] درُوب [dru:b] *pl:* I met him on the street. لاقَيتَه بِالشّارِع [la:gi:tah bišša:riʕ]

streetcar • **1.** ترام [tra:m] ترامات [tra:ma:t] *pl:* تراموای [tra:mwa:y] تراموايات [tra:mwa:ya:t] *pl:*

street light • **1.** ضَوَة شارِع [ðuwat ša:riʕ] ضُوايات شَوارِع [ðuwa:ya:t šawa:riʕ] *pl:* أَضويَة شارِع [ʔaðwiyat ša:riʕ] *pl:* The street lights go on at dark. ضُوايات الشَّوارِع تِشتِعِل لَمّا تصِير ظَلمَة [ðuwa:ya:t ʔiššawa:riʕ tištiʕil lamma tṣi:r ðalma]

strength • **1.** قُوَّة [quwwa, guwwa] *pl:* I don't have the strength to do my work. ما عِندِي قُوَّة حَتَّى أَسَوِّي شُغلِي [ma: ʕindi quwwa ħatta ʔasawwi šuɣli] I've lost all my strength. فِقَدِت كُلّ قُوتِي [fiqadit kull quwwti] The strength of the enemy surprised us. قُوَّة العَدُو أدهِشَتنا [quwwat ʔilʕadu ʔadhišatna]

*** He doesn't know his own strength.** • **1.** ما يعرُف نَفسَه شقَدّ قَوِي [ma: yiʕruf nafsah šgadd qawi]

on the strength of • **1.** بِناءاً عَلَى [bina:ʔan ʕala] We hired him on the strength of your recommendation. شَغَّلناه بِناءاً عَلَى تَوصِيتَك [šaɣɣalna:h bina:ʔan ʕala tawṣi:tak]

strenuous • **1.** مُتعِب [mutʕib] مُجهِد [mujhid] That's a strenuous job. هَذِي فَدّ شَغلَة مُتعِبَة [ha:ði fadd šayla mutʕiba] That's a strenuous job. هَذِي فَدّ شَغلَة تِشلَع القَلب [ha:ði fadd šayla tišlaʕ ʔilgalub]

S

stress • **1.** تَشدِيد [tašdi:d] The stress is on the second syllable of the word. التَّشدِيد عَلَى المَقطَع الثّانِي مِن الكَلِمَة [ʔittašdi:d ʕala ʔilmaqtaʕ ʔiθθa:ni min ʔalkalima]

to stress • **1.** أَكَّد [ʔakkad] تَأكِيد [taʔki:d] *vn:* تَأكَّد [tʔakkad] *p:* شَدَّد عَلَى [šaddad ʕala] تَشدِيد [tašdi:d] *vn:* تشَدَّد [tšaddad] *p:* She stressed the importance of honesty. أَكَّدَت عَلَى أَهَمِّيَّة الأَمانَة [ʔakkidat ʕala ʔahammiyyat ʔilʔama:na] • **2.** شَدَّد [šaddad] *sv* i. We stress the second syllable of the word. نشَدِّد عَلَى المَقطَع الثّانِي مِن الكَلِمَة [nšaddid ʕala ʔilmaqtaʕ ʔiθθa:ni min ʔalkalima]

stretch • **1.** مَسافَة [masa:fa] مَسافات [masa:fa:t] *pl:* قِسِم [qisim] أَقسام [ʔaqsa:m] *pl:* We had to run the last stretch. اِنجِبَرنا نِركُض المَسافَة الأَخِيرَة [ʔinǰibarna nirkuḍ ʔilmasa:fa ʔilʔaxi:ra]

at a stretch • **1.** عَلَى فَدّ جَرَّة [ʕala fadd ǰarra] بَلا وَقفَة [bala wagfa] He works about ten hours at a stretch. يِشتِغُل حَوالِي عَشِر ساعات عَلَى فَدّ جَرَّة [yištiɣul ħawa:li ʕašir sa:ʕa:t ʕala fadd ǰarra]

to stretch • **1.** كَبَّر [kabbar] تَكبِير [takbi:r] *vn:* تكَبَّر [tkabbar] *p:* Can you stretch my shoes a little bit. تِقدَر تكَبُّر قُندَرتِي شوَيَّة [tigdar tkabbur qundarti šwayya] • **2.** تكَبَّر [tkabbar] تكَبُّر [takabbur] *vn: sv* a. The gloves will stretch. الكفُوف تِتكَبَّر [ʔiččfu:f titkabbar] • **3.** مَطَّى [matta:] تَمطِيَة [tamtiya] *vn:* تمَطَّى [tmatta:] *p:* You stretched the elastic too much. مَطَّيت اللّاستِيك هوايَة [matti:t ʔilla:sti:k hwa:ya] • **4.** تمَطَّى [tmatta:] تَمَطِّي [tamatti] *vn: sv* a. تمَغَّط [tmaɣɣat] تَمَغُّط [tamaɣɣut] *vn: sv* a. The lion yawned and stretched. السَّبِع تثاوَب وَتمَطَّى [ʔissabiʕ tθa:wab wtmatta:]

*** The wheat fields stretch out for miles.**

• **1.** حُقُول الحُنطَة مِمتَدَّة لِعِدَّة أَميال [ħuqu:l ʔilħunta mimtadda lʕiddat ʔamya:l]

to stretch out • **1.** مَدّ [madd] مَدّ [madd] *vn:* اِنمَدّ [ʔinmadd] *p:* He stretched out his hand. مَدّ إِيدَه [madd ʔi:dah]

stretcher • **1.** نَقّالَة [naqqa:la] نَقّالات [naqqa:la:t] *pl:* مَحَفَّة [maħaffa] مَحَفّات [maħaffa:t] *pl:* سَديَة [sadya] سَديات [sadya:t] *pl:* They took him to the hospital on a stretcher. شالَوه لِلمُستَشفَى بِالنَّقّالَة [ša:lu:h lilmustašfa binnaqqa:la]

strict • **1.** مِتشَدِّد [mitšaddid] His father is very strict. أَبُوه كُلِّش مِتشَدِّد [ʔabu:h kulliš mitšaddid]

strike • **1.** إضراب [ʔiḍra:b] إضرابات [ʔiḍra:ba:t] *pl:* How long did the strike last? الإِضراب شقَدّ طَوَّل؟ [ʔalʔiḍra:b šgadd tawwal?]

to go on strike • **1.** سَوَّى إِضراب، أَضرَب [sawwa: ʔiḍra:b, ʔaḍrab] تَسوِيَة إِضراب [taswiyat ʔiḍra:b] *vn: sv* i. أَضرَب [ʔaḍrab] إِضراب [ʔiḍra:b] *vn: sv* i. We're going on strike tomorrow. راح نسَوِّي إِضراب باكِر [ra:ħ nsawwi ʔiḍra:b ba:čir]

to strike • **1.** ضِرَب [ḍirab] ضَرُب [ḍarub] *vn:* اِنضِرَب [ʔinḍirab] *p:* Who struck you? مِنُو ضِرَبَك؟ [minu ḍirabak?] • **2.** طَخّ ب [taxx b-] طَخّ [taxx] *vn: sv* u. The ship struck a rock. السَّفِينَة طَخَّت بِصَخرَة [ʔissafi:na taxxat bṣaxra] • **3.** وُقَع عَلَى [wugaʕ ʕala] وُقُوع [wugu:ʕ] *vn: sv* a. ضِرَب [ḍirab] ضَرُب [ḍarub] *vn:* اِنضِرَب [ʔinḍirab] *p:* Lightning struck the tree. الصّاعِقَة وُقعَت عَلَى الشَّجَرَة [ʔiṣṣa:ʕiqa wugʕat ʕala ʔiššaǰara] • **4.** دَقّ [dagg] دَقّ [dagg] *vn: sv* u. The clock just struck ten. السّاعَة هَسَّة دَقَّت عَشرَة [ʔissa:ʕa hassa daggat ʕašra] • **5.** شِعَل [šiʕal] Strike a match. إِشعِل شِخّاطَة [ʔišʕil šixxa:ta] • **6.** لِقَى [liga:] لَقِي [lagy] *vn: sv* i. The government struck oil in the north. الحُكُومَة لِقَت نَفُط بِالشِّمال [ʔilħuku:ma ligat nafuṭ biššima:l] • **7.** عِقَد [ʕiqad] عَقِد [ʕaqid] *vn:* اِنعِقَد [ʔinʕiqad] *p:* Did you strike a bargain? عِقَدِت صَفقَة؟ [ʕiqadit ṣafqa?] • **8.** لِفَت [lifat] لَفِت [lafit] *vn:* اِنلِفَت [ʔinlifat] *p:* That was the first thing that struck my eye. هَذا كان أَوَّل شِي لِفَت نَظَرِي [ha:ða ča:n ʔawwal ši lifat naḍari]

*** It strikes me he's acting very strangely.**

• **1.** يبَيِّن عَلَيه دَيتصَرَّف بصُورَة غَير طَبِيعِيَّة [ybayyin ʕali:h dayitṣarraf bṣu:ra ɣayr tabi:ʕiyya]

*** Does that strike a familiar note?**

• **1.** هَذا يجِيب شِي ببالَك؟ [ha:ða yǰi:b ši biba:lak?] / هَذا يذَكِّرَك بشِي؟ [ha:ða yðakkrak bši?]

to strike off • **1.** شِطَب [šiṭab] شَطُب [šaṭub] *vn:* اِنشِطَب [ʔinšiṭab] *p:* Strike his name off the list. إِشطُب إِسمَه مِن القائِمَة [ʔištub ʔismah min ʔilqa:ʔima]

to strike out • **1.** شِطَب [šiṭab] شَطُب [šaṭub] *vn:* اِنشِطَب [ʔinšiṭab] *p:* حِذَف [ħiðaf] حَذِف [ħaðif] *vn:* اِنحِذَف [ʔinħiðaf] *p:* Strike out the first paragraph. إِشطُب الفَقرَة الأُولَى [ʔištub ʔilfaqara ʔilʔu:la] • **2.** تحَرَّك [tħarrak] حَرَكَ [ħaraka] *vn: sv* a. The patrol struck out into the desert. الدَّورِيَّة تحَرَّكَت بِالصَّحراء [ʔiddawriyya tħarrikat biṣṣaħra:ʔ]

to strike up a friendship • **1.** تصادَق [tṣa:daq] تَصادُق [taṣa:duq] *vn: sv* a. The two of them struck up a friendship very quickly. ثْنَينهُم تصادقَوا بسُرعَة [θnaynhum tṣa:dqaw bsurʕa]

striker • **1.** مُضرِب [muḍrib] مُضرِبِين [muḍribi:n] *pl:* The strikers have agreed to negotiate. المُضرِبِين وافقَوا يِتفاوضُون [ʔilmuḍribi:n wa:fqaw yitfa:wḍu:n]

striking • **1.** زاهِي [za:hi] She likes to wear striking colors. تحِبّ تِلبَس أَلوان زاهيَة [tħibb tilbas ʔalwa:n za:hya] • **2.** عَجِيب [ʕaǰi:b] There's a striking resemblance between the two. أَكُو شَبَه عَجِيب بَيناتهُم [ʔaku šabah ʕaǰi:b bayna:thum]

string • **1.** خِيط [xi:t] خيُوط [xyu:t] *pl:* This string is too short. هَالخَيط كُلِّش قصَيِّر [halxi:t kulliš gṣayyir] • **2.** وَتَر [watar] أَوتار [ʔawta:r] *pl:* I have to buy a new string for my violin. لازِم أَشتِرِي وَتَر جِدِيد لِلكَمَنجَة مالتِي [la:zim ʔaštiri watar ǰidi:d lilkamanǰa ma:lti]

*** He's still attached to his mother's apron strings.**

• **1.** بَعدَه تَحَت سَيطَرَة أُمَّه [baʕdah taħat saytarat ʔummah] / بَعدَه لازِق بأُمَّه [baʕdah la:zig bʔummah]

to string • **1.** لِضَم [liðam] لَضُم [laðum] *vn:* اِنلِضَم [ʔinliðam] *p:* Where can I have my pearls strung? وين أقدَر ألضُم اللّيلو مالي؟ [wiːn ʔagdar ʔalðum ʔilliːluː maːli?] • **2.** وَصَّل [waṣṣal] تَوصِيل [tawṣiːl] *vn:* توَصَّل [twaṣṣal] *p:* How are you going to string the wire to the garage? شلُون راح توَصِّل الوايِر لِلكَراج؟ [šluːn raːħ twaṣṣil ʔilwaːyir lilgaraːǰ?]

string bean • **1.** فاصُولِيَّة [faṣuːliyya] فاصُولِيّات [faːṣuːliyyaːt] *pl:* فاصُوليَا [faṣuːlya] *Collective:*

to strip • **1.** سَلَّخ [sallax] تَصلِيخ [taṣliːx] *vn:* تصَلَّخ [tṣallax] *p:* They strip the cars of everything valuable before they scrap them. يصَلِّخُون السَّيّارات مِن كُلّشِي اللّي يِسوَى قَبُل ما يسَكرَبُوها [yṣallixuːn ʔissayyaːraːt min kullši ʔilli yiswaː gabul maː ysakrabuːha] • **2.** شِلَع [šilaʕ] شَلِع [šaliʕ] *vn:* اِنشِلَع [ʔinšilaʕ] *p:* The captain stripped the medals from his chest. الرَّئِيس شِلَع المَداليات مِن صَدرَه [ʔirraʔiːs šilaʕ ʔilmadaliyyaːt min ṣadrah] • **3.** جَرَّد [ǰarrad] تَجرِيد [tajriːd] *vn:* تجَرَّد [tǰarrad] *p:* They stripped the king of all his privileges. جَرِّدَوا المَلِك مِن كُلّ أمتِيازاتَه [ǰarridaw ʔilmalik min kull ʔimtiyaːzaːtah]

to strip off • **1.** نِزَع [nizaʕ] نَزِع [naziʕ] *vn: sv* a. She stripped off her clothes. نِزعَت هدُومها [nizʕat hduːmha] She stripped off her clothes. تسَلّخَت [tsallxat]

stripe • **1.** قَلَم [qalam] أقلام [ʔaqlaːm] *pl:* The tie has red and white stripes. البُوينباغ بِيه أقلام حُمُر وَبِيض [ʔilbuyinbaːɣ biːh ʔaqlaːm ħumur wbiːð] • **2.** خَيط [xiːṭ] خيُوط [xyuːṭ] *pl:* If you get drunk again, we'll take your stripes away. إذا سكَرِت مَرَّة اللُّخ، ناخُذ خيُوطَك مِنَّك [ʔiða skarit marra ʔillux, naːxuð xyuːṭak minnak]

striped • **1.** مقَلَّم [mqallam] She's wearing a striped dress. لابسَة نَفنُوف مقَلَّم [laːbsah nafnuːf mqallam]

stroke • **1.** اِنفِجار بِالدَماغ [ʔinfiǰaːr biddamaːɣ] اِنفِجارات بِدَّماغ [ʔinfiǰaːraːt biddamaːɣ] *pl:* He died of a stroke. مات مِن أثَر اِنفِجار بِالدَّماغ [maːt min ʔaθar ʔinfiǰaːr biddamaːɣ] • **2.** ضَربَة [ðarba] ضَربات [ðarbaːt] *pl:* With a few strokes of the oars, he was in midstream. بكَم ضَربَة مِجداف، وُصَل لِنُصّ الشَّطّ [bčam ðarbat miǰdaːf, wuṣal linuṣṣ ʔiššaṭṭ] • **3.** With a stroke of the pen, he was sentenced to hang. بِجَرَّة قَلَم، اِنحِكَم عَلِيه بِالإعدام [bǰarrat qalam, ʔinħikam ʕaliːh bilʔiʕdaːm]

*** It was a real stroke of luck to get this apartment.**
• **1.** تَحصِيل هَالشُقَّة كان حَظّ عَدِل [taħṣiːl haššaqqa čaːn ħaðð ʕadil]

*** At one stroke everything was changed.**
• **1.** كُلّش تبَدَّل فَدّ نَوبَة [kullši tbaddal fadd nawba]

*** He arrived at the stroke of four.**
• **1.** وُصَل الساعَة أربَعَة بِالضَبُط [wuṣal ʔissaːʕa ʔarbaʕa biððabuṭ]

to stroke • **1.** مَسَّد ل- [massad l-] تَمسِيد [tamsiːd] *vn:* تمَسَّد [tmassad] *p:* Our cat loves to be stroked. بَزُّونَتنا تحِبّ يِتمَسَّد إلها [bazzuːnatna tħibb yitmassad ʔilha]

stroll • **1.** مَشيَة [mašya] مَشيات [mašyaːt] *pl:* A short stroll won't tire you much. مَشيَة صغَيّرَة ما تتَعّبَك هوايَة [mašya ṣɣayyra maː ʔittaʕʕbak hwaːya]

*** I'd like to take a stroll around the square.**
• **1.** أرِيد أتمَشّى حَول الساحَة [ʔariːd ʔatmaššaː ħawl ʔissaːħa]

to stroll • **1.** تمَشّى [tmaššaː] تمَشّي [tmašši] *vn: sv* a. Let's stroll through the town, خَلّي نِتمَشّى بِالمَدِينَة [xalli nitmaššaː bilmadiːna]

strong • **1.** قَوي [qawi, guwi] He has strong hands. عِندَه إيدَين قَوِيَّة [ʕindah ʔiːdayn qawiyya] • **2.** شَدِيد [šadiːd] قَوي [qawi, guwi] There is a strong wind blowing today. أكُو هَوا شَدِيد دَيهِبّ اليُوم [ʔaku hawa šadiːd dayhibb ʔilyuːm]

struggle • **1.** مَشَقَّة [mašaqqa] مَشَقّات [mašaqqaːt] *pl:* I only beat him after a hard struggle. ما غلَبتَه إلّا بمَشَقَّة [maː ɣilabtah ʔilla bmašaqqa] • **2.** مُكافَحَة [mukaːfaħa] The struggle against illiteracy in Iraq has made progress. مُكافَحَة الأمِّيَّة بِالعِراق تقَدّمَت [mukaːfaħat ʔilʔummiyya bilʕiraːq tqaddimat] • **3.** كِفاح [kifaːħ] مُكافَحَة [mukaːfaħa] مُكافَحات [mukaːfaħaːt] *pl:* They got their freedom through a long struggle. حَصّلَوا عَلَى اِستِقلالهُم بكِفاح طَوِيل [ħaṣṣlaw ʕala ʔistiqlaːlhum bkifaːħ ṭuwiːl] • **4.** تباطَح [tbaːṭaħ] تَباطُح [tabaːṭuħ] *vn: sv* a. I've been struggling with this problem for some time. صارلِي مُدَّة دَأتباطَح ويّا هَالمُشكِلَة [ṣaːrli mudda daʔatbaːṭaħ wiyya halmuškila] • **5.** جاهَد [ǰaːhad] جِهاد [ǰihaːd] *vn: sv* i. The government is struggling to improve economic conditions. الحُكُومَة دَتجاهِد حَتّى تحَسِّن الأحوال الاقتِصادِيَّة [ʔilħukuːma dadǰaːhid ħatta tħassin ʔilʔaħwaːl ʔilʔiqtiṣaːdiyya]

to struggle against • **1.** كافَح [kaːfaħ] مُكافَحَة [mukaːfaħa] *vn:* تكافَح [tkaːfaħ] *p:* We had to struggle against the current. اِضطَرّينا نكافِح التَّيّار [ʔiðṭarriːna nkaːfiħ ʔittayyaːr]

*** We had a hard struggle to get the piano up to the second floor.** • **1.** مِتنا قَبُل ما نصَعِّد البِيانُو لِلطّابِق الثانِي [mitna gabul maː nṣaʕʕid ʔilpyaːnuː liṭṭaːbiq ʔiθθaːni]

stubborn • **1.** عنادِي [ʕnaːdi] عنُودِي [ʕnuːdi] عنادِيِّين [ʕnaːdiyyiːn] *pl:* He's terribly stubborn. هُوَّ كُلّش عنادِي [huwwa kulliš ʕnaːdi]

to get stuck • **1.** اِنحِصَر [ʔinħiṣar] اِنحِصار [ʔinħiṣaːr] *vn: sv* i. I got stuck in the chair. اِنحِصَرِت بِالكُرسِي [ʔinħiṣarit bilkursi] • **2.** طُمَس [ṭumas] طَمُس [ṭamus] *vn: sv* u. اِنحِصَر [ʔinħiṣar] اِنحِصار [ʔinħiṣaːr] *vn: sv* i. My car got stuck in the mud. سَيّارتِي طُمسَت بِالطِّين [sayyaːrti ṭumsat biṭṭiːn] • **3.** توَرَّط [twarraṭ] تَوَرُّط [tawarruṭ] *vn: sv* a.

S

تخوزق [txawzaq] تَخَوزُق [taxawzuq] *vn: sv* a. I got stuck with this car. توَرَّطِت بهَالسَّيّارَة [twarraṭit bhassayya:ra]

*** I got stuck on this passage. • 1.** عِصَت عَلَيّا هاي الجُملَة [ʕiṣat ʕalayya ha:y ʔiǰǰumla]

stuck-up • 1. مِتكَبُّر [mitkabbur] She is stuck-up هِيَّ مِتكَبّرَة [hiyya mitkabbra] She is stuck-up شايلَة خَشِمها [ša:yla xašimha]

student • 1. تِلمِيذ [tilmi:ð] تَلامِيذ [tala:mi:ð] *pl:* طالِب [ṭa:lib] طُلّاب [ṭulla:b] *pl:* How many students are there at the medical school? كَم تِلمِيذ أَكُو بكُلِّيَّة الطِّب؟ [čam tilmi:ð ʔaku bkulliyyat ʔiṭṭibb?]

studio • 1. ستوديُو [stu:dyu] ستوديُوات [stu:dyuwa:t] *pl:* I've got to see a man at the Iraqi Broadcasting Studios. لازِم أَشُوف فَدّ رِجّال بإِستَوديُوات الإذاعَة العِراقِيَّة [la:zim ʔašu:f fadd rijja:l bistu:dyuwa:t ʔilʔiða:ʕa ʔilʕira:qiyya]

study • 1. دِراسَة [dira:sa] Has he finished his studies? خَلَّص دِراستَه؟ [xallaṣ dira:stah?] **• 2.** بَحِث [baħiθ] بُحُوث، أَبحاث [buħu:θ, ʔabħa:θ] *pl:* He has published several studies in that field. نِشَر عِدَّة أَبحاث بهَالمَوضُوع [nišar ʕiddat ʔabħa:θ bhalmawđu:ʕ]

to study • 1. دِرَس [diras] دِراسَة [dira:sa] *vn:* اِندِرَس [ʔindiras] *p:* We studied the map before we started our trip. دِرَسنا الخَرِيطَة قَبُل ما نِبدِي سَفرَتنا [dirasna ʔilxari:ṭa gabul ma: nibdi safratna] He's studying Chinese. دَيِدرُس صِينِي [dayidrus ṣi:ni] **• 2.** بَحَث [biħaθ] بَحِث [baħiθ] *vn:* اِنبِحَث [ʔinbiħaθ] *p:* دِرَس [diras] دَرِس [daris] *vn:* اِندِرَس [ʔindiras] *p:* The government is studying the problem. الحُكُومَة دَتِبحَث المُشكِلَة [ʔilħuku:ma datibħaθ ʔilmuškila]

stuff • 1. غَراض [ɣara:đ] أَشياء [ʔašya:ʔ] Throw that old stuff away! ذِبّ هَالغَراض العَتِيقَة [ðibb halɣara:đ ʔilʕati:ga]

*** Now we'll see what sort of stuff he's made of. • 1.** هَسَّة نشُوف شِنُو مَعدَنَه [hassa nšu:f šinu maʕdanah]

to stuff • 1. حَنَّط [ħannaṭ] تَحنِيط [taħni:ṭ] *vn: sv* i. He stuffs animals for the museum. يحَنِّط حَيوانات لِلمَتحَف [yħanniṭ ħaywa:na:t lilmatħaf] **• 2.** حَشَّى [ħašša:] تَحشِيَة [taħšiya] *vn:* تحَشَّى [tħašša:] *p:* عَبَّى [ʕabba:] تَعبِيَة [taʕbiya] *vn:* تعَبَّى [tʕabba:] *p:* Stuff cotton in your ears. حَشِّي قُطُن بإذنَك [ħašši guṭun bʔiðnak] Can you stuff all these things in one suitcase? تِقدَر تعَبِّي كُل هَالغَراض بفَدّ جَنطَة؟ [tigdar tʕabbi kull halɣara:đ bfadd ǰanṭa?] **• 3.** تِرَس [tiras] تَرِس [taris] *vn:* اِنتِرَس [ʔintiras] *p:* دَكّ [dačč] دَكّ [dačč] *vn:* اِندَكّ [ʔindačč] *p:* We stuffed our bellies with food. دَكَّينا بطُوننا بالأَكِل [dačči:na bṭu:nna bilʔakil]

stuffed • 1. مَسدُود [masdu:d] My nose is all stuffed up. خَشمِي مَسدُود [xašmi masdu:d] **• 2.** مَحشِي [maħši] اِنحَشَّى [ʔinħašša:] We had stuffed turkey for lunch. تغَدَّينا دِيك هِندِي مَحشِي [tɣaddi:na di:č hindi maħši]

to stumble • 1. عِثَر [ʕiθar] عَثِر [ʕaθir] *vn: sv* a. I stumbled over a stone. عِثَرت بحجارَة [ʕiθarit bħǰa:ra]

stupid • 1. غَبِي [ɣabi] أَغبِياء [ʔaɣbiya:ʔ] *pl:* بَلِيد [bali:d] He isn't at all stupid. هُوَّ مُو غَبِي أَبَداً [huwwa mu: ɣabi ʔabadan] **• 2.** سَخِيف [saxi:f] That's a stupid idea. هاي فِكرَة سَخِيفَة [ha:y fikra saxi:fa]

sty • 1. حِدِقدِقَة [ħidigdiga] حِدِقدِقات [ħidigdiga:t] *pl:* I'm getting a sty on my left eye. دَتِطلَعلِي حَدِقدِقَة بعَينِي اليِسرَى [datiṭlaʕli ħadigdiga bʕayni ʔilyisra]

style • 1. إسلُوب [ʔislu:b] أَسالِيب [ʔasa:li:b] *pl:* His style of writing is very poor. إسلُوبَه بالكِتابَة كُلِّش ضَعِيف [ʔislu:bah bilkita:ba kulliš đaʕi:f] **• 2.** مُودَة [mu:da] مُودات [mu:da:t] *pl:* It's the latest style. هاي آخِر مُودَة [ha:y ʔa:xir mu:da] She's always in style. هِيَّ عَالمُودَة دائِماً [hiyya ʕalmu:da da:ʔiman]

subject • 1. مَوضُوع [mawđu:ʕ] مَواضِيع [mawa:đi:ʕ] *pl:* قَضِيَّة [qađiyya] قَضايا [qađa:ya] *pl:* I don't know anything about that subject. ما أَعرُف شِي عَن هَذا المَوضُوع [ma: ʔaʕruf ši ʕan ha:ða ʔilmawđu:ʕ] **• 2.** رَعِيَّة [raʕiyya] رَعايا [raʕa:ya] *pl:* He is a British subject. هُوَّ مِن رَعايا إنكِلتَرا [huwwa min raʕa:ya ʔingiltara] **• 3.** مُبتَدِئ [mubtadiʔ] مُبتَدِئِين [mubtadiʔi:n] *pl:* The subject of this sentence is the word 'Ali'. المُبتَدَأ بهَالجُملَة هُوَّ الكَلِمَة "عَلِي" [ʔilmubtadaʔ bihaǰǰumla huwwa ʔilkalima "ʕali"] **• 4.** مُعَرَّض [muʕarrađ] This schedule is subject to change. هَذا الجَّدوَل مُعَرَّض لِلتَّغيِير [ha:ða ʔiǰǰadwal muʕarrađ littaɣyi:r]

*** I'm always subject to colds. • 1.** آنِي أَنَّشِل بسُرعَة [ʔa:ni ʔannišil bsurʕa]

to subject • 1. أَخضَع [ʔaxđaʕ] خُضُوع [xuđu:ʕ] *vn: sv* i. The Mongols subjected all of Asia to their rule. المَغُول أَخضِعَوا كُلّ آسيا لِحُكُمهُم [ʔilmaɣu:l ʔaxđiʕaw kull ʔa:sya liħukumhum]

to submit • 1. قَدَّم [qaddam] تَقدِيم [taqdi:m] *vn:* تقَدَّم [tqaddam] *p:* I'll submit my report on Monday. راح أَقَدِّم تَقرِيرِي يوم الإثنَين [ra:ħ ʔaqaddim taqri:ri yu:m ʔilʔiθnayn] **• 2.** رِضَخ [riđax] رِضُوخ [riđu:x] *vn: sv* u. The criminal submitted to search. المُجرِم رِضَخ لِلتَّفتِيش [ʔilmuǰrim riđax littafti:š] **• 3.** خِضَع [xiđaʕ] خُضُوع [xuđu:ʕ] *vn: sv* a. the boss forces everyone to submit to his ideas. الرَّئِيس يِجبُر الكُلّ يخضَعُون لآرائَه [ʔirraʔi:s yiǰbur ʔilkull yixđaʕu:n lʔa:ra:ʔah] **• 4.** اِستَسلَم [ʔistaslam] اِستِسلَم [ʔistislam] *vn: sv* i. His mother had to submit to an operation. أُمَّه اِضطَرَّت تِستَسلِم لِعَمَلِيَّة [ʔummah ʔiđṭarrat tistaslim liʕamaliyya]

S

to subscribe • **1.** اِشتِرَك [ʔištirak] اِشتِراك [ʔištira:k] *vn: sv* i. I subscribed to both papers. اِشتِرَكِت بِالجَرِيدتَين [ʔištirakit bijjari:dti:n] • **2.** شارَك [ša:rak] مُشارَكَة [muša:raka] *vn:* تشارَك [tša:rak] *p:* I don't subscribe to your opinion. ما أشارگك برأيَك [ma: ʔaša:rkak braʔyak]

substantial • **1.** كبير [čbi:r] ضَخُم [ðaxum] He lost a substantial sum of money. خِسَر كَمِّيَّة كبيرَة مِن الفلوس [xiṣar kammiyya čbi:ra min ʔiliflu:s] He lost a substantial sum of money. خِسَر مَبلَغ ضَخُم [xiṣar mablaɣ ðaxum] • **2.** جَوهَري [jawhari] I don't see any substantial difference. ما أشُوف أيّ فَرَق جَوهَري [ma: ʔašu:f ʔayy faraq jawhari] • **3.** تُكمَة [tukma] Don't use that ladder; it's not substantial. لا تِستَعمِل هَالدَّرَج؛ هَذا مُو تُكمَة [la: tistaʕmil haddaraj; ha:ða mu: tukma]

substantially • **1.** جَوهَرِياً [jawhariyyan] The two are substantially alike. الثنَين جَوهَرِياً يِتشابهُون [liθnayn jawhariyyan yitša:bhu:n]

substitute • **1.** بَدَل [badal] عِوَض [ʕiwað] Vegetable oil is occasionally used as a substitue for animal fat. الدِّهِن النَّباتِي أحياناً يُستَعمَل كَبَدَل لِلدِّهِن الحَيواني [ʔiddihin ʔinnaba:ti ʔaħya:nan yustaʕmal kabadal liddihin ʔilħaywa:ni] • **2.** بِدال، بَدَل [bida:l, badal] If you can't be here tomorrow, send a substitute. إذا ما تِقدَر تكُون هنا باكِر، دِزّ واحِد بدالَك [ʔiða ma: tigdar tku:n hna ba:čir, dizz wa:ħid bda:lak]

to substitute for • **1.** عَوَّض [ʕawwað] تَعوِيض [taʕwi:ð] *vn:* تعَوَّض [tʕawwað] *p:* I'll substitute red for green. راح أعَوُّض أحمَر بمَكان الأخضَر [ra:ħ ʔaʕawwuð ʔaħmar bmaka:n ʔilʔaxðar] • **2.** أخَذ [ʔaxað] *sv* u. Can you substitute for me today? تِقدَر تاخُذ مَكانِي اليُوم؟ [tigdar ta:xuð maka:ni ʔilyu:m?]

to subtract • **1.** طِرَح [ṭirah] طَرح [tariħ] *vn:* اِنطِرَح [ʔinṭirah] *p:* He subtracted six from ten. طِرَح سِتَّة مِن عَشرَة [ṭirah sitta min ʕašra]

subtraction • **1.** طَرِح [ṭariħ]

suburb • **1.** ضاحِيَة [ða:ħiya] ضَواحِي [ðawa:ħi] *pl:* Their house is in the suburbs of the city. بَيتهُم بِضَواحِي المَدِينَة [baythum bðawa:ħi ʔilmadi:na]

to succeed • **1.** جا وَرَا [ja: wara] مَجِيئ وَرَا [maji:ʔ wara] *vn: sv* i. Who succeeded him in office? مِنُو جا وَراه بالوَظِيفَة [minu ja: wara:h bilwaði:fa] • **2.** نِجَح [nijaħ] نَجاح [naja:ħ] *vn: sv* a. He succeeds in everything he undertakes. يِنجَح بِكُلّما ياخُذ عَلَى عاتقَه [yinjaħ bkullma ya:xuð ʕala ʕa:tqah]

success • **1.** نَجاح [naja:ħ] نَجاحات [naja:ħa:t] *pl:* Congratulations on your success! تَهانِينا عَلَى نَجاحَك [taha:ni:na ʕala naja:ħak] The play wasn't much of a success. التَّمثِيلِيَّة ما حَصّلَت عَلَى نَجاح هوايَة [ʔittamθi:liyya ma: ħaṣṣlat ʕala naja:ħ hwa:ya]

successful • **1.** ناجِح [na:jiħ] He's a successful businessman. هُوَّ رَجُل أعمال ناجِح [huwwa rajul ʔaʕma:l na:jiħ]

successor • **1.** خَلَف [xalaf] (hereditary) . The sheik's oldest son becomes his successor. أكبَر أولاد الشَّيخ يصِير خَلَفَه [ʔakbar ʔawla:d ʔaššayx yṣi:r xalafah]

such • **1.** هِيكِي [hi:či] مِثِل هَذا [miθil ha:ða] Such statements are hard to prove. هِيكِي عِبارات يِصعَب بَرهَنَتها [hi:či ʕiba:ra:t yisʕab barhanatha] I've never heard such nonsense before. ما سِمَعت مِثِل هَاللَّغوَة قَبُل [ma: simaʕit miθil hallaɣwa gabul] I heard such thing. سِمَعِت هِيكِي شِي [simaʕit hi:či ši] I heard such thing. سِمَعِت شِي مِن هَذا القَبِيل [simaʕit ši min ha:ða ʔilqabi:l] • **2.** هَالقَدّ [halgadd] Don't be in such a hurry. لا تِستَعجِل هَالقَدّ [la: tistaʕjil halgadd] It was such a long movie that we didn't get out till midnight. هَل قَدّ ما كان فِلِم طُوِيل، ما طلَعنا إلّا لنُصّ اللَّيل [halgadd ma: ča:n filim ṭuwi:l, ma: ṭlaʕna ʔilla lnuṣṣ ʔillayl]

as such • **1.** بحَدّ ذات [bħadd ða:t-] The work as such isn't difficult. الشُّغُل بحَدّ ذاته مُو صَعُب [ʔiššuɣul bħadd ða:tah mu: ṣaʕub]

such as • **1.** مِثِل [miθil] We sell things such as hats and shirts. نبِيع أشياء مِثِل شَفقات وثياب [nbi:ʕ ʔašya:ʔ miθil šafqa:t wθya:b]

to suck • **1.** مَصّ [maṣṣ] مَصّ [maṣṣ] *vn:* اِنمَصّ [ʔinmaṣṣ] *p:* Our baby sucks his thumb. طِفِلنا يمُصّ إبهامَه [ṭifilna ymuṣṣ ʔibha:mah]

suction • **1.** مَصّ [maṣṣ] اِمتِصاص [ʔimtiṣa:ṣ]

Sudan • **1.** السُّودان [ʔissu:da:n]

Sudanese • **1.** سُوداني [su:da:ni]

sudden • **1.** فُجائِي [fuja:ʔi] There's been a sudden change in the weather. صار تَبَدُّل فُجائِي بِالجَوّ [ṣa:r tabaddul fuja:ʔi bijjaww]

all of a sudden • **1.** فَجأةً [fajʔatan] عَلَى غَفلَة [ʕala ɣafla] بَغتاً [baɣtan] All of a sudden I remembered that I had to mail a letter. فُجأةً تذَكَّرت لازِم أذِبّ رِسالَة بِالبَرِيد [fujʔatan dðakkarit la:zim ʔaðibb risa:la bilbari:d]

to sue • **1.** اِشتِكَى [ʔištika:] شِكايَة [šika:ya] *vn: sv* i. We sued him for damages. اِشتِكَينا عَلِيه بطَلَب التَّعوِيض [ʔištiki:na ʕali:h bṭalab ʔittaʕwi:ð] • **2.** طِلَب [ṭilab] طَلَب [ṭalab] *vn: sv* u. They'll sue for peace. راح يطُلبُون الصُّلُح [ra:ħ yṭulbu:n ʔaṣṣuluħ]

Suez • **1.** السُّوَيس [ʔissuwi:s]

S

to suffer • 1. تعَذَّب [tʕaððab] عَذاب [ʕaða:b] *vn: sv* a. قاسَى [qa:sa:] مقاسات [muqa:sa:t] *vn: sv* i. Did she suffer very much? تعَذَّبَت هوايَة؟ [tʕaððbat hwa:ya?] • **2.** تكَبَّد [tkabbad] تكَبُّد [takabbud] *vn: sv* a. They suffered heavy losses. تكَبَّدَوا خسايِر فادِحَة [tkabbdaw xasa:yir fa:diħa]

sufficient • 1. كافِي [ka:fi]

to suffocate • 1. اِختِنَق [ʔixtinag] اِختِناق [ʔixtina:q] *vn: sv* i. I nearly suffocated. تقرِيباً اِختِنَقِت [taqri:ban ʔixtinagit]

sugar • 1. شَكَر [šakar] Please pass me the sugar. أرجُوك، عَبُّرلِي الشَّكَر [ʔarǰu:k, ʕabburli ʔiššakar]

to suggest • 1. اِقتِرَح [ʔiqtiraħ] اِقتِراح [ʔiqtira:ħ] *vn: sv* i. I suggest that we go to the movies. أقتِرِح نرُوح لِلسِّينَما [ʔaqtiriħ nru:ħ lissinama] • **2.** لَمَّح [lammaħ] تَلمِيح [talmi:ħ] *vn: sv* i. Are you suggesting that I'm wrong? دَتلَمِّح بِأنِّي غَلطان [datlammiħ biʔanni ɣalṭa:n] • **3.** ذَكَّر ب [ðakkar b-] تَذكِير [taðki:r] *vn: sv* i. جاب [ǰa:b] جَيب [ǰi:b] *vn: sv* i. Does this suggest anything to you? هَذا يذَكِّرَك بشِي؟ [ha:ða yðakkrak bši?] Does this suggest anything to you? هَذا يجِيب شِي ببالَك؟ [ha:ða yǰi:b ši bba:lak?]

suggestion • 1. اِقتِراح [ʔiqtira:ħ] اِقتِراحات [ʔiqtira:ħa:t] *pl:* Your suggestion is very reasonable. اِقتِراحَك كُلِّش مَعقُول [ʔiqtira:ħak kulliš maʕqu:l]

suicide • 1. اِنتِحار [ʔintiħa:r] اِنتِحارات [ʔintiħa:ra:t] *pl:* Suicide cases are rare here. حَوادِث الانتِحار نادرَة هنا [ħawa:diθ ʔilʔintiħa:r na:dra hna]

to commit suicide • 1. اِنتِحَر [ʔintiħar] اِنتِحار [ʔintiħa:r] *vn: sv* i. He committed suicide because he owed a lot of money. اِنتِحَر لِأنّ كان مَطلُوب فلُوس هوايَة [ʔintiħar liʔann ča:n maṭlu:b flu:s hwa:ya]

suit • 1. قاط [qa:ṭ] قُوط [qu:ṭ] *pl:* بَدلَة [badla] بَدلات [badla:t] *pl:* He needs a new suit. يِحتاج قاط جِدِيد [yiħta:ǰ qa:ṭ ǰidi:d] • **2.** دَعوَة [daʕwa] دَعوات، دَعاوِي [daʕwa:t, daʕa:wi] *pl:* If you don't pay today, we shall bring suit. إذا ما تِدفَع الفلُوس اليُوم، نقِيم دَعوَة عَلِيك [ʔiða ma: tidfaʕ ʔilflu:s ʔilyu:m, nqi:m daʕwa ʕali:k] • **3.** نوع [nawʕ] أنواع [ʔanwa:ʕ] *pl:* قِسِم [qisim] أقسام [ʔaqsa:m] *pl:* The four suits in cards are hearts, diamonds, spades and clubs. أنواع الوَرَق الأربَعَة هِيَّ كُوبَة ودِينار وَماجَة وَسِنَك [ʔanwa:ʕ ʔilwaraq ʔilʔarbaʕa hiyya ku:pa wdina:r wma:ča wsinak]

*** If he takes one, I'll follow suit.** • **1.** إذا ياخُذ واحِد، آنِي أسَوِّي مِثلَه [ʔiða ya:xuð wa:ħid, ʔa:ni ʔasawwi miθlah]

to suit • 1. رَضَّة [raḍḍa] رَضّات [raḍḍa:t] *pl:* تَرضِيَة [tarḍiya] *vn: sv* i. It's hard to suit everybody. صَعُب تَرَضِّي كُلّ النّاس [ṣaʕub traḍḍi kull ʔinna:s] • **2.** ناسَب [na:sab] مُناسَبَة [muna:saba] *vn:* تناسَب [tna:sab] *p:* والَم [wa:lam] مُوالَمَة [mu:wa:lama] *vn:* توالَم [twa:lam] *p:* These books are suited to the age of the children. هَالكُتُب تناسِب عُمر الأطفال [halkutub tna:sib ʕumr ʔilʔaṭfa:l] • **3.** وافَق [wa:faq] مُوافَقَة [muwa:faqa] *vn: sv* i. ناسَب [na:sab] *sv* i. والَم [wa:lam] *sv* i. Does this suit your taste? هَذا يوافِق ذَوقَك؟ [ha:ða ywa:fiq ðawqak?] Which day would suit you best? يا يوم يوافقَك أحسَن؟ [ya: yawm ywa:fqak ʔaħsan?] • **4.** لاق ل [la:g l-] لَوق [lu:g] *vn: sv* u. Red doesn't suit you. الأحمَر ما يلُوقلَك [ʔilʔaħmar ma: ylu:glak]

to be suited • 1. لاق [la:g] *sv* u. Is she suited for this kind of work? هِيَّ لايقَة لِهالوَظِيفَة؟ [hiyya la:yga lhalwaḍi:fa?] • **2.** صِلَح [ṣilaħ] صَلاحِيَّة [ṣala:ħiyya] *vn: sv* a. This land isn't suited for growing wheat. هَالأرض ما تِصلَح لِزراعَة الحُنطَة [halʔarḍ ma: tiṣlaħ lzira:ʕat ʔilħunṭa] • **3.** لائَم [la:ʔam] مُلائَمَة [mula:ʔama] *vn: sv* i. This climate isn't suited for people with TB. هَالمَناخ ما يلائِم المَسلُولِين [halmana:x ma: yla:ʔim ʔilmaslu:li:n]

*** Suit yourself. • 1.** كَيفَك [kayfak]

suitable • 1. مناسِب [mna:sib] صالِح [ṣa:liħ] مُلائِم [mula:ʔim] We can't find a suitable apartment. ما نِقدَر نِلقِي بَيت مُناسِب [ma: nigdar nilgi bayt muna:sib]

suitcase • 1. جُنطَة [ǰunṭa] جُنَط، جَنطات [ǰunaṭ, ǰanṭa:t] *pl:* I have three suitcases and one trunk. عِندِي ثلاث جُنَط وَصَندُوق واحِد [ʕindi tlaθ ǰunaṭ wṣandu:g wa:ħid]

sullen • 1. عَبُوس [ʕabu:s] معَبِّس [mʕabbis]

sultan • 1. سُلطان [sulṭa:n] سَلاطِين [sala:ṭi:n] *pl:*

sultanate • 1. سَلطَنَة [salṭana] سَلطَنات [salṭana:t] *pl:*

sultry • 1. شَرجِي [šarǰi] It's awfully sultry today. اليُوم الهَوا كُلِّش شَرجِي [ʔilyu:m ʔilhawa kulliš šarǰi]

sum • 1. مَجمُوع [majmu:ʕ] مَجمُوعات [majmu:ʕa:t] *pl:* Just tell me the full sum. بَسّ قُلِّي المَجمُوع [bass gulli ʔilmajmu:ʕ] • **2.** مَبلَغ [mablaɣ] مَبالِغ [maba:liɣ] *pl:* I still owe him a small sum. بَعَدنِي مَديُونلَه مَبلَغ صغَيِّر [baʕadni madyu:n lah mablaɣ ṣɣayyir]

to sum up • 1. لَخَّص [laxxaṣ] تَلخِيص [talxi:ṣ] *vn:* تلَخَّص [tlaxxaṣ] *p:* Let me sum up briefly. خَلِّي ألَخِّص بِاختِصار [xalli ʔalaxxiṣ bixtiṣa:r]

Sumeria • 1. سومَر [su:mar]

Sumerian • 1. سَومَرِي [sawmari] سَومَرِيِّين [sawmari:yyi:n] *pl:* The Sumerians lived in lower Iraq. السُّومَرِيِّين سِكنَوا جنُوب العِراق [ʔissamariyyi:n siknaw ǰinu:b ʔilʕira:q]

S

summary • **1.** خُلاصَة [xulaːṣa] خُلاصات [xulaːṣaːt] *pl:* مُلَخَّص [mulaxxaṣ] مُلَخَّصات [mulaxxaṣaːt] *pl:* Read the book and give me a summary. إقرا الكِتاب وَإنطِينِي المُلَخَّص [ʔiqra ʔilkitaːb wʔinṭiːni ʔilmulaxxaṣ]

summer • **1.** صِيف [ṣayf, ṣiːf] أصياف [ʔaṣyaːf] *pl:* I spent three summers in the mountains. بِقيت ثلَث أصياف بِالجِبال [biqiːt tlaθ ʔiṣyaːf bij̆j̆ibaːl] Does it get hot here in summer? تصِير حارَّة هنا بالصَّيف؟ [tṣiːr ħaːrra hnaː biṣṣayf?] • **2.** I need a new summer suit. يرّادلي بَدلَة صَيفِيَّة جدِيدَة [yirraːdli badlat ṣayfiyya j̆idiːda]

summer resort • **1.** مَصِيف [maṣiːf] مَصايِف [maṣaːyif] *pl:*

to summon • **1.** صاح [ṣaːħ] صَيح [ṣayħ] *vn:* اِنصاح [ʔinṣaːħ] *p:* The boss summoned me to his office. الرَّئِيس صاحنِي لغُرُفتَه [ʔirraʔiːs ṣaːħni lɣuruftah]

to summon up • **1.** اِستَجمَع [ʔistaj̆maʕ] He couldn't summon up the courage to enter the cold water. ما قِدَر يِستَجمِع شَجاعتَه حَتَّى يخُشّ بِالماي البارِد [maː gidar yistaj̆miʕ šaj̆aːʕtah ħatta yxušš bilmaːy ʔilbaːrid]

sun • **1.** شَمِس [šamis] شمُوس [šmuːs] *pl:* The sun has just gone down. الشَّمِس تَوّها غُربَت [ʔiššamis tawwha ɣurbat]

to sun • **1.** شَمَّس [šammas] تشِمِّس [tšimmis] *vn:* *sv* i. تشَمَّس [tšammas] تشِمِّس [tšimmis] *vn:* *sv* a. We saw a snake sunning himself on a rock. شِفنا فَدّ حَيَّة دَتشَمِّس نَفِسها عَلَى صَخرَة [šifna fadd ħayya datšammis nafisha ʕala ṣaxra]

sunbeam • **1.** شُعاع شَمِس [šuʕaːʕ šamis] أشِعَّة شَمِس [ʔašiʕʕat šamis] *pl:*

Sunday • **1.** يَوم الأحَّد [yawm ʔilʔaħħad] أيّام الأحَّد [ʔayyaːm ʔilʔaħħad] *pl:*

sundown • **1.** مُغرُب، مِغرِب [muɣrub, miɣrib] He usually comes home around sundown. عادَةً يِجِي لِلبَيت وَقِت المِغرِب [ʕaːdatan yij̆i lilbayt wakit ʔilmiɣrib]

sunlight • **1.** ضُوء الشَمِس [ðuwʔ ʔiššamis]

Sunna • **1.** سُنَّة [sunna] The Sunna consists of the deeds and sayings of the Prophet. السُّنَّة هِيَّ أفعال وَأحادِيث النَّبِي [ʔissunna hiyya ʔafʕaːl wʔaħaːdiːθ ʔinnabi]

Sunni, Sunnite • **1.** سُنِّي [sunni] سُنَّة، سُنِّيِّين [sunna, sunniyyiːn] *pl:*

sunny • **1.** مُشمِس [mušmis] The front rooms are sunny. الغُرَف الأمامِيَّة مِشمِسَة [ʔilɣuraf ʔilʔamaːmiyya mišmisa] • **2.** صاحِي [ṣaːħi] We'll have a sunny day tomorrow. باكِر الدِّنيا راح تصِير صاحيَة [baːčir ʔiddinya raːħ tṣiːr ṣaːħya]

sunrise • **1.** شُرُوق [šuruːq]

sunset • **1.** غُرُوب [ɣuruːb]

sunshine • **1.** أشِعَّة الشَمِس [ʔašiʕʕat ʔiššamis] ضُوء شَمِس [ðuwʔ šamis] The sunshine is strong today. أشِعَّة الشَّمِس قَوِيَّة اليُوم [ʔašiʕʕat ʔiššamis qawiyya ʔilyuːm]

sunstroke • **1.** ضَربَة شَمِس [ðarbat šamis] ضَربَات شَمِس [ðarbataːt šamis] *pl:* He died of sunstroke. مات مِن ضَربَة شَمِس [maːt min ðarbat šamis]

superior • **1.** رَئِيس [raʔiːs] رُؤَساء [ruʔasaːʔ] *pl:* Is he your superior on the job? هُوَّ رَئِيسَك بِالشُّغُل؟ [huwwa raʔiːsak biššuɣul?] • **2.** مُمتاز [mumtaːz] This is of superior quality. هَذا مِن نُوع مُمتاز [haːða min nawʕ mumtaːz]

superiority • **1.** تَفَوُّق [tafawwuq] Their superiority in numbers is weakened by their lack of experience. تَفَوُّقهُم بالعَدَد قَلَّت أهَمِّيتَه لعَدَم خِبرَتهُم [tafawwuqhum bilʕadad qallat ʕahammiːtah lʕadam xibrathum]

superiority complex • **1.** مُرَكَّب الشُعُور بِالعَظَمَة [murakkab ʔiššuʕuːr bilʕaðama] He has a superiority complex. عِندَه مُرَكَّب الشُّعُور بِالعَظَمَة [ʕindah murakkab ʔiššuʕuːr bilʕaðama]

superstition • **1.** خُرافَة [xuraːfa] خُرافات [xuraːfaːt] *pl:*

superstitious • **1.** * He's terribly superstitious. هوايَة يِعتِقِد بِالخُرافات [hwaːya yiʕtiqid bilxuraːfaːt]

supervision • **1.** إشراف [ʔišraːf] They are under constant supervision. هُمَّ تَحَت إشراف مُستَمِرّ [humma taħat ʔišraːf mustamirr]

supper • **1.** عَشا [ʕašaː] عَشاوات [ʕašawaːt] *pl:* I've been invited for supper. آنِي مَعزُوم عَلَى عَشا [ʔaːni maʕzuːm ʕala ʕaša]

to have supper • **1.** تعَشَّى [tʕaššaː] تَعَشِّي [taʕašši] *vn:* *sv* a. Would you like to have supper with us tonight? تحِبّ تِتعَشَّى ويّانا هاللَّيلَة؟ [tħibb titʕaššaː wiyyaːna hallayla?]

supplement • **1.** مُلحَق [mulħaq] مَلاحِق [malaːħiq] *pl:* The supplement to the phone book is small this year. مُلحَق دَلِيل التِّلِفُون هالسَّنَة صغَيِّر [mulħaq daliːl ʔittilifuːn hassana ṣɣayyir] • **2.** إضافَة [ʔiðaːfa] إضافات [ʔiðaːfaːt] *pl:* The doctor recommended using vitamins as a supplement to the diet. الطَّبِيب وُصَف اِستِعمال الفِيتامِينات كَإضافَة إلَى الغِذاء [ʔiṭṭabiːb wuṣaf ʔistiʕmaːl ʔilfiːtaːmiːnaːt kaʔiðaːfa ʔila ʔilɣiðaːʔ]

S

supply • **1.** كَمِّيَّة [kammiyya] كَمِّيّات [kammiyya:t] *pl:* We still have a big supply of bicycles. بَعَد عِدنا كَمِّيَّة كِبِيرَة مِن البايسِكلات [baʕad ʕidna kammiyya čibi:ra min ʔilba:ysikla:t] • **2.** ذَخِيرَة [ðaxi:ra] ذَخاير [ðaxa:yir] *pl:* مَخزُون [maxzu:n] مَخزُونات [maxzu:na:t] *pl:* Our potato supply is almost gone. ذَخِيرَتنا مِن البُتَيتَة تَقرِيباً خِلصَت [ðaxi:ratna min ʔilputayta taqri:ban xilṣat] • **3.** تَجهِيز [tajhi:z] تَجهِيزات [tajhi:za:t] *pl:* The hospital needs more medical supplies. المُستَشفى يحتاج تَجهِيزات طِبِّيَّة أَكثَر [ʔilmustašfa yiħta:ǰ tajhi:za:t ṭibbiyya ʔakθar]

to supply • **1.** جَهَّز [ǰahhaz] تَجهِيز [tajhi:z] *vn:* تجَهَّز [tǰahhaz] *p:* Our bakery supplies all the big hotels. مَخبَزنا يجَهِّز كُلّ الأُوتِيلات الكِبِيرَة [maxbazna yǰahhiz kull ʔilʔuti:la:t ʔiččibi:ra] • **2.** زَوَّد [zawwad] تَزوِيد [tazwi:d] *vn:* تزَوَّد [tzawwad] *p:* He always supplies us with cigarettes. هُوَّ دائِماً يزَوِّدنا بالجِّكايِر [huwwa da:ʔiman yzawwidna bijǰiga:yir] • **3.** مَوَّن [mawwan] تَموِين [tamwi:n] *vn:* تمَوَّن [tmawwan] *p:* We have a contract to supply the police with ammunition. عِدنا قُنطَرات نمَوِّن الشُّرطَة بالعِتاد [ʕidna qunṭara:t nmawwin ʔiššurṭa bilʕita:d]

support • **1.** تَأيِيد [taʔyi:d] You can count on my support. تِقدَر تِعتِمِد عَلَى تَأيِيدي [tigdar tiʕtimid ʕala taʔyi:di] • **2.** دِنگَة [dinga] دِنگات، دِنَگ [dinga:t, dinag] *pl:* We've got to put supports under the bridge. لازِم نخَلِّي دِنَگ جَوَّة الجِّسِر [la:zim nxalli dinag ǰawwa ʔiǰǰisir]

in support of • **1.** تَأيِيداً لِ [taʔyi:dan l-] Can you offer any evidence in support of your statement. تِقدَر تقَدِّم أَيّ بُرهان تَأيِيداً لعِبارتَك [tigdar tqaddim ʔayy burha:n taʔyi:dan lʕiba:rtak]

to support • **1.** أَيَّد [ʔayyad] تَأيِيد [taʔyi:d] *vn:* تأَيَّد [tʔayyad] *p:* سِنَد [sinad] سَنِد [sanid] *vn:* اِنسِنَد [ʔinsinad] *p:* All the parties are supporting him. كُلّ الأَحزاب دَتأَيِّدَه [kull ʔilʔaħza:b datʔayyidah] I'll support your election campaign. راح أَسنِد حَملتَك الانتِخابِيَّة [ra:ħ ʔasnid ħamiltak ʔilʔintixa:biyya] • **2.** عال [ʕa:l] إعالَة [ʔiʕa:la] *vn:* اِنعال [ʔinʕa:l] *p:* عَيَّش [ʕayyaš] تَعيِيش [taʕyi:š] *vn:* تعَيَّش [tʕayyaš] *p:* He has to support his parents. لازِم يعِيل أُمَّه وأَبُوه [la:zim yʕi:l ʔummah wʔabu:h] • **3.** دِعَم [diʕam] دَعِم [daʕim] *vn:* اِندِعَم [ʔindiʕam] *p:* Have you got evidence to support your claim? عِندَك دَلِيل يِدعَم اِدِّعائَك؟ [ʕindak dali:l yidʕam ʔiddiʕa:ʔak?]

to support oneself • **1.** قام بنَفسَه [qa:m bnafsah] قِيام [qiya:m] *vn: sv* u. I have supported myself ever since I was fifteen. قُمِت بنَفسِي مِن كان عُمرِي خمُسطَعَش سَنَة [qumit bnafsi min ča:n ʕumri xmusṭaʕaš sana]

to suppose • **1.** فُرَض [furaḍ] فَرَض [faraḍ] *vn: sv* u. اِفتِرَض [ʔiftiraḍ] اِفتِراض [ʔiftira:ḍ] *vn: sv* i. Let's suppose that I'm right. خَلِّي نِفرُض آنِي صَحِيح [xalli nifruḍ ʔa:ni ṣaħi:ħ] • **2.** ظَنّ [ḍann] ظَنّ [ḍann] *vn: sv* i. I suppose so. أَظِنّ هِيكِي [ʔaḍinn hi:či]

supposed to • **1.** مَفرُوض [mafru:ḍ] He's supposed to be rich. المَفرُوض هُوَّ غَنِي [ʔilmafru:ḍ huwwa ɣani] • **2.** لازِم [la:zim] I was supposed to go out tonight, but I'm too tired. كان لازِم أَطلَع هاللَّيلَة، لَكِن آنِي كُلِّش تَعبان [ča:n la:zim ʔaṭlaʕ hallayla, la:kin ʔa:ni kulliš taʕba:n]

supposing • **1.** عَلَى فَرِض [ʕala fariḍ] فَرضاً [farḍan] Supposing he doesn't come tonight, what'll we do? عَلَى فَرِض ما يِجِي هاللَّيلَة، شِنسَوِّي؟ [ʕala fariḍ ma: yiji hallayla, šinsawwi?]

sure • **1.** أَكِيد [ʔaki:d] مُؤَكَّد [muʔakkad] That's a sure thing. هَذا شِي أَكِيد [ha:ða ši ʔaki:d] • **2.** طَبعاً [ṭabʕan] مَعلُوم [maʕlu:m] أَكِيد [ʔaki:d] مُؤَكَّد [muʔakkad] Sure, I'd be glad to. طَبعاً، عَلَى عِينِي [ṭabʕan, ʕala ʕi:ni] • **3.** وَالله [wallah, wʔallah] I'd sure like to see him again. وَالله أَرِيد أَشُوفَه مَرَّة اللُّخ [wallah ʔari:d ʔašu:fah marra ʔillux] • **4.** مِتأَكِّد [mitʔakkid] Are you sure of that? إنتَ مِتأَكِّد مِن ذاك؟ [ʔinta mitʔakkid min ða:k?]

for sure • **1.** بالتَّأكِيد [bittaʔki:d] Be there by five o'clock for sure. كُون هناك ساعَة خَمسَة بالتَّأكِيد [ku:n hna:k sa:ʕa xamsa bittaʔki:d]

sure enough • **1.** فِعلاً [fiʕlan] You thought it would rain, and sure enough it did. إنتَ قِلِت راح تُمطُر، وَفِعلاً مُطرَت [ʔinta gilit ra:ħ tumṭur, wfiʕlan muṭrat]

to be sure • **1.** تأَكَّد [tʔakkad] تَأَكُّد [taʔakkud] *vn: sv* a. Be sure to come tomorrow. إتأَكَّد تِجِي باكِر [ʔitʔakkad tiji ba:čir]

*** He's sure to be back up nine o'clock.**

• **1.** بالتَّأكِيد راح يرجَع ساعَة تِسعَة [bittaʔki:d ra:ħ yirǰaʕ sa:ʕa tisʕa]

to make sure • **1.** تأَكَّد [tʔakkad] تَأَكُّد [taʔakkud] *vn: sv* a. تحَقَّق [tħaqqaq] تَحَقُّق [taħaqquq] *vn: sv* a. Make sure that you take everything with you. إتأَكَّد تاخُذ كُلشِي وِيّاك [ʔitʔakkad ta:xuð kullši wiyya:k] I just wanted to make sure that nothing was wrong. بَسّ رِدِت أَتحَقَّق ماكُو شِي [bass ridit ʔatħaqqaq ma:ku ši]

surely • **1.** بالتَّأكِيد [bittaʔki:d] أَكِيد [ʔaki:d] Will you be there? Surely. راح تكُون هناك؟ بالتَّأكِيد [ra:ħ tku:n hna:k? bittaʔki:d] He can surely do that. بالتَّأكِيد يِقدَر يسَوِّي هَذا [bittaʔki:d yigdar ysawwi ha:ða]

*** I surely thought it would be finished.**

• **1.** كِنِت مِتأَكِّد راح تِخلَص [činit mitʔakkid ra:ħ tixlaṣ]

surface • **1.** سَطِح [saṭiħ] سُطُوح [suṭu:ħ] *pl:* وُجِه [wuǰih] وُجُوه [wuǰu:h] *pl:*

surgeon • **1.** جَرّاح [ǰarra:ħ] جَرّاحِين [ǰarra:ħi:n] *pl:*

surgery • **1.** جِراحَة [ǰira:ħa]

surplus • **1.** زِيادَة [ziya:da] There is a surplus in the wheat crop this year that they don't know what to do with.

أكو زيادة بمحصول الحنطة هالسنة ما يدرون شيسوون بيها [ʔaku ziya:da bmaħṣu:l ʔilħunṭa hassana ma: yidru:n šysawwu:n bi:ha] • **2.** زايد [za:yid] The Labor Office has forbidden the company to discharge its surplus employees. مديرية شؤون العمال منعت الاستغناء عن العمال الزايدين [mudi:riyyat šuʔu:n ʔilʕumma:l minʕat ʔilistiɣna:ʔ ʕann ʔilʕumma:l ʔizza:ydi:n]

surprise • **1.** مفاجأة [mufa:ǰaʔa] مفاجآت [mufa:ǰaʔa:t] *pl:* I've got a surprise for you. عندي مفاجأة إلك [ʕindi mufa:ǰaʔa ʔilak] • **2.** دهشة [dahša] You'll get the surprise of your life. راح تندهش دهشة ما صار مثلها [ra:ħ tindihiš dahša ma: ṣa:r miθilha] You'll get the surprise of your life. راح تندهش أكبر دهشة بحياتك [ra:ħ tindihiš ʔakbar dahša bħaya:tak]

to catch by surprise • **1.** فاجئ [fa:ǰaʔ] مفاجأة [mufa:ǰaʔa] *vn:* تفاجأ [tfa:ǰaʔ] *p:* باغت [ba:ɣat] مباغتة [muba:ɣata] *vn:* اتباغت [tba:ɣat] *p:* The rain caught me by surprise. المطر فاجئني [ʔilmuṭar fa:ǰaʔni] The rain caught me by surprise. المطر باغتني [ʔilmuṭar ba:ɣatni]

to take by surprise • **1.** أخذ على غفلة، باغت [ʔaxað ʕala ɣafla, ba:ɣat] *sv* u. باغت [ba:ɣat] مباغتة [muba:ɣata] *vn:* اتباغت [tba:ɣat] *p:* You took me by surprise. أخذتني على غفلة [ʔaxaðitni ʕala ɣafla] You took me by surprise. باغتتني تماماً [ba:ɣatitni tama:man]

to surprise • **1.** أدهش [ʔadhaš] دهشة [dahša] *vn:* اندهش [ʔindihaš] *p:* عجب [ʕaǰǰab] عجب [ʕaǰab] *vn:* تعجب [tʕaǰǰab] *p:* I wanted to surprise you. ردت أدهشك [ridit ʔadihšak] I wanted to surprise you. ردت أعجبك [ridit ʔaʕaǰǰbak] Nothing surprises me any more. ماكو شي يعجبني بعد [ma:ku ši yʕaǰǰibni baʕad] I'm surprised at you. آني متعجب عليك [ʔa:ni mitʕaǰǰib ʕali:k] I'm not surprised at anything you do. شما تسوي ما يدهشني [šma: tsawwi ma: yidhišni]

to surrender • **1.** سلم [sallam] تسليم [tasli:m] *vn:* تسلم [tsallam] *p:* He surrendered to the police. سلم للشرطة [sallam liššurṭa] • **2.** استسلم [ʔistaslam] استسلام [ʔistisla:m] *vn: sv* i. The enemy surrendered. العدو استسلم [ʔilʕadu ʔistaslam]

to surround • **1.** أحاط [ʔaħa:ṭ] إحاطة [ʔiħa:ṭa] *vn:* انحاط [ʔinħa:ṭ] *p:* A high fence surrounds the house. سياج عالي يحيط البيت [siya:ǰ ʕa:li yħi:ṭ ʔilbayt] • **2.** طوق [ṭawwaq] تطويق [taṭwi:q] *vn:* تطوق [tṭawwaq] *p:* حاصر [ħa:ṣar] حصار، محاصرة [ħiṣa:r, muħa:ṣra] *vn:* تحاصر [tħa:ṣar] *p:* We're surrounded. إحنا مطوقين [ʔiħna mṭawwaqi:n]

suspect • **1.** مشبوه [mašbu:h] He's a suspect in that case. هو مشبوه بذيك القضية [huwwa mašbu:h bði:č ʔilqaðiyya]

to suspect • **1.** شك ب [šakk b-] شك [šakk] *vn: sv* u. ارتاب ب [ʔirta:b b-] ارتياب [ʔirtiya:b] *vn: sv* a. اشتبه [ʔištibah] اشتباه [ʔištiba:h] *vn: sv* i. Do you suspect anything? تشك بشي؟ [tšukk bši?] Do you suspect anything? ترتاب بشي؟ [tirta:b bši?]

to suspend • **1.** وقف [waqqaf] توقيف [tawqi:f] *vn:* توقف [twaqqaf] *p:* The bank has suspended payment due to the robbery. البنك وقف الدفع بسبب البوقة [ʔilbank waqqaf ʔiddafiʕ bsabab ʔilbawga] • **2.** فصل [fuṣal] فصل [faṣil] *vn:* انفصل [ʔinfuṣal] *p:* طرد [ṭirad] طرد [ṭarid] *vn:* انطرد [ʔinṭirad] *p:* He was suspended for a year. انفصل لمدة سنة [ʔinfuṣal lmuddat sana] He was suspended from school for a week. انطرد من المدرسة لمدة إسبوع [ʔinṭirad min ʔilmadrasa limuddat ʔisbu:ʕ] • **3.** سحب [siħab] سحب [saħib] *vn:* انسحب [ʔinsiħab] *p:* وقف [waqqaf] *sv* i. The department of health suspended the restaurant's license for a month. وزارة الصحة سحبت إجازة المطعم لمدة شهر [wiza:rat ʔiṣṣiħħa siħbat ʔiǰa:zat ʔilmaṭʕam lmuddat šahar] • **4.** سد [sadd] سد [sadd] *vn:* انسد [ʔinsadd] *p:* عطل [ʕaṭṭal] تعطيل [taʕṭi:l] *vn: sv* i. The government suspended the newspaper. الحكومة سدت الجريدة [ʔilħuku:ma saddat ʔiǰǰari:da] • **5.** علق [ʕallag] تعليق [taʕli:g] *vn:* تعلق [tʕallag] *p:* The worksmen suspended the chandelier from the ceiling by a heavy chain. العمال علقوا الثرية من السقف بسلسلة قوية [ʔilʕumma:l ʕalligaw ʔiθθurayya min ʔissaguf bsilsila qawiyya]

suspense • **1.** حيرة [ħi:ra] I can't stand the suspense any longer. ما أتحمل الحيرة بعد [ma: ʔatħammal ʔilħi:ra baʕad]

suspicion • **1.** شك [šakk] What aroused your suspicion? شنو أثار شكك؟ [šinu ʔaθa:r šakkak?] What aroused your suspicion? شخلاك ترتاب؟ [šxalla:k tirta:b?]

suspicious • **1.** مريب [muri:b] That place looks suspicious. هالمحل يبين مريب [halmaħall yibayyin muri:b] • **2.** شكاك [šakka:k] شكاكين [šakka:ki:n] *pl:* My husband is very suspicious. رجلي كلش شكاك [rajli kulliš šakka:k]

*** I immediately got suspicious.** • **1.** حالاً شكيت [ħa:lan šakki:t] / حالاً إرتابيت [ħa:lan ʔirta:bi:t]

swallow • **1.** جرعة [ǰurʕa] جرع [ǰuraʕ] جرعات [ǰurʕa:t] *pl:* I only took one swallow. شربت بس جرعة وحدة [širabit bass ǰurʕa wiħda] • **2.** The swallows come in the spring and build their nests. بنات سند وهند يجون بالربيع ويبنون عشوشهم [bana:t sind whind yiǰu:n birrabi:ʕ wyibnu:n ʕšu:šhum]

to swallow • **1.** بلع [bilaʕ] بلع [baliʕ] *vn:* انبلع [ʔinbilaʕ] *p:* My throat hurts me so much I can't swallow anything. بلعومي هالقد يوجعني ما أقدر أبلع شي [balʕu:mi halgadd yu:ǰaʕni ma: ʔagdar ʔablaʕ ši]

*** He swallowed the bait hook, line and sinker.** • **1.** الحيلة عبرت عليه [ʔilħi:la ʕubrat ʕali:h]

S

swamp • **1.** هُور [huːr hawr] أهوار [ʔahwaːr] *pl:* مُستَنقَع [mustanqaʕ] مُستَنقَعات [mustanqaʕaːt] *pl:* How far does the swamp go? الهَور شقَدّ يمتَدّ؟ [ʔilhawr šgadd yimtadd?]

to swamp • **1.** غِرَق [ɣirag] غَرِق [ɣarig] *vn: sv* a. I was swamped with work last week. غِرَقِت بِالشُّغُل الإسبُوع اللِّي فات [ɣiragit biššuɣul ʔilʔisbuːʕ ʔilli faːt] • **2.** تِرَس [tiras] تَرِس [taris] *vn:* اِنتِرَس [ʔintiras] *p:* A large wave swamped our boat. فَدّ مَوجَة كِبِيرَة تِرسَت بَلَمنا ماي [fadd mawǰa čibiːra tirsat balamna maːy]

swarm • **1.** جَماعَة [ǰamaːʕa] جَماعات [ǰamaːʕaːt] *pl:* They saw a swarm of bees. شافَوا جَماعَة نَحَل [šaːfaw ǰamaːʕat naħal]

to swarm • **1.** عَجّ [ʕaǰǰ] عَجّ [ʕaǰǰ] *vn: sv* i. The swamp is swarming with mosquitoes. المُستَنقَع يعِجّ بِالبَق [ʔilmustanqaʕ yʕiǰǰ bilbagg]

to sway • **1.** اِهتَزّ [ʔihtazz] اِهتِزاز [ʔihtizaːz] *vn: sv* a. The trees swayed in the wind. الأَشجار اِهتَزَّت بِالهَوا [ʔilʔašǰaːr ʔihtazzat bilhawa] • **2.** أَثَّر عَلَى [ʔaθθar ʕala] تَأثِير [taʔθiːr] *vn:* تأَثَّر [tʔaθθar] *p:* No one can sway him once his mind is made up. مَحَّد يقدَر يأَثِّر عَليه بَعَد ما يسَوِّي فِكرَه [maħħad yigdar yʔaθθir ʕaliːh baʕad maː ysawwi fikrah]

to swear • **1.** حِلَف [ħilaf] حَلِف [ħalif] *vn:* اِنحِلَف [ʔinħilaf] *p:* أَقسَم [ʔaqsam] قَسَم [qasam] *vn: sv* i. She swears she's telling the truth. تِحلِف دَتقُول الصُّدُق [tiħlif datguːl ʔiṣṣudug] Do you swear to that? تِحلِف عَلَى هَذا؟ [tiħlif ʕala haːða?] Do you swear to that? تِقسِم عَلَى هَذا؟ [tiqsim ʕala haːða?] • **2.** شَتَّم [šattam] تَشتِيم [taštiːm] *vn:* تشَتَّم [tšattam] *p:* سَبّ [sabb] سَبّ [sabb] *vn:* اِنسَبّ [ʔinsabb] *p:* He swears constantly. يشَتِّم عَلَى طُول [yšattim ʕala ṭuːl] He swears constantly. يسِبّ عَلَى طُول [yisibb ʕala ṭuːl]

to swear in • **1.** حَلَّف [ħallaf] تَحلِيف [taħliːf] *vn: sv* i. They swore the witness in on the Koran, and later began asking him questions. حَلِّفوا الشّاهِد بالقُرآن وَبَعدين قامَوا يسألُوه أَسئِلَة [ħallifaw ʔiššaːhid bilqurʔaːn wbaʕdayn gaːmaw yisʔaluːh ʔasʔila]

S

sweat • **1.** عَرَق [ʕarag] He wiped the sweat from his brow. مِسَح العَرَق مِن قُصّتَه [misaħ ʔilʕarag min guṣṣtah]

to sweat • **1.** عِرَق [ʕirag] عَرَق [ʕarag] *vn: sv* a. This kind of work makes you sweat. هَالنَّوع مِن الشُّغُل يخَلِّيك تِعرَق [hannuːʕ min ʔiššuɣul yxalliːk tiʕrag]

sweaty • **1.** عَرقان [ʕargaːn] I'm sweaty all over. آني عَرقان مِن فُوق لِجَوَّة [ʔaːni ʕargaːn min fuːg liǰawwa]

to sweep • **1.** كِنَس [kinas] كَنِس [kanis] *vn:* اِنكِنَس [ʔinkinas] *p:* Did you sweep the bedroom? كِنَستِي غُرفَة النَّوم؟ [kinasti ɣurfat ʔinnawm?] • **2.** سِحَل ب [siħal b-] سَحِل [saħil] *vn:* اِنسِحَل [ʔinsiħal] *p: sv* a. Her dress sweeps the ground. نَفنُوفها دَيِسحَل بِالقاع [nafnuːfha dayisħal bilgaːʕ]

to sweep away • **1.** اِكتِسَح [ʔiktisaħ] اِكتِساح [ʔiktisaːħ] *vn: sv* i. The flood waters swept away the town. ماي الفَيَضان اِكتِسَح الوِلايَة [maːy ʔilfayaðaːn ʔiktisaħ ʔilwilaːya]

sweet • **1.** حِلو [ħilw] The dates are very sweet. التَّمُر حِلو كُلِّش [ʔittamur ħilw kulliš] • **2.** حَبُّوب [ħabbuːb] She is a sweet girl. هِيَّ بِنت حَبُّوبَة [hiyya bint ħabbuːba]

sweetheart • **1.** حَبِيب [ħabiːb] أَحِبَّة، أحباب [ʔaħibba, ʔaħbaːb] *pl:* She's his sweetheart. هِيَّ حَبِيبتَه [hiyya ħabiːbtah]

sweets • **1.** حَلَوِيّات [ħalawiyyaːt] I don't care much for sweets. ما أَحِبّ الحَلَوِيّات [maː ʔaħibb ʔilħalawiyyaːt]

swell • **1.** خُوش [xawš, xuːš] She's a swell person. هِيَّ خُوش آدمِيَّة [hiyya xuːš ʔaːdmiyya]

to swell • **1.** وُرَم [wuram] وَرَم [waram] *vn: sv* a. My finger is all swollen. إصبعِي كُلَّه وارُم [ʔiṣibʕi kullah waːrum]

swelling • **1.** وَرَم [waram] Has the swelling gone down? الوَرَم نِزَل؟ [ʔilwaram nizal?]

to swim • **1.** سِبَح [sibaħ] سِبِح، سِباحَة [sibiħ, sibaːħa] *vn: sv* a. Do you know how to swim? تُعرُف تِسبَح؟ [tuʕruf tisbaħ?]

swimming • **1.** سِباحَة [sibaːħa] سِباحات [sibaːħaːt] *pl:* Swimming is the only sport I enjoy. السِّباحَة هِيَّ الرِّياضَة الوَحِيدَة اللِّي أَتوَنَّس بِيها [ʔissibaːħa hiyya ʔirriyaːða ʔilwaħiːda ʔilli ʔatwannas biːha]

swimming pool • **1.** مَسبَح [masbaħ] مَسابِح [masaːbiħ] *pl:*

swing • **1.** مَرجِيحَة [marǰiːħa] مَرجُوحَة [marǰuːħa] مَراجِيح [maraːǰiːħ] *pl:* We have a swing in our garden. عِدنا مَرجُوحَة بحَدِيقَتنا [ʕidna marǰuːħa bħadiːqatna]

in full swing • **1.** أَوج [ʔawǰ] The party is in full swing. الحَفلَة بأَوجها [ʔilħafla bʔawiǰha]

to swing • **1.** مَرجَح [marǰaħ] تمِرجِح، مَرجَحَة [tmirǰiħ, marǰaħa] *vn:* تمَرجَح [tmarǰaħ] *p:* You swing me, and then I'll swing you. إنتَ مَرجِحنِي وَبَعدين آني أَمَرجِحَك [ʔinta marǰiħni wbaʕdayn ʔaːni ʔamarǰiħak] • **2.** تمَرجَح [tmarǰaħ] تَمَرجُح [tamarǰuħ] *vn: sv* a. You'll fall off if you swing so hard. تُوقَع إذا تِتمَرجَح هَالقَدّ حيل [tuːgaʕ ʔiða titmarǰaħ halgadd ħiːl] • **3.** هَزّ [hazz] هَزّ [hazz] *vn:* اِنهَزّ [ʔinhazz] *p:* She swings her arms when she walks. تهِزّ إيدَيها لَمّا تِمشِي [thizz ʔiːdiːha lamma timši]

to swing around • **1.** فَرّ [farr] فَرّ [farr] *vn:* اِنفَرّ [ʔinfarr] *p:* دَيوَر [diːwar] تَدَيوُر [tdiːwur] *vn: sv* u. Swing the car around. فُرّ السَّيّارَة [furr ʔissayyaːra]

switch • **1.** سوِيچ [swiːč] سوِيچات [swiːčaːt] *pl:* The light switch is next to the door. سوِيچ الضُّوَة يَمّ الباب [swiːč ʔiððuwa yamm ʔilbaːb] • **2.** مُقَصّ [mugaṣṣ]

مُقَصّات [mugaṣṣa:t] *pl:* The last car jumped the track at the switch. آخِر فارقون طِلَع مِن السِّكَّة يَمّ المُقَص [ʔa:xir fa:rgu:n ṭilaʕ min ʔissikka yamm ʔilmugaṣṣ]

to switch • **1.** حَوَّل [ħawwal] تَحويل [taħwi:l] *vn:* تحَوَّل [tħawwal] *p:* The train was switched to another track. القِطار تحَوَّل إلَى غير سِكَّة [ʔilqiṭa:r tħawwal ʔila ɣayr sičča] • **2.** دار [da:r] دَير [di:r] *vn:* اِندار [ʔinda:r] *p:* Switch the radio to short wave. دير الرّاديُو عالمَوجَة القَصِيرَة [di:r ʔirra:dyu ʕalmawǰa ʔilqaṣi:ra] • **3.** بادَل [ba:dal] مُبادَلَة [muba:dala] *vn:* تبادَل [tba:dal] *p:* Let's switch places. خَلّي نِتبادَل بمُكاناتنا [xalli nitba:dal bmuka:na:tna]

*** I don't know how we switched coats.**
• **1.** ما أعرُف شلَون أخَذنا قبُوط واحِد لاخ بالغَلَط [ma: ʔaʕruf šlu:n ʔaxaðna qappu:ṭ wa:ħid la:x bilɣalaṭ]

to switch off • **1.** طَفَّى [ṭaffa:] تَطفِيَة [taṭfiya] *vn:* تطَفَّى [tṭaffa:] *p:* Switch off the light. طَفِّي الضُوا [ṭaffi ʔiðḍuwa]

to switch on • **1.** شِعَل [šiʕal] شَعِل [šaʕil] *vn:* اِنشِعَل [ʔinšiʕal] *p:* Switch on the light. إشعِل الضُّوَة [ʔišʕil ʔiðḍuwa]

sword • **1.** سَيف [sayf, si:f] سيُوف [syu:f] *pl:*

syllable • **1.** مَقطَع [maqṭaʕ] مَقاطِع [maqa:ṭiʕ] *pl:* The accent is on the first syllable. التَّأكِيد عَلَى المَقطَع الأوَّل [ʔittaʔki:d ʕala ʔilmaqṭaʕ ʔilʔawwal]

symbol • **1.** رَمِز [ramiz] رُمُوز [rumu:z] *pl:*

symbolic • **1.** رَمزي [ramzi] That sign has the same symbolic meaning all over the world. هالإشارَة بِيها نَفس المَعنَى الرَّمزي بِكُلّ العالَم [halʔiša:ra bi:ha nafs ʔilmaʕna ʔirramzi bkull ʔilʕa:lam]

to symbolize • **1.** رِمَز [rimaz] رَمِز [ramiz] *vn: sv* i. The statue over there symbolizes our struggle against imperialism. هَالتِّمثال يِرمِز إلَى مُكافَحَتنا لِلإستِعمار [hattimθa:l yirmiz ʔila muka:faħatna lilʔistiʕma:r]

to sympathize with • **1.** شارَك بِشعُور [ša:rkak bšuʕu:r] مُشارَكَة [muša:raka] *vn: sv* i. I sympathize with you. أشارَكَك بشعُورَك [ʔaša:rkak bšuʕu:rak] • **2.** عِطَف عَلَى [ʕiṭaf ʕala] عَطُف [ʕaṭuf] *vn: sv* u. I sympathize with the flood victims. أعطُف عَلَى المُتَضَرِّرين بالفَيَضان [ʔaʕṭuf ʕala ʔilmutaðarriri:n bilfayaḍa:n]

sympathy • **1.** عَطُف [ʕaṭuf] I have no sympathy for her. ما عِندي أيّ عَطُف عَليها [ma: ʕindi ʔayy ʕaṭuf ʕali:ha] I have no sympathy for her. قَلبِي ما ينكِسِر عَليها [galbi ma: yinkisir ʕali:ha]

Syria • **1.** سُوريا [su:rya]

Syrian • **1.** سُوري [su:ri] شامي [ša:mi] شامِيِّين [ša:miyyi:n] *pl:* There were a number of Syrians on the boat. كان أكُو عِدَّة سُورِيِّين بالمَركَب [ča:n ʔaku ʕiddat su:riyyi:n bilmarkab] • **2.** سُوري [su:ri] شامِ [ša:mi] He speaks the Syrian dialect very well. يِحكِي اللَّهجَة السُّورِيَّة كُلِّش زين [yiħči ʔillahǰa ʔissu:riyya kulliš zi:n]

system • **1.** نِظام [niḍa:m] أنظِمَة [ʔanḍima] *pl:* They're hoping to change their system of government. دَيتأمَّلُون يبَدِّلُون نِظام حُكُومَتهُم [dayitʔammalu:n ybaddilu:n niḍa:m ħuku:mathum] • **2.** جِهاز [ǰiha:z] أجهِزَة [ʔaǰhiza] *pl:* We're studying the respiratory system. دَندرُس جهاز التَّنَفُّس [danidrus ǰiha:z ʔittanaffus] • **3.** إسلُوب [ʔislu:b] أساليب [ʔasa:li:b] *pl:* I have a better system. عِندي إسلُوب أحسَن [ʕindi ʔislu:b ʔaħsan] • **4.** جِسِم [ǰisim] أجسام [ʔaǰsa:m] *pl:* My system can't take it. جِسمِي ما يتحَمَّلَه [ǰismi ma: yitħammalah]

systematic • **1.** مَنظَّم [mnaḍḍam] He's very systematic. هُوَّ كُلِّش مَنظَم [huwwa kulliš mnaḍḍam]

systematically • **1.** بصُورَة مَنظَّمَة [bṣu:ra mnaḍḍama] You'll have to work more systematically. لازِم تِشتُغُل بِصُورَة مَنظَّمَة أكثَر [la:zim tištuɣul bṣu:ra mnaḍḍama ʔakθar]

S

T

tab • **1.** عَلامَة [ʕala:ma] عَلامات، عَلائِم [ʕala:ma:t, ʕala:ʔim] *pl:* The tab on this file is worn out. العَلامَة مال هالفايِل مشَقِّقَة [ʔilʕala:ma ma:l halfa:yil mšaggiga] • **2.** حساب [ħsa:b] How much is the tab? شقَدّ الحساب؟ [šgadd ʔilħsa:b?]

to keep tabs on • **1.** راقَب [ra:qab] مُراقَبَة [mura:qaba] *vn: sv* i. The police are keeping tabs on him. الشُرطَة دَيراقبُوه [ʔiššurṭa dayra:qbu:h]

table • **1.** مَيز [mayz, mi:z] مِيُوزَة [myu:za] *pl:* Put the table in the middle of the room. حُطّ المِيز بِنُصّ القُبَّة [ħuṭṭ ʔilmi:z bnuṣṣ ʔilgubba] • **2.** جَدوَل [jadwal] جَداوِل [jada:wil] *pl:* The figures are given in the table on page 20. الأرقام مَوجُودَة بِالجَدوَل بِصَفحَة عِشرِين [ʔilʔarqa:m mawju:da biljadwal bṣafħa ʕišri:n]

*** The tables are turned.** • **1.** اِنعِكسَت الآيَة [ʔinʕiksat ʔilʔa:ya]

to table • **1.** أَجَّل النَّظَر بِ [ʔajjal ʔannaðar bi-] *sv* i. Why has the committee tabled the motion? لَوِيش اللَّجنَة أَجِّلَت النَّظَر بِالإقتِراح؟ [lwi:š ʔillajna ʔajjilat ʔinnaðar bilʔiqtira:ħ?]

tablecloth • **1.** شَرشَف مَيز [čarčaf mayz] شَراشِف مَيز [čara:čif mayz] *pl:* مشَمَّع [mšammaʕ] مشَمَّعات [mšammaʕa:t] *pl:*

table of contents • **1.** فِهرَس [fihras] فَهارِس [faha:ris] *pl:* جَدوَل المُحتَويات [jadwal ʔilmuħtawiya:t] جَداوِل المُحتَويات [jada:wil ʔilmuħtawiya:t] *pl:*

tablespoon • **1.** خاشُوقَة أَكِل [xa:šu:gat ʔakil] خواشِيق مال أَكِل [xwa:ši:g ma:l ʔakil] *pl:* خاشُوقَة مال أَكِل [xa:šu:ga ma:l ʔakil] خواشِيق مال أَكِل [xwa:ši:g ma:l ʔakil] *pl:*

tablet • **1.** دَفتَر مِسوَدَّة [daftar miswadda] دَفاتِر مِسوَدَّة [dafa:tir miswadda] *pl:* I've used a whole tablet of paper on this case. خَلَّصِت دَفتَر مِسوَدَّة كامِل عَلَى هالقَضِيَّة [xallaṣit daftar miswadda ka:mil ʕala halqaðiyya] • **2.** حَبّايَة [ħabba:ya] حَبّايات [ħabba:ya:t] *pl:* حُبُوب [ħubu:b] حَبّايات [ħabba:ya:t] *pl:* حَبّ [ħabb] *Collective*

table tennis • **1.** بِنك بَونك [ping pu:ng]

taboo • **1.** مُحَرَّم [muħarram] It's taboo for girls to go out alone at night. مُحَرَّم عالبَنات يطِلعُون باللَّيل وَحَّدهُم [muħarram ʕalbana:t ytilʕu:n billayl waħħadhum]

tack • **1.** دَنبُوس [danbu:s] دَنابِيس [dana:bi:s] *pl:* Tacks don't hold well on this bulletin board. الدَّنابِيس ما تِلزَم زين عَلَى هَاللَّوحَة مال الإعلانات [ʔiddana:bi:s ma: tilzam zi:n ʕala hallawħa ma:l ʔilʔiʕla:na:t] • **2.** بِسمار [bisma:r] بَسامِير [basa:mi:r] *pl:* This tack came out of the sofa. اِنشِلَع هالبِسمار مِن القَنَفَة [ʔinšilaʕ halbisma:r min ʔilqanafa]

to tack • **1.** دَنبَس [danbas] The tailor tacked the sleeve on the coat during the last fitting. الخَيّاط دَنبَس الرِّدان بِالسِّترَة بِآخِر براوَة [ʔilxayya:ṭ danbas ʔirrida:n bissitra bʔa:xir pra:wa] Tack this notice on the bulletin board. دَنبِس هَالإعلان بِلَوحَة الإعلانات [danbis halʔiʕla:n blawħat ʔilʔiʕla:na:t]

tackle • **1.** غَراض [ɣara:ð] I brought my fishing tackle along. جِبِت غَراض صَيد السِّمَك ويّايا [jibit ɣara:ð ṣayd ʔissimač wiyya:ya]

to tackle • **1.** عالَج [ʕa:laj] مُعالَجَة [muʕa:laja] *vn: sv* i. You've tackled the problem the wrong way. عالَجِت المُشكِلَة بطَرِيقَة مُو صَحِيحَة [ʕa:lajit ʔilmuškila bṭari:qa mu: ṣaħi:ħa] You've tackled the problem the wrong way. عالَجت المُشكِلَة غَلَط [ʕa:lajt ʔilmuškila ɣalaṭ]

*** The policeman tackled the thief outside the house.** • **1.** الشُرطِي كُمَش الحَرامِي ووَقَّعَه بَرَّة البَيت [ʔiššurṭi kumaš ʔilħara:mi wawaggaʕah barra lbayt]

tact • **1.** لَباقَة [laba:qa] This situation calls for a certain amount of tact. هَالحالَة تِتطَلَّب شوَيَّة لَباقَة [halħa:la tiṭṭallab šwayya laba:qa]

tactic • **1.** تَكتِيك [takti:k] تَكتِيكات [takti:ka:t] *pl:* إسلُوب [ʔislu:b] أَسالِيب [ʔasa:li:b] *pl:* He's still using the same old tactics to get his own way. بَعدَه دَيستَعمِل نَفس التَّكتِيكات حَتَّى يحَصِّل اللّي يرِيدَه [baʕdah dayistaʕmil nafs ʔittakti:ka:t ħatta yħaṣṣil ʔilli yri:dah] The commander changed his tactics to deal with guerrilla warfare. القائِد بَدَّل أَسالِيبَه الحَربِيَّة حَتَّى تلائِم حَرب العِصابات [ʔilqa:ʔid baddal ʔasa:li:bah ʔilħarbiyya ħatta tla:ʔim ħarib ʔilʕiṣa:ba:t]

tag • **1.** بِطاقَة [biṭa:qa] بِطاقات، بِطايِق [biṭa:qa:t, biṭa:yiq] *pl:* Put a tag on the package. حُطّ بِطاقَة عالرُّزمَة [ħuṭṭ biṭa:qa ʕarruzma]

to tag after • **1.** لِحَق [liħag] لَحِق [laħig] *vn: sv* a. His son has been tagging after him all day. إبنَه لِحَقَه طُول النَّهار [ʔibnah liħagah ṭu:l ʔinnaha:r]

*** Can I tag along?** • **1.** أَقدَر أرُوح وِيّاك؟ [ʔagdar ʔaru:ħ wiyya:k?]

tail • **1.** ذَيل [ðayl] ذيُول، ذيُولَة [ðyu:l, ðyu:la] *pl:* My dog has a short tail. كَلبِي عِندَه ذَيل قصَيِّر [čalbi ʕindah ðayl gṣayyir] • **2.** ذِيال [ðiya:l] ذيالات [ðya:la:t] *pl:* Put your shirt tail inside your pants. خَشِّش ذيال ثوبَك بِالبَنطِرُون [xaššiš ðya:l θu:bak bilpanṭiru:n]

T

*** I can't make head or tail of what he says. • 1.** حكايتَه مَا بِيها لا راس ولا كَعَب [ħča:ytah ma: bi:ha la: ra:s wala čaʕab]

*** Heads or tails? • 1.** طُرَّة لَو كِتبَة؟ [ṭurra law kitba?] / شِير لَو خَطّ؟ [ši:r law xaṭṭ?]

at the tail end • 1. آخِر [ʔa:xir] أَواخِر [ʔawa:xir] *pl:* كَعَب [čaʕab] كعُوب [čʕu:b] *pl:* We arrived at the tail end of the first act. وُصَلنا بآخِر الفَصل الأَوَّل [wuṣalna bʔa:xir ʔilfaṣl ʔilʔawwal] We were at the tail end of the line. كِنّا بكَعَب خَطّ الانتِظار [činna bčaʕab xaṭṭ ʔilintiða:r]

to tail • 1. تِبَع [tibaʕ] تَبع [tabiʕ] *vn:* اِنتِبَع [ʔintibaʕ] *p:* لِحَق [liħag] لَحِق [laħig] *vn:* اِنلِحَق [ʔinliħag] *p:* There's a car tailing us! أَكُو سَيّارَة دَتِتبَعنا [ʔaku sayya:ra datitbaʕna]

tail light • 1. باكلايت [bakla:yt] ضُوَة وَرّانِي [ðuwa warra:ni] ضُوايات وَرّانِيَّة [ðuwa:ya:t warra:niyya] *pl:* I'm having the tail light on my car fixed. دَأَصَلِّح الباكلايت مال سَيّارتِي [daaṣalliħ ʔilba:kla:yt ma:l sayya:rti]

tailor • 1. خَيّاط [xayya:ṭ] خَيّاطِين [xayya:ṭi:n] *pl:* Where is there a good tailor? وين أَكُو خَيّاط زين؟ [wi:n ʔaku xayya:ṭ zi:n?]

to tailor • 1. خَيَّط [xayyaṭ] خِياطَة [xiya:ṭa] *vn:* تخَيَّط [txayyaṭ] *p:* He tailored the suit the way I wanted it. خَيَّط البَدلَة مِثلما رِدتها [xayyaṭ ʔilbadla miθilma: riditha]

tailoring • 1. خياطَة [xya:ṭa] خياط [xya:ṭ] Tailoring is a trade which brings in good money. الخياطَة مِهنَة تجِيب خُوش فلُوس [ʔalxya:ṭa mihna dʒi:b xu:š flu:s] The tailoring costs much more than the material. الخياطَة تكَلِّف هوايَة أَكثَر مِن القماش [ʔalxya:ṭa tkallif hwa:ya ʔakθar min ʔalqma:š]

tailor-made • 1. تِفصال [tifṣa:l] All his clothes are tailormade. كُلّ هدُومَه تِفصال [kull hdu:mah tifṣa:l]

tails • 1. فراك [fra:k] We have to wear tails to the party this evening. لازِم نِلبَس فراك بِالحَفلَة هاللَّيلَة [la:zim nilbas fra:k bilħafla hallayla]

taint • 1. صنان [ṣna:n] The milk has an onion taint to it. الحَلِيب بِيه صنان بُصَل [ʔilħali:b bi:h ṣna:n buṣal] **• 2.** لَطخَة [laṭxa] لَطخات [laṭxa:t] *pl:* This will be a taint on my reputation. هَذِي راح تصِير لَطخَة بِسُمُعتِي [ha:ði ra:ħ tṣi:r laṭxa bsumuʕti]

*** Cover the butter or the onions will taint it. • 1.** غَطِّي الزِبد حَتَّى لا ياخُذ طَعَم بُصَل [ɣaṭṭi ʔizzibid ħatta: la: ya:xuð ṭaʕam buṣal]

take • 1. The take ran to fifty thousand dollars. الدَّخَل وَصَّل إِلَى خَمسِين أَلِف دُولار [ʔiddaxal waṣṣal ʔila xamsi:n ʔalif du:la:r]

to take • 1. أَخَذ مِن، أَخَذ عَلَى [ʔaxað min, ʔaxað ʕala] أَخِذ [ʔaxið] *vn:* اِنأَخَذ [ʔinʔaxað] *p:* Who took my ties? مِنُو أَخَذ بُوينباغاتِي؟ [minu ʔaxað buyinba:ɣa:ti?] Take my advice. اِقبَل نَصِيحتِي [ʔiqbal naṣi:ħti] Don't take it so seriously! لا تاخُذها هَالقَدّ جِدّ [la: ta:xuðha halgadd ǰidd] That takes too much time. هاي تاخُذ هوايَة وَقِت [ha:y ta:xuð hwa:ya wakit] That takes too much time. هاي تِحتاج هوايَة وَقِت [ha:y tiħta:ǰ hwa:ya wakit] He takes too many liberties. ياخُذ حُرِّيتَه أَكثَر مِن اللّازِم [ya:xuð ħurri:tah ʔakθar min ʔilla:zim] We'll take the room with twin beds. راح ناخُذ الغُرفَة أُمّ فراشَين [ra:ħ na:xuð ʔilɣurfa ʔumm fra:šayn] My rook will take your pawn. قَلِعتِي راح تاخُذ الجُندي مالَك [qaliʕti ra:ħ ta:xuð ʔiǰǰundi ma:lak] My rook will take your pawn. راح أَقتُل الجُندي مالَك بالقَلعَة [ra:ħ ʔagtul ʔiǰǰundi ma:lak bilqalʕa] Take my advice. أُخُذ نَصِيحتِي [ʔuxuð naṣi:ħti] We've taken all the necessary precautions. أَخَذنا كُلّ الاحتِياطات اللّازمَة [ʔaxaðna kull ʔilʔiħtiya:ṭa:t ʔilla:zma] Who took first prize? مِنُو أَخَذ الجّائزَة الأُولَى؟ [minu ʔaxað ʔiǰǰa:ʔiza ʔilʔu:la?] You can take it back; I won't need it any more. تِقدَر تاخُذها؛ بَعَد ما أَحتاجها [tigdar ta:xuðha; baʕad ma: ʔaħta:ǰha] I'm taking Ahmed to the movies with me. آنِي ماخِذ أَحمَد لِلسِّينَما وِيّايا [ʔa:ni ma:xið ʔaħmad lissinama wiyya:ya] We took many pictures. أَخَذنا هواي صُوَر [ʔaxaðna hwa:y ṣuwar] Take the measurements of this table. أُخُذ قِياسات هَالمِيز [ʔuxuð qiya:sa:t halmi:z] We always take a nap after lunch. إحنا دائِماً ناخُذ غَفوَة بَعد الغدا [ʔiħna da:ʔiman na:xuð ɣafwa baʕd ʔilɣada] Did the doctor take your temperature this morning? الطَّبِيب أَخَذ حَرارتَك هَاليُوم الصُّبُح؟ [ʔiṭṭabi:b ʔaxað ħara:rtak halyu:m ʔiṣṣubuħ?] Let's take a quick dip. خَلِّي ناخُذ إلنا فَدّ غَطَّة [xalli na:xuð ʔilna fadd ɣaṭṭa] Did you take these figures from the latest report? أَخَذِت هالأَرقام مِن التَّقرِير الأَخِير؟ [ʔaxaðit halʔarqa:m min ʔittaqri:r ʔilʔaxi:r?] **• 2.** بِلَع [bilaʕ] بَلِع [baliʕ] *vn:* اِنبِلَع [ʔinbilaʕ] *p:* Take one pill before each meal. إبلَع حَبّايَة قَبُل كُلّ وَجبَة أَكِل [ʔiblaʕ ħabba:ya gabul kull waǰbat ʔakil] **• 3.** طَوَّل [ṭawwal] تَطويل [taṭwi:l] *vn: sv* i. How long will the trip from here to the market take? الرَّوحَة مِن هِنا لِلسُّوق شقَدّ تطَوِّل؟ [ʔirrawħa min hna lissu:g šgadd ṭṭawwil?] **• 4.** فِهَم [fiham] فَهِم [fahim] *vn: sv* a. أَوَّل [ʔawwal] تَأوِيل [taʔwi:l] *vn: sv* i. He took my remark the wrong way. فِهَم قَصدِي بِالغَلَط [fiham qaṣdi bilɣalaṭ] He took my remark the wrong way. أَوَّل حكايتِي بالغَلَط [ʔawwal ħča:yti bilɣalaṭ] **• 5.** اِنراد [ʔinra:d] *sv* a. It won't take much gas to get there. ما ينراد هوايَة بَنزِين حَتَّى نُوصَل لِهناك [ma: yinra:d hwa:ya banzi:n ħatta nu:ṣul lihna:k] That doesn't take much brains. هاي ما ينرادِلها هوايَة مُخّ [ha:y ma: yinra:dilha hwa:ya muxx] **• 6.** لِزَم [lizam] لَزِم [lazim] *vn: sv* a. She took the child by the hand and led him across the street. لِزمَت إيد الجّاهِل وَعَبّرتَه الشّارِع [lizmat ʔi:d ʔiǰǰa:hil wʕabbratah ʔišša:riʕ]

T

• **7.** وَدَّى [wadda:] *sv* i. What else do you want to take along with you? بَعَد شِتريد توَدِّي وِيَّاك؟ [baʕad šitri:d twaddi wiyya:k?] • **8.** شال [ša:l] شَيل [šayl] *vn: sv* i. My last smallpox vaccination didn't take. آخِر مَرَّة ضِرَبِت جِدرِي ما شال [ʔa:xir marra ð̣irabit ǰidri ma: ša:l] • **9.** سَوَّى [sawwa:] تَسوِيَة [taswiya] *vn: sv* i. The government is going to take a census next year. الحُكُومَة راح تسَوِّي إحصاء نفُوس السَّنَة الجّايَة [ʔilħuku:ma ra:ħ tsawwi ʔiħṣa:ʔ nfu:s ʔissana ʔiǰǰa:yya] • **10.** لِقَى [liga:] إلقاء [ʔilqa:ʔ] *vn: sv* i. Why don't you take a look at the house and tell me what you think? لِيش ما تِلقِي نَظرَة عَالبَيت وَتقُلِّي رَأيَك؟ [li:š ma: tilqi nað̣ra ʕalbayt wtgulli raʔayak?] • **11.** تحَمَّل [tħammal] تَحَمُّل [taħammul] *vn: sv* a. I'll take the responsibility. آنِي راح أتحَمَّل المَسؤُلِيَّة [ʔa:ni ra:ħ ʔatħammal ʔilmasʔuliyya] Why should I take the blame for his mistake? لِيش لازِم أتحَمَّل اللَّوم عَن أغلاطَه؟ [li:š la:zim ʔatħammal ʔillawm ʕan ʔaɣla:ṭah?] • **12.** رِكَب ب [rikab b-] رِكِب [rikib] *vn: sv* u. راح ب [ra:ħ b-] رَوح [ru:ħ] *vn: sv* u. Why don't you take the bus? لِيش ما تِركَب بِالباص؟ [li:š ma: tirkab bilpa:ṣ?]

*** Take it easy! You've got all day.**
• **1.** لا تِستَعجِل عِندَك اليَوم كُلَّه [la: tistaʕǰil ʕindak ʔilyu:m kullah]

*** Take it easy! Don't let that upset you.**
• **1.** لا تدِير بالَك لا تخَلِّي هَذا يزعِجَك [la: tdi:r ba:lak la: txalli ha:ða yziʕǰak]

*** He took me at my word.** • **1.** سَوَّى حكايتِي مال [sawwa: ħča:yti ma:l]

*** How did he take to your suggestion?**
• **1.** عِجَبَه اِقتِراحَك؟ [ʕiǰabah ʔiqtira:ħak?] / قِطَع عَقلَه بإقتِراحَك؟ [giṭaʕ ʕaqlah bʔiqtira:ħak?] / شكان رأيَه بإقتِراحَك؟ [šča:n raʔyah bʔiqtira:ħak?]

*** I take it you're in trouble again.**
• **1.** يبَيِّن إنتَ مورِّط نَفسَك مَرَّة لُخ [ybayyin ʔinta mwarriṭ nafsak marra lux]

*** I took him down a peg or two.**
• **1.** خَلَّيتَه يُعرُف قَدرَه شِنُو [xallaytah yuʕruf qadrah šinu] / كِسَرِت خَشمَه شوَيَّة [kisarit xašmah šwayya]

*** She took the stand as witness for the defense.**
• **1.** وُقفَت كَشاهدَة للدِّفاع [wugfat kaša:hda liddifa:ʕ]

*** Take a look! Isn't that a beautiful horse?**
• **1.** باوِع هَالحِصان مُو حِلو؟ [ba:wiʕ haliħṣa:n mu: ħilu?]

*** They took the town by storm.**
• **1.** هِجمَوا فَدّ هَجمَة واحتَلُّوا الولايَة [hiǰmaw fadd haǰma wʔiħtallaw ʔilwla:ya]

*** How much will you take for your car?**
• **1.** شقَدّ ترِيد بسَيّارتَك؟ [šgadd tri:d bsayya:rtak?]

to take after • **1.** طِلَع عَلَى [ṭilaʕ ʕala] طلُوع [ṭulu:ʕ] *vn: sv* a. He takes after his father. طالِع عَلَى أَبُوه [ṭa:liʕ ʕala ʔabu:h] • **2.** رِكَض وَرا [rikað wara] She took after the dog with a stick. شالَت العُودَة وَرِكضَت وَرا الكَلِب [ša:lat ʔilʕu:da wrikað̣at wara ʔiččalib]

to take away • **1.** أخَذ مِن، أخَذ عَلَى [ʔaxað min, ʔaxað ʕala] أخِذ [ʔaxið] *vn:* اِنأخَذ [ʔinʔaxað] *p:* وَدَّى [wadda:] *sv* i. The police took him away. الشُّرطَة أخذُوه [ʔiššurṭa ʔaxðuwh] The police took him away. الشُّرطَة وَدُّوه [ʔiššurṭa waddu:h] She took my books away with her. وَدَّت كُتبِي وِيّاها [waddat kutbi wiyya:ha] • **2.** وَخَّر [waxxar] تَوخِير [tawxi:r] *vn:* توَخَّر [twaxxar] *p:* Please take the dog away from the table. بالله وَخِّر الكَلِب مِن المَيز [ballah waxxir ʔiččalib min ʔalmayz] • **3.** طِرَح [ṭiraħ] طَرِح [ṭariħ] *vn: sv* a. Take three away from five. إطرَح ثلاثَة مِن خَمسَة [ʔiṭraħ tla:θa min xamsa] • **4.** شال [ša:l] شَيل [ši:l] *vn: sv* i. Please take those dirty cups away. بالله ما تشِيل هَالكوابَة الوَسخَة [ballah ma: tši:l halkwa:ba ʔilwasxa] • **5.** حَطّ [ħaṭṭ] حَطّ [ħaṭṭ] *vn: sv* u. His eccentric behavior takes away from his prestige among the students. تَصَرُّفَه الشّاذّ يحُطّ مِن قَدرَه بين التَّلامِيذ [taṣarrufah ʔiššaðð yħuṭṭ min qadrah bayn ʔittala:mi:ð]

to take back • **1.** سِحَب [siħab] سَحِب [saħib] *vn: sv* a. I take back what I said. أسحَب كَلامِي [ʔasħab kala:mi] • **2.** رَجَّع [raǰǰaʕ] تَرجِيع [tarǰi:ʕ] *vn:* ترَجَّع [traǰǰaʕ] *p:* You can take it back to the tailor. تِقدَر ترَجِّعها لِلخَيّاط [tigdar traǰǰiʕha lilxayya:ṭ] We already hired someone else, so we can't take him back now. عَيَّنّا واحِد غيرَه وَبَعَد ما نِقدَر نرَجّعَه [ʕayyanna: wa:ħid ɣayrah wabaʕad ma: nigdar nraǰǰʕah]

*** This music takes me back to my days in Paris.** • **1.** هَالمُوسِيقَى تذَكّرنِي بأيّام بارِيس [halmusi:qa tðakkirni bʔayya:m pa:ri:s]

to take down • **1.** نَزَّل [nazzal] تَنزِيل [tanzi:l] *vn:* تنَزَّل [tnazzal] *p:* Take the picture down from the wall. نَزِّل الصُّورَة مِن عَالحايِط [nazzil ʔiṣṣu:ra min ʕalħa:yiṭ] • **2.** سَجَّل [saǰǰal] تَسجِيل [tasǰi:l] *vn:* تسَجَّل [tsaǰǰal] *p:* Take down my address. سَجِّل عِنوانِي [saǰǰil ʕinwa:ni] • **3.** ضُبَط [ð̣ubaṭ] ضَبُط [ð̣abuṭ] *vn:* اِنضُبَط [ʔinð̣ubaṭ] *p:* Who's taking down the minutes? مِنُو دَيِضبُط الجَّلسَة؟ [minu dayið̣buṭ ʔiǰǰalsa?]

to take for • **1.** تصَوَّر [tṣawwar] تَصَوُّر [taṣawwur] *vn: sv* a. Sorry, I took you for someone else. العَفو، تصَوَّرتَك غير واحِد [ʔilʕafw, tṣawwartak ɣayr wa:ħid] Sorry, I took you for someone else. العَفو، عَبالِي غير واحِد [ʔilʕafw, ʕaba:li ɣayr wa:ħid] What do you take me for? A liar? شدَتِتصَوَّرنِي؟ كَذّاب؟ [šdatitṣawwarni? čaðða:b?] What do you take me for? A liar? شعَبالَك؟ آنِي كَذّاب؟ [šʕaba:lak? ʔa:ni čaðða:b?]

to take in • **1.** سَوَّى [sawwa:] تَسوِيَة [taswiya] *vn: sv* i. We take in about 30 dinars a day. دَنسَوِّي حَوالِي ثلاثِين دِينار بِاليُوم [dansawwi ħawa:li tla:θi:n dina:r bilyu:m] • **2.** قَصَّف [gaṣṣaf] تَقصِيف [tagṣi:f] *vn: sv* i. Will you take this dress in at the waist? بالله ما تقَصّفِين هَالنَّفنُوف مِن يَمّ الخَصِر؟ [ballah ma: tgaṣṣfi:n hannafnu:f min yamm ʔalxaṣir?] • **3.** تكَلَّف [tkallaf] تَكَلُّف [takalluf] *vn: sv* a. Our uncle took us in after our parents died. عَمّنا تكَلَّف بِينا بَعَد ما ماتَوا أَبُونا وَأُمّنا

[ʕammna tkallaf bi:na baʕad ma: ma:taw ʔabu:na w̄ʔummna] • **4.** تقشمَر [tqašmar] قَشمَرَة [qašmara] *vn: sv* a. Have you been taken in again? تقشمَرت مَرَّة لُخ؟ [tqašmarit marra lux?] • **5.** راقَب [ra:qab] مُراقَبَة [mura:qaba] *vn: sv* i. لاحَظ [la:ħaḍ] مُلاحَظَة [mula:ħaḍa] *vn: sv* i. He sat there, taking it all in. قِعَد هناك يراقِب كُلّشِي [giʕad hna:k yra:qib kullši] • **6.** أَخَذ مِن، أَخَذ عَلَى [ʔaxað min, ʔaxað ʕala] أَخِذ [ʔaxið] *vn:* اِنأخَذ [ʔinʔaxað] *p:* The police took him in for questioning. الشُرطَة أخذُوه لِلمَركَز لِلتَّحقِيق [ʔiššurṭa ʔaxðawh lilmarkaz littaħqi:q]

to take off • **1.** أَخَذ إجازَة [ʔaxað ʔiǰa:za] *sv* u. I'm taking off for the rest of the day. راح آخُذ إجازَة بَقِيَّة النَّهار [ra:ħ ʔa:xuð ʔiǰa:za baqiyat ʔinnaha:r] • **2.** طار [ṭa:r] طَيَران [ṭayara:n] *vn: sv* i. When does the plane take off? شوَقت تطِير الطَّيّارَة؟ [šwakit ʔiṭṭi:r ʔiṭṭiyya:ra?] • **3.** نِزَع [nizaʕ] نَزِع [naziʕ] *vn: sv* a. I'm going to take off my coat. راح أنزَع القَبُّوط مالِي [ra:ħ ʔanzaʕ ʔilqappu:ṭ ma:li] • **4.** نَزَّل [nazzal] تَنزِيل [tanzi:l] *vn: sv* i. نَقَّص [naggaṣ] تَنقِيص [tangi:ṣ] *vn: sv* i. He took a few dollars off the price for me. نَزَّلِّي كَم دُولار مِن السِّعِر [nazzalli čam dula:r min ʔissiʕir]

to take on • **1.** لِزَم [lizam] لَزِم [lazim] *vn:* اِنلِزَم [ʔinlizam] *p:* I took on a new job yesterday. لِزَمِت شَغلَة جِدِيدَة البارحَة [lizamit šaɣla ǰidi:da ʔilba:rħa] • **2.** شَغَّل [šaɣɣal] تَشغِيل [tašɣi:l] *vn:* تشَغَّل [tšaɣɣal] *p:* عَيَّن [ʕayyan] تَعيِين [taʕyi:n] *vn:* تعَيَّن [tʕayyan] *p:* I hear the factory is taking on some new men. سمَعِت المَعمَل راح يشَغِّل عُمّال جِدَّد [smaʕit ʔilmaʕmal ra:ħ yšaɣɣil ʕumma:l ǰiddad] • **3.** أَخَذ [ʔaxað] أَخِذ [ʔaxið] *vn: sv* u. The situation has taken on a new aspect since then. مِن ذاك الوَقِت لِهَسَّة الحالَة أخذَت مَظهَر جِدِيد [min ða:k ʔilwakit lilhassa ʔilħa:la ʔaxðat maðhar ǰidi:d] • **4.** ضاف [ḍa:f] إضافَة [ʔiḍa:fa] *vn:* اِنضاف [ʔinḍa:f] *p:* We'll take on two more coaches at the next station. راح نضِيف فَرقُونَين لُخ بِالمَحَطَّة الجّايَّة [ra:ħ nḍi:f fargu:nayn lux bilmaħaṭṭa ʔiǰǰa:yya]

*** I'll take him on any day!** • **1.** آنِي أنازلَه أيّ يوم [ʔa:ni ʔana:zlah ʔayy yu:m] / آنِي مِستَعِدَّة لَه شوَقت ما يرِيد [ʔa:ni mistaʕidda:lah šwakit ma: yri:d]

to take out • **1.** طَلَّع [ṭallaʕ] تَطلِيع [taṭli:ʕ] *vn:* تطَلَّع [tṭallaʕ] *p:* Did you take the meat out of the refrigerator? طَلَّعِت اللَّحم مِن الثَّلّاجَة؟ [ṭallaʕit ʔillaħam min ʔiθθalla:ǰa?] Why do you take it out on me? لِيش دَتطَلّعها براسِي؟ [li:š daṭṭalliʕha bra:si?] Why do you take it out on me? لِيش دَتطَلِّع حَيفَك بِيّا [li:š daṭṭalliʕ ħayfak biyya] • **2.** وَدَّى ب [wadda: b-] *sv* i. When did he take his children out last? شوَقت كانَت آخِر مَرَّة وَدَّى جهالَه بِفَدّ مُكان؟ [šwakit ča:nat ʔa:xir marra wadda: ǰha:lah bfadd muka:n?]

to take over • **1.** اِستِلَم [ʔistilam] اِستِلام [ʔistila:m] *vn: sv* i. He took over my job. اِستِلَم شُغلِي [ʔistilam šuɣli] Who has taken over the management of the factory? مِنُو اِستِلَم إدارَة المَعمَل؟ [minu ʔistilam ʔida:rat ʔilmaʕmal?]

to take up • **1.** أَخَذ [ʔaxað] أَخِذ [ʔaxið] *vn: sv* u. That takes up a lot of space. هاي تاخُذ هوايَة مَكان [ha:y ta:xuð hwa:ya maka:n] • **2.** صَعَّد [ṣaʕʕad] تَصعِيد [taṣʕi:d] *vn: sv* i. Please take this book up with you when you go. بالله ما تصَعِّد هَالكِتاب وِيّاك مِن ترُوح فُوق؟ [ballah ma: tṣaʕʕid halkita:b wiyya:k min tru:ħ fu:g?] • **3.** عاشَر [ʕa:šar] مُعاشَرَة [muʕa:šara] *vn: sv* i. I wouldn't take up with those people if I were you. آنِي لَو بمَكانَك ما أعاشِر ذُولَة [ʔa:ni law bmaka:nak ma: ʔaʕa:šir ðu:la] I wouldn't take up with those people if I were you. آنِي لَو بمَكانَك ما أمشِي وِيّا ذُولَة النّاس [ʔa:ni law bmaka:nak ma: ʔamši wiyya ðu:la ʔinna:s] I wouldn't take up with those people if I were you. آنِي لَو بمَكانَك ما أتعاشَر وِيّا ذُولَة النّاس [ʔa:ni law bmaka:nak ma: ʔatʕa:šar wiyya ðu:la ʔinna:s] • **4.** بِدا [bida:] بَدأ [badʔ] *vn: sv* i. Can you take up where he left off? تِقدَر تِبدِي منَين ما بَطَّل؟ [tigdar tibdi mni:n ma: baṭṭal?] • **5.** تذاكَر عَن [dða:kar ʕan] تَذاكُر [taða:kur] *vn: sv* i. You'll have to take that matter up with someone else. لازِم تِتذاكَر وِيّا غَيرِي عَن هَالمَوضُوع [la:zim tidða:kar wiyya ɣayri ʕan halmawḍu:ʕ]

taken • **1.** مَأخُوذ [maʔxu:ð] All seats on the bus were taken. كُلّ المَقاعِد بِالباص مأخُوذَة [kull ʔalmaqa:ʕid bilpa:ṣ maʔxu:ða] All seats on the bus were taken. الباص مقَبَّط [ʔilpa:ṣ mqabbuṭ] • **2.** مَحجُوز [maħǰu:z] All seats are taken for tonight's performance. كُلّ المَقاعِد لِحفلَة هاللَّيلَة مَحجُوزَة [kull ʔalmaqa:ʕid liħaflat hallayla maħǰu:za] • **3.** مُغرَم [muɣram] She's really taken with that dress. هِيَّ حَقِيقَةً مُغرَمَة بذاك النَّفنُوف [hiyya ħaqi:qatan muɣrama bða:k ʔinnafnu:f]

taking • **1.** أَخِذ [ʔaxið] Taking pictures is forbidden here. أَخِذ الصُّوَر مَمنُوع هنا [ʔaxið ʔiṣṣuwar mamnu:ʕ hna]
*** She has very taking ways.** • **1.** تَصَرُّفاتها تِسحَر الواحِد [taṣarrufa:tha tisħar ʔilwa:ħid]

tale • **1.** سالفَة [sa:lfa] سوالِف [swa:lif] *pl:* سالُوفَة [sa:lu:fa] سالُوفات، سُوالِيف [sa:lu:fa:t, suwa:li:f] *pl:* سوالِيف [swa:li:f] Children love to listen to fairy tales. الجّهال يحِبُّون يِسمَعُون سوالِف [ʔiǰǰiha:l yħibbu:n yismaʕu:n swa:lif] • **2.** قُصَّة [quṣṣa] قُصَص [quṣaṣ] *pl:* She made up that tale to get even with them. اِختِرعَت هَالقُصَّة حَتَّى تاخُذ حَيفها مِنهُم [ʔixtirʕat halquṣṣa ħatta ta:xuð ħi:fha minhum]

talebearer • **1.** فَتّان [fatta:n] فَتّانِين [fatta:ni:n] *pl:* واشِي [wa:ši] واشِين، وُشات [wa:ši:n, wuš a:t] *pl:*

talent • **1.** مَوهِبَة [mawhiba] مَواهِب [mawa:hib] *pl:* He has a talent for mathematics. عِندَه مَوهِبَة بِالرِّياضِيّات [ʕindah mawhiba birriya:ḍiyya:t] She discovered her

T

artistic talent late in life. اِكتِشفَت مَوهِبتها الفَنِّيَّة بأواخِر عُمُرها [ʔiktišfat mawhibatha ʔalfanniyya bʔawa:xir ʕumurha] • 2. قابلِيَّة [qa:bliyya] قابلِيّات [qa:bliyya:t] *pl:* He has a talent for getting into trouble. عِندَه قابلِيَّة لِخَلق المَشاكِل لنفسَه [ʕindah qa:bliyya lxalq ʔilmaša:kil lnafsah] He has a talent for getting into trouble. يوَقِّع نَفسَه بمَشاكِل [ywaggiʕ nafsah bmaša:kil]

*** I never saw so much talent on one program.** • **1.** بعُمري ما شايِف هَلقَدّ ناس مَوهُوبين بفَدّ مَنهَج [bʕumri ma: ša:yif halgadd na:s mawhu:bi:n bfadd manhaǰ]

talk • **1.** حَديث [ħadi:θ] His talk was much too long. حَديثَه كان أَطوَل مِن اللّازِم [ħadi:θah ča:n ʔaṭwal min ʔilla:zim] Her marriage is the talk of the town. زَواجها صار حَديث المَجالِس [zawa:ǰha ṣa:r ħadi:θ ʔilmaǰa:lis] • **2.** حَكِي [ħači] Oh, that's just talk! هَذا بَسّ حَكِي [ha:ða bass ħači] What kind of talk is that? هَذا شلُون حَكِي؟ [ha:ða šlu:n ħači?] What kind of talk is that? شِنُو هَالحَكِي؟ [šinu: halħači?]

to have a talk with • **1.** حِكَى وِيّا [ħiča: wiyya] حَكِي وِيّا [ħači wiyya] *vn: sv* i. حاكَى [ħa:ča] *sv* i. I had a long talk with him. حَكِيت وِيّاه حَكِي طُويل [ħači:t wiyya:h ħači ṭuwi:l] / حاكَيتَه فَدّ مُدَّة طوِيلَة [ħa:či:tah fadd mudda ṭwi:la]

*** I'd like to have a talk with you.** • **1.** أَرد أَحكِي وِيّاك شوَيَّة [ʔard ʔaħči wiyya:k šwayya] / أَرِيد أَتحاكَى وِيّاك شوَيَّة [ʔari:d ʔatħa:ča: wiyya:k šwayya]

to talk • **1.** حِكَى [ħiča:] حَكِي [ħači] *vn: sv* i. Don't you think he talks too much? ما تِعتِقِد هُوَّ يِحكِي هوايَة؟ [ma: tiʕtiqid huwwa yiħči hwa:ya?] How can he talk with food stuffed in his mouth? شلُون يِقدَر يحكِي وَحَلقَه مَترُوس أكِل؟ [šlu:n yigdar yiħči wħalgah matru:s ʔakil?]

to talk into • **1.** قَنَّع [qannaʕ] تَقنِيع [taqni:ʕ] *vn: sv* i. سَوَّى [sawwa:] *sv* i. Do you suppose we can talk them into coming with us? تِعتِقِد نِقدَر نقَنِّعهُم يِجُون وِيّانا؟ [tiʕtiqid nigdar nqanniʕhum yiǰu:n wiyya:na?] Do you suppose we can talk them into coming with us? تِعتِقِد نِقدَر نسَوِّيلهُم واهِس يِجُون وِيّانا؟ [tiʕtiqid nigdar nsawwi:lhum wa:his yiǰu:n wiyya:na?]

to talk nonsense • **1.** لِغَى [liɣa:] لَغوَة، لَغِي [laɣwa, laɣy] *vn: sv* i. Don't talk nonsense! لا تِلغِي [la: tilɣi] Don't talk nonsense! لا تِحكِي حَكِي فارِغ [la: tiħči ħači fa:riɣ]

to talk over • **1.** بِحَث [biħaθ] بَحِث [baħiθ] *vn: sv* a. دانَش [da:naš] مُدانَشَة [muda:naša] *vn: sv* i. تذاكَر [dða:kar] مُذاكَرَة [muða:kara] *vn: sv* a. Talk the matter over with him. إبحَث المَوضُوع وِيّاه [ʔibħaθ ʔilmawðu:ʕ wiyya:h] Talk the matter over with him. تذاكَر وِيّاه بالمَوضُوع [dða:kar wiyya:h bilmawðu:ʕ] Let's talk it over. خَلّي نِتدانَش بِيها [xalli: nidda:naš bi:ha]

talkative • **1.** ثَرثار [θarθa:r] ثَرثارِين [θarθa:ri:n] *pl:* لَغوي [laɣwi] I don't like real talkative people. ما أَحِبّ الثَّرثارِين [ma: ʔaħibb ʔiθθarθa:ri:n]

*** Our son knows how to speak, but he's just not talkative.** • **1.** إبِننا يُعرُف يِحكِي، بَسّ ما يِحكِي هوايَة [ʔibinna yuʕruf yiħči, bass ma: yiħči hwa:ya]

tall • **1.** طُويل [ṭuwi:l] طوال [ṭwa:l] *pl:* She's tall and thin. هِيَّ طوِيلَة وَضعِيفَة [hiyya ṭwi:la wðiʕi:fa] • **2.** عالِي [ʕa:li] There aren't many tall buildings in that city. ماكُو هوايَة بنايات عاليَة بذيك الوِلايَة [ma:ku hwa:ya bna:ya:t ʕa:lya bði:č ʔilwila:ya]

*** He's one meter, and sixty centimeters tall.** • **1.** طُولَه مَتِر وستِّين سَنتِمَتِر [ṭu:lah matir wsitti:n santimatir]

*** How tall are you?** • **1.** شقَدّ طُولَك؟ [šgadd ṭu:lak?]

tallow • **1.** شَحَم [šaħam] شُحُوم [šuħu:m] *pl:*

to tally • **1.** عَدّ [ʕadd] عَدّ [ʕadd] *vn:* اِنعَدّ [ʔinʕadd] *p:* They have a machine to tally the votes. عِدهُم مَكِينَة لعَدّ الأَصوات [ʕidhum maki:na lʕadd ʔilʔaṣwa:t]

tamarind • **1.** تَمُر هِند [tamur hind] Tamarind makes a refreshing drink. شَربَت تَمُر هِند كُلِّش مُنعِش [šarbat tamur hind kulliš munʕiš]

tambourine • **1.** دَفّ [daff] دفُوف [dfu:f] *pl:*

tame • **1.** أَلِيف [ʔali:f] The birds there are so tame they eat out of your hand. الطِّيُور هناك هَالقَدّ أَلِيفَة تاكُل مِن إيد الواحِد [ʔiṭṭuyu:r hna:k halgadd ʔali:fa ta:kul min ʔi:d ʔilwa:ħid] • **2.** هادِئ [ha:diʔ] All in all, it was a pretty tame evening. بصُورَة عامَّة كانَت فَدّ لَيلَة هادئَة [bṣu:ra ʕa:mma ča:nat fadd layla ha:dʔa]

to become tame • **1.** إلَف [ʔilaf] أُلفَة [ʔulfa] *vn: sv* i. Birds become tame if you feed them every day. الطِّيُور يألِفُون إذا تطَعَّمهُم يَومِيّاً [ʔiṭṭuyu:r yiʔlifu:n ʔiða ṭṭaʕʕumhum yawmiyyan]

to tame • **1.** رَوَّض [rawwað] تَروِيض [tarwi:ð] *vn:* تَرَوَّض [trawwað] *p:* He tames wild animals. يرَوِّض حَيوانات وَحشِيَّة [yrawwið ħaywa:na:t waħšiyya] Lions are easily tamed. السِّباع تِترَوَّض بسُهُولَة [ʔissiba:ʕ titrawwað bsuhu:la]

to tame down • **1.** عِقَل [ʕiqal, ʕigal] عَقِل [ʕaqil] *vn: sv* a. هِدَأ [hidaʔ] هُدُوء [hudu:ʔ] *vn: sv* a. He's tamed down a lot since he left school. عِقَل هوايَة بَعَد ما تِرَك المَدرَسَة [ʕiqal hwa:ya baʕad ma: tirak ʔilmadrasa]

to tamp • **1.** دَكّ [dačč] دَكّ [dačč] *vn:* اِندَكّ [ʔindačč] *p:* Tamp the earth down well before you lay the tile. دِكّ القاع زين قَبُل ما تحُطّ الكاشِي [dičč ʔilga:ʕ zi:n gabul ma: tħuṭṭ ʔilka:ši]

tamper • **1.** مَدَقَّة [madagga] مَدَقّات [madagga:t] *pl:* Do you have a tamper I can borrow? عِندَك مَدَقَّة أَقدَر أَتدايَنها؟ [ʕindak madagga ʔagdar ʔadda:yanha?]

T

to tamper • **1.** لِعَب [liʕab] لِعِب [liʕib] *vn: sv* a. We caught him tampering with the mail. لِزَمناه يِلعَب بِالمَكاتِيب [lizamna:h yilʕab bilmaka:ti:b] Don't tamper with the radio. لا تِلعَب بِالرّاديُو [la: tilʕab birra:dyu]

tan • **1.** سَمار [sama:r] Where did you get that nice tan? مْنين جاك هَالسَّمار؟ [mni:n ǰa:k hassama:r?] • **2.** قَهوائِي آجُغ [gahwa:ʔiy ʔa:čuɣ] جَوزِي آجُغ [ǰawzi ʔa:čuɣ] I lost my tan gloves. ضَيَّعِت كفُوفِي القَهوائِيَّة آجُغ [ḍayyaʕit čfu:fi ʔilgahwa:ʔiyya ʔa:čuɣ]

to tan • **1.** دُبَغ [dubaɣ] دباغَة، دَبُغ [dba:ɣa, dabuɣ] *vn: sv* u. دَبَّغ [dabbaɣ] تدُبُّغ [tdubbuɣ] *vn: sv* u. What do you use when you tan hides? شتِستَعمِلُون مِن تدبغُون الجِّلُود؟ [štistaʕmilu:n min ddibɣu:n ʔiǰǰilu:d?] • **2.** قَهوائِي آجُغ [ʔismarr] اِسمِرار [ʔismira:r] *vn: sv* a. She tans easily. تِسمَرّ بسُهُولَة [tismarr bsuhu:la]

*** I'll tan your hide if you don't behave!**

• **1.** تَرَة أهرِي جِلدَك إذا ما راح تصِير آدمِي [tara ʔahri ǰildak ʔiða: ma: ra:ħ tṣi:r ʔa:dami] / تَرَة أدَبُّغ جِلدَك إذا ما راح تصِير آدَمِي [tara ʔadabbuɣ ǰildak ʔiða ma: ra:ħ tṣi:r ʔa:dami]

tangerine • **1.** لالَنكِيَّة [la:langiyya] لالَنكِيّات [la:langiyya:t] *pl:* لالِنكِي [la:lingi] *Collective*

Tangier • **1.** طَنجَة [ṭanǰa]

tangle • **1.** شَربَكَة [šarbaka] شَربَكات [šarbaka:t] *pl:* This tangle in the strings can't be undone. هَالشَّربَكَة بِالخِيُوط ما تِنفَكّ [haššarbaka bilixyu:ṭ ma: tinfakk] • **2.** وَرطَة [warṭa] وَرطات [warṭa:t] *pl:* You've certainly got yourself in a tangle this time. صُدُق وَقَّعِت نَفسَك بوَرطَة هَالمَرَّة [ṣudug waggaʕit nafsak bwarṭa halmarra]

to tangle • **1.** عَقَّد [ʕaggad] تَعقِيد [taʕgi:d] *vn:* تعَقَّد [tʕaggad] *p:* شَربَك [šarbak] شَربَكَة [šarbaka] *vn:* إتشَربَك [tšarbak] *p:* The cat tangled the string. البَزُّونَة عَقَّدَت الخيط [ʔilbazzu:na ʕaggidat ʔilxi:ṭ] • **2.** وَرَّط [warraṭ] تَوريط [tawri:ṭ] *vn:* توَرَّط [twarraṭ] *p:* Don't tangle with him! لا توَرِّط نَفسَك وِيّاه [la: twarriṭ nafsak wiyya:h]

tangled • **1.** معَقَّد [mʕaggad] The yarn is tangled. الصُّوف معَقَّد [ʔiṣṣu:f mʕaggad] • **2.** مَكفُوش [makfu:š] His hair is tangled. شَعرَه مَكفُوش [šaʕrah makfu:š]

tank • **1.** تانكِي [ta:nki] تانكِيّات [ta:nki:ya:t] *pl:* He took a few fish out of the tank. أخَذ كَم سِمكَة مِن التّانكِي [ʔaxað čam simča min ʔitta:nki] Fill up the tank with gas. إملِي التّانكِي بانزِين [ʔimli: ʔitta:nki banzi:n] • **2.** دَبّابَة [dabba:ba] دَبّابات [dabba:ba:t] *pl:* A column of tanks led the attack. رَتِل مِن الدَّبّابات تصَدّرَت الهِجُوم [ratil min ʔiddabba:ba:t tṣaddrat ʔalhiǰu:m] • **3.** عُنبار [ʕunba:r] عُنبارات [ʕunba:ra:t] *pl:* تانكِي [ta:nki] تانكِيّات [ta:nkiyya:t] *pl:* Every house in Baghdaad has a water tank on the roof. بِكُلّ بَيت بِبَغداد أكُو عَنبار ماي بِالسَّطِح [bkull bayt bibaɣda:d ʔaku ʕanba:r ma:y bissaṭiħ] • **4.** جِدِر [ǰidir] جدُور [ǰdu:r] *pl:* جدُورَة [ǰdu:ra] جدُور [ǰdu:r] *pl:* The hot-water tank is rusty. جِدِر الحَمّام مالنَا مزَنجَر [ǰidir ʔilħamma:m ma:lna mzanǰar]

tanning • **1.** دِباغَة، دباغَة [diba:ɣa, dba:ɣa] Mosul has a tanning factory. المَوصِل بِيها مَعمَل دِباغَة [ʔilmu:ṣil bi:ha maʕmal diba:ɣa]

*** His father gave him a good tanning.**

• **1.** أبُوه بُسَطَه بَسطَة زَينَة [ʔabu:h buṣaṭah basṭa zayna]

tap • **1.** دَقَّة [dagga] دَقّات [dagga:t] *pl:* I heard two taps on the window. سمَعِت دَقّتَين عَالشِّبّاك [smaʕit daggtayn ʕaššibba:č] • **2.** مزَمبِلَة [mzambila] مزَمبِلات [mzambila:t] *pl:* حَنَفِيَّة [ħanafiyya] حَنَفِيّات [ħanafiyya:t] *pl:* The tap on the barrel is dripping. المزَمبِلَة مال البَرمِيل دَتنقُّط [ʔilmzambila ma:l ʔilbarmi:l datnaggiṭ] • **3.** نَعَلجَة [naʕalča] نَعَلجات [naʕalča:t] *pl:* Please put taps on these shoes. بالله دُقّ لِهَالقُندَرَة نَعَلجات [ballah dugg lhalqundara naʕalčsa:t]

*** He always has some story on tap.**

• **1.** عِندَه دائماً حكايات حاضرَة [ʕindah da:ʔiman ħča:ya:t ħa:ðra]

to tap • **1.** نِقَر [nigar] نَقِر [nagir] *vn: sv* u. دَقّ [dagg] دَقّ [dagg] *vn: sv* u. He tapped on the window. نِقَر عالشَّبّاك [nigar ʕaššabba:č] • **2.** حَطّ [ħaṭṭ] حَطّ [ħaṭṭ] *vn:* اِنحَطّ [ţinħaṭṭ] *p:* The police tapped his telephone. الشُّرطَة حَطّوا رَقابَة عَلَى تِلفُونَه [ʔiššurṭa ħaṭṭaw raqa:ba ʕala tilifu:nah] • **3.** دَقّ [dagg] دَقّ [dagg] *vn: sv* u. She tapped me on the shoulder. دَقّت عَلَى كِتفِي [daggat ʕala čitfi]

*** They tapped the water main for the new house.** • **1.** جَرّوا ماي مِن الأبِّي لِلبَيت الجِّدِيد [ǰarraw ma:y min ʔilʔabbi lilbayt ʔiǰǰidi:d]

tape • **1.** شَرِيط [šari:ṭ] أشرِطَة، شَرائِط [ʔašriṭa, šara:yiṭ] *pl:* He has several tapes of Iraqi music. عِندَه كَم شَرِيط مِن المَوسِيقَى العِراقِيَّة [ʕindah čam šari:ṭ min ʔilmusi:qa ʔilʕira:qiyya] I'd like five yards of the white tape. أرِيد خَمِس ياردات مِن الشَّرِيط الأبيَض [ʔari:d xamis ya:rda:t min ʔiššari:ṭ ʔilʔabyað]

*** Getting through this red tape will take a long time.** • **1.** اِجتِياز هَالرَسمِيّات ياخُذ وَقِت هوايَة [ʔiǰtiya:z harrasmiyya:t ya:xuð wakit hwa:ya]

to tape • **1.** لِزَق [lizag] لَزِق [lazig] *vn: sv* i. Please tape an address label on that package. بالله إلزِق بِطاقَة عِنوان عَلَى ذِيك الرُّزمَة [ballah ʔilzig biṭa:qat ʕinwa:n ʕala ði:č ʔirruzma] • **2.** سَجَّل [sajjal] تَسجِيل [tasji:l] *vn:* تسَجَّل [tsajjal] *p:* Last night we taped the President's speech. البارحَة بالليل سَجَّلنا حَدِيث الرَّئِيس [ʔilba:rħa billayl sajjalna ħadi:θ ʔirraʔi:s]

tape measure • **1.** شَرِيط قِياس [šari:ṭ qiya:s] شَرايِط قِياس [šara:yiṭ qiya:s] *pl:*

T

tape recorder • **1.** مُسَجِّل [musajjil] مُسَجِّلِين [musajjili:n] *pl:*

tapeworm • **1.** دُودَة وَحِيدَة [du:da waħi:da] دِيدان وَحِيدَة [di:da:n waħi:da] *pl:*

tar • **1.** قِير [gi:r, ǰi:r] جِير [ǰi:r]

target • **1.** نِيشان [ni:ša:n] هَدَف [hadaf] أهداف [ʔahda:f] *pl:* Did you set up the target? نِصَبت الهَدَف؟ [niṣabt ʔilhadaf?] • **2.** غَرَض [ɣarað] أغراض [ʔaɣra:ð] *pl:* هَدَف [hadaf] أهداف [ʔahda:f] *pl:* Our target for this month is to sell 1,000 suits. غَرَضنا هَالشَّهَر نبِيع ألف بَدلَة [ɣaraḍna haššahar nbi:ʕ ʔalf badla]

tariff • **1.** جُمرُك [gumruk] رَسِم [rasim] رسُوم [rsu:m] *pl:* تَعرِيفَة، تَعرِيفَة جُمرُكِيَّة [taʕri:fa, taʕri:fa gumrugiyya] The tariff on silk is high. الجُمرُك عالحَرِير عالِي [ʔilgumrug ʕalħari:r ʕa:li]

tarnish • **1.** سَواد [sawa:d] Clean the tarnish from those spoons. نَظُّف السَّواد مِن هَالخواشِيق [naḍḍuf ʔissawa:d min halxwa:ši:g] • **2.** زنجار [zinǰa:r] Clean the tarnish off the brass tray. نَظُّف الزِّنجار مِن الصِّينِيَّة اِلبِرنج [naḍḍuf ʔizzinǰa:r min ʔiṣṣi:niyya ʔilprinǰ]

to tarnish • **1.** اِسوَدّ [ʔiswadd] سَواد [sawa:d] *vn: sv* a. The silverware will tarnish if you don't keep it in its box. الفُضِّيّات تِسوَدّ إذا ما تضُمّها بِصَندُوقها [ʔilfuḍḍiyya:t tiswadd ʔiða ma: dḍummha bṣandu:gha] • **2.** زَنجَر [zanǰar] زِنجار [zinǰa:r] *vn: sv* i. That brass doorknob will tarnish quickly. يَدَّة الباب البرنج تزَنجِر بِالعَجَل [yaddat ʔilba:b ʔilprinǰ dzanǰir bilʕaǰal]

tarpaulin • **1.** جادِر [ča:dir] جوادِر [čwa:dir] *pl:* Cover the load with a tarpaulin. غَطِّي الحِمِل بِجادِر [ɣaṭṭi ʔilħimil bča:dir]

tart • **1.** حامُض [ħa:muḍ] The apples have a tart taste. التِّفّاح بِيه طَعُم حامُض [ʔittiffa:ħ bi:h ṭaʕum ħa:muḍ]

task • **1.** شَغلَة [šaɣla] شَغلات [šaɣla:t] *pl:* He is equal to his task. يِطلَع مِن حَقّ هَالشَّغلَة [yiṭlaʕ min ħagg haššaɣla]

to take to task • **1.** زَفّ [zaff] زَفّ [zaff] *vn:* اِنزَفّ [ʔinzaff] *p:* We'll have to take him to task for his laziness. لازِم نزِفَّه عَلَى كَسَلَه [la:zim nziffah ʕala kasalah]

taste • **1.** طَعَم [ṭaʕam] This meat has a peculiar taste. هَاللَّحَم بِيه فَدّ طَعُم غَرِيب [hallaħam bi:h fadd ṭaʕum ɣari:b] I have a bad taste in my mouth. أَكُو فَدّ طَعُم ما طَيِّب بِحَلقِي [ʔaku fadd ṭaʕum ma: ṭayyib bħalgi] • **2.** ذَوق [ðawq] أذواق [ʔaðwa:q] *pl:* I'd have given you credit for better taste. تصَوَّرِت ذَوقَك أحسَن مِن هَذا [tṣawwarit ðawqak ʔaħsan min ha:ða]

*** Let me have a taste of it.** • **1.** خَلِّي أَذُوقَه [xalli ʔaðu:gah]

to have a taste for • **1.** اِستَذوَق [ʔistaðwaq] اِستِذواق [ʔistiðwa:q] *vn: sv* i. He has a taste for classical music. يِستَذوِق المُوسِيقَى الكلاسِيكِيَّة [yistaðwiq ʔilmusi:qa ʔilkla:sikiyya]

to taste • **1.** ذاق [ḍa:g] ذَوق [ðawq] *vn: sv* u. Just taste this coffee! بَسّ ذُوق هَالقَهوَة [bass ðu:g halgahwa]

*** The soup tastes good.** • **1.** الشَّوربَة طَعَمها طَيِّب [ʔiššu:rba ṭaʕamha ṭayyib] It tastes of vinegar. طَعَمها يِنطِي عَلَى خَلّ [ṭaʕamha yinṭi ʕala xall] It tastes of vinegar. بِيه طَعُم خَلّ [bi:h ṭaʕum xall]

tasteless • **1.** ما بِيه طَعَم [ma: bi:h ṭaʕam] The food is tasteless. الأكِل ما بِيه طَعُم [ʔilʔakil ma: bi:h ṭaʕum] • **2.** ما بِيه ذَوق [ma: bi:h ðawq] Her clothes are tasteless. لِبِسها ما بِيه ذَوق [libisha ma: bi:h ðawq]

tasty • **1.** لَذِيذ [laði:ð] طَيِّب [ṭayyib] This food is very tasty. هَالأكِل كُلِّش لَذِيذ [halʔakil kulliš laði:ð]

tavern • **1.** مَيخانَة [mayxa:na] مَيخانات [mayxa:na:t] *pl:*

tax • **1.** ضَرِيبَة [ḍari:ba] ضَرائِب [ḍara:ʔib, ḍara:yib] *pl:* Have you paid your taxes yet? دِفَعِت الضَّرايِب مالتَك لَو بَعَد؟ [difaʕt ʔiḍḍara:yib ma:ltak law baʕad?]

to tax • **1.** فُرَض ضَرِيبَة [furað ḍari:ba] فَرِض [fariḍ] *vn:* اِنفُرَض [ʔinfuraḍ] *p:* Everybody was taxed two dinars. اِنفُرضَت ضَرِيبَة دِينارَين عَلَى كُلّ واحِد [ʔinfurḍat ḍari:bat dina:rayn ʕala kull wa:ħid] It is not governmental policy to tax essential commodities. مُو مِن سِياسَة الحُكُومَة تُفرُض ضَرِيبَة عالسِّلَع الضَّرُورِيَّة [mu: min siya:sat ʔilħuku:ma tufruḍ ḍari:ba ʕassilaʕ ʔiḍḍaru:riyya]

tax collector • **1.** جابِي ضَرِيبَة [ǰa:bi ḍari:ba] جُباة ضَرِيبَة [ǰuba:t ḍari:ba] *pl:*

taxi • **1.** تَكسِي [taksi] تَكسِيّات [taksiyya:t] *pl:* I took a taxi from the station. أخَذِت تاكسِي مِن المَحَطَّة [ʔaxaðit ta:ksi min ʔilmaħaṭṭa]

taxi driver • **1.** سايِق تاكسِي [sa:yiq ta:ksi] سُوّاق تاكسِي [suwwa:q ta:ksi] *pl:*

taxpayer • **1.** دافِع ضَرِيبَة [da:fiʕ ḍari:ba] دافِعِين ضَرِيبَة [da:fiʕi:n ḍari:ba] *pl:*

tea • **1.** شاي [ča:y] شايات [ča:ya:t] *pl:* In Iraq they serve tea in small glasses. بِالعِراق يقَدّمُون الشّاي بِاستِكانات [bilʕira:q yqaddmu:n ʔičča:y bʔistika:na:t]

to teach • **1.** عَلَّم [ʕallam] تَعلِيم [taʕli:m] *vn:* تعَلَّم [tʕallam] *p:* دَرَّس [darras] تَدرِيس [tadri:s] *vn:* تدَرَّس [tdarras] *p:*

Will you teach me German! تعَلِّمني ألماني؟ [tʕallimni ʔalmaːni?] He teaches in a boys' school. هُوَّ يدَرِّس بمَدرسَة مال ولِد [huwwa ydarris bmadrasa maːl wilid] • **2.** عَلَّم [ʕallam] *sv* i. I'll teach him not to disturb me! راح أعَلّمَه بَعَد ما يز عِجني [raːħ ʔaʕallmah baʕad maː yizʕiǰni]

teacher • **1.** مُعَلِّم [muʕallim] مُدَرِّس [mudarris] He always wanted to be a teacher. دائماً راد يصير مُعَلِّم [daːʔiman raːd yṣiːr muʕallim]

teaching • **1.** تَدرِيس [tadriːs] تَعلِيم [taʕliːm] Teaching Arabic isn't too hard. تَدرِيس العَرَبِي مُو كُلِّش صَعُب [tadriːs ʔilʕarabi muː kulliš ṣaʕub]

teachings • **1.** تَعالِيم [taʕaːliːm] Muslims follow the teachings of the Koran. المُسلِمِين يتبَعُون تَعالِيم القُرآن [ʔilmuslimiːn yitbaʕuːn taʕaːliːm ʔilqurʔaːn]

tea cup • **1.** كُوب شاي [kuːb čaːy] أكوَاب [ʔakwaːb čaːy] *pl:*

tea glass • **1.** إستِكان [ʔistikaːn] إستِكانات [ʔistikaːnaːt] *pl:*

tea house • **1.** شايخانَة [čaːyxaːna] شايخانات [čaːyxaːnaːt] *pl:*

teak • **1.** صاج [ṣaːǰ] صاجات، صُوج [ṣaːǰaːt, ṣuːǰ] *pl:* Our dining room table is teak. مَيز أكِلنا مِن صاج [mayz ʔakilna min ṣaːǰ]

tea kettle • **1.** كِتلِي [kitli] كِتلِيّات، كتالِي [kitliyyaːt, ktaːli] *pl:*

team • **1.** فِرقَة، فَرِيق [firqa, fariːq] فِرَق [firaq] *pl:* Our team has won every football game it entered this year. فِرقَتنا غُلبَت كُلّ سِباق كُرَة قَدَم دِخلَت بِيه هالسَّنَة [firqatna ɣulbat kull sibaːq kurat qadam dixlat biːh hassana] • **2.** زَوج [zawǰ] زواج [zwaːǰ] *pl:* مَجمُوعَة [majmuːʕa] مَجمُوعات [majmuːʕaːt] *pl:* That carriage sports a beautiful team of horses. ذِيك العَرَبانَة بِيها خُوش زوج خَيل بَدِيعَة [ðiːč ʔilʕarabaːna biːha xuːš zuːǰ xayl badiːʕa]

to team up • **1.** تجَمَّع [dǰammaʕ] تَجَمُّع [tajammuʕ] *vn: sv* a. They teamed up against me. تجَمّعَوا عَلَيّا [dǰammʕaw ʕalayya] We teamed up in groups of six to play volley ball. نِتجَمَّع كُلّ سِتَّة سُوَة حَتَّى نِلعَب كُرَة الطّائِرَة [nidǰammaʕ kull sitta suwa ħatta nilʕab kurat ʔiṭṭaːʔira]

team mate • **1.** عُضُو فِرقَة [ʕuðw firqa] أعضاء فِرقَة [ʔaʕðaːʔ firqa] *pl:* He's one of my team mates. هُوَّ واحِد مِن أعضاء فِرقَتِي [huwwa waːħid min ʔaʕðaːʔ firaqti]

teamwork • **1.** تَكاتُف [takaːtuf] تَضامُن [taðaːmun] Good teamwork allowed us to finish the job ahead of time. التَّكاتُف خَلّانا نخَلِّص الشُّغُل قَبِل المَوعِد [ʔittakaːtuf xallaːna nxalliṣ ʔiššuɣul gabil ʔilmawʕid]

tea pot • **1.** قُورِي [quːri] قُورِيّات، قُوارِي [quːriyyaːt, quwaːri] *pl:*

tear • **1.** شَقّ [šagg] شقُوق [šguːg] *pl:* Can this tear be mended? هَالشَّقّ مُمكِن يتخَيَّط [haššagg mumkin yitxayyaṭ]

to tear • **1.** شَقّ [šagg] شَقّ [šagg] *vn:* اِنشَقّ [ʔinšagg] *p:* Don't tear the paper! لا تشِقّ الوَرقَة [laː tšigg ʔilwarqa] • **2.** اِنشَقّ [ʔinšaqq] *sv* a. Careful, the canvas is tearing! دِير بالَك، الجّادِر دَينشَقّ [diːr baːlak, ʔiččaːdir dayinšagg] • **3.** نِتَش [nitaš] نَتِش [natiš] *vn:* اِنّتَش [ʔinnitaš] *p:* She tore the letter out of his hand. نِتشَت المَكتُوب مِن إيدَه [nitšat ʔilmaktuːb min ʔiːdah] • **4.** قَصّ [gaṣṣ] قَصّ [gaṣṣ] *vn:* اِنقَصّ [ʔingaṣṣ] *p:* قِطَع [giṭaʕ] قَطِع [gaṭiʕ] *vn:* اِنقِطَع [ʔingiṭaʕ] *p:* Tear the coupon out of the magazine. قُصّ الكُوبَون مِن المَجَلَّة [guṣṣ ʔilkuːpuːn min ʔilmajalla] The button tore off. الدُّقمَة اِنقِطعَت [ʔiddugma ʔingiṭʕat] • **5.** شِلَع [šilaʕ] *sv* a. Who tore this page out of the book? مِنُو شِلَع هَالصَّفحَة مِن الكِتاب؟ [minu šilaʕ haṣṣafħa min ʔilkitaːb?]

to tear down • **1.** فَلَّش [fallaš] تَفلِيش، تفلِّش [tafaliːš, tfilliš] *vn:* تفَلَّش [tfallaš] *p:* He tore his house down. فَلَّش بَيتَه [fallaš baytah]

to tear open • **1.** فَكّ [fakk] فَكّ [fakk] *vn: sv* u. فِتَح [fitaħ] فَتِح [fatiħ] *vn: sv* a. Who tore the package open? مِنُو فَكّ الحُزمَة؟ [minu fakk ʔilħuzma?]

to tear up • **1.** شَقَّق [šaggag] تَشقِيق [tašgiːg] *vn: sv* i. I hope you tore that letter up. أتأمَّل إنتَ شَقَّقِت ذاك المَكتُوب [ʔatʔammal ʔinta šaggagit ðaːk ʔilmaktuːb] • **2.** فَكّ [fakk] فَكّ [fakk] *vn: sv* u. حَفَّر [ħaffar] تحُفُّر [tħuffur] *vn: sv* u. The workmen tore up the street in front of the house. العُمّال فَكَّوا الشّارِع قبال البَيت [ʔilʕummaːl fakkaw ʔiššaːriʕ gbaːl ʔilbayt]

tear • **1.** دَمعَة [damʕa] دَمعات [damʕaːt] *pl:* دمُوع [dmuːʕ] *Collective:* Tears ran down her cheeks. الدِّمُوع اِنحِدرَت عَلَى خدُودها [ʔiddimuːʕ ʔinħidrat ʕala xduːdha]

*** Tears won't help you.** • **1.** البِكَى ما يفِيدِك [ʔilbiča maː yfiːdič]

to tear • **1.** دَمَّع [dammaʕ] تَدمِيع [tadmiːʕ] *vn: sv* i. My eyes are tearing. عيُونِي دَتدَمِّع [ʕyuːni daddammiʕ]

tear gas • **1.** غاز مُسِيل لِلدُمُوع [ɣaːz musiːl liddumuːʕ]

to tease • **1.** داهَر [daːhar] دُهُر، مُداهَرَة [duhur, mudaːhara] *vn: sv* i. Everyone teases him. الكُلّ يداهرُوه [ʔilkull ydaːhruːh] Don't tease the dog. لا تداهِر الكَلِب [laː ddaːhir ʔiččalib]

tea shop • **1.** شايخانَة [čaːyxaːna] شايخانات [čaːyxaːnaːt] *pl:*

teasing • **1.** مداهَرَة [mdaːhara] I don't like this kind of teasing. ما يعجِبنِي هِيكِي مداهَرَة [maː yiʕǰibni hiːči mdaːhara]

tea spoon • **1.** خاشُوقَة شاي [xaːšuːgat čaːy] خواشِيق شاي [xwaːšiːg čaːy] *pl:*

T

technical • **1.** فَنِّي [fanni] The broadcast was called off for technical reasons. توَقّفت الإذاعَة لأسباب فَنِّيَّة [twaqqfat ʔilʔiðaːʕa lʔasbaːb fanniyya] There are several technical institutes in Iraq. أكُو عِدَّة مَعاهِد فَنِّيَّة بِالعِراق [ʔaku ʕiddat maʕaːhid fanniyya bilʕiraːq]

technicality • **1.** سَبَب فَنِّي [sabab fanni] أسباب فَنِّيَّة [ʔasbaːb fanniyya] *pl:* We lost the game due to a technicality. خسَرنا السِّباق لِسَبَب فَنِّي [xsarna ʔissibaːq lsabab fanni]

technician • **1.** فَنِّي [fanni]

technique • **1.** طَرِيقَة [ṭariːqa] طُرُق [ṭuruq] *pl:* أسلُوب [ʔusluːb] أساليب [ʔasaːliːb] *pl:* We'll have to improve our teaching techniques. لازِم نحَسِّن طَرِيقَتنا بِالتَّدرِيس [laːzim nħassin ṭariːqatna bittadriːs]

tedious • **1.** مُمِلّ [mumill] مُضَوِّج [muḍawwiǰ]

teen-ager • **1.** مُراهِق [muraːhiq] مُراهِقِين [muraːhiqiːn] *pl:*

to telecast • **1.** عِرَض بِالتَّلَفِيزيُون [ʕirað̣ bittalifizyuːn] عَرِض بِالتَّلَفِيزيُون [ʕarið̣ bittalifizyuːn] *vn: sv* i.

telegram • **1.** بَرقِيَّة [barqiyya] بَرقِيّات [barqiyyaːt] *pl:* I want to send a telegram. أَرِيد أدِزّ بَرقِيَّة [ʔariːd ʔadizz barqiyya]

telegraph • **1.** بَرق [barq] Where's the telegraph office? وين دائِرَة البَرق؟ [wiːn daːʔirat ʔilbarq?]

to telegraph • **1.** أبرَق [ʔabraq] إبراق [ʔibraːq] *vn: sv* i. Did he telegraph you? أبرَقلَك؟ [ʔabraqlak?]

telegraph operator • **1.** مَأمُور بَرق [maʔmuːr barq] مَأمُورِين بَرق [maʔmuːriːn barq] *pl:*

telephone • **1.** تِلِفَون [tilifuːn] تِلِفُونات [tilifuːnaːt] *pl:* May I use your telephone, please? تِسمَحلِي أستَعمِل تَلِفُونَك مِن فَضلَك؟ [tismaħli ʔastaʕmil talifuːnak min fað̣lak?]

to telephone • **1.** خابَر [xaːbar] مُخابَرَة [muxaːbara] *vn: sv* u. Did anybody telephone? أحَّد خابَر؟ [ʔaħħad xaːbar?]

telephone booth • **1.** مَقصُورَة تِلِفَون [maqṣuːrat tilifuːn] مَقصُورات تِلِفَون [maqṣuːraːt tilifuːn] *pl:*

telephone call • **1.** مُخابَرَة [muxaːbara] مُخابَرات [muxaːbaraːt] *pl:* I have to pay for every telephone call. لازِم أدفَع عَلَى كُلّ مُخابَرَة [laːzim ʔadfaʕ ʕala kull muxaːbara]

telephone directory • **1.** دَلِيل تِلِفَون [daliːl tilifuːn] أدِلَّة تِلِفَون [ʔadillat tilifuːn] *pl:* His name is in the telephone directory. إسمَه بِدَلِيل التِّلِفُون [ʔismah bdaliːl ʔittilifuːn]

telephoning • **1.** مُخابَرَة [muxaːbara] مُخابَرات [muxaːbaraːt] *pl:* Telephoning won't take much time. المُخابَرَة ما تاخُذ هوايَة وَقِت [ʔilmuxaːbara maː taːxuð hwaːya wakit]

telescope • **1.** تِلِسكُوب [talískuːp] تِلِسكُوبات [taliskuːpaːt] *pl:*

teletype • **1.** تِلِتايب [talitaːyp]

to televise • **1.** عِرَض بِالتَّلَفِيزيُون [ʕirað̣ bittalifizyuːn] عَرِض بِالتَّلَفِيزيُون [ʕarið̣ bittalafizyuːn] *vn: sv* i.

television • **1.** تِلِفِزيُون [tilifizyuːn] تَلَفِزيُونات [talifizyuːnaːt] *pl:*

to tell • **1.** قال [gaːl] قَول [gawl] *vn: sv* u. Tell him your name. قُلَّه شاسِمَك [gullah šʔismak] Tell me, what are you doing tonight? قُلِّي شراح تسَوِّي هاللَّيلَة [gulli šraːħ tsawwi hallayla] • **2.** حِچَى [ħičaː] حَكِي [ħači] *vn: sv* i. قال [gaːl] *sv* u. I wish I could tell you the whole story. يا رَيت أقدَر أحكِيلَك القُصَّة كُلّها [yaː riːt ʔagdar ʔaħčiːlak ʔilquṣṣa kullha] • **3.** عِرَف [ʕiraf] *sv* u. You can tell by his voice that he has a cold. تِقدَر تُعرُف مِن حِسَّه إنُّو مَنشُول [tigdar tuʕruf min ħissah ʔinnu manšuːl] • **4.** حِزَر [ħizar] حَزِر [ħazir] *vn: sv* i. Nobody could have told that in advance. مَحَّد كان يِقدَر يحزِر هاي لِقِدّام [maħħad čaːn yigdar yiħzir haːy ligiddaːm] • **5.** فَرَّق [farraq] تَفرِيق [tafriːq] *vn: sv* i. I can't tell one from the other. ما أقدَر أفَرِّق واحِد مِن اللّاخ [maː ʔagdar ʔafarriq waːħid min ʔillaːx] • **6.** سَبَّح [sabbaħ] تَسبِيح [tasbiːħ] *vn: sv* i. That old man is always telling his beads. الشَّيخ دائِماً يسَبِّح بمَسبَحتَه [ʔiššiːx daːʔiman ysabbiħ bmasbaħtah]

*** Can your little boy tell time yet?**
• **1.** إبنَك يِقدَر يقرا الساعَة لَو بَعَد؟ [ʔibnak yigdar yiqraː ʔissaːʕa law baʕad?]

*** To tell the truth, I don't know.** • **1.** بِالحَقِيقَة، آنِي ما أدرِي [bilħaqiːqa, ʔaːni maː ʔadri] والله ما أعرُف [wʔallah, maː ʔaʕruf]

*** You can tell by looking at him that he's been working hard.** • **1.** يبَيِّن عَلَيه كان دَيِشتُغُل بهِمَّة [ybayyin ʕaliːh čaːn dayištuɣul bhimma]

to tell a lie • **1.** كِذَب [čiðab] كِذِب [čiðib] *vn: sv* i. I told her a lie to get out of going to the party. كِذَبِت عَليها حَتَّى لا أرُوح لِلحَفلَة [kiðabit ʕaliːha ħatta laː ʔaruːħ lilħafla] • **2.** كَذَّب [čaððab, kaððab] *sv* i. He's always telling lies. عَلَى طُول يكَذِّب [ʕala ṭuːl yčaððib]

to tell apart • **1.** فَرَّق بَين، مَيَّز [farraq biːn, mayyaz] تَفرِيق تَميِيز [tafriːq, biːn, tamyiːz] *vn: sv* i. مَيَّز [mayyaz] تَميِيز [tamyiːz] *vn: sv* i. I can't tell these two materials apart. ما أقدَر أفَرِّق بين هَالقماشَين [maː ʔagdar ʔafarriq bayn halqmaːšayn]

teller • **1.** صَرّاف [ṣarraːf] صَرّافِين، صَرارِيف [ṣarraːfiːn, ṣaraːriːf] *pl:* He has worked ten years as teller in that bank.

اِشتِغَل صَرّاف عَشِر سنين بِذاك البَنك [ʔištiɣal ṣarra:f ʕašir sni:n bða:k ʔilbang]

temper • **1.** طَبُع [ṭabuʕ] He has an even temper. طَبعَه هادِي [ṭabʕah ha:di] • **2.** صَلابَة [ṣala:ba] This steel has more temper than iron. هَالفُولاذ بِيه صَلابَة أزيَد مِن الحَدِيد [halfu:la:ð bi:h ṣala:ba ʔazyad min ʔilħadi:d]

to lose one's temper • **1.** اِحتَدّ [ʔiħtadd] اِحتِداد [ʔiħtida:d] *vn: sv* a. He loses his temper easily. يِحتَدّ بِالعَجَل [yiħtadd bilʕaǰal]

to temper • **1.** سِقَى [siga:] سَقِي [sagy] *vn: sv* i. In Damascus they have tempered steel for hundreds of years. بِالشّام يِسقُون الفُولاذ صارِلهُم مِئات سنين [biššа:m yisgu:n ʔilfu:la:ð ṣa:rilhum miʔa:t sni:n]

temperamental • **1.** عَصَبِي [ʕaṣabi] She's very temperamental. هِيَّ كُلِّش عَصَبِيَّة [hiyya kulliš ʕaṣabiyya] / خُلُقها ضَيِّق [xulugha ḍayyig]

temperance • **1.** اِعتِدال [ʔiʕtida:l] He lives by temperance. يِعِيش بِاعتِدال [yiʕi:š biʕtida:l]

temperate • **1.** مُعتَدِل [muʕtadil] He is very temperate in his habits. هُوَّ كُلِّش مُعتَدِل بِعاداتَه [huwwa kulliš muʕtadil bʕa:da:tah] Europe is situated in the temperate zone. أورُبّا واقعَة بِالمَنطِقَة المُعتَدِلَة [ʔu:ruppa wa:qʕa bilmanṭiqa ʔalmuʕtadila]

temperature • **1.** سخُونَة [sxu:na] دَرَجَة حَرارَة [daraǰat ħara:ra] Her temperature went down today. سخُونَتها نِزلَت اليُوم [sxu:natha nizlat ʔilyu:m] • **2.** دَرَجَة حَرارَة [daraǰat ħara:ra] What was the highest temperature yesterday? شقَدّ كانَت أعلَى دَرَجَة حَرارَة البارحَة؟ [šgadd ča:nat ʔaʕla: daraǰat ħara:ra ʔilba:rħa?]

temple • **1.** مَعبَد [maʕbad] مَعابِد [maʕa:bid] *pl:* This church is built on the ruins of a Roman temple. هَالكَنِيسَة اِنبِنَت عَلَى خَرايِب مَعبَد رُومانِي [halkani:sa ʔinbinat ʕala xara:yib maʕbad ru:ma:ni] • **2.** تَوراة [tu:ra:t] I love to spend Friday night in the temple. أحِبّ أقضِي مَساء الجُمعَة بِالتَّورات [ʔaħibb ʔagḍi masa:ʔ ʔiǰǰumʕa bittu:ra:t] • **3.** صابِر [ṣa:bir] صَوابِر [ṣawa:bir] *pl:* The bullet struck him in the temple. الرِّصاصَة ضُربَتَه بِصابرَه [ʔirriṣa:ṣa ḍurbatah bṣa:brah]

temporary • **1.** مُوَقَّت [muwaqqat] وَقتِي [waqti] This is only a temporary solution. هَالحَلّ مُوَقَّت بَسّ [halħall muʔaqqat bass]

to tempt • **1.** غرا [ɣira:, ɣara:] إغراء [ʔiɣra:ʔ] *vn: sv* i. That doesn't tempt me. هَذا ما يِغرِينِي [ha:ða ma: yiɣri:ni] That doesn't tempt me. هَذا ما يسَوِّيلِي واهِس [ha:ða ma: ysawwi:li wa:his]

*** I was tempted to tell him the truth.** • **1.** صارلِي واهِس أقُلَّه الحَقِيقَة [ṣa:rli wa:his ʔagullah ʔilħaqi:qa]

temptation • **1.** إغراء [ʔiɣra:ʔ]

tempting • **1.** مُغرِي [muɣri] He made me a very tempting offer. عِرَض عَلَيّا عَرِض مُغرِي [ʕirað ʕalayya ʕarið muɣri]

ten • **1.** عَشرَة [ʕašra] It's ten o'clock. السّاعَة بِالعَشرَة [ʔissa:ʕa bilʕašra] • **2.** عَشرَة [ʕašra] عَشرات [ʕašra:t] *pl:* We're going on a vacation in ten days. رايحِين بإجازَة بَعَد عَشرَة أيّام [ra:yħi:n bʔiǰa:za baʕad ʕašrat ʔayya:m] • **3.** عَشِر [ʕašir] He has ten men working for him. عِندَه عَشِر رَياجِيل يِشتَغلُولَه [ʕindah ʕašir raya:ǰi:l yištaɣlu:lah]

tenacious • **1.** مُصِرّ [muṣirr] عَنُود [ʕanu:d]

tenaciously • **1.** بإصرار [bʔiṣra:r] He holds to his opinion tenaciously. مِتمَسِّك بِرَأيَه بإصرار [mitmassik braʔyah bʔiṣra:r]

tenant • **1.** مِستَأجِر [mistaʔǰir] مِستَأجِرِين [mistaʔǰiri:n] *pl:* He has been our tenant for ten years. هُوَّ مِستَأجِر عِدنا صارلَه عَشِر سنين [huwwa mistaʔǰir ʕidna ṣa:rlah ʕašir sni:n]

to tend • **1.** مال [ma:l] مَيَلان [mayala:n] *vn: sv* i. He tends to be partial in his judgments. يمِيل لِلتَّحَيُّز بِقَرَدار بال [ymi:l littaħayyuz bqara:ra:tah] • **2.** دار بال [da::r ba:l] *sv* i. Tend to your own business! دِير بالَك عَلَى شُغلَك [di:r ba:lak ʕala šuɣlak] Who's going to tend to the furnace? مِنُو راح يدِير بالَه عالفِرِن؟ [minu ra:ħ ydi:r ba:la ʕalfirin?]

tendency • **1.** مَيل، ميلان [mayl, mi:l, miyla:n] He has a tendency to exaggerate. عِندَه مَيل لِلمُبالَغَة [ʕindah mayl lilmuba:laɣa] • **2.** مَيل [mayl] مِيُول [myu:l] *pl:* اِتِّجاه [ʔittiǰa:h] اِتِّجاهات [ʔittiǰa:ha:t] *pl:* He has leftist tendencies. عِندَه مِيُول يَسارِيَّة [ʕindah myu:l yasa:riyya]

tender • **1.** فَرقُون وُقُود [fargu:n wuqu:d] فَرقُونات وُقُود [fargu:na:t wuqu:d] *pl:* Only the locomotive and the tender were derailed. بَسّ المَكِينَة وَفارقُون الوُقُود طِلعَوا مِن السِّكَّة [bass ʔilmaki:na wfa:rgu:n ʔilwuqu:d ṭilʕaw min ʔissičča] • **2.** طَرِي [ṭari] The meat is so tender you can cut it with a fork. اللَّحَم هَالقَدّ طَرِي الواحِد يقُصَّه بالجَّطَل [ʔillaħam halgadd ṭari ʔilwa:ħid yguṣṣah biččaṭal] • **3.** حَسّاس [ħassa:s] The bruise is still tender. الرَّضّ بَعدَه حَسّاس [ʔirraḍḍ baʕdah ħassa:s]

tendon • **1.** وَتَر [watar] أوتار [ʔawta:r] *pl:*

tenement • **1.** بَيت نِزِل [bayt nizil] بيُوت نِزِل [byu:t nizil] *pl:*

tennis • **1.** تَنِس [tanis]

tennis court • **1.** ساحَة تَنِس [sa:ħat tanis] ساحات تَنِس [sa:ħa:t tanis] *pl:*

tennis racquet • **1.** رَكِت [rakit] رَكِتات [rakita:t] *pl:*

tennis shoes • **1.** قُندَرَة لاستيك [qundarat la:sti:g] قَنادِر لاستِيك [qana:dir la:sti:g] *pl:* قُندَرَة رِياضَة [qundarat riya:ða] قَنادِر رِياضَة [qana:dir riya:ða] *pl:*

tense • **1.** مِتوَتِّر [mitwattir] The situation was tense. الحالَة كانَت مِتوَتِّرَة [ʔilħa:la ča:nat mitwattra] He's very tense these days. أعصابَه كُلِّش مِتوَتِّرَة هَالأيّام [ʔaʕṣa:bah kulliš mitwattra halʔayya:m] • **2.** صِيغَة [ṣi:ɣa] That verb is in the past tense. هَالفِعل بصِيغَة الماضِي [halfiʕil bṣi:ɣat ʔilma:ði]

tension • **1.** تَوَتُّر [tawattur] The world is in a state of tension these days. العالَم بحالَة تَوَتُّر هَالأيّام [ʔilʕa:lam bħa:lat tawattur halʔayya:m]

*** Those are high tension power lines.**

• **1.** هَالوايَرات بِيها قُوَّة كَهرَبائِيَّة عالِيَة [halwa:yara:t bi:ha quwwa kahraba:ʔiyya ʕa:lya]

tent • **1.** خَيمَة [xayma, xi:ma] خِيَم، خيام [xiyam, xya:m] *pl:* چادِر [ča:dir] چوادِر [čwa:dir] *pl:* The tent is made of canvas. الخَيمَة مَعمُولَة مِن الجُنفاص [ʔilxi:ma maʕmu:la min ʔilǰunfa:ṣ]

tenth • **1.** عاشِر [ʕa:šir] This is the tenth year I've been working at the same job. هاي السَّنَة العاشرَة آني أشتُغُل نَفس الشُّغُل [ha:y ʔissana ʔilʕa:šra ʔa:ni ʔaštuɣul nafs ʔiššuɣul] • **2.** عُشُر [ʕušur] أعشار [ʔaʕša:r] *pl:* It's not even one tenth finished. أصلاً عُشُرها ما خِلَص [ʔaṣlan ʕušurha ma: xilaṣ]

*** We get paid on the tenth of the month.**

• **1.** نِقبُض رَواتِبنا يَوم عَشرَة بالشَّهَر [niqbuð rawa:tibna yu:m ʕašra biššahar]

term • **1.** شَرط [šarṭ] شُرُوط [šuru:ṭ] *pl:* He gave us very good terms. إنطانا شُرُوط مُمتازَة [ʔinṭa:na šuru:ṭ mumta:za] • **2.** فَصِل [faṣil] فُصُول [fuṣu:l] *pl:* When does the fall school term begin? شوَقت يِبدي فَصل الدِّراسَة لِلخَريف؟ [šwakit yibdi faṣl ʔiddira:sa lilxari:f?] • **3.** مُدَّة [mudda] مُدَد [mudad] *pl:* He spent a four-year term in the presidency. قِضى مُدَّة أربَع سنِين بِالرِّئاسَة [giða: muddat ʔarbaʕ sni:n birriʔa:sa] • **4.** اِصطِلاح [ʔiṣṭila:ħ] اِصطِلاحات [ʔiṣṭila:ħa:t] *pl:* Do you know the technical term for it? تُعرُف الاصطِلاح الفَنِّي مالها؟ [tuʕruf ʔiliṣṭila:ħ ʔilfanni ma:lha?] • **5.** عِبارَة [ʕiba:ra] عِبارات [ʕiba:ra:t] *pl:* I told him in no uncertain terms what I think of him. قِتلَه رَأيي بِيه بِعِبارات صَرِيحَة [gitlah raʔyi bi:h bʕiba:ra:t ṣari:ħa] • **6.** عِلاقَة [ʕila:qa] عِلاقات [ʕila:qa:t] *pl:* We're on bad terms. عِلاقاتنا مُو زينَة [ʕila:qa:tna mu: zi:na]

*** We have been trying to come to terms for months now.** • **1.** صار إلنا أشهُر دَنرِيد نِتفاهَم [ṣa:rinna ʔašhur danri:d nitfa:ham] / صار إلنا أشهُر دَنرِيد نُوصَل إلَى اِتِّفاق [ṣa:r ʔilna ʔašhur danri:d nu:ṣal ʔila ʔittifa:q]

terminal • **1.** مَحَطَّة [maħaṭṭa] مَحَطّات [maħaṭṭa:t] *pl:* We have to pick up the trunks at the freight terminal. لازِم ناخُذ جُنَطنا مِن مَحَطَّة الشَّحِن [la:zim na:xuð ǰunaṭna min maħaṭṭat ʔiššaħin] • **2.** راس [ra:s] رُوس [ru:s] *pl:* The terminals of the battery are corroded. رُؤوس الباتري مزَنجِرَة [ruʔu:s ʔilpa:tri mzanǰira] • **3.** نِهائِي [niha:ʔi] You receive a month's terminal pay when you resign. تاخُذ راتِب شَهَر نِهائِي عِندَما تِستَقِيل [ta:xuð ra:tib šahar niha:ʔi ʕindama tistaqi:l]

to terminate • **1.** أنهَى [ʔanha:] إنهاء [ʔinha:ʔ] *vn: sv* i. فُسَخ [fusax] فَسِخ [fasix] *vn: sv* u. The company terminated his services. الشَّرِكَة أنهَت خَدَماتَه [ʔiššarika ʔanhat xadama:tah] The landlord terminated our lease. صاحِب المُلك فُسَخ عَقد الإيجار مالنا [ṣa:ħib ʔilmuluk fusax ʕaqd ʔilʔi:ǰa:r ma:lna] • **2.** خِلَص [xilaṣ] *sv* a. اِنتِهَى [ʔintiha:] اِنتِهاء [ʔintiha:ʔ] *vn: sv* i. My lease terminates in June. عَقد الإيجار مالِي يِخلَص بحُزَيران [ʕaqd ʔilʔi:ǰa:r ma:li yixlaṣ bħuzi:ra:n]

terminology • **1.** اِصطِلاح [ʔiṣṭila:ħ] Their terminology is not clear. مُصطَلَاحاتهُم مُو واضحَة [muṣṭala:ħa:thum mu: wa:ðħa]

termites • **1.** أرضَة [ʔarða] Our house has termites. بَيتنا بِيه أرضَة [baytna bi:h ʔarða]

terrace • **1.** طَرمَة [ṭarma] طَرامِي، طَرمات [ṭara:mi, ṭarma:t] *pl:* Let's all go sit on the terrace. خَلِّي نرُوح كُلنا نُقعُد بالطَّرمَة [xalli nru:ħ kullna nugʕud biṭṭarma]

terrain • **1.** أرض [ʔarð] أراضِي [ʔara:ði] *pl:* Around Baghdad the terrain is level. يَمّ بَغداد الأراضِي مِنبَسطَة [yamm baɣda:d ʔilʔara:ði minbasṭa]

terrible • **1.** فَظِيع [faði:ʕ] There was a terrible accident this morning. كان أكُو اِصطِدام فَظِيع اليَوم الصُّبُح [ča:n ʔaku ʔiṣṭida:m faði:ʕ ʔilyu:m ʔiṣṣubuħ] • **2.** مخَربَط [mxarbaṭ] The weather is terrible. الجَّوّ كُلِّش مخَربَط [ʔiǰǰaww kulliš mxarbaṭ] الجَّوّ كُلِّش مُو زين [ʔiǰǰaww kulliš mu: zi:n]

terribly • **1.** كُلِّش [kulliš] I'm terribly sorry. آني كُلِّش مِتأسِّف [ʔa:ni kulliš mitʔassif]

terrific • **1.** عَظِيم [ʕaði:m] عُظَماء [ʕuðama:ʔ] *pl:* His poetry is terrific. قَصِيدتَه عَظِيمَة [qaṣi:dtah ʕaði:ma] • **2.** هائِل [ha:ʔil] شَدِيد [šadi:d] Did you hear that terrific explosion today? سِمَعت الإنفِجار الهائِل اليَوم؟ [simaʕt ʔilʔinfiǰa:r ʔilha:ʔil ʔilyu:m?] He's under terrific pressure. هُوَّ تَحَت ضَغِط شَدِيد [huwwa taħat ðaɣiṭ šadi:d]

T

to terrify • **1.** رُعُب [ruʕub] إرعاب [ʔirʕaːb] *vn: sv* i. He brought me news that terrified me. جابلِي خَبَر رِعَبنِي بِيه [ǰaːbli xabar riʕabni biːh]

to be terrified • **1.** اِرتِعَب [ʔirtiʕab] *sv* i. I was terrified. اِرتِعَبِت [ʔirtiʕabit] I was terrified. مِتِت مِن الخُوف [mitit min ʔilxuːf]

terrifying • **1.** مُخِيف [muxiːf] مُرعِب [murʕib]

territory • **1.** أراضِي [ʔaraːḍ̣i] We will defend our territory. راح ندافِع عَن أراضِينا [raːħ ndaːfiʕ ʕan ʔaraːḍ̣iːna]

terror • **1.** خَوف [xuːf] رُعُب [ruʕub] We were speechless with terror. كِنّا جامدِين مِن الخُوف [činna ǰaːmdiːn min ʔilxuːf]

terrorism • **1.** إرهاب [ʔirhaːb] The dictator ruled through terrorism. الدِّكتاتُور حِكَم بالإرهاب [ʔiddiktatuːr ħikam bilʔirhaːb]

terrorist • **1.** إرهابِي [ʔirhaːbi]

to terrorize • **1.** أرهَب [ʔarhab] إرهاب [ʔirhaːb] *vn: sv* i. The bandits terrorized the countryside. قُطّاع الطُّرُق أرهِبَوا النّاس بالأرياف [quṭṭaːʕ ʔiṭṭuruq ʔarhibaw ʔinnaːs bilʔaryaːf]

test • **1.** اِمتِحان [ʔimtiħaːn] اِمتِحانات [ʔimtiħaːnaːt] *pl:* You have to take a test before you get a driver's license. لازِم تاخُذ اِمتِحان قَبُل ما تحَصِّل عَلَى إجازَة سِياقة [laːzim taːxuð ʔimtiħaːn gabul maː tħaṣṣil ʕala ʔiǰaːzat siyaːqa] Did you pass all your tests? نِجَحِت بكُلّ اِمتِحاناتَك؟ [niǰaħit bkull ʔimtiħaːnaːtak?] • **2.** فَحِص [faħiṣ] فُحُوص، فُحُوصات [fuħuːṣ, fuħuːṣaːt] *pl:* I had an eye test today. كان عِندِي فَحص عيُون اليُوم [čaːn ʕindi faħṣ ʕyuːn ʔilyuːm] • **3.** اِختِبار [ʔixtibaːr] اِختِبارات [ʔixtibaːraːt] *pl:* He made several tests during his experiment. سَوَّى عِدَّة اِختِبارات أثناء تَجرُبتَه [sawwaː ʕiddat ʔixtibaːraːt ʔaθnaːʔ taǰrubtah]

to test • **1.** اِمتِحَن [ʔimtiħan] اِمتِحان [ʔimtiħaːn] *vn: sv* i. I'll test half the class today. راح أمتِحِن نُصّ الصَّفّ اليُوم [raːħ ʔamtiħin nuṣṣ ʔiṣṣaff ʔilyuːm] I was tested in arithmetic today. اِمتِحَنِت بالحِساب هاليُوم [ʔimtiħanit bilħisaːb halyuːm] • **2.** فَحَص [fuħaṣ] فَحِص [faħiṣ] *vn: sv* a. Test the brakes. إفحَص البريك [ʔifħaṣ ʔilbrayk] Test this urine for sugar. إفحَص البُول وشُوف إذا بِيه سُكَّر [ʔifħaṣ ʔilbuːl wšuːf ʔiða biːh sukkar]

testicle • **1.** خُصوَة [xuṣwa] خَصاوِي، خِصيان [xaṣaːwi, xiṣyaːn] *pl:*

to testify • **1.** بَيَّن [bayyan] بَيان [bayaːn] *vn: sv* i. Have you anything further to testify? عِندَك بَعَد شِي تبَيّنَه [ʕindak baʕad ši tbayynah] • **2.** شِهَد [šihad] شَهادَة [šahaːda] *vn: sv* a. Can you testify to his honesty? تِقدَر تِشهَد بأمانتَه؟ [tigdar tišhad bʔamaːntah?]

testimony • **1.** شَهادَة [šahaːda] شَهادات [šahaːdaːt] *pl:* Can you add anything further to your testimony? أكُو بَعَد شِي تضِيفَه لِشَهادتَك [ʔaku baʕad ši dḍ̣iːfah lšahaːdtak]

testing • **1.** اِمتِحان [ʔimtiħaːn] اِمتِحانات [ʔimtiħaːnaːt] *pl:* The system of testing in this school is excellent. طَرِيقَة الامتِحان بهَالمَدرَسَة مُمتازَة [ṭariːqat ʔilʔimtiħaːn bhalmadrasa mumtaːza] • **2.** تَجرُبَة [taǰruba] تَجارُب [taǰaːrub] *pl:* We're about ready to resume atomic testing. إحنا عَلَى وَشَك نعِيد التَّجارُب الذَّرِّيَّة [ʔiħna ʕala wašak nʕiːd ʔittaǰaːrub ʔiððarriyya]

test tube • **1.** إنبُوبَة اِختِبار [ʔinbuːba ʔixtibaːr] أنابِيب اِختِبار [ʔanaːbiːb ʔixtibaːr] *pl:*

tetanus • **1.** كزّاز [gazzaːz, guzzaːz]

text • **1.** نَصّ [naṣṣ] نُصُوص [nuṣuːṣ] *pl:* The text of the speech is on page two. نَصّ الخِطاب مَوجُود بصَفحَة ثنَين [naṣṣ ʔilxiṭaːb mawǰuːd bṣafħa θnayn]

textbook • **1.** كتاب مَدرَسِي [ktaːb madrasi] كُتُب مَدرَسِيَّة [kutub madrasiyya] *pl:* كتاب مُقَرَّر [ktaːb muqarrar] كُتُب مُقَرَّرَة [kutub muqarrara] *pl:*

textile • **1.** نَسِيج [nasiːǰ] أنسِجَة [ʔansiǰa] *pl:* There is a new textile plant in Mosul. أكُو مَعمَل نَسِيج جِدِيد بالمُوصِل [ʔaku maʕmal nasiːǰ ǰidiːd bilmuːṣil] • **2.** قماش [qmaːš] قماشات، أقمِشَة [qmaːšaːt, ʔaqmiša] *pl:* نَسِيج [nasiːǰ] أنسِجَة [ʔansiǰa] *pl:* Egypt is famous for its cotton textiles. مَصِر مَشهُورَة بأقمِشَتها القُطنِيَّة [maṣir mašhuːra bʔaqmišatha ʔilquṭniyya]

texture • **1.** مَلمَس [malmas] مَلامِس [malaːmis] *pl:* Silk has a smooth texture. الحَرِير مَلمَسَه ناعِم [ʔalħariːr malmasah naːʕim]

than • **1.** مِن [min] He's older than his brother. هُوَّ أكبَر مِن أخُوه [huwwa ʔakbar min ʔaxuːh] I appreciate him more than ever. أقَدّرَه أزيَد مِن قَبُل [ʔaqaddrah ʔazyad min gabul] • **2.** بَدَلما [badalma] بدال ما [bidal maː] I'd rather stay home than go to that dull play. أفَضِّل أبقَى بالبَيت بَدَل ما أرُوح بهَالرُّوايَة اللِّي تضَوِّج [ʔafaḍ̣ḍ̣il ʔabqaː bilbayt badalma ʔaruːħ bharruwaːya ʔilli dḍ̣awwiǰ]

to thank • **1.** شِكَر [šikar] شُكُر [šukur] *vn: sv* u. I haven't even thanked him yet. بَعَد لهَسَّة ما شكَرتَه [baʕad lhassa maː škartah]

*** Thank goodness!** • **1.** الحَمدُ لِله [ʔilħamdu lillaːh]

thankful • **1.** مَمنُون [mamnuːn] شاكِر [šaːkir] We are very thankful to you. إحنا هوايَة مَمنُونِين [ʔiħna hwaːya mamnuːniːn]

T

thanks • **1.** شُكُر [šukur] I don't expect any thanks or praise. ما اَنتِظِر أَيّ شُكُر أَو ثَناء [maː ʔantiðir ʔayy šukur ʔaw θanaːʔ] • **2.** فَضِل [faḍil] It's no thanks to him that I'm here. الفَضِل مُو إِلَه بِجَيتِي [ʔilfaḍil muː ʔilah bǰayti]

* **Thanks a lot.** • **1.** شُكراً جَزِيلاً [šukran ǰaziːlan]

that • **1.** ذاك [ðaːk] ذُوك، ذُولاك [ðuːk, ðuːlaːk] *pl:* ذِيك [ðiːč] *Feminine:* هَذاك [haːðaːk] هَذِيك [haðiːč] *Feminine:* What's that? ذاك شِنُو؟ [ðaːk šinu?] What's that? شِنُو هَذاك؟ [šinuː haðaːk?] That girl is my sister. ذِيك البِنت أُختِي [ðiːč ʔilbint ʔuxti] That girl is my sister. ذِيك البَنَيَّة أُختِي [ðiːč ʔilbnayya ʔuxti] What does that mean? شِنُو مَعنى ذاك؟ [šinuː maʕnaː ðaːk?] What does that mean? ذِيك شتِعنِي؟ [ðiːč štiʕni?] • **2.** اللّي ,ال- [ʔil, ʔilli] Do you know the story that he told us? تُعرُف الحكايَة اللِي حِكالنا إيّاها؟ [tuʕruf ʔilhčaːya ʔilli hičaːlna ʔiyyaːha?] Who's the man that just came in? مِنُو الرِّجّال اللّي إجا هَسَّة؟ [minu ʔirrijǰaːl ʔilli ʔiǰa hassa?] • **3.** أَنّ [ʔann] They told me that you were ill. قالُولِي إِنَّك كِنِت وِجعان [gaːluːli ʔinnak činit wiǰʕaːn] • **4.** هَل [hal] I don't want that much milk. ما أَرِيد هَالقَدّ حَلِيب [maː ʔariːd halgadd haliːb]

at that • **1.** وَلَو هِيكِي [walaw hiːči] Even at that I wouldn't pay more. وَلَو هِيكِي آنِي ما أَدفَع أَزيَد [walaw hiːči ʔaːni maː ʔadfaʕ ʔazyad] • **2.** مَعَ هَذا [maʕa haːða] At that it costs only two dinars. مَعَ هَذا، يكَلِّف دِينارَين بَسّ [maʕa haːða, ykallif dinaːrayn bass] • **3.** عَلَى هَالحَطَّة [ʕala halhaṭṭa] عَلَى هَالشِكِل [ʕala haššikil] We'll leave it at that. خَلِّي نخَلِّيها عَلَى هَالحَطَّة [xalli nxalliːha ʕala halhaṭṭa]

that is • **1.** يَعنِي [yaʕni] I'll come tomorrow, that is, if it doesn't rain. أَجِي باكِر، يَعنِي، إذا ما مُطرَت [ʔaǰi baːčir, yaʕni, ʔiða maː muṭrat]

thaw • **1.** ذَوَبان ثَلِج [ðawabaːn θaliǰ] مَوع ثَلِج [mawʕ θaliǰ] This year the thaw set in rather early. ذَوَبان الثَّلِج بِدا مِن وَقِت هالسَّنَة [ðawabaːn ʔiθθaliǰ bidaː min wakit hassana]

to thaw • **1.** ذاب الثَّلِج، ماع الثَّلِج [ðaːb ʔiθθilǰ, maːʕ ʔiθθilǰ] *sv* u. ماع [maːʕ] *sv* u. It's thawing. الثَّلِج دَيذُوب [ʔiθθaliǰ dayðuːb] Has the refrigerator thawed out yet? ماع الثَّلِج اللّي بِالثَّلّاجَة؟ [maːʕ ʔiθθaliǰ ʔilli biθθallaːǰa?]

the • **1.** ال [ʔil] The house is big. البَيت كِبِير [ʔilbayt čibiːr] Please pass me the butter. بالله ناوُشنِي الزِّبِد [ballah naːwušni ʔizzibid]

* **The sooner we're paid the better.**

• **1.** كُلّما يِنطُونا فلُوسنا مِن وَقِت، أَحسَن [kullma yinṭuːna fluːsna min wakit, ʔahsan]

theater • **1.** قاعَة تَمثِيل [qaːʕat tamθiːl] قاعات تَمثِيل [qaːʕaːt tamθiːl] *pl:* Our theater has a modern stage. قاعَة التَّمثِيل مالتِنا بِيها مَسرَح عَصرِي [qaːʕat ʔittamθiːl maːlatna biːha masrah ʕaṣri] • **2.** سِينَما [sinama] سِينَمات [sinamaːt] *pl:* Most movie theaters in Baghdad are in Bab el Sharji. أَكثَر السِّينَمات بِبَغداد بِباب الشَّرجِي [ʔakθar ʔissinamaːt bibaydaːd bibaːb ʔiššarǰi]

theft • **1.** بُوقَة [buːga] بَوقات [bawgaːt] *pl:* سَرِقَة [sariqa] سَرِقات [sariqaːt] *pl:* The theft was discovered the next morning. اِكتِشفَوا البَوقَة ثانِي يوم الصُّبُح [ʔiktišfaw ʔilbawga θaːni yuːm ʔiṣṣubuh]

their • **1.** هُم [hum] Do you know their address? تُعرُف عِنوانهُم؟ [tuʕruf ʕinwaːnhum?]

theirs • **1.** مالهُم [maːlhum] This book is theirs. هَالكِتاب مالهُم [halkitaːb maːlhum] • **2.** مال، مالَة [maːl, maːla(t)] [ʔamwaːl] *pl:* We'll go in our car, and they'll take theirs. نرُوح بسَيّارَتنا، وهُمَّة يرُوحُون بمالَتهُم [nruːh bsayyaːratna, whumma yruːhuːn bmaːlathum]

* **Our house isn't as big as theirs.** • **1.** بَيتنَا مُو بقَدّ بَيتهُم [baytna muːbgadd baythum]

* **Are you a friend of theirs?** • **1.** إِنتَ صَدِيقهُم؟ [ʔinta ṣadiːqhum?]

them • **1.** هُم [hum] I don't want to have anything to do with them. ما أَرِيد أَدَخِّل نَفسِي وِيّاهُم [maː ʔariːd ʔadaxxil nafsi wiyyaːhum] • **2.** -ها [-ha] The papers are on the floor; will you please pick them up? الأوراق بِالقاع؛ ما تشِيلها بالله؟ [ʔilʔawraːq bilgaːʕ; maː tšiːlha ballah?]

theme • **1.** مَوضُوع [mawḍuːʕ] مَواضِيع [mawaːḍiːʕ] *pl:* Why did you pick that theme? لوَيش اِنتِخَبِت هَالمَوضُوع؟ [lwiːš ʔintixabit halmawḍuːʕ?] • **2.** إِنشاء [ʔinšaːʔ] إِنشاءات [ʔinšaːʔaːt] *pl:* Have you finished your theme for tomorrow? كِتَبِت الإِنشاء مالَك مال باكِر؟ [kitabit ʔilʔinšaːʔ maːlak maːl baːčir?]

themselves • **1.** نَفِس [nafis] نفُوس، أَنفُس [nufuːs, ʔanfus] *pl:* They did it themselves. هُمَّ سَوُّوها بِنَفِسهُم [humma sawwuːha bnafishum]

* **The pair divided the money between themselves.**

• **1.** ثنَينهُم تقاسمَوا الفلُوس بَينهُم [θnaynhum tqaːsmaw ʔilifluːs baynhum]

then • **1.** بَعدَين [baʕdayn] تالِي [taːli] تُوالِي [tuwaːli] *pl:* What did he do then? وبَعدين شسَوَّى؟ [wbaʕdiːn ššawwaːʔ?] • **2.** لَعَد [laʕad] Then everything is O. K. لَعَد كُلّشِي زين [laʕad kullši ziːn] Well, then, let's go. زين، لَعَد خَلِّي نرُوح [ziːn, laʕad xalli nruːh] • **3.** عُود [ʕuːd] ذاك الوَقِت [ðaːk ʔilwakit] Call Tuesday. We'll know by then. خابُر الثَّلاثاء، عُود يصِير عِدنا مَعلُوم [xaːbur ʔiθθilaːθaːʔ, ʕuːd yṣiːr ʕidna maʕluːm] • **4.** ذاك الوَقِت [ðaːk ʔilwakit] He did it right then, rather than waiting. سَوّاها بذاك الوَقِت، بَدَل ما يِنتِظِر [sawwaːha bðaːk ʔilwakit, badalma yintiðir]

* **We go to the movies now and then.**

• **1.** نرُوح لِلسِينَما بَين مُدَّة ومُدَّة [nruːh lissinama bayn mudda wmudda]

then and there • **1.** رَأساً [raʔsan] Why didn't you take it then and there? لِيش ما أَخَذتها رَأساً؟ [liːš maː ʔaxaðitha raʔsan?]

theoretical • **1.** نَظَرِي [naðari] That's a theoretical solution. هَذَا حَلّ نَظَرِي [haːða ħall naðari]

theoretically • **1.** نَظَرِيّاً [naðariyyan] Theoretically the experiment should turn out all right. نَظَرِيّاً التَّجرُبَة لازِم تِنجَح [naðariyyan ǰittaǰruba laːzim tinǰaħ]

theory • **1.** نَظَرِيَّة [naðariyya] نَظَرِيّات [naðariyyaːt] *pl:*

there • **1.** هناك [hnaːk] Have you ever been there? بعُمرَك رايِح هناك؟ [bʕumrak raːyiħ hnaːk?]

*** I'm afraid he's not quite all there.** • **1.** يبَيِّن مَشخُوط [ybayyin mašxuːṭ]

*** There you are! I was looking all over for you.** • **1.** هِيّاتَك، كِنِت دادَوِّر عَلَيك بكُلّ مَكان [hiyyaːtak, činit daːdawwir ʕaliːk bkull makaːn]

there is, are • **1.** أكُو [ʔaku] There are a few good hotels in town. أكُو كَم أُوتَيل زين بالوِلايَة [ʔaku čam ʔutiːl ziːn bilwilaːya] Are there such people? أكُو هِيكِي ناس؟ [ʔaku hiːči naːs?] There aren't enough chairs. ماكُو سكَملِيّات كافيَة [maːku skamliyyaːt kaːfya]

thereabouts • **1.** ذِيك الأطراف [ðiːč ʔilʔaṭraːf] Are there any banks thereabouts? أكُو بَنك بذِيك الأطراف؟ [ʔaku bang bðiːč ʔilʔaṭraːf?]

therefore • **1.** لِذلِك [liðaːlik] لِهَذا [lihaːða] Therefore I assume it is so. لِذلِك أعتقِد هِيَّ هَالشَّكِل [liðaːlik ʔaʕtiqid hiyya haššikil]

thermometer • **1.** ثَرمُومَتِر [θarmumaːtir] ثَرمُومَترات [θarmumaːtraːt] *pl:*

these • **1.** ذُولَة [ðuːla] هَذُولَة [haðuːla] I like these better. ذُولَة يعجبُونِي أزيَد [ðuːla yʕiǰbuːni ʔazyad] These are good workmen. هذُولَة خُوش عُمّال [hðuːla xuːš ʕummaːl] • **2.** هَل [hal] These boys are good students. هالوُلِد خُوش تِلمِيذ [halwulid xuːš tilmiːð] These cigarettes are Turkish. هَالجِكايِر تُركِيَّة [halǰigaːyir turkiyya] Everything is very expensive these days. كُلّشِي غالِي هَالأيّام [kullši ɣaːli halʔayyaːm]

*** I'll attend to it one of these days.** • **1.** راح أسَوِّيها يَوم مِن الأيّام [raːħ ʔasawwiːha yuːm min ʔilʔayyaːm]

thesis • **1.** نَظَرِيَّة [naðariyya] نَظَرِيّات [naðariyyaːt] *pl:* فَرَضِيَّة [faraðiyya] فَرَضِيّات [faraðiyyaːt] *pl:* His thesis proved to be right. نَظَرِيتَه اِنثِبتَت صِحَّتها [naðariːtah ʔinθibtat ṣiħħatha] • **2.** أُطرُوحَة [ʔuṭruːħa] أُطرُوحات [ʔuṭruwħaːt] *pl:* He wrote an excellent master's thesis. كِتَب أُطرُوحَة مُمتازَة لشِهادَة الماجِستِير [kitab ʔuṭruːħa mumtaːza lšihaːdat ʔilmaːǰistiːr]

they • **1.** هُمَّة، هُمَّ [humma] They're my friends. هُمَّ أصدِقائِي [humma ʔaṣdiqaːʔi]

*** They're leaving tomorrow.** • **1.** مسافرِين باكِر [msaːfriːn baːčir]

*** They work for me.** • **1.** يِشتِغلُولِي [yištiɣluːli]

thick • **1.** ثِخِين [θixiːn] The soup is too thick. الشَّوربَة كُلّش ثِخِينَة [ʔiššuːrba kulliš θixiːna] This board isn't that thick. هَاللَّوحَة ما هَالقَدّ ثِخِينَة [hallawħa maː halgadd θixiːna] He's too thick to understand that. هَذا دَماغَه ثخِين؛ ما يِفهَم هِيكِي أشياء [haːða damaːɣah θxiːn; maː yifham hiːči ʔašyaːʔ]

*** The crowd was very thick at the scene of the accident.** • **1.** كان قَلَبالِغ بمَحَلّ الحادِث [čaːn qalabaːliɣ bmaħall ʔilħaːdiθ]

*** I'll go through thick and thin for him.** • **1.** أتحَمَّل المُرّ والحامُض عَلَى مُودَه [ʔatħammal ʔilmurr wilħaːmuð ʕala muːdah]

*** Wherever there's a fight, he's in the thick of it.** • **1.** وَينما أكُو عَركَة، تِلقِيه بنُصّها [waynma ʔaku ʕarka, tilgiːh bnuṣṣha]

to thicken • **1.** ثِخَن [θixan] ثُخُونَة [θuxuːna] *vn: sv* a. The sauce will thicken if you leave it on the fire to boil. المَرقَة راح تِثخَن إذا تخَلِّيها عَالنّار تفَوُّر [ʔalmarga raːħ tiθxan ʔiða txalliːha ʕannaːr tfawwur] • **2.** ثَخَّن [θaxxan] تَثخِين [taθxiːn] *vn:* تثَخَّن [tθaxxan] *p:* Thicken the sauce with tomato paste. ثَخِّن المَرقَة بمَعجُون طَماطَة [θaxxin ʔilmarga bmaʕǰuːn ṭamaːṭa]

thicket • **1.** دَغَل [daɣal]

thickness • **1.** ثُخُن [θuxun] What is the thickness of that cardboard? شقَدّ ثُخُن هَالمقَوّايَة؟ [šgadd θuxun halimqawwaːya?]

thickset • **1.** مرَصرَص [mraṣraṣ] He's quite thickset. هَذا كُلّش مرَصرَص [haːða kulliš mraṣraṣ]

thick-skinned • **1.** سَفِيه [safiːh] She's thick-skinned, so she didn't mind the insult. هَذِي سَفِيحَة، وَما دارَت بال لِلإهانَة [haːði safiːħa, wama daːrat baːl lilʔihaːna]

thief • **1.** حَرامِي [ħaraːmi] حَرامِيَّة [ħaraːmiyya] *pl:* Stop, thief! إلزَمُوا الحَرامِي [ʔilzamuː ʔilħaraːmi]

thievery • **1.** بَوق [bawg, buːg]

thigh • **1.** فُخُذ [fuxuð] أفخاذ [ʔafxaːð] *pl:*

thimble • **1.** كُشتُبان [kuštubaːn, kištibaːn, kišitbaːn] كِشِتبانات [kišitbaːnaːt] *pl:*

thin • **1.** خَفِيف [xafiːf] The paper is too thin. هَالوَرقَة كُلّش خَفِيفَة [halwarqa kulliš xafiːfa] That soup is rather thin. الشَّوربَة خَفِيفَة شوَيَّة [ʔiššuːrba xafiːfa šwayya] • **2.** ضعِيف [ðʕiːf] ضَعفان [ðaʕfaːn] *pl:* She's gotten thin.

T

صايرَة ضعِيفَة [ṣaːyra ðiʕiːfa] She's gotten thin. ضُعفَت [ðuʕfat] Her face has gotten very thin. وجِهها صاير كُلّش ضعِيف [wiččha ṣaːyir kulliš ðiʕiːf] • **3.** رفِيع [rifiːʕ] That stick's too thin. هَالعُودَة كُلّش رفِيعَة [halʕuːda kulliš rifiːʕa] • **4.** واهي [waːhi] That's a pretty thin excuse. هَذا فَدّ عُذُر كُلّش واهي [haːða fadd ʕuður kulliš waːhi]

*** I'll go through thick and thin for him.** • **1.** أتحَمَّل المُرّ والحامُض عَلَى مُودَه [ʔatħammal ʔilmurr wilħaːmuð ʕala muːdah]

to get thin • **1.** ضعَف [ðiʕaf] ضُعُف [ðuʕuf] *vn: sv* a. You've gotten thin. ضعَفِت [ðiʕafit]

to thin • **1.** خَفّ [xaff] خَفّ [xaff] *vn: sv* u. His hair is thinning. شَعرَه دَيخُفّ [šaʕrah dayxuff] • **2.** خَفَّف [xaffaf] تَخفِيف [taxfiːf] *vn: sv* u. Thin this paint. خَفّف هَالصُّبُغ [xaffuf haṣṣubuɣ]

to thin out • **1.** خَفّ [xaff] خَفّ [xaff] *vn: sv* u. Let's wait until this crowd thins out. خَلّي نِنتِظِر إلَى أن يخُفّ الازدِحام [xalli nintiðir ʔila ʔan yxuff ʔilʔizdiħaːm]

thing • **1.** شِي [ši] أشياء [ʔašyaːʔ] *pl:* حاجَة [ħaːja] حاجات، حَوايِج [ħaːjaːt, ħawaːyij] *pl:* Some funny things have been going on here. شوَيَّة أشياء غَرِيبَة دَتصِير هنا [šwayya ʔašyaːʔ ɣariːba datṣiːr hna] I don't know the first thing about it. ما أعرُف أيّ شِي عَنها [maː ʔaʕruf ʔayy ši ʕanha] We've heard a lot of nice things about you. سمَعنا هوايَة أشياء زينَة عَنَّك [simaʕna hwaːya ʔašyaːʔ ziːna ʕannak] It all adds up to the same thing. أوَّل وتالِي كُلّها فَدّ شِي [ʔawwal wtaːli kullha fadd ši] That's an entirely different thing. هَذا فَدّ شِي يختِلِف تَماماً [haːða fadd ši yixtilif tamaːman]

*** I didn't have a thing to do with it.** • **1.** ما كان إلي أيّ عَلاقَة بهَذا [maː čaːn ʔili ʔayy ʕalaːqa bhaːða]

the real thing • **1.** مِن صُدُق [min ṣudug] This time it's the real thing. هَالنَّوبَة مِن صُدُق [hannawba min ṣudug]

the thing (to do, etc.) • **1.** أحسَن شِي [ʔaħsan ši] The thing to do is to go home. أحسَن شِي واحِد يرُوح لِلبَيت [ʔaħsan ši waːħid yiruːħ lilbayt]

things • **1.** هدُوم [hduːm] Put on your things and let's go for a walk. إلبَس هدُومَك وَخَلّي نِطلَع نِتمَشّى [ʔilbas hduːmak wxalli niṭlaʕ nitmaššaː] • **2.** أمُر [ʔamur] أوامِر [ʔawaːmir] *pl:* حال [ħaːl] أحوال [ʔaħwaːl] *pl:* Things have got to improve. الأمُور لازِم تِتحَسَّن [ʔilʔumuːr laːzim titħassan] • **3.** غراض [ɣaraːð] Have you packed your things yet? لَمَّيت غراضَك لَو بَعَد؟ [lammayt ɣaraːðak law baʕad?]

of all things • **1.** عَجِيب [ʕajiːb] Well of all things, what are you doing here? عَجِيب، إنتَ شدَتسَوِّي هنا؟ [ʕajiːb, ʔinta šdatsawwi hna?]

to see things • **1.** تخَيَّل [txayyal] تَخَيُّل [taxayyul] *vn: sv* a. You're just seeing things. إنتَ بَسّ دَتِتخَيَّل [ʔinta bass datitxayyal]

to think • **1.** افتِكَر [ʔiftikar] افتِكار [ʔiftikaːr] *vn: sv* i. فَكَّر [fakkar] تَفكِير [tafkiːr] *vn: sv* i. Don't you think it's too warm? ما تِفتِكِر الدِّنيا كُلّش حارَّة؟ [maː tiftikir ʔiddinya kulliš ħaːrra?] • **2.** اعتِقَد [ʔiʕtiqad] اعتِقاد [ʔiʕtiqaːd] *vn: sv* i. I think he stated it plainly. أعتِقِد هُوَّ بَيَّنها بوُضُوح [ʔaʕtiqid huwwa bayyanha biwuðuːħ] He thinks his son is clever. يعتِقِد إبنَه كُلّش شاطِر [yiʕtiqid ʔibnah kulliš šaːṭir] • **3.** ظَنّ [ðann] ظَنّ [ðann] *vn: sv* i. I thought you were from the country. ظَنَّيت إنتَ مِن سُكّان الأرياف [ðanniːt ʔinta min sukkaːn ʔilʔaryaːf] I don't think I'll go. ما أظُنّ راح أرُوح [maː ʔaðunn raːħ ʔaruːħ] • **4.** شاف [šaːf] شَوف [šawf] *vn: sv* u. I don't think it's in your interest to do this. ما أشُوف مِن مَصلَحتَك تسَوِّي هاي [maː ʔašuːf min maṣlaħtak tsawwi haːy]

*** He's never really learned how to think.** • **1.** أبَد ما تعَلَّم يستَعمِل فِكرَه [ʔabad maː tʕallam yistaʕmil fikrah]

*** That's what you think, but you're wrong!** • **1.** هَذا رَأيَك، لَكِن إنتَ غَلطان [haːða raʔyak, laːkin ʔinta ɣalṭaːn]

*** Now he thinks differently.** • **1.** هَسَّة تبَدَّل فِكرَه [hassa tbaddal fikrah]

*** He thinks nothing of driving all night.** • **1.** ما يهِمَّه لَو ساق اللَّيل كُلَّه [maː yhimma law saːq ʔillayl kullah]

to think about • **1.** فَكَّر [fakkar] تَفكِير [tafkiːr] *vn: sv* i. I've been thinking about it all afternoon. صارلِي النَّهار كُلَّه دَأفَكِّر بِيها [ṣaːrli ʔinnahaːr kullah daʔafakkir biːha] They're thinking about getting married. دَيفَكّرُون بالزَّواج [dayfakkruːn bizzawaːj]

to think out • **1.** تبَصَّر ب [tbaṣṣar b-] تَبَصُّر [tabaṣṣur] *vn: sv* a. He doesn't think things out very far. ما يتبَصَّر هوايَة بالأمُور [maː yitbaṣṣar hwaːya bilʔumuːr]

to think over • **1.** فَكَّر [fakkar] تَفكِير [tafkiːr] *vn: sv* i. دانَش [daːnaš] مُدانَشَة [mudaːnaša] *vn: sv* i. He's still thinking it over. بَعدَه دَيدانِش فِكرَه [baʕdah daydaːniš fikrah] He's still thinking it over. بَعدَه دَيفَكّر بِيها [baʕdah dayfakkir biːha]

thinker • **1.** مُفَكِّر [mufakkir] مُفَكّرِين [mufakkiriːn] *pl:* Plato was a great thinker. أفلاطُون كان مُفَكِّر عَظِيم [ʔaflaṭuːn čaːn mufakkir ʕaðiːm]

thinking • **1.** تَفكِير [tafkiːr] Thinking about it won't help. التَّفكِير بِيها ما بِيه فائِدَة [ʔattafkiːr biːha maː biːh faːʔida]

*** That's wishful thinking.** • **1.** هَذِي تَمَنِّيات [haːði tamanniyaːt]

thinly • **1.** * Put the paint on thinly. لا تكَثّر الصُّبُغ [laː tkaθθir ʔiṣṣubuɣ] * The valley is thinly forested. هَالوادِي بِيه شوَيَّة أشجار [halwaːdi biːh šwayya ʔašjaːr] * This area is thinly settled. هَالمَنطِقَة ما مِزدَحمَة بالسُّكّان [halmanṭiqa maː mizdaħma bissukkaːn]

thinner • **1.** أضعَف [ʔaðʕaf] He's thinner than his brother. هُوَّ أضعَف مِن أخُوه [huwwa ʔaðʕaf min ʔaxuːh] • **2.** أخفَف

[ʔaxfaf] Can you make it a little thinner? ما تسَوِّي شوَيَّة أَخَفّ؟ [maː tsawwi šwayya ʔaxaff?] • **3.** أرفَع [ʔarfaʕ] أضعَف [ʔaðʕaf] It'll have to be thinner to fit. لازِم تكُون أرفَع حَتَّى ترهَم [laːzim tkuːn ʔarfaʕ ħatta tirham]

to get thinner • 1. ضَعَّف نَفسَه [ðaʕʕaf nafsah] تَضعِيف نفس [taðʕiːf nafs] *vn: sv* u. She wants to get thinner. ترِيد تضعُّف نَفِسها [triːd dðaʕʕuf nafisha]

thinness • 1. ضُعُف [ðuʕuf] Her thinness worries me. ضُعُفها دَيقِلقنِي [ðuʕufha dayiqliqni]

third • 1. ثِلِث [θiliθ, θuluθ] أثلاث [ʔaθlaːθ] *pl:* A third of that will be enough. ثُلث هاي يكَفِّي [θuluθ haːy ykaffi] • **2.** ثالِث [θaːliθ] We couldn't stay for the third act. ما قدَرنا نِبقى لِلفَصل الثّالِث [maː gidarna nibqaː lilfaṣl ʔiθθaːliθ]

third-class • 1. دَرَجَة ثالثَة [daraǰa θaːlθa] Give me one third-class ticket to Basra. إنطِينِي تِكِت دَرَجَة ثالثَة لِلبَصرَة [ʔinṭiːni tikit daraǰa θaːlθa lilbaṣra] • **2.** ثالِث باب [θaːliθ baːb] ثالِث دَرَج [θaːliθ daraǰa] This wool is third class. هَالصُّوف ثالِث باب [haṣṣuːf θaːliθ baːb]

thirdly • 1. ثالِثاً [θaːliθan] First of all it's expensive, secondly it's impractical, and thirdly it's difficult to get. أوَّلاً غالية، ثانِياً مُو عَمَلِيَّة، وَثالِثاً صَعُب تَحصِيلها [ʔawwalan ɣaːlya, θaːniyan muː ʕamaliyya, wθaːliθan ṣaʕub taħṣiːlha]

thirst • 1. عَطَش [ʕaṭaš] I can't quench my thirst. ما دَأقدَر أروِي عَطَشِي [maː daʔagdar ʔarwi ʕaṭaši]

*** He still has his thirst for adventure.**

• **1.** بَعدَه يحِبّ المُغامَرات [baʕdah yħibb ʔilmuɣaːmaraːt]

thirsty • 1. عَطشان [ʕaṭšaːn] عَطاشَة، عَطشانِين [ʕaṭaːša, ʕaṭšaːniːn] pl: I'm very thirsty. آني كُلِّش عَطشان [ʔaːni kulliš ʕaṭšaːn] We all are very thirsty. كُلّنا كِنّا عطاشَة [kullna činna ʕṭaːša]

thirteen • 1. ثلَطَّعَش [tlaṭṭaʕaš]

thirteenth • 1. الثّلَطَّعَش [ʔ itlaṭṭaʕaš] He came on the thirteenth. جا يوم الثّلَطَّعَش [ǰaː yuːm ʔitlaṭṭaʕaš] I stopped reading after the thirteenth page. بَطَّلت القِرايَة بَعد الصَّحِيفَة الثّلَطَّعَش [baṭṭalt ʔilqiraːya baʕd ʔiṣṣaħiːfa ʔitlaṭṭaʕaš] Who was thirteenth in the class? مِنُو طِلَع تلَطَّعَش بِالصَّفّ؟ [minu ṭilaʕ tlaṭṭaʕaš biṣṣaff?]

thirtieth • 1. الثلاثِين [ʔiθθlaːθiːn, ʔittlaːθiːn]

thirty • 1. ثلاثِين [θlaːθiːn, tlaːθiːn] This month has thirty days. هَالشَّهَر بِيه ثلاثِين يوم [haššahar biːh tlaːθiːn yuːm] • **2.** نُصّ [nuṣṣ] It's three thirty. السّاعَة ثلاثَة ونُصّ [ʔissaːʕa tlaːθa wnuṣṣ]

this • 1. هَذا [haːða] هَل [hal] هاذِي [haːði] *Feminine:* هاي [haːy] هَذِي [haːði] *Feminine:* Do you know this man? تُعرُف هَالرِّجّال؟ [tuʕruf harriǰǰaːl?] Is this the same tie I saw? هَذا نَفس الرِّباط اللّي شِفتَه؟ [haːða nafs ʔirribaːṭ ʔilli šiftah?] This is on me. هاي عَلَى حسابِي [haːy ʕala ħsaːbi] This is on me. هَذا عَلَيّا [haːða ʕalayya] What's this? شِنُو هاي؟ [šinuː haːy?] What's this? هاي شِنُو؟ [haːy šinu?] This is just what I wanted to avoid. هاي اللّي كِنِت دَأرِيد أتفاداها [haːy ʔilli činit daʔariːd ʔatfaːdaːha]

*** I'm going to see him this afternoon.**

• **1.** راح أشُوفَه اليَوم العَصِر [raːħ ʔašuːfah ʔilyuːm ʔilʕaṣir]

*** They talked about this and that.**

• **1.** حِكَوا عَالأكُو والماكُو [ħičaw ʕalʔakuː wilmaːkuː]

thorn • 1. شوكَة [šawka] شوكات [šawkaːt] *pl:* شَوك [šawk] *Collective:* The tree is full of thorns. الشَّجَرَة مَترُوسَة شُوك [ʔiššaǰara matruːsa šuːk]

thorny • 1. بِيه شَوك [biːh šuːk] Watch out, that plant is thorny. دِير بالَك، هَالزَّرِع بِيه شُوك [diːr baː lak, hazzariʕ biːh šuːk] • **2.** شائِك [šaːʔik] مُحرِج [muħrij] That is a very thorny question. هَذا فَدّ مَوضُوع شائِك [haːða fadd mawðuːʕ šaːʔik]

thorough • 1. مُتقَن [mutqan] He's very thorough in everything he does. هُوَّ كُلِّش مُتقَن بِكُلشِي اللّي يسَوِّيه [huwwa kulliš mutqan bkullši ʔilli ysawwiːh] • **2.** شامِل [šaːmil] كامِل [kaːmil] He submitted a thorough report. قَدَّم تَقرِير شامِل [qaddam taqriːr šaːmil]

*** He gave him a thorough beating. • 1.** بِسَطَه بَسطَة زَينَة [bisaṭah basṭa zayna]

thoroughbred • 1. أصِيل [ʔaṣiːl] Those horses are thoroughbreds. هَالخَيل أصِيلَة [halxayl ʔaṣiːla]

thoroughfare • 1. شارِع [šaːriʕ] شَوارِع [šawaːriʕ] *pl:* Rashid St. is the main thoroughfare in Baghdad. شارِع الرَّشِيد هُوَّ الشّارِع الرَّئِيسِي بِبَغداد [šaːriʕ ʔirrašiːd huwwa ʔiššaːriʕ ʔirraʔiːsi bibaɣdaːd]

thoroughly • 1. بدِقَّة [bdiqqa] Read it thoroughly. إقرا بدِقَّة [ʔiqraː bdiqqa] • **2.** تَماماً [tamaːman] I'm thoroughly convinced he's wrong. آنِي مِقتِنِع تَماماً إنُّو غَلطان [ʔaːni miqtiniʕ tamaːman ʔinnu ɣalṭaːn]

those • 1. ذَولاك [ðuːlaːk] ذولَة [ðuːla] Who are those people you were talking to? مِنُو هُمَّ ذَولاك اللّي كِنِت دَتحكِي وِيّاهُم؟ [minu humma ðuːlaːk ʔilli činit datiħči wiyyaːhum?]

though • 1. مَعَ أنّ [maʕa ʔann] ولَو [walaw] Though he knew it, he didn't tell me anything about it. مَعَ إنُّو يُعرُفها، ما قَلِّي عَنها [maʕa ʔinnu yuʕrufha, maː galli ʕanha] I bought several shirts, though I didn't need them. إشتِرَيت كَم ثُوب ولَو ما أحتاجهُم [ʔištiriːt čam θuːb wlaw maː

T

ʔaħta:ǰhum] • **2.** لَكِن [la:kin] بَسّ [bass] All right, I'll do it! Not now, though. زين، عُود أسَوِّيها بَسّ مُو هَسَّة [zi:n, ʕu:d ʔasawwi:ha bass mu: hassa] • **3.** مَعَ هَذا [maʕa ha:ða] عَلَى كُلّ حال [ʕala kull ħa:l] You've ordered it, though, haven't you? إنتَ وَصَّيت عَليه، مَعَ هَذا، مُو؟ [ʔinta waṣṣi:t ʕali:h, maʕa ha:ða, mu:?]

as though • **1.** عَبالَك [ʕaba:lak] It looks as though it may rain. شِكِلها عَبالَك راح تُمطُر [šikilha ʕaba:lak ra:ħ tumṭur]

thought • **1.** تَفكِير [tafki:r] The very thought of it makes me sick. مُجَرَّد التَّفكِير بِيه يلَعِّب النَّفِس [muǰarrad ʔittafki:r bi:h ylaʕʕib ʔinnafis] • **2.** فِكرَة [fikra] فِكرات، فِكِر، أفكار [fikra:t, fikir, ʔafka:r.] *pl:* The thought occurred to me. الفِكرَة خِطرَتلِي [ʔilfikra xiṭratli] The thought occurred to me. الفِكرَة جَتّي عَلَى بالِي [ʔilfikra ǰatti ʕala ba:li] • **3.** مُراعاة [mura:ʕa: (t)] Can't you show a little thought for others? ما تبَيِّن شوَيَّة مُراعاة لِلآخَرين؟ [ma: tbayyin šwayya mura:ʕa:t lilʔa:xari:n?]

to be lost in thought • **1.** صُفَن [ṣufan] صَفنَة [ṣafna] *vn: sv* u. He was lost in thought. كان صافُن [ča:n ṣa:fun]

give thought • **1.** فَكَّر [fakkar] تَفكِير [tafki:r] *vn: sv* u. I'll have to give this matter some thought. لازِم أفَكِّر بِهَالمَوضُوع [la:zim ʔafakkir bhalmawðu:ʕ]

*** Don't give it another thought!** • **1.** لا تدَوِّخ راسَك بِيها [la: tdawwix ra:sak bi:ha] / لا يُبقَى بالَك يَمّها [la: yubqa: ba:lak yammha]

thoughtful • **1.** صافُن [ṣa:fun] Why do you look so thoughtful? شبِيك صافُن؟ [šbi:k ṣa:fun?]

*** It's very thoughtful of you to bring me flowers.** • **1.** هَذا فَدّ شعُور كُلِّش لَطِيف مِنَّك تجِيبلِي وَرِد [ha:ða fadd šuʕu:r kullis laṭi:f minnak tǰi:bli warid]

thoughtless • **1.** طايِش [ṭa:yiš] That was a thoughtless act. هَذا فَدّ تَصَرُّف طايِش [ha:ða fadd taṣarruf ṭa:yiš]

*** She's so thoughtless.** • **1.** ما تراعِي شعُور الآخِرين [ma: tra:ʕi šuʕu:r ʔilʔa:xiri:n]

thousand • **1.** ألِف [ʔalif] آلاف، ألُوف [ʔa:la:f, ʔulu:f] *pl:*

thousandth • **1.** الألف [ʔilʔalf] This is our thousandth shipment. هَذِي إرسالِيَّتنا الألف [ha:ði ʔirsa:liyyatna ʔilʔalf] • **2.** واحِد مِن الألف [wa:ħid min ʔilʔalf] I own a thousandth of the company. أملُك واحِد مِن الألف مِن هَالشَّرِكَة [ʔamluk wa:ħid min ʔilʔalf min haššarika]

thrashing • **1.** بَسطَة [basṭa] بَسطات [basṭa:t] *pl:* Did he ever get a thrashing! الصُّدُق أكَل بَسطَة [ʔiṣṣudug ʔakal basṭa]

thread • **1.** خَيط [xayṭ, xi:ṭ] خيُوط [xyu:ṭ] *pl:* Have you a needle and thread? عِندِك أبرَة وخَيط؟ [ʕindič ʔubra wxayṭ?] • **2.** سِنّ [sinn] أسنان [ʔasna:n] *pl:* The thread on this screw is worn out. سِنّ هَالبُرغِي سايِف [sinn halburγi sa:yif]

to thread • **1.** لِضَم [liðam] لَضُم [laðum] *vn: sv* u. I'll thread the needle for you. آنِي ألضُملِك الأبرَة [ʔa:ni ʔalðumlič ʔilʔubra] • **2.** طَلَّع [ṭallaʕ] *sv* i. Would you thread this pipe for me? بالله ما تطَلِّعلِي سِنّ لِهَالبُورِي؟ [ballah ma: ṭṭalliʕli sinn lihalbu:ri?]

threat • **1.** تَهدِيد [tahdi:d] تَهدِيدات [tahdi:da:t] *pl:* Your threats don't scare me. تَهدِيداتَك ما يخَوُّفنِي [tahdi:da:tak ma: yxawwufni]

to threaten • **1.** هَدَّد [haddad] تَهدِيد [tahdi:d] *vn: sv* i. He threatened to leave if they didn't increase his salary. هَدَّد يبَطِّل إذا ما يزَيدُون مَعاشَه [haddad ybaṭṭil ʔiða ma: yzayydu:n maʕa:šah] The epidemic threatened the whole city. المَرَض هَدَّد الوِلايَة كُلّها [ʔilmarað haddad ʔilwila:ya kullha]

three • **1.** ثلاثَة [θla:θa] Three and three equals six. ثلاثَة وثلاثَة تساوِي سِتَّة [tla:θa wtla:θa tsa:wi sitta] • **2.** ثلَث [tlaθ] I've been here three days. كِنِت هنا ثلَث أيّام [činit hna tlaθ ʔayya:m] • **3.** ثلَث, ثلاث [tlaθ, tla:θ] He brought three books. جاب ثلَث كُتُب [ǰa:b tlaθ kutub]

to thresh • **1.** دِرَس [diras] دراس [dra:s] *vn:* اِندِرَس [ʔindiras] *p:* داس [da:s] *sv* u. In northern Iraq, they still thresh grain by oxen. بِشِمال العِراق، بَعَدهُم يدِرسُون الحُبُوب بِالثِّيران [bšima:l ʔilʕira:q, baʕadhum ydirsu:n ʔilħubu:b biθθi:ra:n]

threshing machine • **1.** مَكِينَة دِراس [maki:nat dira:s] مَكايِن دِراس [maka:yin dira:s] *pl:*

threshold • **1.** عِتبَة [ʕitba] عِتبات [ʕitba:t] *pl:*

thrift • **1.** اِقتِصاد [ʔiqtiṣa:d] Scotsmen are known for their thrift. الإسكُتلَندِيِّين مَشهُورِين بالاِقتِصاد [ʔilʔiskutlandiyyi:n mašhu:ri:n bilʔiqtiṣa:d]

thrifty • **1.** مقتَصِد [miqtiṣid] She's a thrifty housewife. هِيَّ فَدّ أمّ بَيت مُقتَصدَة [hiyya fadd ʔumm bayt muqtaṣda]

to thrill • **1.** طُرَب، طرَب [ṭurab, ṭrab] طَرَب [ṭarab] *vn: sv* i. The music thrilled him. طُربَتَه المُوسِيقَى [ṭurbatah ʔilmusi:qa] • **2.** أثار [ʔaθa:r] إثارَة [ʔiθa:ra] *vn: sv* i. Seeing the site of Sumer for the first time thrilled me. شُوفَة مَوقِع سُومَر الأوَّل مَرَّة أثار مَشاعري [šawfat mawqiʕ su:mar lʔawwal marra ʔaθa:r maša:ʕri]

to be thrilled • **1.** طار عَقِل بـ [ṭa:r ʕaqil bi-] *sv* i. Jamil was thrilled with his present. جَمِيل عَقلَه طار بالهَدِيَّة [ǰami:l ʕaqlah ṭa:r bilhadiyya]

thrilling • **1.** رايِع [ra:yiʕ] This is a thrilling view! هَذا فَدّ مَنظَر رايِع [ha:ða fadd manðar ra:yiʕ]

 i, interjection; p, passive; pl, plural; sv, stem vowel; vn, verbal noun

to thrive • **1.** اِنتِعَش [ʔintiʕaš] اِنتِعاش [ʔintiʕaːš] *vn: sv* i. The economy is thriving. الوَضع الاقتِصادي دَيِنتِعِش [ʔalwaðʕ ʔilʔiqtiṣaːdi dayintiʕiš] • **2.** نِمَى [nimaː] نِمُو [nimuw] *vn: sv* u. Cattle thrive here. البَقَر يِنمُو بِهَالمَنطَقَة [ʔilbaqar yinmuw bhalmanṭaqa] • **3.** تَرَعرَع [traʕraʕ] تَرَعرُع [taraʕruʕ] *vn: sv* a. The children are thriving. الجِّهال دَيِترَعرَعُون [ʔijjihaːl dayitraʕraʕuːn]

throat • **1.** زَردُوم [zarduːm] زَرادِيم [zaraːdiːm] *pl:* بَلعُوم [balʕuːm] بلاعِيم [blaːʕiːm] *pl:* The doctor painted my throat with iodine. الطَّبِيب دِهَن زَردُومِي بِيَود [ʔiṭṭabiːb dihan zarduːmi byuːd]

* **He'd cut your throat for two cents.**
• **1.** يقُصّ رُقُبتَك عَلَى فِلسَين [yguṣṣ rugubtak ʕala filsayn]
* **He jumped down my throat.** • **1.** مِهَرنِي [miharni] / زَفنِي [zaffni]
* **She wanted to say something, but the words stuck in her throat.** • **1.** رادَت تقُول فَدّ شِي بَسّ عِصَت الكِلمَة بحَلقِها [raːdat tguːl fadd ši bass ʕiṣat ʔiččilma bħaligha]

to throb • **1.** نُبَض [nubað] نَبُض [nabuð] *vn: sv* u. The blood is throbbing in my veins. الدَّمّ دَيِنبُض بِدَماراتِي [ʔiddamm dayinbuð bdamaraːti]

throne • **1.** عَرِش [ʕariš] عُرُوش [ʕuruːš] *pl:*

through • **1.** بَين [bayn] The president's party drove through cheering crowds. الرَّئِيس وَحاشِيتَه مَرَّوا بسَيّاراتهُم بين الجَّماهِير الهاتفَة [ʔirraʔiːs wħaːšiːtah marraw bsayyaːraːthum biːn ʔijjamaːhiːr ʔilhaːtfa] • **2.** مِن [min] You have to go through the hall to get to the kitchen. لازم تفُوت مِن الهَول حَتَّى ترُوح لِلمَطبَخ [laːzim tfuːt min ʔilhuːl ħatta truːħ lilmaṭbax] • **3.** عَن طَرِيق [ʕan ṭariːq] You'll have to go through the sergeant to see the captain. لازم ترُوح عَن طَرِيق العَرِيف حَتَّى تشُوف الرَّئِيس [laːzim truːħ ʕan ṭariːq ʔilʕariːf ħatta tšuːf ʔirraʔiːs] • **4.** بسَبَب [bsabab] نَتِيجَة [natiːja] نَتائِج [nataːʔij] *pl:* The work was held up two weeks through his negligence. وُقَف الشُّغُل مُدَّة إسبُوعَين بِسَبَب إهمالَه [wugaf ʔiššuɣul muddat ʔisbuːʕayn bsabab ʔihmaːlah]

* **We went through the woods.** • **1.** اِختِرَقنا الغابَة [ʔixtiragna ʔilɣaːba] / قطَعنا الغابَة فَدّ صَفحَة لِلّخ [gṭaʕna ʔilɣaːba fadd ṣafħa lillux]
* **The carpenter bored a hole through the wood.**
• **1.** النَّجّار زِرَف زُرُف بِالخِشبَة [ʔinnajjaːr ziraf zuruf bilxišba]
* **The deal fell through.** • **1.** الصَفقَة ما نِجحَت [ʔiṣṣafqa maː nijħat]
* **There's no through train from Kirkuk to Basra.**
• **1.** ماكُو قِطار يرُوح فَدّ راس مِن كَركُوك لِلبَصرَة [maːkuː qiṭaːr yruːħ fadd raːs min karkuːk lilbaṣra]
* **Is this a through street?** • **1.** هَذا شارِع يخَرِّج؟ [haːða šaːriʕ yxarrij?]

through and through • **1.** مِن الأساس [min ʔilʔasaːs] مِن العِرق [min ʔilʕirig] He's bad through and through. هَذا مُو خُوش آدَمِي مِن الأساس [haːða muː xuːš ʔaːdami min ʔalʔasaːs] • **2.** مِن فَوق لِجَوَّة [min fawg lijawwa] We were soaked through and through. تنَقَّعنا مِن فُوق لِجَوَّة [tnaggaʕna min fuːg lijawwa]

to be through • **1.** خَلَّص [xallaṣ] *sv* i. I'll be through work at five o'clock. أخَلِّص مِن الشُّغُل السّاعَة خَمسَة [ʔaxalliṣ min ʔiššuɣul ʔissaːʕa xamsa]

* **I am through with it.** • **1.** مالِي لازِم بِيه [maːli laːzim biːh baʕad]
* **If you ever do that again, we're through.**
• **1.** تَرَة إذا تسَوِّي هاي مَرَّة لُخ، وَلا أشُوف وِجَّك بَعَد [tara ʔiða tsawwi haːy marra lux, walaː ʔašuːf wiččak baʕad]

throughout • **1.** طُول [ṭuːl] You can get these vegetables throughout the year. تِقدَر تِلقِي هَالخُضرَة طُول السَّنَة [tigdar tilgi halxuðra ṭuːl ʔissana] • **2.** بكُلّ أنحاء [bkull ʔanħaːʔ] This hotel is famous throughout the world. هَالأوتيل مَعرُوف بكُلّ أنحاء العالَم [halʔutiːl maʕruːf bkull ʔanħaːʔ ʔilʕaːlam]

throw • **1.** شَمرَة [šamra] شَمرات [šamraːt] *pl:* ذَبَّة [ðabba] ذَبّات [ðabbaːt] *pl:* That was some throw! هاي شلُون شَمرَة حِلوَة [haːy šluːn šamra ħilwa]

to throw • **1.** شُمَر [šumar] شَمُر [šamur] *vn: sv* u. ذَبّ [ðabb] ذَبّ [ðabb] *vn: sv* i. Let's see how far you can throw the ball. خَلِّي نشُوف شبِعِد تِقدَر تِشمُر الطُّوبَة [xalli nšuːf šbiʕid tigdar tišmur ʔiṭṭuːba] He throws himself into it heart and soul. ذابِب نَفسَه عَليها مِن كُلّ قَلبَه [ðaːbib nafsah ʕaliːha min kull galbah] • **2.** وَقَّع [waggaʕ] *sv* i. شُمَر [šumar] *sv* u. The horse threw him. الحِصان وَقَّعَه [ʔilħiṣaːn waggaʕah] • **3.** بُطَح [buṭaħ] بَطِح [baṭiħ] *vn: sv* a. He threw his opponent in a few seconds. بُطَح خَصمَه بكَم ثانيَة [buṭaħ xaṣmah bčam θaːniya] • **4.** وَجَّه [wajjah] *sv* i. Throw that light this way, please. بالله وَجِّه الضُّوَة لِهَالصَّفحَة [ballah wajjih ʔiðḍuwa lhaṣṣafħa]

to throw away • **1.** ذَبّ [ðabb] ذَبّ [ðabb] *vn: sv* i. Throw the papers away. ذِبّ هَالأوراق [ðibb halʔawraːq] He's just throwing his money away. دَيذِبّ فلُوسَه بِالشَّطّ [dayðibb fluːsah biššaṭṭ]

to throw back • **1.** ذَبّ [ðabb] ذَبّ [ðabb] *vn:* اِنذَبّ [ʔinðabb] *p:* Throw the fish back in the river. ذِبّ السِّمكَة بِالشَّطّ [ðibb ʔissimča biššaṭṭ]

to throw down • **1.** شَمَّر [šammar] *sv* u. شُمَر [šumar] شَمُر [šamur] *vn: sv* u. Don't throw your things down so carelessly. لا تشَمُّر غَراضَك هَالشِّكِل بَلا اِهتِمام [laː tšammur ɣaraːðak haššikil bala ʔihtimaːm]

to throw in • **1.** كَمَّل [čammal] تكِمِّل [tčimmil] *vn: sv* i. The baker threw in a few extra loaves of bread. الخَبّاز كَمَّل كَم صَمُّونَة [ʔilxabbaːz čammal čam ṣammuːna]

* **Ahmed threw in the towel.** • **1.** أحمَد سَلَّم [ʔaħmad sallam] / أحمَد اِستَسلَم [ʔaħmad ʔistaslam]

to throw off • **1.** نِزَع [nizaʕ] He threw off his coat and joined the fight. نِزَع سِترتَه وَاِشتِرَك بِالعَركَة

T

[nizaʕ sitirtah wištirak bilʕarka] • **2.** تخَلَّص [txallaṣ] *sv* a. How did you manage to throw off your cold? شلون قدَرت تِتخَلَّص مِن النَّشلَة؟ [šluːn gdarit titxallaṣ min ʔinnašla?]

to throw out • **1.** ذَبّ [ðabb] ذَبّ [ðabb] *vn:* اِنذَبّ [ʔinðabb] *p:* I threw my old shoes out. ذَبّيت قَنادري العَتيقَة [ðabbiːt qanaːdri ʔilʕatiːga] • **2.** طِرَد [ṭirad] طَرِد [ṭarid] *vn:* اِنطِرَد [ʔinṭirad] *p:* جَلَّق [čallaq] تَجليق [tačliːq] *vn:* تجَلَّق [tčallaq] *p:* She almost threw me out. يَعني إلّا شوَيَّة كان طِردَتني [yaʕni ʔilla šwayya čaːn ṭirdatni] / بَعَد شوَيَّة تجَلِّقني [baʕad šwayya tčalliqni]

*** The judge threw the case out of court for lack of evidence.** • **1.** الحاكِم رَدّ الدَعوَة لعَدَم وُجود أدِلَّة [ʔilħaːkim radd ʔiddaʕwa lʕadam wujuːd ʔadilla]

to throw up • **1.** طَقّ [tagg] *sv* u. That's the second time you've thrown that up to me. هاي المَرَّة الثّانيَة تطُقّها بوِجهي [haːy ʔilmarra ʔiθθaːnya ttuggha bwičči] • **2.** زاع [zaːʕ] زَوع [zawʕ] *vn: sv* u. زَوَّع [zawwaʕ] تَزويع [tazwiːʕ] *vn: sv* i. I throw up whenever I see blood. كُلما أشوف دَمّ أزُوع [kullma ʔašuːf damm ʔazuːʕ] • **3.** بَطَّل [baṭṭal] *sv* i. He threw up a good job to run for the election. بَطَّل مِن شَغلَة زينَة حَتّى يرَشِّح نَفسَه لِلانتِخاب [baṭṭal min šaɣla ziːna ħatta yraššiħ nafsah lilʔintixaːb]

thud • **1.** طَبَّة [ṭabba] طَبّات [ṭabbaːt] *pl:* I heard a thud in the next room. سِمَعِت طَبَّة بغُرفَة اللّخ [simaʕit ṭabba bɣurufat ʔillux]

thumb • **1.** إبهام [ʔibhaːm] إبهامات [ʔibhaːmaːt] *pl:* I burned my thumb. حرَقِت إبهامي [ħragit ʔibhaːmi]

*** I'm all thumbs today.** • **1.** شما أسَوّي بإيدي اليَوم ما يطلَع تمام [šma ʔasawwi bʔiːdi ʔilyuːm maː yitlaʕ tamaːm] / آني مخَربُط اليُوم [ʔaːni mxarbuṭ ʔilyuːm]

*** He's too much under his wife's thumb.** • **1.** يِمشي بحُكُم مَرتَه أكثَر مِن اللازِم [yimši bħukum martah ʔakθar min ʔillaːzim] / مَرتَه راكبتَه [martah raːkbatah]

*** He sticks out like a sore thumb.** • **1.** ذاكُوّ مبَيِّن [ðaːkuwwa mbayyin]

to thumb through • **1.** وَرَّق [warraq] *sv* i. I thumbed through the telephone book. وَرَّقِت بدَليل التِّلِفُون [warraqit bdaliːl ʔittilifuːn]

thumb tack • **1.** دَنبُوس [danbuːs] دنابيس [dnaːbiːs] *pl:* We put up the notice with thumb tacks. عَلَّقنا الإعلان بدَنابيس [ʕallaqna ʔilʔiʕlaːn bdanaːbiːs]

thunder • **1.** قَرقُوعَة [garguːʕa] قَراقيع [garaːgiːʕ] *pl:* رَعَد [raʕad] [.] *pl:* Did you hear the thunder last night? سمَعت القَراقيع البارحَة باللَّيل؟ [smaʕt ʔilgaraːgiːʕ ʔilbaːrħa billayl?]

*** A thunder of applause greeted the speaker.** • **1.** اِستَقبلَوا الخَطيب بفَدّ عاصِفَة مِن التَّصفيق [ʔistaqbilaw ʔilxaṭiːb bfadd ʕaːṣifa min ʔittaṣfiːq]

to thunder • **1.** قَرقَع [gargaʕ] قَرقَعَة [gargaʕa] *vn: sv* i. رِعَد [riʕad] رَعَد [raʕad] *vn: sv* i. It's beginning to thunder. بِدَت تقَرقِع [bidat dgargiʕ] It's beginning to thunder. بِدَت الدِّنيا ترِعِد [bidat ʔiddinya tirʕid]

*** You shouldn't have let him thunder at you like that.** • **1.** ما كان لازِم تخَلّيه يرِعِد ويزبِد عَلَيك هَالشِكِل [maː čaːn laːzim txalliːh yirʕid wyizbid ʕaliːk haššikil]

thunderstorm • **1.** عاصِفَة [ʕaːṣifa] عَواصِف [ʕawaːṣif] *pl:* We missed the thunderstorm. العاصِفَة ما جَتّي عَلينا [ʔilʕaːṣifa maː jatti ʕaliːna]

Thursday • **1.** يَوم الخَميس [yuːm ʔilxamiːs] That can wait till Thursday. خَلّيهَا إلَى يوم الخَميس [xalliːha ʔila yuːm ʔilxamiːs] That can wait till Thursday. خَلّيهَا لِلخَميس [xalliːha lilxamiːs]

to thwart • **1.** خَيَّب [xayyab] *sv* u. His action thwarted our plans. تَصَرُّفَه خَيَّب خُطَطنا [taṣarrufah xayyab xuṭaṭna]

thyme • **1.** زَعتَر [zaʕtar]

tick • **1.** قَرادَة [garaːda] قَرادات [garaːdaːt] *pl:* قَراد [garaːd] *Collective:* The dog is covered with ticks. الكَلِب مَليان قَراد [ʔiččalib malyaːn garaːd] • **2.** دَوشَك [duːšag] دواشِك [dwaːšig] *pl:* We had to sleep on straw ticks. اِضطَرَّينا ننام عَلَى دواشِك مال حَلفَة [ʔiðṭarrayna ʔinnaːm ʕala dwaːšig maːl ħalfa] • **3.** دَقَّة [dagga] دَقّات [daggaːt] *pl:* The room is so quiet you can hear the tick of the clock. القُبَّة هيكِي صَنتَة تِقدَر تِسمَع دَقّات السّاعَة [ʔilgubba hiːči ṣanta tigdar tismaʕ daggaːt ʔissaːʕa]

to tick • **1.** دَقّ [dagg] دَقَّة [dagga] *vn: sv* u. I can hear the watch tick. دَأقدَر أسمَع السّاعَة تدُقّ [daʔagdar ʔasmaʕ ʔissaːʕa ddugg]

ticket • **1.** بطاقَة [biṭaːqa] بطاقات، بطايِق [biṭaːqaːt, biṭaːyiq] *pl:* تِكِت [tikit] تِكِتات [tikitaːt] *pl:* Can you get us three tickets for the play? تِقدَر تدَبُّر إلنا ثلاث بطاقات لِلرِّوايَة؟ [tigdar ddabbur ʔilna tlaːθ biṭaːqaːt lirriwaːya?] You can buy a ticket on the train. تِقدَر تِشتِري تِكِت بالقِطار [tigdar tištiri tikit bilqiṭaːr] • **2.** قائمَة مُرَشَّحين [qaːʔimat muraššaħiːn] The National Party has a good ticket. الحِزب الوَطَني عِندَه قائمَة مُرَشَّحين زينَة [ʔilħizb ʔilwaṭani ʕindah qaːʔimat muraššaħiːn ziːna]

ticking • **1.** خام الشام [xaːm ʔiššaːm] How much is this ticking a yard? هَالخام الشّام بيش الذِّراع؟ [halxaːm ʔiššaːm biyš ʔiððiraːʕ?] • **2.** طَقطَقَة [ṭagṭaga] I just heard a strange ticking in the machine. هَسَّة سمَعِت طَقطَقَة غَريبَة بِالمَكينَة [hassa smaʕit ṭagṭaga ɣariːba bilmakiːna]

tickle • **1.** شَخطَة [šaxṭa] شَخطات [šaxṭaːt] *pl:* I've a tickle in my throat. عِندي فَدّ شَخطَة بزَردُومي [ʕindi fadd šaxṭa bzarduːmi]

to tickle • **1.** دَغدَغ [daɣdaɣ] دَغدَغَة [daɣdaɣa] *vn:* تدَغدَغ [tdaɣdaɣ] *p:* He doesn't laugh even if you tickle him. ما يِضحَك حَتّى لَو دَغدَغتَه [maː yiðhak ħatta law daɣdaɣtah]

ticklish • **1.** حَسّاس [ħassaːs] That's a ticklish question. هَذا فَدّ مَوضُوع حَسّاس [haːða fadd mawðuːʕ ħassaːs]

*** Are you ticklish?** • **1.** تغار بسُهُولَة؟ [tɣaːr bsuhuːla?] / الدَّغدَغَة تأثِّر بِيك؟ [ʔiddaɣdaɣa tʔaθθir biːk?]

tide • **1.** * The tide is coming in. البَحَر راح يِرتِفِع [ʔilbaħar raːħ yirtifiʕ]

high tide • **1.** مَدّ [madd] It was high tide when the ship came up the river. السَّفِينَة دِخلَت النَّهَر وَقِت المَدّ [ʔissafiːna dixlat ʔinnahar wakit ʔilmadd]

low tide • **1.** جَزِر [ǰazir] You can walk out to the island at low tide. وَقِت الجَّزِر تِقدَر تِمشِي لِلجَّزِيرَة [wakit ʔiǰǰazir tigdar timši liǰǰaziːra]

to tide over • **1.** طَلَّع [ṭallaʕ] تَطلِيع [taṭliːʕ] *vn: sv* i. دَبَّر أَمُر [dabbar ʔamur] *sv* u. Two dinars will tide me over until Monday. دِينارَين تطَلِّعني لِيُوم الإثنَين [dinaːrayn ṭṭalliʕni lyuːm ʔilʔiθnayn]

tidy • **1.** مهَندَم [mhandam] منَظَّم [mnaððam] مرَتَّب [mrattab] He is a very tidy person. هُوَّ فَدّ واحِد كُلِّش مهَندَم [huwwa fadd waːħid kulliš mhandam] • **2.** مرَتَّب [mrattab] منَظَّم [mnaððam] Her room is always tidy. غُرفَتها دائِماً مرَتّبَة زين [ɣurfatha daːʔiman mrattba ziːn] • **3.** كبِير [čibiːr] He's inherited a tidy fortune. وِرَث ثَروَة كبِيرَة [wiraθ θarwa čbiːra]

tie • **1.** صِلَة [ṣila] صِلات [ṣilaːt] *pl:* رابِطَة [raːbiṭa] رَوابِط [rawaːbiṭ] *pl:* The two countries are bound by economic and military ties. الدَّولَتَين مُرتَبطِين بِصِلات اِقتِصادِيَّة وَعَسكَرِيَّة [ʔiddawultayn murtabṭiːn bṣilaːt ʔiqtiṣaːdiyya wʕaskariyya] • **2.** رابِطَة [raːbiṭa] رَوابِط [rawaːbiṭ] *pl:* Family ties are stronger in the Middle East than in the West. الرَّوابِط العائِلِيَّة بِالشَّرق الأوسَط أقوى مِن الغَرب [ʔirrawaːbiṭ ʔilʕaːʔiliyya biššarq ʔilʔawsaṭ ʔaqwaː min ʔalɣarb] • **3.** بَوِينباغ [buyinbaːɣ] بَوِينباغات [buyinbaːɣaːt] *pl:* رِباط [ribaːṭ] أربِطَة [ʔarbiṭa] *pl:* He wears expensive ties. يِلبَس بُوِينباغات غالِيَة [yilbas buyinbaːɣaːt ɣaːlya] • **4.** لُوق [luːg] لُوقات [luːqaːt] *pl:* The ties on this line need replacing. اللُّوقات مال هَالسِّكَّة يِنرادِلها تَغيِر [ʔilluːgaːt maːl hassičča yinraːdilha taɣyiːr] • **5.** تَعادُل [taʕaːdul] The game ended in a tie. السِّباق اِنتِهَى بِتَعادُل [ʔissibaːq ʔintihaː btaʕaːdul]

to tie • **1.** شَدّ [šadd] شَدّ [šadd] *vn: sv* i. I have to tie my shoelaces. خَلّي أشِدّ قِيطان قُندَرتِي [xalli ʔašidd qiːṭaːn qundarti] • **2.** تعادَل [tʕaːdal] تَعادُل [taʕaːdul] *vn: sv* a. They tied us in the last minute's play. تعادلَوا وِيّانا بِآخِر لَحظَة مِن اللِّعِب [tʕaːdlaw wiyyaːna bʔaːxir laħða min ʔilliʕib] • **3.** عِقَد [ʕigad] عَقِد [ʕagid] *vn: sv* u. Tie that knot securely. أُعقُد هَالعُقدَة زين [ʔuʕgud halʕugda ziːn]

*** My hands are tied.** • **1.** آنِي مكَتَّف [ʔaːni mčattaf]

to tie down • **1.** رِبَط [ribaṭ] رَبُط [rabuṭ] *vn: sv* u. I don't want to tie myself down. آنِي ما أرِيد أربُط نَفسِي [ʔaːni maː ʔariːd ʔarbuṭ nafsi]

to tie in • **1.** رِهَم [riham] رَهُم [rahum] *vn: sv* a. This ties in nicely with what we know. هَذا يِرهَم زين ويّا اللّي نُعرفَه [haːða yirham ziːn wiyya ʔilli nuʕurfah]

to tie on • **1.** شَدّ [šadd] شَدّ [šadd] *vn: sv* i. رُبَط ب [rubaṭ b-] رَبَط [rabaṭ] *vn: sv* u. Tie on another piece of string. شِدّ بِيها وُصلَة لُخ خيط [šidd biːha wuṣla lux xiːṭ]

to tie up • **1.** رُبَط [rubaṭ] رَبَط [rabaṭ] *vn: sv* u. شَدّ [šadd] شَدّ [šadd] *vn: sv* i. Please tie up these papers for me. أرجُوك أربُطلِي هَالأوراق بخَيط [ʔarǰuːk ʔurbuṭli halʔawraːq bxayṭ] Did you tie up the boat? رِبطتَه لِلبَلَم؟ [rbaṭṭah lilbalam?] • **2.** شَغَّل [šaɣɣal] تَشغِيل [tašɣiːl] *vn: sv* i. He's tied up all his money in real estate. شَغَّل كُلّ فلُوسَه بِمُعامَلات الأملاك [šaɣɣal kull fluːsah bmuʕaːmalaːt ʔilʔamlaːk] • **3.** عَطَّل [ʕaṭṭal] تَعطِيل [taʕṭiːl] *vn: sv* i. The accident tied up traffic. الحادِث عَطَّل المُرُور [ʔilħaːdiθ ʕaṭṭal ʔilmuruːr]

tied up • **1.** مِرتبِط [mirtibiṭ] Are you tied up this evening? إنتَ مِرتبِط بشِي هاللَّيلَة؟ [ʔinta mirtibiṭ bši hallayla?] • **2.** مَشغُول [mašɣuːl] I was tied up all afternoon. كِنِت مَشغُول تَماماً طُول وَرا الظُّهُر [činit mašɣuːl tamaːman ṭuːl wara ʔiððuhur] • **3.** مشَغَّل [mšaɣɣal] I'm sorry, my money's tied up right now. مِتأسِّف فلُوسِي مشَغَّلَة هَسَّة [mitʔassif fluːsi mšaɣɣila hassa]

*** Rashid St. is generally tied up at noontime.** • **1.** شارِع الرَّشِيد عادَةً ما يِنفات بِيه مِن الخَبصَة الظُّهرِيَّة [šaːriʕ ʔirrašiːd ʕaːdataːn maː yinfaːt biːh min ʔilxabṣa ʔiððuhriyya]

tiger • **1.** نِمِر [nimir] نُمُور [numuːr] *pl:* We're going to hunt tigers. راح نصِيد نمُور [raħ nṣiːd nmuːr]

tight • **1.** حَيل [ħayl, ħiːl] Shut your eyes tight. سِدّ عيُونَك حيل [sidd ʕyuːnak ħiːl] Hold tight to the horse's neck. كَلِّب بِرقبَة الحصان حيل [čallib brugbat ʔilħṣaːn ħiːl] • **2.** ضَبّ [ðabb] ضباب [ðbaːb] *pl:* مَضبُوب [maðbuːb] I tied my shoelaces too tight. شَدَّيت قِيطان قُندَرتِي ضَبّ [šaddiːt qiːṭaːn qundarti ðabb] Is the jar sealed tight? قَبَغ الشِّيشَة مَضبُوب زين؟ [qabaɣ ʔiššiːša maðbuːb ziːn?] / قَبَغ الشِّيشَة مَسدُود ضَبّ؟ [qabaɣ ʔiššiːša masduːd ðabb?] • **3.** ضَيِّق [ðayyig] This jacket is too tight for me. هَالسِّترَة كُلِّش ضَيقَة عَلَيّا [hassitra kulliš ðayyga ʕalayya] • **4.** سَكران [sakraːn] سكارَة [skaːra] *pl:* Boy was I tight last night! أمّا آنِي صُدُق كِنِت سَكران البارحَة باللَّيل [ʔamma ʔaːni ṣudug činit sakraːn ʔilbaːrħa billayl] • **5.** بَخِيل [baxiːl] He's very tight with his money. هُوَّ كُلِّش بَخِيل بِفلُوسَه [huwwa kulliš baxiːl bfluːsah] • **6.** شاحّ [šaːħħ] Money is very tight now. الفلُوس شاحَّة هَسَّة [ʔilfluːs šaːħħa hassa]

*** I've been in many a tight spot before.** • **1.** آنِي يا ما واقِع بوَرطَة قَبُل [ʔaːni yaː maː waːgiʕ bwarṭa gabul] / آنِي مارّ بأيّام عَصِيبَة قَبُل [ʔaːni maːrr bʔayyaːm ʕaṣiːba gabul]

T

to sit tight • **1.** صُبَر [ṣubar] صَبُر [ṣabur] *vn: sv* u. You just sit tight; and we'll be with you in half an hour. إصبُر بمَكانَك؛ إحنا راح نكُون يَمَّك بَعَد نُصّ ساعَة [ʔiṣbur bmaka:nak; ʔiħna ra:ħ nku:n yammak baʕad nuṣṣ sa:ʕa]

to tighten • **1.** ضَبّ [ðabb] ضَبّ [ðabb] *vn: sv* u. Tighten the rope. ضُبّ الحَبِل [ðubb ʔilħabil]

tightlipped • **1.** سكُوتِي [sku:ti] سكُوتِيِّين، سكُوتِيَّة [sku:tiyyi:n, sku:tiyya] *pl:* كَتُوم [katu:m] كَتُومِين [katuwmi:n] *pl:* Nuri is quite tightlipped. نُورِي كُلِّش سكُوتِي [nu:ri kulliš sku:ti]

tightly • **1.** ضَبّ [ðabb] حَيل [ħayl, ħi:l] He tied the package tightly. شَدّ الرُّزمَة ضَبّ [šadd ʔirruzma ðabb]

Tigris River • **1.** نَهَر دِجلَة [nahar dijla]

tile • **1.** كاشِيَّة [ka:šiyya] كاشِيّات [ka:šiyya:t] *pl:* كاشِي [ka:ši] *Collective:* A tile fell off the bathroom wall. كاشِيَّة وُقعَت مِن حايِط الحَمّام [ka:šiyya wugʕat min ħa:yiṭ ʔilħamma:m]

to tile • **1.** طَبَّق بكاشِي [ṭabbag bka:ši] تَطبِيق [taṭbi:g] *vn:* تطَبَّق [tṭabbag] *p:* We have to tile the kitchen floor. لازِم نطَبُّق قاع المَطبَخ بالكاشِي [la:zim nṭabbug ga:ʕ ʔilmaṭbax bilka:ši]

till • **1.** دَخَل [daxal] Is there any money in the till? أَكُو فلُوس بِالدَّخَل؟ [ʔaku flu:s biddaxal?] • **2.** إلَى أَن [ʔila: ʔan] حَتَّى [ħatta] Wait till I come back. اِنتِظِر إلَى أَن أرجَع [ʔintiðir ʔila ʔan ʔarjaʕ] • **3.** إلَى [ʔila] حَتَّى [ħatta] I won't be able to see you till next week. ما راح أقدَر أشُوفَك إلَى الإسبُوع الجّاي [ma: ra:ħ ʔagdar ʔašu:fak ʔila ʔilʔisbu:ʕ ʔijja:y]

tilt • **1.** مَيلَة [mayla] مَيلات [mayla:t] *pl:* The telephone pole has taken on a bad tilt. عَمُود التِّلِفُون مال مَيلَة قَوِيَّة [ʕamu:d ʔittilifu:n ma:l mayla qawiyya]

at a tilt • **1.** مايِل [ma:yil] منَكَّس [mnakkas] The Iraqi cap is worn at a tilt. السِّدارَة العِراقِيَّة تِنلِبِس مايلَة [ʔissida:ra ʔilʕira:qiyya tinlibis ma:yla]

to tilt • **1.** مَيَّل [mayyal] تمِيِّل [tmiyyil] *vn: sv* i. نَكَّس [nakkas] تَنكِيس [tanki:s] *vn: sv* i. If you tilt the bottle, you may be able to get it out of the refrigerator. لَو تمَيِّل البُوطِل مُحتَمَل تِقدَر تطَلّعَه مِن الثَّلاجَة [law tmayyil ʔilbuṭul muħtamal tigdar tṭallʕah min ʔiθθilla:ja] Tilt your hat forward a bit. نَكِّس شَفقتَك شوَيَّة [nakkis šafuqtak šwayya] Tilt the flag forward during the parade. نَكِّس العَلَم أثناء الاستِعراض [nakkis ʔilʕalam ʔaθna:ʔ ʔilʔistiʕra:ð] • **2.** حِنَى [ħina:] حَنِي [ħany] *vn: sv* i. مَيَّل [mayyal] *sv* i. I can't tilt my head to either side. ما أقدَر أحنِي راسِي لِلصَّفحَة [ma: ʔagdar ʔaħni ra:si liṣṣafħa]

timber • **1.** أشجار مال خِشَب [ʔašja:r ma:l xišab] Iraq has little timber. العِراق ما بِيه هوايَة أشجار مال خِشَب [ʔilʕira:q ma: bi:h hwa:ya ʔašja:r ma:l xišab] • **2.** دَلَق [dalag] دَلَقات [dalaga:t] *pl:* جِذع [jiðiʕ] جِذُوع [jiðu:ʕ] *pl:* The timbers on our roof are rotting. الدَّلَقات بسَقُفنا خايسَة [ʔiddalaga:t bsagufna xa:ysa]

time • **1.** وَقِت [wakit] أوقات [ʔawqa:t] *pl:* It's time to leave. صار وَقِت الرَّوحَة [ṣa:r wakit ʔirrawħa] What time are we to go? شوَقِت راح نرُوح [šwakit ra:ħ nru:ħ] These are hard times. هاي أوقات عَصِيبَة [ha:y ʔawqa:t ʕaṣi:ba] These are hard times. هَذِي مُو خُوش أيّام [ha:ði mu: xu:š ʔayya:m] • **2.** مَرَّة [marra] مَرّات [marra:t] *pl:* نوبَة [nu:ba] نوبات [nu:ba:t] *pl:* This is my first time here. هاي أوَّل مَرَّة أجِي هنا [ha:y ʔawwal marra ʔaji hna] Four times five equals twenty. أربَع مَرّات خَمسَة، عِشرِين [ʔarbaʕ marra:t xamsa, ʕišri:n] Four times five equals twenty. أربَعَة بخَمسَة يساوِي عِشرِين [ʔarbaʕa bxamsa ysa:wi ʕišri:n] Two times two equals four. مَرّتَين إثنَين يساوِي أربَعَة [marrtayn ʔiθnayn ysa:wi ʔarbaʕa] • **3.** يوم [yawm] أيّام [ʔayya:m] *pl:* زَمَن [zaman] أزمِنَة [ʔazmina] *pl:* Time will tell. الأيّام تِكشِفها [ʔilʔayya:m tikšifha] • **4.** مُدَّة [mudda] مُدَد [mudad] *pl:* The time is up tomorrow. المُدَّة تِخلَص باكِر [ʔilmudda tixlaṣ ba:čir] I worked a long time. اِشتِغَلِت مُدَّة طوِيلَة [ʔištiɣalit mudda ṭwi:la] He comes to see us from time to time. يِجِي يشُوفنا بين مُدَّة وَمُدَّة [yiji yšu:fna bi:n mudda wmudda] He comes to see us from time to time. يِجِي يشُوفنا بين حِين وآخَر [yiji yšu:fna bi:n ħi:n wʔa:xar] • **5.** تَوقِيت [tawqi:t] تَواقِيت [tawa:qi:t] *pl:* The news in Arabic is broadcast from London at 6 P. M. Greenwich time or 9 P. M. Baghdad local time. الأخبار بِالعَرَبِي تِنذاع مِن لَندَن باللَّيل ساعَة سِتَّة حَسَب تَوقِيت غرِينتش أو ساعَة تِسعَة حَسَب تَوقِيت بَغداد المَحَلِّي [ʔilʔaxba:r bilʕarabi tinða:ʕ min landan billayl sa:ʕa sitta ħasab tawqi:t gri:nij ʔaw sa:ʕa tisʕa ħasab tawqi:t bayda:d ʔilmaħalli] • **6.** تَوقِيع [tawqi:ʕ] The drum beats the time in music. الدُّمبُك يضبُط التَّوقِيع بِالمُوسِيقَى [ʔiddumbuk yiðbuṭ ʔittawqi:ʕ bilmusi:qa] • **7.** زَمَن [zaman] أزمِنَة [ʔazmina] *pl:* أوان [ʔawa:n] آوِنَة [ʔa:wina] *pl:* That research is ahead of the times. هَالبُحُوث غالبَة الزَّمَن [halbuħu:θ ɣa:lba ʔizzaman] That design was too far ahead of its time. هَالتَّصمِيم سابِق أوانَه [hattaṣmi:m sa:biq ʔawa:nah] • **8.** مُوَقَّت [muwaqqat] The revolutionaries set a time bomb in the plane. الثُّوّار حَطّوا قُنبُلَة موَقّتَة بِالطَّيّارَة [ʔiθθuwwa:r ħaṭṭaw qunbula mwaqqita biṭṭayya:ra]

* **Would you know what time of day it is?** • **1.** تُعرُف الساعَة بَيش؟ [tuʕruf ʔissa:ʕa bi:š?]

* **They gave him a bad time.** • **1.** ضَوَّجُوه [ðawwju:h] أذّوه هوايَة / [ʔaððu:h hwa:ya]

a long time ago • **1.** مِن زَمان [min zama:n] قَبُل مُدَّة طوِيلَة [gabul mudda ṭwi:la] I met her a long time ago. تعَرَّفِت بِيها مِن زَمان [tʕarrafit bi:ha min zama:n] She left a long time ago. راحَت مِن زَمان [ra:ħat min zama:n] She left a long time ago. صارِلها هوايَة مِن راحَت [ṣa:rilha hwa:ya min ra:ħat]

all the time • **1.** عَلَى طُول [ʕala ṭu:l] دائِماً [da:ʔiman] We had good weather all the time. كان الجَّو مُمتاز عَلَى طُول

[čaːn ʔijjaww mumtaːz ʕala ṭuːl] He's here all the time. هُوَّ دائماً هنا [huwwa daːʔiman hna]

at times • **1.** أحياناً [ʔaħyaːnan] دَورات [dawraːt] At times I work fourteen hours at a stretch. أحياناً أشتُغُل أربَطَعَش ساعَة عَلَى فَدّ جَرَّة [ʔaħyaːnan ʔaštuɣul ʔarbaːṭaʕaš saːʕa ʕala fadd ǰarra] I see him at times. أشُوفَه دَورات [ʔašuːfah dawraːt]

for the time being • **1.** بهالأثناء [bhalʔaθnaːʔ] مُوَقَّتَن [muwaqqatan] Stay here for the time being. إبقَى هنا بهالأثناء [ʔibqaː hna bhalʔaθnaːʔ]

in good time • **1.** بوَقِتها [bwakitha] You'll know it in good time. عُود تُعرُفها بوَقِتها [ʕuːd tuʕrufha bwakitha]

in time • **1.** بنَتِيجَة [bnatiːǰa] أخِيراً [ʔaxiːran] بِالوَقت المُناسِب [bilwakt ʔilmunaːsib] I'm sure we'll come to an agreement in time. آنِي مِتأكِّد راح نوصَل لِفَدّ اِتِّفاق بِالنَّتِيجَة [ʔaːni mitʔakkid raːħ nawṣal lfadd ʔittifaːq binnatiːǰa] • **2.** بِالوَقت المُناسِب [bilwakt ʔilmunaːsib] The doctor arrived in time to save her. الدِّكتُور وُصَل بالوَقت المُناسِب حَتَّى يِنقُذها [ʔiddiktuːr wuṣal bilwakt ʔilmunaːsib ħatta yinquðha]

on time • **1.** عَالوَقِت [ʕalwakit] Please be on time. باللّه كُون عالوَقِت [ballah kuːn ʕalwakit] • **2.** قُسُط [qusuṭ, qisiṭ] أقساط [ʔaqsaːṭ] *pl:* He bought the car on time. اِشتِرَى السَّيّارَة بالأقساط [ʔištiraː ʔissayyaːra bilʔaqsaːṭ]

time after time • **1.** مَرَّة عَلَى مَرَّة [marra ʕala marra] ياما وياما [yaːma wyaːma] مَرّات [marraːt] I've asked him time after time not to do it. ياما وَياما رِدِت مِنَّه ما يسَوِّيها [yaːma wyaːmaː ridit minnah maː ysawwiːha]

to have a good time • **1.** توَنَّس [twannas] وِنسَة [winsa] *vn: sv* a. Did you have a good time? توَنَّسِت؟ [twannasit?]

to time • **1.** عَيَّن وَقِت [ʕayyan wakit] تعيين وَقِت [taʕyiːn wakit] *vn: sv* i. We timed the conference to start after the holiday. عَيَّنّا وَقِت المُؤتَمَر حَتَّى يِبدِي وَرا العُطلَة [ʕayyannaː wakit ʔilmuʔtamar ħatta yibdi wara ʔilʕuṭla] • **2.** لِزَم [lizam] *sv* a. ضُبَط [ḍubaṭ] *sv* u. Who timed the race? مِنُو لِزَم وَقِت السِّباق؟ [minu lizam wakit ʔissibaːq?]

time keeper • **1.** مُوَقِّت [muwaqqit] مُوَقِّتِين [muwaqqitiːn] *pl:*

timely • **1.** وَقِت [waqit, wakit] أوقات [ʔawqaːt] *pl:* That's a timely article. هَذا فَدّ مَقال بوَقتَه [haːða fadd maqaːl bwaktah]

timer • **1.** مُوَقِّت [muwaqqit] مُوَقِّتات [muwaqqitaːt] *pl:* Set the timer for 5 minutes. اِنصُب المُوَقِّت إلَى خَمِس دَقايِق [ʔinṣub ʔilmuwaqqit ʔila xamis daqaːyiq]

timesaver • **1.** * Canned foods are great timesavers. المُعَلَّبات تخَلِّي الواحِد يِقتِصِد بالوَقِت [ʔilmuʕallabaːt txalli ʔilwaːħid yiqtiṣid bilwakit]

timetable • **1.** جَدوَل أوقات [ǰadwal ʔawqaːt] جَداوِل أوقات [ǰadaːwil ʔawqaːt] *pl:*

timid • **1.** مِتوَهوِه [mitwahwih] خَجُول [xaǰuːl] Don't be so timid! لا تصِير هَالقَدّ مِتوَهوِه [laː tṣiːr halgadd mitwahwih]

timing • **1.** تَوقِيت [tawqiːt] The hold-up relied on precise timing. السَّرِقَة اِعتِمدَت عَلَى تَوقِيت دَقِيق [ʔissariqa ʔiʕtimdat ʕala tawqiːt daqiːq]

*** The timing of his speech was excellent.**
• **1.** خِطابَه جا بِالوَقت المُناسِب [xiṭaːbah ǰaː bilwakt ʔilmunaːsib]

tin • **1.** تَنَك [tanak] The price of tin went up last week. أسعار التَّنَك صِعدَت بالإسبُوع اللِّي فات [ʔasʕaːr ʔittanak ṣiʕdat bilʔisbuːʕ ʔilli faːt] • **2.** قُوطِيَّة [quːṭiyya] قواطِي [qwaːṭi] *pl:* Give me a tin of tobacco. إنطِينِي قُوطِيَّة تِتِن [ʔinṭiːni quːṭiyyat titin]

tinder • **1.** عِلقَة [ʕilga] عِلقات [ʕilgaːt] *pl:* Bring a little tinder so I can start the fire. جِيبلِي شوَيَّة عِلقَة حَتَّى أشعِل النّار [ǰiːbli šwayyat ʕilga ħatta ʔašʕil ʔinnaːr]

to tingle • **1.** نَمَّل [nammal] *sv* i. My foot's tingling. رِجلِي منَمّلَة [riǰli mnammla]

to tinkle • **1.** طَقطَق [ṭagṭag] طَقطَقَة [ṭagṭaga] *vn: sv* i. The ice cubes tinkle in the glass. الثَّلِج دَيطَقطِق بالكلاص [ʔiθθaliǰ dayṭagṭig bilglaːṣ]

tinsmith • **1.** تَنَكچِي [tanakči] تَنَكچِيَّة [tanakčiyya] *pl:*

tint • **1.** لَون [luːn] ألوان [ʔalwaːn] *pl:* Use a lighter tint for the wall. اِستَعمِل لُون أفتَح لهَذا الحايِط [ʔistaʕmil luːn ʔaftaħ lhaðaː ʔilħaːyiṭ]

to tint • **1.** صُبَغ [ṣubaɣ] *sv* u. I want my hair tinted blond. أرِيد أصبُغ شَعرِي أشقَر [ʔariːd ʔaṣbuɣ šaʕri ʔašgar] • **2.** لَوَّن [lawwan] تَلوِين [talwiːn] *vn: sv* i. We've tinted one of the photographs. لَوَّنّا واحِد مِن الرُّسُوم [lawwanna waːħid min ʔirrusuːm]

tiny • **1.** صغَيِّر [ṣɣayyir] Where'd you get such a tiny radio? وين لِقيت هِيكِي رادِيُو صغَيِّر؟ [wiːn ligiːt hiːči raːdyu ṣɣayyir?]

tip • **1.** راس [raːs] رُوس [ruːs] *pl:* They landed on the northern tip of the island. نِزلَوا براس الجَّزِيرَة الشِّمالِي [nizlaw braːs ʔiǰǰaziːra ʔiššimaːli] My shoes are worn at the tips. قُندَرتِي سافَت مِن الرّاس [qundarti saːfat min ʔirraːs] • **2.** طَرَف [ṭaraf] أطراف [ʔaṭraːf] *pl:* The word is on the tip of my tongue. الكِلمَة عَلَى طَرَف لِسانِي [ʔiččilma ʕala ṭarf lisaːni] • **3.** زَبانَة [zabaːna] زَبايِن [zabaːyin] *pl:* Do you have cigarettes with tips? عِندَك جِگايِر أمّ الزَّبانَة؟ [ʕindak ǰigaːyir ʔumm ʔizzabaːna?] • **4.** نَصِيحَة [naṣiːħa] نَصايِح [naṣaːyiħ] *pl:* Let me give you a tip. خَلِّي أنطِيك فَدّ نَصِيحَة [xalli ʔanṭiːk fadd naṣiːħa]

T

• **5.** إخبارِيَّة [ʔixbaːriyya] The police found him through a tip. الشُّرطَة لِقوه عَن طَريق إخبارِيَّة [ʔiššurṭa liguːh ʕan ṭariːq ʔixbaːriyya] • **6.** بَخشِيش [baxšiːš] How much of a tip shall I give the waiter? شقَدّ أنطِي بَخشِيش لِلبُوي؟ [šgadd ʔanṭi baxšiːš lilbuːy?]

to tip • **1.** نِطَى بَخشِيش [niṭaː baxšiːš] *sv* i. Did you tip the porter? إنطَيته بَخشِيش لِلحَمّال؟ [ʔinṭiːtah baxšiːš lilħammaːl?]

to tip off • **1.** نِطَى مَعلُومَات [niṭaː maʕluːmaːt] *sv* i. إخبارِيَّة [ʔixbaːriyya] Who tipped you off? مِنُو إنطاك المَعلُومات؟ [minu ʔinṭaːk ʔilmaʕluːmaːt?]

to tip over • **1.** قِلَب [gilab] قَلُب [galub] *vn:* إنقِلَب [ʔingilab] *p:* The maid tipped the chair over. الخادمَة قُلبَت الإسكَملِي [ʔilxaːdma gulbat ʔilʔiskamli] • **2.** اِنقِلَب [ʔingilab] اِنقِلاب [ʔingilaːb] *vn: sv* u. The boat tipped over. البَلَم اِنقِلَب [ʔilbalam ʔingilab]

tiptoe • **1.** أطراف أصابع [ʔaṭraːf ʔaṣaːbiʕ] The children came in on tiptoe. الجِّهال خَشّوا عَلَى أطراف الأصابع [ʔiǰǰihaːl xaššaw ʕala ʔaṭraːf ʔilʔaṣaːbiʕ]

tiptop • **1.** مُمتاز [mumtaːz] My car's in tiptop condition. سَيّارتِي بِحالَة مُمتازَة [sayyaːrti biħaːla mumtaːza]

tire • **1.** تايَر [taːyir] تايَرات [taːyiraːt] *pl:* Did you put air in the tires? نفَخت التّايَرات؟ [nfaxt ʔittaːyiraːt?]

to tire • **1.** تَعَّب [taʕʕab] تَتعِيب [tatʕiːb] *vn: sv* i. The long journey tired us thoroughly. السَّفرَة الطّويلَة تَعّبَتنا كُلِّش [ʔissafra ʔiṭṭwiːla taʕʕbatna kulliš] • **2.** تِعَب [tiʕab] تَعَب، تَعبان [taʕab, taʕbaːn] *vn: sv* a. I tire very easily in this hot weather. آنِي أتعَب بالعَجَل بِهَالجَوّ الحارّ [ʔaːni ʔatʕab bilʕaǰal bhaǰǰaww ʔilħaːrr] • **3.** مَلّ [mall] مَلَل [malal] *vn: sv* i. ضاج [ðaːǰ] ضَوج، ضَوَجان، ضَوجَة [ðawj, ðawaǰaːn, ðuːǰa] *vn: sv* u. I'm tired of her nagging. مَلّيت مِن نَقنَقتها [malliːt min nagnagatha]

tired • **1.** تَعبان [taʕbaːn] He looks tired. يبَيِّن تَعبان [yibayyin taʕbaːn]

tiresome • **1.** مُمِلّ [mumill] What a tiresome person he is! هٰذا صُدُق فَدّ شَخِص مُمِلّ [haːða ṣudug fadd šaxiṣ mumill] • **2.** مُتعِب [mutʕib] This is very tiresome work. هالشُّغُل كُلِّش مُتعِب [haššuɣul kulliš mutʕib]

tissue • **1.** نَسِيج [nasiːǰ] أنسِجَة [ʔansiǰa] *pl:* Was there much tissue injured? كان أكُو هوايَة أنسِجه متأذّايَة؟ [čaːn ʔaku hwaːya ʔansiǰah mitʔaððaːya?] • **2.** كَفِّيَّة وَرَق [čaffiyya waraq] كفافِي وَرَق [čfaːfi waraq] *pl:* Buy me a box of tissues. اِشتِرِيلِي قُوطِيَّة كفافِي وَرَق [ʔištiriːli quːṭiyya čfaːfi waraq]

tissue paper • **1.** وَرَق خَفِيف [waraq xafiːf] Wrap it in tissue paper. لِفّها بوَرَق خَفِيف [liffha bwaraq xafiːf]

title • **1.** إسِم [ʔisim] أسامِي، أسماء [ʔasaːmi, ʔasmaːʔ] *pl:* Do you know the title of the book? تُعرُف إسم الكِتاب؟ [tuʕruf ʔism ʔilkitaːb?] • **2.** لَقَب [laqab] ألقاب [ʔalqaːb] *pl:* What's his title? شِنُو لَقَبَه؟ [šinu laqabah?] • **3.** عِنوان [ʕinwaːn] What's the title of your position? شِنُو عِنوان وَظِيفتَك؟ [šinu ʕinwaːn waðiːftak?] The title page is missing from this book. صَفحَة العِنوان ضايعَة مِن هَالكِتاب. [ṣafħat ʔilʕinwaːn ðaːyʕa min halkitaːb] • **4.** مُلكِيَّة [mulkiyya] مُلكِيّات [mulkiyyaːt] *pl:* Whose name is the title of the car in? بإسِم مَن مُلكِيَة السَّيّارَة؟ [bisim man mulkiyat ʔissayyaːra?]

to • **1.** ال [ʔil] إلَى [ʔila] I have to go to the library. لازم أرُوح لِلمَكتَبَة [laːzim ʔaruːħ lilmaktaba] He went through his fortune to the last cent. صِرَف كُلّ ثَروتَه لآخِر فِلِس [ṣiraf kull θaruːtah lʔaːxir filis] • **2.** ب [b] I told him that to his face. قِلتِله إيّاه بوُجهَه [giltilh ʔiyyaːh bwuččah] What do you say to this? شتِقُول بهاي [šitguːl bhaːy] • **3.** ويّا [wiyya] Did you talk to him? حكَيت وِيّاه؟ [ħčiːt wiyyaːh?] • **4.** عَلَى [ʕala] Apply this ointment to the inflamed area. حُطّ هالمَرهَم عالمَنطَقَة المِلتَهبَة [ħuṭṭ halmarham ʕalmanṭiqa ʔilmiltahba]

* **I'm trying to help you.** • **1.** آنِي بَسّ دَأرِيد أعاونَك [ʔaːni bass daʔariːd ʔaʕaːwnak]

* **I must go to bed.** • **1.** لازِم أنام [laːzim ʔanaːm]

* **It doesn't mean much to him.** • **1.** ما يهِمَّه [maː yhimmah]

* **It's ten minhutes to four.** • **1.** الساعَة أربَعَة إلّا عَشرَة [ʔissaːʕa ʔarbaʕa ʔilla ʕašra]

toad • **1.** عُقرُقَّة [ʕugrugga] عَقارِيق [ʕagaːriːg] عُقرُقّات [ʕugruggaːt] *pl:* عُقرُقّ [ʕugrugg] *Collective:* عُقرُقَّة [ʕugrugga] عُقرُقات [ʕugrugaːt] *pl:* عُقرُقّ [ʕugrugg] *Collective*

toadstool • **1.** راس فطِرّ [raːs fṭirr] رُوس فطِرّ [ruːs fṭirr] *pl:* فطِرّ [fṭirr] *Collective*

toast • **1.** نَخَب [naxab] أنخاب [ʔanxaːb] *pl:* Let's drink a toast to the newlyweds. خَلِّي نِشرَب نَخَب العُرُوس وَالعِرِّيس [xalliː nišrab naxab ʔilʕuruːs wilʕirriːs]

to toast • **1.** حَمَّص [ħammaṣ] تحمِيص [taħmiːṣ] *vn: sv* i. Shall I toast the bread? تريدنِي أحَمِّص الخُبُز؟ [triːdni ʔaħammiṣ ʔilxubuz?] • **2.** شِرَب [širab] *sv* a. Let's toast the host. خَلِّي نِشرَب نَخَب الدّاعِي [xalliː nišrab naxab ʔiddaːʕi]

tobacco • **1.** تِتِن [titin]

tobacco dealer • **1.** تِتِنچِي [titinči, tatanči] تَتَنچِيَّة [tatančiyya] *pl:*

tobacco shop • **1.** مَخزَن سِجايِر [maxzan ǰigaːyir] مَخازِن سِجايِر [maxaːzin ǰigaːyir] *pl:*

today • **1.** يوم [yawm] أيّام [ʔayyaːm] *pl:* اليوم [ʔilyawm] What's on the menu today? شكُو عِدكُم أكِل هاليُوم؟ [šaku ʕidkum ʔakil halyuːm?] I haven't read today's paper yet. بَعَدني ما قرَيت جَريدَة اليُوم [baʕadni maː qriːt ǰariːdat ʔilyuːm]

toe • **1.** إصبع رِجِل [ʔiṣbiʕ rijil] أصابِع رِجِل [ʔaṣaːbiʕ rijil] *pl:* أصابِيع رِجِل [ʔaṣaːbiːʕ rijil] أصابِع رِجِل [ʔaṣaːbiʕ rijil] *pl:* My toes are frozen. أصابِيع رِجلِي مثَلّجَة [ʔaṣaːbiːʕ rijli mθallja]

*** I didn't mean to stop on anybody's toes.**

• **1.** ما قصَدِت الإساءَة لأحَّد [maː qṣadit ʔilʔisaːʔa lʔaħħad] / ما قِصَدِت أتعَرَّض لِأحَّد [maː qṣadit ʔatʕarraḍ lʔaħħad]

*** I have to be on my toes all the time.**

• **1.** لازم أفُكّ عيُونِي عَلَى طُول [laːzim ʔafukk ʕyuːni ʕala ṭuːl] / لازِم أكُون مِتيَقِّظ عَلَى طُول [laːzim ʔakuːn mityaqqiḍ ʕala ṭuːl]

together • **1.** سُوَة، سُوا [suwa] We work together. نِشتُغُل سُوَة [ništuɣul suwa] I saw my friend and his wife walking together. شِفِت صَدِيقِي وَمَرتَه يِتمَشّون سُوَة [šifit ṣadiːqi wmartah yitmaššuːn suwa]

to get together • **1.** اِجتِمَع [ʔiǰtimaʕ] اِجتِماع [ʔiǰtimaːʕ] *vn: sv* i. Can we get together some evening? نِقدَر نِجتِمِع فَدّ لَيلَة؟ [nigdar niǰtimiʕ fadd layla?]

to stick together • **1.** تعاضَد [tʕaːḍad] تَعاضُد [taʕaːḍud] *vn: sv* a. Let's stick together in this matter. خَلّي نِتعاضَد بِهالمَسألَة [xalli nitʕaːḍad bhalmasʔala]

toilet • **1.** مِرحاض [mirħaːḍ] مَراحِيض [maraːħiːḍ] *pl:* خَلاء [xalaːʔ] خَلاءات [xalaːʔaːt] *pl:* Where's the toilet? وين المِرحاض؟ [wiːn ʔilmirħaːḍ?]

toilet paper • **1.** وَرَق مَراحِيض [waraq maraːħiːḍ] وَرَق خَلاء [waraq xalaːʔ] Muslims use water instead of toilet paper. المِسلِمِين يِستَعمِلُون ماي بِدال وَرَق المَراحِيض [ʔilmisilmiːn yistaʕmiluːn maːy bidaːl waraq ʔilmaraːħiːḍ]

token • **1.** دَلِيل [daliːl] دَلائِل [dalaːʔil] *pl:* عَلامَة [ʕalaːma] عَلامات، عَلائِم [ʕalaːmaːt, ʕalaːʔim] *pl:* تِذكار [tiðkaːr] تِذكارات [tiðkaːraːt] *pl:* He gave it to me as a token of his friendship. إنطانِي إيّاها كَدَلِيل عَلَى صَداقتَه [ʔinṭaːniː ʔiyyaːha kadaliːl ʕala ṣadaːqtah] • **2.** إسمِي [ʔismi] We may be able to satisfy them with a token payment. يِمكِن نِقدَر نِرضِيهُم بفَدّ مَبلَغ إسمِي [yimkin nigdar nirḍiːhum bfadd mablaɣ ʔismi]

tolerance • **1.** تَحَمُّل [taħammul] This steel has high tolerance for heat. هَالفُولاذ عِندَه تَحَمُّل قَوِي لِلحَرارَة [halfuːlaːð ʕindah taħammul qawi lilħaraːra] • **2.** تَسامُح [tasaːmuħ] Tolerance is difficult in religion and politics. التَّسامُح بِالدِّين وَبالسِّياسَة صَعُب [ʔittasaːmuħ biddiːn wbissiyaːsa ṣaʕub]

tolerant • **1.** مِتسامِح [mitsaːmiħ] Our boss is very tolerant. مُدِيرنا كُلِّش مِتسامِح [mudiːrna kulliš mitsaːmiħ]

to tolerate • **1.** تسامَح ب [tsaːmaħ b-] *sv* a. I won't tolerate inefficiency. ما راح أتسامَح بحالَة عَدَم الكَفاءَة [maː raːħ ʔatsaːmaħ bħaːlat ʕadam ʔilkafaːʔa]

toll • **1.** عِبرِيَّة [ʕibriyya] عِبريّات [ʕibriyyaːt] *pl:* You have to pay a toll on this bridge. لازِم تِدفَع عِبرِيَّة عَلَى هَالجِسِر [laːzim tidfaʕ ʕibriyya ʕala halǰisir] • **2.** عَدَد [ʕadad] The plane crash took a heavy toll of life. راح عَدَد كِبِير مِن الضَّحايا بحادِث الطِّيّارَة [raːħ ʕadad čibiːr min ʔiððaħaːya bħaːdiθ ʔiṭṭiyyaːra]

toll bridge • **1.** * This is a toll bridge. هَذا الجِّسِر ياخذُون عَليه عِبرِيَّة [haːða ʔiǰǰisir yaːxðuːn ʕaliːh ʕibriyya]

tomato • **1.** طَماطايَة [ṭamaːṭaːya] طَماطايات [ṭamaːṭaːyaːt] *pl:* طَماطَة [ṭamaːṭa] *Collective:* Make the salad with tomatoes and cucumbers. سَوِّي الزَّلاطَة مِن طَماطَة وَخيار [sawwi ʔizzalaːṭa min ṭamaːṭa wxyaːr]

tomato juice • **1.** عَصِير طَماطَة [ʕaṣiːr ṭamaːṭa]

tomato sauce • **1.** مَعجُون طَماطَة [maʕǰuːn ṭamaːṭa]

tomb • **1.** قَبُر [gabur] قبُور [gbuːr] *pl:* He placed a wreath on the tomb of the unknown soldier. حَطّ إكلِيل عَلَى قَبر الجُّندِي المَجهُول [ħaṭṭ ʔikliːl ʕala qabr ʔiǰǰundi ʔilmaǰhuːl] • **2.** ضَرِيح [ḍariːħ] ضَرايِح، أضرِحَة [ḍaraːyiħ, ʔaḍriħa] *pl:* They went to visit Husayn's tomb in Karbala. راحَوا يزُورُون ضَرِيح الحُسَين بِكَربَلاء [raːħaw yzuːruːn ḍariːħ ʔilħusayn bkarbala]

tomcat • **1.** هِرّ [hirr] هرُورَة [hruːra] *pl:*

tomorrow • **1.** باكِر [baːčir] I'll be back tomorrow. راح أرجَع باكِر [raːħ ʔarǰaʕ baːčir] It'll be in tomorrow's paper. تِطلَع بجَرِيدَة باكِر [tiṭlaʕ bǰariːdat baːčir] I won't see him till tomorrow morning. ما راح أشُوفَه قَبُل باكِر الصُّبُح [maː raːħ ʔašuːfah gabul baːčir ʔiṣṣubuħ]

ton • **1.** طَنّ [ṭann] أطنان [ʔaṭnaːn] *pl:* We order a ton of coal. وَصَّينا عَلَى طَنّ فَحَم [waṣṣiːna ʕala ṭann faħam] That's a ten-ton truck. هَاللُّورِي أبُو عَشِر طنُون [halluːri ʔabu ʕašir ṭnuːn]

tone • **1.** لَهجَة [lahǰa] لَهجات [lahǰaːt] *pl:* صُوت [ṣuːt] أصوات [ʔaṣwaːt] *pl:* You shouldn't speak to her in such a rough tone. ما لازِم تِحكِي وِيّاها بهِيكِي لَهجَة حادَّة [maː laːzim tiħči wiyyaːha bhiːči lahǰa ħaːdda] • **2.** صُوت [ṣuːt] أصوات [ʔaṣwaːt] *pl:* This violin has a beautiful tone. هَالكَمَنجَة صُوتها كُلِّش حِلو [halkamanǰa ṣuːtha kulliš ħilw] • **3.** لَون [lawn] ألوان [ʔalwaːn] *pl:* His car is two-tone. سَيّارتَه لَونَين [sayyaːrtah lawnayn]

T

to tone down • **1.** هِدَأ [hidaʔ] هُدُوء [huduːʔ] *vn: sv* a. عِقَل [ʕiqal] عَقِل [ʕaqil] *vn: sv* a. He's toned down a lot since he came here. هِدَأ هوايَة مِن إجا لِهنا [hidaʔ hwaːya min ʔiǰa lihna]

tongs • **1.** ماشَة [maːša] ماشات [maːšaːt] *pl:* Use tongs to stir the coals. حَرِّك الجَّمُر بِالماشَة [ħarrik ʔiǰǰamur bilmaːša] • **2.** مِلقَط [milgaṭ] مَلاقِط [malaːgiṭ] *pl:* He picked up a lump of sugar with the tongs. شال فُصّ شَكَر بِالمِلقَط [šaːl fuṣṣ šakar bilmilgaṭ]

tongue • **1.** لِسان [lisaːn, lsaːn] لِسِن [lisin] لِسانات [lisaːnaːt] ألسِنَة [ʔalsina] *pl:* Let me see your tongue. خَلِّي أشُوف لِسانَك [xalliː ʔašuːf lisaːnak] She has a sharp tongue. عِدها لسان حادّ [ʕidha lsaːn ħaːdd] She has a sharp tongue. لسانها مِثِل السِّكِّين [lsaːnha miθl ʔissiččiːn] The tongue on my shoe is torn off. اِنقِطَع لِسان قُندَرتي [ʔingiṭaʕ lisaːn qundarti]

tonic • **1.** مُقَوِّي [muqawwi] مُقَوِّيات [muqawwiyyaːt] *pl:* What you need is a good tonic. يِنرادلَك فَدّ مُقَوِّي زين [yinraːdlak fadd muqawwi ziːn] • **2.** تونِك [tuːnik] Do you like gin and tonic? يِعجِبَك جِن وَتُونِك؟ [yiʕiǰbak ǰin wtuːnik?] • **3.** دِهِن [dihin] The barber put some tonic on my hair. المِزَيِّن حَطّ دِهِن بِشَعرِي [ʔilmzayyin ħaṭṭ dihin bšaʕri]

tonight • **1.** هَاللَيلَة [hallayla] اللَيلَة [ʔillayla] What shall we do tonight? شِنسَوّي هاللَّيلَة؟ [šinsawwi hallayla?] Have you seen tonight's paper? شِفت الجَّرِيدَة مالَت هاللَّيلَة؟ [šift ʔiǰǰariːda maːlat hallayla?]

tonnage • **1.** طَنّ حُمُولَة [ṭann ħumuːla] What's the tonnage of that vessel? كَم طَنّ حُمُولَة ذِيك الباخِرَة؟ [čam ṭann ħumuːlat ðiːč ʔilbaːxira?]

tonsil • **1.** لَوزَة [lawza, luːza] لَوزَات [lawzaːt] *pl:* My tonsils are swollen. لَوزتَينِي مِلتَهبَة [lawztayni miltahba]

tonsilitis • **1.** اِلتِهاب اللَّوزتَين [ʔiltihaːb ʔillawztayn]

too • **1.** هَمّ [hamm] هَمِّين [hammiːn] May I come, too? أقدَر آني هَمّ أجِي؟ [ʔagdar ʔaːni hamm ʔaǰi?]
 * **This is too hot.** • **1.** هاي كُلِّش حارّ [haːy kulliš ħaːrra]
 * **Don't stay away too long.** • **1.** لا تطَوِّل بَرَّة هوايَة [laː ttawwil barra hwaːya]
 * **This board is too long.** • **1.** هَاللَّوحَة أطوَل مِن اللازِم [hallawħa ʔaṭwal min ʔillaːzim]
 * **The play was none too good.** • **1.** الرُّوايَة ما كانَت كُلِّش زَينَة [ʔirruwaːya maː čaːnat kulliš ziːna]

tool • **1.** أداة [ʔadaːt] أدَوات [ʔadawaːt] *pl:* آلَة [ʔaːla] آلات [ʔaːlaːt] *pl:* Be careful with those new tools. دِير بالَك عَلَى هَالأدَوات الجِّدِيدَة [diːr baːlak ʕala halʔadawaːt ʔiǰǰidiːda] • **2.** آلَة [ʔaːla] آلات [ʔaːlaːt] *pl:* The mayor is only a tool in the hands of his party. رَئِيس البَلَدِيَّة مُو أزيَد مِن آلَة بإيد الحِزب مالَه [raʔiːs ʔilbaladiyya muː ʔazyad min ʔaːla bʔiːd ʔilħizib maːlah]

tooled leather • **1.** جِلِد مَشغُول [ǰilid mašɣuːl] جِلِد مَنقُوش [ǰilid manquːš]

to toot • **1.** طَوَّط [ṭawwaṭ] تطُوُّط [tṭuwwuṭ] *vn: sv* u. دَقّ [dagg] *sv* u. Toot your horn at this corner. طَوُّط بهَذا المَفرَق [ṭawwuṭ bhaːða ʔilmafrag]

tooth • **1.** سِنّ [sinn] سنُون [snuːn] *pl:* This tooth hurts. هَالسِّنّ يوَجِّع [hassinn ywaǰǰiʕ] The saw has a broken tooth. المِنشار بِيه سِنّ مَكسُور [ʔilminšaːr biːh sinn maksuːr]
 * **She has a sweet tooth.** • **1.** تحِبّ الحَلا هوايَة [tħibb ʔilħala hwaːya]
 * **We fought against it tooth and nail.** • **1.** قاوَمناها بكُلّ شِدَّة [qaːwamnaːha bkull šidda]

toothache • **1.** وَجَع [waǰaʕ sinn] I have a toothache. عِندِي وَجَع سِنّ [ʕindi waǰaʕ sinn]

toothbrush • **1.** فِرشَة سنُون [firčat snuːn] فِرَش سنُون [firač snuːn] *pl:*

tooth paste • **1.** مَعجُون سِنُون [maʕǰuːn snuːn]

top • **1.** راس [raːs] رُوس [ruːs] *pl:* The storm broke off the top of our palm tree. العاصِفَة كِسرَت راس النَّخلَة مالَتنا [ʔilʕaːṣifa kisrat raːs ʔinnaxla maːlatna] You'll find that passage at the top of page 32. تشُوف هَالفَقَرَة براس صَفحَة ثنَين وَثلاثِين [tšuːf halfaqara braːs ṣafħa θnayn wtlaːθiːn] • **2.** قِمَّة [qimma, qumma] قِمَم [qimam, qumam] *pl:* How far is it to the top of the mountain? شقَدّ المَسافَة لقِمَّة هَالجِّبَل؟ [šgadd ʔilmasaːfa lqimmat haǰǰibal?] • **3.** عِلو [ʕilw] أعلَى [ʔaʕla] She shouted at the top of her voice. صاحَت بِعِلو حِسّها [ṣaːħat bʕilw ħissha] She shouted at the top of her voice. صاحَت بكُلّ حِسّها [ṣaːħat bkull ħissha] • **4.** فَوقانِي [fawgaːni] There's still one room vacant on the top floor. لهَسَّة أكُو غُرفَة فارغَة بِالقاط الفَوقانِي [lhassa ʔaku ɣurfa faːrɣa bilqaːṭ ʔilfawgaːni] Your handkerchiefs are in the top drawer. كفافِيك بِالمَجَرّ الفَوقانِي [čfaːfiyyak bilmaǰarr ʔilfugaːni] • **5.** تَنتَة [tanta] تَنتات [tantaːt] *pl:* It's such nice weather, let's put the top down. الجَّوّ كُلِّش لَطِيف، خَلِّي ننَزِّل التَنتَة [ʔiǰǰaww kulliš laṭiːf, xalli ʔinnazzil tanta] • **6.** مُصرَع [muṣraʕ] مُصارِع [muṣaːriʕ] *pl:* Do you know how to spin a top? تُعرُف تِلعَب مُصرَع؟ [tuʕruf tilʕab muṣraʕ?] • **7.** فَوق [fawg] The book is lying on top. الكِتاب مَحطُوط لِفُوق [ʔilkitaːb maħṭuːṭ lifuːg] We searched the house from top to bottom. فَتَّشنا البَيت مِن فَوق لِجَوَّة [fattašna ʔilbayt min fuːg liǰawwa] • **8.** أقصَى [ʔaqṣa] We drove at top speed all the way down here. سِقنا بأقصَى سُرعَة طُول الطَّرِيق لِهنا [siqna bʔaqṣa surʕa ṭuːl ʔiṭṭariːq lihna]

*** I don't know why he blew his top.**
• **1.** ما أدري لَيش هاج [ma: ʔadri li:š ha:ǰ]
*** I slept like a top last night.**
• **1.** نِمت مِثل الحجارَة البارحَة بِاللَيل [nimit miθl ʔiliħǰa:ra ʔilba:rħa billayl]
to top off • **1.** أنهَى [ʔanha:] *sv* i. خَلَّص [xallaṣ] *sv* i. Let's top off the evening with a glass of wine. خَلّي نِنهي اللَّيلَة بِفَدّ كلاص شَراب [xalli ninhi ʔillayla bfadd gla:ṣ šara:b]
*** To top it all off, he stole my wallet.**
• **1.** وكمالَة، باق الجِّزدان مالِي [wičma:la, ba:g ʔiǰǰizda:n ma:li] فَوقاها، باق جِزدانِي [fawga:ha, ba:g ǰizda:ni]

topic • **1.** مَوضُوع [mawḍu:ʕ] مَواضِيع [mawa:ḍi:ʕ] *pl:* This is quite a timely topic. هَذا فَدّ مَوضُوع بوَقتَه [ha:ða fadd mawḍu:ʕ bwaktah]

topsoil • **1.** زِميج [zimi:ǰ] The rains are washing away the topsoil. الأمطار دَتِجرُف الزِّمِيج [ʔilʔamṭa:r datiǰruf ʔizzimi:ǰ]

topsy-turvy • **1.** راس عَلَى عَقِب [ra:s ʕala ʕaqib] Everything was topsy-turvy. كُلّشِي كان مَقلُوب راس عَلَى عَقِب [kullši ča:n maglu:b ra:s ʕala ʕaqib]

torch • **1.** مَشعَل [mašʕal] مشاعِيل [mša:ʕil] *pl:*

torment • **1.** عَذاب [ʕaða:b] I can't stand the torment anymore. ما أتحَمَّل العَذاب بَعَد [ma: ʔatħammal ʔilʕaða:b baʕad]
to torment • **1.** أذَّى [ʔaðða:] *sv* i. Stop tormenting that cat! بَسّ عاد تأذّي هَالبَزّونَة [bass ʕa:d tʔaðði halbazzu:na] • **2.** مَرمَر ل [marmar l-] تمَرمُر [tmurmur] *vn: sv* u. عَذَّب [ʕaððab] تَعذِيب [taʕði:b] *vn: sv* i. She tormented her father all day. هِيَّ مَرمُرَتَه لِأبُوها طُول النَّهار [hiyya marmuratah lʔabu:ha ṭu:l ʔinnaha:r] She tormented her father all day. عَذّبَت أبُوها طُول النَّهار [ʕaððibat ʔabu:ha ṭu:l ʔinnaha:r]

torn • **1.** مَشقُوق [mašgu:g] Which pocket is torn? يا جِيب مَشقُوق؟ [ya: ǰi:b mašgu:g?]

tornado • **1.** فَتّالَة [fatta:la] فَتّالات [fatta:la:t] *pl:*

torpedo • **1.** تُوربِيد [tu:rbi:d] تُوربِيدات [tu:rbi:da:t] *pl:*

torrent • **1.** سَيل [sayl] سِيُول [siyu:l] *pl:* The heavy rain caused several small torrents. المُطَر القَوِي سَبَّب عِدَّة سِيُول صغَيّرَة [ʔilmuṭar ʔilqawi sabbab ʕiddat siyu:l ṣɣayyra]
*** The rain came down in torrents.**
• **1.** المُطَر قام يِنزِل مِثل القِرَب [ʔilmuṭar ga:m yinzil miθl ʔilgirab]

torrid zone • **1.** المَنطِقَة الإستِوائِيَّة [ʔilmanṭiqa ʔilʔistiwa:ʔiyya] Most of Africa lies within the torrid zone. مُعظَم أفرِيقيا واقعَة بِالمَنطِقَة الاستِوائِيَّة [muʕḍam ʔafri:qya wa:qʕa bilmanṭiqa ʔalʔistiwa:ʔiyya]

tortoise • **1.** سُلحَفاة [sulħafa:t] سَلاحِف [sala:ħif] *pl:* رَقَّة [ragga] رَقّات [ragga:t] *pl:*

torture • **1.** عَذاب، تَعذِيب [ʕaða:b, taʕði:b] مَرمَرَة [marmara] Life with her is just torture. الحَياة ويّاها عَذاب بَسّ [ʔilħaya:t wiyya:ha ʕaða:b bass] • **2.** تَعذِيب [taʕði:b] Confessions obtained by torture are illegal. الاعتِرافات اللّي تِتحَصَّل بِالتَّعذِيب مُو قانُونِيَّة [ʔiliʕtira:fa:t ʔilli titħaṣṣal bittaʕði:b mu: qa:nu:niyya]
to torture • **1.** عَذَّب [ʕaððab] تَعذِيب [taʕði:b] *vn: sv* i. The police tortured him to get a confession. الشُّرطَة عَذّبُوه حَتَّى ياخذُون مِنَّه اِعتِراف [ʔiššurṭa ʕaððibu:h ħatta ya:xðu:n minnah ʔiʕtira:f]

to toss • **1.** شُمَر [šumar] شَمُر [šamur] *vn: sv* u. Toss me the ball over here. إشمُرلِي الطّوبَة لِهنا [ʔišmurli ʔiṭṭu:ba lihna] • **2.** تقَلَّب [tgallab] تقُلُّب [tgullub] *vn: sv* u. Last night I tossed and turned all night long. البارحَة باللّيل ظَلّيت أتقَلَّب بفراشِي [ʔilba:rħa billayl ḍalli:t ʔatgallab bifra:ši]

tot • **1.** صغَيرُون [zɣayru:n] صغار [zɣa:r] *pl:* She's just a tiny tot. بَعَدها صغَيّرُونَة [baʕadha zɣayyru:na]

total • **1.** مَجمُوع [majmu:ʕ] مَجامِيع [maǰa:mi:ʕ] *pl:* Subtract ten from the total. إطرَح عَشرَة مِن المَجمُوع [ʔiṭraħ ʕašra min ʔilmajmu:ʕ] My total earnings for this month were two hundred dollars. المَجمُوع اللّي حَصَّلتَه هَالشَّهَر مِيتَين دُولار [majmu:ʕ ʔilli ħaṣṣaltah haššahar mitayn dula:r]
to total • **1.** وَصَّل [waṣṣal] *sv* i. His income totals two thousand dollars a year. دَخلَه يوَصِّل ألفَين دُولار بِالسَّنَة [daxlah ywaṣṣil ʔalfayn dula:r bissana] • **2.** حِسَب [ħisab] حساب [ħsa:b] *vn: sv* i. جِمَع [ǰimaʕ] جَمِع [ǰamiʕ] *vn: sv* a. Let's total up our expenses for the month. خَلّي نِحسِب مَصرُوفاتنا مال الشَّهَر [xalli niħsib maṣru:fa:tna ma:l ʔiššahar]

to totter • **1.** تمايَل [tma:yal] تَمايُل [tama:yul] *vn: sv* a. The old man got up and tottered toward the door. الشّايِب قام وَتمايَل لِلباب [ʔašša:yib ga:m wtma:yal lilba:b]

tottering • **1.** مِتداعِي [mitda:ʕi] The bridge is tottering. الجِّسِر مِتداعِي [ʔiǰǰisir midda:ʕi]

touch • **1.** طَخَّة [ṭaxxa] طَخّات [ṭaxxa:t] *pl:* She jumps at the slightest touch. تُقمُز مِن أقَلّ طَخَّة [tugmuz min ʔaqall ṭaxxa] She jumps at the slightest touch. تُقمُز بَسّ واحِد يجِيسها [tugmuz bass wa:ħid ygi:sha] • **2.** مَلمَس [malmas] Silk is soft to the touch. الحَرِير ناعِم المَلمَس [ʔalħari:r na:ʕim ʔilmalmas] • **3.** نُقطَة [nugṭa, nuqṭa] نُقَط [nugaṭ, nuqaṭ] *pl:* The soup still needs a touch of salt. الشّوربَة بَعَدها تِحتاج فَدّ نُقطَة مِلح

T

[ʔiššu:rba baʕadha tiħta:ǰ fadd nugṭat miliħ] • **4.** أَثَر [ʔaθar] آثار [ʔa:θa:r] *pl:* The patient has a touch of fever. المَرِيض عِندَه أَثَر سُخُونَة [ʔilmari:ð̣ ʕindah ʔaθar ṣuxu:na]

*** The game was touch and go towards the end.** • **1.** نَتِيجَة السِباق كانَت معَلَّقَة [nati:ǰat ʔissiba:q ča:nat mʕalliga]

to get in touch with • **1.** اِتِّصَل [ʔittiṣal] اِتِّصال [ʔittiṣa:l] *vn: sv* i. I have to get in touch with him right away. لازِم أَتِّصِل بِيه حالاً [la:zim ʔattiṣil bi:h ħa:lan]

to touch • **1.** جاس [ga:s] *sv* i. طَخّ [ṭaxx] طَخّ [ṭaxx] *vn: sv* u. Please don't touch that! بالله لا تجِيسها لِهاي [ballah la: tgi:sha lha:y] He won't touch liquor. ما يجِيس المَشرُوب [ma: ygi:s ʔilmašru:b]

*** I touched him for two dinars.** • **1.** شِلَعِت مِنَّه دِينارَين [šilaʕit minnah dina:rayn] / تدايَنِت مِنَّه دِينارَين [dda:yanit minnah dina:rayn]

to touch off • **1.** أَدَّى إِلَى [ʔadda: ʔila] تَأدِيَة إِلَى [taʔdiya ʔila] *vn: sv* i. His remarks touched off a violent argument. مُلاحَظاتَه أَدَّت إِلَى فَدّ جَدَل عَنِيف [mula:ħað̣a:tah ʔaddat ʔila fadd ǰadal ʕani:f]

to touch on • **1.** شار إِلَى، تطَرَّق إِلَى [ša:r ʔila, ttarraq ʔila] *sv* i. تطَرَّق [ṭṭarraq] *sv* a. The speaker touched on many points during his talk. المُحاضِر شار إِلَى عِدَّة نُقاط بحَدِيثَه [ʔilmuħa:ð̣ir ša:r ʔila ʕiddat nuqa:ṭ bħadi:θah] • **2.** وُصَل [wuṣal] وُصُول [wuṣu:l] *vn: sv* a. His remarks touch on blasphemy. حَكيَه يُوصَل إِلَى دَرَجَة الكُفُر [ħačyah yu:ṣal ʔila daraǰat ʔilkufur]

to touch up • **1.** سَوَّى رِطُوش لِ [sawwa: riṭu:š li-] *sv* i. They haven't touched up the picture yet. بَعَد لهَسَّة ما سَوّالها رِتُوش لِلصُّورَة [baʕad lhassa ma: sawwa:lha ritu:š liṣṣu:ra]

touched • **1.** مَشخُوط [mašxu:ṭ] Don't mind him! He's a little touched. لا تدِيرلَه بال، هَذا مَشخُوط [la: ddi:rlah ba:l, ha:ða mašxu:ṭ]

to be touched • **1.** تأَثَّر [tʔaθθar] تَأَثُّر [taʔaθθur] *vn: sv* i. She was deeply touched by the story. تأَثّرَت كُلِّش مِن الحِكايَة [tʔaθθrat kulliš min ʔiliħča:ya]

*** I was deeply touched by his kindness.** • **1.** لُطفَه أَخجَلنِي [luṭfah ʔaxǰalni]

touchy • **1.** مِتنَرفِز [mitnarfiz] She's very touchy. هِيَّ كُلِّش مِتنَرفِزَة [hiyya kulliš mitnarfiza] • **2.** حَسّاس [ħassa:s] That's a very touchy subject. هَذا فَدّ مَوضُوع كُلِّش حَسّاس [ha:ða fadd mawð̣u:ʕ kulliš ħassa:s]

tough • **1.** قَوِي [qawi, guwi] The meat is awfully tough. اللَّحَم كُلِّش قَوِي [ʔillaħam kulliš qawi] • **2.** زَحِم [zaħim] That's a tough assignment. هاي فَدّ شَغلَة زَحمَة [ha:y fadd šaɣla zaħma] • **3.** لَرّ [larr] He's a real tough character. هُوَّ فَدّ واحِد أَبُو جاسِم لَرر [huwwa fadd wa:ħid ʔabu ǰa:sim larr] • **4.** سُوء [su:ʔ] He's had tough luck. جابَه سُوء حَظّ [ǰa:bah su:ʔ ħað̣ð̣]

*** That's a tough nut to crack.** • **1.** هاي فَدّ مُشكِلَة ما تِنحَلّ [ha:y fadd muškila ma: tinħall]

to toughen • **1.** عَلَّم عَالخُشُونَة [ʕallam ʕalxušu:na] *sv* i. A year in the army will toughen him. فَدّ سَنَة بِالجَيش تعَلّمَه عالخُشُونَة [fadd sana biǰǰayš tʕallmah ʕalxušu:na]

tour • **1.** جَولَة [ǰawla] جَولات [ǰawla:t] *pl:* He made a tour through Europe and Asia. سَوَّى جَولَة بأَورُبّا وبآسيا [sawwa: ǰawla bʔawruppa: wibʔa:sya]

to tour • **1.** جال [ǰa:l] جَولَة [ǰawla] *vn: sv* u. The troupe is now touring South America. الفِرقَة هَسَّة دَتجُول أَمرِيكا الجَنُوبِيَّة [ʔilfirqa hassa dadǰu:l ʔamri:ka ʔiǰǰinu:biyya]

tourist • **1.** سايِح [sa:yiħ] سِيّاح، سُوّاح [siyya:ħ, suwwa:ħ] *pl:* Many tourists come here during the summer. هوايَة سُوّاح يجُون هنا أَثناء الصَّيف [hwa:ya suwwa:ħ yiǰu:n hna: ʔaθna:ʔ ʔiṣṣayf]

tourist class • **1.** دَرَجَة السِياحَة [daraǰat ʔissiya:ħa] دَرَجَة ثانيَة [daraǰa θa:nya]

to tow • **1.** جَرّ [ǰarr] جَرّ [ǰarr] *vn: sv* u. Can you tow my boat over to that side? بالله تِقدَر تجُرّ البَلَم مالِي لِذاك الصُّوب؟ [ballah tigdar dǰurr ʔilbalam ma:li lða:k ʔiṣṣu:b?]

toward(s) • **1.** اِتِّجاه [ʔittiǰa:h] اِتِّجاهات [ʔittiǰa:ha:t] *pl:* عَلَى اِتِّجاه [ʕala ʔittiǰa:h] He drove off toward Karrada. ساق بِاتِّجاه الكَرّادَة [sa:q bʔittiǰa:h ʔilkarra:da] • **2.** قَرِيب [qari:b] I'll be there towards evening. أَكُون هناك قَرِيب المِغرب [ʔaku:n hna:k qari:b ʔilmiɣrib] • **3.** وِيّا [wiyya] نَحُو [naħw] He was very nice toward me. كان كُلِّش لَطِيف وِيّايا [ča:n kulliš laṭi:f wiyya:ya]

towel • **1.** بَشكِير [baški:r] بَشاكِير [baša:ki:r] *pl:* خاولِي [xa:wli] خاولِيّات [xa:wli:yya:t] *pl:* مَنشَفَة [manšafa] مَناشِف [mana:šif] *pl:*

tower • **1.** بُرِج [buriǰ] بُرُوج، أَبراج [buru:ǰ, ʔabra:ǰ] *pl:* Lightning struck the tower last night. الصّاعِقَة نِزلَت عالبُرِج البارحَة باللَّيل [ʔiṣṣa:ʕiqa nizlat ʕalburiǰ ʔilba:rħa billayl]

town • **1.** مَدِينَة [madi:na] مُدُن [mudun] *pl:* بَلدَة [balda] بَلدات [balda:t] *pl:* What's the name of this town? هَالولايَة شِسِمها؟ [halwla:ya šisimha?] • **2.** بَلَدِي [baladi] He's a member of the town council. هُوَّ عُضو مَجلِس بَلَدِي [huwwa ʕuð̣w maǰlis baladi]

tow rope • **1.** حَبِل جَرّ [ħabil ǰarr] حبال مال جَرّ [ħba:l ma:l ǰarr] *pl:*

tow truck • **1.** سَاحِبَة [saːħiba] ساحِبات [saːħibaːt] *pl:* Send me the tow truck دِزّلِي السّاحِبَة [dizzli ʔissaːħiba]

toxic • **1.** سامّ [saːmm] These fumes are toxic. هَالغازات سامَّة [halɣaːzaːt saːmma]

toy • **1.** مَلاعِيب [malaːʕiːb] لَعّابَة [laʕʕaːba] لَعّابات [laʕʕaːbaːt] *pl:* لَعّاب [laʕʕaːb] *Collective:* I'll bring him some toys. راح أَجِيبلَه مَلاعِيب [raːħ ʔajiːblah malaːʕiːb]

to toy • **1.** صُفَن [ṣufan] *sv* u. I was toying with this idea. كِنِت دَأصفُن بِهَالفِكرَة [činit daʔaṣfun bhalfikra]

trace • **1.** أَثَر [ʔaθar] آثار [ʔaːθaːr] *pl:* The police found traces of poison in the food. الشُّرطَة لِقَوا أَثَر سَمّ بِالأَكِل [ʔiššurṭa ligaw ʔaθar samm bilʔakil] He disappeared without leaving a trace. اِختِفَى بَلا ما يِترُك أَثَر [ʔixtifaː bala maː yitruk ʔaθar]

to trace • **1.** اِتَّبَع [ʔittabbaʕ] تَتَبُّع [tatabbuʕ] *vn: sv* a. اِقتِفَى [ʔiqtifaː] اِقتِفاء [ʔiqtifaːʔ] *vn: sv* i. They traced him by his footsteps. اِتّبّعُوه بِآثار أَقدامَه [ʔittabbiʕuːh bʔaːθaːr ʔaqdaːmah] They traced him by his footsteps. اِقتِفَوا آثار أَقدامَه [ʔiqtifaw ʔaːθaːr ʔaqdaːmah] • **2.** نِسَب [nisab] نِسبَة [nisba] *vn: sv* i. We traced the story to him. نِسَبنا الحكايَة إِلَه [nisabna ʔilħčaːya ʔilah] • **3.** اِستَنسَخ [ʔistansax] اِستِنساخ [ʔistinsaːx] *vn: sv* i. Did you trace the floor plan? اِستَنسَختِ مُخَطَّط البِنايَة؟ [ʔistansaxit muxaṭṭaṭ ʔilbinaːya?]

tracer • **1.** تَأكِيد [taʔkiːd] تَأكِيدات [taʔkiːdaːt] *pl:* We'll send a tracer after that letter. راح ندِزّ تَأكِيد عَلَى ذاك الكِتاب [raːħ ndizz tʔakiːd ʕala ðaːk ʔilkitaːb]

trachoma • **1.** تراخوما [traːxuːma]

tracing paper • **1.** وَرَق اِستِنساخ [waraq ʔistinsaːx]

track • **1.** أَثَر [ʔaθar] آثار [ʔaːθaːr] *pl:* There were many animal tracks around the spring. كان أَكُو آثار حَيوانات هوايَة حَول العَين [čaːn ʔaku ʔaːθaːr ħaywaːnaːt hwaːya ħawl ʔilʕayn] • **2.** دَرُب [darub] درُوب [druːb] *pl:* There is an old track in the desert which leads to the well. أَكُو دَرُب عَتِيق بِالصَّحراء يأَدِّي لِلبِير [ʔaku darub ʕatiːg biṣṣaħraːʔ yʔaddi lilbiːr] • **3.** خَطّ [xaṭṭ] خُطُوط [xuṭuːṭ] *pl:* سَكّ [sačč] The train will arrive on Track Two. القِطار يُوصَل عالخَطّ الثّانِي [ʔilqiṭaːr yuːṣal ʕalxaṭṭ ʔiθθaːni] The tracks between Hilla and Kufa are being repaired. السِّكَّة بين الحِلَّة وَالكُوفَة دَتِتصَلَّح [ʔissičča biːn ʔilħilla wilkuːfa datitṣallaħ] • **4.** زَنجِيل [zanjiːl] زناجِيل [znaːjiːl] *pl:* The left track on the tractor is broken. الزَّنجِيل الصَفحَة اليِسرَة مال التراكتَر مَقطُوع [ʔizzanjiːl ʔilṣafħat ʔilyisra maːl ʔittraktar magṭuːʕ] • **5.** اِتِّجاه [ʔittijaːh] اِتِّجاهات [ʔittijaːhaːt] *pl:* You're on the right track. إِنتَ مِتِّجِه بِالإتِّجاه الصَّحِيح [ʔinta mittijih bilʔittijaːh ʔiṣṣaħiːħ] You're on the right track. إِنتَ ماشِي زين [ʔinta maːši ziːn]

*** I'm afraid you're entirely off the track.** • **1.** أَعتِقِد إِنتَ ماشِي غَلَط [ʔaʕtiqid ʔinta maːši ɣalaṭ]

to keep track of • **1.** ضُبَط [ðubaṭ] ضَبُط [ðabuṭ] *vn: sv* u. Keep close track of your expenses. إِضبُط مَصرُوفاتَك [ʔiðbuṭ maṣruːfaːtak] • **2.** راقَب [raːqab] مُراقَبَة [muraːqaba] *vn: sv* i. The police kept track of him. الشُّرطَة راقبَتَه [ʔiššurṭa raːqbatah]

to track • **1.** اِتَّبَع أَثَر [ʔittabbaʕ ʔaθar] تَتَبُّع أَثَر [tatabbuʕ ʔaθar] *vn: sv* a. We tracked the fox to his lair. اِتَّبَعنا أَثَر الثَّعلَب لِلغار مالَه [ʔittabbiʕna ʔaθar ʔiθθaʕlab lilɣaːr maːlah]

to track up • **1.** وَسَّخ [wassax] *sv* i. You're tracking up the kitchen with your feet. إِنتَ دَاِتوَسِّخ قاع المَطبَخ برجلَك [ʔinta datwassix gaːʕ ʔilmaṭbax brijlak]

tract • **1.** قِطعَة [qiṭʕa] قِطَع [qiṭaʕ] *pl:* مُقاطَعَة [muqaːṭaʕa] مُقاطَعات [muqaːṭaʕaːt] *pl:* Several oil companies are prospecting in this tract. عِدَّة شَرِكات نَفُط دَتنَقِّب بِهَالمُقاطَعَة [ʕiddat šarikaːt nafuṭ datnaqqib bhalmuqaːṭaʕa] • **2.** كُرّاسَة [kurraːsa] كُرّاسات [kurraːsaːt] *pl:* The chamber of commerce published a tract on the oil question. غُرفَة التِّجارَة نِشرَت كُرّاسَة عَن مُشكِلَة النَّفُط [ɣurfat ʔittijaːra nišrat kurraːsa ʕan muškilat ʔinnafuṭ] • **3.** جِهاز [jihaːz] أَجهِزَة [ʔajhiza] *pl:* Her digestive tract is weak. جِهاز الهَضُم مالها ضَعِيف [jihaːz ʔilhaðum maːlha ðaʕiːf]

traction • **1.** سَحِب [saħib] Rear-engined cars have better traction than others. السَّيّارات اللِّي مَكِينَتها لوَرا سَحِبها أَحسَن مِن غيرها [ʔissayyaːraːt ʔilli makiːnatha lwara saħibha ʔaħsan min ɣayrha]

tractor • **1.** ترَكتَر [traktar] ترَكتَرات [traktaraːt] *pl:*

trade • **1.** تِجارَة [tijaːra] Our trade with the Far East has fallen off. تِجارَتنا وِيّا الشَّرق الأَقصَى قَلَّت [tijaːratna wiyya ʔiššarq ʔilʔaqṣaː qallat] • **2.** صَنعَة [ṣanʕa] صَنايِع [ṣanaːyiʕ] *pl:* مِهنَة [mihna] مِهَن [mihan] *pl:* The boy has to learn a trade. الوَلَد لازِم يِتعَلَّم فَدّ صَنعَة [ʔilwalad laːzim yitʕallam fadd ṣanʕa] I'm a butcher by trade مِهنَتِي قَصّاب [mihinti gaṣṣaːb] • **3.** شُغُل [šuɣul] مَعمِيل [maʕmiːl, miʕmiːl] مَعامِيل [maʕaːmiːl] *pl:* He's taking away my trade. كَسَّد عَلَيّا شُغلِي [kassad ʕalayya šuɣli] • **4.** تِجارِي [tijaːri] They published new trade regulations. أَصدِرَوا أَنظِمَة تِجارِيَّة جِدِيدَة [ʔaṣdiraw ʔanðima tijaːriyya jidiːda]

to trade • **1.** بَدَّل [baddal] تَبدِيل [tabdiːl] *vn: sv* i. I've traded my typewriter for a bicycle. بَدَّلِت الآلَة الطّابعَة مالتِي بِبايسِكِل [baddalit ʔilʔaːla ʔiṭṭaːbiʕa maːlti bpaːysikil] • **2.** تاجَر [taːjar] تِجارَة [tijaːra] *vn: sv* i. Iraq trades mostly with England. العِراق يتاجِر عالأَكثَر وِيّا إِنكِلترا [ʔilʕiraːq ytaːjir ʕalʔakθar wiyya ʔingiltara]

T

trader • **1.** تاجِر [ta:ǰir] تُجّار [tuǰǰa:r] *pl:*

tradesman • **1.** دُكّانجِي [dukka:nči] دُكّانجِيَّة [dukka:nčiyya] *pl:*

trade wind • **1.** رِيح تِجارِي [ri:ħ tiǰa:ri] رِياح تِجارِيَّة [riya:ħ tiǰa:riyya] *pl:*

tradition • **1.** تَقلِيد [taqli:d] تَقالِيد [taqa:li:d] *pl:* This is a tradition we have been following for centuries. هَذا فَدّ تَقلِيد إحنا تابعِيه مِن عُصُور [ha:ða fadd taqli:d ʔiħna ta:bʕi:h min ʕuṣu:r]

traditional • **1.** تَقلِيدِي [taqli:di]

traffic • **1.** مُرُور [muru:r] Traffic is heavy on Rashid Street. المُرُور قَوِيَّة بشارِع الرَّشِيد [ʔilmuru:r qawiyya bša:riʕ ʔirraši:d] • **2.** تِجارَة [tiǰa:ra] The United Nations is trying to control the traffic in narcotics. هَيئَة الأمِن ترِيد تُضبُط تِجارَة المُخَدَّرات [hayʔat ʔilʔamin tri:d tuðbuṭ tiǰa:rat ʔilmuxaddara:t]

* **This street is closed to traffic.** • **1.** هاذَ شارِع مَسدُود [ha:ða ša:riʕ masdu:d]

traffic jam • **1.** اِزدِحام سَيّارات [ʔizdiħa:m sayya:ra:t] اِزدِحامات سَيّارات [ʔizdiħa:ma:t sayya:ra:t] *pl:*

traffic light • **1.** أضوِيّات مُرُور [ʔaðwiya:t muru:r] ضُوأضوِيّات مُرُور [ʔaðwiyya:t muru:r] *pl:*

tragedy • **1.** فاجِعَة [fa:ǰiʕa] فَواجِع [fawa:ǰiʕ] *pl:* What a tragedy the accident was! شلُون فاجِعَة كان الحادِث [šlu:n fa:ǰiʕa ča:n ʔilħa:diθ] • **2.** رُوايَة مُحزِنَة [ruwa:ya muħzina] رُوايات مُحزِنَة [ruwa:ya:t muħzina] *pl:* The Baghdad Theatre Group is presenting a tragedy this week. الفِرقَة التَّمثِيلِيَّة البَغدادِيَّة راح تقَدِّم رُوايَة مُحزِنَة هَالإسبُوع [ʔilfirqa ʔittamθi:liyya ʔilbaɣda:diyya ra:ħ tqaddim ruwa:ya muħzina halʔisbu:ʕ]

tragic • **1.** مُؤلِم [muʔlim] مُفجِع [mufǰiʕ] That accident was tragic. ذاك الحادِث كان مُؤلِم [ða:k ʔilħa:diθ ča:n muʔlim]

trail • **1.** طَرِيق [ṭari:q] طُرُق [ṭuruq] *pl:* The trail leads into the woods. الطَّرِيق يأدِّي لِداخِل الغابَة [ʔiṭṭari:q yʔaddi lda:xil ʔilɣa:ba] • **2.** أثَر [ʔaθar] آثار [ʔa:θa:r] *pl:* A trail of blood caught their eye. أثَر مِن الدَّم لِفَت نَظَرهُم [ʔaθar min ʔiddamm lifat naðarhum]

* **The police are on his trail.** • **1.** الشُّرطَة معَقّبَتَه [ʔiššurṭa mʕaqqbatah] / الشُّرطَة وَراه [ʔiššurṭa wara:h]

to trail • **1.** لِحَق [liħag] *sv* a. Somebody trailed me all the way home. فَدّ واحِد لِحَقنِي طُول الطَّرِيق لِلبَيت [fadd wa:ħid liħagni ṭu:l ʔiṭṭari:q lilbayt]

train • **1.** قِطار [qiṭa:r] قِطارات [qiṭa:ra:t] *pl:* When does the train leave? شوَقِت يِتحَرَّك القِطار؟ [šwakit yitħarrak ʔilqiṭa:r?] • **2.** ذيال [ðya:l] ذيالات [ðya:la:t] *pl:* The bride wore a dress with a long train. العَرُوس لِبسَت بَدلَة بِيها ذيال طُوِيل [ʔilʕaru:s libsat badla bi:ha ðya:l ṭuwi:l]

to train • **1.** دَرَّب [darrab] تَدرِيب [tadri:b] *vn: sv* u. He trains the new employees. هُوَّ يدَرُّب المُوَظَّفِين الجِّدَّد [huwwa ydarrub ʔilmuwaððafi:n ʔiǰǰiddad] • **2.** تمَرَّن [tmarran] تَمرِين [tamri:n] *vn: sv* a. He's been training for the fight for weeks. صارلَه أسابِيع دَيتمَرَّن لِلمُلاكَمَة [ṣa:rlah ʔasa:bi:ʕ dayitmarran lilmula:kama]

trainer • **1.** مُدَرِّب [mudarrib] He's a boxing trainer. هَذا مُدَرِّب مُلاكَمَة [ha:ða mudarrib mula:kama] • **2.** طَيّارَة تَدرِيب [ṭiyya:rat tadri:b] طَيّارات مال تَدرِيب [ṭiyya:ra:t ma:l tadri:b] *pl:* That's a trainer for new pilots. هاي طَيّارَة مال تَدرِيب لِلطَّيّارِين الجِّدَد [ha:y ṭiyya:ra ma:l tadri:b liṭṭayya:ri:n ʔaǰǰiddad]

training • **1.** تَمرِين [tamri:n] تَدرِيب [tadri:b] He's still in training. بَعدَه تَحت التَّمرِين [baʕdah taħt ʔiltamri:n] • **2.** تَدرِيب [tadri:b] The Post Office Department maintains a training school for its employees. مُدِيرِيَّة البَرِيد عِدها مَدرَسَة تَدرِيب لِمُستَخدَمِيها [mudi:riyyat ʔilbari:d ʕidha madrasat tadri:b limustaxdami:ha]

trait • **1.** صِفَة [ṣifa] صِفات [ṣifa:t] *pl:* خِصلَة [xiṣla] خِصلات، خِصال، خُصَل، خِصَل [xiṣla:t, xiṣa:l, xuṣal, xiṣal] *pl:* She has many fine traits. عِدها هوايَة صِفات زينَة [ʕidha hwa:ya ṣifa:t zi:na]

traitor • **1.** خائِن [xa:ʔin] خائِنِين، خَوَنَة [xa:ʔini:n, xawana] *pl:*

tramp • **1.** مهتَلَف [mhatlaf] مهتَلَفِين [mhatlafi:n] *pl:* متشَرِّد [mitšarrid] متشَرِّدِين [mitšarridi:n] *pl:* He looks like a tramp. هُوَّ عَبالَك فَدّ واحِد مهتَلَف [huwwa ʕaba:lak fadd wa:ħid mhatlaf]

to trample • **1.** دَوَّس [dawwas] تَدوِيس [tadwi:s] *vn:* تدَوَّس [tdawwas] *p:* The horses trampled the children. الخيل دَوِّسَت الأطفال [ʔilxayl dawwisat ʔilʔaṭfa:l]

transaction • **1.** مُعامَلَة [muʕa:mala] We completed the transaction in the lawyer's office. كَمَّلنا المُعامَلَة بمَكتَب المُحامِي [kammalna ʔilmuʕa:mala bmaktab ʔilmuħa:mi]

to transcribe • **1.** اِستَنسَخ [ʔistansax] اِستِنساخ [ʔistinsa:x] *vn: sv* i. Can you transcribe this into Roman script? تِقدَر تِستَنسِخ هَذا إلَى حرُوف لاتِينِيَّة؟ [tigdar tistansix ha:ða ʔila ħru:f la:tiniyya?]

transcript • **1.** وَثِيقَة [waθi:qa] وَثايِق [waθa:yiq] *pl:* The registrar requires a transcript of my studies in Baghdad. مُسَجِّل الجّامعَة طِلَب وَثِيقَة بِدِراستِي بِبَغداد [musaǰǰil ʔiǰǰa:miʕa ṭilab waθi:qa bdira:sti bibaɣda:d]

transfer • **1.** نَقِل [naqil, nagil] I have asked for a transfer to Baghdad. طلَبِت نَقِل لِبَغداد [ṭlabit naqil lbaɣdaːd]

to transfer • **1.** بَدَّل [baddal] تَبدِيل [tabdiːl] *vn: sv* i. Where do we transfer buses? وِين نبَدِّل الباص؟ [wiːn nbaddil ʔilpaːṣ?] • **2.** نِقَل [niqal, nigal] نَقِل [naqil] *vn:* اِنّقَل [ʔinniqal] *p:* حَوَّل [ħawwal] تَحوِيل [taħwiːl] *vn: sv* i. The commander transferred half his forces to the front. القائِد نِقَل نُصّ قُوّاته لِلجَّبهَة [ʔilqaːʔid niqal nuṣṣ quwwaːtah lijǰabha] He transferred the property to her name. حَوَّل مِلكِيَّة المُلُك إلها [ħawwal milkiyyat ʔilmuluk ʔilha] He'd like to be transferred. يرِيد يِنّقِل [yriːd yinniqil]

to transform • **1.** حَوَّل [ħawwal] تَحوِيل [taħwiːl] *vn: sv* i. This station transforms oil fuel into electric energy. هَالمُحَطَّة تحَوِّل الطّاقَة الحَرارِيَّة مال النَّفُط إلَى قُوَّة كَهرَبائِيَّة [halmuħaṭṭa tħawwil ʔiṭṭaːqa ʔilħaraːriyya maːl ʔinnafuṭ ʔila quwwa kahrabaːʔiyya]

transformer • **1.** مُحَوِّلَة [muħawwila] مُحَوِّلات [muħawwilaːt] *pl:* The transformer in my radio is burnt out. المُحَوِّل بِالرّادِيُو مالِي اِحتِرَق [ʔilmuħawwil birraːdyu maːli ʔiħtirag]

transfusion • **1.** نَقِل دَمّ [naqil damm] The patient needs a blood transfusion. المَرِيض يِنرادلَه نَقِل دَمّ [ʔilmariːð yinraːdlah naqil damm]

transient • **1.** مارّ [maːrr] مارِّين [maːrriːn] *pl:* عابِر [ʕaːbir] عابِرِين [ʕaːbiriːn] *pl:* The airport has sleeping and dining facilities for transients. المَطار مجَهَّز بِمَحَلّ نُوم وَأكِل لِلرُّكّاب المارِّين [ʔilmaṭaːr mǰahhaz bimaħall nuːm wʔakil lirrukkaːb ʔilmaːrriːn]

transit • **1.** ترانسِيت [transiːt] These goods are in transit. هالبِضاعَة ترانسِيت [halbiðaːʕa transiːt]

transition • **1.** اِنتِقال [ʔintiqaːl] Our country is in a period of transition. بِلادنا بفَترَة اِنتِقال [bilaːdna bfatrat ʔintiqaːl]

to translate • **1.** تَرجَم [tarǰam] تَرجَمَة [tarǰama] *vn: sv* u. How do you translate this? شلُون تتَرجُم هاي؟ [šluːn ʔittarǰum haːy?]

translation • **1.** تَرجَمَة [tarǰama, tarǰuma] تَراجِم [taraːǰim] *pl:*

translator • **1.** مُتَرجِم [mutarǰim] مُتَرجِمِين [mutarǰimiːn] *pl:*

transmission • **1.** قِير، كِير [giːr] قِيرات، كِيرات [giːraːt] *pl:* تَرَنسمِشِن [transmišin] تَرَنسمِشِنات [transmišinaːt] *pl:* Something seems to be wrong with the transmission of my car. الكِير مال سَيّارتِي بِيه شِي [ʔilgiːr maːl sayyaːrti biːh ši]

transmitter • **1.** مُرسِلَة [mursila] مُرسِلات [mursilaːt] *pl:* The Baghdad Radio transmitters are at Abu-Ghrayb. مُرسِلات مَحَطَّة إذاعَة بَغداد بِأبُو غرَيب [mursilaːt maħaṭṭat ʔiðaːʕat baɣdaːd biʔabu ɣrayb]

transparent • **1.** شَفّاف [šaffaːf] The water is quite transparent here. الماي شَفّاف هنا [ʔilmaːy šaffaːf hna] • **2.** مَكشُوف [makšuːf] His methods are transparent. أسالِيبَه مَكشُوفَة [ʔasaːliːbah makšuːfa]

to transplant • **1.** نِقَل [niqal] نَقِل [naqil] *vn: sv* u. I'm going to transplant the seedlings today. راح أنقُل الشّتُول اليُوم [raːħ ʔanqul ʔišštuːl ʔilyuːm]

transport • **1.** تَسفِير [tasfiːr] Our primary concern was the transport of troops. هَمّنا الأوَّل كان تَسفِير الجَّيُوش [hammna ʔilʔawwal čaːn tasfiːr ʔiǰǰiyuːš] • **2.** مَركَب نَقِل [markab naqil] مَراكِب نَقِل [maraːkib naqil] *pl:* Two transports were sunk by submarines. الغَوّاصات غِرقَوا مَركَبَين نَقِل [ʔilɣawwaːṣaːt ɣirgaw markabayn naqil] • **3.** طَيّارَة نَقِل [ṭayyaːrat naqil] طَيّارات نَقِل [ṭayyaːraːt naqil] *pl:* He's piloting a transport. دَيقُود طَيّارَة نَقِل [dayquːd ṭayyaːrat naqil]

to transport • **1.** نِقَل [niqal] نَقِل [naqil] *vn: sv* u. The Navy will transport these troops. البَحرِيَّة راح تُنقُل هَالجَّيُوش [ʔilbaħriyya raːħ tunqul haǰǰiyuːš]

transportation • **1.** واسطَة نَقِل [waːsṭat naqil] I'll need some transportation. يِنرادلِي واسطَة نَقِل [yinraːdli waːsṭat naqil]

trap • **1.** فَخّ [faxx] أفخاخ [ʔafxaːx] *pl:* شَرَك [šarak] أشراك [ʔašraːk] *pl:* The police set a trap for him. الشُّرطَة نِصبُولَه فَخّ [ʔiššurṭa niṣbuːlah faxx] • **2.** مَصيَدَة، مِصيادَة [maṣyada, miṣyaːda] مِصيادات [miṣyaːdaːt] *pl:* We caught three rats in the trap. صِدنا ثلاث جرَيدِيَّة بِالمِصيادَة [ṣidna tlaːθ ǰriːdiyya bilmiṣyaːda]

to trap • **1.** حِصَر [ħiṣar] حَصِر [ħaṣir] *vn: sv* i. The boys trapped the cat in a corner. الوُلِد حِصرَوا البَزّونَة بِالزُّوِيَّة [ʔilwulid ħiṣraw ʔilbazzuːna bizzuwiyya]

trash • **1.** زِبِل [zibil] زبالات [zbaːlaːt] *pl:* Burn the trash! إحرِق الزِّبِل [ʔiħrig ʔizzibil] We don't buy such trash. إحنا ما نِشتِرِي هِيكِي زبالات [ʔiħna maː ništiri hiːči zbaːlaːt]

travel • **1.** سَفَر [safar] Travel in winter is difficult. السَّفَر صَعُب بِالشِّتا [ʔissafar ṣaʕub biššita] Let him tell you about his travels. خَلِّيه يِحكِيلَك عَلَى سَفراتَه [xalliːh yiħčiːlak ʕala safraːtah]

to travel • **1.** سافَر [saːfar] سَفَر [safar] *vn: sv* i. I traveled a lot when I was in the Army. سافَرت هوايَة مِن كِنِت بِالجَّيش [saːfart hwaːya min činit biǰǰayš] • **2.** اِفتَرّ [ʔiftarr] فتَرّ [ftarr] *vn: sv* a. دار [daːr] دَوَران [dawaraːn] *vn: sv* u. He has traveled all over Europe. فتَرّ كُلّ أورُبّا [ftarr kull

ʔuːruppa] • **3.** ساح [saːħ] سِياحَة [siyaːħa] *vn: sv* i. She has been traveling for a month. صارِلها شَهَر دَتسِيح [ṣaːrilha šahar datsiːħ]
*** He must have been traveling sixty miles an hour.** • **1.** لازِم كان دَيسُوق سِتِّين مِيل بالساعَة [laːzim čaːn daysuːq sittiːn miːl bissaːʕa]

traveller • **1.** مُسافِر [musaːfir] مُسافِرين [musaːfiriːn] *pl:*

travelling salesman • **1.** بَيّاع [bayyaːʕ] بايِع مِتجَوِّل [baːyiʕ mitǰawwil] بَيّاعَة مِتجَوِّلِين [bayyaːʕa mitǰawwiliːn] *pl:*

tray • **1.** صِينِيَّة [ṣiːniyya] صواني [ṣwaːniː] *pl:* Put the cups on the tray. حُطّ الكوابَة بالصِّينِيَّة [ħuṭṭ ʔilkwaːba biṣṣiːniyya]

treason • **1.** خِيانَة [xiyaːna]

treasure • **1.** كَنز [kanz] كُنُوز [kunuːz, knuːz] *pl:*

treasurer • **1.** أَمِين صَندُوق [ʔamiːn ṣanduːg] أُمَناء صَندُوق [ʔumanaːʔ ṣanduːg] *pl:*

treasury • **1.** خَزِينَة [xaziːna] خَزايِن [xazaːyin] خَزينات [xaziːnaːt] *pl:* The country's treasury is almost empty. خَزِينَة الدَّولَة تَقرِيباً فارغَة [xaziːnat ʔiddawla taqriːban faːrɣa] • **2.** مالِيَّة [maːliyya] He works in the Treasury Department. يِشتُغُل بوِزارَة المالِيَّة [yištuɣul bwizaːrat ʔilmaːliyya]

treat • **1.** لَذَّة [laðða] لَذّات [laððaːt] *pl:* It's a treat to read his books. قرايَة كُتبَه لَذَّة [qraːyat kutbah laðða]
*** This time the treat's on me.** • **1.** هالمَرَّة عَلَيّا [halmarra ʕalayya] / هالمَرَّة عَلَى حسابِي [halmarra ʕala ħsaːbi]
to treat • **1.** عامَل [ʕaːmal] مُعامَلَة [muʕaːmala] *vn: sv* i. He treats me like a child. يعامِلنِي عَبالَك طِفل [yʕaːmilni ʕabaːlak ṭifil] • **2.** عالَج [ʕaːlaǰ] مُعالَجَة [muʕaːlaǰa] *vn: sv* i. Dr. Ahmad is treating me. الدِّكتُور أحمَد دَيعالِجنِي [ʔiddiktuːr ʔaħmad dayʕaːliǰni] • **3.** دِفَع عَلَى [difaʕ ʕala] دَفِع [dafiʕ] *vn: sv* a. He treated everybody. دِفَع عالكُلّ [difaʕ ʕalkull]
to treat lightly • **1.** إستَخَفّ [ʔistaxaff] إستِخفاف [ʔistixfaːf] *vn: sv* i. إستَهوَن [ʔistahwan] إستِهانَة [ʔistihaːna] *vn: sv* i. You shouldn't treat that so lightly. ما لازِم تِستِخِفّ بهَذا [maː laːzim tistixiff bhaːða]

treatment • **1.** تَداوِي [tadaːwi] مُعالَجَة [muʕaːlaǰa] مُعالَجات [muʕaːlaǰaːt] *pl:* I'm going to the doctor's tomorrow for treatment. آنِي رايِح لِلطَّبِيب باكِر لِلتَّداوِي [ʔaːni raːyiħ littabiːb baːčir littadaːwi] • **2.** مُعامَلَة [muʕaːmala] I don't like that kind of treatment. ما تِعجِبنِي هِيكِي مُعامَلَة [maː tiʕǰibni hiːči muʕaːmala]

treaty • **1.** مُعاهَدَة [muʕaːhada] مُعاهَدات [muʕaːhadaːt] *pl:* The treaty has to be ratified by the Senate. المُعاهَدَة لازِم تِتصَدَّق مِن مَجلِس الأَعيان [ʔilmuʕaːhada laːzim titṣaddaq min maǰlis ʔalʔaʕyaːn]

tree • **1.** شَجَرَة [šaǰara] شَجَرات، أَشجار [šaǰaraːt, ʔašǰaːr] *pl:* شَجَر [šaǰar] *Collective:* We have a tree in front of our house. عِدنا شَجَرَة قِدّام البَيت [ʕidna šaǰara giddaːm ʔilbayt]

trellis • **1.** قَمَرِيَّة [qamariyya] قَمَرِيّات [qamariyyaːt] *pl:*

to tremble • **1.** رِجَف [riǰaf] رَجِف [raǰif] *vn: sv* i. He trembled with fear. رِجَف مِن الخُوف [riǰaf min ʔilxuːf]

tremendous • **1.** هائِل [haːʔil] عَظِيم [ʕaðiːm] عُظَماء [ʕuðamaːʔ] *pl:* That's a tremendous undertaking. هَذا مَشرُوع هائِل [haːða mašruːʕ haːʔil] There's a tremendous difference between them. أَكُو إختِلاف عَظِيم بَيناتهُم [ʔaku ʔixtilaːf ʕaðiːm biːnaːthum] • **2.** عَظِيم [ʕaðiːm] عُظَماء [ʕuðamaːʔ] *pl:* They've just got out a tremendous new record. طَلّعَوا إسطِوانَة جِدِيدَة عَظِيمَة [ṭallʕaw ʔisṭiwaːna ǰidiːda ʕaðiːma]

tremendously • **1.** كُلِّش هوايَة [kulliš hwaːya] Social conditions have changed tremendously. الأَحوال الاجتِماعِيَّة تغَيِّرَت كُلِّش هوايَة [ʔilʔaħwaːl ʔilʔiǰtimaːʕiyya tɣayyrat kulliš hwaːya]

tremor • **1.** هَزَّة [hazza] هَزّات [hazzaːt] *pl:* Several weak earth tremors took place yesterday. عِدَّة هَزّات أَرضِيَّة خَفِيفَة صارَت البارحَة [ʕiddat hazzaːt ʔarðiyya xafiːfa ṣaːrat ʔilbaːrħa] • **2.** رَعشَة [raʕša] رَعشات [raʕšaːt] *pl:* إرتِعاش [ʔirtiʕaːš] إرتِعاشات [ʔirtiʕaːšaːt] *pl:* He has a tremor in his hand. عِندَه رَعشَة بإيدَه [ʕindah raʕša bʔiːdah]

trench • **1.** خَندَق [xandaq] خَنادِق [xanaːdiq] *pl:* Civilians were forced to dig trenches. المَدَنِيِّين إنجُبرَوا يُحفُرُون خَنادِق [ʔilmadaniyyiːn ʔinǰubraw yuħufruːn xanaːdiq]

trend • **1.** إتِّجاه [ʔittiǰaːh] إتِّجاهات [ʔittiǰaːhaːt] *pl:* The trend in Iraq is to wear Western suits. الاتِّجاه بالعِراق هَسَّة نَحو لِبس المَلابِس الغَربِيَّة [ʔilʔittiǰaːh bilʕiraːq hassa naħw libis ʔilmalaːbis ʔalɣarbiyya]

to trespass • **1.** تعَدَّى [tʕaddaː] *sv* a. You were trespassing on my property. إنتَ كِنت دَتِتعَدَّى مِن قاعِي [ʔinta činit datitʕadda min gaːʕi]

trestle • **1.** سكَلَّة [skalla] سكَلات [skallaːt] *pl:* The workmen set up a trestle. العُمّال نُصبَوا سكَلَّة [ʔilʕummaːl nuṣbaw skalla]

trial • **1.** مُحاكَمَة [muħa:kama] مُحاكَمات [muħa:kama:t] *pl:* The case was never brought to trial. الدَّعوَة أَبَداً ما اِنعِرضَت لِلمُحاكَمَة [ʔiddaʕwa ʔabadan ma: ʔinʕirðat lilmuħa:kama] He's on trial for murder. هُوَّ هَسَّة تَحت المُحاكَمَة عَن قَضِيَّة قَتِل [huwwa hassa taħt ʔilmuħa:kama ʕan qaðiyyat qatil] • **2.** تَجرُبَة [tajruba] تَجارُب [taja:rub] *pl:* He's been through a lot of trial and tribulation. مَرّ بهوايَة تَجارُب وَشَدائِد [marr bhwa:ya taja:rub wšada:ʔid] Children learn through trial and error. الأَطفال يِتعَلّمُون بِالتَّجرُبَة [ʔilʔatfa:l yitʕallmu:n bittajruba] I took the radio on trial. قبَلِت الرّاديُو عَلَى شَرط التَّجرُبَة [qbalit ʔirra:dyu ʕala šart ʔittajruba]

to give a trial • **1.** جَرَّب [jarrab] *sv* u. Why don't you give the car a trial? لِيش ما تجَرُّب السَّيّارَة فَدّ مُدَّة؟ [li:š ma: djarrub ʔissayya:ra fadd mudda?] We'll give you a week's trial. راح نجَرّبَك فَدّ إسبُوع [ra:ħ njarrbak fadd ʔisbu:ʕ]

triangle • **1.** مُثَلَّث [muθallaθ] A triangle has three sides. المُثَلَّث بِيه ثلاث أَضاع [ʔilmuθallaθ bi:h tlaθ ʔaða:ʕ]

triangular • **1.** مُثَلَّث الشِكِل [muθallaθ ʔiššikil] The race was run on a triangular course. السِّباق جِرَى عَلَى ساحَة مُثَلَّثَة الشِّكِل [ʔissiba:q jira: ʕala sa:ħa muθallaθat ʔiššikil]

tribal • **1.** عَشائِري [ʕaša:ʔiri] The group is studying tribal customs. الجَماعَة دَتِدرُس العادات العَشائِرِيَّة [ʔijjama:ʕa datidrus ʔilʕa:da:t ʔilʕaša:ʔiriyya]

tribe • **1.** عَشِيرَة [ʕaši:ra] عَشاير [ʕaša:yir] *pl:* قَبِيلَة [qabi:la] قَبائِل [qaba:ʔil] *pl:* He's the head of a tribe from the South. هُوَّ شَيخ عَشِيرَة بِالجِنُوب [huwwa ši:x ʕaši:ra bijjinu:b]

tribesman • **1.** إبن عَشاير [ʔibin ʕaša:yir]

tribunal • **1.** هَيئَة تَحكِيم [hayʔa taħki:m] هَيئات تَحكِيم [hayʔa:t taħki:m] *pl:* We'll take the dispute to an international tribunal. راح ناخُذ هَالنِّزاع لِهَيئَة تَحكِيم دَولِيَّة [ra:ħ na:xuð hanniza:ʕ lhayʔat taħki:m dawliyya]

tributary • **1.** رافِد [ra:fid] رَوافِد [rawa:fid] *pl:* The Diyala river is a tributary of the Tigris. نَهر ديالَة مِن رَوافِد نَهَر دِجلَة [nahr dya:la: min rawa:fid nahar dijla]

tribute • **1.** خاوَة [xa:wa] جِزيَة [jizya] جِزيات [jizya:t] *pl:* The Assyrians exacted tribute from many nations. الآشُورِيِّين فُرضوا خاوَة مِن هوايَة دُوَل [ʔilʔašu:riyyi:n furðaw xa:wa min hwa:ya duwal] • **2.** مَدِح [madiħ] He paid you a fine tribute. مِدَحَك مَدِح زين [midaħak madiħ zi:n] He paid you a fine tribute. أَثنَى عَلِيك [ʔaθna: ʕali:k]

trick • **1.** حِيلَة [ħi:la] حِيَل [ħiyal] *pl:* I'm on to his tricks. آني أعرُف حِيَلَه [ʔa:ni ʔaʕruf ħiyalah] Do you know any card tricks? تُعرُف حِيلَة مال وَرَق؟ [tuʕruf ħi:la ma:l waraq?] • **2.** شَطارَة [šata:ra] Don't try your tricks on me! لا تحاوِل تبِيع شَطارتَك بِراسِي [la: tħa:wil tbi:ʕ šata:rtak bra:si] • **3.** نُكتَة [nukta] نُكَت [nukat] *pl:* He played a trick on us. سَوَّى بِينا نُكتَة [sawwa: bi:na nukta] • **4.** واوي [wa:wi] واوِيَّة [wa:wiyya] *pl:* Watch out, there's a trick to that! دِير بالَك هاي بِيها واوي [di:r ba:lak ha:y bi:ha wa:wi] • **5.** دَرُب [darub] درُوب [dru:b] *pl:* He knows all the tricks. يِندَلّ كُلّ الدرُوب [yindall kull ʔiddru:b] • **6.** فَنّ [fann] فنُون [fnu:n] *pl:* There's a trick to fixing this dish. طَبُخ هَالأَكلَة يِنرادلَه فَنّ [tabux halʔakla yinra:dlah fann] • **7.** سِحري [siħri] Have you seen Ali's trick box? شِفت الصَّندُوق السِّحري مال عَلِي؟ [šift ʔissandu:g ʔissiħri ma:l ʕali?]

*** I've got a trick knee.** • **1.** رُكُبتِي مَعيُوبَة [rukubti maʕyu:ba]

*** There's no trick to it.** • **1.** هاي ما يِنراد إلها شِي [ha:y ma: yinra:d ʔilha ši] / هاي سَهلَة [ha:y sahla] / هاي بَسِيطَة [ha:y basi:ta]

to trick • **1.** قَشمَر [qašmar] قَشمَرَة [qašmara] *vn: sv* u. He tricked me again. قَشمَرنِي مَرَّة اللُّخ [qašmarni marrat ʔillux] They tricked us into signing. قَشمَرَونا وَخَلُّونا نِمضِي [qašmaru:na wxallu:na nimði]

to trickle • **1.** خَرّ [xarr] خَرّ [xarr] *vn: sv* u. The water trickled out of the faucet. الماي خَرّ مِن البُوري [ʔilma:y xarr min ʔilbu:ri]

trickster • **1.** غَشّاش [ɣašša:š] غَشّاشَة [ɣašša:ša] *pl:* حَيّال [ħayya:l] حَيّالِين [ħayya:li:n] *pl:* He has a reputation for being a trickster. هَذا مَشهُور بِكَونَه غَشّاش [ha:ða mašhu:r bkawnah ɣašša:š]

tricky • **1.** دَقِيق [daqi:q] That's a tricky question. هَذا فَدّ مَوضُوع دَقِيق [ha:ða fadd mawðu:ʕ daqi:q]

trifle • **1.** شَقَا [šaqa] لِعِب [liʕib] That's no trifle. هاي مُو شَقَة [ha:y mu: šaqa] • **2.** شِي طَفِيف [ši: tafi:f] أَشياء طَفِيفَة [ʔašya:ʔ tafi:fa] *pl:* شِي تافِه [ši ta:fih] أَشياء تافِهَة [ʔašya:ʔ ta:fha] *pl:* Don't bother about trifles. لا تِهتَمّ بالأَشياء الطَّفِيفَة [la: tihtamm bilʔašya:ʔ ʔittafi:fa] • **3.** شوَيَّة [šwayya] إسماً [ʔisman] شَعرَة [šaʕra] شَعرات [šaʕra:t] *pl:* The trousers are a trifle too long. البَنطَرُون شوَيَّة طويل [ʔilpantaru:n šwayya twi:l] The food was good but just a trifle salty. الأَكِل كان زين بَسّ إسماً مالِح [ʔilʔakil ča:n zi:n bass ʔisman ma:liħ]

*** He's was only trifling with her.** • **1.** كان دَيلعَب براسها [ča:n dayilʕab bra:sha]

*** He's no man to trifle with.** • **1.** هَذا فَدّ واحِد يِنحِسِبلَه حساب [ha:ða fadd wa:ħid yinħisiblah ħsa:b]

trifling • **1.** طَفِيف [tafi:f] تافِه [ta:fih] That's such a trifling matter! هَذا شِي كُلّش طَفِيف [ha:ða ši kulliš tafi:f]

T

trigger • **1.** زناد [zna:d] زنادات [zna:da:t] *pl:* The trigger on this pistol has a light pull. الزناد مال هَالمُسَدَّس سَهِل يِنداس [ʔilzna:d ma:l halmusaddas sahil yinda:s]

trigonometry • **1.** عِلم المُثَلَّثات [ʕilm ʔilmuθallaθa:t] حساب المُثَلَّثات [ħsa:b ʔilmuθallaθa:t]

trim • **1.** حاشِيَة [ħa:šiya] حَواشِي [ħawa:ši] *pl:* Most cars now have chrome trim. أَكثَر السَّيّارات بِيها حواشِي مِن نِيكَل [ʔakθar ʔissayya:ra:t bi:ha ħwa:ši min ni:kal] • **2.** تَعدِيل [taʕdi:l] تَعدِيلات [taʕdi:la:t] *pl:* My hair isn't long, but it needs a trim. شَعرِي مُو طُوِيل، لَكِن يِحتاج تَعدِيل [šaʕri mu: ṭuwi:l, la:kin yiħta:ǰ taʕdi:l] • **3.** مرَتَّب [mrattab] She always looks very trim. هِيَّ دائِماً كُلِّش مرَتَّبَة [hiyya da:ʔiman kulliš mrattba] • **4.** نَحِيف [naħi:f] She has a trim figure. عِدها قِوام نَحِيف [ʕidha qiwa:m naħi:f]

to trim • **1.** عَدَّل [ʕaddal] *sv* i. Just trim my hair a little. هَسّ عَدِّل شَعرِي شوَيَّة [hass ʕaddil šaʕri šwayya] • **2.** قَرطَف [garṭaf] قَرطَفَة [garṭafa] *vn: sv* u. I'm trimming my mustache. دَأقَرطُف شوارِبي [daʔagarṭuf šwa:rbi] • **3.** زَوَّق [zawwag] زواقَة [zwa:ga] *vn:* تزَوَّق [tzawwag] *p:* She trimmed her hat with feathers. زَوّقَت شَفقَتها بِالرِّيش [zawwgat šafqatha birri:š]

trimming • **1.** نَقِش [naqiš] The trimming or her dress is red. النَّقِش عَلَى بَدلَتها أحمَر [ʔinnaqiš ʕala badlatha ʔaħmar] • **2.** حباشَة [ħba:ša] حباشات [ħba:ša:t] *pl:* We had turkey and all the trimmings. أَكَلنا دِيك هِندِي وحباشاتَه [ʔakalna di:č hindi wħba:ša:tah]

*** He gave me a trimming.** • **1.** بُسَطنِي بَسطَة زَينَة [busaṭni basṭa zayna]

*** We really got a trimming in our last game.** • **1.** صُدُق تدَمَّرنا بلِعبَتنا الأخِيرَة [ṣudug tdammarna bliʕbatna ʔilʔaxi:ra]

trip • **1.** سَفرَة [safra] سَفرات [safra:t] *pl:* How was your trip? شلُون كانَت سَفِرتَك؟ [šlu:n ča:nat safirtak?] Have a pleasant trip. أتمَنّالَك سَفرَة زينَة [ʔatmanna:lak safra zi:na] • **2.** رُوحَة [rawħa] رُوحات [rawħa:t] *pl:* رَجعَة [raǰʕa] رَجعات [raǰʕa:t] *pl:* The trip there was quicker than the trip back. الرَّوحَة كانَت أسهَل مِن الرَّجعَة [ʔirrawħa ča:nat ʔashal min ʔirraǰʕa]

to trip • **1.** عِثَر [ʕiθar] عَثِر [ʕaθir] *vn: sv* a. Be careful not to trip on the stairs. دِير بالَك لا تِعثَر بِالدَّرَج [di:r ba:lak la: tiʕθar biddaraǰ] • **2.** ضِرَب بَند [ḍirab band] *sv* u. He tripped me. ضِرَبنِي بَند [ḍirabni band]

to trip up • **1.** لِقَف [ligaf] لَقُف [laguf] *vn: sv* u. صاد [ṣa:d] صَيد [ṣayd] *vn: sv* i. My professor tripped me up on that question. الأستاذ لِقَفنا بِهَالسُّؤال [ʔilʔusta:ð ligafna bhassuʔa:l] • **2.** غِلَط [ɣilaṭ] غَلَط [ɣalaṭ] *vn: sv* a. I must have tripped up somewhere. لازِم غلَطِت بِفَدّ مَكان [la:zim ɣlaṭit bfadd maka:n]

tripe • **1.** كَرِش [kariš] كرُوش [kru:š] *pl:* I can't eat tripe. ما أَقدَر آكُل الكَرشَة [ma: ʔagdar ʔa:kul ʔilkarša] • **2.** لَغوَة [laɣwa] لَغوات، لَغاوِي [laɣwa:t, laɣa:wi:] *pl:* حَكِي فاصِخ [ħači fa:ṣix] That's just tripe! هَذِي لَغوَة [ha:ði laɣwa]

to triple • **1.** ضاعَف تلاث مَرّات [ḍa:ʕaf tla:θ marra:t] *sv* u. He tripled his earnings. ضاعَف أرباحَه ثلاث مَرّات [ḍa:ʕaf ʔarba:ħah tlaθ marra:t]

triplet • **1.** * She had triplets. جابَت ثلاثَة [ǰa:bat tla:θa]

tripod • **1.** سَيبايَة [saypa:ya] سَيبايات [saypa:ya:t] *pl:*

trite • **1.** بايخ [ba:yix] That joke's too trite. هَالنُّكتَة صارَت بايخَة [hannukta ṣa:rat ba:yxa]

triumph • **1.** اِنتِصار [ʔintiṣa:r] اِنتِصارات [ʔintiṣa:ra:t] *pl:*

triumphant • **1.** مُنتَصِر [muntaṣir]

trivial • **1.** تافِه [ta:fih] طَفِيف [ṭafi:f] That's a trivial matter. هاي فَدّ شِي تافِه [ha:y fadd ši ta:fih]

trolley • **1.** ترام [tra:m] ترامات [tra:ma:t] *pl:* In Cairo they still have trolleys. بَعَد أكُو ترامات بالقاهِرَة [baʕad ʔaku tra:ma:t blqa:hira]

troop • **1.** فِرقَة، فَرِيق [firqa, fari:q] فِرَق [firaq] *pl:* My nephew is in a boy scout troop. اِبن أخُويا بِفِرقَة الكَشّافَة [ʔibin ʔaxu:ya bfirqat ʔilkašša:fa] • **2.** جُندِي [ǰundi] جنُود [ǰinu:d] *pl:* Get the troops out of the sun! خَلِّي الجُنُود لا يُوقفُون بِالشَّمِس [xalli ʔiǰǰunu:d la: yu:gfu:n biššamis]

to troop in • **1.** خَشّ [xašš] خَشّ [xašš] *vn: sv* u. The students all trooped in when the bell rang. التَّلامِيذ خَشَّوا كُلّهُم مِن دَقّ الجَّرَس [ʔittala:mi:ð xaššaw kullhum min dagg ʔiǰǰaras]

trophy • **1.** كَأس [kaʔs] كُؤُوس [kuʔu:s] *pl:* Our school took the trophy this year. مَدرَستنا أخذَت الكَأس هالسَّنَة [madrasatna ʔaxðat ʔilkaʔs hassana]

Tropic of Cancer • **1.** مَدار السَّرَطان [mada:r ʔissaraṭa:n]

Tropic of Capricorn • **1.** مَدار الجَدي [mada:r *ʔiǰǰady*]

tropical • **1.** اِستِوائِي [ʔistiwa:ʔi] Central Africa has a tropical climate. أفرِيقِيا الوُسطَى جَوّها اِستِوائِي [ʔafri:qya: ʔilwusṭa ǰawwha ʔistiwa:ʔi]

tropics • **1.** المَنطِقَة الاِستِوائِيَّة [ʔilmanṭiqa ʔilistiwa:ʔiyya] Much of Africa lies within the tropics. أكثَر أفرِيقِيا واقعَة بِالمَنطِقَة الاستِوائِيَّة [ʔakθar ʔafri:qya: wa:qʕa bilmanṭiqa ʔalʔistiwa:ʔiyya]

trot • **1.** خَبَب [xabab] That horse has a nice trot. هَالحِصان خَبَبَه حِلو [halħiṣa:n xababah ħilw]

to trot • **1.** خَبّ [xabb] خَبّ [xabb] *vn: sv* u. The horse trotted around the field. الحصان خَبّ حَول السّاحَة [ʔilħṣa:n xabb ħawl ʔissa:ħa]

trouble • **1.** مُشكِلَة [muškila] مَشاكِل [maša:kil] *pl:* What's your trouble? شِنُو مُشكِلتَك؟ [šinu muškiltak?] What's your trouble? شبِيك؟ [šbi:k?] • **2.** إزعاج [ʔizʕa:ǰ] إزعاجات [ʔizʕa:ǰa:t] *pl:* This trouble is quite unnecessary. هَذا فَدّ إزعاج أبَد ما إلَه مُوجِب [ha:ða fadd ʔizʕa:ǰ ʔabad ma: ʔilah mu:ǰib] • **3.** اِضطِراب [ʔiðṭira:b] اِضطِرابات [ʔiðṭira:ba:t] *pl:* There's been trouble up at Mosul. أكُو اِضطِرابات بِالمُوصِل [ʔaku ʔiðṭira:ba:t bilmu:ṣil] • **4.** زَحمَة [zaħma] زَحمات [zaħma:t] *pl:* Don't put yourself to any trouble. لا تجُرّ زَحمَة [la: dǰurr zaħma] Don't put yourself to any trouble. لا تِتكَلَّف [la: titkallaf] • **5.** وَرطَة [warṭa] وَرطات [warṭa:t] *pl:* He's in trouble again. هَمّ وُقَع بوَرطَة [hamm wugaʕ bwarṭa] He's in trouble again. هَمِّينَة توَرَّط [hammi:na twarraṭ]

*** What's the trouble?** • **1.** إش صار؟ [ʔiš ṣa:r?]

to trouble • **1.** أزعَج [ʔazʕaǰ] إزعاج [ʔizʕa:ǰ] *vn: sv* i. دَوَّخ [dawwax] تدُوُّخ [tduwwux] *vn: sv* u. I'm sorry, but I'll have to trouble you again. مِتأسِّف بَسّ آنِي مِضطَرّ أزعِجَك مَرَّة لُخ [mitʔassif bass ʔa:ni miðṭarr ʔaziʕǰak marra lux] • **2.** شَوَّش [šawwaš] تَشوِيش [tašwi:š] *vn:* تشَوَّش [tšawwaš] *p:* The news troubled me very much. الأخبار شَوّشَتنِي كُلِّش [ʔilʔaxba:r šawwšatni kulliš] • **3.** قِلَق [qilaq] قَلَق [qalaq] *vn: sv* i. What's troubling you? Is it some bad news? شِنُو اللّي قَلّقَك أكُو أخبار مُو زينَة؟ [šinu: ʔilli qallqak, ʔaku ʔaxba:r mu: zi:na?] What's troubling you? Is it some bad news? شبِيك مِتشَوِّش، أكُو أخبار مُو زينَة؟ [šbi:k mitšawwiš, ʔaku ʔaxba:r mu: zi:na?] • **4.** أذَّى [ʔaðða:] أذِيَّة [ʔaðiyya] *vn: sv* i. My arm has been troubling me ever since my accident. إيدِي دَتأذِّينِي مِن صار الحادِث لهَسَّة [ʔi:di dataʔaðði:ni min ṣa:r ʔilħa:diθ lhassa]

*** What's troubling you? Is it your eyes again?** • **1.** شبِيك، هَمّ عيُونَك؟ [šbi:k, hamm ʕyu:nak?] بِيك مَزعُوج، هَمّ عيُونَك؟ [šbi:k mazʕu:ǰ, hamm ʕyu:nak?]

*** May I trouble you for a match?** • **1.** تِسمَحلِي بشِخّاطَة؟ [tismaħli bšixxa:ṭa?]

troubled • **1.** عَسِير [ʕasi:r] عَصِيب [ʕaṣi:b] We are living in troubled times. دَنعِيش بأيّام عَسِيرَة [danʕi:š bʔayya:m ʕasi:ra] We are living in troubled times. دَنعِيش بفَدّ زَمَن عَصِيب [danʕi:š bfadd zaman ʕaṣi:b] • **2.** قِلِق [qaliq] I've been very troubled about his health lately. صِرِت كُلِّش قلِق عَلَى صِحّتَه بِالمُدَّة الأخِيرَة [ṣirit kulliš qaliq ʕala ṣiħħtah bilmudda ʔilʔaxi:ra]

troublesome • **1.** مدَوِّخ [mdawwix] My tooth has been troublesome. سِنِّي مدَوِّخنِي [sinni mdawwixni] • **2.** مُزعِج [muzʕiǰ] قَلّاق [qalla:q] That pupil is troublesome today. هَالتِّلمِيذ مُزعِج اليُوم [hattilmi:ð muzʕiǰ ʔilyu:m]

trough • **1.** حَوض سَقِي [ħu:ð saqy] أحواض سَقِي [ʔaħwa:ð saqy] *pl:* The watering trough leaks. حَوض السَّقِي دَيخُرّ [ħawð ʔissagy dayxurr] • **2.** مَعلَف [maʕlaf] مَعالِف [mʕa:lif] *pl:* Throw some more food in the trough. حُطّ بَعَد عَلَف بِالمِعلَف [ħuṭṭ baʕad ʕalaf bilmiʕlaf]

trousers • **1.** بَنطَرُون [panṭaru:n] بَنطَرُونات [panṭaru:na:t] *pl:*

trousseau • **1.** جِهاز [ǰiha:z] أجهِزَة [ʔaǰhiza] *pl:*

trowel • **1.** مالَج [ma:laǰ] موالِج [mwa:liǰ] *pl:* حَفّارَة [ħaffa:ra] حَفّارات [ħaffa:ra:t] *pl:*

truce • **1.** هُدنَة [hudna] هُدنات، هُدَن [hudna:t, hudan] *pl:* The two countries agreed to a truce. الدَّولَتَين اِتّفقَوا عَلَى هُدنَة [ʔiddawiltayn ʔittifqaw ʕala hudna]

truck • **1.** لَورِي [lu:ri] لَورِيّات [lu:riyya:t] *pl:*

to truck • **1.** نِقَل بِاللُّورِي [niqal billu:ri] *sv* u. وَدَّى [wadda:] *sv* i. He trucks his produce to the warehouse. دَينقُل المخَضَّر مالَه لِلعَلوَة بِاللُّورِي [dayinqul ʔilmxaððar ma:lah lilʕalwa billu:ri]

trucker • **1.** سايِق لَورِي [sa:yiq lu:ri] سُوّاق لَورِيّات [suwwa:q lu:riyya:t] *pl:* The truckers went on strike today. سُوّاق اللُّورِيّات سَوّوا إضراب اليُوم [suwwa:q ʔillu:riyya:t sawwaw ʔiðra:b ʔilyu:m]

truck farm • **1.** مَزرَعَة خُضَر [mazraʕat xuðar] مَزارِع خُضَر [maza:riʕ xuðar] *pl:*

truck farmer • **1.** زَرّاع خُضَر [zarra:ʕ xuðar]

truck farming • **1.** زَرِع خُضَر [zariʕ xuðar]

true • **1.** صُدُق [ṣudug] صَحِيح [ṣaħi:ħ] Is that story true? هَالحكايَة صُدُق؟ [halħča:ya ṣudug?] He is a true scholar. هُوَّ طالِب عِلم مِن صُدُق [huwwa ṭa:lib ʕilim min ṣudug] • **2.** مُخلِص [muxliṣ] صُدُق [ṣudug] He's a true friend. هُوَّ صَدِيق مُخلِص [huwwa ṣadi:q muxlaṣ] He stayed true to his principles. بُقَى مُخلِص لِمَبادئَه [buqa: muxliṣ limaba:dʔah] • **3.** طِبق الأصِل [ṭibq ʔilʔaṣil] I swear this is a true copy. أشهَد بأن هاي نُسخَة طِبق الأصِل [ʔašhad bʔan ha:y nusxa ṭibq ʔilʔaṣil]

truffle • **1.** كِمايَة [čima:ya] كِمايات [čima:ya:t] *pl:* كِمَة [čima] *Collective*

truly • **1.** حَقِيقَةً [ħaqi:qatan] بِالحَقِيقَة [bilħaqi:qa] I am truly sorry. آنِي مِتأسِّف حَقِيقَةً [ʔa:ni mitʔassif ħaqi:qatan]

T

trumpet • **1.** بُوق [buːq] بواق [bwaːq] *pl:* بُوري [buːri] بُوريّات، بُواري [buːriyyaːt, bwaːri] *pl:*

trunk • **1.** جِذِع [ǰiðiʕ] جذُوع [ǰðuːʕ] *pl:* The trunk of the tree is completely hollow. جِذع الشَّجَرَة كُلّه فارِغ [ǰiðʕ ʔiššaǰara kullah faːriɣ] The human body consists of head, trunk, and limbs. جِسِم الإنسان يِتكَوَّن مِن راس وَجِذِع وَأطراف [ǰisim ʔilʔinsaːn yitkawwan min raːs wǰiðiʕ wʔaṭraːf] • **2.** صَندُوق [ṣanduːg] صَنادِيق [ṣanaːdiːg] *pl:* Are the trunks packed yet? الصَّنادِيق كُلّها مَترُوسَة لَو بَعَد؟ [ʔiṣṣanaːdiːg kullha matruːsa law baʕad?] • **3.** كِسوَة رِياضَة [čiswat riyaːðạ] *pl:* بَنطَرُون رِياضَة [panṭaruːn riyaːðạ] بَنطرونات رِياضَة [panṭaruːn riyaːðạ] *pl:* These trunks are too tight. هَالكِسوَة كُلِّش ضَيقَة [halčiswa kulliš ðayyga] • **4.** رَئِيسِي [raʔiːsi] The Karbala branch joins the trunk line at Hindiyya. الخطّ الفَرعِي مال كَربَلاء يِتَّصِل بِالخَطّ الرَّئِيسِي بِسَدَّة الهِندِيَّة [ʔilxaṭṭ ʔilfarʕi maːl karbala yittiṣil bilxaṭṭ ʔirraʔiːsi bsaddat ʔilhindiyya]

truss • **1.** حزام [ħzaːm] حِزِم [ħizim] *pl:* He has to wear a truss. لازِم يِلبَس حزام [laːzim yilbas ħzaːm] • **2.** رَبّاط [rabbaːṭ] رَبّاطات [rabbaːṭaːt] *pl:* The new bridge is built with steel trusses. الجِّسِر الجِّدِيد مَبنِي عَلَى رَبّاطات مِن فُولاذ [ʔiǰǰisir ʔiǰǰidiːd mabni ʕala rabbaːṭaːt min fuːlaːð]

trust • **1.** ثِقَة [θiqa] I'm putting my trust in you. آنِي حاطّ ثِقتِي بِيك [ʔaːni ħaːṭṭ θiqati biːk] • **2.** وِصايَة [wiṣaːya] وِصايات [wiṣaːyaːt] *pl:* That orphan's money is in a trust. فلُوس هَاليَتِيم مَحطُوطَة تَحت الوِصايَة [fluːs halyatiːm maħṭuːṭa taħt ʔalwiṣaːya] • **3.** إئتِمان [ʔiʔtimaːn] I'm investing my money in a trust company. دَأشَغِّل فلُوسِي بشَرِكَة إئتِمان [daʔašaɣɣil fluːsi bšarikat ʔiʔtimaːn]

to trust • **1.** وِثَق ب [wiθaq b-] ثِقَة [θiqa] *vn: sv* a. أَمَّن ب [ʔamman b-] تَأمِين [taʔmiːn] *vn: sv* i. I don't trust him. آنِي ما أثِق بِيه [ʔaːni maː ʔaθiq biːh] Can you trust me until payday? تِقدَر تأمِّن بِيّا لِيُوم المَعاش؟ [tigdar tʔammin biyya liyuːm ʔilmaʕaːš?] • **2.** تأمَّل [tʔammal] I trust you slept well. أتأمَّل نِمِت زين [ʔatʔammal nimit ziːn]

to trust to • **1.** اِعتِمَد عَلَى [ʔiʕtimad ʕala] *sv* i. You shouldn't trust too much to your memory. ما لازِم هَالقَدّ تِعتِمِد عَلَى ذاكِرتَك [maː laːzim halgadd tiʕtimid ʕala ðaːkirtak]

trustee • **1.** وَصِيّ [waṣiyy] أَوصِياء [ʔawṣiyyaːʔ] *pl:* The judge appointed Ahmad as trustee for his nephew's estate. القاضِي عَيَّن أحمَد وَصِيّ عَلَى أملاك إبن أخُوه [ʔilqaːðị ʕayyan ʔaħmad waṣiyy ʕala ʔamlaːk ʔibin ʔaxuːh]

trusteeship • **1.** وِصايَة [wiṣaːya] This country was under trusteeship a long time. هَالدَّولَة كانَت تَحت الوِصايَة مُدَّة طُويلَة [haddawla čaːnat taħt ʔalwiṣaːya mudda ṭuwiːla]

trustful • **1.** *no equivalent* • * He's too trustful. يأمِّن بِالنّاس هوايَة [yʔammin binnaːs hwaːya]

trustworthy • **1.** أَمِين [ʔamiːn] That man isn't very trustworthy. هذا الرِّجال مُو كُلِّش أَمِين [haːða ʔirriǰaːl muː kulliš ʔamiːn]

truth • **1.** صُدُق [ṣudug] حَقِيقَة [ħaqiːqa] حَقايِق، حَقائِق [ħaqaːyiq, ħaqaːʔiq] *pl:* صَحِيح [ṣaħiːħ] صِحَّة [ṣiħħa] That's the truth. هَذا الصُّدُق [haːða ʔiṣṣudug] I told him the plain truth. قِتلَه الحَقِيقَة مِثلِما هِيَّ [gittlah ʔilħaqiːqa miθilmaː hiyya]

truthful • **1.** صادِق [ṣaːdiq, ṣaːdig] Ali is very truthful. عَلِي كُلِّش صادِق [ʕali kulliš ṣaːdiq]

truthfulness • **1.** صِدِق [ṣidiq] His truthfulness is beyond question. صِدقَه ما بِيه شَكّ [ṣidqah maː biːh šakk] • **2.** صِحَّة [ṣiħħa] I'm not challenging the truthfulness of that statement. ما دَأناقِش صِحَّة التَّصرِيح [maː daʔanaːqiš ṣiħħat ʔittaṣriːħ]

try • **1.** مُحاوَلَة [muħaːwala] مُحاوَلات [muħaːwalaːt] *pl:* They reached the mountaintop on the first try. وُصلَوا لقِمَّة الجِّبَل بأوَّل مُحاوَلَة [wuṣlaw lqummat ʔiǰǰibal bʔawwal muħaːwala]

to try • **1.** جَرَّب [ǰarrab] تَجرُبَة [taǰruba] *vn:* تجَرَّب [tǰarrab] *p:* I'd like to try it. يعجِبنِي أجَرُّبها [yiʕǰibni ʔaǰarrubha] Have you tried this medicine yet? جَرَّبِت هَالدُّوا لَو بَعَد؟ [ǰarrabit hadduwaː law baʕad?] • **2.** حاوَل [ħaːwal] مُحاوَلَة [muħaːwala] *vn: sv* i. Try to reach him in his office. حاوِل تِتِّصِل بِيه بدائِرتَه [ħaːwil tittiṣil biːh bdaːʔirtah] • **3.** ذاق [ðaːq] ذَوق [ðawq] *vn:* اِنذاق [ʔinðaːg] *p:* Try some of the peppers. I think you'll like them prepared this way. ذُوق شوَيَّة مِن الفِلفِل، أظِنّ يعجبَك مَطبُوخ هِيكِي [ðuːg šwayya min ʔilfilfil, ʔaðinn yiʕiǰbak maṭbuːx hiːči] • **4.** حاكَم [ħaːkam] مُحاكَمَة [muħaːkama] *vn: sv* u. Who's going to try the accused? مِنُو راح يحاكِم المُتَّهَم؟ [minu raːħ yħaːkim ʔilmuttaham?] • **5.** شاف [šaːf] شَوف [šawf] *vn: sv* u. نَظَر [naðar] أنظار [ʔanðaːr] *pl: sv* u. Which judge is trying the case? يا حاكِم دَيشُوف الدَّعوَة؟ [yaː ħaːkim dayšuːf ʔiddaʕwa?]

to try on • **1.** قَدَّر [gaddar] *sv* i. I'd like to try that suit on again. أرِيد أقَدِّر هَالقاط مَرَّة لُخ [ʔariːd ʔagaddir halqaːṭ marra lux] I'd like to try that suit on again. أرِيد أشُوف مَرَّة لُخ شلُون القاط يُقعُد عَلَيّا [ʔariːd ʔašuːf marra lux šluːn ʔilqaːṭ yugʕud ʕalayya]

to try out • **1.** جَرَّب [ǰarrab] تَجرُبَة [taǰruba] *vn:* تجَرَّب [tǰarrab] *p:* I'm going to try out a new car. راح أجَرُّب فَدّ سَيّارَة جِدِيدَة [raːħ ʔaǰarrub fadd sayyaːra ǰidiːda]

trying • **1.** عَصِيب [ʕaṣiːb] Those were trying times. هاي أوقات عَصِيبَة [haːy ʔawqaːt ʕaṣiːba]

tub • **1.** طَشِت [ṭašit] طشُوت [ṭšuːt] *pl:* The wash is still in the tub. الهِدُوم بَعَدها بِالطَّشِت [ʔilhduːm baʕadha biṭṭašit]

T

• **2.** بانيُو [baːnyu] بانيُوات [baːnyuwaːt] *pl:* Did you wash out the bath tub after you took a bath? غِسَلت البانيُو بَعَد ما أخَذِت حَمّام؟ [ɣisalt ʔalbaːnyuː baʕad maː ʔaxaðit ħammaːm?]

tube • **1.** إنبُوبَة [ʔinbuːba] إنبُوبات [ʔinbuːbaːt] *pl:* بُوري [buːri] بُوريّات، بُواري [buːriːyyaːt, bwaːriː] *pl:* They had to feed him through a tube. اِضطَرّوا يِنطُوه أكَل بِأنبُوبَة [ʔiðṭarraw yinṭuːh ʔakal biʔanbuːba] • **2.** جُوب [čuːb] جُوبات، جواب، جوابَة [čuːbaːt, čwaːb, čwaːba] *pl:* I need a new tube for my bicycle. أحتاج كُوب جِديد لِلبايسِكِل مالِي [ʔaħtaːǰ čuːb ǰidiːd lilpaːysikil maːli] • **3.** تيُوب [tyuːb] تيُوبات [tyuːbaːt] *pl:* دَبَّة [dabba] دَبّات [dabbaːt] *pl:* I want a large tube of tooth paste. أريد فَدّ تيُوب كِبير مَعجُون مال سنُون [ʔariːd fadd tyuːb čibiːr maʕǰuːn maːl snuːn] • **4.** لَمبَة [lamba] لَمبات [lambaːt] *pl:* My radio needs a new tube. الرّاديُو مالِي يِنرادلَه لَمبَة جِديدَة [ʔirraːdyu maːli yinraːdlah lampa ǰidiːda]

tubercular • **1.** مَسلُول [masluːl]

tuberculosis • **1.** سِلّ [sill]

tubing • **1.** بُوري [buːri] بُوريّات، بُواري [buːriyyaːt, bwaːri] *pl:* I need two hundred meters of tubing. أحتاج مِيتَين مَتِر بُوري [ʔaħtaːǰ mitayn matir buːri]

tubular • **1.** عَلَى شِكِل إنبُوب [ʕala šikil ʔinbuːb] عَلَى شِكِل بُوري [ʕala šikil buːri]

tuck • **1.** كَسرَة [kasra] كَسرات [kasraːt] *pl:* طَويَة [ṭawya] طَويات [ṭawyaːt] *pl:* The dress needs some tucks at the waist. النَّفنُوف يِنرادلَه كَم كَسرَة مِن الخِصِر [ʔannafnuːf yinraːdlah čam kasra min ʔilxiṣir]

to tuck in • **1.** لَفلَف [laflaf] تلِفلِف [tliflif] *vn: sv* i. Mother used to tuck us in at night. أمّي كانَت تلَفلِفنا بِاللِّحفان باللَّيل [ʔummi čaːnat tlaflifna billiħfaːn billayl] • **2.** خَشَّش [xaššaš] تَخشِيش [taxšiːš] *vn:* تخَشَّش [txaššaš] *p:* Your shirt tail is out; tuck it in your pants. ثوبَك طالِع؛ خَشِّشَه بِالبَنطُرُون [θuːbak ṭaːliʕ; xaššišah bilpanṭuruːn]

to tuck up • **1.** شال [šaːl] شَيل [šayl] *vn:* اِنشال [ʔinšaːl] *p:* She tucked up her skirts and ran. شالَت ذيالها وَركضَت [šaːlat ðyaːlha wrikðat]

Tuesday • **1.** يَوم الثِّلاثاء [yawm ʔiθθilaːθaːʔ, yawm ʔittilaːθa] I'll be back on Tuesday. أرجَع يوم الثَّلاثاء [ʔarǰaʕ yuːm ʔiθθilaːθaːʔ]

tuft • **1.** كَفشَة [kafša] كَفشات [kafšaːt] *pl:* The squirrel has only one tuft of hair on its tail. السِّنجاب عِندَه بَسّ كَفشَة شَعَر وِحدَة بِذَيلَه [ʔissinǰaːb ʕindah bass kafšat šaʕar wiħda biðiːlah] • **2.** كَومَة [kawma] كُوَم [kuwam] *pl:* There's a rabbit behind that tuft of grass. أكُو أرنَب وَرا كُومَة الحَشِيش ذِيك [ʔaku ʔarnab wara kuːmat ʔilħašiːš ðiːč] • **3.** كَعكُولَة [kaʕkuːla] كَعكُولات [kaʕkuːlaːt] *pl:* كَعاكِيل [kaʕaːkiːl] This type of pigeon has a tuft on its head. هَالنّوع حَمام عِندَه كَعكُولَة [hannawʕ ħamaːm ʕindah kaʕkuːla]

tug • **1.** ماطَور [maːṭuːr] ماطَورات [maːṭuːraːt] *pl:* Two tugs are towing the barge. ماطَورَين دَيجَرّون الدُّوبَة [maːṭuːrayn dayǰarruːn ʔidduːba]

to tug • **1.** سَحسَل [saħsal] تسِحسِل [tsiħsil] *vn: sv* i. جَرجَر [ǰarǰar] تجِرجِر [tǰirǰir] *vn: sv* i. Stop tugging at me! بَسّ عاد تسَحسِل بِيّا [bass ʕaːd tsaħsil biyya]

tug of war • **1.** جَرّ الحَبِل [ǰarr ʔilħabil] Who won the tug of war? مِنُو غِلَب بِجَرّ الحَبِل؟ [minu ɣilab bǰarr ʔilħabil?]

tuition • **1.** أجُور الدِراسَة [ʔuǰuːr ʔiddiraːsa] Have you paid your tuition yet? دفَعِت أجُور الدِّراسَة لَو بَعَد؟ [dfaʕit ʔuǰuːr ʔiddiraːsa law baʕad?]

tumble • **1.** وَقعَة [wagʕa] وَقعات [wagʕaːt] *pl:* شُقلُمبَة، جُقلُمبَة [čuqlumba] شُقلُمبات، جُقلُمبات [čuqlumbaːt] *pl:* She took quite a tumble yesterday. تشَقلِبَت فَدّ شُقلُمبَة زينَة البارحَة [tčaqlibat fadd čuqlumba ziːna ʔilbaːrħa]

to tumble down • **1.** تشَقلَب، تجَقلَب [tčaqlab] تشِقلِب [tčiqlib] *vn: sv* a. تدَعبَل [tdaʕbal] تدِعبِل [tdiʕbil] *vn: sv* a. He tumbled down the stairs. تشَقلَب مِن الدَّرَج [tčaqlab min ʔiddaraǰ]

tumbler • **1.** كلاص [glaːṣ] كلاصات [glaːṣaːt] *pl:* بَرداغ [bardaːɣ] بَراديغ [baraːdiːɣ] *pl:* He brought me some water in a tumbler. جابلِي شوَيَّة ماي بِبَرداغ [ǰaːbli šwayya maːy bbardaːɣ]

tumor • **1.** وَرَم [waram] أورام [ʔawraːm] *pl:*

tune • **1.** نَغمَة [naɣma] نَغمات [naɣmaːt] *pl:* لَحِن [laħin] ألحان [ʔalħaːn] *pl:* Do you know that tune? تُعرُف هَاللَّحِن؟ [tuʕruf hallaħin?]

*** He keeps harping on the same tune.** • **1.** يضِلّ يدُقّ عَلَى نَفس الوَتَر [yðill ydugg ʕala nafs ʔilwatar]

in tune • **1.** مَنصُوب [manṣuːb] Is your violin in tune? الكَمَنجَة مالتَك مَنصُوبَة؟ [ʔilkamanǰa maːltak manṣuːba?]

*** Their government is in tune with the times.** • **1.** نِظام الحُكُم مالهُم يِتلائَم وِيّا الزَّمان [niðaːm lħukum maːlhum yitlaːʔam wiyya ʔazzamaːn]

out of tune • **1.** نَشاز [našaːz] She always sings out of tune. دائِماً تغَنّي نَشاز [daːʔiman tɣanni našaːz] • **2.** ما مَنصُوب [maː manṣuːb] The lute is out of tune. العُود ما مَنصُوب [ʔilʕuːd maː manṣuːb]

to tune in • **1.** طَلَّع [ṭallaʕ] *sv* i. You haven't tuned the station in properly. إنتَ ما طَلَّعت المَحَطَّة زين [ʔinta maː ṭallaʕt ʔalmaħaṭṭa ziːn] You haven't tuned the station in properly. الرّاديُو مُو عالمَحَطَّة [ʔirraːdyu muː ʕalmaħaṭṭa]

T

to tune up • **1.** نَصَب آلات [niṣab ʔaːlaːt] نَصُب آلات [naṣub ʔaːlaːt] *vn: sv* u. The orchestra is tuning up. الفِرقَة دَتِنصُب آلاتها [ʔilfirqa datinṣub ʔaːlaːtha] • **2.** ضُبَط [ðubaṭ] ضَبُط [ðabuṭ] *vn:* اِنضُبَط [ʔinðubaṭ] *p:* قَسَّم [qassam] تَقسِيم [taqsiːm] *vn:* تقَسَّم [tqassam] *p:* Did you tune up the motor? ضُبَطت المَكِينَة؟ [ðubaṭt ʔilmakiːna?]

tuning • **1.** نَصُب [naṣub] The piano needs tuning. البيانُو يِنرادلَه نَصُب [ʔilpyaːnuː yinraːdlah naṣub]

Tunis • **1.** تُونِس [tuːnis]

Tunisia • **1.** تُونِس [tuːnis]

Tunisian • **1.** تُونِسِي [tuːnisi] تُونِسِيِّين [tuːnisiyyiːn] *pl:*

tunnel • **1.** نَفَق [nafaq] أنفاق [ʔanfaːq] *pl:*

turban • **1.** عمامَة [ʕmaːma] عمايِم [ʕmaːyim] لَفَّة [laffa] لَفّات [laffaːt] *pl:* عمامَة [ʕmaːma] *Collective:* جَرّاوِيَّة [čarraːwiyya] جَرّاوِيّات [čarraːwiyyaːt] *pl:*

turbine • **1.** تَربِين [tarbiːn] تَربِينات [tarbiːnaːt] *pl:*

turbulence • **1.** اِضطِراب [ʔiðṭiraːb] There's some turbulence ahead so we'll change course. راح نبَدِّل اِتِّجاهنا لِأَنّ أَكُو اِضطِراب بِالجَوّ قِدّامنا [raːħ nbaddil ʔittiǰaːhna liʔann ʔaku ʔiðṭiraːb biǰǰaww giddaːmna]

turbulent • **1.** مِضطِرِب [miðṭirib] It is a very turbulent situation. الحالَة كانَت مِضطَرِبَة كُلِّش [ʔilħaːla čaːnat miðṭarba kulliš]

Turcoman • **1.** تُركمانِي [turkmaːni] تُركمان [turkmaːn] *pl:* Most Turcomans in Iraq live around Kirkuk. أكثَر التُّركمان بِالعِراق بمَنطِقَة كَركُوك [ʔakθar ʔitturkumaːn bilʕiraːq bmanṭiqat karkuːk]

turf • **1.** عِشِب [ʕišib]

Turk • **1.** تُركِي [turki] تُرُك، أتراك [turuk, ʔatraːk] *pl:*

Turkey • **1.** تُركِيا [turkiya]

turkey • **1.** دِيك هِندِي [diːč hindi] دِيُوكَة هِندِيَّة [dyuːča hindiyya] *pl:* عَلِي عَلِيشِيش [ʕališiːš] عَلِيشِيشات [ʕališiːšaːt] *pl:*

Turkish • **1.** تُركِي [turki] أتراك [ʔatraːk] *pl:* Is he a Turkish citizen? هُوَّ جِنسِيتَه تُركِي [huwwa ǰinsiːtah turki] How do you say it in Turkish? شلُون تقُولها بالتُّركِي؟ [šluːn tguːlha bitturki?] I stopped by the Turkish bath to see Ali. مَرِّيت بِالحَمّام التُّركِي حَتَّى أشُوف عَلِي [marriːt bilħammaːm ʔitturki ħatta ʔašuːf ʕali]

Turkish delight • **1.** حَلقُوم [ħalquːm] لُقُم [luqum]

Turkish towel • **1.** خاولِي [xaːwli] خاولِيّات [xaːwliːyyaːt] *pl:* بَشكِير [paškiːr] بَشاكِير [pašaːkiːr] *pl:*

turn • **1.** فَرَّة [farra] فَرّات [farraːt] *pl:* He gave the wheel a half turn. فَرّ الچَرخ نُصّ فَرَّة [farr ʔilčarix nuṣṣ farra] Give the valve three turns to the right. فُرّ الصَّمّام ثلَث فَرّات لِليَمِين [furr ʔiṣṣammaːm tlaθ farraːt lilyamiːn] • **2.** لَوفَة [luːfa] Take the first turn to the right. دُور بأَوَّل لُوفَة عاليَمِين [duːr bʔawwal luːfa ʕalyamiːn] • **3.** نوبَة [nuːba] نوبات [nuːbaːt] *pl:* دَور [dawr, duːr] أدوار [ʔadwaːr] *pl:* It's my turn now. هَسَّة نُوبتِي [hassa nuːbti] You will be called up in turn. راح تِنصاح بِالدُّور [raːħ tinṣaːħ bidduːr]

* **We encountered difficulties at every turn.** • **1.** اِعتِرضَتنا صُعُوبات مِن كُلّ ناحِيَة [ʔiʕtirðatna ṣuʕuːbaːt min kull naːħiya]

* **The meat is cooked to a turn.** • **1.** اللَّحَم مَطبُوخ عَالأُصُول [ʔillaħam maṭbuːx ʕalʔuṣuːl]

* **Last night he took a turn for the worse.** • **1.** البارحَة بِاللَّيل صِحّتَه تدَهوُرَت [ʔilbaːrħa billayl ṣiħħtah tdahwurat]

* **The political situation has taken a turn for the better.** • **1.** الحالَة السِياسِيَّة صار بِيها تَحَسُّن [ʔilħaːla ʔissiyaːsiyya ṣaːr biːha taħassun]

good turn • **1.** مَعرُوف [maʕruːf] زِينِيَّة [zayniyya] زِينِيّات [zayniyyaːt] *pl:* Ali did me a good turn. عَلِي سَوّالِي زِينِيَّة [ʕali sawwaːli zayniyya]

to take turns • **1.** تناوَب [tnaːwab] تَناوُب [tanaːwub] *vn: sv* a. We'll take turns driving. راح نِتناوَب بِالسِّياقَة [raːħ nitnaːwab bissiyaːqa]

to turn • **1.** دار [daːr] دَير [dayr] *vn: sv* i. فَرّ [farr] فَرّ [farr] *vn: sv* u. I can't turn the key. ما دَأقدَر أدِير المِفتاح [maː daʔagdar ʔadiːr ʔilmiftaːħ] She turned her back on me. دارَتلِي ظَهَرها [daːratli ðaharha] Turn your chair to the light. فُرّ الكُرسِي مالَك عالضَوا [furr ʔilkursi maːlak ʕaððuwa] • **2.** اِنقِلَب [ʔingilab] *sv* u. The tide of battle will turn. مَجرَى المَعرَكَة راح ينقُلُب [maǰraː ʔilmaʕraka raːħ yingulub] The tide of battle will turn. الآيَة راح تِنقُلُب [ʔilʔaːya raːħ tingulub] • **3.** لَوَى [luwaː] لَوي [lawy] *vn:* إنلِوَى [ʔinliwaː] *p:* It's the second time today that I turned my ankle. هاي ثانِي مَرَّة هَاليُوم ألوِي رِجلِي [haːy θaːni marra halyuːm ʔalwi rijli] • **4.** توَجَّه [twaǰǰah] تَوَجُّه [tawaǰǰuh] *vn: sv* i. I don't know who to turn to. ما أدرِي إلمَن أتوَجَّه [maː ʔadri ʔilman ʔatwaǰǰah] • **5.** تحَوَّل [tħawwal] تَحَوُّل [taħawwul] *vn: sv* a. The water turned to steam. الماي تحَوَّل إلَى بُخار [ʔilmaːy tħawwal ʔila buxaːr] • **6.** چِرَخ [čirax] چَرخ، چِراخَة [čarix, čiraːxa] *vn:* اِنچِرَخ [ʔinčirax] *p:* He turned these chess pieces on a lathe. چِرَخ قُطَع هَالشِّطرَنج بِالتُّورنَة [čirax quṭaʕ haššiṭranǰ bittuːrna] • **7.** قَلَّب [gallab] تَقلِيب [tagliːb] *vn:* تقَلَّب [tgallab] *p:* She turned the pages slowly. قَلِّبَت الصَّحايِف عَلَى كَيفها [gallubat ʔiṣṣaħaːyif ʕala kiːfha] The police turned the room upside down. الشُّرطَة قَلْبَوا الغُرفَة مِن فُوگ لِجَوَّة [ʔiššurṭa gallibaw ʔilɣurfa min fuːg lijawwa] The police turned the room upside down. الشُّرطَة نَبَّشَوا الغُرفَة [ʔiššurṭa nabbišaw ʔilɣurfa] • **8.** لَعَّب [laʕʕab] تَلعِيب [talʕiːb] *vn: sv* i. The sight turned my stomach. المَنظَر لَعَّب نَفسِي [ʔilmanðar laʕʕab nafsi] • **9.** وَجَّه [wajjah] تَوجِيه [tawjiːh] *vn:* تَوَجَّه [twajjah] *p:* Turn the hose on the fire! وَجِّه البُورِي عَالنّار [wajjih ʔilbuːri ʕannaːr] • **10.** صار [ṣaːr] *sv* i. He's just turned fifty today. صار عُمرَه خَمسِين سَنَة اليُوم [ṣaːr ʕumrah xamsiːn sana ʔilyuːm] They turned traitor. صارَوا خَوَنَة [ṣaːraw xawana] • **11.** قِلَب [gilab] قَلُب [galub] *vn:* اِنقِلَب [ʔingilab] *p:* بَدَّل [baddal] تَبدِيل [tabdiːl] *vn:* I want to turn these stocks into cash. أرِيد أَقلُب هَالسَّندات إِلَى نَقِد [ʔariːd ʔaglub hassandaːt ʔila naqid] • **12.** اِفتَرّ [ʔiftarr] فَرّ [farr] *vn: sv* a. The wheels turned slowly. الجرُوخ اِفتَرَّت يَواش [ʔilčruːx ʔiftarrat yawaːš] • **13.** اِلتِفَت [ʔiltifat] اِلتِفات [ʔiltifaːt] *vn: sv* i. She turned to look at him. اِلتِفتَت حَتَّى تباوِع عَليه [ʔiltiftat ħatta tbaːwiʕ ʕaliːh]

*** She turned red.** • **1.** حمَرَّت [ħmarrat]

*** The milk turned sour.** • **1.** الحَلِيب حمَضّ [ʔilħaliːb ʔiħmaðð]

*** They turned pale when they heard the news.** • **1.** صفَرَّوا مِن سِمعَوا الخَبَر [ṣfarraw min simʕaw ʔilxabar]

to turn around • **1.** اِندار [ʔindaːr] *sv* a. Turn around and let me see the back of your jacket. اِندار وَخَلِّي أَشُوف ظَهر سِترتَك [ʔindaːr wxalli ʔašuːf ðahir sitirtak] • **2.** دَيوَر [daywar] دَيوَرَة [diːwara] *vn:* تدَيوَر [tdiːwar] *p:* Turn around, the street is closed. دَيوُر، الشّارِع مَسدُود [diːwur, ʔiššaːriʕ masduːd]

to turn back • **1.** رِجَع [rijaʕ] رُجُوع [rujuːʕ] *vn: sv* a. Let's turn back. خَلِّي نِرجَع [xalliː nirjaʕ]

to turn down • **1.** رُفَض [rufað] رَفُض [rafuð] *vn:* اِنرُفَض [ʔinrufað] *p:* رَدّ [radd] رَدّ [radd] *vn:* اِنرَدّ [ʔinradd] *p:* The management turned down my application. الإدارَة رُفضَت طَلَبِي [ʔilʔidaːra rufðat ṭalabi] • **2.** طَوَّى [ṭawwaː] *sv* i. عِوَج [ʕiwaj] *sv* i. Please don't turn down the corners of my book. لا تِعوِج حَواشِي الوَرَق بِكتابِي [laː tiʕwij ħawaːši ʔilwaraq biktaːbi] • **3.** نَصَّة [naṣṣa] نَصّات [naṣṣaːt] *pl:* تَنصِيَة [tanṣiya] *vn: sv* i. نَزَّل [nazzal] تَنزِيل [tanziːl] *vn: sv* i. Will you turn down the radio, please? نَصِّي الرّادِيُو، مِن فَضلَك [naṣṣi ʔirraːdyu, min faðlak] • **4.** فات ب [faːt b-] فَوت [fawt] *vn:* اِنفات [ʔinfaːt] *p:* دَيوَر [daywar] دَيوَرَة [daywara] *vn:* تدَيوَر [tdaywar] *p:* Turn down this road. فُوت بِهالطَّرِيق [fuːt bhaṭṭariːq]

to turn in • **1.** خَشّ مِن [xašš min] خَشّ [xašš] *vn: sv* u. فات [faːt] فَوت [fuːt] *vn: sv* u. Driver, turn in here! سايِق، خُشّ مِن هنا [saːyiq, xušš min hna] • **2.** نام [naːm] نَوم [nawm] *vn: sv* a. We ought to turn in early tonight. لازِم نِنام عَلَى وَقِت هاللَّيلَة [laːzim ʔinnaːm ʕala wakit hallayla] • **3.** وِشَى [wišaː] وِشايَة [wišaːya] *vn: sv* i. We turned him in to the police. وِشِينا بِيه بِالشُّرطَة [wišiːna biːh biššurṭa]

• **4.** قَدَّم [qaddam] تَقدِيم [taqdiːm] *vn: sv* i. He turned in his resignation. قَدَّم اِستِقالتَه [qaddam ʔistiqaːltah] • **5.** سَلَّم [sallam] تَسلِيم [tasliːm] *vn: sv* i. You must turn your gun in to the police. لازِم تسَلِّم بُندُقِيتَك لِلشُّرطَة [laːzim tsallim bunduqiːtak liššurṭa]

to turn into • **1.** صار [ṣaːr] *sv* i. اِنقِلَب [ʔingilab] اِنقِلاب [ʔinqilaːb] *vn: sv* i. The wine turned into vinegar. الشَّراب اِنقِلَب إِلَى خَلّ [ʔiššaraːb ʔingilab ʔila xall] He has turned into a poet. اِنقِلَب شاعِر [ʔingilab šaːʕir] He has turned into a poet. صار شاعِر [ṣaːr šaːʕir]

to turn loose • **1.** فَكّ [fakk] فَكّ [fakk] *vn: sv* u. هَدّ [hadd] هَدّ [hadd] *vn: sv* i. He turned his dog loose. فَكّ كَلبَه [fakk čalbah]

to turn off • **1.** سَدّ [sadd] سَدّ [sadd] *vn:* اِنسَدّ [ʔinsadd] *p:* قِطَع [qiṭaʕ] قَطِع [qaṭiʕ] *vn:* اِنقِطَع [ʔinqiṭaʕ] *p:* Did you turn off the gas? سَدَّيت الغاز؟ [saddayt ʔilɣaːz?] • **2.** طَفَّى [ṭaffaː] تَطفِيَة [taṭfiya] *vn: sv* i. Turn off the radio. طَفِّي الرّادِيُو [ṭaffi ʔirraːdyu]

to turn on • **1.** شِعَل [šiʕal] شَعِل [šaʕil] *vn:* اِنشِعَل [ʔinšiʕal] *p:* Why don't you turn on the light? لِيش ما تِشعِل الضُّوَة؟ [liːš maː tišʕil ʔiððuwa?] • **2.** فَكّ [fakk] فَكّ [fakk] *vn:* اِنفَكّ [ʔinfakk] *p:* Who turned on the radio? مِنُو فَكّ الرّادِيُو؟ [minu fakk ʔirraːdyu?]

to turn out • **1.** طِرَد [ṭirad] طَرِد [ṭarid] *vn:* اِنطِرَد [ʔinṭirad] *p:* They turned me out of my room in the hotel. طِردَونِي مِن غُرُفتِي بالأُوتِيل [ṭirduːni min ɣurufti bilʔutiːl] • **2.** قِلَب [gilab] قَلُب [galub] *vn:* اِنقِلَب [ʔingilab] *p:* Turn the right side of the material out. أَقلُب القماش عَلَى وُجَّه [ʔuglub ʔilqmaːš ʕala wuččah] • **3.** طَلَّع [ṭallaʕ] تَطلِيع [taṭliːʕ] *vn:* تطَلَّع [tṭallaʕ] *p:* أَنتَج [ʔantaj] إنتاج [ʔintaːj] *vn: sv* i. The factory turns out 500 pairs of shoes a day. المَعمَل يطَلِّع خَمِس مِيَّة زوج قَنادِر بِاليُوم [ʔilmaʕmal yṭalliʕ xamis miyyat zawj qanaːdir bilyuːm] • **4.** طِلَع [ṭilaʕ] طُلُوع [ṭuluːʕ] *vn:* اِنطِلَع [ʔinṭilaʕ] *p:* How did the elections turn out? شلُون طِلعَت نَتِيجَة الانتِخابات؟ [šluːn ṭilʕat natiːjat ʔilintixaːbaːt?] The snapshots didn't turn out right. الصُّوَر ما طِلعَت زين [ʔiṣṣuwar maː ṭilʕat ziːn] • **5.** حِضَر [ħiðar] حُضُور [ħuðuːr] *vn: sv* a. A large crowd turned out for the meeting. جَماعَة كِبِيرَة مِن النّاس حِضرَت الاِجتِماع [jamaːʕa čibiːra min ʔinnaːs ħiðrat ʔilʔijtimaːʕ]

to turn over • **1.** قِلَب [gilab] قَلُب [galub] *vn:* اِنقِلَب [ʔingilab] *p:* I nearly turned over the table. بَعَد شوَيَّة أَقلُب المِيز [baʕad šwayya ʔaglub ʔilmiːz] • **2.** اِنقِلَب [ʔingilab] اِنقِلاب [ʔinqilaːb] *vn: sv* u. Our boat turned over. بَلَمنا اِنقِلَب [balamna ʔingilab] • **3.** سَلَّم [sallam] تَسلِيم [tasliːm] *vn:* تسَلَّم [tsallam] *p:* Everyone has to turn over his weapons to the police. الكُلّ لازِم يسَلّمُون أَسلِحَتهُم لِلشُّرطَة [ʔilkull laːzim ysallmuːn ʔasliħathum liššurṭa] He turned his business over to his son. سَلَّم شُغلَه لِإبنَه [sallam šuɣlah lʔibnah] • **4.** قَلَّب [gallab] تَقلِيب [tagliːb] *vn: sv* u. Turn it over in your mind before you give me your answer.

T

قَلُّبها بِعَقلَك زين قَبُل ما تِنطِينِي جَواب [gallubha bʕaqlak ziːn gabul maː tinṭiːni ǰawaːb]

to turn up • 1. ظِهَر [ðihar] ظُهُور [ðuhuːr] *vn: sv* a. طِلَع [ṭilaʕ] طُلُوع [ṭuluːʕ] *vn: sv* a. I guess the file will probably turn up when we are not looking for it. أَعتِقِد هالفايِل عَلَى الأَكثَر راح يِظهَر مِن ما دَندَوِّر عَليه [ʔaʕtiqid halfaːyil ʕala ʔilʔakθar raːħ yiðhar min maː dandawwir ʕaliːh] • **2.** نُبَص [nubaṣ] نَبُص [nabuṣ] *vn: sv* u. ظِهَر [ðihar] ظُهُور [ðuhuːr] *vn: sv* a. The missing man suddenly turned up here in Baghdad. الرِّجّال الضّايِع فُجأةً نُبَص هنا بِبَغداد [ʔirrijjaːl ʔiððaːyiʕ fujʔatan nubaṣ hna bibaɣdaːd]

turning • 1. تَحَوُّل [taħawwul] That was the turning point. هاي كانَت نُقطَة التَّحَوُّل [haːy čaːnat nuqṭat ʔittaħawwul] • **2.** تَراجُع [taraːjuʕ] نُقُوص [nuquːṣ] There'll be no turning back now. ماكُو مَجال لِلتَّراجُع [maːku majaːl littaraːjuʕ]

turnip • 1. شَلغَمَة [šalɣama] شَلغَمات [šalɣamaːt] *pl:* شَلغَم [šalɣam] *Collective*

turnkey • 1. سَجّان [sajjaːn] سَجّانِين [sajjaːniːn] *pl:*

turnover • 1. تَغيِير [taɣyiːr] تَغيِيرات [taɣyiːraːt] *pl:* There's a big turnover of employees in this office. أَكُو هوايَة تَغِير بِالمُوَظَّفِين بِهالدّائِرَة [ʔaku hwaːya taɣyiːr bilmuwaððafiːn bhaddaːʔira] • **2.** بَيع ووشِرا [bayʕ wšira] My uncle's store has a big turnover. أَكُو هوايَة بَيع وَشِرَى بِدُكّان عَمِّي [ʔaku hwaːya bayʕ wšira bdukkaːn ʕammi] • **3.** كليجايَة [kliːčaːya] كليجايات [kliːčaːyaːt] *pl:* كلَيجَة [kliːča] *Collective:* They served date turnovers with tea. قَدّمَوا كلَيجَة مال تَمُر ويّا شاي [qaddmaw kliːča maːl tamur wiyya čaːy]

turpentine • 1. تَربَنتِين [tarpantiːn]

turquoise • 1. فَيرُوز [fayruːz] شَذِر [šaðir] My sister has a turquoise stone in her ring. أُختِي عِدها فَصّ فَيرُوز بِالمِحبَس مالها [ʔuxti ʕidha faṣṣ fayruːz bilmiħbas maːlha]

turret • 1. بُرِج [burij] بُرُوج، أَبراج [buruːj, ʔabraːj] *pl:* The old castle has turrets on the walls. القَلعَة العَتِيقَة بِيها أَبراج بِالحياطِين [ʔalqalʕa ʔilʕatiːga biːha ʔabraːj biliħyaːṭiːn] The tank returned with a turret damaged. الدَّبّابَة رِجعَت بِبُرِج مَحَطَّم [ʔiddabbaːba rijʕat bburij mħaṭṭam]

turtle • 1. رَقَّة [ragga] رَقّات [raggaːt] *pl:* رَقّ [ragg] *Collective:* سُلحَفات [sulħafaːt] سَلاحِف [salaːħif] *pl:* رَفِش [rafiš] رُفُوش [rufuːš] *pl:*

turtledove • 1. فُختايَة [fuxtaːya] فُختايات [fuxtaːyaːt] *pl:*

turtleneck sweater • 1. بلُوز رُقبَة [bluːz rugba] بلُوزات أَبُو رُقبَة [bluːzaːt ʔabuː rugba] *pl:* He's wearing a turtleneck sweater. يِلبَس بلُوز أَبُو رُقبَة [yilbas bluːz ʔabu rugba]

tusk • 1. ناب [naːb] أَنياب [ʔanyaːb] *pl:*

tutor • 1. مُعَلِّم خُصُوصِي [muʕallim xuṣuːṣi] مُعَلِّمِين خُصُوصِيِّين [muʕallimiːn xuṣuːṣiyyiːn] *pl:* You need a tutor in mathematics. يِنرادلَك مُعَلِّم خُصُوصِي بِالرِّياضِيّات [yinraːdlak muʕallim xuṣuːṣi birriyaːðiyyaːt]

tuxedo • 1. قاط سمَوكِن [qaːṭ smuːkin] قُوط سمَوكِن [quːṭ smuːkin] *pl:*

twang • 1. خَنَّة [xanna] He talks with a twang. عِندَه خَنَّة بِحَكيَه [ʕindah xanna bħačyah]

tweezers • 1. مِنقاش [mingaːš] مِنقاشات [mingaːšaːt] *pl:* مِناقِيش [minaːgiːš] *pl:*

twelfth • 1. الثنَعَش [ʔiθθinaʕaš]

twelve • 1. ثنَعَش [θnaʕaš]

twentieth • 1. العِشرِين [ʔilʕišriːn]

twenty • 1. عِشرِين [ʕišriːn]

twice • 1. مَرّتَين [marrtayn] نَوبتَين [nawbtayn] I was invited there twice. آنِي مَرّتَين مَعزُوم هناك [ʔaːni marrtayn maʕzuːm hnaːk] • **2.** ضِعِف [ðiʕif] أَضعاف [ʔaðʕaːf] *pl:* That way will take twice as long. هَالطَّرِيق ياخُذ ضِعف المُدَّة [haṭṭariːq yaːxuð ðiʕf ʔilmudda] I paid twice as much. دفَعِت ضِعف هالمِقدار [dfaʕit ðiʕf halmiqdaːr]

twig • 1. غُصُن صغَيِّر [ɣuṣun ṣɣayyir] أَغصان صغَيّرَة [ʔaɣṣaːn ṣɣayyra] *pl:*

twin • 1. تَوم [tawm] تَوامَة [twaːma] *pl:* Those two boys are twins. هَالوَلَدَين تَوم [halwaladayn tawm] She's his twin sister. هِيَّ أُختَه التَّوم [hiyya ʔuxtah ʔattawm]

twine • 1. سُوتلِي [suːtli] I need some more twine to tie this package. أَرِيد شوَيَّة لاخ سُوتلِي حَتَّى أَشِدّ الرُّزمَة [ʔariːd šwayya laːx suːtli ħatta ʔašidd ʔirruzma]

to twine • 1. تسَلَّق [tsallaq] تَسَلُّق [tasalluq] *vn: sv* a. The grapevine twines around the trellis. عَرَق العِنَب يِتسَلَّق عَلَى ذِيك القَمَرِيَّة [ʕarag ʔilʕinab yitsallaq ʕala ðiːč ʔilqamariyya]

twinge • 1. نَغزَة [naɣza] نَغزات [naɣzaːt] *pl:* I just felt a twinge in my side. حَسَّيت فَدّ نَغزَة بخاصِرتِي [ħassiːt fadd naɣza bxaːṣirti]

to twinkle • 1. تلَألَأ [tlaʔlaʔ] تَلَألُؤ [talaʔluʔ] *vn: sv* a. The stars were twinkling. النِّجُوم كانَت دَتِتلَألَأ [ʔinnijuːm čaːnat datitlaʔlaʔ]

T

to twirl • **1.** فَرّ [farr] فَرّ [farr] *vn: sv* u. He twirled his umbrella. فَرّ شَمسِيتَه [farr šamsi:tah] • **2.** اِفتَرّ [ʔiftarr] *sv* a. The pencil twirled on the end of the string. القَلَم المعَلّق بِالخَيط قام يِفتَرّ [ʔilqalam ʔilmʕallag bilxi:ṭ ga:m yiftarr] • **3.** فِتَل [fital] فَتِل [fatil] *vn: sv* i. بُرَم [buram] بَرُم [barum] *vn: sv* u. The officer twirled his moustache. الضّابُط فِتَل شوارِبَه [ʔiḍḍa:buṭ fital šwa:rbah]

twist • **1.** بَرمَة [barma] بَرمات [barma:t] *pl:* He gave the donkey's tail a good twist. بُرَم ذَيل الزّمال بَرمَة قَوِيَّة [buram ðayl ʔizzuma:l barma qawiyya] • **2.** وُصلَة [wuṣla] وُصَل [wuṣal] *pl:* Add a twist of lemon peel. حُطّ فَدّ وُصلَة قِشِر نُومِي حامُض [ḥuṭṭ fadd wuṣlat gišir nu:mi ḥa:muð]

to twist • **1.** لُوَى [luwa:] لَوي [lawi] *vn:* اِنلُوَى [ʔinluwa:] *p:* He twisted my arm until it hurt. لُوَى إيدَيَّة إلَى أن قامَت تُوجَعنِي [luwa: ʔi:dayya ʔila ʔan ga:mat tu:ǰaʕni] I nearly twisted my ankle. لُوَيت رِجلِي إلّا شوَيَّة [luwi:t rijli ʔilla šwayya] Twist the two ends of the wire together. إلوِي نِهايتَين الوايَر سُوَة [ʔilwi niha:ytayn ʔilwa:yar suwa] • **2.** فَرّ [farr] فَرّ [farr] *vn:* اِنفَرّ [ʔinfarr] *p:* Twist the screw two more turns to the right. فُرّ البُرغِي مَرّتَين لُخ لِليِمنَى [furr ʔilburɣi marrtayn lux lilyimna] • **3.** تلَوَّى [tlawwa:] تَلَوِّي [talawwi] *vn: sv* a. The road twists through the mountains. الطَّرِيق يِتلَوَّى بين الجِّبال [ʔiṭṭari:q yitlawwa: bi:n ʔiǰǰiba:l]

*** She twisted him around her little finger.** • **1.** لَبِستَه بإصبَعها مِثل المِحبَس [labistah bişbaʕha miθl ʔilmiḥbas]

twister • **1.** فِتّيلَة [fitti:la] فِتّيلات [fitti:la:t] *pl:* The twister blew off the garage roof. الفِتّيلَة طَيّرَت سَقُف الكَراج [ʔilfitti:la ṭayyrat saguf ʔilgara:ǰ]

to twitch • **1.** رَفّ [raff] رَفّ [raff] *vn: sv* u. My eye is twitching. عينِي دَترُفّ [ʕi:ni datruff]

to twitter • **1.** وَصوَص [waṣwaṣ] وَصوَصَة [waṣwaṣa] *vn: sv* i. The sparrows are twittering. العَصافِير دَتوَصوِص [ʔilʕaṣa:fi:r datwaṣwiṣ]

two • **1.** ثنَين [θnayn, θni:n] ثِنتَين [θintayn] There's no one here but the two of us. ماكُو أَحَّد هنا غير إحنا الثّنَين [ma:ku ʔaḥḥad hna ɣayr ʔiḥna ʔiθθnayn] It is two o'clock. السّاعَة ثِنتَين [ʔissa:ʕa θintayn] The two of you come here! ثنَينكُم تعالُوا هنا [θnaynkum taʕa:lu: hna] They came in by twos. دِخلَوا إثنَين إثنَين [dixlaw ʔiθnayn ʔiθnayn] • **2.** ين [- i:n] He owns two houses and two cars. يِملُك بَيتَين وَسَيّارتَين [yimluk baytayn wsayya:rti:n] A two-passenger car is not big enough for our family. سَيّارَة مال نَفَرَين ما كافيَة لِعائِلَتنا [sayya:ra ma:l nafarayn ma: ka:fya lʕa:ʔilatna]

two-faced • **1.** أَبُو وجهَين [ʔabu: wiǰhi:n] He's two-faced and sneaky; don't trust him. هَذا أَبُو وِجهَين وَحَيّال؛ لا تِثِق بِيه [ha:ða ʔabu wiǰhayn wḥayya:l; la: taθiq bi:h]

two hundred • **1.** مِيتَين [mi:tayn, miti:n]

type • **1.** نوع [nawʕ] أنواع [ʔanwa:ʕ] *pl:* شِكِل [šikil] أشكال، شكُول [ʔaška:l, šku:l] *pl:* What type of shoe did you have in mind? أيّ نُوع قُندَرَة عَقلَك قاطِع بِيه [ʔayy nu:ʕ qundara ʕaqlak qa:ṭiʕ bi:h] • **2.** فَصِيلَة [faṣi:la] فَصائِل [faṣa:ʔil] *pl:* Do you remember your blood type? تِتذَكَّر مِن أيّ فَصِيلَة دَمَّك؟ [tidðakkar min ʔayy faṣi:la dammak?] • **3.** حَرُف [ḥaruf] حُرُوف [ḥuru:f] *pl:* Which kind of type do you want? أيّ نُوع مِن الحرُوف ترِيد؟ [ʔayy nu:ʕ min ʔiliḥru:f tri:d?] • **4.** صِنِف [ṣinif] أصناف، صُنُوف [ʔaṣna:f, ṣunu:f] *pl:* He's not my type. هَذا مُو مِن صِنفِي [ha:ða mu: min ṣinfi]

to type • **1.** طِبَع [ṭubaʕ] طَبُع [ṭabuʕ] *vn:* اِنطُبَع [ʔinṭubaʕ] *p:* Can you type? تِقدَر تِطبَع؟ [tigdar tiṭbaʕ?] • **2.** صَنَّف [ṣannaf] تَصنِيف [taṣni:f] *vn:* تصَنَّف [tṣannaf] *p:* Nurse, have you typed that blood yet? يا مُمَرِّضَة، صَنَّفتِي هالدَّم لَو بَعَد؟ [ya: mumarriða, ṣannafti haddamm law baʕad?]

typewriter • **1.** طابِعَة [ṭa:biʕa] Bring the typewriter here. جِيب الطّابِعَة هنا [ǰi:b ʔiṭṭa:biʕa hna]

typewriting • **1.** طَبُع [ṭabuʕ] طِباعَة [ṭiba:ʕa] Do they teach typewriting at this school? يعَلّمُون طَبُع بهالمَدرَسَة؟ [yʕallimu:n ṭabuʕ bhalmadrasa?]

typhoid • **1.** تِيفُو [ti:fu]

typhus • **1.** تِيفُوس [ti:fu:s]

typical • **1.** أصلِي [ʔaṣli] This is a typical example of an old Iraqi house. هَذا نَمُوذَج أصلِي لِلبَيت العِراقِي القَدِيم [ha:ða namu:ðaǰ ʔaṣli lilbayt ʔilʕira:qi ʔilqadi:m] • **2.** صَمِيم [ṣami:m] He's a typical Iraqi. هُوَّ عِراقِي صَمِيم [huwwa ʕira:qi ṣami:m]

*** That's typical of him.** • **1.** هَذِي دَقّاتَه [ha:ði dagga:tah]

typist • **1.** كاتِب طابِعَة [ka:tib ṭa:biʕa] كُتّاب طابِعَة [kutta:b ṭa:biʕa] *pl:* He's a good typist. هَذا خُوش كاتِب طابِعَة [ha:ða xu:š ka:tib ṭa:biʕa]

tyranny • **1.** ظُلُم [ðulum] اِستِبداد [ʔistibda:d]

tyrant • **1.** ظالِم [ða:lim] ظُلّام [ðulla:m] *pl:* مُستَبِدّ [mustabidd] مُستَبِدِّين [mustabiddi:n] *pl:* He's a tyrant in the office, but he's active in community welfare. هَذا ظالِم بِالدّائِرَة لَكِن يسَوِّي خير هوايَة لِلمُجتَمَع [ha:ða ða:lim bidda:ʔira, la:kin ysawwi xi:r hwa:ya lilmuǰtamaʕ]

T

U

udder • **1.** ديس [di:s] ديُوس [dyu:s] *pl:* ضَرِع [ḍariʕ] ضرُوع [ḍru:ʕ] *pl:* ثَدي [θady] ثِدايَة [θida:ya] *pl:*

uglier • **1.** أبشَع [ʔabšaʕ] أقبَح [ʔaqbaħ] She's uglier than her sister. هِيَّ أبشَع مِن أُختها [hiyya ʔabšaʕ min ʔuxutha]

ugly • **1.** قَبِيح [qabi:ħ] بَشِع [bašiʕ] She's so ugly! هِيَّ كُلِّش قَبِيحَة [hiyya kulliš qabi:ħa] • **2.** مُغرِض [muɣriḍ] قَبِيح [qabi:ħ] They're spreading ugly rumors about him. دَيشَيّعُون إشاعات مُغرِضَة عَنّه [dayšayyʕu:n ʔiša:ʕa:t muɣriḍa ʕannah]

ulcer • **1.** قُرحَة [qurħa] قُرَح، قُرحات [qurah, qurħa:t] *pl:*

ulterior • **1.** خَفِي [xafi] I think there is an ulterior motive behind his action. أعتقِد أكُو غَرَض خَفِي بعَمَلَه [ʔaʕtiqid ʔaku ɣaraḍ xafi bʕamalah]

ultimate • **1.** نِهائِي [niha:ʔi] أخِير [ʔaxi:r] آخَر [ʔa:xar] Is this your ultimate goal? هاي غايتَك النِّهائِيَّة؟ [ha:y ɣa:ytak ʔinniha:ʔiyya?] Is this your ultimate goal? هَذِي آخَر غايَة تريدها؟ [ha:ði ʔa:xar ɣa:ya tri:dha?]

ultimatum • **1.** إنذار نِهائِي [ʔinḍa:r niha:ʔi] إنذارات نِهائِيَّة [ʔinða:ra:t niha:ʔiyya] *pl:* We issued an ultimatum to the enemy. دَزَّينا إنذار نِهائِي لِلعَدو [dazzi:na ʔinða:r niha:ʔi lilʕadu]

ultra • **1.** مِتطَرِّف [mittarrif] He is ultra-Conservative. هُوَّ مُحافِظ مِتطَرِّف [huwwa muħa:fiḍ mittarrif] • **2.** فَوق [fawq] We studied ultra-violet rays in physics. دِرَسنا الأشِعَّة فَوق البَنَفسَجِيَّة بِالفِيزِياء [dirasna ʔilʔašiʕʕa fawq ʔilbanafsajiyya bilfi:zya:ʔ]

umbilical cord • **1.** حَبِل الصُرَّة [ħabil ʔiṣṣurra] حبال الصُرَّة [ħba:l ʔiṣṣurra] *pl:*

umbrella • **1.** شَمسِيَّة [šamsiyya] شَمسِيّات [šamsiyya:t] *pl:* شَماسِي [šama:si] شَمسِيّات [šamsiyya:t] *pl:*

umpire • **1.** حَكَم [ħakam] حُكّام، حَكَمِيَّة [ħukka:m, ħakamiyya] *pl:* مُحَكِّم [muħakkim] مُحَكِّمِين [muħakkimi:n] *pl:*

un • **1.** ما [ma:-, ma-] مُو [mu:] غير [ɣi:r] This is an unusual situation. هَذِي حالَة مُو إعتِيادِيَّة [ha:ði ħa:la mu: ʔiʕtiya:diyya] Last night we had unexpected company. البارحَة باللَّيل جُونا خُطّار ما مُتوَقَّعِين [ʔilba:rħa billi:l ǰu:na xuṭṭa:r ma: mutwaqqaʕi:n] That's very unlikely. هاي كُلِّش ما مُحتَمَلَة [ha:y kulliš ma: muħtamala] I am uncomfortable here! آنِي مُو مِرتاح هنا [ʔa:ni mu: mirta:ħ hna] His trip is still uncertain. سَفِرتَه بَعَدها مُو أكِيدَة [safirtah baʕadha mu: ʔaki:da] I'm still uncertain as to whether I'll go. آني لهَسَّة غير مِتأكِّد إذا راح أرُوح [ʔa:ni lhassa ɣi:r mitʔakkid ʔiða ra:ħ ʔaru:ħ] The climate here is unhealthy. الجَّوّ هنا غير صِحِّي [ʔiǰǰaww hna: ɣi:r ṣiħħi] • **2.** ما [ma:] It's quite unlike anything I've seen before. هَذا ما يِشبَه أيّ شِي آني شايفَه قَبُل [ha:ða ma: yišbah ʔayy ši ʔa:ni ša:yfah gabul] This is undesirable. هِيكِي شِي ما يِنراد [hi:či ši ma: yinra:d] This is unfit to eat. هَذا ما يِصلَح لِلأكِل [ha:ða ma: yiṣlaħ lilʔakil] • **3.** بِدُون [bidu:n] بِلا [bila] This radio has an unconditional guarantee. هَالرّاديُو بِيه تَعَهُّد بِدُون شَرط [harra:dyu bi:h taʕahhud bidu:n šarṭ] That's undoubtedly the reason he quit. هَذا بِلا شَكّ سَبَب طَلِعتَه [ha:ða bila šakk sabab ṭaliʕtah] The fort was left unmanned. القَلعَة اِنترِكَت بِدُون جُنُود [ʔalqalʕa ʔintirkat bidu:n ǰunu:d] He did it unconsciously. سَوّاها بلا شُعُور [sawwa:ha bila šuʕu:r] • **4.** خِلاف [xila:f] That's quite unlike him. هاي تَماماً خِلاف عادتَه [ha:y tama:man xila:f ʕa:dtah] • **5.** ما إل [ma: ʔil-] That remark is uncalled for. هَالحكايَة ما إلها مُوجِب [halħča:ya ma: ʔilha mu:ǰib] Your fears are unfounded. خوفَك ما إلَه مُوجِب [xawfak ma: ʔilah mu:ǰib] The statement is unfounded. هَالحكايَة ما إلها أساس [halħča:ya ma: ʔilha ʔasa:s] It was an unparalleled success. كان فَدّ نَجاح ما إلَه مَثِيل [ča:n fadd naǰa:ħ ma: ʔilah maθi:l]

*** She's been so unfortunate.**

• **1.** عَلَى طُول هِيَّ ما كانَت مَحظُوظَة [ʕala ṭu:l hiyya ma: ča:nat maħðu:ða]

*** He was unfaithful to his wife.** • **1.** كان دَيخُون زَوُجتَه [ča:n dayxu:n zawuǰtah] / ما كان مُخلِص لزَوُجتَه [ma: ča:n muxliṣ lizawuǰtah]

*** He is unusually bright.** • **1.** ذَكائَه أكثَر مِن الإعتِيادِي [ðaka:ʔah ʔakθar min ʔilʔiʕtiya:di]

to un • **1.** فَكّ [fakk] فَكّ [fakk] *vn: sv* u. I can't unlatch the door. ما أقدَر أفُكّ اللِّسان مال الباب [ma: ʔagdar ʔafukk ʔillisa:n ma:l ʔilba:b] He unbuttoned his shirt. فَكّ الدُّقمَة مال ثوبَه [fakk ʔiddugma ma:l θu:bah] He unbuttoned his shirt. فَكّ ثوبَه [fakk θu:bah] They uncoupled the engine at Hindiyya. فَكّوا مَكِينَة القِطار بِالهِندِيَّة [fakkaw maki:nat ʔilqiṭa:r bilhindiyya] He unbuckled his belt. فَكّ حزامَه [fakk ħza:mah]

unabridged • **1.** كامِل [ka:mil] This is the unabridged edition of his book. هَذِي النُّسخَة الكامِلَة مِن كِتابَه [ha:ði ʔannusxa ʔilka:mila min kita:bah]

unanimous • **1.** إجماعِي [ʔiǰma:ʕi] It needs unanimous approval. تِحتاج إلَى مُوافَقَة إجماعِيَّة [tiħta:ǰ ʔila muwa:faqa ʔiǰma:ʕiyya]

unanimously • **1.** إجماع [ʔijma:ʕ] They elected him unanimously. اِنتِخَبوه بِالإجماع [ʔintixabawh bilʔijma:ʕ]

unarmed • **1.** أعزَل [ʔaʕzal] The robber was unarmed. الحَرامِي كان أعزَل [ʔilħara:mi ča:n ʔaʕzal]

unbeliever • **1.** كافِر [ka:fir] كَفَرَة، كُفّار [kafara, kuffa:r] *pl:*

uncertainty • **1.** حِيرَة [ħi:ra] Don't leave us in such uncertainty. لا تخَلِّينا بهِيكِي حِيرَة [la: txalli:na bhi:či ħi:ra]

uncivil • **1.** خَشِن [xašin] جافّ [ǰa:ff] He was very uncivil to us. كان كُلِّش خَشِن وِيّانا [ča:n kulliš xašin wiyya:na]

uncle • **1.** عَمّ [ʕamm] عمام، عمُومَة [ʕma:m, ʕmu:ma.] *pl:*

unclean • **1.** نَجِس [najis] I can't pray now; I'm unclean. هَسَّة ما أقدَر أصَلِّي لِأنِّي نَجِس [hassa ma: ʔagdar ʔaṣalli liʔanni nagis]

uncomfortable • **1.** مِتضايِق [mitða:yiq] I felt uncomfortable when my father was there. حَسَّيت نَفسِي مِتضايِق مِن أبُويا كان هناك [ħassi:t nafsi midða:yiq min ʔabu:ya ča:n hna:k]

uncompromising • **1.** مِتعَنِّت [mitʕannit] مِتعَنِّتِين [mitʕanniti:n] *pl:* معانِد [mʕa:nid] معانِدِين [mʕa:nidi:n] *pl:* The union leaders are very uncompromising. زُعَماء النَّقابَة كُلِّش مِتعَنِّتِين [zuʕama:ʔ ʔinnaqa:ba kulliš mitʕanniti:n]

unconscious • **1.** غايبَة رُوحها [ɣa:yba ru:ħha] He's still unconscious. بَعدَه غايِب رُوحَه [baʕdah ɣa:yib ru:ħah]

uncouth • **1.** خَشِن [xašin]

to uncover • **1.** كَشَّف [kaššaf] تَكشِيف، تكِشِّف [takši:f, tkiššif] *vn: sv* i. Don't uncover that pot. لا تكَشِّف الجِّدِر [la: tkaššif ʔiǰǰidir] • **2.** اِكتِشَف [ʔiktišaf] اِكتِشاف [ʔiktiša:f] *vn: sv* i. I uncovered something new in that case. اِكتِشَفِت فَدّ شِي جدِيد بِالدَّعوَى [ʔiktišafit fadd ši ǰdi:d biddaʕwa]

uncovered • **1.** مَكشُوف [makšu:f] مكَشَّف [mkaššaf] Their heads are uncovered. رُوسهُم مَكشُوفَة [ru:shum makšu:fa]

under • **1.** جَوَّة [ǰawwa] تَحَت [taħat] The slippers are under the bed. النَّعَل جَوَّة الجَّرپايَة [ʔinnaʕal ǰawwa ʔiččarpa:ya] Can you swim under water? تِقدَر تِسبَح جَوَّة الماي؟ [tigdar tisbaħ ǰawwa ʔilma:y?] • **2.** تَحَت [[taħat, taħt] Are you under medical treatment? إنتَ تَحت التَّداوِي هَسَّة؟ [ʔinta taħt ʔittada:wi hassa?] The police put him under surveillance. الشُّرطَة حَطّوه تَحت المُراقَبَة [ʔiššurṭa ħaṭṭu:h taħt ʔilmura:qaba] • **3.** ب [b] Under the new system, there will be elections soon. بِالنِّظام الجِّدِيد راح تصِير اِنتِخابات قَرِيباً [binniða:m ʔiǰǰidi:d ra:ħ tṣi:r ʔintixa:ba:t qari:ban] Under these circumstances that could never happen. بهِيكِي الظُّرُوف ذِيك أبَد ما تصِير [bhi:či ʔiððuru:f ði:č ʔabad ma: tṣi:r] • **4.** أقَلّ مِن [ʔaqall min] تَحَت [taħt] جَوَّة [ǰawwa] This meat weighs under a kilo. هَاللَّحَم وَزنَه أقَلّ مِن كِيلُو [hallaħam waznah ʔaqall min ki:lu] They cannot vote since they are under legal age. ما يقدرُون يصَوّتُون لِأنّ جَوَّة السِّنّ القانُونِي [ma: ygidru:n yṣawwtu:n liʔann ǰawwa ʔissinn ʔilqa:nu:ni] • **5.** جَوّانِي [ǰawwa:ni] Their underclothing is wool. هدُومهُم الجَّوّانِيَّة مِن صُوف [hdu:mhum ʔiǰǰawwa:niyya min ṣu:f] • **6.** نائِب [na:ʔib] نُوّاب [nuwwa:b] *pl:* He's the under-secretary of defense. هُوَّ نائِب وَزِير الدِّفاع [huwwa na:ʔib wazi:r ʔiddifa:ʕ]

*** I'm under contract with the government.**
• **1.** آنِي ماضِي عَقِد وِيّا الحُكُومَة [ʔa:ni ma:ḍi ʕaqid wiyya ʔilħuku:ma]
*** Don't forget you are under oath.**
• **1.** لا تِنسَى إنتَ حالِف يَمِين [la: tinsa: ʔinta ħa:lif yami:n]
*** Is the fire under control?** • **1.** النار مسَيطَر عَلَيها؟ [ʔinna:r msayṭar ʕali:ha?]

underarm • **1.** أبُط [ʔubuṭ] أباط [ʔuba:ṭ] *pl:* This salve will prevent underarm perspiration. هَالدِّهِن يِمنَع العَرَق مِن الأبُط [haddihin yimnaʕ ʔilʕarag min ʔilʔubuṭ]

underdog • **1.** مِسكِين [miski:n] مَساكِين [masa:ki:n] *pl:* He always helps the underdog. هُوَّ دائِماً يعاوُن المَساكِين [huwwa da:ʔiman yʕa:wun ʔilmasa:ki:n]

underground • **1.** جَوَّة القاع [ǰawwa ʔilga:ʕ] The city has underground telephone lines. أسلاك التِّلِفُون مال هَالوِلايَة جَوَّة القاع [ʔasla:k ʔittilifu:n ma:l halwla:ya ǰawwa ʔilga:ʕ] • **2.** مُقاوَمَة سِرِّيَّة [muqa:wama sirriyya] He served with the underground during the war. خِدَم وِيّا المُقاوَمَة السِّرِّيَّة أثناء الحَرب [xidam wiyya ʔilmuqa:wama ʔissirriyya ʔaθna:ʔ ʔilħarb]

underhand • **1.** مِن جَوَّة [min ǰawwa] Throw the ball underhand. أشمُر الطُّوبَة مِن جَوَّة [ʔušmur ʔiṭṭu:ba min ǰawwa]

underlying • **1.** أساسِي [ʔasa:si] Do you understand the underlying causes? تُعرُف الأسباب الأساسِيَّة؟ [tuʕruf ʔilʔasba:b ʔilʔasa:siyya?]

to undermine • **1.** حُفَر [ħufar] حَفُر [ħafur] *vn:* اِنحُفَر [ʔinħufar] *p:* The river undermined the wall and brought it down. النَّهَر حُفَر جَوَّة الحايِط وَوَقَّعَه [ʔinnahar ħufar ǰawwa ʔilħa:yiṭ wwaggaʕah] He undermined my position and got me fired. هُوَّ اللِّي حُفَر جَوّايَة وَخَلّانِي أنطِرِد [huwwa ʔilli ħufar ǰawwa:ya wxalla:ni ʔanṭirid]

underneath • **1.** جَوَّة [ǰawwa] I found the ball underneath the bed. لِقيت الطُّوبَة جَوَّة الجَّربايَة [ligi:t ʔiṭṭu:ba ǰawwa ʔiččarpa:ya]

undernourishment • **1.** سُوء تَغذِيَة [su:ʔ taɣðiya]

underpants • **1.** لِباس [liba:s] لباسات [lba:sa:t] *pl:* لِبسان [libsa:n] pl:

underprivileged • **1.** مَحرُوم [mahru:m] He built a hospital for underprivileged children. بِنَى مُستَشفى لِلأطفال المَحرُومِين [bina: mustašfa lilʔaṭfa:l ʔilmahru:mi:n]

to underrate • **1.** اِستَخَفّ ب [ʔistaxaff b-] اِستِخفاف [ʔistixfa:f] *vn: sv* i. قَلَّل مِن [qallal min] تَقلِيل [taqli:l] *vn: sv* i. We underrated his strength. اِستَخَفِّينا بِقُوَّتَه [ʔistaxaffi:na bquwwtah]

to undersell • **1.** كِسَر [kisar] *sv* i. That store undersold us. ذاك المَحَلّ كِسَرنا [ða:k ʔilmahall kisarna]

undershirt • **1.** فانِيلَّة [fani:lla] فانِيلّات [fanilla:t] *pl:*

to understand • **1.** اِفتِهَم [ʔiftiham] فِهِم [fihim] *vn: sv* i. فِهَم [fiham] فَهِم [fahim] *vn: sv* a. He doesn't understand Russian. ما يِفتِهِم رُوسِي [ma: yiftihim ru:si] I understand from his letter that he likes his work. أَفهَم مِن مَكتُوبَه الشَّغلَة عِجبَتَه [ʔafham min maktu:bah ʔiššaɣla ʕiǰbatah]

understanding • **1.** إدراك [ʔidra:k] He has keen understanding. عِندَه خُوش إدراك [ʕindah xu:š ʔidra:k] • **2.** تَفاهُم [tafa:hum] There's a close understanding between them. أَكُو بَينَاتهُم تَفاهُم زين [ʔaku bayna:thum tafa:hum zi:n] • **3.** مُدرِك [mudrik] He's a very understanding man. هُوَّ فَدّ واحِد مُدرِك [huwwa fadd wa:hid mudrik]

* **They've reached an understanding on the Berlin question.** • **1.** تفاهمَوا عَلَى قَضِيَّة بَرلِين [tfa:hmaw ʕala qaḍiyyat barli:n]

understood • **1.** مَفهُوم [mafhu:m] Of course that's understood! طَبعاً هاي مَفهُومَة [ṭabʕan ha:y mafhu:ma]

to undertake • **1.** قام بِـ [qa:m bi-] قِيام [qiya:m] *vn: sv* u. I hope you're not planning to undertake that trip alone. أتأمَّل إنتَ ما راح تقُوم بِهَالسَّفرَة وَحدَك [ʔatʔammal ʔinta ma: ra:h tqu:m bhassafra wahdak] • **2.** تكَفَّل [tkaffal] تَكَفُّل [takafful] *vn: sv* a. He undertook to pay for his nephew's education. تكَفَّل بمَصاريف تَثقِيف إبِن أخُوه [tkaffal bmaṣa:ri:f taθqi:f ʔibin ʔaxu:h]

undertaking • **1.** تَحَمُّل [tahammul] His undertaking that responsibility was a big favor. تَحَمُّلَه هَالمَسؤُولِيَّة كان فَدّ لُطُف كِبِير [tahammulah halmasʔu:liyya ča:n fadd luṭuf čibi:r] • **2.** مَشرُوع [mašru:ʕ] مَشارِيع [maša:ri:ʕ] *pl:* The government is encouraging industrial undertakings. الحُكُومَة دَتشَجِّع المَشارِيع الصِّناعِيَّة [ʔilhuku:ma datšaǰǰiʕ ʔilmaša:ri:ʕ ʔiṣṣina:ʕiyya]

undertaker • **1.** مغَسِّل [mɣassil] مغَسِّلِين [mɣassili:n] *pl:*

underwear • **1.** هدُوم جَوّانِيَّة [hdu:m ǰawwa:niyya]

underworld • **1.** مُحِيط إجرام [muhi:ṭ ʔiǰra:m] He grew up in the underworld. نِشَأ بمُحِيط الإجرام [niša? bmuhi:ṭ ʔilʔiǰra:m]

to underwrite • **1.** ضِمَن [ḍiman] ضَمان [ḍama:n] *vn:* *sv* i. Will the International Bank underwrite this loan? البَنك الدَّولِي راح يُضمُن هالقَرض؟ [ʔilbank ʔiddawli ra:h yuḍmun halqariḍ?]

to undo • **1.** حَلّ [hall] حَلّ [hall] *vn: sv* i. فَلّ [fall] فَلّ [fall] *vn: sv* i. فَكّ [fakk] فَكّ [fakk] *vn: sv* u. Help me undo this knot. عاوِنِّي نحِلّ هَالعُقدَة [ʕa:winni nhill halʕugda] • **2.** عَدَّل [ʕaddal] تَعدِيل [taʕdi:l] *vn: sv* i. We'll need a week to undo this mess. يِنراد إلنا إسبُوع حَتَّى نعَدِّل هالخَربَطَة [yinra:d ʔilna ʔisbu:ʕ hatta nʕaddil halxarbaṭa]

* **Now it's happened; it can't be undone.**
• **1.** هَسَّة بَعَد صارَت وماكُو مَجال لِلتَّراجُع [hassa baʕad ṣa:rat wma:ku maǰa:l littara:ǰuʕ]

undoing • **1.** خَراب [xara:b] Drink was the cause of his undoing. الشُّرُب كان سَبَب خَرابَه [ʔiššurub ča:n sabab xara:bah]

to undress • **1.** نَزَّع [nazzaʕ] تنزِّع، تَنزِيع [tnizziʕ, tanzi:ʕ] *vn: sv* i. I'll undress the children. آني راح أنَزِّعهُم لِلجِّهال [ʔa:ni ra:h ʔanazziʕhum liǰǰiha:l] • **2.** نِزَع [nizaʕ] نَزِع [naziʕ] *vn: sv* a. The phone rang just as I was undressing. دَقّ التَّلِفون أوَّل ما بدَيت أنزَع هدُومِي [dagg ʔittalifu:n ʔawwal ma: bdi:t ʔanzaʕ hdu:mi]

undulent fever • **1.** حُمَّة مالطا [hummat ma:lṭa]

unduly • **1.** أكثَر مِن اللازِم [ʔakθar min ʔilla:zim] You are unduly severe. إنتَ قاسِي أكثَر مِن اللّازِم [ʔinta qa:si ʔakθar min ʔilla:zim]

undying • **1.** إلَى الأبَد [ʔila ʔilʔabad] You have my undying gratitude. راح أبقَى مَمنُون إلَك إلَى الأبَد [ra:h ʔabqa: mamnu:n ʔilak ʔila ʔilʔabad]

uneasily • **1.** بِقَلَق [bqalaq] He sat waiting there uneasily. قِعَد دَينتِظِر بِقَلَق [giʕad dayintiḍir bqalaq]

U

uneasy • **1.** مِتقَيِّد [mitqayyid] I feel uneasy in his company. أَحِسّ مِتقَيِّد مِن أَكُون وِيّاه [ʔaħiss mitqayyid min ʔakuːn wiyyaːh] I feel uneasy in his company. ما آخُذ حُرِّيتِي هَالقَدّ مِن أَكُون وِيّاه [maː ʔaːxuð ħurriːti halgadd min ʔakuːn wiyyaːh] • **2.** ما مُستِقِرّ [maː mustaqirr] This is an uneasy situation. هَالوَضِع ما مِستِقِرّ [halwaðiʕ maː mistiqirr] • **3.** مِتشَوِّش [mitšawwiš] He left his wife very uneasy. خَلَّى مَرتَه مِتشَوّشَة كُلِّش [xallaː martah mitšawwša kulliš]

unemployed • **1.** عاطِل [ʕaːṭil] بَطّال [baṭṭaːl] He's unemployed now. هُوَّ هَسَّة عاطِل [huwwa hassa ʕaːṭil]

unemployment • **1.** عَطالَة [ʕaṭaːla] بَطالَة [baṭaːla] Unemployment this year is less than before. العَطالَة هالسَّنَة أَقَلّ مِن قَبُل [ʔilʕaṭaːla hassana ʔaqall min gabul]

UNESCO • **1.** يُونَسكُو [yuːnisku]

unexpectedly • **1.** عَلَى غَفلَة [ʕala ɣafla] The accident occurred unexpectedly. الحادِث صار عَلَى غَفلَة [ʔilħaːdiθ ṣaːr ʕala ɣafla]

unfinished • **1.** عَالنُّصّ [ʕannuṣṣ] ما خَلصان [maː xalṣaːn] ناقِص [naːgiṣ] The contractor left the work unfinished. القُنطَرجِي تِرَك الشُّغُل عَالنُّصّ [ʔilqunṭarči tirak ʔiššuɣul ʕannuṣṣ]

unfortunate • **1.** مُؤسِف [muʔsif] That's an unfortunate mistake! هَذِي غَلطَة مُؤسِفَة [haːði ɣalṭa muʔsifa]

unfortunately • **1.** لِسُوء الحَظّ [lisuːʔ ʔilħaðð] Unfortunately, negotiations aren't advancing very well. لِسُوء الحَظّ، المُفاوَضات ما دَتِتقَدَّم هَالقَدّ زين [lisuːʔ ʔilħaðð, ʔilmufaːwaðaːt maː datitqaddam halgadd ziːn]

ungrateful • **1.** ناكِر الجَمِيل [naːkir ʔiǰǰamiːl] ناكِرِين الجَمِيل [naːkiriːn ʔiǰǰamiːl] *pl:* He's an ungrateful boy. هَالوَلَد ناكِر الجَمِيل [halwalad naːkir ʔiǰǰamiːl]

unharmed • **1.** سَلامات [salaːmaːt] He escaped unharmed. طِلَع سَلامات [ṭilaʕ salaːmaːt]

to unhitch • **1.** حَلّ [ħall] حَلّ [ħall] *vn: sv* i. فَكّ [fakk] فَكّ [fakk] *vn: sv* u. They unhitched the horses from the carriage. حَلّوا الخَيل مِن العَرَبانَة [ħallaw ʔilxayl min ʔilʕarabaːna]

to unhook • **1.** فَكّ [fakk] فَكّ [fakk] *vn: sv* u. Unhook the garden gate, please. بالله ما تفُكّ باب الحَدِيقَة [ballah maː tfukk baːb ʔilħadiːqa]

unification • **1.** تَوحِيد [tawħiːd] The foreign ministers are considering unification of the country. وُزَراء الخارِجِيَّة دَيدُرسُون تَوحِيد البَلَد [wuzaraːʔ ʔilxaːriǰiyya daydursuːn tawħiːd ʔilbalad]

uniform • **1.** بَدلَة رَسمِيَّة [badla rasmiyya] بَدلات رَسمِيَّة [badlaːt rasmiyya] *pl:* They gave us new uniforms. إنطُونا بَدلات رَسمِيَّة جِدِيدَة [ʔinṭuːna badlaːt rasmiyya ǰidiːda] • **2.** عَلَى نَمَط واحِد [ʕala namaṭ waːħid] Their products aren't of very uniform quality. مُنتَجاتهُم مُو عَلَى نَمَط واحِد [muntaǰaːthum muː ʕala namaṭ waːħid]

uniformity • **1.** تَناسُق [tanaːsuq] We need more uniformity in our administrative practices. نِحتاج إِلَى تَناسُق أَكثَر بِالإدارَة [niħtaːǰ ʔila tanaːsuq ʔakθar bilʔidaːra]

to unify • **1.** وَحَّد [waħħad] تَوحِيد [tawħiːd] *vn: sv* i. Bismarck unified Germany. بِسمارك وَحَّد أَلمانيَا [bismaːrk waħħad ʔalmaːnya]

unilateral • **1.** مِن جانِب واحِد [min ǰaːnib waːħid] We will not accept any unilateral decision. ما نِقبَل قَرار مِن جانِب واحِد [maː niqbal qaraːr min ǰaːnib waːħid]

union • **1.** اِتِّحاد [ʔittiħaːd] اِتِّحادات [ʔittiħaːdaːt] *pl:* Racial segregation is still in vogue in the Union of South Africa, unfortunately. التَّميِيز العُنصُري بَعدَه مَوجُود بِاِتِّحاد جَنُوب أَفرِيقِيا لِسُوء الحَظّ [ʔittamyiːz ʔilʕunṣuri baʕdah mawǰuːd bʔittiħaːd ǰanuːb ʔafriːqya lisuːʔ ʔilħaðð] • **2.** نَقابَة [naqaːba] نَقابات [naqaːbaːt] *pl:* Are you a member of the union? إِنتَ عُضُو بِالنَّقابَة؟ [ʔinta ʕuðw binnaqaːba?]

unique • **1.** وَحِيد [waħiːd] It was a unique experience. كانَت تَجرُبَة وَحِيدَة مِن نَوعها [čaːnat taǰruba waħiːda min nawʕha]

unison • **1.** صَوت واحِد [ṣawt waːħid] Repeat this statement in unison. عِيدُوا هَالجُملَة بصُوت واحِد [ʕiːduː halǰumla bṣuːt waːħid]

unit • **1.** قِسِم [qisim] أَقسام [ʔaqsaːm] *pl:* This book is divided into twelve units. الكِتاب مقَسَّم إِلَى ثنَعَش قِسِم [ʔilkitaːb mqassam ʔila θnaʕaš qisim] • **2.** وحدَة [wiħda] He's been assigned to another unit. اِنّقَل لِغير وحدَة [ʔinniqal lɣayr wiħda]

to unite • **1.** اِتِّحَد [ʔittiħad] اِتِّحاد [ʔittiħaːd] *vn: sv* i. Egypt and Syria united to form the UAR. مَصِر وَسُوريا اِتَّحدَوا وسَوَّوا الجَمهُورِيَّة العَرَبِيَّة المُتَّحِدَة [maṣir wsuːrya ʔitiħdaw wsawwaw ʔiǰǰamhuːriyya ʔilʕarabiyya ʔilmuttaħida] • **2.** وَحَّد [waħħad] تَوحِيد [tawħiːd] *vn: sv* i.

U

United Arab Republic • **1.** الجُمهُورِيَّة العَرَبِيَّة المُتَّحِدَة [ʔijǰamhuːriyya ʔilʕarabiyya ʔilmuttaħida]

United Nations • **1.** الأُمَم المُتَّحِدَة [ʔilʔumam ʔilmuttaħida]

United States • **1.** الوِلايات المُتَّحِدَة [ʔilwilaːyaːt ʔilmuttaħida]

unity • **1.** اِتِّحاد [ʔittiħaːd] The Arabs need unity. العَرَب يِنراد إلهُم اِتِّحاد [ʔilʕarab yinraːd ʔilhum ʔittiħaːd] • **2.** وحدَة [wiħda] Arab unity is the goal of many parties. الوحدَة العَرَبِيَّة غايَة هوايَة أحزاب [ʔilwiħda ʔilʕarabiyya ɣaːyat hwaːya ʔaħzaːb]

universal • **1.** عامّ [ʕaːmm] There is universal agreement on that. أكُو اِتِّفاق عامّ عَلَى هاي [ʔaku ʔittifaːq ʕaːmm ʕala haːy] • **2.** عالَمِي [ʕaːlami] Gandhi had a universal message. غاندِي رِسالتَه كانَت عالَمِيَّة [ɣaːndi risaːltah čaːnat ʕaːlamiyya]

universe • **1.** عالَم [ʕaːlam] الكَون [kawn] دِنيا [dinya]

university • **1.** جامِعَة [ǰaːmiʕa] جامِعات [ǰaːmiʕaːt] *pl:* How many students are there at this university? شقَدّ أكُو طُلّاب بِهالجّامِعَة [šgadd ʔaku ṭullaːb bhajǰaːmiʕa?] • **2.** بِهالجّامِعَة [ǰaːmiʕiy] University life is loads of fun. الحَياة الجّامِعِيَّة كُلّش لَطِيفَة [ʔilħayaːt ʔijǰaːmiʕiyya kulliš laṭiːfa]

unknown • **1.** مَجهُول [majhuːl] We visited the grave of the unknown soldier. زِرنا قَبر الجُندِي المَجهُول [zirna qabr ʔijǰundi ʔilmajhuːl]

unless • **1.** إلّا إذا [ʔilla ʔiða] We're coming, unless it rains. إحنا جايّين اللّهُمَّ إلّا إذا تُمطُر الدِّنيا [ʔiħna ǰaːyyiːn ʔallahumma ʔilla ʔiða tumṭur ʔiddinya] • **2.** إذا ما [ʔiðaː maː] Unless you tell me why, I won't do it. إذا ما تقُلِّي لِيش، تَرَة آني ما أسَوِّيها [ʔiða maː tgulli liːš, tara ʔaːni maː ʔasawwiːha]

to unload • **1.** فَرَّغ [farraɣ] تَفرِيغ [tafriːɣ] *vn:* تفَرَّغ [tfarraɣ] *p:* They haven't unloaded the ship's cargo yet. بَعَد ما فَرّغوا حُمُولَة المَركَب [baʕad maː farrɣaw ħumuːlat ʔilmarkab] Unload your gun before you go in the car. فَرِّغ التُّفَقَة مالتَك قَبُل ما تخُشّ بِالسَّيّارَة [farriɣ ʔittufga maːltak gabul maː txušš bissayyaːra]

unlucky • **1.** مَشؤُوم [mašʔuːm] It was an unlucky coincidence. كانَت فَدّ صِدفَة مَشؤُومَة [čaːnat fadd ṣidfa mašʔuːma] • **2.** ما مَحظُوض [maː maħðuːð̣] I don't know why I'm so unlucky. ما أدرِي لِيش آنِي هَالقَدّ ما مَحظُوظ [maː ʔadri liːš ʔaːni halgadd maː maħðuːð̣]

to unmask • **1.** بَيَّن [bayyan] تَبيِين [tabyiːn] *vn: sv* i. كِشَف [kišaf] كَشِف [kašif] *vn: sv* i. They unmasked the traitor. بَيّنَوا الخائِن [bayynaw ʔilxaːʔin]

unoccupied • **1.** فارِغ [faːriɣ] That house is unoccupied. ذاك البَيت فارِغ [ðaːk ʔilbayt faːriɣ]

unpleasant • **1.** مُزعِج [muzʕij] I got some unpleasant news today. جَتنِي شوَيَّة أخبار مُزعِجَة اليُوم [ǰatni šwayya ʔaxbaːr muzʕiǰa ʔilyuːm]

unrest • **1.** قَلاقِل [qalaːqil] We heard there's unrest in Najaf. سمَعنا أكُو قَلاقِل بِالنَّجَف [simaʕna ʔaku qalaːqil binnaǰaf]

unruly • **1.** وَقِيح [wakiːħ] وُقَّح [wukkaħ] *pl:* وَقِح [wakiħ] He's an unruly child. هُوَّ وَلَد وَقِيح [huwwa walad wakiːħ]

unstable • **1.** قَلِق [qaliq] This chemical compound is unstable. هَالمُرَكَّب الكِيمياوِي قَلِق [halmurakkab ʔilkiːmyaːwi qaliq]

to untangle • **1.** حَلّ [ħall] حَلّ [ħall] *vn: sv* i. فَكّ [fakk] فَكّ [fakk] *vn: sv* u. Can you please untangle this string? بالله ما تحِلّ هَالخيُوط المكَبّنَة [ballah maː tħill halxyuːṭ ʔilmčabbina] • **2.** فَضّ [fað̣ð̣] فَضّ [fað̣ð̣] *vn: sv* u. The police untangled the traffic jam. شُرطَة المُرُور فَضّوا اِزدِحام السَّيّارات [šurṭat ʔilmuruːr fað̣ð̣aw ʔizdiħaːm ʔissayyaːraːt]

untidy • **1.** مخَربَط [mxarbaṭ] His wife is very untidy. مَرتَه كُلّش مخَربَطَة [martah kulliš mxarbaṭa]

to untie • **1.** فَكّ [fakk] فَكّ [fakk] *vn: sv* u. Can you untie this knot for me? تِقدَر تفُكّلِي هَالعُقدَة؟ [tigdar tfukkli halʕuqda?] Wait till I untie the package. اِنتِظِر إلَى أن أفُكّ الرُّزمَة [ʔintið̣ir ʔila ʔan ʔafukk ʔirruzma]

until • **1.** إلَى إل- [ʔila, ʔil-] حَتَّى [ħatta] Wait until tomorrow. اِنتِظِر لِباكِر [ʔintið̣ir lbaːčir] • **2.** إلَى أن [ʔilaː ʔan] حَتَّى [ħatta] Wait until he comes. اِنتِظِر إلَى أن يِجِي [ʔintið̣ir ʔila ʔan yiǰi]

to unveil • **1.** زاح سِتّار عَن [zaːħ sitaːr ʕan] *sv* i. The president will unveil the monument next week. رَئِيس الجُمهُورِيَّة راح يزِيح السِّتار عَن النَّصُب التِّذكارِي الإسبُوع الجّاي [raʔiːs ʔijǰumhuːriyya raːħ yziːħ ʔissitaːr ʕan ʔinnaṣub ʔittiðkaːri ʔilʔisbuːʕ ʔijǰaːy]

up • **1.** فَوق [fuːg] I'm up here. آنِي فُوق هنا [ʔaːni fuːg hna] Would you please put it up there? بالله ما تحُطَّه فُوق هناك؟ [ballah maː tħuṭṭah fuːg hnaːk?] You can find a nice room for a dinar and up. تِقدَر تِلقِي غُرفَة زينَة هنا مِن دِينار وفُوق [tigdar tilgi ɣurfa ziːna hna min dinaːr wfuːg] • **2.** قاعِد [gaːʕid] Is he up already? هُوَّ مِن هَسَّة قاعِد مِن النُّوم؟ [huwwa min hassa gaːʕid min ʔinnuːm?] • **3.** عَكِس [ʕakis] Shall we head up the river? خَلِّي نِتّجِه عَكِس الماي؟ [xalliː nittiǰih ʕakis ʔilmaːy?] • **4.** مَترُوك [matruːk] عَلَى [ʕala] The decision is up to you. القَرار مَترُوك إِلَك [ʔilqara:r matru:k ʔilak] The decision is up to you. القَرار عَلِيك [ʔilqara:r ʕali:k]

*** Your time is up.** • **1.** خِلَص وَقتَك [xilaṣ waktak]

*** He was walking up and down the room.** • **1.** كان دَيرُوح ويِجِي بِالقُبَّة [ča:n dayru:ħ wyiǰi bilgubba]

*** We all have our ups and downs.** • **1.** هاي الدنيا، يَوم إِلَك ويَوم عَلَيك [ha:y ʔiddinya, yawm ʔilak wyawm ʕali:k] هاي الدِّنيا، يَوم تِصعَد يوم تِنزِل [ha:y ʔiddinya, yawm tiṣʕad yawm tinzil]

up to • **1.** لحَدّ [lħadd] Because of the storm, trains were up to two hours late. بِسَبَب العاصِفَة القِطارات كانَت مِتأَخرَة لِحَدّ ساعتِين [bsabab ʔilʕa:ṣifa ʔilqiṭa:ra:t ča:nat mitʔaxxra liħadd sa:ʕtayn] • **2.** قَدّ [gadd] He isn't up to the job. هُوَّ مُو قَدّ هَالشَّغلَة [huwwa mu: gadd haššaɣla]

*** What's he up to this time?** • **1.** هَالنَوبَة شَكُو عِندَه؟ [hannu:ba šaku: ʕindah?]

up to now • **1.** لِهَسَّة [lhassa] Up to now he hasn't answered. بَعَد لهَسَّة ما جاوَب [baʕad lhassa ma: ǰa:wab]

uphill • **1.** * This road goes uphill for a mile and then descends. هَالطَّرِيق يِصعَد فَدّ مِيل وَبَعدين يِنزِل [haṭṭari:q yiṣʕad fadd mi:l wbaʕdi:n yinzil]

upkeep • **1.** صِيانَة [ṣiya:na] My car requires a lot of expenses for upkeep. سَيّارتي يِنرادِلها هوايَة مَصارِيف لِلصِّيانَة [sayya:rti yinra:dilha hwa:ya maṣa:ri:f liṣṣiya:na]

upper • **1.** فَوقانِي [fawga:ni] The fire started on the upper floor. النّار بِدَت مِن القاط الفَوقانِي [ʔinna:r bidat min ʔilqa:ṭ ʔilfuga:ni]

*** Write the page number in the upper right-hand corner.** • **1.** حُطّ أَرقام الصَفحات الفَوق بِالجِهَة اليِمنَة [ħuṭṭ ʔarqa:m ʔiṣṣafħa:t ʔilfawg biǰǰiha ʔilyimna]

to uproot • **1.** شِلَع [šilaʕ] شَلع [šaliʕ] *vn: sv* a. قِلَع [qilaʕ] قَلِع [qaliʕ] *vn: sv* a. The storm uprooted several trees. العاصِفَة شِلعَت كَم شَجَرَة [ʔilʕa:ṣifa šilʕat čam šaǰara]

upset • **1.** مَقلُوق [maqlu:q] مِتشَوِّش [mitšawwiš] He was all upset. كان كُلِّش مَقلُوق [ča:n kulliš maqlu:q] • **2.** مِتخَربُط [mitxarbuṭ] I have an upset stomach. مِعِدتي مِتخَربُطَة [miʕidti mitxarbuṭa]

to upset • **1.** قِلَب [gilab] قَلُب [galub] *vn: sv* u. وَقَّع [waggaʕ] توُقِّع [twuggiʕ] *vn: sv* i. Be careful or you'll upset the pitcher. دِير بالَك، تَرَة راح تُقلُب الدَّولكَة [di:r ba:lak, tara ra:ħ tuglub ʔiddu:lka] You're upsetting the boat! إِنتَ راح تُقلُب البَلَم [ʔinta ra:ħ tuglub ʔilbalam] • **2.** خَربَط [xarbaṭ] *sv* u. Nothing ever upsets him. ماكُو فَدّ شِي يخَربُطَه [ma:ku fadd ši yxarbuṭah]

upside down • **1.** بِالمَقلُوب [bilmaglu:b] That picture is upside down. هَالصُّورَة مَحطُوطَة بِالمَقلُوب [haṣṣu:ra maħṭu:ṭa bilmaglu:b]

to turn upside down • **1.** قِلَب [gilab] قَلُب [galub] *vn: sv* u. They turned the whole house upside down. قُلبَوا البَيت كُلَّه [gulbaw ʔilbayt kullah]

upstairs • **1.** فَوقانِي [fawga:ni] The upstairs apartment is vacant. الشَّقَّة الفُوقانِيَّة فارغَة [ʔaššiqqa ʔalfu:ga:niyya fa:rɣa] • **2.** فَوق [fawg, fu:g] He's upstairs. هُوَّ فَوق [huwwa fu:g] • **3.** فَوق [fu:g, fu:q] لِفَوق [lifawq] Bring our bags upstairs. صَعِّد جِنَطنا لِفُوق [ṣaʕʕid ǰinaṭna lifu:g]

up-to-date • **1.** عَلَى آخِر طَرز [ʕala ʔa:xir ṭarz] عَلَى آخِر طِراز [ʕala ʔa:xir ṭira:z] حَدِيث [ħadi:θ] She has an up-to-date kitchen. عِدها مَطبَخ عَلَى آخِر طِراز [ʕidha maṭbax ʕala ʔa:xir ṭira:z] • **2.** لحَدّ اليَوم [lħadd ʔilyu:m] My books are posted up to date. دَفاتري التِّجارِيَّة مَنظَّمَة لِحَدّ اليُوم [dafa:tri ʔittiǰa:riyya mnaðˤðˤma liħadd ʔilyu:m]

urge • **1.** دافِع [da:fiʕ] دَوافِع [dawa:fiʕ] *pl:* I felt the urge to tell him what I thought of him. حَسَّيت بِفَدّ دافِع أَقُلَّه رَأيِي بِيه [ħassi:t bfadd da:fiʕ ʔagullah raʔyi bi:h]

to urge • **1.** حَثّ [ħaθθ] *sv* i. If you urge her a bit, she'll do it. هِيَّ تسَوِّيها لَو شوَيَّة تحِثّها [hiyya tsawwi:ha law šwayya tħiθθha] • **2.** شَجَّع [šaǰǰaʕ] تَشجِيع [tašǰi:ʕ] *vn: sv* i. She urged us to stay longer. شَجّعَتنا نِبقى مُدَّة أَطوَل [šaǰǰʕatna nibqa: mudda ʔaṭwal] • **3.** حَرَّض [ħarraðˤ] تَحرِيض [taħri:ðˤ] *vn: sv* i. His mother urged him to commit the crime. أُمَّه حَرِّضَتَه يسَوِّي هَالجَّرِيمَة [ʔummah ħarriðˤatah ysawwi haǰǰari:ma]

urgent • **1.** مُستَعجَل [mustaʕǰal] I have an urgent request. عِندِي فَدّ طَلَب مُستَعجَل [ʕindi fadd ṭalab mustaʕǰal]

use • **1.** اِستِعمال [ʔistiʕma:l] How long has this method been in use? شقَدّ صارِلها هَالطَّرِيقَة بِالإِستِعمال [šgadd ṣa:rilha haṭṭari:qa bilʔistiʕma:l] • **2.** فائِدَة [fa:ʔida] Will that be of any use to you? هاي بِيها فائِدَة إِلَك؟ [ha:y bi:ha fa:ʔida ʔilak?] Will that be of any use to you? هاي تفِيدَك؟ [ha:y tfi:dak?] What's the use of arguing? شِنُو الفائِدَة مِن المُجادَلَة؟ [šinu ʔilfa:ʔida min ʔilmuǰa:dala?] • **3.** حاجَة [ħa:ǰa] حاجات، حَوايِج [ħa:ǰa:t, ħawa:yiǰ] *pl:* I have no use for that. مالِي حاجَة بهاي [ma:li ħa:ǰa bha:y] I have no use for that. ما أَحتاج هاي [ma: ʔaħta:ǰ ha:y]

*** It's no use, we've got to do it.** • **1.** ماكُو جارَة، إِحنا لازِم نسَوِّيها [ma:ku: ča:ra, ʔiħna la:zim nsawwi:ha]

to make use of • **1.** اِستَغَلّ [ʔistaɣall] اِستِغلال [ʔistiɣla:l] *vn: sv* i. He made good use of the opportunity. اِستَغَلّ الفُرصَة زين [ʔistaɣall ʔilfurṣa zi:n]

to use • **1.** اِستَعمَل [ʔistaʕmal] اِستِعمال [ʔistiʕma:l] *vn: sv* i. I can't use that. ما أَقدَر أَستَعمِل هاي [ma: ʔagdar ʔastaʕmil ha:y] What toothpaste do you use? يا مَعجُون سنُون تِستَعمِل؟ [ya: maʕǰu:n snu:n tistaʕmil?] We'll use this room as a classroom. راح نِستَعمِل هَالغُرفَة كَصَف [ra:ħ nistaʕmil halɣurfa kaṣaff]

U

to use up • **1.** اِستَهلَك [ʔistahlak] اِستِهلاك [ʔistihlaːk] *vn:* *sv* i. اِستَنفَذ [ʔistanfað] اِستِنفاذ [ʔistinfaːð] *vn:* *sv* i. خَلَّص [xallaṣ] تَخلِيص [taxliːṣ] *vn:* *sv* i. صِرَف [ṣiraf] صَرُف [ṣaruf] *vn:* *sv* u. We've used up all our supplies. اِستَنفَذنا كُلّ المَوجُود اللِّي عِدنا [ʔistanfaðna kull ʔilmawǰuːd ʔilli ʕidna] His car uses up a lot of gasoline. سَيّارتَه تِستَهلِك هوايَة بَنزِين [sayyaːrtah tistahlik hwaːya banziːn]

used • **1.** كان [čaːn] I used to live here. كِنِت أَسكُن هنا [činit ʔaskun hna] He used to eat in restaurants before he got married. كان دَياكُل بالمَطاعِم قَبُل ما تزَوَّج [čaːn dayaːkul bilmaṭaːʕim gabul maː dzawwaǰ] • **2.** مِتعَوِّد [mitʕawwid] I'm not used to hard work. آنِي ما مِتعَوِّد عَلَى الشُّغُل الصَّعُب [ʔaːni maː mitʕawwid ʕala ʔiššuɣul ʔiṣṣaʕub]

to get used to • **1.** تعَوَّد عَلَى [tʕawwad ʕala] *sv* a. She's gotten used to getting up at seven o'clock. هِيَّ تعَوّدَت عالقَعدَة السّاعَة سَبعَة [hiyya tʕawwdat ʕalgaʕda ʔissaːʕa sabʕa]

useful • **1.** مُفِيد [mufiːd] نافِع [naːfiʕ] A maid is useful around the house. الخَدّامَة مُفِيدَة بالبَيت [ʔilxaddaːma mufiːda bilbayt] I've found this book very useful. شِفِت هَالكِتاب كُلِّش نافِع [šifit halkitaːb kulliš naːfiʕ]

useless • **1.** ماكُو فائِدَة [maːku faːʔida] ما بِيه فائِدَة [maː biːh faːʔida] It's useless to try to convince him. ماكُو فائِدَة تحاوِل تقَنّعَه [maːku faːʔida tħaːwil tqannʕah] This map is useless to me. هَالخَرِيطَة ما بِيها فائِدَة إلِي [halxariːṭa maː biːha faːʔida ʔili]

usher • **1.** تَشرِيفاتِي [tašriːfaːti] تَشرِيفاتِيَّة [tašriːfaːtiyya] *pl:* دَلِيل [daliːl] دَلِيلِين [daliːliːn] *pl:* أَدِلّاء [ʔadillaːʔ] The usher will show you your seats. التَّشرِيفاتِي راح يراوِيكُم مَقاعِدكُم [ʔittašriːfaːti raːħ yraːwiːkum maqaːʕidkum]

to usher • **1.** دَلَّى [dallaː] *pl:* تدِلِّي [tdilli] *vn:* تدَلَّى [tdallaː] *p:* We were ushered to our seats. تدَلّينا عَلَى مَقاعِدنا [ddalliːna ʕala maqaːʕidna]

usual • **1.** اِعتِيادِي [ʔiʕtiyaːdi] Our usual hours are from 8 to 3. دَوامنا الاعتِيادِي مِن الثَّمانيَة إلَى الثَّلاثَة [dawaːmna ʔilʔiʕtiyaːdi min ʔiθθamaːnya ʔila ʔiθθalaːθa] We'll meet at the usual place. راح نِلتِقِي بِالمُكان الاعتِيادِي [raːħ niltiqi bilmukaːn ʔilʔiʕtiyaːdi]

as usual • **1.** عادَة [ʕaːda] عَالعادَة [ʕalʕaːda] It's raining, as usual. دَتُمطُر كَالعادَة [datumṭur kalʕaːda] Everything went along as usual. كُلْشِي مِشَى عالعادَة [kullši mišaː ʕalʕaːda]

usually • **1.** عادَةً [ʕaːdatan] I usually visit them twice a week. عادَةً أَزُورهُم مَرّتَين بِالإسبُوع [ʕaːdatan ʔazuːrhum marrtayn bilʔisbuːʕ]

utensil • **1.** أَداة [ʔadaːt] أَدَوات [ʔadawaːt] *pl:* We bought some new cooking utensils. اِشتِرَينا أَدَوات طَبُخ جِدِيدَة [ʔištiriːna ʔadawaːt ṭabux ǰidiːda]

utmost • **1.** كُلِّش [kulliš] The matter is of the utmost importance. القَضِيَّة كُلِّش مُهِمَّة [ʔilqaðiyya kulliš muhimma] • **2.** أَقصَى [ʔaqṣa] He expended the utmost energy. بِذَل أَقصَى جُهدَه [biðal ʔaqṣa ǰuhdah]

utter • **1.** كُلِّش [kulliš] Things are in a state of utter confusion in the office. الأُمُور كُلِّش مخَربُطَة بِالدّائِرَة [ʔilʔumuːr kulliš mxarbuṭa biddaːʔira]

to utter • **1.** قال [gaːl] قَول [gawl] *vn:* *sv* u. I couldn't utter a single word. ما قِدَرت أَقُول وَلا كِلمَة [maː gidart ʔaguːl wala čilma]

U

V

vacant • **1.** فارِغ [fa:riɣ] خالِي [xa:li] The house has been vacant for a week. البَيت صارلَه إسبُوع فارِغ [ʔilbayt ṣa:rlah ʔisbu:ʕ fa:riɣ] Next to our house there is still a vacant lot. يَمّ بَيتنا أكُو ساحَة فارغَة [yamm baytna ʔaku sa:ħa fa:rɣa] • **2.** شاغِر [ša:ɣir] شَواغِر [šawa:ɣir] *pl:* We have no position vacant at the moment. ما عِدنا وَظِيفَة شاغرَة هَسَّة [ma: ʕidna waðʼi:fa ša:ɣra hassa]

to vacate • **1.** فَرَّغ [farraɣ] تَفرِيغ [tafri:ɣ] *vn: sv* i. طِلَع [ṭilaʕ] طُلُوع [ṭulu:ʕ] *vn: sv* a. When are you going to vacate the house? شوَقِت راح تفَرِّغ البَيت؟ [šwakit ra:ħ tfarriɣ ʔilbayt?]

vacation • **1.** عُطلَة [ʕuṭla] عُطلات [ʕuṭla:t] *pl:* The children are looking forward to their vacation. الجَّهال دَينتَظرُون عُطلَتهُم بفارِغ الصَّبُر [ʔijjaha:l dayintaðʼru:n ʕuṭlathum bfa:riɣ ʔiṣṣabur]

on vacation • **1.** مُجاز [muja:z] إجازَة [ʔija:za] إجازات [ʔija:za:t] *pl:* Ali is on vacation. عَلِي مُجاز [ʕali muja:z]

vague • **1.** مُبهَم [mubham] مُو واضِح [mu: wa:ðʼiħ] He gave me a vague answer. جاوَبنِي جَواب مُبهَم [ja:wabni jawa:b mubham]

vaguely • **1.** مُو بوُضُوح [mu: bwuðʼu:ħ] I remember him vaguely. ما أتذَكَّرَه بِوُضُوح [ma: ʔadðakkarah biwuðʼu:ħ]

vain • **1.** مَغرُور [maɣru:r] شايِف نَفسَه [ša:yif nafsah] She's terribly vain. هِيَّ كُلّش مَغرُورَة [hiyya kulliš maɣru:ra]

in vain • **1.** عَبَثاً [ʕabaθan] The doctor tried in vain to save the boy's life. الدِّكتور عَبَثاً حاوَل يِنقُذ حَياة الوَلَد [ʔiddiktu:r ʕabaθan ħa:wal yinquð ħaya:t ʔilwalad]

valid • **1.** صَحِيح [ṣaħi:ħ] I don't think your argument is valid. ما أعتِقِد جَدَلَك صَحِيح [ma: ʔaʕtiqid jadalak ṣaħi:ħ] • **2.** صالِح [ṣa:liħ] نافِذ المَفعُول [na:fið ʔilmafʕu:l] Is my license still valid? إجازتِي بَعَدها صالحَة؟ [ʔija:zti baʕadha ṣa:lħa?]

*** Your passport isn't valid any more.**

• **1.** باسبُورتَك خِلصَت المُدَّة مالتَه [pa:ṣpurtak xilṣat ʔilmudda ma:ltah]

valley • **1.** وادِي [wa:di] وِديان [widya:n] *pl:*

valuable • **1.** ثَمِين [θami:n] نَفِيس [nafi:s] That's a valuable ring. هَذا مِحبَس ثَمِين [ha:ða miħbas θami:n]

valuables • **1.** أشياء ثَمِينَة [ʔašya:ʔ θami:na] You'd better lock your valuables in the safe. أحسَن لَو تحُطّ أشيائك الثَّمِينَة بِالقاصَة [ʔaħsan law tħuṭṭ ʔašya:ʔak ʔiθθami:na bilqa:ṣa]

value • **1.** قِيمَة [qi:ma] قِيَم [qiyam] *pl:* This coin has no value. هالقِطعَة النُّقُود ما إلها قِيمَة [halqiṭʕat ʔinnuqu:d ma: ʔilha qi:ma] Even though it's rare, it's of no value to me. وَلَو هِيَّ نادرَة، بَسّ ما إلها قِيمَة بِالنِّسبَة إلِي [walaw hiyya na:dra, bass ma: ʔilha qi:ma binnisba ʔili] • **2.** وَزِن [wazin] I don't attach any value to his opinions. ما أنطِي أيّ وَزِن لآرائه [ma: ʔanṭi ʔayy wazin lʔa:ra:ʔah]

to value • **1.** إعتَزّ ب [ʔiʕtazz b-] إعتِزاز [ʔiʕtiza:z] *vn: sv* a. قَدَّر [qaddar] تَقدِير [taqdi:r] *vn: sv* i. I value his friendship very highly. هوايَة أعتَزّ بِصَداقتَه [hwa:ya ʔaʕtazz bṣada:qtah] • **2.** ثَمَّن [θamman] تَثمِين [taθmi:n] *vn: sv* i. سام [sa:m] سَوم [sawm] *vn: sv* u. What do you value your house at? بيش تثَمِّن بَيتَك؟ [biyš tθammin baytak?] What do you value your house at? شتِفتِكِر بَيتَك يِسوَى؟ [štiftikir baytak yiswa:?]

valve • **1.** صَمّام [ṣamma:m] صَمّامات [ṣamma:ma:t] *pl:* The worker opened a valve to let oil into the pipeline. العامِل فَكّ الصَّمّام حَتَّى النَّفُط يِجرِي بِالبُورِي [ʔilʕa:mil fakk ʔiṣṣamma:m ħatta ʔinnafuṭ yijri bilbu:ri] • **2.** وَلف [walf] وَلفات [walfa:t] *pl:* Your valves need adjusting. الوَلفات يِنرادِلها ضَبُط [ʔilwalfa:t yinra:dilha ðʼabuṭ]

to vanish • **1.** اِختِفَى [ʔixtifa:] اِختِفاء [ʔixtifa:ʔ] *vn: sv* i. My pencil has vanished. قَلَمِي اِختِفَى [qalami ʔixtifa:]

vapor • **1.** بُخار [buxa:r] On sunny days a lot of vapor goes into the atmosphere. بِالأيّام المُشمِسَة هوايَة بُخار يِصعَد لِلجَّوّ [bilʔayya:m ʔilmušmisa hwa:ya buxa:r yiṣʕad lijjaww]

variable • **1.** مُو ثابِت [mu: θa:bit] The weather is variable these days. الجَّوّ مُو ثابِت هَالأيّام [ʔijjaww mu: θa:bit halʔayya:m]

variety • **1.** تَشكِيلَة [taški:la] تَشكِيلات [taški:la:t] *pl:* We have a wide variety of shirts. عِدنا تَشكِيلَة كبِيرَة مِن الثِّياب [ʕidna taški:la čbi:ra min ʔiθθiya:b] • **2.** نوع [nawʕ] أنواع [ʔanwa:ʕ] *pl:* How many varieties of apples grow in your orchard? كَم نُوع مِن التِّفّاح عِندَك بِبُستانَك؟ [čam nu:ʕ min ʔattiffa:ħ ʕindak bibusta:nak?] • **3.** تَنَوُّع [tanawwuʕ] There's not much variety in my life. ماكُو تَنَوُّع بِحَياتِي [ma:ku tanawwuʕ bħaya:ti]

various • **1.** مِختِلِف [mixtilif] I have various reasons. عِندِي أسباب مِختَلفَة [ʕindi ʔasba:b mixtalfa]

varnish • **1.** وَرنِيش [warni:š] How long does it take the varnish to dry? شقَدّ يطَوِّل الوارنِيش حَتَّى يِيبَس؟ [šgadd yṭawwil ʔilwarni:š ħatta yi:bas?]

to varnish • **1.** ضِرَب وَارنِيش [ðirab warni:š] ضَرُب [ðarub] *vn: sv* u. We just varnished the doors. تَوّنا ضِرَبنا البُوب وارنِيش [tawwna ðirabna ʔilbu:b wa:rni:š]

to vary • **1.** اِختِلَف [ʔixtilaf] اِختِلاف [ʔixtila:f] *vn: sv* i. The length varies in each case. الطُّول يِختِلِف بِكُلّ حالَة [ʔiṭṭu:l yixtilif bkull ħa:la]

vase • **1.** مَزهَرِيَّة [mazhariyya] مَزهَرِيّات [mazhariyya:t] *pl:*

veal • **1.** لَحَم عِجِل [laħam ʕiǰil]

vegetable • **1.** مخَضَّر [mxaððar] مخَضَّرات، مخَاضِير [mxaððara:t, mxa:ði:r] *pl:*

vehicle • **1.** عَجَلَة [ʕaǰala]

veil • **1.** بُوشِي [pu:ši] بُوشِيّات، بوش [pu:ši:yya:t, pu:š] *pl:* بُوشِيَّة [pu:šiyya] بُوشِيّات [pu:šiyya:t] *pl:* Many Iraqi women still wear veils. هوايَة نِسوان عِراقِيّات بَعَدهُم يِلِبسُون بُوشِيَّة [hwa:ya niswa:n ʕira:qiyya:t baʕadhum yilibsu:n pu:šiyya]

vein • **1.** دَمار [dama:r] دَمارات [dama:ra:t] *pl:* وَرِيد [wari:d] أَورِدَة [ʔawrida] *pl:* The medicine has to be injected into the vein. الدُّوا لازِم يِنضُرُب بِالدَّمار [ʔidduwa la:zim yinðurub biddama:r]

velvet • **1.** قَدِيفَة [qadi:fa]

venereal disease • **1.** مَرَض زُهرِي [marað zuhri] أَمراض زُهرِيَّة [ʔamra:ð zuhriyya] *pl:* Gonorrhea is a venereal disease. السَّيَلان مَرَض زُهرِي [ʔissayala:n marað zuhri]

Venice • **1.** البُندُقِيَّة [ʔilbunduqiyya]

venom • **1.** سَمّ [samm] سمُوم [sumu:m] *pl:*

vent • **1.** مَجرَى هَوا [maǰra hawa] مَجارِي هَوا [maǰa:ri hawa] *pl:* مَنفَذ هَوا [manfað hawa] مَنافِذ هَوا [mana:fið hawa] *pl:* بادقِير [ba:dgi:r] بادقِيرات [ba:dgi:ra:t] *pl:* Open the vent! فُكّ مَجرَى الهَوا [fukk maǰra ʔilhawa]

to give vent • **1.** نَفَّس [naffas] تَنفِيس [tanfi:s] *vn: sv* i. She gave vent to her anger. نَفِّسَت عَن قَلُبها [naffisat ʕan galubha]

ventilation • **1.** تَهوِيَة [tahwiya] This room needs ventilation. هَالغُرفَة يِنرادِلها تَهوِيَة [halɣurfa yinra:dilha tahwiya]

venture • **1.** مُجازَفَة [muǰa:zafa] مُجازَفات [muǰa:zafa:t] *pl:* مُخاطَرَة [muxa:ṭara] مُخاطَرات [muxa:ṭara:t] *pl:* It was a dangerous venture. كانَت مُجازَفَة خَطرَة [ča:nat muǰa:zafa xaṭra] I'm going into a new business venture. راح أَسَوِّي فَدّ مُجازَفَة تِجارِيَّة [ra:ħ ʔasawwi fadd muǰa:zafa tiǰa:riyya]

to venture • **1.** خاطَر [xa:ṭar] مُخاطَرَة [muxa:ṭara] *vn: sv* i. جازَف [ǰa:zaf] مُجازَفَة [muǰa:zafa] *vn: sv* i. I wouldn't venture to go out in this weather. ما أَرِيد أَخاطِر أَطلَع بِهِيكِي جَوّ [ma: ʔari:d ʔaxa:ṭir ʔaṭlaʕ bhi:či ǰaww] • **2.** جازَف [ǰa:zaf] مُجازَفَة [muǰa:zafa] *vn: sv* i. Nothing ventured, nothing gained. ما تجازِف، كُلّشِي ما تحَصِّل [ma: dǰa:zif, kullši ma: tħaṣṣil]

verb • **1.** فِعِل [fiʕil] أفعال [ʔafʕa:l] *pl:*

verbal • **1.** شَفَهِي [šafahi] شَفَوِي [šafawi] We have a verbal agreement. بَيناتنا عَقِد شَفَهِي [bayna:tna ʕaqid šafahi]

verdict • **1.** حُكُم [ħukum] أَحكام [ʔaħka:m] *pl:* قَرار [qara:r] قَرارات [qara:ra:t] *pl:* The court issued the verdict. المَحكَمَة صَدّرَت الحُكُم [ʔilmaħkama ṣaddrat ʔilħukum]

verge • **1.** حافَّة [ħa:ffa] She's on the verge of a breakdown. هِيَّ عَلَى حافَّة الإنهِيار العَصَبِي [hiyya ʕala ħa:ffat ʔilʔinhiya:r ʔilʕaṣabi] • **2.** وَشَك [wašak] I was on the verge of telling him. كِنِت عَلَى وَشَك أَقُلَّه [činit ʕala wašak ʔagullah]

verse • **1.** شِعِر [šiʕir] The play is written in verse. الرِّوايَة عَلَى شِكِل شِعِر [ʔirruwa:ya ʕala šikil šiʕir] • **2.** بَيت [bayt] بيُوت [biyu:t] *pl:* Let's read the first verse of the poem. خَلِّي نِقرا أَوَّل بَيت مِن القَصِيدَة [xalli niqra: ʔawwal bayt min ʔilqaṣi:da] • **3.** قِسِم [qisim] أَقسام [ʔaqsa:m] *pl:* Let's sing only the first verse. خَلِّي نغَنِّي أَوَّل قِسِم بَسّ [xalli nɣanni ʔawwal qisim bass]

version • **1.** رُوايَة [ruwa:ya, riwa:ya] رُوايات [ruwa:ya:t] *pl:* I heard another version. سِمَعِت رُوايَة لُخ [simaʕit ruwa:ya lux]

versus • **1.** ضِدّ [ðidd] أَضداد [ʔaðda:d] *pl:* This is the case of the cotton company versus the ministry of agriculture. هَذِي دَعوَة شَرِكَة القُطِن ضِدّ وِزارَة الزِّراعَة [ha:ði daʕwat šarikat ʔilguṭin ðidd wiza:rat ʔizzira:ʕa]

vertical • **1.** عَمُودِي [ʕamu:di] The Nabi Shiit minaret in Mosul isn't vertical. مَنارَة النَّبِي شِيت اللِّي بِالمَوصِل مُو عَمُودِيَّة [mana:rat ʔinnabi ši:t ʔilli bilmu:ṣil mu: ʕamu:diyya]

very • **1.** كُلّش [kulliš] The bank is not very far from here. البَنك مُو كُلِّش بِعِيد مِن هِنَا [ʔilbank mu: kulliš biʕi:d min hna] We're very satisfied with the new cook.

V

إحنا كُلِّش مِرتاحِين مِن الطَّبّاخ الجِّدِيد [ʔiħna kulliš mirtaːħiːn min ʔiṭṭabbaːx ʔijjidiːd] • **2.** بِالضَبُط [biðḍabuṭ] نَفِس [nafis] نُفُوس، أَنفُس [nufuːs, ʔanfus] *pl:* بِالذات [biððaːt] That's the very thing I want. هَذا الشِّي اللِّي أَرِيدَه بِالضَبُط [haːða ʔišši ʔilli ʔariːdah biððabuṭ] • **3.** نَفس [nafs] بِالذات [biððaːt] She left that very day. راحَت بنَفِس اليُوم [raːħat bnafis ʔilyuːm]

*** He came the very next day.** • **1.** ما طَوَّل لِثانِي يَوم وإجا [maː ṭawwal liθaːni yawm wʔijaː]

vessel • **1.** سَفِينَة [safiːna] سُفُن [sufun] *pl:* مَركَب [markab] مَراكُب [maraːkub] *pl:* Several large vessels were docked in the harbor. عِدَّة سُفُن كبار وَكّت بالمِيناء [ʕiddat sufun kbaːr waččat bilmiːnaːʔ]

vest • **1.** يَلَك [yalag] يَلَكات [yalagaːt] *pl:* زَخمَة [zaxma, zixma] زَخمات، زِخَم [zaxmaːt, zixam] *pl:* He usually wears a vest. عادَةً يِلبَس يَلَك [ʕaːdatan yilbas yalag]

vestige • **1.** أَثَر [ʔaθar] آثار [ʔaːθaːr] *pl:*

veteran • **1.** مُحارِب [muħaːrib] مُحارِبِين [muħaːribiːn] *pl:* He's an old veteran. هَذا مُحارِب قَدِيم [haːða muħaːrib qadiːm] • **2.** مدَرَّب [mdarrab] مدَرَّبِين [mdarrabiːn] *pl:* مُحَنَّك [muħannak] مُحَنَّكِين [muħannakiːn] *pl:* He's a veteran politician. هُوَّ سِياسِي مدَرَّب [huwwa siyaːsi mdarrab]

*** He's a veteran of the North African campaign of World War II.** • **1.** حارَب بشِمال أفرِيقيا بِالحَرب الثانِيَة [ħaːrab bšimaːl ʔafriːqya bilħarb ʔiθθaːnya]

veterinarian • **1.** بَيطَرِي [bayṭari] بَيطَرِيَّة [bayṭariːyya] *pl:* بَيطار [bayṭaːr] بَياطرَة [bayaːṭra] *pl:* The veterinarian can tell you what's wrong with your horse. البَيطَرِي يِقدَر يقُلَّك شبِيه الحصان مالَك [ʔilbayṭari yigdar yugullak šbiːh ʔilħṣaːn maːlak]

viaduct • **1.** جِسِر [jisir] جسُور [jsuːra] *pl:*

to vibrate • **1.** اِهتَزّ [ʔihtazz] اِهتِزاز [ʔihtizaːz] *vn: sv* a. رِجَف [rijaf] رَجِف [rajif] *vn: sv* i. Pluck the string and watch it vibrate. أُضرُب الوَتَر وشُوف شلُون يِهتَزّ [ʔuðrub ʔilwatar wšuːf šluːn yihtazz] The steering wheel vibrates at high speed. السِّتيرِن يِرجِف مِن تسُوق بسُرعَة [ʔalstiːrin yirjif min tsuːq bsurʕa]

vice • **1.** رَذِيلَة [raðiːla] رَذايِل [raðaːyil] *pl:* Gambling is a vice. لِعِب القمار رَذِيلَة [liʕib ʔilqmaːr raðiːla] • **2.** نائِب [naːʔib] نُوّاب [nuwwaːb] *pl:* He's the vice-president. هُوَّ نائِب الرَّئِيس [huwwa naːʔib ʔirraʔiːs]

vicinity • **1.** مَنطِقَة [manṭiqa] Is there a tailor in this vicinity? أَكُو خَيّاط بِهالمَنطِقَة؟ [ʔaku xayyaːṭ bhalmanṭiqa?] Is there a tailor in this vicinity? أَكُو خَيّاط قَرِيب مِن هنا [ʔaku xayyaːṭ qariːb min hna] • **2.** حَوالِي [ħawaːli] The weather is bad in the vicinity of Washington. الجَّوّ مُو زين حَوالِي واشِنطَن [ʔijjaww muː ziːn ħawaːli waːšinṭun]

vicious • **1.** شَرِس [šaris] خَبِيث [xabiːθ] The dog is vicious. الكَلِب شَرِس [ʔiččalib šaris]

*** She has a vicious tongue.** • **1.** لسانها وَسِخ [lsaːnha wasix] / لسانها يقُصّ [lsaːnha yguṣṣ]

victim • **1.** ضَحِيَّة [ḍaħiyya] ضَحايا [ḍaħayaː] *pl:* He was the victim of an auto accident. راح ضَحِيَّة حادِث تَصادُم [raːħ ḍaħiyyat ħaːdiθ taṣaːdum]

victor • **1.** مِنتِصِر [mintiṣir] مِنتِصِرِين [mintiṣriːn] *pl:* We were the victors in that struggle. إحنا كِنّا المِنتِصرِين بِذاك الكِفاح [ʔiħna činna ʔilmintiṣriːn bðaːk ʔilkifaːħ]

victorious • **1.** مُنتَصِر [muntaṣir] The victorious army entered the city. الجَّيش المُنتَصِر دِخَل الوِلايَة [ʔijjayš ʔilmuntaṣir dixal ʔilwilaːya]

victory • **1.** اِنتِصار [ʔintiṣaːr] اِنتِصارات [ʔintiṣaːraːt] *pl:* نَصِر [naṣir] That was a great victory. كان فَدّ اِنتِصار عَظِيم [čaːn fadd ʔintiṣaːr ʕaðiːm]

view • **1.** مَنظَر [manḍar] مَناظِر [manaːḍir] *pl:* You have a nice view from here. عِندَك خُوش مَنظَر مِن هنا [ʕindak xuːš manḍar min hna] • **2.** رَأي [raʔy] آراء [ʔaːraːʔ] *pl:* Our views differ. آرائنا تِختِلِف [ʔaːraːʔna tixtilif] • **3.** نَظَر [naḍar] أنظار [ʔanḍaːr] *pl:* In view of these developments, we'll have to change our plans. بِالنَّظَر إلَى هَالتَّطَوُّرات، لازِم نغَيِّر خُطَطنا [binnaḍar ʔila hattaṭawwuraːt, laːzim nɣayyir xuṭaṭna] Here's my point of view. هاي وُجهَة نَظَري [haːy wujhat naḍari]

in view • **1.** مبَيِّن [mbayyin] Is the ship in view? السَّفِينَة مبَيّنَة؟ [ʔissafiːna mbayyna?]

to come into view • **1.** بَيَّن [bayyan] *sv* i. The ship finally came into view. السَّفِينَة تالِيها بَيَّنَت [ʔissafiːna taːliːha bayynat]

vile • **1.** قَذِر [qaðir] قَذِرِين [qaðiriːn] *pl:* سافِل [saːfil] سَفَلَة [safala] *pl:* He's really a vile person. هُوَّ فَدّ واحِد كُلِّش قَذِر [huwwa fadd waːħid kulliš qaðir] • **2.** مُزعِج [muzʕij] What vile weather we're having! غير جَوّ مُزعِج هَذا [ɣiːr jaww muzʕij haːða]

village • **1.** قَريَة [qarya] قُرَى [quraː] *pl:* He lives in the village. دَيسكُن بِالقَريَة [dayiskun bilqarya]

vinegar • **1.** خَلّ [xall]

to violate • **1.** خالَف [xaːlaf] مُخالَفَة [muxaːlafa] *vn: sv* i. That's not the first time he's violated the law. هاي مُو أَوَّل مَرَّة يخالِف بِيها القانُون [haːy muː ʔawwal marra yxaːlif biːha ʔilqaːnuːn]

V

violation • **1.** مُخالَفَة [muxa:lafa] مُخالَفات [muxa:lafa:t] *pl:* He has three violations on his record. عِندَه ثلاث مُخالَفات [ʕindah tla:θ muxa:lafa:t]

violent • **1.** عَنِيف [ʕani:f] He's a violent person. هُوَّ فَدّ واحِد كُلِّش عَنِيف [huwwa fadd wa:ħid kulliš ʕani:f] • **2.** حادّ [ħa:dd] We had a violent argument. صارَت بَيناتنا مُناقَشَة حادَّة [ṣa:rat bayna:tna muna:qaša ħa:dda] • **3.** فَظِيع [faðị:ʕ] He died a violent death. مُوتَه كانَت فَظِيعَة [mu:tah ča:nat faðị:ʕa]

violet • **1.** وَردَة بَنَفشَة [wardat banafša] وَردات بَنَفشَة [warda:t banafša] *pl:* وَرِد بَنَفشَة [warid banafša] *Collective:* We have violets in our garden. عِدنا وَرِد بَنَفسَج بحَدِيقَتنا [ʕidna warid banafsaǰ bħadi:qatna] • **2.** بَنَفسَجِي [banafsaǰi] Her dress is violet. بَدلَتها بَنَفسَجِيَّة [badlatha banafsaǰiyya]

violin • **1.** كَمَنجَة [kamanǰa] كَمَنجات [kamanǰa:t] *pl:*

virgin • **1.** باكِر، باكِرَة [ba:kir, ba:kra] بَواكِر [bawa:kir] *pl:* بنَيَّة [bnayya] بنَيّات [bnayya:t] *pl:* She's a virgin. هِيَّ باكِر [hiyya ba:kir] • **2.** عَذراء [ʕaðra:ʔ] عَذارَى، عَذرات [ʕaða:ra, ʕaðra:t] *pl:* He told the story of the Virgin Mary. حِكَى قُصَّة مَريَم العَذراء [ħiča: quṣṣat maryam ʔilʕaðra:ʔ]

virtue • **1.** حَسَنَة [ħasana] حَسَنات [ħasana:t] *pl:* His virtues are undeniable. حَسَناتَه ما تُنكَر [ħasana:tah ma: tunkar] • **2.** فَضِل [faðịl] He has risen to this position by virtue of his education. وُصَل لِهالمَنصَب بفَضِل ثَقافتَه [wuṣal lihalmanṣab bfaðịl θaqa:ftah]

visa • **1.** فِيزَة [fi:za] فِيزات [fi:za:t] *pl:* تَأشِيرَة [taʔši:ra] تَأشِيرات [taʔši:ra:t] *pl:*

vise • **1.** مَنگَنَة [mangana] مَنگَنات [mangana:t] *pl:*

visibility • **1.** مَدَي الرُّؤيا [mada ʔirruʔya] The visibility is limited today. مَدَى الرُّؤيَا مَحدُودَة هَاليُوم [mada: ʔirruʔya: maħdu:da halyu:m]

visible • **1.** مبَيِّن [mbayyin] واضِح [wa:ðịħ] The ship isn't visible yet. الباخِرَة بَعَد لهَسَّة ما مبَيِّنَة [ʔilba:xira baʕad lhassa ma: mbayyna]

vision • **1.** نَظَر [naðar] أنظار [ʔanða:r] *pl:* His vision is getting poor. نَظَرَه دَيضعَف [naðarah dayiðʕaf] He's a man of great vision. هُوَّ فَدّ واحِد عِندَه نَظَر بَعِيد [huwwa fadd wa:ħid ʕindah naðar baʕi:d]

visit • **1.** زِيارَة [ziya:ra] That was an unexpected visit. ذِيك كانَت فَدّ زِيارَة ما مُتَوَقَّعَة [ði:č ča:nat fadd ziya:ra ma: mutawaqqaʕa]

to pay a visit • **1.** زار [za:r] زِيارَة [ziya:ra] *vn:* انزار [ʔinza:r] *p:* He paid me a visit last week. زارنِي بالإسبُوع اللِّي فات [za:rni bilʔisbu:ʕ ʔilli fa:t]
to visit • **1.** زار [za:r] زِيارَة [ziya:ra] *vn: sv* u. He wanted to visit you. راد يزُورَك [ra:d yzu:rak] Have you visited our museum yet? زِرت المَتحَف مالنَا لَو بَعَد؟ [zirt ʔalmatħaf ma:lna law baʕad?]

visitor • **1.** خُطّار [xuṭṭa:r] زائِر [za:ʔir] زُوّار [zuwwa:r] *pl:* We're having visitors tonight. عِدنا خُطّار هاللَّيلَة [ʕidna xiṭṭa:r hallayla] No visitors are allowed in this ward. الزُّوّار مَمنُوع يدُخلُون بهَالرَّدهَة [ʔizzuwwa:r mamnu:ʕ yduxlu:n bharradha]

vital • **1.** حَيَوِي [ħayawi] It's of vital importance to me. هَذا فَدّ شِي حَيَوِي بالنِّسبَة إلِي [ha:ða fadd ši ħayawi binnisba ʔili] • **2.** مُهِمّ [muhimm] He's well posted on the vital issues of the day. هُوَّ مِتطِلِع عَلَى كُلّ الأشياء المُهِمَّة اللِّي تصِير [huwwa miṭṭiliʕ ʕala kull ʔilʔašya:ʔ ʔilmuhimma ʔilli tṣi:r]

vitality • **1.** حَيَوِيَّة [ħayawiyya] He has a lot of vitality. عِندَه حَيَوِيَّة مُمتازَة [ʕindah ħayawiyya mumta:za]

vitamin • **1.** فِيتامِين [fitami:n] فِيتامِينات [fitamina:t] *pl:*

vivid • **1.** خَصِب [xaṣib] He has a vivid imagination. عِندَه خَيال خَصِب [ʕindah xaya:l xaṣib] • **2.** بَرّاق [barra:q] زاهِي [za:hi] He uses vivid colors in his paintings. يِستَعمِل ألوان بَرّاقَة بالرِّسُوم مالتَه [yistaʕmil ʔalwa:n barra:qa birrisu:m ma:ltah] • **3.** واضِح [wa:ðịħ] He gave us a vivid description of his experience. اِنطانا وَصُف واضِح عَن تَجارُبَه [ʔinṭa:na waṣuf wa:ðịħ ʕan taǰa:rubah]

vocal cords • **1.** حبال صَوتِيَّة [ħba:l ṣawtiyya]

voice • **1.** صَوت [ṣawt, ṣu:t] أصوات [ʔaṣwa:t] *pl:* حِسّ [ħiss] His voice carries well. حِسَّه يِنسِمِع زين [ħissah yinsimiʕ zi:n]
to voice • **1.** جاهَر [ǰa:har] مُجاهَرَة [muǰa:hara] *vn: sv* i. Don't be afraid to voice your opinions. لا تخاف تجاهِر بمُعارَضتَك [la: txa:f dǰa:hir bmuʕa:raðṭak]

void • **1.** مَلغِي [malɣi] باطِل [ba:ṭil] This check is void. هَالصَّكّ مَفعُولَه باطِل [haṣṣakk mafʕu:lah ba:ṭil] The contract is null and void. العَقِد مَفعُولَه باطِل [ʔilʕaqid mafʕu:lah ba:ṭil]
to void • **1.** بَطَّل [baṭṭal] تَبطِيل [tabṭi:l] *vn: sv* i. I'll void the check. راح أبَطِّل الشَّيك [ra:ħ ʔabaṭṭil ʔičči:k]

volcano • **1.** بُركان [burka:n] بَراكِين [bara:ki:n] *pl:*

volley-ball • **1.** الكُرَة الطائِرَة [ʔilkura ʔiṭṭa:ʔira]

V

volt • **1.** فولت [fu:lt]

volume • **1.** جُزء [ǰuzuʔ] أجزاء [ʔaǰza:ʔ] *pl:* مُجَلَّد [muǰallad] The book was published in two volumes. الكِتاب اِنْشَر بجُزئَين [ʔilkita:b ʔinnišar bǰuzʔayn] • **2.** حَجِم [ħaǰim] حُجُوم، أحجام [ħuǰu:m, ʔaħǰa:m] *pl:* What's the volume of this tank? شِنُو حَجِم هَالعُمبار؟ [šinu: ħaǰim halʕumba:r?] • **3.** جُملَة [ǰumla] جُمَل [ǰumal] *pl:* The factory's producing clothing in volume. المَعمَل دَينتِج هِدُوم بِالجُملَة [ʔilmaʕmal dayintiǰ hidu:m biǰǰumla]

voluntarily • **1.** بِاختِيار [bʔixtiya:r] مِن كَيف [min kayf] He did it voluntarily. سَوّاها بِاختِيارَه [sawwa:ha bʔixtiya:rah]

voluntary • **1.** اِختِياري [ʔixtiya:ri] Education is voluntary after 16. الدِّراسَة اِختِيارِيَّة بَعَد سِنّ السِّتطَعَش [ʔiddira:sa ʔixtiya:riyya baʕad sinn ʔissiṭṭaʕaš]

volunteer • **1.** مِتطَوِّع [miṭṭawwiʕ] مِتطَوِّعِين [miṭṭawwiʕi:n] *pl:* Can you get some volunteers to do it? تِقدَر تِلقِي فَدّ كَم مِتطَوِّع يسَوُّوها؟ [tigdar tilgi fadd čam miṭṭawwiʕ ysawwu:ha?]

to volunteer • **1.** عِرَض [ʕirað] عَرِض [ʕarið] *vn:* *sv* u. تبَرَّع ب [tbarraʕ b-] تَبَرُّع [tabarruʕ] *vn:* *sv* a. He volunteered his services. عِرَض خَدَماتَه [ʕirað xadama:tah] • **2.** تطَوَّع [ṭṭawwaʕ] تَطَوُّع [taṭawwuʕ] *vn:* *sv* a. Who'll volunteer for this job? مِنُو يِتطَوَّع لِهَالشَّغلَة؟ [minu yiṭṭawwaʕ lihaššaɣla?]

to vomit • **1.** زاع [za:ʕ] زَوع [zawʕ] *vn:* *sv* u. زَوَّع [zawwaʕ] تَزويع [tazwi:ʕ] *vn:* *sv* i. ذَبّ [ðabb] ذَبّ [ðabb] *vn:* *sv* i. قِلَب [gilab] قَلُب [galub] *vn:* *sv* u. He got drunk and vomited. سِكَر وزَوَّع [sikar wzawwaʕ]

vote • **1.** صُوت [ṣawt] أصوات [ʔaṣwa:t] *pl:* They elected him by a majority of 2000 votes. اِنتِخبَوه بِأكثَرِيَّة ألفَين صُوت [ʔintixbu:h biʔakθariyyat ʔalfayn ṣuwt] • **2.** تَصويت [taṣwi:t] Minors have no vote. الصغار ما عِدهُم حَقّ التَّصويت [ʔilṣɣa:r ma: ʕidhum ħaqq ʔittaṣwi:t] The motion was put to a vote. حَطّوا الاقتِراح بِالتَّصويت [ħaṭṭaw ʔilʔiqtira:ħ bittaṣwi:t]

to vote • **1.** اِنتِخَب [ʔintixab] اِنتِخاب [ʔintixa:b] *vn:* *sv* i. صَوَّت [ṣawwat] تَصويت [taṣwi:t] *vn:* *sv* i. I couldn't vote in the last elections. ما قِدَرت أنتِخِب بِالإنتِخابات اللّي فاتَت [ma: gidart ʔantixib bilʔintixa:ba:t ʔilli fa:tat] Who'd you vote for? اِلمَن اِنتِخَبِت؟ [ʔilman ʔintixabit?] • **2.** صَوَّت [ṣawwat] تَصويت [taṣwi:t] *vn:* *sv* i. Shall we vote on it? اِنصَوِّت بِيها؟ [ʔinṣawwit bi:ha?] • **3.** قَرَّر [qarrar] تَقرِير [taqri:r] *vn:* *sv* i. The board voted five hundred dinars for relief. المَجلِس قَرَّر تَخصِيص خَمِس مِيَّة دِينار لِلإعانات [ʔilmaǰlis qarrar taxṣi:ṣ xamis miyyat dina:r lilʔiʕa:na:t]

to vote down • **1.** رُفَض بِالتَّصويت [rufað bittaṣwi:t] *sv* u. They voted down the proposal. رُفضَوا الاقتِراح بِالتَّصويت [rufðaw ʔilʔiqtira:ħ bittaṣwi:t]

voter • **1.** ناخِب [na:xib] ناخِبِين [na:xibi:n] *pl:* مُنتَخِب [muntaxib] مُنتَخِبِين [muntaxibi:n] *pl:* We have 200 voters in this section. عِدنا مِيتَين ناخِب بهَالمُحَلَّة [ʕidna mitayn na:xib bhalmuħalla]

to vouch • **1.** شِهَد [šihad] شَهادَة [šaha:da] *vn:* *sv* a. I vouch for him. آني أشهَدلَه [ʔa:ni ʔašhadlah]

to vow • **1.** تعَهَّد [tʕahhad] تَعَهُّد [taʕahhud] *vn:* *sv* a. He vowed not to do it again. تعَهَّد ما يسَوِّيها بَعَد [tʕahhad ma: ysawwi:ha baʕad] • **2.** حِلَف [ħilaf] حَلِف [ħalif] *vn:* *sv* i. He vowed to avenge his brother's death. حِلَف ياخُذ ثار أخُوه اللّي مات [ħilaf ya:xuð θa:r ʔaxu:h ʔilma:t]

voyage • **1.** سَفرَة [safra] سَفرات [safra:t] *pl:*

vulgar • **1.** بَذِيء [baði:ʔ] He uses vulgar language. يِستَعمِل حَكِي بَذِيء [yistaʕmil ħači baði:ʔ] • **2.** فَضّ [faðð] خَشِن [xašin] He's a vulgar person. هَذا فَدّ واحِد فَضّ [ha:ða fadd wa:ħid faðð]

vulnerable • **1.** عُرضَة [ʕurða] Our position is vulnerable to attack. مَوقِفنا عُرضَة لِلهِجُوم [mawqifna ʕurðah lilhiǰu:m]

vulture • **1.** حدَيَّة [ħdayya] حدَيّات [ħdayya:t] *pl:* Vultures eat only carrion. الحِدَيّات ياكلُون فطايِس بَسّ [ʔilħidayya:t ya:klu:n fṭa:yis bass]

vulva • **1.** فَرج [fariǰ] فرُوج [fru:ǰ] *pl:* كُسّ [kuss] كساسَة [ksa:sa] *pl:*

V

W

to wad • **1.** كَعبَر [kaʕbar] كَعبَرَة [kaʕbara] *vn: sv* u. He wadded up the paper and threw it away. كَعبَر الوَرَق وَذَبَّه [kaʕbar ʔilwaraq wðabbah]

to waddle • **1.** تدَعبَل [tdaʕbal] تدِعبِل [tdiʕbil] *vn: sv* a. The duck waddled over to the water. البَطَّة تدَعبِلَت لِلمَيّ [ʔilbaṭṭa ddaʕbilat lilmayy]

to wade • **1.** خاض [xaːð̣] خَوض [xawð] *vn:* اِنخاض [ʔinxaːð̣] *p:* The soldiers waded ashore. الجِّنُود خاضَوا لِلسّاحِل [ʔijjinuːd xaːð̣aw lissaːħil] We waded across the stream. قِطَعنا الشَّطّ خُوض [giṭaʕna ʔiššaṭṭ xuːð̣] • **2.** ذَبّ [ðabb] ذَبّ [ðabb] *vn: sv* i. I waded into my work. ذَبِّيت نَفسِي عالشُّغُل [ðabbiːt nafsi ʕaššuɣul]

waders • **1.** أَحذِيَة خَوض [ʔaħðiyat xawð] He bought a pair of waders to go fishing. اِشتِرَى أَحذِيَة خُوض حَتَّى يِصِيد سِمَك [ʔištiraː ʔaħðiyat xuːð̣ ħatta yiṣiːd simač]

to wag • **1.** هَزّ ب [hazz b-] هَزّ [hazz] *vn:* اِنهَزّ [ʔinhazz] *p:* The dog wagged its tail. الكَلِب هَزّ بذَيلَه [ʔiččalib hazz bðiːlah]

wage • **1.** أُجرَة [ʔuǰra] أُجُور [ʔuǰuːr] *pl:* They're not paying a decent wage. ما يِدفِعُون أُجرَة زِينَة [maː ydifʕuːn ʔuǰra ziːna]

to wage • **1.** ثار [θaːr] إثارَة [ʔiθaːra] *vn: sv* i. They can't wage a long war. ما يِقدرُون يثِيرُون حَرب طَوِيلَة [maː ygidruːn yθiːruːn ħarib ṭwiːla]

wage rates • **1.** مُستَوَى أُجُور [mustawa ʔuǰuːr] Wage rates are rising. مُستَوَى الأُجُور دَيِرتِفِع [mustawaː ʔalʔuǰuːr dayirtifiʕ]

wagon • **1.** عَرَبانَة [ʕarabaːna] عَرَبانات [ʕarabaːnaːt] *pl:* Hitch the horses to the new wagon. شِدّ الخَيل بِالعَرَبانَة الجِّدِيدَة [šidd ʔilxayl bilʕarabaːna ʔijǰidiːda]

waist • **1.** خِصِر [xiṣir] خُصُور [xuṣuːr] *pl:* خاصرَة [xaːṣra] خَواصِر [xawaːṣir] *pl:* I took the pants in at the waist. قَصَّفِت البَنطَرُون مِن يَمّ الخِصِر [gaṣṣafit ʔilpanṭaruːn min yamm ʔalxiṣir]

wait • **1.** اِنتِظار [ʔintiðaːr] The hour's wait was aggravating. ساعَة الانتِظار كانَت مُزعِجَة [saːʕat ʔilʔintiðaːr čaːnat muzʕiǰa]

to lie in wait • **1.** ترَصَّد [traṣṣad] تَرَصُّد [taraṣṣud] *vn: sv* a. They were lying in wait for us. كانَوا مِترَصّدِين إلنا [čaːnaw mitraṣṣdiːn ʔilna]

to wait • **1.** اِنتِظَر [ʔintiðar] اِنتِظار [ʔintiðaːr] *vn: sv* i. اِصطبَر [ʔiṣṭubar] اِصطِبار، صَبُر [ʔiṣṭibaːr, ṣabur] *vn: sv* u. Wait a moment. اِنتِظِر شوَيَّة [ʔintiðir šwayya] Have you been waiting long? صارلَك هوايَة مِنتِظِر؟ [ṣaːrlak hwaːya mintiðir?] I can hardly wait to see him. ما دَأقدَر أَصطبُر عَلَى شُوفتَه [maː daʔagdar ʔaṣṭubur ʕala šuːftah] • **2.** تأَجَّل [tʔaǰǰal] تَأَجُّل [taʔaǰǰul] *vn: sv* a. Can that business wait till tomorrow? هالمَسألَة مُمكِن تِتأَجَّل لِباكِر؟ [halmasʔala mumkin titʔaǰǰal lbaːčir?] • **3.** عَطَّل [ʕaṭṭal] تَعطِيل [taʕṭiːl] *vn:* تعَطَّل [tʕaṭṭal] *p:* We'll wait dinner for him. عُود نعَطِّل العَشا عَلَى مُودَه [ʕuːd nʕaṭṭil ʔilʕašaː ʕala muːdah] • **4.** صُبَر [ṣubar] صَبُر [ṣabur] *vn: sv* u. I can't wait till that day comes. ما دَأقدَر أَصبُر إلَى أَن يِجِي ذاك اليُوم [maː daʔagdar ʔaṣbur ʔila ʔan yiǰi ðaːk ʔilyuːm]

to wait for • **1.** اِنتِظَر [ʔintiðar] اِنتِظار [ʔintiðaːr] *vn: sv* i. I'll wait for you until five o'clock. أَنتِظرَك الساعَة خَمسَة [ʔantiðrak lissaːʕa xamsa] Wait for his answer. اِنتِظِر جَوابَه [ʔintiðir ǰawaːbah]

to wait on • **1.** شاف شُغُل [šaːf šuɣul] *sv* u. Will you please wait on me now? بالله ما تشُوف شُغلِي عاد؟ [ballah maː tšuːf šuɣli ʕaːd?]

waiter • **1.** بُوي [buːy] بُويات [buːyaːt] *pl:* He's a waiter in a restaurant. هُوَّ بُوي مال مَطعَم [huwwa buːy maːl maṭʕam]

waiting room • **1.** غُرفَة اِنتِظار [ɣurfat ʔintiðaːr] غُرَف اِنتِظار [ɣuraf ʔintiðaːr] *pl:* Is there a waiting room at the airport? أَكُو غُرفَة اِنتِظار بِالمَطار؟ [ʔaku ɣurfat ʔintiðaːr bilmaṭaːr?]

to wake • **1.** قَعَّد [gaʕʕad] تقِعِّد [tgiʕʕid] *vn: sv* i. Please wake me at seven o'clock. بالله قَعِّدنِي ساعَة سَبعَة [ballah gaʕʕidni saːʕa sabʕa]

to wake up • **1.** فَزّز مِن النُّوم، قَعَّد مِن النُّوم [fazzaz min ʔinnuːm, gaʕʕad min ʔinnuːm] *sv* i. قَعَّد [gaʕʕad] *sv* i. The noise woke me up in the middle of the night. الصُّوت فَزَّزنِي مِن النُّوم بنُصّ اللَّيل [ʔiṣṣuːt fazzazni min ʔannuːm bnuṣṣ ʔillayl] • **2.** قِعَد [giʕad] *sv* u. I didn't wake up until eight this morning. ما قعَدت مِن النُّوم إلّا ساعَة ثمانيَة الصُّبُح [maː gʕadt min ʔinnuːm ʔilla saːʕa θmaːnya ʔiṣṣubuħ]

*** It's high time you wake up to the fact that....** • **1.** لازِم تفُكّ عَينَك مُو ثِخنَت [laːzim tfukk ʕawnak muː θixnat...]

walk • **1.** مَشيَة [mašya] مَشيات [mašyaːt] *pl:* Did you have a nice walk? أَخَذِتلَك خُوش مَشيَة؟ [ʔaxaðitlak xuːš mašya?] You can recongnize him by his walk. تِقدَر تعُرفَه مِن مَشِيتَه [tigdar tʕurfah min mašiːtah]

to go for a walk • **1.** تمَشّى [tmašša:] تَمَشّي [tamašši] *vn: sv* a. Let's go for a walk. خَلّي نِتمَشّى [xalli nitmašša:]

to walk • **1.** مِشَى [miša:] مَشِي [mašy] *vn: sv* i. Shall we walk or take the bus? راح نِمشِي لَو ناخُذ باص؟ [ra:ħ nimši law na:xuð pa:ṣ?] Can the baby walk yet? الجّاهِل يِقدَر يِمشِي لَو بَعَد؟ [ʔijja:hil yigdar yimši law baʕad?] • **2.** مَشّيت الكَلِب [maššiːt ʔiččalib]

to walk down • **1.** نِزَل [nizal] *sv* i. We were walking down the stairs. كِنّا دَنِنزِل الدَّرَج [činna daninzil ʔiddaraj]

to walk out on • **1.** طِلَع [ṭilaʕ] *sv* a. بَطَّل [baṭṭal] *sv* i. Our girl walked out on us. الخَدّامَة طِلعَت [ʔilxadda:ma ṭilʕat]

to walk up • **1.** صِعَد [ṣiʕad] صُعُود [ṣuʕu:d] *vn: sv* a. He can't walk up the stairs. ما يِقدَر يِصعَد الدَّرَج [ma: yigdar yiṣʕad ʔiddaraj]

wall • **1.** حايِط [ħa:yiṭ] حِيطان، حيَاطِين [ħi:ṭa:n, hyaṭi:n] *pl:* Hang the picture on this wall. عَلِّق الصُّورَة عَلَى هَالحايِط [ʕallig ʔiṣṣu:ra ʕala halħa:yiṭ] Only the walls are still standing. بَسّ الحِياطِين بَعَدها باقيَة [bass ʔilħiya:ṭi:n baʕadha ba:qya]

to wall up • **1.** بِنَى [bina:] بِنايَة [bina:ya] *vn: sv* i. They're walling up the doorways and windows in that building. دَيبنُون الشَّبابِيك وَالإبواب مال هَالبِنايَة [daybnu:n ʔiššaba:bi:č wilʔibwa:b ma:l halbina:ya]

wallet • **1.** جِزدان [jizda:n] جِزدانات، جَزادِين [jizda:na:t, jaza:di:n] *pl:* جَزادِين [jaza:di:n] I lost my wallet. ضَيَّعِت جَزداني [ðayyaʕit jazda:ni]

walnut • **1.** جَوزَة [jawza] جَوزات [jawza:t] *pl:* جَوز [jawz] *Collective:* Let's buy some walnuts. خَلّي نِشتِري جُوز [xalli: ništiri ju:z] • **2.** خِشَب جَوز [xišab jawz] This table is made of walnut. هَالميز مسَوَّى مِن خِشَب جُوز [halmi:z msawwa: min xišab ju:z]

walnut tree • **1.** جَوزَة [ju:za] جَوزات [ju:za:t] *pl:* شَجرَة جَوز [šajrat jawz] شَجَرات جَوز [šajara:t ju:z] *pl:* We have a walnut tree in our garden. عِدنا جُوزَة بحَدِيقَتنا [ʕidna ju:za bħadi:qatna]

want • **1.** مَطلَب [maṭlab] مَطالِيب [maṭa:li:b] *pl:* My wants are very modest. مَطالِيبي بَسِيطَة [maṭa:li:bi basi:ṭa]

*** I'll take it for want of something better.** • **1.** راح أقبَلها لِأَن ماكُو شِي أحسَن [ra:ħ ʔaqbalha liʔan ma:ku ši ʔaħsan]

to want • **1.** راد [ra:d] إرادَة [ʔira:da] *vn:* اِنراد [ʔinra:d] *p:* He knows what he wants. يُعرُف شِيرِيد [yuʕruf šiyri:d] I want two sandwiches. أرِيد سَندويجتَين [ʔari:d sandwi:čtayn] How much do you want for your furniture? شقَدّ ترِيد أنطِيك بِهالأثاث؟ [šgadd tri:d ʔanṭi:k bhalʔaθa:θ?] I want to go swimming. أرِيد أسبَح [ʔari:d ʔasbaħ]

want ad • **1.** إعلان [ʔiʕla:n] إعلانات [ʔiʕla:na:t] *pl:*

wanted • **1.** مَطلُوب [maṭlu:b] He is wanted by the police. هُوَّ مَطلُوب مِن الشُّرطَة [huwwa maṭlu:b min ʔiššurṭa]

war • **1.** حَرُب [ħarub] حُرُوب [ħuru:b] *pl:* Where were you during the last war? وين كِنِت أثناء الحَرب الأخِيرَة؟ [wi:n činit ʔaθna:ʔ ʔilħarb ʔilʔaxi:ra?]

holy war • **1.** جِهاد [jiha:d]

ward • **1.** قاوُوش [qa:wu:š] قَواوِيش [qawa:wi:š] *pl:* رَدهَة [radha] رَدهات [radha:t] *pl:* They had to put him in the ward because all the rooms were taken. اِضطَرّوا يحُطُّوه بالقاوُوش لِأَنّ كُلّ الغُرَف مَشغُولَة [ʔiðṭarraw yħuṭṭu:h bilqa:wu:š liʔann kull ʔilɣuraf mašɣu:la]

warden • **1.** مُدِير السِجِن [mudi:r ʔissijin] مُدَراء السِجِن [mudara:ʔ ʔissijin] *pl:*

wardrobe • **1.** قَنطُور [qanṭu:r, kantu:r] قَنطُورات [kanṭu:ra:t] *pl:* What are your clothes doing in my wardrobe? عَجَب حاطّ هدُومَك بِالكَنتُور مالي؟ [ʕajab ħa:ṭṭ hdu:mak bilkantu:r ma:li?] • **2.** طَخُم هدُوم [ṭaxum hdu:m] She bought herself a complete wardrobe. اِشتِرَت طَخُم كامِل هِدُوم [ʔištirat ṭaxum ka:mil hidu:m]

warehouse • **1.** مَخزَن [maxzan] مَخازِن [maxa:zin] *pl:*

warm • **1.** دافِي [da:fi] It's warm today. الجَوّ دافِي اليُوم [ʔijjaww da:fi ʔilyu:m] • **2.** دَفيان [dafya:n] Are you warm enough? إنتَ دَفيان زين؟ [ʔinta dafya:n zi:n?]

to warm • **1.** دَفَّى [daffa:] *sv* i. Come in and warm yourself by the fire. تَعال جَوَّة ودَفِّي نَفسَك يَمّ النّار [taʕa:l jawwa wdaffi nafsak yamm ʔinna:r] • **2.** حِمَى [ħima:] حَمِي [ħamy] *vn:* اِنحِمَى [ʔinħima:] *p:* Please warm up the soup for me. بالله حَمِّيلي الشَّوربَة [ballah ħammi:ly ʔiššu:rba]

to warm up • **1.** مال [ma:l] *sv* i. I can't warm up to him. ما أقدَر أمِيل إلَه [ma: ʔagdar ʔami:l ʔilah]

warmth • **1.** حَماوَة [ħama:wa] The warmth of the fire reached me over here. جَتنِي حَماوَة النّار لِهنا [jatni ħama:wat ʔinna:r lihna]

to warn • **1.** حَذَّر [ħaððar] تَحذِير [taħði:r] *vn: sv* i. They warned me about him. حَذِّرُونِي مِنَّه [ħaððru:ni minnah] • **2.** نِذَر [niðar] أنذَر [ʔanðar] إنذار [ʔinða:r] *vn: sv* i. The government warned that demonstrators would be jailed. الحُكُومَة أنذِرَت بِحَبس اللّي يسَوُّون مُظاهَرات [ʔilħuku:ma ʔanðirat bħabs ʔilli ysawwu:n muða:hara:t]

warning • **1.** تَحذِير [taħði:r] The government broadcast a warning about the flood. الحُكُومَة أذاعَت تَحذِير عَن الفَيضان [ʔilħuku:ma ʔaða:ʕat taħði:r ʕan ʔilfayða:n]

W

to warp • **1.** عَكَّف [ʕakkaf] *sv* u. This wood will warp. هَالنّوع مِن الخِشَب يعَكُّف [hannu:ʕ min ʔilxišab yʕakkuf] • **2.** تعَوَّج [tʕawwaǰ] *sv* a. The records will be warped in the heat. الإسطِوانات تِتعَوَّج بالحَرارَة [ʔilʔiṣṭiwa:na:t titʕawwaǰ bilħara:ra]

wash • **1.** هدُوم مَغسُولَة [hdu:m maɣsu:la] The maid hung the wash on the line. الخَدّامَة شَرَّت الهدُوم المَغسُولَة عَالحَبَل [ʔilxadda:ma šarrat ʔilhdu:m ʔilmaɣsu:la ʕalħabil]

to wash • **1.** غِسَل [ɣisal, xisal] غَسِل [ɣasil] *vn:* اِنغِسَل [ʔinɣisal] *p:* Wash these shirts, please. بالله، غِسلِي هالهدُوم [ballah, ɣisli halhdu:m] This floor hasn't been washed yet. القاع بَعَدها ما اِنغِسلَت [ʔilga:ʕ baʕadha ma: ʔinɣislat] • **2.** غَسَّل [ɣassal, xassal] *sv* i. غِسَل [ɣisal] *sv* i. Did you wash your face? غَسِّلِت وُجهَك؟ [ɣassalit wuǰhak?]

to wash away • **1.** جِرَف [ǰiraf] جَرُف [ǰaruf] *vn:* اِنجِرَف [ʔinǰiraf] *p:* Last year the flood washed away the bridge. السَّنَة اللّي فاتَت الفَيَضان جِرَف الجِّسِر [ʔissanat ʔilli fa:tat ʔilfayaða:n ǰiraf ʔiǰǰisir]

to wash up • **1.** غَسَّل [ɣassal] *sv* i. غِسَل [ɣisal] *sv* i. I'd like to wash up before supper. أرِيد أغَسِّل قَبُل الأكِل [ʔari:d ʔaɣassil gabul ʔilʔakil]

* **He's washed up.** • **1.** اِنتِهَى أمرَه [ʔintiha: ʔamrah]

* **Our plans for a trip are all washed up.** • **1.** مَشرُوعنا مال السَفرَة فِشَل [mašru:ʕna ma:l ʔissafra fišal]

waste • **1.** تَبدِيد [tabdi:d] That's plain waste. هَذا تَبدِيد واضِح [ha:ða tabdi:d wa:ðiħ] • **2.** مَضيَعَة [maðyaʕa] It's a waste of time and energy. هاي مَضيَعَة لِلوَقِت وَالجَّهد [ha:y maðyaʕa lilwakit wiǰǰahid]

* **Haste makes waste.** • **1.** العَجَلَة مِن الشَيطان [ʔilʕaǰala min ʔiššayṭa:n]

to go to waste • **1.** بار [ba:r] بَور [bu:r] *vn: sv* u. A good cook doesn't let anything go to waste. الطَّبّاخَة الزَّينَة ما تخَلّي شِي يبُور [ʔiṭṭabba:xa ʔizzayna ma: txalli ši ybu:r] • **2.** راح [ra:ħ] *sv* u. ضاع [ða:ʕ] ضِياع [ðiya:ʕ] *vn: sv* i. His talents are going to waste. قابلِيّاتَه رايحَة عَبَث [qa:bliyya:tah ra:yħa ʕabaθ]

to lay waste • **1.** دُمَر [dumar] دَمُر [damur] *vn:* اِندُمَر [ʔindumar] *p:* The storm has laid waste the entire area. العاصِفَة دُمرَت المَنطَقَة كُلّها [ʔilʕa:ṣifa dumrat ʔilmanṭaqa kullha]

to waste • **1.** ضَيَّع [ðayyaʕ] تَضيِيع [taðyi:ʕ] *vn: sv* i. He wastes a lot of time talking. يضَيِّع هوايَة وَقِت بِالحَكي [yiðayyiʕ hwa:ya wakit bilħači]

wastebasket • **1.** سَلَّة مُهمَلات [sallat muhmala:t] سلال مُهمَلات [sla:l muhmala:t] *pl:*

watch • **1.** ساعَة [sa:ʕa] ساعات [sa:ʕa:t] *pl:* By my watch it's five. بِالخَمسَة حَسَب ساعَتِي [bilxamsa ħasab sa:ʕati]

to watch • **1.** تفَرَّج عَلَي [tfarraǰ ʕala] *sv* i. I've been watching this program for about an hour. صارلِي حَوالِي ساعَة دَأتفَرَّج عَلَى هالمَنهَج [ṣa:rli ħawa:li sa:ʕa daʔatfarraǰ ʕala halmanhaǰ] • **2.** باوَع [ba:waʕ] مُباوَعَة [muba:waʕa] *vn: sv* i. شاف [ša:f] *sv* u. Watch how I do it. باوِع شلُون دَأسَوِّيها [ba:wiʕ šlu:n daʔasawwi:ha] • **3.** دار بَال [da:r ba:l] *sv* i. Who's going to watch the children? مِنُو راح يدِير بالَه عَالجُّهال؟ [minu ra:ħ ydi:r ba:la ʕaǰǰaha:l?] • **4.** راقَب [ra:qab] مُراقَبَة [mura:qaba] *vn: sv* u. That fellow needs close watching. هَذا واحِد لازِم يراقبَه زين [ha:ða wa:ħid la:zim yra:qbah zi:n] • **5.** فَكّ [fakk] *sv* u. دار بَال [da:r ba:l] *sv* i. Watch yourself with him. فُكّ عينَك زين ويّاه [fukk ʕaynak zi:n wiyya:h]

to watch out • **1.** دار بَال [da:r ba:l] *sv* i. Watch out when you cross the street. دِير بالَك مِن تُعبُر الشّارِع [di:r ba:lak min tuʕbur ʔišša:riʕ]

to watch out for • **1.** ترَقَّب [traqqab] *sv* a. I'll be watching out for you to arrive at the station. راح أترَقَّب وُصُولَك لِلمَحَطَّة [ra:ħ ʔatraqqab wuṣu:lak lilmaħaṭṭa]

watchmaker • **1.** ساعَجِي [sa:ʕači] ساعَجِيَّة [sa:ʕačiyya] *pl:*

watchman • **1.** حارِس [ħa:ris] حُرّاس [ħurra:s] *pl:*

water • **1.** ماي [ma:y] مَيّ [mayy] Please give me a glass of water. بالله إنطِينِي كلاص ماي [ballah ʔinṭi:ni gla:ṣ ma:y]

to water • **1.** سِقَى [siga:] سَقِي [sagi] *vn:* اِنسِقَى [ʔinsiga:] *p:* I water the garden every day. آنِي أسقِي الحَدِيقَة يَومِيّاً [ʔa:ni ʔasgi ʔilħadi:qa yawmiyyan] Have the horses been watered yet? سقِيت الخَيل لَو بَعَد؟ [sgi:t ʔilxayl law baʕad?] • **2.** دَمَّع [dammaʕ] تَدمِيع [tadmi:ʕ] *vn: sv* i. My eyes are watering. عيُونِي دَتدَمِّع [ʕyu:ni daddammiʕ] • **3.** سال [sa:l] سَيل [sayl] *vn: sv* i. The cake makes my mouth water. الكَيكَة خَلَّت لُعابِي يسِيل [ʔilkayka xallat luʕa:bi ysi:l]

waterfall • **1.** شَلّال [šalla:l] شَلّالات [šalla:la:t] *pl:*

watermelon • **1.** رَقِّيَّة [raggiyya] رَقِّيات [raggiyya:t] *pl:* رَقِّي [raggi] *Collective*

waterproof • **1.** ضِدّ المُطَر [ðidd ʔilmuṭar] Is this coat waterproof? هَالمِعطَف ضِدّ المُطَر؟ [halmiʕṭaf ðidd ʔilmuṭar?] • **2.** ضِدّ المَيّ [ðidd ʔilmayy] Is this watch waterproof? هَالسّاعَة ضِدّ المَيّ [hassa:ʕa ðidd ʔilmayy]

wave • **1.** مُوجَة [mu:ǰa] أمواج [ʔamwa:ǰ] *pl:* مَوج [mu:ǰ] *Collective:* The waves are very high today. المُوج كُلّش عالِي اليُوم [ʔilmu:ǰ kulliš ʕa:li ʔilyu:m] • **2.** مَوجَة [mawǰa] مَوجات [mawǰa:t] *pl:* A wave of enthusiasm swept the country. فَدّ مَوجَة مِن الحَماس إجتاحَت البَلَد [fadd mawǰa min ʔilħama:s ʔiǰta:ħat ʔilbalad]

W

to wave • **1.** رَفرَف [rafraf] رَفرَفَة [rafrafa] *vn:* ترَفرَف [trafraf] *p:* The flags were waving in the breeze. الإعلام كانَت دَترَفرف بالهَوا [ʔiliʕlaːm čaːnat datrafrif bilhawa] • **2.** أشَّر [ʔaššar] تَأشِير [taʔšiːr] *vn: sv* i. I waved to him with my hand. أشَّرِتلَه بِيدِي [ʔaššaritlah biːdi]

wax • **1.** شَمِع [šamiʕ]

way • **1.** طَرِيق [ṭariːq] طُرُق [ṭuruq] *pl:* Is this the way to Baghdad? هَذا الطَّرِيق لِبَغداد؟ [haːða ʔiṭṭariːq lbaydaːd?] Are you going my way? رايِح عَلَى طَرِيقِي؟ [raːyiħ ʕala ṭariːqi?] • **2.** طَرِيقَة [ṭariːqa] طُرُق [ṭuruq] *pl:* That's just his way of dealing with employees. هَذِي عادَةً طَرِيقَة مُعامَلتَه لِلمُوَظَّفِين [haːði ʕaːdatan ṭariːqat muʕaːmaltah lilmuwaððafiːn] There are different ways of doing things. أكُو عِدَّة طُرُق [ʔaku ʕiddat ṭuruq] • **3.** شِكِل [šikil] You shouldn't treat people this way. ما لازِم تعامِل النّاس بِهَالشِّكِل [maː laːzim tʕaːmil ʔinnaːs bhaššikil] That's the way he wants it. يرِيدها هَالشِّكِل [yriːdha haššikil] • **4.** دَرُب [darub] Do you know your way around here? تُعرُف دَربَك بِهَالمَنطِقَة؟ [tuʕruf darbak bhalmanṭiqa?] Do you know your way around here? تِندَلّ هَالمَنطِقَة؟ [tindall halmanṭiqa?] • **5.** مَصارِيف [maṣaːriːf] He paid my way. هُوَّ دِفَع المَصارِيف مالتِي [huwwa difaʕ ʔilmaṣaːriːf maːlti] I paid my own way at college. دفَعت مَصارِيف دِراستِي مِن جِيبِي الخاصّ [dfaʕit maṣaːriːf diraːsti min jiːbi ʔilxaːṣṣ] • **6.** أمُر [ʔamur] أوامِر [ʔawaːmir] *pl:* He'll make his way wherever he is. يِقدَر يدَبُّر أمرَه وَين ما تذِبَّه [yigdar ydabbur ʔamrah wiːn maː dðibbah]

* **Everything is going along (in) the same old way.** • **1.** كُلشِي بَعدَه مِثِلما كان [kullši baʕdah miθilma čaːn]

* **Everything turned out the way they wanted.** • **1.** كُلشِي صار مِثِلما رادَوا [kullši ṣaːr miθilma raːdaw]

* **Have it your own way!** • **1.** مِثِلما ترِيد [miθilmaː triːd] / كَيفَك [kayfak]

* **I'm afraid he's in a bad way.** • **1.** أخاف حالتَه مُو زَينَة [ʔaxaːf ħaːltah muː zayna]

* **I don't see my way clear to do it now.** • **1.** ما أشُوف مِن المُناسَبَة أسَوِّيها هَسَّة [maː ʔašuːf min ʔilmunaːsaba ʔasawwiːha hassa]

* **Christmas is still a long way off.** • **1.** بَعَد هوايَة لِكرِسمَس [baʕad hwaːya likrismas]

a long way • **1.** بعِيد [biʕiːd] The school is a long way from our house. المَدرَسَة بِعِيدَة عَن بَيتنا [ʔilmadrasa biʕiːda ʕan baytna]

by the way • **1.** بِالمُناسَبَة [bilmunaːsaba] By the way, are you coming with us tonight? بِالمُناسَبَة إنتَ جاي وِيّانا هاللَّيلَة؟ [bilmunaːsaba ʔinta ǰaːy wiyyaːna hallayla?]

by way of • **1.** عَلَى طَرِيق [ʕala ṭariːq] We went by way of Damascus. رِحنا عَلَى طَرِيق الشّام [riħna ʕala ṭariːq ʔiššaːm] • **2.** عَلَى سَبِيل [ʕala sabiːl] He said it by way of a joke. قالها عَلَى سَبِيل النُّكتَة [gaːlha ʕala sabiːl ʔinnukta]

in a way • **1.** مِن جِهَة [min ǰiha] نَوعاً ما [nuːʕan maː] In a way he's right. مِن جِهَة هُوَّ صَحِيح [min ǰiha huwwa ṣaħiːħ]

in no way • **1.** أبَداً [ʔabadan] This is in no way better than what you had before. هاي أبَداً مُو أحسَن مِن اللِّي كانَت عِندَك قَبُل [haːy ʔabadan muː ʔaħsan min ʔilli čaːnat ʕindak gabul]

in the way of • **1.** مِن [min] What have you got in the way of radios? شَكُو عِدكُم مِن الرّادِيُوات؟ [šaku ʕidkum min ʔirraːdyuwaːt?]

in what way • **1.** شلَون [šluːn] In what way is that better? شلُون هاي أحسَن؟ [šluːn haːy ʔaħsan?]

out of the way • **1.** مُو عالرِجل [muː ʕarriǰil] This place is somewhat out of the way. هَالمَحَلّ شوَيَّة مُو عالرِّجِل [halmuħall šwayya muː ʕarriǰil]

right of way • **1.** طَرِيق [ṭariːq] You shouldn't have gone through, I had the right of way. ما كان لازِم تفُوت، الطَّرِيق كان إلِي [maː čaːn laːzim tfuːt, ʔiṭṭariːq čaːn ʔili]

to get under way • **1.** تقَدَّم [tqaddam] *sv* a. إبتِدَى [ʔibtida] *sv* i. The project is slowly getting under way. المَشرُوع دَيِتقَدَّم شوَيَّة شوَيَّة [ʔilmašruːʕ dayitqaddam šwayya šwayya]

to give way • **1.** إنقِطَع [ʔingiṭaʕ] *sv* i. The rope's giving way. الحَبِل دَينقِطِع [ʔilħabil dayingiṭiʕ]

to go out of one's way • **1.** تكَلَّف [tkallaf] *sv* a. I don't want you to go out of your way for my sake. ما أرِيدَك تِتكَلَّف عَلَى مُودِي [maː ʔariːdak titkallaf ʕala muːdi] • **2.** بِذَل [biðal] بَذِل [baðil] *vn: sv* i. We went out of our way to make him comfortable. بذَلنا جُهُودنا حَتَّى نخَلِّيه يرتاح [bðalna ǰuhuːdna ħatta nxalliːh yirtaːħ]

way out • **1.** مَخرَج [maxraǰ] مَخارِج [maxaːriǰ] *pl:* I don't see any way out of this mess. ما دَأشُوف أيّ مَخرَج مِن هَالوُرطَة [maː daʔašuːf ʔayy maxraǰ min halwurṭa]

we • **1.** إحنَا [ʔiħna] We're not the ones responsible. إحنا مُو المَسؤُولِين [ʔiħna muː ʔilmasʔuliːn]

* **We have a house in Najef.** • **1.** عِدنا بَيت بِالنَّجَف [ʕidna bayt binnaǰaf]

* **We haven't seen him.** • **1.** ما شِفناه [maː šifnaːh]

Weak • **1.** خَفِيف [xafiːf] Would you like your tea weak or strong? ترِيد شايَك خَفِيف لَو طُوخ؟ [triːd čaːyak xafiːf law ṭuːx?] • **2.** ضَعِيف [ðaʕiːf] He's still weak from his illness. بَعدَه ضَعِيف مِن المَرَض [baʕdah ðaʕiːf min ʔilmarað] The bridge is weak. الجِّسِر ضَعِيف [ʔiǰǰisir ðaʕiːf]

to weaken • **1.** ضَعَّف [ðaʕʕaf] *sv* u. The flood weakened the bridge. الفَيَضان ضَعَّف الجِّسِر [ʔilfayaðaːn ðaʕʕaf ʔiǰǰisir] • **2.** أضعَف [ʔaðʕaf] إضعاف [ʔiðʕaːf] *vn: sv* u. Aspirin weakens you. الأسبَرِين يضعِفَك [ʔalʔaspariːn yðiʕfak]

weakness • **1.** نُقطَة ضُعُف [nuqṭat ðuʕuf] نُقاط ضُعُف [nuqaːṭ ðuʕuf] *pl:* That's his biggest weakness. هَذِي أهَمّ نُقطَة ضُعُف عِندَه [haːði ʔahamm nuqṭat ðuʕuf ʕindah]

W

wealth • **1.** ثَروَة [θarwa] They wasted the wealth of the nation. ضَيّعَوا ثَروَة البَلَد [ðayyʕaw θarwat ʔilbalad]

wealthy • **1.** زَنكِين [zangi:n] زَناكِين [zana:gi:n] *pl:* غَنِي [ɣani] أغنِياء [ʔaɣniya:ʔ] *pl:* She married a wealthy merchant. تزَوّجَت فَدّ تاجِر زَنكِين [dzawwǰat fadd ta:ǰir zangi:n]

weapon • **1.** سلاح [sla:ħ] أسلِحَة [ʔasliħa] *pl:* All weapons have to be turned over to the police. كُلّ الأسلِحَة لازِم تِتسَلَّم لِلشُّرطَة [kull ʔilʔasliħa la:zim titsallam liššurṭa]

wear • **1.** هدُوم [hdu:m] I'm sorry, we carry only men's wear. مِتأسِّف، عِدنا هدُوم رِياجِيل بَسّ [mitʔassif, ʕidna hdu:m riya:ǰi:l bass] • **2.** لِبِس [libis] There's still a lot of wear left in this suit. هَالقاط بَعَد بِيه لِبِس هوايَة [halqa:ṭ baʕad bi:h libis hwa:ya]

*** The cuffs are showing signs of wear.**
• **1.** الردانات مبَيّنَة سايفَة [ʔirrida:na:t mbayyna sa:yfa]

to wear • **1.** لِبَس [libas] لِبِس [libis] *vn:* اِنلِبَس [ʔinlibas] *p:* He never wears a hat. أبَد ما يِلبَس شَفقَة [ʔabad ma: yilbas šafqa] What did she wear? شلِبسَت؟ [šlibsat?] • **2.** طَوَّل [ṭawwal] *sv* i. This coat didn't wear well. هَالمِعطَف ما طَوَّل هوايَة [halmiʕṭaf ma: ṭawwal hwa:ya]

*** She wears her hair short.** • **1.** هِيَّ تقُصّ شَعَرها قصَيِّر [hiyya tguṣṣ šaʕarha gṣayyir]

to wear down • **1.** قام [ga:m] *sv* u. These heels are all worn down. هَالكعُوبَة مال قنادِر كُلّها قامَت [haličʕu:ba ma:l qna:dir kullha ga:mat]

*** We finally wore him down.** • **1.** تالِيها نَزَّلنا عَن بَغِلتَه [ta:li:ha nazzalna ʕan baɣiltah]

to wear off • **1.** بُرَد [burad] *sv* a. Wait till the excitement wears off. اِنتِظِر إلَى أن تبرَد الهَوسَة [ʔintiðir ʔila ʔan tibrad ʔilhu:sa] • **2.** راح [ra:ħ] *sv* u. The paint has worn off my car in several spots. الصُّبُغ مال سَيّارتي راح مِن كَم مَكان [ʔiṣṣubuɣ ma:l sayya:rti ra:ħ min čam maka:n]

to wear out • **1.** اِستَهلَك [ʔistahlak] اِستِهلاك [ʔistihla:k] *vn:* *sv* a. The tires are all worn out. التّايَرات كُلّها اِستَهلكَت [ʔatta:yira:t kullha ʔistahilkat] Our furniture is worn out. أثاثنا اِستَهلَك [ʔaθa:θna ʔistahlak] • **2.** شَقَّق [šaggag] تشَقَّق [tšaggag] *p:* He wore out his shoes quickly. شَقَّق قُندَرتَه بِالعَجَل [šaggag qundartah bilʕaǰal] • **3.** هِلَك [hilak] هَلاك [hala:k] *vn:* *sv* i. Just don't wear yourself out! لا تِهلِك نَفسَك [la: tihlik nafsak]

weather • **1.** جَوّ [ǰaww] أجواء [ʔaǰwa:ʔ] *pl:* طَقِس [ṭaqis] مَناخ [mana:x] How is the weather today? شلُون الجَّوّ اليُوم؟ [šlu:n ʔiǰǰaww ʔilyu:m?]

*** I'm a little under the weather today.**
• **1.** ما دَأحِسّ هَالقَدّ زَين هَاليَوم [ma: daʔaħiss halgadd zayn halyu:m]

to weather • **1.** دَبَّر أمر [dabbar ʔamr] تَدبِير أمر [tadbi:r ʔamr] *vn:* *sv* i. How did you weather the flood? شلُون دَبَّرت أمرَك بِالفَيَضان [šlu:n dabbarit ʔamrak bilfayaða:n]

to weave • **1.** حاك [ħa:k, ħa:č] حَوك، حياكَة [ħu:k, ħya:ka] *vn:* اِنحاك [ʔinħa:k] *p:* The children wove this rug at school. الأطفال حاكَوا هَالبساط بِالمَدرَسَة [ʔilʔaṭfa:l ħa:kaw halbsa:ṭ bilmadrasa]

weaver • **1.** حايِك [ħa:yik, ħa:yič] حِيّاك [ħiyya:k, ħiyya:č] *pl:* He's a weaver. هُوَّ حايِك [huwwa ħa:yik]

wedding • **1.** عِرِس [ʕiris] أعراس [ʔaʕra:s] *pl:* I was at the wedding but not at the reception. كِنِت بِالعِرِس بَسّ مُو بِالحَفلَة [činit bilʕiris bass mu: bilħafla]

Wednesday • **1.** الأربِعاء [ʔilʔarbiʕa:ʔ]

weeds • **1.** حَشِيش [ħaši:š] The whole garden is full of weeds. الحَدِيقَة مَترُوسَة حَشِيش [ʔilħadi:qa matru:sa ħaši:š]

to weed • **1.** شِلَع حَشِيش [šilaʕ ħaši:š] شَلِع حَشِيش [šaliʕ ħaši:š] *vn:* *sv* a. I've got to weed the garden. لازِم أشلَع الحَشِيش مِن الحَدِيقَة [la:zim ʔašlaʕ ʔilħaši:š min ʔilħadi:qa]

week • **1.** إسبُوع [ʔisbu:ʕ] أسابِيع [ʔasa:bi:ʕ] *pl:* I'll be back in three weeks. راح أرجَع بخِلال ثلَث أسابِيع [ra:ħ ʔarǰaʕ bxila:l tlaθ ʔasa:bi:ʕ]

by the week • **1.** إسبُوعِيَّة [ʔisbu:ʕiyya] They pay by the week. يدفعُون إسبُوعِيَّة [ydifʕu:n ʔisbu:ʕiyya]

weekend • **1.** عُطلَة إسبُوع [ʕuṭlat ʔisbu:ʕ] عُطَل أسابِيع [ʕuṭal ʔasa:bi:ʕ] *pl:* We decided to spend the weekend at the lake. قَرَّرنا نِقضِي عُطلَة الإسبُوع بالبُحَيرَة [qarrarna nigði ʕuṭlat ʔilʔisbu:ʕ bilbuħayra]

weekly • **1.** إسبُوعِي [ʔisbu:ʕi] He publishes a weekly newspaper. يطَلِّع جَرِيدَة إسبُوعِيَّة [yṭalliʕ ǰari:da ʔisbu:ʕiyya] • **2.** مَرَّة بِالإسبُوع [marra bilisbu:ʕ] أسبُوعِيّاً [ʔusbu:ʕiyyan] This magazine appears weekly. هالمَجَلَّة تِطلَع مَرَّة بِالإسبُوع [halmaǰalla tiṭlaʕ marra bilʔisbu:ʕ]

to weep • **1.** بِكَى [biča:] *sv* i. She wept bitter tears. بِكَت بحُرقَة [bičat bħurga]

to weigh • **1.** وُزَن [wuzan] وَزِن [wazin] *vn:* اِنوُزَن [ʔinwuzan] *p:* Please weigh this package for me. بالله أوزِنلي هَالرُّزمَة [ballah ʔu:zinli harruzma] He always weighs his words carefully. دائِماً يُوزِن حكاياتَه زين [da:ʔiman yu:zin ħča:ya:tah zi:n]

*** This piece of meat weighs four pounds.**
• **1.** هَالوُصلَة اللَّحَم وَزِنها أربَع كَيلُوات [halwuṣlat ʔillaħam wazinha ʔarbaʕ ki:luwa:t]

W

*** The responsibility weighs heavily on me.**
• **1.** هَالمَسؤُولِيَّة كُلِّش زَحمَة [halmasʔuːliyya kulliš zaħma]

weight • **1.** عِيار [ʕiyaːr] The weights are under the scale. العِيارات جَوَّة المِيزان [ʔilʕyaːraːt ǰawwa ʔilmiːzaːn] • **2.** وَزِن [wazin] ثُقُل [θugul] Did you put down the weight of the package? سَجَّلِت وَزِن الرُّزمَة؟ [saǰǰalit wazin ʔirruzma?] Don't attach much weight to what he says. لا تِنطِي هوايَة وَزِن لِحَكيَه [laː tinṭi hwaːya wazin lħačyah] • **3.** حساب [ħsaːb] وَزِن [wazin] His opinion carries great weight. رأيَه يِنحِسِبلَه حساب [raʔyah yinħisiblah ħsaːb] His opinion carries great weight. رأيَه إلَه وَزِن [raʔyah ʔilah wazin]

weird • **1.** غَرِيب [ɣariːb] That's a weird story. هاي حِكايَة غَرِيبَة [haːy ħčaːya ɣariːba]

welcome • **1.** اِستِقبال [ʔistiqbaːl] اِستِقبالات [ʔistiqbaːlaːt] *pl:* They gave us a warm welcome. اِستَقبِلُونا اِستِقبال حارّ [ʔistaqbiluːna ʔistiqbaːl ħaːrr] They gave us a warm welcome. رَحِّبَوا بِينا زين [raħħibaw biːna ziːn] • **2.** عَالمَرام [ʕalmaraːm] This is a welcome change in government policy. هَالتَّغيير بِسِياسَة الحُكُومَة كان عَالمَرام [hattaɣyiːr bsiyaːsat ʔilħukuːma čaːn ʕalmaraːm]

*** You're always welcome here.**
• **1.** شوَقِت ما تِجِي أهلاً وَسَهلاً [šwakit maː tiǰi ʔahlan wasahlan] / هَذا مِثِل بَيتكُم [haːða miθil baytkum]
*** You're welcome.** • **1.** أهلاً وَسَهلاً [ʔahlan wasahlan] / مَمنُون [mamnuːn]
to welcome • **1.** اِستَقبَل [ʔistaqbal] *sv* i. رَحَّب ب [raħħab b-] *sv* i. They welcomed us warmly. اِستَقبِلُونا بِالتِّرحاب [ʔistaqbiluːna bittirħaːb] They welcomed us warmly. رَحِّبَوا بِينا [raħħibaw biːna]

to weld • **1.** لِحَم [liħam] لَحِم [laħim] *vn: sv* i. He's welding the bumper on my car. دَيِلحِم الدَّعّامِيَّة مال سَيّارتِي [dayilħim ʔiddaʕʕaːmiyya maːl sayyaːrti]

welfare • **1.** رَخاء [raxaːʔ] The welfare of the country depends on this project. رَخاء البِلاد يِعتِمِد عَلَى هَذا المَشرُوع [raxaːʔ ʔilbilaːd yiʕtimid ʕala haːða ʔilmašruːʕ]

well • **1.** بير [biːr] بيارَة، آبار [byaːr, ʔaːbaːr] *pl:* They're digging a well back of the house. دَيحَفرُون بير وَرا البَيت [dayħaffruːn biːr wara ʔilbayt] • **2.** زَين [ziːn] Do you know him well? تعُرفَه زين؟ [tʕurfah ziːn?] I'm not feeling well today. آنِي ما دَأحِسّ هَالقَدّ زين اليُوم [ʔaːni maː daʔaħiss halgadd ziːn ʔilyuːm] The new business is doing very well. الشُّغُل زين دَيمشِي [ʔiššuɣul ziːn dayimši] Please let me do it. Very well. بالله خَلِّينِي أسَوِّيها زين [ballah xalliːni ʔasawwiːha ziːn] • **3.** هوايَة [hwaːya] There were well over 1000 people. كانَوا هوايَة أزيَد مِن ألف واحِد [čaːnaw hwaːya ʔazyad min ʔalf waːħid] • **4.** ها [haː] Well, where did you come from? ها، منِين جِيت؟ [ha, mniːn ǰiːt?]

*** Best for you leave to leave her as she is**
• **1.** أحسَنلَك تخَلِّيها مِثلما هِيَّ
[ʔaħsanlak txalliːha miθilmaː hiyya]
as well as • **1.** مِثلما [miθilma] مِثِل [miθil] He talks Arabic as well as I do. يِحكِي عَرَبِي مِثلما أحكِي آنِي [yiħči ʕarabi miθilma ʔaħči ʔaːni] He talks Arabic as well as I do. يِحكِي عَرَبِي مِثلِي [yiħči ʕarabi miθli]
*** He knows Arabic as well as several other languages.**
• **1.** يُعرُف عَرَبِي ويُعرُف لُغات أُخرَى [yuʕruf ʕarabi wyuʕruf luɣaːt ʔuxra]
*** He couldn't very well refuse to come.**
• **1.** ما كان أكُو مَجال يِرفُض الدَّعوَة [maː čaːn ʔaku maǰaːl yirfuð ʔiddaʕwa]
*** He could very well change his mind.**
• **1.** أكُو اِحتِمال كَبِير يبَدِّل فِكرَه [ʔaku ʔiħtimaːl čabiːr ybaddil fikrah]
to get well • **1.** طاب [ṭaːb] *sv* i. صار [ṣaːr] *sv* i. First I must get well again. خَلِّي أطِيب أوَّل [xalli ʔaṭiːb ʔawwal] I hope you get well soon! إن شاء الله تصِير زين عَن قَرِيب [ʔinšaːllah tṣiːr ziːn ʕan qariːb]

well-behaved • **1.** عاقِل [ʕaːqil] مأدَّب [mʔaddab] She's a well-behaved child. هاي فَدّ طِفلَة كُلِّش عاقلَة [haːy fadd ṭifla kulliš ʕaːqla]

well-done • **1.** مَطبُوخ زَين [maṭbuːx zayn] مِستوِي زَين [mistiwiː zayn] The meat is well-done. اللَّحَم مَطبُوخ زين [ʔillaħam maṭbuːx ziːn]

well-to-do • **1.** زَنكِين [zangiːn] زَناكِين [zanaːgiːn] *pl:* His family is well-to-do. عائِلتَه زَنكِينَة [ʕaːʔiltah zangiːna]

west • **1.** غَرب [ɣarb] The wind is from the west. الهَوا مِن الغَرب [ʔilhawa min ʔalɣarb] The sign points west. السَّهِم يأشِّر عالغَرب [ʔissahim yiʔaššir ʕalɣarb] • **2.** غَربِي [ɣarbi] There's a west wind today. أكُو هَوا غَربِي اليُوم [ʔaku hawa ɣarbi ʔilyuːm]

western • **1.** غَربِي [ɣarbi] The Syrian Desert extends into the western part of Iraq. بادِيَة الشّام تِمتَدّ لِلقِسم الغَربِي مِن العِراق [baːdiyat ʔiššaːm timtadd lilqism ʔilɣarbi min ʔilʕiraːq]

westward • **1.** غَرب [ɣarb] They headed westward. اتِّجهَوا لِلغَرب [ʔittiǰhaw lilɣarb]

wet • **1.** مبَلَّل [mballal] مِتنَقِّع [mitnaggiʕ] منَقَّع [mnaggaʕ] My socks are wet. جوارِيبِي مبَلّلَة [ǰwaːriːbi mballila] I'm wet through and through. آنِي مِتنَقِّع مِن فُوق لِجَوَّة [ʔaːni mitnaggiʕ min fuːg liǰawwa] • **2.** رَطِب [raṭib] We had a wet summer. مَرّ عَلينا صَيف رَطِب [marr ʕaliːna ṣayf raṭib] • **3.** جدِيد [ǰidiːd] The paint is still wet. الصُّبُغ بَعدَه جدِيد [ʔiṣṣubuɣ baʕdah ǰdiːd] The paint is still wet. الصُّبُغ بَعدَه ما يابِس [ʔiṣṣubuɣ baʕdah maː yaːbis]
to get wet • **1.** تنَقَّع [tnaggaʕ] تنِقِّع [tniggiʕ] *vn: sv* a. تبَلَّل [tballal] *sv* a. I got wet yesterday in the rain. تنَقَّعِت مِن المُطَر البارحَة [tnaggaʕit min ʔilmuṭar ʔilbaːrħa]

W

to wet • **1.** بال [ba:l] بَول [bu:l] *vn: sv* u. The baby wet his pants. الطِّفِل بال بِلباسَه [ʔiṭṭifil ba:l bilba:sah]

whale • **1.** حُوتَة [ħu:ta] حُوتات [ħu:ta:t] *pl:* حُوت [ħu:t] *Collective*

what • **1.** ش [š-] What would you like to eat? شيعِجبَك تاكُل؟ [šyʕiǰbak ta:kul?] • **2.** شِنُو [šinu] What things are missing? شِنُو الأَشياء النّاقصَة؟ [šinu: ʔilʔašya:ʔ ʔinna:gṣa?] What's the color of the gloves? شِنُو لُون الكفُوف؟ [šinu: lu:n ʔilčfu:f?] • **3.** شلُون [šlu:n] شقَدّ [šgadd] What beautiful flowers you have in your garden! شلُون حِلو هَالوَرِد اللِّي عِندَك بِالحَدِيقَة [šlu:n ħilw halwarid ʔilli ʕindak bilħadi:qa] What nonsense! شلُون لَغوَة [šlu:n laɣwa] • **4.** بَيش [bi:š] What time is it? السّاعَة بيش؟ [ʔissa:ʕa biyš?] • **5.** يا [ya:] Do you know what train we're supposed to take? تُعرُف يا قِطار لازِم ناخُذ؟ [tuʕruf ya: qiṭa:r la:zim na:xuð?] • **6.** اللِّي [ʔilli] That's just what I wanted to avoid. هَذا الشّي اللِّي رِدِت أتحاشاه [ha:ða ʔišši ʔilli ridit ʔatħa:ša:h]

*** He certainly knows what's what.**
• **1.** مُؤَكَّد هُوَّ يُعرُف شَكُو شماكُو [muʔakkad huwwa yuʕruf šaku šma:ku]

*** He didn't get there in time, but what of it?**
• **1.** ما وُصَل لِهناك عَالوَقِت، بَسّ شيهِمّ؟ [ma: wuṣal lihna:k ʕalwakit, bass šyhimm?]

*** What about me?** • **1.** وآني؟ [wʔa:ni?]

what ... for • **1.** إلوَيش [ʔilwi:š] لَيش [li:š] لُوَيش [luwi:š] What did you do that for? لُويش سَوَّيتها هاي؟ [luwi:š sawwi:tha ha:y?]

what's more • **1.** بِالإضافَة [bilʔiða:fa] And what's more, he is very efficient. وَبِالإضافَة لِهذا، هُوَّ قَدِير [wbʔilʔiða:fa lha:ða, huwwa qadi:r] • **2.** هَمّ [hamm] I'm leaving, and what's more, I'm taking the furniture. راح أرُوح وآخُذ الأثاث هَمّ [ra:ħ ʔaru:ħ wa:xuð ʔilʔaθa:θ hamm]

whatever • **1.** شما [šma] Whatever he does is all right with me. شما يسَوِّي ما يخالِف [šma: ysawwi ma: yxa:lif] Do whatever you want. سَوِّي شما ترِيد [sawwi šma tri:d] She's lost whatever respect she had for him. ضَيّعَت شما كان عِدها مِن الإحتِرام إلَه [ðayyʕat šma: ča:n ʕidha min ʔilʔiħtira:m ʔilah] • **2.** ش [š-] Whatever made you do that? شخَلّاك تسَوِّي هاي؟ [šxalla:k tsawwi ha:y?] • **3.** أبَداً [ʔabadan] I have no money whatever. ما عِندِي فلُوس أبَداً [ma: ʕindi flu:s ʔabadan]

whatsoever • **1.** أبَداً [ʔabadan] I have no money whatsoever. ما عِندِي فلُوس أبَداً [ma: ʕindi flu:s ʔabadan]

wheat • **1.** حُنطَة [ħunṭa] They raise a lot of wheat in Iraq. يزرعُون هوايَة حُنطَة بِالعِراق [yzirʕu:n hwa:ya ħunṭa bilʕira:q]

wheel • **1.** چَرخ [čarix] چرُوخ [čru:x] *pl:* This wheel on that wagon is broken. الچَرخ مال هَالعَرَبانَة مَكسُور [ʔilčarix ma:l halʕaraba:na maksu:r]

to wheel • **1.** دِفَع [difaʕ] دَفِع [dafiʕ] *vn:* اِندِفَع [ʔindifaʕ] *p:* Wheel the baby carriage into the garage. إدفَع عَرَبانَة الجّاهِل لِلكَراج [ʔidfaʕ ʕaraba:nat ʔiǰǰa:hil lilgara:ǰ]

to wheel around • **1.** اِفتَرّ [ʔiftarr] *sv* a. He wheeled around suddenly and fired. عَلَى غَفلَة فتَرّ وَشَوَّت [ʕala ɣafla ftarr wšawwat]

when • **1.** وَقِت [waqit, wakit] أوقات [ʔawqa:t] *pl:* يَمتَى [yamta] When can I see you again? شوَقِت أشُوفَك مَرَّة لُخ؟ [šwakit ʔašu:fak marra lux?] • **2.** مِن [min] لَمّا [lamma] لَمّات [lamma:t] *pl:* لَمَّن [lamman] When he calls up tell him I'm not here. مِن يخابُر قُلَّه آنِي ما هنا [min yxa:bur gullah ʔa:ni ma: hna] When the work is done you can go. تِقدَر ترُوح مِن يِخلَص الشُّغُل [tigdar tru:ħ min yixlaṣ ʔiššuɣul] I wasn't home when he called. ما كِنِت بِالبَيت لَمّا خابَر [ma: činit bilbayt lamma xa:bar]

*** There are times when I enjoy being alone.**
• **1.** تِجِي أوقات يعجِبنِي أكُون لوَحدِي [tiǰi ʔawqa:t yiʕǰibni ʔaku:n lwaħdi]

whenever • **1.** وَقتما [wakit ma:] Come to see us whenever you have time. زُورنا شوَقِت ما يصِير عِندَك وَقِت [zu:rna šwakit ma: yṣi:r ʕindak wakit] • **2.** كُلّ ما، كُلّما [kull ma:, kullma] Whenever we have a picnic it rains. كُلّما نسَوِّي سَفرَة، تقُوم تُمطُر [kullma: nsawwi safra, tgu:m tumṭur]

*** Whenever did you find time to write?**
• **1.** شلُون دَبَّرِت وَقِت حَتَّى تِكتِب؟ [šlu:n dabbarit wakit ħatta tiktib?]

where • **1.** وين [wi:n] Where is the nearest hotel? وين أقرَب أوتيل؟ [wi:n ʔaqrab ʔuti:l?] Where does the difference lie? وين الاختِلاف؟ [wi:n ʔilʔixtila:f?] • **2.** اللِّي [ʔilli] We found him just where we expected him to be. لِقَينا بِالمَكان اللِّي توَقَّعنا نِلقِيه بِيه [lgi:nah bilmaka:n ʔilli twaqqaʕna nilgi:h bi:h] They will send them where they're needed most. عُود يدِزُّوهُم لِلمَكان اللِّي يِحتاجُوهُم بِيه هوايَة [ʕu:d ydizzu:hum lilmaka:n ʔilli yiħta:ǰu:hum bi:h hwa:ya]

where ... from • **1.** إمنِين، منِين، مِن وَين [ʔimni:n, mni:n, min wayn] Where does your friend come from? صَدِيقَك منِين؟ [ṣadi:qak mni:n?]

wherever • **1.** وَين ما [wi:n ma:] Wherever you are, don't forget to write me. لا تِنسَى تِكتِبلِي وَين ما تكُون [la: tinsa: tiktibli wi:n ma: tku:n] Wherever you go in this country you'll find good roads. وَين ما ترُوح بهَالبَلَد، كُلّ الطُّرُق زينَة [wayn ma: tru:ħ bhalbalad, kull ʔiṭṭuruq zi:na]

whether • **1.** إذا [ʔiða] لَو [law, luː] I'd like to know whether he's coming. أرِيد أعرُف إذا راح يِجِي لَو لا [ʔariːd ʔaʕruf ʔiða raːħ yiǰi law laː]

whey • **1.** رُوبَة [ruːba]

which • **1.** أيّ، أي [ʔayy] يا [yaː] Which bag did you pick out? يا جَنطَة أخَذتِي؟ [yaː ǰanṭa ʔaxaðti?] • **2.** ياهُو [yaːhu] Which is yours? ياهُو مالَك؟ [yaːhu maːlak?] • **3.** اللّي [ʔilli] Please return the book which you borrowed. بالله رَجِّع الكِتاب اللّي طلَبتَه [ballah rajjiʕ ʔilkitaːb ʔilli ṭlabtah]

whichever • **1.** أيّ [ʔayy] Take whichever one you want. أُخُذ أيّ واحِد ترِيدَ [ʔuxuð ʔayy waːħid triːda]

while • **1.** شوَيَّة [šwayya] فَدّ مُدَّة [fadd mudda] فَدّ فترَة [fadd fatra] You'll have to wait a while. لازم تِنتِظِر شوَيَّة [laːzim tintiðir šwayya] • **2.** مِن [min] لَمّا [lamma] بِأثناء ما [bʔaθnaːʔ maː] He came while we were out. إجا مِن كِنّا طالعِين [ʔiǰa min činna ṭaːlʕiːn] • **3.** بَينَما [baynama] Some people live in luxury, while others are dying of starvation. بَعَض النّاس يعِيشُون بِبَذَخ بَينَما غير هُم مَيّتِين مِن الجُوع [baʕað ʔinnaːs yʕiːšuːn bbaðax baynama ɣiːrhum mayytiːn min ʔilǰuːʕ] • **4.** ما دام [maː daːm] I want to go in while it's still light. أرِيد أرُوح ما دام بَعَدها ضاوية [ʔariːd ʔaruːħ maː daːm baʕadha ðaːwya]

to while away • **1.** قِضَى [giðaː] قِضيان [giðyaːn] *vn: sv* i. I while away my time reading. دَأقضِي وَقتِي أقرا [daʔagði wakti ʔaqraː]

whip • **1.** قَمچِي [qamči] قماچِي [qmaːči] *pl:* The driver snapped the whip. العَرَبَنچِي طَقّ القَمچِي مالَه [ʔilʕarabanči ṭagg ʔilqamči maːlah]

to whip • **1.** ضِرَب بِالقَمچِي [ðirab bilqamči] *sv* u. He whipped the horse mercilessly. ضِرَب الخَيل مالتَه بالقَمچِي بَلا رَحَم [ðirab ʔilxayl maːltah bilqamči bala raħam]

whisky • **1.** وِيسكِي [wiski]

whisper • **1.** هَمس [hams] I heard a whisper in the next room. سمَعِت هَمِس بالغُرفَة اللّي يَمنَا [smaʕit hamis bilɣurfa ʔilli yamna]

in a whisper • **1.** مُشاوَرَة [mušaːwara] They spoke in a whisper so that no one would hear them. حِچَوا مشاورَة حَتَّى لا حَدّ يِسمَعهُم [ħičaw mšaːwra ħatta laː ħadd yismaʕhum]

to whisper • **1.** هِمَس [himas] *sv* i. شاوَر [šaːwar] مُشاوَرَة [mušaːwara] *vn: sv* i. She whispered the word in my ear. هِمسَت الكِلمَة بِإذنِي [himsat ʔiččilma bʔiðni] She whispered the word in my ear. شاورَتنِي بِالكِلمَة [šaːwratni biččilma]

whistle • **1.** صافِرَة [ṣaːfira] صافِرات [ṣaːfiraːt] *pl:* The policeman lost his whistle. الشُّرطِي ضَيَّع الصّافِرَة مالتَه [ʔiššurṭi ðayyaʕ ʔiṣṣaːfira maːltah] • **2.** ماصُولَة [maːṣuːla] ماصُولات [maːṣuːlaːt] *pl:* The boy broke his whistle. الوَلَد كِسَر الماصُولَة مالتَه [ʔilwalad kisar ʔilmaːṣuːla maːltah] • **3.** صَوفرَة [ṣawfra] صَوفرات [ṣawfraːt] *pl:* The signal was one long and two short whistles. الإشارَة كانَت صَوفرَة طوِيلَة وَصَوفِرتَين قصار [ʔilʔišaːra čaːnat ṣuːfra ṭwiːla wṣuːfirtayn gṣaːr]

to whistle • **1.** صَوفَر [ṣawfar] صَوفَرَة [ṣawfara] vn: sv i He whistled as he walked along. كان دَيِمشِي وَيصَوفِر [čaːn dayimši wyṣuːfir] He whistled to the cab. صَوفَرلَه لِلتَّكسِي [ṣuːfarlah littaksi]

white • **1.** أبيَض [ʔabyað] بِيض [biːð] *pl:* بَيضَة [bayða] *Feminine:* She wore a white dress at the party. لِبسَت نَفنُوف أبيَض بِالحَفلَة [libsat nafnuːf ʔabyað bilħafla] • **2.** بَياض [bayaːð] I put the whites of four eggs in the cake. حَطّيت بَياض أربَع بَيضات بِالكَيكَة [ħaṭṭiːt bayaːð ʔarbaʕ bayðaːt bilkayka]

whitewash • **1.** بَياض [bayaːð] The whitewash is peeling off the walls. البَياض مال الحايط دَيُوقَع [ʔilbayaːð maːl ʔilħaːyiṭ dayuːgaʕ]

to whitewash • **1.** بَيَّض [bayyað] تَبيِيض [tabyiːð] *vn:* تبَيَّض [tbayyað] *p:* How long will it take you to whitewash the garage? شقَدّ مُدَّة يِنرادلَك حَتَّى تبَيِّض الكَراج؟ [šgadd mudda yinraːdlak ħatta tbayyið ʔilgaraːǰ?]

who • **1.** مِنُو [minu] Who used this book last? مِنُو آخِر واحِد إستَعمَل هَالكِتاب؟ [minu ʔaːxir waːħid ʔistaʕmal halkitaːb?] • **2.** اللّي [ʔilli] Did you notice the man who just passed by? لاحَظتَ الرِّجّال اللّي مَرّ مِن هنا هَسَّة؟ [laːħaðat ʔirriǰǰaːl ʔilli marr min hna hassa?] • **3.** مَن [man] Who did you give it to? إلمَن إنطَيتها؟ [ʔilman ʔinṭiːtha?]

who ... for • **1.** عَلَى مَن [ʕala man] Who are you looking for? عَلَى مَن دَتدَوُّر؟ [ʕala man daddawwur?]

whoever • **1.** مِنُو ما [minuː maː] Whoever wants it may have it. مِنُو ما يرِيدها خَلّي ياخُذها [minuː maː yriːdha xalliː yaːxuðha]

whole • **1.** كامِل [kaːmil] كُلّ [kull] I intend to stay a whole week. بنِيَّتِي أبقَى إسبُوع كامِل [bniyyti ʔabqaː ʔisbuːʕ kaːmil] He ate the whole thing himself. أكَل كُلّشِي وَحدَه [ʔakal kullši waħdah]

on the whole • **1.** بصُورَة عامَّة [bṣuːra ʕaːmma] شِي عَلَى شِي [ši ʕala ši] On the whole, I agree with you. بصُورَة عامَّة آنِي أتّفِق وِيّاك [bṣuːra ʕaːmma ʔaːni ʔattifiq wiyyaːk]

wholesale • **1.** بِالجُملَة [biǰǰumla] They sell only wholesale. ما يبِيعُون غير بِالجُملَة [maː ybiːʕuːn ɣiːr biǰǰumla] The president gave out wholesale pardons. رَئِيس الجَمهُورِيَّة طَلَّع عفو بِالجُملَة [raʔiːs ʔiǰǰamhuːriyya ṭallaʕ ʕafw biǰǰumla]

W

wholesale price • **1.** سِعِر الجُملَة [siʕir ʔijǰumla] What's the wholesale price? شِنُو سِعِر الجُملَة؟ [šinu siʕir ʔijǰumla?]

whooping cough • **1.** سُعال دِيكِي [suʕaːl diːki] My kids all have whooping cough. وِلدِي كُلّهُم عِدهُم سُعال دِيكِي [wildi kullhum ʕidhum suʕaːl diːki]

whore • **1.** قَحبَة [gaħba] قَحبات، قحَاب [gaħbaːt, għaːb] *pl:*

whose • **1.** مال مَن [maːl man] Whose watch is this? مال مَن هَالسّاعَة؟ [maːl man hassaːʕa?] • **2.** اللِّي [ʔilli] There's the lady whose bag you found yesterday. هَذِي المرَيَّة اللِّي لقَيت جَنطَتها البارحَة [haːði ʔilmrayya ʔilli lgiːt ǰanṭatha ʔilbaːrħa]

why • **1.** لُوَيش [luwiːš] لَيش [liːš] إلوَيش [ʔilwiːš] Why is the train so crowded this morning? لُويش القِطار هَالقَدّ خَبصَة اليُوم؟ [luwiːš ʔilqiṭaːr halgadd xabṣa ʔilyuːm?]

*** Why, what do you mean?** • **1.** ها شتُقصُد؟ [haː štuqṣud?]

*** Why there he is!** • **1.** ها هِيّاتَه [haː hiyyaːtah]

that's why • **1.** لِهَذا [lihaːða] لِهالسَّبَب [lihassabab] That's why I didn't call you. لهَذا ما خابَرتَك [lhaðaː maː xaːbartak]

wick • **1.** فِتِيلَة [fitiːla] فِتِيلات، فَتايِل [fitiːlaːt, , fataːyil] *pl:*

wide • **1.** عَرِيض [ʕariːð̣] The garage doorway isn't wide enough. الباب مال الگَراج مُو هَالقَدّ عَرِيض [ʔilbaːb maːl ʔilgaraːǰ muː halgadd ʕariːð̣a] The window is very wide. الشُّبّاك عَرِيض هوايَة [ʔiššubbaːč ʕariːð̣ hwaːya] • **2.** كبِير [čbiːr] واسِع [waːsiʕ] We have a wide selection of shoes. عِدنا مَجمُوعَة كبِيرَة مِن الأَحذِيَة [ʕidna majmuːʕa čbiːra min ʔalʔaħðiya] • **3.** واسِع [waːsiʕ] Our firm has wide commercial connections. شَرِكَتنا عِدها عِلاقات تِجارِيَّة واسعَة [šarikatna ʕidha ʕilaːqaːt tiǰaːriyya waːsʕa]

*** The window is two feet wide.** • **1.** شبّاك عُرضَه فُوتَين [ššibbaːč ʕurð̣ah fuːtayn]

wide-awake • **1.** صاحِي [ṣaːħi] I'm wide awake. آنِي صاحِي تَماماً [ʔaːni ṣaːħi tamaːman]

*** He's a wide-awake fellow.** • **1.** عَينَه مَفكُوكَة زَين [ʕiːnah mafkuːka zayn]

wide-eyed • **1.** * He looked at me wide-eyed. فَكّ عيُونَه مِتعَجِّب [fakk ʕyuːnah mitʕaǰǰib]

to widen • **1.** عَرَّض [ʕarrað̣] تَعرِيض [taʕriːð̣] *vn:* تعَرَّض [tʕarrað̣] *p:* They're going to widen our street. راح يعَرّضُون شارِعنا [raːħ yʕarrð̣uːn šaːriʕna]

wide open • **1.** عَلَى قفاها [ʕala gfaːha] He left the door wide open. خَلَّى الباب مَفكُوك عَلَى قفاها [xallaː ʔilbaːb mafkuːk ʕala gfaːha]

widespread • **1.** مِنتِشِر [mintišir] How widespread is this opinion? شقَدّ مِنتَشرَة هَالفِكرَة؟ [šgadd mintašra halfikra?] • **2.** شايِع [šaːyiʕ] This custom is widespread here. هَالعادَة شايعَة هنا [halʕaːda šaːyʕa hna] • **3.** واسِع [waːsiʕ] شامِل [šaːmil] The hailstorm caused widespread damage. الحالُوب سَبَّب ضَرَر واسِع [ʔilħaːluːb sabbab ð̣arar waːsiʕ]

widow • **1.** أَرمَلَة [ʔarmala] أَرامِل [ʔaraːmil] *pl:*

widower • **1.** * That man is a widower. هَالرِّجّال مَرتَه مَيِّتَة [harriǰǰaːl martah mayyta]

width • **1.** عُرُض [ʕuruð̣] عُرُوض [ʕuruːð̣] *pl:* What's the width of this window? شقَدّ عُرُض هَالشِّبّاك؟ [šgadd ʕuruð̣ haššibbaːč?] The room is nine feet in width. الغُرفَة عُرُضها تِسِع فُوتات [ʔilɣurfa ʕuruð̣ha tisiʕ fuːtaːt] We need double-width material for the drapes. نِحتاج قماش أَبُو عُرضَين لِلبَردات [niħtaːǰ qmaːš ʔabu ʕurðayn lilpardaːt]

wife • **1.** زَوجَة [zawǰa] زَوجات [zawǰaːt] *pl:* She's the wife of the prime minister. هاي زَوجَة رَئِيس الوُزَراء [haːy zawǰat raʔiːs ʔilwuzaraːʔ]

wild • **1.** وَحشِي [waħši] There are no wild animals in this area. ماكُو حَيوانات وَحشِيَّة بِهَالمَنطَقَة [maːku ħaywaːnaːt waħšiyya bhalmanṭaqa] • **2.** وَقِيح ,وَقِح [wakiːħ, wakiħ] وُقَّح [wukkaħ] *pl:* وَقِح [wakiħ] The children are too wild. الوُلِد كُلِّش وُقَّح [ʔilwulid kulliš wukkaħ] • **3.** مِتحَمِّس [mitħammis] I'm not wild about it. آنِي مُو كُلِّش مِتحَمِّس عَليها [ʔaːni muː kulliš mitħammis ʕaliːha]

*** He lead a wild life when he was young.** • **1.** كان طايِش مِن كان صغَيِّر [čaːn ṭaːyiš min čaːn ṣɣayyir]

*** My boy is wild about ice cream.** • **1.** إبنِي يمُوت عَالدَونَدرمَة [ʔibni ymuːt ʕadduːndirma]

to go wild • **1.** تحَمَّس [tħammas] The crowd went wild when they heard the news. النّاس تحَمّسَوا مِن سِمعَوا الأَخبار [ʔinnaːs tħammsaw min simʕaw ʔilʔaxbaːr] • **2.** هاج [haːǰ] *sv* i. The crowd went wild and attacked the embassy. النّاس هاجَوا وهِجمَوا عالسَّفارَة [ʔinnaːs haːǰaw whiǰmaw ʔassafaːra]

to run wild • **1.** اِنهَدّ [ʔinhadd] *sv* a. The dog has run wild since his master died. الكَلِب اِنهَدّ مِن مات صاحبَه [ʔiččalib ʔinhadd min maːt ṣaːħbah]

wilderness • **1.** جَول [čuːl] جوَال [čwaːl] *Pl:* They wandered in the wilderness. تاهَوا بِالجّوال [taːhaw biǰ ǰwaːl]

wilds • **1.** * Their house is way out in the wilds. بَيتهُم بِآخِر الدِّنيا [baythum biʔaːxir ʔiddinya]

will • **1.** إرادَة [ʔiraːda] He has a strong will. عِندَه إرادَة قَوِيَّة [ʕindah ʔiraːda qawiyya] • **2.** وَصِيَّة [waṣiyya, wuṣiyya]

وُصِيّات، وَصايا [wuṣiyyaːt, waṣaːya] *pl:* He died without making a will. مات بَلا ما يِكتِب وَصِيَّة [maːt bala maː yiktib waṣiyya]

at will • **1.** كَيف [kayf] They come and go at will. يرُوحُون ويجُون بِكيفهُم [yruːħuːn wyiǰuːn bkayfhum]

to will • **1.** وَصَّى [waṣṣaː] تَوصِيَة [tawṣiya] *vn: sv* i. He willed all his property to the hospital. وَصَّى كُلّ أملاكَه لِلمُستَشفَى [waṣṣaː kull ʔamlaːkah lilmustašfa]

will • **1.** عُود [ʕuːd] I'll meet you at three o'clock. عُود أشُوفَك ساعَة ثلاثَة [ʕuːd ʔašuːfak saːʕa tlaːθa] We'll see what can be done. عُود نشُوف شنِقدَر نسَوِّي [ʕuːd nšuːf šnigdar nsawwi] • **2.** راح [raːħ] They'll be surprised to see you here. راح يِتعَجّبُون مِن يشُوفُوك هنا [raːħ yitʕaǰǰbuːn min yšuːfuːk hna] I thought that would happen. تصَوَّرِت هِيكِي شِي راح يصِير [tṣawwarit hiːči ši raːħ yṣiːr] I won't be able to do that. ما راح أقدَر أسَوِّي هاي [maː raːħ ʔagdar ʔasawwi haːy] He won't get anywhere that way. ما راح يَوصَل النَّتِيجَة بِهَالطَّرِيقَة [maː raːħ yuːṣal ʔinnatiːǰa bhaṭṭariːqa]

*** Won't you come in for a minute?**
• **1.** بالله ما تخُشّ شوَيَّة؟ [ballah maː txušš šwayya?]

*** Will you please reserve a room for me.**
• **1.** بالله ما تِحجِز إلِي غُرفَة [ballah maːtiħǰiz ʔili ɣurfa]

*** This hall will hold a thousand people.**
• **1.** هَالقاعَة تِلزَم ألِف واحِد [halqaːʕa tilzam ʔalif waːħid]

*** What would you like to drink?** • **1.** شيعجبَك تِشرَب؟ [šyʕiǰbak tišrab?]

*** We would rather live outside of town.**
• **1.** إحنا نفَضِّل نِسكُن خارِج الوِلايَة [ʔiħna nfaðððil niskun xaːriǰ ʔilwlaːya]

*** Would you rather go to the theater?**
• **1.** تفَضِّل ترُوح لِلسِينَما؟ [tfaðððil truːħ lissinama?]

*** He would never take the job.** • **1.** أبَد ما يِقبَل هَالشغُل [ʔabad maːm yiqbal haššɣul]

*** He'll go for days without smoking.**
• **1.** أحياناً يِبقَى عِدَّة أيّام بَلا ما يدَخِّن [ʔaħyaːnan yibqaː ʕiddat ʔayyaːm balaː maː ydaxxin]

willing • **1.** * I'm willing to try anything. ما عِندِي مانِع شما يكُون [maː ʕindi maːniʕ šmaː ykuːn]
* I'm willing to try anything. أقبَل أسَوِّي كُلّشِي [ʔaqbal ʔasawwi kullši]

will power • **1.** قُوَّة إرادَة [quwwat ʔiraːda] He has amazing will power. عِندَه قُوَّة إرادَة عَجِيبَة [ʕindah quwwat ʔiraːda ʕajiːba]

to wilt • **1.** ذِبَل [ðibal] ذَبِل [ðabil] *vn: sv* a. The flowers have wilted. الوَرِد ذِبَل [ʔilwarid ðibal]

to win • **1.** غِلَب [ɣilab] غُلُب [ɣulub] *vn: sv* u. I'm going to win this time. راح أغلُب هَالمَرَّة [raːħ ʔaɣlub halmarra] Which team do you think will win? يا فَرِيق تِتصَوَّر راح تُغلُب؟ [yaː fariːq titṣawwar raːħ tuɣlub?] • **2.** رِبَح [ribaħ] رَبِح [rabiħ] *vn: sv* a. I won five hundred fils. رُبَحِت خَمِس مِيَّة فِلِس [rubaħit xamis miyyat filis]

to win over • **1.** إستَمال [ʔistamaːl] *sv* i. Can you win him over to our side? تِقدَر تِستِمِيلَه لِجانِبنا؟ [tigdar tistimiːlah liǰaːnibna?] Can you win him over to our side? تِقدَر تقَنّعَه يصِير ويّانا؟ [tigdar tqannʕah yṣiːr wiyyaːna?]

winch • **1.** بَكرَة [bakra] بَكرات، بَكَر [bakraːt, bakar.] *pl:*

wind • **1.** هَوا [hawa] There was a violent wind last night. كان أكُو هَوا كُلِّش عالِي البارحَة باللَّيل [čaːn ʔaku hawa kulliš ʕaːli ʔilbaːrħa billayl]

*** There's something in the wind.** • **1.** يبَيِّن أكُو شِي بالجَوّ [ybayyin ʔaku šiː biǰǰaww]

*** I took the wind out of his sails.** • **1.** فَشَّيت جرابَه [faššayt ǰraːbah]

to get wind of • **1.** حَسّ [ħass] *sv* i. عِرَف ب [ʕiraf b-] *sv* u. I got wind of the story yesterday. حَسَّيت بِالقُصَّة البارحَة [ħassayt bilquṣṣa ʔilbaːrħa]

to wind • **1.** تعَرَّج [tʕarraǰ] تعَرُّج [taʕarruǰ] *vn: sv* a. The road winds through the mountains. الطَّرِيق يِتعَرَّج بين الجِّبال [ʔiṭṭariːq yitʕarraǰ biːn ʔiǰǰibaːl] • **2.** لَفّ [laff] لَفّ [laff] *vn:* اِنلَفّ [ʔinlaff] *p:* Wind it around my finger. لِفّها داير ما داير إصبِعِي [liffha daːyir maː daːyir ʔiṣibʕi] • **3.** كَوَّك [kawwak] تَكوِيك [takwiːk] *vn:* تكَوَّك [tkawwak] *p:* I forgot to wind my watch. نسَيت أكَوُّك ساعتِي [nsayt ʔakawwuk saːʕti]

to wind up • **1.** لَفّ [laff] لَفّ [laff] *vn:* اِنلَفّ [ʔinlaff] *p:* Will you help me wind up this yarn? ما تعاوُنِّي ألِفّ هَالصُّوف؟ [maː tʕaːwunni ʔaliff haṣṣuːf?] • **2.** رَتَّب [rattab] تَرتِيب [tartiːb] *vn: sv* i. They gave him two weeks' time in which to wind up his affairs. إنطُوه إسبُوعَين حَتَّى يرَتِّب أمُورَه [ʔinṭuːh ʔisbuːʕayn ħatta yrattib ʔumuːrah]

to get winded • **1.** نِهَت [nihat] *sv* a. I get winded easily when I run. أنهَت بِالعَجَل مِن أركُض [ʔanhat bilʕaǰal min ʔarkuð]

winding sheet • **1.** كِفَن [čifan] كفانَة [čfaːna] *pl:*

windmill • **1.** طاحُونَة هَوا [ṭaːħuːna hawa] طواحِين هَوا [ṭwaːħiːn hawa] *pl:* مَكِينَة هَوائِيَّة [makiːna hawaːʔiyya] مَكايِن هَوائِيَّة [makaːyin hawaːʔiyya] *pl:*

window • **1.** شِبّاك [šibbaːč, šibbaːk] شبابِيك [šbaːbiːč, šbaːbiːk] *pl:* Please open the windows. بالله فُكّ الشِّبابِيك [ballah fukk ʔiššibaːbiːč] • **2.** جامخانَة [ǰaːmxaːna] جامخانات [ǰaːmxaːnaːt] *pl:* Put these on display in the window. إعرِض هَالأشياء بِالجّامخانَة [ʔiʕrið halʔašyaːʔ biǰǰaːmxaːna]

W

windowpane • **1.** جامَة [ǰa:ma] جامات [ǰa:ma:t] *pl:* The stone broke the windowpane. الحجارَة كِسرَت الجّامَة [ʔilħǰa:ra kisrat ʔiǰǰa:ma]

windpipe • **1.** قَصَبَة هَوائِيَّة [qaṣaba hawa:ʔiyya] قَصَبات هَوائِيَّة [qaṣaba:t hawa:ʔiyya] *pl:*

windshield • **1.** جامَة قِدّامِيَّة [ǰa:ma gidda:miyya] جامات قِدّامِيَّة [ǰa:ma:t gidda:miyya] *pl:*

windy • **1.** It's windy today. أكُو هَوا هوايَة اليُوم [ʔaku hawa hwa:ya ʔilyu:m]

wine • **1.** شَراب [šara:b] Do you have aged wine? عِندَك شَراب مُعَتَّق؟ [ʕindak šara:b muʕattaq?]

wing • **1.** جناح [ǰina:ħ] جناحات، أجنِحَة [ǰina:ħa:t, ʔaǰniħa] *pl:* The pigeon broke its wing. الطِّير اِنكِسَر جناحَه [ʔiṭṭi:r ʔinkisar ǰna:ħah] The office is in the left wing of the building. الدّائِرَة بِالجِّناح اللّي عَاليِسرَة مِن البِنايَة [ʔidda:ʔira biǰǰina:ħ ʔilli ʕalyisra min ʔilbina:ya] • **2.** حِمايَة [ħima:ya] She took him under her wing. شِملَتَه بِحِمايَتَه [šimlatah bħima:yatha]

*** I watched the play from the wings.**
• **1.** تفَرَّجِت عَالرُّوايَة مِن صَفحَة المَسرَح وَرا البَردَة [tfarraǰit ʕarruwa:ya min ṣafħat ʔilmasraħ wara ʔilparda]

wink • **1.** غَمزَة [ɣamza] غَمزات [ɣamza:t] *pl:* She gave me a knowing wink. غُمزَتلِي غَمزَة واحِد يِدري [ɣumzatli ɣamzat wa:ħid yidri] • **2.** لَحظَة [laħḏa] لَحظات [laħḏa:t] *pl:* I didn't sleep a wink. ما غُمضَت عيني وَلا لَحظَة [ma: ɣumḏat ʕi:ni wala laħḏa]

*** He was gone in a wink.** • **1.** غاب مِثِل لَمح البَصَر [ɣa:b miθil lamħ ʔilbaṣar]

to wink • **1.** غُمَز [ɣumaz] غُمُز [ɣamuz] *vn: sv* u. Did she wink at you? غُمزَتلَك؟ [ɣumzatlak?]

winter • **1.** شِتا [šita] شِتايات [šita:ya:t] *pl:* We don't travel in winter. ما نسافِر بِالشِّتا [ma: nsa:fir biššita]

to wipe • **1.** نَشَّف [naššaf] تَنشِيف [tanši:f] *vn:* تنَشَّف [tnaššaf] *p:* I'll wash the dishes if you wipe them. أغسِل المواعِين إذا إنتَ تنَشِّفهُم [ʔaɣsil ʔilmwa:ʕi:n ʔiða ʔinta tnaššifhum]

to wipe off • **1.** مِسَح [misaħ] مَسِح [masiħ] *vn:* اِنمِسَح [ʔinmisaħ] *p:* First let me wipe off the dust. خَلّي أمسَح التُّراب أوَّل [xalli ʔamsaħ ʔittira:b ʔawwal]

to wipe out • **1.** قِضَى عَلَى [qiḏa:, giḏa: ʕala] قَضاء [qaḏa:ʔ] *vn:* اِنقِضَى [ʔinqiḏa:] *p:* The earthquake wiped out the whole town. الزِّلزال قِضَى عالولايَة كُلها [ʔizzilza:l giḏa: ʕalwla:ya kullha]

wire • **1.** سِلك [silk] أسلاك [ʔasla:k] *pl:* سِيم [si:m] سيُومَ [syu:ma] *pl:* وايِر [wa:yir] وايِرات [wa:yira:t] *pl:* The wire isn't strong enough. السِّلك مُو هَالقَدّ قَوي [ʔissilk mu: halgadd qawi] • **2.** بَرقِيَّة [barqiyya] بَرقِيّات [barqiyya:t] *pl:* Send him a wire. دِزّلَه بَرقِيَّة [dizzlah barqiyya]

by wire • **1.** بَرقِيّاً [barqiyyan] I'll let you know by wire. عُود أخَبّرَك بَرقِيّاً [ʕu:d ʔaxabbrak barqiyyan]

to wire • **1.** دَزّ بَرقِيَّة لِ [dazz barqiyya li-] He wired me to meet him at the station. دَزّلِي بَرقِيَّة ألاقِيه بِالمَحطَّة [dazzli barqiyya ʔala:gi:h bilmaħṭṭa]

wisdom • **1.** عَقِل [ʕaqil] That needs courage and wisdom. هاي يِنرادِلها شَجاعَة وَعَقِل [ha:y yinra:dilha šaǰa:ʕa wʕaqil]

wise • **1.** عاقِل [ʕa:qil] He's a very wise man. هُوَّ فَدّ واحِد كُلِّش عاقِل [huwwa fadd wa:ħid kulliš ʕa:qil]

*** When are you going to get wise to yourself?**
• **1.** شَوَقِت راح يِجِي عَقلَك براسَك؟ [šwakit ra:ħ yiji ʕaqlak bra:sak?]

*** Don't be such a wise guy.** • **1.** إثقَل شوَيَّة [ʔiθgal šwayya]

to put one wise • **1.** فَهَّم [fahham] تَفهِيم [tafhi:m] *vn:* تفَهَّم [tfahham] *p:* Don't you think we ought to put him wise? ما تِعتِقِد أحسَن نفَهّمَه شَكُو شماكُو؟ [ma: tiʕtiqid ʔaħsan nfahhimah šaku šma:ku?]

wish • **1.** رَغبَة [raɣba] رَغبات [raɣba:t] *pl:* My wishes are easily satisfied. رَغباتِي سَهل تَحقِيقها [raɣba:ti sahil taħqi:qha] • **2.** تَمَنِّيات [tamanniya:t] *pl:* Best wishes for the New Year! أطيَب التَّمَنِّيات بمُناسَبَة راس السَّنَة [ʔaṭyab ʔittamanniya:t bmuna:sabat ra:s ʔissana]

to wish • **1.** تمَنَّى [tmanna:] تَمَنِّي [tamanni] *vn: sv* a. We wished him luck on his trip. تمَنَّيناله سَفرَة موَفَّقَة [tmannayna:lah safra mwaffqa] I wish I could stay here longer. أتمَنَّى لَو أقدَر أبقَى مُدَّة أطوَل [ʔatmanna: law ʔagdar ʔabqa: mudda ʔaṭwal] I wouldn't wish it on my worse enemy. ما أتمَنّاها لعَدُوّي [ma: ʔatmanna:ha lʕaduwwi]

*** I wish I'd done that.** • **1.** يارَيت سَوَّيتها [ya:ri:t sawwaytha]

to wish for • **1.** تمَنَّى [tmanna:] تَمَنِّي [tamanni] *vn: sv* a. What do you wish for most? شتِتمَنَّى هَسَّة أزيَد شِي؟ [štitmanna: hassa ʔazyad ši?]

witch • **1.** سَحّارَة [saħħa:ra] سَحّارات [saħħa:ra:t] *pl:* ساحِرَة [sa:ħira] ساحِرات [sa:ħira:t] *pl:*

with • **1.** وِيّا [wiyya] مَعَ [maʕa] I'll have lunch with him today. راح أتغَدَّى وِيّاه اليُوم [ra:ħ ʔadɣadda: wiyya:h ʔilyu:m] Do you want something to drink with your meal? يِعجبَك تِشرَب شِي وِيّا الأكِل؟ [yiʕiǰbak tišrab ši wiyya ʔilʔakil?] He took the book with him. أخَذ الكِتاب وِيّاه [ʔaxað ʔilkita:b wiyya:h] • **2.** مَعَ [maʕa] ب [b] With pleasure! مَعَ المَمنُونِيَّة [maʕa ʔilmamnu:niyya] • **3.** ب [b] With all the money he's spent he should have a better house than that. بهالفلوس اللّي صِرَفها كان لازِم يكُون عِندَه بَيت أَحسَن مِن هَذا [bhaliflu:s ʔilli ṣirafha ča:n la:zim yku:n ʕindah bayt ʔaħsan min ha:ða] The house was crawling with ants. البَيت كان يرُوش بِالنَّمِل [ʔilbayt ča:n yru:š binnamil] • **4.** بالنِسبَة إِلي [binnisba ʔili] With him it's all a matter of money. بِالنِّسبَة إِلَه هِيَّ مَوضُوع فلُوس بَسّ [binnisba ʔilah hiyya mawḍu:ʕ flu:s bass] • **5.** رَغُم [rayum] With all the work he's done he still isn't finished. رَغُم كُلّ الشُّغُل اللّي سَوّاه هُوَّ لهَسَّة بَعَد ما مخَلِّص [rayum kull ʔiššuyul ʔilli sawwa:h huwwa lhassa baʕad ma: mxalliṣ] • **6.** عِند [ʕind] He's staying with us. هُوَّ نازِل عِدنا [huwwa na:zil ʕidna] • **7.** مِن [min] She was beaming with happiness. وِجهَها كان دَيِضحَك مِن الفَرَح [wiččha ča:n dayiḍħak min ʔilfaraħ]

to withdraw • **1.** سِحَب [siħab] سَحِب [saħib] *vn:* انسِحَب [ʔinsiħab] *p:* I withdraw the motion. أَسحَب الاقتِراح [ʔasħab ʔilʔiqtira:ħ] • **2.** اِنسِحَب [ʔinsiħab] اِنسِحاب [ʔinsiħa:b] *vn: sv* i. Because of health reasons I will withdraw from the elections. آني راح أنسِحِب مِن الإنتِخابات لأسباب صِحِّيَّة [ʔa:ni ra:ħ ʔansiħib min ʔilʔintixa:ba:t liʔasba:b ṣiħħiyya]

to wither • **1.** ذِبَل [ðibal] *sv* a. Her face is withered. وِجهَها ذَبلان [wiččha ðabla:n]

within • **1.** خِلال [xila:l] I expect an answer within three days. أَتوَقَّع جَواب خِلال ثلَث أيّام [ʔatwaqqaʕ ǰawa:b xila:l tlaθ ʔayya:m] • **2.** ضِمِن [ḍimin] Speeding is forbidden within the city limits. السُّرعَة مَمنُوعَة ضِمِن حُدُود الوِلايَة [ʔissurʕa mamnu:ʕa ḍimin ħidu:d ʔilwila:ya] This is within my authority. هاي ضِمِن سُلطاتي [ha:y ḍimin sulṭa:ti] • **3.** خِلال [xila:l] The letters came within a short period. المَكاتِيب وُصلَت بخِلال فَترَة قَصِيرَة [ʔilmaka:ti:b wuṣlat bxila:l fatra qaṣi:ra]

*** We're within 3 miles of the city.**

• **1.** إحنا بِبعِد تلَث أميال مِن الوِلايَة [ʔiħna bibiʕid itlaθ amya:l min ʔilwla:ya]

without • **1.** بلَيّا [blayya] بِلا [bila] بِدُون [bidu:n] مِن غَير [min yayr] Can I get in without a ticket? أَقدَر أَخُشّ بلَيّا تِكِت؟ [ʔagdar ʔaxušš blayya: tikit?] He left without permission. طِلَع بِدُون إجازَة [ṭilaʕ bidu:n ʔiǰa:za] She left the room without saying a word. تِركَت الغُرفَة بلَيّا ما تقُول وَلا كِلمَة [tirkat ʔilyurfa blayya: ma: dgu:l wala čilma]

witness • **1.** شاهِد [ša:hid] شُهُود [šuhu:d] *pl:* The witnesses haven't been examined yet. الشُّهُود بَعَد ما اِنسِئلَوا لهَسَّة [ʔiššuhu:d baʕad ma: ʔinsiʔlaw lhassa]

to witness • **1.** شِهَد عَلَى [šihad ʕala] *sv* a. We witnessed his signature. شهَدنا عَلَى تَوقِيعَه [šhadna ʕala tawqi:ʕah] • **2.** شاف [ša:f] شَوف [šawf] *vn: sv* u. Did you witness the accident? شِفت الحادِث مِن صار؟ [šift ʔilħa:diθ min ṣa:r?] • **3.** تفَرَّج عَلَى [tfarraǰ ʕala] تَفَرُّج [tafarruǰ] *vn: sv* a. A huge crowd witnessed the game. هوايَة ناس تفَرّجوا عالسِّباق [hwa:ya na:s tfarrǰaw ʕassiba:q]

witty • **1.** منَكِّت لاذِع [mnakkit la:ðiʕ] He's very witty. هُوَّ منَكِّت لاذِع [huwwa mnakkit la:ðiʕ]

wolf • **1.** ذِيب [ði:b] ذِياب [ðiya:b] *pl:* The wolves have been killing our sheep. الذِّياب دَياكلُون خُرفانّا [ʔiððiya:b daya:klu:n xurfa:nna]

*** He's a wolf in sheep's clothing.**

• **1.** بالوُجِه مرايَة وبالقُفَة سِلايَة [bilwuǰih mra:ya wbilgufa silla:ya]

woman • **1.** مَرَة [mara] نِسوان [niswa:n] *pl:* مرَيَّة [mrayya] مرَيّات [mrayya:t] *pl:* That woman is selling yoghurt. ذِيك المَرَة دَتبِيع لِبَن [ði:č ʔilmara datbi:ʕ liban]

womb • **1.** رَحَم [raħam] أرحام [ʔarħa:m] *pl:*

wonder • **1.** مُعجِزَة [muʕǰiza] مُعجِزات [muʕǰiza:t] *pl:* The medicine works wonders. هَالدُّوا يسَوِّي مُعجِزات [hadduwa ysawwi muʕǰiza:t] It's a wonder that you got here at all. وُصُولَك هنا بحَدّ ذاتَه كان مُعجِزَة [wuṣu:lak hna: bħadd ða:tah ča:n muʕǰiza]

*** No wonder it's cold with the window open.**

• **1.** طَبعاً تصِير بارِدَة إذا الشِّبّاك مَفكُوك [ṭabʕan tṣi:r ba:rda ʔiða ʔiššibba:č mafku:k]

to wonder • **1.** اِستَغرَب [ʔistayrab] اِستِغراب [ʔistiyra:b] *vn: sv* u. I shouldn't wonder if it were true. ما أَستَغرُب إذا كانَت صُدُق [ma: ʔastayrub ʔiða ča:nat ṣudug]

*** I was wondering where you were.**

• **1.** رِدِت أعرُف عَجَباً إنتَ وَين [ridit ʔaʕruf ʕaǰaban ʔinta wayn]

*** I wonder what he'll do now.** • **1.** عَجَباً شراح يسَوِّي هَسَّة [ʕaǰaban šra:ħ ysawwi hassa]

wonderful • **1.** مُمتاز [mumta:z] That's a wonderful book. هَذا كِتاب مُمتاز [ha:ða kita:b mumta:z]

wood • **1.** خِشَب [xišab] What kind of wood is this? شِنُو نُوع هالخِشَب؟ [šinu nu:ʕ halxišab?] • **2.** حَطَب [ħaṭab] Those people are collecting wood for the fire. ذُولَة دَيلِمُّون حَطَب لِلنّار [ðu:la daylimmu:n ħaṭab linna:r]

wooden • **1.** مِن خِشَب [min xišab] The pan has a wooden handle. الطّاوَة بِيها يَدَّة مِن خِشَب [ʔiṭṭa:wa bi:ha yadda min xišab] The room is divided by a wooden partition. الغُرفَة مَقسُومَة بِحاجِز مِن خِشَب [ʔilyurfa maqsu:ma bħa:ǰiz min xišab]

W

woods • **1.** غابَة [ɣa:ba] غابات [ɣa:ba:t] *pl:* Is there a path through the woods? أكُو طَرِيق مِن الغابَة؟ [ʔaku ṭari:q min ʔilɣa:ba?]

*** We're not out of the woods yet.**

• **1.** بَعَدها حالَتنا ما مِستَقِرَّة [baʕadha ħa:latna ma: mistaqirra]

wool • **1.** صُوف [ṣu:f] أصواف [ʔaṣwa:f] *pl:* The blanket is made of pure wool. هالبَطّانِيَّة صُوف خالِص [halbaṭṭa:niyya ṣu:f xa:liṣ]

woolen • **1.** مِن صُوف [min ṣu:f] I bought a woolen sweater. اِشتِرَيت بلُوز مِن صُوف [ʔištiri:t blu:z min ṣu:f]

woolens • **1.** صُوفِي [ṣu:fi] Did you put moth balls in your woolens? حَطِّيت نَفتالِين وِيّا الصُّوفِيّات مالتَك؟ [ħaṭṭi:t naftali:n wiyya ʔiṣṣu:fiyya:t ma:ltak?]

word • **1.** كِلمَة [čilma] كَلِمَة [kalima, kilma] كَلِمات [kalima:t, čilma:t] *pl:* We have to learn fifty new words between now and tomorrow. لازِم نِحفُظ خَمسِين كِلمَة مِن هنا لباكِر [la:zim niħfuð̣ xamsi:n čilma min hna lba:čir] How do you spell that word? شلُون تِتهَجّى هالكِلمَة؟ [šlu:n tithajja: haččilma?] I don't want to hear another word about this. ما أرِيد أسمَع وَلا كِلمَة بَعَد عَن هالمَوضُوع [ma: ʔari:d ʔasmaʕ wala čilma baʕad ʕan halmawð̣u:ʕ] I remember the tune, but I forget the words. أتذَكَّر اللَّحَن بَسّ ناسِي الكَلِمات [ʔadðakkar ʔillaħan bass na:si ʔilkalima:t] • **2.** وَعَد [waʕad] He gave his word that he would finish the job in time. نِطَى وَعَد يخَلِّص الشُّغُل بوَقتَه [niṭa: waʕad yxalliṣ ʔiššuɣul bwaktah] • **3.** خَبَر [xabar] Try to send them word we need reinforcements. حاوِل تدِزّلهُم خَبَر عَن حاجَتنا لِلمُساعَدَة [ħa:wil ddizzilhum xabar ʕan ħa:jatna lilmusa:ʕada]

*** You can take his word for it.** • **1.** اِعتِمِد عَلَى حكايتَه [ʔiʕtimid ʕala ħča:ytah]

*** He doesn't let you get a word in edgewise.**

• **1.** ما يخَلِّي أحَّد يِحكِي [ma: yxalli ʔaħħad yiħči]

*** In a word, no.** • **1.** مُختَصَر مُفِيد، لا [muxtaṣar mufi:d, la:]

to word • **1.** رَتَّب كَلِمات [rattab kalima:t] تَرتِيب كَلِمات [tarti:b kalima:t] *vn: sv* i. How do you want to word the telegram? شلُون ترِيد ترَتِّب كَلِمات البَرقِيَّة؟ [šlu:n tri:d trattib kalima:t ʔilbarqiyya?]

wording • **1.** * The wording of this sentence is bad. عِبارات هالجُملَة ما مرَتّبَة [ʕiba:ra:t halǰumla ma: mrattba]

work • **1.** شُغُل [šuɣul] أشغال [ʔašɣa:l] *pl:* The Department of Public Works is being reorganized. أعادَوا تَنظِيم مُدِيرِيَّة الأشغال العامَّة [ʔaʕa:daw tanði:m mudi:riyyat ʔilʔašɣa:l ʔilʕa:mma] The work is boring. الشُّغُل يضَوِّج [ʔiššuɣul yð̣awwij] He's been out of work since the factory closed. هُوَّ قاعِد بِلا شُغُل مِن سَدَّوا المَعمَل [huwwa ga:ʕid bila šuɣul min saddaw ʔilmaʕmal] • **2.** مُؤَلَّفَة [muʔallafa] مُؤَلَّفات [muʔallafa:t] *pl:* All of that author's works are very popular. كُلّ مُؤَلَّفات هالكاتِب ناجحَة [kull muʔallafa:t halka:tib na:jħa] • **3.** عَمَل [ʕamal] عَملَة [ʕamla] *Feminine:* All that painter's works are very popular. كُلّ أعمال هَذا الرَّسّام ناجحَة [kull ʔaʕma:l ha:ða ʔirrassa:m na:jħa] • **4.** قِطعَة [qiṭʕa] قِطَع [qiṭaʕ] *pl:* That work of art is in the Egyptian museum. هالقِطعَة الفَنِّيَّة بالمَتحَف المِصرِي [halqiṭʕa ʔalfanniyya bilmatħaf ʔilmiṣri]

*** It took a lot of work to convince him we were right.**

• **1.** تعَبنا يَالله قَنَّعناه [tʕabna yallah qannaʕna:h]

to work • **1.** اِشتِغَل [ʔištiɣal] اِشتِغال [ʔištiɣa:l] *vn: sv* u. I work from eight to five. أشتُغُل مِن الثَّمانيَة لِلخَمسَة [ʔaštuɣul min ʔiθθima:nya lilxamsa] The elevator doesn't work. المَصعَد ما يِشتُغُل [ʔilmaṣʕad ma: yištuɣul] • **2.** شَغَّل [šaɣɣal] He works his employees very hard. يشَغِّل عُمّالَه كُلِّش هوايَة [yšaɣɣil ʕumma:lah kulliš hwa:ya] Do you know how to work an adding machine? تُعرُف شلُون تشَغِّل مَكِينَة حسابات؟ [tuʕruf šlu:n tšaɣɣil maki:nat ħsa:ba:t?] • **3.** نِجَح [nijaħ] نَجاح [naja:ħ] *vn: sv* a. This trick doesn't always work. هاللِّعبَة مُو دائماً تِنجَح [halliʕba mu: da:ʔiman tinjaħ] • **4.** فَكّ [fakk] *sv* u. I had to work my way through the crowd. اِضطَرَّيت أفَكِّلي طَرِيق بين النّاس بِالتِدِفِّع [ʔið̣ṭarrayt ʔafukkli ṭari:q bi:n ʔinna:s biltidiffiʕ]

to work loose • **1.** رِخَى [rixa:] *sv* a. Several screws have worked loose on the machine. كَم بُرغِي رِخَت بِالمَكِينَة [čam burɣi rixat bilmaki:na]

to work on • **1.** قَنَّع [qannaʕ] *sv* i. We're working on him to give us the day off. دَنقَنّعَه حَتَّى يِنطِينا يوم عُطلَة [danqanniʕah ħatta yinṭi:na yu:m ʕuṭla] • **2.** اِشتِغَل ب [ʔištiɣal b-] *sv* u. The mechanic is just working on your car now. المِيكانِيكِي دَيِشتُغُل بسَيّارتَك هَسَّة [ʔilmi:kani:ki dayištuɣul bsayya:rtak hassa]

to work out • **1.** رَتَّب [rattab] تَرتِيب [tarti:b] *vn:* ترَتَّب [trattab] *p:* هَيَّأ [hayyaʔ] تَهَيُّء [tahayyuʔ] *vn:* تهَيَّئ [thayyaʔ] *p:* The plan is well worked out. المَشرُوع مِترَتِّب زين [ʔilmašru:ʕ mitrattib zi:n] • **2.** نِجَح [nijaħ] نَجاح [naja:ħ] *vn: sv* a. How do you think this idea would work out? شقَدّ تِتصَوَّر هالفِكرَة راح تِنجَح؟ [šgadd titṣawwar halfikra ra:ħ tinjaħ?] • **3.** مِشَى [miša:] مَشِي [mašy] *vn: sv* i. How did things work out? شلُون مِشَت الأمُور؟ [šlu:n mišat ʔilʔumu:r?]

worker • **1.** عامِل [ʕa:mil] عُمّال [ʕumma:l] *pl:* He's the best worker in my factory. هَذا أحسَن عامِل بالمَعمَل مالِي [ha:ða ʔaħsan ʕa:mil bilmaʕmal ma:li]

*** He's a hard worker.** • **1.** هَذا كُلِّش شَغُول [ha:ða kulliš šaɣu:l]

working hours • **1.** دَوام [dawa:m] May I call you during working hours? أقدَر أخابرَك أثناء الدَّوام؟ [ʔagdar ʔaxa:brak ʔaθna:ʔ ʔiddawa:m?]

workman • **1.** عامِل [ʕa:mil] عُمّال [ʕumma:l] *pl:*

W

works • **1.** مَكِينَة [maki:na] مَكاين [maka:yin] *pl:* The works of that clock need repairing. المَكِينَة مال هَالسّاعَة يِنرادِلها تَصلِيح [ʔilmaki:na ma:l hassa:ʕa yinra:dilha taşli:ħ]

water works • **1.** إسالَة ماء [ʔisa:lat ma:ʔ] The water works are outside the city. إسالَة الماء بَرَّة الوِلايَة [ʔisa:lat ʔilma:ʔ barra ʔilwila:ya]

world • **1.** دِنيا [dinya] He's traveled all over the world. دار الدِّنيا كُلّها [da:r ʔiddinya kullha] I wouldn't hurt him for anything in the world. ما أذِّيه لَو يِنطُونِي مُلك الدِّنيا [ma: ʔaʔaði:h law yintu:ni mulk ʔiddinya] • **2.** عالَم [ʕa:lam] The Red Cross is a world-wide organization. مُؤَسَّسَة الصَّلِيب الأَحمَر مِنتَشرَة بكُلّ العالَم [muʔassasat ʔişşali:b ʔilʔaħmar mintašra bkull ʔilʕa:lam]

*** Where in the world have you been?**

• **1.** بيا زوِيَّة كِنِت ضامُم نَفسَك؟ [bya: zwiyya činit ða:mum nafsak?]

*** It will do him a world of good to go somewhere else.** • **1.** هوايَة لمَصلَحتَه لَو يرُوح لغَير مَكان [hwa:ya lmaşlaħtah law yru:ħ lɣayr maka:n]

*** My father thinks the world of you.**

• **1.** أبُويا يقَدّرَك كُلِّش هوايَة [ʔabu:ya yqaddrak kulliš hwa:ya]

worm • **1.** دُودَة [du:da] دُودات [du:da:t] *pl:* دُود [du:d] *Collective:* Do you use worms for bait? إنتَ تِستَعمِل دُود لِلطُّعُم؟ [ʔinta tistaʕmil du:d littuʕum?]

wormy • **1.** مدَوِّد [mdawwid] These dates are wormy. هَالتَّمُر كُلّه مدَوِّد [hattamur kullah mdawwid]

worn • **1.** مِستَهلِك [mistahlik] قايِم [ga:yim] My coat is pretty worn. سِترتي مِستَهلِكَة [sitirti mistahlika]

worn-out • **1.** تَعبان كُلِّش [taʕba:n kulliš] He looks worn-out. يبَيِّن عَليه تَعبان كُلِّش [yibayyin ʕali:h taʕba:n kulliš]

worry • **1.** دَوخَة راس [dawxat ra:s] قَلَق [qalaq] Her son gave her a great deal of worry. إبنها سَبَّب إلها هوايَة دَوخَة راس [ʔibinha sabbab ʔilha hwa:ya dawxat ra:s]

to worry • **1.** شَوَّش [šawwaš] *sv* u. قِلَق [qilaq] قَلَق [qalaq] *vn:* اِنقِلَق [ʔinqilaq] *p:* His silence worries me. سُكُوتَه دَيشَوُّشني [suku:tah dayšawwušni] • **2.** تشَوَّش [tšawwaš] *sv* a. I'm worried about him. فِكري مِتشَوِّش عَليه [fikri mitšawwiš ʕali:h]

*** I won't let that worry me.** • **1.** ما أدَوِّخ راسِي بهاي [ma: ʔadawwux ra:si bha:y]

*** The future doesn't worry him.** • **1.** ما يخاف مِن المُستَقبَل [ma: yxa:f min ʔilmustaqbal]

*** I don't have time to worry about that.**

• **1.** الصِدُق ما عِندِي وَقت إلهاي [ʔişşidug ma: ʕindi wakt ʔilha:y]

worse • **1.** أمَرّ [ʔamarr] أنجَس [ʔangas] He's feeling worse this morning. هَاليُوم صِحّتَه بَعَد أمَرّ [halyu:m şiħħtah baʕad ʔamarr] The weather is worse now than it was in the morning. الجَّوّ هَسَّة أنجَس مِن الصُّبُح [ʔijjaww hassa ʔangas min ʔişşubuħ] • **2.** أسوَء [ʔaswaʔ] His business is going from bad to worse. شُغلَه دَيتطَوَّر مِن سَيِّئ إلَى أسوَء [šuɣlah dayittawwar min sayyiʔ ʔila ʔaswaʔ] • **3.** أتعَس [ʔatʕas] He's even worse off now. حالتَه هَسَّة بَعَد أتعَس [ħa:ltah hassa baʕad ʔatʕas]

*** He's none the worse for it.**

• **1.** ما صابَه أي ضَرَر مِن وَراها [ma: şa:bah ʔayy ðarar min wara:ha]

*** Her condition is getting worse and worse.**

• **1.** حالتَها دَتِتدَهوَر [ħa:latha datitdahwar]

worship • **1.** عِبادَة [ʕiba:da] The worship of idols was prevalent before Islam. عِبادَة الأصنام كانَت مَوجُودَة قَبِل الإسلام [ʕiba:dat ʔilʔaşna:m ča:nat mawju:da gabil ʔilʔisla:m]

to worship • **1.** عِبَد [ʕibad] عبادَة [ʕba:da] *vn:* اِنعِبَد [ʔinʕibad] *p:* He worships his wife. يِعبِدها لمَرتَه [yiʕbidha lmartah]

worst • **1.** أسوَء [ʔaswaʔ] But wait, I haven't told you the worst. يَواش، بَعَد ما قِتلَك أسوَء شِي [yawa:š, baʕad ma: gitlak ʔaswaʔ ši] • **2.** أنجَس [ʔangas] I got the worst piece. جَتنِي أنجَس وُصلَة [jatni ʔangas wuşla] • **3.** أتعَس [ʔatʕas] That's the worst accident I've seen in my life. ذاك أتعَس حادِث تَصادُم شايفَه بعُمرِي [ða:k ʔatʕas ħa:diθ taşa:dum ša:yfah bʕumri]

*** I get the worst of it when I argue with him.**

• **1.** كُلّما أتناقَش ويّاه، آني آكُلها [kullma ʔatna:qaš wiyya:h, ʔa:ni ʔa:kulha]

*** We're over the worst of it.** • **1.** شَرّهَا فات [šarrha fa:t]

at worst • **1.** بأتعَس الحالات [bʔatʕas ʔilħa:la:t] At worst, the storm won't last longer than a week. بأتعَس الحالات، العاصِفَة ما تطَوِّل أزيَد مِن إسبُوع [bʔatʕas ʔilħa:la:t, ʔilʕa:şifa ma: ttawwil ʔazyad min ʔisbu:ʕ]

worth • **1.** قِيمَة [qi:ma] قِيَم [qiyam] *pl:* He didn't appreciate her true worth. ما قَدَّر قِيمَتها الحَقِيقِيَّة [ma: qaddar qi:matha ʔilħaqi:qiyya] • **2.** حَقّ [ħagg] Give me 10 fils worth of peanuts. إنطِينِي حَقّ عَشِر فلُوس فِستِق عَبِيد [ʔinti:ni ħagg ʕašir flu:s fistiq ʕabi:d]

*** Give me fifty fils worth of almonds.**

• **1.** إنطِينِي بخَمسِين فِلِس لَوز [ʔinti:ni bxamsi:n filis lawz]

*** Did you get your money's worth in the night club last night?** • **1.** عاد طَلَّعت فلُوسَك اللِّي حَطَّيتها بالمَلهى البارحَة باللّيل؟ [ʕa:d tallaʕt flu:sak ʔilli ħatti:tha bilmalha: ʔilba:rħa billayl?]

to be worth • **1.** يِسوَى [yiswa:] *sv* a. It's worth the trouble. تِسوَى دَوخَة الرّاس [tiswa: dawxat ʔirra:s] That horse is worth five hundred dinars. هَالحِصان يِسوَى خَمِس مِيَّة دِينار [halħişa:n yiswa: xamis miyyat dina:r] • **2.** اِستَحَقّ [ʔistaħaqq] اِستِحقاق [ʔistiħqa:q] *vn:* *sv* i. His idea is worth trying. فِكِرتَه تِستِحِقّ التَّجرُبَة [fikirtah tistiħiqq ʔittajruba]

W

*** Pay him what he's worth.** • **1.** إنطِيه عَلَى قَدّ تَعَبَه [ʔinṭi:h ʕala gadd taʕabah]

*** He's worth about two million dinars.**

• **1.** يِملِكلَه فَدّ مِليَونَين دِينار [yimliklah fadd milyu:nayn dina:r]

*** I'll make it worth your while.** • **1.** أَرَضّيك [ʔaraðði:k] / ما تِتنَدَّم [ma: titnaddam]

worthless • **1.** ما إلَه قِيمَة [ma: ʔilah qi:ma] That money is worthless now. هَالفِلُوس بَعَد ما إلها قِيمَة [halfilu:s baʕad ma: ʔilha qi:ma]

*** The painting is practically worthless.**

• **1.** هَالصُورَة ما تِسوَى شِي [haṣṣu:ra ma: tiswa ši]

worthy • **1.** نَبِيل [nabi:l] They did it for a worthy cause. سَوُّوها لِغايَة نَبِيلَة [sawwu:ha liɣa:ya nabi:la]

wound • **1.** جَرِح [ǰariħ] جرُوح [ǰru:ħ] *pl:* It will be a couple of months before the wound in his leg is healed. يِنرادلَه شَهرَين حَتَّى الجَّرِح اللّي برِجلَه يطِيب [yinra:dlah šahrayn ħatta ʔiǰǰariħ ʔilli briǰlah yṭi:b]

to wound • **1.** جِرَح [ǰirah] جَرِح [ǰariħ] *vn:* اِنجِرَح [ʔinǰirah] *p:* جَرَّح [ǰarrah] تَجرِيح [tarǰri:ħ] *vn: sv* i. Several men were wounded in the action. كَم واحِد اِنجِرحَوا بِذاك الهِجُوم [čam wa:hid ʔinǰirħaw bða:k ʔalhiǰu:m] The explosion wounded three soldiers. الاِنفِجار جِرَح ثلَث جِنُود [ʔilʔinfiǰa:r ǰirah tlaθ ǰinu:d]

to wrap • **1.** لَفّ [laff] لَفّ [laff] *vn:* اِنلَفّ [ʔinlaff] *p:* غَلَّف [ɣallaf] *sv* i. Shall I wrap it up for you? ترِيد أَلِفّلَك إيّاها؟ [tri:d ʔalifflak ʔiyya:ha?]

*** He's all wrapped up in his work.**

• **1.** ذابِب نَفسَه عَالشُغُل [ða:bib nafsah ʕaššuɣul] / مِنهِمِك بِالشُغُل [minhimik biššuɣul] / طامُس بِالشُغُل [ṭa:mus biššuɣul]

wrapping paper • **1.** وَرَق تَغلِيف [waraq taɣli:f]

wreath • **1.** إكلِيل [ʔikli:l] أَكالِيل [ʔaka:li:l] *pl:*

wreck • **1.** أَنقاض [ʔanqa:ð] The bodies are still buried in the wreck. الجِّثَث بَعَدها مَدفُونَة بِالأنقاض [ʔiǰǰiθaθ baʕadha madfu:na bilʔanqa:ð] • **2.** حادِث [ħa:diθ] حَوادِث [ħawa:diθ] *pl:* Was anybody killed in the wreck? أَحَّد مات بِالحادِث؟ [ʔaħħad ma:t bilħa:diθ?]

*** He's a complete wreck.** • **1.** أَعصابَه مِنهارَة [ʔaʕṣa:bah minha:ra]

to wreck • **1.** حَطَّم [ħaṭṭam] تَحطِيم [taħṭi:m] *vn: sv* u. The collision wrecked the car. التَّصادُم حَطَّمها لِلسَّيّارَة [ʔittaṣa:dum ħaṭṭamha lissayya:ra] • **2.** دَمَّر [dammar] تَدمِير [tadmi:r] *vn: sv* u. The explosion wrecked the whole plant. الاِنفِجار دَمَّر المَعمَل [ʔilʔinfiǰa:r dammar ʔilmaʕmal] • **3.** دُمَر [dumar] دَمُر [damur] *vn:* اِندُمَر [ʔindumar] *p:* The strike wrecked his business. الإضراب دَمَر شُغلَه [ʔalʔiðra:b damar šuɣlah]

wrench • **1.** سبانَة [spa:na] سبانات، سباين [spa:na:t, spa:yin] *pl:*

to wrestle • **1.** تصارَع [tṣa:raʕ] تَصارُع [taṣa:ruʕ] *vn: sv* a. He likes to wrestle better than box. يعِجبَه يِتصارَع أَزيَد مِن ما يِتلاكَم [yʕiǰbah yitṣa:raʕ ʔazyad min ma: yitla:kam] • **2.** عالَج [ʕa:laǰ] مُعالَجَة [muʕa:laǰa] *vn:* تعالَج [tʕa:laǰ] *p:* I've been wrestling with this problem for hours. صارلِي ثلاث ساعات دَأعالِج هَالقَضِيَّة [ṣa:rli tlaθ sa:ʕa:t daʔaʕa:liǰ halqaðiyya]

wretched • **1.** ضايِج [ða:yiǰ] I still feel wretched. بَعَدنِي ضايِج [baʕadni ða:yiǰ]

to wring • **1.** عِصَر [ʕiṣar] عَصِر [ʕaṣir] *vn: sv* u. Wring out the clothes. إعصُر الهدُوم [ʔiʕṣur ʔilhdu:m] • **2.** لُوَى [luwa:] لَوِي [lawy] *vn: sv* i. She wrung the chicken's neck. لُوَت رُقبَة الدِّجاجَة [luwat rugbat ʔiddiǰa:ǰa]

wringer • **1.** عصّارَة [ʕaṣṣa:ra, ʕuṣṣa:ra] عصّارات [ʕaṣṣa:ra:t, ʕuṣṣa:ra:t] *pl:* The wringer on my washing machine is broken. عَصّارَة الغَسّالَة مالتِي مَكسُورَة [ʕaṣṣa:rat ʔilɣassa:la ma:lti maksu:ra]

wrinkle • **1.** تَجعِيد [taǰʕi:d] تَجاعِيد [taǰa:ʕi:d] *pl:* Her face is full of wrinkles. وِجهَها مَترُوس تَجاعِيد [wiččha matru:s taǰa:ʕi:d]

to wrinkle • **1.** عَكنَش [ʕaknaš] تعِكنِش [tʕikniš] *vn:* تعَكنَش [tʕaknaš] *p:* He wrinkled his forehead. عَكنَش وُجَّه [ʕaknaš wuččah] • **2.** تعَقَّج [tʕaqqač] تَعَقِّج [taʕaqqič] *vn: sv* a. This silk wrinkles easily. هَالحَرِير يِتعَقَّج بِالعَجَل [halħari:r yitʕaqqač bilʕaǰal]

wrist • **1.** رُسُغ [rusuɣ] أَرساغ [ʔarsa:ɣ] *pl:* You've got a sprained wrist. أَكُو عِندَك رُسُغ مَفسُوخ [ʔaku ʕindak rusuɣ mafsu:x]

wrist watch • **1.** ساعَة إيد [sa:ʕa ʔi:d] ساعات إيد [sa:ʕa:t ʔi:d] *pl:*

to write • **1.** كِتَب [kitab] كِتبَة، كِتابَة [kitba, kita:ba] *vn:* اِنكِتَب [ʔinkitab] *p:* Write your name on the first line. إكتِب إسمَك عَلَى أَوَّل سَطِر [ʔiktib ʔismak ʕala ʔawwal saṭir]

to write down • **1.** سَجَّل [saǰǰal] تَسجِيل [tasǰi:l] *vn: sv* i. Write down that telephone number before you forget it. سَجِّل هَالرَّقَم مال التَّلِفُون قَبُل ما تِنسَى [saǰǰil harraqam ma:l ʔittilifu:n gabul ma: tinsa:]

to write off • **1.** حِسَب [ħisab] حساب [ħsa:b] *vn:* اِنحِسَب [ʔinħisab] *p:* You'd better write that off as a bad debt. أَحسَنلَك إحسِب هَالدَّين مَيِّت [ʔaħsanlak ʔiħsib haddayn mayyit]

W

writer • **1.** كاتِب [ka:tib] كُتّاب [kutta:b] *pl:* My son wants to become a story writer. إبنِي يريد يصِير كاتِب قُصَصِي [ʔibni yri:d yṣi:r ka:tib quṣaṣi]

writing • **1.** كِتبَة [kitba] كِتابَة [kita:ba] كِتابات [kita:ba:t] *pl:* I can't read his writing. ما أقدَر أقرا كِتابتَه [ma: ʔagdar ʔaqra: kita:btah]

*** I don't get around to writing.**

• **1.** ما دَيصِير عِندِي وَقِت أكتِب [ma: dayṣi:r ʕindi wakit ʔaktib]

in writing • **1.** مَكتُوب [maktu:b] I'd like to have that in writing. أرِيد هاي مَكتُوبَة [ʔari:d ha:y maktu:ba]

writings • **1.** كِتابَة [kita:ba] كِتابات [kita:ba:t] *pl:* I don't understand his writings. ما أقدَر أفتِهِم كِتاباتَه [ma: ʔagdar ʔaftihim kita:ba:tah]

wrong • **1.** غَلَط [ɣalaṭ] He admitted that he was in the wrong. اِعتِرَف بغَلَطَه [ʔiʕtiraf byalaṭah] I must have added the figures up wrong again. لازِم هَمّ جمَعِت الأرقام غَلَط [la:zim hamm ǰmaʕit ʔilʔarqa:m ɣalaṭ] You're heading in the wrong direction. اِتِّجاهَك مُو صَحِيح [ʔittiǰa:hak mu: ṣaḥi:ḥ] You're heading in the wrong direction. اِتِّجاهَك غَلَط [ʔittiǰa:hak ɣalaṭ] • **2.** غَلطان [ɣalṭa:n] I'm afraid you're wrong. أعتِقِد إنتَ غَلطان [ʔaʕtiqid ʔinta ɣalṭa:n] I'll admit that I was completely wrong about him. أعتِرِف آنِي كِنِت غَلطان برأيِي بِيه [ʔaʕtirif ʔa:ni činit ɣalṭa:n braʔyi bi:h] • **3.** مُو تَمام [mu: tama:m] Something is wrong with the telephone. أكُو شِي مُو تَمام بهَالتَّلِفُون [ʔaku ši mu: tama:m bhattalifu:n]

*** He got out on the wrong side of the bed.**

• **1.** هَاليَوم وُجهَه مَقلُوب [halyawm wuǰǰah maglu:b]

*** Is anything wrong with you?** • **1.** يَوجعَك شِي؟ [yu:ǰʕak ši?]

*** What's wrong with you?** • **1.** شبِيك؟ [šbi:k?]

to do wrong • **1.** غِلَط [ɣilaṭ] غَلَط [ɣalaṭ] *vn: sv* a. He thinks he can do no wrong. يِعتِقِد هُوَّ أبَد ما يِغلَط [yiʕtiqid huwwa ʔabad ma: yiɣlaṭ]

to wrong • **1.** ظِلَم [ðilam] ظُلُم [ðulum] *vn:* اِنظِلَم [ʔinðilam] *p:* غِدَر [ɣidar] غَدِر [ɣadir] *vn:* اِنغِدَر [ʔinɣidar] *p:* He thinks he's been wronged. يِعتِقِد إنُّو هُوَّ مَظلُوم [yiʕtiqid ʔinnu huwwa maðlu:m]

wrongfully • **1.** ظُلماً و عِدواناً [ðulman wʕidwa:nan] بالتَّعَدِّي [biltaʕaddi] He was wrongfully accused of incompetence. اِتِّهمُوه بعَدَم القابلِيَّة ظُلماً وَعِدواناً [ʔittihmu:h bʕadam ʔilqa:bliyya ðulman wʕidwa:nan]

W

X

X-ray • **1.** أَشِعَّة أَيكس [ʔašiʕʕat ʔiːks] أَشِعّات أَيكس [ʔašiʕʕaːt ʔiːks] *pl:* Who discovered the X-ray? مِنُو اِكتِشَف أَشِعَّة أَيكس؟ [minu ʔiktišaf ʔašiʕʕat ʔiːks?] • **2.** أَشِعَّة [ʔašiʕʕa] أَشِعّات [ʔašiʕʕaːt] *pl:* May I see the X-ray? أَقدَر أَشُوف الأَشِعَّة؟ [ʔagdar ʔašuːf ʔilʔašiʕʕa?]

to X-ray • **1.** أَخَذ أَشِعَّة لِ [ʔaxað ʔašiʕʕa li-]
The dentist X-rayed my teeth.
طَبِيب الأَسنان أَخَذ أَشِعَّة لِسنُونِي
[ṭabiːb ʔilʔasnaːn ʔaxað ʔašiʕʕa lsnuːni]

X

Y

yard • **1.** I'd like to have five yards of this material. أَرِيد خَمِس ياردات مِن هَالقُماش [ʔariːd xamis yaːrdaːt min halqumaːš] • **2.** ساحَة [saːħa] ساحات [saːħaːt] *pl:* The house has a yard for the children to play in. البَيت بِيه ساحَة يِلعبُون بِيها الجِّهال [ʔilbayt biːh saːħa yliʕbuːn biːha ʔiǰǰihaːl] • **3.** سكَلَّة [skalla] سكَلات [skallaːt] *pl:* You may be able to get that at the lumber yard. بَلكِي تِقدَر تِلقِيها بالإسكَلَّة مال خِشَب [balki tigdar tilgiːha bilʔiskalla maːl xišab]

yarn • **1.** غَزِل [ɣazil] I'll take six balls of that green yarn. أَرِيد خَمِس لَفّات مِن ذاك الغَزِل الأَخضَر [ʔariːd xamis laffaːt min ðaːk ʔilɣazil ʔilʔaxðar]

to yawn • **1.** تثاوَب [tθaːwab] تَثاوُب [taθaːwub] *vn: sv* a. He began to yawn from drowsiness. بِدا يِتثاوُب مِن النَّعَس [bidaː yitθaːwub min ʔinnaʕas]

year • **1.** سَنَة [sana] سَنَوات [sanawaːt] *pl:* He's thirty years old. عُمرَه ثلاثِين سَنَة [ʕumrah tlaːθiːn sana] I haven't seen him for years. صارلِي سنِين ما شايفَه [ṣaːrli sniːn maː šaːyfah]

*** Year in, year out, the same routine.**

• **1.** سَنَة تخُشّ، سَنَة تِطلَع، ماكُو تَغيِير [sana txušš, sana tiṭlaʕ, maːku taɣyiːr]

yearly • **1.** سَنَوِي [sanawi] How much is the yearly rent? شقَدّ الأَجار السَّنَوِي؟ [šgadd ʔilʔaǰaːr ʔissanawi?]

*** My uncle pays us a yearly visit.**

• **1.** عَمِّي يزُورنا مَرَّة بِالسَّنَة [ʕammi yzuːrna marra bissana]

yeast • **1.** خُمرَة [xumra] خُمرات [xumraːt] *pl:* خَمِيرَة [xamiːra] خَمِيرات [xamiːraːt] *pl:*

yell • **1.** عَيطَة [ʕayṭa] عَيطات [ʕayṭaːt] *pl:* He let out a yell and died. عاط فَدّ عَيطَة وَمات [ʕaːṭ fadd ʕayṭa wmaːt]

to yell • **1.** عَيَّط [ʕayyaṭ] تَعيِيط [taʕyiːṭ] *vn: sv* i. Don't yell; you'll wake the neighbors. لا تعَيِّط، راح تقَعِّد الجُّوارين [laː tʕayyiṭ, raːħ tgaʕʕid ʔiǰǰuwaːriːn]

yellow • **1.** أَصفَر [ʔaṣfar] صُفُر، صَفرِين [ṣufur, safriːn] *pl:* صَفرَة [ṣafra] *Feminine:* She's wearing a yellow dress. لابسَة نَفنُوف أَصفَر [laːbsah nafnuːf ʔaṣfar]

*** He's yellow.** • **1.** هَذا جَبان [haːða ǰabaːn]

yes • **1.** إي [ʔiː] نَعَم [naʕam] بَلِي [bali] Yes, I'll be glad to go. إي، أَرُوح مَعَ المَمنُونِيَّة [ʔi, ʔaruːħ maʕa ʔilmamnuːniyya]

yes man • **1.** أَبُو بَلِي [ʔabu bali] He's a yes man. هَذا أَبُو بَلِي [haːða ʔabu bali]

yesterday • **1.** البارحَة [ʔilbaːrħa] I saw him yesterday. شِفتَه البارحَة [šiftah ʔilbaːrħa]

yet • **1.** بَعَد [baʕad] (with negative) . Haven't you read the book yet? ما قرَيت الكِتاب بَعَد؟ [maː qrayt ʔilkitaːb baʕad?] He hasn't come yet. ما جا بَعَد [maː ǰaː baʕad] • **2.** لَو بَعَد [law baʕad] Did you see the new play yet? شِفت التَّمثِيلِيَّة الجِّدِيدَة لَو بَعَد؟ [šift ʔittamθiːliyya ʔiǰǰidiːda law baʕad?] Have you selected anything yet? اِستَنقَيت شِي لَو بَعَد؟ [ʔistanayt ši law baʕad?] • **3.** لَكِن [laːkin] بَسّ [bass] He didn't want to go, yet he had to. ما راد يرُوح لَكِن اِضطَرّ [maː raːd yiruːħ laːkin ʔiðṭarr] • **4.** مَعَ هَذا [maʕa haːða] And yet you can't help liking him. مَعَ هَذا ما تِقدَر إلّا تحِبَّه [maʕa haːða maː tigdar ʔilla tħibbah]

to yield • **1.** طَلَّع [ṭallaʕ] تَطلِيع [taṭliːʕ] *vn:* تطَلَّع [tṭallaʕ] *p:* جاب [ǰaːb] جَيب [ǰayb] *vn: sv* i. His business doesn't yield much profit. مَصلَحتَه ما تطَلِّع هوايَة رِبح [maṣlaħtah maː tṭalliʕ hwaːya ribiħ] • **2.** نِتَج [nitaǰ] إنتاج [ʔintaːǰ] *vn:* اِنِّتَج [ʔinnitaǰ] *p:* This farm yields a pretty good income. هَالمَزرَعَة تِنتِج خُوش وارد [halmazraʕa tintiǰ xuːš waːrid] • **3.** خِضَع [xiðaʕ] خُضُوع [xuðuːʕ] *vn: sv* a. أَذعَن [ʔaðʕan] إذعان [ʔiðʕaːn] *vn: sv* i. رِضَخ [riðax] رُضُوخ [ruðuːx] *vn: sv* a. We'll never yield to force. أَبَداً ما نِخضَع لِلقُوَّة [ʔabadan maː nixðaʕ lilquwwa]

yoghurt • **1.** لِبَن [liban]

yolk • **1.** صَفار [ṣafaːr]

you • **1.** إنتَ [ʔinta] إنتُم [ʔintum] *pl:* Are you the new clerk? إنتَ الكاتِب الجِّدِيد؟ [ʔinta ʔilkaːtib ʔiǰǰidiːd?] • **2.** ك [ak] كُم [kum] *pl:* كِ [ič] *Feminine:* I haven't seen you in a long time. ما شِفتَك مِن زَمان [maː šiftak min zamaːn]

young • **1.** جاهِل [ǰaːhil] Who's that young man? مِنُو ذاك الرِّجّال الجّاهِل؟ [minu ðaːk ʔirriǰǰaːl ʔiǰǰaːhil?] She's very young for her age. تبَيِّن جاهلَة بِالنِّسبَة لعُمرها [tbayyin ǰaːhla binnisba lʕumurha]

*** The night is still young.** • **1.** اللَّيل بَعدَه بأَوَّلَه [ʔillayl baʕdah bʔawwalah]

young people • **1.** شَباب [šabaːb] The young people had a lot of fun. الشَّباب توَنّسَوا هوايَة [ʔiššabaːb twannsaw hwaːya]

yours • **1.** (مال كَ، كِ، كُم) [maːl- (-ak, -ič, kum)] This hat is yours, sir. هَالشَّفقَة مالَك، يا أُستاذ [haššafqa maːlak, yaː ʔustaːð] This doll is yours. هَاللَّعابَة مالتِك [hallaʕʕaːba maːltič] My bag is bigger than yours. جِنُطتِي أَكبَر مِن مالتَك [ǰinutti ʔakbar min maːltak]

*** Is he a friend of yours, Mr. Smith?** • **1.** هَذا مِن أَصدِقائك، يا مِستِر سمِث؟ [ha:ða min ʔaṣdiqa:ʔak, ya: mistir smiθ?]

yourself • **1.** نَفِس [nafis] نُفُوس، أَنفُس [nufu:s, ʔanfus] *pl:* Did you hurt yourself? أَذَّيت نَفسَك؟ [ʔaððiːt nafsak?]

youth • **1.** شَباب [šaba:b] He had to work hard in his youth. اِضطَرّ يِشتُغُل هوايَة بِشَبابَه [ʔiðṭarr yištuɣul hwa:ya bšaba:bah]

yo-yo • **1.** يويَو [yu:yu] يَويَووات [yu:yu:wa:t] *pl:*

Y

Z

zebra • **1.** زيبرا [ziːbra] زِيبرات [ziːbraːt] *pl:*

zero • **1.** صِفِر [ṣifir] صفارَة [ṣfaːra] *pl:* Add another zero. حُطّ صِفِر لاخ [ħuṭṭ ṣifir laːx] The temperature is zero. دَرَجَة الحَرارَة صِفِر [darağat ʔilħaraːra ṣifir]

zinc • **1.** قَصدِير [qaṣdiːr]

Zion • **1.** صَهيُون [ṣahyuːn]

Zionism • **1.** صَّهيُونِيَّة [ṣahyuːniyya]

Zionist • **1.** صَهيُونِي [ṣahyuːni]

zipper • **1.** زَنجِيل [zanǰiːl] زَناجِيل [zanaːǰiːl] *pl:* I broke the zipper on my sweater. كِسَرِت الزَّنجِيل مال بلُوزِي [kisarit ʔizzanǰiːl maːl bluːzi]

zither • **1.** قانُون [qaːnuːn] قَوانِين [qawaːniːn] *pl:*

zone • **1.** مَنطِقَة [manṭiqa, manṭaqa] مَناطِق [manaːṭiq, manaːṭig] *pl:* Iraq is located in the temperate zone. العِراق واقِع بِالمَنطِقَة المُعتَدِلَة [ʔilʕiraːq waːqiʕ bilmanṭiqa ʔalmuʕtadila]

zoo • **1.** حَدِيقَة حَيوانات [ħadiːqa ħaywaːnaːt] حَدايِق حَيوانات [ħadaːyiq ħaywaːnaːt] *pl:*

zoology • **1.** عِلِم الحَيوانات [ʕilim ʔilħaywaːnaːt]

Z